D1567655

the MACARTHUR STUDY BIBLE

SECOND EDITION

PRESENTED TO

BY

ON

Your word is a lamp to my feet and a light to my path.

PSALM 119:105

the MacArthur STUDY BIBLE

THOMAS NELSON

NEW AMERICAN STANDARD VERSION™

the MACARTHUR STUDY BIBLE

SECOND EDITION

JOHN MACARTHUR

AUTHOR AND GENERAL EDITOR

THOMAS NELSON

Since 1798

www.ThomasNelson.com

THE MACARTHUR STUDY BIBLE, 2nd Edition

Library of Congress Control Number: 2019953007

Cover art and design by Kate Armstrong.

Typesetting and interior design by Esther Moody and Matthew Van Zomeren.

Published by Thomas Nelson, Inc., in Nashville, TN. Thomas Nelson is a registered trademark of HarperCollins Christian Publishing, Inc.

Printed in China

24 25 26 27 28 29 30 /DSC/ 15 14 13 12 11 10 9 8 7

TABLE OF

CONTENTS

INDEX OF

CHARTS AND MAPS

BY BOOK OF THE BIBLE

— INTRODUCTION TO —

THE BIBLE

The Bible is a collection of 66 documents inspired by God. These documents are gathered into two testaments, the Old (39) and the New (27). Prophets, priests, kings, and leaders from the nation of Israel wrote the OT books in Hebrew (with two passages in Aramaic). The apostles and their associates wrote the NT books in Greek.

The OT record starts with the creation of the universe and closes about 400 years before the first coming of Jesus Christ.

The flow of history through the OT moves along the following lines:

- Creation of the universe
- Fall of man
- Judgment flood over the earth
- Abraham, Isaac, Jacob (Israel)—fathers of the chosen nation
- The history of Israel
    - Exile in Egypt—430 years
    - Exodus and wilderness wanderings—40 years
    - Conquest of Canaan—7 years
    - Era of Judges—350 years
    - United Kingdom—Saul, David, Solomon—110 years
    - Divided Kingdom—Judah/Israel—350 years
    - Exile in Babylon—70 years
    - Return and rebuilding the land—140 years

The details of this history are explained in the 39 books divided into 5 categories:

- The Law—5 (Genesis—Deuteronomy)
- History—12 (Joshua—Esther)
- Wisdom—5 (Job—Song of Solomon)
- Major Prophets—5 (Isaiah—Daniel)
- Minor Prophets—12 (Hosea—Malachi)

After the completion of the OT, there were 400 years of silence, during which no prophet spoke or wrote any Scripture. That silence was broken by the arrival of John the Baptist announcing that the promised Lord Savior had come. The NT records the rest of the story from the birth of Christ to the culmination of all history and the final eternal state; so the two testaments go from creation to consummation, eternity past to eternity future.

While the 39 OT books major on the history of Israel and the promise of the coming Savior, the 27 NT books major on the person of Christ and the establishment of the church. The four Gospels give the record of His birth, life, death, resurrection, and ascension. Each of the four writers views the greatest and most important event of history, the coming of the God-man, Jesus Christ, from a different perspective. Matthew looks at Him through the perspective of His kingdom; Mark through the perspective of His servanthood; Luke through the perspective of His humanness; and John through the perspective of His deity.

The book of Acts tells the story of the impact of the life, death, and resurrection of Jesus Christ, the Lord Savior—from His ascension, the consequent coming of the Holy Spirit, and the birth of the church, through the early years of gospel preaching by the apostles and their associates. Acts records the establishment of the church in Judea, Samaria, and into the Roman Empire.

The 21 epistles were written to churches and individuals to explain the significance of the person and work of Jesus Christ, with its implications for life and witness until He returns.

The NT closes with Revelation, which starts by picturing the current church age, and culminates with Christ's return to establish His earthly kingdom, bringing judgment on the ungodly and glory and blessing for believers. Following the millennial reign of the Lord Savior will be the last judgment, leading to the eternal state. All believers of all history enter the ultimate eternal glory prepared for them, and all the ungodly are consigned to hell to be punished forever.

To understand the Bible, it is essential to grasp the sweep of that history from creation to consummation. It is also crucial to keep in focus the unifying theme of Scripture. The one constant theme unfolding throughout the whole Bible is this: God for His own glory has chosen to create and gather to Himself a group of people to be the subjects of His eternal kingdom, to praise, honor, and serve Him forever and through whom He will display His wisdom, power, mercy, grace, and glory. To gather His chosen ones, God must redeem them from sin. The Bible reveals God's plan for this redemption from its inception in eternity past to its completion in eternity future. Covenants, promises, and epochs are all secondary to the one continuous plan of redemption.

There is one God. The Bible has one Creator. It is one book. It has one plan of grace, recorded from initiation, through execution, to consummation. From predestination to glorification, the Bible is the story of God redeeming His chosen people for the praise of His glory.

As God's redemptive purposes and plan unfold in Scripture, five recurring motifs are constantly emphasized:

- the character of God
- the judgment for sin and disobedience
- the blessing for faith and obedience
- the Lord Savior and sacrifice for sin
- the coming kingdom and glory

Everything revealed on the pages of both the OT and NT is associated with those five categories. Scripture is always teaching or illustrating: 1) the character and attributes of God; 2) the tragedy of sin and disobedience to God's holy standard; 3) the blessedness of faith and obedience to God's standard; 4) the need for a Savior by whose righteousness and substitution sinners can be forgiven, declared just, and transformed to obey God's standard; and 5) the coming glorious end of redemptive history in the Lord Savior's earthly kingdom and the subsequent eternal reign and glory of God and Christ. It is essential as one studies Scripture to grasp these recurring categories like great hooks on which to hang the passages. While reading through the Bible, one should be able to relate each portion of Scripture to these dominant topics, recognizing that what is introduced in the OT is also made more clear in the NT.

Looking at these five categories separately gives an overview of the Bible.

1. THE REVELATION OF THE CHARACTER OF GOD

Above all else, Scripture is God's self-revelation. He reveals Himself as the sovereign God of the universe who has chosen to make man and to make Himself known to man. In that self-revelation is established His standard of absolute holiness. From Adam and Eve through Cain and Abel and to everyone before and after the law of Moses, the standard of righteousness was established and is sustained to the last page of the NT. Violation of it produces judgment, temporal and eternal.

In the OT, it is recorded that God revealed Himself by the following means:

- creation—primarily through man—who was made in His image
- angels
- signs, wonders, and miracles
- visions
- spoken words by prophets and others
- theophanies
- written Scripture (OT)

In the NT, it is recorded that God revealed Himself again by the same means, but more clearly and fully:

- creation—the God-man, Jesus Christ, who was the very image of God
- angels
- signs, wonders, and miracles
- visions
- spoken words by apostles and prophets
- written Scripture (NT)

2. THE REVELATION OF DIVINE JUDGMENT FOR SIN AND DISOBEDIENCE

Scripture repeatedly deals with the matter of man's sin, which leads to divine judgment. Account after account in Scripture demonstrates the deadly effects in time and eternity of violating God's standard. There are 1,189 chapters in the Bible. Only four of them don't involve a fallen world: the first two and the last two—before the Fall and after the creation of the new heaven and new earth. The rest is the chronicle of the tragedy of sin.

In the OT, God showed the disaster of sin—starting with Adam and Eve, to Cain and Abel, the patriarchs, Moses and Israel, the kings, priests, some prophets, and Gentile nations. Throughout the OT is the relentless record of continual devastation produced by sin and disobedience to God's law.

In the NT, the tragedy of sin becomes more clear. The preaching and teaching of Jesus and the apostles begin and end with a call to repentance. King Herod, the Jewish leaders, and the nation of Israel—along with Pilate, Rome, and the rest of the world—all reject the Lord Savior, spurn the truth of God, and thus condemn themselves. The chronicle of sin continues unabated to the end of the age and the return of Christ in judgment. In the NT, disobedience is even more flagrant than OT disobedience because it involves the rejection of the Lord Savior Jesus Christ in the brighter light of NT truth.

3. THE REVELATION OF DIVINE BLESSING FOR FAITH AND OBEDIENCE

Scripture repeatedly promises wonderful rewards in time and eternity that come to people who trust God and seek to obey Him. In the OT, God showed the blessedness of repentance from sin, faith in Himself, and obedience to His Word—from Abel, through the patriarchs, to the remnant in Israel—and even Gentiles who believed (such as the people of Nineveh).

God's standard for man, His will, and His moral law were always made known. To those who faced their inability to keep God's standard, recognized their sin, confessed their impotence to please God by their own effort and works, and asked Him for forgiveness and grace—there came merciful redemption and blessing for time and eternity.

In the NT, God again showed the full blessedness of redemption from sin for repentant people. There were those who responded to the preaching of repentance by John the Baptist. Others repented at the preaching of Jesus. Still others from Israel obeyed the gospel through the apostles' preaching. And finally, there were Gentiles all over the Roman Empire who believed the gospel. To all those and to all who will believe through all of history, there is blessing promised in this world and the world to come.

4. THE REVELATION OF THE LORD SAVIOR AND SACRIFICE FOR SIN

This is the heart of both the OT, which Jesus said spoke of Him in type and prophecy, and the NT, which gives the biblical record of His coming. The promise of blessing is dependent on grace and mercy given to the sinner. Grace means that sin is not held against the sinner. Such forgiveness is dependent on a payment of sin's penalty to satisfy holy justice. That requires a substitute—one to die in the sinner's place. God's chosen substitute—the only one who qualified—was Jesus. Salvation is always by the same gracious means, whether during OT or NT times. When any sinner comes to God, repentant and convinced he has no power to save himself from the deserved judgment of divine wrath, and pleads for mercy, God's promise of forgiveness is granted. God then declares him righteous because the sacrifice and obedience of Christ is put to his account. In the OT, God justified sinners that same way, in anticipation of Christ's atoning work. There is, therefore, a continuity of grace and salvation through all of redemptive history. Various covenants, promises, and epochs do not alter that fundamental continuity, nor does the discontinuity between the OT witness nation, Israel, and the NT witness people, the church. A fundamental continuity is centered in the cross, which was no interruption in the plan of God, but is the very thing to which all else points.

Throughout the OT, the Savior and sacrifice are promised. In Genesis, He is the seed of the woman who will destroy Satan. In Zechariah, He is the pierced one to whom Israel turns and by whom God opens the fountain of forgiveness to all who mourn over their sin. He is the very One symbolized in the sacrificial system of the Mosaic law. He is the suffering substitute spoken of by the prophets. Throughout the OT, He is the Messiah who would die for the transgressions of His people; from beginning to end in the OT, the theme of the Lord Savior as a sacrifice for sin is presented. It is solely because of His perfect sacrifice for sin that God graciously forgives repentant believers.

In the NT, the Lord Savior came and actually provided the promised sacrifice for sin on the cross. Having fulfilled all righteousness by His perfect life, He fulfilled justice by His death. Thus God Himself atoned for sin, at a cost too great for the human mind to fathom. Now He graciously supplies on their behalf all the merit necessary for His people to be the objects of His favor. That is what Scripture means when it speaks of salvation by grace.

5. THE REVELATION OF THE KINGDOM AND GLORY OF THE LORD SAVIOR

This crucial component of Scripture brings the whole story to its God-ordained consummation. Redemptive history is controlled by God, so as to culminate in His eternal glory. Redemptive history will end with the same precision and exactness with which it began. The truths of eschatology are neither vague nor unclear—nor are they unimportant. As in any book, how the story ends is the most crucial and compelling part—so with the Bible. Scripture notes several very specific features of the end planned by God.

In the OT, there is repeated mention of an earthly kingdom ruled by the Messiah, Lord Savior, who will come to reign. Associated with that kingdom will be the salvation of Israel, the salvation of Gentiles, the renewal of the earth from the effects of the curse, and the bodily resurrection of God's people who have died. Finally, the OT predicts that there will be the "uncreation" or dissolution of the universe, and the creation of a new heaven and new earth—which will be the eternal state of the godly—and a final hell for the ungodly.

In the NT, these features are clarified and expanded. The King was rejected and executed, but He promised to come back in glory, bringing judgment, resurrection, and His kingdom for all who believe. Innumerable Gentiles from every nation will be included among the redeemed. Israel will be saved and grafted back into the root of blessing from which she has been temporarily excised.

Israel's promised kingdom will be enjoyed, with the Lord Savior reigning on the throne, in the renewed earth, exercising power over the whole world, having taken back His rightful authority, and receiving due honor and worship. Following that kingdom will come the dissolution of the renewed, but still sin-stained creation, and the subsequent creation of a new heaven and new earth—which will be the eternal state, separate forever from the ungodly in hell.

Those are the five topics that fill up the Bible. To understand them at the start is to know the answer to the question that continually arises—Why does the Bible tell us this? Everything fits into this glorious pattern. As you read, hang the truth on these five hooks and the Bible will unfold, not as 66 separate documents, or even two separate testaments—but one book, by one divine Author, who wrote it all with one overarching theme.

My prayer is that the magnificent and overwhelming theme of the redemption of sinners for the glory of God will carry every reader with captivating interest from beginning to end of the story. Christian—this is your story. It is from God for you—about you. It tells what He planned for you, why He made you, what you were, what you have become in Christ, and what He has prepared for you in eternal glory.

John MacArthur

PERSONAL NOTES

Why write a study Bible? The answer to that question comes in a conversation between Philip and an Ethiopian recorded in Acts 8:30, 31:

> Philip ran up and heard him reading Isaiah the prophet, and said, "Do you understand what you are reading?"
> And he said, "Well, how could I, unless someone guides me?"
> And he invited Philip to come up and sit with him.

As Philip did with the eunuch, I want to sit with you and explain the Scriptures. This Study Bible allows me that intimate opportunity.

Although I personally bear full responsibility for all the notes in The MacArthur Study Bible because they all have come from me and through me, a work of this magnitude with the responsibility to be accurate could only have been done with a team of supportive co-workers who committed themselves to assist me by arduous labor with loving devotion and commitment to excellence. Many friends have participated in the team—all of whom deserve to be commended and thanked.

My highest gratitude belongs to my friend and ministry partner, Dr. Richard Mayhue, Senior Vice President and Dean of The Master's Seminary. He has worked next to me through the whole project, laboring beyond anyone while serving as project manager, OT and NT researcher, editor, and counselor. His exceptional gift for management, along with his vast knowledge of Scripture and doctrine, coupled with our one-mindedness theologically, plus his writing skill, have made for a more effective partnership.

Gratitude in abundance must be given to the faculty of the Master's Seminary for their assistance in original research and carefully prepared first draft material for the study notes on the Old Testament. Using the foundation of that original research and material, I worked and re-worked the study notes into their final form.

Never have I been so challenged and blessed at the same time as during the two intense years of finalizing this work. Studying along in my private place, perusing every word of Scripture, plus being challenged to understand each phrase and verse has yielded richness to my life and ministry like nothing I have undertaken before.

I have always been committed to the Scriptures as inspired, inerrant, infallible, sufficient and eternal. I have always preached the Bible expositionally, verse by verse, book by book. After this enterprise, I feel even more strongly about the necessity of preaching every pure word of Scripture (Ps 12:6). I have been profoundly enriched in my own life, as never before, because of the sheer force of so much divine truth pouring through me daily. For many months I spent eight or more hours every day working in the word, not so much because I had to, but because I could not leave the text—its riches held me captive.

My thanks to you, the reader, for loving Scripture enough to be a serious student. This work is an additional way of fulfilling my calling as a pastor-teacher mandated " to equip his people for works of service, so that the body of Christ may be built up" (Eph. 4:12).

A special word of thanks is certainly in order for my beloved wife, Patricia, who supported me with her prayers and encouragement, and endured my times of isolation with understanding.

With gratitude most of all to our glorious God who gave us his precious word, do I pray that he will be honored by this effort to explain what his word means by what it says.

John MacArthur

HOW WE GOT
THE BIBLE

Ever since Eve encountered Satan's barrage of doubt and denial (Ge 3:1–7), mankind has continued to question God's Word. Unfortunately, Eve had little or no help in sorting through her intellectual obstacles to full faith in God's self-disclosure (Ge 2:16, 17).

Now the Scripture certainly has more than enough content to be interrogated, considering that it's comprised of 66 books, 1,189 chapters, 31,173 verses, and 774,746 words. When you open your English translation to read or study, you might have asked in the past or are currently asking, "How can I be sure this is the pure and true Word of God?"

A question of this kind is not altogether bad, especially when one seeks to learn with a teachable mind (Ac 17:11). The Scripture invites the kinds of queries that a sincere student asks. A whole host of questions can flood the mind, such as:

- Where did the Bible come from?
- Whose thinking does it reflect?
- Did any books of the Bible get lost in time past?
- What does the Scripture claim for itself?
- Does it live up to its claims?
- Who wrote the Bible—God or man?
- Has Scripture been protected from human tampering over the centuries?
- How close to the original manuscripts are today's translations?
- How did the Bible get to our time and in our language?
- Is there more Scripture to come, beyond the current 66 books?
- Who determined, and on what basis, that the Bible would be composed of the traditional list of 66 books?
- If the Scriptures were written over a period of 1,500 years (ca. 1405 B.C. to A.D. 95), passed down since then for almost 2,000 years, and translated into several thousand languages, what prevented the Bible from being changed by the carelessness or ill motives of men?
- Does today's Bible really deserve the title "The Word of God"?

Undoubtedly, these questions have bombarded the minds of many. A study of the Scriptures alone settles all questions to the extent that there is no need to be bothered by them again. Scripture gives this assurance.

SCRIPTURE'S SELF-CLAIMS

Take the Bible and let it speak for itself. Does it claim to be God's Word? Yes! Over 2,000 times in the Old Testament alone, the Bible asserts that God spoke what is written within its pages. From the beginning (Ge 1:3) to the end (Mal 4:3) and continually throughout, this is what Scripture claims.

The phrase "the Word of God" occurs over 40 times in the New Testament. It is equated with the Old Testament (Mk 7:13). It is what Jesus preached (Lk 5:1). It was the message the apostles taught (Ac 4:31; 6:2). It was the Word the Samaritans received (Ac 8:14) as given by the apostles (Ac 8:25). It was the message the Gentiles received as preached by Peter (Ac 11:1). It was the word Paul preached on his first missionary journey (Ac 13:5, 7, 44, 48, 49; 15:35, 36). It was the message preached on Paul's second missionary journey (Ac 16:32; 17:13; 18:11). It was the message Paul preached on his third missionary journey (Ac 19:10). It was the focus of Luke in the book of Acts in that it spread rapidly and widely (Ac 6:7; 12:24; 19:20). Paul was careful to tell the Corinthians that he spoke the Word as it was given from God, that it had not been adulterated, and that it was a manifestation of truth (2Co 2:17; 4:2). Paul acknowledged that it was the source of his preaching (Col 1:25; 1Th 2:13).

Psalms 19 and 119, plus Proverbs 30:5–6, make powerful statements about God's Word which set it apart from any other religious instruction ever known in the history of mankind. These passages make the case for the Bible being called "sacred" (2Ti 3:15) and "holy" (Ro 1:2).

The Bible claims ultimate spiritual authority in doctrine, reproof, correction, and instruction in righteousness because it represents the inspired Word of Almighty God (2Ti 3:16, 17). Scripture asserts its spiritual sufficiency, so much so that it claims exclusivity for its teaching (cf. Is 55:11; 2Pe 1:3, 4).

God's Word declares that it is *inerrant* (Pss 12:6; 119:140; Pr 30:5a; Jn 10:35) and *infallible* (2Ti 3:16, 17). In other words, it is true and therefore trustworthy. All of these qualities are dependent on the fact that Scripture is God-given (2Ti 3:16; 2Pe 1:20, 21), which guarantees its quality at the Source and at its original writing.

In Scripture, the person of God and the Word of God are everywhere interrelated, so much so that whatever is true about the character of God is true about the nature of God's Word. God is true, impeccable, and reliable; therefore, so is His Word. What a person thinks about God's Word, in reality, reflects what a person thinks about God.

Thus, the Scripture can make these demands on its readers.

> He humbled you and let you be hungry, and fed you with manna which you did not know, nor did your fathers know, that He might make you understand that man does not live by bread alone, but man lives by everything that proceeds out of the mouth of the Lord.
>
> DEUTERONOMY 8:3

> I have not departed from the command of His lips; I have treasured the words of His mouth more than my necessary food.
>
> JOB 23:12

THE PUBLISHING PROCESS

The Bible does not expect its reader to speculate on how these divine qualities were transferred from God to His Word, but rather anticipates the questions with convincing answers. Every generation of skeptics has assailed the self-claims of the Bible, but its own explanations and answers have been more than equal to the challenge. The Bible has gone through God's publishing process in being given to and distributed among the human race. Its several features are discussed below.

REVELATION

God took the initiative to disclose or reveal Himself to mankind (Heb 1:1). The vehicles varied; sometimes it was through the created order, at other times through visions/dreams or speaking prophets. However, the most complete and understandable self-disclosures were through the propositions of Scripture (1Co 2:6–16). The revealed and written Word of God is unique in that it is the only revelation of God that is complete and that so clearly declares man's sinfulness and God's provision of the Savior.

INSPIRATION

The revelation of God was captured in the writings of Scripture by means of "inspiration." This has more to do with the process by which God revealed Himself than the fact of His self-revelation. "All Scripture is inspired by God..." (2Ti 3:16) makes the claim. Peter explains the process, " ... know this first of all, that no prophecy of Scripture is *a matter* of one's own interpretation, for no prophecy was ever made by an act of human will, but men moved by the Holy Spirit spoke from God" (2Pe 1:20, 21). By this means, the Word of God was protected from human error in its original record by the ministry of the Holy Spirit (cf. Dt 18:18; Mt 1:22). A section of Zec 7:12 describes it most clearly, " ... the law and the words which the LORD of hosts had sent by His Spirit through the former prophets." This ministry of the Spirit extended to both the part (the words) and to the whole in the original writings.

CANONICITY

We must understand that the Bible is actually one book with one Divine Author, though it was written over a period of 1,500 years through the pens of almost 40 human writers. The Bible began with the creation account of Ge 1, 2, written by Moses about 1405 B.C., and extends to the eternity future account of Rev 21, 22, written by the apostle John about A.D. 95. During this time, God progressively revealed Himself and His purposes in the inspired Scriptures. But this raises a significant question: "How do we know what supposed sacred writings were to be included in the canon of Scripture and which ones were to be excluded?"

Over the centuries, 3 widely recognized principles were used to validate those writings which came as a result of divine revelation and inspiration. First, the writing had to have a recognized prophet or apostle as its author (or one associated with them, as in the case of Mark, Luke, Hebrews, James, and Jude). Second, the writing could not disagree with or contradict previous Scripture. Third, the writing had to have general consensus by the church as an inspired book. Thus, when various councils met in church history to consider the canon, they did not vote for the canonicity of a book but rather recognized, after the fact, what God had already written.

With regard to the Old Testament, by the time of Christ all of the Old Testament had been written and accepted in the Jewish community. The last book, Malachi, had been completed about 430 B.C. Not only does the Old Testament canon of Christ's day conform to the Old Testament which has since been used throughout the centuries, but it does not contain the uninspired and spurious Apocrypha, that group of 14 rogue writings which were written after Malachi and attached to the Old Testament about 200–150 B.C. in the Greek translation of the Hebrew Old Testament called the Septuagint (LXX), appearing to this very day in some versions of the Bible. However, not one passage from the Apocrypha is cited by any New Testament writer, nor did Jesus affirm any of it as He recognized the Old Testament canon of His era (cf. Lk 24:27, 44).

THE HEBREW OLD TESTAMENT

Law	Prophets	Writings
1. Genesis 2. Exodus 3. Leviticus 4. Numbers 5. Deuteronomy	A. *Former Prophets* 6. Joshua 7. Judges 8. Samuel (1 & 2) 9. Kings (1 & 2) B. *Latter Prophets* 10. Isaiah 11. Jeremiah 12. Ezekiel 13. The Twelve (minor prophets)	A. *Poetical Books* 14. Psalms 15. Proverbs 16. Job B. *Five Rolls (Megilloth)* 17. Song of Solomon 18. Ruth 19. Lamentations 20. Ecclesiastes 21. Esther C. *Historical Books* 22. Daniel 23. Ezra-Nehemiah 24. Chronicles (1 & 2)

By Christ's time, the Old Testament canon had been divided up into two lists of 22 or 24 books respectively, each of which contained all the same material as the 39 books of our modern versions. In the 22 book canon, Jeremiah and Lamentations were considered as one, as were Judges and Ruth. The table on page xx shows how the 24 book format was divided.

The same 3 key tests of canonicity that applied to the Old Testament also applied to the New Testament. In the case of Mark and Luke/Acts, the authors were considered to be, in effect, the penmen for Peter and Paul respectively. James and Jude were written by Christ's half-brothers. While Hebrews is the only New Testament book whose authorship is unknown for certain, its content is so in line with both the Old Testament and New Testament, that the early church concluded it must have been written by an apostolic associate. The 27 books of the New Testament have been universally accepted since ca. A.D. 350–400 as inspired by God.

PRESERVATION

How can one be sure that the revealed and inspired, written Word of God, which was recognized as canonical by the early church, has been handed down to this day without any loss of material? Furthermore, since one of the Devil's prime concerns is to undermine the Bible, have the Scriptures survived this destructive onslaught? In the beginning, he denied God's Word to Eve (Ge 3:4). Satan later attempted to distort the Scripture in his wilderness encounter with Christ (Mt 4:6, 7). Through King Jehoiakim, he even attempted to literally destroy the Word (Jer 36:23). The battle for the Bible rages, but Scripture has and will continue to outlast its enemies.

God anticipated man's and Satan's malice towards the Scripture with divine promises to preserve His Word. The very continued existence of Scripture is guaranteed in Is 40:8, "The grass withers, the flower fades, but the word of our God stands forever" (cf. 1Pe 1:25). This even means that no inspired Scripture has been lost in the past and still awaits rediscovery.

The actual content of Scripture will be perpetuated, both in heaven (Ps 119:89) and on earth

(Is 59:21). Thus the purposes of God, as published in the sacred writings, will never be thwarted, even in the least detail (cf. Mt 5:18; 24:25; Mk 13:31; Lk 16:17).

> So will My word be which goes forth from My mouth; it will not return to Me empty, without accomplishing what I desire, and without succeeding in the matter for which I sent it.
> ISAIAH 55:11

TRANSMISSION

Since the Bible has frequently been translated into multiple languages and distributed throughout the world, how can we be sure that error has not crept in, even if it was unintentional? As Christianity spread, it is certainly true that people desired to have the Bible in their own language, which required translations from the original Hebrew and Aramaic languages of the Old Testament and the Greek of the New Testament. Not only did the work of translators provide an opportunity for error, but publication, which was done by hand copying until the printing press arrived ca. A.D. 1450, also afforded continual possibilities of error.

Through the centuries, the practitioners of textual criticism, a precise science, have discovered, preserved, catalogued, evaluated, and published an amazing array of biblical manuscripts from both the Old and New Testaments. In fact, the number of existing biblical manuscripts dramatically outdistances the existing fragments of any other ancient literature. By comparing text with text, the textual critic can confidently determine what the original prophetic/apostolic, inspired writing contained.

Although existing copies of the main, ancient Hebrew text (Masoretic) date back only to the tenth century A.D., two other important lines of textual evidence bolster the confidence of textual critics that they have reclaimed the originals. First, the tenth century A.D. Hebrew Old Testament can be compared to the Greek translation called the Septuagint or LXX (written ca. 200–150 B.C.; the oldest existing manuscripts date to ca. A.D. 325). There is amazing consistency between the two, which speaks of the accuracy in copying the Hebrew text for centuries. Second, the discovery of the Dead Sea Scrolls in 1947–1956 (manuscripts that are dated ca. 200–100 B.C.) proved to be monumentally important. After comparing the earlier Hebrew texts with the later ones, only a few slight variants were discovered, none of which changed the meaning of any passage. Although the Old Testament had been translated and copied for centuries, the latest version was essentially the same as the earlier ones.

The New Testament findings are even more decisive because a much larger amount of material is available for study; there are over 5,000 Greek New Testament manuscripts that range from the whole testament to scraps of papyri which contain as little as part of one verse. A few existing fragments date back to within 25–50 years of the original writing. New Testament textual scholars have generally concluded that 1) 99.99 percent of the original writings have been reclaimed, and 2) of the remaining one hundredth of one percent, there are no variants substantially affecting any Christian doctrine.

With this wealth of biblical manuscripts in the original languages and with the disciplined activity of textual critics to establish with almost perfect accuracy the content of the autographs, any errors which have been introduced and/or perpetuated by the thousands of translations over the centuries can be identified and corrected by comparing the translation or copy with the reassembled original. By this providential means, God has made good His promise to preserve the Scriptures. We can rest assured that there are translations available today which indeed are worthy of the title, The Word of God.

The history of a full, English translation Bible essentially began with John Wycliffe (ca. A.D. 1330–1384), who made the first English translation of the whole Bible. Later, William Tyndale was associated with the first complete, printed New Testament in English, ca. A.D. 1526. Myles Coverdale followed in A.D. 1535, by delivering the first complete Bible printed in English. By A.D. 1611, the King James Version (KJV) had been completed. Since then, hundreds of translations have been made—some better, some worse. Today, the better English translations of the Hebrew and Greek Scriptures include: 1) New American Standard Bible (NASB); 2) English Standard Version (ESV); and 3) New King James Version (NKJV).

SUMMING IT UP

God intended His Word to abide forever (preservation). Therefore His written, propositional, self-disclosure (revelation) was protected from error in its original writing (inspiration) and collected in 66 books of the Old and New Testaments (canonicity).

Through the centuries, tens of thousands of copies and thousands of translations have been made (transmission) which did introduce some error. Because there is an abundance of existing ancient Old Testament and New Testament manuscripts, however, the exacting science of textual criticism has been able to reclaim the content of the original writings (revelation and inspiration) to the extreme degree of 99.99 percent, with the remaining one hundredth of one percent having no effect on its content (preservation).

The sacred book which we read, study, obey, and preach deserves to unreservedly be called The Bible or "The Book without peer," since its author is God and it bears the qualities of total truth and complete trustworthiness, as also characterizes its divine source.

IS THERE MORE TO COME?

How do we know that God will not amend our current Bible with a 67th inspired book? Or, in other words, "Is the canon forever closed?"

Scripture texts warn that no one should delete from or add to Scripture (Dt 4:2; 12:32; Pr 30:6). Realizing that additional canonical books actually came after these words of warning, we can only conclude that while no deletions whatsoever were permitted, in fact, authorized, inspired writings were permitted to be added in order to complete the canon protected by those passages.

The most compelling text on the closed canon is the Scripture to which nothing has been added for 1,900 years.

> I testify to everyone who hears the words of the prophecy of this book: if anyone adds to them, God will add to him the plagues which are written in this book; and if anyone takes away from the words of the book of this prophecy, God will take away his part from the tree of life and from the holy city, which are written in this book.
>
> REVELATION 22:18, 19

Several significant observations, when taken together, have convinced the church over the centuries that the canon of Scripture is actually closed, never to be reopened.

1. The book of Revelation is unique to the Scripture in that it describes with unparalleled detail the end-time events which precede eternity future. As Genesis began Scripture by bridging the gap from eternity past into our time/space existence with the only detailed creation account (Ge 1, 2), so Revelation transitions out of time/space back into eternity future (Rev 20–22). Genesis and Revelation, by their contents, are the perfectly matched bookends of Scripture.
2. Just as there was prophetic silence after Malachi completed the Old Testament canon, so there was a parallel silence after John delivered Revelation. This leads to the conclusion that the New Testament canon was then closed also.
3. Since there have not been, nor now are, any authorized prophets or apostles in either the Old Testament or New Testament sense, there are not any potential authors of future inspired, canonical writings. God's Word, "once for all handed down to the saints," is never to be added to, but to be earnestly contended for (Jude 3).
4. Of the 4 exhortations not to tamper with Scripture, only the one in Rev 22:18, 19 contains warnings of severe Divine judgment for disobedience. Further, Revelation is the only book of the New Testament to end with this kind of admonition and was the last New Testament book to be written. Therefore, these facts strongly suggest that Revelation was the last book of the canon and that the Bible is complete; to either add or delete would bring God's severe displeasure.
5. Finally, the early church, those closest in time to the apostles, believed that Revelation concluded God's inspired writings, the Scriptures.

So we can conclude, based on solid Biblical reasoning, that the canon is and will remain closed. There will be no future 67th book of the Bible.

WHERE DO WE STAND?

In April 1521, Martin Luther appeared before his ecclesiastical accusers at the Diet of Worms. They had given him the ultimatum to repudiate his unwavering faith in the sufficiency and perspicuity of the Scriptures. Luther is said to have responded, "Unless I am convicted by Scripture and plain reason—I do not accept the authority of popes and councils, for they have contradicted each other—my conscience is captive to the Word of God.... God help me! Here I stand."

Like Martin Luther, may we rise above the doubts within and confront the threats without when God's Word is assailed. God help us to be loyal contenders of the faith. Let us stand with God and the Scripture alone.

THE BIBLE

This book contains: the mind of God, the state of man, the way of salvation, the doom of sinners, and the happiness of believers.

Its doctrine is holy, its precepts are binding, its histories are true, and its decisions are immutable. Read it to be wise, believe it to be saved, and practice it to be holy.

It contains light to direct you, food to support you, and comfort to cheer you. It is the traveler's map, the pilgrim's staff, the pilot's compass, the soldier's sword, and the Christian's charter. Here heaven is open, and the gates of hell are disclosed.

Christ is the grand subject, our good its design, and the glory of God its end. It should fill the memory, rule the heart, and guide the feet.

Read it slowly, frequently, and prayerfully. It is a mine of wealth, health to the soul, and a river of pleasure. It is given to you here in this life, will be opened at the judgment, and is established forever.

It involves the highest responsibility, will reward the greatest labor, and condemn all who trifle with its contents.

> For this reason we also constantly thank God that when you received the word of God which you heard from us, you accepted it not as the word of men, but for what it really is, the word of God, which also performs its work in you who believe.
>
> 1 THESSALONIANS 2:13

THE PROGRESS OF REVELATION

Old Testament		
Book	Approximate Writing Date	Author
1. Job	Unknown	Anonymous
2. Genesis	1445–1405 B.C.	Moses
3. Exodus	1445–1405 B.C.	Moses
4. Leviticus	1445–1405 B.C.	Moses
5. Numbers	1445–1405 B.C.	Moses
6. Deuteronomy	1445–1405 B.C.	Moses
7. Psalms	1410–450 B.C.	Multiple Authors
8. Joshua	1405–1385 B.C.	Joshua
9. Judges	ca. 1043 B.C.	Samuel
10. Ruth	ca. 1030–1010 B.C.	Samuel (?)
11. Song of Solomon	971–965 B.C.	Solomon
12. Proverbs	971–686 B.C.	Solomon primarily
13. Ecclesiastes	940–931 B.C.	Solomon
14. 1 Samuel	931–722 B.C.	Anonymous
15. 2 Samuel	931–722 B.C.	Anonymous
16. Obadiah	850–840 B.C.	Obadiah
17. Joel	835–796 B.C.	Joel
18. Jonah	ca. 760 B.C.	Jonah
19. Amos	ca. 755 B.C.	Amos
20. Hosea	755–710 B.C.	Hosea
21. Micah	735–710 B.C.	Micah
22. Isaiah	700–681 B.C.	Isaiah
23. Nahum	ca. 650 B.C.	Nahum
24. Zephaniah	635–625 B.C.	Zephaniah
25. Habakkuk	615–605 B.C.	Habakkuk
26. Ezekiel	590–570 B.C.	Ezekiel
27. Lamentations	586 B.C.	Jeremiah
28. Jeremiah	586–570 B.C.	Jeremiah

29. 1 Kings	561–538 B.C.	Anonymous
30. 2 Kings	561–538 B.C.	Anonymous
31. Daniel	536–530 B.C.	Daniel
32. Haggai	ca. 520 B.C.	Haggai
33. Zechariah	480–470 B.C.	Zechariah
34. Ezra	457–444 B.C.	Ezra
35. 1 Chronicles	450–430 B.C.	Ezra (?)
36. 2 Chronicles	450–430 B.C.	Ezra (?)
37. Esther	450–331 B.C.	Anonymous
38. Malachi	433–424 B.C.	Malachi
39. Nehemiah	424–400 B.C.	Ezra

New Testament		
Book	**Approximate Writing Date**	**Author**
1. James	A.D. 44–49	James
2. Galatians	A.D. 49–50	Paul
3. Matthew	A.D. 50–60	Matthew
4. Mark	A.D. 50–60	Mark
5. 1 Thessalonians	A.D. 51	Paul
6. 2 Thessalonians	A.D. 51–52	Paul
7. 1 Corinthians	A.D. 55	Paul
8. 2 Corinthians	A.D. 55–56	Paul
9. Romans	A.D. 56	Paul
10. Luke	A.D. 60–61	Luke
11. Ephesians	A.D. 60–62	Paul
12. Philippians	A.D. 60–62	Paul
13. Colossians	A.D. 60–62	Paul
14. Philemon	A.D. 60–62	Paul
15. Acts	A.D. 62	Luke
16. 1 Timothy	A.D. 62–64	Paul
17. Titus	A.D. 62–64	Paul
18. 1 Peter	A.D. 64–65	Peter
19. 2 Timothy	A.D. 66–67	Paul
20. 2 Peter	A.D. 67–68	Peter
21. Hebrews	A.D. 67–69	Unknown
22. Jude	A.D. 68–70	Jude
23. John	A.D. 80–90	John
24. 1 John	A.D. 90–95	John
25. 2 John	A.D. 90–95	John
26. 3 John	A.D. 90–95	John
27. Revelation	A.D. 94–96	John

—— HOW TO STUDY——

THE BIBLE

Here are tips on how to get the most out of the study of this "divine handbook." These pointers will help answer the most crucial question of all, "How can a young man keep his way pure?" The psalmist responds, "By keeping it according to Your word" (Ps 119:9).

WHY IS IT IMPORTANT TO STUDY THE BIBLE?

Why is God's Word so important? Because it contains God's mind and will for your life (2Ti 3:16, 17). It is the only source of absolute divine authority for you as a servant of Jesus Christ.

It is infallible in its totality: "The law of the LORD is perfect, restoring the soul; the testimony of the LORD is sure, making wise the simple" (Ps 19:7).

It is inerrant in its parts: "Every word of God is tested; He is a shield to those who take refuge in Him. Do not add to His words or He will reprove you, and you will be proved a liar" (Pr 30:5, 6).

It is complete: "I testify to everyone who hears the words of the prophecy of this book: if anyone adds to them, God will add to him the plagues which are written in this book; and if anyone takes away from the words of the book of this prophecy, God will take away his part from the tree of life and from the holy city, which are written in this book." (Rev 22:18, 19).

It is authoritative and final: "Forever, O LORD, Your word is settled in heaven" (Ps 119:89).

It is totally sufficient for your needs: " … so that the man of God may be adequate, equipped for every good work" (2Ti 3:16, 17).

It will accomplish what it promises: "So will My word be which goes forth from My mouth; it will not return to Me empty, without accomplishing what I desire, and without succeeding in the matter for which I sent it" (Is 55:11).

It provides the assurance of your salvation: "He who is of God hears the words of God…" (Jn 8:47; cf. 20:31).

HOW WILL I BENEFIT FROM STUDYING THE BIBLE?

Millions of pages of material are printed every week. Thousands of new books are published each month. This would not be surprising to Solomon who said, " … be warned: the writing of many books is endless" (Ecc 12:12).

Even with today's wealth of books and computer helps, the Bible remains the only source of divine revelation and power that can sustain Christians in their "daily walk with God." Note these significant promises in the Scripture.

The Bible is the source of truth: "Sanctify them in the truth; Your word is truth" (Jn 17:17).

The Bible is the source of God's blessing when obeyed: "But He said, 'On the contrary, blessed are those who hear the word of God and observe it' " (Lk 11:28).

The Bible is the source of victory: " … the sword of the Spirit, which is the word of God" (Eph 6:17).

The Bible is the source of growth: " … like newborn babies, long for the pure milk of the word, so that by it you may grow" (1Pe 2:2).

The Bible is the source of power: "For I am not ashamed of the gospel, for it is the power of God for salvation to everyone who believes, to the Jew first and also to the Greek" (Ro 1:16).

The Bible is the source of guidance: "Your word is a lamp to my feet and a light to my path" (Ps 119:105).

WHAT SHOULD BE MY RESPONSE TO THE BIBLE?

Because the Bible is so important and because it provides unparalleled eternal benefits, then these should be your responses:

- Believe it (Jn 6:68, 69)
- Obey it (1Jn 2:5)
- Preach it (2Ti 4:2)
- Honor it (Job 23:12)
- Guard it (1Ti 6:20)
- Study it (Ezr 7:10)
- Love it (Ps 119:97)
- Fight for it (Jude 3)

WHO CAN STUDY THE BIBLE?

Not everyone can be a Bible student. Check yourself on these necessary qualifications for studying the Word with blessing:

- Are you saved by faith in Jesus Christ (1Co 2:14–16)?
- Are you hungering for God's Word (1Pe 2:2)?
- Are you searching God's Word with diligence (Ac 17:11)?
- Are you seeking holiness (1Pe 1:14–16)?
- Are you Spirit-filled (Eph 5:18)?

The most important question is the first. If you have never invited Jesus Christ to be your personal Savior and the Lord of your life, then your mind is blinded by Satan to God's truth (2Co 4:4).

If Christ is your need, stop reading right now and, in your own words with prayer, turn away from sin and turn toward God: "For by grace you have been saved through faith; and that not of yourselves, it is the gift of God; not as a result of works, so that no one may boast" (Eph 2:8, 9).

WHAT ARE THE BASICS OF BIBLE STUDY?

Personal Bible study, in precept, is simple. I want to share with you 5 steps to Bible study which will give you a pattern to follow.

STEP 1—READING.

Read a passage of Scripture repeatedly until you understand its theme, meaning the main truth of the passage. Isaiah said, "To whom would He teach knowledge, and to whom would He interpret the message? Those *just* weaned from milk? Those *just* taken from the breast? For He says, 'Order on order, order on order, line on line, line on line, a little here, a little there' " (Is 28:9, 10).

Develop a plan on how you will approach reading through the Bible. Unlike most books, you will probably not read it straight through from cover to cover. There are many good Bible reading plans available, but here is one that I have found helpful.

Read through the Old Testament at least once a year. As you read, note in the margins any truths you particularly want to remember, and write down separately anything you do not immediately understand. Often as you read you will find that many questions are answered by the text itself. The questions to which you cannot find answers become the starting points for more in-depth study using commentaries or other reference tools.

Follow a different plan for reading the New Testament. Read one book at a time repetitiously for a month or more. This will help you to retain what is in the New Testament and not always have to depend on a concordance to find things.

If you want to try this, begin with a short book, such as 1 John, and read it through in one sitting every day for 30 days. At the end of that time, you will know what is in the book. Write on index cards the major theme of each chapter. By referring to the cards as you do your daily reading, you will begin to remember the content of each chapter. In fact, you will develop a visual perception of the book in your mind.

Divide longer books into short sections and read each section daily for 30 days. For example, the gospel of John contains 21 chapters. Divide it into 3 sections of 7 chapters. At the end of 90 days, you will finish John. For variety, alternate short and long books, and in less than 3 years you will have finished the entire New Testament—and you will really know it!

STEP 2—INTERPRETING.

In Ac 8:30, Philip asked the Ethiopian eunuch, "Do you understand what you are reading?" Or put another way, "What does the Bible mean by what it says?" It is not enough to read the text and jump directly to the application; we must first determine what it means, otherwise the application may be incorrect.

As you read Scripture, always keep in mind one simple question: "What does this mean?" To answer that question requires the use of the most basic principle of interpretation, called the analogy of faith, which tells the reader to "interpret the Bible with the Bible." Letting the Holy Spirit be your teacher (1Jn 2:27), search the Scripture He has authored, using cross references, comparative passages, concordances, indexes, and other helps. For those passages that yet remain unclear, consult your pastor or godly men who have written in that particular area.

ERRORS TO AVOID

As you interpret Scripture, several common errors should be avoided.

1. Do not draw any conclusions at the price of proper interpretation. That is, do not make the Bible say what you want it to say, but rather let it say what God intended when He wrote it.
2. Avoid superficial interpretation. You have heard people say, "To me, this passage means," or "I feel it is saying...." The first step in interpreting the Bible is to recognize the four gaps we have to bridge: language, culture, geography, and history (see below).
3. Do not spiritualize the passage. Interpret and understand the passage in its normal, literal, historical, grammatical sense, just as you would understand any other piece of literature you were reading today.

GAPS TO BRIDGE

The books of the Bible were written many centuries ago. For us to understand today what God was communicating then, there are several gaps that need to be bridged: the language gap, the cultural gap, the geographical gap, and the historical gap. Proper interpretation, therefore, takes time and disciplined effort.

1. **Language.** The Bible was originally written in Greek, Hebrew, and Aramaic. Often, understanding the meaning of a word or phrase in the original language can be the key to correctly interpreting a passage of Scripture.
2. **Culture.** The culture gap can be tricky. Some people try to use cultural differences to explain away the more difficult biblical commands. Realize that Scripture must first be viewed in the context of the culture in which it was written. Without an understanding of first-century Jewish culture, it is difficult to understand the gospels. Acts and the Epistles must be read in light of the Greek and Roman cultures.
3. **Geography.** A third gap that needs to be closed is the geography gap. Biblical geography makes the Bible come alive. A good Bible atlas is an invaluable reference tool that can help you comprehend the geography of the Holy Land.
4. **History.** We must also bridge the history gap. Unlike the scriptures of most other world religions, the Bible contains the records of actual historical persons and events. An understanding of Bible history will help us place the people and events in it in their proper historical perspective. A good Bible dictionary or Bible encyclopedia is useful here, as are basic historical studies.

PRINCIPLES TO UNDERSTAND

Four principles should guide us as we interpret the Bible: literal, historical, grammatical, and synthesis.

1. **The Literal Principle.** Scripture should be understood in its literal, normal, and natural sense. While the Bible does contain figures of speech and symbols, they were intended to convey literal truth. In general, however, the Bible speaks in literal terms, and we must allow it to speak for itself.
2. **The Historical Principle.** This means that we interpret a passage in its historical context. We must ask what the text meant to the people to whom it was first written. In this way we can develop a proper contextual understanding of the original intent of Scripture.
3. **The Grammatical Principle.** This requires that we understand the basic grammatical structure of each sentence in the original language. To whom do the pronouns refer? What is the tense of the main verb? You will find that when you ask some simple questions like those, the meaning of the text immediately becomes clearer.
4. **The Synthesis Principle.** This is what the Reformers called the *analogia scriptura*. It means that the Bible does not contradict itself. If we arrive at an interpretation of a pas-

sage that contradicts a truth taught elsewhere in the Scriptures, our interpretation cannot be correct. Scripture must be compared with Scripture to discover its full meaning.

STEP 3—EVALUATING.

You have been reading and asking the question, "What does the Bible say?" Then you have interpreted, asking the question, "What does the Bible mean?" Now it is time to consult others to ensure that you have the proper interpretation. Remember, the Bible will never contradict itself.

Read Bible introductions, commentaries, and background books which will enrich your thinking through that illumination which God has given to other men and to you through their books. In your evaluation, be a true seeker. Be one who accepts the truth of God's Word even though it may cause you to change what you always have believed, or cause you to alter your life pattern.

STEP 4—APPLYING.

The next question is: "How does God's truth penetrate and change my own life?" Studying Scripture without allowing it to penetrate to the depths of your soul would be like preparing a banquet without eating it. The bottom-line question to ask is, "How do the divine truths and principles contained in any passage apply to me in terms of my attitude and actions?"

Jesus made this promise to those who would carry their personal Bible study through to this point: "If you know these things, you are blessed if you do them" (Jn 13:17).

Having read and interpreted the Bible, you should have a basic understanding of what the Bible says, and what it means by what it says. But studying the Bible does not stop there. The ultimate goal should be to let it speak to you and enable you to grow spiritually. That requires personal application.

Bible study is not complete until we ask ourselves, "What does this mean for my life and how can I practically apply it?" We must take the knowledge we have gained from our reading and interpretation and draw out the practical principles that apply to our personal lives.

If there is a command to be obeyed, we obey it. If there is a promise to be embraced, we claim it. If there is a warning to be followed, we heed it. This is the ultimate step: we submit to Scripture and let it transform our lives. If you skip this step, you will never enjoy your Bible study, and the Bible will never change your life.

Here is the spring where waters flow,
  To quench our heat of sin:
Here is the tree where truth doth grow,
  To lead our lives therein:
Here is the judge that stints the strife,
  When men's devices fail:
Here is the bread that feeds the life
  That death cannot assail.
The tidings of salvation dear,
  Comes to our ears from hence:
The fortress of our faith is here,
  And shield of our defense.
Then be not like the swine that hath
  A pearl at his desire,
And takes more pleasure from the trough
  And wallowing in the mire.
Read not this book in any case,
  But with a single eye:
Read not but first desire God's grace,
  To understand thereby.
Pray still in faith with this respect,
  To bear good fruit therein,
That knowledge may bring this effect,
  To mortify your sin.
Then happy you shall be in all your life,
What so to you befalls:
Yes, double happy you shall be,
  When God by death you calls.

(From the first Bible printed in Scotland—1576)

STEP 5—CORRELATING.

This last stage connects the doctrine you have learned in a particular passage or book with divine truths and principles taught elsewhere in the Bible to form the big picture. Always keep in mind that the Bible is one book in 66 parts, and it contains a number of truths and principles, taught over and over again in a variety of ways and circumstances. By correlating and cross-referencing, you will begin to build a sound doctrinal foundation by which to live.

WHAT NOW?

The psalmist said, "How blessed is the man who does not walk in the counsel of the wicked, nor stand in the path of sinners, nor sit in the seat of scoffers! But his delight is in the law of the LORD, and in His law he meditates day and night" (Ps 1:1, 2).

It is not enough just to study the Bible. We must meditate upon it. In a very real sense we are giving our brain a bath; we are washing it in the purifying solution of God's Word.

> This book of the law shall not depart from your mouth, but you shall meditate on it day and night, so that you may be careful to do according to all that is written in it; for then you will make your way prosperous, and then you will have success.
>
> JOSHUA 1:8

— PREFACE TO THE —

NEW AMERICAN STANDARD BIBLE

Scriptural Promise

"The grass withers, the flower fades, but the word of our God stands forever."
ISAIAH 40:8

The New American Standard Bible has been produced with the conviction that the words of Scripture as originally penned in the Hebrew, Aramaic, and Greek were inspired by God. Since they are the eternal Word of God, the Holy Scriptures speak with fresh power to each generation, to give wisdom that leads to salvation, that men may serve Christ to the glory of God.

The purpose of the Editorial Board in making this translation was to adhere as closely as possible to the original languages of the Holy Scriptures, and to make the translation in a fluent and readable style according to current English usage.

THE FOURFOLD AIM OF THE LOCKMAN FOUNDATION

1. These publications shall be true to the original Hebrew, Aramaic, and Greek.
2. They shall be grammatically correct.
3. They shall be understandable.
4. They shall give the Lord Jesus Christ His proper place, the place which the Word gives Him; therefore, no work will ever be personalized.

PREFACE TO THE NEW AMERICAN STANDARD BIBLE

In the history of English Bible translations, the King James Version is the most prestigious. This time-honored version of 1611, itself a revision of the Bishops' Bible of 1568, became the basis for the English Revised Version appearing in 1881 (New Testament) and 1885 (Old Testament). The American counterpart of this last work was published in 1901 as the American Standard Version. The ASV, a product of both British and American scholarship, has been highly regarded for its scholarship and accuracy. Recognizing the values of the American Standard Version, The Lockman Foundation felt an urgency to preserve these and other lasting values of the ASV by incorporating recent discoveries of Hebrew and Greek textual sources and by rendering it into more current English. Therefore, in 1959 a new translation project was launched, based on the time-honored principles of translation of the ASV and KJV. The result is the New American Standard Bible.

Translation work for the NASB was begun in 1959. In the preparation of this work numerous other translations have been consulted along with the linguistic tools and literature of biblical scholarship. Decisions about English renderings were made by consensus of a team composed of educators and pastors. Subsequently, review and evaluation by other Hebrew and Greek scholars outside the Editorial Board were sought and carefully considered.

The Editorial Board has continued to function since publication of the complete Bible in 1971. This edition of the NASB represents revisions and refinements recommended over the last several years as well as thorough research based on modern English usage.

PRINCIPLES OF TRANSLATION

Modern English Usage: The attempt has been made to render the grammar and terminology in contemporary English. When it was felt that the word-for-word literalness was unacceptable to the modern reader, a change was made in the direction of a more current English idiom. In the instances where this has been done, the more literal rendering has been indicated in the notes. There are a few exceptions to this procedure. In particular, frequently "And" is not translated at the beginning of sentences because of differences in style between ancient and modern writing. Punctuation is a relatively modern invention, and ancient writers often linked most of their sentences with "and" or other connectives. Also, the Hebrew idiom "answered and said" is sometimes reduced to "answered" or "said" as demanded by the context. For current English the idiom "it came about that" has not been translated in the New Testament except when a major transition is needed.

ALTERNATIVE READINGS:
In addition to the more literal renderings, notations have been made to include alternate translations, reading of variant manuscripts and explanatory equivalents of the text. Only such notations have been used as have been felt justified in assisting the reader's comprehension of the terms used by the original author.

HEBREW TEXT:
In the present translation the latest edition of Rudolf Kittel's BIBLIA HEBRAICA has been employed together with the most recent light from lexicography, cognate languages, and the Dead Sea Scrolls.

HEBREW TENSES:
Consecution of tenses in Hebrew remains a puzzling factor in translation. The translators have been guided by the requirements of a literal translation, the sequence of tenses, and the immediate and broad contexts.

THE PROPER NAME OF GOD IN THE OLD TESTAMENT:
In the Scriptures, the name of God is most significant and understandably so. It is inconceivable to think of spiritual matters without a proper designation for the Supreme Deity. Thus the most common name for the Deity is God, a translation of the original *Elohim*. One of the titles for God is Lord, a translation of *Adonai*. There is yet another name which is particularly assigned to God as His special or proper name, that is, the four letters YHWH (Exodus 3:14 and Isaiah 42:8). This name has not been pronounced by the Jews because of reverence for the great sacredness of the divine name. Therefore, it has been consistently translated LORD. The only exception to this translation of YHWH is when it occurs in immediate proximity to the word Lord, that is, *Adonai*. In that case it is regularly translated GOD in order to avoid confusion.

It is known that for many years YHWH has been transliterated as Yahweh, however no complete certainty attaches to this pronunciation.

GREEK TEXT:
Consideration was given to the latest available manuscripts with a view to determining the best Greek text. In most instances the 26th edition of Eberhard Nestle's NOVUM TESTAMENTUM GRAECE was followed.

GREEK TENSES:
A careful distinction has been made in the treatment of the Greek aorist tense (usually translated as the English past, "He did") and the Greek imperfect tense (normally rendered either as English past progressive, "He was doing"; or, if inceptive, as "He began to do" or "He started to do"; or else if customary past, as "He used to do"). "Began" is italicized if it renders an imperfect tense, in order to distinguish it from the Greek verb for "begin." In some contexts the difference between the Greek imperfect and the English past is conveyed better by the choice of vocabulary or by other words in the context, and in such cases the Greek imperfect may be rendered as a simple past tense (e.g. "had an illness for many years" would be preferable to "was having an illness for many years" and would be understood in the same way).

On the other hand, not all aorists have been rendered as English pasts ("He did"), for some of them are clearly to be rendered as English perfects ("He has done"), or even as past perfects ("He had done"), judging from the context in which they occur. Such aorists have been rendered as perfects or past perfects in this translation.

As for the distinction between aorist and present imperatives, the translators have usually rendered these imperatives in the customary manner, rather than attempting any such fine distinction as "Begin to do!" (for the aorist imperative), or, "Continually do!" (for the present imperative).

As for sequence of tenses, the translators took care to follow English rules rather than Greek in translating Greek presents, imperfects and aorists. Thus, where English says, "We knew that he was doing," Greek puts it, "We knew that he does"; similarly, "We knew that he had done" is the Greek, "We knew that he did." Likewise, the English, "When he had come, they met him," is represented in Greek by, "When he came, they met him." In all cases a consistent transfer has been made from the Greek tense in the subordinate clause to the appropriate tense in English.

In the rendering of negative questions introduced by the particle *mē* (which always expects the answer "No") the wording has been altered from a mere, "Will he not do this?" to a more accurate, "He will not do this, will he?"

THE LOCKMAN FOUNDATION

—EXPLANATION OF—

GENERAL FORMAT

QUOTATION MARKS are used in the text in accordance with modern English usage.

ITALICS are used in the text to indicate words which are not found in the original Hebrew, Aramaic, or Greek but implied by it. Italics are used in the marginal notes to signify alternate readings for the text. Roman text in the marginal alternate readings is the same as italics in the Bible text.

"THOU," "THEE," AND "THY" are not used in this edition and have been rendered as "YOU" and "YOUR."

NOTES AND CROSS REFERENCES are placed below the text on the page and listed under verse numbers to which they refer. *Superior lower case, italic letters* refer to literal renderings, alternate translations, or explanations. *Superior upper case, bold letters* refer to cross references. Cross references in italics are parallel passages.

SMALL CAPS in the New Testament are used in the text to indicate Old Testament quotations or obvious references to Old Testament texts. Variations of Old Testament wording are found in New Testament citations depending on whether the New Testament writer translated from a Hebrew text, used existing Greek or Aramaic translations, or paraphrased the material. It should be noted that modern rules for the indication of direct quotation were not used in biblical times; thus, the ancient writer would use exact quotations or references to quotation without specific indication of such.

14 "You are [A]the light of the world. A city set on a
[a]hill cannot be hidden; 15 [A]nor does *anyone* light a
lamp and put it under a [a]basket, but on the lampstand, and it gives light to all who are in the house.
16 Let your light shine before men in such a way that
they may [A]see your good works, and [B]glorify your
Father who is in heaven.
17 "Do not think that I came to abolish the [A]Law
or the Prophets; I did not come to abolish but to
fulfill. 18 For truly I say to you, [A]until heaven and
earth pass away, not [a]the smallest letter or stroke
shall pass from the Law until all is accomplished.
19 Whoever then annuls one of the least of these
commandments, and teaches [a]others *to do* the same,
shall be called least [A]in the kingdom of heaven; but
whoever [b]keeps and teaches *them*, he shall be called
great in the kingdom of heaven.
20 "For I say to you that unless your [A]righteous-
ness surpasses *that* of the scribes and Pharisees,
you will not enter the kingdom of heaven.

PERSONAL RELATIONSHIPS

21 "[A]You have heard that [a]the ancients were told,
'[B]YOU SHALL NOT COMMIT MURDER' and 'Whoever
commits murder shall be [b]liable to [c]the court.' 22 But

5:14 [a]Or *mountain* [A]Prov 4:18; John 8:12; 9:5; 12:36 5:15 [a]Or *peck-measure* [A]Mark
5:18 [a]Lit *one iota* (Heb yodh) or *one projection of a letter* (serif) [A]Matt 24:35; Luke 16:17
was said to the ancients [b]Or *guilty before* [A]Matt 5:27, 33, 38, 43 [B]Ex 20:13; Deut 5:17
Aram *reqa* [c]Lit *the Sanhedrin* [d]Lit *Gehenna of fire* [A]Deut 16:18; 2 Chr 19:5f [B]Matt 10:
23:1; 24:20 [C]Matt 5:29f; 10:28; 18:9; 23:15, 33; Mark 9:43ff; Luke 12:5; James 3:6 5
Luke 12:58 5:26 [a]Lit *quadrans* (equaling two mites); i.e. 1/64 of a daily wage [A]Luk
Job 31:1; Matt 15:19; James 1:14, 15 5:29 [a]I.e. sin [b]Lit *that one…be lost* [C]L

5:16 light shine. A godly life gives convincing testimony of the saving power of God. That brings Him glory. Cf. 1Pe 2:12.

5:17 Do not think … abolish the Law or the Prophets. Jesus was neither giving a new law nor modifying the old, but rather explaining the true significance of the moral content of Moses' law and the rest of the OT. "The Law and the Prophets" speaks of the entirety of the OT Scriptures, not the rabbinical interpretations of them. fulfill. This speaks of fulfillment in the same sense that prophecy is fulfilled. Christ was indicating that He is the fulfillment of the law in all its aspects. He fulfilled the moral law by keeping it perfectly. He fulfilled the ceremonial law by being the embodiment of everything the law's types and symbols pointed to. And He fulfilled the

mark or an apostrophe.
extension on a Heb. let
modern typefaces.

5:19 shall be callec
called great. The consec
or teaching disobedience
is to be called least in the
(see note on Jas 2:10). Det
kingdom of heaven is en
tive (cf. Mt 20:23), and Je
will hold those in lowest
Word in low esteem. The
believers who disobey,
God's law (see note on
does not refer to loss
from the fact that, thou
called least, they will sti
of heaven. The positive

that these stones become bread." [4] But He answered
and said, "It is written, '[A]MAN SHALL NOT LIVE ON
BREAD ALONE, BUT ON EVERY WORD THAT PROCEEDS
OUT OF THE MOUTH OF GOD.' "
[5] Then the devil *took Him into [A]the holy city
and had Him stand on the pinnacle of the temple,
[6] and *said to Him, "If You are the Son of God, throw
Yourself down; for it is written,

'[A]HE WILL COMMAND HIS ANGELS
CONCERNING YOU';

and

'ON *their* HANDS THEY WILL
BEAR YOU UP,
SO THAT YOU WILL NOT STRIKE YOUR
FOOT AGAINST A STONE.' "

[7] Jesus said to him, "[a]On the other hand, it is written, '[A]YOU SHALL NOT PUT THE LORD YOUR GOD TO
THE TEST.' "
[8] [A]Again, the devil *took Him to a very high
mountain and *showed Him all the kingdoms of
the world and their glory; [9] and he said to Him,
"[A]All these things I will give You, if You fall down
and [a]worship me." [10] Then Jesus *said to him, "Go,
Satan! For it is written, '[A]YOU SHALL WORSHIP THE
LORD YOUR GOD, AND [a]SERVE HIM ONLY.' " [11] Then
the devil *left Him; and behold, [A]angels came and
began to minister to Him.

4:4 [A]Deut 8:3 4:5 [A]Neh 11:1, 18; Dan 9:24; Matt 27:53 4:6 [A]Ps 91:11, 12 4:7 [a]Lit
[A]1 Cor 10:20f 4:10 [a]*Or fulfill religious duty to Him* [A]Deut 6:13; 10:20 4:11 [A]Ma
[B]Mark 1:14; Luke 4:14; John 1:43; 2:11 4:13 [A]Matt 11:23; Mark 1:21; 2:1; Luke 4:23, 31; Joh
4:16 [A]Is 9:2; 60:1-3; Luke 2:32 4:17 [a]*Or proclaim* [A]Mark 1:14, 15 [B]Matt 3:2 4:18 [A]J
John 6:1 [C]Matt 10:2; 16:18; John 1:40-42 4:19 [a]Lit *Come here after Me* 4:21 [a]*Or Jc*

4:4 It is written. All 3 of Jesus' replies to the Devil were taken from Deuteronomy. This one, from Dt 8:3, states that God allowed Israel to hunger, so that He might feed them with manna and teach them to trust Him to provide for them. So the verse is directly applicable to Jesus' circumstances and a fitting reply to Satan's temptation. every word that proceeds out of the mouth of God. A more important source of sustenance than food, it nurtures our spiritual needs in a way that benefits us eternally, rather than merely pro-

of this world" (2Co 4:4). T
in his power (1Jn 5:19). Th
10:13 (*see note there*), wh
controlled the kingdom
demon is called the pri
of Persia.

4:10 For it is writte
citing and paraphrasing
these relate to the Israe
periences. Christ, like th
wilderness to be tested
them. He withstood eve

PERSONAL PRONOUNS are capitalized when pertaining to Deity.

ASTERISKS are used to mark verbs that are historical presents in the Greek which have been translated with an English past tense in order to conform to modern usage. The translators recognized that in some contexts the present tense seems more unexpected and unjustified to the English reader than a past tense would have been. But Greek authors frequently used the present tense for the sake of heightened vividness, thereby transporting their readers in imagination to the actual scene at the time of occurrence. However, the translators felt that it would be wise to change these historical presents to English past tenses.

ABBREVIATIONS

AND SPECIAL MARKINGS

A.D.	in the year of our Lord
a.k.a.	also known as
A.M.	midnight to noon
ANE	Ancient Near Eastern
Arab.	Arabic
Aram.	Aramaic
B.C.	before Christ
ca.	about, approximately
cf.	compare
chap., chaps.	chapter, chapters
contra.	contrast
DOL	Day of the Lord
DSS	Dead Sea Scrolls
E	East
e.g.	for example
et al.	and others
etc.	and so forth
fem.	feminine
f., ff.	following verse, following verses
Gr.	Greek
Heb.	Hebrew
i.e.	that is
Kt.	Kethib (literally, in Aramaic, "written")—the written words of the Hebrew Old Testament preserved by the Masoretes (see "Qr.")
Lat.	Latin
lit.	literally
LXX	Septuagint—an ancient translation of the Old Testament into Greek
Macc.	1 and 2 Maccabees—two historical books in the noncanonical Apocrypha
masc.	masculine
mg	Refers to a marginal reading on another verse
mi.	mile/miles
ms., mss.	manuscript, manuscripts
M.T.	Masoretic text
Mt.	mount
N	North
NT	New Testament
Or	An alternate translation justified by the Hebrew, Aramaic, or Greek
OT	Old Testament
pl.	plural
P.M.	noon to midnight
Qr.	Qere (literally, in Aramaic, "read")—certain words read aloud, differing from the written words, in the Masoretic tradition of the Hebrew Old Testament (see "Kt.")
S	South
Sam.	Samaritan Pentateuch—a variant Hebrew edition of the books of Moses, used by the Samaritan community
sing.	singular
Syr.	Syriac
Tg.	Targum—an Aramaic paraphrase of the Old Testament
v., vv.	verse, verses
vss.	versions—ancient translations of the Bible
Vg.	Vulgate—an ancient translation of the Bible into Latin, translated and edited by Jerome
W	West
[ ]	In text, brackets indicate words probably not in the original writings
[ ]	In margin, brackets indicate references to a name, place or thing similar to, but not identical with that in the text

KEY TO PARENTHETICAL REFERENCES

( )	exact text
(cf.)	corroborative text
(see)	amplifying/clarifying text
(contra.)	contrasting text

THE

OLD TESTAMENT

INTRODUCTION TO THE

PENTATEUCH

The first 5 books of the Bible (Genesis, Exodus, Leviticus, Numbers, Deuteronomy) form a complete literary unit called the Pentateuch, meaning "five scrolls." The five independent books of the Pentateuch were written as an unbroken unity in content and historical sequence, with each succeeding book beginning where the former left off.

Genesis' first words, "In the beginning God created ..." (Ge 1:1) imply the reality of God's eternal or "before time" existence and announce the spectacular transition to time and space. While the exact date of creation cannot be determined, it certainly would be estimated to be thousands of years ago, not millions. Starting with Abraham (ca. 2165–1990 B.C.) in Ge 11, this book of beginnings spans over 300 years to the death of Joseph in Egypt (ca. 1804 B.C.). There is then another gap of almost 300 years until the birth of Moses in Egypt (ca. 1525 B.C.; Ex 2).

Exodus begins with the words "Now these are the names" (Ex 1:1), listing those of the family of Jacob who went down to Egypt to be with Joseph toward the end of Genesis (Ge 46ff.). The second book of the Pentateuch, which records the escape of the Israelites from Egypt, concludes when the cloud which led the people through the wilderness descends upon the newly constructed tabernacle.

The first Hebrew words of Leviticus may be translated, "Then the LORD called to Moses" (Lv 1:1). From the cloud of God's Presence in the tabernacle of meeting (Lv 1:1), God summons Moses in order to prescribe to him the ceremonial law which told Israel how they must approach their Holy Lord. Leviticus concludes with, "These are the commandments which the LORD commanded Moses for the sons of Israel at Mount Sinai" (Lv 27:34).

Numbers, much like Leviticus, commences with God commissioning Moses at the tabernacle of meeting, this time to take a census in preparation for war against Israel's enemies. The book's title in the Hebrew Bible accurately represents the content—"Wilderness." Due to lack of trust in God, Israel did not want to engage its enemies militarily in order to claim the Promised Land. After forty additional years in the wilderness for their rebellion, Israel arrived on the plains of Moab.

Despite the fact that "It is eleven days' *journey* from Horeb by the way of Mount Seir to Kadesh-barnea" (Dt 1:2), the journey took Israel forty years due to their rebellion against God. Moses preached the book of Deuteronomy as a sermon on the Plains of Moab in preparation for God's people to enter the land of covenant promise (Ge 12:1–3). The title Deuteronomy is from the Gr. phrase *deuteros nomos*, meaning "second law." The book focuses on the restatement and, to some extent, the reapplication of the law to Israel's new circumstances.

Moses was the human author of the Pentateuch (Ex 17:14; 24:4; Nu 33:1, 2; Dt 31:9; Jos 1:8; 2Ki 21:8); thus, another title for the collection is "The Books of Moses." Through Moses, God revealed Himself, His former works, Israel's family history, and its role in His plan of redemption for mankind. The Pentateuch is foundational to all the rest of Scripture.

Quoted or alluded to thousands of times in the OT and in the NT, the Pentateuch was Israel's first inspired body of Scripture. For many years, this alone was Israel's Bible. Another common title for this section of Scripture is *Torah* or Law, nomenclature which looks at the didactic nature of these books. The Israelites were to meditate upon it (Jos 1:8), teach it to their children (Dt 6:4–8), and read it publicly (Ne 8:1ff.). Just before his death and Israel's move into the Promised Land, Moses set forth the process by which public reading would make its way into human hearts and change their relationship with God, and ultimately their conduct:

> Assemble the people, the men and the women and the children and the alien who is in your town, so that they may hear and learn and fear the LORD your God, and be careful to observe all the words of this law.
>
> DEUTERONOMY 31:12

The relationships between the commands are important. The people must: 1) gather to hear the law in order to learn what is required of them and what it has to say about God; 2) learn about the Lord in order to fear Him based on a correct understanding of who He is; and 3) fear God in order to be correctly motivated to obedience and good works. Good works performed for any other reason will be improperly motivated. The priests taught the law to the families (Mal 2:4–7), and the parents instructed the children within the home (Dt 6:4ff.). Instruction in the law, in short, would provide the right foundation for the OT believer's relationship with God.

Because the Israelites' knowledge of the world in which they lived came through the Egyptians, as well as their ancestors the Mesopotamians, there was much confusion about the creation of the world, how it got to its present state, and how Israel had come into existence. Ge 1–11 helped Israel understand the origin and nature of creation, human labor, sin, marriage, murder, death, bigamy, judgment, the multiplicity of languages, cultures, etc. These chapters established the worldview which explained the remainder of Israel's first Bible, the Pentateuch.

The later portion of Genesis explained to Israel who they were, including the purpose God had for them as a people. In Ge 12:1–3, God had appeared to Abraham and made a three-fold promise to give them a land, descendants, and blessing. Years later, in a ceremony typical to Abraham's culture, God recast the three-fold promise into a covenant (Ge 15:7ff.). The remainder of Genesis treats the fulfillment of all three promises, but focuses especially on the seed or descendants. The barrenness of each of the patriarchs' chosen wives taught Israel the importance of trust and patience in waiting for children from God.

The rest of the Pentateuch looks at the way in which the promises of Ge 12:1–3 expand in the Abrahamic Covenant and achieve their initial stages of fulfillment. Exodus and Leviticus focus more on the blessing of relationship with God. In Exodus, Israel meets the God of their fathers and is led forth by Him from Egypt to the Promised Land. Leviticus underscores the meticulous care with which the people and priests were to approach God in worship and every dimension of their lives. Holiness and cleanness come together in simple and practical ways. Numbers and Deuteronomy focus on the journey to and preparation for the Land. The Pentateuch treats many issues related to Israel's relationship with their God. But the underlying theme of the Pentateuch is the initial, unfolding fulfillments of God's promises made to Abraham.

CHRONOLOGY OF THE OLD TESTAMENT PATRIARCHS AND JUDGES

2075 2050 2025 2000 1975 1950 1925 1900 1875 1850 1825 1800 1775 1750 1725 1700 1675 1650 1625 1600 1575
PATRIARCHS & JUDGES
Abraham
Ishmael
Isaac
Jacob
Levi
Joseph
EGYPTIAN RULERS
Neb-ku-re
(10th Dynasty at Heracleoplis began 2133 B.B.)
Mery-ku-re
Menthu-hotep III
MIDDLE KINGDOM (12th Dynasty)
Menthu-hotep II
Senusret I
Senusret II
Amenemhet III
Queen Sebek-neferu-re
(Period of Political disintegration in Egypt)
Hyksos kings at Avaris (Zoan)
Amenemhet I
Amenemhet II
Senusret III
Amenemhet IV
(11th Dynasty at Thebes began 2134 B.C.

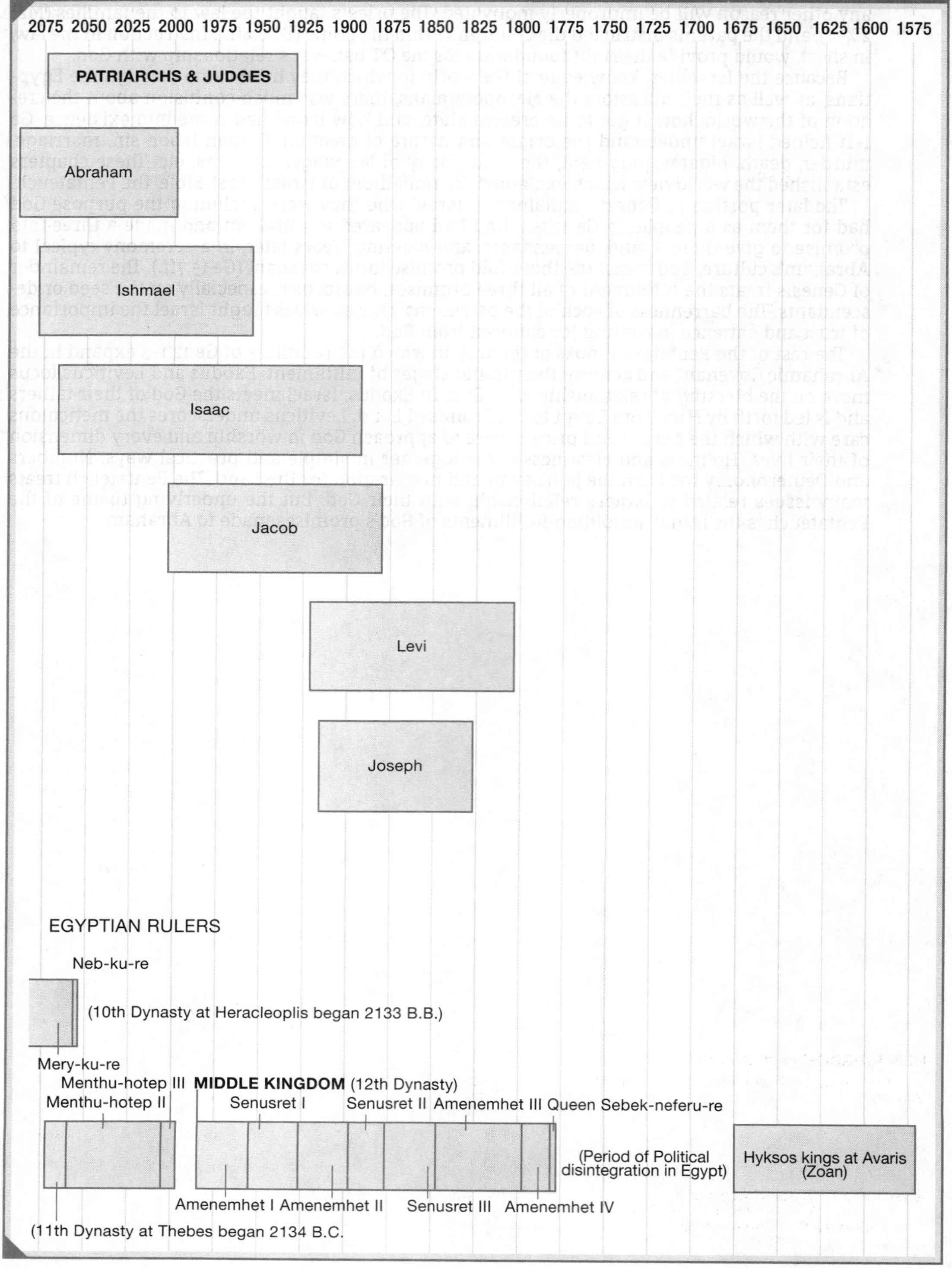

CHRONOLOGY OF THE OLD TESTAMENT PATRIARCHS AND JUDGES

1550 1525 1500 1475 1450 1425 1400 1375 1350 1325 1300 1275 1250 1225 1200 1175 1150 1125 1100 1075 1050

Aaron

Cushan-rishathaim of Mesopotamia
Eglon of Moad
Deborah & Barak
Tola
Jephthah
Elon

Moses
Othniel
Ehud
Gideon
Jair

1445
The Exodus
Joshua
Elders
Jabin of Hazor (in North)
Abimelech
Ibzan
Abdon

Birth of Eli
Eli

Shamgar

1105
Birth of Samuel
Samuel

Joel & Abijah

Samson (West)

NEW KINGDOM (18th Dynasty)
Thutmose I
Amose I
Thutmose III
(Pharaoh of The Oppression)
Amenhotep III
Amenhotep IV
(19th Dynasty)
Rameses I
Sethi I
Merneptah
(20th Dynasty)
Rameses III
Rameses II
Period of political weakness in Egypt (Rameses IV-XI)
Amenhotep I
Queen Hatshepsut & Thutmose III
Thutmose II
Amenhotep II
(Pharaoh of The Exodus)
Thutmose IV
Ay
Tutankhamon
Horemheb
(Period of Confusion)

A HARMONY OF THE BOOKS OF SAMUEL, KINGS, AND CHRONICLES

I. THE KINGSHIP OF GOD (1Sa 1:1–7:17; 1Ch 1:1–9:44)
- A. Genealogical Tables (1Ch 1:1–9:44)
  - 1. Genealogies of the Patriarchs (1Ch 1:1–2:2)
  - 2. Genealogies of the Tribes of Israel (1Ch 2:3–9:44)
- B. The Close of the Theocracy (1Sa 1:1–7:17)
  - 1. The Early Life of Samuel (1Sa 1:1–4:1a)
    - a. Samuel's birth and infancy (1Sa 1:1–2:11)
    - b. Samuel at Shiloh (1Sa 2:12–4:1a)
  - 2. The Period of National Disaster (1Sa 4:1b–7:2)
    - a. Israel's defeat and loss of the ark (1Sa 4:1b–11a)
    - b. Fall of the house of Eli (1Sa 4:11b–22)
    - c. The ark of God (1Sa 5:1–7:2)
  - 3. Samuel, the Last of the Judges (1Sa 7:3–17)

II. THE KINGSHIP OF SAUL (1Sa 8:1–31:13; 1Ch 10:1–14)
- A. Establishment of Saul as First King of Israel (1Sa 8:1–10:27)
- B. Saul's Reign until His Rejection (1Sa 11:1–15:35)
- C. The Decline of Saul and the Rise of David (1Sa 16:1–31:13)
  - 1. David's Early History (1Sa 16:1–23)
  - 2. David's Advancement and Saul's Growing Jealousy (1Sa 17:1–20:42)
    - a. David and Goliath (1Sa 17:1–51)
    - b. David at the court of Saul (1Sa 18:1–20:42)
  - 3. David's Life of Exile (1Sa 21:1–28:2)
    - a. David's flight (1Sa 21:1–22:5)
    - b. Saul's vengeance on the priests of Nob (1Sa 22:6–23)
    - c. David's rescue of Keilah (1Sa 23:1–13)
    - d. David's last meeting with Jonathan (1Sa 23:14–18)
    - e. David's betrayal by the Ziphites (1Sa 23:19–24a)
    - f. David's escape from Saul in the Wilderness of Maon (1Sa 23:24b–28)
    - g. David's flight from Saul; David's mercy on Saul's life in the cave (1Sa 23:29–24:22)
    - h. Samuel's death (1Sa 25:1)
    - i. David's wedding to Abigail (1Sa 25:2–44)
    - j. David's mercy on Saul's life again (1Sa 26:1–25)
    - k. David's joining with the Philistines (1Sa 27:1–28:2)
  - 4. Saul's Downfall in War with the Philistines (1Sa 28:3–31:13; 1Ch 10:1–14)
    - a. Saul's fear of the Philistines (1Sa 28:3–6)
    - b. Saul's visit to the witch of En-dor (1Sa 28:7–25)
    - c. David leaves the Philistines; defeats the Amalekites (1Sa 29:1–30:31)
    - d. Saul and his sons slain (1Sa 31:1–13; 1Ch 10:1–14)

III. THE KINGSHIP OF DAVID (2Sa 1:1–24:25; 1Ki 1:1–2:11; 1Ch 10:14–29:30)
- A. David's Victories (2Sa 1:1–10:19; 1Ch 10:14–20:8)
  - 1. The Political Triumphs of David (2Sa 1:1–5:25; 1Ch 10:14–12:40)
    - a. David is king of Judah (2Sa 1:1–4:12; 1Ch 10:14–12:40)
    - b. David is king over all Israel (2Sa 5:1–25)
  - 2. The Spiritual Triumphs of David (2Sa 6:1–7:29; 1Ch 13:1–17:27)
    - a. The ark of the covenant (2Sa 6:1–23; 1Ch 13:1–16:43)
    - b. The temple and the Davidic Covenant (2Sa 7:1–29; 1Ch 17:1–27)
  - 3. The Military Triumphs of David (2Sa 8:1–10:19; 1Ch 18:1–20:8)
- B. David's Sins (2Sa 11:1–27)
  - 1. David's Adultery with Bathsheba (2Sa 11:1–5)

2. David's Murder of Uriah the Hittite (2Sa 11:6–27)
C. David's Problems (2Sa 12:1–24:25; 1Ch 21:1–27:34)
1. David's House Suffers (2Sa 12:1–13:36)
a. Nathan's prophecy against David (2Sa 12:1–14)
b. David's son dies (2Sa 12:15–25)
c. Joab's loyalty to David (2Sa 12:26–31)
d. Amnon's incest (2Sa 13:1–20)
e. Amnon's murder (2Sa 13:21–36)
2. David's Kingdom Suffers (2Sa 13:37–24:25; 1Ch 21:1–27:34)
a. Absalom's rebellion (2Sa 13:37–17:29)
b. Absalom's murder (2Sa 18:1–33)
c. David's restoration as king (2Sa 19:1–20:26)
d. David's kingship evaluated (2Sa 21:1–23:39)
e. David's numbering of the people (2Sa 24:1–25; 1Ch 21:1–30)
D. David's Preparation and Organization for the Temple (1Ch 22:1–27:34)
E. David's Last Days (1Ki 1:1–2:11; 1Ch 28:1–29:30)
1. David's Failing Health: Abishag the Shunammite (1Ki 1:1–4)
2. Adonijah's Attempt to Seize the Kingdom (1Ki 1:5–9)
3. Solomon's Anointing as King (1Ki 1:10–40; 1Ch 29:20–25)
4. Adonijah's Submission (1Ki 1:41–53)
5. David's Last Words (1Ki 2:1–9; 1Ch 28:1–29:25)
a. David's words for Israel (1Ch 28:1–8)
b. David's words for Solomon (1Ki 2:1–9; 1Ch 28:9–29:19)
c. David's dedication to the temple (1Ch 29:1–20)
6. David's Death (1Ki 2:10, 11; 1Ch 29:26–30)

IV. THE KINGSHIP OF SOLOMON (1Ki 2:12–11:43; 1Ch 29:21–2Ch 9:31)
A. Solomon's Kingship Begins (1Ki 2:12–4:34; 1Ch 29:21–2Ch 1:17)
1. Solomon's Kingship Established (1Ki 2:12; 1Ch 29:21–2Ch 1:1)
2. Solomon's Adversaries Removed (1Ki 2:13–46)
3. Solomon's Wedding to Pharaoh's Daughter (1Ki 3:1)
4. Solomon's Spiritual Condition (1Ki 3:2, 3)
5. Solomon's Sacrifice at Gibeon (1Ki 3:4; 2Ch 1:2–6)
6. Solomon's Dream and Prayer for Wisdom (1Ki 3:5–15; 2Ch 1:7–12)
7. Solomon's Judging of the Harlots with God's Wisdom (1Ki 3:16–28)
8. Solomon's Officers, His Power, Wealth, and Wisdom (1Ki 4:1–34; 2Ch 1:13–17)
B. Solomon's Splendor (1Ki 5:1–8:66; 2Ch 2:1–7:22)
1. Preparations for the Building of the Temple (1Ki 5:1–18; 2Ch 2:1–18)
2. The Building of the Temple (1Ki 6:1–38; 2Ch 3:1–14)
3. The Building of the Royal Palace (1Ki 7:1–12)
4. The Making of the Vessels for the Temple (1Ki 7:13–51; 2Ch 3:15–5:1)
5. The Dedication and Completion of the Temple (1Ki 8:1–66; 2Ch 5:2–7:22)
C. Solomon's Demise (1Ki 9:1–11:43; 2Ch 8:1–9:31)
1. Davidic Covenant Repeated (1Ki 9:1–9)
2. Solomon's Disobedience to the Covenant (1Ki 9:10–11:8; 2Ch 8:1–9:28)
3. Solomon's Chastening for Breaking the Covenant (1Ki 11:9–40)
4. Solomon's Death (1Ki 11:41–43; 2Ch 9:29–31)

V. THE KINGDOM DIVIDED (1Ki 12:1–22:53; 2Ki 1:1–17:41; 2Ch 10:1–28:27)
A. The Kingdom Divides (1Ki 12:1–14:31)
1. The Division's Cause (1Ki 12:1–24)
2. Jeroboam, King of Israel (1Ki 12:25–14:20)
3. Rehoboam, King of Judah (1Ki 14:21–31; 2Ch 10:1–12:16)
B. Judah's Two Kings (1Ki 15:1–24; 2Ch 13:1–16:14)
1. Abijam, a.k.a., Joram, King of Judah (1Ki 15:1–8; 2Ch 13:1–22)
2. Asa, King of Judah (1Ki 15:9–24; 2Ch 14:1–16:14)
C. Israel's Five Kings (1Ki 15:25–16:28)
1. Nadab, King of Israel (1Ki 15:25–31)
2. Baasha, King of Israel (1Ki 15:32–16:7)
3. Elah, King of Israel (1Ki 16:8–14)
4. Zimri, King of Israel (1Ki 16:15–20)
5. Omri, King of Israel (1Ki 16:21–28)
D. Ahab, King of Israel (1Ki 16:29–22:40)
1. Ahab's Sin (1Ki 16:29–34)
2. Elijah the Prophet (1Ki 17:1–19:21)
3. Wars with Syria (1Ki 20:1–43)
4. Naboth Swindled and Killed (1Ki 21:1–16)
5. Ahab's Death (1Ki 21:17–22:40)

INTRODUCTION TO THE PROPHETS

The writing prophets of the OT fall into two groups: the 4 major prophets—Isaiah, Jeremiah, Ezekiel, and Daniel—and the 12 minor prophets—Hosea, Joel, Amos, Obadiah, Jonah, Micah, Nahum, Habakkuk, Zephaniah, Haggai, Zechariah, and Malachi. Lamentations falls into the major-prophet grouping because of its connection with Jeremiah

Besides these, the OT regarded others as prophets. Such prophets as Gad, Nathan, Elijah, and Elisha were typical of the nonwriting prophets. In a sense, John the Baptist as a forerunner of Jesus was a prophet who belonged to the OT era.

The following table gives the sequence and approximate dates and direction of ministry for the writing prophets, with "Israel" designating the northern kingdom and "Judah" the southern:

PROPHETS ORGANIZED BY DATE AND DIRECTION OF MINISTRY

Prophet	Ministered To	In the Years
Obadiah	Edom	850–840 B.C.
Joel	Judah	835–796 B.C.
Jonah	Nineveh	784–760 B.C.
Amos	Israel	763–755 B.C.
Hosea	Israel	755–710 B.C.
Isaiah	Judah	739–680 B.C.
Micah	Judah	735–710 B.C.
Nahum	Nineveh	650–630 B.C.
Zephaniah	Judah	635–625 B.C.
Jeremiah	Judah	627–570 B.C.
Habakkuk	Judah	620–605 B.C.
Daniel	Babylon	605–536 B.C.
Ezekiel	Babylon	593–570 B.C.
Haggai	Judah	520–505 B.C.
Zechariah	Judah	520–470 B.C.
Malachi	Judah	437–417 B.C.

CHRONOLOGY OF THE OLD TESTAMENT KINGS AND PROPHETS

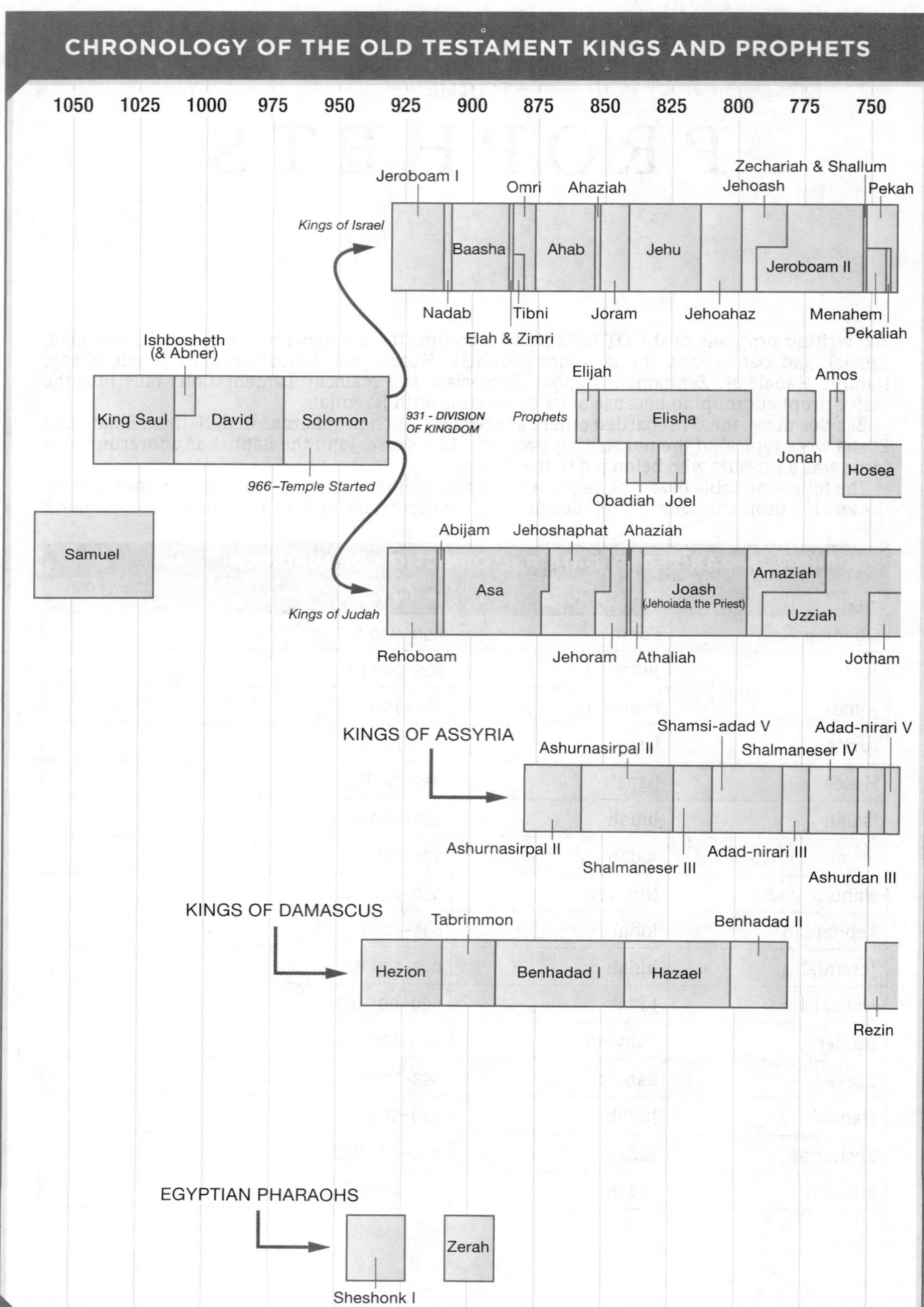
1050
1025
1000
975
950
925
900
875
850
825
800
775
750
Kings of Israel
Jeroboam I
Omri
Ahaziah
Zechariah & Shallum
Jehoash
Pekah
Baasha
Ahab
Jehu
Jeroboam II
Nadab
Tibni
Joram
Jehoahaz
Menahem
Elah & Zimri
Pekahiah
Ishbosheth
(& Abner)
King Saul
David
Solomon
931 - DIVISION
OF KINGDOM
966–Temple Started
Prophets
Elijah
Elisha
Amos
Jonah
Hosea
Obadiah
Joel
Samuel
Kings of Judah
Abijam
Jehoshaphat
Ahaziah
Asa
Joash
(Jehoiada the Priest)
Amaziah
Uzziah
Rehoboam
Jehoram
Athaliah
Jotham
KINGS OF ASSYRIA
Shamsi-adad V
Adad-nirari V
Ashurnasirpal II
Shalmaneser IV
Ashurnasirpal II
Shalmaneser III
Adad-nirari III
Ashurdan III
KINGS OF DAMASCUS
Tabrimmon
Benhadad II
Hezion
Benhadad I
Hazael
Rezin
EGYPTIAN PHARAOHS
Zerah
Sheshonk I

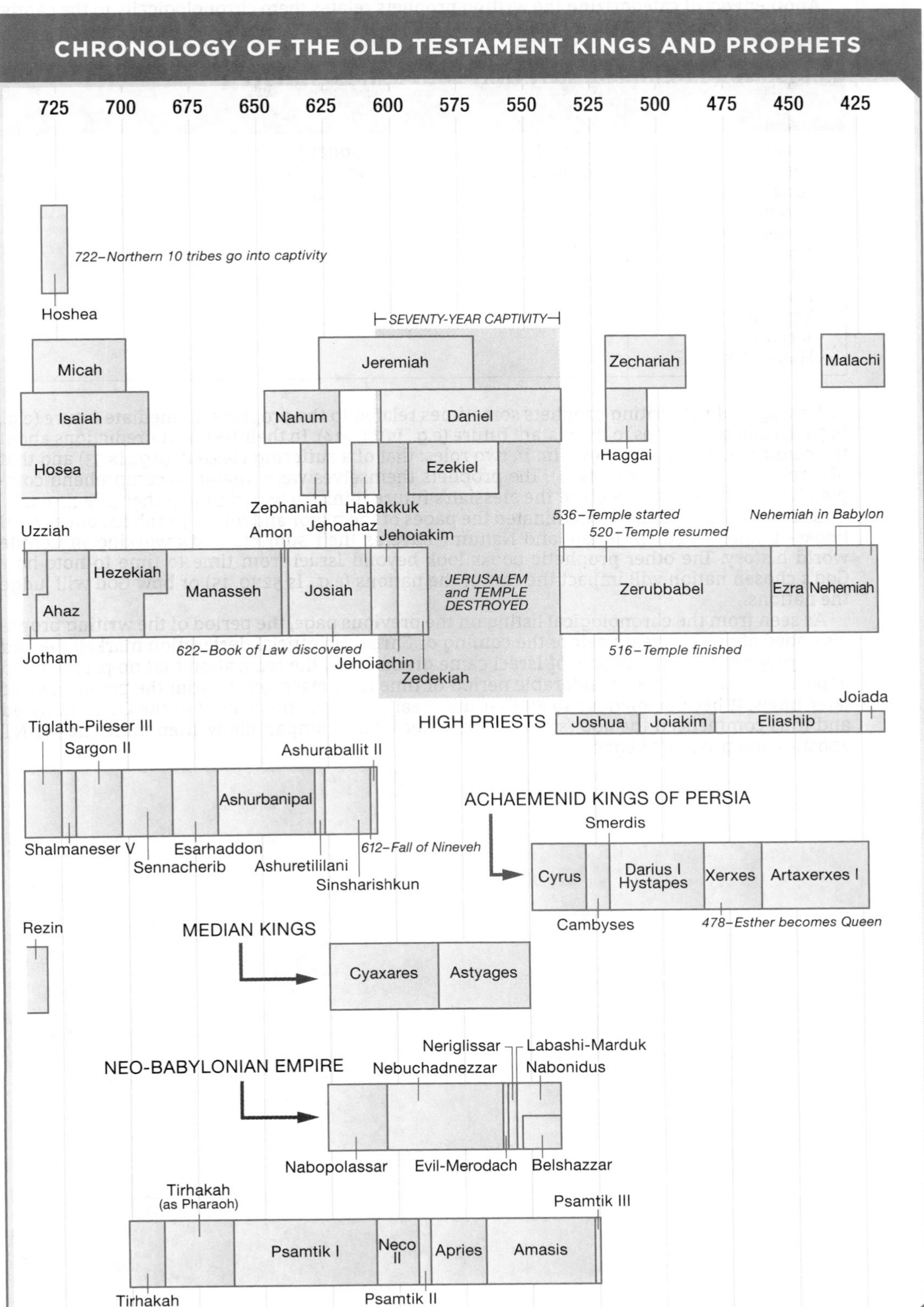
CHRONOLOGY OF THE OLD TESTAMENT KINGS AND PROPHETS
725
700
675
650
625
600
575
550
525
500
475
450
425
722–Northern 10 tribes go into captivity
Hoshea
SEVENTY-YEAR CAPTIVITY
Micah
Jeremiah
Zechariah
Malachi
Isaiah
Nahum
Daniel
Hosea
Ezekiel
Haggai
Zephaniah
Habakkuk
536–Temple started
Nehemiah in Babylon
Uzziah
Amon
Jehoahaz
Jehoiakim
520–Temple resumed
Hezekiah
Manasseh
Josiah
JERUSALEM and TEMPLE DESTROYED
Zerubbabel
Ezra
Nehemiah
Ahaz
Jotham
622–Book of Law discovered
Jehoiachin
516–Temple finished
Zedekiah
Joiada
HIGH PRIESTS
Joshua
Joiakim
Eliashib
Tiglath-Pileser III
Sargon II
Ashuraballit II
Ashurbanipal
ACHAEMENID KINGS OF PERSIA
Smerdis
Shalmaneser V
Esarhaddon
612–Fall of Nineveh
Sennacherib
Ashuretililani
Sinsharishkun
Cyrus
Darius I Hystapes
Xerxes
Artaxerxes I
Rezin
Cambyses
478–Esther becomes Queen
MEDIAN KINGS
Cyaxares
Astyages
Neriglissar
Labashi-Marduk
NEO-BABYLONIAN EMPIRE
Nebuchadnezzar
Nabonidus
Nabopolassar
Evil-Merodach
Belshazzar
Tirhakah (as Pharaoh)
Psamtik III
Psamtik I
Neco II
Apries
Amasis
Tirhakah
Psamtik II

Another way of categorizing the writing prophets relates them chronologically to the captivities of Israel (ca. 722 B.C.) and Judah (ca. 586 B.C.):

PROPHETS ORGANIZED BY WRITING DATE AND CAPTIVITY

Pre-Exilic	Exilic	Post-Exilic
· Obadiah · Joel · Jonah · Amos · Hosea · Isaiah · Micah · Nahum · Zephaniah · Jeremiah · Habakkuk	· Daniel · Ezekiel	· Haggai · Zechariah · Malachi

Messages of the writing prophets sometimes related to the prophets' immediate future (e.g., Is 7:1–11) and sometimes to the distant future (e.g., Is 7:12–14). In their frequent predictions about the coming Messiah, they saw Him in two roles: that of a suffering Messiah (e.g., Is 53) and that of a reigning Messiah (e.g., Is 11). The prophets themselves were unable to comprehend completely how these two aspects of the Messiah's future ministry would fit together (1Pe 1:10–12).

God's dealings with Israel dominated the pages of the major and minor prophets, but several books—Daniel, Obadiah, Jonah, and Nahum—have as their subjects God's working in Gentile world history. The other prophetic books look beyond Israel from time to time to note how God's chosen nation will impact the rest of the nations (e.g., Is 52:10, 15) or how God will judge the nations.

As seen from the chronological listing on the previous page, the period of the writing prophets ended about 400 years before the coming of Christ. No official declaration marked the end of OT prophecy, but the people of Israel came gradually to the realization that no prophet had appeared in Israel for a considerable period of time (cf. 1 Macc. 9:27). From the perspective of later times, it became obvious to all that the great prophetic movement of the OT terminated and thus commenced the 400 "silent years," after which comparable written ministries of NT apostles and prophets began.

THE FIRST BOOK
OF MOSES CALLED

GENESIS

TITLE

The English title, Genesis, comes from the Greek translation (Septuagint, LXX) meaning "origins"; whereas, the Hebrew title is derived from the Bible's very first word, translated "in the beginning." Genesis serves to introduce the Pentateuch (the first 5 books of the OT) and the entire Bible. The influence of Genesis in Scripture is demonstrated by its being quoted over 35 times in the NT and hundreds of allusions appearing in both Testaments. The story line of salvation which begins in Ge 3 is not completed until Rev 21, 22, where the eternal kingdom of redeemed believers is gloriously pictured.

AUTHOR AND DATE

While 1) the author does not identify himself in Genesis and 2) Genesis ends almost 3 centuries before Moses was born, both the OT (Ex 17:14; Nu 33:2; Jos 8:31; 1Ki 2:3; 2Ki 14:6; Ezr 6:18; Ne 13:1; Da 9:11, 13; Mal 4:4) and the NT (Mt 8:4; Mk 12:26; Lk 16:29; 24:27, 44; Jn 5:46; 7:22; Ac 15:1; Ro 10:19; 1Co 9:9; 2Co 3:15) ascribe this composition to Moses, who is the fitting author in light of his educational background (cf. Ac 7:22). No compelling reasons have been forthcoming to challenge Mosaic authorship. Genesis was written after the Exodus (ca. 1445 B.C.), but before Moses' death (ca. 1405 B.C.). For a brief biographical sketch of Moses read Ex 1–6.

BACKGROUND AND SETTING

The initial setting for Genesis is eternity past. God then, by willful act and divine Word, spoke all creation into existence, furnished it, and finally breathed life into a lump of dirt which He fashioned in His image to become Adam. God made mankind the crowning point of His creation, i.e., His companions who would enjoy fellowship with Him and bring glory to His name.

The historical background for the early events in Genesis is clearly Mesopotamian. While it is difficult to pinpoint precisely the historical moment for which this book was written, Israel first heard Genesis sometime prior to crossing the Jordan River and entering the Promised Land (ca. 1405 B.C.).

Genesis has 3 distinct, sequential geographical settings: 1) Mesopotamia (chaps. 1–11); 2) the Promised Land (chaps. 12–36); and 3) Egypt (chaps. 37–50). The time frames of these 3 segments are: 1) Creation to ca. 2090 B.C.; 2) 2090–1897 B.C.; and 3) 1897–1804 B.C. Genesis covers more time than the remaining books of the Bible combined.

HISTORICAL AND THEOLOGICAL THEMES

In this book of beginnings, God revealed Himself and a worldview to Israel which contrasted, at times sharply, with the worldview of Israel's neighbors. The author made no attempt to defend the existence of God or to present a systematic discussion of His person and works. Rather, Israel's God distinguished Himself clearly from the alleged gods of her neighbors. Theological foundations are revealed which include God the Father, God the Son, God the Holy Spirit, man, sin, redemption, covenant, promise, Satan and angels, kingdom, revelation, Israel, judgment, and blessing.

Genesis 1–11 (primeval history) reveals the origins of the universe, i.e., the beginnings of time and space and many of the firsts in human experience, such as marriage, family, the Fall, sin, redemption, judgment, and nations. Genesis 12–50 (patriarchal history) explained to Israel how they came into existence as a family, whose ancestry could be traced to Eber (hence the "Hebrews"; Ge 10:24, 25) and even more remotely to Shem, the son of Noah (hence the "Semites"; Ge 10:21). God's people came to understand not only their ancestry and family history, but also the origins of their institutions, customs, languages, and different cultures, especially basic human experiences such as sin and death.

Because they were preparing to enter Canaan and dispossess the Canaanite inhabitants of their homes and properties, God revealed their enemies' background. In addition, they needed to understand the actual basis of the war they were about to declare in light of the immorality of killing, consistent with the other 4 books that Moses was writing (Exodus, Leviticus, Numbers, and Deuteronomy). Ultimately, the Jewish nation would understand a selected portion of preceding world history and the inaugural background of

Israel as a basis by which they would live in their new beginnings under Joshua's leadership in the land which had previously been promised to their original patriarchal forefather, Abraham.

Genesis 12:1–3 established a primary focus on God's promises to Abraham. This narrowed their view from the entire world of peoples in Ge 1–11 to one small nation, Israel, through whom God would progressively accomplish His redemptive plan. This underscored Israel's mission to be "a light to the nations" (Is 42:6). God promised land, descendants (seed), and blessing. This 3-fold promise became, in turn, the basis of the covenant with Abraham (Ge 15:1–20). The rest of Scripture bears out the fulfillment of these promises.

On a larger scale, Ge 1–11 set forth a singular message about the character and works of God. In the sequence of accounts which make up these chapters of Scripture, a pattern emerges which reveals God's abundant grace as He responded to the willful disobedience of mankind. Without exception, in each account God increased the manifestation of His grace. But also without exception, man responded in greater sinful rebellion. In biblical words, the more sin abounded the more did God's grace abound (cf. Ro 5:20).

One final theme of both theological and historical significance sets Genesis apart from other books of Scripture, in that the first book of Scripture corresponds closely with the final book. In the book of Revelation, the paradise which was lost in Genesis will be regained. The apostle John clearly presented the events recorded in his book as future resolutions to the problems which began as a result of the curse in Ge 3. His focus is upon the effects of the Fall in the undoing of creation and the manner in which God rids His creation of the curse effect. In John's own words, "There will no longer be any curse" (Rev 22:3). Not surprisingly, in the final chapter of God's Word, believers will find themselves back in the Garden of Eden, the eternal paradise of God, eating from the tree of life (Rev 22:1–14). At that time, they will partake, wearing robes washed in the blood of the Lamb (Rev 22:14).

INTERPRETIVE CHALLENGES

Grasping the individual messages of Genesis which make up the larger plan and purpose of the book presents no small challenge, since both the individual accounts and the book's overall message offer important lessons to faith and works. Genesis presents creation by divine fiat, *ex nihilo*, i.e., "out of nothing." Three traumatic events of epic proportions, namely the Fall, the universal Flood, and the Dispersion of nations are presented as historical backdrop in order to understand world history. From Abraham on, the pattern is to focus on God's redemption and blessing.

The customs of Genesis often differ considerably from those of our modern day. They must be explained against their ancient Near Eastern background. Each custom must be treated according to the immediate context of the passage before any attempt is made to explain it based on customs recorded in extrabiblical sources or even elsewhere in Scripture.

OUTLINE

Genesis by content is comprised of two basic sections: 1) Primitive history (Ge 1–11) and 2) Patriarchal history (Ge 12–50). Primitive history records 4 major events: 1) Creation (Ge 1, 2); 2) the Fall (Ge 3–5); 3) the Flood (Ge 6–9); and 4) the Dispersion (Ge 10, 11). Patriarchal history spotlights 4 great men: 1) Abraham (Ge 12:1–25:8); 2) Isaac (Ge 21:1–35:29); 3) Jacob (Ge 25:21–50:14); and 4) Joseph (Ge 30:22–50:26).

The literary structure of Genesis is built on the frequently recurring phrase "*the records of* the generations of" and is the basis for the following outline.

I. The Creation of Heaven and Earth (1:1–2:3)

II. The Generations of the Heavens and the Earth (2:4–4:26)
- A. Adam and Eve in Eden (2:4–25)
- B. The Fall and Its Outcomes (chap. 3)
- C. Murder of a Brother (4:1–24)
- D. Hope in the Descendants of Seth (4:25, 26)

III. The Generations of Adam (5:1–6:8)
- A. Genealogy—Seth to Noah (chap. 5)
- B. Rampant Sin Prior to the Flood (6:1–8)

IV. The Generations of Noah (6:9–9:29)
- A. Preparation for the Flood (6:9–7:9)
- B. The Flood and Deliverance (7:10–8:19)
- C. God's Noahic Covenant (8:20–9:17)
- D. The History of Noah's Descendants (9:18–29)

V. The Generations of Shem, Ham, and Japheth (10:1–11:9)
- A. The Nations (chap. 10)
- B. Dispersion of the Nations (11:1–9)

VI. The Generations of Shem: Genealogy of Shem to Terah (11:10–26)

VII. The Generations of Terah (11:27–25:11)
- A. Genealogy (11:27–32)
- B. The Abrahamic Covenant: His Land and People (12:1–22:19)
  1. Journey to the Promised Land (12:1–9)

2. Redemption from Egypt (12:10–20)
3. Division of the land (chap. 13)
4. Victory over the kings (chap. 14)
5. The covenant ratified (chap. 15)
6. Rejection of Hagar and Ishmael (chap. 16)
7. The covenant confirmed (chap. 17)
8. Birth of Isaac foretold (18:1–15)
9. Sodom and Gomorrah (18:16–19:38)
10. Philistine encounter (chap. 20)
11. Isaac's birth (chap. 21)
12. Abraham's act of faith with Isaac (22:1–19)

C. Abraham's Promised Seed (22:20–25:11)
1. Rebekah's background (22:20–24)
2. Death of Sarah (chap. 23)
3. Isaac's marriage to Rebekah (chap. 24)
4. Isaac the only heir (25:1–6)
5. Death of Abraham (25:7–11)

VIII. The Generations of Ishmael (25:12–18)

IX. The Generations of Isaac (25:19–35:29)

A. Competition Between Esau and Jacob (25:19–34)
B. Covenant Blessings to Isaac (chap. 26)
C. Jacob's Deception for the Blessing (27:1–40)
D. Blessing on Jacob in a Foreign Land (27:41–32:32)
1. Jacob sent to Laban (27:41–28:9)
2. Angel at Bethel (28:10–22)
3. Disagreements with Laban (29:1–30)
4. Promised seed (29:31–30:24)
5. Departure from Aram (30:25–31:55)
6. Angels at Mahanaim and Penuel (chap. 32)

E. Esau's Reunion and Reconciliation with Jacob (33:1–17)
F. Events and Deaths from Shechem to Mamre (33:18–35:29)

X. The Generations of Esau (36:1–37:1)

XI. The Generations of Jacob (37:2–50:26)

A. Joseph's Dreams (37:2–11)
B. Family Tragedy (37:12–38:30)
C. Vice Regency over Egypt (chaps. 39–41)
D. Reunion with Family (chaps. 42–45)
E. Transition to Exodus (chaps. 46–50)
1. Journey to Egypt (46:1–27)
2. Occupation in Goshen (46:28–47:31)
3. Blessings on the twelve tribes (48:1–49:28)
4. Death and burial of Jacob in Canaan (49:29–50:14)
5. Death of Joseph in Egypt (50:15–26)

THE CREATION

1 [A]In the beginning [B]God [C]created the heavens and
the earth. 2 The earth was [a,A]formless and void,
and [B]darkness was over the [b]surface of the deep,
and [C]the Spirit of God [D]was [c]moving over the [b]sur-
face of the waters. 3 Then [A]God said, "Let there be
light"; and there was light. 4 God saw that the light
was [A]good; and God [B]separated the light from the
darkness. 5 [A]God called the light day, and the darkness He called night. And [B]there was evening and
there was morning, one day.
6 Then God said, "Let there be [a]an [A]expanse in the
midst of the waters, and let it separate the waters
from the waters." 7 God made the [a]expanse, and separated [A]the waters which were below the [a]expanse
from the waters [B]which were above the [a]expanse; and
it was so. 8 God called the [a]expanse heaven. And there
was evening and there was morning, a second day.
9 Then God said, "[A]Let the waters below the heavens be gathered into one place, and let [B]the dry land
appear"; and it was so. 10 God called the dry land
earth, and the [A]gathering of the waters He called
seas; and God saw that it was good. 11 Then God said,
"Let the earth sprout [a,A]vegetation, [b]plants yielding
seed, *and* fruit trees on the earth bearing fruit after
[c]their kind [d]with seed in them"; and it was so. 12 The
earth brought forth [a]vegetation, [b]plants yielding
seed after [c]their kind, and trees bearing fruit [d]with
seed in them, after [c]their kind; and God saw that
it was good. 13 There was evening and there was
morning, a third day.
14 Then God said, "Let there be [a,A]lights in the
[b,B]expanse of the heavens to separate the day from
the night, and let them be for [C]signs and for [D]sea-
sons and for days and years; 15 and let them be for
[a]lights in the [b]expanse of the heavens to give light
on the earth"; and it was so. 16 God made the two
[a]great lights, the [A]greater [b]light [c]to govern the day,
and the lesser [b]light [c]to govern the night; *He made*
[B]the stars also. 17 [A]God placed them in the [a]expanse

1:1 [A]Ps 102:25; Is 40:21; John 1:1, 2; Heb 1:10 [B]Ps 89:11; 90:2; Acts 17:24; Rom 1:20; Heb 11:3 [C]Job 38:4; Is 42:5; 45:18; Rev 4:11 1:2 [a]*Or a waste and emptiness* [b]*Lit face of* [c]*Or hovering* [A]Jer 4:23 [B]Job 38:9 [C]Ps 104:30; Is 40:13, 14 [D]Deut 32:11; Is 31:5 1:3 [A]Ps 33:6, 9; 2 Cor 4:6 1:4 [A]Ps 145:9, 10 [B]Is 45:7 1:5 [A]Ps 74:16 [B]Ps 65:8 1:6 [a]*Or a firmament* [A]Is 40:22; Jer 10:12; 2 Pet 3:5 1:7 [a]*Or firmament* [A]Job 38:8-11 [B]Ps 148:4 1:8 [a]*Or firmament* 1:9 [A]Ps 104:6-9; Jer 5:22; 2 Pet 3:5 [B]Ps 24:1, 2; 95:5 1:10 [A]Ps 33:7; 95:5; 146:6 1:11 [a]*Or grass* [b]*Or herbs* [c]*Lit its* [d]*Lit in which is its seed* [A]Ps 65:9-13; 104:14; Heb 6:7 1:12 [a]*Or grass* [b]*Or herbs* [c]*Lit its* [d]*Lit in which is its seed* 1:14 [a]*Or luminaries, light-bearers* [b]*Or firmament* [A]Ps 74:16; 136:7 [B]Ps 19:1; 150:1 [C]Jer 10:2 [D]Ps 104:19 1:15 [a]*Or luminaries, light-bearers* [b]*Or firmament* 1:16 [a]*Or luminaries, light-bearers* [b]*Or luminary, light-bearer* [c]*Lit for the dominion of* [A]Ps 136:8, 9 [B]Job 38:7; Ps 8:3; Is 40:26 1:17 [a]*Or firmament* [A]Jer 33:20, 25

1:1–2:3 This description of God creating heaven and earth is understood to be: 1) recent, i.e., thousands not millions of years ago; 2) *ex nihilo,* i.e., out of nothing; and 3) special, i.e., in 6 consecutive 24-hour periods called "days" and further distinguished as such by this phrase, "the evening and the morning." Scripture does not support a creation date earlier than about 10,000 years ago. **In the beginning.** While God exists eternally (Ps 90:2), this marked the beginning of the universe in time and space. In explaining Israel's identity and purpose to her on the plains of Moab, God wanted His people to know about the origin of the world in which they found themselves. **God.** Elohim is a general term for deity and a name for the True God, though used also at times for pagan gods (31:30), angels (Ps 8:5), men (Ps 82:6), and judges (Ex 21:6). Moses made no attempt to defend the existence of God, which is assumed, or explain what He was like in person and works, which is treated elsewhere (cf. Is 43:10, 13). Both are to be believed by faith (cf. Heb 11:3, 6). **created.** This word is used here of God's creative activity alone, although it occasionally is used elsewhere of matter which already existed (Is 65:18). Context demands in no uncertain terms that this was a creation without preexisting material (as does other Scripture: cf. Is 40:28; 45:8, 12, 18; 48:13; Jer 10:16; Ac 17:24). **the heavens and the earth.** All of God's creation is incorporated into this summary statement which includes all 6 consecutive days of creation.

1:2 formless and void. This means "not finished in its shape and as yet uninhabited by creatures" (cf. Is 45:18, 19; Jer 4:23). God would quickly (in 6 days) decorate His initial creation (1:2–2:3). **deep.** Sometimes referred to as primordial waters, this is the term used to describe the earth's water-covered surface before the dry land emerged (1:9, 10). Jonah used this word to describe the watery abyss in which he found himself submerged (Jon 2:5). **Spirit of God.** Not only did God the Holy Spirit participate in creation, but so did God the Son (cf. Jn 1:1–3; Col 1:16; Heb 1:2).

1:3 God said. God effortlessly spoke light into existence (cf. Pss 33:6; 148:5). This dispelled the darkness of v. 2. **light.** The greater and lesser lights (the sun and moon) were created later (1:14–19) on the fourth day. Here, God was the provider of light (2Co 4:6) and will in eternity future be the source of light (cf. Rev 21:23).

1:4 good. Good for the purposes it was intended to serve (cf. 1:31).

1:4, 5 separated ... called. After the initial creation, God continued to complete His universe. Once God separated certain things, He then named them. Separating and naming were acts of dominion and served as a pattern for man, who would also name a portion of God's creation over which God gave him dominion (2:19, 20).

1:5 one day. God established the pattern of creation in 7 days which constituted a complete week. "Day" can refer to: 1) the light portion of a 24-hour period (1:5, 14); 2) an extended period of time (2:4); or 3) the 24-hour period which basically refers to a full rotation of the earth on its axis, called evening and morning. This cannot mean an age, but only a day, reckoned by the Jews from sunset to sunset (vv. 8, 13, 19, 23, 31). "Day" with numerical adjectives in Hebrew always refers to a 24-hour period. Comparing the order of the week in Ex 20:8–11 with the creation week confirms this understanding of the time element. Such a cycle of light and dark means that the earth was rotating on its axis, so that there was a source of light on one side of the earth, though the sun was not yet created (v. 16).

1:6 expanse. The portion of God's creation named "heavens," that which man saw when he looked up, i.e., the atmospheric and stellar heaven.

1:7 below the expanse. Refers to subterranean reservoirs (cf. 7:11). **above the expanse.** This could possibly have been a canopy of water vapor which acted to make the earth like a hothouse, provided uniform temperature, inhibited mass air movements, caused mist to fall, and filtered out ultraviolet rays, thus extending life.

1:9, 10 dry land. This was caused by a tremendous, cataclysmic upheaval of the earth's surface, and the rising and sinking of the land, which caused the waters to plunge into the low places, forming the seas, the continents and islands, the rivers and lakes (cf. Job 38:4–11; Ps 104:6–9).

1:11, 12 after their kind. God set in motion a providential process whereby the vegetable kingdom could reproduce through seeds which would maintain each one's unique characteristics. The same phrase is used to describe the perpetuating reproduction of animals within their created species (vv. 21, 24, 25), and indicates that evolution, which proposes reproduction across species lines, is a false explanation of origins.

1:11 with seed in them. The principle of reproduction that marks all life (cf. vv. 22, 24, 28).

1:14 lights. Cf. v. 16. For 3 days there had been light (v. 4) in the day as though there were a sun, and lesser light at night as though there were the moon and stars. God could have left it that way, but did not. He created the "lights, sun, moon, and stars," not for light, but to serve as markers for signs, seasons, days, and years. **signs.** Certainly to include: 1) weather (Mt 16:2, 3); 2) testimony to God (Pss 8, 19; Ro 1:14–20; 3) divine judgment (Joel 2:30, 31; Mt 24:29); and 4) navigation (Mt 2:1, 2). **seasons.** It is the earth's movement in relation to the sun and moon that determines the seasons and the calendar.

1:15–18 two great lights ... to separate the light from the darkness. It was God (not some other deity) who created the lights. Israel had originally come from Mesopotamia, where the celestial bodies were worshiped,

of the heavens to give light on the earth, 18 and [a]to
[A]govern the day and the night, and to separate the
light from the darkness; and God saw that it was
good. 19 There was evening and there was morning,
a fourth day.
20 Then God said, "Let the waters [a]teem with
swarms of living creatures, and let birds fly above
the earth [b]in the open [c]expanse of the heavens."
21 God created [A]the great sea monsters and every
living creature that moves, with which the waters
swarmed after their kind, and every winged bird
after its kind; and God saw that it was good. 22 God
blessed them, saying, "Be fruitful and multiply, and
fill the waters in the seas, and let birds multiply
on the earth." 23 There was evening and there was
morning, a fifth day.
24 [A]Then God said, "Let the earth bring forth living creatures after [a]their kind: cattle and creeping
things and beasts of the earth after [a]their kind";
and it was so. 25 God made the [A]beasts of the earth
after [a]their kind, and the cattle after [a]their kind, and
everything that creeps on the ground after its kind;
and God saw that it was good.
26 Then God said, "Let [A]Us make [B]man in Our image, according to Our likeness; and let them [C]rule
over the fish of the sea and over the birds of the
[a]sky and over the cattle and over all the earth, and
over every creeping thing that creeps on the earth."
27 God created man [A]in His own image, in the image of God He created him; [B]male and female He
created them. 28 God blessed them; and God said to
them, "[A]Be fruitful and multiply, and fill the earth,
and subdue it; and rule over the fish of the sea and
over the birds of the [a]sky and over every living thing
that [b]moves on the earth." 29 Then God said, "Behold,
[A]I have given you every plant yielding seed that
is on the [a]surface of all the earth, and every tree
[b]which has fruit yielding seed; it shall be food for
you; 30 and [A]to every beast of the earth and to every
bird of the [a]sky and to every thing that [b]moves on
the earth [c]which has life, *I have given* every green
plant for food"; and it was so. 31 God saw all that He
had made, and behold, it was very [A]good. And there
was evening and there was morning, the sixth day.

THE CREATION OF MAN AND WOMAN

2 Thus the heavens and the earth were completed,
and all [A]their hosts. 2 By [A]the seventh day God
completed His work which He had done, and [B]He
rested on the seventh day from all His work which
He had done. 3 Then God blessed the seventh day
and sanctified it, because in it He rested from all
His work which God had created [a]and made.
4 [a,A]This is the account of the heavens and the
earth when they were created, in [B]the day that the
LORD God made earth and heaven. 5 [A]Now no shrub

1:18 [a]Lit *for the dominion of* [A]Jer 31:35 1:20 [a]Or *swarm* [b]Lit *on the face of* [c]Or *firmament* 1:21 [A]Ps 104:25-28 1:24 [a]Lit *its* [A]Gen 2:19; 6:20; 7:14; 8:19 1:25 [a]Lit *its* [A]Gen 7:21, 22; Jer 27:5 1:26 [a]Lit *heavens* [A]Gen 3:22; 11:7 [B]Gen 5:1; 9:6; 1 Cor 11:7; Eph 4:24; James 3:9 [C]Ps 8:6-8 1:27 [A]Gen 5:1f; 1 Cor 11:7; Eph 4:24; Col 3:10 [B]Matt 19:4; Mark 10:6 1:28 [a]Lit *heavens* [b]Or *creeps* [A]Gen 9:1, 7; Lev 26:9; Ps 127:3, 5 1:29 [a]Lit *face of* [b]Lit *in which is the fruit of a tree yielding seed* [A]Ps 104:14; 136:25 1:30 [a]Lit *heavens* [b]Or *creeps* [c]Lit *in which is a living soul* [A]Ps 145:15, 16; 147:9 1:31 [A]Ps 104:24, 28; 119:68; 1 Tim 4:4 2:1 [A]Deut 4:19; 17:3 2:2 [A]Ex 20:8-11; 31:17 [B]Heb 4:4, 10 2:3 [a]Lit *to make* 2:4 [a]Lit *These are the generations* [A]Job 38:4-11 [B]Gen 1:3-31 2:5 [A]Gen 1:11

and more recently from Egypt, where the sun was worshiped as a primary deity. God was revealing to them that the very stars, moons, and planets which Israel's neighbors had worshiped were the products of His creation. Later, they became worshipers of the "host of heaven" (*see note on 2Ki 17:16*), which led to their being taken captive out of the Promised Land.

1:20 living creatures. These creatures, including the extraordinarily large ones, included all sorts of fish and mammals, even dinosaurs (*see notes on Job 40:15–41:1*).

1:22 blessed. This is the first occurrence of the word "bless" in Scripture. God's admonition to "be fruitful and multiply" was the substance of the blessing.

1:24, 25 cattle … beasts. This probably represents all kinds of large, four-legged animals.

1:24 beasts of the earth. Different from and larger than the clan of cattle, this would include dinosaurs like Behemoth (Job 40:15ff.).

1:26 Us … Our. The first clear indication of the triunity of God (cf. 3:22; 11:7). The very name of God, Elohim (1:1), is a plural form of El. **man.** The crowning point of creation, a living human, was made in God's image to rule creation. **Our image.** This defined man's unique relation to God. Man is a living being capable of embodying God's communicable attributes (cf. 9:6; Ro 8:29; Col 3:10; Jas 3:9). In his rational life, he was like God in that he could reason and had intellect, will, and emotion. In the moral sense, he was like God because he was good and sinless.

1:26–28 rule over. This defined man's unique relation to creation. Man was God's representative in ruling over the creation. The command to rule separated him from the rest of living creation and defined his relationship as above the rest of creation (cf. Ps 8:6–8).

1:27 male and female. Cf. Mt 19:4; Mk 10:6. While these two persons equally shared God's image and together exercised dominion over creation, they were by divine design physically diverse in order to accomplish God's mandate to multiply, i.e., neither one could reproduce offspring without the other.

1:28 blessed. This second blessing (cf. 1:22) involved reproduction and dominion. **Be fruitful and multiply, and fill the earth, and subdue it.** God, having just created the universe, created His representative (rule over) and representation (cf. image and likeness). Man would fill the earth and oversee its operation. "Subdue" does not suggest a wild and unruly condition for the creation because God Himself pronounced it "good." Rather, it speaks of a productive ordering of the earth and its inhabitants to yield its riches and accomplish God's purposes.

1:29, 30 food for you … for food. Prior to the curse (3:14–19), both mankind and beasts were vegetarians.

1:31 very good. What had been pronounced good individually (vv. 4, 10, 12, 18, 21, 25) was now called "very good" collectively. The words anticipated God's conclusion that it was "not good" for a man to be alone (2:18), which occurred on the sixth day.

2:1–3 These words affirm that God had completed His work. Four times it is said that He finished His work, and 3 times it is said that this included all His work. Present processes in the universe reflect God sustaining that completed creation, not more creation (cf. Heb 1:3).

2:2 completed … rested. God certainly did not rest due to weariness; rather, establishing the pattern for man's work cycle, He only modeled the need for rest. Later, the Sabbath ordinance of Moses found its basis in the creation week (cf. Ex 20:8–11). The Sabbath was God's sacred ordained day in the weekly cycle. Jesus said, "The Sabbath was made for man" (Mk 2:27), and Ge 2:3 stated that God "sanctified" or set apart the Sabbath day because He rested in it. Later, it was set aside for a day of worship in the Mosaic law (*see note on Ex 20:8*). Hebrews 4:4 distinguishes between physical rest and the redemptive rest to which it pointed. Colossians 2:16 makes it clear that the Mosaic "Sabbath" has no symbolic or ritual place in the New Covenant. The church began worshiping on the first day of the week to commemorate the resurrection of Christ (Ac 20:7).

2:4–4:26 The history of the heavens and the earth (v. 4).

2:4–25 This section fills in the details of man's creation on day six. How did Moses obtain this account, so different from the absurd fictions of the pagans? Not from any human source, for man was not in existence to witness it. Not from the light of reason, for though intellect can know the eternal power of the Godhead (Ro 1:18–20) and that God made all things, it cannot know how. None but the Creator Himself could give this data and, therefore, it is through faith that one understands that the worlds were formed by the Word of God (Heb 11:3).

of the field was yet in the earth, and no plant of the
field had yet sprouted, [B]for the LORD God had not
sent rain upon the earth, and there was no man
to [a]cultivate the ground. 6 But a [a]mist used to rise
from the earth and water the whole [b]surface of the
ground. 7 Then the LORD God formed man of [A]dust
from the ground, and breathed into his nostrils
the breath of life; and [B]man became a living [a]be-
ing. 8 The LORD God planted a [A]garden toward the
east, in Eden; and there He placed the man whom
He had formed. 9 Out of the ground the LORD God
caused to grow [A]every tree that is pleasing to the
sight and good for food; [B]the tree of life also in the
midst of the garden, and the tree of the knowledge
of good and evil.
10 Now a [A]river [a]flowed out of Eden to water the
garden; and from there it divided and became four
[b]rivers. 11 The name of the first is Pishon; it [a]flows
around the whole land of [A]Havilah, where there is
gold. 12 The gold of that land is good; the bdellium
and the onyx stone are there. 13 The name of the
second river is Gihon; it [a]flows around the whole
land of Cush. 14 The name of the third river is [a,A]Ti-
gris; it [b]flows east of Assyria. And the fourth river
is the [c,B]Euphrates.
15 Then the LORD God took the man and put him
into the garden of Eden to cultivate it and keep it.
16 The LORD God [A]commanded the man, saying,
"From any tree of the garden you may eat freely;
17 but from the tree of the knowledge of good and
evil you shall not [a]eat, for in the day that you eat
from it [A]you will surely die."
18 Then the LORD God said, "It is not good for the
man to be alone; [A]I will make him a helper [a]suitable
for him." 19 [A]Out of the ground the LORD God formed
every beast of the field and every bird of the [a]sky,
and [B]brought *them* to the man to see what he would
call them; and whatever the man called a living
creature, that was its name. 20 The man gave names
to all the cattle, and to the birds of the [a]sky, and to
every beast of the field, but for [b]Adam there was
not found [A]a helper [c]suitable for him. 21 So the LORD
God caused a [A]deep sleep to fall upon the man, and
he slept; then He took one of his ribs and closed up
the flesh at that place. 22 The LORD God [a]fashioned
into a woman [A]the rib which He had taken from the
man, and brought her to the man. 23 The man said,

"[A]This is now bone of my bones,
And flesh of my flesh;

2:5 [a]Lit *work, serve* [B]Ps 65:9, 10; Jer 10:12, 13 2:6 [a]Or *flow* [b]Lit *face of* 2:7 [a]Lit *soul* [A]Gen 3:19 [B]1 Cor 15:45 2:8 [A]Gen 13:10; Is 51:3; Ezek 28:13 2:9 [A]Ezek 47:12 [B]Gen 3:22; Rev 2:7; 22:2, 14 2:10 [a]Lit *was going out* [b]Lit *heads* [A]Ps 46:4 2:11 [a]Lit *surrounds* [A]Gen 25:18 2:13 [a]Lit *is the one surrounding* 2:14 [a]Heb *Hiddekel* [b]Lit *is the one going* [c]Heb *Perath* [A]Dan 10:4 [B]Gen 15:18 2:16 [A]Gen 3:2, 3 2:17 [a]Lit *eat from it* [A]Deut 30:15, 19, 20; Rom 6:23; 1 Tim 5:6; James 1:15 2:18 [a]Lit *corresponding to* [A]1 Cor 11:9 2:19 [a]Lit *heavens* [A]Gen 1:24 [B]Gen 1:26 2:20 [a]Lit *heavens* [b]Or *man* [c]Lit *corresponding to* [A]Gen 2:18 2:21 [A]Gen 15:12 2:22 [a]Lit *built* [A]1 Cor 11:8, 9 2:23 [A]Gen 29:14; Eph 5:28, 29

2:6 mist . . . rise from the earth. "Mist" should be translated "flow." It indicates that water came up from beneath the ground as springs and spread over the whole earth in an uninterrupted cycle of water. After the fall, rain became the primary means of watering the earth and allowed for floods and droughts that did not exist originally. Rains also allowed for God to judge through floods and droughts.

2:7 formed. Many of the words used in this account of the creation of man picture a master craftsman at work shaping a work of art to which he gives life (1Co 15:45). This adds detail to the statement of fact in 1:27 (cf. 1Ti 2:13). Cf. Ps 139:14. Made from dirt, a man's value is not in the physical components that form his body, but in the quality of life which forms his soul (see Job 33:4).

2:8 garden . . . Eden. The Babylonians called the lush green land from which water flowed *edenu;* today, the term "oasis" describes such a place. This was a magnificent garden paradise, unlike any the world has seen since, where God fellowshiped with those He created in His image. The exact location of Eden is unknown; if "toward the east" was used in relationship to where Moses was when he wrote, then it could have been in the area of Babylon, the Mesopotamian Valley.

2:9 tree of life. A real tree, with special properties to sustain eternal life. It was placed in the center of the garden, where it must have been observed by Adam, and its fruit perhaps eaten by him, thus sustaining his life (2:16). Such a tree, symbolic of eternal life, will be in the new heavens and new earth (*see note on Rev 22:2*). **tree . . . knowledge.** Cf. 2:16; 3:1–6, 11, 22. It was perhaps given that title because it was a test of obedience by which our first parents were tried, whether they would be good or bad—obey God or disobey His command.

2:10 out of. That is to say "the source," and likely refers to some great spring gushing up inside the garden from some subterranean reservoir. There was no rain at that time.

2:11 Pishon . . . Havilah. Locations are uncertain. This represents pre-Flood geography, now dramatically altered.

2:12 bdellium. A gum resin. This refers more to appearance than color, i.e., it had the appearance of a pale resin.

2:13 Gihon . . . Cush. The river location is uncertain. Cush could be modern-day Ethiopia.

2:14 Tigris . . . Assyria. The post-Flood Tigris River runs NW to SE east of the city of Babylon through the Mesopotamian Valley. **Euphrates.** A river that runs parallel (NW to SE) to the Tigris and empties into the Persian Gulf after joining the Tigris.

2:15 cultivate it and keep it. Work was an important and dignified part of representing the image of God and serving Him, even before the Fall. Cf. Rev 22:3.

2:17 surely die. To "die" has the basic idea of separation. It can mean spiritual separation, physical separation, and/or eternal separation. At the moment of their sin, Adam and Eve died spiritually, but because God was merciful they did not die physically until later (5:5). There is no reason given for this prohibition, other than it was a test (*see note on v. 9*). There was nothing magical about that tree, but eating from it after it had been forbidden by God would indeed give man the knowledge of evil—since evil can be defined as disobeying God. Man already had the knowledge of good.

2:18 not good. When God saw His creation as very good (1:31), He viewed it as being to that point the perfect outcome to His creative plan. However, in observing man's state as not good, He was commenting on his incompleteness before the end of the sixth day because the woman, Adam's counterpart, had not yet been created. The words of this verse emphasize man's need for a companion, a helper, and an equal. He was incomplete without someone to complement him in fulfilling the task of filling, multiplying, and taking dominion over the earth. This points to Adam's inadequacy, not Eve's insufficiency (cf. 1Co 11:9). Woman was made by God to meet man's deficiency (cf. 1Ti 2:14).

2:19 This was not a new creation of animals. They were created before man on the fifth and sixth days (1:20–25). Here the Lord God was calling attention to the fact that He created them "out of the ground" as He did man, but man, who was a living soul in the image of God, was to name them, signifying his rule over them.

2:20 gave names to. Naming is an act of discerning something about the creature so as to appropriately identify it and also an act of leadership or authority over that which was named. There is no kinship with any animal since none was a fitting companion for Adam.

2:21 one of his ribs. This could also be "sides," including surrounding flesh ("flesh of my flesh," v. 23). Divine surgery by the Creator presented no problems. This would also imply the first act of healing in Scripture.

2:23 bone of my bones. Adam's poem focuses on naming the delight of his heart in this newly found companion. The man (ish) names her "woman" (isha) because she had her source in him (the root of the word "woman" is "soft"). She truly was made of bone from his bones and flesh from his flesh. Cf. 1Co 11:8. The English words man/woman

[a]She shall be called [b]Woman,
Because [a]she was taken out of [c]Man."

24 [A]For this reason a man shall leave his father and
his mother, and be joined to his wife; and they shall
become one flesh. 25 [A]And the man and his wife were
both naked and were not ashamed.

THE FALL OF MAN

3 Now [A]the serpent was more crafty than any
beast of the field which the LORD God had made.
And he said to the woman, "Indeed, has God said,
'You shall not eat from [a]any tree of the garden'?"
2 The woman said to the serpent, "[A]From the fruit
of the trees of the garden we may eat; 3 but from
the fruit of the tree which is in the middle of the
garden, God has said, 'You shall not eat from it or
touch it, or you will die.'" 4 [A]The serpent said to the
woman, "You surely will not die! 5 For God knows
that in the day you eat from it your eyes will be
opened, and [A]you will be like God, knowing good
and evil." 6 [A]When the woman saw that the tree was
good for food, and that it was a delight to the eyes,
and that the tree was desirable to make *one* wise,
she took from its fruit and ate; and she gave also to
her husband with her, and he ate. 7 Then the eyes
of both of them were opened, and they [A]knew that
they were naked; and they sewed fig leaves together
and made themselves [a]loin coverings.
8 They heard the sound of [A]the LORD God walking
in the garden in the [a]cool of the day, [B]and the man
and his wife hid themselves from the presence of
the LORD God among the trees of the garden. 9 Then
the LORD God called to the man, and said to him,
"[A]Where are you?" 10 He said, "[A]I heard the sound
of You in the garden, and I was afraid because I
was naked; so I hid myself." 11 And He said, "Who
told you that you were naked? Have you eaten from
the tree of which I commanded you not to eat?"
12 [A]The man said, "The woman whom You gave *to*
be with me, she gave me from the tree, and I ate."
13 Then the LORD God said to the woman, "What is

2:23 [a]Lit *This one* [b]Heb *Ishshah* [c]Heb *Ish* 2:24 [A]Matt 19:5; Mark 10:7, 8; 1 Cor 6:16; Eph 5:31 2:25 [A]Gen 3:7, 10, 11 3:1 [a]Or *every* [A]2 Cor 11:3; Rev 12:9; 20:2 3:2 [A]Gen 2:16, 17 3:4 [A]John 8:44; 2 Cor 11:3 3:5 [A]Is 14:14; Ezek 28:2, 12-17 3:6 [A]Rom 5:12-19; 1 Tim 2:14; James 1:14, 15; 1 John 2:16 3:7 [a]Or *girdles* [A]Is 47:3; Lam 1:8 3:8 [a]Lit *wind, breeze* [A]Gen 18:33; Lev 26:12; Deut 23:14 [B]Job 31:33; Ps 139:1-12; Hos 10:8; Amos 9:3; Rev 6:15-17 3:9 [A]Gen 4:9; 18:9 3:10 [A]Ex 20:18, 19; Deut 5:25 3:12 [A]Job 31:33; Prov 28:13

sustain the same relationship as the Hebrew words, hinting at that original creation.

2:24 leave ... be joined to. The marital relationship was established as the first human institution. The responsibility to honor one's parents (Ex 20:12) does not cease with leaving and the union of husband with wife (Mt 19:5; Mk 10:7, 8; 1Co 6:16; Eph 5:31), but does represent the inauguration of a new and primary responsibility. "Joined" carries the sense of a permanent or indissoluble union, so that divorce was not considered (cf. 3:16). "One flesh" speaks of a complete unity of parts making a whole, e.g., one cluster, many grapes (Nu 13:23) or one God in 3 persons (Dt 6:4); thus this marital union was complete and whole with two people. This also implies their sexual completeness. One man and one woman constitute the pair to reproduce. The "one flesh" is primarily seen in the child born of that union, the one perfect result of the union of two. Cf. uses of this verse in Mt 19:5, 6; Mk 10:8; 1Co 6:16; Eph 5:31. Permanent monogamy was and continues to be God's design and law for marriage.

2:25 both naked ... not ashamed. With no knowledge of evil before the Fall, even nakedness was shameless and innocent. They found their complete gratification in the joy of their one union and their service to God. With no inward principle of evil to work on, the solicitation to sin had to come from without, and it did.

3:1 the serpent. The word means "snake." The apostle John identified this creature as Satan (cf. Rev 12:9; 20:2) as did Paul (2Co 11:3). The serpent, a manifestation of Satan, appears for the first time before the Fall of man. The rebellion of Satan, therefore, had occurred sometime after 1:31 (when everything in creation was good), but before 3:1. Cf. Eze 28:11–15 for a possible description of Satan's dazzling beauty and Is 14:13, 14 for Satan's motivation to challenge God's authority (cf. 1Jn 3:8). Satan, being a fallen archangel and, thus, a supernatural spirit, had possessed the body of a snake in its pre-Fall form (cf. 3:14 for post-Fall form). **more crafty.** Deceitful; cf. Mt 10:16. **to the woman.** She was the object of his attack, being the weaker one and needing the protection of her husband. He found her alone and unfortified by Adam's experience and counsel. Cf. 2Ti 3:6. Though sinless, she was temptable and seducible. **has God said...?** In effect Satan said, "Is it true that He has restricted you from the delights of this place? This is not like one who is truly good and kind. There must be some mistake." He insinuated doubt as to her understanding of God's will, appearing as an angel of light (2Co 11:14) to lead her to the supposed true interpretation. She received him without fear or surprise, but as some credible messenger from heaven with the true understanding, because of his cunning.

3:2, 3 In her answer, Eve extolled the great liberty that they had; with only one exception, they could eat all the fruit.

3:3 not ... touch it. An addition to the original prohibition as recorded (cf. Ge 2:17). Adam may have so instructed her for her protection.

3:4, 5 not die! Satan, emboldened by her openness to him, spoke this direct lie. This lie actually led her and Adam to spiritual death (separation from God). So, Satan is called a liar and murderer from the beginning (Jn 8:44). His lies always promise great benefits (as in v. 5). Eve experienced this result—she and Adam did know good and evil; but by personal corruption, they did not know as God knows in perfect holiness.

3:6 good ... delight ... desirable. She decided that Satan was telling the truth and she had misunderstood God, but she didn't know what she was doing. It was not overt rebellion against God, but seduction and deception to make her believe her act was the right thing to do (cf. v. 13). The NT confirms that Eve was deceived (2Co 11:3; 1Ti 2:14; Rev 12:9). **he ate.** A direct transgression without deception (*see note on 1Ti 2:13, 14*).

3:7 opened ... knew ... sewed. The innocence noted in 2:25 had been replaced by guilt and shame (vv. 8–10), and from then on they had to rely on their conscience to distinguish between good and their newly acquired capacity to see and know evil.

3:8 God appeared, as before, in tones of goodness and kindness, walking in some visible form (perhaps Shekinah light as He later appeared in Ex 33:18–23; 34:5–8, 29; 40:34–38). He came not in fury, but in the same condescending way He had walked with Adam and Eve before.

3:9 Where are you? The question was God's way of bringing man to explain why he was hiding, rather than expressing ignorance about man's location. Shame, remorse, confusion, guilt, and fear all led to their clandestine behavior. There was no place to hide; there never is. See Ps 139:1–12.

3:10 the sound of You. The sound of 3:8, which probably was God calling for Adam and Eve. Adam responded with the language of fear and sorrow, but not confession.

3:11 Adam's sin was evidenced by his new knowledge of the evil of nakedness, but God still waited for Adam to confess to what God knew they had done. The basic reluctance of sinful people to admit their iniquity is here established. Repentance is still the issue. When sinners refuse to repent, they suffer judgment; when they do repent, they receive forgiveness.

3:12 The woman whom You gave. Adam pitifully put the responsibility on God for giving him Eve. That only magnified the tragedy in that Adam had knowingly transgressed God's prohibition, but still would not be open and confess his sin, taking full responsibility for his action, which was not made under deception (1Ti 2:14).

3:13 The serpent deceived me. The woman's desperate effort to pass the blame to the serpent, which was partially true (1Ti 2:14), did not absolve her of the responsibility for her distrust and disobedience toward God.

this you have done?" And the woman said, "[A]The
serpent deceived me, and I ate." 14 The LORD God
said to the serpent,

"[A]Because you have done this,
Cursed are you more than all cattle,
And more than every beast of the field;
On your belly you will go,
And [B]dust you will eat
All the days of your life;
15 And I will put [A]enmity
Between you and the woman,
And between your seed and her seed;
[B]He shall [a]bruise you on the head,
And you shall bruise him on the heel."

16 To the woman He said,

"I will greatly multiply
Your pain [a]in childbirth,
In pain you will [A]bring forth children;
Yet your desire will be for your husband,
And [B]he will rule over you."

17 Then to Adam He said, "Because you have listened
to the voice of your wife, and have eaten from the
tree about which I commanded you, saying, 'You
shall not eat from it';

[A]Cursed is the ground because of you;
[B]In [a]toil you will eat of it
All the days of your life.
18 "Both thorns and thistles it
shall grow for you;
And you will eat the [a]plants of the field;
19 By the sweat of your face
You will eat bread,
Till you [A]return to the ground,
Because [B]from it you were taken;
For you are dust,
And to dust you shall return."

20 Now the man called his wife's name [a],[A]Eve,
because she was the mother of all *the* living. 21 The
LORD God made garments of skin for Adam and his
wife, and clothed them.
22 Then the LORD God said, "Behold, the man
has become like one of [A]Us, knowing good and
evil; and now, he might stretch out his hand, and
take also from [B]the tree of life, and eat, and live
forever"— 23 therefore the LORD God sent him out
from the garden of Eden, to cultivate the ground
from which he was taken. 24 So [A]He drove the man
out; and at the [B]east of the garden of Eden He
stationed the [C]cherubim and the flaming sword
which turned every direction to guard the way to
[D]the tree of life.

3:13 [A]2 Cor 11:3; 1 Tim 2:14 3:14 [A]Deut 28:15-20 [B]Is 65:25; Mic 7:17 3:15 [a]Or *crush* [A]Rev 12:17 [B]Rom 16:20 3:16 [a]Lit *and your pregnancy, conception* [A]John 16:21; 1 Tim 2:15 [B]1 Cor 14:34 3:17 [a]Or *sorrow* [A]Gen 5:29; Rom 8:20-22; Heb 6:8 [B]Job 5:7; 14:1; Eccl 2:23 3:18 [a]Lit *plant* 3:19 [A]Ps 90:3; 104:29; Eccl 12:7 [B]Gen 2:7 3:20 [a]I.e. living; or life [A]2 Cor 11:3; 1 Tim 2:13 3:22 [A]Gen 1:26 [B]Gen 2:9; Rev 22:14 3:24 [A]Ezek 31:11 [B]Gen 2:8 [C]Ex 25:18-22; Ps 104:4; Ezek 10:1-20; Heb 1:7 [D]Gen 2:9

3:14 to the serpent. The cattle and all the rest of creation were cursed (see Ro 8:20–23; cf. Jer 12:4) as a result of Adam and Eve's eating, but the serpent was uniquely cursed by being made to slither on its belly. It probably had legs before this curse. Now snakes represent all that is odious, disgusting, and low. They are branded with infamy and avoided with fear. Cf. Is 65:25; Mic 7:17.

3:15 After cursing the physical serpent, God turned to the spiritual serpent, the lying seducer, Satan, and cursed him. **bruise you on the head ... bruise him on the heel.** This "first gospel" is prophetic of the struggle and its outcome between "your seed" (Satan and unbelievers, who are called the Devil's children in Jn 8:44) and her seed (Christ, a descendant of Eve, and those in Him), which began in the garden. In the midst of the curse passage, a message of hope shone forth—the woman's offspring called "He" is Christ, who will one day defeat the Serpent. Satan could only "bruise" Christ's heel (cause Him to suffer), while Christ will bruise Satan's head (destroy him with a fatal blow). Paul, in a passage strongly reminiscent of Ge 3, encouraged the believers in Rome, "And the God of peace will soon crush Satan under your feet" (Ro 16:20). Believers should recognize that they participate in the crushing of Satan because, along with their Savior and because of His finished work on the cross, they also are of the woman's seed. For more on the destruction of Satan, see Heb 2:14, 15; Rev 20:10.

3:16 pain in childbirth. This is a constant reminder that a woman gave birth to sin in the human race and passes it on to all her children. She can be delivered from this curse by raising godly children, as indicated in 1Ti 2:15 (*see note there*). **your desire ... he will rule.** Just as the woman and her seed will engage in a war with the serpent, i.e., Satan and his seed (v. 15), because of sin and the curse, the man and the woman will face struggles in their own relationship. Sin has turned the harmonious system of God-ordained roles into distasteful struggles of self-will. Lifelong companions, husbands and wives, will need God's help in getting along as a result. The woman's desire will be to lord it over her husband, but the husband will rule by divine design (Eph 5:22–25). This interpretation of the curse is based upon the identical Hebrew words and grammar being used in 4:7 (*see note there*) to show the conflict man will have with sin as it seeks to rule him.

3:17 Because you have listened. The reason given for the curse on the ground and human death is that man turned his back on the voice of God, to follow his wife in eating that from which God had ordered him to abstain. The woman sinned because she acted independently of her husband, disdaining his leadership, counsel, and protection. The man sinned because he abandoned his leadership and followed the wishes of his wife. In both cases, God's intended roles were reversed.

3:17, 18 Cursed is the ground because of you. God cursed the object of man's labor and made it reluctantly, yet richly, yield his food through hard work.

3:19 return to the ground. I.e., to die (cf. 2:7). Man, by sin, became mortal. Although he did not die the moment he ate (by God's mercy), he was changed immediately and became liable to all the sufferings and miseries of life, to death, and to the pains of hell forever. Adam lived 930 years (5:5).

3:21 garments of skin. The first physical deaths should have been the man and his wife, but it was an animal—a shadow of the reality that God would someday kill a substitute to redeem sinners.

3:22 like one of Us. *See note on 1:26.* This was spoken out of compassion for the man and woman, who only in limited ways were like the Trinity, knowing good and evil—not by holy omniscience, but by personal experience (cf. Is 6:3; Hab 1:13; Rev 4:8).

3:22, 23 and live forever. *See note on 2:9.* God told man that he would surely die if he ate of the forbidden tree. But God's concern may also have been that man not live forever in his pitifully cursed condition. Taken in the broader context of Scripture, driving the man and his wife out of the garden was an act of merciful grace to prevent them from being sustained forever by the tree of life.

3:24 cherubim. Later in Israel's history, two cherubim or angelic figures guarded the ark of the covenant and the Holy of Holies in the tabernacle (Ex 25:18–22), where God communed with His people. **flaming sword.** An unexplainable phenomenon, perhaps associated directly with the cherubim or the flaming, fiery Shekinah presence of God Himself.

CAIN AND ABEL

4 Now the man [a]had relations with his wife Eve,
and she conceived and gave birth to [b]Cain, and
she said, "I have gotten a [c]manchild with *the help*
of the LORD." 2 Again, she gave birth to his brother
Abel. And [A]Abel was [B]a keeper of flocks, but Cain
was a tiller of the ground. 3 So it came about [a]in
the course of time that Cain brought an offering to
the LORD of the fruit of the ground. 4 [A]Abel, on his
part also brought of the firstlings of his flock and
of their fat portions. And [B]the LORD had regard for
Abel and for his offering; 5 but [A]for Cain and for his
offering He had no regard. So [B]Cain became very
angry and his countenance fell. 6 Then the LORD
said to Cain, "[A]Why are you angry? And why has
your countenance fallen? 7 [A]If you do well, [a]will not
your countenance be lifted up? [B]And if you do not
do well, sin is crouching at the door; and its desire
is for you, [C]but you must master it." 8 Cain [a]told Abel
his brother. And it came about when they were in
the field, that Cain rose up against Abel his brother
and [A]killed him.
9 Then the LORD said to Cain, "[A]Where is Abel
your brother?" And he said, "I do not know. Am I
my brother's keeper?" 10 He said, "What have you
done? [A]The voice of your brother's blood is crying
to Me from the ground. 11 Now [A]you are cursed from
the ground, which has opened its mouth to receive
your brother's blood from your hand. 12 [A]When
you cultivate the ground, it will no longer yield
its strength to you; [B]you will be a vagrant and a
wanderer on the earth." 13 Cain said to the LORD,
"My punishment is too great to bear! 14 Behold,
You have [A]driven me this day from the face of the
ground; and from Your face I will be hidden, and
[B]I will be a vagrant and a wanderer on the earth,
and [C]whoever finds me will kill me." 15 So the LORD
said to him, "Therefore whoever kills Cain, vengeance will be taken on him [A]sevenfold." And the
LORD [a,B]appointed a sign for Cain, so that no one
finding him would slay him.
16 Then Cain went out from the presence [A]of the
LORD, and [a]settled in the land of [b]Nod, east of Eden.
17 Cain [a]had relations with his wife and she conceived, and gave birth to Enoch; and he built a
city, and called the name of the city Enoch, after
the name of his son. 18 Now to Enoch was born
Irad, and Irad [a]became the father of Mehujael, and
Mehujael [a]became the father of Methushael, and
Methushael [a]became the father of Lamech. 19 Lamech took to himself [A]two wives: the name of the
one was Adah, and the name of the other, Zillah.
20 Adah gave birth to Jabal; he was the father of
those who dwell in tents and *have* livestock. 21 His
brother's name was Jubal; he was the father of all
those who play the lyre and pipe. 22 As for Zillah,
she also gave birth to Tubal-cain, the forger of all
implements of bronze and iron; and the sister of
Tubal-cain was Naamah.
23 Lamech said to his wives,

4:1 [a]Lit *knew* [b]I.e. gotten one [c]Or *man, the LORD* 4:2 [A]Luke 11:50, 51 [B]Gen 46:32; 47:3 4:3 [a]Lit *at the end of days* 4:4 [A]Heb 11:4 [B]1 Sam 15:22 4:5 [A]1 Sam 16:7 [B]Is 3:9; Jude 11 4:6 [A]Jon 4:4 4:7 [a]Or *surely you will be accepted* [A]Jer 3:12; Mic 7:18 [B]Num 32:23 [C]Job 11:14, 15; Rom 6:12, 16 4:8 [a]Lit *said to* [A]Matt 23:35; Luke 11:51; 1 John 3:12-15; Jude 11 4:9 [A]Gen 3:9 4:10 [A]Num 35:33; Deut 21:1-9; Heb 12:24; Rev 6:9, 10 4:11 [A]Gen 3:14; Deut 28:15-20; Gal 3:10 4:12 [A]Deut 28:15-24; Joel 1:10-20 [B]Lev 26:17, 36 4:14 [A]Gen 3:24; Jer 52:3 [B]Deut 28:64-67 [C]Num 35:19 4:15 [a]Or *set a mark on* [A]Gen 4:24 [B]Ezek 9:4, 6 4:16 [a]Lit *dwelt* [b]I.e. wandering [A]2 Kin 24:20; Jer 23:39; 52:3 4:17 [a]Lit *knew* 4:18 [a]Lit *begot* 4:19 [A]Gen 2:24

4:1 had relations with his wife. The act of sexual intercourse was considered the only means by which God Himself gave children. He was acknowledged as the sovereign giver of all life.

4:2 Again, she gave birth. Some think the boys may have been twins, since no time element intervenes between vv. 1, 2. **keeper of flocks … tiller of the ground.** Both occupations were respectable; in fact, most people subsisted through a combination of both. God's focus was not on their vocation, but on the nature of their respective offerings.

4:3 fruit of the ground. Produce in general.

4:4 firstlings … fat. The best animals.

4:4, 5 Abel's offering was acceptable (cf. Heb 11:4), not just because it was an animal, nor just because it was the very best of what he had, nor even that it was the culmination of a zealous heart for God; but, because it was in every way obediently given according to what God must have revealed (though not recorded in Genesis). Cain, disdaining the divine instruction, just brought what he wanted to bring: some of his crop.

4:5, 6 angry. Rather than being repentant for his sinful disobedience, he was hostile toward God, whom he could not kill, and jealous of his brother, whom he could kill (cf. 1Jn 3:12; Jude 11).

4:7 do well … *countenance* be lifted up. God reminded Cain that if he had obeyed God and offered the animal sacrifices God had required, his sacrifices would have been acceptable. It wasn't personal preference on God's part, or disdain for Cain's vocation, or the quality of his produce that caused God to reject his sacrifice. **sin is crouching at the door.** God told Cain that if he chose not to obey His commands, ever-present sin, crouched and waiting to pounce like a lion, would fulfill its desire to overpower him (cf. 3:16).

4:8 The first murder in Scripture (cf. Mt 23:35; Lk 11:51; Heb 12:24). Cain rejected the wisdom spoken to him by God Himself, rejected doing well, refused to repent, and thus crouching sin pounced and turned him into a killer. Cf. 1Jn 3:10–12.

4:9 Am I my brother's keeper? Cain's sarcasm was a play on words, based on the fact that Abel was the "keeper" of sheep. Lying was the third sin resulting from Cain's attitude of indifference to God's commands. Sin was ruling over him (v. 7).

4:10 voice … blood. A figure of speech to indicate that Abel's death was well known to God.

4:11 cursed from the ground. A second curse came from God affecting just the productivity of the soil Cain would till. To a farmer like Cain, this curse was severe, and meant that Cain would all his life be a wanderer, "a vagrant and a wanderer" (vv. 12, 14).

4:14 whoever … kill me. This shows that the population of the earth was, by then, greatly increased. As a wanderer and scavenger in an agrarian world, Cain would be easy prey for those who wanted his life.

4:15 sign. While not described here, it involved some sort of identifiable mark that he was under divine protection which was mercifully given to Cain by God. At the same time, the mark that saved him was the lifelong sign of his shame.

4:16 Nod. An unknown location.

4:17 Cain had relations with his wife. Cain's wife obviously was one of Adam's later daughters (5:4). By Moses' time, this kind of close marriage was forbidden (Lv 18:7–17), because of genetic decay. **Enoch.** His name means "initiation," and was symbolic of the new city where Cain would try to mitigate his curse.

4:19 two wives. No reason is given on Lamech's part for the first recorded instance of bigamy. He led the Cainites in open rebellion against God (cf. 2:24) by his violation of marriage law.

4:20 Jabal. He invented tents and the nomadic life of herdsmen so common in the Middle East and elsewhere.

4:21 Jubal. He invented both stringed and wind instruments.

4:22 Tubal-cain. He invented metallurgy.

4:23, 24 Lamech killed someone in self-defense. He told his wives that they need not fear any harm coming to them for the killing because if anyone tried to retaliate, he would retaliate and kill them. He thought that if God promised 7-fold vengeance on anyone killing Cain, He would give 77-fold vengeance on anyone attacking Lamech.

"Adah and Zillah,
Listen to my voice,
You wives of Lamech,
Give heed to my speech,
[A]For I [a]have killed a man for wounding me;
And a boy for striking me;
24 If Cain is avenged [A]sevenfold,
Then Lamech seventy-sevenfold."

25 [A]Adam [a]had relations with his wife again; and
she gave birth to a son, and named him [b]Seth, for,
she said, "God [c]has appointed me another [d]offspring
in place of Abel, [B]for Cain killed him." 26 To Seth, to
him also [A]a son was born; and he called his name
Enosh. Then *men* began [B]to call [a]upon the name
of the LORD.

DESCENDANTS OF ADAM

5 This is the book of the generations of Adam. In
the day when God created man, He made him
[A]in the likeness of God. 2 He created them [A]male and
female, and He [B]blessed them and named them [a]Man
in the day when they were created.
3 When Adam had lived one hundred and thirty
years, he [a]became the father of *a son* in his own
likeness, according to his image, and named him
Seth. 4 Then the days of Adam after he became the
father of Seth were eight hundred years, and he
had *other* sons and daughters. 5 So all the days that
Adam lived were nine hundred and thirty years,
and he died.
6 Seth lived one hundred and five years, and became the father of Enosh. 7 Then Seth lived eight
hundred and seven years after he became the father
of Enosh, and he had *other* sons and daughters. 8 So
all the days of Seth were nine hundred and twelve
years, and he died.
9 Enosh lived ninety years, and became the father
of Kenan. 10 Then Enosh lived eight hundred and
fifteen years after he became the father of Kenan,
and he had *other* sons and daughters. 11 So all the
days of Enosh were nine hundred and five years,
and he died.
12 Kenan lived seventy years, and became the
father of Mahalalel. 13 Then Kenan lived eight hundred and forty years after he became the father of
Mahalalel, and he had *other* sons and daughters.
14 So all the days of Kenan were nine hundred and
ten years, and he died.
15 Mahalalel lived sixty-five years, and became
the father of Jared. 16 Then Mahalalel lived eight
hundred and thirty years after he became the father
of Jared, and he had *other* sons and daughters. 17 So
all the days of Mahalalel were eight hundred and
ninety-five years, and he died.
18 Jared lived one hundred and sixty-two years,
and became the father of Enoch. 19 Then Jared lived
eight hundred years after he became the father
of Enoch, and he had *other* sons and daughters.
20 So all the days of Jared were nine hundred and
sixty-two years, and he died.
21 Enoch lived sixty-five years, and became the
father of Methuselah. 22 Then Enoch [A]walked with
God three hundred years after he became the father
of Methuselah, and he had *other* sons and daughters.
23 So all the days of Enoch were three hundred and
sixty-five years. 24 [A]Enoch walked with God; and he
was not, for God [B]took him.
25 Methuselah lived one hundred and eighty-sev-
en years, and became the father of Lamech. 26 Then
Methuselah lived seven hundred and eighty-two
years after he became the father of Lamech, and
he had *other* sons and daughters. 27 So all the days
of Methuselah were nine hundred and sixty-nine
years, and he died.
28 Lamech lived one hundred and eighty-two
years, and became the father of a son. 29 Now he
called his name Noah, saying, "This one will [a]give
us rest from our work and from the toil of our
hands *arising* from [A]the ground which the LORD
has cursed." 30 Then Lamech lived five hundred
and ninety-five years after he became the father of

4:23 [a]Or *kill* [A]Ex 20:13; Lev 19:18; Deut 32:35; Ps 94:1 4:24 [A]Gen 4:15 4:25 [a]Lit *knew* [b]Heb *Sheth* [c]Heb *shath* [d]Lit *seed* [A]Gen 5:3 [B]Gen 4:8 4:26 [a]Or *by* [A]Luke 3:38 [B]Gen 12:8; 26:25; 1 Kin 18:24; Ps 116:17; Joel 2:32; Zeph 3:9; 1 Cor 1:2 5:1 [A]Gen 1:26, 27; Eph 4:24; Col 3:10 5:2 [a]Lit *Adam* [A]Matt 19:4; Mark 10:6 [B]Gen 1:28 5:3 [a]Lit *begot*, and so throughout the ch 5:22 [A]Gen 6:9; 17:1; 24:40; 48:15; Mic 6:8; Mal 2:6; 1 Thess 2:12 5:24 [A]2 Kin 2:11; Jude 14 [B]2 Kin 2:10; Ps 49:15; 73:24; Heb 11:5 5:29 [a]Lit *comfort us in* [A]Gen 3:17-19; 4:11

4:25 Seth. With Cain removed as the older brother and heir of the family blessing, and with Abel dead, God graciously gave Adam and Eve a godly son through whom the seed of redemption (3:15) would be passed all the way to Jesus Christ (Lk 3:38).

4:26 *men* began to call upon the name of the LORD. As men realized their inherent sinfulness with no human means to appease God's righteous indignation and wrath over their multiplied iniquities, they turned to God for mercy and grace in hopes of a restored personal relationship.

5:1–6:8 generations of Adam. Ten specific families are mentioned. Most likely, in accord with other biblical genealogies, this listing is representative rather than complete (cf. Ru 4:18–22).

5:1–32 Adam … Noah. The genealogy connects Adam to the Noahic family which not only survived the Flood, but also became first in God's re-creation. Two recurring phrases carry redemption history forward: "… he had *other* sons and daughters," "… and he died." These lines, which get repeated for each successive descendant of Adam, echo two contrasting realities; God had said "you will surely die" (2:17), but He had also commanded them to "be fruitful and multiply" (1:28).

5:1 the likeness of God. *See notes on 1:26.*

5:2 named them Man. In naming man, God declared His own dominion over all creation (Mt 19:4; Mk 10:6).

5:3 in his own likeness, according to his image. The human image and likeness in which God created mankind was procreatively passed to the second generation and to all generations which follow.

5:5 nine hundred and thirty years. These are literal years marking unusual length of life, accounted for by the pre-Flood environment. The earth was under a canopy of water that filtered out the ultraviolet rays of the sun, producing a much more moderate and healthful condition. *See notes on 1:7; 2:6.* **and he died.** God told Adam that if he ate of the tree he would surely die (2:17). It included spiritual death immediately and then physical death later.

5:24 walked with God … was not, for God took him. Enoch is the only break in the chapter from the incessant comment, "and he died." Cf. 4:17, 18; 1Ch 1:3; Lk 3:37; Heb 11:5; Jude 14. Only one other man is said to have enjoyed this intimacy of relationship in walking with God, Noah (6:9). Enoch experienced being taken to heaven alive by God, as did Elijah later (2Ki 2:1–12).

5:25–27 Methuselah. The man who lived the longest life on record. He died the year of the flood judgment (cf. 7:6).

5:29 This one will give us rest. Comfort and rest would come through the godly life

Noah, and he had *other* sons and daughters. 31 So
all the days of Lamech were seven hundred and
seventy-seven years, and he died.
32 Noah was [A]five hundred years old, and Noah
became the father of Shem, Ham, and Japheth.

THE CORRUPTION OF MANKIND

6 Now it came about, when men began to multiply on the face of the land, and daughters were
born to them, 2 that the sons of God saw that the
daughters of men were [a]beautiful; and they took
wives for themselves, whomever they chose. 3 Then
the LORD said, "[A]My Spirit shall not [a]strive with man
forever, [b,B]because he also is flesh; [c]nevertheless
his days shall be one hundred and twenty years."
4 The [A]Nephilim were on the earth in those days,
and also afterward, when the sons of God came in
to the daughters of men, and they bore *children* to
them. Those were the mighty men who *were* of old,
men of renown.
5 Then the LORD saw that the wickedness of man
was great on the earth, and that [A]every intent of
the thoughts of his heart was only evil continually.
6 [A]The LORD was sorry that He had made man on
the earth, and He was [B]grieved [a]in His heart. 7 The
LORD said, "[A]I will blot out man whom I have created
from the face of the land, from man to animals to
creeping things and to birds of the [a]sky; for [B]I am
sorry that I have made them." 8 But [A]Noah [B]found
favor in the eyes of the LORD.
9 These are *the records of* the generations of
Noah. Noah was a [A]righteous man, [a,B]blameless in
his [b]time; Noah [C]walked with God. 10 Noah [a]became
the father of three sons: Shem, Ham, and Japheth.
11 Now the earth was [A]corrupt in the sight of God,
and the earth was [B]filled with violence. 12 God looked
on the earth, and behold, it was corrupt; for [A]all flesh
had corrupted their way upon the earth.
13 Then God said to Noah, "[A]The end of all flesh has
come before Me; for the earth is filled with violence
because of them; and behold, I am about to destroy
them with the earth. 14 Make for yourself an ark of
gopher wood; you shall make the ark with rooms,
and shall [a]cover it inside and out with pitch. 15 This
is how you shall make it: the length of the ark three
hundred [a]cubits, its breadth fifty [a]cubits, and its
height thirty [a]cubits. 16 You shall make a [a]window
for the ark, and finish it to a cubit from [b]the top;
and set the door of the ark in the side of it; you
shall make it with lower, second, and third decks.
17 Behold, [A]I, even I am bringing the flood of water
upon the earth, to destroy all flesh in which is the
breath of life, from under heaven; everything that is
on the earth shall perish. 18 But I will establish [A]My
covenant with you; and [B]you shall enter the ark—you
and your sons and your wife, and your sons' wives

5:32 [A]Gen 7:6 6:2 [a]Lit *good* 6:3 [a]Or *rule in;* some ancient versions read *abide in* [b]Or *in his going astray he is flesh* [c]Or *therefore* [A]Gal 5:16, 17; 1 Pet 3:20 [B]Ps 78:39 6:4 [A]Num 13:33 6:5 [A]Gen 8:21; Ps 14:1-3; Prov 6:18; Matt 15:19; Rom 1:28-32 6:6 [a]Lit *to* [A]Gen 6:7; Jer 18:7-10 [B]Is 63:10; Eph 4:30 6:7 [a]Lit *heavens* [A]Deut 28:63; 29:20 [B]Gen 6:6; Amos 7:3, 6 6:8 [A]Matt 24:37; Luke 17:26; 1 Pet 3:20 [B]Gen 19:19; Ex 33:17; Luke 1:30 6:9 [a]Lit *complete, perfect;* or *having integrity* [b]Lit *generations* [A]Ps 37:39; 2 Pet 2:5 [B]Gen 17:1; Deut 18:13; Job 1:1 [C]Gen 5:24 6:10 [a]Lit *begot* 6:11 [A]Deut 31:29; Judg 2:19 [B]Ezek 8:17 6:12 [A]Ps 14:1-3 6:13 [A]Is 34:1-4; Ezek 7:2, 3; Amos 8:2; 1 Pet 4:7 6:14 [a]Or *pitch* 6:15 [a]I.e. One cubit equals approx 18 in. 6:16 [a]Or *roof* [b]Lit *above* 6:17 [A]2 Pet 2:5 6:18 [A]Gen 9:9-16; 17:7 [B]Gen 7:7

of Noah, who is an "heir of the righteousness which is according to faith" (Heb 11:7).

6:1–4 The account that follows records an act of degradation that reveals the end-point of God's patience.

6:1 Such long lifespans as indicated in the record of chap. 5 caused massive increase in earth's population.

6:2 **sons of God ... daughters of men.** The sons of God, identified elsewhere almost exclusively as angels (Job 1:6; 2:1; 38:7), saw and took wives of the human race. This produced an unnatural union which violated the God-ordained order of human marriage and procreation (Ge 2:24). Some have argued that the sons of God were the sons of Seth who cohabited with the daughters of Cain; others suggest they were perhaps human kings wanting to build harems. But the passage puts strong emphasis on the angelic vs. human contrast. The NT places this account in sequence with other Genesis events and identifies it as involving fallen angels who indwelt men (*see notes on 2Pe 2:4, 5; Jude 6*). Matthew 22:30 does not necessarily negate the possibility that angels are capable of procreation, but just that they do not marry. To procreate physically, they had to possess human, male bodies.

6:3 **My Spirit.** Cf. Ge 1:2. The Holy Spirit played a most active role in the OT. The Spirit had been striving to call men to repentance and righteousness, especially as Scripture notes, through the preaching of Enoch and Noah (1Pe 3:20; 2Pe 2:5; Jude 14). **one hundred and twenty.** The span of time until the Flood (cf. 1Pe 3:20), in which man was given opportunity to respond to the warning that God's Spirit would not always be patient.

6:4 **Nephilim.** This word is from a root meaning "to fall," indicating that they were strong men who "fell" on others in the sense of overpowering them (the only other use of this term is in Nu 13:33). They were already in the earth when the "mighty men" and "men of renown" were born. The fallen ones are not the offspring from the union in 6:1, 2.

6:5 **his heart was only evil continually.** This is one of the strongest and clearest statements about man's sinful nature. Sin begins in the thought-life (*see notes on Jas 1:13–15*). The people of Noah's day were exceedingly wicked, from the inside out. Cf. Jer 17:9, 10; Mt 12:34, 35; 15:18, 19; Mk 7:21; Lk 6:45.

6:6 **sorry ... grieved.** Sin sorrowed God who is holy and without blemish (Eph 4:30). Cf. Ex 32:14; 1Sa 15:11; Jer 26:3.

6:7 God promised total destruction when His patience ran out (cf. Ecc 8:11).

6:8 **But Noah found favor.** Lest one believe that Noah was spared because of his good works alone (cf. Heb 11:7), God makes it clear that Noah was a man who believed in God as Creator, Sovereign, and the only Savior from sin. He found grace for himself, because he humbled himself and sought it (cf. 4:26). *See notes on Is 55:6, 7*; he was obedient, as well (6:22; 7:5; Jas 4:6–10).

6:9–9:29 The generations of Noah.

6:9 **a righteous man ... blameless ... walked.** Cf. Eze 14:14, 20; 2Pe 2:5. The order is one of increasing spiritual quality before God: "righteous" is to live by God's righteous standards; "blameless" sets him apart by a comparison with those of his day; and that he "walked with God" puts him in a class with Enoch (5:24).

6:11 **corrupt ... filled with violence.** Cf. 6:3, 5. The seed of Satan, the fallen rejectors of God, deceitful and destructive, had dominated the world.

6:13 **I am about to destroy them with the earth.** Destroy did not mean annihilation, but rather referred to the flood judgment, both of the earth and its inhabitants.

6:14 **ark.** A hollow chest, a box designed to float on water (Ex 2:3). **gopher wood.** Probably cedar or cypress trees, abundant in the mountains of Armenia.

6:15, 16 While the ark was not designed for beauty or speed, these dimensions provided extraordinary stability in the tumultuous floodwaters. A cubit was about 18 inches long, making the ark 450 feet long, 75 feet wide, and 45 feet high. A gigantic box of that size would be very stable in the water, impossible to capsize. The volume of space in the ark was 1.4 million cubic feet, equal to the capacity of 522 standard railroad box cars, which could carry 125,000 sheep. It had 3 stories, each 15 feet high; each deck was equipped with various rooms (lit. "nests"). "Pitch" was a resin substance to seal the seams and cracks in the wood. The "window" may have actually been a low wall around the flat roof to catch water for all on the ark.

6:17 **flood of water.** Other notable Scriptures on the worldwide flood brought by God include: Job 12:15; 22:16; Ps 29:10; Is 54:9; Mt 24:37–39; Lk 17:26, 27; Heb 11:7; 1Pe 3:20; 2Pe 2:5; 3:5, 6.

6:18 **But I will establish My covenant with you.** In contrast with the rest of the created

with you. 19 [A]And of every living thing of all flesh,
you shall bring two of every *kind* into the ark, to
keep *them* alive with you; they shall be male and
female. 20 [A]Of the birds after their kind, and of the
animals after their kind, of every creeping thing
of the ground after its kind, two of every *kind* will
come to you to keep *them* alive. 21 As for you, take
for yourself some of all [A]food which is edible, and
gather *it* to yourself; and it shall be for food for you
and for them." 22 [A]Thus Noah did; according to all
that God had commanded him, so he did.

THE FLOOD

7 Then the LORD said to Noah, "Enter the ark, you
and all your household, for you *alone* I have seen
to be [A]righteous before Me in this [a]time. 2 You shall take
[a]with you of every [A]clean animal [b]by sevens, a male
and his female; and of the animals that are not clean
two, a male and his female; 3 also of the birds of the
[a]sky, [b]by sevens, male and female, to keep [c]offspring
alive on the face of all the earth. 4 For after [A]seven
more days, I will send rain on the earth [B]forty days and
forty nights; and I will blot out from the face of the
land [C]every living thing that I have made." 5 [A]Noah did
according to all that the LORD had commanded him.
6 Now Noah was [A]six hundred years old when the
flood of water [a]came upon the earth. 7 Then [A]Noah
and his sons and his wife and his sons' wives with
him entered the ark because of the water of the flood.
8 [A]Of clean animals and animals that are not clean
and birds and everything that creeps on the ground,
9 there went into the ark to Noah [a]by twos, male and
female, as God had commanded Noah. 10 It came about
after [A]the seven days, that the water of the flood [a]came
upon the earth. 11 In the [A]six hundredth year of Noah's
life, in the second month, on the seventeenth day of
the month, on the same day all [B]the fountains of the
great deep burst open, and the [a]floodgates of the sky
were opened. 12 [A]The rain [a]fell upon the earth for forty
days and forty nights.
13 On the very same day [A]Noah and Shem and
Ham and Japheth, the sons of Noah, and Noah's wife
and the three wives of his sons with them, entered
the ark, 14 they and every beast after its kind, and all
the cattle after [a]their kind, and every creeping thing
that creeps on the earth after its kind, and every bird

6:19 [A]Gen 7:2, 14, 15 6:20 [A]Gen 7:3 6:21 [A]Gen 1:29, 30 6:22 [A]Gen 7:5; Heb 11:7 7:1 [a]Lit *generation* [A]Gen 6:9 7:2 [a]Lit *to* [b]Lit *seven seven* [A]Lev 11:1-31; Deut 14:3-20 7:3 [a]Lit *heavens* [b]Lit *seven seven* [c]Lit *seed* 7:4 [A]Gen 7:10 [B]Gen 7:12, 17 [C]Gen 6:7, 13 7:5 [A]Gen 6:22 7:6 [a]Lit *was* [A]Gen 5:32 7:7 [A]Gen 6:18; 7:13; Matt 24:38f; Luke 17:27 7:8 [A]Gen 6:19, 20; 7:2, 3 7:9 [a]Lit *two two* 7:10 [a]Lit *were* [A]Gen 7:4 7:11 [a]Or *windows of the heavens* [A]Gen 7:6 [B]Gen 8:2 7:12 [a]Lit *was* [A]Gen 7:4, 17 7:13 [A]Gen 6:18; 7:7 7:14 [a]Lit *its*

order which God was to destroy, Noah and his family were not only to be preserved, but they were to enjoy the provision and protection of a covenant relationship with God. This is the first mention of "covenant" in Scripture. This pledged covenant is actually made and explained in 9:9–17 (*see notes there*).

6:19, 20 There are less than 18,000 species living on earth today. This number may have been doubled to allow for now extinct creatures. With two of each, a total of 72,000 creatures is reasonable as indicated in the note on 6:15, 16; the cubic space could hold 125,000 sheep, and since the average size of land animals is less than a sheep, perhaps less than 60 percent of the space was used. The very large animals were surely represented by young. There was ample room also for the one million species of insects, as well as food for a year for everyone (v. 21).

7:1 righteous. Cf. 6:9; Job 1:1.

7:2, 3 sevens ... sevens. The extra 6 pairs of clean animals and birds would be used for sacrifice (8:20) and food (9:3).

7:3 to keep offspring alive. So that God could use them to replenish the earth.

7:4 God allowed one more week for sinners to repent. **rain ... forty days and forty nights.** A worldwide rain for this length of time is impossible in post-Flood atmospheric conditions, but not then. The canopy that covered the whole earth (*see note on 1:7*), a thermal water blanket encircling the earth, was to be condensed and dumped all over the globe (v. 10).

7:11 month ... day. The calendar system of Noah's day is unknown, although it appears that one month equaled 30 days. If calculated by the Jewish calendar of Moses' day, it would be about May. This period of God's grace was ended (cf. 6:3, 8; 7:4). **all the fountains of the great deep burst open.** The subterranean waters sprang up from inside the earth to form the seas and rivers (1:10; 2:10–14), which were not produced by rainfall (since there was none), but by deep fountains in the earth. **the floodgates of the sky.** The celestial waters in the canopy encircling the globe were dumped on the earth and joined with the terrestrial and the subterranean waters (cf. 1:7). This ended the water canopy surrounding the earth and unleashed the water in the earth; together these phenomena began the new system of hydrology that has since characterized the earth (see Job 26:8; Ecc 1:7; Is 55:10; Am 9:6). The sequence in this verse, indicating that the earth's crust breaks up first, then the heavens drop their water, is interesting because the volcanic explosions that would have occurred when the earth fractured would have sent magma and dust into the atmosphere, along

THE FLOOD CHRONOLOGY
1. In the 600th year of Noah (second month, tenth day), Noah entered the ark (Ge 7:4, 10, 11).
2. In the 600th year of Noah (second month, seventeenth day), the flood began (Ge 7:11).
3. The waters flooded the earth for 150 days (five months of thirty days each), including the forty days and forty nights of rain (Ge 7:12, 17, 24; 8:1), plus the initial receding.
4. The waters further receded to the point that (600th year, seventh month, seventeenth day) the ark rested on Ararat (Ge 8:3, 4).
5. The waters continued to abate so that (600th year, tenth month, first day) the tops of the mountains were visible (Ge 8:5).
6. Forty days later (600th year, eleventh month, tenth day) Noah sent out a raven and a dove (Ge 8:6). Over the next fourteen days, Noah sent out two more doves (Ge 8:10, 12). In all, this took sixty-one days, or two months and one day.
7. By Noah's 601st year on the first month, the first day, the water had dried up (Ge 8:12, 13).
8. Noah waited one month and twenty-six days before he disembarked in the second month, the twenty-seventh day, of his 601st year. From beginning to end, the Flood lasted one year and ten days from Ge 7:11 to Ge 8:14.

after its kind, [b]all sorts of birds. 15 So they went into
the ark to Noah, [A]by twos of all flesh in which was
the breath of life. 16 Those that entered, male and
female of all flesh, entered as God had commanded
him; and the LORD closed *it* behind him.
17 Then the flood [a]came upon the earth for [A]forty
days, and the water increased and lifted up the ark,
so that it rose above the earth. 18 The water prevailed and increased greatly upon the earth, and
the ark [a]floated on the [b]surface of the water. 19 The
water prevailed more and more upon the earth, so
that all the high mountains [a]everywhere under the
heavens were covered. 20 The water prevailed fifteen
[a]cubits higher, [A]and the mountains were covered.
21 [A]All flesh that [a]moved on the earth perished, birds
and cattle and beasts and every swarming thing
that swarms upon the earth, and all mankind; 22 of
all that was on the dry land, all [A]in whose nostrils
was the breath of the spirit of life, died. 23 Thus He
blotted out [a]every living thing that was upon the
face of the land, from man to animals to creeping
things and to birds of the [b]sky, and they were blotted out from the earth; and only [A]Noah was left,
together with those that were with him in the ark.
24 [A]The water prevailed upon the earth one hundred
and fifty days.

THE FLOOD SUBSIDES

8 But [A]God remembered Noah and all the beasts
and all the cattle that were with him in the ark;
and [B]God caused a wind to pass over the earth, and
the water subsided. 2 Also [A]the fountains of the deep
and the [a]floodgates of the sky were closed, and [B]the
rain from the sky was restrained; 3 and the water
receded steadily from the earth, and at the end [A]of
one hundred and fifty days the water decreased.
4 In the seventh month, on the seventeenth day of
the month, [A]the ark rested upon the mountains of

7:14 [b]Lit *every bird, every wing* 7:15 [A]Gen 6:19; 7:9 7:17 [a]Lit *was* [A]Gen 7:4 7:18 [a]Lit *went* [b]Lit *face* 7:19 [a]Lit *which were under all the heavens* 7:20 [a]I.e. One cubit equals approx 18 in. [A]Gen 8:4 7:21 [a]Or *crept* [A]Gen 6:7, 13, 17; 7:4 7:22 [A]Gen 2:7 7:23 [a]Lit *all existence* [b]Lit *heavens* [A]Matt 24:38, 39; Luke 17:26, 27; Heb 11:7; 1 Pet 3:20; 2 Pet 2:5 7:24 [A]Gen 8:3 8:1 [A]Gen 19:29; Ex 2:24; 1 Sam 1:19; Ps 105:42 [B]Ex 14:21; 15:10; Job 12:15; Ps 29:10; Is 44:27; Nah 1:4 8:2 [a]Or *windows of the heavens* [A]Gen 7:11 [B]Gen 7:4, 12 8:3 [A]Gen 7:24 8:4 [A]Gen 7:20

with gigantic sprays of water, gas, and air—all penetrating the canopy and triggering its downpour.

7:16 the LORD closed *it* behind him. No small event is spared in the telling of this episode, although the details are sparse.

7:19 all the high mountains. This describes the extent of the Flood as global. Lest there be any doubt, Moses adds "under the heavens" (cf. 2Pe 3:5–7). There are over 270 flood stories told in cultures all over the earth, which owe their origin to this one global event.

7:20 The highest mountains were at least 22.5 feet under water, so that the ark floated freely above the peaks. This would include the highest peak in that area, Mt. Ararat (8:4), which is ca. 17,000 feet high. That depth further proves it was not a local flood, but a global one.

7:24 one hundred and fifty days. These days included the 40 day and night period of rain (7:12, 17). The Flood rose to its peak at that point (cf. 8:3). It then took over 2 1/2 months before the water receded to reveal other mountain peaks (8:4, 5), over 4 1/2 months before the dove could find dry land (8:8–12), and almost 8 months before the occupants could leave the ark (8:14).

8:1 But God remembered Noah. God's covenant with Noah brought provision and protection in the midst of severe judgment. The remnant was preserved and God initiated steps toward reestablishing the created order on earth. **the waters subsided.** God used the wind to dry the ground; evaporation returned water to the atmosphere.

8:4 the mountains of Ararat. These were in the region of the Caucasus, also known as

MAJOR MOUNTAINS OF THE BIBLE
Mt. Ararat (in modern Turkey), where Noah's ark came to rest (Ge 8:4).
Mt. Carmel, where Elijah was victorious over the prophets of Baal (1Ki 18:9–42).
Mt. Ebal (opposite Mt. Gerizim), where Moses commanded that an altar be built after the Hebrews entered the Promised Land (Dt 27:4).
Mt. Gerizim, where Jesus talked with the Samaritan woman at the well (Jn 4:20).
Mt. Gilboa, where King Saul and his sons were killed in a battle with the Philistines (1Ch 10:1, 8).
Mt. Hermon, a mountain range that marked the northern limit of the conquest of Canaan (Jos 11:3, 17).
Mt. Lebanon, the source of cedar wood for Solomon's temple in Jerusalem (1Ki 5:14, 18).
Mt. Moriah, where Abraham brought Isaac for sacrifice (Ge 22:2) and the location of Solomon's temple (2Ch 3:1).
Mt. Olivet, or Mt. of Olives, where Jesus gave the discourse on His Second Coming (Mt 24:3).
Mt. Pisgah, or Nebo, where Moses viewed the Promised Land (Dt 34:1).
Mt. Seir, south of the Dead Sea, the location to which Esau moved after Isaac's death (Ge 36:8).
Mt. Sinai, or Horeb (near Egypt), where the law was given to Moses (Ex 19:2–25).
Mt. Tabor, six miles east of Nazareth, served as a boundary between Issachar and Zebulun; also Barak launched his attack on Sisera from Tabor (Jdg 4:6–15).
Mt. Zion, originally limited to the SW sector (2Sa 5:7), was later used of all Jerusalem (La 1:4).

Ararat. 5 The water decreased steadily until the tenth
month; in the tenth month, on the first day of the
month, the tops of the mountains became visible.
6 Then it came about at the end of forty days, that
Noah opened the [A]window of the ark which he had
made; 7 and he sent out a raven, and it [a]flew here
and there until the water was dried up [b]from the
earth. 8 Then he sent out a dove from him, to see
if the water was abated from the face of the land;
9 but the dove found no resting place for the sole of
her foot, so she returned to him into the ark, for the
water was on the [a]surface of all the earth. Then he
put out his hand and took her, and brought her into
the ark to himself. 10 So he waited yet another seven
days; and again he sent out the dove from the ark.
11 The dove came to him toward [a]evening, and behold, in her [b]beak was a freshly picked olive leaf. So
Noah knew that the water was abated from the earth.
12 Then he waited yet another seven days, and sent
out [A]the dove; but she did not return to him again.
13 Now it came about in the [A]six hundred and first
year, in the first *month,* on the first of the month,
the water was dried up [a]from the earth. Then Noah
removed the covering of the ark, and looked, and
behold, the [b]surface of the ground was dried up.
14 In the second month, on the twenty-seventh day
of the month, the earth was dry. 15 Then God spoke
to Noah, saying, 16 "Go out of the ark, you and your
wife and your sons and your sons' wives with you.
17 Bring out with you every living thing of all flesh
that is with you, birds and animals and every creeping thing that creeps on the earth, that they may
[a,A]breed abundantly on the earth, and be fruitful
and multiply on the earth." 18 So Noah went out,
and his sons and his wife and his sons' wives with
him. 19 Every beast, every creeping thing, and every
bird, everything that moves on the earth, went out
[a]by their families from the ark.
20 Then Noah built [A]an altar to the LORD, and took
of every [B]clean animal and of every clean bird and
offered [C]burnt offerings on the altar. 21 The LORD
[A]smelled the soothing aroma; and the LORD said [a]to
Himself, "I will never again [B]curse the ground on
account of man, for [C]the [b]intent of man's heart is
evil from his youth; [D]and I will never again [c]destroy
every living thing, as I have done.

22 "While the earth remains,
Seedtime and harvest,
And cold and heat,
And [A]summer and winter,
And [B]day and night
Shall not cease."

COVENANT OF THE RAINBOW

9 And God blessed Noah and his sons and said
to them, "[A]Be fruitful and multiply, and fill the
earth. 2 The fear of you and the terror of you will
be on every beast of the earth and on every bird of
the [a]sky; with everything that creeps on the ground,
and all the fish of the sea, into your hand they are
given. 3 Every moving thing that is alive shall be
food for you; I give all to you, [A]as *I gave* the green
plant. 4 Only you shall not eat flesh with its life, *that
is,* [A]its blood. 5 Surely I will require [a,A]your lifeblood;
[b,B]from every beast I will require it. And [b]from *every* man, [b]from every man's brother I will require
the life of man.

6 "[A]Whoever sheds man's blood,
By man his blood shall be shed,
For [B]in the image of God
He made man.
7 "As for you, [A]be fruitful and multiply;
[a]Populate the earth abundantly
and multiply in it."

8 Then God spoke to Noah and to his sons with
him, saying, 9 "Now behold, [A]I Myself do establish
My covenant with you, and with your [a]descendants

8:6 [A]Gen 6:16 8:7 [a]Lit *went out, going and returning* [b]Lit *from upon* 8:9 [a]Lit *face* 8:11 [a]Lit *the time of evening* [b]Lit *mouth* 8:12 [A]Jer 48:28 8:13 [a]Lit *from upon* [b]Lit *face* [A]Gen 7:6 8:17 [a]Or *swarm* [A]Gen 1:22, 28 8:19 [a]Or *according to their kind* 8:20 [A]Gen 12:7, 8; 13:18; 22:9 [B]Gen 7:2; Lev 11:1-47 [C]Gen 22:2; Ex 10:25 8:21 [a]Lit *to His heart* [b]Or *inclination* [c]Lit *smite* [A]Ex 29:18, 25 [B]Gen 3:17; 6:7, 13, 17; Is 54:9 [C]Gen 6:5; Ps 51:5; Jer 17:9; Rom 1:21; 3:23; Eph 2:1-3 [D]Gen 9:11, 15 8:22 [A]Ps 74:17 [B]Jer 33:20, 25 9:1 [A]Gen 1:28; 9:7 9:2 [a]Lit *heavens* 9:3 [A]Gen 1:29 9:4 [A]Lev 7:26f; 17:10-16; 19:26; Deut 12:16, 23; 15:23; 1 Sam 14:34; Acts 15:20, 29 9:5 [a]Lit *your blood of your lives* [b]Lit *from the hand of* [A]Ex 20:13; 21:12 [B]Ex 21:28, 29 9:6 [A]Ex 21:12-14; Lev 24:17; Num 35:33; Matt 26:52 [B]Gen 1:26, 27 9:7 [a]Lit *Swarm in the earth* [A]Gen 9:1 9:9 [a]Lit *seed* [A]Gen 6:18

ancient Urartu, where the elevation exceeded 17,000 feet.

8:7–12 a raven …. dove. Ravens survive on a broad range of food types. If any food was available outside the ark, the raven could survive. In contrast, a dove is much more selective in its food choices. The dove's choice of food would indicate that new life had begun to grow; thus Noah and his family could also survive outside the ark.

8:14–16 Noah and his family had been in the ark for 378 days (cf. 7:4, 10, 11).

8:17–19 be fruitful and multiply. In the process of replenishing the created order that He had judged with destruction, God repeated the words of the blessing which He had put upon nonhuman creatures (1:22). Noah faced a new world where longevity of life began to decline immediately; the earth was subject to storms and severe weather, blazing heat, freezing cold, seismic action, and natural disasters.

8:20 built an altar. This was done as an act of worship in response to God's covenant faithfulness in sparing him and his family.

8:21 smelled the soothing aroma. God accepted Noah's sacrifice. **curse … destroy.** Regardless of how sinful mankind would become in the future, God promised not to engage in global catastrophe by flood again (cf. 9:11). *See notes on 2Pe 3:3–10* for how God will destroy the earth in the future.

8:22 While the earth remains. With many alterations from the global flood, God reestablished the cycle of seasons after the catastrophic interruption.

9:1 blessed Noah … Be fruitful and multiply, and fill the earth. God blessed Noah and recommissioned him to fill the earth (cf. 1:28).

9:2, 3 The fear of you. Man's relationship to the animals appears to have changed, in that man is free to eat animals for sustenance (v. 3).

9:4 blood. Raw blood was not to be consumed as food. It symbolically represented life. To shed blood symbolically represented death (cf. Lv 17:11). The blood of animals, representing their life, was not to be eaten. It was, in fact, that blood that God designed to be a covering for sin (Lv 17:11).

9:5 beast … man. Capital punishment was invoked upon every animal (Ex 21:28) or man who took human life unlawfully. Cf. Jn 19:11; Ac 25:11; Ro 13:4 for clear NT support for this punishment.

9:6 For in the image of God. The reason man could kill animals, but neither animals nor man could kill man, is because man alone was created in God's image.

9:9–17 This is the first covenant God made with man, afterwards called the Noahic Covenant.

9:9, 10 with you … with your descendants … with every living creature. The

after you; 10 and with every living creature that is
with you, the birds, the cattle, and every beast of
the earth with you; of all that comes out of the ark,
even every beast of the earth. 11 I establish My covenant with you; and all flesh shall [A]never again be
cut off by the water of the flood, [B]neither shall there
again be a flood to destroy the earth." 12 God said,
"This is [A]the sign of the covenant which I am making between Me and you and every living creature
that is with you, for [a]all successive generations; 13 I
set My [A]bow in the cloud, and it shall be for a sign
of a covenant between Me and the earth. 14 It shall
come about, when I bring a cloud over the earth,
that the bow will be seen in the cloud, 15 and [A]I will
remember My covenant, which is between Me and
you and every living creature of all flesh; and [B]never
again shall the water become a flood to destroy all
flesh. 16 When the bow is in the cloud, then I will
look upon it, to remember the [A]everlasting covenant
between God and every living creature of all flesh
that is on the earth." 17 And God said to Noah, "This
is the sign of the covenant which I have established
between Me and all flesh that is on the earth."

18 Now the sons of Noah who came out of the
ark were Shem and Ham and Japheth; and [A]Ham
was the father of Canaan. 19 These three *were* the
sons of Noah, and [A]from these the whole earth was
[a]populated.

20 Then Noah began [a]farming and planted a vineyard. 21 He drank of the wine and [A]became drunk,
and uncovered himself inside his tent. 22 Ham, the
father of Canaan, [A]saw the nakedness of his father,
and told his two brothers outside. 23 But Shem and
Japheth took a garment and laid it upon both their
shoulders and walked backward and covered the nakedness of their father; and their faces were [a]turned
away, so that they did not see their father's nakedness. 24 When Noah awoke from his wine, he knew
what his youngest son had done to him. 25 So he said,

"[A]Cursed be Canaan;
[a,B]A servant of servants
He shall be to his brothers."

26 He also said,

"[A]Blessed be the LORD,
The God of Shem;
And let Canaan be [a]his servant.
27 "[A]May God enlarge Japheth,
And let him dwell in the tents of Shem;
And let Canaan be [a]his servant."

28 Noah lived three hundred and fifty years after
the flood. 29 So all the days of Noah were nine hundred and fifty years, and he died.

DESCENDANTS OF NOAH

10 Now these are *the records of* the generations
of Shem, Ham, and Japheth, the sons of Noah;
and sons were born to them after the flood.
2 [A]The sons of Japheth *were* [B]Gomer and Magog
and [C]Madai and [D]Javan and Tubal and [E]Meshech
and Tiras. 3 The sons of Gomer *were* [A]Ashkenaz and
[a]Riphath and [B]Togarmah. 4 The sons of Javan *were*
Elishah and [A]Tarshish, Kittim and [a]Dodanim. 5 From

9:11 [A]Gen 8:21 [B]Is 54:9 9:12 [a]Or *everlasting generations* [A]Gen 9:13, 17; 17:11 9:13 [A]Ezek 1:28 9:15 [A]Lev 26:42, 45; Deut 7:9; Ezek 16:60 [B]Gen 9:11 9:16 [A]Gen 17:13, 19; 2 Sam 23:5 9:18 [A]Gen 9:25-27; 10:6 9:19 [a]Lit *scattered* [A]Gen 9:1, 7; 10:32; 1 Chr 1:4 9:20 [a]Lit to be *a farmer* 9:21 [A]Prov 20:1 9:22 [A]Hab 2:15 9:23 [a]Lit *backward* 9:25 [a]I.e. The lowest of servants [A]Deut 27:16 [B]Josh 9:23 9:26 [a]Or *their* [A]Gen 14:20; 24:27 9:27 [a]Or *their* [A]Gen 10:2-5; Is 66:19 10:2 [A]1 Chr 1:5-7 [B]Ezek 38:2, 6 [C]2 Kin 17:6 [D]Is 66:19 [E]Ezek 38:2 10:3 [a]I.e. In 1 Chr 1:6, *Diphath* [A]Jer 51:27 [B]Ezek 27:14 10:4 [a]I.e. In 1 Chr 1:7, *Rodanim* [A]Ezek 27:12, 25

covenant with Noah included living creatures as was first promised in 6:19.

9:11 by the water. The specific promise of this covenant, never to destroy the world again by water, was qualified by the means, for God has since promised to destroy the earth with fire one day (2Pe 3:10, 11; Rev 20:9; 21:1).

9:12 the sign of the covenant. The rainbow is the perpetual, symbolic reminder of this covenant promise, just as circumcision of all males would be for the Abrahamic Covenant (17:10, 11).

9:15 I will remember. Not simple recognition, but God's commitment to keep the promise.

9:16 the everlasting covenant. This covenant with Noah is the first of 5 divinely originated covenants in Scripture explicitly described as "everlasting." The other 4 include: 1) Abrahamic (Ge 17:7); 2) Priestly (Nu 25:10–13); 3) Davidic (2Sa 23:5); and 4) New (Jer 32:40). The term "everlasting" can mean either 1) to the end of time and/or 2) through eternity future. It never looks back to eternity past. Of the 6 explicitly mentioned covenants of this kind in Scripture, only the Mosaic or Old Covenant was nullified.

9:18 Ham was the father of Canaan. Canaan's offspring, the idolatrous enemies of Israel whose land Abraham's descendants would later take (15:13–16), became a primary focus in chap. 10. This notation is important since Moses was writing the Pentateuch just before the Israelites took Canaan (see Introduction: Author and Date, Background and Setting).

9:19 from these the whole earth. All men who have ever lived since the Flood came from these 3 sons of Noah (cf. 10:32). The "one man" (Ac 17:26) from whom all nations came is Adam through Noah. All physical characteristics of the whole race were present in the genetics of Noah, his sons, and their wives.

9:21 became drunk. Fermentation, which leads to drunkenness, may have been caused by changed ecological conditions as a result of the Flood. Noah may have taken off his clothes because of the heat, or been involuntarily exposed due to his drunkenness.

9:22 saw the nakedness. There is no reasonable support for the notion that some perverse activity, in addition to seeing nakedness, occurred. But clearly, the implication is that Ham looked with some sinful thought, if only for a while until he left to inform his brothers. Perhaps he was glad to see his father's dignity and authority reduced to such weakness. He thought his brothers might share his feelings so he eagerly told them. They did not, however, share his attitude (v. 23).

9:25–27 Cursed be Canaan. The shift from Ham to his son Canaan established the historic legitimacy of Israel's later conquest of the Canaanites. These were the people with whom Israel had to do battle shortly after they first heard Moses' reading of this passage. Here, God gave Israel the theological basis for the conquest of Canaan. The descendants of Ham had received a sentence of judgment for the sins of their progenitor. In 10:15–20, the descendants of Canaan are seen to be the earlier inhabitants of the land later promised to Abraham.

9:26 let Canaan be his servant. Conquered peoples were called servants, even if they were not household or private slaves. Shem, the ancestor of Israel, and the other "Semites" were to be the masters of Ham's descendants, the Canaanites. The latter would give their land to the former.

9:27 dwell in the tents. This means that spiritual blessings would come to the Japhethites through the God of Shem (v. 26) and the line of Shem from which Messiah would come.

10:1–11:9 The genealogy of Shem, Ham, and Japheth (v. 1).

10:1–32 See the map "The Nations of Genesis 10" for the locations of Noah's descendants.

10:5 were separated . . . according to his

these the coastlands of the nations [a]were separated
into their lands, every one according to his language, according to their families, into their nations.
6 [A]The sons of Ham *were* Cush and Mizraim and
Put and Canaan. 7 The sons of Cush *were* [A]Seba and
Havilah and Sabtah and [B]Raamah and Sabteca; and
the sons of Raamah *were* [B]Sheba and [C]Dedan. 8 Now
Cush [a]became the father of Nimrod; he [b]became a
mighty one on the earth. 9 He was a mighty hunter
before the LORD; therefore it is said, "Like Nimrod a
mighty hunter before the LORD." 10 The beginning
of his kingdom was [a,A]Babel and Erech and Accad
and Calneh, in the land of [B]Shinar. 11 From that land
he went forth [A]into Assyria, and built Nineveh and
Rehoboth-Ir and Calah, 12 and Resen between Nineveh and Calah; that is the great city. 13 Mizraim
[a]became the father of [A]Ludim and Anamim and
Lehabim and Naphtuhim 14 and [A]Pathrusim and
Casluhim (from which came the Philistines) and
Caphtorim.
15 Canaan [a]became the father of [A]Sidon, his firstborn, and [B]Heth 16 and [A]the Jebusite and the Amorite
and the Girgashite 17 and the Hivite and the Arkite
and the Sinite 18 and the Arvadite and the Zemarite
and the Hamathite; and afterward the families of
the Canaanite were spread abroad. 19 [A]The territory of the Canaanite [a]extended from Sidon as you
go toward Gerar, as far as Gaza; as you go toward
[B]Sodom and Gomorrah and Admah and Zeboiim, as
far as Lasha. 20 These are the sons of Ham, according
to their families, according to their languages, by
their lands, by their nations.
21 Also to Shem, the father of all the children of
Eber, *and* the [a]older brother of Japheth, children
were born. 22 [A]The sons of Shem *were* [B]Elam and
Asshur and [C]Arpachshad and [D]Lud and Aram. 23 The
sons of Aram *were* [A]Uz and Hul and Gether and
Mash. 24 Arpachshad [a]became the father of [A]She-
lah; and Shelah [a]became the father of Eber. 25 [A]Two
sons were born to Eber; the name of the one *was*
[a]Peleg, for in his days the earth was divided; and
his brother's name *was* Joktan. 26 Joktan [a]became
the father of Almodad and Sheleph and Hazarmaveth and Jerah 27 and Hadoram and Uzal and Diklah
28 and [a]Obal and Abimael and Sheba 29 and Ophir
and Havilah and Jobab; all these were the sons of
Joktan. 30 Now their [a]settlement [b]extended from
Mesha as you go toward Sephar, the hill country of
the east. 31 These are the sons of Shem, according
to their families, according to their languages, by
their lands, according to their nations.
32 These are the families of the sons of Noah,
according to their genealogies, by their nations;
and [A]out of these the nations were separated on
the earth after the flood.

UNIVERSAL LANGUAGE, BABEL, CONFUSION

11 Now the whole earth [a]used the same language
and [b]the same words. 2 It came about as they

10:5 [a]Or *separated themselves* 10:6 [A]1 Chr 1:8-10 10:7 [A]Is 43:3 [B]Ezek 27:22 [C]Ezek 27:15, 20 10:8 [a]Lit *begot* [b]Lit *began to be* 10:10 [a]Or *Babylon* [A]Gen 11:9 [B]Gen 11:2; 14:1 10:11 [A]Mic 5:6 10:13 [a]Lit *begot* [A]Jer 46:9 10:14 [A]1 Chr 1:12 10:15 [a]Lit *begot* [A]1 Chr 1:13; Jer 47:4 [B]Gen 23:3 10:16 [A]Gen 15:19-21 10:19 [a]Lit *was* [A]Num 34:2-12 [B]Gen 14:2, 3 10:21 [a]Or *the brother of Japheth the elder* 10:22 [A]1 Chr 1:17 [B]Gen 14:1, 9 [C]Gen 11:10 [D]Is 66:19 10:23 [A]Job 1:1; Jer 25:20 10:24 [a]Lit *begot* [A]Gen 11:12; Luke 3:35 10:25 [a]I.e. division [A]1 Chr 1:19 10:26 [a]Lit *begot* 10:28 [a]In 1 Chr 1:22, *Ebal* 10:30 [a]Lit *dwelling* [b]Lit *was* 10:32 [A]Gen 9:19 11:1 [a]Lit *was one lip* [b]Or *few* or *one set of words*

language. This act describes the situation after the Tower of Babel account in chap. 11.

10:6–20 The sons of Ham. Many of whom were Israel's enemies.

10:8–10 Nimrod. This powerful leader was evidently the force behind the building of Babel (see 11:1–4).

10:10 Babel. The beginning of what later would prove to be Babylon, the destroyer of God's people and His city Jerusalem (ca. 605–539 B.C.).

10:11 into Assyria, and built Nineveh. This was Israel's primary enemy from the East. Nimrod was Israel's prototypical ancient enemy warrior, whose name in Heb. means "rebel" (cf. Mic 5:6).

10:15–19 Canaan. A notable shift occurs in this section away from place names to the inhabitants themselves (note the "ite" ending). These are not only the cursed people of Canaan's curse for the scene at Noah's drunkenness, but also they are those who possess the Promised Land which Israel as a nation needed to conquer. But the Noahic curse alone did not determine their guilt, for God said to Abram that the iniquity of the Amorites must first be complete before his descendants could occupy the Promised Land (15:16).

10:21–31 The sons of Shem, i.e., Semitic people.

10:21 older brother of Japheth. Shem was the oldest of Noah's 3 sons.

10:25 the earth was divided. This looks ahead to the dispersion of nations at Babel (11:1–9).

11:1 same language and the same words. God, who made man as the one creature with whom He could speak (1:28), was to take the gift of language and use it to divide the race, for the apostate worship at Babel indicated that man had turned against God in pride (11:8, 9).

11:2 as they journeyed east. God had restated His commission for man to "be

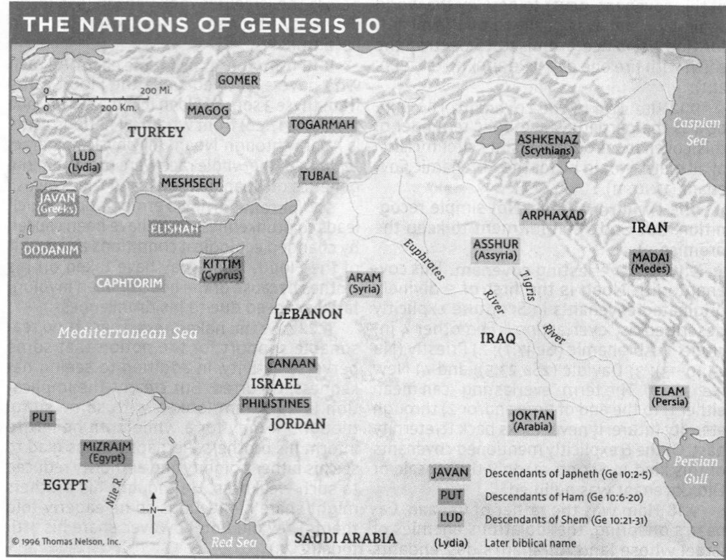

journeyed east, that they found a plain in the land [A]of
Shinar and [a]settled there. 3 They said to one another,
"Come, let us make bricks and burn *them* thoroughly."
And they used brick for stone, and they used [A]tar for
mortar. 4 They said, "Come, let us build for ourselves
a city, and a tower whose top [A]*will reach* into heaven,
and let us make for ourselves [B]a name, otherwise we
[C]will be scattered abroad over the face of the whole
earth." 5 [A]The LORD came down to see the city and the
tower which the sons of men had built. 6 The LORD
said, "Behold, they are one people, and they all have
[a,A]the same language. And this is what they began to
do, and now nothing which they purpose to do will
be [b]impossible for them. 7 Come, [A]let Us go down and
there [B]confuse their [a]language, so that they will not
understand one another's [a]speech." 8 So the LORD
[A]scattered them abroad from there over the face of
the whole earth; and they stopped building the city.
9 Therefore its name was called [a,A]Babel, because there
the LORD confused the [b]language of the whole earth;
and from there the LORD scattered them abroad over
the face of the whole earth.

DESCENDANTS OF SHEM

10 [A]These are *the records of* the generations of
Shem. Shem was one hundred years old, and [a]be-
came the father of Arpachshad two years after the
flood; 11 and Shem lived five hundred years after he
became the father of Arpachshad, and he had *other*
sons and daughters.
12 Arpachshad lived thirty-five years, and became
the father of Shelah; 13 and Arpachshad lived four
hundred and three years after he became the father
of Shelah, and he had *other* sons and daughters.
14 Shelah lived thirty years, and became the father of Eber; 15 and Shelah lived four hundred and
three years after he became the father of Eber, and
he had *other* sons and daughters.
16 Eber lived thirty-four years, and became the
father of Peleg; 17 and Eber lived four hundred and
thirty years after he became the father of Peleg,
and he had *other* sons and daughters.
18 Peleg lived thirty years, and became the father
of Reu; 19 and Peleg lived two hundred and nine
years after he became the father of Reu, and he
had *other* sons and daughters.
20 Reu lived thirty-two years, and became the
father of Serug; 21 and Reu lived two hundred and
seven years after he became the father of Serug,
and he had *other* sons and daughters.
22 Serug lived thirty years, and became the father of Nahor; 23 and Serug lived two hundred
years after he became the father of Nahor, and
he had *other* sons and daughters.
24 Nahor lived twenty-nine years, and became
the father of [A]Terah; 25 and Nahor lived one hundred and nineteen years after he became the father
of Terah, and he had *other* sons and daughters.
26 Terah lived seventy years, and became [A]the
father of Abram, Nahor and Haran.
27 Now these are *the records of* the generations
of Terah. Terah became the father of Abram, Nahor
and Haran; and [A]Haran became the father of [B]Lot.
28 Haran died [a]in the presence of his father Terah
in the land of his birth, in [A]Ur of the Chaldeans.
29 Abram and [A]Nahor took wives for themselves.
The name of Abram's wife was [B]Sarai; and the
name of Nahor's wife was [C]Milcah, the daughter
of Haran, the father of Milcah [a]and Iscah. 30 [A]Sarai
was barren; she had no child.
31 Terah took Abram his son, and Lot the son
of Haran, his grandson, and Sarai his daughter-
in-law, his son Abram's wife; and they went out
[a]together from [A]Ur of the Chaldeans in order to
enter the land of Canaan; and they went as far
as Haran, and [b]settled there. 32 The days of Terah

11:2 [a]Lit *dwelt* [A]Gen 10:10; 14:1; Dan 1:2 11:3 [A]Gen 14:10 11:4 [A]Deut 1:28; 9:1; Ps 107:26 [B]Gen 6:4; 2 Sam 8:13 [C]Deut 4:27 11:5 [A]Gen 18:21; Ex 3:8; 19:11, 18, 20 11:6 [a]Lit *one lip* [b]Lit *withheld from* [A]Gen 11:1 11:7 [a]Lit *lip* [A]Gen 1:26 [B]Gen 42:23; Ex 4:11; Deut 28:49; Is 33:19; Jer 5:15 11:8 [A]Gen 11:4; Ps 92:9; Luke 1:51 11:9 [a]Or *Babylon;* cf Heb *balal,* confuse [b]Lit *lip* [A]Gen 10:10 11:10 [a]Lit *begot,* and so throughout the ch [A]Gen 10:22-25 11:24 [A]Josh 24:2 11:26 [A]Josh 24:2 11:27 [A]Gen 11:31; 12:4 [B]Gen 13:10; 14:12; 19:1, 29 11:28 [a]Or *during the lifetime of* [A]Gen 11:31 11:29 [a]Lit *and the father of* [A]Gen 24:10 [B]Gen 17:15; 20:12 [C]Gen 22:20, 23; 24:15 11:30 [A]Gen 16:1 11:31 [a]Lit *with them* [b]Lit *dwelt* [A]Gen 15:7; Neh 9:7; Acts 7:4

fruitful and multiply; populate the earth" (9:7). It was in the course of spreading out that the events of this account occurred.

11:3, 4 let us make bricks … build for ourselves a city, and a tower … make for ourselves a name. While dispersing, a portion of the post-Flood group, under the leading of the powerful Nimrod (10:8–10), decided to stop and establish a city as a monument to their pride and for their reputation. The tower, even though it was a part of the plan, was not the singular act of rebellion. Human pride was, which led these people to defy God. They were refusing to move on, i.e., scattering to fill the earth as they had been instructed. In fact, this was Nimrod's and the people's effort to disobey the command of God in 9:1, and thus defeat the counsel of heaven. They had to make bricks, since there were few stones on the plain.

11:4 whose top *will reach* into heaven. Not that the tower would actually reach to the abode of God and not that the top would represent the heavens. They wanted it to be a high tower as a monument to their abilities, one that would enhance their fame. In this endeavor, they disobeyed God and attempted to steal His glory.

11:6 nothing … will be impossible. They were so united that they would do all they desired to do.

11:7 let Us. *See note on 1:26* (cf. 3:22).

11:8 scattered them abroad. God addressed their prideful rebellion at the first act. They had chosen to settle; He forced them to scatter. This account tells how it was that the families of the earth "were separated … every one according to his language" (10:5) and "were separated on the earth after the flood" (10:32).

11:9 its name was called Babel. This is linked to a Heb. word meaning "to confuse." From this account, Israel first understood not only how so many nations, peoples, and languages came about, but also the rebellious origins of their archetypal enemy, Babylon (cf. 10:5, 20, 31). **scattered them.** Because they would not fill the earth as God had commanded them, God confused their language so that they had to separate and collect in regions where their own language was spoken.

11:10–26 Shem … Abram. The genealogy of Shem (v. 10). Israel, upon hearing this section read, learned how the generation who survived the Flood related to their own father, Abram (v. 26), later known as Abraham (cf. 17:5). The shortening of life-spans was in effect.

11:14 Eber. Progenitor of the Hebrews (i.e., Eber's descendants).

11:26 seventy years. The age that Terah began to father children. Abram was born later when Terah was 130 (ca. 2165 B.C.). Cf. 11:32 with 12:4.

11:27–25:11 The genealogy of Terah (v. 27).

11:27 Abram. The name means "exalted father." Cf. 17:5.

11:28 Ur of the Chaldeans. A prosperous, populous city in Mesopotamia.

11:31 from Ur … as far as Haran. Cf. Ac 7:2–4; Heb 11:8–10. Abram traveled along the Euphrates to Haran, a crossroads trading town in northern Mesopotamia or Syria, the best route from which to come down into Canaan

were two hundred and five years; and Terah died in Haran.

ABRAM JOURNEYS TO EGYPT

12 Now [A]the LORD said to Abram,

"[a]Go forth from your country,
And from your relatives
And from your father's house,
To the land which I will show you;
2 And [A]I will make you a great nation,
And [B]I will bless you,
And make your name great;
And so [a,C]you shall be a blessing;
3 And [A]I will bless those who bless you,
And the one who [a]curses
you I will [b]curse.
[B]And in you all the families of
the earth will be blessed."

4 So Abram went forth as the LORD had spoken to
him; and [A]Lot went with him. Now Abram was seventy-five years old when he departed from Haran.
5 Abram took Sarai his wife and Lot his nephew, and
all their [A]possessions which they had accumulated,
and [B]the [a]persons which they had acquired in Haran, and they [b]set out for the land of Canaan; [C]thus
they came to the land of Canaan. 6 Abram passed
through the land as far as the site of [A]Shechem, to
the [a]oak of Moreh. Now the Canaanite *was* then
in the land. 7 The LORD [A]appeared to Abram and
said, "[B]To your [a]descendants I will give this land."
So he built [C]an altar there to the LORD who had appeared to him. 8 Then he proceeded from there to
the mountain on the east of Bethel, and pitched his
tent, with [A]Bethel on the west and Ai on the east;
and there he built an altar to the LORD and [B]called
upon the name of the LORD. 9 Abram journeyed on,
continuing toward [A]the [a]Negev.

12:1 [a]Lit *Go for yourself* [A]Gen 15:7; Acts 7:3; Heb 11:8 12:2 [a]Lit *be a blessing* [A]Gen 17:4-6; 18:18; 46:3; Deut 26:5 [B]Gen 22:17 [C]Zech 8:13 12:3 [a]Or *reviles* [b]Or *bind under a curse* [A]Gen 24:35; 27:29; Num 24:9 [B]Gen 22:18; 26:4; 28:14; Acts 3:25; Gal 3:8 12:4 [A]Gen 11:27, 31 12:5 [a]Lit *souls* [b]Lit *went forth to go to* [A]Gen 13:6 [B]Gen 14:14; Lev 22:11 [C]Gen 11:31; Heb 11:8 12:6 [a]Or *terebinth* [A]Gen 35:4; Deut 11:30 12:7 [a]Lit *seed* [A]Gen 17:1; 18:1 [B]Gen 13:15; 15:18; Deut 34:4; Ps 105:9-12; Acts 7:5; Gal 3:16 [C]Gen 13:4, 18; 22:9 12:8 [A]Josh 8:9, 12 [B]Gen 4:26; 21:33 12:9 [a]I.e. South country [A]Gen 13:1, 3; 20:1; 24:62

and avoid crossing the great desert with all his people and animals (see 12:4).

12:1–3 the LORD ... to Abram. This passage is the promise whose fulfillment extends all through Scripture (either in fact or in expectation) to Rev 20. The actual Abrahamic Covenant is introduced in 12:1–3, actually made in 15:18–21, reaffirmed in 17:1–21, then renewed also with Isaac (26:2–5) and Jacob (28:10–17). It is an everlasting covenant (17:7, 8; 1Ch 16:17; Ps 105:7–12; Is 24:5) which contains 4 elements: 1) seed (17:2–7; cf. Gal 3:8, 16, where it referred to Christ); 2) land (15:18–21; 17:8); 3) a nation (12:2; 17:4); plus 4) divine blessing and protection (12:3). This covenant is unconditional in the sense of its ultimate fulfillment of a kingdom and salvation for Israel (*see notes on Ro 11:1–27*), but conditional in terms of immediate fulfillment (cf. 17:14). Its national importance to Israel is magnified by its repeated references and point of appeal throughout the OT (cf. 2Ki 13:23; 1Ch 16:15–22; Ne 9:7, 8). Its importance spiritually to all believers is expounded by Paul (*see notes on Gal 3, 4*). Stephen quoted 12:1 in Ac 7:3.

12:1 To the land. Abram was still in Haran (11:31) when the call was repeated (Ac 7:2) to go to Canaan.

12:2 name great. Abram's magnificent reputation and legacy was fulfilled materially (13:2; 24:35), spiritually (21:22), and socially (23:6).

12:3 the one who curses you I will curse. Those who "curse" Abram and his descendants are those who treat him lightly, despise him, or treat him with contempt. God's curse for such lack of respect and disdain was to involve the most harsh of divine judgments. The opposite was to be true for those who bless him and his people. **in you all the families of the earth will be blessed.** Paul identified these words as "the gospel beforehand to Abraham" (Gal 3:8).

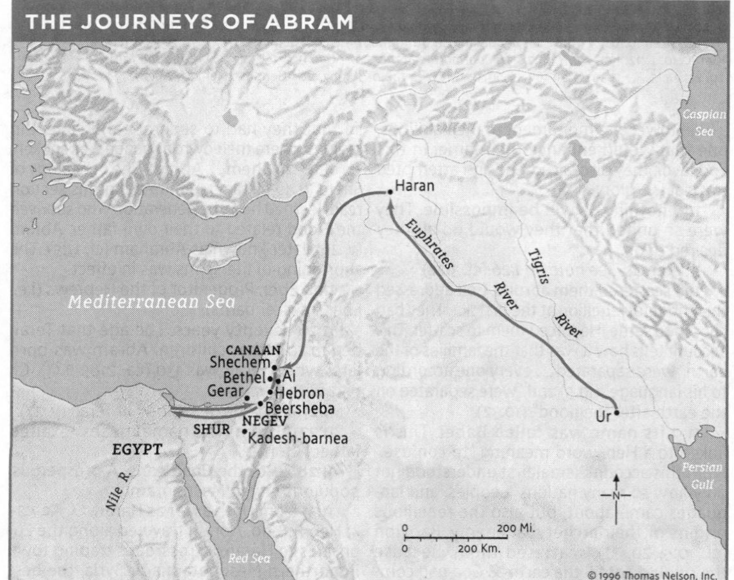

12:4 Haran. *See note on 11:31.* They must have been there for some time because they accumulated a group of people (probably servants).

12:5 they came to ... Canaan. Ca. 2090 B.C.

12:6 Shechem. A Canaanite town located in the valley between Mt. Ebal and Mt. Gerizim (cf. Dt 27:4, 12) W of the Jordan about 15 mi. and N of Jerusalem about 30 mi. Moreh was most likely a resident of the area for whom the tree was named. **Canaanite *was* then in the land.** Moses was writing approximately 700 years after Abram entered the land (ca. 1405 B.C.). The Canaanites, of whom he wrote, were soon to be the opponents of Israel as they entered Canaan.

12:7 I will give this land. Cf. 13:15; 15:18; 17:7, 8; Gal 3:16. God was dealing with Abram, not in a private promise, but with a view toward high and sacred interests long into the future, i.e., the land which his posterity was to inhabit as a peculiar people. The seeds of divine truth were to be sown there for the benefit of all mankind. It was chosen as the most appropriate land for the coming of divine revelation and salvation for the world. **altar ... to the LORD.** By this act, Abram made an open confession of his religion, established worship of the true God, and declared his faith in God's promise. This was the first true place of worship ever erected in the Promised Land. Isaac would later build an altar also to commemorate the Lord's appearance to him (26:24, 25), and Jacob also built one in Shechem (33:18–20).

12:8 Bethel ... Ai. Bethel, 7 mi. N of Jerusalem, was named later by Abraham (28:19). Ai was 2 mi. E of Bethel, where Joshua later fought (Jos 7, 8).

12:9 toward the Negev. Abram moved toward the Negev into a less desirable area for raising crops but better for his vocation as

10 Now there was [A]a famine in the land; so Abram
went down to Egypt to sojourn there, for the famine was [B]severe in the land. 11 It came about when
he [a]came near to Egypt, that he said to Sarai his
wife, “See now, I know that you are a [b,A]beautiful
woman; 12 [A]and when the Egyptians see you, they
will say, ‘This is his wife’; and they will kill me,
but they will let you live. 13 Please say that you are
[A]my sister so that it may go well with me because
of you, and that [a,B]I may live on account of you.”
14 It came about when Abram came into Egypt, the
Egyptians [a]saw that the woman was very beautiful.
15 Pharaoh’s officials saw her and praised her to
Pharaoh; and [A]the woman was taken into Pharaoh’s
house. 16 Therefore [A]he treated Abram well for her
sake; and [a,B]gave him sheep and oxen and donkeys
and male and female servants and female donkeys
and camels.

17 But the LORD [A]struck Pharaoh and his house
with great plagues because of Sarai, Abram’s wife.
18 Then Pharaoh called Abram and said, “[A]What is
this you have done to me? Why did you not tell me
that she was your wife? 19 Why did you say, ‘She
is my sister,’ so that I took her for my wife? Now
then, [a]here is your wife, take her and go.” 20 Pharaoh commanded *his* men concerning him; and they
[a]escorted him away, with his wife and all that belonged to him.

ABRAM AND LOT

13 So Abram went up from Egypt to [A]the [a]Negev,
he and his wife and all that belonged to him,
and Lot with him.
2 Now Abram was [A]very rich in livestock, in silver
and in gold. 3 He went [a]on his journeys from the
[b]Negev as far as Bethel, to the place where his tent
had been at the beginning, [A]between Bethel and Ai,
4 to the place of the [A]altar which he had made there
formerly; and there Abram called on the name of the
LORD. 5 Now [A]Lot, who went with Abram, also had
flocks and herds and tents. 6 And [A]the land could not
[a]sustain them [b]while dwelling together, [B]for their
possessions were so great that they were not able
to remain together. 7 [A]And there was strife between
the herdsmen of Abram’s livestock and the herdsmen of Lot’s livestock. Now [B]the Canaanite and the
Perizzite were dwelling then in the land.

8 [A]So Abram said to Lot, “Please let there be no
strife between you and me, nor between my herdsmen and your herdsmen, for we are brothers. 9 Is
not the whole land before you? Please separate from
me; if *to* the left, then I will go to the right; or if *to*
the right, then I will go to the left.” 10 Lot lifted up
his eyes and saw all the [a,A]valley of the Jordan, that it
was well watered everywhere—*this was* before the
LORD [B]destroyed Sodom and Gomorrah—like [C]the
garden of the LORD, [D]like the land of Egypt as you go

12:10 [A]Gen 26:1 [B]Gen 43:1 12:11 [a]Lit *drew near to enter* [b]Lit *woman of beautiful appearance* [A]Gen 26:7; 29:17 12:12 [A]Gen 20:11 12:13 [a]Lit *my soul* [A]Gen 20:2, 5, 12; 26:7 [B]Jer 38:17, 20 12:14 [a]Lit *saw the woman that she was* 12:15 [A]Gen 20:2 12:16 [a]Lit *he had* [A]Gen 20:14 [B]Gen 13:2 12:17 [A]Gen 20:18; 1 Chr 16:21; Ps 105:14 12:18 [A]Gen 20:9, 10; 26:10 12:19 [a]Or *behold* 12:20 [a]Lit *sent* 13:1 [a]I.e. South country [A]Gen 12:9 13:2 [A]Gen 24:35 13:3 [a]Lit *by his stages* [b]I.e. South country [A]Gen 12:8 13:4 [A]Gen 12:7, 8 13:5 [A]Gen 12:5 13:6 [a]Lit *bear* [b]Lit *to dwell* [A]Gen 36:7 [B]Gen 12:5, 16; 13:2 13:7 [A]Gen 26:20 [B]Gen 12:6; 15:20, 21 13:8 [A]Prov 15:18; 20:3 13:10 [a]Lit *circle* [A]Gen 19:17-29; Deut 34:3 [B]Gen 19:24 [C]Gen 2:8, 10 [D]Gen 47:6

a herdsman, perhaps engaging also in merchant activity.

12:10 a famine in the land. Famine was not an unusual phenomenon in Canaan; two other major food shortages also occurred during the patriarchal period (26:1; 41:56). The severity and timing of this one forced Abram, soon after his arrival and travel in the Promised Land (vv. 5–9), to emigrate to Egypt, where food was usually in abundant supply. Still holding to God’s promise, he did not return to Ur, though matters were extremely difficult (cf. Heb 11:15).

12:11 beautiful woman. At 65, Sarai was still young and exceptionally attractive, being only half the age she was to be when she died (127). The patriarchs lived long; Abram was 175 when he died.

12:12, 13 Abram’s fear of Sarai’s being taken to Pharaoh’s harem and his being killed led him to disguise his true relationship to her *(cf. 20:13). Abram sought on his own initiative* to take care of his future, thinking to assist God in fulfilling His promises.

12:13 sister. This was a lying half-truth, since Sarai was Abram’s half-sister (20:12).

12:15 taken into Pharaoh’s house. Egyptian officials did take notice of Sarai and informed their monarch of her beauty. The result was not unexpected; she ended up in Pharaoh’s harem!

12:17 the LORD struck Pharaoh … with great plagues. The separation of Abram and Sarai was critical enough to evoke the Lord’s personal and dramatic intervention. Abram engineered the ruse to protect himself (v. 13, “that I may live”) apparently without too much thought being given to Sarai; but God’s reaction focused upon the protection of Sarai (“because of Sarai”).

12:18, 19 What is this you have done to me? … take her and go. Somehow, and it remains unexplained, the plagues uncovered the deceit of Abram for Pharaoh. The monarch of Egypt humiliated Abram with his questions, showing more character than Abram gave him credit for and sending Abram out of his country.

12:20 escorted him away. Abram’s lie brought him and his extended family to an ignominious exit from Egypt—one which the servants must have talked about among themselves, with some loss to Abram’s integrity and reputation in their eyes. *See note on 13:9.*

13:1–4 Significantly, after the disastrous situation in Egypt, Abram journeyed back to where he had erected an altar and there he again worshiped (see 12:8).

13:5 flocks and herds. Wealth in the ancient world was measured not by land owned but by the size of one’s herds and the possession of silver, gold, and jewels (cf. v. 2; Job 1:1–3).

13:6, 7 Not unexpectedly, conflict occurred because of crowded conditions and limited grazing space. Both uncle and nephew had accrued much on the slow trip from Ur via Haran and Egypt to the Bethel/Ai region.

13:7 Perizzite. A Canaanite tribe. Cf. 34:30; Dt 7:1; Jdg 1:4; 3:5, 6; 1Ki 9:20, 21; Ezr 9:1.

13:8 we are brothers. Abram’s whole reaction in resolving the strife between the two households and their personnel portrayed a different Abram than seen in Egypt; one whose attitude was not self-centered. Waving his right to seniority, he gave the choice to his nephew, Lot.

13:9 Is not the whole land before you? Abram gladly called on Lot to select for himself (vv. 10, 11) what he desired for his household and flocks. After Lot’s choice had been exercised, then Abram would accept what was left for him. Perhaps this did much to restore, in the eyes of the servants, Abram’s integrity and reputation (*see note on 12:20*).

13:10 before the LORD destroyed Sodom and Gomorrah. When Moses was writing (700 years after Abram came to Canaan) the devastation of that region had long before occurred by divinely initiated catastrophe (19:23–29), totally obliterating any evidence of its agricultural richness. **like the garden of the LORD, like … Egypt.** This 2-fold appraisal of the Jordan Valley, with its meadows on either side of the river to which Lot was so strongly attracted, highlighted its lush and fertile nature. Moses, reading this to the Jews about to enter Canaan and likening it to the Garden of Eden, referred hearer and reader to God’s revelatory description of it (Ge 2:8–15). Likening it to an obviously well-known and well-irrigated region of Egypt referred them to a place the Jews had likely known well in their sojourn in Egypt. **Zoar.** Cf. 4:2. A town located at the S end of the Dead Sea, whose name means “small place” (see 19:22).

to [E]Zoar. 11 So Lot chose for himself all the [a]valley of
the Jordan, and Lot journeyed eastward. Thus they
separated from each other. 12 Abram [a]settled in the
land of Canaan, while Lot [a]settled in [A]the cities of
the [b]valley, and moved his tents as far as Sodom.
13 Now [A]the men of Sodom were wicked [a]exceedingly
and [B]sinners against the LORD.

14 The LORD said to Abram, after Lot had separated from him, "[A]Now lift up your eyes and look
from the place where you are, [B]northward and
southward and eastward and westward; 15 [A]for all
the land which you see, [B]I will give it to you and to
your [a]descendants forever. 16 I will make your [a]de-
scendants [A]as the dust of the earth, so that if anyone
can number the dust of the earth, then your [a]descen-
dants can also be numbered. 17 Arise, [A]walk about
the land through its length and breadth; for [B]I will
give it to you." 18 Then Abram moved his tent and
came and dwelt by the [a,A]oaks of Mamre, which are
in Hebron, and there he built [B]an altar to the LORD.

WAR OF THE KINGS

14 And it came about in the days of Amraphel
king of [A]Shinar, Arioch king of Ellasar, Chedorlaomer king of [B]Elam, and Tidal king of [a]Goiim,
2 *that* they made war with Bera king of Sodom,
and with Birsha king of Gomorrah, Shinab king
of [A]Admah, and Shemeber king of [B]Zeboiim, and
the king of Bela (that is, [C]Zoar). 3 All these [a]came
as allies to [A]the valley of Siddim (that is, [B]the Salt
Sea). 4 Twelve years they had served Chedorlaomer, but the thirteenth year they rebelled. 5 In the
fourteenth year Chedorlaomer and the kings that
were with him, came and [a]defeated the [A]Rephaim
in [B]Ashteroth-karnaim and the Zuzim in Ham
and the Emim in [b,C]Shaveh-kiriathaim, 6 and the
[A]Horites in their Mount Seir, as far as [B]El-paran,
which is by the wilderness. 7 Then they turned back
and came to En-mishpat (that is, [A]Kadesh), and
[a]conquered all the country of the Amalekites, and
also the Amorites, who lived in [B]Hazazon-tamar.
8 And the king of Sodom and the king of Gomorrah
and the king of Admah and the king of Zeboiim and
the king of Bela (that is, Zoar) came out; and they
arrayed for battle against them in [A]the valley of
Siddim, 9 against Chedorlaomer king of Elam and
Tidal king of [a]Goiim and Amraphel king of Shinar
and Arioch king of Ellasar—four kings against five.
10 Now the valley of Siddim was full of tar pits;
and [A]the kings of Sodom and Gomorrah fled, and
they fell [a]into them. But those who survived fled
to the [B]hill country. 11 Then they took all the goods
of Sodom and Gomorrah and all their food supply, and departed. 12 They also took Lot, [A]Abram's
nephew, and his possessions and departed, [B]for he
was living in Sodom.

13 Then [a]a fugitive came and told Abram the [A]He-
brew. Now he was [b]living by the [c,B]oaks of Mamre
the Amorite, brother of Eshcol and brother of Aner,
and these were [d,C]allies with Abram. 14 When Abram
heard that [A]his [a]relative had been taken captive, he
[b]led out his trained men, [B]born in his house, three
hundred and eighteen, and went in pursuit as far
as [C]Dan. 15 [A]He divided [a]his forces against them by
night, he and his servants, and [b]defeated them, and
pursued them as far as Hobah, which is [c]north of

13:10 [E]Gen 14:2, 8; 19:22; Deut 34:3 13:11 [a]Lit *circle* 13:12 [a]Lit *dwelt* [b]Lit *circle* [A]Gen 14:2; 19:24, 25, 29 13:13 [a]Lit *wicked and sinners exceedingly* [A]Gen 18:20; Ezek 16:49 [B]Gen 39:9; Num 32:23; 2 Pet 2:7, 8 13:14 [A]Deut 3:27; 34:1-4; Is 49:18 [B]Gen 28:14 13:15 [a]Lit *seed* [A]Gen 12:7 [B]Gen 13:17; 15:7; 17:8; 2 Chr 20:7; Acts 7:5 13:16 [a]Lit *seed* [A]Gen 16:10; 28:14; Num 23:10 13:17 [A]Num 13:17-24 [B]Gen 13:15 13:18 [a]Or *terebinths* [A]Gen 14:13 [B]Gen 8:20; 12:7, 8 14:1 [a]Or *nations* [A]Gen 10:10; 11:2 [B]Gen 10:22; Is 11:11; Dan 8:2 14:2 [A]Gen 10:19 [B]Deut 29:23 [C]Gen 13:10; 19:22 14:3 [a]Lit *joined together* [A]Gen 14:8, 10 [B]Num 34:12; Deut 3:17; Josh 3:16 14:5 [a]Lit *smote* [b]Or *the plain of Kiriathaim* [A]Deut 3:11, 13 [B]Deut 1:4; Josh 9:10 [C]Num 32:37 14:6 [A]Gen 36:20; Deut 2:12, 22 [B]Gen 21:21; Num 10:12 14:7 [a]Lit *smote* [A]Num 13:26 [B]2 Chr 20:2 14:8 [A]Gen 14:3 14:9 [a]Or *nations* 14:10 [a]Lit *there* [A]Gen 14:17, 21, 22 [B]Gen 19:17 14:12 [A]Gen 11:27 [B]Gen 13:12 14:13 [a]Lit *the* [b]Lit *abiding* [c]Or *terebinths* [d]Lit *possessors of the covenant* [A]Gen 40:15; Ex 3:18 [B]Gen 13:18; 14:24 [C]Gen 21:27, 32 14:14 [a]Lit *brother* [b]Or *mustered* [A]Gen 14:12 [B]Gen 12:5; 15:3; 17:27; Eccl 2:7 [C]Deut 34:1; Judg 18:29; 1 Kin 15:20 14:15 [a]Lit *himself* [b]Lit *smote* [c]Lit *on the left* [A]Judg 7:16

13:11, 12 An excellent yet selfish choice, from a worldly point of view, but disastrous spiritually because it drew him into the wickedness of Sodom (v. 13).

13:13 the men of Sodom were wicked exceedingly. Lot's decisions put him in dangerous proximity to those cities whose names would become a byword for perversion and unbridled wickedness. Their evil is the theme of chap. 19.

13:14–17 With Lot gone, the Lord reaffirmed His covenant promise with Abram (Ge 12:1–3). Strikingly and unmistakably, the Lord deeded the Land (v. 14—look in all directions, and v. 17—walk in all directions) in perpetuity to Abram and his descendants, whom He declared would be definitely innumerable (v. 16—as the dust).

13:18 the oaks of Mamre. A distinctively large grove of trees owned by Mamre the Amorite (14:13) located ca. 19 mi. SW of Jerusalem at Hebron whose elevation exceeds 3,000 feet. **built an altar.** Cf. 12:7, 8; 13:4. He was devoted to the worship of God.

14:1–12 Raiding, conquering, and making other kings and city-states subservient vassals were all part of the world of the Fertile Crescent in Abraham's day. These locations mentioned range from Shinar in the east (the region of Babylon in Mesopotamia) to the region S of the Salt Sea (Dead Sea) to the Jordan Valley, to the land of Moab, SW of the Dead Sea to Mt. Seir (later Edom). Amalekites (*see note on Ex 17:8*) did not yet exist in Abram's time (cf. 36:12), but they did when Moses wrote. Amorites scattered throughout Canaan became Canaanites. Vassal states, when they thought they could throw off the yoke of their suzerain with impunity, rebelled by not paying the assessed tribute and waited for any military response. This time rebellion evoked a major military excursion by the offended suzerain Chedorlaomer and his allies (vv. 5–7); in the ensuing confrontation with Sodom and Gomorrah and their allies (vv. 8–10), the vassals miscalculated and they lost. Lot, by then a resident of Sodom, was taken captive.

14:10 valley of Siddim. Perhaps this was the large peninsula that comes out into the Dead Sea from the eastern shore. In Abram's time, it may have come all the way across to the western shore (near Masada), so the bottom third of the current Dead Sea formed this dry valley. **tar pits.** These pits provided sealants for all sorts of uses.

14:13 a fugitive. One of the survivors who had fled from the invaders to the mountains (v. 10) went farther and located Lot's uncle (the people knew who was related to whom). One as wealthy as Abram would not be hard to find, and was obviously thought to be one who could do something about the crisis which had affected his own close relatives. **the Hebrew.** For the first time in the biblical record, this ethnic appellation, "descended from Eber" (cf. 11:15–17), is accorded to Abram. Foreigners used it of Israelites and Israelites used it of themselves in the presence of foreigners (cf. 34:14; 40:15; 43:32). **oaks of Mamre.** *See note on 13:18.*

14:14 trained men. Abram's private militia, members of his extended family ("born in his house") totaling 318, were highly skilled bodyguards and the protective force for his possessions. These, together with the trained men of his allies (vv. 13, 24), were mustered and set off in pursuit of the military kidnappers, lest their captives be taken away to the E, to Shinar (the early name for Mesopotamia) or farther E, to Elam.

14:15, 16 divided ... defeated ... pursued ... brought back. A battle-wise Abram, no stranger to military strategy, pursued the

[B]Damascus. 16 He [A]brought back all the goods, and
also brought back [B]his [a]relative Lot with his possessions, and also the women, and the people.

GOD'S PROMISE TO ABRAM

17 Then after his return from the [a]defeat of Chedorlaomer and the kings who were with him, [A]the
king of Sodom went out to meet him at the valley
of Shaveh (that is, [B]the King's Valley). 18 And [A]Mel-
chizedek king of Salem brought out [B]bread and
wine; now he was a [C]priest of [a]God Most High. 19 He
blessed him and said,

"Blessed be Abram of [a]God Most High,
[b,A]Possessor of heaven and earth;
20 And blessed be [a]God Most High,
Who has delivered your enemies
into your hand."

[A]He gave him a tenth of all. 21 The king of Sodom
said to Abram, "Give the [a]people to me and take
the goods for yourself." 22 Abram said to the king
of Sodom, "I have [a]sworn to the LORD [b,A]God Most
High, [c,B]possessor of heaven and earth, 23 that [A]I will
not take a thread or a sandal thong or anything
that is yours, for fear you would say, 'I have made
Abram rich.' 24 [a]I will take nothing except what the
young men have eaten, and the share of the men
who went with me, [A]Aner, Eshcol, and Mamre; let
them take their share."

ABRAM PROMISED A SON

15 After these things [A]the word of the LORD came
to Abram in a vision, saying,

"[B]Do not fear, Abram,
I am [C]a shield to you;
[a]Your [D]reward shall be very great."

2 Abram said, "O Lord [a]GOD, what will You give me,
since I [b]am childless, and the [c]heir of my house is
Eliezer of Damascus?" 3 And Abram said, "[a]Since
You have given no [b]offspring to me, [c]one [A]born in
my house is my heir." 4 Then behold, the word of the
LORD came to him, saying, "This man will not be
your heir; [A]but one who will come forth from your
own [a]body, he shall be your heir." 5 And He took him
outside and said, "Now look toward the heavens,
and [A]count the stars, if you are able to count them."
And He said to him, "[B]So shall your [a]descendants
be." 6 [A]Then he believed in the LORD; and He reckoned it to him as righteousness. 7 And He said to
him, "I am the LORD who brought you out of [A]Ur
of the Chaldeans, to [B]give you this land to [a]possess
it." 8 He said, "O Lord [a]GOD, [A]how may I know that
I will [b]possess it?" 9 So He said to him, "[a]Bring Me
a three year old heifer, and a three year old female
goat, and a three year old ram, and a turtledove,
and a young pigeon." 10 Then he [a]brought all these
to Him and [A]cut them [b]in two, and laid each half
opposite the other; but he [B]did not cut the birds.

14:15 [B]Gen 15:2 14:16 [a]Lit *brother* [A]1 Sam 30:8, 18, 19 [B]Gen 14:12, 14 14:17 [a]Lit *smiting* [A]Gen 14:10 [B]2 Sam 18:18 14:18 [a]Heb *El Elyon* [A]Heb 7:1-10 [B]Ps 104:15 [C]Ps 110:4; Heb 5:6, 10 14:19 [a]Heb *El Elyon* [b]Or *Creator* [A]Gen 14:22 14:20 [a]Heb *El Elyon* [A]Heb 7:4 14:21 [a]Lit *soul* 14:22 [a]Lit *lifted up my hand* [b]Heb *El Elyon* [c]Or *Creator* [A]Gen 14:19 [B]Ps 24:1 14:23 [A]2 Kin 5:16 14:24 [a]Lit *Not to me except* [A]Gen 14:13 15:1 [a]Or *Your very great reward* [A]Gen 15:4; 46:2; 1 Sam 15:10 [B]Gen 21:17; 26:24; Is 41:10 [C]Deut 33:29 [D]Num 18:20; Ps 58:11 15:2 [a]Heb *YHWH*, usually rendered *LORD* [b]Lit *go* [c]Lit *son of acquisition* 15:3 [a]Lit *Behold* [b]Lit *seed* [c]Lit *and behold, a son of* [A]Gen 14:14 15:4 [a]Lit *inward parts* [A]Gal 4:28 15:5 [a]Lit *seed* [A]Gen 22:17; 26:4; Deut 1:10 [B]Ex 32:13; Rom 4:18; Heb 11:12 15:6 [A]Rom 4:3, 20-22; Gal 3:6; James 2:23 15:7 [a]Or *inherit* [A]Gen 11:31 [B]Gen 13:15, 17 15:8 [a]Heb *YHWH*, usually rendered *LORD* [b]Or *inherit* [A]Judg 6:36-40; Luke 1:18 15:9 [a]Lit *Take* 15:10 [a]Lit *took* [b]Lit *in the midst* [A]Gen 15:17 [B]Lev 1:17

enemy for over 150 mi. (N of Damascus) and defeated the marauding consortium, being totally successful in his objective.

14:17 the valley of Shaveh. *See note on 2Sa 18:18.* The liberated king of Sodom went to meet Abram near Jerusalem.

14:18 Melchizedek king of Salem. The lack of biographical and genealogical particulars for this ruler, whose name meant "righteous king" and who was a king-priest over ancient Jerusalem, allowed for later revelation to use him as a type of Christ (cf. Ps 110:4; Heb 7:17, 21). His superior status in Abram's day is witnessed 1) by the king of Sodom, the first to meet Abram returning in victory, deferring to Melchizedek before continuing with his request (vv. 17, 21) and 2) by Abram, without demur, both accepting a blessing from and also giving a tithe to this priest-king (vv. 19, 20). Cf. Heb 7:1, 2. **priest of God Most High.** The use of El Elyon (Sovereign Lord) for God's name indicated that Melchizedek, who used this title two times (vv. 18, 19), worshiped, served, and represented no Canaanite deity, but the same one whom Abram also called Yahweh El Elyon (v. 22). That this was so is confirmed by the added description, "Possessor of heaven and earth," being used by both Abram and Melchizedek (vv. 19, 22).

14:20 Who has delivered your enemies into your hand. Credit for victory over a superior military coalition correctly went to the Sovereign Lord (El Elyon) and not to Abram's prowess (*see note at vv. 15, 16*). To Melchizedek, and to Abram too, this amounted to true worship of the true God. **a tenth.** This is the first mention in Scripture of giving 10 percent (cf. 28:22). This 10-percent offering was purely voluntary, and may only have been a tenth of the best, not a tenth of the total (*see note on Heb 7:4*). This tenth is not like the required tenths given to Israel in the Mosaic law (*see notes on Nu 18:21–24; Dt 14:22; 26:12*).

14:21–24 If Abram acceded to the king of Sodom's request, he would have allowed that wicked king to attribute Abram's wealth to the king's generosity, thus distorting the clear testimony of the Lord's blessings on his life. To accept such payment would belie his trust in God! Such a personal commitment would not be foisted upon his allies, who could make their own decisions. As for his own servants, their meals taken from the spoils was sufficient compensation. Undoubtedly, the servants remembered their master's reaction and testimony; it overcame much of the negative aspects in the memory of the earlier exit from Egypt (see 12:20).

15:1 I am a shield. God served Abram as his divine protector (cf. Pss 7:10; 84:9).

15:2 I am childless. In response to God's encouragement and admonition (v. 1), Abram showed what nagged at him. How could God's promise of many descendants (13:16) and of being a great nation (12:2) come about when he had no children? **Eliezer of Damascus.** To Abram, God's promise had stalled; so adoption of a servant as the male heir—a well known contemporary Mesopotamian custom—was the best officially recognizable arrangement to make it come to pass, humanly speaking.

15:3–5 The question, "What will You give me?" (v. 2) became an accusation, "You have given no offspring to me!" (v. 3). The Lord's rejection of Abram's solution (v. 4) preceded God's reiterated promise of innumerable descendants (v. 5).

15:5 Cf. Ro 4:18.

15:6 believed ... reckoned ... as righteousness. The Apostle Paul quoted these words as an illustration of faith over and against works (Ro 4:3, 9, 22; Gal 3:6; Jas 2:23). Abram was justified by faith! *See notes on Ro 4 and Gal 3* for a fuller discussion of justification by faith.

15:7 to give you this land to possess it. That a specifically identifiable land (see vv. 18–21) was intimately linked with Abram's having many descendants in God's purpose and in the Abrahamic Covenant was clearly revealed and, in a formal ceremony (vv. 9–21), would be placed irrevocably beyond dispute.

15:8 how may I know that I will possess it? A question not of veiled accusation at the delayed fulfillment but of genuine request for information and assurance. In response, God affirmed His covenant with Abram in a remarkable ceremony (vv. 9–21).

15:9, 10 cut them in two. The sign of ancient covenants often involved the cutting in

11 The birds of prey came down upon the carcasses,
and Abram drove them away.
12 Now when the sun was going down, [A]a deep
sleep fell upon Abram; and behold, [a]terror *and* great
darkness fell upon him. 13 *God* said to Abram, "Know
for certain that [A]your [a]descendants will be strangers
in a land that is not theirs, [b]where [B]they will be enslaved and oppressed [C]four hundred years. 14 But I
will also judge the nation whom they will serve, and
afterward they will come out [A]with [a]many possessions. 15 As for you, [A]you shall go to your fathers in
peace; you will be buried at a good old age. 16 Then
in [A]the fourth generation they will return here, for
[B]the iniquity of the Amorite is not yet complete."
17 It came about when the sun had set, that it was
very dark, and behold, *there appeared* a smoking
oven and a flaming torch which [A]passed between
these pieces. 18 On that day the LORD made a covenant
with Abram, saying,

"[A]To your [a]descendants I have given this land,
From [B]the river of Egypt as far as the
great river, the river Euphrates:

19 [A]the Kenite and the Kenizzite and the Kadmonite
20 and the Hittite and the Perizzite and the Rephaim
21 and the Amorite and the Canaanite and the Girgashite and the Jebusite."

SARAI AND HAGAR

16 Now [A]Sarai, Abram's wife had borne him
no *children,* and she had [B]an Egyptian maid
whose name was Hagar. 2 So Sarai said to Abram,
"Now behold, the LORD has prevented me from
bearing *children.* [A]Please go in to my maid; perhaps
I will [a]obtain children through her." And Abram listened to the voice of Sarai. 3 After Abram had [a]lived
[A]ten years in the land of Canaan, Abram's wife Sarai
took Hagar the Egyptian, her maid, and gave her
to her husband Abram as his wife. 4 He went in to
Hagar, and she conceived; and when she saw that
she had conceived, her mistress was despised in her
sight. 5 And Sarai said to Abram, "[A]May the wrong
done me be upon you. I gave my maid into your
[a]arms, but when she saw that she had conceived,
I was despised in her [b]sight. [B]May the LORD judge
between [c]you and me." 6 But Abram said to Sarai,
"Behold, your maid is in your [a]power; do to her what
is good in your [b]sight." So Sarai treated her harshly,
and [A]she fled from her presence.
7 Now [A]the angel of the LORD found her by a
spring of water in the wilderness, by the spring
on the way to [B]Shur. 8 He said, "Hagar, Sarai's maid,
[A]where have you come from and where are you going?" And she said, "I am fleeing from the presence
of my mistress Sarai." 9 Then the angel of the LORD
said to her, "Return to your mistress, and submit
yourself [a]to her authority." 10 Moreover, the [A]angel
of the LORD said to her, "[B]I will greatly multiply
your [a]descendants so that [b]they will be too many to
count." 11 The angel of the LORD said to her further,

"Behold, you are with child,
And you will bear a son;

15:12 [a]Or *a terror of great darkness* [A]Gen 2:21; 28:11; Job 33:15 15:13 [a]Lit *seed* [b]Lit *and shall serve them; and they shall afflict them* [A]Acts 7:6, 17 [B]Ex 1:11; Deut 5:15 [C]Ex 12:40; Gal 3:17 15:14 [a]Lit *great* [A]Ex 12:32-38 15:15 [A]Gen 25:8; 47:30 15:16 [A]Gen 15:13 [B]Lev 18:24-28 15:17 [A]Jer 34:18, 19 15:18 [a]Lit *seed* [A]Gen 17:8; Josh 21:43; Acts 7:5 [B]Ex 23:31; Num 34:1-15; Deut 1:7, 8 15:19 [A]Ex 3:17; 23:28; Josh 24:11; Neh 9:8 16:1 [A]Gen 11:30 [B]Gen 12:16 16:2 [a]Lit *be built from her* [A]Gen 30:3, 4, 9, 10 16:3 [a]Lit *dwelt* [A]Gen 12:4 16:5 [a]Lit *bosom* [b]Lit *eyes* [c]Lit *me and you* [A]Jer 51:35 [B]Gen 31:53; Ex 5:21 16:6 [a]Lit *hand* [b]Lit *eyes* [A]Gen 16:9 16:7 [A]Gen 21:17, 18; 22:11, 15; 31:11 [B]Gen 20:1; 25:18 16:8 [A]Gen 3:9; 1 Kin 19:9, 13 16:9 [a]Lit *under her hands* 16:10 [a]Lit *seed* [b]Or *it shall not be counted for multitude* [A]Gen 22:15-18 [B]Gen 17:20

half of animals, so that the pledging parties could walk between them, affirming that the same should happen to them if they broke the covenant (see Jer 34:18, 19).

15:12 sleep. God put him to sleep, because the covenant did not involve any promise on his part. He would not walk through the pieces as a pledge (see v. 17).

15:13, 14 The words of God in the covenant ceremony assured Abram that his descendants would definitely be in the land, although a painful detour into Egypt would delay fulfillment until long after his demise. Cf. Ac. 7:6, 7.

15:13 four hundred years. This represents an approximated number which is precisely 430 years (cf. Ex 12:40).

15:16 the iniquity of the Amorite is not yet complete. A delay in judgment occasioned the delay in covenant fulfillment. Judgment on Egypt (v. 14) would mark the departure of Abram's descendants for their Land, and judgment on the Canaanites (broadly defined ethnically as Amorites) would mark their entrance to that Land.

15:17 smoking oven ... flaming torch. Cf. Ex 13:21. These items symbolized the presence of God, who solemnly promised by divine oath to fulfill His promises to Abram by alone passing through the animal pieces (vv. 9–11).

15:18–21 river of Egypt as far as ... Euphrates. Scripture records both general (Ex 23:31; Nu 13:21; Dt 11:24; 1Ki 8:65; 2Ki 14:25; Is 27:12) and specific (Nu 34:1–12; Jos 15:1, 2; Eze 47:15–20; 48:1, 28) descriptions of the Promised Land, centering on the ancient land of Canaan. Such precise geographic demarcation will not allow for any redefinitions which would emasculate God's promise of its specificity. The river of Egypt was most probably what became known as the Wadi El Arish, the southern border of Judah. **Kenite ... Jebusite.** The various peoples who inhabited the land are named. Such precise detailing of the nations in the land of Canaan attests again to the specificity of the Promised Land in God's promises.

16:1 See Gal 4:21–31, where Paul uses Hagar as an illustration.

16:3 gave her to her husband. After 10 childless years (cf. 12:4), Sarai resorted to the custom of the day by which a barren wife could get a child through one of her own maidservants (v. 2, "I will obtain children through her"). Abram, ignoring divine reaction and assurance in response to his earlier attempt to appoint an heir (cf. 15:2–5), sinfully yielded to Sarai's insistence, and Ishmael was born (v. 15).

16:5 wrong done me be upon you .... I was despised. Sarai, not anticipating contemptuous disregard by Hagar (v. 4) as the result of her solution for barrenness, blamed Abram for her trouble and demanded judgment to rectify the broken mistress-servant relationship. Abram transferred his responsibility to Sarai, giving her freedom to react as she wished (v. 6, "your maid is in your power..."). Sarai treated her so badly, she left.

16:7 the angel of the LORD. This special individual spoke as though He were distinct from Yahweh, yet also spoke in the first person as though He were indeed to be identified as Yahweh Himself, with Hagar recognizing that in seeing this Angel, she had seen God (v. 13). Others had the same experience and came to the same conclusion (cf. 22:11–18; 31:11–13; Ex 3:2–5; Nu 22:22–35; Jdg 6:11–23; 13:2–5; 1Ki 19:5–7). The Angel of the Lord, who does not appear after the birth of Christ, is often identified as the preincarnate Christ. *See note on Ex 3:2.* **Shur.** South of Canaan and east of Egypt, which meant that Hagar attempted to return home to Egypt.

16:8 Hagar, Sarai's maid. Both the salutation and the instruction (v. 9, "Return ... submit...") given by the Angel and the response by Hagar treated the mistress-servant relationship as if it were still intact. Rebelling and absconding was not the solution (v. 9)!

16:10 I will greatly multiply. A servant she might have been, but mother of many she would also become, thus making Abram the father of two groups of innumerable descendants (see 13:16; 15:5).

16:11 call his name Ishmael. With her son's name meaning "God hears," Hagar the servant

And you shall call his name [a]Ishmael,
Because [A]the LORD [b]has given
heed to your affliction.
12 "He will be a [A]wild donkey of a man,
His hand *will be* against everyone,
And everyone's hand *will be* against him;
And he will [a]live [b,B]to the east
of all his brothers."

13 Then she called the name of the LORD who spoke
to her, "[a]You are [b]a God who sees"; for she said,
"[A]Have I even [c]remained alive here after seeing
Him?" 14 Therefore the well was called [a]Beer-lahai-roi;
behold, it is between [A]Kadesh and Bered.
15 So Hagar bore Abram a son; and Abram called
the name of his son, whom Hagar bore, Ishmael.
16 Abram was [A]eighty-six years old when Hagar
bore Ishmael to [a]him.

ABRAHAM AND THE COVENANT OF CIRCUMCISION

17 Now when Abram was ninety-nine years old,
[A]the LORD appeared to Abram and said to him,

"I am [a]God [B]Almighty;
Walk before Me, and be [b,C]blameless.
2 "I will [a]establish My [A]covenant
between Me and you,
And I will [B]multiply you exceedingly."

3 Abram [A]fell on his face, and God talked with him,
saying,

4 "As for Me, behold, My
covenant is with you,
And you will be the father of a
[A]multitude of nations.
5 "No longer shall your name
be called [a]Abram,
But [A]your name shall be [b]Abraham;
For [B]I have made you the father
of a multitude of nations.

6 I will make you exceedingly fruitful, and I will
make nations of you, and [A]kings will come forth
from you. 7 I will establish My covenant between Me
and you and your [a]descendants after you throughout their generations for an [A]everlasting covenant,
[B]to be God to you and [C]to your [a]descendants after
you. 8 [A]I will give to you and to your [a]descendants
after you, the land of your sojournings, all the land
of Canaan, for an everlasting possession; and [B]I will
be their God."
9 God said further to Abraham, "Now as for you,
[A]you shall keep My covenant, you and your [a]de-
scendants after you throughout their generations.
10 [A]This is My covenant, which you shall keep, between Me and you and your [a]descendants after
you: every male among you shall be circumcised.
11 And [A]you shall be circumcised in the flesh of your
foreskin, and it shall be the sign of the covenant
between Me and you. 12 And every male among
you who is [A]eight days old shall be circumcised
throughout your generations, a *servant* who is born
in the house or who is bought with money from any

16:11 [a]I.e. God hears [b]Lit *has heard* [A]Ex 2:23, 24; 3:7, 9 16:12 [a]Lit *dwell* [b]Lit *before the face of;* or *in defiance of* [A]Job 24:5; 39:5-8 [B]Gen 25:18 16:13 [a]Or *You, God, see me* [b]Heb *Elroi* [c]Lit *seen here after the one who saw me* [A]Gen 32:30; Ps 139:1-12 16:14 [a]I.e. the well of the living one who sees me [A]Gen 14:7 16:16 [a]Lit *Abram* [A]Gen 12:4; 16:3 17:1 [a]Heb *El Shaddai* [b]Lit *complete, perfect;* or *having integrity* [A]Gen 12:7; 18:1 [B]Gen 28:3; 35:11 [C]Gen 6:9; Deut 18:13 17:2 [a]Lit *give* [A]Gen 15:18 [B]Gen 13:16; 15:5 17:3 [A]Gen 17:17; 18:2 17:4 [A]Gen 35:11; 48:19 17:5 [a]I.e. exalted father [b]I.e. father of a multitude [A]Neh 9:7 [B]Rom 4:17 17:6 [A]Gen 17:16; 35:11 17:7 [a]Lit *seed* [A]Gen 17:13, 19; Ps 105:9, 10; Luke 1:55 [B]Gen 26:24; Lev 11:45; 26:12, 45; Heb 11:16 [C]Gen 28:13; Gal 3:16 17:8 [a]Lit *seed* [A]Gen 12:7; 13:15, 17; Acts 7:5 [B]Ex 6:7; 29:45; Lev 26:12; Deut 29:13; Rev 21:7 17:9 [a]Lit *seed* [A]Ex 19:5 17:10 [a]Lit *seed* [A]John 7:22; Acts 7:8; Rom 4:11 17:11 [A]Ex 12:48; Deut 10:16; Acts 7:8; Rom 4:11 17:12 [A]Lev 12:3

could not ever forget how God had heard her cry of affliction.

16:12 a wild donkey of a man. The untameable desert onager (wild donkey) best described the fiercely aggressive and independent nature Ishmael would exhibit, along with his Arabic descendants.

16:13 You are a God who sees. Recognizing the Angel as God and ascribing this new name to Him arose from Hagar's astonishment at having been the object of God's gracious attention. The theophany and revelation led her to call Him also "the living one who sees me" (v. 14).

16:15 his son . . . Ishmael. Ca. 2079 B.C.

16:16 eighty-six years old. Abram was 75 when he left Haran (12:4). There would be a 13 year interval until 17:1 picks up the narrative again.

17:2 My covenant between Me and you. Another reaffirmation of His unilateral covenant with Abram, which did not mean that there would be no responsibilities falling upon its recipients. *See notes on vv. 7–9 below and on 12:1–3; 15:18–21.*

17:4 a multitude of nations. The 3-fold reaffirmation of the divine promise of many descendants, perhaps including Isaac's and Ishmael's, brackets the change of name (vv. 4–6), giving it significant emphasis.

17:5 your name shall be Abraham. Cf. 11:27. The name meaning "father of many nations" reflected Abraham's new relationship to God as well as his new identity based on God's promise of seed. Cf. Ro 4:17.

17:6 kings will come forth from you. This promise highlights the reality of more than one people group, or nation in its own right, coming from Abraham.

17:7 I will establish My covenant. This relationship was set up at God's initiative and also designated as an "everlasting covenant" (v. 7), thus applying to Abraham's posterity with equal force and bringing forth the declaration "I will be their God" (v. 8). This pledge became the dictum of the covenant relationship between Yahweh, i.e., Jehovah, and Israel.

17:8 all the land of Canaan. God's reaffirmation of His covenant promises to Abraham did not occur without mention of the land being deeded by divine right to him and his descendants as "an everlasting possession." Cf. Ac 7:5.

17:9 you shall keep My covenant. Despite repeated disobedience by the patriarchs and the nation, God's faithfulness to His covenant commitment never wavered (e.g., Dt 4:25–31; 30:1–9; 1Ch 16:15–18; Jer 30:11; 46:27, 28; Am 9:8; Lk 1:67–75; Heb 6:13–18). Divine attestations of Abraham's obedience (22:16–18; 26:3–5) were pronounced years after the formal establishment of His covenant (12:1–3; 15:12–18). Though the nation was apostate, there was always an obedient remnant of faithful Israelites (see Zep 3:12, 13).

17:11 the sign of the covenant. Circumcision (cutting away the male foreskin) was not entirely new in this period of history, but the special religious and theocratic significance then applied to it was entirely new, thus identifying the circumcised as belonging to the physical and ethnical lineage of Abraham (cf. Ac 7:8; Ro 4:11). Without divine revelation, the rite would not have had this distinctive significance, thus it remained a theocratic distinctive of Israel (cf. v. 13). There was a health benefit, since disease could be kept in the folds of the foreskin, so that removing it prevented that. Historically, Jewish women have had the lowest rate of cervical cancer. But the symbolism had to do with the need to cut away sin and be cleansed. It was the male organ which most clearly demonstrated the depth of depravity because it carried the seed that produced depraved sinners. Thus, circumcision symbolized the need for a profoundly deep cleansing to reverse the effects of depravity.

17:12 eight days old. This same time frame was repeated in Lv 12:3.

foreigner, who is not of your [a]descendants. 13 A *ser-*
vant who is born in your house or [A]who is bought
with your money shall surely be circumcised; thus
shall My covenant be in your flesh for an everlasting covenant. 14 But an uncircumcised male who
is not circumcised in the flesh of his foreskin, that
person shall be [A]cut off from his people; he has
broken My covenant."
15 Then God said to Abraham, "As for Sarai your
wife, you shall not call her name Sarai, but [a]Sarah
shall be her name. 16 I will bless her, and indeed I
will give you [A]a son by her. Then I will bless her, and
she shall be *a mother of* nations; [B]kings of peoples
will [a]come from her." 17 Then Abraham [A]fell on his
face and laughed, and said in his heart, "Will a child
be born to a man one hundred years old? And [B]will
Sarah, who is ninety years old, bear *a child?*" 18 And
Abraham said to God, "Oh that Ishmael might live
before You!" 19 But God said, "No, but Sarah your wife
will bear you [A]a son, and you shall call his name
[a]Isaac; and [B]I will establish My covenant with him
for an everlasting covenant for his [b]descendants after him. 20 As for Ishmael, I have heard you; behold,
I will bless him, and [A]will make him fruitful and
will multiply him exceedingly. [B]He shall [a]become
the father of twelve princes, and I will make him
a [C]great nation. 21 But My covenant I will establish
with [A]Isaac, whom [B]Sarah will bear to you at this
season next year." 22 When He finished talking with
him, [A]God went up from Abraham.
23 Then Abraham took Ishmael his son, and all *the*
servants who were [A]born in his house and all who
were bought with his money, every male among the
men of Abraham's household, and circumcised the
flesh of their foreskin in the very same day, [B]as God
had said to him. 24 Now Abraham was ninety-nine
years old when [A]he was circumcised in the flesh of
his foreskin. 25 And [A]Ishmael his son was thirteen
years old when he was circumcised in the flesh of
his foreskin. 26 In the very same day Abraham was
circumcised, and Ishmael his son. 27 All the men
of his household, who were [A]born in the house or
bought with money from a foreigner, were circumcised with him.

BIRTH OF ISAAC PROMISED

18 Now [A]the LORD appeared to him by the [a,B]oaks
of Mamre, while he was sitting at the tent door
in the heat of the day. 2 When he lifted up his eyes
and looked, behold, three [A]men were standing opposite him; and when he saw *them,* he ran from the
tent door to meet them and bowed himself to the
earth, 3 and said, "[a]My Lord, if now I have found favor in Your sight, please do not [b]pass Your servant
by. 4 Please let a little water be brought and [A]wash
your feet, and [a]rest yourselves under the tree; 5 and
I will [a,A]bring a piece of bread, that you may [b]refresh
yourselves; after that you may go on, since you have
[c]visited your servant." And they said, "So do, as you
have said." 6 So Abraham hurried into the tent to
Sarah, and said, "[a]Quickly, prepare three [b]measures of
fine flour, knead *it* and make bread cakes." 7 Abraham
also ran to the herd, and took a tender and [a]choice
calf and gave *it* to the servant, and he hurried to prepare it. 8 He took curds and milk and the calf which
he had prepared, and placed *it* before them; and he
was standing by them under the tree [a]as they ate.
9 Then they said to him, "Where is Sarah your
wife?" And he said, "There, in the tent." 10 He said,
"[A]I will surely return to you [a]at this time next year;
and behold, Sarah your wife will have a son." And
Sarah was listening at the tent door, which was
behind him. 11 Now [A]Abraham and Sarah were old,
advanced in age; Sarah was [B]past [a]childbearing.
12 Sarah laughed [a]to herself, saying, "[A]After I have
become old, shall I have pleasure, my [B]lord being

17:12 [a]Lit *seed* 17:13 [A]Ex 12:44 17:14 [A]Ex 4:24-26 17:15 [a]I.e. princess 17:16 [a]Lit *be* [A]Gen 18:10 [B]Gen 17:6; 36:31 17:17 [A]Gen 17:3; 18:12; 21:6 [B]Gen 21:7 17:19 [a]I.e. he laughs [b]Lit *seed* [A]Gen 17:16; 18:10; 21:2 [B]Gen 26:2-5 17:20 [a]Lit *beget twelve princes* [A]Gen 16:10 [B]Gen 25:12-16 [C]Gen 21:18 17:21 [A]Gen 17:19; 18:10, 14 [B]Gen 21:2 17:22 [A]Gen 18:33; 35:13 17:23 [A]Gen 14:14 [B]Gen 17:9-11 17:24 [A]Rom 4:11 17:25 [A]Gen 16:16 17:27 [A]Gen 14:14 18:1 [a]Or *terebinths* [A]Gen 12:7; 17:1 [B]Gen 13:18; 14:13 18:2 [A]Gen 18:16, 22; 32:24; Josh 5:13; Judg 13:6-11; Heb 13:2 18:3 [a]Or *O Lord* [b]Lit *pass away from Your servant* 18:4 [a]Lit *support* [A]Gen 19:2; 24:32; 43:24 18:5 [a]Lit *take* [b]Lit *sustain your heart* [c]Lit *come to* [A]Judg 6:18, 19; 13:15, 16 18:6 [a]Lit *Hasten three measures* [b]Heb *seah;* i.e. one seah equals approx eleven qts 18:7 [a]Lit *good* 18:8 [a]Lit *and* 18:10 [a]Lit *when the time revives* [A]Gen 21:2; Rom 9:9 18:11 [a]Lit *the manner of women* [A]Gen 17:17; Rom 4:19 [B]Heb 11:11 18:12 [a]Lit *within* [A]Gen 17:17; Luke 1:18 [B]1 Pet 3:6

17:14 shall be cut off from his people. Being cut off from the covenant community meant loss of temporal benefits stemming from being part of the special, chosen, and theocratic nation, even to the point of death by divine judgment.

17:15 Sarai … Sarah. Fittingly, since Sarai ("my princess") would be the ancestress of the promised nations and kings, God changed her name to Sarah, taking away the limiting personal pronoun "my," and calling her "princess" (v. 16).

17:16 *mother of* nations. Cf. 17:5.

17:17 fell on his face and laughed, and said in his heart. A proper reaction of adoration over God's promises was marred by the incredulity of Abraham. He knew he was to be a father (12:2; 15:4), but this was the first mention that his barren, old wife was to be the mother.

17:18 Oh that Ishmael might live before You! Abraham's plea for a living son to be the designated beneficiary of God's promises betrayed just how impossible it was for him and Sarah to have children (cf. Ro 4:17).

17:19–21 Again, patiently but firmly rejecting Abraham's alternative solution, God emphatically settled the matter by bracketing His gracious bestowal of much posterity to Ishmael (see 25:12–18) with affirmations that indeed Sarah's son would be the heir of the "everlasting covenant." For the first time God named the son.

17:19 call his name Isaac. The name of the promised son meant "he laughs," an appropriate reminder to Abraham of his initial, faithless reaction to God's promise.

17:23–27 the very same day. Without delay, Abraham fully carried out God's command on himself, on "every male," and on "all the men of his household" (vv. 23, 27).

18:1 the LORD appeared. Another instance of a theophany, although Abraham perhaps did not recognize at first that one of his visitors, whom he humbly greeted and entertained (vv. 2–8) and properly sent on their way (v. 16), was Yahweh. **oaks of Mamre.** *See note on 13:18.*

18:3 My Lord. Although perhaps first used as the customary respectful address of a host to a visitor, later in their interchange it was used knowingly by Abraham of his true and sovereign Lord, whom he must have recognized when the visitor spoke of Himself as "LORD" (v. 14).

18:9–13 Despite a promise clearly reminiscent of God's words to Abraham, Sarah reacted with similar incredulity as her husband had done (cf. 17:17). She was not thinking of divine miracle but of divine providence working only within the normal course of life, being convinced that, at their age, bearing children was just not naturally possible.

18:10, 14 Cf. Ro 9:9.

old also?" 13 And the LORD said to Abraham, "Why did Sarah laugh, saying, 'Shall I indeed [a]bear *a child,* when I am *so* old?' 14 [A]Is anything too [a]difficult for the LORD? At the [B]appointed time I will return to you, [b]at this time next year, and Sarah will have a son." 15 Sarah denied *it* however, saying, "I did not laugh"; for she was afraid. And He said, "No, but you did laugh."

16 Then [A]the men rose up from there, and looked down toward Sodom; and Abraham was walking with them to send them off. 17 [A]The LORD said, "Shall I hide from Abraham [B]what I am about to do, 18 since Abraham will surely become a great and [a]mighty nation, and in him [A]all the nations of the earth will be blessed? 19 For I have [a,A]chosen him, so that he may [B]command his children and his household after him to [C]keep the way of the LORD by doing righteousness and justice, so that the LORD may bring upon Abraham [D]what He has spoken about him." 20 And the LORD said, "[A]The outcry of Sodom and Gomorrah is indeed great, and their sin is exceedingly grave. 21 I will [A]go down now, and see if they have done entirely according to its outcry, which has come to Me; and if not, I will know."

22 Then [A]the men turned away from there and went toward Sodom, while Abraham was still standing before [B]the LORD. 23 Abraham came near and said, "[A]Will You indeed sweep away the righteous with the wicked? 24 Suppose there are fifty righteous within the city; will You indeed sweep *it* away and not [a]spare the place for the sake of the fifty righteous who are in it? 25 Far be it from You to do [a]such a thing, to slay the righteous with the wicked, so that the righteous and the wicked are *treated* alike. Far be it from You! Shall not [A]the Judge of all the earth [b]deal justly?" 26 So the LORD said, "[A]If I find in Sodom fifty righteous within the city, then I will [a]spare the whole place on their account." 27 And Abraham replied, "Now behold, I have [a]ventured to speak to the Lord, although I am *but* [A]dust and ashes. 28 Suppose the fifty righteous are lacking five, will You destroy the whole city because of five?" And He said, "I will not destroy *it* if I find forty-five there." 29 He spoke to Him yet again and said, "Suppose forty are found there?" And He said, "I will not do *it* on account of the forty." 30 Then he said, "Oh may the Lord not be angry, and I shall speak; suppose thirty are found there?" And He said, "I will not do *it* if I find thirty there." 31 And he said, "Now behold, I have [a]ventured to speak to the Lord; suppose twenty are found there?" And He said, "I will not destroy *it* on account of the twenty." 32 Then he said, "[A]Oh may the Lord not be angry, and I shall speak only this once; suppose ten are found there?" And He said, "I will not destroy *it* on account of the ten." 33 As soon as He had finished speaking to Abraham [A]the LORD departed, and Abraham returned to his place.

THE DOOM OF SODOM

19 Now the [A]two angels came to Sodom in the evening as Lot was sitting in the gate of Sodom. When [B]Lot saw *them,* he rose to meet them and [a]bowed down *with his* face to the ground. 2 And he said, "Now behold, my lords, please turn aside into your servant's house, and spend the night, and wash your feet; then you may rise early and go on your way." They said however, "No, but we shall spend the night in the square." 3 Yet he urged them strongly, so they turned aside to him and entered his house; [A]and he prepared a feast for them, and baked unleavened

18:13 [a]Lit *surely bear* 18:14 [a]Or *wonderful* [b]Lit *when the time revives* [A]Jer 32:17, 27; Zech 8:6; Matt 19:26; Luke 1:37; Rom 4:21 [B]Gen 17:21; 18:10 18:16 [A]Gen 18:2, 22; 19:1 18:17 [A]Gen 18:22, 26, 33; Amos 3:7 [B]Gen 18:21; 19:24 18:18 [a]Or *populous* [A]Gen 12:3; 22:18; Acts 3:25; Gal 3:8 18:19 [a]Lit *known* [A]Neh 9:7; Amos 3:2 [B]Deut 6:6, 7 [C]Gen 17:9 [D]Gen 12:2, 3 18:20 [A]Gen 19:13; Ezek 16:49, 50 18:21 [A]Gen 11:5; Ex 3:8; Ps 14:2 18:22 [A]Gen 18:16; 19:1 [B]Gen 18:1, 17 18:23 [A]Ex 23:7; Num 16:22; 2 Sam 24:17; Ps 11:4-7 18:24 [a]Or *forgive* 18:25 [a]Lit *after this manner* [b]Lit *do justice* [A]Deut 1:16, 17; 32:4; Job 8:3, 20; Ps 58:11; 94:2; Is 3:10, 11; Rom 3:5, 6 18:26 [a]Or *forgive* [A]Jer 5:1 18:27 [a]Lit *undertaken* [A]Gen 3:19; Job 30:19; 42:6 18:31 [a]Lit *undertaken* 18:32 [A]Judg 6:39 18:33 [A]Gen 17:22; 35:13 19:1 [a]Lit *bowed himself* [A]Gen 18:2, 22 [B]Gen 18:2-5 19:3 [A]Gen 18:6-8

18:14, 15 A rhetorical question ("Is anything too difficult…?") and divine declaration ("At the appointed time…"), coupled with obvious knowledge of her thoughts ("laughed to herself"), made Sarah fearfully perceive her total misperception of God's working.

18:17, 18 Shall I hide from Abraham what I am about to do, since…? The Lord's reason for permitting Abraham to know of judgment in advance underscored his special role in the plan of God and the certain outcome of His covenant with Abraham—many offspring and great blessing.

18:18 Cf. Gal 3:8.

18:19 For I have chosen him, so that he may command. An expression of divine confidence, i.e., a tribute to faithfulness, obedience, and consistency.

18:20 The outcry … is indeed great. The iniquity of the two cities, by then complete (cf. 15:16), had reached the point of no return before the Lord, who demonstrated before Abraham how justly He assessed the time for judgment (v. 21, "I will go down now, and see…").

18:23 Will You indeed sweep away the righteous with the wicked? The intercession for the two wicked cities began with a question that portrayed Abraham's acute awareness of God's mercy toward the righteous and the distinction He made between the good and the bad (v. 25).

18:24 fifty righteous. Among the righteous was Lot (see 2Pe 2:7, 8).

18:25 Shall not the Judge of all the earth deal justly? Abraham's clear understanding of God's character being able only to do what is good and totally above reproach was affirmed with this rhetorical question.

18:27 I am *but* dust and ashes. Abraham's negotiation, far from being crassly or selfishly manipulative, humbly and compassionately expressed his concern for people (cf. 13:8, 9) and particularly interceded for the place where his nephew Lot and his family lived. Neither did he intend to anger the Lord by his repeated requests (vv. 28, 30, 32).

18:32 on account of the ten. That the number of righteous people necessary to forestall judgment had been reduced from 50 to 10 may have reflected Abraham's awareness both of the intense wickedness of the cities as well as Lot's ineffective witness there. Abraham probably had the whole of Lot's family in mind.

18:33 the LORD departed, and Abraham returned to his place. Nothing more could be done; the judgment was inevitable!

19:1 two angels. These were the angels who, with God, had visited Abraham (18:22). They had taken human form (v. 10; called "men"). **Lot was sitting in the gate.** Since city officials and other prominent citizens conducted the community's affairs at the gate, Lot participated there as a judge (v. 9).

19:2 please turn aside into your servant's house. Lot's invitation to the two angels (vv. 1–3) to partake themselves of his hospitality was most likely not just courtesy, but an effort to protect them from the known perversity of the Sodomites.

19:3 he urged them strongly. Such was Lot's concern for these strangers that their stated preference to pass the night in the town square could not be permitted.

bread, and they ate. 4 Before they lay down, [A]the men
of the city, the men of Sodom, surrounded the house,
both young and old, all the people [a]from every quarter; 5 and they called to Lot and said to him, "[A]Where
are the men who came to you tonight? Bring them
out to us that we may [a]have relations with them."
6 But Lot went out to them at the doorway, and shut
the door behind him, 7 and said, "Please, my brothers, do not act wickedly. 8 Now behold, [A]I have two
daughters who have not [a]had relations with man;
please let me bring them out to you, and do to them
[b]whatever you like; only do nothing to these men,
inasmuch as they have come under the [c]shelter of
my roof." 9 But they said, "Stand aside." Furthermore,
they said, "This one came in [a]as an alien, and already
[A]he is acting like a judge; now we will treat you worse
than them." So they pressed hard against [b]Lot and
came near to break the door. 10 But [A]the men reached
out their [a]hands and brought Lot into the house
[b]with them, and shut the door. 11 [A]They [a]struck the
men who were at the doorway of the house with
blindness, both small and great, so that they wearied
themselves trying to find the doorway.

12 Then the *two* men said to Lot, "Whom else have
you here? A son-in-law, and your sons, and your
daughters, and whomever you have in the city,
bring *them* out of the place; 13 for we are about to
destroy this place, because [A]their outcry has become
so great before the LORD that [B]the LORD has sent
us to destroy it." 14 Lot went out and spoke to his
sons-in-law, who [a]were to marry his daughters, and
said, "Up, [A]get out of this place, for the LORD will
destroy the city." [B]But he appeared to his sons-in-law
[b]to be jesting.

15 When morning dawned, the angels urged Lot,
saying, "Up, take your wife and your two daughters
who are here, or you will be swept away in the [a]pun-
ishment of the city." 16 But he hesitated. So the men
[A]seized his hand and the hand of his wife and the
[a]hands of his two daughters, for [B]the compassion
of the LORD *was* upon him; and they brought him
out, and put him outside the city. 17 When they had
brought them outside, [a]one said, "[A]Escape for your
life! [B]Do not look behind you, and do not stay [b]any-
where in the [c]valley; escape to [D]the [c]mountains, or
you will be swept away." 18 But Lot said to them, "Oh
no, my lords! 19 Now behold, your servant has found
favor in your sight, and you have magnified your
lovingkindness, which you have shown me by saving
my life; but I cannot escape to the [a]mountains, for
the disaster will overtake me and I will die; 20 now
behold, this town is near *enough* to flee to, and it is
small. Please, let me escape there (is it not small?)
[a]that my life may be saved." 21 He said to him, "Behold, I grant you this [a]request also, not to overthrow
the town of which you have spoken. 22 Hurry, escape
there, for I cannot do anything until you arrive there."
Therefore the name of the town was called [a,A]Zoar.

23 The sun had risen over the earth when Lot
came to Zoar. 24 Then the LORD [A]rained on Sodom
and Gomorrah brimstone and fire from the LORD
out of heaven, 25 and [A]He overthrew those cities,
and all the [a]valley, and all the inhabitants of the
cities, and what grew on the ground. 26 But his wife,

19:4 [a]Or *without exception;* lit *from every end* [A]Gen 13:13; 18:20 19:5 [a]I.e. have intercourse [A]Lev 18:22; Judg 19:22 19:8 [a]I.e. had intercourse [b]Lit *as is good in your sight* [c]Lit *shadow* [A]Judg 19:24 19:9 [a]Lit *to sojourn* [b]Lit *the man, against Lot* [A]Ex 2:14 19:10 [a]Lit *hand* [b]Lit *to* [A]Gen 19:1 19:11 [a]Lit *smote* [A]Deut 28:28, 29; 2 Kin 6:18; Acts 13:11 19:13 [A]Gen 18:20 [B]Lev 26:30-33; Deut 4:26; 28:45; 1 Chr 21:15 19:14 [a]Or *had married;* lit *were taking* [b]Lit *like one who was jesting* [A]Num 16:21, 45; Rev 18:4 [B]Jer 43:1, 2 19:15 [a]Or *iniquity* 19:16 [a]Lit *hand* [A]Deut 5:15; 6:21; 7:8; 2 Pet 2:7 [B]Ex 34:7; Ps 32:10; 33:18, 19 19:17 [a]Lit *he* [b]Lit *in all the circle* [c]Lit *mountain* [A]Jer 48:6 [B]Gen 19:26 [C]Gen 13:10 [D]Gen 14:10 19:19 [a]Lit *mountain* 19:20 [a]Lit *and my soul will live* 19:21 [a]Lit *thing* 19:22 [a]I.e. small [A]Gen 13:10; 14:2 19:24 [A]Deut 29:23; Ps 11:6; Is 13:19; Ezek 16:49, 50; Luke 17:29; Jude 7 19:25 [a]Lit *circle* [A]Deut 29:23; Ps 107:34; Is 13:19; Lam 4:6; 2 Pet 2:6

19:4 the men of the city ... all the people. Both the size of the lustful mob of men boisterously milling around Lot's house and the widespread nature of Sodom's moral perversion received emphasis both from the additional qualifiers used ("all the people from every quarter" and "both young and old") and the request made (v. 5, "have relations with them"). Even acknowledging legitimate exaggeration in this use of "all" would not detract from this emphasis—this was indeed a wicked city!

19:5 have relations with them. They sought homosexual relations with the visitors. God's attitude toward this vile behavior became clear when He destroyed the city (vv. 23–29). Cf. Lv 18:22, 29; 20:13; Ro 1:26; 1Co 6:9; 1Ti 1:10 where all homosexual behavior is prohibited and condemned by God.

19:6–8 Lot's response betrayed tension in his ethics; his offer to gratify their sexual lust contradicted his plea not to act "wickedly." Such contradiction made clear also the vexation of spirit under which he lived in wicked Sodom (cf. 2Pe 2:6, 7).

19:8 do to them whatever you like. The constraints of Eastern hospitality and the very purpose for which Lot had invited the visitors in (vv. 2, 3) compelled Lot to offer his daughters for a less deviant (*see notes on Ro 1:24–27*) kind of wickedness, so as to protect his guests. This foolish effort shows that while Lot was right with God (2Pe 2:7, 8), he had contented himself with some sins and weak faith rather than leaving Sodom. But God was gracious to him because he was righteous, by faith, before God.

19:9 acting like a judge. Their accusation suggests Lot had made moral pronouncements before, but his evaluation was no longer tolerable. **pressed hard.** Homosexual deviation carries an uncontrollable lust that defies restraint. Even when blinded, they tried to fulfill their lust (v. 11).

19:10, 11 Lot was now being protected by those whom he had earlier sought to protect!

19:13 the LORD has sent us to destroy it. With the wickedness of the city so graphically confirmed (vv. 4–11), divine judgment was the only outcome, but Lot's family could escape it (vv. 12, 13). Cf. Jude 7.

19:14 appeared ... to be jesting. Lot's warning of imminent judgment fell within the category of jesting, so concluded his sons-in-law (or perhaps his daughters' fiancés).

19:16 compassion of the LORD *was* upon him. This reason, elsewhere described as God having remembered Abraham (v. 29), is why, in the face of Lot's seeming reluctance to leave ("hesitated"), the angels personally and forcefully escorted him and his family beyond the city's precincts.

19:17–21 An urbanized lifestyle was apparently superior to a lonely one in the mountains and might be why Lot, playing upon the mercy already shown him, negotiated for an alternative escape destination—another city! The angel's reply (v. 21) indicated that this city was included in the original judgment plan, but would be spared for Lot's sake.

19:24 brimstone ... from the LORD out of heaven. When morning came (v. 23) judgment fell. Any natural explanation about how the Lord used combustible sulfur deposits to destroy that locale falters on this emphatic indication of miraculous judgment. "Brimstone" could refer to any inflammable substance; perhaps a volcanic eruption and an earthquake with a violent electrical storm "overthrew" (v. 25) the area. That area is now believed to be under the south end of the Dead Sea. Burning gases, sulfur, and magma blown into the air all fell to bury the region.

19:26 his wife ... looked *back*. Lot's wife paid the price of disregarding the angelic warning to flee without a backward glance (v. 17). In so doing, she became not only encased in salt, but a poignant example of disobedience producing unwanted reaction at judgment day (cf. Lk 17:29–32), even as her home cities became bywords of God's judgment on sin (cf. Is 1:9; Ro 9:29; 2Pe 2:5, 6).

from behind him, [A]looked *back,* and she became a
pillar of salt.
27 Now Abraham arose early in the morning *and*
went to [A]the place where he had stood before the
LORD; 28 and he looked down toward Sodom and
Gomorrah, and toward all the land of the [a]valley,
and he saw, and behold, [A]the smoke of the land ascended like the smoke of a [b]furnace.
29 Thus it came about, when God destroyed the
cities of the [a]valley, that [A]God remembered Abraham, and [B]sent Lot out of the midst of the overthrow,
when He overthrew the cities in which Lot lived.

LOT IS DEBASED

30 Lot went up from Zoar, and [a,A]stayed in the
[b]mountains, and his two daughters with him; for
he was afraid to [c]stay in Zoar; and he [a]stayed in a
cave, he and his two daughters. 31 Then the firstborn said to the younger, "Our father is old, and
there is not a man [a]on earth to [A]come in to us after
the manner of the earth. 32 Come, [A]let us make our
father drink wine, and let us lie with him that we
may preserve [a]our family through our father." 33 So
they made their father drink wine that night, and
the firstborn went in and lay with her father; and
he did not know when she lay down or when she
arose. 34 On the following day, the firstborn said to
the younger, "Behold, I lay last night with my father;
let us make him drink wine tonight also; then you
go in and lie with him, that we may preserve [a]our
family through our father." 35 So they made their
father drink wine that night also, and the younger
arose and lay with him; and he did not know when
she lay down or when she arose. 36 Thus both the
daughters of Lot were with child by their father.
37 The firstborn bore a son, and called his name
[A]Moab; he is the father of the Moabites to this day.
38 As for the younger, she also bore a son, and called
his name Ben-ammi; he is the father of the [a]sons of
[A]Ammon to this day.

ABRAHAM'S TREACHERY

20 Now Abraham journeyed from [A]there toward the land of [B]the [a]Negev, and [b]settled
between Kadesh and Shur; then he sojourned in
[C]Gerar. 2 Abraham said of Sarah his wife, "[A]She is my
sister." So [B]Abimelech king of Gerar sent and took
Sarah. 3 [A]But God came to Abimelech in a dream of
the night, and said to him, "Behold, [B]you are a dead
man because of the woman whom you have taken,
for she is [a]married." 4 Now Abimelech had not come
near her; and he said, "Lord, [A]will You slay a nation,
even *though* [a]blameless? 5 Did he not himself say to
me, 'She is my sister'? And she [A]herself said, 'He is
my brother.' In [B]the integrity of my heart and the
innocence of my [a]hands I have done this." 6 Then
God said to him in the dream, "Yes, I know that in
the integrity of your heart you have done this, and
I also [a,A]kept you from sinning against Me; therefore I did not let you touch her. 7 Now therefore,
restore the man's wife, for [A]he is a prophet, and he
will pray for you and you will live. But if you do not
restore *her,* know that you shall surely die, you and
all who are yours."
8 So Abimelech arose early in the morning and
called all his servants and told all these things in
their hearing; and the men were greatly frightened.
9 [A]Then Abimelech called Abraham and said to him,
"What have you done to us? And [a]how have I sinned
against you, that you have brought on me and on my
kingdom [B]a great sin? You have done to me [b]things
that ought not to be done." 10 And Abimelech said to
Abraham, "What have you [a]encountered, that you
have done this thing?" 11 Abraham said, "Because I
thought, surely there is no [A]fear of God in this place,
and [B]they will kill me because of my wife. 12 Besides,

19:26 [A]Gen 19:17; Luke 17:32 19:27 [A]Gen 18:22 19:28 [a]Lit *circle* [b]Lit *kiln* [A]Rev 9:2; 18:9 19:29 [a]Lit *circle* [A]Deut 7:8; 9:5, 27 [B]2 Pet 2:7 19:30 [a]Lit *dwelt* [b]Lit *mountain* [c]Lit *dwell* [A]Gen 19:17, 19 19:31 [a]Or *in the land* [A]Gen 16:2, 4; 38:8; Deut 25:5 19:32 [a]Lit *seed from our father* [A]Luke 21:34 19:34 [a]Lit *seed from our father* 19:37 [A]Deut 2:9 19:38 [a]Heb *Bene-Ammon* [A]Deut 2:19 20:1 [a]I.e. South country [b]Lit *dwelt* [A]Gen 18:1 [B]Gen 12:9 [C]Gen 26:1, 6 20:2 [A]Gen 12:11-13; 20:12; 26:7 [B]Gen 12:15 20:3 [a]Lit *married to a husband* [A]Gen 12:17, 18 [B]Gen 20:7 20:4 [a]Lit *righteous* [A]Gen 18:23-25 20:5 [a]Lit *palms* [A]Gen 20:13 [B]1 Kin 9:4; Ps 7:8; 26:6 20:6 [a]Lit *restrained* [A]1 Sam 25:26, 34 20:7 [A]1 Sam 7:5; 2 Kin 5:11; Job 42:8 20:9 [a]Lit *what* [b]Lit *deeds* [A]Gen 12:18 [B]Gen 39:9 20:10 [a]Lit *seen* 20:11 [A]Neh 5:15; Prov 16:6 [B]Gen 12:12; 26:7

19:29 **the cities of the valley.** The best archeological evidence locates Sodom and Gomorrah at the south of the Dead Sea region, i.e., in the area south of the Lisan Peninsula that juts out on the east (*see note on 14:10*). **God remembered Abraham.** Cf. 18:23–33.

19:30 **afraid to stay in Zoar.** Perhaps because the people there felt he was responsible for all the devastation, or he feared more judgment on the region might hit the city (vv. 17–23).

19:31–36 The immoral philosophy of Sodom and Gomorrah had so corrupted the thinking of Lot's daughters that they unhesitatingly contrived to be impregnated by their own father! They were virgins (v. 8), the married daughters were dead (v. 14) and there were no men left for husbands (v. 25). In fearing they would have no children, they conceived the gross iniquity.

19:37, 38 The two sons born of incest became the progenitors of Moab and Ammon, Israel's longstanding enemies.

20:1 **Gerar.** A Philistine city on the border between Canaan and Egypt, about 10 mi. S of Gaza.

20:2 **She is my sister.** Twenty-five years after leaving Egypt in disgrace because of lying about his wife (12:10–20), Abraham reverted to the same ploy. **Abimelech.** This king who took Sarah into his harem was most likely the father or grandfather of the Abimelech encountered by Isaac. *See note on 26:1.*

20:3 **God came . . . in a dream.** Again Abraham's Lord intervened to protect Sarah, who had joined in the lie of her husband (v. 5), deceiving a king who earnestly protested his innocence and integrity before God (vv. 4–6) and who, together with his aides, demonstrated proper submission to the warning of God (v. 8).

20:6 **kept you from sinning.** Notwithstanding God's restraint of Abimelech, he was still required to restore Sarah to forestall judgment.

20:7 **he is a prophet.** Abraham, in spite of his lie, still served as God's intermediary and intercessor for Abimelech (cf. vv. 17, 18). This is the first time the Hebrew term for "prophet" is used in Scripture. Here it identified Abraham as recognized by God to speak to Him on behalf of Abimelech. Usually it is used to describe not one who speaks to God on behalf of someone, but one who speaks to someone on behalf of God.

20:9 **things that ought not to be done.** The confrontation between prophet and king attested the grievous nature of Abraham's actions. How humiliating for the prophet of God to be so rebuked by a heathen king.

20:11–13 Abraham offered 3 reasons for his lie: 1) his perception from the horrible vices in Sodom that all other cities had no fear of God, including Gerar; 2) his fear of death as a mitigating factor for what he had done; and 3) his wife actually being his half-sister as justification for lying and hiding their marital status. Abraham didn't need fraud to protect himself. God was able to provide safety for him.

she actually is my sister, the daughter of my father, but not the daughter of my mother, and she
became my wife; 13 and it came about, when [A]God
caused me to wander from my father's house, that
I said to her, 'This is [a]the kindness which you will
show to me: [b]everywhere we go, [B]say of me, "He is
my brother." ' " 14 [A]Abimelech then took sheep and
oxen and male and female servants, and gave them
to Abraham, and restored his wife Sarah to him.
15 Abimelech said, "[A]Behold, my land is before you;
[a]settle wherever [b]you please." 16 To Sarah he said,
"Behold, I have given your [A]brother a thousand
pieces of silver; behold, it is [a]your vindication before all who are with you, and before all men you
are cleared." 17 [A]Abraham prayed to God, and God
healed Abimelech and his wife and his maids, so
that they bore *children.* 18 [A]For the LORD had closed
fast all the wombs of the household of Abimelech
because of Sarah, Abraham's wife.

ISAAC IS BORN

21 [A]Then the LORD took note of Sarah as He had
said, and the LORD did for Sarah as He had
[a]promised. 2 [A]So Sarah conceived and bore a son to
Abraham in his old age, at [B]the appointed time of
which God had spoken to him. 3 Abraham called the
name of his son who was born to him, whom Sarah
bore to him, [A]Isaac. 4 Then Abraham circumcised
his son Isaac when he was [A]eight days old, as God
had commanded him. 5 Now Abraham was [A]one
hundred years old when his son Isaac was born
to him. 6 Sarah said, "God has made [A]laughter for
me; everyone who hears will laugh [a]with me." 7 And
she said, "[A]Who would have said to Abraham that
Sarah would nurse children? Yet I have borne him
a son in his old age."
8 The child grew and was weaned, and Abraham made a great feast on the day that Isaac was
weaned.

SARAH TURNS AGAINST HAGAR

9 Now Sarah saw [A]the son of Hagar the Egyptian, whom she had borne to Abraham, [a,B]mocking.
10 Therefore she said to Abraham, "[A]Drive out this
maid and her son, for the son of this maid shall not
be an heir with my son [a]Isaac." 11 [A]The matter [a]dis-
tressed Abraham greatly because of his son. 12 But
God said to Abraham, "[a]Do not be distressed because
of the lad and your maid; whatever Sarah tells you,
listen to her, for [A]through Isaac [b]your descendants
shall be named. 13 And of [A]the son of the maid I will
make a nation also, because he is your [a]descendant."
14 So Abraham rose early in the morning and took
bread and a [a]skin of water and gave *them* to Hagar,
putting *them* on her shoulder, and *gave her* the boy,
and sent her away. And she departed and wandered
about in the wilderness of Beersheba.
15 When the water in the skin was used up, she [a]left
the boy under one of the bushes. 16 Then she went
and sat down opposite him, about a bowshot away,
for she said, "Do not let me [a]see the boy die." And she
sat opposite him, and [A]lifted up her voice and wept.
17 God [A]heard the lad crying; and the angel of God
called to Hagar from heaven and said to her, "What
is the matter with you, Hagar? [B]Do not fear, for God
has heard the voice of the lad where he is. 18 Arise,
lift up the lad, and hold him by [a]the hand, [A]for I will
make a great nation of him." 19 Then God [A]opened her
eyes and she saw [B]a well of water; and she went and
filled the [a]skin with water and gave the lad a drink.
20 [A]God was with the lad, and he grew; and he
[a]lived in the wilderness and became an archer. 21 [A]He
[a]lived in the wilderness of Paran, and his mother
took a wife for him from the land of Egypt.

COVENANT WITH ABIMELECH

22 Now it came about at that time that [A]Abimelech
and Phicol, the commander of his army, spoke to
Abraham, saying, "[B]God is with you in all that you

20:13 [a]Lit *your* [b]Lit *at every place where* [A]Gen 12:1-9 [B]Gen 12:13; 20:5 20:14 [A]Gen 12:16 20:15 [a]Lit *dwell* [b]Lit *it is good in your sight* [A]Gen 13:9; 34:10; 47:6 20:16 [a]Lit *for you a covering of the eyes* [A]Gen 20:5 20:17 [A]Num 12:13; 21:7; James 5:16 20:18 [A]Gen 12:17 21:1 [a]Lit *spoken* [A]Gen 17:16, 21; 18:10, 14; Gal 4:23 21:2 [A]Acts 7:8; Gal 4:22; Heb 11:11 [B]Gen 17:21; 18:10, 14 21:3 [A]Gen 17:19, 21 21:4 [A]Gen 17:12; Acts 7:8 21:5 [A]Gen 17:17 21:6 [a]Lit *for* [A]Gen 18:13; Ps 126:2; Is 54:1 21:7 [A]Gen 18:11, 13 21:9 [a]Or *playing* [A]Gen 16:1, 4, 15 [B]Gal 4:29 21:10 [a]Lit *with Isaac* [A]Gal 4:30 21:11 [a]Lit *was very grievous in Abraham's sight* [A]Gen 17:18 21:12 [a]Lit *Do not let it be grievous in your sight* [b]Lit *your seed will be called* [A]Rom 9:7; Heb 11:18 21:13 [a]Lit *seed* [A]Gen 16:10; 21:18; 25:12-18 21:14 [a]I.e. a skin used as a bottle 21:15 [a]Lit *cast* 21:16 [a]Lit *look upon the death of the child* [A]Jer 6:26; Amos 8:10 21:17 [A]Ex 3:7; Deut 26:7; Ps 6:8 [B]Gen 26:24 21:18 [a]Lit *your* [A]Gen 16:10; 21:13; 25:12-16 21:19 [a]V 14, note 1 [A]Num 22:31; 2 Kin 6:17 [B]Gen 16:7, 14 21:20 [a]Lit *dwelt* [A]Gen 28:15; 39:2, 3, 21 21:21 [a]Lit *dwelt* [A]Gen 25:18 21:22 [A]Gen 20:2, 14; 26:26 [B]Gen 26:28; Is 8:10

20:16 cleared. This is better translated "justified."

21:1 the LORD took note of Sarah. To the aged couple (vv. 2, 5, 7), exactly as promised, a son was born and the 25 year suspense was finally over with the laughter of derision turning to rejoicing (v. 6). The barrenness of Sarah (11:30) had ended.

21:4 circumcised. *See note on 17:11.*

21:5 Isaac … born to him. Ca. 2065 B.C. God fulfilled His promise to Abraham (12:2; 15:4, 5; 17:7).

21:8 weaned. This usually occurred in the second or third year.

21:9 the son of Hagar … mocking. The celebration of Isaac's passage from infancy to childhood witnessed the laughter of ridicule (an intensive form of the Hebrew for laughing) and offended Sarah, causing her to demand the expulsion of Ishmael and his mother from the encampment (v. 10).

21:10 Drive out … not be an heir. Legal codes of Abraham's day—e.g., of Nuzi and of Hammurabi—forbade the putting out of a handmaiden's son if a rightful, natural heir was born. Sarah's request, thus, offended social law, Abraham's sensibilities, and his love for Ishmael (v. 11). Abraham, however, was given divine approval and assurances to overcome his scruples before sending Hagar and Ishmael out into the wilderness (vv. 12–15). Cf. Gal 4:22–31.

21:12 Cf. Ro 9:7; Heb 11:18.

21:13 Cf. v. 18; *see notes on 16:11, 12.* Ishmael was about 17 years old, a customary time for sons to go out to set up their own lives.

21:14 wilderness of Beersheba. A wide, extensive desert on the southern border of Palestine.

21:17 God heard the lad crying. When desperation turned the lad's voice of scoffing into a cry of anguish at probable death from thirst (vv. 15, 16), God heard him whose name had been given years before when God had heard Hagar's cries (16:11). It reminded the mother of the promise made to Abraham about her son (17:20). **angel of God.** Same person as the Angel of the Lord. *See note on Ex 3:2.*

21:18 *See note on v. 13.*

21:21 wilderness of Paran. Located in the NE section of the Sinai Peninsula, the area called Arabia.

21:22–34 A parity treaty formally struck between Abimelech and Abraham guaranteed the proper control and sharing of the region's limited water resources and also assured the king of the patriarch's fair and equitable treatment for years to come.

do; 23 now therefore, [A]swear to me here by God that
you will not deal falsely with me or with my offspring or with my posterity, but according to the
kindness that I have shown to you, you shall show
to me and to the land in which you have sojourned."
24 Abraham said, "I swear it." 25 But Abraham [a]com-
plained to Abimelech because of the well of water
which the servants of Abimelech [A]had seized. 26 And
Abimelech said, "I do not know who has done this
thing; you did not tell me, nor did I hear of it [a]until
today."

27 Abraham took sheep and oxen and gave them
to Abimelech, and [A]the two of them made a covenant. 28 Then Abraham set seven ewe lambs of the
flock by themselves. 29 Abimelech said to Abraham,
"What do these seven ewe lambs mean, which you
have set by themselves?" 30 He said, "You shall take
these seven ewe lambs from my hand so that it may
be a [A]witness to me, that I dug this well." 31 Therefore he called that place [A]Beersheba, because there
the two of them took an oath. 32 So they made a
covenant at Beersheba; and Abimelech and Phicol,
the commander of his army, arose and returned to
the land of the Philistines. 33 *Abraham* planted a
tamarisk tree at Beersheba, and there [A]he called on
the name of the LORD, the [B]Everlasting God. 34 And
Abraham sojourned [A]in the land of the Philistines
for many days.

THE OFFERING OF ISAAC

22 Now it came about after these things, that
[A]God tested Abraham, and said to him,
"[B]Abraham!" And he said, "Here I am." 2 He said,
"Take now [A]your son, your only son, whom you love,
Isaac, and go to the land of [B]Moriah, and offer him
there as a [C]burnt offering on one of the mountains
of which I will tell you." 3 So Abraham rose early in
the morning and saddled his donkey, and took two
of his young men with him and Isaac his son; and
he split wood for the burnt offering, and arose and
went to the place of which God had told him. 4 On
the third day Abraham raised his eyes and saw the
place from a distance. 5 Abraham said to his young
men, "Stay here with the donkey, and I and the lad
will go over there; and we will worship and return
to you." 6 Abraham took the wood of the burnt offering and [A]laid it on Isaac his son, and he took in
his hand the fire and the knife. So the two of them
walked on together. 7 Isaac spoke to Abraham his
father and said, "My father!" And he said, "Here I
am, my son." And he said, "Behold, the fire and the
wood, but where is the [A]lamb for the burnt offering?" 8 Abraham said, "God will [a]provide for Himself
the lamb for the burnt offering, my son." So the two
of them walked on together.

9 Then they came to [A]the place of which God
had told him; and Abraham built [B]the altar there
and arranged the wood, and bound his son Isaac
and [C]laid him on the altar, on top of the wood.
10 Abraham stretched out his hand and took the
knife to slay his son. 11 But [A]the angel of the LORD
called to him from heaven and said, "Abraham,
Abraham!" And he said, "Here I am." 12 He said,
"Do not stretch out your hand against the lad, and
do nothing to him; for now [A]I know that you [a]fear
God, since you have not withheld [B]your son, your
only son, from Me." 13 Then Abraham raised his
eyes and looked, and behold, behind *him* a ram
caught in the thicket by his horns; and Abraham
went and took the ram and offered him up for a
burnt offering in the place of his son. 14 Abraham
called the name of that place [a]The LORD Will Provide, as it is said to this day, "In the mount of the
LORD [A]it will [b]be provided."

15 Then the angel of the LORD called to Abraham
a second time from heaven, 16 and said, "[A]By Myself
I have sworn, declares the LORD, because you have
done this thing and have not withheld your son,

21:23 [A]Josh 2:12; 1 Sam 24:21 21:25 [a]Lit *reproved* [A]Gen 26:15, 18, 20-22 21:26 [a]Lit *except* 21:27 [A]Gen 26:31 21:30 [A]Gen 31:48 21:31 [A]Gen 21:14; 26:33 21:33 [A]Gen 12:8 [B]Ex 15:18; Deut 32:40; Ps 90:2; 93:2; Is 40:28; Jer 10:10; Hab 1:12; Heb 13:8 21:34 [A]Gen 22:19 22:1 [A]Deut 8:2, 16; Heb 11:17; James 1:12-14 [B]Gen 22:11 22:2 [A]Gen 22:12, 16; John 3:16; 1 John 4:9 [B]2 Chr 3:1 [C]Gen 8:20 22:6 [A]John 19:17 22:7 [A]Ex 29:38-42; John 1:29, 36; Rev 13:8 22:8 [a]Lit *see* 22:9 [A]Gen 22:2 [B]Gen 12:7, 8; 13:18 [C]Heb 11:17-19; James 2:21 22:11 [A]Gen 16:7-11; 21:17, 18 22:12 [a]Or *reverence;* lit *are a fearer of God* [A]James 2:21, 22 [B]Gen 22:2, 16 22:14 [a]Heb *YHWH-jireh* [b]Lit *be seen* [A]Gen 22:8 22:16 [A]Ps 105:9; Luke 1:73; Heb 6:13, 14

21:31 Beersheba. This site is about 45 mi. SW of Jerusalem.

21:32 the land of the Philistines. Abraham had contact with early migrations of Aegean traders who settled along the SW coastal regions of Canaan and who were the predecessors of the 12th century B.C. influx of Philistines, the future oppressors of Israel.

21:33 tamarisk tree. This tree functioned as a reminder of the treaty concluded between two well known contemporaries, and also as a marker of one of Abraham's worship sites. **the Everlasting God.** A divine name appropriately signifying to Abraham the unbreakable and everlasting nature of the covenant God had made with him, notwithstanding his being only a resident alien and a sojourner in the Land (cf. 23:4).

22:1 God tested Abraham. This was not a temptation; rather God examined Abraham's heart (cf. Jas 1:2–4, 12–18).

22:2 Take ... your son ... and offer him. These startling commands activated a special testing ordeal for Abraham, i.e., to sacrifice his "only son" (repeated 3 times by God, vv. 2, 12, 16). This would mean killing the son (over 20 years old) and with that, ending the promise of the Abrahamic Covenant. Such action would seem irrational, yet Abraham obeyed (v. 3). **Moriah.** Traditionally associated with Jerusalem, and the site on which Solomon's temple would be built later (cf. 2Ch 3:1).

22:4 third day. With no appearance of reluctance or delay, Abraham rose early (v. 3) for the two-day trip from Beersheba to Moriah, one of the hills around Jerusalem.

22:5 I and the lad will go ... we will worship and return. The 3-day journey (v. 4) afforded much time of reflection upon God's commands but, without wavering or questioning the morality of human sacrifice or the purposes of God, Abraham confidently assured his servants of his and Isaac's return and went ahead with arrangements for the sacrifice (v. 6). Hebrews 11:17–19 reveals that he was so confident in the permanence of God's promise, that he believed if Isaac were to be killed, God would raise him from the dead (*see notes*), or God would provide a substitute for Isaac (v. 8).

22:9, 10 Abraham's preparations to kill his only son could not have placed his trust in God in sharper focus. Cf. Heb 11:17–19.

22:11 angel of the LORD. *See note on Ex 3:2.*

22:12 now I know. Abraham passed the test (v. 1). He demonstrated faith that God responds to with justification. *See note on Jas 2:21.*

22:13 in the place of his son. The idea of substitutionary atonement is introduced, which would find its fulfillment in the death of Christ (Is 53:4–6; Jn 1:29; 2Co 5:21).

22:15–18 In this formal reaffirmation of His Abrahamic Covenant, the Lord mentioned the 3 elements of land, seed, and blessing, but with attention directed graphically to the conquest of the Land promised (v. 17, "shall possess the gate of their enemies").

22:16, 17 Cf. 12:1–3; 15:13–18; 17:2, 7, 8, 9; Heb 6:13, 14.

your only son, 17 indeed I will greatly bless you, and
I will greatly [A]multiply your [a]seed as the stars of the
heavens and as [B]the sand which is on the seashore;
and [C]your [a]seed shall possess the gate of [b]their enemies. 18 [A]In your [a]seed all the nations of the earth
shall [b]be blessed, because you have [B]obeyed My
voice." 19 [A]So Abraham returned to his young men,
and they arose and went together to Beersheba;
and Abraham lived at Beersheba.

20 Now it came about after these things, that it
was told Abraham, saying, "Behold, [A]Milcah [a]also
has borne children to your brother Nahor: 21 Uz
his firstborn and Buz his brother and Kemuel the
father of Aram 22 and Chesed and Hazo and Pil-
dash and Jidlaph and Bethuel." 23 Bethuel [a]became
the father of [A]Rebekah; these eight Milcah bore to
Nahor, Abraham's brother. 24 His concubine, whose
name was Reumah, [a]also bore Tebah and Gaham
and Tahash and Maacah.

DEATH AND BURIAL OF SARAH

23 Now [a]Sarah lived one hundred and twen-
ty-seven years; *these were* the years of the
life of Sarah. 2 Sarah died in [A]Kiriath-arba (that is,
Hebron) in the land of Canaan; and Abraham [a]went in
to mourn for Sarah and to weep for her. 3 Then Abraham rose from before his dead, and spoke to the [A]sons
of Heth, saying, 4 "I am [A]a stranger and a sojourner
among you; [B]give me [a]a [C]burial site among you that
I may bury my dead out of my sight." 5 The sons of
Heth answered Abraham, saying to him, 6 "Hear us,
my lord, you are a [a,A]mighty prince among us; bury
your dead in the choicest of our graves; none of us
will refuse you his grave for burying your dead." 7 So
Abraham rose and bowed to the people of the land,
the sons of Heth. 8 And he spoke with them, saying,
"If it is your [a]wish *for me* to bury my dead out of
my sight, hear me, and approach [A]Ephron the son
of Zohar for me, 9 that he may give me the cave of
Machpelah which he owns, which is at the end of his
field; for the full price let him give it to me in [a]your
presence for [b]a burial site." 10 Now Ephron was sitting
among the sons of Heth; and Ephron the Hittite answered Abraham in the hearing of the sons of Heth;
even [A]of all who went in at the gate of his city, saying,
11 "No, my lord, hear me; [A]I give you the field, and I
give you the cave that is in it. In the presence of the
sons of my people I give it to you; bury your dead."
12 And Abraham bowed before the people of the land.
13 He spoke to Ephron in the hearing of the people
of the land, saying, "If you will only please listen to
me; I will give the price of the field, accept *it* from
me that I may bury my dead there." 14 Then Ephron
answered Abraham, saying to him, 15 "My lord, listen
to me; a piece of land worth four hundred [A]shekels
of silver, what is that between me and you? So bury
your dead." 16 Abraham listened to Ephron; and Abraham [A]weighed out for Ephron the silver which he
had named in the [a]hearing of the sons of Heth, four
hundred shekels of silver, [b]commercial standard.

17 So [A]Ephron's field, which was in Machpelah,
which faced Mamre, the field and cave which was
in it, and all the trees which were in the field, that
were [a]within all the confines of its border, [b]were
deeded over 18 to Abraham for a possession [A]in the
presence of the sons of Heth, before all who went in
at the gate of his city. 19 After this, Abraham buried
Sarah his wife in the cave of the field at Machpelah facing Mamre (that is, Hebron) in the land of
Canaan. 20 So the field and the cave that is in it,

22:17 [a]Or *descendants* [b]Lit *his* [A]Gen 15:5; 26:4; Jer 33:22; Heb 11:12 [B]Gen 32:12 [C]Gen 24:60 22:18 [a]Or *descendants* [b]Or *bless themselves* [A]Gen 12:3; 18:18; Acts 3:25; Gal 3:8, 16 [B]Gen 18:19; 22:3, 10; 26:5 22:19 [A]Gen 22:5 22:20 [a]Lit *she also* [A]Gen 11:29 22:23 [a]Lit *begot* [A]Gen 24:15 22:24 [a]Lit *she also* 23:1 [a]Lit *the life of Sarah was* 23:2 [a]Or *proceeded* [A]Josh 14:15; 15:13; 21:11 23:3 [A]Gen 10:15; 15:20 23:4 [a]Lit *possession of a grave* [A]Gen 17:8; Lev 25:23; 1 Chr 29:15; Ps 39:12; 105:12; 119:19; Heb 11:9, 13 [B]Acts 7:16 [C]Gen 49:30 23:6 [a]Lit *prince of God* [A]Gen 14:14; 20:7 23:8 [a]Lit *soul* [A]Gen 25:9 23:9 [a]Lit *the midst of you* [b]Lit *possession of a burial place* 23:10 [A]Gen 23:18; 34:20, 24; Ruth 4:1, 11 23:11 [A]2 Sam 24:21-24 23:15 [A]Ex 30:13; Ezek 45:12 23:16 [a]Lit *ears* [b]Lit *current according to the merchant* [A]2 Sam 14:26; Jer 32:9, 10; Zech 11:12 23:17 [a]Lit *in all its border around* [b]Or *were ratified* [A]Gen 25:9; 49:29, 30; 50:13 23:18 [A]Gen 23:10

22:17 possess the gate of their enemies. Cf. 24:60. Refers to conquering enemies, so as to control their city.

22:18 Cf. Ac 3:25.

22:20–24 it was told. This is clear indication that, despite geographical separation, information about family genealogies flowed back and forth in the Fertile Crescent region. This update advised most notably of a daughter, Rebekah, born to Isaac's cousin, Bethuel (v. 23). It also reminds the readers that Abraham and Sarah had not lost all ties with their original home. Abraham's brother, Nahor, still lived back in Mesopotamia, though he had not seen him for about 60 years.

23:1, 2 Although Sarah's age—the only woman's age at death recorded in Scripture—might suggest her importance in God's plan, it more importantly reminds of the birth of her only son well beyond childbearing age (at 90 years of age, cf. 17:17) and of God's intervention to bring about the fulfillment of His word to her and Abraham. Sarah's death occurred ca. 2028 B.C.

23:2 Hebron. *See note on 13:18.*

23:3 the sons of Heth. A settlement of Hittites whose original home was in Anatolia (modern-day Turkey), who had already been established in Canaan far from their homeland.

23:4 give me a burial site. Negotiations for the purchase ("give" signifies here "sell") of Hittite property was properly conducted in accordance with contemporary Hittite custom, with Abraham wanting to pay the market value for it (v. 9).

23:6 a mighty prince among us. Rank and reputation accorded Abraham a place of leadership and respect, leading his neighbors (the Hittites) to freely offer their best sepulchers to him. They went on and arranged for Abraham to purchase a cave that belonged to a wealthy neighbor called Ephron (vv. 7–9), unknown to Abraham.

23:10 sitting. Ephron was probably sitting at the city gate where business was usually transacted.

23:11 I give you the field. This suggests not that Ephron felt generous, but that he was constrained by Hittite feudal polity, which tied ownership of land with service to the ruler. Passing the land to Abraham would pass also feudal responsibilities to Abraham, making him liable for all taxes and duties. This Ephron was apparently anxious to do, thus the offer to give the land.

23:16 shekels of silver, commercial standard. Precious metals were not made into coins for exchange until centuries later. Merchants maintained the shekel as the standard weight of value for business transactions. A shekel weighed less than one half ounce.

23:17, 18 With the words of the transaction, the careful description of the property, and the payment of the stated price all done before witnesses and at the proper place of business, ownership of the land officially passed to Abraham. It was still binding years later in the time of Jacob (49:29–32; 50:12, 13).

23:19 After this. Once the purchase had been made, Abraham buried Sarah. Moses notes the place is Hebron in Canaan, to which his initial readers were soon headed.

23:20 So the field and the cave … were deeded. This is an important summary, because finally, after years of nomadic wandering, Abraham owned a small piece of real estate in the midst of all the land divinely promised to him and his descendants. The cave also became many years later the family burial plot for Abraham, Isaac, Rebekah, Leah, and Jacob (cf. 25:9; 49:31; 50:13), with Rachel being the exception (35:19).

[a]were [A]deeded over to Abraham for [b]a burial site
by the sons of Heth.

A BRIDE FOR ISAAC

24 Now [A]Abraham was old, advanced in age;
and the LORD had [B]blessed Abraham in every way. 2 Abraham said to his servant, the oldest
of his household, who had [A]charge of all that he
owned, "[B]Please place your hand under my thigh,
3 and I will make you swear by the LORD, [A]the God
of heaven and the God of earth, that you [B]shall not
take a wife for my son from the daughters of [C]the
Canaanites, among whom I live, 4 but you will go
to [A]my country and to my relatives, and take a wife
for my son Isaac." 5 The servant said to him, "Suppose the woman is not willing to follow me to this
land; should I take your son back to the land from
where you came?" 6 Then Abraham said to him,
"[A]Beware that you do not take my son back there!
7 [A]The LORD, the God of heaven, who took me from
my father's house and from the land of my birth,
and who spoke to me and who swore to me, saying, '[B]To your [a]descendants I will give this land,' He
will send [C]His angel before you, and you will take
a wife for my son from there. 8 But if the woman
is not willing to follow you, then you will [A]be free
from this my oath; [B]only do not take my son back
there." 9 So the servant [A]placed his hand under the
thigh of Abraham his master, and swore to him
concerning this matter.
10 Then the servant took ten camels from the
camels of his master, and set out with a variety of
[A]good things of his master's in his hand; and he
arose and went to [a]Mesopotamia, to [B]the city of
Nahor. 11 He made the camels kneel down outside
the city by [A]the well of water at evening time, [B]the
time when women go out to draw water. 12 He said,
"[A]O LORD, the God of my master Abraham, please
[a,B]grant me success today, and show lovingkindness
to my master Abraham. 13 Behold, [A]I am standing
by the [a]spring, and the daughters of the men of the
city are coming out to draw water; 14 now may it be
that the girl to whom I say, 'Please let down your
jar so that I may drink,' and [a]who answers, 'Drink,
and I will water your camels also'—*may* she *be the*
one whom You have appointed for Your servant
Isaac; and by this I will know that You have shown
lovingkindness to my master."

REBEKAH IS CHOSEN

15 [A]Before he had finished speaking, behold, [B]Re-
bekah who was born to Bethuel the son of [C]Milcah,
the wife of Abraham's brother Nahor, came out
with her jar on her shoulder. 16 The girl was [A]very
beautiful, a virgin, and no man had [a]had relations
with her; and she went down to the spring and
filled her jar and came up. 17 Then the servant ran
to meet her, and said, "[A]Please let me drink a little
water from your jar." 18 [A]She said, "Drink, my lord";
and she quickly lowered her jar to her hand, and
gave him a drink. 19 Now when she had finished
giving him a drink, [A]she said, "I will draw also for
your camels until they have finished drinking."
20 So she quickly emptied her jar into the trough,
and ran back to the well to draw, and she drew for
all his camels. 21 [A]Meanwhile, the man was gazing
at her [a]in silence, to know whether the LORD had
made his journey successful or not.
22 When the camels had finished drinking, the
man took a [A]gold ring weighing a half-shekel and
two bracelets for her [a]wrists weighing ten shekels in
gold, 23 and said, "Whose daughter are you? Please
tell me, is there room for us to lodge in your father's
house?" 24 She said to him, "[A]I am the daughter of
Bethuel, the son of Milcah, whom she bore to Nahor."
25 Again she said to him, "We have plenty of both

23:20 [a]Or *were ratified* [b]Lit *possession of a burial place* [A]Jer 32:10-14 24:1 [A]Gen 18:11 [B]Gen 12:2; 13:2; 24:35; Gal 3:9 24:2 [A]Gen 39:4-6 [B]Gen 24:9; 47:29 24:3 [A]Gen 14:19, 22 [B]Deut 7:3; 2 Cor 6:14-17 [C]Gen 10:15-19; 26:34, 35; 28:1, 8 24:4 [A]Gen 12:1; Heb 11:15 24:6 [A]Gen 24:8 24:7 [a]Lit *seed* [A]Gen 24:3 [B]Gen 12:7; 13:15; 15:18; Ex 32:13 [C]Gen 16:7; 21:17; 22:11; Ex 23:20, 23 24:8 [A]Josh 2:17-20 [B]Gen 24:6 24:9 [A]Gen 24:2 24:10 [a]Heb *Aram-naharaim, Aram of the two rivers* [A]Gen 24:22, 53 [B]Gen 11:31, 32 24:11 [A]Gen 24:42 [B]Ex 2:16; 1 Sam 9:11 24:12 [a]Lit *cause to occur for me* [A]Gen 24:27, 42, 48; 26:24; Ex 3:6, 15 [B]Gen 27:20 24:13 [a]Lit *fountain of water* [A]Gen 24:43 24:14 [a]Lit *she will say* 24:15 [A]Gen 24:45 [B]Gen 22:20, 23 [C]Gen 11:29 24:16 [a]Lit *known* [A]Gen 12:11; 26:7; 29:17 24:17 [A]John 4:7 24:18 [A]Gen 24:14, 46 24:19 [A]Gen 24:14 24:21 [a]Lit *keeping silent* [A]Gen 24:12-14, 27, 52 24:22 [a]Lit *hands* [A]Gen 24:47; Ex 32:2, 3 24:24 [A]Gen 24:15

24:2 **servant, the oldest of his household.** Eliezer, at 85 years of age, had risen to steward, or "chief of staff," a position of substantial authority (indicated in v. 10). He would have received all Abraham's wealth if he had no son (see 15:1, 2), yet when Isaac was born the inheritance became Isaac's. So, not only had he loyally served his master despite having been displaced by another heir (cf. 15:2–4), but he also faithfully served that heir (v. 67).

24:2–4 **place your hand under my thigh, and . . . swear.** *See note on v. 9.* A solemn pledge mentioning the Lord's name and formalized by an accepted customary gesture indicated just how serious an undertaking this was in Abraham's eyes. At his age (v. 1), Abraham was concerned to perpetuate his people and God's promise through the next generation, so he covenanted with his servant to return to Mesopotamia and bring back a wife for Isaac.

24:3, 4 Matrimonial arrangements were made by parents, and chosen partners were to come from one's own tribe. It was apparently customary to marry one's first cousin. But Abraham's higher motive was to prevent Isaac from marrying a Canaanite pagan after Abraham's death, thus possibly leading the people away from the true God.

24:6, 7 **do not take my son back there!** Should the expected scenario not materialize (v. 5) then the dictates of the oath were lifted (v. 8), but the option of Isaac going was summarily rejected because it suggested a nullification of God's promise and calling for the land of promise (v. 7).

24:7 **He will send His angel before you.** A statement of Abraham's faith that the 450 mile expedition to Mesopotamia was clearly under divine oversight.

24:9 **his hand under the thigh.** An ancient Near Eastern custom by which an intimate touch affirmed an oath (cf. 47:29).

24:10 **city of Nahor.** No doubt the home of Abraham's brother, Nahor (22:20).

24:12–14 The steward's prayer manifests not only his trust in God to direct affairs but also the selflessness with which he served Abraham. His patience after prayer (v. 21), his worship at answered prayer (v. 26), and his acknowledgment of divine guidance (v. 27) also portrayed his faith.

24:14 **water your camels also.** Hospitality required giving water to a thirsty stranger, but not to animals. A woman who would do that was unusually kind and served beyond the call of duty. Rebekah's servant attitude was revealed (vv. 15–20) as was her beauty and purity (v. 16).

24:20 **all his camels.** A single camel can hold up to 25 gallons and he had 10 of them. Serving them was a great task as she filled them all (v. 22).

24:22 **shekels.** *See note on 23:14, 16.*

24:24 **I am the daughter of.** In formal introductions, an abbreviated genealogy provided for specific identification (cf. 22:23). She was Isaac's cousin.

straw and feed, and room to lodge in." 26 Then the
man [A]bowed low and worshiped the LORD. 27 He
said, "[A]Blessed be the LORD, the God of my master
Abraham, who has not forsaken [B]His lovingkindness and His truth toward my master; as for me,
[C]the LORD has guided me in the way to the house
of my master's brothers."
28 Then [A]the girl ran and told her mother's household about these things. 29 Now Rebekah had a
brother whose name was [A]Laban; and Laban ran
outside to the man at the spring. 30 When he saw
the ring and the bracelets on his sister's [a]wrists,
and when he heard the words of Rebekah his sister, saying, "[b]This is what the man said to me," he
went to the man; and behold, he was standing by
the camels at the spring. 31 And he said, "[A]Come in,
[B]blessed of the LORD! Why do you stand outside
since [C]I have prepared the house, and a place for
the camels?" 32 So the man entered the house. Then
[a,A]Laban unloaded the camels, and he gave straw
and feed to the camels, and water to wash his feet
and the feet of the men who were with him. 33 But
when *food* was set before him to eat, he said, "I will
not eat until I have told my business." And he said,
"Speak on." 34 So he said, "I am [A]Abraham's servant.
35 The LORD has greatly [A]blessed my master, so that
he has become [a]rich; and He has given him [B]flocks
and herds, and silver and gold, and servants and
maids, and camels and donkeys. 36 Now [A]Sarah my
master's wife bore a son to my master [a]in her old
age, and [B]he has given him all that he has. 37 [A]My
master made me swear, saying, 'You shall not take
a wife for my son from the daughters of the Canaanites, in whose land I [a]live; 38 but you shall go
to my father's house and to my relatives, and take
a wife for my son.' 39 [A]I said to my master, 'Suppose
the woman does not follow me.' 40 He said to me,
'[A]The LORD, before whom I have [B]walked, will send
[C]His angel with you to make your journey successful, and you will take a wife for my son from my
relatives and from my father's house; 41 [A]then you
will be free from my oath, when you come to my
relatives; and if they do not give her to you, you
will be free from my oath.'
42 "So [A]I came today to the spring, and said,
'O LORD, the God of my master Abraham, if now
You will make my journey on which I go [B]successful;
43 behold, [A]I am standing by the [a]spring, and may
it be that the maiden who comes out to draw, and
to whom I say, "[B]Please let me drink a little water
from your jar"; 44 and she will say to me, "You drink,
and I will draw for your camels also"; let her be
the woman whom the LORD has appointed for my
master's son.'
45 "Before I had finished [A]speaking in my heart,
behold, [B]Rebekah came out with her jar on her shoulder, and went down to the spring and drew, and
[C]I said to her, 'Please let me drink.' 46 She quickly
lowered her jar from her *shoulder,* and said, '[A]Drink,
and I will water your camels also'; so I drank, and
she watered the camels also. 47 [A]Then I asked her,
and said, 'Whose daughter are you?' And she said,
'The daughter of Bethuel, Nahor's son, whom Milcah
bore to him'; and I put the [B]ring on her nose, and
the bracelets on her [a]wrists. 48 And I [A]bowed low
and worshiped the LORD, and blessed the LORD,
the God of my master Abraham, [B]who had guided
me in the right way to take the daughter of my
master's [a]kinsman for his son. 49 So now if you are
going to [a,A]deal kindly and truly with my master,
tell me; and if not, let me know, that I may turn to
the right hand or the left."
50 Then Laban and Bethuel replied, "[A]The matter
comes from the LORD; [B]*so* we cannot speak to you
bad or good. 51 Here is Rebekah before you, take *her*
and go, and let her be the wife of your master's son,
as the LORD has spoken."
52 When Abraham's servant heard their words,
he [A]bowed himself to the ground [a]before the LORD.
53 The servant brought out [A]articles of silver and
articles of gold, and garments, and gave them to
Rebekah; he also gave precious things to her brother
and to her mother. 54 Then he and the men who
were with him ate and drank and spent the night.
When they arose in the morning, he said, "[A]Send
me away to my master." 55 But her brother and her
mother said, "[A]Let the girl stay with us *a few* days,
say ten; afterward she may go." 56 He said to them,
"Do not delay me, since [A]the LORD has prospered
my way. Send me away that I may go to my master."
57 And they said, "We will call the girl and [a]consult
her wishes." 58 Then they called Rebekah and said
to her, "Will you go with this man?" And she said, "I
will go." 59 Thus they sent away their sister Rebekah

24:26 [A]Gen 24:48, 52; Ex 4:31 24:27 [A]Gen 24:12, 42, 48; Ex 18:10; Ruth 4:14; 1 Sam 25:32; 2 Sam 18:28; Luke 1:68 [B]Gen 32:10; Ps 98:3 [C]Gen 24:21, 48 24:28 [A]Gen 29:12 24:29 [A]Gen 29:5, 13 24:30 [a]Lit *hands* [b]Lit *Thus the man* 24:31 [A]Gen 29:13 [B]Gen 26:29; Ruth 3:10; Ps 115:15 [C]Gen 18:3-5; 19:2, 3 24:32 [a]Lit *he* [A]Gen 43:24; Judg 19:21 24:34 [A]Gen 24:2 24:35 [a]Lit *great* [A]Gen 24:1 [B]Gen 13:2 24:36 [a]Lit *after she was old* [A]Gen 21:1-7 [B]Gen 25:5 24:37 [a]Lit *dwell* [A]Gen 24:2-4 24:39 [A]Gen 24:5 24:40 [A]Gen 24:7 [B]Gen 5:22, 24; 17:1 [C]Ex 23:20 24:41 [A]Gen 24:8 24:42 [A]Gen 24:11, 12 [B]Neh 1:11 24:43 [a]Lit *fountain of water* [A]Gen 24:13 [B]Gen 24:14 24:45 [A]1 Sam 1:13 [B]Gen 24:15 [C]Gen 24:17 24:46 [A]Gen 24:18, 19 24:47 [a]Lit *hands* [A]Gen 24:23, 24 [B]Ezek 16:11, 12 24:48 [a]Lit *brother* [A]Gen 24:26, 52 [B]Gen 24:27; Ps 32:8; 48:14; Is 48:17 24:49 [a]Lit *show lovingkindness and truth* [A]Gen 47:29; Josh 2:14 24:50 [A]Ps 118:23; Mark 12:11 [B]Gen 31:24, 29 24:52 [a]Lit *to* [A]Gen 24:26, 48 24:53 [A]Gen 24:10, 22; Ex 3:22; 11:2; 12:35 24:54 [A]Gen 24:56, 59; 30:25 24:55 [A]Judg 19:4 24:56 [A]Gen 24:40 24:57 [a]Lit *ask her mouth*

24:29–31 Laban. From what is revealed about his character (chap. 29), there is reason to believe that his sight of all the presents and the camels generated the welcome.

24:33 I will not eat until. The first order of business was to identify his master and to explain his assignment, but not without stressing the blessings of God upon his master and upon his trip (vv. 34–48) and also not without immediately seeking to conclude his task and return home (vv. 49, 54–56). This is the portrait of a committed, faithful, and selfless servant!

24:49 right ... left. An expression indicating the matter of which way to go next.

24:50, 51 The servant's conviction and focus was obvious and intense, precluding anything but immediate acknowledgment of God's leading and anything less than a full compliance with his request from Rebekah's father and brother.

24:53 By this dowry, Rebekah was betrothed to Isaac.

24:54 Send me away to my master. Protocol and courtesy demanded a messenger be dismissed by the addressee.

24:57, 58 Will you go with this man? Commendably, Rebekah concurred with an immediate departure, and showed her confident acceptance of what was providentially coming about in her life.

24:59 her nurse. See 35:8.

and [A]her nurse with Abraham's servant and his men.
60 They blessed Rebekah and said to her,

"May you, our sister,
[A]Become thousands of ten thousands,
And may [B]your [a]descendants possess
The gate of those who hate them."

61 Then Rebekah arose with her maids, and they
mounted the camels and followed the man. So the
servant took Rebekah and departed.

ISAAC MARRIES REBEKAH

62 Now Isaac had come from going to [A]Beer-lahai-
roi; for he [a]was living in [B]the [b]Negev. 63 Isaac went
out [A]to [a]meditate in the field toward evening; and
[B]he lifted up his eyes and looked, and behold, camels were coming. 64 Rebekah lifted up her eyes, and
when she saw Isaac she dismounted from the camel.
65 She said to the servant, "Who is that man walking
in the field to meet us?" And the servant said, "He
is my master." Then she took her [a]veil and covered
herself. 66 The servant told Isaac all the things that
he had done. 67 Then Isaac brought her into his
mother Sarah's tent, and [A]he took Rebekah, and she
became his wife, and [B]he loved her; thus Isaac was
comforted after [C]his mother's death.

ABRAHAM'S DEATH

25 Now Abraham took another wife, [a]whose
name was Keturah. 2 [A]She bore to him Zimran and Jokshan and Medan and Midian and Ishbak
and Shuah. 3 Jokshan [a]became the father of Sheba
and Dedan. And the sons of Dedan were Asshurim
and Letushim and Leummim. 4 The sons of Midian
were Ephah and Epher and Hanoch and Abida and
Eldaah. All these *were* the sons of Keturah. 5 [A]Now
Abraham gave all that he had to Isaac; 6 but to the
sons of [a]his concubines, Abraham gave gifts while
he was still living, and [A]sent them away from his
son Isaac eastward, to the land of the east.
7 These are [a]all the years of Abraham's life that
he lived, [A]one hundred and seventy-five years.
8 Abraham breathed his last and died [A]in a [a]ripe
old age, an old man and satisfied *with life;* and he
was [B]gathered to his people. 9 Then his sons Isaac
and Ishmael buried him in [A]the cave of Machpelah,
in the field of Ephron the son of Zohar the Hittite,
facing Mamre, 10 [A]the field which Abraham purchased from the sons of Heth; there Abraham was
buried with Sarah his wife. 11 It came about after the
death of Abraham, that [A]God blessed his son Isaac;
and Isaac [a]lived by [B]Beer-lahai-roi.

DESCENDANTS OF ISHMAEL

12 Now these are *the records of* the generations of
[A]Ishmael, Abraham's son, whom Hagar the Egyptian, Sarah's maid, bore to Abraham; 13 and these are
the names of [A]the sons of Ishmael, by their names,
[a]in the order of their birth: Nebaioth, the firstborn of
Ishmael, and Kedar and Adbeel and Mibsam 14 and
Mishma and Dumah and Massa, 15 Hadad and Tema,
Jetur, Naphish and Kedemah. 16 These are the sons
of Ishmael and these are their names, by their villages, and by their camps; [A]twelve princes according
to their [a]tribes. 17 These are the years of the life of
Ishmael, [A]one hundred and thirty-seven years; and
he breathed his last and died, and was [B]gathered to
his people. 18 They [a]settled from [A]Havilah to [B]Shur
which is [b]east of Egypt [c]as one goes toward Assyria;
[C]he [d]settled in defiance of all his [e]relatives.

ISAAC'S SONS

19 Now these are *the records of* [A]the generations
of Isaac, Abraham's son: Abraham [a]became the
father of Isaac; 20 and Isaac was forty years old

24:59 [A]Gen 35:8 24:60 [a]Lit *seed* [A]Gen 17:16 [B]Gen 22:17 24:62 [a]Lit *was dwelling* [b]I.e. South country [A]Gen 16:14; 25:11 [B]Gen 20:1 24:63 [a]Or *stroll;* meaning uncertain [A]Josh 1:8; Ps 1:2; 77:12; 119:15, 27, 48; 143:5; 145:5 [B]Gen 18:2 24:65 [a]Or *shawl* 24:67 [A]Gen 25:20 [B]Gen 29:18 [C]Gen 23:1, 2 25:1 [a]Lit *and her name* 25:2 [A]1 Chr 1:32, 33 25:3 [a]Lit *begot* 25:5 [A]Gen 24:35, 36 25:6 [a]Lit *concubines which belonged to Abraham* [A]Gen 21:14 25:7 [a]Lit *the days of* [A]Gen 12:4 25:8 [a]Lit *good* [A]Gen 15:15; 47:8, 9 [B]Gen 25:17; 35:29; 49:29, 33 25:9 [A]Gen 23:17, 18; 49:29, 30; 50:13 25:10 [A]Gen 23:3-16 25:11 [a]Lit *dwelt* [A]Gen 12:2, 3; 22:17; 26:3 [B]Gen 16:14; 24:62 25:12 [A]Gen 16:15 25:13 [a]Lit *in regard to their generations* [A]1 Chr 1:29-31 25:16 [a]Or *peoples* [A]Gen 17:20 25:17 [A]Gen 16:16 [B]Gen 25:8; 49:33 25:18 [a]Lit *dwelt* [b]Lit *before* [c]Lit *as you go* [d]Lit *fell over against* [e]Lit *brothers* [A]1 Sam 15:7 [B]Gen 20:1 [C]Gen 16:12 25:19 [a]Lit *begot* [A]Matt 1:2

24:60 They blessed Rebekah and said. Little did they realize that their conventional prayer wishing numerous offspring to Rebekah fitted in nicely with God's promises of many descendants to Abraham through Sarah and Isaac. They also wished for her offspring to be victorious over their enemies ("possess their gates"), perhaps echoing God's promises of possession of the land of the Canaanites (13:17; 15:7, 16; 17:8).

24:62 Beer-lahai-roi. See 16:14. Located on the Canaan-Egypt border, about 25 mi. NW of Kadesh-barnea. Isaac lived there after Abraham's death (25:11).

24:63 to meditate. How God drew Isaac from home to where Hagar encountered the Angel of the Lord (cf. 16:14) remains unknown, but he was in the right place to meet the caravan returning with his fiancée. Perhaps he was prayerfully contemplating the circumstances of his life and the void left by his mother's death (v. 67), as well as thinking about and hoping the steward would not return from a failed mission.

24:65 she took her veil and covered herself. Convention demanded the designated bride veil her face in the presence of her betrothed until the wedding day.

24:67 his mother Sarah's tent. He thus established his acceptance of her as his wife before he had seen her beauty. When he did see her, "he loved her."

25:1–4 Abraham's sons through Keturah, (a concubine, cf. v. 6; 1Ch 1:32) a wife of lower status than Sarah, became the progenitors of various Arab tribes to the east of Canaan.

25:5, 6 Conferring gifts upon these other sons, then sending them away, and also conferring the estate upon Isaac ensured that Isaac would be considered as the rightful heir without competition or threat from his half-brothers. The steward, Eliezer, had informed Rebekah's relatives that all of Abraham's estate was Isaac's (cf. 24:36).

25:8 gathered to his people. A euphemism for death, but also an expression of personal continuance beyond death, which denoted a reunion with previously departed friends (ca. 1990 B.C.). Cf. Mt 8:11; Lk 16:22, 23.

25:9, 10 his sons ... buried him. Abraham's funeral brought together two sons who would perhaps otherwise have remained somewhat estranged from each other (cf. 35:29). He was buried in the place which he had purchased at Hebron (chap. 23).

25:12–18 the generations of Ishmael. With the death of Abraham and the focus shifting to Isaac, the record confirms God's promise of 12 princes to Ishmael (cf. 17:20, 21).

25:13–16 Arab tradition has it that these are their earliest ancestors.

25:16 by their villages, and by their camps. In addition to serving as a testimony to God's promises (17:20), information such as this genealogy helped Israel to understand the origins of their neighbors in central and northern Arabia.

25:19–35:29 The genealogy of Isaac.

25:20 Paddan-aram. The "plain of Aram" in upper Mesopotamia near Haran to the NNE of Canaan.

when he took [A]Rebekah, the [B]daughter of Bethuel
the [a]Aramean of Paddan-aram, the [C]sister of Laban
the [a]Aramean, to be his wife. 21 Isaac prayed to the
LORD on behalf of his wife, because she was barren;
and [A]the LORD [a]answered him and Rebekah his wife
[B]conceived. 22 But the children struggled together
within her; and she said, "If it is so, why then am
I *this way?*" So she went to [A]inquire of the LORD.
23 The LORD said to her,

"[A]Two nations are in your womb;
[B]And two peoples will be
separated from your body;
And one people shall be
stronger than the other;
And [C]the older shall serve the younger."

24 When her days to be delivered were fulfilled, behold, there were twins in her womb. 25 Now the first
came forth red, [A]all over like a hairy garment; and
they named him Esau. 26 Afterward his brother came
forth with [A]his hand holding on to Esau's heel, so
[B]his name was called [a]Jacob; and Isaac was [C]sixty
years old when she gave birth to them.
27 When the boys grew up, Esau became a skillful
hunter, a man of the field, but Jacob was a [a]peace-
ful man, [b,A]living in tents. 28 Now Isaac loved Esau,
because [a]he had [A]a taste for game, [B]but Rebekah
loved Jacob. 29 When Jacob had cooked [A]stew, Esau
came in from the field and he was [a]famished; 30 and
Esau said to Jacob, "Please let me have a swallow of
[a]that red stuff there, for I am [b]famished." Therefore
his name was called [c]Edom. 31 But Jacob said, "[a]First
sell me your [A]birthright." 32 Esau said, "Behold, I am
about to die; so of what *use* then is the birthright
to me?" 33 And Jacob said, "[a]First swear to me"; so
he swore to him, and [A]sold his birthright to Jacob.
34 Then Jacob gave Esau bread and lentil stew; and
he ate and drank, and rose and went on his way.
Thus Esau despised his birthright.

ISAAC SETTLES IN GERAR

26 Now there was [A]a famine in the land, besides
the previous famine that had occurred in the
days of Abraham. So Isaac went to Gerar, to [B]Abime-
lech king of the Philistines. 2 The LORD [A]appeared to
him and said, "Do not go down to Egypt; [a,B]stay in the
land of which I shall tell you. 3 Sojourn in this land
and [A]I will be with you and [B]bless you, for [C]to you
and to your [a]descendants I will give all these lands,
and I will establish [D]the oath which I swore to your
father Abraham. 4 [A]I will multiply your [a]descendants
as the stars of heaven, and will give your [a]descen-
dants all these lands; and [B]by your [a]descendants all
the nations of the earth [b]shall be blessed; 5 because
Abraham [a,A]obeyed Me and kept My charge, My commandments, My statutes and My laws."
6 So Isaac [a]lived in Gerar. 7 When the men of the
place asked about his wife, he said, "[A]She is my sister," for he was [B]afraid to say, "my wife," *thinking,*
"[a]the men of the place might kill me on account of
Rebekah, for she is [C]beautiful." 8 It came about, when

25:20 [a]I.e. Syrian [A]Gen 24:15, 29, 67 [B]Gen 22:23 [C]Gen 24:29 25:21 [a]Lit *was entreated of him* [A]1 Sam 1:17; 1 Chr 5:20; 2 Chr 33:13; Ezra 8:23; Ps 127:3 [B]Rom 9:10 25:22 [A]1 Sam 9:9; 10:22 25:23 [A]Gen 17:4-6, 16; Num 20:14; Deut 2:4, 8 [B]Gen 27:29 [C]Gen 27:40; Mal 1:2, 3; Rom 9:12 25:25 [A]Gen 27:11 25:26 [a]I.e. one who takes by the heel or supplants [A]Hos 12:3 [B]Gen 27:36 [C]Gen 25:20 25:27 [a]Lit *complete* [b]Lit *dwelling* [A]Heb 11:9 25:28 [a]Lit *game was in his mouth* [A]Gen 27:19 [B]Gen 27:6-10 25:29 [a]Lit *weary* [A]2 Kin 4:38 25:30 [a]Lit *the red, this red* [b]Lit *weary* [c]I.e. red 25:31 [a]Lit *Today* [A]Deut 21:16, 17; 1 Chr 5:1, 2 25:33 [a]Lit *Today* [A]Heb 12:16 26:1 [A]Gen 12:10 [B]Gen 20:1, 2 26:2 [a]Lit *dwell* [A]Gen 12:7; 17:1; 18:1 [B]Gen 12:1 26:3 [a]Lit *seed* [A]Gen 26:24; 28:15; 31:3 [B]Gen 12:2 [C]Gen 12:7; 13:15; 15:18 [D]Gen 22:16-18; Ps 105:9 26:4 [a]Lit *seed* [b]Or *bless themselves* [A]Gen 15:5; 22:17; Ex 32:13 [B]Gen 22:18; Gal 3:8 26:5 [a]Lit *hearkened to My voice* [A]Gen 22:16 26:6 [a]Lit *dwelt* 26:7 [a]Lit *lest...place* [A]Gen 12:13; 20:2, 12 [B]Prov 29:25 [C]Gen 12:11; 24:16; 29:17

25:21 she was barren. Confronted by 20 years of his wife's barrenness (vv. 20, 26), Isaac rose to the test and earnestly turned to God in prayer, obviously acknowledging thereby God's involvement and timing in the seed-promise.

25:22 struggled together within her. The very uncomfortable condition of her pregnancy ("why then am I *this way?*") prompted Rebekah, undoubtedly following the example of her husband, to turn earnestly to God in prayer. She learned directly from the Lord that the severe jostling in her womb prefigured the future antagonism between the two nations to arise from her twin sons (v. 23).

25:23 the older shall serve the younger. This was contrary to the custom in patriarchal times when the elder son enjoyed the privileges of precedence in the household and at the father's death received a double share of the inheritance and became the recognized head of the family (cf. Ex 22:29; Nu 8:14–17; Dt 21:17). Grave offenses could annul such primogeniture rights (cf. Ge 35:22; 49:3, 4; 1Ch 5:1) or the birthright could be sacrificed or legally transferred to another in the family, as in this case (vv. 29–34). In this case, God declared otherwise since His sovereign elective purposes did not necessarily have to follow custom (cf. Ro 9:10–14, esp. v. 12).

25:24 days . . . were fulfilled. Esau and Jacob were born ca. 2005 B.C.

25:25 red. This would be the linguistic basis for calling Esau's country "Edom" (cf. v. 30).

25:27, 28 The difference between the two sons manifested itself in several areas: 1) as progenitors—Esau of Edom and Jacob of Israel; 2) in disposition—Esau a rugged, headstrong hunter preferring the outdoors and Jacob a plain, amiable man preferring the comforts of home; and 3) in parental favoritism—Esau by his father and Jacob by his mother. These were the ingredients for conflict and heartache!

25:30 Edom. In a play upon words to forever recall that Esau was born red and hairy (v. 25) and had sold his birthright for red stew, he was also named Edom, i.e., "Red."

25:31 birthright. A double portion of the inheritance (Dt 21:17) and the right to be family chief and priest (Ex 4:22).

25:34 despised his birthright. The final evaluation of the verbal tussle and bartering which took place between the twins, all of which was indicative of prior discussions or arguments sufficient for Jacob to conclude how little Esau valued it. He became, therefore, known as irreligious, i.e., "a godless person" (Heb 12:16).

26:1 a famine in the land. Once again the Land of Promise forced the beneficiaries of the covenant to move so as to escape the effects of a famine. **Abimelech.** Most probably a Philistine dynastic title, with this being a different king from the one who had met Abraham (chap. 20). *See note on 20:2.* **Philistines.** This tribe of people who originally sailed the Mediterranean Sea became fierce enemies of Israel when they settled along the SW coast of Canaan. Friendly to Isaac, they were forerunners of hostile descendant enemies.

26:2–11 Obedience and deceit were in juxtaposition. Obeying God to dwell in the land (vv. 2, 3, 6), yet lying about his wife to the people of the land (vv. 7–11) reflected familiar shades of Abraham's strategy for survival (see 12:10–14; 20:1–4).

26:3–5 God confirmed the Abrahamic Covenant with Isaac, stressing the same 3 elements as before: land, seed, and blessing. He appended specific honorable mention of Abraham's obedient response to all of God's words. *See notes on 12:1–3; 15:13–21; 17:2, 7, 8, 9.* Although Abraham was commended for his deeds, the Abrahamic Covenant was an unconditional covenant grounded in God's sovereign will (cf. Lv 26:44, 45).

26:4 Cf. Ac 3:25.

26:6–9 Unlike his ancestor to whom God sovereignly revealed the relationship between Abraham and Sarah (20:3), this king providentially discovered Rebekah's relationship to Isaac by just happening to look out of a window and witnessing caresses indicative of marriage and intimacy.

he had been there a long time, that Abimelech king of
the Philistines looked out through a window, and saw,
and behold, Isaac was caressing his wife Rebekah.
9 Then Abimelech called Isaac and said, "Behold, certainly she is your wife! How then did you say, 'She is
my sister'?" And Isaac said to him, "Because I said,
'I might die on account of her.' " 10 [A]Abimelech said,
"What is this you have done to us? One of the people
might easily have lain with your wife, and you would
have brought guilt upon us." 11 So Abimelech charged
all the people, saying, "He who [A]touches this man or
his wife shall surely be put to death."
12 Now Isaac sowed in that land and [a]reaped in
the same year a hundredfold. And [A]the LORD blessed
him, 13 and the man [A]became rich, and continued
to grow [a]richer until he became very [a]wealthy;
14 for [A]he had possessions of flocks [a]and herds and
a great household, so that the Philistines envied
him. 15 Now [A]all the wells which his father's servants had dug in the days of Abraham his father,
the Philistines stopped up [a]by filling them with
earth. 16 Then Abimelech said to Isaac, "Go away
from us, for you are [a,A]too powerful for us." 17 And
Isaac departed from there and camped in the valley
of Gerar, and [a]settled there.

QUARREL OVER THE WELLS

18 Then Isaac dug again the wells of water which
[a]had been dug in the days of his father Abraham, for
the Philistines had stopped them up after the death
of Abraham; and he [b]gave them the same names
which his father had [c]given them. 19 But when Isaac's
servants dug in the valley and found there a well of
[a]flowing water, 20 the herdsmen of Gerar [A]quarreled
with the herdsmen of Isaac, saying, "The water is
ours!" So he named the well [a]Esek, because they
contended with him. 21 Then they dug another well,
and they quarreled over it too, so he named it [a]Sit-
nah. 22 He moved away from there and dug another
well, and they did not quarrel over it; so he named it
[a]Rehoboth, for he said, "[b,A]At last the LORD has made
[c]room for us, and we will be [B]fruitful in the land."
23 Then he went up from there to [A]Beersheba.
24 The LORD [A]appeared to him the same night and
said,

"[B]I am the God of your father Abraham;
[C]Do not fear, for I am with you.
I [D]will bless you, and multiply
your [a]descendants,
For the sake of My servant Abraham."

25 So he built an [A]altar there and called upon the
name of the LORD, and pitched his tent there; and
there Isaac's servants dug a well.

COVENANT WITH ABIMELECH

26 Then [A]Abimelech came to him from Gerar [a]with
his adviser Ahuzzath and Phicol the commander of
his army. 27 Isaac said to them, "[A]Why have you come
to me, since you hate me and have sent me away from
you?" 28 They said, "We see plainly [A]that the LORD has
been with you; so we said, 'Let there now be an oath
between us, *even* between [a]you and us, and let us
make a covenant with you, 29 that you will do us no
harm, just as we have not touched you [a]and have done
to you nothing but good and have sent you away in
peace. You are now the [A]blessed of the LORD.' " 30 Then
[A]he made them a feast, and they ate and drank. 31 In
the morning they arose early and [a,A]exchanged oaths;
then Isaac sent them away and they departed from
him in peace. 32 Now it came about on the same day,
that Isaac's servants came in and told him about the
well which they had dug, and said to him, "We have
found water." 33 So he called it Shibah; therefore the
name of the city is [A]Beersheba to this day.
34 When Esau was forty years old [A]he [a]married
Judith the daughter of Beeri the Hittite, and Basemath the daughter of Elon the Hittite; 35 and [A]they
[a]brought grief to Isaac and Rebekah.

26:10 [A]Gen 20:9 26:11 [A]Ps 105:15 26:12 [a]Lit *found* [A]Gen 24:1; 26:3; Job 42:12; Prov 10:22 26:13 [a]Lit *great* [A]Prov 10:22 26:14 [a]Lit *and possessions of herds* [A]Gen 24:35; 25:5 26:15 [a]Lit *and filled them* [A]Gen 21:25, 30 26:16 [a]Lit *much mightier than we* [A]Ex 1:9 26:17 [a]Lit *dwelt* 26:18 [a]Lit *they had dug* [b]Lit *called their names as the names* [c]Lit *called* 26:19 [a]Lit *living* 26:20 [a]I.e. contention [A]Gen 21:25 26:21 [a]I.e. enmity 26:22 [a]I.e. broad places [b]Lit *Truly now* [c]Or *broad* [A]Ps 4:1; Is 54:2, 3 [B]Gen 17:6; Ex 1:7 26:23 [A]Gen 22:19 26:24 [a]Lit *seed* [A]Gen 26:2 [B]Gen 17:7, 8; 24:12; Ex 3:6; Acts 7:32 [C]Gen 15:1 [D]Gen 22:17; 26:3, 4 26:25 [A]Gen 12:7, 8; 13:4, 18; Ps 116:17 26:26 [a]Lit *and his confidential friend* [A]Gen 21:22 26:27 [A]Judg 11:7 26:28 [a]Lit *us and you* [A]Gen 21:22, 23 26:29 [a]Lit *and just as we* [A]Gen 24:31; Ps 115:15 26:30 [A]Gen 19:3 26:31 [a]Lit *swore one to another* [A]Gen 21:31 26:33 [A]Gen 21:31 26:34 [a]Lit *took as wife* [A]Gen 28:8; 36:2 26:35 [a]Lit *were a bitterness of spirit to* [A]Gen 27:46

26:11 charged all the people ... be put to death. A pagan king imposing the death penalty on anyone troubling Isaac or Rebekah suggests God was at work to preserve His chosen seed (cf. vv. 28, 29). Cf. Ps 105:14, 15.

26:12–14 Isaac was content to stay in that place and farm some land. His efforts were blessed by God, but envied by the Philistines!

26:15 all the wells ... stopped up. Water was so precious in that desert land that wells were essential. Plugging someone's well was ruinous to them and constituted serious aggression, often leading to war. Isaac could have retaliated, but he did not; rather he dug new wells (vv. 16–19).

26:22 Rehoboth. The word means "room enough." Finally a well was dug without a quarrel erupting (vv. 20, 21). Now that they were no longer perceived as encroaching upon another's territory, Isaac selected an appropriate place-name which reflected how he saw God providentially working out their situation.

26:24, 25 This abbreviated reaffirmation of the Abrahamic Covenant was designed to assuage Isaac's anxiety at facing envy, quarrels, and hostility (vv. 14, 20, 27), and to assure Isaac that he had reasoned right—fruitfulness in posterity would prevail. That it was a significant reminder to Isaac is seen in a response reminiscent of his father—he built an altar of worship to mark the spot of God's appearance to him (12:7).

26:26 Abimelech ... and Phicol. Because 90 years had passed since Abraham was visited by men with the same names, they must have been titles rather than proper names (cf. 21:22). *See note on v. 1.*

26:28 an oath .... covenant. In a mirror image of a former occasion (21:22–32), Abimelech in the company of a friend and the highest ranking officer in his army (v. 26) sought after a treaty with one they estimated to be superior and stronger than themselves and a possible threat (v. 29). Isaac, on the other hand, perceived them as hostile (v. 27). The outcome was most desirable for both—peace between them (v. 31).

26:30 Ratification of a covenant often involved a banquet.

26:33 Beersheba. Lit. "the well of the oath." The very place where his father Abraham had made an oath with another Abimelech and Phicol (*see note on v. 26*) and which Abraham had named Beersheba (21:32).

26:35 brought grief. Esau's choice of wives from among neighboring Hittite women saddened his parents. His action had deliberately ignored the standard set by Abraham for Isaac (24:3). Cf. 27:46.

JACOB'S DECEPTION

27 Now it came about, when Isaac was old and
[A]his eyes were too dim to see, that he called
his [B]older son Esau and said to him, "My son." And
he said to him, "Here I am." 2 [a,A]Isaac said, "Behold
now, I am old *and* I do not know the day of my death.
3 Now then, please take your gear, your quiver and
your bow, and go out to the field and [A]hunt game
for me; 4 and prepare a savory dish for me such as
I love, and bring it to me that I may eat, so that [A]my
soul may bless you before I die."
5 Rebekah was listening while Isaac spoke to his
son Esau. So when Esau went to the field to hunt
for game to bring *home,* 6 [A]Rebekah said to her son
Jacob, "Behold, I heard your father speak to your
brother Esau, saying, 7 'Bring me *some* game and
prepare a savory dish for me, that I may eat, and
bless you in the presence of the LORD before my
death.' 8 Now therefore, my son, [A]listen to [a]me [b]as
I command you. 9 Go now to the flock and [a]bring
me two choice [b]young goats from there, that I may
prepare them *as* a savory dish for your father, such
as he loves. 10 Then you shall bring *it* to your father,
that he may eat, so that he may bless you before
his death." 11 Jacob [a]answered his mother Rebekah,
"Behold, Esau my brother is a [A]hairy man and I
am a smooth man. 12 [A]Perhaps my father will feel
me, then I will be as a [a]deceiver in his sight, and I
will bring upon myself a curse and not a blessing."
13 But his mother said to him, "Your curse be on me,
my son; only [A]obey my voice, and go, get *them* for
me." 14 So he went and got *them,* and brought *them*
to his mother; and his mother made savory food
such as his father loved. 15 Then Rebekah took the
[a]best [A]garments of Esau her elder son, which were
with her in the house, and put them on Jacob her
younger son. 16 And she put the skins of the [a]young
goats on his hands and on the smooth part of his
neck. 17 She also gave the savory food and the bread,
which she had made, [a]to her son Jacob.
18 Then he came to his father and said, "My father."
And he said, "Here I am. Who are you, my son?"
19 Jacob said to his father, "I am Esau your firstborn; I have done as you told me. [A]Get up, please,
sit and eat of my game, that [a,B]you may bless me."
20 Isaac said to his son, "How is it that you have *it* so
quickly, my son?" And he said, "[A]Because the LORD
your God caused *it* to happen to me." 21 Then Isaac
said to Jacob, "Please come close, that [A]I may feel
you, my son, whether you are really my son Esau or
not." 22 So Jacob came close to Isaac his father, and
he felt him and said, "The voice is the voice of Jacob,
but the hands are the hands of Esau." 23 He did not
recognize him, because his hands were [A]hairy like
his brother Esau's hands; so he blessed him. 24 And
he said, "Are you really my son Esau?" And he said,
"I am." 25 So he said, "Bring *it* to me, and I will eat
of my son's game, that [a,A]I may bless you." And he
brought *it* to him, and he ate; he also brought him
wine and he drank. 26 Then his father Isaac said to
him, "Please come close and kiss me, my son." 27 So
he came close and kissed him; and when he smelled
the smell of his garments, he [A]blessed him and said,

"See, [B]the smell of my son
Is like the smell of a field [C]which
the LORD has blessed;
28 Now may [A]God give you of
the dew of heaven,
And of the [B]fatness of the earth,
And an abundance of grain
and new wine;

27:1 [A]Gen 48:10; 1 Sam 3:2 [B]Gen 25:25, 33, 34 27:2 [a]Lit *He* [A]Gen 47:29 27:3 [A]Gen 25:28 27:4 [A]Gen 27:19, 25, 31; 48:9, 15, 16; Deut 33:1; Heb 11:20 27:6 [A]Gen 25:28 27:8 [a]Lit *my voice* [b]Lit *according to what* [A]Gen 27:13, 43 27:9 [a]Lit *take* [b]Lit *kids of goats* 27:11 [a]Lit *said to* [A]Gen 25:25 27:12 [a]Lit *mocker* [A]Gen 27:21, 22 27:13 [A]Gen 27:8 27:15 [a]Lit *desirable;* or *choice* [A]Gen 27:27 27:16 [a]Lit *kids of the goats* 27:17 [a]Lit *into the hand of* 27:19 [a]Lit *your soul* [A]Gen 27:31 [B]Gen 27:4 27:20 [A]Gen 24:12 27:21 [A]Gen 27:12 27:23 [A]Gen 27:16 27:25 [a]Lit *my soul* [A]Gen 27:4 27:27 [A]Heb 11:20 [B]Song 4:11 [C]Ps 65:10 27:28 [A]Gen 27:39; Deut 33:13, 28; Prov 3:20; Zech 8:12 [B]Num 18:12

27:1 Isaac was old. Blind Isaac evidently thought he was near death (v. 2) and would not live much beyond his current 137 years, which was the age of Ishmael when he died (25:17). He certainly did not expect to live another 43 years as he actually did (35:28; cf. 30:24, 25; 31:41; 41:46, 47; 45:6; 47:9 to calculate Isaac's age at 137 and his twin sons' ages at 77 years old).

27:4 my soul may bless you. Ignoring the words of God to Rebekah (25:23), forgetting Esau's bartered birthright (25:33), and overlooking Esau's grievous marriages (26:35), Isaac was still intent on treating Esau as the eldest and granting him the blessing of birthright, and so arranged for his favorite meal before bestowing final fatherly blessing on his favorite son.

27:5 Rebekah was listening. Desperation to secure patriarchal blessing for Jacob bred deception and trickery, with Rebekah believing her culinary skills could make goat's meat taste and smell like choice venison (vv. 8–10) and make Jacob seem like Esau (vv. 15–17).

27:12 a deceiver in his sight. To his credit, Jacob at first objected. The differences between him and Esau would surely not fool his father and might result in blessing being replaced with a curse as a fitting punishment for deception.

27:13 Your curse be on me. With his mother accepting full responsibility for the scheme and bearing the curse should it occur, Jacob acquiesced and followed Rebekah's instructions.

27:15 best garments of ... her elder son. Esau, having been married for 37 years (cf. v. 1; 26:35), would have had his own tents and his own wives to do for him; so how and why Rebekah came by some of his best clothes in her tent is unknown. Perhaps these garments were the official robes associated with the priestly functions of the head of the house, kept in her house until passed on to the oldest son. Perhaps Esau had, on occasion, worn them, thus their smell of the field (v. 27).

27:20 the LORD your God caused *it* to happen to me. Isaac's perfectly legitimate question in v. 20 (hunting took time and Jacob had come so quickly with goats from the pen) afforded Jacob an escape route—confess and stop the deceit! Instead, Jacob, with consummate ease, knowing he needed Isaac's irrevocable confirmation even though he had bought the birthright, ascribed success in the hunt to God's providence. A lie had to sustain a lie, and a tangled web had begun to be woven (vv. 21–24). Although Jacob received Isaac's blessing that day, the deceit caused severe consequences: 1) he never saw his mother after that; 2) Esau wanted him dead; 3) Laban, his uncle, deceived him; 4) his family life was full of conflict; and 5) he was exiled for years from his family. By the promise of God he would have received the birthright (25:23). He didn't need to scheme this deception with his mother.

27:27–29 Finally, with all lingering doubts removed, Isaac pronounced the blessing upon Jacob, although the opening words show he thought the one receiving it was Esau, the man of the field. His prayer-wish called for prosperity and superiority and ended with a repeat of God's words to Abraham (v. 29c; cf. 12:1–3). The words indicated that Isaac thought the covenantal line should have continued through his eldest son, Esau.

29 [A]May peoples serve you,
And nations bow down to you;
[B]Be master of your brothers,
[C]And may your mother's sons
bow down to you.
[D]Cursed be those who curse you,
And blessed be those
who bless you."

THE STOLEN BLESSING

30 Now it came about, as soon as Isaac had finished blessing Jacob, and Jacob had hardly gone
out from the presence of Isaac his father, that
Esau his brother came in from his hunting. 31 Then
he also made savory food, and brought it to his
father; and he said to his father, "[A]Let my father
arise and eat of his son's game, that [a,B]you may
bless me." 32 Isaac his father said to him, "[A]Who
are you?" And he said, "I am your son, [B]your firstborn, Esau." 33 Then Isaac [a]trembled violently, and
said, "[A]Who was he then that hunted game and
brought *it* to me, so that I ate of all *of it* before
you came, and blessed him? [B]Yes, and he shall
be blessed." 34 When Esau heard the words of his
father, [A]he cried out with an exceedingly great
and bitter cry, and said to his father, "Bless me,
even me also, O my father!" 35 And he said, "[A]Your
brother came deceitfully and has taken away your
blessing." 36 Then he said, "[a]Is he not rightly named
[A]Jacob, for he has supplanted me these two times?
He took away my birthright, and behold, now he
has taken away my blessing." And he said, "Have
you not reserved a blessing for me?" 37 But Isaac
replied to Esau, "Behold, I have made him [A]your
master, and all his [a]relatives I have given to him
[b]as servants; and with grain and new wine I have
sustained him. Now as for you then, what can I do,
my son?" 38 Esau said to his father, "Do you have
only one blessing, my father? Bless me, *even* me
also, O my father." So Esau lifted his voice and
[A]wept.

39 Then [A]Isaac his father answered and said to
him,

"Behold, [a,B]away from the [b]fertility of
the earth shall be your dwelling,
And [a]away from the dew of
heaven from above.
40 "By your sword you shall live,
And your brother [A]you shall serve;
But it shall come about [B]when
you become restless,
That you will [a]break his yoke
from your neck."

41 So Esau [A]bore a grudge against Jacob because of
the blessing with which his father had blessed him;
and Esau said [a]to himself, "[B]The days of mourning
for my father are near; then I will kill my brother
Jacob." 42 Now when the words of her elder son Esau
were reported to Rebekah, she sent and called her
younger son Jacob, and said to him, "Behold your
brother Esau is consoling himself concerning you *by*
planning to kill you. 43 Now therefore, my son, [A]obey
my voice, and arise, [a]flee to [B]Haran, to my brother
[C]Laban! 44 Stay with him [A]a few days, until your
brother's fury [a]subsides, 45 until your brother's anger [a]against you subsides and he forgets [A]what you
did to him. Then I will send and get you from there.
Why should I be bereaved of you both in one day?"
46 Rebekah said to Isaac, "I am tired of [a]living
because of [A]the daughters of Heth; [B]if Jacob takes
a wife from the daughters of Heth, like these, from
the daughters of the land, what good will my life
be to me?"

JACOB IS SENT AWAY

28 So Isaac called Jacob and [A]blessed him and
charged him, and said to him, "[B]You shall not
take a wife from the daughters of Canaan. 2 Arise,
go to Paddan-aram, to the house of [A]Bethuel your
mother's father; and from there take to yourself a

27:29 [A]Gen 25:23; Is 45:14; 49:7, 23; 60:12, 14 [B]Gen 9:26, 27; 27:37 [C]Gen 37:7, 10 [D]Gen 12:3; Num 24:9 27:31 [a]Lit *your soul* [A]Gen 27:19 [B]Gen 27:4 27:32 [A]Gen 27:18 [B]Gen 25:33, 34 27:33 [a]Lit *trembled with a very great trembling* [A]Gen 27:35 [B]Gen 25:23; 28:3, 4; Num 23:20 27:34 [A]Heb 12:17 27:35 [A]Gen 27:19 27:36 [a]Or *Was he then named Jacob that he has* [A]Gen 25:26, 32-34 27:37 [a]Lit *brothers* [b]Lit *for* [A]Gen 27:28, 29 27:38 [A]Heb 12:17 27:39 [a]Or *of* [b]Lit *fatness* [A]Heb 11:20 [B]Gen 27:28; Deut 33:13, 28 27:40 [a]Lit *tear off* [A]Gen 25:23; 27:29 [B]2 Kin 8:20-22 27:41 [a]Lit *in his heart* [A]Gen 32:3-11; 37:4, 8 [B]Gen 50:2-4, 10 27:43 [a]Lit *flee for yourself* [A]Gen 27:8, 13 [B]Gen 11:31 [C]Gen 24:29 27:44 [a]Lit *turns away* [A]Gen 31:41 27:45 [a]Lit *turns away from you* [A]Gen 27:12, 19, 35 27:46 [a]Lit *my life* [A]Gen 26:34, 35; 28:8 [B]Gen 24:3 28:1 [A]Gen 27:33 [B]Gen 24:3, 4 28:2 [A]Gen 25:20

27:33 Isaac trembled violently. Visibly shocked when the scandal was uncovered by the entrance of Esau, the father, remembering the Lord's words to Rebekah (25:23), refused to withdraw the blessing and emphatically affirmed its validity—"yes, and he shall be blessed" and a little later "Behold, I have made him your master" and also "your brother you shall serve" (vv. 37, 40). Sudden realization at having opposed God's will all those years likely made the shock more severe.

27:34 Bless me, *even* me also. Esau fully expected to receive the blessing, for he had identified himself to his father as the firstborn (v. 32). Anguished at losing this important paternal blessing and bitterly acting as the innocent victim (v. 36), Esau shifted the blame for the loss of birthright and blessing to Jacob and pleaded for some compensating word of blessing from his father (vv. 36, 38).

27:39, 40 The prayer-wish called for prosperity and inferiority, i.e., maintaining the validity of the words to Jacob and replacing "be master of your brothers" with "your brother you shall serve" (vv. 29, 40). This secondary blessing would not and could not undo the first one.

27:40 you will break his yoke from your neck. In later history, the Edomites, who descended from the line of Esau, fought time and again with Israel and shook off Israelite control on several occasions (2Ki 8:20; 2Ch 21:8–10; 28:16, 17).

27:41 The days of mourning for my father. Evidently Esau also thought his father was on the verge of death (27:1) and so, out of respect for his aged father, he postponed murder. Isaac lived another 43 years (*see note on 27:1*).

27:45 bereaved of you both in one day. Rebekah understood she stood to lose both her sons since, after the murder of Jacob, the avenger of blood, i.e., the next nearest relative, would track down and execute Esau.

27:46 daughters of Heth. Local Hittite women. *See note on 26:35.*

28:1, 2 from there take to yourself a wife. Anxious for the safety of her son, Rebekah easily convinced her husband that the time had come for him to seek a non-Canaanite wife back in their homeland and preferably from near kinsmen (vv. 2, 5), just as Rebekah had been sought for Isaac (see 24:1–4).

28:2 Paddan-aram. *See note on 25:20.*

wife from the daughters of Laban your mother's brother. 3 May [a,A]God Almighty [B]bless you and [C]make you fruitful and [D]multiply you, that you may become a [E]company of peoples. 4 May He also give you the [A]blessing of Abraham, to you and to your [a]descendants with you, that you may [B]possess the land of your [C]sojournings, which God gave to Abraham." 5 Then [A]Isaac sent Jacob away, and he went to Paddan-aram to Laban, son of Bethuel the Aramean, the brother of Rebekah, the mother of Jacob and Esau.

6 Now Esau saw that Isaac had blessed Jacob and sent him away to Paddan-aram to take to himself a wife from there, *and that* when he blessed him he charged him, saying, "[A]You shall not take a wife from the daughters of Canaan," 7 and that Jacob had obeyed his father and his mother and had gone to Paddan-aram. 8 So Esau saw that [A]the daughters of Canaan displeased [a]his father Isaac; 9 and Esau went to Ishmael, and [a]married, [A]besides the wives that he had, Mahalath the daughter of Ishmael, Abraham's son, the sister of Nebaioth.

JACOB'S DREAM

10 Then Jacob departed from [A]Beersheba and went toward [B]Haran. 11 He [a]came to [b]a [A]certain place and spent the night there, because the sun had set; and he took one of the stones of the place and put it [c]under his head, and lay down in that place. 12 [A]He had a dream, and behold, a ladder was set on the earth with its top reaching to heaven; and behold, [B]the angels of God were ascending and descending on it. 13 And behold, [A]the LORD stood [a]above it and said, "I am the LORD, [B]the God of your father Abraham and the God of Isaac; the land on which you lie, I will give it [C]to you and to [D]your [b]descendants. 14 Your [a]descendants will also be like [A]the dust of the earth, and you will [b]spread out [B]to the west and to the east and to the north and to the south; and [C]in you and in your [a]descendants shall all the families of the earth be blessed. 15 Behold, [A]I am with you and [B]will keep you wherever you go, and [C]will bring you back to this land; for [D]I will not leave you until I have done what I have [a]promised you." 16 Then Jacob [A]awoke from his sleep and said, "[B]Surely the LORD is in this place, and I did not know it." 17 He was afraid and said, "[A]How awesome is this place! This is none other than the house of God, and this is the gate of heaven."

18 So Jacob rose early in the morning, and took [A]the stone that he had put [a]under his head and set it up as a pillar and poured oil on its top. 19 He called the name of that place [a,A]Bethel; however, [b]previously the name of the city had been [B]Luz. 20 Then Jacob [A]made a vow, saying, "[B]If God will be with me and will keep me on this journey that I [a]take, and will give me [b,C]food to eat and garments to wear, 21 and [A]I return to my father's house in [a]safety, [B]then the LORD will be my God. 22 This stone, which I have set up as a pillar, [A]will be God's house, and [B]of all that You give me I will surely give a tenth to You."

JACOB MEETS RACHEL

29 Then Jacob [a]went on his journey, and came to the land of [A]the sons of the east. 2 He looked, and [a]saw [A]a well in the field, and behold, three flocks

28:3 [a]Heb *El Shaddai* [A]Gen 17:1; 35:11; 48:3 [B]Gen 22:17 [C]Gen 17:6, 20 [D]Gen 17:2; 26:4, 24 [E]Gen 35:11; 48:4 28:4 [a]Lit *seed* [A]Gen 12:2; 22:17 [B]Gen 15:7, 8; 17:8 [C]1 Chr 29:15; Ps 39:12 28:5 [A]Gen 27:43 28:6 [A]Gen 28:1 28:8 [a]Lit *in the eyes of his* [A]Gen 24:3; 26:34, 35; 27:46 28:9 [a]Lit *took for his wife* [A]Gen 26:34; 36:2 28:10 [A]Gen 26:23 [B]Gen 12:4, 5; 27:43 28:11 [a]Lit *lighted on* [b]Lit *the place* [c]Lit *at his head-place* [A]Gen 28:19 28:12 [A]Gen 41:1; Num 12:6 [B]John 1:51 28:13 [a]Or *beside him* [b]Lit *seed* [A]Gen 35:1; Amos 7:7 [B]Gen 26:3, 24 [C]Gen 13:15, 17; 26:3 [D]Gen 12:7; 15:18 28:14 [a]Lit *seed* [b]Lit *break through* [A]Gen 13:16; 22:17 [B]Gen 13:14, 15 [C]Gen 12:3; 18:18; 22:18; 26:4 28:15 [a]Lit *spoken to* [A]Gen 26:3, 24; 31:3 [B]Num 6:24; Ps 121:5, 7, 8 [C]Gen 48:21; Deut 30:3 [D]Num 23:19; Deut 7:9; 31:6, 8 28:16 [A]1 Kin 3:15; Jer 31:26 [B]Ex 3:4-6; Josh 5:13-15; Ps 139:7-12 28:17 [A]Ps 68:35 28:18 [a]Lit *at his head-place* [A]Gen 28:11; 35:14 28:19 [a]I.e. the house of God [b]Lit *at the first* [A]Judg 1:23 [B]Gen 35:6; 48:3 28:20 [a]Lit *go* [b]Lit *bread* [A]Gen 31:13; Judg 11:30; 2 Sam 15:8 [B]Gen 28:15 [C]1 Tim 6:8 28:21 [a]Lit *peace* [A]Judg 11:31 [B]Deut 26:17 28:22 [A]Gen 35:7 [B]Lev 27:30; Deut 14:22 29:1 [a]Lit *lifted up his feet* [A]Judg 6:3, 33 29:2 [a]Lit *behold* [A]Gen 24:10, 11; Ex 2:15, 16

28:3, 4 This extra patriarchal blessing unveiled where Isaac was in his thinking. He had come to understand that the divine blessings would go through Jacob, to whom the Abrahamic Covenant promises of posterity and land also applied—quite the reversal of prior wishes and understanding (cf. 27:27–29). The lack of land possession at that time, described by the phrase "the land of your sojournings," did not deter at all from the certainty of God's promise.

28:3 God Almighty. Significantly, El Shaddai was the name Isaac chose to employ when blessing Jacob. It was the name of sovereign power with which God had identified Himself to Abraham in covenant reaffirmation (17:1) which must have been an encouraging factor to both him and his son.

28:5 Isaac sent Jacob away. Ca. 1928 B.C. This must have been a hard departure for the domestic Jacob.

28:9 Esau went to Ishmael. Marrying back into the line of Abraham through the family of Ishmael seemed to have been a ploy to gain favor with his father (vv. 6, 8), and show an obedience similar to his brother's (v. 7). He hoped by such gratifying of his parents to atone for past delinquencies, and maybe have his father change the will. He actually increased iniquity by adding to his pagan wives (26:34, 35) a wife from a family God had rejected.

28:10–15 For the first time, and significantly while Jacob was on his way out of the land of Canaan, God revealed Himself to Jacob and confirmed the Abrahamic Covenant with him in all of its 3 elements of land, seed, and blessing (vv. 13, 14). Later, God would remind Jacob of this event when He instructed him to return to the land (31:13) and Jacob would remind his household of it when he instructed them to cleanse their homes before they could return to Bethel (35:3).

28:10 Haran. *See note on 11:31.*

28:11 a certain place. Identified in v. 19 as Bethel, about 50 mi. N of Beersheba, and about 6 mi. N of Jerusalem. There he spent the night in an open field.

28:12 a ladder ... angels of God were ascending and descending. A graphic portrayal of the heavenly Lord's personal involvement in the affairs of earth, and here especially as they related to divine covenant promises in Jacob's life (vv. 13–15). This dream was to encourage the lonely traveler. God's own appointed angelic messengers ensured the carrying out of His will and plans. More than likely, the angels traversed a stairway rather than a ladder.

28:15 will keep you ... will bring you back. A most timely, comforting, and assuring promise which remained engraved on Jacob's heart during his sojourn in Haran (see 30:25). His forced departure from Canaan did not and would not abrogate any of God's promises to him.

28:18–21 a pillar. Marking a particular site as of special religious significance by means of a stone pillar was a known practice. A libation offering, a change of place-name, and a vow of allegiance to the Lord in exchange for promised protection and blessing completed Jacob's ceremonial consecration of Bethel, i.e., "House of God."

28:22 a tenth. Tithing, though not commanded by God, was obviously already known and voluntarily practiced, and served to acknowledge God's providential beneficence in the donor's life (*see note on 14:20*). Jacob may have been bargaining with God, as if to buy His favor rather than purely worshiping God with his gift, but it is best to translate the "if" (v. 20) as "since" and see Jacob's vow and offering as genuine worship based on confidence in God's promise (vv. 13–15).

29:1–4 Conveniently meeting, at his destination, shepherds who knew both Laban and Rachel reflected the directing hand of God upon his life, just as promised (28:15).

29:2, 3 stone ... was large. Perhaps due to the fact that this well of precious stored

of sheep were lying there beside it, for from that
well they watered the flocks. Now the stone on the
mouth of the well was large. 3 When all the flocks
were gathered there, they would then roll the stone
from the mouth of the well and water the sheep,
and put the stone back in its place on the mouth
of the well.
4 Jacob said to them, "My brothers, where are
you from?" And they said, "We are from [A]Haran."
5 He said to them, "Do you know Laban the [A]son of
Nahor?" And they said, "We know *him*." 6 And he
said to them, "Is it well with him?" And they said,
"It is well, and here is [A]Rachel his daughter coming
with the sheep." 7 He said, "Behold, it is still high
day; it is not time for the livestock to be gathered.
Water the sheep, and go, pasture them." 8 But they
said, "We cannot, until all the flocks are gathered,
and they roll the stone from the mouth of the well;
then we water the sheep."
9 While he was still speaking with them, Rachel
came with her father's sheep, for she was a shepherdess. 10 When Jacob saw Rachel the daughter of
Laban his mother's brother, and the sheep of Laban
his mother's brother, Jacob went up and rolled the
stone from the mouth of the well and watered the
flock of Laban his mother's brother. 11 Then Jacob
[A]kissed Rachel, and lifted his voice and wept. 12 Jacob told Rachel that he was a [a,A]relative of her father
and that he was Rebekah's son, and [B]she ran and
told her father.
13 So when [A]Laban heard the news of Jacob his
sister's son, he ran to meet him, and [B]embraced him
and kissed him and brought him to his house. Then
he related to Laban all these things. 14 Laban said to
him, "Surely you are [A]my bone and my flesh." And
he stayed with him a month.
15 Then Laban said to Jacob, "Because you are
my [a]relative, should you therefore serve me for
nothing? Tell me, what shall [A]your wages be?"
16 Now Laban had two daughters; the name of the
older was Leah, and the name of the younger was
Rachel. 17 And Leah's eyes were weak, but Rachel was
[A]beautiful of form and [a]face. 18 Now Jacob [A]loved
Rachel, so he said, "[B]I will serve you seven years
for your younger daughter Rachel." 19 Laban said,
"It is better that I give her to you than to give her
to another man; stay with me." 20 So Jacob served
seven years for Rachel and they seemed to him but
a few days [A]because of his love for her.

LABAN'S TREACHERY

21 Then Jacob said to Laban, "Give *me* my wife,
for my [a]time is completed, that I may [A]go in to her."
22 Laban gathered all the men of the place and made
a feast. 23 Now in the evening he took his daughter
Leah, and brought her to him; and *Jacob* went in
to her. 24 Laban also gave his maid Zilpah to his
daughter Leah as a maid. 25 So it came about in the
morning that, behold, it was Leah! And he said to
Laban, "[A]What is this you have done to me? Was it
not for Rachel that I served with you? Why then have
you [B]deceived me?" 26 But Laban said, "It is not [a]the
practice in our place to [b]marry off the younger before the firstborn. 27 Complete the week of this one,
and we will give you the other also for the service
which [A]you shall serve with me for another seven
years." 28 Jacob did so and completed her week,
and he gave him his daughter Rachel as his wife.
29 Laban also gave his maid Bilhah to his daughter
Rachel as her maid. 30 So *Jacob* went in to Rachel
also, and indeed [A]he loved Rachel more than Leah,
and he served with [a]Laban for [B]another seven years.
31 Now the LORD saw that Leah was [a]unloved,
and He opened her womb, but Rachel was barren.
32 Leah conceived and bore a son and named him
[a]Reuben, for she said, "Because the LORD has [b,A]seen

29:4 [A]Gen 28:10 29:5 [A]Gen 24:24, 29 29:6 [A]Ex 2:16 29:11 [A]Gen 33:4 29:12 [a]Lit *brother* [A]Gen 28:5 [B]Gen 24:28 29:13 [A]Gen 24:29-31 [B]Gen 33:4 29:14 [A]Gen 2:23; Judg 9:2; 2 Sam 5:1; 19:12, 13 29:15 [a]Lit *brother* [A]Gen 31:41 29:17 [a]Lit *beautiful of appearance* [A]Gen 12:11, 14; 26:7 29:18 [A]Gen 24:67 [B]Hos 12:12 29:20 [A]Song 8:7 29:21 [a]Lit *days are* [A]Judg 15:1 29:25 [A]Gen 12:18; 20:9; 26:10 [B]1 Sam 28:12 29:26 [a]Lit *done thus in* [b]Lit *give* 29:27 [A]Gen 31:41 29:30 [a]Lit *him* [A]Gen 29:17, 18 [B]Gen 31:41 29:31 [a]Lit *hated* 29:32 [a]I.e. see, a son [b]Lit *looked upon* [A]Gen 16:11; 31:42; Ex 3:7; 4:31; Deut 26:7; Ps 25:18

water could evaporate rapidly in the sun, or be filled with blowing dust, or used indiscriminately, it had been covered and its use regulated (vv. 7, 8).

29:5 Laban the son of Nahor. Genealogical fluidity in the use of "son," meaning male descendant, occurred in Jacob's inquiry after Laban, for he was actually Nahor's grandson (cf. 22:20–23).

29:6–8 It appears that Jacob was trying to get these men to water their sheep immediately and leave, so he could be alone with Rachel for the meeting.

29:9 speaking with them. The language of Haran was Aramaic or Chaldee and evidently was known by Abraham and his sons. There is no comment on how these patriarchs spoke with the Canaanites and Egyptians in their travels, but it is reasonable to assume they had become skilled linguists, knowing more than Hebrew and Aramaic.

29:10–14 Customary greetings and personal introductions ended 97 years of absence since Rebekah had left (*see notes on 25:21; 27:1*), and Laban's nephew was welcomed home.

29:14 a month. Tradition in that ancient area allowed a stranger to be cared for 3 days. On the fourth he was to tell his name and mission. After that he could remain if he worked in some agreed-upon way (v. 15).

29:17 eyes were weak. Probably means that they were a pale color rather than the dark and sparkling eyes most common. Such paleness was viewed as a blemish.

29:18–30 Love and working to provide his service as a dowry (vv. 18–20) combined to make Jacob happily remain during the first 7 years in Laban's household, almost as an adopted son rather than a mere employee. But Jacob, the deceiver (27:1–29), was about to be deceived (vv. 22–25). Local marriage customs (v. 26), love for Rachel, and more dowry desired by Laban (vv. 27–30) all conspired to give Jacob not only 7 more years of labor under Laban, but two wives who were to become caught up in jealous childbearing competition (30:1–21).

29:23 The deception was possible because of the custom of veiling the bride and the dark of the night (v. 25).

29:23, 30 went in to. This is a euphemism for consummating marriage.

29:27, 30 It appears that Laban agreed to give Jacob Rachel after the week of wedding celebration for Leah's marriage to him, and before the 7 years of labor.

29:28 Rachel as his wife. Such consanguinity was not God's will (*see note on Ge 2:24*), and the Mosaic code later forbade it (Lv 18:18). Polygamy always brought grief, as in the life of Jacob.

29:31 Leah was unloved ... Rachel was barren. There was quite a contrast when the one dearly beloved (vv. 18, 20, 30) had no children, whereas the one rejected did. Jacob might have demoted Leah, but God took action on her behalf. Leah had also prayed about her husband's rejection (v. 33) and had been troubled by it, as seen in the names given to her first 4 sons (vv. 32–35).

my affliction; surely now my husband will love me."
33 Then she conceived again and bore a son and said,
"[A]Because the LORD has [a]heard that I am [b]unloved,
He has therefore given me this *son* also." So she
named him Simeon. 34 She conceived again and
bore a son and said, "Now this time my husband will
become [a]attached to me, because I have borne him
three sons." Therefore he was named [A]Levi. 35 And
she conceived again and bore a son and said, "This
time I will [a]praise the LORD." Therefore she named
him [b,A]Judah. Then she stopped bearing.

THE SONS OF JACOB

30 Now when Rachel saw that [A]she bore Jacob
no children, [a]she became jealous of her sister; and she said to Jacob, "[B]Give me children, or else
I die." 2 Then Jacob's anger burned against Rachel,
and he said, "Am I in the place of God, who has
[A]withheld from you the fruit of the womb?" 3 She
said, "[A]Here is my maid Bilhah, go in to her that she
may [B]bear on my knees, that [a,A]through her I too
may have children." 4 So [A]she gave him her maid
Bilhah as a wife, and Jacob went in to her. 5 Bilhah
conceived and bore Jacob a son. 6 Then Rachel said,
"God has [a,A]vindicated me, and has indeed heard
my voice and has given me a son." Therefore she
named him [b]Dan. 7 Rachel's maid Bilhah conceived
again and bore Jacob a second son. 8 So Rachel said,
"With [a]mighty wrestlings I have [b]wrestled with my
sister, *and* I have indeed prevailed." And she named
him Naphtali.
9 When Leah saw that she had stopped bearing, she took her maid Zilpah and gave her to
Jacob as a wife. 10 Leah's maid Zilpah bore Jacob
a son. 11 Then Leah said, "[a]How fortunate!" So she
named him [b]Gad. 12 Leah's maid Zilpah bore Jacob
a second son. 13 Then Leah said, "[a]Happy am I!
For women [A]will call me happy." So she named
him [b]Asher.
14 Now in the days of wheat harvest Reuben went
and found [A]mandrakes in the field, and brought
them to his mother Leah. Then Rachel said to Leah,
"Please give me some of your son's mandrakes."
15 But she said to her, "Is it a small matter for you
to take my husband? And would you take my son's
mandrakes also?" So Rachel said, "Therefore he may
lie with you tonight in return for your son's mandrakes." 16 When Jacob came in from the field in the
evening, then Leah went out to meet him and said,
"You must come in to me, for I have surely hired
you with my son's mandrakes." So he lay with her
that night. 17 God gave heed to Leah, and she conceived and bore Jacob a fifth son. 18 Then Leah said,
"God has given me my [a]wages because I gave my
maid to my husband." So she named him Issachar.
19 Leah conceived again and bore a sixth son to Jacob. 20 Then Leah said, "God has endowed me with
a good gift; now my husband [a]will dwell with me,
because I have borne him six sons." So she named
him Zebulun. 21 Afterward she bore a daughter and
named her Dinah.
22 Then [A]God remembered Rachel, and God gave
heed to her and [B]opened her womb. 23 So she conceived and bore a son and said, "God has [A]taken
away my reproach." 24 She named him Joseph, saying, "[A]May the LORD [a]give me another son."

JACOB PROSPERS

25 Now it came about when Rachel had borne
Joseph, that Jacob said to Laban, "[A]Send me away,
that I may go to my own place and to my own
country. 26 Give *me* my wives and my children [A]for
whom I have served you, and let me depart; for you
yourself know my service which I have [a]rendered

29:33 [a]Heb *shama,* related to Simeon [b]Lit *hated* [A]Deut 21:15 29:34 [a]Heb *lavah,* related to Levi [A]Gen 49:5 29:35 [a]Heb *Jadah,* related to Judah [b]Heb *Jehudah* [A]Gen 49:8; Matt 1:2 30:1 [a]Lit *Rachel* [A]Gen 29:31 [B]1 Sam 1:5, 6 30:2 [A]Gen 20:18; 29:31 30:3 [a]Lit *from her I too may be built* [A]Gen 16:2 [B]Gen 50:23; Job 3:12 30:4 [A]Gen 16:3, 4 30:6 [a]Lit *judged* [b]I.e. He judged [A]Ps 35:24; 43:1; Lam 3:59 30:8 [a]Lit *wrestlings of God* [b]Heb *niphtal,* related to Naphtali 30:11 [a]Lit *With fortune!* Some versions read *Fortune has come* [b]I.e. Fortune 30:13 [a]Lit *With my happiness!* [b]I.e. happy [A]Luke 1:48 30:14 [A]Song 7:13 30:18 [a]Heb *sachar,* related to Issachar 30:20 [a]Heb *zabal,* related to Zebulun. Some translate *will honor* 30:22 [A]1 Sam 1:19, 20 [B]Gen 29:31 30:23 [A]Is 4:1; Luke 1:25 30:24 [a]Lit *add to me;* Heb *Joseph* [A]Gen 35:17 30:25 [A]Gen 24:54, 56 30:26 [a]Lit *served* [A]Gen 29:18, 20, 27; Hos 12:12

30:1 or else I die. A childless woman in ancient Near Eastern culture was no better than a dead wife and became a severe embarrassment to her husband (see v. 23).

30:2 Am I in the place of God…? Although spoken in a moment of frustration with Rachel's pleading for children and the envy with which it was expressed, Jacob's words do indicate an understanding that ultimately God opened and closed the womb.

30:3 on my knees. When the surrogate gave birth while actually sitting on the knees of the wife, it symbolized the wife providing a child for her husband.

30:1–21 The competition between the two sisters/wives is demonstrated in using their maids as surrogate mothers (vv. 3, 7, 9, 12), in declaring God had judged the case in favor of the plaintiff (v. 6), in bartering for time with the husband (vv. 14–16), in accusing one of stealing her husband's favor (v. 15), and in the name given to one son—"wrestled with my sister" (Naphtali, v. 8). The race for children was also accompanied by prayers to the Lord or by acknowledgment of His providence (vv. 6, 17, 20, 22; also 29:32, 33, 35). This bitter and intense rivalry, all the more fierce though they were sisters, and even though they occupied different dwellings with their children as customary, shows that the evil lay in the system itself (bigamy), which as a violation of God's ordinance (Ge 2:24) could not yield happiness.

30:14 mandrakes. Jacob had 8 sons by then from 3 women and about 6 years had elapsed since his marriages. The oldest son, Reuben, was about 5. Playing in the field during wheat harvest, he found this small, orange-colored fruit and "brought them to his mother Leah." These were superstitiously viewed in the ancient world as "love-apples," an aphrodisiac or fertility-inducing narcotic.

30:15, 16 This odd and desperate bargain by Rachel was an attempt to become pregnant with the aid of the mandrakes, a folk remedy which failed to understand that God gives children (vv. 6, 17, 20, 22).

30:20 now my husband will dwell with me. The plaintive cry of one still unloved (cf. 29:31) as confirmed by Jacob's frequent absence from her home. She hoped that having 6 children for Jacob would win his permanent residence with her. **Zebulun.** The name means "dwelling," signifying her hope of Jacob's dwelling with her.

30:21 Dinah. Although not the only daughter to be born to Jacob (cf. 37:35; 46:7), her name is mentioned in anticipation of the tragedy at Shechem (chap. 34).

30:22 Then God remembered Rachel. All the desperate waiting (see 30:1) and pleading climaxed at the end of 7 years with God's response. Then Rachel properly ascribed her delivery from barrenness to the Lord, whom she also trusted for another son (vv. 23, 24).

30:24 Joseph. Ca. 1914 B.C. His name means "he will add" or "may he add," indicating both her thanks and her faith that God would give her another son.

30:25 Send me away … to my own country. Fourteen years of absence had not dulled Jacob's acute awareness of belonging to the land God had given to him. Since Mesopotamia was not his home and his contract with Laban was up, he desired to return to "my own place" and "my own country." Jacob's wish to return to Canaan was not hidden from Laban (v. 30).

you." 27 But Laban said to him, "If now [a]it pleases
you, *stay with me;* I have divined [A]that the LORD
has blessed me on your account." 28 He [a]contin-
ued, "[A]Name me your wages, and I will give it."
29 But he said to him, "[A]You yourself know how I
have served you and how your cattle have [a]fared
with me. 30 For you had little before [a]I came and
it has [b]increased to a multitude, and the LORD has
blessed you [c]wherever I turned. But now, when
shall I provide for my own household also?" 31 So
he said, "What shall I give you?" And Jacob said,
"You shall not give me anything. If you will do
this *one* thing for me, I will again pasture *and*
keep your flock: 32 let me pass through your entire
flock today, removing from there every [A]speckled
and spotted sheep and every black [a]one among
the lambs and the spotted and speckled among
the goats; and *such* shall be my wages. 33 So my
[a]honesty will answer for me later, when you come
concerning my [b]wages. Every one that is not speckled and spotted among the goats and black among
the lambs, *if found* with me, will be considered
stolen." 34 Laban said, "[a]Good, let it be according
to your word." 35 So he removed on that day the
striped and spotted male goats and all the speckled
and spotted female goats, every one with white
in it, and all the black ones among the sheep, and
gave them into the [a]care of his sons. 36 And he put
a distance of three days' journey between himself and Jacob, and Jacob fed the rest of Laban's
flocks.

37 Then Jacob [a]took fresh rods of poplar and almond and plane trees, and peeled white stripes in
them, exposing the white which *was* [b]in the rods.
38 He set the rods which he had peeled in front of the
flocks in the gutters, *even* in the watering troughs,
where the flocks came to drink; and they [a]mated
when they came to drink. 39 So the flocks [a]mated
by the rods, and the flocks brought forth striped,
speckled, and spotted. 40 Jacob separated the lambs,
and [a]made the flocks face toward the striped and all
the black in the flock of Laban; and he put his own
herds apart, and did not put them with Laban's flock.
41 Moreover, whenever the [a]stronger of the flock
[b]were mating, Jacob would place the rods in the
sight of the flock in the gutters, so that they might
[c]mate by the rods; 42 but when the flock was feeble,
he did not put *them* in; so the feebler were Laban's
and the [a]stronger Jacob's. 43 So [A]the man [a]became
exceedingly prosperous, and had large flocks and
female and male servants and camels and donkeys.

JACOB LEAVES SECRETLY FOR CANAAN

31 Now [a]Jacob heard the words of Laban's sons,
saying, "Jacob has taken away all that was our
father's, and from what belonged to our father he
has made all this [b]wealth." 2 Jacob saw the [a]attitude
of Laban, and behold, it was not *friendly* toward him
as formerly. 3 Then the LORD said to Jacob, "[A]Return
to the land of your fathers and to your relatives, and
[B]I will be with you." 4 So Jacob sent and called Rachel

30:27 [a]Lit *I have found favor in your eyes* [A]Gen 26:24; 39:3, 5; Is 61:9 30:28 [a]Lit *said* [A]Gen 29:15; 31:7, 41 30:29 [a]Lit *been* [A]Gen 31:6 30:30 [a]Lit *me* [b]Lit *broken forth* [c]Lit *at my foot* 30:32 [a]Lit *sheep* [A]Gen 31:8 30:33 [a]Lit *righteousness* [b]Lit *wages which are before you* 30:34 [a]Lit *Behold, would that it might be* 30:35 [a]Lit *hand* 30:37 [a]Lit *took to himself* [b]Lit *on* 30:38 [a]Or *conceived* 30:39 [a]Or *conceived* 30:40 [a]Lit *set the faces* 30:41 [a]Lit *bound ones;* i.e. firm and compact [b]Or *conceived* [c]Or *conceive* 30:42 [a]Lit *bound ones;* i.e. firm and compact 30:43 [a]Lit *broke forth* [A]Gen 12:16; 13:2; 24:35; 26:13, 14; 30:30 31:1 [a]Lit *he* [b]Lit *glory* 31:2 [a]Lit *face* 31:3 [A]Gen 32:9 [B]Gen 28:15

30:27 I have divined. *See note on Dt 18:9–12.*

30:28 Name me your wages. On the two occasions that Laban asked this of Jacob it was to urge him to stay. The first time (29:15) Laban had sought to reward a relative, but this time it was because he had been rewarded since "the LORD has blessed me on your account" (v. 27). Jacob readily confirmed Laban's evaluation in that "little" had indeed become "a multitude" (v. 30) since he had come on the scene. Laban's superficial generosity should not be mistaken for genuine goodness (see 31:7). He was attempting to deceive Jacob into staying because it was potentially profitable for him.

30:31–36 What shall I give you? Laban wanted Jacob to stay and asked what it would take for him to do so. Jacob wanted nothing except to be in a position for God to bless him. He was willing to stay, but not be further indebted to the scheming and selfish Laban. He offered Laban a plan that could bless him while costing Laban nothing. He would continue to care for Laban's animals, as he had been doing. His pay would consist of animals not yet born, animals which would seem the less desirable to Laban because of their markings and color. None of the solid color animals would be taken by Jacob, and if any were born into Jacob's flocks, Laban could take them (they were considered as stolen). Only those animals born speckled, spotted, striped, or abnormally colored would belong to Jacob. Evidently, most of the animals were white (sheep), black (goats), and brown (cattle). Few were in the category of Jacob's request. Further, Jacob would not even use the living speckled or abnormally colored animals to breed more like them. He would separate them into a flock of their own kind, apart from the normally colored animals. Only the spotted and abnormally colored offspring born in the future to the normally colored would be his. Since it seemed to Laban that the birth of such abnormally marked animals was unlikely to occur in any significant volume from the normally colored, he agreed. He believed this a small and favorable concession on his part to maintain the skills of Jacob to further enlarge his herds and flocks. Jacob, by this, put himself entirely in God's hands. Only the Lord could determine what animals would be Jacob's. To make sure Jacob didn't cheat on his good deal, Laban separated the abnormally marked from the normal animals in Jacob's care (vv. 34–36).

30:37–42 rods. Jacob was knowledgeable about sheep, goats, and cattle, having kept his father's animals for most of his 90 years, and Laban's for the last 14 years. He knew that when one uncommonly marked animal was born (with a recessive gene), he could then begin to breed that gene selectively to produce flocks and herds of abnormally marked animals, which were in no way inferior physically to the normally marked. Once he began this breeding process, he sought to stimulate it by some methods that may appear superstitious and foolish to us (as the mandrakes in v. 14). But it is most likely that he had learned that, when the bark was peeled, there was some stimulant released into the water that stimulated the animals to sexual activity. In v. 38, the word "mated" is literally, in Heb., "to be hot," or as is said of animals, "to be in heat." His plan was successful (v. 39), and he kept his own flock separate from the normally colored ones of Laban. His system worked to his own advantage, not that of Laban (v. 42) who had for years taken advantage of him. Jacob gave God the credit for the success of his efforts (31:7, 9).

31:1, 2 Of materialistic bent and envious at Jacob's success, Laban's sons grumbled at what they saw as the depleting of their father's assets, thus hurting their own inheritance. If Jacob heard of this, so did Laban, and that knowledge rankled him to the point of surliness toward his son-in-law (cf. 31:20). Profiting from God's blessings through Jacob (30:27, 30) was one thing, but seeing only Jacob blessed was quite another matter and elicited no praise or gratitude to God from Laban.

31:3 Return to the land. When Jacob sought to leave at the end of his contract (30:25), the timing was not in accord with God's plan. Six years later, God providentially directed Jacob's departure and assured him of His presence. Jacob served his father-in-law a total of twelve years (vv. 38–41).

31:4 called ... in the field. In the privacy of the open field, Jacob's plans could be confidentially shared with his wives.

and Leah to his flock in the field, 5 and said to them, "[A]I see your father's [a]attitude, that it is not *friendly* toward me as formerly, but [B]the God of my father has been with me. 6 [A]You know that I have served your father with all my strength. 7 Yet your father has [A]cheated me and [B]changed my wages ten times; however, [C]God did not allow him to hurt me. 8 If [A]he spoke thus, 'The speckled shall be your wages,' then all the flock brought forth speckled; and if he spoke thus, 'The striped shall be your wages,' then all the flock brought forth striped. 9 Thus God has [A]taken away your father's livestock and given *them* to me. 10 And it came about at the time when the flock were [a]mating that I lifted up my eyes and saw in a dream, and behold, the male goats which were [b]mating *were* striped, speckled, and mottled. 11 Then [A]the angel of God said to me in the dream, 'Jacob,' and I said, 'Here I am.' 12 He said, 'Lift up now your eyes and see *that* all the male goats which are [a]mating are striped, speckled, and mottled; for [A]I have seen all that Laban has been doing to you. 13 I am [A]the God *of* Bethel, where you [B]anointed a pillar, where you made a vow to Me; now arise, [a]leave this land, and [C]return to the land of your birth.' " 14 Rachel and Leah said to him, "Do we still have any portion or inheritance in our father's house? 15 Are we not reckoned by him as foreigners? For [A]he has sold us, and has also [a]entirely consumed [b]our purchase price. 16 Surely all the wealth which God has taken away from our father belongs to us and our children; now then, do whatever God has said to you."

17 Then Jacob arose and put his children and his wives upon camels; 18 and he drove away all his livestock and all his property which he had gathered, his acquired livestock which he had gathered in Paddan-aram, [A]to go to the land of Canaan to his father Isaac. 19 When Laban had gone to shear his flock, then Rachel stole the [a,A]household idols that were her father's. 20 And Jacob [a]deceived Laban the Aramean by not telling him that he was fleeing. 21 So he fled with all that he had; and he arose and crossed the *Euphrates* River, and set his face toward the hill country of [A]Gilead.

LABAN PURSUES JACOB

22 When it was told Laban on the third day that Jacob had fled, 23 then he took his [a]kinsmen with him and pursued him *a distance of* seven days' journey, and he overtook him in the hill country of Gilead. 24 [A]God came to Laban the Aramean in a [B]dream of the night and said to him, "[a,C]Be careful that you do not speak to Jacob either good or bad."

25 Laban caught up with Jacob. Now Jacob had pitched his tent in the hill country, and Laban with his [a]kinsmen camped in the hill country of Gilead. 26 Then Laban said to Jacob, "What have you done [a]by deceiving me and carrying away my daughters like captives of the sword? 27 Why did you flee secretly and [a]deceive me, and did not tell me so that I might have sent you away with joy and with songs, with [A]timbrel and with [B]lyre; 28 and did not allow me [A]to kiss my sons and my daughters? Now you have done foolishly. 29 It is in [a]my power to do you harm, but [A]the God of your father spoke to me last night, saying, '[b,B]Be careful not to speak either good or bad to Jacob.' 30 Now you have indeed gone away because you longed greatly for your father's house; *but* why did you steal [A]my gods?" 31 Then Jacob replied to Laban,

31:5 [a]Lit *face* [A]Gen 31:2 [B]Gen 21:22; 28:13, 15; 31:29, 42, 53; Is 41:10; Heb 13:5 31:6 [A]Gen 30:29 31:7 [A]Gen 29:25 [B]Gen 31:41 [C]Gen 15:1; 31:29 31:8 [A]Gen 30:32 31:9 [A]Gen 31:1, 16 31:10 [a]Or *conceiving* [b]Lit *leaping upon the flock* 31:11 [A]Gen 16:7-11; 22:11, 15; 31:13; 48:16 31:12 [a]Lit *leaping upon the flock* [A]Ex 3:7 31:13 [a]Lit *go out from* [A]Gen 28:13, 19 [B]Gen 28:18, 20 [C]Gen 28:15; 32:9 31:15 [a]I.e. enjoyed the benefit of [b]Lit *our money* [A]Gen 29:20, 23, 27 31:18 [A]Gen 35:27 31:19 [a]Heb *teraphim* [A]Gen 31:30, 34; 35:2; Judg 17:5; 1 Sam 19:13; Hos 3:4 31:20 [a]Lit *stole the heart of* 31:21 [A]Gen 37:25 31:23 [a]Lit *brothers* 31:24 [a]Lit *Take heed to yourself* [A]Gen 20:3; 31:29 [B]Gen 20:3, 6; 31:11 [C]Gen 24:50; 31:7, 29 31:25 [a]Lit *brothers* 31:26 [a]Lit *and you have stolen my heart* 31:27 [a]Lit *steal me* [A]Ex 15:20 [B]Gen 4:21 31:28 [A]Gen 31:55 31:29 [a]Lit *the power of my hand* [b]Lit *Take heed to yourself* [A]Gen 31:5, 24, 42, 53 [B]Gen 31:24 31:30 [A]Gen 31:19; Josh 24:2; Judg 18:24

31:5 your father's . . . my father. A contrast, perhaps not intentional, but nevertheless noticeable since their father signaled rejection toward him, whereas the God of his father had accepted him.

31:6–9 As Jacob explained it, his unstinting service to their father had been met by Laban with wage changes intended to cripple his son-in-law's enterprise, but God had intervened by blocking the intended hurt (v. 7) and overriding the wage changes with great prosperity (v. 9).

31:10–12 *See notes on 30:37–42.*

31:11 the angel of God. Cf. 21:17. The same as the Angel of the Lord (16:11; 22:11, 15). *See note on Ex 3:2.*

31:13 I am the God *of* Bethel. The Angel of God (v. 11) clearly identified Himself as the Lord, pointing back as He did so to the earlier critical encounter with God in Jacob's life (28:10–22).

31:14–16 The two wives concurred that, in the context of severely strained family relationships, their inheritance might be in question since the ties that bind no longer held them there. They also agreed that God's intervention had, in effect, refunded what their father had wrongfully withheld and spent.

31:19 household idols. Lit. teraphim (cf. 2Ki 23:24; Eze 21:21). These images or figurines of varying sizes, usually of nude goddesses with accentuated sexual features, either signaled special protection for, inheritance rights for, or guaranteed fertility for the bearer. Or, perhaps possession by Rachel would call for Jacob to be recognized as head of the household at Laban's death. *See notes on vv. 30, 44.*

31:20 Jacob deceived Laban. Because of fear at what Laban might do (v. 31), Jacob dispensed with the expected courtesy he had not forgotten before (30:25) and clandestinely slipped away at an appropriate time (v. 19). With all his entourage, this was not a simple exit. Laban's gruffness (vv. 1, 2) exuded enough hostility for Jacob to suspect forceful retaliation and to react by escaping what danger he could not know for sure.

31:21 the *Euphrates* River . . . hill country of Gilead. The area S of Galilee to the E of the Jordan River respectively.

31:23 seven days' journey. That it took so long for Laban's band to catch up with a much larger group burdened with possessions and animals indicates a forced march was undertaken by Jacob's people, probably motivated by Jacob's fear.

31:24 Be careful . . . either good or bad. God again sovereignly protected, as He had done for Abraham and Isaac (12:17–20; 20:3–7; 26:8–11), to prevent harm coming to His man. In a proverbial expression (cf. Ge 24:50; 2Sa 13:22) Laban is cautioned not to use anything in the full range of options open to him, "from the good to the bad," to alter the existing situation and bring Jacob back.

31:26 my daughters like captives. Laban evidently did not believe that his daughters could have possibly agreed with the departure and must have left under duress.

31:27–29 Laban's questions protested his right to have arranged a proper send-off for his family and functioned as a rebuke of Jacob's thoughtlessness toward him.

31:30 why did you steal my gods? Longing to return to Canaan (cf. 30:25) might excuse his leaving without notice, but it could not excuse the theft of his teraphim (31:19). Laban's thorough search for these idols (vv. 33–35) also marked how important they were to him as a pagan worshiper. *See notes on vv. 19, 44.*

31:31 afraid. A reasonable fear is experienced by Jacob, who had come to find a wife and stayed for at least 20 years (v. 38) under the selfish compulsions of Laban.

"Because I was afraid, for I thought that you would
take your daughters from me by force. 32 [A]The one
with whom you find your gods shall not live; in the
presence of our [a]kinsmen [b]point out what is yours
[c]among my belongings and take *it* for yourself." For
Jacob did not know that Rachel had stolen them.
33 So Laban went into Jacob's tent and into Leah's
tent and into the tent of the two maids, but he did
not find *them.* Then he went out of Leah's tent and
entered Rachel's tent. 34 Now Rachel had taken the
[a]household idols and put them in the camel's saddle,
and she sat on them. And Laban felt through all the
tent but did not find *them.* 35 She said to her father,
"Let not my lord be angry that I cannot [A]rise before
you, for the manner of women is upon me." So he
searched but did not find the [a,B]household idols.
36 Then Jacob became angry and contended with
Laban; and Jacob said to Laban, "What is my transgression? What is my sin that you have hotly pursued me? 37 Though you have felt through all my
goods, what have you found of all your household
goods? Set *it* here before my [a]kinsmen and your
[a]kinsmen, that they may decide between us two.
38 These twenty years I *have been* with you; your
ewes and your female goats have not miscarried,
nor have I eaten the rams of your flocks. 39 That
which was torn *of beasts* I did not bring to you; I
bore the loss of it myself. You required it of my hand
whether stolen by day or stolen by night. 40 *Thus* I
was: by day the [a]heat consumed me and the frost
by night, and my sleep fled from my eyes. 41 These
twenty years I have been in your house; [A]I served
you fourteen years for your two daughters and six
years for your flock, and you [B]changed my wages
ten times. 42 If [A]the God of my father, the God of
Abraham, and the fear of Isaac, had not been for
me, surely now you would have sent me away empty-handed. [B]God has seen my affliction and the toil
of my hands, so He [C]rendered judgment last night."

THE COVENANT OF MIZPAH

43 Then Laban replied to Jacob, "The daughters
are my daughters, and the children are my children,
and [A]the flocks are my flocks, and all that you see is
mine. But what can I do this day to these my daughters or to their children whom they have borne?

31:32 [a]Lit *brothers* [b]Lit *recognize* [c]Lit *with me* [A]Gen 44:9 31:34 [a]Heb *teraphim* 31:35 [a]Heb *teraphim* [A]Lev 19:32 [B]Gen 31:19 31:37 [a]Lit *brothers* 31:40 [a]Or *drought* 31:41 [A]Gen 29:27, 30 [B]Gen 31:7 31:42 [A]Gen 31:5, 29, 53 [B]Gen 29:32; Ex 3:7 [C]Gen 31:24, 29 31:43 [A]Gen 31:1

31:34, 35 One dishonest deed needed further dishonesty and trickery to cover it up.

31:35 the manner of women. Rachel claimed she was having her menstrual period.

31:37 decide between us two. Rachel's theft and dishonest cover-up had precipitated a major conflict between her father and her husband which could only be resolved by judicial inquiry before witnesses.

31:38–42 Jacob registered his complaint that he had unfairly borne the losses normally carried by the owner and had endured much discomfort in fulfilling his responsibility. Jacob also delivered his conclusion that except for the oversight of God, Laban may very well have fleeced him totally.

31:42 fear of Isaac. Also see "the fear of his father Isaac" (v. 53). This was another divine name, signifying Jacob's identification of the God who caused Isaac to reverence Him.

31:43 Laban pled his case, amounting to nothing more than the manifestation of his grasping character, by claiming everything was his.

FALSE GODS IN THE OLD TESTAMENT
1. Rachel's household gods (Ge 31:19)
2. The golden calf at Sinai (Ex 32)
3. Nanna, the moon god of Ur, worshiped by Abraham before his salvation (Jos 24:2)
4. Asherah, or Ashtaroth, the chief goddess of Tyre, referred to as the lady of the sea (Jdg 6:24–32)
5. Dagon, the chief Philistine agriculture and sea god and father of Baal (Jdg 16:23–30; 1Sa 5:1–7)
6. Ashtaroth, a Canaanite goddess, another consort of Baal (1Sa 7:3, 4)
7. Molech, the god of the Ammonites and the most horrible idol in the Scriptures (1Ki 11:7; 2Ch 28:14; 33:6)
8. The two golden images made by King Jeroboam, set up at the shrines of Dan and Bethel (1Ki 12:28–31)
9. Baal, the chief deity of Canaan (1Ki 18:17–40; 2Ki 10:28; 11:18)
10. Rimmon, the Syrian god of Naaman the leper (2Ki 5:15–19)
11. Nisroch, the Assyrian god of Sennacherib (2Ki 19:37)
12. Nebo, the Babylonian god of wisdom and literature (Is 46:1)
13. Merodach, also called Marduk, the chief god of the Babylonian pantheon (Jer 50:2)
14. Tammuz, the husband and brother of Ishtar (Asherah), goddess of fertility (Eze 8:14)
15. The golden image in the plain of Dura (Da 3)

44 So now come, let us [A]make a covenant, [a]you and I, and [B]let it be a witness between [b]you and me." 45 Then Jacob took [A]a stone and set it up *as* a pillar. 46 Jacob said to his [a]kinsmen, "Gather stones." So they took stones and made a heap, and they ate there by the heap. 47 Now Laban [A]called it [a]Jegar-sahadutha, but Jacob called it [b]Galeed. 48 Laban said, "[A]This heap is a witness between [a]you and me this day." Therefore it was named Galeed, 49 and [a,A]Mizpah, for he said, "May the LORD watch between [b]you and me when we are [c]absent one from the other. 50 If you mistreat my daughters, or if you take wives besides my daughters, *although* no man is with us, see, [A]God is witness between [a]you and me." 51 Laban said to Jacob, "Behold this heap and behold the pillar which I have set between [a]you and me. 52 This heap is a witness, and the pillar is a witness, that I will not pass by this heap to you for harm, and you will not pass by this heap and this pillar to me, for harm. 53 [A]The God of Abraham and the God of Nahor, the God of their father, [B]judge between us." So Jacob swore by [C]the fear of his father Isaac. 54 Then Jacob [A]offered a sacrifice on the mountain, and called his [a]kinsmen to [b]the meal; and they ate [c]the meal and spent the night on the mountain. 55 [a]Early in the morning Laban arose, and [A]kissed his sons and his daughters and blessed them. Then Laban departed and returned to his place.

JACOB'S FEAR OF ESAU

32 Now as Jacob went on his way, [A]the angels of God met him. 2 Jacob said when he saw them, "This is God's [a]camp." So he named that place [b,A]Mahanaim.

3 Then Jacob [A]sent messengers before him to his brother Esau in the land of [B]Seir, the [a]country of [C]Edom. 4 He also commanded them saying, "Thus you shall say to my lord Esau: 'Thus says your servant Jacob, "I have sojourned with Laban, and [A]stayed until now; 5 [A]I have oxen and donkeys *and* flocks and male and female servants; and I have sent to tell my lord, [B]that I may find favor in your sight." ' "

6 The messengers returned to Jacob, saying, "We came to your brother Esau, and furthermore [A]he is coming to meet you, and four hundred men are with him." 7 Then Jacob was [A]greatly afraid and distressed; and he divided the people who were with him, and the flocks and the herds and the camels, into two companies; 8 for he said, "If Esau comes to the one company and [a]attacks it, then the company which is left will escape."

9 Jacob said, "O [A]God of my father Abraham and God of my father Isaac, O LORD, who said to me, '[B]Return to your country and to your relatives, and I will [a]prosper you,' 10 [a]I am unworthy [A]of all the lovingkindness and of all the [b]faithfulness which You have shown to Your servant; for with my staff *only* I crossed this Jordan, and now I have become two companies. 11 [A]Deliver me, I pray, [B]from the hand of my brother, from the hand of Esau; for I fear him, that he will come and [a]attack me *and* the [C]mothers with the children. 12 For You said, '[A]I will surely [a]prosper you and [B]make your [b]descendants as the sand of the sea, which is too great to be numbered.' "

13 So he spent the night there. Then he [a]selected from what [b]he had with him a [A]present for his brother Esau: 14 two hundred female goats and twenty male goats, two hundred ewes and twenty rams, 15 thirty milking camels and their colts, forty cows and ten bulls, twenty female donkeys and ten male donkeys. 16 He delivered *them* into the hand of his servants, every drove by itself, and said to his servants, "Pass on before me, and put a space

31:44 [a]Lit *I and you* [b]Lit *me and you* [A]Gen 21:27, 32; 26:28 [B]Josh 24:27 31:45 [A]Gen 28:18; Josh 24:26, 27 31:46 [a]Lit *brothers* 31:47 [a]I.e. the heap of witness, in Aram [b]I.e. the heap of witness, in Heb [A]Josh 22:34 31:48 [a]Lit *me and you* [A]Josh 24:27 31:49 [a]Lit *the Mizpah;* i.e. the watchtower [b]Lit *me and you* [c]Lit *hidden* [A]Judg 11:29; 1 Sam 7:5, 6 31:50 [a]Lit *me and you* [A]Jer 29:23; 42:5 31:51 [a]Lit *me and you* 31:53 [A]Gen 28:13 [B]Gen 16:5 [C]Gen 31:42 31:54 [a]Lit *brothers* [b]Lit *eat bread* [c]Lit *bread* [A]Ex 18:12 31:55 [a]Ch 32:1 in Heb [A]Gen 31:28, 43 32:1 [A]2 Kin 6:16, 17; Ps 34:7 32:2 [a]Or *company* [b]I.e. Two Camps, or Two Companies [A]Josh 21:38; 2 Sam 2:8 32:3 [a]Lit *field* [A]Gen 27:41, 42; 32:7, 11 [B]Gen 14:6; 33:14 [C]Gen 25:30; 36:8, 9 32:4 [A]Gen 31:41 32:5 [A]Gen 30:43 [B]Gen 33:8 32:6 [A]Gen 33:1 32:7 [A]Gen 32:11 32:8 [a]Lit *smites* 32:9 [a]Lit *do good with you* [A]Gen 28:13; 31:42 [B]Gen 28:15; 31:3, 13 32:10 [a]Lit *I am less than all* [b]Or *truth* [A]Gen 24:27 32:11 [a]Lit *smite* [A]Ps 59:1, 2 [B]Gen 27:41, 42; 33:4 [C]Hos 10:14 32:12 [a]Lit *do good with* [b]Lit *seed* [A]Gen 28:14 [B]Gen 22:17 32:13 [a]Lit *took* [b]Lit *had come to his hand* [A]Gen 43:11

31:44 let us make a covenant. Although Laban did regard all in Jacob's hands as his—after all Jacob had arrived 20 years before with nothing—nevertheless, the matter was clearly ruled in Jacob's favor, since Laban left with nothing. A treaty was struck in the customary fashion (vv. 45–51) in which they covenanted not to harm each other again (v. 52). With heaps of stones as testaments to the treaty named and in place (vv. 47–49), with the consecration meals having been eaten (vv. 46, 54), and with the appropriate oaths and statements made in the name of their God (vv. 50, 53), the agreement was properly sanctioned and concluded and thus they parted company. All contact between Abraham's kin in Canaan and Mesopotamia appears to have ended at this point.

31:47–49 Jegar-sahadutha … Galeed … Mizpah. The first two words mean in Aramaic and also Hebrew, "heap of witnesses." The third word means "watchtower."

31:53 God of Nahor. Laban's probable syncretistic paralleling of the God of Abraham with that of Nahor and Terah, his brother and father respectively, elicited Jacob again using "the fear of Isaac," a reference to the true God (v. 42), for he certainly could not give credence to any of Laban's syncretistic allusions.

32:1 the angels of God. With one crisis behind him and before him the suspense of having to face Esau, Jacob was first met by an angelic host, who must have reminded him of Bethel, which served also as a timely reminder and encouragement of God's will being done on earth (28:11–15).

32:2 God's camp … Mahanaim. Meaning "double camp," i.e., one being God's and one being his own. It was located E of the Jordan River in Gilead near the River Jabbok.

32:3 Seir … Edom. The territory of Esau S of the Dead Sea.

32:7 greatly afraid and distressed. He had sought reconciliation with Esau (vv. 4, 5), but the report of the returning envoys (v. 6) only confirmed his deepest suspicions that Esau's old threat against him (27:41, 42) had not abated over the years, and his coming with force betokened only disaster (vv. 8, 11). He prepared for the attack by dividing his company of people and animals.

32:9–12 Commendably, notwithstanding the plans to appease his brother (vv. 13–21), Jacob prayed for deliverance, rehearsing God's own commands and covenant promise (v. 12; see 28:13–15), acknowledging his own anxiety, and confessing his own unworthiness before the Lord. This was Jacob's first recorded prayer since his encounter with God at Bethel en route to Laban (28:20–22).

32:13–21 The logistics of Jacob's careful

between droves." 17 He commanded the [a]one in
front, saying, "When my brother Esau meets you
and asks you, saying, 'To whom do you belong,
and where are you going, and to whom do these
animals in front of you belong?' 18 then you shall
say, '*These* belong to your servant Jacob; it is a
present sent to my lord Esau. And behold, he also
is behind us.' " 19 Then he commanded also the
second and the third, and all those who followed
the droves, saying, "After this manner you shall
speak to Esau when you find him; 20 and you shall
say, 'Behold, your servant Jacob also is behind us.' "
For he said, "I will appease him with the present
that goes before me. Then afterward I will see his
face; perhaps he will accept me." 21 So the present
passed on before him, while he himself spent that
night in the camp.
22 Now he arose that same night and took his two
wives and his two maids and his eleven children,
and crossed the ford of the [A]Jabbok. 23 He took them
and sent them across the stream. And he sent across
whatever he had.

JACOB WRESTLES

24 Then Jacob was left alone, and a man [A]wrestled
with him until daybreak. 25 When he saw that he had
not prevailed against him, he touched the socket of
his thigh; so the socket of Jacob's thigh was dislocated while he wrestled with him. 26 Then he said,
"Let me go, for the dawn is breaking." But he said, "[A]I
will not let you go unless you bless me." 27 So he said
to him, "What is your name?" And he said, "Jacob."
28 [A]He said, "Your name shall no longer be Jacob,
but [a]Israel; for you have striven with God and with
men and have prevailed." 29 Then [A]Jacob asked him
and said, "Please tell me your name." But he said,
"Why is it that you ask my name?" And he blessed
him there. 30 So Jacob named the place [a]Peniel, for
he said, "[A]I have seen God face to face, yet my [b]life
has been preserved." 31 Now the sun rose upon him
just as he crossed over [A]Penuel, and he was limping
on his thigh. 32 Therefore, to this day the sons of Israel do not eat the sinew of the hip which is on the
socket of the thigh, because he touched the socket
of Jacob's thigh in the sinew of the hip.

32:17 [a]Lit *first* 32:22 [A]Deut 3:16; Josh 12:2 32:24 [A]Hos 12:3, 4 32:26 [A]Hos 12:4 32:28 [a]I.e. he who strives with God; or God strives [A]Gen 35:10; 1 Kin 18:31 32:29 [A]Judg 13:17, 18 32:30 [a]I.e. the face of God [b]Lit *soul* [A]Gen 16:13; Ex 24:10, 11; 33:20; Num 12:8; Judg 6:22; 13:22 32:31 [A]Judg 8:8

appeasement strategy (550 animals Esau would prize) may highlight his ability to plan but it highlights even more, given the goal statement at the end (v. 20), his failure to pray and believe that God would change Esau's heart.

32:22–32 This unique, nightlong wrestling match at Peniel ends with the 97 year old Jacob having a change of name (v. 28) and the place having a new name assigned to it (v. 30) in order to memorialize it for Jacob and later generations. The limp with which he emerged from the match (vv. 25, 31) also served to memorialize this event.

32:22 Jabbok. A stream, 60–65 mi. long, E of the Jordan which flows into that river midway between the Sea of Galilee and the Dead Sea (ca. 45 mi. S of the Sea of Galilee).

32:24 a man wrestled. The site name, Peniel, or "face of God," given by Jacob (v. 30) and the commentary given by Hosea (Hos 12:4) identifies this man with whom Jacob wrestled as the Angel of the Lord who is also identified as God, a pre-incarnate appearance of the Lord Jesus Christ. *See note on Ex 3:2.*

32:28 no longer ... Jacob, but Israel. Jacob's personal name changed from one meaning "heel-catcher" or "deceiver" to one meaning "God's fighter" or "he struggles with God" (cf. 35:10). **with God and with men.** An amazing evaluation of what Jacob had accomplished, i.e., emerging victorious from the struggle. In the record of his life, "struggle" did indeed dominate: 1) with his brother Esau (chaps. 25–27); 2) with his father (chap. 27); 3) with his father-in-law (chaps. 29–31); 4) with his wives (chap. 30); and 5) with God at Peniel (v. 28).

32:30 Peniel. *See note on v. 24.*

32:32 not eat the sinew of the hip. This might refer to the sciatic muscle/tendon. The observation that up to Moses' time ("to this day") the nation of Israel did not eat this part of a hindquarter intrigues because it bears no mention elsewhere in the OT, nor is it enshrined in the Mosaic law. It does find mention in the Jewish Talmud as a sacred law.

JACOB RETURNS TO CANAAN

After 20 years in northern Mesopotamia, Jacob returned to Canaan. On the way, he encountered God face-to-face at Penuel (32:30, 31).

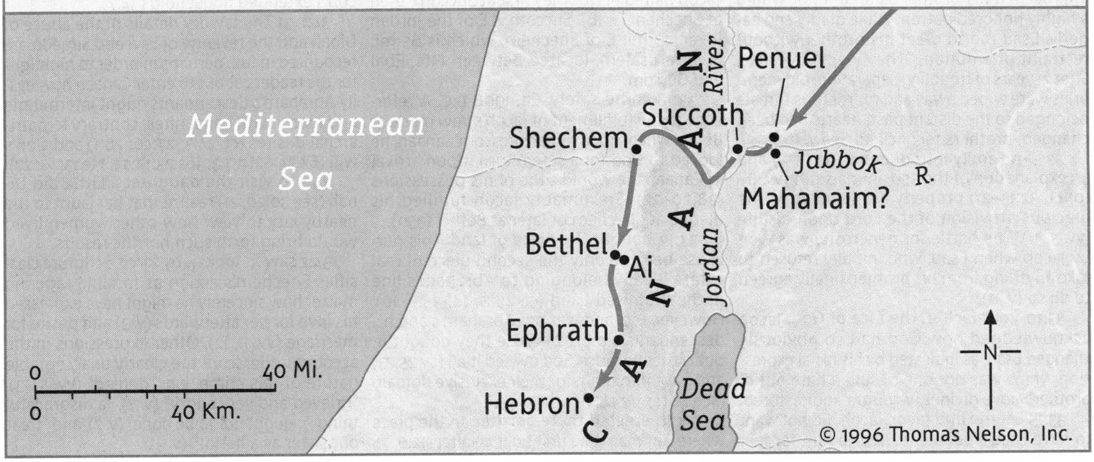

JACOB MEETS ESAU

33 Then Jacob lifted his eyes and looked, and
behold, [A]Esau was coming, and four hundred
men with him. So he divided the children [a]among
Leah and Rachel and the two maids. 2 He put the
maids and their children [a]in front, and Leah and her
children [b]next, and Rachel and Joseph [b]last. 3 But
he himself passed on ahead of them and [A]bowed
down to the ground seven times, until he came
near to his brother.
4 Then Esau ran to meet him and embraced him,
and [A]fell on his neck and kissed him, and they wept.
5 He lifted his eyes and saw the women and the children, and said, "[a]Who are these with you?" So he
said, "[A]The children whom God has graciously given
your servant." 6 Then the maids came near [a]with
their children, and they bowed down. 7 Leah likewise came near with her children, and they bowed
down; and afterward Joseph came near with Rachel,
and they bowed down. 8 And he said, "What do you
mean by [A]all this company which I have met?" And
he said, "[B]To find favor in the sight of my lord." 9 But
Esau said, "[A]I have plenty, my brother; let what
you have be your own." 10 Jacob said, "No, please,
if now I have found favor in your sight, then take
my present from my hand, [a]for I see your face as
one sees the face of God, and you have received me
favorably. 11 Please take my [a,A]gift which has been
brought to you, [B]because God has dealt graciously
with me and because I have [b]plenty." Thus he urged
him and he took *it*.
12 Then [a]Esau said, "Let us take our journey and
go, and I will go before you." 13 But he said to him,
"My lord knows that the children are frail and that
the flocks and herds which are nursing are [a]a care
to me. And if they are driven hard one day, all the
flocks will die. 14 Please let my lord pass on before
his servant, and I will proceed at my leisure, according to the pace of the cattle that are before me and
according to the pace of the children, until I come
to my lord at [A]Seir."
15 Esau said, "Please let me leave with you some
of the people who are with me." But he said, "[a]What
need is there? [A]Let me find favor in the sight of my
lord." 16 So Esau returned that day on his way to
Seir. 17 Jacob journeyed to [a,A]Succoth, and built for
himself a house and made booths for his livestock;
therefore the place is named Succoth.

JACOB SETTLES IN SHECHEM

18 Now Jacob came safely to the city of [A]Shechem,
which is in the land of Canaan, when he came from
[B]Paddan-aram, and camped before the city. 19 [A]He
bought the piece of land where he had pitched his
tent from the hand of the sons of Hamor, Shechem's
father, for one hundred [a]pieces of money. 20 Then he
erected there an altar and called it [a]El-Elohe-Israel.

THE TREACHERY OF JACOB'S SONS

34 Now [A]Dinah the daughter of Leah, whom
she had borne to Jacob, went out to [a]visit the
daughters of the land. 2 When Shechem the son of
Hamor [A]the Hivite, the prince of the land, saw her,
he took her and lay with her [a]by force. 3 [a]He was
deeply attracted to Dinah the daughter of Jacob,
and he loved the girl and [b]spoke tenderly to her. 4 So

33:1 [a]Or *to* [A]Gen 32:6 33:2 [a]Lit *first* [b]Lit *behind* 33:3 [A]Gen 42:6; 43:26 33:4 [A]Gen 45:14, 15 33:5 [a]Or *What relation are these to you?* [A]Gen 48:9; Ps 127:3; Is 8:18 33:6 [a]Lit *they and* 33:8 [A]Gen 32:13-16 [B]Gen 32:5 33:9 [A]Gen 27:39, 40 33:10 [a]Lit *for therefore I have seen your face like seeing God's face* 33:11 [a]Lit *blessing* [b]Lit *all* [A]1 Sam 25:27 [B]Gen 30:43 33:12 [a]Lit *he* 33:13 [a]Lit *upon me* 33:14 [A]Gen 32:3 33:15 [a]Lit *Why this?* [A]Ruth 2:13 33:17 [a]I.e. booths [A]Josh 13:27; Judg 8:5, 14; Ps 60:6 33:18 [A]Gen 12:6; Josh 24:1; Judg 9:1 [B]Gen 25:20; 28:2 33:19 [a]Heb *qesitah* [A]Josh 24:32; John 4:5 33:20 [a]I.e. God, the God of Israel 34:1 [a]Lit *see* [A]Gen 30:21 34:2 [a]Lit *and humbled her* [A]Gen 34:30 34:3 [a]Lit *His soul clung* [b]Lit *spoke to the heart of the girl*

33:1, 2 Esau was coming. Jacob hastily divided his family into 3 groups (cf. 32:7) and went ahead of them to meet his brother. The division and relative location of his family in relationship to the perceived danger gives tremendous insight into whom Jacob favored.

33:3, 4 Fearfully and deferentially, Jacob approached his brother as an inferior would a highly honored patron, while gladly and eagerly, Esau ran to greet his brother without restraint of emotion. "They wept" because, after 21 years of troubling separation, old memories were wiped away and murderous threats belonged to the distant past; hearts had been changed, brothers reconciled! See v. 10.

33:5–11 Family introductions (vv. 5–7) and an explanation of the 550 animals gift (vv. 8–10; cf. 32:13–21) properly acknowledged the gracious provision of the Lord upon his life (vv. 5, 11). The battle for generosity was won by Jacob when Esau, who initially refused to take anything from his brother, finally agreed to do so (v. 11).

33:10 your face ... the face of God. Jacob acknowledged how God had so obviously changed Esau, as indicated by his facial expression which was not one of sullen hate but of brotherly love divinely wrought and restored.

33:15 Let me find favor. Jacob did not want to have Esau's people loaned to him for fear something might happen to again fracture their relationship.

33:16, 17 to Seir ... to Succoth. With Esau's planned escort courteously dismissed, they parted company. Jacob's expressed intention to meet again in Seir (*see note on 32:3*), for whatever reason, did not materialize. Instead, Jacob halted his journey first at Succoth, then at Shechem (v. 18). Succoth is E of the Jordan River, 20 mi. E of Shechem, which is 65 mi. N of Jerusalem, located between Mts. Ebal and Gerizim.

33:18 came safely. Ca. 1908 B.C. A reference to the fulfillment of Jacob's vow made at Bethel when, upon departure from Canaan, he looked to God for a safe return. Upon arrival in Canaan, he would tithe of his possessions (28:20–22). Presumably Jacob fulfilled his pledge at Shechem or later at Bethel (35:1).

33:19 bought the piece of land. This purchase became only the second piece of real estate legally belonging to Abraham's line in the Promised Land (cf. 23:17, 18; 25:9, 10). However, the land was not Abraham's and his descendants simply because they bought it, but rather because God owned it all (Lv 25:23) and gave it to them for their exclusive domain (*see notes on 12:1–3*).

33:20 erected there an altar. In the place where Abraham had first built an altar (12:6, 7), Jacob similarly marked the spot with a new name, incorporating his own new name (32:28), "God, the God of Israel," declaring that he worshiped the "Mighty One." "Israel" perhaps foreshadowed its use for the nation with which it rapidly became associated, even when it consisted of not much more than Jacob's extended household (34:7).

34:1–31 The tawdry details of the abuse of Dinah and the revenge of Levi and Simeon are recounted in full, perhaps in order to highlight for the readers about to enter Canaan how easily Abraham's descendants might intermingle and marry with Canaanites, contrary to patriarchal desires (cf. 24:3; 27:46; 28:1) and God's will (Ex 34:6; Dt 7:3; Jos 23:12, 13; Ne 13:26, 27).

34:1 to visit the daughters. Little did Dinah (see 30:20, 21) realize that her jaunt to the nearby city to view how other women lived would bring forth such horrific results.

34:2 saw ... took ... by force. Scripture classifies Shechem's action as forcible rape, no matter how sincerely he might have expressed his love for her afterwards (v. 3) and desire for marriage (vv. 11, 12). Other expressions in the account underscore the clearly unacceptable nature of this crime, e.g. "defiled" (vv. 5, 13), "grieved and very angry" (v. 7), "a disgraceful thing ... ought not to be done" (v. 7), and "treat our sister as a harlot" (v. 31).

Shechem [A]spoke to his father Hamor, saying, "Get me this young girl for a wife." 5 Now Jacob heard that he had defiled Dinah his daughter; but his sons were with his livestock in the field, so Jacob kept silent until they came in. 6 Then Hamor the father of Shechem went out to Jacob to speak with him. 7 Now the sons of Jacob came in from the field when they heard *it;* and the men were grieved, and they were very angry because he had done a [a,A]disgraceful thing in Israel [b]by lying with Jacob's daughter, for such a thing ought not to be done.

8 But Hamor spoke with them, saying, "The soul of my son Shechem longs for your daughter; please give her to him [a]in marriage. 9 Intermarry with us; give your daughters to us and take our daughters for yourselves. 10 Thus you shall [a]live with us, and [A]the land shall be *open* before you; [a]live and [B]trade in it and [C]acquire property in it." 11 Shechem also said to her father and to her brothers, "If I find favor in your sight, then I will give whatever you say to me. 12 Ask me ever so much bridal payment and gift, and I will give according as you say to me; but give me the girl [a]in marriage."

13 But Jacob's sons answered Shechem and his father Hamor with deceit, because he had defiled Dinah their sister. 14 They said to them, "We cannot do this thing, to give our sister to [A]one who is uncircumcised, for that would be a disgrace to us. 15 Only on this *condition* will we consent to you: if you will become like us, in that every male of you be circumcised, 16 then we will give our daughters to you, and we will take your daughters for ourselves, and we will [a]live with you and become one people. 17 But if you will not listen to us to be circumcised, then we will take our daughter and go."

18 Now their words seemed [a]reasonable to Hamor and Shechem, Hamor's son. 19 The young man did not delay to do the thing, because he was delighted with Jacob's daughter. Now he was more respected than all the household of his father. 20 So Hamor and his son Shechem came to the [A]gate of their city and spoke to the men of their city, saying, 21 "These men are [a]friendly with us; therefore let them [b]live in the land and trade in it, for behold, the land is [c]large enough for them. Let us take their daughters [d]in marriage, and give our daughters to them. 22 Only on this *condition* will the men consent to us to [a]live with us, to become one people: that every male among us be circumcised as they are circumcised. 23 Will not their livestock and their property and all their animals be ours? Only let us consent to them, and they will [a]live with us." 24 [A]All who went out of the gate of his city listened to Hamor and to his son Shechem, and every male was circumcised, all who went out of the gate of his city.

25 Now it came about on the third day, when they were in pain, that two of Jacob's sons, [A]Simeon and Levi, Dinah's brothers, each took his sword and came upon the city unawares, and killed every male. 26 They killed Hamor and his son Shechem with the edge of the sword, and took Dinah from Shechem's house, and went forth. 27 Jacob's sons came upon the slain and looted the city, because they had defiled their sister. 28 They took their flocks and their herds and their donkeys, and that which was in the city and that which was in the field; 29 and they captured and looted all their wealth and all their little ones and their wives, even all that *was* in the houses. 30 Then Jacob said to Simeon and Levi, "You have [A]brought trouble on me by [B]making me odious among the inhabitants of the land, among [C]the Canaanites and the Perizzites; and [a,D]my men being few in number, they will gather together against me and [b]attack me and I will be destroyed, I and my household." 31 But they said, "Should he [a]treat our sister as a harlot?"

JACOB MOVES TO BETHEL

35 Then God said to Jacob, "Arise, go up to [A]Bethel and [a]live there, and make an altar there to [B]God, who appeared to you [C]when you fled [b]from your brother Esau." 2 So Jacob said to his

34:4 [A]Judg 14:2 34:7 [a]Lit *senseless* [b]Lit *to lie* [A]Deut 22:20-30; Judg 20:6; 2 Sam 13:12 34:8 [a]Lit *for a wife* 34:10 [a]Lit *dwell* [A]Gen 13:9; 20:15 [B]Gen 42:34 [C]Gen 47:27 34:12 [a]Lit *for a wife* 34:14 [A]Gen 17:14 34:16 [a]Lit *dwell* 34:18 [a]Lit *good* 34:20 [A]Ruth 4:1; 2 Sam 15:2 34:21 [a]Lit *peaceful* [b]Lit *dwell* [c]Lit *wide of hands before them* [d]Lit *to us for wives* 34:22 [a]Lit *dwell* 34:23 [a]Lit *dwell* 34:24 [A]Gen 23:10 34:25 [A]Gen 49:5-7 34:30 [a]Lit *I, few in number* [b]Lit *smite* [A]Josh 7:25 [B]Ex 5:21; 1 Sam 13:4; 2 Sam 10:6 [C]Gen 13:7; 34:2 [D]Gen 46:26, 27; Deut 4:27; 1 Chr 16:19; Ps 105:12 34:31 [a]Or *make* 35:1 [a]Lit *dwell* [b]Lit *from the face of* [A]Gen 28:19 [B]Gen 28:13 [C]Gen 27:43

34:5 **Jacob kept silent.** In the absence of further data, Jacob's reticence to respond should not be criticized. Wisdom dictated that he wait and counsel with his sons, but their reaction, grief, anger, and vengeance hijacked the talks between Jacob and Hamor (v. 6) and led finally to Jacob's stern rebuke (v. 30).

34:6–10 The prince of Shechem painted a picture of harmonious integration (v. 16, "become one people"). However, Shechemite self-interest and enrichment actually prevailed (v. 23).

34:7 **in Israel.** Already Jacob's household is being called by the name God had given him as father of the coming nation (32:28).

34:13–17 Feigning interest in the proposals put forward and misusing, if not abusing, the circumcision sign of the Abrahamic Covenant (*see notes on 17:11–14*), Jacob's sons conned both father and son into convincing all the men to submit to circumcision because the outcome would be to their favor with marriages (v. 9) and social, economic integration (v. 10).

34:19 **he was more respected.** Meaning that the men agreed to such an excruciating surgery (vv. 24, 25) because they had so much respect for him and because they anticipated mercenary benefit (v. 23).

34:20 **gate of their city.** The normal place for public gatherings.

34:25–29 A massacre of all males and the wholesale plunder of the city went way beyond the reasonable, wise, and justly deserved punishment of one man; this was a considerably more excessive vengeance than the Mosaic law would later legislate (cf. Dt 22:28, 29).

34:27 **Jacob's sons.** Simeon and Levi set in motion the barbarity of that day and attention validly falls upon them in the narrative (vv. 25, 30; cf. 49:5–7), but their brothers joined in the looting, thereby approving murder and mayhem as justifiable retribution for the destroyed honor of their sister (v. 31).

34:30 **You have brought trouble on me.** Vengeance exacted meant retaliation expected. Total loss of respect ("making me odious") and of peaceful relations (v. 21) put both him and them in harm's way with survival being highly unlikely. This threat tested God's promise of safety, giving Jacob cause for great concern (28:15; 32:9, 12). **Perizzites.** *See note on 13:7.*

35:1 **Bethel.** This was the place where God confirmed the Abrahamic Covenant to Jacob (28:13–15).

35:2–4 **Put away the foreign gods.** Moving to Bethel necessitated spiritual preparation beyond the level of an exercise in logistics. Possession of idolatrous symbols such as figurines, amulets, or cultic charms (v. 4, "rings ... in their ears") were no longer tolerable, including Rachel's troubling teraphim (31:19). Idols buried

[A]household and to all who were with him, "Put away
[B]the foreign gods which are among you, and [C]purify
yourselves and change your garments; 3 and let us
arise and go up to Bethel, and I will make [A]an altar
there to God, [B]who answered me in the day of my
distress and [C]has been with me [a]wherever I have
gone." 4 So they gave to Jacob all the foreign gods
which [a]they had and the rings which were in their
ears, and Jacob hid them under the [b]oak which was
near Shechem.
5 As they journeyed, there was [a,A]a great terror
upon the cities which were around them, and they
did not pursue the sons of Jacob. 6 So Jacob came
to [A]Luz (that is, Bethel), which is in the land of Canaan, he and all the people who were with him. 7 [A]He
built an altar there, and called the place [a]El-bethel,
because there God had revealed Himself to him
when he fled [b]from his brother. 8 Now [A]Deborah,
Rebekah's nurse, died, and she was buried below
Bethel under the oak; it was named [a]Allon-bacuth.

JACOB IS NAMED ISRAEL

9 Then God appeared to Jacob again when he
came from Paddan-aram, and He [A]blessed him.
10 [A]God said to him,

"Your name is Jacob;
[a]You shall no longer be called Jacob,
But Israel shall be your name."

Thus He called [b]him Israel. 11 God also said to him,

"I am [a,A]God Almighty;
[B]Be fruitful and multiply;
A nation and a [C]company of nations
shall [b]come from you,
And [D]kings shall [b]come forth from [c]you.
12 "[A]The land which I gave to
Abraham and Isaac,
I will give it to you,
And I will give the land to your
[a]descendants after you."

13 Then [A]God went up from him in the place where
He had spoken with him. 14 Jacob set up [A]a pillar in
the place where He had spoken with him, a pillar
of stone, and he poured out a drink offering on it;
he also poured oil on it. 15 So Jacob named the place
where God had spoken with him, [a,A]Bethel.
16 Then they journeyed from Bethel; and when
there was still some distance to go to [A]Ephrath, Rachel
began to give birth and she [a]suffered severe labor.
17 When she was in severe labor the midwife said to
her, "Do not fear, for now [A]you have another son." 18 It
came about as her soul was departing (for she died),
that she named him [a]Ben-oni; but his father called
him [b]Benjamin. 19 So [A]Rachel died and was buried
on the way to [B]Ephrath (that is, Bethlehem). 20 Jacob
set up a pillar over her grave; that is the [A]pillar of
Rachel's grave to this day. 21 Then Israel journeyed
on and pitched his tent beyond the [a,A]tower of [b]Eder.
22 It came about while Israel was dwelling in that
land, that [A]Reuben went and lay with Bilhah his
father's concubine, and Israel heard *of it.*

THE SONS OF ISRAEL

Now there were twelve sons of Jacob— 23 [A]the sons
of Leah: Reuben, Jacob's firstborn, then Simeon and
Levi and Judah and Issachar and Zebulun; 24 [A]the sons
of Rachel: Joseph and Benjamin; 25 and [A]the sons of Bilhah, Rachel's maid: Dan and Naphtali; 26 and [A]the sons
of Zilpah, Leah's maid: Gad and Asher. These are the
sons of Jacob who were born to him in Paddan-aram.
27 Jacob came to his father Isaac at [A]Mamre of
[B]Kiriath-arba (that is, Hebron), where Abraham
and Isaac had sojourned.
28 Now the days of Isaac were [A]one hundred and
eighty years. 29 Isaac breathed his last and died
and was [A]gathered to his people, an [B]old man [a]of
ripe age; and [C]his sons Esau and Jacob buried him.

35:2 [A]Gen 18:19; Josh 24:15 [B]Gen 31:19, 30, 34 [C]Ex 19:10, 14 35:3 [a]Lit *in the way which* [A]Gen 28:20-22 [B]Ps 107:6 [C]Gen 28:15; 31:3, 42 35:4 [a]Lit *were in their hand* [b]Or *terebinth* 35:5 [a]Or *a terror of God* [A]Ex 15:16; 23:27; Deut 2:25 35:6 [A]Gen 28:19; 48:3 35:7 [a]I.e. the God of Bethel [b]Lit *from the face of* [A]Gen 35:3 35:8 [a]I.e. oak of weeping [A]Gen 24:59 35:9 [A]Gen 32:29 35:10 [a]Lit *Your name* [b]Lit *his name* [A]Gen 17:5; 32:28 35:11 [a]Heb *El Shaddai* [b]Or *come into being* [c]Lit *your loins* [A]Gen 17:1; 28:3; Ex 6:3 [B]Gen 9:1, 7 [C]Gen 48:4 [D]Gen 17:6, 16; 36:31 35:12 [a]Lit *seed* [A]Gen 12:7; 13:15; 26:3, 4; 28:13; Ex 32:13 35:13 [A]Gen 17:22; 18:33 35:14 [A]Gen 28:18, 19; 31:45 35:15 [a]I.e. the house of God [A]Gen 28:19 35:16 [a]Lit *had difficulty in her giving birth* [A]Gen 35:19; 48:7; Ruth 4:11; Mic 5:2 35:17 [A]Gen 30:24 35:18 [a]I.e. the son of my sorrow [b]I.e. the son of the right hand 35:19 [A]Gen 48:7 [B]Ruth 1:2; 4:11; Mic 5:2 35:20 [A]1 Sam 10:2 35:21 [a]Heb *Migdal-eder* [b]Or *flock* [A]Mic 4:8 35:22 [A]Gen 49:4; 1 Chr 5:1 35:23 [A]Gen 29:31-35; 30:18-20; 46:8; Ex 1:1-4 35:24 [A]Gen 30:22-24; 35:18 35:25 [A]Gen 30:5-8 35:26 [A]Gen 30:10-13 35:27 [A]Gen 13:18; 18:1; 23:19 [B]Josh 14:15 35:28 [A]Gen 25:26 35:29 [a]Lit *and satisfied with days* [A]Gen 25:8; 49:33 [B]Gen 15:15 [C]Gen 25:9

out of sight, plus bathing and changing to clean clothes, all served to portray both cleansing from defilement by idolatry and consecration of the heart to the Lord. It had been 8 or 10 years since his return to Canaan and, appropriately, time enough to clean up all traces of idolatry.

35:4 oak … near Shechem. Possibly this was the same tree as in Abraham's day (12:6).

35:5 a great terror. A supernaturally induced fear of Israel rendered the surrounding city-states unwilling and powerless to intervene and made Jacob's fear of their retaliation rather inconsequential (34:30).

35:7 built an altar there. Through this act of worship, fulfillment of his vow (28:20–22), and renaming the site, Jacob reconfirmed his allegiance to God, who also affirmed His commitment to Jacob by re-appearing to him, repeating the change of name (v. 10; cf. 32:28), and rehearsing the Abrahamic promises (vv. 11, 12). In response, Jacob also repeated the rite he had performed when he first met God at Bethel (v. 14) and reaffirmed its name (v. 15).

35:11 kings shall come forth from you. God's words, here included for the first time since His promises at Abraham's circumcision (17:6, 16), served as a reminder of future royalty.

35:13 went up. The presence of God was there in some visible form.

35:14 A commonly done way to make a covenant (*see note on 28:18–21*).

35:16 Ephrath. A more ancient name for Bethlehem (v. 19; 48:7; cf. Micah 5:2).

35:18 Ben-oni … Benjamin. The dying mother appropriately named her newly born son "Son of my sorrow," but the grieving father named him "Son of my right hand," thus assigning him a place of honor in the home. Her prayer at the birth of her firstborn was answered (30:24).

35:20 The memorial to Rachel could still be seen in Moses' day, about one mi. N of Bethlehem.

35:21 tower of Eder. Likely a watchtower for shepherds, near Bethlehem.

35:22 twelve sons of Jacob. The birth of Benjamin in Canaan (v. 18) furnished reason to simply review the sons born outside of Canaan, with only one sad note preceding it, i.e., the sin of Reuben, which tainted the qualifier "Jacob's firstborn" in the listing (see 49:3, 4; Dt 22:30; 1Ch 5:1, 2).

35:27 Mamre … Hebron. *See note on 13:18.*

35:29 his sons Esau and Jacob. Ca. 1885 B.C. Isaac's funeral brought his two sons back together, as Abraham's funeral had done for Isaac and Ishmael (25:9). Jacob, back in the land before his father's death, fulfilled yet another part of his Bethel vow (28:21, "return to my father's house in safety").

ESAU MOVES

36 Now these are *the records of* the generations
of [A]Esau (that is, Edom).
2 Esau [A]took his wives from the daughters of Canaan: Adah the daughter of Elon the Hittite, and
[B]Oholibamah the daughter of Anah and the [C]grand-
daughter of Zibeon the Hivite; 3 also Basemath, Ishmael's daughter, the sister of Nebaioth. 4 Adah bore
[A]Eliphaz to Esau, and Basemath bore Reuel, 5 and
Oholibamah bore Jeush and Jalam and Korah. These
are the sons of Esau who were born to him in the
land of Canaan.
6 [A]Then Esau took his wives and his sons and his
daughters and all [a]his household, and his livestock
and all his cattle and all his goods which he had acquired in the land of Canaan, and went to *another*
land away from his brother Jacob. 7 [A]For their property had become too great for them to [a]live together,
and the [B]land where they [C]sojourned could not sustain them because of their livestock. 8 So Esau lived
in the hill country of [A]Seir; Esau is [B]Edom.

DESCENDANTS OF ESAU

9 These then are *the records of* the generations of
Esau the father of [a]the Edomites in the hill country
of Seir. 10 These are the names of Esau's sons: Eliphaz
the son of Esau's wife Adah, Reuel the son of Esau's
wife Basemath. 11 The sons of Eliphaz were Teman,
Omar, [a]Zepho and Gatam and Kenaz. 12 Timna was
a concubine of Esau's son Eliphaz and she bore
[A]Amalek to Eliphaz. These are the sons of Esau's
wife Adah. 13 These are the sons of Reuel: Nahath
and Zerah, Shammah and Mizzah. These were the
sons of Esau's wife Basemath. 14 These were the
sons of Esau's wife Oholibamah, the daughter of
Anah and the [a]granddaughter of Zibeon: [b]she bore
to Esau, Jeush and Jalam and Korah.
15 These are the chiefs of the sons of Esau. The sons
of Eliphaz, the firstborn of Esau, are chief Teman,
chief Omar, chief Zepho, chief Kenaz, 16 chief Korah,
chief Gatam, chief Amalek. These are the chiefs [a]de-
scended from Eliphaz in the land of Edom; these are
the sons of Adah. 17 These are the sons of Reuel, Esau's
son: chief Nahath, chief Zerah, chief Shammah, chief
Mizzah. These are the chiefs [a]descended from Reuel
in the land of Edom; these are the sons of Esau's
wife Basemath. 18 These are the sons of Esau's wife
Oholibamah: chief Jeush, chief Jalam, chief Korah.
These are the chiefs [a]descended from Esau's wife
Oholibamah, the daughter of Anah. 19 These are the
sons of Esau (that is, Edom), and these are their chiefs.
20 These are the sons of Seir [A]the Horite, the inhabitants of the land: Lotan and Shobal and Zibeon
and Anah, 21 and Dishon and Ezer and Dishan. These
are the chiefs [a]descended from the Horites, the sons
of Seir in the land of Edom. 22 The sons of Lotan were
Hori and [a]Hemam; and Lotan's sister was Timna.
23 These are the sons of Shobal: [a]Alvan and Manahath and Ebal, [b]Shepho and Onam. 24 These are
the sons of Zibeon: Aiah and Anah—he is the Anah
who found the hot springs in the wilderness when
he was pasturing the donkeys of his father Zibeon.
25 These are the children of Anah: Dishon, and Oholibamah, the daughter of Anah. 26 These are the sons
of [a,A]Dishon: [b]Hemdan and Eshban and Ithran and
Cheran. 27 These are the sons of Ezer: Bilhan and
Zaavan and [a]Akan. 28 These are the sons of Dishan:
Uz and Aran. 29 These are the chiefs [a]descended from
the Horites: chief Lotan, chief Shobal, chief Zibeon,
chief Anah, 30 chief Dishon, chief Ezer, chief Dishan.
These are the chiefs [a]descended from the Horites,
according to their *various* chiefs in the land of Seir.
31 Now these are the kings who reigned in the land
of Edom before any [A]king reigned over the sons of
Israel. 32 [a,A]Bela the son of Beor reigned in Edom,
and the name of his city was Dinhabah. 33 Then
Bela died, and Jobab the son of Zerah of Bozrah
became king in his place. 34 Then Jobab died, and
Husham of the land of the Temanites became king
in his place. 35 Then Husham died, and Hadad the
son of Bedad, who [a]defeated Midian in the field of
Moab, became king in his place; and the name of his
city was Avith. 36 Then Hadad died, and Samlah of
Masrekah became king in his place. 37 Then Samlah
died, and Shaul of Rehoboth on the *Euphrates* River
became king in his place. 38 Then Shaul died, and
Baal-hanan the son of Achbor became king in his
place. 39 Then Baal-hanan the son of Achbor died,

36:1 [A]Gen 25:30 36:2 [A]Gen 28:9 [B]Gen 36:25 [C]Gen 36:24 36:4 [A]1 Chr 1:35 36:6 [a]Lit *the souls of his house* [A]Gen 12:5 36:7 [a]Lit *dwell* [A]Gen 13:6 [B]Gen 17:8; Heb 11:9 [C]1 Chr 29:15; Ps 39:12 36:8 [A]Gen 32:3 [B]Gen 36:1, 19 36:9 [a]Lit *Edom* 36:11 [a]In 1 Chr 1:36, *Zephi* 36:12 [A]Ex 17:8-16; Num 24:20; Deut 25:17-19; 1 Sam 15:2, 3 36:14 [a]Gr *son* [b]Lit *and she* 36:16 [a]Lit *of Eliphaz* 36:17 [a]Lit *of Reuel* 36:18 [a]Lit *of Oholibamah, Esau's wife* 36:20 [A]Gen 14:6; Deut 2:12, 22; 1 Chr 1:38-42 36:21 [a]Lit *of the Horites* 36:22 [a]In 1 Chr 1:39, *Homam* 36:23 [a]In 1 Chr 1:40, *Alian* [b]In 1 Chr 1:40, *Shephi* 36:26 [a]Heb *Dishan* [b]In 1 Chr 1:41, *Hamran* [A]1 Chr 1:41 36:27 [a]In 1 Chr 1:42, *Jaakan* 36:29 [a]Lit *of the Horites* 36:30 [a]Lit *of the Horites* 36:31 [A]Gen 17:6, 16; 35:11; 1 Chr 1:43 36:32 [a]Lit *And Bela* [A]1 Chr 1:43 36:35 [a]Or *smote*

36:1–37:1 The genealogy of Esau (v. 1).

36:1–19 The taking up of the history of Jacob (37:2), the next patriarch, is preceded by a fairly detailed genealogy of Esau, to which is appended both the genealogy of Seir the Horite (vv. 20–30), whose descendants were the contemporary inhabitants of Edom, and a listing of Edomite kings and chiefs. Jacob's and Esau's posterities, as history would go on to show, would not be in isolation from each other as originally intended (vv. 6–8). They were to become bitter enemies engaged with each other in war.

36:1 Edom. Cf. v. 8; *see note on 25:30;* see Introduction to Obadiah.

36:7 too great for them to live together. Crowded grazing and living conditions finally clinched the decision by Esau to move permanently to Edom, where he had already established a home (cf. 32:3; 33:14, 16). Since it was Abraham's descendants through Isaac and Jacob who would possess the land, it was fitting for God to work out the circumstances providentially of keeping Jacob's lineage in the land and moving Esau's lineage out. It is not revealed if Esau had understood and come to accept the promises of God to Jacob, although his descendants surely sought to deny Israel any right to their land or their life.

36:8 hill country of Seir. This was divinely assigned as Esau's place (Dt 2:5; Jos 24:4).

36:10–14 Cf. 1Ch 1:35–37.

36:15 the chiefs. This term, "ruler of a thousand," apart from one exception (Zec 12:5, 6), is used exclusively for the tribal princes or clan leaders, the political/military leaders in Edom. It may suggest a loosely formed tribal confederacy.

36:20–28 Cf. 1Ch 1:38–42.

36:31–39 kings ... before any king ... of Israel. Sandwiched in the genealogical details of Edom is a statement prophetically pointing to kingship in Israel (17:6, 16; 35:11; 49:10; Nu 24:7, 17, 18; Dt 17:14–20). The kings' list does not introduce a dynasty, each ruler not being the son of his predecessor. "Kings" more likely suggests rule over a more settled people than tribal groups.

and [a]Hadar became king in his place; and the name
of his city was [b]Pau; and his wife's name was Mehetabel, the daughter of Matred, daughter of Mezahab.
40 Now these are the names of the chiefs [a]descended
from Esau, according to their families *and* their local-
ities, by their names: chief Timna, chief [b]Alvah, chief
Jetheth, 41 chief Oholibamah, chief Elah, chief Pinon,
42 chief Kenaz, chief Teman, chief Mibzar, 43 chief Magdiel, chief Iram. These are the chiefs of Edom (that is,
Esau, the father of [a]the Edomites), according to their
habitations in the land of their possession.

JOSEPH'S DREAM

37 Now Jacob lived in [A]the land [a]where his father
had sojourned, in the land of Canaan. 2 These
are *the records of* the generations of Jacob.
Joseph, when [A]seventeen years of age, was pasturing the flock with his brothers while he was *still* a
youth, along with [B]the sons of Bilhah and the sons of
Zilpah, his father's wives. And Joseph brought back
a [C]bad report about them to their father. 3 Now Israel
loved Joseph more than all his sons, because he was
[A]the son of his old age; and he made him a [a,B]varicol-
ored tunic. 4 His brothers saw that their father loved
him more than all his brothers; and *so* they [A]hated
him and could not speak to him [a]on friendly terms.
5 Then Joseph [a,A]had a dream, and when he told
it to his brothers, they hated him even more. 6 He
said to them, "Please listen to this dream which I
have [a]had; 7 for behold, we were binding sheaves in
the field, and lo, my sheaf rose up and also stood
erect; and behold, your sheaves gathered around and
[A]bowed down to my sheaf." 8 Then his brothers said
to him, "[A]Are you actually going to reign over us? Or
are you really going to rule over us?" So they hated
him even more for his dreams and for his words.
9 Now he [a]had still another dream, and related it to
his brothers, and said, "Lo, I have [a]had still another
dream; and behold, the sun and the moon and eleven
stars were bowing down to me." 10 He related *it* to his
father and to his brothers; and his father rebuked
him and said to him, "What is this dream that you
have [a]had? Shall I and your mother and [A]your brothers actually come to bow ourselves down before you
to the ground?" 11 [A]His brothers were jealous of him,
but his father [B]kept the saying *in mind.*
12 Then his brothers went to pasture their father's
flock in Shechem. 13 Israel said to Joseph, "Are not
your brothers pasturing *the flock* in [A]Shechem? Come,
and I will send you to them." And he said to him, "[a]I
will go." 14 Then he said to him, "Go now and see about
the welfare of your brothers and the welfare of the
flock, and bring word back to me." So he sent him
from the valley of [A]Hebron, and he came to Shechem.
15 A man found him, and behold, he was wandering
in the field; and the man asked him, "[a]What are you
looking for?" 16 He said, "I am looking for my brothers;
please tell me where they are pasturing *the flock.*"
17 Then the man said, "They have moved from here;
for I heard *them* say, 'Let us go to [A]Dothan.'" So Joseph
went after his brothers and found them at Dothan.

THE PLOT AGAINST JOSEPH

18 [a]When they saw him from a distance and before
he came close to them, they [A]plotted against him to
put him to death. 19 They said to one another, "[a]Here
comes this dreamer! 20 Now then, come and let us
kill him and throw him into one of the pits; and [A]we
will say, 'A wild beast devoured him.' Then let us see
what will become of his dreams!" 21 But [A]Reuben
heard *this* and rescued him out of their hands and
said, "Let us not [a]take his life." 22 Reuben further
said to them, "Shed no blood. Throw him into this
pit that is in the wilderness, but do not lay hands on
him"—that he might rescue him out of their hands, to
restore him to his father. 23 So it came about, when

36:39 [a]In 1 Chr 1:50, *Hadad* [b]In 1 Chr 1:50, *Pai* 36:40 [a]Lit *of Esau* [b]In 1 Chr 1:51, *Aliah* 36:43 [a]Heb *Edom* 37:1 [a]Lit *of his father's sojournings* [A]Gen 17:8; 28:4 37:2 [A]Gen 41:46 [B]Gen 35:25, 26 [C]1 Sam 2:22-24 37:3 [a]Or *full-length robe* [A]Gen 44:20 [B]Gen 37:23, 32 37:4 [a]Lit *in peace* [A]Gen 27:41; 1 Sam 17:28 37:5 [a]Lit *dreamed* [A]Gen 28:12; 31:10, 11, 24 37:6 [a]Lit *dreamed* 37:7 [A]Gen 42:6, 9; 43:26; 44:14 37:8 [A]Gen 49:26; Deut 33:16 37:9 [a]Lit *dreamed* 37:10 [a]Lit *dreamed* [A]Gen 27:29 37:11 [A]Acts 7:9 [B]Dan 7:28; Luke 2:19, 51 37:13 [a]Lit *Behold me* [A]Gen 33:18-20 37:14 [A]Gen 13:18; 23:2, 19; 35:27; Josh 14:14, 15; Judg 1:10 37:15 [a]Lit *saying, "What...?"* 37:17 [A]2 Kin 6:13 37:18 [a]Or *And* [A]Ps 31:13; 37:12, 32; Mark 14:1; John 11:53; Acts 23:12 37:19 [a]Lit *Behold, this master of dreams comes* 37:20 [A]Gen 37:32, 33 37:21 [a]Lit *smite his soul* [A]Gen 42:22

36:43 father of the Edomites. The closing title of the genealogy calls attention to the Lord's words to Rebekah at the birth of her sons, "two nations are in your womb" (25:23); here was the nation from the older.

37:1 land where his father had sojourned. This by-line into the story of Jacob's son, Joseph, informs the reader that Jacob's father, Isaac, hence his sons as well, though in the land, had not yet entered into possession of their inheritance. They were still alien residents. **land of Canaan.** Actually Jacob and his family were in Hebron (v. 14). *See note on 13:18.*

37:2–50:26 The genealogy of Jacob (v. 2).

37:2 Joseph, when seventeen years of age. Eleven years had passed since he had entered the land of Canaan with his family (cf. 30:22–24), since Joseph was born 6 years before departing from Haran. **a bad report.** Whether Joseph brought this at his own initiative or reported back at the father's demand on 4 of his brothers (e.g., v. 14) is not elaborated upon, nor specifically cited as the cause of the brothers' intense dislike of Joseph (cf. vv. 4, 5, 8, 11, 18, 19).

37:3, 4 Overt favoritism of Joseph and tacit appointment of him as the primary son by the father (*see note on 37:3*) conspired to estrange him from his brothers. They hated and envied him (vv. 4, 5, 11) and could not interact with him without conflict and hostility. Joseph must have noticed the situation.

37:3 a varicolored tunic. The Septuagint (LXX) favored this translation of the Heb. phrase used by Moses, although some prefer "a long-sleeved robe" or "an ornamented tunic." It marked the owner as the one whom the father intended to be the future leader of the household, an honor normally given to the firstborn son.

37:5–10 The content of the dreams which Joseph recounted exacerbated fraternal hostility, with the second one also incurring paternal rebuke. The dream symbolism needed no special interpretation to catch its significant elevation of the favored son to ruling status over his brothers (vv. 8–10).

37:11 kept the saying *in mind.* Unlike the brothers, who immediately rejected any meaning to Joseph's words yet still allowed the dream to sorely irritate them into greater resentment of their brother (v. 19), the father, notwithstanding his public admonishment of Joseph, continued to ponder the meaning of the dreams.

37:12–17 The assignment to Shechem brought Joseph providentially to Dothan, a site more convenient for contact with merchants using the main trade route on their way to Egypt.

37:12, 14 Shechem ... Hebron. Shechem (*see note on 12:6*) was located ca. 50 mi. N of Hebron (*see note on 13:18*).

37:17 Dothan. Almost 15 mi. N of Shechem.

37:18–27 The brothers' plans for murder and cover-up, the fruit of hate and envy, were forestalled by two brothers: first by Reuben, who intended to effect a complete rescue (vv. 21, 22), and then by Judah who, prompted by a passing merchants' caravan, proposed a profitable alternative to fratricide (vv. 25–27).

Joseph [a]reached his brothers, that they stripped
Joseph of his [b]tunic, the varicolored tunic that was
on him; 24 and they took him and threw him into the
pit. Now the pit was empty, without any water in it.
25 Then they sat down to eat [a]a meal. And as they
raised their eyes and looked, behold, a caravan of
[A]Ishmaelites was coming from Gilead, with their
camels bearing [b,B]aromatic gum and [c,C]balm and
[d]myrrh, [e]on their way to bring *them* down to Egypt.
26 Judah said to his brothers, "What profit is it for us
to kill our brother and [A]cover up his blood? 27 [A]Come
and let us sell him to the Ishmaelites and not lay
our hands on him, for he is our brother, our *own*
flesh." And his brothers listened *to him.* 28 Then
some [A]Midianite traders passed by, so they pulled
him up and lifted Joseph out of the pit, and [B]sold
[a]him to the Ishmaelites for twenty *shekels* of silver.
Thus [C]they brought Joseph into Egypt.
29 Now Reuben returned to the pit, and behold,
Joseph was not in the pit; so he [A]tore his garments.
30 He returned to his brothers and said, "[A]The boy is
not *there;* as for me, where am I to go?" 31 So [A]they
took Joseph's tunic, and slaughtered a male goat
and dipped the tunic in the blood; 32 and they sent
the varicolored tunic and brought it to their father
and said, "We found this; please [a]examine *it* to *see*
whether it is your son's tunic or not." 33 Then he [a]ex-
amined it and said, "It is my son's tunic. [A]A wild beast
has devoured him; [B]Joseph has surely been torn to
pieces!" 34 So Jacob [A]tore his clothes, and put sackcloth on his loins and mourned for his son many
days. 35 Then all his sons and all his daughters arose
to comfort him, but he refused to be comforted. And
he said, "Surely I will [A]go down to Sheol in mourning
for my son." So his father wept for him. 36 Meanwhile,
the [a]Midianites [A]sold him in Egypt to Potiphar, Pharaoh's officer, the captain of the bodyguard.

JUDAH AND TAMAR

38 And it came about at that time, that Judah
[a]departed from his brothers and [b]visited
a certain [A]Adullamite, whose name was Hirah.

37:23 [a]Lit *came to* [b]Or *full-length robe* 37:25 [a]Lit *bread* [b]Or *ladanum spice* [c]Or *mastic* [d]Or *resinous bark* [e]Lit *going* [A]Gen 16:11, 12; 37:28; 39:1 [B]Gen 43:11 [C]Jer 8:22; 46:11 37:26 [A]Gen 37:20 37:27 [A]Gen 42:21 37:28 [a]Lit *Joseph* [A]Gen 37:25; Judg 6:1-3; 8:22, 24 [B]Gen 45:4, 5; Ps 105:17; Acts 7:9 [C]Gen 39:1 37:29 [A]Gen 37:34; 44:13 37:30 [A]Gen 42:13, 36 37:31 [A]Gen 37:3, 23 37:32 [a]Or *recognize* 37:33 [a]Or *recognized* [A]Gen 37:20 [B]Gen 44:28 37:34 [A]Gen 37:29 37:35 [A]Gen 25:8; 35:29; 42:38; 44:29, 31 37:36 [a]Lit *Medanites* [A]Gen 39:1 38:1 [a]Lit *went down* [b]Lit *turned aside to* [A]Josh 15:35; 1 Sam 22:1

37:25 Ishmaelites. Also known as Midianites (cf. vv. 28, 36; 39:1). The descendants of Ishmael and of Abraham through Keturah and Midian (25:1, 2) were sufficiently intermarried or were such inveterate travelers and traders that they were viewed as synonymous groups. These were coming W from Gilead. **Gilead.** *See note on 31:21.*

37:27 This criminal behavior would later be prohibited by the Mosaic legislation (Ex 21:16; Dt 24:7)

37:28 twenty *shekels* of silver. This was the average price of a slave at that time in the second millennium B.C. Although most slaves were part of the booty of military conquest, private and commercial slave-trading was also common. Joseph was sold into slavery ca. 1897 B.C.

37:29 Reuben ... tore his garments. Although he was absent at the time of the sale, he would be held responsible for the treachery, and so joined in the cover-up (vv. 30–35). His grief manifested how much he had actually wanted to rescue Joseph (see 42:22).

37:31–35 The deceiver of Isaac (27:18–29) was deceived by his own sons' lie. Sin's punishment is often long delayed.

37:35 Sheol. This is the first OT use of this term for the abode of the dead (in 35:20 the word "grave" is used to refer to an earthly burial plot). It is a general Hebrew term meaning the place of the dead (used 65 times in the OT), referring to either the body in its decaying form or the soul in its conscious afterlife.

37:36 Potiphar. He was a prominent court official and high-ranking officer in Egypt, perhaps captain of the royal bodyguard (cf. 40:3, 4). His name, a most unusual grammatical form for that period, either meant "the one whom the god Ra has given" or "the one who is placed on earth by Ra," making it a descriptive epithet more than a personal name. *See note on 40:3, 4.*

38:1–30 The Judah-Interlude, as it is sometimes known, is bracketed by references to the sale of Joseph to Potiphar (37:36; 39:1). Such a parenthesis in the Joseph story demands some reason why a chapter laced with wickedness, immorality, and subterfuge should of necessity be placed in this spot. The answer is that the events recorded are chronologically in the right place, being contemporary with the time of Joseph's slavery in Egypt (v. 1, "at that time"). The account is also genealogically in the right place, i.e., with Joseph gone (seemingly for good), with Reuben, Simeon, and Levi out of favor (for incest and for treachery), Judah would most likely accede to firstborn status. It provides a contrast because it also demonstrates the immoral character of Judah, as compared with the virtue of Joseph. Canaanite syncretistic religion and inclusivism threatened to absorb the fourth and later generations of Abraham's heirs, but Egyptian exile and racial exclusivism produced not loss of their ethnic identity, but preservation of it.

38:1 Adullamite. Adullam was a town about 1 mi. NW of Hebron.

JOSEPH AND HIS BROTHERS

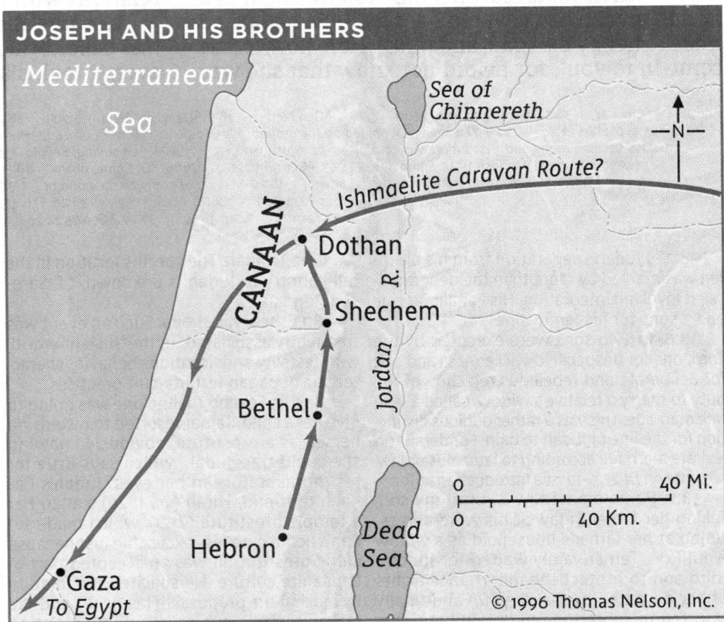

Joseph followed his shepherd brothers from Hebron to Dothan, where they sold him to a caravan of Ishmaelites on their way to Egypt.

2 Judah saw there a daughter of a certain Canaanite whose name was [A]Shua; and he took her and went in to her. 3 So she conceived and bore a son and he named him [A]Er. 4 Then she conceived again and bore a son and named him [A]Onan. 5 She bore still another son and named him [A]Shelah; and it was at Chezib [a]that she bore him.

6 Now Judah took a wife for Er his firstborn, and her name *was* Tamar. 7 But [A]Er, Judah's firstborn, was evil in the sight of the LORD, so the LORD took his life. 8 Then Judah said to Onan, "[A]Go in to your brother's wife, and perform your duty as a brother-in-law to her, and raise up [a]offspring for your brother." 9 Onan knew that the [a,A]offspring would not be his; so when he went in to his brother's wife, he [b]wasted his seed on the ground in order not to give [a]offspring to his brother. 10 But what he did was displeasing in the sight of the LORD; so He [A]took his life also. 11 Then Judah said to his daughter-in-law Tamar, "[A]Remain a widow in your father's house until my son Shelah grows up"; for he [a]thought, "*I am afraid* that he too may die like his brothers." So Tamar went and lived in her father's house.

12 Now [a]after a considerable time Shua's daughter, the wife of Judah, died; and when [b]the time of mourning was ended, Judah went up to his sheepshearers at [A]Timnah, he and his friend Hirah the Adullamite. 13 It was told to Tamar, "[a]Behold, your father-in-law is going up to [A]Timnah to shear his sheep." 14 So she [a]removed her widow's garments and [A]covered *herself* with a [b]veil, and wrapped herself, and sat in the gateway of [c]Enaim, which is on the road to Timnah; for she saw that Shelah had grown up, and [B]she had not been given to him as a wife. 15 When Judah saw her, he thought she *was* a harlot, for she had covered her face. 16 So he turned aside to her by the road, and said, "[a]Here now, let me come in to you"; for he did not know that she was his daughter-in-law. And she said, "What will you give me, that you may come in to me?" 17 He said, therefore, "I will send you a [a]young goat from the flock." She said, moreover, "Will you give a pledge until you send *it?*" 18 He said, "What pledge shall I give you?" And she said, "[A]Your seal and your cord, and your staff that is in your hand." So he gave *them* to her and went in to her, and she conceived by him. 19 Then she arose and departed, and [a]removed her [b]veil and put on her widow's garments.

20 When Judah sent the [a]young goat by his friend the Adullamite, to receive the pledge from the woman's hand, he did not find her. 21 He asked the men of her place, saying, "Where is the temple prostitute who was by the road at Enaim?" But they said, "There has been no temple prostitute here." 22 So he returned to Judah, and said, "I did not find her; and furthermore, the men of the place said, 'There has been no temple prostitute here.'" 23 Then Judah said, "Let her [a]keep them, otherwise we will become a laughingstock. [b]After all, I sent this young goat, but you did not find her."

24 Now it was about three months later that Judah was informed, "[a]Your daughter-in-law Tamar has played the harlot, and behold, she is also with child by harlotry." Then Judah said, "Bring her out and [A]let her be burned!" 25 It was while she was being brought out that she sent to her father-in-law, saying, "I am with child by the man to whom these things belong." And she said, "[A]Please examine and see, whose signet ring and cords and staff are these?" 26 Judah recognized *them,* and said, "[A]She is more righteous than I, inasmuch as [B]I did not give her to my son Shelah." And he did not [a]have relations with her again.

27 It came about at the time she was giving birth, that behold, there were [A]twins in her womb. 28 Moreover, it took place while she was giving birth, one

38:2 [A]1 Chr 2:3 38:3 [A]Gen 46:12; Num 26:19 38:4 [A]Gen 46:12 38:5 [a]Lit *when* [A]Num 26:20 38:7 [A]Gen 46:12; Num 26:19; 1 Chr 2:3 38:8 [a]Lit *seed* [A]Deut 25:5, 6; Matt 22:24 38:9 [a]Lit *seed* [b]Lit *spilled on the ground* [A]Deut 25:6 38:10 [A]Gen 46:12; Num 26:19 38:11 [a]Lit *said* [A]Ruth 1:12, 13 38:12 [a]Lit *the days became many and* [b]Lit *Judah was comforted, he* [A]Josh 15:10, 57 38:13 [a]Lit *saying, Behold* [A]Josh 15:10, 57; Judg 14:1 38:14 [a]Lit *removed from herself* [b]Or *shawl* [c]In Josh 15:34, *Enam* [A]Gen 24:65 [B]Gen 38:11, 26 38:16 [a]Or *Come, now* 38:17 [a]Lit *kid of goats* 38:18 [A]Gen 38:25; 41:42 38:19 [a]Lit *removed from herself* [b]Or *shawl* 38:20 [a]Lit *kid of goats by the hand of* 38:23 [a]Lit *take for herself* [b]Lit *Behold* 38:24 [a]Lit *saying, Your* [A]Lev 21:9 38:25 [A]Gen 37:32 38:26 [a]Lit *know her yet again* [A]1 Sam 24:17 [B]Gen 38:14 38:27 [A]Gen 25:24-26

38:2–5 Judah's separation from his brethren was marked by more than the geographical; it involved integration. His Canaanite wife had 3 sons for his family line.

38:6–10 Two sons were executed by the Lord, one for unspecified wickedness and one for deliberate and rebellious rejection of the duty to marry a relative's widow, called a levirate marriage. This was a rather dubious distinction for the line of Judah to gain. For details on levirate marriage according to later Mosaic law, *see note on Dt 25:5–10;* see Introduction to Ruth.

38:11 Remain a widow … until my son. Taking her father-in-law at his word and residing at her father's household as a widow would do, Tamar vainly waited for Judah's third son to protect the inheritance rights of her deceased husband (v. 14) and finally resorted to subterfuge to obtain her rights (vv. 13–16). In so doing, she may have been influenced by Hittite inheritance practices which wickedly called the father-in-law into levirate marriage in the absence of sons to do so.

38:12 Timnah. The specific location in the hill country of Judah is unknown. Cf. Samson, Jdg 14:1.

38:13 shear his sheep. Such an event was frequently associated, in the ancient world, with festivity and licentious behavior characteristic of pagan fertility-cult practices.

38:14, 15 Feeling that no one was going to give her a child, Tamar resorted to disguising herself as a prostitute, obviously knowing she could trap Judah, which says little for his moral stature in her eyes. Judah's Canaanite friend, Hirah (vv. 1, 20), called her a temple prostitute (v. 21), which made Judah's actions no less excusable just because cultic prostitution was an accepted part of Canaanite culture. He solicited the iniquity by making the proposal to her (v. 16), and she played the role of a prostitute, negotiating the price (v. 17).

38:18 Your seal and your cord, and your staff. A prominent man in the ancient Near East endorsed contracts with the cylinder seal he wore on a cord around his neck. Her request for the walking stick suggests it also had sufficient identifying marks on it (cf. v. 25, "whose … are these?"). The custom of using 3 pieces of identification is attested to in Ugaritic (Canaanite) literature.

38:20–23 It was not good for one's reputation to keep asking for the whereabouts of a prostitute.

38:24 let her be burned! Double standards prevailed in that Judah, no less guilty than Tamar, commanded her execution for immorality. Later Mosaic legislation would prescribe this form of the death penalty for a priest's daughter who prostituted herself or for those guilty of certain forms of incest (Lv 20:14; 21:9).

38:26 more righteous than I. This was not an accolade for her moral character and faith, but a commendation by Judah for her attention to inheritance rights of her family line and his shameful neglect thereof. Her death sentence was rescinded.

put out a hand, and the midwife took and tied a scarlet *thread* on his hand, saying, "This one came out first." 29 But it came about as he drew back his hand, that behold, his brother came out. Then she said, "What a breach you have made for yourself!" So he was named [a,A]Perez. 30 Afterward his brother came out who had the scarlet *thread* on his hand; and he was named [a,A]Zerah.

JOSEPH'S SUCCESS IN EGYPT

39 Now Joseph had been taken down to Egypt; and Potiphar, an Egyptian officer of Pharaoh, the captain of the bodyguard, bought him [a]from the [A]Ishmaelites, who had taken him down there. 2 [A]The LORD was with Joseph, so he became a [a]successful man. And he was in the house of his master, the Egyptian. 3 Now his master [A]saw that the LORD was with him and *how* the LORD [B]caused all that he did to prosper in his hand. 4 So Joseph [A]found favor in his sight and [a]became his personal servant; and he made him overseer over his house, and [B]all that he owned he put in his [b]charge. 5 It came about that from the time he made him overseer in his house and over all that he owned, the LORD [A]blessed the Egyptian's house on account of Joseph; thus [B]the LORD'S blessing was upon all that he owned, in the house and in the field. 6 So he left everything he owned in Joseph's [a]charge; and with him *there* he did not [b]concern himself with anything except the [c]food which he [d]ate.

Now Joseph was [A]handsome in form and appearance. 7 It came about after these events [A]that his master's wife [a]looked with desire at Joseph, and she said, "[B]Lie with me." 8 But [A]he refused and said to his master's wife, "Behold, with me *here,* my master [a]does not concern himself with anything in the house, and he has put all that he owns in my [b]charge. 9 [a,A]There is no one greater in this house than I, and he has withheld nothing from me except you, because you are his wife. How then could I do this great evil and [B]sin against God?" 10 As she spoke to Joseph day after day, he did not listen to her to lie beside her *or* be with her. 11 Now it happened [a]one day that he went into the house to do his work, and none of the men of the household was there inside. 12 She caught him by his garment, saying, "Lie with me!" And he left his garment in her hand and fled, and went outside. 13 [a]When she saw that he had left his garment in her hand and had fled outside, 14 she called to the men of her household and said to them, "See, he has brought in a [a]Hebrew to us to make sport of us; he came in to me to lie with me, and I [b]screamed. 15 When he heard that I raised my voice and [a]screamed, he left his garment beside me and fled and went outside." 16 So she [a]left his garment beside her until his master came home. 17 Then she [A]spoke to him [a]with these words, "[b]The Hebrew slave, whom you brought to us, came in to me to make sport of me; 18 and as I raised my voice and [a]screamed, he left his garment beside me and fled outside."

JOSEPH IMPRISONED

19 Now when his master heard the words of his wife, which she spoke to him, saying, "[a]This is what your slave did to me," [A]his anger burned. 20 So Joseph's master took him and [A]put him into the jail, the place where the king's prisoners were confined; and

38:29 [a]I.e. a breach [A]Gen 46:12; Ruth 4:12 38:30 [a]I.e. a dawning or brightness [A]1 Chr 2:4 39:1 [a]*Lit from the hand of* [A]Gen 37:25, 28, 36; Ps 105:17 39:2 [a]*Or prosperous* [A]Gen 39:3, 21, 23; Acts 7:9 39:3 [A]Gen 21:22; 26:28 [B]Ps 1:3 39:4 [a]*Or ministered to him* [b]Lit *hand* [A]Gen 18:3; 19:19 [B]Gen 24:2; 39:8, 22 39:5 [A]Gen 30:27 [B]Deut 28:3, 4, 11 39:6 [a]Lit *hand* [b]Lit *know* [c]Lit *bread* [d]*Or used to eat* [A]Gen 29:17; 1 Sam 16:12 39:7 [a]Lit *lifted up her eyes at* [A]Prov 7:15-20 [B]2 Sam 13:11 39:8 [a]Lit *does not know what is in the house* [b]Lit *hand* [A]Prov 6:23, 24 39:9 [a]*Or He is not greater* [A]Gen 41:40 [B]Gen 20:6; 42:18; 2 Sam 12:13; Ps 51:4 39:11 [a]Lit *about this day* 39:13 [a]Lit *And it came about when* 39:14 [a]Lit *Hebrew man* [b]Lit *called with a great voice* 39:15 [a]Lit *called out* 39:16 [a]Lit *let…lie beside* 39:17 [a]Lit *according to* [b]Lit *saying, "The* [A]Ex 23:1; Prov 26:28 39:18 [a]Lit *called out* 39:19 [a]Lit *According to these things your slave* [A]Prov 6:34 39:20 [A]Gen 40:3; Ps 105:18

38:29 Perez. This first of the twins, born of prostitution and incest to Tamar, nevertheless came into the messianic line, which went through Boaz and Ruth to King David (Ru 4:18–22; Mt 1:3). His name means "breach" or "pushing through."

39:1 Potiphar. *See note on 37:36.* **Ishmaelites.** *See note on 37:25.*

39:2 The LORD was with Joseph. Any and all ideas that Joseph, twice a victim of injustice, had been abandoned by the Lord are summarily banished by the employment of phrases highlighting God's oversight of his circumstances, e.g. "with him" (vv. 3, 21), "caused all he did to prosper" (vv. 3, 23), "found/gave him favor" (vv. 4, 21), "blessed/blessing" (v. 5), and "extended kindness to him" (v. 21). Neither being unjustly sold into slavery and forcibly removed from the Land (37:28), nor being unjustly accused of sexual harassment and imprisoned (vv. 13–18) were events signaling even a temporary loss of divine superintendence of Joseph's life and God's purpose for His people, Israel.

39:2–4 successful … overseer over his house. This involved the authority and trust as the steward of the whole estate (v. 5, "house and field" and v. 9, "no one greater"), one of the criteria for which was trust. No doubt Joseph was conversant in the Egyptian language (*see note on 29:9*).

39:5 the LORD's blessing. Joseph was experiencing fulfillment of the Abrahamic Covenant, even at that time before Israel was in the Land (see 12:1–3).

39:6 except the food which he ate. Since Joseph proved trustworthy enough to need no oversight, his master concerned himself only with his own meals or his very own personal affairs. Joseph himself remarked that Potiphar had delegated to him so much that he no longer knew the full extent of his own business affairs (v. 8); in fact, he knew only what was set before him (v. 6).

39:9 this great evil. Joseph explained, when first tempted, that adultery would be a gross violation of his ethical convictions which demanded 1) the utmost respect for his master and 2) a life of holiness before his God. Far more was involved than compliance with the letter of an ancient Near Eastern law-code, many of which did forbid adultery, but rather obedience to the moral standards belonging to one who walked with God, and that long before Mosaic law-code prescriptions applied (cf. Ps 51:4).

39:10–18 Her incessant efforts to seduce Joseph failed in the face of his strong convictions not to yield or be compromised. At flashpoint, Joseph fled! Based on false accusations, Joseph was deemed guilty and imprisoned. Cf. 2Ti 2:22 for a NT picture of Joseph's attitude.

39:12 his garment. See 37:31–35 for the other time one of Joseph's cloaks was used in a conspiracy against him.

39:17 Hebrew slave. This term was used by Potiphar's wife as a pejorative, intended to heap scorn upon someone considered definitely unworthy of any respect. Its use may also suggest some latent attitudes toward dwellers in Canaan, which could be aggravated to her advantage. Potiphar's wife also neatly shifted the blame onto her husband for having hired the Hebrew in the first place (vv. 16–18) and stated this also before the servants (v. 14).

39:19, 20 The death penalty for adultery may not have applied to a charge of attempted adultery, attempted seduction or rape (cf. vv. 14, 18), so Potiphar consigned Joseph to the prison reserved for royal servants, from where, in the providence of God, he would be summoned into Pharaoh's presence and begin the next stage of his life (cf. chaps. 40, 41). *See note on 40:3, 4.*

he was there in the jail. 21 But [A]the LORD was with Joseph and extended kindness to him, and [B]gave him favor in the sight of the chief jailer. 22 The chief jailer [A]committed to Joseph's [a]charge all the prisoners who were in the jail; so that whatever was done there, he was [b]responsible *for it.* 23 [A]The chief jailer did not supervise anything under [a]Joseph's charge because [B]the LORD was with him; and whatever he did, [C]the LORD made to prosper.

JOSEPH INTERPRETS A DREAM

40 Then it came about after these things, [A]the cupbearer and the baker for the king of Egypt offended their lord, the king of Egypt. 2 Pharaoh was [A]furious with his two officials, the chief cupbearer and the chief baker. 3 So he put them in confinement in the house of the [A]captain of the bodyguard, in the jail, the *same* place where Joseph was imprisoned. 4 The captain of the bodyguard put Joseph in charge of them, and he [a]took care of them; and they were in confinement for [b]some time. 5 Then the cupbearer and the baker for the king of Egypt, who were confined in jail, both had a dream the same night, each man with his *own* dream *and* each dream with its *own* interpretation. 6 [a]When Joseph came to them in the morning and observed them, [b]behold, they were dejected. 7 He asked Pharaoh's officials who were with him in confinement in his master's house, "[a,A]Why are your faces so sad today?" 8 Then they said to him, "[A]We have [a]had a dream and there is no one to interpret it." Then Joseph said to them, "[B]Do not interpretations belong to God? Tell *it* to me, please."

9 So the chief cupbearer told his dream to Joseph, and said to him, "In my dream, [a]behold, *there was* a vine in front of me; 10 and on the vine *were* three branches. And as it was budding, its blossoms came out, *and* its clusters produced ripe grapes. 11 Now Pharaoh's cup was in my hand; so I took the grapes and squeezed them into Pharaoh's cup, and I put the cup into Pharaoh's [a]hand." 12 Then Joseph said to him, "This is the [A]interpretation of it: the three branches are three days; 13 within three more days Pharaoh will [a]lift up your head and restore you to your [b]office; and you will put Pharaoh's cup into his hand according to your former custom when you were his cupbearer. 14 Only [a]keep me in mind when it goes well with you, and please [A]do me a kindness [b]by mentioning me to Pharaoh and get me out of this house. 15 For [A]I was in fact kidnapped from the land of the Hebrews, and even here I have done nothing that they should have put me into the [a]dungeon."

16 When the chief baker saw that he had interpreted favorably, he said to Joseph, "I also *saw* in my dream, and behold, *there were* three baskets of white bread on my head; 17 and in the top basket *there were* some of all [a]sorts of baked food for Pharaoh, and the birds were eating them out of the basket on my head." 18 Then Joseph answered and said, "This is its interpretation: the three baskets are three days; 19 within three more days Pharaoh will lift up your head from you and will hang you on a tree, and the birds will eat your flesh off you."

20 Thus it came about on the third day, *which was* [A]Pharaoh's birthday, that he made a feast for all his servants; [B]and he lifted up the head of the chief cupbearer and the head of the chief baker among his servants. 21 He restored the chief cupbearer to his [a]office, and [A]he put the cup into Pharaoh's [b]hand; 22 but [A]he hanged the chief baker, just as Joseph had interpreted to them. 23 Yet the chief cupbearer did not remember Joseph, but [A]forgot him.

39:21 [A]Gen 39:2; Ps 105:19; Acts 7:9 [B]Ex 3:21; 11:3; 12:36 39:22 [a]Lit *hand* [b]Lit *the doer* [A]Gen 39:4; 40:3, 4 39:23 [a]Lit *his hand* [A]Gen 39:3, 8 [B]Gen 39:2, 3 [C]Gen 39:3 40:1 [A]Gen 40:11, 13; Neh 1:11 40:2 [A]Prov 16:14 40:3 [A]Gen 39:1, 20 40:4 [a]Lit *ministered to* [b]Lit *days* 40:6 [a]Or *And* [b]Lit *and behold* 40:7 [a]Lit *saying, Why* [A]Neh 2:2 40:8 [a]Lit *dreamed* [A]Gen 41:15 [B]Gen 41:16; Dan 2:27, 28 40:9 [a]Lit *and behold* 40:11 [a]Lit *palm* 40:12 [A]Dan 2:36; 4:18, 19 40:13 [a]Or possibly *forgive you* [b]Lit *place* 40:14 [a]Lit *remember me with yourself* [b]Lit *and mention* [A]Josh 2:12; 1 Sam 20:14; 1 Kin 2:7 40:15 [a]Or *pit* [A]Gen 37:26-28 40:17 [a]Lit *food for Pharaoh made by a baker* 40:20 [A]Matt 14:6 [B]2 Kin 25:27; Jer 52:31 40:21 [a]Lit *wine-pouring* [b]Lit *palm* [A]Gen 40:13 40:22 [A]Gen 40:19; Esth 7:10 40:23 [A]Job 19:14; Ps 31:12; Eccl 9:15

39:21 extended kindness to him. God did not permit this initial painful imprisonment to continue (cf. Ps 105:18, 19).

39:22, 23 Once again Joseph, though in circumstances considerably less comfortable than Potiphar's home, rose to a position of trust and authority and proved to be trustworthy enough not to need any oversight.

40:1 the king of Egypt. To be identified as Senusert II, ca. 1894–1878 B.C.

40:2 the chief cupbearer and the chief baker. Both these occupations and ranks in Pharaoh's court are attested in existing ancient Egyptian documents. The cupbearer gave him his drinks. The baker cooked his bread. Both had to be trustworthy and beyond the influence of the monarch's enemies.

40:3, 4 captain of the bodyguard. *See note on 37:36.* If this was Potiphar, the captain of the guard, then Joseph's former master directed him to attend to the two royal servants remanded into his custody until sentence was past. This prison was also called "the house of the captain of the bodyguard" (v. 3), "his master's house" (v. 7), and "dungeon" (40:15; 41:14), unless Joseph had been moved to another penal facility.

40:5 dream. Oneiromancy, the science or practice of interpreting dreams, flourished in ancient Egypt because dreams were thought to determine the future. Both Egypt and Babylon developed a professional class of dream interpreters. Deuteronomy 13:1–5 shows that such dream interpreters were part of ancient false religion and to be avoided by God's people. By some 500 years later, a detailed manual of dream interpretation had been compiled. Unlike Joseph, neither cupbearer nor baker understood the significance of their dreams (cf. 37:5–11).

40:8 Do not interpretations belong to God? Joseph was careful to give credit to his Lord (cf. 41:16). Daniel, the only other Hebrew whom God allowed to accurately interpret revelatory dreams, was just as careful to do so (Da 2:28). Significantly, God chose both men to play an important role for Israel while serving pagan monarchs and stepping forward at the critical moment to interpret their dreams and reveal their futures.

40:9–13 the chief cupbearer. Consistent with his duty as the cupbearer to the king, he dreamed of a drink prepared for Pharaoh. It was a sign that he would be released and returned to his position (v. 13).

40:14, 15 keep me in mind. A poignant appeal to the cupbearer, whose future was secure, to speak a word for Joseph's freedom, because he knew cupbearers had the ear of kings. The cupbearer quickly forgot Joseph (v. 23) until his memory was prompted just at the right moment two years later (41:1, 9).

40:15 the land of the Hebrews. Giving this designation to the land of Canaan indicates that Joseph understood the land promise of the Abrahamic Covenant.

40:16 interpreted favorably. The chief baker, noting some similarity in the dreams, was encouraged to request interpretation of his dream.

40:20 Pharaoh's birthday. The Rosetta Stone (discovered in A.D. 1799, this is a trilingual artifact from Egyptian antiquity, ca. 196 B.C., whose Greek inscription enabled linguists to understand the language of hieroglyphics) records a custom of releasing Pharaoh's prisoners, but at this party held for his servants, Pharaoh rendered two very different kinds of judgment (vv. 21, 22).

PHARAOH'S DREAM

41 Now it happened at the end of two full years that Pharaoh had a dream, and behold, he was standing by the Nile. 2 And lo, from the Nile there came up seven cows, sleek and [a]fat; and they grazed in the [A]marsh grass. 3 Then behold, seven other cows came up after them from the Nile, ugly and [a]gaunt, and they stood by the *other* cows on the bank of the Nile. 4 The ugly and [a]gaunt cows ate up the seven sleek and fat cows. Then Pharaoh awoke. 5 He fell asleep and dreamed a second time; and behold, seven ears of grain came up on a single stalk, plump and good. 6 Then behold, seven ears, thin and scorched by the east wind, sprouted up after them. 7 The thin ears swallowed up the seven plump and full ears. Then Pharaoh awoke, and behold, *it was* a dream. 8 Now in the morning [A]his spirit was troubled, so he sent and called for all the [a,B]magicians of Egypt, and all its [C]wise men. And Pharaoh told them his [b]dreams, but [D]there was no one who could interpret them to Pharaoh.

9 Then the chief cupbearer spoke to Pharaoh, saying, "I would make mention today of [A]my *own* [a]offenses. 10 Pharaoh was [A]furious with his servants, and [B]he put me in confinement in the house of the captain of the bodyguard, *both* me and the chief baker. 11 [A]We had a dream [a]on the same night, [b]he and I; each of us dreamed according to the interpretation of his *own* dream. 12 Now a Hebrew youth *was* with us there, a [A]servant of the captain of the bodyguard, and we related *them* to him, and [B]he interpreted our dreams for us. To each one he interpreted according to his *own* dream. 13 And just [A]as he interpreted for us, so it happened; he restored me in my [a]office, but he hanged him."

JOSEPH INTERPRETS

14 Then Pharaoh sent and [A]called for Joseph, and they [B]hurriedly brought him out of the dungeon; and when he had shaved himself and changed his clothes, he came to Pharaoh. 15 Pharaoh said to Joseph, "I have had a dream, [A]but no one can interpret it; and [B]I have heard [a]it said about you, that [b]when you hear a dream you can interpret it." 16 Joseph then answered Pharaoh, saying, "[a,A]It is not in me; [B]God will [b]give Pharaoh a favorable answer." 17 So Pharaoh spoke to Joseph, "In my dream, behold, I was standing on the bank of the Nile; 18 and behold, seven cows, [a]fat and sleek came up out of the Nile, and they grazed in the marsh grass. 19 Lo, seven other cows came up after them, poor and very ugly and [a]gaunt, such as I had never seen for [b]ugliness in all the land of Egypt; 20 and the lean and [a]ugly cows ate up the first seven fat cows. 21 Yet when they had [a]devoured them, it could not be [b]detected that they had [a]devoured them, [c]for they were just as ugly as [d]before. Then I awoke. 22 I saw also in my dream, and behold, seven ears, full and good, came up on a single stalk; 23 and lo, seven ears, withered, thin, *and* scorched by the east wind, sprouted up after them; 24 and the thin ears swallowed the seven good ears. Then [A]I told it to the [a]magicians, but there was no one who could explain it to me."

25 Now Joseph said to Pharaoh, "Pharaoh's [a]dreams are one *and the same;* [A]God has told to Pharaoh what He is about to do. 26 The seven good cows are seven years; and the seven good ears are seven years; the [a]dreams are one *and the same.* 27 The seven lean and ugly cows that came up after them are seven years, and the seven thin ears scorched by the east wind [A]will be seven years of famine. 28 [a]It is as I have spoken to Pharaoh: [A]God has shown to Pharaoh what He is about to do. 29 Behold, [A]seven years of great abundance are coming in all the land of Egypt; 30 and after them [A]seven years of famine will [a]come, and all the abundance will be forgotten in the land of Egypt, and the famine will [b]ravage the land. 31 So the abundance will be unknown in the land because of that subsequent famine; for it *will be* very severe. 32 Now as for the repeating of the dream to Pharaoh twice, *it means* that [A]the matter is determined by God, and God will quickly bring it about. 33 Now let Pharaoh look for a man [A]discerning and wise, and set him over the land of Egypt. 34 Let Pharaoh take action to appoint overseers [a]in charge of the land, and let him exact a fifth *of the produce* of the land of Egypt in the seven years of abundance. 35 Then let them [A]gather all the food of these good years that are coming, and store up the grain for food in the cities under

41:2 [a]Lit *fat of flesh* [A]Job 8:11; Is 19:6, 7 41:3 [a]Lit *lean of flesh* 41:4 [a]Lit *lean of flesh* 41:8 [a]Or *soothsayer priests* [b]Lit *dream* [A]Dan 2:1, 3 [B]Ex 7:11, 22; Dan 1:20; 2:2 [C]Matt 2:1 [D]Dan 2:27; 4:7 41:9 [a]Or *sins* [A]Gen 40:14, 23 41:10 [A]Gen 40:2, 3 [B]Gen 39:20 41:11 [a]Lit *one night* [b]Lit *I and he* [A]Gen 40:5 41:12 [A]Gen 37:36 [B]Gen 40:12 41:13 [a]Lit *place* [A]Gen 40:21, 22 41:14 [A]Ps 105:20 [B]Dan 2:25 41:15 [a]Lit *about you, saying* [b]Lit *you hear a dream to interpret it* [A]Gen 41:8 [B]Dan 5:16 41:16 [a]Lit *Apart from me* [b]Lit *answer the peace of Pharaoh* [A]Dan 2:30; Zech 4:6; Acts 3:12; 2 Cor 3:5 [B]Gen 40:8; 41:25, 28, 32; Deut 29:29; Dan 2:22, 28, 47 41:18 [a]Lit *fat of flesh* 41:19 [a]Lit *lean of flesh* [b]Lit *badness* 41:20 [a]Lit *bad* 41:21 [a]Lit *entered their inward parts* [b]Or *known* [c]Lit *and* [d]Lit *in the beginning* 41:24 [a]Or *soothsayer priests* [A]Is 8:19; Dan 4:7 41:25 [a]Lit *dream is* [A]Gen 41:28, 32; Dan 2:28, 29, 45 41:26 [a]Lit *dream is* 41:27 [A]2 Kin 8:1 41:28 [a]Lit *That is the thing which I spoke* [A]Gen 41:25, 32 41:29 [A]Gen 41:47 41:30 [a]Lit *arise* [b]Lit *destroy* [A]Gen 41:54, 56; 47:13; Ps 105:16 41:32 [A]Gen 41:25, 28 41:33 [A]Gen 41:39 41:34 [a]Lit *over* 41:35 [A]Gen 41:48

41:1 the Nile. This river dominated Egyptian life.

41:8 no one who could interpret. The combined expertise of a full council of Pharaoh's advisers and dream experts, all of whom had been summoned into his presence, failed to provide an interpretation of the two disturbing dreams. Without knowing it, they had just set the stage for Joseph's entrance on the scene of Egyptian history.

41:9 Then the chief cupbearer spoke. With memory suitably prompted, the butler apologized for his neglect ("my *own* offenses"), and apprised Pharaoh of the Hebrew prisoner and his accurate interpretation of dreams two years earlier (vv. 10–13).

41:14 Then Pharaoh sent and called for Joseph. The urgent summons had Joseph in front of Pharaoh with minimum delay, in prized, clean-shaven Egyptian style for a proper appearance.

41:16 It is not in me; God will give. Deprecating any innate ability, Joseph advised at the very outset that the answer Pharaoh desired could only come from God.

41:25 God has told. Joseph's interpretation kept the focus fixed upon what God had determined for Egypt (vv. 28, 32).

41:33–36 After interpreting the dream, Joseph told Pharaoh how to survive the next 14 years. Incongruously, Joseph, a slave and a prisoner, appended to the interpretation a long-term strategy for establishing reserves to meet the future need, and included advice on the quality of the man to head up the project. Famines had ravaged Egypt before, but this time divine warning permitted serious and sustained advance planning.

Pharaoh's authority, and let them guard *it.* 36 Let
the food become as a reserve for the land for the
seven years of famine which will occur in the land
of Egypt, so that the land will not perish during
the famine."
37 Now the [a]proposal seemed good [b]to Pharaoh
and [b]to all his servants.

JOSEPH IS MADE A RULER OF EGYPT

38 Then Pharaoh said to his servants, "Can we
find a man like this, [A]in whom is a divine spirit?"
39 So Pharaoh said to Joseph, "Since God has informed you of all this, there is no one so [A]dis-
cerning and wise as you are. 40 [A]You shall be over
my house, and according to your [a]command all
my people shall [b]do homage; only in the throne
I will be greater than you." 41 Pharaoh said to Joseph, "See, I have set you [A]over all the land of
Egypt." 42 Then Pharaoh [A]took off his signet ring
from his hand and put it on Joseph's hand, and
clothed him in garments of fine linen and [B]put
the gold necklace around his neck. 43 He had him
ride in [a]his second chariot; and they proclaimed
before him, "[b]Bow the knee!" And he set him over
all the land of Egypt. 44 Moreover, Pharaoh said
to Joseph, "*Though* I am Pharaoh, yet [A]without
[a]your permission no one shall raise his hand or
foot in all the land of Egypt." 45 Then Pharaoh
named Joseph [a]Zaphenath-paneah; and he gave
him Asenath, the daughter of Potiphera priest of
[b,A]On, as his wife. And Joseph went forth over the
land of Egypt.
46 Now Joseph was [A]thirty years old when he
[a]stood before Pharaoh, king of Egypt. And Joseph
went out from the presence of Pharaoh and went
through all the land of Egypt. 47 During the seven
years of plenty the land brought forth [a]abundantly.
48 So he gathered all the food of *these* seven years
which occurred in the land of Egypt and placed the
food in the cities; he placed in every city the food
from its own surrounding fields. 49 Thus Joseph
stored up grain [a]in great abundance like the sand
of the sea, until he stopped [b]measuring *it,* for it was
[c]beyond measure.

THE SONS OF JOSEPH

50 Now before the year of famine came, [A]two sons
were born to Joseph, whom Asenath, the daughter of
Potiphera priest of [a]On, bore to him. 51 Joseph named
the firstborn [a]Manasseh, "For," *he said,* "God has
made me forget all my trouble and all my father's
household." 52 He named the second [a]Ephraim, "For,"
he said, "[A]God has made me fruitful in the land of
my affliction."
53 When the seven years of plenty which had been
in the land of Egypt came to an end, 54 and [A]the
seven years of famine began to come, just as Joseph
had said, then there was famine in all the lands, but
in all the land of Egypt there was bread. 55 So when
all the land of Egypt was famished, the people cried
out to Pharaoh for bread; and Pharaoh said to all
the Egyptians, "Go to Joseph; [A]whatever he says to
you, you shall do." 56 When the famine was *spread*
over all the face of the earth, then Joseph opened
all [a]the storehouses, and sold to the Egyptians; and
the famine was severe in the land of Egypt. 57 *The
people of* all the earth came to Egypt to buy grain
from Joseph, because [A]the famine was severe in
all the earth.

JOSEPH'S BROTHERS SENT TO EGYPT

42 Now [A]Jacob saw that there was grain in
Egypt, and Jacob said to his sons, "Why are
you staring at one another?" 2 He said, "Behold,

41:37 [a]Lit *word* [b]Lit *in the sight of* 41:38 [A]Job 32:8; Dan 4:8, 9, 18; 5:11, 14 41:39 [A]Gen 41:33 41:40 [a]Lit *mouth* [b]Lit *kiss* [A]Ps 105:21; Acts 7:10 41:41 [A]Gen 42:6; Ps 105:21; Dan 6:3; Acts 7:10 41:42 [A]Esth 3:10; 8:2 [B]Dan 5:7, 16, 29 41:43 [a]Lit *the second...which was his* [b]Heb *Abreck: Attention* or *Make way* 41:44 [a]Lit *you no one* [A]Ps 105:22 41:45 [a]Probably Egyptian for "God speaks; he lives" [b]Or *Heliopolis* [A]Jer 43:13; Ezek 30:17 41:46 [a]Or *entered the service of* [A]Gen 37:2 41:47 [a]Lit *by handfuls* 41:49 [a]Lit *very much* [b]Lit *numbering* [c]Or *without number* 41:50 [a]Or *Heliopolis* [A]Gen 48:5 41:51 [a]I.e. making to forget 41:52 [a]I.e. fruitfulness [A]Gen 17:6; 28:3; 49:22 41:54 [A]Gen 41:30; Ps 105:16; Acts 7:11 41:55 [A]John 2:5 41:56 [a]Lit *that which was in them* 41:57 [A]Gen 12:10 42:1 [A]Acts 7:12

41:37–41 To Pharaoh and his royal retinue, no other candidate but Joseph qualified for the task of working out this good plan, because they recognized that he spoke God-given revelation and insight (v. 39). Joseph's focus on his Lord had taken him from prison to the palace quickly (v. 41).

41:38 a divine spirit. The Egyptians did not understand about the third person of the triune Godhead. They merely meant that God had assisted Joseph.

41:41 set you over all the land of Egypt. The country-wide jurisdiction accorded to Joseph receives frequent mention in the narrative (vv. 43, 44, 46, 55; 42:6; 45:8).

41:42 signet ring ... garments ... gold necklace. Emblems of office and a reward of clothing and jewelry suitable to the new rank accompanied Pharaoh's appointment of Joseph as vizier, or prime minister, the second-in-command (v. 40; 45:8, 26). Joseph wore the royal seal on his finger, authorizing him to transact the affairs of state on behalf of Pharaoh himself.

41:43–45 Other awards appropriate to promotion were also bestowed upon Joseph, namely official and recognizable transportation (v. 43), an Egyptian name (v. 45), and an Egyptian wife (v. 45). Further, the populace was commanded to show deference for their vizier (v. 43, "Bow the knee"). All these dreams had been revealed by God, in a rare display of manifesting truth through pagans, so that Joseph would be established in Egypt as a leader and, thus elevated, could be used for the preservation of God's people when the famine came to Canaan. Thus, God cared for His people and fulfilled His promises (*see note on 45:1–8*).

41:43 his second chariot. This signified to all that Joseph was second-in-command.

41:45 Zaphenath-paneah. This name probably means "The Nourisher of the Two Lands, the Living One" but various other proposals have also been suggested (see marginal note); certainty of that meaning still eludes scholars. Foreigners are known to have been assigned an Egyptian name.

41:46 thirty years old. Ca. 1884 B.C. Only 13 years had elapsed since his involuntary departure from "the land of the Hebrews" (cf. 40:15). Joseph had been 17 when the narrative commenced (37:2).

41:50 On. One of the 4 great Egyptian cities, also called Heliopolis, which was known as the chief city of the sun god, Ra. It was located ca. 19 mi. N of ancient Memphis.

41:51, 52 Manasseh ... Ephraim. The names, meaning "forgetful" and "fruitful," assigned to his sons together with their explanations depict the centrality of God in Joseph's worldview. Years of suffering, pagan presence, and separation from his own family had not harmed his faith.

41:54–57 Use of hyperbole with "all" (vv. 54, 56, 57) emphatically indicates the widespread ravaging impact of famine far beyond Egypt's borders. She had become indeed the "breadbasket" of the ancient world.

41:55, 56 Go to Joseph. After 7 years, Joseph's authority remained intact, and Pharaoh still fully trusted his vizier. He dispensed the food supplies by sale to Egyptians and others (v. 47).

42:1–3 Jacob's sons were paralyzed in the famine, and Jacob was reluctant to let his family return to Egypt, not knowing what would happen to them (v. 4). But, with no other choice left, he dispatched them to buy grain in Egypt (v. 2).

[A]I have heard that there is grain in Egypt; go down
there and buy *some* for us [a]from that place, [B]so that
we may live and not die." 3 Then ten brothers of
Joseph went down to buy grain from Egypt. 4 But
Jacob did not send Joseph's brother [A]Benjamin with
his brothers, for he said, "[B]I am afraid that harm
may befall him." 5 So the sons of Israel came to buy
grain among those who were coming, [A]for the famine was in the land of Canaan *also.*

6 Now [A]Joseph was the ruler over the land; he was
the one who sold to all the people of the land. And
Joseph's brothers came and [B]bowed down to him
with *their* faces to the ground. 7 When Joseph saw
his brothers he recognized them, but he disguised
himself to them and [A]spoke to them harshly. And
he said to them, "Where have you come from?" And
they said, "From the land of Canaan, to buy food."

8 But Joseph had recognized his brothers, although [A]they did not recognize him. 9 Joseph [A]re-
membered the dreams which he [a]had about them,
and said to them, "You are spies; you have come to
look at the [b]undefended parts of our land." 10 Then
they said to him, "No, [A]my lord, but your servants
have come to buy food. 11 We are all sons of one
man; we are [A]honest men, your servants are not
spies." 12 Yet he said to them, "No, but you have
come to look at the [a]undefended parts of our land!"
13 But they said, "Your servants are twelve brothers
in all, the sons of one man in the land of Canaan;
and behold, the youngest is with [A]our father today, and [B]one is no longer alive." 14 Joseph said to
them, "It is as I said [a]to you, you are spies; 15 by
this you will be tested: [A]by the life of Pharaoh, you
shall not go from this place unless your youngest
brother comes here! 16 Send one of you that he may
get your brother, while you remain confined, that
your words may be tested, whether there is [A]truth
in you. But if not, by the life of Pharaoh, surely you
are spies." 17 So he put them all together in [A]prison
for three days.

18 Now Joseph said to them on the third day, "Do
this and live, for [A]I fear God: 19 if you are honest
men, let one of your brothers be confined in [a]your
prison; but as for *the rest of* you, go, carry grain
for the famine of your households, 20 and [A]bring
your youngest brother to me, so your words may
be verified, and you will not die." And they did so.
21 Then they said to one another, "[A]Truly we are
guilty concerning our brother, because we saw the
distress of his soul when he pleaded with us, yet we
would not listen; therefore this distress has come
upon us." 22 Reuben answered them, saying, "[A]Did
I not tell [a]you, 'Do not sin against the boy'; and you
would not listen? [b,B]Now comes the reckoning for his
blood." 23 They did not know, however, that Joseph
understood, for there was an interpreter between
them. 24 He turned away from them and [A]wept. But
when he returned to them and spoke to them, he
[B]took Simeon from them and bound him before their
eyes. 25 [A]Then Joseph gave orders to fill their bags
with grain and to restore every man's money in his
sack, and to give them provisions for the journey.
And thus it was done for them.

26 So they loaded their donkeys with their grain
and departed from there. 27 As one *of them* opened
his sack to give his donkey fodder at the lodging
place, he saw his [A]money; and behold, it was in the
mouth of his sack. 28 Then he said to his brothers,
"My money has been returned, and behold, it is
even in my sack." And their hearts [a]sank, and they
turned [b]trembling to one another, saying, "[A]What
is this that God has done to us?"

SIMEON IS HELD HOSTAGE

29 When they came to their father Jacob in the
land of Canaan, they told him all that had happened
to them, saying, 30 "The man, the lord of the land,
[A]spoke harshly with us, and took us for spies of the
country. 31 But we said to him, 'We are [A]honest men;
we are not spies. 32 We are twelve brothers, sons of

42:2 [a]Lit *from there* [A]Acts 7:12 [B]Gen 43:8; Ps 33:18, 19 42:4 [A]Gen 35:24 [B]Gen 42:38 42:5 [A]Gen 12:10; 26:1; 41:57; Acts 7:11 42:6 [A]Gen 41:41, 55 [B]Gen 37:7-10; 41:43; Is 60:14 42:7 [A]Gen 42:30 42:8 [A]Gen 37:2; 41:46 42:9 [a]Lit *had dreamed* [b]Lit *nakedness of the land* [A]Gen 37:6-9 42:10 [A]Gen 37:8 42:11 [A]Gen 42:16, 19, 31, 34 42:12 [a]Lit *nakedness of the land* 42:13 [A]Gen 43:7 [B]Gen 37:30; 42:32; 44:20 42:14 [a]Lit *to you, saying* 42:15 [A]1 Sam 17:55 42:16 [A]Gen 42:11 42:17 [A]Gen 40:4, 7 42:18 [A]Gen 39:9; Lev 25:43; Neh 5:15 42:19 [a]Lit *the house of your prison* 42:20 [A]Gen 42:34; 43:5; 44:23 42:21 [A]Gen 37:26-28; 45:3; Hos 5:15 42:22 [a]Lit *you saying* [b]Lit *And behold, his blood also is required* [A]Gen 37:21, 22 [B]Gen 9:5, 6; 1 Kin 2:32; 2 Chr 24:22; Ps 9:12 42:24 [A]Gen 43:30; 45:14, 15 [B]Gen 43:14, 23 42:25 [A]Gen 44:1; Rom 12:17, 20, 21; 1 Pet 3:9 42:27 [A]Gen 43:21, 22 42:28 [a]Lit *went out* [b]Lit *trembled* [A]Gen 43:23 42:30 [A]Gen 42:7 42:31 [A]Gen 42:11

42:4 Benjamin. See 35:16–19. He was the youngest of all, the second son of Rachel, Jacob's beloved, and the favorite of his father since he thought Joseph was dead.

42:6 bowed down. Without their appreciating it at the time, Joseph's dream became reality (37:5–8). Recognition of Joseph was unlikely because: 1) over 15 years had elapsed and the teenager sold into slavery had become a mature adult; 2) he had become Egyptian in appearance and dress; 3) he treated them without a hint of familiarity (vv. 7, 8); and 4) they thought he was dead (v. 13).

42:9–22 The brothers' final evaluation after being imprisoned for 3 days, after protesting the charge of espionage, and after hearing the royal criterion for establishing their innocence (vv. 15, 20), revealed their guilty conscience and their understanding that vengeance for their wrongdoing to Joseph had probably arrived (vv. 21, 22). Calling themselves "honest men" (v. 10) was hardly an accurate assessment.

42:9 remembered the dreams. Joseph remembered his boyhood dreams about his brothers bowing down to him (37:9) as they were coming true.

42:15 by the life of Pharaoh. Speaking an oath in the name of the king would most likely have masked Joseph's identity from the brothers. Perhaps it also prevented them from grasping the significance of his declaration, "I fear God" (v. 18). **unless your youngest brother comes here!** Joseph wanted to find out if they had done the same or a similar thing to Benjamin as to himself.

42:19, 20 if you are honest men. Joseph took their assessment of themselves at face value when exhorting them to respond to his proposals, but still asked for a hostage.

42:21 distress of his soul. The brothers had steeled their hearts when selling Joseph to the Midianites (37:28, 29), but they could not forget the fervent pleading and terror-filled voice of the teenager dragged away as a slave from home. Reuben reminded them of his warning at that time and the consequence.

42:22 reckoning for his blood. This declaration referred to the death penalty (9:5).

42:24 took Simeon. He kept hostage not Reuben the firstborn, but Simeon, the oldest brother, who willingly participated in the crime against Joseph (37:21–31).

42:28 God has done. Their guilty conscience and fear of vengeance from God surfaced again in this response to the money with which they had purchased the grain being returned and found in the one sack which had been opened. Later, upon discovering all their money had been returned, their fear increased even further (v. 35).

our father; one is no longer alive, and the youngest
is with our father today in the land of Canaan.' 33 The
man, the lord of the land, said to us, '[A]By this I will
know that you are honest men: leave one of your
brothers with me and take *grain for* the famine of
your households, and go. 34 But bring your youngest brother to me that I may know that you are not
spies, but [a]honest men. I will give your brother to
you, and you may [A]trade in the land.' "
35 Now it came about as they were emptying their
sacks, that behold, [A]every man's bundle of money
was in his sack; and when they and their father saw
their bundles of money, they were dismayed. 36 Their
father Jacob said to them, "You have [A]bereaved me
of my children: Joseph is no more, and Simeon is
no more, and you would take Benjamin; all these
things are against me." 37 Then Reuben spoke to his
father, saying, "You may put my two sons to death if
I do not bring him *back* to you; put him in my [a]care,
and I will return him to you." 38 But [a]Jacob said, "My
son shall not go down with you; for his [A]brother is
dead, and he alone is left. [B]If harm should befall him
on the journey [b]you are taking, then you will [C]bring
my gray hair down to Sheol in sorrow."

THE RETURN TO EGYPT

43 [A]Now the famine was severe in the land. 2 So it
came about when they had finished eating the
grain which they had brought from Egypt, that their
father said to them, "Go back, buy us a little food."
3 Judah spoke to him, however, saying, "[A]The man solemnly warned [a]us, 'You shall not see my face unless
your brother is with you.' 4 If you send our brother
with us, we will go down and buy you food. 5 But if
you do not send *him,* we will not go down; for the
man said to us, 'You will not see my face unless your
brother is with you.' " 6 Then Israel said, "Why did you
treat me so badly [a]by telling the man whether you
still had *another* brother?" 7 But they said, "The man
questioned particularly about us and our relatives,
saying, '[A]Is your father still alive? Have you *another*
brother?' So we [a]answered his questions. Could we
possibly know that he would say, 'Bring your brother
down'?" 8 Judah said to his father Israel, "Send the
lad with me and we will arise and go, [A]that we may
live and not die, we as well as you and our little ones.
9 [A]I myself will be surety for him; [a]you may hold me
responsible for him. If I do not bring him *back* to you
and set him before you, then [b]let me bear the blame
before you forever. 10 For if we had not delayed, surely
by now we could have returned twice."
11 Then their father Israel said to them, "If *it must
be* so, then do this: take some of the best products of
the land in your [a]bags, and carry down to the man
[A]as a present, a little [b,B]balm and a little honey, [c]aro-
matic gum and [d]myrrh, pistachio nuts and almonds.
12 Take double *the* money in your hand, and take back
in your hand [A]the money that was returned in the
mouth of your sacks; perhaps it was a mistake. 13 Take
your brother also, and arise, return to the man; 14 and
may [a,A]God Almighty [B]grant you compassion in the
sight of the man, so that he will release to you [C]your
other brother and Benjamin. And as for me, [D]if I am
bereaved of my children, I am bereaved." 15 So the
men took [A]this present, and they took double *the*
money in their hand, and Benjamin; then they arose
and went down to Egypt and stood before Joseph.

JOSEPH SEES BENJAMIN

16 When Joseph saw Benjamin with them, he said
to his [A]house steward, "Bring the men into the house,
and slay an animal and make ready; for the men are
to dine with me at noon." 17 So the man did as Joseph
said, and [a]brought the men to Joseph's house. 18 Now
the men were afraid, because they were brought to
Joseph's house; and they said, "*It is* because of the
money that was returned in our sacks the first time
that we are being brought in, that he may [a]seek
occasion against us and fall upon us, and take us
for slaves with our donkeys." 19 So they came near
to Joseph's house steward, and spoke to him at the
entrance of the house, 20 and said, "Oh, my lord, we
indeed came down the first time to buy food, 21 and
it came about when we came to the lodging place,
that we opened our sacks, and behold, [A]each man's
money was in the mouth of his sack, our money
in [a]full. So [B]we have brought it back in our hand.
22 We have also brought down other money in our
hand to buy food; we do not know who put our
money in our sacks." 23 He said, "[a]Be at ease, do not
be afraid. [A]Your God and the God of your father has
given you treasure in your sacks; [b]I had your money."
Then [B]he brought Simeon out to them. 24 Then the
man brought the men into Joseph's house and

42:33 [A]Gen 42:19, 20 42:34 [a]Lit *you are honest* [A]Gen 34:10 42:35 [A]Gen 43:12, 15, 21 42:36 [A]Gen 43:14 42:37 [a]Lit *hand* 42:38 [a]Lit *he* [b]Lit *on which you are going* [A]Gen 37:33, 34; 42:13; 44:27, 28 [B]Gen 42:4 [C]Gen 37:35; 44:29, 31 43:1 [A]Gen 12:10; 26:1; 41:56, 57 43:3 [a]Lit *us, saying* [A]Gen 43:5; 44:23 43:6 [a]Lit *to tell* 43:7 [a]Lit *told him according to these words* [A]Gen 42:13; 43:27 43:8 [A]Gen 42:2 43:9 [a]Lit *from my hand you may require him* [b]Lit *I shall have sinned before you all the days* [A]Gen 42:37; 44:32; Philem 18, 19 43:11 [a]Or *vessels* [b]Or *mastic* [c]Or *ladanum spice* [d]Or *resinous bark* [A]Gen 32:20; 43:25, 26 [B]Gen 37:25; Jer 8:22; Ezek 27:17 43:12 [A]Gen 42:25, 35; 43:21, 22 43:14 [a]Heb *El Shaddai* [A]Gen 17:1; 28:3; 35:11 [B]Ps 106:46 [C]Gen 42:24 [D]Gen 42:36 43:15 [A]Gen 43:11 43:16 [A]Gen 44:1 43:17 [a]Lit *the man brought* 43:18 [a]Lit *roll himself upon us* 43:21 [a]Lit *its weight* [A]Gen 42:27, 35 [B]Gen 43:12, 15 43:23 [a]Lit *Peace be to you* [b]Lit *your money had come to me* [A]Gen 42:28 [B]Gen 42:24

42:36 Jacob could not handle the prospect of losing another son, and didn't trust the brothers who had already divested him of two sons by what he may have thought were their intrigues. **all ... against me.** The whole situation overwhelmed Jacob who complained against his sons (cf. 43:6) and would not release Benjamin (v. 38).

42:37 The always salutary Reuben generously made his father an offer easy to refuse—killing his grandsons!

43:3 solemnly warned us. The seriousness of Joseph's words portended failure for another mission to buy food, unless the criterion he had set down was strictly met.

43:9 I myself will be surety for him. Reuben's offer to guarantee the safety of Benjamin had been rejected (42:37, 38), but Judah's was accepted (v. 11) because of the stress of the famine and the potential death of all (v. 8) if they waited much longer (v. 10).

43:11 a little. Likely, this was a significant present because they had little left. But there was no future at all past the little if they did not get grain in Egypt.

43:14 Jacob's acquiescence to let Benjamin go (v. 13) ended with prayer for the brothers' and Benjamin's safety and with a cry of being a helpless victim of circumstances. Pessimism had apparently set into his heart and deepened after the loss of Joseph.

43:23 Your God ... has given. An indication of Joseph's steward either having come to faith in God or having become very familiar with how Joseph talked of his God and life. So concerned were the brothers to protest their ignorance of the means of the money

[A]gave them water, and they [B]washed their feet; and
he gave their donkeys fodder. 25 So they prepared
[A]the present [a]for Joseph's coming at noon; for they
had heard that they were to eat [b]a meal there.
26 When Joseph came home, they brought into the
house to him the present which was in their hand
and [A]bowed to the ground before him. 27 Then he
asked them about their welfare, and said, "[A]Is your
old father well, of whom you spoke? Is he still alive?"
28 They said, "Your servant our father is well; he is
still alive." [A]They bowed down [a]in homage. 29 As
he lifted his eyes and saw his brother Benjamin,
his mother's son, he said, "Is this [A]your youngest
brother, of whom you spoke to me?" And he said,
"[B]May God be gracious to you, my son." 30 Joseph hurried *out* for [a,A]he was deeply stirred over his brother,
and he sought *a place* to weep; and he entered his
chamber and [B]wept there. 31 Then he washed his face
and came out; and he [A]controlled himself and said,
"[a]Serve the meal." 32 So they served him by himself,
and them by themselves, and the Egyptians who
ate with him by themselves, because the Egyptians
could not eat bread with the Hebrews, for that is
[a,A]loathsome to the Egyptians. 33 Now they [a]were
seated before him, [A]the firstborn according to his
birthright and the youngest according to his youth,
and the men looked at one another in astonishment.
34 He took portions to them from [a]his own table, [A]but
Benjamin's portion was five times as much as any
of theirs. So they feasted and drank freely with him.

THE BROTHERS ARE BROUGHT BACK

44 [A]Then he commanded his house steward,
saying, "Fill the men's sacks with food, as
much as they can carry, and put each man's money
in the mouth of his sack. 2 Put my cup, the silver cup,
in the mouth of the sack of the youngest, and his
money for the grain." And he did [a]as Joseph had told
him. 3 [a]As soon as it was light, the men were sent
away, they with their donkeys. 4 They had *just* gone
out of [A]the city, *and* were not far off, when Joseph
said to his house steward, "Up, follow the men; and
when you overtake them, say to them, 'Why have
you repaid evil for good? 5 Is not this the one from
which my lord drinks and which he indeed uses for
[A]divination? You have done wrong in doing this.' "
6 So he overtook them and spoke these words to
them. 7 They said to him, "Why does my lord speak
such words as these? Far be it from your servants
to do such a thing. 8 Behold, [A]the money which we
found in the mouth of our sacks we have brought
back to you from the land of Canaan. How then
could we steal silver or gold from your lord's house?
9 [A]With whomever of your servants it is found, let
him die, and we also will be my lord's [B]slaves." 10 So
he said, "Now let it also be according to your words;
he with whom it is found shall be my slave, and *the
rest of* you shall be innocent." 11 Then they hurried,
each man lowered his sack to the ground, and each
man opened his sack. 12 He searched, beginning
with the oldest and ending with the youngest, and
[A]the cup was found in Benjamin's sack. 13 Then they
[A]tore their clothes, and when each man loaded his
donkey, they returned to [B]the city.
14 When Judah and his brothers came to Joseph's
house, he was still there, and [A]they fell to the ground
before him. 15 Joseph said to them, "What is this deed
that you have done? Do you not know that such a
man as I can indeed practice [A]divination?" 16 So Judah said, "What can we say to my lord? What can we

43:24 [A]Gen 18:4; 19:2; 24:32 [B]Luke 7:44; John 13:5; 1 Tim 5:10 43:25 [a]Lit *until* [b]Lit *bread* [A]Gen 43:11, 15 43:26 [A]Gen 37:7, 10 43:27 [A]Gen 43:7; 45:3 43:28 [a]Lit *and prostrated themselves* [A]Gen 37:7, 10 43:29 [A]Gen 42:13 [B]Num 6:25; Ps 67:1 43:30 [a]Lit *his compassion grew warm* [A]1 Kin 3:26 [B]Gen 42:24; 45:2, 14, 15; 46:29 43:31 [a]Lit *Set on bread* [A]Gen 45:1 43:32 [a]Lit *an abomination* [A]Gen 46:34; Ex 8:26 43:33 [a]Lit *sat* [A]Gen 42:7 43:34 [a]Lit *his face* [A]Gen 35:24; 45:22 44:1 [A]Gen 42:25 44:2 [a]Or *according to the word* 44:3 [a]Lit *The morning was light* 44:4 [A]Gen 44:13 44:5 [A]Gen 30:27; 44:15; Lev 19:26; Deut 18:10-14 44:8 [A]Gen 43:21 44:9 [A]Gen 31:32 [B]Gen 44:16 44:12 [A]Gen 44:2 44:13 [A]Gen 37:29, 34; Num 14:6; 2 Sam 1:11 [B]Gen 44:4 44:14 [A]Gen 37:7, 10 44:15 [A]Gen 44:5

being returned and to express their desire to settle this debt (vv. 20–22), that they missed the steward's clear reference to the God of Israel ("the God of your father") and his oversight of events in which he had played a part ("I had your money").

43:26 bowed to the ground. Again, Joseph's boyhood dream (37:5–8) had become reality (cf. 42:6).

43:29 God be gracious. Joseph easily used the name of God in his conversation, but the brothers did not hear the name of their own covenant God being spoken by one who looked just like an Egyptian (cf. 42:18).

43:30 to weep. Joseph was moved to tears on several occasions (42:24; 45:2, 14, 15; 46:29).

43:32 not eat bread with the Hebrews. Exclusivism kept the Egyptians sensitive to the social stigma attached to sharing a meal table with foreigners (cf. 46:34). Discrimination prevailed at another level too: Joseph ate alone, his rank putting him ahead of others and giving him his own meal-table and setting.

43:33 the firstborn … the youngest. To be seated at the table in birth order in the house of an Egyptian official was startling—how did he know this of them? Enough clues had been given in Joseph's previous questions about the family and his use of God's name for them to wonder about him and his personal knowledge of them. Obviously, they simply did not believe Joseph was alive (44:20) and certainly not as a personage of such immense influence and authority. They had probably laughed through the years at the memory of Joseph's dreams of superiority.

43:34 Benjamin's portion. Favoritism shown to Rachel's son silently tested their attitudes; any longstanding envy, dislike, or animosity could not be easily masked. None surfaced.

44:2 my cup, the silver cup. Joseph's own special cup, also described as one connected with divination (vv. 5, 15) or hydromancy (interpreting the water movements), was a sacred vessel symbolizing the authority of his office of Egyptian vizier. Mention of its superstitious nature and purpose need not demand Joseph be an actual practitioner of pagan religious rites. *See note on v. 15.*

44:5 divination. *See note on Dt 18:9–12.*

44:7–9 The brothers, facing a charge of theft, protested their innocence by pointing first to their integrity in returning the money from the last trip, and then by declaring death on the perpetrator and slavery for themselves.

44:12 beginning with the oldest. Again, there was a display of inside knowledge of the family, which ought to have signaled something to the brothers. *See note on 43:33.*

44:13 tore their clothes. A well known ancient Near Eastern custom of visibly portraying the pain of heart being experienced. They were very upset that Benjamin might become a slave in Egypt (v. 10). Benjamin appears to have been speechless. They had passed a second test of devotion to Benjamin (the first in v. 34).

44:14 fell … before him. Again the dream had become reality (cf. 37:5–8; 42:6); but now prostrate before him, they had come to plead for mercy both for their youngest brother Benjamin and for their father Jacob (vv. 18–34).

44:15 practice divination. *See notes on vv. 2, 5.* Joseph, still disguising himself as an Egyptian official before his brothers, permitted them to think it so.

44:16 So Judah said. Judah stepped forward as the family spokesman since it was he who came with his brothers to Joseph's house and he who pled with him (cf. vv. 14, 18); Reuben, the firstborn, had been eclipsed. **God has found out the iniquity.** Judah, showing how his heart

speak? And how can we justify ourselves? God has
found out the iniquity of your servants; behold, we
are my lord's [A]slaves, both we and the one in whose
[a]possession the cup has been found." 17 But he said,
"Far be it from me to do this. The man in whose
[a]possession the cup has been found, he shall be my
slave; but as for you, go up in peace to your father."
18 Then Judah approached him, and said, "Oh my
lord, may your servant please speak a word in my
lord's ears, and [a,A]do not be angry with your servant;
for [B]you are equal to Pharaoh. 19 [A]My lord asked his
servants, saying, 'Have you a father or a brother?'
20 We said to my lord, 'We have an old father and [A]a
little child of *his* old age. Now [B]his brother is dead,
so he alone is left of his mother, and his father loves
him.' 21 Then you said to your servants, '[A]Bring him
down to me that I may set my eyes on him.' 22 But we
said to my lord, 'The lad cannot leave his father, for
if he should leave his father, [a]his father would die.'
23 You said to your servants, however, '[A]Unless your
youngest brother comes down with you, you will
not see my face again.' 24 Thus it came about when
we went up to your servant my father, we told him
the words of my lord. 25 [A]Our father said, 'Go back,
buy us a little food.' 26 But we said, 'We cannot go
down. If our youngest brother is with us, then we
will go down; for we cannot see the man's face unless our youngest brother is with us.' 27 Your servant
my father said to us, 'You know that [A]my wife bore
me two sons; 28 and the one went out from me, and
[A]I said, "Surely he is torn in pieces," and I have not
seen him since. 29 If you take this one also from [a]me,
and harm befalls him, you will [A]bring my gray hair
down to Sheol in [b]sorrow.' 30 Now, therefore, when I
come to your servant my father, and the lad is not
with us, since [a,A]his life is bound up in the lad's life,
31 when he sees that the lad is not *with us,* he will
die. Thus your servants will [A]bring the gray hair of
your servant our father down to Sheol in sorrow.
32 For your servant [A]became surety for the lad to
my father, saying, 'If I do not bring him *back* to
you, then [a]let me bear the blame before my father
forever.' 33 Now, therefore, please let your servant
remain instead of the lad a slave to my lord, and let
the lad go up with his brothers. 34 For how shall I go
up to my father if the lad is not with me—for fear
that I see the evil that would [a]overtake my father?"

JOSEPH DEALS KINDLY WITH HIS BROTHERS

45 Then Joseph could not control himself before
all those who stood by him, and he cried,
"Have everyone go out from me." So there [a]was no
man with him [A]when Joseph made himself known to
his brothers. 2 [A]He [a]wept so loudly that the Egyptians
heard *it,* and the household of Pharaoh heard *of it.*
3 Then Joseph said to his brothers, "[A]I am Joseph! [B]Is
my father still alive?" But his brothers could not answer him, for [C]they were dismayed at his presence.
4 Then Joseph said to his brothers, "Please come
[a]closer to me." And they came [a]closer. And he said, "I
am your brother Joseph, whom you [A]sold into Egypt.
5 Now do not be grieved or angry [a]with yourselves,
because [A]you sold me here, for [B]God sent me before
you to preserve life. 6 For the famine *has been* in the
land [A]these two years, and there are still five years
in which there will be neither plowing nor harvesting. 7 [A]God sent me before you to preserve for you a
remnant in the earth, and to keep you alive by a great
[a]deliverance. 8 Now, therefore, it was not you who sent
me here, but God; and He has made me a [A]father to
Pharaoh and lord of all his household and ruler over
all the land of Egypt. 9 Hurry and go up to my father,
and [A]say to him, 'Thus says your son Joseph, "God has
made me lord of all Egypt; come down to me, do not
delay. 10 You shall [a]live in the land of [A]Goshen, and
you shall be near me, you and your children and your
children's children and your flocks and your herds
and all that you have. 11 There I will also [A]provide for
you, for there are still five years of famine *to come,*
and you and your household and all that you have
would be impoverished." ' 12 Behold, your eyes see,
and the eyes of my brother Benjamin *see,* that it is
my mouth which is speaking to you. 13 Now you must
tell my father of all my splendor in Egypt, and all
that you have seen; and you must hurry and [A]bring
my father down here." 14 Then he fell on his brother
Benjamin's neck and [A]wept, and Benjamin wept on
his neck. 15 He kissed all his brothers and wept on
them, and afterward his brothers talked with him.

44:16 [a]Lit *hand* [A]Gen 44:9 44:17 [a]Lit *hand* 44:18 [a]Lit *let not your anger burn against* [A]Gen 18:30, 32; Ex 32:22 [B]Gen 37:7, 8; 41:40-44 44:19 [A]Gen 43:7 44:20 [A]Gen 37:3; 43:8; 44:30 [B]Gen 37:33; 42:13, 38 44:21 [A]Gen 42:15, 20 44:22 [a]Lit *he would* 44:23 [A]Gen 43:3, 5 44:25 [A]Gen 43:2 44:27 [A]Gen 46:19 44:28 [A]Gen 37:31-35 44:29 [a]Lit *my face* [b]Lit *evil* [A]Gen 42:38; 44:31 44:30 [a]Lit *his soul is bound with his soul* [A]1 Sam 18:1 44:31 [A]Gen 44:29 44:32 [a]Lit *and I shall have sinned for all the days before my father* [A]Gen 43:9 44:34 [a]Lit *find* 45:1 [a]Lit *stood* [A]Acts 7:13 45:2 [a]Lit *gave forth his voice in weeping* [A]Gen 45:14, 15; 46:29 45:3 [A]Acts 7:13 [B]Gen 43:27 [C]Gen 37:20-28; 42:21, 22 45:4 [a]Lit *near* [A]Gen 37:28 45:5 [a]Lit *in your eyes* [A]Gen 37:28 [B]Gen 45:7, 8; 50:20; Ps 105:17 45:6 [A]Gen 37:2; 41:46, 53 45:7 [a]Lit *escaped company* [A]Gen 45:5 45:8 [A]Judg 17:10 45:9 [A]Acts 7:14 45:10 [a]Lit *dwell* [A]Gen 46:28, 34; 47:1 45:11 [A]Gen 47:12 45:13 [A]Acts 7:14 45:14 [A]Gen 45:2

had changed, acknowledged the providence of God in uncovering their guilt (note the "we" in the questions), and did not indulge in any blame shifting, even onto Benjamin.

44:18–34 An eloquent and contrite plea for mercy, replete with reference to the aged father's delight in and doting upon the youngest son (vv. 20, 30) and the fatal shock should he be lost (vv. 22, 29, 31, 34). Judah's evident compassion for Jacob and readiness to substitute himself for Benjamin in slavery finally overwhelmed Joseph—these were not the same brothers of yesteryear (45:1).

45:1–8 Stunned by the revelation of who it really was with whom they dealt, the brothers then heard expressed a masterpiece of recognition of and submission to the sovereignty of God, i.e., His providential rule over the affairs of life, both good and bad. *See note on 41:43–45.*

45:6 these two years. Joseph would have been 39 years old and away from his brothers for 22 years (37:2).

45:7 to preserve .... remnant. Words reflecting, on Joseph's part, an understanding of the Abrahamic Covenant and its promise of a nation (cf. chaps. 12; 15; 17).

45:8 father to Pharaoh. A title which belonged to viziers and which designated one who, unrelated to Pharaoh, nevertheless performed a valuable function and held high position, which in Joseph's case was "lord of all Egypt" (v. 9). A new and younger Pharaoh now reigned, Senusret III, ca. 1878–1841 B.C.

45:10 land of Goshen. This area, located in the NE section of the Egyptian Delta region, was appropriate for grazing the herds of Jacob (cf. 47:27; 50:8). Over 400 years later, at the time of the Exodus, the Jews still lived in Goshen (cf. Ex 8:22; 9:26).

45:14, 15 Reconciliation was accomplished with much emotion, which clearly showed that Joseph held no grudges and had forgiven them,

16 Now when [A]the [a]news was heard in Pharaoh's
house [b]that Joseph's brothers had come, it [c]pleased
Pharaoh and his servants. 17 Then Pharaoh said to Joseph, "Say to your brothers, 'Do this: load your beasts
and [a]go to the land of Canaan, 18 and take your father
and your households and come to me, and [A]I will
give you the [a]best of the land of Egypt and you will
eat the fat of the land.' 19 Now you are ordered, 'Do
this: [a]take [A]wagons from the land of Egypt for your
little ones and for your wives, and bring your father
and come. 20 Do not [a]concern yourselves with your
goods, for the [b]best of all the land of Egypt is yours.' "
21 Then the sons of Israel did so; and Joseph gave
them [A]wagons according to the [a]command of Pharaoh, and gave them provisions for the journey. 22 To
[a]each of them he gave [A]changes of garments, but
to Benjamin he gave three hundred *pieces of* silver
and [B]five changes of garments. 23 To his father he
sent [a]as follows: ten donkeys loaded with the [b]best
things of Egypt, and ten female donkeys loaded
with grain and bread and sustenance for his father
[c]on the journey.
24 So he sent his brothers away, and [a]as they departed, he said to them, "Do not [b]quarrel on the
journey." 25 Then they went up from Egypt, and came
to the land of Canaan to their father Jacob. 26 They
told him, saying, "Joseph is still alive, and indeed
he is ruler over all the land of Egypt." But [a]he was
stunned, for [A]he did not believe them. 27 When they
told him all the words of Joseph that he had spoken
to them, and when he saw the [A]wagons that Joseph
had sent to carry him, the spirit of their father Jacob
revived. 28 Then Israel said, "It is enough; my son Joseph is still alive. I will go and see him before I die."

JACOB MOVES TO EGYPT

46 So Israel set out with all that he had, and
came to [A]Beersheba, and offered sacrifices
to the [B]God of his father Isaac. 2 [A]God spoke to Israel
[a]in visions of the night and said, "[B]Jacob, Jacob." And
he said, "Here I am." 3 He said, "[A]I am God, the God of
your father; do not be afraid to go down to Egypt,
for I will [B]make you a great nation there. 4 [A]I will go
down with you to Egypt, and [B]I will also surely bring
you up again; and [C]Joseph will [a]close your eyes."
5 Then Jacob arose from Beersheba; and the sons
of Israel carried their father Jacob and their little
ones and their wives in the [A]wagons which Pharaoh had sent to carry him. 6 They took their livestock and their property, which they had acquired
in the land of Canaan, and [A]came to Egypt, Jacob
and all his [a]descendants with him: 7 his sons and his
grandsons with him, his daughters and his grand-
daughters, and all his [a]descendants he brought
with him to Egypt.

THOSE WHO CAME TO EGYPT

8 Now these are the [A]names of the sons of Israel,
Jacob and his sons, who went to Egypt: Reuben,
Jacob's firstborn. 9 The sons of Reuben: Hanoch and
Pallu and Hezron and Carmi. 10 The [A]sons of Simeon:
[a]Jemuel and Jamin and Ohad and [b]Jachin and [c]Zohar
and Shaul the son of a Canaanite woman. 11 The sons
of Levi: [a]Gershon, Kohath, and Merari. 12 The sons of
Judah: Er and Onan and Shelah and Perez and Zerah
(but Er and Onan died in the land of Canaan). And
the [A]sons of Perez were Hezron and Hamul. 13 The
sons of Issachar: Tola and [a]Puvvah and [b]Iob and
Shimron. 14 The sons of Zebulun: Sered and Elon
and Jahleel. 15 These are the sons of Leah, whom she
bore to Jacob in Paddan-aram, with his daughter
Dinah; [a]all his sons and his daughters *numbered*
thirty-three. 16 The [A]sons of Gad: [a]Ziphion and Haggi,
Shuni and [b]Ezbon, Eri and [c]Arodi and Areli. 17 The
[A]sons of Asher: Imnah and Ishvah and Ishvi and Beriah and their sister Serah. And the [B]sons of Beriah:
Heber and Malchiel. 18 These are the sons of Zilpah,
whom Laban gave to his daughter Leah; and she
bore to Jacob these sixteen persons. 19 The sons of
Jacob's wife Rachel: Joseph and Benjamin. 20 [A]Now to
Joseph in the land of Egypt were born Manasseh and
Ephraim, whom Asenath, the daughter of Potiphera,
priest of On, bore to him. 21 The [A]sons of Benjamin:
Bela and Becher and Ashbel, Gera and Naaman, [a]Ehi
and Rosh, [b]Muppim and [c]Huppim and Ard. 22 These
are the sons of Rachel, who were born to Jacob; *there*

45:16 [a]Lit *voice* [b]Lit *saying, "Joseph's brothers have come"* [c]Lit *was good in the eyes of* [A]Acts 7:13 45:17 [a]Lit *come, go* 45:18 [a]Lit *good* [A]Gen 27:28 45:19 [a]Lit *take for yourselves* [A]Gen 45:21, 27; 46:5; Num 7:3-8 45:20 [a]Lit *let your eye look with regret upon your vessels* [b]Lit *good* 45:21 [a]Lit *mouth* [A]Gen 45:19 45:22 [a]Lit *all of them he gave each man* [A]2 Kin 5:5 [B]Gen 43:34 45:23 [a]Lit *like this* [b]Lit *good* [c]Lit *for* 45:24 [a]Lit *they departed; and he said* [b]Lit *be agitated* 45:26 [a]Lit *his heart grew numb* [A]Gen 37:31-35 45:27 [A]Gen 45:19 46:1 [A]Gen 21:31; 28:10 [B]Gen 26:24; 28:13; 31:42 46:2 [a]Lit *in the visions* [A]Gen 15:1; Num 12:6; Job 33:14, 15 [B]Gen 22:11; 31:11 46:3 [A]Gen 17:1; 28:13 [B]Gen 12:2; Ex 1:9; Deut 26:5 46:4 [a]Lit *put his hand on* [A]Gen 28:15; 48:21 [B]Gen 50:24; Ex 3:8 [C]Gen 50:1 46:5 [A]Gen 45:21 46:6 [a]Lit *seed* [A]Deut 26:5; Josh 24:4; Ps 105:23; Is 52:4; Acts 7:15 46:7 [a]Lit *seed* 46:8 [A]Ex 1:1-4; Num 26:4, 5; 1 Chr 2:1ff 46:10 [a]In Num 26:12 and 1 Chr 4:24, *Nemuel* [b]In 1 Chr 4:24, *Jarib* [c]In Num 26:13 and 1 Chr 4:24, *Zerah* [A]Ex 6:15 46:11 [a]In 1 Chr 6:16, *Gershom* 46:12 [A]1 Chr 2:5 46:13 [a]In Num 26:23, *Puvah;* in 1 Chr 7:1, *Puah* [b]In Num 26:24 and 1 Chr 7:1, *Jashub* 46:15 [a]Lit *all the souls of* 46:16 [a]In Num 26:15, *Zephon* [b]In Num 26:16, *Ozni* [c]In Num 26:17, *Arod* [A]Num 26:15-18 46:17 [A]1 Chr 7:30 [B]1 Chr 7:31 46:20 [A]Gen 41:50-52 46:21 [a]In Num 26:38, *Ahiram* [b]In Num 26:39, *Shephupham;* in 1 Chr 7:12, *Shuppim* [c]In Num 26:39, *Hupham* [A]1 Chr 7:6

evidencing the marks of a spiritually mature man. *See note on 50:15–18.* It had been 22 years since the brothers sold Joseph into slavery.

45:16 it pleased Pharaoh. The final seal of approval for Joseph's relatives to immigrate to Egypt came unsought from Pharaoh (vv. 17–20).

45:24 Do not quarrel on the journey. A needed admonition because they would have so much sin to think about as they readied their confession to their father.

45:26 he was stunned. Like his sons (v. 3), Jacob was shocked by the totally unexpected good news. Even though the record is silent on the matter, this was the appropriate occasion for the sons to confess their crime to their father.

46:1 offered sacrifices. The route to Egypt for Jacob went via Beersheba, a notable site about 25 mi. SW of Hebron and favorite place of worship for both Abraham and Isaac (21:33; 26:25).

46:2–4 God spoke ... in visions. Jacob's anxiety about his departure to Egypt was allayed by the Lord's approval and confirmation of his descendants returning as a nation. God had previously appeared/spoken to Jacob in 28:10–17; 32:24–30; 35:1, 9–13.

46:4 close your eyes. A promise of dying peacefully in the presence of his beloved son (cf. 49:33).

46:6 came to Egypt. Ca. 1875 B.C. They remained 430 years (Ex 12:40) until the Exodus in 1445 B.C.

46:8–27 The genealogical register, separately listing and totaling the sons per wife and handmaid, is enveloped by notification that it records the sons/persons of Jacob who went to Egypt (vv. 8, 27). Ancient Near Eastern genealogies could include historical notes as is true here, namely the death of Er and Onan (v. 12), and that Laban gave the handmaids to his daughters (vv. 18, 25).

46:8 the sons of Israel. This was the first time that author Moses referred to the family as a whole in this way, although "in Israel" had been used by the sons of Jacob before (cf. 34:7).

were fourteen persons in all. 23 The sons of Dan: [a]Hu-
shim. 24 The sons of Naphtali: [a]Jahzeel and Guni and
Jezer and [b]Shillem. 25 These are the [A]sons of Bilhah,
whom [B]Laban gave to his daughter Rachel, and she
bore these to Jacob; *there were* seven persons in all.
26 [A]All the persons belonging to Jacob, who came to
Egypt, [a]his direct descendants, not including the
wives of Jacob's sons, *were* sixty-six persons in all,
27 and the sons of Joseph, who were born to him in
Egypt were [a]two; [A]all the persons of the house of
Jacob, who came to Egypt, *were* seventy.

28 Now he sent Judah before him to Joseph, to
point out *the way* before him to [A]Goshen; and they
came into the land of Goshen. 29 Joseph [a]prepared
his chariot and went up to Goshen to meet his father Israel; as soon as he appeared [b]before him, he
fell on his neck and [A]wept on his neck a long time.
30 Then Israel said to Joseph, "Now let me die, since I
have seen your face, that you are still alive." 31 Joseph
said to his brothers and to his father's household, "[A]I
will go up and tell Pharaoh, and will say to him, 'My
brothers and my father's household, who *were* in the
land of Canaan, have come to me; 32 and the men are
shepherds, for they have been [a]keepers of livestock;
and they have brought their flocks and their herds
and all that they have.' 33 When Pharaoh calls you
and says, '[A]What is your occupation?' 34 you shall say,
'Your servants have been [a,A]keepers of livestock from
our youth even until now, both we and our fathers,'
that you may [b]live in the land of [B]Goshen; for every
shepherd is [c,C]loathsome to the Egyptians."

JACOB'S FAMILY SETTLES IN GOSHEN

47 Then [A]Joseph went in and told Pharaoh, and
said, "My father and my brothers and their
flocks and their herds and all that they have, have
come out of the land of Canaan; and behold, they
are in the land of [B]Goshen." 2 He took five men from
among his brothers and [A]presented them to Pharaoh. 3 Then Pharaoh said to his brothers, "[A]What is
your occupation?" So they said to Pharaoh, "Your
servants are [B]shepherds, both we and our fathers."
4 They said to Pharaoh, "[A]We have come to sojourn
in the land, for there is no pasture for your servants' flocks, for [B]the famine is severe in the land
of Canaan. Now, therefore, please let your servants
[a,C]live in the land of Goshen." 5 Then Pharaoh said
to [a]Joseph, "Your father and your brothers have
come to you. 6 The land of Egypt is [a]at your disposal;
[b]settle your father and your brothers in [A]the best of
the land, let them [c]live in the land of Goshen; and
if you know any [B]capable men among them, then
[d]put them in charge of my livestock."

7 Then Joseph brought his father Jacob and [a]pre-
sented him to Pharaoh; and Jacob [A]blessed Pharaoh.
8 Pharaoh said to Jacob, "How many [a]years have you
lived?" 9 So Jacob said to Pharaoh, "The [a,A]years of
my sojourning are one hundred and [b]thirty; few
and [c]unpleasant have been the [a]years of my life, nor
have they [d]attained [B]the [a]years [e]that my fathers lived
during the days of their sojourning." 10 And Jacob
[A]blessed Pharaoh, and went out from [a]his presence.
11 So Joseph [a]settled his father and his brothers and
gave them a possession in the land of Egypt, in [A]the
best of the land, in the land of [B]Rameses, as Pharaoh
had ordered. 12 Joseph [A]provided his father and his
brothers and all his father's household with [a]food,
according to their little ones.

13 Now there was no [a]food in all the land, because
the famine was very severe, so that [A]the land of
Egypt and the land of Canaan languished because
of the famine. 14 [A]Joseph gathered all the money that

46:23 [a]In Num 26:42, *Shuham* 46:24 [a]In 1 Chr 7:13, *Jahziel* [b]In 1 Chr 7:13, *Shallum* 46:25 [A]Gen 30:5, 7 [B]Gen 29:29 46:26 [a]Lit *who came out of his loins* [A]Ex 1:5 46:27 [a]Lit *two souls* [A]Ex 1:5; Deut 10:22; Acts 7:14 46:28 [A]Gen 45:10 46:29 [a]Lit *tied, harnessed* [b]Lit *to* [A]Gen 45:14, 15 46:31 [A]Gen 47:1 46:32 [a]Lit *men* 46:33 [A]Gen 47:2, 3 46:34 [a]Lit *men* [b]Lit *dwell* [c]Lit *an abomination* [A]Gen 13:7, 8; 26:20; 37:2 [B]Gen 45:10, 18; 47:6, 11 [C]Gen 43:32; Ex 8:26 47:1 [A]Gen 46:31 [B]Gen 45:10; 46:28 47:2 [A]Acts 7:13 47:3 [A]Gen 46:33 [B]Gen 46:34 47:4 [a]Lit *dwell* [A]Gen 15:13; Deut 26:5; Ps 105:23 [B]Gen 43:1; Acts 7:11 [C]Gen 46:34 47:5 [a]Lit *Joseph, saying* 47:6 [a]Lit *before you* [b]Lit *cause them to dwell* [c]Lit *dwell* [d]Lit *appoint them rulers* [A]Gen 45:10, 18; 47:11 [B]Ex 18:21, 25; 1 Kin 11:28; Prov 22:29 47:7 [a]Lit *set him before* [A]Gen 47:10; 2 Sam 14:22; 1 Kin 8:66 47:8 [a]Lit *are the days of the years of your life* 47:9 [a]Lit *days of the years* [b]Lit *thirty years* [c]Lit *evil* [d]Lit *reached* [e]Lit *of the life of my fathers* [A]Heb 11:9, 13 [B]Gen 25:7; 35:28 47:10 [a]Lit *Pharaoh's* [A]Gen 47:7 47:11 [a]Lit *caused to dwell* [A]Gen 47:6, 27 [B]Ex 1:11; 12:37 47:12 [a]Or *bread* [A]Gen 45:11 47:13 [a]Or *bread* [A]Gen 41:30; Acts 7:11 47:14 [A]Gen 41:56

46:26 sixty-six persons. The total of vv. 8–25 is 70, from which Er, Onan, Manasseh, and Ephraim need to be deleted.

46:27 seventy. Jacob, Joseph, Manasseh, and Ephraim should be added to the 66. The 75 of Ac 7:14 included an additional 5 people, born in the land, which were added in the LXX reading of 46:8–27 (cf. Ex 1:5; Dt 10:22). These 5 included two sons of Manasseh, two sons of Ephraim, and one grandson of the latter. *See note on Ex 1:5.*

46:28 sent Judah before him. Once again Judah was the leader going ahead as Jacob's representative, not Reuben. *See note on 44:16.* **Goshen.** *See note on 45:10.*

46:31–34 Joseph's instructions about his preparatory interview with Pharaoh were designed to secure his relatives a place somewhat separate from the mainstream of Egyptian society. The social stigma regarding the Hebrews (43:32), who were shepherds also (v. 34), played a crucial role in protecting Israel from intermingling and losing their identity in Egypt. *See note on 43:32.*

47:1–6 in the land of Goshen. By informing Pharaoh of where he had located his family (cf. 45:10; 46:28) and then by having the family's 5 representatives courteously request permission to reside in Goshen (vv. 2, 4), Joseph, wise to court procedures, paved the way for Pharaoh's confirmation and approval (v. 6).

47:7, 10 Jacob blessed Pharaoh. The aged patriarch's salutations pronounced, undoubtedly in the name of God, a benediction on Pharaoh Senusert III (*see note on 45:8*) for his generosity and his provision of a safe place for Jacob's family. Though Senusert III had ascended to the throne before the famine ended, he honored his father's commitments.

47:9 my sojourning ... few and unpleasant. Since neither Jacob nor his fathers had actually possessed the land of Canaan, describing life as a sojourning was a fitting evaluation to give. In addition, his years seemed few in contrast to those of the two who had visited Egypt long before him, Abraham and Isaac (175 and 180 years respectively). And still overshadowed with pessimism, the days were "unpleasant," in the sense of toil and trouble, of many sorrows, distresses, and crises. *See note on 48:15.*

47:11 land of Rameses. An alternative designation for Goshen (cf. 46:34; 47:1, 6), with this name perhaps used later to more accurately describe the region for Moses' contemporary readers. *See note on Ex 1:11* regarding the name Rameses ("Raamses" being the alternate spelling in Exodus). This region is also called Zoan elsewhere (cf. Ps 78:12, 43).

47:12 according to their little ones. A rationing system was evidently in operation.

47:13–24 When the famine finally exhausted the Egyptians' supply of money, Joseph accepted animals in exchange for grain (v. 17). After the animals ran out, the people were desperate enough to exchange their land (vv. 19, 20). Eventually, Pharaoh owned all the land, except what was the priests' (v. 22), though the people were allowed to work the land and pay one-fifth of its yield to Pharaoh (v. 24). Whatever may have been

was found in the land of Egypt and in the land of
Canaan for the grain which they bought, and Joseph
brought the money into Pharaoh's house. 15 When
the money was all spent in the land of Egypt and in
the land of Canaan, all the Egyptians came to Joseph
[a]and said, "Give us [b]food, for [A]why should we die
in your presence? For *our* money [c]is gone." 16 Then
Joseph said, "Give up your livestock, and I will give
you *food* for your livestock, since *your* money [a]is
gone." 17 So they brought their livestock to Joseph,
and Joseph gave them [a]food in exchange for the
horses and the [b]flocks and the herds and the donkeys; and he [c]fed them with [a]food in exchange for
all their livestock [d]that year. 18 When that year was
ended, they came to him the [a]next year and said to
him, "We will not hide from my lord that our money
is all spent, and the [b]cattle are my lord's. There is
nothing left [c]for my lord except our bodies and our
lands. 19 Why should we die before your eyes, both
we and our land? Buy us and our land for [a]food, and
we and our land will be slaves to Pharaoh. So give
us seed, that we may live and not die, and that the
land may not be desolate."

RESULT OF THE FAMINE

20 So Joseph bought all the land of Egypt for Pharaoh, for [a]every Egyptian sold his field, because the
famine was severe upon them. Thus the land became Pharaoh's. 21 As for the people, he removed
them to the cities from one end of Egypt's border to
the other. 22 Only the land of the priests he did not
buy, for the priests had an allotment from Pharaoh,
and they [a]lived off the allotment which Pharaoh
gave them. Therefore, they did not sell their land.
23 Then Joseph said to the people, "Behold, I have
today bought you and your land for Pharaoh; now,
here is seed for you, and you may sow the land. 24 [a]At
the harvest you shall give a [A]fifth to Pharaoh, and
[b]four-fifths shall be your own for seed of the field
and for your food and for those of your households
and as food for your little ones." 25 So they said, "You
have saved our lives! Let us find favor in the sight of
my lord, and we will be Pharaoh's slaves." 26 Joseph
made it a statute concerning the land of Egypt *valid*
to this day, that Pharaoh should have the fifth; [A]only
the land of the priests [a]did not become Pharaoh's.
27 Now Israel [a]lived in the land of Egypt, in [b]Go-
shen, and they [A]acquired property in it and [B]were
fruitful and became very numerous. 28 Jacob lived in
the land of Egypt [A]seventeen years; so the [a]length of
Jacob's life was one hundred and forty-seven years.
29 When [a,A]the time for Israel to die drew near,
he called his son Joseph and said to him, "Please,
if I have found favor in your sight, [B]place now your
hand under my thigh and [C]deal with me in kindness
and [b]faithfulness. Please do not bury me in Egypt,
30 but when I [A]lie down with my fathers, you shall
carry me out of Egypt and bury me in [B]their burial
place." And he said, "I will do as you have said."
31 He said, "[A]Swear to me." So he swore to him. Then
[B]Israel bowed *in worship* at the head of the bed.

ISRAEL'S LAST DAYS

48 Now it came about after these things that [a]Jo-
seph was told, "Behold, your father is sick."
So he took his two sons [A]Manasseh and Ephraim
with him. 2 When [a]it was told to Jacob, "Behold, your
son Joseph has come to you," Israel [b]collected his
strength and sat [c]up in the bed. 3 Then Jacob said to
Joseph, "[a,A]God Almighty appeared to me at [B]Luz in
the land of Canaan and blessed me, 4 and He said to
me, 'Behold, I will make you fruitful and numerous,
and I will make you a company of peoples, and will
give this land to your [a]descendants after you for [A]an
everlasting possession.' 5 Now your two sons, who
were born to you in the land of Egypt before I came
to you in Egypt, are mine; [A]Ephraim and Manasseh
shall be mine, as [B]Reuben and Simeon are. 6 But
your offspring that [a]have been born after them
shall be yours; they shall be called by the [b]names
of their brothers in their inheritance. 7 Now as for
me, when I came from [A]Paddan, [B]Rachel died, [a]to
my sorrow, in the land of Canaan on the journey,
when there was still some distance to go to Ephrath;

47:15 [a]Lit *saying* [b]Or *bread* [c]Lit *ceases* [A]Gen 47:19 47:16 [a]Lit *ceases* 47:17 [a]Or *bread* [b]Lit *livestock of the flocks and livestock of the herds* [c]Lit *led them as a shepherd* [d]Lit *in that year* 47:18 [a]Lit *second* [b]Lit *livestock of the cattle* [c]Lit *in the presence of* 47:19 [a]Or *bread* 47:20 [a]Lit *Egypt, every man* 47:22 [a]Lit *ate their allotment* 47:24 [a]Lit *It shall come about...that you shall* [b]Lit *four parts* [A]Gen 41:34 47:26 [a]Lit *alone did* [A]Gen 47:22 47:27 [a]Lit *dwelt* [b]Lit *in the land of Goshen* [A]Gen 47:11 [B]Gen 17:6; 26:4; 35:11; Ex 1:7; Deut 26:5; Acts 7:17 47:28 [a]Lit *days of Jacob, the years of his life* [A]Gen 47:9 47:29 [a]Lit *the days of Israel to die drew near* [b]Lit *truth* [A]Deut 31:14; 1 Kin 2:1 [B]Gen 24:2 [C]Gen 24:49 47:30 [A]Gen 15:15; Deut 31:16 [B]Gen 23:17-20; 25:9, 10; 35:29; 49:29-32; 50:5, 13; Acts 7:15, 16 47:31 [A]Gen 21:23, 24; 24:3; 31:53; 50:25 [B]1 Kin 1:47 48:1 [a]Lit *one said to Joseph* [A]Gen 41:51, 52; Josh 14:4 48:2 [a]Lit *one told Jacob and said* [b]Lit *strengthened himself* [c]Lit *upon the bed* 48:3 [a]Heb *El Shaddai* [A]Gen 28:13f; 35:9-12 [B]Gen 28:19; 35:6 48:4 [a]Lit *seed* [A]Gen 17:8 48:5 [A]Gen 41:50-52; 46:20; 48:1; Josh 14:4 [B]1 Chr 5:1, 2 48:6 [a]Lit *you have begotten* [b]Lit *name* 48:7 [a]Lit *upon me* [A]Gen 33:18 [B]Gen 35:19, 20

the land tenure system at that time, some private land ownership did at first exist, but finally, as in a feudal system, all worked their land for Pharaoh. Landed nobility did lose out and declined during major social reforms undertaken under Senusert III. This is the first record in Scripture of a national income tax, and the amount was 20 percent. Later, after the Exodus, God would prescribe tithes for Israel as national income taxes to support the theocracy (see Mal 3:10).

47:15 When the money was all spent. The severity of the famine finally bankrupted all in Egypt and Canaan. With no monetary instruments available as a medium of exchange, a barter system was established (vv. 16–18).

47:16–18 Land soon replaced animals as the medium of exchange.

47:25, 26 The extra measures imposed by Joseph to control the impact of the famine, i.e., moving parts of the population into cities (v. 21) and demanding a one-fifth tax on crop yields (v. 24), did not affect his approval ratings (v. 25). Whatever the gain to Pharaoh, the people obviously understood that Joseph had not enriched himself at their expense.

47:27, 28 fruitful and ... numerous. For 17 years, Jacob was witness to the increase; he had a glimpse of God's promise to Abraham, Isaac, and himself in the process of being fulfilled.

47:29 your hand under my thigh. Cf. Abraham and Eliezer in Ge 24:9. do not bury me in Egypt. With the customary sign of an oath in that day, Joseph sincerely promised to bury Jacob, at his request, in the family burial cave in Canaan (cf. 49:29–32).

47:31 Cf. Heb 11:21.

48:3–6 After summarizing God's affirmation of the Abrahamic Covenant to himself, Jacob/Israel, in gratitude for Joseph's great generosity and preservation of God's people, formally proclaimed adoption of Joseph's sons on a par with Joseph's brothers in their inheritance, thus granting to Rachel's two sons (Joseph and Benjamin) 3 tribal territories in the Land (cf. v. 16). This may explain why the new name, Israel, was used throughout the rest of the chapter.

48:4 Cf. Ac 7:5.

and I buried her there on the way to Ephrath (that
is, Bethlehem)."
8 When Israel [A]saw Joseph's sons, he said, "Who
are these?" 9 Joseph said to his father, "[A]They are my
sons, whom God has given me here." So he said, "Bring
them to me, please, that [B]I may bless them." 10 Now
[A]the eyes of Israel were *so* dim from age *that* he could
not see. Then [a]Joseph brought them close to him, and
he [B]kissed them and embraced them. 11 Israel said to
Joseph, "I never [a]expected to see your face, and behold,
God has let me see your [b]children as well." 12 Then Joseph [a]took them from his knees, and [A]bowed with his
face to the ground. 13 Joseph took them both, Ephraim
with his right hand toward Israel's left, and Manasseh
with his left hand toward Israel's right, and brought
them close to him. 14 But Israel stretched out his right
hand and laid it on the head of Ephraim, who was
the younger, and his left hand on Manasseh's head,
[a]crossing his hands, [b]although [A]Manasseh was the
firstborn. 15 He blessed Joseph, and said,

"[A]The God before whom my fathers
Abraham and Isaac walked,
[B]The God who has been my shepherd
[a]all my life to this day,
16 [A]The angel who has redeemed
me from all evil,
[B]Bless the lads;
And may my name [a]live on in them,
And the [b]names of my fathers
Abraham and Isaac;
And [C]may they grow into a multitude
in the midst of the earth."

17 When Joseph saw that his father [A]laid his right
hand on Ephraim's head, it displeased him; and
he grasped his father's hand to remove it from
Ephraim's head to Manasseh's head. 18 Joseph said to
his father, "Not so, my father, for this one is the firstborn. Place your right hand on his head." 19 But his
father refused and said, "I know, my son, I know; he
also will become a people and he also will be great.
However, his younger brother shall be greater than
he, and [A]his [a]descendants shall become a [b]multitude
of nations." 20 [A]He blessed them that day, saying,

"By you Israel will pronounce
blessing, saying,
'May God make you like Ephraim
and Manasseh!'"

Thus he put Ephraim before Manasseh. 21 Then Israel said to Joseph, "Behold, I am about to die, but
[A]God will be with you, and [B]bring you back to the
land of your fathers. 22 I give you one [a]portion more
than your brothers, [A]which I took from the hand of
the Amorite with my sword and my bow."

ISRAEL'S PROPHECY CONCERNING HIS SONS

49 Then Jacob summoned his sons and said,
"Assemble yourselves that I may tell you
what will befall you [A]in the [a]days to come.

2 "Gather together and hear, O sons of Jacob;
And [A]listen to Israel your father.

3 "Reuben, you are my firstborn;
My might and [A]the beginning
of my strength,
[a]Preeminent in dignity and
[a]preeminent in power.

48:8 [A]Gen 48:10 48:9 [A]Gen 33:5 [B]Gen 27:4 48:10 [a]Lit *he* [A]Gen 27:1 [B]Gen 27:27 48:11 [a]Lit *meditated, judged* [b]Lit *seed* 48:12 [a]Lit *made them come out* [A]Gen 42:6 48:14 [a]Or *consciously directing* [b]Lit *when* [A]Gen 41:51, 52 48:15 [a]Lit *from the continuance of me* [A]Gen 17:1 [B]Gen 49:24 48:16 [a]Lit *be called* [b]Lit *name* [A]Gen 22:11, 15-18; 28:13-15; 31:11 [B]Heb 11:21 [C]Gen 28:14; 46:3 48:17 [A]Gen 48:14 48:19 [a]Lit *seed* [b]Lit *fullness* [A]Gen 28:14; 46:3 48:20 [A]Heb 11:21 48:21 [A]Gen 26:3 [B]Gen 28:15; 46:4; 50:24 48:22 [a]Or *ridge;* lit *shoulder;* Heb *Shechem* [A]Josh 24:32; John 4:5 49:1 [a]Lit *end of the days* [A]Num 24:14 49:2 [A]Ps 34:11 49:3 [a]Lit *preeminence* [A]Deut 21:17; Ps 78:51; 105:36

48:8 Who are these? Blind Jacob asked for identification of Joseph's sons before he would pronounce their blessings. Perhaps, at this point, he recollected the time of blessing before his own father and the trick played on blind Isaac (27:1–29).

48:14 crossing his hands. Intentionally crossing his hands, Jacob altered what Joseph expected to happen and placed his right hand on the youngest, not on the firstborn. When Joseph attempted to correct Jacob's mistake (vv. 17, 18), he learned that Jacob knew exactly what he was doing (vv. 19, 20). The patriarchal blessing took on prophetic significance with such action and words, since Ephraim would be the most influential of the two to the extent that Ephraim would become a substitute name for Israel (*see note on 48:19*).

48:15 blessed Joseph. With hands on the sons' heads, Jacob uttered the prayer-wish for Joseph, which indicated by his wording that these two would be taking his son's place under Abraham and Isaac. *See note on vv. 3–6.*

48:15, 16 Pessimism no longer overshadowed Jacob's testimony; he recognized that every day had been under God's hand or that of His Angel (*see note on 16:13*). This was a different evaluation of his life than previously given (47:9).

48:16 redeemed me. This is the first mention of God as redeemer, deliverer, or Savior.

48:19 younger brother shall be greater. Ephraim did indeed become the dominant tribe of the 10 northern tribes, eventually being used as the national designate for the 10 tribes in the prophets (Is 7:2, 5, 9, 17; Hos 9:3–16).

48:21 bring you back. Dying Jacob gave voice to his undying trust in God's taking his descendants back to Canaan.

48:22 one portion … with my sword. Jacob's history does not record any conquest of Amorite land. He did purchase property from the children of Hamor (Ge 33:19) but that was not by conquest. At some time this military event had actually occurred, but for some unknown reason it finds no other mention in God's revelation.

49:1–28 With Judah and Joseph receiving the most attention (vv. 8–12, 22–26), the father's blessing portrayed the future history of each son, seemingly based upon their characters up to that time. The cryptic nature of the poetry demands rigorous analysis for correlating tribal history with Jacob's last word and testament. See Moses' blessing on the tribes in Dt 33, ca. 1405 B.C.

49:1 in the days to come. The key expression leading into the poetic content of Jacob's prediction for each son often signifies the last days in prophetic literature (Is 2:2; Eze 38:16) or points more generally to "the latter days" (Dt 4:30; 31:29), i.e., in the sense of "in subsequent days."

49:2–27 The names of the sons are not given in birth order (cf. 29:32–30:24; 35:18), nor in the pattern of wife, then handmaid (cf. 46:8–25). The order is as per the mother: 1) the 6 sons of Leah; 2) one son of Bilhah; 3) two sons of Zilpah; 4) one son of Bilhah; and 5) the two sons of Rachel. Other than the reversal of Leah's fifth and sixth sons, the others remain in chronological order in relation to their mothers. No other pattern is discernible. It may have been nothing more than a mnemonic device, or just how Jacob personally had come to recall them to mind.

49:3, 4 The seriousness of Reuben's sin (35:22) was not forgotten. Its consequences erased his birthright (1Ch 5:1–3), and whatever dignity and majesty he might have had, his tribe received scant mention in Israelite history and produced not one judge, prophet, military

4 “[a]Uncontrolled as water, you shall
not have preeminence,
[A]Because you went up to your father’s bed;
Then you defiled *it*—he went up to my couch.

5 “[A]Simeon and Levi are brothers;
Their swords are implements of violence.
6 “[A]Let my soul not enter into their council;
Let not my glory be united
with their assembly;
Because in their anger they slew [a]men,
And in their self-will they lamed [b]oxen.
7 “Cursed be their anger, for it is fierce;
And their wrath, for it is cruel.
[A]I will [a]disperse them in Jacob,
And scatter them in Israel.

8 “Judah, your brothers shall praise you;
Your hand shall be on the
neck of your enemies;
[A]Your father’s sons shall bow down to you.
9 “Judah is a [A]lion’s whelp;
From the prey, my son, you have gone up.
[B]He [a]couches, he lies down as a lion,
And as a [b]lion, who [c]dares rouse him up?
10 “[A]The scepter shall not depart from Judah,
Nor the ruler’s staff from between his feet,
[a]Until Shiloh comes,
And [B]to him *shall be* the
obedience of the peoples.
11 “[a,A]He ties *his* foal to the vine,
And his donkey’s colt to the choice vine;
[B]He washes his garments in wine,
And his robes in the blood of grapes.
12 “His eyes are [a]dull from wine,
And his teeth [b]white from milk.

13 “[A]Zebulun will dwell at the seashore;
And he *shall be* [a]a haven for ships,
And his flank *shall be* toward Sidon.

14 “Issachar is [a]a strong donkey,
[A]Lying down between the [b]sheepfolds.
15 “When he saw that a resting place was good
And that the land was pleasant,
He bowed his shoulder to bear *burdens*,
And became a slave at forced labor.

16 “[A]Dan shall [B]judge his people,
As one of the tribes of Israel.
17 “Dan shall be a serpent in the way,
A horned snake in the path,
That bites the horse’s heels,
So that his rider falls backward.
18 “[A]For Your salvation I wait, O LORD.

19 “[A]As for Gad, [a]raiders shall raid him,
But he will raid *at* their [b]heels.

20 “[a,A]As for [B]Asher, his [b]food shall be [c]rich,
And he will yield royal dainties.

21 “[A]Naphtali is a doe let loose,
He gives beautiful words.

22 “[A]Joseph is a fruitful [a]bough,
A fruitful [a]bough by a spring;
Its [b]branches run over a wall.

49:4 [a]Or *Boiling over;* lit *Recklessness* [A]Gen 35:22; Deut 27:20; 1 Chr 5:1 49:5 [A]Gen 34:25-30 49:6 [a]Lit *a man* [b]Lit *an ox* [A]Ps 64:2 49:7 [a]Lit *divide* [A]Josh 19:1, 9; 21:1-42 49:8 [A]Gen 27:29; 1 Chr 5:2 49:9 [a]Lit *bows down* [b]Or *lioness* [c]Lit *shall* [A]Ezek 19:5-7; Mic 5:8 [B]Num 24:9 49:10 [a]Or *Until he comes to Shiloh;* or *Until he comes to whom it belongs* [A]Num 24:17; Ps 60:7; 108:8 [B]Ps 2:6-9; 72:8-11; Is 42:1, 4; 49:6 49:11 [a]Lit *Binding of* [A]Deut 8:7, 8; 2 Kin 18:32 [B]Is 63:2 49:12 [a]Or *darker than* [b]Or *whiter than* 49:13 [a]Lit *for a shore of ships* [A]Deut 33:18, 19 49:14 [a]Lit *a donkey of bone* [b]Or *saddlebags* [A]Judg 5:16; Ps 68:13 49:16 [A]Deut 33:22; Judg 18:26, 27 [B]Gen 30:6 49:18 [A]Ex 15:2; Ps 25:5; 40:1-3; 119:166, 174; Is 25:9; Mic 7:7 49:19 [a]Lit *a raiding band* [b]Lit *heel* [A]Deut 33:20 49:20 [a]Lit *From* [b]Or *bread* [c]Lit *fat* [A]Deut 33:24, 25 [B]Gen 30:13 49:21 [A]Deut 33:23 49:22 [a]Lit *son* [b]Lit *daughters* [A]Deut 33:13-17

leader, or other important person (cf. Jdg 5:15; 1Ch 5:1). Moses prayed for this tribe not to die out (Dt 33:6). “Uncontrolled as water” lit. means “boiling” and shows instability.

49:5–7 The cruelty and anger of Simeon and Levi at Shechem were not forgotten (34:25). Their consequences affected Simeon who: 1) became the smallest tribe in the second census of Moses (Nu 26:14); 2) was omitted from the blessing of Moses (Dt 33:8); and 3) later shared territory with Judah (Jos 19:1–9). Levi was “scattered” (v. 7) throughout Israel; they became, by God’s grace and through their loyalty to God (Ex 32:26), the priestly tribe and residents of the cities of refuge. Neither possessed their own designated region in the Land, although Levi’s priestly position was certainly a privileged one (cf. Dt 33:8–11; Jos 21:1–3). “Lamed” means to cut the leg tendons as a means of destroying the animal’s usefulness.

49:8–12 As strong as a young lion and entrenched as an old lion, to Judah’s line belonged national prominence and kingship, including David, Solomon, and their dynasty (640 years after this), as well as “the one to whom the scepter belongs” i.e., Shiloh, the cryptogram for the Messiah, the one also called the “Lion from the Tribe of Judah” (Rev 5:5). On the march through the wilderness, Judah went first (Nu 10:14) and had the largest population in Moses’ census (cf. Nu 1:27; 26:22). This language (vv. 11, 12) describes prosperity so great that people will tie a donkey to a choice vine, letting it eat because there is such abundance; wine will be as plentiful as water and everyone will be healthy. This is likely a millennial prophecy.

49:13 Although Zebulun’s territory did not border the Mediterranean nor the Sea of Galilee, the tribe was situated to benefit from the important trade route, the Via Maris, traversed by sea traders moving through her territory.

49:14, 15 Issachar, an industrious, robust, hardy, and stalwart tribe, lived up to the name of their founder whose name meant “man of wages” (cf. 1Ch 7:1–5; 12:32).

49:16–18 Dan, whose name meant “Judge,” fathered an aggressive tribe that would also judge in the nation but would not be known for moral stature or religious faithfulness (cf. Jdg 13:2; 18:1ff.; 1Ki 12:28–30; 2Ki 10:29). Dan would later abandon its land allotment (Jos 19:40–48) and migrate to the extreme north of Israel (Jdg 18:1–31). Jacob’s closing cry expressed hope for Dan in the day when salvation would indeed come to Israel. Dan, however, is omitted in the list of tribes in Rev 7:4–8.

49:19 Settling in Transjordan exposed Gad’s people to invasions, making them valiant fighters worthy of victory and commendation (cf. 1Ch 5:18–22; 12:8–15).

49:20 Asher benefited much from occupying the agriculturally rich coastal region N of Carmel, and provided gourmet delights for the palace. Cf. Jos 19:24–31.

49:21 Deer-like speed and agility marked Naphtali’s military prowess (cf. Jdg 4:6; 5:18). The song of Deborah and Barak, who hailed from Naphtali (Jdg 4:6), is representative of his eloquent words (Jdg 5).

49:22–26 Addressed to Joseph, but applicable to his two sons (cf. 48:15–20), these words thrust forth a contrasting experience of growth and prosperity alongside hostility and conflict. Verses 23, 24 may be a biography of Joseph. No other tribe had such direct reference to the Lord God (vv. 24, 25) in their blessing as addressed to Joseph. The 4 names for God well reflect Joseph’s

23 “The archers bitterly attacked him,
And shot *at him* and harassed him;
24 But his [A]bow remained [a]firm,
And [b,B]his arms were agile,
From the hands of the
[C]Mighty One of Jacob
(From there is [D]the Shepherd,
[E]the Stone of Israel),
25 From [A]the God of your father
who helps you,
And [a,B]by the [b]Almighty who blesses you
With [C]blessings of heaven above,
Blessings of the deep that lies beneath,
Blessings of the breasts and of the womb.
26 “The blessings of your father
Have surpassed the blessings
of my ancestors
Up to the [a]utmost bound of
[A]the everlasting hills;
May they be on the head of Joseph,
And on the crown of the head of the one
distinguished among his brothers.

27 “Benjamin is a [a]ravenous wolf;
In the morning he devours the prey,
And in the evening he divides the spoil.”

28 All these are the twelve tribes of Israel, and this
is what their father said to them [a]when he blessed
them. He blessed them, every one [b]with the blessing appropriate to him. 29 Then he charged them
and said to them, “I am about to be [A]gathered to
my people; [B]bury me with my fathers in the cave
that is in [C]the field of Ephron the Hittite, 30 in the
[A]cave that is in the field of Machpelah, which is before Mamre, in the land of Canaan, which Abraham
bought along with the field from Ephron the Hittite
for a [a]burial site. 31 There they buried [A]Abraham
and his wife [B]Sarah, there they buried [C]Isaac and
his wife Rebekah, and there I buried Leah— 32 the
field and the cave that is in it, purchased from the
sons of Heth.” 33 When Jacob finished charging his
sons, he drew his feet into the bed and [A]breathed
his last, and was [B]gathered to his people.

THE DEATH OF ISRAEL

50 Then Joseph fell on his father’s face, and
wept over him and kissed him. 2 Joseph commanded his servants the physicians to embalm his
father. So the physicians [A]embalmed Israel. 3 Now
forty days were [a]required for [b]it, for [c]such is the
period required for embalming. And the Egyptians
[A]wept for him seventy days.
4 When the days of [a]mourning for him were past,
Joseph spoke to the household of Pharaoh, saying,
“If now I have found favor in your sight, please
speak [b]to Pharaoh, saying, 5 ‘[A]My father made me
swear, saying, “Behold, I am about to die; in my
grave [B]which I dug for myself in the land of Canaan,
there you shall bury me.” Now therefore, please let
me go up and bury my father; then I will return.’ ”
6 Pharaoh said, “Go up and bury your father, as he
made you swear.”
7 So Joseph went up to bury his father, and with
him went up all the servants of Pharaoh, the elders
of his household and all the elders of the land of
Egypt, 8 and all the household of Joseph and his
brothers and his father’s household; they left only
their little ones and their flocks and their herds
in the land of Goshen. 9 There also went up with
him both chariots and horsemen; and it was a very
great company. 10 When they came to the [a]thresh-
ing floor of Atad, which is beyond the Jordan, they
[A]lamented there with a very great and [b]sorrowful
lamentation; and he [c]observed seven days mourning for his father. 11 Now when the inhabitants of

49:24 [a]I.e. in an unyielding position [b]Lit *the arms of his hands* [A]Job 29:20 [B]Ps 18:34; 73:23; Is 41:10 [C]Ps 132:2, 5; Is 1:24; 49:26 [D]Ps 23:1; 80:1 [E]Ps 118:22; Is 28:16; 1 Pet 2:6-8 49:25 [a]Or *with* [b]Heb *Shaddai* [A]Gen 28:13; 32:9 [B]Gen 28:3; 48:3 [C]Gen 27:28 49:26 [a]Lit *limit; or desire* [A]Deut 33:15, 16 49:27 [a]Lit *a wolf that tears* 49:28 [a]Lit *and* [b]Lit *according to his blessing* 49:29 [A]Gen 25:8 [B]Gen 47:30 [C]Gen 23:16-20; 50:13 49:30 [a]Lit *possession of a burial place* [A]Gen 23:3-20 49:31 [A]Gen 25:9 [B]Gen 23:19 [C]Gen 35:29 49:33 [A]Gen 25:8; Acts 7:15 [B]Gen 49:29 50:2 [A]Gen 50:26; 2 Chr 16:14; Matt 26:12; Mark 16:1; John 19:39, 40 50:3 [a]Lit *fulfilled* [b]Or *him* [c]Lit *so are fulfilled the days of embalming* [A]Gen 50:10; Num 20:29; Deut 34:8 50:4 [a]Lit *weeping* [b]Lit *In the ears of* 50:5 [A]Gen 47:29-31 [B]2 Chr 16:14; Is 22:16; Matt 27:60 50:10 [a]Heb *Goren ha-Atad* [b]Lit *heavy* [c]Lit *made a mourning for seven days* [A]Acts 8:2

emphasis on the sovereignty of his God, no matter the misfortune and grief which attended his way (cf. v. 23). Samuel was from Ephraim, Gideon from Manasseh.

49:27 The warlike nature of the small tribe of Benjamin became well known, as exhibited in their archers and slingers (Jdg 20:16; 1Ch 8:40; 12:2; 2Ch 14:8; 17:17) and in their brazen defense of their wickedness in Gibeah (Jdg 19, 20). Both Sauls in the Bible were from this tribe: the first king in Israel (1Sa 9:1, 2) and the Apostle Paul (Php 3:5).

49:29–32 Jacob’s dying instructions were fully carried out (cf. 50:12–14). See 23:6–20.

49:31 there I buried Leah. Honor was finally accorded to Leah in death and in Jacob’s request to be buried alongside his wife, as were his fathers. Burial alongside Rachel, the beloved wife, was not requested.

49:33 Jacob … breathed his last. Ca. 1858 B.C. **gathered to his people.** *See note on 25:8.*

50:2, 3 physicians to embalm. Joseph summoned medical men, who were fully capable of embalming, rather than the religious embalmers in order to avoid the magic and mysticism associated with their practices. Usually in Egypt, mummifying was a 40-day process, which included gutting the body, drying it, and wrapping it.

50:3–6 Once normal embalming and mourning had been properly observed according to Egyptian custom, Joseph was free to seek permission to conduct a funeral in Canaan.

50:7–11 Out of respect for Joseph, a substantial escort accompanied him and all his relatives into the land of Canaan. This extraordinary event gave assurance to later generations because the bodies of the 3 patriarchs were in Canaan and Joseph’s bones awaited transport there when, as per Joseph’s last words, God’s promises to the 3 began to be fulfilled.

ADAM TO ISRAEL’S TWELVE TRIBES

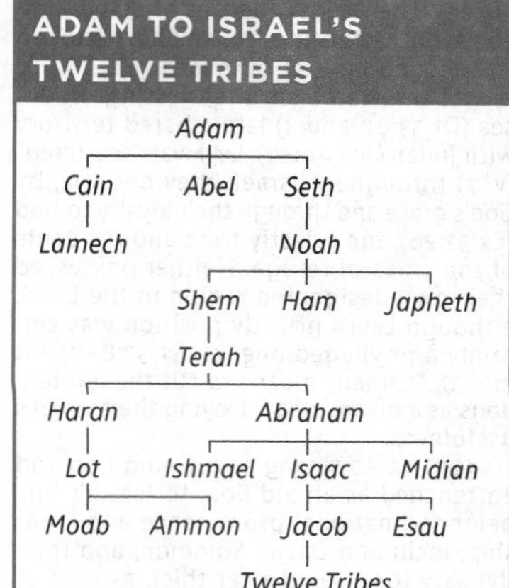

the land, the Canaanites, saw the mourning at [a]the
threshing floor of Atad, they said, "This is a [b]griev-
ous [c]mourning for the Egyptians." Therefore it was
named [d]Abel-mizraim, which is beyond the Jordan.

BURIAL AT MACHPELAH

12 Thus his sons did for him as he had charged
them; 13 for his sons carried him to the land of Canaan and buried him in [A]the cave of the field of
Machpelah before Mamre, which Abraham had
bought along with the field for a [a]burial site from
Ephron the Hittite. 14 After he had buried his father,
Joseph returned to Egypt, he and his brothers, and
all who had gone up with him to bury his father.

15 When Joseph's brothers saw that their father was dead, they said, "[A]What if Joseph bears a
grudge against us and pays us back in full for all
the wrong which we did to him!" 16 So they [a]sent *a*
message to Joseph, saying, "Your father charged
before he died, saying, 17 'Thus you shall say to Joseph, "Please forgive, I beg you, the transgression
of your brothers and their sin, for they did you
wrong." ' And now, please forgive the transgression of the servants of the God of your father." And
Joseph wept when they spoke to him. 18 Then his
brothers also came and [A]fell down before him and
said, "Behold, we are your servants." 19 But Joseph
said to them, "Do not be afraid, for am I in God's
place? 20 As for you, [A]you meant evil against me,
but God meant it for good in order to bring about
[a]this present result, to preserve many people alive.
21 So therefore, do not be afraid; [A]I will provide for
you and your little ones." So he comforted them
and spoke [a]kindly to them.

DEATH OF JOSEPH

22 Now Joseph stayed in Egypt, he and his father's household, and Joseph lived one hundred
and ten years. 23 Joseph saw the third generation
of Ephraim's sons; also the sons of Machir, the son
of Manasseh, were [A]born on Joseph's knees. 24 Joseph said to his brothers, "[A]I am about to die, but
God will surely [a]take care of you and bring you up
from this land to the land which He [b]promised on
oath to [B]Abraham, to [C]Isaac and to [D]Jacob." 25 Then
Joseph made the sons of Israel swear, saying, "God
will surely [a]take care of you, and [A]you shall carry my
bones up from here." 26 So Joseph died at the age of
one hundred and ten years; and [a]he was [A]embalmed
and placed in a coffin in Egypt.

50:11 [a]Heb *Goren ha-Atad* [b]Lit *heavy* [c]Heb *ebel* [d]I.e. the meadow (or mourning) of Egypt 50:13 [a]Lit *possession of a burial place* [A]Gen 23:16-20; Acts 7:16 50:15 [A]Gen 37:28; 42:21, 22 50:16 [a]Lit *commanded* 50:18 [A]Gen 37:8-10; 41:43 50:20 [a]Lit *as it is this day* [A]Gen 37:26, 27; 45:5, 7 50:21 [a]Lit *to their heart* [A]Gen 45:11; 47:12 50:23 [A]Gen 30:3 50:24 [a]Or *visit* [b]Lit *swore* [A]Gen 48:21; Ex 3:16, 17; Heb 11:22 [B]Gen 13:15, 17; 15:7, 8, 18 [C]Gen 26:3 [D]Gen 28:13; 35:12 50:25 [a]Or *visit* [A]Gen 47:29, 30; Ex 13:19; Josh 24:32; Heb 11:22 50:26 [a]Lit *they embalmed him* [A]Gen 50:2

50:15–18 The brothers' guilty consciences reasserted themselves and caused them to seriously underestimate the genuineness of Joseph's forgiveness and affection for them. Jacob's concern to plead on his sons' behalf equally underestimated Joseph's words and actions toward his brethren.

50:19 **am I in God's place?** This concise question tweaked their memory of his explanation of how God had put him where he was (cf. 45:3–8), in the place God intended him to be at that time.

50:20 ***but* God meant it for good.** Joseph's wise, theological answer has gone down in history as the classic statement of God's sovereignty over the affairs of men. *See note on 45:1–8.*

50:24 **God will surely take care of you.** Joseph died just as he had lived, firmly trusting in God to carry out His promises (cf. Heb 11:22). Almost 4 centuries later, Moses took Joseph's remains out of Egypt (Ex 13:19) and Joshua buried them at Shechem (Jos 24:32). **to Abraham, to Isaac and to Jacob.** The death of Jacob had finally allowed for the 3 patriarchs to be mentioned together.

50:26 **age of one hundred and ten years.** Ca. 1804 B.C. Joseph's span of life was considered, at that time in Egypt, an ideal lifespan. Amenemhet III (ca. 1841–1792 B.C.) was the reigning Pharaoh. Exodus picked up the historical narrative, after a 280-year silence, ca. 1525 B.C. with the birth of Moses. *See note on Ex 1:6–8.*

JOSEPH—A TYPE OF CHRIST

Joseph	Parallels	Jesus
37:2	A shepherd of his father's sheep	Jn 10:11, 27–29
37:3	His father loved him dearly	Mt 3:17
37:4	Hated by his brothers	Jn 7:4, 5
37:13, 14	Sent by father to brothers	Heb 2:11
37:20	Others plotted to harm them	Jn 11:53
37:23	Robes taken from them	Jn 19:23, 24
37:26	Taken to Egypt	Mt 2:14, 15
37:28	Sold for the price of a slave	Mt 26:15
39:7	Tempted	Mt 4:1
39:16–18	Falsely accused	Mt 26:59, 60
39:20	Bound in chains	Mt 27:2
40:2, 3	Placed with two other prisoners, one who was saved and the other lost	Lk 23:32
41:41	Exalted after suffering	Php 2:9–11
41:46	Both 30 years old at the beginning of public recognition	Lk 3:23
42:24; 45:2, 14, 15; 46:29	Both wept	Jn 11:35
45:1–15	Forgave those who wronged them	Lk 23:34
45:7	Saved their nation	Mt 1:21
50:20	What men did to hurt them, God turned to good	1Co 2:7, 8

THE SECOND BOOK OF MOSES CALLED

EXODUS

TITLE

The Greek Septuagint (LXX) and the Latin Vulgate versions of the OT assigned the title "Exodus" to this second book of Moses, because the departure of Israel from Egypt is the dominant historical fact in the book (19:1). In the Hebrew Bible, the opening words, "And (or Now) these are the names," served as the title of the book. The opening "And" or "Now" in the Hebrew title suggests that this book was to be accepted as the obvious sequel to Genesis, the first book of Moses. Hebrews 11:22 commends the faith of Joseph who, while on his deathbed (ca. 1804 B.C.), spoke of the "exodus" of the sons of Israel, looking ahead over 350 years to the Exodus (ca. 1445 B.C.).

AUTHOR AND DATE

Mosaic authorship of Exodus is unhesitatingly affirmed. Moses followed God's instructions and "wrote down all the words of the LORD" (24:4), which included at the least the record of the battle with Amalek (17:14), the Ten Commandments (34:4, 27–29), and the Book of the Covenant (20:22–23:33). Similar assertions of Mosaic writing occur elsewhere in the Pentateuch: Moses is identified as the one who recorded the "starting places according to their journeys" (Nu 33:2) and who "wrote this law" (Dt 31:9).

The OT corroborates Mosaic authorship of the portions mentioned above (see Jos 1:7, 8; 8:31, 32; 1Ki 2:3; 2Ki 14:6; Ne 13:1; Da 9:11–13; and Mal 4:4). The NT concurs by citing Ex 3:6 as part of "the book of Moses" (Mk 12:26), by assigning Ex 13:2 to "the law of Moses," which is also referred to as "the Law of the Lord" (Lk 2:22, 23), by ascribing Ex 20:12 and 21:17 to Moses (Mk 7:10), by attributing the law to Moses (Jn 7:19; Ro 10:5), and by Jesus' specifically declaring that Moses had written of Him (Jn 5:46, 47).

At some time during his 40-year tenure as Israel's leader, beginning at 80 years of age and ending at 120 (7:7; Dt 34:7), Moses wrote down this second of his 5 books. More specifically, it would have been after the Exodus and obviously before his death on Mt. Nebo in the plains of Moab. The date of the Exodus (ca. 1445 B.C.) dictates the date of the writing in the 15th century B.C.

Scripture dates Solomon's fourth year of reign, when he began to build the temple (ca. 966/65 B.C.), as being 480 years after the Exodus (1Ki 6:1), establishing the early date of 1445 B.C. Jephthah noted that, by his day, Israel had possessed Heshbon for 300 years (Jdg 11:26). Calculating backward and forward from Jephthah, and taking into account different periods of foreign oppression, judgeships and kingships, the wilderness wanderings, and the initial entry and conquest of Canaan under Joshua, this early date is confirmed and amounts to 480 years.

Scripture also dates the entry of Jacob and his extended family into Egypt (ca. 1875 B.C.) as being 430 years before the Exodus (12:40), thus placing Joseph in what archeologists have designated as the 12th Dynasty, the Middle Kingdom period of Egyptian history, and placing Moses and Israel's final years of residence and slavery in what archeologists have designated as the 18th Dynasty, or New Kingdom period. Further, Joseph's stint as vizier over all of Egypt (Ge 45:8) precludes his having served under the Hyksos (ca. 1730–1570 B.C.), the foreign invaders who ruled during a period of confusion in Egypt and who never controlled all of the country. They were a mixed Semitic race who introduced the composite bow. These implements of war made possible their expulsion from Egypt.

BACKGROUND AND SETTING

Eighteenth Dynasty Egypt, the setting for Israel's dramatic departure, was not a politically or economically weak and obscure period of Egyptian history. Thutmose III, for example, the Pharaoh of the Oppression has been called the "Napoleon of Ancient Egypt," the sovereign who expanded the boundaries of Egyptian influence far beyond natural borders. This was the dynasty which over a century before, under the leadership of Amose I, had expelled the Hyksos kings from the country and redirected the country's economic, military, and diplomatic growth. At the time of the Exodus, Egypt was strong, not weak.

Moses, born in 1525 B.C. (80 years old in 1445 B.C.), became "educated in all the learning of the Egyptians" (Ac 7:22) while growing up in the courts of Pharaohs Thutmose I and II and Queen Hatshepsut for his first 40 years (Ac 7:23). He was in self-imposed, Midianite exile during the reign of Thutmose III for another 40 years (Ac 7:30), and returned at God's direction to be Israel's leader early in the reign of

Amenhotep II, the Pharaoh of the Exodus. God used both the educational system of Egypt and his exile in Midian to prepare Moses to represent his people before a powerful pharaoh and to guide his people through the wilderness of the Sinai Peninsula during his final 40 years (Ac 7:36). Moses died on Mt. Nebo when he was 120 years old (Dt 34:1–6), as God's judgment was on him for his anger and disrespect (Nu 20:1–13). While he looked on from afar, Moses never entered the Promised Land. Centuries later he appeared to the disciples on the Mt. of Transfiguration (Mt 17:3).

HISTORICAL AND THEOLOGICAL THEMES

In God's timing, the Exodus marked the end of a period of oppression for Abraham's descendants (Ge 15:13), and constituted the beginning of the fulfillment of the covenant promise to Abraham that his descendants would not only reside in the Promised Land, but would also multiply and become a great nation (Ge 12:1–3, 7). The purpose of the book may be expressed like this: to trace the rapid growth of Jacob's descendants from Egypt to the establishment of the theocratic nation.

At appropriate times, on Mt. Sinai and in the plains of Moab, God also gave the Israelites that body of legislation, the law, which they needed for living properly in Israel as the theocratic people of God. By this, they were distinct from all other nations (Dt 4:7, 8; Ro 9:4, 5).

By God's self-revelation, the Israelites were instructed in the sovereignty and majesty, the goodness and holiness, and the grace and mercy of their Lord, the one and only God of heaven and earth (see especially Ex 3, 6, 33, 34). The account of the Exodus and the events that followed are also the subject of other major biblical revelation (cf. Pss 105:25–45; 106:6–27; Ac 7:17–44; 1Co 10:1–13; Heb 9:1–6; 11:23–29).

INTERPRETIVE CHALLENGES

The absence of any Egyptian record of the devastation of Egypt by the 10 plagues and the major defeat of Pharaoh's elite army at the Red Sea should not give rise to speculation on whether the account is historically authentic. Egyptian historiography did not permit records of their pharaohs' embarrassments and ignominious defeats to be published. In recording the Conquest under Joshua, Scripture specifically notes the three cities which Israel destroyed and burned (Jos 6:24; 8:28; 11:11–13). The Conquest, after all, was one of takeover and inhabitation of property virtually intact, not a war designed to destroy. The date of Israel's march into Canaan will not be confirmed, therefore, by examining extensive burn levels at city-sites of a later period.

Despite the absence of any extrabiblical, ancient Near Eastern records of the Hebrew bondage, the plagues, the Exodus, and the Conquest, archeological evidence corroborates the early date. All the pharaohs, for example, of the 15th century left evidence of interest in building enterprises in Lower Egypt. These projects were obviously accessible to Moses in the Delta region near Goshen.

The typological significance of the tabernacle has occasioned much reflection. Ingenuity in linking every item of furniture and every piece of building material to Christ may appear most intriguing, but if NT statements and allusions do not support such linkage and typology then hermeneutical caution must rule. The tabernacle's structure and ornamentation for efficiency and beauty are one thing, but finding hidden meaning and symbolism is unfounded. How the sacrificial and worship system of the tabernacle and its parts meaningfully typify the redeeming work of the coming Messiah must be left to those NT passages which treat the subject.

OUTLINE

I. Israel in Egypt (1:1–12:36)

- A. The Population Explosion (1:1–7)
- B. The Oppression Under the Pharaohs (1:8–22)
- C. The Maturation of a Deliverer (2:1–4:31)
- D. The Confrontation with Pharaoh (5:1–11:10)
- E. The Preparation for Departure (12:1–36)

II. Israel on the Road to Sinai (12:37–18:27)

- A. Exiting Egypt and Panicking (12:37–14:14)
- B. Crossing the Red Sea and Rejoicing (14:15–15:21)
- C. Traveling to Sinai and Grumbling (15:22–17:16)
- D. Meeting with Jethro and Learning (18:1–27)

III. Israel Encamped at Sinai (19:1–40:38)

- A. The Law of God Prescribed (19:1–24:18)
- B. The Tabernacle of God Described (25:1–31:18)
- C. The Worship of God Defiled (32:1–35)
- D. The Presence of God Confirmed (33:1–34:35)
- E. The Tabernacle of God Constructed (35:1–40:38)

ISRAEL MULTIPLIES IN EGYPT

1 Now these are the [A]names of the sons of Israel
who came to Egypt with Jacob; they came each
one [a]with his household: 2 Reuben, Simeon, Levi and
Judah; 3 Issachar, Zebulun and Benjamin; 4 Dan and
Naphtali, Gad and Asher. 5 All the [a]persons who came
from the loins of Jacob were [A]seventy [b]in number,
but Joseph was *already* in Egypt. 6 [A]Joseph died, and
all his brothers and all that generation. 7 But the
sons of Israel [A]were fruitful and [a]increased greatly,
and multiplied, and became exceedingly [b]mighty,
so that the land was filled with them.
8 Now a new [A]king arose over Egypt, who did not
know Joseph. 9 [A]He said to his people, "Behold, the
people of the sons of Israel are [a]more and mightier
than we. 10 Come, let us [A]deal wisely with them, or
else they will multiply and [a]in the event of war, they
will also join themselves to those who hate us, and
fight against us and [b]depart from the land." 11 So they
appointed [A]taskmasters over them to afflict them
with [a,B]hard labor. And they built for Pharaoh [C]storage cities, Pithom and [D]Raamses. 12 But the more
they afflicted them, [A]the more they multiplied and
the more they [a]spread out, so that they were in dread
of the sons of Israel. 13 The Egyptians compelled the
sons of Israel [A]to labor rigorously; 14 and they made
[A]their lives bitter with hard labor in mortar and
bricks and at all *kinds* of labor in the field, all their
labors which they rigorously [a]imposed on them.
15 Then the king of Egypt spoke to the Hebrew
midwives, one of whom [a]was named Shiphrah and
the other [a]was named Puah; 16 and he said, "When
you are helping the Hebrew women to give birth and
see *them* upon the birthstool, [A]if it is a son, then you
shall put him to death; but if it is a daughter, then she
shall live." 17 But the midwives [a,A]feared God, and [B]did
not do as the king of Egypt had [b]commanded them,
but let the boys live. 18 So the king of Egypt called for
the midwives and said to them, "Why have you done
this thing, and let the boys live?" 19 The midwives
said to Pharaoh, "Because the Hebrew women are
not as the Egyptian women; for they are vigorous
and give birth before the midwife [a]can get to them."
20 So [A]God was good to the midwives, and [B]the people
multiplied, and became very [a]mighty. 21 Because the
midwives [a,A]feared God, He [b,B]established [c]households
for them. 22 Then Pharaoh commanded all his people,
saying, "[A]Every son who is born [a]you are to cast into
[B]the Nile, and every daughter you are to keep alive."

THE BIRTH OF MOSES

2 Now a man from [A]the house of Levi went and
[a]married a daughter of Levi. 2 The woman
conceived and bore a son; and when she saw

1:1 [a]Lit *and* [A]Gen 46:8-27 1:5 [a]Lit *souls* [b]Lit *as to souls* [A]Gen 46:26, 27; Deut 10:22 1:6 [A]Gen 50:26 1:7 [a]Lit *swarmed* [b]Or *numerous* [A]Gen 12:2; 28:3; 35:11; 46:3; 47:27; 48:4; Deut 26:5; Ps 105:24; Acts 7:17 1:8 [A]Acts 7:18, 19 1:9 [a]Or *too many and too mighty for us* [A]Ps 105:24, 25 1:10 [a]Lit *it came about when war befalls that* [b]Lit *go up from* [A]Acts 7:19 1:11 [a]Lit *their burdens* [A]Gen 15:13; Ex 3:7; 5:6 [B]Ex 1:14; 2:11; 5:4-9; 6:6f [C]1 Kin 9:19; 2 Chr 8:4 [D]Gen 47:11 1:12 [a]Lit *broke forth* [A]Ex 1:7 1:13 [A]Gen 15:13; Deut 4:20 1:14 [a]Lit *worked through them* [A]Ex 2:23; 6:9; Num 20:15; Acts 7:19 1:15 [a]Lit *the name was* 1:16 [A]Acts 7:19 1:17 [a]Or *revered* [b]Lit *spoken to* [A]Ex 1:21; Prov 16:6 [B]Acts 4:18-20; 5:29 1:19 [a]Lit *comes to* 1:20 [a]Or *numerous* [A]Prov 11:18; Eccl 8:12; Heb 6:10 [B]Ex 1:12; Is 3:10 1:21 [a]Or *revered* [b]Lit *made* [c]Or *families* [A]Ex 1:17 [B]1 Sam 2:35; 2 Sam 7:11, 27; 1 Kin 2:24; 11:38 1:22 [a]Some versions insert *to the Hebrews* [A]Acts 7:19 [B]Gen 41:1 2:1 [a]Lit *took* [A]Ex 6:16, 18, 20

1:1–12:36 This section recounts Israel's final years in Egypt before the Exodus.

1:1–5 Genesis also reported the names and the number of Jacob's descendants who came to Egypt (Ge 35:23–26; 46:8–27).

1:5 seventy in number. Cf. Ge 46:8–27. Ac 7:14 reports 75 with the addition of 5 relatives of Joseph included in the LXX, but not the Heb. text.

1:6–8 This summary of a lengthy period of time moves the record from the death of Joseph (ca. 1804 B.C.), the last recorded event in Genesis, to the radical change in Israel's history, i.e., from favor before Egypt's pharaoh to disfavor and enslavement (ca. 1525–1445 B.C.).

1:7 The growth of the nation (cf. 12:37) was phenomenal! It grew from 70 men to 603,000 males, 20 years of age and older, thus allowing for a total population of about 2 million (Nu 1:46) departing from Egypt. The seed of Abraham was no longer an extended family, but a nation. The promise that his descendants would be fruitful and multiply (Ge 35:11, 12) had indeed been fulfilled in Egypt.

1:8 a new king arose. This king is either to be identified as one of the Hyksos kings (see Introduction) during a period of political disintegration, or as Pharaoh Ahmose I, founder of what archeologists have designated as the 18th Dynasty of the New Kingdom period in Egyptian history. It is probably best to take this new king, who did not know Joseph, as a Hyksos ruler. Furthermore, the term "arose" signifies "rose against," which accords well with a foreign seizure of the Egyptian throne. The Hyksos (ca. 1730–1570 B.C.) came from outside Egypt (cf. Ac 7:18).

1:9–12 Another summary of a fairly lengthy period of time, as indicated by the population continuing to grow in spite of increasing hardship imposed on Israel.

1:9 the people. An Egyptian pharaoh designated Israel as a nation, marking the first time the term "people" or "nation" is used of them.

1:10, 11 join … those who hate us … appointed taskmasters over them. Israel was assessed both as a threat to national security and as an economic asset—slavery would, therefore, control the danger and maximize their usefulness.

1:11 storage cities, Pithom and Raamses. Places where both provisions and military hardware were stored. Archeological identification has not been finally definitive, with some 3 to 5 options being put forward for them. Pithom is usually taken as a center of solar worship in northern Egypt, and Raamses as Qantir in the eastern Delta region. In addition, the city might very well have been renamed under the reign of the later, powerful pharaoh, and that name was better known to Israel later on (cf. the case of Laish, or Leshem, renamed Dan in Ge 14:14, Jos 19:47, and Jdg 18:29).

1:13 The Egyptians. The native inhabitants continued to enslave Israel. Between vv. 12 and 13 a major change in Egyptian history took place—the Hyksos were driven out (ca. 1570 B.C.).

1:14 hard labor in mortar and bricks. Archeologists have uncovered reliefs and paintings confirming the Egyptian practice of imposing forced labor on prisoners and slaves. These paintings also show foremen and guards watching construction work while scribes registered data on tablets.

1:15–17 the midwives feared God. These brave, older women reverenced their God and thus obeyed Him and not man. They obviously understood that children were a gift from God and that murder was wrong. The two midwives mentioned by name were probably the leading representatives of their profession, for it is unlikely that such a burgeoning population had only two midwives to deal with all the births.

1:15, 16 The failure of rigorous bondage to suppress population growth necessitated that different measures be taken; hence, the royal order to the Hebrew midwives to murder male infants at birth.

1:16 birthstool. Lit. "two stones" on which the women sat to deliver.

1:19, 20 Rather than trying to argue for a justifiable lie on the part of midwives seeking to protect God's people, take it as a statement of what was true: God was directly involved in this affair of birth and national growth. That's the key to understanding why no decree of Pharaoh would work out as he intended it, and why Hebrew women were so healthy and gave birth with ease.

1:22 The failure of the extermination program demanded of the midwives finally caused Pharaoh to demand that all his subjects get involved in murdering newborn boys.

2:1, 2 Since Moses was born soon after the general decree of 1:22 was given (ca. 1525 B.C.), the issuer of the decree was Thutmose I.

[a]that he was [b,A]beautiful, she hid him for three
months. 3But when she could hide him no longer,
she got him a [a,A]wicker [b]basket and covered it over
with tar and pitch. Then she put the child into it
and set *it* among the [B]reeds by the bank of the Nile.
4[A]His sister stood at a distance to [a]find out what
would [b]happen to him.
5The daughter of Pharaoh came down [A]to bathe
at the Nile, with her maidens walking alongside the
Nile; and she saw the [a]basket among the reeds and
sent her maid, and she brought it *to her.* 6When
she opened *it,* she [a]saw the child, and behold, *the*
[b]boy was crying. And she had pity on him and
said, "This is one of the Hebrews' children." 7Then
his sister said to Pharaoh's daughter, "Shall I go
and call [a]a nurse for you from the Hebrew women
that she may nurse the child for you?" 8Pharaoh's
daughter said to her, "Go *ahead.*" So the girl went
and called the child's mother. 9Then Pharaoh's
daughter said to her, "Take this child away and
nurse him for me and I will give *you* your wages."
So the woman took the child and nursed him.
10The child grew, and she brought him to Pharaoh's daughter and [A]he became her son. And she
named him [a]Moses, and said, "Because I [b]drew
him out of the water."
11Now it came about in those days, [A]when Moses
had grown up, that he went out to his brethren and
looked on their [a,B]hard labors; and [C]he saw an Egyptian beating a Hebrew, one of his brethren. 12So he
[a]looked this way and that, and when he saw there
was no one *around,* he [A]struck down the Egyptian
and hid him in the sand. 13He went out [A]the next
day, and behold, two Hebrews were [a]fighting with
each other; and he said to the [b]offender, "Why are
you striking your companion?" 14But he said, "[A]Who
made you a [a]prince or a judge over us? Are you [b]in-
tending to kill me as you killed the Egyptian?" Then
Moses was afraid and said, "Surely the matter has
become known."

MOSES ESCAPES TO MIDIAN

15When Pharaoh heard of this matter, he tried
to kill Moses. But [A]Moses fled from the presence of
Pharaoh and [a]settled in the land of Midian, and he
sat down [B]by a well.
16Now [A]the priest of Midian had seven daughters;
and [B]they came to draw water and filled the troughs
to water their father's flock. 17Then the shepherds
came and drove them away, but [A]Moses stood up
and helped them and watered their flock. 18When
they came to [A]Reuel their father, he said, "Why have
you come *back* so soon today?" 19So they said, "An
Egyptian delivered us from the hand of the shepherds, and what is more, he even drew the water for
us and watered the flock." 20He said to his daughters,
"Where is he then? Why is it that you have left the
man behind? Invite him [a]to have something to eat."
21[A]Moses was willing to dwell with the man, and he
gave his daughter [B]Zipporah to Moses. 22Then she
gave birth to [A]a son, and he named him [a]Gershom, for
he said, "I have been [B]a [b]sojourner in a foreign land."
23Now it came about in *the course of* those many
days that the king of Egypt died. And the sons of Israel [A]sighed because of the bondage, and they cried
out; and [B]their cry for help because of *their* bondage
rose up to God. 24So [A]God heard their groaning; and
God remembered [B]His covenant with Abraham,
Isaac, and Jacob. 25[A]God saw the sons of Israel, and
God [a]took notice *of them.*

THE BURNING BUSH

3 Now Moses was pasturing the flock of [A]Jethro
his father-in-law, the priest of Midian; and
he led the flock to the [a]west side of the wilderness and came to [B]Horeb, the [C]mountain of God.

2:2 [a]Lit *him that* [b]Lit *good* [A]Acts 7:20; Heb 11:23 2:3 [a]I.e. papyrus reeds [b]Or *chest* [A]Is 18:2 [B]Is 19:6 2:4 [a]Lit *know* [b]Lit *be done* [A]Ex 15:20; Num 26:59 2:5 [a]Or *chest* [A]Ex 7:15; 8:20 2:6 [a]Heb *saw it, the child* [b]Or *lad* 2:7 [a]Lit *a woman giving suck* 2:10 [a]Heb *Mosheh,* from *mashah* [b]Heb *mashah* [A]Acts 7:21 2:11 [a]Lit *burdens* [A]Acts 7:23; Heb 11:24-26 [B]Ex 1:11; 5:4, 5; 6:6, 7 [C]Acts 7:24 2:12 [a]Lit *turned* [A]Acts 7:24, 25 2:13 [a]Or *quarreling* [b]Or *the guilty one* [A]Acts 7:26-28 2:14 [a]Lit *man, a prince* [b]Lit *saying in your heart* [A]Gen 19:9; Acts 7:27, 28 2:15 [a]Lit *dwelt* [A]Acts 7:29; Heb 11:27 [B]Gen 24:11; 29:2 2:16 [A]Ex 3:1; 18:12 [B]Gen 24:11, 13, 19; 29:9, 10; 1 Sam 9:11 2:17 [A]Gen 29:3, 10 2:18 [A]Ex 3:1; Num 10:29 2:20 [a]Lit *that he may eat bread* 2:21 [A]Acts 7:29 [B]Ex 4:25; 18:2 2:22 [a]Cf Heb *ger sham, a stranger there* [b]Heb *ger* [A]Ex 4:20; 18:3, 4 [B]Gen 23:4; Lev 25:23; Acts 7:29; Heb 11:13, 14 2:23 [A]Ex 6:5, 9 [B]Ex 3:7, 9; Deut 26:7; James 5:4 2:24 [A]Ex 6:5; Acts 7:34 [B]Gen 15:13f; 22:16-18; 26:2-5; 28:13-15; Ps 105:8, 42 2:25 [a]Lit *knew* them [A]Ex 3:7; 4:31; Acts 7:34 3:1 [a]Or *rear part* [A]Ex 2:18; 4:18; 18:12; Num 10:29 [B]Ex 3:12; 17:6; 33:6; 1 Kin 19:8 [C]Ex 4:27; 18:5; 24:13

2:3, 4 The careful actions of Moses' mother to construct the ark of bulrushes, to set Moses afloat close to the royal bathing place, and to have his sister watch to see what would happen, indicate a hope that something would work out right for the child.

2:5 The daughter of Pharaoh. Identified possibly as Hatshepsut or another princess; in either case a princess whom God providentially used to override Pharaoh's death decree and protect the life of His chosen leader for the Israelites.

2:10 became her son. The position of "son" undoubtedly granted Moses special privileges belonging to nobility, but none of these persuaded Moses to relinquish his native origin. Rather, as the NT advises, his spiritual maturity was such that when he came of age, he "refused to be called the son of Pharaoh's daughter" (Heb 11:24). The formal education in the court of that time meant that Moses would have learned reading, writing, arithmetic, and perhaps one or more of the languages of Canaan. He would also have participated in various outdoor sports, e.g., archery and horseback riding, two favorites of the 18th Dynasty court.

2:11 when Moses had grown up. The narrative skips over all details of Moses' life as the adopted son of a princess prior to the event which led to his flight into Midian.

2:11, 12, 16–21 Two injustices aroused Moses' indignation with different consequences: one resulted in his leaving home, having killed an Egyptian who beat an Israelite; the other resulted in his finding a new home as an Egyptian who helped the Midianite daughters of Reuel, and in his finding a wife. Undoubtedly, Reuel and his family soon discovered Moses was not really an Egyptian.

2:14 Cf. Ac 7:27, 28, 35.

2:15 Midian. The Midianites, who were descendants of Abraham and Keturah (Ge 25:1–4), settled in the Arabian Peninsula along the eastern shore of the Gulf of Aqabah.

2:18 Reuel. He was also known as Jethro (3:1), who may very well have been a worshiper of the true God (cf. 18:12–23), notwithstanding his being also the priest of Midian.

2:21–23 The narrative skips over the unimportant details of this 40-year period and moves the record quickly to the finding of a new home and family and to the moment when Moses returned to his people.

2:23–25 The hardship imposed upon Israel finally brought forth a collective cry for relief. The response of God is presented in 4 words: "heard," "remembered," "saw," and "took notice." This signaled that a response was forthcoming.

2:24 remembered His covenant. The unilateral covenant God made with Abraham (Ge 12:1–3; 15:1–21; 17:1–22) and confirmed with Isaac (Ge 26:2–5) and with Jacob (Ge 28:10–15; 35:9–15) specifically promised a geographically recognizable territory to the descendants of Abraham through Isaac and Jacob. Through them, too, the world would be blessed.

3:1 Moses was pasturing the flock. Moses worked as a shepherd while living with his

2 [A]The angel of the LORD appeared to him in a blazing fire from the midst of [a]a [B]bush; and he looked,
and behold, the bush was burning with fire, yet the
bush was not consumed. 3 So Moses said, "[a,A]I must
turn aside now and see this [b]marvelous sight, why
the bush is not burned up." 4 When the LORD saw
that he turned aside to look, [A]God called to him
from the midst of the bush and said, "Moses, Moses!" And he said, "Here I am." 5 Then He said, "Do
not come near here; [A]remove your sandals from
your feet, for the place on which you are standing
is holy ground." 6 He said also, "[A]I am the God of
your father, the God of Abraham, the God of Isaac,
and the God of Jacob." [B]Then Moses hid his face, for
he was [C]afraid to look at God.
7 The LORD said, "I have surely [A]seen the affliction
of My people who are in Egypt, and have given heed
to their cry because of their taskmasters, for I am
aware of their sufferings. 8 So I have come down
[A]to deliver them from the [a]power of the Egyptians,
and to bring them up from that land to a [B]good and
spacious land, to a land flowing with milk and honey,
to the place of [C]the Canaanite and the Hittite and the
Amorite and the Perizzite and the Hivite and the
Jebusite. 9 Now, behold, [A]the cry of the sons of Israel
has come to Me; furthermore, I have seen the oppression with which the Egyptians are oppressing them.

THE MISSION OF MOSES

10 Therefore, come now, and I will send you to
Pharaoh, [A]so that you may bring My people, the
sons of Israel, out of Egypt." 11 But Moses said to
God, "[A]Who am I, that I should go to Pharaoh, and
that I should bring the sons of Israel out of Egypt?"

3:2 [a]Lit *the* [A]Gen 16:7-11; 21:17; 22:11, 15; Ex 3:4-11, 16; Judg 13:13-21; Acts 7:30 [B]Deut 33:16; Mark 12:26; Luke 20:37; Acts 7:30 3:3 [a]Lit *Let me turn* [b]Lit *great* [A]Acts 7:31 3:4 [A]Ex 4:5 3:5 [A]Josh 5:15; Acts 7:33 3:6 [A]Gen 28:13; Ex 3:16; 4:5; Matt 22:32; Mark 12:26; Luke 20:37 [B]Acts 7:32 [C]Judg 13:22; Rev 1:17 3:7 [A]Ex 2:25; Neh 9:9; Ps 106:44; Is 63:9; Acts 7:34 3:8 [a]Lit *hand* [A]Gen 15:13-16; 46:4; 50:24, 25; Ex 6:6-8; 12:51 [B]Ex 3:17; 13:5; Num 13:27; Deut 1:25; 8:7-9; Jer 11:5; Ezek 20:6 [C]Gen 15:19-21; Josh 24:11 3:9 [A]Ex 2:23 3:10 [A]Gen 15:13, 14; Ex 12:40, 41; Mic 6:4; Acts 7:6, 7 3:11 [A]Ex 4:10; 6:12; 1 Sam 18:18

father-in-law, a life and occupation quite different from the privilege and prestige associated with his life in Pharaoh's court. **Horeb.** An alternative name for Mt. Sinai (cf. 19:11; Dt 4:10). Traditionally, this mountain has been identified with Jebel Musa, "the mountain of Moses." "Horeb" is the Heb. for the non-Semitic place-name, Sinai, located in the southern part of the Sinai Peninsula. **the mountain of God.** This is known as such because of what took place there later in Israel's history. This name for the mountain suggests that the book of Exodus was written by Moses after the events at Sinai. Others suggest that it was already known as a sacred mountain prior to the call of Moses; but it seems best to relate the name to what God did for Israel there.

3:2–4 Moses' attention was drawn to a most unusual sight, that of a burning bush which was not being consumed by the fire within. A supernatural event is the only viable explanation. Natural explanations of certain types of flowers with gaseous pods or oil glands fail, in that, after 40 years of work in the desert, Moses would surely have ignored something normal. This was so different that it aroused his curiosity and demanded further examination. God was in the bush speaking, clearly a miraculous event.

3:2 The angel of the LORD. Lit. "messenger of Yahweh" who, in context, turns out to be the Lord Himself talking to Moses (cf. Ac 7:30).

3:5–10 Cf. Ac 7:33, 34.

3:5 Do not come near ... remove your sandals. A sign of reverence in a holy place, one set apart from the norm because God was present there. These commands prevented Moses from rashly intruding, unprepared, into God's presence.

3:6 I am the God of your father. God's opening words, although important for Moses to hear, point the reader back to 2:24—showing that the God of Israel has remembered His people and has begun to take action (cf. Mt 22:32; Mk 12:26; Lk 20:37; Ac 3:13; 7:32). **Moses hid his face.** A fitting reaction of reverent fear in the presence of the Divine was modeled by Moses.

3:7, 8 I have surely seen ... have given heed. An emphasis on God's having been well aware of the desperate situation of Israel. The result: He promised to deliver them from Egyptian oppression. Here, and in the next two verses, the repetitive manner in describing what God saw and would do, served to underscore all the more His personal involvement in the history of His people whom He had sent into Egypt.

3:8 to a good and spacious land, to a land ... to the place. Three descriptions of the land to which Israel was going to be taken emphatically underscored the land promise of the Abrahamic Covenant. **flowing with milk and honey.** A formal and graphic way of describing a fertile land of bounteous provision. **the Canaanite and the Hittite.** A specific identification of the territory to which Israel was going; her Promised Land was currently inhabited by other peoples.

3:10 I will send you. The divine summons made Moses both leader/deliverer of Israel and ambassador of God before Pharaoh.

3:11 Who am I...? The first response is an objection from Moses to the divine summons, an expression of inadequacy for such a serious mission. It sounded reasonable, for after 40 years of absence from Egypt, what could he, a mere shepherd in Midian, do upon return?

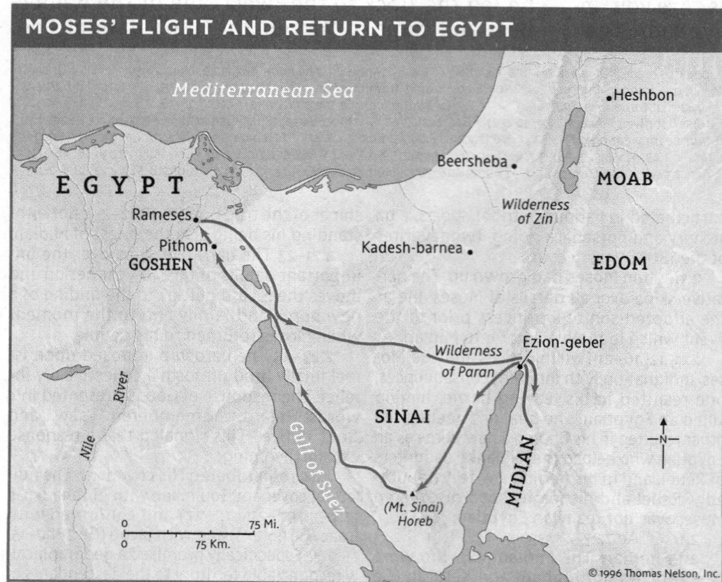

After killing an Egyptian, Moses fled through the Sinai and settled in Midian, where he married Zipporah. God spoke to Moses at the burning bush at Horeb, after which Moses returned to Egypt to assist the Israelites.

12 And He said, "Certainly [A]I will be with you, and
this shall be the sign to you that it is I who have
sent you: [B]when you have brought the people out
of Egypt, [C]you shall [a]worship God at this mountain."
13 Then Moses said to God, "Behold, I am going to
the sons of Israel, and I will say to them, 'The God
of your fathers has sent me to you.' Now they may
say to me, 'What is His name?' What shall I say to
them?" 14 God said to Moses, "[a,A]I AM WHO [a]I AM";
and He said, "Thus you shall say to the sons of Israel,
'[a]I AM has sent me to you.' " 15 God, furthermore,
said to Moses, "Thus you shall say to the sons of
Israel, '[A]The LORD, the God of your fathers, the God
of Abraham, the God of Isaac, and the God of Jacob,
has sent me to you.' This is My name forever, and
this is My [B]memorial-name [a]to all generations. 16 Go
and [A]gather the elders of Israel together and say to
them, '[B]The LORD, the God of your fathers, the God
of Abraham, Isaac and Jacob, has appeared to me,
saying, "[a,C]I am indeed concerned about you and
what has been done to you in Egypt. 17 So [A]I said, I
will bring you up out of the affliction of Egypt to
the land of [B]the Canaanite and the Hittite and the
Amorite and the Perizzite and the Hivite and the
Jebusite, to a land [C]flowing with milk and honey." '
18 [A]They will [a]pay heed to what you say; and [B]you
with the elders of Israel will come to the king of
Egypt and you will say to him, 'The LORD, the God
of the Hebrews, has met with us. So now, please,
let us go a [C]three days' journey into the wilderness,
that we may sacrifice to the LORD our God.' 19 But I
know that the king of Egypt [A]will not permit you to
go, [B]except [a]under compulsion. 20 So I will stretch
out [A]My hand and strike Egypt with all My [B]miracles
which I shall do in the midst of it; and [C]after that
he will let you go. 21 I will grant this people [A]favor
in the sight of the Egyptians; and it shall be that
when you go, you will not go empty-handed. 22 But
every woman [A]shall ask of her neighbor and the
woman who lives in her house, articles of silver
and articles of gold, and clothing; and you will put
them on your sons and daughters. Thus you will
[B]plunder the Egyptians."

MOSES GIVEN POWERS

4 Then Moses said, "What if they will not believe
me or [A]listen [a]to what I say? For they may say,
'[B]The LORD has not appeared to you.' " 2 The LORD
said to him, "What is that in your hand?" And he
said, "[A]A staff." 3 Then He said, "Throw it on the
ground." So he threw it on the ground, and [A]it became a serpent; and Moses fled from it. 4 But the
LORD said to Moses, "Stretch out your hand and
grasp *it* by its tail"—so he stretched out his hand and
caught it, and it became a staff in his [a]hand— 5 "that
[A]they may believe that [B]the LORD, the God of their
fathers, the God of Abraham, the God of Isaac, and
the God of Jacob, has appeared to you."

3:12 [a]Or *serve* [A]Gen 31:3; Ex 4:12, 15; 33:14-16; Deut 31:23; Josh 1:5; Is 43:2 [B]Ex 19:1 [C]Ex 19:2, 3; Acts 7:7 3:14 [a]Related to the name of God, *YHWH*, rendered *LORD*, which is derived from the verb *HAYAH, to be* [A]Ex 6:3; John 8:24, 28, 58; Heb 13:8; Rev 1:8; 4:8 3:15 [a]Lit *to generation of generation* [A]Ex 3:6, 13 [B]Ps 30:4; 97:12; 102:12; 135:13; Hos 12:5 3:16 [a]Lit *Visiting I have visited* [A]Ex 4:29 [B]Gen 28:13; 48:15; Ex 3:2, 6; 4:5 [C]Ex 4:31; Ps 33:18f 3:17 [A]Gen 15:13-21; 46:4; 50:24, 25 [B]Josh 24:11 [C]Ex 3:8 3:18 [a]Lit *hear your voice* [A]Ex 4:31 [B]Ex 5:1 [C]Ex 5:3; 8:27 3:19 [a]Lit *by a strong hand* [A]Ex 5:2 [B]Ex 6:1 3:20 [A]Ex 6:1; 7:4, 5; 9:15; 13:3, 9, 14 [B]Ex 7:3; 15:11; Deut 6:22; Neh 9:10; Ps 105:27; 135:9; Jer 32:20; Acts 7:36 [C]Ex 11:1; 12:31-33 3:21 [A]Ex 11:3; 12:36; 1 Kin 8:50; Ps 105:37f; 106:46; Prov 16:7 3:22 [A]Gen 15:14; Ex 11:2; 12:35 [B]Ezek 39:10 4:1 [a]Lit *to my voice* [A]Ex 3:18; 6:30 [B]Ex 3:15, 16 4:2 [A]Ex 4:17, 20 4:3 [A]Ex 7:10-12 4:4 [a]Lit *palm* 4:5 [A]Ex 4:31; 19:9 [B]Gen 28:13; 48:15; Ex 3:6, 15

3:12 Certainly I will be with you. The divine promise, one given also to the patriarchs, Abraham, Isaac, and Jacob, should have been sufficient to quell all the chosen agent's fears and sense of inadequacy for the task. **you shall worship God at this mountain.** A second divine promise signified the future success of the mission, suggesting that Israel would not be delivered simply out of bondage and oppression, but rescued to worship (cf. Ac 7:7).

3:13 Then Moses said. Was Moses at this point crossing the line from reasonable inquiry to unreasonable doubt? God's patient replies instructing Moses on what He would do and what the results would be, including Israel's being viewed with favor by the Egyptians (3:21), ought to caution the reader from hastily classifying Moses' attitude as altogether wrong from the very beginning of the interaction between him and the Lord. A response of divine anger comes only in 4:14 at the very end of Moses' questions and objections. *See note on 4:1.* **What is His name?** Moses raised a second objection. Israel might ask for God's name in validation of Moses' declaration that he had been sent by the God of their fathers. Significantly, the question was not "Who is this God?" The Hebrews understood the name Yahweh had been known to the patriarchs (which Genesis well indicates). Asking "what" meant they sought for the relevancy of the name to their circumstances. "Who?" sought after title, name, and identity, whereas "What?" inquired into the character, quality, or essence of a person.

3:14 I AM WHO I AM. This name for God points to His self-existence and eternality; it denotes "I am the One who is/will be," which is decidedly the best and most contextually suitable option from a number of theories about its meaning and etymological source. The significance in relation to "God of your fathers" is immediately discernible: He's the same God throughout the ages! The consonants from the Heb. word *YHWH*, combined with the vowels from the divine name *Adonai* (Master or Lord), gave rise to the name "Jehovah" in English. Since the name *Yahweh* was considered so sacred that it should not be pronounced, the Massoretes inserted the vowels from *Adonai* to remind themselves to pronounce it when reading instead of saying *Yahweh*. Technically, this combination of consonants is known as the "tetragrammaton."

3:15–22 Having provided Moses with His name in response to his second inquiry, God then furnished him with two speeches, one for Israel's elders (vv. 16, 17) and one for Pharaoh (v. 18b). Also included was notification of the elders' positive response to Moses' report (v. 18a), of Pharaoh's refusal to grant them their request (v. 19), of God's miraculous, judgmental reaction (v. 20), and of Israel's plundering of the Egyptians, who found themselves responding favorably to the departing nation's request for silver, gold, and clothing (vv. 21, 22). The last of these harkens back to God's promise to Abraham that his descendants would come out of the land of their affliction with great possessions (Ge 15:14).

3:15 Cf. Mt 22:32; Mk 12:26; Ac 3:13.

3:16 elders. Lit. "bearded ones," which indicated the age and wisdom needed to lead.

3:17 land of. *See notes on 3:8.*

3:18 three days' journey. The request for a 3-day journey to worship, in the light of 1) direct promises of deliverance from Egypt, 2) worship at Horeb, and 3) entrance into Canaan, was not a ruse to get out and then not return, but an initial, moderate request to highlight the intransigence of Pharaoh—he just would not let these slaves leave under any conditions (v. 19)!

3:22 *See note on 12:36.*

4:1 Then Moses said. In a third objection, Moses gave an unworthy response, after the lengthy explanation by God to Moses in 3:14–22. At this point, the hypothetical situation proposed became more objection than reasonable inquiry.

4:2–9 In response to the hypothetical situation of Israel's rejecting God as having appeared to him, Moses was given 3 signs to accredit him as the chosen spokesman and leader. Note the purpose stated: "That they may believe that the LORD … appeared to you" (v. 5). Two of these signs personally involved Moses right then and there—the rod to snake and back, the hand leprous and healed. No matter what the situation Moses could envision himself facing, God had sufficient resources to authenticate His man, and Moses was not to think otherwise.

6 The LORD furthermore said to him, "Now put
your hand into your bosom." So he put his hand
into his bosom, and when he took it out, behold,
his hand was [A]leprous like snow. 7 Then He said,
"Put your hand into your bosom again." So he put
his hand into his bosom again, and when he took
it out of his bosom, behold, [A]it was restored like
the rest of his flesh. 8 "If they will not believe you
or [a]heed the [b]witness of the first sign, they may
believe the [b]witness of the last sign. 9 But if they
will not believe even these two signs or heed what
you say, then you shall take some water from the
Nile and pour it on the dry ground; and the water
which you take from the Nile [A]will become blood
on the dry ground."

10 Then Moses said to the LORD, "Please, Lord, [A]I
have never been [a]eloquent, neither [b]recently nor
in time past, nor since You have spoken to Your
servant; for I am [c]slow of speech and [c]slow of
tongue." 11 The LORD said to him, "Who has made
man's mouth? Or [A]who makes *him* mute or deaf, or
seeing or blind? Is it not I, the LORD? 12 Now then go,
and [A]I, even I, will be with your mouth, and [B]teach
you what you are to say." 13 But he said, "Please, Lord,
now [a]send *the message* by whomever You will."

AARON TO BE MOSES' MOUTHPIECE

14 Then the anger of the LORD burned against
Moses, and He said, "Is there not your brother
Aaron the Levite? I know that [a]he speaks fluently.
And moreover, behold, [A]he is coming out to meet
you; when he sees you, he will be glad in his heart.
15 You are to speak to him and [A]put the words in his
mouth; and I, even I, will be with your mouth and
his mouth, and I will teach you what you are to do.
16 Moreover, [A]he shall speak for you to the people;
and he will be as a mouth for you and you will be
as God to him. 17 You shall take in your hand [A]this
staff, [B]with which you shall perform the signs."

18 Then Moses departed and returned to [a]Jethro
[A]his father-in-law and said to him, "Please, let me
go, that I may return to my brethren who are in
Egypt, and see if they are still alive." And Jethro
said to Moses, "Go in peace." 19 Now the LORD said to
Moses in Midian, "Go [a]back to Egypt, for [A]all the men
who were seeking your life are dead." 20 So Moses
took his wife and his [A]sons and mounted them on
a donkey, and returned to the land of Egypt. Moses
also took the [B]staff of God in his hand.

21 The LORD said to Moses, "When you go [a]back
to Egypt see that you perform before Pharaoh all
[A]the wonders which I have put in your [b]power; but
[B]I will harden his heart so that he will not let the
people go. 22 Then you shall say to Pharaoh, 'Thus
says the LORD, "[A]Israel is My son, My firstborn. 23 So
I said to you, '[A]Let My son go that he may serve Me';
but you have refused to let him go. Behold, [B]I will
kill your son, your firstborn." ' "

24 Now it came about at the lodging place on the
way that the LORD met him and [A]sought to put him

4:6 [A]Num 12:10; 2 Kin 5:27 4:7 [A]Num 12:13-15; Deut 32:39; 2 Kin 5:14; Matt 8:3; Luke 17:12-14 4:8 [a]Lit *listen to* [b]Lit *voice* 4:9 [A]Ex 7:19, 20 4:10 [a]Lit *a man of words* [b]Lit *yesterday* [c]Lit *heavy* [A]Ex 3:11; 4:1; 6:12; Jer 1:6 4:11 [A]Ps 94:9; 146:8; Matt 11:5; Luke 1:20, 64 4:12 [A]Ex 4:15, 16; Deut 18:18; Is 50:4; Jer 1:9 [B]Matt 10:19, 20; Mark 13:11; Luke 12:11, 12; 21:14, 15 4:13 [a]Lit *send by the hand which You send* 4:14 [a]Lit *speaking he speaks* [A]Ex 4:27 4:15 [A]Ex 4:12, 30; 7:1f; Num 23:5, 12, 16; Deut 18:18; Is 51:16; 59:21; Jer 1:9 4:16 [A]Ex 7:1, 2 4:17 [A]Ex 4:2, 20; 17:9 [B]Ex 7:9-20; 14:16 4:18 [a]Heb *Jether* [A]Ex 2:21; 3:1 4:19 [a]Lit *return* [A]Ex 2:15, 23 4:20 [A]Ex 18:3, 4; Acts 7:29 [B]Ex 4:17; 17:9; Num 20:8, 9, 11 4:21 [a]Lit *to return* [b]Lit *hand* [A]Ex 3:20; 11:9, 10 [B]Ex 7:3, 13; 9:12, 35; 10:1, 20, 27; 14:4, 8; Deut 2:30; Josh 11:20; 1 Sam 6:6; Is 63:17; John 12:40; Rom 9:18 4:22 [A]Is 63:16; 64:8; Jer 31:9; Hos 11:1; Rom 9:4 4:23 [A]Ex 5:1; 6:11; 7:16 [B]Ex 11:5; 12:29; Ps 105:36; 135:8; 136:10 4:24 [A]Num 22:22

4:10 I have never been eloquent. With his fourth argument, Moses focused on his speech disability, describing himself lit. as not being "a man of words," as being "heavy in mouth and heavy in tongue," i.e., unable to articulate his thoughts in fluent, flowing speech. An ancient document, *The Tale of the Eloquent Peasant,* suggests that eloquence was important in Egyptian culture, something which Moses would have well known from his time in the court. **neither recently nor in time past.** This is a pointed and inappropriate, if not impolite, criticism that somehow in all the discussion God had overlooked Moses' speech disability. Unless this disability changed, Moses believed that he could not undertake the assigned task (cf. 6:12).

4:11, 12 Who has made man's mouth? Three rhetorical questions from God shut the door on any complaints or criticisms about being clumsy of speech. The follow-up command, "Now then go!" including its promise of divine help in speech forbade all such objections.

4:13–16 Moses' fifth and final statement, notwithstanding the opening supplication, "Please Lord," was a polite way of bluntly saying, "Choose someone else, not me!" The anger of God toward this overt expression of reluctance was appropriate, yet the Lord still provided another way for His plan to move forward unhindered. Providentially (v. 27), Aaron would meet his brother Moses, and positively respond to being the spokesman.

4:15 and I will teach you. The plural pronoun "you" means that God had promised to assist both of them in their newly appointed duties.

4:16 you will be as God to him. Aaron would speak to the people for Moses, even as Moses would speak to Aaron for the Lord.

4:17 this staff, with which you shall perform the signs. Moses, despite God's anger at his unwillingness, retained superiority in that he had the instrument by which miracles would be done so that it was identified as "the staff of God" (v. 20).

4:18 Please, let me go. Courtesy toward the father-in-law for which he worked was not overlooked because of the divine call to service as national leader. Exactly how much was explained of the encounter at the burning bush remains unknown, but the purpose for the return, "and see if they are still alive," suggests that specific details of the call for him to be leader/deliverer were left unsaid, in contrast to the full explanation given to Aaron (v. 28).

4:20 sons. Gershom (2:22) and Eliezer (18:4).

4:21 I will harden his heart. The Lord's personal and direct involvement in the affairs of men so that His purposes might be done is revealed as God informed Moses what would take place. Pharaoh was also warned that his own refusal would bring judgment on him (v. 23). Previously Moses had been told that God was certain of Pharaoh's refusal (3:19). This interplay between God's hardening and Pharaoh's hardening his heart must be kept in balance. Ten times (4:21; 7:3; 9:12; 10:1, 20, 27; 11:10; 14:4, 8, 17) the historical record notes specifically that God hardened the king's heart, and ten times (7:13, 14, 22; 8:15, 19, 32; 9:7, 34, 35; 13:15) the record indicates the king hardened his own heart. The Apostle Paul used this hardening as an example of God's inscrutable will and absolute power to intervene as He chooses, yet obviously never without loss of personal responsibility for actions taken (Ro 9:16–18). The theological conundrum posed by such interplay of God's acting and Pharaoh's acting can only be resolved by accepting the record as it stands and by taking refuge in the omniscience and omnipotence of the God who planned and brought about His deliverance of Israel from Egypt, and in so doing also judged Pharaoh's sinfulness. *See note at 9:12.*

4:22 My son, My firstborn. To the ancient Egyptians, the firstborn son was special and sacred, and the Pharaoh considered himself the only son of the gods. Now he heard of a whole nation designated as God's firstborn son, meaning "declared and treated as first in rank, preeminent, with the rights, privileges, and responsibilities of being actually the firstborn." The Lord pointedly referred to the nation collectively in the singular in order to

to death. 25 Then Zipporah took [A]a flint and cut off
her son's foreskin and [a]threw it at Moses' feet, and
she said, "You are indeed a bridegroom of blood to
me." 26 So He let him alone. At that time she said,
"*You are* a bridegroom of blood"—[a]because of the
circumcision.
27 [A]Now the LORD said to Aaron, "Go to meet Moses in the wilderness." So he went and met him at
the [B]mountain of God and kissed him. 28 [A]Moses
told Aaron all the words of the LORD with which
He had sent him, and [B]all the signs that He had
commanded him *to do.* 29 Then Moses and Aaron
went and [A]assembled all the elders of the sons of
Israel; 30 and [A]Aaron spoke all the words which the
LORD had spoken to Moses. He then performed
the [B]signs in the sight of the people. 31 So [A]the people believed; and when they heard that the LORD
[a,B]was concerned about the sons of Israel and that
He had seen their affliction, then [C]they bowed low
and worshiped.

ISRAEL'S LABOR INCREASED

5 And afterward Moses and Aaron came and said
to Pharaoh, "[A]Thus says the LORD, the God of
Israel, '[B]Let My people go that they may celebrate a
feast to Me in the wilderness.' " 2 But Pharaoh said,
"[A]Who is the LORD that I should obey His voice to
let Israel go? I do not know the LORD, and besides,
[B]I will not let Israel go." 3 Then they said, "[A]The God
of the Hebrews has met with us. Please, let us go a
three days' journey into the wilderness that we may
sacrifice to the LORD our God, otherwise He will fall
upon us with pestilence or with the sword." 4 But the
king of Egypt said to them, "Moses and Aaron, why
do you [a]draw the people away from their [b]work?
Get *back* to your [c,A]labors!" 5 Again Pharaoh said,
"Look, [A]the people of the land are now many, and
you would have them cease from their labors!" 6 So
the same day Pharaoh commanded [A]the taskmasters over the people and their [B]foremen, saying,
7 "You are no longer to give the people straw to
make brick as previously; let them go and gather
straw for themselves. 8 But the quota of bricks which
they were making previously, you shall impose on
them; you are not to reduce any of it. Because they
are [A]lazy, therefore they cry out, '[a]Let us go and
sacrifice to our God.' 9 Let the labor be heavier on
the men, and let them work at it so that they will
pay no attention to false words."
10 So [A]the taskmasters of the people and their
foremen went out and spoke to the people, saying, "Thus says Pharaoh, 'I am not going to give
you *any* straw. 11 You go *and* get straw for yourselves wherever you can find *it,* but none of your
labor will be reduced.' " 12 So the people scattered
through all the land of Egypt to gather stubble for
straw. 13 The taskmasters pressed them, saying,
"Complete your [a]work quota, [b]*your* daily amount,
just as when [c]you had straw." 14 Moreover, [A]the
foremen of the sons of Israel, whom Pharaoh's
taskmasters had set over them, [B]were beaten [a]and
were asked, "Why have you not completed your required amount either yesterday or today in making
brick as previously?"
15 Then the foremen of the sons of Israel came
and cried out to Pharaoh, saying, "Why do you deal
this way with your servants? 16 There is no straw
given to your servants, yet they keep saying to us,
'Make bricks!' And behold, your servants are being
beaten; but it is the fault of your *own* people." 17 But
he said, "You are [A]lazy, *very* lazy; therefore you say,
'Let us go *and* sacrifice to the LORD.' 18 So go now
and work; for you will be given no straw, yet you
must deliver the quota of bricks." 19 The foremen
of the sons of Israel saw that they were in trouble
[a]because they were told, "You must not reduce [b]*your*

4:25 [a]Lit *made it touch at his feet* [A]Gen 17:14; Josh 5:2, 3 4:26 [a]Lit *with reference to* 4:27 [A]Ex 4:14 [B]Ex 3:1; 18:5; 24:13 4:28 [A]Ex 4:15f [B]Ex 4:8f 4:29 [A]Ex 3:16 4:30 [A]Ex 4:15, 16 [B]Ex 4:1-9 4:31 [a]Lit *had visited* [A]Ex 3:18; 4:8f; 19:9 [B]Gen 50:24; Ex 3:16 [C]Gen 24:26; Ex 12:27; 1 Chr 29:20 5:1 [A]Ex 3:18 [B]Ex 4:23; 6:11; 7:16 5:2 [A]2 Kin 18:35; 2 Chr 32:14; Job 21:15 [B]Ex 3:19 5:3 [A]Ex 3:18 5:4 [a]Lit *loose* [b]Lit *works* [c]Lit *burdens* [A]Ex 1:11; 2:11; 6:5-7 5:5 [A]Ex 1:7, 9 5:6 [A]Ex 1:11; 3:7; 5:10, 13, 14 [B]Ex 5:10, 14, 15, 19 5:8 [a]Lit *saying, 'Let* [A]Ex 5:17 5:10 [A]Ex 1:11; 3:7; 5:6 5:13 [a]Lit *works* [b]Lit *the matter of a day in its day* [c]Lit *there was* 5:14 [a]Lit *saying* [A]Ex 5:6 [B]Is 10:24 5:17 [A]Ex 5:8 5:19 [a]Lit *saying* [b]Lit *from your bricks the matter of a day in its day*

show that He was a father in what He would do, i.e., bring a nation into existence, then nurture and lead him (cf. Dt 14:1, 2). Divine sonship, as in the pagan world's perverted concept of a sexual union between the gods and women, was never so much as hinted at in the way God used the term to express His relationship with Israel, who were His people, a treasured possession, a kingdom of priests, and a holy nation (cf. 6:7; 19:4–6).

4:24–26 The presence of Zipporah's name indicates that the personal pronouns refer to Moses. She, judging by her action of suddenly and swiftly circumcising her son, understood that the danger to her husband's life was intimately connected to the family's not bearing the sign of the covenant given to Abraham for all his descendants (Ge 17:10–14). Her evaluation, "You are indeed a bridegroom of blood to me," suggests her own revulsion with this rite of circumcision, which Moses should have performed. The result, however, was God's foregoing the threat and letting Moses go (v. 26a). The reaction of God at this point dramatically underscored the seriousness of the sign He had prescribed. *See note on Jer 4:4.*

4:29, 30 The "leadership team" functioned as instructed: Aaron told all and Moses performed all the signs given to him (vv. 2–9).

4:31 So the people believed … then they bowed … and worshiped. Just as God predicted, they responded in belief at the signs and in worship at the explanation of God's awareness of their misery.

5:1 Let My people go. With this command from Israel's Lord, the confrontation between Pharaoh and Moses, between Pharaoh and God, commenced. It was a command Pharaoh would hear often in the days leading up to the Exodus.

5:2 Who is the LORD…? In all likelihood Pharaoh knew of Israel's God, but his interrogative retort insolently and arrogantly rejected Him as having any power to make demands of Egypt's superior ruler.

5:3–5 As a follow-up to Pharaoh's rejection, the spokesmen rephrase more specifically their request, together with a warning of possible divine judgment upon Israel for their failure to obey their God. Pharaoh saw this simply as a ruse to reduce the hours put in by his slave workforce.

5:6–9 Showing his authority to give orders to Israel, Pharaoh immediately increased their workload and the severity of their bondage. By adding, "they will pay no attention to false words," he showed his negative evaluation of God's words.

5:10 taskmasters … and their foremen. When combined with "foremen of the sons of Israel" (v. 15), a 3-level command structure is seen to have been in place—Egyptian section leaders and labor gang bosses, and Israelite foremen.

5:11 straw. Ancient documents from Egypt show that straw was used as a necessary component of bricks—it helped bind the clay together.

5:15–19 The formal labor complaint at the highest level was rejected with an emphatic evaluation of laziness on the part of Israel and a demand that production not slack.

daily amount of bricks." 20 When they left Pharaoh's
presence, they met Moses and Aaron as they were
[a]waiting for them. 21 [A]They said to them, "[B]May
the LORD look upon you and judge *you*, for you
have [C]made [a]us odious in Pharaoh's sight and in
the sight of his servants, to put a sword in their
hand to kill us."

22 Then Moses returned to the LORD and said,
"[A]O Lord, why have You brought harm to this people? Why did You ever send me? 23 Ever since I came
to Pharaoh to speak in Your name, he has done
harm to this people, [A]and You have not delivered
Your people at all."

GOD PROMISES ACTION

6 Then the LORD said to Moses, "Now you shall
see what I will do to Pharaoh; for [a,A]under compulsion he will let them go, and [a]under compulsion
he will drive them out of his land."

2 God spoke further to Moses and said to him, "I
am [A]the LORD; 3 and I appeared to Abraham, Isaac,
and Jacob, as [a,A]God Almighty, but *by* [B]My name,
[b]LORD, I did not make Myself known to them. 4 I
also established [A]My covenant with them, to give
them the land of Canaan, the [a]land in which they
sojourned. 5 Furthermore I have [A]heard the groaning of the sons of Israel, because the Egyptians are
holding them in bondage, and I have remembered
My covenant. 6 Say, therefore, to the sons of Israel, '[A]I
am the LORD, and [B]I will bring you out from under
the burdens of the Egyptians, and I will deliver you
from their bondage. I will also [C]redeem you with
[D]an outstretched arm and with great judgments.
7 Then I will take you [a,A]for My people, and [B]I will be
[b]your God; and [C]you shall know that I am the LORD
your God, who brought you out from under the
burdens of the Egyptians. 8 I will bring you to the
land which [A]I [a]swore to give to Abraham, Isaac, and
Jacob, and [B]I will give it to you *for* a possession; [C]I
am the LORD.' " 9 So Moses spoke thus to the sons of
Israel, but they did not listen to Moses on [A]account
of *their* [a]despondency and cruel bondage.

10 Now the LORD spoke to Moses, saying, 11 "[A]Go,
[a]tell Pharaoh king of Egypt [b]to let the sons of Israel go out of his land." 12 But Moses spoke before
the LORD, saying, "Behold, the sons of Israel have
not listened to me; [A]how then will Pharaoh listen
to me, for I am [a,B]unskilled in speech?" 13 Then the
LORD spoke to Moses and to Aaron, and gave them
a charge to the sons of Israel and to Pharaoh king
of Egypt, to bring the sons of Israel out of the
land of Egypt.

THE HEADS OF ISRAEL

14 These are the heads of their fathers' households. [A]The sons of Reuben, Israel's firstborn: Hanoch and Pallu, Hezron and Carmi; these are the
families of Reuben. 15 The [A]sons of Simeon: Jemuel
and Jamin and Ohad and Jachin and Zohar and
Shaul the son of a Canaanite woman; these are the
families of Simeon. 16 These are the names of [A]the
sons of Levi according to their generations: Gershon
and Kohath and Merari; and the [a]length of Levi's
life was one hundred and thirty-seven years. 17 [A]The
sons of Gershon: [a]Libni and Shimei, according to
their families. 18 [A]The sons of Kohath: Amram and
Izhar and Hebron and Uzziel; and the [a]length of Kohath's life was one hundred and thirty-three years.

5:20 [a]Lit *standing to meet* 5:21 [a]Lit *our savor to stink* [A]Ex 14:11; 15:24; 16:2 [B]Gen 16:5; 31:53 [C]Gen 34:30; 1 Sam 13:4; 27:12; 2 Sam 10:6; 1 Chr 19:6 5:22 [A]Num 11:11; Jer 4:10 5:23 [A]Ex 3:8 6:1 [a]Lit *by a strong hand* [A]Ex 3:19, 20; 7:4, 5; 11:1; 12:31, 33, 39; 13:3 6:2 [A]Ex 3:14, 15 6:3 [a]Heb *El Shaddai* [b]Heb *YHWH*, usually rendered *LORD* [A]Gen 17:1; 35:11; 48:3 [B]Ps 68:4; 83:18; Is 52:6; Jer 16:21; Ezek 37:6, 13 6:4 [a]Lit *land of their sojournings in which...* [A]Gen 12:7; 15:18; 17:4, 7; 26:3, 4; 28:4, 13 6:5 [A]Ex 2:24 6:6 [A]Ex 13:3, 14; 20:2; Deut 6:12 [B]Ex 3:17; 7:4; 12:51; 16:6; 18:1; Deut 26:8; Ps 136:11 [C]Ex 15:13; Deut 7:8; 1 Chr 17:21; Neh 1:10 [D]Deut 4:34; 5:15; 26:8; Ps 136:11f 6:7 [a]Lit *to Me for a people* [b]Lit *to you for a God* [A]Ex 19:5; Deut 4:20; 7:6; 2 Sam 7:24 [B]Gen 17:7f; Ex 29:45f; Lev 11:45; 26:12, 13, 45; Deut 29:13 [C]Ex 16:12; Is 41:20; 49:23, 26; 60:16 6:8 [a]Lit *lifted up My hand* [A]Gen 15:18; 26:3; Num 14:30; Neh 9:15; Ezek 20:5, 6 [B]Josh 24:13; Ps 136:21, 22 [C]Ex 6:6 6:9 [a]Lit *shortness of spirit* [A]Ex 2:23 6:11 [a]Lit *speak to* [b]Lit *that he let* [A]Ex 4:22, 23 6:12 [a]Lit *uncircumcised of lips* [A]Ex 4:1, 10; 6:30 [B]Jer 1:6 6:14 [A]Gen 46:9; Num 26:5-11; 1 Chr 5:3 6:15 [A]Gen 46:10; 1 Chr 4:24 6:16 [a]Lit *years* [A]Gen 46:11; Num 3:17; 26:57f; 1 Chr 6:1, 16-19 6:17 [a]In 1 Chr 23:7, *Ladan* [A]Num 3:18-20; 1 Chr 6:17-19 6:18 [a]Lit *years* [A]Num 3:19; 1 Chr 6:2, 18

5:20–21 The leadership team evidently knew of the lodging of the formal labor complaint and waited outside the royal hall in order to meet Israel's representatives. The meeting was definitely not a cordial one, with accusations raised both about the propriety of and the authority of the words and actions of Aaron and Moses toward Pharaoh.

5:22, 23 Moses returned to the LORD. Whether Moses and his brother remonstrated with the foremen about their strong and wrong evaluation remains a moot point. Rather, the focus is upon Moses, who remonstrated with the Lord in prayer. Evidently, Moses did not anticipate what effect Pharaoh's refusal and reaction would have upon his own people. Confrontation with Pharaoh so far had provoked both angry resentment of Israel by the Egyptians and of Moses by Israel—this was not the expected scenario!

6:1 Now you shall see. The Lord announced in response to Moses' prayer that finally the stage had been set for dealing with Pharaoh, who, in consequence, would only be able to urge Israel to leave.

6:2–5 God spoke to Moses and reminded him of His promises to the patriarchs. Once again the focal point of the covenant was the land of Canaan deeded to their descendants by divine decree. The fact that this covenant was remembered meant obvious removal from Egypt!

6:2, 3 I am the LORD. The same self-existent, eternal God, Yahweh, had been there in the past with the patriarchs; no change had occurred in Him, either in His covenant or promises.

6:3 God Almighty ... LORD ... not make Myself known. Since the name Yahweh was spoken before the Flood (Ge 4:26) and later by the patriarchs (Ge 9:26; 12:8; 22:14; 24:12), the special significance of Yahweh, unknown to them, but to be known by their descendants, must arise from what God would reveal of Himself in keeping the covenant and in redeeming Israel. *See notes on 3:13, 14.*

6:4 My covenant. The Abrahamic Covenant (cf. Ge 15:1–21; 17:1–8).

6:6–8 God instructed Moses to remind Israel of what they had previously been told: of God's remembering the covenant with Abraham, of His seeing their misery, of His delivering them from it, of His granting to them the land of Canaan, and thus taking them there. The repetitive "I will" (7 times) marked God's personal, direct involvement in Israel's affairs. Bracketed, as they were, by the declaration, "I am Yahweh," denoted certainty of fulfillment.

6:9 on account of *their* despondency. The bondage was so great that it blocked out even the stirring words Moses had just delivered to them (vv. 6–8).

6:12 unskilled in speech. *See notes on 4:10.*

6:14–27 The genealogical information formally identified Moses and Aaron as descendants of Levi, third son of Jacob by Leah. It also listed Aaron's son, Eleazar, and grandson, Phinehas, both of whom would become Israel's High Priests. Mention of Levi in company with Reuben and Simeon recalled, perhaps, the unsavory background belonging to these three tribal fathers (Ge 49:3–7) and emphasized that the choice of Moses and Aaron was not due to an exemplary lineage. This is intended to be a representative genealogy, not a complete one.

19 [A]The sons of Merari: Mahli and Mushi. These are the
families of the Levites according to their generations.
20 [A]Amram [a]married his father's sister Jochebed, and
she bore him Aaron and Moses; and the [b]length of
Amram's life was one hundred and thirty-seven
years. 21 [A]The sons of Izhar: Korah and Nepheg and
Zichri. 22 [A]The sons of Uzziel: Mishael and [a]Elzaphan
and Sithri. 23 Aaron [a]married Elisheba, the daughter
of [A]Amminadab, the sister of [B]Nahshon, and she bore
him [C]Nadab and Abihu, Eleazar and Ithamar. 24 The
[A]sons of Korah: Assir and Elkanah and [a]Abiasaph;
these are the families of the Korahites. 25 Aaron's
son [A]Eleazar [a]married one of the daughters of Putiel,
and she bore him [B]Phinehas. These are the heads of
the fathers' *households* of the Levites according to
their families. 26 It was *the same* Aaron and Moses to
whom the LORD said, "[A]Bring out the sons of Israel
from the land of Egypt according to their [B]hosts."
27 They were the ones [A]who spoke to Pharaoh king
of Egypt [a]about bringing out the sons of Israel from
Egypt; it was *the same* Moses and Aaron.
28 Now it came about on the day when the LORD
spoke to Moses in the land of Egypt, 29 that the LORD
spoke to Moses, saying, "[A]I am the LORD; [B]speak to
Pharaoh king of Egypt all that I speak to you." 30 But
Moses said before the LORD, "Behold, I am [a,A]unskilled
in speech; how then will Pharaoh listen to me?"

"I WILL STRETCH OUT MY HAND"

7 Then the LORD said to Moses, "[A]See, I make you
as God to Pharaoh, and your brother Aaron shall
be your prophet. 2 You shall speak all that I command
you, and your brother [A]Aaron shall speak to Pharaoh
that he let the sons of Israel go out of his land. 3 But [A]I
will harden Pharaoh's heart that I may [B]multiply My
signs and My wonders in the land of Egypt. 4 When
[A]Pharaoh does not listen to you, then I will lay My
hand on Egypt and [B]bring out My hosts, My people
the sons of Israel, from the land of Egypt by [C]great
judgments. 5 [A]The Egyptians shall know that I am
the LORD, when I [B]stretch out My hand on Egypt and
bring out the sons of Israel from their midst." 6 So
Moses and Aaron did *it;* [A]as the LORD commanded
them, thus they did. 7 Moses was [A]eighty years old
and Aaron [a]eighty-three, when they spoke to Pharaoh.

AARON'S ROD BECOMES A SERPENT

8 Now the LORD spoke to Moses and Aaron, saying, 9 "When Pharaoh speaks to you, saying, '[a,A]Work
a miracle,' then you shall say to Aaron, '[B]Take your
staff and throw *it* down before Pharaoh, *that* it may
become a serpent.' " 10 So Moses and Aaron came
to Pharaoh, and thus they did just as the LORD had
commanded; and Aaron threw his staff down before
Pharaoh and [a]his servants, and it [A]became a serpent.
11 Then Pharaoh also [A]called for *the* wise men and
the sorcerers, and they also, the [a,B]magicians of
Egypt, did [b]the same with [C]their secret arts. 12 For
each one threw down his staff and they turned into
serpents. But Aaron's staff swallowed up their staffs.
13 Yet [A]Pharaoh's heart was [a]hardened, and he did
not listen to them, as the LORD had said.

WATER IS TURNED TO BLOOD

14 Then the LORD said to Moses, "Pharaoh's heart
is [a]stubborn; he refuses to let the people go. 15 Go to

6:19 [A]Num 3:20; 1 Chr 6:19; 23:21 6:20 [a]Lit *took to him to wife* [b]Lit *years* [A]Ex 2:1, 2; Num 26:59 6:21 [A]Num 16:1; 1 Chr 6:37, 38 6:22 [a]In Num 3:30, *Elizaphan* [A]Lev 10:4; Num 3:30 6:23 [a]Lit *took to him to wife* [A]Ruth 4:19, 20; 1 Chr 2:10 [B]Num 1:7; 2:3 [C]Lev 10:1; Num 3:2; 26:60; 1 Chr 6:3; 24:1 6:24 [a]In 1 Chr 6:23 and 9:19, *Ebiasaph* [A]Num 26:11; 1 Chr 6:22, 23, 37 6:25 [a]Lit *took to him to wife* [A]Josh 24:33 [B]Num 25:7-13; Josh 24:33; Ps 106:30 6:26 [A]Ex 3:10; 6:13 [B]Ex 7:4; 12:17, 51 6:27 [a]Lit *to bring out* [A]Ex 5:1 6:29 [A]Ex 6:2, 6, 8 [B]Ex 6:11; 7:2 6:30 [a]Lit *uncircumcised of lips* [A]Ex 4:10; 6:12; Jer 1:6 7:1 [A]Ex 4:16 7:2 [A]Ex 4:15 7:3 [A]Ex 4:21 [B]Ex 11:9; Acts 7:36 7:4 [A]Ex 3:19, 20; 7:13, 16, 22; 8:15, 19; 9:12; 11:9 [B]Ex 12:51; 13:3, 9 [C]Ex 6:6 7:5 [A]Ex 7:17; 8:19, 22; 10:7; 14:4, 18, 25 [B]Ex 3:20 7:6 [A]Gen 6:22; 7:5; Ex 7:2 7:7 [a]Lit *83 years old* [A]Deut 29:5; 31:2; 34:7; Acts 7:23, 30 7:9 [a]Lit *Show a wonder for yourselves* [A]Is 7:11; John 2:18; 6:30 [B]Ex 4:2, 17 7:10 [a]Lit *before his* [A]Ex 4:3; 7:9 7:11 [a]Or *soothsayer priests* [b]Lit *thus* [A]Dan 2:2; 4:6; 5:7 [B]Gen 41:8; Ex 7:22; Dan 2:2; 2 Tim 3:8 [C]Ex 7:22; 8:7, 18; 2 Tim 3:9; Rev 13:13, 14 7:13 [a]Lit *strong* [A]Ex 4:21; 7:3, 22; 8:15, 19, 32; 9:7, 12, 34, 35; 10:1, 20, 27 7:14 [a]Or *hard;* lit *heavy*

6:28–7:5 A summary of the mission to Egypt resumes the narrative after the genealogical aside on Moses and Aaron.

7:1 **as God to Pharaoh.** Moses, as the spokesman and ambassador for God, would speak with authority and power. **your prophet.** Aaron, as the divinely appointed spokesman for Moses, would forthrightly deliver the message given to him. Cf. Ac 14:11–13, where Barnabas and Paul were so perceived in a similar situation.

7:4 **My hosts, My people.** The first term in this double-barreled designation of Israel occurred originally in 6:26. The nation was seen as organized like an army with its different divisions (its tribes) and also as God's military instrument upon the Canaanites. The second term with its possessive pronoun revealed the incongruity of Pharaoh's acting as though these people belonged to him.

7:5 **know that I am the LORD.** This purpose of the Exodus finds repeated mention in God's messages to Pharaoh and in God's descriptions of what He was doing (cf. 7:16; 8:10, 22; 9:14, 16, 29; 14:4, 18). Some of the Egyptians did come to understand the meaning of the name Yahweh, for they responded appropriately to the warning of the seventh plague (9:20), and others accompanied Israel into the wilderness (12:38). In the final analysis, Egypt would not be able to deny the direct involvement of the God of Israel in their rescue from bondage and the destruction of Egypt's army.

7:9 **Work a miracle.** Pharaoh's desire for accreditation would not go unanswered. That which God had done for Moses with the staff (4:2–9), and Moses had copied for Israel (4:30, 31), also became the sign of authority before Pharaoh (cf. 7:10).

7:11 **magicians.** Magic and sorcery played a major role in the pantheistic religion of Egypt. Its ancient documents record the activities of the magicians, one of the most prominent being the charming of serpents. These men were also styled "wise men" and "sorcerers," i.e., the learned men of the day and the religious as well (the word for sorcery being derived from a word meaning "to offer prayers"). Two of these men were named Jannes and Jambres (cf. 2Ti 3:8). Any supernatural power came from Satan (cf. 2Co 11:13–15). **secret arts.** By means of their "witchcraft," the wise men, sorcerers, and magicians demonstrated their abilities to perform a similar feat. Whether by optical illusion, sleight of hand, or learned physical manipulation of a snake, all sufficiently skillful enough to totally fool Pharaoh and his servants, or by evil supernaturalism, the evaluation given in the inspired record is simply "they also … did the same." However, the turning of rods into snakes, and later turning water into blood (7:22) and calling forth frogs (8:7), were not the same as trying to create gnats from inanimate dust (8:18–19). At that point, the magicians had no option but to confess their failure.

7:12 **Aaron's staff swallowed up their staffs.** The loss of the magicians' staffs in this fashion gave evidence of the superiority of God's power when Aaron's staff gulped down theirs.

7:14–10:29 The obvious miraculous nature of the 10 plagues cannot be explained by identifying them with natural occurrences to which Moses then applied a theological interpretation. The specific prediction of, as well as the intensity of, each plague moved it beyond being normal, natural phenomena. The notification of the specific discriminatory nature of some of the plagues, distinguishing between Hebrew and Egyptian (cf. 8:23; 9:4, 6; 10:23), or Goshen and the rest of the land (cf. 8:22; 9:26), as they did, also marks the supernatural nature of these events.

7:15 **in the morning.** Apparently, Pharaoh habitually went to the river for washing or,

Pharaoh in the morning [a]as [A]he is going out to the
water, and station yourself to meet him on the bank
of the Nile; and you shall take in your hand [B]the staff
that was turned into a serpent. 16 [A]You shall say to
him, 'The LORD, the God of the Hebrews, sent me
to you, saying, "[B]Let My people go, that they may
serve Me in the wilderness. But behold, you have
not listened until now." 17 Thus says the LORD, "[A]By
this you shall know that I am the LORD: behold, I
will strike [a]the water that is in the Nile with the
staff that is in my hand, and [B]it will be turned to
blood. 18 [A]The fish that are in the Nile will die, and
the Nile will [a]become foul, and the Egyptians will
[b,B]find difficulty in drinking water from the Nile." ' "
19 Then the LORD said to Moses, "Say to Aaron, 'Take
your staff and [A]stretch out your hand over the waters of Egypt, over their rivers, over their [a]streams,
and over their pools, and over all their reservoirs of
water, that they may become blood; and there will
be blood throughout all the land of Egypt, both in
vessels of wood and in *vessels of* stone.' "
20 So Moses and Aaron did even as the LORD had
commanded. And he lifted up [a,A]the staff and struck
the water that *was* in the Nile, in the sight of Pharaoh and in the sight of his servants, and [B]all the
water that *was* in the Nile was turned to blood.
21 The fish that *were* in the Nile died, and the Nile
[a]became foul, so that the Egyptians could not drink
water from the Nile. And the blood was through all
the land of Egypt. 22 [A]But the [a]magicians of Egypt
did [b]the same with their secret arts; and Pharaoh's
heart was [c]hardened, and he did not listen to them,
as the LORD had said. 23 Then Pharaoh turned and
went into his house [a]with no concern even for this.
24 So all the Egyptians dug around the Nile for water to drink, for they could not drink of the water
of the Nile. 25 Seven days [a]passed after the LORD
had struck the Nile.

FROGS OVER THE LAND

8 [a]Then the LORD said to Moses, "Go to Pharaoh
and say to him, 'Thus says the LORD, "[A]Let My
people go, that they may serve Me. 2 But if you refuse to let *them* go, behold, I will smite your whole
territory with frogs. 3 The Nile will [A]swarm with
frogs, which will come up and go into your house

7:15 [a]Lit *behold* [A]Ex 2:5; 8:20 [B]Ex 4:2, 3; 7:10 7:16 [A]Ex 3:13, 18; 4:22; 5:1 [B]Ex 4:23; 5:1, 3 7:17 [a]Lit *upon the waters* [A]Ex 5:2; 7:5; 10:2; Ps 9:16; Ezek 25:17 [B]Ex 4:9; 7:20; Rev 11:6; 16:4, 6 7:18 [a]I.e. have a bad smell [b]Or *be weary of* [A]Ex 7:21 [B]Ex 7:24 7:19 [a]Or *canals* [A]Ex 8:5, 6, 16; 9:22; 10:12, 21; 14:21, 26 7:20 [a]Lit *with the staff* [A]Ex 17:5 [B]Ps 78:44; 105:29 7:21 [a]I.e. had a bad smell 7:22 [a]Or *soothsayer priests* [b]Lit *thus* [c]Lit *strong* [A]Ex 7:11; 8:7 7:23 [a]Lit *and he did not set his heart even to this* 7:25 [a]Lit *were fulfilled* 8:1 [a]Ch 7:26 in Heb [A]Ex 3:18; 4:23; 5:1, 3 8:3 [A]Ps 105:30

more likely, for the performance of some religious rite. Three times Moses would meet him at this early morning rendezvous to warn of plagues, i.e., the first, fourth, and seventh (8:20; 9:13). **on the bank of the Nile.** The first confrontation of the plague cycle took place on the banks of the Nile, the sacred waterway of the land, whose annual ebb and flow contributed strategically and vitally to the agricultural richness of Egypt. Hymns of thanksgiving were often sung for the blessings brought by the Nile, the country's greatest, single economic resource.

7:17 blood. The Heb. word does not denote red coloring such as might be seen when red clay is washed downstream, but denotes actual substance, i.e., blood.

7:19, 20 the waters … all their reservoirs of water. The use of different words, "waters, streams, rivers, pools, and reservoirs," indicates graphically the extent of the plague. Even buckets of wood and stone filled with water and kept inside the homes could not escape the curse of their contents being turned into blood.

7:22 the magicians … did the same with their secret arts. How ludicrous and revealing that the magicians resorted to copycat methodology instead of reversing the plague. What they did, bringing just more blood, did serve, however, to bolster Pharaoh's stubbornness.

7:24 dug around the Nile. The only recourse was to tap into the natural water table, the subterranean water supply. Evidently this was the water which was available to the magicians to use (v. 22).

7:25 Seven days. An interval of time occurred before another warning was delivered, indicating that the plagues did not occur rapidly in uninterrupted succession.

8:1 Go to Pharaoh. The warning for the second plague was delivered to Pharaoh, presumably at his palace. Warnings for the fifth (9:1) and eighth (10:1) plagues also occurred at the palace.

8:2 smite. The verb God used also meant "to plague." Various terms (lit. from the Heb.), namely "plagues" (9:14), "strike" (12:13), and "pestilence" (9:3, 15), were employed to impress them with the severity of what was happening in Egypt. **frogs.** That Egyptians favored frogs was seen in the wearing of amulets in the shape of a frog and in the prohibition against intentionally killing frogs, who were considered sacred animals. The croaking of frogs from the river and pools of water signaled to farmers that the gods who controlled the Nile's flooding and receding had once again made the land fertile. The god Hapi was venerated on this occasion because he had caused alluvial

THE TEN PLAGUES ON EGYPT

The Plague	Egyptian Deity	The Effect
1. Blood (7:20)	Hapi	Pharaoh hardened (7:22)
2. Frogs (8:6)	Heqt	Pharaoh begs relief, promises freedom (8:8), but is hardened (8:15)
3. Gnats (8:17)	Hathor, Nut	Pharaoh hardened (8:19)
4. Flies (8:24)	Shu, Isis	Pharaoh bargains (8:28), but is hardened (8:32)
5. Livestock diseased (9:6)	Apis	Pharaoh hardened (9:7)
6. Boils (9:10)	Sekhmet	Pharaoh hardened (9:12)
7. Hail (9:23)	Geb	Pharaoh begs relief (9:27), promises freedom (9:28), but is hardened (9:35)
8. Locusts (10:13)	Serapis	Pharaoh bargains (10:11), begs relief (10:17), but is hardened (10:20)
9. Darkness (10:22)	Ra	Pharaoh bargains (10:24), but is hardened (10:27)
10. Death of firstborn (12:29)		Pharaoh and Egyptians beg Israel to leave Egypt (12:31–33)

and into your bedroom and on your bed, and into
the houses of your servants and on your people,
and into your ovens and into your kneading bowls.
4 So the frogs will come up on you and your people
and all your servants." ' " 5 [a]Then the LORD said to
Moses, "Say to Aaron, '[A]Stretch out your hand with
your staff over the rivers, over the [b]streams and
over the pools, and make frogs come up on the
land of Egypt.' " 6 So Aaron stretched out his hand
over the waters of Egypt, and the [a,A]frogs came up
and covered the land of Egypt. 7 [A]The [a]magicians
did [b]the same with their secret arts, [c]making frogs
come up on the land of Egypt.
8 Then Pharaoh [A]called for Moses and Aaron and
said, "[B]Entreat the LORD that He remove the frogs
from me and from my people; and [C]I will let the
people go, that they may sacrifice to the LORD."
9 Moses said to Pharaoh, "[a]The honor is yours to tell
me: when shall I entreat for you and your servants
and your people, that the frogs be [b]destroyed from
you and your houses, *that* they may be left only in
the Nile?"
10 Then he said, "Tomorrow." So he said, "*May it
be* according to your word, that you may know that
there is [A]no one like the LORD our God. 11 The [A]frogs
will depart from you and your houses and your
servants and your people; they will be left only in
the Nile." 12 Then Moses and Aaron went out from
Pharaoh, and [A]Moses cried to the LORD concerning
the frogs which He had [a]inflicted upon Pharaoh.
13 The LORD did according to the word of Moses, and
the frogs died out of the houses, the courts, and the
fields. 14 So they piled them in heaps, and the land
[a]became foul. 15 But when Pharaoh saw that there
was relief, he [a]hardened his heart and [A]did not listen
to them, as the LORD had said.

THE PLAGUE OF INSECTS

16 Then the LORD said to Moses, "Say to Aaron,
'Stretch out your staff and strike the dust of the
earth, that it may become [a]gnats through all the
land of Egypt.' " 17 They did so; and Aaron stretched
out his hand with his staff, and struck the dust
of the earth, and there were [a]gnats on man and
beast. All the dust of the earth became [a,A]gnats
through all the land of Egypt. 18 The [a]magicians
tried with their secret arts to bring forth [b]gnats,
but [A]they could not; so there were [b]gnats on man
and beast. 19 Then the [a]magicians said to Pharaoh,
"[A]This is the finger of God." But Pharaoh's heart
was [b]hardened, and he did not listen to them, as
the LORD had said.
20 Now the LORD said to Moses, "[A]Rise early in the
morning and present yourself before Pharaoh, [a]as
[B]he comes out to the water, and say to him, 'Thus
says the LORD, "[C]Let My people go, that they may
serve Me. 21 For if you do not let My people go, behold, I will send swarms of flies on you and on
your servants and on your people and into your
houses; and the houses of the Egyptians will be full
of swarms of flies, and also the ground on which
they *dwell*. 22 [A]But on that day I will set apart the
land of Goshen, where My people are [a]living, so
that no swarms of flies will be there, in order that
you may know that [b,B]I, the LORD, am in the midst
of the land. 23 I will [a]put a division between My

8:5 [a]Ch 8:1 in Heb [b]Or *canals* [A]Ex 7:19 8:6 [a]Lit *frog* [A]Ps 78:45; 105:30 8:7 [a]Or *soothsayer priests* [b]Lit *thus* [c]Lit *and made* [A]Ex 7:11, 22 8:8 [A]Ex 8:25; 9:27; 10:16 [B]Ex 8:28; 9:28; 10:17; Num 21:7; 1 Kin 13:6 [C]Ex 8:15, 29, 32 8:9 [a]Lit *Glory over me* [b]Lit *cut off* 8:10 [A]Ex 9:14; Deut 4:35, 39; 33:26; 2 Sam 7:22; 1 Chr 17:20; Ps 86:8; Is 46:9; Jer 10:6, 7 8:11 [A]Ex 8:13 8:12 [a]Lit *placed* [A]Ex 8:30; 9:33; 10:18 8:14 [a]I.e. had a bad smell 8:15 [a]Lit *made heavy* [A]Ex 7:4 8:16 [a]Or *lice* 8:17 [a]Or *lice* [A]Ps 105:31 8:18 [a]Or *soothsayer priests* [b]Or *lice* [A]Ex 7:11, 12; 8:7; 9:11 8:19 [a]Or *soothsayer priests* [b]Lit *strong* [A]Ex 7:5; 10:7; Ps 8:3; Luke 11:20 8:20 [a]Lit *behold* [A]Ex 7:15; 9:13 [B]Ex 2:5; 7:15 [C]Ex 3:18; 4:23; 5:1, 3; 8:1 8:22 [a]Lit *standing* [b]Or *I am the LORD in the midst of the earth* [A]Ex 9:4, 6, 24; 10:23; 11:7 [B]Ex 9:29; 19:5; 20:11 8:23 [a]Lit *set a ransom*

deposits to come downstream. Further, the frog was the representation, the image, of the goddess Heqt, the wife of the god Khum, and the symbol of resurrection and fertility. The presence of frogs in such abundance, all over everywhere outside and inside the houses (vv. 3, 13), however, brought only frustration, dismay, and much discomfort, rather than the normal signal that the fields were ready for cultivating and harvesting.

8:7 The magicians did the same. Once again, instead of reversing the plague, the magicians in demonstrating the power of their secret arts only appeared to increase the frog population to the added discomfort of the people. Their power was not sufficient enough to do more than play "copycat." That the magicians could duplicate but not eradicate the problem was, however, sufficient to solidify royal stubbornness.

8:8 Entreat the LORD. Using the Lord's name and begging for relief through His intervention was more a point in negotiation and not a personal or official recognition of Israel's Lord.

8:9 left only in the Nile. A specific detail like this in Moses' question indicates that the Nile and the waters had returned to normal and again continued to support life.

8:10 Tomorrow. Having been granted the privilege to set the time when the Lord would answer Moses' prayer for relief, Pharaoh requested a cessation only on the next day. Presumably he hoped something else would happen before then so that he would not have to acknowledge the Lord's power in halting the plague, nor be obligated to Moses and his God. But God answered the prayer of Moses, and Pharaoh remained obstinate (v. 15).

8:16 Without prior warning, the third plague descended on the country. The same absence of warning occurred for the sixth (9:8, 9) and the ninth (10:21) plagues. A 3-fold pattern surfaces: prior warning at the river, then at the palace, and then no warning given. **gnats.** The Heb. term is preferably taken to designate tiny, stinging insects barely visible to the naked eye. Those priests, who fastidiously kept themselves religiously pure by frequent washing and by shaving off body hair, were afflicted and rendered impure in their duties.

8:17 All the dust of the earth . . . through all the land. The record stresses by its repetition of "all" and "land" the tremendous extent and severity of this pestilence.

8:19 This is the finger of God. The failure of the magicians to duplicate this plague elicited from them this amazing evaluation, not only among themselves, but publicly before Pharaoh, who nevertheless remained recalcitrant, unwilling to acknowledge the power of God.

8:21 swarms. The LXX translates "swarms" as "dog-fly," a bloodsucking insect. The ichneumon fly, which deposited its eggs on other living things so the larvae could feast upon it, was considered the manifestation of the god Uatchit. "The land was laid waste because of the swarms" (v. 24) is hardly an evaluation propitious for any insect-god! Whatever the specific type of fly might have been, the effect of the plague was intense and distressful.

8:22 set apart the land of Goshen. For the first time in connection with the plagues, God specifically noted the discrimination to be made—Israel would be untouched! The term "sign" (v. 23) describes the distinction which was being drawn and which was also specifically noted for the fifth, seventh, ninth, and tenth plagues. Coupled with the repeated emphasis on "My people" in God's pronouncements, the specific distinguishing between Israel in Goshen and Egypt itself highlighted both God's personal and powerful oversight of His people.

8:23 Tomorrow. The plague-warning on this occasion stated exactly when it would strike, giving Pharaoh and his people opportunity to repent or yield. "Tomorrow" was also

people and your people. Tomorrow this sign will
occur.” ’ ” 24 Then the LORD did so. And there came
[a]great swarms of flies into the house of Pharaoh
and the houses of his servants and the land was
[A]laid waste because of the swarms of flies in all
the land of Egypt.
25 Pharaoh [A]called for Moses and Aaron and
said, “[B]Go, sacrifice to your God within the land.”
26 But Moses said, “It is not right to do so, for we
will sacrifice to the LORD our God [a]what is [A]an
abomination to the Egyptians. If we sacrifice [a]what
is an abomination to the Egyptians before their
eyes, will they not then stone us? 27 We must go a
[A]three days’ journey into the wilderness and sacrifice to the LORD our God as He [a]commands us.”
28 Pharaoh said, “[A]I will let you go, that you may
sacrifice to the LORD your God in the wilderness;
only you shall not go very far away. [B]Make supplication for me.” 29 Then Moses said, “Behold, I am
going out from you, and I shall make supplication
to the LORD that the swarms of flies may depart
from Pharaoh, from his servants, and from his
people tomorrow; only do not let Pharaoh [A]deal
deceitfully again in not letting the people go to
sacrifice to the LORD.”
30 So [A]Moses went out from Pharaoh and made
supplication to the LORD. 31 The LORD did [a]as Moses
asked, and removed the swarms of flies from Pharaoh, from his servants and from his people; not one
remained. 32 But Pharaoh [a]hardened his heart this
time also, and [A]he did not let the people go.

EGYPTIAN CATTLE DIE

9 Then the LORD said to Moses, “Go to Pharaoh
and speak to him, ‘Thus says the LORD, the God
of the Hebrews, “[A]Let My people go, that they may
serve Me. 2 For [A]if you refuse to let *them* go and
[a]continue to hold them, 3 behold, [A]the hand of the
LORD [a]will come *with* a very severe pestilence on
your livestock which are in the field, on the horses,
on the donkeys, on the camels, on the herds, and on
the flocks. 4 [A]But the LORD will make a distinction
between the livestock of Israel and the livestock of
Egypt, so that [B]nothing will die of all that belongs to
the sons of Israel.” ’ ” 5 The LORD set a definite time,
saying, “Tomorrow the LORD will do this thing in
the land.” 6 So the LORD did this thing on the next
day, and [A]all the livestock of Egypt died; [B]but of the
livestock of the sons of Israel, not one died. 7 Pharaoh sent, and behold, there was not even one of the
livestock of Israel dead. But [A]the heart of Pharaoh
was [a]hardened, and he did not let the people go.

THE PLAGUE OF BOILS

8 Then the LORD said to Moses and Aaron, “Take
for yourselves handfuls of soot from a kiln, and let
Moses throw it toward the sky in the sight of Pharaoh. 9 It will become fine dust over all the land of
Egypt, and will become [A]boils breaking out with
sores on man and beast through all the land of
Egypt.” 10 So they took soot from a kiln, and stood
before Pharaoh; and Moses threw it toward the sky,
and it became boils breaking out with sores on man

8:24 [a]Lit *heavy* [A]Ps 78:45; 105:31 8:25 [A]Ex 8:8; 9:27; 10:16 [B]Ex 9:28; 10:8, 24; 12:31 8:26 [a]Lit *the abomination of Egypt* [A]Gen 43:32; 46:34; Deut 7:25f 8:27 [a]Lit *says to us* [A]Ex 3:18; 5:3 8:28 [A]Ex 8:8, 15, 29, 32 [B]Ex 8:8; 9:28; 1 Kin 13:6 8:29 [A]Ex 8:8, 15 8:30 [A]Ex 8:12 8:31 [a]Lit *according to the word of Moses* 8:32 [a]Lit *made heavy* [A]Ex 4:21; 8:8, 15 9:1 [A]Ex 4:23; 8:1 9:2 [a]Lit *still hold* [A]Ex 8:2 9:3 [a]Lit *will be* [A]Ex 7:4; 1 Sam 5:6; Ps 39:10; Acts 13:11 9:4 [A]Ex 8:22 [B]Ex 9:6 9:6 [A]Ex 9:19, 20, 25; Ps 78:48 [B]Ex 9:4 9:7 [a]Lit *heavy* [A]Ex 7:14; 8:32 9:9 [A]Deut 28:27; Rev 16:2

the due time for the fifth, seventh, and eighth plagues (9:5, 18; 10:4), and “about midnight” was the stated time for the tenth plague to commence (11:4). *See note on 11:4.*

8:26 sacrifice ... what is an abomination to the Egyptians. An attempt at appeasement by compromise on the part of Pharaoh—“Go, sacrifice ... within the land”—was countered by Moses’ pointing out that Israel’s sacrifices would not be totally acceptable to the Egyptians, who might even react violently—“will they not then stone us?” This evaluation Pharaoh immediately understood. Either their strong dislike of shepherds and sheep (Ge 46:34) or Israel’s sacrificial animals being sacred ones in their religion brought about Egyptian aversion to Israel’s sacrifices.

8:27–29 We must go .... will let you go. The first declaration showed the decision to travel no less than 3 days beyond Egyptian borders was a nonnegotiable item. The second declaration showed Pharaoh trying to keep that decision to travel and sacrifice strictly under his authority and not as a response to the Lord’s request for His people.

8:28 Make supplication for me. An abbreviated request, applying not only to himself but also for the removal of the plague as previously asked in connection with the second plague (8:8).

8:29 do not let Pharaoh deal deceitfully. Moses’ closing exhortation underscored the deceptive nature of the king’s words.

8:31 not one remained. This declaration of the total divine removal of the flies—a demonstration of God’s answering Moses’ entreaty—did not persuade Pharaoh at all. Once again, removed from the humiliating effects of a plague, his stubborn resistance resurfaced (v. 32).

9:3 in the field. Apparently stabled livestock did not succumb to the pestilence. Although incredibly severe, some animals were still alive afterwards for Egypt to continue without total loss to an economy which depended upon domesticated animals. A few months later, when the seventh plague struck, there were still some cattle, which, if left in the field, would have died (9:19). **horses ... camels.** Horses, which were common in the period, had been brought into military service by the Hyksos. See Introduction: Author and Date. Camels were a domesticated animal by this time in the 15th century B.C. **a very severe pestilence.** In listing the different kinds of livestock, the severe nature of the plague was emphatically underscored as one which would for the first time target personal property. Egyptian literature and paintings substantiate how valuable livestock was to them. Whatever the exact nature of this pestilence—anthrax, murrain, or other livestock disease—it was clearly contagious and fatal. Religious implications were obvious: Egypt prized the bull as a sacred animal with special attention and worship being given to the Apis bull, the sacred animal of the god Ptah. Heliopolis venerated the bull, Mnevis. Further, the goddess Hathor, represented by a cow, or a cow-woman image, was worshiped in several cities.

9:4 nothing will die. The additional declaration on the safety of Israel’s livestock graphically underscored the miraculous nature of what God was about to do as He declared for the second time the distinction being made between Israel and Egypt. It underscored Israel’s protection and to whom she really belonged.

9:5 set a definite time. The prophetic and miraculous nature of this plague is highlighted by stating “tomorrow” and, by noting “on the next day,” it happened as predicted (v. 6).

9:6 of the livestock of ... Israel, not one died. The distinction being made received added emphasis with this double declaration that Israelites suffered absolutely no loss in livestock.

9:7 Pharaoh sent. This time the king had to check on the veracity of the protection afforded Israel. Whatever his own rationalizations or theories about it might have been, they only confirmed him in his resistance and disobedience, despite finding out that there was “not even one ... dead.”

9:9 boils breaking out with sores on man and beast. For the first time human health was targeted.

9:10 soot from a kiln. Aaron and Moses took two handfuls of soot, not just from any furnace, but from a lime-kiln or brick-making

and beast. 11[A]The [a]magicians could not stand before
Moses because of the boils, for the boils were on the
magicians [b]as well as on all the Egyptians. 12And
[A]the LORD [a]hardened Pharaoh's heart, and he did not
listen to them, just as the LORD had spoken to Moses.
13Then the LORD said to Moses, "[A]Rise up early in
the morning and stand before Pharaoh and say to
him, 'Thus says the LORD, the God of the Hebrews,
"[B]Let My people go, that they may serve Me. 14For
this time I will send all My plagues [a]on you and your
servants and your people, so that [A]you may know
that there is no one like Me in all the earth. 15For *if*
by now I had put forth My hand and struck you and
your people with pestilence, you would then have
been cut off from the earth. 16But, indeed, [A]for this
reason I have allowed you to [a]remain, in order to
show you My power and in order to proclaim My
name through all the earth. 17Still you exalt yourself
against My people [a]by not letting them go.

THE PLAGUE OF HAIL

18Behold, about this time tomorrow, [A]I will [a]send
a very heavy hail, such as has not been *seen* in Egypt
from the day it was founded [b]until now. 19Now
therefore send, bring [A]your livestock and whatever
you have in the field to safety. [B]Every man and beast
that is found in the field and is not brought home,
when the hail comes down on them, will die."'"
20[A]The one among the servants of Pharaoh who
[a]feared the word of the LORD made his servants
and his livestock flee into the houses; 21but he who
[a]paid no regard to the word of the LORD [b]left his
servants and his livestock in the field.
22Now the LORD said to Moses, "Stretch out your
hand toward the sky, that [a,A]hail may fall on all the
land of Egypt, on man and on beast and on every
plant of the field, throughout the land of Egypt."
23Moses stretched out his staff toward the sky, and
the LORD [a]sent [b]thunder and [A]hail, and fire ran down
to the earth. And the LORD rained hail on the land
of Egypt. 24So there was hail, and fire [a]flashing continually in the midst of the hail, very severe, such as
had not been in all the land of Egypt since it became
a nation. 25[A]The hail struck all that was in the field
through all the land of Egypt, both man and beast; the
hail also struck every plant of the field and shattered
every tree of the field. 26[A]Only in the land of Goshen,
where the sons of Israel *were,* there was no hail.
27Then Pharaoh [a,A]sent for Moses and Aaron, and
said to them, "[B]I have sinned this time; the LORD
is the righteous one, and I and my people are the
wicked ones. 28[A]Make supplication to the LORD, for
there has been enough of God's [a]thunder and hail;
and [B]I will let you go, and you shall stay no longer."
29Moses said to him, "As soon as I go out of the
city, I will [A]spread out my [a]hands to the LORD; the
[b]thunder will cease and there will be hail no longer,
that you may know that [B]the earth is the LORD'S.

9:11 [a]Or *soothsayer priests* [b]Lit *and on all* [A]Ex 8:18 9:12 [a]Lit *made strong* [A]Ex 4:21; 10:1, 20; 14:8; Josh 11:20; John 12:40 9:13 [A]Ex 8:20 [B]Ex 4:23 9:14 [a]Lit *to your heart* [A]Ex 8:10; Deut 3:24; 2 Sam 7:22; 1 Chr 17:20; Ps 86:8; Is 45:5-8; 46:9; Jer 10:6, 7 9:16 [a]Lit *stand* [A]Prov 16:4; Rom 9:17 9:17 [a]Lit *so as not to let* 9:18 [a]Lit *cause to rain* [b]Lit *and until now* [A]Ex 9:23, 24 9:19 [A]Ex 9:6 [B]Ex 9:25 9:20 [a]Or *revered* [A]Prov 13:13 9:21 [a]Lit *did not set his heart to* [b]Lit *then left* 9:22 [a]Lit *there may be hail* [A]Rev 16:21 9:23 [a]Lit *gave* [b]Lit *sounds* [A]Gen 19:24; Josh 10:11; Ps 18:13; 78:47; 105:32; Is 30:30; Ezek 38:22; Rev 8:7 9:24 [a]Lit *taking hold of itself* 9:25 [A]Ex 9:19; Ps 78:47, 48; 105:32, 33 9:26 [A]Ex 8:22; 9:4, 6; 11:7 9:27 [a]Lit *sent and called* [A]Ex 8:8 [B]Ex 10:16, 17; 2 Chr 12:6; Ps 129:4; 145:17; Lam 1:18 9:28 [a]Lit *sounds* [A]Ex 8:8, 28; 10:17 [B]Ex 8:25; 10:8, 24 9:29 [a]Lit *palms* [b]Lit *sounds* [A]1 Kin 8:22, 38; Ps 143:6; Is 1:15 [B]Ex 8:22; 19:5; 20:11; Ps 24:1; 1 Cor 10:26

furnace. That which participated so largely in their oppressive labor became the source of a painful health hazard for the oppressors!

9:11 magicians could not stand. A side comment indicates that these men (who in Egyptian eyes were men of power) had been so sorely afflicted that they could not stand, either physically or vocationally, before God's spokesmen. Although they are not mentioned after the third plague, they apparently had continued to serve before Pharaoh and were undoubtedly there when plagues 4 and 5 were announced. Their powerlessness had not been sufficient as yet for Pharaoh to dispense with their services—an outward symbol, perhaps, of Pharaoh's unwillingness to grant the God of Israel total sovereignty.

9:12 the LORD hardened. For the first time, apart from the words to Moses before the plagues began (cf. Ex 4:21; 7:3), the statement is made that God hardened Pharaoh's heart. In the other instances, the record observes that Pharaoh hardened his own heart. Each instance records "as the LORD commanded," so what happened did so from two closely related perspectives: 1) God was carrying out His purpose through Pharaoh, and 2) Pharaoh was personally responsible for his actions as the command of v. 13 implies. *See note on 4:21.*

9:14 My plagues. God's use of the possessive pronoun specified what should have become abundantly clear to Pharaoh by then, namely, that these were God's own workings.

9:14–19 After sounding again the customary demand to release God's people for worship (v. 13), and after delivering a warning of how His plagues would really have an impact (v. 14), God provided more information and issued certain preliminary instructions: (1) A 3-fold purpose pertained to the plagues; namely, the Egyptians would recognize that Yahweh was incomparable, that His power would be demonstrated through them, and that His name, character, attributes, and power would be known everywhere. As a result of the plagues, Egypt could not keep her humiliation hidden from other nations. (2) A declaration that whatever royal authority Pharaoh had, it had been because of God's sovereign and providential control of world affairs, which included putting Pharaoh on his throne. This was a telling reminder that He was what He declared Himself to be, the one and only true and immanent Lord. (3) A reminder of the worst scenario for Egypt if Yahweh had chosen, in lieu of the preceding plagues, to strike the people first—they would have perished. In other words, God had been gracious and longsuffering in the progression of the plagues. (4) A declaration that the weather about to be unleashed by the incomparable God was unlike anything previously recorded in Egypt's entire history, or "since its founding" or "since it became a nation." (5) An instruction as to how the Egyptians could avoid severe storm damage and loss of property. Grace was once again afforded them!

9:16 See Ro 9:17 where Paul indicates God's sovereignty over Pharaoh.

9:20, 21 who feared … who paid no regard. Some heard the instruction and obeyed; others, like their national leader, "paid no regard to the word of the LORD," a graphic expression of refusal to heed divine instruction.

9:23, 24 fire ran down to the earth … fire flashing. The violent, electrical thunderstorm brought with it unusual lightning, or "fireballs," which zigzagged (lit. "fire taking hold of itself") to and fro on the ground with the hail.

9:26 Only in the land of Goshen. The discriminatory nature of this plague was unannounced beforehand, but the national distinction previously declared and observed again prevailed. Although unstated, those who were in the strife-torn regions and who obeyed instructions obviously found their livestock equally safe and sound.

9:27 I have sinned this time. Any improvement in Pharaoh's theological understanding, notwithstanding the following confession of a righteous Lord and of a wicked people, was rendered suspect by the face-saving caveat "this time." Lacking repentance, it brushed aside all previous reaction and disobedience as having no significance.

9:28 there has been enough. Moses' reply (v. 30) indicated that such an evaluation was not one of repentance nor one of fearing the Lord and acknowledging His power.

30 [A]But as for you and your servants, I know that
[B]you do not yet [a]fear [b]the LORD God." 31 (Now the
flax and the [A]barley were [a]ruined, for the barley
was in the ear and the flax was in bud. 32 But the
wheat and the spelt were not [a]ruined, for they *ripen*
late.) 33 [A]So Moses went out of the city from Pharaoh, and spread out his [a]hands to the LORD; and the
[b]thunder and the hail ceased, and rain [c]no longer
poured on the earth. 34 But when Pharaoh saw that
the rain and the hail and the [a]thunder had ceased,
he sinned again and [b]hardened his heart, he and his
servants. 35 Pharaoh's heart was [a]hardened, and he
did not let the sons of Israel go, just as the [A]LORD
had spoken through Moses.

THE PLAGUE OF LOCUSTS

10 Then the LORD said to Moses, "Go to Pharaoh,
for [A]I have [a]hardened his heart and the heart
of his servants, that I may [b]perform these signs of
Mine [c]among them, 2 and [A]that you may tell in the
[a]hearing of your son, and of your grandson, how I
made a mockery of the Egyptians and how I [b]per-
formed My signs among them, [B]that you may know
that I am the LORD."

3 Moses and Aaron went to Pharaoh and said to
him, "Thus says the LORD, the God of the Hebrews,
'How long will you refuse to [A]humble yourself before Me? [B]Let My people go, that they may serve Me.
4 For if you refuse to let My people go, behold, tomorrow I will bring locusts into your territory. 5 They
shall cover the surface of the land, so that no one
will be able to see the land. [A]They will also eat the
rest of what has escaped—what is left to you from
the hail—and they will eat every tree which sprouts
for you out of the field. 6 Then [A]your houses shall
be filled and the houses of all your servants and
the houses of all the Egyptians, *something* which
neither your fathers nor your grandfathers have
seen, from the day that they [a]came upon the earth
until this day.'" And he turned and went out from
Pharaoh. 7 [A]Pharaoh's servants said to him, "How
long will this man be [B]a snare to us? Let the men
go, that they may serve the LORD their God. Do you
not [a]realize that Egypt is destroyed?" 8 So Moses and
Aaron [A]were brought back to Pharaoh, and he said
to them, "[B]Go, serve the LORD your God! [a]Who are
the ones that are going?" 9 Moses said, "[A]We shall
go with our young and our old; with our sons and
our daughters, [B]with our flocks and our herds we
shall go, for we [a]must hold a feast to the LORD."
10 Then he said to them, "Thus may the LORD be
with you, [a]if ever I let you and your little ones go!
Take heed, for evil is [b]in your mind. 11 Not so! Go
now, the men *among you,* and serve the LORD, for
[a]that is what you desire." So [A]they were driven out
from Pharaoh's presence.

12 Then the LORD said to Moses, "[A]Stretch out
your hand over the land of Egypt for the locusts,
that they may come up on the land of Egypt and
[B]eat every plant of the land, *even* all that the hail
has left." 13 So Moses stretched out his staff over the
land of Egypt, and the LORD directed an east wind
on the land all that day and all that night; and when
it was morning, the east wind [a]brought the [A]locusts.

9:30 [a]*Or reverence* [b]*Lit before the LORD* [A]Ex 8:29 [B]Is 26:10 9:31 [a]*Lit smitten* [A]Ruth 1:22; 2:23 9:32 [a]*Lit smitten* 9:33 [a]*Lit palms* [b]*Lit sounds* [c]*Lit was not poured* [A]Ex 8:12; 9:29 9:34 [a]*Lit sounds* [b]*Lit made heavy* 9:35 [a]*Lit strong* [A]Ex 4:21 10:1 [a]*Lit made heavy* [b]*Lit put* [c]*Lit in his midst* [A]Ex 4:21; 7:13; Josh 11:20; John 12:40; Rom 9:18 10:2 [a]*Lit ears* [b]*Lit put* [A]Ex 12:26, 27; 13:8, 14, 15; Deut 4:9; Ps 44:1; 78:5; Joel 1:3 [B]Ex 7:5, 17 10:3 [A]1 Kin 21:29; 2 Chr 34:27; James 4:10; 1 Pet 5:6 [B]Ex 4:23 10:5 [A]Joel 1:4; 2:25 10:6 [a]*Lit were* [A]Ex 8:3, 21 10:7 [a]*Lit know* [A]Ex 7:5; 8:19; 12:33 [B]Ex 23:33; Josh 23:13; 1 Sam 18:21; Eccl 7:26 10:8 [a]*Lit Who and who are* [A]Ex 8:8 [B]Ex 8:25 10:9 [a]*Lit have a feast* [A]Ex 12:37, 38 [B]Ex 10:26 10:10 [a]*Lit when I* [b]*Lit before your face* 10:11 [a]*Lit you desire it* [A]Ex 10:28 10:12 [A]Ex 7:19 [B]Ex 10:5, 15 10:13 [a]*Lit carried* [A]Ps 78:46; 105:34

9:31, 32 flax and the barley were ruined ... the wheat and the spelt were not ruined. A very brief bulletin on which crops were damaged and which were not placed this plague in Feb. All 4 crops mentioned were important economic resources. Wheat would be harvested only a month later than flax and barley together with the aftercrop "spelt" or "rye." God's timing of the disaster to two crops left room for Pharaoh to repent before the other crops might be destroyed.

9:34 sinned again. Pharaoh's culpability increased because when he saw God answer Moses' prayer—an entreaty he had requested (v. 28)—still all his admissions and promises were promptly swept aside. **he and his servants.** For the first time mention is made of the stubborn resistance of Pharaoh's entourage, all of whom had hardened their hearts. The striking contrast emerges in God's directions to Moses for the next plague: He had hardened their hearts for a purpose (10:1).

10:2 that you may tell ... that you may know. The release from Egypt, accompanied by these great acts of God, was designed to become an important and indelible part in recounting the history of Israel to succeeding generations. It would tell just who their God was and what He had done. **make a mockery.** Lit. "to deal harshly with" or "to make sport of," and describing an action by which shame and disgrace is brought upon its object.

10:3 How long will you refuse...? The question asked of Pharaoh struck a contrast with the opening words of God to Moses (v. 1), "I have hardened his heart." What God did cannot erase personal responsibility from Pharaoh to hear, repent, and submit. Under the cumulative weight of 7 plagues, the time had come to deliver a challenge to reconsider and obey. This is God's grace operating parallel with His own sovereign purposes.

10:4–6 The extent and intensity of the locust plague was such that it would be unique in Egyptian history—nothing like any locust problem during the previous two generations, nor like any locust swarm in the future (v. 14). Locust invasions were feared in Egypt, to the point that the farmers often prayed to the locust god to ensure the safety of their crops. The humiliation of their god was total, as was the damage: "Nothing green was left" (v. 15).

10:7 How long will this man...? The first "How long?" question in this encounter dealt with the desired response from Pharaoh (v. 3), whereas this second "How long?" question pointed out their impatience at Pharaoh's intransigence. Their advice—to give in—was the best choice. **Egypt is destroyed.** The advisers negatively evaluated the state of the country after 7 plagues, and suggested that Pharaoh was refusing to acknowledge how desperate the situation really was even before the agriculture was completely destroyed. Stubborn resistance did not necessarily rob them of all reason, and the better part of wisdom this time demanded acquiescence to Moses' request.

10:8 Who are the ones that are going? For the first time Pharaoh tried to negotiate a deal before the threatened plague struck. Adroitly, he suggested in his question that only representatives of Israel, perhaps only the men (v. 11), need go out to worship.

10:10 may the LORD be with you. Sarcastic threats demonstrated the unyielding and unreasonable obstinacy of Pharaoh. Egyptian women did accompany their men in religious celebration, but in Israel's case if the men went out then the women and children were in effect hostages bidding them return.

10:11 driven out. For the first time, God's two spokesmen were angrily dismissed from the throne room.

10:12 all that the hail has left. This reminder of the previous plague in which God had graciously restrained the extent of agricultural damage appeared also in the warning of the plague given to Pharaoh and his advisers (v. 5) and in the description of the damage done by the locusts (v. 15).

10:13 an east wind. God used natural means, most probably the spring hot wind,

14 [A]The locusts came up over all the land of Egypt
and settled in all the territory of Egypt; *they were*
very [a]numerous. There had never been so *many*
[b]locusts, nor would there be so *many* [c]again. 15 For
they covered the surface of the whole land, so that
the land was darkened; and they [A]ate every plant
of the land and all the fruit of the trees that the hail
had left. Thus nothing green was left on tree or plant
of the field through all the land of Egypt. 16 Then
Pharaoh hurriedly [A]called for Moses and Aaron, and
he said, "[B]I have sinned against the LORD your God
and against you. 17 Now therefore, please forgive
my sin only this once, and [A]make supplication to
the LORD your God, that He would only remove
this death from me." 18 [A]He went out from Pharaoh
and made supplication to the LORD. 19 So the LORD
shifted *the wind* to a very strong west wind which
took up the locusts and drove them into the [a]Red
Sea; not one locust was left in all the territory of
Egypt. 20 But [A]the LORD [a]hardened Pharaoh's heart,
and he did not let the sons of Israel go.

DARKNESS OVER THE LAND

21 Then the LORD said to Moses, "[A]Stretch out
your hand toward the sky, that there may be darkness over the land of Egypt, even a darkness [B]which
may be felt." 22 So Moses stretched out his hand
toward the sky, and there was [A]thick darkness in
all the land of Egypt for three days. 23 They did
not see one another, nor did anyone rise from
his place for three days, [A]but all the sons of Israel had light in their dwellings. 24 Then Pharaoh
[A]called to Moses, and said, "Go, serve the LORD;
only let your flocks and your herds be detained.
Even [B]your little ones may go with you." 25 But
Moses said, "You must also [a]let us have sacrifices
and burnt offerings, that we may [b]sacrifice *them*
to the LORD our God. 26 [A]Therefore, our livestock
too shall go with us; not a hoof shall be left behind,
for we shall take some of them to serve the LORD
our God. And until we arrive there, we ourselves
do not know with what we shall serve the LORD."
27 But [A]the LORD [a]hardened Pharaoh's heart, and
he was not willing to let them go. 28 Then Pharaoh
said to him, "[A]Get away from me! [a]Beware, do not
see my face again, for in the day you see my face
you shall die!" 29 Moses said, "You are right; [A]I shall
never see your face again!"

THE LAST PLAGUE

11 Now the LORD said to Moses, "One more plague
I will bring on Pharaoh and on Egypt; [A]after
that he will let you go from here. When he lets you
go, he will surely drive you out from here completely. 2 Speak now in the [a]hearing of the people
that [A]each man ask from his neighbor and each
woman from her neighbor for articles of silver and
articles of gold." 3 [A]The LORD gave the people favor
in the sight of the Egyptians. [B]Furthermore, the man
Moses *himself* was [a]greatly esteemed in the land of
Egypt, *both* in the sight of Pharaoh's servants and
in the sight of the people.
4 Moses said, "Thus says the LORD, 'About [A]mid-
night I am going out into the midst of Egypt,

10:14 [a]Lit *heavy* [b]Lit *locusts like them before them* [c]Lit *after them* [A]Deut 28:38; Ps 78:46; 105:34; Joel 1:4, 7; 2:1-11; Rev 9:3 10:15 [A]Ex 10:5; Ps 105:34f 10:16 [A]Ex 8:8 [B]Ex 9:27 10:17 [A]Ex 8:8, 28; 9:28; 1 Kin 13:6 10:18 [A]Ex 8:30 10:19 [a]Lit *Sea of Reeds* 10:20 [a]Lit *made strong* [A]Ex 4:21; 11:10 10:21 [A]Ex 9:22 [B]Deut 28:29 10:22 [A]Ps 105:28; Rev 16:10 10:23 [A]Ex 8:22 10:24 [A]Ex 8:8, 25 [B]Ex 10:10 10:25 [a]Lit *give into our hand* [b]Lit *make* 10:26 [A]Ex 10:9 10:27 [a]Lit *made strong* [A]Ex 4:21; 10:20; 14:4, 8 10:28 [a]Lit *Take heed to yourself* [A]Ex 10:11 10:29 [A]Ex 11:8; Heb 11:27 11:1 [A]Ex 12:31, 33, 39 11:2 [a]Lit *ears* [A]Ex 3:22; 12:35, 36 11:3 [a]Lit *very great* [A]Ex 3:21; 12:36; Ps 106:46 [B]Deut 34:10-12 11:4 [A]Ex 12:29

or "sirocco," to bring the locusts into the country from the Arabian Peninsula.

10:16 hurriedly. A recognition on the part of Pharaoh that his country now faced a crisis brought forth a hurried confession to Aaron and Moses, which again was merely an expedient course of action.

10:17 forgive my sin. Again, an attempt to sound earnest in his response, and again with an appeal for Moses to pray for removal of the plague. He referred to it this time as "this death," or "deadly plague," phrases which highlighted the severity of Egypt's condition.

10:19 west wind. In answer to prayer, wind direction reversed as the Lord caused the locusts to be blown eastward out of the country. The completeness of their removal received emphasis. That none remained in the country was apparently something unusual, perhaps somewhat distinct from previously known locust invasions. The absence of locusts was a challenging reminder of the power of the Lord who had brought it all to pass.

10:21, 22 darkness … felt … thick darkness. Such a description of the ninth plague, which occurred without warning, pointed to the most unusual nature of the three-day darkness that now prevented any from leaving their homes. That Israel had light in their dwellings and went about their normal activity stresses the supernatural nature of this plague. It takes attention away from trying to explain the darkness solely in terms of the Khamsin, the swirling sandstorms of the day. The LXX did, however, string together 3 Gr. words, two for darkness and one for storm, to portray the nuance of the Heb. In so doing, it may unwittingly have given some credence to a severe sandstorm. Theologically, such thick darkness directly challenged the faithfulness of the sun god, Ra, to provide warmth and sunshine from day to day, and also prevented any daily worship rituals from taking place.

10:24 Go … little ones may go with you. Pharaoh's deceitful and manipulative negotiating skills rose to the occasion: Let the people go but keep back their livestock as the hostage forcing their return. He had not yet understood that partial obedience to the Lord's directions was unacceptable.

10:25 See 3:18 for remarks on the request to leave for worship, which suggests something less than permanent departure.

10:28 Get away from me! … you shall die! Pharaoh's obstinacy and resistance reached a new height when he summarily dismissed Moses and Aaron and this time added a death threat.

10:29 never see your face again! Moses concurred, but from another perspective than that of Pharaoh. All negotiations and requests ceased immediately. Moses would be summoned to see Pharaoh again after the tenth plague (12:31), but that would be to hear him finally concede defeat.

11:1–3 Now the LORD said. Read as "the Lord had said." In a parenthetical paragraph, the narrative recorded that which God had already said to Moses during the 3 days of darkness, priming him for Pharaoh's summons, and priming Israel to receive Egyptian jewelry and other goods. An aside explained Egyptian generosity as occasioned by divine intervention (cf. 12:35, 36). This also included a healthy respect by Egypt's leaders and people for Israel's leader.

11:4–8 Moses said. Moses' response to Pharaoh's threat continued with his giving warning of the final plague and leaving with great indignation. The death threat delivered by Pharaoh evoked one from God. The "get out!" from Pharaoh to Israel's and God's spokesmen would be met by the "get out" from the Egyptians to Israel.

11:4 About midnight. The day was not specified, as in previous plagues by "tomorrow." It took place either the same day of the final confrontation with Pharaoh or a few days later. If the instructions for the Passover (12:1–20) were not given during the days of darkness, then 4 days minimum would be required to set the stage for that special feast day, i.e., from the tenth to the fourteenth day (12:3, 6). *See note on 8:23.* **I am going out.** God was, of course, involved in all previous plagues

5 and [A]all the firstborn in the land of Egypt shall
die, from the firstborn of the Pharaoh who sits on
his throne, even to the firstborn of the slave girl
who is behind the millstones; all the firstborn of
the cattle as well. 6 Moreover, there shall be [A]a great
cry in all the land of Egypt, such as there has not
been *before* and such as shall never be again. 7 [A]But
against any of the sons of Israel a dog will not *even*
[a]bark, whether against man or beast, that you may
[b]understand how the LORD makes a distinction between Egypt and Israel.' 8 [A]All these your servants
will come down to me and bow themselves [a]before
me, saying, 'Go out, you and all the people who [b]fol-
low you,' and after that I will go out." [B]And he went
out from Pharaoh in hot anger.

9 Then the LORD said to Moses, "[A]Pharaoh will
not listen to you, so [B]that My wonders will be multiplied in the land of Egypt." 10 [A]Moses and Aaron
performed all these wonders before Pharaoh; yet
[B]the LORD [a]hardened Pharaoh's heart, and he did
not let the sons of Israel go out of his land.

THE PASSOVER LAMB

12 Now the LORD said to Moses and Aaron in the
land of [a]Egypt, 2 "[A]This month shall be the beginning of months for you; it is to be the first month
of the year to you. 3 Speak to all the congregation of
Israel, saying, 'On the tenth of this month they are
each one to take a [a]lamb for themselves, according to their fathers' households, a [a]lamb for [b]each
household. 4 Now if the household is too small for a
[a]lamb, then he and his neighbor nearest to his house
are to take one according to the [b]number of persons
in them; according to [c]what each man should eat,
you are to [d]divide the lamb. 5 Your [a]lamb shall be
[A]an unblemished male a year old; you may take it

11:5 [A]Ex 12:12, 29; Ps 78:51; 105:36; 135:8; 136:10 11:6 [A]Ex 12:30 11:7 [a]Lit *sharpen his tongue* [b]Lit *know* [A]Ex 8:22; Josh 10:21 11:8 [a]Lit *to* [b]Lit *are at your feet* [A]Ex 12:31-33 [B]Heb 11:27 11:9 [A]Ex 7:4 [B]Ex 7:3 11:10 [a]Lit *made strong* [A]Ex 4:21 [B]Ex 7:3; 9:12; 10:20, 27; Josh 11:20; Is 63:17; John 12:40 12:1 [a]Lit *Egypt, saying* 12:2 [A]Ex 13:4; 23:15; 34:18; Deut 16:1 12:3 [a]Or *kid* [b]Lit *the* 12:4 [a]Or *kid* [b]Or *amount* [c]Lit *each man's eating* [d]Lit *compute for* 12:5 [a]Or *kid* [A]Lev 22:18-21; 23:12; Heb 9:14; 1 Pet 1:19

through whatever means He chose to use, but this time, to warrant personal attention, God stated that He Himself (emphatic personal pronoun used) would march throughout the land. Note the repeated "I will" statements in the Passover instructions (12:12, 13).

11:5 the firstborn. The firstborn held a particularly important position in the family and society, not only inheriting a double portion of the father's estate, but also representing special qualities of life and strength (cf. Ge 49:3). In Egypt, the firstborn would ascend to the throne and continue the dynasty. Whatever significance might have been attached religiously, politically, dynastically, and socially, it was all stripped away by the extent and intensity of the plague—namely the execution of all the firstborn of all classes of the population including their animals.

11:6 So drastic was this plague that its uniqueness in Egypt's history, already past and yet to come, was noted in the warning.

11:7 In contrast to the turmoil and grief experienced in Egyptian territory, all remained tranquil in Israelite territory—so much so that not even a dog barked. That the Lord had made and was making a sharp distinction between the two peoples was a fact to which none could be blind.

12:1 the LORD said. Most probably, the instructions on the Passover (vv. 1–20) were also given during the 3 days of darkness in order to fully prepare Israel for the grand finale, their Exodus from Egypt. **in the land.** Later, while Israel was in the wilderness, Moses wrote (23:14–17; Dt 16:1–8) and indicated that the detailed instructions for this very special feast day in Israel's religious calendar were not like those of the other special days, all which were given after the nation had already left Egypt. This one, the Passover, was inextricably linked to what took place in the Exodus, and that connection was never to be forgotten. It became indelibly entrenched in Israel's tradition and has always marked the day of redemption from Egypt.

12:2 This month. The month of Abib (Mar./Apr.) by divine decree became the beginning of the religious calendar, marking the start of Israel's life as a nation. Later in Israel's history, after the Babylonian captivity, Abib would become Nisan (cf. Ne 2:1; Est 3:7).

12:3–14 The detailed instructions for the Passover included what animal to select, when to kill it, what to do with its blood, how to cook it, what to do with leftovers, how to dress for the meal, the reason why it was being celebrated "in haste," and what the shed blood signified.

12:5 Your lamb … unblemished. A kid goat was an alternative choice. Any flaw would

CHRONOLOGY OF THE EXODUS

Date	Event	Reference
Fifteenth day, first month, first year	Exodus	Exodus 12
Fifteenth day, second month, first year	Arrival in Wilderness of Sin	Exodus 16:1
Third month, first year	Arrival in Wilderness of Sinai	Exodus 19:1
First day, first month, second year	Erection of Tabernacle	Exodus 40:1, 17
	Dedication of Altar	Numbers 7:1
	Consecration of Levites	Numbers 8:1–26
Fourteenth day, first month, second year	Passover	Numbers 9:5
First day, second month, second year	Census	Numbers 1:1, 18
Fourteenth day, second month, second year	Supplemental Passover	Numbers 9:11
Twentieth day, second month, second year	Departure from Sinai	Numbers 10:11
First month, fortieth year	In Wilderness of Zin	Numbers 20:1, 22–29; 33:38
First day, fifth month, fortieth year	Death of Aaron	Numbers 20:22–29; 33:38
First day, eleventh month, fortieth year	Moses' Address	Deuteronomy 1:3

from the sheep or from the goats. 6 [a]You shall keep
it until the [A]fourteenth day of the same month, then
the whole assembly of the congregation of Israel
is to kill it [b,B]at twilight. 7 [A]Moreover, they shall take
some of the blood and put it on the two doorposts
and on the lintel [a]of the houses in which they eat it.
8 They shall eat the flesh [A]that *same* night, [B]roasted
with fire, and they shall eat it with [C]unleavened
bread [a,D]and bitter herbs. 9 Do not eat any of it raw
or boiled at all with water, but rather [A]roasted with
fire, *both* its head and its legs along with [B]its entrails. 10 [A]And you shall not leave any of it over until
morning, but whatever is left of it until morning,
you shall burn with fire. 11 Now you shall eat it in
this manner: *with* your loins girded, your sandals
on your feet, and your staff in your hand; and you
shall eat it in haste—it is [A]the LORD'S Passover. 12 For
[A]I will go through the land of Egypt on that night,
and will strike down all the firstborn in the land
of Egypt, both man and beast; and [B]against all the
gods of Egypt I will execute judgments—[C]I am the
LORD. 13 [A]The blood shall be a sign for you on the
houses where you [a]live; and when I see the blood
I will pass over you, and no plague will befall you
[b]to destroy *you* when I strike the land of Egypt.

FEAST OF UNLEAVENED BREAD

14 'Now [A]this day will be [B]a memorial to you, and
you shall celebrate it *as* a feast to the LORD; throughout your generations you are to celebrate it *as* [a,C]a
permanent ordinance. 15 [A]Seven days you shall eat unleavened bread, but on the first day you shall [a]remove
leaven from your houses; for whoever eats anything
leavened from the first day until the seventh day, [B]that
[b]person shall be cut off from Israel. 16 [A]On the first
day you shall have a holy assembly, and *another* holy
assembly on the seventh day; no work at all shall be
done on them, except what must be eaten [a]by every
person, that alone may be [b]prepared by you. 17 You
shall also observe [A]the *Feast of* Unleavened Bread,
for on this [B]very day I brought your hosts out of the
land of Egypt; therefore you shall observe this day
throughout your generations as [C]a [a]permanent ordinance. 18 [A]In the first *month,* on the fourteenth day
of the month at evening, you shall eat unleavened
bread, until the twenty-first day of the month at evening. 19 [A]Seven days there shall be no leaven found in
your houses; for whoever eats what is leavened, that
[a,B]person shall be cut off from the congregation of
Israel, whether *he is* an alien or a native of the land.
20 You shall not eat anything leavened; in all your
dwellings you shall eat unleavened bread.' "

21 Then [A]Moses called for all the elders of Israel
and said to them, "[a]Go and [B]take for yourselves
[b]lambs according to your families, and slay [C]the
Passover *lamb.* 22 [A]You shall take a bunch of hyssop
and dip it in the blood which is in the basin, and
[a]apply some of the blood that is in the basin to the
lintel and the two doorposts; and none of you shall
go outside the door of his house until morning.

A MEMORIAL OF REDEMPTION

23 For [A]the LORD will pass through to smite the
Egyptians; and when He sees the blood on the lintel
and on the two doorposts, the LORD will pass over
the door and will [B]not allow the [C]destroyer to come
in to your houses to smite *you.* 24 And [A]you shall observe this event as an ordinance for you and your
children forever. 25 When you enter the land which
the LORD will give you, as He has [a]promised, you
shall observe this [b]rite. 26 [A]And when your children
say to you, '[a]What does this rite mean to you?' 27 you
shall say, 'It is a Passover sacrifice to [A]the LORD
[a]who passed over the houses of the sons of Israel in
Egypt when He smote the Egyptians, but [b]spared our
homes.' " [B]And the people bowed low and worshiped.

12:6 [a]Lit *It shall be to you for a guarding* [b]Lit *between the two evenings* [A]Ex 12:14, 17; Lev 23:5; Num 9:1-3, 11; 28:16 [B]Ex 16:12; Deut 16:4, 6 12:7 [a]Lit *upon* [A]Ex 12:22 12:8 [a]Lit *in addition to* [A]Ex 34:25; Num 9:12 [B]Deut 16:7 [C]Deut 16:3, 4; 1 Cor 5:8 [D]Num 9:11 12:9 [A]Ex 12:8 [B]Ex 29:13, 17, 22 12:10 [A]Ex 16:19; 23:18; 34:25 12:11 [A]Ex 12:13, 21, 27, 43 12:12 [A]Ex 11:4, 5 [B]Num 33:4; Ps 82:1 [C]Ex 6:2 12:13 [a]Lit *are* [b]Lit *for destruction* [A]Heb 11:28 12:14 [a]Or *an eternal* [A]Ex 12:6; Lev 23:4, 5; 2 Kin 23:21 [B]Ex 13:9 [C]Ex 12:17, 24; 13:10 12:15 [a]Lit *cause to cease* [b]Lit *soul* [A]Ex 13:6, 7; 23:15; 34:18; Lev 23:6; Num 28:17; Deut 16:3, 8 [B]Gen 17:14; Ex 12:19; Num 9:13 12:16 [a]Lit *pertaining to* [b]Lit *done* [A]Lev 23:7, 8; Num 28:18, 25 12:17 [a]Or *eternal* [A]Deut 16:3-8 [B]Ex 12:41 [C]Ex 12:14; 13:3, 10 12:18 [A]Ex 12:2; Lev 23:5-8; Num 28:16-25 12:19 [a]Lit *soul* [A]Ex 12:15; 23:15; 34:18 [B]Num 9:13 12:21 [a]Lit *Draw out* [b]Lit *sheep* [A]Num 9:4; Heb 11:28 [B]Ex 12:3 [C]Ex 12:11 12:22 [a]Lit *cause to touch* [A]Ex 12:7 12:23 [A]Ex 11:4; 12:12, 13 [B]Rev 7:3; 9:4 [C]1 Cor 10:10; Heb 11:28 12:24 [A]Ex 12:14, 17; 13:5, 10 12:25 [a]Lit *spoken* [b]Lit *service* 12:26 [a]Lit *What is this service to you?* [A]Ex 10:2; 13:8, 14, 15; Deut 32:7; Josh 4:6; Ps 78:6 12:27 [a]Lit *because He* [b]Lit *delivered* [A]Ex 12:11 [B]Ex 4:31

render it unfit to represent a pure, wholesome sacrifice given to Yahweh.

12:6 at twilight. Lit. "between the two evenings." Since the new day was reckoned from sunset, the sacrificing of the lamb or kid was done before sunset while it was still day 14 of the first month. "Twilight" has been taken to signify either that time between sunset and the onset of darkness, or from the decline of the sun until sunset. Later Moses would prescribe the time for the sacrifice as "in the evening at sunset" (Dt 16:6). According to Josephus, it was customary in his day to kill the lamb at about 3:00 p.m. This was the time of day that Christ, the Christian's Passover lamb (1Co 5:7), died (Lk 23:44–46).

12:9 Do not eat any of it raw. A prohibition with health implications which also distinguished them from pagan peoples who often ate raw flesh in their sacred festivals.

12:12 against all the gods. The tenth plague was a judgment against all Egyptian deities. The loss of the firstborn of men and beasts had far-reaching theological implications, namely, the impotence of the pagan deities, many of whom were represented by animals, to protect their devotees from such nationwide tragedies. The great cry of grief (11:6; 12:30) may also have bemoaned the incapability of the nation's gods.

12:14 a memorial. The details of how this Passover Day was to be memorialized in future years were laid down (vv. 14–20), and then repeated in the instructions to the elders (vv. 21–27). Prescribing the eating of unleavened bread for 7 days, demanding a thorough housecleaning from leaven (v. 15), issuing a stern warning of banishment for eating leaven (v. 15), and bracketing the 7 days with special holy days (v. 16), served to proclaim the high importance of the nation's remembering this event.

12:19 an alien. Provision was made right at the beginning for non-Israelites to be included in the nation's religious festivals. Failure to comply with the regulations on leaven would result in banishment for the alien as well.

12:22 bunch of hyssop. Certain identification is impossible, but this could be the marjoram plant. **lintel … the two doorposts.** The top and two sides of the doorway.

12:23 the destroyer. This is most likely the Angel of the Lord (cf. 2Sa 24:16; Is 37:36). *See note on 3:2.*

12:25 The promise of entering the land again received emphasis. Israel was not to think of the Exodus as merely a departure from Egypt, but rather as a departure from one land in order to enter another land, which would be their own, in strict accordance with the specifics of the Abrahamic Covenant for his descendants through Isaac and Jacob (cf. Ge 17:7, 8).

12:26, 27 In the annual commemoration of the Passover, parents were obligated to teach their children its meaning. It became

28 Then the sons of Israel went and did *so;* just
as the LORD had commanded Moses and Aaron,
so they did.
29 Now it came about at [A]midnight that [B]the LORD
struck all [C]the firstborn in the land of Egypt, from
the firstborn of Pharaoh who sat on his throne to
the firstborn of the captive who was in the dungeon, and all the firstborn of [D]cattle. 30 Pharaoh
arose in the night, he and all his servants and all
the Egyptians, and there was [A]a great cry in Egypt,
for there was no home where there was not someone dead. 31 Then [A]he called for Moses and Aaron
at night and said, "Rise up, [B]get out from among
my people, both you and the sons of Israel; and go,
[a]worship the LORD, as you have said. 32 Take [A]both
your flocks and your herds, as you have said, and
go, and bless me also."

EXODUS OF ISRAEL

33 [A]The Egyptians urged the people, to send them
out of the land in haste, for they said, "We will all
be dead." 34 So the people took [A]their dough before
it was leavened, *with* their kneading bowls bound
up in the clothes on their shoulders.
35 [A]Now the sons of Israel had done according
to the word of Moses, for they had requested from
the Egyptians articles of silver and articles of gold,
and clothing; 36 and the LORD had given the people
favor in the sight of the Egyptians, so that they let
them have their request. Thus they [A]plundered the
Egyptians.
37 Now the [A]sons of Israel journeyed from [B]Rame-
ses to Succoth, about [C]six hundred thousand men on
foot, aside from children. 38 A [A]mixed multitude also
went up with them, [a]along with flocks and herds, a
[B]very large number of livestock. 39 They baked the
dough which they had brought out of Egypt into
cakes of unleavened bread. For it had not become
leavened, since they were [A]driven out of Egypt and
could not delay, nor had they [a]prepared any provisions for themselves.
40 Now the time [a]that the sons of Israel lived in
Egypt was [A]four hundred and thirty years. 41 And
at the end of four hundred and thirty years, [a]to [A]the
very day, [B]all the hosts of the LORD went out from
the land of Egypt.

ORDINANCE OF THE PASSOVER

42 [A]It is a night [a]to be observed for the LORD for
having brought them out from the land of Egypt;
this night is for the LORD, [a]to be observed [b]by all
the sons of Israel throughout their generations.
43 The LORD said to Moses and Aaron, "This is
the ordinance of [A]the Passover: no [a,B]foreigner is
to eat of it; 44 but every man's [A]slave purchased
with money, after you have circumcised him, then
he may eat of it. 45 [A]A sojourner or a hired servant
shall not eat of it. 46 It is to be eaten in a single
house; you are not to bring forth any of the flesh
outside of the house, [A]nor are you to break any bone
of it. 47 [A]All the congregation of Israel are to [a]cele-
brate this. 48 But [A]if a [a]stranger sojourns with you,
and [b]celebrates the Passover to the LORD, let all his
males be circumcised, and then let him come near
to [c]celebrate it; and he shall be like a native of the
land. But no uncircumcised person may eat of it.
49 [a,A]The same law shall [b]apply to the native as to
the [c]stranger who sojourns among you."
50 Then all the sons of Israel did *so;* they did just
as the LORD had commanded Moses and Aaron.
51 And on that same day [A]the LORD brought the sons
of Israel out of the land of Egypt [a,B]by their hosts.

12:29 [A]Ex 11:4, 5 [B]Num 8:17; 33:4; Ps 135:8; 136:10 [C]Ex 4:23; Ps 78:51; 105:36 [D]Ex 9:6 12:30 [A]Ex 11:6 12:31 [a]Or *serve* [A]Ex 8:8 [B]Ex 8:25 12:32 [A]Ex 10:9, 26 12:33 [A]Ex 10:7; 11:1; 12:39; Ps 105:38 12:34 [A]Ex 12:39 12:35 [A]Ex 3:21, 22; 11:2, 3; Ps 105:37 12:36 [A]Ex 3:22 12:37 [A]Num 33:3, 5 [B]Gen 47:11 [C]Ex 38:26; Num 1:46; 2:32; 11:21; 26:51 12:38 [a]Lit *and* [A]Num 11:4 [B]Ex 17:3; Num 20:19; 32:1; Deut 3:19 12:39 [a]Lit *made* [A]Ex 6:1; 11:1; 12:31-33 12:40 [a]Or *of the sons of Israel who dwelt* [A]Gen 15:13, 16; Acts 7:6; Gal 3:17 12:41 [a]Lit *that it happened on this very day* [A]Ex 12:17 [B]Ex 3:8, 10; 6:6 12:42 [a]Or *of vigil* [b]Lit *to the sons* [A]Ex 13:10; 34:18; Deut 16:1 12:43 [a]Lit *son of a stranger* [A]Ex 12:11; Num 9:14 [B]Ex 12:48 12:44 [A]Gen 17:12, 13; Lev 22:11 12:45 [A]Lev 22:10 12:46 [A]Num 9:12; Ps 34:20; John 19:33, 36 12:47 [a]Lit *do* [A]Ex 12:6; Num 9:13, 14 12:48 [a]Lit *sojourner* [b]Lit *does* [c]Lit *do* [A]Num 9:14 12:49 [a]Lit *One law* [b]Lit *be* [c]Lit *sojourner* [A]Lev 24:22; Num 15:15, 16, 29 12:51 [a]Lit *according to* [A]Ex 12:41 [B]Ex 6:26

customary for the youngest child of a Jewish family to elicit the father's formal explanation of what happened in connection with the original observance of the meal in Egypt.

12:31 Rise up, get out ... worship the LORD. Finally, Pharaoh's response to the repeated "Let My people go!" became "Leave my people!" with no attempt at further negotiation, but total acquiescence. His subjects, fearing more deaths, concurred and hastened Israel's departure (v. 33), driving them out with no time wasted (v. 39).

12:32 bless me also. Undoubtedly, this final request from Pharaoh, whose heart was certainly not repentant (14:8), temporarily conceded defeat and acknowledged Moses and his God as the victors and as those who had the power and resources to bless him.

12:36 they plundered the Egyptians. Cf. Ge 15:14; Ex 3:20, 21. This was not done with deceit, but rather a straightforward request (cf. 11:2, 3).

12:37–18:27 This section recounts the march of the Israelites from Egypt to Mt. Sinai.

12:37 Rameses to Succoth. One of the cities Israel built (1:11) headed up the itinerary for the journey through the wilderness to Canaan. Succoth is first mentioned in Ge 33:17 as an encampment designated by the word *Succoth,* which means "booth." Although there is later a town by that name E of the Jordan (cf. Jdg 8:5–16), this is rather a place near Egypt (cf. 13:20; Nu 33:5, 6). **six hundred thousand men on foot.** A conservative estimate based on the number of men, probably the fighting men 20 years of age and above, would give a population of 2 million. Israel's population had exploded from the 70 who entered with Jacob in 1875 B.C. to the 2 million who left with Moses in 1445 B.C. *See note on 1:7.*

12:38 A mixed multitude. Other Semitic peoples, other races, and perhaps some native Egyptians accompanied the departing nation. They preferred to be identified with the victorious nation and Jehovah God. Later, some of these became the troublemakers with whom Moses had to deal (Nu 11:4).

12:40, 41 four hundred and thirty years. Abraham had been told that his descendants would be aliens mistreated in a foreign land for 400 years, using a figure rounded to hundreds (Ge 15:13).

12:43–51 Additional regulations given for the holding of the Passover contained prohibitions on any uncircumcised foreigner, stranger, or hired servant being a valid participant. To partake of this meal, non-Israelites had to be "like a native of the land" (v. 48). *See note on Jer 4:4.*

12:46 break any bone. Christ, the Christian's Passover lamb (1Co 5:7), had no bones broken (Jn 19:36).

12:50 all ... did so. On two occasions (see also v. 28) Moses emphasized the complete obedience of the nation in response to the Lord's commands to them: a contrast to the disobedience they would demonstrate in the very near future.

12:51 on that same day. What would be for the nation in their new land a special Sabbath day, was for them at that time the day on which their journey began.

CONSECRATION OF THE FIRSTBORN

13 Then the LORD spoke to Moses, saying,
2 "[A]Sanctify to Me every firstborn, the first
[a]offspring of every womb among the sons of Israel,
both of man and beast; it belongs to Me."
3 Moses said to the people, "[A]Remember this
day in which you went out from Egypt, from the
house of [a]slavery; for [B]by [b]a powerful hand the LORD
brought you out from this place. [C]And nothing leavened shall be eaten. 4 On this day in the [A]month of
Abib, you are about to go forth. 5 It shall be when
the LORD [A]brings you to the land of the Canaanite,
the Hittite, the Amorite, the Hivite and the Jebusite, which [B]He swore to your fathers to give you,
a land flowing with milk and honey, [C]that you shall
[a]observe this rite in this month. 6 For [A]seven days
you shall eat unleavened bread, and on the seventh
day there shall be a feast to the LORD. 7 Unleavened
bread shall be eaten throughout the seven days; and
[A]nothing leavened shall be seen [a]among you, nor
shall any leaven be seen [a]among you in all your borders. 8 [A]You shall tell your son on that day, saying,
'It is because of what the LORD did for me when I
came out of Egypt.' 9 And [A]it shall [a]serve as a sign
to you on your hand, and as a reminder [b]on your
forehead, that the law of the LORD may be in your
mouth; for with [B]a powerful hand the LORD brought
you out of Egypt. 10 Therefore, you shall [A]keep this
ordinance at its appointed time from [a]year to year.
11 "Now when [A]the LORD brings you to the land
of the Canaanite, as [B]He swore to you and to your
fathers, and gives it to you, 12 [A]you shall [a]devote to
the LORD the first [b]offspring of every womb, and
[c]the first offspring of every beast that you own; the
males belong to the LORD. 13 But [A]every first [a]off-
spring of a donkey you shall redeem with a lamb,
but if you do not redeem *it,* then you shall break
its neck; and [B]every firstborn of man among your
sons you shall redeem. 14 [A]And it shall be when your
son asks you in time to come, saying, 'What is this?'
then you shall say to him, '[B]With a [a]powerful hand
the LORD brought us out of Egypt, from the house
of [b]slavery. 15 It came about, when Pharaoh was
stubborn about letting us go, that the [A]LORD killed
every firstborn in the land of Egypt, both the firstborn of man and the firstborn of beast. Therefore, I
sacrifice to the LORD the males, the first [a]offspring
of every womb, but every firstborn of my sons I redeem.' 16 So [A]it shall [a]serve as a sign on your hand
and as [b]phylacteries [c]on your forehead, for with a
[d]powerful hand the LORD brought us out of Egypt."

GOD LEADS THE PEOPLE

17 Now when Pharaoh had let the people go, God
did not lead them by the way of the land of the
Philistines, even though it was near; for God said,
"[A]The people might change their minds when they
see war, and return to Egypt." 18 Hence God led the
people around by the way of the wilderness to the
[a]Red Sea; and the sons of Israel went up [A]in martial
array from the land of Egypt. 19 Moses took [A]the
bones of Joseph with him, for he had made the sons
of Israel solemnly swear, saying, "God will surely
[a]take care of you, and you shall carry my bones from

13:2 [a]Lit *opening* [A]Ex 13:12, 13, 15; 22:29; Lev 27:26; Num 3:13; 8:16f; 18:15; Deut 15:19; Luke 2:23 13:3 [a]Lit *slaves* [b]Lit *strength of hand* [A]Ex 12:42; Deut 16:3 [B]Ex 3:20; 6:1 [C]Ex 12:19 13:4 [A]Ex 12:2; 23:15; 34:18; Deut 16:1 13:5 [a]Lit *serve this service* [A]Ex 3:8, 17; Josh 24:11 [B]Ex 6:8 [C]Ex 12:25 13:6 [A]Ex 12:15-20 13:7 [a]Lit *to* [A]Ex 12:19 13:8 [A]Ex 10:2; 12:26f; 13:14; Ps 44:1 13:9 [a]Lit *be for* [b]Lit *between your eyes* [A]Ex 12:14; 13:16; Num 15:39; Deut 6:8; 11:18 [B]Ex 13:3 13:10 [a]Lit *days to days* [A]Ex 12:24, 25; 13:5 13:11 [A]Ex 13:5 [B]Gen 15:18; 17:8; 28:15; Ps 105:42-45 13:12 [a]Lit *cause to pass over* [b]Lit *opening* [c]Lit *every issue the offspring of a beast* [A]Ex 13:1, 2; 22:29; 34:19; Lev 27:26; Num 18:15; Ezek 44:30; Luke 2:23 13:13 [a]Lit *opening* [A]Ex 34:20; Num 18:15 [B]Num 3:46 13:14 [a]Lit *strength of hand* [b]Lit *slaves* [A]Ex 10:2; 12:26, 27; 13:8; Deut 6:20; Josh 4:6, 21 [B]Ex 13:3, 9 13:15 [a]Lit *opening* [A]Ex 12:29 13:16 [a]Lit *be for* [b]Or *frontlet-bands* [c]Lit *between your eyes* [d]Lit *strength of hand* [A]Ex 13:9; Deut 6:8 13:17 [A]Ex 14:11, 12; Num 14:1-4; Deut 17:16 13:18 [a]Lit *Sea of Reeds* [A]Josh 1:14; 4:12, 13 13:19 [a]Lit *visit* [A]Gen 50:24, 25; Josh 24:32; Acts 7:15, 16

13:2–10 Further explanation tied their departure to the divine promise of entrance and residence in a new land where commemoration of the Exodus would occur through annual observance of this 7 day feast. Again the pedagogical opportunity afforded was not to be overlooked (vv. 8, 16).

13:2 Sanctify to Me every firstborn. Since the firstborn of Israel, of both man and animal, were untouched by the tenth plague, it was fitting that they be set aside as special unto God. Note the closing emphasis: "It belongs to Me." Further instruction followed on the law relating to the firstborn males once they were in their assigned territory (vv. 11–16). This divine demand was closely linked to the day of departure (12:51, "on that same day") and the Feast of Unleavened Bread (v. 3, "this day" and v. 4, "on this day … in the month of Abib"). See Lk 2:7, where Christ was referred to as Mary's firstborn.

13:8 for me when I. A personalized application of God's working belonged to the first generation who experienced the Exodus. Later generations could only say "for us, when we …." in the sense of "our nation," but without loss to the significance of how God had brought about such an important day in the nation's history. Note the personalized application of the law of the firstborn as well (v. 15, "I sacrifice … my sons I redeem").

13:9 Later generations would translate this figurative and proverbial expression (cf. Pr 3:3; 6:21) into the physical reality of phylacteries—the leather prayer-boxes which were strapped on the left arm and on the forehead. Four strips of parchment inscribed with certain words (13:1–16; Dt 6:4–9; 11:13–21) were placed inside these boxes. The imagery of the proverbial mode of speech signified that their conduct was to be that of someone who could verbally recall what God's law demanded of them. Yahweh, who had rescued them, had also provided the standards of life for them!

13:12, 15 See Lk 2:23.

13:17 by the way of the land of the Philistines. Travelers going E and NE out of Egypt had two good options: "the way of the sea," or "the way of Shur." The first route, the most direct and shortest, was dotted with Egyptian fortresses which monitored arrivals and departures to and from Egypt. A little further N, Philistine territory also presented a military threat. The lack of battle-readiness on Israel's part deleted the first option, and God chose the second option (v. 18; 15:22). In any case, God had told Moses to lead the people to Horeb or Sinai, the mountain of God (3:1), and not to take them immediately into Canaan (3:12).

13:18 the Red Sea. An alternative designation, quite in accord with the Heb. term, would be "Sea of Reeds," or perhaps "of papyrus marshes." The difficulty of precisely locating other names associated with the crossing of the Red Sea (see 14:2) has occasioned much debate on the location of the crossing. Four views have generally emerged: It was located 1) in the northeastern region of the Delta—but this would have been in effect "the way of the sea" and would not have been 3 days' journey from Marah (15:22, 23); 2) in the northern end of the Gulf of Suez—but this rules out entry into the wilderness of Shur (15:22); 3) in the vicinity of Lake Timsah or the southern extension of present-day Lake Menzaleh—but probably more than 3 days from Marah; and 4) in the Bitter Lakes region, satisfying, in terms of geography and time, all objections to the other options.

13:19 the bones of Joseph. In fulfillment of their solemnly sworn duty and responsibility (Ge 50:24–26), the Israelites took Joseph's coffin with them. Some 360 years earlier he had foreseen the day when God would bring about the Exodus, and his instructions about his bones being carried to the Promised Land indicated just how certain he was of Israel's departure for Canaan (cf. Ge 50:24–26; Heb 11:22). After the years of wilderness wanderings, Joseph's remains reached their final resting place in Shechem (Jos 24:32).

here with you." [20]Then they set out from [A]Succoth and camped in Etham on the edge of the wilderness. [21][A]The LORD was going before them in a pillar of cloud by day to lead them on the way, and in a pillar of fire by night to give them light, that they might [a]travel by day and by night. [22][a]He [A]did not take away the pillar of cloud by day, nor the pillar of fire by night, from before the people.

PHARAOH IN PURSUIT

14 Now the LORD spoke to Moses, saying, [2]"Tell the sons of Israel to turn back and camp before [A]Pi-hahiroth, between [B]Migdol and the sea; you shall camp in front of Baal-zephon, opposite it, by the sea. [3]For Pharaoh will say of the sons of Israel, 'They are wandering aimlessly in the land; the wilderness has shut them in.' [4]Thus [A]I will [a]harden Pharaoh's heart, and [B]he will chase after them; and I will be honored through Pharaoh and all his army, and [C]the Egyptians will know that I am the LORD." And they did so.

[5]When the king of Egypt was told that the people had fled, [a]Pharaoh and his servants had a change of heart toward the people, and they said, "What is this we have done, that we have let Israel go from serving us?" [6]So he made his chariot ready and took his people with him; [7]and he took six hundred select chariots, and all the *other* chariots of Egypt with officers over all of them. [8][A]The LORD [a]hardened the heart of Pharaoh, king of Egypt, and he chased after the sons of Israel as the sons of Israel were going out [b,B]boldly. [9]Then [A]the Egyptians chased after them *with* all the horses *and* chariots of Pharaoh, his horsemen and his army, and they overtook them camping by the sea, [B]beside Pi-hahiroth, in front of Baal-zephon.

[10]As Pharaoh drew near, the sons of Israel [a]looked, and behold, the Egyptians were marching after them, and they became very frightened; [A]so the sons of Israel cried out to the LORD. [11]Then [A]they said to Moses, "Is it because there were no graves in Egypt that you have taken us away to die in the wilderness? Why have you dealt with us in this way, [a]bringing us out of Egypt? [12][A]Is this not the word that we spoke to you in Egypt, saying, '[a]Leave us alone that we may serve the Egyptians'? For it would have been better for us to serve the Egyptians than to die in the wilderness."

THE SEA IS DIVIDED

[13]But Moses said to the people, "[A]Do not fear! [a]Stand by and see [B]the salvation of the LORD which He will accomplish for you today; for the Egyptians whom you have seen today, you will never see them

13:20 [A]Ex 12:37; Num 33:6   13:21 [a]Lit *go* [A]Ex 14:19, 24; 33:9, 10; Num 9:15; 14:14; Deut 1:33; Neh 9:12; Ps 78:14; 99:7; 105:39; Is 4:5; 1 Cor 10:1   13:22 [a]Or *The pillar of cloud by day and the pillar of fire by night did not depart* [A]Neh 9:19   14:2 [A]Num 33:7 [B]Jer 44:1   14:4 [a]Lit *make strong* [A]Ex 4:21; 7:3; 14:17 [B]Ex 14:23 [C]Ex 7:5; 14:25   14:5 [a]Lit *the heart of Pharaoh...was changed*   14:8 [a]Lit *made strong* [b]Lit *with a high hand* [A]Ex 14:4 [B]Num 33:3; Acts 13:17   14:9 [A]Ex 15:9; Josh 24:6 [B]Ex 14:2   14:10 [a]Lit *lifted up their eyes* [A]Josh 24:7; Neh 9:9; Ps 34:17; 107:6   14:11 [a]Lit *so as to bring* [A]Ex 5:21; 15:24; 16:2; Ps 106:7, 8   14:12 [a]Lit *Cease from us* [A]Ex 6:9   14:13 [a]Or *Take your stand* [A]Gen 15:1; 46:3; Ex 20:20; 2 Chr 20:15, 17; Is 41:10, 13, 14 [B]Ex 14:30; 15:2

13:20 Etham on the edge of the wilderness. The Heb. name of this place may be a transliteration of the Egyptian word *Khetem* meaning "fortress." A line of fortresses (*see note on v. 17*) stretched from the Mediterranean Sea to the Gulf of Suez. Even if the site remains unknown so that pinpointing it is not possible, it was surely a place bordering on the desert area to the E of Egypt.

13:21 a pillar of cloud …. pillar of fire. This was the means by which God led the people. It was a single column, being cloud by day and fire by night (cf. 14:24) and was associated with the Angel of God (14:19; 23:20–23) or the Angel of God's presence (Is 63:8, 9). *See note on 3:2.* It was the pillar from which the Lord also spoke to Moses (33:9–11).

14:3, 4 Pharaoh will say …. will harden. Pharaoh was kept abreast of Israelite progress, and when he heard of the change of direction, he assumed they were lost in unfamiliar territory and were trapped, closed in by desert, sea, and marsh. God intervened again, and the stage was set for the final confrontation and final display of divine power.

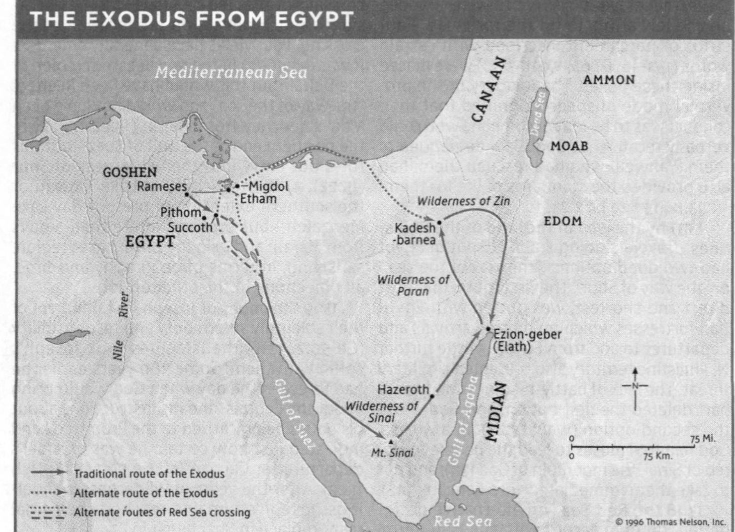

14:5 What is this we have done…? Hardened hearts lost all sensitivity to the recent tragedy and focused instead on the loss of the economic benefit Israel's enslavement had provided. Those who had urged the Israelites to quickly leave now had the urge to force them to return!

14:7 six hundred select chariots. Chariots, introduced by the Hyksos (see Introduction: Author and Date), featured prominently in the army of Egypt, and these "select" ones belonged to an elite, specialized unit.

14:8 sons of Israel were going out boldly. The confidence shown by Israel in their departure is in sharp contrast to the fear they exhibited when they became aware of the pursuing force (v. 10).

14:10 cried out to the LORD. The initial reaction of the people on seeing the approach was to turn to the Lord in anxious prayer. But prayer soon turned to complaints with Moses as the target of their dismay.

14:11 no graves in Egypt. In the light of Egypt's excessive preoccupation with death and various funerary and mortuary rituals, the bitter irony of Israel's questions marked how easily they had forgotten both bondage and rescue.

14:12 serve the Egyptians. Just how much they conveniently forgot the degree of enslavement came out in their "We told you so" attitude. The comment of being better off living and serving than dying perhaps summarized their earlier reaction to Moses and Aaron outside the royal chambers (5:20, 21).

14:13 Do not fear! Moses' exhortation turned attention to the Lord, whose power they had

again forever. 14 [A]The LORD will fight for you while
[B]you keep silent."
15 Then the LORD said to Moses, "Why are you
crying out to Me? Tell the sons of Israel to go forward. 16 As for you, lift up [A]your staff and stretch
out your hand over the sea and divide it, and the
sons of Israel shall [a]go through the midst of the sea
on dry land. 17 As for Me, behold, [A]I will [a]harden the
hearts of the Egyptians so that they will go in after
them; and I will be honored through Pharaoh and
all his army, through his chariots and his horsemen.
18 [A]Then the Egyptians will know that I am the LORD,
when I am honored through Pharaoh, through his
chariots and his horsemen."
19 [A]The angel of God, who had been going before
the camp of Israel, moved and went behind them;
and the pillar of cloud moved from before them and
stood behind them. 20 So it came between the camp of
Egypt and the camp of Israel; and there was the cloud
[a]along with the darkness, yet it gave light at night.
Thus the one did not come near the other all night.
21 [A]Then Moses stretched out his hand over the
sea; and the LORD [a]swept the sea *back* by a strong
east wind all night and turned the sea into [B]dry land,
so [C]the waters were divided. 22 [A]The sons of Israel
[a]went through the midst of the sea on the dry land,
and [B]the waters *were like* a wall to them on their
right hand and on their left. 23 Then [A]the Egyptians
took up the pursuit, and all Pharaoh's horses, his
chariots and his horsemen went in after them into
the midst of the sea. 24 At the morning watch, [A]the
LORD looked down on the [a]army of the Egyptians
[b]through the pillar of fire and cloud and brought the
[a]army of the Egyptians into confusion. 25 He [a]caused
their chariot wheels to swerve, and He made them
drive with difficulty; so the Egyptians said, "Let [b]us
flee from Israel, [A]for the LORD is fighting for them
against the Egyptians."
26 Then the LORD said to Moses, "[A]Stretch out
your hand over the sea so that the waters may come
back over the Egyptians, over their chariots and
their horsemen." 27 So Moses stretched out his hand
over the sea, and [A]the sea returned to its normal
state at daybreak, while the Egyptians were fleeing
[a]right into it; then the LORD [b,B]overthrew the Egyptians in the midst of the sea. 28 The waters returned
and covered the chariots and the horsemen, [a]even
Pharaoh's entire army that had gone into the sea
after them; [A]not even one of them remained. 29 But
the sons of Israel walked on [A]dry land through the
midst of the sea, and the waters *were like* a wall to
them on their right hand and on their left.
30 [A]Thus the LORD saved Israel that day from the
hand of the Egyptians, and Israel [B]saw the Egyptians dead on the seashore. 31 When Israel saw the
great [a]power which the LORD had [b]used against the
Egyptians, the people [c]feared the LORD, and [A]they
believed in the LORD and in His servant Moses.

THE SONG OF MOSES AND ISRAEL

15 [A]Then Moses and the sons of Israel sang this
song to the LORD, [a]and said,

14:14 [A]Ex 14:25; 15:3; Deut 1:30; 3:22; Josh 23:3; 2 Chr 20:29; Neh 4:20 [B]Is 30:15 14:16 [a]Lit *enter the* [A]Ex 4:17, 20; 7:19; 14:21, 26; 17:5, 6, 9; Num 20:8, 9, 11; Is 10:26 14:17 [a]Lit *make strong* [A]Ex 14:4, 8 14:18 [A]Ex 14:25 14:19 [A]Ex 13:21, 22 14:20 [a]Lit *and the darkness* 14:21 [a]Lit *caused to go* [A]Ex 7:19; 14:16 [B]Ps 66:6; 106:9; 136:13, 14 [C]Ex 15:8; Josh 3:16; 4:23; Neh 9:11; Ps 74:13; 78:13; 114:3, 5; Is 63:12, 13 14:22 [a]Lit *entered the* [A]Ex 15:19; Josh 3:17; 4:22; Neh 9:11; Ps 66:6; 78:13; Heb 11:29 [B]Ex 14:29; 15:8 14:23 [A]Ex 14:4, 17 14:24 [a]Lit *camp* [b]Or *in* [A]Ex 13:21 14:25 [a]Or *removed* [b]Lit *me* [A]Ex 14:4, 14, 18 14:26 [A]Ex 14:16 14:27 [a]Lit *to meet it* [b]Lit *shook off* [A]Josh 4:18 [B]Ex 15:1, 7; Deut 11:4; Neh 9:11; Ps 78:53; Heb 11:29 14:28 [a]Lit *in respect to* [A]Ps 78:53; 106:11 14:29 [A]Ex 14:22; Ps 66:6; Is 11:15 14:30 [A]Ex 14:13; Ps 106:8, 10; Is 63:8, 11 [B]Ps 58:10; 59:10 14:31 [a]Lit *hand* [b]Lit *done* [c]Or *revered* [A]Ex 4:31; 19:9; Ps 106:12; John 2:11; 11:45 15:1 [a]Lit *and said, saying* [A]Ps 106:12; Rev 15:3

already seen dramatically in action, and whose deliverance they were about to witness and personally experience. All they needed to do was stand by and watch their God at work, fighting on their side. Euphemistically, Moses informed his people of the certain death of the Egyptian soldiers—you will not see them again! Expressing and experiencing fear did not mean Israel was less than 600,000 fighting men in number, as some have objected. The poorly trained, inadequately equipped, militarily unprepared, and inexperienced Israelites (13:17) were no match for Pharaoh's experienced troops and his highly trained and mobilized chariot force.

14:14 The LORD will fight. This has been and will be true throughout the history of Israel (cf. 1Sa 17:47; 2Ch 14:10, 11; 20:15; Ps 24:8; Zec 14:3).

14:15 Why are you crying out to Me? … go forward. The Lord's promise of deliverance overruled all despair and sense of hopelessness.

14:16, 17 lift up your staff. For the grand, triumphant finale, the staff which had previously been used to bring in different plagues on the Egyptians now divided the water, opening up a valley through which Israel would walk and in which Egypt's army would drown.

14:19 stood behind them. The Angel of the Lord, and the pillar of cloud and fire, moved from being advance guard to being rear guard, from leading to protecting. *See note on 3:2.*

14:21 strong east wind. God's use of natural phenomena does not detract in any way from the miraculous nature of what took place that night. The psalmist recorded this event as the Lord dividing the sea by His strength (Ps 74:13). The wind walled up the waters on either side of the pathway then opened (v. 22; 15:8; Ps 78:13).

14:24 the morning watch. The last of three 4-hour night watches (2:00–6:00 a.m.) ended about sunrise.

14:24, 25 the LORD looked down … brought the army … into confusion. Not only was the Lord fully aware of exactly what was happening—after all, He hardened Egyptian hearts to pursue Israel—He also brought havoc among them. Entrapped in the valley between the walls of water and in total disarray, they acknowledged that the Lord was fighting for their enemy. Not only were they swept aside by the returning waters (vv. 26–28), they were also hindered from driving their chariots forward by a sudden cloudburst (Ps 77:17–19).

14:29–31 The stark difference between Israel and Egypt is again rehearsed: one nation is obstinate and defeated, their dead on the shores of the sea, having acknowledged the Lord victorious; the other nation is alive on the shores, having traversed the sea on dry ground, acknowledging the work of the Lord, reverencing and believing Him and His servant, Moses.

15:1–18 The structure of the song now sung by the nation contains 4 stanzas (vv. 1–5; 6–10; 11–13; and 14–17) and a one-line closing declaration (v. 18). Stanzas one and two end with "They went down" and "They sank…," a refrain emphasizing the finality of the enemy army's defeat. Stanzas three and four end with reference to God's Holy Place (vv. 13, 17). More is involved than in easily observing these break points of the song. The flow of thought and emphasis is also interesting. Stanza one briefly introduces God's powerful victory (vv. 1–5). Stanza two graphically repeats the victory and then inserts the arrogant and vengeful assertions of victory by the enemy to show how puny they were (vv. 6–10). Stanza three concisely summarizes the victory after asking an appropriate question (vv. 11–13). Further, since the victory was essential for Israel's rescue, the stanza also introduces them. Stanza four picks up and expands on Yahweh's leading His people to their divinely assigned home and the consequent fear by other nations as they hear of Israel's dramatic rescue from such a powerful enemy nation (vv. 14–17). The closing line sums it all up: "The LORD shall reign forever and ever." A narrative interlude (vv. 19, 20) reminds of the theme behind the song, and introduces the antiphonal response of Miriam and her band of women (v. 21).

15:1 I will sing. The Israelites began their song in the first person, effectively personalizing the community's song as individually relevant, each person heralding Yahweh's victory and declaring who and what He was to them (note the possessive pronouns in v. 2).

"[b,B]I will sing to the LORD, for
He [c]is highly exalted;
[C]The horse and its rider He has
hurled into the sea.
2 "[a,A]The LORD is my strength and song,
And He has become my salvation;
[B]This is my God, and I will praise Him;
[C]My father's God, and I will [D]extol Him.
3 "[A]The LORD is a warrior;
[a,B]The LORD is His name.
4 "[A]Pharaoh's chariots and his army
He has cast into the sea;
And the choicest of his officers are
[a]drowned in the [b]Red Sea.
5 "The deeps cover them;
[A]They went down into the
depths like a stone.
6 "[A]Your right hand, O LORD, is
majestic in power,
[B]Your right hand, O LORD,
shatters the enemy.
7 "And in the greatness of Your
[a]excellence You [A]overthrow those
who rise up against You;
[B]You send forth Your burning anger,
and it [C]consumes them as chaff.
8 "[A]At the blast of Your nostrils the
waters were piled up,
[B]The flowing waters stood up like a heap;
The deeps were congealed in
the heart of the sea.
9 "[A]The enemy said, 'I will pursue, I will
overtake, I will [B]divide the spoil;
My [a]desire shall be [b]gratified against them;
I will draw out my sword, my
hand will [c]destroy them.'
10 "[A]You blew with Your wind, the
sea covered them;
[B]They sank like lead in the [a]mighty waters.
11 "[A]Who is like You among the gods, O LORD?
Who is like You, [B]majestic in holiness,
[C]Awesome in praises, [D]working wonders?
12 "[A]You stretched out Your right hand,
The earth swallowed them.
13 "In Your lovingkindness You have [A]led the
people whom You have [B]redeemed;
In Your strength You have guided
them [C]to Your holy habitation.
14 "[A]The peoples have heard, they tremble;
Anguish has gripped the
inhabitants of Philistia.
15 "Then the [A]chiefs of Edom were dismayed;
[B]The leaders of Moab,
trembling grips them;
[C]All the inhabitants of Canaan
have melted away.
16 "[A]Terror and dread fall upon them;
[B]By the greatness of Your arm they
are motionless as stone;
Until Your people pass over, O LORD,
Until the people pass over whom
You [C]have purchased.
17 "[A]You will bring them and [B]plant them in
[C]the mountain of Your inheritance,
[D]The place, O LORD, which You have
made for Your dwelling,
[E]The sanctuary, O Lord, which Your
hands have established.
18 "[A]The LORD shall reign forever and ever."

19 [A]For the horses of Pharaoh with his chariots
and his horsemen went into the sea, and the LORD
brought back the waters of the sea on them, but
the sons of Israel walked on [B]dry land through the
midst of the sea.
20 [A]Miriam the prophetess, Aaron's sister, took
the [B]timbrel in her hand, and all the women went
out after her with timbrels and with [a,C]dancing.
21 Miriam answered them,

"[A]Sing to the LORD, for He [a]is highly exalted;
The horse and his rider He has
hurled into the sea."

THE LORD PROVIDES WATER

22 [A]Then Moses [a]led Israel from the [b]Red Sea, and
they went out into [B]the wilderness of [C]Shur; and
they went three days in the wilderness and found
no water. 23 When they came to [A]Marah, they could
not drink the waters [a]of Marah, for they were [b]bit-
ter; therefore it was named [c]Marah. 24 So the people
[A]grumbled at Moses, saying, "What shall we drink?"

15:1 [b]Or *Let me sing* [c]Or *triumphed gloriously* [B]Is 12:5; 42:10-12 [C]Jer 51:21 15:2 [a]Heb *YAH* [A]Ps 18:1, 2; Is 12:2; Hab 3:18f [B]Ps 48:14 [C]Ex 3:6, 15, 16 [D]2 Sam 22:47; Ps 99:5; Is 25:1 15:3 [a]Heb *YHWH*, usually rendered *LORD* [A]Ex 14:14; Rev 19:11 [B]Ex 3:15; 6:2, 3, 7, 8; Ps 24:8; 83:18 15:4 [a]Lit *sunk* [b]Lit *Sea of Reeds* [A]Ex 14:6, 7, 17, 28 15:5 [A]Ex 15:10; Neh 9:11 15:6 [A]Ex 3:20; 6:1 [B]Ps 118:15, 16 15:7 [a]Or *exaltation* [A]Ex 14:27 [B]Ps 78:49, 50 [C]Deut 4:24; Is 5:24; Heb 12:29 15:8 [A]Ex 14:22, 29; Job 4:9 [B]Ps 78:13 15:9 [a]Lit *soul* [b]Lit *be filled with them* [c]Or *dispossess, bring to ruin* [A]Ex 14:5, 8, 9 [B]Judg 5:30; Is 53:12; Luke 11:22 15:10 [a]Or *majestic* [A]Ex 14:27, 28 [B]Ex 15:5 15:11 [A]Ex 8:10; 9:14; Deut 3:24; 2 Sam 7:22; 1 Kin 8:23; Ps 71:19; 86:8; Mic 7:18 [B]Is 6:3; Rev 4:8 [C]Ps 22:23 [D]Ps 72:18; 136:4 15:12 [A]Ex 15:6 15:13 [A]Neh 9:12; Ps 77:20 [B]Ex 15:16; Ps 77:15 [C]Ex 15:17; Ps 78:54 15:14 [A]Deut 2:25; Hab 3:7 15:15 [A]Gen 36:15, 40 [B]Num 22:3, 4 [C]Josh 2:9, 11, 24; 5:1 15:16 [A]Ex 23:27; Deut 2:25; Josh 2:9 [B]Ex 15:5, 6 [C]Ex 15:13; Ps 74:2; Is 43:1; Jer 31:11; Titus 2:14; 2 Pet 2:1 15:17 [A]Ex 23:20; 32:34 [B]Ps 44:2; 80:8, 15 [C]Ps 2:6; 78:54, 68 [D]Ps 68:16; 76:2; 132:13, 14 [E]Ps 78:69 15:18 [A]Ps 10:16; 29:10; Is 57:15 15:19 [A]Ex 14:23, 28 [B]Ex 14:22, 29 15:20 [a]Lit *dances* [A]Ex 2:4; Num 26:59; 1 Chr 6:3; Mic 6:4 [B]Judg 11:34; 1 Sam 18:6; 1 Chr 15:16; Ps 68:25; 81:2; 149:3; Jer 31:4 [C]Judg 11:34; 21:21; 1 Sam 18:6; Ps 30:11; 150:4 15:21 [a]Or *has triumphed gloriously* [A]Ex 15:1 15:22 [a]Lit *caused Israel to journey* [b]Lit *Sea of Reeds* [A]Ps 77:20; 78:52, 53 [B]Num 33:8 [C]Gen 16:7; 20:1; 25:18 15:23 [a]Lit *from* [b]Heb *Marim* [c]I.e. bitterness [A]Num 33:8; Ruth 1:20 15:24 [A]Ex 14:11; 16:2; Ps 106:13

15:6 O LORD. The forthright declarations of the opening stanza (vv. 1–5) are most appropriately followed by this vocative form of address in the rest of the song (vv. 6, 11, 16, 17), since the focus of attention is on His working and intervention.

15:15 Edom ... Moab ... Canaan. Edom and Moab were on the eastern border of the Jordan; Canaan is to the west.

15:16, 17 An expression of confidence in the promises that God had made to Abraham 700 years earlier (see Ge 12, 15, 17).

15:18 reign forever. This speaks of the eternal, universal kingship of the Lord (cf. Ps 145:13).

15:20 the prophetess. Miriam was the first woman to be given this honor. She herself claimed the Lord had spoken through her (Nu 12:2). She apparently played an important role in these rescue events because the prophet Micah states that God delivered Israel by the hand of Moses, Aaron, and Miriam (Mic 6:4). Other women to receive this rare honor were Deborah (Jdg 4:4); Huldah (2Ki 22:14); Isaiah's wife (Is 8:3); Anna (Lk 2:36); and Philip's four daughters (Ac 21:9).

15:24 grumbled at Moses. Israelite memory of victory displayed a remarkable brevity. The personalized declarations of their ode to the Lord sung 3 days earlier vanished into thin air. Their belief of Moses faded out of the picture (14:31). Their question about drinking water roughly brushed aside all recent affirmations of God's being worthy of praise because He

25 Then he [A]cried out to the LORD, and the LORD
showed him [B]a tree; and he threw *it* into the waters,
and the waters became sweet.

There He [C]made for them a statute and regulation, and there He [D]tested them. 26 And He said,
"[A]If you will give earnest heed to the voice of the
LORD your God, and do what is right in His sight,
and give ear [B]to His commandments, and keep all
His statutes, [C]I will put none of the diseases on you
which I have put on the Egyptians; for I, [D]the LORD,
am your healer."

27 Then they came to [A]Elim where there *were*
twelve springs of water and seventy date palms,
and they camped there beside the waters.

THE LORD PROVIDES MANNA

16 Then they set out from Elim, and all the congregation of the sons of Israel came to the
wilderness of [A]Sin, which is between Elim and Sinai,
on [B]the fifteenth day of the second month after their
departure from the land of Egypt. 2 The whole congregation of the sons of Israel [A]grumbled against
Moses and Aaron in the wilderness. 3 The sons of
Israel said to them, "[A]Would that we had died by
the LORD'S hand in the land of Egypt, [B]when we sat
by the pots of [a]meat, when we ate bread to the full;
for you have brought us out into this wilderness to
kill this whole assembly with hunger."

4 Then the LORD said to Moses, "Behold, [A]I will
rain bread from heaven for you; and the people shall
go out and gather a day's portion every day, that I
may [B]test them, whether or not they will walk in My
[a]instruction. 5 [A]On the sixth day, when they prepare
what they bring in, it will be twice as much as they
gather daily." 6 So Moses and Aaron said to all the
sons of Israel, "At evening [a,A]you will know that the
LORD has brought you out of the land of Egypt; 7 and
in the morning [a]you will see [A]the glory of the LORD,
for [B]He hears your grumblings against the LORD;
and [C]what are we, that you grumble against us?"

THE LORD PROVIDES MEAT

8 Moses said, "*This will happen* when the LORD
gives you [a]meat to eat in the evening, and bread
to the full in the morning; for the LORD hears your
grumblings which you grumble against Him. And
what are we? Your grumblings are [A]not against us
but against the LORD."

9 Then Moses said to Aaron, "Say to all the congregation of the sons of Israel, '[A]Come near before the
LORD, for He has heard your grumblings.' " 10 It came
about as Aaron spoke to the whole congregation of
the sons of Israel, that they [a]looked toward the wilderness, and behold, [A]the glory of the LORD appeared
in the cloud. 11 And the LORD spoke to Moses, saying,
12 "[A]I have heard the grumblings of the sons of Israel;
speak to them, saying, '[a]At twilight you shall eat [b]meat,
and in the morning you shall be filled with bread;
and [B]you shall know that I am the LORD your God.' "

13 So it came about at evening that [A]the quails
came up and covered the camp, and in the morning [B]there was a layer of dew around the camp.

15:25 [A]Ex 14:10 [B]Ezek 47:7, 8 [C]Josh 24:25 [D]Ex 16:4; Deut 8:2, 16; Judg 2:22; 3:1, 4; Ps 66:10 15:26 [A]Ex 19:5, 6; Deut 7:12 [B]Ex 20:2-17 [C]Deut 7:15; 28:58, 60 [D]Ex 23:25; Deut 32:39; Ps 41:3, 4; 103:3; 147:3 15:27 [A]Num 33:9 16:1 [A]Num 33:10, 11; Ezek 30:15 [B]Ex 12:6, 51; 19:1 16:2 [A]Ex 14:11; 15:24; Ps 106:25; 1 Cor 10:10 16:3 [a]Or *flesh* [A]Ex 17:3; Num 14:2, 3; 20:3; Lam 4:9 [B]Num 11:4, 5 16:4 [a]Or *law* [A]Neh 9:15; Ps 78:23-25; 105:40; John 6:31; 1 Cor 10:3 [B]Ex 15:25; Deut 8:2, 16 16:5 [A]Ex 16:22 16:6 [a]Lit *and you* [A]Ex 6:7 16:7 [a]Lit *and you* [A]Ex 16:10, 12; Is 35:2; 40:5; John 11:4, 40 [B]Num 14:27; 17:5 [C]Num 16:11 16:8 [a]Or *flesh* [A]1 Sam 8:7; Luke 10:16; Rom 13:2; 1 Thess 4:8 16:9 [A]Num 16:16 16:10 [a]Lit *turned* [A]Ex 13:21; 16:7; Num 16:19; 1 Kin 8:10f 16:12 [a]Lit *Between the two evenings* [b]Or *flesh* [A]Ex 16:8; Num 14:27 [B]Ex 6:7; 16:7; 1 Kin 20:28; Joel 3:17 16:13 [A]Num 11:31; Ps 78:27-29; 105:40 [B]Num 11:9

had done wonders and was clearly taking them to their land.

15:25 waters became sweet. Since there is no known tree which would naturally make unpalatable water drinkable, this must have been a miracle by which God demonstrated His willingness and ability to look after His people in a hostile environment. Marah is usually associated with modern day Ain Hawarah, where the waters still remain brackish and unpleasant. **tested them.** "To subject to difficulty in order to prove the quality of someone or something" is one way to explain the meaning of the Heb. word used. Later, at Rephidim (17:1–7), at Sinai (20:20), and at Taberah (Nu 11:1–3; 13:26–33), God did just that to Israel. This is something which no one can do to God Himself (Dt 6:16)—He needs no testing in character or deed, but man certainly does need proving.

15:26 the LORD ... your healer. Since this is what He is, Jehovah-Rapha, obedience to divine instruction and guidance will obviously bring healing, not the consequence of plagues like those visited upon Egypt. This promise is limited in context to Israel, most likely for the duration of the Exodus only.

15:27 Elim. The next stopping place, most probably in modern day Wadi Garandel, had an abundant water supply—God would and did lead them aright!

16:1 wilderness of Sin. More details of the camp sites in the journey from Rameses to Succoth and beyond are found in Nu 33:5–11. That itinerary also lists the next stop as having been Dophkah (Nu 33:12). Identifying it with modern Debbet er Ramleh locates it in the SW of the Sinai Peninsula on a direct line between Elim and Sinai. **fifteenth day ... second month.** Thirty days after their departure from Rameses.

16:2 The whole congregation ... grumbled. What characterized them as a whole was this attitude of negativism. Faced with the scarcity of resources in the wilderness, they hankered after the abundant resources they had experienced in Egypt. The country which had enslaved them looked good in comparison to the wilderness. Again, their complaining so soon after benefiting from the miracles done by the Lord on their behalf points only to their short-term memory and self-centeredness.

16:3 died by the LORD's hand. Incredibly, Israel's complaint still acknowledged the intervention of the Lord in their affairs. Sarcastically, they voiced a preference for dying in Egypt. The hand of the Lord which they had glorified in song (15:6) only a month beforehand, they now pretended would have been better used to kill them in Egypt.

16:4 I will rain bread. God's gracious answer to their complaining was to promise an abundance of the bread they missed. God's directions on how to gather it would also test their obedience to Him (vv. 4, 5, 16, 26–28). *See note on 16:31.*

16:5 The same principle on a larger scale would feed the nation during and after the sabbatical year (cf. Lv 25:18–22).

16:6 you will know. Israel's short-term memory loss would be short-lived because that very day of complaint would witness not only God's provision for them but also would powerfully remind them of who had brought them out of Egypt, namely, the Lord their God (cf. vv. 11, 12).

16:7 the glory of the LORD. In seeing the start of the provision of daily bread on the next day, Israel would also see the Lord's glory, an appropriate term to use because what He did showed His presence with them. "Glory" typically refers to God's manifested presence, which makes Him impressive and leads to worship. **your grumblings.** Set in the context of instruction on how the Lord would act to provide for them, the 4-fold repetition of this phrase (vv. 6–9) served to highlight God's gracious response in contrast to their ungracious grumbling against Him. For an effective poetic presentation of this contrast, refer to Ps 78:17–25.

16:13 quails. The psalmist removed all doubt about whether these birds of the partridge family were not real birds but something else, for he called them "winged fowl" and in the preceding line of the parallelism referred to the coming of the quails as God having "rained meat" on them (Ps 78:27). Upon return to their former habitat, these migratory birds would often fall to the ground, exhausted from prolonged flight. In

14 [A]When the layer of dew [a]evaporated, behold, on the
[b]surface of the wilderness [B]there was a fine flake-like
thing, fine as the frost on the ground. 15 When the sons
of Israel saw *it,* they said to one another, "[a]What is it?"
For they did not know what it was. And Moses said
to them, "[A]It is the bread which the LORD has given
you to eat. 16 This is [a]what the LORD has commanded,
'Gather of it every man [b]as much as he should eat; you
shall take [c,A]an omer apiece according to the number
of persons each of you has in his tent.' " 17 The sons
of Israel did so, and *some* gathered much and *some*
little. 18 When they measured it with an omer, [A]he
who had gathered much had no excess, and he who
had gathered little had no lack; every man gathered
[a]as much as he should eat. 19 Moses said to them,
"[A]Let no man leave any of it until morning." 20 But
they did not listen to Moses, and some left part of it
until morning, and it bred worms and became foul;
and Moses was angry with them. 21 They gathered
it morning by morning, every man [a]as much as he
should eat; but when the sun grew hot, it would melt.

THE SABBATH OBSERVED

22 [A]Now on the sixth day they gathered twice as
much bread, two omers for each one. When all the
[B]leaders of the congregation came and told Moses, 23 then he said to them, "This is what the LORD
[a]meant: [A]Tomorrow is a sabbath observance, a holy
sabbath to the LORD. Bake what you will bake and
boil what you will boil, and [B]all that is left over [b]put
aside to be kept until morning." 24 So they [a]put it
aside until morning, as Moses had ordered, and [A]it
did not become foul nor was there any worm in it.
25 Moses said, "Eat it today, for today is a sabbath
to the LORD; today you will not find it in the field.
26 [A]Six days you shall gather it, but on the seventh
day, *the* sabbath, there will be [a]none."

27 It came about on the seventh day that some
of the people went out to gather, but they found
none. 28 Then the LORD said to Moses, "[A]How long
do you refuse to keep My commandments and My
[a]instructions? 29 See, [a]the LORD has given you the
sabbath; therefore He gives you bread for two days
on the sixth day. Remain every man in his place;
let no man go out of his place on the seventh day."
30 So the people rested on the seventh day.

31 The house of [A]Israel named it [a]manna, and it
was like [B]coriander seed, white, and its taste was
like wafers with honey. 32 Then Moses said, "This is
[a]what the LORD has commanded, 'Let an omerful of
it be kept throughout your generations, that they
may see the bread that I fed you in the wilderness,
when I brought you out of the land of Egypt.' " 33 Moses said to Aaron, "[A]Take a jar and put an omerful
of manna in it, and place it before the LORD to be
kept throughout your generations." 34 As the LORD
commanded Moses, so Aaron placed it before [A]the
Testimony, to be kept. 35 [A]The sons of Israel ate the
manna forty years, until they came to an inhabited
land; they ate the manna until they came to the
border of the land of Canaan. 36 (Now [A]an omer is
a tenth of an [a]ephah.)

WATER IN THE ROCK

17 Then all the congregation of the sons of Israel journeyed by [a]stages from the wilderness of [A]Sin, according to the [b]command of the
LORD, and camped at [B]Rephidim, and there was
no water for the people to drink. 2 Therefore the
people [A]quarreled with Moses and said, "Give us
water that we may drink." And Moses said to them,
"[B]Why do you quarrel with me? [C]Why do you test
the LORD?" 3 But the people thirsted there for water; and [a]they [A]grumbled against Moses and said,
"Why, now, have you brought us up from Egypt,
to kill [b]us and [c]our children and [c,B]our livestock
with thirst?" 4 So Moses cried out to the LORD,
saying, "What shall I do to this people? A [A]little

16:14 [a]Lit *had gone up* [b]Lit *face of* [A]Num 11:7-9 [B]Ex 16:31; Neh 9:15; Ps 78:24; 105:40 16:15 [a]Heb *Man hu,* cf v 31 [A]Ex 16:4; Neh 9:15; Ps 78:24; John 6:31; 1 Cor 10:3 16:16 [a]Lit *the thing which* [b]Lit *according to his eating* [c]Lit *an omer for a head* [A]Ex 16:32, 36 16:18 [a]Lit *according to his eating* [A]2 Cor 8:15 16:19 [A]Ex 12:10; 16:23; 23:18 16:21 [a]Lit *according to his eating* 16:22 [A]Ex 16:5 [B]Ex 34:31 16:23 [a]Lit *spoke* [b]Lit *lay up for you* [A]Gen 2:3; Ex 20:8-11; 23:12; 31:15; 35:2; Lev 23:3; Neh 9:13, 14 [B]Ex 16:19 16:24 [a]Lit *laid it up* [A]Ex 16:20 16:26 [a]Lit *none on it* [A]Ex 20:9, 10 16:28 [a]Or *laws* [A]2 Kin 17:14; Ps 78:10; 106:13 16:29 [a]Lit *for the LORD* 16:31 [a]Heb *man,* cf v 15 [A]Num 11:7-9; Deut 8:3, 16 [B]Ex 16:14 16:32 [a]Lit *the thing which* 16:33 [A]Heb 9:4; Rev 2:17 16:34 [A]Ex 25:16, 21; 27:21; 40:20; Num 17:10 16:35 [A]Deut 8:2f; Josh 5:12; Neh 9:20, 21 16:36 [a]I.e. Approx one bu [A]Ex 16:16 17:1 [a]Lit *their journeyings* [b]Lit *mouth* [A]Ex 16:1; Num 33:12 [B]Ex 19:2; Num 33:14 17:2 [A]Ex 14:11; Num 20:2, 3, 13 [B]Ex 16:8 [C]Deut 6:16; Ps 78:18, 41; Matt 4:7; 1 Cor 10:9 17:3 [a]Lit *the people* [b]Lit *me* [c]Lit *my* [A]Ex 16:2, 3 [B]Ex 12:38 17:4 [A]Num 14:10; 1 Sam 30:6

ancient Egyptian paintings, people were shown catching quails by throwing nets over the brush where they were nesting.

16:16, 32 omer. Slightly more than two quarts.

16:18 See 2Co 8:15, where Paul applies this truth to Christian giving.

16:22–30 The provision of manna on 6 days only but none on the seventh was a weekly lesson on the nature of the Sabbath as a different day. It taught the people to keep the Sabbath properly, and acted as a challenge to obey God's commands.

16:31 manna. The arrival of the quails in much quantity (v. 13) was totally overshadowed by the arrival of manna the next morning. Despite the different descriptions given for its form and taste (vv. 14, 31), the name chosen for it derived from the question they asked. "Manna" was an older form of their question, "What is it?" The psalmist referred to manna as the "food from heaven" and "bread of angels" which rained down after God had opened the windows of heaven (Ps 78:23–25). Natural explanations for the manna, such as lichen growing on rocks or insect-excreted granules on tamarisk thickets, are totally inadequate to explain its presence in sufficient quantity on the ground under the dew every day except the Sabbath for the next 40 years (v. 35) to satisfy every family's hunger. It was supernaturally produced and supernaturally sustained to last for the Sabbath!

16:32–36 place it before the LORD. Provision was made for memorializing the giving of the manna. When the tabernacle was finally constructed, the pot of manna was placed inside the ark. Succeeding generations would be reminded, when they came for worship, of the faithfulness of the Lord in caring for His people (cf. Heb 9:4).

17:1 Rephidim. To be identified as modern day Wadi Refayid.

17:2 the people quarreled. This time the people, reacting to Moses' leading them to a waterless site, quarreled with him or laid a charge against him. So intense was their reaction that Moses thought he was about to be stoned (v. 4). Significantly, the nation had not come to Rephidim without divine guidance (v. 1), portrayed by the column of fire and cloud. The people, in the midst of their emotional response, simply could not see that right before their eyes was the evidence of God's leading.

17:4 Moses cried out to the LORD. The leader turned to God in prayer, whereas the people, instead of following his example, turned on their leader. Moses' petition was not an isolated incident. His life was characterized by prayer (cf. 15:25; 32:30–32; Nu 11:2, 11; 12:13; 14:13, 19) and by turning to God for solutions to problems and crises.

more and they will stone me." 5 Then the LORD
said to Moses, "Pass before the people and take
with you some of [A]the elders of Israel; and take
in your hand your staff with which [B]you struck
the Nile, and go. 6 Behold, I will stand before you
there on the rock at [A]Horeb; and [B]you shall strike
the rock, and water will come out of it, that the
people may drink." And Moses did so in the sight
of the elders of Israel. 7 He named the place [a,A]Mas-
sah and [b,B]Meribah because of the quarrel of the
sons of Israel, and because they [C]tested the LORD,
saying, "Is the LORD among us, or not?"

AMALEK FOUGHT

8 Then [A]Amalek came and fought against Israel
at [B]Rephidim. 9 So Moses said to [A]Joshua, "Choose
men for us and go out, fight against Amalek. Tomorrow I will station myself on the top of the hill
with [B]the staff of God in my hand." 10 Joshua did as
Moses [a]told him, [b]and fought against Amalek; and
Moses, Aaron, and [A]Hur went up to the top of the
hill. 11 So it came about when Moses held his hand
up, that Israel prevailed, and when he let his hand
[a]down, Amalek prevailed. 12 But Moses' hands were
heavy. Then they took a stone and put it under him,
and he sat on it; and Aaron and Hur [A]supported
his hands, one on one side and one on the other.
Thus his hands were steady until the sun set. 13 So
Joshua [a]overwhelmed Amalek and his people with
the edge of the sword.

14 Then the LORD said to Moses, "[A]Write this in [a]a
book as a memorial and [b]recite it to Joshua, [c]that [B]I
will utterly blot out the memory of Amalek from
under heaven." 15 Moses built an [A]altar and named
it [B]The LORD is My Banner; 16 and he said, "[a,A]The
LORD has sworn; the LORD will have war against
Amalek from generation to generation."

JETHRO, MOSES' FATHER-IN-LAW

18 Now [A]Jethro, the priest of Midian, Moses'
father-in-law, heard of all that God had done
for Moses and for Israel His people, how the LORD
had brought Israel out of Egypt. 2 Jethro, Moses'
father-in-law, took Moses' wife [A]Zipporah, after he

17:5 [A]Ex 3:16, 18 [B]Ex 7:20 17:6 [A]Ex 3:1 [B]Num 20:10, 11; Deut 8:15; Neh 9:15; Ps 78:15; 105:41; 114:8; 1 Cor 10:4 17:7 [a]I.e. test [b]I.e. quarrel [A]Deut 6:16; 9:22; Ps 95:8 [B]Num 20:13, 24; 27:14; Ps 81:7 [C]Num 14:22; Deut 33:8 17:8 [A]Gen 36:12; Num 24:20; Deut 25:17-19; 1 Sam 15:2 [B]Ex 17:1 17:9 [A]Ex 24:13 [B]Ex 4:20 17:10 [a]Lit *said to* [b]Lit *to fight* [A]Ex 24:14; 31:2 17:11 [a]Lit *rest* 17:12 [A]Is 35:3 17:13 [a]Lit *weakened* 17:14 [a]Lit *the book* [b]Lit *place it in the ears of* [c]Or *for* [A]Ex 24:4; 34:27; Num 33:2 [B]Deut 25:19; 1 Sam 15:3 17:15 [A]Ex 24:4 [B]Gen 22:14; Judg 6:24 17:16 [a]Or *Because a hand is against the throne of the LORD;* lit *Because a hand upon the throne of YAH* [A]Gen 22:16 18:1 [A]Ex 2:16, 18; 3:1 18:2 [A]Ex 2:21; 4:25

17:5, 6 **Pass before the people .... will stand before you.** By these words in His instructions to Moses, the Lord reinforced both the position of Moses as leader and Himself as present to act. He answered the people's charge against Moses and their underlying challenge of His presence (v. 7). In fact, He intervened miraculously!

17:7 **Massah and Meribah.** Appropriate names, "Testing" and "Contending," were assigned to this place; a disappointing culmination to all they had experienced of God's miraculous care and guidance (cf. Ps 95:7, 8; Heb 3:7, 8).

17:8 **Amalek came and fought.** The Amalekites took their name from Amalek, the grandson of Esau, and dwelt as a nomadic people in the Negev. Israel first encountered their military at Rephidim in the wilderness (Ex 17:8–13; Dt 25:17, 18). As a result, the Amalekites were doomed to annihilation by God (17:14; Nu 24:20; Dt 25:19) but it would not be immediate (17:16). The Amalekites defeated disobedient Israel at Hormah (Nu 14:43–45). Saul failed to destroy them as God ordered (1Sa 15:2, 3, 9). David later fought and defeated the Amalekites (1Sa 30:1–20). In Hezekiah's day, the Amalekite remnant in the land was finally destroyed by Hezekiah (ca. 716–687 B.C.). The final descendants of Agag (Est 3:1), the Amalekite king in Saul's day, were destroyed in Persia at the time of Esther and Mordecai (ca. 473 B.C.; Est 2:5, 8–10).

17:9–13 Through the circumstances they experienced, Israel had learned how God provided food and water. They had to learn through warfare that God would also bring about defeat of hostile neighbors.

17:9 **Joshua.** The name of Moses' aide-de-camp, or personal minister (24:13; 33:11; Jos 1:1) appears here for the first time in Exodus. His assignment to muster a task force was part of his being groomed for military leadership in Israel. Actually, at this stage his name was still Hoshea, which later changed to Joshua at Kadesh just before the reconnaissance mission in Canaan (Nu 13:16). At this stage, Israel could not be described as a seasoned army and was not even militarily well prepared and trained. See Introduction to Joshua. **the staff of God.** The staff which Moses held up in his hands was no magic wand. Rather it had been previously used to initiate, via His chosen leader, the miracles which God did and about which He had informed Moses in advance. It became, therefore, the symbol of God's personal and powerful involvement, with Moses' outstretched arms perhaps signifying an appeal to God. The ebb and flow of battle in correlation with Moses' uplifted or drooping arms imparted more than psychological encouragement as the soldiers looked up to their leader on the hilltop, and more than Moses' interceding for them. It demonstrated and acknowledged their having to depend upon God for victory in battle and not upon their own strength and zeal. It also confirmed the position of Moses both in relation to God and the nation's well-being and safety. They had angrily chided him for their problems, but God confirmed his appointment as leader.

17:10 **Hur.** Caleb's son and the grandfather of Bezalel, the artisan (cf. 31:2–11; 1Ch 2:19, 20).

17:14 **Write this ... as a memorial and recite it.** Moses would have learned writing and record-keeping in Pharaoh's school of government. Official Hebrew records other than Scripture were also to be kept, and in this case especially for the purpose of remembering the victory in the very first battle in which they nationally engaged. God referred to "a book," so Moses had evidently already begun it. This was not, then, the initial entry into what perhaps became known as the "Book of the Wars of the LORD" (Nu 21:14). Writing it was essential, so the facts could be verified and needed not to depend upon human memory or solely oral tradition. **blot out the memory.** The sentence of national extinction which the Amalekites proclaimed for Israel (cf. Ps 83:4–7) passed by divine decree upon the Amalekites. The sentence was partially realized in Saul's and David's day (cf. 1Sa 15:1–9 and 2Sa 1:1; 8:11, 12), after which it is scarcely mentioned again. However, due to Saul's disobedience in sparing Agag, the Amalekite king and some of his people (1Sa 15:7–9), he lost his throne (v. 23). Samuel killed Agag (v. 33), but some Amalekites remained to return a few years later to raid Israel's southern territory, even capturing David's family (1Sa 30:1–5). David killed all but 400 (1Sa 30:16, 17) who escaped. It was a descendant of Agag, Haman, who tried to exterminate the Jews later in Esther's day (cf. Est 3:1, 6).

17:15 **The LORD is My Banner.** By titling the altar with this designation for the Lord, Yahweh-Nissi, Moses declared the Lord Himself to be the standard of His people.

17:16 **The LORD has sworn.** The difficulty of the Heb. text permits an alternative translation: "a hand is upon/toward/against the throne/banner of Yahweh," with the sense of supplication, or of taking an oath. Contextually, the significance is clear, whatever the translation adopted: The ongoing problem with Amalek was not merely one nation hostile toward another, it was a war between God and Amalek.

18:1 **Jethro ... heard of all.** The intelligence-gathering ability of ancient peoples should not be underestimated. Quickly and thoroughly the news of significant events in other lands passed from one place to another, very often via the merchant caravans which traversed the Fertile Crescent, or through ambassadors and other official contacts between nations. In Jethro's case, whatever knowledge he had gleaned of Israel's progress had been supplemented with information from Zipporah and her sons after Moses sent them ahead to her home (v. 2).

had sent her away, 3 and her [A]two sons, of whom
[a]one was named Gershom, for Moses said, "I have
been [B]a [b]sojourner in a foreign land." 4 [a]The other
was named [b,A]Eliezer, for *he said,* "[B]The God of my
father was my help, and delivered me from the
sword of Pharaoh."
5 Then Jethro, Moses' father-in-law, came with
his sons and his wife to Moses [a]in the wilderness
where he was camped, at [A]the mount of God. 6 He
[a]sent word to Moses, "I, your father-in-law Jethro,
am coming to you with your wife and her two
sons with her." 7 Then Moses went out to meet his
father-in-law, and [A]he bowed down and [B]kissed him;
and they [C]asked each other of their welfare and
went into the tent. 8 Moses told his father-in-law
all that the LORD had done to Pharaoh and to the
Egyptians [A]for Israel's sake, all the [B]hardship that
had befallen them on the journey, and *how* [C]the
LORD had delivered them. 9 Jethro rejoiced over
all [A]the goodness which the LORD had done to
Israel, [a]in delivering [b]them from the hand of the
Egyptians. 10 So Jethro said, "[A]Blessed be the LORD
who delivered you from the hand of the Egyptians
and from the hand of Pharaoh, *and* who delivered
the people from under the hand of the Egyptians.
11 Now I know that [A]the LORD is greater than all
the gods; [a]indeed, [B]it was proven when they dealt
proudly against [b]the people." 12 [A]Then Jethro, Moses' father-in-law, took a burnt offering and sacrifices for God, and Aaron came with all the elders
of Israel to eat [a]a meal with Moses' father-in-law
before God.
13 It came about the next day that Moses sat to
judge the people, and the people stood about Moses
from the morning until the evening. 14 Now when
Moses' father-in-law saw all that he was doing for
the people, he said, "What is this thing that you are
doing for the people? Why do you alone sit *as judge*
and all the people stand about you from morning
until evening?" 15 Moses said to his father-in-law,
"Because the people come to me [A]to inquire of God.
16 When they have a [a,A]dispute, it comes to me, and
I judge between a man and his neighbor and make
known the statutes of God and His laws."

JETHRO COUNSELS MOSES

17 Moses' father-in-law said to him, "The thing that
you are doing is not good. 18 [A]You will surely wear
out, both yourself and [a]these people who are with
you, for the [b]task is too heavy for you; [B]you cannot do
it alone. 19 Now listen to [a]me: I will give you counsel,
and God be with you. [b]You be the people's representative before God, and you [A]bring the [c]disputes to
God, 20 [A]then teach them the statutes and the laws,
and make known to them [B]the way in which they are
to walk and the work they are to do. 21 Furthermore,
you shall [a]select out of all the people [A]able men [B]who
fear God, men of truth, those who [C]hate dishonest
gain; and you shall place *these* over them *as* leaders
of thousands, [b]of hundreds, [b]of fifties and [b]of tens.
22 Let them judge the people at all times; and let it
be [A]that every major [a]dispute they will bring to you,
but every minor [a]dispute they themselves will judge.
So it will be easier for you, and [B]they will bear *the
burden* with you. 23 If you do this thing and God *so*
commands you, then you will be able to [a]endure, and
all [b]these people also will go to [c]their place in peace."
24 So Moses listened [a]to his father-in-law and did
all that he had said. 25 Moses chose [A]able men out
of all Israel and made them heads over the people,
leaders of thousands, [a]of hundreds, [a]of fifties and
[a]of tens. 26 They judged the people at all times; [A]the
difficult [a]dispute they would bring to Moses, but
every minor [a]dispute they themselves would judge.
27 Then Moses [a,A]bade his father-in-law farewell, and
he went his way into his own land.

MOSES ON SINAI

19 [A]In the third month after the sons of Israel had
gone out of the land of Egypt, [a]on that very
day they came into the wilderness of [B]Sinai. 2 When
they set out from [A]Rephidim, they came to the wilderness of Sinai and camped in the wilderness;
and there Israel camped in front of [B]the mountain.

18:3 [a]Lit *the name of the one was* [b]Heb *ger* [A]Ex 2:22; 4:20; Acts 7:29 [B]Ex 2:22 18:4 [a]Lit *The name of the other was* [b]Heb *El-ezer;* i.e. my God is help [A]1 Chr 23:15, 17 [B]Gen 49:25 18:5 [a]Lit *unto* [A]Ex 3:1, 12; 4:27; 24:13 18:6 [a]Lit *said* 18:7 [A]Gen 43:26, 28 [B]Gen 29:13; Ex 4:27 [C]Gen 43:27; 2 Sam 11:7 18:8 [A]Ex 4:23; 7:4, 5 [B]Num 20:14; Neh 9:32 [C]Ex 15:6, 16 18:9 [a]Lit *in that He had delivered* [b]Lit *him* [A]Is 63:7-14 18:10 [A]Gen 14:20; 2 Sam 18:28; 1 Kin 8:56; Ps 68:19, 20 18:11 [a]Lit *indeed, in the thing in which they* [b]Lit *them* [A]Ex 12:12; 15:11; 2 Chr 2:5; Ps 95:3; 97:9; 135:5 [B]Luke 1:51 18:12 [a]Lit *bread* [A]Gen 31:54; Ex 24:5 18:15 [A]Num 9:6, 8; 27:5; Deut 17:8-13 18:16 [a]Lit *matter* [A]Ex 24:14 18:18 [a]Lit *this* [b]Lit *matter* [A]Num 11:14, 17; Deut 1:12 [B]Deut 1:9 18:19 [a]Lit *my voice* [b]Lit *You be for the people in front of God* [c]Lit *matters* [A]Num 27:5 18:20 [A]Deut 1:18; 4:1, 5; 5:1 [B]Ps 143:8 18:21 [a]Lit *see* [b]Lit *leaders of* [A]Ex 18:25; Deut 1:13, 15; 2 Chr 19:5-10; Ps 15:1-5; Acts 6:3 [B]Gen 42:18; 2 Sam 23:3 [C]Deut 16:19 18:22 [a]Lit *matter* [A]Deut 1:17, 18 [B]Num 11:17 18:23 [a]Lit *stand* [b]Lit *this* [c]Lit *his* 18:24 [a]Lit *to the voice of* 18:25 [a]Lit *leaders of* [A]Ex 18:21; Deut 1:15 18:26 [a]Lit *matter* [A]Ex 18:22 18:27 [a]Lit *sent off his father-in-law* [A]Num 10:29, 30 19:1 [a]Lit *on this day* [A]Ex 12:6, 51; 16:1 [B]Deut 1:6; 4:10, 15; 5:2 19:2 [A]Ex 17:1; Num 33:15 [B]Ex 3:1, 12; 18:5

18:7–12 Moses' testimony elicited responses of praise and sacrifice from Jethro; evidence of his belief. Further, he understood fully the incomparability of Yahweh (v. 11). The priest of Midian (v. 1) was surely no worshiper of Midian's gods! Since Midianites were generally regarded as idolaters (cf. Nu 25:17, 18; 31:2, 3, 16), Jethro must be viewed as remarkably different from his contemporaries; a difference highlighted by Aaron and the elders worshiping and fellowshiping together with him (v. 12).

18:12 for God. Since the name Yahweh is always used in connection with sacrifices prescribed for Israel in the Pentateuch, the switch to Elohim must have some significance here, particularly after Jethro had himself used the name of Yahweh in his response to Moses. Despite the strong declaration of his faith and understanding, Jethro was a believing Gentile, therefore, a proselyte, and an alien. In this situation the Lord was relating to the Israelite and Gentile world simultaneously, thus the use of Elohim rather than Yahweh, the unique covenant name for Israel.

18:13–27 Jethro's practical wisdom was of immense benefit to Moses and Israel, and has been lauded as an example of delegation and management organization by efficiency experts for centuries—and still is. Woven into Jethro's advice were statements about God and the virtues of godly men that cause one to respect this man as having his newfound faith well integrated into his thinking. Indeed, he fully recognized that Moses needed divine permission to enact his advice (v. 23). Moses apparently did not immediately implement Jethro's solution, but waited until the law had been given (cf. Dt 1:9–15).

18:21 These same spiritual qualities were required of NT leaders (see Ac. 6:3; 1Ti 3:1–7; Titus 1:6–9).

19:1–40:38 This section outlines Israel's activities during their approximately 11-month stay at Sinai (cf. 19:1 with Nu 10:11).

3 Moses went up to God, and [A]the LORD called to him
from the mountain, saying, "Thus you shall say to
the house of Jacob and tell the sons of Israel: 4 '[A]You
yourselves have seen what I did to the Egyptians,
and *how* I bore you on [B]eagles' wings, and brought
you to Myself. 5 Now then, [A]if you will indeed obey
My voice and [B]keep My covenant, then you shall be
[C]My [a]own possession among all the peoples, for
[D]all the earth is Mine; 6 and you shall be to Me [A]a
kingdom of priests and [B]a holy nation.' These are
the words that you shall speak to the sons of Israel."
7 [A]So Moses came and called the elders of the
people, and set before them all these words which
the LORD had commanded him. 8 [A]All the people
answered together and said, "All that the LORD has
spoken we will do!" And Moses brought back the
words of the people to the LORD. 9 The LORD said to
Moses, "Behold, I will come to you in [A]a thick cloud,
so that the [B]people may hear when I speak with you
and may also believe in you forever." Then Moses
told the words of the people to the LORD.
10 The LORD also said to Moses, "Go to the people
and [A]consecrate them today and tomorrow, and let
them [B]wash their garments; 11 and let them be ready
for the third day, for on [A]the third day the LORD will
come down on Mount Sinai in the sight of all the
people. 12 You shall set bounds for the people all
around, saying, '[a]Beware that you do not go up on
the mountain or touch the border of it; [A]whoever
touches the mountain shall surely be put to death.
13 No hand shall touch him, but [A]he shall surely be
stoned or [a]shot through; whether beast or man, he
shall not live.' When the ram's horn sounds a long
blast, they shall come up to [B]the mountain." 14 So
Moses went down from the mountain to the people
and consecrated the people, and they washed their
garments. 15 He said to the people, "Be ready for the
third day; do not go near a woman."
16 [A]So it came about on the third day, when it was
morning, that there were [a]thunder and lightning
flashes and a thick cloud upon the mountain and a
very loud trumpet sound, so that all the people who
were in the camp trembled. 17 And Moses brought
the people out of the camp to meet God, and they
stood at the [a]foot of the mountain.

THE LORD VISITS SINAI

18 [A]Now Mount Sinai *was* all in smoke because the
LORD descended upon it [B]in fire; and its smoke ascended like [C]the smoke of a furnace, and [D]the whole
mountain [a]quaked violently. 19 When the sound of
the trumpet grew louder and louder, Moses spoke
and [A]God answered him with [a]thunder. 20 [A]The LORD
came down on Mount Sinai, to the top of the mountain; and the LORD called Moses to the top of the
mountain, and Moses went up. 21 Then the LORD
spoke to Moses, "Go down, [a]warn the people, so that
[A]they do not break through to the LORD to gaze, and
many of them [b]perish. 22 Also let the [A]priests who
come near to the LORD consecrate themselves, or
else the LORD will break out against them." 23 Moses said to the LORD, "The people cannot come up
to Mount Sinai, for You [a]warned us, saying, '[A]Set
bounds about the mountain and consecrate it.' "

19:3 [A]Ex 3:4 19:4 [A]Deut 29:2 [B]Deut 32:11; Rev 12:14 19:5 [a]Or *special treasure* [A]Ex 15:26; Deut 5:2f [B]Ps 78:10 [C]Deut 4:20; 7:6; 14:2; 26:18; Ps 135:4; Titus 2:14; 1 Pet 2:9 [D]Ex 9:29; Deut 10:14; Job 41:11; Ps 50:12; 1 Cor 10:26 19:6 [A]1 Pet 2:5, 9; Rev 1:6; 5:10 [B]Deut 7:6; 14:21; 26:19; Is 62:12 19:7 [A]Ex 4:29, 30 19:8 [A]Ex 4:31; 24:3, 7; Deut 5:27; 26:17 19:9 [A]Ex 19:16; 24:15, 16; Deut 4:11; Ps 99:7 [B]Deut 4:12, 36 19:10 [A]Lev 11:44, 45 [B]Gen 35:2; Lev 15:5; Num 8:7, 21; 19:19; Rev 22:14 19:11 [A]Ex 19:16 19:12 [a]Lit *Take heed to yourselves* [A]Heb 12:20 19:13 [a]I.e. with arrows [A]Heb 12:20 [B]Ex 19:17 19:16 [a]Lit *sounds* [A]Heb 12:18, 19, 21 19:17 [a]Lit *lower part* 19:18 [a]Or *trembled* [A]Deut 4:11; Ps 104:32; 144:5 [B]Ex 3:2; 24:17; Deut 5:4; 2 Chr 7:1-3; Heb 12:18 [C]Gen 15:17; 19:28 [D]Judg 5:5; Ps 68:7, 8; Jer 4:24 19:19 [a]Or *a voice;* lit *a sound* [A]Ps 81:7 19:20 [A]Neh 9:13 19:21 [a]Lit *testify to* [b]Lit *fall* [A]Ex 3:5; 1 Sam 6:19 19:22 [A]Ex 19:24; 24:5; Lev 10:3; 21:6-8 19:23 [a]Lit *testified to* [A]Ex 19:12

19:3–8 The Israelites discerned the familiar pattern, in shortened form, of a suzerainty (superior-subordinate relationship) treaty in God's words: a preamble (v. 3), a historical prologue (v. 4), certain stipulations (v. 5a), and blessings (vv. 5b–6a). The acceptance in solemn assembly would normally be recorded in the final treaty document. Here it follows upon presentation of the treaty to them (vv. 7, 8). *See note on 24:7.*

19:3 from the mountain. The sign which the Lord had given particularly to Moses when he was still in Midian (3:12), that God had indeed sent him, was now fulfilled; he was with the people before the mountain of God. **house of Jacob … sons of Israel.** In employing this dual designation for the nation, the Lord reminded them of their humble beginnings as descendants of Abraham through Isaac and Jacob, who had been with them in Egypt, and of their status now as a nation (children = people).

19:4 bore you on eagles' wings. With a most appropriate metaphor, God described the Exodus and the journey to Sinai. Eagles were known to have carried their young out of the nests on their wings and taught them to fly, catching them when necessary on their outspread wings. Moses, in his final song, employed this metaphor of God's care for Israel and especially noted that there was only one Lord who did this (Dt 32:11–12).

19:5, 6 Three titles for Israel, "My own possession," "a kingdom of priests," and "a holy nation," were given by the Lord to the nation, contingent upon their being an obedient and covenant-keeping nation. These titles summarized the divine blessings which such a nation would experience: belonging especially to the Lord, representing Him in the earth and being set apart unto Him for His purposes. These expanded ethnically and morally what it meant to have brought them to Himself. "For all the earth is Mine," in the midst of the titles, laid stress upon the uniqueness and sovereignty of the Lord and had to be understood as dismissing all other claims by so-called other gods of the nations. It was more than the power of one god over another in Israel's situation; it was the choice and power of the only Lord! See 1Pe 2:9, where Peter uses these terms in the sense of God's spiritual kingdom of the redeemed.

19:8 All the people answered together. Presented with the details of God's bilateral, conditional covenant (note the "if you will obey … then you shall be" in v. 5), the people, briefed by their elders, responded with positive enthusiasm. The Lord's response to them does not take it as a rash promise by the people (cf. Dt 5:27–29).

19:9 believe in you forever. The Lord designed the upcoming encounter with Him so as to forestall any later accusation that Moses had himself compiled the law and had not met with the Lord on the mountain. It would also lead to great deference being accorded Moses by the people.

19:10 consecrate them. How serious this step was for the nation was emphasized for them by two days of special preparation. The inward preparation for meeting with God was mirrored in the outward actions of maintaining bodily cleanliness.

19:12, 13 The proper approach to a holy God could not have been better stressed than by imposing a death penalty upon those who violated the arbitrary boundaries which God had set around the mountain. Even animals could not encroach upon this sacred area (cf. Heb 12:20).

19:15 do not go near a woman. This was so they would be ceremonially clean (see Lv 15:16–18).

19:16 thunder and lightning. The dramatic visual presentation of God's presence on the mountain, accompanied by thick cloud and trumpet blast, more than impressed the onlookers with God's majesty and power—they trembled, but so did Moses (Heb 12:21). The unusual was happening, not the usual phenomena from volcanic activity, as some writers have proposed.

24 Then the LORD said to him, "[a]Go down and come
up *again,* [A]you and Aaron with you; but do not let
the [B]priests and the people break through to come
up to the LORD, or He will break forth upon them."
25 So Moses went down to the people and told them.

THE TEN COMMANDMENTS

20 Then God spoke all these words, saying,
2 "[A]I am the LORD your God, [B]who brought
you out of the land of Egypt, out of the house of
[a]slavery.
3 "[A]You shall have no other [B]gods [a]before Me.
4 "[A]You shall not make for yourself [a]an idol, or
any likeness of what is in heaven above or on the
earth beneath or in the water under the earth. 5 [A]You
shall not worship them or serve them; for I, the
LORD your God, am a [B]jealous God, [C]visiting the
iniquity of the fathers on the children, on the third
and the fourth generations of those who hate Me,
6 but showing lovingkindness to [A]thousands, to
those who love Me and keep My commandments.
7 "[A]You shall not take the name of the LORD your
God in vain, for the LORD will not [a]leave him unpunished who takes His name in vain.
8 "Remember [A]the sabbath day, to keep it holy.
9 [A]Six days you shall labor and do all your work,
10 but the seventh day is a sabbath of the LORD your
God; *in it* [A]you shall not do any work, you or your son
or your daughter, your male or your female servant
or your cattle or your sojourner who [a]stays with you.

19:24 [a]Lit *Go, descend* [A]Ex 24:1, 9, 12 [B]Ex 19:22 20:2 [a]Lit *slaves* [A]Lev 26:1; Deut 5:6; Ps 81:10 [B]Ex 13:3; 15:13, 16; Deut 7:8 20:3 [a]Or *besides Me* [A]Deut 6:14; 2 Kin 17:35; Jer 25:6; 35:15 [B]Ex 15:11; 20:23 20:4 [a]Or *a graven image* [A]Lev 19:4; 26:1; Deut 4:15-19; 27:15 20:5 [A]Ex 23:24; Josh 23:7; 2 Kin 17:35 [B]Ex 34:14; Deut 4:24; Josh 24:19; Nah 1:2 [C]Ex 34:6, 7; Num 14:18, 33; Deut 5:9, 10; 1 Kin 21:29; Jer 32:18 20:6 [A]Deut 7:9 20:7 [a]Or *hold him guiltless* [A]Lev 19:12; Deut 6:13; 10:20 20:8 [A]Ex 23:12; 31:13-16; Lev 26:2; Deut 5:12 20:9 [A]Ex 34:21; 35:2, 3; Lev 23:3; Deut 5:13; Luke 13:14 20:10 [a]Lit *is in your gates* [A]Neh 13:16-19

19:24 the priests. With the law still to be given, no priesthood had been established in Israel. These priests must have been the firstborn in each family who served as family priests because they had been dedicated to the Lord (cf. 13:2; 24:5). Their place would be taken over later by the Levites (Nu 3:45).

20:1 all these words. This general description of the commands to follow also received from Moses the title "Ten Commandments" (34:28; Dt 4:13). By this emphasis on God Himself speaking these words (cf. Dt 5:12, 15, 16, 22, 32, 33), all theories on Israel's borrowing legal patterns or concepts from the nations around them are unacceptable.

20:3–17 The Ten Commandments, also known as the Decalogue, which follow upon the opening historical prologue (v. 2), are formed as a precept or direct command given in the second person. This form was something rather uncommon in that day. Ancient Near Eastern law codes for the most part were casuistic, or case-law, in form, i.e., an "if ... then" construction written in the third person wherein a supposed offense was followed by a statement of the action to be taken or penalty to be exacted. The Ten Commandments may also be grouped into two broad categories: the vertical, namely man's relationship to God (vv. 2–11), and the horizontal, namely man's relationship to the community (vv. 12–17). Concisely listed prohibitions mark the second category, with only one exception—an imperative plus its explanation (v. 12). Explanation or reason appended to a prohibition marks the first category. By these Ten Commandments, true theology and true worship, the name of God, the Sabbath, family honor, life, marriage, property, truth, and virtue are well protected. *See note on 24:7.*

20:3 before Me. Meaning "over against Me," this is a most appropriate expression in the light of the next few verses. All false gods stand in opposition to the true God, and the worship of them is incompatible with the worship of Yahweh. When Israel departed from the worship of the only one and true God, she plunged into religious confusion (Jdg 17, 18).

20:4–6 The mode or fashion of worship appropriate to only one Lord forbids any attempt to represent or caricature Him by use of anything He has made. Total censure of artistic expression was not the issue; the absolute censure of idolatry and false worship was the issue. Violation would seriously affect succeeding generations because the Lord demanded full and exclusive devotion, i.e., He is a jealous God (cf. 34:14; Dt 4:24; 5:9). The worship of man-made representations was nothing less than hatred of the true God.

20:5, 6 on the third and the fourth generations ... thousands. Moses had made it clear that children were not punished for the sins of their parents (Dt 24:16; see Eze 18:19–32), but children would feel the impact of breaches of God's law by their parents' generation as a natural consequence of its disobedience, its hatred of God. Children reared in such an environment would imbibe and then practice similar idolatry, thus themselves expressing hateful disobedience. The difference in consequence served as both a warning and a motivation. The effect of a disobedient generation was to plant wickedness so deeply that it took several generations to reverse.

20:7 take the name ... in vain. To use God's name in such a way as to bring disrepute upon His character or deeds was to irreverently misuse His name. To fail to perform an oath in which His name had been legitimately uttered (cf. 22:10, 11; Lv 19:12; Dt 6:13) was to call into question His existence, since the guilty party evidently had no further thought of the God whose name he had used to improve his integrity. For the believer in the church age, however, the use of the name of God is not a needed verification of his intention and trustworthiness, since his life is to exhibit truth on all occasions, with his "yes" meaning "yes" and his "no" meaning "no" (Mt 5:37; Jas 5:12).

20:8 sabbath. Cf. 31:12–17. Each seventh day belonged to the Lord and would not be a work day but one set apart (i.e., holy) for rest and for time devoted to the worship of Yahweh. The term "Sabbath" is derived from "to rest or cease from work." The historical precedent for such a special observance was the creation week; a span of time equal to what man copied in practice. Each Sabbath day should have reminded the worshiper that the God whom he praised had indeed made everything in both realms of existence in 6 twenty-four-hour days. The Sabbath would

THE TEN COMMANDMENTS

Commandment	OT Statement	OT Death Penalty	NT Restatement
1st Polytheism	Ex 20:3	Ex 22:20; Dt 6:13–15	Ac 14:15
2nd Idols	Ex 20:4	Dt 27:15	1Jn 5:21
3rd Swearing	Ex 20:7	Lv 24:15, 16	Jas 5:12
4th Sabbath	Ex 20:8	Nu 15:32–36	Col 2:16 nullifies
5th Obedience to parents	Ex 20:12	Ex 21:15–17	Eph 6:1
6th Murder	Ex 20:13	Ex 21:12	1Jn 3:15
7th Adultery	Ex 20:14	Lv 20:10	1Co 6:9, 10
8th Theft	Ex 20:15	Ex 21:16	Eph 4:28
9th False Witness	Ex 20:16	Dt 18:16–21	Col 3:9, 10
10th Coveting	Ex 20:17	———	Eph 5:3

11 [A]For in six days the LORD made the heavens and
the earth, the sea and all that is in them, and rested
on the seventh day; therefore the LORD blessed the
sabbath day and made it holy.
12 "[A]Honor your father and your mother, that your
[B]days may be prolonged in the land which the LORD
your God gives you.
13 "[A]You shall not murder.
14 "[A]You shall not commit adultery.
15 "[A]You shall not steal.
16 "[A]You shall not bear false witness against your
[B]neighbor.
17 "[A]You shall not covet your neighbor's house;
[B]you shall not covet your neighbor's wife or his
male servant or his female servant or his ox or his
donkey or anything that belongs to your neighbor."
18 [A]All the people perceived the [a]thunder and the
lightning flashes and the sound of the trumpet and
the mountain smoking; and when the people saw
it, they trembled and stood at a distance. 19 [A]Then
they said to Moses, "Speak [a]to us yourself and we
will listen; but let not God speak [a]to us, or we will
die." 20 Moses said to the people, "[A]Do not be afraid;
for God has come in order [B]to test you, and in order that [C]the fear of Him may [a]remain with you, so
that you may not sin." 21 So the people stood at a
distance, while Moses approached [A]the thick cloud
where God *was.*
22 Then the LORD said to Moses, "Thus you shall
say to the sons of Israel, 'You yourselves have seen
that [A]I have spoken [a]to you from heaven. 23 [A]You
shall not make *other gods* besides Me; [B]gods of silver or gods of gold, you shall not make for yourselves. 24 You shall make [A]an altar of earth for Me,
and you shall sacrifice on it your [B]burnt offerings
and your [C]peace offerings, [D]your sheep and your
oxen; in every place [E]where I cause My name to be
remembered, I will come to you and bless you. 25 If
you make an altar of stone for Me, [A]you shall not
build it of cut stones, for if you wield your tool on
it, you will profane it. 26 And you shall not go up by
steps to My altar, so that [A]your nakedness will not
be exposed on it.'

ORDINANCES FOR THE PEOPLE

21 "Now these are the [A]ordinances which you are
to set before them:

20:11 [A]Gen 2:2, 3; Ex 31:17 20:12 [A]Lev 19:3; Deut 27:16; Matt 15:4; 19:19; Mark 7:10; 10:19; Luke 18:20; Eph 6:2 [B]Deut 5:16, 33; 6:2; 11:8, 9; Jer 35:7 20:13 [A]Gen 9:6; Ex 21:12; Lev 24:17; Matt 5:21; 19:18; Mark 10:19; Luke 18:20; Rom 13:9; James 2:11 20:14 [A]Lev 20:10; Deut 5:18; Matt 5:27; 19:18; Rom 13:9 20:15 [A]Ex 21:16; Lev 19:11, 13; Matt 19:18; Rom 13:9 20:16 [A]Ex 23:1, 7; Deut 5:20; Matt 19:18 [B]Lev 19:18 20:17 [A]Deut 5:21; Rom 7:7; 13:9; Eph 5:3, 5 [B]Prov 6:29; Matt 5:28 20:18 [a]Lit *sounds* [A]Ex 19:16, 18; Heb 12:18, 19 20:19 [a]Lit *with* [A]Deut 5:5, 23-27; Gal 3:19; Heb 12:19 20:20 [a]Lit *be before* [A]Ex 14:13; Is 41:10, 13 [B]Ex 15:25; Deut 13:3 [C]Deut 4:10; 6:24; Prov 3:7; 16:6; Is 8:13 20:21 [A]Ex 19:16; Deut 5:22 20:22 [a]Lit *with* [A]Deut 4:36; 5:24, 26; Neh 9:13 20:23 [A]Ex 20:3 [B]Ex 32:1, 2, 4; Deut 29:17 20:24 [A]Ex 20:25; 27:1-8 [B]Ex 10:25; 18:12 [C]Ex 24:5; Lev 1:2 [D]Deut 12:5; 16:6, 11; 26:2; 2 Chr 6:6 [E]Deut 12:5; 26:2 20:25 [A]Deut 27:5, 6; Josh 8:31 20:26 [A]Ex 28:42, 43 21:1 [A]Ex 24:3, 4; Deut 4:14; 6:1

also stand, therefore, as a counter to evolutionary ideas prevalent in false religion. Moses, in the review of the Decalogue, also linked the observance of the Sabbath with Israel's exodus from Egypt and specified that this was why Israel was to keep it (Dt 5:12–15). Significantly, the command for the Sabbath is not repeated in the NT, whereas the other 9 are. In fact, it is nullified (cf. Col 2:16, 17). Belonging especially to Israel under the Mosaic economy, the Sabbath could not apply to the believer of the church age, for he is living in a new economy.

20:12–16 Cf. Mt 19:18–19; Mk 10:19; Lk 18:20.

20:12 Honor your father and your mother. The key to societal stability is reverence and respect for parents and their authority. The appended promise primarily related the command to life in the Promised Land and reminded the Israelite of the program God had set up for him and his people. Within the borders of their territory, God expected them not to tolerate juvenile delinquency, which at heart is overt disrespect for parents and authority. Severe consequences, namely capital punishment, could apply (cf. Dt 21:18–21). One of the reasons for the Babylonian exile was a failure to honor parents (Eze 22:7, 15). The Apostle Paul individualized this national promise when he applied the truth to believers in his day (cf. Mt 15:4; Mk 7:10; Eph 6:1–3).

20:13–15 Cf. Ro 13:9.

20:13 murder. The irreversible nature of the divinely imposed sentence of death on every manslayer who killed another intentionally (cf. 21:12; Nu 35:17–21) stands without parallel in ancient Near Eastern literature and legal codes (cf. Ge 9:5, 6). Further, the sacredness of human life stands out in the passages dealing with unintentional manslaughter. The accident of death still carried with it a penalty of banishment to the city of refuge until the death of the High Priest for the one who killed someone unintentionally. Careful appraisal of the word Moses used (one of 7 different Heb. words for killing, and one used only 47 times in the OT) suggests a broad translation of "to kill, slay" but denoting the taking of life under a legal system where he would have to answer to the stipulations of a legal code, no matter whether he killed unintentionally or intentionally. By this command, men would be reminded and exhorted to strive after carefulness in the affairs of life so that on the person-to-person level no one would die by their hand. *See note on 21:12–14* (cf. Mt 5:21; Jas 2:11).

20:14 adultery. Applicable to both men and women, this command protected the sacredness of the marriage relationship. God had instituted marriage at the creation of man and woman (Ge 2:24) and had blessed it as the means of filling the earth (Ge 1:28). The penalty for infidelity in the marital relationship was death (Lv 20:10). Adultery was also referred to as "a great sin" (Ge 20:9) and a "great evil and sin against God" (cf. Ge 39:9; Mt 5:27; Jas 2:11).

20:15 steal. Any dishonest acquiring of another's goods or assets greatly disturbs the right to ownership of private property, which is an important principle for societal stability.

20:16 false witness. Justice is not served by any untruthful testimony. Practically all societies have recognized this principle and adjure all witnesses in courts to tell the truth and nothing but the truth.

20:17 covet. The thoughts and desires of the heart do not escape attention. A strong longing to have what another has is wrong. This tenth command suggests that none of the previous 9 commandments are only external acts with no relation to internal thoughts (cf. Mt 15:19; Ro 7:7; 13:9).

20:18 trembled and stood at a distance. The people fearfully withdrew from the cluster of phenomena accompanying this theophany, this appearance of God on the mountain. They instinctively placed Moses in the position of mediator between them and God, because such was the gap between them and their holy God that they feared they were not fit to live in His presence (v. 19).

20:19 let not God speak. Fearing for their lives, the nation asked Moses to be their mediator (cf. Heb 12:18–21).

20:20 Instructed not to respond to the phenomena with fear, they were also told that proper fear, i.e., awe and reverence of God, deterred sin.

20:22–26 Sacrifices, offerings, and altars were not unknown to Israel and were already part of certain worship ceremonies. Neither the earthen nor stone altars would have even a hint of being shaped to represent something more specific, so the restrictions on the form and the method of building would ensure the appropriateness and propriety of their worship. Leviticus 1–7 outlines the Mosaic sacrifices.

21:1 ordinances. A combination of casuistic (case-law) and apodictic (direct command) precepts laid down, as a detailed enlargement of the Decalogue, the framework for judging and resolving civil disputes in Israel. Such a combination continued to confirm the uniqueness of Israel's law among the different ancient Near Eastern law-codes. Later in a special ceremony, God entitled these precepts the Book of the Covenant (24:7).

2 "If you buy [A]a Hebrew slave, he shall serve for
six years; but on the seventh he shall go out as a
free man without payment. 3 If he comes [a]alone,
he shall go out [a]alone; if he is the husband of a
wife, then his wife shall go out with him. 4 If his
master gives him a wife, and she bears him sons or
daughters, the wife and her children shall belong
to her master, and he shall go out [a]alone. 5 But [A]if
the slave plainly says, 'I love my master, my wife
and my children; I will not go out as a free man,'
6 then his master shall bring him to [a]God, then he
shall bring him to the door or the doorpost. And
his master shall pierce his ear with an awl; and he
shall serve him permanently.
7 "[A]If a man sells his daughter as a female slave,
she is not to [a]go free [B]as the male slaves [a]do. 8 If
she is [a]displeasing in the eyes of her master [b]who
designated her for himself, then he shall let her be
redeemed. He does not have authority to sell her to
a foreign people because of his [c]unfairness to her.
9 If he designates her for his son, he shall deal with
her according to the custom of daughters. 10 If he
takes to himself another woman, he may not reduce
her [a]food, her clothing, or [A]her conjugal rights. 11 If
he will not do these three *things* for her, then she
shall go out for nothing, without *payment of* money.

PERSONAL INJURIES

12 "[A]He who strikes a man so that he dies shall
surely be put to death. 13 [A]But [a]if he did not lie in wait
for him, but [B]God let *him* fall into his hand, then I
will appoint you a place to which he may flee. 14 [A]If,
however, a man acts presumptuously toward his
neighbor, so as to kill him craftily, you are to take
him *even* from My altar, that he may die.
15 "He who strikes his father or his mother shall
surely be put to death.
16 "[A]He who [a]kidnaps a man, whether he sells
him or he is found in his [b]possession, shall surely
be put to death.
17 "[A]He who curses his father or his mother shall
surely be put to death.
18 "If men have a quarrel and one strikes the other
with a stone or with *his* fist, and he does not die but
[a]remains in bed, 19 if he gets up and walks around
outside on his staff, then he who struck him shall
go unpunished; he shall only pay for his [a]loss of
time, and [b]shall take care of him until he is completely healed.
20 "If a man strikes his male or female slave with
a rod and he dies [a]at his hand, he shall [b]be punished. 21 If, however, he [a]survives a day or two, no
vengeance shall be taken; [A]for he is his [b]property.
22 "If men struggle with each other and strike a
woman with child so that [a]she gives birth prematurely, yet there is no injury, he shall surely be fined
as the woman's husband [b]may demand of him, and
he shall [A]pay [c]as the judges *decide.* 23 But if there
is *any further* injury, [A]then you shall appoint *as a
penalty* life for life, 24 [A]eye for eye, tooth for tooth,
hand for hand, foot for foot, 25 burn for burn, wound
for wound, [a]bruise for bruise.
26 "If a man strikes the eye of his male or female
slave, and destroys it, he shall let him go free on
account of his eye. 27 And if he [a]knocks out a tooth
of his male or female slave, he shall let him go free
on account of his tooth.
28 "If an ox gores a man or a woman [a]to death, [A]the
ox shall surely be stoned and its flesh shall not be
eaten; but the owner of the ox shall go unpunished.
29 If, however, an ox was previously in the habit of
goring and its owner has been warned, yet he does
not confine it and it kills a man or a woman, the ox
shall be stoned and its owner also shall be put to

21:2 [A]Lev 25:39-43; Deut 15:12-18; Jer 34:14 21:3 [a]Lit *by himself* 21:4 [a]Lit *by himself* 21:5 [A]Deut 15:16, 17 21:6 [a]Or *the judges who acted in God's name* 21:7 [a]Lit *go out* [A]Neh 5:5 [B]Ex 21:2, 3 21:8 [a]Lit *bad* [b]Another reading is *so that he did not designate her* [c]Lit *dealing treacherously* 21:10 [a]Lit *flesh* [A]1 Cor 7:3, 5 21:12 [A]Gen 9:6; Lev 24:17; Num 35:30; Matt 26:52 21:13 [a]Lit *he who* [A]Num 35:10-34; Deut 19:1-13; Josh 20:1-9 [B]1 Sam 24:4, 10, 18 21:14 [A]Deut 19:11, 12; 1 Kin 2:28-34 21:16 [a]Lit *steals* [b]Lit *hand* [A]Deut 24:7 21:17 [A]Lev 20:9; Prov 20:20; Matt 15:4; Mark 7:10 21:18 [a]Lit *lies* 21:19 [a]Lit *his sitting* [b]Lit *healing, he shall cause to be healed* 21:20 [a]Lit *under* [b]Lit *suffer vengeance* 21:21 [a]Lit *stands* [b]Lit *money* [A]Lev 25:44-46 21:22 [a]Or *an untimely birth occurs;* lit *her children come out* [b]Lit *lays on him* [c]Lit *by arbitration* [A]Ex 21:30; Deut 22:18, 19 21:23 [A]Lev 24:19; Deut 19:21 21:24 [A]Lev 24:20; Deut 19:21; Matt 5:38 21:25 [a]Lit *welt* 21:27 [a]Lit *causes to fall* 21:28 [a]Lit *so that he dies* [A]Gen 9:5; Ex 21:32

21:2–11 The law of the slave guaranteed freedom after a specified period of 6 years unless the slave himself elected permanent servitude, but this would be service in a context not of abuse but of love (v. 5). Any permanent, involuntary servitude for a Hebrew slave to a Hebrew master was obviously undesirable for Israelite society and was unknown in Israel (cf. Lv 25:39–55). Provision was also made to ensure the proper treatment of female slaves, who could not deliberately be left destitute by wrongful action on the part of their master.

21:12–14 The laws relating to personal injury (vv. 15–36) from man or animal were preceded by the most serious of injuries, homicide. The death penalty was prescribed for intentional homicide only (see 20:13), whereas for unintentional homicide the penalty was banishment to an appointed place, which later God revealed were the cities of refuge (cf. Nu 35:6–24; Dt 19:1–13). No degree of sanctuary applied to one guilty of premeditated murder. Death by accident at the hand of another is something unplanned by man but which God let happen. The law did afford sanctuary but away from home and vengeful relatives, often for life, because there the one guilty of involuntary manslaughter remained until the death of the High Priest (Nu 35:25, 28).

21:15, 17 Disrespect for parents seen in physical and verbal abuse of them by their children was so serious it was designated a capital offense. Commandment 5 was a serious matter! Other ancient law-codes, e.g., the Code of Hammurabi, also respected parental authority and prescribed severe consequences, although not the death penalty.

21:17 Cf. Mt 15:4; Mk 7:10.

21:20, 21, 26, 27 Punishment of slaves was considered the right of the owner (Pr 10:13; 13:24), but did not allow for violence. Judges were to decide the appropriate punishment if the slave died (v. 20). If the slave lived a few days it was evidence that the owner had no intent to kill, and the loss of the slave was punishment enough (v. 21). A beating without death immediately ensuing was construed as a disciplinary matter, not a homicidal one. Any permanent personal injury brought freedom and loss of a master's investment. The master's power over the slave was thus limited, which made this law unprecedented in the ancient world.

21:22 Compensation was mandatory for accidentally causing a premature birth, even if no injury resulted to either mother or child. Judges were brought into the legal process so that damages awarded were fair and were not calculated out of vengeance.

21:23, 24 Cf. Lv 24:19, 20; Dt 19:21. The principle of retaliation, or *lex talionis,* applied if injury did occur to either mother or child. The punishment matched, but did not exceed, the damage done to the victim. The welfare of a pregnant woman was protected by this law so that unintentional maltreatment constituted culpable negligence. Significantly for the abortion debate, the fetus was considered a person; thus, someone was held accountable for its death or injury.

21:24 Cf. Mt 5:38.

death. 30 If a ransom is [a]demanded of him, then he
shall give for the redemption of his life whatever
is [a]demanded of him. 31 Whether it gores a son or
[a]a daughter, it shall be done to him according to
[b]the same rule. 32 If the ox gores a male or female
slave, [a]the owner shall give his *or her* master [A]thirty
shekels of silver, and the ox shall be stoned.
33 "If a man opens a pit, or [a]digs a pit and does
not cover it over, and an ox or a donkey falls into
it, 34 the owner of the pit shall make restitution; he
shall [a]give money to its owner, and the dead *animal*
shall become his.
35 "If one man's ox hurts another's so that it dies,
then they shall sell the live ox and divide its price
equally; and also they shall divide the dead *ox*. 36 Or
if it is known that the ox was previously in the habit
of goring, yet its owner has not confined it, he shall
surely pay ox for ox, and the dead *animal* shall
become his.

PROPERTY RIGHTS

22 "[a]If a man steals an ox or a sheep and slaughters it or sells it, he shall pay five oxen for
the ox and [A]four sheep for the sheep.
2 "[a]If the [A]thief is [b]caught while breaking in and
is struck so that he dies, there will be no bloodguiltiness on his account. 3 *But* if the sun has risen on
him, there will be bloodguiltiness on his account.
He shall surely make restitution; if he owns nothing,
then he shall be [A]sold for his theft. 4 If what he stole
is actually found alive in his [a]possession, whether
an ox or a donkey or a sheep, [A]he shall pay double.
5 "If a man lets a field or vineyard be grazed *bare*
and lets his animal loose so that it grazes in another
man's field, he shall make restitution from the best
of his own field and the best of his own vineyard.
6 "If a fire breaks out and spreads to thorn bushes,
so that stacked grain or the standing grain or the
field *itself* is consumed, he who started the fire shall
surely make restitution.
7 "[A]If a man gives his neighbor money or goods to
keep *for him* and it is stolen from the man's house, if
the thief is [a]caught, he shall pay double. 8 If the thief
is not [a]caught, then the owner of the house shall
[b]appear before [c,A]the judges, *to* determine whether
he [d]laid his hands on his neighbor's property. 9 For
every [a]breach of trust, *whether it is* for ox, for donkey, for sheep, for clothing, *or* for any lost thing
about which one says, 'This is it,' the [b]case of both
parties shall come before [c,A]the judges; he whom [c]the
judges condemn shall pay double to his neighbor.
10 "If a man gives his neighbor a donkey, an ox, a
sheep, or any animal to keep *for him,* and it dies or is
hurt or is driven away while no one is looking, 11 an
[A]oath before the LORD shall be made by the two of
them [a]that he has not [b]laid hands on his neighbor's
property; and its owner shall accept *it,* and he shall
not make restitution. 12 But if it is actually stolen from
him, he shall make restitution to its owner. 13 If it is all
torn to pieces, let him bring it as evidence; he shall
not make restitution for what has been torn to pieces.
14 "If a man [a]borrows *anything* from his neighbor,
and it is injured or dies while its owner is not with
it, he shall make full restitution. 15 If its owner is
with it, he shall not make restitution; if it is hired,
it came for its hire.

SUNDRY LAWS

16 "[A]If a man seduces a virgin who is not engaged,
and lies with her, he must pay a dowry for her *to
be* his wife. 17 If her father absolutely refuses to
give her to him, he shall [a]pay money equal to the
[A]dowry for virgins.
18 "You shall not allow a [A]sorceress to live.
19 "[A]Whoever lies with an animal shall surely be
put to death.
20 "[A]He who sacrifices to [a]any god, other than to
the LORD alone, shall be [b]utterly destroyed.
21 "[A]You shall not wrong a stranger or oppress
him, for you were strangers in the land of Egypt.
22 [A]You shall not afflict any widow or orphan. 23 If
you afflict him at all, *and* [A]if he does cry out to Me,
[B]I will surely hear his cry; 24 and My anger will be
kindled, and I will kill you with the sword, [A]and
your wives shall become widows and your children fatherless.

21:30 [a]Lit *laid on him* 21:31 [a]Lit *gores a daughter* [b]Lit *this judgment* 21:32 [a]Lit *he* [A]Zech 11:12; Matt 26:15; 27:3, 9 21:33 [a]Lit *if a man digs* 21:34 [a]Lit *give back* 22:1 [a]Ch 21:37 in Heb [A]2 Sam 12:6; Luke 19:8 22:2 [a]Ch 22:1 in Heb [b]Lit *found* [A]Matt 6:19; 24:43; 1 Pet 4:15 22:3 [A]Matt 18:25 22:4 [a]Lit *hand* [A]Ex 22:7 22:7 [a]Lit *found* [A]Lev 6:1-7 22:8 [a]Lit *found* [b]Lit *approach to* [c]Or *God* [d]Lit *stretched his hand* [A]Ex 22:9; Deut 17:8, 9; 19:17 22:9 [a]Or *matter of transgression* [b]Lit *matter* [c]Or *God* [A]Ex 22:8, 28; Deut 25:1 22:11 [a]Lit *whether* [b]Lit *stretched his hand* [A]Heb 6:16 22:14 [a]Lit *asks* 22:16 [A]Deut 22:28, 29 22:17 [a]Lit *weigh out silver* [A]Gen 34:12; 1 Sam 18:25 22:18 [A]Lev 19:31; 20:6, 27; Deut 18:10, 11; 1 Sam 28:3; Jer 27:9, 10 22:19 [A]Lev 18:23; 20:15, 16; Deut 27:21 22:20 [a]Lit *the gods* [b]Lit *put under the ban* [A]Ex 32:8; 34:15; Lev 17:7; Num 25:2; Deut 17:2, 3, 5; 1 Kin 18:40; 2 Kin 10:25 22:21 [A]Ex 23:9; Lev 19:33, 34; 25:35; Deut 1:16; 10:19; 27:19; Zech 7:10 22:22 [A]Deut 24:17, 18; Prov 23:10, 11; Jer 7:6, 7 22:23 [A]Deut 15:9; Job 35:9; Luke 18:7 [B]Deut 10:18; Job 34:28; Ps 10:14, 17, 18; 18:6; 68:5; James 5:4 22:24 [A]Ps 109:2, 9

21:30 Animal owners were held responsible for death or injuries caused by their animals. Since the owner was guilty of negligence and not of an intentional crime, he was able to make payment to escape the death penalty. Again, judges are brought into the process to ensure that no vengeful decisions are made.

21:32 shekels. A shekel weighs .4 oz.; 30 shekels would weigh 12 oz. Christ was betrayed for the price of a slave (Zec 11:12, 13; Mt 26:14, 15).

22:3 if the sun has risen on him. The culpability of a householder's actions against an intruder depended on whether the break-in (lit. "digging through" the mud walls) was at night or in the daytime. At night quick evaluation of an intruder's intentions was not as clear as it might be in daytime, nor would someone be awake and on hand to help.

22:11 an oath before the LORD. Presumably an oath of innocence which would bind the two parties to a dispute over lost goods and preclude any further legal action being taken.

22:16 If a man seduces ... pay a dowry. The male was held accountable for premarital intercourse and the victim was seen as having been exploited by him, for which he paid a price (cf. Dt 22:22–29).

22:18 sorceress. A woman who practices occultism.

22:19 The degree of sexual perversion in Canaanite culture was such that bestiality was fairly commonplace (cf. Lv 18:23, 24). Hittite laws, for example, even permitted cohabitation with certain animals.

22:20 utterly destroyed. Lit. meaning "put to the ban" or "devoted to sacred use," which in this case meant death (cf. Jos 7:2ff.).

22:22 widow or orphan. God reserved His special attention for widows and orphans who often had no one to care for them. He also reserved a special reaction, His wrath, for those abusing and exploiting them. This wrath would work out in military invasions as the sword reduced the abusers' families to the same status of being without spouse or parents.

25 “[A]If you lend money to My people, to the poor
[a]among you, you are not to [b]act as a creditor to him;
you shall not [c]charge him [B]interest. 26 If you ever
take your neighbor’s cloak [A]as a pledge, you are to
return it to him before the sun sets, 27 for that is his
only covering; it is his cloak for his [a]body. What else
shall he sleep in? And it shall come about that [A]when
he cries out to Me, I will hear *him,* for [B]I am gracious.
28 “You shall not [a,A]curse God, [B]nor curse a ruler
of your people.
29 “[A]You shall not delay *the offering from* [a]your
harvest and your vintage. [B]The firstborn of your
sons you shall give to Me. 30 [A]You shall do the same
with your oxen *and* with your sheep. It shall be with
its mother seven days; [B]on the eighth day you shall
give it to Me.
31 “[A]You shall be holy men to Me, therefore [B]you
shall not eat *any* flesh torn to pieces in the field;
you shall throw it to the dogs.

SUNDRY LAWS

23 “[A]You shall not bear a false report; do not join
your hand with a wicked man to be a [B]mali-
cious witness. 2 You shall not follow [a]the masses in
doing evil, nor shall you [b]testify in a dispute so as
to turn aside after [a]a multitude in order to [A]pervert
justice; 3 [A]nor shall you [a]be partial to a poor man in
his dispute.
4 “[A]If you meet your enemy’s ox or his donkey
wandering away, you shall surely return it to him.
5 [A]If you see the donkey of one who hates you lying
helpless under its load, you shall refrain from leaving it to him, you shall surely release *it* with him.
6 “[A]You shall not pervert the justice *due* to your
needy *brother* in his dispute. 7 [A]Keep far from a
false charge, and [B]do not kill the innocent or the
righteous, for [C]I will not acquit the guilty.
8 “[A]You shall not take a bribe, for a bribe blinds
the clear-sighted and [a]subverts the cause of the just.
9 “[A]You shall not oppress a [a]stranger, since you
yourselves know the [b]feelings of a [a]stranger, for you
also were [a]strangers in the land of Egypt.

THE SABBATH AND LAND

10 “[A]You shall sow your land for six years and
gather in its yield, 11 but *on* the seventh year you
shall let it [a]rest and lie fallow, so that the needy of
your people may eat; and whatever they leave the
beast of the field may eat. You are to do the same
with your vineyard *and* your olive grove.
12 “[A]Six days you are to do your work, but on the
seventh day you shall cease *from labor* so that your
ox and your donkey may rest, and the son of your
female slave, as well as [a]your stranger, may refresh
themselves. 13 Now [A]concerning everything which
I have said to you, be on your guard; and [B]do not
mention the name of other gods, nor let *them* be
heard [a]from your mouth.

THREE NATIONAL FEASTS

14 “[A]Three times a year you shall celebrate a feast
to Me. 15 You shall observe [A]the Feast of Unleavened
Bread; for seven days you are to eat unleavened
bread, as I commanded you, at the appointed time
in the [B]month Abib, for in it you came out of Egypt.
And [a,C]none shall appear before Me empty-handed.
16 Also *you shall observe* [A]the Feast of the Harvest
of the first fruits of your labors *from* what you sow
in the field; also the Feast of the Ingathering at the
end of the year [B]when you gather in *the fruit of* your

22:25 [a]Lit *with* [b]Lit *be* [c]Lit *lay upon* [A]Lev 25:35-37; Deut 15:7-11 [B]Deut 23:19, 20; Neh 5:7; Ps 15:5; Ezek 18:8 22:26 [A]Deut 24:6, 10-13; Job 24:3; Prov 20:16; Amos 2:8 22:27 [a]Lit *skin* [A]Ex 22:23 [B]Ex 34:6 22:28 [a]Or *revile* [A]Lev 24:15, 16 [B]Eccl 10:20; Acts 23:5 22:29 [a]Lit *your fullness and your tears* [A]Ex 23:16, 19; Deut 26:2-11; Prov 3:9 [B]Ex 13:2, 12 22:30 [A]Deut 15:19; Lev 22:27 [B]Gen 17:12; Lev 12:3 22:31 [A]Ex 19:6; Lev 11:44; 19:2 [B]Lev 7:24; 17:15; Ezek 4:14 23:1 [A]Ex 20:16; Lev 19:11f; Deut 5:20; Ps 101:5; Prov 10:18 [B]Deut 19:16-21; Ps 35:11; Prov 19:5; Acts 6:11 23:2 [a]Lit *many men* [b]Or *answer* [A]Deut 16:19; 24:17 23:3 [a]Lit *honor* [A]Ex 23:6; Lev 19:15; Deut 1:17; 16:19 23:4 [A]Deut 22:1-4 23:5 [A]Deut 22:4 23:6 [A]Ex 23:2, 3; Lev 19:15 23:7 [A]Ex 20:16; Ps 119:29; Eph 4:25 [B]Ex 20:13; Deut 27:25 [C]Ex 34:7; Deut 25:1; Rom 1:18 23:8 [a]Or *distorts the words* [A]Deut 10:17; 16:19; Prov 15:27; 17:8, 23; Is 5:22, 23 23:9 [a]Or *sojourner(s)* [b]Lit *soul* [A]Ex 22:21; Lev 19:33f; Deut 24:17f; 27:19 23:10 [A]Lev 25:1-7 23:11 [a]Lit *drop* 23:12 [a]Lit *the sojourner* [A]Ex 20:8-11; 31:15; 34:21; 35:2, 3; Lev 23:3; Deut 5:13f 23:13 [a]Lit *on* [A]Deut 4:9, 23; 1 Tim 4:16 [B]Josh 23:7; Ps 16:4; Hos 2:17 23:14 [A]Ex 23:17; 34:22-24; Deut 16:16 23:15 [a]Lit *they...not* [A]Ex 12:14-20; Lev 23:6-8; Num 28:16-25 [B]Ex 12:2; 13:4 [C]Ex 22:29; 34:20 23:16 [A]Ex 34:22; Lev 23:10; Num 28:26 [B]Lev 23:39

22:25 interest. One way in which the people showed their concern for the poor and needy was to take no business advantage of them. Charging interest was allowable (Lv 25:35–37; Dt 23:19, 20), but not when it was exorbitant or worsened the plight of the borrower. The psalmist identified a righteous man as one who lends money without interest (Ps 15:5).

22:28 See Ac 23:5, where Paul apparently violated this law, not knowing to whom he spoke.

22:31 holy men to Me. All these laws and regulations caused Israel to be set apart in conduct, not just in name. The special calling as Yahweh’s firstborn son (4:22) and as His treasured possession, a kingdom of priests and a holy nation (19:5, 6) mandated ethical uprightness. **not eat *any* flesh torn.** Flesh of an animal killed by another and lying in the field became unclean by coming into contact with unclean carnivores and insects and with putrefaction by not having had the blood drained properly from it. A set-apart lifestyle impacted every area of life, including from where one collected his meat.

23:1–9 A list of miscellaneous laws, which includes the protection of equitable and impartial justice for all. False testimony, undiscerningly following a majority, favoring one over another, and accepting bribes, all contribute to the perversion of true justice. The attitude of impartiality was to include the helping of another with his animals regardless of whether he be friend or foe. If no help was given, his livelihood could very well be adversely affected, which was a situation others in the community could not allow to happen.

23:10, 11 seventh year. A sabbatical year of rest after 6 years of farming benefited both the land and the poor. This pattern of letting a field lie fallow appears to have been unique with Israel.

23:13 Idolatry was to be avoided right down to the level of not causing the name of other deities to be remembered. This perhaps served also as a prohibition of intermarriage with other nations, for in the marriage contract recognition was given to the deities of the parties involved, which would have had the effect of putting God on a par with pagan gods.

23:14–19 Requiring all males to be present for 3 specified feasts at a central sanctuary would have had a socially and religiously uniting effect on the nation. The men must trust the Lord to protect their landholdings while on pilgrimage to the tabernacle (cf. 34:23, 24). All 3 feasts were joyful occasions, being a commemoration of the Exodus (the Feast of Unleavened Bread), an expression of gratitude to God for all the grain He had provided (the Feast of the Harvest), and a thanksgiving for the final harvest (the Feast of Ingathering). Alternative names appear in the biblical record for the second and third feasts: the Feast of Weeks (34:22) or Firstfruits (34:22; Ac 2:1), and the Feast of Tabernacles or Booths (Lv 23:33–36). For additional discussions, see, Lv 23:1–24:9; Nu 28, 29; Dt 16.

labors from the field. 17 [A]Three times a year all your males shall appear before the Lord [a]GOD.

18 "[A]You shall not offer the blood of My sacrifice with leavened bread; [B]nor is the fat of My [a]feast to remain overnight until morning.

19 "You shall bring [A]the choice first fruits of your soil into the house of the LORD your God.

"[B]You are not to boil a young goat in the milk of its mother.

CONQUEST OF THE LAND

20 "Behold, I am going to send [A]an angel before you to guard you along the way and [B]to bring you into the place which I have prepared. 21 Be on your guard before him and obey his voice; [A]do not be rebellious toward him, for he will not pardon your transgression, since [B]My name is in him. 22 But if you truly obey his voice and do all that I say, then [A]I will be an enemy to your enemies and an adversary to your adversaries. 23 [A]For My angel will go before you and bring you in to *the land of* the Amorites, the Hittites, the Perizzites, the Canaanites, the Hivites and the Jebusites; and I will completely destroy them. 24 [A]You shall not worship their gods, nor serve them, nor do according to their deeds; [B]but you shall utterly overthrow them and break their [C]*sacred* pillars in pieces. 25 [A]But you shall serve the LORD your God, [a]and He will bless your bread and your water; and [B]I will remove sickness from your midst. 26 There shall be no one miscarrying or [A]barren in your land; [B]I will fulfill the number of your days. 27 I will [A]send My terror ahead of you, and [B]throw into confusion all the people among whom you come, and I will [C]make all your enemies turn *their* backs to you. 28 I will send [A]hornets ahead of you so that they will [B]drive out the Hivites, the Canaanites, and the Hittites before you. 29 [A]I will not drive them out before you in a single year, that the land may not become desolate and the beasts of the field become too numerous for you. 30 I will drive them out before you [A]little by little, until you become fruitful and take possession of the land. 31 [A]I will fix your boundary from the [a]Red Sea to the sea of the Philistines, and from the wilderness to the River *Euphrates;* [B]for I will deliver the inhabitants of the land into your hand, and you will [C]drive them out before you. 32 [A]You shall [a]make no covenant with them [B]or with their gods. 33 [A]They shall not live in your land, because they will make you sin against Me; for *if* you serve their gods, [B]it will surely be a snare to you."

PEOPLE AFFIRM THEIR COVENANT WITH GOD

24 Then He said to Moses, "[A]Come up to the LORD, you and Aaron, [B]Nadab and Abihu and [C]seventy of the elders of Israel, and you shall worship at a distance. 2 Moses alone, however, shall come near to the LORD, but they shall not come near, nor shall the people come up with him."

3 Then Moses came and recounted to the people all the words of the LORD and all the [a]ordinances; and all the people answered with one voice and said, "[A]All the words which the LORD has spoken we will do!" 4 [A]Moses wrote down all the words of the LORD. Then he arose early in the morning, and built an [B]altar [a]at the foot of the mountain with twelve pillars for the twelve tribes of Israel.

23:17 [a]Heb *YHWH*, usually rendered *LORD* [A]Ex 23:14; 34:23; Deut 16:16 23:18 [a]Or *festival* [A]Ex 34:25; Lev 2:11 [B]Ex 12:10; Lev 7:15; Deut 16:4 23:19 [A]Ex 22:29; 34:26; Deut 26:2, 10; Neh 10:35; Prov 3:9 [B]Deut 14:21 23:20 [A]Ex 3:2; 14:19; 23:23; 32:34; 33:2 [B]Ex 15:16, 17 23:21 [A]Deut 9:7; Ps 78:40, 56 [B]Ex 3:14; 6:3; 34:5-7 23:22 [A]Gen 12:3; Num 24:9; Deut 30:7 23:23 [A]Ex 23:20; Josh 24:8, 11 23:24 [A]Ex 20:5; 23:13, 33; Deut 12:30f [B]Num 33:52; Deut 7:5; 12:3; 2 Kin 18:4 [C]Ex 34:13; Lev 26:1; 2 Kin 3:2 23:25 [a]Or *that He may bless* [A]Lev 26:3-13; Deut 6:13; 10:12; 28:1-14; Josh 22:5; 1 Sam 12:20; Matt 4:10 [B]Ex 15:26; Deut 7:15 23:26 [A]Deut 7:14 [B]Deut 4:40; Job 5:26 23:27 [A]Gen 35:5; Ex 15:16; Deut 2:25; Josh 2:9 [B]Deut 7:23 [C]Ps 18:40; 21:12 23:28 [A]Deut 7:20; Josh 24:12 [B]Ex 33:2; 34:11 23:29 [A]Deut 7:22 23:30 [A]Deut 7:22 23:31 [a]Lit *Sea of Reeds* [A]Gen 15:18; Deut 1:7, 8; 11:24 [B]Deut 2:36; Josh 21:44 [C]Josh 24:12, 18 23:32 [a]Lit *cut* [A]Ex 34:12; Deut 7:2 [B]Ex 23:13, 24 23:33 [A]Deut 7:1-5, 16 [B]Ex 34:12; Deut 12:30; Josh 23:13; Judg 2:3; Ps 106:36 24:1 [A]Ex 19:24 [B]Ex 6:23; 28:1; Lev 10:1, 2 [C]Num 11:16 24:3 [a]Or *judgments* [A]Ex 19:8; 24:7; Deut 5:27 24:4 [a]Lit *under* [A]Ex 17:14; 34:27; Deut 31:9 [B]Ex 17:15

23:19 not to boil a young goat. Canaanite ritual, according to excavations at Ras Shamra (ancient Ugarit), called for sacrificial kids to be boiled in milk, but the damaged Ugaritic text does not clearly specify mother's milk. If it were so, then it is understandable that Israel was being prevented from copying pagan idolatrous ritualism. Another option suggests that the dead kid was being boiled in the very substance which had sustained its life; hence the prohibition. Until more archeological information comes to light, the specific religious or cultural reason remains as supposition.

23:23 My angel. Usually taken to be a reference to the Angel of Yahweh, who is distinguished from the Lord who talks about Him as another person. *See note on 3:2.* Yet, He is identified with Him by reason of His forgiving sin and the Lord's name being in Him (v. 21). Neither Moses nor some other messenger or guide qualifies for such descriptions. The key to victory in the upcoming takeover of the land would not be Israel's military skill but the presence of this Angel, who is the pre-incarnate Christ.

23:24 *sacred* pillars. Stone markers of pagan shrines were absolutely intolerable once the land had been taken from the tribes just mentioned in the previous verse.

23:25, 26 Proper worship brought with it due rewards, not only good harvests and a good water supply, but also physical health, including fertility and safe pregnancies.

23:28 hornets. This figurative expression of the panic-producing power of God parallels "My terror" (v. 27), which was the obvious effect of "My angel" having been the advance guard to the conquest (v. 23). In anticipation of the conquest of their land, Israel was being given another reminder that victory depended on God and not their own efforts alone. Fear and panic did play a strategic role in the victories in Transjordan and Canaan (Nu 22:3; Jos 2:9, 11; 5:1; 9:24). An alternative nonfigurative view is based upon the bee or wasp being a heraldic symbol of Egyptian pharaohs whose steady succession of military strikes into Canaan year after year God providentially used to weaken Canaan prior to the invasion by Israel.

23:29, 30 The occupation would be a gradual but effective process taking longer than a year to accomplish, but ensuring full control of a land in good condition and not left desolate by a sweeping and destructive warfare. The reference to the multiplication of wild beasts if the land was desolated underscores the fertility of the land and its ability to support life.

23:31 I will fix your boundary. God gave both broad and more detailed geographic descriptions of the land. Even limited demarcation of borders was sufficient to lay out the extent of their possession. It would extend from the Gulf of Aqabah to the Mediterranean and from the desert in the Negev to the river of the northern boundary.

23:32 make no covenant. International diplomacy, with its parity or suzerainty treaties, was not an option open to Israel in dealing with the tribes living within the designated borders of the Promised Land (Dt 7:1, 2). All these treaties were accompanied by the names of the nations' gods, so it was fitting to deliver a charge not to make a treaty (covenant) with them, nor to serve their pagan gods. The situation with other nations outside the land being given to Israel was different (cf. Dt 20:10–18).

24:4 twelve pillars. Unlike pagan stone markers (23:24), these were built to represent the 12 tribes and were placed alongside the altar Moses had erected in preparation for a covenant ratification ceremony. They did not mark the worship site of a pagan deity.

5 He sent young men of the sons of Israel, [A]and they
offered burnt offerings and sacrificed young bulls
as peace offerings to the LORD. 6 [A]Moses took half
of the blood and put *it* in basins, and the *other* half
of the blood he sprinkled on the altar. 7 Then he
took [A]the book of the covenant and read *it* in the
hearing of the people; and they said, "[B]All that the
LORD has spoken we will do, and we will be obedient!" 8 So [A]Moses took the blood and sprinkled *it*
on the people, and said, "Behold [B]the blood of the
covenant, which the LORD has [a]made with you [b]in
accordance with all these words."

9 Then Moses went up [a]with Aaron, [A]Nadab and
Abihu, and seventy of the elders of Israel, 10 and
[A]they saw the God of Israel; and under His feet
[a,B]there appeared to be a pavement of sapphire,
[b]as clear as the sky itself. 11 Yet He did not stretch
out His hand against the nobles of the sons of Israel; and [A]they saw God, and they ate and drank.

12 Now the LORD said to Moses, "Come up to Me
on the mountain and [a]remain there, and [A]I will give
you the stone tablets [b]with the law and the commandment which I have written for their instruction." 13 So Moses arose [a]with [A]Joshua his [b]servant,
and Moses went up to [B]the mountain of God. 14 But
to the elders he said, "[A]Wait here for us until we return to you. And behold, [B]Aaron and Hur are with
you; whoever [a]has a legal matter, let him approach
them." 15 Then Moses went up to the mountain, and
[A]the cloud covered the mountain. 16 [A]The glory of
the LORD [a]rested on Mount Sinai, and the cloud
covered it for six days; and on the seventh day He
[B]called to Moses from the midst of the cloud. 17 [A]And
to the eyes of the sons of Israel the appearance of
the glory of the LORD was like a [B]consuming fire on
the mountain top. 18 Moses entered the midst of the
cloud [a]as he went up to the mountain; and Moses
was on the mountain [A]forty days and forty nights.

OFFERINGS FOR THE SANCTUARY

25 Then the LORD spoke to Moses, saying, 2 "[A]Tell
the sons of Israel to [a]raise a [b]contribution for
Me; [B]from every man whose heart moves him you
shall [a]raise My [b]contribution. 3 This is the [a]contribu-
tion which you are to [b]raise from them: gold, silver
and bronze, 4 [a,A]blue, purple and scarlet *material,*
fine linen, goat *hair,* 5 rams' skins dyed red, porpoise
skins, acacia wood, 6 [A]oil for lighting, [B]spices for the

24:5 [A]Ex 18:12 24:6 [A]Heb 9:18 24:7 [A]Ex 24:4; Heb 9:19 [B]Ex 24:3 24:8 [a]Lit *cut* [b]Lit *on all* [A]Heb 9:19, 20 [B]Zech 9:11; Matt 26:28; Mark 14:24; Luke 22:20; 1 Cor 11:25; Heb 13:20 24:9 [a]Lit *and* [A]Ex 24:1 24:10 [a]Lit *like a pavement* [b]Lit *and as* [A]Ex 24:11; Num 12:8; Is 6:5; John 1:18; 6:46 [B]Ezek 1:26; 10:1; Rev 4:3 24:11 [A]Gen 16:13; 32:30; Ex 24:10 24:12 [a]Lit *be* [b]Lit *and* [A]Ex 31:18; 32:15; Deut 5:22 24:13 [a]Lit *and* [b]Or *minister* [A]Ex 17:9-14; 33:11 [B]Ex 3:1 24:14 [a]Lit *is a master of matters* [A]Gen 22:5 [B]Ex 17:10, 12 24:15 [A]Ex 19:9 24:16 [a]Lit *dwelt* [A]Ex 16:10; Num 14:10 [B]Ps 99:7 24:17 [A]Ex 3:2; Ezek 1:28 [B]Deut 4:24; 9:3; Heb 12:29 24:18 [a]Lit *and* [A]Ex 34:28; Deut 9:9; 10:10 25:2 [a]Lit *take* [b]Or *heave offering* [A]Ex 35:4-9 [B]Ex 35:21; 1 Chr 29:3, 5, 9; Ezra 2:68; 2 Cor 8:11, 12; 9:7 25:3 [a]Or *heave offering* [b]Lit *take* 25:4 [a]Or *violet* [A]Ex 28:5, 6, 8 25:6 [A]Ex 27:20 [B]Ex 30:23f

24:5 young men. Most probably a reference to firstborn children who officiated until the law appointed the Levites in their place.

24:7 the book of the covenant. Civil, social, and religious laws were received by Moses on Mt. Sinai, orally presented (v. 3), then written down (v. 4), and read to the people. This book contained not only this detailed enlargement of the Decalogue (20:22–23:33), but also the Ten Commandments themselves (20:1–17) and the preliminary abbreviated presentation of the treaty (19:3–6). *See notes on 19:3–8; 20:3–17.*

24:8 sprinkled *it* on the people. By this act, Moses, in response to the positive acceptance and assertion of obedience by the people after hearing the Book of the Covenant read to them, officially sealed the treaty with blood; a not uncommon custom (cf. Ge 15:9–13, 17). Half of the blood used had been sprinkled on the altar as part of the consecration ceremony. The representatives of Israel were thereby qualified to ascend the mountain and participate in the covenant meal with Yahweh (24:11; cf. Heb 9:20).

24:9–11 they saw the God of Israel. The representatives accompanying Moses up the mountain, as per God's instructions, were privileged to have seen God without being consumed by His holiness. Precisely what they saw must remain a moot point and must stay within the description given, which focuses only on what was under His feet. This perhaps indicates that only a partial manifestation took place such as would occur before Moses (33:20), or that the elders, in the presence of divine majesty, beauty, and strength (cf. Ps 96:6), did not dare raise their eyes above His footstool.

24:10 pavement of sapphire. The description sounds like a comparison with lapis lazuli, an opaque blue precious stone much used in Mesopotamia and Egypt at that time.

24:12 stone tablets. For the first time, mention is made of what form the revelation of the law would take: tablets of stone. They were also called the "tablets of the testimony" (31:18) and the "tablets of the covenant" (Dt 9:9).

24:14 Hur. *See note on 17:10.*

24:16–18 This was the first (ending in 32:6) of two (40 days and 40 nights each) trips to Sinai (cf. 34:2–28). The awe-inspiring sight of God's glory cloud, the Shekinah, resting on the mountain and into which Moses disappeared for 40 days and nights, impressed everyone with the singular importance of this event in Israel's history. During these days Moses received all the instructions on the tabernacle and its furnishings and accoutrements (chaps. 25–31). The settling of the Shekinah upon the tabernacle at its completion impressed the Israelites with the singular importance of this structure in Israel's worship of and relationship to Yahweh (40:34–38).

25:1–40:38 The primary focus of attention in the closing chapters is upon the design and construction of the central place of worship for the nation. In preparation for occupation of their land, they had been given a system of law to regulate individual and national life, to prevent exploitation of the poor and the stranger, and to safeguard against polytheism and idolatry. That these safeguards were needed was confirmed by the idolatrous golden calf incident (32:1–35). The very detailed and divinely given blueprint of the tabernacle removes all speculation about whether it has any comparison with, or was somehow derived from, the little portable sanctuaries belonging to various tribal deities. The origin of the tabernacle was found in God and delivered to Moses by special revelation (cf. 25:9, 40; 26:30; Heb 8:5).

25:2 My contribution. Voluntarily and freely the people were given opportunity to personally contribute to the nation's worship center from the list of 14 components and materials needed to build the tabernacle. One wonders how much of their contribution came originally from Egyptian homes and had been thrust into the hands of the Israelites right before the Exodus (cf. 12:35, 36). The people so responded with joy and enthusiasm that they finally had to be restrained from bringing any more gifts (35:21–29; 36:3–7). A similar response occurred centuries later, when King David requested gifts to build the temple (1Ch 29:1–9).

25:4 blue, purple, and scarlet *material*. These colors were produced by dying the thread: blue from a shellfish, purple from the secretion of a murex snail, and crimson from powdered eggs and bodies of certain worms, which attached themselves to holly plants. Deriving different colored dyes from different natural sources demonstrates a substantial degree of technical sophistication with textiles and fabrics. **fine linen.** Egypt had a reputation for excellence in producing finely twined linens.

25:5 rams' skins dyed red. With all the wool removed and then dyed, it resembled moroccan leather. **acacia wood.** A hard, durable, close-grained, and aromatic desert wood avoided by wood-eating insects. It was considered good for cabinet making, and could also be found in sufficient quantities in the Sinai Peninsula.

25:6 spices. For the many years of Bible history, Arabia was highly respected for the variety of balsams she exported.

anointing oil and for the fragrant incense, 7 onyx stones and setting stones for the [A]ephod and for the [a,B]breastpiece. 8 Let them [A]construct a sanctuary for Me, [B]that I may dwell among them. 9 [A]According to all that I am going to show you, *as* the pattern of the tabernacle and the pattern of all its furniture, just so you shall construct *it*.

ARK OF THE COVENANT

10 "[A]They shall construct an ark of acacia wood two and a half [a]cubits [b]long, and one and a half cubits [c]wide, and one and a half cubits [d]high. 11 You shall [A]overlay it with pure gold, inside and out you shall overlay it, and you shall make a gold molding [a]around it. 12 You shall cast four gold rings for it and [a]fasten them on its four feet, and two rings shall be on one side of it and two rings on the other side of it. 13 You shall make poles of acacia wood and overlay them with gold. 14 You shall put the poles into the rings on the sides of the ark, to carry the ark with them. 15 The [A]poles shall [a]remain in the rings of the ark; they shall not be removed from it. 16 You shall [A]put into the ark the testimony which I shall give you.

17 "You shall [A]make a [a]mercy seat of pure gold, two and a half [b]cubits [c]long and one and a half cubits [d]wide. 18 You shall make two cherubim of gold, make them of hammered work [a]at the two ends of the mercy seat. 19 Make one cherub [a]at one end and one cherub [a]at the other end; you shall make the cherubim *of one piece* with the mercy seat at its two ends. 20 [A]The cherubim shall have *their* wings spread upward, covering the mercy seat with their wings and [a]facing one another; the faces of the cherubim are to be *turned* toward the mercy seat. 21 [A]You shall put the mercy seat [a]on top of the ark, and [B]in the ark you shall put the testimony which I will give to you. 22 [A]There I will meet with you; and from above the mercy seat, from [B]between the two cherubim which are upon the ark of the testimony, I will speak to you about all that I will give you in commandment for the sons of Israel.

THE TABLE OF SHOWBREAD

23 "[A]You shall make a table of acacia wood, two cubits [a]long and one cubit [b]wide and one and a half cubits [c]high. 24 You shall overlay it with pure gold and make a gold [A]border around it. 25 You shall make for it a rim of a handbreadth around *it;* and you shall make a gold border for the rim around it. 26 You shall make four gold rings for it and put rings on the four corners which are on its four feet. 27 The rings shall be close to the rim as holders for the poles to carry the table. 28 You shall make the poles of acacia wood and overlay them with gold, so that with them the table may be carried. 29 You shall make its [a,A]dishes and its pans and its jars and its [b]bowls with which to pour drink offerings; you shall make them of pure gold. 30 You shall set [A]the bread of the [a]Presence on the table before Me [b]at all times.

THE GOLDEN LAMPSTAND

31 "[A]Then you shall make a lampstand of pure gold. The lampstand *and* its base and its shaft are to be made of hammered work; its cups, its [a]bulbs and its flowers shall be *of one piece* with it. 32 [A]Six branches shall go out from its sides; three branches of the lampstand from its one side and three branches of the lampstand from its [a]other side.

25:7 [a]*Or pouch* [A]Ex 28:4, 6-14 [B]Ex 28:4, 15-30 25:8 [A]Ex 36:1-5 [B]Ex 29:45, 46; Num 5:3; Deut 12:11; 1 Kin 6:13; 2 Cor 6:16; Rev 21:3 25:9 [A]Ex 25:40; 26:30; Acts 7:44; Heb 8:2, 5 25:10 [a]I.e. One cubit equals approx 18 in. [b]Lit *its length* [c]Lit *its width* [d]Lit *its height* [A]Ex 37:1-9; Deut 10:3; Heb 9:4 25:11 [a]Lit *on it round about* [A]Heb 9:4 25:12 [a]*Or put* 25:15 [a]Lit *be* [A]1 Kin 8:8 25:16 [A]Ex 40:20; Deut 10:2; 31:26; 1 Kin 8:9; Heb 9:4 25:17 [a]Lit *propitiatory,* and so through v 22 [b]I.e. One cubit equals approx 18 in. [c]Lit *its length* [d]Lit *its width* [A]Ex 37:6 25:18 [a]Lit *from* 25:19 [a]Lit *from* 25:20 [a]Lit *their faces to* [A]1 Kin 8:7; 1 Chr 28:18; Heb 9:5 25:21 [a]Lit *above, upon* [A]Ex 26:34; 40:20 [B]Ex 25:16 25:22 [A]Ex 29:42, 43; 30:6, 36; Lev 16:2; Num 17:4 [B]Num 7:89; 1 Sam 4:4; 2 Sam 6:2; 2 Kin 19:15; Ps 80:1; Is 37:16 25:23 [a]Lit *its length* [b]Lit *its width* [c]Lit *its height* [A]Ex 37:10-16 25:24 [A]Ex 25:11 25:29 [a]*Or platters* [b]Lit *libation bowls* [A]Ex 37:16; Num 4:7 25:30 [a]Lit *Face* [b]*Or continually* [A]Ex 39:36; 40:23; Lev 24:5-9 25:31 [a]*Or calyx* [A]Ex 37:17-24; 1 Kin 7:49; Zech 4:2 25:32 [a]Lit *second* [A]Ex 37:18

25:7 onyx stones. Sometimes thought to be chrysoprase quartz, a product known to the Egyptians and with which Israel was no doubt familiar. The LXX translated it as beryl.

25:8 I may dwell. The tabernacle, a noun derived from the verb "to dwell," was an appropriate designation for that which was to be the place of God's presence with His people. His presence would be between the cherubim and from there He would meet with Moses (v. 22).

25:9 tabernacle. The Pentateuch records 5 different names for the tabernacle: 1) "sanctuary," denoting a sacred place or set apart, i.e., holy, place; 2) "tent," denoting a temporary or collapsible dwelling; 3) "tabernacle," from "to dwell," denoting the place of God's presence (as well as other titles); 4) "tabernacle of the congregation, or meeting"; and 5) "tabernacle of the testimony."

25:11 pure gold. The technology of the day was sufficient to refine gold.

25:16 the testimony. This designation for the two tablets of stone containing the Ten Commandments which were placed inside the ark explains why it was also called "the ark of the testimony" (v. 22), and shows why it was appropriate to call the whole structure "the tabernacle" or "the tent of the testimony." "The ark of the covenant of the LORD of all the earth" (Jos 3:11) and "the holy ark" (2Ch 35:3) were alternative designations.

25:17 mercy seat. The lid or cover of the ark was the "mercy seat" or the place at which atonement took place. Between the Shekinah glory cloud above the ark and the tablets of law inside the ark was the blood-sprinkled cover. Blood from the sacrifices stood between God and the broken law of God!

25:18 cherubim. Forged as one with the golden cover of the ark were two angelic beings rising up on each end and facing each other, their wings stretching up and over forming an arch. Cherubim, associated with the majestic glory and presence of God (cf. Eze 10:1–22), were appropriately woven into the tabernacle curtains and the veil for the Holy of Holies (26:1, 31), for this place was where God was present with His people. Scripture reveals them as the bearers of God's throne (1Sa 4:4; Is 37:16) and the guardians of the Garden of Eden and the Tree of Life (Ge 3:24).

25:30 bread of the Presence. Each week a new batch of 12 loaves of bread was laid on a table on the N side of the Holy Place. The utensils for this table were also made of refined gold (v. 29). This "Bread of His Presence" was not set out in order to feed Israel's God, unlike food placed in pagan shrines and temples, but to acknowledge that the 12 tribes were sustained constantly under the watchful eye and care of their Lord. The bread was eaten in the Holy Place each Sabbath by the priests on duty (Lv 24:5–9). The bread of the Presence is understood to typify the Lord Jesus Christ as the Bread which came from heaven (Jn 6:32–35).

25:31 lampstand. Situated opposite the table of the bread of the Presence on the S side of the Holy Place stood an ornate lampstand, or menorah, patterned after a flowering almond tree. It provided light for the priests serving in the Holy Place. Care was taken, according to God's instructions (27:20, 21; 30:7, 8; Lv 24:1–4), to keep it well supplied with pure olive oil so that it would not be extinguished. The lampstand is seen as typifying the Lord Jesus Christ, who was the true Light which came into the world (Jn 1:6–9; 8:12).

33 [A]Three cups *shall be* shaped like almond *blos-*
soms in the one branch, a [a]bulb and a flower, and
three cups shaped like almond *blossoms* in the
[b]other branch, a [a]bulb and a flower—so for six
branches going out from the lampstand; 34 and
[A]in the lampstand four cups shaped like almond
blossoms, its [a]bulbs and its flowers. 35 [A]A [a]bulb
shall be under the *first* pair of branches *coming*
out of it, and a [a]bulb under the *second* pair of
branches *coming* out of it, and a [a]bulb under the
third pair of branches *coming* out of it, for the six
branches coming out of the lampstand. 36 [A]Their
[a]bulbs and their branches *shall be of one piece*
with it; all of it shall be one piece of hammered
work of pure gold. 37 Then you shall make its lamps
seven *in number;* and [A]they shall [a]mount its lamps
so as to shed light on the space in front of it. 38 Its
snuffers and [a]their trays *shall be* of pure gold. 39 It
shall be made from a talent of pure gold, with all
these utensils. 40 [A]See that you make *them* [B]after
the pattern for them, which was shown to you on
the mountain.

CURTAINS OF LINEN

26 "[A]Moreover you shall make the tabernacle
with ten curtains of fine twisted linen and
[a]blue and purple and scarlet *material;* you shall
make them with cherubim, the work of a skillful
workman. 2 The length of each curtain shall be
twenty-eight [a]cubits, and the width of each curtain
four [a]cubits; all the curtains shall have [b]the same
measurements. 3 Five curtains shall be [a]joined to
one another, and *the other* five curtains *shall be*
[a]joined to one another. 4 You shall make loops of
[a]blue on the edge of the [b]outermost curtain in the
first set, and likewise you shall make *them* on the
edge of the curtain that is outermost in the second
[c]set. 5 You shall make fifty loops in the one curtain,
and you shall make fifty loops on the [a]edge of the
curtain that is in the second [b]set; the loops shall be

25:33 [a]Or *calyx* [b]Lit *one branch* [A]Ex 37:19 25:34 [a]Or *calyxes* [A]Ex 37:20 25:35 [a]Or *calyx* [A]Ex 37:21 25:36 [a]Or *calyxes* [A]Ex 37:22 25:37 [a]Lit *raise up* [A]Num 8:2 25:38 [a]Lit *its snuff dishes* 25:40 [A]Heb 8:5 [B]Ex 25:9; 26:30; Num 8:4; Acts 7:44 26:1 [a]Or *violet* [A]Ex 36:8-19 26:2 [a]I.e. One cubit equals approx 18 in. [b]Lit *one measure* 26:3 [a]Or *coupled* 26:4 [a]Or *violet* [b]Lit *one curtain from the end in the coupling* [c]Lit *coupling* 26:5 [a]Lit *end* [b]Lit *coupling*

25:39 talent. Approximately 75 pounds.
25:40 Cf. Heb 8:5.
26:1 ten curtains. The beauty of these curtains could be seen only from the inside, the thick outer protective covering of goats' hair drapes, and ram and porpoise skins (v. 14) hiding them from the view of anyone except the priests who entered.

THE PLAN OF THE TABERNACLE

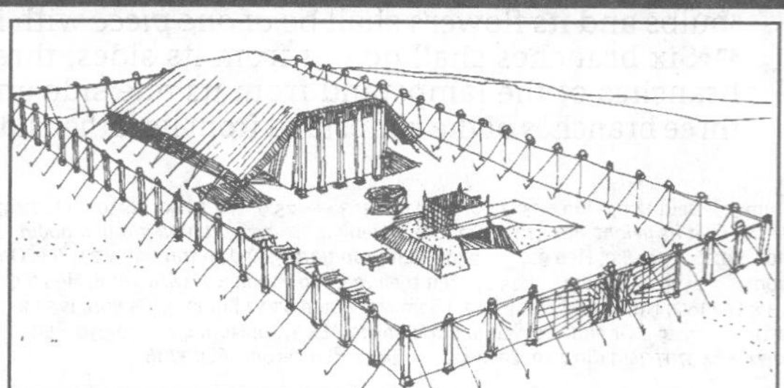

The tabernacle was to provide a place where God might dwell among His people. The term *tabernacle* sometimes refers to the tent, including the holy place and the holy of holies, which was covered with embroidered curtains. But in other places it refers to the entire complex, including the curtained court in which the tent stood.

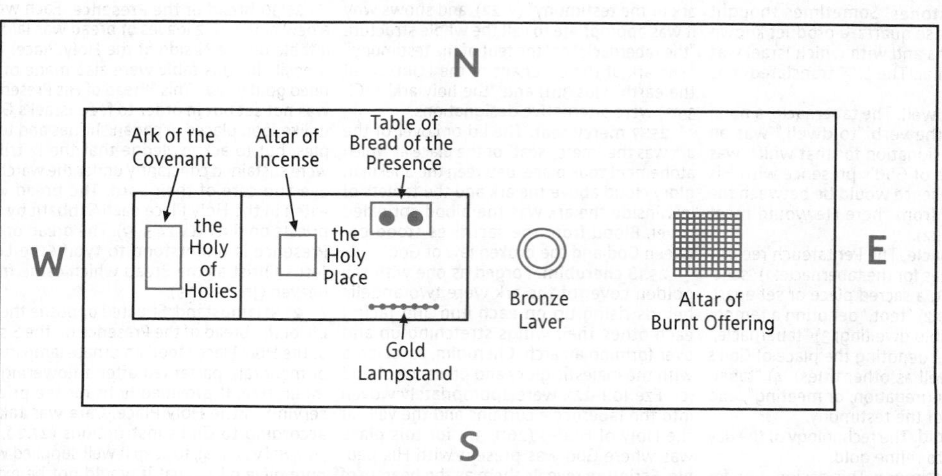

This illustration shows relative positions of the tabernacle furniture used in Israelite worship. The tabernacle is enlarged for clarity.

opposite each other. 6 You shall make fifty clasps of
gold, and [a]join the curtains to one another with the
clasps so that the [b]tabernacle will be a unit.

CURTAINS OF GOATS' HAIR

7 "Then [A]you shall make curtains of goats' *hair* for
a tent over the tabernacle; you shall make eleven
curtains in all. 8 The length of each curtain *shall be*
thirty [a]cubits, and the width of each curtain four
cubits; the eleven curtains shall have [b]the same
measurements. 9 You shall [a]join five curtains by
themselves and the *other* six curtains by themselves, and you shall double over the sixth curtain
[b]at the front of the tent. 10 You shall make fifty loops
on the edge of the [a]curtain that is outermost in the
first [b]set, and fifty loops on the edge of the curtain
that is outermost in the second [b]set.
11 "You shall make fifty clasps of [a]bronze, and you
shall put the clasps into the loops and [b]join the tent
together so that it will be [c]a unit. 12 The [a]overlapping
part that is left over in the curtains of the tent, the
half curtain that is left over, shall lap over the back of
the tabernacle. 13 The cubit on one side and the cubit
on the other, of what is left over in the length of the
curtains of the tent, shall lap over the sides of the
tabernacle on one side and on the other, to cover it.
14 [A]You shall make a covering for the tent of rams' skins
[a]dyed red and a covering of porpoise skins above.

BOARDS AND SOCKETS

15 "Then you shall make [A]the boards for the tabernacle of acacia wood, standing upright. 16 Ten cubits
shall be the length of [a]each board and one and a
half cubits the width of each board. 17 *There shall be*
two tenons for each board, [a]fitted to one another;
thus you shall do for all the boards of the tabernacle. 18 You shall make the boards for the tabernacle:
twenty boards [a]for the south side. 19 You shall make
forty [a,A]sockets of silver under the twenty boards,
two [a]sockets under one board for its two tenons
and two [a]sockets under another board for its two
tenons; 20 and for the second side of the tabernacle,
on the north side, twenty boards, 21 and their forty
[a]sockets of silver; two [a]sockets under one board and
two [a]sockets under another board. 22 For the [a]rear
of the tabernacle, to the west, you shall make six
boards. 23 You shall make two boards for the corners
of the tabernacle at the [a]rear. 24 They shall be double
beneath, and together they shall be complete [a]to
its top [b]to the first ring; thus it shall be with both
of them: they shall form the two corners. 25 There
shall be eight boards with their [a]sockets of silver,
sixteen [a]sockets; two [a]sockets under one board and
two [a]sockets under another board.
26 "Then you shall make [A]bars of acacia wood, five
for the boards of one side of the tabernacle, 27 and
five bars for the boards of the [a]other side of the tabernacle, and five bars for the boards of the side of the
tabernacle for the [b]rear *side* to the west. 28 The middle
bar in the [a]center of the boards shall pass through
from end to end. 29 You shall overlay the boards with
gold and make their rings of gold *as* holders for the
bars; and you shall overlay the bars with gold. 30 Then
you shall erect the tabernacle [A]according to its plan
which you have been shown in the mountain.

THE VEIL AND SCREEN

31 "You shall make [A]a veil of [a]blue and purple and
scarlet *material* and fine twisted linen; it shall be
made with cherubim, the work of a skillful workman. 32 You shall [a]hang it on four pillars of acacia
overlaid with gold, their hooks *also being of* gold,
on four [b]sockets of silver. 33 You shall [a]hang up the
veil under the clasps, and shall bring in [A]the ark
of the testimony there within the veil; and the veil
shall [b]serve for you as a partition [B]between the holy
place and the holy of holies. 34 [A]You shall put the
mercy seat on the ark of the testimony in the holy
of holies. 35 [A]You shall set the table outside the veil,
and the [B]lampstand opposite the table on the side
of the tabernacle toward the south; and you shall
put the table on the north side.
36 "[A]You shall make a screen for the doorway of
the tent of [a]blue and purple and scarlet *material* and
fine twisted linen, the work of a [b]weaver. 37 [A]You shall
make five pillars of acacia for the screen and overlay them with gold, their hooks *also being of* gold;
and you shall cast five [a]sockets of [b]bronze for them.

THE BRONZE ALTAR

27 "And you shall make [A]the altar of acacia
wood, five [a]cubits long and five cubits
wide; the altar shall be square, and its height
shall be three cubits. 2 You shall make [A]its horns
on its four corners; its horns shall be of one piece
with it, and you shall overlay it with [a]bronze.

26:6 [a]Or *couple* [b]Or *dwelling place,* and so throughout the ch 26:7 [A]Ex 36:14 26:8 [a]I.e. One cubit equals approx 18 in. [b]Lit *one measure* 26:9 [a]Or *couple* [b]Lit *toward the front of the face of the tent* 26:10 [a]Lit *one curtain* [b]Lit *coupling* 26:11 [a]Or *copper* [b]Or *couple* [c]Lit *one* 26:12 [a]Lit *excess* 26:14 [a]Or *tanned* [A]Ex 36:19 26:15 [A]Ex 36:20-34 26:16 [a]Lit *the* 26:17 [a]Lit *bound* 26:18 [a]Lit *toward the side of the Negev to the south* 26:19 [a]Or *bases* [A]Ex 38:27 26:21 [a]Or *bases* 26:22 [a]Lit *extreme parts* 26:23 [a]Lit *extreme parts* 26:24 [a]Or *at its head* [b]Or *with reference to* 26:25 [a]Or *bases* 26:26 [A]Ex 36:31 26:27 [a]Lit *second* [b]Lit *extreme parts* 26:28 [a]Lit *midst* 26:30 [A]Ex 25:9, 40; Acts 7:44; Heb 8:5 26:31 [a]Or *violet* [A]Ex 36:35, 36; 2 Chr 3:14; Matt 27:51; Heb 9:3 26:32 [a]Lit *put* [b]Or *bases* 26:33 [a]Lit *put* [b]Lit *separate for you between* [A]Ex 25:16; 40:21 [B]Heb 9:2f 26:34 [A]Ex 25:21; 40:20; Lev 16:2 26:35 [A]Ex 40:22 [B]Ex 40:24 26:36 [a]Or *violet* [b]Lit *variegator;* i.e. a weaver in colors [A]Ex 36:37 26:37 [a]Or *bases* [b]Or *copper* [A]Ex 36:38 27:1 [a]I.e. One cubit equals approx 18 in. [A]Ex 38:1-7 27:2 [a]Or *copper,* and so for *bronze* throughout the ch [A]Ps 118:27

26:7 eleven curtains. The extra length of the outer drapes doubled as a covering for the front and back of the tabernacle structure (vv. 9–13).

26:15–29 The frame or trellis work, on which the curtains and outer coverings were draped, also received precise instructions. The portability of the whole structure was obvious. Throughout the wilderness wanderings, it could be quickly dismantled and readied for transport, and just as rapidly reerected.

26:30 according to its plan. Again (cf. 25:40) the warning was sounded that the blueprint must be carefully followed. Nothing was to be left to human guesswork, no matter how skilled the craftsmen might have been.

26:31–34 A veil, similar in design to the inner curtains (*see note on 26:1*), divided the tabernacle into the Holy Place and the Most Holy, or lit. the Holy of Holies.

26:36 screen. Another curtain or veil, without the embroidered cherubim motif, was made to cover the entrance way into the Holy Place.

27:1 altar. The largest piece of equipment, also known as the "altar of burnt offering" (Lv 4:7, 10, 18), was situated in the courtyard of

3 You shall make its pails for removing its ashes, and
its shovels and its basins and its forks and its firepans; you shall make all its utensils of bronze. 4 You
shall make for it a grating of network of bronze,
and on the net you shall make four bronze rings
[a]at its four corners. 5 You shall put it beneath, under the ledge of the altar, so that the net will reach
halfway up the altar. 6 You shall make poles for the
altar, poles of acacia wood, and overlay them with
bronze. 7 Its poles shall be inserted into the rings, so
that the poles shall be on the two sides of the altar
[A]when it is carried. 8 You shall make it hollow with
planks; [A]as it was shown to you in the mountain,
so they shall make *it*.

COURT OF THE TABERNACLE

9 "You shall make [A]the court of the [a]tabernacle. [b]On
the south side *there shall be* hangings for the court
of fine twisted linen one hundred cubits long for
one side; 10 and its pillars *shall be* twenty, with their
twenty [a]sockets of bronze; the hooks of the pillars and
their [b]bands *shall be* of silver. 11 Likewise for the north
side in length *there shall be* hangings one hundred
cubits long, and its twenty pillars with their twenty
[a]sockets of bronze; the hooks of the pillars and their
bands *shall be* of silver. 12 *For* the width of the court
on the west side *shall be* hangings of fifty cubits *with*
their ten pillars and their ten [a]sockets. 13 The width
of the court on the [a]east side *shall be* fifty cubits.
14 The hangings for the *one* [a]side *of the gate shall be*
fifteen cubits *with* their three pillars and their three
[b]sockets. 15 And for the [a]other [b]side *shall be* hangings
of fifteen cubits *with* their three pillars and their
three [c]sockets. 16 For the gate of the court *there shall*
be a screen of twenty cubits, of [a]blue and purple and
scarlet *material* and fine twisted linen, the work of a
[b]weaver, *with* their four pillars and their four [c]sockets.
17 All the pillars around the court shall be furnished
with silver bands *with* their hooks of silver and their
[a]sockets of bronze. 18 The length of the court *shall be*
one hundred cubits, and the width fifty throughout,
and the height five cubits of fine twisted linen, and
their [a]sockets of bronze. 19 All the utensils of the tabernacle *used* in all its service, and all its pegs, and all
the pegs of the court, *shall be* of bronze.
20 "You shall charge the sons of Israel, that they
bring you [A]clear oil of beaten olives for the [a]light,
to make a lamp [b]burn continually. 21 In the [A]tent of
meeting, outside [B]the veil which is before the testimony, [C]Aaron and his sons shall keep it in order
from evening to morning before the LORD; *it shall*
be a perpetual [D]statute throughout their generations
[a]for the sons of Israel.

GARMENTS OF THE PRIESTS

28 "Then [A]bring near to yourself Aaron your
brother, and his sons with him, from among
the sons of Israel, to minister as priest to Me—Aaron,
[B]Nadab and Abihu, Eleazar and Ithamar, Aaron's
sons. 2 You shall make [A]holy garments for Aaron your
brother, for glory and for beauty. 3 You shall speak
to all the [a,A]skillful persons [B]whom I have endowed
with [b]the spirit of wisdom, that they make Aaron's
garments to consecrate him, that he may minister
as priest to Me. 4 These are the garments which they
shall make: a [a,A]breastpiece and an ephod and a robe
and a tunic of checkered work, a turban and a sash,
and they shall make holy garments for Aaron your
brother and his sons, that he may minister as priest
to Me. 5 They shall take [A]the gold and the [a]blue and
the purple and the scarlet *material* and the fine linen.
6 "They shall also make [A]the ephod of gold, of
[a]blue and purple *and* scarlet *material* and fine
twisted linen, the work of the skillful workman.
7 It shall have two shoulder pieces joined to its two
ends, that it may be joined. 8 The skillfully woven
band, which is on it, shall be like its workmanship,
[a]of the same material: of gold, of [b]blue and purple

27:4 [a]Lit *on* 27:7 [A]Num 4:15 27:8 [A]Ex 25:40; 26:30; Acts 7:44; Heb 8:5 27:9 [a]Or *dwelling place* [b]Lit *For the side of the Negev to the south* [A]Ex 38:9-20 27:10 [a]Or *bases* [b]Or *fillets, rings* 27:11 [a]Or *bases* 27:12 [a]Or *bases* 27:13 [a]Lit *east side eastward* 27:14 [a]Lit *shoulder* [b]Or *bases* 27:15 [a]Lit *second* [b]Lit *shoulder* [c]Or *bases* 27:16 [a]Or *violet* [b]Lit *variegator;* i.e. a weaver in colors [c]Or *bases* 27:17 [a]Or *bases* 27:18 [a]Or *bases* 27:20 [a]Or *luminary* [b]Lit *ascend* [A]Ex 35:8, 28; Lev 24:1-4 27:21 [a]Lit *from* [A]Ex 25:22; 29:42; 30:36 [B]Ex 26:31, 33 [C]Ex 30:8; 1 Sam 3:3; 2 Chr 13:11 [D]Ex 28:43; 29:9; Lev 3:17; 16:34; Num 18:23; 19:21; 1 Sam 30:25 28:1 [A]Num 18:7; Ps 99:6; Heb 5:1, 4 [B]Ex 24:1, 9 28:2 [A]Ex 29:5, 29; 31:10; 39:1-31; Lev 8:7-9, 30 28:3 [a]Lit *wise of heart* [b]I.e. artistic skill [A]Ex 31:6; 35:25, 31-35; 36:1 [B]Ex 31:3; Is 11:2; 1 Cor 12:7-11; Eph 1:17 28:4 [a]Or *pouch* [A]Ex 28:15-43 28:5 [a]Or *violet* [A]Ex 25:3 28:6 [a]Or *violet* [A]Ex 39:2-7; Lev 8:7 28:8 [a]Lit *from it* [b]Or *violet*

the tabernacle. It was covered, not in gold as the items inside the Holy Place, but in bronze. Like the other pieces of furniture and equipment, it was also built to be carried by poles (vv. 6, 7).

27:3 All the altar's utensils and accessories were also made of bronze, not gold.

27:9 the court of the tabernacle. The dimensions of the rectangular courtyard space, bordered by curtains and poles around the tabernacle were also precisely given (vv. 9–19; 150 ft. by 75 ft.). The outer hangings were high enough, 5 cubits or 7.5 ft., to block all view of the interior of the courtyard (v. 18). Entry into the courtyard of God's dwelling place was not gained just generally and freely from all quarters.

27:16 gate of the court. The curtain forming the covering for the entranceway into the courtyard was colored differently from that which surrounded the oblong courtyard. Clearly there was only one way to enter this very special place where God had chosen to place the evidence of His dwelling with His people.

27:20, 21 clear oil of beaten olives. The clear oil from crushed unripened olives granted almost a smoke-free light. The people were to provide the fuel to maintain the light needed by the High Priest and his priestly staff in the Holy Place.

28:1 minister as priest to Me. The 3-fold repetition of this phrase in the opening words about Aaron's priestly wardrobe would appear to stress the importance of his role in the religious life of the nation. Aaron's sons were part of the priesthood being set up. The Heb. text groups the sons in two pairs, the first pair being Nadab and Abihu, both of whom died because of wanton disregard of God's instructions (Lv 10:1, 2). Aaron and his descendants, as well as the tribe of Levi, were selected by God to be Israel's priests—they did not appoint themselves to the position. The law clearly defined their duties for worship and the sacrifices in the tabernacle and for the individual worshiper and the nation's covenantal relationship to God.

28:2 for glory and for beauty. The garments were designed to exalt the office and function of the priesthood, vividly marking out Aaron as a special person playing a special mediatorial role—they were "holy" vestments. In the OT priestly system for the nation of Israel, such dress maintained the priest-laity distinction.

28:3 skillful persons. This was the first reference in God's instructions to Moses that certain men would be especially empowered by Him to work skillfully on this construction project.

28:5–13 ephod. Whenever Aaron entered the sanctuary, he carried with him on his shoulders the badge and the engraved stones that were representative of the 12 tribes.

and scarlet *material* and fine twisted linen. 9 You
shall take two onyx stones and engrave on them the
names of the sons of Israel, 10 six of their names on
the one stone and the names of the remaining six
on the [a]other stone, according to their birth. 11 [a]As a
jeweler engraves a signet, you shall engrave the two
stones according to the names of the sons of Israel;
you shall [b]set them in filigree *settings* of gold. 12 You
shall put the two stones on the shoulder pieces of
the ephod, *as* stones of memorial for the sons of
Israel, and Aaron shall [A]bear their names before
the LORD on his two shoulders [B]for a memorial.
13 [A]You shall make filigree *settings* of gold, 14 and
two chains of pure gold; you shall make them of
twisted cordage work, and you shall put the corded
chains on the filigree *settings.*

15 "[A]You shall make a [a]breastpiece of judgment,
the work of a skillful workman; like the work of
the ephod you shall make it: of gold, of [b]blue and
purple and scarlet *material* and fine twisted linen
you shall make it. 16 It shall be square *and* folded
double, a span [a]in length and a span [a]in width. 17 You
shall [a]mount on it four rows of stones; the first row
shall be a row of ruby, topaz and emerald; 18 and the
second row a turquoise, a sapphire and a diamond;
19 and the third row a jacinth, an agate and an amethyst; 20 and the fourth row a beryl and an onyx
and a jasper; they shall be [a]set in gold filigree. 21 The
stones shall be according to the names of the sons of
Israel: twelve, according to their names; they shall
be *like* the engravings of a seal, each [A]according to
his name for the twelve tribes. 22 You shall make
on the [a]breastpiece chains of twisted cordage work
in pure gold. 23 You shall make on the breastpiece
two rings of gold, and shall put the two rings on
the two ends of the breastpiece. 24 You shall put the
two cords of gold on the two rings at the ends of the
breastpiece. 25 You shall put the *other* two ends of
the two cords on the two filigree *settings,* and put
them on the shoulder pieces of the ephod, at the
front of it. 26 You shall make two rings of gold and
shall place them on the two ends of the breastpiece,
on the edge of it, which is toward the inner side of
the ephod. 27 You shall make two rings of gold and
put them on the bottom of the two shoulder pieces
of the ephod, on the front of it close to the place
where it is joined, above the skillfully woven band
of the ephod. 28 They shall bind the breastpiece by
its rings to the rings of the ephod with a [a]blue cord,
so that it will be on the skillfully woven band of the
ephod, and that the breastpiece will not come loose
from the ephod. 29 Aaron shall carry the names of
the sons of Israel in the breastpiece of judgment
over his heart when he enters the holy place, for a
memorial before the LORD continually. 30 [A]You shall
put in the breastpiece of judgment the [a,B]Urim and
the Thummim, and they shall be over Aaron's heart
when he goes in before the LORD; and Aaron shall
carry the judgment of the sons of Israel over his
heart before the LORD continually.

31 "[A]You shall make the robe of the ephod all of
[a]blue. 32 There shall be an opening [a]at its top in the
middle of it; around its opening there shall be a
binding of woven work, like the opening of a coat
of mail, so that it will not be torn. 33 You shall make
on its hem pomegranates of blue and purple and
scarlet *material,* all around on its hem, and bells of
gold between them all around: 34 a golden bell and
a pomegranate, a golden bell and a pomegranate,
all around on the hem of the robe. 35 It shall be on
Aaron [a]when he ministers; and [b]its tinkling shall
be heard when he enters and [c]leaves the holy place
before the LORD, so that he will not die.

36 "You shall also make [A]a plate of pure gold and
shall engrave on it, like the engravings of a seal,
'[B]Holy to the LORD.' 37 You shall [a]fasten it on a [b]blue
cord, and it shall be on the turban; it shall be at the
front of the turban. 38 It shall be on Aaron's forehead,
and Aaron shall [a,A]take away the iniquity of the holy
things which the sons of Israel consecrate, with
regard to all their holy gifts; and it shall always be
on his forehead, that [B]they may be accepted before
the LORD.

39 "You shall weave [A]the tunic of checkered work
of fine linen, and shall make a turban of fine linen,
and you shall make a sash, the work of a [a]weaver.

28:10 [a]Lit *second* 28:11 [a]Lit *A work of a lapidary, engravings of a seal* [b]Lit *make them to be surrounded* 28:12 [A]Ex 28:29; 39:6f [B]Ex 39:7; Lev 24:7; Num 31:54; Josh 4:7; 1 Cor 11:24f 28:13 [A]Ex 39:16-18 28:15 [a]Or *pouch* [b]Or *violet* [A]Ex 39:8-21 28:16 [a]Lit *its* 28:17 [a]Lit *fill in a setting of stones, four rows of stones* 28:20 [a]Lit *interwoven with gold in their settings* 28:21 [A]Rev 7:4-8; 21:12 28:22 [a]Or *pouch,* and so through v 30 28:28 [a]Or *violet* 28:30 [a]I.e. lights and perfections [A]Lev 8:8 [B]Num 27:21; Deut 33:8; Ezra 2:63; Neh 7:65 28:31 [a]Or *violet* [A]Ex 39:22-26 28:32 [a]Or *for his head* 28:35 [a]Lit *for ministering* [b]Lit *its sound* [c]Lit *comes out* from 28:36 [A]Ex 39:30, 31; Lev 8:9 [B]Zech 14:20 28:37 [a]Lit *place* [b]Or *violet* 28:38 [a]Or *bear* [A]Lev 10:17; 22:16; Num 18:1 [B]Lev 1:4; 22:27; 23:11; Is 56:7 28:39 [a]Lit *variegator;* i.e. a weaver in colors [A]Ex 39:27-29

28:15–30 breastpiece of judgment. The 12 precious stones, each engraved with a tribe's name, colorfully and ornately displayed Aaron's representative role of intercession for the tribes before the Lord. The breastpiece was to be securely fastened to the ephod so as not to come loose from it (v. 28 and 39:21). Thus, to speak of the ephod after this was done would be to speak of the whole ensemble.

28:30 Urim and the Thummim. The etymological source of these two terms, as well as the material nature of the objects represented by them, cannot be established with any degree of finality. Clearly two separate objects were inserted into the breastpiece and became thereby an essential part of the High Priest's official regalia. Aaron and his successors bore over their heart "the judgment of the sons of Israel," i.e., "judgment" in the sense of giving a verdict or decision. The passages in which the terms appear (Lv 8:8; Nu 27:21; Dt 33:8; 1Sa 28:6; Ezr 2:63; Ne 7:65) and those which record inquiries of the Lord when a High Priest with the ephod was present (Jos 9:14; Jdg 1:1, 2; 20:18; 1Sa 10:22; 23:2, 4, 10–12; 1Ch 10:14) allow for the following conclusions: 1) that these two objects represented the right of the High Priest to request guidance for the acknowledged leader who could not approach God directly, as Moses had done, but had to come via the God-ordained priestly structure, and 2) that the revelation then received gave specific direction for an immediate problem or crisis, and went beyond what could be associated with some sort of sacred lots providing merely a wordless "yes" and "no" response.

28:31–35 robe. The priest's outer garment.

28:32 coat of mail. A flexible metal covering used by the Egyptians for protection in battle.

28:33 bells of gold. The sound of the tinkling bells sewn on the hem of the High Priest's robe signaled those waiting outside the Holy Place that their representative ministering before the Lord was still alive and moving about, fulfilling his duties.

28:36–38 turban. The headdress carried the declaration essential to worship and priestly representation, namely the holiness of the Lord, and in so doing reminded the High Priest and all others that their approach to God must be done with reverence.

28:39 tunic ... sash. An undergarment.

40 "For Aaron's sons you shall make [A]tunics; you
shall also make sashes for them, and you shall make
[a,B]caps for them, for glory and for beauty. 41 You shall
put them on Aaron your brother and on his sons
with him; and you shall [A]anoint them and [a]ordain
them and consecrate them, that they may serve Me
as priests. 42 You shall make for them [A]linen breeches
to cover *their* bare flesh; they shall [a]reach from the
loins even to the thighs. 43 They shall be on Aaron
and on his sons when they enter the tent of meeting, or [A]when they approach the altar to minister
in the holy place, so that they do not incur [a]guilt
and die. [B]It *shall be* a statute forever to him and to
his [b]descendants after him.

CONSECRATION OF THE PRIESTS

29 "[A]Now this is [a]what you shall do to them to
consecrate them to minister as priests to Me:
take one young bull and two rams without blemish, 2 and [A]unleavened bread and unleavened cakes
mixed with oil, and unleavened wafers [a]spread with
oil; you shall make them of fine wheat flour. 3 You
shall put them in one basket, and present them in
the basket along with the bull and the two rams.
4 Then [A]you shall bring Aaron and his sons to the
doorway of the tent of meeting and wash them
with water. 5 You shall take the garments, and put
on Aaron the [A]tunic and [B]the robe of the ephod and
[C]the ephod and [D]the [a]breastpiece, and gird him with
the skillfully [E]woven band of the ephod; 6 and you
shall set the [A]turban on his head and put [B]the holy
crown on the turban. 7 Then you shall take [A]the
anointing oil and pour it on his head and anoint
him. 8 You shall bring his sons and put [A]tunics on
them. 9 You shall gird them with [A]sashes, Aaron and
his sons, and bind [a]caps on them, and they shall
have [B]the priesthood by a perpetual statute. So you
shall [b,C]ordain Aaron and his sons.

THE SACRIFICES

10 "Then you shall bring the bull before the tent
of meeting, and Aaron and his sons shall [A]lay their
hands on the head of the bull. 11 You shall slaughter
the bull before the LORD at the doorway of the tent
of meeting. 12 You shall [A]take some of the blood of
the bull and put *it* on [B]the horns of the altar with
your finger; and you shall pour out all the blood at
the base of the altar. 13 You shall [A]take all the fat that
covers the entrails and the [a]lobe of the liver, and the
two kidneys and the fat that is on them, and offer
them up in smoke on the altar. 14 But [A]the flesh of
the bull and its hide and its refuse, you shall burn
with fire outside the camp; it is a sin offering.
15 "[A]You shall also take the one ram, and Aaron and
his sons shall lay their hands on the head of the ram;
16 and you shall slaughter the ram and shall take its
blood and sprinkle it around on the altar. 17 Then you
shall cut the ram into its pieces, and wash its entrails
and its legs, and put *them* [a]with its pieces and [b]its
head. 18 You shall offer up in smoke the whole ram
on the altar; it is a burnt offering to the LORD: [A]it is
a soothing aroma, an offering by fire to the LORD.
19 "Then [A]you shall take the [a]other ram, and Aaron
and his sons shall lay their hands on the head of the
ram. 20 You shall slaughter the ram, and take some
of its blood and put *it* on the lobe of Aaron's right
ear and on the lobes of his sons' right ears and on
the thumbs of their right hands and on the big toes
of their right feet, and sprinkle the *rest of the* blood
around on the altar. 21 Then you shall take some of the
blood that is on the altar and some of the [A]anointing
oil, and sprinkle *it* on Aaron and on his garments and
on his sons and on his sons' garments with him; so
he and his garments shall be consecrated, as well as
his sons and his sons' garments with him.
22 "You shall also take the fat from the ram and
the fat tail, and the fat that covers the entrails and
the [a]lobe of the liver, and the two kidneys and the
fat that is on them and the right thigh (for it is a
ram of [b]ordination), 23 and one cake of bread and
[A]one cake of bread *mixed with* oil and one wafer
from the basket of unleavened bread which is *set*
before the LORD; 24 and you shall put [a]all these [b]in
the [c]hands of Aaron and [b]in the [c]hands of his sons,
and shall wave them as a wave offering before the
LORD. 25 [A]You shall take them from their hands, and
offer them up in smoke on the altar on the burnt
offering for a soothing aroma before the LORD; it
is an offering by fire to the LORD.
26 "Then you shall take [A]the breast of Aaron's ram
of [a]ordination, and wave it as a wave offering before
the LORD; and it shall be your portion. 27 You shall
consecrate the breast of the wave offering and the
thigh of the heave offering which was waved and
which was [a]offered from the ram of [b]ordination,
from the one which was for Aaron and from the
one which was for his sons. 28 It shall be for Aaron
and his sons as *their* portion forever from the sons

28:40 [a]Lit *headgear* [A]Ex 28:4; 39:27, 41 [B]Ex 29:9; 39:28; Lev 8:13; Ezek 44:18 28:41 [a]Lit *fill their hand* [A]Ex 29:7, 9; 30:30; 40:15; Lev 8:1-36; 10:7 28:42 [a]Lit *be* [A]Ex 39:28; Lev 6:10; 16:4; Ezek 44:18 28:43 [a]Or *iniquity* [b]Lit *seed* [A]Ex 20:26 [B]Ex 27:21 29:1 [a]Lit *the thing which* [A]Lev 8:1-34 29:2 [a]Or *anointed* [A]Lev 2:4; 6:19-23 29:4 [A]Ex 40:12; Lev 8:6 29:5 [a]Or *pouch* [A]Ex 28:39; Lev 8:7 [B]Ex 28:31 [C]Ex 28:6 [D]Ex 28:15 [E]Ex 28:8 29:6 [A]Ex 28:4, 39 [B]Ex 28:36, 37; Lev 8:9 29:7 [A]Ex 30:25; Lev 8:12; 21:10; Num 35:25; Ps 133:2 29:8 [A]Ex 28:39, 40; Lev 8:13 29:9 [a]Lit *headgear* [b]Lit *fill the hand of* [A]Ex 28:40 [B]Ex 40:15; Num 3:10; 18:7; 25:13; Deut 18:5 [C]Ex 28:41; Lev 8:1-36 29:10 [A]Lev 1:4; 8:14 29:12 [A]Lev 8:15 [B]Ex 27:2; 30:2 29:13 [a]Or *appendage on* [A]Lev 3:3, 4 29:14 [A]Lev 4:11, 12, 21; Heb 13:11 29:15 [A]Lev 8:18 29:17 [a]Lit *on* [b]Lit *on its* 29:18 [A]Gen 8:21; Ex 29:25 29:19 [a]Lit *second* [A]Lev 8:22f 29:21 [A]Ex 30:25, 31; Lev 8:30 29:22 [a]Or *appendage on* [b]Lit *filling* 29:23 [A]Lev 8:26 29:24 [a]Lit *the whole* [b]Lit *on* [c]Lit *palms* 29:25 [A]Lev 8:28 29:26 [a]Lit *filling* [A]Lev 7:31, 34; 8:29 29:27 [a]Lit *heaved; or lifted up* [b]Lit *filling*

28:40–43 The rest of the priests also had distinctive dress to wear, visually setting them apart from the ordinary citizen. Failure to comply with the dress regulations when serving in the sanctuary brought death. Such a severe consequence stressed the importance of their duties and should have motivated the priests not to consider their priestly role as a mundane, routine, and thankless task.

29:1–18 **consecrate.** The ones chosen to begin the priesthood could not enter into office without Moses' conducting a solemn, 7-day investiture (vv. 4–35 and Lv 8:1–36), involving washing, dressing, anointing, sacrificing, daubing and sprinkling with blood, and eating.

29:19, 20 Daubing blood on the right ear, hand, and big toe symbolically sanctified the ear to hear the Word of God, the hand to do the work of God, and the foot to walk in the way of God.

29:27, 28 **wave offering ... heave offering.** *See note on Lv 7:30–32.*

of Israel, for it is a heave offering; and it shall be
a heave offering from the sons of Israel from the
sacrifices of their peace offerings, *even* their heave
offering to the LORD.
29 "[A]The holy garments of Aaron shall be for his
sons after him, [a]that in them they may be anointed
and ordained. 30 For seven days the one of his sons
who is priest in his stead shall put them on when
he enters the tent of meeting to minister in the
holy place.

FOOD OF THE PRIESTS

31 "You shall take the ram of [a]ordination and [A]boil
its flesh in a holy place. 32 Aaron and his sons shall eat
the flesh of the ram and the bread that is in the basket,
at the doorway of the tent of meeting. 33 Thus [A]they
shall eat [a]those things by which atonement was made
[b]at their ordination *and* consecration; but a [c,B]layman
shall not eat *them*, because they are holy. 34 [A]If any of
the flesh of [a]ordination or any of the bread remains
until morning, then you shall burn the remainder
with fire; it shall not be eaten, because it is holy.
35 "Thus you shall do to Aaron and to his sons,
according to all that I have commanded you; you
shall [a]ordain them through [A]seven days. 36 [A]Each day
you shall offer a bull as a sin offering for atonement,
and you shall [a]purify the altar when you make atonement [b]for it, and [B]you shall anoint it to consecrate it.
37 For seven days you shall make atonement [a]for the
altar and consecrate it; then [A]the altar shall be most
holy, *and* whatever touches the altar shall be holy.
38 "Now [A]this is what you shall offer on the altar:
two one year old lambs each day, continuously.
39 The [A]one lamb you shall offer in the morning and
the [a]other lamb you shall offer at [b]twilight; 40 and
there *shall be* one-tenth *of an ephah* of fine flour
mixed with one-fourth of a hin of beaten oil, and
one-fourth of a hin of wine for a drink offering with
one lamb. 41 The [a]other lamb you shall offer at [b]twi-
light, and shall offer with it [c]the same grain offering
and [d]the same drink offering as in the morning, for
a soothing aroma, an offering by fire to the LORD.
42 It shall be a continual burnt offering throughout your generations at the doorway of the tent of
meeting before the LORD, [A]where I will meet with
you, to speak to you there. 43 I will meet there with
the sons of Israel, and it shall be consecrated by My
glory. 44 I will consecrate the tent of meeting and
the altar; I will also consecrate Aaron and his sons
to minister as priests to Me. 45 [A]I will dwell among
the sons of Israel and will be their God. 46 They shall
know that [A]I am the LORD their God who brought
them out of the land of Egypt, that I might dwell
among them; I am the LORD their God.

THE ALTAR OF INCENSE

30 "Moreover, you shall make [A]an altar as a place
for burning incense; you shall make it of acacia wood. 2 Its length *shall be* a [a]cubit, and its width
a cubit, it shall be square, and its height *shall be* two
cubits; its horns *shall be* [b]of one piece with it. 3 You
shall overlay it with pure gold, its top and its [a]sides
all around, and its horns; and you shall make a gold
molding all around for it. 4 You shall make two gold
rings for it under its molding; you shall make *them*
on its two side walls—on [a]opposite sides—and [b]they
shall be holders for poles with which to carry it. 5 You
shall make the poles of acacia wood and overlay them
with gold. 6 You shall put [a]this altar in front of the
veil that is [b]near the ark of the testimony, in front of
the [c,A]mercy seat that is over *the ark of* the testimony,
where I will meet with you. 7 Aaron shall burn fragrant incense on it; he shall burn it every morning
when he trims the lamps. 8 When Aaron [a]trims the
lamps at [b]twilight, he shall burn incense. *There shall
be* perpetual incense before the LORD throughout
your generations. 9 You shall not offer any strange
incense on [a]this altar, or burnt offering or meal offering; and you shall not pour out a drink offering on it.
10 Aaron shall [A]make atonement on its horns once a
year; he shall make atonement on it with the blood of
the sin offering of atonement once a year throughout
your generations. It is most holy to the LORD."
11 The LORD also spoke to Moses, saying, 12 "When you
take [A]a [a]census of the sons of Israel [b]to number them,
then each one of them shall give [B]a ransom for [c]himself
to the LORD, when you [d]number them, so that there
will be no plague among them when you [d]number

29:29 [a]Lit *for anointing in them and filling their hand in them* [A]Num 20:26, 28 29:31 [a]Lit *filling* [A]Lev 8:31 29:33 [a]Lit *them* [b]Lit *to fill their hand to sanctify them* [c]Lit *stranger* [A]Lev 10:14 [B]Lev 22:10, 13 29:34 [a]Lit *filling* [A]Ex 12:10; 23:18; 34:25; Lev 8:32 29:35 [a]Lit *fill their hand* [A]Lev 8:33 29:36 [a]Or *offer a sin offering on the altar* [b]Lit *upon* [A]Heb 10:11 [B]Ex 40:10 29:37 [a]Lit *upon* [A]Ex 30:28f 29:38 [A]Num 28:3-31; 29:6-38 29:39 [a]Lit *second* [b]Lit *between the two evenings* [A]Ezek 46:13-15 29:41 [a]Lit *second* [b]Lit *between the two evenings* [c]Lit *according to the grain offering of the morning* [d]Lit *according to its* 29:42 [A]Ex 25:22; Num 17:4 29:45 [A]Ex 25:8; Lev 26:12; Num 5:3; Deut 12:11; Zech 2:10; 2 Cor 6:16; Rev 21:3 29:46 [A]Ex 20:2 30:1 [A]Ex 37:25-29 30:2 [a]I.e. One cubit equals approx 18 in. [b]Lit *from itself* 30:3 [a]Lit *walls* 30:4 [a]Lit *its two* [b]Lit *it* 30:6 [a]Lit *it* [b]Lit *upon or over* [c]Lit *propitiatory* [A]Ex 25:21f 30:8 [a]Lit *causes to ascend* [b]Lit *between the two evenings* 30:9 [a]Lit *it* 30:10 [A]Lev 16:18 30:12 [a]Lit *sum* [b]Lit *for their being mustered* [c]Lit *his soul* [d]Lit *muster* [A]Ex 38:25, 26; Num 1:2; 26:2 [B]Num 31:50

29:40 *ephah* ... **hin.** Four to six gallons and six to eight pints respectively.

29:42 throughout your generations. Perhaps this phrase intends a prophetic reminder or confirmation of a long history for Israel.

29:45 I will dwell. That He would be their God and they would be His people was one thing, but that He would also dwell or tabernacle with them was a very important reality in the experience of the new nation. They were to understand not only the transcendence of their God, whose dwelling place was in the heaven of heavens, but also the immanence of their God, whose dwelling place was with them. Their redemption from Egypt was for this purpose (v. 46).

30:1–10 altar ... incense. The design for this piece of furniture for the Holy Place was not given with the other two (25:23–40) but follows the instructions about the priesthood perhaps because it was the last piece to which the High Priest came before he entered the Holy of Holies once a year. Right after Aaron's consecration ceremony had been noted, his duties of 1) ensuring proper incense was offered continually upon this altar and that 2) he was also once a year to cleanse it with blood from the atonement offering (v. 10) received attention.

30:6 in front of the veil. This places the altar outside of the Holy of Holies in the Holy Place. Heb 9:3, 4 speaks of the altar in the Holy of Holies in the sense of its proximity to the ark and in relation to its cleansing on the Day of Atonement. The priests could not go beyond it on any other day.

30:9 strange incense. See v. 38.

30:12 census. The reason for the numbering of all males of military age (v. 14) was not stated, but its seriousness surfaces in the dire warning given about a plague and the use of the term "ransom" in connection with it (cf. 1Ch 21).

them. 13 This is what everyone who [a]is numbered shall give: half a shekel according to the shekel of the sanctuary ([A]the shekel is twenty gerahs), half a shekel as a [b]contribution to the LORD. 14 Everyone who [a]is numbered, from twenty years old and over, shall give the [b]contribution to the LORD. 15 The rich shall not pay more and the poor shall not pay less than the half shekel, when you give the [a]contribution to the LORD to make atonement for [b]yourselves. 16 You shall take the atonement money from the sons of Israel and shall give it for the service of the tent of meeting, that it may be a memorial for the sons of Israel before the LORD, to make atonement for [a]yourselves."

17 The LORD spoke to Moses, saying, 18 "You shall also make [A]a laver of [a]bronze, with its base of bronze, for washing; and you shall [B]put it between the tent of meeting and the altar, and you shall put water in it. 19 Aaron and his sons shall [A]wash their hands and their feet from it; 20 when they enter the tent of meeting, they shall wash with water, so that they will not die; or when they approach the altar to minister, by offering up in smoke a fire *sacrifice* to the LORD. 21 So they shall wash their hands and their feet, so that they will not die; and [A]it shall be a perpetual statute for them, for [a]Aaron and his [b]descendants throughout their generations."

THE ANOINTING OIL

22 Moreover, the LORD spoke to Moses, saying, 23 "Take also for yourself the finest of spices: of flowing myrrh five hundred *shekels,* and of fragrant cinnamon half as much, two hundred and fifty, and of fragrant cane two hundred and fifty, 24 and of cassia five hundred, according to the shekel of the sanctuary, and of olive oil a hin. 25 You shall make [a]of these a holy anointing oil, a perfume mixture, the work of a perfumer; it shall be [A]a holy anointing oil. 26 With it [A]you shall anoint the tent of meeting and the ark of the testimony, 27 and the table and all its utensils, and the lampstand and its utensils, and the altar of incense, 28 and the altar of burnt offering and all its utensils, and the laver and its stand. 29 You shall also consecrate them, that they may be most holy; whatever touches them shall be holy. 30 [A]You shall anoint Aaron and his sons, and consecrate them, that they may minister as priests to Me. 31 You shall speak to the sons of Israel, saying, 'This shall be a holy anointing oil to Me throughout your generations. 32 It shall not be poured on [a]anyone's body, nor shall you make *any* like it in [b]the same proportions; [A]it is holy, *and* it shall be holy to you. 33 [A]Whoever shall mix *any* like it or whoever puts any of it on a [a]layman [b,B]shall be cut off from his people.' "

THE INCENSE

34 Then the LORD said to Moses, "Take for yourself spices, stacte and onycha and galbanum, spices with pure frankincense; there shall be an equal part of each. 35 With it you shall make incense, a perfume, the work of a perfumer, salted, pure, *and* holy. 36 You shall beat some of it very fine, and put part of it before the testimony in the tent of meeting [A]where I will meet with you; it shall be most holy to you. 37 The incense which you shall make, [A]you shall not make in [a]the same proportions for yourselves; it shall be holy to you for the LORD. 38 [A]Whoever shall make *any* like it, to [a]use as perfume, [b]shall be cut off from his people."

THE SKILLED CRAFTSMEN

31 [A]Now the LORD spoke to Moses, saying, 2 "See, I have called by name Bezalel, the [A]son of Uri, the son of Hur, of the tribe of Judah. 3 I have [A]filled him with the Spirit of God in wisdom, in understanding, in knowledge, and in all *kinds of* [a]craftsmanship, 4 to [a]make artistic designs for work in gold, in silver, and in [b]bronze, 5 and in the cutting of stones [a]for settings, and in the carving of wood, that he may work in all *kinds of* [b]craftsmanship. 6 And behold, I Myself have [a]appointed with him [A]Oholiab, the son of Ahisamach, of the tribe of Dan; and in the hearts of all who are [b]skillful I have put [c]skill, that they may make all that I have commanded you: 7 [A]the tent of meeting, and [B]the ark of testimony, and [C]the [a]mercy seat upon it, and all the furniture of the tent, 8 [A]the table also and its [a]utensils, and the [B]pure *gold* lampstand with all its [a]utensils, and [C]the altar

30:13 [a]Lit *passes over to those who are mustered* [b]Lit *heave offering* [A]Lev 27:25; Num 3:47; Ezek 45:12 30:14 [a]V 13, note 1 [b]Lit *heave offering of the LORD* 30:15 [a]Lit *heave offering of the LORD* [b]Lit *your souls* 30:16 [a]Lit *your souls* 30:18 [a]Or *copper* [A]Ex 38:8 [B]Ex 40:30 30:19 [A]Ex 40:31f; Is 52:11 30:21 [a]Lit *him* [b]Lit *seed* [A]Ex 28:43 30:25 [a]Lit *it* [A]Ex 37:29; 40:9; Lev 8:10 30:26 [A]Ex 40:9; Lev 8:10; Num 7:1 30:30 [A]Ex 29:7; Lev 8:12 30:32 [a]Lit *the flesh of man* [b]Lit *its proportion* [A]Ex 30:25, 37 30:33 [a]Lit *stranger* [b]Lit *even he shall* [A]Ex 30:38 [B]Gen 17:14; Ex 12:15; Lev 7:20f 30:36 [A]Ex 29:42 30:37 [a]Lit *its proportion* [A]Ex 30:32 30:38 [a]Lit *smell of it* [b]Lit *even he shall* [A]Ex 30:33 31:1 [A]Ex 35:30-36:1 31:2 [A]1 Chr 2:20 31:3 [a]Or *workmanship* [A]Ex 35:31; 1 Kin 7:14; 1 Cor 12:4-8 31:4 [a]Lit *devise devices* [b]Or *copper* 31:5 [a]Lit *to fill in (for a setting)* [b]Or *workmanship* 31:6 [a]Lit *given* [b]Lit *wise of heart* [c]Lit *wisdom* [A]Ex 35:34 31:7 [a]Lit *propitiatory* [A]Ex 36:8-38 [B]Ex 37:1-5 [C]Ex 37:6-9 31:8 [a]Or *vessels* [A]Ex 37:10-16 [B]Ex 37:17-24; Lev 24:4 [C]Ex 37:25-29

30:13 shekel of the sanctuary. A shekel weighed about .4 oz. (cf. Lv 5:15; 27:3, 25; Nu 3:47; 7:13ff.).

30:18–21 laver of bronze. The washing of hands and feet was mandatory before engaging in priestly duties. Again, the seriousness of being ceremonially purified is seen in the warning of death if this washing was neglected. Nothing casual was being done in the sanctuary or out in the courtyard!

30:22–33 Nothing was left to chance or to human ingenuity. The ingredients for making the anointing oil were carefully spelled out. Anything different was totally unacceptable and brought with it the penalty of death (v. 33). This was to be a unique blend! Using it for any other purpose also erased its holy status as set apart for use in the tabernacle and made it no different from the ordinary and the mundane.

30:25, 35 work of a perfumer. The skill of the perfumer was obviously already well known in Israel, a trade which they undoubtedly observed in Egypt.

30:34–38 incense. God also listed the ingredients for the unique blend of incense prescribed for use at the altar of incense. Making anything different would have been to make "strange incense" (v. 9) and would also result in death (v. 38). Personal use rendered its holy status null and void. Nadab and Abihu were executed for violating this command (cf. Lv 10:1, 2).

31:1–11 God identified two men by name as specially chosen and divinely endued with ability, or Spirit-filled, to make all He had revealed to Moses (cf. 28:3; 36:1). None of the craftsmen were left untouched by divinely bestowed understanding in the intricacy of their work. They were called "craftsmen," suggesting previously developed skill. They were to make all that is prescribed in Ex 25–30.

of incense, 9 [A]the altar of burnt offering also with
all its [a]utensils, and [B]the laver and its stand, 10 the
[a,A]woven garments as well, and the holy garments
for Aaron the priest, and the garments of his sons,
with which to [b]carry on their priesthood; 11 [A]the
anointing oil also, and the [B]fragrant incense for
the holy place, they are to make *them* according to
all that I have commanded you."

THE SIGN OF THE SABBATH

12 The LORD spoke to Moses, saying, 13 "But as for
you, speak to the sons of Israel, saying, '[A]You shall
surely observe My sabbaths; for *this* is [B]a sign between Me and you throughout your generations,
that you may know that I am the LORD who sanctifies you. 14 Therefore you are to observe the sabbath,
for it is holy to you. [A]Everyone who profanes it shall
surely be put to death; for whoever does any work
on it, that person shall be cut off from among his
people. 15 [A]For six days work may be done, but on
the seventh day there is a [B]sabbath of complete rest,
holy to the LORD; [C]whoever does any work on the
sabbath day shall surely be put to death. 16 So the
sons of Israel shall observe the sabbath, to [a]cele-
brate the sabbath throughout their generations as a
perpetual covenant.' 17 [A]It is a sign between Me and
the sons of Israel forever; [B]for in six days the LORD
made heaven and earth, but on the seventh day He
ceased *from labor,* and was refreshed."

18 When He had finished speaking with him upon
Mount Sinai, He gave Moses [A]the two tablets of the testimony, tablets of stone, [B]written by the finger of God.

THE GOLDEN CALF

32 Now when the people saw that Moses [A]delayed
to come down from the mountain, the people
assembled about Aaron and said to him, "Come,
[B]make us [a]a god who will go before us; as for [C]this
Moses, the man who brought us up from the land
of Egypt, we do not know what has become of him."
2 Aaron said to them, "[A]Tear off the gold rings which
are in the ears of your wives, your sons, and your
daughters, and bring *them* to me." 3 Then all the people tore off the gold rings which were in their ears
and brought *them* to Aaron. 4 He took *this* from their
hand, and fashioned it with a graving tool and made
it into a [A]molten calf; and they said, "[a]This is your
god, O Israel, who brought you up from the land of
Egypt." 5 Now when Aaron saw *this,* he built an altar
before it; and Aaron made a proclamation and said,
"Tomorrow *shall be* a feast to the LORD." 6 So the next
day they rose early and [A]offered burnt offerings, and
brought peace offerings; and [B]the people sat down
to eat and to drink, and rose up [C]to play.

7 Then the LORD spoke to Moses, "Go [a]down at once,
for your people, whom [A]you brought up from the
land of Egypt, have [B]corrupted *themselves.* 8 They
have quickly turned aside from the way which I commanded them. [A]They have made for themselves a molten calf, and have worshiped it and [B]have sacrificed to
it and said, '[a,C]This is your god, O Israel, who brought
you up from the land of Egypt!' " 9 [A]The LORD said
to Moses, "I have seen this people, and behold, they
are [a,B]an obstinate people. 10 Now then [A]let Me alone,
that My anger may burn against them and that I may
destroy them; and [B]I will make of you a great nation."

MOSES' ENTREATY

11 Then [A]Moses entreated the LORD his God, and
said, "O LORD, why does Your anger burn against
Your people whom You have brought out from the
land of Egypt with great power and with a mighty
hand? 12 Why should [A]the Egyptians speak, saying,
'With evil *intent* He brought them out to kill them
in the mountains and to destroy them from the face
of the earth'? Turn from Your burning anger and
change Your mind about *doing* harm to Your people.
13 Remember Abraham, Isaac, and Israel, Your servants to whom You [A]swore by Yourself, and said to
them, 'I will [B]multiply your [a]descendants as the stars
of the heavens, and [C]all this land of which I have
spoken I will give to your [a]descendants, and they

31:9 [a]Or *vessels* [A]Ex 38:1-7 [B]Ex 38:8 31:10 [a]Or *service garments* [b]Lit *minister as priests* [A]Ex 39:1 31:11 [A]Ex 30:23-32 [B]Ex 30:34-38 31:13 [A]Ex 20:8 [B]Ex 31:17; Ezek 20:12, 20 31:14 [A]Ex 31:15; 35:2; Num 15:32, 35; John 7:23 31:15 [A]Ex 20:9-11; 23:12; 34:21; 35:2; Lev 23:3; Deut 5:12-14 [B]Gen 2:2f; Ex 16:23; 20:8; 35:2, 3 [C]Ex 31:14 31:16 [a]Lit *do* 31:17 [A]Ex 31:13; Ezek 20:12 [B]Gen 1:31; 2:2, 3; Ex 20:11 31:18 [A]Ex 24:12; 34:29; Deut 4:13; 5:22; 9:10f [B]Ex 32:15, 16; 34:1, 28; Deut 9:10 32:1 [a]Or *gods* [A]Ex 24:18; Deut 9:11, 12 [B]Acts 7:40 [C]Ex 14:11 32:2 [A]Ex 35:22 32:4 [a]Or *These are your gods* [A]Deut 9:16; Neh 9:18; Ps 106:19; Acts 7:41 32:6 [A]Acts 7:41 [B]1 Cor 10:7 [C]Ex 32:17-19; Num 25:2 32:7 [a]Lit *go down* [A]Ex 32:4, 11; Deut 9:12 [B]Gen 6:11f 32:8 [a]Or *These are your gods* [A]Ex 20:3, 4, 23 [B]Ex 22:20; 34:15; Deut 32:17 [C]1 Kin 12:28 32:9 [a]Or *a stiff-necked* [A]Num 14:11-20 [B]Ex 33:3, 5; 34:9; Is 48:4; Acts 7:51 32:10 [A]Deut 9:14 [B]Num 14:12 32:11 [A]Deut 9:18, 26 32:12 [A]Num 14:13-19; Deut 9:28; Josh 7:9 32:13 [a]Lit *seed* [A]Gen 22:16-18; Heb 6:13 [B]Gen 15:5; 26:4 [C]Gen 12:7; 13:15; 15:18; 17:8; 35:12; Ex 13:5, 11; 33:1

31:12–17 *See note on 20:8.*

31:18 two tablets of the testimony. *See note on 25:16.* **written by the finger of God.** A figurative way of attributing the law to God.

32:1 make us a god. Such was the influence of the polytheistic world in which they lived that the Israelites, in a time of panic or impatience, succumbed to a pagan worldview. What made it even more alarming was the rapidity with which pagan idolatry swept in despite recent real-life demonstrations of God's greatness and goodness toward them. But they weren't just requesting gods, but gods to lead them forward—"who will go before us." The pagan world view had robbed them of seeing God as having led them out of Egypt and instead they scornfully attributed the Exodus to Moses (cf. Ac. 7:40).

32:4 a molten calf. The young bull, which Aaron caused to be fashioned, was a pagan religious symbol of virile power. A miniature form of the golden calf, although made of bronze and silver, was found at the site of the ancient Philistine city of Ashkelon. Since it dates to about 1550 B.C. it indicates that calf worship was known not only in Egypt, but also in Canaan prior to the time of Moses. In worshiping the calf, the Israelites violated the first 3 commandments (20:3–7).

32:5 feast to the LORD. Syncretism brought about the ludicrous combination of an idol, an altar, and a festal celebration held in a bizarre attempt to honor the true God.

32:6 rose up to play. The Heb. word allows for the inclusion of drunken and immoral activities so common to idolatrous fertility cults in their revelry (see the description in vv. 7, 25). Syncretism had robbed the people of all ethical alertness and moral discernment (cf. 1Co 10:7).

32:7 your people. In alerting Moses to the trouble in the camp, God designated Israel as Moses' people, a change of possessive pronoun Moses could not have missed. Beforehand God had acknowledged them as "My people." In pleading with God for Israel and in responding to God's offer to make of him a great nation (v. 10), Moses maintained what he knew to be true, given the Exodus and the divine promises to the patriarchs (vv. 12, 13), and designated them correctly as "Your people" (v. 11).

32:10 make of you a great nation. God could have consumed all the people and started over again with Moses, just as He had earlier with Abraham (Ge 12).

32:13 Israel. Another name for Jacob, which means "one who strives with God" (cf. Ge 32:28).

shall inherit *it* forever.' " 14 [A]So the LORD changed
His mind about the harm which He said He would
do to His people.
15 [A]Then Moses turned and went down from the
mountain with the two tablets of the testimony in
his hand, [B]tablets which were written on both [a]sides;
they were written on one *side* and the other. 16 The
tablets were God's work, and the writing was God's
writing engraved on the tablets. 17 Now when Joshua
heard the sound of the people [a]as they shouted,
he said to Moses, "There is a sound of war in the
camp." 18 But he said,

"It is not the sound of the cry of triumph,
Nor is it the sound of the cry of defeat;
But the sound of singing I hear."

MOSES' ANGER

19 It came about, as soon as [a]Moses came near
the camp, that [A]he saw the calf and *the* dancing;
and Moses' anger burned, and [B]he threw the tablets
from his hands and shattered them [b]at the foot of
the mountain. 20 [A]He took the calf which they had
made and burned *it* with fire, and ground it to powder, and scattered it over the surface of the water
and made the sons of Israel drink *it*.
21 Then Moses said to Aaron, "What did this people do to you, that you have brought *such* great sin
upon them?" 22 Aaron said, "Do not let the anger of
my lord burn; you know the people yourself, [A]that
they are [a]prone to evil. 23 For [A]they said to me, 'Make
[a]a god for us who will go before us; for this Moses,
the man who brought us up from the land of Egypt,
we do not know what has become of him.' 24 I said
to them, 'Whoever has any gold, let them tear it off.'
So they gave *it* to me, and [A]I threw it into the fire,
and out came this calf."
25 Now when Moses saw that the people were [a]out
of control—for Aaron had [A]let them [b]get out of control
to be a derision among [c]their enemies— 26 then Moses stood in the gate of the camp, and said, "Whoever
is for the LORD, *come* to me!" And all the sons of Levi
gathered together to him. 27 He said to them, "Thus
says the LORD, the God of Israel, 'Every man *of you*
put his sword upon his thigh, and go back and forth
from gate to gate in the camp, and kill every man his
brother, and every man his friend, and every man
his [a]neighbor.' " 28 So [A]the sons of Levi did [a]as Moses
instructed, and about three thousand men of the
people fell that day. 29 Then Moses said, "[a]Dedicate
yourselves today to the LORD—for every man has
been against his son and against his brother—in
order that He may bestow a blessing upon you today."
30 On the next day Moses said to the people, "[A]You
yourselves have [a]committed a great sin; and now
I am going up to the LORD, perhaps I can [B]make
atonement for your sin." 31 Then Moses returned
to the LORD, and said, "Alas, this people has [a]com-
mitted a great sin, and they have made [b]a [A]god of
gold for themselves. 32 But now, if You will, forgive
their sin—and if not, please blot me out from Your
[A]book which You have written!" 33 The LORD said to
Moses, "Whoever has sinned against Me, [A]I will blot
him out of My book. 34 But go now, lead the people
[A]where I told you. Behold, [B]My angel shall go before
you; nevertheless [C]in the day when I [a]punish, [D]I will
[b]punish them for their sin." 35 [A]Then the LORD smote
the people, because of [B]what they did with the calf
which Aaron had made.

THE JOURNEY RESUMED

33 Then the LORD spoke to Moses, "Depart, go
up from here, you and the people whom you
have brought up from the land of Egypt, to the land
of which [A]I swore to Abraham, [B]Isaac, and [C]Jacob,
saying, '[D]To your [a]descendants I will give it.' 2 I will
send [A]an angel before you and [B]I will drive out the
Canaanite, the Amorite, the Hittite, the Perizzite, the

32:14 [A]Ps 106:45 32:15 [a]Lit *their sides* [A]Deut 9:15 [B]Ex 31:18 32:17 [a]Lit *in its shouting* 32:19 [a]Lit *he* [b]Lit *beneath* [A]Ex 32:6; Deut 9:16 [B]Deut 9:17 32:20 [A]Deut 9:21 32:22 [a]Lit *in evil* [A]Deut 9:24 32:23 [a]Or *gods* [A]Ex 32:1-4 32:24 [A]Ex 32:4 32:25 [a]Lit *let loose* [b]Lit *go loose* [c]Lit *those who rise against them* [A]1 Kin 12:28-30; 14:16 32:27 [a]Or *kin* 32:28 [a]Lit *according to Moses' word* [A]Num 25:7-13; Deut 33:9 32:29 [a]Lit *Fill your hand* 32:30 [a]Lit *sinned* [A]1 Sam 12:20, 23 [B]Num 25:13 32:31 [a]Lit *sinned* [b]Or *gods* [A]Ex 20:23 32:32 [A]Ps 69:28; Is 4:3; Dan 12:1; Mal 3:16, 17; Phil 4:3; Rev 3:5; 21:27 32:33 [A]Ex 17:14; Deut 29:20; Ps 9:5; Rev 3:5 32:34 [a]Lit *visit* [b]Lit *visit their sin upon them* [A]Ex 3:17 [B]Ex 23:20 [C]Deut 32:35; Rom 2:5, 6 [D]Ps 99:8 32:35 [A]Ex 32:28 [B]Ex 32:4, 24 33:1 [a]Lit *seed* [A]Ex 32:13 [B]Gen 26:1-3 [C]Gen 28:10 [D]Gen 12:7 33:2 [A]Ex 32:34 [B]Ex 23:27-31; Josh 24:11

32:14 the LORD changed His mind about the harm. Moses' appeal for God to change His mind, to relent, succeeded because God had only threatened judgment, not decreed it. A divine intention is not an unchangeable divine decree. Decrees or sworn declarations (cf. Ge 22:16–18; Ps 110:4) or categorical statements of not changing or relenting (cf. Jer 4:28; Eze 24:14; Zec 8:14, 15) are unconditional and bind the speaker to the stated course of action regardless of the circumstances or reactions of the listeners. Intentions retain a conditional element and do not necessarily bind the speaker to a stated course of action (cf. Jer 15:6; 18:8–10; 26:3, 13, 19; Joel 2:13; Jon 3:9, 10; 4:2).

32:19 shattered them. Moses pictured the nation breaking God's commandments by actually breaking the tablets on which they were written.

32:22–24 Aaron, held responsible by Moses for what had taken place in the camp (vv. 21, 25), endeavored to avoid responsibility for the people's actions by shifting the blame to their propensity to do evil, and also for the presence of the golden calf by ridiculously representing it as having just popped out of the fire all by itself!

32:23 See Ac. 7:40.

32:26 Whoever is for the LORD. Only the tribe of Levi responded to the call to take action in response to this situation which demanded judgment be inflicted. They had understood that neutrality could not exist in the open confrontation between good and evil. Family and national ties were superseded by submission to the Lord to do His will, which in this situation was to wield the sword of God's judgment to preserve His honor and glory.

32:28 They apparently killed those who persisted in idolatry and immorality (cf. Nu 25:6–9).

32:32 blot me out from Your book. Nothing more strongly marked the love of Moses for his people than his sincere willingness to offer up his own life rather than see them disinherited and destroyed. The book to which Moses referred, the psalmist entitled "the book of life" (Ps 69:28). Untimely or premature death would constitute being blotted out of the book. The Apostle Paul displayed a similar passionate devotion for his kinsmen (Ro 9:1–3).

33:2–6 Good news included bad news! Entry into the Promised Land was not forfeited, but God's presence on the way was withdrawn. What was a sworn covenant-promise to the patriarchs just could not be broken: what was assured—the divine presence on the way—could be set aside because of sin (cf. 23:20–23). Removal of their jewelry depicted outwardly the people's sorrow of heart. It was a response analogous to donning sackcloth and ashes.

33:2 *See notes on 3:8.*

Hivite and the Jebusite. 3 *Go up* to a land [A]flowing with milk and honey; for I will not go up in your midst, because you are [a,B]an obstinate people, and [C]I might destroy you on the way."

4 When the people heard this [a]sad word, [A]they went into mourning, and none of them put on his ornaments. 5 For the LORD had said to Moses, "Say to the sons of Israel, 'You are [a,A]an obstinate people; should I go up in your midst for one moment, I would destroy you. Now therefore, put off your ornaments from you, that I may know what I shall do with you.' " 6 So the sons of Israel stripped themselves of their ornaments, from Mount Horeb *onward.*

7 Now Moses used to take [A]the tent and pitch it outside the camp, a good distance from the camp, and he called it the tent of meeting. And [B]everyone who sought the LORD would go out to the tent of meeting which was outside the camp. 8 And it came about, whenever Moses went out to the tent, that all the people would arise and stand, each at the entrance of his tent, and gaze after Moses until he entered the tent. 9 Whenever Moses entered the tent, [A]the pillar of cloud would descend and stand at the entrance of the tent; [B]and [a]the LORD would speak with Moses. 10 When all the people saw the pillar of cloud standing at the entrance of the tent, all the people would arise and worship, each at the entrance of his tent. 11 Thus [A]the LORD used to speak to Moses face to face, just as a man speaks to his friend. When [a]Moses returned to the camp, [B]his servant Joshua, the son of Nun, a young man, would not depart from the tent.

MOSES INTERCEDES

12 Then Moses said to the LORD, "See, You say to me, '[A]Bring up this people!' But You Yourself have not let me know [B]whom You will send with me. [C]Moreover, You have said, 'I have known you by name, and you have also found favor in My sight.' 13 Now therefore, I pray You, if I have found favor in Your sight, [A]let me know Your ways that I may know You, so that I may find favor in Your sight. [B]Consider too, that this nation is Your people." 14 And He said, "[A]My presence shall go *with you,* and [B]I will give you rest." 15 Then he said to Him, "[A]If Your presence does not go *with us,* do not lead us up from here. 16 For how then can it be known that I have found favor in Your sight, I and Your people? Is it not by Your going with us, so that [A]we, I and Your people, may be distinguished from all the *other* people who are upon the face of the [a]earth?"

17 The LORD said to Moses, "I will also do this thing of which you have spoken; [A]for you have found favor in My sight and I have known you by name." 18 [A]Then [a]Moses said, "I pray You, show me Your glory!" 19 And He said, "[A]I Myself will make all My goodness pass before you, and will proclaim the name of the LORD before you; and [B]I will be gracious to whom I will be gracious, and will show compassion on whom I will show compassion." 20 But He said, "You cannot see My face, [A]for no man can see Me and live!" 21 Then the LORD said, "Behold, there is a place [a]by Me, and [A]you shall stand *there* on the rock; 22 and it will come about, while My glory is passing by, that I will put you in the cleft of the rock and [A]cover you with My hand until I have passed by. 23 Then I will take My hand away and you shall see My back, but [A]My face shall not be seen."

THE TWO TABLETS REPLACED

34 Now the LORD said to Moses, "Cut out for yourself [A]two stone tablets like the former ones, and [B]I will write on the tablets the words that were on the former tablets which you shattered. 2 So be ready by morning, and come up in the morning to [A]Mount Sinai, and [a]present yourself there to Me on the top of the mountain. 3 [A]No man is to come up with you, nor let any man be seen [a]anywhere on the mountain; even the flocks and the herds may not graze in front of that mountain." 4 So he cut out [A]two stone tablets like the former ones, and Moses rose up early in the morning and went up to Mount Sinai, as the LORD had commanded him, and he took two stone tablets in his hand. 5 [A]The LORD descended in the cloud and stood there with him as [a]he called upon the name of the LORD. 6 Then the LORD passed by in front of him and proclaimed, "The LORD, the LORD God, [A]compassionate and gracious, slow to anger, and abounding in lovingkindness and [a]truth; 7 who [A]keeps lovingkindness for thousands, who forgives iniquity, transgression and sin; yet He [B]will by no means leave *the guilty* unpunished, [C]visiting the iniquity of fathers on the children and on the

33:3 [a]Lit *a stiff-necked* [A]Ex 3:8, 17 [B]Ex 32:9; 33:5 [C]Ex 32:10 33:4 [a]Lit *evil* [A]Num 14:1, 39 33:5 [a]Lit *a stiff-necked* [A]Ex 33:3 33:7 [A]Ex 18:7, 12-16 [B]Ex 29:42f 33:9 [a]Lit *He* [A]Ex 13:21 [B]Ps 99:7 33:11 [a]Lit *he* [A]Num 12:8; Deut 34:10 [B]Ex 24:13 33:12 [A]Ex 3:10; 32:34 [B]Ex 33:2 [C]Ex 33:17 33:13 [A]Ps 25:4; 27:11; 51:13; 86:11; 119:33 [B]Ex 3:7, 10; 5:1; 32:12, 14; Deut 9:26, 29 33:14 [A]Deut 4:37; Is 63:9 [B]Deut 12:10; 25:19; Josh 21:44; 22:4 33:15 [A]Ps 80:3, 7, 19 33:16 [a]Lit *ground* [A]Lev 20:24, 26 33:17 [A]Ex 33:12 33:18 [a]Lit *he* [A]Ex 33:20-23 33:19 [A]Ex 34:6, 7 [B]Rom 9:15 33:20 [A]Is 6:5; 1 Tim 6:16 33:21 [a]Lit *with* [A]Ps 18:2, 46; 27:5; 61:2; 62:7 33:22 [A]Ps 91:1, 4; Is 49:2; 51:16 33:23 [A]Ex 33:20; John 1:18 34:1 [A]Ex 24:12; 31:18; 32:16, 19 [B]Deut 10:2, 4 34:2 [a]Or *place yourself before* [A]Ex 19:11, 18, 20 34:3 [a]Lit *on all* [A]Ex 19:12, 13 34:4 [A]Ex 34:1 34:5 [a]Or *he called out with the name of the LORD* [A]Ex 19:9; 33:9 34:6 [a]Or *faithfulness* [A]Num 14:18; Deut 4:31; Neh 9:17; Ps 86:15; 103:8; 108:4; 145:8; Joel 2:13; Rom 2:4 34:7 [A]Ex 20:5, 6; Deut 5:10; 7:9; Ps 103:3; 130:3, 4; 1 John 1:9 [B]Ex 23:7; Deut 7:10; Job 10:14; Nah 1:3 [C]Deut 5:9

33:7 the tent of meeting. In the time prior to the construction of the tabernacle, Moses' tent became the special meeting place for Moses to talk intimately, "face to face" (v. 11), with God. No doubt the people watching from afar were reminded of the removal of God's immediate presence.

33:12–17 Again Moses entered earnestly and confidently into the role of intercessor before God for the nation whom he again referred to as "Your people" (vv. 13, 16). Moses clearly understood that without God's presence they would not be a people set apart from other nations, so why travel any farther? Moses' favored standing before the Lord comes out in the positive response to his intercession (v. 17).

33:18–23 Cautionary measures were needed for God to respond only in part to Moses' request to see more of Him than he was already experiencing (cf. Nu 12:8)—otherwise he would die. Notwithstanding God's being gracious and compassionate to whomever He chose, Moses could not see God's face and live. Whatever he saw of God's nature transformed into blazing light is referred to as "God's back" and was never subsequently described by Moses (cf. Jn 1:18; 1Jn 4:12).

33:19 See Ro 9:15.

34:1 Cut ... two stone tablets. Renewal of the covenant meant replacement of the broken original tablets on which God had personally written the Ten Commandments (cf. 32:19).

34:2–28 Moses' second period of 40 days and nights on Mt. Sinai (cf. chaps. 25–32).

34:6, 7 Here is one of the testimonies to the character of God.

34:7 *See note on 20:5, 6.*

grandchildren to the third and fourth generations."
8 Moses made haste [a,A]to bow low toward the earth
and worship. 9 He said, "[A]If now I have found favor
in Your sight, O Lord, I pray, let the Lord go along
in our midst, even though [a,B]the people are so obstinate, and [C]pardon our iniquity and our sin, and
[D]take us as Your own [b]possession."

THE COVENANT RENEWED

10 Then [a]God said, "Behold, [A]I am going to make
a covenant. Before all your people [B]I will perform
miracles which have not been [b]produced in all the
earth nor among any of the nations; and all the
people [c]among whom you live will see the working
of the LORD, for it is a fearful thing that I am going
to perform with you.
11 "[a]Be sure to observe what I am commanding
you this day: behold, [A]I am going to drive out the
Amorite before you, and the Canaanite, the Hittite,
the Perizzite, the Hivite and the Jebusite. 12 [A]Watch
yourself that you make no covenant with the inhabitants of the land into which you are going, or it will
become a snare in your midst. 13 [A]But *rather,* you are
to tear down their altars and smash their *sacred*
pillars and cut down their [a,B]Asherim 14 —for [A]you
shall not worship any other god, for the LORD, whose
name is Jealous, is a jealous God— 15 otherwise you
might make a covenant with the inhabitants of the
land and they would play the harlot with their gods
and [A]sacrifice to their gods, and someone [B]might
invite you [a]to eat of his sacrifice, 16 and [A]you might
take some of his daughters for your sons, and his
daughters might play the harlot with their gods and
cause your sons *also* to play the harlot with their
gods. 17 [A]You shall make for yourself no molten gods.
18 "You shall observe [A]the Feast of Unleavened
Bread. For [B]seven days you are to eat unleavened
bread, [a]as I commanded you, at the appointed time
in the [C]month of Abib, for in the month of Abib you
came out of Egypt.
19 "[A]The first offspring from every womb belongs
to Me, and all your male livestock, the first offspring
from [a]cattle and sheep. 20 [A]You shall redeem with a
lamb the [a]first offspring from a donkey; and if you
do not redeem *it,* then you shall break its neck. You
shall redeem [B]all the firstborn of your sons. [b,C]None
shall appear before Me empty-handed.
21 "You shall work [A]six days, but on the seventh
day you shall rest; *even* during plowing time and
harvest you shall rest. 22 You shall celebrate [A]the
Feast of Weeks, *that is,* the first fruits of the wheat
harvest, and the Feast of Ingathering at the turn of
the year. 23 [A]Three times a year all your males are
to appear before the Lord [a]GOD, the God of Israel.
24 For I will [a,A]drive out nations before you and enlarge your borders, and no man shall covet your
land when you go up three times a year to appear
before the LORD your God.
25 "[A]You shall not [a]offer the blood of My sacrifice
with leavened bread, [B]nor is the sacrifice of the
Feast of the Passover to [b]be left over until morning.
26 "You shall bring [A]the very first of the first fruits
of your soil into the house of the LORD your God.
"You shall not boil a young goat in its mother's
milk."
27 Then the LORD said to Moses, "[A]Write [a]down
these words, for in accordance with these words I
have made [B]a covenant with you and with Israel."
28 So he was there with the LORD [A]forty days and
forty nights; he did not eat bread or drink water.
And [a,B]he wrote on the tablets the words of the covenant, [C]the Ten [b]Commandments.

MOSES' FACE SHINES

29 It came about when Moses was coming down
from Mount Sinai (and the [A]two tablets of the testimony *were* in Moses' hand as he was coming down
from the mountain), that Moses did not know that
[B]the skin of his face shone because of his speaking
with Him. 30 So when Aaron and all the sons of Israel
saw Moses, behold, the skin of his face shone, and
[A]they were afraid to come near him. 31 Then Moses
called to them, and Aaron and all the rulers in the
congregation returned to him; and Moses spoke to
them. 32 Afterward all the sons of Israel came near,
and he commanded them *to do* everything that the
LORD had spoken [a]to him on Mount Sinai. 33 When
Moses had finished speaking with them, [A]he put

34:8 [a]Lit *and bowed...worshiped* [A]Ex 4:31 34:9 [a]Lit *it is a people stiff-necked* [b]Or *inheritance* [A]Ex 33:13 [B]Ex 32:9 [C]Ex 34:7 [D]Deut 4:20; 9:26, 29; 32:9; Ps 33:12 34:10 [a]Lit *He* [b]Lit *created* [c]Lit *in whose midst you are* [A]Ex 34:27, 28; Deut 5:2 [B]Deut 4:32; Ps 72:18; 136:4 34:11 [a]Lit *Observe for yourself* [A]Ex 33:2 34:12 [A]Ex 23:32, 33 34:13 [a]I.e. wooden symbols of a female deity [A]Ex 23:24; Deut 12:3 [B]Deut 16:21; Judg 6:25, 26; 2 Kin 18:4; 2 Chr 34:3f 34:14 [A]Ex 20:3, 5; Deut 4:24 34:15 [a]Lit *and you eat* [A]Ex 22:20; 32:8 [B]Num 25:1, 2; Deut 32:37, 38 34:16 [A]Deut 7:3; Josh 23:12, 13; 1 Kin 11:1-4 34:17 [A]Ex 20:4, 23; Lev 19:4; Deut 5:8 34:18 [a]Or *which* [A]Ex 12:17; Lev 23:6; Num 28:16f [B]Ex 12:15, 16 [C]Ex 12:2; 13:4 34:19 [a]Or *oxen* [A]Ex 13:2; 22:29f 34:20 [a]Lit *first opening of* [b]Lit *They shall not* [A]Ex 13:13 [B]Ex 13:15; Num 3:45 [C]Ex 22:29; 23:15; Deut 16:16 34:21 [A]Ex 20:9f; 23:12; 31:15; 35:2; Lev 23:3; Deut 5:13f 34:22 [A]Ex 23:16; Num 28:26 34:23 [a]Heb *YHWH*, usually rendered *LORD* [A]Ex 23:14-17 34:24 [a]Or *dispossess* [A]Ex 33:2; Ps 78:55 34:25 [a]Lit *slaughter* [b]Lit *remain overnight* [A]Ex 23:18 [B]Ex 12:10 34:26 [A]Ex 23:19; Deut 26:2 34:27 [a]Lit *for yourself* [A]Ex 17:14; 24:4 [B]Ex 34:10 34:28 [a]Or *He*, i.e. The LORD [b]Lit *Words* [A]Ex 24:18 [B]Ex 31:18; 34:1 [C]Deut 4:13; 10:4 34:29 [A]Ex 32:15 [B]Matt 17:2; 2 Cor 3:7 34:30 [A]2 Cor 3:7 34:32 [a]Lit *with* 34:33 [A]2 Cor 3:13

34:11 *See note on 3:8.*

34:12–17 *See note on 23:32.* This time the admonition on international treaties included a warning of how idolatry could easily ensnare them by seemingly innocent invitations to join the festivities like a good neighbor or by intermarriage, because these events would require recognition of the contracting parties' deities. Their future history demonstrated the urgency of such instruction and the disaster of disobeying it.

34:18 *See note on 12:14.*

34:19, 20 *See note on 13:2.*

34:21 *See note on 20:8.*

34:22, 23, 26 *See note on 23:14–19.*

34:29–35 The first time on the mount (24:12–32:14), unlike the second, had not left Moses with a face which was reflecting some radiance associated with being in the presence of the Lord for an extended period of time. On the first occasion, mere mention was made of Moses' being gone 40 days and nights (24:18). On the second, mention was made of the 40 day and night absence but adding that Moses had been there with the Lord, neither eating nor drinking (v. 28), appears to draw attention to the different nature of the second visit. It, in comparison with the first, was not interrupted by the Lord's sending Moses away because of sin in the camp (32:7–10). A compliant and not defiant people feared the evidence of God's presence. When not speaking to the Lord or authoritatively on His behalf to the people, Moses veiled his face. The Apostle Paul advised that the veil prevented the people from seeing a fading glory and related it to the inadequacy of the old covenant and the blindness of the Jews in his day (*see notes on 2Co 3:7–18*).

a veil over his face. 34 But whenever Moses went
in before the LORD to speak with Him, [A]he would
take off the veil until he came out; and whenever
he came out and spoke to the sons of Israel what he
had been commanded, 35 [A]the sons of Israel would
see the face of Moses, that the skin of Moses' face
shone. So Moses would replace the veil over his face
until he went in to speak with Him.

THE SABBATH EMPHASIZED

35 Then Moses assembled all the congregation of the sons of Israel, and said to them,
"[A]These are the things that the LORD has commanded *you* to [a]do:

2 "[A]For six days work may be done, but on the
seventh day you shall have a holy *day,* [B]a sabbath of
complete rest to the LORD; [C]whoever does any work
on it shall be put to death. 3 [A]You shall not kindle a
fire in any of your dwellings on the sabbath day."

4 Moses spoke to all the congregation of the sons
of Israel, saying, "This is the thing which the LORD
has commanded, saying, 5 '[A]Take from among you
a [a]contribution to the LORD; whoever is of a willing heart, let him bring it as the LORD'S [a]contribu-
tion: gold, silver, and [b]bronze, 6 and [a]blue, purple
and scarlet *material,* fine linen, goats' *hair,* 7 and
rams' skins [a]dyed red, and porpoise skins, and acacia wood, 8 and oil for lighting, and spices for the
anointing oil, and for the fragrant incense, 9 and
onyx stones and setting stones for the ephod and
for the [a]breastpiece.

TABERNACLE WORKMEN

10 '[A]Let every skillful man among you come, and
make all that the LORD has commanded: 11 the [a,A]tab-
ernacle, its tent and its covering, its hooks and its
boards, its bars, its pillars, and its [b]sockets; 12 the
[A]ark and its poles, the [a]mercy seat, and the curtain of the screen; 13 the [A]table and its poles, and all
its [a]utensils, and the bread of the [b]Presence; 14 the
[A]lampstand also for the light and its utensils and
its lamps and the oil for the light; 15 and the [A]altar
of incense and its poles, and the [B]anointing oil and
the [C]fragrant incense, and the screen for the doorway at the [a]entrance of the tabernacle; 16 [A]the altar
of burnt offering with its [a]bronze grating, its poles,
and all its [b]utensils, the [c]basin and its stand; 17 [A]the
hangings of the court, its pillars and its [a]sockets,
and the screen for the gate of the court; 18 the pegs
of the tabernacle and the pegs of the court and their
cords; 19 the [a,A]woven garments for ministering in
the holy place, the holy garments for Aaron the
priest and the garments of his sons, to minister
as priests.' "

GIFTS RECEIVED

20 Then all the congregation of the sons of Israel departed from Moses' presence. 21 [A]Everyone
whose heart [a]stirred him and everyone whose spirit
[b]moved him came *and* brought the LORD'S [c]contri-
bution for the work of the tent of meeting and for
all its service and for the holy garments. 22 Then all
[a]whose hearts moved them, both men and women,
came *and* brought brooches and [b]earrings and signet rings and bracelets, all articles of gold; so *did*
every man who [c]presented an offering of gold to
the LORD. 23 Every man, [a]who had in his possession
[b]blue and purple and scarlet *material* and fine linen
and goats' *hair* and rams' skins [c]dyed red and porpoise skins, brought them. 24 Everyone who could
make a [a]contribution of silver and [b]bronze brought
the LORD'S [a]contribution; and every man [c]who had
in his possession acacia wood for any work of the
service brought it. 25 All the [a]skilled women spun
with their hands, and brought what they had spun,
in [b]blue and purple *and* scarlet *material* and *in* fine
linen. 26 All the women whose heart [a]stirred with
a skill spun the goats' *hair.* 27 The rulers brought
the onyx stones and the stones for setting for the
ephod and for the [a]breastpiece; 28 and [A]the spice
and the oil for the light and for the anointing oil
and for the fragrant incense. 29 The [a]Israelites, all
the men and women, whose heart [b]moved them to
bring *material* for all the work, which the LORD had
commanded through Moses to be done, brought a
[A]freewill offering to the LORD.

30 [A]Then Moses said to the sons of Israel, "See,
the LORD has called by name Bezalel the son of
Uri, the son of Hur, of the tribe of Judah. 31 And He
has filled him with the Spirit of God, in wisdom, in
understanding and in knowledge and in all [a]crafts-
manship; 32 [a]to make designs for working in gold
and in silver and in [b]bronze, 33 and in the cutting
of stones for settings and in the carving of wood,
so as to perform in every inventive work. 34 He also
has put in his heart to teach, both he and [A]Oholiab,
the son of Ahisamach, of the tribe of Dan. 35 [A]He has
filled them with [a]skill to perform every work of an
engraver and of a designer and of an embroiderer,
in [b]blue and in purple *and* in scarlet *material,* and in
fine linen, and of a weaver, as performers of every
work and makers of designs.

34:34 [A]2 Cor 3:16 34:35 [A]2 Cor 3:13 35:1 [a]*Lit do them* [A]Ex 34:32 35:2 [A]Ex 20:9, 10; 23:12; 31:15; 34:21; Lev 23:3; Deut 5:13f [B]Ex 16:23 [C]Num 15:32-36 35:3 [A]Ex 12:16; 16:23 35:5 [a]*Or heave offering* [b]*Or copper* [A]Ex 25:1-9 35:6 [a]*Or violet* 35:7 [a]*Or tanned* 35:9 [a]*Or pouch* 35:10 [A]Ex 31:6 35:11 [a]*Lit dwelling place* [b]*Or bases* [A]Ex 26:1-30 35:12 [a]*Lit propitiatory* [A]Ex 25:10-22 35:13 [a]*Or vessels* [b]*Lit Face* [A]Ex 25:23-30 35:14 [A]Ex 25:31ff 35:15 [a]*Or doorway* [A]Ex 30:1-6 [B]Ex 30:25 [C]Ex 30:34-38 35:16 [a]*Or copper* [b]*Or vessels* [c]*Or laver* [A]Ex 27:1-8 35:17 [a]*Or bases* [A]Ex 27:9-18 35:19 [a]*Or service garments* [A]Ex 31:10; 39:1 35:21 [a]*Lit lifted up* [b]*Or made him willing* [c]*Or heave offering* [A]Ex 25:2; 35:5, 22, 26, 29; 36:2 35:22 [a]*Or who were willing-hearted* [b]*Or nose rings* [c]*Lit waved a wave offering* 35:23 [a]*Lit with whom was found* [b]*Or violet* [c]*Or tanned* 35:24 [a]*Or heave offering* [b]*Or copper* [c]*Lit with whom was found* 35:25 [a]*Lit women wise of heart* [b]*Or violet* 35:26 [a]*Lit lifted them up in wisdom* 35:27 [a]*Or pouch* 35:28 [A]Ex 30:23ff 35:29 [a]*Lit sons of Israel* [b]*Lit made them willing* [A]Ex 35:21; 1 Chr 29:9 35:30 [A]Ex 31:1-6 35:31 [a]*Or work* 35:32 [a]*Lit devise devices* [b]*Or copper* 35:34 [A]Ex 31:6 35:35 [a]*Lit wisdom of heart* [b]*Or violet* [A]Ex 31:3, 6; 35:31; 1 Kin 7:14

35:1–40:38 In this section, the Israelites constructed the tabernacle as God so prescribed in 25:1–31:18.

35:1–3 *See note on 20:8.* This time, however, an extra admonition forbids the making of a fire on the Sabbath.

35:4–9 *See note on 25:2.*

35:10–19 *See notes on 25:11–28:43.*

35:20–29 *See note on 25:2.*

35:30–36:1 The Lord also gave the two named craftsmen skill in teaching their trades. This substantiates that they were most probably the supervisors or leaders of the construction teams. *See notes on 28:3; 31:1–11.*

THE TABERNACLE UNDERWRITTEN

36 "Now Bezalel and Oholiab, and every [a]skillful
person in whom the LORD has put [b]skill and
understanding to know how to perform all the work
[c]in the construction of the sanctuary, shall perform in
accordance with all that the LORD has commanded."
2 Then Moses called Bezalel and Oholiab and every [a]skillful person in [b]whom the LORD had put
[c]skill, [A]everyone whose heart stirred him, to come to
the work to perform it. 3 They received from Moses
all the [a]contributions which the sons of Israel had
brought [b]to perform the work [c]in the construction
of the sanctuary. And they still *continued* bringing
to him freewill offerings every morning. 4 And all
the [a]skillful men who were performing all the work
of the sanctuary came, each from [b]the work which
[c]he was performing, 5 and they said to [a]Moses, "[A]The
people are bringing much more than enough for the
[b]construction work which the LORD commanded *us*
to [c]perform." 6 So Moses issued a command, and a
[a]proclamation was circulated throughout the camp,
saying, "Let no man or woman any longer perform
work for the [b]contributions of the sanctuary." Thus
the people were restrained from bringing *any more.*
7 [A]For the [a]material they had was sufficient and
more than enough for all the work, to perform it.

CONSTRUCTION PROCEEDS

8 [A]All the [a]skillful men among those who were
performing the work made the [b]tabernacle with ten
curtains; of fine twisted linen and [c]blue and purple
and scarlet *material,* with cherubim, the work of a
skillful workman, [d]Bezalel made them. 9 The length
of each curtain was twenty-eight [a]cubits and the
width of each curtain four [a]cubits; all the curtains
had [b]the same measurements. 10 He [a]joined five
curtains to one another and *the other* five curtains
he [a]joined to one another. 11 He made loops of [a]blue
on the edge of the [b]outermost curtain in the first
[c]set; he did likewise on the edge of the curtain that
was [b]outermost in the second [c]set. 12 He made [A]fifty
loops in the one curtain and he made fifty loops on
the [a]edge of the curtain that was in the second [b]set;
the loops were opposite each other. 13 He made [A]fifty
clasps of gold and [a]joined the curtains to one another with the clasps, so the tabernacle was [b]a unit.
14 Then [A]he made curtains of goats' *hair* for a
tent over the tabernacle; he made eleven curtains
[a]in all. 15 The length of each curtain *was* thirty cubits and four cubits the width of each curtain; the
eleven curtains had [a]the same measurements. 16 He
[a]joined five curtains by themselves and *the other* six
curtains by themselves. 17 Moreover, he made fifty
loops on the edge of the curtain that was outermost
in the *first* [a]set, and he made fifty loops on the edge
of the curtain *that was outermost in* the second [a]set.
18 He made fifty clasps of [a]bronze to [b]join the tent
together so that it would be [c]a unit. 19 He made a
covering for the tent of rams' skins [a]dyed red, and
a covering of porpoise skins above.
20 [A]Then he made the boards for the tabernacle
of acacia wood, standing upright. 21 Ten cubits *was*
the length of [a]each board and one and a half cubits
the width of each board. 22 *There were* two tenons
for each board, [a]fitted to one another; thus he did
for all the boards of the tabernacle. 23 He made the
boards for the tabernacle: twenty boards [a]for the
south side; 24 and he made forty [a]sockets of silver
under the twenty boards; two [a]sockets under one
board for its two tenons and two [a]sockets under
another board for its two tenons. 25 Then for the
second side of the tabernacle, on the north side,
he made twenty boards, 26 and their forty [a]sockets
of silver; two [a]sockets under one board and two
[a]sockets under another board. 27 For the [a]rear of the
tabernacle, to the west, he made six boards. 28 He
made two boards for the corners of the [a]taberna-
cle at the [b]rear. 29 They were double beneath, and
together they were complete to its [a]top [b]to the first
ring; thus he did with both of them for the two corners. 30 There were eight boards with their [a]sockets
of silver, sixteen [a]sockets, [b]two under every board.
31 Then he made [A]bars of acacia wood, five for the
boards of one side of the tabernacle, 32 and five bars
for the boards of the [a]other side of the tabernacle,
and five bars for the boards of the tabernacle for
the [b]rear *side* to the west. 33 He made the middle bar
to pass through in the [a]center of the boards from
end to end. 34 He overlaid the boards with gold and
made their rings of gold *as* holders for the bars, and
overlaid the bars with gold.
35 [A]Moreover, he made the veil of [a]blue and purple
and scarlet *material,* and fine twisted linen; he made
it with cherubim, the work of a skillful workman.
36 He made four pillars of acacia for it, and overlaid
them with gold, with their hooks of gold; and he cast
four [a]sockets of silver for them. 37 He made a [A]screen
for the doorway of the tent, of [a]blue and purple and
scarlet *material,* and fine twisted linen, the work of
a [b]weaver; 38 and *he made* its [A]five pillars with their

36:1 [a]Lit *man wise of heart* [b]Lit *wisdom* [c]Or *connected with the service of;* lit *of the service of* 36:2 [a]Lit *man wise of heart* [b]Lit *whose heart* [c]Lit *wisdom* [A]Ex 35:21, 26 36:3 [a]Lit *lifted offering* [b]Lit *to perform it for the work* [c]Lit *of the service of* 36:4 [a]Lit *wise* [b]Lit *his* [c]Lit *they were* 36:5 [a]Lit *Moses, saying,* [b]Lit *service for the work* [c]Lit *perform it* [A]2 Chr 24:14; 31:6-10 36:6 [a]Lit *voice* [b]Lit *heave offering* 36:7 [a]Lit *work* [A]1 Kin 8:64 36:8 [a]Lit *wise of heart* [b]Lit *dwelling place* [c]Or *violet* [d]Lit *he* [A]Ex 26:1-14 36:9 [a]I.e. One cubit equals approx 18 in. [b]Lit *one measure* 36:10 [a]Or *coupled* 36:11 [a]Or *violet* [b]Lit *one curtain from the end in the coupling* [c]Lit *coupling* 36:12 [a]Lit *end* [b]Lit *coupling* [A]Ex 26:5 36:13 [a]Or *coupled* [b]Lit *one* [A]Ex 26:6 36:14 [a]Lit *in number* [A]Ex 26:7-14 36:15 [a]Lit *one measure* 36:16 [a]Or *coupled* 36:17 [a]Lit *coupling* 36:18 [a]Or *copper* [b]Or *couple* [c]Lit *one* 36:19 [a]Or *tanned* 36:20 [A]Ex 26:15-29 36:21 [a]Lit *the* 36:22 [a]Lit *bound* 36:23 [a]Lit *to the side of the Negev, to the south* 36:24 [a]Or *bases* 36:26 [a]Or *bases* 36:27 [a]Lit *extreme parts* 36:28 [a]Lit *dwelling place* [b]Lit *extreme parts* 36:29 [a]Or *head* [b]Or *with reference to* 36:30 [a]Or *bases* [b]Lit *two sockets* 36:31 [A]Ex 26:26-29 36:32 [a]Or *second* [b]Lit *extreme parts* 36:33 [a]Lit *midst* 36:35 [a]Or *violet* [A]Ex 26:31-37 36:36 [a]Or *bases* 36:37 [a]Or *violet* [b]Lit *variegator;* i.e. a weaver in colors [A]Ex 26:36 36:38 [A]Ex 26:37

36:2–7 The people, stubborn and disobedient at times, nevertheless rose to the occasion and voluntarily brought much more than was needed for the building of the tabernacle. *See note on 25:2.*

36:8–39:43 The report of the work done is repeated in the past tense. This report also highlighted how careful the workers were in carrying out the instructions and blueprints received. Note the repeated refrain on doing all just as the Lord had commanded Moses (39:1, 5, 7, 21, 26, 29, 31, 32, 42, 43 and 40:19, 21, 23, 25, 27, 29, 32).

36:8–37 *See notes on chap. 26.*

hooks, and he overlaid their tops and their [a]bands
with gold; but their five [b]sockets were of [c]bronze.

CONSTRUCTION CONTINUES

37 [A]Now Bezalel made the ark of acacia wood;
its length was two and a half [a]cubits, and
its width one and a half cubits, and its height one
and a half cubits; 2 and he overlaid it with pure
gold inside and out, and made a gold molding for
it all around. 3 He cast four rings of gold for it on
its four feet; even two rings on one side of it, and
two rings on the [a]other side of it. 4 He made poles
of acacia wood and overlaid them with gold. 5 He
put the poles into the rings on the sides of the ark,
to carry [a]it. 6 He made a [a]mercy seat of pure gold,
two and a half cubits [b]long and one and a half cubits
[c]wide. 7 He made two cherubim of gold; he made
them of hammered work [a]at the two ends of the
mercy seat; 8 one cherub [a]at the one end and one
cherub [a]at the other end; he made the cherubim *of
one piece* with the mercy seat [a]at the two ends. 9 The
cherubim had *their* wings spread upward, covering
the [a]mercy seat with their wings, with their faces
toward each other; the faces of the cherubim were
toward the mercy seat.
10 [A]Then he made the table of acacia wood, two
[a]cubits [b]long and a cubit [c]wide and one and a half
cubits [d]high. 11 He overlaid it with pure gold, and
made a gold molding for it all around. 12 He made a
rim for it of a handbreadth all around, and made a
gold molding for its rim all around. 13 He cast four
gold rings for it and put the rings on the four corners that were on its four feet. 14 Close by the rim
were the rings, the holders for the poles to carry the
table. 15 He made the poles of acacia wood and overlaid them with gold, to carry the table. 16 He made
the utensils which were on the table, its [a]dishes and
its pans and its [b]bowls and its jars, with which to
pour out drink offerings, of pure gold.
17 [A]Then he made the lampstand of pure gold. He
made the lampstand of hammered work, its base
and its shaft; its cups, its [a]bulbs and its flowers were
of one piece with it. 18 There were six branches going
out of its sides; three branches of the lampstand
from the one side of it and three branches of the
lampstand from the [a]other side of it; 19 three cups
shaped like almond *blossoms,* a [a]bulb and a flower
in one branch, and three cups shaped like almond
blossoms, a [a]bulb and a flower in the other branch—
so for the six branches going out of the lampstand.
20 In the lampstand *there were* four cups shaped
like almond *blossoms,* its [a]bulbs and its flowers;
21 and a [a]bulb was under the *first* pair of branches
coming out of it, and a [a]bulb under the *second* pair
of branches *coming* out of it, and a [a]bulb under the
third pair of branches *coming* out of it, for the six
branches coming out of the lampstand. 22 Their
[a]bulbs and their branches were *of one piece* with it;
the whole of it *was* a single hammered work of pure
gold. 23 He made its seven lamps with its snuffers
and its [a]trays of pure gold. 24 He made it and all its
utensils from a talent of pure gold.
25 [A]Then he made the altar of incense of acacia
wood: a cubit [a]long and a cubit [b]wide, square, and
two cubits [c]high; its horns were *of one piece* with
it. 26 He overlaid it with pure gold, its top and its
[a]sides all around, and its horns; and he made a gold
molding for it all around. 27 He made two golden
rings for it under its molding, on its two sides—on
opposite sides—as holders for poles with which
to carry it. 28 He made the poles of acacia wood
and overlaid them with gold. 29 [A]And he made the
holy anointing oil and the pure, fragrant incense
of spices, the work of a perfumer.

THE TABERNACLE COMPLETED

38 [A]Then he made the altar of burnt offering
of acacia wood, five [a]cubits [b]long, and five
cubits [c]wide, square, and three cubits [d]high. 2 He
made its horns on its four corners, its horns [a]being
of one piece with it, and he overlaid it with [b]bronze.
3 He made all the utensils of the altar, the pails and
the shovels and the basins, the flesh hooks and the
firepans; he made all its utensils of bronze. 4 He
made for the altar a grating of bronze network
beneath, under its ledge, reaching halfway up. 5 He
cast four rings on the four ends of the bronze grating *as* holders for the poles. 6 He made the poles of
acacia wood and overlaid them with bronze. 7 He
inserted the poles into the rings on the sides of
the altar, with which to carry it. He made it hollow
with planks.
8 [A]Moreover, he made the laver of bronze with
its base of bronze, [a]from the mirrors of the serving women who served at the doorway of the tent
of meeting.
9 [A]Then he made the court: [a]for the south side the
hangings of the court were of fine twisted linen, one
hundred cubits; 10 their twenty pillars, and their
twenty [a]sockets, *made* of bronze; the hooks of the
pillars and their [b]bands *were* of silver. 11 For the north
side *there were* one hundred cubits; their twenty
pillars and their twenty [a]sockets *were* of bronze, the
hooks of the pillars and their [b]bands *were* of silver.
12 For the west side *there were* hangings of fifty cubits *with* their ten pillars and their ten [a]sockets; the
hooks of the pillars and their [b]bands *were* of silver.
13 For the [a]east side fifty cubits. 14 The hangings for

36:38 [a]Or *fillets, rings* [b]Or *bases* [c]Or *copper* 37:1 [a]I.e. One cubit equals approx 18 in. [A]Ex 25:10-20 37:3 [a]Lit *second* 37:5 [a]Lit *the ark* 37:6 [a]Lit *propitiatory* [b]Lit *its length* [c]Lit *its width* 37:7 [a]Lit *from* 37:8 [a]Lit *from* 37:9 [a]Lit *propitiatory* 37:10 [a]I.e. One cubit equals approx 18 in. [b]Lit *its length* [c]Lit *its width* [d]Lit *its height* [A]Ex 25:23-29 37:16 [a]Or *platters* [b]Lit *libation bowls* 37:17 [a]Or *calyxes* [A]Ex 25:31-39 37:18 [a]Lit *second* 37:19 [a]Or *calyx* 37:20 [a]Or *calyxes* 37:21 [a]Or *calyx* 37:22 [a]Or *calyxes* 37:23 [a]Lit *snuff dishes* 37:25 [a]Lit *its length* [b]Lit *its width* [c]Lit *its height* [A]Ex 30:1-5 37:26 [a]Lit *walls* 37:29 [A]Ex 30:23-25, 34, 35 38:1 [a]I.e. One cubit equals approx 18 in. [b]Lit *its length* [c]Lit *its width* [d]Lit *its height* [A]Ex 27:1-8 38:2 [a]Lit *were* [b]Or *copper,* and so for *bronze* throughout the ch 38:8 [a]Lit *with* [A]Ex 30:18 38:9 [a]Lit *to the side of the Negev, to the south* [A]Ex 27:9-19 38:10 [a]Or *bases* [b]Or *fillets, rings* 38:11 [a]Or *bases* [b]Or *fillets, rings* 38:12 [a]Or *bases* [b]Or *fillets, rings* 38:13 [a]Lit *east side, eastward*

37:1–9 *See notes on 25:16, 17, 18.*
37:10–16 *See note on 25:30.*
37:17–24 *See note on 25:31.*
37:25–28 *See note on 30:1–10.*
37:29 *See notes on 30:22–33, 34–38.*
38:1–7 *See note on 27:1.*
38:8 *See note on 30:18–21.*
38:9–20 *See notes on 27:9, 16.*

the *one* [a]side *of the gate were* fifteen cubits, *with* their three pillars and their three [b]sockets, 15 and so for the [a]other [b]side. [c]On both sides of the gate of the court *were* hangings of fifteen cubits, *with* their three pillars and their three [d]sockets. 16 All the hangings of the court all around *were* of fine twisted linen. 17 The [a]sockets for the pillars *were* of [b]bronze, the hooks of the pillars and their [c]bands, of silver; and the overlaying of their tops, of silver, and all the pillars of the court were furnished with silver [c]bands. 18 The screen of the gate of the court was the work of the [a]weaver, of [b]blue and purple and scarlet *material* and fine twisted linen. And the length *was* twenty cubits and the [c]height *was* five cubits, corresponding to the hangings of the court. 19 Their four pillars and their four [a]sockets *were* of bronze; their hooks *were* of silver, and the overlaying of their tops and their [b]bands *were* of silver. 20 All the pegs of the [a]tabernacle and of the court all around *were* of bronze.

THE COST OF THE TABERNACLE

21 [a]This is the number of the things for the [b]tabernacle, the [b]tabernacle of the testimony, as they were [c]numbered according to the [d]command of Moses, for the service of the Levites, by the hand of Ithamar the son of Aaron the priest. 22 Now [A]Bezalel the son of Uri, the son of Hur, of the tribe of Judah, made all that the LORD had commanded Moses. 23 With him *was* [A]Oholiab the son of Ahisamach, of the tribe of Dan, an engraver and a skillful workman and a [a]weaver in [b]blue and in purple and in scarlet *material,* and fine linen.

24 All the gold that was used for the work, in all the work of the sanctuary, even the gold of the wave offering, was 29 talents and 730 shekels, according to [A]the shekel of the sanctuary. 25 [A]The silver of those of the congregation who were [a]numbered was 100 talents and 1,775 shekels, according to the shekel of the sanctuary; 26 [A]a beka a head (*that is,* half a shekel according to the shekel of the sanctuary), for each one who passed over to those who were [a]numbered, from twenty years old and upward, for [B]603,550 men. 27 The hundred talents of silver were for casting the [a]sockets of the sanctuary and the [a]sockets of the veil; one hundred [a]sockets for the hundred talents, a talent for a [a]socket. 28 Of the 1,775 *shekels,* he made hooks for the pillars and overlaid their tops and made [a]bands for them. 29 The bronze of the wave offering was 70 talents and 2,400 shekels. 30 With it he made the [a]sockets to the doorway of the tent of meeting, and the bronze altar and its bronze grating, and all the utensils of the altar, 31 and the [a]sockets of the court all around and the [a]sockets of the gate of the court, and all the pegs of the [b]tabernacle and all the pegs of the court all around.

THE PRIESTLY GARMENTS

39 Moreover, from the [a,A]blue and purple and scarlet *material,* they made finely [B]woven garments for ministering in the holy place [b]as well as the holy garments which were for Aaron, just as the LORD had commanded Moses.

2 [A]He made the ephod of gold, *and* of [a]blue and purple and scarlet *material,* and fine twisted linen. 3 Then they hammered out gold sheets and cut *them* into threads [a]to be woven in *with* the [b]blue and the purple and the scarlet *material,* and the fine linen, the work of a skillful workman. 4 They made attaching shoulder pieces for [a]the ephod; it was attached at its two *upper* ends. 5 The skillfully woven band which was on it was like its workmanship, [a]of the same material: of gold *and* of [b]blue and purple and scarlet *material,* and fine twisted linen, just as the LORD had commanded Moses.

6 [A]They made the onyx stones, set in gold filigree *settings;* they were engraved *like* the engravings of a signet, according to the names of the sons of Israel. 7 And [A]he placed them on the shoulder pieces of the ephod, *as* memorial stones for the sons of Israel, just as the LORD had commanded Moses.

8 [A]He made the breastpiece, the work of a skillful workman, like the workmanship of the ephod: of gold *and* of [a]blue and purple and scarlet *material* and fine twisted linen. 9 It was square; they made the breastpiece folded double, a span [a]long and a span [b]wide when folded double. 10 And they [a]mounted four rows of stones on it. The first row *was* a row of ruby, topaz, and emerald; 11 and the second row, a turquoise, a sapphire and a diamond; 12 and the third row, a jacinth, an agate, and an amethyst; 13 and the fourth row, a beryl, an onyx, and a jasper. They were set in gold filigree *settings* when they were [a]mounted. 14 The stones were corresponding to the names of the sons of Israel; they were

38:14 [a]Lit *shoulder* [b]Or *bases* 38:15 [a]Lit *second* [b]Lit *shoulder* [c]Lit *On this side and on that side* [d]Or *bases* 38:17 [a]Or *bases* [b]Or *copper* [c]Or *fillets, rings* 38:18 [a]Lit *variegator;* i.e. a weaver in colors [b]Or *violet* [c]Lit *height in width* 38:19 [a]Or *bases* [b]Or *fillets, rings* 38:20 [a]Lit *dwelling place* 38:21 [a]Lit *These are the appointed things of the tabernacle* [b]Lit *dwelling place* [c]Lit *appointed* [d]Lit *mouth* 38:22 [A]Ex 31:2 38:23 [a]Lit *variegator;* i.e. a weaver in colors [b]Or *violet* [A]Ex 31:6 38:24 [A]Ex 30:13; Lev 27:25; Num 3:47; 18:16 38:25 [a]Lit *mustered* [A]Ex 30:11-16 38:26 [a]Lit *mustered* [A]Ex 30:13, 15 [B]Ex 12:37; Num 1:46; 26:51 38:27 [a]Or *bases* 38:28 [a]Or *fillets, rings* 38:30 [a]Or *bases* 38:31 [a]Or *bases* [b]Lit *dwelling place* 39:1 [a]Or *violet* [b]Lit *and they made* [A]Ex 35:23 [B]Ex 31:10; 35:19 39:2 [a]Or *violet* [A]Ex 28:6-12 39:3 [a]Lit *to work* [b]Or *violet* 39:4 [a]Lit *it* 39:5 [a]Lit *from it* [b]Or *violet* 39:6 [A]Ex 28:9-11 39:7 [A]Ex 28:12 39:8 [a]Or *violet* [A]Ex 28:15-28 39:9 [a]Lit *its length* [b]Lit *its width* 39:10 [a]Lit *filled* 39:13 [a]Lit *filled*

38:21–31 The inventory taken calculates out at half a shekel (cf. 30:13–16) per man 20 years old and up to equal 603,550 men (cf. Nu 1:46 and the first census). Talents were about 75 pounds and shekels about half an ounce.

39:1, 2 **they made ... He made.** The third-person plural, "they," dominating the manufacturing report (vv. 2–31), is interrupted 4 times by the singular "he" (vv. 2, 7, 8, 22). The plural undoubtedly refers to Bezalel and/or his associates in operation, whereas the singular marks out what Bezalel worked on by himself.

39:1 **as the LORD had commanded Moses.** This repetitive refrain (vv. 1, 5, 7, 21, 26, 29, 31), a quality-control statement, signals to the reader of every age, or to the listener in Israel back then, that God's detailed instructions to Moses on the fabricating of the ephod (vv. 2–7), breastpiece (vv. 8–21), and priestly garments (vv. 22–31) were followed to the letter. Obedience in every detail was taken seriously by Israel's artisans.

39:2 **He made the ephod.** *See note on 28:5–13.*

39:3 **they hammered out gold sheets and cut *them* into threads.** The process adopted to get the delicate strips for braided chains or gold embroidery work conformed well with contemporary Egyptian methods of gold-working.

39:8 **He made the breastpiece.** *See notes on 28:15–30.* The Urim and Thummim were inserted into the breastpiece and became an essential part of it, or were seen as a permanent connection with it.

twelve, corresponding to their names, *engraved with* the engravings of a signet, each with its name for the twelve tribes. 15 They made on the breastpiece chains like cords, of twisted cordage work in pure gold. 16 They made two gold filigree *settings* and two gold rings, and put the two rings on the two ends of the breastpiece. 17 Then they put the two gold cords in the two rings at the ends of the breastpiece. 18 They put the *other* two ends of the two cords on the two filigree *settings*, and put them on the shoulder pieces of the ephod at the front of it. 19 They made two gold rings and placed *them* on the two ends of the breastpiece, on its inner edge which was next to the ephod. 20 Furthermore, they made two gold rings and placed them on the bottom of the two shoulder pieces of the ephod, on the front of it, close to the place where it joined, above the woven band of the ephod. 21 They bound the breastpiece by its rings to the rings of the ephod with a [a]blue cord, so that it would be on the woven band of the ephod, and that the breastpiece would not come loose from the ephod, just as the LORD had commanded Moses.

22 [A]Then he made the robe of the ephod of woven work, all of [a]blue; 23 [A]and the opening of the robe was *at the top* in the center, as the opening of a coat of mail, with a binding all around its opening, so that it would not be torn. 24 They made pomegranates of [a]blue and purple and scarlet *material and* twisted *linen* on the hem of the robe. 25 They also made bells of pure gold, and put the bells between the pomegranates all around on the hem of the [a]robe, 26 [a]alternating a bell and a pomegranate all around on the hem of the robe for the service, just as the LORD had commanded Moses.

27 [A]They made the tunics of finely woven linen for Aaron and his sons, 28 and the turban of fine linen, and the decorated [a]caps of fine linen, and the linen breeches of fine twisted linen, 29 and the sash of fine twisted linen, and [a]blue and purple and scarlet *material*, the work of the [b]weaver, just as the LORD had commanded Moses.

30 [A]They made the plate of the holy crown of pure gold, and [a]inscribed it like the engravings of a signet, "Holy to the LORD." 31 They [a]fastened a [b]blue cord to it, to [a]fasten it on the turban above, just as the LORD had commanded Moses.

32 Thus all the work of the [a]tabernacle of the tent of meeting was completed; and the sons of Israel did according to all that the LORD had commanded Moses; so they did. 33 They brought the tabernacle to Moses, the tent and all its [a]furnishings: its clasps, its boards, its bars, and its pillars and its [b]sockets; 34 and the covering of rams' skins [a]dyed red, and the covering of porpoise skins, and the screening veil; 35 the ark of the testimony and its poles and the [a]mercy seat; 36 the table, all its utensils, and the bread of the [a]Presence; 37 the pure *gold* lampstand, [a]with its arrangement of lamps and all its utensils, and the oil for the light; 38 and the gold altar, and the anointing oil and the fragrant incense, and the veil for the doorway of the tent; 39 the [a]bronze altar and its [a]bronze grating, its poles and all its utensils, the laver and its stand; 40 the hangings for the court, its pillars and its [a]sockets, and the screen for the gate of the court, its cords and its pegs and all the [b]equipment for the service of the tabernacle, for the tent of meeting; 41 the woven garments for ministering in the holy place and the holy garments for Aaron the priest and the garments of his sons, to minister as priests. 42 So the sons of Israel did all the work according to all that the LORD had commanded Moses. 43 And Moses [a]examined all the work and behold, they had done it; just as the LORD had commanded, this they had done. So Moses [A]blessed them.

THE TABERNACLE ERECTED

40 Then the LORD spoke to Moses, saying, 2 "[A]On the first day of the first month you shall set up the [a]tabernacle of the tent of meeting. 3 [A]You shall

39:21 [a]Or *violet* 39:22 [a]Or *violet* [A]Ex 28:31, 34 39:23 [A]Ex 28:32 39:24 [a]Or *violet* 39:25 [a]Lit *robe, between the pomegranates* 39:26 [a]Lit *a bell and a pomegranate, a bell...* 39:27 [A]Ex 28:39, 40, 42 39:28 [a]Lit *headgear* 39:29 [a]Or *violet* [b]Lit *variegator;* i.e. a weaver in colors 39:30 [a]Lit *wrote on it a writing* [A]Ex 28:36, 37 39:31 [a]Lit *put* [b]Or *violet* 39:32 [a]Lit *dwelling place* 39:33 [a]Or *utensils* [b]Or *bases* 39:34 [a]Or *tanned* 39:35 [a]Lit *propitiatory* 39:36 [a]Lit *Face* 39:37 [a]Lit *its lamps, the lamps set in order* 39:39 [a]Or *copper* 39:40 [a]Or *bases* [b]Or *utensils* 39:43 [a]Lit *saw* [A]Lev 9:22, 23; Num 6:23-26 40:2 [a]Lit *dwelling place* [A]Ex 19:1; 40:17; Num 1:1 40:3 [A]Ex 26:33; 40:21; Num 4:5

39:22 he made the robe of the ephod. *See note on 28:31–35.*

39:27 They made the tunics ... for Aaron and his sons. *See notes on 28:39–43.*

39:30 They made the plate of the holy crown. *See note on 28:36–38* on this special plate engraved with its message of God's purity and separation from all the profane and impure.

39:32 Thus all the work ... was completed. Finally the moment arrived when all the different tasks assigned to different craftsmen were all completed, and the great task on which they embarked was ready for formal presentation to Israel's leader. **and the sons of Israel.** No individual artisan is singled out for special mention or award; instead the whole nation was represented as doing everything in accordance with the Lord's instructions to Moses. **so they did.** In what is almost an offhanded aside, emphasis is placed on the strict attention paid to the official, divine specifications for all parts of the work for the tabernacle.

39:33 They brought the tabernacle to Moses. Attestations of obedience and accuracy provide, as it were, an envelope (vv. 32, 42, 43) for the concise inventory of all the parts included in that presentation to Moses. None of the individual parts listed, nor the sum of them, reflect just human ingenuity in designing something they wanted to have, but reflect instead just what their Lord required them to have. It was fully His architecture and His design at every level of the undertaking.

39:42, 43 The double repetition of the same quality-control refrain found earlier in the chapter together with the 2 additional phrases emphasizing exact conformity (note "behold" and "just as") to all specifications combine to formally mark the closing of these great God-initiated preparations for the place of His presence and the site of their worship. Israel's skillful craftsmen had done their work with zero tolerance for error in mind!

39:43 Moses examined all the work. Fittingly enough, the one who had been with God on the mount and had passed on to the people the blueprints for everything connected with the Lord's tabernacle personally inspected the work and confirmed its successful completion. The term "work" is to be taken as "the end result of professional and skilled craftsmen." **So Moses blessed them.** By this act, Moses set his final and formal seal of approval on the outcome of their earnestness and diligence, and expressed his prayer-wish that good would result to them from their God. This is the only instance recorded in Exodus of Moses' pronouncing a blessing upon his people. The other appearances of the verb "to bless" occur 3 times with God as the subject of the verb (20:11, 24; 23:25) and one time with Pharaoh requesting Moses to bless him (12:32).

40:1–33 Finally the time arrived for the tabernacle to be erected with the Holy of Holies and its accompanying Holy Place to the W, and the courtyard entrance to the E.

place the ark of the testimony there, and you shall
screen the ark with the veil. 4 You shall [A]bring in the
table and [a,B]arrange what belongs on it; and you
shall [C]bring in the lampstand and [b]mount its lamps.
5 Moreover, you shall [A]set the gold altar of incense
before the ark of the testimony, and set up the veil
for the doorway to the tabernacle. 6 You shall set
the altar of burnt offering in front of the doorway
of the tabernacle of the tent of meeting. 7 You shall
[A]set the laver between the tent of meeting and the
altar and put water [a]in it. 8 You shall set up the court
all around and [a]hang up the veil for the gateway of
the court. 9 Then you shall take the anointing oil and
[A]anoint the tabernacle and all that is in it, and shall
consecrate it and all its [a]furnishings; and it shall be
holy. 10 You shall anoint the altar of burnt offering
and all its utensils, and consecrate the altar, and [A]the
altar shall be most holy. 11 You shall anoint the laver
and its stand, and consecrate it. 12 Then you shall
[A]bring Aaron and his sons to the doorway of the
tent of meeting and wash them with water. 13 [A]You
shall put the holy garments on Aaron and anoint
him and consecrate him, that he may minister as
a priest to Me. 14 You shall bring his sons and put
tunics on them; 15 and you shall anoint them even
as you have anointed their father, that they may
minister as priests to Me; and their anointing will
[a]qualify them for a [A]perpetual priesthood throughout their generations." 16 Thus Moses did; according
to all that the LORD had commanded him, so he did.
17 Now [A]in the first month [a]of the second year,
on the first *day* of the month, the [b]tabernacle was
erected. 18 Moses erected the tabernacle and [a]laid
its [b]sockets, and set up its boards, and [a]inserted its
bars and erected its pillars. 19 He spread the tent over
the tabernacle and put the covering of the tent [a]on
top of it, just as the LORD had commanded Moses.
20 Then he took [A]the testimony and put *it* into the
ark, and [a]attached the poles to the ark, and put the
[b]mercy seat [c]on top of the ark. 21 He brought the ark
into the tabernacle, and [A]set up a veil for the screen,
and screened off the ark of the testimony, just as
the LORD had commanded Moses. 22 Then he [A]put
the table in the tent of meeting on the north side
of the tabernacle, outside the veil. 23 He set the arrangement of [A]bread in order on it before the LORD,
just as the LORD had commanded Moses. 24 Then he
placed the lampstand in the tent of meeting, opposite the table, on the south side of the tabernacle.
25 He [A]lighted the lamps before the LORD, just as the
LORD had commanded Moses. 26 Then he [A]placed the
gold altar in the tent of meeting in front of the veil;
27 and he [A]burned fragrant incense on it, just as the
LORD had commanded Moses. 28 Then he set up the
[a]veil for the doorway of the tabernacle. 29 He [A]set
the altar of burnt offering *before* the doorway of the
tabernacle of the tent of meeting, and [B]offered on
it the burnt offering and the meal offering, just as
the LORD had commanded Moses. 30 He placed the
laver between the tent of meeting and the altar and
put water in it for washing. 31 [A]From it Moses and
Aaron and his sons washed their hands and their
feet. 32 When they entered the tent of meeting, and
when they approached the altar, they washed, just
as the LORD had commanded Moses. 33 He [A]erected
the court all around the [a]tabernacle and the altar,
and [b]hung up the veil for the gateway of the court.
Thus Moses finished the work.

THE GLORY OF THE LORD

34 [A]Then the cloud covered the tent of meeting, and
the [B]glory of the LORD filled the tabernacle. 35 Moses
[A]was not able to enter the tent of meeting because
the cloud had settled on it, and the glory of the LORD
filled the tabernacle. 36 Throughout all their journeys
[A]whenever the cloud was taken up from over the
tabernacle, the sons of Israel would set out; 37 but [A]if
the cloud was not taken up, then they did not set out
until the day when it was taken up. 38 For throughout
all their journeys, [A]the cloud of the LORD was on the
tabernacle by day, and there was fire in it by night,
in the sight of all the house of Israel.

40:4 [a]Lit *arrange its arrangement* [b]Or *light* [A]Ex 26:35; 40:22 [B]Ex 25:30; 40:23 [C]Ex 40:24f 40:5 [A]Ex 40:26 40:7 [a]Lit *there* [A]Ex 30:18; 40:30 40:8 [a]Lit *put the screen* 40:9 [a]Or *utensils* [A]Ex 30:26; Lev 8:10 40:10 [A]Ex 29:37 40:12 [A]Lev 8:1-6 40:13 [A]Ex 28:41; Lev 8:13 40:15 [a]Lit *be for them* [A]Ex 29:9; Num 25:13 40:17 [a]Lit *in* [b]Lit *dwelling place* [A]Ex 40:2 40:18 [a]Lit *put* [b]Or *bases* 40:19 [a]Lit *over it above* 40:20 [a]Lit *set* [b]Lit *propitiatory* [c]Lit *over the ark above* [A]Ex 25:16; Deut 10:5; 1 Kin 8:9; 2 Chr 5:10; Heb 9:4 40:21 [A]Ex 26:33 40:22 [A]Ex 26:35 40:23 [A]Ex 25:30; Lev 24:5, 6 40:25 [A]Ex 25:37; 40:4 40:26 [A]Ex 30:6; 40:5 40:27 [A]Ex 30:7 40:28 [a]Or *screen* 40:29 [A]Ex 40:6 [B]Ex 29:38-42 40:31 [A]Ex 30:19, 20 40:33 [a]Or *dwelling place* [b]Lit *put the screen* [A]Ex 27:9-18; 40:8 40:34 [A]Num 9:15-23 [B]1 Kin 8:11; Ezek 43:4f; Rev 15:8 40:35 [A]1 Kin 8:11; 2 Chr 5:13, 14 40:36 [A]Num 9:17; Neh 9:19 40:37 [A]Num 9:19-22 40:38 [A]Ex 13:21; Num 9:12, 15; Ps 78:14; Is 4:5

In terms of pagan religions and their worship of the sun god, some polemic significance might be seen in the High Priest worshiping God with his back to the rising sun. All who entered the courtyard also turned their backs to the rising sun as they came in to sacrifice and worship.

40:17 The tabernacle was completed almost one year after the Exodus from Egypt. The people were at the foot of Mt. Sinai at that time, where the book of Leviticus was given in the first month of that second year. The record of Numbers begins with the people still at Mt. Sinai in the second month of that second year after leaving Egypt (cf. Nu 1:1).

40:34 the cloud covered … the glory of the LORD filled. This was the final confirmation for Moses and the people that all the work for setting up God's dwelling place had been properly done and all the tedious instructions obediently followed.

40:36 taken up. This first occurred (as recorded in Nu 10:11) 50 days after the tabernacle was finished and erected.

THE THIRD BOOK
OF MOSES CALLED

LEVITICUS

TITLE

The original Hebrew title of this third book of the law is taken from the first word, translated "And He called." Several OT books derive their Hebrew names in the same manner (e.g., Genesis, "In the beginning"; Exodus, "Now these are the names"). The title "Leviticus" comes from the Latin Vulgate version of the Greek OT (LXX) *Leuitikon* meaning "matters of the Levites" (25:32, 33). While the book addresses issues of the Levites' responsibilities, much more significantly all the priests are instructed in how they are to assist the people in worship, and the people are informed about how to live a holy life. New Testament writers quote the book of Leviticus over 15 times.

AUTHOR AND DATE

Authorship and date issues are resolved by the concluding verse of the book, "These are the commandments which the LORD commanded Moses for the sons of Israel at Mount Sinai" (27:34; cf. 7:38; 25:1; 26:46). The fact that God gave these laws to Moses (cf. 1:1) appears 56 times in Leviticus' 27 chapters. In addition to recording detailed prescriptions, the book chronicles several historical accounts relating to the laws (see 8–10; 24:10–23). The Exodus occurred in 1445 B.C. (see Introduction to Exodus: Author and Date) and the tabernacle was finished one year later (Ex 40:17). Leviticus picks up the record at that point, probably revealed in the first month (Abib/Nisan) of the second year after the Exodus. The book of Numbers begins after that in the second month (Ziv; cf. Nu 1:1).

BACKGROUND AND SETTING

Before the year that Israel camped at Mt. Sinai: 1) the presence of God's glory had never formally resided among the Israelites; 2) a central place of worship, like the tabernacle, had never existed; 3) a structured and regulated set of sacrifices and feasts had not been given; and 4) a High Priest, a formal priesthood, and a cadre of tabernacle workers had not been appointed. As Exodus concluded, features one and two had been accomplished, thereby requiring that elements three and four be inaugurated, which is where Leviticus fits in. Exodus 19:6 called Israel to be "a kingdom of priests and a holy nation." Leviticus in turn is God's instruction for His newly redeemed people, teaching them how to worship and obey Him.

Israel had, up to that point, only the historical records of the patriarchs from which to gain their knowledge of how to worship and live before their God. Having been slaves for centuries in Egypt, the land of a seemingly infinite number of gods, their concept of worship and the godly life was severely distorted. Their tendency to hold on to polytheism and pagan ritual is witnessed in the wilderness wanderings, e.g., when they worshiped the golden calf (cf. Ex 32). God would not permit them to worship in the ways of their Egyptian neighbors, nor would He tolerate Egyptian ideas about morality and sin. With the instructions in Leviticus, the priests could lead Israel in worship appropriate to the Lord.

Even though the book contains a great deal of law, it is presented in a historical format. Immediately after Moses supervised the construction of the tabernacle, God came in glory to dwell there; this marked the close of the book of Exodus (40:34–38). Leviticus begins with God calling Moses from the tabernacle and ends with God's commands to Moses in the form of binding legislation. Israel's King had occupied His palace (the tabernacle), instituted His law, and declared Himself a covenant partner with His subjects.

No geographical movement occurs in this book. The people of Israel stay at the foot of Sinai, the mountain where God came down to give His law (25:1; 26:46; 27:34). They were still there one month later when the record of Numbers began (cf. Nu 1:1).

HISTORICAL AND THEOLOGICAL THEMES

The core ideas around which Leviticus develops are the holy character of God and the will of God for Israel's holiness. God's holiness, mankind's sinfulness, sacrifice, and God's presence in the sanctuary are the book's most common themes. With a clear, authoritative tone, the book sets forth instruction toward personal holiness at the urging of God (11:44, 45; 19:2; 20:7, 26; cf. 1Pe 1:14–16). Matters pertaining to Israel's life of faith tend to focus on purity in ritual settings, but not to the exclusion of concerns regarding Israel's personal purity. In fact, there is a continuing emphasis on personal holiness in response to the holiness of God (cf. this emphasis in chaps. 17–27). On over 125 occasions, Leviticus indicts mankind for uncleanness and/or instructs on how to be purified. The motive for such holiness is stated in two repeated phrases: "I am the Lord" and "I am holy." These are used over 50 times. *See note on 11:44, 45.*

The theme of the conditional Mosaic Covenant resurfaces throughout the book, but particularly in chap. 26. This contract for the new nation not only details the consequences for obedience or disobedience to the covenant stipulations, but it does so in a manner scripted for determining Israel's history. One cannot help but recognize prophetic implications in the punishments for disobedience; they sound like the events of the much later Babylonian deportment, captivity, and subsequent return to the land almost 900 years after Moses wrote Leviticus (ca. 538 B.C.). The eschatological implications for Israel's disobedience will not conclude until Messiah comes to introduce His kingdom and end the curses of Lv 26 and Dt 28 (cf. Zec 14:11).

The 5 sacrifices and offerings were symbolic. Their design was to allow the truly penitent and thankful worshiper to express faith in and love for God by the observance of these rituals. When the heart was not penitent and thankful, God was not pleased with the ritual. Cf. Am 5:21–27. The offerings were burnt, symbolizing the worshiper's desire to be purged of sin and sending up the fragrant smoke of true worship to God. The myriad of small details in the execution of the rituals was to teach exactness and precision that would extend to the way the people obeyed the moral and spiritual laws of God and the way they revered every facet of His Word.

INTERPRETIVE CHALLENGES

Leviticus is both a manual for the worship of God in Israel and a theology of Old Covenant ritual. Comprehensive understanding of the ceremonies, laws, and ritual details prescribed in the book is difficult today because Moses assumed a certain context of historical understanding. Once the challenge of understanding the detailed prescriptions has been met, the question arises as to how believers in the church should respond to them, since the NT clearly abrogates OT ceremonial law (cf. Ac 10:1–16; Col 2:16, 17), the levitical priesthood (cf. 1Pe 2:9; Rev 1:6; 5:10; 20:6), and the sanctuary (cf. Mt 27:51), as well as instituting the New Covenant (cf. Mt 26:28; 2Co 3:6–18; Heb 7–10). Rather than try to practice the old ceremonies or look for some deeper spiritual significance in them, the focus should be on the holy and divine character behind them. This may partly be the reason that explanations which Moses often gave in the prescriptions for cleanness offer greater insight into the mind of God than do the ceremonies themselves. The spiritual principles in which the rituals were rooted are timeless because they are embedded in the nature of God. The NT makes it clear that from Pentecost forward (cf. Ac 2), the church is under the authority of the New Covenant, not the Old (cf. Heb 7–10).

The interpreter is challenged to compare features of this book with NT writers who present types or analogies based on the tabernacle and the ceremonial aspects of the law, so as to teach valuable lessons about Christ and New Covenant reality. Though the ceremonial law served only as a shadow of the reality of Christ and His redemptive work (Heb 10:1), excessive typology is to be rejected. Only that which NT writers identify as types of Christ should be so designated (cf. 1Co 5:7, "Christ our Passover").

The most profitable study in Leviticus is that which yields truth in the understanding of sin, guilt, substitutionary death, and atonement by focusing on features which are not explained or illustrated elsewhere in OT Scripture. Later OT authors, and especially NT writers, build on the basic understanding of these matters provided in Leviticus. The sacrificial features of Leviticus point to their ultimate, one-time fulfillment in the substitutionary death of Jesus Christ (Heb 9:11–22).

OUTLINE

Leviticus 1–16 explains how to have personal access to God through appropriate worship and Leviticus 17–27 details how to be spiritually acceptable to God through an obedient walk.

OUTLINE

I. Laws Pertaining to Sacrifice (1:1–7:38)
- A. Legislation for the Laity (1:1–6:7)
  1. Burnt offerings (chap. 1)
  2. Grain offerings (chap. 2)
  3. Peace offerings (chap. 3)
  4. Sin offerings (4:1–5:13)
  5. Guilt offerings (5:14–6:7)
- B. Legislation for the Priesthood (6:8–7:38)
  1. Burnt offerings (6:8–13)
  2. Grain offerings (6:14–23)
  3. Sin offerings (6:24–30)
  4. Guilt offerings (7:1–10)
  5. Peace offerings (7:11–36)
  6. Concluding remarks (7:37, 38)

II. Beginnings of the Priesthood (8:1–10:20)

A. Ordination of Aaron and His Sons (chap. 8)
B. First Sacrifices (chap. 9)
C. Execution of Nadab and Abihu (chap. 10)

III. Prescriptions for Uncleanness (11:1–16:34)

A. Unclean Animals (chap. 11)
B. Uncleanness of Childbirth (chap. 12)
C. Unclean Diseases (chap. 13)
D. Cleansing of Diseases (chap. 14)
E. Unclean Discharges (chap. 15)
F. Purification of the Tent of Meeting from Uncleanness (chap. 16)

IV. Guidelines for Practical Holiness (17:1–27:34)

A. Sacrifice and Food (chap. 17)
B. Proper Sexual Behavior (chap. 18)
C. Neighborliness (chap. 19)
D. Capital/Grave Crimes (chap. 20)
E. Instructions for Priests (chaps. 21, 22)
F. Religious Festivals (chap. 23)
G. The Tabernacle (24:1–9)
H. An Account of Blasphemy (24:10–23)
I. Sabbatical and Jubilee Years (chap. 25)
J. Exhortation to Obey the Law: Blessings and Curses (chap. 26)
K. Redemption of Votive Gifts (chap. 27)

THE LAW OF BURNT OFFERINGS

1 Then [A]the LORD called to Moses and spoke to
him from the tent of meeting, saying, 2 "Speak to
the sons of Israel and say to them, 'When any man
of you brings an [a,A]offering to the LORD, you shall
bring your [a]offering of animals from [B]the herd or
the flock. 3 If his offering is a [A]burnt offering from
the herd, he shall offer it, a male [B]without defect; he
shall offer it [C]at the doorway of the tent of meeting,
that he may be accepted before the LORD. 4 [A]He shall
lay his hand on the head of the burnt offering, that
it may be accepted for him to make [B]atonement on
his behalf. 5 [A]He shall slay the [a]young bull before
the LORD; and Aaron's sons the priests shall offer up [B]the blood and [C]sprinkle the blood around
on the altar that is at the doorway of the tent of
meeting. 6 [A]He shall then skin the burnt offering
and cut it into its pieces. 7 [A]The sons of Aaron the
priest shall put fire on the altar and arrange wood
on the fire. 8 Then Aaron's sons the priests shall
arrange the pieces, the head and the [A]suet over
the wood which is on the fire that is on the altar.

1:1 [A]Ex 19:3; 25:22; Num 7:89 1:2 [a]Heb *qorban* [A]Mark 7:11 [B]Lev 22:18f 1:3 [A]Lev 6:8-13 [B]Ex 12:5; Lev 22:20-24; Deut 15:21; 17:1 [C]Lev 17:8, 9; Deut 12:5, 6, 11 1:4 [A]Ex 29:10, 15, 19; Lev 3:2, 8 [B]Ex 29:33; Lev 4:20, 26, 31; 2 Chr 29:23, 24 1:5 [a]Or *one of the herd;* lit *son of the herd* [A]Ex 29:11, 16, 20 [B]Lev 17:11 [C]Lev 1:11; 3:2, 8, 13; Heb 12:24; 1 Pet 1:2 1:6 [A]Lev 7:8 1:7 [A]Lev 6:8-13 1:8 [A]Lev 1:12; 3:3, 4; 8:20

1:1–7:38 This section provides laws pertaining to sacrifice. For the first time in Israel's history, a well-defined set of sacrifices was given to them, although people had offered sacrifices since the time of Abel and Cain (cf. Ge 4:3, 4). This section contains instructions for the people (1:1–6:7) and the priests (6:8–7:38). For a comparison with the millennial kingdom sacrifices, *see notes on Eze 45, 46.*

1:1–6:7 God had taken the nation at its word, "All that the LORD has spoken we will do" (Ex 19:8; 24:3–8), and gave detailed instructions as to how they were to sacrifice to Him. Five sacrifices were outlined: the first 3 were voluntary, the last 2 compulsory. They were: 1) burnt offering (1:1–17); 2) grain offering (2:1–16); 3) peace offering (3:1–17); 4) sin offering (4:1–5:13); and 5) trespass or guilt offering (5:14–6:7). All these offerings were forms of worship to God, to give expression of the penitent and thankful heart. Those who were truly God's by faith gave these offerings with an attitude of worship; for the rest, they were external rituals only.

1:1 the LORD called to Moses. Leviticus begins where Exodus left off (see Introduction: Author and Date; Background and Setting). No sooner did the glory cloud come down to rest on the tabernacle in the concluding verses of Exodus than God instructed Moses with the content in Leviticus. The question of how to use the tabernacle in worship is answered here by an audible voice from the Divine Glory over the ark in the Holy of Holies (cf. Ex 40:34; Nu 7:89; Ps 80:1). **tent of meeting.** This is so named since it was the place where Israel would gather to meet the Lord (cf. Ex 25:8, 22; 26:1–37). See Ex 25–32 for a detailed description of the tabernacle.

1:2 Speak to the sons of Israel. This is essential revelation, with reference to their spiritual life, for all the descendants of Jacob, who was also called Israel (cf. Ge 32:28). **When any man of you brings.** These were completely voluntary and freewill offerings with no specific number or frequency given (1:3). The regulation excluded horses, dogs, pigs, camels, and donkeys, which were used in pagan sacrifices, as well as rabbits, deer, beasts, and birds of prey. The sacrifice had to be from the offerer's herd, or he had to purchase it. **an offering.** The Pharisees manipulated this simple concept so that adult children could selfishly withhold the material goods which would help their parents, under the guise of *Corban,* that it was dedicated to the Lord (cf. Mk 7:8–13). **herd ... flock.** These terms refer to the cattle (1:3), sheep, or goats (1:10) respectively. Only domestic animals could be sacrificed.

1:3–17 See 6:8–13 for the priests' instructions. The burnt offerings were the first sacrifices revealed because these were the ones to be most frequently offered: every morning and evening (Nu 28:1–8), every Sabbath (Nu 28:9, 10), the first day of each month (Nu 28:11–15), and at the special feasts (Nu 28:16–29:40). This offering signified voluntary and complete dedication and consecration to the Lord. It was an offering of repentance for sins committed, with the desire to be purged from the guilt of sinful acts. Designed to demonstrate the sinner's penitence and obedience, it indicated his self-dedication to the worship of God. The most costly animal was mentioned first; the least costly last. The singing of psalms later became a part of this ritual (cf. Pss 4; 5; 40; 50; 66).

1:3–9 This section describes the sacrifice of bulls (1:5).

1:3 burnt offering. This offering is so called because it required that the animal be completely consumed by the fire, except for the crop of feathers of a bird (1:16) or skin of the bull, which went to the priest (1:6; 7:8). **a male without defect.** Since no animal with any deformity or defect was permitted, the priests would inspect each animal, perhaps using a method which the Egyptians employed in their sacrifices, calling for all inspected and approved animals to have a certificate attached to the horns and sealed with wax. A male without defect was required, as it was the choicest offering of the flock. **at the doorway ... before the LORD.** This entrance to the courtyard around the tabernacle where the altar of burnt offering stood (Ex 40:6) would place the one offering a sacrifice on the N side of the altar (cf. 1:11). God's presence in the cloud rested upon the mercy seat of the ark in the Holy of Holies inside the tabernacle proper (*see note on 1:1*). The offering was brought to and offered before the Lord, not before man.

1:4 lay his hand on the head. This symbolic gesture pictured the transfer of the sacrificer's sin to the sacrificial animal and was likely done with a prayer of repentance and request for forgiveness (cf. Ps 51:18, 19). **make atonement.** The word means "cover." The psalmist defines it by saying, "Blessed is he whose transgression is forgiven, whose sin *is* covered" (Ps 32:1). Theologically, the "atonement" of the OT covered sin only temporarily, but it did not eliminate sin or later judgment (Heb 10:4). The one time sacrifice of Jesus Christ fully atoned for sin, thus satisfying God's wrath forever and insuring eternal salvation (cf. Heb 9:12; 1Jn 2:2), even to those who put saving faith in God for their redemption before Christ's death on the cross (cf. Ro 3:25, 26; Heb 9:15). **on his behalf.** This was a substitutionary sacrifice that prefigured the ultimate substitute—Jesus Christ (cf. Is 53; *see note on 2Co 5:21*).

1:5 He shall slay. Making vivid and dramatic the consequences of sin, the person offering the sacrifice killed and butchered the animal (cf. v. 6). **Aaron's sons.** This refers to the immediate descendants of Aaron, i.e., Nadab, Abihu, Eleazar, and Ithamar (cf. Ex 28:1). In the beginning, there were 5 priests, including Aaron, who served as the High Priest. **shall offer up ... sprinkle the blood.** The priest had to collect the blood in a basin and then offer it to God as a sacrifice to indicate that a life had been taken, i.e., death occurred (cf. 17:11, 14). The price of sin is always death (cf. Ge 2:17; Ro 6:23). **the altar.** The altar of burnt offering (cf. Ex 27:1–8; 38:1–7), which is in the courtyard outside of the tabernacle proper. The

CHRIST IN THE LEVITICAL OFFERINGS

Offering	Christ's Provision	Christ's Character
1. Burnt Offering (Lv 1:3–17; 6:8–13)	atonement	Christ's sinless nature
2. Grain Offering (Lv 2:1–16; 6:14–23)	dedication/consecration	Christ was wholly devoted to the Father's purposes
3. Peace Offering (Lv 3:1–17; 7:11–36)	reconciliation/fellowship	Christ was at peace with God
4. Sin Offering (Lv 4:1–5:13; 6:24–30)	propitiation	Christ's substitutionary death
5. Guilt Offering (Lv 5:14–6:7; 7:1–10)	repentance	Christ paid it all for redemption

9 Its [A]entrails, however, and its legs he shall wash
with water. And [B]the priest shall offer up in smoke
all of it on the altar for a burnt offering, an offering
by fire of [C]a soothing aroma to the LORD.
10 'But if his offering is from the flock, of the sheep
or of the goats, for a burnt offering, he shall offer it
a [A]male without defect. 11 [A]He shall slay it on the side
of the altar northward before the LORD, and Aaron's
sons the priests shall sprinkle its blood around on
the altar. 12 He shall then cut it into its pieces with its
head and its [A]suet, and the priest shall arrange them
on the wood which is on the fire that is on the altar.
13 The entrails, however, and the legs he shall wash
with water. And [A]the priest shall offer all of it, and
offer it up in smoke on the altar; it is a burnt offering,
an offering by fire of a soothing aroma to the LORD.
14 'But if his offering to the LORD is a burnt offering of birds, then he shall bring his offering
from the [A]turtledoves or from young pigeons. 15 The
priest shall bring it to the altar, and wring off its
head and offer it up in smoke on the altar; and its
blood is to be drained out [A]on the side of the altar.
16 He shall also take away its crop with its feathers
and cast it beside the altar eastward, to the place
of the [a,A]ashes. 17 Then he shall tear it by its wings,
but [A]shall not sever *it*. And the priest shall offer it
up in smoke on the altar on the wood which is on
the fire; [B]it is a burnt offering, an offering by fire
of a soothing aroma to the LORD.

THE LAW OF GRAIN OFFERINGS

2 'Now when anyone presents a [A]grain offering
as an offering to the LORD, his offering shall
be of fine flour, and he shall pour oil on it and put
frankincense on it. 2 He shall then bring it to Aaron's
sons the priests; and shall take from it [A]his handful
of its fine flour and of its oil with all of its frankincense. And the priest shall offer *it* up in smoke
as its [B]memorial portion on the altar, an offering
by fire of a soothing aroma to the LORD. 3 [A]The remainder of the grain offering belongs to [B]Aaron
and his sons: a thing most holy, of the offerings to
the LORD by fire.
4 'Now when you bring an offering of a grain
offering baked in an oven, *it shall be* [A]unleavened
cakes of fine flour mixed with oil, or unleavened
wafers [a]spread with oil. 5 If your offering is a grain
offering *made* [A]on the griddle, *it shall be* of fine
flour, unleavened, mixed with oil; 6 you shall break
it into bits and pour oil on it; it is a grain offering.
7 Now if your offering is a grain offering *made*
[A]in a [a]pan, it shall be made of fine flour with oil.
8 When you bring in the grain offering which is
made of these things to the LORD, it shall be presented to the priest and he shall bring it to the
altar. 9 The priest then shall take up from the grain
offering [A]its memorial portion, and shall offer *it*
up in smoke on the altar *as* an offering by fire of
a soothing aroma to the LORD. 10 [A]The remainder
of the grain offering belongs to Aaron and his
sons: a thing most holy of the offerings to the
LORD by fire.
11 '[A]No grain offering, which you bring to the
LORD, shall be made with leaven, for you shall not
offer [a]up in smoke any leaven or any honey as an
[B]offering by fire to the LORD. 12 [A]As an offering of

1:9 [A]Ex 12:9 [B]Num 15:8-10; 28:11-14 [C]Gen 8:21; Ex 29:18, 25; Lev 1:13; Num 15:3; Eph 5:2 1:10 [A]Ex 12:5; Lev 1:3; Ezek 43:22; 1 Pet 1:19 1:11 [A]Ex 24:6; Lev 1:5; 8:19; 9:12 1:12 [A]Lev 3:3, 4 1:13 [A]Num 15:4-7; 28:11-14 1:14 [A]Gen 15:9; Lev 5:7, 11; 12:8; Luke 2:24 1:15 [A]Lev 5:9 1:16 [a]Or *fat ashes* [A]Lev 6:10 1:17 [A]Gen 15:10; Lev 5:8 [B]Lev 9:13 2:1 [A]Lev 6:14-18; Num 15:4 2:2 [A]Lev 5:12; 6:15 [B]Lev 2:9, 16; 5:12; 24:7; Acts 10:4 2:3 [A]Lev 2:10; 6:16 [B]Lev 10:12, 13 2:4 [a]Lit *anointed* [A]Ex 29:2 2:5 [A]Lev 6:21; 7:9 2:7 [a]Lit *lidded cooking pan* [A]Lev 7:9 2:9 [A]Lev 2:2, 16; 5:12 2:10 [A]Lev 2:3; 6:16 2:11 [a]Lit *up from it* [A]Ex 23:18; 34:25; Lev 6:16, 17 [B]Ex 29:25; Lev 1:13 2:12 [A]Ex 34:22; Lev 7:13; 23:10, 17, 18

prototype experience, before the tabernacle was constructed, is remembered in Ex 24:1–8.

1:9 wash. This allowed the one sacrificing to cleanse the animal of excrement and thus make it clean. **a soothing aroma.** The pleasant smell of burning meat signified the sacrifice of obedience which was pleasing to the Lord. While the costly ritual recognized God's anger for sin committed (cf. 1:13, 17), the penitent heart behind the sacrifice made it acceptable. That was far more significant than the sacrifice itself (cf. Ge 8:21; 1Sa 15:22). This is the first of 3 freewill offerings to please the Lord; cf. the grain offering (2:2) and the peace offering (3:5).

1:10–13 from the flock. This section describes the sacrifice of sheep and goats.

1:11 side … northward. This placed the one sacrificing in front of the tabernacle door (cf. 1:3).

1:14–17 of birds. This section describes the sacrifice of birds. God does not ask the poor to bring the same burnt offering as those financially well off because the relative cost to the one sacrificing was an important factor. This is the kind of sacrifice brought by Joseph and Mary on the eighth day after Christ's birth for Mary's purification (cf. 12:8; Lk 2:22–24).

1:15 The priest … wring off. Unlike the livestock being killed by the one offering the sacrifice, the bird was killed by the priest.

1:16 crop … feathers. This refers to the neck or gullet of a bird, where food was stored. **eastward … place of the ashes.** This was the closest side to the entrance of the tabernacle compound and provided for the easiest removal of the ashes outside (cf. 6:10–11).

2:1–16 See 6:14–23 for the priests' instructions. The grain offering signified homage and thanksgiving to God as a voluntary offering which was offered along with a burnt offering and a drink offering at the appointed sacrifices (cf. Nu 28:1–15). Three variations were prescribed: 1) uncooked flour (2:1–3); 2) baked flour (2:4–13); or 3) roasted firstfruit grain from the harvest (2:14–16). This was the only non-animal sacrifice of the 5 and shows that there was a place for offering from the fruit of the soil (as in the case of Cain in Ge 4).

2:1–3 fine flour. The first variation consisted of uncooked flour whose quality of "fine" paralleled the "unblemished" animal in the burnt offering. A portion of this offering was to support the priests (v. 3). Like the drink offering or "libation," the grain offering was added to the burnt offering (cf. Nu 28:1–15).

2:1 oil. *See note on 2:4.* **frankincense.** *See note on 2:15.*

2:2 handful. Unlike the whole burnt offering (1:9), only a representative or memorial portion was given to the Lord. **soothing aroma.** *See note on 1:9.*

2:3 Aaron and his sons. Unlike the burnt offering (cf. 1:9, 13, 17), this offering supplies provision for the priests. **most holy.** This was unique from the others because it was not limited to God alone, like the burnt offering, nor eaten in part by the worshiper, like the peace offering. Only the priest could eat the portion not burned (see 7:9). The sin offering (6:17, 25) and the trespass offering (6:17; 7:1) are also called "most holy."

2:4–13 This variation of the grain offering involved baked flour. The kinds of containers discussed are: 1) oven (2:4); 2) griddle (2:5, 6); and 3) covered pan (2:7–10). The manner of preparation is discussed in 2:11–13.

2:4 unleavened cakes. The notion of leaven as a symbol representing the presence of sin remains valid beyond the context of the Passover and continues to the NT (cf. Mt 16:6; 1Co 5:6, 7). **spread with oil.** Literally, "anointed with oil." Anointing is usually reserved for human appointments by God. Here, it was applied to the preparation of a holy sacrifice, set apart as a memorial to the Lord.

2:11 This applies to the offerings of 2:4–10, all of which were to be burned on the altar. **not … leaven or … honey.** Both yeast and honey were edible foods, but were never to be used with a grain offering, since both could induce fermentation, which symbolized sin (*see note on 2:4*).

2:12 This applies to the offering of 2:14–16,

first fruits you shall bring them to the LORD, but
they shall not ascend for a soothing aroma on the
altar. 13 Every grain offering of yours, moreover,
you shall season with salt, so that [A]the salt of the
covenant of your God shall not be lacking from
your grain offering; with all your offerings you
shall offer salt.
14 'Also if you bring a grain offering of early ripened things to the LORD, you shall bring [A]fresh
heads of grain roasted in the fire, grits of new
growth, for the grain offering of your early ripened things. 15 You shall then put oil on it and lay
incense on it; it is a grain offering. 16 The priest shall
offer up in smoke [A]its memorial portion, part of its
grits and its oil with all its incense as an offering
by fire to the LORD.

THE LAW OF PEACE OFFERINGS

3 'Now if his offering is a [A]sacrifice of peace offerings, if he is going to offer out of the herd,
whether male or female, he shall offer it [B]without
defect before the LORD. 2 [A]He shall lay his hand on
the head of his offering and [B]slay it at the doorway
of the tent of meeting, and Aaron's sons the priests
shall sprinkle the blood around on the altar. 3 From
the sacrifice of the peace offerings he shall present
an offering by fire to the LORD, the fat that covers
the entrails and all the fat that is on the entrails,
4 and the two kidneys with the fat that is on them,
which is on the loins, and the [a]lobe of the liver,
which he shall remove with the kidneys. 5 Then
[A]Aaron's sons shall offer *it* up in smoke on the altar
[B]on the burnt offering, which is on the wood that
is on the fire; [C]it is an offering by fire of a soothing
aroma to the LORD. 6 But if his offering for a sacrifice
of peace offerings to the LORD is from the flock, he
shall offer it, male or female, [A]without defect. 7 If
he is going to offer [A]a lamb for his offering, then
he shall offer it [B]before the LORD, 8 and [A]he shall
lay his hand on the head of his offering and [B]slay
it before the tent of meeting, and Aaron's sons shall
[C]sprinkle its blood around on the altar. 9 From the
[A]sacrifice of peace offerings he shall bring as an
offering by fire to the LORD, its fat, [a]the entire fat
tail which he shall remove close to the backbone,
and the fat that covers the entrails and all the fat
that is on the entrails, 10 and the two kidneys with
the fat that is on them, which is on the loins, and
the [a]lobe of the liver, which he shall remove [A]with
the kidneys. 11 Then the priest shall offer *it* up in
smoke [A]on the altar *as* [B]food, an offering by fire
to the LORD.
12 'Moreover, if his offering is [A]a goat, then he
shall offer it before the LORD, 13 and he shall lay
his hand on its head and slay it before the tent
of meeting, and the sons of Aaron shall sprinkle
its blood around on the altar. 14 From it he shall
present his offering as an offering by fire to the
LORD, the fat that covers the entrails and all the
fat that is on the entrails, 15 and the two kidneys
with the fat that is on them, which is on the loins,
and the [a]lobe of the liver, which he shall remove
[A]with the kidneys. 16 The priest shall offer them up
in smoke on the altar *as* food, an offering by fire
for a soothing aroma; [A]all fat is the LORD'S. 17 It is
a [A]perpetual statute throughout your generations
in all your dwellings: you shall not eat any fat [B]or
any blood.' "

THE LAW OF SIN OFFERINGS

4 Then the LORD spoke to Moses, saying, 2 "Speak
to the sons of Israel, saying, 'If a person sins [A]un-
intentionally in any of the [a]things which the LORD
has [B]commanded not to be done, and commits any

2:13 [A]Num 18:19; 2 Chr 13:5; Ezek 43:24 2:14 [A]Lev 23:14 2:16 [A]Lev 2:2 3:1 [A]Lev 7:11-34; 17:5 [B]Lev 1:3; 22:20-24 3:2 [A]Lev 1:4 [B]Ex 29:11, 16, 20 3:4 [a]*Or appendage on* 3:5 [A]Lev 7:28-34 [B]Ex 29:38-42; Num 28:3-10 [C]Num 15:8-10; 28:12-14 3:6 [A]Lev 3:1; 22:20-24 3:7 [A]Num 15:4, 5; 28:4-8 [B]Lev 17:8, 9; 1 Kin 8:62 3:8 [A]Lev 1:4 [B]Lev 3:2 [C]Lev 1:5 3:9 [a]*Lit the fat tail, entire* [A]Lev 17:5; Num 7:88; 1 Sam 10:8; 2 Sam 6:17; 1 Kin 3:15; 8:63, 64; 1 Chr 16:1 3:10 [a]*Or appendage on* [A]Lev 3:4, 15 3:11 [A]Lev 3:5 [B]Lev 3:16; 21:6, 8, 17, 22 3:12 [A]Num 15:6-11 3:15 [a]*Or appendage on* [A]Lev 3:4; 7:4 3:16 [A]Lev 7:23-25 3:17 [A]Lev 6:18, 22; 7:34, 36; 10:9, 15; 16:29; 17:7; 23:14, 21; 24:3 [B]Lev 7:26; 17:10-16 4:2 [a]*Lit commands of the LORD which are not to be done* [A]Lev 4:22, 27; 5:15-18; 22:14 [B]Lev 4:13

which was not to be burned on the altar, but rather roasted by the worshiper (v. 14) before going to the tabernacle.

2:13 the salt of the covenant. This was included in all of the offerings in 2:4–10, 14–16 since salt was emblematic of permanence or loyalty to the covenant.

2:14 early ripened things. These would be offered at the Feast of Firstfruits (23:9–14) and the Feast of Weeks (23:15–22).

2:15 incense. A gum resin with a pungent, balsamic odor, used in the tabernacle sacrifices (cf. Ex 30:34).

3:1–17 See 7:11–36 for the priests' instructions. The peace offering symbolizes the peace and fellowship between the true worshiper and God (as a voluntary offering). It was the third freewill offering resulting in a sweet aroma to the Lord (3:5), which served as the appropriate corollary to the burnt offering of atonement and the grain offering of consecration and dedication. It symbolized the fruit of redemptive reconciliation between a sinner and God (cf. 2Co 5:18).

3:1–5 Pertains to cattle, i.e., the herd, used in the peace offering.

3:1, 2 male or female. This is similar to the burnt offering in manner of presentation (cf. 1:3–9), but different in that a female was allowed.

3:4 the fat. All of the fat was dedicated to the Lord (3:3–5, 9–11, 14–16).

3:6–11 Pertains to sheep used in the peace offering.

3:11 *as* food. The sacrifice was intended to symbolize a meal between God and the one offering it, where peace and friendship were epitomized by sharing that meal together.

3:12–16 Pertains to goats used in the peace offering.

3:17 not eat . . . fat or . . . blood. The details given in the chapter distinctly define which fat was to be burned and not eaten, so that whatever adhered to other parts or was mixed with them might be eaten. As with many facets of the Mosaic legislation, there were underlying health benefits also.

4:1–6:7 The sin (4:1–5:13) and guilt (5:14–6:7) offerings differed from the previous 3 in that the former were voluntary and these were compulsory. The sin offering differed from the guilt offering in that the former involved iniquity where restitution was not possible, while in the latter it was possible.

4:1–5:13 See 6:24–30 for the priests' instructions. The sin offering atoned for sins committed unknowingly where restitution was impossible. This was a required sacrifice, as was the guilt offering (5:14–6:7). Unintentional sins of commission (4:1–35) and unintentional sins of omission (5:1–13) are discussed. Leviticus 4:1–35 indicates the person committing the sin: 1) the High Priest (vv. 3–12); 2) the congregation (vv. 13–21); 3) a leader (vv. 22–26); and 4) an individual (vv. 27–35). Leviticus 5:1–13 unfolds according to the animal sacrificed: 1) lamb/goat (vv. 1–6); 2) bird (vv. 7–10); and 3) flour (vv. 11–13).

4:2 unintentionally. The intended meaning is to stray into a sinful situation, but not necessarily to be taken completely by surprise. Nu 15:30, 31 illustrates the defiant

of them, 3 [A]if the anointed priest sins so as to bring
guilt on the people, then let him offer to the LORD a
[a]bull without defect as a sin offering for the sin he has
[b]committed. 4 He shall bring the bull to the doorway
of the tent of meeting before the LORD, and [A]he shall
lay his hand on the head of the bull and slay the bull
before the LORD. 5 Then the [A]anointed priest is to take
some of the blood of the bull and bring it to the tent
of meeting, 6 and the priest shall dip his finger in the
blood and sprinkle some of the blood seven times
before the LORD, in front of [A]the veil of the sanctuary.
7 The priest shall also put some of the blood on the
horns of [A]the altar of fragrant incense which is before
the LORD in the tent of meeting; and all the blood of
the bull he shall pour out at the base of the altar of
burnt offering which is at the doorway of the tent of
meeting. 8 [A]He shall remove from it all the fat of the
bull of the sin offering: the fat that covers the entrails,
and all the fat which is on the entrails, 9 and the two
kidneys with the fat that is on them, which is on the
loins, and the [a]lobe of the liver, which he shall remove
[A]with the kidneys 10 (just as it is removed from the ox
of the sacrifice of peace offerings), and the priest is to
offer them up in smoke on the altar of burnt offering.
11 But [A]the hide of the bull and all its flesh with its head
and its legs and its entrails and its refuse, 12 [a]that is,
all *the rest of* the bull, he is to bring out to [A]a clean
place outside the camp where the [b]ashes are poured
out, and burn it on wood with fire; where the [b]ashes
are poured out it shall be burned.

13 'A Now if the whole congregation of Israel commits error and the matter [a]escapes the notice of
the assembly, and they commit any of the [b]things
which the LORD has commanded not to be done,
and they become guilty; 14 [A]when the sin [a]which
they have [b]committed becomes known, then the
assembly shall offer [B]a [c]bull of the herd for a sin
offering and bring it before the tent of meeting.
15 Then [A]the elders of the congregation shall lay their
hands on the head of the bull before the LORD, and
the bull shall be slain [B]before the LORD. 16 Then the
anointed priest is to bring some of the blood of the
bull to the tent of meeting; 17 and [A]the priest shall dip
his finger in the blood and sprinkle *it* seven times
before the LORD, in front of the veil. 18 He shall put
some of the blood on the horns of [A]the altar which
is before the LORD [a]in the tent of meeting; and all
the blood he shall pour out at the base of the altar
of burnt offering which is at the doorway of the
tent of meeting. 19 [A]He shall remove all its fat from
it and offer it up in smoke on the altar. 20 He shall
also do with the bull just as he did with [A]the bull
of the sin offering; thus he shall do with it. So [B]the
priest shall make atonement for them, and they will
be forgiven. 21 Then he is to bring out the bull to *a
place* outside the camp and burn it as he burned
the first bull; it is [A]the sin offering for the assembly.
22 'When [A]a leader [B]sins and unintentionally does
any one of all the [a]things which the LORD his God
has commanded not to be done, and he becomes

4:3 [a]*Or bull of the herd* [b]Lit *sinned* [A]Lev 4:14, 23, 28 4:4 [A]Lev 1:4; 4:15; Num 8:12 4:5 [A]Lev 4:3, 17 4:6 [A]Ex 40:21, 26 4:7 [A]Lev 4:18, 25, 30, 34; 8:15; 9:9; 16:18 4:8 [A]Lev 3:3, 4 4:9 [a]*Or appendage on* [A]Lev 3:4 4:11 [A]Lev 9:11; Num 19:5 4:12 [a]Lit *and* [b]*Or fat ashes are* [A]Lev 4:21; 6:10, 11; 16:27 4:13 [a]Lit *is hidden from the eyes of* [b]Lit *commands of the LORD which are not to be done* [A]Num 15:24-26 4:14 [a]Lit *concerning which* [b]Lit *sinned* [c]Lit *son of the herd* [A]Lev 4:3 [B]Lev 4:3, 23, 28 4:15 [A]Lev 8:14, 18, 22; Num 8:10, 12 [B]Lev 1:3 4:17 [A]Lev 4:6 4:18 [a]Lit *which is in* [A]Lev 4:7, 25, 30, 34 4:19 [A]Lev 4:8 4:20 [A]Lev 4:8, 21 [B]Num 15:25, 28 4:21 [A]Lev 4:13f; 16:15-17; Num 15:24-26 4:22 [a]Lit *commands of the LORD which are not to be done* [A]Num 31:13; 32:2 [B]Lev 4:2, 27

attitude of intentional sin. **not to be done … commits any.** Sins of commission.

4:3–12 Sacrifices for the sin of the High Priest are given.

4:3 the anointed priest. See Ex 29:29 and Lv 16:32, which defined this person as the High Priest. **bring guilt on the people.** Only the High Priest, due to his representative position, was capable of this type of guilt infusion. For example, Achan had brought about the defeat of Israel when he held back the spoils, but the entire nation was not executed, as was his family (cf. Jos 7:22–26).

4:5 to the tent of meeting. He actually went into the Holy Place.

4:6 seven times. The number of completion or perfection, indicating the nature of God's forgiveness (Ps 103:12). **the veil of the sanctuary.** The veil marked the entry into the very presence of God in the Holy of Holies.

4:7 altar of fragrant incense. See Ex 30:1–10. This altar was in the tabernacle proper before the veil. It was so close to the ark that Hebrews speaks of it as actually being in the Holy of Holies (Heb 9:4). This altar was also sprinkled with blood on the Day of Atonement (Ex 30:10). **Altar of burnt offering.** The altar in the courtyard on which blood was normally splashed.

4:10 peace offerings. *See note on 3:1–17.*

4:11 refuse. This term identifies the major internal organs of an animal, including the intestines' waste content.

4:12 bring … outside the camp. This was a symbolic gesture of removing the sin from the people (cf. Heb 13:11–13 in reference to Christ).

4:13–21 Sacrifices for the sin of the congregation were to follow essentially the same procedure as that for the sin of priests (4:3–12).

4:16 the anointed priest. *See note on 4:3.*

4:22–26 These are sacrifices for the sin of a ruler. The blood of the sacrifice was not sprinkled in the Holy Place, as for the priest or congregation (4:6, 17), but only on the altar of burnt offering.

OLD TESTAMENT SACRIFICES COMPARED TO CHRIST'S SACRIFICE

Leviticus		Hebrews
1. Old Covenant (temporary)	Heb 7:22; 8:6, 13; 10:20	1. New Covenant (permanent)
2. Obsolete promises	Heb 8:6–13	2. Better promises
3. A shadow	Heb 8:5; 9:23, 24; 10:1	3. The reality
4. Aaronic priesthood (many)	Heb 6:19–7:25	4. Melchizedekian priesthood (one)
5. Sinful priesthood	Heb 7:26, 27; 9:7	5. Sinless priest
6. Limited-by-death priesthood	Heb 7:16, 17, 23, 24	6. Forever priesthood
7. Daily sacrifices	Heb 7:27; 9:12, 25, 26; 10:9, 10, 12	7. Once-for-all sacrifice
8. Animal sacrifices	Heb 9:11–15, 26; 10:4–10, 19	8. Sacrifice of God's Son
9. Ongoing sacrifices	Heb 10:11–14, 18	9. Sacrifices no longer needed
10. Once-a-year atonement	Heb 7:25; 9:12, 15; 10:1–4, 12	10. Eternal propitiation

guilty, 23 [a,A]if his sin [b]which he has committed is
made known to him, he shall bring for his offering
a [c,B]goat, [C]a male without defect. 24 He shall lay his
hand on the head of the male goat and slay it in the
place where [a]they slay the burnt offering before
the LORD; it is a sin offering. 25 Then the priest is to
take some of the blood of the sin offering with his
finger and put it on [A]the horns of the altar of burnt
offering; and *the rest of* its blood he shall pour out
at the base of the altar of burnt offering. 26 [A]All its
fat he shall offer up in smoke on the altar as *in the
case of* the fat of the sacrifice of peace offerings.
Thus [B]the priest shall make atonement for him in
regard to his sin, and he will be forgiven.

27 'Now if [a]anyone of [b]the common people sins
[A]unintentionally in doing any of the [c]things which
the LORD has commanded not to be done, and becomes guilty, 28 [a,A]if his sin which he has [b]committed
is made known to him, then he shall bring for his
offering a [c,B]goat, a [C]female without defect, for his
sin which he has [b]committed. 29 [A]He shall lay his
hand on the head of the sin offering and [B]slay the
sin offering at the place of the burnt offering. 30 The
priest shall take some of its blood with his finger
and put it on the horns of [A]the altar of burnt offering; and [B]all *the rest of* its blood he shall pour out
at the base of the altar. 31 [A]Then he shall remove all
its fat, just as the fat was removed from the sacrifice of peace offerings; and the priest shall offer it
up in smoke on the altar for [B]a soothing aroma to
the LORD. Thus the priest shall make atonement for
him, [a]and he will be forgiven.

32 'But if he brings [A]a lamb as his offering for a
sin offering, he shall bring it, a female without defect. 33 [A]He shall lay his hand on the head of the sin
offering and slay it for a sin offering [B]in the place
where [a]they slay the burnt offering. 34 The priest is
to take some of the blood of the sin offering with his
finger and put it on the horns of [A]the altar of burnt
offering, and [B]all *the rest of* its blood he shall pour
out at the base of the altar. 35 Then he shall remove
[A]all its fat, just as the fat of the lamb is removed
from the sacrifice of the peace offerings, and the
priest shall offer them up in smoke on the altar, on
the offerings by fire to the LORD. Thus [B]the priest
shall make atonement for him in regard to his sin
which he has [a]committed, and he will be forgiven.

THE LAW OF GUILT OFFERINGS

5 'Now if a person sins after he hears a [a]public [A]ad-
juration *to testify* when he is a witness, whether
he has seen or *otherwise* known, if he does not
tell *it*, then he will bear his [b]guilt. 2 Or if a person
touches [A]any unclean thing, whether a carcass of
an unclean beast or the carcass of unclean cattle
or a carcass of unclean swarming things, though it
is hidden from him and he is unclean, then he will
be guilty. 3 Or if he touches human uncleanness, of
whatever *sort* his uncleanness *may* be with which
he becomes unclean, and it is hidden from him, and
then he comes to know *it*, he will be guilty. 4 Or if
a person [A]swears thoughtlessly with his lips to do
evil or to do good, in whatever matter a man may
speak thoughtlessly with an oath, and it is hidden
from him, and then he comes to know *it*, he will be
guilty in one of these. 5 So it shall be when he becomes guilty in one of these, that he shall [A]confess
that in which he has sinned. 6 He shall also bring
his guilt offering to the LORD for his sin which he
has [a]committed, [A]a female from the flock, a lamb
or a [b]goat as a sin offering. So the priest shall make
atonement on his behalf for his sin.

7 'But if [a]he cannot afford a lamb, then he shall
bring to the LORD his guilt offering for that in which
he has sinned, two turtledoves or two young pigeons, [A]one for a sin offering and the other for a
burnt offering. 8 He shall bring them to the priest,
who shall offer first that which is for the sin offering
and shall nip its head at the front of its neck, but
he [A]shall not sever *it*. 9 He shall also sprinkle some
of the blood of the sin offering [A]on the side of the
altar, while the rest of the blood shall be drained out
[B]at the base of the altar: it is a sin offering. 10 The
second he shall then prepare as a burnt offering
[A]according to the ordinance. [B]So the priest shall
make atonement on his behalf for his sin which he
has [a]committed, and it will be forgiven him.

11 'But [A]if his [a]means are insufficient for two turtledoves or two young pigeons, then for his offering
for that which he has sinned, he shall bring the tenth
of an [b]ephah of fine flour for a sin offering; [B]he shall
not put oil on it or place incense on it, for it is a sin
offering. 12 He shall bring it to the priest, and the
priest shall take his handful of it as its memorial
portion and offer *it* up in smoke on the altar, [a]with

4:23 [a]Lit *or* [b]Lit *in which he has sinned* [c]Lit *buck of the goats* [A]Lev 4:3 [B]Lev 4:3, 14, 28 [C]Lev 4:28 4:24 [a]Lit *one slays* 4:25 [A]Lev 4:7, 18, 30, 34 4:26 [A]Lev 4:19 [B]Lev 4:20, 31; 5:10, 13, 16, 18; 6:7 4:27 [a]Lit *one soul* [b]Lit *the people of the land* [c]Lit *commands of the LORD which are not to be done* [A]Lev 4:2; Num 15:27 4:28 [a]Lit *or* [b]Lit *sinned* [c]Or *female goat* [A]Lev 4:3 [B]Lev 4:3, 14, 23, 32 [C]Lev 4:23 4:29 [A]Lev 1:4; 4:4, 24 [B]Lev 1:5, 11 4:30 [A]Lev 4:7, 18, 25, 34 [B]Lev 4:7 4:31 [a]Or *so that he may be* [A]Lev 4:8 [B]Gen 8:21; Ex 29:18; Lev 1:9, 13; 2:2, 9, 12 4:32 [A]Lev 4:28 4:33 [a]Lit *one slays* [A]Lev 1:4, 5 [B]Lev 4:29 4:34 [A]Lev 4:7, 18, 25, 30 [B]Lev 4:7 4:35 [a]Lit *sinned* [A]Lev 4:26, 31 [B]Lev 4:20 5:1 [a]Lit *voice of an oath* [b]Or *iniquity* [A]Prov 29:24; Jer 23:10 5:2 [A]Lev 11:8, 11, 24-40; Num 19:11-16; Deut 14:8 5:4 [A]Num 30:6, 8; Ps 106:33 5:5 [A]Lev 16:21; 26:40; Num 5:7; Prov 28:13 5:6 [a]Lit *sinned* [b]Lit *female goat* [A]Lev 4:28, 32 5:7 [a]Lit *his hand does not reach enough for* [A]Lev 12:6, 8; 14:22, 30, 31 5:8 [A]Lev 1:17 5:9 [A]Lev 1:15 [B]Lev 4:7, 18 5:10 [a]Lit *sinned* [A]Lev 1:14-17 [B]Lev 4:20, 26; 5:13, 16 5:11 [a]Lit *hand does not reach* [b]I.e. Approx one bu [A]Lev 14:21-32; 27:8 [B]Lev 2:1, 2 5:12 [a]Lit *upon*

4:27–35 These are sacrifices for the sin of an individual. Either a goat (4:27–31) or a lamb (4:32–35) could be sacrificed in much the same manner as the offering for a ruler (4:22–26).

5:1–13 Dealing with unintentional sins continues with an emphasis on sins of omission (vv. 1–4). Lambs/goats (v. 6), birds (vv. 7–10), or flour (vv. 11–13) were acceptable sacrifices.

5:1–5 This call to confession named a few examples of violations for which penitence was the right response: 1) withholding evidence (v. 1); 2) touching something unclean (vv. 2, 3); and 3) rash oath making (v. 4).

5:1 public adjuration ... witness. A witness who did not come forward to testify was sinning when he had actually seen a violation or had firsthand knowledge, such as hearing the violator confess to the sin.

5:4 swears. "Speaking thoughtlessly" suggests a reckless oath for good or bad, i.e., an oath the speaker should not or could not keep.

5:5 he shall confess. Confession must accompany the sacrifice as the outward expression of a repentant heart which openly acknowledged agreement with God concerning sin. Sacrifice minus true faith, repentance, and obedience was hypocrisy (cf. Ps 26:4; Is 9:17; Am 5:21–26).

5:7 burnt offering. *See notes on 1:3–17.*

5:11 ephah. About 6 gallons. **not put oil ... incense.** Contrast the grain offering (2:2).

the offerings of the LORD by fire: it is a sin offering.
13 So the priest shall make atonement for him concerning his sin which he has [a]committed from [A]one
of these, and it will be forgiven him; then [B]*the rest*
shall become the priest's, like the grain offering.' "
14 Then the LORD spoke to Moses, saying, 15 "[A]If a
person acts unfaithfully and sins [B]unintentionally
against the LORD'S holy things, then he shall bring
his [C]guilt offering to the LORD: [D]a ram without defect
from the flock, according to your valuation in silver
by shekels, in *terms of* the [E]shekel of the sanctuary, for
a guilt offering. 16 [A]He shall make restitution for that
which he has sinned against the holy thing, and shall
add to it a fifth part of it and give it to the priest. [B]The
priest shall then make atonement for him with the
ram of the guilt offering, and it will be forgiven him.
17 "Now if a person sins and does any of the things
[a]which the LORD has commanded not to be done,
[A]though he was unaware, still he is guilty and shall
bear his punishment. 18 He is then to bring to the
priest [A]a ram without defect from the flock, according to your valuation, for a guilt offering. So the
priest shall make atonement for him concerning his
error in which he sinned [B]unintentionally and did
not know *it,* and it will be forgiven him. 19 It is a guilt
offering; he was certainly guilty before the LORD."

GUILT OFFERING

6 [a]Then the LORD spoke to Moses, saying, 2 "[A]When
a person sins and acts unfaithfully against the
LORD, and deceives his companion in regard to a
deposit or a security entrusted *to him,* or through
robbery, or *if* he has extorted from his companion,
3 or [A]has found what was lost and lied about it and
sworn falsely, so that he sins in regard to any one of
the things a man may do; 4 then it shall be, when he
sins and becomes guilty, that he shall [A]restore what
he took by robbery or what he got by extortion, or the
deposit which was [a]entrusted to him or the lost thing
which he found, 5 or anything about which he swore
falsely; [A]he shall make restitution for it [a]in full and
add to it one-fifth more. [B]He shall give it to the one
to whom it belongs on the day *he presents* his guilt
offering. 6 Then he shall bring to the priest his guilt
offering to the LORD, [A]a ram without defect from the
flock, according to your valuation, for a guilt offering, 7 and [A]the priest shall make atonement for him
before the LORD, and he will be forgiven for any one
of the things which he may have done to incur guilt."

THE PRIEST'S PART IN THE OFFERINGS

8 [a]Then the LORD spoke to Moses, saying, 9 "Command Aaron and his sons, saying, 'This is [A]the law
for the burnt offering: the burnt offering itself *shall*
remain on the hearth on the altar all night until
the morning, and [B]the fire on the altar is to be kept
burning on it. 10 The priest is to put on [A]his linen
robe, and he shall put on undergarments next to
his flesh; and he shall take up the [a]ashes *to* which
the fire [b]reduces the burnt offering on the altar and
place them beside the altar. 11 Then he shall take off
his garments and put on other garments, and carry
the [a]ashes outside the camp to a clean place. 12 The
fire on the altar shall be kept burning on it. It shall
not go out, but the priest shall burn wood on it every morning; and he shall lay out the burnt offering
on it, and offer up in smoke the fat portions of the
peace offerings [A]on it. 13 Fire shall be kept burning
continually on the altar; it is not to go out.
14 'Now this is the law of the grain offering: the
sons of Aaron shall present it before the LORD in
front of the altar. 15 [A]Then one *of them* shall lift up
from it a handful of the fine flour of the grain offering, [a]with its oil and all the incense that is on the
grain offering, and he shall offer *it* up in smoke on
the altar, a soothing aroma, as its memorial offering
to the LORD. 16 [A]What is left of it Aaron and his sons
are to eat. It shall be eaten as unleavened cakes in a
holy place; they are to eat it in the court of the tent of
meeting. 17 [A]It shall not be baked with leaven. I have
given it as their share from My offerings by fire; [B]it is
most holy, like the sin offering and [C]the guilt offering.

5:13 [a]Lit *sinned* [A]Lev 5:4, 5 [B]Lev 2:3 5:15 [A]Num 5:5-8 [B]Lev 4:2; 22:14 [C]Lev 7:1-10 [D]Lev 6:6 [E]Ex 30:13 5:16 [A]Lev 6:5; 22:14; Num 5:7, 8 [B]Lev 7:2-7 5:17 [a]Lit *the commands of the LORD which are* [A]Lev 4:2; 5:19 5:18 [A]Lev 5:15 [B]Lev 5:17 6:1 [a]Ch 5:20 in Heb 6:2 [A]Ex 22:7-15 6:3 [A]Ex 23:4; Deut 22:1-4 6:4 [a]Or *deposited with* [A]Lev 24:18, 21 6:5 [a]Lit *in its sum* [A]Lev 5:16 [B]Num 5:8 6:6 [A]Lev 5:15 6:7 [A]Lev 7:2-5 6:8 [a]Ch 6:1 in Heb 6:9 [A]Ex 29:38-42; Num 28:3-10 [B]Lev 6:12, 13 6:10 [a]Or *fat ashes* [b]Lit *consumes* [A]Ex 28:39, 42; 39:27, 28 6:11 [a]Or *fat ashes* 6:12 [A]Lev 3:5 6:15 [a]Lit *and some of* [A]Lev 2:2, 9 6:16 [A]Lev 2:3; 10:12-14; Ezek 44:29 6:17 [A]Lev 2:11 [B]Ex 40:10; Lev 6:25, 26, 29, 30; Num 18:9 [C]Lev 7:7; 10:16-18

5:13 grain offering. *See notes on 2:1–16.*

5:14–6:7 See 7:1–10 for the priests' instructions. The trespass or guilt offering symbolized an atonement for sin unknowingly committed where restitution was possible. Like the sin offering (4:1–5:13), this one was compulsory. For sins against the Lord's property, restitution was made to the priest (5:14–19), while restitution was made to the person who suffered loss in other instances (6:1–7).

5:15 shekel of the sanctuary. This amounted to 20 gerahs (Ex 30:13; Lv 27:25; Nu 3:47) or 2 bekas (Ex 38:26), which is the equivalent of four-tenths of one ounce. God fixed the value of a shekel.

5:16 a fifth part. The offender was required to make a 120 percent restitution, which was considerably lower than that prescribed elsewhere in the Mosaic law, e.g., Ex 22:7, 9. Perhaps this is accounted for by a voluntary confession in contrast to an adjudicated and forced conviction.

6:1–7 While all sins are against God (cf. Ps 51:4), some are direct (5:14–19) and others are indirect, involving people (6:1–7), as here. These violations are not exhaustive, but representative samples used to establish and illustrate the principle.

6:6 your valuation. The priest served as an appraiser to give appropriate value to the goods in question.

6:8–7:38 These were laws of sacrifice for the priesthood. Leviticus 1:1–6:7 has dealt with 5 major offerings from the worshiper's perspective. Here instructions for the priests are given, with special attention to the priests' portion of the sacrifice.

6:8–13 The burnt offering. *See notes on 1:3–17.*

6:9 on the hearth on the altar all night. This resulted in the complete incineration of the sacrifice, picturing it as totally given to the Lord, with the smoke arising as a sweet aroma to Him (1:9, 13, 17).

6:10, 11 ashes. This described both the immediate (v. 10) and final (v. 11) disposition of the ash remains, i.e., that which is worthless.

6:12 fat . . . peace offerings. *See note on 3:4.*

6:13 burning continually. The perpetual flame indicated a continuous readiness on the part of God to receive confession and restitution through the sacrifice.

6:14–23 The grain offering. *See notes on 2:1–16.*

6:15 handful. *See note on 2:2.*

6:16–18 Unlike the burnt offering, the grain offering provided food for the priests and their male children, i.e., future priests.

6:16 in a holy place. This was to be eaten only in the courtyard of the tabernacle.

18 [A]Every male among the sons of Aaron may eat it;
it is a permanent ordinance throughout your generations, from the offerings by fire to the LORD.
[B]Whoever touches them will become consecrated.' "
19 Then the LORD spoke to Moses, saying, 20 "This
is the offering which Aaron and his sons are to present to the LORD on the day when he is anointed;
the tenth of an [A]ephah of fine flour as [B]a [a]regular
grain offering, half of it in the morning and half of
it in the evening. 21 It shall be prepared with oil on a
[A]griddle. When it is *well* stirred, you shall bring it.
You shall present the grain offering in baked pieces
as a soothing aroma to the LORD. 22 The anointed
priest who will be in his place [a]among his sons
shall [b]offer it. By a permanent ordinance it shall
be entirely offered up in smoke to the LORD. 23 So
every grain offering of the priest shall be burned
entirely. It shall not be eaten."
24 Then the LORD spoke to Moses, saying, 25 "Speak
to Aaron and to his sons, saying, 'This is the law of
the sin offering: [A]in the place where the burnt offering is slain the sin offering shall be slain before
the LORD; it is most holy. 26 [A]The priest who offers
it for sin shall eat it. It shall be eaten in a holy place,
in the court of the tent of meeting. 27 [A]Anyone who
touches its flesh will become consecrated; and when
any of its blood [a]splashes on a garment, in a holy
place you shall wash what was splashed on. 28 Also
[A]the earthenware vessel in which it was boiled shall
be broken; and if it was boiled in a bronze vessel,
then it shall be scoured and rinsed in water. 29 [A]Ev-
ery male among the priests may eat of it; [B]it is most
holy. 30 But no sin offering [A]of which any of the
blood is brought into the tent of meeting to make
atonement [B]in the holy place shall be eaten; [C]it shall
be burned with fire.

THE PRIEST'S PART IN THE OFFERINGS

7 'Now this is the law of the [A]guilt offering; it is
most holy. 2 In [A]the place where they slay the
burnt offering they are to slay the guilt offering,
and he shall sprinkle its blood around on the altar.
3 Then he shall offer from it all its fat: the [A]fat tail
and the fat that covers the entrails, 4 and the two
kidneys with the fat that is on them, which is on
the loins, and the lobe on the liver he shall remove
[A]with the kidneys. 5 The priest shall offer them up
in smoke on the altar as an offering by fire to the
LORD; it is a guilt offering. 6 [A]Every male among
the priests may eat of it. It shall be eaten in a holy
place; it is most holy. 7 The guilt offering is like the
[A]sin offering, there is one law for them; the [B]priest
who makes atonement with it [a]shall have it. 8 Also
the priest who presents any man's burnt offering,
[a]that priest shall have for himself the skin of the
burnt offering which he has presented. 9 Likewise,
every grain offering that is baked in the oven and
everything prepared in a [a]pan or on a [A]griddle [b]shall
belong to the priest who presents it. 10 Every grain
offering, mixed with oil or dry, shall [a]belong to all
the sons of Aaron, [b]to all alike.
11 'Now this is the law of the [A]sacrifice of peace
offerings which shall be presented to the LORD. 12 If
he offers it by way of [A]thanksgiving, then along
with the sacrifice of thanksgiving he shall offer
[B]unleavened cakes mixed with oil, and unleavened
wafers [a]spread with oil, and cakes *of well* stirred
fine flour mixed with oil. 13 With the sacrifice of his
peace offerings for thanksgiving, he shall present
his offering with cakes of [A]leavened bread. 14 Of [a]this
he shall present one of every offering as a [b]contri-
bution to the LORD; [A]it shall [c]belong to the priest
who sprinkles the blood of the peace offerings.
15 '[A]Now *as for* the flesh of the sacrifice of his
thanksgiving peace offerings, it shall be eaten on
the day of his offering; he shall not leave any of
it over until morning. 16 But if the sacrifice of his
offering is a [A]votive or a freewill offering, it shall
be eaten on the day that he offers his sacrifice, and
on the [a]next day what is left of it may be eaten;
17 [A]but what is left over from the flesh of the sacrifice on the third day shall be burned with fire.
18 So if any of the flesh of the sacrifice of his peace
offerings should *ever* be eaten on the third day, he
who offers it will not be accepted, *and* it will not
be reckoned to his *benefit*. It shall be an [A]offensive
thing, and the person who eats of it will bear his
own iniquity.

6:18 [A]Lev 6:29; 7:6; Num 18:10; 1 Cor 9:13 [B]Lev 6:27 6:20 [a]Lit *grain offering continually* [A]Lev 5:11 [B]Num 4:16 6:21 [A]Lev 2:5 6:22 [a]Lit *from among* [b]Lit *do* 6:25 [A]Lev 1:11 6:26 [A]Lev 6:29 6:27 [a]Lit *one sprinkles* [A]Lev 7:19 6:28 [A]Lev 11:33; 15:12 6:29 [A]Lev 6:18 [B]Lev 6:17, 25 6:30 [A]Lev 4:1-21 [B]Lev 4:7, 18 [C]Lev 4:11, 12, 21 7:1 [A]Lev 5:14-6:7 7:2 [A]Lev 1:11 7:3 [A]Lev 3:9 7:4 [A]Lev 3:4 7:6 [A]Lev 6:18, 29; Num 18:9 7:7 [a]Lit *it shall be for him* [A]Lev 6:25, 26, 30 [B]1 Cor 9:13; 10:18 7:8 [a]Lit *for the priest, it shall be for him* 7:9 [a]Lit *lidded cooking pan* [b]Lit *for the priest, it shall be for him* [A]Lev 2:5 7:10 [a]Lit *be* [b]Lit *a man as his brother* 7:11 [A]Lev 3:1 7:12 [a]Or *anointed* [A]Lev 7:15 [B]Lev 2:4; Num 6:15 7:13 [A]Lev 2:12; 23:17, 18; Amos 4:5 7:14 [a]Lit *it* [b]Or *heave offering* [c]Lit *be for* [A]Num 18:8, 11, 19 7:15 [A]Lev 22:29, 30 7:16 [a]Lit *morrow and what* [A]Lev 19:5-8 7:17 [A]Ex 12:10 7:18 [A]Lev 19:7; Prov 15:8

6:19–23 Aaron, as High Priest, was to make a daily grain offering at morning and night on behalf of his priestly family.

6:20 he is anointed. See 8:7–12. **ephah.** *See note on 5:11.*

6:22, 23 The anointed priest … in his place. The High Priests who succeed Aaron are in view here. **burned entirely.** The priests' offering was to be given completely, with nothing left over.

6:24–30 The sin offering. *See notes on 4:1–5:13.*

6:25 burnt offering. *See notes on 1:3–17.* **most holy.** *See note on 2:3.*

6:26 priest … eat. The priest putting the offering on the brazen altar could use it for food, if the sacrifice was for a ruler (4:22–26) or the people (4:27–35).

6:27, 28 Instructions on the cleanness of the priest's garments as they relate to blood.

6:30 no sin offering … eaten. Those sacrifices made on behalf of a priest (4:3–12) or the congregation (4:13–21) could be eaten.

7:1–10 The trespass or guilt offering. *See notes on 5:14–6:7.* Verses 7–10 provide a brief excursus on what may be eaten by the priests.

7:1 most holy. *See note on 2:3.*

7:7 *See note on 6:26.*

7:10 mixed with oil or dry. Both were acceptable options.

7:11–36 The peace offering. *See notes on 3:1–17.* The purposes for the peace offering are given in vv. 11–18. Special instructions which prevented a priest from being "cut off" (vv. 19–27) and the allotment to Aaron and his sons (vv. 28–36) are enumerated.

7:11–15 A peace offering for thanksgiving shall also be combined with a grain offering (see 2:1–16). The meat had to be eaten that same day, probably for the reason of health since it would rapidly spoil and for the purpose of preventing people from thinking that such meat had some spiritual presence in it, thus developing some superstitions.

7:13 leavened bread. Contrast the unleavened grain offering (see 2:11).

7:16–18 votive … freewill offering. The priest could eat the meat the same day or

19 'Also the flesh that touches anything unclean
shall not be eaten; it shall be burned with fire. [a]As
for *other* flesh, anyone who is clean may eat *such*
flesh. 20 [A]But the person who eats the flesh of the
sacrifice of peace offerings which belong to the
LORD, [a]in his uncleanness, that person [B]shall be
cut off from his people. 21 [A]When anyone touches
anything unclean, whether human uncleanness,
or an unclean animal, or any unclean [a]detestable
thing, and eats of the flesh of the sacrifice of peace
offerings which belong to the LORD, that person
shall be cut off from his people.' "
22 Then the LORD spoke to Moses, saying,
23 "Speak to the sons of Israel, saying, 'You shall
not eat [A]any fat *from* an ox, a sheep or a goat.
24 Also the fat of *an animal* which dies and the fat
of an animal [A]torn *by beasts* may be put to any
other use, but you must certainly not eat it. 25 For
whoever eats the fat of the animal from which [a]an
offering by fire is offered to the LORD, even the
person who eats shall be cut off from his people.
26 [A]You are not to eat any blood, either of bird or
animal, in any of your dwellings. 27 Any person
who eats any blood, even that person shall be cut
off from his people.' "
28 Then the LORD spoke to Moses, saying, 29 "Speak
to the sons of Israel, saying, 'He who offers [A]the
sacrifice of his peace offerings to the LORD shall
bring his offering to the LORD from the sacrifice of
his peace offerings. 30 His own hands are to bring
offerings by fire to the LORD. He shall bring the fat
with the breast, that the [A]breast may be [a]presented
as a wave offering before the LORD. 31 The priest
shall offer up the fat in smoke on the altar, but [A]the
breast shall belong to Aaron and his sons. 32 You
shall give [A]the right thigh to the priest as a [a]contri-
bution from the sacrifices of your peace offerings.
33 The one among the sons of Aaron who offers the
blood of the peace offerings and the fat, the right
thigh shall be his as *his* portion. 34 For I have taken
[A]the breast of the wave offering and the thigh of
the [a]contribution from the sons of Israel from the
sacrifices of their peace offerings, and have given
them to Aaron the priest and to his sons as *their*
due forever from the sons of Israel.
35 'This is [a]that which is consecrated to Aaron
and [a]that [A]which is consecrated to his sons from
the offerings by fire to the LORD, in that day when
he presented them to serve as priests to the LORD.
36 [a]These the LORD had commanded to be given
them from the sons of Israel in the day that He
[A]anointed them. It is *their* due forever throughout
their generations.' "
37 This is the law of the burnt offering, the grain
offering and the sin offering and the guilt offering
and [A]the ordination offering and the sacrifice of
peace offerings, 38 [A]which the LORD commanded
Moses at Mount Sinai in the day that He commanded
the sons of Israel to [a]present their offerings to the
LORD in the wilderness of Sinai.

THE CONSECRATION OF AARON AND HIS SONS

8 Then the LORD spoke to Moses, saying, 2 "[A]Take
Aaron and his sons with him, and the [B]garments
and [C]the anointing oil and the bull of the sin offering, and the two rams and the basket of unleavened
bread, 3 and assemble all the congregation at the
doorway of the tent of meeting." 4 So Moses did just
as the LORD commanded him. When the congregation was assembled at the doorway of the tent of
meeting, 5 Moses said to the congregation, "This is
the thing which the LORD has commanded to do."
6 Then [A]Moses had Aaron and his sons come near
and [B]washed them with water. 7 He [A]put the tunic
on him and girded him with the sash, and clothed
him with the robe and put the ephod on him; and
he girded him with the artistic band of the ephod,
[a]with which he tied *it* to him. 8 He then placed the
[a]breastpiece on him, and in the [a]breastpiece he put
[b,A]the Urim and the Thummim. 9 He also placed the
turban on his head, and on the turban, at its front,
he placed [A]the golden plate, the holy crown, just as
the LORD had commanded Moses.
10 Moses then took [A]the anointing oil and
anointed the [a]tabernacle and all that was in it, and

7:19 [a]Lit *And the flesh* 7:20 [a]Lit *and his uncleanness is on him* [A]Lev 22:3-7; Num 19:13 [B]Lev 7:25 7:21 [a]Some mss read *swarming thing* [A]Lev 5:2, 3 7:23 [A]Lev 3:17 7:24 [A]Ex 22:31; Lev 17:15; 22:8 7:25 [a]Lit *he offers an offering by fire* 7:26 [A]Gen 9:4; Lev 17:10-16; 19:26; Deut 12:23; 1 Sam 14:33; Acts 15:20 7:29 [A]Lev 3:1 7:30 [a]Lit *waved* [A]Ex 29:26, 27; Lev 8:29; Num 6:20 7:31 [A]Num 18:11; Deut 18:3 7:32 [a]Or *heave offering* [A]Ex 29:27; Lev 7:34; 9:21; Num 6:20 7:34 [a]Or *heave offering* [A]Ex 29:27; Lev 10:14, 15; Num 18:18 7:35 [a]Lit *the anointed portion of* [A]Num 18:8 7:36 [a]Lit *Which* [A]Ex 40:13-15; Lev 8:12, 30 7:37 [A]Ex 29:22-34; Lev 8:22, 23 7:38 [a]Or *offer* [A]Lev 1:1; 26:46; 27:34; Deut 4:5 8:2 [A]Ex 28:1 [B]Lev 6:10 [C]Ex 30:25 8:6 [A]Ex 29:4-6 [B]Ex 30:19, 20; Ps 26:6; 1 Cor 6:11; Eph 5:26 8:7 [a]Lit *and with it* [A]Ex 28:4 8:8 [a]Lit *pouch* [b]I.e. the lights and perfections [A]Ex 28:30; Num 27:21; Deut 33:8; 1 Sam 28:6; Ezra 2:63; Neh 7:65 8:9 [A]Ex 28:36 8:10 [a]Or *dwelling place* [A]Ex 30:26-29; Lev 8:2

next day, but eating on the third day brought punishment.

7:19–21 **cut off.** Uncleanness was punishable by death. See chap. 22 for more details.

7:22–27 *See note on 3:17.*

7:27 **cut off.** *See note on 7:19–21.*

7:29 **offering ... sacrifice.** The worshiper made a peace offering from his sacrifice so that the Lord received the blood (v. 33) and the fat (v. 33). The priests received the breast (vv. 30, 31) and right thigh (v. 33). The worshiper could use the rest for himself.

7:30–32 **wave offering.** This was a symbolic act indicating the offering was for the Lord. Bread (Ex 29:23–24), meat (Ex 29:22–24), gold (Ex 38:24), oil (Lv 14:12), and grain (Lv 23:11) all served as wave offerings. Another type of offering was the heave offering. Jewish tradition portrayed the wave offering as being presented with a horizontal motion and the heave offering with a vertical motion, as suggested by Lv 10:15.

7:36 **He anointed them.** See 8:30.

7:37, 38 Moses gives a summary conclusion of 1:3–7:36.

7:37 **ordination offering.** This refers to the offerings at the ordination of Aaron and his sons (see 8:14–36; Ex 29:1–46).

8:1–10:20 Beginnings of the Aaronic priesthood are discussed in this section. Before the time of Aaron, the patriarchs (Ge 4:3, 4) and the fathers (Job 1:5) had offered sacrifices to God, but with Aaron came the fully prescribed priestly service.

8:1–36 Aaron and his sons were consecrated before they ministered to the Lord. The consecration of Aaron and his sons had been ordered long before (*see notes on Ex 29:1–28*), but is here described with all the ceremonial details as it was done after the tabernacle was completed and the regulations for the various sacrifices enacted.

8:2 **the garments.** *See notes on Ex 28:1–43.* **the anointing oil.** Oil was used for ceremonial anointing (8:12, 30). **sin offering.** *See notes on 4:1–5:13, esp. 4:3–12.*

8:6–9 *See notes on Ex 28:1–43.*

8:8 **the Urim and the Thummim.** A feature on the breastpiece of the High Priest by which God's people were given His decision on matters which required a decision. *See note on Ex 28:30.*

consecrated them. 11 He sprinkled some of it on the
altar seven times and anointed the altar and all its
utensils, and the basin and its stand, to [A]consecrate
them. 12 Then he poured some of the [A]anointing oil
on Aaron's head and anointed him, to consecrate
him. 13 [A]Next Moses had Aaron's sons come near
and clothed them with tunics, and girded them
with sashes and bound [a]caps on them, just as the
LORD had commanded Moses.

14 Then he brought [A]the bull of the sin offering,
and Aaron and his sons laid their hands on the head
of the bull of the sin offering. 15 Next [a]Moses slaughtered *it* and took the blood and with his finger [A]put
some of it around on the horns of the altar, and
purified the altar. Then he poured out *the rest of* the
blood at the base of the altar and consecrated it, to
make atonement for it. 16 He also [A]took all the fat that
was on the entrails and the [a]lobe of the liver, and the
two kidneys and their fat; and Moses offered it up in
smoke on the altar. 17 [A]But the bull and its hide and
its flesh and its refuse he burned in the fire outside
the camp, just as the LORD had commanded Moses.

18 Then he presented [A]the ram of the burnt offering, and Aaron and his sons laid their hands on
the head of the ram. 19 [a]Moses slaughtered *it* and
sprinkled the blood around on the altar. 20 When
he had cut the ram into its pieces, Moses [A]offered
up the head and the pieces and the suet in smoke.
21 After he had washed the entrails and the legs with
water, Moses [A]offered up the whole ram in smoke
on the altar. It was a burnt offering for a soothing
aroma; it was an offering by fire to the LORD, just
as the LORD had commanded Moses.

22 Then he presented the second ram, [A]the ram
of [a]ordination, and Aaron and his sons laid their
hands on the head of the ram. 23 [a]Moses slaughtered *it* and took some of its blood and [A]put it on
the lobe of Aaron's right ear, and on the thumb of
his right hand and on the big toe of his right foot.
24 He also had Aaron's sons come near; and Moses
put some of the blood on the lobe of their right ear,
and on the thumb of their right hand and on the
big toe of their right foot. Moses then [A]sprinkled
the rest of the blood around on the altar. 25 He took
the fat, and the fat tail, and all the fat that was on
the entrails, and the [a]lobe of the liver and the two
kidneys and their fat and the right thigh. 26 [A]From
the basket of unleavened bread that was before the
LORD, he took one unleavened cake and one cake
of bread *mixed with* oil and one wafer, and placed
them on the portions of fat and on the right thigh.
27 He then [A]put all *these* on the hands of Aaron and
on the hands of his sons and presented them as
a wave offering before the LORD. 28 Then Moses
[A]took them from their hands and offered them up
in smoke on the altar with the burnt offering. They
were an ordination offering for [B]a soothing aroma;
it was an offering by fire to the LORD. 29 Moses also
took [A]the breast and presented it for a wave offering
before the LORD; it was [B]Moses' portion of the ram of
ordination, just as the LORD had commanded Moses.

30 So Moses [A]took some of the anointing oil and
some of the blood which was on the altar and sprinkled it on Aaron, on his garments, on his sons, and
on the garments of his sons with him; and he consecrated Aaron, his garments, and his sons, and the
garments of his sons with him.

31 Then Moses said to Aaron and to his sons, "[A]Boil
the flesh at the doorway of the tent of meeting, and
eat it there together with the bread which is in the
basket of the ordination offering, just as I commanded, [B]saying, 'Aaron and his sons shall eat it.'
32 [A]The remainder of the flesh and of the bread you
shall burn in the fire. 33 [A]You shall not go outside
the doorway of the tent of meeting for seven days,
until the day that the period of your ordination
is fulfilled; for he will [a]ordain you through seven
days. 34 The LORD has commanded to do as has been
done this day, to make atonement on your behalf.
35 At the doorway of the tent of meeting, moreover,
you shall remain day and night for seven days and
[A]keep the charge of the LORD, so that you will not
die, for so I have been commanded." 36 Thus Aaron
and his sons did all the things which the LORD had
commanded through Moses.

AARON OFFERS SACRIFICES

9 Now it came about [A]on the eighth day that Moses
called Aaron and his sons and the elders of Israel;
2 and he said to Aaron, "[A]Take for yourself a calf, a
bull, for a sin offering and a ram for a burnt offering,
both without defect, and offer *them* before the LORD.
3 Then to the sons of Israel you shall speak, saying,
'Take a male goat for a sin offering, and a calf and a
lamb, both one year old, without defect, for a burnt
offering, 4 and an ox and a ram for peace offerings, to
sacrifice before the LORD, and a grain offering mixed
with oil; for today [A]the LORD will appear to you.' " 5 So

8:11 [A]Ex 29:36, 37; 30:29 8:12 [A]Ex 29:7; 30:30; Lev 21:10, 12; Ps 133:2 8:13 [a]Lit *headgear* [A]Ex 29:8, 9 8:14 [A]Ex 29:10; Lev 4:4; Ps 66:15; Ezek 43:19 8:15 [a]Lit *he slaughtered it and Moses took* [A]Ex 29:12; Lev 4:7; Ezek 43:20 8:16 [a]Or *appendage on* [A]Ex 29:13 8:17 [A]Ex 29:14; Lev 4:11, 12 8:18 [A]Ex 29:15; Lev 8:2 8:19 [a]Lit *He slaughtered it and Moses sprinkled* 8:20 [A]Lev 1:8 8:21 [A]Ex 29:18 8:22 [a]Lit *filling*, and so throughout the ch [A]Ex 29:31; Lev 8:2 8:23 [a]Lit *He slaughtered it and Moses took* [A]Ex 29:20, 21 8:24 [A]Heb 9:18-22 8:25 [a]Or *appendage on* 8:26 [A]Ex 29:23 8:27 [A]Ex 29:24 8:28 [A]Ex 29:25 [B]Gen 8:21 8:29 [A]Lev 7:31-34 [B]Ex 29:26; Ps 99:6 8:30 [A]Ex 29:21 8:31 [A]Ex 29:31 [B]Ex 29:32 8:32 [A]Ex 29:34 8:33 [a]Lit *fill your hands* [A]Ex 29:35 8:35 [A]Num 3:7; 9:19; Deut 11:1; 1 Kin 2:3; Ezek 48:11 9:1 [A]Ezek 43:27 9:2 [A]Ezek 29:1; Lev 4:3 9:4 [A]Ex 29:43

8:11 seven times. *See note on 4:6.*

8:12 to consecrate him. This act was to ceremonially set Aaron apart from the congregation to be a priest unto God, and from the other priests to be High Priest.

8:14–17 *See notes on 4:3–12.*

8:17 refuse. *See note on 4:11.*

8:18–21 *See notes on 1:3–17.*

8:23, 24 right ear ... right hand ... right foot. Using a part to represent the whole, Aaron and his sons were consecrated to listen to God's holy Word, to carry out His holy assignments, and to live holy lives.

8:29 wave offering. *See note on 7:30–32.*

8:35 keep the charge of the LORD. The commandment of God ordered Aaron and his sons to do exactly as the Lord had spoken through Moses. Disobedience would meet with death.

9:1–24 Since the priests had been consecrated and appropriate sacrifices offered on their behalf, they were prepared to fulfill their priestly duties on behalf of the congregation as they carried out all of the prescribed sacrifices in Lv 1–7 and rendered them to the Lord.

9:2–4 sin ... burnt ... peace ... grain offering. *See notes on 4:1–5:13; 1:3–17; 3:1–17; and 2:1–16* respectively.

9:4, 6 the glory of the LORD. The Lord's manifestation or presence was going to appear to them to show acceptance of the

they took what Moses had commanded to the front
of the tent of meeting, and the whole congregation
came near and stood before the LORD. [6] Moses said,
"This is the thing which the LORD has commanded
you to do, that [A]the glory of the LORD may appear to
you." [7] Moses then said to Aaron, "Come near to the
altar and [a,A]offer your sin offering and your burnt
offering, that you may make atonement for yourself
and for the people; then make the offering [b]for the
people, that you may make atonement for them, just
as the LORD has commanded."

[8] [A]So Aaron came near to the altar and slaughtered the calf of the sin offering which was for himself. [9] [A]Aaron's sons presented the blood to him; and
he dipped his finger in the blood and [B]put *some* on
the horns of the altar, and poured out *the rest of*
the blood at the base of the altar. [10] The fat and the
kidneys and the [a]lobe of the liver of the sin offering,
he then offered up in smoke on the altar just as the
LORD had commanded Moses. [11] [A]The flesh and the
skin, however, he burned with fire outside the camp.

[12] Then he slaughtered the burnt offering; and
Aaron's sons handed the blood to him and he sprinkled it around on the altar. [13] They handed the burnt
offering to him in [a]pieces, with the head, and he
offered *them* up in smoke on the altar. [14] He also
washed the entrails and the legs, and offered *them*
up in smoke with the burnt offering on the altar.

[15] Then he presented the people's offering, and
took the [A]goat of the sin offering which was for the
people, and slaughtered it and offered it for sin, like
the first. [16] He also presented the burnt offering, and
[a]offered it according to [A]the ordinance. [17] Next he
presented [A]the grain offering, and filled his [a]hand
with some of it and offered *it* up in smoke on the
altar, [B]besides the burnt offering of the morning.

[18] Then [A]he slaughtered the ox and the ram, the
sacrifice of peace offerings which was for the people; and Aaron's sons handed the blood to him and
he sprinkled it around on the altar. [19] As for the portions of fat from the ox and from the ram, the fat
tail, and the *fat* [A]covering, and the kidneys and the
[a]lobe of the liver, [20] they now placed the portions
of fat on the breasts; and he offered [a]them up in
smoke on the altar. [21] But [A]the breasts and the right
thigh Aaron [a]presented as a wave offering before
the LORD, just as Moses had commanded.

[22] Then Aaron lifted up his hands toward the
people and [A]blessed them, and he stepped down
after making the sin offering and the burnt offering
and the peace offerings. [23] Moses and Aaron went
into the tent of meeting. When they came out and
blessed the people, [A]the glory of the LORD appeared
to all the people. [24] [A]Then fire came out from before
the LORD and consumed the burnt offering and the
portions of fat on the altar; and when all the people
saw *it,* they shouted and fell on their faces.

THE SIN OF NADAB AND ABIHU

10 Now [A]Nadab and Abihu, the sons of Aaron,
took their respective [B]firepans, and after putting fire in them, placed incense on it and offered
strange fire before the LORD, which He had not
commanded them. [2] [A]And fire came out from the
presence of the LORD and consumed them, and they
died before the LORD. [3] Then Moses said to Aaron,
"It is what the LORD spoke, saying,

> 'By those who [A]come near Me I
> [a,B]will be treated as holy,
> And before all the people I
> will [C]be honored.' "

So Aaron, therefore, kept silent.

[4] Moses called also to [A]Mishael and Elzaphan,
the sons of Aaron's uncle Uzziel, and said to them,
"Come forward, carry your [a]relatives away from the
front of the sanctuary to the outside of the camp."

9:6 [A]Ex 24:16; Lev 9:23 9:7 [a]Lit *make* [b]Lit *of* [A]Heb 5:3; 7:27 9:8 [A]Lev 4:1-12 9:9 [A]Lev 9:12, 18 [B]Lev 4:7 9:10 [a]Or *appendage on* 9:11 [A]Lev 4:11, 12; 8:17 9:13 [a]Lit *its pieces* 9:15 [A]Lev 4:27-31 9:16 [a]Lit *made* [A]Lev 1:1-13 9:17 [a]Lit *palm* [A]Lev 2:1-3 [B]Lev 3:5 9:18 [A]Lev 3:1-11 9:19 [a]Or *appendage on* [A]Lev 3:9 9:20 [a]Lit *the portions of fat* 9:21 [a]Lit *waved* [A]Ex 29:26, 27; Lev 7:30-34 9:22 [A]Num 6:22-26; Deut 21:5; Luke 24:50 9:23 [A]Lev 9:6; Num 16:19 9:24 [A]1 Kin 18:38, 39; 2 Chr 7:1 10:1 [A]Ex 24:1, 9; Num 3:2; 26:61 [B]Lev 16:12 10:2 [A]Num 3:4; 16:35; 26:61 10:3 [a]Or *will show Myself holy* [A]Ex 19:22; Lev 21:6 [B]Ex 30:30; Ezek 38:16 [C]Ex 14:4, 17; Is 49:3; Ezek 28:22 10:4 [a]Lit *brothers* [A]Ex 6:22

sacrifices. *See notes on vv. 23, 24,* where that appearance is recorded.

9:8–21 Aaron presented sacrifices on his own behalf (vv. 8–14) and on behalf of the people (vv. 15–21).

9:17 burnt offering … morning. See Ex 29:41; Nu 28:4.

9:21 wave offering. *See note on 7:30–32.*

9:22 lifted up his hand toward the people. The High Priest gave a symbolic gesture for blessing, perhaps pronouncing the priestly blessing (Nu 6:24–26; cf. 2Co 13:14).

9:23 the glory of the LORD appeared. The Bible speaks often of the glory of God—the visible appearance of His beauty and perfection reduced to blazing light. His glory appeared to Moses in a burning bush in Midian (Ex 3:1–6), in a cloud on Mt. Sinai (Ex 24:15–17), and in a rock on Mt. Sinai (Ex 33:18–23). The glory of God also filled the tabernacle (Ex 40:34), led the people as a pillar of fire and cloud (Ex 40:35–38), and also filled the temple in Jerusalem (1Ki 8:10, 11). When Aaron made the first sacrifice in the wilderness, as a priest, the "glory of the LORD appeared to all the people." In these manifestations, God was revealing His righteousness, holiness, truth, wisdom, and grace—the sum of all He is. However, nowhere has God's glory been more perfectly expressed than in His Son, the Lord Jesus Christ (Jn 1:14). It will be seen on earth again when He returns (Mt 24:29–31; 25:31).

9:24 fire came out … consumed. This fire miraculously signified that God had accepted their offering (cf. 1Ki 18:38, 39), and the people shouted for joy because of that acceptance and worshiped God.

10:1 Nadab and Abihu. These were the two oldest sons of Aaron. **firepans.** The vessels in which the incense was burned in the Holy Place (its features are unknown) was to be used only for holy purposes. **strange fire.** Though the exact infraction is not detailed, in some way they violated the prescription for offering incense (cf. Ex 30:9, 34–38), probably because they were drunk (see vv. 8, 9). Instead of taking the incense fire from the brazen altar, they had some other source for the fire and thus perpetrated an act, which, considering the descent of the miraculous fire they had just seen and their solemn duty to do as God told them, betrayed carelessness, irreverence, and lack of consideration for God. Such a tendency had to be punished for all priests to see as a warning.

10:2 fire came out. The same divine fire that accepted the sacrifices (9:24) consumed the errant priests. That was not unlike the later deaths of Uzzah (2Sa 6:6, 7) or Ananias and Sapphira (Ac 5:5, 10).

10:3 treated as holy … be honored. Nadab and Abihu were guilty of violating both requirements of God's absolute standard. The priests had received repeated and solemn warnings as to the necessity of reverence before God (see Ex 19:22; 29:44). **Aaron … kept silent.** In spite of losing his two sons, he did not complain, but submitted to the righteous judgment of God.

10:4 Mishael … Elzaphan. See Ex 6:22 for their lineage. This procedure prevented the

5 So they came forward and carried them still in
their [A]tunics to the outside of the camp, as Moses
had said. 6 Then Moses said to Aaron and to his sons
Eleazar and Ithamar, "[A]Do not [a]uncover your heads
nor tear your clothes, so that you will not die and
that He will not [B]become wrathful against all the
congregation. But your [b]kinsmen, the whole house
of Israel, shall bewail the burning which the LORD
has [c]brought about. 7 You shall not even go out from
the doorway of the tent of meeting, or you will die;
for [A]the LORD'S anointing oil is upon you." So they
did according to the word of Moses.
8 The LORD then spoke to Aaron, saying, 9 "[A]Do
not drink wine or strong drink, neither you nor
your sons with you, when you come into the tent of
meeting, so that you will not die—it is a perpetual
statute throughout your generations— 10 and [A]so
as to make a distinction between the holy and the
profane, and between the unclean and the clean,
11 and [A]so as to teach the sons of Israel all the statutes
which the LORD has spoken to them through Moses."
12 Then Moses spoke to Aaron, and to his surviving sons, [A]Eleazar and Ithamar, "[B]Take the grain
offering that is left over from the LORD'S offerings
by fire and eat it unleavened beside the altar, for it
is most holy. 13 You shall eat it, moreover, in a holy
place, because it is your due and your sons' due out
of the LORD'S offerings by fire; for thus I have been
commanded. 14 [A]The breast of the wave offering,
however, and the thigh of the offering you may
eat in a clean place, you and your sons and your
daughters with you; for they have been given as
your due and your sons' due out of the sacrifices
of the peace offerings of the sons of Israel. 15 [A]The
thigh offered by lifting up and the breast offered
by waving they shall bring along with the offerings by fire of the portions of fat, to present as a
wave offering before the LORD; so it shall be a thing
perpetually due you and your sons with you, just
as the LORD has commanded."
16 But Moses searched carefully for the [A]goat of the
sin offering, and behold, it had been burned up! So
he was angry with Aaron's surviving sons Eleazar
and Ithamar, saying, 17 "Why [A]did you not eat the sin
offering at the holy place? For it is most holy, and
[a]He gave it to you to bear away [B]the guilt of the congregation, to make atonement for them before the
LORD. 18 Behold, [A]since its blood had not been brought
inside, into the sanctuary, you should certainly have
[B]eaten it in the sanctuary, just as I commanded." 19 But
Aaron spoke to Moses, "Behold, this very day they
[A]presented their sin offering and their burnt offering
before the LORD. When things like these happened to
me, if I had eaten a sin offering today, would it have
been good in the sight of the LORD?" 20 When Moses
heard *that,* it seemed good in his sight.

LAWS ABOUT ANIMALS FOR FOOD

11 The LORD spoke again to Moses and to Aaron,
saying to them, 2 "Speak to the sons of Israel,
saying, '[A]These are the creatures which you may eat
from all the animals that are on the earth. 3 Whatever divides a hoof, thus making split hoofs, *and*
chews the cud, among the animals, that you may eat.
4 Nevertheless, [A]you are not to eat of these, among
those which chew the cud, or among those which

10:5 [A]Ex 29:5; Lev 8:13 10:6 [a]Lit *unbind* [b]Lit *brothers* [c]Lit *burned* [A]Lev 21:1-5, 10-12 [B]Num 1:53; 16:22, 46; 18:5; Josh 7:1; 22:18, 20; 2 Sam 24:1 10:7 [A]Ex 28:41; Lev 21:12 10:9 [A]Prov 20:1; 31:5; Is 28:7; Ezek 44:21; Hos 4:11; Luke 1:15; Eph 5:18; 1 Tim 3:3; Titus 1:7 10:10 [A]Lev 11:47; 20:25; Ezek 22:26 10:11 [A]Deut 17:10, 11; 33:10 10:12 [A]Ex 6:23; Num 3:2 [B]Lev 6:14-18 10:14 [A]Lev 7:30-34; Num 18:11 10:15 [A]Lev 7:34 10:16 [A]Lev 9:3, 15 10:17 [a]Or *was given* [A]Lev 6:24-30 [B]Ex 28:38; Lev 22:16; Num 18:1 10:18 [A]Lev 6:30 [B]Lev 6:26 10:19 [A]Lev 9:8, 12 11:2 [A]Deut 14:3-21 11:4 [A]Acts 10:14

priests from defiling themselves by handling the dead bodies (Lv 21:1), and allowed the whole congregation to see the result of such disregard for the holiness of God. **outside of the camp.** As this was done with the ashes of sacrificed animals (6:11), so it was done with the remains of these two priests who received God's wrath.

10:6 Eleazar and Ithamar. Aaron's youngest sons who yet lived. Later, the line of Eleazar would be designated as the unique line of the High Priest (cf. Nu 25:10–13).

10:6, 7 This prohibition against the customary signs of mourning was usually reserved for the High Priest only as prescribed in 21:10–12. Here, Moses applies it to Eleazar and Ithamar also.

10:8, 9 Do not drink wine or strong drink. Taken in its context, this prohibition suggests that intoxication led Nadab and Abihu to perform their blasphemous act. Cf. Pr 23:20–35; 1Ti 3:3; Titus 1:7.

10:11 teach the sons of Israel. It was essential that alcohol not hinder the clarity of their minds, since the priests were to teach God's law to all of Israel. They were the expositors of the Scripture, alongside the prophets who generally received the Word directly from the Lord. Ezra would become the supreme example of a commendable priest (Ezr 7:10).

10:12–15 *See notes on the peace offering in 3:1–17; 7:11–36.*

10:16–20 The sin offering had not been eaten as prescribed in 6:26, but rather it was wholly burned. It was the duty of the priests to have eaten the meat after the blood was sprinkled on the altar, but instead of eating it in a sacred feast, they had burned it outside the camp. Moses discovered this disobedience, probably from a dread of some further judgment, and challenged, not Aaron, whose heart was too torn in the death of his sons, but the two surviving sons in the priesthood to explain their breach of ritual duty. Aaron, who heard the charge, however, and by whose direction the violation had occurred, gave the explanation. His reason was that they had done all the ritual sacrifice correctly up to the point of eating the meat, but omitted eating because he was too dejected for a feast in the face of the appalling judgments that had fallen. He was wrong, because God had specifically commanded the sin offering to be eaten in the Holy Place. God's law was clear, and it was sin to deviate from it at all. Moses sympathized with Aaron's grief, however, and having made his point, dropped the issue.

11:1–16:34 Prescriptions for uncleanness are covered in this section. God used the tangible issues of life which He labeled clean/unclean to repeatedly impress upon Israel the difference between what was holy and unholy. "Clean" means acceptable to God; "unclean" means unacceptable to God. Leviticus 11–15 details the code of cleanness; Lv 16 returns to sacrifices on the Day of Atonement.

11:1–47 This section contains further legislation on the consumption of animals. Abel's offering hints at a "post-Fall/pre-Flood" diet of animals (Ge 4:4). After the Noahic flood, God specifically had granted man permission to eat meat (Ge 9:1–4), but here spelled out the specifics as covenant legislation. All of the reasons for the prohibitions are not specified. The major points were: 1) that Israel was to obey God's absolute standard, regardless of the reason for it, or the lack of understanding of it; and 2) such a unique diet was specified that Israel would find it difficult to eat with the idolatrous people around and among them. Their dietary laws served as a barrier to easy socialization with idolatrous peoples. Dietary and hygienic benefits were real, but only secondary to the divine purposes of obedience and separation.

11:3–23 This section is repeated in Dt 14:3–20 in almost the exact same wording. The subject matter includes animals (vv. 3–8), water life (vv. 9–12), birds (vv. 13–19), and insects (vv. 20–23).

11:4 camel. The camel has a divided foot of two large parts, but the division is not complete and the two toes rest on an elastic pad.

divide the hoof: the camel, for though it chews cud,
it does not divide the hoof, it is unclean to you.
5 Likewise, the [a]shaphan, for though it chews cud,
it does not divide the hoof, it is unclean to you; 6 the
[a]rabbit also, for though it chews cud, it does not
divide the hoof, it is unclean to you; 7 and the pig,
for though it divides the hoof, thus making a split
hoof, it does not chew cud, it is unclean to you. 8 You
shall not eat of their flesh nor touch their carcasses;
they are unclean to you.
9 '[A]These you may eat, whatever is in the water:
all that have fins and scales, those in the water, in
the seas or in the rivers, you may eat. 10 [A]But whatever is in the seas and in the rivers that does not
have fins and scales among all the teeming life of
the water, and among all the living creatures that
are in the water, they are detestable things to you,
11 and they shall be [a]abhorrent to you; you may not
eat of their flesh, and their carcasses you shall detest. 12 Whatever in the water does not have fins and
scales is [a]abhorrent to you.

AVOID THE UNCLEAN

13 'These, moreover, [A]you shall detest among the
birds; they are [a]abhorrent, not to be eaten: the [b]ea-
gle and the vulture and the [c]buzzard, 14 and the kite
and the falcon in its kind, 15 every raven in its kind,
16 and the ostrich and the owl and the sea gull and
the hawk in its kind, 17 and the little owl and the cormorant and the [a]great owl, 18 and the white owl and
the [a]pelican and the carrion vulture, 19 and the stork,
the heron in its kinds, and the hoopoe, and the bat.
20 'All the [a]winged insects that walk on *all* fours
are detestable to you. 21 Yet these you may eat
among all the [a]winged insects which walk on *all*
fours: those which have above their feet jointed
legs with which to jump on the earth. 22 These of
them you may eat: the locust in its kinds, and the
devastating locust in its kinds, and the cricket in
its kinds, and the grasshopper in its kinds. 23 But
all other [a]winged insects which are four-footed are
detestable to you.
24 'By these, moreover, you will be made unclean:
whoever touches their carcasses becomes unclean
until evening, 25 and [A]whoever picks up any of their
carcasses shall wash his clothes and be unclean
until evening. 26 Concerning all the animals which
divide the hoof but do not make a split *hoof,* or
which do not chew cud, they are unclean to you:
whoever touches them becomes unclean. 27 Also
whatever walks on its paws, among all the creatures
that walk on *all* fours, are unclean to you; whoever
touches their carcasses becomes unclean until evening, 28 and the one who picks up their carcasses
shall wash his clothes and be unclean until evening;
they are unclean to you.
29 'Now these are to you the unclean among the
swarming things which swarm on the earth: the
mole, and the mouse, and the [a]great lizard in its
kinds, 30 and the gecko, and the [a]crocodile, and the
lizard, and the [b]sand reptile, and the chameleon.
31 These are to you the unclean among all the swarming things; whoever touches them when they are
dead becomes unclean until evening. 32 Also anything on which one of them may fall when they
are dead becomes unclean, including any wooden
article, or clothing, or a skin, or a sack—any article
[a]of which use is made—[A]it shall be put in the water
and be unclean until evening, then it becomes clean.
33 As for any [A]earthenware vessel into which one of
them may fall, whatever is in it becomes unclean
and you shall break [a]the vessel. 34 Any of the [a]food
which may be eaten, on which water comes, shall
become unclean, and any [a]liquid which may be
drunk in every vessel shall become unclean. 35 Everything, moreover, on which part of their carcass
may fall becomes unclean; an oven or a [a]stove shall
be smashed; they are unclean and shall continue as
unclean to you. 36 Nevertheless a spring or a cistern
[a]collecting water shall be clean, though the one who
touches their carcass shall be unclean. 37 If a part
of their carcass falls on any seed for sowing which
is to be sown, it is clean. 38 Though if water is put
on the seed and a part of their carcass falls on it, it
is unclean to you.
39 'Also if one of the animals dies which you have
for food, the one who touches its carcass becomes
unclean until evening. 40 [A]He too, who eats some of
its carcass shall wash his clothes and be unclean
until evening, and the one who picks up its carcass
shall wash his clothes and be unclean until evening.
41 '[A]Now every swarming thing that swarms on
the earth is detestable, not to be eaten. 42 Whatever crawls on its belly, and whatever walks on *all*
fours, whatever has many feet, in respect to every
swarming thing that swarms on the earth, you
shall not eat them, for they are detestable. 43 [A]Do
not render [a]yourselves detestable through any of
the swarming things that swarm; and you shall not
make yourselves unclean with them so that you

11:5 [a]A small, shy, furry animal *(Hyrax syriacus)* found in the peninsula of the Sinai, northern Israel, and the region round the Dead Sea; KJV *coney,* orig NASB *rock badger* 11:6 [a]Or *hare* 11:9 [A]Deut 14:9 11:10 [A]Deut 14:10 11:11 [a]Lit *detestable things* 11:12 [a]Lit *detestable things* 11:13 [a]Lit *a detestable thing* [b]Or *vulture* [c]Or *black vulture* [A]Deut 14:12-19 11:17 [a]Specifically, *great horned owl* 11:18 [a]Or *owl or jackdaw* 11:20 [a]Lit *swarming things with wings* 11:21 [a]V 20, note 1 11:23 [a]V 20, note 1 11:25 [A]Lev 11:40 11:29 [a]Or *thorn-tailed lizard* 11:30 [a]Or *lizard* [b]Species as yet undefined 11:32 [a]Lit *with which work is done* [A]Lev 15:12 11:33 [a]Lit *it* [A]Lev 6:28; 15:12 11:34 [a]I.e. if touched by a carcass; cf vv 29-32 11:35 [a]Lit *hearth for supporting (two) pots* 11:36 [a]Lit *of a gathering of* 11:40 [A]Lev 17:15; 22:8; Deut 14:21; Ezek 44:31 11:41 [A]Lev 11:29 11:43 [a]Lit *your souls* [A]Lev 20:25

11:5, 6 **shaphan … rabbit.** While not true ruminating animals, the manner in which these animals processed their food gave the distinct appearance of "chewing the cud."

11:9 **fins and scales.** Much like the cud and hoof characteristics, the "no fin and scales" guidelines ruled out a segment of water life commonly consumed by ancient people.

11:13 **among the birds.** Rather than unifying characteristics as in the hoof-cud and no fin-scales descriptions, the forbidden birds were simply named.

11:21 This describes the locust (v. 22), which was allowed for food.

11:24–43 This section deals with separation from other defiling things.

11:26, 27 These prohibited animals would include horses and donkeys, which have a single hoof, and lion and tigers, which have paws.

11:30 **gecko.** A type of lizard.

11:36 **a spring or a cistern.** The movement and quantity of water determined the probability of actual contamination. Water was scarce also, and it would have been a threat to the water supply if all water touched by these prohibited carcasses was forbidden for drinking.

become unclean. 44 For [A]I am the LORD your God.
Consecrate yourselves therefore, and [B]be holy, for I
am holy. And you shall not make yourselves unclean
with any of the swarming things that swarm on the
earth. 45 [A]For I am the LORD who brought you up
from the land of Egypt to be your God; thus [B]you
shall be holy, for I am holy.' "
46 This is the law regarding the animal and the
bird, and every living thing that moves in the waters and everything that swarms on the earth, 47 [A]to
make a distinction between the unclean and the
clean, and between the edible creature and the creature which is not to be eaten.

LAWS OF MOTHERHOOD

12 Then the LORD spoke to Moses, saying, 2 "Speak
to the sons of Israel, saying:
'When a woman [a]gives birth and bears a male
child, then she shall be unclean for seven days, [A]as
in the days of [b]her menstruation she shall be unclean. 3 On [A]the eighth day the flesh of his foreskin
shall be circumcised. 4 Then she shall remain in
the blood of *her* purification for thirty-three days;
she shall not touch any consecrated thing, nor enter the sanctuary until the days of her purification
are completed. 5 But if she bears a female *child,*
then she shall be unclean for two weeks, as in her
[a]menstruation; and she shall remain in the blood
of *her* purification for sixty-six days.
6 '[A]When the days of her purification are completed, for a son or for a daughter, she shall bring
to the priest at the doorway of the tent of meeting a
one year old lamb for a burnt offering and a young
pigeon or a turtledove [B]for a sin offering. 7 Then he
shall offer it before the LORD and make atonement
for her, and she shall be cleansed from the [a]flow of
her blood. This is the law for her who bears *a child,*
whether a male or a female. 8 But if [a]she cannot
afford a lamb, then she shall take [A]two turtledoves
or two young pigeons, [B]the one for a burnt offering
and the other for a sin offering; and the [C]priest shall
make atonement for her, and she will be clean.' "

THE TEST FOR LEPROSY

13 Then the LORD spoke to Moses and to Aaron,
saying, 2 "When a man has on the skin of his
[a]body a swelling or a scab or a bright spot, and it
becomes [b]an infection of leprosy on the skin of his
[a]body, [A]then he shall be brought to Aaron the priest
or to one of his sons the priests. 3 The priest shall
look at the mark on the skin of the [a]body, and if
the hair in the infection has turned white and the
infection appears to be deeper than the skin of his
[a]body, it is an infection of leprosy; when the priest

11:44 [A]Ex 6:7; 16:12; 23:25; Is 43:3; 51:15 [B]Lev 19:2; 1 Pet 1:16 11:45 [A]Ex 6:7; 20:2; Lev 22:33; 25:38; 26:45 [B]Lev 19:2; 1 Pet 1:16 11:47 [A]Lev 10:10; Ezek 22:26; 44:23 12:2 [a]Lit *produces seed* [b]Lit *the impurity of her sickness* [A]Lev 15:19; 18:19 12:3 [A]Gen 17:12; Luke 1:59; 2:21 12:5 [a]Lit *impurity* 12:6 [A]Luke 2:22 [B]Lev 5:7 12:7 [a]Lit *fountain* 12:8 [a]Lit *her hand does not find a sufficiency of a lamb* [A]Luke 2:22-24 [B]Lev 5:7 [C]Lev 4:26 13:2 [a]Lit *flesh* [b]Lit *a mark, stroke,* and so throughout the ch [A]Deut 24:8 13:3 [a]Lit *flesh*

11:44, 45 Consecrate yourselves … be holy, for I am holy. In all of this, God is teaching His people to live antithetically. That is, He is using these clean and unclean distinctions to separate Israel from other idolatrous nations who have no such restrictions, and He is illustrating by these prescriptions that His people must learn to live His way. Through dietary laws and rituals, God is teaching them the reality of living His way in everything. They are being taught to obey God in every seemingly mundane area of life, so as to learn how crucial obedience is. Sacrifices, rituals, diet, and even clothing and cooking are all carefully ordered by God to teach them that they are to live differently from everyone else. This is to be an external illustration for the separation from sin in their hearts. Because the Lord is their God, they are to be utterly distinct. In v. 44, for the first time the statement "I am the LORD your God" is made, as a reason for the required separation and holiness. After this verse, that phrase is mentioned about 50 more times in this book, along with the equally instructive claim, "I am holy." Because God is holy and is their God, the people are to be holy in outward ceremonial behavior as an external expression of the greater necessity of heart holiness. The connection between ceremonial holiness carries over into personal holiness. The only motivation given for all these laws is to learn to be holy because God is holy. The holiness theme is central to Leviticus (see 10:3; 19:2; 20:7, 26; 21:6–8).

12:1–8 Uncleanness is related to the mother's afterbirth, not the child.

12:2 menstruation. *See note on 15:19–24.*

12:3 eighth day. Joseph and Mary followed these instructions at the birth of Christ (Lk 2:21). **circumcised.** The sign of the Abrahamic (Ge 17:9–14) Covenant was incorporated into the laws of Mosaic cleanness. Cf. Ro 4:11–13. (For a discussion on circumcision, *see note on Jer 4:4.*)

12:5 two weeks … sixty-six days. Apparently mothers were unclean twice as long (80 days) after the birth of a daughter as a son (40 days), which reflected the stigma on women for Eve's part in the Fall. This stigma is removed in Christ (*see notes on 1Ti 2:13–15*).

12:6 burnt offering … sin offering. Though the occasion was joyous, the sacrifices required were to impress upon the mind of the parent the reality of original sin and that the child had inherited a sin nature. The circumcision involved a cutting away of the male foreskin, which could carry infections and diseases in its folds. This cleansing of the physical organ so as not to pass on disease (Jewish women have historically had the lowest incidence of cervical cancer) was a picture of the deep need for cleansing from depravity, which is most clearly revealed by procreation, as men produce sinners and only sinners. Circumcision points to the fact that cleansing is needed at the very core of a human being, a cleansing God offers to the faithful and penitent through the sacrifice of Christ to come.

12:8 turtledoves … pigeons. Cf. Lv 1:14–17; 5:7–10. These were the offerings of Joseph and Mary after Christ's birth (cf. Lk 2:24), when they presented Jesus as their firstborn to the Lord (Ex 13:2; Lk 2:22). Birds, rather than livestock, indicated a low economic situation, though one who was in total poverty could offer flour (5:11–13).

13:1–14:57 This section covers laws pertaining to skin diseases.

13:2 bright spot. This probably refers to inflammation. **leprosy.** This is a term referring to various ancient skin disorders that were sometimes superficial, sometimes serious. It may have included modern leprosy (Hansen's disease). The symptoms described in vv. 2, 6, 10, 18, 30, and 39 are not sufficient for a diagnosis of the clinical condition. For the protection of the people, observation and isolation were demanded for all suspected cases of what could be a contagious disease. This biblical leprosy involved some whiteness (v. 3; Ex 4:6), which disfigured its victim but did not disable him. Naaman was able to exercise his functions as general of Syria's army, although a leper (2Ki 5:1, 27). Both OT and NT lepers went almost everywhere, indicating that this disease was not the leprosy of today that cripples. A victim of this scaly disease was unclean as long as the infection was partial. Once the body was covered with it, he was clean and could enter the place of worship (see vv. 12–17). Apparently the complete covering meant the contagious period was over. The allusion to a boil (vv. 18–28) with inflamed or raw areas and whitened hairs may refer to a related infection that was contagious. When lepers were cured by Christ, they were neither lame nor deformed. They were never brought on beds. Similar skin conditions are described in vv. 29–37 and vv. 38–44 (some inflammation from infection). The aim of these laws was to protect the people from disease, but more importantly, to inculcate into them by vivid object lessons how God desired purity, holiness, and cleanness among His people.

has looked at him, he shall pronounce him unclean.
4 But if the bright spot is white on the skin of his
[a]body, and [b]it does not appear to be deeper than the
skin, and the hair on it has not turned white, then
the priest shall [c]isolate *him who has* the infection
for seven days. 5 The priest shall look at him on the
seventh day, and if in his eyes the infection [a]has not
changed *and* the infection has not spread on the
skin, then the priest shall [b]isolate him for seven
more days. 6 The priest shall look at him again on
the seventh day, and if the infection has faded and
the mark has not spread on the skin, then the priest
shall pronounce him clean; it is *only* a scab. And he
shall [A]wash his clothes and be clean.

7 "But if the scab spreads farther on the skin after
he has shown himself to the priest for his cleansing,
he shall appear again to the priest. 8 The priest shall
look, and if the scab has spread on the skin, then the
priest shall pronounce him unclean; it is leprosy.

9 "When the infection of leprosy is on a man, then
he shall be brought to the priest. 10 The priest shall
then look, and if there is a [A]white swelling in the skin,
and it has turned the hair white, and there is quick
raw flesh in the swelling, 11 it is [a]a chronic leprosy on
the skin of his [b]body, and the priest shall pronounce
him unclean; he shall not [c]isolate him, for he is unclean. 12 If the leprosy breaks out farther on the skin,
and the leprosy covers all the skin of *him who has*
the infection from his head even to his feet, [a]as far as
the priest can see, 13 then the priest shall look, and behold, *if* the leprosy has covered all his [a]body, he shall
pronounce clean *him who has* the infection; it has
all turned white *and* he is clean. 14 But whenever raw
flesh appears on him, he shall be unclean. 15 The priest
shall look at the raw flesh, and he shall pronounce
him unclean; the raw flesh is unclean, it is leprosy.
16 Or if the raw flesh turns again and is changed to
white, then he shall [A]come to the priest, 17 and the
priest shall look at him, and behold, *if* the infection
has turned to white, then the priest shall pronounce
clean *him who has* the infection; he is clean.

18 "When the [a]body has a boil on its skin and it
is healed, 19 and in the place of the boil there is a
white swelling or a reddish-white, bright spot, then
it shall be shown to the priest; 20 and the priest shall
look, and behold, *if* [a]it appears to be lower than
the skin, and the hair on it has turned white, then
the priest shall pronounce him unclean; it is the
infection of leprosy, it has broken out in the boil.
21 But if the priest looks at it, and behold, there are
no white hairs in it and it is not lower than the skin
and is faded, then the priest shall [a]isolate him for
seven days; 22 and if it spreads farther on the skin,
then the priest shall pronounce him unclean; it is
an infection. 23 But if the bright spot remains in
its place and does not spread, it is *only* the scar of
the boil; and the priest shall pronounce him clean.

24 "Or if the [a]body sustains in its skin a burn by
fire, and the raw *flesh* of the burn becomes a bright
spot, reddish-white, or white, 25 then the priest shall
look at it. And if the hair in the bright spot has
[A]turned white and it appears to be deeper than the
skin, it is leprosy; it has broken out in the burn.
Therefore, the priest shall pronounce him unclean;
it is an infection of leprosy. 26 But if the priest looks
at it, and indeed, there is no white hair in the bright
spot and it is no [a]deeper than the skin, but is dim,
then the priest shall [b]isolate him for seven days;
27 and the priest shall look at him on the seventh
day. If it spreads farther in the skin, then the priest
shall pronounce him unclean; it is an infection of
leprosy. 28 But if the bright spot remains in its place
and has not spread in the skin, but is dim, it is the
swelling from the burn; and the priest shall pronounce him clean, for it is *only* the scar of the burn.

29 "Now if a man or woman has an infection on
the head or on the beard, 30 then the priest shall
look at the infection, and if it appears to be deeper
than the skin and there is thin yellowish hair in it,
then the priest shall pronounce him unclean; it is a
scale, it is leprosy of the head or of the beard. 31 But
if the priest looks at the infection of the scale, and
indeed, it appears to be no deeper than the skin
and there is no black hair in it, then the priest shall
[a]isolate *the person* with the scaly infection for seven
days. 32 On the seventh day the priest shall look at
the infection, and if the scale has not spread and
no yellowish hair has [a]grown in it, and the appearance of the scale is no deeper than the skin, 33 then
he shall shave himself, but he shall not shave the
scale; and the priest shall [a]isolate *the person* with
the scale seven more days. 34 Then on the seventh
day the priest shall look at the scale, and if the scale
has not spread in the skin and it appears to be no
deeper than the skin, the priest shall pronounce him
clean; and he shall wash his clothes and be clean.
35 But if the scale spreads farther in the skin after his
cleansing, 36 then the priest shall look at him, and
if the scale has spread in the skin, the priest need
not seek for the yellowish hair; he is unclean. 37 If
in his sight the scale has remained, however, and
black hair has grown in it, the scale has healed, he
is clean; and the priest shall pronounce him clean.

38 "When a man or a woman has bright spots on
the skin of the [a]body, *even* white bright spots, 39 then
the priest shall look, and if the bright spots on the
skin of their [a]bodies are a faint white, it is [b]eczema
that has broken out on the skin; he is clean.

40 "Now if a [a]man loses the hair of his head, he
is [A]bald; he is clean. 41 If his head becomes bald at
the [a]front and sides, he is bald on the forehead; he
is clean. 42 But if on the bald head or the bald forehead, there occurs a reddish-white infection, it is
leprosy breaking out on his bald head or on his bald
forehead. 43 Then [A]the priest shall look at him; and
if the swelling of the infection is reddish-white on
his bald head or on his bald forehead, like the appearance of leprosy in the skin of the [a]body, 44 he is

13:4 [a]*Lit flesh* [b]*Lit the appearance of it is not deeper* [c]*Lit shut up* 13:5 [a]*Lit has stood* [b]*Lit shut up* 13:6 [A]Lev 11:25; 14:8 13:10 [A]Num 12:10; 2 Kin 5:27; 2 Chr 26:19, 20 13:11 [a]*Lit an old* [b]*Lit flesh* [c]*Lit shut up* 13:12 [a]*Lit with regard to the whole sight of the priest's eyes* 13:13 [a]*Lit flesh* 13:16 [A]Luke 5:12-14 13:18 [a]*Lit flesh* 13:20 [a]*Lit the appearance of it is lower* 13:21 [a]*Lit shut up* 13:24 [a]*Lit flesh* 13:25 [A]Ex 4:6; Num 12:10; 2 Kin 5:27 13:26 [a]*Lit lower* [b]*Lit shut up* 13:31 [a]*Lit shut up* 13:32 [a]*Lit been* 13:33 [a]*Lit shut up* 13:38 [a]*Lit flesh* 13:39 [a]*Lit flesh* [b]*Lit tetter* 13:40 [a]*Lit man's head becomes bald* [A]2 Kin 2:23; Is 15:2; Amos 8:10 13:41 [a]*Lit border of his face* 13:43 [a]*Lit flesh* [A]Lev 10:10; Ezek 22:26

a leprous man, he is unclean. The priest shall surely
pronounce him unclean; his infection is on his head.
45 "As for the leper who has the infection, his
clothes shall be torn, and [A]the hair of his head shall
be [a]uncovered, and he shall [B]cover his mustache and
cry, '[C]Unclean! Unclean!' 46 He shall remain unclean
all the days during which he has the infection; he
is unclean. He shall live alone; his dwelling shall
be [A]outside the camp.
47 "When a garment has a [a]mark of leprosy in it,
whether it is a wool garment or a linen garment,
48 whether in [a]warp or woof, of linen or of wool,
whether in leather or in any article made of leather,
49 if the mark is greenish or reddish in the garment
or in the leather, or in the [a]warp or in the woof, or in
any article of leather, it is a leprous mark and shall
be shown to the priest. 50 Then [A]the priest shall look
at the mark and shall [a]quarantine the article with
the mark for seven days. 51 He shall then look at the
mark on the seventh day; if the mark has spread in
the garment, whether in the warp or in the woof, or
in the leather, whatever the purpose for which the
leather is used, the mark is a [a]leprous malignancy, it
is unclean. 52 So he shall burn the garment, whether
the warp or the woof, in wool or in linen, or any article of leather in which the mark occurs, for it is a
[a]leprous malignancy; it shall be burned in the fire.
53 "But if the priest shall look, and indeed the mark
has not spread in the garment, either in the warp or
in the woof, or in any article of leather, 54 then the
priest shall order them to wash the thing in which
the mark occurs and he shall [a]quarantine it for
seven more days. 55 After the article with the mark
has been washed, the priest shall again look, and
if the mark has not changed its appearance, even
though the mark has not spread, it is unclean; you
shall burn it in the fire, whether an eating away has
produced bareness on the top or on the front of it.
56 "Then if the priest looks, and if the mark has
faded after it has been washed, then he shall tear
it out of the garment or out of the leather, whether
from the warp or from the woof; 57 and if it appears
again in the garment, whether in the warp or in the
woof, or in any article of leather, it is an outbreak;
the article with the mark shall be burned in the fire.
58 The garment, whether the warp or the woof, or
any article of leather from which the mark has departed when you washed it, it shall then be washed
a second time and will be clean."
59 This is the law for the mark of leprosy in a garment of wool or linen, whether in the warp or in the
woof, or in any article of leather, for pronouncing
it clean or unclean.

LAW OF CLEANSING A LEPER

14 Then the LORD spoke to Moses, saying, 2 "This
shall be the law of the leper in the day of his
cleansing. [A]Now he shall be brought to the priest,
3 and the priest shall go [A]out to the outside of the
camp. Thus the priest shall look, and if the [a]infection
of leprosy has been healed in the leper, 4 then the
priest shall give orders to take two live clean birds
and [A]cedar wood and a [a]scarlet string and hyssop
for the one who is to be cleansed. 5 The priest shall
also give orders to slay the one bird in an earthenware vessel over [a]running water. 6 *As for* the live
bird, he shall take it together with [A]the cedar wood
and the [a]scarlet string and the [B]hyssop, and shall dip
them and the live bird in the blood of the bird that
was slain over the [b]running water. 7 [A]He shall then
sprinkle seven times the one who is to be cleansed
from the leprosy and shall pronounce him clean,
and shall let the live bird go free over the open field.
8 [A]The one to be cleansed shall then wash his clothes
and shave off all his hair and bathe in water and [B]be
clean. Now afterward, he may enter the camp, but
he [C]shall stay outside his tent for seven days. 9 It will
be on the seventh day that he shall shave off all his
hair: he shall shave his head and his beard and his
eyebrows, even all his hair. He shall then wash his
clothes and bathe his [a]body in water and [A]be clean.
10 "Now on the eighth day he is to take two male
lambs without defect, and a yearling ewe lamb
without defect, and three-tenths *of an* [a]*ephah* of fine
flour mixed with oil for a grain offering, and one
[b,A]log of oil; 11 and the priest who pronounces him
clean shall present the man to be cleansed and the
[a]aforesaid before the LORD at the doorway of the

13:45 [a]Or *disheveled* [A]Lev 10:6 [B]Ezek 24:17, 22; Mic 3:7 [C]Lam 4:15 13:46 [A]Num 5:1-4; 12:14 13:47 [a]Lit *infection,* and so throughout the ch 13:48 [a]Or *weaving or texture* 13:49 [a]Or *weaving or texture* 13:50 [a]Lit *shut up* [A]Ezek 44:23 13:51 [a]Lit *malignant leprosy* 13:52 [a]Lit *malignant leprosy* 13:54 [a]Lit *shut up* 14:2 [A]Matt 8:4; Mark 1:44; Luke 5:14; 17:14 14:3 [a]Lit *mark, stroke,* and so throughout the ch [A]Lev 13:46 14:4 [a]Lit *scarlet color and* [A]Lev 14:6, 49, 51, 52; Num 19:6 14:5 [a]Lit *living* 14:6 [a]Lit *scarlet color and* [b]Lit *living* [A]Lev 14:4 [B]Ps 51:7 14:7 [A]Ezek 36:25 14:8 [A]Lev 11:25; 13:6; Num 8:7 [B]Lev 14:9, 20 [C]Num 5:2, 3; 12:14, 15; 2 Chr 26:21 14:9 [a]Lit *flesh* [A]Lev 14:8, 20 14:10 [a]I.e. Approx one bu [b]I.e. Approx one pt [A]Lev 14:12, 15, 21, 24 14:11 [a]Lit *them*

13:45 "Unclean! Unclean!" Here are the symbols of grief and isolation. This same cry is heard from the survivors of Jerusalem's destruction (cf. La 4:15).

13:47–59 Deals with garments worn by infected persons.

13:59 pronouncing it clean or unclean. The primary purpose of this legislation was to assist the priest in determining the presence of contagious skin disease. The language of the passage indicates disease that affects the clothes as it did the person. This provided more illustrations of the devastating infection of sin and how essential cleansing was spiritually.

14:1–32 This section explains the cleansing ritual for healed persons.

14:2 the law of the leper. The sense of this law is a prescription, not for healing from leprosy and other such diseases, but rather for the ceremonial cleansing, which needed to be performed after the person was declared clean.

14:3 outside of the camp. The leper was not allowed to return to society immediately. Before the person could enter the camp, some priest skilled in the diagnoses of disease needed to examine him and assist with the ritual of the two birds (vv. 4–7).

14:4–7 The bundle of cedar and hyssop tied with scarlet included the living bird. It was all dipped 7 times into the blood of the killed bird mixed with water to symbolize purification. The bird was then set free to symbolize the leper's release from quarantine.

14:4 hyssop. *See note on Ex 12:22* (cf. Lv 14:6, 49, 51).

14:8 outside his tent. The movement was progressive until finally he could enter and dwell in his own tent, giving dramatic indication of the importance of thorough cleansing for fellowship with God's people. This was a powerful lesson from God on the holiness He desired for those who lived among His people. This has not changed (see 2Co 7:1).

14:10–20 As part of the leper's ceremonial cleansing ritual, trespass or guilt (5:14–6:7), sin (4:1–5:13), burnt (1:3–17), and grain (2:1–16) offerings were to be made.

14:10 one log of oil. Less than one pint.

tent of meeting. 12 Then the priest shall take the one
male lamb and bring it for a [A]guilt offering, with
the [a,B]log of oil, and present them as a [C]wave offering before the LORD. 13 Next he shall slaughter the
male lamb in [A]the place where they slaughter the
sin offering and the burnt offering, at the place of
the sanctuary—for the guilt offering, [B]like the sin
offering, belongs to the priest; it is most holy. 14 The
priest shall then take some of the blood of the [A]guilt
offering, and the priest shall put *it* on [B]the lobe of the
right ear of the one to be cleansed, and on the thumb
of his right hand and on the big toe of his right foot.
15 The priest shall also take some of the [a,A]log of oil,
and pour *it* into his left palm; 16 the priest shall then
dip his right-hand finger into the oil that is in his
left palm, and with his finger sprinkle some of the
oil seven times before the LORD. 17 Of the remaining
oil which is in his palm, the priest shall put some
on the right ear lobe of the one to be cleansed, and
on the thumb of his right hand, and on the big toe
of his right foot, on the blood of the guilt offering;
18 while the rest of the oil that is in the priest's palm,
he shall put on the head of the one to be cleansed.
So the priest shall make [A]atonement on his behalf
before the LORD. 19 The priest shall next offer the
[A]sin offering and make atonement for the one to be
cleansed from his uncleanness. Then afterward, he
shall slaughter the burnt offering. 20 The priest shall
offer up the burnt offering and the grain offering
on the altar. Thus the priest shall make atonement
for him, and [A]he will be clean.

21 "[A]But if he is poor and his [a]means are insufficient, then he is to take one male lamb for a [B]guilt
offering as a wave offering to make atonement
for him, and one-tenth *of an* [b]*ephah* of fine flour
mixed with oil for a grain offering, and a [c,C]log of
oil, 22 and two turtledoves or two young pigeons
which [a]are within his means, [A]the one shall be a [B]sin
offering and the other a burnt offering. 23 [A]Then the
eighth day he shall bring them for his cleansing to
the priest, at the doorway of the tent of meeting,
before the LORD. 24 The priest shall take the lamb
of the guilt offering and [A]the [a]log of oil, and the
priest shall offer them for a wave offering before
the LORD. 25 Next he shall slaughter the lamb of the
guilt offering; and the priest is to take some of the
blood of the guilt offering and put *it* on [A]the lobe
of the right ear of the one to be cleansed and on
the thumb of his right hand and on the big toe of
his right foot. 26 The priest shall also pour some of
the oil into his left palm; 27 and with his right-hand
finger the priest shall sprinkle some of the oil that
is in his left palm seven times before the LORD.
28 The priest shall then put some of the oil that is
in his palm on the lobe of the right ear of the one
to be cleansed, and on the thumb of his right hand
and on the big toe of his right foot, on the place
of the blood of the guilt offering. 29 Moreover, the
rest of the oil that is in the priest's palm he shall
put on the head of the one to be cleansed, to make
atonement on his behalf before the LORD. 30 He
shall then offer one of the turtledoves or young
pigeons, [a]which are within his means. 31 *He shall
offer* what [a]he can afford, [A]the one for a sin offering and the other for a burnt offering, together
with the grain offering. So the priest shall make
atonement before the LORD on behalf of the one
to be cleansed. 32 This is the law *for him* in whom
there is an infection of leprosy, whose [a]means are
limited for his cleansing."

CLEANSING A LEPROUS HOUSE

33 The LORD further spoke to Moses and to Aaron,
saying:
34 "[A]When you enter the land of Canaan, which
I give you for a possession, and I put a mark of
leprosy on a house in the land of your possession,
35 then the one who owns the house shall come
and tell the priest, saying, '*Something* like [A]a mark
of leprosy has become visible to me in the house.'
36 The priest shall then command that they empty
the house before the priest goes in to look at the
mark, so that everything in the house need not
become unclean; and afterward the priest shall
go in to look at the house. 37 So he shall look at the
mark, and if the mark on the walls of the house has
greenish or reddish depressions and appears deeper
than the [a]surface, 38 then the priest shall come out
of the house, to the [a]doorway, and [b]quarantine the
house for seven days. 39 The priest shall return on
the seventh day and [a]make an inspection. If the
mark has indeed spread in the walls of the house,
40 then the priest shall order them to tear out the
stones with the mark in them and throw them away
[a]at an unclean place outside the city. 41 He shall have
the house scraped all around [a]inside, and they shall
dump the plaster that they scrape off at an unclean
place outside the city. 42 Then they shall take other

14:12 [a]I.e. Approx one pt [A]Lev 5:6, 18; 6:6; 14:19 [B]Lev 14:10 [C]Ex 29:22-24, 26 14:13 [A]Ex 29:11; Lev 1:11; 4:24 [B]Lev 6:24-30; 7:7 14:14 [A]Lev 14:19 [B]Ex 29:20; Lev 8:23, 24 14:15 [a]I.e. Approx one pt [A]Lev 14:10 14:18 [A]Lev 4:26; Num 15:28; Heb 2:17 14:19 [A]Lev 14:12 14:20 [A]Lev 14:8, 9 14:21 [a]Lit *hand is not reaching* [b]I.e. Approx one bu [c]I.e. Approx one pt [A]Lev 5:11; 12:8; 27:8 [B]Lev 14:22 [C]Lev 14:10 14:22 [a]Lit *his hand reaches* [A]Lev 5:7 [B]Lev 14:21, 24, 25 14:23 [A]Lev 14:10, 11 14:24 [a]I.e. Approx one pt [A]Lev 14:10 14:25 [A]Lev 14:14 14:30 [a]Lit *from those which his hand can reach* 14:31 [a]Lit *his hand can reach* [A]Lev 5:7 14:32 [a]Lit *hand does not reach* 14:34 [A]Gen 17:8; Num 32:22; Deut 7:1; 32:49 14:35 [A]Ps 91:10 14:37 [a]Lit *wall* 14:38 [a]Lit *doorway of the house* [b]Lit *shut up* 14:39 [a]Lit *look* 14:40 [a]Lit *to* 14:41 [a]Lit *from the house around*

14:12 wave offering. *See note on 7:30–32.*

14:17 right ear ... right hand ... right foot. *See note on 8:23, 24.*

14:18 put on the head. This would not have been understood as an anointing for entry into an office, but rather a symbolic gesture of cleansing and healing. There could be a connection with the NT directive to anoint the sick for healing (Mk 6:13; 16:18; Jas 5:14).

14:33–57 This section covers contaminated houses which most likely involved some kinds of infectious bacteria, fungus, or mold.

14:34 I put a mark of leprosy. God's sovereign hand is acknowledged in the diseases that were in Canaan (cf. Ex 4:11; Dt 32:39). He had His purposes for these afflictions, as He always does. Uniquely, in Israel's case, they allowed for object lessons on holiness.

14:37 greenish or reddish depressions. The disease would appear to be some sort of contagious mildew. Leprosy (Hansen's disease), as we know it today, is not the problem here since it is a disease related to the human senses, i.e., the destruction of feeling due to the dysfunction of the nerves. It is not known to be contagious either, and it couldn't be developed in a house. The matter of cleansing such houses is delineated in vv. 38–53.

stones and replace *those* stones, and he shall take other plaster and replaster the house.

43 "If, however, the mark breaks out again in the house after he has torn out the stones and scraped the house, and after it has been replastered, 44 then the priest shall come in and [a]make an inspection. If he sees that the mark has indeed spread in the house, it is [A]a malignant mark in the house; it is unclean. 45 He shall therefore tear down the house, its stones, and its timbers, and all the plaster of the house, and he shall take *them* outside the city to an [A]unclean place. 46 Moreover, whoever goes into the house during the time that he has [a]quarantined it, becomes [A]unclean until evening. 47 Likewise, whoever lies down in the house shall wash his clothes, and whoever eats in the house shall wash his clothes.

48 "If, on the other hand, the priest comes in and [a]makes an inspection and the mark has not indeed spread in the house after the house has been replastered, then the priest shall pronounce the house clean because the mark has [b]not reappeared. 49 To cleanse the house then, he shall take [A]two birds and cedar wood and a [a]scarlet string and hyssop, 50 and he shall slaughter the one bird in an earthenware vessel over [a]running water. 51 Then he shall take the cedar wood and the [A]hyssop and the [a]scarlet string, with the live bird, and dip them in the blood of the slain bird as well as in the [b]running water, and sprinkle the house seven times. 52 He shall thus cleanse the house with the blood of the bird and with the [a]running water, along with the live bird and with the cedar wood and with the hyssop and with the [b]scarlet string. 53 However, he shall let the live bird go free outside the city into the open field. So he shall make atonement for the house, and it will be clean."

54 This is the law for any mark of leprosy—even for a [A]scale, 55 and for the [A]leprous garment or house, 56 and [A]for a swelling, and for a scab, and for a bright spot— 57 to teach [a]when they are unclean and [b]when they are clean. This is the law of leprosy.

CLEANSING UNHEALTHINESS

15 The LORD also spoke to Moses and to Aaron, saying, 2 "Speak to the sons of Israel, and say to them, '[A]When any man has a discharge from his [a]body, [b]his discharge is unclean. 3 This, moreover, shall be his uncleanness in his discharge: it is his uncleanness whether his body allows its discharge to flow or whether his body obstructs its discharge. 4 Every bed on which the person with the discharge lies becomes unclean, and everything on which he sits becomes unclean. 5 Anyone, moreover, who touches his bed shall wash his clothes and bathe in water and be unclean until evening; 6 and whoever sits on the thing on which the man with the discharge has been sitting, shall wash his clothes and bathe in water and be unclean until evening. 7 Also whoever touches the [a]person with the discharge shall wash his clothes and bathe in water and be unclean until evening. 8 Or if the man with the discharge spits on one who is clean, he too shall wash his clothes and bathe in water and be unclean until evening. 9 Every saddle on which the person with the discharge rides becomes unclean. 10 Whoever then touches any of the things which were under him shall be unclean until evening, and he who carries them shall wash his clothes and bathe in water and be unclean until evening. 11 Likewise, whomever the one with the discharge touches without having rinsed his hands in water shall wash his clothes and bathe in water and be unclean until evening. 12 However, an [A]earthenware vessel which the person with the discharge touches shall be broken, and every wooden vessel shall be rinsed in water.

13 'Now when the man with the discharge becomes cleansed from his discharge, then he [A]shall count off for himself seven days for his cleansing; he shall then wash his clothes and bathe his body in [a]running water and will become clean. 14 Then on the eighth day he shall take for himself [A]two turtledoves or two young pigeons, and come before the LORD to the doorway of the tent of meeting and give them to the priest; 15 and the priest shall offer them, [A]one for a sin offering and the other for a burnt offering. So [B]the priest shall make atonement on his behalf before the LORD because of his discharge.

16 '[A]Now if a [a]man has a seminal emission, he shall bathe all his body in water and be unclean until evening. 17 As for any garment or any leather on which there is seminal emission, it shall be washed with water and be unclean until evening. 18 If a man lies with a woman *so that* there is a seminal emission, they shall both bathe in water and be [A]unclean until evening.

19 '[A]When a woman has a discharge, *if* her discharge in her body is blood, she shall continue in her menstrual impurity for seven days; and whoever touches her shall be unclean until evening. 20 Everything also on which she lies during her menstrual impurity shall be unclean, and everything on which she sits shall be unclean. 21 Anyone who touches

14:44 [a]Lit *look* [A]Lev 13:51 14:45 [A]Lev 14:41 14:46 [a]Lit *shut up* [A]Num 19:7, 10, 21, 22 14:48 [a]Lit *looks* [b]Lit *healed* 14:49 [a]Lit *scarlet color* [A]Lev 14:4 14:50 [a]Lit *living* 14:51 [a]Lit *scarlet color* [b]Lit *living* [A]1 Kin 4:33; Ps 51:7 14:52 [a]Lit *living* [b]Lit *scarlet color* 14:54 [A]Lev 13:30 14:55 [A]Lev 13:47-52 14:56 [A]Lev 13:2 14:57 [a]Lit *in the day of uncleanness* [b]Lit *in the day of cleanness* 15:2 [a]Lit *flesh,* and so throughout the ch [b]Or *by his discharge, he is unclean* [A]Lev 22:4; Num 5:2; 2 Sam 3:29 15:7 [a]Lit *flesh* 15:12 [A]Lev 6:28; 11:33 15:13 [a]Lit *living* [A]Lev 8:33; 14:8 15:14 [A]Lev 14:22, 23 15:15 [A]Lev 5:7; 14:31 [B]Lev 14:19, 31 15:16 [a]Lit *man's...goes out from him* [A]Lev 22:4; Deut 23:10, 11 15:18 [A]1 Sam 21:4 15:19 [A]Lev 12:2

14:57 to teach when they are unclean … clean. The priest needed instruction in identifying and prescribing the course for disease such as that described herein, to teach people the importance of distinguishing holy things.

15:1–33 This section deals with purification for bodily discharges. Several types of discharges by men (vv. 1–18) and women (vv. 19–30) are identified and given prescribed treatment.

15:2–15 These verses describe secretions related to some disease of the male sexual organs. After he became well, he was required to make both a sin and a burnt offering (v. 15).

15:16–18 These verses refer to natural sexual gland secretions for which no offerings were required.

15:19–24 These verses concern the natural menstrual discharge of a woman for which no offerings were required.

her bed shall wash his clothes and bathe in water
and be unclean until evening. 22 Whoever touches
any thing on which she sits shall wash his clothes
and bathe in water and be unclean until evening.
23 Whether it be on the bed or on the thing on which
she is sitting, when he touches it, he shall be unclean
until evening. 24 [A]If a man actually lies with her so
that her menstrual impurity is on him, he shall be
unclean seven days, and every bed on which he lies
shall be unclean.

25 '[A]Now if a woman has a discharge of her blood
many days, not at the period of her menstrual impurity, or if she has a discharge beyond [a]that period, all the days of her impure discharge she shall
continue as though [b]in her menstrual impurity;
she is unclean. 26 Any bed on which she lies all the
days of her discharge shall be to her like [a]her bed
at menstruation; and every thing on which she sits
shall be unclean, like [b]her uncleanness at that time.
27 Likewise, whoever touches them shall be unclean
and shall wash his clothes and bathe in water and
be unclean until evening. 28 When she becomes
clean from her discharge, she shall count off for
herself seven days; and afterward she will be clean.
29 Then on the eighth day she shall take for herself
two turtledoves or two young pigeons and bring
them in to the priest, to the doorway of the tent of
meeting. 30 The priest shall offer the [A]one for a sin
offering and the other for a burnt offering. So the
priest shall make atonement on her behalf before
the LORD because of her impure discharge.'

31 "Thus you shall keep the sons of Israel separated from their uncleanness, so that they will
not die in their uncleanness by their [A]defiling My
[a]tabernacle that is among them." 32 This is the law
for the one with a discharge, and for the man [a]who
has a seminal emission so that he is unclean by it,
33 and for the woman who is ill because of menstrual impurity, and for the one who has a discharge,
whether a male or a female, or a man who lies with
an unclean woman.

LAW OF ATONEMENT

16 Now the LORD spoke to Moses after [A]the death
of the two sons of Aaron, when they had approached the presence of the LORD and died. 2 The
LORD said to Moses:

"Tell your brother Aaron that he shall not enter
[A]at any time into the holy place inside the veil,
before the [a]mercy seat which is on the ark, or he
will die; for [B]I will appear in the cloud over the
[a]mercy seat. 3 Aaron shall enter the holy place with
this: with a [a]bull for a [A]sin offering and a ram for
a burnt offering. 4 He shall put on the [A]holy linen
tunic, and the linen undergarments shall be next
to his [a]body, and he shall be girded with the linen
sash and attired with the linen turban (these are
holy garments). Then he shall [B]bathe his [a]body in
water and put them on. 5 He shall take from the
congregation of the sons of Israel [A]two male goats
for a sin offering and one ram for a burnt offering. 6 Then [A]Aaron shall offer the bull for the sin
offering which is for himself, that he may make
atonement for himself and for his household. 7 He
shall take the two goats and present them before
the LORD at the doorway of the tent of meeting.

15:24 [A]Lev 18:19; 20:18 15:25 [a]Lit *her menstrual impurity* [b]Lit *in the days of* [A]Matt 9:20; Mark 5:25; Luke 8:43 15:26 [a]Lit *the bed of her menstrual impurity* [b]Lit *the uncleanness of her menstrual impurity* 15:30 [A]Lev 5:7 15:31 [a]Or *dwelling place* [A]Lev 20:3; Num 19:13, 20; Ezek 5:11; 36:17 15:32 [a]Lit *whose seminal emission goes out from him* 16:1 [A]Lev 10:1, 2 16:2 [a]Lit *propitiatory* [A]Ex 30:10; Heb 6:19; 9:7, 25 [B]Ex 25:21, 22; 40:34; 1 Kin 8:10-12 16:3 [a]Or *bull of the herd* [A]Lev 4:1-12; 16:6; Heb 9:7 16:4 [a]Lit *flesh* [A]Ex 28:39, 42 [B]Ex 30:20; Lev 16:24; Heb 10:22 16:5 [A]Lev 4:13-21; 2 Chr 29:21; Ezek 45:22 16:6 [A]Heb 5:3

15:25–30 These verses deal with some secretion of blood indicating disease, not menstruation, requiring a sin and burnt offering after she is well.

15:31–33 In all these instructions, God was showing the Israelites that they must have a profound reverence for holy things; and nothing was more suited to that purpose than to bar from the tabernacle all who were polluted by any kind of uncleanness, ceremonial as well as natural, physical as well as spiritual. In order to mark out His people as dwelling before Him in holiness, He required of them complete purity and didn't allow them to come before Him when defiled, even by involuntary or secret impurities. And when one considers that God was training a people to live in His presence, it becomes apparent that these rules for the maintenance of personal purity, pointing to the necessity of purity in the heart, were neither too stringent nor too minute.

16:1–34 This section covers the Day of Atonement (cf. Ex 30:10; Lv 23:26–32; Nu 29:7–11; Heb 9:1–28), which was commanded to be observed annually (v. 34) to cover the sins of the nation, both corporately and individually (v. 17). Even with the most scrupulous observance of the required sacrifices, many sins and defilements still remained unacknowledged and, therefore, without specific expiation. This special inclusive sacrifice was designed to cover all that (v. 33). The atonement was provided, but only those who were genuine in faith and repentance received its benefit, the forgiveness of God. That forgiveness was not based on any animal sacrifice, but on the One all sacrifices pictured—the Lord Jesus Christ and His perfect sacrifice on the cross (cf. Heb 10:1–10). This holiest of all Israel's festivals occurred in Sept./Oct. on the tenth day of the seventh month (v. 29). It anticipated the ultimate High Priest and the perfect sacrificial Lamb.

16:1 The death of the two sons of Aaron. Cf. 10:1–3.

16:2 Common priests went every day to burn incense on the golden altar in the part of the tabernacle sanctuary outside the veil, where the lampstand, table, and bread of the Presence were. None except the High Priest was allowed to enter inside the veil (cf. v. 12), into the Holy Place, actually called the Holy of Holies, where the ark of the covenant rested. This arrangement was designed to inspire a reverence for God at a time when His presence was indicated by visible symbols. **appear in the cloud.** This cloud was likely the smoke of the incense which the High Priest burned on his annual entrance into the Holy of Holies. It was this cloud that covered the mercy seat on the ark of the covenant (see v. 13). **the mercy seat.** See Ex 25:17–22. It lit. means "place of atonement" and referred to the throne of God between the cherubim (cf. Is 6). It is so named because it was where God manifested Himself for the purpose of atonement.

16:3 sin ... burnt offering. For these offerings brought by Aaron the High Priest, *see notes on 4:1–5:13; 6:24–30 and 1:3–17; 6:8–13,* respectively. The bull was sacrificed first as a sin offering (16:11–14) and later the ram as a burnt offering (16:24).

16:4 For a description of the priests' normal clothing, see Ex 28:1–43 and Lv 8:6–19. He wore them later for the burnt offering (cf. v. 24). These humbler clothes were less ornate, required for the Day of Atonement to portray the High Priest as God's humble servant, himself in need of atonement (vv. 11–14).

16:5 two ... goats. See 16:7–10, 20–22. One animal would be slain to picture substitutionary death and the other sent to the wilderness to represent removal of sin. **one ram.** Along with the High Priest's ram (v. 3), these were to be offered as burnt offerings (v. 24).

16:6–28 The following sequence describes the activities of the High Priest and those who assisted him on the Day of Atonement: 1) The High Priest (HP) washed at the basin in the courtyard and dressed in the tabernacle (v. 4). 2) The HP offered the bull as a sin offering for himself and his family (vv. 3, 6, 11). 3) The HP entered the Holy of Holies (HH) with the

8 Aaron shall cast lots for the two goats, one lot for the LORD and the other lot for the [a]scapegoat. 9 Then Aaron shall offer the goat on which the lot for the LORD fell, and make it a sin offering. 10 But the goat on which the lot for the [a]scapegoat fell shall be presented alive before the LORD, to make [A]atonement upon it, to send it into the wilderness as the [a]scapegoat.

11 "Then Aaron shall offer the bull of the sin offering [A]which is for himself and make atonement for himself and [B]for his household, and he shall slaughter the bull of the sin offering which is for himself. 12 He shall take a [A]firepan full of coals of fire from upon the altar before the LORD and [a]two handfuls of finely ground [B]sweet incense, and bring *it* inside the veil. 13 He shall put the incense on the fire before the LORD, that the cloud of incense may cover the [a,A]mercy seat that is on *the ark of* the testimony, [B]otherwise he will die. 14 Moreover, [A]he shall take some of the blood of the bull and sprinkle *it* [B]with his finger on the [a]mercy seat on the east *side;* also in front of the [a]mercy seat he shall sprinkle some of the blood with his finger seven times.

15 "Then he shall slaughter the goat of the sin offering [A]which is for the people, and bring its blood inside the veil and do with its blood as he did with the blood of the bull, and sprinkle it on the [a]mercy seat and in front of the [a]mercy seat. 16 [A]He shall make atonement for the holy place, because of the impurities of the sons of Israel and because of their transgressions in regard to all their sins; and thus he shall do for the tent of meeting which abides with them in the midst of their impurities. 17 When he goes in to make atonement in the holy place, no one shall be in the tent of meeting until he comes out, that he may make atonement for himself and for his household and for all the assembly of Israel. 18 Then he shall go out to the altar that is before the LORD and make atonement for it, and shall take some of the blood of the bull and of the blood of the goat and [A]put it on the horns of the altar on all sides. 19 [A]With his finger he shall sprinkle some of the blood on it seven times and cleanse it, and from the impurities of the sons of Israel consecrate it.

20 "When he finishes atoning for the holy place and the tent of meeting and the altar, he shall offer the live goat. 21 Then Aaron shall lay both of his hands on the head of the live goat, and [A]confess over it all the iniquities of the sons of Israel and all their transgressions [a]in regard to all their sins; and he shall lay them on the head of the goat and send *it* away into the wilderness by the hand of a man who *stands* in readiness. 22 The goat shall bear on itself all their iniquities to a solitary land; and he shall release the goat in the wilderness.

23 "Then Aaron shall come into the tent of meeting and take off [A]the linen garments which he put on when he went into the holy place, and shall leave them there. 24 [A]He shall bathe his [a]body with water in a holy place and put on [B]his clothes, and come forth and offer his burnt offering and the burnt offering of the people and make atonement for himself and for the people. 25 Then he shall offer up in smoke the fat of the sin offering on the altar. 26 The one who released the goat as the [a]scapegoat [A]shall wash his clothes and bathe his [b]body with water; then afterward he shall come into the camp. 27 But the bull of the sin offering and the goat of the sin offering, [A]whose blood was brought in to make atonement in the holy place, shall be taken outside the camp, and they shall burn their hides, their flesh, and their refuse in the fire. 28 Then the [A]one who burns them shall wash his clothes and bathe his body with water, then afterward he shall come into the camp.

16:8 [a]Lit *goat of removal,* or else a name: *Azazel* 16:10 [a]Lit *goat of removal,* or else a name: *Azazel* [A]Is 53:4-10; Rom 3:25; 1 John 2:2 16:11 [A]Heb 7:27; 9:7 [B]Lev 16:33 16:12 [a]Lit *the filling of the hollow of his hands* [A]Lev 10:1; Num 16:18 [B]Ex 30:34-38 16:13 [a]Lit *propitiatory* [A]Ex 25:21 [B]Ex 28:43; Lev 22:9; Num 4:15, 20 16:14 [a]Lit *propitiatory* [A]Heb 9:25 [B]Lev 4:6, 17 16:15 [a]Lit *propitiatory* [A]Heb 7:27; 9:7, 12 16:16 [A]Ex 29:36, 37; 30:10; Heb 2:17 16:18 [A]Lev 4:25; Ezek 43:20, 22 16:19 [A]Lev 16:14; Ezek 43:20 16:21 [a]Lit *in addition to* [A]Lev 5:5 16:23 [A]Lev 16:4; Ezek 42:14; 44:19 16:24 [a]Lit *flesh* [A]Lev 16:4 [B]Ex 28:40, 41 16:26 [a]Lit *goat of removal,* or else a name: *Azazel* [b]Lit *flesh* [A]Lev 11:25, 40 16:27 [A]Lev 6:30; Heb 13:11 16:28 [A]Num 19:8

bull's blood, incense, and burning coals from the altar of burnt offering (vv. 12, 13). 4) The HP sprinkled the bull's blood on the mercy seat 7 times (v. 14). 5) The HP went back to the courtyard and cast lots for the two goats (vv. 7, 8). 6) The HP sacrificed one goat as a sin offering for the people (vv. 5, 9, 15). 7) The HP reentered the HH to sprinkle blood on the mercy seat and also the Holy Place (cf. Ex 30:10; vv. 15–17). 8) The HP returned to the altar of burnt offering and cleansed it with the blood of the bull and goat (vv. 11, 15, 18, 19). 9) The scapegoat was dispatched to the wilderness (vv. 20–22). 10) Afterward, the goatkeeper cleansed himself (v. 26). 11) The HP removed his special Day of Atonement clothing, rewashed, and put on the regular HP clothing (vv. 23, 24). 12) The HP offered two rams as burnt offerings for himself and the people (vv. 3, 5, 24). 13) The fat of the sin offering was burned (v. 25). 14) The bull-and-goat sin offerings were carried outside the camp to be burned (v. 27). 15) The one who burned the sin offering cleansed himself (v. 28).

16:8 cast lots. *See note on Pr 16:33.* **the scapegoat.** Cf. vv. 10, 26. This goat (lit. *Azazel* or "escape goat") pictured the substitutionary bearing and total removal of sin which would later be fully accomplished by Jesus Christ (cf. Mt 20:28; Jn 1:29; 2Co 5:21; Gal 1:4; 3:13; Heb 9:28; 10:1–10; 1Pe 2:24; 1Jn 2:2). *See notes on vv. 20–22.*

16:9, 10 *See notes on vv. 20–22.*

16:12 inside the veil. *See note on v. 2.* The veil separated all from the holy and consuming presence of God. It was this veil in Herod's temple that was torn open from top to bottom at the death of Christ, signifying access into God's presence through Jesus Christ (see Mt 27:51; Mk 15:38; Lk 23:45).

16:13 cloud. *See note on v. 2.* **on the ... testimony.** The Testimony included the tablets of stone, upon which were written the Ten Commandments (Ex 25:16; 31:18), located in the ark under the mercy seat.

16:14 seven times. This number symbolically indicated completion or perfection (cf. v. 19).

16:16 atonement for the holy place. The object of this solemn ceremony was to impress the minds of the Israelites with the conviction that the whole tabernacle was stained by the sins of a guilty people. By those sins, they had forfeited the privileges of the presence of God and worship of Him, so that an atonement had to be made for their sins as the condition of God remaining with them.

16:17 himself ... his household ... assembly. The Day of Atonement was necessary for everyone since all had sinned, including the High Priest.

16:20–22 This "sin offering of atonement" portrayed Christ's substitutionary sacrifice (vv. 21, 22) with the result that the sinner's sins were removed (v. 22). *See notes on Is 52:13–53:12* for another discussion of these truths. Christ lived out this representation when He cried from the cross, "My God, My God, why have You forsaken Me?" (Mt 27:46).

16:21, 22 hands on the head of the live goat. This act was more than a symbolic gesture; it was a picture of the ultimate "substitutionary atonement" fulfilled by the Lord Jesus Christ (cf. Is 53:5, 6, 10, 12; *see note on 2Co 5:21*).

16:27 outside the camp. This represents the historical reality of Christ's death outside of Jerusalem (cf. Heb 13:10–14).

AN ANNUAL ATONEMENT

29 "*This* shall be a permanent statute for you: [A]in
the seventh month, on the tenth day of the month,
you shall humble your souls and not [B]do any work,
whether the native, or the alien who sojourns
among you; 30 for it is on this day that [a]atonement
shall be made for you to [A]cleanse you; you will be
clean from all your sins before the LORD. 31 It is to
be a sabbath of solemn rest for you, that you may
[A]humble your souls; it is a permanent statute. 32 So
the priest who is anointed and [a]ordained to serve
as priest in his father's place shall make atonement:
he shall thus put on [A]the linen garments, the holy
garments, 33 and make atonement for the holy sanctuary, and he shall make atonement for the tent
of meeting and for the altar. He shall also make
atonement for [A]the priests and for all the people
of the assembly. 34 Now you shall have this as a
[A]permanent statute, to [B]make atonement for the
sons of Israel for all their sins once every year." And
just as the LORD had commanded Moses, *so* he did.

BLOOD FOR ATONEMENT

17 Then the LORD spoke to Moses, saying, 2 "Speak
to Aaron and to his sons and to all the sons of
Israel and say to them, 'This is what the LORD has
commanded, saying, 3 "Any man from the house of
Israel who slaughters an ox or a lamb or a goat in
the camp, or who slaughters it outside the camp,
4 and [A]has not brought it to the doorway of the tent
of meeting to present *it* as an offering to the LORD
before the [a]tabernacle of the LORD, bloodguiltiness
is to be reckoned to that man. He has shed blood and
that man shall be cut off from among his people.
5 [a]The reason is so that the sons of Israel may bring
their sacrifices which they were sacrificing in the
open field, that they may bring them in to the LORD,
at the doorway of the tent of meeting to the priest,
and sacrifice them as sacrifices of peace offerings
to the LORD. 6 The priest shall sprinkle the blood on
the altar of the LORD at the doorway of the tent of
meeting, and [A]offer up the fat in smoke as a soothing
aroma to the LORD. 7 [A]They shall no longer sacrifice
their sacrifices to the [a]goat demons with which they
play the harlot. This shall be a permanent statute
to them throughout their generations." '

8 "Then you shall say to them, 'Any man from
the house of Israel, or from the aliens who sojourn
among them, who offers a burnt offering or sacrifice, 9 and [A]does not bring it to the doorway of the
tent of meeting to [a]offer it to the LORD, that man
also shall be cut off from his people.

10 '[A]And any man from the house of Israel, or from
the aliens who sojourn among them, who eats any
blood, [B]I will set My face against that person who eats
blood and will cut him off from among his people.
11 For [A]the [a]life of the flesh is in the blood, and I have
given it to you on the altar to make atonement for
your souls; for [B]it is the blood by reason of the [a]life
that makes atonement.' 12 Therefore I said to the sons
of Israel, 'No person among you may eat blood, nor
may any alien who sojourns among you eat blood.'
13 So when any man from the sons of Israel, or from
the aliens who sojourn among them, [a]in hunting
catches a beast or a bird which may be eaten, [A]he
shall pour out its blood and cover it with earth.

14 "[A]For *as for the* [a]life of all flesh, its blood is
identified with its [a]life. Therefore I said to the sons
of Israel, 'You are not to eat the blood of any flesh,
for the [a]life of all flesh is its blood; whoever eats it
shall be cut off.' 15 [A]When any person eats *an animal*
which dies or is torn *by beasts,* whether he is a native or an alien, he shall wash his clothes and bathe
in water, and remain unclean until evening; then he
will become clean. 16 But if he does not wash *them*
or bathe his body, then [A]he shall bear his [a]guilt."

LAWS ON IMMORAL RELATIONS

18 Then the LORD spoke to Moses, saying, 2 "Speak
to the sons of Israel and say to them, '[A]I am

16:29 [A]Lev 23:27; Num 29:7 [B]Ex 31:14, 15 16:30 [a]Lit *he shall make atonement* [A]Ps 51:2; Jer 33:8; Eph 5:26 16:31 [A]Lev 23:32; Ezra 8:21; Is 58:3, 5; Dan 10:12 16:32 [a]Lit *whose hand is filled* [A]Lev 16:4 16:33 [A]Lev 16:11 16:34 [A]Lev 23:31 [B]Heb 9:7 17:4 [a]Lit *dwelling place* [A]Deut 12:5-21 17:5 [a]Lit *In order that* 17:6 [A]Num 18:17 17:7 [a]Or *goat-idols* [A]Ex 22:20; 32:8; 34:15; Deut 32:17; 2 Chr 11:15; Ps 106:37f; 1 Cor 10:20 17:9 [a]Lit *do* [A]Ex 20:24; Lev 17:4 17:10 [A]Gen 9:4; Lev 3:17; 7:26, 27; Deut 12:16, 23-25; 1 Sam 14:33 [B]Lev 20:3, 6; Jer 44:11 17:11 [a]Lit *soul* [A]Gen 9:4; Lev 17:14 [B]Heb 9:22 17:13 [a]Lit *who in hunting* [A]Deut 12:16 17:14 [a]Lit *soul* [A]Gen 9:4; Lev 17:11 17:15 [A]Ex 22:31; Lev 7:24; 22:8; Deut 14:21 17:16 [a]Or *iniquity* [A]Num 19:20 18:2 [A]Ex 6:7; Lev 11:44; Ezek 20:5

16:29 seventh month. Tishri is Sept./Oct. **humble your souls.** This act of denying oneself was probably with respect to food, making the Day of Atonement the only day of prescribed fasting in Israel's annual calendar.

16:30 clean from all your sins. See Ps 103:12; Is 38:17; Mic 7:19. This day provided ceremonially cleansing for one year, and pictured the forgiveness of God available to all who believed and repented. Actual atonement was based on cleansing through the sacrifice of Christ (cf. Ro 3:25, 26; Heb 9:15).

16:34 once every year. The better sacrifice of Jesus Christ was offered once-for-all, never to be repeated (cf. Heb 9:11–10:18). Upon that sacrifice all forgiveness of sin is based, including that of OT believers.

17:1–27:34 Guidelines for practical holiness are detailed throughout this section.

17:1–22:33 Holiness issues that pertain to the individual are enumerated.

17:1–16 Miscellaneous laws relating to sacrifice are discussed.

17:1–9 The Lord warns against sacrificing anywhere other than at the door of the tabernacle of meeting (cf. vv. 5–7).

17:4 bloodguiltiness. An unauthorized sacrifice could result in death.

17:5 peace offerings. *See notes on 3:1–17; 7:11–34.*

17:10–16 Warnings against the misuse of blood are issued (cf. 7:26, 27; Dt 12:16, 23–25; 15:23; 1Sa 14:32–34).

17:11 life of the flesh is in the blood. This phrase is amplified by "its blood is *identified* with its life" (17:14). Blood carries life-sustaining elements to all parts of the body; therefore it represents the essence of life. In contrast, the shedding of blood represents the shedding of life, i.e., death (cf. Ge 9:4). NT references to the shedding of the blood of Jesus Christ are references to His death. **blood . . . that makes atonement.** Since it contains the life, blood is sacred to God. Shed blood (death) from a substitute atones for or covers the sinner, who is then allowed to live.

17:13, 14 It was customary with heathen hunters, when they killed any game, to pour out the blood as an offering to the god of the hunt. The Israelites, to the contrary, were enjoined by this directive and banned from all such superstitious acts of idolatry.

17:15, 16 This cleansing was necessary because these animals would not have had the blood drained properly. Cf. Ex 22:31; Dt 14:21.

18:1–30 Laws are given, relating to sexual practices, which would eliminate the abominations being practiced by the heathen in the land (18:27; cf. Lv 20:10–21; Dt 22:13–30). These specific laws assume the general prohibition of adultery (Ex 20:14) and a father incestuously engaging his daughter. They do not necessarily invalidate the special case of a levirate marriage (cf. Dt 25:5). The penalties for such outlawed behavior are detailed in 20:10–21.

the LORD your God. 3 You shall not do [a]what is [A]done
in the land of Egypt where you lived, nor are you
to do [a]what is [B]done in the land of Canaan where I
am bringing you; you shall not walk in their statutes. 4 You are to perform My judgments and keep
My statutes, [a]to live in accord with them; [A]I am the
LORD your God. 5 So you shall keep My statutes and
My judgments, [A]by which a man may live if he does
them; I am the LORD.
6 'None of you shall approach any blood relative [a]of his to uncover nakedness; I am the LORD.
7 [A]You shall not uncover the nakedness of your
father, that is, the nakedness of your mother. She
is your mother; you are not to uncover her nakedness. 8 [A]You shall not uncover the nakedness
of your father's wife; it is your father's nakedness.
9 [A]The nakedness of your sister, *either* your father's
daughter or your mother's daughter, whether born
at home or born outside, their nakedness you
shall not uncover. 10 The nakedness of your son's
daughter or your daughter's daughter, their nakedness you shall not uncover; for [a]their nakedness
is yours. 11 The nakedness of your father's wife's
daughter, [a]born to your father, she is your sister,
you shall not uncover her nakedness. 12 [A]You shall
not uncover the nakedness of your father's sister;
she is your father's blood relative. 13 You shall not
uncover the nakedness of your mother's sister,
for she is your mother's blood relative. 14 [A]You
shall not uncover the nakedness of your father's
brother; you shall not approach his wife, she is
your aunt. 15 [A]You shall not uncover the nakedness of your daughter-in-law; she is your son's
wife, you shall not uncover her nakedness. 16 [A]You
shall not uncover the nakedness of your brother's
wife; it is your brother's nakedness. 17 [A]You shall
not uncover the nakedness of a woman and of her
daughter, nor shall you take her son's daughter
or her daughter's daughter, to uncover her nakedness; they are blood relatives. It is [a]lewdness.
18 You shall not [a]marry a woman in addition to
[b]her sister [c]as a rival while she is alive, to uncover
her nakedness.
19 '[A]Also you shall not approach a woman to uncover her nakedness during her [B]menstrual impurity. 20 [A]You shall not have intercourse with your
neighbor's wife, to be defiled with her. 21 You shall
not give any of your offspring [A]to [a]offer them to
Molech, nor shall you [B]profane the name of your
God; I am the LORD. 22 [A]You shall not lie with a male
as [a]one lies with a female; it is an abomination.
23 [A]Also you shall not have intercourse with any
animal to be defiled with it, nor shall any woman
stand before an animal to [a]mate with it; it is a perversion.
24 'Do not defile yourselves by any of these
things; for by all these [A]the nations which I am
casting out before you have become defiled. 25 For
the land has become defiled, [A]therefore I have
brought its [a]punishment upon it, so the land [B]has
spewed out its inhabitants. 26 But as for you, you
are to keep My statutes and My judgments and
shall not do any of these abominations, *neither*
the native, nor the alien who sojourns among you
27 (for the men of the land who have been before
you have done all these abominations, and the land
has become defiled); 28 so that the land will not
spew you out, should you defile it, as it has spewed
out the nation which has been before you. 29 For
whoever does any of these abominations, [a]those
persons who do *so* shall be cut off from among
their people. 30 Thus you are to keep [A]My charge,
that you do not practice any of the abominable
customs which have been practiced before you,
so as not to defile yourselves with them; [B]I am the
LORD your God.' "

18:3 [a]Lit *according to the deed of* [A]Ezek 20:7, 8 [B]Lev 18:24-30; 20:23 18:4 [a]Lit *to walk in them* [A]Lev 18:2 18:5 [A]Neh 9:29; Ezek 18:9; 20:11; Luke 10:28; Rom 10:5; Gal 3:12 18:6 [a]Lit *of his flesh* 18:7 [A]Lev 20:11; Deut 27:20; Ezek 22:10 18:8 [A]Lev 20:11; Deut 22:30; 27:20; 1 Cor 5:1 18:9 [A]Lev 18:11; 20:17; Deut 27:22 18:10 [a]Lit *they are your nakedness* 18:11 [a]Lit *begotten of* 18:12 [A]Lev 20:19 18:14 [A]Lev 20:20 18:15 [A]Lev 20:12 18:16 [A]Lev 20:21 18:17 [a]Or *wickedness* [A]Lev 20:14 18:18 [a]Lit *take a wife* [b]Or *another* [c]Lit *to be* 18:19 [A]Lev 15:24; 20:18 [B]Lev 12:2 18:20 [A]Lev 20:10; Prov 6:29; Matt 5:27, 28; 1 Cor 6:9; Heb 13:4 18:21 [a]Lit *cause to pass over* [A]Lev 20:2-5; Deut 12:31 [B]Lev 19:12; 20:3; 21:6; Ezek 36:20; Mal 1:12 18:22 [a]Lit *those who lie* [A]Lev 20:13; Deut 23:18 mg; Rom 1:27 18:23 [a]Or *lie* [A]Ex 22:19; Lev 20:15, 16; Deut 27:21 18:24 [A]Lev 18:3; Deut 18:12 18:25 [a]Lit *iniquity* [A]Lev 20:23; Deut 9:5; 18:12 [B]Lev 18:28; 20:22 18:29 [a]Or *and the* 18:30 [A]Lev 22:9; Deut 11:1 [B]Lev 18:2

18:3 not do what is done. Repeating the sexual practices or customs of the Egyptians and Canaanites was forbidden by God.

18:4 I am the LORD your God. This phrase, used over 50 times, asserts the uniqueness of the One True and Living God, who calls His people to holiness as He is holy, and calls them to reject all other gods.

18:5 a man may live if he does them. Special blessing was promised to the Israelites on the condition of their obedience to God's law. This promise was remarkably verified in particular eras of their history, in the national prosperity they enjoyed when pure and undefiled religion prevailed among them. Obedience to God's law always insures temporal blessings, as this verse indicates. But these words have a higher reference to spiritual life as indicated by the Lord (cf. Lk 10:28) and Paul (cf. Ro 10:5). Obedience does not save from sin and hell, but it does mark those who are saved (cf. Eph 2:8, 9; *see notes on Ro 2:6–10*).

18:6–18 This section deals with consanguinity, i.e., the sins of incest.

18:6 uncover nakedness. This is a euphemism for sexual relations.

18:8 your father's wife. Actually a stepmother is in mind here (cf. v. 7).

18:11 your sister. Here he is forbidden to marry a stepsister.

18:18 while she is alive. The principle on which the prohibitions are made changes slightly. Instead of avoiding sexual involvement because it would violate a relational connection, this situation defaults to the principle of one person at a time, or while the other is still alive, i.e., it forbids polygamy. Commonly in Egyptian, Chaldean, and Canaanite culture, sisters were taken as wives in polygamous unions. God forbids such, as all polygamy is forbidden by the original law of marriage (see Ge 2:24, 25). Moses, because of hard hearts, tolerated it, as did others in Israel in the early stages of that nation. But it always led to tragedy.

18:19 menstrual impurity. Cf. 15:24.

18:21 Molech. This Semitic false deity (god of the Ammonites) was worshiped with child sacrifice (cf. Lv 20:2–5; 1Ki 11:7; 2Ki 23:10; Jer 32:35). Since this chapter deals otherwise with sexual deviation, there is likely an unmentioned sexual perversion connected with this pagan ritual. Jews giving false gods homage gave foreigners occasion to blaspheme the true God.

18:22 not lie with a male. This outlaws all homosexuality (cf. 20:13; Ro 1:27; 1Co 6:9; 1Ti 1:10). *See notes on Ge 19:1–29.*

18:23 intercourse with any animal. This outlaws the sexual perversion of bestiality.

18:29 cut off. All the sexual perversions discussed in this chapter were worthy of death, indicating their loathsomeness before God.

18:30 practiced before you. Not in their presence, but by the people who inhabited the land before them in time (cf. v. 27), were such sins committed.

IDOLATRY FORBIDDEN

19 Then the LORD spoke to Moses, saying:
2 "Speak to all the congregation of the sons
of Israel and say to them, '[A]You shall be holy, for
I the LORD your God am holy. 3 Every one of you
[A]shall reverence his mother and his father, and
you shall keep [B]My sabbaths; [C]I am the LORD your
God. 4 Do not turn to [A]idols or make for yourselves
molten [B]gods; I am the LORD your God.
5 'Now when you offer a sacrifice of peace offerings to the LORD, you shall offer it so that you may
be accepted. 6 It shall be eaten the same day you
offer *it,* and the next day; but what remains until the
third day shall be burned with fire. 7 So if it is eaten
at all on the third day, it is an offense; it will not be
accepted. 8 Everyone who eats it will bear his iniquity, for he has profaned the holy thing of the LORD;
and that person shall be cut off from his people.

SUNDRY LAWS

9 '[A]Now when you reap the harvest of your land,
you shall not reap to the very corners of your field,
nor shall you gather the gleanings of your harvest.
10 Nor shall you glean your vineyard, nor shall you
gather the fallen fruit of your vineyard; you shall
leave them for the needy and for the stranger. I am
the LORD your God.
11 '[A]You shall not steal, nor deal falsely, [B]nor lie
to one another. 12 [A]You shall not swear falsely by
My name, so as to [B]profane the name of your God;
I am the LORD.
13 '[A]You shall not oppress your neighbor, nor rob
him. [B]The wages of a hired man are not to remain
with you all night until morning. 14 You shall not
curse a deaf man, nor [A]place a stumbling block
before the blind, but you shall revere your God; I
am the LORD.
15 '[A]You shall do no injustice in judgment; you
shall not be partial to the poor nor defer to the great,
but you are to judge your neighbor fairly. 16 You shall
not go about as [A]a slanderer among your people,
and you are not to [a]act against the [b,B]life of your
neighbor; I am the LORD.
17 'You [A]shall not hate your [a]fellow countryman in
your heart; you [B]may surely reprove your neighbor,
but shall not incur sin because of him. 18 [A]You shall
not take vengeance, [B]nor bear any grudge against
the sons of your people, but [C]you shall love your
neighbor as yourself; I am the LORD.
19 'You are to keep My statutes. You shall not breed
together two kinds of your cattle; [A]you shall not sow
your field with two kinds of seed, nor wear a garment
upon you of two kinds of material mixed together.
20 '[A]Now if a man lies carnally with a woman who
is a slave acquired for *another* man, but who has in
no way been redeemed nor given her freedom, there
shall be punishment; they shall not, *however,* be put
to death, because she was not free. 21 He shall bring
his guilt offering to the LORD to the doorway of the
tent of meeting, [A]a ram for a guilt offering. 22 The
priest shall also make atonement for him with the
ram of the guilt offering before the LORD for his
sin which he has committed, and the sin which he
has committed will be forgiven him.
23 'When you enter the land and plant all kinds
of trees for food, then you shall count their fruit
as [a]forbidden. Three years it shall be [a]forbidden to
you; *it* shall not be eaten. 24 But in the fourth year
all its fruit shall be holy, an offering of praise to
the LORD. 25 In the fifth year you are to eat of its
fruit, that its yield may increase for you; I am the
LORD your God.
26 'You shall not eat *anything* [A]with the blood, nor
practice [B]divination or soothsaying. 27 [A]You shall not
round off the side-growth of your heads nor harm
the edges of your beard. 28 You shall not make any
cuts in your [a]body for the [b]dead nor make any tattoo
marks on yourselves: I am the LORD.

19:2 [A]Ex 19:6; Lev 11:44; 20:7, 26; Eph 1:4; 1 Pet 1:16 19:3 [A]Ex 20:12; 31:13; Deut 5:16 [B]Ex 20:8 [C]Lev 11:44 19:4 [A]Lev 26:1; Ps 96:5; 115:4-7 [B]Ex 20:23; 34:17 19:9 [A]Lev 23:22; Deut 24:20-22 19:11 [A]Ex 20:15, 16 [B]Jer 9:3-5; Eph 4:25 19:12 [A]Ex 20:7; Deut 5:11; Matt 5:33 [B]Lev 18:21 19:13 [A]Ex 22:7-15, 21-27 [B]Deut 24:15; James 5:4 19:14 [A]Deut 27:18 19:15 [A]Ex 23:3, 6; Deut 1:17; 10:17; 16:19 19:16 [a]Lit *stand* [b]Lit *blood* [A]Ps 15:3; Jer 6:28; 9:4; Ezek 22:9 [B]Ex 23:7; Deut 27:25 19:17 [a]Lit *brother* [A]1 John 2:9, 11; 3:15 [B]Matt 18:15; Luke 17:3 19:18 [A]Deut 32:35; Rom 12:19; Heb 10:30 [B]Ps 103:9 [C]Matt 19:19; Mark 12:31; Luke 10:27; Rom 13:9; Gal 5:14; James 2:8 19:19 [A]Deut 22:9, 11 19:20 [A]Deut 22:23-27 19:21 [A]Lev 6:1-7 19:23 [a]Lit *uncircumcised* 19:26 [A]Gen 9:4; Lev 7:26f; 17:10; Deut 12:16, 23 [B]Deut 18:10; 2 Kin 17:17 19:27 [A]Lev 21:5; Deut 14:1 19:28 [a]Lit *flesh* [b]Lit *soul*

19:1–37 Here are practical applications of holy conduct in society.

19:2 I the LORD your God am holy. This basic statement, which gives the reason for holy living among God's people, is the central theme in Leviticus (cf. 20:26). *See note on 11:44, 45.* Cf. 1Pe 1:16. Israel had been called to be a holy nation, and the perfectly holy character of God (cf. Is 6:3) was the model after which the Israelites were to live (cf. 10:3; 20:26; 21:6–8).

19:3 reverence his mother and his father. The fifth commandment (cf. Ex 20:12) to honor one's father and mother is amplified by the use of a different word, "reverence." Because they revered (an attitude), they could then honor (an action).

19:3, 4 In addition to the fifth commandment, the fourth (19:3b), the first (19:4a), and the second (19:4b) were commanded as illustrations of holy behavior (cf. Ex 20:3–6, 8–11).

19:5–8 peace offerings. *See notes on 3:1–17; 7:11–34.*

19:9, 10 This was the law of gleaning (cf. 23:22; Dt 24:19–22), a practice seen in Ru 2:8–23.

19:11 Commandments from Ex 20 are again repeated.

19:12 Cf. Mt 5:33.

19:13 wages . . . not to remain with you all night. Hired workers were to be paid at the end of a work day. Unsalaried day workers depended on pay each day for their sustenance. *See notes on Mt 20:1, 2.*

19:14 deaf . . . blind. Israel's God of compassion always demonstrated a concern for the disabled.

19:16 act against the life. This refers to doing anything that would wrongfully jeopardize the life of a neighbor.

19:18 This, called the second great commandment, is the most often quoted OT text in the NT (Mt 5:43; 19:19; 22:39; Mk 12:31, 33; Lk 10:27; Ro 13:9; Gal 5:14; Jas 2:8).

19:19 These mixtures may have been characteristic of some idolatrous practices.

19:20–22 In the case of immorality with a betrothed slave, the couple was to be punished (possibly by scourging), but not killed. Afterward, a trespass or guilt offering (*see notes on 5:14–6:7*) was to be rendered with appropriate reparation. This is an exception to the norm (cf. Dt 22:23, 24).

19:23–25 forbidden. They could not eat from the fruit trees of Canaan for 4 years after entering the land because the fruit of the first 3 years was to be considered unclean, and the fourth year the fruit was to be offered to the Lord. Some gardeners say preventing a tree from bearing fruit in the first years, by cutting off the blossoms, makes it more productive.

19:26 divination or soothsaying. Attempting to tell the future with the help of snakes and clouds was a common ancient way of foretelling good or bad future. These were forbidden forms of witchcraft which involved demonic activity. *See note on Dt 18:9–12.*

19:27, 28 These pagan practices were most likely associated with Egyptian idolatry and were therefore to be avoided. The practice of making deep gashes on the face and arms or

29 '[A]Do not [a]profane your daughter by making
her a harlot, so that the land will not fall to harlotry
and the land become full of lewdness. 30 You shall
[A]keep My sabbaths and [B]revere My sanctuary; I am
the LORD.
31 'Do not turn to [a,A]mediums or spiritists; do not
seek them out to be defiled by them. I am the LORD
your God.
32 '[A]You shall rise up before the grayheaded and
honor the [a]aged, and you shall revere your God; I
am the LORD.
33 '[A]When a stranger resides with you in your land,
you shall not do him wrong. 34 The stranger who resides with you shall be to you as the native among
you, and [A]you shall love him as yourself, for you were
aliens in the land of Egypt; I am the LORD your God.
35 '[A]You shall do no wrong in judgment, in measurement of weight, or capacity. 36 You shall have
[A]just balances, just weights, a just [a]ephah, and a just
[b]hin; I am the LORD your God, who brought you out
from the land of Egypt. 37 You shall thus observe all
My statutes and all My ordinances and do them; I
am the LORD.' "

ON HUMAN SACRIFICE AND IMMORALITIES

20 Then the LORD spoke to Moses, saying, 2 "You
shall also say to the sons of Israel:
'Any man from the sons of Israel or from the
aliens sojourning in Israel [A]who gives any of his
[a]offspring to Molech, shall surely be put to death;
[B]the people of the land shall stone him with stones.
3 I will also set My face against that man and will
cut him off from among his people, because he
has given some of his [a]offspring to Molech, [A]so
as to defile My sanctuary and [B]to profane My holy
name. 4 If the people of the land, however, [a]should
ever disregard that man when he gives any of his
[b]offspring to Molech, so as not to put him to death,
5 then I Myself will set My face against that man and
against his family, and I will cut off from among
their people both him and all those who play the
harlot after him, by playing the harlot after Molech.
6 'As for the person who turns to [a,A]mediums and
to spiritists, to play the harlot after them, I will also
set My face against that person and will cut him
off from among his people. 7 You shall consecrate
yourselves therefore and [A]be holy, for I am the LORD
your God. 8 [A]You shall keep My statutes and practice
them; I am the LORD who sanctifies you.
9 '[A]If *there is* anyone who curses his father or
his mother, he shall surely be put to death; he has
cursed his father or his mother, his bloodguiltiness
is upon him.
10 '[A]If *there is* a man who commits adultery with
another man's wife, one who commits adultery with
his friend's wife, the adulterer and the adulteress
shall surely be put to death. 11 [A]If *there is* a man who
lies with his father's wife, he has uncovered his
father's nakedness; both of them shall surely be put
to death, their bloodguiltiness is upon them. 12 [A]If
there is a man who lies with his daughter-in-law,
both of them shall surely be put to death; they have
committed [a]incest, their bloodguiltiness is upon
them. 13 [A]If *there is* a man who lies with a male as
those who lie with a woman, both of them have
committed a detestable act; they shall surely be
put to death. Their bloodguiltiness is upon them.
14 [A]If *there is* a man who [a]marries a woman and her
mother, it is immorality; both he and they shall be
burned with fire, so that there will be no immorality in your midst. 15 [A]If *there is* a man who lies
with an animal, he shall surely be put to death; you
shall also kill the animal. 16 If *there is* a woman who
approaches any animal to [a]mate with it, you shall
kill the woman and the animal; they shall surely be
put to death. Their bloodguiltiness is upon them.
17 '[A]If *there is* a man who takes his sister, his father's daughter or his mother's daughter, so that he
sees her nakedness and she sees his nakedness, it
is a disgrace; and they shall be cut off in the sight
of the sons of their people. He has uncovered his
sister's nakedness; he bears his guilt. 18 [A]If *there is*
a man who lies with a [a]menstruous woman and
uncovers her nakedness, he has laid bare her flow,
and she has [b]exposed the flow of her blood; thus

19:29 [a]Or *degrade* [A]Lev 21:9; Deut 22:21; 23:17, 18 19:30 [A]Lev 19:3 [B]Lev 26:2 19:31 [a]Or *ghosts or spirits* [A]Lev 20:6, 27; Deut 18:11; 1 Sam 28:3; Is 8:19 19:32 [a]Lit *face of the aged* [A]Prov 23:22; Lam 5:12; 1 Tim 5:1 19:33 [A]Ex 22:21; Deut 24:17, 18 19:34 [A]Lev 19:18 19:35 [A]Deut 25:13-16; Ezek 45:10 19:36 [a]I.e. Approx one bu [b]I.e. Approx one gal. [A]Deut 25:13-15; Prov 20:10 20:2 [a]Lit *seed* [A]Lev 18:21 [B]Lev 20:27; 24:14-23; Num 15:35, 36; Deut 21:21 20:3 [a]Lit *seed* [A]Lev 15:31 [B]Lev 18:21 20:4 [a]Lit *hiding they hide their eyes from* [b]Lit *seed* 20:6 [a]Or *ghosts and spirits* [A]Lev 19:31 20:7 [A]Eph 1:4; 1 Pet 1:16 20:8 [A]Ex 31:13 20:9 [A]Ex 21:17; Deut 27:16 20:10 [A]Ex 20:14; Lev 18:20; Deut 5:18 20:11 [A]Lev 18:7, 8; Deut 27:20 20:12 [a]Lit *confusion;* i.e. a violation of divine order [A]Lev 18:15 20:13 [A]Lev 18:22 20:14 [a]Lit *takes* [A]Lev 18:17; Deut 27:23 20:15 [A]Lev 18:23; Deut 27:21 20:16 [a]Lit *lie* 20:17 [A]Lev 18:9; Deut 27:22 20:18 [a]Lit *sick* [b]Or *uncovered* [A]Lev 15:24; 18:19

legs, in times of grief, was universal among pagans. It was seen as a mark of respect for the dead, as well as a sort of propitiatory offering to the gods who presided over death. The Jews learned this custom in Egypt and, though weaned from it, relapsed into the old superstition (cf. Is 22:12; Jer 16:6; 47:5). Tattoos also were connected to names of idols, and were permanent signs of apostasy.

19:29 profane your daughter. Even the pagans of ancient Assyria at this time forbade such horrendous means of monetary gain.

19:30 sabbaths. *See note on 19:3, 4.*

19:31 mediums or spiritists. Mediums are humans who act as "go-betweens" to supposedly contact/communicate with the spirits of the dead, who are actually impersonated by demons. Cf. 20:6, 27.

19:32 rise ... honor. Showing respect for the older man acknowledged God's blessing of long life and the wisdom that comes with it (cf. Is 3:5).

19:33, 34 stranger. Cf. Ex 22:21.

19:36 ephah ... hin. These dry and liquid measures respectively were equal approximately to 4 to 6 gallons and 6 to 8 pints.

20:1–27 Here capital and other grave crimes are discussed. Many of the same issues from chap. 18, 19 are elaborated, with the emphasis on the penalty paid for the violation.

20:2 gives any of his offspring to Molech. Molech (Moloch), the Ammonite god of the people surrounding Israel, required human (especially child) sacrifice. *See note on 18:21.*

20:5, 6 cut off. This means to kill. It is synonymous with "put to death" in v. 9.

20:5 play the harlot. This speaks figuratively of spiritual idolatry.

20:6 mediums ... spiritists. *See note on 19:31.* "Spiritists" refers to demons (cf. 20:27).

20:9 curses his father or his mother. Doing the very opposite of the command to honor or to revere (cf. 19:3) had fatal consequences. See Mk 7:10, where Jesus referred to this text.

20:10–21 Here are the punishments for violating the prohibitions of sexual sins detailed in 18:1–30; see Dt 22:13–30.

both of them shall be cut off from among their people. 19 [A]You shall also not uncover the nakedness of
your mother's sister or of your father's sister, for
such a one has made naked his [a]blood relative; they
will bear their guilt. 20 [A]If *there is* a man who lies
with his uncle's wife he has uncovered his uncle's
nakedness; they will bear their sin. They will die
childless. 21 [A]If *there is* a man who takes his brother's
wife, it is [a]abhorrent; he has uncovered his brother's
nakedness. They will be childless.

22 'You are therefore to keep all My statutes and
all My ordinances and do them, so that the land to
which I am bringing you to [a]live will not [A]spew you
out. 23 Moreover, you shall not [a]follow [A]the customs
of the nation which I will drive out before you, for
they did all these things, and [B]therefore I have abhorred them. 24 Hence I have said to you, "[A]You are
to possess their land, and I Myself will give it to you
to possess it, a land flowing with milk and honey."
I am the LORD your God, who has [B]separated you
from the peoples. 25 [A]You are therefore to make a
distinction between the clean animal and the unclean, and between the unclean bird and the clean;
and you shall not make [a]yourselves detestable by
animal or by bird or by anything [b]that creeps on
the ground, which I have separated for you as unclean. 26 Thus you are to be holy to Me, for I the
LORD am holy; and I [A]have set you apart from the
peoples to be Mine.

27 'Now a man or a woman [A]who is a medium
or a [a]spiritist shall surely be put to death. They
shall be stoned with stones, their bloodguiltiness
is upon them.' "

REGULATIONS CONCERNING PRIESTS

21 Then the LORD said to Moses, "Speak to the
priests, the sons of Aaron, and say to them:
'[A]No one shall defile himself for a *dead* person
among his people, 2 [A]except for his relatives who are
nearest to him, his mother and his father and his
son and his daughter and his brother, 3 also for his
virgin sister, who is near to him [a]because she has
had no husband; for her he may defile himself. 4 He
shall not defile himself as a [a]relative by marriage
among his people, and so profane himself. 5 [A]They
shall not make any baldness on their heads, [B]nor
shave off the edges of their beards, [C]nor make any
cuts in their flesh. 6 They shall be holy to their God
and [A]not profane the name of their God, for they
present the offerings by fire [a]to the LORD, [B]the food
of their God; so they shall be holy. 7 [A]They shall not
take a woman who is profaned by harlotry, nor shall
they take a woman divorced from her husband; for
he is holy to his God. 8 You shall consecrate him,
therefore, for he offers [A]the food of your God; he
shall be holy to you; for I the LORD, who sanctifies
you, am holy. 9 [A]Also the daughter of any priest, if
she profanes herself by harlotry, she profanes her
father; she shall be burned with fire.

10 'The priest who is the highest among his
brothers, on whose head the anointing oil has been
poured and [a]who has been consecrated to wear the
garments, [A]shall not [b]uncover his head nor tear his
clothes; 11 [A]nor shall he approach any dead person,
nor defile himself *even* for his father or his mother;
12 [A]nor shall he go out of the sanctuary nor profane
the sanctuary of his God, for [B]the consecration of the
anointing oil of his God is on him; I am the LORD.
13 He shall take a wife in her virginity. 14 [A]A widow,
or a divorced woman, or one who is profaned by
harlotry, these he may not take; but rather he is to
[a]marry a virgin of his own people, 15 so that he will
not profane his [a]offspring among his people; for I
am the LORD who sanctifies him.' "

16 Then the LORD spoke to Moses, saying, 17 "Speak
to Aaron, saying, 'No man of your [a]offspring
throughout their generations who has a defect shall
approach to offer the [A]food of his God. 18 [A]For no one
who has a defect shall approach: a blind man, or
a lame man, or he who has a [a,A]disfigured *face*, or
any deformed *limb*, 19 or a man who has a broken
foot or broken hand, 20 or a hunchback or a dwarf,
or *one who has* a [a]defect in his eye or eczema or
scabs or [A]crushed testicles. 21 No man among the
[a]descendants of Aaron the priest who has a defect
is to come near to offer the LORD'S offerings by fire;

20:19 [a]Lit *flesh* [A]Lev 18:12, 13 20:20 [A]Lev 18:14 20:21 [a]Or *an impure deed* [A]Lev 18:16 20:22 [a]Lit *dwell in it* [A]Lev 18:28 20:23 [a]Lit *walk in the statutes* [A]Lev 18:3 [B]Lev 18:25 20:24 [A]Ex 13:5; 33:1-3 [B]Ex 33:16; Lev 20:26 20:25 [a]Lit *your souls* [b]Lit *with which the ground creeps* [A]Lev 10:10; 11:1-47; Deut 14:3-21 20:26 [A]Lev 20:24 20:27 [a]Lit *spiritist among them* [A]Lev 19:31 21:1 [A]Lev 19:28; Ezek 44:25 21:2 [A]Lev 21:11 21:3 [a]Or *whom no man has had* 21:4 [a]Lit *husband among* 21:5 [A]Deut 14:1; Ezek 44:20 [B]Lev 19:27 [C]Deut 14:1 21:6 [a]Lit *of* [A]Lev 18:21 [B]Lev 3:11 21:7 [A]Lev 21:13, 14 21:8 [A]Lev 21:6 21:9 [A]Gen 38:24; Lev 19:29 21:10 [a]Lit *whose hand has been filled* [b]Lit *unbind* [A]Lev 10:6 21:11 [A]Lev 19:28; Num 19:14 21:12 [A]Lev 10:7 [B]Ex 29:6, 7 21:14 [a]Lit *take as wife* [A]Lev 21:7; Ezek 44:22 21:15 [a]Lit *seed* 21:17 [a]Lit *seed* [A]Lev 21:6 21:18 [a]Lit *slit* [A]Lev 22:19-25 21:20 [a]Lit *obscurity* [A]Deut 23:1; Is 56:3-5 21:21 [a]Lit *seed*

20:22 will not spew you out. God told Israel repeatedly that remaining in the land required obedience to the Mosaic Covenant (cf. 18:25, 28).

20:27 medium ... spiritist. *See note on 19:31.*

21:1–24 Laws for the priests are given, which demanded a higher standard of holy conduct than for the general Israelite.

21:1 defile himself. Coming into contact with a corpse (Nu 19:11) or being in the same room with one (Nu 19:14) made one unclean. The exceptions were the dead from the priest's own family (vv. 2–4).

21:5 baldness ... edges ... cuts in their flesh. These were the superstitious marks of grief. *See note on 19:27, 28.* Cf. 1Ki 18:28.

21:6 the food of their God. This phrase appears 5 times in Lv 21 (cf. vv. 8, 17, 21, 22). It most likely refers to the bread of the Presence in the Holy Place (cf. Ex 25:30; 39:36; 40:23; Lv 24:5–9).

21:7, 8 The priest was allowed to marry, but only in the purest of circumstances. A holy marriage union pictured the holy union between God and His people. See 21:13, 14. The priests were to be living models of that holy union. Cf. Paul's words regarding pastors in 1Ti 3:2, 4; Titus 1:6.

21:9 The priests' children were to live a holy life. The common punishment of stoning (cf. Dt 22:21) is replaced with burning by fire. Cf. 1Ti 3:4; Titus 1:6.

21:10–15 Here is a summary of the standards for the High Priest which were the highest and most holy in accord with his utmost sacred responsibility.

21:10 shall not uncover his head nor tear his clothes. Acts associated with mourning or anguish (cf. the violation in Christ's trial, Mt 26:65; Mk 14:63).

21:16–23 defect. Just as the sacrifice had to be without blemish, so did the one offering the sacrifice. As visible things exert strong impressions on the minds of people, any physical impurity or malformation tended to distract from the weight and authority of the sacred office, failed to externally exemplify the inward wholeness God sought, and failed to be a picture of Jesus Christ, the Perfect High Priest to come (cf. Heb 7:26).

since he has a defect, he shall not come near to offer
[A]the food of his God. 22 He may eat [A]the food of his
God, *both* of the most holy and of the holy, 23 only
he shall not go in to the veil or come near the altar
because he has a defect, so that he will not profane
My sanctuaries. For I am the LORD who sanctifies
them.' " 24 So Moses spoke to Aaron and to his sons
and to all the sons of Israel.

SUNDRY RULES FOR PRIESTS

22 Then the LORD spoke to Moses, saying, 2 "Tell
Aaron and his sons to be careful with the
holy *gifts* of the sons of Israel, which they dedicate
to Me, so as not to profane My holy name; I am
the LORD. 3 Say to them, '[A]If any man among all
your [a]descendants throughout your generations
approaches the holy *gifts* which the sons of Israel
dedicate to the LORD, while he has an uncleanness,
that person shall be cut off from before Me; I am
the LORD. 4 [A]No man of the [a]descendants of Aaron,
who is a leper or who has a discharge, may eat of
the holy *gifts* until he is clean. [B]And if one touches
anything made unclean by a corpse or if [C]a man
has a seminal emission, 5 or [A]if a man touches any
teeming things by which he is made unclean, or
any man by whom he is made unclean, whatever
his uncleanness; 6 a [a]person who touches any such
shall be unclean until evening, and shall not eat
of the holy *gifts* unless he has bathed his [b]body
in water. 7 But when the sun sets, he will be clean,
and afterward he shall eat of the holy *gifts,* for [A]it is
his [a]food. 8 He shall not eat [A]*an animal* which dies
or is torn *by beasts,* becoming unclean by it; I am
the LORD. 9 They shall therefore keep [A]My charge,
so that [B]they will not bear sin because of it and die
thereby because they profane it; I am the LORD who
sanctifies them.

10 '[A]No [a]layman, however, is to eat the holy *gift;* a
sojourner with the priest or a hired man shall not
eat of the holy *gift.* 11 [A]But if a priest buys a [a]slave as
his property with his money, [b]that one may eat of it,
and those who are born in his house may eat of his
[c]food. 12 If a priest's daughter is married to a [a]layman,
she shall not eat of the [b]offering of the *gifts.* 13 But if
a priest's daughter becomes a widow or divorced,
and has no child and returns to her father's house
as in her youth, she shall eat of her father's [a]food;
[A]but no [b]layman shall eat of it. 14 [A]But if a man eats
a holy *gift* unintentionally, then he shall add to it a
fifth of it and shall give the holy *gift* to the priest.
15 [A]They shall not profane the holy *gifts* of the sons of
Israel which they offer to the LORD, 16 and *so* cause
them [A]to bear [a]punishment for guilt by eating their
holy *gifts;* for I am the LORD who sanctifies them.' "

FLAWLESS ANIMALS FOR SACRIFICE

17 Then the LORD spoke to Moses, saying, 18 "Speak
to Aaron and to his sons and to all the sons of Israel
and say to them, '[A]Any man of the house of Israel
or of the aliens in Israel who presents his offering,
whether it is any of their [a]votive or any of their
freewill offerings, which they present to the LORD
for a burnt offering— 19 [A]for you to be accepted—*it
must be* a male without defect from the cattle, the
sheep, or the goats. 20 [A]Whatever has a defect, you
shall not offer, for it will not be accepted for you.
21 When a man offers a sacrifice of peace offerings
to the LORD [A]to [a]fulfill a special vow or for a freewill offering, of the herd or of the flock, it must be
perfect to be accepted; there shall be no defect in
it. 22 Those *that are* blind or fractured or maimed or
having a running sore or eczema or scabs, you shall
not offer to the LORD, nor make of them an offering
by fire on the altar to the LORD. 23 In respect to an
ox or a lamb which has an [a]overgrown or stunted
member, you may present it for a freewill offering,
but for a vow it will not be accepted. 24 Also [A]any-
thing *with its testicles* bruised or crushed or torn
or cut, you shall not offer to the LORD, or [a]sacrifice
in your land, 25 nor shall you accept any such from
the hand of a foreigner for offering [A]as the [a]food
of your God; for their corruption is in them, they
have a defect, they shall not be accepted for you.' "

26 Then the LORD spoke to Moses, saying, 27 "When
an ox or a sheep or a goat is born, it shall [a]remain
[A]seven days [b]with its mother, and from the eighth
day on it shall be accepted as a sacrifice of an offering by fire to the LORD. 28 [A]But, *whether* it is an ox
or a sheep, you shall not kill *both* it and its young in
one day. 29 When you sacrifice [A]a sacrifice of thanksgiving to the LORD, you shall sacrifice it so that you
may be accepted. 30 It shall be eaten on the same
day, you shall leave none of it until morning; I am
the LORD. 31 [A]So you shall keep My commandments,
and do them; I am the LORD.

32 "You shall not profane My holy name, but I
will be sanctified among the sons of Israel; I am
the LORD who sanctifies you, 33 [A]who brought you
out from the land of Egypt, to be your God; I am
the LORD."

21:21 [A]Lev 21:6 21:22 [A]1 Cor 9:13 22:3 [a]*Lit seed* [A]Lev 7:20, 21; Num 19:13 22:4 [a]*Lit seed* [A]Lev 14:1-32 [B]Lev 11:24-28, 39, 40 [C]Lev 15:16, 17 22:5 [A]Lev 11:23-28 22:6 [a]*Lit soul* [b]*Lit flesh* 22:7 [a]*Lit bread* [A]Num 18:11 22:8 [A]Lev 7:24; 11:39, 40; 17:15 22:9 [A]Lev 18:30 [B]Ex 28:43; Lev 22:16; Num 18:22 22:10 [a]*Lit stranger* [A]Ex 29:33; Lev 22:13; Num 3:10 22:11 [a]*Lit soul* [b]*Lit he may* [c]*Lit bread* [A]Gen 17:13; Ex 12:44 22:12 [a]*Lit stranger* [b]*Lit heave offering* 22:13 [a]*Lit bread* [b]*Lit stranger* [A]Lev 22:10 22:14 [A]Lev 5:15, 16 22:15 [A]Num 18:32 22:16 [a]*Or iniquity requiring a guilt offering* [A]Lev 10:17; 22:9 22:18 [a]*Lit vows* [A]Num 15:14 22:19 [A]Lev 21:18-21; Deut 15:21 22:20 [A]Deut 15:21; 17:1; Mal 1:8, 14; Heb 9:14; 1 Pet 1:19 22:21 [a]*Or make a special votive offering* [A]Num 15:3, 8 22:23 [a]*Or a deformed* 22:24 [a]*Lit do* [A]Lev 21:20 22:25 [a]*Lit bread* [A]Lev 21:22 22:27 [a]*Lit be* [b]*Lit under* [A]Ex 22:30 22:28 [A]Deut 22:6, 7 22:29 [A]Lev 7:12 22:31 [A]Lev 19:37; Num 15:40; Deut 4:40 22:33 [A]Lev 11:45

22:1–33 These are additional instructions on ceremonial cleanness for the priests, beginning with a death threat (v. 3, "cut off") to those who might violate these rules.

22:4 leper. Cf. 13:1–14:32; *see note on 13:2.* **discharge.** *See notes on 15:1–33.*

22:5 teeming things. See 11:29–38.

22:7 he will be clean. In the same manner, much water is not made unclean by a small contamination. Time was essential for ceremonial purification.

22:10, 11 buys a slave ... with his money. This portion of the sacrifice assigned to the support of the priests was restricted to the use of his family. However, an indentured servant or slave was to be treated as one of the priest's family, pertaining to eating the consecrated food. See the laws of release, which show this to be a temporary indenture (25:10; Ex 21:2–11; Dt 15:12–18).

22:17–30 This section describes the unacceptable and acceptable sacrifices.

22:31–33 The motive behind obedience to God was His holy nature and grace in delivering the nation.

LAWS OF RELIGIOUS FESTIVALS

23 The LORD spoke again to Moses, saying,
2 "Speak to the sons of Israel and say to them,
'[A]The LORD'S appointed times which you shall [B]pro-
claim as holy convocations—My appointed times
are these:
3 '[A]For six days work may be done, but on the
seventh day there is a sabbath of complete rest, a
holy convocation. You shall not do any work; it is a
sabbath to the LORD in all your dwellings.
4 'These are the [A]appointed times of the LORD,
holy convocations which you shall proclaim at the
times appointed for them. 5 [A]In the first month, on
the fourteenth day of the month [a]at twilight is the
LORD'S Passover. 6 Then on the fifteenth day of the
same month there is the [A]Feast of Unleavened Bread
to the LORD; for seven days you shall eat unleavened bread. 7 On the first day you shall have a holy
convocation; you shall [A]not do any laborious work.
8 But for seven days you shall present an offering
by fire to the LORD. On the seventh day is a holy
convocation; you shall not do any laborious work.' "
9 Then the LORD spoke to Moses, saying, 10 "Speak
to the sons of Israel and say to them, 'When you
enter the land which I am going to give to you and
[A]reap its harvest, then you shall bring in the sheaf
of the first fruits of your harvest to the priest. 11 He
shall wave the sheaf before the LORD for you to be
accepted; on the day after the sabbath the priest
shall wave it. 12 Now on the day when you wave
the sheaf, you shall offer a male lamb one year old
without defect for a burnt offering to the LORD. 13 Its
[A]grain offering shall then be two-tenths *of an ephah*
of fine flour mixed with oil, an offering by fire to the
LORD *for* a soothing aroma, with its drink offering, a
fourth of a [a]hin of wine. 14 Until this same day, until
you have brought in the offering of your God, [A]you
shall eat neither bread nor roasted grain nor new
growth. It is to be a perpetual statute throughout
your generations in all your dwelling places.
15 '[A]You shall also count for yourselves from
the day after the sabbath, from the day when you
brought in the sheaf of the wave offering; there
shall be seven complete sabbaths. 16 You shall count
fifty days to the day after the seventh sabbath;
then you shall present a [A]new grain offering to
the LORD. 17 You shall bring in from your dwelling
places two *loaves* of bread for a wave offering,
made of two-tenths *of an* [a]*ephah;* they shall be of
a fine flour, baked [A]with leaven as first fruits to
the LORD. 18 Along with the bread you shall present seven one year old male lambs without defect,
and a bull of the herd and two rams; they are to
be a burnt offering to the LORD, with their grain
offering and their drink offerings, an offering by
fire of a soothing aroma to the LORD. 19 You shall
also offer [A]one male goat for a sin offering and two
male lambs one year old for a sacrifice of peace offerings. 20 The priest shall then wave them with the
bread of the first fruits for a wave offering with two
lambs before the LORD; they are to be holy to the
LORD for the priest. 21 On this same day you shall
[A]make a proclamation as well; you are to have a
holy convocation. You shall do no laborious [B]work.
It is to be a perpetual statute in all your dwelling
places throughout your generations.

23:2 [A]Lev 23:4, 37, 44; Num 29:39 [B]Lev 23:21 23:3 [A]Ex 20:9, 10; 23:12; 31:13-17; 35:2, 3; Lev 19:3; Deut 5:13, 14 23:4 [A]Ex 23:14; Lev 23:2 23:5 [a]Lit *between the two evenings* [A]Ex 12:18, 19; Num 28:16-25; Deut 16:1; Josh 5:10 23:6 [A]Ex 12:14-20; 23:15; 34:18; Deut 16:3-8 23:7 [A]Lev 23:8, 21, 25, 35, 36 23:10 [A]Ex 23:19; 34:26 23:13 [a]I.e. Approx one gal. [A]Lev 6:20 23:14 [A]Ex 34:26; Num 15:20, 21 23:15 [A]Num 28:26-31; Deut 16:9-12 23:16 [A]Num 28:26 23:17 [a]I.e. Approx one bu [A]Lev 2:12; 7:13 23:19 [A]Lev 4:23; Num 28:30 23:21 [A]Lev 23:2, 4 [B]Lev 23:7

23:1–27:34 Holiness issues that pertain to the nation collectively are outlined.

23:1–24:9 The special feasts of Israel are explained. Cf. Ex 23:14–17; Nu 28:1–29:40; Dt 16:1–17.

23:1–44 This section points to days which are sacred to the Lord. After the Sabbath (v. 3), the feasts are given in the order of the calendar (vv. 4–44).

23:2 proclaim as holy convocations. These festivals did not involve gatherings of all Israel in every case. Only the feasts of 1) Unleavened Bread; 2) Weeks; and 3) Tabernacles required that all males gather in Jerusalem (cf. Ex 23:14–17; Dt 16:16, 17).

23:3 sabbath of complete rest. The Mosaic ordinance of the fourth commandment came first (cf. Ge 2:1–3; Ex 20:8–11).

23:4–22 Three events were commemorated in Mar./Apr.: 1) Passover on the 14th (v. 5); 2) Feast of Unleavened Bread on the 15th-21st (vv. 6–8); and Feast of Firstfruits on the day after the Sabbath of Unleavened Bread week (vv. 9–14).

23:5 the LORD's Passover. The festival commemorated God's deliverance of Israel from Egypt (cf. Ex 12:1–14, 43–49; Nu 28:16; Dt 16:1, 2).

23:6–8 Feast of Unleavened Bread. This festival connected with the Passover commemorated Israel's hurried departure from Egypt and the associated hardships (cf. Ex 12:15–20; 13:3–10; Nu 28:17–25; Dt 16:3–8).

23:9–14 the first fruits of your harvest. This festival dedicated the initial part of the barley harvest in Mar./Apr. and was celebrated on the day after the Sabbath of Unleavened Bread week. It involved presenting to the Lord a sheaf of barley (cf. 23:10, 11) accompanied by burnt, grain, and drink offerings (cf. Ex 29:40). Firstfruits symbolized the consecration of the whole harvest to God, and was a pledge of the whole harvest to come (cf. Ro 8:23; 11:16; 1Co 15:20; Jas 1:18).

23:15–22 fifty days. The Feast of Weeks (May/June) dedicated the firstfruits of the wheat harvest (cf. Ex 23:16; Nu 28:26–31; Dt 16:9–12). It occurred on the 50th day after the Sabbath preceding the Feast of Firstfruits. It is also known as the Feast of Harvest (Ex 23:16) and Pentecost, Gr. for 50 (Ac 2:1).

CHRIST FULFILLS ISRAEL'S FEASTS

The Feasts (Lv 23)	Christ's Fulfillment
Passover (March/April)	Death of Christ (1Co 5:7)
Unleavened Bread (March/April)	Sinlessness of Christ (1Co 5:8)
First fruits (March/April)	Resurrection of Christ (1Co 15:23)
Pentecost (May/June)	Outpouring of Spirit of Christ (Ac 1:5; 2:4)
Trumpets (Sept./Oct.)	Israel's Regathering by Christ (Mt 24:31)
Atonement (Sept./Oct.)	Substitutionary Sacrifice by Christ (Ro 11:26)
Booths (Sept./Oct.)	Rest and Reunion with Christ (Zec 14:16–19)

22 '[A]When you reap the harvest of your land,
moreover, you shall not reap to the very corners
of your field nor gather the gleaning of your harvest; you are to leave them for the needy and the
alien. I am the LORD your God.' "
23 Again the LORD spoke to Moses, saying,
24 "Speak to the sons of Israel, saying, '[A]In the seventh month on the first of the month you shall have
a [a]rest, a [B]reminder by blowing *of trumpets,* a holy
convocation. 25 You shall [A]not do any laborious
work, but you shall present an offering by fire to
the LORD.' "

THE DAY OF ATONEMENT

26 The LORD spoke to Moses, saying, 27 "On exactly [A]the tenth day of this seventh month is [B]the
day of atonement; it shall be a holy convocation for
you, and you shall humble your souls and present
an offering by fire to the LORD. 28 You shall not do
any work on this same day, for it is a [A]day of atonement, [B]to make atonement on your behalf before
the LORD your God. 29 If there is any [a]person who
will not humble himself on this same day, [A]he shall
be cut off from his people. 30 As for any person who
does any work on this same day, that person I will
destroy from among his people. 31 You shall do no
work at all. It is to be a perpetual statute throughout
your generations in all your dwelling places. 32 It
is to be a sabbath of complete rest to you, and you
shall humble your souls; on the ninth of the month
at evening, from evening until evening you shall
keep your sabbath."

33 Again the LORD spoke to Moses, saying,
34 "Speak to the sons of Israel, saying, 'On [A]the fifteenth of this seventh month is the [B]Feast of Booths
for seven days to the LORD. 35 On the first day is a
holy convocation; you shall do [A]no laborious work
of any kind. 36 [A]For seven days you shall present
an offering by fire to the LORD. On [B]the eighth day
you shall have a holy convocation and present an
offering by fire to the LORD; it is an assembly. You
shall do no laborious work.
37 'These are [A]the appointed times of the LORD
which you shall proclaim as holy convocations, to
present offerings by fire to the LORD—burnt offerings and grain offerings, sacrifices and drink offerings, [B]*each* day's matter on its own day— 38 besides
those of the sabbaths of the LORD, and besides your
gifts and besides all your [a]votive and freewill offerings, which you give to the LORD.
39 'On exactly the fifteenth day of the seventh
month, [A]when you have gathered in the crops of
the land, you shall celebrate the feast of the LORD
for seven days, with a [a]rest on the first day and a
[a]rest on the eighth day. 40 Now on the first day you
shall take for yourselves the [a]foliage of beautiful
trees, palm branches and boughs of leafy trees and
willows of the brook, and you shall rejoice before
the LORD your God for seven days. 41 You shall thus
celebrate it *as* a feast to the LORD for seven days
in the year. It *shall be* a perpetual statute throughout your generations; you shall celebrate it in the
seventh month. 42 You shall [a]live [A]in booths for
seven days; all the native-born in Israel shall [a]live

23:22 [A]Lev 19:9, 10; Deut 24:19; Ruth 2:15f 23:24 [a]Lit *sabbath rest* [A]Num 29:1 [B]Num 10:9, 10 23:25 [A]Lev 23:21 23:27 [A]Lev 16:29; 25:9; Num 29:7 [B]Ex 30:10; Lev 16:30; 23:28; Num 29:7-11 23:28 [A]Lev 23:27 [B]Lev 16:34 23:29 [a]Lit *soul* [A]Gen 17:14; Lev 13:46; Num 5:2 23:34 [A]Num 29:12 [B]Lev 23:42, 43; Deut 16:13, 16; Ezra 3:4; Neh 8:14; Zech 14:16; John 7:2 23:35 [A]Lev 23:25 23:36 [A]Num 29:12-34 [B]Num 29:35-38 23:37 [A]Lev 23:2 [B]Num 28:1-29:38 23:38 [a]Lit *vows, and besides all your* 23:39 [a]Lit *sabbath rest* [A]Ex 23:16 23:40 [a]Lit *products, fruit* 23:42 [a]Lit *dwell* [A]Lev 23:34

23:23–43 Three events were commemorated in Sept./Oct.: 1) Feast of Trumpets on the 1st (vv. 23–25); 2) Day of Atonement on the 10th (vv. 26–32); and 3) Feast of Booths or Tabernacles on the 15th-21st (vv. 33–43).

23:23–25 **reminder by blowing *of trumpets*.** This feast, called the Feast of Trumpets, consecrated the seventh month (Sept./Oct.) as a sabbatical month (cf. Nu 29:1–6).

23:26–32 **day of atonement.** The annual Day of Atonement pointed to the forgiveness and cleansing of sin for the priests, the nation, and the tabernacle (*see notes on 16:1–34*).

23:33–43 **Feast of Booths.** This festival commemorated God's deliverance, protection, and provision during the wilderness wanderings of the Exodus (cf. Ex 23:16; Nu 29:12–38; Dt 16:13–15). It is also known as the Feast of Tabernacles and Feast of Ingathering (Ex 23:16). The people lived in booths or huts made from limbs (cf. Ne 8:14–18), remembering their wilderness experience. It also celebrated the autumn harvest and will be celebrated in the Millennium (cf. Zec 14:16).

JEWISH FEASTS

Feast of	Month on Jewish Calendar	Day	Corre-sponding Month	References
Passover	Nisan	14	Mar.–Apr.	Ex 12:1–14; Mt 26:17–20
*Unleavened Bread	Nisan	15–21	Mar.–Apr.	Ex 12:15–20
First fruits	Nisan	16	Mar.–Apr.	Lv 23:9–14
	or Sivan	6	May–June	Nu 28:26
*Pentecost (Harvest or Weeks)	Sivan	6 (50 days after barley harvest)	May–June	Dt 16:9–12; Ac 2:1
Trumpets, Rosh Hashanah	Tishri	1, 2	Sept.–Oct.	Nu 29:1–6
Day of Atonement, Yom Kippur	Tishri	10	Sept.–Oct.	Lv 23:26–32; Heb 9:7
*Booths (Tabernacles or Ingathering)	Tishri	15–21	Sept.–Oct.	Ne 8:13–18; Jn 7:2
Dedication (Lights), Hanukkah	Chislev	25 (8 days)	Nov.–Dec.	Jn 10:22
Purim (Lots)	Adar	14, 15	Feb.–Mar.	Est 9:18–32

**The three major feasts for which all males of Israel were required to travel to the temple in Jerusalem (Ex 23:14–19).*

in booths, 43 so that [A]your generations may know
that I had the sons of Israel live in booths when I
brought them out from the land of Egypt. I am the
LORD your God.' " 44 So Moses declared to the sons
of Israel [A]the appointed times of the LORD.

THE LAMP AND THE BREAD OF THE SANCTUARY

24 Then the LORD spoke to Moses, saying,
2 "Command the sons of Israel that they bring
to you [A]clear oil from beaten olives for the [a]light, to
make a lamp [b]burn continually. 3 Outside the veil of
testimony in the tent of meeting, Aaron shall keep
it in order from evening to morning before the
LORD continually; *it shall be* a perpetual statute
throughout your generations. 4 He shall keep the
lamps in order on the [A]pure *gold* lampstand before
the LORD continually.
5 "[A]Then you shall take fine flour and bake twelve
cakes with it; two-tenths *of an ephah* shall be *in* each
cake. 6 You shall set them *in* two rows, six *to* a row,
on the [A]pure *gold* table before the LORD. 7 You shall
put pure frankincense on each row that it may be
[A]a memorial portion for the bread, *even* an offering
by fire to the LORD. 8 [A]Every sabbath day he shall
set it in order before the LORD [B]continually; it is
an everlasting covenant [a]for the sons of Israel. 9 [A]It
shall be for Aaron and his sons, and they shall eat
it in a holy place; for it is most holy to him from
the LORD'S offerings by fire, *his* portion forever."
10 Now the son of an Israelite woman, whose father was an Egyptian, went out among the sons of
Israel; and the Israelite woman's son and a man of
Israel struggled with each other in the camp. 11 The
son of the Israelite woman blasphemed the [A]Name
and cursed. So they brought him to Moses. (Now
his mother's name was Shelomith, the daughter of
Dibri, of the tribe of Dan.) 12 They put him in [a]cus-
tody [b]so that [A]the command of the LORD might be
made clear to them.
13 Then the LORD spoke to Moses, saying, 14 "Bring
the one who has cursed outside the camp, and let all
who heard him [A]lay their hands on his head; then
[B]let all the congregation stone him. 15 You shall speak
to the sons of Israel, saying, '[A]If anyone curses his
God, then he will bear his sin. 16 Moreover, the one
who [A]blasphemes the name of the LORD shall surely
be put to death; all the congregation shall certainly
stone him. The alien as well as the native, when he
blasphemes the Name, shall be put to death.

"AN EYE FOR AN EYE"

17 '[A]If a man [a]takes the life of any human being,
he shall surely be put to death. 18 [A]The one who
[a]takes the life of an animal shall make it good, life
for life. 19 If a man [a]injures his neighbor, just as he
has done, so it shall be done to him: 20 [A]fracture
for fracture, [B]eye for eye, tooth for tooth; just as he
has [a]injured a man, so it shall be [b]inflicted on him.
21 Thus the one who [a]kills an animal shall make it
good, but [A]the one who [a]kills a man shall be put to
death. 22 There shall be [A]one [a]standard for you; it
shall be for the stranger as well as the native, for
I am the LORD your God.' " 23 Then Moses spoke to
the sons of Israel, and they brought the one who
had cursed outside the camp and stoned him with
stones. Thus the sons of Israel did, just as the LORD
had commanded Moses.

THE SABBATIC YEAR AND YEAR OF JUBILEE

25 The LORD then spoke to Moses [a]at Mount Sinai,
saying, 2 "Speak to the sons of Israel and say
to them, 'When you come into the land which I shall
give you, then the land shall have a sabbath to the
LORD. 3 [A]Six years you shall sow your field, and six
years you shall prune your vineyard and gather in
its crop, 4 but during [A]the seventh year the land shall
have a sabbath rest, a sabbath to the LORD; you shall
not sow your field nor prune your vineyard. 5 Your
harvest's [a]aftergrowth you shall not reap, and your
grapes of untrimmed vines you shall not gather;
the land shall have a sabbatical year. 6 [A]All of you
shall have the sabbath *products* of the land for food;
yourself, and your male and female slaves, and your
hired man and your foreign resident, those who live
as aliens with you. 7 Even your cattle and the animals
that are in your land shall have all its crops to eat.
8 'You are also to count off seven sabbaths of
years for yourself, seven times seven years, so that

23:43 [A]Deut 31:13; Ps 78:5f 23:44 [A]Lev 23:37 24:2 [a]Or *luminary* [b]Lit *ascend* [A]Ex 27:20, 21 24:4 [A]Ex 25:31; 31:8; 37:17 24:5 [A]Ex 25:30; 39:36; 40:23 24:6 [A]Ex 25:24; 1 Kin 7:48 24:7 [A]Lev 2:2, 9, 16 24:8 [a]Lit *from* [A]Matt 12:5 [B]Ex 25:30; Num 4:7; 2 Chr 2:4 24:9 [A]Matt 12:4; Mark 2:26; Luke 6:4 24:11 [A]Ex 3:15; 22:28; Job 2:5, 9; Is 8:21 24:12 [a]Or *prison* [b]Lit *to declare distinctly to them according to the mouth of the LORD* [A]Ex 18:15; Num 15:34 24:14 [A]Deut 13:9; 17:7 [B]Lev 20:2, 27; Deut 21:21 24:15 [A]Ex 22:28 24:16 [A]1 Kin 21:10; Matt 12:31; Mark 3:28f 24:17 [a]Lit *smites* [A]Gen 9:6; Ex 21:12; Num 35:30, 31; Deut 27:24 24:18 [a]Lit *smites* [A]Lev 24:21 24:19 [a]Lit *gives a blemish* 24:20 [a]Lit *given a blemish* [b]Lit *given* [A]Ex 21:23; Deut 19:21 [B]Matt 5:38 24:21 [a]Lit *smites* [A]Lev 24:17 24:22 [a]Lit *judgment* [A]Ex 12:49; Num 9:14; 15:15, 16, 29 25:1 [a]Or *on* 25:3 [A]Ex 23:10, 11 25:4 [A]Lev 25:20 25:5 [a]Lit *growth from spilled kernels* 25:6 [A]Lev 25:20, 21

24:1–9 These are additional instructions for the tabernacle relating to the lamps (vv. 1–4) and the bread (vv. 5–9). See Ex 25:31–40; 27:20, 21; 37:17–24 and Ex 25:23–30; 39:36; 40:23, respectively.

24:5 Each loaf was made with 4 quarts of flour.

24:10–23 This portion relates to the sin of blasphemy. Cf. Ex 20:7; 22:28.

24:10–14, 23 Now the son. Here is another historical example of blasphemy along similar lines as the Nadab and Abihu account (10:1, 2). The blasphemer was one of the "many other people." The people transferred the guilt of them all to him.

24:12 put him in custody. There were no jails in Israel since incarceration was not a penalty for crime. They had merely restrained him, probably in a pit of some sort, until they could establish his punishment. Punishments were corporal, banishment, or, in severe cases, death. Those who lived through the punishment worked to secure restitution for those they had violated.

24:20 Cf. Mt 5:38. This law of retaliation established the principle that the punishment should fit the crime, but not go beyond it.

25:1–55 Proper care for the Lord's property is prescribed for the sabbatical year (25:1–7) and the Jubilee year (25:8–55).

25:1–7 This involves revitalization of the land. The seventh year of rest would invigorate and replenish the nutrients in the soil. Whatever grew naturally was free to all for the taking (vv. 6, 7).

25:8–55 The Year of Jubilee involved a year of release from indebtedness (vv. 23–38) and bondage of all sorts (vv. 39–55). All prisoners and captives were set free, slaves released, and debtors absolved. All property reverted to original owners. This plan curbed inflation and moderated acquisitions. It also gave new opportunity to people who had fallen on hard times.

25:8–17 These are general instructions for Jubilee.

you have the time of the seven sabbaths of years, *namely,* forty-nine years. 9 You shall then sound a ram's horn abroad on [A]the tenth day of the seventh month; on the day of atonement you shall sound a horn all through your land. 10 You shall thus consecrate the fiftieth year and [A]proclaim [a]a release through the land to all its inhabitants. It shall be a jubilee for you, [b]and [B]each of you shall return to his own property, [b]and each of you shall return to his family. 11 You shall have the fiftieth year as a jubilee; you shall not sow, nor reap its aftergrowth, nor gather in *from* its untrimmed vines. 12 For it is a jubilee; it shall be holy to you. You shall eat its crops out of the field.

13 '[A]On this year of jubilee each of you shall return to his own property. 14 If you make a sale, moreover, to your friend or buy from your friend's hand, [A]you shall not wrong one another. 15 Corresponding to the number of years after the jubilee, you shall buy from your [a]friend; he is to sell to you according to the number of years of crops. 16 [A]In proportion to the [a]extent of the years you shall increase its price, and in proportion to the fewness of the years you shall diminish its price, for *it is* a number of crops he is selling to you. 17 So [A]you shall not wrong one another, but you shall [a]fear your God; for I am the LORD your God.

18 'You shall thus observe My statutes and keep My judgments, so as to carry them out, that [A]you may live securely on the land. 19 Then the land will yield its produce, so that you can eat your fill and live securely on it. 20 But if you say, "[A]What are we going to eat on the seventh year [a]if we do not sow or gather in our crops?" 21 then [A]I will so order My blessing for you in the sixth year that it will bring forth the crop for three years. 22 When you are sowing the eighth year, you can still eat [A]old things from the crop, eating *the old* until the ninth year when its crop comes in.

THE LAW OF REDEMPTION

23 'The land, moreover, shall not be sold permanently, for [A]the land is Mine; for [B]you are *but* aliens and sojourners with Me. 24 Thus for every [a]piece of your property, you are to provide for the redemption of the land.

25 '[A]If a [a]fellow countryman of yours becomes so poor he has to sell part of his property, then his nearest kinsman is to come and buy back what his [a]relative has sold. 26 Or in case a man has no kinsman, but so [a]recovers his means as to find sufficient for its redemption, 27 [A]then he shall calculate the years since its sale and refund the balance to the man to whom he sold it, and so return to his property. 28 But if [a]he has not found sufficient means to get it back for himself, then what he has sold shall remain in the hands of its purchaser until the year of jubilee; but at the jubilee it shall [b]revert, that [A]he may return to his property.

29 'Likewise, if a man sells a dwelling house in a walled city, then his redemption right remains valid until a full year from its sale; his right of redemption lasts a full year. 30 But if it is not bought back for him within the space of a full year, then the house that is in the walled city passes permanently to its purchaser throughout his generations; it does not [a]revert in the jubilee. 31 The houses of the villages, however, which have no surrounding wall shall be considered [a]as open fields; they have redemption rights and [b]revert in the jubilee. 32 As for [A]cities of the Levites, the Levites have a permanent right of redemption for the houses of the cities which are their possession. 33 What, therefore, [a]belongs to the Levites may be redeemed and a house sale [b]in the city of this possession [c]reverts in the jubilee, for the houses of the cities of the Levites are their possession among the sons of Israel. 34 [A]But pasture fields of their cities shall not be sold, for that is their perpetual possession.

OF POOR COUNTRYMEN

35 '[A]Now in case a [a]countryman of yours becomes poor and his [b]means with regard to you falter, then you are to sustain him, like a stranger or a sojourner, that he may live with you. 36 [A]Do not take [a]usurious interest from him, but revere your God, that your [b]countryman may live with you. 37 You shall not give

25:9 [A]Lev 23:27 25:10 [a]Or *liberty* [b]Or *when* [A]Jer 34:8, 15, 17 [B]Lev 25:13, 28, 54 25:13 [A]Lev 25:10; 27:24 25:14 [A]Lev 25:17 25:15 [a]Lit *friend's hands* 25:16 [a]Lit *multitude* [A]Lev 25:27, 51, 52 25:17 [a]Or *reverence* [A]Lev 25:14; Prov 14:31; 22:22; Jer 7:5, 6; 1 Thess 4:6 25:18 [A]Lev 26:5; Deut 12:10; Jer 23:6 25:20 [a]Or *behold* [A]Lev 25:4 25:21 [A]Deut 28:8 25:22 [A]Lev 26:10 25:23 [A]Ex 19:5 [B]Gen 23:4; 1 Chr 29:15; Ps 39:12; Heb 11:13; 1 Pet 2:11 25:24 [a]Lit *land* 25:25 [a]Lit *brother* [A]Ruth 2:20; 4:4, 6 25:26 [a]Lit *his hand reaches* 25:27 [A]Lev 25:16 25:28 [a]Lit *his hand has not found sufficient to* [b]Lit *go out* [A]Lev 25:10, 13 25:30 [a]Lit *go out* 25:31 [a]Lit *according to* [b]Lit *go out* 25:32 [A]Num 35:1-8; Josh 21:2 25:33 [a]Lit *is from* [b]Lit *and* [c]Lit *goes out* 25:34 [A]Num 35:2-5 25:35 [a]Lit *brother* [b]Lit *hand* [A]Deut 15:7-11; 24:14, 15 25:36 [a]Lit *interest and usury* [b]Lit *brother* [A]Ex 22:25; Deut 23:19, 20

25:9 ram's horn. This was blown on the tenth day of the seventh month to start the 50th year of universal redemption.

25:10 proclaim a release. Not only must they let the land lie fallow, but the people were allowed a one-year break from their labor. Those bound by a work contract were released from their commitments and there was the release of indentured servants.

25:14–16 The Jubilee year had an effect on the value of land, which was to be considered in all transactions.

25:17 you shall not wrong one another. No one should take advantage of or abuse another person, because cruelty is against the very character of God. Penalties for crime were to be swift and exact.

25:18–22 God's provision in the year of no planting was given, which on a smaller scale had been true for the Sabbath day during the Exodus (cf. Ex 16:5).

25:20, 21 crop for three years. When the important query was asked, God responded by promising to supply enough to last.

25:23–34 Various regulations regarding real estate are outlined.

25:23 the land is Mine. God owns the earth and all that is in it (cf. Ps 24:1). The people of Israel were, in fact, only tenants on the land by the Lord's grace. Therefore ownership of property was temporary, not permanent.

25:33 cities of the Levites. Cf. Nu 35:1–8; Jos 21.

25:34 pasture fields. These were fields that the village/city-at-large used to grow crops.

25:35–38 Instructions on dealing with the poor are outlined.

25:35 like a stranger or a sojourner. The law required gleanings (leftovers after harvest) for the Israelite as well as the stranger (cf. 19:9, 10; 23:22; Dt 24:19–21).

25:36 usurious interest. Usury or excessive interest was prohibited for all (Ps 15:5). Even fair interest was otherwise prohibited in dealing with the poor (*see notes on Dt 23:19, 20; 24:10–13*). The basics of life were to be given, not loaned, to the poor.

him your silver at interest, nor your food for gain.
38 [A]I am the LORD your God, who brought you out
of the land of Egypt to give you the land of Canaan
and [B]to be your God.
39 'A If a [a]countryman of yours becomes so poor
with regard to you that he sells himself to you,
you shall not subject him to a slave's service. 40 He
shall be with you as a hired man, as [A]if he were a
sojourner; he shall serve with you until the year
of jubilee. 41 He shall then go out from you, he and
his sons with him, and shall go back to his family,
that he may return to the property of his forefathers. 42 For they are My servants whom I brought
out from the land of Egypt; they are not to be sold
in a slave sale. 43 [A]You shall not rule over him with
severity, but are to revere your God. 44 As for your
male and female slaves whom you may have—you
may acquire male and female slaves from the pagan nations that are around you. 45 Then, too, *it is*
out of the sons of the sojourners who live as aliens
among you that you may gain acquisition, and out
of their families who are with you, whom they will
have [a]produced in your land; they also may become
your possession. 46 You may even bequeath them to
your sons after you, to receive as a possession; you
can use them as permanent slaves. [A]But in respect
to your [a]countrymen, the sons of Israel, you shall
not rule with severity over one another.

OF REDEEMING A POOR MAN

47 'Now if the [a]means of a stranger or of a sojourner with you becomes sufficient, and a [b]countryman
of yours becomes so poor with regard to him as to
sell himself to a stranger who is sojourning with
you, or to the descendants of a stranger's family,
48 then he shall have redemption right after he has
been sold. One of his brothers may redeem him, 49 or
his uncle, or his uncle's son, may redeem him, or one
of his blood relatives from his family may redeem
him; or [a,A]if he prospers, he may redeem himself.
50 He then with his purchaser shall calculate from
the year when he sold himself to him up to the year
of jubilee; and the price of his sale shall correspond
to the number of years. *It is* like the days of a hired
man *that* he shall be with him. 51 If there are still
many years, [A]he shall refund part of his purchase
price in proportion to them for his own redemption;
52 and if few years remain until the year of jubilee,
he shall so calculate with him. In proportion to his
years he is to refund *the amount for* his redemption.
53 Like a man hired year by year he shall be with
him; [A]he shall not rule over him with severity in
your sight. 54 Even if he is not redeemed by [a]these
means, [A]he shall still go out in the year of jubilee, he
and his sons with him. 55 For the sons of Israel are
My servants; they are My servants whom I brought
out from the land of Egypt. I am the LORD your God.

BLESSINGS OF OBEDIENCE

26 'You shall not make for yourselves [a,A]idols, nor
shall you set up for yourselves [B]an image or
[C]a *sacred* pillar, nor shall you place a [D]figured stone
in your land to bow down [b]to it; for I am the LORD
your God. 2 [A]You shall keep My sabbaths and reverence My sanctuary; I am the LORD. 3 [A]If you walk in
My statutes and keep My commandments so as to
carry them out, 4 then [A]I shall give you rains in their
season, so that the land will yield its produce and the
trees of the field will bear their fruit. 5 [A]Indeed, your
threshing will last for you until grape gathering, and
grape gathering will last until sowing time. You will
thus eat your [a]food to the full and [B]live securely in
your land. 6 [A]I shall also grant peace in the land, so
that [B]you may lie down with no one making *you*
tremble. [C]I shall also eliminate harmful beasts from
the land, and [D]no sword will pass through your land.
7 But you will chase your enemies and they will fall
before you by the sword; 8 [A]five of you will chase a
hundred, and a hundred of you will chase ten thousand, and your enemies will fall before you by the
sword. 9 So I will turn toward you and [A]make you
fruitful and multiply you, and I will [B]confirm My

25:38 [A]Lev 11:45 [B]Gen 17:7 25:39 [a]Lit *brother* [A]Ex 21:2-6; Deut 15:12-18; 1 Kin 9:22 25:40 [A]Ex 21:2 25:43 [A]Ex 1:13, 14; Lev 25:46, 53; Ezek 34:4; Col 4:1 25:45 [a]Lit *begotten* 25:46 [a]Lit *brothers* [A]Lev 25:43 25:47 [a]Lit *hand...reaches* [b]Lit *brother* 25:49 [a]Lit *if his hand has reached and* [A]Lev 25:26, 27 25:51 [A]Lev 25:16 25:53 [A]Lev 25:43 25:54 [a]Or *these years* [A]Lev 25:10, 13, 28 26:1 [a]Or *graven images* [b]Lit *over* [A]Lev 19:4; Deut 5:8 [B]Ex 20:4; Deut 16:21f [C]Ex 23:24 [D]Num 33:52 26:2 [A]Lev 19:30 26:3 [A]Deut 7:12-26; 11:13; 28:1-14 26:4 [A]Deut 11:14 26:5 [a]Lit *bread* [A]Deut 11:15; Joel 2:19, 26; Amos 9:13 [B]Lev 25:18, 19; Ezek 34:25 26:6 [A]Ps 29:11; 85:8; 147:14 [B]Zeph 3:13 [C]Lev 26:22 [D]Lev 26:25 26:8 [A]Deut 32:30 26:9 [A]Gen 17:6; 22:17; 48:4 [B]Gen 17:7

25:38 to give you the land of Canaan. The Lord cites His generosity in giving them a land that was not theirs as a motive for their generosity toward their countrymen.

25:39–55 The principles for dealing with slavery are laid out.

25:42 For they are My servants. The spirit of OT slavery is revealed in these words. God, in effect, ordered that slaves be treated like family, i.e., better than employees, because they are His slaves whom He redeemed out of the slave markets of Egypt. God owned not only the land (v. 23), but also the people.

25:44–46 from the pagan nations. These slaves included people whom Israel was to either drive out or destroy (i.e., slavery was a humane option) and those who came to Israel in the Exodus from Egypt.

25:47–55 This section deals with an alien who has an Israelite slave.

25:48 redemption right. Redemption, a contractual agreement which existed in the slave culture, offered the potential for emancipation to indentured individuals under certain conditions. Slaves could be bought out of slavery or some other sort of indentured status by family members or other interested parties who would pay the ransom price.

25:51–54 *amount for* his redemption. The cost of buying him out of slavery was affected by the Jubilee year, when he could be set free.

25:55 The Israelites emancipated from Egypt by God were all God's servants; therefore, they were to treat their own slaves with the same grace and generosity as God had granted them.

26:1–46 The covenant blessings for obedience (26:3–13) and curses for disobedience (26:14–39) are elaborated (cf. Dt 28). A provision for repentance is also offered (26:40–45).

26:1, 2 A representative summary of the Ten Commandments (Ex 20:3–17) was set forth as the standard by which Israel's obedience or disobedience would be measured.

26:1 image ... pillar ... figured stone. Israel's neighbors used all of these devices for the worship of their gods.

26:3–13 These blessings will reward obedience.

26:4 rains in their season. If the rains did not come at the right times, the people experienced crop failure and famine (cf. 1Ki 17, 18).

26:6 harmful beasts. Dangerous animals such as lions and bears existed in that area. Joseph's brothers claimed that such an animal had killed him (Ge 37:20).

26:7 chase your enemies. God provided victories repeatedly in the conquest of Canaan (cf. Jos 8–12).

26:9 make you fruitful and multiply you ... confirm My covenant with you. What God commanded at Creation and repeated after the Flood was contained in the covenant

covenant with you. 10 [A]You will eat the old supply
and clear out the old because of the new. 11 [A]More-
over, I will make My [a]dwelling among you, and My
soul will not [b]reject you. 12 [A]I will also walk among
you and be your God, and you shall be My people.
13 [A]I am the LORD your God, who brought you out
of the land of Egypt so that *you* would not be their
slaves, and [B]I broke the bars of your yoke and made
you walk erect.

PENALTIES OF DISOBEDIENCE

14 '[A]But if you do not obey Me and do not carry out
all these commandments, 15 if, instead, you [A]reject My
statutes, and if your soul abhors My ordinances so
as not to carry out all My commandments, *and* so
[B]break My covenant, 16 I, in turn, will do this to you: I
will appoint over you a [A]sudden terror, consumption
and fever that will waste away the eyes and cause
the [B]soul to pine away; also, [C]you will sow your seed
uselessly, for your enemies will eat it up. 17 I will set
My face against you so that you will be struck down
before your enemies; and [A]those who hate you will
rule over you, and [B]you will flee when no one is pursuing you. 18 If also after these things you do not obey
Me, then I will punish you [A]seven times more for your
sins. 19 I will also [A]break down your pride of power; I
will also make your sky like iron and your earth like
bronze. 20 [A]Your strength will be spent uselessly, for
your land will not yield its produce and the trees of
the land will not yield their fruit.

21 'If then, you [a,A]act with hostility against Me and
are unwilling to obey Me, I will increase the plague
on you [B]seven times according to your sins. 22 [A]I will
let loose among you the beasts of the field, which
will bereave you of your children and destroy your
cattle and reduce your number so that [B]your roads
lie deserted.

23 '[A]And if by these things you are not turned
to Me, but act with hostility against Me, 24 then I
will [A]act with hostility against you; and I, even I,
will strike you [B]seven times for your sins. 25 I will
also bring upon you a sword which will execute
[A]vengeance for the covenant; and when you gather
together into your cities, I will send [B]pestilence
among you, so that you shall be delivered into enemy hands. 26 [A]When I break your staff of bread, ten
women will bake your bread in one oven, and they
will bring back your bread [a]in rationed amounts,
so that you will [B]eat and not be satisfied.

27 'Yet if in spite of this you do not obey Me, but
act with hostility against Me, 28 then [A]I will act with
wrathful hostility against you, and I, even I, will
punish you seven times for your sins. 29 Further,
[A]you will eat the flesh of your sons and the flesh of
your daughters you will eat. 30 I then [A]will destroy
your high places, and cut down your [B]incense altars,
and heap your [a]remains on the [a]remains of your
idols, for My soul shall abhor you. 31 I will [a]lay [A]waste
your cities as well and will make your [B]sanctuaries
desolate, and I will not [C]smell your soothing aromas.
32 I will make [A]the land desolate [B]so that your enemies who settle in it will be appalled over it. 33 You,
however, I [A]will scatter among the nations and will
draw out a sword after you, as your land becomes
desolate and your cities become waste.

34 '[A]Then the land will [a]enjoy its sabbaths all
the days of the desolation, while you are in your
enemies' land; then the land will rest and [a]enjoy
its sabbaths. 35 All the days of *its* desolation it will
observe the rest which it did not observe on your
sabbaths, while you were living on it. 36 As for those
of you who may be left, I will also bring [A]weakness
into their hearts in the lands of their enemies. And
the sound of a driven leaf will chase them, and
even when no one is pursuing they will flee [a]as
though from the sword, and they will fall. 37 [A]They
will therefore stumble over each other as if *running*
from the sword, although no one is pursuing; and
you will have *no strength* [a]to stand up before your
enemies. 38 But [A]you will perish among the nations,

26:10 [A]Lev 25:22 26:11 [a]Or *tabernacle* [b]Lit *abhor* [A]Ex 25:8; 29:45, 46; Ezek 37:26 26:12 [A]Gen 3:8; Deut 23:14; 2 Cor 6:16 26:13 [A]Ex 20:2 [B]Ezek 34:27 26:14 [A]Deut 28:15-68; Josh 23:15 26:15 [A]Lev 26:11; 2 Kin 17:15 [B]Lev 26:9 26:16 [A]Deut 28:22; Ps 78:33 [B]1 Sam 2:33; Ezek 24:23; 33:10 [C]Judg 6:3-6; Job 31:8 26:17 [A]Ps 106:41 [B]Lev 26:36, 37; Ps 53:5; Prov 28:1 26:18 [A]Lev 26:21, 24, 28 26:19 [A]Is 28:1-3; Ezek 24:21 26:20 [A]Ps 127:1; Is 17:10, 11; 49:4; Jer 12:13 26:21 [a]Lit *walk,* and so throughout the ch [A]Lev 26:23, 27, 40 [B]Lev 26:18 26:22 [A]2 Kin 17:25 [B]Judg 5:6 26:23 [A]Lev 26:21; Jer 5:3 26:24 [A]Lev 26:28, 41 [B]Lev 26:21 26:25 [A]Jer 50:28; 51:11 [B]Num 14:12 26:26 [a]Lit *by weight* [A]Is 3:1; Ezek 4:16, 17; 5:16 [B]Mic 6:14 26:28 [A]Lev 26:24, 41; Is 59:18 26:29 [A]2 Kin 6:29 26:30 [a]Lit *corpses* [A]2 Kin 23:20; Ezek 6:3, 6; Amos 7:9 [B]2 Chr 34:4, 7; Is 27:9 26:31 [a]Lit *give desolation to* [A]Neh 2:3; Jer 44:2, 6, 22 [B]Is 63:18; Lam 2:7 [C]Amos 5:21 26:32 [A]Jer 9:11; 12:11; 25:11; 33:10 [B]Jer 18:16; 19:8 26:33 [A]Deut 4:27; 28:64; Ps 44:11; 106:27; Jer 31:10; Ezek 12:15; 20:23; Zech 7:14 26:34 [a]Lit *satisfy* [A]Lev 26:43; 2 Chr 36:21 26:36 [a]Lit *the flight of the sword* [A]Is 30:17; Lam 1:3, 6; 4:19; Ezek 21:7 26:37 [a]Lit *you will stand* [A]Jer 6:21; Nah 3:3 26:38 [A]Deut 4:26

promise of seed (Ge 12:1–3), which He will fulfill to the nation of Israel as promised to Abraham (Ge 15:5, 6).

26:12 your God ... My people. The promise of an intimate covenant relationship with the God of the universe is given (cf. 2Co 6:16).

26:14–39 These punishments will repay disobedience.

26:15 break My covenant. By disobeying the commandments and the various laws of the Mosaic Covenant, Israel broke this conditional covenant. Unlike the ultimate provisions of the unconditional covenant made with Abraham, all blessings in the covenant of Mosaic law were conditioned upon obedience (cf. Lv 26:25).

26:16 consumption. Perhaps tuberculosis or leprosy is in view (the subject of much legislation in Lv 13, 14), but no certain identification is possible. **your enemies will eat it.** They will be conquered by their enemies at a time when those enemies will enjoy Israel's harvest.

26:22 roads lie deserted. The activity on a nation's roadway, i.e., messengers, merchants, and people traveling, reflected the well-being of that country. This is a picture of extreme economic siege.

26:25 vengeance for the covenant. God's retribution for Israel's breaking the conditional Mosaic Covenant is pledged.

26:29 eat the flesh. There will be widespread famine in the land and thus the people will even resort to cannibalism, which actually came to pass (cf. 2Ki 6:28, 29; Jer 19:9; La 2:20; 4:10).

26:30 high places. These were natural shrines for the worship of idols. Solomon disobeyed God by worshiping Him on the high places (1Ki 3:4), and not long afterward, he was serving the gods of his foreign wives (1Ki 11:1–9).

26:31–35 All this occurred in the terrible invasion of the northern kingdom of Israel in 722 B.C. by the Assyrians and the destruction of the southern kingdom of Judah in 605–586 B.C. by the Babylonians. In the case of Judah, it was a 70-year captivity to rest the land for all the Sabbath years that had been violated. See 2Ch 36:17–21.

26:35 rest which it did not observe. By implication, because they had violated the Sabbath repeatedly. This violation became the basis of the later 70-year Babylonian captivity (cf. 2Ch 36:20–21).

26:38 The 10 tribes of the northern kingdom of Israel never returned directly from captivity. See 2Ki 17:7–23; *see note on Ac 26:7.*

and your enemies' land will consume you. 39 [A]So those of you who may be left will rot away because of their iniquity in the lands of your enemies; and also because of the iniquities of their forefathers they will rot away with them.

40 '[A]If they confess their iniquity and the iniquity of their forefathers, in their unfaithfulness which they committed against Me, and also in their acting with hostility against Me— 41 I also was acting with hostility against them, to bring them into the land of their enemies—[A]or if their uncircumcised heart becomes humbled so that [B]they then make amends for their iniquity, 42 then I will remember [A]My covenant with Jacob, and I will remember also [B]My covenant with Isaac, and [C]My covenant with Abraham as well, and I will remember the land. 43 [A]For the land will be abandoned by them, and will make up for its sabbaths while it is made desolate without them. They, meanwhile, will be making amends for their iniquity, [a]because they rejected My ordinances and their [B]soul abhorred My statutes. 44 Yet in spite of this, when they are in the land of their enemies, I will not reject them, nor will I so [A]abhor them as [B]to destroy them, [C]breaking My covenant with them; for I am the LORD their God. 45 But I will remember for them the [A]covenant with their ancestors, whom I brought out of the land of Egypt in the sight of the nations, that [B]I might be their God. I am the LORD.' "

46 [A]These are the statutes and ordinances and laws which the LORD established between Himself and the sons of Israel [a]through Moses at Mount Sinai.

RULES CONCERNING VALUATIONS

27 Again, the LORD spoke to Moses, saying, 2 "Speak to the sons of Israel and say to them, '[A]When a man makes a difficult vow, he *shall be valued* according to your valuation of persons belonging to the LORD. 3 If your valuation is of the male from twenty years even to sixty years old, then your valuation shall be fifty shekels of silver, after [A]the shekel of the sanctuary. 4 Or if it is a female, then your valuation shall be thirty shekels. 5 If it be from five years even to twenty years old then your valuation for the male shall be twenty shekels and for the female ten shekels. 6 But if *they are* from a month even up to five years old, then your valuation shall be [A]five shekels of silver for the male, and for the female your valuation shall be three shekels of silver. 7 If *they are* from sixty years old and upward, if it is a male, then your valuation shall be fifteen shekels, and for the female ten shekels. 8 But if he is poorer than your valuation, then he shall be placed before the priest and the priest shall value him; [A]according to [a]the means of the one who vowed, the priest shall value him.

9 'Now if it is an animal of the kind which [a]men can present as an offering to the LORD, any such that one gives to the LORD shall be holy. 10 [A]He shall not replace it or exchange it, a good for a bad, or a bad for a good; or if he does exchange animal for animal, then both it and its substitute shall become holy. 11 If, however, it is any unclean animal of the kind which [a]men do not present as an offering to the LORD, then he shall place the animal before the priest. 12 The priest shall value it [a]as either good or bad; as you, the priest, value it, so it shall be. 13 But if he should ever *wish to* redeem it, then he shall add one-fifth of it to your valuation.

14 'Now if a man consecrates his house as holy to the LORD, then the priest shall value it [a]as either good or bad; as the priest values it, so it shall stand. 15 Yet if the one who consecrates it should *wish to* redeem his house, then he shall add one-fifth of your valuation price to it, so that it may be his.

16 'Again, if a man consecrates to the LORD part of the fields of his own property, then your valuation shall be [a]proportionate to the seed needed for it: a homer of barley seed at fifty shekels of silver. 17 If he consecrates his field as of the year of jubilee, according to your valuation it shall stand. 18 If he consecrates his field after the jubilee, however, then the priest shall calculate the price for [a]him [b]proportionate to the years that are left until the year of jubilee; and it shall be deducted from your valuation. 19 If the one who consecrates it should ever wish to redeem the field, then he shall add one-fifth of your valuation price to it, so that it may pass to him. 20 Yet if he will not redeem the field, [a]but has sold the field to another man, it may no longer be redeemed; 21 and when it [a]reverts in the jubilee, the field shall be holy to the LORD, like a field [b]set apart; [A]it shall be for the priest as his [c]property. 22 Or if he consecrates to the LORD a field which he has bought, which is not a part of the field of his own [a]property, 23 then the priest shall calculate for [a]him the amount of your valuation up to the year of jubilee; and he shall on that day give your valuation as holy to the LORD. 24 In the year of jubilee the field shall return to the one from whom he bought it, to whom the possession of the land belongs. 25 Every valuation of yours, moreover, shall be after [A]the shekel of the sanctuary. The shekel shall be twenty gerahs.

26:39 [A]Ezek 4:17; 33:10 26:40 [A]Jer 3:12-15; 14:20; Hos 5:15 26:41 [A]Jer 4:4; 9:25, 26; Ezek 44:7, 9; Acts 7:51 [B]Ezek 20:43 26:42 [A]Gen 28:13-15; 35:11, 12 [B]Gen 26:2-5 [C]Gen 22:15-18 26:43 [a]Lit *because and by the cause* [A]Lev 26:34 [B]Lev 26:11 26:44 [A]Lev 26:11 [B]Deut 4:31; Jer 30:11 [C]Jer 33:20-26 26:45 [A]Ex 6:6-8 [B]Gen 17:7 26:46 [a]Lit *by the hand of* [A]Lev 7:38; 27:34; Deut 4:5; 29:1 27:2 [A]Num 6:2; Deut 23:21-23 27:3 [A]Ex 30:13; Lev 27:25; Num 3:47; 18:16 27:6 [A]Num 18:16 27:8 [a]Lit *what the hand reaches* [A]Lev 5:11; 14:21-24 27:9 [a]Lit *they* 27:10 [A]Lev 27:33 27:11 [a]Lit *they* 27:12 [a]Lit *between* 27:14 [a]Lit *between good* 27:16 [a]Lit *according to its seed* 27:18 [a]Or *it* [b]Lit *according to the years* 27:20 [a]Or *if he* 27:21 [a]Lit *goes out* [b]Or *devoted, banned* [c]Lit *possession* [A]Num 18:14; Ezek 44:29 27:22 [a]Lit *possession* 27:23 [a]Or *it* 27:25 [A]Ex 30:13; Lev 27:3; Num 3:47; 18:16

26:40–42 **If they confess …. will remember My covenant.** God's covenant was rooted in the relationship He had initiated with His people. True repentance would be honored by Him.

26:42 **Jacob … Isaac … Abraham.** The reverse order is a look in retrospect as opposed to the actual historical sequence.

26:46 Much of the content of Leviticus came during Moses' two "forty day and night" visits to Sinai (cf. Ex 24:16–32:6; 34:2–28; Lv 7:37, 38; 25:1; 27:34).

27:1–34 Standard legislation is given for dedicated persons, animals, houses, and lands.

27:2–7 **makes a … vow.** This sets the gift apart from the rest of his household and possessions as a gift to the Lord and His service.

27:3 **the shekel of the sanctuary.** *See note on 5:15.*

26 '[A]However, a firstborn among animals, which
as a firstborn belongs to the LORD, no man may
consecrate it; whether ox or sheep, it is the LORD'S.
27 But if *it is* among the unclean animals, then he
shall [a]redeem it according to your valuation and
add to it one-fifth of it; and if it is not redeemed,
then it shall be sold according to your valuation.
28 'Nevertheless, [A]anything which a man [a]sets
apart to the LORD out of all that he has, of man or
animal or of the fields of his own property, shall not
be sold or redeemed. Anything [b]devoted to destruction
is most holy to the LORD. 29 No [a]one who may
have been [b]set apart among men shall be ransomed;
he shall surely be put to death.

30 'Thus [A]all the tithe of the land, of the seed of
the land or of the fruit of the tree, is the LORD'S; it
is holy to the LORD. 31 If, therefore, a man wishes
to redeem part of his tithe, he shall add to it
one-fifth of it. 32 For every tenth part of herd or
flock, whatever [A]passes under the rod, the tenth
one shall be holy to the LORD. 33 [A]He is not to be
concerned whether *it is* good or bad, nor shall he
exchange it; or if he does exchange it, then both
it and its substitute shall become holy. It shall not
be redeemed.' "
34 [A]These are the commandments which the LORD
commanded Moses for the sons of Israel at Mount
Sinai.

27:26 [A]Ex 13:2 27:27 [a]Or *ransom* 27:28 [a]Lit *anything devoted;* or *banned* [b]Or *puts under the ban* [A]Num 18:14; Josh 6:17-19 27:29 [a]Lit *one devoted;* or *banned* [b]Or *put under the ban* 27:30 [A]Gen 28:22; 2 Chr 31:5; Neh 13:12 27:32 [A]Jer 33:13; Ezek 20:37 27:33 [A]Lev 27:10 27:34 [A]Lev 26:46; Deut 4:5

27:26 a firstborn. The firstborn already belonged to the Lord (Ex 13:2), so the worshiper could not dedicate it a second time.

27:29 No one … set apart. A person under the ban, like Achan in Jos 7.

27:30–32 tithe. This general tithe was given to the Levites. Cf. Nu 18:21–32. This is the only mention of tithe or 10 percent in Leviticus. However, along with this offering, there were two other OT tithes which totaled about 23 percent annually (cf. the second tithe—Dt 14:22; and the third tithe every 3 years—Dt 14:28, 29; 26:12).

THE FOURTH BOOK OF MOSES CALLED

NUMBERS

TITLE

The English title "Numbers" comes from the Greek (LXX) and Latin (Vg.) versions. This designation is based on the numberings that are a major focus of chaps. 1–4 and 26. The most common Hebrew title comes from the fifth word in the Hebrew text of 1:1, "in the wilderness [of]." This name is much more descriptive of the total contents of the book, which recount the history of Israel during almost 39 years of wandering in the wilderness. Another Hebrew title, favored by some early church Fathers, is based on the first word of the Hebrew text of 1:1, "and He spoke." This designation emphasizes that the book records the Word of God to Israel.

AUTHOR AND DATE

The first 5 books of the Bible, called the Law, of which Numbers is the fourth, are ascribed to Moses throughout Scripture (Jos 8:31; 2Ki 14:6; Ne 8:1; Mk 12:26; Jn 7:19). The book of Numbers itself refers to the writing of Moses in 33:2 and 36:13.

Numbers was written in the final year of Moses' life. The events from 20:1 to the end occur in the 40th year after the Exodus. The account ends with Israel poised on the eastern side of the Jordan River across from Jericho (36:13), which is where the conquest of the land of Canaan began (Jos 3–6). The book of Numbers must be dated ca. 1405 B.C., since it is foundational to the book of Deuteronomy, and Deuteronomy is dated in the 11th month of the 40th year after the Exodus (Dt 1:3).

BACKGROUND AND SETTING

Most of the events of the book are set "in the wilderness." The word "wilderness" is used 48 times in Numbers. This term refers to land that contains little vegetation or trees, and because of a sparsity of rainfall, it cannot be cultivated. This land is best used for tending flocks of animals. In 1:1–10:10, Israel encamped in "the wilderness of Sinai." It was at Sinai that the Lord had entered into the Mosaic Covenant with them (Ex 19–24). From 10:11–12:16, Israel traveled from Sinai to Kadesh. In 13:1–20:13, the events took place in and around Kadesh, which was located in "the wilderness of Paran" (12:16; 13:3, 26), "the wilderness of Zin" (13:21; 20:1). From 20:14–22:1, Israel traveled from Kadesh to the "plains of Moab." All the events of 22:2–36:13 occurred while Israel was encamped in the plain to the N of Moab. That plain was a flat and fertile piece of land in the middle of the wasteland (21:20; 23:28; 24:1).

The book of Numbers concentrates on events that take place in the second and fortieth years after the Exodus. All incidents recorded in 1:1–14:45 occur in 1444 B.C., the year after the Exodus. Everything referred to after 20:1 is dated ca. 1406/1405 B.C., the 40th year after the Exodus. The laws and events found in 15:1–19:22 are undated, but probably all should be dated ca. 1443 to 1407 B.C. The lack of material devoted to this 37 year period, in comparison with the other years of the journey from Egypt to Canaan, communicates how wasted these years were because of Israel's rebellion against the Lord and His consequent judgment.

HISTORICAL AND THEOLOGICAL THEMES

Numbers chronicles the experiences of two generations of the nation of Israel. The first generation participated in the Exodus from Egypt. Their story begins in Ex 2:23 and continues through Leviticus and into the first 14 chapters of Numbers. This generation was numbered for the war of conquest in Canaan (1:1–46). However, when the people arrived at the southern edge of Canaan, they refused to enter the land (14:1–10). Because of their rebellion against the Lord, all the adults 20 and over (except Caleb and Joshua) were sentenced to die in the wilderness (14:26–38). In chaps. 15–25, the first and second generations overlap; the first died out as the second grew to adulthood. A second numbering of the people commenced the history of this second generation (26:1–56). These Israelites did go to war (26:2) and inherited the land (26:52–56). The story of this second generation, beginning in Numbers 26:1, continues through the books of Deuteronomy and Joshua.

Three theological themes permeate Numbers. First, the Lord Himself communicated to Israel through Moses (1:1; 7:89; 12:6–8), so the words of Moses had divine authority. Israel's response to Moses mirrored her obedience or disobedience to the Lord. Numbers contains three distinct divisions based on Israel's response to the word of the Lord: obedience (chaps. 1–10), disobedience (chaps. 11–25), and renewed obedience (chaps. 26–36). The second theme is that the Lord is the God of judgment. Throughout Numbers, the "anger" of the Lord was aroused in response to Israel's sin (11:1, 10, 33; 12:9; 14:18; 25:3, 4; 32:10, 13, 14). Third, the faithfulness of the Lord to keep His promise to give the seed of Abraham the land of Canaan is emphasized (15:2; 26:52–56; 27:12; 33:50–56; 34:1–29).

INTERPRETIVE CHALLENGES

Four major interpretive challenges face the reader of Numbers. First, is the book of Numbers a separate book, or is it a part of a larger literary whole, the Pentateuch? The biblical books of Genesis, Exodus, Leviticus, Numbers, and Deuteronomy form the Torah. The remainder of the Scripture always views these 5 books as a unit. The ultimate meaning of Numbers cannot be divorced from its context in the Pentateuch. The first verse of the book speaks of the Lord, Moses, the tabernacle, and the Exodus from Egypt. This assumes that the reader is familiar with the 3 books that precede Numbers. Still, every Hebrew manuscript available divides the Pentateuch in exactly the same way as the present text. In them the book of Numbers is a well defined unit, with a structural integrity of its own. The book has its own beginning, middle, and ending, even as it functions within a larger whole. Thus, the book of Numbers is also to be viewed with singular identity.

The second interpretive question asks, "Is there a sense of coherence in the book of Numbers?" It is readily evident that Numbers contains a wide variety of literary materials and forms. Census lists, genealogies, laws, historical narratives, poetry, prophecy, and travel lists are found in this book. Nevertheless, they are all blended to tell the story of Israel's journey from Mt. Sinai to the plains of Moab. The coherence of Numbers is reflected in the outline that follows.

A third issue deals with the large numbers given for the tribes of Israel in 1:46 and 26:51. These two lists of Israel's men of war, taken 39 years apart, both put the number over 600,000. These numbers demand a total population for Israel in the wilderness of around 2.5 million at any one time. From a natural perspective, this total seems too high for the wilderness conditions to sustain. However, it must be recognized that the Lord supernaturally took care of Israel for 40 years (Dt 8:1–5). Therefore, the large numbers must be accepted at face value (*see note on 1:46*).

The fourth interpretive challenge concerns the heathen prophet Balaam, whose story is recorded in 22:2–24:25. Even though Balaam claimed to know the Lord (22:18), Scripture consistently refers to him as a false prophet (2Pe 2:15, 16, Jude 11). The Lord used Balaam as His mouthpiece to speak the true words He put in his mouth (*see notes on 22:2–24:25*).

OUTLINE

I. The Experience of the First Generation of Israel in the Wilderness (1:1–25:18)
- A. The Obedience of Israel toward the Lord (1:1–10:36)
  1. The organization of Israel around the tabernacle of the Lord (1:1–6:27)
  2. The orientation of Israel toward the tabernacle of the Lord (7:1–10:36)
- B. The Disobedience of Israel toward the Lord (11:1–25:18)
  1. The complaining of Israel on the journey (11:1–12:16)
  2. The rebellion of Israel and its leaders at Kadesh (13:1–20:29)
     - a. The rebellion of Israel and the consequences (13:1–19:22)
     - b. The rebellion of Moses and Aaron and the consequences (20:1–29)
  3. The renewed complaining of Israel on the journey (21:1–22:1)
  4. The blessing of Israel by Balaam (22:2–24:25)
  5. The final rebellion of Israel with Baal of Peor (25:1–18)

II. The Experience of the Second Generation of Israel in the Plains of Moab: The Renewed Obedience of Israel toward the Lord (26:1–36:13)
- A. The Preparations for the Conquest of the Land (26:1–32:42)
- B. The Review of the Journey in the Wilderness (33:1–49)
- C. The Anticipation of the Conquest of the Land (33:50–36:13)

THE CENSUS OF ISRAEL'S WARRIORS

1 Then the LORD spoke to Moses in the wilderness
of Sinai, in the tent of meeting, on [A]the first of the
second month, in the second year after they had come
out of the land of Egypt, saying, 2 "[A]Take a [a]census of
all the congregation of the sons of Israel, by their
families, by their fathers' households, according to
the number of names, every male, head by head 3 from
[A]twenty years old and upward, whoever *is able to* go
out to war in Israel, you and Aaron shall [a]number
them by their armies. 4 With you, moreover, there
shall be a man of each tribe, [A]each one head of his
father's household. 5 These then are the names of the
men who shall stand with you: [A]of Reuben, Elizur the
son of Shedeur; 6 of Simeon, Shelumiel the son of Zurishaddai; 7 of Judah, [A]Nahshon the son of Amminadab;
8 of Issachar, Nethanel the son of Zuar; 9 of Zebulun,
Eliab the son of Helon; 10 of the sons of Joseph: of
Ephraim, Elishama the son of Ammihud; of Manasseh,
Gamaliel the son of Pedahzur; 11 of Benjamin, Abidan
the son of Gideoni; 12 of Dan, Ahiezer the son of Ammishaddai; 13 of Asher, Pagiel the son of Ochran; 14 of
Gad, Eliasaph the son of [A]Deuel; 15 of Naphtali, Ahira
the son of Enan. 16 These are they who were [A]called of
the congregation, the leaders of their fathers' tribes;
they were the [B]heads of [a]divisions of Israel."
17 So Moses and Aaron took these men who had
been designated by name, 18 and they assembled all
the congregation together on the [A]first of the second
month. Then they registered by [B]ancestry in their
families, by their fathers' households, according to the
number of names, from twenty years old and upward,
head by head, 19 just as [A]the LORD had commanded Moses. So he numbered them in the wilderness of Sinai.
20 [A]Now the sons of Reuben, Israel's firstborn,
their genealogical registration by their families, by
their fathers' households, according to the number
of names, head by head, every male from twenty
years old and upward, whoever *was able to* go out
to war, 21 their numbered men of the tribe of Reuben *were* 46,500.
22 [A]Of the sons of Simeon, their genealogical registration by their families, by their fathers' households, their numbered men, according to the number of names, head by head, every male from twenty
years old and upward, [B]whoever *was able to* go
out to war, 23 their numbered men of the tribe of
Simeon *were* 59,300.
24 [A]Of the sons of Gad, their genealogical registration by their families, by their fathers' households,
according to the number of names, from twenty
years old and upward, whoever *was able to* go out
to war, 25 their numbered men of the tribe of Gad
were 45,650.
26 [A]Of the sons of Judah, their genealogical registration by their families, by their fathers' households, according to the number of names, from
twenty years old and upward, whoever *was able to*
go out to war, 27 their numbered men of the tribe
of Judah *were* 74,600.
28 [A]Of the sons of Issachar, their genealogical registration by their families, by their fathers' households, according to the number of names, from
twenty years old and upward, whoever *was able to*
go out to war, 29 their numbered men of the tribe
of Issachar *were* 54,400.
30 [A]Of the sons of Zebulun, their genealogical registration by their families, by their fathers' households, according to the number of names, from
twenty years old and upward, whoever *was able to*
go out to war, 31 their numbered men of the tribe of
Zebulun *were* 57,400.
32 [A]Of the sons of Joseph, *namely,* of the sons of
Ephraim, their genealogical registration by their

1:1 [A]Ex 40:2, 17 1:2 [a]Lit *sum* [A]Ex 12:37; 38:25, 26; Num 26:2 1:3 [a]Lit *muster,* and so throughout the ch [A]Ex 30:14; 38:26 1:4 [A]Ex 18:21, 25; Num 1:16; Deut 1:15 1:5 [A]Gen 29:32; Ex 1:2; Deut 33:6; Rev 7:5 1:7 [A]Ruth 4:20; 1 Chr 2:10; Luke 3:32 1:14 [A]Num 2:14 1:16 [a]Lit *thousands;* or *clans* [A]Ex 18:21; Num 7:2; 16:2; 26:9 [B]Ex 18:25 1:18 [A]Num 1:1 [B]Ezra 2:59; Heb 7:3 1:19 [A]2 Sam 24:1 1:20 [A]Num 26:5-7 1:22 [A]Num 26:12-14 [B]Ps 144:1 1:24 [A]Gen 30:11; Num 26:15-18; Josh 4:12; Jer 49:1 1:26 [A]Gen 29:35; Num 26:19-22; 2 Sam 24:9; Ps 78:68; Matt 1:2 1:28 [A]Num 26:23-25 1:30 [A]Num 26:26, 27 1:32 [A]Num 26:35-37; Deut 33:13-17; Jer 7:15; Obad 19

1:1–10:36 The first 10 chapters of Numbers record the final preparations of Israel necessary for their conquest of the land of Canaan. In this section, the Lord spoke to Israel through Moses (1:1; 2:1; 3:1, 5, 11, 14, 44; 4:1, 17, 21; 5:1, 5, 11; 6:1, 22; 7:4; 8:1, 5, 23; 9:1, 9; 10:1), and Moses and Israel responded with obedience (1:19, 54; 2:33, 34; 3:16, 42, 51; 4:49; 7:2, 3; 8:3; 9:5, 18, 23; 10:13, 14–28 [in accordance with 2:34]). These chapters divide into two parts (1:1–6:27 and 7:1–10:36), which both end with an invocation of the Lord's blessing on Israel (6:22–27 and 10:35, 36).

1:1–6:27 These 6 chapters chronologically follow the events recorded in 7:1–10:10. The ordering of Israel around the tabernacle (1:1–4:49) and the purity of the camp of Israel (5:1–6:27) were the final results of the Lord's commands that began in Ex 25:1. Obeying God's instructions transformed an impure (Ex 32:7, 8) and disorderly (Ex 32:25) Israel into a people ready to march into Canaan.

1:1 Then the LORD spoke to Moses. This connects the revelation given here by the Lord with Ex 25:1ff. and Lv 1:1ff. The word from God directed everything that was done by Israel. **the wilderness of Sinai.** Israel had been encamped there for 11 months. See Ex 19:1. **the tent of meeting.** The tabernacle, where the Lord's glory resided in the cloud, had been erected one month earlier (Ex 40:17). This was God's dwelling place in the midst of His people. In Nu 1:1–6:27, Israel was organized with the tabernacle as the central feature. **the second year.** Numbers begins in the 14th month (377 days) after the Exodus from Egypt.

1:2 a census. In Ex 30:11–16, the Lord had commanded that a census of the males in Israel over 20 (excluding the Levites) be taken for the purpose of determining the ransom money for the service of the tabernacle. The result of that census is recorded in Ex 38:25–28. The total number, 603,550 (Ex 38:26), equals the number in 1:46.

1:3 go out to war. The purpose of this census was to form a roster of fighting men. The book of Numbers looks ahead to the invasion of the land promised to Abraham (cf. Ge 12:1–3).

1:4 a man. One leader from each of the 12 tribes was to assist Moses and Aaron in the numbering of the men. These same leaders are mentioned in Nu 2:1–34 and 10:14–28 as the heads of tribes and in 7:1–88 they bring gifts to the tabernacle.

1:17–46 The numbers from the tribes were:

Reuben	46,500 (v. 21)
Simeon	59,300 (v. 23)
Gad	45,650 (v. 25)
Judah	74,600 (v. 27)
Issachar	54,400 (v. 29)
Zebulun	57,400 (v. 31)
Ephraim	40,500 (v. 33)
Manasseh	32,200 (v. 35)
Benjamin	35,400 (v. 37)
Dan	62,700 (v. 39)
Asher	41,500 (v. 41)
Naphtali	53,400 (v. 43)
Total	603,550 (v. 46)

The tribal order follows the pattern of Jacob's wives: first, the sons of Leah; second, the sons of Rachel; and third, the sons of the maids, except Gad (born of Leah's maid), who replaced Levi in the third-born position (cf. Ge 29:31–30:24; 35:16–20).

families, by their fathers' households, according to
the number of names, from twenty years old and
upward, whoever *was able to* go out to war, 33 their
numbered men of the tribe of Ephraim *were* 40,500.
34 [A]Of the sons of Manasseh, their genealogical registration by their families, by their fathers'
households, according to the number of names,
from twenty years old and upward, whoever *was*
able to go out to war, 35 their numbered men of the
tribe of Manasseh *were* 32,200.
36 [A]Of the sons of Benjamin, their genealogical
registration by their families, by their fathers'
households, according to the number of names,
from twenty years old and upward, whoever *was*
able to go out to war, 37 their numbered men of the
tribe of Benjamin *were* 35,400.
38 [A]Of the sons of Dan, their genealogical registration by their families, by their fathers' households,
according to the number of names, from twenty years
old and upward, whoever *was able to* go out to war,
39 their numbered men of the tribe of Dan *were* 62,700.
40 [A]Of the sons of Asher, their genealogical registration by their families, by their fathers' households, according to the number of names, from
twenty years old and upward, whoever *was able*
to go out to war, 41 their numbered men of the tribe
of Asher *were* 41,500.
42 [A]Of the sons of Naphtali, their genealogical registration by their families, by their fathers' households, according to the number of names, from
twenty years old and upward, whoever *was able to*
go out to war, 43 their numbered men of the tribe of
Naphtali *were* 53,400.
44 These are the ones who were numbered, whom
Moses and Aaron numbered, with the leaders of Israel, twelve men, each of whom was of his father's
household. 45 So all the numbered men of the sons of
Israel by their fathers' households, from twenty years
old and upward, whoever *was able to* go out to war in
Israel, 46 even all the numbered men were [A]603,550.

LEVITES EXEMPTED

47 [A]The Levites, however, were not numbered
among them by their fathers' tribe. 48 For the LORD
had spoken to Moses, saying, 49 "Only the tribe of
Levi [A]you shall not number, nor shall you take their
[a]census among the sons of Israel. 50 But you shall
[A]appoint the Levites over the [a]tabernacle of the testimony, and over all its furnishings and over all that
belongs to it. They shall carry the tabernacle and
all its furnishings, and they shall take care of it;
they shall also camp around the [a]tabernacle. 51 [A]So
when the tabernacle is to set out, the Levites shall
take it down; and when the tabernacle encamps, the
Levites shall set it up. But [B]the [a]layman who comes
near shall be put to death. 52 [A]The sons of Israel shall
camp, each man by his own camp, and each man by
his own standard, according to their armies. 53 [A]But
the Levites shall camp around the tabernacle of the
testimony, so that there will be [B]no wrath on the
congregation of the sons of Israel. [C]So the Levites
shall keep charge of the tabernacle of the testimony."
54 Thus the sons of Israel did; according to all which
the LORD had commanded Moses, so they did.

ARRANGEMENT OF THE CAMPS

2 Now the LORD spoke to Moses and to Aaron,
saying, 2 "[A]The sons of Israel shall camp, each
by his own standard, with the [a]banners of their fathers' households; they shall camp around the tent
of meeting [b]at a distance. 3 Now those who camp
on the east side toward the sunrise *shall be* of the
standard of the camp of Judah, by their armies, and
the leader of the sons of Judah: [A]Nahshon the son of
Amminadab, 4 and his army, even their [a]numbered
men, 74,600. 5 Those who camp next to him *shall be*
the tribe of Issachar, and the leader of the sons of
Issachar: [A]Nethanel the son of Zuar, 6 and his army,
even their numbered men, 54,400. 7 *Then comes*
the tribe of Zebulun, and the leader of the sons of
Zebulun: [A]Eliab the son of Helon, 8 and his army,
even his numbered men, 57,400. 9 The total of the
numbered men of the camp of Judah: 186,400, by
their armies. [A]They shall set out first.
10 "On the south side *shall be* the standard of the
camp of Reuben by their armies, and the leader of the
sons of Reuben: [A]Elizur the son of Shedeur, 11 and his
army, even their numbered men, 46,500. 12 Those who

1:34 [A]Num 26:28-34 1:36 [A]Gen 49:27; Num 26:38-41; 2 Chr 17:17; Rev 7:8 1:38 [A]Gen 30:6; 46:23; Num 2:25; 26:42, 43 1:40 [A]Num 26:44-47 1:42 [A]Num 26:48-50 1:46 [A]Ex 12:37; 38:26; Num 2:32; 26:51 1:47 [A]Num 2:33; 3:14-39; 4:49; 26:57-64 1:49 [a]Lit *sum* [A]Num 26:62 1:50 [a]Lit *dwelling place,* and so throughout the ch [A]Ex 38:21; Num 3:6-8, 25-37; 4:15, 25-27, 31, 32 1:51 [a]Lit *stranger* [A]Num 4:1-33 [B]Num 3:10, 38; 4:15, 19, 20 1:52 [A]Num 2:2, 34 1:53 [A]Num 3:23, 29, 35, 38 [B]Lev 10:6; Num 16:46; 18:5 [C]Num 8:24; 18:2-4; 1 Chr 23:32 2:2 [a]Lit *signs* [b]Or *facing it* [A]Num 1:52; 24:2 2:3 [A]Num 1:7; 10:14; Ruth 4:20; 1 Chr 2:10; Luke 3:32, 33 2:4 [a]Lit *mustered,* and so throughout the ch 2:5 [A]Num 1:8; 7:18, 23 2:7 [A]Num 1:9 2:9 [A]Num 10:14 2:10 [A]Num 1:5

1:46 six hundred and three thousand five hundred and fifty. This number, combined with the 22,000 Levite males a month old and above (3:39), allows for a total population of over 2,000,000 Israelites. Since this number seems too high for the wilderness conditions and relatively few firstborn sons (3:43), some have reinterpreted the plain meaning of the text by 1) saying "thousand" means "clan" or "chief" here, or 2) stating the numbers are symbolic. However, if "thousand" is not the meaning in this chapter, 1:46 would read 598 "clans" or "chiefs" with only 5,500 individuals. Thus, the meaning "thousand" must be retained. Further, there is no textual indication that these numbers are symbolic. The only conclusion is that God took care of over 2,000,000 people in the wilderness during the period of 40 years (cf. Dt 8:3, 4). Tampering with the number is tampering with God's purpose for these numbers—to show His power in behalf of Israel.

1:50 appoint the Levites. The tribe of Levi, including Moses and Aaron, was not included in this census because it was exempt from military service. The Levites were to serve the Lord by carrying and attending to the tabernacle (cf. 3:5–13; 4:1–33, 46–49).

1:51 the layman. This word often refers to the "alien" or "stranger." The non-Levite Israelite was like a "foreigner" to the transporting of the tabernacle and had to keep his distance lest he die.

1:53 no wrath. The purpose of setting the Levites apart and arranging them around the tabernacle was to keep the wrath of the Lord from consuming Israel (cf. Ex 32:10, 25–29).

2:2 standard ... banners. The banners were flags identifying the individual tribes (probably with some sort of insignia). The standards were flags marking each of the 4 encampments of 3 tribes each. **tent of meeting.** For details see Ex 25–30.

2:3 on the east side ... Judah. Judah occupied the place of honor to the E. Genesis 49:8–12 highlights the role and centrality Judah would have in the defeat of Israel's enemies. Judah was the tribe through which the Messiah would be born. **Nahshon.** Nahshon appears in the later genealogies of the messianic line (cf. Ru 4:20; Mt 1:4).

camp next to him *shall be* the tribe of Simeon, and the
leader of the sons of Simeon: [A]Shelumiel the son of Zurishaddai, 13 and his army, even their numbered men,
59,300. 14 Then *comes* the tribe of Gad, and the leader of
the sons of Gad: [A]Eliasaph the son of [a]Deuel, 15 and his
army, even their numbered men, 45,650. 16 The total of
the numbered men of the camp of Reuben: 151,450 by
their armies. And [A]they shall set out second.
17 "[A]Then the tent of meeting shall set out *with*
the camp of the Levites in the midst of the camps;
just as they camp, so they shall set out, every man
in his place by their standards.
18 "On the west side *shall be* the standard of the
camp of [A]Ephraim by their armies, and the leader
of the sons of Ephraim *shall be* [B]Elishama the son
of Ammihud, 19 and his army, even their numbered
men, 40,500. 20 Next to him *shall be* the tribe of
Manasseh, and the leader of the sons of Manasseh:
[A]Gamaliel the son of Pedahzur, 21 and his army, even
their numbered men, 32,200. 22 Then *comes* the tribe
of [A]Benjamin, and the leader of the sons of Benjamin: [B]Abidan the son of Gideoni, 23 and his army,
even their numbered men, 35,400. 24 The total of the
numbered men of the camp of Ephraim: 108,100, by
their armies. And [A]they shall set out third.
25 "On the north side *shall be* the standard of the
camp of Dan by their armies, and the leader of the sons
of Dan: [A]Ahiezer the son of Ammishaddai, 26 and his
army, even their numbered men, 62,700. 27 Those who
camp next to him *shall be* the tribe of Asher, and the
leader of the sons of Asher: [A]Pagiel the son of Ochran,
28 and his army, even their numbered men, 41,500.
29 Then *comes* the tribe of [A]Naphtali, and the leader
of the sons of Naphtali: [B]Ahira the son of Enan, 30 and
his army, even their numbered men, 53,400. 31 The
total of the numbered men of the camp of Dan *was*
157,600. [A]They shall set out last by their standards."
32 These are the numbered men of the sons of Israel by their fathers' households; the total of the numbered men of the camps by their armies, [A]603,550.
33 [A]The Levites, however, were not numbered among
the sons of Israel, just as the LORD had commanded
Moses. 34 Thus the sons of Israel did; according to all
that the LORD commanded Moses, so they camped
by their standards, and so they set out, every one
by his family according to his father's household.

LEVITES TO BE PRIESTHOOD

3 [A]Now these are *the records of* the generations
of Aaron and Moses at the time when the LORD

2:12 [A]Num 1:6 2:14 [a]Many mss read *Reuel* [A]Num 1:14; 7:42 2:16 [A]Num 10:18 2:17 [A]Num 1:53 2:18 [A]Gen 48:14-20; Jer 31:9, 18-20 [B]Num 1:10 2:20 [A]Num 1:10 2:22 [A]Ps 68:27 [B]Num 1:11 2:24 [A]Num 10:22 2:25 [A]Num 1:12 2:27 [A]Num 1:13 2:29 [A]Gen 30:8 [B]Num 1:15 2:31 [A]Num 10:25 2:32 [A]Ex 38:26; Num 1:46 2:33 [A]Num 1:47; 26:57-62 3:1 [A]Ex 6:20-27

2:14 Deuel. See marginal note. The letters R and D are similar in Heb. and were easily confused by the scribes who copied the text.

2:17 set out. As the tribes marched, the tabernacle was transported in the middle of the tribes of Israel, 6 in front and 6 behind.

2:32 *See note on 1:46.*

3:1 Aaron and Moses. Because Aaron and his sons are emphasized in this chapter, Aaron

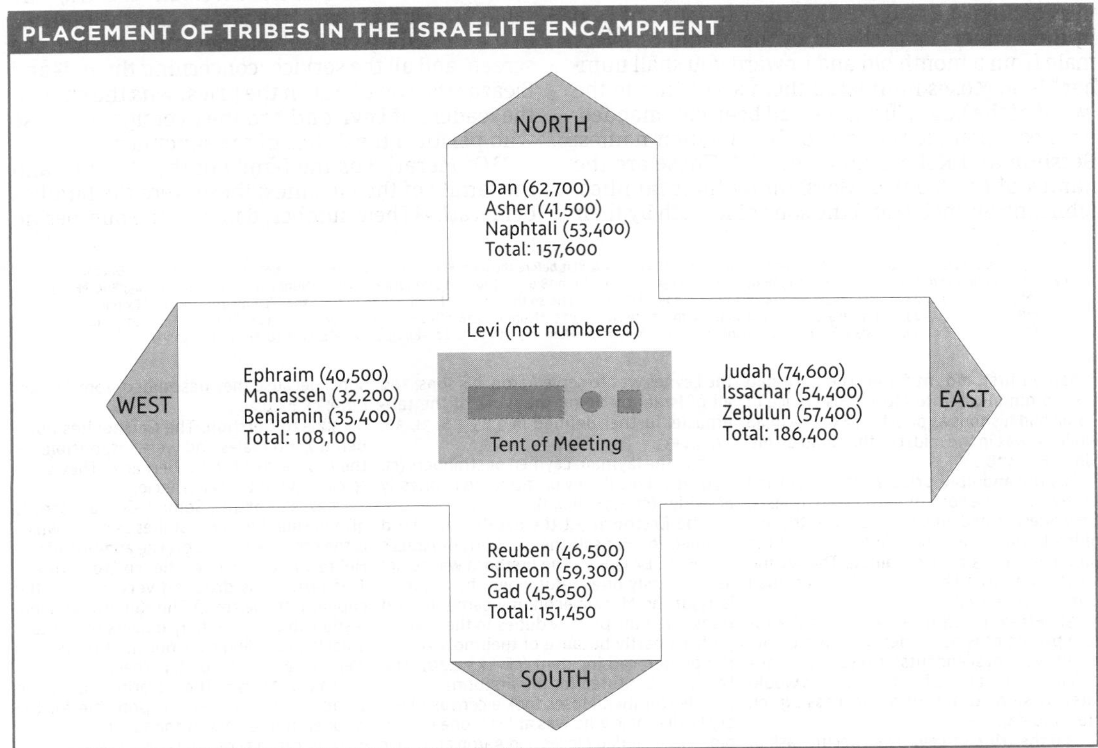

spoke with Moses on Mount Sinai. 2 [A]These then are
the names of the sons of Aaron: Nadab the firstborn,
and Abihu, Eleazar and Ithamar. 3 These are the
names of the sons of Aaron, the [A]anointed priests,
whom he [a]ordained to serve as priests. 4 [A]But Nadab
and Abihu died before the LORD when they offered
strange fire before the LORD in the wilderness of
Sinai; and they had no children. So Eleazar and
Ithamar served as priests [a]in the lifetime of their
father Aaron.
5 Then the LORD spoke to Moses, saying, 6 "[A]Bring
the tribe of Levi near and set them before Aaron the
priest, that they may serve him. 7 They shall perform
the duties for [a]him and for the whole congregation
before the tent of meeting, to do the [A]service of the
tabernacle. 8 They shall also keep all the furnishings
of the tent of meeting, along with the duties of the
sons of Israel, to do the service of the tabernacle.
9 You shall thus [A]give the Levites to Aaron and to
his sons; they are wholly given to him from among
the sons of Israel. 10 So you shall appoint Aaron and
his sons that [A]they may keep their priesthood, but
[B]the [a]layman who comes near shall be put to death."
11 Again the LORD spoke to Moses, saying, 12 "Now,
behold, I [A]have taken the Levites from among the
sons of Israel instead of every [B]firstborn, the first
issue of the womb among the sons of Israel. So the
Levites shall be Mine. 13 For [A]all the firstborn are
Mine; on the day that I struck down all the firstborn
in the land of Egypt, I sanctified to Myself all the
firstborn in Israel, from man to beast. They shall
be Mine; I am the LORD."
14 Then the LORD spoke to Moses [A]in the wilderness of Sinai, saying, 15 "[a,A]Number the sons of Levi
by their fathers' households, by their families; every
male from a month old and upward you shall number." 16 So Moses numbered them according to the
[a]word of the LORD, just as he had been commanded.
17 [A]These then are the sons of Levi by their names:
Gershon and Kohath and Merari. 18 These are the
names of the [A]sons of Gershon by their families:
Libni and Shimei; 19 and the sons of Kohath by their
families: Amram and Izhar, Hebron and Uzziel;
20 and the sons of Merari by their families: Mahli
and Mushi. These are the families of the Levites
according to their fathers' households.
21 Of Gershon *was* the family of the Libnites and
the family of the Shimeites; these *were* the families
of the Gershonites. 22 Their numbered men, in the
numbering of every male from a month old and
upward, *even* their numbered men *were* 7,500. 23 The
families of the Gershonites were to camp behind
the [a]tabernacle westward, 24 and the leader of the
fathers' households of the Gershonites *was* Eliasaph
the son of Lael.

DUTIES OF THE PRIESTS

25 Now [A]the duties of the sons of Gershon in the
tent of meeting *involved* the tabernacle and [B]the
tent, its covering, and [C]the screen for the doorway
of the tent of meeting, 26 and [A]the hangings of the
court, and [B]the screen for the doorway of the court
which is around the tabernacle and the altar, and its
cords, according to all the service [a]concerning them.
27 Of Kohath *was* the family of the Amramites
and the family of the Izharites and the family of
the Hebronites and the family of the Uzzielites;
these were the families of the Kohathites. 28 In the
numbering of every male from a month old and
upward, *there were* 8,600, performing the duties of
the sanctuary. 29 The families of the sons of Kohath
were to camp on the southward side of the tabernacle, 30 and the leader of the fathers' households
of the Kohathite families was [a]Elizaphan the son of
Uzziel. 31 Now [A]their duties *involved* [B]the ark, [C]the
table, [D]the lampstand, [E]the altars, and the utensils
of the sanctuary with which they minister, and the
screen, and all the service [a]concerning them; 32 and
Eleazar the son of Aaron the priest *was* the chief of
the leaders of Levi, *and had* the oversight of those
who perform the duties of the sanctuary.
33 Of Merari *was* the family of the Mahlites and
the family of the Mushites; these *were* the families
of Merari. 34 Their numbered men in the numbering

3:2 [A]Ex 6:23; Num 26:60 3:3 [a]Lit *filled their hand* [A]Ex 28:41 3:4 [a]Lit *before the face* [A]Lev 10:1, 2; Num 26:61 3:6 [A]Num 8:6-22; 18:1-7; Deut 10:8 3:7 [a]Lit *him and the duties of the whole congregation* [A]Num 1:50 3:9 [A]Num 18:6 3:10 [a]Lit *stranger* [A]Ex 29:9 [B]Num 1:51 3:12 [A]Num 3:45; 8:14 [B]Ex 13:2 3:13 [A]Ex 13:2; Lev 27:26; Neh 10:36 3:14 [A]Ex 19:1 3:15 [a]Lit *muster,* and so throughout the ch [A]Num 1:47 3:16 [a]Lit *mouth* 3:17 [A]Ex 6:16-22 3:18 [A]Ex 6:17 3:23 [a]Lit *dwelling place,* and so throughout the ch 3:25 [A]Num 4:24-26 [B]Ex 26:1, 7, 14 [C]Ex 26:36 3:26 [a]Lit *of it* [A]Ex 27:9, 12, 14, 15 [B]Ex 27:16 3:30 [a]In Ex 6:22, *Elzaphan* 3:31 [a]Lit *of it* [A]Num 4:15 [B]Ex 25:10-22 [C]Ex 25:23-28 [D]Ex 25:31-40 [E]Ex 27:1, 2; 30:1-5

is named first. **Mount Sinai.** The Lord had first communicated to Moses His choice of Aaron and his sons as priests in Ex 28:1–29:46 while he was in the midst of the cloud on Mt. Sinai (Ex 24:18).

3:3 the anointed priests. Of all the tribe of Levi, only the sons of Aaron were priests. Only priests could offer the sacrifices; the rest of the Levites aided them in the work of the tabernacle (cf. 3:7–9). **ordained.** The setting apart of Aaron and his sons to the priesthood is recorded in Lv 8:1–9:24.

3:4 Eleazar and Ithamar. All of the future priests of Israel under the Mosaic Covenant were descendants of these two sons of Aaron. Eleazar and his descendants would later be singled out for great blessing (cf. Nu 25:10–13).

3:6 the tribe of Levi. The specific task of the Levites was to serve Aaron, his sons, and all of Israel by doing the work of the tabernacle, further defined in 3:25, 26, 31, 36, 37; 4:4–33.

3:10 the layman. Laymen or strangers (cf. 1:51) would die if they participated in priestly activities (cf. 3:38; 16:40).

3:12 firstborn. At the Exodus, the Lord claimed for Himself the firstborn of Israel's males (cf. Ex 13:1, 2). The firstborn was to act as the family priest. But when the full ministry of the Mosaic economy came in, God transferred the priestly duties to the Levites, perhaps partly because of their holy zeal in the golden calf incident (cf. Ex 32:29). The Levites substituted for the firstborn.

3:15 Number. Moses took a census of every Levite male who was at least one month old. This included Moses and Aaron and their sons, because they descended from Amram (3:19; cf. Ex 6:20).

3:21–26 Gershon. The Gershonites numbered 7,500 males and were responsible for the coverings of the tabernacle. They were to camp W of the tabernacle.

3:27–32 Kohath. Some LXX manuscripts give the number of Kohathites as 8,300, which is the preferred reading. (The addition of one Hebrew letter changes the "six" to a "three." This letter was dropped very early in the copying of the text.) The Kohathites were responsible for the holy objects of the tabernacle (including transporting the ark) and were to camp S of the tabernacle.

3:33–37 Merari. The Merarites numbered 6,200 males and were responsible for the wooden framework of the tabernacle. They were to camp N of the tabernacle.

of every male from a month old and upward, *were* 6,200. 35 The leader of the fathers' households of the families of Merari *was* Zuriel the son of Abihail. They *were* to [A]camp on the northward side of the tabernacle. 36 Now the appointed duties of the sons of Merari *involved* the frames of the tabernacle, its bars, its pillars, its sockets, all its equipment, and the service concerning them, 37 and the pillars around the court with their sockets and their pegs and their cords.

38 Now those who were to [A]camp before the tabernacle eastward, before the tent of meeting toward the sunrise, are Moses and Aaron and his sons, performing the duties of the sanctuary for the obligation of the sons of Israel; but [B]the [a]layman coming near was to be put to death. 39 All the numbered men of the Levites, whom Moses and Aaron numbered at the [a]command of the LORD by their families, every male from a month old and upward, *were* [A]22,000.

FIRSTBORN REDEEMED

40 Then the LORD said to Moses, "[A]Number every firstborn male of the sons of Israel from a month old and upward, and [a]make a list of their names. 41 You [A]shall take the Levites for Me, I am the LORD, instead of all the firstborn among the sons of Israel, and the cattle of the Levites instead of all the firstborn among the cattle of the sons of Israel." 42 So Moses numbered all the firstborn among the sons of Israel, just as the LORD had commanded him; 43 and all the firstborn males by the number of names from a month old and upward, for their numbered men were [A]22,273.

44 Then the LORD spoke to Moses, saying, 45 "[A]Take the Levites instead of all the firstborn among the sons of Israel and the cattle of the Levites. And the Levites shall be Mine; I am the LORD. 46 [A]For the ransom of the 273 of the firstborn of the sons of Israel who are in excess beyond the Levites, 47 you shall take [A]five shekels apiece, per head; you shall take *them* in [B]terms of the shekel of the sanctuary ([C]the shekel is twenty [a]gerahs), 48 and give the money, the ransom of those who are in excess among them, to Aaron and to his sons." 49 So Moses took the ransom money from those who were in excess, beyond those ransomed by the Levites; 50 from the firstborn of the sons of Israel he took the money in terms of the shekel of the sanctuary, 1,365. 51 Then Moses gave the ransom money to Aaron and to his sons, at the [a]command of the LORD, just as the LORD had commanded Moses.

DUTIES OF THE KOHATHITES

4 Then the LORD spoke to Moses and to Aaron, saying, 2 "Take [a]a census of the [b]descendants of Kohath from among the sons of Levi, by their families, by their fathers' households, 3 from [A]thirty years and upward, even to fifty years old, all who enter the service to do the work in the tent of meeting. 4 This is the work of the [a]descendants of Kohath in the tent of meeting, *concerning* the most holy things.

5 "When the camp sets out, Aaron and his sons shall go in and they shall take down [A]the veil of the screen and cover the [B]ark of the testimony with it; 6 and they shall lay a [A]covering of porpoise skin on it, and shall spread over *it* a cloth of pure [a]blue, and shall insert its poles. 7 Over the table of the bread of the Presence they shall also spread a cloth of [a]blue and put on it the dishes and the pans and the sacrificial bowls and the jars for the drink offering, and [A]the continual bread shall be on it. 8 They shall spread over them a cloth of scarlet *material,* and cover the same with a covering of porpoise skin, and they shall insert its poles. 9 Then they shall take a [a]blue cloth and cover the [A]lampstand for the light, [B]along with its lamps and its snuffers, and its [b]trays and all its oil vessels, by which they serve it; 10 and they shall put it and all its utensils in a covering of porpoise skin, and shall put it on the carrying bars. 11 Over the golden altar they shall spread a [a]blue cloth and cover it with a covering of porpoise skin, and shall insert its poles; 12 and they shall take all the utensils of service, with which they serve in the sanctuary, and put them in a [a]blue cloth and cover them with a covering of porpoise skin, and put them on the carrying bars. 13 Then they shall take away the [a]ashes from the [A]altar, and spread a purple cloth over it. 14 They shall also put on it all its utensils by which they serve in connection with it: the firepans, the forks and shovels and the basins, all the utensils of the altar; and they shall spread a cover of porpoise skin over it and insert its poles. 15 When Aaron and his sons have finished covering the holy *objects* and all the furnishings of the sanctuary, when the camp is to set out, after that the sons of Kohath shall come to carry *them,* so that they will not touch the holy *objects* [A]and die. These are the [a]things in the tent of meeting which the sons of Kohath are to carry.

16 "The responsibility of Eleazar the son of Aaron the priest is [A]the oil for the light and the [B]fragrant incense and [C]the continual grain offering and [D]the anointing oil—the responsibility of all the [a]tabernacle

3:35 [A]Num 1:53; 2:25 3:38 [a]Lit *stranger* [A]Num 1:53; 2:3 [B]Num 1:51 3:39 [a]Lit *word* [A]Num 3:43; 4:48; 26:62 3:40 [a]Lit *take the number* [A]Num 3:15 3:41 [A]Num 3:12, 45 3:43 [A]Num 3:39 3:45 [A]Num 3:12 3:46 [A]Ex 13:13, 15; Num 18:15, 16 3:47 [a]I.e. A gerah equals approx one-fortieth oz [A]Lev 27:6; Num 18:16 [B]Ex 30:13 [C]Lev 27:25; Ezek 45:12 3:51 [a]Lit *mouth* 4:2 [a]Lit *the sum* [b]Lit *sons* 4:3 [A]Num 4:23, 30, 35; 8:24; 1 Chr 23:3, 24, 27; Ezra 3:8 4:4 [a]Lit *sons* 4:5 [A]Ex 40:5; Lev 16:2; 2 Chr 3:14; Matt 27:51; Heb 9:3 [B]Ex 25:10-16 4:6 [a]Or *violet* [A]Num 4:25 4:7 [a]Or *violet* [A]Ex 25:30; Lev 24:5-9 4:9 [a]Or *violet* [b]Lit *snuff dishes* [A]Ex 25:31 [B]Ex 25:37, 38 4:11 [a]Or *violet* 4:12 [a]Or *violet* 4:13 [a]Or *fat ashes;* i.e. soaked with fat [A]Ex 27:1-8 4:15 [a]Lit *burden...of the sons* [A]Num 1:51; 4:19, 20; 2 Sam 6:6, 7 4:16 [a]Lit *dwelling place,* and so throughout the ch [A]Lev 24:1-3 [B]Ex 30:34-38 [C]Lev 6:20 [D]Ex 30:22-33

3:38 **Moses ... Aaron.** Moses and Aaron and his sons were given the place of honor on the east of the tabernacle and gave overall supervision to the Levites. Eleazar oversaw the Kohathites (3:32), and Ithamar oversaw the Gershonites and Merarites (4:28, 33).

3:43 **twenty-two thousand two hundred and seventy-three.** This was the total number of Israelite firstborn males arriving in the 12 1/2 months since the Exodus. The Levites took the place of the first 22,000 firstborns, and the rest (273) were redeemed with 1,365 silver shekels (about 170 lbs.).

4:1–49 For a discussion of the tabernacle and contents, *see notes on Ex 25–30.*

4:3 **thirty ... to fifty.** This second census of the Levites determined those who would carry the tabernacle on the coming journey to Canaan. Only those between the ages of 30 and 50 were called by the Lord for this task (*see note on 8:24*).

4:4–16 **Kohath.** The Kohathites carried the furnishings of the tabernacle only after they had been covered by Aaron and his sons. If the Kohathites touched (4:15) or saw (4:20) any of the holy things, they would die.

and of all that is in it, with the sanctuary and its furnishings."
17 Then the LORD spoke to Moses and to Aaron, saying, 18 "Do not let the tribe of the families of the Kohathites be cut off from among the Levites. 19 But do this to them that they may live and [A]not die when they approach the most holy *objects:* Aaron and his sons shall go in and assign each of them to his work and to his load; 20 but [A]they shall not go in to see the holy *objects* even for a moment, or they will die."

DUTIES OF THE GERSHONITES

21 Then the LORD spoke to Moses, saying, 22 "Take [a]a census of the sons of Gershon [b]also, by their fathers' households, by their families; 23 from [A]thirty years and upward to fifty years old, you shall [a]number them; all who enter to perform the service to do the work in the tent of meeting. 24 This is the service of the families of the Gershonites, in serving and in carrying: 25 they shall carry [A]the curtains of the tabernacle and the tent of meeting *with* its covering and [B]the covering of porpoise skin that is on top of it, and the screen for the doorway of the tent of meeting, 26 and [A]the hangings of the court, and the screen for the doorway of the gate of the court which is around the tabernacle and the altar, and their cords and all the equipment for their service; and all that is to be done, [a]they shall perform. 27 All the service of the sons of the Gershonites, in all their loads and in all their work, shall be *performed* at the [a]command of Aaron and his sons; and you shall assign to them as a duty all their loads. 28 This is the service of the families of the sons of the Gershonites in the tent of meeting, and their duties *shall be* [a]under the direction of Ithamar the son of Aaron the priest.

DUTIES OF THE MERARITES

29 "*As for* the sons of Merari, you shall number them by their families, by their fathers' households; 30 from [A]thirty years and upward even to fifty years old, you shall number them, everyone who enters the service to do the work of the tent of meeting. 31 Now this is the duty of their loads, for all their service in the tent of meeting: the boards of the tabernacle and its bars and its pillars and its [a]sockets, 32 and the pillars around the court and their [a]sockets and their pegs and their cords, with all their equipment and with all their service; and you shall assign *each man* by name the items [b]he is to carry. 33 This is the service of the families of the sons of Merari, according to all their service in the tent of meeting, [a]under the direction of Ithamar the son of Aaron the priest."
34 So Moses and Aaron and the leaders of the congregation numbered the sons of the Kohathites by their families and by their fathers' households, 35 from [A]thirty years and upward even to fifty years old, everyone who entered the service for work in the tent of meeting. 36 Their numbered men by their families were 2,750. 37 These are the numbered men of the Kohathite families, everyone who was serving in the tent of meeting, whom Moses and Aaron numbered according to the [a]commandment of the LORD [b]through Moses.
38 The numbered men of the sons of Gershon by their families and by their fathers' households, 39 from thirty years and upward even to fifty years old, everyone who entered the service for work in the tent of meeting. 40 Their numbered men by their families, by their fathers' households, were 2,630. 41 These are the numbered men of the families of the sons of Gershon, everyone who was serving in the tent of meeting, whom Moses and Aaron numbered according to the [a]commandment of the LORD.
42 The numbered men of the families of the sons of Merari by their families, by their fathers' households, 43 from [A]thirty years and upward even to fifty years old, everyone who entered the service for work in the tent of meeting. 44 Their numbered men by their families were 3,200. 45 These are the numbered men of the families of the sons of Merari, whom Moses and Aaron numbered according to the [a]commandment of the LORD [b]through Moses.
46 All the numbered men of the Levites, whom Moses and Aaron and the leaders of Israel numbered, by their families and by their fathers' households, 47 from thirty years and upward even to fifty years old, everyone who could enter to do the work of service and the work of carrying in the tent of meeting. 48 Their numbered men were [A]8,580. 49 According to the [a]commandment of the LORD [b]through Moses, they [A]were numbered, everyone by his serving or carrying; thus *these were* his numbered men, just as the LORD had commanded Moses.

ON DEFILEMENT

5 Then the LORD spoke to Moses, saying, 2 "Command the sons of Israel that they [A]send away from the camp every leper and everyone having a [B]discharge and everyone who is [C]unclean because of a *dead* person. 3 You shall send away both male and female; you shall send them outside the camp so that they will not defile their camp where I dwell

4:19 [A]Num 4:15 4:20 [A]Ex 19:21; 1 Sam 6:19 4:22 [a]Lit *the sum* [b]Lit *also them* 4:23 [a]Lit *muster,* and so throughout the ch [A]Num 4:3; 1 Chr 23:3, 24, 27 4:25 [A]Ex 40:19 [B]Ex 26:14; Num 4:6 4:26 [a]Lit *so they shall serve* [A]Ex 38:9 4:27 [a]Lit *mouth* 4:28 [a]Lit *in the hand* 4:30 [A]Num 4:3; 8:24-26 4:31 [a]Or *bases* 4:32 [a]Or *bases* [b]Lit *of the duty of their loads* 4:33 [a]Lit *in the hand* 4:35 [A]1 Chr 23:24 4:37 [a]Lit *mouth* [b]Lit *by the hand of* 4:41 [a]Lit *mouth* 4:43 [A]Num 8:24-26 4:45 [a]Lit *mouth* [b]Lit *by the hand of* 4:48 [A]Num 3:39 4:49 [a]Lit *mouth* [b]Lit *by the hand of* [A]Num 1:47 5:2 [A]Lev 13:8, 46; Num 12:10, 14, 15 [B]Lev 15:2 [C]Lev 21:1; Num 9:6-10; 19:11

4:21–28 **Gershon.** *See note on 3:21–26.*

4:29–33 **Merari.** *See note on 3:33–37.*

4:34–49 **numbered.** The Kohathites totaled 2,750 (4:36), the Gershonites 2,630 (4:40), the Merarites 3,200 (4:44). All the Levites from 30–50 years old in service added up to 8,580 (4:48).

5:1–4 These verses deal with outward, visible defects.

5:2 **leper.** One having an infectious skin disease (cf. Lv 13:1–14:57). **discharge.** A bodily emission indicative of disease, primarily from the sex organs (cf. Lv 15:1–33). ***dead* person.** Physical contact with a dead body (cf. Lv 21:11). All of these prohibitions had sensible health benefits as well as serving to illustrate the need for moral cleanliness when approaching God.

5:3 **outside the camp ... where I dwell in their midst.** God's holy presence in the cloud in the tabernacle demanded cleanness.

[A]in their midst." 4 The sons of Israel did so and sent
them outside the camp; just as the LORD had spoken
to Moses, thus the sons of Israel did.
5 Then the LORD spoke to Moses, saying, 6 "Speak
to the sons of Israel, '[A]When a man or woman commits any of the sins of mankind, acting unfaithfully
against the LORD, and that person is guilty, 7 then
[a]he shall [A]confess [b]his sins which [c]he has committed,
and he [B]shall make restitution in full for his wrong
and add to it one-fifth of it, and give *it* to him whom
he has wronged. 8 But if the man has no [a]relative
to whom restitution may be made for the wrong,
the restitution which is made for the wrong *must
go* to the LORD for the priest, besides the ram of
atonement, by which atonement is made for him.
9 [A]Also every [a]contribution pertaining to all the
holy *gifts* of the sons of Israel, which they offer to
the priest, shall be his. 10 So every man's holy *gifts*
shall be his; whatever any man gives to the priest,
it [A]becomes his.' "

THE ADULTERY TEST

11 Then the LORD spoke to Moses, saying, 12 "Speak
to the sons of Israel and say to them, 'If any man's
wife [A]goes astray and is unfaithful to him, 13 and a
man has [A]intercourse with her and it is hidden from
the eyes of her husband and she is [a]undetected,
although she has defiled herself, and there is no
witness against her and she has not been caught
in the act, 14 [a]if a spirit of [A]jealousy comes over him
and he is jealous of his wife when she has defiled
herself, or if a spirit of jealousy comes over him
and he is jealous of his wife when she has not defiled herself, 15 the man shall then bring his wife
to the priest, and shall bring *as* [a]an offering for
her one-tenth of an [b]ephah of barley meal; he shall
not pour oil on it nor put frankincense on it, for it
is a grain offering of jealousy, a grain offering of
memorial, [A]a reminder of iniquity.
16 'Then the priest shall bring her near and have
her stand before the LORD, 17 and the priest shall take
holy water in an earthenware vessel; and [a]he shall
take some of the dust that is on the floor of the tabernacle and put *it* into the water. 18 The priest shall
then have the woman stand before the LORD and let
the hair of the woman's head go loose, and place the
grain offering of memorial [a]in her hands, which is
the grain offering of jealousy, and in the hand of the
priest is to be the water of bitterness that brings a
curse. 19 The priest shall have her take an oath and
shall say to the woman, "If no man has lain with you
and if you have not [A]gone astray into uncleanness,
being under *the authority of* your husband, be [a]im-
mune to this water of bitterness that brings a curse;
20 if you, however, have [A]gone astray, *being* under *the
authority of* your husband, and if you have defiled
yourself and a man other than your husband has
had intercourse with you" 21 (then the priest shall
have the woman [A]swear with the oath of the curse,
and the priest shall say to the woman), "the LORD
make you a curse and an oath among your people
by the LORD'S making your thigh [a]waste away and
your abdomen swell; 22 and this water that brings
a curse shall go into your [a]stomach, and make your
abdomen swell and your thigh [b]waste away." And
the woman [A]shall say, "Amen. Amen."
23 'The priest shall then write these curses on a
scroll, and he shall [a]wash them off into the water of
bitterness. 24 Then he shall make the woman drink
the water of bitterness that brings a curse, so that
the water which brings a curse will go into her [a]and
cause bitterness. 25 The priest shall take the grain
offering of jealousy from the woman's hand, and he
shall wave the grain offering before the LORD and
bring it to the altar; 26 and [A]the priest shall take a
handful of the grain offering as its memorial offering
and offer *it* up in smoke on the altar, and afterward
he shall make the woman drink the water. 27 When
he has made her drink the water, then it shall come
about, if she has defiled herself and has been unfaithful to her husband, that the water which brings
a curse will go into her [a]and *cause* bitterness, and
her abdomen will swell and her thigh will [b]waste
away, and the woman will become [A]a curse among

5:3 [A]Lev 26:12; Num 35:34 5:6 [A]Lev 5:14-6:7 5:7 [a]Lit *they* [b]Lit *their* [c]Lit *they have* [A]Lev 5:5; 26:40, 41; Josh 7:19 [B]Lev 6:4, 5 5:8 [a]Lit *redeemer* 5:9 [a]Lit *heave offering* [A]Lev 7:32, 34; 10:14, 15 5:10 [A]Lev 10:13 5:12 [A]Num 5:19-21, 29 5:13 [a]Lit *concealed* [A]Lev 18:20; 20:10 5:14 [a]Lit *and* [A]Prov 6:34; Song 8:6 5:15 [a]Lit *her* [b]I.e. Approx one bu [A]1 Kin 17:18; Ezek 29:16 5:17 [a]Lit *the priest* 5:18 [a]Lit *on her palms* 5:19 [a]Lit *free from* [A]Num 5:12 5:20 [A]Num 5:12 5:21 [a]Lit *fall* [A]Josh 6:26; 1 Sam 14:24; Neh 10:29 5:22 [a]Or *inward parts* [b]Lit *fall* [A]Deut 27:15 5:23 [a]Lit *wipe* 5:24 [a]Lit *to* 5:26 [A]Lev 2:2, 9 5:27 [a]Lit *to* [b]Lit *fall* [A]Jer 29:18; 42:18; 44:12

Therefore, all the unclean were barred from the encampment of Israel.

5:5–10 These verses deal with personal sins, which are not as outwardly visible as the uncleanness of 5:1–4.

5:6 **against the LORD.** A sin committed against God's people was considered a sin committed against God Himself. There was a need for confession and restitution in addition to the trespass offering (cf. Lv 5:14–6:7).

5:8 **no relative.** A supplement to Lv 6:1–7. If the injured party had died and there was no family member to receive the restitution called for in v. 7, it was to go to the priest as the Lord's representative.

5:11–31 These verses deal with the most intimate of human relationships and the most secret of sins. Adultery was to be determined and dealt with to maintain the purity of the camp. To accomplish that purity, God called for a very elaborate and public trial. If adultery was proven, it was punished with death, and this ceremony made guilt or innocence very apparent. It was not a trial with normal judicial process, since such sins are secret and lack witnesses, but it was effective. The ceremony was designed to be so terrifying and convicting that the very tendencies of human nature would make it clear if the person was guilty.

5:14 **a spirit of jealousy.** A mood of suspicion came over the husband that his wife had defiled herself with another man. The accuracy of the suspicion was determined to be right or wrong.

5:15 **a reminder of iniquity.** The purpose of the husband's offering was to bring the secret iniquity (if it was present) to light. How this was done is explained in 5:18, 25–26.

5:18 **before the LORD.** The woman was brought to a priest at the tabernacle. There she was in the presence of the Lord, who knew her guilt or innocence. ***hair ... go loose.*** Lit. "unbind the head." In Lv 10:6; 13:45; 21:10, this phrase signifies mourning. This seems to signify the expectation of judgment and consequent mourning if the woman was proven to be guilty. **water of bitterness.** This water included dust from the tabernacle floor (5:17) and the ink used to write the curses (5:23). The woman was to drink the water (5:26). If the woman was guilty, the water would make her life bitter by carrying out the curse of making her thigh rot and her belly swell (5:21, 27). The public, frightening nature of this test could not fail to make guilt or innocence appear when the conscience was so assaulted.

her people. 28 But if the woman has not defiled herself and is clean, she will then be free and conceive [a]children.

29 'This is the law of jealousy: when a wife, *being* under *the authority of* her husband, [A]goes astray and defiles herself, 30 or when a spirit of jealousy comes over a man and he is jealous of his wife, he shall then make the woman stand before the LORD, and the priest shall apply all this law to her. 31 Moreover, the man will be free from [a]guilt, but that woman shall [A]bear her [a]guilt.' "

LAW OF THE NAZIRITES

6 Again the LORD spoke to Moses, saying, 2 "Speak to the sons of Israel and say to them, 'When a man or woman makes a [a]special vow, the vow of [A]a [b]Nazirite, to [c]dedicate himself to the LORD, 3 he shall [A]abstain from wine and strong drink; he shall drink no vinegar, whether made from wine or strong drink, nor shall he drink any grape juice nor eat fresh or dried grapes. 4 All the days of his [a]separation he shall not eat anything that is produced by the grape vine, from *the* seeds even to *the* skin.

5 'All the days of his vow of separation [A]no razor shall pass over his head. He shall be holy until the days are fulfilled for which he separated himself to the LORD; he shall let the locks of hair on his head grow long.

6 '[A]All the days of his separation to the LORD he shall not go near to a dead person. 7 He [A]shall not make himself unclean for his father or for his mother, for his brother or for his sister, when they die, because his separation to God is on his head. 8 All the days of his separation he is holy to the LORD.

9 'But if a man dies very suddenly beside him and he defiles his dedicated head *of hair,* then [A]he shall shave his head on the day when he becomes clean; [B]he shall shave it on the seventh day. 10 Then on the eighth day he shall bring [A]two turtledoves or two young pigeons to the priest, to the doorway of the tent of meeting. 11 The priest shall offer [A]one for a sin offering and *the* other for a burnt offering, and make atonement for him [a]concerning his sin because of the *dead* person. And that same day he shall consecrate his head, 12 and shall dedicate to the LORD his days [a]as a [b]Nazirite, and shall bring a male lamb a year old for a guilt offering; but the former days will be void because his separation was defiled.

13 'Now this is the law of the Nazirite [A]when the days of his separation are fulfilled, he shall bring [a]the offering to the doorway of the tent of meeting. 14 He shall present his offering to the LORD: one male lamb a year old without defect for a burnt offering and one [A]ewe-lamb a year old without defect for a sin offering and one ram without defect for a peace offering, 15 and a basket of [A]unleavened cakes of fine flour mixed with oil and unleavened wafers spread with oil, along with [B]their grain offering and their drink offering. 16 Then the priest shall present *them* before the LORD and shall offer his sin offering and his burnt offering. 17 He shall also offer the ram for a sacrifice of peace offerings to the LORD, together with the basket of unleavened cakes; the priest shall likewise offer its grain offering and its drink offering. 18 [A]The Nazirite shall then shave his dedicated head *of hair* at the doorway of the tent of meeting, and take the dedicated hair of his head and put *it* on the fire which is under the sacrifice of peace offerings. 19 [A]The priest shall take the ram's shoulder *when it has been* boiled, and one unleavened cake out of the basket and one unleavened wafer, and shall put *them* on the [a]hands of the Nazirite after he has shaved his [b]dedicated *hair.* 20 Then the priest shall wave them for a wave offering before the LORD. It is holy for the priest, together with the breast offered by waving and the thigh offered by lifting up; and [A]afterward the Nazirite may drink wine.'

21 "This is the law of the Nazirite who vows his offering to the LORD according to his separation, in addition to what *else* [a]he can afford; according to his vow which he takes, so he shall do according to the law of his separation."

AARON'S BENEDICTION

22 Then the LORD spoke to Moses, saying, 23 "Speak to Aaron and to his sons, saying, 'Thus [A]you shall bless the sons of Israel. You shall say to them:

5:28 [a]Lit *seed* 5:29 [A]Num 5:12 5:31 [a]Or *iniquity* [A]Lev 20:17 6:2 [a]Or *difficult* [b]I.e. one separated [c]Or *live as a Nazirite* [A]Judg 13:5; 16:17; Amos 2:11, 12 6:3 [A]Luke 1:15 6:4 [a]Or *living as a Nazirite,* and so through v 21 6:5 [A]1 Sam 1:11 6:6 [A]Lev 21:1-3; Num 19:11-22 6:7 [A]Num 9:6 6:9 [A]Lev 14:8, 9 [B]Num 6:18 6:10 [A]Lev 5:7; 14:22 6:11 [a]Lit *because of that which he sinned* [A]Lev 5:7 6:12 [a]Or *of dedication* [b]I.e. one separated 6:13 [a]Lit *it* [A]Acts 21:26 6:14 [A]Lev 14:10; Num 15:27 6:15 [A]Ex 29:2; Lev 2:4 [B]Num 15:1-7 6:18 [A]Num 6:9; Acts 21:23, 24 6:19 [a]Lit *palms* [b]Or *separated* [A]Lev 7:28-34 6:20 [A]Eccl 9:7 6:21 [a]Lit *his hand can reach* 6:23 [A]1 Chr 23:13

5:28 conceive children. The penalty for the guilty wife was obvious, since the death penalty was called for. In contrast, the innocent wife was assured she would live to bring forth children.

6:1–21 Whereas 5:1–31 dealt with the cleansing of the camp by dealing with the unclean and sinful, 6:1–21 showed how consecration to the Lord was possible for every Israelite. Although only the family of Aaron could be priests, any man or woman could be "priestly" (i.e., dedicated to God's service) for a time (from a month to a lifetime) by means of the vow of a Nazirite. Such a vow was made by people unusually devout toward God and dedicated to His service.

6:2 the vow of a Nazirite. The word "vow" here is related to the word "wonder," which signifies something out of the ordinary. "Nazirite" transliterates a Heb. term meaning "dedication by separation." The Nazirite separated himself to the Lord by separating himself from 1) grape products (6:3, 4), 2) the cutting of one's hair (6:5), and 3) contact with a dead body (6:6, 7). The High Priest was also forbidden 1) to drink wine while serving in the tabernacle (Lv 10:9), and 2) to touch dead bodies (Lv 21:11). Further, both the High Priest's crown (Ex 29:6; 39:30; Lv 8:9) and the Nazirite's head (6:9, 18) are referred to by the same Heb. word. The Nazirite's hair was like the High Priest's crown. Like the High Priest, the Nazirite was holy to the Lord (6:8; cf: Ex 28:36) all the days (6:4, 5, 6, 8) of his vow.

6:9 dies . . . suddenly. If the Nazirite inadvertently came in contact with a dead body, he was to shave his head, on the eighth day bring the prescribed offerings, and begin the days of his vow again. This is a good illustration of the fact that sin can become mingled with the best intentions, and is not always premeditated. When sin is mixed with the holiest actions, it calls for a renewed cleansing.

6:13 fulfilled. At the end of the determined time, the Nazirite was released from his vow through offerings and the shaving of his head. His hair was to be brought to the sanctuary at the time of those offerings (cf. Ac 18:18).

6:22–27 Obedient Israel, organized before and consecrated to the Lord, was the recipient of God's blessing (i.e., His favor) pronounced by the priests.

24 The LORD [A]bless you, and [B]keep you;

25 The LORD [A]make His face shine on you,
And [B]be gracious to you;

26 The LORD [A]lift up His countenance on you,
And [B]give you peace.'

27 So they shall [a,A]invoke My name on the sons of
Israel, and I *then* will bless them."

OFFERINGS OF THE LEADERS

7 Now on [A]the day that Moses had finished setting
up the tabernacle, he [B]anointed it and consecrated it with all its furnishings and the altar and
all its utensils; he anointed them and consecrated
them also. 2 Then [A]the leaders of Israel, the heads of
their fathers' households, [B]made an offering (they
were the leaders of the tribes; they were the ones
who [a]were over the [b]numbered men). 3 When they
brought their offering before the LORD, six [A]covered
carts and twelve oxen, a cart for *every* two of the
leaders and an ox for each one, then they presented
them before the tabernacle. 4 Then the LORD spoke
to Moses, saying, 5 "Accept *these things* from them,
that they may be [a]used in the service of the tent of
meeting, and you shall give them to the Levites, *to*
each man according to his service." 6 So Moses took
the carts and the oxen and gave them to the Levites. 7 Two carts and four oxen he gave to the sons
of Gershon, according to [A]their service, 8 and four
carts and eight oxen he gave to the sons of Merari,
according to [A]their service, under the [a]direction of
Ithamar the son of Aaron the priest. 9 But he did not
give *any* to the sons of Kohath because theirs *was*
[A]the service of the holy *objects, which* they carried
on the shoulder.
10 The leaders offered the dedication *offering*
[a]for the altar [b]when [A]it was anointed, so the leaders
offered their offering before the altar. 11 Then the
LORD said to Moses, "Let them present their offering,
one leader each day, for the dedication of the altar."
12 Now the one who presented his offering on
the first day was Nahshon the son of Amminadab,
of the tribe of Judah; 13 and his offering *was* one
silver [a,A]dish whose weight *was* one hundred and
thirty *shekels,* one silver bowl of seventy shekels,
[B]according to [b]the shekel of the sanctuary, both of
them full of fine flour mixed with oil for a grain
offering; 14 one gold pan of ten *shekels,* full of incense; 15 one [a]bull, one ram, one male lamb one
year old, for a burnt offering; 16 [A]one male goat for
a sin offering; 17 and for the sacrifice of peace offerings, two oxen, five rams, five male goats, five
male lambs one year old. This *was* the offering of
[A]Nahshon the son of Amminadab.
18 On the second day Nethanel the son of Zuar,
leader of Issachar, presented *an offering;* 19 he presented as his offering one silver dish whose weight
was one hundred and thirty *shekels,* one silver bowl
of seventy shekels, according to the shekel of the
sanctuary, both of them full of fine flour mixed
with oil for a grain offering; 20 one gold pan of ten
shekels, full of incense; 21 one bull, one ram, one
male lamb one year old, for a burnt offering; 22 one
male goat for a sin offering; 23 and for the sacrifice
of [A]peace offerings, two oxen, five rams, five male
goats, five male lambs one year old. This *was* the
offering of Nethanel the son of Zuar.
24 On the third day *it was* Eliab the son of Helon,
leader of the sons of Zebulun; 25 his offering *was*
one silver dish whose weight *was* one hundred and
thirty *shekels,* one silver bowl of seventy shekels,
according to the shekel of the sanctuary, both of
them full of fine flour mixed with oil for a grain
offering; 26 one gold pan of ten *shekels,* full of incense; 27 one young bull, one ram, one [A]male lamb
one year old, for a burnt offering; 28 one male goat
for a sin offering; 29 and for the sacrifice of peace
offerings, two oxen, five rams, five male goats, five
male lambs one year old. This *was* the offering of
Eliab the son of Helon.
30 On the fourth day *it was* Elizur the son of Shedeur, leader of the sons of Reuben; 31 his offering
was one silver dish whose weight *was* one hundred and thirty *shekels,* one silver bowl of seventy
shekels, according to the shekel of the sanctuary,
both of them full of fine flour mixed with oil for a
grain offering; 32 one gold pan of ten *shekels,* full
of incense; 33 one bull, one ram, one [A]male lamb
one year old, for a burnt offering; 34 one male goat
for a sin offering; 35 and for the sacrifice of peace

6:24 [A]Deut 28:3-6; Ps 28:9 [B]1 Sam 2:9; Ps 17:8 6:25 [A]Ps 80:3, 7, 19 [B]Ps 86:16 6:26 [A]Ps 4:6; 44:3 [B]Ps 29:11; 37:37 6:27 [a]Lit *put* [A]2 Sam 7:23; 2 Chr 7:14 7:1 [A]Ex 40:17 [B]Ex 40:9-11; Num 7:10, 84, 88 7:2 [a]Lit *stood* [b]Lit *mustered* [A]Num 1:5-16 [B]2 Chr 35:8 7:3 [A]Is 66:20 7:5 [a]Lit *for serving* 7:7 [A]Num 4:24-26 7:8 [a]Lit *hand* [A]Num 4:31, 32 7:9 [A]Num 4:5-15 7:10 [a]Lit *of* [b]Lit *in the day that* [A]Num 7:1; 2 Chr 7:9 7:13 [a]Or *platter,* and so through v 85 [b]I.e. Approx one-half oz, and so through v 86 [A]Ex 25:29; 37:16 [B]Num 3:47 7:15 [a]Or *bull of the herd,* and so through v 81 7:16 [A]Lev 4:23 7:17 [A]Luke 3:32, 33 7:23 [A]Lev 7:11-13 7:27 [A]Is 53:7; John 1:29; 1 Pet 1:19 7:33 [A]Heb 9:28

6:24 bless. The Lord's blessing was described as His face (i.e., His presence) shining on His people (v. 25) and looking at them (v. 26). God shone forth in benevolence on Israel and looked on them for good. **keep.** The results of the Lord's blessing were His preservation of Israel ("keep"), His kindness toward her ("be gracious," v. 25), and her total well-being ("peace," v. 26).

6:27 invoke My name. The name of the Lord represented His person and character. The priests were to call for God to dwell among His people and meet all their needs.

7:1–10:36 These 4 chapters show how the Lord spoke to Moses (7:89) and led Israel (9:22; 10:11, 12) from the tabernacle. As Israel was properly oriented toward the Lord and obeyed His word, God gave them victory over their enemies (10:35).

7:1–89 As the people of Israel had been generous in giving to the construction of the tabernacle (see Ex 35:4–29), they showed the same generosity in its dedication.

7:1 finished setting up the tabernacle. According to Ex 40:17, the tabernacle was raised up on the first day of the first month of the second year. Thus the tabernacle was set up 11 1/2 months after the Exodus from Egypt.

7:2 the leaders of Israel. The leaders of the 12 tribes were those named in 1:5–15 who oversaw the numbering of the people. The order of the presentation by tribe of their offerings to the tabernacle was the same as the order of march given in 2:3–32.

7:6 the carts and the oxen. These were to be used in the transportation of the tabernacle. According to v. 9, the sons of Kohath did not receive a cart because they were to carry the holy things of the tabernacle on their shoulders.

7:12 the first day. I.e., the first day of the first month. The gifts of the leaders to the tabernacle were given over 12 successive days.

offerings, two oxen, five rams, five male goats, five male lambs one year old. This *was* the offering of Elizur the son of Shedeur.

36 On the fifth day *it was* Shelumiel the son of Zurishaddai, leader of the children of Simeon; 37 his offering *was* one silver dish whose weight *was* one hundred and thirty *shekels,* one silver bowl of seventy shekels, according to the shekel of the sanctuary, both of them full of fine flour mixed with oil for a grain offering; 38 one gold pan of ten *shekels,* full of incense; 39 one bull, one ram, one male lamb one year old, for a burnt offering; 40 one male goat for a sin offering; 41 and for the sacrifice of peace offerings, two oxen, five rams, five male goats, five male lambs one year old. This *was* the offering of Shelumiel the son of Zurishaddai.

42 On the sixth day *it was* [A]Eliasaph the son of Deuel, leader of the sons of Gad; 43 his offering *was* one silver dish whose weight *was* one hundred and thirty *shekels,* one silver bowl of seventy shekels, according to the shekel of the sanctuary, both of them full of [A]fine flour mixed with oil for a grain offering; 44 one gold pan of ten *shekels,* full of incense; 45 [A]one bull, one ram, one male lamb one year old, for a burnt offering; 46 one male goat for a sin offering; 47 and for the sacrifice of peace offerings, two oxen, five rams, five male goats, five male lambs one year old. This *was* the offering of Eliasaph the son of Deuel.

48 On the seventh day *it was* [A]Elishama the son of Ammihud, leader of the sons of Ephraim; 49 his offering *was* one silver dish whose weight *was* one hundred and thirty *shekels,* one silver bowl of seventy shekels, according to the shekel of the sanctuary, both of them full of fine flour mixed with oil for a grain offering; 50 one gold pan of ten *shekels,* full of [A]incense; 51 [A]one bull, one ram, one male lamb one year old, for a burnt offering; 52 one male goat for a sin offering; 53 and for the sacrifice of peace offerings, two oxen, five rams, five male goats, five male lambs one year old. This *was* the offering of Elishama the son of Ammihud.

54 On the eighth day *it was* [A]Gamaliel the son of Pedahzur, leader of the sons of Manasseh; 55 his offering *was* one silver dish whose weight *was* one hundred and thirty *shekels,* one silver bowl of seventy shekels, according to the shekel of the sanctuary, both of them full of fine flour mixed with oil for a grain offering; 56 one gold pan of ten *shekels,* full of [A]incense; 57 one bull, one ram, one [A]male lamb one year old, for a burnt offering; 58 one male goat for a sin offering; 59 and for the [A]sacrifice of peace offerings, two oxen, five rams, five male goats, five male lambs one year old. This *was* the offering of Gamaliel the son of Pedahzur.

60 On the ninth day *it was* [A]Abidan the son of Gideoni, leader of the sons of Benjamin; 61 his offering *was* one silver dish whose weight *was* one hundred and thirty *shekels,* one silver bowl of seventy shekels, according to the shekel of the sanctuary, both of them full of fine flour mixed with oil for a grain offering; 62 one gold pan of ten *shekels,* full of [A]incense; 63 one bull, one ram, one male lamb one year old, for a burnt offering; 64 one male goat for a [A]sin offering; 65 and for the sacrifice of [A]peace offerings, two oxen, five rams, five male goats, five male lambs one year old. This *was* the offering of Abidan the son of Gideoni.

66 On the tenth day *it was* [A]Ahiezer the son of Ammishaddai, leader of the sons of Dan; 67 his offering *was* one silver dish whose weight *was* one hundred and thirty *shekels,* one silver bowl of seventy shekels, according to the [A]shekel of the sanctuary, both of them full of fine flour mixed with oil for a grain offering; 68 one gold pan of ten *shekels,* full of [A]incense; 69 one bull, one ram, one male lamb one year old, for a burnt offering; 70 one male goat for a sin offering; 71 and for the sacrifice of peace offerings, two oxen, five rams, five male goats, five male lambs one year old. This *was* the offering of Ahiezer the son of Ammishaddai.

72 On the eleventh day *it was* [A]Pagiel the son of Ochran, leader of the sons of Asher; 73 his offering *was* one silver dish whose weight *was* one hundred and thirty *shekels,* one silver bowl of seventy shekels, according to the shekel of the sanctuary, both of them full of fine flour mixed with oil for a grain offering; 74 one gold pan of ten *shekels,* full of [A]incense; 75 one bull, one ram, one male lamb one year old, for a burnt offering; 76 one male goat for a sin offering; 77 and for the sacrifice of peace offerings, two oxen, five rams, five male goats, five male lambs one year old. This *was* the offering of Pagiel the son of Ochran.

78 On the twelfth day *it was* [A]Ahira the son of Enan, leader of the sons of Naphtali; 79 his offering *was* one [A]silver dish whose weight *was* one hundred and thirty *shekels,* one silver bowl of seventy shekels, according to the shekel of the sanctuary, both of them full of fine flour mixed with oil for a grain offering; 80 one gold pan of ten *shekels,* full of incense; 81 one bull, one ram, one male lamb one year old, for a burnt offering; 82 one male goat for a sin offering; 83 and for the sacrifice of peace offerings, two oxen, five rams, five male goats, five male lambs one year old. This *was* the offering of Ahira the son of Enan.

84 This *was* [A]the dedication *offering* [a]for the altar from the leaders of Israel [b]when [B]it was anointed: twelve silver dishes, twelve silver bowls, twelve gold pans, 85 each silver dish *weighing* one hundred and thirty *shekels* and each bowl seventy; all the silver of the utensils *was* 2,400 *shekels,* according to the shekel of the sanctuary; 86 the twelve gold pans, full of incense, *weighing* ten *shekels* apiece, according to the [A]shekel of the sanctuary, all the gold of the pans

7:42 [A]Num 1:14; 10:20 7:43 [A]Lev 2:5; 14:10 7:45 [A]Ps 50:8-14; Is 1:11 7:48 [A]Num 1:10; 2:18; 1 Chr 7:26 7:50 [A]Deut 33:10; Ezek 8:11; Luke 1:10 7:51 [A]Mic 6:6-8 7:54 [A]Num 2:20 7:56 [A]Ex 30:7 7:57 [A]Ex 12:5; Acts 8:32; Rev 5:6 7:59 [A]Lev 3:1-17 7:60 [A]Num 1:11; 2:22 7:62 [A]Rev 5:8; 8:3, 4 7:64 [A]2 Cor 5:21 7:65 [A]Col 1:20 7:66 [A]Num 1:12; 2:25 7:67 [A]Ex 30:13; Lev 27:25 7:68 [A]Ps 141:2 7:72 [A]Num 1:13; 2:27 7:74 [A]Mal 1:11 7:78 [A]Num 1:15; 2:29 7:79 [A]Ezra 1:9, 10; Dan 5:2 7:84 [a]Lit *of* [b]Lit *in the day that* [A]Num 7:10 [B]Num 7:1 7:86 [A]Ex 30:13

7:84–88 Each of the leaders gave the same offerings to the tabernacle. Here the total of all the gifts was given.

120 *shekels;* 87 all the oxen for the burnt offering twelve bulls, *all* the rams twelve, the male lambs one year old with their grain offering twelve, and the male goats for a sin offering twelve; 88 and all the oxen for the sacrifice of peace offerings 24 bulls, *all* the rams 60, the male goats 60, the male lambs one year old 60. [A]This *was* the dedication *offering* for the altar after it was anointed.

89 Now when [A]Moses went into the tent of meeting to speak with Him, he heard the voice speaking to him from above [B]the [a]mercy seat that was on the ark of the testimony, from [C]between the two cherubim, so He spoke to him.

THE SEVEN LAMPS

8 Then the LORD spoke to Moses, saying, 2 "Speak to Aaron and say to him, 'When you [a]mount the lamps, the seven lamps will [A]give light in the front of the lampstand.' " 3 Aaron therefore did so; he [a]mounted its lamps at the front of the lampstand, just as the LORD had commanded Moses. 4 [A]Now this was the workmanship of the lampstand, hammered work of gold; from its base to its flowers it was hammered work; [B]according to the pattern which the LORD had shown Moses, so he made the lampstand.

CLEANSING THE LEVITES

5 Again the LORD spoke to Moses, saying, 6 "Take the Levites from among the sons of Israel and [A]cleanse them. 7 Thus you shall do to them, for their [a]cleansing: *sprinkle* [b]purifying [A]water on them, and let them [c,B]use a razor over their whole [d]body and [C]wash their clothes, and they will be clean. 8 Then let them take a [a]bull with [A]its grain offering, fine flour mixed with oil; and a second [a]bull you shall take for a sin offering. 9 So [A]you shall present the Levites before the tent of meeting. [B]You shall also assemble the whole congregation of the sons of Israel, 10 and present the Levites before the LORD; and the sons of Israel [A]shall lay their hands on the Levites. 11 Aaron then shall [a]present the Levites before the LORD as a [A]wave offering from the sons of Israel, that they may [b]qualify to perform the service of the LORD. 12 Now [A]the Levites shall lay their hands on the heads of the bulls; then offer the one for a sin offering and the other for a burnt offering to the LORD, to make atonement for the Levites. 13 You shall have the Levites stand before Aaron and before his sons so as to present them as a wave offering to the LORD.

14 "Thus you shall separate the Levites from among the sons of Israel, and [A]the Levites shall be Mine. 15 Then after that the Levites may go in to serve the tent of meeting. But you shall cleanse them and [A]present them as a wave offering; 16 for they are [A]wholly given to Me from among the sons of Israel. I have taken them for Myself [B]instead of every first issue of the womb, the firstborn of all the sons of Israel. 17 For [A]every firstborn among the sons of Israel is Mine, among the men and among the animals; on the day that I struck down all the firstborn in the land of Egypt I sanctified them for Myself. 18 But I have taken the Levites instead of every firstborn among the sons of Israel. 19 [A]I have given the Levites as [a]a gift to Aaron and to his sons from among the sons of Israel, to perform the service of the sons of Israel at the tent of meeting and to make atonement on behalf of the sons of Israel, so that there will be no [B]plague among the sons of Israel by [b]their coming near to the sanctuary."

20 Thus did Moses and Aaron and all the congregation of the sons of Israel to the Levites; according to all that the LORD had commanded Moses concerning the Levites, so the sons of Israel did to them. 21 [A]The Levites, too, purified themselves from sin and washed their clothes; and Aaron presented them as a wave offering before the LORD. Aaron also made atonement for them to cleanse them. 22 Then after that the Levites went in to perform their service in the tent of meeting before Aaron and before his sons; just as the LORD had commanded Moses concerning the Levites, so they did to them.

RETIREMENT

23 Now the LORD spoke to Moses, saying, 24 "This is what *applies* to the Levites: from [A]twenty-five years old and upward [a]they shall enter to perform service in the work of the tent of meeting. 25 But at the age of fifty years they shall [a]retire from service

7:88 [A]Num 7:1, 10 7:89 [a]Lit *propitiatory* [A]Ex 40:34, 35 [B]Ex 25:21, 22 [C]Ps 80:1; 99:1 8:2 [a]Lit *raise up* [A]Ex 25:37; Lev 24:2, 4 8:3 [a]Lit *raised up* 8:4 [A]Ex 25:31-40 [B]Ex 25:9, 31-40; 26:30; 37:17-24 8:6 [A]Is 52:11 8:7 [a]Lit *this their cleansing* [b]Lit *water of sin* [c]Lit *cause to pass* [d]Lit *flesh* [A]Num 19:9, 13, 20 [B]Lev 14:8, 9 [C]Num 8:21 8:8 [a]Or *bull of the herd* [A]Lev 2:1; Num 15:8-10 8:9 [A]Ex 29:4; 40:12 [B]Lev 8:3 8:10 [A]Lev 1:4 8:11 [a]Lit *wave,* and so throughout the ch [b]Lit *be able* [A]Lev 7:30, 34 8:12 [A]Ex 29:10 8:14 [A]Num 3:12; 16:9 8:15 [A]Ex 29:24 8:16 [A]Num 3:9 [B]Ex 13:2; Num 3:12, 45 8:17 [A]Ex 13:2, 12, 13, 15; Luke 2:23 8:19 [a]Lit *given ones* [b]Lit *the sons of Israel's* [A]Num 3:9 [B]Num 1:53; 16:46 8:21 [A]Num 8:7 8:24 [a]Lit *he* [A]Num 4:3; 1 Chr 23:3, 24, 27 8:25 [a]Lit *return*

7:89 He spoke to him. With the completion of the tabernacle, the Lord communicated His Word to Moses from the mercy seat in the Holy of Holies (see Lv 1:1; Nu 1:1).

8:1–4 Exodus 25:32–40 recorded the instructions for the making of the golden lampstand and Ex 37:17–24 reported its completion. Here, as a part of the dedication of the tabernacle, the 7 lamps of the lampstand were lit.

8:5–26 This ceremony set apart the Levites to the service of the Lord. Their dedication was a feature of the overall description of the dedication of the tabernacle.

8:6 cleanse. In contrast to the priests who were consecrated (Ex 29:1, 9), the Levites were cleansed. According to v. 7, this cleansing was accomplished by first, the sprinkling of water; second, the shaving of the body; and third, the washing of the clothes. This cleansing of the Levites made them pure so they might come into contact with the holy objects of the tabernacle. Similar requirements were given for the cleansing of the leper in Lv 14:8, 9.

8:9 the whole congregation. Since the Levites took the place of the firstborn, who had acted as family priests among the people of Israel (see vv. 16–18), all of the congregation of Israel showed their identification with the Levites by the laying on of their hands.

8:19 a gift to Aaron. The Levites were given by God to assist the priests. **no plague.** *See note on 1:53.*

8:24 twenty-five years old. The Levites were to begin their service in helping the priests at age 25. However, in 4:3 the age of commencement is 30. A rabbinic suggestion was that the Levites were to serve a 5-year apprenticeship. A better solution can be discovered by noting the differing tasks in the two chapters. Numbers 4 dealt with the carrying of the tabernacle, while here they helped in the service in the tabernacle. A Levite began serving in the tabernacle at 25 and carrying the tabernacle at 30. In both cases, his service ended at age 50. David later lowered the age to 20 (see 1Ch 23:24, 27; cf. Ezr 3:8).

in the work and not work any more. 26 They may,
however, [a]assist their brothers in the tent of meeting, [A]to keep an obligation, but they *themselves* shall
do no work. Thus you shall deal with the Levites
concerning their obligations."

THE PASSOVER

9 Thus the LORD spoke to Moses in the wilderness
of Sinai, in [A]the first month of the second year
after they had come out of the land of Egypt, saying,
2 "Now, let the sons of Israel observe the Passover
at [A]its appointed time. 3 On the fourteenth day of
this month, [a]at twilight, you shall observe it at its
appointed time; you shall observe it according to
all its statutes and according to all its ordinances."
4 So Moses [a]told the sons of Israel to observe the
Passover. 5 [A]They observed the Passover in the first
month, on the fourteenth day of the month, at twilight, in the wilderness of Sinai; [B]according to all
that the LORD had commanded Moses, so the sons
of Israel did. 6 But there were *some* men who were
[A]unclean because of *the* [a]dead person, so that they
could not observe Passover on that day; so [B]they
came before Moses and Aaron on that day. 7 Those
men said to him, "*Though* we are unclean because
of *the* [a]dead person, why are we restrained from
presenting the offering of the LORD at its appointed
time among the sons of Israel?" 8 Moses therefore
said to them, "[a,A]Wait, and I will listen to what the
LORD will command concerning you."
9 Then the LORD spoke to Moses, saying, 10 "Speak
to the sons of Israel, saying, 'If any one of you or
of your generations becomes unclean because of
a *dead* [a]person, or is on a distant journey, he may,
however, observe the Passover to the LORD. 11 In
the second month on the [A]fourteenth day at twilight, they shall observe it; they [B]shall eat it with
unleavened bread and bitter herbs. 12 They [A]shall
leave none of it until morning, [B]nor break a bone of
it; according to all the statute of the Passover they
shall observe it. 13 [A]But the man who is clean and is
not on a journey, and yet [a]neglects to observe the
Passover, that [b]person shall then be cut off from his
people, for he did not present the offering of the
LORD at its appointed time. That man [B]will bear his
sin. 14 [A]If an alien sojourns among you and [a]observes
the Passover to the LORD, according to the statute
of the Passover and according to its ordinance, so
he shall do; you shall have [B]one statute, both for the
alien and for the native of the land.' "

THE CLOUD ON THE TABERNACLE

15 Now on [A]the day that the tabernacle was erected
[B]the cloud covered the tabernacle, the [C]tent of the
testimony, and [D]in the evening it was like the appearance of fire over the tabernacle, until morning.
16 So it was continuously; [A]the cloud would cover it
by day, and the appearance of fire by night. 17 [A]When-
ever the cloud was lifted from over the tent, afterward the sons of Israel would then set out; and in
the place where the cloud settled down, there the
sons of Israel would camp. 18 At the [a]command of
the LORD the sons of Israel would set out, and at
the [a]command of the LORD they would camp; [A]as
long as the cloud settled over the tabernacle, they
remained camped. 19 Even when the cloud lingered
over the tabernacle for many days, [a]the sons of Israel
would keep the LORD'S charge and not set out. 20 If
[a]sometimes the cloud remained a few days over the
tabernacle, [A]according to the [b]command of the LORD
they remained camped. Then according to the [b]com-
mand of the LORD they set out. 21 If [a]sometimes the
cloud [b]remained from evening until morning, when
the cloud was lifted in the morning, they would
move out; or *if it remained* in the daytime and at
night, whenever the cloud was lifted, they would set
out. 22 Whether it was two days or a month or a year
that the cloud lingered over the tabernacle, staying
above it, the sons of Israel remained camped and
did not set out; but [A]when it was lifted, they did set
out. 23 [A]At the [a]command of the LORD they camped,
and at the [a]command of the LORD they set out; they
kept the LORD'S charge, according to the [a]command
of the LORD through Moses.

8:26 [a]Lit *serve* [A]Num 1:53 9:1 [A]Ex 40:2, 17; Num 1:1 9:2 [A]Ex 12:6; Lev 23:5; Deut 16:1, 2 9:3 [a]Lit *between the two evenings,* and so throughout the ch 9:4 [a]Lit *spoke to* 9:5 [A]Josh 5:10 [B]Ex 12:1-13 9:6 [a]Lit *soul of man* [A]Num 5:2; 19:11-22 [B]Ex 18:15; Num 27:2 9:7 [a]Lit *soul of man* 9:8 [a]Lit *Stand* [A]Ex 18:15; Ps 85:8 9:10 [a]Lit *soul* 9:11 [A]2 Chr 30:2, 15 [B]Ex 12:8 9:12 [A]Ex 12:10 [B]Ex 12:46; John 19:36 9:13 [a]Or *ceases* [b]Lit *soul* [A]Gen 17:14; Ex 12:15, 47 [B]Num 5:31 9:14 [a]Or *would observe* [A]Ex 12:48 [B]Ex 12:49; Lev 24:22; Num 15:15, 16, 29 9:15 [A]Ex 40:2, 17 [B]Ex 40:34 [C]Num 17:7 [D]Ex 13:21, 22 9:16 [A]Ex 40:34; Neh 9:12 9:17 [A]Ex 40:36-38; Num 10:11, 12 9:18 [a]Lit *mouth* [A]1 Cor 10:1 9:19 [a]Lit *and the* 9:20 [a]Lit *it was that* [b]Lit *mouth* [A]Ps 48:14; Prov 3:5, 6 9:21 [a]Lit *it was that* [b]Lit *was* 9:22 [A]Ex 40:36, 37 9:23 [a]Lit *mouth* [A]Ps 73:24; 107:7; Is 63:14

9:1–14 The call from the Lord to keep the Passover led to an inquiry from those whose uncleanness kept them from obeying. This request led to an amplification of the requirement by the Lord. This was the second Passover.

9:1 the first month. The events recorded in these verses precede the beginning of the census in chap. 1, but follow the dedication of the tabernacle in chap. 7.

9:3 twilight. The time between the end of one day and the beginning of the next. See Ex 12:6.

9:6 unclean. Ceremonially unclean because of contact with a dead body. *See note on 5:2.*

9:10 any one ... of your generations. This word from the Lord was not only for the current situation, but it was a continuing ordinance for Israel. If a man was unable to eat the Passover because of uncleanness or because he was away from the land, he could partake of the Passover on the fourteenth day of the second month.

9:12 This text is alluded to in Jn 19:36.

9:13 cut off. If any Israelite did not keep the Passover at the appointed time and was not unclean or away from the land, he was to be "cut off," which implies that he was to be killed.

9:14 one statute. A non-Israelite who wished to participate in the Passover would be required to be circumcised.

9:15–23 See Ex 40:34–38. The cloud, the visible symbol of the Lord's presence, was continually sitting above the tabernacle. The movement of the cloud was the signal to Israel that they were to travel on their journey.

9:15 tabernacle was erected. The presence of the Lord arrived when the tabernacle was completed and raised up on the first day of the first month of the second year after they had come out of Egypt.

9:16 cloud ... fire. The presence of the Lord which was seen in the cloud by day became a fire that was seen at night (cf. Lv 16:2).

9:23 command ... command. The text emphasizes that Israel obeyed the Lord at this point in her experience. Throughout the wilderness wanderings, the Israelites could only journey as the cloud led them. When it did not move, they stayed encamped where they were.

THE SILVER TRUMPETS

10 The LORD spoke further to Moses, saying,
2 “Make yourself two trumpets of silver, of
hammered work you shall make them; and you
shall use them for [A]summoning the congregation
and for having the camps set out. 3 [A]When both are
blown, all the congregation shall gather themselves
to you at the doorway of the tent of meeting. 4 Yet
if *only* one is blown, then the [A]leaders, the heads of
the [a]divisions of Israel, shall assemble before you.
5 But when you blow an alarm, the camps that are
pitched [A]on the east side shall set out. 6 When you
blow an alarm the second time, the camps that are
pitched on [A]the south side shall set out; an alarm
is to be blown for them to set out. 7 When conven-
ing the assembly, however, you shall blow without
[A]sounding an alarm. 8 [A]The priestly sons of Aaron,
moreover, shall blow the trumpets; and [a]this shall
be for you a perpetual statute throughout your
generations. 9 When you go to war in your land
against the adversary who [A]attacks you, then you
shall sound an alarm with the trumpets, that you
may be [B]remembered before the LORD your God,
and be saved from your enemies. 10 Also in the day
of your gladness and in your appointed [a]feasts, and
on the first *days* of your months, [A]you shall blow
the trumpets over your burnt offerings, and over
the sacrifices of your peace offerings; and they shall
be as a reminder of you before your God. I am the
LORD your God.”

THE TRIBES LEAVE SINAI

11 Now in [A]the second year, in the second month,
on the twentieth of the month, the cloud was lifted
from over the [a]tabernacle of the testimony; 12 and
the sons of Israel set out on [A]their journeys from
the wilderness of Sinai. Then the cloud settled down
in the [B]wilderness of Paran. 13 [A]So they moved out
for the first time according to the [a]commandment
of the LORD through Moses. 14 The standard of the
camp of the sons of Judah, according to their armies,
[A]set out first, with Nahshon the son of Amminadab,
over its army, 15 and Nethanel the son of Zuar, over
the tribal army of the sons of Issachar; 16 and Eliab
the son of Helon over the tribal army of the sons
of Zebulun.
17 [A]Then the tabernacle was taken down; and
the sons of Gershon and the sons of Merari, who
were carrying the tabernacle, set out. 18 Next [A]the
standard of the camp of Reuben, according to their
armies, set out with Elizur the son of Shedeur, over
its army, 19 and Shelumiel the son of Zurishaddai
over the tribal army of the sons of Simeon, 20 and
Eliasaph the son of Deuel was over the tribal army
of the sons of Gad.
21 [A]Then the Kohathites set out, carrying the holy
objects; and [B]the tabernacle was set up before their
arrival. 22 [A]Next the standard of the camp of the sons
of Ephraim, according to their armies, was set out,
with Elishama the son of Ammihud over its army,
23 and Gamaliel the son of Pedahzur over the tribal
army of the sons of Manasseh; 24 and Abidan the
son of Gideoni over the tribal army of the sons of
Benjamin.
25 [A]Then the standard of the camp of the sons of
Dan, according to their armies, *which formed* the
[B]rear guard for all the camps, set out, with Ahiezer
the son of Ammishaddai over its army, 26 and Pagiel the son of Ochran over the tribal army of the
sons of Asher; 27 and Ahira the son of Enan over the
tribal army of the sons of Naphtali. 28 [a]This was the
order of march of the sons of Israel by their armies
as they set out.
29 Then Moses said to [A]Hobab the son of [B]Reuel
the Midianite, Moses’ father-in-law, “We are setting
out to the place of which the LORD said, ‘[C]I will give
it to you’; [D]come with us and we will do you good,
for the LORD [E]has [a]promised good concerning Israel.” 30 But he said to him, “[A]I will not come, but
rather will go to my *own* land and relatives.” 31 Then

10:2 [A]Is 1:13 10:3 [A]Jer 4:5; Joel 2:15 10:4 [a]Lit *thousands;* or *clans* [A]Ex 18:21; Num 1:16; 7:2 10:5 [A]Num 10:14 10:6 [A]Num 10:18 10:7 [A]Joel 2:1 10:8 [a]Lit *it* [A]Num 31:6; Josh 6:4; 2 Chr 13:12 10:9 [A]Judg 2:18; 1 Sam 10:18; Ps 106:42 [B]Gen 8:1; Ps 106:4 10:10 [a]Or *times* [A]Ps 81:3-5 10:11 [a]Lit *dwelling place,* and so throughout the ch [A]Ex 40:17 10:12 [A]Ex 40:36 [B]Gen 21:21; Num 12:16 10:13 [a]Lit *mouth* [A]Deut 1:6 10:14 [A]Num 2:3-9 10:17 [A]Num 4:21-32 10:18 [A]Num 2:10-16 10:21 [A]Num 4:4-20 [B]Num 10:17 10:22 [A]Num 2:18-24 10:25 [A]Num 2:25-31 [B]Josh 6:9, 13 10:28 [a]Lit *These are the settings out of the sons* 10:29 [a]Lit *spoken* [A]Judg 4:11 [B]Ex 2:18; 3:1; 18:12 [C]Gen 12:7; Ex 6:4-8 [D]Ps 95:1-7; 100:1-5 [E]Deut 4:40; 30:5 10:30 [A]Judg 1:16; Matt 21:28, 29

10:1–10 Israel was also to be guided by the blowing of the two silver trumpets made by Moses. Both a call to gather and a call to march were communicated with the trumpets.

10:2 **trumpets.** According to a Jewish tradition, these instruments were between 12 and 20 in. long and had a narrow tube that was flared at the end. **hammered work.** The same description is given concerning the cherubim above the mercy seat. See Ex 25:18; 37:7.

10:3, 4 **both ... one.** The first function of the trumpets was to gather the people to the tabernacle. When both trumpets were blown, all adult males of the congregation were to gather. If only one trumpet was blown, the leaders were to come.

10:5 **set out.** The second purpose of the trumpets was to give a signal indicating that the tribes were to begin their march. The exact difference between the blowing for the gathering at the tabernacle and for the march is not known. Jewish tradition said the convocation sound was a long steady blast, while the advance signal was a succession of 3 shorter notes.

10:8 **a perpetual statute.** The blowing of the horns was to be a perpetual ordinance in Israel, calling the people to worship or to war.

10:11–36 Finally, in an orderly and obedient fashion, Israel departed from Sinai as the Lord commanded through Moses.

10:11 **second year ... twentieth of the month.** Only 13 months after the Exodus from Egypt and 11 months after the arrival at Sinai, Israel began to march toward Canaan.

10:12 **the wilderness of Sinai.** According to 13:26, Kadesh was in the Wilderness of Paran, probably at its northern border. This verse gives a summary of God’s leading from Sinai to Kadesh.

10:14–28 The order of march followed by Israel in these verses is in exact conformity to the details given in 2:1–34.

10:14 **standard.** *See note on 2:2.* **Nahshon.** For the fourth, and final time in the book of Numbers, the 12 leaders of the first generation of Israel were noted (see chaps. 1, 2 and 7). In accordance with Ge 49:8–12, the tribe of Judah was given preeminence as the ruling tribe. It led the march into the Promised Land.

10:29 **Hobab.** As the son of Reuel, Hobab was Moses’ brother-in-law. **Reuel.** Reuel was the father-in-law of Moses (see Ex 2:18). **come with us.** Moses sought Hobab’s help in leading Israel through the wilderness. He promised Hobab a portion of the inheritance of Israel within the land if he would come. The text of Numbers does not explicitly state whether Hobab responded to Moses or not. But Jdg 1:16 implies that Hobab agreed to Moses’ request. Later, he joined with Judah in the conquest of the land and did receive the blessing of dwelling in the land.

he said, "Please do not leave us, inasmuch as you
know where we should camp in the wilderness, and
you [A]will be as eyes for us. 32 So it will be, if you go
with us, that [a,A]whatever good the LORD [b]does for
us, [B]we will [c]do for you."
33 [A]Thus they set out from the mount of the LORD
three days' journey, with [B]the ark of the covenant of
the LORD journeying in front of them for the [a]three
days, to seek out [C]a resting place for them. 34 [A]The
cloud of the LORD was over them by day when they
set out from the camp.
35 Then it came about when the ark set out that
Moses said,

"[A]Rise up, O LORD!
And let Your enemies be scattered,
And let those [B]who hate You
flee [a]before You."

36 When it came to rest, he said,

"[A]Return, O LORD,
To the myriad [B]thousands of Israel."

THE PEOPLE COMPLAIN

11 Now the people became like [A]those who complain of adversity [B]in the hearing of the LORD;
and when the LORD heard *it,* His anger was kindled,
and the fire of the LORD burned among them and
consumed *some* of the outskirts of the camp. 2 [A]The
people therefore cried out to Moses, and Moses
prayed to the LORD and the fire [a]died out. 3 So the
name of that place was called [a,A]Taberah, because
the fire of the LORD burned among them.
4 The [A]rabble who were among them [a]had greedy
desires; and also the sons of Israel wept again and
said, "[B]Who will give us [b]meat to eat? 5 [A]We remember the fish which we used to eat free in Egypt, the
cucumbers and the melons and the leeks and the
onions and the garlic, 6 but now [A]our [a]appetite is
gone. There is nothing at all [b]to look at except this
manna."
7 [A]Now the manna was like coriander seed, and
its appearance like that of [B]bdellium. 8 The people
would go about and gather *it* and grind *it* [a]between
two millstones or beat *it* in the mortar, and boil *it*
in the pot and make cakes with it; and its taste was
as the taste of [b]cakes baked with oil. 9 [A]When the
dew fell on the camp at night, the manna would
fall [a]with it.

THE COMPLAINT OF MOSES

10 Now Moses heard the people weeping throughout their families, each man at the doorway of his
tent; and the anger of the LORD was kindled greatly,
and [a]Moses was displeased. 11 [A]So Moses said to the
LORD, "Why have You [a]been so hard on Your servant? And why have I not found favor in Your sight,
that You have laid the burden of all this people on
me? 12 Was it I who conceived all this people? Was
it I who brought them forth, that You should say to
me, 'Carry them in your bosom as a [a,A]nurse carries
a nursing infant, to the land which [B]You swore to
their fathers'? 13 Where am I to get meat to give to [A]all
this people? For they weep before me, saying, 'Give
us meat that we may eat!' 14 [A]I alone am not able to
carry all this people, because it is too [a]burdensome
for me. 15 [A]So if You are going to deal thus with me,
please kill me at once, if I have found favor in Your
sight, and do not let me see my wretchedness."

SEVENTY ELDERS TO ASSIST

16 The LORD therefore said to Moses, "Gather for
Me [A]seventy men from the elders of Israel, [B]whom
you know to be the elders of the people and their
officers and bring them to the tent of meeting, and
let them take their stand there with you. 17 [A]Then
I will come down and speak with you there, and I
will take of [B]the Spirit who is upon you, and will
put *Him* upon them; and they shall bear the burden of the people with you, so that you will not
bear *it* all alone. 18 Say to the people, '[A]Consecrate
yourselves for tomorrow, and you shall eat meat;
for you have wept [B]in the ears of the LORD, saying,

10:31 [A]Job 29:15 10:32 [a]Lit *that good which* [b]Lit *does good* [c]Lit *do good* [A]Ps 22:27-31; 67:5-7 [B]Lev 19:34; Deut 10:18 10:33 [a]Lit *three days' journey* [A]Num 10:12 [B]Deut 1:33 [C]Is 11:10 10:34 [A]Num 9:15-23 10:35 [a]Or *from Your presence* [A]Ps 68:1, 2; Is 17:12-14 [B]Deut 7:10; 32:41 10:36 [A]Is 63:17 [B]Deut 1:10 11:1 [A]Num 14:2; 16:11; 17:5 [B]Num 11:18; 14:28 11:2 [a]Lit *sank down* [A]Num 12:11, 13; 21:7 11:3 [a]I.e. burning [A]Deut 9:22 11:4 [a]Lit *desired a desire* [b]Lit *flesh,* and so throughout the ch [A]Ex 12:38; 1 Cor 10:6 [B]Ps 78:20 11:5 [A]Ex 16:3 11:6 [a]Lit *soul is dried up* [b]Lit *for our eyes* [A]Num 21:5 11:7 [A]Ex 16:31 [B]Gen 2:12 11:8 [a]Lit *with* [b]Lit *juice of oil* 11:9 [a]Lit *on* [A]Ex 16:13, 14 11:10 [a]Lit it was *evil in Moses' sight* 11:11 [a]Lit *dealt ill with* [A]Ex 5:22; Deut 1:12 11:12 [a]Or *foster-father* [A]2 Kin 10:1, 5; Is 49:23 [B]Gen 24:7; Ex 13:5, 11; 33:1 11:13 [A]Num 11:21, 22; John 6:5-9 11:14 [a]Lit *heavy* [A]Ex 18:18; Deut 1:12 11:15 [A]Ex 32:32 11:16 [A]Ex 24:1, 9 [B]Ex 18:25 11:17 [A]Num 11:25 [B]1 Sam 10:6; Joel 2:28 11:18 [A]Ex 19:10, 22 [B]Num 11:1

10:33 journey … three days. The Israelites traveled for 3 days from Sinai before they encamped for more than one night.

10:35, 36 As Israel traveled and encamped, Moses prayed that the Lord would give victory and that His presence would be among her.

11:1–25:18 In contrast to Nu 1–10, a major change takes place at 11:1. Obedient Israel became complaining (11:1; 14:2, 27, 29, 36; 16:1–3, 41; 17:5) and rebellious (14:9; 17:10) Israel. Ultimately, Moses and Aaron rebelled against the Lord as well (20:10, 24). In response to Israel's disobedience, the Lord's anger was aroused (11:1, 10, 33; 12:9; 14:18; 25:3, 4) and He plagued His people (14:37; 16:46, 47, 48, 49, 50; 25:8, 9, 18) as He had Pharaoh and the Egyptians (Ex 9:14; 12:13; 30:12). Nevertheless, even though God judged that generation of Israel, He will still fulfill His promises to Abraham in the future (23:5–24:24).

11:1–12:16 The complaining of the people and leaders began on the journey from Sinai to Kadesh.

11:1 the LORD heard *it*. Their complaining was outward and loud. **the outskirts of the camp.** God in His grace consumed only those who were on the very edges of the encampment of Israel.

11:4 The rabble. The word only occurs here in the OT. However, another word, "multitude," was used in Ex 12:38. The "rabble" here are non-Israelites who left Egypt with Israel in the Exodus. **meat.** After over a year of eating manna in the wilderness, the mixed multitude wanted the spicy food of Egypt once again.

11:7 manna. See Ex 16:14. **bdellium.** This refers more to appearance than color, i.e., it had the appearance of a pale resin.

11:13, 14 Moses confessed to God that he was not able to provide meat for the people as they demanded. Their complaining was discouraging him so that because of this great burden, Moses desired death from the hand of the Lord.

11:16–30 In response to Moses' despair in leading the people, the Lord gave him 70 men to help.

11:16 seventy men. These aides to Moses might be the same 70 referred to in Ex 18:21–26.

11:17 the Spirit. This refers to the Spirit of God. It was by means of the Holy Spirit that Moses was able to lead Israel. In v. 25, the Lord gave the Spirit to the 70 men in fulfillment of the word He gave to Moses.

"Oh that someone would give us meat to eat! For we
were well-off in Egypt." Therefore the LORD will give
you meat and you shall eat. 19 You shall eat, not one
day, nor two days, nor five days, nor ten days, nor
twenty days, 20 [a]but a whole month, until it comes
out of your nostrils and becomes loathsome to you;
because [A]you have rejected the LORD who is among
you and have wept before Him, saying, "Why did
we ever leave Egypt?" ' " 21 But Moses said, "The
people, among whom I am, are 600,000 on foot;
yet You have said, 'I will give them meat, so that
they may eat for a whole month.' 22 Should flocks
and herds be slaughtered for them, to be sufficient
for them? Or should all the fish of the sea be gathered together for them, to be sufficient for them?"
23 The LORD said to Moses, "Is [A]the LORD'S [a]power
limited? Now you shall see whether [B]My word will
[b]come true for you or not."

24 So Moses went out and [A]told the people the
words of the LORD. Also, he gathered seventy men of
the elders of the people, and stationed them around
the tent. 25 [A]Then the LORD came down in the cloud
and spoke to him; and He took of the Spirit who
was upon him and placed *Him* upon the seventy
elders. And when the Spirit rested upon them, they
prophesied. But they did not do *it* again.

26 But two men had remained in the camp; the
name of one was Eldad and the name of the [a]other
Medad. And [A]the Spirit rested upon them (now
they were among those who had been registered,
but had not gone out to the tent), and they prophesied in the camp. 27 So a young man ran and told
Moses and said, "Eldad and Medad are prophesying in the camp." 28 Then [A]Joshua the son of Nun,
the attendant of Moses from his youth, said, "[B]Mo-
ses, my lord, restrain them." 29 But Moses said to
him, "Are you jealous for my sake? [A]Would that all
the LORD'S people were prophets, that the LORD
would put His Spirit upon them!" 30 Then Moses
[a]returned to the camp, *both* he and the elders
of Israel.

THE QUAIL AND THE PLAGUE

31 [A]Now there went forth a wind from the LORD
and it brought quail from the sea, and let *them* fall
beside the camp, about a day's journey on this side
and a day's journey on the other side, all around the
camp and [a]about two [b]cubits *deep* on the surface
of the ground. 32 The people [a]spent all day and all
night and all the next day, and gathered the quail
(he who gathered least gathered ten [b,A]homers) and
they spread *them* out for themselves all around the
camp. 33 [A]While the meat was still between their
teeth, before it was chewed, the anger of the LORD
was kindled against the people, and the LORD struck
the people with a very severe plague. 34 So the name
of that place was called [a,A]Kibroth-hattaavah, because there they buried the people who had been
greedy. 35 From Kibroth-hattaavah [A]the people set
out for Hazeroth, and they [a]remained at Hazeroth.

THE MURMURING OF MIRIAM AND AARON

12 Then Miriam and Aaron spoke against Moses
because of the Cushite woman whom he had
married (for he had married a [A]Cushite woman);
2 [A]and they said, "Has the LORD indeed spoken only
through Moses? Has He not spoken through us as
well?" And the LORD heard it. 3 (Now the man Moses
was [A]very humble, more than any man who was on
the face of the earth.) 4 Suddenly the LORD said to
Moses and Aaron and to Miriam, "You three come
out to the tent of meeting." So the three of them
came out. 5 [A]Then the LORD came down in a pillar
of cloud and stood at the doorway of the tent, and
He called [a]Aaron and Miriam. When they had both
come forward, 6 He said,

"Hear now My words:
If there is a prophet among you,
I, the LORD, shall make Myself
known to him in a [A]vision.
I shall speak with him in a [B]dream.

11:20 [a]Lit *until* [A]Josh 24:27; 1 Sam 10:19 11:23 [a]Lit *hand short* [b]Lit *befall you* [A]Is 50:2; 59:1 [B]Ezek 12:25; 24:14 11:24 [A]Num 11:16 11:25 [A]Num 11:17; 12:5 11:26 [a]Lit *second* [A]Num 24:2; 1 Sam 10:6; 2 Chr 15:1; Neh 9:30 11:28 [A]Ex 33:11; Josh 1:1 [B]Mark 9:38-40 11:29 [A]1 Cor 14:5 11:30 [a]Lit *removed himself* 11:31 [a]Or from *about two cubits above* [b]I.e. One cubit equals approx 18 in. [A]Ex 16:13; Ps 78:26-28; 105:40 11:32 [a]Lit *rose* [b]I.e. One homer equals approx 11 bu [A]Ezek 45:11 11:33 [A]Ps 78:29-31; 106:15 11:34 [a]I.e. the graves of greediness [A]Deut 9:22 11:35 [a]Lit *were* [A]Num 33:17 12:1 [A]Ex 2:21 12:2 [A]Num 16:3 12:3 [A]Matt 11:29 12:5 [a]Or *"Aaron and Miriam!"* [A]Ex 19:9; 34:5 12:6 [A]Gen 46:2; 1 Sam 3:15 [B]Gen 31:11; 1 Kin 3:5, 15

11:21 six hundred thousand. Moses rounded off the 603,550 of 1:46; 2:32.

11:23 Is the LORD's power limited? The Lord indicated He was able to do as He had said and provide meat for the 600,000 men of Israel and their families for one month.

11:25 prophesied. Here the prophesying refers to the giving of praise and similar expressions of worship to the Lord without prior training. The text is clear that this was a one-time event as far as these men were concerned.

11:29 that the LORD would put His Spirit upon them! Moses desired and anticipated the day when all of God's people would have His Spirit within them. By this, he looked forward to the New Covenant. See Eze 36:22–27; Jer 31:31ff.; Joel 2:28.

11:31 a day's journey. The Lord, using a wind, brought a great quantity of quail that surrounded the encampment within one day's journey. **about two cubits *deep* on the ... ground.** The birds flew at a height of about 3 ft. where they were able to be easily captured or clubbed to the ground by the people.

11:32 ten homers. About 60–70 bu.

12:1–16 The brother and sister of Moses opposed his leadership. The immediate occasion was the prophesying of the elders. Moses' position as the spokesman for God to Israel was called into question.

12:1 Cushite. Ethiopia (also known as Cush), S of Egypt, was inhabited by the descendants of Cush, the firstborn son of Ham (Ge 10:6, 7). Although the term "Cushite" could have been used concerning Zipporah, Moses' first wife, it seems more likely that Moses had remarried after the death of Zipporah. The marriage to the Ethiopian woman had been recent and furnished the pretext for the attack of Miriam and Aaron. Since Miriam is mentioned first, she probably was the instigator of the attack against Moses.

12:2 spoken only through Moses. Miriam and Aaron asserted that God had spoken to them in the same way that He had spoken to Moses.

12:3 very humble. This statement is often cited as evidence that Moses could not have written the book of Numbers, for he would not have boasted in his own humility. However, the Holy Spirit certainly could inspire Moses to make an accurate statement about himself, probably against his own natural inclination. In this context, Moses was asserting there was nothing that he had done to provoke this attack by Miriam and Aaron.

12:5 the LORD came down. As in Ge 11:5, this clause states that the Lord knows and deals with situations on earth. Here the Lord came down and, in v. 10, departed. This was God's answer to the attack against Moses.

7 "Not so, with [A]My servant Moses,
[B]He is faithful in all My household;
8 [A]With him I speak mouth to mouth,
Even openly, and not in dark sayings,
And he beholds [B]the form of the LORD.
Why then were you not afraid
To speak against My servant,
against Moses?"

9 So the anger of the LORD burned against them and [A]He departed. 10 But when the cloud had withdrawn from over the tent, behold, [A]Miriam *was* leprous, as [B]*white as* snow. As Aaron turned toward Miriam, behold, she *was* leprous. 11 Then Aaron said to Moses, "Oh, my lord, I beg you, [A]do not account *this* sin to us, in which we have acted foolishly and in which we have sinned. 12 Oh, do not let her be like one dead, whose flesh is half eaten away when he comes from his mother's womb!" 13 Moses cried out to the LORD, saying, "O God, [A]heal her, I pray!" 14 But the LORD said to Moses, "If her father had but [A]spit in her face, would she not bear her shame for seven days? Let her be shut up for seven days [B]outside the camp, and afterward she may be received again." 15 So [A]Miriam was shut up outside the camp for seven days, and the people did not move on until Miriam was received again.

16 Afterward, however, the people moved out from Hazeroth and camped in the wilderness of Paran.

SPIES VIEW THE LAND

13 Then [A]the LORD spoke to Moses saying, 2 "[A]Send out for yourself men so that they may spy out the land of Canaan, which I am going to give to the sons of Israel; you shall send a man from each of their fathers' tribes, every one a leader among them." 3 So Moses sent them from the wilderness of Paran at the [a]command of the LORD, all of them men who were heads of the sons of Israel. 4 These then *were* their names: from the tribe of Reuben, Shammua the son of Zaccur; 5 from the tribe of Simeon, Shaphat the son of Hori; 6 from the tribe of Judah, [A]Caleb the son of Jephunneh; 7 from the tribe of Issachar, Igal the son of Joseph; 8 from the tribe of Ephraim, [A]Hoshea the son of Nun; 9 from the tribe of Benjamin, Palti the son of Raphu; 10 from the tribe of Zebulun, Gaddiel the son of Sodi; 11 from the tribe of Joseph, from the tribe of Manasseh, Gaddi the son of Susi; 12 from the tribe of Dan, Ammiel the son of Gemalli; 13 from the tribe of Asher, Sethur the son of Michael; 14 from the tribe of Naphtali, Nahbi the son of Vophsi; 15 from the tribe of Gad, Geuel the son of Machi. 16 These are the names of the men whom Moses sent to spy out the land; but Moses called [A]Hoshea the son of Nun, Joshua.

17 When Moses sent them to spy out the land of Canaan, he said to them, "Go up [a]there into [A]the [b]Negev; then go up into the hill country. 18 See what the land is like, and whether the people who live in it are strong *or* weak, whether they are few or many. 19 How is the land in which they live, is it good or bad? And how are the cities in which they live, are *they* [a]like *open* camps or with fortifications? 20 [A]How is the land, is it fat or lean? Are there trees in it or not? [a]Make an [B]effort then to get some of the fruit of the land." Now the time was the time of the first ripe grapes.

21 So they went up and spied out the land from [A]the wilderness of Zin as far as Rehob, [a,B]at Lebo-hamath. 22 When they had gone up into [A]the Negev, [a]they came to Hebron where [B]Ahiman, Sheshai and Talmai, the [b]descendants of [C]Anak were. (Now Hebron was built seven years before [D]Zoan in Egypt.) 23 Then they came to the [a]valley of [b,A]Eshcol and from there cut down a branch with a single cluster

12:7 [A]Josh 1:1 [B]Heb 3:2, 5 12:8 [A]Deut 34:10; Hos 12:13 [B]Ex 20:4; 24:10, 11; Deut 5:8; Ps 17:15 12:9 [A]Gen 17:22; 18:33 12:10 [A]Deut 24:9 [B]Ex 4:6; 2 Kin 5:27 12:11 [A]2 Sam 19:19; 24:10 12:13 [A]Ps 30:2; 41:4; Is 30:26; Jer 17:14 12:14 [A]Deut 25:9; Job 17:6; 30:10; Is 50:6 [B]Num 5:1-4 12:15 [A]Deut 24:9 13:1 [A]Deut 1:22, 23 13:2 [A]Deut 1:22; 9:23 13:3 [a]Lit *mouth* 13:6 [A]Num 14:6, 30; Josh 14:6 13:8 [A]Num 13:16; Deut 32:44 13:16 [A]Num 13:8; Deut 32:44 13:17 [a]Lit *here* [b]I.e. South country, and so throughout the ch [A]Gen 12:9; 13:1, 3 13:19 [a]Lit *in* 13:20 [a]Lit *Use your strength* [A]Deut 1:24, 25 [B]Deut 31:6, 23 13:21 [a]Or *to the entrance of Hamath* [A]Num 20:1; 27:14; 33:36 [B]Josh 13:5 13:22 [a]Lit Most mss read *one came* [b]Lit *children* [A]Num 13:17 [B]Josh 15:14 [C]Num 13:28, 33 [D]Ps 78:12, 43 13:23 [a]Or *wadi* [b]I.e. cluster [A]Gen 14:13; Num 13:24; 32:9; Deut 1:24

12:7 **My servant Moses.** This phrase is also repeated in v. 8. A servant of the Lord in the OT is one who responded in faith by obedience to the Word of the Lord. **faithful in all My household.** A reference to Moses' loyal performance of his role as covenant mediator between the Lord and Israel.

12:8 **mouth to mouth.** God spoke to Moses without mediation. Also the Lord did not speak to Moses through visions and dreams, but plainly. It was not that Moses saw the full glory of God (cf. Jn 1:18), but rather that he had the most explicit, intimate encounters (cf. Dt 34:10). **the form of the LORD.** This is the likeness or representation of the Lord which Moses was privileged to see. See Ex 33:23.

12:10 **leprous.** In judgment of Miriam's opposition to Moses, the Lord struck her with leprosy. For the treatment of a leper, see Lv 13–14. A public sin required a public response from the Lord.

12:16 **wilderness of Paran.** *See note on 10:12.*

13:1–14:45 These chapters record the massive failure of Israel at Kadesh. The people failed to believe the Lord (14:11) and take the Promised Land. Their lack of faith was open rebellion against the Lord (14:9). The NT looks back to these times as an illustration of apostasy (cf. 1Co 10:5; Heb 3:16–19).

13:1 **the LORD spoke to Moses.** According to Dt 1:22, 23, the people had first requested the spies be sent out after Moses challenged them to take the land. Here, the Lord affirmed the peoples' desire and commanded Moses to send them.

13:2 **spy out the land of Canaan.** The spies were specifically called to explore the land that God had promised to Israel. This exploration gave valuable information to Moses for the conquest of the land.

13:3 **heads of the sons of Israel.** These leaders were different from those mentioned in Nu 1, 2, 7, 10. Presumably the tribal leaders in the 4 earlier lists were older men. The task for the spies called for some leaders who were younger, probably about 40 years of age, based on the ages of Caleb and Joshua.

13:16 **Hoshea ... Joshua.** For reasons not made clear, Moses changed the name of Hoshea, meaning "desire for salvation," to Joshua, meaning "the Lord is salvation."

13:17–20 The spies were to determine the nature of the land itself, as well as the strengths and weaknesses of the people.

13:20 **the time of the first ripe grapes.** Midsummer (mid to late July).

13:21 **from the wilderness of Zin as far as Rehob.** These were the southernmost and northernmost borders of the land.

13:22 **Hebron.** The first major city the spies came to in Canaan. Abram had earlier built an altar to the Lord here (cf. Ge 13:18). Abraham and Isaac were buried here (Ge 49:31). The city had been fortified at about 1730 B.C., 7 years before the building of Zoan in Egypt, and later became the inheritance of Caleb (Jos 14:13–15) and then David's capital when he reigned over Judah (2Sa 2:1–4). **the descendants of Anak.** Cf. 13:28. Anak was probably the ancestor of Ahiman, Sheshiai, and Talmai, who were living at Hebron. They were noted for their height (Dt 2:21; 9:2).

13:23 **the valley of Eshcol.** Eshcol means "cluster."

of grapes; and they carried it on a pole between two *men,* with some of the pomegranates and the figs. 24 That place was called the valley of [a]Eshcol, because of the cluster which the sons of Israel cut down from there.

THE SPIES' REPORTS

25 When they returned from spying out the land, at the end of forty days, 26 they proceeded to come to Moses and Aaron and to all the congregation of the sons of Israel [a]in the wilderness of Paran, at [A]Kadesh; and they brought back word to them and to all the congregation and showed them the fruit of the land. 27 Thus they told him, and said, "We went in to the land where you sent us; and [A]it certainly does flow with milk and honey, and [B]this is its fruit. 28 Nevertheless, [A]the people who live in the land are strong, and the cities are fortified *and* very large; and moreover, we saw [B]the [a]descendants of Anak there. 29 Amalek is living in the land of [A]the Negev and the Hittites and the Jebusites and [B]the Amorites are living in the hill country, and [C]the Canaanites are living by the sea and by the side of the Jordan."

30 Then Caleb quieted the people [a]before Moses and said, "We should by all means go up and take possession of it, for we will surely overcome it." 31 But the men who had gone up with him said, "[A]We are not able to go up against the people, for they are too strong for us." 32 So they gave out to the sons of Israel [A]a bad report of the land which they had spied out, saying, "The land through which we have gone, in spying it out, is [B]a land that devours its [a]inhabitants; and [C]all the people whom we saw in it are men of *great* size. 33 There also we saw the [A]Nephilim (the sons of Anak are part of the Nephilim); and [B]we became like grasshoppers in our own sight, and so we were in their sight."

THE PEOPLE REBEL

14 Then all the congregation [a]lifted up their voices and cried, and the people wept [b]that night. 2 All the sons of Israel [A]grumbled against Moses and Aaron; and the whole congregation said to them, "[B]Would that we had died in the land of Egypt! Or would that we had died in this wilderness! 3 Why is the LORD bringing us into this land, [A]to fall by the sword? [B]Our wives and our little ones will become plunder; would it not be better for us to return to Egypt?" 4 So they said to one another, "[A]Let us appoint a leader and return to Egypt."

5 [A]Then Moses and Aaron fell on their faces in the presence of all the assembly of the congregation of the sons of Israel. 6 Joshua the son of Nun and Caleb the son of Jephunneh, of those who had spied out the land, tore their clothes; 7 and they spoke to all the congregation of the sons of Israel, saying, "[A]The land which we passed through to spy out is an exceedingly good land. 8 [A]If the LORD is pleased with us, then He will bring us into this land and give it to us—[B]a land which flows with milk and honey. 9 Only [A]do not rebel against the LORD; and do not [B]fear the people of the land, for they will be our [a]prey. Their [b]protection has been removed from them, and the LORD is with us; do not fear them." 10 [A]But all the congregation said to stone them with stones. Then [B]the glory of the LORD appeared in the tent of meeting to all the sons of Israel.

MOSES PLEADS FOR THE PEOPLE

11 [A]The LORD said to Moses, "How long will this people spurn Me? And how long will [B]they not believe in Me, despite all the signs which I have performed in their midst? 12 I will smite them with [a,A]pestilence and dispossess them, and I [B]will make you into a nation greater and mightier than they."

13 [A]But Moses said to the LORD, "Then the Egyptians will hear of it, for by Your strength You brought up this people from their midst, 14 and they will tell *it* to the inhabitants of this land. They have heard that You, O LORD, are in the midst of this people, for [A]You, O LORD, are seen eye to eye, while Your cloud stands over them; and You go before them in a pillar of cloud by day and in a pillar of fire by night. 15 Now if You slay this people as one man, [A]then the nations who

13:24 [a]I.e. cluster 13:26 [a]Lit *to* [A]Num 20:1, 14; 32:8 13:27 [A]Ex 3:8, 17; 13:5 [B]Deut 1:25 13:28 [a]Lit *born ones* [A]Deut 1:28; 9:1, 2 [B]Num 13:33 13:29 [A]Num 13:17; 14:25, 45 [B]Josh 10:6 [C]Num 14:43, 45 13:30 [a]Lit *toward* 13:31 [A]Deut 1:28; 9:1-3 13:32 [a]Or *settlers* [A]Num 14:36, 37; Ps 106:24 [B]Ezek 36:13, 14 [C]Amos 2:9 13:33 [A]Gen 6:4 [B]Deut 1:28; 9:2; Josh 11:21 14:1 [a]Lit *lifted and gave their voice* [b]Lit *in that* 14:2 [A]Num 11:1 [B]Num 11:5; 16:13; 20:3, 4; 21:5 14:3 [A]Ex 5:21; 16:3 [B]Num 14:31; Deut 1:39 14:4 [A]Neh 9:17 14:5 [A]Num 16:4 14:7 [A]Num 13:27; Deut 1:25 14:8 [A]Deut 10:15 [B]Ex 3:8; Num 13:27 14:9 [a]Lit *food* [b]Lit *shadow* [A]Deut 1:26; 9:23, 24 [B]Deut 1:21, 29 14:10 [A]Ex 17:4 [B]Ex 16:10; Lev 9:23 14:11 [A]Ex 32:9-13 [B]Ps 106:24 14:12 [a]Lit *the pestilence* [A]Lev 26:25; Deut 28:21 [B]Ex 32:10 14:13 [A]Ex 32:11-14; Ps 106:23 14:14 [A]Ex 13:21; Deut 5:4 14:15 [A]Ex 32:12

13:28 the people … are strong. The spies reported that the land was good; however, the people were too strong to be conquered.

13:30 Caleb quieted the people. The verb "quieted" usually occurs in the form of the interjection "Hush!" This implies that the spies' report evoked a vocal reaction from the people. Caleb concurred with the report of the other spies, but called the people to go up and take the land, knowing that with God's help they were able to overcome the strong people.

13:32 a bad report. The report of the 10 spies was evil because it exaggerated the dangers of the people in the land, sought to stir up and instill fear in the people of Israel and, most importantly, it expressed their faithless attitude toward God and His promises.

13:33 Nephilim. This term was used in Ge 6:4 for a group of strong men who lived on the earth before the Flood. The descendants of Anak were, in exaggeration, compared to these giants, which led the spies to view themselves as grasshoppers before them.

14:1 all the congregation … wept. All of Israel bewailed the circumstances.

14:2 grumbled. The term means "to murmur." Specifically, they wished they had died in Egypt or the wilderness.

14:4 appoint a leader and return to Egypt. The faithless people were ready to reject God's leader, Moses.

14:6 tore their clothes. This was an indication of distress (see Ge 37:29).

14:7–9 Joshua and Caleb reaffirmed their appraisal that the land was good and their confidence that the Lord would deliver it and its people into their hands.

14:10 the glory of the LORD appeared. In response to the people's violent rejection of Joshua and Caleb's challenge, God appeared.

14:11 spurn … not believe in Me. They had refused to trust or rely on God and His power to give them the land of Canaan in spite of the signs that He had done in their midst.

14:12 I will make you into a nation. As in Ex 32:9, 10, God threatened to wipe out the people and start over again with Moses' "son." This justifiable threat showed the seriousness with which God took rebellion on the part of His people.

14:13–19 As in Ex 32:11–13, Moses interceded for Israel to protect the Lord's reputation with the Egyptians, who would charge the Lord with inability to complete His deliverance of Israel and thus deny His power. Second, the Lord's loyal love was the basis on which the Lord could forgive His people.

have heard of Your fame will [a]say, 16 'Because the
LORD [A]could not bring this people into the land which
He promised them by oath, therefore He slaughtered
them in the wilderness.' 17 But now, I pray, let the
power of the Lord be great, just as You have [a]declared,
18 '[A]The LORD is slow to anger and abundant in lovingkindness, forgiving iniquity and transgression;
but [B]He will by no means clear *the guilty,* [C]visiting the
iniquity of the fathers on the children [a]to the third
and the fourth *generations.*' 19 [A]Pardon, I pray, the
iniquity of this people according to the greatness of
Your lovingkindness, just as You also have forgiven
this people, from Egypt even until now."

THE LORD PARDONS AND REBUKES

20 So the LORD said, "[A]I have pardoned *them* according to your word; 21 but indeed, [A]as I live, [a,B]all
the earth will be filled with the glory of the LORD.
22 Surely [A]all the men who have seen My glory and
My signs which I performed in Egypt and in the
wilderness, yet [B]have put Me to the test these ten
times and have not listened to My voice, 23 [A]shall by
no means see the land which I swore to their fathers,
nor shall any of those who spurned Me see it. 24 But
My servant Caleb, [A]because he has had a different
spirit and has followed Me fully, [a,B]I will bring into the
land [b]which he entered, and his [c]descendants shall
take possession of it. 25 [A]Now the Amalekites and the
Canaanites live in the valleys; turn tomorrow and
set out to the wilderness by the way of the [a]Red Sea."
26 The LORD spoke to Moses and Aaron, saying,
27 "How long *shall I bear* with this evil congregation who are [A]grumbling against Me? I have heard
the complaints of the sons of Israel, which they are
[a]making against Me. 28 Say to them, '[A]As I live,' says
the LORD, 'just as [B]you have spoken in My hearing, so
I will surely do to you; 29 [A]your corpses will fall in this
wilderness, even all [B]your [a]numbered men, according
to your complete number from twenty years old and
upward, who have grumbled against Me. 30 Surely
you shall not come into the land in which I [a]swore
to settle you, [A]except Caleb the son of Jephunneh and
Joshua the son of Nun. 31 [A]Your children, however,
whom you said would become a prey—I will bring
them in, and they will know the land which you have
rejected. 32 [A]But as for you, your corpses will fall in this
wilderness. 33 Your sons shall be shepherds for [A]forty
years in the wilderness, and they will [a]suffer *for* your
[b]unfaithfulness, until your corpses [c]lie in the wilderness. 34 According to the [A]number of days which you
spied out the land, forty days, for every day you shall
bear your [a]guilt a year, *even* forty years, and you will
know My opposition. 35 [A]I, the LORD, have spoken,
surely this I will do to all this evil congregation who
are gathered together against Me. In this wilderness
they shall be destroyed, and there they will die.' "
36 [A]As for the men whom Moses sent to spy out
the land and who returned and made all the congregation grumble against him by bringing out a
bad report concerning the land, 37 even [A]those men
who brought out the very bad report of the land died
by a [B]plague before the LORD. 38 But Joshua the son
of Nun and Caleb the son of Jephunneh remained
alive out of those men who went to spy out the land.

ISRAEL REPULSED

39 When Moses spoke [A]these words to all the sons
of Israel, [B]the people mourned greatly. 40 In the
morning, however, they rose up early and went up
to the [a]ridge of the hill country, saying, "[A]Here we
are; [b]we have indeed sinned, but we will go up to the
place which the LORD has promised." 41 But Moses
said, "[A]Why then are you transgressing the [a]com-
mandment of the LORD, when it will not succeed?
42 [A]Do not go up, or you will be struck down before
your enemies, for the LORD is not among you. 43 For
the Amalekites and the Canaanites will be there in
front of you, and you will fall by the sword, inasmuch
as you have turned back from following the LORD.
And the LORD will not be with you." 44 But they went
up heedlessly to the [a]ridge of the hill country; neither
[A]the ark of the covenant of the LORD nor Moses left
the camp. 45 Then the Amalekites and the Canaanites who lived in that hill country came down, and
struck them and beat them down as far as [A]Hormah.

LAWS FOR CANAAN

15 Now the LORD spoke to Moses, saying,
2 "[A]Speak to the sons of Israel and say to them,
'When you enter the land [a]where you are to live,

14:15 [a]Lit *speak, saying* 14:16 [A]Josh 7:7 14:17 [a]Lit *spoken, saying* 14:18 [a]Lit *on* [A]Ex 20:6; 34:6, 7; Deut 5:10; 7:9; Ps 103:8; 145:8; Jon 4:2 [B]Ex 20:5; Deut 5:9; 7:10 [C]Ex 34:7 14:19 [A]Ex 32:32; 34:9 14:20 [A]Mic 7:18-20 14:21 [a]Lit *and all* [A]Num 14:28; Deut 32:40; Is 49:18 [B]Is 6:3; Hab 2:14 14:22 [A]1 Cor 10:5 [B]Ex 5:21; 14:11; 15:24; 16:2; 17:2, 3; 32:1; Num 11:1, 4; 12:1; 14:2 14:23 [A]Num 26:65; 32:11; Heb 3:18 14:24 [a]Lit *him I* [b]Lit *where* [c]Lit *seed* [A]Num 14:6-9 [B]Num 26:65; 32:12; Deut 1:36; Josh 14:6-15 14:25 [a]Lit *Sea of Reeds* [A]Num 13:29 14:27 [a]Lit *complaining* [A]Num 11:1 14:28 [A]Num 14:21 [B]Num 14:2; Deut 2:14, 15; Heb 3:17 14:29 [a]Lit *mustered* [A]Heb 3:17 [B]Num 1:45, 46 14:30 [a]Lit *raised My hand* [A]Num 14:24 14:31 [A]Num 14:3 14:32 [A]Num 26:64, 65; 32:13; 1 Cor 10:5 14:33 [a]Lit *bear* [b]Lit *fornications* [c]Lit *are finished* [A]Deut 2:7; 8:2, 4; 29:5 14:34 [a]Or *iniquities* [A]Num 13:25 14:35 [A]Num 23:19 14:36 [A]Num 13:4-16, 32 14:37 [A]1 Cor 10:10; Heb 3:17, 18 [B]Num 16:49 14:39 [A]Num 14:28-35 [B]Ex 33:4 14:40 [a]Or *top of the mountain* [b]Or *and we will go up…for we have sinned* [A]Deut 1:41-44 14:41 [a]Lit *mouth* [A]2 Chr 24:20 14:42 [A]Deut 1:42 14:44 [a]Or *top of the mountain* [A]Num 31:6 14:45 [A]Num 21:3 15:2 [a]Lit *of your dwellings* [A]Lev 23:10

14:22 ten times. Taken literally this includes: 1) Ex 14:10–12; 2) Ex 15:22–24; 3) Ex 16:1–3; 4) Ex 16:19, 20; 5) Ex 16:27–30; 6) Ex 17:1–4; 7) Ex 32:1–35; 8) Nu 11:1–3; 9) Nu 11:4–34; 10) Nu 14:3.

14:24 My servant Caleb. Since Caleb was recognized as one who feared and trusted the Lord, He later rewarded his faith (cf. Jos 14).

14:25 turn … and set out to the wilderness. Because of Israel's refusal to enter the land, instead of continuing northward, God commanded they move southward toward the Gulf of Aqabah.

14:26–35 The Lord granted the Israelites their wish, i.e., their judgment was that they would die in the wilderness (vv. 29, 35: cf. v. 2). Their children, however, whom they thought would become victims (v. 3), God would bring into the land of Canaan (vv. 30–32). The present generation of rebels would die in the wilderness until 40 years were completed. The 40 years were calculated as one year for each day the spies were in Canaan.

14:37 died by a plague. As an indication of the certainty of the coming judgment, the 10 spies who undermined the people's faith were struck by the plague and died.

14:44 they went up heedlessly to the … hill country. With characteristic obstinacy, the people rejected Moses' counsel and the Lord's command and went to attack the Amalekites in the hill country. Since the Lord was not with them, they were defeated.

15:1–41 Even though the Israelites had rebelled against the Lord and were under His judgment, the Lord still planned to give the land of Canaan to them. These laws assumed Israel's entrance into the land (15:2, 17).

15:1–16 The law of the grain offering recorded here differs from that given in Lv 2.

which I am giving you, 3 then make [A]an offering by
fire to the LORD, a burnt offering or a sacrifice to
[a,B]fulfill a special vow, or as a freewill offering or in
your [C]appointed times, to make a [D]soothing aroma
to the LORD, from the herd or from the flock. 4 [A]The
one who presents his offering shall present to the
LORD a grain offering of one-tenth *of an ephah* of
fine flour mixed with one-fourth of a [a]hin of oil,
5 and you shall prepare wine for the drink offering, one-fourth of a hin, with the burnt offering or
for the sacrifice, for [A]each lamb. 6 Or for a ram you
shall prepare as a grain offering two-tenths *of an
ephah* of fine flour mixed with one-third of a hin
of oil; 7 and for the drink offering you shall offer
one-third of a hin of wine as a soothing aroma to
the LORD. 8 When you prepare [A]a bull as a burnt offering or a sacrifice, to [a]fulfill a special vow, or for
peace offerings to the LORD, 9 then you shall offer
with the bull a grain offering of three-tenths *of an
ephah* of fine flour mixed with one-half a hin of oil;
10 and you shall offer as the drink offering one-half
a hin of wine as an offering by fire, as a soothing
aroma to the LORD.
11 'Thus it shall be done for each ox, or for each
ram, or for each of the male lambs, or of the goats.
12 According to the number that you prepare, so
you shall do for everyone according to their number. 13 All who are native shall do these things in
this manner, in presenting an offering by fire, as a
soothing aroma to the LORD.

LAW OF THE SOJOURNER

14 If an alien sojourns with you, or one who may
be among you throughout your generations, and
he *wishes to* make an offering by fire, as a soothing
aroma to the LORD, just as you do so he shall do.
15 *As for* the assembly, there shall be [A]one statute
for you and for the alien who sojourns *with you*,
a perpetual statute throughout your generations;
as you are, so shall the alien be before the LORD.
16 There is to be [A]one law and one ordinance for you
and for the alien who sojourns with you.' "
17 Then the LORD spoke to Moses, saying, 18 "Speak
to the sons of Israel and say to them, 'When you enter the land where I bring you, 19 then it shall be, that
when you eat of the [a,A]food of the land, you shall lift
up [b]an offering to the LORD. 20 [A]Of the first of your
[a]dough you shall lift up a cake as an [b]offering; as [B]the
[b]offering of the threshing floor, so you shall lift it
up. 21 From the first of your [a]dough you shall give to
the LORD an [b]offering throughout your generations.
22 'But when you [A]unwittingly fail and do not
observe all these commandments, which the LORD
has spoken to Moses, 23 *even* all that the LORD has
commanded you [a]through Moses, from the day
when the LORD gave commandment and onward
throughout your generations, 24 then it shall be, if
it is done [A]unintentionally, [a]without the knowledge
of the congregation, that all the congregation shall
offer one bull for a burnt offering, as a soothing
aroma to the LORD, [B]with its grain offering and
its drink offering, according to the ordinance, and
one male goat for a sin offering. 25 Then [A]the priest
shall make atonement for all the congregation of the
sons of Israel, and they will be forgiven; for it was
an error, and they have brought their offering, an
offering by fire to the LORD, and their sin offering
before the LORD, for their error. 26 So all the congregation of the sons of Israel will be forgiven, with the
alien who sojourns among them, for *it happened*
to all the people through [A]error.
27 'Also if one person sins [A]unintentionally, then
he shall offer a one year old female goat for a sin
offering. 28 [A]The priest shall make atonement before
the LORD for the person who goes astray when he
sins unintentionally, making atonement for him
[a]that he may be forgiven. 29 You shall have one law
for him who does *anything* unintentionally, for
him who is native among the sons of Israel and
for the alien who sojourns among them. 30 But the
person who does *anything* [A]defiantly, whether he
is native or an alien, that one is blaspheming the
LORD; and that person shall be cut off from among
his people. 31 Because he has [A]despised the word of
the LORD and has broken His commandment, that
person shall be completely cut off; [B]his [a]guilt *will
be* on him.' "

SABBATH-BREAKING PUNISHED

32 Now while the sons of Israel were in the wilderness, they found a man [A]gathering wood on the
sabbath day. 33 Those who found him gathering
wood brought him to Moses and Aaron and to all
the congregation; 34 and they put him in [a]custody
[A]because it had not been [b]declared what should be
done to him. 35 Then the LORD said to Moses, "The

15:3 [a]*Or make a special votive offering* [A]Lev 1:2, 3 [B]Lev 22:21 [C]Lev 23:1-44 [D]Gen 8:21; 2 Cor 2:15, 16; Phil 4:18 15:4 [a]I.e. Approx one gal., and so through v 10 [A]Num 28:1-29:40 15:5 [A]Lev 1:10; 3:6; Num 15:11 15:8 [a]*Or make a special votive offering* [A]Lev 1:3; 3:1 15:15 [A]Num 9:14; 15:29 15:16 [A]Lev 24:22 15:19 [a]*Lit bread* [b]*Or a heave offering* [A]Josh 5:11, 12 15:20 [a]*Or coarse meal* [b]*Or heave offering* [A]Ex 34:26; Lev 23:14 [B]Deut 14:22, 23; 16:13 15:21 [a]*Or coarse meal* [b]*Or offering lifted up* 15:22 [A]Lev 4:2 15:23 [a]*Lit by the hand of* 15:24 [a]*Lit from the eyes of the congregation* [A]Lev 4:2, 22, 27; 5:15, 18 [B]Num 15:8-10 15:25 [A]Lev 4:20; Heb 2:17 15:26 [A]Num 15:24 15:27 [A]Lev 4:27-31; Luke 12:48 15:28 [a]*Or and he shall* [A]Lev 4:35 15:30 [A]Num 14:40-44; Deut 1:43; 17:12, 13 15:31 [a]*Or iniquity* [A]2 Sam 12:9; Prov 13:13 [B]Ezek 18:20 15:32 [A]Ex 31:14, 15; 35:2, 3 15:34 [a]*Or prison* [b]*Lit declared distinctly* [A]Num 9:8

The grain offerings in Leviticus were offered separately as a gift to the Lord. Here, for the first time, grain and drink offerings were allowed to be offered along with either a burnt or a peace offering.

15:4 ***ephah* ... hin.** Measurements equal to 4 to 6 gallons and 6 to 8 pints.

15:17–21 This regulation pertained to the offering of the firstfruits of the harvest. When the people entered the land of Canaan and began to enjoy its produce, they were to show their devotion to the Lord by presenting to Him a cake baked from the first cuttings of the grain.

15:22 unwittingly fail. Sin offerings were prescribed whenever any of the Lord's commands were disobeyed accidentally, i.e., by unintentional neglect or omission. In vv. 24–26, the offerings for the whole community were given. In vv. 27–29, the offerings for the individual person who sinned unintentionally were stated.

15:30 does *anything* defiantly. Lit. "with a high hand." These sins, committed knowingly and deliberately were described as blasphemous because they were an arrogant act of insubordination against the Lord. Anyone guilty of presumptuous sin was to be excommunicated from Israel and put to death.

15:32–36 This was an illustration of defiant sin. When it was determined that there was a premeditated violation of the Sabbath law, death was required.

man shall surely be put to death; [A]all the congregation shall stone him with stones outside the camp." 36 So all the congregation brought him outside the camp and stoned him [a]to death with stones, just as the LORD had commanded Moses.

37 The LORD also spoke to Moses, saying, 38 "Speak to the sons of Israel, and tell them that they shall make for themselves [A]tassels on the corners of their garments throughout their generations, and that they shall put on the tassel of each corner a cord of blue. 39 It shall be a tassel for you [a]to look at and [A]remember all the commandments of the LORD, so as to do them and not [b]follow after your own heart and your own eyes, after which you played the harlot, 40 so that you may remember to do all My commandments and [A]be holy to your God. 41 I am the LORD your God who brought you out from the land of Egypt to be your God; I am the LORD your God."

KORAH'S REBELLION

16 Now [A]Korah the son of Izhar, the son of Kohath, the son of Levi, with [B]Dathan and Abiram, the sons of Eliab, and On the son of Peleth, sons of Reuben, took *action,* 2 and they rose up before Moses, [a]together with some of the sons of Israel, two hundred and fifty leaders of the congregation, [b,A]chosen in the assembly, men of renown. 3 They assembled together [A]against Moses and Aaron, and said to them, "[a,B]You have gone far enough, for all the congregation are holy, every one of them, and [C]the LORD is in their midst; so why do you exalt yourselves above the assembly of the LORD?"

4 When Moses heard *this,* [A]he fell on his face; 5 and he spoke to Korah and all his company, saying, "Tomorrow morning the LORD will show who is His, and [A]who is holy, and will bring *him* near to Himself; even [B]the one whom He will choose, He will bring near to Himself. 6 Do this: take censers for yourselves, Korah and all [a]your company, 7 and put fire in them, and lay incense upon them in the presence of the LORD tomorrow; and the man whom the LORD chooses *shall be* the one who is holy. [a,A]You have gone far enough, you sons of Levi!"

8 Then Moses said to Korah, "Hear now, you sons of Levi, 9 [A]is it [a]not enough for you that the God of Israel has separated you from the *rest of* the congregation of Israel, [B]to bring you near to Himself, to do the service of the tabernacle of the LORD, and to stand before the congregation to minister to them; 10 and that He has brought you near, *Korah,* and all your brothers, sons of Levi, with you? And are you [A]seeking for the priesthood also? 11 Therefore you and all your company are gathered together [A]against the LORD; but as for Aaron, [a]who is he that [B]you grumble against him?"

12 Then Moses sent [a]a summons to Dathan and Abiram, the sons of Eliab; but they said, "We will not come up. 13 Is it [a]not enough that you have brought us up out of a [A]land flowing with milk and honey [B]to have us die in the wilderness, but you would also lord it over us? 14 Indeed, you have not brought us [A]into a land flowing with milk and honey, nor have you given us an inheritance of [B]fields and vineyards. Would you [a,C]put out the eyes of [b]these men? We will not come up!"

15 Then Moses became very angry and said to the LORD, "[A]Do not regard their offering! [B]I have not taken a single donkey from them, nor have I done harm to any of them." 16 Moses said to Korah, "You and all your company be present before the LORD tomorrow, both you and they along with Aaron. 17 Each of you take his firepan and put incense on [a]it, and each of you bring his censer before the LORD, two hundred and fifty firepans; also you and Aaron *shall* each *bring* his firepan." 18 So they each took his *own* censer and put fire on [a]it, and laid incense on [a]it; and they stood at the doorway of the tent of meeting, with Moses and Aaron. 19 Thus Korah assembled all the congregation against them at the doorway of the tent of meeting. And [A]the glory of the LORD appeared to all the congregation.

20 Then the LORD spoke to Moses and Aaron, saying, 21 "[A]Separate yourselves from among this congregation, [B]that I may consume them instantly." 22 But they fell on their faces and said, "O God, [A]God of the spirits of all flesh, [B]when one man sins, will You be angry with the entire congregation?"

15:35 [A]Lev 20:2, 27; 24:14-23; Deut 21:21 15:36 [a]Lit *with stones and he died* 15:38 [A]Deut 22:12; Matt 23:5 15:39 [a]Lit *and you shall look at it* [b]Lit *seek* [A]Deut 4:23; 6:12; 8:11, 14, 19 15:40 [A]Lev 11:44, 45 16:1 [A]Ex 6:21; Jude 11 [B]Num 26:9; Deut 11:6 16:2 [a]Lit *and men from* [b]Lit *called ones of* [A]Num 1:16; 26:9 16:3 [a]Lit *It is much for you* [A]Num 12:2; Ps 106:16 [B]Num 16:7 [C]Num 5:3 16:4 [A]Num 14:5 16:5 [A]Lev 10:3; Ps 65:4 [B]Num 17:5, 8 16:6 [a]Lit *his* 16:7 [a]Lit *It is much for you* [A]Num 16:3 16:9 [a]Or *too little for you* [A]Is 7:13 [B]Num 3:6, 9; Deut 10:8 16:10 [A]Num 3:10; 18:1-7 16:11 [a]Lit *what* [A]Ex 16:7 [B]1 Cor 10:10 16:12 [a]Lit *to call* 16:13 [a]Lit *a little thing* [A]Ex 16:3; Num 11:4-6 [B]Num 14:2, 3 16:14 [a]Lit *bore out* [b]Lit *those* [A]Num 13:27; 14:8 [B]Ex 22:5; 23:10, 11; Num 20:5 [C]Judg 16:21; 1 Sam 11:2 16:15 [A]Gen 4:4, 5 [B]1 Sam 12:3 16:17 [a]Lit *them* 16:18 [a]Lit *them* 16:19 [A]Num 14:10; 16:42; 20:6 16:21 [A]Num 16:45 [B]Ex 32:10, 12 16:22 [A]Num 27:16 [B]Gen 18:23-32; Lev 4:3

15:37, 38 tassels. These blue tassels were in the form of a flower or petal and were attached to the garments of the Israelites to remind them of their need to trust and obey God's commands.

15:41 the LORD. This reminder harkens back to Moses' first encounter with the Lord in the desert (Ex 3:13–22).

16:1–18:32 In 16:1–40, Korah (a Levite), allied with some Reubenites and other leaders of Israel, instigated an organized opposition to the authority of Aaron and the priests. Their argument against Moses and Aaron was that by claiming the unique right and responsibility to represent the people before God, they exalted themselves based on the promise that "all the congregation are holy, every one of them, and the LORD is in their midst" (16:3). The Lord dealt with these rebels (16:4–40) and reaffirmed His choice of Aaron (16:41–17:13). Finally, the Lord restated the duties and support of both the priests and Levites (18:1–32). These events took place at some unidentified place and time during Israel's wilderness wanderings.

16:1 Korah. Korah was descended from Levi through Kohath. Being a son of Kohath, he already had significant duties at the tabernacle (see 4:1–20). However, he desired further to be a priest (see v. 10).

16:8 sons of Levi. Other Levites were involved in this rebellion with Korah.

16:12 Dathan and Abiram. These two men of the tribe of Reuben despised Moses, blaming him for taking Israel out of the land of Egypt and failing to bring them into the land of Canaan. Because of Moses' perceived failure, they attacked him, joining with Korah in the rebellion against Moses and Aaron.

16:15 nor have I done harm to any of them. Moses pled his innocence before the Lord, claiming to have been a true servant-leader. This confirms that Nu 12:3 could have been written by Moses.

16:16–35 God judged those who rebelled against Moses and Aaron by putting them to death.

16:21 The Lord answered Moses' intercession by calling the people to depart from the tents of the rebels so that only they would be judged.

16:22 God of the spirits of all flesh. This phrase appears only here and in 27:16. Moses

23 Then the LORD spoke to Moses, saying, 24 "Speak to the congregation, saying, '[A]Get back from around the dwellings of Korah, Dathan and Abiram.' "

25 Then Moses arose and went to Dathan and Abiram, with the elders of Israel following him, 26 and he spoke to the congregation, saying, "[A]Depart now from the tents of these wicked men, and touch nothing that belongs to them, [B]or you will be swept away in all their sin." 27 So they got back from around the dwellings of Korah, Dathan and Abiram; and Dathan and Abiram came out *and* stood at the doorway of their tents, along with their wives and [A]their sons and their little ones. 28 Moses said, "By this you shall know that [A]the LORD has sent me to do all these deeds; for this is not [a]my doing. 29 If these men die [a]the death of all men or [b]if they suffer the [A]fate of all men, *then* the LORD has not sent me. 30 But [A]if the LORD [a]brings about an entirely new thing and the ground opens its mouth and swallows them up with all that is theirs, and they [B]descend alive into [b]Sheol, then you will understand that these men have spurned the LORD."

31 As he finished speaking all these words, the ground that was under them split open; 32 and [A]the earth opened its mouth and swallowed them up, and their households, and [B]all the men who belonged to Korah with *their* possessions. 33 So they and all that belonged to them went down alive to [a]Sheol; and the earth closed over them, and they perished from the midst of the assembly. 34 All Israel who *were* around them fled at their [a]outcry, for they said, "The earth may swallow us up!" 35 [A]Fire also came forth from the LORD and consumed the [B]two hundred and fifty men who were offering the incense.

36 [a]Then the LORD spoke to Moses, saying, 37 "Say to Eleazar, the son of Aaron the priest, that he shall take up the censers out of the midst of the [a]blaze, for they are holy; and you scatter the [b]burning coals abroad. 38 As for the censers of these [a]men who have sinned at the cost of their lives, let them be made into hammered sheets for a plating of the altar, since they did present them before the LORD and they are holy; and [A]they shall be for a sign to the sons of Israel." 39 So Eleazar the priest took the bronze censers which the men who were burned had offered, and they hammered them out as a plating for the altar, 40 as a [a]reminder to the sons of Israel that [A]no [b]layman who is not of the [c]descendants of Aaron should come near [B]to burn incense before the LORD; so that he will not become like Korah and his company—just as the LORD had spoken to him [d]through Moses.

MURMURING AND PLAGUE

41 But on the next day all the congregation of the sons of Israel [A]grumbled against Moses and Aaron, saying, "You are the ones who have caused the death of the LORD'S people." 42 It came about, however, when the congregation had assembled against Moses and Aaron, that they turned toward the tent of meeting, and behold, the cloud covered it and [A]the glory of the LORD appeared. 43 Then Moses and Aaron came to the front of the tent of meeting, 44 and the LORD spoke to Moses, saying, 45 "[a,A]Get away from among this congregation, that I may consume them instantly." Then they fell on their faces. 46 Moses said to Aaron, "Take your censer and put in it fire from the altar, and lay incense *on it;* then bring it quickly to the congregation and [A]make atonement for them, for [B]wrath has gone forth from the LORD, the plague has begun!" 47 Then Aaron took *it* as Moses had spoken, and ran into the midst of the assembly, for behold, the plague had begun among the people. [A]So he put *on* the incense and made atonement for the people. 48 He took his stand between the dead and the living, so that the plague was checked. 49 [A]But those who died by the plague were 14,700, besides those who [B]died on account of Korah. 50 Then Aaron returned to Moses at the doorway of the tent of meeting, for the plague had been checked.

AARON'S ROD BUDS

17 [a]Then the LORD spoke to Moses, saying, 2 "Speak to the sons of Israel, and get from them a rod for each father's household: twelve rods, from all their leaders according to their fathers' households. You shall write each name on his rod, 3 and write Aaron's name on the rod of Levi; for there is one rod for the head *of each* of their fathers' households. 4 You shall then deposit them in the tent of meeting in front of [A]the testimony, where I meet with you. 5 It will come about that the rod of [A]the man whom I choose will sprout. Thus I will lessen from

16:24 [A]Num 16:45 16:26 [A]Is 52:11 [B]Gen 19:15, 17 16:27 [A]Num 26:11 16:28 [a]Lit *from my heart* [A]Ex 3:12-15; 4:12, 15 16:29 [a]Lit *like the death* [b]Lit *the visitation of all men be visited upon them* [A]Eccl 3:19 16:30 [a]Lit *creates a new creation* [b]I.e. the nether world [A]Job 31:2, 3 [B]Ps 55:15 16:32 [A]Num 26:10; Deut 11:6; Ps 106:17 [B]Num 26:11 16:33 [a]I.e. the nether world 16:34 [a]Or *voice* 16:35 [A]Num 11:1-3; 26:10 [B]Num 16:2 16:36 [a]Ch 17:1 in Heb 16:37 [a]Or *place of burning* [b]Lit *the fire* 16:38 [a]Lit *sinners against their lives* [A]Ezek 14:8; 2 Pet 2:6 16:40 [a]Or *memorial* [b]Lit *stranger* [c]Lit *seed* [d]Lit *by the hand of* [A]Num 1:51 [B]Ex 30:7-10 16:41 [A]Num 16:3 16:42 [A]Num 16:19 16:45 [a]Or *Arise* [A]Num 16:21, 24 16:46 [A]Num 25:13; Is 6:6, 7 [B]Num 18:5; Deut 9:22 16:47 [A]Num 25:6-8, 13 16:49 [A]Num 25:9 [B]Num 16:32, 35 17:1 [a]Ch 17:16 in Heb 17:4 [A]Ex 25:16, 21, 22; Num 17:7 17:5 [A]Num 16:5

called on omniscient God who knows the heart of everyone to judge those who had sinned, and those only.

16:30 **an entirely new thing.** This supernatural opening of the earth to swallow the rebels was a sign of God's wrath and the vindication of Moses and Aaron.

16:32 **their households.** Numbers 26:11 indicates that this did not include their children.

16:36–40 The 250 leaders of Israel had brought censers filled with fire before the Lord (16:17, 18). The censers were holy to the Lord since they had been used in the tabernacle. Therefore, Eleazar was commanded to hammer out the metal censers into a covering for the altar. That covering was to be a perpetual reminder that God had chosen Aaron and his descendants for the priesthood.

16:41–50 Instead of bringing about the repentance of the people, the Lord's wrath only led to more complaining. Though the children of Israel held Moses and Aaron accountable for the people who had been killed by the Lord, it was the intervention of Moses and Aaron for the entire nation that saved them from destruction because of their opposition to God.

16:46 **incense.** Incense was symbolic of prayer. Aaron interceded in prayer and the plague stopped (v. 48).

16:49 **fourteen thousand seven hundred.** See 1Co 10:10.

17:2 **twelve rods.** These sticks of wood were to bear the names of the 12 tribes, with the tribe of Levi replaced by the name Aaron.

17:4 **in front of the testimony.** The Testimony is the Ten Commandments written on two stone tablets kept in the ark of the covenant. The phrase "in front of the testimony" is synonymous with "before the ark."

upon Myself the grumblings of the sons of Israel,
who are grumbling against you." 6 Moses therefore
spoke to the sons of Israel, and all their leaders gave
him a rod apiece, for each leader according to their
fathers' households, twelve rods, with the rod of
Aaron among their rods. 7 So Moses deposited the
rods before the LORD in [A]the tent of the testimony.
8 Now on the next day Moses went into the tent
of the testimony; and behold, [A]the rod of Aaron for
the house of Levi had sprouted and put forth buds
and produced blossoms, and it bore ripe almonds.
9 Moses then brought out all the rods from the presence of the LORD to all the sons of Israel; and they
looked, and each man took his rod. 10 But the LORD
said to Moses, "Put back the rod of Aaron [A]before the
testimony [a]to be kept as a sign against the [b,B]rebels,
that you may put an end to their grumblings against
Me, so that they will not die." 11 Thus Moses did; just
as the LORD had commanded him, so he did.
12 Then the sons of Israel spoke to Moses, saying,
"[A]Behold, we perish, we are dying, we are all dying!
13 [A]Everyone who comes near, who comes near to
the tabernacle of the LORD, must die. Are we to
perish completely?"

DUTIES OF LEVITES

18 So the LORD said to Aaron, "You and your
sons and your father's household with you
shall [A]bear the guilt [a]in connection with the sanctuary, and you and your sons with you shall bear
the guilt [b]in connection with your priesthood. 2 But
bring with you also your brothers, the tribe of Levi,
the tribe of your father, that they may be [A]joined
with you and serve you, while you and your sons
with you are before the tent of the testimony. 3 And
they shall thus attend to your obligation and the
obligation of all the tent, but [A]they shall not come
near to the furnishings of the sanctuary and [B]the
altar, or both they and you will die. 4 They shall be
joined with you and attend to the obligations of the
tent of meeting, for all the service of the tent; but
an [a]outsider may not come near you. 5 So you shall
attend to the [A]obligations of the sanctuary and the
obligations of the altar, [B]so that there will no longer
be wrath on the sons of Israel. 6 Behold, I Myself
[A]have taken your [a]fellow Levites from among the
sons of Israel; they are [B]a gift to you, [b]dedicated
to the LORD, to perform the service for the tent of
meeting. 7 But you and your sons with you shall [A]at-
tend to your priesthood for everything concerning
the altar and inside the veil, and you are to perform
service. I am giving you the priesthood as [B]a [a]be-
stowed service, but [C]the [b]outsider who comes near
shall be put to death."

THE PRIESTS' PORTION

8 Then the LORD spoke to Aaron, "Now behold,
I Myself have given you charge of My [a,A]offerings,
even all the holy gifts of the sons of Israel I have
given them to you as a portion and to your sons as
a perpetual allotment. 9 This shall be yours from
the most holy *gifts reserved* from the fire; every
offering of theirs, even [A]every grain offering and
every [B]sin offering and every guilt offering, which
they shall render to Me, shall be most holy for you
and for your sons. 10 As the most holy *gifts* you shall
eat it; every male shall eat it. It shall be holy to you.
11 This also is yours, [A]the offering of their gift, even
all the wave offerings of the sons of Israel; I have
[B]given them to you and to your sons and daughters
with you as a perpetual allotment. Everyone of
your household who is clean may eat it. 12 [A]All the
[a]best of the fresh oil and all the [a]best of the fresh
wine and of the grain, the first fruits of those which
they give to the LORD, I give them to you. 13 [A]The
first ripe fruits of all that is in their land, which
they bring to the LORD, shall be yours; everyone of
your household who is clean may eat it. 14 [A]Every
devoted thing in Israel shall be yours. 15 [a,A]Every
first issue of the womb of all flesh, whether man
or animal, which they offer to the LORD, shall be
yours; nevertheless the firstborn of man you shall
surely redeem, and the firstborn of unclean animals
you shall redeem. 16 As to their redemption price,
from a month old you shall redeem them, by your
valuation, five [a]shekels in silver, according to the
[a]shekel of the sanctuary, which is twenty gerahs.
17 But [A]the firstborn of an ox or the firstborn of a
sheep or the firstborn of a goat, you shall not redeem; they are holy. [B]You shall sprinkle their blood
on the altar and shall offer up their fat in smoke
as an offering by fire, for a soothing aroma to the

17:7 [A]Num 1:50, 53; 9:15 17:8 [A]Ezek 17:24; Heb 9:4 17:10 [a]Lit *for preserving* [b]Lit *sons of rebellion* [A]Num 17:4 [B]Deut 9:7, 24 17:12 [A]Is 6:5 17:13 [A]Num 1:51 18:1 [a]Lit *of the sanctuary* [b]Lit *of your priesthood* [A]Ex 28:38; Lev 10:17; 22:16 18:2 [A]Num 3:5-10 18:3 [A]Num 4:15-20 [B]Num 1:51; 18:7 18:4 [a]Lit *a stranger* 18:5 [A]Ex 27:21; Lev 24:3 [B]Num 16:46 18:6 [a]Lit *brethren the* [b]Lit *given* [A]Num 3:12, 45 [B]Num 3:9 18:7 [a]Lit *service of gift* [b]Lit *stranger* [A]Ex 29:9 [B]Num 18:20; Deut 18:2; Matt 10:8; 1 Pet 5:2, 3 [C]Num 1:51 18:8 [a]Lit *heave offerings*, and so throughout the ch [A]Lev 6:16, 18; 7:28-34 18:9 [A]Lev 2:1-16 [B]Lev 6:30 18:11 [A]Num 18:1; Deut 18:3 [B]Lev 22:1-16 18:12 [a]Lit *fat* [A]Deut 18:4; 32:14; Ps 81:16; 147:14 18:13 [A]Ex 22:29; 23:19; 34:26 18:14 [A]Lev 27:1-33 18:15 [a]Lit *Everything that opens* [A]Ex 13:13, 15; Num 3:46 18:16 [a]I.e. A shekel equals approx one-half oz 18:17 [A]Deut 15:19 [B]Lev 3:2

17:8 the rod of Aaron. God had stated that the stick of the man He had chosen would blossom (17:5). The stick of Aaron had not only blossomed, but had yielded ripe almonds. Thus God had exceeded the demands of the test, so there would be no uncertainty of the fact that Aaron had been chosen as High Priest.

17:10 a sign. Aaron's rod that blossomed and brought forth fruit was to be kept as an indication of God's choice in order to permanently stop the murmuring of the rebellious Israelites.

17:12 Behold, we perish. Finally, the people realized their sin in challenging Aaron's role.

17:13 comes near. The people's fear of going near to God led to a reaffirmation of the priesthood of Aaron and his sons in chap. 18.

18:1–7 Only Aaron and his family could minister with the holy articles of the sanctuary of God.

18:1 the LORD said to Aaron. Only here in vv. 1–25 and in Lv 10:8 does the Lord speak directly to Aaron alone. **bear the guilt.** Aaron and his sons from this point forward were responsible for any offense against the holiness of the tabernacle or violations of the rules of priesthood.

18:7 bestowed service. Even though the priesthood demanded much, the priests were to view it as a gift from the Lord.

18:8–20 In return for their service to the Lord, the priests were to receive a portion of the offerings which the people presented in worship. They could keep all of the parts of the sacrifices not consumed on the altar by fire. Also, the offerings of firstfruits and everything devoted to the Lord were theirs as well.

LORD. 18 Their [a]meat shall be yours; it shall be yours like the [A]breast of a wave offering and like the right thigh. 19 [A]All the offerings of the holy *gifts,* which the sons of Israel offer to the LORD, I have given to you and your sons and your daughters with you, as a perpetual allotment. It is [B]an everlasting covenant of salt before the LORD to you and your [a]descendants with you." 20 Then the LORD said to Aaron, "[A]You shall have no inheritance in their land nor own any portion among them; [B]I am your portion and your inheritance among the sons of Israel.

21 "To the sons of Levi, behold, I have given all the [A]tithe in Israel for an inheritance, in return for their service which they perform, the service of the tent of meeting. 22 [A]The sons of Israel shall not come near the tent of meeting again, or they will bear sin and die. 23 Only the Levites shall perform the service of the tent of meeting, and they shall [A]bear their iniquity; it shall be a perpetual statute throughout your generations, and among the sons of Israel [B]they shall have no inheritance. 24 For the tithe of the sons of Israel, which they offer as an offering to the LORD, I have given to the Levites for an inheritance; therefore I have said concerning them, '[A]They shall have no inheritance among the sons of Israel.' "

25 Then the LORD spoke to Moses, saying, 26 "Moreover, you shall speak to the Levites and say to them, 'When you take from the sons of Israel [A]the tithe which I have given you from them for your inheritance, then you shall present an offering from it to the LORD, a [B]tithe of the tithe. 27 Your offering shall be reckoned to you as the grain from the threshing floor or the full produce from the wine vat. 28 So you shall also present an offering to the LORD from your tithes, which you receive from the sons of Israel; and from it you shall give the LORD'S offering to Aaron the priest. 29 Out of all your gifts you shall present every offering due to the LORD, from all the [a]best of them, [b]the sacred part from them.' 30 You shall say to them, 'When you have [a]offered from it the best of it, then *the rest* shall be reckoned to the Levites as the product of the threshing floor, and as the product of the wine vat. 31 You may eat it anywhere, you and your households, for it is your compensation in return for your service in the tent of meeting. 32 You will bear no sin by reason of it when you have [a]offered the [b]best of it. But you shall not [A]profane the sacred gifts of the sons of Israel, or you will die.' "

ORDINANCE OF THE RED HEIFER

19 Then the LORD spoke to Moses and Aaron, saying, 2 "This is the statute of the law which the LORD has commanded, saying, 'Speak to the sons of Israel that they bring you an [A]unblemished red heifer in which is no defect *and* [B]on which a yoke has never [a]been placed. 3 You shall give it to [A]Eleazar the priest, and it shall [B]be brought outside the camp and be slaughtered in his presence. 4 Next Eleazar the priest shall take some of its blood with his finger and [A]sprinkle some of its blood toward the front of the tent of meeting seven times. 5 Then the heifer shall be burned in his sight; [A]its hide and its flesh and its blood, with its refuse, shall be burned. 6 The priest shall take [A]cedar wood and hyssop and scarlet *material* and cast it into the midst of the [a]burning heifer. 7 The priest [A]shall then wash his clothes and bathe his [a]body in water, and afterward come into the camp, but the priest shall be unclean until evening. 8 The one who burns it shall also wash his clothes in water and bathe his [a]body in water, and shall be unclean until evening. 9 Now a man who is clean shall gather up the ashes of the heifer and deposit them outside the camp in a clean place, and [a]the congregation of the sons of Israel shall keep it as [A]water to remove impurity; it is [b]purification from sin. 10 The one who gathers the ashes of the heifer [A]shall wash his clothes and be unclean until evening; and it shall be a perpetual statute to the sons of Israel and to the alien who sojourns among them.

11 '[A]The one who touches the corpse of any [a]person shall be unclean for seven days. 12 That one shall [A]purify himself from uncleanness with [a]the water on the third day and on the seventh day, *and then* he will be clean; but if he does not purify himself on the third day and on the seventh day, he will

18:18 [a]Lit *flesh* [A]Lev 7:31 18:19 [a]Lit *seed* [A]Num 18:11 [B]2 Chr 13:5 18:20 [A]Deut 10:9; 12:12; 14:27, 29 [B]Deut 18:2; Josh 13:33; Ezek 44:28 18:21 [A]Lev 27:30-33; Deut 14:22-29 18:22 [A]Num 1:51 18:23 [A]Num 18:1 [B]Num 18:20 18:24 [A]Deut 10:9 18:26 [A]Num 18:21 [B]Neh 10:38 18:29 [a]Lit *fat* [b]Lit *its* 18:30 [a]Lit *lifted* 18:32 [a]Lit *lifted* [b]Lit *fat* [A]Lev 22:15, 16 19:2 [a]Lit *come up* [A]Lev 22:20-25 [B]Deut 21:3 19:3 [A]Num 3:4 [B]Lev 4:11, 12, 21; Num 19:9 19:4 [A]Lev 4:6, 17; 16:14 19:5 [A]Ex 29:14; Lev 4:11, 12 19:6 [a]Lit *burning of the heifer* [A]Lev 14:4 19:7 [a]Lit *flesh* [A]Lev 16:26, 28; 22:6 19:8 [a]Lit *flesh* 19:9 [a]Lit *it shall be to the congregation…Israel, for a guarding as water of impurity* [b]Or *a sin offering* [A]Num 8:7; 31:23 19:10 [A]Num 19:7 19:11 [a]Lit *soul of man* [A]Lev 21:1, 11; Num 5:2; 6:6; Acts 21:26, 27 19:12 [a]Lit *it* [A]Num 19:19; 31:19

18:19 an everlasting covenant of salt. Salt, which does not burn, was a metaphor to speak of durability. As salt keeps its flavor, so the Lord's covenant with the priesthood was durable. The Lord would provide through the offerings of His people for His priests forever.

18:21–24 The Levites received the tithes from the people. This was their source of income and compensation for their tabernacle service.

18:25–32 As the Levites themselves received the tithe, they were also required to present a tithe (a tenth) of what they received to the Lord.

19:1–22 Over a period of 38 1/2 years, over 1.2 million people died in the wilderness because of God's judgment. The Israelites were continually coming into contact with dead bodies, which led to ceremonial uncleanness. Therefore, the Lord provided a means of purification so that those who came into contact with dead bodies might be cleansed.

19:1–10 The provision given for the preparation of the "water of purification" (cf. Lv 12–15).

19:2 an unblemished red heifer. A reddish brown cow, probably young since no yoke had been laid on it. This cow was burned and its ashes were used as the agent of purification (see v. 9).

19:3 Eleazar. The son of Aaron was a deputy High Priest who was in charge of the slaughter of the red cow. **outside the camp.** The red cow was killed outside the camp of Israel, and its ashes were stored there as well (see v. 9). Hebrews 13:11–13 picks up the image of "outside the camp" as it relates to Christ's death outside of Jerusalem.

19:6 cedar wood and hyssop and scarlet. The cow was totally consumed by the fire along with these 3 materials, which were also used in the ritual of purification of skin disease (Lv 14:1–9). The ashes of all these and the cow were mixed to make the agent by which cleansing could take place.

19:11–22 A general statement regarding the use of the "water of purification" (vv. 11–13) is followed by a more detailed explanation of the procedure to be followed.

not be clean. [13] [A]Anyone who touches a corpse, the [a]body of a man who has died, and does not purify himself, [B]defiles the [b]tabernacle of the LORD; and that person shall be cut off from Israel. Because the water for impurity was not [c,C]sprinkled on him, he shall be unclean; his uncleanness is still on him.

[14] 'This is the law when a man dies in a tent: everyone who comes into the tent and everyone who is in the tent shall be unclean for seven days. [15] Every open vessel, which has no covering [a]tied down on it, shall be unclean. [16] [A]Also, anyone who in the open field touches one who has been slain with a sword or who has died *naturally,* or a human bone or a grave, shall be unclean for seven days. [17] Then for the unclean *person* they shall take some of the [a]ashes of the [b]burnt [c,A]purification from sin and [d]flowing water shall be [e]added to them in a vessel. [18] A clean person shall take hyssop and dip *it* in the water, and sprinkle *it* on the tent and on all the furnishings and on the persons who were there, and on the one who touched the bone or the one slain or the one dying *naturally* or the grave. [19] Then the clean *person* [A]shall sprinkle on the unclean on the third day and on the seventh day; and on the seventh day he shall purify him from uncleanness, and he shall wash his clothes and bathe *himself* in water and shall be clean by evening.

[20] 'But the man who is unclean and does not purify himself from uncleanness, that person shall be cut off from the midst of the assembly, because he has [A]defiled the sanctuary of the LORD; the water for impurity has not been sprinkled on him, he is unclean. [21] So it shall be a perpetual statute for them. And he [A]who sprinkles the water for impurity shall wash his clothes, and he who touches the water for impurity shall be unclean until evening. [22] [A]Furthermore, anything that the unclean *person* touches shall be unclean; and the person who touches *it* shall be unclean until evening.' "

DEATH OF MIRIAM

20 Then the sons of Israel, the whole congregation, came to the [A]wilderness of Zin in the first month; and the people stayed at Kadesh. Now Miriam died there and was buried there.

[2] [A]There was no water for the congregation, [B]and they assembled themselves against Moses and Aaron. [3] [A]The people thus contended with Moses and spoke, saying, "[B]If only we had perished [C]when our brothers perished before the LORD! [4] [A]Why then have you brought the LORD'S assembly into this wilderness, for us and our beasts to die [a]here? [5] Why have you made us come up from Egypt, to bring us in to this wretched place? [A]It is not a place of [a]grain or figs or vines or pomegranates, nor is there water to drink." [6] Then Moses and Aaron came in from the presence of the assembly to the doorway of the tent of meeting and [A]fell on their faces. Then the glory of the LORD appeared to them; [7] and the LORD spoke to Moses, saying,

THE WATER OF MERIBAH

[8] "Take [A]the rod; and you and your brother Aaron assemble the congregation and speak to the rock before their eyes, that it may yield its water. You shall thus bring forth water for them out of the rock and let the congregation and their beasts drink."

[9] So Moses took the rod [A]from before the LORD, just as He had commanded him; [10] and Moses and Aaron gathered the assembly before the rock. And he said to them, "[A]Listen now, you rebels; shall we bring forth water for you out of this rock?" [11] Then Moses lifted up his hand and struck the rock twice with his rod; and [A]water came forth abundantly, and the congregation and their beasts drank. [12] But the LORD said to Moses and Aaron, "[A]Because you have not believed Me, to treat Me as holy in the sight of the sons of Israel, therefore you shall not bring this assembly into the land which I have given them."

19:13 [a]Lit *soul* [b]Lit *dwelling place* [C]Or *thrown* [A]Lev 7:21; 22:3-7 [B]Lev 15:31; 20:3; Num 19:20 [C]Num 19:19 19:15 [a]Lit *cord* 19:16 [A]Num 31:19 19:17 [a]Lit *dust* [b]Lit *burning of the* [c]Or *sin offering* [d]Lit *living* [e]Lit *put* [A]Num 19:9 19:19 [A]Ezek 36:25; Heb 10:22 19:20 [A]Num 19:13 19:21 [A]Num 19:7 19:22 [A]Lev 5:2, 3; 7:21; 22:5, 6 20:1 [A]Num 13:21; 27:14; 33:36 20:2 [A]Ex 17:1 [B]Num 16:19, 42 20:3 [A]Ex 17:2 [B]Num 14:2, 3 [C]Num 16:31-35 20:4 [a]Lit *there* [A]Ex 17:3 20:5 [a]Lit *seed* [A]Num 16:14 20:6 [A]Num 14:5 20:8 [A]Ex 4:17, 20; 17:5, 6 20:9 [A]Num 17:10 20:10 [A]Ps 106:33 20:11 [A]Ps 78:16; Is 48:21; 1 Cor 10:4 20:12 [A]Num 20:24; 27:14; Deut 1:37; 3:26, 27

19:18 A clean person. Any clean person, not just priests, could sprinkle the unclean with the water of purification.

20:1–22:1 These chapters record the beginning of the transition from the old generation (represented by Miriam and Aaron) to the new generation (represented by Eleazar). Geographically, Israel moves from Kadesh (20:1) to the plains of Moab (22:1) from where the conquest of the land would be launched. There is an interval of 37 years between 19:22 and 20:1.

20:1–13 Just as the children of Israel failed to trust in the Lord (14:11) and thus were not allowed to go into the Promised Land (14:30), Israel's leaders, Moses and Aaron, would also not go into the land because of failure to trust in the Lord.

20:1 the first month. The year is not stated. However, at the end of this chapter, there is a report of the death of Aaron. According to Nu 33:38, Aaron died on the first day of the fifth month of the fortieth year after the Exodus from Egypt. Thus, the first month here must be of the fortieth year. Most of the older generation had died in the wilderness. **Kadesh.** As the people had begun their wilderness wanderings at Kadesh (13:26), so they ended them there. Kadesh was located on the northern boundary of the wilderness of Paran (13:26) and on the SE border of the wilderness of Zin. **Miriam died.** Miriam, who led Israel in celebrating the victory over Egypt at the Red Sea (Ex 15:20, 21), also led the attack against Moses recorded in Nu 12:1–15. Her death served as a symbol that the old generation would not enter Canaan.

20:2 no water. During Israel's 40 years in the wilderness, water was their greatest physical need. The Lord had provided it continually, beginning at Horeb (Ex 17:1–7). The present lack of water stirred the people to contend with Moses.

20:3 If only we had perished when our brothers perished. The situation was so desperate in the people's mind that they wished they had been among those who died in Korah's rebellion (16:41–50).

20:6 fell on their faces. As he had done in the past, Moses sought the Lord's counsel (see 14:5; 16:4).

20:8 speak to the rock. Though God told Moses to take his rod with which He had performed many wonders in the past (Ex 4:1–5; 7:19–21; 14:16; 17:5, 6), he was only to speak to the rock for it to yield water.

20:10 you rebels. Instead of speaking to the rock, Moses spoke to the people, accusing them of being rebels against God. By his actions, Moses joined the people in rebellion against God (see 27:14).

20:12 you have not believed Me. The Lord's evaluation of Moses was that he failed to take God at His word and thus to treat Him as holy to the people. Moses here failed in the same way as Israel had at Kadesh 38 years previously (14:11). **you shall not bring this assembly into the land.** God's judgment upon Moses for his sin of striking the rock was that he would not take Israel into the land of Canaan. The inclusion of Aaron demonstrated his partnership with Moses in the action against the Lord.

13 Those *were* the waters of [a,A]Meribah, [b]because
the sons of Israel contended with the LORD, and
He proved Himself holy among them.
14 From Kadesh Moses then sent messengers to
[A]the king of Edom: "Thus your brother Israel has
said, 'You [B]know all the hardship that has befall-
en us; 15 that our fathers went down to Egypt, and
we stayed in Egypt a long time, and the Egyptians
treated us and our fathers badly. 16 But [A]when we
cried out to the LORD, He heard our voice and sent
[B]an angel and brought us out from Egypt; now behold, we are at Kadesh, a town on the edge of your
territory. 17 Please [A]let us pass through your land.
We will not pass through field or through vineyard;
we will not even drink water from a well. We will
go along the king's highway, not turning to the
right or left, until we pass through your territory.' "
18 [A]Edom, however, said to him, "You shall not
pass through [a]us, or I will come out with the sword
against you." 19 Again, the sons of Israel said to him,
"We will go up by the highway, and if I and [A]my
livestock do drink any of your water, [B]then I will
[a]pay its price. Let me only pass through on my feet,
[b]nothing *else*." 20 But he said, "[A]You shall not pass
through." And Edom came out against him with a
heavy [a]force and with a strong hand. 21 [A]Thus Edom
refused to allow Israel to pass through his territory;
[B]so Israel turned away from him.
22 Now when they set out from [A]Kadesh, the sons of
Israel, the whole congregation, came to Mount Hor.

DEATH OF AARON

23 Then the LORD spoke to Moses and Aaron at
[A]Mount Hor by the border of the land of Edom, saying, 24 "Aaron will be [A]gathered to his people; for he
shall not enter the land which I have given to the
sons of Israel, because [B]you rebelled against My
[a]command at the waters of Meribah. 25 Take Aaron
and his son [A]Eleazar and bring them up to Mount
Hor; 26 and strip Aaron of his garments and put
them on his son Eleazar. So Aaron will be [A]gathered
to his people, and will die there." 27 So Moses did just
as the LORD had commanded, and they went up
to Mount Hor in the sight of all the congregation.
28 After Moses had stripped Aaron of his garments
and [A]put them on his son Eleazar, [B]Aaron died there
on the mountain top. Then Moses and Eleazar came
down from the mountain. 29 When all the congregation saw that Aaron had died, all the house of
Israel wept for Aaron thirty [A]days.

ARAD CONQUERED

21 When the Canaanite, the king of [A]Arad, who
lived in the [a]Negev, heard that Israel was coming by the way of [b]Atharim, then he fought against
Israel and took some of them captive. 2 So [A]Israel
made a vow to the LORD and said, "If You will indeed
deliver this people into my hand, then I will [a]utterly
destroy their cities." 3 The LORD heard the voice of
Israel and delivered up the Canaanites; then they
[a]utterly destroyed them and their cities. Thus the
name of the place was called [b,A]Hormah.
4 Then they set out from Mount Hor by the way
of the [a]Red Sea, to [A]go around the land of Edom;
and the [b]people became impatient because of the
journey. 5 The people spoke against God and Moses,
"[A]Why have you brought us up out of Egypt to die in
the wilderness? For there is no [a]food and no water,
and [b,B]we loathe this miserable food."

THE BRONZE SERPENT

6 [A]The LORD sent fiery serpents among the people
and [B]they bit the people, so that [C]many people of
Israel died. 7 [A]So the people came to Moses and said,
"We have sinned, because we have spoken against
the LORD and you; [B]intercede with the LORD, that
He may remove the serpents from us." And Moses
interceded for the people. 8 Then the LORD said to

20:13 [a]I.e. contention [b]Or *where* [A]Ex 17:7; Ps 95:8 20:14 [A]Gen 36:31-39; Deut 2:4 [B]Josh 2:9, 10; 9:9, 10, 24 20:16 [A]Ex 2:23; 3:7 [B]Ex 14:19 20:17 [A]Num 21:22 20:18 [a]Lit *me* [A]Num 24:18 20:19 [a]Lit *give* [b]Or *no great thing* [A]Ex 12:38 [B]Deut 2:6, 28 20:20 [a]Lit *people* [A]Judg 11:17 20:21 [A]Judg 11:17 [B]Deut 2:8 20:22 [A]Num 20:1, 14 20:23 [A]Num 33:37 20:24 [a]Lit *mouth* [A]Gen 25:8 [B]Num 20:5, 10 20:25 [A]Num 3:4 20:26 [A]Num 20:24 20:28 [A]Ex 29:29 [B]Num 33:38; Deut 10:6; 32:50 20:29 [A]Gen 1:5; 50:3, 10; Deut 34:8 21:1 [a]I.e. South country [b]Or *the spies* [A]Num 33:40; Josh 12:14; Judg 1:16 21:2 [a]Lit *devote to destruction* [A]Gen 28:20; Judg 11:30 21:3 [a]Lit *devoted to destruction* [b]I.e. a devoted thing; or Destruction [A]Num 14:45 21:4 [a]Lit *Sea of Reeds* [b]Lit *soul of the people was short* [A]Deut 2:8 21:5 [a]Lit *bread* [b]Lit *our soul loathes* [A]Num 14:2, 3 [B]Num 11:6 21:6 [A]Deut 8:15 [B]Jer 8:17 [C]1 Cor 10:9 21:7 [A]Num 11:2; Ps 78:34; Is 26:16; Hos 5:15 [B]Ex 8:8; 1 Sam 12:19; Acts 8:24

20:13 Meribah. Lit. "contention, quarreling." The same name was used earlier at the first occasion of bringing water from the rock (Ex 17:7).

20:14–21 Moses' attempt to pass through the territory of Edom was rejected by the king.

20:14 your brother Israel. The people of Edom were descended from Esau, the brother of Jacob (see Ge 36:1).

20:17 the king's highway. The major N-S trade route from the Gulf of Aqabah N to Damascus, which passed through the Edomite city of Sela.

20:20 with a heavy force and with a strong hand. The king of Edom sent out his army to intercept Israel. Since Israel was forbidden by the Lord to engage in warfare with Edom (Dt 2:4–6), they turned away from Edom's border.

20:22–29 Eleazar succeeded his father, Aaron, as High Priest. Aaron's death further marked the passing of the first generation.

20:22 Mount Hor. Likely a mountain to the NE of Kadesh on the border of Edom.

20:24 because you rebelled against My command. Aaron had joined Moses in rebellion against God (v. 12). Aaron's death foreshadowed the death of Moses.

20:29 wept … thirty days. This was the same mourning period as for Moses (Dt 34:8). Since the normal time for mourning was 7 days (see Ge 50:10), the length of this mourning showed the importance of Aaron and the loss to Israel.

21:1–3 Israel's first victory over the Canaanites occurred at Hormah, the place they had previously been defeated (see 14:45).

21:1 king of Arad. This raiding king came from a Canaanite city in the S (i.e., the Negev).

21:3 they utterly destroyed them. Israel vowed to the Lord that if He would give them victory over Arad, they would completely destroy them, not claiming the spoils of victory for themselves. The Lord responded to this vow and gave victory.

21:4–9 After their victory over Arad, Israel showed again their lack of obedience toward the Lord.

21:4 by the way of the Red Sea. Cf. Dt 2:1. Since the way through Edom was barred, Moses turned to the S to take Israel around Edom. Thus, Israel journeyed toward Elath on the coast of the Gulf of Aqabah. This long, circuitous route led to impatience and frustration on the part of Israel.

21:5 this miserable food. The people's impatience led them to despise the manna (see 11:6).

21:6 fiery serpents. So called because these snake bites inflicted a fiery inflammation.

21:7 We have sinned. The people confessed their iniquity and asked that they might be released from the judgment God had sent.

Moses, "[a]Make a [A]fiery *serpent,* and set it on a standard; and it shall come about, that everyone who is
bitten, when he looks at it, he will live." 9 And Moses
made a [A]bronze serpent and set it on the standard;
and it came about, that if a serpent bit any man,
when he looked to the bronze serpent, he lived.
10 [A]Now the sons of Israel moved out and camped
in Oboth. 11 They journeyed from Oboth and camped
at Iye-abarim, in the wilderness which is opposite
Moab, to the [a]east. 12 [A]From there they set out and
camped in [a]Wadi Zered. 13 From there they journeyed
and camped on the other side of the Arnon, which
is in the wilderness that comes out of the border of
the Amorites, [A]for the Arnon is the border of Moab,
between Moab and the Amorites. 14 Therefore it is
said in the Book of the Wars of the LORD,

"Waheb in Suphah,
And the wadis of the Arnon,
15 And the slope of the wadis
That extends to the site of [A]Ar,
And leans to the border of Moab."

16 [A]From there *they continued* to [a]Beer, that is the
well where the LORD said to Moses, "Assemble the
people, that I may give them water."

17 [A]Then Israel sang this song:

"Spring up, O well! Sing to it!
18 "The well, which the leaders sank,
Which the nobles of the people dug,
With the scepter *and* with their staffs."

And from the wilderness *they continued* to Mattanah, 19 and from Mattanah to Nahaliel, and from
Nahaliel to Bamoth, 20 and from Bamoth to the valley that is in the land of Moab, at the top of Pisgah
which overlooks the [a]wasteland.

TWO VICTORIES

21 [A]Then Israel sent messengers to Sihon, king of
the Amorites, saying, 22 "[A]Let me pass through your
land. We will not turn off into field or vineyard; we
will not drink water from wells. We will go by the
king's highway until we have passed through your
border." 23 [A]But Sihon would not permit Israel to pass
through his border. So Sihon gathered all his people
and went out against Israel in the wilderness, and
came to [B]Jahaz and fought against Israel. 24 Then
[A]Israel [a]struck him with the edge of the sword, and
took possession of his land from the Arnon to the
Jabbok, as far as the sons of Ammon; for the [B]border

21:8 [a]Lit *Make for yourself* [A]Is 14:29; 30:6; John 3:14 21:9 [A]2 Kin 18:4; John 3:14, 15 21:10 [A]Num 33:43, 44 21:11 [a]Lit *sunrise* 21:12 [a]I.e. a dry ravine except during rainy season [A]Num 33:45 21:13 [A]Num 22:36; Judg 11:18 21:15 [A]Num 21:28; Deut 2:9, 18, 29 21:16 [a]I.e. a well [A]Num 33:46-49 21:17 [A]Ex 15:1; Ps 105:2 21:20 [a]Or *Jeshimon* 21:21 [A]Deut 2:26-37; Judg 11:19 21:22 [A]Num 20:16, 17 21:23 [A]Num 20:21 [B]Deut 2:32 21:24 [a]Lit *smote,* so with Gr and Lat [A]Amos 2:9 [B]Deut 2:37

21:9 a bronze serpent. One had to fix his gaze upon this snake, a definite act of the will, if he wanted to be healed and live. See the typological use of this incident in Jn 3:14, 15.

21:10–20 Israel circled around both Edom and Moab and encamped on the N side of the Arnon River in the territory of the Amorites.

21:14 the Book of the Wars of the LORD. This was apparently a book of victory songs that was current at the time of Moses, possibly written by Moses or a contemporary. The work is cited here as evidence that the Arnon River was the northern boundary of Moab.

21:16 Beer. Lit. "well." Here God provided water for Israel. In response, Israel praised the Lord with a song which might have also come from "the Book of the Wars of the LORD" (vv. 17, 18).

21:21–32 As with Edom (20:14–19), Israel requested passage through the land of Sihon, a king of the Amorites. Since there was no requirement from the Lord not to engage the Amorites in warfare as there had been for Edom, when Sihon brought out his army, he was attacked and defeated by Israel. Israel thus took the land bounded by the Arnon River on the S, the Dead Sea and Jordan River on the W, the Jabbok River on the N, and the land of the Ammonites on the E.

21:27 those who use proverbs say. These words came from the wise men, probably among the Amorites. The words of vv. 27–30 describe the Amorites' defeat of the Moabites N of the Arnon River. Ironically, as the Amorites had taken the land from the Moabites, the Israelites had taken the land from the Amorites. The purpose of these words cited by Moses was to substantiate Israel's right to this land. According to God's commandments, the territory belonging to the Moabites was not to be taken by Israel because the Moabites were descendants of Lot (Dt 2:9). However, what belonged to the Amorites had been promised to Israel and was theirs for the taking.

HYMNS AND SONGS OF THE OLD TESTAMENT

The earliest recorded song in the Bible is referred to as the Song of Moses (see Ex. 15). This hymn was sung by the people to celebrate God's miraculous deliverance of the Hebrews from the Egyptian army at the Red Sea (Ex. 14:3–30). Other significant hymns and songs of the Old Testament include the following:

Personality	Description	Biblical Reference
Israelites	Sung by the people as they dug life-saving wells in the wilderness	Nu 21:14–18
Moses	A song of praise to God by Moses just before his death	Dt 32:1–44
Deborah and Barak	A victory song after Israel's defeat of the Canaanites	Jdg 5:1–31
Israelite Women	A song to celebrate David's defeat of Goliath	1Sa 18:6, 7
Levite Singers	A song of praise at the dedication of the temple in Jerusalem	2Ch 5:12–14
Levite Singers	A song of praise, presented as a marching song as the army of Israel prepared for battle	2Ch 20:20–23
Levite Singers	A song at the temple restoration ceremony during Hezekiah's reign	2Ch 29:25–30

of the sons of Ammon *was* [b]Jazer. 25 Israel took
all these cities and [A]Israel lived in all the cities of
the Amorites, in Heshbon, and in all her [a]villages.
26 For Heshbon was the city of Sihon, king of the
Amorites, who had fought against the former king
of Moab and had taken all his land out of his hand,
as far as the Arnon. 27 Therefore those who use
proverbs say,

"Come to Heshbon! Let it be built!
So let the city of Sihon be established.
28 "[A]For a fire went forth from Heshbon,
A flame from the town of Sihon;
It devoured [B]Ar of Moab,
The [a,C]dominant [b]heights of the Arnon.
29 "[A]Woe to you, O Moab!
You are ruined, O people of [B]Chemosh!
[C]He has given his sons as fugitives,
[D]And his daughters into captivity,
To an Amorite king, Sihon.
30 "But we have cast them down,
Heshbon is ruined as far as [A]Dibon,
Then we have laid waste even to Nophah,
Which *reaches* to Medeba."

31 Thus Israel lived in the land of the Amorites.
32 Moses sent to spy out [A]Jazer, and they captured
its villages and dispossessed the Amorites who
were there.
33 [A]Then they turned and went up by the way of
Bashan, and Og the king of Bashan went out [a]with
all his people, for battle at [B]Edrei. 34 But the LORD
said to Moses, "[A]Do not fear him, for I have given
him into your hand, and all his people and his land;
and you shall do to him as you did to Sihon, king
of the Amorites, who lived at Heshbon." 35 So [A]they
[a]killed him and his sons and all his people, until
there was no remnant left him; and they possessed
his land.

BALAK SENDS FOR BALAAM

22 [A]Then the sons of Israel journeyed, and
camped in the plains of Moab beyond the
Jordan *opposite* Jericho.
2 Now [A]Balak the son of Zippor saw all that Israel
had done to the Amorites. 3 [A]So Moab was in great
fear because of the people, for they were numerous;
and Moab was in dread of the sons of Israel. 4 Moab
said to the elders of [A]Midian, "Now this [a]horde will
lick up all that is around us, as the ox licks up the
grass of the field." And Balak the son of Zippor was
king of Moab at that time. 5 So he sent messengers
to [A]Balaam the son of Beor, at [B]Pethor, which is near
the [a]River, *in* the land of the sons of his people,
to call him, saying, "Behold, a people came out of
Egypt; behold, they cover the surface of the land,
and they are living opposite me. 6 [A]Now, therefore,
please come, [B]curse this people for me since they
are too [a]mighty for me; perhaps I may be able to
[b]defeat them and drive them out of the land. For
I know that he whom you bless is blessed, and he
whom you curse is cursed."
7 So the elders of Moab and the elders of Midian
departed with the *fees for* [A]divination in their hand;
and they came to Balaam and [a]repeated Balak's
words to him. 8 He said to them, "Spend the night
here, and I will bring word back to you as the LORD
may speak to me." And the leaders of Moab stayed
with Balaam. 9 Then [A]God came to Balaam and said,
"Who are these men with you?" 10 Balaam said to
God, "Balak the son of Zippor, king of Moab, has
sent *word* to me, 11 'Behold, there is a people who
came out of Egypt and they cover the surface of the
land; now come, curse them for me; perhaps I may
be able to fight against them and drive them out.'"
12 God said to Balaam, "Do not go with them; [A]you
shall not curse the people, for they [B]are blessed."
13 So Balaam arose in the morning and said to
Balak's leaders, "Go back to your land, for the LORD

21:24 [b]M.T. reads *strong* 21:25 [a]Lit *daughters* [A]Amos 2:10 21:28 [a]Lit *lords of the* [b]Or *Bamoth* [A]Jer 48:45 [B]Num 21:15 [C]Num 22:41; Is 15:2; 16:12 21:29 [A]Jer 48:46 [B]Judg 11:24; 1 Kin 11:33; 2 Kin 23:13 [C]Is 15:5 [D]Is 16:2 21:30 [A]Num 32:3, 34; Jer 48:18, 22 21:32 [A]Num 32:1, 3, 35; Jer 48:32 21:33 [a]Lit *he and* [A]Deut 3:1-7 [B]Josh 13:12 21:34 [A]Deut 3:2 21:35 [a]Lit *smote* [A]Deut 3:3, 4 22:1 [A]Num 33:48, 49 22:2 [A]Judg 11:25 22:3 [A]Ex 15:15 22:4 [a]Lit *assembly* [A]Num 25:15-18; 31:1-3 22:5 [a]I.e. Euphrates [A]Josh 24:9; 2 Pet 2:15f; Jude 11 [B]Deut 23:4 22:6 [a]Or *numerous* [b]Lit *smite* [A]Num 22:17; 23:7, 8 [B]Num 22:12; 24:9 22:7 [a]Lit *spoke* [A]Num 23:23; 24:1; Josh 13:22 22:9 [A]Gen 20:3 22:12 [A]Num 23:8; 24:9 [B]Gen 12:2; 22:17

21:33–35 The land N of the Jabbok River was under the control of Og, another Amorite king. Og attacked Israel and suffered a devastating defeat. Thus, all of the land in the Transjordan from the Arnon River in the S to the heights of Bashan in the N came under Israelite control.

22:1 With their control of Transjordan secured, Israel moved unimpeded to the plains of Moab in preparation for assaulting Canaan.

22:2–24:25 The narrative changes to center on Balaam, a pagan prophet. His oracles reassert the faithfulness of the Lord to the Abrahamic Covenant and His purpose to bless Israel. In 22:2–40, the events leading to Balaam's words are recorded. This is followed in 22:41–24:24 with the words of his prophecies, and the conclusion is in 24:25.

22:3 Moab was in great fear. The Moabites were descendants of Lot (see Ge 19:36, 37). Balak, their king, had seen how the Israelites destroyed the Amorites. Not knowing that Israel was forbidden by God to attack Moab, he was terrified that the same end awaited him and his people (Dt 2:9).

22:4 Midian. The Midianites were descendants of Abraham through Keturah (see Ge 25:1–4), who lived S of Moab's border. When Moab communicated to the elders of Midian that they were in danger of being destroyed by Israel as well, they joined with Moab in an alliance to defeat Israel.

22:5 Balaam. Balaam was from Pethor, a city on the Euphrates River, perhaps near Mari, where the existence of a cult of prophets whose activities resembled those of Balaam have been found. Balaam practiced magic and divination (24:1) and eventually led Israel into apostasy (31:16). Later Scripture identifies Balaam as a false prophet (Dt 23:3–6; Jos 13:22; 24:9, 10; Ne 13:1–3; Mic 6:5; 2Pe 2:15, 16; Jude 11; Rev 2:14).

22:6 curse this people. Knowing that Israel was too strong to defeat militarily, Balak called for Balaam to come and curse Israel. A curse was a spoken word that was believed to bring misfortune upon the one it was spoken against. Balak acknowledged that Balaam had the reputation of pronouncing curses that actually worked.

22:8 as the LORD may speak to me. Throughout these chapters Balaam himself used the name "Lord," i.e., Israel's God (22:13, 18–19; 23:3, 12; 24:13). In 22:18 he even called the Lord, "the LORD my God." In this verse it must be assumed that Balaam expected the God of Israel to speak to him. As a pagan prophet he would anticipate making contact with the gods of any people.

22:9 God came to Balaam. Israel's God did communicate to Balaam. However, rather than using the term "Lord," which indicates a covenant relationship, God consistently used the word "God" when He spoke to him (22:9, 12, 20). Though Balaam used the word "Lord," the biblical text makes it clear that he did not have a relationship with Israel's God.

22:12 they are blessed. Balaam could not curse Israel because the Lord had determined to give them blessing only.

has refused to let me go with you." 14 The leaders of Moab arose and went to Balak and said, "Balaam refused to come with us."

15 Then Balak again sent leaders, more numerous and more distinguished than [a]the former. 16 They came to Balaam and said to him, "Thus says Balak the son of Zippor, 'Let nothing, I beg you, hinder you from coming to me; 17 for I will indeed honor you richly, and I will do whatever you say to me. [A]Please come then, curse this people for me.' " 18 Balaam replied to the servants of Balak, "[A]Though Balak were to give me his house full of silver and gold, I could not do anything, either small or great, contrary to the [a]command of the LORD my God. 19 Now please, you also stay here tonight, and I will find out what else the LORD will speak to me." 20 God came to Balaam at night and said to him, "If the men have come to call you, rise up *and* go with them; but [A]only the word which I speak to you shall you do."

21 [A]So Balaam arose in the morning, and saddled his donkey and went with the leaders of Moab.

THE ANGEL AND BALAAM

22 But God was angry because he was going, [A]and the angel of the LORD took his stand in the way as an adversary against him. Now he was riding on his donkey and his two servants were with him. 23 When the donkey saw the angel of the LORD standing in the way with his drawn sword in his hand, the donkey turned off from the way and went into the field; but Balaam struck the donkey to turn her back into the way. 24 Then the angel of the LORD stood in a narrow path of the vineyards, *with* a wall on this side and a wall on that side. 25 When the donkey saw the angel of the LORD, she pressed herself to the wall and pressed Balaam's foot against the wall, so he struck her again. 26 The angel of the LORD went further, and stood in a narrow place where there was no way to turn to the right hand or the left. 27 When the donkey saw the angel of the LORD, she lay down under Balaam; so [A]Balaam was angry and struck the donkey with his stick. 28 And [A]the LORD opened the mouth of the donkey, and she said to Balaam, "What have I done to you, that you have struck me these three times?" 29 Then Balaam said to the donkey, "Because you have made a mockery of me! If there had been a sword in my hand, [A]I would have killed you by now." 30 The donkey said to Balaam, "Am I not your donkey on which you have ridden all your life to this day? Have I ever been accustomed to do so to you?" And he said, "No."

31 Then the LORD opened the eyes of Balaam, and he saw [A]the angel of the LORD standing in the way with his drawn sword in his hand; and he bowed [a]all the way to the ground. 32 The angel of the LORD said to him, "Why have you struck your donkey these three times? Behold, I have come out as an adversary, because your way was [a,A]contrary to me. 33 But the donkey saw me and turned aside from me these three times. If she had not turned aside from me, I would surely have killed you just now, and let her live." 34 Balaam said to the angel of the LORD, "[A]I have sinned, for I did not know that you were standing in the way against me. Now then, if it is displeasing to you, I will turn back." 35 But the angel of the LORD said to Balaam, "Go with the men, but [A]you shall speak only the word which I [a]tell you." So Balaam went along with the leaders of Balak.

36 When Balak heard that Balaam was coming, he went out to meet him at the city of Moab, which is on the Arnon border, [a]at the extreme end of the border. 37 Then Balak said to Balaam, "Did I not urgently send to you to call you? Why did you not come to me? Am I really unable to honor you?" 38 So Balaam said to Balak, "Behold, I have come now to you! [A]Am I able to speak anything at all? The word that God puts in my mouth, that I shall speak." 39 And Balaam went with Balak, and they came to Kiriath-huzoth. 40 Balak sacrificed oxen and sheep, and sent *some* to Balaam and the leaders who were with him.

41 Then it came about in the morning that Balak took Balaam and brought him up to [a,A]the high places of Baal, and he saw from there [b]a [B]portion of the people.

THE PROPHECIES OF BALAAM

23 Then Balaam said to Balak, "Build seven altars for me here, and prepare seven bulls and seven rams for me here." 2 Balak did just as Balaam had spoken, and Balak and Balaam offered up a bull and a ram on each altar. 3 Then Balaam said to Balak, "Stand beside your burnt offering, and I will go; perhaps the LORD will come to meet me, and whatever He shows me I will tell you." So he went to a bare hill.

22:15 [a]Lit *these* 22:17 [A]Num 22:6 22:18 [a]Lit *mouth* [A]Num 22:38; 24:13; 1 Kin 22:14; 2 Chr 18:13 22:20 [A]Num 22:35; 23:5, 12, 16, 26; 24:13 22:21 [A]2 Pet 2:15 22:22 [A]Ex 23:20 22:27 [A]James 1:19 22:28 [A]2 Pet 2:16 22:29 [A]Prov 12:10; Matt 15:19 22:31 [a]Lit *and prostrated himself to his face* [A]Josh 5:13-15 22:32 [a]Lit *reckless* [A]2 Pet 2:15 22:34 [A]Num 14:40 22:35 [a]Or *speak to* [A]Num 22:20 22:36 [a]Lit *which is at* 22:38 [A]Num 22:18 22:41 [a]Or *Bamoth-baal* [b]Lit *the end of the camp* [A]Num 21:28 [B]Num 23:13

22:20 only the word which I speak to you. Because of his great desire for the material wealth that would come to him, Balaam desired to go to Balak. He implored the Lord even after God had told him not to go. God acceded to Balaam's request to let him go, but told him that he could speak only the true message from God.

22:22 because he was going. Even though God had given Balaam permission to go (v. 20), He knew that his motive was not right. Thus the anger of the Lord burned against Balaam because God knew that he was not yet submissive to what He required. The result of God's confrontation with Balaam was a reaffirmation of the word given in v. 20, repeated in v. 35, that he was to speak only the words that God wanted him to speak. That Balaam got the message is explicitly stated in v. 38. **the angel of the LORD.** The Angel of the Lord was a manifestation of the presence of the Lord Himself. He was equated with deity (see Ge 16:7; 18:1, 2; Ex 3:1–6). *See note on Ex 3:2.*

22:28 the LORD opened the mouth of the donkey. Balaam's donkey was able to see the Angel of the Lord with His drawn sword (v. 23, 25, 27). Realizing the danger to herself, she sought to avoid the Angel. In doing this, she preserved Balaam as well. Miraculously, the donkey was able to communicate with Balaam.

22:31 the LORD opened the eyes of Balaam. The Lord allowed Balaam to see things as they really were, especially those things that are not ordinarily visible to humans, and to be submissive to His will as he went to Balak.

22:41–23:12 Balaam's first oracle emphatically stated that Israel could not be cursed (23:8). She was unlike all the other nations of the world (23:9). Balaam even wished to share in her blessing (23:10).

4 Now God met Balaam, and he said to Him, "I
have set up the seven altars, and I have offered up
a bull and a ram on each altar." 5 Then the LORD
[A]put a word in Balaam's mouth and said, "Return to
Balak, and you shall speak thus." 6 So he returned to
him, and behold, he was standing beside his burnt
offering, he and all the leaders of Moab. 7 He took
up his [a]discourse and said,

"From [A]Aram Balak has brought me,
Moab's king from the
mountains of the East,
'[B]Come curse Jacob for me,
And come, denounce Israel!'
8 "[A]How shall I curse whom God
has not cursed?
And how can I denounce whom the
LORD has not denounced?
9 "As I see him from the top of the rocks,
And I look at him from the hills;
[A]Behold, a people *who* dwells apart,
And will not be reckoned
among the nations.
10 "[A]Who can count the dust of Jacob,
Or number the fourth part of Israel?
[B]Let [a]me die the death of the upright,
[C]And let my end be like his!"

11 Then Balak said to Balaam, "What have you
done to me? [A]I took you to curse my enemies, but
behold, you have actually blessed them!" 12 He replied, "Must I not be careful to speak [A]what the LORD
puts in my mouth?"
13 Then Balak said to him, "Please come with me
to another place from where you may see them,
although you will only see the extreme end of them
and will not see all of them; and curse them for me
from there." 14 So he took him to the field of Zophim,
to the top of Pisgah, and built seven altars and offered a bull and a ram on *each* altar. 15 And he said to
Balak, "Stand here beside your burnt offering while
I myself meet *the LORD* over there." 16 Then the LORD
met Balaam and [A]put a word in his mouth and said,
"Return to Balak, and thus you shall speak." 17 He
came to him, and behold, he was standing beside
his burnt offering, and the leaders of Moab with
him. And Balak said to him, "What has the LORD
spoken?" 18 Then he took up his [a]discourse and said,

"Arise, O Balak, and hear;
Give ear to me, O son of Zippor!
19 "[A]God is not a man, that He should lie,
Nor a son of man, that He should repent;
[B]Has He said, and will He not do it?
Or has He spoken, and will
He not make it good?
20 "Behold, I have received *a*
command to bless;
[A]When He has blessed, then
[B]I cannot revoke it.
21 "[A]He has not observed [a]misfortune in Jacob;
[B]Nor has He seen trouble in Israel;
[C]The LORD his God is with him,
[D]And the shout of a king is among them.
22 "[A]God brings them out of Egypt,
He is for them like the [B]horns
of the wild ox.
23 "[A]For there is no omen against Jacob,
Nor is there any divination against Israel;
At the proper time it shall
be said to Jacob
And to Israel, what God has done!
24 "[A]Behold, a people rises like a lioness,
And as a lion it lifts itself;
It will not lie down until it
devours the prey,
And drinks the blood of the slain."

25 Then Balak said to Balaam, "Do not curse them
at all nor bless them at all!" 26 But Balaam replied
to Balak, "Did I not tell you, '[a,A]Whatever the LORD
speaks, that I must do'?"
27 Then Balak said to Balaam, "Please come, I
will take you to another place; perhaps it will be
[a]agreeable with God that you curse them for me
from there." 28 So Balak took Balaam to the top of
Peor which overlooks the [a]wasteland. 29 Balaam
said to Balak, "Build seven altars for me here and
prepare seven bulls and seven rams for me here."
30 Balak did just as Balaam had said, and offered up
a bull and a ram on *each* altar.

THE PROPHECY FROM PEOR

24 When Balaam saw that it [a]pleased the LORD
to bless Israel, he did not go as at other times
to [b]seek [A]omens but he set his face toward the [B]wil-
derness. 2 And Balaam lifted up his eyes and saw

23:5 [A]Num 22:20; Deut 18:18; Jer 1:9 23:7 [a]Lit *parable* [A]Num 22:5; Deut 23:4 [B]Num 22:6 23:8 [A]Num 22:12 23:9 [A]Deut 32:8; 33:28 23:10 [a]Lit *my soul* [A]Gen 13:16; 28:14 [B]Is 57:1 [C]Ps 37:37 23:11 [A]Neh 13:2 23:12 [A]Num 22:20 23:16 [A]Num 22:20 23:18 [a]Lit *parable* 23:19 [A]1 Sam 15:29 [B]Is 40:8; 55:11 23:20 [A]Gen 12:2; 22:17; Num 22:12 [B]Is 43:13 23:21 [a]Or *iniquity* [A]Num 14:18, 19, 34; Ps 32:2, 5 [B]Deut 9:24; 32:5; Jer 50:20 [C]Ex 3:12; Deut 31:23 [D]Deut 33:5; Ps 89:15-18 23:22 [A]Num 24:8 [B]Deut 33:17 23:23 [A]Num 22:7; 24:1; Josh 13:22 23:24 [A]Gen 49:9; Nah 2:11, 12 23:26 [a]Lit *saying, Whatever* [A]Num 22:18 23:27 [a]Lit *right in the sight of God* 23:28 [a]Or *Jeshimon* 24:1 [a]Lit *was good in the eyes of* [b]Lit *encounter* [A]Num 22:7; 23:23 [B]Num 23:28

23:5 the LORD put a word in Balaam's mouth. Even though Balak and Balaam offered sacrifices on pagan altars, it was the Lord who gave Balaam his oracle.

23:7 He took up his discourse. This statement introduces each of Balaam's speeches (vv. 7, 18; 24:3, 20, 21, 23).

23:10 Who can count the dust of Jacob. Here is Oriental hyperbole signifying a very populous nation as Jacob's posterity was to be (cf. Gen 13:16; 28:14). **fourth part of Israel.** The camp was divided into 4 parts, one on each side of the tabernacle. If one could not count the part, certainly no one could count the whole.

23:13–26 Balaam's second oracle reaffirmed the Lord's determination to bless Israel. The iniquity in Israel was mercifully set aside by the Lord (23:21) and therefore would not stop His plan. The God who supernaturally brought Israel out of Egypt (23:22) would give victory over all her enemies (23:24).

23:19 God is not a man. In contrast to the unreliability of man, so well seen in Balaam himself, God is reliable and immutable. He does not change; therefore, His words always come to pass.

23:27–24:14 Balaam's third oracle focused on the ultimate King (the "Messiah"), who would bring the blessings of the Abrahamic Covenant both to Israel and the nations.

23:28 Peor. Also named Beth-peor (Dt 3:29), it was the location of a temple to Baal (25:3).

24:2 the Spirit of God came upon him. This terminology was regularly used in the OT for those whom God uniquely prepared

Israel [a]camping tribe by tribe; and [A]the Spirit of God
came upon him. 3 He took up his [a]discourse and said,

"[A]The oracle of Balaam the son of Beor,
And the oracle of the man
whose eye is opened;
4 The oracle of him who [A]hears
the [a]words of God,
Who sees the [B]vision of [b]the Almighty,
Falling down, yet having
his eyes uncovered,
5 How fair are your tents, O Jacob,
Your dwellings, O Israel!
6 "Like [a]valleys that stretch out,
Like gardens beside the river,
Like [A]aloes planted by the LORD,
Like [B]cedars beside the waters.
7 "Water will flow from his buckets,
And his seed *will be* by many waters,
And his king shall be higher than [A]Agag,
[B]And his kingdom shall be exalted.
8 "[A]God brings him out of Egypt,
He is for him like the horns of the wild ox.
[B]He will devour the nations *who*
are his adversaries,
And will crush their bones in pieces,
And shatter *them* with his [C]arrows.
9 "[A]He [a]couches, he lies down as a lion,
And as a [b]lion, who [c]dares rouse him?
[B]Blessed is everyone who blesses you,
And cursed is everyone who curses you."

10 Then Balak's anger burned against Balaam,
and he struck his [a]hands together; and Balak said
to Balaam, "I called you to curse my enemies, but
behold, you have persisted in blessing them these
three times! 11 Therefore, [a]flee to your place now. I
said I would honor you greatly, but behold, the LORD
has held you back from honor." 12 Balaam said to
Balak, "[A]Did I not tell your messengers whom you
had sent to me, saying, 13 'Though Balak were to give
me his house full of silver and gold, I could not do
anything contrary to the [a]command of the LORD,
either good or bad, [A]of my own [b]accord. [B]What the
LORD speaks, that I will speak'? 14 And now, behold,
[A]I am going to my people; come, *and* I will advise
you what this people will do to your people in the
[a]days to come."
15 He took up his discourse and said,

"[A]The oracle of Balaam the son of Beor,
And the oracle of the man
whose eye is opened,
16 The oracle of him who hears
the [a]words of God,
And knows the knowledge
of the [b]Most High,
Who sees the vision of [c]the Almighty,
Falling down, yet having
his eyes uncovered.
17 "I see him, but not now;
I behold him, but not near;
A star shall come forth from Jacob,
[A]A scepter shall rise from Israel,
[B]And shall crush through the
[a]forehead of Moab,
And [b]tear down all the sons of [c]Sheth.
18 "[A]Edom shall be a possession,
[B]Seir, its enemies, also will
be a possession,
While Israel performs valiantly.
19 "One from Jacob shall have dominion,
And will destroy the remnant
from the city."

20 And he looked at Amalek and took up his discourse and said,

"Amalek was the first of the nations,
[A]But his end *shall be* [a]destruction."

21 And he looked at the [A]Kenite, and took up his
discourse and said,

"Your dwelling place is enduring,
And your nest is set in the cliff.
22 "Nevertheless Kain will be consumed;
How long will [A]Asshur [a]keep you captive?"

24:2 [a]Lit *dwelling* [A]Num 11:26; 1 Sam 19:20; Rev 1:10 24:3 [a]Lit *parable,* and so throughout the ch [A]Num 24:15, 16 24:4 [a]Lit *sayings* [b]Heb *Shaddai* [A]Num 22:20 [B]Gen 15:1; Num 12:6 24:6 [a]Or possibly *palm trees* [A]Ps 45:8 [B]Ps 1:3 24:7 [A]Num 24:20; 1 Sam 15:8 [B]Ps 145:11-13 24:8 [A]Num 23:22 [B]Num 23:24; Ps 2:9 [C]Ps 45:5 24:9 [a]Lit *bows down* [b]Or *lioness* [c]Lit *shall* [A]Gen 49:9; Num 23:24 [B]Gen 12:3; 27:29 24:10 [a]Lit *palms* 24:11 [a]Lit *flee for yourself* 24:12 [A]Num 22:18 24:13 [a]Lit *mouth* [b]Lit *heart* [A]Num 16:28 [B]Num 22:20 24:14 [a]Lit *end of the days* [A]Num 31:8, 16; Josh 13:22 24:15 [A]Num 24:3, 4 24:16 [a]Lit *sayings* [b]Heb *Elyon* [c]Heb *Shaddai* 24:17 [a]Lit *corners* [b]Another reading is *the crown of the head of* [c]I.e. tumult [A]Gen 49:10 [B]Num 21:29; Is 15:1-16:14 24:18 [A]Gen 27:29; Amos 9:11, 12 [B]Gen 32:3 24:20 [a]Lit *to destroying* [A]Num 24:24 24:21 [A]Gen 15:19 24:22 [a]Lit *take* [A]Gen 10:21, 22

to do His work (see Jdg 3:10). Unlike the previous two oracles, Balaam does not involve himself in divination before giving this third oracle. He is empowered with the Holy Spirit to utter God's message accurately.

24:3 whose eye is opened. His inner eye of understanding had been opened by God's Spirit.

24:7 Agag. In 1Sa 15:32, 33, an Amalekite king bore this name. The Amalekites were the first people to attack Israel after they left Egypt (see Ex 17:8–15). "Agag" may be a proper name or a title of Amalekite rulers, like "Pharaoh" in Egypt.

24:8 God brings him out of Egypt. Because of the verbal similarities between 24:8 and 9, with 23:22 and 24, the "him" in this verse is usually interpreted to be Israel. However, since the "him" is sing. and the closest reference in v. 7 is to the coming king, it is better to see vv. 8 and 9 as referring to Israel's king. Numbers 24:9 is a direct quote from Ge 49:9, which speaks of the ultimate King who will come from Judah—the Messiah.

24:9 Blessed is everyone who blesses you. These words refer to Ge 12:3. The ultimate fulfillment of the Abrahamic Covenant centers around the coming Messiah. It is the one who blesses Israel who will ultimately reap God's blessing in the future.

24:14 in the days to come. Lit. "at the end of days." This term is rightfully used in the OT for the distant future. Balaam's fourth oracle takes the truth communicated in the third and applies it to Moab.

24:15–19 Balaam's fourth oracle predicted the future coming of Israel's king, who would "crush through the forehead of Moab" and conquer Edom. He will have total dominion.

24:20–24 Balaam's final 3 oracles look at the future of the nations. First, Amalek will come to an end (24:20). Second, the Kenites, identical to or a part of the Midianites, will be carried away by Asshur, i.e., Assyria (24:21, 22). Third, Assyria and Eber, probably Israel herself (Ge 10:21), will be afflicted by Cyprus or Kittim (Kittim came to represent the Mediterranean region W of Canaan and in Da 11:30 refers to Rome), until Cyprus comes to ruin.

23 Then he took up his discourse and said,

"Alas, who can live except
God has ordained it?
24 "But ships *shall come* from
the coast of [A]Kittim,
And they shall afflict Asshur
and will afflict [B]Eber;
[C]So they also *will come* to destruction."

25 Then Balaam arose and departed and returned
to [A]his place, and Balak also went his way.

THE SIN OF PEOR

25 While Israel remained at [A]Shittim, the people
began [B]to play the harlot with the daughters
of Moab. 2 For [A]they invited the people to the sacrifices of their gods, and the people ate and bowed
down to their gods. 3 So [A]Israel joined themselves
to [a]Baal of Peor, and the LORD was angry against
Israel. 4 The LORD said to Moses, "Take all the leaders
of the people and execute them [a]in broad daylight
before the LORD, [A]so that the fierce anger of the
LORD may turn away from Israel." 5 So Moses said
to the judges of Israel, "Each of you [A]slay his men
who have joined themselves to [a]Baal of Peor."
6 Then behold, one of the sons of Israel came and
brought to his [a]relatives a [A]Midianite woman, in the
sight of Moses and in the sight of all the congregation of the sons of Israel, [B]while they were weeping at the doorway of the tent of meeting. 7 [A]When
Phinehas the son of Eleazar, the son of Aaron the
priest, saw it, he arose from the midst of the congregation and took a spear in his hand, 8 and he went
after the man of Israel into the [a]tent and pierced
both of them through, the man of Israel and the
woman, through the [b]body. [A]So the plague on the
sons of Israel was checked. 9 [A]Those who died by
the plague were 24,000.

THE ZEAL OF PHINEHAS

10 Then the LORD spoke to Moses, saying, 11 "[A]Phin-
ehas the son of Eleazar, the son of Aaron the priest,
has turned away My wrath from the sons of Israel in
that he was jealous with My jealousy among them,
so that I did not destroy the sons of Israel [B]in My
jealousy. 12 Therefore say, '[A]Behold, I give him My
[B]covenant of peace; 13 and it shall be for him and his
[a]descendants after him, a covenant of a [A]perpetual
priesthood, because he was jealous for his God and
[B]made atonement for the sons of Israel.' "
14 Now the name of the [a]slain man of Israel who was
[a]slain with the Midianite woman, was Zimri the son
of Salu, a leader of a father's household among the
Simeonites. 15 The name of the Midianite woman who
was [a]slain was [A]Cozbi the daughter of [B]Zur, [b]who was
head of the people of a father's household in Midian.
16 Then the LORD spoke to Moses, saying, 17 "[A]Be hostile to the Midianites and strike them; 18 for they have
been hostile to you with their tricks, with which they
have deceived you in the affair of Peor and in the affair
of Cozbi, the daughter of the leader of Midian, their sister
who was slain on the day of the plague because of Peor."

CENSUS OF A NEW GENERATION

26 [a]Then it came about after the [A]plague, [b]that
the LORD spoke to Moses and to Eleazar the
son of Aaron the priest, saying, 2 "[A]Take a [a]census of
all the congregation of the sons of Israel from twenty
years old and upward, by their fathers' households,
whoever is able to go out to war in Israel." 3 So Moses and Eleazar the priest spoke with them [A]in the
plains of Moab by the Jordan at Jericho, saying,
4 "*Take a census of the people* from twenty years old
and upward, as the LORD has commanded Moses."
Now the sons of Israel who came out of the land
of Egypt *were:*
5 Reuben, Israel's firstborn, the sons of Reuben:
of Hanoch, the family of the Hanochites; of Pallu,

24:24 [A]Gen 10:4; Ezek 27:6 [B]Gen 10:21 [C]Num 24:20 24:25 [A]Num 24:14 25:1 [A]Num 33:49; Josh 2:1 [B]Num 31:16; 1 Cor 10:8; Rev 2:14 25:2 [A]Ex 34:15; Deut 32:38 25:3 [a]Or *Baal-peor* [A]Ps 106:28, 29; Hos 9:10 25:4 [a]Lit *in front of the sun* [A]Deut 13:17 25:5 [a]Or *Baal-peor* [A]Ex 32:27 25:6 [a]Lit *brothers* [A]Num 22:4 [B]Joel 2:17 25:7 [A]Ps 106:30 25:8 [a]Or *inner rooms* [b]Or *belly* [A]Num 16:46-48 25:9 [A]Num 14:37; 16:48-50; 31:16 25:11 [A]Ps 106:30 [B]Ex 20:5 25:12 [A]Ps 106:30, 31 [B]Is 54:10; Ezek 34:25; 37:26 25:13 [a]Lit *seed* [A]Ex 29:9 [B]Num 16:46 25:14 [a]Lit *smitten* 25:15 [a]Lit *smitten* [b]Lit *he* [A]Num 25:18 [B]Num 31:8 25:17 [A]Num 25:1; 22:4; 31:1-3 26:1 [a]Ch 25:19 in Heb [b]Ch 26:1 in Heb [A]Num 25:9 26:2 [a]Lit *sum* [A]Ex 30:11-16; 38:25, 26; Num 1:2 26:3 [A]Num 22:1; 33:48; 35:1

25:1–18 The final failure of Israel before the conquest of Canaan occurred in the plains of Moab. According to 31:16, the incident was brought about by the counsel of Balaam. Failing to be able to curse Israel, he gave the Moabites and Midianites direction in how to provoke the Lord's anger against His people.

25:1 **Shittim.** The region across the Jordan River from Jericho where Israel invaded the land of Canaan (see Jos 2:1).

25:3 **joined themselves to Baal of Peor.** Israel engaged in acts of sexual immorality with the women of Moab. Since this was part of the pagan cult that was worshiped by the Moabites, the Israelites joined in these idolatrous practices. The Israelites yoked themselves to the false god of the Moabites and the Midianites, referred to as Baal of Peor. This was a violation of the first commandment.

25:6 Cf. vv. 14, 15.

25:9 **twenty-four thousand.** This is to be differentiated from the plague over the golden calf where 23,000 died (cf. Ex 32:1–14, 28; 1Co 10:8).

25:10–13 Because of Phinehas' zeal for God's holiness, the Lord made "a covenant of a perpetual priesthood" with him so that through his family line would come all future, legitimate High Priests (cf. Ps 106:30, 31). This promise will extend even into the millennial kingdom (cf. Eze 40:46; 44:10, 15; 48:11).

25:17 **Be hostile to the Midianites.** Because the Midianites had attacked Israel by their schemes of sexual and idolatrous seduction, the Lord called Israel to attack them in return. This attack is recorded in 31:1–24.

26:1–36:13 The final major section of Numbers records the renewed obedience of Israel. God continued to speak (26:1, 2, 52; 27:6, 12, 18; 28:1; 31:1, 25; 33:50; 34:1, 16; 35:1, 9), and the second generation of Israel obeyed. Most of the commandments in this section related to Israel's life after they entered the Land.

26:1–32:42 These chapters begin and end speaking of going to war (26:2; 32:20, 29, 32) and the ensuing inheritance of Canaan (26:52–56; 32:32). Israel was being prepared for the conquest of the Promised Land.

26:1–51 This second census, like the first taken over 38 years earlier (1:1–46), counted all the men 20 years of age and older, fit for military service.

26:5–51 The numbers for each tribe with the net gain or loss were as follows:

Tribe	Number	Verse	Gain/Loss
Reuben	43,730	(v. 7)	-2,770
Simeon	22,200	(v. 14)	-37,100
Gad	40,500	(v. 18)	-5,150
Judah	76,500	(v. 22)	+1,900
Issachar	64,300	(v. 25)	+9,900
Zebulun	60,500	(v. 27)	+3,100
Manasseh	52,700	(v. 34)	+20,500
Ephraim	32,500	(v. 37)	-8,000
Benjamin	45,600	(v. 41)	+10,200
Dan	64,400	(v. 43)	+1,700
Asher	53,400	(v. 47)	+11,900
Naphtali	45,400	(v. 50)	-8,000
Total	601,730	(v. 51)	-1,820

The great decline in the tribe of Simeon might be due to its participation in the sin of Baal of Peor (see 25:14).

the family of the Palluites; 6 of Hezron, the family of
the Hezronites; of Carmi, the family of the Carmites.
7 These are the families of the Reubenites, and those
who were numbered of them were [A]43,730. 8 The
son of Pallu: Eliab. 9 The sons of Eliab: Nemuel and
Dathan and Abiram. These are the Dathan and Abiram who were [A]called by the congregation, who contended against Moses and against Aaron in the company of Korah, when they contended against
the LORD, 10 and [A]the earth opened its mouth and
swallowed them up along with Korah, when that company died, [B]when the fire devoured 250 men, so
that they became a [a]warning. 11 [A]The sons of Korah,
however, did not die.

12 The sons of Simeon according to their families: of [a]Nemuel, the family of the Nemuelites; of Jamin, the family of the Jaminites; of [b]Jachin, the
family of the Jachinites; 13 of [a]Zerah, the family of
the Zerahites; of Shaul, the family of the Shaulites.
14 These are the families of the Simeonites, [A]22,200.
15 The sons of Gad according to their families: of
[a]Zephon, the family of the Zephonites; of Haggi, the family of the Haggites; of Shuni, the family of the
Shunites; 16 of [a]Ozni, the family of the Oznites; of
Eri, the family of the Erites; 17 of [a]Arod, the family
of the Arodites; of Areli, the family of the Arelites.
18 These are the families of the sons of Gad according to those who were numbered of them, [A]40,500.
19 The [A]sons of Judah *were* Er and Onan, but Er
and Onan died in the land of Canaan. 20 The [A]sons
of Judah according to their families were: of Shelah, the family of the Shelanites; of Perez, the family of the Perezites; of Zerah, the family of the Zerahites.
21 The sons of Perez were: of Hezron, the family of
the Hezronites; of Hamul, the family of the Hamulites. 22 These are the families of Judah according to
those who were numbered of them, [A]76,500.
23 The [A]sons of Issachar according to their families: *of* Tola, the family of the Tolaites; of [a]Puvah,
the family of the Punites; 24 of [a]Jashub, the family
of the Jashubites; of Shimron, the family of the
Shimronites. 25 These are the families of Issachar according to those who were numbered of them, [A]64,300.
26 The [A]sons of Zebulun according to their families: of Sered, the family of the Seredites; of Elon, the family of the Elonites; of Jahleel, the family of the
Jahleelites. 27 These are the families of the Zebulunites according to those who were numbered of them, [A]60,500.
28 The [A]sons of Joseph according to their families:
Manasseh and Ephraim. 29 The sons of Manasseh:
of Machir, the family of the Machirites; and [A]Machir [a]became the father of Gilead: of Gilead, the family
of the Gileadites. 30 These are the sons of Gilead:
of [a]Iezer, the family of the [A]Iezerites; of Helek, the
family of the Helekites; 31 and *of* Asriel, the family of the Asrielites; and *of* Shechem, the family of
the Shechemites; 32 and *of* Shemida, the family of
the Shemidaites; and *of* Hepher, the family of the
Hepherites. 33 Now Zelophehad the son of Hepher
had no sons, but only daughters; and [A]the names of the daughters of Zelophehad were Mahlah, Noah,
Hoglah, Milcah and Tirzah. 34 These are the families of Manasseh; and those who were numbered of them were [A]52,700.
35 These are the sons of Ephraim according to their families: of Shuthelah, the family of the Shuthelahites; of [a]Becher, the family of the Becherites; of Tahan, the family of the Tahanites. 36 These
are the sons of Shuthelah: of Eran, the family of
the Eranites. 37 These are the families of the sons of
Ephraim according to those who were numbered of them, [A]32,500. These are the sons of Joseph according to their families.
38 The sons of Benjamin according to their families: of Bela, the family of the Belaites; of Ashbel, the family of the Ashbelites; of [a]Ahiram, the family
of the Ahiramites; 39 of [a]Shephupham, the family
of the Shuphamites; of [b]Hupham, the family of the
Huphamites. 40 The sons of Bela were [a]Ard and Naaman: *of Ard,* the family of the Ardites; of Naaman,
the family of the Naamites. 41 These are the sons of
Benjamin according to their families; and those who were numbered of them were [A]45,600.
42 These are the sons of Dan according to their families: of [a]Shuham, the family of the Shuhamites. These are the families of Dan according to
their families. 43 All the families of the Shuhamites, according to those who were numbered of them, were [A]64,400.
44 The [A]sons of Asher according to their families: of Imnah, the family of the Imnites; of Ishvi, the family of the Ishvites; of Beriah, the family of the
Beriites. 45 Of the sons of Beriah: of Heber, the family of the Heberites; of Malchiel, the family of the
Malchielites. 46 The name of the daughter of Asher
was Serah. 47 These are the families of the sons of
Asher according to those who were numbered of them, [A]53,400.
48 The [A]sons of Naphtali according to their families: of Jahzeel, the family of the Jahzeelites; of Guni,
the family of the Gunites; 49 of Jezer, the family of the
Jezerites; of [A]Shillem, the family of the Shillemites.

26:7 [A]Num 1:21 26:9 [A]Num 1:16; 16:2 26:10 [a]Lit *sign* [A]Num 16:32 [B]Num 16:35, 38 26:11 [A]Num 16:27, 33; Deut 24:16 26:12 [a]In Gen 46:10 and Ex 6:15, *Jemuel* [b]In 1 Chr 4:24, *Jarib* 26:13 [a]In Gen 46:10, *Zohar* 26:14 [A]Num 1:23 26:15 [a]In Gen 46:16, *Ziphion* 26:16 [a]In Gen 46:16, *Ezbon* 26:17 [a]In Gen 46:16, *Arodi* 26:18 [A]Num 1:25 26:19 [A]Gen 38:2; 46:12 26:20 [A]Gen 49:8; 1 Chr 2:3; Rev 7:5 26:22 [A]Num 1:27 26:23 [a]In Gen 46:13, *Puvvah;* in 1 Chr 7:1, *Puah* [A]Gen 46:13; 1 Chr 7:1 26:24 [a]In Gen 46:13, *Iob* 26:25 [A]Num 1:29 26:26 [A]Gen 46:14 26:27 [A]Num 1:31 26:28 [A]Gen 46:20; Deut 33:16f 26:29 [a]Lit *begot* [A]Josh 17:1; 1 Chr 7:14f 26:30 [a]In Josh 17:2, *Abiezer* [A]Judg 6:11, 24, 34 26:33 [A]Num 27:1 26:34 [A]Num 1:35 26:35 [a]In 1 Chr 7:20, *Bered* 26:37 [A]Num 1:33 26:38 [a]In Gen 46:21, *Ehi;* in 1 Chr 8:1, *Aharah* 26:39 [a]In Gen 46:21, *Muppim;* in 1 Chr 7:12, *Shuppim* [b]In Gen 46:21, *Muppim* and *Huppim* 26:40 [a]In 1 Chr 8:3, *Addar* 26:41 [A]Num 1:37 26:42 [a]In Gen 46:23, *Hushim* 26:43 [A]Num 1:39 26:44 [A]Gen 46:17; 1 Chr 7:30 26:47 [A]Num 1:41 26:48 [A]Gen 46:24; 1 Chr 7:13 26:49 [A]1 Chr 7:13

26:9 Dathan and Abiram. These were singled out for special mention because of their part in the rebellion recorded in 16:1–40. Mention of them was a reminder of God's judgment against rebellion.

26:11 The sons of Korah. These sons of Korah were spared judgment because they separated themselves from their father's house (see 16:26).

26:19 Er and Onan. These two sons of Judah did not receive an inheritance in the land because of their great evil (see Ge 38:1–10).

26:33 Zelophehad. The mentioning of Zelophehad having no sons, but only daughters, laid the basis for the laws of inheritance stated in 27:1–11; 36:1–12.

50 These are the families of Naphtali according to
their families; and those who were numbered of
them were [A]45,400.
51 These are those who were numbered of the
sons of Israel, [A]601,730.
52 Then the LORD spoke to Moses, saying,
53 "[a]Among these the land shall be divided for an
inheritance according to the number of names.
54 [A]To the larger *group* you shall increase their
inheritance, and to the smaller *group* you shall
diminish their inheritance; each shall be given
their inheritance according to those who were
numbered of them. 55 But the land shall be [A]di-
vided by lot. They shall [a]receive their inheritance
according to the names of the tribes of their fathers. 56 According to the selection by lot, their
inheritance shall be divided between the larger
and the smaller *groups*."
57 [A]These are those who were numbered of the
Levites according to their families: of Gershon, the
family of the Gershonites; of Kohath, the family of
the Kohathites; of Merari, the family of the Merarites. 58 These are the families of Levi: the family
of the Libnites, the family of the Hebronites, the
family of the Mahlites, the family of the Mushites,
the family of the Korahites. [A]Kohath [a]became the
father of Amram. 59 The name of Amram's wife [A]was
Jochebed, the daughter of Levi, who was born to
Levi in Egypt; and she bore to Amram: Aaron and
Moses and their sister Miriam. 60 [A]To Aaron were
born Nadab and Abihu, Eleazar and Ithamar. 61 [A]But
Nadab and Abihu died when they offered strange
fire before the LORD. 62 Those who were numbered
of them were [A]23,000, every male from a month old
and upward, for [B]they were not numbered among
the sons of Israel [C]since no inheritance was given
to them among the sons of Israel.
63 These are those who were numbered by Moses
and Eleazar the priest, who numbered the sons of
Israel in the plains of Moab by the Jordan at Jericho.
64 [A]But among these there was not a man of those
who were numbered by Moses and Aaron the priest,
who numbered the sons of Israel in the wilderness
of Sinai. 65 For the LORD had said [a]of them, "[A]They
shall surely die in the wilderness." And not a man
was left of them, [B]except Caleb the son of Jephunneh
and Joshua the son of Nun.

A LAW OF INHERITANCE

27 Then [A]the daughters of Zelophehad, the son of
Hepher, the son of Gilead, the son of Machir,
the son of Manasseh, of the families of Manasseh
the son of Joseph, came near; and these are [B]the
names of his daughters: Mahlah, Noah and Hoglah
and Milcah and Tirzah. 2 They stood before Moses
and before Eleazar the priest and before the leaders and all the congregation, at the doorway of the
tent of meeting, saying, 3 "Our father [A]died in the
wilderness, yet he was not among the company of
those who gathered themselves together against
the LORD in the company of Korah; but he died in
his own sin, and [B]he had no sons. 4 Why should the
name of our father be withdrawn from among his
family because he had no son? Give us a possession
among our father's brothers." 5 [A]So Moses brought
their case before the LORD.
6 Then the LORD spoke to Moses, saying, 7 "[A]The
daughters of Zelophehad are right in *their* statements. You shall surely give them a hereditary
possession among their father's brothers, and you
shall transfer the inheritance of their father to them.
8 Further, you shall speak to the sons of Israel, saying, 'If a man dies and has no son, then you shall
transfer his inheritance to his daughter. 9 If he has
no daughter, then you shall give his inheritance to
his brothers. 10 If he has no brothers, then you shall
give his inheritance to his father's brothers. 11 If his
father has no brothers, then you shall give his inheritance to his nearest relative in his own family,
and he shall possess it; and it shall be a [A]statutory
ordinance to the sons of Israel, just as the LORD
commanded Moses.' "
12 [A]Then the LORD said to Moses, "Go up to this
[B]mountain of Abarim, and see the land which I have
given to the sons of Israel. 13 When you have seen it,
you too [A]will be gathered to your people, [B]as Aaron
your brother [a]was; 14 for in the wilderness of Zin,
during the strife of the congregation, [A]you rebelled
against My [a]command [b]to treat Me as holy before
their eyes at the water." (These are the waters of
Meribah of Kadesh in the wilderness of Zin.)

JOSHUA TO SUCCEED MOSES

15 Then Moses spoke to the LORD, saying, 16 "[A]May
the LORD, the God of the spirits of all flesh, appoint a

26:50 [A]Num 1:43 26:51 [A]Ex 12:37; 38:26; Num 1:46; 11:21 26:53 [a]Lit *To* 26:54 [A]Num 33:54 26:55 [a]Lit *inherit according to* [A]Num 33:54; 34:13 26:57 [A]Gen 46:11; Ex 6:16; 1 Chr 6:1, 16 26:58 [a]Lit *begot* [A]Ex 6:20 26:59 [A]Ex 2:1, 2; 6:20 26:60 [A]Num 3:2 26:61 [A]Lev 10:1, 2; Num 3:4 26:62 [A]Num 3:39 [B]Num 1:47 [C]Num 18:23, 24 26:64 [A]Num 14:29-35; Deut 2:14-16; Heb 3:17 26:65 [a]Or *to* [A]Num 14:26-35; Ps 90:3-10; 1 Cor 10:5 [B]Deut 1:36; Josh 14:6-10 27:1 [A]Num 26:33; 36:1 [B]Num 26:33 27:3 [A]Num 26:64, 65 [B]Num 26:33 27:5 [A]Num 9:8; 27:21 27:7 [A]Num 36:2; Josh 17:4 27:11 [A]Num 35:29 27:12 [A]Deut 3:23-27; 32:48-52 [B]Num 33:47, 48 27:13 [a]Lit *was gathered* [A]Num 31:2 [B]Num 20:24, 28; Deut 10:6 27:14 [a]Lit *mouth* [b]Lit *for My sanctity* [A]Num 20:12; Deut 32:51; Ps 106:32 27:16 [A]Num 16:22

26:52–56 These census numbers would be used to decide the size of each tribe's inheritance in the land. The exact locations would be determined by lot (see Jos 13:1–7; 14:1–19:51 for the outworking of these words).

26:57–65 As in the first census (3:14–39), the Levites were counted separately. The total number of Levites was 23,000 (v. 62), an increase of 1,000 over the previous census (see 3:39).

27:1–11 The coming distribution of the land of Canaan presented a dilemma for the family of Zelophehad since he had no sons. His 5 daughters boldly asked that they inherit their father's name and his inheritance (vv. 1–4). The Lord's decision that the daughters should receive his inheritance became the basis of a perpetual statute in Israel governing inheritances (vv. 5–11).

27:3 he died in his own sin. Zelophehad had not been involved in Korah's rebellion. Instead, he had died under God's judgment in the wilderness, like the rest of the faithless Exodus generation.

27:8–11 The following is the order of inheritance: son, daughter, brother, paternal uncle, and closest relative in the family. This same order (with the exception of the daughter) was followed in Lv 25:48, 49 dealing with the various cases of redemption of the land in the Jubilee year.

27:12–14 God reaffirmed that Moses could not enter the land of Canaan, although he was able to see it from Mt. Nebo, across from Jericho (see Dt 32:49).

27:15–17 Moses' greatest concern was that Israel have a good leader who was like a shepherd. The Lord answered his request in the man Joshua.

man over the congregation, 17 who [A]will go out [a]and come in before them, and who will lead them out and [b]bring them in, so that the congregation of the LORD will not be [B]like sheep which have no shepherd." 18 So the LORD said to Moses, "[a]Take Joshua the son of Nun, a man [A]in whom is the Spirit, and [B]lay your hand on him; 19 and have him stand before Eleazar the priest and before all the congregation, and [A]commission him in their sight. 20 You shall put some of your [a]authority on him, in order that all the congregation of the sons of Israel may obey *him.* 21 Moreover, he shall stand before Eleazar the priest, who shall inquire for him [A]by the judgment of the Urim before the LORD. At his [a]command they shall go out and at his [a]command they shall come in, *both* he and the sons of Israel with him, even all the congregation." 22 Moses did just as the LORD commanded him; and he took Joshua and set him before Eleazar the priest and before all the congregation. 23 Then he laid his hands on him and [A]commissioned him, just as the LORD had spoken [a]through Moses.

LAWS FOR OFFERINGS

28 Then the LORD spoke to Moses, saying, 2 "Command the sons of Israel and say to them, 'You shall [a]be careful to present My offering, My [A]food for My offerings by fire, of a soothing aroma to Me, at their appointed time.' 3 [A]You shall say to them, 'This is the offering by fire which you shall offer to the LORD: two male lambs one year old without defect *as* a continual burnt offering every day. 4 You shall offer the one lamb in the morning and the other lamb you shall offer [a]at twilight; 5 also [A]a tenth of an ephah of fine flour for a [B]grain offering, mixed with a fourth of a hin of beaten oil. 6 It is a continual burnt offering which was ordained in Mount Sinai as a soothing aroma, an offering by fire to the LORD. 7 Then the drink offering with it *shall be* a fourth of a hin for each lamb, [A]in the holy place you shall pour out a drink offering of strong drink to the LORD. 8 The other lamb you shall offer [a]at twilight; as the grain offering of the morning and as its drink offering, you shall offer it, an offering by fire, a soothing aroma to the LORD.

9 'Then on the sabbath day two male lambs one year old without defect, and two-tenths *of an* [a]*ephah* of fine flour mixed with oil as a grain offering, and its drink offering: 10 *This is* the burnt offering of every sabbath in addition to the [A]continual burnt offering and its drink offering.

11 'Then [A]at the beginning of each of your months you shall present a burnt offering to the LORD: two [a]bulls and one ram, seven male lambs one year old without defect; 12 [A]and three-tenths *of an* [a]*ephah* of fine flour mixed with oil for a grain offering, for each bull; and two-tenths of fine flour mixed with oil for a grain offering, for the one ram; 13 and a tenth *of an* [a]*ephah* of fine flour mixed with oil for a grain offering for each lamb, for a burnt offering of a soothing aroma, an offering by fire to the LORD. 14 Their drink offerings shall be half a hin of wine for a bull and a third of a hin for the ram and a fourth of a hin for a lamb; this is the burnt offering of each month throughout the months of the year. 15 And one male goat for a sin offering to the LORD; it shall be offered with its drink offering in addition to the [A]continual burnt offering.

16 '[A]Then on the fourteenth day of the first month shall be the LORD'S Passover. 17 [A]On the fifteenth day of this month *shall be* a [B]feast, unleavened bread *shall be* eaten for seven days. 18 On the [A]first day *shall be* a holy convocation; you shall do no laborious work. 19 You shall present an offering by fire, a burnt offering to the LORD: two [a]bulls and one ram and seven male lambs one year old, [A]having them without defect. 20 For their grain offering, you shall offer fine flour mixed with oil: three-tenths *of an* [a]*ephah* for a bull and two-tenths for the ram. 21 A tenth *of an* [a]*ephah* you shall offer for [b]each of the seven lambs; 22 and one male goat for a [A]sin offering to make atonement for you. 23 You shall present these besides [A]the burnt offering of the morning, which is for a continual burnt offering. 24 After this manner you shall present daily, for seven days, [A]the food of the offering by fire, of a soothing aroma to the LORD; it shall be presented with its drink offering in addition to the [B]continual burnt offering. 25 On the seventh day you shall have a holy convocation; [A]you shall do no laborious work.

26 'Also on [A]the day of the first fruits, when you present a new grain offering to the LORD in your *Feast of* Weeks, you shall have a holy convocation; [B]you shall do no laborious work. 27 You shall offer

27:17 [a]Lit *before them and who will* [b]Lit *who will bring* [A]Deut 31:2; 2 Chr 1:10 [B]1 Kin 22:17; Ezek 34:5; Matt 9:36; Mark 6:34 27:18 [a]Lit *Take for yourself* [A]Num 11:25-29; Deut 34:9 [B]Num 27:23 27:19 [A]Deut 3:28; 31:3, 7, 8, 23 27:20 [a]Lit *majesty* 27:21 [a]Lit *mouth* [A]Ex 28:30; 1 Sam 28:6 27:23 [a]Lit *by the hand of* [A]Deut 31:23 28:2 [a]Lit *watch* [A]Lev 3:11 28:3 [A]Ex 29:38-42 28:4 [a]Lit *between the two evenings* 28:5 [A]Ex 16:36; Num 15:4 [B]Lev 2:1 28:7 [A]Ex 29:42 28:8 [a]Lit *between the two evenings* 28:9 [a]I.e. Approx one bu 28:10 [A]Num 28:3 28:11 [a]Lit *bulls of the herd* [A]Num 10:10; Ezek 46:6, 7 28:12 [a]I.e. Approx one bu [A]Num 15:4-12 28:13 [a]I.e. Approx one bu 28:15 [A]Num 28:3 28:16 [A]Ex 12:1-20; Lev 23:5-8; Deut 16:1-8 28:17 [A]Lev 23:6 [B]Ex 23:15; 34:18; Deut 16:3-8 28:18 [A]Lev 23:7 28:19 [a]Or *bulls of the herd* [A]Deut 15:21 28:20 [a]I.e. Approx one bu 28:21 [a]I.e. Approx one bu [b]Lit *each lamb* 28:22 [A]Lev 16:18; Rom 8:3; Gal 4:4f 28:23 [A]Num 28:3 28:24 [A]Lev 3:11 [B]Num 28:3 28:25 [A]Num 28:18 28:26 [A]Ex 23:16; 34:22; Lev 23:15-21; Deut 16:9-12 [B]Num 28:18

27:18 lay your hand on him. Joshua already had the inner endowment for leadership. He was empowered by the Holy Spirit. This inner endowment was to be recognized by an external ceremony. Moses publicly laid his hands upon Joshua. This act signified the transfer of Moses' leadership to Joshua. The laying on of hands can accompany a dedication to an office (see Nu 8:10).

27:20 put some of your authority. Moses was to pass on some of the "honor" or "majesty" that he had to Joshua. See Jos 3:7.

27:21 Eleazar ... shall inquire for him. Moses had been able to communicate directly with God (12:8), but Joshua would receive the Word from the Lord through the High Priest. **Urim.** *See note on Ex 28:30* for this part of the High Priest's breastpiece (Ex 39:8–21) as a means of determining God's will (cf. Dt 33:8; 1Sa 28:6).

28:1–29:40 Instructions concerning the regular celebrations in Israel's worship calendar had been given previously. Now, poised to enter the land, Moses gave an orderly reiteration and summary of the regular offerings for each time of celebration, adding some additional offerings.

28:3–8 See Ex 29:38–42.

28:9, 10 These were newly revealed offerings for the Sabbath.

28:11–15 These were newly revealed offerings for the "beginning of ... your months."

28:16–25 See Lv 23:5–8.

28:26–31 See Lv 23:18.

a burnt offering for a soothing aroma to the LORD: two young bulls, one ram, seven male lambs one year old; 28 and their grain offering, fine flour mixed with oil: three-tenths *of an* [a]*ephah* for each bull, two-tenths for the one ram, 29 a tenth for [a]each of the seven lambs; 30 *also* one male goat to make atonement for you. 31 [A]Besides the continual burnt offering and its grain offering, you shall present *them* with their drink offerings. They shall be [a]without defect.

OFFERINGS OF THE SEVENTH MONTH

29 '[A]Now in the seventh month, on the first day of the month, you shall also have a holy convocation; [B]you shall do no laborious work. It will be to you a day for blowing trumpets. 2 You shall offer a burnt offering as a soothing aroma to the LORD: one [a]bull, one ram, *and* seven male lambs one year old without defect; 3 also their grain offering, fine flour mixed with oil: three-tenths *of an* [a]*ephah* for the bull, two-tenths for the ram, 4 and one-tenth for [a]each of the seven lambs. 5 *Offer* one male goat for a sin offering, to make atonement for you, 6 [A]besides the burnt offering of the new moon and its grain offering, and the [B]continual burnt offering and its grain offering, and their drink offerings, according to their ordinance, for a soothing aroma, an offering by fire to the LORD.

7 'Then on [A]the tenth day of this seventh month you shall have a holy convocation, and you shall humble yourselves; you shall not do any work. 8 You shall present a burnt offering to the LORD *as* a soothing aroma: one bull, one ram, seven male lambs one year old, [A]having them without defect; 9 and their grain offering, fine flour mixed with oil: three-tenths *of an* [a]*ephah* for the bull, two-tenths for the one ram, 10 a tenth for each of the seven lambs; 11 one male goat for a sin offering, besides [A]the sin offering of atonement and [B]the continual burnt offering and its grain offering, and their drink offerings.

12 'Then on [A]the fifteenth day of the seventh month you shall have a holy convocation; you [B]shall do no laborious work, and you shall observe a feast to the LORD for seven days. 13 You shall present a burnt offering, an offering by fire as a soothing aroma to the LORD: thirteen bulls, two rams, fourteen male lambs one year old, which are without defect; 14 and their grain offering, fine flour mixed with oil: three-tenths *of an* [a]*ephah* for [b]each of the thirteen bulls, two-tenths for [c]each of the two rams, 15 and a tenth for each of the fourteen lambs; 16 and one male goat for a sin offering, [A]besides the continual burnt offering, its grain offering and its drink offering.

17 'Then on [A]the second day: twelve bulls, two rams, fourteen male lambs one year old without defect; 18 and their grain offering and their drink offerings for the bulls, for the rams and for the lambs, by their number [A]according to the ordinance; 19 and one male goat for a sin offering, [A]besides the continual burnt offering and its grain offering, and their drink offerings.

20 'Then on the third day: eleven bulls, two rams, fourteen male lambs one year old without defect; 21 and their grain offering and their drink offerings for the bulls, for the rams and for the lambs, by their number according to the ordinance; 22 and one male goat for a sin offering, besides the continual burnt offering and its grain offering and its drink offering.

23 'Then on the fourth day: ten bulls, two rams, fourteen male lambs one year old without defect; 24 their grain offering and their drink offerings for the bulls, for the rams and for the lambs, by their number according to the ordinance; 25 and one male goat for a sin offering, besides the continual burnt offering, its grain offering and its drink offering.

26 'Then on the fifth day: nine bulls, two rams, fourteen male lambs one year old [A]without defect; 27 and their grain offering and their drink offerings for the bulls, for the rams and for the lambs, by their number according to the ordinance; 28 and one male goat for a sin offering, besides the continual burnt offering and its grain offering and its drink offering.

29 'Then on the sixth day: eight bulls, two rams, fourteen male lambs one year old without defect; 30 and their grain offering and their drink offerings for the bulls, for the rams and for the lambs, by their number according to the ordinance; 31 and one male goat for a sin offering, besides the continual burnt offering, its grain offering and its drink offerings.

32 'Then on the seventh day: seven bulls, two rams, fourteen male lambs one year old without defect; 33 and their grain offering and their drink offerings for the bulls, for the rams and for the lambs, by their number according to the ordinance; 34 and one male goat for a sin offering, besides the continual burnt offering, its grain offering and its drink offering.

35 '[A]On the eighth day you shall have a solemn assembly; you shall do no laborious work. 36 But you shall present a burnt offering, an offering by fire, as a soothing aroma to the LORD: one bull, one ram, seven male lambs one year old without defect; 37 their grain offering and their drink offerings for the bull, for the ram and for the lambs, by their number according to the ordinance; 38 and one male goat for a sin offering, besides the continual burnt offering and its grain offering and its drink offering.

39 'You shall present these to the LORD at your [A]appointed times, besides your [a]votive offerings and your freewill offerings, for your burnt offerings and for your grain offerings and for your drink offerings and for your peace offerings.' " 40 [a]Moses spoke to the sons of Israel in accordance with all that the LORD had commanded Moses.

28:28 [a]I.e. Approx one bu 28:29 [a]Lit *each lamb* 28:31 [a]Lit *without defect to you* [A]Num 28:3 29:1 [A]Ex 23:16; 34:22; Lev 23:23-25 [B]Num 28:26 29:2 [a]Or *bull of a herd,* and so throughout the ch 29:3 [a]I.e. Approx one bu 29:4 [a]Lit *each lamb,* and so throughout the ch 29:6 [A]Num 28:27 [B]Num 28:3 29:7 [A]Lev 16:29-34; 23:26-32 29:8 [A]Lev 22:20; Deut 15:21; 17:1 29:9 [a]I.e. Approx one bu 29:11 [A]Lev 16:3, 5 [B]Num 28:3 29:12 [A]Lev 23:33-35; Deut 16:13-15 [B]Num 29:1 29:14 [a]I.e. Approx one bu [b]Lit *each bull* [c]Lit *each ram* 29:16 [A]Num 28:3 29:17 [A]Lev 23:36 29:18 [A]Lev 2:1-16 29:19 [A]Num 28:8 29:26 [A]Heb 7:26 29:35 [A]Lev 23:36 29:39 [a]Lit *vows* [A]Lev 23:2 29:40 [a]Ch 30:1 in Heb

29:1–6 See Lv 23:23–25. **29:7–11** See Lv 23:26–32. **29:12–38** See Lv 23:33–43.

THE LAW OF VOWS

30 Then Moses spoke to [A]the heads of the tribes of the sons of Israel, saying, "This is the word which the LORD has commanded. 2 [A]If a man makes a vow to the LORD, or takes an oath to bind himself with a binding obligation, he shall not violate his word; he shall do according to all that proceeds out of his mouth.

3 "Also if a woman makes a vow to the LORD, and binds herself by an obligation in her father's house in her youth, 4 and her father hears her vow and her obligation by which she has bound herself, and her father [a]says nothing to her, then all her vows shall stand and every obligation by which she has bound herself shall stand. 5 But if her father should forbid her on the day he hears *of it,* none of her vows or her obligations by which she has bound herself shall stand; and the LORD will forgive her because her father had forbidden her.

6 "However, if she should [a]marry while [b]under her vows or the rash statement of her lips by which she has bound herself, 7 and her husband hears of it and says nothing to her on the day he hears *it,* then her vows shall stand and her obligations by which she has bound herself shall stand. 8 But if on the day her husband hears *of it,* he forbids her, then he shall annul her vow which [a]she is under and the rash statement of her lips by which she has bound herself; and the LORD will forgive her.

9 "But the vow of a widow or of a divorced woman, everything by which she has bound herself, shall stand against her. 10 However, if she vowed in her husband's house, or bound herself by an obligation with an oath, 11 and her husband heard *it,* but said nothing to her *and* did not forbid her, then all her vows shall stand and every obligation by which she bound herself shall stand. 12 But if her husband indeed annuls them on the day he hears *them,* then whatever proceeds out of her lips concerning her vows or concerning the obligation of herself shall not stand; her husband has annulled them, and the LORD will forgive her.

13 "Every vow and every binding oath to humble herself, her husband may confirm it or her husband may annul it. 14 But if her husband indeed says nothing to her from day to day, then he confirms all her vows or all her obligations which are on her; he has confirmed them, because he said nothing to her on the day he heard them. 15 But if he indeed annuls them after he has heard them, then he shall bear her guilt."

16 These are the statutes which the LORD commanded Moses, *as* between a man and his wife, *and as* between a father and his daughter, *while she is* in her youth in her father's house.

THE SLAUGHTER OF MIDIAN

31 Then the LORD spoke to Moses, saying, 2 "[A]Take full vengeance for the sons of Israel on the Midianites; afterward you will be [B]gathered to your people." 3 Moses spoke to the people, saying, "Arm men from among you for the war, that they may [a]go against Midian to execute [A]the LORD'S vengeance on Midian. 4 A thousand from each tribe of all the tribes of Israel you shall send to the war." 5 So there were [a]furnished from the thousands of Israel, a thousand from each tribe, twelve thousand armed for war. 6 Moses sent them, a thousand from each tribe, to the war, and Phinehas the son of Eleazar the priest, to the war with them, [A]and the holy vessels and [B]the trumpets for the alarm in his hand. 7 So they made war against Midian, just as the LORD had commanded Moses, and [A]they killed every male. 8 They killed the kings of Midian along with the *rest of* their slain: [A]Evi and Rekem and [B]Zur and Hur and Reba, the five kings of Midian; they also killed [C]Balaam the son of Beor with the sword. 9 The sons of Israel captured the women of Midian and their little ones; and all their cattle and all their flocks and all their goods they plundered. 10 Then they burned all their cities where they lived and all their camps with fire. 11 [A]They took all the spoil and all the prey, both of man and of beast. 12 They brought the captives and the prey and the spoil to Moses, and to Eleazar the priest and to the congregation of the sons of Israel, to the camp at the plains of Moab, which are by the Jordan *opposite* Jericho.

13 Moses and Eleazar the priest and all the leaders of the congregation went out to meet them outside the camp. 14 Moses was angry with the officers of the army, the captains of thousands and the captains of hundreds, who had come from service in the war. 15 And Moses said to them, "Have you [a]spared [A]all the women? 16 [A]Behold, these [a]caused the sons of Israel, through the [b]counsel of [B]Balaam, to [c]trespass against the LORD in the matter of Peor, so the plague was among the congregation of the LORD.

30:1 [A]Num 1:4, 16; 7:2 30:2 [A]Deut 23:21-23; Matt 5:33 30:4 [a]Lit *is silent to her,* and so throughout the ch 30:6 [a]Lit *be to a husband* [b]Lit *her vows are on her* 30:8 [a]Lit *is on her* 31:2 [A]Num 25:1, 16, 17 [B]Num 20:24, 26; 27:13 31:3 [a]Lit *be* [A]Lev 26:25 31:5 [a]Lit *delivered* 31:6 [A]Num 14:44 [B]Num 10:8, 9 31:7 [A]Deut 20:13; Judg 21:11; 1 Kin 11:15, 16 31:8 [A]Josh 13:21 [B]Num 25:15 [C]Num 31:16; Josh 13:22 31:11 [A]Deut 20:14 31:15 [a]Lit *let...live* [A]Deut 20:14 31:16 [a]Lit *were to* [b]Lit *word* [c]*Possibly defect from the Lord* [A]Num 25:1-9 [B]Num 31:8

30:1–16 This chapter added clarification to the laws regarding vows given in Lv 27:1–33. The basic principle for men is restated in v. 2. Then, it was asserted that a man was also responsible for the vows made by women in his household (vv. 3–16). A father or husband could overrule the vow of a daughter or wife, but a man's silence, if he knew of the vow, meant it must be accomplished.

30:2 a vow .... binding obligation. A promise to do something or a promise not to do something. Christ could have had this text in mind (Mt 5:33).

30:9 a widow or .... divorced woman. These were not viewed as being under a man's authority, so the word of the woman alone sufficed.

31:1–54 This chapter has many links with previous passages in Numbers: vengeance on Midian (vv. 2, 3; 25:17, 18); Zur the Midianite (v. 8; 25:15); Balaam (vv. 8, 16; 22:2–24:25); Peor (v. 16; 25:1–9, 14, 15); purification after contact with the dead (vv. 19–24; 19:11–19); care for the priests and Levites (vv. 28–47; 18:8–32). This battle with the Midianites modeled God's requirements for holy war when Israel took vengeance on His enemies (see Dt 20:1–18).

31:1–11 Israel was commanded by the Lord to take vengeance on Midian because they were responsible for corrupting Israel at Peor (25:1–18).

31:2 gathered to your people. A euphemism for death (see Ge 25:8, 17; 35:29).

31:12–24 All the Midianites, except the virgin women, were to be put to death. Both the soldiers and the spoil needed to be cleansed.

17 [A]Now therefore, kill every male among the little
ones, and kill every woman who has known man
[a]intimately. 18 But all the [a]girls who have not known
man [b]intimately, [c]spare for yourselves. 19 [A]And you,
camp outside the camp seven days; whoever has
killed any person and whoever has touched any
slain, purify yourselves, you and your captives, on
the third day and on the seventh day. 20 You shall
purify for yourselves every garment and every article of [a]leather and all the work of goats' *hair,* and
all articles of wood."

21 Then Eleazar the priest said to the men of war
who had gone to battle, "This is the statute of the
law which the LORD has commanded Moses: 22 only
the gold and the silver, the bronze, the iron, the
tin and the lead, 23 everything that can stand the
fire, you shall pass through the fire, and it shall
be clean, but it shall be purified with [A]water for
impurity. But whatever cannot stand the fire you
shall pass through the water. 24 And you shall wash
your clothes on the seventh day and be clean, and
afterward you may enter the camp."

DIVISION OF THE BOOTY

25 Then the LORD spoke to Moses, saying, 26 "You
and Eleazar the priest and the heads of the fathers'
households of the congregation take a count of the
booty [a]that was captured, both of man and of animal; 27 and [A]divide the booty between the warriors
who went out to battle and all the congregation.
28 [A]Levy a tax for the LORD from the men of war
who went out to battle, one [a]in five hundred of the
persons and of the cattle and of the donkeys and of
the sheep; 29 take it from their half and give it to Eleazar the priest, as an [a]offering to the LORD. 30 From
the sons of Israel's half, you shall take one drawn
out of every fifty of the persons, of the cattle, of the
donkeys and of the sheep, from all the animals, and
give them to the Levites who [A]keep charge of the
tabernacle of the LORD." 31 Moses and Eleazar the
priest did just as the LORD had commanded Moses.

32 Now the booty that remained from the spoil
which the [a]men of war had plundered was 675,000
sheep, 33 and 72,000 cattle, 34 and 61,000 donkeys,
35 and of human beings, of the women who had not
known man [a]intimately, all the persons were 32,000.

36 The half, the portion of those who went out
to war, was *as follows:* the number of sheep was
337,500, 37 and the LORD'S levy of the sheep was 675;
38 and the cattle were 36,000, from which the LORD'S
levy was 72; 39 and the donkeys were 30,500, from
which the LORD'S levy was 61; 40 and the human
beings were 16,000, from whom the LORD'S levy
was 32 persons. 41 Moses gave the levy *which was*
the LORD'S offering to Eleazar the priest, just [A]as
the LORD had commanded Moses.

42 As for the sons of Israel's half, which Moses
[a]separated from the men who had gone to war—
43 now the congregation's half was 337,500 sheep,
44 and 36,000 cattle, 45 and 30,500 donkeys, 46 and the
human beings were 16,000— 47 and from the sons
of Israel's half, Moses took one drawn out of every
fifty, both of man and of animals, and gave them
to the Levites, who kept charge of the tabernacle of
the LORD, just as the LORD had commanded Moses.

48 Then the officers who were over the thousands
of the army, the captains of thousands and the captains of hundreds, approached Moses, 49 and they
said to Moses, "Your servants have taken a census
of men of war who are in our charge, and no man of
us is missing. 50 So we have brought as an offering
to the LORD what each man found, articles of gold,
armlets and bracelets, signet rings, earrings and
necklaces, [A]to make atonement for ourselves before
the LORD." 51 Moses and Eleazar the priest took the
gold from them, all kinds of wrought articles. 52 All
the gold of the offering which they offered up to
the LORD, from the captains of thousands and the
captains of hundreds, was 16,750 shekels. 53 [A]The
men of war had taken booty, every man for himself.
54 So Moses and Eleazar the priest took the gold from
the captains of thousands and of hundreds, and
brought it to the tent of meeting as [A]a memorial
for the sons of Israel before the LORD.

REUBEN AND GAD SETTLE IN GILEAD

32 Now the sons of Reuben and the sons of Gad
had an [A]exceedingly large number of livestock. So when they saw the land of [B]Jazer and the
land of Gilead, that [a]it was indeed a place suitable
for livestock, 2 the sons of Gad and the sons of Reuben came and spoke to Moses and to Eleazar the
priest and to the leaders of the congregation, saying,
3 "[A]Ataroth, Dibon, Jazer, Nimrah, Heshbon, Elealeh,
Sebam, Nebo and Beon, 4 the land [A]which the LORD
[a]conquered before the congregation of Israel, is a
land for livestock, and your servants have livestock."
5 They said, "If we have found favor in your sight, let
this land be given to your servants as a possession;
do not take us across the Jordan."

6 But Moses said to the sons of Gad and to the
sons of Reuben, "Shall your brothers go to war

31:17 [a]Lit *by lying with a man* [A]Deut 7:2; 20:16-18 31:18 [a]Lit *female children* [b]Lit *by lying with a man* [c]Lit *keep alive* 31:19 [A]Num 19:11-22 31:20 [a]Or *skin* 31:23 [A]Num 19:9, 17 31:26 [a]Lit *of captives* 31:27 [A]Josh 22:8 31:28 [a]Lit *soul from* [A]Num 18:21-30 31:29 [a]Lit *heave offering,* and so throughout the ch 31:30 [A]Num 3:7, 8, 25, 26, 31, 36, 37; 18:3, 4 31:32 [a]Lit *people* 31:35 [a]Lit *by lying with a man* 31:41 [A]Num 5:9, 10; 18:19 31:42 [a]Or *divided* 31:50 [A]Ex 30:12-16 31:53 [A]Num 31:32; Deut 20:14 31:54 [A]Ex 30:16 32:1 [a]Lit *behold, the place, a place for* [A]Ex 12:38 [B]Num 21:32 32:3 [A]Num 32:34-38 32:4 [a]Lit *smote* [A]Num 21:34

31:17 The execution of all male children and women of childbearing age ensured the extermination of the Midianites and prevented them from ever again seducing Israel to sin. Reference to Midianites later (Jdg 6:1–6) was to a different clan. It was the Midianites living in Moab who were destroyed here.

31:25–54 The plunder was divided equally between those who went and fought and those who stayed.

32:1–42 The tribes of Reuben and Gad desired to live in the land already conquered because they possessed much livestock and the land was good for grazing. Moses gave them, along with the half tribe of Manasseh, portions of the land only on the condition that they would fully participate in the conquest of Canaan.

32:3 Ataroth ... Beon. The places mentioned here cannot be identified, but all lie between the Arnon River to the S and the Jabbok River to the N.

while you yourselves sit here? 7 [A]Now why are you
[a]discouraging the sons of Israel from crossing over
into the land which the LORD has given them?
8 [a]This is what your fathers did when I sent them
from [A]Kadesh-barnea to see the land. 9 For when
they went up to [A]the [a]valley of Eshcol and saw the
land, they [b]discouraged the sons of Israel so that
they did not go into the land which the LORD had
given them. 10 So [A]the LORD'S anger burned in that
day, and He swore, saying, 11 '[A]None of the men who
came up from Egypt, from twenty years old and
upward, shall see the land which I swore to Abraham, to Isaac and to Jacob; for they did not follow
Me fully, 12 except Caleb the son of Jephunneh the
Kenizzite and Joshua the son of Nun, [A]for they have
followed the LORD fully.' 13 [A]So the LORD'S anger
burned against Israel, and He made them wander
in the wilderness forty years, until the entire generation of those who had done evil in the sight of
the LORD was destroyed. 14 Now behold, you have
risen up in your fathers' place, a brood of sinful
men, to add still more to the burning [A]anger of
the LORD against Israel. 15 For if you [A]turn away
from following Him, He will once more abandon
them in the wilderness, and you will destroy all
these people."

16 Then they came near to him and said, "We
will build here sheepfolds for our livestock and
cities for our little ones; 17 [A]but we ourselves will
be armed ready *to go* before the sons of Israel,
until we have brought them to their place, while
our little ones live in the fortified cities because of
the inhabitants of the land. 18 [A]We will not return
to our homes until every one of the sons of Israel
has possessed his inheritance. 19 For we will not
have an inheritance with them on the other side
of the Jordan and beyond, because our inheritance
has fallen to us [A]on this side of the Jordan toward
the east."

20 [A]So Moses said to them, "If you will do [a]this,
if you will arm yourselves before the LORD for the
war, 21 and all of you armed men cross over the
Jordan before the LORD until He has driven His
enemies out from before Him, 22 [A]and the land
is subdued before the LORD, then afterward you
shall return and be free of obligation toward the
LORD and toward Israel, and this land shall be
yours for a possession before the LORD. 23 But if
you will not do so, behold, you have sinned against
the LORD, and be sure [A]your sin will find you out.
24 Build yourselves cities for your little ones, and
sheepfolds for your sheep, and [A]do [a]what you have
promised."

25 The sons of Gad and the sons of Reuben spoke
to Moses, saying, "Your servants will do just as my
lord commands. 26 [A]Our little ones, our wives, our
livestock and all our cattle shall [a]remain there in
the cities of Gilead; 27 while your servants, everyone who is armed for war, will [A]cross over in the
presence of the LORD to battle, just as my lord
says."

28 So Moses gave command concerning them to
Eleazar the priest, and to Joshua the son of Nun,
and to the heads of the fathers' *households* of the
tribes of the sons of Israel. 29 Moses said to them,
"If the sons of Gad and the sons of Reuben, everyone who is armed for battle, will cross with you
over the Jordan in the presence of the LORD, and
the land is subdued before you, then you shall give
them the land of Gilead for a possession; 30 but
if they will not cross over with you armed, they
shall have possessions among you in the land of
Canaan." 31 The sons of Gad and the sons of Reuben
answered, saying, "As the LORD has said to your
servants, so we will do. 32 We ourselves will cross
over armed in the presence of the LORD into the
land of Canaan, and the possession of our inheritance *shall remain* with us across the Jordan."

33 [A]So Moses gave to them, to the sons of Gad
and to the sons of Reuben and to the half-tribe
of Joseph's son Manasseh, the kingdom of Sihon,
king of the Amorites and the kingdom of Og, the
king of Bashan, the land with its cities with *their*
[a]territories, the cities of the surrounding land.
34 The sons of Gad built Dibon and Ataroth and
[A]Aroer, 35 and Atroth-shophan and Jazer and Jogbehah, 36 and [A]Beth-nimrah and Beth-haran as
fortified cities, and sheepfolds for sheep. 37 The
sons of Reuben built Heshbon and Elealeh and
Kiriathaim, 38 and [A]Nebo and Baal-meon—*their*
names being changed—and Sibmah, and they gave
other names to the cities which they built. 39 The
sons of [A]Machir the son of Manasseh went to Gilead
and took it, and dispossessed the Amorites who
were in it. 40 So Moses gave [A]Gilead to Machir the
son of Manasseh, and he lived in it. 41 Jair the son
of Manasseh went and took its [a]towns, and called
them [b,A]Havvoth-jair. 42 Nobah went and took Kenath and its villages, and called it Nobah after [A]his
own name.

32:7 [a]Lit *restraining the hearts of* [A]Num 13:27-14:4 32:8 [a]Lit *Thus your fathers* [A]Num 13:3, 26; Deut 1:19-25 32:9 [a]Or *wadi* [b]Lit *restrained the hearts of* [A]Num 13:24; Deut 1:24 32:10 [A]Num 14:11f; Deut 1:34 32:11 [A]Num 14:28-30 32:12 [A]Deut 1:36; Josh 14:8f 32:13 [A]Num 14:33-35 32:14 [A]Deut 1:34f 32:15 [A]Deut 30:17, 18; 2 Chr 7:19, 20 32:17 [A]Josh 4:12, 13 32:18 [A]Josh 22:1-4 32:19 [A]Josh 12:1; 13:8 32:20 [a]Lit *this thing* [A]Deut 3:18 32:22 [A]Deut 3:20 32:23 [A]Gen 4:7; 44:16; Is 59:12 32:24 [a]Lit *that which has come out of your mouth* [A]Num 30:2 32:26 [a]Lit *be* [A]Josh 1:14 32:27 [A]Josh 4:12 32:33 [a]Lit *borders* [A]Deut 3:8-17; Josh 12:1-6 32:34 [A]Deut 2:36 32:36 [A]Num 32:3 32:38 [A]Is 46:1 32:39 [A]Gen 50:23 32:40 [A]Deut 3:12, 13, 15; Josh 17:1 32:41 [a]Lit *tent villages* [b]I.e. the towns of Jair [A]Deut 3:14; Judg 10:4 32:42 [A]2 Sam 18:18; Ps 49:11

32:8 This is what your fathers did. Moses feared that if these two tribes were comfortably settled, they would not join with the other 10 tribes in conquering Canaan, and that could be the beginning of a general revolt against entering the land. As the 10 spies had dissuaded the people at Kadesh nearly 40 years earlier from conquering the land (vv. 9–13; 13:26–14:4), the refusal of these two tribes could cause the people to fail again (v. 15).

32:23 your sin will find you out. The two tribes committed themselves to provide their warriors for the conquest of the land. This agreement satisfied Moses, although he added that nonparticipation would be sin, and God would certainly find and judge the tribes for their sin.

32:33 half-tribe of … Manasseh. Once the agreement was reached with Reuben and Gad concerning settlement on the E side of the Jordan, the half tribe of Manasseh, also rich with flocks, joined in seeking land in that territory. However, vv. 39–42 indicate that Manasseh conquered cities not yet taken and settled in the northern area of Gilead.

REVIEW OF THE JOURNEY FROM EGYPT TO JORDAN

33 These are the journeys of the sons of Israel, by which they came out from the land of Egypt by their armies, under [A]the [a]leadership of Moses and Aaron. 2 Moses recorded their starting places according to their journeys by the [a]command of the LORD, and these are their journeys according to their starting places. 3 [A]They journeyed from Rameses in the first month, on the fifteenth day of the first month; on the [a]next day after the Passover the sons of Israel [B]started out [b]boldly in the sight of all the Egyptians, 4 while the Egyptians were burying all their firstborn whom the LORD had struck down among them. The LORD had also executed judgments [A]on their gods.

5 Then [A]the sons of Israel journeyed from Rameses and camped in Succoth. 6 [A]They journeyed from Succoth and camped in Etham, which is on the edge of the wilderness. 7 [A]They journeyed from Etham and turned back to Pi-hahiroth, which faces Baal-zephon, and they camped before Migdol. 8 [A]They journeyed [a]from before Hahiroth and passed through the midst of the sea into the wilderness; and [B]they went three days' journey in the wilderness of Etham and camped at Marah. 9 [A]They journeyed from Marah and came to Elim; and in Elim there were twelve springs of water and seventy palm trees, and they camped there. 10 They journeyed from Elim and camped by the [a]Red Sea. 11 They journeyed from the [a]Red Sea and camped in [A]the wilderness of Sin. 12 They journeyed from the wilderness of Sin and camped at Dophkah. 13 They journeyed from Dophkah and camped at Alush. 14 They journeyed from Alush and camped [A]at Rephidim; now it was there that the people had no water to drink. 15 They journeyed from Rephidim and camped in [A]the wilderness of Sinai. 16 They journeyed from the wilderness of Sinai and camped at [A]Kibroth-hattaavah.

17 They journeyed from Kibroth-hattaavah and camped at [A]Hazeroth. 18 They journeyed from Hazeroth and camped at Rithmah. 19 They journeyed from Rithmah and camped at Rimmon-perez. 20 They journeyed from Rimmon-perez and camped at [A]Libnah. 21 They journeyed from Libnah and camped at Rissah. 22 They journeyed from Rissah and camped in Kehelathah. 23 They journeyed from Kehelathah and camped at Mount Shepher. 24 They journeyed from Mount Shepher and camped at Haradah. 25 They journeyed from Haradah and camped at Makheloth. 26 They journeyed from Makheloth and camped at Tahath. 27 They journeyed from Tahath and camped at Terah. 28 They journeyed from Terah and camped at Mithkah. 29 They journeyed from Mithkah and camped at Hashmonah. 30 They journeyed from Hashmonah and camped at [A]Moseroth. 31 They journeyed from Moseroth and camped at Bene-jaakan. 32 They journeyed from [A]Bene-jaakan and camped at Hor-haggidgad. 33 They journeyed from Hor-haggidgad and camped at [A]Jotbathah. 34 They journeyed from Jotbathah and camped at Abronah. 35 They journeyed from Abronah and camped at [A]Ezion-geber. 36 They journeyed from Ezion-geber and camped in the wilderness of [A]Zin, that is, Kadesh. 37 They journeyed from Kadesh and camped at [A]Mount Hor, [B]at the edge of the land of Edom.

38 [A]Then Aaron the priest went up to Mount Hor at the [a]command of the LORD, and died there in the fortieth year after the sons of Israel had come from the land of Egypt, on the first *day* in the fifth month. 39 Aaron was one hundred twenty-three years old when he died on Mount Hor.

40 Now the Canaanite, the king of [A]Arad [a]who lived in the [b]Negev in the land of Canaan, heard of the coming of the sons of Israel.

41 Then they journeyed from Mount Hor and camped at Zalmonah. 42 They journeyed from Zalmonah and camped at Punon. 43 They journeyed from Punon and camped at [A]Oboth. 44 They journeyed from Oboth and camped at Iye-abarim, at the border of Moab. 45 They journeyed from Iyim and camped at Dibon-gad. 46 They journeyed from Dibon-gad and camped at Almon-diblathaim. 47 They journeyed from Almon-diblathaim and camped in the mountains of [A]Abarim, before Nebo. 48 They journeyed from the mountains of Abarim and [A]camped in the plains of Moab by the Jordan *opposite* Jericho. 49 They camped by the Jordan, from Beth-jeshimoth as far as [A]Abel-shittim in the plains of Moab.

LAW OF POSSESSING THE LAND

50 Then the LORD spoke to Moses in the plains of Moab by the Jordan *opposite* Jericho, saying, 51 "Speak to the sons of Israel and say to them, '[A]When you cross over the Jordan into the land of Canaan, 52 then you shall drive out all the inhabitants of the land from before you, and [A]destroy all their figured stones, and destroy all their molten images and demolish all their high places; 53 [A]and you shall take possession of the land and live in it, for I have given the land to you to possess it. 54 [A]You shall inherit the land by lot according to

33:1 [a]Lit *hand* [A]Ps 77:20; 105:26; Mic 6:4 33:2 [a]Lit *mouth* 33:3 [a]Lit *morrow* [b]Lit *with a high hand* [A]Ex 12:37 [B]Ex 14:8 33:4 [A]Ex 12:12 33:5 [A]Ex 12:37 33:6 [A]Ex 13:20 33:7 [A]Ex 14:1, 2 33:8 [a]Many mss read *from Pi-hahiroth* [A]Ex 14:22 [B]Ex 15:22, 23 33:9 [A]Ex 15:27 33:10 [a]Lit *Sea of Reeds* 33:11 [a]Lit *Sea of Reeds* [A]Ex 16:1 33:14 [A]Ex 17:1 33:15 [A]Ex 19:1 33:16 [A]Num 11:34 33:17 [A]Num 11:35 33:20 [A]Deut 1:1 33:30 [A]Deut 10:6 33:32 [A]Gen 36:27; Deut 10:6; 1 Chr 1:42 33:33 [A]Deut 10:7 33:35 [A]Deut 2:8 33:36 [A]Num 20:1 33:37 [A]Num 20:22 [B]Num 20:16 33:38 [a]Lit *mouth* [A]Num 20:28; Deut 10:6 33:40 [a]Lit *and he* [b]I.e. South country [A]Num 21:1 33:43 [A]Num 21:10, 11 33:47 [A]Num 27:12 33:48 [A]Num 22:1 33:49 [A]Num 25:1 33:51 [A]Josh 3:17 33:52 [A]Ex 23:24; Lev 26:1; Deut 7:5; 12:3, 30; Ps 106:34-36 33:53 [A]Deut 11:31; 17:14; Josh 21:43 33:54 [A]Num 26:53-56

33:1–49 The Lord commanded Moses to write a list of Israel's encampments between Egypt and the plains of Moab. Significantly, 40 places were mentioned (not including Rameses and the plains of Moab), reflecting the 40 years spent in the wilderness. Some sites recorded earlier are not listed, and other sites are only mentioned here. The God who would lead the Israelites in the conquest of Canaan (33:50–56) was the One who had led them through the wilderness.

33:50–36:13 The Promised Land had been Israel's goal from the beginning of Numbers. This last part of the book anticipated the settlement of Canaan.

33:50–56 God commanded that all of the Canaanites were to be exterminated, along with all their idolatrous symbols.

33:52 their high places. Hills on which

your families; to the larger you shall give more
inheritance, and to the smaller you shall give less
inheritance. Wherever the lot falls to anyone, that
shall be his. You shall inherit according to the tribes
of your fathers. 55 But if you do not drive out the
inhabitants of the land from before you, then it
shall come about that those whom you let remain
of them *will become* [A]as pricks in your eyes and as
thorns in your sides, and they will trouble you in
the land in which you live. 56 And as I plan to do to
them, so I will do to you.' "

INSTRUCTION FOR APPORTIONING CANAAN

34 Then the LORD spoke to Moses, saying,
2 "Command the sons of Israel and say to
them, 'When you enter [A]the land of Canaan, this
is the land that shall fall to you as an inheritance,
even the land of Canaan according to its borders.
3 [A]Your southern [a]sector shall [b]extend from the wilderness of Zin along the side of Edom, and your
southern border shall [b]extend from the end of the
Salt Sea [B]eastward. 4 Then your border shall turn
direction from the south to the ascent of Akrabbim
and [a]continue to Zin, and its [b]termination shall be
to the south of [A]Kadesh-barnea; and it shall [c]reach
Hazaraddar and [a]continue to Azmon. 5 The border
shall turn *direction* from Azmon to the brook of
Egypt, and its termination shall be at [A]the sea.
6 'As for the western border, you shall have the
Great Sea, that is, *its* [a]coastline; this shall be your
west border.
7 '[A]And this shall be your north border: you shall
draw your *border* line from the Great Sea to Mount

33:55 [A]Josh 23:13 34:2 [A]Gen 17:8; Ps 78:54, 55; 105:11 34:3 [a]Lit *side* [b]Lit *be* [A]Josh 15:1-3 [B]Josh 15:5 34:4 [a]Lit *pass along* [b]Lit *goings out,* and so throughout the ch [c]Lit *go forth to* [A]Num 32:8 34:5 [A]Josh 15:4 34:6 [a]Lit *border* 34:7 [A]Ezek 47:15-17

Canaanite altars and shrines were placed.

33:56 as I plan to do to them, so I will do to you. If Israel failed to obey God, she would be the object of God's punishment in exactly the same way as the Canaanites were.

34:1–15 God gave precise instruction to Israel concerning the boundaries of the land of Canaan. Sadly, the actual conquest of the land fell far short of these boundaries.

FROM THE WILDERNESS TO CANAAN

The attempt 40 years earlier to move from Kadesh-barnea north into Canaan had been rebuffed. This time Moses wanted to go east through Edom and north through Moab toward Canaan. However, the Hebrews were refused passage through both territories despite kinship with the peoples. Instead, Moses went south to Elath, then north and east, bypassing Edom and Moab. North of the Arnon River, they defeated the Amorites and were poised to cross the Jordan from the east to enter Canaan.

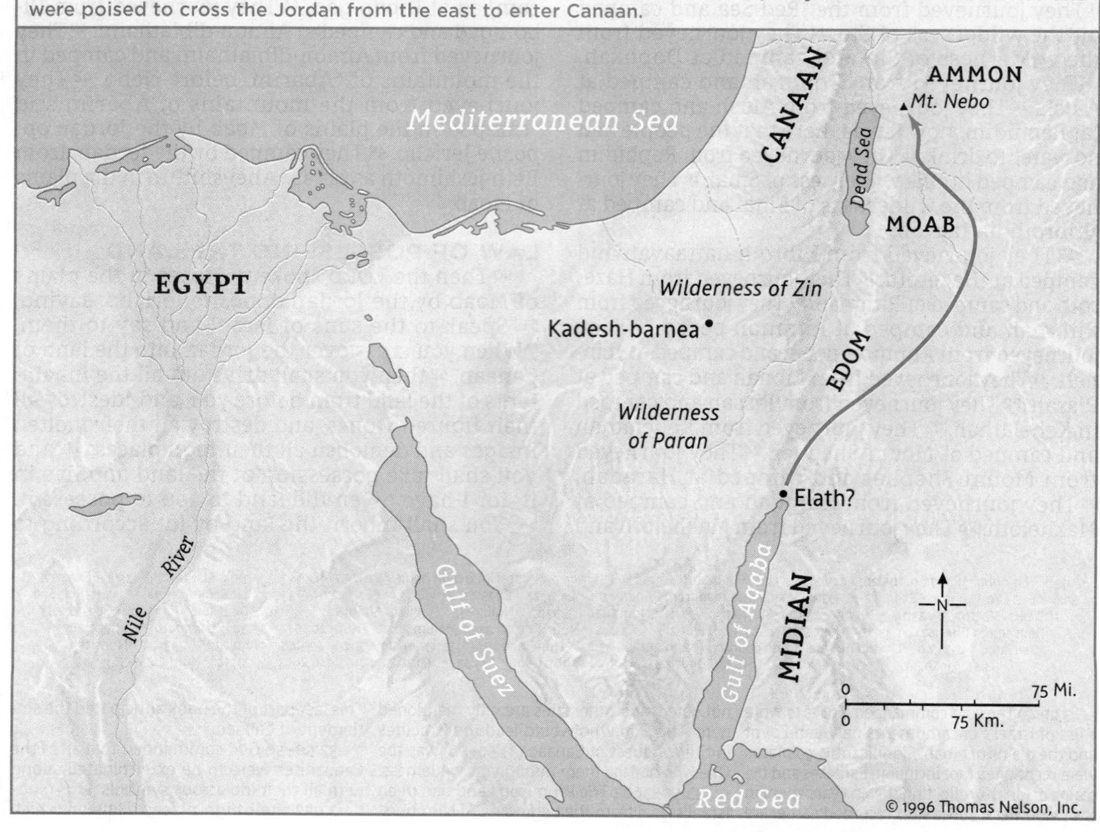

Hor. 8 You shall draw a line from Mount Hor to [A]the [a]Lebo-hamath, and the termination of the border shall be at Zedad; 9 and the border shall proceed to Ziphron, and its termination shall be at Hazar-enan. This shall be your north border.

10 'For your eastern border you shall also draw a line from Hazar-enan to Shepham, 11 and the border shall go down from Shepham to [A]Riblah on the east side of Ain; and the border shall go down and reach to the [a]slope on the east side of the Sea of [B]Chinnereth. 12 And the border shall go down to the Jordan and its termination shall be at the Salt Sea. This shall be your land according to its borders all around.' "

13 So Moses commanded the sons of Israel, saying, "[A]This is the land that you are to apportion by lot among you as a possession, which the LORD has commanded to give to the nine and a half tribes. 14 [A]For the tribe of the sons of Reuben have received *theirs* according to their fathers' households, and the tribe of the sons of Gad according to their fathers' households, and the half-tribe of Manasseh have received their possession. 15 The two and a half tribes have received their possession across the Jordan opposite Jericho, eastward toward the sunrising."

16 Then the LORD spoke to Moses, saying, 17 "[A]These are the names of the men who shall apportion the land to you for inheritance: Eleazar the priest and Joshua the son of Nun. 18 You shall take one leader of every tribe to apportion the land for inheritance. 19 These are the names of the men: of the tribe of [A]Judah, [B]Caleb the son of Jephunneh. 20 Of the tribe of the sons of [A]Simeon, Samuel the son of Ammihud. 21 Of the tribe of [A]Benjamin, Elidad the son of Chislon. 22 Of the tribe of the sons of Dan a leader, Bukki the son of Jogli. 23 Of the sons of Joseph: of the tribe of the sons of Manasseh a leader, Hanniel the son of Ephod. 24 Of the tribe of the sons of Ephraim a leader, Kemuel the son of Shiphtan. 25 Of the tribe of the sons of Zebulun a leader, Elizaphan the son of Parnach. 26 Of the tribe of the sons of Issachar a leader, Paltiel the son of Azzan. 27 Of the tribe of the sons of Asher a leader, Ahihud the son of Shelomi. 28 Of the tribe of the sons of Naphtali a leader, Pedahel the son of Ammihud." 29 These are those whom the LORD commanded to apportion the inheritance to the sons of Israel in the land of Canaan.

CITIES FOR THE LEVITES

35 [A]Now the LORD spoke to Moses in the plains of Moab by the Jordan *opposite* Jericho, saying, 2 "Command the sons of Israel that they give to the Levites from the inheritance of their possession cities to live in; and you shall give to the Levites pasture lands around the cities. 3 The cities shall be theirs to live in; and their pasture lands shall be for their cattle and for their herds and for all their beasts.

4 "The pasture lands of the cities which you shall give to the Levites *shall extend* from the wall of the city [a]outward a thousand cubits around. 5 You shall also measure outside the city on the east side two thousand cubits, and on the south side two thousand cubits, and on the west side two thousand cubits, and on the north side two thousand cubits, with the city in the center. This shall become theirs as pasture lands for the cities.

CITIES OF REFUGE

6 The cities which you shall give to the Levites *shall be* the [A]six cities of refuge, which you shall give for the manslayer to flee to; and in addition to them you shall give forty-two cities. 7 All the cities which you shall give to the Levites *shall be* [A]forty-eight cities, [a]together with their pasture lands. 8 [A]As for the cities which you shall give from the possession of the sons of Israel, you shall take more from the larger and you shall take less from the smaller; each shall give some of his cities to the Levites in proportion to his possession which he inherits."

9 Then the LORD spoke to Moses, saying, 10 "[A]Speak to the sons of Israel and say to them, 'When you cross the Jordan into the land of Canaan, 11 [A]then you shall select for yourselves cities to be your [B]cities of refuge, that the manslayer who has [a]killed any person [C]unintentionally may flee there. 12 [A]The cities shall be to you as a refuge from the avenger, so that the manslayer will not die until he stands before the congregation for [a]trial. 13 The cities which you are to give shall be your six cities of refuge. 14 You [A]shall give three cities across the Jordan and three cities [a]in the land of Canaan; they are to be cities of refuge. 15 These six cities shall be for refuge for the sons of Israel, and for the alien and for the sojourner among them; that anyone who [a]kills a person [A]unintentionally may flee there.

34:8 [a]Or *entrance of Hamath* [A]Josh 13:5 34:11 [a]Lit *shoulder* [A]2 Kin 23:33 [B]Deut 3:17; Josh 13:27 34:13 [A]Gen 15:18; Num 26:52-56; Deut 11:24; Josh 14:1-5 34:14 [A]Num 32:33 34:17 [A]Josh 14:1, 2 34:19 [A]Gen 29:35; Deut 33:7; Ps 60:7 [B]Num 13:6, 30; 26:65; Deut 1:36 34:20 [A]Gen 29:33; 49:5; Ezek 48:24 34:21 [A]Gen 49:27; Deut 33:12; Ps 68:27 35:1 [A]Lev 25:32-34 35:4 [a]Lit *and outward* 35:6 [A]Josh 20:7-9 35:7 [a]Lit *them* [A]Josh 21:41 35:8 [A]Lev 25:32-34; Num 26:54; 33:54; Josh 21:1-42 35:10 [A]Josh 20:1-9 35:11 [a]Lit *smote* [A]Deut 19:1-13 [B]Josh 20:2f [C]Ex 21:13; Lev 4:2f, 22f; Num 35:22-25 35:12 [a]Lit *judgment* [A]Deut 19:4-6; Josh 20:2, 3 35:14 [a]Lit *you shall give in* [A]Deut 4:41 35:15 [a]Lit *smites* [A]Num 35:11

34:13 give to the nine and a half tribes. The land to be conquered was to be given to the 9 1/2 tribes. The other 2 1/2 tribes already had their inheritance in Transjordan (32:1–42).

34:16–29 The Lord appointed the men who were to assign the portions of the land of Canaan: Eleazar the priest (20:25, 26), Joshua the commander (27:18–23), and the leaders of each of the 10 tribes which were to receive an inheritance. None of these men were sons of the leaders listed in 1:5–15.

35:1–8 Forty-eight cities throughout the land were to be given to the Levites. The tribe of Levi did not receive a tribal allotment, but lived among the other tribes. Joshua 21:1–42 gave the list of these 48 cities.

35:2 from the inheritance of their possession. According to 18:23, the Levites were to have no land as inheritance in Canaan, so the Levites did not inherit these towns; they only lived in them. **pasture lands around the cities.** The Levites were also given grazing land around the cities so that their animals might feed.

35:9–34 Six of the Levitical cities were to be established as "cities of refuge" (see Dt 19:1–13). These cities were to be havens giving protection to any person who accidentally killed another person (manslaughter).

35:12 the avenger. The meaning of this term is "near of kin." It refers to the person chosen by a family to deal with a loss suffered in that family. Here the close relative of a homicide victim would seek to avenge his death, but not until proper judgment was made.

16 '[A]But if he struck him down with an iron object,
so that he died, he is a murderer; the murderer shall
surely be put to death. 17 If he struck him down with
a stone in the hand, by which he will die, and *as a*
result he died, he is a murderer; the murderer [A]shall
surely be put to death. 18 Or if he struck him with
a wooden object in the hand, by which he might
die, and *as a result* he died, he is a murderer; the
murderer shall surely be put to death. 19 The blood
avenger himself shall put the murderer to death;
he shall put him to death when he meets him. 20 [A]If
he pushed him of hatred, or threw something at
him [B]lying in wait and *as a result* he died, 21 or if
he struck him down with his hand in enmity, and
as a result he died, the one who struck him shall
surely be put to death, he is a murderer; the blood
avenger shall put the murderer to death when he
meets him.

22 '[A]But if he pushed him suddenly without enmity, or threw something at him without lying in
wait, 23 or with any [a]deadly object of stone, and
without seeing it dropped on him so that he died,
while he was not his enemy nor seeking his injury,
24 then [A]the congregation shall judge between the
slayer and the blood avenger according to these
ordinances. 25 The congregation shall deliver the
manslayer from the hand of the blood avenger, and
the congregation shall restore him to his city of
refuge to which he fled; and he shall live in it until
the death of the high priest who was anointed with
the holy oil. 26 But if the manslayer at any time goes
beyond the border of his city of refuge to which he
may flee, 27 and the blood avenger finds him outside the border of his city of refuge, and the blood
avenger kills the manslayer, he will not be guilty
of blood 28 because he should have remained in his
city of refuge until the death of the high priest. But
after the death of the high priest the manslayer shall
return to the land of his possession.

29 'These things shall be for a [A]statutory ordinance to you throughout your generations in all
your dwellings.

30 '[A]If anyone kills a person, the murderer shall
be put to death at the [a]evidence of witnesses, but
[B]no person shall be put to death on the testimony of
one witness. 31 Moreover, you shall not take ransom
for the life of a murderer who is guilty of death, but
he shall surely be put to death. 32 You shall not take
ransom for him who has fled to his city of refuge,
that he may return to live in the land [a]before the
death of the priest. 33 [A]So you shall not pollute the
land in which you are; for blood pollutes the land
and no expiation can be made for the land for the
blood that is shed on it, except [B]by the blood of
him who shed it. 34 You shall not [A]defile the land in
which you live, in the midst of which [B]I dwell; for
I the LORD am dwelling in the midst of the sons
of Israel.' "

INHERITANCE BY MARRIAGE

36 [A]And the heads of the fathers' *households*
of the family of the sons of Gilead, the son
of Machir, the son of Manasseh, of the families of
the sons of Joseph, came near and spoke before
Moses and before the leaders, the heads of the fathers' *households* of the sons of Israel, 2 and they
said, "The LORD commanded my lord to give the
land by lot to the sons of Israel as an inheritance,
and my lord [A]was commanded by the LORD to give
the inheritance of Zelophehad our brother to his
daughters. 3 But if they [a]marry one of the sons of
the *other* tribes of the sons of Israel, their inheritance will be withdrawn from the inheritance of
our fathers and will be added to the inheritance
of the tribe to which they belong; thus it will be
withdrawn from our allotted inheritance. 4 When
the [A]jubilee of the sons of Israel [a]comes, then their
inheritance will be added to the inheritance of the
tribe to which they belong; so their inheritance will
be withdrawn from the inheritance of the tribe of
our fathers."

5 Then Moses commanded the sons of Israel
according to the [a]word of the LORD, saying, "The
tribe of the sons of Joseph are right in *their* statements. 6 [A]This is [a]what the LORD has commanded
concerning the daughters of Zelophehad, saying,
'Let them marry [b]whom they wish; only they must
marry within the family of the tribe of their father.' 7 Thus [A]no inheritance of the sons of Israel
shall [a]be transferred from tribe to tribe, for the
sons of Israel shall each [b]hold to the inheritance
of the tribe of his fathers. 8 [A]Every daughter who
comes into possession of an inheritance of any
tribe of the sons of Israel shall be wife to one of
the family of the tribe of her father, so that the
sons of Israel each may possess the inheritance of

35:16 [A]Ex 21:12, 14; Lev 24:17 35:17 [A]Num 35:31 35:20 [A]Gen 4:8; 2 Sam 3:27; 20:10 [B]Ex 21:14; Deut 19:11 35:22 [A]Num 35:11 35:23 [a]Lit *by which he may die* 35:24 [A]Josh 20:6 35:29 [A]Num 27:11 35:30 [a]Lit *mouth* [A]Num 35:16 [B]Deut 17:6; 19:15; Matt 18:16; John 7:51; 8:17, 18 35:32 [a]Or *until* 35:33 [A]Deut 21:7, 8; Ps 106:38 [B]Gen 9:6 35:34 [A]Lev 18:24, 25 [B]Num 5:3 36:1 [A]Num 27:1 36:2 [A]Num 27:5-7 36:3 [a]Lit *become wives to*, in this ch 36:4 [a]Lit *shall be* [A]Lev 25:10 36:5 [a]Lit *mouth* 36:6 [a]Lit *the thing which* [b]Lit *to the good one in their eyes* [A]Num 27:7 36:7 [a]Lit *turn about* [b]Lit *cleave* [A]1 Kin 21:3 36:8 [A]1 Chr 23:22

35:19 Swift retribution according to the law of Ge 9:5, 6.

35:24 judge between the slayer and the blood avenger. The congregation was called to decide the motive of the killer, whether it was with or without hostility. If there was evil intent, the killer was turned over to the avenger to be put to death. If, however, hostility could not be proven to exist between the killer and the victim, then the killer was allowed to remain in the city of refuge.

35:25 until the death of the high priest. The manslayer without evil intent was to remain in the city of refuge until the death of the High Priest. The death of the High Priest marked the end of an old era and the beginning of a new one for the manslayer.

35:30 witnesses. No one could be judged guilty of death on the testimony of only one witness. Two or more witnesses were required in all capital cases (cf. Dt 17:6; 19:15).

35:33 blood pollutes the land. Though murder and inadvertent killing polluted the land, murder was atoned for by the death of the murderer. Failure to observe these principles would make the land unclean. If the whole land became unclean, then the Lord would no longer be able to dwell in their midst.

36:1–13 The issue raised here stemmed from a decision regarding female inheritance in 27:1–11. Since a tribe would lose an allotted inheritance in the year of Jubilee if an inheriting woman had married into another tribe, the woman of any tribe who inherited land must marry within her own tribe.

his fathers. 9 Thus no inheritance shall [a]be transferred from one tribe to another tribe, for the
tribes of the sons of Israel shall each [b]hold to his
own inheritance."
10 Just as the LORD had commanded Moses, so
the daughters of Zelophehad did: 11 [A]Mahlah, Tirzah, Hoglah, Milcah and Noah, the daughters of
Zelophehad married their uncles' sons. 12 They
married *those* from the families of the sons of
Manasseh the son of Joseph, and their inheritance
[a]remained with the tribe of the family of their
father.
13 [A]These are the commandments and the ordinances which the LORD commanded to the sons of
Israel through Moses in the plains of Moab by the
Jordan *opposite* Jericho.

36:9 [a]Lit *turn about* [b]Lit *cleave* 36:11 [A]Num 26:33 36:12 [a]Lit *was* 36:13 [A]Lev 26:46; 27:34; Num 22:1

36:12 married *those* from ... Manasseh. The daughters of Zelophehad exemplified the obedience to God's commandments that should have been practiced by all of Israel. Their inheritance was a direct result of their obedience to the Lord—a basic lesson stressed throughout the whole book of Numbers.

THE FIFTH BOOK OF MOSES CALLED

DEUTERONOMY

TITLE

The English title "Deuteronomy" comes from the Greek Septuagint (LXX) mistranslation of "copy of this law" in 17:18 as "second law," which was rendered *Deuteronomium* in the Latin version (Vulgate). The Hebrew title of the book is translated "These are the words," from the first two Hebrew words of the book. The Hebrew title is a better description of the book since it is not a "second law," but rather the record of Moses' words of explanation concerning the law. Deuteronomy completes the five-part literary unit called the Pentateuch.

AUTHOR AND DATE

Moses has been traditionally recognized as the author of Deuteronomy, since the book itself testifies that Moses wrote it (1:1, 5; 31:9, 22, 24). Both the OT (1Ki 2:3; 8:53; 2Ki 14:6; 18:12) and the NT (Ac 3:22, 23; Ro 10:19) support the claim of Mosaic authorship. While Dt 32:48–34:12 was added after Moses' death (probably by Joshua), the rest of the book came from Moses' hand just before his death in 1405 B.C.

The majority of the book is comprised of farewell speeches that the 120-year-old Moses gave to Israel, beginning on the first day of the 11th month of the 40th year after the Exodus from Egypt (1:3). These speeches can be dated Jan.–Feb., 1405 B.C. In the last few weeks of Moses' life, he committed these speeches to writing and gave them to the priests and elders for the coming generations of Israel (31:9, 24–26).

BACKGROUND AND SETTING

Like Leviticus, Deuteronomy does not advance historically, but takes place entirely in one location over about one month of time (cf. Dt 1:3 and 34:8 with Jos 5:6–12). Israel was encamped in the central rift valley to the E of the Jordan River (Dt 1:1). This location was referred to in Nu 36:13 as "the plains of Moab," an area N of the Arnon River across the Jordan River from Jericho. It had been almost 40 years since the Israelites had exited Egypt.

The book of Deuteronomy concentrates on events that took place in the final weeks of Moses' life. The major event was the verbal communication of divine revelation from Moses to the people of Israel (1:1–30:20; 31:30–32:47; 33:1–29). The only other events recorded were: 1) Moses' recording the law in a book and his commissioning of Joshua as the new leader (31:1–29); 2) Moses' viewing of the land of Canaan from Mt. Nebo (32:48–52; 34:1–4); and 3) his death (34:5–12).

The original recipients of Deuteronomy, both in its verbal and written presentations, were the second generation of the nation of Israel (except Joshua and Caleb, who were older). All of that generation, from 40 to 60 years of age, had been born in Egypt and had participated as children or teens in the Exodus. Those under 40 had been born and reared in the wilderness. Together, they comprised the generation that was on the verge of conquering the land of Canaan under Joshua, 40 years after they had left Egypt (1:34–39).

HISTORICAL AND THEOLOGICAL THEMES

Like Leviticus, Deuteronomy contains much legal detail, but with an emphasis on the people rather than the priests. As Moses called the second generation of Israel to trust the Lord and be obedient to His covenant made at Horeb (Sinai), he illustrated his points with references to Israel's past history. He reminded Israel of her rebellion against the Lord at Horeb (9:7–10:11) and at Kadesh (1:26–46), which brought devastating consequences. He also reminded her of the Lord's faithfulness in giving victory over her enemies (2:24–3:11; 29:2, 7, 8). Most importantly, Moses called the people to take the land that God had promised by oath to their forefathers Abraham, Isaac, and Jacob (1:8; 6:10; 9:5; 29:13; 30:20; 34:4; cf. Ge 15:18–21; 26:3–5; 35:12). Moses not only looked back, he also looked ahead and saw that Israel's future failure to obey God would lead to her being scattered among the nations before the fulfillment of His oath to the patriarchs would be completed (4:25–31; 29:22–30:10; 31:26–29).

The book of Deuteronomy, along with Psalms and Isaiah, reveals much about the attributes of God. Thus, it is directly quoted over 40 times in the NT (exceeded only by Psalms and Isaiah) with many more allusions to its content. Deuteronomy reveals that the Lord is the only God (4:39; 6:4), and that He is jealous (4:24), faithful (7:9), loving (7:13), merciful (4:31), yet angered by sin (6:15). This is the God who called

Israel to Himself. Over 250 times, Moses repeated the phrase, "the Lord your God" to Israel. Israel was called to obey (28:2), fear (10:12), love (10:12), and serve (10:12) her God by walking in His ways and keeping His commandments (10:12, 13). By obeying Him, the people of Israel would receive His blessings (28:1–14). Obedience and the pursuit of personal holiness is always based upon the character of God. Because of who He is, His people are to be holy (cf., 7:6–11; 8:6, 11, 18; 10:12, 16, 17; 11:13; 13:3, 4; 14:1, 2).

INTERPRETIVE CHALLENGES

Three interpretive challenges face the reader of Deuteronomy. First, is the book a singular record, or is it only a part of the larger literary whole, the Pentateuch? The remainder of the Scripture always views the Pentateuch as a unit, and the ultimate meaning of Deuteronomy cannot be divorced from its context in the Pentateuch. The book also assumes the reader is already familiar with the 4 books that precede it; in fact, Deuteronomy brings into focus all that had been revealed in Genesis to Numbers, as well as its implications for the people as they entered the land. However, every available Hebrew manuscript divides the Pentateuch in exactly the same way as the present text, indicating that the book is a well-defined unit recounting the final speeches of Moses to Israel, so it may also be viewed as a singular record.

Second, is the structure of Deuteronomy based on the secular treaties of Moses' day? During the last 35 years, many evangelical scholars have supported the Mosaic authorship of Deuteronomy by appealing to the similarities between the structure of the book and the ancient Near Eastern treaty form of the mid-second millennium B.C. (the approximate time of Moses). These secular suzerainty treaties (i.e., a ruler dictating his will to his vassals) followed a set pattern not used in the mid-first millennium B.C. These treaties usually contained the following elements: 1) preamble—identifying the parties to the covenant; 2) historical prologue—a history of the king's dealing with his vassals; 3) general and specific stipulations; 4) witnesses; 5) blessings and curses; and 6) oaths and covenant ratification. Deuteronomy, it is believed, approximates this basic structure. While there is agreement that 1:1–5 is a preamble, 1:5–4:43 a historical prologue, and chaps. 27, 28 feature blessings and cursings, there is no consensus as to how the rest of Deuteronomy fits this structure. While there might have been a covenant renewal on the plains of Moab, this is neither clearly explicit nor implicit in Deuteronomy. It is best to take the book for what it claims to be: the explanation of the law given by Moses for the new generation. The structure follows the speeches given by Moses. See Outline.

Third, what was the covenant made in the land of Moab (29:1)? The majority opinion posits this covenant as a renewal of the Sinaitic Covenant made nearly 40 years before with the first generation. Here, Moses supposedly updated and renewed this same covenant with the second generation of Israel. The second view sees this covenant as a Palestinian Covenant which guarantees the nation of Israel's right to the land, both at that time and in the future. A third position is that Moses in chaps. 29, 30 anticipated the New Covenant, since he knew Israel would fail to keep the Sinaitic Covenant. The third view seems the best.

OUTLINE

I. Introduction: The Historical Setting of Moses' Speeches (1:1–4)

II. The First Address by Moses: A Historical Prologue (1:5–4:43)
- A. A Historical Review of God's Gracious Acts from Horeb to Beth-peor (1:5–3:29)
- B. An Exhortation to Obey the Law (4:1–40)
- C. The Setting Apart of Three Cities of Refuge (4:41–43)

III. The Second Address by Moses: The Stipulations of the Sinaitic Covenant (4:44–28:68)
- A. Introduction (4:44–49)
- B. The Basic Elements of Israel's Relationship with the Lord (5:1–11:32)
  1. The Ten Commandments (5:1–33)
  2. The total commitment to the Lord (6:1–25)
  3. Separation from the gods of other nations (7:1–26)
  4. A warning against forgetting the Lord (8:1–20)
  5. Illustrations of Israel's rebellion in the past (9:1–10:11)
  6. An admonition to fear and love the Lord and obey His will (10:12–11:32)
- C. The Specific Stipulations for Life in the New Land (12:1–26:19)
  1. Instructions for the life of worship (12:1–16:17)
  2. Instructions for leadership (16:18–18:22)
  3. Instructions for societal order (19:1–23:14)
  4. Instructions from miscellaneous laws (23:15–25:19)
  5. The first fruits and tithes in the land (26:1–15)
  6. The affirmation of obedience (26:16–19)
- D. The Blessings and Curses of the Covenant (27:1–28:68)

IV. The Third Address by Moses: Another Covenant (29:1–30:20)

V. The Concluding Events (31:1–34:12)
- A. The Change of Leadership (31:1–8)
- B. The Future Reading of the Law (31:9–13)

- C. The Song of Moses (31:14–32:47)
  - 1. The anticipation of Israel's failure (31:14–29)
  - 2. The witness of Moses' song (31:30–32:43)
  - 3. The communicating of Moses' song (32:44–47)
- D. The Final Events of Moses' Life (32:48–34:12)
  - 1. The directives for Moses' death (32:48–52)
  - 2. The blessing of Moses (33:1–29)
  - 3. The death of Moses (34:1–12)

ISRAEL'S HISTORY AFTER THE EXODUS

1 These are the words which Moses spoke to all Israel
[A]across the Jordan in the wilderness, in the [B]Ara-
bah opposite [a]Suph, between Paran and Tophel and
Laban and Hazeroth and Dizahab. 2 It is eleven days'
journey from [A]Horeb by the way of Mount [B]Seir to
[C]Kadesh-barnea. 3 In the [A]fortieth year, on the first *day*
of the eleventh month, Moses spoke to the children
of Israel, [B]according to all that the LORD had commanded him *to give* to them, 4 after he had [a,A]defeated
Sihon the king of the Amorites, who lived in Heshbon,
and [B]Og the king of Bashan, who lived in [C]Ashtaroth
[b]and Edrei. 5 Across the Jordan in the land of Moab,
Moses undertook to expound this law, saying,

6 "The LORD our God [A]spoke to us at Horeb, saying,
'You have [a]stayed long enough at this mountain.
7 Turn and set your journey, and go to [A]the hill country
of the Amorites, and to all their neighbors in the Arabah, in the hill country and in the lowland and in [B]the
[a]Negev and by the seacoast, the land of the Canaanites, and Lebanon, as far as the great river, the river
Euphrates. 8 See, I have placed the land before you;
go in and possess the land which the LORD [A]swore
to give to your fathers, to Abraham, to Isaac, and to
Jacob, to them and their [a]descendants after them.'

9 "I spoke to you at that time, saying, '[A]I am not able
to bear *the burden* of you alone. 10 The LORD your God
has [A]multiplied you, and behold, you are this day like
the stars of heaven in number. 11 May the LORD, the
God of your fathers, increase you a thousand-fold
more than you are and bless you, [A]just as He has
[a]promised you! 12 How can I alone bear the load and
burden of you and your strife? 13 [a,A]Choose wise and
discerning and experienced men from your tribes,
and I will appoint them as your heads.' 14 You answered me and said, 'The thing which you have said
to do is good.' 15 So I took the heads of your tribes, wise
and experienced men, and [a]appointed them heads
over you, leaders of thousands and [b]of hundreds,
[b]of fifties and [b]of tens, and officers for your tribes.

16 "Then I charged your judges at that time, saying, 'Hear *the cases* between your [a]fellow countrymen, and [A]judge righteously between a man and his
[b]fellow countryman, or the alien who is with him.
17 [A]You shall not show partiality in judgment; you
shall hear the small and the great alike. You shall
[B]not fear [a]man, for the judgment is God's. [C]The case

1:1 [a]Perhaps Red Sea [A]Deut 4:46 [B]Deut 2:8 1:2 [A]Ex 3:1; 17:6 [B]Gen 32:3 [C]Num 13:26; 32:8; Deut 9:23 1:3 [A]Num 33:38 [B]Deut 4:1, 2 1:4 [a]Lit *smitten* [b]So with ancient versions; M.T. omits *and* [A]Num 21:21-26; Deut 2:26-35; Josh 13:10; Neh 9:22 [B]Num 21:33-35; Josh 13:12 [C]Josh 12:4 1:6 [a]Lit *dwelt* [A]Num 10:11-13 1:7 [a]I.e. South country [A]Gen 15:18; Deut 11:24; Josh 10:40 [B]Gen 12:9 1:8 [a]Lit *seed* [A]Gen 12:7; 26:3; 28:13; Ex 33:1; Num 14:23; 32:11; Heb 6:13, 14 1:9 [A]Ex 18:18, 24; Num 11:14 1:10 [A]Gen 15:5; 22:17; Ex 32:13; Deut 7:7; 10:22; 26:5; 28:62 1:11 [a]Lit *spoken to* [A]Deut 1:8, 10 1:13 [a]Lit *Give for yourselves* [A]Ex 18:21 1:15 [a]Lit *gave* [b]Lit *leaders of* 1:16 [a]Lit *brothers* [b]Lit *brother* [A]Deut 16:18; John 7:24 1:17 [a]Lit *because of man* [A]Deut 10:17; 16:19; 24:17; 2 Chr 19:5, 6; Prov 24:23-26; Acts 10:34; James 2:1, 9 [B]Prov 29:25 [C]Ex 18:22, 26

1:1–4 This introduction gives the setting of Deuteronomy and its purpose.

1:1 the words which Moses spoke. Almost all of Deuteronomy consists of speeches given by Moses at the end of his life. According to v. 3, Moses acted upon the authority of God since his inspired words were in accordance with the commandments that God had given. **to all Israel.** This expression is used 12 times in this book and emphasizes the unity of Israel, and the universal applications of these words. **the Arabah opposite Suph.** Except for Jordan and the Arabah (see marginal note), the exact location of the places named in 1:1 is not known with certainty, although they may have been along Israel's route N from the Gulf of Aqabah (cf. Nu 33). The plain referred to is the large rift valley that extends from the Sea of Galilee in the N to the Gulf of Aqabah in the S. Israel was encamped to the E of the Jordan River in this valley.

1:2 eleven days' *journey*. The distance from Horeb to Kadesh-barnea was about 150 mi. Kadesh was on the southern border of the Promised Land. This trip took 11 days on foot, but for Israel lasted 38 more years. **Horeb.** The usual name in Deuteronomy for Mt. Sinai means "desolation," a fitting name since the area around Sinai is barren and uninviting. **Mount Seir.** South of the Dead Sea in Edom.

1:3 the fortieth year. The 40th year after the Exodus from Egypt. The years of divine judgment (Nu 14:33, 34) were ending. **the eleventh month.** Jan.-Feb., 1405 B.C. Numbers 20–36 records the events of the 40th year.

1:4 Sihon ... Og. The two kings of the Amorites whom the Jews defeated in Transjordan (see 2:24–3:11; Nu 21:21–35).

1:5–4:43 These verses are mainly Moses' first speech. Moses introduced his explanation of the law with a call to enter the land of Canaan (vv. 6–8), which had been promised by the Abrahamic Covenant from God (cf. Ge 15:18–21). Throughout this book, he refers to that covenant promise (1:35; 4:31; 6:10, 18, 23; 7:8, 12; 8:1, 18; 9:5; 10:11; 11:9, 21; 13:17; 19:8; 26:3, 15; 27:3; 28:11; 29:13; 30:20; 31:7, 20–23; 34:4). He then gave a historical review of God's gracious acts (1:9–3:29) and a call to Israel for obedience to the covenant given to them by the Lord at Sinai (4:1–40). This introductory section ends with a brief narrative recounting the appointment of the 3 cities of refuge E of the Jordan (4:41–43).

1:5 expound. To make clear, distinct, or plain. The purpose of the book was to make the sense and purpose of the law clear to the people as they entered the land. It was to be their guide to the law while living in the land. Moses did not review what happened at Horeb (Sinai), which is recorded by him in Exodus, Leviticus, and Numbers (cf. Ex 20:1–Nu 10:10), but rather gave Israel instruction in how to walk with God and how to fulfill God's will in the land and be blessed.

1:7, 8 the land. The land which the Lord set before Israel to go in and possess was clearly described in v. 7. The hill country of the Amorites referred to the mountainous territory W of the Dead Sea. The Arabah was the land in the rift valley from the Sea of Galilee in the N to the Dead Sea in the S. The hill country referred to the hills that run through the center of the land N and S. These hills are to the W of the Sea of Galilee and the Jordan River. The lowland referred to the low rolling hills that sloped toward the Mediterranean coast (Shephelah). The Negev described the dry wasteland stretching southward from Beersheba to the wilderness. The seacoast referred to the land along the Mediterranean Sea. The boundaries of the land of the Canaanites were given in Nu 34:1–15. Lebanon to the N marked the northwestern boundary on the coast. The NE boundary of the land was the Euphrates River. Cf. Nu 34:1–12.

1:8 the LORD swore. God's command to take possession of this land by conquest was based upon the promise of the land that had been given in a covenant to Abraham (Ge 15:18–21) and reiterated to Isaac and Jacob (Ge 26:3–5; 28:13–15; 35:12). These 3 patriarchs are mentioned 7 times in Deuteronomy (1:8; 6:10; 9:5, 27; 29:13; 30:20; 34:4). The Lord sealed His promise to the patriarchs with an oath (swore) indicating that He would never change His plan (cf. Ps 110:4).

1:9–18 *See notes on Ex 18* for the background.

1:10 the stars of heaven. The Lord had promised Abraham that his descendants would be as numerous as the stars in the sky (see Ge 15:5; 22:17). The nation's growth proved both God's intention and ability to fulfill His original promises to Abraham.

1:11 a thousand-fold. A Semitic way of saying "an infinitely large number."

1:13 Choose wise ... men. The fulfillment of God's promise to give to Abraham such a large posterity created a problem for Moses. The nation had become too large for Moses to govern effectively. The solution was the appointment by Moses of men to help him lead the people (see Ex 18:13–27). These men were to be 1) wise, i.e., men who knew how to apply their knowledge; 2) discerning, i.e., those who had understanding and so were able to judge; and 3) experienced, i.e., knowledgeable and respected. Cf. Ex 18:21.

that is too hard for you, you shall bring to me, and
I will hear it.' 18 [A]I commanded you at that time all
the things that you should do.
19 "Then we set out from [A]Horeb, and went
through all that [B]great and terrible wilderness
which you saw on the way to the [C]hill country of
the Amorites, just as the LORD our God had commanded us; and we came to [A]Kadesh-barnea. 20 I
said to you, 'You have come to the hill country of
the Amorites which the LORD our God is about to
give us. 21 See, the LORD your God has placed the
land before you; go up, take possession, as the LORD,
the God of your fathers, has spoken to you. [A]Do not
fear or be dismayed.'
22 "[A]Then all of you approached me and said, 'Let
us send men before us, that they may search out
the land for us, and bring back to us word of the
way by which we should go up and the cities which
we shall enter.' 23 The thing pleased me and I took
twelve of your men, one man for each tribe. 24 [A]They
turned and went up into the hill country, and came
to the valley of Eshcol and spied it out. 25 Then they
took *some* of the fruit of the land in their hands and
brought it down to us; and they brought us back a
report and said, 'It is a good land which the LORD
our God is about to give us.'
26 "[A]Yet you were not willing to go up, but [B]re-
belled against the [a]command of the LORD your God;
27 and [A]you grumbled in your tents and said, 'Because the LORD hates us, He has brought us out of
the land of Egypt to deliver us into the hand of the
Amorites to destroy us. 28 Where can we go up? Our
brethren have made our hearts melt, saying, "The
people are bigger and taller than we; the cities are
large and fortified to heaven. And besides, we saw
[A]the sons of the Anakim there." ' 29 Then I said to
you, 'Do not be shocked, nor fear them. 30 The LORD
your God who goes before you will [A]Himself fight
on your behalf, [a]just as He did for you in Egypt
before your eyes, 31 and in the wilderness where you
saw how [A]the LORD your God carried you, just as a
man carries his son, in all the way which you have
walked until you came to this place.' 32 But [a,A]for all
this, you did not trust the LORD your God, 33 [A]who
goes before you on *your* way, [B]to seek out a place
for you to encamp, in fire by night and cloud by
day, to show you the way in which you should go.
34 "Then the LORD heard the sound of your words,
and He was angry and [A]took an oath, saying, 35 '[A]Not
one of these men, this evil generation, shall see the
good land which I swore to give your fathers, 36 except Caleb the son of Jephunneh; he shall see it, and
[A]to him and to his sons I will give the land on which
he has set foot, because he has followed the LORD
fully.' 37 [A]The LORD was angry with me also on your
account, saying, '[B]Not even you shall enter there.
38 Joshua the son of Nun, who stands before you, [A]he
shall enter there; encourage him, for [B]he will cause
Israel to inherit it. 39 Moreover, [A]your little ones who
you said would become a prey, and your sons, who
this day have [B]no knowledge of good or evil, shall
enter there, and I will give it to them and they shall
possess it. 40 But as for you, [A]turn around and set
out for the wilderness by the way to the [a]Red Sea.'
41 "[A]Then you said to me, 'We have sinned against
the LORD; we will indeed go up and fight, just as the
LORD our God commanded us.' And every man of
you girded on his weapons of war, and regarded it as
easy to go up into the hill country. 42 [A]And the LORD
said to me, 'Say to them, "Do not go up nor fight, for
I am not among you; otherwise you will be [a]defeated
before your enemies." ' 43 So I spoke to you, but you
would not listen. Instead [A]you rebelled against the
[a]command of the LORD, and acted presumptuously
and went up into the hill country. 44 [A]The Amorites
who [a]lived in that hill country came out against
you and chased you [B]as bees do, and crushed you
from Seir to Hormah. 45 Then you returned and wept

1:18 [A]Ex 18:20 1:19 [A]Deut 1:2 [B]Deut 2:7; 8:15; 32:10; Jer 2:6 [C]Deut 1:7 1:21 [A]Josh 1:6, 9 1:22 [A]Num 13:1-3 1:24 [A]Num 13:21-25 1:26 [a]Lit *mouth* [A]Num 14:1-4 [B]Deut 9:23 1:27 [A]Deut 9:28; Ps 106:25 1:28 [A]Num 13:28, 33; Deut 9:2 1:30 [a]Lit *according to all that* [A]Ex 14:14; Deut 3:22; 20:4; Neh 4:20 1:31 [A]Deut 32:10-12; Is 46:3, 4; 63:9; Hos 11:3; Acts 13:18 1:32 [a]Lit *in this matter* [A]Num 14:11; Ps 106:24; Heb 3:19; 4:2; Jude 5 1:33 [A]Ex 13:21; Num 9:15-23; Neh 9:12; Ps 78:14 [B]Num 10:33 1:34 [A]Num 14:28-30; Heb 3:18 1:35 [A]Ps 95:11; 106:26; Ezek 20:15; 1 Cor 10:5; Heb 3:14-19 1:36 [A]Num 14:24; Josh 14:9 1:37 [A]Num 20:12; Deut 3:26; 4:21 [B]Num 27:13, 18 1:38 [A]Num 14:30 [B]Num 34:17; Deut 3:28; 31:7; Josh 11:23 1:39 [A]Num 14:3, 31 [B]Is 7:15, 16 1:40 [a]Lit *Sea of Reeds* [A]Num 14:25 1:41 [A]Num 14:40 1:42 [a]Lit *smitten* [A]Num 14:41-43 1:43 [a]Lit *mouth* [A]Num 14:40 1:44 [a]Lit *dwelt* [A]Num 14:45 [B]Ps 118:12

1:19–21 *See notes on Nu 10:11–12:16* for the background.

1:22–46 *See notes on Nu 13, 14* for the background.

1:22 Let us send men before us. When challenged by Moses to take the land (vv. 20, 21), the people requested that spies be sent first. Moses, it seems, took their request to the Lord, who also approved their plan and commanded Moses to appoint the spies (Nu 13:1, 2). Thus, Moses selected 12 men who went to see what the land was like (Nu 13:17–20).

1:26 but rebelled. Israel, at Kadesh-barnea, deliberately and defiantly refused to respond to God's command to take the land (Nu 14:1–9).

1:27 you grumbled. Israel complained in their tents that the Lord hated them. They assumed the Lord brought them from Egypt to have them destroyed by the Amorites.

1:28 the Anakim. Lit. "sons of the Anakim" (i.e., the Anakites). The Anakites were early inhabitants of Canaan described as "great and tall" (2:10, 21; 9:2; Nu 13:32, 33). They were larger than the Israelites and were especially feared because of their military power.

1:32 you did not trust the LORD your God. The failure of the people to take the land at the beginning of their time in the wilderness was explained here in the same way as in Nu 14:11. Israel did not take the Lord at His Word and, therefore, did not obey His command. The Israelites' lack of obedience is explained as the outcome of their lack of faith in the Lord.

1:33 in fire … and cloud. The cloud by day and the fire by night were the means of God's direction for Israel in the wilderness (Ex 13:21; Nu 9:15–23). The Lord who guided Israel through the wandering journey was the same Lord who had already searched out a place for Israel in the land. As He had directed them in the past, He would direct them also in the future.

1:36–38 Caleb … Joshua. They were excluded from this judgment because of exemplary faith and obedience (cf. Nu 14:24; Jos 14:8, 9).

1:37 The LORD was angry with me. Although his disobedience occurred almost 39 years after the failure of Israel at Kadesh (Nu 20:1–13), Moses included it here with Israel's disobedience to the Lord because his disobedience was of the same kind. Moses, like Israel, failed to honor the Word of the Lord and thus, in rebellion for self glory, disobeyed God's clear command and struck the rock rather than speaking to it. Thus, he suffered the same result of God's anger and, like Israel, was not allowed to go into the land (Nu 20:12).

1:41–45 Israel's further defiance of the Lord's command was shown by their presumption in seeking to go into the land after God said they should not. This time they rebelled by attempting to go in and conquer

before the LORD; but the [A]LORD did not listen to your voice nor give ear to you. 46 So you remained in [A]Kadesh many days, [a]the days that you spent *there.*

WANDERINGS IN THE WILDERNESS

2 "[A]Then we turned and set out for the wilderness by the way to the [a]Red Sea, as the LORD spoke to me, and circled [B]Mount Seir for many days. 2 And the LORD spoke to me, saying, 3 'You have circled this mountain long enough. *Now* turn north, 4 [A]and command the people, saying, "You will pass through the [B]territory of your brothers the sons of Esau who live in Seir; and [C]they will be afraid of you. So be very careful; 5 do not [a]provoke them, for I will not give you any of their land, even *as little as* a [b]footstep [A]because I have given Mount Seir to Esau as a possession. 6 You shall buy food from them with money so that you may eat, and you shall also purchase water from them with money so that you may drink. 7 For the LORD your God has blessed you in all [a]that you have done; He has known your [b]wanderings through this [A]great wilderness. These [B]forty years the LORD your God has been with you; you have not lacked a thing." '

8 "So we passed beyond our brothers the sons of Esau, who live in Seir, away from the [A]Arabah road, away from Elath and [B]from Ezion-geber. And we turned and passed through by the way of the wilderness of Moab. 9 Then the LORD said to me, 'Do not harass Moab, nor provoke them to war, for I will not give you any of [a]their land as a possession, because I have given [A]Ar to [B]the sons of Lot as a possession.' 10 (The [A]Emim lived there formerly, a people as great, numerous, and tall as the Anakim. 11 Like the Anakim, they are also regarded as [A]Rephaim, but the Moabites call them Emim. 12 [A]The Horites formerly lived in Seir, but the sons of Esau dispossessed them and destroyed them from before them and settled in their place, [B]just as Israel did to the land of [a]their possession which the LORD gave to them.) 13 'Now arise and cross over the [a]brook Zered yourselves.' So we crossed over the [a]brook Zered. 14 Now the [a]time that it took for us to come from Kadesh-barnea until we crossed over the [b]brook Zered was [A]thirty-eight years, until [B]all the generation of the men of war perished from within the camp, as [C]the LORD had sworn to them. 15 [A]Moreover the hand of the LORD was against them, to destroy them from within the camp until they all perished.

16 "So it came about when [A]all the men of war had finally perished from among the people, 17 that the LORD spoke to me, saying, 18 'Today you shall cross over [A]Ar, the border of Moab. 19 When you come opposite the [A]sons of Ammon, do not harass them nor provoke them, for I will not give you any of the land of the sons of Ammon as a possession, because I have given it to [B]the sons of Lot as a possession.' 20 (It is also regarded as the land of the [A]Rephaim, *for* Rephaim formerly lived in it, but the Ammonites call them Zamzummin, 21 a people as great, numerous, and tall as the Anakim, but the LORD destroyed them before them. And they dispossessed them and settled in their place, 22 just as He did for the sons of Esau, who [A]live in Seir, when He destroyed [B]the Horites from before them; they dispossessed them and settled in their place even to this day.

1:45 [A]Job 27:8, 9; Ps 66:18; John 9:31 1:46 [a]Lit *as the days* [A]Num 20:1, 22; Deut 2:7, 14; Judg 11:17 2:1 [a]Lit *Sea of Reeds* [A]Num 21:4 [B]Deut 1:2 2:4 [A]Num 20:14-21 [B]Gen 36:8 [C]Ex 15:15, 16 2:5 [a]*Or engage in strife with* [b]Lit *treading of a sole of a foot* [A]Gen 36:8; Josh 24:4 2:7 [a]Lit *the work of your hand* [b]Lit *goings* [A]Deut 1:19 [B]Num 14:33, 34; 32:13; Deut 2:14 2:8 [A]Deut 1:1 [B]Num 33:35; 1 Kin 9:26 2:9 [a]Lit *his* [A]Num 21:15, 28; Deut 2:18, 29 [B]Gen 19:36, 37 2:10 [A]Gen 14:5 2:11 [A]Gen 14:5; Deut 2:20 2:12 [a]Lit *his* [A]Gen 36:20; Deut 2:22 [B]Num 21:25, 35 2:13 [a]Or *wadi* 2:14 [a]Lit *days in which we went* [b]Or *wadi* [A]Deut 2:7 [B]Num 14:29-35; 26:64, 65; Ps 106:26; 1 Cor 10:5 [C]Deut 1:34, 35 2:15 [A]Jude 5 2:16 [A]Deut 2:14 2:18 [A]Deut 2:9 2:19 [A]Gen 19:38 [B]Deut 2:9 2:20 [A]Deut 2:11 2:22 [A]Gen 36:8; Deut 2:5 [B]Deut 2:12

the land, only to be chased back by the Amorites. The Lord showed His displeasure by not helping them or sympathizing with their defeat, and for that generation there was no escape from death in the desert during the next 38 years (cf. Nu 15–19).

1:46 you remained in Kadesh many days. These words suggest that Israel spent a large part of the 38 years in the wilderness around Kadesh-barnea.

2:1–3:11 *See notes on Nu 20:14–21:35* for the background.

2:1–23 This section deals with encounters with Israel's relatives, the Edomites (vv. 1–8), Moabites (vv. 9–18), and Ammonites (vv. 19–23).

2:1 the way to the Red Sea. Cf. Nu 21:4. After spending a long time at Kadesh, the Israelites set out once again at the command of the Lord through Moses. They traveled away from their Promised Land in a southeasterly direction from Kadesh toward the Gulf of Aqabah on the road to the Red Sea. Thus began the wanderings that were about to end. **circled Mount Seir.** Israel spent many days wandering in the vicinity of Mt. Seir, the mountain range of Edom, S of the Dead Sea and extending down the eastern flank of the Arabah.

2:3 turn north. The departure from Kadesh had been in a southeasterly direction away from the Promised Land, until the Lord commanded Israel to turn again northward in the direction of the Promised Land.

2:4 your brothers the sons of Esau. Esau was the brother of Jacob (Ge 25:25, 26). The Edomites, the descendants of Esau, lived in Mt. Seir. According to Nu 20:14–21, the Edomites refused to allow Israel to pass through their land. Verse 8, reflecting this refusal, states that the Israelites went around the border of the descendants of Esau, i.e., to the E of their territory.

2:5 I will not give you any of their land. God had granted to the descendants of Esau an inheritance (Mt. Seir was their possession). In v. 9, the same is said about the Moabites and in v. 19, about the Ammonites.

2:8 from Elath and from Ezion-geber. Two towns located just N of the Gulf of Aqabah. Israel passed to the E of Edom and to the E of Moab on their journey northward.

2:10 The Emim. Apparently a Moabite term (see v. 11) meaning "terrible ones." This people, numerous and tall, were the pre-Moabite occupants of the land of Moab.

2:12 their possession which the LORD gave to them. The Horites were Hurrians, a people who lived in various places in Syria and Canaan. Those living in the region of Seir had been displaced by the descendants of Esau. The displacement of the Horites by the Edomites was analogous to the Israelites' possession of their own land.

2:13 Zered. A brook that ran into the Dead Sea from the SE. It seems to have constituted the southern boundary of Moab. In contrast to the disobedience associated with Kadesh, the people obeyed the command to cross over the brook Zered. There was a new spirit of obedience toward the Lord among the people.

2:14 thirty-eight years. From 1444–1406 B.C. These were the years from the failure at Kadesh to the obedience at Zered. It was during this time that the rebellious generation, who had been denied access to the Promised Land by the oath of the Lord, had all died.

2:20 Zamzummin. Apparently an Ammonite term used to describe their precursors in their land. They were characterized as being as tall as the Anakim. But the Lord had destroyed them and given their land to the Ammonites. This was an encouragement to the Israelites that God could also defeat the Anakim in the land of Canaan and give that land to Israel.

23And the [A]Avvim, who lived in villages as far as
Gaza, the [a,B]Caphtorim who came from [b,C]Caphtor,
destroyed them and lived in their place.) 24'Arise, set
out, and pass through the [a,A]valley of Arnon. Look!
I have given Sihon the Amorite, king of Heshbon,
and his land into your hand; begin to take possession and contend with him in battle. 25This day I
will begin to put [A]the dread and fear of you [a]upon
the peoples [b]everywhere under the heavens, who,
when they hear the report of you, [B]will tremble and
be in anguish because of you.'
26"[A]So I sent messengers from the wilderness of
Kedemoth to Sihon king of Heshbon with words of
peace, saying, 27'Let me pass through your land, I
will [a]travel only on the highway; I will not turn aside
to the right or to the left. 28You will sell me food
for money so that I may eat, and give me water for
money so that I may drink, [A]only let me pass through
on [a]foot, 29just as the sons of Esau who live in Seir
and the Moabites who live in [A]Ar did for me, until I
cross over the Jordan into the land which the LORD
our God is giving to us.' 30But [A]Sihon king of Heshbon
was not willing for us to pass [a]through his land; for
the [B]LORD your God hardened his spirit and made
his heart obstinate, in order to deliver him into your
hand, as *he is* today. 31The LORD said to me, 'See, I
have begun to deliver Sihon and his land [a]over to
you. Begin to [b]occupy, that you may possess his land.'
32"Then Sihon [a]with all his people came out to
meet us in battle at Jahaz. 33[A]The LORD our God
delivered him [a]over to us, and we [b,B]defeated him
with his sons and all his people. 34So we captured
all his cities at that time and [a,A]utterly destroyed [b]the
men, women and children of every city. We left no
survivor. 35We took [A]only the animals as our booty
and the spoil of the cities which we had captured.
36From [A]Aroer which is on the edge of the [a]valley
of Arnon and *from* the city which is in the [a]valley,
even to Gilead, there was no city that was too high
for us; the LORD our God delivered all [b]over to us.
37[A]Only you did not go near to the land of the sons
of Ammon, all along the [a]river [B]Jabbok and the cities of the hill country, and wherever the LORD our
God had commanded us.

CONQUESTS RECOUNTED

3 "[A]Then we turned and went up the road to Bashan,
and Og, king of Bashan, [a]with all his people came
out to meet us in battle at Edrei. 2But the LORD said to
me, 'Do not fear him, for I have delivered him and all
his people and his land into your hand; and you shall
do to him just as you did to Sihon king of the Amorites,
who lived at Heshbon.' 3So the LORD our God delivered
Og also, king of Bashan, with all his people into our
hand, and we smote [a]them until no survivor was [b]left.
4We captured all his cities at that time; there was not
a city which we did not take from them: sixty cities, all
the region of [A]Argob, the kingdom of Og in Bashan.
5All these were cities fortified with high walls, gates
and bars, besides a great many [a]unwalled towns. 6We
[a]utterly destroyed them, as we did to [A]Sihon king of
Heshbon, [b,B]utterly destroying [c]the men, women and
children of every city. 7[A]But all the animals and the
spoil of the cities we took as our booty.
8"[A]Thus we took the land at that time from the
hand of the two kings of the Amorites who were
beyond the Jordan, from the [a]valley of Arnon to
Mount Hermon 9(Sidonians [A]call Hermon [B]Sirion,
and the Amorites call it [C]Senir): 10all the cities of
the plateau and all Gilead and [A]all Bashan, as far as
Salecah and Edrei, cities of the kingdom of Og in
Bashan. 11(For only Og king of Bashan was left of
the remnant of the [A]Rephaim. Behold, his [a]bedstead
was an iron [a]bedstead; it is in [B]Rabbah of the sons
of Ammon. Its length was nine cubits and its width
four cubits [b]by ordinary cubit.)

2:23 [a]I.e. Philistines [b]I.e. Crete [A]Josh 13:3 [B]Gen 10:14; 1 Chr 1:12 [C]Jer 47:4; Amos 9:7 2:24 [a]Or *wadi* [A]Num 21:13, 14; Judg 11:18 2:25 [a]Lit *in front of* [b]Lit *under all the heavens* [A]Ex 23:27; Deut 11:25; Josh 2:9 [B]Ex 15:14-16 2:26 [A]Num 21:21-32; Deut 1:4; Judg 11:19-21 2:27 [a]Lit *go by the way* 2:28 [a]Lit *my feet* [A]Num 20:19 2:29 [A]Deut 2:9 2:30 [a]Lit *by him* [A]Num 21:23 [B]Ex 4:21; Josh 11:20 2:31 [a]Lit *before you* [b]Lit *possess* 2:32 [a]Lit *he and* 2:33 [a]Lit *before us* [b]Lit *smote* [A]Ex 23:31; Deut 7:2 [B]Deut 29:7 2:34 [a]Or *put under the ban* [b]Lit *every city of man...* [A]Deut 3:6; 7:2 2:35 [A]Deut 3:7 2:36 [a]Or *wadi* [b]Lit *before us* [A]Deut 3:12; 4:48; Josh 12:2; 13:9 2:37 [a]Or *wadi* [A]Deut 2:19 [B]Gen 32:22; Num 21:24; Deut 3:16 3:1 [a]Lit *he and* [A]Num 21:33-35 3:3 [a]Lit *him* [b]Lit *left to him* 3:4 [A]Deut 3:13, 14; 1 Kin 4:13 3:5 [a]Or *rural* 3:6 [a]Or *put them under the ban* [b]Or *putting under the ban* [c]Lit *every city of men...* [A]Deut 1:4 [B]Deut 2:34 3:7 [A]Deut 2:35 3:8 [a]Or *wadi* [A]Num 32:33; Josh 12:1-7; 13:8-12 3:9 [A]Deut 4:48; Josh 11:17; Ps 42:6; 133:3 [B]Ps 29:6 [C]1 Chr 5:23 3:10 [A]Josh 13:11 3:11 [a]Or *couch* [b]Lit *by a man's forearm* [A]Gen 14:5; Deut 2:11, 20 [B]2 Sam 11:1; 12:26; Jer 49:2

2:23 the Avvim. The ancient village dwellers of southwestern Palestine along the Mediterranean coast as far as the city of Gaza. **the Caphtorim.** Caphtor probably refers to Crete and may be a reference to an early Philistine group from that island who invaded the coast of Palestine, defeated the Avvim, and then dwelt there. These Caphtorim were precursors to the later, greater Philistine invasion of ca. 1200 B.C.

2:24–3:29 Moses continues the historical survey detailing the defeat of two Amorite kings, Sihon and Og, and the takeover of their territory.

2:24 the valley of Arnon. The northern boundary of Moab. Israel was allowed to attack Sihon the Amorite because the Amorites were not relatives of Israel.

2:25 fear of you. As the conquest began, God put the fear of Israel into the hearts of their enemies.

2:26 the wilderness of Kedemoth. Kedemoth means "eastern regions." It was probably a few mi. N of the Arnon River and near to the eastern border of the Amorite state.

2:27 Let me pass through. As with the Edomites previously (Nu 20:17), Moses asked to pass peacefully through the territory of Sihon.

2:30 hardened his spirit. Sihon, by his own conscious will, refused Israel's request to journey through his land. God confirmed what was already in Sihon's heart, namely arrogance against the Lord and His people Israel, so that He might defeat him in battle and give his land to Israel.

2:32 Jahaz. The place of battle between Sihon and the Israelites, probably a few mi. to the N of Kedemoth (v. 26).

3:1 Bashan. A fertile region located E of the Sea of Galilee and the Jordan River extending from Mt. Hermon in the N to the Yarmuk River in the S. Israel met King Og and his army in battle at Edrei, a city on the Yarmuk River. The Amorite king ruled over 60 cities (vv. 4–10; Jos 13:30), which were taken by Israel; this kingdom was assigned to the Transjordanic tribes, especially the half-tribe of Manasseh (v. 13).

3:8 beyond the Jordan. East of the Jordan River, Israel controlled the territory from the Arnon River to Mt. Hermon, a length of about 150 mi. Note that the perspective of the speaker was to the E of the Jordan; the W of the Jordan still needed to be conquered. This statement helps date these speeches as preconquest.

3:11 an iron bedstead. The bedstead may actually have been a coffin, which would have been large enough to also hold tomb objects. The size of the "bedstead," 13 1/2 by 6 ft., emphasized the largeness of Og, who was a giant (the last of the Rephaim, a race of giants). As God had given Israel victory over the giant Og, so He would give them victory over the giants in the land.

12"So we took possession of this land at that time.
From [A]Aroer, which is by the [a]valley of Arnon, and
half the hill country of [B]Gilead and its cities I gave
to the Reubenites and to the Gadites. 13The rest of
Gilead and all Bashan, the kingdom of Og, I gave to
the half-tribe of Manasseh, all the region of Argob
(concerning all Bashan, it is called the land of Rephaim. 14[A]Jair the son of Manasseh took all the region
of Argob as far as the border of the Geshurites and
the Maacathites, and called [a]it, *that is,* Bashan, after
his own name, [b]Havvoth-jair, *as it is* to this day.)
15[A]To Machir I gave Gilead. 16To the Reubenites
and to the Gadites I gave from Gilead even as far as
the [a]valley of Arnon, the middle of the [a]valley [b]as a
border and as far as the [a]river [A]Jabbok, the border
of the sons of Ammon; 17the Arabah also, with the
Jordan [a]as *a* border, from [b,A]Chinnereth [B]even as far
as the sea of the Arabah, [C]the Salt Sea, [c]at the foot
of the slopes of Pisgah on the east.
18"Then I commanded you at that time, saying,
'[A]The LORD your God has given you this land to possess it; [B]all you valiant men shall cross over armed
before your brothers, the sons of Israel. 19[A]But your
wives and your little ones and your livestock (I know
that you have [B]much livestock) shall remain in your
cities which I have given you, 20[A]until the LORD
gives rest to your fellow countrymen as to you, and
they also possess the land which the LORD your God
will give them beyond the Jordan. [B]Then you may
return every man to his possession which I have
given you.' 21I commanded Joshua at that time,
saying, 'Your eyes have seen all that the LORD your
God has done to these two kings; so the LORD shall
do to all the kingdoms into which you are about to
cross. 22Do not fear them, for the LORD your God
[A]is the one fighting for you.'
23"I also pleaded with the LORD at that time, saying, 24'O Lord [a]GOD, You have begun to show Your
servant [A]Your greatness and Your strong hand;
for what [B]god is there in heaven or on earth who
can do such works and mighty acts as Yours? 25Let
me, I pray, cross over and see the [A]fair land that
is beyond the Jordan, [a]that good hill country and
Lebanon.' 26But [A]the LORD was angry with me on
your account, and would not listen to me; and the
LORD said to me, '[a]Enough! Speak to Me no more
of this matter. 27Go up to the top of [A]Pisgah and lift
up your eyes to the west and north and south and
east, and see *it* with your eyes, [B]for you shall not
cross over this Jordan. 28[A]But charge Joshua and
encourage him and strengthen him, [B]for he shall go
across [a]at the head of this people, and he will give
them as an inheritance the land which you will see.'
29So we remained in the valley opposite [A]Beth-peor.

ISRAEL URGED TO OBEY GOD'S LAW

4 "Now, O Israel, listen to the statutes and the judgments which [A]I am teaching you to perform, so
that [B]you may live and go in and take possession of
the land which the LORD, the God of your fathers, is
giving you. 2[A]You shall not add to the word which
[B]I am commanding you, nor take away from it, that
you may keep the commandments of the LORD your
God which I command you. 3[A]Your eyes have seen
what the LORD has done in the case of Baal-peor,
for all the men who followed Baal-peor, the LORD
your God has destroyed [a]them from among you.
4But you who held fast to the LORD your God are
alive today, every one of you.
5"See, I have taught you statutes and judgments
[A]just as the LORD my God commanded me, that you
should do thus in the land where you are entering
to possess it. 6So keep and do *them,* [A]for that is your
wisdom and your understanding in the sight of the
peoples who will hear all these statutes and say,
'Surely this great nation is a wise and understanding

3:12 [a]Or *wadi* [A]Deut 2:36 [B]Num 32:32-38; Josh 13:8-13 3:14 [a]Lit *them* [b]I.e. the towns of Jair [A]Num 32:41; 1 Chr 2:22 3:15 [A]Num 32:39, 40 3:16 [a]Or *wadi* [b]Lit *and* [A]Num 21:24; Deut 2:37 3:17 [a]Lit *and* [b]I.e. the Sea of Galilee [c]Lit *under* [A]Num 34:11; Josh 13:27 [B]Josh 12:3 [C]Gen 14:3; Josh 3:16 3:18 [A]Josh 1:13 [B]Num 32:20; Josh 4:12, 13 3:19 [A]Josh 1:14 [B]Ex 12:38 3:20 [A]Josh 1:15 [B]Josh 22:4 3:22 [A]Ex 14:14; Deut 1:30; 20:4; Neh 4:20 3:24 [a]Heb *YHWH*, usually rendered *LORD* [A]Deut 11:2 [B]Ex 8:10; 15:11; 2 Sam 7:22; Ps 71:19; 86:8 3:25 [a]Lit *this* [A]Deut 4:22 3:26 [a]Lit *Enough for you* [A]Deut 1:37 3:27 [A]Num 23:14; 27:12 [B]Deut 1:37 3:28 [a]Lit *before this people* [A]Num 27:18; Deut 31:3, 7, 8, 23 [B]Deut 1:38 3:29 [A]Num 25:1-3; Deut 4:46; 34:6 4:1 [A]Deut 1:3 [B]Lev 18:5; Deut 5:33; 8:1; 16:20; 30:16, 19; Ezek 20:11; Rom 10:5 4:2 [A]Deut 12:32; Prov 30:6; Rev 22:18 [B]Deut 4:5, 14, 40 4:3 [a]Lit *him* [A]Num 25:1-9 4:5 [A]Lev 26:46; 27:34 4:6 [A]Deut 30:19, 20; 32:46, 47; Job 28:28; Ps 19:7; 111:10; Prov 1:7; 2 Tim 3:15

3:12–20 *See notes on Nu 32:1–42; 34:13–15* for background.

3:20 rest. A peaceful situation with the land free from external threat and oppression. The eastern 2 1/2 tribes had the responsibility to battle alongside their western brethren until the conquest was complete (cf. Jos 22).

3:22 the LORD your God … fighting for you. Moses commanded Joshua not to be afraid because the Lord Himself would provide supernatural power and give them the victory (cf. 1:30; 31:6–8; Jos 1:9).

3:23 I … pleaded with the LORD. With the victories over Sihon and Og, Moses made one final passionate plea to the Lord to be allowed to enter the Promised Land. However, the Lord would not allow Moses that privilege. He did, however, allow Moses to go to the top of Pisgah and see the land (cf. Dt 32:48–52; 34:1–4).

3:26 the LORD was angry. *See note on 1:37*; cf. 4:21–24.

3:29 Beth-peor. Located E of the Jordan River, probably opposite Jericho (*see notes on Nu 22–25* for the background).

4:1 O Israel, listen. Moses called the people to hear and obey the rules of conduct that God had given them to observe. Successful conquest and full enjoyment of life in the land was based on submission to God's law. **the statutes and the judgments.** The first are permanent rules for conduct fixed by the reigning authority, while the second deal with judicial decisions which served as precedents for future guidance.

4:2 You shall not add … nor take away from. The Word that God had given to Israel through Moses was complete and sufficient to direct the people. Thus, this law, the gift of God at Horeb, could not be supplemented or reduced. Anything that adulterated or contradicted God's law would not be tolerated (cf. 12:32; Pr 30:6; Rev 22:18, 19).

4:3, 4 Moses used the incident at Baal-peor (Nu 25:1–9) to illustrate from the Israelites' own history that their very lives depended on obeying God's law. Only those who had held fast to the Lord by obeying His commands were alive that day to hear Moses.

4:6 the peoples. Israel's obedience to God's law would provide a testimony to the world that God was near to His people and that His laws were righteous. One purpose of the law was to make Israel morally and spiritually unique among all the nations and, therefore, draw those nations to the one true and living God. They were from their beginnings to be a witness nation. Though they failed and have been temporarily set aside, the prophets revealed that in the future kingdom of Messiah they will be a nation of faithful witnesses (cf. Is 45:14; Zec 8:23). **a wise and understanding people.** The nations would see 3 things in Israel (vv. 6–8). First, the Israelites would know how to apply God's knowledge so as to have discernment and to be able to judge matters accurately.

people.' 7 For [A]what great nation is there that has a
god [B]so near to it as is the LORD our God [C]whenever
we call on Him? 8 Or what great nation is there that
has [A]statutes and judgments as righteous as this
whole law which I am setting before you today?
9 "Only [A]give heed to yourself and keep your soul
diligently, so that you do not forget the things which
your eyes have seen and they do not depart from
your heart [B]all the days of your life; but [C]make them
known to your sons and your grandsons. 10 *Remember* the day you stood before the LORD your God at
Horeb, when the LORD said to me, 'Assemble the
people to Me, that I may let them hear My words
[A]so they may learn to [a]fear Me all the days they live
on the earth, and that they may [B]teach their children.' 11 You came near and stood at the foot of the
mountain, [A]and the mountain burned with fire to
the *very* heart of the heavens: darkness, cloud and
thick gloom. 12 Then the LORD spoke to you from the
midst of the fire; you heard the sound of words, but
you saw no form—only a voice. 13 So He declared
to you His covenant which He commanded you to
perform, *that is,* [A]the Ten [a]Commandments; and
[B]He wrote them on two tablets of stone. 14 The LORD
commanded me at that time to teach you statutes
and judgments, that you might perform them in
the land where you are going over to possess it.
15 "So [A]watch yourselves carefully, since you did
not see any [B]form on the day the LORD spoke to you
at Horeb from the midst of the fire, 16 so that you
do not [A]act corruptly and [B]make a graven image for
yourselves in the form of any figure, the likeness
of male or female, 17 the likeness of any animal that
is on the earth, the likeness of [A]any winged bird
that flies in the sky, 18 the likeness of anything that
creeps on the ground, the likeness of any fish that
is in the water below the earth. 19 And *beware* not
to lift up your eyes to heaven and see the sun and
the moon and the stars, [A]all the host of heaven,
[B]and be drawn away and worship them and serve
them, those which the LORD your God has allotted
to all the peoples under the whole heaven. 20 But
the LORD has taken you and brought you out of
[A]the iron furnace, from Egypt, to [B]be a people for
His own possession, as today.
21 "[A]Now the LORD was angry with me on your
account, and swore that I would not cross the Jordan, and that I would not enter the good land which
the LORD your God is giving you as an inheritance.
22 For [A]I will die in this land, I shall not cross the
Jordan, but you shall cross and take possession of
this [B]good land. 23 So watch yourselves, [A]that you
do not forget the covenant of the LORD your God
which He made with you, and [B]make for yourselves a
graven image in the form of anything *against* which
the LORD your God has commanded you. 24 For the
LORD your God is a [A]consuming fire, a [B]jealous God.
25 "When you [a]become the father of children and
children's children and have remained long in the
land, and [A]act corruptly, and [B]make an [b]idol in the
form of anything, and [C]do that which is evil in the
sight of the LORD your God *so as* to provoke Him to
anger, 26 I [A]call heaven and earth to witness against
you today, that you will [B]surely perish quickly from
the land where you are going over the Jordan to
possess it. You shall not [a]live long on it, but will
be utterly destroyed. 27 The LORD will [A]scatter you
among the peoples, and you will be left few in number among the nations where the LORD drives you.
28 [A]There you will serve gods, the work of man's
hands, [B]wood and stone, [C]which neither see nor
hear nor eat nor smell. 29 [A]But from there you will
seek the LORD your God, and you will find *Him* if
you search for Him [B]with all your heart and all your

4:7 [A]Deut 4:32-34; 2 Sam 7:23 [B]Ps 34:17, 18; 145:18; 148:14; Is 55:6 [C]Ps 34:18; 85:9 4:8 [A]Ps 89:14; 97:2; 119:144, 160, 172 4:9 [A]Deut 4:23; 6:12; 8:11, 14, 19; Prov 4:23; 23:19 [B]Deut 6:2; 12:1; 16:3 [C]Gen 18:19; Deut 4:10; 6:7, 20-25; 11:19; 32:46; Ps 78:5, 6; Prov 22:6; Eph 6:4 4:10 [a]Or *reverence* [A]Deut 14:23; 17:19; 31:12, 13 [B]Deut 4:9 4:11 [A]Ex 19:18; Heb 12:18, 19 4:13 [a]Lit *Words* [A]Ex 34:28; Deut 10:4 [B]Ex 31:18; 34:1, 28 4:15 [A]Josh 23:11 [B]Is 40:18 4:16 [A]Deut 4:25; 9:12; 31:29 [B]Ex 20:4; Lev 26:1; Deut 5:8, 9; 27:15; Rom 1:23 4:17 [A]Rom 1:23 4:19 [A]Gen 2:1; Deut 17:3; 2 Kin 17:16; 21:3 [B]Deut 13:5, 10; Job 31:26-28 4:20 [A]1 Kin 8:51; Jer 11:4 [B]Ex 19:5; Deut 7:6; 14:2; 26:18; Titus 2:14; 1 Pet 2:9 4:21 [A]Num 20:12; Deut 1:37 4:22 [A]Num 27:13, 14 [B]Deut 3:25 4:23 [A]Deut 4:9 [B]Deut 4:16 4:24 [A]Ex 24:17; Deut 9:3; Is 30:27; 33:14; Heb 12:29 [B]Deut 5:9; 6:15 4:25 [a]Lit *beget* [b]Or *a graven image* [A]Deut 4:16 [B]Deut 4:23 [C]2 Kin 17:17 4:26 [a]Lit *prolong your days* [A]Deut 30:19; 31:28; 32:1; Is 1:2; Mic 6:2 [B]Deut 7:4; 8:19, 20 4:27 [A]Lev 26:33; Deut 28:64; 29:28; Neh 1:8 4:28 [A]Deut 28:36, 64; Jer 16:13 [B]Deut 29:17 [C]Ps 115:4-8; 135:15-18; Is 44:12-20 4:29 [A]Deut 30:1-3, 10; 2 Chr 15:4; Is 55:6; Jer 29:13 [B]Deut 6:5; 10:12

4:7 a god so near to it. Second, faithfulness to the Lord would allow the nations to see that the Lord had established intimacy with Israel.

4:8 statutes and judgments as righteous. Third, the nations would see that Israel's law was distinctive, for its source was the Lord indicating its character was righteous.

4:9–31 This section carries the most basic lesson for Israel to learn—to fear and reverence God.

4:9 make them known to your sons. Deuteronomy stresses the responsibility of parents to pass on their experiences with God and the knowledge they have gained from Him to their children (cf. 6:7; 11:19).

4:10 *Remember* the day. One experience of Israel to be passed on from generation to generation was the great theophany (the self-revelation of God in physical form) which took place at Horeb (cf. Ex 19:9–20:19).

4:12 no form. Israel was to remember that when God revealed Himself at Sinai, His presence came through His voice, i.e., the sound of His words. They did not see Him. God is Spirit (Jn 4:24), which rules out any idolatrous representation of God in any physical form (vv. 16–18) or any worship of the created order (v. 19).

4:13 the Ten Commandments. Lit. "ten statements," from which comes the term "Decalogue." These summarize and epitomize all the commandments the Lord gave to Israel through Moses. Though the phrase occurs only here, in 10:4, and in Ex 34:28, there are 26 more references to it in Deuteronomy (*see notes on Mt 19:16–21; 22:35–40; Mk 10:17–22; Ro 13:8–10*).

4:15–19 This is a strong emphasis on commandments one and two (cf. Ro 1:18–23).

4:20 the iron furnace. A fire was used to heat iron sufficiently to be hammered into different shapes or welded to other objects. The iron furnace here suggests that Israel's time in Egypt was a period of ordeal, testing, and purifying for the Hebrews, readying them for usefulness as God's witness nation.

4:24 a jealous God. God is zealous to protect what belongs to Him. He will not allow another to have the honor that is due to Him alone (cf. Is 42:8; 48:11).

4:25–31 Cf. 8:18, 19. In fact, this briefly outlined the future judgment of Israel, which culminated in the northern 10 tribes being exiled to Assyria (ca. 722 B.C.; 2Ki 17) and the southern two tribes being deported to Babylon (ca. 605–586 B.C.; 2Ki 24, 25). Although the Jews returned in the days of Ezra and Nehemiah (ca. 538–445 B.C.), they never regained their autonomy or dominance. Thus, the days of promised restoration and return look forward to Messiah's return to set up the millennial kingdom.

4:27 the LORD will scatter you. Moses warned Israel that the judgment for idolatry would be their dispersion among the nations by the Lord (see 28:64–67).

soul. 30 When you [A]are in distress and all these things
have come upon you, [B]in the latter days [C]you will
return to the LORD your God and listen to His voice.
31 For the LORD your God is a [A]compassionate God;
[B]He will not fail you nor [C]destroy you nor [D]forget the
covenant with your fathers which He swore to them.

32 "Indeed, [A]ask now concerning the former days
which were before you, since the [B]day that God created [a]man on the earth, and *inquire* [C]from one end of
the heavens to the other. [D]Has *anything* been done
like this great thing, or has *anything* been heard like
it? 33 [A]Has *any* people heard the voice of God speaking from the midst of the fire, as you have heard *it,*
and survived? 34 [A]Or has a god tried to go to take
for himself a nation from within *another* nation [B]by
trials, by signs and wonders and by war and [C]by a
mighty hand and by an outstretched arm and by
great terrors, [a]as the LORD your God did for you in
Egypt before your eyes? 35 To you it was shown that
you might know that the LORD, He is God; [A]there is
no other besides Him. 36 [A]Out of the heavens He let
you hear His voice [B]to discipline you; and on earth
He let you see His great fire, and you heard His
words from the midst of the fire. 37 [a,A]Because He
loved your fathers, therefore He chose [b]their descendants after them. And He [c,B]personally brought you
from Egypt by His great power, 38 driving out from
before you nations greater and mightier than you,
to bring you in *and* [A]to give you their land for an
inheritance, as it is today. 39 Know therefore today,
and take it to your heart, that [A]the LORD, He is God
in heaven above and on the earth below; there is
no other. 40 [A]So you shall keep His statutes and His
commandments which I am [a]giving you today, that
[B]it may go well with you and with your children
after you, and [C]that you may [b]live long on the land
which the LORD your God is giving you for all time."

41 [A]Then Moses set apart three cities across the
Jordan to the [a]east, 42 that a manslayer might flee
there, who unintentionally slew his neighbor without having enmity toward him in time past; and by
fleeing to one of these cities he might live: 43 [A]Bezer
in the wilderness on the plateau for the Reubenites,
and Ramoth in Gilead for the Gadites, and Golan in
Bashan for the Manassites.

44 Now this is the law which Moses set before
the sons of Israel; 45 these are the testimonies and
the statutes and the ordinances which Moses spoke
to the sons of Israel, when they came out from
Egypt, 46 across the Jordan, in the valley [A]opposite
Beth-peor, in the land of [B]Sihon king of the Amorites who lived at Heshbon, whom Moses and the
sons of Israel [a]defeated when they came out from
Egypt. 47 They took possession of his land and the
land of [A]Og king of Bashan, the two kings of the
Amorites, *who were* across the Jordan to the [a]east,
48 from [A]Aroer, which is on the edge of the [a]valley of
Arnon, even as far as [B]Mount Sion (that is, Hermon),
49 with all the Arabah across the Jordan to the east,
even as far as the sea of the Arabah, [a]at the foot of
the slopes of Pisgah.

THE TEN COMMANDMENTS REPEATED

5 Then Moses summoned all Israel and said to
them:

"Hear, O Israel, the statutes and the ordinances
which I am speaking today in your [a]hearing, that
you may learn them and observe [b]them carefully.

4:30 [A]Ps 18:6; 59:16; 107:6, 13 [B]Deut 31:29; Jer 23:20; Hos 3:5; Heb 1:2 [C]Jer 4:1, 2 4:31 [A]Ex 34:6; 2 Chr 30:9; Neh 9:31; Ps 103:8; 111:4; 116:5; Jon 4:2 [B]Deut 31:6, 8; Josh 1:5; 1 Chr 28:20; Heb 13:5 [C]Jer 30:11 [D]Lev 26:45 4:32 [a]Or *Adam* [A]Deut 32:7; Job 8:8 [B]Gen 1:27; Is 45:12 [C]Deut 28:64; Matt 24:31 [D]Deut 4:7; 2 Sam 7:23 4:33 [A]Ex 20:22; Deut 5:24, 26 4:34 [a]Lit *according to all that* [A]Ex 14:30; Deut 33:29 [B]Deut 7:19 [C]Deut 5:15; 6:21; Ps 136:12 4:35 [A]Ex 8:10; 9:14; Deut 4:39; 32:12, 39; 1 Sam 2:2; Is 43:10-12; 44:6-8; 45:5-7; Mark 12:32 4:36 [A]Ex 19:9, 19; 20:18, 22; Deut 4:33; Neh 9:13; Heb 12:25 [B]Deut 8:5 4:37 [a]Lit *And instead, because* [b]Lit *his seed* [c]Lit *with His presence* [A]Deut 7:7, 8; 10:15; 33:3 [B]Ex 33:14; Is 63:9 4:38 [A]Num 32:4; 34:14, 15 4:39 [A]Deut 4:35; Josh 2:11 4:40 [a]Lit *commanding* [b]Lit *prolong your days* [A]Lev 22:31; Deut 4:2; Ps 105:45 [B]Deut 4:1; 5:16, 29, 33; 6:3, 18; 12:25, 28; 22:7 [C]Ex 23:26; Deut 32:47 4:41 [a]Lit *sunrise* [A]Num 35:6; Deut 19:2-13; Josh 20:7-9 4:43 [A]Josh 20:8 4:46 [a]Lit *smote* [A]Deut 3:29 [B]Num 21:21-25 4:47 [a]Lit *sunrise* [A]Deut 1:4; 3:3, 4 4:48 [a]Or *wadi* [A]Deut 2:36; 3:12 [B]Deut 3:9; Ps 133:3 4:49 [a]Lit *under* 5:1 [a]Lit *ears* [b]Lit *to do them*

4:30 the latter days. Lit. "the end of days." Moses saw in the distant future a time when repentant Israel would turn again to the Lord and obey Him. Throughout the Pentateuch, "the latter days" refers to the time when Messiah will establish His kingdom (see Ge 49:1, 8–12; Nu 24:14–24; Dt 32:39–43).

4:31 the covenant with your fathers. God mercifully, not because they deserve it, will fulfill the covenant He made with Abraham, Isaac, and Jacob with repentant Israel in the future. God will not forget the Word that He has given to Abraham and his seed (cf. Ro 11:25–27).

4:32–40 A historical apologetic, appealing for the nation's obedience to God's law.

4:32–39 since the day that God created man on the earth. In all of human history, no other nation has had the privilege that Israel had of hearing God speak, as He did in giving the law at Mt. Sinai, and surviving such an awesome experience. Nor had any other people been so blessed, chosen and delivered from bondage by such mighty miracles as Israel saw. God did this to reveal to them that He alone is God (vv. 35, 39).

4:37 He personally. Lit. "His face." God Himself had brought Israel out of Egypt. The Exodus resulted from the electing love that God had for the patriarchs and their descendants.

4:40 Such gracious privilege, as remembered in vv. 32–39, should elicit obedience, particularly in view of the unconditional promise that the Land will be theirs permanently ("for all time") as is detailed in chaps. 29, 30.

4:41–43 These 3 verses are a narrative insertion at the end of Moses' speech. The setting aside of 3 cities on the E side of the Jordan by Moses showed that Moses willingly obeyed the commandments God gave him. He was an example of the type of obedience that God was calling for in 4:1–40 (cf. Nu 35:14; Jos 20:8–9).

4:44–28:68 The heart of Deuteronomy is found in this long second speech of Moses. "Now this is the law" (4:44) which Moses explained to Israel (cf. 1:5). After a brief introduction (4:44–49), Moses gave the people a clear understanding of what the law directed concerning their relationship with the Lord in the land (5:1–26:19), then concluded by recounting the blessings or the curses which would come upon the nation as a consequence of their response to the stipulations of this law (27:1–28:68).

4:45 testimonies ... statutes ... ordinances. God's instruction to Israel was set forth in: 1) the testimonies, the basic covenant stipulations (5:6–21); 2) statutes, words that were inscribed and therefore fixed; and 3) ordinances, the decisions made by a judge on the merits of the situation. This law was given to Israel when they came out of Egypt. Moses is not giving further law, he is now explaining that which has already been given.

4:48 Mount Sion. This reference to Mt. Hermon is not to be confused with Mt. Zion in Jerusalem.

4:49 sea of the Arabah. The Dead Sea.

5:1–11:32 As Moses began his second address to the people of Israel, he reminded them of the events and the basic commands from God that were foundational to the Sinaitic Covenant (5:1–33; see Ex 19:1–20:21). Then, in 6:1–11:32, Moses expounded and applied the first 3 of the Ten Commandments to the present experience of the people.

5:1 Hear, O Israel. The verb "hear" carried the sense "obey." A hearing that leads to obedience was demanded of all the people (cf. 6:4; 9:1; 20:3; 27:9).

2 The LORD our God made [A]a covenant with us at
Horeb. 3 [A]The LORD did not make this covenant with
our fathers, but with us, *with* all those of [a]us alive
here today. 4 The LORD spoke to you [A]face to face
at the mountain [B]from the midst of the fire, 5 *while*
[A]I was standing between the LORD and you at that
time, to declare to you the word of the LORD; [B]for
you were afraid because of the fire and did not go
up the mountain. [a]He said,
6 '[A]I am the LORD your God who brought you out
of the land of Egypt, out of the house of [a]slavery.
7 '[A]You shall have no other gods [a]before Me.
8 '[A]You shall not make for yourself [a]an idol, *or* any
likeness *of* what is in heaven above [b]or on the earth
beneath [b]or in the water under the earth. 9 You shall
not worship them or serve them; for I, the LORD
your God, am a jealous God, [A]visiting the iniquity
of the fathers on the children, and on the third and
the fourth *generations* of those who hate Me, 10 but
[A]showing lovingkindness to thousands, to those
who love Me and keep My commandments.
11 '[A]You shall not take the name of the LORD your
God in vain, for the LORD will not [a]leave him unpunished who takes His name in vain.
12 '[A]Observe the sabbath day to keep it holy, as
the LORD your God commanded you. 13 Six days you
shall labor and do all your work, 14 but [A]the seventh
day is a sabbath of the LORD your God; *in it* you shall
not do any work, you or your son or your daughter or your male servant or your female servant
or your ox or your donkey or any of your cattle or
your sojourner who [a]stays with you, so that your
male servant and your female servant may rest as
well as you. 15 [A]You shall remember that you were
a slave in the land of Egypt, and the LORD your God
brought you out of there by a mighty hand and by
an outstretched arm; therefore the LORD your God
commanded you to observe the sabbath day.
16 '[A]Honor your father and your mother, as the
LORD your God has commanded you, [B]that your days
may be prolonged and that it may go well with you
on the land which the LORD your God gives you.
17 '[A]You shall not murder.
18 '[A]You shall not commit adultery.
19 '[A]You shall not steal.
20 '[A]You shall not bear false witness against your
neighbor.
21 '[A]You shall not covet your neighbor's wife,
and you shall not desire your neighbor's house,
his field or his male servant or his female servant,
his ox or his donkey or anything that belongs to
your neighbor.'

MOSES INTERCEDED

22 "These words the LORD spoke to all your assembly at the mountain from the midst of the fire,
of the cloud and *of* the thick gloom, with a great
voice, and He added no more. [A]He wrote them on
two tablets of stone and gave them to me. 23 And
when you heard the voice from the midst of the
darkness, while the mountain was burning with fire,
you came near to me, all the heads of your tribes

5:2 [A]Ex 19:5; Mal 4:4 5:3 [a]Lit *us ourselves* [A]Jer 31:32; Heb 8:9 5:4 [A]Num 14:14; Deut 34:10 [B]Deut 4:33 5:5 [a]Lit *saying* [A]Gal 3:19 [B]Ex 19:16, 21-24; 20:18; Heb 12:18-21 5:6 [a]Lit *slaves* [A]Ex 20:2-17; Lev 26:1; Deut 6:4; Ps 81:10 5:7 [a]Or *besides* [A]Ex 20:3 5:8 [a]Or *a graven image* [b]Lit *or what is* [A]Ex 20:4-6; Lev 26:1; Deut 4:15-18; 27:15; Ps 97:7 5:9 [A]Ex 34:7; Num 14:18; Deut 7:10 5:10 [A]Num 14:18; Deut 7:9; Jer 32:18 5:11 [a]Or *hold him guiltless* [A]Ex 20:7; Lev 19:12; Deut 6:13; 10:20; Matt 5:33 5:12 [A]Ex 16:23-30; 20:8-11; 31:13f; Mark 2:27f 5:14 [a]Lit *is in your gates* [A]Gen 2:2; Heb 4:4 5:15 [A]Ex 20:11 5:16 [A]Ex 20:12; Lev 19:3; Deut 27:16; Matt 15:4; 19:19; Mark 7:10; 10:19; Luke 18:20; Eph 6:2, 3; Col 3:20 [B]Deut 4:40 5:17 [A]Gen 9:6; Ex 20:13; Lev 24:17; Matt 5:21f; 19:18; Mark 10:19; Rom 13:9; James 2:11 5:18 [A]Ex 20:14; Lev 20:10; Matt 5:27f; 19:18; Mark 10:19; Luke 18:20; Rom 13:9; James 2:11 5:19 [A]Ex 20:15; Lev 19:11 5:20 [A]Ex 20:16; 23:1; Matt 19:18 5:21 [A]Ex 20:17; Rom 7:7; 13:9 5:22 [A]Ex 24:12; 31:18; Deut 4:13

5:2 a covenant with us at Horeb. The second generation of Israel, while children, received the covenant that God made with Israel at Sinai.

5:3 did not make this covenant with our fathers. The "fathers" were not the people's immediate fathers, who had died in the wilderness, but their more distant ancestors, the patriarchs (see 4:31, 37; 7:8, 12; 8:18). The Sinaitic or Mosaic Covenant was in addition to and distinct from the Abrahamic Covenant made with the patriarchs.

5:6–21 The first 4 commandments involve relationship with God, the last 6 deal with human relationships. Together they were the foundation of Israel's life before God. Moses here reiterated them as given originally at Sinai. Slight variations from the Exodus text are accounted for by Moses' explanatory purpose in Deuteronomy. *See notes on Ex 20:1–17* for an additional explanation of these commands.

5:7 no other gods. Cf. Ex 20:3. "Other gods" were nonexistent pagan gods, which were made in the form of idols and shaped by the minds of their worshipers. The Israelite was to be totally faithful to the God to whom he was bound by covenant. Cf. Mt 16:24–27; Mk 8:34–38; Lk 9:23–26; 14:26–33.

5:8 an idol ... any likeness. Cf. Ex 20:4, 5. Reducing the infinite God to any physical likeness was intolerable, as the people found out in their attempt to cast God as a golden calf (cf. Ex 32).

5:9, 10 third and the fourth *generations* ... thousands. *See note on Ex 20:5, 6* for an explanation of this often misunderstood text. **those who hate Me ... love Me.** Disobedience is equal to hatred of God, as love is equal to obedience (cf. Mt 22:34–40; Ro 13:8–10).

5:11 take the name ... in vain. Cf. Ex 20:7. Attach God's name to emptiness. Cf. Ps 111:9; Mt 6:9; Lk 1:49; Jn 17:6, 26.

5:12 as the LORD your God commanded you. Cf. Ex 20:8–10. These words are missing from Ex 20:8, but refer back to this commandment given to Israel at Sinai 40 years earlier.

5:15 brought you out of there. Here an additional reason is given for God's rest after creation (i.e., for the observance of the Sabbath; see Ex 20:11)—God's deliverance of the people from Egypt. While the Israelites had been slaves in Egypt, they were not allowed rest from their continual labor, so the Sabbath was also to function as a day of rest in which their deliverance from bondage would be remembered with thanksgiving as the sign of their redemption and continual sanctification (cf. Ex 31:13–17; Eze 20:12).

5:16–20 Cf. Mt 19:18–19; Mk 10:19; Lk 18:20.

5:16 that your days may be prolonged. Cf. Ex 20:12; Mt 15:4; Mk 7:10; Eph 6:2, 3. Paul indicated that this was the first commandment with a promise attached (Eph 6:2). Jesus also had much to say about honoring parents (see Mt 10:37; 19:29; Lk 2:49–51; Jn 19:26, 27).

5:17 murder. Cf. Ex 20:13; Mt 5:21; Jas 2:11.

5:18 adultery. Cf. Ex 20:14; Mt 5:27.

5:19 steal. Cf. Ex 20:15; Eph 4:28.

5:20 bear false witness. Cf. Ex 20:16; Col 3:9.

5:21 covet ... desire. Cf. Ex 20:17. Both the lusting after a neighbor's wife and a strong desire for a neighbor's property were prohibited by the tenth commandment (cf. Ro 7:7).

5:22 and He added no more. These Ten Commandments alone were identified as direct quotations by God. The rest of the stipulations of the covenant were given to Moses, who in turn gave them to the Israelites. These basic rules, which reflect God's character, continue to be a means by which God reveals the sinful deeds of the flesh (cf. Ro 7:7–14; Gal 3:19–24; 5:13–26). They are also a holy standard for conduct that the saved live by through the Spirit's power, with the exception of keeping the Sabbath (cf. Col 2:16, 17). **two tablets of stone.** The tablets were written on both sides (see Ex 32:15).

5:22–27 The frightening circumstances of God's presence at Sinai caused the people to have enough fear to ask Moses to receive the words from God and communicate those words to them, after which they promised to obey all that God said (see v. 27).

and your elders. 24 You said, 'Behold, the LORD our
God has shown us His glory and His greatness, and
we have heard His voice from the midst of the fire;
we have seen today that God speaks with man, yet
he lives. 25 [A]Now then why should we die? For this
great fire will consume us; if we hear the voice
of the LORD our God any longer, then we will die.
26 For [A]who is there of all flesh who has heard the
voice of the living God speaking from the midst of
the fire, as we *have,* and lived? 27 [a]Go near and hear
all that the LORD our God says; then speak to us all
that the LORD our God speaks to you, and we will
hear and do *it.*'

28 "The LORD heard the voice of your words when
you spoke to me, [A]and the LORD said to me, 'I have
heard the voice of the words of this people which
they have spoken to you. They have done well in all
that they have spoken. 29 [A]Oh that they had such a
heart in them, that they would fear Me and [B]keep
all My commandments always, that [C]it may be well
with them and with their sons forever! 30 Go, say
to them, "Return to your tents." 31 [A]But as for you,
stand here by Me, that I may speak to you all the
commandments and the statutes and the judgments
which you shall teach them, that they may observe
them in the land which I give them to possess.' 32 So
you shall observe to do just as the LORD your God
has commanded you; [A]you shall not turn aside to
the right or to the left. 33 [A]You shall walk in all the
way which the LORD your God has commanded you,
[B]that you may live and that it may be well with you,
and that you may prolong *your* days in the land
which you will possess.

OBEY GOD AND PROSPER

6 "Now this is the commandment, the statutes
and the judgments which the LORD your God
has commanded *me* to teach you, that you might do
them in the land where you are going over to possess it, 2 so that you and your son and your grandson might [A]fear the LORD your God, to keep all His
statutes and His commandments which I command
you, [B]all the days of your life, and that your days
may be prolonged. 3 O Israel, you should listen and
[a]be careful to do *it,* that [A]it may be well with you and
that you may multiply greatly, just as the LORD, the
God of your fathers, has promised you, *in* [B]a land
flowing with milk and honey.

4 "[A]Hear, O Israel! The LORD is our God, the [B]LORD
is one! 5 [A]You shall love the LORD your God [B]with all
your heart and with all your soul and with all your
might. 6 [A]These words, which I am commanding
you today, shall be on your heart. 7 [A]You shall teach
them diligently to your sons and shall talk of them
when you sit in your house and when you walk by
the way and when you lie down and when you rise
up. 8 [A]You shall bind them as a sign on your hand
and they shall be as [a]frontals [b]on your forehead.
9 [A]You shall write them on the doorposts of your
house and on your gates.

10 "Then it shall come about when the LORD your
God brings you into the land which He swore to
your fathers, Abraham, Isaac and Jacob, to give
you, [A]great and splendid cities which you did not
build, 11 and houses full of all good things which
you did not fill, and hewn cisterns which you did
not dig, vineyards and olive trees which you did
not plant, and [A]you eat and are satisfied, 12 then
watch yourself, that [A]you do not forget the LORD
who brought you from the land of Egypt, out of the
house of [a]slavery. 13 [A]You shall [a]fear *only* the LORD
your God; and you shall [b]worship Him and [B]swear
by His name. 14 [A]You shall not follow other gods,
any of the gods of the peoples who surround you,

5:25 [A]Ex 20:18, 19; Deut 18:16 5:26 [A]Deut 4:33 5:27 [a]Lit *Go yourself* 5:28 [A]Deut 18:17 5:29 [A]Ps 81:13; Is 48:18 [B]Deut 11:1 [C]Deut 5:16, 33 5:31 [A]Ex 24:12 5:32 [A]Deut 17:20; 28:14; Josh 1:7; 23:6; Prov 4:27 5:33 [A]Deut 10:12; Jer 7:23; Luke 1:6 [B]Deut 4:1, 40; 12:25, 28; 22:7; Eph 6:3 6:2 [A]Ex 20:20; Deut 10:12; Ps 111:10; 128:1; Eccl 12:13 [B]Deut 4:9 6:3 [a]Lit *keep* [A]Deut 5:33 [B]Ex 3:8, 17 6:4 [A]Matt 22:37; Mark 12:29, 30; Luke 10:27 [B]Deut 4:35, 39; John 10:30; 1 Cor 8:4; Eph 4:6 6:5 [A]Matt 22:37; Mark 12:30; Luke 10:27 [B]Deut 4:29; 10:12 6:6 [A]Deut 11:18 6:7 [A]Deut 4:9; 11:19; Eph 6:4 6:8 [a]Or *frontlet bands* [b]Lit *between your eyes* [A]Ex 12:14; 13:9, 16; Deut 11:18; Prov 3:3; 6:21; 7:3 6:9 [A]Deut 11:20 6:10 [A]Deut 9:1; 19:1; Josh 24:13; Ps 105:44 6:11 [A]Deut 8:10; 11:15; 14:29 6:12 [a]Lit *slaves* [A]Deut 4:9 6:13 [a]Or *reverence* [b]Or *serve* [A]Deut 13:4; Matt 4:10; Luke 4:8 [B]Deut 5:11; 10:20; Ps 63:11; Matt 5:33 6:14 [A]Jer 25:6

5:28, 29 God affirmed that the pledge to be obedient was the right response (v. 28), and then expressed His loving passion for them to fulfill their promise so they and their children would prosper.

5:30–33 They asked to be given all God's Word (v. 27), so God dismissed the people and told Moses He was going to give the law to him to teach the people (v. 31). At stake was life and prosperity in the Land of Promise.

6:1–3 **days … prolonged.** Moses' concern is that successive generations maintain the obedience to God's laws that ensures life and prosperity.

6:3 **a land flowing with milk and honey.** A description that included the richness of the land which the Israelites were soon to possess (see 11:9; 26:9, 15; 27:3; 31:20).

6:4, 5 Cf. Mk 12:29, 30, 32, 33.

6:4 **Hear, O Israel!** See 5:1. Deuteronomy 6:4–9, known as the *Shema* (Heb. for "hear"), has become the Jewish confession of faith, recited twice daily by the devout, along with 11:13–21 and Nu 15:37–41. **The LORD … LORD is one!** The intent of these words was to give a clear statement of the truth of monotheism, that there is only one God. Thus, it has also been translated "the Lord is our God, the Lord alone." The word used for "one" in this passage does not mean "singleness," but "unity." The same word is used in Ge 2:24, where the husband and wife were said to be "one flesh." Thus, while this verse was intended as a clear and concise statement of monotheism, it does not exclude the concept of the Trinity.

6:5–9 **You shall love the LORD your God.** First in the list of all that was essential for the Jew was unreserved, wholehearted commitment expressed in love to God. Since this relationship of love for God could not be represented in any material way as with idols, it had to be demonstrated in obedience to God's law in daily life. Cf. 11:16–21; Mt 22:37; Lk 10:27.

6:6 **These words … on your heart.** The people were to think about these commandments and meditate on them so that obedience would not be a matter of formal legalism, but a response based upon understanding. The law written upon the heart would be an essential characteristic of the later New Covenant (see Jer 31:33).

6:7 **teach them diligently to your sons.** The commandments were to be the subject of conversation, both inside and outside the home, from the beginning of the day to its end.

6:8 **hand … frontals on your forehead.** The Israelite was to continually meditate upon and be directed by the commandments that God had given to him. Later in Jewish history, this phrase was taken literally and the people tied phylacteries (boxes containing these verses) to their hands and foreheads with thongs of leather.

6:10, 11 **the LORD your God brings you into the land.** God reiterated that He was going to give Israel the land in fulfillment of the promises that He had made to Abraham, Isaac, and Jacob, both with title and prosperity.

6:13 **swear by His name.** An oath was a solemn pledge to affirm something said as absolutely true. The invoking of the Lord's name in the oath meant that one was bound

15 for the LORD your God in the midst of you is a
[A]jealous God; otherwise the anger of the LORD your
God will be kindled against you, and He will [a]wipe
you off the face of the earth.
16 "[A]You shall not put the LORD your God to the
test, [B]as you tested *Him* at Massah. 17 [A]You should diligently keep the commandments of the LORD your
God, and His testimonies and His statutes which He
has commanded you. 18 You shall do what is right
and good in the sight of the LORD, that [A]it may be
well with you and that you may go in and possess
the good land which the LORD swore to *give* your
fathers, 19 by driving out all your enemies from
before you, as the LORD has spoken.
20 "[A]When your son asks you in time to come,
saying, 'What *do* the testimonies and the statutes
and the judgments *mean* which the LORD our God
commanded you?' 21 then you shall say to your son,
'We were slaves to Pharaoh in Egypt, and the LORD
brought us from Egypt with a mighty hand. 22 Moreover, the LORD showed great and distressing signs
and wonders before our eyes against Egypt, Pharaoh and all his household; 23 He brought us out
from there in order to bring us in, to give us the
land which He had sworn to our fathers.' 24 So the
LORD commanded us to observe all these statutes,
[A]to fear the LORD our God for our good always and
[B]for our survival, as *it is* today. 25 [A]It will be righteousness for us if we [a]are careful to observe all
this commandment before the LORD our God, just
as He commanded us.

WARNINGS

7 "[A]When the LORD your God brings you into
the land where you are entering to possess it,
and clears away many nations before you, the Hittites and the Girgashites and the Amorites and the
Canaanites and the Perizzites and the Hivites and
the Jebusites, [B]seven nations greater and stronger
than you, 2 and when the LORD your God delivers
them before you and you [a]defeat them, [A]then you
shall [b]utterly destroy them. [B]You shall make no covenant with them [C]and show no favor to them. 3 Furthermore, [A]you shall not intermarry with them; you
shall not give your [a]daughters to [b]their sons, nor
shall you take [c]their daughters for your [d]sons. 4 For
[a]they will turn your [b]sons away from [c]following Me
to serve other gods; then the anger of the LORD will
be kindled against you and [A]He will quickly destroy
you. 5 But thus you shall do to them: [A]you shall tear
down their altars, and smash their *sacred* pillars,
and hew down their [a]Asherim, and burn their grav-
en images with fire. 6 For you are [A]a holy people to
the LORD your God; the LORD your God has chosen
you to be [B]a people for His [a]own possession out of
all the peoples who are on the face of the [b]earth.
7 "[A]The LORD did not set His love on you nor
choose you because you were more in number than
any of the peoples, for you were the fewest of all
peoples, 8 but because the LORD loved you and kept
the [A]oath which He swore to your forefathers, [B]the
LORD brought you out by a mighty hand and redeemed you from the house of [a]slavery, from the
hand of Pharaoh king of Egypt. 9 Know therefore
that the LORD your God, [A]He is God, [B]the faithful
God, [C]who keeps [a]His covenant and [a]His lovingkindness to a thousandth generation with those
who [D]love Him and keep His commandments; 10 but
[A]repays those who hate Him to [a]their faces, to destroy [b]them; He will not delay [c]with him who hates
Him, He will repay him to his face. 11 Therefore,
you shall keep the commandment and the statutes
and the judgments which I am commanding you
today, to do them.

6:15 [a]Lit *destroy* [A]Deut 4:24; 5:9 6:16 [A]Matt 4:7; Luke 4:12 [B]Ex 17:7 6:17 [A]Deut 11:22; Ps 119:4 6:18 [A]Deut 4:40 6:20 [A]Ex 13:8, 14 6:24 [A]Deut 10:12; Jer 32:39 [B]Ps 41:2; Luke 10:28 6:25 [a]Lit *keep* [A]Deut 24:13; Rom 10:3 7:1 [A]Deut 20:16-18 [B]Acts 13:19 7:2 [a]Lit *smite* [b]Lit *surely devote to the ban* [A]Num 31:17; Josh 11:11 [B]Ex 23:32 [C]Deut 7:16; 13:8 7:3 [a]Lit *daughter* [b]Lit *his son* [c]Lit *his daughter* [d]Lit *son* [A]Ex 34:15, 16; Josh 23:12; Ezra 9:2 7:4 [a]Lit *he* [b]Lit *son* [c]Lit *after* [A]Deut 4:26 7:5 [a]I.e. wooden symbols of a female deity [A]Ex 23:24; 34:13; Deut 12:3 7:6 [a]Or *special treasure* [b]Lit *ground* [A]Ex 19:6; Deut 14:2, 21; Ps 50:5; Jer 2:3 [B]Ex 19:5; Deut 4:20; 14:2; 26:18; Ps 135:4; Titus 2:14; 1 Pet 2:9 7:7 [A]Deut 4:37 7:8 [a]Lit *slaves* [A]Ex 32:13 [B]Ex 13:3 7:9 [a]Lit *the* [A]Deut 4:35, 39 [B]Is 49:7; 1 Cor 1:9; 1 Thess 5:24; 2 Tim 2:13 [C]Ex 20:6; Dan 9:4 [D]Deut 5:10 7:10 [a]Lit *his face* [b]Lit *him* [c]Lit *to* [A]Is 59:18; Nah 1:2

under obligation before God to fulfill that word (cf. Mt 4:10; Lk 4:8).

6:15 a jealous God. *See note on 4:24.*

6:16 Massah. This name actually means "testing" (cf. Ex 17:1–7; Mt 4:7; Lk 4:12).

6:20 When your son asks you in time to come. When a young son asked the meaning of the law, his father was to use the following pattern in explaining it to him. First, the Israelites were in bondage in Egypt (v. 21a). Second, God miraculously delivered the Israelites and judged the Egyptians (v. 21b). Third, this work was in accord with His promise to the patriarchs (v. 23). Fourth, God gave His law to Israel that His people might obey it (vv. 24, 25).

6:25 righteousness for us. A true and personal relationship with God that would be manifest in the lives of the people of God. There was no place for legalism or concern about the external since the compelling motive for this righteousness was to be love for God (v. 5).

7:1–26 This section discusses how the Israelites should relate to the inhabitants of Canaan including their destruction, the forbidding of intermarriage, and the elimination of all altars and idols. It was God's time for judgment on that land.

7:1 seven nations. These 7 groups controlled areas of land usually centered around one or more fortified cities. Together they had greater population and military strength than Israel. Six of these 7 are mentioned elsewhere (see Ex 3:8). The unique nation here is the Girgashites, who are referred to in Ge 10:16; Jos 3:10; 24:11; 1Ch 1:14, and in Ugaritic texts. They may have been tribal people living in the N of Canaan.

7:2 utterly destroy them. All the men, women and children were to be put to death. Even though this action seems extreme, the following need to be kept in mind: 1) the Canaanites deserved to die for their sin (9:4, 5; cf. Ge 15:16); 2) the Canaanites persisted in their hatred of God (7:10); and 3) the Canaanites constituted a moral cancer that had the potential of introducing idolatry and immorality which would spread rapidly among the Israelites (20:17, 18).

7:3 not intermarry. Because of the intimate nature of marriage, the idolatrous spouse could lead her mate astray (see 1Ki 11:1–8 for the example of Solomon).

7:5 tear down their altars. This destructive action would remove any consequent temptation for the Israelites to follow the religious practices of the nations they were to displace from the Land.

7:6 a holy people to the LORD your God. The basis for the command to destroy the Canaanites is found in God's election of Israel. God had set apart Israel for His own special use and they were His treasured possession. As God's people, Israel needed to be separated from the moral pollution of the Canaanites.

7:8 loved you … kept the oath. The choosing of Israel as a holy nation set apart for God was grounded in God's love and His faithfulness to the promises He had made to the patriarchs, not in any merit or intrinsic goodness in Israel.

7:9 a thousandth generation. *See note on 1:11.*

PROMISES OF GOD

12 "[A]Then it shall come about, because you listen
to these judgments and keep and do them, that the
LORD your God will keep with you [a]His covenant
and [a]His lovingkindness which He swore to your
forefathers. 13 He will [A]love you and bless you and
[B]multiply you; He will also bless the fruit of your
womb and the fruit of your ground, your grain and
your new wine and your oil, the increase of your
herd and the young of your flock, [a]in the land which
He swore to your forefathers to give you. 14 You shall
be blessed above all peoples; there will be no male
or female [A]barren among you or among your cattle.
15 [A]The LORD will remove from you all sickness; and
He will not put on you any of the harmful diseases
of Egypt which you have known, but He will lay
them on all who hate you. 16 You shall consume all
the peoples whom the LORD your God will deliver
to you; [A]your eye shall not pity them, nor shall you
serve their gods, for that *would be* [B]a snare to you.

17 "If you should say in your heart, 'These nations
are greater than I; how can I [A]dispossess them?'
18 you shall not be afraid of them; you shall well
[A]remember what the LORD your God did to Pharaoh and to all Egypt: 19 [A]the great trials which your
eyes saw and the signs and the wonders and the
mighty hand and the outstretched arm by which
the LORD your God brought you out. So shall the
LORD your God do to all the peoples of whom you
are afraid. 20 Moreover, the LORD your God will send
[A]the hornet against them, until those who are left
and hide themselves from you perish. 21 You shall
not dread [a]them, for [A]the LORD your God is in your
midst, [B]a great and awesome God. 22 [A]The LORD
your God will clear away these nations before you
little by little; you will not be able to put an end to
them quickly, for the [a]wild beasts would grow too
numerous for you. 23 [A]But the LORD your God will
deliver them before you, and will [a]throw them into
great confusion until they are destroyed. 24 [A]He
will deliver their kings into your hand so that you
will make their name perish from under heaven;
[B]no man will be able to stand before you until you
have destroyed them. 25 The graven images of their
gods you are to [A]burn with fire; you shall [B]not covet
the silver or the gold that is on them, nor take it
for yourselves, or you will be [C]snared by it, for it
is an [D]abomination to the LORD your God. 26 You
shall not bring an abomination into your house,
and like it come under the [A]ban; you shall utterly
detest it and you shall utterly abhor it, for it is
something banned.

GOD'S GRACIOUS DEALINGS

8 "All the commandments that I am commanding
you today you shall be careful to do, that you
[A]may live and multiply, and go in and possess the
land which the LORD swore *to give* to your forefathers. 2 [A]You shall remember all the way which the
LORD your God has [B]led you in the wilderness these
forty years, that He might humble you, [C]testing you,
to know what was in your heart, whether you would
keep His commandments or not. 3 He humbled you
and let you be hungry, and fed you with manna
which you did not know, nor did your fathers know,
that He might make you [a]understand that [A]man does
not live by bread alone, but man lives by everything
that proceeds out of the mouth of the LORD. 4 [A]Your
clothing did not wear out on you, nor did your foot
swell these forty years. 5 [A]Thus you are to know in
your heart that the LORD your God was disciplining
you just as a man disciplines his son. 6 Therefore,
you shall keep the commandments of the LORD
your God, to walk in His ways and to [a]fear Him.

7:12 [a]Lit *the* [A]Lev 26:3-13; Deut 28:1-14 7:13 [a]Lit *on the ground* [A]Ps 146:8; Prov 15:9; John 14:21 [B]Lev 26:9; Deut 13:17; 30:5 7:14 [A]Ex 23:26 7:15 [A]Ex 15:26 7:16 [A]Deut 7:2 [B]Ex 23:33; Judg 8:27; Ps 106:36 7:17 [A]Num 33:53 7:18 [A]Ps 105:5 7:19 [A]Deut 4:34 7:20 [A]Ex 23:28; Josh 24:12 7:21 [a]Lit *from before them* [A]Ex 29:45; Josh 3:10 [B]Deut 10:17; Neh 1:5; 9:32 7:22 [a]Lit *beasts of the field* [A]Ex 23:29, 30 7:23 [a]Lit *confuse them with* [A]Ex 23:27; Josh 10:10 7:24 [A]Josh 6:2; 10:23-25 [B]Deut 11:25; Josh 1:5; 10:8; 23:9 7:25 [A]Ex 32:20; Deut 12:3; 1 Chr 14:12 [B]Ex 20:17 [C]Deut 7:16; Judg 8:27 [D]Deut 17:1 7:26 [A]Lev 27:28f 8:1 [A]Deut 4:1 8:2 [A]Deut 8:16 [B]Ps 136:16; Amos 2:10 [C]Ex 15:25; 20:20; 2 Chr 32:31 8:3 [a]Lit *know* [A]Matt 4:4; Luke 4:4 8:4 [A]Deut 29:5; Neh 9:21 8:5 [A]Deut 4:36; 2 Sam 7:14; Prov 3:12; Heb 12:6; Rev 3:19 8:6 [a]Or *reverence*

7:12–15 The Lord promised Israel particular blessings for their obedience, which are further enumerated in 28:1–14.

7:12 **the LORD your God will keep with you His covenant.** If Israel was obedient to the Lord, they would experience His covenantal mercy. However, the people could forfeit the blessings of the covenant through their own disobedience.

7:13 **grain ... new wine ... oil.** These were the 3 principal food products of Palestine. "Grain" included wheat and barley. "New wine" was the grape juice as it came from the presses. The "oil" was the olive oil used in cooking and in the lamps.

7:15 **the harmful diseases of Egypt.** Some virulent and malignant diseases such as elephantiasis, ophthalmia, and dysentery were common in Egypt.

7:20 **God will send the hornet.** The hornet or wasp was a large insect, common in Canaan, that may have had a potentially fatal sting. Here the reference was probably figurative in the sense of a great army sent into panic when the Lord would inflict His sting on them (see 11:25). *See note on Ex 23:28.*

7:22 **little by little.** Even though the Lord promised that the defeat of the people of the land would be quick (4:26; 9:3), the process of settlement would be more gradual to avoid the danger of the land returning to a primitive state of natural anarchy.

7:26 **You shall utterly detest it and ... utterly abhor it.** "Detest" and "abhor" were strong words of disapproval and rejection. Israel was to have the same attitude toward the idols of the Canaanites as did God Himself. **it is something banned.** The images or idols were to be set aside for destruction.

8:2 **remember.** The people were to recall what God had done for them (cf. 5:15; 7:18; 8:18; 9:7; 15:15; 16:3, 12; 24:9, 18; 25:17), and not forget (cf. 4:9, 23, 31; 6:12; 8:11, 14, 19; 9:7; 25:19; 26:13). **to know what was in your heart.** Israel's 40 years in the wilderness was a time of God's affliction and testing so that the basic attitude of the people toward God and His commandments could be made known. God chose to sustain His hungry people in the wilderness by a means previously unknown to them. Through this miraculous provision, God both humbled the people and tested their obedience.

8:3 **manna which you did not know.** God sustained the people in the wilderness with a food previously unknown to them. See Ex 16:15 for the beginning of the giving of the manna and Jos 5:12 for its cessation. **man does not live by bread alone.** Israel's food in the wilderness was decreed by the Word of God. They had manna because it came by God's command; therefore, ultimately it was not bread that kept them alive, but God's Word (cf. Mt 4:4; Lk 4:4).

8:4 **Your clothing did not wear out.** This miraculous provision is also mentioned in 29:5.

8:5 **the LORD your God was disciplining you.** Israel's sojourn in the wilderness was viewed as a time of God's discipline of His children. He was seeking to correct their wayward attitude so that they might be prepared to obediently go into the land.

8:6–10 An extensive description of God's abundant blessings for Israel in the land (cf. 7:7–9).

7 For [A]the LORD your God is bringing you into a good land, a land of brooks of water, of fountains and springs, flowing forth in valleys and hills; 8 a land of wheat and barley, of vines and fig trees and pomegranates, a land of olive oil and honey; 9 a land where you will eat food without scarcity, in which you will not lack anything; a land whose stones are iron, and out of whose hills you can dig copper. 10 When [A]you have eaten and are satisfied, you shall bless the LORD your God for the good land which He has given you.

11 "[a]Beware that you do not [A]forget the LORD your God by not keeping His commandments and His ordinances and His statutes which I am commanding you today; 12 otherwise, [A]when you have eaten and are satisfied, and have built good houses and lived *in them,* 13 and when your herds and your flocks multiply, and your silver and gold multiply, and all that you have multiplies, 14 then your heart will become [a]proud and you will [A]forget the LORD your God who brought you out from the land of Egypt, out of the house of [b]slavery. 15 He led you through [A]the great and terrible wilderness, *with its* [B]fiery serpents and scorpions and thirsty ground where there was no water; He [C]brought water for you out of the rock of flint. 16 In the wilderness He fed you manna [A]which your fathers did not know, that He might humble you and that He might [B]test you, to do good for you [a]in the end. 17 Otherwise, [A]you may say in your heart, 'My power and the strength of my hand made me this wealth.' 18 But you shall remember the LORD your God, for [A]it is He who is giving you power to make wealth, that He may confirm His covenant which He swore to your fathers, as *it is* this day. 19 It shall come about if you ever forget the LORD your God and go after other gods and serve them and worship them, [A]I testify against you today that you will surely perish. 20 Like the nations that the LORD makes to perish before you, so [A]you shall perish; because you would not listen to the voice of the LORD your God.

ISRAEL PROVOKED GOD

9 "Hear, O Israel! You are crossing over the Jordan today to go in to dispossess [A]nations greater and mightier than you, great cities [a,B]fortified to heaven, 2 a people great and tall, the sons of the Anakim, whom you know and of whom you have heard *it said,* '[A]Who can stand before the sons of Anak?' 3 Know therefore today that [A]it is the LORD your God who is crossing over before you as [B]a consuming fire. He will destroy them and He will subdue them before you, so that [C]you may drive them out and destroy them quickly, just as the LORD has spoken to you.

4 "[A]Do not say in your heart when the LORD your God has driven them out before [a]you, 'Because of my righteousness the LORD has brought me in to possess this land,' but *it is* [B]because of the wickedness of these nations *that* the LORD is dispossessing them before you. 5 It is [A]not for your righteousness or for the uprightness of your heart that you are going to possess their land, but *it is* because of the wickedness of these nations *that* the LORD your God is driving them out before you, in order to confirm [B]the [a]oath which the LORD swore to your fathers, to Abraham, Isaac and Jacob.

6 "Know, then, *it is* not because of your righteousness *that* the LORD your God is giving you this good land to possess, for you are [A]a [a]stubborn people. 7 Remember, do not forget how you provoked the LORD your God to wrath in the wilderness; [A]from the day that you left the land of Egypt until you arrived at this place, you have been rebellious against the

8:7 [A]Deut 11:9-12; Jer 2:7 8:10 [A]Deut 6:11 8:11 [a]Lit *Take heed to yourself* [A]Deut 4:9 8:12 [A]Prov 30:9; Hos 13:6 8:14 [a]Lit *lifted up* [b]Lit *slaves* [A]Deut 8:11; Ps 106:21 8:15 [A]Deut 1:19; Jer 2:6 [B]Num 21:6 [C]Ex 17:6; Num 20:11; Deut 32:13; Ps 78:15; 114:8 8:16 [a]Lit *at your end* [A]Ex 16:15 [B]Deut 8:2 8:17 [A]Deut 9:4 8:18 [A]Prov 10:22; Hos 2:8 8:19 [A]Deut 4:26; 30:18 8:20 [A]Ezek 5:5-17 9:1 [a]Lit *and fortified* [A]Deut 4:38; 7:1; 11:23 [B]Deut 1:28 9:2 [A]Num 13:22, 28, 33; Josh 11:21, 22 9:3 [A]Deut 31:3; Josh 3:11 [B]Deut 4:24; Heb 12:29 [C]Ex 23:31; Deut 7:24 9:4 [a]Lit *you saying* [A]Deut 8:17; 9:7, 24; 31:27 [B]Lev 18:3, 24-30; Deut 12:31; 18:9-14 9:5 [a]Lit *word* [A]Titus 3:5 [B]Gen 12:7; 13:15; 15:7; 17:8; 26:4; 28:13 9:6 [a]Or *stiff-necked* [A]Deut 9:13; 10:16; 31:27 9:7 [A]Ex 14:10f; Num 14:22

8:7 a good land. In contrast to the desolation of the wilderness, vv. 7–9 describe the abundance of Israel's new land.

8:9 iron … copper. The mountains of southern Lebanon and the region E of the Sea of Galilee and S of the Dead Sea contained iron. Both copper and iron were found in the Rift Valley S of the Dead Sea.

8:11 do not forget the LORD your God. Sufficient food would lead to the satisfaction of Israel in the land (vv. 10, 12). This satisfaction and security could lead to Israel forgetting God. Forgetting God means no longer having Him in the daily thoughts of one's life. This forgetfulness would lead to a disobedience of His commandments. Whereas, in the wilderness, Israel had to depend on God for the necessities of life, in the rich land there would be a tempting sense of self-sufficiency.

8:14 then your heart will become proud. Pride was viewed as the root of forgetfulness. In their prosperity, the people might claim that their power and strength had produced their wealth (v. 17).

8:15 water … out of the rock. Cf. Nu 20:9–13.

8:16 to do good for you in the end. God designed the test of the wilderness so that Israel might be disciplined to obey Him. Through her obedience, she received the blessing of the land. Thus, God's design was to do good for Israel at the end of the process.

8:18, 19 *See note on 4:25–31.*

8:19 if you ever forget. Forgetting God would lead to worshiping other gods, which in turn would result in certain destruction. As God destroyed the Canaanites for their idolatry, so also would He judge Israel.

9:1–10:11 This part of Moses' speech rehearses the sins of the Israelites at Horeb (cf. Ex 32).

9:2 the Anakim. Moses remembered the people's shock when they heard the original report of the 12 spies concerning the size, strength, and number of the inhabitants of Canaan (Nu 13:26–14:6). Therefore, he emphasized that from a purely military and human point of view, their victory was impossible. The fear of the spies and the people focused on the Anakim, a tall, strong people who lived in the land of Canaan (*see note on 1:28*).

9:3 a consuming fire. The Lord was pictured as a fire which burned everything in its path. So the Lord would go over into Canaan and exterminate Canaanites. **destroy them quickly.** Israel was to be the human agent of the Lord's destruction of the Canaanites. The military strength of the Canaanites would be destroyed quickly (see Jos 6:1–11:23), though the complete subjugation of the land would take time (see 7:22; Jos 13:1).

9:4 Because of my righteousness. Three times in vv. 4–6, Moses emphasized that the victory was not because of Israel's goodness, but was entirely the work of God. It was the wickedness of the Canaanites that led to their expulsion from the land (cf. Ro 10:6).

9:6 a stubborn people. Lit. "hard of neck." An expression for the stubborn, intractable, obdurate, and unbending attitude of Israel. In vv. 7–29, Moses illustrated Israel's rebellious attitude and actions toward the Lord.

9:7 Remember. Moses challenged Israel to call to mind the long history of their stubbornness and provocation of God which had extended from the time of the Exodus from

LORD. 8 Even [A]at Horeb you provoked the LORD to wrath, and the LORD was so angry with you that He would have destroyed you. 9 When I went up to the mountain to receive the tablets of stone, the tablets of the covenant which the LORD had made with you, then I remained on the mountain forty days and nights; [A]I neither ate bread nor drank water. 10 The LORD gave me the two tablets of stone [A]written by the finger of God; and on them *were* all the words which the LORD had spoken with you at the mountain from the midst of the fire on the day of the assembly. 11 It came about [A]at the end of forty days and nights that the LORD gave me the two tablets of stone, the tablets of the covenant. 12 [A]Then the LORD said to me, 'Arise, go down from here quickly, for your people whom you brought out of Egypt have acted corruptly. They have [B]quickly turned aside from the way which I commanded them; they have made a molten image for themselves.' 13 The [A]LORD spoke further to me, saying, 'I have seen this people, and indeed, it is a [a,B]stubborn people. 14 [A]Let Me alone, that I may destroy them and [B]blot out their name from under heaven; and I will make of you a nation mightier and greater than they.'

15 "[A]So I turned and came down from the mountain while the mountain was burning with fire, and the two tablets of the covenant were in my two hands. 16 And I saw that you had indeed sinned against the LORD your God. You had made for yourselves a molten calf; you had turned aside quickly from the way which the LORD had commanded you. 17 I took hold of the two tablets and threw them from my hands and smashed them before your eyes. 18 [A]I fell down before the LORD, [B]as at the first, forty days and nights; [C]I neither ate bread nor drank water, [D]because of all your sin which you had committed in doing what was evil in the sight of the LORD to provoke Him to anger. 19 For [A]I was afraid of the anger and hot displeasure with which the LORD was wrathful against you in order to destroy you, [B]but the LORD listened to me that time also. 20 The LORD was angry enough with Aaron to destroy him; so I also prayed for Aaron at the same time. 21 [A]I took your [a]sinful *thing*, the calf which you had made, and burned it with fire and crushed it, grinding it very small until it was as fine as dust; and I threw its dust into the brook that came down from the mountain.

22 "Again at [A]Taberah and at [B]Massah and at [C]Kibroth-hattaavah you provoked the LORD to wrath. 23 When the LORD sent you from [A]Kadesh-barnea, saying, '[B]Go up and possess the land which I have given you,' then you rebelled against the [a]command of the LORD your God; [C]you neither believed Him nor listened to His voice. 24 [A]You have been rebellious against the LORD from the day I knew you.

25 "[A]So I fell down before the LORD the forty days and nights, which I [a]did because the LORD had said He would destroy you. 26 [A]I prayed to the LORD and said, 'O Lord GOD, do not destroy Your people, even Your inheritance, whom You have redeemed through Your greatness, whom You have brought out of Egypt with a mighty hand. 27 Remember Your servants, Abraham, Isaac, and Jacob; do not look at the stubbornness of this people or at their wickedness or their sin. 28 Otherwise the land from which You brought us may say, "[A]Because the LORD was not able to bring them into the land which He had [a]promised them and because He hated them He has brought them out to slay them in the wilderness." 29 Yet they are Your people, even [A]Your inheritance, whom You have brought out by Your [B]great power and Your outstretched arm.'

THE TABLETS REWRITTEN

10 "At that time the LORD said to me, '[A]Cut out for yourself two tablets of stone like the former ones, and come up to Me on the mountain, and [B]make an ark of wood for yourself. 2 [A]I will write on the tablets the words that were on the former tablets which you shattered, and [B]you shall put them in the ark.' 3 So [A]I made an ark of acacia wood and [B]cut out two tablets of stone like the former ones, and went

9:8 [A]Ex 32:7-10; Ps 106:19 9:9 [A]Ex 24:18; 34:28; Deut 8:3; 9:18 9:10 [A]Deut 4:13 9:11 [A]Deut 9:9 9:12 [A]Ex 32:7, 8 [B]Judg 2:17 9:13 [a]Or *stiff-necked* [A]Ex 32:9 [B]Deut 10:16; 31:27; 2 Kin 17:14 9:14 [A]Ex 32:10 [B]Ps 9:5; 109:13 9:15 [A]Ex 32:15-19 9:18 [A]Ex 34:28 [B]Deut 10:10 [C]Deut 9:9 [D]Ex 34:9 9:19 [A]Ex 32:10f; Heb 12:21 [B]Ex 34:10; Deut 10:10 9:21 [a]Lit *sin* [A]Ex 32:20 9:22 [A]Num 11:3 [B]Ex 17:7 [C]Num 11:34 9:23 [a]Lit *mouth* [A]Deut 1:2 [B]Deut 1:21 [C]Deut 1:26; Ps 106:24 9:24 [A]Deut 9:7; 31:27 9:25 [a]Lit *fell down* [A]Deut 9:18 9:26 [A]Ex 32:11-13; 1 Sam 7:9; Jer 15:1 9:28 [a]Lit *spoken to* [A]Ex 32:12; Num 14:16 9:29 [A]Deut 4:20; 1 Kin 8:51; Neh 1:10; Ps 106:40 [B]Deut 4:34 10:1 [A]Ex 34:1 [B]Ex 25:10 10:2 [A]Deut 4:13 [B]Ex 25:16 10:3 [A]Ex 25:5; 37:1-9 [B]Ex 34:4

Egypt for 40 years until the present moment on the plains of Moab.

9:10 the finger of God. God Himself had written the Ten Commandments on the two tablets of stone at Mt. Sinai (see Ex 31:18).

9:14 blot out their name from under heaven. God threatened to destroy the people of Israel so completely that He pictured it as an obliteration of all memory of them from the world of men. This threat was taken by Moses as an invitation to intercede for the children of Israel (Nu 14:11–19).

9:19 Cf. Heb 12:21.

9:20 I also prayed for Aaron. Moses interceded on behalf of Aaron, on whom the immediate responsibility for the Israelites' sin of the golden calf rested. Aaron had thus incurred the wrath of God, and his life was in danger (see Ex 32:1–6). This is the only verse in the Pentateuch which specifically states that Moses prayed for Aaron.

9:22 Taberah ... Massah ... Kibroth-hattaavah. These 3 places were all associated with Israel's rebellion against the Lord. Taberah, "burning," was where the people had complained of their misfortunes (Nu 11:1–3). At Massah, "testing," they had found fault with everything and in presumption had put God to the test (Ex 17:1–7). At Kibroth-hattaavah, "graves of craving," the people had again incurred God's anger by complaining about their food (Nu 11:31–35).

9:23 Kadesh-barnea. There they sinned by both lack of faith in God and disobedience (cf. Nu 13, 14).

9:24 You have been rebellious against the LORD. Moses concluded that his dealings with Israel as God's mediator had been one of continual rebellion on Israel's part, which led to his intercession (vv. 25–29).

9:28 the land from which You brought us. Moses' prayer of intercession to the Lord on behalf of Israel appealed to the Lord to forgive His people because the Egyptians could have interpreted God's destruction of Israel as His inability to fulfill His promise and His hate for His people.

10:1–3 two tablets of stone like the former ones. God had listened to Moses' intercession and dealt mercifully with the Israelites who had broken the covenant by rewriting the Ten Commandments on two tablets prepared for that purpose by Moses. The second tablets were made of the same material and were the same size as the first.

10:1 an ark of wood. This refers to the ark of the covenant. Moses telescoped the events in these verses. Later, at the construction of the ark of the covenant, Moses placed the two new stone tablets within that ark (see Ex 37:1–9).

up on the mountain with the two tablets in my hand.
4 He wrote on the tablets, like the former writing,
[A]the Ten [a]Commandments [B]which the LORD had
spoken to you on the mountain from the midst of
the fire [C]on the day of the assembly; and the LORD
gave them to me. 5 Then I turned and [A]came down
from the mountain and [B]put the tablets in the ark
which I had made; [C]and there they are, as the LORD
commanded me."
6 (Now the sons of Israel set out from [a]Beeroth
[A]Bene-jaakan to Moserah. [B]There Aaron died and
there he was buried and Eleazar his son ministered as priest in his place. 7 [A]From there they
set out to Gudgodah, and from Gudgodah to Jotbathah, a land of brooks of water. 8 [A]At that time
the LORD set apart the tribe of Levi to carry the
ark of the covenant of the LORD, to stand before
the LORD [B]to serve Him and to bless in His name
until this day. 9 [A]Therefore, Levi does not have
a portion or inheritance with his brothers; the
LORD is his inheritance, just as the LORD your
God spoke to him.)
10 "[A]I, moreover, stayed on the mountain forty
days and forty nights like the first time, and the
LORD listened to me that time also; the LORD was
not willing to destroy you. 11 Then the LORD said
to me, 'Arise, proceed on your journey ahead of
the people, that they may go in and possess the
land which I swore to their fathers to give them.'
12 "[A]Now, Israel, what does the LORD your God
require from you, but to [a]fear the LORD your God,
to walk in all His ways and [B]love Him, and to serve
the LORD your God with [C]all your heart and with
all your soul, 13 *and* to keep the LORD'S commandments and His statutes which I am commanding
you today for your good? 14 Behold, [A]to the LORD
your God belong heaven and the [a]highest heavens,
[B]the earth and all that is in it. 15 [A]Yet on your fathers did the LORD set His affection to love them,
and He chose their [a]descendants after them, *even*
you above all peoples, as *it is* this day. 16 [A]So circumcise [a]your heart, and [B]stiffen your neck no
longer. 17 [A]For the LORD your God is the God of gods
and the [B]Lord of lords, the great, the mighty, and
the awesome God [C]who does not show partiality
nor [D]take a bribe. 18 He executes justice for [A]the
orphan and the widow, and shows His love for
the alien by giving him food and clothing. 19 [A]So
show your love for the alien, for you were aliens
in the land of Egypt. 20 You shall fear the LORD
your God; you shall serve Him and [A]cling to Him,
and [B]you shall swear by His name. 21 He is [A]your
praise and He is your God, who has done these
great and awesome things for you which your
eyes have seen. 22 [A]Your fathers went down to
Egypt seventy persons *in all,* [B]and now the LORD
your God has made you as numerous as the stars
of heaven.

REWARDS OF OBEDIENCE

11 "You shall therefore [A]love the LORD your God,
and always [B]keep His charge, His statutes, His
ordinances, and His commandments. 2 Know this
day [A]that I *am* not *speaking* with your sons who
have not known and who have not seen the [a]dis-
cipline of the LORD your God—His greatness, His
mighty hand and His outstretched arm, 3 and [A]His
signs and His works which He did in the midst of
Egypt to Pharaoh the king of Egypt and to all his
land; 4 and what He did to Egypt's army, to its horses
and its chariots, [A]when He made the water of the
[a]Red Sea to [b]engulf them while they were pursuing
you, and the LORD [c]completely destroyed them;
5 and what He did to you in the wilderness until you

10:4 [a]Lit *Words* [A]Ex 34:28; Deut 4:13 [B]Ex 20:1 [C]Deut 9:10; 18:16 10:5 [A]Ex 34:29 [B]Ex 40:20 [C]1 Kin 8:9 10:6 [a]Or *the wells of the sons of Jaakan* [A]Num 33:30, 31 [B]Num 20:25-28; 33:38 10:7 [A]Num 33:33, 34 10:8 [A]Num 3:6; 18:1-7; Deut 31:9 [B]Deut 17:12; 18:5; 21:5 10:9 [A]Num 18:20, 24; Deut 18:1, 2; Ezek 44:28 10:10 [A]Ex 34:28; Deut 9:18 10:12 [a]Or *reverence* [A]Mic 6:8 [B]Deut 6:5; Matt 22:37; 1 Tim 1:5 [C]Deut 4:29 10:14 [a]Lit *heaven of heavens* [A]1 Kin 8:27; Neh 9:6; Ps 68:33; 115:16 [B]Ps 24:1 10:15 [a]Lit *seed* [A]Deut 4:37 10:16 [a]Lit *the foreskin of your heart* [A]Lev 26:41; Jer 4:4 [B]Deut 9:6 10:17 [A]Josh 22:22; Ps 136:2; Dan 2:47; 1 Tim 6:15; Rev 19:16 [B]Rev 17:14 [C]Deut 1:17; Acts 10:34; Rom 2:11; Gal 2:6; Eph 6:9 [D]Deut 16:19 10:18 [A]Ex 22:22-24; Ps 68:5; 146:9 10:19 [A]Lev 19:34; Ezek 47:22, 23 10:20 [A]Deut 11:22; 13:4 [B]Deut 5:11; 6:13; Ps 63:11 10:21 [A]Ps 109:1; 148:14; Jer 17:14 10:22 [A]Gen 46:27 [B]Gen 15:5; 22:17; Deut 1:10 11:1 [A]Deut 6:5; 10:12 [B]Lev 18:30; 22:9 11:2 [a]Or *instruction* [A]Deut 4:34 11:3 [A]Ex 7:8-21 11:4 [a]Lit *Sea of Reeds* [b]Lit *flow over their faces* [c]Lit *to this day* [A]Ex 14:28; Deut 1:40; 2:1

10:6–9 These verses show that the priesthood of Aaron and service of the Levites were restored after the incident of the golden calf.

10:6 **Moserah. There Aaron died.** Aaron was not killed at Sinai, but lived until the 40th year of the Exodus, which shows the effectiveness of Moses' intercession before the Lord (cf. Nu 20:22–29; 33:38, 39). After Aaron's death, the priestly ministry continued in the appointment of Eleazar. Moserah is the district in which Mt. Hor stands, on which Aaron died (cf. Nu 20:27, 28; 33:38).

10:8 **At that time.** This refers to the time that Israel was at Mt. Sinai.

10:9 **not have a portion.** The family of Levi received no inheritance in the land of Canaan (see Nu 18:20, 24).

10:10, 11 Because of Moses' intercession, not because of their righteousness, the Israelites were encamped on the banks of the Jordan, ready to enter the Promised Land.

10:12, 13 **what does the LORD … require from you…?** This rhetorical question led into Moses' statement of the 5 basic requirements that God expected of His people (cf. Mic 6:8): 1) **to fear the LORD your God.** To hold God in awe and submit to Him; 2) **to walk in all His ways.** To conduct life in accordance with the will of God; 3) **to … love Him.** To choose to set one's affections on the Lord and on Him alone; 4) **to serve the LORD your God.** To have the worship of the Lord as the central focus of life; 5) **to keep the LORD's commandments.** To obey the requirements the Lord had imposed.

10:14, 15 God, with the same sovereignty by which He controls all things, had chosen the patriarchs and the nation of Israel to be His special people.

10:16 **So circumcise your heart.** Moses called the Israelites to cut away all the sin in their hearts, as the circumcision surgery cut away the skin. This would leave them with a clean relationship to God (cf. 30:6; Lv 26:40, 41; Jer 4:4; 9:25; Ro 2:29). *See note on Jer 4:4.*

10:18 **He executes justice.** The sovereign, authoritative God is also impartial (v. 17), as seen in His concern for the orphan, the widow, and the alien (cf. Lv 19:9–18; Jas 1:27).

10:20 **cling to Him.** The verb means "to stick to" or "to hold on to." As a husband is to be united to his wife (Ge 2:24), so Israel was to cling intimately to her God.

10:22 **seventy persons.** See Ex 1:5. One of the great and awesome things God had done for Israel was multiplying the 70 people who went to Egypt into a nation of over two million people.

11:2 **your sons.** Moses distinguished between the adults and the children in his audience. The adults were those who had seen the Exodus from Egypt as children and had experienced the Lord's discipline in the wilderness. It was to these adults that Moses could say, "Your own eyes have seen all the great work of the LORD which He did" (v. 7). It was that specially blessed generation of adults that were called to pass on the teaching of what they had learned to their children (v. 19).

came to this place; 6 and [A]what He did to Dathan
and Abiram, the sons of Eliab, the son of Reuben,
when the earth opened its mouth and swallowed
them, their households, their tents, and [B]every living
thing that [a]followed them, among all Israel— 7 but
your own eyes have seen all the great work of the
LORD which He did.
8 "You shall therefore keep every commandment
which I am commanding you today, [A]so that you
may be strong and go in and possess the land into
which you are about to cross to possess it; 9 [A]so that
you may prolong *your* days on the land which the
LORD swore to your fathers to give to them and to
their [a]descendants, [B]a land flowing with milk and
honey. 10 For the land, into which you are entering to
possess it, is not like the land of Egypt from which
you came, where you used to sow your seed and
water it with your [a]foot like a vegetable garden.
11 But [A]the land into which you are about to cross
to possess it, a land of hills and valleys, drinks water from the rain of heaven, 12 a land for which the
LORD your God cares; [A]the eyes of the LORD your
God are always on it, from the [a]beginning even to
the end of the year.
13 "It shall come about, [A]if you listen obediently
to my commandments which I am commanding
you today, [B]to love the LORD your God and to serve
Him [C]with all your heart and all your soul, 14 that
[a,A]He will give the rain for your land in its season,
the [b,B]early and [c]late rain, that you may gather in
your grain and your new wine and your oil. 15 [a,A]He
will give grass in your fields for your cattle, and
[B]you will eat and be satisfied. 16 [a,A]Beware that your
hearts are not deceived, and that you do not turn
away and serve other gods and worship them. 17 Or
[A]the anger of the LORD will be kindled against you,
and He will [B]shut up the heavens [C]so that there will
be no rain and the ground will not yield its fruit;
and [D]you will perish quickly from the good land
which the LORD is giving you.
18 "[A]You shall therefore [a]impress these words of
mine on your heart and on your soul; and you shall
bind them as a sign on your hand, and they shall be
as [b]frontals [c]on your forehead. 19 [A]You shall teach
them to your sons, talking of them when you sit in
your house and when you walk along the road and
when you lie down and when you rise up. 20 [A]You
shall write them on the doorposts of your house and
on your gates, 21 so that [A]your days and the days of
your sons may be multiplied on the land which the
LORD swore to your fathers to give them, as [a,B]long
as the heavens *remain* above the earth. 22 For if you
are [A]careful to keep all this commandment which I
am commanding you to do, [B]to love the LORD your
God, to walk in all His ways and [C]hold fast to Him,
23 then the LORD will [A]drive out all these nations
from before you, and you will [B]dispossess nations
greater and mightier than you. 24 [A]Every place on
which the sole of your foot treads shall be yours;
[B]your border will be from the wilderness to Lebanon, *and* from the river, the river Euphrates, as far
as [a]the western sea. 25 [A]No man will be able to stand
before you; the LORD your God will lay the dread
of you and the fear of you on all the land on which
you set foot, as He has spoken to you.
26 "[A]See, I am setting before you today a blessing and a curse: 27 the [A]blessing, if you listen to the
commandments of the LORD your God, which I am
commanding you today; 28 and the [A]curse, if you
do not listen to the commandments of the LORD
your God, but turn aside from the way which I am
commanding you today, [a]by following other gods
which you have not known.
29 "It shall come about, when the LORD your God
brings you into the land where you are entering
to possess it, [A]that you shall place the blessing on

11:6 [a]Lit *was at their feet* [A]Num 16:1-35; Ps 106:16-18 [B]Num 26:10, 11 11:8 [A]Deut 31:6, 7, 23; Josh 1:6, 7 11:9 [a]Lit *seed* [A]Deut 4:40; 5:16, 33; 6:2; Prov 10:27 [B]Ex 3:8
11:10 [a]I.e. probably a treadmill 11:11 [A]Deut 8:7 11:12 [a]Lit *beginning of the year* [A]1 Kin 9:3 11:13 [A]Lev 26:3; Deut 7:12 [B]Deut 11:1 [C]Deut 4:29 11:14 [a]So some ancient versions; M.T. reads *I* [b]I.e. autumn [c]I.e. spring [A]Lev 26:4; Deut 28:12 [B]Joel 2:23; James 5:7 11:15 [a]So some ancient versions; M.T. reads *I* [A]Ps 104:14 [B]Deut 6:11
11:16 [a]Lit *Watch yourselves* [A]Job 31:27 11:17 [A]Deut 6:15; 9:19 [B]1 Kin 8:35; 2 Chr 6:26; 7:13 [C]Deut 28:24 [D]Deut 4:26 11:18 [a]Lit *put* [b]Lit *frontlet bands* [c]Lit *between your eyes* [A]Ex 13:9, 16; Deut 6:8 11:19 [A]Deut 4:9, 10; 6:7; Prov 22:6 11:20 [A]Deut 6:9 11:21 [a]Lit *the days of the heavens* [A]Prov 3:2; 4:10; 9:11 [B]Ps 72:5
11:22 [A]Deut 6:17 [B]Deut 11:1 [C]Deut 10:20 11:23 [A]Deut 4:38 [B]Deut 9:1 11:24 [a]I.e. the Mediterranean [A]Josh 1:3; 14:9 [B]Gen 15:18; Ex 23:31; Deut 1:7, 8
11:25 [A]Ex 23:27; Deut 7:24 11:26 [A]Deut 30:1, 19 11:27 [A]Deut 28:1-14 11:28 [a]Lit *to follow* [A]Deut 28:15-68 11:29 [A]Deut 27:12; Josh 8:33

11:6 Dathan and Abiram. These two sons of Eliab, of the tribe of Reuben, had rebelled against the authority of Moses, the Lord's chosen leader. The basis of their complaint was that Moses had brought Israel out of Egypt, a fertile and prosperous land, and not brought them into Canaan. Because of their rebellion against Moses, God had judged them by having the earth open and swallow them up (see Nu 16:12–14, 25–27, 31–33). God's judgment of their rebellion was spoken of here by Moses in the context of his contrast between the land of Egypt and the land of Canaan (vv. 10–12).

11:10, 11 the land, into which you are entering to possess it. The land of Canaan was different from Egypt. The land of Egypt depended upon the Nile River for its fertility. By contrast, the land of Canaan depended upon the rains that came from heaven for its fertility.

11:10 water it with your foot. Probably a reference to carrying water to each garden or the practice of indenting the ground with foot-dug channels through which irrigating water would flow.

11:13 Cf. 6:5.

11:14 He will give the rain for your land. Since the land of Canaan was dependent upon the rainfall for its fertility, God promised in response to Israel's obedience to give them the rain necessary for that fertility (vv. 16, 17). **the early and late rain.** The early rain was the autumn rain from Oct. to Jan. The latter rain was the spring rain which came through Mar./Apr.

11:18–21 For the children and all subsequent generations, God's great acts had not been seen "with their own eyes," as had been the case for that first generation. God's acts were to be "seen" for them in the Word of Scripture. It was to be in Moses' words that the acts of God would be put before the eyes of their children. The first priority, therefore, was given to Scripture as the means of teaching the law and grace of God (cf. 6:6–9).

11:24 Every place … your foot treads. In response to the obedience of Israel (vv. 22, 23), the Lord promised to give to Israel all of the land they personally traversed to the extent of the boundaries that He had given. This same promise was repeated in Jos 1:3–5. Had Israel obeyed God faithfully, her boundaries would have been enlarged to fulfill the promise made to Abraham (Ge 15:18). But because of Israel's disobedience, the complete promise of the whole land still remains, to be fulfilled in the future kingdom of Messiah (cf. Eze 36:8–38).

11:26–32 As a final motive for driving home the importance of obedience and trust in God, Moses gave instruction for a ceremony which the people were to carry out when they entered the land. They were to read the blessings and the curses of the covenant on Mt. Gerizim and Mt. Ebal (see 27:1–14) as they actually would do later (Jos 8:30–35).

Mount Gerizim and the curse on Mount Ebal. 30 Are
they not across the Jordan, west of the way toward
the sunset, in the land of the Canaanites who live
in the Arabah, opposite [A]Gilgal, beside [B]the [a]oaks
of Moreh? 31 For you are about to cross the Jordan
to go in to possess the land which the LORD your
God is giving you, and [A]you shall possess it and
live in it, 32 and you shall be careful to do all the
statutes and the judgments which I am setting
before you today.

LAWS OF THE SANCTUARY

12 "These are the statutes and the judgments
which you shall carefully observe in the land
which the LORD, the God of your fathers, has given
you to possess [a,A]as long as you live on the [b]earth.
2 You shall utterly destroy all the places where the
nations whom you shall dispossess serve their gods,
on the [A]high mountains and on the hills and under
every green tree. 3 [A]You shall tear down their altars and smash their *sacred* pillars and burn their
[a]Asherim with fire, and you shall cut down the
engraved images of their gods and [B]obliterate their
name from that place. 4 You shall not act like this
toward the LORD your God. 5 [A]But you shall seek
the LORD at the place which the LORD your God
will choose from all your tribes, to establish His
name there for His dwelling, and there you shall
come. 6 There you shall bring your burnt offerings,
your sacrifices, [A]your tithes, the [a]contribution of
your hand, your votive offerings, your freewill offerings, and the firstborn of your herd and of your
flock. 7 There also you and your households shall
eat before the LORD your God, and [A]rejoice in all
[a]your undertakings in which the LORD your God
has blessed you.
8 "You shall not do at all what we are doing here
today, [A]every man *doing* whatever is right in his own
eyes; 9 for you have not as yet come to [A]the resting
place and the [B]inheritance which the LORD your God
is giving you. 10 When you cross the Jordan and live
in the land which the LORD your God is giving you
to inherit, and [A]He gives you rest from all your enemies around *you* so that you live in security, 11 [A]then
it shall come about that the place in which the LORD
your God will choose for His name to dwell, there
you shall bring all that I command you: your burnt
offerings and your sacrifices, your tithes and the
[a]contribution of your hand, and all your choice votive
offerings which you will vow to the LORD. 12 And you

11:30 [a]Lit *terebinths* [A]Josh 4:19 [B]Gen 12:6 11:31 [A]Deut 17:14; Josh 21:43 12:1 [a]Lit *all the days* [b]Lit *ground* [A]Deut 4:9, 10; 1 Kin 8:40 12:2 [A]2 Kin 16:4; 17:10, 11 12:3 [a]I.e. wooden symbols of a female deity [A]Num 33:52; Deut 7:5; Judg 2:2 [B]Ex 23:13; Ps 16:4; Zech 13:2 12:5 [A]Ex 20:24; Deut 12:11, 13; 2 Chr 7:12; Ps 78:68 12:6 [a]Or *heave offering* [A]Deut 14:22 12:7 [a]Lit *the putting forth of your hand* [A]Lev 23:40; Deut 12:12, 18; 14:26; 28:47; Eccl 3:12, 13; 5:18-20 12:8 [A]Judg 17:6; 21:25 12:9 [A]Deut 3:20; 25:19; Ps 95:11 [B]Deut 4:21 12:10 [A]Josh 11:23 12:11 [a]Or *heave offering* [A]Deut 12:5; 15:20; 16:2; 17:8; 18:6

12:1–26:19 Having delineated the general principles of Israel's relationship with the Lord (5:1–11:32), Moses then explained specific laws that would help the people subordinate every area of their lives to the Lord. These instructions were given for Israel to "observe in the land" (12:1).

12:1–16:17 The first specific instructions that Moses gives deal with the public worship of the Lord by Israel as they come into the land.

12:1–32 Moses begins by repeating his instructions concerning what to do with the false worship centers after Israel had taken possession of the land of the Canaanites (see 7:1–6). They were to destroy them completely.

12:2 the high mountains … hills … every green tree. The Canaanite sanctuaries to be destroyed were located in places believed to have particular religious significance. The mountain or hill was thought to be the home of a god and by ascending the mountain, the worshiper was in some symbolic sense closer to the deity. Certain trees were considered to be sacred and symbolized fertility, a dominant theme in Canaanite religion.

12:3 their altars … pillars … engraved images. These were elements of Canaanite worship, which included human sacrifice (v. 31). If they remained, the people might mix the worship of God with those places (v. 4).

12:5 the place which the LORD your God will choose. Cf. vv. 11, 18, 21. Various places of worship were chosen after the people settled in Canaan, such as Mt. Ebal (27:1–8; Jos 8:30–35), Shechem (Jos 24:1–28) and Shiloh (Jos 18:1), which was the center of worship through the period of Judges (Jdg 21:19). The tabernacle, the Lord's dwelling place, was located in Canaan, where the Lord chose to dwell. The central importance of the tabernacle was in direct contrast to the multiple places (see v. 2) where the Canaanites practiced their worship of idols. Eventually, the tabernacle was brought to Jerusalem by David (cf. 2Sa 6:12–19).

12:6 *See notes on Lv 1–7* for descriptions of these various ceremonies.

12:7 eat … rejoice. Some of the offerings were shared by the priests, Levites, and the worshipers (cf. Lv 7:15–18). The worship of God was to be holy and reverent, yet full of joy.

12:8 every man *doing* whatever is right in his own eyes. There seems to have been some laxity in the offering of the sacrifices in the wilderness which was not to be allowed when Israel came into the Promised Land. This self-centered attitude became a major problem in the time of Judges (cf. Jdg 17:6; 21:25).

ISRAEL'S CALENDAR

Month Pre-/Post-Exilic	Of Year Sacred/Civil	Modern Equivalent	Characteristics
Abib/Nisan	1/7	March/April	Latter Rains; Barley Harvest
Ziv/Iyyar	2/8	April/May	Dry Season Begins
Sivan	3/9	May/June	Wheat Harvest; Early Figs
Tammuz	4/10	June/July	Hot Season; Grape Harvest
Ab	5/11	July/August	Olive Harvest
Elul	6/12	August/September	Dates, Summer Figs
Ethanim/Tishri	7/1	September/October	Former Rains; Plowing Time
Bul/Heshvan	8/2	October/November	Rains; Wheat, Barley Sown
Chislev	9/3	November/December	Winter Begins
Tebeth	10/4	December/January	Rains
Shebat	11/5	January/February	Almond Trees Blossom
Adar	12/6	February/March	Latter Rains Begin; Citrus Harvest

shall [A]rejoice before the LORD your God, you and your
sons and daughters, your male and female servants,
and the [B]Levite who is within your gates, since [C]he
has no portion or inheritance with you.
13 "[A]Be careful that you do not offer your burnt
offerings in every *cultic* place you see, 14 but in the
place which the LORD chooses in one of your tribes,
there you shall offer your burnt offerings, and there
you shall do all that I command you.
15 "[A]However, you may slaughter and eat meat
within any of your gates, [a]whatever you desire, according to the blessing of the LORD your God which
He has given you; the unclean and the clean may
eat of it, as of [B]the gazelle and the deer. 16 [A]Only you
shall not eat the blood; [B]you are to pour it out on
the ground like water. 17 [A]You are not allowed to eat
within your gates the tithe of your grain or new wine
or oil, or the firstborn of your herd or flock, or any of
your votive offerings which you vow, or your freewill
offerings, or the [a]contribution of your hand. 18 But
[A]you shall eat them before the LORD your God in [B]the
place which the LORD your God will choose, you and
your son and daughter, and your male and female
servants, and the [C]Levite who is within your gates;
and you shall [D]rejoice before the LORD your God in
all [a]your undertakings. 19 [A]Be careful that you do not
forsake the Levite [a]as long as you live in your land.
20 "When the LORD your God extends your border [A]as He has promised you, and you say, 'I will
eat meat,' because [a]you desire to eat meat, *then*
you may eat meat, [b]whatever you desire. 21 If the
place which the LORD your God chooses to put His
name is too far from you, then you may slaughter
of your herd and flock which the LORD has given
you, as I have commanded you; and you may eat
within your gates [a]whatever you desire. 22 Just as
a gazelle or a deer is eaten, so you will eat it; the
unclean and the clean alike may eat of it. 23 Only
be sure [A]not to eat the blood, for the blood is the
[a]life, and you shall not eat the [a]life with the flesh.
24 You shall not eat it; you shall pour it out on the
ground like water. 25 You shall not eat it, so that [A]it
may be well with you and your sons after you, for
[B]you will be doing what is right in the sight of the
LORD. 26 [A]Only your holy things which you may have
and your votive offerings, you shall take and go to
the place which the LORD chooses. 27 And [A]you shall
offer your burnt offerings, the flesh and the blood,
on the altar of the LORD your God; and the blood
of your sacrifices shall be poured out on the altar
of the LORD your God, and [B]you shall eat the flesh.
28 "Be careful to listen to all these words which I
command you, so that [A]it may be well with you and
your sons after you forever, for you will be doing what
is good and right in the sight of the LORD your God.
29 "When [A]the LORD your God cuts off before you
the nations which you are going in to dispossess,
and you dispossess them and dwell in their land,
30 beware that you are not ensnared [a]to follow them,
after they are destroyed before you, and that you do
not inquire after their gods, saying, 'How do these
nations serve their gods, that I also may do likewise?'
31 [A]You shall not behave thus toward the LORD your
God, for every abominable act which the LORD hates
they have done for their gods; for [B]they even burn
their sons and daughters in the fire to their gods.
32 "[a,A]Whatever I command you, you shall be careful to do; [B]you shall not add to nor take away from it.

SHUN IDOLATRY

13 "[a,A]If a prophet or a dreamer of dreams arises
among you and gives you a sign or a wonder,
2 and the sign or the wonder comes true, concerning which he spoke to you, saying, '[A]Let us go after
other gods (whom you have not known) and let
us serve them,' 3 you shall not listen to the words

12:12 [A]Deut 12:7 [B]Deut 12:18, 19; 26:11-13 [C]Deut 10:9; 14:29 12:13 [A]Deut 12:5, 11 12:15 [a]Lit *in every desire of your soul* [A]Deut 12:20-23 [B]Deut 12:22; 14:5; 15:22 12:16 [A]Gen 9:4; Lev 7:26; 17:10-12; 1 Sam 14:33f; Acts 15:20, 29 [B]Deut 15:23 12:17 [a]Lit *heave offering* [A]Deut 12:26 12:18 [a]Lit *the putting forth of your hand* [A]Deut 14:23 [B]Deut 12:5 [C]Deut 12:12 [D]Deut 12:7; Eccl 3:12f; 5:18-20 12:19 [a]Lit *all your days upon your land* [A]Deut 14:27 12:20 [a]Lit *your soul desires* [b]Lit *in every desire of your soul* [A]Gen 15:18; Deut 11:24; 19:8 12:21 [a]Lit *in every desire of your soul* 12:23 [a]Lit *soul* [A]Gen 9:4; Lev 17:10-14; Deut 12:16 12:25 [A]Deut 4:40; Is 3:10 [B]Ex 15:26; 1 Kin 11:38 12:26 [A]Num 5:9f; 18:19; Deut 12:17 12:27 [A]Lev 1:9, 13 [B]Lev 3:1-17 12:28 [A]Deut 4:40; Eccl 8:12 12:29 [A]Josh 23:4 12:30 [a]Lit *after them* 12:31 [A]Deut 9:5 [B]Lev 18:21; Deut 18:10; Ps 106:37; Jer 32:35 12:32 [a]Lit *Everything that* [A]Deut 4:2; Josh 1:7 [B]Prov 30:6; Rev 22:18 13:1 [a]Ch 13:2 in Heb [A]Matt 24:24; Mark 13:22; 2 Thess 2:9 13:2 [A]Deut 13:6, 13

12:15 slaughter … within any of your gates. While sacrificial offerings were brought to the appointed centers for worship as well as the central sanctuary, the killing and eating of meat for regular eating could be engaged in anywhere. The only restriction on eating nonsacrificial meat was the prohibition of the blood and the fat.

12:17–19 All sacrifices and offerings had to be brought to the place chosen by God.

12:21 If the place … is too far. Moses envisioned the enlarging of the borders of Israel according to God's promise. This meant that people would live farther and farther away from the central sanctuary. Except for sacrificial animals, all others could be slaughtered and eaten close to home.

12:23 the blood is the life. See Ge 9:4–6 and Lv 17:10–14. The blood symbolized life. By refraining from eating blood, the Israelite demonstrated respect for life and ultimately for the Creator of life. Blood, representing life, was the ransom price for sins. So blood was sacred and not to be consumed by the people. This relates to atonement in Lv 16; Heb 9:12–14; 1Pe 1:18, 19; 1Jn 1:7.

12:29, 30 Cf. 2Co 6:14–7:1, where Paul gives a similar exhortation.

12:31 they even burn their sons and daughters. One of the detestable practices of Canaanite worship was the burning of their sons and daughters in the fire as sacrifices to Molech (cf. Lv 18:21; 20:2–5; 1Ki 11:7; 2Ki 23:10; Jer 32:35).

12:32 you shall not add to nor take away. *See note on 4:2.*

13:1–18 After the general prohibition of involvement in Canaanite worship (12:29–31), Moses discussed 3 ways in which the temptation to idolatry was likely to come to Israel: 1) through a false prophet (vv. 1–5); 2) through a family member (vv. 6–11); or 3) through apostates in some Canaanite city (vv. 12–18).

13:2 the sign or the wonder comes true. Miraculous signs alone were never meant to be a test of truth (cf. Pharaoh's magicians in Ex 7–10). A prophet or a dreamer's prediction may come true, but if his message contradicted God's commands, the people were to trust God and His Word rather than such experience. **Let us go after other gods.** The explicit temptation was to renounce allegiance to the Lord and go after other gods. The result of this apostasy would be the serving of these false gods by worshiping them, which would be in direct contradiction to the first commandment (5:7).

13:3 the LORD your God is testing you. God, in His sovereignty, allowed the false prophets to entice the people to apostasy to test the true disposition of the hearts of the Israelites. And while the temptation was dangerous, the overcoming of that temptation would strengthen the people in their love for God and obedience to His commandments. Cf. 6:5.

of that prophet or that dreamer of dreams; for the
LORD your God is [A]testing you to find out if [B]you
love the LORD your God with all your heart and
with all your soul. 4 [A]You shall follow the LORD your
God and fear Him; and you shall keep His commandments, listen to His voice, serve Him, and
[B]cling to Him. 5 But that prophet or that dreamer of
dreams shall be [A]put to death, because he has [a]coun-
seled [b]rebellion against the LORD your God who
brought you from the land of Egypt and redeemed
you from the house of [c]slavery, [B]to seduce you from
the way in which the LORD your God commanded
you to walk. [C]So you shall purge the evil from
among you.
6 "[A]If your brother, your mother's son, or your
son or daughter, or the wife [a]you cherish, or your
friend who is as your own soul, entice you secretly,
saying, '[B]Let us go and serve other gods' (whom
neither you nor your fathers have known, 7 of the
gods of the peoples who are around you, near you
or far from you, from one end of the earth to the
other end), 8 [A]you shall not yield to him or listen
to him; [B]and your eye shall not pity him, nor shall
you spare or conceal him. 9 [A]But you shall surely kill
him; [B]your hand shall be first against him to put
him to death, and afterwards the hand of all the
people. 10 So you shall stone him [a]to death because
he has sought [A]to seduce you from the LORD your
God who brought you out from the land of Egypt,
out of the house of [b]slavery. 11 Then [A]all Israel will
hear and be afraid, and will never again do such a
wicked thing among you.
12 "If you hear in one of your cities, which the
LORD your God is giving you to live in, *anyone* saying *that* 13 some worthless men have gone out from
among you and have seduced the inhabitants of
their city, saying, '[A]Let us go and serve other gods'
(whom you have not known), 14 then you shall investigate and search out and inquire thoroughly.
If it is true *and* the matter established that this
abomination has been done among you, 15 [A]you
shall surely strike the inhabitants of that city with
the edge of the sword, [a]utterly destroying it and
all that is in it and its cattle with the edge of the
sword. 16 [A]Then you shall gather all its booty into
the middle of its open square and burn the city
and all its booty with fire as a whole burnt offering to the LORD your God; and it shall be a [a,B]ruin
forever. It shall never be rebuilt. 17 Nothing from
that which is put under the ban shall cling to your
hand, in order that the LORD may turn from [A]His
burning anger and [B]show mercy to you, and have
compassion on you and [C]make you increase, just
[D]as He has sworn to your fathers, 18 [a]if you will listen to the voice of the LORD your God, [b]keeping all
His commandments which I am commanding you
today, [c]and doing what is right in the sight of the
LORD your God.

13:3 [A]Ex 20:20; Deut 8:2, 16; 1 Cor 11:19 [B]Deut 6:5 13:4 [A]2 Kin 23:3; 2 Chr 34:31; 2 John 6 [B]Deut 10:20 13:5 [a]Lit *spoken* [b]Lit *turning aside* [c]Lit *slaves* [A]Deut 13:9, 15; 17:5; 1 Kin 18:40 [B]Deut 4:19; 13:10 [C]1 Cor 5:13 13:6 [a]Lit *of your bosom* [A]Deut 17:2-7; 29:18 [B]Deut 13:2 13:8 [A]Prov 1:10 [B]Deut 7:2 13:9 [A]Deut 13:5 [B]Lev 24:14; Deut 17:7 13:10 [a]Lit *with stones so that he dies* [b]Lit *slaves* [A]Deut 13:5 13:11 [A]Deut 19:20 13:13 [A]Deut 13:2 13:15 [a]Or *putting it under the ban* [A]Deut 13:5 13:16 [a]Lit *mound* [A]Deut 7:25, 26 [B]Josh 8:28; Is 17:1; 25:2; Jer 49:2 13:17 [A]Ex 32:12; Num 25:4 [B]Deut 30:3 [C]Deut 7:13 [D]Gen 22:17; 26:4, 24; 28:14 13:18 [a]Or *for* [b]Lit *to keep* [c]Lit *to do*

13:5 purge the evil from among you. The object of the severe penalty was not only the punishment of the evildoer, but also the preservation of the community. Paul must have had this text in mind when he gave a similar command to the Corinthian church (cf. 1Co 5:13; also Dt 17:7; 19:19; 21:21; 22:21; 24:7).

13:6 your brother … friend. The temptation to idolatry might also come from a member of the immediate family or from an intimate friend. While the temptation from the false prophet would be made openly based on a sign or wonder, this temptation would be made secretly and would be based upon the intimacy of relationship.

13:10 stone him to death. The convicting witness cast the first stone. Love for family and friends must not take precedence over devotion to God (cf. Lk 14:26).

13:12 one of your cities. He has in mind an entire city of Canaan given by God to the Israelites, yet enticed to idolatry.

13:13 worthless men. Lit. "sons of Belial (worthlessness)." *Belial* is used of Satan in 2Co 6:15. It is a way to describe evil, worthless, or wicked men (Jdg 19:22; 1Sa 2:12; 1Ki 21:10, 13).

THE DEATH PENALTY

Crime	Scripture Reference
1. Premeditated Murder	Genesis 9:6; Exodus 21:12–14, 22, 23
2. Kidnapping	Exodus 21:16; Deuteronomy 24:7
3. Striking or Cursing Parents	Exodus 21:15; Leviticus 20:9; Proverbs 20:20; Matthew 15:4; Mark 7:10
4. Magic and Divination	Exodus 22:18
5. Bestiality	Exodus 22:19; Leviticus 20:15, 16
6. Sacrificing to False Gods	Exodus 22:20
7. Profaning the Sabbath	Exodus 35:2; Numbers 15:32–36
8. Offering Human Sacrifice	Leviticus 20:2
9. Adultery	Leviticus 20:10–21; Deuteronomy 22:22
10. Incest	Leviticus 20:11, 12, 14
11. Homosexuality	Leviticus 20:13
12. Blasphemy	Leviticus 24:11–14, 16, 23
13. False Prophecy	Deuteronomy 13:1–10
14. Incorrigible Rebelliousness	Deuteronomy 17:12; 21:18–21
15. Fornication	Deuteronomy 22:20, 21
16. Rape of Betrothed Virgin	Deuteronomy 22:23–27

CLEAN AND UNCLEAN ANIMALS

14 "You are [A]the sons of the LORD your God; [B]you
shall not cut yourselves nor [a]shave your forehead for the sake of the dead. 2 For you are [A]a holy
people to the LORD your God, and the LORD has chosen you to be a [B]people for His [a]own possession out
of all the peoples who are on the face of the earth.
3 "[A]You shall not eat any detestable thing. 4 [A]These
are the animals which you may eat: the ox, the sheep,
the goat, 5 [a]the deer, the gazelle, the roebuck, the wild
goat, the ibex, the antelope and the mountain sheep.
6 Any animal that divides the hoof and has the hoof
split in [a]two *and* [b]chews the cud, among the animals,
that you may eat. 7 Nevertheless, you are not to eat of
these among those which [a]chew the cud, or among
those that divide the hoof in [b]two: the camel and the
[c]rabbit and the [d]shaphan, for though they [a]chew the
cud, they do not divide the hoof; they are unclean for
you. 8 The pig, because it divides the hoof but *does*
not *chew* the cud, it is unclean for you. You shall
not eat any of their flesh nor touch their carcasses.
9 "These you may eat of all that are in water: anything that has fins and scales you may eat, 10 but
anything that does not have fins and scales you
shall not eat; it is unclean for you.
11 "You may eat any clean bird. 12 But [A]these are
the ones which you shall not eat: the [a]eagle and
the vulture and the [b]buzzard, 13 and the red kite,
the falcon, and the kite in their kinds, 14 and every
raven in its kind, 15 and the ostrich, the owl, the sea
gull, and the hawk in their kinds, 16 the little owl, the
[a]great owl, the white owl, 17 the pelican, the carrion
vulture, the cormorant, 18 the stork, and the heron
in their kinds, and the hoopoe and the bat. 19 And all
the [a]teeming life with wings are unclean to you; they
shall not be eaten. 20 You may eat any clean bird.
21 "[A]You shall not eat anything which dies *of itself*.
You may give it to the alien who is in your [a]town, so
that he may eat it, or you may sell it to a foreigner,
for you are [B]a holy people to the LORD your God.
[C]You shall not boil a young goat in its mother's milk.
22 "You [A]shall surely tithe all the produce from
[a]what you sow, which comes out of the field every
year. 23 You shall eat in the presence of the LORD
your God, [A]at the place where He chooses to establish His name, the tithe of your grain, your new
wine, your oil, and the firstborn of your herd and
your flock, so that you may [B]learn to fear the LORD
your God always. 24 If the [a]distance is so great
for you that you are not able to [b]bring *the tithe*,
since the place where the LORD your God chooses
[A]to set His name is too far away from you when
the LORD your God blesses you, 25 then you shall
[a]exchange *it* for money, and bind the money in
your hand and go to the place which the LORD
your God chooses. 26 You may spend the money for
whatever your [a]heart desires: for oxen, or sheep,
or wine, or strong drink, or whatever your [a]heart
[b]desires; and [A]there you shall eat in the presence
of the LORD your God and rejoice, you and your
household. 27 Also you shall not neglect [A]the Levite who is in your [a]town, [B]for he has no portion
or inheritance among you.
28 "[A]At the end of every third year you shall bring
out all the tithe of your produce in that year, and
shall deposit *it* in your [a]town. 29 The Levite, [A]because
he has no portion or inheritance among you, and
[B]the alien, the [a]orphan and the widow who are in
your [b]town, shall come and [C]eat and be satisfied,
in order that [D]the LORD your God may bless you in
all the work of your hand which you do.

THE SABBATIC YEAR

15 "[A]At the end of *every* seven years you shall
[a]grant a remission *of debts*. 2 This is the manner of remission: every creditor shall release what

14:1 [a]Lit *make a baldness between your eyes* [A]Rom 8:16; 9:8, 26; Gal 3:26; 1 John 3:1 [B]Lev 19:28; 21:5; Jer 16:6; 41:5 14:2 [a]Or *special treasure* [A]Lev 20:26; Deut 7:6; Rom 12:1 [B]Ex 19:5; Deut 4:20; 26:18; Titus 2:14; 1 Pet 2:9 14:3 [A]Ezek 4:14 14:4 [A]Lev 11:2-45; Acts 10:14 14:5 [a]Exact identification of these animals is uncertain 14:6 [a]Lit *two hoofs* [b]Lit *brings up* 14:7 [a]Lit *brings up* [b]Lit *a cleaving* [c]Or *hare* [d]A small, shy, furry animal *(Hyrax syriacus)* found in the peninsula of the Sinai, northern Israel, and the region round the Dead Sea; KJV *coney*, orig NASB *rock-badger* 14:12 [a]Or *vulture* [b]Or *black vulture* [A]Lev 11:13 14:16 [a]Or *great horned owl* 14:19 [a]I.e. flying insects 14:21 [a]Lit *gates* [A]Lev 17:15; 22:8; Ezek 4:14; 44:31 [B]Deut 14:2 [C]Ex 23:19; 34:26 14:22 [a]Lit *your seed* [A]Lev 27:30; Deut 12:6, 17; Neh 10:37 14:23 [A]Deut 12:5 [B]Deut 4:10; Ps 2:11; 111:10; 147:11; Is 8:13; Jer 32:38-40 14:24 [a]Lit *way* [b]Lit *carry* it [A]Deut 12:5, 21 14:25 [a]Lit *give in money* 14:26 [a]Lit *soul* [b]Lit *asks of you* [A]Deut 12:7 14:27 [a]Lit *gates* [A]Deut 12:12 [B]Num 18:20; Deut 10:9; 18:12 14:28 [a]Lit *gates* [A]Deut 26:12 14:29 [a]Or *fatherless* [b]Lit *gates* [A]Deut 10:9 [B]Deut 16:11, 14; 24:19-21; 26:12; Ps 94:6; Is 1:17 [C]Deut 6:11 [D]Deut 15:10; Mal 3:10 15:1 [a]Lit *make a release* [A]Deut 31:10

14:1 you shall not cut … nor shave. The two practices, lacerating the body and shaving the head, were associated with mourning customs of foreign religions. Though the actions could in themselves appear to be innocent, they were associated with practices and beliefs reprehensible to the Lord. Cf. Lv 19:27, 28; 21:5; 1Ki 18:28; 1Co 3:17.

14:2 you are a holy people to the LORD your God. Again comes the important reminder of their peculiar relation to God. Over 250 times, Moses emphasized to Israel, "the LORD *your* God."

14:3–21 This summary of clean and unclean animals is drawn from the list in Lv 11:2–23. The ground for the allowances and prohibitions of the eating of certain animals was that Israel was to be holy to the Lord (vv. 2, 21). These special dietary laws were to separate them from social mixing with pagan idolatrous people, to prevent them from being lured into idolatry.

14:21 anything which dies *of itself*. Eating the meat of an animal that had died a natural death was prohibited because the animal had not been killed in the proper fashion and the blood drained out (*see note on 12:23*). The animal, however, could be eaten by "the alien who is in your town." *See notes on Lv 17:10–16.* **a young goat in its mother's milk.** This prohibition no doubt reflected a common practice in Canaanite religion which was superstitiously observed hoping that fertility and productivity would be increased (cf. Ex 23:19; 34:26).

14:22 tithe. A tenth. The tithe specified in these verses was only that of the agricultural produce which the land would provide. This was a second tithe to be used for the celebration of convocations of worship at the sanctuary (vv. 23–26), in addition to the first tithe mentioned, known as the Levitical tithe, which went to support the priests and Levites who served the people. Cf. Lv 27:30–33 and Nu 18:21–32. A third welfare tithe was also offered every 3 years (*see notes on 14:28; 26:12*).

14:23 eat in the presence of the LORD. The tithe was to be taken to the central sanctuary where the worshipers were to eat a portion in fellowship with the Lord.

14:24 If the distance is so great. If certain Israelites lived too far from the sanctuary for it to be practical for them to carry their agricultural tithe there, then they could exchange the tithe locally for silver and subsequently convert the money back into substance at the sanctuary.

14:26 wine, or strong drink. *See notes on Pr 20:1; 23:29–35; 31:4–7.*

14:28 At the end of every third year. In year 3 and year 6 of the 7 year sabbatical cycle, rather than taking this tithe to the central sanctuary, it was instead stored up within the individual cities in the land. This tithe was used to feed the Levites, the orphan, the widow, and the stranger (i.e., foreigner) who lived with the Israelites. Cf. 26:12; Nu 18:26–32.

15:1 At the end of *every* seven years … grant a remission *of debts*. The sabbatical

he has loaned to his neighbor; he shall not exact
it of his neighbor and his brother, because the
LORD'S remission has been proclaimed. 3 [A]From
a foreigner you may exact *it,* but your hand shall
release whatever of yours is with your brother.
4 However, there will be no poor among you, since
[A]the LORD will surely bless you in the land which
the LORD your God is giving you as an inheritance
to possess, 5 if only you listen obediently to the
voice of the LORD your God, to observe carefully
all this commandment which I am commanding
you today. 6 [A]For the LORD your God will bless
you as He has promised you, and you will lend
to many nations, but you will not borrow; and
you will rule over many nations, but they will
not rule over you.

7 "If there is [A]a poor man with you, one of your
brothers, in any of your [a]towns in your land which
the LORD your God is giving you, [B]you shall not
harden your heart, nor close your hand from your
poor brother; 8 but [A]you shall freely open your hand
to him, and shall generously lend him sufficient for
his need *in* whatever he lacks. 9 Beware that there is
no base [a]thought in your heart, saying, '[A]The seventh
year, the year of remission, is near,' and [B]your eye is
hostile toward your poor brother, and you give him
nothing; then he [C]may cry to the LORD against you,
and it will be a sin in you. 10 You shall generously
give to him, and your heart shall not be grieved
when you give to him, because [A]for this thing the
LORD your God will bless you in all your work and
in all [a]your undertakings. 11 [A]For the poor will never
cease *to be* [a]in the land; therefore I command you,
saying, 'You shall freely open your hand to your
brother, to your needy and poor in your land.'

12 "[A]If your [a]kinsman, a Hebrew man or woman,
is sold to you, then he shall serve you six years,
but in the seventh year you shall set him [b]free.
13 When you set him [a]free, you shall not send him
away empty-handed. 14 You shall furnish him liberally from your flock and from your threshing
floor and from your wine vat; you shall give to
him as the LORD your God has blessed you. 15 You
shall remember that you were a slave in the land
of Egypt, and the LORD your God redeemed you;
therefore I command you [a]this today. 16 It shall
come about [A]if he says to you, 'I will not go out
from you,' because he loves you and your household, since he fares well with you; 17 then you shall
take an awl and pierce it through his ear into the
door, and he shall be your servant forever. Also
you shall do likewise to your maidservant.

18 "It shall not seem hard to you when you set
him [a]free, for he has given you six years *with*
[b]double the service of a hired man; so the LORD
your God will bless you in whatever you do.

19 "[A]You shall consecrate to the LORD your God
all the firstborn males that are born of your herd
and of your flock; you shall not work with the
firstborn of your herd, nor shear the firstborn
of your flock. 20 [A]You and your household shall
eat it every year before the LORD your God in
the place which the LORD chooses. 21 [A]But if it
has any [a]defect, *such as* lameness or blindness,
or any serious [a]defect, you shall not sacrifice it
to the LORD your God. 22 You shall eat it within
your gates; [A]the unclean and the clean alike *may*
eat it, as [A]a gazelle or a deer. 23 Only [A]you shall
not eat its blood; you are to pour it out on the
ground like water.

15:3 [A]Deut 23:20 15:4 [A]Deut 28:8 15:6 [A]Deut 28:12, 13 15:7 [a]Lit *gates* [A]Lev 25:35; Deut 15:11 [B]1 John 3:17 15:8 [A]Matt 5:42; Luke 6:34; Gal 2:10 15:9 [a]Lit *word* [A]Deut 15:1 [B]Matt 20:15 [C]Ex 22:23; Deut 24:15; Job 34:28; Ps 12:5; James 5:4 15:10 [a]Lit *the putting forth of your hand* [A]Deut 14:29; Ps 41:1; Prov 22:9 15:11 [a]Lit *in the midst of* [A]Matt 26:11; Mark 14:7; John 12:8 15:12 [a]Lit *brother* [b]Lit *free from you* [A]Ex 21:2-6; Lev 25:39-43; Jer 34:14 15:13 [a]Lit *free from you* 15:15 [a]Lit *this thing* 15:16 [A]Ex 21:5, 6 15:18 [a]Lit *free from you* [b]Lit *double the amount* 15:19 [A]Ex 13:2, 12 15:20 [A]Lev 7:15-18; Deut 12:5; 14:23 15:21 [a]Lit *blemish* [A]Lev 22:19-25; Deut 17:1 15:22 [A]Deut 12:15, 16, 22 15:23 [A]Gen 9:4; Lev 7:26; 17:10; 19:26; Deut 12:16, 23

year was established and described in Ex 23:10, 11 and Lv 25:1–7. However, while these texts stated that in the seventh year the land was to lie fallow without any crops being planted, only here did Moses prescribe a cancellation of debts. On the basis of vv. 9–11, the debt was canceled completely and permanently, not just a cancellation of payment during that year.

15:3 From a foreigner you may exact *it*. The provision for sabbatical release of debts was not intended for one who stayed only temporarily in the land. That foreigner was still responsible to pay his debts.

15:4 there will be no poor. Idealistically, there was the possibility that poverty would be eradicated in the land "since the LORD will surely bless you in the land." The fullness of that blessing, however, would be contingent on the completeness of Israel's obedience. Thus, vv. 4–6 were an encouragement to strive for a reduction of poverty while at the same time they stressed the abundance of the provision God would make in the Promised Land.

15:8 generously lend him sufficient for his need. The attitude of the Israelites toward the poor in their community was to be one of warmth and generosity. The poor were given whatever was necessary to meet their needs, even with the realization that such "loans" would never need to be paid back. *See note on 23:19, 20.*

15:11 For the poor will never cease *to be* in the land. Realistically (in contrast to v. 4), the disobedience toward the Lord on Israel's part meant that there would always be poor people in the land of Israel. Jesus repeated this truism in Mt 26:11.

15:12 If your kinsman … is sold. In the context of vv. 1–11, the reason for the sale would be default, an alternative repayment of a debt, and a period of servitude would substitute for that repayment. The Hebrew slave would serve his master 6 years following the sale with freedom being declared in the seventh year.

15:13 you shall not send him away empty-handed. When a slave had completed his time of service, his former owner was to make ample provision for him so that he would not begin his state of new freedom in destitution.

15:15 remember. The Israelites, formerly enslaved in Egypt, were to treat their own slaves as God had treated them.

15:17 an awl … through his ear. In certain circumstances, a slave might prefer to remain with the family after the required 6 years of servitude. He would then be marked with a hole in his ear and become a servant forever (cf. Ex 21:5, 6).

15:18 double the service of a hired man. The slave was worth double to his owner because the owner not only had the service of the slave, but he also did not have to pay out anything for that service as he would have for a hired hand.

15:19 consecrate … all the firstborn. The firstborn was the first to be produced during the bearing life of an animal. It was to be consecrated to the Lord. The firstborn would be sacrificed annually, and the offerers would participate in the sacrificial meal (see 14:23). **nor shear.** The firstborn ox or bull was not to be worked, nor the firstborn sheep or goat shorn in the time before their sacrifice to the Lord.

15:21 any defect. An imperfect firstborn animal was not acceptable as a sacrifice. It was to be treated like any other nonsacrificial animal (see 12:15, 16) and eaten at home (cf. Mal 1:6–14).

THE FEASTS OF PASSOVER, OF WEEKS, AND OF BOOTHS

16 "Observe [A]the month of Abib and [a,B]celebrate
the Passover to the LORD your God, for in the
month of Abib the LORD your God brought you out
of Egypt by night. 2 You shall sacrifice the Passover
to the LORD your God from the flock and the herd, in
the place where the LORD chooses to establish His
name. 3 [A]You shall not eat leavened bread with it;
seven days you shall eat with it unleavened bread,
the bread of affliction (for you came out of the land
of Egypt in haste), so that you may remember [B]all
the days of your life the day when you came out of
the land of Egypt. 4 For seven days no leaven shall
be seen with you in all your territory, and [A]none
of the flesh which you sacrifice on the evening of
the first day shall remain overnight until morning.
5 You are not allowed to sacrifice the Passover in any
of your [a]towns which the LORD your God is giving
you; 6 but [A]at the place where the LORD your God
chooses to establish His name, you shall sacrifice
the Passover in the evening at sunset, at the time
that you came out of Egypt. 7 You shall [A]cook and
eat *it* in the place which the LORD your God chooses.
In the morning you are to return to your tents. 8 Six
days you shall eat unleavened bread, and [A]on the
seventh day there shall be [B]a solemn assembly to
the LORD your God; you shall do no work *on it.*

9 "[A]You shall count seven weeks for yourself; you
shall begin to count seven weeks from the time you
begin to put the sickle to the standing grain. 10 Then
you shall [a]celebrate the Feast of Weeks to the LORD
your God with a tribute of a freewill offering of your
hand, which you shall give just as the LORD your God
blesses you; 11 and you shall [A]rejoice before the LORD
your God, you and your son and your daughter and
your male and female servants and [B]the Levite who is
in your [a]town, and [C]the stranger and the [b]orphan and
the widow who are in your midst, in the place where
the LORD your God chooses to establish His name.
12 [A]You shall remember that you were a slave in Egypt,
and you shall be careful to observe these statutes.

13 "[A]You shall [a]celebrate the Feast of Booths seven
days after you have gathered in from your threshing
floor and your wine vat; 14 and you shall [A]rejoice in
your feast, you and your son and your daughter and
your male and female servants and the Levite and
the stranger and the [a]orphan and the widow who
are in your [b]towns. 15 Seven days you shall celebrate
a feast to the LORD your God in the place which the
LORD chooses, because the LORD your God will bless
you in all your produce and in all the work of your
hands, so that you will be altogether joyful.

16 "[A]Three times in a year all your males shall appear before the LORD your God in the place which
He chooses, at the Feast of Unleavened Bread and
at the Feast of Weeks and at the Feast of Booths,
and [B]they shall not appear before the LORD empty-handed. 17 Every man [a]shall give as he is able,
according to the blessing of the LORD your God
which He has given you.

18 "You shall appoint for yourself judges and officers in all your [a]towns which the LORD your God is
giving you, according to your tribes, and they shall
judge the people with righteous judgment. 19 [A]You
shall not distort justice; [B]you shall not [a]be partial,
and [C]you shall not take a bribe, for a bribe blinds
the eyes of the wise and perverts the words of the
righteous. 20 Justice, *and only* justice, you shall pursue, that [A]you may live and possess the land which
the LORD your God is giving you.

21 "[A]You shall not plant for yourself an [a]Asherah
of any kind of tree beside the altar of the LORD your
God, which you shall make for yourself. 22 [A]You shall
not set up for yourself a *sacred* pillar which the
LORD your God hates.

16:1 [a]Lit *perform* [A]Ex 12:2 [B]Num 28:16 16:3 [A]Ex 12:8, 15, 19, 39; 13:3; 34:18 [B]Deut 4:9 16:4 [A]Ex 12:8, 10; 34:25 16:5 [a]Lit *gates* 16:6 [A]Deut 12:5 16:7 [A]Ex 12:8; 2 Chr 35:13 16:8 [A]Num 28:25 [B]Ex 12:16; 13:6; Lev 23:8, 36 16:9 [A]Ex 23:16; 34:22; Lev 23:15; Num 28:26 16:10 [a]Lit *perform* 16:11 [a]Lit *gates* [b]Or *fatherless* [A]Deut 12:7 [B]Deut 12:12 [C]Deut 14:29 16:12 [A]Deut 15:15 16:13 [a]Lit *perform* [A]Lev 23:34-43 16:14 [a]Or *fatherless* [b]Lit *gates* [A]Deut 16:11 16:16 [A]Ex 23:14-17; 34:23, 24 [B]Ex 34:20 16:17 [a]Lit *according to the gift of his hand* 16:18 [a]Lit *gates* 16:19 [a]Lit *regard persons* [A]Ex 23:2; Lev 19:15; Deut 1:17; 10:17 [B]Prov 24:23 [C]Ex 23:8; Prov 17:23; Eccl 7:7 16:20 [A]Deut 4:1 16:21 [a]I.e. wooden symbol of a female deity [A]Deut 7:5; 2 Kin 17:16; 21:3; 2 Chr 33:3 16:22 [A]Lev 26:1

16:1–17 Moses discusses the feasts during which all the men over 20 years of age were to appear before the Lord at the central worship site. If possible, their families were to go as well (see vv. 11, 14). Cf. Ex 23; Lv 23; Nu 28, 29.

16:1 the month of Abib. Abib (which was later called Nisan) occurred in the spring (approximately Mar. or Apr.).

16:1–8 celebrate the Passover. The offering of Passover itself was to be only a lamb (Ex 12:3–11). However, additional offerings were also to be made during the Passover and the subsequent 7 days of the Feast of Unleavened Bread (cf. Ex 12:15–20; 13:3–10; Lv 23:6–8; Nu 28:19–25). Therefore, sacrifices from both the flock and the herd were used in keeping the Passover.

16:3 remember. This was the key word at Passover time as it is for the Lord's Supper today (cf. Mt 26:26–30; Lk 22:14–19; 1Co 11:23–26).

16:5, 6 at the place ... God chooses. The Passover sacrifices could no longer be slain by every family in their house (see Ex 12:46). From this point on, the Passover sacrifices must be killed at the central place of worship.

16:7 In the morning ... return to your tents. After the sacrifice of the Passover animal and the eating and the night vigil which followed, in the morning the people would return to their lodgings or tents where they were staying for the duration of the feast.

16:10–12 the Feast of Weeks. Seven weeks later this second feast was celebrated. It was also called the "Feast of the Harvest" (Ex 23:16) or the "day of the first fruits" (Lv 23:9–22; Nu 28:26–31) and later came to be known as "Pentecost" (Ac 2:1). With the grain harvest completed, this one-day festival was a time of rejoicing. The outpouring of the Holy Spirit, 50 days after the death of Christ at the Passover, was on Pentecost and gives special meaning to that day for Christians (cf. Joel 2:28–32; Ac 2:14–18).

16:13–15 the Feast of Booths. This was also called the "Feast of Ingathering" and the "Feast of Tabernacles" (cf. Ex 23:16; 34:22; Lv 23:33–43; Nu 29:12–39).

16:18–18:22 This section deals with the responsibilities of the officials who were to maintain pure worship within the land and to administer justice impartially.

16:18 appoint ... judges and officers. Moses had appointed leaders at Sinai to help him in the administration of the people (1:13). Here he specified that such important leadership should continue in each city. "Judges" were those who adjudicated cases with the application of the law. "Officers" were subordinate leaders of various kinds.

16:19 a bribe blinds the eyes. Accepting a bribe was wrong since it perverted the ability of judges to act in fairness to the parties in litigation.

16:21, 22 Asherah ... *sacred* pillar. Asherah was the name of a Canaanite goddess, represented by a wooden pole, image or tree. A stone pillar symbolic of male fertility was prevalent in the Canaanite religion. These were forbidden by the first two commandments (Ex 20:3–6; Dt 5:7–10).

ADMINISTRATION OF JUSTICE

17 "[A]You shall not sacrifice to the LORD your God
an ox or a sheep which has a blemish *or* any
[a]defect, for that is a detestable thing to the LORD
your God.
2 "[A]If there is found in your midst, in any of your
[a]towns, which the LORD your God is giving you, a
man or a woman who does what is evil in the sight
of the LORD your God, by transgressing His covenant, 3 and has gone and [A]served other gods and
worshiped them, [B]or the sun or the moon or any of
the heavenly host, [C]which I have not commanded,
4 and if it is told you and you have heard of it, then
you shall inquire thoroughly. Behold, if it is true
and the thing certain that this detestable thing has
been done in Israel, 5 then you shall bring out that
man or that woman who has done this evil deed to
your gates, *that is,* the man or the woman, and [A]you
shall stone them to [a]death. 6 [A]On the [a]evidence of
two witnesses or three witnesses, he who is to die
shall be put to death; he shall not be put to death
on the [a]evidence of one witness. 7 [A]The hand of the
witnesses shall be first against him to put him to
death, and afterward the hand of all the people. [B]So
you shall purge the evil from your midst.
8 "[A]If any case is too difficult for you to decide,
between [a]one kind of homicide or another, between
[b]one kind of lawsuit or another, and between [c]one
kind of assault or another, being cases of dispute in
your [d]courts, then you shall arise and go up to [B]the
place which the LORD your God chooses. 9 So you
shall come to [A]the Levitical priest or the judge who
is *in office* in those days, and you shall inquire *of
them* and they will declare to you the verdict in the
case. 10 You shall do according to the [a]terms of the
verdict which they declare to you from that place
which the LORD chooses; and you shall be careful
to observe according to all that they teach you.
11 [A]According to the [a]terms of the law which they
teach you, and according to the verdict which they
tell you, you shall do; you shall not turn aside from
the word which they declare to you, to the right or
the left. 12 The man who acts [A]presumptuously by
not listening to the priest who stands there to serve
the LORD your God, nor to the judge, that man shall
die; thus you shall purge the evil from Israel. 13 Then
all the people will hear and be afraid, and will not
act [A]presumptuously again.
14 "When you enter the land which the LORD your
God gives you, and you [A]possess it and live in it,
and you say, '[B]I will set a king over me like all the
nations who are around me,' 15 you shall surely set
a king over you whom the LORD your God chooses,
one [A]from among your [a]countrymen you shall set
as king over yourselves; you may not put a foreigner over yourselves who is not your [a]country-
man. 16 [A]Moreover, he shall not multiply horses for
himself, nor shall he [B]cause the people to return to
Egypt to multiply horses, since [C]the LORD has said
to you, 'You shall never again return that way.' 17 [A]He
shall not multiply wives for himself, [a]or else his
heart will turn away; nor shall he greatly increase
silver and gold for himself.
18 "Now it shall come about when he sits on the
throne of his kingdom, he shall write for himself a
copy of this law on a scroll [a,A]in the presence of the
Levitical priests. 19 It shall be with him and he shall
read it [A]all the days of his life, that he may learn to
fear the LORD his God, [a]by carefully observing all the
words of this law and these statutes, 20 that his heart
may not be lifted up above his [a]countrymen [A]and
that he may not turn aside from the commandment,
to the right or the left, so that he and his sons may
continue long in his kingdom in the midst of Israel.

17:1 [a]Lit *evil thing* [A]Deut 15:21 17:2 [a]Lit *gates* [A]Deut 13:6-11 17:3 [A]Ex 22:20 [B]Job 31:26-28 [C]Jer 7:22 17:5 [a]Lit *death with stones* [A]Lev 24:14; Josh 7:25 17:6 [a]Lit *mouth* [A]Num 35:30; Deut 19:15; Matt 18:16; John 8:17; 2 Cor 13:1; 1 Tim 5:19; Heb 10:28 17:7 [A]Lev 24:14; Deut 13:9 [B]1 Cor 5:13 17:8 [a]Lit *blood to blood* [b]Lit *judgment to judgment* [c]Lit *stroke to stroke* [d]Lit *gates* [A]2 Chr 19:10; Hag 2:11 [B]Deut 12:5; Ps 122:5 17:9 [A]Deut 19:17 17:10 [a]Lit *mouth* 17:11 [a]Lit *mouth* [A]Deut 25:1 17:12 [A]Num 15:30; Deut 1:43; 17:13; 18:20; Hos 4:4 17:13 [A]Deut 17:12 17:14 [A]Deut 11:31; Josh 21:43 [B]1 Sam 8:5, 19, 20; 10:19 17:15 [a]Lit *brother(s)* [A]Jer 30:21 17:16 [A]1 Kin 4:26; 10:26-29; Ps 20:7 [B]Is 31:1; Ezek 17:15 [C]Ex 13:17, 18; Hos 11:5 17:17 [a]Lit *nor* [A]2 Sam 5:13; 12:11; 1 Kin 11:3, 4 17:18 [a]Lit *from before* [A]Deut 31:24-26 17:19 [a]Lit *to keep to do them* [A]Deut 4:9, 10; Josh 1:8 17:20 [a]Lit *brothers* [A]Deut 5:32; 1 Kin 15:5

17:1 any … defect. To bring a defective sacrifice to the Lord was to bring something into the sanctuary that was forbidden. Such a sacrifice was an abomination to the Lord. To offer less than the best to God was to despise His name (see Mal 1:6–8). Offering a less than perfect sacrifice was, in effect, failing to acknowledge God as the ultimate provider of all that was best in life.

17:3–7 served other gods. The local judges were to see that false worshipers were executed, so that idolatry was dealt with severely.

17:6, 7 two … or three witnesses. The execution of the idolater could not take place on the basis of hearsay. There had to be at least two valid witnesses against the accused person in order for a case to be established. One witness was not sufficient in a case of this severity; this standard avoided false testimony. The way in which the execution was carried out emphasized the burden of responsibility for truthful testimony that rested on the witnesses in a case involving capital punishment. The witnesses, by casting the first stone, accepted responsibility for their testimony (cf. 19:15; 1Co 5:13).

17:8–13 any case … too difficult for you to decide. If a judge thought a case was too difficult for him to decide, he could take it to a central tribunal, consisting of priests and an officiating chief judge, to be established at the future site of the central sanctuary. The decision of that tribunal would be final, and anyone refusing to abide by that court's decision was subject to the death penalty.

17:14 a king. The office of kingship was anticipated by Moses in the Pentateuch (see Ge 17:16; 35:11; 49:9–12; Nu 24:7, 17). He anticipated the time when the people would ask for a king and here gave explicit instruction concerning the qualifications of that future king.

17:15 from among your countrymen. How the Lord would make that choice was not said, but the field was narrowed by the specification that he must be a brother Israelite.

17:16, 17 multiply … multiply … multiply. Restrictions were placed on the king: 1) he must not acquire many horses; 2) he must not take multiple wives; and 3) he must not accumulate much silver and gold. The king was not to rely on military strength, political alliances, or wealth for his position and authority, but he was to look to the Lord. Solomon violated all of those prohibitions, while his father, David, violated the last two. Solomon's wives brought idolatry into Jerusalem, which resulted in the kingdom being divided (1Ki 11:1–43).

17:18 write …. copy of this law. The ideal set forth was that of the king who was obedient to the will of God, which he learned from reading the law. The result of his reading of the Pentateuch would be fear of the Lord and humility. The king was pictured as a scribe and scholar of Scripture. Josiah reinstituted this approach at a bleak time in Israel's history (cf. 2Ki 22).

17:20 his heart may not be lifted up above his countrymen. The king was not to be above God's law, any more than any other Israelite.

PORTION OF THE LEVITES

18 “[A]The Levitical priests, the whole tribe of
Levi, shall have no portion or inheritance
with Israel; they shall eat the LORD’S offerings by
fire and His [a]portion. 2 [A]They shall have no inheritance among their [a]countrymen; the LORD is their
inheritance, as He [b]promised them.
3 “[A]Now this shall be the priests’ due from the
people, from those who offer a sacrifice, either an
ox or a sheep, of which they shall give to the priest
the shoulder and the two cheeks and the stomach.
4 You shall give him the [A]first fruits of your grain,
your new wine, and your oil, and the first shearing
of your sheep. 5 [A]For the LORD your God has chosen
him and his sons from all your tribes, to [B]stand [a]and
serve in the name of the LORD forever.
6 “Now if a Levite comes from any of your [a]towns
throughout Israel where he [A]resides, and comes
[b]whenever he desires to the place which the LORD
chooses, 7 then he shall serve in the name of the LORD
his God, like all his fellow Levites who stand there before the LORD. 8 [A]They shall eat [a]equal portions, except
what they receive from the sale of their fathers’ *estates.*

SPIRITISM FORBIDDEN

9 “When you enter the land which the LORD your
God gives you, you shall not learn to [a,A]imitate the
detestable things of those nations. 10 There shall
not be found among you anyone [A]who makes his
son or his daughter pass through the fire, one who
uses divination, one [B]who practices witchcraft, or
one who interprets omens, or a sorcerer, 11 or one
who casts a spell, [A]or a medium, or a spiritist, or
one who calls up the dead. 12 For whoever does these
things is detestable to the LORD; and [A]because of
these detestable things the LORD your God will drive
them out before you. 13 [A]You shall be [a]blameless before the LORD your God. 14 For those nations, which
you shall dispossess, listen to those who [A]practice
witchcraft and to diviners, but as for you, the LORD
your God has not allowed you *to do* so.
15 “[A]The LORD your God will raise up for you a
prophet like me from among you, from your [a]coun-
trymen, you shall listen to him. 16 This is [A]according
to all that you asked of the LORD your God in Horeb
on the day of the assembly, saying, ‘Let me not hear
again the voice of the LORD my God, let me not see
this great fire anymore, or I will die.’ 17 [A]The LORD
said to me, ‘They have [a]spoken well. 18 I will raise
up a prophet from among their [a]countrymen like
you, and [A]I will put My words in his mouth, and [B]he
shall speak to them all that I command him. 19 [A]It
shall come about that whoever will not listen to My
words which he shall speak in My name, I Myself will
require *it* of him. 20 But the prophet who speaks a
word [A]presumptuously in My name which I have not
commanded him to speak, or [B]which he speaks in the
name of other gods, [a]that prophet shall die.’ 21 [a]You
may say in your heart, ‘How will we know the word
which the LORD has not spoken?’ 22 [A]When a prophet
speaks in the name of the LORD, if the thing does not
come about or come true, that is the thing which
the LORD has not spoken. The prophet has spoken
it [B]presumptuously; you shall not be afraid of him.

CITIES OF REFUGE

19 “[A]When the LORD your God cuts off the nations, whose land the LORD your God gives

18:1 [a]*Or inheritance* [A]Deut 10:9; 1 Cor 9:13 18:2 [a]Lit *brothers* [b]Lit *spoke to* [A]Num 18:20 18:3 [A]Lev 7:32-34; Num 18:11, 12 18:4 [A]Num 18:12 18:5 [a]Lit *to* [A]Ex 29:9 [B]Deut 10:8 18:6 [a]Lit *gates* [b]Lit *with all the desire of his soul* [A]Num 35:2, 3 18:8 [a]Lit *portion like portion* [A]Lev 27:30-33; Num 18:21-24; 2 Chr 31:4; Neh 12:44 18:9 [a]Lit *do according to* [A]Deut 9:5 18:10 [A]Deut 12:31 [B]Ex 22:18; Lev 19:26, 31; 20:6; Jer 27:9, 10; Mal 3:5 18:11 [A]Lev 19:31 18:12 [A]Lev 18:24 18:13 [a]Lit *complete, perfect;* or *having integrity* [A]Gen 6:9; 17:1; Matt 5:48 18:14 [A]2 Kin 21:6 18:15 [a]Lit *brothers* [A]Matt 21:11; Luke 2:25-34; 7:16; 24:19; John 1:21, 25; 4:19; Acts 3:22; 7:37 18:16 [A]Ex 20:18, 19; Deut 5:23-27 18:17 [a]Lit *done well what they have spoken* [A]Deut 5:28 18:18 [a]Lit *brothers* [A]Is 51:16; John 17:8 [B]John 4:25; 8:28; 12:49, 50 18:19 [A]Acts 3:23; Heb 12:25 18:20 [a]Lit *and that* [A]Deut 13:5; 17:12 [B]Deut 13:1, 2; Jer 14:14; Zech 13:3 18:21 [a]Lit *if you say* 18:22 [A]Jer 28:9 [B]Deut 18:20 19:1 [A]Deut 6:10, 11

18:1 the whole tribe of Levi. Unlike the other 12 tribes, none of the tribe of Levi, including the priests, was given an allotment of land to settle and cultivate. The Levites lived in the cities assigned to them throughout the land (Nu 35:1–8; Jos 21) while the priests lived near the central sanctuary, where they went to officiate in their appropriate course (cf. 1Ch 6:57–60). Levites assisted the priests (Nu 3, 4, 8).

18:3–5 the priests’ due. In place of a land inheritance and in recognition of their priestly duties, the priests had a right to specific portions of the animals offered for sacrifices.

18:6–8 a Levite. If a Levite wanted to go to the central sanctuary to minister there in the Lord’s name, he was permitted to do so and to receive equal support along with other Levites.

18:9–12 the detestable things of those nations. Moses gave a strict injunction not to copy, imitate, or do what the polytheistic Canaanites did. Nine detestable practices of the Canaanites were delineated in vv. 10, 11, namely: 1) sacrificing children in the fire (see 12:31); 2) witchcraft, seeking to determine the will of the gods by examining and interpreting omens; 3) soothsaying, attempting to control the future through power given by evil spirits; 4) interpreting omens, telling the future based on signs; 5) sorcery, inducing magical effects by drugs or some other sort of potion; 6) conjuring spells, binding other people by magical muttering; 7) being a medium, one who supposedly communicates with the dead, but actually communicates with demons; 8) being a spiritist, one who has an intimate acquaintance with the demonic, spiritual world; and 9) calling up the dead, investigating and seeking information from the dead. These evil practices were the reason the Lord was going to drive the Canaanites out of the land.

18:15–19 a prophet like me. The singular pronoun emphasizes the ultimate Prophet who was to come. Both the OT (34:10) and the NT (Ac 3:22, 23; 7:37) interpret this passage as a reference to the coming Messiah, who like Moses would receive and preach divine revelation and lead His people (cf. Jn 1:21, 25, 43–45; 6:14; 7:40). In fact, Jesus was like Moses in several other ways: 1) He was spared death as a baby (Ex 2; Mt 2:13–23); 2) He renounced a royal court (Php 2:5–8; Heb 11:24–27); 3) He had compassion on His people (Nu 27:17; Mt 9:36); 4) He made intercession for the people (Dt 9:18; Heb 7:25); 5) He spoke with God face to face (Ex 34:29, 30; 2Co 3:7); and 6) He was the mediator of a covenant (Dt 29:1; Heb 8:6, 7).

18:20–22 he speaks in the name of other gods. In contrast to the true prophet, Moses predicted there would be false prophets who would come to Israel, speaking not in the name of the Lord, but in the name of false gods. How could the people tell if a prophet was authentically speaking for God? Moses said, “if the thing does not come about,” it was not from God. The characteristic of false prophets is the failure of their predictions to always come true. Sometimes false prophets speak and it happens as they said, but they are representing false gods and trying to turn people from the true God—they must be rejected and executed (13:1–5). Other times, false prophets are more subtle and identify with the true God but speak lies. If ever a prophecy of such a prophet fails, he is shown to be false. Cf. Jer 28:15–17; 29:30–32.

19:1–23:14 The statutes explained by Moses in this part of Deuteronomy deal broadly with social and community order. These laws focus on interpersonal relationships.

19:1–13 See Nu 35:9–34 for the purpose of the cities of refuge.

you, and you dispossess them and settle in their
cities and in their houses, 2 [A]you shall set aside three
cities for yourself in the midst of your land, which
the LORD your God gives you to [a]possess. 3 You shall
prepare the [a]roads for yourself, and divide into
three parts the territory of your land which the
LORD your God will give you as a possession, [b]so
that any manslayer may flee there.
4 "[A]Now this is the case of the manslayer who
may flee there and live: when he [a]kills his friend
[b]unintentionally, [c]not hating him previously— 5 as
when *a man* goes into the forest with his friend to
cut wood, and his hand [a]swings the axe to cut down
the tree, and the iron *head* slips off the [b]handle and
[c]strikes his friend so that he dies—he may flee to
one of these cities and live; 6 otherwise the avenger
of blood might pursue the manslayer [a]in the heat
of his anger, and overtake him, because the way is
long, and [b]take his life, though he was not deserving of death, since he had not hated him previously.
7 Therefore, I command you, saying, 'You shall set
aside three cities for yourself.'
8 "If the LORD your God [A]enlarges your territory,
just as He has sworn to your fathers, and gives
you all the land which He [a]promised to give your
fathers— 9 if you [a]carefully observe all this commandment which I command you today, [A]to love
the LORD your God, and to walk in His ways always—[B]then you shall add three more cities for
yourself, besides these three. 10 So innocent blood
will not be shed in the midst of your land which
the LORD your God gives you as an inheritance,
and [A]bloodguiltiness be on you.
11 "But [A]if there is a man who hates his neighbor
and lies in wait for him and rises up against him and
strikes [a]him so that he dies, and he flees to one of
these cities, 12 then the elders of his city shall send and
take him from there and deliver him into the hand of
the avenger of blood, that he may die. 13 [a,A]You shall
not pity him, but [B]you shall purge the blood of the
innocent from Israel, that it may go well with you.

LAWS OF LANDMARK AND TESTIMONY

14 "[A]You shall not move your neighbor's boundary
mark, which the ancestors have set, in your inheritance which you will inherit in the land that the
LORD your God gives you to [a]possess.
15 "[A]A single witness shall not rise up against a
man on account of any iniquity or any sin [a]which
he has committed; on the [b]evidence of two or three
witnesses a matter shall be confirmed. 16 [A]If a malicious witness rises up against a man to [a]accuse
him of [b]wrongdoing, 17 then both the men who have
the dispute shall stand [A]before the LORD, before the
priests and the judges who will be *in office* in those
days. 18 The judges [A]shall investigate thoroughly,
and if the witness is a false witness *and* he has [a]ac-
cused his brother falsely, 19 then [A]you shall do to him
just as he had intended to do to his brother. Thus
you shall purge the evil from among you. 20 [A]The
rest will hear and be afraid, and will never again do
such an evil thing among you. 21 Thus [a,A]you shall
not show pity: [B]life for life, [C]eye for eye, tooth for
tooth, hand for hand, foot for foot.

LAWS OF WARFARE

20 "When you go out to battle against your
enemies and see [A]horses and chariots *and*
people more numerous than you, [B]do not be afraid
of them; for the LORD your God, who brought you up
from the land of Egypt, is with you. 2 When you are
approaching the battle, the priest shall come near
and speak to the people. 3 He shall say to them, 'Hear,
O Israel, you are approaching the battle against
your enemies today. Do not be fainthearted. [A]Do
not be afraid, or panic, or tremble before them,

19:2 [a]Lit *possess it* [A]Deut 4:41; Josh 20:2 19:3 [a]Lit *road* [b]Lit *and it shall be for every manslayer to flee there* 19:4 [a]Lit *smites* [b]Lit *without knowledge* [c]Lit *and he was not hating him previously* [A]Num 35:9-34 19:5 [a]Lit *is thrust with* [b]Lit *wood* [c]Lit *finds* 19:6 [a]Lit *while his heart is hot* [b]Lit *smite him in the soul* 19:8 [a]Lit *spoke* [A]Gen 15:18 19:9 [a]Lit *keep…to do it* [A]Deut 6:5 [B]Josh 20:7 19:10 [A]Num 35:33; Deut 21:1-9 19:11 [a]Lit *him in the soul* [A]Ex 21:12; Num 35:16; 1 John 3:15 19:13 [a]Lit *Your eye* [A]Deut 7:2 [B]1 Kin 2:31 19:14 [a]Lit *possess it* [A]Deut 27:17; Job 24:2; Prov 22:28; Hos 5:10 19:15 [a]Lit *in any sin, which he sins* [b]Lit *mouth of two witnesses, or by the mouth of three* [A]Num 35:30; Deut 17:6; Matt 18:16; John 8:17; 2 Cor 13:1; 1 Tim 5:19; Heb 10:28 19:16 [a]Lit *testify against* [b]Lit *turning aside* [A]Ex 23:1; Ps 27:12 19:17 [A]Deut 17:9 19:18 [a]Lit *testified against* [A]Deut 25:1 19:19 [A]Prov 19:5 19:20 [A]Deut 17:13; 21:21 19:21 [a]Lit *your eye* [A]Deut 19:13 [B]Ex 21:23; Lev 24:20 [C]Matt 5:38 20:1 [A]Deut 3:22; 7:18; 31:6, 8; Ps 20:7; Is 31:1 [B]2 Chr 32:7, 8; Ps 23:4; Is 41:10 20:3 [A]Deut 20:1; Josh 23:10

19:2 three cities. Three cities of refuge were to be set aside in Canaan after the conquest of the land (see Jos 20:7 for Israel's obedience to this command). These 3 cities to the W of the Jordan River were in addition to the 3 already established E of it (see 4:41–43 for the eastern cities of refuge).

19:9 add three more cities. If the Israelites had been faithful in following the Lord fully, then He would have enlarged their territory to the boundaries promised in the Abrahamic Covenant (Ge 15:18–21). In that case, 3 more cities of refuge, for a total of 9, would have been needed.

19:14 your neighbor's boundary mark. These "boundary marks" referred to stones bearing inscriptions which identified the owner of the property. Moving a neighbor's boundary stone was equivalent to stealing his property (cf. Pr 22:28; 23:10).

19:15 on the evidence of two or three witnesses. More than one witness was necessary to convict a man of a crime. This principle was to act as a safeguard against the false witness who might bring an untruthful charge against a fellow Israelite. By requiring more than one witness, greater accuracy and objectivity was gained (cf. Dt 17:6; Mt 18:15–17; 2Co 13:1).

19:16–19 a malicious witness. In some cases, there would only be one witness who brought a charge against someone. When such a case was taken to the central tribunal of priests and judges for trial, and upon investigation the testimony of the witness was found to be false, the accuser received the punishment appropriate for the alleged crime.

19:20 hear and be afraid. When the fate of the false witness became known in Israel, it would serve as a deterrent against giving false testimony in Israel's courts.

19:21 eye for eye. This principle of legal justice (called *lex talionis,* "law of retaliation") was given to encourage appropriate punishment of a criminal in cases where there might be a tendency to be either too lenient or too strict (*see notes on Ex 21:23, 24; Lv 24:20*). Jesus confronted the Jews of His day for taking this law out of the courts and using it for purposes of personal vengeance (cf. Mt 5:38–42).

20:1–20 The humanitarian principles applicable in war under Mosaic law are in stark contrast to the brutality and cruelty of other nations.

20:1 do not be afraid. When Israelites went into battle, they were never to fear an enemy's horses or chariots because the outcome of a battle would never be determined by mere military strength. The command not to be afraid was based on God's power and faithfulness, which had already been proved to Israel in their deliverance from Egypt.

20:2–4 the priest shall … speak to the people. The role of the priest in battle was to encourage the soldiers by God's promise,

4 for the LORD your God [A]is the one who goes with
you, to fight for you against your enemies, to save
you.' 5 The officers also shall speak to the people,
saying, 'Who is the man that has built a new house
and has not [A]dedicated it? Let him depart and return
to his house, otherwise he might die in the battle
and another man would dedicate it. 6 Who is the
man that has planted a vineyard and has not [a]be-
gun to use its fruit? Let him depart and return to
his house, otherwise he might die in the battle and
another man [a]would begin to use its fruit. 7 [A]And
who is the man that is engaged to a woman and
has not [a]married her? Let him depart and return to
his house, otherwise he might die in the battle and
another man [b]would marry her.' 8 Then the officers
shall speak further to the people and say, '[A]Who is
the man that is afraid and fainthearted? Let him
depart and return to his house, so that [a]he might
not make his brothers' hearts melt like his heart.'
9 When the officers have finished speaking to the
people, they shall appoint commanders of armies
at the head of the people.

10 "When you approach a city to fight against
it, you shall [a]offer it terms of peace. 11 If it [a]agrees
to make peace with you and opens to you, then all
the people who are found in it shall become your
[A]forced labor and shall serve you. 12 However, if
it does not make peace with you, but makes war
against you, then you shall besiege it. 13 When the
LORD your God gives it into your hand, [A]you shall
strike all the [a]men in it with the edge of the sword.
14 Only the women and the children and [A]the animals and all that is in the city, all its spoil, you shall
take as booty for yourself; and you shall [a]use the
spoil of your enemies which the LORD your God has
given you. 15 Thus you shall do to all the cities that
are very far from you, which are not of the cities of
these nations [a]nearby. 16 [A]Only in the cities of these
peoples that the LORD your God is giving you as
an inheritance, you shall not leave alive anything
that breathes. 17 But you shall [a]utterly destroy them,
the Hittite and the Amorite, the Canaanite and the
Perizzite, the Hivite and the Jebusite, as the LORD
your God has commanded you, 18 so that they may
not teach you to do [A]according to all their detestable
things which they have done for their gods, so that
you would [B]sin against the LORD your God.

19 "When you besiege a city a long time, to make
war against it in order to capture it, you shall not
destroy its trees by swinging an axe against them;
for you may eat from them, and you shall not cut
them down. [a]For is the tree of the field a man, that
it should [b]be besieged by you? 20 Only the trees
which you know [a]are not fruit trees you shall destroy
and cut down, that you may construct siegeworks
against the city that is making war with you until
it falls.

EXPIATION OF A CRIME

21 "If a slain person is found lying in the open
country in the land which the LORD your God
gives you to [a]possess, *and* it is not known who has
struck him, 2 then your elders and your judges shall
go out and measure *the distance* to the cities which
are around the slain one. 3 It shall be that the city
which is nearest to the slain man, that is, the elders
of that city, shall take a heifer of the herd, which
has not been worked and which has not pulled in
a yoke; 4 and the elders of that city shall bring the
heifer down to a valley with running water, which
has not been plowed or sown, and shall break the
heifer's neck there in the valley. 5 Then [A]the priests,
the sons of Levi, shall come near, for the LORD your
God has chosen them to serve Him and to bless in
the name of the LORD; and every dispute and every
[a]assault [b]shall be settled by them. 6 All the elders
of that city [a]which is nearest to the slain man shall
[A]wash their hands over the heifer whose neck was
broken in the valley; 7 and they shall answer and
say, 'Our hands did not shed this blood, nor did
our eyes see *it*. 8 [a]Forgive Your people Israel whom
You have redeemed, O LORD, and do not place the

20:4 [A]Deut 1:30; 3:22; Josh 23:10 20:5 [A]Neh 12:27 20:6 [a]Lit *treat(ed) it as common* 20:7 [a]Lit *taken* [b]Lit *take* [A]Deut 24:5 20:8 [a]So with Gr and other ancient versions [A]Judg 7:3 20:10 [a]Lit *call to it for peace* 20:11 [a]Lit *answers peace* [A]1 Kin 9:21 20:13 [a]Lit *males* [A]Num 31:7 20:14 [a]Lit *eat* [A]Josh 8:2 20:15 [a]Lit *here* 20:16 [A]Ex 23:31-33; Num 21:2, 3; Deut 7:1-5; Josh 11:14 20:17 [a]Or *put them under the ban* 20:18 [A]Ex 34:12-16; Deut 7:4; 9:5; 12:30, 31 [B]Ex 23:33; 2 Kin 21:3-15; Ps 106:34-41 20:19 [a]Read as interrogative with ancient versions [b]Lit *come before you in the siege* 20:20 [a]Lit *they are not trees for food* 21:1 [a]Lit *possess it* 21:5 [a]Lit *stroke* [b]Lit *shall be according to their mouth* [A]Deut 17:9-11; 19:17; 1 Chr 23:13 21:6 [a]Lit *who are* [A]Matt 27:24 21:8 [a]Lit *Cover over, atone for*

presence, and power to be strong in faith. A lack of trust in God's ability to fight for them would affect the strength of their will so that they would become fainthearted. Victory was linked to their faith in God.

20:5–8 Let him depart and return to his house. Four exemptions from service in Israel's volunteer army were cited to illustrate the principle that anyone whose heart was not in the fight should not be there. Those who had other matters on their minds or were afraid were allowed to leave the army and return to their homes, since they would be useless in battle and even influence others to lose courage (v. 8).

20:10–15 terms of peace. Cities outside of Canaan were not under the judgment of total destruction, so to them Israel was to offer a peace treaty. If the city agreed to become a vassal to Israel, then the people would become tributary subjects. However, if the offer of peace was rejected, Israel was to besiege and take the city, killing the men and taking possession of the rest of the people and animals as spoils of war. Note here the principle that the proclamation of peace preceded judgment (cf. Mt 10:11–15).

20:16–18 utterly destroy. The Canaanite cities were to be totally destroyed, i.e., nothing was to be spared, in order to destroy their influence toward idolatry (cf. 7:22–26).

20:19, 20 you shall not destroy its trees. When besieging a city, armies in the ancient world would cut down the trees to build ramps and weapons, as well as facilities for the long siege. However, Israel was not to use fruit trees in the siege of a city so they could enjoy the fruit of the land God had given to them (7:12, 13).

21:1–9 it is not known who has struck him. This law, which dealt with an unsolved homicide, was not given elsewhere in the Pentateuch. In the event that the guilty party was unknown, justice could not adequately be served. However, the people were still held responsible to deal with the crime. The elders of the city closest to the place where the body of a dead man was found were to accept responsibility for the crime. This precluded inter-city strife, in case relatives sought revenge. They would go to a valley (idol altars were always on high places, so this avoided association with idolatry) and there break the neck of a heifer, indicating that the crime deserved to be punished. But the handwashing of the elders (v. 6) would show that, although they accepted responsibility for what had happened, they were nevertheless free from the guilt attached to the crime.

21:5 This distinctly indicates that final judicial authority in the theocracy of Israel rested with the priests.

guilt of [A]innocent blood in the midst of Your people
Israel.' And the bloodguiltiness shall be [b]forgiven
them. 9 [A]So you shall remove the guilt of innocent
blood from your midst, when you do what is right
in the eyes of the LORD.

DOMESTIC RELATIONS

10 "When you go out to battle against your enemies, and [A]the LORD your God delivers them into
your hands and you take them away captive, 11 and
see among the captives a beautiful woman, and
have a desire for her and would take her as a wife
for yourself, 12 then you shall bring her home to
your house, and she shall [A]shave her head and [a]trim
her nails. 13 She shall also [a]remove the clothes of
her captivity and shall remain in your house, and
[A]mourn her father and mother a full month; and
after that you may go in to her and be her husband
and she shall be your wife. 14 It shall be, if you are
not pleased with her, then you shall let her go [a]wher-
ever she wishes; but you shall certainly not sell her
for money, you shall not [b]mistreat her, because you
have [A]humbled her.

15 "If a man has two wives, the one loved and
[A]the other [a]unloved, and *both* the loved and the
[a]unloved have borne him sons, if the firstborn son
belongs to the [a]unloved, 16 then it shall be in the day
he [a]wills what he has to his sons, he cannot make
the son of the loved the firstborn before the son of
the [b]unloved, who is the firstborn. 17 But he shall
acknowledge the firstborn, the son of the [a]unloved,
by giving him a double portion of all that [b]he has,
for he is the [A]beginning of his strength; [B]to him
belongs the right of the firstborn.

18 "If any man has a stubborn and rebellious son
who will [A]not obey his father or his mother, and
when they chastise him, he will not even listen
to them, 19 then his father and mother shall seize
him, and bring him out to the elders of his city [a]at
the gateway of his hometown. 20 They shall say to
the elders of his city, 'This son of ours is stubborn
and rebellious, he will not obey us, he is a glutton
and a drunkard.' 21 [A]Then all the men of his city
shall stone him to death; so [B]you shall remove
the evil from your midst, and [C]all Israel will hear
of it and fear.

22 "If a man has committed a sin [A]worthy of death
and he is put to death, and you hang him on a tree,
23 [A]his corpse shall not hang all night on the tree,
but you shall surely bury him on the same day (for
[B]he who is hanged is [a]accursed of God), so that you
[C]do not defile your land which the LORD your God
gives you as an inheritance.

SUNDRY LAWS

22 "[A]You shall not see your [a]countryman's ox or
his sheep straying away, and [b]pay no attention to them; you shall certainly bring them back to
your countryman. 2 If your countryman is not near
you, or if you do not know him, then you shall bring
it home to your house, and it shall remain with you
until your countryman looks for it; then you shall
restore it to him. 3 Thus you shall do with his donkey, and you shall do the same with his garment,
and you shall do likewise with anything lost by
your countryman, which he has lost and you have
found. You are not allowed to [a]neglect *them*. 4 You
shall not see your countryman's donkey or his ox

21:8 [b]Lit *covered over, atoned for* [A]Num 35:33, 34; Jon 1:14 21:9 [A]Deut 19:13 21:10 [A]Josh 21:44 21:12 [a]Lit *do* [A]Lev 14:8, 9; Num 6:9 21:13 [a]Lit *remove from her* [A]Ps 45:10 21:14 [a]Lit *according to her soul* [b]Or *enslave* [A]Gen 34:2 21:15 [a]Lit *hated* [A]Gen 29:33 21:16 [a]Lit *makes to inherit* [b]Lit *hated* 21:17 [a]Lit *hated* [b]Lit *is found with him* [A]Gen 49:3 [B]Gen 25:31 21:18 [A]Ex 20:12; Lev 19:3; Prov 1:8; Eph 6:1-3 21:19 [a]Lit *and to the gate of his place* 21:21 [A]Lev 20:2, 27; 24:14-23; Num 15:25, 36 [B]Deut 19:19 [C]Deut 13:11 21:22 [A]Deut 22:26; Matt 26:66; Mark 14:64; Acts 23:29 21:23 [a]Lit *the curse of God* [A]Josh 8:29; 10:26, 27; John 19:31 [B]Gal 3:13 [C]Lev 18:25; Num 35:34 22:1 [a]Lit *brother,* and so through v 4 [b]Lit *hide yourself from them* [A]Ex 23:4, 5; Prov 27:10; Zech 7:9 22:3 [a]Lit *hide yourself*

21:11–14 a beautiful woman. According to ancient war customs, a female captive became the servant of the victors. Moses was given instruction to deal in a kind way with such issues. In the event her conquerors were captivated by her beauty and contemplated marriage with her, one month was required to elapse, during which her troubled feelings might settle, her mind would be reconciled to the new conditions of conquest, and she could sorrow over the loss of her parents as she left home to marry a stranger. One month was the usual mourning period for Jews, and the features of this period, e.g., shaving the head, trimming the nails, and removing her lovely clothes (ladies on the eve of captivity dressed to be attractive to their captors), were typical signs of Jewish grief. This action was important to show kindness to the woman and to test the strength of the man's affection. After the 30 days, they could marry. If later he decided divorce was appropriate (based on the provisions of 24:1–4), he could not sell her as a slave. She was to be set completely free because "you have humbled her." This phrase clearly refers to sexual activity, in which the wife has fully submitted herself to her husband (cf. 22:23, 24, 28, 29). It should be noted that divorce appears to have been common among the people, perhaps learned from their time in Egypt, and tolerated by Moses because of their "hard hearts" (*see notes on Dt 24:1–4; Mt 19:8*).

21:11, 12 among the captives a beautiful woman. Such a woman would be from a non-Canaanite city that Israel had captured (see 20:14) since all the Canaanites were to be killed (20:16). These discarded items were symbolic of the casting off of her former life and carried purification symbolism (cf. Lv 14:18; Nu 8:7).

21:15–17 has two wives. In the original, the words are rendered "has had two wives," referring to events that have already taken place, evidently intimating that one wife is dead and another has taken her place. Moses, then, is not legislating on a polygamous case where a man has two wives at the same time, but on that of a man who has married twice in succession. The man may prefer the second wife and be exhorted by her to give his inheritance to one of her sons. The issue involves the principle of the inheritance of the firstborn (the right of primogeniture). The firstborn son of the man, whether from the favorite wife or not, was to receive the double portion of the inheritance. The father did not have the authority to transfer this right to another son. This did not apply to sons of a concubine (Ge 21:9–13) or in cases of misconduct (Ge 49:3, 4).

21:18–21 a stubborn and rebellious son. Cf. 27:16. The long-term pattern of rebellion and sin of a child who was incorrigibly disobedient is in view. No hope remained for such a person who flagrantly violated the fifth commandment (Ex 20:12), so he was to be stoned to death.

21:22, 23 hang him on a tree. After an execution, the body was permitted to hang on a tree for the rest of the day as a public display of the consequences of disobedience. However, the body was not to remain on the tree overnight, but was to be properly buried before sunset. Cf. Gal 3:13, where Paul quotes this text in regard to the death of the Lord Jesus Christ.

22:1–26:19 While loving God was the first duty (cf. 6:5), loving one's neighbor came next (cf. Mt 22:37–40). In this section, the law of loving one's neighbor is applied to domestic and social relationships.

22:1–4 pay no attention. The Israelite must not hide his eyes from such an obvious loss. It was his duty to pursue and bring back the lost property of his neighbor.

fallen down on the way, and [a]pay no attention to
them; you shall certainly help him to raise *them* up.
5 "A woman shall not wear man's clothing, nor
shall a man put on a woman's clothing; for whoever does these things is an abomination to the
LORD your God.
6 "If you happen to come upon a bird's nest along
the way, in any tree or on the ground, with young
ones or eggs, and the mother sitting on the young
or on the eggs, [A]you shall not take the mother with
the young; 7 you shall certainly let the mother go,
but the young you may take for yourself, [A]in order
that it may be well with you and that you may prolong your days.
8 "When you build a new house, you shall make
a parapet for your roof, so that you will not bring
bloodguilt on your house if anyone falls from it.
9 "[A]You shall not sow your vineyard with two
kinds of seed, or [a]all the produce of the seed which
you have sown and the increase of the vineyard
will become defiled.
10 "[A]You shall not plow with an ox and a donkey
together.
11 "[A]You shall not wear a material mixed of wool
and linen together.
12 "[A]You shall make yourself tassels on the four
corners of your garment with which you cover
yourself.

LAWS ON MORALITY

13 "[A]If any man takes a wife and goes in to her
and *then* [a]turns against her, 14 and charges her with
shameful deeds and [a]publicly defames her, and says,
'I took this woman, *but* when I came near her, I did
not find her a virgin,' 15 then the girl's father and
her mother shall take and bring out the *evidence*
of the girl's virginity to the elders of the city at the
gate. 16 The girl's father shall say to the elders, 'I
gave my daughter to this man for a wife, but he
[a]turned against her; 17 and behold, he has charged
her with shameful deeds, saying, "I did not find
your daughter a virgin." But [a]this is the evidence
of my daughter's virginity.' And they shall spread
the garment before the elders of the city. 18 So [A]the
elders of that city shall take the man and chastise
him, 19 and they shall fine him a hundred *shekels*
of silver and give it to the girl's father, because he
[a]publicly defamed a virgin of Israel. And she shall
remain his wife; he cannot [b]divorce her all his days.
20 "But if this [a,A]charge is true, that the girl was not
found a virgin, 21 then they shall bring out the girl
to the doorway of her father's house, and the men
of her city shall stone her [a]to death because she has
[A]committed an act of folly in Israel by playing the
harlot in her father's house; thus [B]you shall purge
the evil from among you.
22 "[A]If a man is found lying with a married
woman, then both of them shall die, the man who
lay with the woman, and the woman; thus you shall
purge the evil from Israel.
23 "[A]If there is a girl who is a virgin engaged to
a man, and *another* man finds her in the city and
lies with her, 24 then you shall bring them both out
to the gate of that city and you shall stone them
[a]to death; the girl, because she did not cry out in
the city, and the man, because he has violated his
neighbor's wife. Thus you shall purge the evil from
among you.
25 "But if in the field the man finds the girl who
is engaged, and the man forces her and lies with
her, then only the man who lies with her shall die.
26 But you shall do nothing to the girl; there is no sin
in the girl worthy of death, for just as a man rises
against his neighbor and murders him, so is this
case. 27 When he found her in the field, the engaged
girl cried out, but there was no one to save her.

22:4 [a]Lit *hide yourself from them* 22:6 [A]Lev 22:28 22:7 [A]Deut 4:40 22:9 [a]Lit *the fullness* [A]Lev 19:19 22:10 [A]2 Cor 6:14-16 22:11 [A]Lev 19:19 22:12 [A]Num 15:37-41; Matt 23:5 22:13 [a]Lit *hates her* [A]Gen 29:21; Deut 24:1; Judg 15:1 22:14 [a]Lit *causes an evil name to go out against her* 22:16 [a]Lit *hated her* 22:17 [a]Lit *these are* 22:18 [A]Ex 18:21; Deut 1:9-18 22:19 [a]Lit *caused an evil name to go out against a virgin* [b]Lit *send her away* 22:20 [a]Lit *matter* [A]Deut 17:4 22:21 [a]Lit *with stones so that she dies* [A]Gen 34:7; Lev 19:29; 21:9; Deut 23:17, 18; Judg 20:5-10; 2 Sam 13:12, 13 [B]Deut 13:5; 17:7; 19:19 22:22 [A]Lev 20:10; Ezek 16:38; Matt 5:27, 28; John 8:5; 1 Cor 6:9; Heb 13:4 22:23 [A]Lev 19:20-22; Matt 1:18, 19 22:24 [a]Lit *with stones so that they die*

22:5 nor shall a man put on a woman's clothing. Found only here in the Pentateuch, this statute prohibited a man from wearing any item of feminine clothing or ornamentation, or a woman from wearing any item of masculine clothing or ornamentation. The same word translated "abomination" was used to describe God's view of homosexuality (Lv 18:22; 20:13). This instance specifically outlawed transvestism. The creation order distinctions between male and female were to be maintained without exception (cf. Ge 1:27).

22:6 a bird's nest. Found only here in the Pentateuch, this law showed that God cared for the long-term provisions for His people. By letting the mother go, food could be acquired without killing the source of future food.

22:8 a parapet. Found only here in the Pentateuch, this refers to the roof of a home in ancient Israel, which was flat and usually reached by outside stairs. To prevent injury or death from falling, a fence was to be built around the roof. This, too, expressed love for those who might otherwise be injured or killed.

22:9 two kinds of seed. The aim of the legislation seems to be to maintain healthy crops by keeping the seeds separate from one another. *See note on Lv 19:19.*

22:10 an ox and a donkey together. According to the dietary laws prescribed earlier (14:1–8), the ox was a "clean" animal, but the donkey was "unclean." Even more compelling was the fact that these two different animals couldn't together plow a straight furrow. Their temperaments, natural instincts, and physical characteristics made it impossible. As with the seed (v. 9), God is protecting His people's food.

22:11 material . . . wool and linen. *See note on Lv 19:19.*

22:12 make . . . tassels. See Nu 15:38–40 for the purpose of these tassels.

22:13–30 This section is on family life (cf. Lv 18:1–30; 20:10–21).

22:13–21 An Israelite who doubted the virginity of his bride was to make a formal accusation to the "elders of the city." If her parents gave proof of virginity showing the accusation was false, the husband was to pay a penalty and was prohibited from divorcing the woman. However, if she was found not to be a virgin, then she was to be put to death.

22:15 the *evidence* of the girl's virginity. Probably a blood-stained garment or a bed sheet from the wedding night.

22:19 *shekels*. This word is not in the Hebrew text, but the context suggests it. A shekel weighed .4 oz., so the total fine would be about 2.5 lbs. of silver.

22:22–29 Adultery was punished by death for the two found in the act. If the adulterous persons were a man with a woman who was pledged to be married to someone else, this consentual act led to the death of both parties (vv. 23, 24). However, if the man forced (i.e., raped) the woman, then only the man's life was required (vv. 25–27). If the woman was a virgin not pledged in marriage, then the man had to pay a fine, marry the girl, and keep her as his wife as long as he lived (vv. 28, 29).

28 "[A]If a man finds a girl who is a virgin, who is not engaged, and seizes her and lies with her and they are discovered, 29 then the man who lay with her shall give to the girl's father fifty *shekels* of silver, and she shall become his wife because he has violated her; he cannot divorce her all his days.

30 "[a,A]A man shall not take his father's wife so that he will not uncover his father's skirt.

PERSONS EXCLUDED FROM THE ASSEMBLY

23 "[A]No one who is [a]emasculated or has his male organ cut off shall enter the assembly of the LORD. 2 No one of illegitimate birth shall enter the assembly of the LORD; none of his *descendants,* even to the tenth generation, shall enter the assembly of the LORD. 3 [A]No Ammonite or Moabite shall enter the assembly of the LORD; none of their *descendants,* even to the tenth generation, shall ever enter the assembly of the LORD, 4 [A]because they did not meet you with [a]food and water on the way when you came out of Egypt, and because they hired against you [B]Balaam the son of Beor from Pethor of [b]Mesopotamia, to curse you. 5 Nevertheless, the LORD your God was not willing to listen to Balaam, but the LORD your God [A]turned the curse into a blessing for you because the LORD your God [B]loves you. 6 [A]You shall never seek their peace or their prosperity all your days.

7 "You shall not detest an Edomite, for [A]he is your brother; you shall not detest an Egyptian, [B]because you were an alien in his land. 8 The sons of the third generation who are born to them may enter the assembly of the LORD.

9 "When you go out as [a]an army against your enemies, you shall keep yourself from every evil thing.

10 "[A]If there is among you any man who is unclean because of a nocturnal emission, then he must go outside the camp; he may not [a]reenter the camp. 11 But it shall be when evening approaches, he shall bathe himself with water, and at sundown he may [a]reenter the camp.

12 "You shall also have a place outside the camp and go out there, 13 and you shall have a [a]spade among your tools, and it shall be when you sit down outside, you shall dig with it and shall turn [b]to cover up your excrement. 14 Since [A]the LORD your God walks in the midst of your camp to deliver you and to [a]defeat your enemies before you, therefore your camp must be [B]holy; and He must not see [b]anything indecent among you [c]or He will turn away from you.

15 "[A]You shall not hand over to his master a slave who has [a]escaped from his master to you. 16 He shall live with you in your midst, in the place which he shall choose in one of your [a]towns where it pleases him; [A]you shall not mistreat him.

17 "[A]None of the daughters of Israel shall be a cult prostitute, [B]nor shall any of the sons of Israel be a cult prostitute. 18 You shall not bring the hire of a harlot or the wages of a [a,A]dog into the house of the LORD your God for any votive offering, for both of these are an abomination to the LORD your God.

19 "[A]You shall not charge interest to your [a]countrymen: interest on money, food, *or* anything that may be loaned at interest. 20 [A]You may charge interest to a foreigner, but to your [a]countrymen you shall not charge interest, so that [B]the LORD your God may bless you in all [b]that you undertake in the land which you are about to enter to [c]possess.

22:28 [A]Ex 22:16 22:30 [a]Ch 23:1 in Heb [A]Lev 18:8; 20:11; Deut 27:20; 1 Cor 5:1 23:1 [a]Lit *wounded by crushing* of testicles [A]Lev 21:20; 22:24 23:3 [A]Neh 13:1, 2 23:4 [a]Lit *bread* [b]Heb *Aram-naharaim* [A]Neh 13:2 [B]Num 22:5; 23:7; Josh 24:9; 2 Pet 2:15; Jude 11 23:5 [A]Prov 26:2 [B]Deut 4:37 23:6 [A]Ezra 9:12 23:7 [A]Gen 25:24-26; Obad 10, 12 [B]Ex 22:21; 23:9; Lev 19:34; Deut 10:19 23:9 [a]Or *a camp* 23:10 [a]Lit *come to the midst of* [A]Lev 15:16 23:11 [a]Lit *come to the midst of* 23:13 [a]Lit *peg* [b]Lit *and* 23:14 [a]Lit *give* [b]Lit *nakedness of anything* [c]Lit *and* [A]Lev 26:12 [B]Ex 3:5 23:15 [a]Lit *delivered himself* [A]1 Sam 30:15 23:16 [a]Lit *gates* [A]Ex 22:21; Prov 22:22 23:17 [A]Lev 19:29; Deut 22:21 [B]Gen 19:5; 2 Kin 23:7 23:18 [a]I.e. male prostitute, sodomite [A]Lev 18:22; 20:13 23:19 [a]Lit *brother* [A]Ex 22:25; Lev 25:35-37; Neh 5:2-7; Ps 15:5 23:20 [a]Lit *brother* [b]Lit *the putting forth of your hand* [c]Lit *possess it* [A]Deut 28:12 [B]Deut 15:10

22:30 A man shall not take his father's wife. In no case was a man to marry his father's wife or have sexual relations with her. This probably has relations with a stepmother in view, though incest was certainly forbidden (cf. Lv 18:6–8).

23:1 the assembly of the LORD. From the sanctification of the home and marriage in the previous chapter, Moses proceeds to the sanctification of their union as a congregation and speaks of the right of citizenship, including being gathered before the presence of the Lord to worship Him. Most likely, this law did not exclude one from residence in the area where Israel was to live, but from public offices and honors, intermarriage, and participation in the religious rites at the tabernacle plus later at the temple. The emasculated (v. 1), the illegitimate (v. 2), and the Ammonites and Moabites (vv. 3–6) were not allowed to worship the Lord. The general rule was that strangers and foreigners, for fear of friendship or marriage connections which would lead Israel into idolatry, were not admissible until their conversion to God and the Jewish faith. This purge, however, describes some limitations to the general rule. Eunuchs, illegitimate children, and people from Ammon and Moab were excluded. Eunuchs were forbidden because such willful mutilation (lit. in Heb., by crushing, which was the way such an act was generally performed) violated God's creation of man, was associated with idolatrous practices, and was done by pagan parents to their children so that they might serve as eunuchs in the homes of the great (cf. 25:11, 12). The illegitimate were excluded so as to place an indelible stigma as a discouragement to shameful sexual misconduct. People from Ammon and Moab were excluded, not because they were born out of incest (cf. Ge 19:30ff.), but on account of their vicious hostility toward God and His people Israel. Many of the Israelites were settled E of the Jordan in the immediate neighborhood of these people, so God raised this wall to prevent the evils of idolatrous influence. Individuals from all 3 of these outcast groups are offered grace and acceptance by Isaiah upon personal faith in the true God (cf. Is 56:1–8). Ruth the Moabitess serves as a most notable example (cf. Ru 1:4, 16).

23:2, 3 to the tenth generation. The use of the words "shall ever" and "never" in vv. 3, 6 seems to indicate that this phrase is an idiom denoting permanent exclusion from the worshiping community of Israel. In contrast, an Edomite or Egyptian might worship in Israel in the third generation (see vv. 7, 8). Though these nations had also been enemies, Edom was a near relative, coming from Jacob's family, while individual Egyptians had shown kindness to the Israelites at the Exodus (cf. Ex 12:36).

23:9–14 Because the camp of Israelite soldiers was a place of God's presence (v. 14), the camp was to be kept clean. Instruction was given concerning nocturnal emission (vv. 10, 11) and defecation (vv. 12, 13). Such instruction for external cleanness illustrated what God wanted in the heart.

23:15–25:19 Moses selected 21 sample laws to further illustrate the nature of the requirements of living under the Sinaitic Covenant.

23:15, 16 A fugitive slave was not to be turned over to his master. Evidently this has in mind a slave from the Canaanites or other neighboring nations who was driven out by oppression or with a desire to know Israel's God.

23:17, 18 Prostitution as a form of worship was forbidden. "Dog" was a reference to male prostitutes (cf. Rev 22:15).

23:19, 20 This prohibition of lending money at interest to a fellow Israelite is qualified by

21 "[A]When you make a vow to the LORD your God,
you shall not delay to pay it, for it would be sin in
you, [a]and the LORD your God will surely require it
of you. 22 However, if you refrain from vowing, it
would not be sin in you. 23 You shall be careful to
perform what goes out from your lips, just as you
have voluntarily vowed to the LORD your God, what
you have [a]promised.
24 "When you enter your neighbor's vineyard,
then you may eat grapes [a]until you are fully satisfied, but you shall not put any in your [b]basket.
25 "[A]When you enter your neighbor's standing
grain, then you may pluck the heads with your hand,
but you shall not wield a sickle in your neighbor's
standing grain.

LAW OF DIVORCE

24 "When a man takes a wife and marries her,
and it happens [a]that she finds no favor in
his eyes because he has found some [A]indecency
in her, and [B]he writes her a certificate of divorce
and puts *it* in her hand and sends her out from
his house, 2 and she leaves his house and goes and
becomes another man's *wife*, 3 and if the latter husband [a]turns against her and writes her a certificate
of divorce and puts *it* in her hand and sends her
out of his house, or if the latter husband dies who
took her to be his wife, 4 *then* her [A]former husband
who sent her away is not allowed to take her again
to be his wife, since she has been defiled; for that
is an abomination before the LORD, and you shall
not bring sin on the land which the LORD your God
gives you as an inheritance.
5 "[A]When a man takes a new wife, he shall not go
out with the army nor be charged with any duty;
he shall be free at home one year and shall [B]give
happiness to his wife whom he has taken.

SUNDRY LAWS

6 "No one shall take a handmill or an upper millstone in pledge, for he would be taking a life in pledge.
7 "[A]If a man is [a]caught kidnapping any of his
[b]countrymen of the sons of Israel, and he deals
with him violently or sells him, then that thief shall
die; so you shall purge the evil from among you.
8 "[A]Be careful against [a]an infection of leprosy,
that you diligently observe and do according to
all that the Levitical priests teach you; as I have
commanded them, so you shall be careful to do.
9 Remember what the LORD your God did [A]to Miriam
on the way as you came out of Egypt.
10 "[A]When you make your neighbor a loan of any
sort, you shall not enter his house to take his pledge.
11 You shall remain outside, and the man to whom
you make the loan shall bring the pledge out to you.
12 If he is a poor man, you shall not sleep with his
pledge. 13 [A]When the sun goes down you shall surely
return the pledge to him, that he may sleep in his
cloak and bless you; and [B]it will be righteousness
for you before the LORD your God.
14 "[A]You shall not oppress a hired servant *who is*
poor and needy, whether *he is* one of your [a]coun-
trymen or one of your aliens who is in your land
in your [b]towns. 15 [A]You shall give him his wages on
his day [a]before the sun sets, for he is poor and sets
his [b]heart on it; so that [B]he will not cry against you
to the LORD and it become sin in you.
16 "[A]Fathers shall not be put to death [a]for *their*
sons, nor shall sons be put to death [a]for *their* fathers; everyone shall be put to death for his own sin.

23:21 [a]Lit *for* [A]Num 30:1, 2; Job 22:27; Ps 61:8; Eccl 5:4, 5; Matt 5:33 **23:23** [a]Lit *spoken with your mouth* **23:24** [a]Lit *according to your satisfaction of your soul* [b]Or *vessel* **23:25** [A]Matt 12:1; Mark 2:23; Luke 6:1 **24:1** [a]Lit *if* [A]Num 5:12, 28; Deut 22:13-21 [B]Matt 5:31; 19:7-9; Mark 10:4, 5 **24:3** [a]Lit *hates her* **24:4** [A]Jer 3:1 **24:5** [A]Deut 20:7 [B]Prov 5:18 **24:7** [a]Lit *found stealing* [b]Lit *brothers* [A]Ex 21:16 **24:8** [a]Lit *a mark* or *stroke* [A]Lev 13:1-14, 57 **24:9** [A]Num 12:10 **24:10** [A]Ex 22:26, 27 **24:13** [A]Ex 22:26 [B]Deut 6:25; Ps 106:31; Dan 4:27 **24:14** [a]Lit *brothers* [b]Lit *gates* [A]Lev 19:13; 25:35-43; Deut 15:7-18; Prov 14:31; Amos 4:1; 1 Tim 5:18 **24:15** [a]Lit *that the sun shall not go down on it* [b]Lit *soul* [A]Lev 19:13; Jer 22:13; James 5:4 [B]Ex 22:23; Deut 15:9; Job 35:9; James 5:4 **24:16** [a]Or *with* [A]2 Kin 14:6; 2 Chr 25:4; Jer 31:29, 30; Ezek 18:20

Ex 22:25 and Lv 25:35, 36, which indicates that it restricts its application to the poor and prevents further impoverishment, but it was allowed for foreigners who were engaged in trade and commerce to enlarge their wealth. According to Dt 15:1, 2, it is also clear that money could be legitimately lent in the normal course of business, subject to forgiveness of all unpaid debt in the sabbatical year (cf. 24:10).

23:21–23 Though vows were made voluntarily, they were to be promptly kept once made. Cf. Nu 30:2.

23:24, 25 Farmers were to share their produce with the people in the land, but the people were not to profit from the farmers' generosity.

24:1–4 This passage does not command, commend, condone, or even suggest divorce. Rather, it recognizes that divorce occurs and permits it only on restricted grounds. The case presented here is designed to convey the fact that divorcing produced defilement. Notice the following sequence: 1) if a man finds an uncleanness (some impurity or something vile, cf. 23:14) in his wife, other than adultery, which was punished by execution (cf. 22:22); 2) if he legally divorces her (although God hates divorce, as Mal 2:16 says; He has designed marriage for life, as Ge 2:24 declares; and He allowed divorce because of hard hearts, as Mt 19:8 reveals); 3) if she then marries another man; 4) if the new husband then dies or divorces her; then that woman could not return to her first husband (v. 4). This is so because she was "defiled" with such a defilement that is an abomination to the Lord and a sinful pollution of the Promised Land. What constitutes that defilement? Only one thing is possible—she was defiled in the remarriage because there was no ground for the divorce. So when she remarried, she became an adulteress (Mt 5:31, 32) and is thus defiled so that her former husband can't take her back. Illegitimate divorce proliferates adultery. *See notes on Mt 5:31, 32; 19:4–9.*

24:5 During the first year of marriage, a man was not held responsible for military service or any other duty. He was to devote that year of marriage to the enjoyment and establishment of his marriage.

24:6 Two millstones were needed to grind grain. Neither was to be taken in pledge because it was indispensable to one's daily subsistence.

24:7 The death penalty would be exacted on kidnappers who kidnaped a brother Israelite for involuntary servitude or as merchandise to sell.

24:8, 9 Moses exhorted the people to follow the commands of the Lord regarding infectious skin diseases (*see notes on Lv 13:1–14:57*).

24:10–13 **his pledge**. This would often be a cloak, an outer garment, which was given in pledge to guarantee the repayment of a loan. God's people were to act righteously in the lending of money. An example of a righteous lender was one who did not forcefully exact payment and who allowed a poor person to retain his pledge (cloak) overnight if it was necessary to keep him warm. Lending to the poor was permitted, but without 1) interest (23:19, 20); 2) coercion to repay; and 3) extension of the loan beyond the sabbatical year (15:1, 2).

24:14, 15 Day laborers were to be paid on the day they labored because they lived day to day on such wages (cf. Lv 19:13; Mt 20:1–16).

24:16 Punishment for a crime was to be borne only by the offender. *See notes on Eze*

17 "[A]You shall not pervert the justice [a]due an
alien *or* [b]an orphan, nor [B]take a widow's garment
in pledge. 18 But you shall remember that you were
a slave in Egypt, and that the LORD your God redeemed you from there; therefore I am commanding you to do this thing.
19 "[A]When you reap your harvest in your field
and have forgotten a sheaf in the field, you shall
not go back to get it; it shall be [B]for the alien, for
the [a]orphan, and for the widow, in order that the
LORD your God [C]may bless you in all the work of
your hands. 20 [A]When you beat your olive tree, you
shall not go over the boughs [a]again; it shall be [B]for
the alien, for the [b]orphan, and for the widow.
21 "When you gather the grapes of your vineyard,
you shall not [a]go over it again; it shall be for the
alien, for the [b]orphan, and for the widow. 22 You shall
remember that you were a slave in the land of Egypt;
therefore I am commanding you to do this thing.

SUNDRY LAWS

25 "[A]If there is a dispute between men and they
go to [a]court, and [b]the judges decide their
case, [B]and they justify the righteous and condemn
the wicked, 2 then it shall be if the wicked man [a,A]de-
serves to be beaten, the judge shall then make him
lie down and be beaten in his presence with the
number of stripes according to his [b]guilt. 3 [A]He may
beat him forty times *but* no more, so that he does
not beat him with many more stripes than these
and your brother is not [B]degraded in your eyes.
4 "[A]You shall not muzzle the ox while he is
threshing.
5 "When brothers live together and one of them
dies and has no son, the wife of the deceased shall
not be *married* outside *the family* to a strange man.
[A]Her husband's brother shall go in to her and take
her to himself as wife and perform the duty of a
husband's brother to her. 6 It shall be that the firstborn whom she bears shall [a]assume the name of his
dead brother, so that [A]his name will not be blotted
out from Israel. 7 [A]But if the man does not desire
to take his brother's wife, then his brother's wife
shall go up to the gate to the elders and say, 'My
husband's brother refuses to establish a name for
his brother in Israel; he is not willing to perform
the duty of a husband's brother to me.' 8 Then the
elders of his city shall summon him and speak to
him. And *if* he persists and says, 'I do not desire
to take her,' 9 [A]then his brother's wife shall come
to him in the sight of the elders, and pull his sandal off his foot and [B]spit in his face; and she shall
[a]declare, 'Thus it is done to the man who does not
build up his brother's house.' 10 In Israel his name
shall be called, 'The house of him whose sandal
is removed.'
11 "If *two* men, a man and his [a]countryman, are
struggling together, and the wife of one comes near
to deliver her husband from the hand of the one who
is striking him, and puts out her hand and seizes his
genitals, 12 then you shall cut off her [a]hand; [b,A]you
shall not show pity.
13 "[A]You shall not have in your bag [a]differing
weights, a large and a small. 14 You shall not have
in your house [a]differing measures, a large and a
small. 15 You shall have a full and just weight; you
shall have a full and just [a]measure, [A]that your days
may be prolonged in the [b]land which the LORD your
God gives you. 16 For [A]everyone who does these
things, everyone who acts unjustly is an abomination to the LORD your God.
17 "[A]Remember what Amalek did to you along
the way when you came out from Egypt, 18 how he
met you along the way and attacked among you
all the stragglers at your rear when you were faint
and weary; and he [A]did not [a]fear God. 19 Therefore
it shall come about when the LORD your God has
given you [A]rest from all your surrounding enemies,
in the land which the LORD your God gives you as
an inheritance to [a]possess, you shall blot out the
memory of Amalek from under heaven; you must
not forget.

24:17 [a]Lit *of* [b]Or *the fatherless* [A]Ex 23:9; Lev 19:33; Deut 1:17; 10:17; 16:19; 27:19 [B]Ex 22:22 24:19 [a]Or *fatherless* [A]Lev 19:9, 10; 23:22 [B]Deut 14:29 [C]Prov 19:17 24:20 [a]Lit *after yourself* [b]Or *fatherless* [A]Lev 19:10 [B]Deut 24:19 24:21 [a]Lit *glean it after yourself* [b]Or *fatherless* 25:1 [a]Lit *the judgment* [b]Lit *they judge them* [A]Deut 17:8-13; 19:17 [B]Deut 1:16, 17 25:2 [a]Lit *is a son of beating* [b]Or *wickedness* [A]Prov 19:29; Luke 12:48 25:3 [A]2 Cor 11:24 [B]Job 18:3 25:4 [A]Prov 12:10; 1 Cor 9:9; 1 Tim 5:18 25:5 [A]Matt 22:24; Mark 12:19; Luke 20:28 25:6 [a]Lit *stand on* [A]Ruth 4:5, 10 25:7 [A]Ruth 4:5, 6 25:9 [a]Lit *answer and say* [A]Ruth 4:7, 8 [B]Num 12:14 25:11 [a]Lit *brother* 25:12 [a]Lit *palm* [b]Lit *your eye* [A]Deut 7:2; 19:13 25:13 [a]Lit *a stone and a stone* [A]Lev 19:35-37; Prov 11:1; 20:23; Ezek 45:10; Mic 6:11 25:14 [a]Lit *an ephah and an ephah* 25:15 [a]Lit *ephah* [b]Lit *ground* [A]Ex 20:12 25:16 [A]Prov 11:1 25:17 [A]Ex 17:8-16 25:18 [a]Or *reverence* [A]Ps 36:1; Rom 3:18 25:19 [a]Lit *possess it* [A]Deut 12:9

18. The death of Saul's 7 grandsons (2Sa 21:5–9) is a striking exception of national proportion grounded in God's sovereign wisdom, as was the death of David and Bathsheba's first son (2Sa 12:14).

24:17, 18 The administration of law should be carried out with equity for all members of society, including those with the least power and influence, e.g., widows, orphans, and immigrants.

24:19–22 The practice of allowing the needy to glean in the field was grounded in the remembrance of Israel's hard service in Egypt (v. 18).

25:1–3 Corporal punishment for crimes committed was to be equitably carried out in the presence of the judges and was limited to 40 stripes.

25:4 A worker must be allowed to enjoy the fruit of his own labor (cf. 1Co 9:9; 1Ti 5:18; 2Ti 2:6).

25:5–10 Levirate marriages (from Latin, *levir,* "husband's brother") provided that the brother of a dead man who died childless was to marry the widow in order to provide an heir. These were not compulsory marriages in Israel, but were applied as strong options to brothers who shared the same estate. Obviously, this required that the brother be unmarried and desired to keep the property in the family by passing it on to a son. Cf. Lv 18:16; 20:21 where adultery with a living brother's wife is forbidden. Though not compulsory, this practice reflected fraternal affection, and if a single brother refused to conform to this practice, he was confronted with contempt and humiliation by the elders. The perpetuation of his name as a member of the covenant people witnessed to the dignity of the individual. Since Nu 27:4–8 gave daughters the right of inheritance when there were no sons in a family, it is reasonable to read "no child" rather than "no son" in v. 5. Cf. Tamar, Ge 38:8–10, and the Boaz-Ruth marriage, Ru 4:1–17.

25:5 Cf. Mt 22:24; Mk 12:19; Lk 20:28.

25:11, 12 The consequence of the immodest act was the only example of punishment by mutilation in the Pentateuch.

25:13–16 The weights and measures of trade were to be kept equitably so people were not cheated. Obedience meant prosperous years in the land.

25:17–19 The admonition to remember the treachery of the Amalekites was repeated to the new generation (*see notes on Ex 17:9–16*). For execution of the command, see 1Sa 15.

OFFERING FIRST FRUITS

26 “Then it shall be, when you enter the land
which the LORD your God gives you as an
inheritance, and you possess it and live in it, 2 that
you shall take some of [A]the first of all the produce
of the ground which you bring in from your land
that the LORD your God gives you, and you shall put
it in a basket and [B]go to the place where the LORD
your God chooses to establish His name. 3 You shall
go to the priest who is in office at that time and say
to him, ‘I declare this day to the LORD [a]my God that
I have entered the land which the LORD swore to
our fathers to give us.’ 4 Then the priest shall take
the basket from your hand and set it down before
the altar of the LORD your God. 5 You shall answer
and say before the LORD your God, ‘[A]My father was
a [a]wandering Aramean, and he went down to Egypt
and [b]sojourned there, [B]few in number; but there he
became a [C]great, mighty and populous nation. 6 And
the [A]Egyptians treated us harshly and afflicted us,
and imposed hard labor on us. 7 Then [A]we cried to
the LORD, the God of our fathers, and the LORD heard
our voice and saw our affliction and our toil and
our oppression; 8 [A]and the LORD brought us out of
Egypt with a mighty hand and an outstretched arm
and with great terror and with signs and wonders;
9 and He has brought us to this place and has given
us this land, [A]a land flowing with milk and honey.
10 Now behold, I have brought the first of the produce of the ground [A]which You, O LORD have given
me.’ And you shall set it down before the LORD your
God, and worship before the LORD your God; 11 and
you and [A]the Levite and the alien who is among you
shall [B]rejoice in all the good which the LORD your
God has given you and your household.
12 “[A]When you have finished [a]paying all the tithe
of your increase in the third year, the year of tithing,
then you shall give it to the Levite, to the stranger,
to the [b]orphan and to the widow, that they may eat
in your [c]towns and be satisfied. 13 You shall say before the LORD your God, ‘I have removed the sacred
portion from *my* house, and also have given it to the
Levite and the alien, the [a]orphan and the widow, according to all Your commandments which You have
commanded me; [A]I have not transgressed or forgotten any of Your commandments. 14 I have not eaten
of it [a]while mourning, nor have I removed any of it
while I was unclean, nor offered any of it to the dead.
I have listened to the voice of the LORD my God; I
have done according to all that You have commanded
me. 15 [A]Look down from Your holy habitation, from
heaven, and bless Your people Israel, and the ground
which You have given us, [B]a land flowing with milk
and honey, as You swore to our fathers.’
16 “This day the LORD your God commands you to
do these statutes and ordinances. You shall therefore be careful to do them [A]with all your heart and
with all your soul. 17 [A]You have today declared the
LORD to be your God, and [a]that you would walk
in His ways and keep His statutes, His commandments and His ordinances, and listen to His voice.
18 The LORD has today declared you to be [A]His people, a treasured possession, as He promised you,
and [a]that you should keep all His commandments;

26:2 [A]Ex 22:29; 23:16, 19; Num 18:13; Prov 3:9 [B]Deut 12:5 26:3 [a]So with Gr; Heb *your* 26:5 [a]Or *perishing* [b]Or *lived as an alien* [A]Gen 43:1-14 [B]Gen 46:27 [C]Deut 1:10; 10:22 26:6 [A]Ex 1:8-11 26:7 [A]Ex 2:23-25; 3:9 26:8 [A]Deut 4:34; 34:11, 12 26:9 [A]Ex 3:8, 17 26:10 [A]Deut 8:18; Prov 10:22 26:11 [A]Deut 12:12 [B]Deut 12:7; 16:11; Eccl 3:12, 13; 5:18-20 26:12 [a]Lit *tithing* [b]Or *fatherless* [c]Lit *gates* [A]Lev 27:30; Num 18:24; Deut 14:28, 29; Heb 7:5, 9, 10 26:13 [a]Or *fatherless* [A]Ps 119:141, 153, 176 26:14 [a]Lit *while in my* 26:15 [A]Ps 80:14; Is 63:15; Zech 2:13 [B]Deut 26:9 26:16 [A]Deut 4:29 26:17 [a]Lit *to walk in* [A]Ps 48:14 26:18 [a]Lit *to keep all* [A]Ex 6:7; 19:5; Deut 4:20; 7:6; 14:2; 28:9; 29:13; Titus 2:14; 1 Pet 2:9

26:1–15 As the stipulation section of Deuteronomy came to an end (chaps. 5–25), Moses commanded the people to keep two rituals when they had conquered the land and began to enjoy its produce. These two rituals were the initial firstfruits offering (26:1–11) and the first third-year special tithe (26:12–15). In both cases, there is an emphasis upon the prayer of confession to be given at the time of the rituals (26:5–10, 13–15). These special offerings were given in order to celebrate Israel's transition from a nomadic existence to a settled agrarian community, made possible by the Lord's blessing.

26:2 **the first of all the produce.** Baskets of the firstfruits of the first harvest reaped by Israel once they were in the land of Canaan were to be taken to the tabernacle (cf. Ex 23:19; 34:26; Nu 18:12–17). This is to be distinguished from the annual Feast of Firstfruits (cf. Lv 23:9–14) celebrated in conjunction with the Passover and the Feast of Unleavened Bread.

26:5 **you shall … say before the LORD your God.** The offering of the firstfruits was to be accompanied by an elaborate confession of the Lord's faithfulness in preserving Israel and bringing the people into the land. The essential aspects of the worshiper's coming to the sanctuary were the presentation of the firstfruits, bowing in worship, and rejoicing in the Lord's goodness. In this manner the visit to the sanctuary was a confession and acknowledgment of God. It was a time of praise and rejoicing because of God's goodness and mercy extended to former generations and evidence of divine sustaining grace at that time. **a wandering Aramean.** This phrase referred to Jacob, who was each Israelite's father or ancestor. When Jacob fled from his home in Beersheba he passed through Syria (Aram) to Mesopotamia (Ge 24:10) to live with Laban his uncle. Returning from there, Jacob was overtaken by Laban after he came through Syria at the Jabbok River, where he not only faced the wrath of Laban but also that of Esau his brother. Later, the famine in Canaan necessitated his migration to Egypt. When the Israelites became populous and powerful, they were oppressed by the Egyptians, but it was God who responded to their prayers and miraculously delivered them out of Egypt. It was God who enabled them to enter and conquer the land from which the firstfruits were presented before the altar.

26:12 **the tithe.** I.e., the tithe collected every third year of Israel in the land of Canaan (see 14:28). Apparently this tithe was not taken to the central sanctuary, but distributed locally to Levites, immigrants, widows, and orphans. For the other regular annual tithes, *see note on 14:22.*

26:13, 14 **You shall say before the LORD your God.** The confession to be made in connection with the offering of this first tithe consisted of a statement of obedience (vv. 13, 14) and a prayer for God's blessing (v. 15). In this manner, the Israelite confessed his continual dependence on God and lived in obedient expectation of God's continued gracious blessing.

26:15 **Look down from … heaven.** This was the first reference to God's dwelling place being in heaven. From His abode in heaven, God had given the Israelites the land flowing with milk and honey as He had promised to the patriarchs. His continued blessing on both the people and the land was requested.

26:16–19 These 4 verses concluded Moses' explanation of the law's stipulations by calling for the total commitment by Israel to the Lord and His commands. These verses can be viewed as the formal ratification of the Sinaitic Covenant between the Lord and the second generation of Israel. In accepting the terms of this agreement, acknowledging that the Lord is their God, and promising wholehearted obedience plus a desire to listen to God's voice, the Israelites were assured that they were His people and the chosen over all other nations to receive His blessings and the calling to witness to His glory to all the world. See Ex 19:5, 6.

26:16 **This day.** I.e., the first day of the 11th month of the 40th year (1:3). Note also, "today" in vv. 17, 18.

19 and [a]that He will [A]set you high above all nations
which He has made, for praise, fame, and honor;
and that you shall be [B]a consecrated people to the
LORD your God, as He has spoken."

THE CURSES OF MOUNT EBAL

27 Then Moses and the elders of Israel charged
the people, saying, "Keep all the commandments which I command you today. 2 [A]So it shall be
on the day when you cross the Jordan to the land
which the LORD your God gives you, that you shall
set up for yourself large stones and coat them with
lime 3 and write on them all the words of this law,
when you cross over, so that you may enter the land
which the LORD your God gives you, [A]a land flowing
with milk and honey, as the LORD, the God of your
fathers, [a]promised you. 4 So it shall be when you
cross the Jordan, you shall set up [A]on Mount Ebal,
these stones, [a]as I am commanding you today, and
you shall coat them with lime. 5 Moreover, you shall
build there an altar to the LORD your God, an altar of
stones; you [A]shall not [a]wield an iron *tool* on them.
6 You shall build the altar of the LORD your God of
[a]uncut stones, and you shall offer on it burnt offerings to the LORD your God; 7 and you shall sacrifice
peace offerings and eat there, and [A]rejoice before
the LORD your God. 8 You shall write on the [a]stones
all the words of this law very distinctly."
9 Then Moses and the Levitical priests spoke to
all Israel, saying, "Be silent and listen, O Israel! This
day you have become a people for the LORD your
God. 10 You shall therefore [a]obey the LORD your God,
and do His commandments and His statutes which
I command you today."
11 Moses also charged the people on that day,
saying, 12 "When you cross the Jordan, these shall
stand on [A]Mount Gerizim to bless the people: [B]Sim-
eon, Levi, Judah, Issachar, Joseph, and Benjamin.
13 For the curse, these shall stand on Mount Ebal:
Reuben, Gad, Asher, Zebulun, Dan, and Naphtali.
14 The Levites shall then answer and say to all the
men of Israel with a loud voice,
15 'Cursed is the man who makes [a,A]an idol or a
molten image, an abomination to the LORD, the
work of the hands of the craftsman, and sets *it* up
in secret.' And [B]all the people shall answer and say,
'Amen.'
16 '[A]Cursed is he who dishonors his father or
mother.' And all the people shall say, 'Amen.'
17 '[A]Cursed is he who moves his neighbor's boundary mark.' And all the people shall say, 'Amen.'
18 '[A]Cursed is he who misleads a blind *person*
on the road.' And all the people shall say, 'Amen.'
19 '[A]Cursed is he who distorts the justice due an
alien, [a]orphan, and widow.' And all the people shall
say, 'Amen.'
20 '[A]Cursed is he who lies with his father's wife,
because he has uncovered his father's skirt.' And
all the people shall say, 'Amen.'
21 '[A]Cursed is he who lies with any animal.' And
all the people shall say, 'Amen.'
22 '[A]Cursed is he who lies with his sister, the
daughter of his father or of his mother.' And all
the people shall say, 'Amen.'

26:19 [a]Lit *to set you* [A]Deut 4:7, 8; 28:1, 13 [B]Ex 19:6; Deut 7:6; Is 62:12; Jer 2:3; 1 Pet 2:9 27:2 [A]Josh 8:30-32 27:3 [a]Lit *spoke to* [A]Deut 26:9 27:4 [a]Lit *which* [A]Deut 11:29; Josh 8:30 27:5 [a]Lit *lift up* [A]Ex 20:25; Josh 8:31 27:6 [a]Lit *whole* 27:7 [A]Deut 26:11 27:8 [a]I.e. stones coated with lime, cf v 4 27:10 [a]Lit *listen to the voice of* 27:12 [A]Deut 11:29 [B]Josh 8:33-35 27:15 [a]Or *a graven image* [A]Ex 20:4, 23; 34:17; Lev 19:4; 26:1; Deut 4:16, 23; 5:8; Is 44:9 [B]1 Cor 14:16 27:16 [A]Ex 20:12; 21:17; Lev 19:3; 20:9; Deut 5:16; Ezek 22:7 27:17 [A]Deut 19:14; Prov 22:28 27:18 [A]Lev 19:14 27:19 [a]Or *fatherless* [A]Ex 22:21; 23:9; Lev 19:33; Deut 10:18; 24:17 27:20 [A]Lev 18:8; 20:11; Deut 22:30; 1 Cor 5:1 27:21 [A]Ex 22:19; Lev 18:23; 20:15 27:22 [A]Lev 18:9; 20:17

27:1–28:68 In these two chapters, Moses explained the curses and the blessings associated with the Sinaitic Covenant. He first called Israel to perform an elaborate ceremony to ratify the covenant when they entered the land (27:1–26; carried out by Joshua in Jos 8:30–35). This was to remind the people that it was essential to obey the covenant and its laws. Then, Moses further explained the blessings for obedience and the curses for disobedience (28:1–68).

27:2, 4 coat them with lime. Upon arrival in the Land of Promise, under Joshua, large stone pillars were to be erected. Following the method used in Egypt, they were to be prepared for writing by whitewashing with plaster. When the law was written on the stones, the white background would make it clearly visible and easily read. These inscribed stones were to offer constant testimony to all people and coming generations of their relationship to God and His law (cf. 31:26; Jos 24:26, 27).

27:3, 8 all the words of this law. Probably a reference to the whole book of Deuteronomy.

27:4 Mount Ebal. A mountain in the center of the Promised Land, just to the N of the city of Shechem. It was at Shechem that the Lord first appeared to Abraham in the land and where Abraham built his first altar to the Lord (Ge 12:6, 7). This mountain, where the stone pillars with the law and the altar (v. 5) were built, was the place where the curses were to be read (v. 13).

27:5–7 build there an altar. In addition to setting up the stones, the Israelites were to build an altar of uncut stones. On this altar the offerings were to be brought to the Lord, and together the people would rejoice in God's presence. This is what was done when the covenantal relationship was established at Mt. Sinai (Ex 24:1–8). The burnt offerings, completely consumed, represented complete devotion to God; the peace offerings expressed thanks to Him.

27:12, 13 these … these. The 12 tribes were divided into two groups of 6 each. The tribe of Levi was to participate in the first group. The tribes of Manasseh and Ephraim were together as the tribe of Joseph.

27:12 Mount Gerizim. This was the mountain just to the S of Mt. Ebal with the city of Shechem in the valley between, from which the blessings were to be read. Perhaps the actual arrangement provided that the priests stood by the ark of the covenant, in the valley between the two mountains, with 6 tribes located northward toward Mt. Ebal and 6 southward toward Mt. Gerizim. The priests and Levites read the curses and blessings with the people responding with the "Amen" of affirmation. **to bless.** The blessings that were to be recited from Mt. Gerizim were not recorded in this passage, no doubt omitted here to stress that Israel did not prove themselves obedient to the covenant and, therefore, did not enjoy the blessings.

27:15–26 Twelve offenses serve as examples of the kind of iniquities that made one subject to the curse. These offenses might have been chosen because they are representative of sins that might escape detection and so remain secret (vv. 15, 24).

27:15 man who makes …. molten image. The first curse concerned idolatry, the breaking of the first and second commandments (5:7–10). **Amen.** To each curse all the people responded, "Amen." The word means "so be it." The people thereby indicated their understanding and agreement with the statement made.

27:16 dishonors his father or mother. The dishonoring of parents was the breaking of the fifth commandment (5:16).

27:17 boundary mark. *See note on 19:14.*

27:18 misleads a blind *person*. This refers to abusing a blind man.

27:19 distorts the justice. The taking advantage of those members of society who could be easily abused.

27:20 lies with his father's wife. Incest. *See note on 22:30.*

27:21 lies with any animal. Bestiality. See Ex 22:19; Lv 18:23; 20:15, 16.

27:22 lies with his sister. The committing of incest with either a full sister or a half sister.

23 '[A]Cursed is he who lies with his mother-in-law.'
And all the people shall say, 'Amen.'
24 '[A]Cursed is he who strikes his neighbor in secret.' And all the people shall say, 'Amen.'
25 '[A]Cursed is he who accepts a bribe to strike
down an innocent person.' And all the people shall
say, 'Amen.'
26 '[A]Cursed is he who does not confirm the words
of this law by doing them.' And all the people shall
say, 'Amen.'

BLESSINGS AT GERIZIM

28 "[A]Now it shall be, if you diligently [a]obey the
LORD your God, being careful to do all His
commandments which I command you today, the
LORD your God [B]will set you high above all the nations of the earth. 2 All these blessings will come
upon you and [A]overtake you if you [a]obey the LORD
your God:
3 "Blessed *shall* you *be* in the city, and blessed
shall you *be* [A]in the [a]country.
4 "Blessed *shall be* the [a]offspring of your [b]body
and the [a]produce of your ground and the [a]offspring
of your beasts, the increase of your herd and the
young of your flock.
5 "Blessed *shall be* your basket and your kneading bowl.
6 "Blessed *shall* you *be* [A]when you come in, and
blessed *shall* you *be* when you go out.
7 "The LORD shall cause your enemies who rise
up against you to be [a]defeated before you; they
will come out against you one way and will flee before you seven ways. 8 The LORD will command the
blessing upon you in your barns and in [A]all that you
put your hand to, and He will bless you in the land
which the LORD your God gives you. 9 [A]The LORD
will establish you as a holy people to Himself, as
He swore to you, if you keep the commandments
of the LORD your God and walk in His ways. 10 So
all the peoples of the earth will see that [a,A]you are
called by the name of the LORD, and they will be
afraid of you. 11 [A]The LORD will make you abound
in prosperity, in the [a]offspring of your [b]body and in
the [a]offspring of your beast and in the [a]produce of
your ground, in the land which the LORD swore to
your fathers to give you. 12 The LORD will open for
you His good storehouse, the heavens, to give rain
to your land in its season and to bless all the work
of your hand; and [A]you shall lend to many nations,
but you shall not borrow. 13 [A]The LORD will make
you the head and not the tail, and you only will be
above, and you will not be underneath, if you listen
to the commandments of the LORD your God, which
I charge you today, to [a]observe *them* carefully, 14 and
[A]do not turn aside from any of the words which I
command you today, to the right or to the left, to
go after other gods to serve them.

CONSEQUENCES OF DISOBEDIENCE

15 "[A]But it shall come about, if you do not [a]obey
the LORD your God, to observe to do all His commandments and His statutes with which I charge

27:23 [A]Lev 20:14 27:24 [A]Ex 21:12; Lev 24:17; Num 35:30, 31 27:25 [A]Ex 23:7; Deut 10:17; Ps 15:5; Ezek 22:12 27:26 [A]Ps 119:21; Jer 11:3; Gal 3:10 28:1 [a]Lit *listen to the voice of* [A]Ex 15:26; 23:22-27; Lev 26:3-13; Deut 7:12-26; 11:13 [B]Deut 28:13; 26:19; 1 Chr 14:2 28:2 [a]Lit *listen to the voice of* [A]Zech 1:6 28:3 [a]Or *field* [A]Gen 39:5 28:4 [a]Lit *fruit* [b]Lit *womb* 28:6 [A]Ps 121:8 28:7 [a]Lit *smitten* 28:8 [A]Deut 15:10 28:9 [A]Ex 19:5 28:10 [a]Lit *the name of the LORD is called upon you* [A]2 Chr 7:14 28:11 [a]Lit *fruit* [b]Or *womb* [A]Deut 28:4; Prov 10:22 28:12 [A]Deut 23:20 28:13 [a]Lit *keep and do* [A]Deut 28:1, 44 28:14 [A]Deut 5:32; Josh 1:7 28:15 [a]Lit *listen to the voice of* [A]Lev 26:14-43; Josh 23:15; Dan 9:11

27:23 lies with his mother-in-law. See Lv 18:17; 20:14.

27:24 strikes his neighbor in secret. A secret attempt to murder a neighbor.

27:25 accepts a bribe. This relates to a paid assassin.

27:26 does not confirm the words of this law. The final curse covered all the rest of God's commandments enunciated by Moses on the plains of Moab (cf. Gal 3:10). Total obedience is demanded by the law and required by God. Only the Lord Jesus Christ accomplished this (2Co 5:21). Amen. All the people agreed to be obedient (cf. Ex 24:1–8), a promise they would soon violate.

28:1–68 In his responsibility as leader and mediator, Moses had previously told the people the promise of God's blessing and the warning that they should not turn to other gods when the covenant was given at Sinai (Ex 23:20–33). After their rebellion against that covenant, Moses warned them (Lv 26) of the divine judgment that would come if they disobeyed. Here, Moses gives an exhortation based upon the blessings and the curses of the covenant (see Lv 26:1–45). The blessings and the curses in this chapter follow the same structure. First, Moses clearly explained that the quality of Israel's future experience would come on the basis of obedience or disobedience to God (28:1, 2, 15). Second, the actual blessings and curses were succinctly stated (28:3–6, 16–19). Third, Moses gave a sermonic elaboration of the basic blessings and curses (28:7–14, 20–68). Just as the curses were given more prominence in the ceremony of 27:11–26, so the curses incurred by disobedience to the covenant were much more fully developed here. The perspective of Moses was that Israel would not prove faithful to the covenant (31:16–18, 27) and so would not enjoy the blessings of the covenant; therefore, the curses received much more attention.

28:1–14 See Jos 21:45; 23:14, 15; 1Ki 8:56 for blessing fulfillment.

28:1, 2 diligently obey the LORD your God. "Diligently obey" stressed the need for complete obedience on the part of Israel. The people could not legally or personally merit God's goodness and blessing, but their constant desire to obey, worship, and maintain a right relation to Him was evidence of their true faith in and love for Him (cf. 6:5). It was also evidence of God's gracious work in their hearts.

28:1 high above all the nations. If Israel obeyed the Lord, ultimate blessing would be given in the form of preeminence above all the nations of the world (see 26:19). The indispensable condition for obtaining this blessing was salvation, resulting in obedience to the Lord, in the form of keeping His commandments. This blessing will ultimately come to pass in the millennial kingdom, particularly designed to exalt Israel's King, the Messiah, and His nation (see Zec 13:1–14:21; Ro 11:25–27).

28:3–6 Blessed. These beatitudes summarize the various spheres where the blessing of God would extend to Israel's life. God's favor is also intended to permeate all their endeavors as emphasized further in the expanded summary in 28:7–14, on the condition of obedience (vv. 1, 2, 9, 13, 14). They will know victory, prosperity, purity, respect, abundance, and dominance—comprehensive blessing.

28:6 come in ... go out. An idiomatic way of referring to the normal everyday activities of life (see 31:2). This is a fitting conclusion to the "blessings and curses" (v. 19) since it sums up everything.

28:10 called by the name of the LORD. Israel's obedience and blessing would cause all the people of the earth to fear Israel because they were clearly the people of God. This was God's intention for them all along, to be a witness to the nations of the one true and living God and draw the Gentiles out of idol worship. They will be that witness nation in the last days (see Rev 7:4–10; 14:1) and in the kingdom (see Zec 8:1–12).

28:13 the head and not the tail. Israel was to be the leader over the other nations ("the head") and not to be in subjection to another nation ("the tail").

28:15–68 The curses are outlined as God warned His people of the price of the absence of love for Him and disobedience.

28:15 Cf. Jos 23:15, 16.

you today, that all these curses will come upon you and overtake you:

16 “[A]Cursed *shall* you *be* in the city, and cursed *shall* you *be* in the [a]country.

17 “[A]Cursed *shall be* your basket and your kneading bowl.

18 “[A]Cursed *shall be* the [a]offspring of your [b]body and the [a]produce of your ground, the increase of your herd and the young of your flock.

19 “[A]Cursed *shall* you *be* when you come in, and cursed *shall* you *be* when you go out.

20 “[A]The LORD will send upon you curses, confusion, and [B]rebuke, in all [a]you undertake to do, until you are destroyed and until [C]you perish quickly, on account of the evil of your deeds, because you have forsaken Me. 21 [A]The LORD will make the pestilence cling to you until He has consumed you from the land where you are entering to possess it. 22 [A]The LORD will smite you with consumption and with fever and with inflammation and with fiery heat and with [a]the sword and [B]with blight and with mildew, and they will pursue you until [C]you perish. 23 [a]The heaven which is over your head shall be bronze, and the earth which is under you, iron. 24 [A]The LORD will make the rain of your land powder and dust; from heaven it shall come down on you until you are destroyed.

25 “[A]The LORD shall cause you to be [a]defeated before your enemies; you will go out one way against them, but you will flee seven ways before them, and you will [B]be *an example of* terror to all the kingdoms of the earth. 26 [A]Your carcasses will be food to all birds of the sky and to the beasts of the earth, and there will be no one to frighten *them* away.

27 “[A]The LORD will smite you with the boils of Egypt and with [B]tumors and with the scab and with the itch, from which you cannot be healed. 28 The LORD will smite you with madness and with blindness and with bewilderment of heart; 29 and you will [a,A]grope at noon, as the blind man gropes in darkness, and you will not prosper in your ways; but you shall only be oppressed and robbed continually, with none to save you. 30 [A]You shall betroth a wife, but another man will violate her; [B]you shall build a house, but you will not live in it; you shall plant a vineyard, but you will not [a]use its fruit. 31 Your ox shall be slaughtered before your eyes, but you will not eat of it; your donkey shall be torn away from you, and will not be restored to you; your sheep shall be given to your enemies, and you will have none to save you. 32 [A]Your sons and your daughters shall be given to another people, while your eyes look on and yearn for them continually; but there will be nothing [a]you can do. 33 [A]A people whom you do not know shall eat up the produce of your ground and all your labors, and you will never be anything but oppressed and crushed continually. 34 You shall be driven mad by the sight of [a]what you see. 35 [A]The LORD will strike you on the knees and legs with sore boils, from which you cannot be healed, from the sole of your foot to the crown of your head. 36 [A]The LORD will bring you and your king, whom you set over you, to a nation which neither you nor your fathers have known, and there you shall serve other gods, [B]wood and stone. 37 [A]You shall become a horror, a proverb, and a taunt among all the people where the LORD drives you.

38 “[A]You shall bring out much seed to the field but you will gather in little, for [B]the locust will consume it. 39 [A]You shall plant and cultivate vineyards, but you will neither drink of the wine nor gather *the grapes,* for the worm will devour them. 40 [A]You shall have olive trees throughout your territory but you will not anoint yourself with the oil, for your olives will drop off. 41 [A]You shall [a]have sons and daughters but they will not be yours, for they will go into captivity. 42 [A]The cricket shall possess all your trees and the produce of your ground. 43 [A]The alien who is among you shall rise above you higher and higher, but you will go down lower and lower. 44 [A]He shall lend to you, but you will not lend to him; [B]he shall be the head, and you will be the tail.

45 “So all these curses shall come on you and pursue you and overtake you [A]until you are destroyed, because you would not [a]obey the LORD your God by

28:16 [a]Or *field* [A]Deut 28:3 28:17 [A]Deut 28:5 28:18 [a]Lit *fruit* [b]Or *womb* [A]Deut 28:4 28:19 [A]Deut 28:6 28:20 [a]Lit *the putting forth of your hand which you do* [A]Deut 28:8; Mal 2:2 [B]Ps 80:16; Is 51:20; 66:15 [C]Deut 4:26 28:21 [A]Lev 26:25; Num 14:12; Jer 24:10; Amos 4:10 28:22 [a]Another reading is *drought* [A]Lev 26:16 [B]Amos 4:9 [C]Deut 4:26 28:23 [a]Lit *Your* 28:24 [A]Deut 11:17; 28:12 28:25 [a]Lit *smitten* [A]Deut 28:7; Is 30:17 [B]2 Chr 29:8; Jer 15:4; 24:9; Ezek 23:46 28:26 [A]Jer 7:33; 16:4; 19:7; 34:20 28:27 [A]Ex 9:9; Deut 7:15; 28:60, 61 [B]1 Sam 5:6 28:29 [a]Lit *be groping* [A]Ex 10:21 28:30 [a]Lit *begin it* [A]Job 31:10; Jer 8:10 [B]Amos 5:11 28:32 [a]Lit *in the power of your hand* [A]Deut 28:41 28:33 [A]Jer 5:15, 17 28:34 [a]Lit *your eyes which you* 28:35 [A]Deut 28:27 28:36 [A]2 Kin 17:4, 6; 24:12, 14; 25:7, 11; 2 Chr 36:1-21; Jer 39:1-9 [B]Deut 4:28; Jer 16:13 28:37 [A]1 Kin 9:7, 8; Jer 19:8; 24:9; 25:9; 29:18 28:38 [A]Is 5:10; Mic 6:15; Hag 1:6 [B]Ex 10:4; Joel 1:4 28:39 [A]Is 5:10; 17:10, 11 28:40 [A]Jer 11:16; Mic 6:15 28:41 [a]Lit *beget* [A]Deut 28:32 28:42 [A]Deut 28:38 28:43 [A]Deut 28:13 28:44 [A]Deut 28:12 [B]Deut 28:13 28:45 [a]Lit *listen to the voice of* [A]Deut 4:25, 26

28:16–19 These are parallels to the blessings in vv. 3–6.

28:20 until you are destroyed. Moses was aware that the Israelites were apt to be unfaithful to God, so he portrays in extended warnings the disastrous results of the loss of their land and their place of worship if they disobeyed God. Destruction was the ultimate calamity for Israel's sin (vv. 20, 21, 24, 45, 48, 51, 61, 63).

28:21 Cf. Jer 14:12; 21:6; Eze 5:12; 6:11.

28:22 Cf. Am 4:9.

28:23 bronze … iron. The heavens would be as bright as bronze, but no rain would fall from them to water the ground. The earth would be as hard as iron, so any rain that would fall would run off and not penetrate (cf. Am 4:7).

28:25 Cf. 2Ch 29:8; Ne 1:8; Jer 15:4.

28:26 Cf. Jer 7:33; 16:4; 19:7; 34:20.

28:27 the boils of Egypt. The disease with which God afflicted the Egyptians prior to the Exodus (see Ex 9:9; Am 4:10).

28:30 These 3 curses were in contrast to the exemptions from military service granted in 20:5–7. The exemptions were possible because God would grant His people victory in battle. Disobedience to the Lord, however, would mean that God would no longer fight for His people. Those normally exempted from military service would be forced to fight and be killed. Consequently, the soldier's betrothed wife would be violated and his house and grapes taken by the foreign invader (cf. Jer 8:10; Am 5:11; Zep 1:13).

28:32 Cf. 2Ch 29:9.

28:35 sole of your foot … head. Diseases of the skin would afflict the people cursed by God. The disease mentioned here is like that from which Job suffered (see Job 2:7).

28:36 your king, whom you set over you. Though they had no king at the time of entering the land, Moses anticipated that Israel would have a king over them when this curse came—a future king of Israel who would be taken with them into exile. **to a nation which neither you nor your fathers have known.** The Israelites would be taken captive to a nation other than Egypt, where they had recently been in bondage. This future nation would be particularly steeped in idolatry (cf. 2Ki 17:41; Jer 16:13).

28:37 Cf. 1Ki 9:8; 2Ch 29:8; Jer 19:8; 25:9, 18; 29:18.

keeping His commandments and His statutes which
He commanded you. 46 They shall become [A]a sign
and a wonder on you and your [a]descendants forever.
47 "[A]Because you did not serve the LORD your God
with joy and a glad heart, for the abundance of all
things; 48 therefore you shall serve your enemies
whom the LORD will send against you, [A]in hunger,
in thirst, in nakedness, and in the lack of all things;
and He [B]will put an iron yoke on your neck until He
has destroyed you.
49 "[A]The LORD will bring a nation against you from
afar, from the end of the earth, [B]as the eagle swoops
down, a nation whose language you shall not understand, 50 a nation of fierce countenance who will
[A]have no respect for the old, nor show favor to the
young. 51 Moreover, it shall eat the [a]offspring of your
herd and the produce of your ground until you are
destroyed, who also leaves you no grain, new wine,
or oil, nor the increase of your herd or the young
of your flock until they have caused you to perish.
52 [A]It shall besiege you in all your [a]towns until your
high and fortified walls in which you trusted come
down throughout your land, and it shall besiege you
in all your [a]towns throughout your land which the
LORD your God has given you. 53 [A]Then you shall eat
the [a]offspring of your own body, the flesh of your
sons and of your daughters whom the LORD your
God has given you, during the siege and the distress
by which your enemy will [b]oppress you. 54 The man
who is [a]refined and very delicate among you [b]shall
be hostile toward his brother and toward the wife
[c]he cherishes and toward the rest of his children
who remain, 55 so that he will not give *even* one of
them any of the flesh of his children which he will
eat, since he has nothing *else* left, during the siege
and the distress by which your enemy will [a]oppress
you in all your [b]towns. 56 [A]The [a]refined and delicate
woman among you, who would not venture to set
the sole of her foot on the ground for delicateness
and [b]refinement, [c]shall be hostile toward the husband [d]she cherishes and toward her son and daughter, 57 and toward her afterbirth which issues from
between her [a]legs and toward her children whom
she bears; for [A]she will eat them secretly for lack of
anything *else,* during the siege and the distress by
which your enemy will [b]oppress you in your [c]towns.
58 "If you are not careful to observe all the words
of this law which are written in this book, to [a,A]fear
this honored and awesome [B]name, [b]the LORD your
God, 59 then the LORD will bring extraordinary
plagues on you and [a]your descendants, even [b]se-
vere and lasting plagues, and miserable and chronic
sicknesses. 60 [A]He will bring back on you all the diseases of Egypt of which you were afraid, and they
will cling to you. 61 Also every sickness and every
plague which, not written in the book of this law,
the LORD will bring on you [A]until you are destroyed.
62 Then you shall be left few in number, [A]whereas
you were as numerous as the stars of heaven, because you did not [a]obey the LORD your God. 63 It shall
come about that as the LORD [A]delighted over you
to prosper you, and multiply you, so the LORD will
[B]delight over you to make you perish and destroy
you; and you will be [C]torn from the land where you
are entering to possess it. 64 Moreover, the LORD
will [A]scatter you among all peoples, from one end
of the earth to the other end of the earth; and there
you shall [B]serve other gods, wood and stone, which
you or your fathers have not known. 65 [A]Among
those nations you shall find no rest, and there will
be no resting place for the sole of your foot; but
there [B]the LORD will give you a trembling heart,

28:46 [a]Lit *seed* [A]Num 26:10; Is 8:18; Ezek 5:15; 14:8 28:47 [A]Deut 12:7; Neh 9:35-37 28:48 [A]Lam 4:4-6 [B]Jer 28:13, 14 28:49 [A]Is 5:26-30; 7:18-20; Jer 5:15; 6:22, 23 [B]Jer 48:40; 49:22; Lam 4:19; Hos 8:1 28:50 [A]Is 47:6 28:51 [a]Lit *fruit* 28:52 [a]Lit *gates* [A]Jer 10:17, 18; Zeph 1:15, 16 28:53 [a]Lit *fruit* [b]Or *distress* [A]Lev 26:29; 2 Kin 6:28, 29; Jer 19:9; Lam 2:20; 4:10 28:54 [a]Lit *tender* [b]Lit *his eye shall be evil toward* [c]Lit *of his bosom* 28:55 [a]Or *distress* [b]Lit *gates* 28:56 [a]Lit *tender* [b]Lit *tenderness* [c]Lit *her eye shall be evil toward* [d]Lit *of her bosom* [A]Lam 4:10 28:57 [a]Lit *feet* [b]Or *distress* [c]Lit *gates* [A]2 Kin 6:28, 29; Lam 4:10 28:58 [a]Or *reverence* [b]Heb *YHWH* [A]Ps 99:3; Mal 1:14 [B]Is 42:8 28:59 [a]Lit *plague on your seed* [b]Lit *great* 28:60 [A]Deut 28:27 28:61 [A]Deut 4:25, 26 28:62 [a]Lit *listen to the voice of* [A]Deut 1:10; Neh 9:23 28:63 [A]Jer 32:41 [B]Prov 1:26 [C]Jer 12:14; 45:4 28:64 [A]Lev 26:33; Deut 4:27; Neh 1:8 [B]Deut 4:28; 29:26; 32:17 28:65 [A]Lam 1:3 [B]Lev 26:36

28:38–40 Cf. Is 5:10; Joel 1:4; Mic 6:15.

28:46 Cf. 2Ch 29:8; Jer 18:6; Eze 14:8.

28:49 a nation ... from the end of the earth. God would raise up a nation to act as His own instrument of judgment against His ungrateful people. This foreign nation was described as coming from a far distance from Israel, a nation that would arise quickly and one that would completely devastate the land. This was fulfilled first by Assyria (Is 5:26; 7:18–20; 28:11; 37:18; Hos 8:1) and second, by Babylon (Jer 5:15; La 4:19; Eze 17:3; Hab 1:6–8).

28:50 Cf. 2Ch 36:17.

28:52–57 Ultimately, an invading nation would besiege all of the cities of Judah (*see note on 28:49*). In vv. 53–57, Moses gave a revolting description of the Israelites' response to those siege conditions. The unthinkable activity of cannibalism is introduced in v. 53 and then illustrated in the verses that follow (see 2Ki 6:28, 29; La 2:20; 4:10).

28:52 Cf. 2Ch 32:10; Jer 10:17, 18; Eze 5:2; Hos 11:6.

28:53 Cf. Jer 19:9.

28:58–63 this honored and awesome name, the LORD your God. Israel's obedience to the law (i.e., the Sinaitic Covenant) would lead to fearing the Lord, whose "name" represents His presence and character. The title "Lord (Yahweh)" revealed the glory and greatness of God (see Ex 3:15). Significantly, the phrase "the LORD your God" is used approximately 280 times in the book of Deuteronomy. The full measure of the divine curse would come on Israel when its disobedience had been hardened into disregard for the glorious and awesome character of God. In vv. 15, 45 Moses described curses for disobedience; hence the worst of the curses come when disobedience is hardened into failure to fear God. Only God's grace would save a small remnant (v. 62), thus keeping Israel from being annihilated (cf. Mal 2:2). In contrast to the promise made to Abraham in Ge 15:5, the physical seed of Abraham under God's curse would be reduced; as God had multiplied the seed of the patriarchs in Egypt (see Ex 1:7), He would decimate their numbers to make them as nothing until His restoration of the nation in a future day (see 30:5).

28:59–61 Cf. Am 4:10.

28:61 the book of this law. A definite, particular written document was meant (see 31:9), referring not just to Deuteronomy (cf. 31:9), but to the Pentateuch, as far as it had been written. This is evident from vv. 60, 61, which indicate that the diseases of Egypt were written in the book of the law, thus referring to Exodus, which records those plagues.

28:63 Cf. Jer 12:14; 45:4.

28:64 the LORD will scatter you. The Jews remaining after the curses fall would be dispersed by the Lord ultimately to serve false gods, restlessly and fearfully throughout all the nations of the earth (cf. Ne 1:8, 9; Jer 30:11; Eze 11:16). This dispersion began with the captivity of the northern kingdom, Israel (722 B.C.), then the southern kingdom, Judah (586 B.C.), and is still a reality today. In the future earthly kingdom of Messiah, Israel will experience its regathering in faith, salvation, and righteousness. See Is 59:19–21; Jer 31:31–34; Eze 36:8–37:14; Zec 12:10–14:21. The unbearable nature of Israel's present condition was emphasized since the people longed for another time (v. 67). Cf. Jer 44:7; Hos 8:13; 9:3; 11:4, 5.

failing of eyes, and despair of soul. 66 So your life shall [a]hang in doubt before you; and you will be in dread night and day, and shall have no assurance of your life. 67 [A]In the morning you shall say, 'Would that it were evening!' And at evening you shall say, 'Would that it were morning!' because of the dread of your heart which you dread, and for the sight of your eyes which you will see. 68 The LORD will bring you back to Egypt in ships, by the way about which I spoke to you, 'You will never see it again!' And there you will offer yourselves for sale to your enemies as male and female slaves, but there will be no buyer."

THE COVENANT IN MOAB

29 [a,A]These are the words of the covenant which the LORD commanded Moses to make with the sons of Israel in the land of Moab, besides the [B]covenant which He had made with them at Horeb.

2 [a]And Moses summoned all Israel and said to them, "You have seen all that the LORD did before your eyes in the land of Egypt to Pharaoh and all his servants and all his land; 3 [A]the great trials which your eyes have seen, those great signs and wonders. 4 Yet to this day [A]the LORD has not given you a heart to know, nor eyes to see, nor ears to hear. 5 I have led you forty years in the wilderness; [A]your clothes have not worn out on you, and your sandal has not worn out on your foot. 6 [A]You have not eaten bread, nor have you drunk wine or strong drink, in order that you might know that I am the LORD your God. 7 [A]When you [a]reached this place, Sihon the king of Heshbon and Og the king of Bashan came out to meet us for battle, but we [b]defeated them; 8 and we took their land and [A]gave it as an inheritance to the Reubenites, the Gadites, and the half-tribe of the Manassites. 9 [A]So keep the words of this covenant to do them, [B]that you may prosper in all that you do.

10 "You stand today, all of you, before the LORD your God: your chiefs, your tribes, your elders and your officers, *even* all the men of Israel, 11 your little ones, your wives, and the alien who is within your camps, from [A]the one who chops your wood to the one who draws your water, 12 that you may enter into the covenant with the LORD your God, and into His oath which the LORD your God is making with you today, 13 in order that He may establish you today as His people and that [A]He may be your God, just as He spoke to you and as He swore to your fathers, to Abraham, Isaac, and Jacob.

14 "Now not with you alone am I [A]making this covenant and this oath, 15 [A]but both with those who stand here with us today in the presence of the LORD our God and with those who are not with us here today 16 (for you know how we lived in the land of Egypt, and how we came through the midst of the nations through which you passed; 17 moreover, you have seen their abominations and their idols *of* [A]wood, stone, silver, and gold, which *they had* with them); 18 [A]so that there will not be among you a man or woman, or family or tribe, whose heart turns away today from the LORD our God, to go and serve the gods of those nations; that there will not be among you [B]a root bearing poisonous

28:66 [a]Lit *be hung for you in front* 28:67 [A]Job 7:4 29:1 [a]Ch 28:69 in Heb [A]Lev 26:46; 27:34 [B]Deut 5:2, 3 29:2 [a]Ch 29:1 in Heb 29:3 [A]Deut 4:34; 7:19 29:4 [A]Is 6:9, 10; Ezek 12:2; Matt 13:14; Acts 28:26, 27; Rom 11:8 29:5 [A]Deut 8:4 29:6 [A]Deut 8:3 29:7 [a]Lit *came to* [b]Lit *smote* [A]Num 21:21-24, 33, 35; Deut 2:26-3:17 29:8 [A]Num 32:32, 33; Deut 3:12, 13 29:9 [A]Deut 4:6; 1 Kin 2:3 [B]Josh 1:7 29:11 [A]Josh 9:21, 23, 27 29:13 [A]Gen 17:7; Ex 6:7 29:14 [A]Jer 31:31; Heb 8:7, 8 29:15 [A]Acts 2:39 29:17 [A]Ex 20:23; Deut 4:28; 28:36 29:18 [A]Deut 13:6 [B]Deut 32:32; Heb 12:15

28:68 but there will be no buyer. Israel would be so abandoned by God that she would not even be able to sell herself into slavery. The curse of God would bring Israel into a seemingly hopeless condition (cf. Hos 8:13; 9:3). The specific mention of Egypt could be symbolic for any lands where the Jews have been taken into bondage or sold as slaves. But it is true that after the destruction of Jerusalem in A.D. 70, which was a judgment on the apostasy of Israel and their rejection and execution of the Messiah, this prophecy was actually fulfilled. The Roman general Titus, who conquered Jerusalem and Israel, sent 17,000 adult Jews to Egypt to perform hard labor there and had those who were under 17 years old publicly sold. Under the Roman emperor Hadrian, countless Jews were sold and suffered such bondage and cruelty.

29:1–30:20 These chapters contain the third address of Moses, which is a contrast between the covenant at Sinai and the covenant he envisioned for Israel in the future. Though the past had seen Israel's failure to keep the covenant and to trust in God, there was hope for the future. It was this hope that Moses emphasized in the content of these chapters focusing clearly on the themes of the New Covenant.

29:1 These are the words. The Heb. text numbers this verse as 28:69 rather than 29:1, seeing it as the conclusion to the second address of Moses. However, as in 1:1, these words introduce what follows, serving as the introduction to Moses' third address. **the covenant . . . in the land of Moab.** The majority of interpreters view the covenant stated here as a reference to the covenant made at Sinai. According to this view, the covenant that God made with Israel at Sinai (Horeb) was renewed in Moab. However, this verse clearly states that the covenant of which Moses now speaks was "besides," or "in addition to," the previous covenant. This was another covenant distinct from the one made at Sinai. This other covenant is viewed by some interpreters as the Palestinian Covenant, which gave Israel the title to the land (see 30:5). However, the emphasis of these two chapters is not on the land, but on the change of Israel's heart (see the contrast between 29:4 and 30:6). It was exactly this change of heart which the later prophets would term "The New Covenant" (see Jer 31:31–34; Eze 36:26, 27). In response to Israel's certain failure under the provisions of the Sinaitic Covenant (29:23–28), Moses anticipated the New Covenant under which Israel would be obedient to the Lord and finally reap His blessings (30:1–10).

29:4 the LORD has not given you . . . eyes to see. In spite of all they had experienced (vv. 2, 3), Israel was spiritually blind to the significance of what the Lord had done for them, lacking spiritual understanding, even as Moses was speaking. This spiritual blindness of Israel continues to the present day (Ro 11:8), and it will not be reversed until Israel's future day of salvation (see Ro 11:25–27). The Lord had not given them an understanding heart, simply because the people had not penitently sought it (cf. 2Ch 7:14).

29:9 keep the words of this covenant. The spiritual experience of God's faithfulness to Israel should have led to obedience to the stipulations of the Sinaitic Covenant in the future, but could not without a transformed heart (vv. 4, 18) and the true knowledge of God (v. 6).

29:10, 11 You stand . . . before the LORD your God. All the people were likely stationed in an orderly way before Moses, but this is not a call to outward order, but inward devotion, to make the covenant a matter of the heart and life.

29:12 enter into the covenant . . . and . . . oath. "Enter into" expresses entire submission in faith and repentance before God, resulting in heart obedience. The people were to bind themselves in an oath to obey the stipulations of God's covenant (cf. Gen 26:28).

29:14, 15 not with you alone. All of Israel, present and future, were to be bound by the stipulations of the covenant to obey God and be blessed. Thus they would be able to lead all nations to the blessedness of salvation (cf. Jn 17:20, 21; Ac 2:39).

29:18 a root bearing poisonous fruit and wormwood. The picture was of a root spreading poison and bitterness into the whole tree. The metaphor indicates permeation of idolatry throughout Israel because of the action of an individual family or tribe, precipitating God's curse and wrath.

fruit and wormwood. 19 It shall be when he hears the
words of this curse, that he will [a]boast, saying, 'I have
peace though I walk in the stubbornness of my heart
in order [b]to destroy the watered *land* with the dry.'
20 The LORD shall never be willing to forgive him, but
rather the anger of the LORD and [A]His jealousy will
[a,B]burn against that man, and every curse which is
written in this book will [b]rest on him, and the LORD
will [C]blot out his name from under heaven. 21 Then
the LORD will single him out for [a]adversity from all
the tribes of Israel, according to all the curses of the
covenant [A]which are written in this book of the law.
22 "Now the generation to come, your sons who
rise up after you and [A]the foreigner who comes from
a distant land, when they see the plagues of the land
and the diseases with which the LORD has [a]afflicted
it, will say, 23 'All its land is [A]brimstone and salt, [B]a
burning waste, [a]unsown and unproductive, and no
grass grows in it, like the overthrow of [C]Sodom and
Gomorrah, Admah and Zeboiim, which the LORD
overthrew in His anger and in His wrath.' 24 All the
nations will say, '[A]Why has the LORD done thus to
this land? Why this great [a]outburst of anger?' 25 Then
men will say, '[A]Because they forsook the covenant of
the LORD, the God of their fathers, which He made
with them when He brought them out of the land
of Egypt. 26 They went and served other gods and
worshiped them, gods whom they have not known
and whom He had not [a]allotted to them. 27 Therefore,
the anger of the LORD burned against that land, [A]to
bring upon it every curse which is written in this
book; 28 and [A]the LORD uprooted them from their
land in anger and in fury and in great wrath, and
cast them into another land, as *it is* this day.'
29 "[A]The secret things belong to the LORD our
God, but [B]the things revealed belong to us and to
our sons forever, that we may observe all the words
of this law.

RESTORATION PROMISED

30 "So it shall be when all of these things have
come upon you, [A]the blessing and the curse
which I have set before you, and you [a]call *them* to
mind [B]in all nations where the LORD your God has
banished you, 2 and you [A]return to the LORD your
God and [a]obey Him [B]with all your heart and soul
according to all that I command you today, you and
your sons, 3 then the LORD your God will [A]restore
[a]you from captivity, and have compassion on you,
and [B]will gather you again from all the peoples
where the LORD your God has [C]scattered you. 4 If
your outcasts are at the ends of the [a]earth, [A]from
there the LORD your God will gather you, and from
there He will [b]bring you back. 5 [A]The LORD your God
will bring you into the land which your fathers possessed, and you shall possess it; and He will prosper
you and [B]multiply you more than your fathers.
6 "Moreover [A]the LORD your God will circumcise
your heart and the heart of your [a]descendants, [B]to
love the LORD your God with all your heart and with
all your soul, so that you may live. 7 [A]The LORD your
God will [a]inflict all these curses on your enemies

29:19 [a]Lit *bless himself in his heart* [b]I.e. to destroy everything 29:20 [a]Lit *smoke* [b]Lit *lie down* [A]Ps 79:5; Ezek 23:25 [B]Ps 74:1; 80:4 [C]Ex 32:33; Deut 9:14; 2 Kin 14:27 29:21 [a]Lit *evil* [A]Deut 30:10 29:22 [a]Lit *made it sick* [A]Jer 19:8; 49:17; 50:13 29:23 [a]Lit *it is not sown and does not cause to sprout* [A]Gen 19:24; Is 34:9; Jer 17:6; Zeph 2:9 [B]Is 1:7; 64:11 [C]Jude 7 29:24 [a]Lit *heat* [A]1 Kin 9:8; Jer 22:8 29:25 [A]2 Kin 17:9-23; 2 Chr 36:13-21 29:26 [a]Lit *portioned* 29:27 [A]Dan 9:11 29:28 [A]2 Chr 7:20; Ps 52:5; Prov 2:22; Ezek 19:12, 13 29:29 [A]Acts 1:7 [B]John 5:39; Acts 17:11; 2 Tim 3:16 30:1 [a]Lit *cause them to return to your heart* [A]Deut 11:26; 30:15, 19 [B]Lev 26:40-45; Deut 28:64; 29:28; 1 Kin 8:47 30:2 [a]Lit *listen to His voice* [A]Deut 4:29, 30; Neh 1:9 [B]Deut 4:29 30:3 [a]Lit *your captivity* [A]Gen 28:15; 48:21; Ps 126:1, 4; Jer 29:14 [B]Ps 147:2; Jer 32:37; Ezek 34:13 [C]Deut 4:27 30:4 [a]Lit *sky* [b]Lit *take you* [A]Neh 1:9; Is 43:6; 48:20; 62:11 30:5 [A]Jer 29:14; 30:3 [B]Deut 7:13; 13:17 30:6 [a]Lit *seed* [A]Deut 10:16 [B]Deut 6:5 30:7 [a]Lit *put* [A]Deut 7:15

29:19 to destroy the watered *land* with the dry. The meaning is that the deceived individual rebel against the Lord follows only his wicked heart and could not hide within the total community. The idolater would stand out and bear the judgment for his idolatry.

29:20 blot out his name from under heaven. The idolater would have no place among God's people, because God would curse him and then kill him (cf. 25:19: Ex 17:14). This very strong language reveals how God feels about idolatry, which is forbidden in the Decalogue (Ex 20:2–7).

29:21 this book of the law. *See note on 31:9.*

29:22 the generation to come ... and the foreigner. In a future day, both Israel and the nations would see the results of God's judgment upon the land of Israel because of Israel's disobedience, as a witness to the holy standard God has established in His law. Cf. Lv 26:31, 32.

29:23 Sodom. The punishment the Lord would bring upon Israel in the future was likened to that of Sodom and her allies whom the Lord buried in fiery brimstone in the time of Abraham and Lot (see Ge 19:24–29). It should be noted that Sodom and vicinity resembled paradise, the garden of God, before its destruction (cf. Ge 13:10).

29:24 This question is answered in vv. 25–28.

29:29 God has not revealed all that could be disclosed from His infinite mind. What He has unveiled stands sufficient for salvation, maturation in the faith, and glorifying God by obedience to His Word. While there are secret things unknown, believers will be held accountable to obey only what they do know accented by the divine threat of judgment for continued sinful disobedience.

30:1–10 The rejection of God by Israel, and of Israel by God and the subsequent dispersion were not the end of the story of God's people. Having anticipated a time when Israel's disobedience would lead to her captivity in a foreign land, Moses looked beyond the destruction of that time of judgment to an even more distant time of restoration and redemption for Israel (cf. Lv 26:40–45). This future restoration and blessing of Israel would take place under the New Covenant (*see notes on Jer 31:31–34; 32:36–41; Eze 36:25–27*). For a comparison of the New Covenant with the Old Covenant, *see notes on 2Co 3:6–18.*

30:1–3 you call *them* to mind. Moses moved to the future when curses would be over and blessings would come. At some future time, after disobedience to the Lord brought upon Israel the curses of the covenant, the people will remember that the circumstances in which they found themselves were the inevitable consequence of their disobedience, and in repentance they will return to the Lord. This repentance will lead to a wholehearted commitment of obedience to God's commandments (v. 8) and the consequent end of Israel's distress (v. 3). This is the ultimate salvation of Israel by faith in Christ, spoken of by Isaiah (54:4–8), Jeremiah (31:31–34; 32:37–42), Ezekiel (36:23–38), Hosea (14:1–9), Joel (3:16–21), Amos (9:11–15), Zephaniah (3:14–20), Zechariah (12:10–13:9), Malachi (3:16–4:4), and Paul (Ro 11:25–27).

30:4, 5 The gathering of Jews out of all the countries of the earth will follow Israel's final redemption. Restoration to the land will be in fulfillment of the promise of the covenant given to Abraham (see Ge 12:7; 13:15; 15:18–21; 17:8) and so often reiterated by Moses and the prophets.

30:6 the LORD ... will circumcise your heart. Cf. 10:16. This work of God in the innermost being of the individual is the true salvation that grants a new will to obey Him in place of the former spiritual insensitivity and stubbornness (cf. Jer 4:4; 9:25; Ro 2:28, 29). This new heart will allow the Israelite to love the Lord wholeheartedly, and is the essential feature of the New Covenant (see 29:4, 18; 30:10, 17; Jer 31:31–34; 32:37–42; Eze 11:19; 36:26). *See note on Jer 4:4.*

30:7 on your enemies. The curses that had fallen on Israel because of disobedience will in the future come upon the nations that

and on those who hate you, who persecuted you.
8 And you shall again [a]obey the LORD, and observe
all His commandments which I command you today. 9 [A]Then the LORD your God will [a]prosper you
abundantly in all the work of your hand, in the [b]off-
spring of your [c]body and in the [b]offspring of your
cattle and in the [b]produce of your ground, for [B]the
LORD will again rejoice over you for good, just as
He rejoiced over your fathers; 10 [a]if you [b]obey the
LORD your God to keep His commandments and
His statutes which [A]are written in this book of the
law, [a]if you turn to the LORD your God [B]with all your
heart and soul.

11 "For this commandment which I command
you today is not too difficult for you, nor is it [a]out
of reach. 12 It is not in heaven, [a]that you should say,
'[A]Who will go up to heaven for us to get it for us and
make us hear it, that we may observe it?' 13 Nor is
it beyond the sea, [a]that you should say, 'Who will
cross the sea for us to get it for us and make us hear
it, that we may observe it?' 14 But the word is very
near you, in your mouth and in your heart, that you
may observe it.

CHOOSE LIFE

15 "See, [A]I have set before you today life and [a]pros-
perity, and death and [b]adversity; 16 in that I command you today [A]to love the LORD your God, to walk
in His ways and to keep His commandments and
His statutes and His judgments, that you [B]may live
and multiply, and that the LORD your God may bless
you in the land where you are entering to possess
it. 17 But if your heart turns away and you will not
obey, but are drawn away and worship other gods
and serve them, 18 I declare to you today that [A]you
shall surely perish. You will not prolong *your* days
in the land where you are crossing the Jordan to
enter [a]and possess it. 19 [A]I call heaven and earth to
witness against you today, that I have set before
you life and death, [B]the blessing and the curse. So
choose life in order that you may live, you and your
[a]descendants, 20 [A]by loving the LORD your God, by
obeying His voice, and [B]by holding fast to Him; [C]for
[a]this is your life and the length of your days, [b]that you
may live in [D]the land which the LORD swore to your
fathers, to Abraham, Isaac, and Jacob, to give them."

MOSES' LAST COUNSEL

31 So Moses went and spoke these words to all
Israel. 2 And he said to them, "I am [A]a hundred
and twenty years old today; [B]I am no longer able to
come and go, and the LORD has said to me, '[C]You
shall not cross this Jordan.' 3 [A]It is the LORD your
God who will cross ahead of you; He will destroy
these nations before you, and you shall dispossess them. [B]Joshua is the one who will cross ahead
of you, just as the LORD has spoken. 4 The LORD
will do to them just as He did to Sihon and Og, the
kings of the Amorites, and to their land, when He
destroyed them. 5 [A]The LORD will deliver them up
before you, and you shall do to them according to all
the commandments which I have commanded you.

30:8 [a]Lit *listen to the voice of* 30:9 [a]Lit *make you have excess for good* [b]Lit *fruit* [c]Lit *womb* [A]Jer 31:27, 28 [B]Jer 32:41 30:10 [a]Or *for you will* [b]Lit *listen to the voice of* [A]Deut 29:21 [B]Deut 4:29 30:11 [a]Lit *far off* 30:12 [a]Lit *to say* [A]Rom 10:6-8 30:13 [a]Lit *to say* 30:15 [a]Lit *good* [b]Lit *evil* [A]Deut 11:26 30:16 [A]Deut 6:5 [B]Deut 4:1; 30:19 30:18 [a]Lit *to* [A]Deut 4:26; 8:19 30:19 [a]Lit *seed* [A]Deut 4:26 [B]Deut 30:1 30:20 [a]Lit *that* [b]Lit *to dwell* [A]Deut 6:5 [B]Deut 10:20 [C]Deut 4:1; 32:47; Acts 17:25, 28 [D]Gen 12:7; 17:1-8 31:2 [A]Deut 34:7 [B]Num 27:17; 1 Kin 3:7 [C]Deut 1:37; 3:27 31:3 [A]Deut 9:3 [B]Num 27:18 31:5 [A]Deut 7:2

have enslaved the Jews. The judgment of God would come upon those who cursed the physical seed of Abraham in fulfillment of Ge 12:3.

30:8, 9 you shall again obey the LORD. With a new heart under the New Covenant, Israel would obey all the commandments of the Lord. This would result in the Lord's blessing, which would bring greater prosperity than Israel had ever previously experienced.

30:10 Here is a renewed enforcement of the indispensable fruit of salvation and another echo of the constant theme of this book.

30:11–14 After remembering the failures of the past and the prospects for the future, Moses earnestly admonished the people to make the right choice. The issue facing them was to enjoy salvation and blessing by loving God so wholeheartedly that they would willingly live in obedience to His Word. The choice was simple, yet profound. It was stated in simple terms so that they could understand and grasp what God expected of them (v. 11). Although God had spoken from heaven, He had spoken through Moses in words every person could understand (v. 12). They did not have to search at some point beyond the sea (v. 13). The truth was there, through Moses, now in their hearts and minds (v. 14). All the truth necessary for choosing to love and obey God and thus avoid disobedience and cursing, they had heard and known (v. 15). Paul quotes vv. 12–14 in Ro 10:6–8.

30:15 Here Moses pinpoints the choice—to love and obey God is life and prosperity, to reject God is death and adversity. If they chose to love God and obey His Word, they would enjoy all God's blessings (v. 16). If they refused to love and obey Him, they would be severely and immediately punished (vv. 17, 18). Paul, in speaking about salvation in the NT, makes use of this appeal made by Moses (Ro 10:1–13). Like Moses, Paul is saying that the message of salvation is plain and understandable.

30:19 choose life. Moses forces the decision, exhorting Israel on the plains of Moab before God (heaven) and man (earth) to choose by believing in and loving God, the life available through the New Covenant (see v. 6). Sadly, Israel failed to respond to this call to the right choice (see 31:16–18, 27–29). Choosing life or death was also emphasized by Jesus. The one who believed in Him had the promise of eternal life; while the one who refused to believe faced eternal death (cf. Jn 3:1–36). Every person faces this same choice.

31:1–34:12 Two themes dominate the last 4 chapters of Deuteronomy: 1) the death of Moses (31:1, 2, 14, 16, 26–29; 32:48–52; 33:1; 34:1–8, 10–12) and 2) the succession of Joshua (31:1–8, 14, 23; 32:44; 34:9). These final chapters are centered around two more speeches by Moses: 1) the Song of Moses (32:1–43), and 2) the Blessings of Moses (33:1–29).

31:1 Moses went and spoke. Though some interpreters view this verse as the conclusion to the foregoing address in chaps. 29, 30, it is better to see these words as an introduction to the words of Moses which follow, based upon the general pattern of Deuteronomy. Verses 2–6 are addressed to every Israelite.

31:2 a hundred and twenty years old. This was the age of Moses at his death. According to Ac 7:30, Moses spent 40 years in Midian tending sheep. Thus, the life of Moses is broken down into three 40-year periods. His first 40 years were spent in Egypt (Ex 2:1–15). The second 40 years were spent in Midian (Ex 2:15–4:19). His final 40 years were spent leading Israel out of Egypt and through the wilderness to the Promised Land. The life and ministry of Moses were completed, but God's work would go on (v. 3a). **come and go.** Here is an idiom for engaging in a normal day's work and activity. Though still strong for his age (cf. 34:7), Moses admitted that he no longer could provide the daily leadership necessary for Israel. Furthermore, God would not allow him to enter the land over the Jordan because of his sin at the waters of Meribah (see 32:51).

31:3 God ... will cross ... Joshua ... will cross. Though Joshua was to be the new human leader over Israel (see 31:3–7, 23), it was the Lord Himself who was the real leader and power. He would cross over ahead of them to enable them to destroy the nations.

31:4 Sihon and Og. Israel was assured that the nations of the land would be destroyed by the Lord in the same way that He had recently defeated the Amorite kings, Sihon and Og, on

6 [A]Be strong and courageous, [B]do not be afraid or
tremble at them, for [C]the LORD your God is the one
who goes with you. [D]He will not fail you or forsake
you."
7 Then Moses called to Joshua and said to him in
the sight of all Israel, "[A]Be strong and courageous,
for you shall go with this people into the land which
the LORD has sworn to their fathers to give them,
and you shall give it to them as an inheritance.
8 [A]The LORD is the one who goes ahead of you; He
will be with you. [B]He will not fail you or forsake
you. Do not fear or be dismayed."
9 So Moses wrote this law and gave it to the
priests, the sons of Levi [A]who carried the ark of
the covenant of the LORD, and to all the elders of
Israel. 10 Then Moses commanded them, saying, "At
the end of *every* seven years, at the time of [A]the year
of remission of debts, at the [B]Feast of Booths, 11 when
all Israel comes [A]to appear before the LORD your
God at [B]the place which He will choose, [C]you shall
read this law in front of all Israel in their hearing.
12 Assemble the people, the men and the women
and children and [a]the alien who is in your [b]town,
so that they may hear and [A]learn and fear the LORD
your God, and be careful to observe all the words
of this law. 13 Their children, who have not known,
will hear and learn to fear the LORD your God, as
long as you live on the land [a]which you are about
to cross the Jordan to [b]possess."

ISRAEL WILL FALL AWAY

14 Then the LORD said to Moses, "Behold, [a,A]the
time for you to die is near; call Joshua, and present yourselves at the tent of meeting, that I may
commission him." [B]So Moses and Joshua went
and presented themselves at the tent of meeting.
15 [A]The LORD appeared in the tent in a pillar of
cloud, and the pillar of cloud stood at the doorway
of the tent. 16 The LORD said to Moses, "Behold,
[A]you are about to lie down with your fathers; and
[B]this people will arise and play the harlot with the
strange gods of the land, into the midst of which
they are going, and [C]will forsake Me and break My
covenant which I have made with them. 17 [A]Then
My anger will be kindled against them in that day,
and [B]I will forsake them and [C]hide My face from
them, and they will be consumed, and many evils
and troubles will come upon them; so that they
will say in that day, '[D]Is it not because our God is
not among us that these evils have come upon
us?' 18 But I will surely hide My face in that day
because of all the evil which they will do, for they
will turn to other gods.
19 "Now therefore, [A]write this song for yourselves,
and teach it to the sons of Israel; put it [a]on their lips,
so that this song may be a witness for Me against
the sons of Israel. 20 [A]For when I bring them into the
land flowing with milk and honey, which I swore
to their fathers, and they have eaten and are satisfied and [B]become [a]prosperous, then they will turn
to other gods and serve them, and spurn Me and
break My covenant. 21 Then it shall come about,
[A]when many evils and troubles have come upon
them, that this song will testify before them as a
witness (for it shall not be forgotten from the [a]lips
of their descendants); for [B]I know their intent which
they are [b]developing today, before I have brought
them into the land which I swore." 22 [A]So Moses
wrote this song the same day, and taught it to the
sons of Israel.

JOSHUA IS COMMISSIONED

23 [A]Then He commissioned Joshua the son of Nun,
and said, "[B]Be strong and courageous, for you shall
bring the sons of Israel into the land which I swore
to them, and [C]I will be with you."

31:6 [A]Josh 10:25; 1 Chr 22:13 [B]Deut 1:29; 7:18; 20:1 [C]Deut 20:4 [D]Josh 1:5; Heb 13:5 31:7 [A]Deut 1:38; 3:28 31:8 [A]Ex 13:21; 33:14 [B]Deut 31:6; Josh 1:5; Heb 13:5 31:9 [A]Num 4:5, 6, 15; Deut 10:8; 31:25, 26; Josh 3:3 31:10 [A]Deut 15:1, 2 [B]Lev 23:34; Deut 16:13 31:11 [A]Deut 16:16 [B]Deut 12:5 [C]Josh 8:34; 2 Kin 23:2 31:12 [a]Lit *your alien* [b]Lit *gates* [A]Deut 4:10 31:13 [a]Lit *where* [b]Lit *possess it* 31:14 [a]Lit *your days to die are* [A]Num 27:12, 13; Deut 4:22; 32:50 [B]Ex 33:9-11 31:15 [A]Ex 33:9 31:16 [A]Gen 15:15 [B]Ex 34:15; Deut 4:25-28; Judg 2:11, 12, 17 [C]Judg 10:6; 1 Kin 18:18; 19:10; Jer 2:13 31:17 [A]Judg 2:14; 6:13 [B]2 Chr 15:2; 24:20 [C]Ps 104:29; Is 8:17 [D]Num 14:42 31:19 [a]Lit *in their mouths* [A]Deut 31:22 31:20 [a]Lit *fat* [A]Deut 6:10-12; 8:10, 19; 11:16, 17 [B]Deut 32:15-17 31:21 [a]Lit *mouth of its seed* [b]Lit *making* [A]Lev 26:41; Deut 4:30 [B]1 Chr 28:9; John 2:24, 25 31:22 [A]Deut 31:19 31:23 [A]Num 27:23; Deut 31:7 [B]Josh 1:6 [C]Ex 3:12

the E side of the Jordan River (see 2:26–3:11). That was a preview of what was to come (v. 5).

31:6–8 Be strong and courageous. The strength and courage of the warriors of Israel would come from their confidence that their God was with them and would not forsake them. In vv. 7, 8, Moses repeated the substance of his exhortation, this time addressing it specifically to Joshua in the presence of the people to encourage him and to remind the people that Joshua's leadership was being assumed with the full approval of God. This principle for faith and confidence is repeated in 31:23; Jos 1:5–7; 2Sa 10:12; 2Ki 2:2; 1Ch 22:11–13; 2Ch 32:1–8; Ps 27:14. The writer of Hebrews quotes vv. 6, 8 in 13:5.

31:9 Moses wrote this law. At the least, Moses, perhaps with the aid of some scribes or elders who assisted him in leading Israel, wrote down the law that he had explained in the first 32 chapters of Deuteronomy (cf. v. 24). However, since the law explained in Deuteronomy had been given in portions of Exodus through Numbers, it seems best to view this written law as all that is presently found in Scripture from Ge 1 through Dt 32:47. After Moses' death, Dt 32:48–34:12 were added to complete the canonical Torah, perhaps by one of the elders who had served with Moses, even Joshua.

31:11 you shall read this law in front of all Israel. The law that Moses wrote down was given to the priests who were required to be its custodians and protectors and to read it in the hearing of all Israel at the Feast of Tabernacles during each sabbatical year. This reading of the law every 7 years was to remind the people to live in submission to their awe-inspiring God.

31:14 the tent of meeting. The Lord told Moses to summon Joshua to the tent where He met Israel, and the presence of the Lord appeared in the pillar of cloud standing at the door of the Holy Place (v. 15). This signaled God's confirmation of Joshua, the former military captain (see Ex 17:9–14) and spy (see Nu 13:16), as Israel's new leader. God's message to Joshua is summed up in vv. 16–22.

31:16–21 they ... will forsake Me and break My covenant. After Moses' death, the Lord Himself predicts that in spite of what He has commanded (30:11, 20), the Israelites would forsake Him by turning to worship other gods and thereby break the Sinaitic Covenant. Having forsaken God, the people would then be forsaken by God with the inevitable result that disaster would fall upon them at every turn. This is one of the saddest texts in the OT. After all God had done, He knew they would forsake Him.

31:19, 22 write this song. The song that the Lord gave Moses to teach the Israelites would be a constant reminder of their disobedience to the Lord and the results of that disobedience. The song was written that same day and is recorded in 32:1–43.

31:23 I will be with you. Joshua was to assume his lonely role of leadership over Israel with an assurance of the companionship and strength of the Lord. God's presence with him was sufficient to enable him to meet boldly every obstacle that the future could bring (see Jos 1:5; 3:7).

24 It came about, when Moses finished writing the
words of this law in a book until they were complete,
25 that Moses commanded the Levites [A]who carried
the ark of the covenant of the LORD, saying, 26 "Take
this book of the law and place it beside the ark of
the covenant of the LORD your God, that it may [a]re-
main there as a witness against you. 27 For I know
[A]your rebellion and [B]your [a]stubbornness; behold,
while I am still alive with you today, you have been
rebellious against the LORD; how much more, then,
after my death? 28 Assemble to me all the elders
of your tribes and your officers, that I may speak
these words in their hearing and [A]call the heavens
and the earth to witness against them. 29 For I know
that after my death you will [A]act corruptly and turn
from the way which I have commanded you; and
evil will befall you in the latter days, for you will
do that which is evil in the sight of the LORD, provoking Him to anger with the work of your hands."
30 Then Moses spoke in the hearing of all the assembly of Israel the words of this song, until they
were complete:

THE SONG OF MOSES

32 "[A]Give ear, O heavens, and let me speak;
And let the earth hear the
words of my mouth.
2 "[A]Let my teaching drop as the rain,
My speech distill as the dew,
[B]As the droplets on the fresh grass
And as the showers on the herb.
3 "[A]For I proclaim the name of the LORD;
[B]Ascribe greatness to our God!
4 "[A]The Rock! His work is perfect,
[B]For all His ways are [a]just;
[C]A God of faithfulness and
without injustice,
Righteous and upright is He.
5 "[a,A]They have acted corruptly toward Him,
They are not His children,
because of their defect;
[B]*But are* a perverse and
crooked generation.
6 "Do you thus [A]repay the LORD,
[B]O foolish and unwise people?
[C]Is not He your Father who
has bought you?
[D]He has made you and established you.
7 "Remember the days of old,
Consider the years of all generations.
[A]Ask your father, and he will inform you,
Your elders, and they will tell you.
8 "[A]When the Most High gave the
nations their inheritance,
When He separated the sons of [a]man,
He set the boundaries of the peoples
[B]According to the number of
the sons of Israel.
9 "[A]For the LORD'S portion is His people;
Jacob is the allotment of His inheritance.

31:25 [A]Deut 31:9 31:26 [a]Lit *be* 31:27 [a]Lit *stiff neck* [A]Deut 9:7, 24 [B]Ex 32:9; Deut 9:6, 13 31:28 [A]Deut 4:26; 30:19; 32:1 31:29 [A]Judg 2:19 32:1 [A]Deut 4:26; Ps 50:4; Is 1:2; Jer 6:19 32:2 [A]Is 55:10, 11 [B]Ps 72:6 32:3 [A]Ex 33:19; 34:5, 6 [B]Deut 3:24; 5:24 32:4 [a]Or *judgment* [A]Deut 32:15, 18, 30; 2 Sam 22:31 [B]Gen 18:25; Dan 4:37 [C]Deut 7:9 32:5 [a]Lit *It has* [A]Deut 4:25; 31:29 [B]Matt 17:17 32:6 [A]Ps 116:12 [B]Deut 32:28 [C]Deut 1:31; Ps 74:2; Is 63:16 [D]Deut 32:15 32:7 [A]Ex 12:26; Ps 78:5-8 32:8 [a]Or *Adam* [A]Acts 17:26 [B]Num 23:9; Deut 33:28 32:9 [A]1 Sam 10:1; 1 Kin 8:51, 53; Jer 10:16

31:24 in a book. The words that Moses had spoken were written down in a book that was placed beside the ark of the covenant (v. 26). Only the Ten Commandments were placed in the ark itself (Ex 25:16; 31:18). The "book of the law" (v. 26) was one of the titles for the Pentateuch in the rest of Scripture (Jos 1:8; 8:34).

31:27 your rebellion and your stubbornness. See 9:6, 13; 10:16. Moses was well acquainted with Israel's obstinate ways even in the most gracious of divine provision.

31:29 you will act corruptly. Dominated by the practice of idolatry (see 4:16, 25; 9:12), the people would become wicked. **evil will befall you in the latter days.** "The latter days" (lit. "at the end of the days") referred to the far distant future. This was the time when the king would come from Judah (Ge 49:8–12) to defeat Israel's enemies (Nu 24:17–19). Here it is revealed that it would also be a time when disaster would fall upon Israel because of evil done, thus bringing the Lord's wrath. The description of God's judgment on Israel and the nations in this song can't be limited to the immediate future of the people as they entered the land, but extends to issues which are eschatological in time and global in extent, as the song indicates (32:1–43).

31:30–32:43 This prophetic, poetic song has as its central theme Israel's apostasy, which brings God's certain judgment. The song begins with a short introduction emphasizing the steadfast God and the fickle nation (vv. 1–6). The song describes God's election of Israel (vv. 8, 9) and His care for them from the time of the wilderness wanderings (vv. 10–12) to their possession and initial enjoyment of the blessings in the land (vv. 13, 14). However, Israel's neglect of God's goodness and her apostasy (vv. 15–18) would bring God's future outpouring of wrath on His people (vv. 19–27) and Israel's continuing blindness in the face of God's wrath (vv. 28–33). Ultimately, God's vengeance would strip Israel of all power and turn the nation from idolatry (vv. 34–38). Then, God would bring His judgment upon the nations, both His enemies and Israel's (vv. 39–42). The song ends with a call to the nations to rejoice with Israel because God would punish His enemies and spiritually heal both Israel and her land (v. 43). Ezekiel 16 should be studied as a comparison to this chapter. It recites similar matters in graphic and picturesque language.

32:1 Give ear, O heavens … and let the earth hear. All of creation was called to be an audience to hear the message to Israel as in 30:19 because the truth Moses was about to proclaim concerned the whole universe. It did so because it involved the honor of God the Creator so disregarded by sinners, the justification of God so righteous in all His ways, and the manifestation in heaven and earth of God's judgment and salvation (v. 43).

32:2 my teaching. Moses imparted instruction that if received would, like rain, dew, raindrops, and showers to the earth, bring benefit to the hearts and the minds of the hearers.

32:3 Ascribe greatness to our God! Cf. 3:24; 5:24; 9:26; 11:2; Ps 150:2. This command refers to the greatness of God revealed in His acts of omnipotence.

32:4 The Rock! This word, representing the stability and permanence of God, was placed at the beginning of the verse for emphasis and was followed by a series of phrases which elaborated the attributes of God as the Rock of Israel. It is one of the principal themes in this song (see vv. 15, 18, 30, 31), stressing the unchanging nature of God in contrast with the fickle nature of the people.

32:5 a perverse and crooked generation. Israel, in contrast to God, was warped and twisted. Jesus used this phrase in Mt 17:17 of an unbelieving generation and Paul in Php 2:15 of the dark world of mankind in rebellion against God.

32:6 your Father. The foolishness and stupidity of Israel would be seen in the fact that they would rebel against God who as a Father had brought them forth and formed them into a nation. As Father, He was the progenitor and originator of the nation and the One who had matured and sustained it. This idea of God as Father of the nation is emphasized in the OT (cf. 1Ch 29:10; Is 63:16; 64:8; Mal 2:10) while the idea of God as Father of individual believers is developed in the NT (cf. Ro 8:15; Gal 4:6).

32:7 Remember the days of old. A call to reflect on past history and to inquire about the lessons to be learned.

32:8, 9 the Most High. This title for God emphasized His sovereignty and authority over all the nations (see Ge 11:9; 10:32; 14:18; Nu 24:16) with the amazing revelation that in

10 “[A]He found him in a desert land,
And in the howling waste of a wilderness;
He encircled him, He cared for him,
He guarded him as [B]the pupil of His eye.
11 “[A]Like an eagle that stirs up its nest,
That hovers over its young,
[B]He spread His wings and caught them,
He carried them on His pinions.
12 “[A]The LORD alone guided him,
[B]And there was no foreign god with him.
13 “[A]He made him ride on the high
places of the earth,
And he ate the produce of the field;
[B]And He made him suck
honey from the rock,
And [C]oil from the flinty rock,
14 Curds of cows, and milk of the flock,
With fat of lambs,
And rams, the breed of Bashan, and goats,
[A]With the finest of the wheat—
And of the [B]blood of grapes
you drank wine.

15 “[A]But [a]Jeshurun grew fat and kicked—
You are grown fat, thick, and sleek—
[B]Then he forsook God [C]who made him,
And scorned [D]the Rock of his salvation.
16 “[A]They made Him jealous
with strange *gods;*
[B]With abominations they
provoked Him to anger.
17 “[A]They sacrificed to demons
who were not God,
[B]To gods whom they have not known,
[C]New *gods* who came lately,
Whom your fathers did not dread.
18 “You neglected [A]the Rock
who begot you,
[B]And forgot the God who
gave you birth.

19 “[A]The LORD saw *this,* and
spurned *them*
[B]Because of the provocation of
His sons and daughters.
20 “Then He said, ‘I will hide
My face from them,
[A]I will see what their end *shall be;*
[B]For they are a perverse generation,
[C]Sons in whom is no faithfulness.
21 ‘[A]They have made Me jealous
with *what* is not God;
They have provoked Me to
anger with their [a,B]idols.
[C]So I will make them jealous with
those who are not a people;
I will provoke them to anger
with a foolish nation,
22 [A]For a fire is kindled in My anger,
And burns to the lowest part of [a]Sheol,
[B]And consumes the earth with its yield,
And sets on fire the foundations
of the mountains.

23 ‘[A]I will heap misfortunes on them;
[B]I will use My arrows on them.

32:10 [A]Deut 1:19 [B]Ps 17:8; Prov 7:2; Zech 2:8 32:11 [A]Ex 19:4; Deut 33:12 [B]Ps 18:10-18 32:12 [A]Deut 4:35, 39 [B]Deut 32:39; Is 43:12 32:13 [A]Is 58:14 [B]Deut 8:8; Ps 81:16 [C]Job 29:6 32:14 [A]Ps 81:16; 147:14 [B]Gen 49:11 32:15 [a]I.e. Israel [A]Deut 31:20 [B]Judg 10:6 [C]Deut 32:6 [D]Deut 32:4; Ps 89:26 32:16 [A]Ps 78:58 [B]Ps 106:29 32:17 [A]Lev 17:7; 1 Cor 10:20 [B]Deut 28:64 [C]Judg 5:8 32:18 [A]Deut 32:4 [B]Ps 106:21 32:19 [A]Lev 26:30; Ps 106:40 [B]Jer 44:21-23 32:20 [A]Deut 31:29 [B]Deut 32:5 [C]Deut 9:23 32:21 [a]Lit *vanities* [A]Deut 32:16; 1 Cor 10:22 [B]Deut 32:17; 1 Kin 16:13, 26 [C]Rom 10:19 32:22 [a]I.e. the nether world [A]Num 16:33-35; Ps 18:7, 8; Lam 4:11 [B]Lev 26:20 32:23 [A]Deut 29:21 [B]Ps 18:14; 45:5

the whole plan for the world, God had as His goal the salvation of His chosen people. God ordained a plan where the number of nations (70 according to Ge 10) corresponded to the number of the children of Israel (70 according to Ge 46:27). Further, as God gave the nations their lands, He established their boundaries, leaving Israel enough land to sustain their expected population.

32:10–14 This whole description of what God did for Israel is figurative. Israel is like a man in the horrible desert in danger of death, without food or water, who is rescued by the Lord.

32:10 **as the pupil of His eye.** Lit. “the apple of His eye.” Just as the pupil of the eye is essential for vision and, therefore, closely protected, especially in a howling wind, so God closely protected Israel. Cf. Ps 17:8; Pr 7:2.

32:11 **hovers over its young.** The Lord exercised His loving care for Israel like an eagle caring for its young, especially as they were taught to fly. As they began to fly and had little strength, they would start to fall. At that point, an eagle would stop their fall by spreading its wings so they could land on them; so the Lord has carried Israel and not let the nation fall. He had been training Israel to fly on His wings of love and omnipotence.

32:12 **no foreign god.** Moses makes clear that God alone carried Israel through all its struggles and victories, thus depriving the people of any excuse for apostasy from the Lord by interest in false gods.

32:13 **honey from the rock.** A reference to honeycombs located in the fissures of the faces of a cliff is used because Canaan had many wild bees. **oil from the flinty rock.** Likely a reference to olive trees growing in rocky places otherwise bereft of fruit-growing trees. These metaphoric phrases regarding honey and oil point to the most valuable products coming out of the most unproductive places.

32:14 **rams … of Bashan.** *See note on 3:1.*

32:15 **Jeshurun.** The word means “righteous” (lit. “the upright one”), i.e., a name for Israel which sarcastically expresses the fact that Israel did not live up to God’s law after entering the land. God uses this name to remind Israel of His calling and to severely rebuke apostasy. **grew fat and kicked.** Like an ox which had become fat and intractable, Israel became affluent because of the bountiful provisions of God but, instead of being thankful and obedient, became rebellious against the Lord (cf. 6:10–15).

32:16 **strange *gods*.** Israel turned to worship the gods of the people in the land. These were gods they had not before acknowledged (v. 17).

32:17 **demons.** Cf. Lv 17:7; 2Ch 11:15; Ps 106:37. The term describes those angels who fell with Satan and constitute the evil force that fights against God and His holy angels. Idol worship is a form of demon worship, as demon spirits impersonate the idol and work their wicked strategies through the system of false religion tied to the false god.

32:18–33 For this foolish apostasy, the Lord will severely judge Israel. This visitation of anger is in the form of a divine resolution to punish Israelites whenever they pursue idols, including the next generation of sons and daughters (v. 19). In vv. 20–22, Moses quotes the Lord Himself.

32:21 **not a people.** As the Lord was provoked to jealousy by Israel’s worship of that which was “not God,” so He would provoke Israel to jealousy and anger by humiliation before a foolish, vile “no-nation.” In Ro 10:19, Paul applied the term “not a nation” to the Gentile nations generally. Jews who worship a “no-god” will be judged by a “no-people.”

32:22 **a fire is kindled … to the lowest part of Sheol.** Cf. 29:20. Once the fire of God’s anger was kindled, it knew no limits in its destructive force, reaching to even those in the grave, an indication of God’s eternal judgment against those who oppose Him.

32:23 **misfortunes … arrows.** The misfortunes (lit. “evil”) are described in v. 24. The arrows represent the enemies who would defeat Israel in war and are further described in vv. 25–27.

24 ‘[A]*They will be* wasted by famine,
and consumed by [a]plague
[B]And bitter destruction;
[C]And the teeth of beasts I will
send upon them,
[D]With the venom of crawling
things of the dust.
25 ‘[A]Outside the sword will bereave,
And inside terror—
[B]Both young man and virgin,
The nursling with the man of gray hair.
26 ‘I would have said, “[A]I will
cut them to pieces,
[B]I will remove the memory
of them from men,”
27 Had I not feared the provocation
by the enemy,
That their adversaries would misjudge,
That they would say, “[A]Our
hand is [a]triumphant,
And the LORD has not done all this.” ’

28 “[A]For they are a nation [a]lacking in counsel,
And there is no understanding in them.
29 “[A]Would that they were wise, that
they understood this,
[B]That they would discern their [a]future!
30 “[A]How could one chase a thousand,
And two put ten thousand to flight,
Unless their [B]Rock had sold them,
And the LORD had given them up?
31 “Indeed their rock is not like our Rock,
[A]Even our enemies [a]themselves
judge this.
32 “For their vine is from the vine of Sodom,
And from the fields of Gomorrah;
Their grapes are grapes of [A]poison,
Their clusters, bitter.
33 “Their wine is the venom of [a]serpents,
And the [b]deadly poison of cobras.
34 ‘[A]Is it not laid up in store with Me,
Sealed up in My treasuries?
35 ‘[A]Vengeance is Mine, and retribution,
[B]In due time their foot will slip;
[C]For the day of their calamity is near,
And the impending things are
hastening upon them.’
36 “[A]For the LORD will vindicate His people,
[B]And will have compassion on His servants,
When He sees that *their* [a]strength is gone,
And there is none *remaining,* bond or free.
37 “And He will say, ‘[A]Where are their gods,
The rock in which they sought refuge?
38 ‘[A]Who ate the fat of their sacrifices,
And drank the wine of their drink offering?
[B]Let them rise up and help you,
Let them be your hiding place!
39 ‘[A]See now that I, I am He,
[B]And there is no god besides Me;
[C]It is I who put to death and give life.
[D]I have wounded and it is I who heal,
[E]And there is no one who can
deliver from My hand.
40 ‘Indeed, [A]I lift up My hand to heaven,
And say, as I live forever,
41 [A]If I sharpen My [a]flashing sword,
And My hand takes hold on justice,
[B]I will render vengeance on My adversaries,
And I will repay those who hate Me.
42 ‘[A]I will make My arrows drunk with blood,
[B]And My sword will devour flesh,
With the blood of the slain and the captives,
From the long-haired [a]leaders
of the enemy.’
43 “[A]Rejoice, O nations, *with* His people;
[B]For He will avenge the blood
of His servants,
[C]And will render vengeance
on His adversaries,
[D]And will atone for His land *and* His people.”

32:24 [a]Lit *burning heat* [A]Deut 28:22, 48 [B]Ps 91:6 [C]Lev 26:22 [D]Amos 5:18, 19 32:25 [A]Lam 1:20; Ezek 7:15 [B]2 Chr 36:17; Lam 2:21 32:26 [A]Deut 4:27; 28:64 [B]Deut 9:14 32:27 [a]Lit *high* [A]Num 15:30 32:28 [a]Lit *perishing* [A]Deut 32:6 32:29 [a]Or *latter end* [A]Deut 5:29 [B]Deut 31:29 32:30 [A]Lev 26:7, 8 [B]Deut 32:4; Ps 44:12 32:31 [a]Lit *are judges* [A]Ex 14:25 32:32 [A]Deut 29:18 32:33 [a]Lit *dragons* [b]Lit *cruel* 32:34 [A]Job 14:17; Jer 44:21 32:35 [A]Ps 94:1; Rom 12:19; Heb 10:30 [B]Jer 23:12 [C]Ezek 7:5-10 32:36 [a]Lit *hand* [A]Ps 135:14; Heb 10:30 [B]Lev 26:43-45; Deut 30:1-3 32:37 [A]Judg 10:14; Jer 2:28 32:38 [A]Num 25:1, 2 [B]Jer 11:12 32:39 [A]Is 41:4; 43:10 [B]Deut 32:12; Is 45:5 [C]1 Sam 2:6; Ps 68:20 [D]Ps 51:8 [E]Ps 50:22 32:40 [A]Ezek 20:5, 6; 21:4, 5 32:41 [a]Or *lightning* [A]Is 34:6-8 [B]Jer 50:28-32 32:42 [a]Lit *head* [A]Deut 32:23 [B]Jer 12:12; 46:10, 14 32:43 [A]Rom 15:10 [B]2 Kin 9:7; Rev 6:10; 19:2 [C]Is 1:24, 25 [D]Ps 65:3; 79:9; 85:1

32:27 Our hand is triumphant. Military arrogance. The only thing that would prevent the Lord from permitting the complete destruction of His people would be His concern that the Gentiles might claim for themselves the honor of victory over Israel.

32:31 rock … Rock. A contrast between the gods of the nations (“rock”) and Israel’s true God (“Rock”). Israel could smite its foes with very little difficulty because of the weakness of their gods, who are not like the Rock Jehovah.

32:32 the vine of Sodom. Employing the metaphor of a vineyard, its grapes and its wine, the wickedness of Israel’s enemies was described as having its roots in Sodom and Gomorrah, the evil cities destroyed by God as recorded in Ge 19:1–29.

32:34 Sealed up in My treasuries. The wicked acts of Israel’s enemies were known to God and are stored up in His storehouse. At the proper time, God will avenge. Paul uses this image in Ro 2:4, 5.

32:35 Vengeance is Mine, and retribution. The manner and timing of the repayment of man’s wickedness is God’s prerogative. This principle is reaffirmed in the NT in Ro 12:19; Heb 10:30.

32:36 This is the promise that the Lord will judge Israel as a nation, but that the nation is composed of righteous and wicked. God actually helps the righteous by destroying the wicked. “His servants” are the righteous, all who in the time of judgment are faithful to the Lord (cf. Mal 3:16–4:3). The Lord has judged Israel, not to destroy the nation, but to punish the sinners and show the folly of their false gods (vv. 37, 38). At the same time, the Lord has always shown compassion for those who have loved and obeyed Him.

32:39 that I, I am He. After showing the worthlessness of false gods (vv. 37, 38), this declaration of the nature of God was presented in contrast to show that the God of Israel is the living God, the only One who can offer help and protection to Israel. He has the power of life and death with regard to Israel (cf. 1Sa 2:6; 2Ki 5:7) and the power to wound and heal them (cf. Is 30:26; 57:17, 18; Jer 17:14; Hos 6:1).

32:40–42 I lift up My hand. God takes an oath to bring vengeance on His enemies. Here (as in Ex 6:8; Nu 14:28) the hand is used anthropomorphically of God, who can swear by no greater than His eternal Self (cf. Is 45:23; Jer 22:5; Heb 6:17).

32:43 Rejoice, O nations, *with* His people. As a result of the execution of God’s vengeance, all nations will be called upon to praise with Israel the Lord who will have provided redemptively for them in Christ and also provided a new beginning in the land. This atonement for the Land is the satisfaction of God’s wrath by the sacrifice of His

44 Then Moses came and spoke all the words of this song in the hearing of the people, he, with [a,A]Joshua the son of Nun. 45 When Moses had finished speaking all these words to all Israel, 46 he said to them, "[A]Take to your heart all the words with which I am warning you today, which you shall command [B]your sons to observe [a]carefully, *even* all the words of this law. 47 For it is not an idle word for you; indeed [A]it is your life. And [B]by this word you will prolong your days in the land, [a]which you are about to cross the Jordan to [b]possess."

48 [A]The LORD spoke to Moses that very same day, saying, 49 "[A]Go up to this mountain of the Abarim, Mount Nebo, which is in the land of Moab [a]opposite Jericho, and look at the land of Canaan, which I am giving to the sons of Israel for a possession. 50 Then die on the mountain where you ascend, and be [A]gathered to your people, as Aaron your brother died on Mount Hor and was gathered to his people, 51 [A]because you broke faith with Me in the midst of the sons of Israel at the waters of Meribah-kadesh, in the [B]wilderness of Zin, because you did not treat Me as holy in the midst of the sons of Israel. 52 [A]For you shall see the land at a distance, but [B]you shall not go there, into the land which I am giving the sons of Israel."

THE BLESSING OF MOSES

33 Now this is the blessing with which Moses [A]the man of God blessed the sons of Israel before his death. 2 He said,

"[A]The LORD came from Sinai,
[B]And [a]dawned on them from Seir;
[C]He shone forth from Mount Paran,
And He came from [D]the [b]midst
of ten thousand holy ones;
[E]At His right hand there was
[c]flashing lightning for them.
3 "[A]Indeed, He loves [a]the people;
[B]All [b]Your holy ones are in Your hand,
[C]And they [c]followed in Your steps;
Everyone receives of Your words.
4 "[A]Moses charged us with a law,
[B]A possession for the assembly of Jacob.
5 "[A]And He was king in Jeshurun,
When the heads of the people
were gathered,
The tribes of Israel together.

6 "[A]May Reuben live and not die,
Nor his men be few."

7 [A]And this regarding Judah; so he said,

"Hear, O LORD, the voice of Judah,
And bring him to his people.
With his hands he contended for [a]them,
And may You be a help against
his adversaries."

8 Of Levi he said,

"*Let* Your [A]Thummim and Your Urim
belong to [a]Your [B]godly man,
[C]Whom You proved at Massah,
With whom You contended at
the waters of Meribah;
9 [A]Who said of his father and his mother,
'I did not consider them';
And he did not acknowledge his brothers,
Nor did he regard his own sons,
For [B]they observed Your word,
And kept Your covenant.

32:44 [a]Lit *Hoshea* [A]Num 13:8, 16 32:46 [a]Lit *to do* [A]Ezek 40:4; 44:5 [B]Deut 4:9 32:47 [a]Lit *where* [b]Lit *possess it* [A]Deut 8:3; 30:20 [B]Deut 4:40; 33:25 32:48 [A]Num 27:12 32:49 [a]Lit *which is opposite* [A]Num 27:12-14; Deut 3:27 32:50 [A]Gen 25:8 32:51 [A]Num 20:12 [B]Num 27:14 32:52 [A]Deut 34:1-3 [B]Deut 1:37; 3:27 33:1 [A]Josh 14:6 33:2 [a]Lit *rose to* [b]Lit *myriads of holiness* [c]Or *a fiery law* [A]Ex 19:18, 20; Ps 68:8, 17 [B]Judg 5:4 [C]Num 10:12; Hab 3:3 [D]Dan 7:10; Acts 7:53 [E]Ex 23:20-22 33:3 [a]Lit *peoples* [b]Lit *His* [c]Or *lie down at Your feet* [A]Deut 4:37; Mal 1:2 [B]Deut 7:6; 14:2 [C]Deut 6:1-9; Luke 10:39 33:4 [A]Deut 4:2; John 7:19 [B]Ps 119:111 33:5 [A]Num 23:21 33:6 [A]Gen 49:3, 4 33:7 [a]Lit *him* [A]Gen 49:8-12 33:8 [a]Lit *him* [A]Ex 28:30; Lev 8:8 [B]Ps 106:16 [C]Ex 17:7; Num 20:13, 24; Deut 6:16 33:9 [A]Ex 32:27-29 [B]Mal 2:5

enemies in judgment. The atonement for the people is by the sacrifice of Jesus Christ on the cross (cf. Ps 79:9). Paul quotes this passage in Ro 15:10, as does the writer of Hebrews (1:6).

32:47 it is your life. Moses reiterated to Israel that obedience to the Lord's commands was to be the key to her living long in the land that God had prepared and called for this song to be a kind of national anthem which the leaders should see is frequently repeated to animate the people to love and obey God.

32:48–34:12 The anticipation of and record of Moses' death (32:48–52; 34:1–12) bracket the recording of Moses' blessing given to Israel before his death. This literary unit was composed and added to the text after the death of Moses.

32:49 Mount Nebo. A peak in the Abarim range of mountains to the E of the N end of the Dead Sea, from where Moses would be able to see across to the Promised Land, which he was not permitted to enter.

32:50 gathered to his people. An idiom for death. See Ge 25:8, 17; 35:29; 49:33; Nu 20:24, 26; 31:2.

33:1–29 The final words of Moses to the people were a listing of the blessings of each of the tribes of Israel, Simeon excluded (vv. 6–25). These blessings were introduced and concluded with passages which praise God (vv. 2–5, 26–29). That these blessings of Moses are presented in this chapter as recorded by someone other than Moses is clear because in v. 1, Moses was viewed as already being dead, and as the words of Moses were presented, the clause "he said" (vv. 2, 7, 8, 12, 13, 18, 20, 22, 23, 24) was used.

33:1 the man of God. The first use of this phrase in Scripture. Subsequently, some 70 times in the OT, messengers of God (especially prophets) are called "a man of God" (1Sa 2:27; 9:6; 1Ki 13:1; 17:18; 2Ki 4:7). The NT uses this title for Timothy (1Ti 6:11; 2Ti 3:17). Moses was viewed among such prophets in this conclusion to the book (see 34:10).

33:2 Sinai ... Seir ... Paran. These are mountains associated with the giving of the law—Sinai on the S, Seir on the NE, and Paran on the N. These mountains provide a beautiful metaphor, borrowed from the dawn. God, like the morning sun, is the Light that rises to give His beams to all the Promised Land. **holy ones.** Probably a reference to the angels who assisted God when the law was mediated to Moses at Mt. Sinai (see Ac 7:53; Gal 3:19; Heb 2:2).

33:3 He loves the people. Notwithstanding the awe-inspiring symbols of majesty displayed at Sinai, the law was given in kindness and love to provide both temporal and eternal blessing to those with a heart to obey it. Cf. Ro 13:8–10.

33:5 king in Jeshurun. *See note on 32:15.* Lit. "he was king." It is possible that this refers back to Moses in v. 4. However, it is more likely speaking of God since: 1) Moses is never called "king" elsewhere in Scripture; 2) Moses was not anointed to be king as were the other human kings of Israel; 3) Israel forsook God as their king when they chose Saul to be king (1Sa 8:7); and 4) God is elsewhere actually declared to be king over Jeshurun (Is 44:1–6).

33:6 Reuben. Here is the prayer that this tribe would survive in large numbers (cf. Nu 1:21; 2:11).

33:7 Judah. Moses prayed that this tribe would be powerful in leading the nation to be victorious in battle through the help of the Lord.

33:8–11 Levi. Moses prays for the Levites to fulfill their tasks, God granting to them

10 "[A]They shall teach Your ordinances to Jacob,
And Your law to Israel.
[B]They shall put incense [a]before You,
And [C]whole burnt offerings on Your altar.
11 "O LORD, bless his substance,
And accept the work of his hands;
Shatter the loins of those who
rise up against him,
And those who hate him, so that
they will not rise *again*."

12 Of Benjamin he said,

"[A]May the beloved of the LORD
dwell in security by Him,
[B]Who shields him all the day,
[C]And he dwells between His shoulders."

13 Of Joseph he said,

"[A]Blessed of the LORD *be* his land,
With the choice things of
heaven, with the dew,
And from the deep lying beneath,
14 And with the choice yield of the sun,
And with the choice produce
of the months.
15 "And with the [a]best things of
[A]the ancient mountains,
And with the choice things of
the everlasting hills,
16 And with the choice things of
the earth and its fullness,
And the favor [A]of Him who
dwelt in the bush.
Let it come to the head of Joseph,
And to the crown of the head of the one
distinguished among his brothers.
17 "As the firstborn of his ox, majesty is his,
And his horns are the horns
of [A]the wild ox;
With them he will [B]push the peoples,
All [a]at once, *to* the ends of the earth.
And those are the ten
thousands of Ephraim,
And those are the thousands
of Manasseh."

18 [A]Of Zebulun he said,

"Rejoice, Zebulun, in your going forth,
And, Issachar, in your tents.
19 "[A]They will call peoples
to the mountain;
There they will offer
[B]righteous sacrifices;
For they will [a]draw out [C]the
abundance of the seas,
And the hidden treasures of the sand."

20 [A]Of Gad he said,

"Blessed is the one who enlarges Gad;
He lies down [B]as a [a]lion,
And tears the arm, also the
crown of the head.
21 "[A]Then he [a]provided the first
part for himself,
[B]For there the ruler's portion
was [b]reserved;
[C]And he came *with* the leaders
of the people;
[D]He executed the justice of the LORD,
And His ordinances with Israel."

22 [A]Of Dan he said,

"Dan is [B]a lion's whelp,
That leaps forth from Bashan."

23 Of Naphtali he said,

"[A]O Naphtali, satisfied with favor,
And full of the blessing of the LORD,
Take possession of the
sea and the south."

24 [A]Of Asher he said,

"More blessed than sons is Asher;
May he be favored by his brothers,
[B]And may he dip his foot in oil.
25 "[A]Your locks will be iron and bronze,
[B]And according to your days, so
will your leisurely walk be.

33:10 [a]Lit *in Your nostrils* [A]Lev 10:11; Deut 31:9-13 [B]Lev 16:12, 13 [C]Ps 51:19 33:12 [A]Deut 4:37f; 12:10 [B]Deut 32:11 [C]Ex 28:12 33:13 [A]Gen 27:27, 28; 49:22-26 33:15 [a]Or *chief* [A]Hab 3:6 33:16 [A]Ex 2:2-6; 3:2, 4 33:17 [a]Or *together* [A]Num 23:22 [B]1 Kin 22:11; Ps 44:5 33:18 [A]Gen 49:13-15 33:19 [a]Lit *suck* [A]Ex 15:17; Ps 2:6; Is 2:3 [B]Ps 4:5; 51:19 [C]Is 60:5 33:20 [a]Or *lioness* [A]Gen 49:19 [B]Gen 49:9 33:21 [a]Lit *saw* [b]Or *covered up* [A]Num 32:1-5 [B]Num 34:14 [C]Josh 4:12 [D]Josh 22:1-3 33:22 [A]Gen 49:16 [B]Ezek 19:2, 3 33:23 [A]Gen 49:21 33:24 [A]Gen 49:20 [B]Job 29:6 33:25 [A]Ps 147:13 [B]Deut 4:40; 32:47

protection from their enemies. Moses omitted Simeon, but that tribe did receive a number of allies in the southern territory of Judah (Jos 19:2–9) and did not lose their identity (cf. 1Ch 4:34–38).

33:12 Benjamin. That this tribe would have security and peace because the Lord would shield them was Moses' request. They were given the land in the N of Judah near Jerusalem.

33:13–17 Joseph. This included both Ephraim and Manasseh (v. 17), who would enjoy material prosperity (vv. 13–16) and military might (v. 17), which would compensate and reward them for the Egyptian slavery of their ancestor (see Ge 49:26). Ephraim would have greater military success in the future than Manasseh as the outworking of Jacob's blessing of the younger over the older (see Ge 48:20).

33:18 Zebulun ... Issachar. Moses prayed that these two tribes from the fifth and sixth sons of Leah would receive God's blessing in their daily lives, particularly through the trade on the seas.

33:20 Gad. This tribe had large territory E of the Jordan and was a leader in gaining the victory in battles in Canaan.

33:22 Dan. Dan had the potential for great energy and strength and leaped from its southern settlement to establish a colony in the N. Cf. Ge 49:17, 18, where Dan is compared to a serpent.

33:23 Naphtali. This tribe would enjoy the favor of God in the fullness of His blessing, having land in the W of Galilee and S of the northern Danites.

33:24 Asher. The request is that this tribe would experience abundant fertility and prosperity, depicted by reference to a foot-operated oil press. Shoes of hard metal suited both country people and soldiers.

26 "[A]There is none like the God of [a]Jeshurun,
[B]Who rides the heavens [b]to your help,
And through the skies in His majesty.
27 "[A]The eternal God is a [a]dwelling place,
[B]And underneath are the everlasting arms;
[C]And He drove out the enemy
from before you,
[D]And said, 'Destroy!'
28 "[A]So Israel dwells in security,
[B]The fountain of Jacob secluded,
[C]In a land of grain and new wine;
[D]His heavens also drop down dew.
29 "[A]Blessed are you, O Israel;
[B]Who is like you, a people
saved by the LORD,
[C]Who is the shield of your help
[D]And the sword of your majesty!
[E]So your enemies will cringe before you,
[F]And you will tread upon
their high places."

THE DEATH OF MOSES

34 [A]Now Moses went up from the plains of Moab
to Mount Nebo, to the top of Pisgah, which is
opposite Jericho. And the LORD [B]showed him all the
land, Gilead as far as Dan, 2 and all Naphtali and the
land of Ephraim and Manasseh, and all the land of
Judah as far as the [a,A]western sea, 3 and the [a]Negev
and the plain in the valley of Jericho, [A]the city of
palm trees, as far as Zoar. 4 Then the LORD said to
him, "This is the land which [A]I swore to Abraham,
Isaac, and Jacob, saying, 'I will give it to your [a]de-
scendants'; I have let you see *it* with your eyes, but
you shall not go over there." 5 So Moses [A]the servant
of the LORD [B]died there in the land of Moab, according to the [a]word of the LORD. 6 And He buried him in
the valley in the land of Moab, [A]opposite Beth-peor;
but [B]no man knows his burial place to this day. 7 Although Moses was [A]one hundred and twenty years
old when he died, [B]his eye was not dim, nor his
vigor abated. 8 So the sons of Israel wept for Moses
in the plains of Moab thirty days; then the days of
weeping *and* mourning for Moses came to an end.
9 Now Joshua the son of Nun was [A]filled with the
spirit of wisdom, for Moses had laid his hands on
him; and the sons of Israel listened to him and did as
the LORD had commanded Moses. 10 Since that time
[A]no prophet has risen in Israel like Moses, whom
[B]the LORD knew face to face, 11 for all the signs and
wonders which the LORD sent him to perform in
the land of Egypt against Pharaoh, all his servants,
and all his land, 12 and for all the mighty [a]power and
for all the great terror which Moses performed in
the sight of all Israel.

33:26 [a]I.e. Israel [b]Lit *in* [A]Ex 15:11; Deut 4:35; Ps 86:8; Jer 10:6 [B]Deut 10:14; Ps 68:33, 34; 104:3; Hab 3:8 33:27 [a]Or *refuge* [A]Ps 90:1, 2 [B]Gen 49:24 [C]Ex 34:11; Josh 24:18 [D]Deut 7:2 33:28 [A]Deut 33:12; Jer 23:6 [B]Num 23:9; Deut 32:8 [C]Gen 27:28, 37 [D]Deut 33:13 33:29 [A]Ps 1:1; 32:1, 2 [B]Deut 4:32; 2 Sam 7:23 [C]Gen 15:1; Ps 33:20; 115:9-11 [D]Ps 68:34 [E]Ps 66:3 [F]Num 33:52 34:1 [A]Deut 32:49 [B]Deut 32:52 34:2 [a]I.e. Mediterranean Sea [A]Deut 11:24 34:3 [a]I.e. South country [A]Judg 1:16; 3:13; 2 Chr 28:15 34:4 [a]Lit *seed* [A]Gen 12:7; 26:3; 28:13 34:5 [a]Lit *mouth* [A]Num 12:7; Josh 1:1, 2 [B]Deut 32:50 34:6 [A]Deut 3:29; 4:46 [B]Jude 9 34:7 [A]Deut 31:2 [B]Gen 27:1; 48:10 34:9 [A]Num 27:18, 23; Is 11:2 34:10 [A]Deut 18:15, 18 [B]Ex 33:11; Num 12:8; Deut 5:4 34:12 [a]Lit *hand*

33:26, 27 the God of Jeshurun. Moses concluded his blessings with a reminder of the uniqueness of Israel's God. For "Jeshurun," *see note on 32:15.*

33:28, 29 This pledge was only partially fulfilled after they entered the land, but it awaits a complete fulfillment in the kingdom of Messiah.

33:28 The fountain of Jacob. This is a euphemism for Jacob's seed, referring to his posterity.

34:1–12 This concluding chapter was obviously written by someone other than Moses (probably the writer of Joshua) to bridge out of Deuteronomy into Joshua.

34:1 Pisgah. The range or ridge of which Mt. Nebo was the highest point.

34:1–4 the LORD showed him. From the top of the mountain, Moses was allowed to see the panorama of the Land the Lord had promised to give (the Land of Canaan) to the patriarchs and their seed in Ge 12:7; 13:15; 15:18–21; 26:4; 28:13, 14.

34:6 He buried him. The context indicates that the Lord is the one who buried Moses, and man did not have a part in it. Cf. Jude 9, which recounts Michael's and Satan's dispute over Moses' body.

34:7 not dim ... abated. Moses' physical vision and physical health were not impaired. It was not death by natural causes that kept Moses from leading Israel into the Promised Land; it was his unfaithfulness to the Lord at Meribah (see Nu 20:12).

34:8 thirty days. The mourning period for Moses conformed to that of Aaron (Nu 20:29).

34:9 spirit of wisdom ... laid his hands. Joshua received 1) confirmation of the military and administrative ability necessary to the task the Lord had given him, as well as, 2) the spiritual wisdom to rely on and to be committed to the Lord through the laying on of Moses' hands.

34:10 no prophet ... like Moses. Moses was the greatest of all the OT prophets, one whom the Lord knew intimately. Not until John the Baptist was there another prophet greater than Moses (see Mt 11:11). After John, the Prophet came of whom Moses wrote (cf. Jn 1:21, 25; 6:14 with Dt 18:15, 18; Ac 3:22; 7:37). Moses next appeared on the Mt. of Transfiguration together with Elijah and Jesus Christ (Mt 17:3; Mk 9:4; Lk 9:30, 31).

THE BOOK OF JOSHUA

TITLE

This is the first of the 12 historical books, and it gained its name from the exploits of Joshua, the understudy whom Moses prayed for and commissioned as a leader in Israel (Nu 27:12–23). "Joshua" means "Jehovah saves," or "the Lord is salvation," and corresponds to the NT name "Jesus." God delivered Israel in Joshua's day when He was personally present as the saving Commander who fought on Israel's behalf (5:14–6:2; 10:42; 23:3, 5; Ac 7:45).

AUTHOR AND DATE

Although the author is not named, the most probable candidate is Joshua, who was the key eyewitness to the events recorded (cf. 18:9; 24:26). An assistant whom Joshua groomed could have finished the book by attaching such comments as those concerning Joshua's death (24:29–33). Some have even suggested that this section was written by the High Priest Eleazar, or his son, Phinehas. Rahab was still living at the time Jos 6:25 was penned. The book was completed before David's reign (15:63; cf. 2Sa 5:5–9). The most likely writing period is ca. 1405–1385 B.C.

Joshua was born in Egyptian slavery, trained under Moses, and by God's choice rose to his key position of leading Israel into Canaan. Distinguishing features of his life include: 1) service (Ex 17:10; 24:13; 33:11; Nu 11:28); 2) soldiering (Ex 17:9–13); 3) scouting (Nu 13, 14); 4) supplication by Moses (Nu 27:15–17); 5) the sovereignty of God (Nu 27:18ff.); 6) the Spirit's presence (Nu 27:18; Dt 34:9); 7) separation by Moses (Nu 27:18–23; Dt 31:7, 8, 13–15); and 8) selflessness in wholly following the Lord (Nu 32:12).

BACKGROUND AND SETTING

When Moses passed the baton of leadership on to Joshua before he died (Dt 34), Israel was at the end of its 40 year wilderness wandering period ca. 1405 B.C. Joshua was approaching 90 years of age when he became Israel's leader. He later died at the age of 110 (24:29), having led Israel to drive out most of the Canaanites and having divided the land among the 12 tribes. Poised on the plains of Moab, E of the Jordan River and the land which God had promised (Ge 12:7; 15:18–21), the Israelites awaited God's direction to conquer the land. They faced peoples on the western side of the Jordan who had become so steeped in iniquity that God would cause the land, so to speak, to spew out these inhabitants (Lv 18:24, 25). He would give Israel the land by conquest, primarily to fulfill the covenant He had pledged to Abraham and his descendants, but also to pass just judgment on the sinful inhabitants (cf. Ge 15:16). Long possession of different parts of the land by various peoples had pre-dated even Abraham's day (Ge 10:15–19; 12:6; 13:7). Its inhabitants had continued on a moral decline in the worship of many gods up to Joshua's time.

HISTORICAL AND THEOLOGICAL THEMES

A keynote feature is God's faithfulness to fulfill His promise of giving the Land to Abraham's descendants (Ge 12:7; 15:18–21; 17:8). By His leading (cf. 5:14–6:2), they inhabited the territories E and W of the Jordan, and so the word "possess" appears nearly 20 times.

Related to this theme is Israel's failure to press their conquest to every part of the Land (13:1). Judges 1–2 later describes the tragic results from this sin. Key verses focus on: 1) God's promise of possession of the Land (1:3, 6); 2) meditation on God's law, which was strategic for His people (1:8); and 3) Israel's actual possession of the Land in part (11:23; 21:45; 22:4).

Specific allotment of distinct portions in the Land was Joshua's task, as recorded in chaps. 13–22. Levites were placed strategically in 48 towns so that God's spiritual services through them would be reasonably within reach of the Israelites, wherever they lived.

God wanted His people to possess the Land: 1) to keep His promise (Ge 12:7); 2) to set the stage for later developments in His kingdom plan (cf. Ge 17:8; 49:8–12), e.g., positioning Israel for events in the periods of the kings and prophets; 3) to punish peoples that were an affront to Him because of extreme sinfulness (Lv 18:25); and 4) to be a testimony to other peoples (Jos 2:9–11), as God's covenant heart reached out to all nations (Ge 12:1–3).

INTERPRETIVE CHALLENGES

Miracles always challenge readers either to believe that the God who created heaven and earth (Ge 1:1) can do other mighty works, too, or to explain them away. As in Moses' day, miracles in this book were a part of God's purpose, such as: 1) His holding back the Jordan's waters (Jos 3:7–17); 2) the fall of Jericho's walls (Jos 6:1–27); 3) the hailstones (Jos 10:1–11); and 4) the long day (Jos 10:12–15).

Other challenges include: 1) How did God's blessing on the harlot Rahab, who responded to Him in faith, relate to her telling a lie (Jos 2)?; 2) Why were Achan's family members executed with him (Jos 7)?; 3) Why was Ai, with fewer men than Israel, hard to conquer (Jos 7–8)?; 4) What does God's sending "the hornet" before Israel mean (Jos 24:12)? These questions will be addressed in the notes.

OUTLINE

I. Entering the Promised Land (1:1–5:15)

II. Conquering the Promised Land (6:1–12:24)
- A. The Central Campaign (6:1–8:35)
- B. The Southern Campaign (9:1–10:43)
- C. The Northern Campaign (11:1–15)
- D. The Summary of Conquests (11:16–12:24)

III. Distributing Portions in the Promised Land (13:1–22:34)
- A. Summary of Instructions (13:1–33)
- B. West of the Jordan (14:1–19:51)
- C. Cities of Refuge (20:1–9)
- D. Cities of the Levites (21:1–45)
- E. East of the Jordan (22:1–34)

IV. Retaining the Promised Land (23:1–24:28)
- A. The First Speech by Joshua (23:1–16)
- B. The Second Speech by Joshua (24:1–28)

V. Postscript (24:29–33)

GOD'S CHARGE TO JOSHUA

1 Now it came about after the death of Moses
the servant of the LORD, that the LORD spoke
to Joshua the son of Nun, Moses' [a]servant, saying,
2 "Moses [A]My servant is dead; now therefore arise,
[B]cross this Jordan, you and all this people, to the
land which I am giving to them, to the sons of Israel.
3 [A]Every place on which the sole of your foot treads, I
have given it to you, just as I spoke to Moses. 4 [A]From
the wilderness and this Lebanon, even as far as the
great river, the river Euphrates, all the land of the
Hittites, and as far as the Great Sea toward the setting of the sun will be your territory. 5 [A]No man will
be able to stand before you all the days of your life.
Just as I have been with Moses, I will be with you;
[B]I will not fail you or forsake you. 6 [A]Be strong and
courageous, for you shall give this people possession
of the land which I swore to their fathers to give
them. 7 Only be strong and very courageous; [a,A]be
careful to do according to all the law which Moses
My servant commanded you; do not turn from it to
the right or to the left, so that you may [b]have success
wherever you go. 8 [A]This book of the law shall not
depart from your mouth, but you shall meditate on
it day and night, so that you may [a]be careful to do
according to all that is written in it; [B]for then you will
make your way prosperous, and then you will [b]have
success. 9 Have I not commanded you? [A]Be strong
and courageous! [B]Do not tremble or be dismayed,
for the LORD your God is with you wherever you go."

JOSHUA ASSUMES COMMAND

10 Then Joshua commanded the officers of the
people, saying, 11 "Pass through the midst of the
camp and command the people, saying, 'Prepare
provisions for yourselves, for within [A]three days
you are to cross this Jordan, to go in to possess
the land which the LORD your God is giving you,
to possess it.' "
12 [A]To the Reubenites and to the Gadites and to the
half-tribe of Manasseh, Joshua [a]said, 13 "Remember
the word which Moses the servant of the LORD commanded you, saying, '[A]The LORD your God gives you
rest and will give you this land.' 14 Your wives, your
little ones, and your cattle shall remain in the land
which Moses gave you beyond the Jordan, but you
shall cross before your brothers in battle array, all
your valiant warriors, and shall help them, 15 until
the LORD gives your brothers rest, as *He gives* you,
and they also possess the land which the LORD
your God is giving them. [A]Then you shall return to
[a]your own land, and possess [b]that which Moses [B]the
servant of the LORD gave you beyond the Jordan
toward the sunrise."
16 They answered Joshua, saying, "All that you
have commanded us we will do, and wherever you
send us we will go. 17 Just as we obeyed Moses in
all things, so we will obey you; only [A]may the LORD
your God be with you as He was with Moses. 18 Anyone who rebels against your [a]command and does
not obey your words in all that you command him,

1:1 [a]Or *minister* 1:2 [A]Num 12:7; Deut 34:5 [B]Josh 1:11 1:3 [A]Deut 11:24 1:4 [A]Gen 15:18; Num 34:3 1:5 [A]Deut 7:24 [B]Deut 31:6, 7; Heb 13:5 1:6 [A]Deut 31:6, 7, 23 1:7 [a]Lit *observe* [b]Or *act wisely* [A]Deut 5:32 1:8 [a]Lit *observe* [b]Or *act wisely* [A]Deut 31:24; Josh 8:34 [B]Deut 29:9; Ps 1:1-3 1:9 [A]Josh 1:7 [B]Deut 31:8 1:11 [A]Josh 3:2 1:12 [a]Lit *said, saying* [A]Num 32:20-22 1:13 [A]Deut 3:18-20 1:15 [a]Lit *the land of your possession* [b]Lit *it* [A]Josh 22:4 [B]Josh 1:1 1:17 [A]Josh 1:5, 9 1:18 [a]Lit *mouth*

1:2 the land which I am giving. This is the land God promised in His covenant with Abraham and often reaffirmed later (Ge 12:7; 13:14–15; 15:18–21).

1:4 Borders of the Promised Land are: *west,* the Mediterranean seacoast; *east,* Euphrates River far to the east; *south,* the wilderness over to the Nile of Egypt; *north,* Lebanon.

1:5 The promise of divine power for Joshua's task.

1:6 I swore to their fathers. Cf. Ge 12:7; 15:18–21; 17:8; 26:3; 28:13; 35:12 to Abraham, Isaac, and Jacob.

1:7 strong and very courageous. *See note on Dt 31:6–8.*

1:8 This book of the law. A reference to Scripture, specifically Genesis through Deuteronomy, written by Moses (cf. Ex 17:14; Dt 31:9–11, 24). **meditate on it.** To read with thoughtfulness, to linger over God's Word. The parts of Scripture they possessed have always been the main spiritual food of those who served Him, e.g., Job (Job 23:12); the psalmist (Ps 1:1–3); Jeremiah (Jer 15:16); and Jesus (Jn 4:34). **prosperous ... success.** The promise of God's blessing on the great responsibility God has given Joshua. The principle here is central to all spiritual effort and enterprise, namely the deep understanding and application of Scripture at all times.

1:9 LORD ... is with you. This assurance has always been the staying sufficiency for His servants such as: Abraham (Ge 15:1); Moses and his people (Ex 14:13); Isaiah (Is 41:10); Jeremiah (Jer 1:7, 8); and Christians through the centuries (Mt 28:20; Heb 13:5).

1:11 within three days. In some cases, events which took place before this announcement and these 3 days (cf. 3:2) are described later on, e.g., Joshua's sending two scouts to check out the Land (2:22).

1:12 half-tribe of Manasseh. In Ge 48 Jacob blessed both sons of Joseph, Ephraim, and Manasseh, so that Joseph actually received a double blessing (Ge 48:22). This allowed for 12 allotments of the land, Levi being excluded because of priestly function.

1:13–18 The LORD ... will give you this land. God gave them these lands directly across the Jordan River on the E (cf. Nu 32). Yet, it was their duty to assist the other tribes

JOSHUA'S PREPARATION FOR MINISTRY

1. Ex 17:9, 10, 13–14	Joshua led the victorious battle against the Amalekites.
2. Ex 24:13	Joshua, the servant of Moses, accompanied the Jewish leader to the mountain of God (cf. 32:17).
3. Nu 11:28	Joshua was the attendant of Moses from his youth.
4. Nu 13:16	Moses changed his name from Hoshea ("salvation") to Joshua ("the Lord saves").
5. Nu 14:6–10, 30, 38	Joshua, along with Caleb, spied out the land of Canaan with 10 others. Only Joshua and Caleb urged the nation to possess the land and, thus, only they of the 12 actually entered Canaan.
6. Nu 27:18	Joshua was indwelt by the Holy Spirit.
7. Nu 27:18–23	Joshua was commissioned for spiritual service the first time, to assist Moses.
8. Nu 32:12	Joshua followed the Lord fully.
9. Dt 31:23	Joshua was commissioned a second time, to replace Moses.
10. Dt 34:9	Joshua was filled with the spirit of wisdom.

shall be put to death; only be strong and courageous."

RAHAB SHELTERS SPIES

2 Then Joshua the son of Nun sent two men as
spies secretly from [A]Shittim, saying, "Go, view
the land, especially Jericho." So they went and came
into the house of [B]a harlot whose name was Rahab,
and [a]lodged there. 2 It was told the king of Jericho,
saying, "Behold, men from the sons of Israel have
come here tonight to search out the land." 3 And the
king of Jericho sent *word* to Rahab, saying, "Bring
out the men who have come to you, who have entered your house, for they have come to search out
all the land." 4 But the [A]woman had taken the two
men and hidden them, and she said, "Yes, the men
came to me, but I did not know where they were
from. 5 It came about when *it was time* to shut the
gate at dark, that the men went out; I do not know
where the men went. Pursue them quickly, for you
will overtake them." 6 But [A]she had brought them
up to the roof and hidden them in the stalks of flax
which she had laid in order on the roof. 7 So the men
pursued them on the road to the Jordan to the fords;
and as soon as those who were pursuing them had
gone out, they shut the gate.
8 Now before they lay down, [a]she came up to them
on the roof, 9 and said to the men, "[A]I know that the
LORD has given you the land, and that the [B]terror
of you has fallen on us, and that all the inhabitants
of the land have [a]melted away before you. 10 [A]For
we have heard how the LORD dried up the water
of the [a]Red Sea before you when you came out of
Egypt, and [B]what you did to the two kings of the
Amorites who were beyond the Jordan, to Sihon
and Og, whom you [b]utterly destroyed. 11 When we
heard *it,* [A]our hearts melted and no [a]courage remained in any man any longer because of you; for
the [B]LORD your God, He is God in heaven above and
on earth beneath. 12 Now therefore, please swear
to me by the LORD, since I have dealt kindly with
you, that you also will deal kindly with my father's
household, and give me a [A]pledge of [a]truth, 13 and
[a]spare my father and my mother and my brothers
and my sisters, with all who belong to them, and
deliver our [b]lives from death." 14 So the men said
to her, "Our [a]life [b]for yours if you do not tell this
business of ours; and it shall come about when the
LORD gives us the land that we will [A]deal kindly and
[c]faithfully with you."

THE PROMISE TO RAHAB

15 Then she let them down by a rope through the
window, for her house was on the city wall, so that
she was living on the wall. 16 She said to them, "[A]Go
to the hill country, so that the pursuers will not
happen upon you, and hide yourselves there for
three days until the pursuers return. Then afterward you may go on your way." 17 The men said to
her, "[A]We *shall be* free from this oath [a]to you which
you have made us swear, 18 [a]unless, when we come
into the land, you tie this cord of scarlet thread in
the window through which you let us down, and
[A]gather to yourself into the house your father and
your mother and your brothers and all your father's
household. 19 It shall come about that anyone who
goes out of the doors of your house into the street,
his blood *shall be* on his own head, and we *shall*
be free; but anyone who is with you in the house,
[A]his blood *shall be* on our head if a hand is *laid* on
him. 20 But if you tell this business of ours, then we
shall be free from the oath which you have made us
swear." 21 She said, "According to your words, so be
it." So she sent them away, and they departed; and
she tied the scarlet cord in the window.
22 They departed and came to the hill country, and
remained there for three days until the pursuers
returned. Now the pursuers had sought *them* [a]all
along the road, but had not found *them.* 23 Then
the two men returned and came down from the
hill country and crossed over and came to Joshua
the son of Nun, and they related to him all that had
happened to them. 24 They said to Joshua, "Surely the
LORD has given all the land into our hands; moreover, [A]all the inhabitants of the land have [a]melted
away before us."

2:1 [a]Lit *lay down* [A]Num 25:1; Josh 3:1 [B]Heb 11:31; James 2:25 2:4 [A]2 Sam 17:19 2:6 [A]James 2:25 2:8 [a]Lit *then she* 2:9 [a]Or *become demoralized* [A]Num 20:24; Josh 9:24 [B]Ex 23:27; Deut 2:25; Josh 9:9, 10 2:10 [a]Lit *Sea of Reeds* [b]Or *put under the ban* [A]Ex 14:21; Num 23:22; 24:8 [B]Num 21:21-35 2:11 [a]Lit *spirit arose* [A]Josh 5:1; 7:5; Ps 22:14; Is 13:7; 19:1 [B]Deut 4:39 2:12 [a]Or *faithfulness* [A]Josh 2:18, 19 2:13 [a]Lit *let live* [b]Lit *souls* 2:14 [a]Lit *soul* [b]Lit *instead of you to die* [c]Or *truly* [A]Gen 24:49 2:16 [A]James 2:25 2:17 [a]Lit *of yours* [A]Gen 24:8 2:18 [a]Lit *behold* [A]Josh 2:12 2:19 [A]Matt 27:25 2:22 [a]Lit *through all the road* 2:24 [a]Or *become demoralized* [A]Josh 2:9

of Israel to invade and conquer their allotted land to the W.

2:1 two men as spies. These scouts would inform Joshua on various features of the topography, food, drinking water, and defenses to be overcome in the invasion. **Shittim ... Jericho.** The grove (cf. 3:1) was situated in foothills about 7 mi. E of the Jordan, and Jericho lay seven mi. W of the river. **house of a harlot.** Their purpose was not impure; rather, the spies sought a place where they would not be conspicuous. Resorting to such a house would be a good cover, from where they might learn something of Jericho. Also, a house on the city wall (v. 15) would allow a quick getaway. In spite of this precaution, their presence became known (vv. 2, 3). God, in His sovereign providence, wanted them there for the salvation of the harlot. She would provide an example of His saving by faith a woman at the bottom of the social strata, as He saved Abraham at the top (cf. Jas 2:18–25). Most importantly, by God's grace she was in the Messianic line (Mt 1:5).

2:2 the king. He was not over a broad domain, but only the city-state. Kings over other city areas appear later during this conquest (cf. 8:23; 12:24).

2:4, 5 Cf. vv. 9–11. Lying is sin to God (Ex 20:16), for He cannot lie (Titus 1:2). God commended her faith (Heb 11:31; Jas 2:25) as expressed in vv. 9–16, not her lie. He never condones any sin, yet none are without some sin (cf. Ro 3:23), thus the need for forgiveness. But He also honors true faith, small as it is, and imparts saving grace (Ex 34:7).

2:6 stalks of flax. These fibers, used for making linen, were stems about 3 feet long, left to sit in water, then piled in the sun or on a level roof to dry.

2:11 God in heaven above and on earth beneath. She confessed the realization that He is the sovereign Creator and Sustainer of all that exists (cf. Dt 4:39; Ac 14:15; 17:23–28), thus the Supreme One.

2:15, 16 Her home was on the city wall, with the Jordan (v. 7) to the E. The rugged mountains to the W provided many hiding places.

2:18 cord. A different word from "rope" (v. 15). Scarlet, unlike drab green, brown, gray, etc., is better seen to mark the house for protection. The color also is fitting for these whose blood (v. 19) was under God's pledge of safety.

ISRAEL CROSSES THE JORDAN

3 Then Joshua rose early in the morning; and he
and all the sons of Israel set out from [A]Shittim
and came to the Jordan, and they lodged there
before they crossed. 2 [A]At the end of three days
the officers went through the midst of the camp;
3 and they commanded the people, saying, "When
you see the [A]ark of the covenant of the LORD your
God with the Levitical priests carrying it, then
you shall set out from your place and go after it.
4 However, there shall be between you and it a
distance of about 2,000 [a]cubits by measure. Do
not come near it, that you may know the way by
which you shall go, for you have not passed this
way before."
5 Then Joshua said to the people, "[A]Consecrate
yourselves, for tomorrow the LORD will do wonders
among you." 6 And Joshua spoke to the priests, saying, "Take up the ark of the covenant and cross over
ahead of the people." So they took up the ark of the
covenant and went ahead of the people.
7 Now the LORD said to Joshua, "This day I will
begin to [A]exalt you in the sight of all Israel, that they
may know that just as I have been with Moses, I will
be with you. 8 You shall, moreover, command the
priests who are carrying the ark of the covenant,
saying, 'When you come to the edge of the waters
of the Jordan, you shall stand *still* in the Jordan.' "
9 Then Joshua said to the sons of Israel, "Come here,
and hear the words of the LORD your God." 10 Joshua
said, "By this you shall know that [A]the living God is
among you, and that He will assuredly [B]dispossess
from before you the Canaanite, the Hittite, the Hivite, the Perizzite, the Girgashite, the Amorite, and
the Jebusite. 11 Behold, the ark of the covenant of [A]the
Lord of all the earth is crossing over ahead of you
into the Jordan. 12 Now then, [A]take for yourselves
twelve men from the tribes of Israel, one man for
each tribe. 13 It shall come about when the soles
of the feet of the priests who carry the ark of the
LORD, the Lord of all the earth, rest in the waters
of the Jordan, the waters of the Jordan will be cut

3:1 [A]Josh 2:1 3:2 [A]Josh 1:11 3:3 [A]Deut 31:9 3:4 [a]I.e. One cubit equals approx 18 in. 3:5 [A]Ex 19:10, 11; Josh 7:13 3:7 [A]Josh 4:14 3:10 [A]Deut 5:26; 1 Thess 1:9 [B]Ex 33:2; Deut 7:1 3:11 [A]Job 41:11; Ps 24:1; Zech 6:5 3:12 [A]Josh 4:2

3:3 the ark. Symbolized God's presence going before His people. Kohathites customarily carried the ark (Nu 4:15; 7:9), but in this unusual case the Levitical priests transported it, as in Jos 6:6 and 1Ki 8:3–6.

3:4 two thousand cubits. 1,000 yards.

3:8 stand ... in the Jordan. The priests were to stand there to permit time for God's words (v. 9) to stimulate reflection on the greatness of God's eminent action in giving the Land as He showed His presence (v. 10). Also, it was a preparation to allow the people following to get set for God's miracle which stopped the waters for a crossing (vv. 13–17).

3:10 Canaanite people to be killed or defeated were sinful to the point of extreme (cf. Ge 15:16; Lv 18:24, 25). God, as moral judge, has the right to deal with all people, as at the end (Rev 20:11–15) or any other time when He deems it appropriate for His purposes. The question is not why God chose to destroy these sinners, but why He had let them live so long, and why all sinners are not destroyed far sooner than they are. It is grace that allows any sinner to draw one more breath of life (cf. Ge 2:17; Eze 18:20; Ro 6:23).

THE PEOPLES AROUND THE PROMISED LAND

(cf. Ex 34:10–17; Dt 20:17; Jos 3:10; 9:1; 24:11)

1. Amalekites	The descendants of Amalek, the grandson of Esau (Ge 36:12), who dwelt S of Canaan in the Negev.
2. Ammonites	The descendants of Ammon, the grandson of Lot by his youngest daughter (Ge 19:38), who lived E of the Jordan River and N of Moab.
3. Amorites	A general term for the inhabitants of the Land, but especially for the descendants of Canaan who inhabited the hill country on both sides of the Jordan.
4. Canaanites	Broadly speaking, these are the descendants of Canaan, son of Ham, son of Noah (cf. Ge 10:15–18), and included many of the other groups named here.
5. Edomites	The descendants of Esau who settled SE of Palestine (cf. Ge 25:30) in the land of Seir.
6. Gebalites	People of the ancient seaport later known as Byblos, about 20 mi. N of modern Beirut (Jos 13:5).
7. Geshurites	The inhabitants of Geshur, E of the Jordan and to the S of Syria (Jos 12:5).
8. Gibeonites	The inhabitants of Gibeon and surrounding area (Jos 9:17).
9. Girgashites	A tribe descended from Canaan, which was included among the general population of the Land without specific geographical identity.
10. Girzites	An obscure group which lived in the NW part of the Negev, before they were destroyed by David (1Sa 27:8, 9).
11. Hittites	Immigrants from the Hittite Empire (in the region of Syria) to the central region of the Land (cf. Ge 23:10; 2Sa 11:3).
12. Hivites	Descendants of Canaan who lived in the northern reaches of the Land.
13. Horites	Ancient residents of Edom from an unknown origin who were destroyed by Esau's descendants (Dt 2:22).
14. Jebusites	Descendants of Canaan who dwelt in the hill country around Jerusalem (cf. Ge 15:21; Ex 3:8).
15. Kenites	A Midianite tribe that originally dwelt in the Gulf of Aqabah region (1Sa 27:10).
16. Moabites	The descendants of Moab, the grandson of Lot by his eldest daughter (Ge 19:37), who lived E of the Dead Sea.
17. Perizzites	People included among the general population of the Land who do not trace their lineage to Canaan. Their exact identity is uncertain.

off, *and* the waters which are [a]flowing down from
above [b]will [A]stand in one heap."
14 So when the people set out from their tents to
cross the Jordan with the priests carrying [A]the ark
of the covenant before the people, 15 and when those
who carried the ark came into the Jordan, and the
feet of the priests carrying the ark were dipped in
the edge of the water (for the [A]Jordan overflows
all its banks all the days of harvest), 16 [A]the waters
which were [a]flowing down from above stood *and*
rose up in [B]one heap, a great distance away at Adam,
the city that is beside Zarethan; and those which
were [a]flowing down toward the sea of the [C]Arabah,
the Salt Sea, were completely cut off. So the people
crossed opposite Jericho. 17 And the priests who
carried the ark of the covenant of the LORD stood
firm [A]on dry ground in the middle of the Jordan
while all Israel crossed on dry ground, until all the
nation had finished crossing the Jordan.

MEMORIAL STONES FROM JORDAN

4 Now when all the nation had finished crossing the
[A]Jordan, the LORD spoke to Joshua, saying, 2 "[A]Take
for yourselves twelve men from the people, one man
from each tribe, 3 and command them, saying, 'Take
up for yourselves twelve stones from here out of
the middle of the Jordan, from the place where the
priests' feet are standing firm, and carry them over
with you and lay them down in [A]the lodging place
where you will lodge tonight.' " 4 So Joshua called the
twelve men whom he had appointed from the sons of
Israel, one man from each tribe; 5 and Joshua said to
them, "[a]Cross again to the ark of the LORD your God
into the middle of the Jordan, and each of you take
up a stone on his shoulder, according to the number
of the tribes of the sons of Israel. 6 [a]Let this be a sign
among you, so that [A]when your children ask [b]later,
saying, 'What do these stones mean to you?' 7 then
you shall say to them, 'Because the [A]waters of the
Jordan were cut off before the ark of the covenant of
the LORD; when it crossed the Jordan, the waters of
the Jordan were cut off.' So these stones shall become
a [B]memorial to the sons of Israel forever."
8 Thus the sons of Israel did as Joshua commanded, and took up twelve stones from the middle of the Jordan, just as the LORD spoke to Joshua,
according to the number of the tribes of the sons
of Israel; and they carried them over with them to
[A]the lodging place and put them down there. 9 Then
Joshua set up twelve [A]stones in the middle of the
Jordan at the place where the feet of the priests
who carried the ark of the covenant were standing,
and they are there to this day. 10 For the priests who
carried the ark were standing in the middle of the
Jordan until everything was completed that the
LORD had commanded Joshua to speak to the people, according to all that Moses had commanded
Joshua. And the people hurried and crossed; 11 and
when all the people had finished crossing, the ark of
the LORD and the priests crossed before the people.
12 [A]The sons of Reuben and the sons of Gad and the
half-tribe of Manasseh crossed over in battle array
before the sons of Israel, just as Moses had spoken to
them; 13 about 40,000 equipped for war, crossed for
battle before the LORD to the desert plains of Jericho.
14 [A]On that day the LORD exalted Joshua in the
sight of all Israel; so that they [a]revered him, just
as they had [a]revered Moses all the days of his life.
15 Now the LORD said to [a]Joshua, 16 "Command the
priests who carry [A]the ark of the testimony that they
come up from the Jordan." 17 So Joshua commanded
the priests, saying, "Come up from the Jordan." 18 It
came about when the priests who carried the ark
of the covenant of the LORD had come up from the
middle of the Jordan, and the soles of the priests'
feet were [a]lifted up to the dry ground, that the waters of the Jordan returned to their place, and went
over all its banks as before.
19 Now the people came up from the Jordan on the
[A]tenth of the first month and camped at Gilgal on
the eastern edge of Jericho. 20 [a,A]Those twelve stones
which they had taken from the Jordan, Joshua set
up [B]at Gilgal. 21 He said to the sons of [a]Israel, "When
your children ask their fathers in time to come,
saying, 'What are these stones?' 22 then you shall
inform your children, saying, 'Israel crossed this
Jordan on [A]dry ground.' 23 For the LORD your God
dried up the waters of the Jordan before you until
you had crossed, just as the LORD your God had done
to the [a]Red Sea, [A]which He dried up before us until
we had crossed; 24 that [A]all the peoples of the earth
may know that the [B]hand of the LORD is mighty, so
that you may [a,C]fear the LORD your God [b]forever."

ISRAEL IS CIRCUMCISED

5 Now it came about when all the kings of the
Amorites who *were* beyond the Jordan to the
west, and all the kings of the [A]Canaanites who *were*

3:13 [a]Lit *going* [b]Lit *and they will* [A]Ex 15:8 3:14 [A]Ps 132:8; Acts 7:44f 3:15 [A]1 Chr 12:15; Jer 12:5; 49:19 3:16 [a]Lit *going* [A]Ps 66:6; 74:15; 114:3, 5 [B]Josh 3:13 [C]Deut 1:1 3:17 [A]Ex 14:21, 22, 29 4:1 [A]Deut 27:2; Josh 3:17 4:2 [A]Josh 3:12 4:3 [A]Josh 4:20 4:5 [a]Lit *Cross before the ark* 4:6 [a]Lit *That this may be* [b]Lit *tomorrow* [A]Ex 12:26; 13:14; Josh 4:21 4:7 [A]Josh 3:13 [B]Ex 12:14; Num 16:40 4:8 [A]Josh 4:20 4:9 [A]Gen 28:18; Josh 24:26f; 1 Sam 7:12 4:12 [A]Num 32:17 4:14 [a]Or *feared* [A]Josh 3:7 4:15 [a]Lit *Joshua, saying* 4:16 [A]Ex 25:16 4:18 [a]Lit *drawn out* 4:19 [A]Deut 1:3 4:20 [a]Lit *these* [A]Josh 4:8 [B]Josh 4:3, 8 4:21 [a]Lit *Israel, saying,* 4:22 [A]Josh 3:17 4:23 [a]Lit *Sea of Reeds* [A]Ex 14:21 4:24 [a]Or *reverence* [b]Lit *all the days* [A]1 Kin 8:42; 2 Kin 19:19; Ps 106:8 [B]Ex 15:16; 1 Chr 29:12; Ps 89:13 [C]Ex 14:31; Ps 76:7f; Jer 10:7 5:1 [A]Num 13:29

3:16 rose up in one heap. The God of all power, who created heaven, earth, and all else according to Ge 1, worked miracles here. The waters were dammed up at Adam, a city 15 mi. N of the crossing, and also in tributary creeks. Once the miracle was completed, God permitted waters to flow again (4:18) after all the people had walked to the other side on dry ground (3:17). As the Exodus had begun (cf. Ex 14), so it ended.

4:1–8 Twelve stones picked up from the riverbed became a memorial to God's faithfulness. They were set up at Gilgal (about 1 1/4 mi. from Jericho), which was Israel's first campsite in the invaded land (vv. 19, 20). Placing 12 stones in the riverbed itself commemorated the place which God dried up, where His ark had been held, and where He showed by a miracle His mighty presence and worthiness of respect (vv. 9–11, 21–24).

4:19 tenth of the first month. March-April. Abib was the term used by pre-exilic Jews; Nisan later came to be used by postexilic Israel.

5:1 heard. Reports of God's supernaturally opening a crossing struck fear into the Canaanites. The miracle was all the more incredible and shocking since God performed it when the Jordan was swollen to flood height (3:15). To the people in the Land, this miracle was a powerful demonstration proving

by the sea, [B]heard how the LORD had dried up the
waters of the Jordan before the sons of Israel until
[a]they had crossed, that their hearts melted, and
there was no spirit in them any longer because of
the sons of Israel.
2 At that time the LORD said to Joshua, "Make for
yourself [A]flint knives and circumcise again the sons
of Israel the second time." 3 So Joshua made himself
flint knives and circumcised the sons of Israel at
[a]Gibeath-haaraloth. 4 This is the reason why Joshua
circumcised them: [A]all the people who came out of
Egypt who were males, all the men of war, died in
the wilderness along the way after they came out
of Egypt. 5 For all the people who came out were
circumcised, but all the people who were born in
the wilderness along the way as they came out of
Egypt had not been circumcised. 6 For the sons of
Israel walked [A]forty years in the wilderness, until all
the nation, *that is,* the men of war who came out of
Egypt, [a]perished because they did not listen to the
voice of the LORD, [B]to whom the LORD had sworn
that He would not let them see the land which the
LORD had sworn to their fathers to give us, a land
flowing with milk and honey. 7 Their children whom
He raised up in their place, Joshua [a]circumcised;
for they were uncircumcised, because they had not
circumcised them along the way.
8 Now when they had finished circumcising all
the nation, they remained in their places in the
camp until they were [a]healed. 9 Then the LORD said
to Joshua, "Today I have rolled away [A]the reproach
of Egypt from you." So the name of that place is
called [a]Gilgal to this day.
10 While the sons of Israel camped at Gilgal [A]they
observed the Passover on the evening of the [B]four-
teenth day of the month on the desert plains of
Jericho. 11 On the [a]day after the Passover, on [b]that
very day, they ate some of the produce of the land,
unleavened cakes and parched *grain.* 12 [A]The manna
ceased on the [a]day after they had eaten some of the
produce of the land, so that the sons of Israel no
longer had manna, but they ate some of the yield
of the land of Canaan during that year.
13 Now it came about when Joshua was by Jericho,
that he lifted up his eyes and looked, and behold,
[A]a man was standing opposite him with his sword
drawn in his hand, and Joshua went to him and said
to him, "Are you for us or for our adversaries?" 14 He
said, "No; rather I indeed come now *as* captain of
the host of the LORD." And Joshua [A]fell on his face to
the earth, and bowed down, and said to him, "What
has my lord to say to his servant?" 15 The captain
of the LORD'S host said to Joshua, "[A]Remove your
sandals from your feet, for the place where you are
standing is holy." And Joshua did so.

THE CONQUEST OF JERICHO

6 Now Jericho was tightly shut because of the
sons of Israel; no one went out and no one
came in. 2 The LORD said to Joshua, "See, I have
given Jericho into your hand, with [A]its king *and*
the valiant warriors. 3 You shall march around the
city, all the men of war circling the city once. You
shall do so for six days. 4 Also seven priests shall
carry seven [A]trumpets of rams' horns before the ark;
then on the seventh day you shall march around
the city seven times, and the priests shall blow the
trumpets. 5 It shall be that when they make a long
blast with the ram's horn, and when you hear the
sound of the trumpet, all the people shall shout
with a great shout; and the wall of the city will fall
down [a]flat, and the people will go up every man
[b]straight ahead."
6 So Joshua the son of Nun called the priests and
said to them, "Take up the ark of the covenant, and
let seven priests carry seven trumpets of rams'
horns before the ark of the LORD." 7 Then [a]he said
to the people, "Go forward, and march around the
city, and let the armed men go on before the ark of
the LORD." 8 And it was *so,* that when Joshua had
spoken to the people, the seven priests carrying
the seven trumpets of rams' horns before the LORD
went forward and blew the trumpets; and the ark
of the covenant of the LORD followed them. 9 The
armed men went before the priests who blew the
trumpets, and [A]the rear guard came after the ark,

5:1 [a]Other mss read *we* [B]Josh 2:10, 11 5:2 [A]Ex 4:25 5:3 [a]I.e. the hill of the foreskins 5:4 [A]Deut 2:14 5:6 [a]Lit *were finished* [A]Deut 2:7, 14 [B]Num 14:29-35; 26:63-65 5:7 [a]Lit *circumcised them* 5:8 [a]Lit *revived* 5:9 [a]I.e. rolling [A]Zeph 2:8 5:10 [A]Ex 12:18 [B]Josh 4:19 5:11 [a]Lit *morrow* [b]Lit *this* 5:12 [a]Lit *morrow* [A]Ex 16:35 5:13 [A]Gen 18:1, 2; 32:24, 30; Num 22:31 5:14 [A]Gen 17:3 5:15 [A]Ex 3:5 6:2 [A]Deut 7:24 6:4 [A]Lev 25:9 6:5 [a]Lit *in its place* [b]Lit *before himself* 6:7 [a]Or *they* 6:9 [A]Josh 6:13; Is 52:12

that God is mighty (4:24). This came on top of reports about the Red Sea miracle (2:10).

5:2 circumcise. God commanded Joshua to see that this was done to all males under 40. These were sons of the generation who died in the wilderness, survivors (cf. vv. 6, 7) from the new generation God spared in Nu 13, 14. This surgical sign of a faith commitment to the Abrahamic Covenant (see Ge 17:9–14) had been ignored during the wilderness trek. Now God wanted it reinstated, so the Israelites would start out right in the land they were possessing. *See note on Jer 4:4.*

5:8 they were healed. This speaks of the time needed to recover from such a painful and potentially infected wound.

5:9 rolled away the reproach. By His miracle of bringing the people into the Land, God removed (rolled away) the ridicule which the Egyptians had heaped on them.

5:10 Passover. Commemorated God's deliverance from Egypt, recorded in Ex 7–12. Such a remembrance was a strengthening preparation for trusting God to work in possessing the new land.

5:12 manna ceased. God had begun to provide this food from the time of Ex 16 and did so for 40 years (Ex 16:35). Since food was plentiful in the land of Canaan, they could provide for themselves with produce such as dates, barley, and olives.

5:13–15 captain. The Lord Jesus Christ (6:2; cf. 5:15 with Ex 3:2, 5) in a pre-incarnate appearance (Christophany). He came as the Angel (Messenger) of the Lord, as if He were a man (cf. the one of 3 "angels," Ge 18). Joshua fittingly was reverent in worship. The captain, sword drawn, showed a posture indicating He was set to give Israel victory over the Canaanites (6:2; cf. 1:3).

6:1 Jericho. The city was fortified by a double ring of walls, the outer 6 ft. thick and the inner 12; timbers were laid across these, supporting houses on the walls. Since Jericho was built on a hill, it could be taken only by mounting a steep incline, which put the Israelites at a great disadvantage. Attackers of such a "fortress" often used a siege of several months to force surrender through starvation.

6:3–21 The bizarre military strategy of marching around Jericho gave occasion for the Israelites to take God at His promise (v. 2). They would also heighten the defenders' uneasiness. Seven is sometimes a number used to signify completeness (cf. 2Ki 5:10, 14).

6:5 God assured Israel of an astounding miracle, just as He had done at the Jordan.

while they continued to blow the trumpets. 10 But
Joshua commanded the people, saying, "You shall
not shout nor let your voice be heard nor let a word
proceed out of your mouth, until the day I tell you,
'Shout!' Then you shall shout!" 11 So he had the ark
of the LORD [a]taken around the city, circling *it* once;
then they came into the camp and spent the night
in the camp.
12 Now Joshua rose early in the morning, and the
priests took up the ark of the LORD. 13 [A]The seven
priests carrying the seven trumpets of rams' horns
before the ark of the LORD went on continually, and
blew the trumpets; and the armed men went before
them and [B]the rear guard came after the ark of the
LORD, while they continued to blow the trumpets.
14 Thus the second day they marched around the
city once and returned to the camp; they did so
for six days.
15 Then on the seventh day they rose early at the
dawning of the day and marched around the city
in the same manner seven times; only on that day
they marched around the city seven times. 16 At the
seventh time, when the priests blew the trumpets,
Joshua said to the people, "[A]Shout! For the LORD
has given you the city. 17 The city shall be [A]under
the ban, it and all that is in it belongs to the LORD;
only Rahab the harlot [a]and all who are with her in
the house shall live, because she hid the messengers
whom we sent. 18 But as for you, only keep yourselves from the things under the ban, so that you do
not [a]covet *them* and [A]take some of the things under
the ban, and make the camp of Israel accursed and
bring trouble on it. 19 [A]But all the silver and gold and
articles of bronze and iron are holy to the LORD;
they shall go into the treasury of the LORD." 20 So the
people shouted, and [a]*priests* blew the trumpets; and
when the people heard the sound of the trumpet,
the people shouted with a great shout and the [A]wall
fell down [b]flat, so that the people went up into the
city, every man straight [c]ahead, and they took the
city. 21 [A]They [a]utterly destroyed everything in the
city, both man and woman, young and old, and ox
and sheep and donkey, with the edge of the sword.
22 Joshua said to the two men who had spied out
the land, "[A]Go into the harlot's house and bring the
woman and all she has out of there, as you have
sworn to her." 23 So the young men who were spies
went in and [A]brought out Rahab and her father and
her mother and her brothers and all she had; they
also brought out all her relatives and placed them
outside the camp of Israel. 24 [A]They burned the city
with fire, and all that was in it. Only the silver and
gold, and articles of bronze and iron, they put into
the treasury of the [a]house of the LORD. 25 However,
[A]Rahab the harlot and her father's household and
all she had, Joshua [a]spared; and she has lived in the
midst of Israel to this day, for [B]she hid the messengers whom Joshua sent to spy out Jericho.
26 Then Joshua made them take an oath at that
time, saying, "[A]Cursed before the LORD is the man
who rises up and builds this city Jericho; with *the
loss of* his firstborn he shall lay its foundation, and
with *the loss of* his youngest son he shall set up its
gates." 27 So [A]the LORD was with Joshua, and his
[B]fame was in all the land.

ISRAEL IS DEFEATED AT AI

7 [A]But the sons of Israel acted unfaithfully in regard to the things under the ban, for Achan, the
son of Carmi, the son of Zabdi, the son of Zerah,
from the tribe of Judah, took some of the things
under the ban, therefore the anger of the LORD
burned against the sons of Israel.
2 Now Joshua sent men from Jericho to Ai, which
is near [A]Beth-aven, east of Bethel, and said to them,
"[a]Go up and spy out the land." So the men went up
and spied out Ai. 3 They returned to Joshua and
said to him, "Do not let all the people go up; *only*
about two or three thousand men need go up [a]to
Ai; do not make all the people toil up there, for they
are few." 4 So about three thousand men from the
people went up there, but [A]they fled [a]from the men
of Ai. 5 The men of Ai struck down about thirty-six
of their men, and pursued them [a]from the gate
as far as Shebarim and struck them down on the
descent, so the [A]hearts of the people melted and
became as water.
6 Then Joshua [A]tore his clothes and fell to the
earth on his face before the ark of the LORD until
the evening, *both* he and the elders of Israel; and
[B]they put dust on their heads. 7 Joshua said, "Alas,
O Lord [a]GOD, why did You ever bring this people
over the Jordan, *only* to deliver us into the hand of
the Amorites, to destroy us? If only we had been
willing [b]to dwell beyond the Jordan! 8 O Lord, what
can I say since Israel has turned *their* [a]back before
their enemies? 9 [A]For the Canaanites and all the inhabitants of the land will hear of it, and they will

6:11 [a]Lit *to go around* 6:13 [A]Josh 6:4 [B]Josh 6:9 6:16 [A]2 Chr 13:14f 6:17 [a]Lit *she and all* [A]Lev 27:28; Deut 20:17 6:18 [a]Lit *devote* [A]Josh 7:1 6:19 [A]Num 31:11, 12, 21-23 6:20 [a]Or *they* [b]Lit *in its place* [c]Lit *before himself* [A]Heb 11:30 6:21 [a]Or *put under the ban* [A]Deut 20:16 6:22 [A]Josh 2:12-19 6:23 [A]Heb 11:31 6:24 [a]I.e. tabernacle [A]Deut 20:16-18 6:25 [a]Lit *let live* [A]Heb 11:31 [B]Josh 2:6 6:26 [A]1 Kin 16:34 6:27 [A]Gen 39:2; Judg 1:19 [B]Josh 9:1, 3 7:1 [A]Josh 6:17-19 7:2 [a]Lit *saying, Go* [A]Josh 18:12; 1 Sam 13:5; 14:23 7:3 [a]Lit *and smite* 7:4 [a]Lit *before* [A]Lev 26:17; Deut 28:25 7:5 [a]Or *before* [A]Lev 26:36; Josh 2:11; Ezek 21:7; Nah 2:10 7:6 [A]Job 2:12 [B]Job 42:6; Lam 2:10; Rev 18:19 7:7 [a]Heb *YHWH*, usually rendered LORD [b]Lit *and had dwelt* 7:8 [a]Lit *neck* 7:9 [A]Ex 32:12; Deut 9:28

6:16 The loud shout in unison expressed an expectation of God's action to fulfill His guaranteed promise (vv. 2, 5, 16).

6:17 under the ban. The Heb. term means "utterly destroyed," as in v. 21; i.e., to ban or devote as spoil for a deity. Here it is stated to be retained for God's possession, a tribute belonging to Him for the purpose of destruction.

6:22–25 Joshua honored the promise of safety to the household of Rahab. The part of the wall securing this house must not have fallen, and all possessions in the dwelling were safe.

6:26 God put a curse on whoever would rebuild Jericho. While the area around it was later occupied to some extent (2Sa 10:5), in Ahab's reign Hiel rebuilt Jericho and experienced the curse by losing his eldest and youngest sons (1Ki 16:34).

6:27 God kept His pledge that He would be with Joshua (1:5–9).

7:1–5 Israel's defeat here is similar to an earlier setback against the Amalekites (Nu 14:39–45).

7:2 Ai. A town situated W of the Jordan, in the hills E of Bethel (cf. Ge 12:8).

7:3 few. The "few" inhabitants of Ai are numbered at 12,000 in 8:25 (cf. 8:3).

7:9 what will You do for Your great name? The main issue is the glory and honor of God (cf. Daniel's prayer in Da 9:16–19).

surround us and cut off our name from the earth.
And what will You do for Your great name?"
10 So the LORD said to Joshua, "Rise up! Why is
it that you have fallen on your face? 11 Israel has
sinned, and [A]they have also transgressed My covenant which I commanded them. And they have
even taken some of the things under the ban and
have both stolen and deceived. Moreover, they have
also put *them* among their own things. 12 Therefore
the [A]sons of Israel cannot stand before their enemies; they turn *their* [a]backs before their enemies,
for they have become accursed. I will not be with
you anymore unless you destroy the things under
the ban from your midst. 13 Rise up! [A]Consecrate
the people and say, 'Consecrate yourselves for tomorrow, for thus the LORD, the God of Israel, has
said, "[B]There are things under the ban in your
midst, O Israel. You cannot stand before your enemies until you have removed the things under
the ban from your midst." 14 In the morning then
you shall come near by your tribes. And it shall be
that the tribe which [A]the LORD takes *by lot* shall
come near by families, and the family which the
LORD takes shall come near by households, and
the household which the LORD takes shall come
near man by man. 15 [A]It shall be that the one who
is taken with the things under the ban shall be
burned with fire, he and all that belongs to him,
because he has transgressed the covenant of the
LORD, and because he [B]has committed a disgraceful
thing in Israel.' "

THE SIN OF ACHAN

16 So Joshua arose early in the morning and
brought Israel near by [a]tribes, and the tribe of Judah was taken. 17 He brought the family of Judah
near, and he took the family of the Zerahites; and
he brought the family of the Zerahites near man
by man, and Zabdi was taken. 18 He brought his
household near man by man; and [A]Achan, son of
Carmi, son of Zabdi, son of Zerah, from the tribe
of Judah, was taken. 19 Then Joshua said to Achan,
"My son, I implore you, [A]give glory to the LORD,
the God of Israel, and give praise to Him; and tell
me now what you have done. Do not hide it from
me." 20 So Achan answered Joshua and said, "Truly,
I have sinned against the LORD, the God of Israel,
and [a]this is what I did: 21 when I saw among the spoil
a beautiful mantle from Shinar and two hundred
shekels of silver and a bar of gold fifty shekels in
weight, then I [A]coveted them and took them; and
behold, they are concealed in the earth inside my
tent with the silver underneath it."
22 So Joshua sent messengers, and they ran to
the tent; and behold, it was concealed in his tent
with the silver underneath it. 23 They took them
from inside the tent and brought them to Joshua
and to all the sons of Israel, and they poured them
out before the LORD. 24 Then Joshua and all Israel
with him, took Achan the son of Zerah, the silver,
the mantle, the bar of gold, his sons, his daughters,
his [a]oxen, his donkeys, his sheep, his tent and all
that belonged to him; and they brought them up
to [A]the valley of [b]Achor. 25 Joshua said, "Why have
you [A]troubled us? The LORD will trouble you this
day." And all Israel stoned [a]them with stones; and
they burned them with fire [b]after they had stoned
them with stones. 26 They raised over him a great
heap of stones that stands to this day, and the LORD
turned from the fierceness of His anger. Therefore
the name of that place has been called [A]the valley
of [a]Achor to this day.

THE CONQUEST OF AI

8 Now the LORD said to Joshua, "[A]Do not fear or
be dismayed. Take all the people of war with
you and arise, go up to Ai; see, [B]I have given into
your hand the king of Ai, his people, his city, and
his land. 2 You shall do to Ai and its king just as you
did to Jericho and its king; you shall [A]take only its
spoil and its cattle as plunder for yourselves. [a]Set
an ambush for the city behind it."
3 So Joshua rose with all the people of war to go up
to Ai; and Joshua chose 30,000 men, valiant warriors,
and sent them out at night. 4 He commanded them,
saying, "See, you are [A]going to ambush the city from
behind [a]it. Do not go very far from the city, but all of
you be ready. 5 Then I and all the people who are with
me will approach the city. And when they come out
to meet us as at the first, [A]we will flee before them.
6 They will come out after us until we have drawn
them away from the city, for they will say, '*They* are
fleeing before us as at the first.' So we will flee before
them. 7 And you shall rise from *your* ambush and
take possession of the city, for the LORD your God
will deliver it into your hand. 8 Then it will be when
you have seized the city, that you shall set the city
on fire. You shall do *it* [A]according to the word of the
LORD. See, I have commanded you." 9 So Joshua sent
them away, and they went to the place of ambush and

7:11 [A]Josh 6:18, 19 7:12 [a]Lit *necks* [A]Num 14:39, 45; Judg 2:14 7:13 [A]Josh 3:5 [B]Josh 6:18 7:14 [A]Prov 16:33 7:15 [A]1 Sam 14:38f [B]Gen 34:7; Judg 20:6 7:16 [a]Lit *its tribes* 7:18 [A]Num 32:23; Acts 5:1-10 7:19 [A]1 Sam 6:5; 2 Chr 30:22; Jer 13:16; John 9:24 7:20 [a]Lit *thus and thus I did* 7:21 [A]Eph 5:5; 1 Tim 6:10 7:24 [a]Or *cattle* [b]I.e. trouble [A]Josh 15:7 7:25 [a]Lit *him* [b]Lit *and they stoned* [A]Josh 6:18 7:26 [a]I.e. trouble [A]Is 65:10; Hos 2:15 8:1 [A]Josh 1:9; 10:8 [B]Josh 6:2 8:2 [a]Lit *Set for yourself* [A]Deut 20:14; Josh 8:27 8:4 [a]Lit *the city* [A]Judg 20:29 8:5 [A]Judg 20:32 8:8 [A]Deut 20:16-18; Josh 8:2

7:15, 24, 25 Achan's family faced execution with him. They were regarded as co-conspirators in what he did. They helped cover up his guilt and withheld information from others. Similarly, family members died in Korah's rebellion (Nu 16), Haman's fall (Est 9:13–14), and after Daniel's escape (Da 6:24).

7:21 **I saw.** There are 4 steps in the progress of Achan's sin: "I saw .... coveted .... took .... concealed." David's sin with Bathsheba followed the same path (2Sa 11; cf. Jas 1:14, 15). **a beautiful mantle from Shinar.** A costly, ornate robe beautified by colored figures of men or animals, woven or done in needlework, and perhaps trimmed with jewels. The word is used for a king's robe in Jon 3:6.

7:24 **Achor.** Lit. "trouble" (cf. Is 65:10; Hos 2:15).

8:3 **thirty thousand men.** Joshua's elite force was far superior to that of Ai, with a mere 12,000 total population (8:25). This time Joshua took no small force presumptuously (cf. 7:3, 4), but had 30,000 to sack and burn Ai, a decoy group to lure defenders out (vv. 5, 6), and a third detachment of about 5,000 to prevent Bethel from helping Ai (v. 12).

8:7 **God will deliver it into your hand.** God had sovereignly caused Israel's defeat earlier due to Achan's disobedience (7:1–5). Yet, this time, despite Israel's overwhelming

remained between Bethel and Ai, on the west side of
Ai; but Joshua spent that night among the people.
10 Now Joshua [A]rose early in the morning and
mustered the people, and he went up with the elders of Israel before the people to Ai. 11 Then all the
people of war who *were* with him went up and drew
near and arrived in front of the city, and camped on
the north side of Ai. Now *there was* a valley between
him and Ai. 12 And he took about 5,000 men and set
them in ambush between [A]Bethel and Ai, on the
west side of the [a]city. 13 So they stationed the people,
all the army that was on the north side of the city,
and its rear guard on the west side of the city, and
Joshua spent that night in the midst of the valley.
14 It came about when the king of Ai saw *it,* that the
men of the city hurried and rose up early and went
out to meet Israel in battle, he and all his people at
the appointed place before the desert plain. But he
did not know that *there was* an ambush against him
behind the city. 15 Joshua and all Israel pretended
to be beaten before them, and fled [A]by the way of
the wilderness. 16 And all the people who were in
the city were called together to pursue them, and
they pursued Joshua and [A]were drawn away from
the city. 17 So not a man was left in Ai or Bethel who
had not gone out after Israel, and they left the city
[a]unguarded and pursued Israel.
18 Then the LORD said to Joshua, "[A]Stretch out
the javelin that is in your hand toward Ai, for I will
give it into your hand." So Joshua stretched out the
javelin that was in his hand toward the city. 19 The
men in ambush rose quickly from their place, and
when he had stretched out his hand, they ran and
entered the city and captured it, and they quickly set
the city on fire. 20 When the men of Ai turned [a]back
and looked, behold, the smoke of the city ascended
to the sky, and they had no place to flee this way
or that, for the people who had been fleeing to the
wilderness turned against the pursuers. 21 When
Joshua and all Israel saw that the *men in* ambush
had captured the city and that the smoke of the city
ascended, they turned back and [a]slew the men of Ai.
22 [a]The others came out from the city to encounter
them, so that they were *trapped* in the midst of Israel, [b]some on this side and some on that side; and
they [c]slew them until [A]no one was left [d]of those who
survived or escaped. 23 But they took alive the king
of Ai and brought him to Joshua.
24 Now when Israel had finished killing all the inhabitants of Ai in the field in the wilderness where
they pursued them, and all of them were fallen by
the edge of the sword until they were destroyed,
then all Israel returned to Ai and struck it with the
edge of the sword. 25 [A]All who fell that day, both
men and women, were 12,000—all the [a]people of Ai.
26 For Joshua [A]did not withdraw his hand with which
he stretched out the javelin until he had [a]utterly
destroyed all the inhabitants of Ai. 27 [A]Israel took
only the cattle and the spoil of that city as plunder
for themselves, according to the word of the LORD
which He had commanded Joshua. 28 So Joshua
burned Ai and made it [A]a heap forever, a desolation
until this day. 29 [A]He hanged the king of Ai on a tree
until evening; and at sunset Joshua gave command
and they took his body down from the tree and
threw it at the entrance of the city gate, and raised
over it a great heap of stones *that stands* to this day.
30 Then Joshua built an altar to the LORD, the God
of Israel, in [A]Mount Ebal, 31 just as Moses the servant
of the LORD had commanded the sons of Israel, as
it is written in the book of the law of Moses, [A]an altar of uncut stones on which no man had wielded
an iron *tool;* and they offered burnt offerings on it
to the LORD, and sacrificed peace offerings. 32 He
[A]wrote there on the stones a copy of the law of Moses, which [a]he had written, in the presence of the
sons of Israel. 33 [A]All Israel with their elders and
officers and their judges were standing on both
sides of the ark before the Levitical priests who
carried the ark of the covenant of the LORD, the
stranger as well as the native. Half of them *stood* in
front of [B]Mount Gerizim and half of them in front of
Mount Ebal, just as Moses the servant of the LORD
had given command at first to bless the people of
Israel. 34 Then afterward he read all the words of
the law, the blessing and the curse, according to
all that is written in [A]the book of the law. 35 There
was not a word of all that Moses had commanded
which Joshua did not read before all the assembly
of Israel [A]with the women and the little ones and
the strangers who were [a]living among them.

GUILE OF THE GIBEONITES

9 Now it came about when [A]all the kings who were
beyond the Jordan, in the hill country and in the
lowland and on all the [B]coast of the Great Sea toward
Lebanon, [C]the Hittite and the Amorite, the Canaanite, the Perizzite, the Hivite and the Jebusite, heard
of it, 2 that they gathered themselves together with
[a,A]one accord to fight with Joshua and with Israel.

8:10 [A]Gen 22:3 8:12 [a]I.e. Ai [A]Gen 12:8; 28:19; Judg 1:22 8:15 [A]Josh 15:61; 16:1; 18:12 8:16 [A]Judg 20:31 8:17 [a]Lit *open* 8:18 [A]Ex 14:16; 17:9-13; Josh 8:26 8:20 [a]Lit *behind them* 8:21 [a]Lit *smote* 8:22 [a]Lit *These came* [b]Lit *these...those* [c]Lit *smote* [d]Lit *for it* [A]Josh 8:8 8:25 [a]Lit *men* [A]Deut 20:16-18 8:26 [a]Or *put under the ban* [A]Ex 17:11, 12 8:27 [A]Josh 8:2 8:28 [A]Deut 13:16 8:29 [A]Deut 21:22, 23 8:30 [A]Deut 27:2-8 8:31 [A]Ex 20:25 8:32 [a]I.e. Moses [A]Deut 27:2, 3, 8 8:33 [A]Deut 27:11-14 [B]Deut 11:29 8:34 [A]Josh 1:8 8:35 [a]Lit *walking* [A]Ex 12:38; Deut 31:12; Zech 8:23 9:1 [A]Num 13:29; Josh 3:10 [B]Num 34:6 [C]Ex 3:17; 23:23 9:2 [a]Lit *one mouth* [A]Ps 83:3, 5

numbers, God was still the sovereign power for this victory (8:7).

8:18 the javelin. Joshua's hoisted javelin represented the go-ahead indicator to occupy Ai. Possibly the raising was even a signal of confidence in God: "for I will give it into your hand." Earlier, Moses' uplifted rod and arms probably signified trusting contact with God for victory over Amalek (Ex 17:8–13).

8:29 the king of Ai. The complete execution of Ai's populace included hanging even the king. This wise move prevented later efforts to muster a Canaanite army. Further, as a wicked king, he was worthy of punishment according to biblical standards (Dt 21:22; Jos 10:26, 27). This carried out the vengeance of God on His enemies.

8:30–35 This ceremony took place in obedience to Dt 27:1–26 at the conclusion of Joshua's central campaign (cf. 6:1–8:35).

8:30, 31 Thanks is offered to God for giving victory. The altar, in obedience to the instruction of Ex 20:24–26, was built of uncut stones, thus keeping worship simple and untainted by man's showmanship. Joshua gave God's Word a detailed and central place.

3 When the inhabitants of [A]Gibeon heard what
Joshua had done to Jericho and to Ai, 4 they also
acted craftily and [a]set out as envoys, and took
worn-out sacks on their donkeys, and wineskins
worn-out and torn and [b]mended, 5 and worn-out and
patched sandals on their feet, and worn-out clothes
on themselves; and all the bread of their provision
was dry *and* had become crumbled. 6 They went to
Joshua to the [A]camp at Gilgal and said to him and to
the men of Israel, "We have come from a far country; now therefore, make a covenant with us." 7 The
men of Israel said to the [A]Hivites, "Perhaps you are
living [a]within our land; [B]how then shall we make a
covenant with you?" 8 But they said to Joshua, "[A]We
are your servants." Then Joshua said to them, "Who
are you and where do you come from?" 9 They said
to him, "Your servants have come from [A]a very far
country because of the [a]fame of the LORD your God;
for [B]we have heard the report of Him and all that He
did in Egypt, 10 and all that He did to the two kings
of the Amorites who were beyond the Jordan, to
Sihon king of Heshbon and to Og king of Bashan
who was at Ashtaroth. 11 So our elders and all the
inhabitants of our country spoke to us, saying, 'Take
provisions in your hand for the journey, and go to
meet them and say to them, "[A]We are your servants;
now then, make a covenant with us."' 12 This our
bread *was* warm *when* we took it for our provisions
out of our houses on the day that we left to come
to you; but now behold, it is dry and has become
crumbled. 13 These wineskins which we filled were
new, and behold, they are torn; and these our clothes
and our sandals are worn out because of the very
long journey." 14 So the men *of Israel* took some of
their provisions, and [A]did not ask for the [a]counsel
of the LORD. 15 [A]Joshua made peace with them and
made a covenant with them, to let them live; and the
leaders of the congregation swore *an oath* to them.
16 It came about at the end of three days after they
had made a covenant with them, that they heard
that they were neighbors and that they were living
[a]within their land. 17 Then the sons of Israel set out
and came to their cities on the third day. Now their
cities *were* [A]Gibeon and Chephirah and Beeroth and
Kiriath-jearim. 18 The sons of Israel did not strike them
because the leaders of the congregation had sworn
to them by the LORD the God of Israel. And the whole
congregation grumbled against the leaders. 19 But
all the leaders said to the whole congregation, "We
have sworn to them by the LORD, the God of Israel,
and now we cannot touch them. 20 This we will do

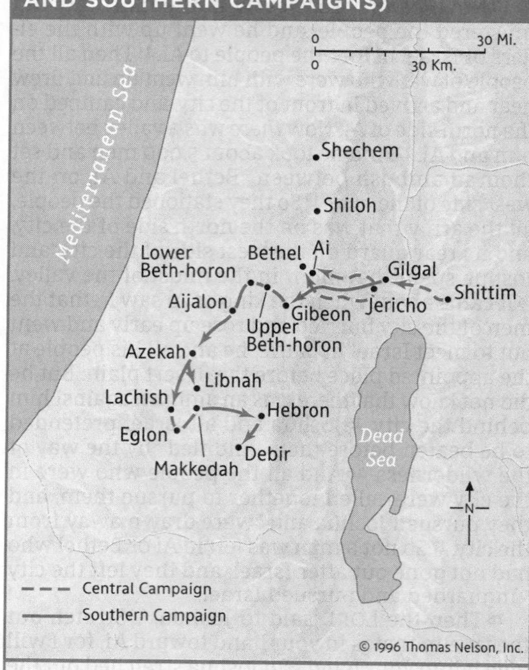

From the camp at Gilgal, Joshua launched two campaigns. The central campaign conquered Jericho, Bethel, and Ai. The southern campaign defeated a coalition of Canaanite kings, pushing as far as Debir.

to them, even let them live, so that wrath will not be
upon us for the oath which we swore to them." 21 The
leaders said to them, "Let them live." So they became
[A]hewers of wood and drawers of water for the whole
congregation, just as the leaders had spoken to them.
22 Then Joshua called for them and spoke to them,
saying, "Why have you deceived us, saying, 'We are
very far from you,' [A]when you are living [a]within our
land? 23 Now therefore, you are [A]cursed, and [a]you
shall never cease being slaves, both hewers of wood
and drawers of water for the house of my God." 24 So
they answered Joshua and said, "[A]Because it was certainly told your servants that the LORD your God had
commanded His servant Moses to give you all the
land, and to destroy all the inhabitants of the land

9:3 [A]Josh 9:17, 22; 10:2; 21:17 9:4 [a]Lit *went and traveled as envoys* [b]Lit *tied up* 9:6 [A]Josh 5:10 9:7 [a]Lit *among us* [A]Josh 9:1; 11:19 [B]Ex 23:32; Deut 7:2 9:8 [A]Deut 20:11; 2 Kin 10:5 9:9 [a]Or *name* [A]Josh 9:16, 17 [B]Josh 2:9; 9:24 9:11 [A]Josh 9:8 9:14 [a]Lit *mouth* [A]Num 27:21 9:15 [A]Ex 23:32 9:16 [a]Lit *among them* 9:17 [A]Josh 18:25 9:21 [A]Deut 29:11 9:22 [a]Lit *among us* [A]Josh 9:16 9:23 [a]Lit *a servant shall not be cut off from you* [A]Gen 9:25 9:24 [A]Josh 9:9

9:3 inhabitants. Gibeon of the Hivites (v. 7), or Horites (cf. Ge 36:2, 20), was NW of Jerusalem and about 7 mi. from the area of Ai. It was a strong city with capable fighting men (10:2). Three other towns were in league with it (9:17).

9:4–15 The Gibeonite plot to trick Israel worked. Israel's sinful failure occurred because they were not vigilant in prayer to assure that they acted by God's counsel (v. 14; cf. Pr 3:5, 6).

9:15 Israel precipitously made peace with the Gibeonites (11:19) who lived nearby, even though God had instructed them to eliminate the people of cities in the Land (Dt 7:1, 2). God permitted peace with cities outside (Dt 20:11–15).

9:21–23 While honoring the pledge of peace with the Gibeonites (v. 19), Joshua made them woodcutters and water carriers because of the deception. This curse extended the perpetual (v. 23) part of "let Canaan be his servant" (Ge 9:26). Gibeon became a part of Benjamin's land area (Jos 18:25). Later, Joshua consigned Gibeon as one of the Levite towns (21:17). Nehemiah had help from some Gibeonites in rebuilding the walls of Jerusalem (Ne 3:7).

before you; therefore we feared greatly for our lives
because of you, and have done this thing. 25 Now behold, [A]we are in your hands; do as it seems good and
right in your sight to do to us." 26 Thus he did to them,
and delivered them from the hands of the sons of
Israel, and they did not kill them. 27 But Joshua made
them that day hewers of wood and drawers of water
for the congregation and for the altar of the LORD,
to this day, [A]in the place which He would choose.

FIVE KINGS ATTACK GIBEON

10 Now it came about when Adoni-zedek king
of Jerusalem heard that Joshua had captured
Ai, and had [a]utterly destroyed it (just [A]as he had
done to Jericho and its king, so he had done to Ai
and its king), and that the inhabitants of Gibeon
had [B]made peace with Israel and were [b]within their
land, 2 that [a]he [A]feared greatly, because Gibeon *was*
a great city, like one of the royal cities, and because
it was greater than Ai, and all its men *were* mighty.
3 Therefore Adoni-zedek king of Jerusalem sent *word*
[A]to Hoham king of Hebron and to Piram king of
Jarmuth and to Japhia king of Lachish and to Debir
king of Eglon, saying, 4 "Come up to me and help
me, and let us [a]attack Gibeon, for it has [A]made peace
with Joshua and with the sons of Israel." 5 So the
five kings of [A]the Amorites, the king of Jerusalem,
the king of Hebron, the king of Jarmuth, the king of
Lachish, *and* the king of Eglon, gathered together
and went up, they with all their armies, and camped
by Gibeon and fought against it.

6 Then the men of Gibeon sent *word* to Joshua to
the camp at Gilgal, saying, "Do not [a]abandon your
servants; come up to us quickly and save us and help
us, for all the kings of the Amorites that live in the
hill country have assembled against us." 7 So Joshua
went up from Gilgal, he and [A]all the people of war
with him and all the valiant warriors. 8 The LORD
said to Joshua, "[A]Do not fear them, for I have given
them into your hands; not [a]one of them shall stand
before you." 9 So Joshua came upon them suddenly
[a]by marching all night from Gilgal. 10 [A]And the LORD
confounded them before Israel, and He [a]slew them
with a great slaughter at Gibeon, and pursued them
by the way of the ascent of Beth-horon and struck
them as far as Azekah and Makkedah. 11 As they fled
from before Israel, *while* they were at the descent
of Beth-horon, [A]the LORD threw large stones from
heaven on them as far as Azekah, and they died;
there were more who died [a]from the hailstones than
those whom the sons of Israel killed with the sword.

12 Then Joshua spoke to the LORD in the day when
the LORD delivered up the Amorites before the sons
of Israel, and he said in the sight of Israel,

"O [A]sun, stand still at Gibeon,
And O moon in the valley of Aijalon."
13 [A]So the sun stood still, and
the moon stopped,
Until the nation avenged
themselves of their enemies.

Is it not written in [B]the book of Jashar? And [C]the
sun stopped in the middle of the sky and did not
hasten to go *down* for about a whole day. 14 There
was no day like that before it or after it, when the
LORD listened to the voice of a man; for [A]the LORD
fought for Israel.

15 Then Joshua and all Israel with him returned
to the camp to Gilgal.

VICTORY AT MAKKEDAH

16 Now these [A]five kings had fled and hidden
themselves in the cave at Makkedah. 17 It was told
Joshua, saying, "The five kings have been found
hidden in the cave at Makkedah." 18 Joshua said,
"Roll large stones against the mouth of the cave, and
assign men by it to guard them, 19 but do not stay
there yourselves; pursue your enemies and [a]attack
them in the rear. Do not allow them to enter their
cities, for the LORD your God has delivered them
into your hand." 20 It came about when Joshua and
the sons of Israel had finished [a]slaying them with a
very great slaughter, [A]until they were destroyed, and
the survivors *who* remained of them [b]had entered
the fortified cities, 21 that all the people returned to
the camp to Joshua at Makkedah in peace. No one
[a]uttered a word against any of the sons of Israel.

22 Then Joshua said, "Open the mouth of the cave
and bring these five kings out to me from the cave."
23 They did so, and [A]brought these five kings out to
him from the cave: the king of Jerusalem, the king

9:25 [A]Gen 16:6 9:27 [A]Deut 12:5 10:1 [a]*Or put under the ban* [b]Lit *among them* [A]Josh 8:21f [B]Josh 9:15 10:2 [a]Lit *they* [A]Ex 15:14-16 10:3 [A]Josh 10:23 10:4 [a]Lit *smite* [A]Josh 9:15 10:5 [A]Num 13:29 10:6 [a]Lit *slacken your hands from* 10:7 [A]Josh 8:1 10:8 [a]Lit *a man* [A]Josh 1:5, 9 10:9 [a]Lit *he went up* 10:10 [a]Lit *struck* [A]Deut 7:23 10:11 [a]Lit *with* [A]Ps 18:12f; Is 28:2 10:12 [A]Hab 3:11 10:13 [A]Hab 3:11 [B]2 Sam 1:18 [C]Is 38:8 10:14 [A]Ex 14:14; Deut 1:30; Josh 10:42 10:16 [A]Josh 10:5 10:19 [a]Lit *smite their tail* 10:20 [a]Lit *striking* [b]Lit *and had* [A]Deut 20:16 10:21 [a]Lit *sharpened his tongue* 10:23 [A]Deut 7:24

10:1–11 Gibeon and 3 other towns (9:17) were attacked by a coalition of 5 cities. Israel came to the rescue, with God giving the victory (v. 10).

10:11 The hailstones were miraculous. Note their: 1) source, God; 2) size, large; 3) slaughter, more by stones than by sword; 4) selectivity, only on the enemy; 5) swath, "as far as Azekah"; 6) situation, during a trek down a slope and while God caused the sun to stand still; and 7) similarity to miraculous stones God will fling down during the future wrath (Rev 16:21).

10:12–14 sun stood still, and the moon stopped. Some say an eclipse hid the sun, keeping its heat from Joshua's worn soldiers and allowing coolness for battle. Others suppose a local (not universal) refraction of the sun's rays such as the local darkness in Egypt (Ex 10:21–23). Another view has it as only language of observation; i.e., it only seemed to Joshua's men that the sun and moon stopped as God helped them do in one literal 24-hour day what would normally take longer. Others view it as lavish poetic description, not literal fact. However, such ideas fail to do justice to 10:12–14, and needlessly question God's power as Creator. This is best accepted as an outright, monumental miracle. Joshua, moved by the Lord's will, commanded the sun to delay (Heb., "be still, silent, leave off"). The earth actually stopped rotating or, more likely, the sun moved in the same way to keep perfect pace with the battlefield. The moon also ceased its orbiting. This permitted Joshua's troops time to finish the battle with complete victory (v. 11).

10:13–15 book of Jashar. *Jashar* means "upright." It may be the same as the book called Wars of the Lord (Nu 21:14). The Book of Jashar is mentioned again in 2Sa 1:18 and a portion is recorded in Jos 10:12–13. The book appears to have been a compilation of Hebrew songs in honor of Israel's leaders and exploits in battle.

of Hebron, the king of Jarmuth, the king of Lachish,
and the king of Eglon. 24 When they brought these
kings out to Joshua, Joshua called for all the men
of Israel, and said to the chiefs of the men of war
who had gone with him, "Come near, [A]put your feet
on the necks of these kings." So they came near and
put their feet on their necks. 25 Joshua then said to
them, "[A]Do not fear or be dismayed! Be strong and
courageous, for thus the LORD will do to all your enemies with whom you fight." 26 So afterward Joshua
struck them and put them to death, and he [A]hanged
them on five trees; and they hung on the trees until evening. 27 It came about at [a]sunset that Joshua
gave a command, and [A]they took them down from
the trees and threw them into the cave where they
had hidden themselves, and put large stones over
the mouth of the cave, to this very day.
28 Now Joshua captured Makkedah on that day,
and struck it and its king with the edge of the sword;
[A]he [a]utterly destroyed [b]it and every [c]person who was
in it. He left no survivor. Thus he did to the king of
Makkedah [B]just as he had done to the king of Jericho.

JOSHUA'S CONQUEST OF SOUTHERN PALESTINE

29 Then Joshua and all Israel with him passed on
from Makkedah to [A]Libnah, and fought against Libnah. 30 The LORD gave it also with its king into the
hands of Israel, and he struck it and every person
who *was* in it with the edge of the sword. He left
no survivor in it. Thus he did to its king just as he
had done to the king of Jericho.
31 And Joshua and all Israel with him passed on
from Libnah to Lachish, and they camped by it and
fought against it. 32 The LORD gave Lachish into the
hands of Israel; and he captured it on the second
day, and struck it and every person who *was* in it
with the edge of the sword, according to all that he
had done to Libnah.
33 Then Horam king of [A]Gezer came up to help
Lachish, and Joshua [a]defeated him and his people
until he had left him no survivor.
34 And Joshua and all Israel with him passed on
from Lachish to Eglon, and they camped by it and
fought against it. 35 They captured it on that day
and struck it with the edge of the sword; and he
[a]utterly destroyed that day every person who *was*
in it, according to all that he had done to Lachish.
36 Then Joshua and all Israel with him went up
from Eglon to [A]Hebron, and they fought against it.
37 They captured it and struck it and its king and all
its cities and all the persons who *were* in it with the
edge of the sword. He left no survivor, according
to all that he had done to Eglon. And he [a]utterly
destroyed it and every person who *was* in it.
38 Then Joshua and all Israel with him returned to
[A]Debir, and they fought against it. 39 He captured it
and its king and all its cities, and they struck them
with the edge of the sword, and [a]utterly destroyed
every person *who was* in it. He left no survivor. Just
as he had done to Hebron, so he did to Debir and
its king, as he had also done to Libnah and its king.
40 Thus Joshua struck all the land, [A]the hill country and the [a]Negev and the lowland and the slopes
and [B]all their kings. He left no survivor, but [C]he [b]ut-
terly destroyed all who breathed, just as the LORD,
the God of Israel, had commanded. 41 Joshua struck
them from Kadesh-barnea even as far as Gaza, and
all the country of [A]Goshen even as far as Gibeon.
42 Joshua captured all these kings and their lands
at one time, because [A]the LORD, the God of Israel,
fought for Israel. 43 So Joshua and all Israel with
him returned to the camp at Gilgal.

NORTHERN PALESTINE TAKEN

11 Then it came about, when Jabin king of [A]Hazor
heard *of it,* that he sent to Jobab king of Madon and to the king of Shimron and to the king of
Achshaph, 2 and to the kings who were of the north
in the hill country, and in the [A]Arabah—south of
[a]Chinneroth and in the lowland and on the [b]heights
of Dor on the west— 3 to the Canaanite on the east
and on the west, and the Amorite and the Hittite
and the Perizzite and the Jebusite in the hill country,
and [A]the Hivite [a]at the foot of [B]Hermon in the land of
[C]Mizpeh. 4 They came out, they and all their armies
with them, [A]*as* many people as the sand that is on
the seashore, with very many horses and chariots.
5 So all of these kings having agreed to meet, came
and encamped together at the waters of Merom, to
fight against Israel.
6 Then the LORD said to Joshua, "[A]Do not be afraid
because of them, for tomorrow at this time I will
deliver all of them slain before Israel; you shall
[B]hamstring their horses and burn their chariots
with fire." 7 So Joshua and all the people of war

10:24 [A]Mal 4:3 10:25 [A]Josh 10:8 10:26 [A]Josh 8:29 10:27 [a]Lit *the time of the going of the sun* [A]Deut 21:22, 23 10:28 [a]Or *put under the ban* [b]Some mss read *them* [c]Lit *soul,* and so throughout the ch [A]Deut 20:16 [B]Josh 6:21 10:29 [A]Josh 15:42; 21:13 10:33 [a]Lit *smote* [A]Josh 16:3, 10; Judg 1:29; 1 Kin 9:16f 10:35 [a]Or *put under the ban* 10:36 [A]Num 13:22; Judg 1:10, 20; 2 Sam 5:1, 3, 5, 13; 2 Chr 11:10 10:37 [a]Or *put it under the ban* 10:38 [A]Josh 15:15; Judg 1:11; 1 Chr 6:58 10:39 [a]Or *put it under the ban* 10:40 [a]I.e. South country [b]Or *put it under the ban* [A]Deut 1:7 [B]Deut 7:24 [C]Deut 20:16 10:41 [A]Josh 11:16; 15:51 10:42 [A]Josh 10:14 11:1 [A]Josh 11:10 11:2 [a]I.e. Sea of Galilee [b]Or *Naphoth-dor* [A]Josh 12:3; 13:27 11:3 [a]Lit *under* [A]Deut 7:1; Judg 3:3, 5; 1 Kin 9:20 [B]Josh 11:17; 13:5, 11 [C]Josh 15:38; 18:26 11:4 [A]Judg 7:12 11:6 [A]Josh 10:8 [B]2 Sam 8:4

10:24 feet on their necks. This gesture 1) symbolized victory and 2) promised assurance of future conquest (v. 25).

10:40–43 A summary of Joshua's southern campaign (cf. 9:1–10:43).

10:42 Tribute belongs to the Lord for all the victories, as "in everything give thanks" (1Th 5:18).

11:1 Hazor. A city 5 mi. SW of Lake Huleh, 10 mi. N of the Sea of Galilee. King Jabin led a coalition of kings from several city-states in Galilee and to the W against Joshua, whose victory reports in the S had spread northward.

11:2 south ... in the lowland. This refers to the deep rift of the Jordan River valley to the S of the Lake of Chinneroth (12:3), later called the Sea of Galilee. Chinneroth was probably a town not far N of the lake. The lowland or foothills are an area somewhat W of the Jordan, toward the Mediterranean Sea. Here also is the plain of Sharon and the heights of Dor, i.e., foothills extending to Mt. Carmel, nearer the Mediterranean coast and Dor, a seaport city.

11:5 Merom. These copious springs a few mi. SW of Lake Huleh, about 13 mi. N from the Lake of Chinneroth, which provided the northern armies a rendezvous point.

11:6 hamstring. They cut the large sinew or ligament at the back of the hock on the rear leg, which crippled the horses, making them useless.

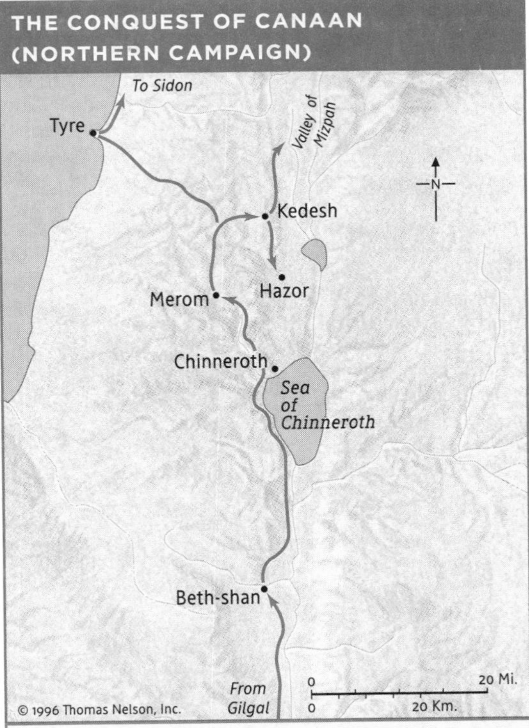

A coalition of kings, including Canaanites, Amorites, Hittites, Perizzites, Jebusites, and Hivites, fought against Joshua at the water of Merom. Joshua's armies pursued some of them toward Tyre and Sidon and others toward Kedesh, while also turning aside to destroy Hazor.

with him came upon them suddenly by the waters
of Merom, and attacked them. 8 The LORD delivered
them into the hand of Israel, so that they [a]defeated
them, and pursued them as far as Great Sidon and
[A]Misrephoth-maim and the valley of [B]Mizpeh to the
east; and they struck them until no survivor was
left to them. 9 Joshua did to them as the LORD had
told him; he [A]hamstrung their horses and burned
their chariots with fire.

10 Then Joshua turned back at that time, and captured [A]Hazor and struck its king with the sword; for
Hazor formerly was the head of all these kingdoms.
11 [A]They struck every person who was in it with the
edge of the sword, [a]utterly destroying *them;* there
was no one left who breathed. And he burned Hazor
with fire. 12 Joshua captured all the cities of these
kings, and all their kings, and he struck them with
the edge of the sword, *and* utterly destroyed them;
just [A]as Moses the servant of the LORD had commanded. 13 However, Israel did not burn any cities
that stood on their mounds, except Hazor alone,
which Joshua burned. 14 [A]All the spoil of these cities and the cattle, the sons of Israel took as their
plunder; but they struck every man with the edge of
the sword, until they had destroyed them. They left
no one who breathed. 15 Just as the LORD had commanded Moses his servant, so Moses commanded
Joshua, and so Joshua did; he left nothing undone
of all that the LORD had commanded Moses.

16 Thus Joshua took all that land: [A]the hill country and all the [a]Negev, all that land of Goshen, the
lowland, [B]the Arabah, the hill country of Israel and
its lowland 17 from [A]Mount Halak, that rises toward
Seir, even as far as Baal-gad in the valley of Lebanon
[a]at the foot of Mount Hermon. And he captured [B]all
their kings and struck them down and put them
to death. 18 Joshua waged war a long time with all
these kings. 19 There was not a city which made
peace with the sons of Israel except [A]the Hivites
living in Gibeon; they took them all in battle. 20 [A]For
it was of the LORD to [a]harden their hearts, to meet
Israel in battle in order that he might [B]utterly destroy them, that they might [b]receive no mercy, but
that he might destroy them, just as the LORD had
commanded Moses.

21 Then Joshua came at that time and cut off [A]the
Anakim from the hill country, from Hebron, from
Debir, from Anab and from all the hill country of
Judah and from all the hill country of Israel. Joshua
utterly destroyed them with their cities. 22 There
were no Anakim left in the land of the sons of Israel; only in Gaza, in [A]Gath, and in [B]Ashdod some
remained. 23 So Joshua took the whole land, according to all that the LORD had spoken to Moses, and
[A]Joshua gave it for an inheritance to Israel according

11:8 [a]Lit *smote* [A]Josh 13:6 [B]Josh 11:3 11:9 [A]Josh 11:6 11:10 [A]Josh 11:1 11:11 [a]Or *putting them under the ban,* and so throughout the ch [A]Deut 20:16 11:12 [A]Num 33:50-52; Deut 7:2; 20:16f 11:14 [A]Num 31:11, 12 11:16 [a]I.e. South country [A]Josh 10:40, 41 [B]Josh 11:2 11:17 [a]Lit *under* [A]Josh 12:7 [B]Deut 7:24 11:19 [A]Josh 9:3, 7 11:20 [a]Lit *make strong* [b]Lit *have* [A]Ex 14:17 [B]Deut 7:16 11:21 [A]Num 13:33; Deut 9:2 11:22 [A]1 Sam 17:4; 1 Kin 2:39; 1 Chr 8:13 11:22 [B]Josh 15:46f; 1 Sam 5:1; Is 20:1 11:23 [A]Deut 1:38

11:8 Great Sidon. A city on the Phoenician coast, N of Hazor. "Great" may refer to surrounding areas along with the city itself. Misrephoth-maim. This location lay W of Hazor and also on the Mediterranean.

11:12–15 A summary of Joshua's northern campaign (11:1–15).

11:16, 17 Joshua took all that land. The sweeping conquest covered much of Canaan. hill country. In the S, in Judah. Negev. South of the Dead Sea. Goshen. Probably the land between Gaza and Gibeon. lowland. Or foothills; refers to an area between the Mediterranean coastal plain and the hills of Judah. Arabah. The rift valley running S of the Dead Sea all the way to the Red Sea's Gulf of Aqabah. The hill country of Israel is distinct from that in 11:16, lying in the northern part of Palestine. The conquest reached from Mt. Halak, about 6 mi. S of the Dead Sea, to Mt. Hermon about 40 mi. NE from the Lake of Chinneroth.

11:18 war a long time. The conquest took approximately 7 years—ca. 1405–1398 B.C. (cf. 14:10). Only Gibeon submitted without a fight (v. 19).

11:20 it was of the LORD to harden their hearts. God turned the Canaanites' hearts to fight in order that Israel might be His judging instrument to destroy them. They were willfully guilty of rejecting the true God with consequent great wickedness, and were as unfit to remain in the Land as vomit spewed out of the mouth (Lv 18:24, 25).

11:21 Anakim. Enemies who dwelt in the southern area which Joshua had defeated. They descended from Anak ("long-necked"), and were related to the giants who made Israel's spies feel small as grasshoppers by comparison (Nu 13:28–33). Compare also Dt 2:10, 11, 21. Their territory was later given to Caleb as a reward for his loyalty (14:6–15).

11:22 Anakim … Gath. Some of them remained in Philistine territory, most notably those who preceded Goliath (cf. 1Sa 17:4).

11:23 the whole land. Here is a key verse for the book which sums up 11:16–22. How does this relate to 13:1, where God tells Joshua

to their divisions by their tribes. [B]Thus the land had
rest from war.

KINGS DEFEATED BY ISRAEL

12 Now these are the [A]kings of the land whom
the sons of Israel [a]defeated, and whose land
they possessed beyond the Jordan toward the sunrise, from the valley of the Arnon as far as Mount
Hermon, and all the Arabah to the east: 2 Sihon
king of the Amorites, who lived in Heshbon, *and*
ruled [A]from Aroer, which is on the edge of the valley of the Arnon, both the middle of the valley and
half of Gilead, even as far as the brook Jabbok, the
border of the sons of Ammon; 3 and the [A]Arabah
as far as the Sea of [a]Chinneroth toward the east,
and as far as the sea of the Arabah, *even* the Salt
Sea, eastward [b]toward [B]Beth-jeshimoth, and on the
south, [c]at the foot of the slopes of Pisgah; 4 and the
territory of Og king of Bashan, one of [A]the remnant
of Rephaim, who lived at [B]Ashtaroth and at Edrei,
5 and ruled over Mount Hermon and [A]Salecah and
all Bashan, as far as [B]the border of the Geshurites
and the Maacathites, and half of Gilead, *as far as*
the border of Sihon king of Heshbon. 6 Moses the
servant of the LORD and the sons of Israel [a]defeated
them; and [A]Moses the servant of the LORD gave it
to the Reubenites and the Gadites and the half-tribe
of Manasseh as a possession.
7 Now these are the kings of the land whom
Joshua and the sons of Israel [a]defeated beyond
the Jordan toward the west, from Baal-gad in the
valley of Lebanon even as far as [A]Mount Halak,
which rises toward Seir; and Joshua gave it to the
tribes of Israel as a possession according to their
divisions, 8 in [A]the hill country, in the lowland, in
the Arabah, on the slopes, and in the wilderness,
and in the [a]Negev; the Hittite, the Amorite and
the Canaanite, the Perizzite, the Hivite and the
Jebusite: 9 the [A]king of Jericho, one; the [B]king of
Ai, which is beside Bethel, one; 10 the [A]king of Jerusalem, one; the king of Hebron, one; 11 the king of
Jarmuth, one; the king of Lachish, one; 12 the king
of Eglon, one; the king of Gezer, one; 13 the king of
Debir, one; the king of Geder, one; 14 the king
of Hormah, one; the king of [A]Arad, one; 15 the king of
Libnah, one; the king of Adullam, one; 16 the king
of Makkedah, one; the king of Bethel, one; 17 the
king of Tappuah, one; the [A]king of Hepher, one;

DIVISION OF LAND AMONG THE TWELVE TRIBES

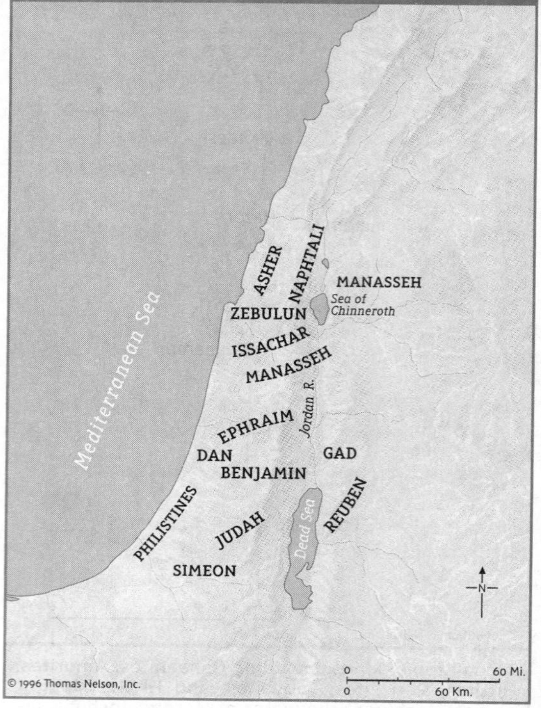

Mediterranean Sea
ASHER
NAPHTALI
MANASSEH
Sea of Chinneroth
ZEBULUN
ISSACHAR
MANASSEH
Jordan R.
EPHRAIM
DAN
GAD
BENJAMIN
PHILISTINES
JUDAH
Dead Sea
REUBEN
SIMEON
N
0 60 Mi.
0 60 Km.

© 1996 Thomas Nelson, Inc.

18 the king of [A]Aphek, one; the king of Lasharon,
one; 19 the king of Madon, one; the king of Hazor,
one; 20 the king of Shimron-meron, one; the king
of Achshaph, one; 21 the king of Taanach, one; the
king of Megiddo, one; 22 the king of [A]Kedesh, one;
the king of Jokneam in Carmel, one; 23 the king of
Dor in the [a]heights of Dor, one; the king of [A]Goiim
in Gilgal, one; 24 the king of Tirzah, one: [A]in all,
thirty-one kings.

CANAAN DIVIDED AMONG THE TRIBES

13 Now [A]Joshua was old *and* advanced in years
when the LORD said to him, "You are old
and advanced in years, and very much of the land
remains to be possessed. 2 This is the land that

11:23 [B]Deut 12:9, 10; 25:19; Heb 4:8 12:1 [a]Lit *smote* [A]Num 32:33; Deut 3:8-17 12:2 [A]Deut 2:36 12:3 [a]I.e. Galilee [b]Lit *the way of* [c]Lit *under* [A]Josh 11:2 [B]Josh 13:20 12:4 [A]Deut 3:11 [B]Deut 1:4 12:5 [A]Deut 3:10; Josh 13:11; 1 Chr 5:11 [B]Deut 3:14; 1 Sam 27:8 12:6 [a]Lit *smote* [A]Num 32:33; Deut 3:12 12:7 [a]Lit *smote* [A]Josh 11:17 12:8 [a]I.e. South country [A]Josh 11:16 12:9 [A]Josh 6:2 [B]Josh 8:29 12:10 [A]Josh 10:23 12:14 [A]Num 21:1 12:17 [A]1 Kin 4:10 12:18 [A]Josh 13:4; 2 Kin 13:17 12:22 [A]Josh 19:37; 20:7; 21:32 12:23 [a]Or *Naphath-dor* [A]Gen 14:1 12:24 [A]Deut 7:24 13:1 [A]Josh 14:10

that he did *not* take the whole land? It may mean that the major battles had been fought and supremacy demonstrated, even if further incidents would occur and not every last pocket of potential resistance had yet been rooted out.

12:1–24 the kings ... defeated. The actual list of 31 kings conquered (v. 24) follows and fills out the summary of "all the land" in 11:16, 17, 23. The roster shows the kings whom "Moses defeated" E of the Jordan earlier (vv. 1–6; cf. Nu 21; Dt 2:24–3:17); then those whom Joshua conquered W of the Jordan—a summary (7, 8); central kings (9); southern kings (10–16); and northern kings (17–24).

12:24 The conquest of all these kings, covering areas up and down the "whole land" (11:23), was due to the Lord's faithful help, which fulfilled His Word. God promised the land in His covenant with Abraham (Ge 12:7), and reaffirmed that He would give success in conquest (Jos 1:3, 6).

13:1 Joshua was old. By this time he was about 95, in comparison to Caleb's 85 years (14:10). In 23:1, he was 110 and near death (24:29).

13:1, 2 much of the land. Some land had not yet actually been occupied by the Israelites through the previous general victories. Pockets or areas in 13:2–6 still lay untouched by specific invasion and occupation (*see note on 11:23*). When Joshua allotted areas to individuals and tribes, they bore the challenge to drive out lingering resisters; if not, they would disobey God's mandate to be resolute in conquest (Dt 11:22, 23). Failure to do this thoroughly is a sad theme in Jdg 1.

remains: all the regions *of* the Philistines and all
those of the [A]Geshurites; 3 from the Shihor which is
[a]east of Egypt, even as far as the border of Ekron
to the north (it is counted as Canaanite); the [A]five
lords of the Philistines: the Gazite, the Ashdodite,
the Ashkelonite, the Gittite, the Ekronite; and the
Avvite 4 [a]to the south, all the land of the Canaanite,
and Mearah that belongs to the Sidonians, as far
as [A]Aphek, to the border of the [B]Amorite; 5 and the
land of the [A]Gebalite, and all of Lebanon, toward
the [a]east, [B]from Baal-gad below Mount Hermon as
far as [b]Lebo-hamath. 6 All the inhabitants of the hill
country from Lebanon as far as [A]Misrephoth-maim,
all the Sidonians, I will [a]drive them out from before
the sons of Israel; [B]only allot it to Israel for an inheritance as I have commanded you. 7 Now therefore,
apportion this land for an inheritance to the nine
tribes and the half-tribe of Manasseh."

8 With [a]the other half-tribe, the Reubenites and the
Gadites received their inheritance which Moses gave
them [A]beyond the Jordan to the east, just as Moses
the servant of the LORD gave to them; 9 from Aroer,
which is on the edge of the valley of the Arnon, with
the city which is in the middle of the valley, and all
the plain of Medeba, as far as Dibon; 10 and all the
cities of Sihon king of the Amorites, who reigned in
Heshbon, as far as the border of the sons of Ammon;
11 and [A]Gilead, and the [a]territory of the Geshurites
and Maacathites, and all Mount Hermon, and all
Bashan as far as Salecah; 12 all the kingdom of [A]Og in
Bashan, who reigned in Ashtaroth and in Edrei (he
alone was left of the remnant of the Rephaim); for
Moses [B]struck them and dispossessed them. 13 But
the sons of Israel did not dispossess the Geshurites
or the Maacathites; for Geshur and Maacath live
among Israel until this day. 14 [A]Only to the tribe of
Levi he did not give an inheritance; the offerings
by fire to the LORD, the God of Israel, are [a]their inheritance, as He spoke to him.

15 So Moses gave *an inheritance* to the tribe of the
sons of Reuben according to their families. 16 Their
[a]territory was [A]from Aroer, which is on the edge of
the valley of the Arnon, with the city which is in the
middle of the valley and all the plain by Medeba;
17 Heshbon, and all its cities which are on the plain:
Dibon and Bamoth-baal and Beth-baal-meon, 18 and
[A]Jahaz and Kedemoth and Mephaath, 19 and [A]Kiria-
thaim and Sibmah and Zereth-shahar on the hill of
the valley, 20 and Beth-peor and the slopes of Pisgah
and Beth-jeshimoth, 21 even all the cities of the plain
and all the kingdom of Sihon king of the Amorites
who reigned in Heshbon, whom Moses struck with
the chiefs of Midian, [A]Evi and Rekem and Zur and
Hur and Reba, the princes of Sihon, who lived in
the land. 22 The sons of Israel also killed [A]Balaam
the son of Beor, the diviner, with the sword among
the rest of their slain. 23 The border of the sons of
Reuben was the [a]Jordan. This was the inheritance
of the sons of Reuben according to their families,
the cities and their villages.

24 Moses also gave *an inheritance* to the tribe of
Gad, to the sons of Gad, according to their families.
25 Their territory was [A]Jazer, and all the cities of
Gilead, and half the land of the sons of Ammon, as
far as Aroer which is before Rabbah; 26 and from
Heshbon as far as Ramath-mizpeh and Betonim,
and from Mahanaim as far as the border of [a]Debir;
27 and in the valley, Beth-haram and Beth-nimrah
and Succoth and Zaphon, the rest of the kingdom
of Sihon king of Heshbon, with the Jordan [a]as a
border, as far as the *lower* end of the Sea of [b,A]Chin-
nereth beyond the Jordan to the east. 28 This is the
inheritance of the sons of Gad according to their
families, the cities and their villages.

29 Moses also gave *an inheritance* to the half-tribe
of Manasseh; and it was for the half-tribe of the sons
of Manasseh according to their families. 30 Their
territory was from Mahanaim, all Bashan, all the
kingdom of Og king of Bashan, and all [A]the [a]towns
of Jair, which are in Bashan, sixty cities; 31 also half
of Gilead, with [A]Ashtaroth and Edrei, the cities of
the kingdom of Og in Bashan, *were* for the sons of
Machir the son of Manasseh, for half of the sons of
Machir according to their families.

32 These are *the territories* which Moses apportioned for an inheritance in the plains of Moab,
beyond the Jordan at Jericho to the east. 33 But [A]to
the tribe of Levi, Moses did not give an inheritance;
the LORD, the God of Israel, is their inheritance, as
He had [a]promised to them.

CALEB'S REQUEST

14 Now these are *the territories* which the sons of
Israel inherited in the land of Canaan, which
[A]Eleazar the priest, and Joshua the son of Nun, and
the heads of the [a]households of the tribes of the sons

13:2 [A]Josh 13:11; 1 Sam 27:8 13:3 [a]Lit *on the face of* [A]1 Sam 6:4, 16 13:4 [a]Or *from the Teman* [A]Josh 12:18; 19:30; 1 Sam 4:1; 1 Kin 20:26, 30 [B]Ezek 16:3; Amos 2:10 13:5 [a]Lit *sunrise* [b]Or *the entrance of Hamath* [A]1 Kin 5:18 [B]Josh 12:7 13:6 [a]Or *dispossess* [A]Josh 11:8 [B]Num 33:54 13:8 [a]Lit *it, the* [A]Josh 12:1-6 13:11 [a]Or *border* [A]Gen 37:25; Num 32:29; Josh 13:25; 17:5f 13:12 [A]Deut 3:11 [B]Num 21:24 13:14 [a]Lit *his* [A]Deut 18:1, 2 13:16 [a]Or *border* [A]Josh 13:9 13:18 [A]Num 21:23; Judg 11:20; Is 15:4; Jer 48:34 13:19 [A]Num 32:37; Jer 48:1, 23; Ezek 25:9 13:21 [A]Num 31:8 13:22 [A]Num 31:8 13:23 [a]Lit *Jordan and border* 13:25 [A]Num 21:32; Josh 21:39; 2 Sam 24:5; 1 Chr 6:81; 26:31; Is 16:8f; Jer 48:32 13:26 [a]Or *Lidebir* 13:27 [a]Lit *and border* [b]I.e. Galilee [A]Num 34:11; Deut 3:17 13:30 [a]Lit *tent villages* [A]Num 32:41 13:31 [A]Josh 9:10; 12:4; 13:12; Judg 10:6; 1 Sam 7:3f; 12:10; 1 Chr 6:71 13:33 [a]Lit *spoken to* [A]Deut 18:1f; Josh 13:14 14:1 [a]Lit *fathers'* [A]Num 34:16-29

13:3 Shihor. Probably related to the Nile (Is 23:3; Jer 2:18), and possibly a name for that river or an eastern tributary of it. The name could also refer to a seasonal rain trough which runs to the Mediterranean, the Wadi-el-Arish in the desert S of Canaan, NE of Egypt.

13:7 apportion this land. God commanded Joshua to devise allotments within boundaries for inheritances as He had prepared for earlier (Nu 32–34). Joshua announced divisions made clear by lot to tribes E of the Jordan (13:8–33), tribes W of the Jordan (Jos 14–19), Caleb (14:6–15; cf. 15:13–19), his own area (19:49–51), cities of refuge (20:1–9), and Levite towns (21).

13:22 Israel also killed Balaam. This Israelite slaying of the infamous false prophet occurred at an unidentified point during the conquest (cf. Nu 21–25; 31:16; Jos 24:9, 10; 2Pe 2:15, 16; Jude 11; Rev 2:14).

13:33 to … Levi … not give an inheritance. God did not give this tribe a normal allotment of land. This suited His choice of Levites for the special ministry of the tabernacle service. Their inheritance consisted in this unique role to share His holy ministrations (18:7). God did assign them cities and adjacent lands (14:4; Nu 35:2, 4, 5), scattered at 48 places (21:41) throughout all the tribes. This made these religious servants accessible to all the people (cf. chap. 21).

14:1 the land of Canaan. The name for the land W of the Jordan.

of Israel apportioned to them for an inheritance, 2 by the [A]lot of their inheritance, as the LORD commanded [a]through Moses, for the nine tribes and the half-tribe. 3 For [A]Moses had given the inheritance of the two tribes and the half-tribe beyond the Jordan; but [B]he did not give an inheritance to the Levites among them. 4 For the sons of Joseph were two tribes, [A]Manasseh and Ephraim, and they did not give a portion to the Levites in the land, except cities to live in, with their pasture lands for their livestock and for their property. 5 Thus the sons of Israel did just [A]as the LORD had commanded Moses, and they divided the land.

6 Then the sons of Judah drew near to Joshua in Gilgal, and [A]Caleb the son of Jephunneh the Kenizzite said to him, "You know the word which the LORD spoke to Moses the man of God concerning [a]you and me in Kadesh-barnea. 7 I was forty years old when [A]Moses the servant of the LORD sent me from Kadesh-barnea to spy out the land, and I brought word back to him as *it was* in my heart. 8 Nevertheless my brethren who went up with me made the heart of the people [a]melt with fear; but [A]I followed the LORD my God fully. 9 So Moses swore on that day, saying, 'Surely [A]the land on which your foot has trodden will be an inheritance to you and to your children forever, because you have followed the LORD my God fully.' 10 Now behold, the LORD has let me live, just as He spoke, these forty-five years, from the time that the LORD spoke this word to Moses, when Israel walked in the wilderness; and now behold, I am eighty-five years old today. 11 [A]I am still as strong today as I was in the day Moses sent me; as my strength was then, so my strength is now, for war and for [B]going out and coming in. 12 Now then, give me this hill country about which the LORD spoke on that day, for you heard on that day that [A]Anakim *were* there, with great fortified cities; perhaps the LORD will be with me, and I will [a]drive them out as the LORD has spoken."

13 So Joshua [A]blessed him and [B]gave Hebron to Caleb the son of Jephunneh for an inheritance. 14 Therefore, Hebron became the inheritance of Caleb the son of Jephunneh the Kenizzite until this day, because he followed the LORD God of Israel fully. 15 Now the name of Hebron was formerly [a]Kiriath-arba; *for Arba* was the greatest man among the Anakim. [A]Then the land had rest from war.

TERRITORY OF JUDAH

15 Now [A]the lot for the tribe of the sons of Judah according to their families [a]reached the [B]border of Edom, southward to the [C]wilderness of Zin at the extreme south. 2 Their south border was from the lower end of the Salt Sea, from the bay that turns to the south. 3 Then it proceeded southward to the ascent of Akrabbim and continued to Zin, then went up by the south of Kadesh-barnea and continued to Hezron, and went up to Addar and turned about to Karka. 4 It [A]continued to Azmon and proceeded to the [a,B]brook of Egypt, and the [b]border ended at the sea. This shall be your south border. 5 The [A]east border *was* the Salt Sea, as far as the [a]mouth of the Jordan. And the [B]border of the north side was from the bay of the sea at the [a]mouth of the Jordan. 6 Then the border went up to Beth-hoglah, and continued on the north of Beth-arabah, and the border went up to the stone of Bohan the son of Reuben. 7 The border went up to Debir from [A]the valley of Achor, and turned northward toward Gilgal which is opposite the ascent of Adummim, which is on the south of the valley; and the border continued to the waters of En-shemesh and [a]it ended at En-rogel. 8 Then the border went up the valley of Ben-hinnom to the slope of the [A]Jebusite on the south (that is, Jerusalem); and the border went up to the top of the mountain which is before the valley of Hinnom to the west, which is at the end of the valley of Rephaim toward the north. 9 From the top of the mountain the border curved to the spring of the waters of Nephtoah and proceeded to the cities of Mount Ephron, then the border curved to [A]Baalah (that is, [B]Kiriath-jearim). 10 The border turned about from Baalah westward to Mount Seir, and continued to the slope of Mount Jearim on the north (that is, Chesalon), and went down to Beth-shemesh and continued through [A]Timnah. 11 The border proceeded to the side of Ekron northward. Then the border curved to Shikkeron and continued to Mount Baalah and proceeded to Jabneel, and the [a]border ended at the sea. 12 The west border *was* [A]at the Great Sea, even *its* [a]coastline. This is the border around the sons of Judah according to their families.

13 Now [A]he gave to Caleb the son of Jephunneh a portion [B]among the sons of Judah, according to the [a]command of the LORD to Joshua, *namely,* [b]Kiriath-arba, *Arba being* the father of Anak (that

14:2 [a]Lit *by the hand of* [A]Num 26:55; 33:54; 34:13 14:3 [A]Num 32:33 [B]Josh 13:14 14:4 [A]Gen 41:51f; 46:20; 48:1, 5; Num 26:28; 2 Chr 30:1 14:5 [A]Num 35:1f; Josh 21:2 14:6 [a]Lit *me and concerning you* [A]Num 13:6, 30; 14:6, 24, 30 14:7 [A]Num 13:1-31 14:8 [a]Lit *become demoralized* [A]Num 14:24; Deut 1:36 14:9 [A]Deut 1:36 14:11 [A]Deut 34:7 [B]Deut 31:2 14:12 [a]Or *dispossess* [A]Num 13:33 14:13 [A]Josh 22:6 [B]Judg 1:20; 1 Chr 6:55f 14:15 [a]I.e. the city of Arba [A]Josh 11:23 15:1 [a]Lit *was to* [A]Num 34:3, 4 [B]Num 20:16 [C]Deut 32:51 15:4 [a]Or *wadi* [b]Lit *goings out of the border were* [A]Num 34:5 [B]Gen 15:18; 1 Kin 8:65 15:5 [a]Lit *end* [A]Num 34:3, 10-12 [B]Josh 18:15-19 15:7 [a]Lit *the goings out of it were* [A]Josh 7:24 15:8 [A]Josh 15:63 15:9 [A]1 Chr 13:6 [B]Judg 18:12 15:10 [A]Gen 38:13; Judg 14:1 15:11 [a]Lit *goings out...were* 15:12 [a]Lit *border* [A]Num 34:6 15:13 [a]Lit *mouth* [b]I.e. the city of Arba [A]Josh 14:13-15 [B]Num 13:6

14:5 Thus the sons of Israel did. They obeyed in some things, but not in all (*see note on 13:1, 2*).

14:6–9 Caleb. This passage reviews what is also recounted in Nu 13, 14. This includes a celebration of God's faithfulness (vv. 7–11), and Caleb's specific inheritance (vv. 12–15). Later, he conquered the area (15:13, 14) and conferred blessing on Othniel and his daughter (15:15–19).

14:10 eighty-five years old. Given 1) that Caleb was 40 at Kadesh-barnea and 2) that the Israelites had wandered in the wilderness 38 years, then the conquering of the Land took 7 years (ca. 1405–1398 B.C.), Caleb was now 85 years old.

14:12–14 Based on His promise (v. 9), God granted Caleb's desire for Hebron because of his faithfulness to believe that God would give the Land to the Israelites as He promised.

14:15 Anakim. See 15:13; *see note on 11:21.*

15:1–12 the lot for ... Judah. The tribe's southern boundary (v. 1) ran from the lower tip of the Salt or Dead Sea in a sweep through the desert over to the Wadi, the brook of Egypt (*see note on 13:3*), and along it to the Mediterranean. The eastern limit (v. 5) ran the length of the Salt Sea itself. On the N, it extended from the N end of the Salt Sea by various lines working to the Mediterranean (vv. 5–11). The Mediterranean coastline served as the western border (v. 12).

is, Hebron). 14 [A]Caleb [a]drove out from there the three
[B]sons of Anak: Sheshai and Ahiman and Talmai, the
children of Anak. 15 Then [A]he went up from there
against the inhabitants of Debir; now the name of
Debir formerly was Kiriath-sepher. 16 And Caleb said,
"The one who [a]attacks Kiriath-sepher and captures
it, [b]I will give him Achsah my daughter as a wife."
17 [A]Othniel the son of Kenaz, the brother of Caleb,
captured it; so he gave him Achsah his daughter as
a wife. 18 [A]It came about that when she came *to him,*
she persuaded him to ask her father for a field. So
she alighted from the donkey, and Caleb said to her,
"What do you want?" 19 Then she said, "Give me a
blessing; since you have given me the land of the
[a]Negev, give me also springs of water." So he gave
her the upper springs and the lower springs.

20 This is the inheritance of the tribe of the sons
of Judah according to their families.

21 Now the cities at the extremity of the tribe of
the sons of Judah toward the border of Edom in
the south were Kabzeel and [A]Eder and Jagur, 22 and
Kinah and Dimonah and Adadah, 23 and Kedesh and
Hazor and Ithnan, 24 Ziph and Telem and Bealoth,
25 and Hazor-hadattah and Kerioth-hezron (that is,
Hazor), 26 Amam and Shema and Moladah, 27 and
Hazar-gaddah and Heshmon and Beth-pelet, 28 and
Hazar-shual and [A]Beersheba and Biziothiah, 29 Baalah and Iim and Ezem, 30 and Eltolad and Chesil
and Hormah, 31 and [A]Ziklag and Madmannah and
Sansannah, 32 and Lebaoth and Shilhim and Ain
and Rimmon; in all, twenty-nine cities with their
villages.

33 In the lowland: [A]Eshtaol and Zorah and Ashnah,
34 and Zanoah and En-gannim, Tappuah and Enam,
35 Jarmuth and [A]Adullam, Socoh and Azekah, 36 and
Shaaraim and Adithaim and Gederah and Gedero-
thaim; fourteen cities with their villages.

37 Zenan and Hadashah and Migdal-gad, 38 and
Dilean and Mizpeh and Joktheel, 39 [A]Lachish and
Bozkath and Eglon, 40 and Cabbon and Lahmas and
Chitlish, 41 and Gederoth, Beth-dagon and Naamah
and Makkedah; sixteen cities with their villages.

42 Libnah and Ether and Ashan, 43 and Iphtah and
Ashnah and Nezib, 44 and Keilah and Achzib and
Mareshah; nine cities with their villages.

45 Ekron, with its towns and its villages; 46 from
Ekron even to the sea, all that were by the [a]side of
Ashdod, with their villages.

47 Ashdod, its towns and its villages; Gaza, its
towns and its villages; as far as [A]the [a]brook of Egypt
and the Great Sea, even *its* [b]coastline.

48 In the hill country: Shamir and Jattir and Socoh, 49 and Dannah and Kiriath-sannah (that is,
Debir), 50 and Anab and Eshtemoh and Anim, 51 and
Goshen and Holon and Giloh; eleven cities with
their villages.

52 Arab and Dumah and Eshan, 53 and Janum and
Beth-tappuah and Aphekah, 54 and Humtah and
Kiriath-arba (that is, Hebron), and Zior; nine cities
with their villages.

55 Maon, Carmel and Ziph and Juttah, 56 and Jezreel and Jokdeam and Zanoah, 57 Kain, Gibeah and
Timnah; ten cities with their villages.

58 Halhul, Beth-zur and Gedor, 59 and Maarath
and Beth-anoth and Eltekon; six cities with their
villages.

60 Kiriath-baal (that is, Kiriath-jearim), and Rabbah; two cities with their villages.

61 In the wilderness: Beth-arabah, Middin and
Secacah, 62 and Nibshan and the City of Salt and
Engedi; six cities with their villages.

63 Now as for the [A]Jebusites, the inhabitants of
Jerusalem, the sons of Judah could not [a]drive them
out; so the Jebusites live with the sons of Judah at
Jerusalem until this day.

TERRITORY OF EPHRAIM

16 Then the lot for the sons of Joseph went from
the Jordan at Jericho to the waters of Jericho
on the east into [A]the wilderness, going up from
Jericho through the hill country to Bethel. 2 It went
from Bethel to Luz, and [A]continued to the border of
the Archites at Ataroth. 3 It went down westward
to the territory of the Japhletites, as far as the territory of lower [A]Beth-horon even to [B]Gezer, and [a]it
ended at the sea.

4 The [A]sons of Joseph, Manasseh and Ephraim,
received their inheritance. 5 Now *this* was the territory of the sons of Ephraim according to their
families: the border of their inheritance eastward
was [A]Ataroth-addar, as far as upper Beth-horon.
6 Then the border went westward at [A]Michmethath
on the north, and the border turned about eastward to Taanath-shiloh and continued *beyond* it
to the east of Janoah. 7 It went down from Janoah
to Ataroth and to [A]Naarah, then reached Jericho

15:14 [a]Or *dispossessed* [A]Josh 11:21, 22 [B]Num 13:33; Deut 9:2 15:15 [A]Josh 10:38 15:16 [a]Lit *smites* [b]Lit *and I* 15:17 [A]Judg 1:13; 3:9 15:18 [A]Judg 1:14 15:19 [a]I.e. South country 15:21 [A]Gen 35:21 15:28 [A]Gen 21:31 15:31 [A]1 Sam 27:6; 30:1 15:33 [A]Judg 13:25; 16:31 15:35 [A]1 Sam 22:1 15:39 [A]Josh 10:3; 2 Kin 14:19 15:46 [a]Lit *hand* 15:47 [a]Or *wadi* [b]Lit *border* [A]Josh 15:4 15:63 [a]Or *dispossess them* [A]Judg 1:21; 2 Sam 5:6; 1 Chr 11:4 16:1 [A]Josh 8:15; 18:12 16:2 [A]Josh 18:13 16:3 [a]Lit *the goings out of it were* [A]Josh 18:13; 1 Kin 9:17 [B]Josh 10:33 16:4 [A]Josh 17:14 16:5 [A]Josh 18:13 16:6 [A]Josh 17:7 16:7 [A]1 Chr 7:28

15:17 Othniel. A conqueror like Caleb, who was his father-in-law, he would later be a judge in Israel (Jdg 3:9–11).

15:18, 19 Caleb's daughter sought blessing and exercised real faith for it—like father, like daughter.

15:20–62 the inheritance of … Judah. Judah's cities are grouped in 4 areas: S (vv. 20–32); lowland or foothills over near the Mediterranean (vv. 33–47); hilly central region (vv. 48–60); Judean wilderness dropping eastward down to the Dead Sea (vv. 61, 62).

15:63 Jebusites. The inhabitants of Jerusalem were descendants from the third son of Canaan (Ge 10:15, 16; 15:21). Joshua killed their king who had joined a pact against Gibeon (Jos 10). Israelites called the area "Jebus" until David ordered Joab and his soldiers to capture the city (2Sa 5:6, 7) and made it his capital. Judges 1:8, 21 show that the Israelites conquered Jebus and burned it, but the Jebusites later regained control until David's day. Melchizedek had been a very early king (Ge 14), a believer in the true God, when the site was "Salem" (cf. Ps 76:2, "Salem" is "Jerusalem").

16:1–4 sons of Joseph. Joseph's territory was double as it was given to his sons Manasseh and Ephraim, who had inheritances stretching over a good portion of the central area in the Promised Land.

16:5–9 territory of … Ephraim. The description is of the land N of Judah's territory, from the Jordan W to the Mediterranean Sea. There was the inclusion of some cities in the territory of Manasseh, since Ephraim's land was small compared to its population.

and came out at the Jordan. 8 From [A]Tappuah the border continued westward to the [a]brook of Kanah, and [b]it ended at the sea. This is the inheritance of the tribe of the sons of Ephraim according to their families, 9 *together* with the cities which were set apart for the sons of Ephraim in the midst of the inheritance of the sons of Manasseh, all the cities with their villages. 10 [A]But they did not [a]drive out the Canaanites who lived in Gezer, so [B]the Canaanites live in the midst of Ephraim to this day, and they became forced laborers.

TERRITORY OF MANASSEH

17 Now *this* was the lot for the tribe of [A]Manasseh, for he was the firstborn of Joseph. To Machir the firstborn of Manasseh, the father of Gilead, [a]were allotted Gilead and Bashan, because he was a man of war. 2 So *the lot* was *made* for the rest of the sons of Manasseh according to their families: for the sons of Abiezer and for the sons of Helek and for the sons of Asriel and for the sons of Shechem and for the sons of Hepher and for the sons of Shemida; these *were* the male [a]descendants of Manasseh the son of Joseph according to their families.

3 However, [A]Zelophehad, the son of Hepher, the son of Gilead, the son of Machir, the son of Manasseh, had no sons, only daughters; and these are the names of his daughters: Mahlah and Noah, Hoglah, Milcah and Tirzah. 4 They came near before Eleazar the priest and before Joshua the son of Nun and before the leaders, saying, "The LORD commanded Moses to give us an inheritance among our brothers." So [A]according to the [a]command of the LORD he gave them an inheritance among their father's brothers. 5 Thus there fell ten portions to Manasseh, besides the land of Gilead and Bashan, which is beyond the Jordan, 6 because the daughters of Manasseh received an inheritance among his sons. And the [A]land of Gilead belonged to the rest of the sons of Manasseh.

7 The border of Manasseh [a]ran from Asher to Michmethath which was east of Shechem; then the border went [b]southward to the inhabitants of En-tappuah. 8 The land of Tappuah belonged to Manasseh, but [A]Tappuah on the border of Manasseh *belonged* to the sons of Ephraim. 9 The [A]border went down to the [a]brook of Kanah, southward of the [a]brook (these cities *belonged* to Ephraim among the cities of Manasseh), and the border of Manasseh *was* on the north side of the [a]brook and [b]it ended at the sea. 10 The south side *belonged* to Ephraim and the north side to Manasseh, and the sea was [a]their border; and they reached to Asher on the north and to Issachar on the east. 11 In Issachar and in Asher, [A]Manasseh had Beth-shean and its towns and Ibleam and its towns, and the inhabitants of Dor and its towns, and the inhabitants of En-dor and its towns, and the inhabitants of Taanach and its towns, and the inhabitants of Megiddo and its towns, the third is [B]Napheth. 12 [A]But the sons of Manasseh could not take possession of these cities, because the Canaanites persisted in living in that land. 13 It came about when the sons of Israel became strong, [A]they put the Canaanites to forced labor, but they did not [a]drive them out completely.

14 Then the [A]sons of Joseph spoke to Joshua, saying, "Why have you given me only one lot and one portion for an inheritance, since I am a numerous people whom the LORD has thus far blessed?" 15 Joshua said to them, "If you are a numerous people, go [a]up to the forest and [b]clear a place for yourself there in the land of the Perizzites and of the Rephaim, since the hill country of Ephraim is too narrow for you." 16 The sons of Joseph said, "The hill country is not enough for us, and all the Canaanites who live in the valley land have [A]chariots of iron, both those who are in Beth-shean and its towns and those who are in the valley of Jezreel." 17 Joshua spoke to the house of Joseph, to Ephraim and Manasseh, saying, "You are a numerous people and have great power; you shall not have one lot *only*, 18 but the hill country shall be yours. For though it is a forest, you shall [a]clear it, and to its [b]farthest borders it shall be yours; for you shall [c]drive out the Canaanites, even though they have [A]chariots of iron *and* though they are strong."

REST OF THE LAND DIVIDED

18 Then the whole congregation of the sons of Israel assembled themselves at [A]Shiloh, and set up the tent of meeting there; and the land was subdued before them.

2 There remained among the sons of Israel seven tribes who had not divided their inheritance. 3 So Joshua said to the sons of Israel, "[A]How long will you put off entering to take possession of the land which the LORD, the God of your fathers, has given

16:8 [a]Or *wadi* [b]Lit *the goings out of it were* [A]Josh 17:8 16:10 [a]Or *dispossess* [A]Judg 1:29; 1 Kin 9:16 [B]Josh 17:12, 13 17:1 [a]Lit *and there was to him* [A]Gen 41:51; 46:20; 48:17f 17:2 [a]Lit *sons* 17:3 [A]Num 26:33; 27:1-7 17:4 [a]Lit *mouth* [A]Num 27:5-7 17:6 [A]Josh 13:30, 31 17:7 [a]Lit *was* [b]Lit *to the right hand* 17:8 [A]Josh 16:8 17:9 [a]Or *wadi* [b]Lit *goings out of it were* [A]Josh 16:8f 17:10 [a]Lit *its* 17:11 [A]1 Chr 7:29 [B]Josh 11:2; 12:23 17:12 [A]Judg 1:27 17:13 [a]Or *dispossess* [A]Josh 16:10 17:14 [A]Num 13:7 17:15 [a]Lit *up for yourself* [b]Lit *cut down* 17:16 [A]Josh 17:18; Judg 1:19; 4:3, 13 17:18 [a]Lit *cut it down* [b]Lit *goings out* [c]Or *dispossess* [A]Josh 17:16 18:1 [A]Judg 21:19; Jer 7:12; 26:6, 9 18:3 [A]Judg 18:9

16:10 Ephraim did not drive the Canaanites from their area. This is the first mention of the fatal policy of neglecting to exterminate the idolaters (cf. Dt 20:16).

17:1–18 Manasseh. The other half-tribe of Manasseh, distinct from the half in 16:4, received its portion of the split inheritance W of the Jordan to the N and E near the Lake of Chinneroth (Galilee).

17:3–6 Zelophehad. In Manasseh's tribe, this man had no sons as heirs, but his 5 daughters received the inheritance. God led Moses to give this right to women (Nu 27:1–11, cited in v. 4).

17:12–18 sons of Manasseh. Tribesmen of Manasseh complained that Joshua did not allot them land sufficient to their numbers and that the Canaanites were too tough for them to drive out altogether. He permitted them extra land in forested hills that they could clear. Joshua told them that they could drive out the Canaanites for God had promised to be with them in victory against chariots (Dt 20:1).

18:1 Shiloh. Israel as a whole, having had their camp first at Gilgal (4:20; 5:9), converged to Shiloh for worship at the tabernacle. Shiloh, about 9 mi. N of Bethel and 20 mi. N of Jerusalem, remained the center of spiritual attention, as in Jdg 18:31 and 1Sa 1:3. Due to Israel's sin, God would later let the Philistines devastate Israel at Shiloh and capture the ark (1Sa 4:10, 17), and He would later use Shiloh as an example of judgment (Jer 7:12).

you? 4 Provide for yourselves three men from [a]each
tribe that I may send them, and that they may arise
and walk through the land and write a description
of it according to their inheritance; then they shall
[b]return to me. 5 They shall divide it into seven portions; [A]Judah shall stay in its territory on the south,
and the house of Joseph shall stay in their territory
on the north. 6 You shall describe the land in seven
divisions, and bring *the description* here to me. [A]I will
cast lots for you here before the LORD our God. 7 For
[A]the Levites have no portion among you, because the
priesthood of the LORD is [a]their inheritance. Gad and
Reuben and the half-tribe of Manasseh also have received their inheritance eastward beyond the Jordan,
which Moses the servant of the LORD gave them."
8 Then the men arose and went, and Joshua commanded those who went to describe the land, saying, "Go and walk through the land and describe it,
and return to me; then I will cast lots for you here
before the LORD in [A]Shiloh." 9 So the men went and
passed through the land, and described it by cities in
seven divisions in a book; and they came to Joshua
to the camp at Shiloh. 10 And [A]Joshua cast lots for
them in Shiloh before the LORD, and there Joshua
divided the land to the sons of Israel according to
their divisions.

THE TERRITORY OF BENJAMIN

11 Now the lot of the tribe of the sons of Benjamin
came up according to their families, and the territory
of their lot [a]lay between the sons of Judah and the
sons of Joseph. 12 [A]Their border on the north side was
from the Jordan, then the border went up to the side
of Jericho on the north, and went up through the hill
country westward, and [a]it ended at the wilderness
of Beth-aven. 13 From there the border continued to
[A]Luz, to the side of Luz (that is, Bethel) southward;
and the border went down to Ataroth-addar, near
the hill which *lies* on the south of [B]lower Beth-horon.
14 The border extended *from there* and turned round
on the west side southward, from the hill which
lies before Beth-horon southward; and [a]it ended at
Kiriath-baal (that is, Kiriath-jearim), a city of the sons
of Judah. This *was* the west side. 15 Then the [A]south
side *was* from the edge of Kiriath-jearim, and the
border went westward and went to the fountain of
the waters of Nephtoah. 16 The border went down to
the edge of the hill which is in the [A]valley of Ben-hinnom, which is in the valley of Rephaim northward;
and it went down to the valley of Hinnom, to the
slope of the Jebusite southward, and went down
to En-rogel. 17 It extended northward and went to
En-shemesh and went to Geliloth, which is opposite
the ascent of Adummim, and it went down to the
[A]stone of Bohan the son of Reuben. 18 It continued
to the side in front of the Arabah northward and
went down to the Arabah. 19 The border continued
to the side of Beth-hoglah northward; and the [a]bor-
der ended at the north bay of the Salt Sea, at the
south end of the Jordan. This *was* the south border.
20 Moreover, the Jordan was its border on the east
side. This *was* the inheritance of the sons of Benjamin, according to their families *and* according to
its borders all around.
21 Now the cities of the tribe of the sons of Benjamin according to their families were Jericho and
Beth-hoglah and Emek-keziz, 22 and Beth-arabah
and Zemaraim and Bethel, 23 and Avvim and Parah
and Ophrah, 24 and Chephar-ammoni and Ophni and
[A]Geba; twelve cities with their villages. 25 Gibeon
and Ramah and Beeroth, 26 and Mizpeh and Chephirah and Mozah, 27 and Rekem and Irpeel and
Taralah, 28 and [A]Zelah, Haeleph and the Jebusite
(that is, Jerusalem), Gibeah, Kiriath; fourteen cities with their villages. This is the inheritance of
the [B]sons of Benjamin according to their families.

TERRITORY OF SIMEON

19 Then the second lot [a]fell to Simeon, to the
tribe of the sons of Simeon according to their
families, and their inheritance was in the midst of
the inheritance of the sons of Judah. 2 So they had as
their inheritance Beersheba or [a]Sheba and Moladah,
3 and Hazar-shual and Balah and Ezem, 4 and Eltolad
and Bethul and Hormah, 5 and Ziklag and Beth-marcaboth and Hazar-susah, 6 and Beth-lebaoth and
Sharuhen; thirteen cities with their villages; 7 Ain,
Rimmon and Ether and Ashan; four cities with their
villages; 8 and all the villages which *were* around
these cities as far as Baalath-beer, Ramah of the
[a]Negev. This *was* the inheritance of the tribe of the
sons of Simeon according to their families. 9 The
inheritance of the sons of Simeon *was taken* from
the portion of the sons of Judah, for the share of the
sons of Judah was too large for them; so the sons
of Simeon received *an* inheritance in the midst of
[a]Judah's inheritance.

TERRITORY OF ZEBULUN

10 Now the third lot came up for the sons of Zebulun according to their families. And the territory
of their inheritance was as far as Sarid. 11 Then their
border went up to the west and to Maralah, it then
[a]touched Dabbesheth and reached to the [b]brook that
is before Jokneam. 12 Then it turned from Sarid to
the east toward the sunrise as far as the border of
Chisloth-tabor, and it proceeded to Daberath and
[a]up to Japhia. 13 From there it continued eastward

18:4 [a]Lit *the* [b]Lit *come* 18:5 [A]Josh 15:1 18:6 [A]Josh 14:2 18:7 [a]Lit *his* [A]Num 18:7, 20; Josh 13:33 18:8 [A]Josh 18:1 18:10 [A]Num 34:16-29; Josh 19:51 18:11 [a]Lit *went out* 18:12 [a]Lit *the goings out of it were* [A]Josh 16:1 18:13 [A]Gen 28:19; Judg 1:23 [B]Josh 16:3 18:14 [a]Lit *the goings out of it were* 18:15 [A]Josh 15:5-9 18:16 [A]2 Kin 23:10 18:17 [A]Josh 15:6 18:19 [a]Lit *goings out of the border were* 18:24 [A]Ezra 2:26; Is 10:29 18:28 [A]2 Sam 21:14 [B]Num 26:38 19:1 [a]Lit *came out* 19:2 [a]In Josh 15:26, *Shema* 19:8 [a]I.e. South country 19:9 [a]Lit *their* 19:11 [a]Or *reached to* [b]Or *wadi* 19:12 [a]Lit *went up*

18:8, 10 Seven tribes were yet to receive land (v. 2). Joshua obtained from their 21 surveyor scouts (vv. 2–4) descriptions of the 7 areas of land, then cast lots to decide the choices. The High Priest Eleazar served him, seeking God's will by casting lots (19:51). This was not some act of mere chance, but a means God used to reveal His will (*see note on Pr 16:33*).

18:11–28 **the lot of … Benjamin**. This inheritance lay between Judah's and Ephraim's, and embraced Jerusalem (v. 28).

19:1–9 **Simeon**. This area was a southern portion of Judah's territory, since that allotment was more than Judah needed (v. 9).

19:10–16 **Zebulun**. This allotment lay W of the Lake of Chinneroth (Sea of Galilee) and ran to the Mediterranean Sea.

toward the sunrise to Gath-hepher, to Eth-kazin,
and it proceeded to Rimmon [a]which stretches to
Neah. 14 The border circled around it on the north
to Hannathon, and [a]it ended at the valley of Iphtahel. 15 *Included* also *were* Kattah and Nahalal and
Shimron and Idalah and Bethlehem; twelve cities
with their villages. 16 This *was* the inheritance of the
sons of Zebulun according to their families, these
cities with their villages.

TERRITORY OF ISSACHAR

17 The fourth lot [a]fell to Issachar, to the sons of Issachar according to their families. 18 Their territory
was to Jezreel and *included* Chesulloth and [A]Shunem,
19 and Hapharaim and Shion and Anaharath, 20 and
Rabbith and Kishion and Ebez, 21 and Remeth and
En-gannim and En-haddah and Beth-pazzez. 22 The
border reached to [A]Tabor and Shahazumah and
Beth-shemesh, and [a]their border ended at the Jordan;
sixteen cities with their villages. 23 This *was* the inheritance of the tribe of the sons of Issachar according to their families, the cities with their villages.

TERRITORY OF ASHER

24 Now the fifth lot [a]fell to the tribe of the sons of
Asher according to their families. 25 Their territory
was Helkath and Hali and Beten and Achshaph,
26 and Allammelech and Amad and Mishal; and it
reached to Carmel on the west and to Shihor-lib-
nath. 27 It turned toward the [a]east to Beth-dagon and
reached to Zebulun, and to the valley of Iphtahel
northward to Beth-emek and Neiel; then it proceeded on [b]north to [A]Cabul, 28 and Ebron and Rehob
and Hammon and Kanah, as far as Great [A]Sidon.
29 The border turned to Ramah and to the fortified
city of Tyre; then the border turned to Hosah, and
[a]it ended at the sea by the region of [A]Achzib. 30 *Included* also *were* Ummah, and Aphek and Rehob;
twenty-two cities with their villages. 31 This *was* the
inheritance of the tribe of the sons of Asher according to their families, these cities with their villages.

TERRITORY OF NAPHTALI

32 The sixth lot [a]fell to the sons of Naphtali; to
the sons of Naphtali according to their families.
33 Their border was from Heleph, from the oak in
Zaanannim and Adami-nekeb and Jabneel, as far
as Lakkum, and [a]it ended at the Jordan. 34 Then the
border turned westward to Aznoth-tabor and proceeded from there to Hukkok; and it reached to
Zebulun on the south and [a]touched Asher on the
west, and to Judah at the Jordan toward the [b]east.
35 The fortified cities *were* Ziddim, Zer and [A]Ham-
math, Rakkath and [B]Chinnereth, 36 and Adamah
and Ramah and Hazor, 37 and Kedesh and Edrei
and En-hazor, 38 and Yiron and Migdal-el, Horem
and Beth-anath and Beth-shemesh; nineteen cities
with their villages. 39 This *was* the inheritance of
the tribe of the sons of Naphtali according to their
families, the cities with their villages.

TERRITORY OF DAN

40 The seventh lot [a]fell to the tribe of the sons of
Dan according to their families. 41 The territory of their
inheritance was Zorah and Eshtaol and Ir-shemesh,
42 and Shaalabbin and Aijalon and Ithlah, 43 and Elon
and Timnah and Ekron, 44 and Eltekeh and Gibbethon and Baalath, 45 and Jehud and Bene-berak and
Gath-rimmon, 46 and Me-jarkon and Rakkon, with the
territory over against [a]Joppa. 47 The territory of the
[A]sons of Dan proceeded [a]beyond them; for the sons of
Dan went up and fought with Leshem and captured
it. Then they struck it with the edge of the sword and
possessed it and [b]settled in it; and they called [c,B]Leshem
Dan after the name of Dan their father. 48 This *was* the
inheritance of the tribe of the sons of Dan according
to their families, these cities with their villages.
49 When they finished apportioning the land for
inheritance by its borders, the sons of Israel gave
an inheritance in their midst to Joshua the son of
Nun. 50 In accordance with the [a]command of the
LORD they gave him the city for which he asked,
[A]Timnath-serah in the hill country of Ephraim. So
he built the city and [b]settled in it.
51 [A]These are the inheritances which Eleazar the
priest, and Joshua the son of Nun, and the heads of
the [a]households of the tribes of the sons of Israel
distributed by lot in Shiloh before the LORD at the
doorway of the tent of meeting. So they finished
dividing the land.

19:13 [a]Or *and is marked off* 19:14 [a]Lit *the goings out of it were* 19:17 [a]Lit *came out* 19:18 [A]1 Sam 28:4; 2 Kin 4:8 19:22 [a]Lit *the goings out of their border were* [A]Judg 4:6; Ps 89:12 19:24 [a]Lit *came out* 19:27 [a]Lit *sunrise* [b]Lit *from the left hand* [A]1 Kin 9:13 19:28 [A]Gen 10:19; Judg 1:31; Acts 27:3 19:29 [a]Lit *the goings out of it were* [A]Judg 1:31 19:32 [a]Lit *came out* 19:33 [a]Lit *the goings out of it were* 19:34 [a]Or *reached to* [b]Lit *sunrise* 19:35 [A]Gen 10:18; 1 Kin 8:65 [B]Deut 3:17 19:40 [a]Lit *came out* 19:46 [a]Heb *Japho* 19:47 [a]Lit *from* [b]Lit *dwelt* [c]I.e. Laish [A]Judg 18:1 [B]Judg 18:29 19:50 [a]Lit *mouth* [b]Lit *dwelt* [A]Num 13:8; Josh 24:30 19:51 [a]Lit *fathers* [A]Josh 18:10

19:17–23 Issachar. The area basically ran just below the Sea of Galilee from the Jordan W over to Mt. Tabor, circling SW almost to Megiddo, N of Manasseh's portion.

19:24–31 Asher. This territory was a long, broad strip flanking the Mediterranean on the W, then Naphtali's and Zebulun's claims on the E, running S to Manasseh's. It reached from Mt. Carmel in the S to the area of Tyre in the N.

19:32–39 Naphtali. This region took in a long stretch of land with a border at the northern edge of all the Israelite inheritances, a line on the W dividing it from Asher, southward to follow Zebulun's northern border. Then it struck eastward toward the Sea of Galilee with land to the W alongside that sea and down to Issachar's claim, over to the Jordan River. The eastern line ran northward, including the city of Hazor and also Dan, then swung N of Dan. Jesus' Galilean ministry would take place largely in this area (Is 9:1, 2; Mt 4:13–17).

19:33 oak. This may have been an oak forest (if taken in a collective sense, as the word possibly means in Ge 12:6) near Kedesh and NW of the waters at Merom. According to Jdg 4:11, it was the site where Jael killed Sisera with a hammer and tent peg (4:21).

19:40–48 Dan. The tribal allotment was a narrow, roughly U-shaped strip just N of Judah's claim and S of Ephraim's. The Mediterranean coast lay on the western arm of the "U." Joppa was on the coast near the N end. Later the Danites, failing to possess their original claim (Jdg 1:34–36), migrated northeastward to a territory by Laish or Leshem (Jos 19:47). They conquered this area N of the Sea of Galilee and Hazor, and renamed it Dan (Jos 19:47, 48; Jdg 18:27–29).

19:49, 50 Joshua received his own inheritance from the children of Israel, an area he preferred in the hills of his tribe, Ephraim (Nu 13:8). He built a city, Timnath-serah, about 16 mi. SW of Shechem. His inheritance was an intrinsic part of God's promise to him, as was also Caleb's inheritance (Nu 14:30).

SIX CITIES OF REFUGE

20 Then the LORD spoke to Joshua, saying,
2 "Speak to the sons of Israel, saying, '[a]Des-
ignate [A]the cities of refuge, of which I spoke to you
[b]through Moses, 3 that the manslayer who [a]kills any
person unintentionally, without premeditation,
may flee there, and they shall become your refuge
from the avenger of blood. 4 He shall flee to one of
these cities, and shall stand at the entrance of the
[A]gate of the city and state his case in the hearing
of the elders of that city; and they shall [a]take him
into the city to them and give him a place, so that
he may dwell among them. 5 Now [A]if the avenger
of blood pursues him, then they shall not deliver
the manslayer into his hand, because he struck
his neighbor without premeditation and did not
hate him beforehand. 6 He shall dwell in that city
[A]until he stands before the congregation for judgment, until the death of the one who is high priest
in those days. Then the manslayer shall [a]return to
his own city and to his own house, to the city from
which he fled.' "
7 So they [a]set apart [A]Kedesh in [b]Galilee in the hill
country of Naphtali and Shechem in the hill country
of Ephraim, and Kiriath-arba (that is, Hebron) in
[B]the hill country of Judah. 8 Beyond the Jordan east
of Jericho, they [a]designated Bezer in the wilderness
on the plain from the tribe of Reuben, and Ramoth
in Gilead from the tribe of Gad, and Golan in Bashan
from the tribe of Manasseh. 9 [A]These were the appointed cities for all the sons of Israel and for the
stranger who sojourns among them, that whoever
[a]kills any person unintentionally may flee there, and
not die by the hand of the avenger of blood until
he stands before the congregation.

FORTY-EIGHT CITIES OF THE LEVITES

21 Then the heads of [a]households of [A]the Levites
approached Eleazar the priest, and Joshua the
son of Nun, and the heads of [a]households of the
tribes of the sons of Israel. 2 They spoke to them at
Shiloh in the land of Canaan, saying, "[A]The LORD
commanded [a]through Moses to give us cities to live
in, with their pasture lands for our cattle." 3 So the
sons of Israel gave the Levites from their inheritance these cities with their pasture lands, according
to the [a]command of the LORD. 4 Then the lot came

CITIES OF REFUGE

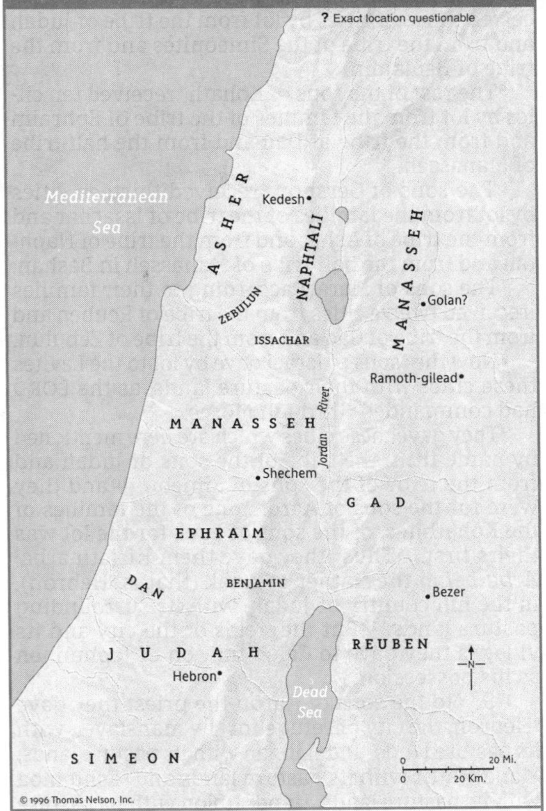

In biblical times tribal bonds were very strong. In the event a person from one tribe killed a member of another tribe, even if by accident, blood vengeance was to be taken by killing a member of the offender's tribe.

The cities of refuge were established at several strategic locations to provide a place of sanctuary for those who had killed someone unintentionally, regardless of tribal affiliation. There they could remain in safety until they had either been judged innocent by the congregation or until the death of the current high priest. At that time, they could return freely to their original home region without fear of reprisal.

20:2 [a]Lit *Set for yourselves* [b]Lit *by the hand of* [A]Num 35:6-34; Deut 4:41-43; 19:2ff 20:3 [a]Lit *smites* 20:4 [a]Lit *gather* [A]Ruth 4:1; Job 5:4; Jer 38:7 20:5 [A]Num 35:12 20:6 [a]Lit *return and come* [A]Num 35:12 20:7 [a]Lit *sanctified* [b]Heb *Galil* [A]Josh 21:32; 1 Chr 6:76 [B]Josh 21:11; Luke 1:39 20:8 [a]Lit *set* 20:9 [a]Lit *smites* [A]Num 35:13ff 21:1 [a]Lit *fathers* [A]Num 35:1-8 21:2 [a]Lit *by the hand of* [A]Num 35:2 21:3 [a]Lit *mouth*

20:2–9 cities of refuge. Moses had spoken God's Word to name 6 cities in Israel as refuge centers. A person who inadvertently killed another could flee to the nearest of these for protection (cf. Nu 35:9–34). Three lay W of the Jordan, and 3 lay to the E, each reachable in a day for those in its area. The slayer could flee there to escape pursuit by a family member seeking to exact private justice. Authorities at the refuge protected him and escorted him to a trial. If found innocent, he was guarded at the refuge until the death of the current High Priest, a kind of statute of limitations (Jos 20:6). He could then return home. If found guilty of murder, he suffered due punishment.

21:1–3 cities to live in. God had given Moses His direction to provide 48 cities for the Levites, dotted throughout Israel's tribal allotments (Nu 35:1–8). Six were to be the cities of refuge (Nu 35:6).

21:3–42 the sons of Israel gave the Levites. These 48 cities (v. 41) are for various branches of the Levite people to live in and have pasture for their livestock (v. 42). People of the other tribes donated the areas, each site giving the Levites a vantage point from which to minister spiritually to the people nearby. In fairness, larger tribes devoted more land, smaller ones less (Nu 35:8). Only the Kohathites were priests, with other branches of Levites assisting in various roles of ritual worship and manual labors.

21:4 Kohathites. Under God's guiding wisdom, these received 13 city areas in the vicinity of Jerusalem or at a reasonable distance within allotments of Judah, Benjamin, and Simeon. This would give them access to carry out priestly functions where God would later have the ark moved and the temple situated (2Sa 6).

out for the families of the Kohathites. And the sons
of Aaron the priest, who were of the Levites, [a]re-
ceived thirteen cities by lot from the tribe of Judah
and from the tribe of the Simeonites and from the
tribe of Benjamin.
5 The rest of the sons of Kohath [a]received ten cities by lot from the families of the tribe of Ephraim
and from the tribe of Dan and from the half-tribe
of Manasseh.
6 The sons of Gershon [a]received thirteen cities
by lot from the families of the tribe of Issachar and
from the tribe of Asher and from the tribe of Naphtali and from the half-tribe of Manasseh in Bashan.
7 The sons of Merari according to their families
[a]received twelve cities from the tribe of Reuben and
from the tribe of Gad and from the tribe of Zebulun.
8 Now the [A]sons of Israel gave by lot to the Levites
these cities with their pasture lands, as the LORD
had commanded [a]through Moses.
9 They gave these cities which are *here* mentioned
by name from the tribe of the sons of Judah and
from the tribe of the sons of Simeon; 10 and they
were for the sons of Aaron, one of the families of
the Kohathites, of the sons of Levi, for the lot was
theirs first. 11 Thus [A]they gave them Kiriath-arba,
Arba being the [B]father of Anak (that is, Hebron),
in the hill country of Judah, with its surrounding
pasture lands. 12 But the fields of the city and its
villages they gave to Caleb the son of Jephunneh
as his possession.
13 So [A]to the sons of Aaron the priest they gave
[B]Hebron, the city of refuge for the manslayer, with
its pasture lands, and [C]Libnah with its pasture lands,
14 and [A]Jattir with its pasture lands and [B]Eshtemoa
with its pasture lands, 15 and [a]Holon with its pasture
lands and [A]Debir with its pasture lands, 16 and [a]Ain
with its pasture lands and [A]Juttah with its pasture
lands *and* [B]Beth-shemesh with its pasture lands;
nine cities from these two tribes. 17 From the tribe
of Benjamin, [A]Gibeon with its pasture lands, [B]Geba
with its pasture lands, 18 Anathoth with its pasture
lands and [a]Almon with its pasture lands; four cities.
19 All the cities of the sons of Aaron, the priests, were
thirteen cities with their pasture lands.
20 Then the cities from the tribe of Ephraim were
allotted to the [A]families of the sons of Kohath, the
Levites, *even to* the rest of the sons of Kohath. 21 They
gave them [A]Shechem, the city of refuge for the manslayer, with its pasture lands, in the hill country of
Ephraim, and Gezer with its pasture lands, 22 and
Kibzaim with its pasture lands and Beth-horon with
its pasture lands; four cities. 23 From the tribe of
Dan, Elteke with its pasture lands, Gibbethon with
its pasture lands, 24 Aijalon with its pasture lands,
Gath-rimmon with its pasture lands; four cities.
25 From the half-tribe of Manasseh, *they allotted*
Taanach with its pasture lands and Gath-rimmon
with its pasture lands; two cities. 26 All the cities
with their pasture lands for the families of the rest
of the sons of Kohath were ten.
27 [A]To the sons of Gershon, one of the families of
the Levites, from the half-tribe of Manasseh, *they
gave* Golan in Bashan, the city of refuge for the
manslayer, with its pasture lands, and Be-eshterah
with its pasture lands; two cities. 28 From the tribe
of Issachar, *they gave* Kishion with its pasture lands,
Daberath with its pasture lands, 29 Jarmuth with its
pasture lands, En-gannim with its pasture lands;
four cities. 30 From the tribe of Asher, *they gave* Mishal with its pasture lands, Abdon with its pasture
lands, 31 Helkath with its pasture lands and Rehob
with its pasture lands; four cities. 32 From the tribe
of Naphtali, *they gave* [A]Kedesh in Galilee, the city
of refuge for the manslayer, with its pasture lands
and Hammoth-dor with its pasture lands and Kartan
with its pasture lands; three cities. 33 All the cities
of the Gershonites according to their families were
thirteen cities with their pasture lands.
34 To the families of [A]the sons of Merari, the rest
of the Levites, *they gave* from the tribe of Zebulun,
Jokneam with its pasture lands and Kartah with its
pasture lands. 35 Dimnah with its pasture lands, Nahalal with its pasture lands; four cities. 36 From the
tribe of Reuben, *they gave* [A]Bezer with its pasture
lands and Jahaz with its pasture lands, 37 Kedemoth
with its pasture lands and Mephaath with its pasture lands; four cities. 38 From the tribe of Gad, *they
gave* [A]Ramoth in Gilead, the city of refuge for the
manslayer, with its pasture lands and [B]Mahanaim
with its pasture lands, 39 Heshbon with its pasture
lands, Jazer with its pasture lands; four cities in
all. 40 All *these were* the cities of the sons of Merari
according to their families, the rest of the families
of the Levites; and their lot was twelve cities.
41 [A]All the cities of the Levites in the midst of the
possession of the sons of Israel were forty-eight
cities with their pasture lands. 42 These cities each
had its surrounding pasture lands; thus *it was* with
all these cities.
43 [A]So the LORD gave Israel all the land which
He had sworn to give to their fathers, and [B]they
possessed it and lived in it. 44 And the LORD [A]gave
them rest on every side, according to all that He
had sworn to their fathers, and [B]no one of all their
enemies stood before them; [C]the LORD gave all their
enemies into their hand. 45 [A]Not [a]one of the good
promises which the LORD had [b]made to the house
of Israel failed; all came to pass.

21:4 [a]Lit *had* 21:5 [a]Lit *had* 21:6 [a]Lit *had* 21:7 [a]Lit *had* 21:8 [a]Lit *by the hand of* [A]Gen 49:5ff 21:11 [A]1 Chr 6:55 [B]Josh 14:15; 15:13 21:13 [A]1 Chr 6:57 [B]Josh 15:54 [C]Josh 15:42 21:14 [A]Josh 15:48 [B]Josh 15:50 21:15 [a]In 1 Chr 6:58, *Hilen* [A]Josh 15:49 21:16 [a]In 1 Chr 6:59, *Ashan* [A]Josh 15:55 [B]Josh 15:10 21:17 [A]Josh 18:25 [B]Josh 18:24 21:18 [a]In 1 Chr 6:60, *Allemeth* 21:20 [A]1 Chr 6:66 21:21 [A]Josh 20:7 21:27 [A]1 Chr 6:71 21:32 [A]Josh 20:7 21:34 [A]1 Chr 6:77 21:36 [A]Deut 4:43; Josh 20:8 21:38 [A]Deut 4:43; 1 Kin 4:13 [B]Gen 32:2; 2 Sam 2:8 21:41 [A]Num 35:7 21:43 [A]Deut 34:4 [B]Num 33:53; Deut 11:31; 17:14 21:44 [A]Josh 1:13; 23:1 [B]Deut 7:24 [C]Ex 23:31 21:45 [a]Lit *a word from every good word* [b]Lit *spoken* [A]Josh 23:14; 1 Kin 8:56

21:43–45 So the LORD gave Israel all the land. This sums up God's fulfillment of His covenant promise to give Abraham's people the Land (Ge 12:7; Jos 1:2, 5–9). God also kept His Word in giving the people rest (Dt 12:9, 10). In a valid sense, the Canaanites were in check, under military conquest as God had pledged (Jos 1:5), not posing an immediate threat. Not every enemy had been driven out, however, leaving some to stir up trouble later. But God's people failed to exercise their responsibility and possess their land to the full degree in various areas.

TRIBES BEYOND JORDAN RETURN

22 [A]Then Joshua summoned the Reubenites and the Gadites and the half-tribe of Manasseh, 2 and said to them, "You have kept all that Moses the servant of the LORD commanded you, [A]and have listened to my voice in all that I commanded you. 3 You have not forsaken your brothers these many days to this day, but have kept the charge of the commandment of the LORD your God. 4 And now [A]the LORD your God has given rest to your brothers, as He spoke to them; therefore turn now and go to your tents, to the land of your possession, which Moses the servant of the LORD gave you beyond the Jordan. 5 Only be very careful to observe the commandment and the law which Moses the servant of the LORD commanded you, to [A]love the LORD your God and walk in all His ways and keep His commandments and hold fast to Him and serve Him [B]with all your heart and with all your soul." 6 So Joshua [A]blessed them and sent them away, and they went to their tents.

7 Now [A]to the one half-tribe of Manasseh Moses had given *a possession* in Bashan, but [B]to the other half Joshua gave *a possession* among their brothers westward beyond the Jordan. So when Joshua sent them away to their tents, he blessed them, 8 and said to [a]them, "Return to your tents with great riches and with very much livestock, with silver, gold, bronze, iron, and with very many clothes; [A]divide the spoil of your enemies with your brothers." 9 The sons of Reuben and the sons of Gad and the half-tribe of Manasseh returned *home* and departed from the sons of Israel at Shiloh which is in the land of Canaan, to go to the [A]land of Gilead, to the land of their possession which they had possessed, according to the [a]command of the LORD [b]through Moses.

THE OFFENSIVE ALTAR

10 When they came to the region of the Jordan which is in the land of Canaan, the sons of Reuben and the sons of Gad and the half-tribe of Manasseh built an altar there by the Jordan, a large altar in appearance. 11 And the sons of Israel heard *it* [a]said, "Behold, the sons of Reuben and the sons of Gad and the half-tribe of Manasseh have [A]built an altar at the [b]frontier of the land of Canaan, in the region of the Jordan, on the side *belonging to* the sons of Israel." 12 When the sons of Israel heard *of it,* the whole congregation of the sons of Israel gathered themselves at [A]Shiloh to go up against them in war.

13 Then the sons of Israel sent to the sons of Reuben and to the sons of Gad and to the half-tribe of Manasseh, into the land of Gilead, [A]Phinehas the son of Eleazar the priest, 14 and with him ten chiefs, one chief for each father's household from each of the tribes of Israel; and [A]each one of them *was* the head of his father's household among the [a]thousands of Israel. 15 They came to the sons of Reuben and to the sons of Gad and to the half-tribe of Manasseh, to the land of Gilead, and they spoke with them saying, 16 "Thus says the whole congregation of the LORD, 'What is this unfaithful act which you have committed against the God of Israel, turning away from following the LORD this day, by [A]building yourselves an altar, to rebel against the LORD this day? 17 Is not [A]the iniquity of Peor [a]enough for us, from which we have not cleansed ourselves to this day, although a plague came on the congregation of the LORD, 18 that you must turn away this day from following the LORD? If you rebel against the LORD today, [A]He will be angry with the whole congregation of Israel tomorrow. 19 If, however, the land of your possession is unclean, then [a]cross into the land of the possession of the LORD, where the LORD'S tabernacle [b]stands, and take possession among us. Only do not rebel against the LORD, or rebel against us by [A]building an altar for yourselves, besides the altar of the LORD our God. 20 Did not [A]Achan the son of Zerah act unfaithfully in the things under the ban, and wrath fall on all the congregation of Israel? And that man did not perish alone in his iniquity.' "

21 Then the sons of Reuben and the sons of Gad and the half-tribe of Manasseh answered and spoke to the heads of the [a]families of Israel. 22 "The [A]Mighty One, God, the LORD, the Mighty One, God, the LORD! [B]He knows, and may Israel itself know. If *it was* in rebellion, or if in an unfaithful act against the LORD do not save us this day! 23 If we have built us an altar to turn away from following the LORD, or if to [A]offer a burnt offering or grain offering on it, or if to offer sacrifices of peace offerings on it, may the LORD Himself require it. 24 But truly we have done this out of concern, [a]for a reason, saying, 'In time to come your sons may say to our [b]sons, "What have you to do with the LORD, the God of Israel? 25 For the LORD has made the Jordan a border between us and you, *you* sons of Reuben and sons of Gad; you have no portion in the LORD." So your sons may make our sons stop fearing the LORD.'

26 "Therefore we said, 'Let us [a]build an altar, not for burnt offering or for sacrifice; 27 rather it shall be [A]a witness between us and you and between our generations after us, that we are to [B]perform the service of the LORD before Him with our burnt

22:1 [A]Num 32:20-22 22:2 [A]Josh 1:12-18 22:4 [A]Num 32:18; Deut 3:20 22:5 [A]Deut 5:10 [B]Deut 4:29 22:6 [A]Gen 47:7; Josh 14:13; 2 Sam 6:18; Luke 24:50 22:7 [A]Num 32:33 [B]Josh 17:1-13 22:8 [a]Lit *them, saying, "Return* [A]Num 31:27; 1 Sam 30:16 22:9 [a]Lit *mouth* [b]Lit *by the hand of* [A]Num 32:1, 26, 29 22:11 [a]Lit *saying* [b]Lit *front* [A]Deut 12:5; Josh 22:19 22:12 [A]Josh 18:1 22:13 [A]Num 25:7, 11; 31:6 22:14 [a]Or *families* [A]Num 1:4 22:16 [A]Josh 22:11 22:17 [a]Lit *little for us* [A]Num 25:1-9 22:18 [A]Num 16:22 22:19 [a]Lit *cross for yourselves* [b]Lit *abides* [A]Josh 22:11 22:20 [A]Josh 7:1-26 22:21 [a]Lit *thousands* 22:22 [A]Deut 10:17 [B]1 Kin 8:39; Job 10:7; Ps 44:21 22:23 [A]Deut 12:11 22:24 [a]Lit *from* [b]Lit *sons, saying* 22:26 [a]Lit *prepare to build for ourselves* 22:27 [A]Gen 31:48; Josh 24:27 [B]Deut 12:6, 11, 26f

22:1 Reubenites ... Gadites ... Manasseh. The tribes from E of the Jordan had helped their people conquer the land W of the river. Now they were ready to go back to their families to the E.

22:4 Moses ... gave you. Clearance from Moses and Joshua for these tribes to possess land E of the Jordan was of God (v. 9; 24:8; Nu 32:30–33).

22:10–34 an altar ... by the Jordan. The special altar built by the 2 1/2 tribes near the river, though well-meant, aroused suspicions among western tribes. They feared rebellion against the Shiloh altar that served all the tribes in unity. When challenged, men of the eastern tribes explained their motives to follow the true God, be in unity with the rest of Israel, and not be regarded as outsiders. The explanation met with other Israelites' approval.

offerings, and with our sacrifices and with our peace offerings, so that your sons will not say to our sons in time to come, "You have no portion in the LORD." ' 28 Therefore we said, 'It shall also come about if they say *this* to us or to our generations in time to come, then we shall say, "See the copy of the altar of the LORD which our fathers made, not for burnt offering or for sacrifice; rather it is a witness between us and you." ' 29 Far be it from us that we should rebel against the LORD and turn away from following the LORD this day, by [A]building an altar for burnt offering, for grain offering or for sacrifice, besides the altar of the LORD our God which is before His [a]tabernacle."

30 So when Phinehas the priest and the leaders of the congregation, even the heads of the [a]families of Israel who *were* with him, heard the words which the sons of Reuben and the sons of Gad and the sons of Manasseh spoke, it pleased them. 31 And Phinehas the son of Eleazar the priest said to the sons of Reuben and to the sons of Gad and to the sons of Manasseh, "Today we know that the [A]LORD is in our midst, because you have not committed this unfaithful act against the LORD; now you have delivered the sons of Israel from the hand of the LORD."

32 Then Phinehas the son of Eleazar the priest and the leaders returned from the sons of Reuben and from the sons of Gad, from the land of Gilead to the land of Canaan, to the sons of Israel, and brought back word to them. 33 The word pleased the sons of Israel, and the sons of Israel [A]blessed God; and they did not speak of going up against them in war to destroy the land in which the sons of Reuben and the sons of Gad were living. 34 The sons of Reuben and the sons of Gad [A]called the altar *Witness;* "For," *they said,* "it is a witness between us that the LORD is God."

JOSHUA'S FAREWELL ADDRESS

23 Now it came about after many days, when the LORD had given [A]rest to Israel from all their enemies [a]on every side, and Joshua was old, advanced in years, 2 that [A]Joshua called for all Israel, for their elders and their heads and their judges and their officers, and said to them, "I am old, advanced in years. 3 And you have seen all that the LORD your God has done to all these nations because of you, for [A]the LORD your God is He who has been fighting for you. 4 See, [A]I have apportioned to you these nations which remain as an inheritance for your tribes, with all the nations which I have cut off, from the Jordan even to the Great Sea toward the setting of the sun. 5 The LORD your God, He will thrust them out from before you and [a,A]drive them from before you; and [B]you will possess their land, just as the LORD your God [b]promised you. 6 [A]Be very firm, then, to keep and do all that is written in the book of the law of Moses, so that you may not turn aside from it to the right hand or to the left, 7 so that you will not [a]associate with these nations, these which remain among you, or [A]mention the name of their gods, or [B]make *anyone* swear *by them,* or [C]serve them, or bow down to them. 8 But you are to cling to the LORD your God, as you have done to this day. 9 [A]For the LORD has [a]driven out great and strong nations from before you; and as for you, [B]no man has stood before you to this day. 10 [A]One of your men puts to flight a thousand, for the LORD your God is [B]He who fights for you, just as He [a]promised you. 11 So take diligent heed to yourselves to love the LORD your God. 12 For if you ever go back and [A]cling to the rest of these nations, these which remain among you, and [B]intermarry with them, so that you [a]associate with them and they with you, 13 know with certainty that the LORD your God will not continue to [a]drive these nations out from before you; but they will be a [A]snare and a trap to you, and a whip on your sides and thorns in your eyes, until you perish from off this good land which the LORD your God has given you.

14 "Now behold, today [A]I am going the way of all the earth, and you know in all your hearts and in all your souls that [B]not one word of all the good words which the LORD your God spoke concerning you has failed; all have [a]been fulfilled for you, not [b]one of them has failed. 15 It shall come about that just as all the good words which the LORD your God spoke to you have come upon you, so [A]the LORD will bring upon you all the threats, until He has destroyed you from off this good land which the LORD your God has given you. 16 [A]When you transgress the covenant of the LORD your God, which He commanded you, and go and serve other gods and bow down to them, then the anger of the LORD will burn against you, and you will perish quickly from off the good land which He has given you."

JOSHUA REVIEWS ISRAEL'S HISTORY

24 Then [A]Joshua gathered all the tribes of Israel to Shechem, and called for the elders of Israel and for their heads and their judges and their officers; and they presented themselves before

22:29 [a]Lit *dwelling place* [A]Deut 12:13f 22:30 [a]Lit *thousands* 22:31 [A]Ex 25:8; Lev 26:11f; 2 Chr 15:2 22:33 [A]1 Chr 29:20; Dan 2:19; Luke 2:28 22:34 [A]Gen 31:47-49 23:1 [a]Lit *from round about* [A]Josh 21:44 23:2 [A]Josh 24:1 23:3 [A]Deut 1:30 23:4 [A]Ex 23:30 23:5 [a]Or *dispossess* [b]Lit *spoke to* [A]Ex 23:20 [B]Num 33:53 23:6 [A]Deut 5:32; Josh 1:7 23:7 [a]Lit *go among* [A]Ex 23:13; Ps 16:4 [B]Deut 6:13; 10:20 [C]Ex 20:5 23:9 [a]Or *dispossessed* [A]Ex 23:23, 30 [B]Deut 7:24 23:10 [a]Lit *spoke to* [A]Lev 26:8; Deut 28:7; 32:20 [B]Deut 3:22; Josh 23:3 23:12 [a]Lit *go among* [A]Ex 34:15, 16; Ps 106:34, 35 [B]Deut 7:3, 4; Ezra 9:2; Neh 13:25 23:13 [a]Or *dispossess* [A]Ex 23:33; 34:12; Deut 7:16 23:14 [a]Lit *come* [b]Lit *one word* [A]1 Kin 2:2 [B]Josh 21:45 23:15 [A]Lev 26:14-33; Deut 28:15 23:16 [A]Deut 4:25, 26 24:1 [A]Josh 23:2

23:1 Joshua was old. A long time had passed since he led the conquest ca. 1405–1398 B.C.; Joshua had grown very old, and was 110 when he died (24:29), ca. 1385–1383 B.C. (*see note on 13:1*).

23:5 the LORD ... will thrust them out. God was ready to help His people drive the remaining Canaanites out so that they could possess their claims more fully. Such moves needed to be gradual (Dt 7:22), but determined, in obedience to God.

23:7, 8 The dangers from being incomplete about possessing all the land included that of intermingling with the godless, as in marriages (v. 12), and committing to their gods, thus drifting from worshiping the true God. The Canaanites would become snares, traps, scourges, and thorns, causing Israelites to eventually lose the Land (vv. 13, 15–16).

23:15, 16 This actually occurred 800 years later, when Babylon exiled the Israelites ca. 605–586 B.C. (cf. 2Ki 24–25).

24:1–25 It was time for worship and thanksgiving for all God had done leading up to and including the conquest of Canaan.

24:1–5 Joshua reviewed the history recorded in Ge 11 to Ex 15.

God. 2 Joshua said to all the people, "Thus says the
LORD, the God of Israel, 'From ancient times your
fathers lived beyond the [a]River, *namely,* [A]Terah,
the father of Abraham and the father of Nahor,
and they served other gods. 3 Then [A]I took your father Abraham from beyond the [a]River, and led him
through all the land of Canaan, and [B]multiplied his
[b]descendants and gave him [C]Isaac. 4 To Isaac I gave
[A]Jacob and Esau, and [B]to Esau I gave Mount Seir
to possess it; but [C]Jacob and his sons went down
to Egypt. 5 Then [A]I sent Moses and Aaron, and I
plagued Egypt [a]by what I did in its midst; and afterward I brought you out. 6 I brought your fathers
out of Egypt, and [A]you came to the sea; and Egypt
pursued your fathers with chariots and horsemen to
the [a]Red Sea. 7 But when they cried out to the LORD,
He put darkness between you and the Egyptians,
and brought the sea upon them and covered them;
and your own eyes saw what I did in Egypt. And
[A]you lived in the wilderness for a long time. 8 Then
[A]I brought you into the land of the Amorites who
lived beyond the Jordan, and they fought with you;
and I gave them into your hand, and you took possession of their land when I destroyed them before
you. 9 Then [A]Balak the son of Zippor, king of Moab,
arose and fought against Israel, and he sent and
summoned Balaam the son of Beor to curse you.
10 But I [A]was not willing to listen to Balaam. So he
had to bless you, and I delivered you from his hand.
11 [A]You crossed the Jordan and came to Jericho; and
the citizens of Jericho fought against you, *and* [B]the
Amorite and the Perizzite and the Canaanite and
the Hittite and the Girgashite, the Hivite and the
Jebusite. Thus [C]I gave them into your hand. 12 Then
I [A]sent the hornet before you and it [a]drove out the
two kings of the Amorites from before you, *but* [B]not
by your sword or your bow. 13 [A]I gave you a land on
which you had not labored, and cities which you
had not built, and you have lived in them; you are
eating of vineyards and olive groves which you
did not plant.'

"WE WILL SERVE THE LORD"

14 "Now, therefore, [a,A]fear the LORD and serve
Him in sincerity and [b]truth; and put away the gods
which your fathers served beyond the [c]River and
in Egypt, and serve the LORD. 15 If it is disagreeable
in your sight to serve the LORD, choose for yourselves today whom you will serve: whether the gods
which your fathers served which were beyond the
River, or [A]the gods of the Amorites in whose land
you are living; but as for me and my house, we will
serve the LORD."

16 The people answered and said, "Far be it from
us that we should forsake the LORD to serve other
gods; 17 for the LORD our God is He who brought us
and our fathers up out of the land of Egypt, from
the house of [a]bondage, and who did these great
signs in our sight and preserved us through all
the way in which we went and among all the peoples through whose midst we passed. 18 The LORD
drove out from before us all the peoples, even the
Amorites who lived in the land. We also will serve
the LORD, for He is our God."

19 Then Joshua said to the people, "You will not
be able to serve the LORD, [A]for He is a holy God.
He is [B]a jealous God; [C]He will not forgive your
transgression or your sins. 20 [A]If you forsake the
LORD and serve foreign gods, then He will turn
and do you harm and consume you after He has
done good to you." 21 The people said to Joshua,
"No, but we will serve the LORD." 22 Joshua said
to the people, "You are witnesses against yourselves that [A]you have chosen for yourselves the
LORD, to serve Him." And they said, "We are witnesses." 23 "Now therefore, put away the foreign
gods which are in your midst, and [A]incline your
hearts to the LORD, the God of Israel." 24 [A]The people said to Joshua, "We will serve the LORD our
God and we will [a]obey His voice." 25 [A]So Joshua
made a covenant with the people that day, and
made for them a statute and an ordinance in Shechem. 26 And Joshua [A]wrote these words in the
book of the law of God; and he took a large stone
and set it up there under the oak that was by the
sanctuary of the LORD. 27 Joshua said to all the
people, "Behold, [A]this stone shall be for a witness
against us, for it has heard all the words of the
LORD which He spoke [a]to us; thus it shall be for
a witness against you, so that you do not deny

24:2 [a]I.e. Euphrates [A]Gen 11:27-32 24:3 [a]I.e. Euphrates [b]Lit *seed* [A]Gen 12:1; 24:7 [B]Gen 15:5 [C]Gen 21:3 24:4 [A]Gen 25:25, 26 [B]Gen 36:8; Deut 2:5 [C]Gen 46:6, 7 24:5 [a]Lit *according to* [A]Ex 4:14-17 24:6 [a]Lit *Sea of Reeds* [A]Ex 14:2-31 24:7 [A]Deut 1:46; 2:14 24:8 [A]Num 21:21-32 24:9 [A]Num 22:2-6 24:10 [A]Deut 23:5 24:11 [A]Josh 3:14-17 [B]Ex 23:23, 28; Deut 7:1 [C]Ex 23:31 24:12 [a]Lit *drove them out* [A]Ex 23:28; Deut 7:20 [B]Ps 44:3 24:13 [A]Deut 6:10, 11 24:14 [a]Or *reverence* [b]Or *faithfulness* [c]I.e. Euphrates [A]Deut 10:12; 18:13; 1 Sam 12:24 24:15 [A]Judg 6:10 24:17 [a]Lit *bondmen* 24:19 [A]Lev 19:2; 20:7, 26 [B]Ex 20:5; 34:14 [C]Ex 23:21 24:20 [A]Deut 4:25, 26 24:22 [A]Ps 119:173 24:23 [A]1 Kin 8:57, 58; Ps 119:36; 141:4 24:24 [a]Lit *listen to* [A]Ex 19:8; 24:3, 7; Deut 5:27 24:25 [A]Ex 24:8 24:26 [A]Deut 31:24 24:27 [a]Lit *with* [A]Josh 22:27, 34

24:2 the River. The Euphrates, where Abraham's family had lived. It is clear here that God's calling of Abraham out to Himself was also a call out of idolatry, as He does with others (cf. 1Th 1:9).

24:6–13 Joshua reviewed the history recorded in Ex 12 to Jos 22.

24:8, 15 Amorites. Sometimes this is used as a general term for the entire pagan populace (cf. v. 11) in Canaan, as elsewhere (Ge 15:16; Jdg 1:34, 35). At other times, the name has a narrower reference to people of the hill country (Nu 13:29), distinct from others.

24:9, 10 Balaam. *See note on Jos 13:22* about the unsavory nature of Balaam in Nu 21–25.

24:12 I sent the hornet before you. This description, as also in Ex 23:28, is a picturesque figure (cf. also 23:13) portraying God's own fighting to assist Israel (23:3, 5, 10, 13). This awesome force put the enemy to flight, as the feared hornets lit. can do (Dt 7:20, 21).

24:15 choose … today whom you will serve. Joshua's fatherly model (reminiscent of Abraham's, Ge 18:19) was for himself and his family to serve the Lord, not false gods. He called others in Israel to this, and they committed themselves to serve the Lord also (vv. 21, 24).

24:18 The population joined Joshua in claiming total commitment to serve the Lord (cf. Ex 19:8).

24:26 book of the law. Joshua expands the first 5 books of Moses, as the canon of revealed Scripture develops. **by the sanctuary.** God's tabernacle, the ark of the covenant, was at Shiloh (21:2). The stone of witness by the holy place (sanctuary) here was at Shechem (24:1). This holy place is not a formal tent or building, but a sacred place by a tree (cf. Ge 12:6; 35:4), as other places had significance in the past for worship to God (Ge 21:33).

your God." 28 Then Joshua dismissed the people, each to his inheritance.

JOSHUA'S DEATH AND BURIAL

29 It came about after these things that Joshua the son of Nun, the servant of the LORD, died, being one hundred and ten years old. 30 And they buried him in the territory of his inheritance in [A]Timnath-serah, which is in the hill country of Ephraim, on the north of Mount Gaash.
31 [A]Israel served the LORD all the days of Joshua and all the days of the elders who [a]survived Joshua, and had known all the deeds of the LORD which He had done for Israel.
32 Now [A]they buried the bones of Joseph, which the sons of Israel brought up from Egypt, at Shechem, in the piece of ground [B]which Jacob had bought from the sons of Hamor the father of Shechem for one hundred [a]pieces of money; and they became the inheritance of Joseph's sons. 33 And Eleazar the son of Aaron died; and they buried him [a]at Gibeah of [A]Phinehas his son, which was given him in the hill country of Ephraim.

24:30 [A]Josh 19:50 24:31 [a]Lit *prolonged days after* [A]Judg 2:6f [B]Gen 33:19; John 4:5; Acts 7:15f 24:32 [a]Heb *qesitah* [A]Gen 50:24, 25; Ex 13:19 24:33 [a]Or *on the hill* [A]Josh 22:13

24:29–33 Joshua ... Eleazar. Three prominent leaders were buried as the conquering generation was passing on: Joseph, Joshua, and the High Priest Eleazar.

24:29 one hundred and ten years old. This was ca. 1383 B.C. (cf. 14:7–10).

24:31 Faithfulness to God extended only one generation (cf. Jdg 2:6–13).

24:32 The bones of Joseph. These had been carried by the Israelites in the Exodus (Ex 13:19) as Joseph had made them promise (Ge 50:25). He wanted his remains to lie in the Land of covenant pledge. So now his people laid them to rest at Shechem, in the Land God had guaranteed (Ge 12:7).

THE BOOK OF JUDGES

TITLE

The book bears the fitting name "Judges," which refers to unique leaders God gave to His people for preservation against their enemies (2:16–19). The Hebrew title means "deliverers" or "saviors," as well as judges (cf. Dt 16:18; 17:9; 19:17). Twelve such judges arose before Samuel; then Eli and Samuel raised the count to 14. God Himself is the higher Judge (11:27). Judges spans about 350 years from Joshua's conquest (ca. 1398 B.C.) until Eli and Samuel judged prior to the establishment of the monarchy (ca. 1043 B.C.).

AUTHOR AND DATE

No author is named in the book, but the Jewish Talmud identifies Samuel, a key prophet who lived at the time these events took place and could have personally summed up the era (cf. 1Sa 10:25). The time was earlier than David's capture of Jerusalem ca. 1004 B.C. (2Sa 5:6, 7) since Jebusites still controlled the site (Jdg 1:21). Also, the writer deals with a time before a king ruled (17:6; 18:1; 21:25). Since Saul began his reign ca. 1043 B.C., a time shortly after his rule began is probably when Judges was written.

BACKGROUND AND SETTING

Judges is a tragic sequel to Joshua. In Joshua, the people were obedient to God in conquering the Land. In Judges, they were disobedient, idolatrous, and often defeated. Judges 1:1–3:6 focuses on the closing days of the book of Joshua. Judges 2:6–9 gives a review of Joshua's death (cf. Jos 24:28–31). The account describes 7 distinct cycles of Israel's drifting away from the Lord starting even before Joshua's death, with a full departure into apostasy afterward. Five basic reasons are evident for these cycles of Israel's moral and spiritual decline: 1) disobedience in failing to drive the Canaanites out of the Land (Jdg 1:19, 21, 35); 2) idolatry (2:12); 3) intermarriage with wicked Canaanites (3:5, 6); 4) not heeding judges (2:17); and 5) turning away from God after the death of the judges (2:19).

A four-part sequence repeatedly occurred in this phase of Israel's history: 1) Israel's departure from God; 2) God's chastisement in permitting military defeat and subjugation; 3) Israel's prayer pleading for deliverance; and 4) God raising up "judges," either civil or sometimes local military champions who led in shaking off the oppressors. Fourteen judges arose, six of them military judges (Othniel, Ehud, Deborah, Gideon, Jephthah, and Samson). Two men were of special significance for contrast in spiritual leadership: 1) Eli, judge and High Priest (not a good example); and 2) Samuel, judge, priest, and prophet (a good example).

HISTORICAL AND THEOLOGICAL THEMES

Judges is thematic rather than chronological; foremost among its themes is God's power and covenant mercy in graciously delivering the Israelites from the consequences of their failures, which were suffered for sinful compromise (cf. 2:18, 19; 21:25). In 7 periods of sin to salvation (cf. Introduction: Outline), God compassionately delivered His people throughout the different geographical areas of tribal inheritances which He had earlier given through Joshua (Jos 13–22). The apostasy covered the whole land, as indicated by the fact that each area is specifically identified: southern (3:7–31); northern (4:1–5:31); central (6:1–10:5); eastern (10:6–12:15); and western (13:1–16:31). His power to faithfully rescue shines against the dark backdrop of pitiful human compromise and sometimes bizarre twists of sin, as in the final summary (Jdg 17–21). The last verse (21:25) sums up the account: "In those days there was no king in Israel; everyone did what was right in his own eyes."

INTERPRETIVE CHALLENGES

The most stimulating challenges are: 1) how to view men's violent acts against enemies or fellow countrymen, whether with God's approval or without it; 2) God's use of leaders who at times do His will and at times follow their own sinful impulses (Gideon, Eli, Jephthah, Samson); 3) how to view Jephthah's vow and offering of his daughter (11:30–40); and 4) how to resolve God's sovereign will with His providential working in spite of human sin (cf. 14:4).

The chronology of the various judges in different sectors of the Land raises questions about how much time passed and how the time totals can fit into the entire time span from the Exodus (ca. 1445 B.C.) to Solomon's fourth year, ca. 967/966 B.C., which is said to be 480 years (1Ki 6:1; *see note on Jdg 11:26*). A reasonable explanation is that the deliverances and years of rest under the judges in distinct parts of the land included overlaps, so that some of them did not run consecutively but rather concurrently during the 480 years. Paul's estimate of "about 450" years in Ac 13:19 is an approximation.

OUTLINE

I. Introduction and Summary—The Disobedience of Israel (1:1–3:6)

A. Incomplete Conquest over the Canaanites (1:1–36)
B. The Decline and Judgment of Israel (2:1–3:6)

II. A Selected History of the Judges—The Deliverance of Israel (3:7–16:31)

A. First Period: Othniel vs. Mesopotamians (3:7–11)
B. Second Period: Ehud and Shamgar vs. Moabites (3:12–31)
C. Third Period: Deborah vs. Canaanites (4:1–5:31)
D. Fourth Period: Gideon vs. Midianites (6:1–8:32)
E. Fifth Period: Tola and Jair vs. Abimelech's Effects (8:33–10:5)
F. Sixth Period: Jephthah, Ibzan, Elon, and Abdon vs. Philistines and Ammonites (10:6–12:15)
G. Seventh Period: Samson vs. Philistines (13:1–16:31)

III. Epilogue—The Dereliction of Israel (17:1–21:25)

A. The Idolatry of Micah and the Danites (17:1–18:31)
B. The Crime at Gibeah and War Against Benjamin (19:1–21:25)

JERUSALEM IS CAPTURED

1 Now it came about after the death of Joshua that
the sons of Israel [A]inquired of the LORD, saying,
"Who shall go up first for us [B]against the Canaanites,
to fight against them?" 2 The LORD said, "[A]Judah
shall go up; behold, I have given the land into his
hand." 3 Then Judah said to Simeon his brother,
"Come up with me into [a]the territory allotted me,
that we may fight against the Canaanites; and [b]I in
turn will go with you into [c]the territory allotted you."
So Simeon went with him. 4 Judah went up, and [A]the
LORD gave the Canaanites and the Perizzites into
their hands, and they [a]defeated ten thousand men
at Bezek. 5 They found Adoni-bezek in Bezek and
fought against him, and they [a]defeated the Canaanites and the Perizzites. 6 But Adoni-bezek fled; and
they pursued him and caught him and cut off his
[a]thumbs and big toes. 7 Adoni-bezek said, "Seventy
kings with their thumbs and their big toes cut off
used to gather up *scraps* under my table; [A]as I have
done, so God has repaid me." So they brought him
to Jerusalem and he died there.
8 Then the sons of Judah fought against [A]Jerusa-
lem and captured it and struck it with the edge of
the sword and set the city on fire. 9 Afterward the
sons of Judah went down to fight against the Canaanites living in the hill country and in the [a]Negev
and in the lowland. 10 [A]So Judah went against the
Canaanites who lived in Hebron (now the name of
Hebron formerly *was* Kiriath-arba); and they struck
Sheshai and Ahiman and Talmai.

CAPTURE OF OTHER CITIES

11 Then [A]from there he went against the inhabitants of Debir (now the name of Debir formerly *was*
Kiriath-sepher). 12 And Caleb said, "The one who
attacks Kiriath-sepher and captures it, I will even
give him my daughter Achsah for a wife." 13 [A]Othniel
the son of Kenaz, Caleb's younger brother, captured
it; so he gave him his daughter Achsah for a wife.
14 Then [A]it came about when she came *to him,* that
she persuaded him to ask her father for a field. Then
she alighted from [a]her donkey, and Caleb said to
her, "What [b]do you want?" 15 She said to him, "Give
me a blessing, since you have given me the land of
the [a]Negev, give me also springs of water." So Caleb
gave her the upper springs and the lower springs.
16 The [a]descendants of [A]the Kenite, Moses' father-in-law, went up from the [B]city of palms with
the sons of Judah, to the wilderness of Judah which
is in the south of [C]Arad; and they went and lived
with the people. 17 Then Judah went with Simeon
his brother, and they struck the Canaanites living
in Zephath, and utterly destroyed it. So the name
of the city was called [A]Hormah. 18 And Judah took
[A]Gaza with its territory and Ashkelon with its territory and Ekron with its territory. 19 Now the LORD
was with Judah, and they took possession of the hill
country; but they could not [a]drive out the inhabitants of the valley because they had [A]iron chariots.
20 Then they gave Hebron to Caleb, [A]as Moses had
[a]promised; and he drove out from there [B]the three
sons of Anak. 21 [A]But the sons of Benjamin did not
drive out the [B]Jebusites who lived in Jerusalem; so
the Jebusites have lived with the sons of Benjamin
in Jerusalem to this day.
22 Likewise the house of Joseph went up against
Bethel, and the LORD was with them. 23 The house of
Joseph spied out Bethel ([A]now the name of the city
was formerly Luz). 24 The spies saw a man coming
out of the city and they said to him, "Please show
us the entrance to the city and [A]we will treat you
kindly." 25 So he showed them the entrance to the
city, and they struck the city with the edge of the
sword, [A]but they let the man and all his family go
free. 26 The man went into the land of the Hittites
and built a city and named it Luz [a]which is its name
to this day.

PLACES NOT CONQUERED

27 [A]But Manasseh did not take possession of
Beth-shean and its villages, or Taanach and its villages, or the inhabitants of Dor and its villages, or
the inhabitants of Ibleam and its villages, or the
inhabitants of Megiddo and its villages; so [B]the Canaanites persisted in living in that land. 28 It came

1:1 [A]Num 27:21 [B]Judg 1:27; 2:21-23; 3:1-6 1:2 [A]Gen 49:8 1:3 [a]Lit *my lot* [b]Lit *I, even I* [c]Lit *your lot* 1:4 [a]Lit *smote them* [A]Ps 44:2; 78:55 1:5 [a]Lit *smote* 1:6 [a]Lit *thumbs of his hands and his feet* 1:7 [A]Lev 24:19 1:8 [A]Josh 15:63; Judg 1:21 1:9 [a]I.e. South country 1:10 [A]Josh 15:13-19 1:11 [A]Josh 15:15 1:13 [A]Judg 3:9 1:14 [a]Lit *the* [b]Lit *for yourself* [A]Josh 15:18 1:15 [a]I.e. South country 1:16 [a]Lit *sons* [A]Num 10:29-32; Judg 4:11 [B]Deut 34:3; Judg 3:13 [C]Num 21:1 1:17 [A]Num 21:3 1:18 [A]Josh 11:22 1:19 [a]Or *dispossess* [A]Josh 17:16; Judg 4:3, 13 1:20 [a]Lit *spoken* [A]Josh 14:9 [B]Josh 15:14; Judg 1:10 1:21 [A]Josh 15:63; Judg 1:8 [B]1 Chr 11:4 1:23 [A]Gen 28:19 1:24 [A]Josh 2:12 1:25 [A]Josh 6:25 1:26 [a]Lit *it* 1:27 [A]Josh 17:12 [B]Judg 1:1

1:1 after the death of Joshua. Ca. 1383 B.C. (cf. Jos 14:7–10 with Jos 24:29). Descriptions of the book's setting in Jdg 1, 2 vary between times after Joshua's death and flashbacks summarizing conditions while he was alive (as 2:2–6). Compare Jos 1:1, "After the death of Moses …."

1:2 Judah shall go up. This tribe received God's first go-ahead to push for a more thorough conquest of its territory. The reason probably lay in God's choice that Judah be the leader among the tribes (Ge 49:8–12; 1Ch 5:1, 2) and set the example for them in the other territories.

1:6, 7 cut off his thumbs and big toes. Removing the king's thumbs hampered effective use of a weapon; taking off his big toes rendered footing unreliable in battle. The Lord Himself is nowhere said to endorse this tactic, but it was an act of retributive justice for what Adoni-bezek had done to others. It appears from his confession that he was acknowledging he deserved it.

1:12–15 Caleb said. This repeats the account of Caleb and his family (cf. Jos 15:13–19).

1:16 the city of palms. Since Jericho was destroyed in the invasion, this refers to the area around Jericho, an oasis of springs and palms (Dt 34:3).

1:19 they could not drive out. "They" of Judah could not. They had been promised by Joshua that they could conquer the lowland (Jos 17:16, 18) and should have remembered Jos 11:4–9. This is a recurring failure among the tribes to rise to full trust and obedience for victory by God's power. Compromising for less than what God was able to give (Jos 1:6–9) began even in Joshua's day (Jdg 2:2–6) and earlier (Nu 13, 14). In another sense, God permitted enemies to hold out as a test to display whether His people would obey Him (2:20–23; 3:1, 4). Another factor involved keeping the wild animal count from rising too fast (Dt 7:22).

1:20 sons of Anak. Anak was an early inhabitant of central Canaan near Hebron from whom came an entire group of unusually tall people called the Anakim (Dt 2:10). They frightened the 10 spies (Nu 13:33; Dt 9:2), but were finally driven out of the land by Caleb (Jos 14:12–15; 15:13–14; 21:11) with the exception of some who resettled with the Philistines (Jos 11:22). "The sons of Anak" was used as a term equivalent to "the Anakim."

about when Israel became strong, that they put the
Canaanites to forced labor, but they did not drive
them out completely.
29 [A]Ephraim did not drive out the Canaanites who
were living in Gezer; so the Canaanites lived in Gezer among them.
30 Zebulun did not drive out the inhabitants of
Kitron, or the inhabitants of [a]Nahalol; so the Canaanites lived among them and became subject
to forced labor.
31 Asher did not drive out the inhabitants of
Acco, or the inhabitants of Sidon, or of Ahlab, or
of Achzib, or of Helbah, or of Aphik, or of Rehob.
32 So the Asherites lived among the Canaanites,
the inhabitants of the land; for they did not drive
them out.
33 Naphtali did not drive out the inhabitants of
Beth-shemesh, or the inhabitants of Beth-anath,
but lived among the Canaanites, the inhabitants of
the land; and the inhabitants of Beth-shemesh and
Beth-anath became forced labor for them.
34 Then the Amorites [a]forced the sons of Dan into
the hill country, for they did not allow them to come
down to the valley; 35 yet the Amorites persisted in
[a]living in Mount Heres, in Aijalon and in Shaalbim;
but when the [b]power of the house of Joseph [c]grew
strong, they became forced labor. 36 The border of
the Amorites ran from the [A]ascent of Akrabbim,
from Sela and upward.

ISRAEL REBUKED

2 Now [A]the angel of the LORD came up from Gilgal
to [B]Bochim. And he said, "[C]I brought you up out of
Egypt and led you into the land which I have sworn
to your fathers; and I said, '[D]I will never break My
covenant with you, 2 and as for you, [A]you shall make
no covenant with the inhabitants of this land; [B]you
shall tear down their altars.' But you have not [a]obeyed
Me; what is this you have done? 3 Therefore I also
said, '[A]I will not drive them out before you; but they
will [a]become [B]*as thorns* in your sides and their gods
will be a snare to you.' " 4 When the angel of the LORD
spoke these words to all the sons of Israel, the people
lifted up their voices and wept. 5 So they named that
place [a]Bochim; and there they sacrificed to the LORD.

JOSHUA DIES

6 [A]When Joshua had dismissed the people, the
sons of Israel went each to his inheritance to possess
the land. 7 The people served the LORD all the days of
Joshua, and all the days of the elders who [a]survived
Joshua, who had seen all the great work of the LORD
which He had done for Israel. 8 Then Joshua the son
of Nun, the servant of the LORD, died at the age of
one hundred and ten. 9 And they buried him in the
territory of [A]his inheritance in Timnath-heres, in
the hill country of Ephraim, north of Mount Gaash.
10 All that generation also were gathered to their
fathers; and there arose another generation after
them who [A]did not know the LORD, nor yet the work
which He had done for Israel.

ISRAEL SERVES BAALS

11 Then the sons of Israel did [A]evil in the sight
of the LORD and [a]served the [B]Baals, 12 and [A]they
forsook the LORD, the God of their fathers, who
had brought them out of the land of Egypt, and
followed other gods from *among* the gods of the
peoples who were around them, and bowed themselves down to them; thus they provoked the LORD
to anger. 13 So they forsook the LORD and [A]served
Baal and the Ashtaroth. 14 [A]The anger of the LORD
burned against Israel, and He gave them into the
hands of plunderers who plundered them; and [B]He
sold them into the hands of their enemies around
them, so that they could no longer stand before
their enemies. 15 Wherever they went, the hand of
the LORD was against them for evil, as the LORD
had spoken and [A]as the LORD had sworn to them,
so that they were severely distressed.
16 [A]Then the LORD raised up judges [a]who delivered them from the hands of those who plundered

1:29 [A]Josh 16:10 1:30 [a]Perhaps same as *Nahalal* 1:34 [a]Lit *pressed* 1:35 [a]Lit *dwelling* [b]Lit *hand* [c]Lit *was heavy* 1:36 [A]Josh 15:3 2:1 [A]Judg 6:11; 13:2-21 [B]Judg 2:5 [C]Ex 20:2 [D]Gen 17:7, 8; Lev 26:42, 44; Deut 7:9 2:2 [a]Lit *listened to My voice* [A]Ex 23:32; Deut 7:2-5 [B]Ex 34:12, 13 2:3 [a]Some ancient mss read *be adversaries, and* [A]Josh 23:13 [B]Num 33:55 2:5 [a]I.e. weepers 2:6 [A]Josh 24:28-31 2:7 [a]Lit *prolonged days after* 2:9 [A]Josh 19:49f 2:10 [A]Ex 5:2; 1 Sam 2:12 2:11 [a]Or *worshiped* [A]Judg 3:7, 12; 4:1; 6:1 [B]Judg 6:25; 8:33; 10:6 2:12 [A]Deut 31:16 2:13 [A]Judg 10:6 2:14 [A]Deut 31:17; Ps 106:40-42 [B]Deut 28:25; 32:30 2:15 [A]Lev 26:14-39; Deut 28:15-68 2:16 [a]Lit *and they* [A]Ps 106:43-45

1:34 Amorites forced … Dan. Like all other tribes, Dan had a territory given them, but they failed to claim the power of God to conquer that territory. Later they capitulated even more by accepting defeat and migrating to another territory in the N, becoming idolatrous (Jdg 18).

2:1 the angel of the LORD. One of 3 preincarnate theophanies by the Lord Jesus Christ in Judges (cf. 6:11–18; 13:3–23). This same Divine Messenger had earlier led Israel out of Egypt (cf. Ex 14:19). *See note on Ex 3:2.* **I will never break My covenant with you.** God would be faithful until the end, but the people would forfeit blessing for trouble, due to their disobedience (cf. v. 3).

2:10 another generation … did not know. The first people in the Land had vivid recollections of all the miracles and judgments and were devoted to faith, duty, and purity. The new generation were ignorant of the experiences of their parents and yielded more easily to corruption. To a marked degree the people of this new generation were not true believers, and were not tuned to the God of miracles and victory. Still, many of the judges did genuinely know the Lord, and some who did not live by faith eventually threw themselves on God's mercy during oppressions.

2:12 they … followed other gods. Idol worship, such as the golden calf in the wilderness (Ex 32), flared up again. Spurious gods of Canaan were plentiful. El was the supreme Canaanite deity, a god of uncontrolled lust and a bloody tyrant, as shown in writings found at Ras Shamra in N Syria. His name means "strong, powerful." Baal, son and successor of El, was "lord of heaven," a farm god of rain and storm, his name meaning "lord, possessor." His cult at Phoenicia included animal sacrifices, ritual meals, and licentious dances. Chambers catered to sacred prostitution by men and women (cf. 1Ki 14:23, 24; 2Ki 23:7). Anath, sister-wife of Baal, also called Ashtoreth (Astarte), patroness of sex and war, was called "virgin" and "holy" but was actually a "sacred prostitute." Many other gods besides these also attracted worship.

2:14 The anger of the LORD burned. Calamities designed as chastisement brought discipline intended to lead the people to repentance.

2:16 the LORD raised up judges. A "judge" or deliverer was distinct from a judge in the English world today. Such a leader guided military expeditions against foes as here and arbitrated judicial matters (cf. 4:5). There was no succession or national rule. They were local deliverers, lifted up to leadership by

them. 17 Yet they did not listen to their judges, for
they played the harlot after other gods and bowed
themselves down to them. They turned aside quickly
from the way [A]in which their fathers had walked in
obeying the commandments of the LORD; they did
not do as *their fathers.* 18 When the LORD raised up
judges for them, [A]the LORD was with the judge and
delivered them from the hand of their enemies all
the days of the judge; for the LORD was [B]moved to
pity by their groaning because of those who oppressed and afflicted them. 19 But it came about
when the judge died, that they would turn back and
act more corruptly than their fathers, in following
other gods to serve them and bow down to them;
they did not abandon their practices or their stubborn ways. 20 [A]So the anger of the LORD burned
against Israel, and He said, "Because this nation
has transgressed My covenant which I commanded
their fathers and has not listened to My voice, 21 [A]I
also will no longer drive out before them any of the
nations which Joshua left when he died, 22 in order
to [A]test Israel by them, whether they will keep the
way of the LORD to walk in it as their fathers [a]did,
or not." 23 So the LORD allowed those nations to
remain, not driving them out quickly; and He did
not give them into the hand of Joshua.

IDOLATRY LEADS TO SERVITUDE

3 [A]Now these are the nations which the LORD
left, to test Israel by them (*that is,* all who
had not [a]experienced any of the wars of Canaan;
2 only in order that the generations of the sons of
Israel might [a]be taught war, [b]those who had not
[c]experienced it formerly). 3 *These nations are:* the
five lords of the Philistines and all the Canaanites
and the Sidonians and [A]the Hivites who lived in
Mount Lebanon, from Mount Baal-hermon as far
as [a]Lebo-hamath. 4 They were for [a,A]testing Israel,
to find out if they would [b]obey the commandments
of the LORD, which He had commanded their fathers [c]through Moses. 5 [A]The sons of Israel lived
among the Canaanites, the Hittites, the Amorites,
the Perizzites, the Hivites, and the Jebusites; 6 and
[A]they took their daughters for themselves as wives,
and gave their own daughters to their sons, and
served their gods.

7 The sons of Israel did [A]what was evil in the sight
of the LORD, and [B]forgot the LORD their God and
[C]served the Baals and the [a]Asheroth. 8 Then the anger of the LORD was kindled against Israel, so that
He sold them into the hands of Cushan-rishathaim
king of [a]Mesopotamia; and the sons of Israel served
Cushan-rishathaim eight years.

2:17 [A]Judg 2:7 2:18 [A]Josh 1:5 [B]Deut 32:36; Ps 106:44 2:20 [A]Judg 2:14 2:21 [A]Josh 23:4, 5, 13 2:22 [a]Lit *kept* [A]Deut 8:2; 13:3 3:1 [a]Lit *known* [A]Judg 1:1; 2:21, 22 3:2 [a]Lit *know, to teach them* [b]Lit *only* [c]Lit *known* 3:3 [a]Or *the entrance of Hamath* [A]Josh 9:7; 11:19 3:4 [a]Lit *testing by them* [b]Lit *hear* [c]Lit *by the hand of* [A]Deut 8:2 3:5 [A]Ps 106:35 3:6 [A]Ex 34:15, 16; Deut 7:3, 4; Josh 23:12 3:7 [a]I.e. wooden symbol of a female deity [A]Judg 2:11 [B]Deut 4:9 [C]Judg 2:13 3:8 [a]Heb *Aram-naharaim*

God when the deplorable condition of Israel in the region around them prompted God to rescue the people.

3:1 nations ... left. The purpose was to use them to test (cf. v. 4) and discipline the sinful Israelites, as well as to aid the young in learning the art of war.

3:5 *See notes on 1:1–20.*

3:6 *See note on 1:19.* The Israelites failed God's test, being enticed into 1) marriages with Canaanites and 2) worship of their gods. Disobedience was repeated frequently through the centuries, and led God to use the Assyrians (2Ki 17) and Babylonians (2Ki 24, 25) to expel them from the land gained here.

THE JUDGES OF ISRAEL

Judge and Tribe	Scripture References	Oppressors	Period of Oppression/ Rest
(1) **Othniel** (Judah), Son of Kenaz, younger brother of Caleb	Jdg 1:11–15; 3:1–11; Jos 15:16–19; 1Ch 4:13	Cushan-rishathaim, king of Mesopotamia	8 years/40 years
(2) **Ehud** (Benjamin), Son of Gera	Jdg 3:12–4:1	Eglon, king of Moab; Ammonites; Amalekites	18 years/80 years
(3) **Shamgar** (Perhaps foreign), Son of Anath	Jdg 3:31; 5:6	Philistines	Not given/Not given
(4) **Deborah** (Ephraim), **Barak** (Naphtali), Son of Abinoam	Jdg 4:1–5:31; Heb 11:32	Jabin, king of Canaan; Sisera, commander of the army	20 years/40 years
(5) **Gideon** (Manasseh), Son of Joash the Abiezrite. Also called: Jerubbaal (6:32; 7:1); Jerubbesheth (2Sa 11:21)	Jdg 6:1–8:32; Heb 11:32	Midianites; Amalekites; "People of the East"	7 years/40 years
(6) **Abimelech** (Manasseh), Son of Gideon by a concubine	Jdg 8:33–9:57; 2Sa 11:21	Civil war	Abimelech ruled over Israel 3 years
(7) **Tola** (Issachar), Son of Puah	Jdg 10:1, 2		Judged Israel 23 years
(8) **Jair** (Gilead-Manasseh)	Jdg 10:3–5		Judged Israel 22 years
(9) **Jephthah** (Gilead-Manasseh), Son of Gilead by a harlot	Jdg 10:6–12:7; Heb 11:32	Philistines; Ammonites; Civil war with the Ephraimites	18 years/Judged Israel 6 years
(10) **Ibzan** (Judah or Zebulun) (Bethlehem-Zebulun; cf. Jos 19:15)	Jdg 12:8–10		Judged Israel 7 years
(11) **Elon** (Zebulun)	Jdg 12:11, 12		Judged Israel 10 years
(12) **Abdon** (Ephraim), Son of Hillel	Jdg 12:13–15		Judged Israel 8 years
(13) **Samson** (Dan), Son of Manoah	Jdg 13:1–16:31; Heb 11:32	Philistines	40 years/Judged Israel 20 years

THE FIRST JUDGE DELIVERS ISRAEL

9 When the sons of Israel cried to the LORD, the
LORD raised up a deliverer for the sons of Israel
to deliver them, [A]Othniel the son of Kenaz, Caleb's
younger brother. 10 [A]The Spirit of the LORD came
upon him, and he judged Israel. When he went out
to war, the LORD gave Cushan-rishathaim king of
[a]Mesopotamia into his hand, so that [b]he prevailed
over Cushan-rishathaim. 11 Then the land had rest
forty years. And Othniel the son of Kenaz died.

12 Now the sons of Israel again [A]did evil in the
sight of the LORD. So [B]the LORD strengthened Eglon
the king of Moab against Israel, because they had
done evil in the sight of the LORD. 13 And he gathered
to himself the sons of Ammon and Amalek; and he
went and [a]defeated Israel, and they possessed [A]the
city of the palm trees. 14 The sons of Israel served
Eglon the king of Moab eighteen years.

EHUD DELIVERS FROM MOAB

15 But when the sons of Israel [A]cried to the LORD,
the LORD raised up a deliverer for them, Ehud the
son of Gera, the Benjamite, a left-handed man. And
the sons of Israel sent tribute by [a]him to Eglon the
king of Moab. 16 Ehud made himself a sword which
had two edges, a cubit in length, and he bound it
on his right thigh under his cloak. 17 He presented
the tribute to Eglon king of Moab. Now Eglon was a
very fat man. 18 It came about when he had finished
presenting the tribute, that he sent away the people
who had carried the tribute. 19 But he himself turned
back from the idols which were at Gilgal, and said, "I
have a secret message for you, O king." And he said,
"Keep silence." And all who attended him left him.
20 Ehud came to him while he was sitting alone in his
cool roof chamber. And Ehud said, "I have a message
from God for you." And he arose from his seat. 21 Ehud
stretched out his left hand, took the sword from his
right thigh and thrust it into his belly. 22 The handle
also went in after the blade, and the fat closed over
the blade, for he did not draw the sword out of his
belly; and the refuse came out. 23 Then Ehud went
out into the vestibule and shut the doors of the roof
chamber behind him, and locked *them.*

24 When he had gone out, his servants came and
looked, and behold, the doors of the roof chamber
were locked; and they said, "[A]He is only [a]relieving
himself in the cool room." 25 They waited until they
[a]became anxious; but behold, he did not open the
doors of the roof chamber. Therefore they took the
key and opened them, and behold, their master had
fallen to the [b]floor dead.

26 Now Ehud escaped while they were delaying,
and he passed by the idols and escaped to Seirah.
27 It came about when he had arrived, that [A]he blew
the trumpet in the hill country of Ephraim; and the
sons of Israel went down with him from the hill country, and he *was* in front of them. 28 He said to them,
"Pursue *them,* for the LORD has given your enemies
the Moabites into your hands." So they went down
after him and seized [A]the fords of the Jordan opposite Moab, and did not allow anyone to cross. 29 They
struck down at that time about ten thousand Moabites, all robust and valiant men; and no one escaped.
30 So Moab was subdued that day under the hand of
Israel. And the land was undisturbed for eighty years.

SHAMGAR DELIVERS FROM PHILISTINES

31 After him came [A]Shamgar the son of Anath,
who struck down six hundred Philistines with an
oxgoad; and he also saved Israel.

DEBORAH AND BARAK DELIVER FROM CANAANITES

4 Then [A]the sons of Israel again did evil in the
sight of the LORD, after Ehud died. 2 And the
LORD sold them into the hand of [A]Jabin king of Canaan, who reigned in Hazor; and the commander
of his army was Sisera, who lived in [B]Harosheth-ha-
goyim. 3 The sons of Israel cried to the LORD; for he
had nine hundred [A]iron chariots, and he oppressed
the sons of Israel severely for twenty years.

4 Now Deborah, a [a]prophetess, the wife of Lappi-
doth, was judging Israel at that time. 5 She used to
[a]sit under the [A]palm tree of Deborah between Ramah
and Bethel in the hill country of Ephraim; and the
sons of Israel came up to her for judgment. 6 Now
she sent and summoned [A]Barak the son of Abinoam
from Kedesh-naphtali, and said to him, "[a]Behold,
the LORD, the God of Israel, has commanded, 'Go
and march to Mount Tabor, and take with you ten

3:9 [A]Judg 1:13 3:10 [a]Heb *Aram* [b]Lit *his hand was strong* [A]Num 11:25-29; 24:2 3:12 [A]Judg 2:11 [B]Judg 2:14 3:13 [a]Lit *smote* [A]Deut 34:3; Judg 1:16 3:15 [a]Lit *his hand* [A]Ps 78:34 3:24 [a]Lit *covering his feet* [A]1 Sam 24:3 3:25 [a]Lit *were ashamed* [b]Lit *earth* 3:27 [A]Judg 6:34; 1 Sam 13:3 3:28 [A]Judg 7:24; 12:5 3:31 [A]Judg 5:6 4:1 [A]Judg 2:19 4:2 [A]Josh 11:1, 10 [B]Judg 4:13, 16 4:3 [A]Judg 1:19 4:4 [a]Lit *woman prophetess* 4:5 [a]Or *live* [A]Gen 35:8 4:6 [a]Or *Has not…commanded…?* [A]Heb 11:32

3:10 The Spirit of the LORD came. Certain judges were expressly said to have the Spirit of the Lord come upon them (6:34; 11:29; 13:25; 14:6, 19; 15:14); others apparently also had this experience. This is a common OT expression signifying a unique act of God which conferred power and wisdom for victory. But this did not guarantee that the will of God would be done in absolutely all details, as is apparent in Gideon (8:24–27, 30), Jephthah (11:34–40), and Samson (16:1).

3:20 "I have a message from God for you." Ehud claimed he came to do God's will in answer to prayer (v. 15). Calmly and confidently, Ehud acted and later credited the defeat of the wicked king to God (v. 28; cf. Ps 75:6, 7, 10; Da 4:25), though it was by means of Ehud, as Jael used her way (4:21) and Israel's armies used the sword (4:16). By God's power, Ehud's army would slay a greater number (v. 29). Men's evil provokes God's judgment (Lv 18:25).

3:24 "He is only relieving himself." The dead king's servants guessed he was indisposed in privacy, lit. "covering his feet," a euphemism for bathroom functions.

3:31 Shamgar. His extraordinary exploit causes one to think of Samson (15:16). **an oxgoad.** This was a stout stick about 8–10 ft. long and 6 in. around, with a sharp metal tip to prod or turn oxen. The other end was a flat, curved blade for cleaning a plow.

4:4 Deborah, a prophetess. She was an unusual woman of wisdom and influence who did the tasks of a judge, except for military leadership. God can use women mightily for civil, religious, or other tasks, e.g., Huldah the prophetess (2Ki 22:14), Philip's daughters in prophesying (Ac 21:8, 9), and Phoebe a deaconess (Ro 16:1). Deborah's rise to such a role is the exception in the book because of Barak's failure to show the courage to lead courageously (vv. 8, 14). God rebuked his cowardice by the pledge that a woman would slay Sisera (v. 9).

thousand men from the sons of Naphtali and from
the sons of Zebulun. 7 I will draw out to you Sisera,
the commander of Jabin's army, with his chariots
and his [a]many *troops* to the river Kishon, and [A]I will
give him into your hand.' " 8 Then Barak said to her,
"If you will go with me, then I will go; but if you
will not go with me, I will not go." 9 She said, "I will
surely go with you; nevertheless, the honor shall
not be yours on the journey that you are about to
take, [A]for the LORD will sell Sisera into the hands of
a woman." Then Deborah arose and went with Barak
to Kedesh. 10 Barak called [A]Zebulun and Naphtali
together to Kedesh, and ten thousand men went
up [a,B]with him; Deborah also went up with him.

11 Now Heber [A]the Kenite had separated himself from the Kenites, from the sons of Hobab the father-in-law of Moses, and had pitched his tent as far away as the [a]oak in [B]Zaanannim, which is near Kedesh.

12 Then they told Sisera that Barak the son of Abinoam had gone up to Mount Tabor. 13 Sisera called
together all his chariots, [A]nine hundred iron chariots, and all the people who *were* with him, from
[B]Harosheth-hagoyim to the river Kishon. 14 Deborah
said to Barak, "Arise! For this is the day in which
the LORD has given Sisera into your hands; [a]behold,
[A]the LORD has gone out before you." So Barak went
down from Mount Tabor with ten thousand men
following him. 15 [A]The LORD [a]routed Sisera and all
his chariots and all *his* army with the edge of the
sword before Barak; and Sisera alighted from *his*
chariot and fled away on foot. 16 But Barak pursued
the chariots and the army as far as Harosheth-ha-
goyim, and all the army of Sisera fell by the edge
of the sword; [A]not even one was left.

17 Now Sisera fled away on foot to the tent of Jael
the wife of Heber the Kenite, for *there was* peace
between Jabin the king of Hazor and the house of
Heber the Kenite. 18 Jael went out to meet Sisera,
and said to him, "Turn aside, my master, turn aside
to me! Do not be afraid." And he turned aside to
her into the tent, and she covered him with a [a]rug.
19 [A]He said to her, "Please give me a little water to
drink, for I am thirsty." So she opened a [a]bottle of
milk and gave him a drink; then she covered him.
20 He said to her, "Stand in the doorway of the tent,
and it shall be if anyone comes and inquires of you,
and says, 'Is there anyone here?' that you shall say,
'No.' " 21 But Jael, Heber's wife, [A]took a tent peg and
[a]seized a hammer in her hand, and went secretly to
him and drove the peg into his temple, and it went
through into the ground; for he was sound asleep
and exhausted. So he died. 22 And behold, as Barak
pursued Sisera, Jael came out to meet him and said
to him, "Come, and I will show you the man whom
you are seeking." And he entered [a]with her, and
behold Sisera was lying dead with the tent peg in
his temple.

23 So [A]God subdued on that day Jabin the king
of Canaan before the sons of Israel. 24 The hand of
the sons of Israel pressed heavier and heavier upon
Jabin the king of Canaan, until they had [a]destroyed
Jabin the king of Canaan.

THE SONG OF DEBORAH AND BARAK

5 [A]Then Deborah and Barak the son of Abinoam sang on that day, saying,

2 "[A]That [a]the leaders led in Israel,
That [B]the people volunteered,
Bless the LORD!
3 "Hear, O kings; give ear, O rulers!
[A]I—to the LORD, I will sing,
I will sing praise to the LORD,
the God of Israel.
4 "[A]LORD, when You went out from Seir,
When You marched from
the field of Edom,
[B]The earth quaked, the
heavens also dripped,
Even the clouds dripped water.
5 "[A]The mountains [a]quaked at the
presence of the LORD,
[B]This Sinai, at the presence of the
LORD, the God of Israel.

6 "In the days of [A]Shamgar the son of Anath,
In the days of [B]Jael, the highways
[a]were deserted,
And travelers [b]went by [c]roundabout ways.
7 "The peasantry ceased, they
ceased in Israel,
Until I, Deborah, arose,
Until I arose, a mother in Israel.
8 "[A]New gods were chosen;
Then war *was* in the gates.
Not a shield or a spear was seen
Among forty thousand in Israel.
9 "My heart *goes out* to [A]the
commanders of Israel,
The volunteers among the people;
Bless the LORD!

4:7 [a]Lit *multitude* [A]Ps 83:9 4:9 [A]Judg 4:21 4:10 [a]Lit *at his feet* [A]Judg 5:18 [B]Judg 4:14; 5:15 4:11 [a]Or *terebinth* [A]Judg 1:16 [B]Josh 19:33 4:13 [A]Judg 4:3 [B]Judg 4:2 4:14 [a]Or *has not the LORD gone...?* [A]Deut 9:3; 2 Sam 5:24; Ps 68:7 4:15 [a]Lit *confused* [A]Deut 7:23; Josh 10:10 4:16 [A]Ex 14:28; Ps 83:9 4:18 [a]Or *blanket* 4:19 [a]I.e. skin container [A]Judg 5:24-27 4:21 [a]Lit *placed* [A]Judg 5:26 4:22 [a]Lit *to* 4:23 [A]Neh 9:24; Ps 18:47 4:24 [a]Lit *cut off* 5:1 [A]Ex 15:1 5:2 [a]Or *locks hung loose in* [A]Judg 5:9 [B]Ps 110:3 5:3 [A]Ps 27:6 5:4 [A]Deut 33:2; Ps 68:7 [B]Ps 68:8, 9 5:5 [a]Lit *flowed* [A]Ex 19:18 [B]Ps 68:8 5:6 [a]Lit *had ceased* [b]Lit *walked* [c]Lit *twisted* [A]Judg 3:31 [B]Judg 4:17 5:8 [A]Deut 32:17 5:9 [A]Judg 5:2

4:11 Hobab the father-in-law of Moses. Nu 10:29 indicates that Reuel (elsewhere called Jethro, cf. Ex. 3:1) is Moses' father-in-law and Hobab is Reuel's son. Both "father-in-law" and "brother-in-law" have the same three consonants in Hebrew, and therefore, here would be better translated "Hobab the brother-in-law of Moses."

4:19, 20 she ... gave him a drink ... covered him. Usually, this was the strongest pledge of protection possible.

4:21 a tent peg and .... hammer. Jael's bold stroke in a tent rather than on a battlefield draws Deborah's and Barak's praise (5:24–27). Her strength and skill had no doubt been toughened by a common Bedouin duty of hammering down pegs to secure tents, or striking them loose to take down tents.

5:1 sang on that day. The song (vv. 1–31) was in tribute to God for victory in Jdg 4:13–24. Various songs praise God for His help, e.g., Moses' (Ex 15), David's (2Sa 23:1–7), and the Lamb's (Rev 15:3, 4).

10 “[A]You who ride on [a]white donkeys,
You who sit on *rich* carpets,
And you who travel on the road—[b]sing!
11 “At the sound of those who divide *flocks*
among [A]the watering places,
There they shall recount [B]the
righteous deeds of the LORD,
The righteous deeds for His
[a]peasantry in Israel.
Then the people of the LORD
went down [C]to the gates.

12 “[A]Awake, awake, Deborah;
Awake, awake, [a]sing a song!
Arise, Barak, and [B]take away your
captives, O son of Abinoam.
13 “Then survivors came down to the nobles;
The people of the LORD came
down to me as warriors.
14 “From Ephraim those whose root
is [A]in Amalek *came down,*
Following you, Benjamin,
with your peoples;
From Machir commanders came down,
And from Zebulun those who
wield the staff of [a]office.
15 “And the [a]princes of Issachar
were with Deborah;
As *was* Issachar, so *was* Barak;
Into the valley they rushed [A]at his [b]heels;
Among the divisions of Reuben
There were great resolves of heart.
16 “Why did you sit among [A]the [a]sheepfolds,
To hear the piping for the flocks?
Among the divisions of Reuben
There were great searchings of heart.
17 “[A]Gilead [a]remained across the Jordan;
And why did Dan stay in ships?
Asher sat at the seashore,
And [a]remained by its landings.
18 “[A]Zebulun *was* a people who despised
their lives *even* to death,
And Naphtali also, on the high
places of the field.

19 “[A]The kings came *and* fought;
Then fought the kings of Canaan
[B]At Taanach near the waters of Megiddo;
[C]They took no plunder in silver.
20 “[A]The stars fought from heaven,
From their courses they
fought against Sisera.
21 “The torrent of Kishon swept them away,
The ancient torrent, the torrent Kishon.
[A]O my soul, march on with strength.
22 “[A]Then the horses' hoofs beat
From the dashing, the dashing
of his [a]valiant steeds.
23 ‘Curse Meroz,’ said the angel of the LORD,
‘Utterly curse its inhabitants;
[A]Because they did not come to
the help of the LORD,
To the help of the LORD
against the warriors.’

24 “[A]Most blessed of women is Jael,
The wife of Heber the Kenite;
Most blessed is she of women in the tent.
25 “He asked for water *and* she
gave him milk;
In a magnificent bowl she
brought him curds.
26 “She reached out her hand for the tent peg,
And her right hand for the
workmen's hammer.
Then she struck Sisera, she
smashed his head;
And she shattered and pierced his temple.
27 “Between her feet he bowed, he fell, he lay;
Between her feet he bowed, he fell;
Where he bowed, there he fell [a]dead.

28 “Out of the window she looked
and lamented,
The mother of Sisera through the [a]lattice,
‘Why does his chariot delay in coming?
Why do the [b]hoofbeats of
his chariots tarry?’
29 “Her wise princesses would answer her,
Indeed she repeats her words to herself,
30 ‘[A]Are they not finding, are they
not dividing the spoil?
A maiden, two maidens
for every warrior;
To Sisera a spoil of dyed work,
A spoil of dyed work embroidered,
Dyed work of double embroidery
on the [a]neck of the spoiler?’

5:10 [a]Or *tawny* [b]Or *declare it* [A]Judg 10:4; 12:14 5:11 [a]Or *rural dwellers* [A]Gen 24:11; 29:2, 3 [B]1 Sam 12:7; Mic 6:5 [C]Judg 5:8 5:12 [a]Or *utter* [A]Ps 57:8 [B]Ps 68:18; Eph 4:8 5:14 [a]Lit *the scribe* [A]Judg 12:15 5:15 [a]So with ancient versions; Heb *My princes* [b]Lit *feet* [A]Judg 4:10 5:16 [a]Or *saddlebags* [A]Num 32:1, 2, 24, 36 5:17 [a]Or *dwelt* [A]Josh 22:9 5:18 [A]Judg 4:6, 10 5:19 [A]Josh 11:1-5; Judg 4:13 [B]Judg 1:27 [C]Judg 5:30 5:20 [A]Josh 10:12-14 5:21 [A]Ex 15:2; Ps 44:5 5:22 [a]Lit *mighty ones* [A]Job 39:19-25 5:23 [A]Judg 5:13 5:24 [A]Judg 4:19-21 5:27 [a]Lit *devastated* 5:28 [a]Or *window* [b]Lit *steps* 5:30 [a]Lit *necks of the spoil* [A]Ex 15:9

5:10 white donkeys. Because of this unusual color, they were a prize of kings and the rich.

5:11 At the sound of those who divide *flocks* among the watering places. The wells were at a little distance from towns in the E, away from the battles and often places for pleasant reflection.

5:14 root is in Amalek. Ephraim as a tribe took the central hill area, which the Amalekites had held with deep roots (cf. 12:15).

5:17 why did Dan stay in ships? Danites migrated from their territory to Laish N of the Lake of Chinneroth (Sea of Galilee) before the Israelite triumph of Jdg 4, though details of it are not given until Jdg 18. They became involved with Phoenicians of the NW in ship commerce (cf. Joppa as a coastal city, Jos 19:46). As with some other tribes, they failed to make the trek to assist in the battle of Jdg 4.

5:20 stars fought. A poetic way to say that God used these heavenly bodies to help Israel. They are bodies representing and synonymous with the heavens, the sky from which He sent a powerful storm and flood (cf. “torrent” of the Kishon River, v. 21) that swept Syrians from their chariots. God also hid the stars by clouds, increasing Syrian ineffectiveness.

5:24–27 Though this act was murder and a breach of honor, likely motivated by her desire for favor with the conquering Israelites, and though it was without regard for God on her part, God's overruling providence caused great blessing to flow from it. Thus the words of vv. 24–27 in the victory song.

31 "[A]Thus let all Your enemies perish, O LORD;
[B]But let those who love Him be like the
rising of the sun in its might."

And the land was undisturbed for forty years.

ISRAEL OPPRESSED BY MIDIAN

6 Then the sons of Israel [A]did what was evil in
the sight of the LORD; and the LORD gave them
into the hands of [B]Midian seven years. 2 The [a]power
of Midian prevailed against Israel. Because of Midian the sons of Israel made for themselves [A]the
dens which were in the mountains and the caves
and the strongholds. 3 For it was when Israel had
sown, that the Midianites would come up with the
Amalekites and the sons of the east and [a]go against
them. 4 So they would camp against them and [A]de-
stroy the produce of the earth [a]as far as Gaza, and
[B]leave no sustenance in Israel as well as no sheep,
ox, or donkey. 5 For they would come up with their
livestock and their tents, they would come in [A]like
locusts for number, both they and their camels were
innumerable; and they came into the land to devastate it. 6 So Israel was brought [A]very low because
of Midian, and the sons of Israel cried to the LORD.
7 Now it came about when the sons of Israel cried
to the LORD on account of Midian, 8 that the LORD
sent a prophet to the sons of Israel, and [A]he said to
them, "Thus says the LORD, the God of Israel, 'It was
I who brought you up from Egypt and brought you
out from the house of [a]slavery. 9 I delivered you from
the hands of the Egyptians and from the hands of
all your oppressors, and dispossessed them before
you and gave you their land, 10 and I said to you,
"I am the LORD your God; you [A]shall not fear the
gods of the Amorites in whose land you live. But
you have not [a]obeyed Me." ' "

GIDEON IS VISITED

11 Then [A]the angel of the LORD came and sat under the [a]oak that was in Ophrah, which belonged to
Joash the [B]Abiezrite as his son [C]Gideon was beating
out wheat in the wine press in order to save *it* from
the Midianites. 12 The angel of the LORD appeared to
him and said to him, "The LORD is with you, O valiant warrior." 13 Then Gideon said to him, "O my
lord, if the LORD is with us, why then has all this
happened to us? And where are all His miracles
which our fathers told us about, saying, 'Did not the
LORD bring us up from Egypt?' But [A]now the LORD
has abandoned us and given us into the hand of
Midian." 14 The LORD [a]looked at him and said, "[A]Go
in this your strength and deliver Israel from the
hand of Midian. Have I not sent you?" 15 [A]He said to
Him, "O Lord, [a]how shall I deliver Israel? Behold,
my family is the least in [B]Manasseh, and I am the
youngest in my father's house." 16 [A]But the LORD
said to him, "Surely I will be with you, and you shall
[a]defeat Midian as one man." 17 So [a]Gideon said to
Him, "If now I have found favor in Your sight, then
show me [A]a sign that it is You who speak with me.
18 Please do not depart from here, until I come *back*
to You, and bring out my offering and lay it before
You." And He said, "I will remain until you return."
19 Then Gideon went in and [A]prepared a young
goat and unleavened bread from an [a]ephah of flour;
he put the meat in a basket [b]and the broth in a pot,
and brought *them* out to him under the [c]oak and
presented *them*. 20 The angel of God said to him,
"Take the meat and the unleavened bread and lay
them on this rock, and pour out the broth." And he
did so. 21 Then the angel of the LORD put out the end
of the staff that was in his hand and touched the
meat and the unleavened bread; and [A]fire sprang
up from the rock and consumed the meat and the
unleavened bread. Then the angel of the LORD [a]van-
ished from his sight. 22 [A]When Gideon saw that he
was the angel of the LORD, [a]he said, "Alas, O Lord
[b]GOD! For now I have seen the angel of the LORD
face to face." 23 The LORD said to him, "Peace to
you, do not fear; you shall not die." 24 Then Gideon
built an altar there to the LORD and named it [a]The
LORD is Peace. To this day it is still [A]in Ophrah of
the Abiezrites.
25 Now on the same night the LORD said to him,
"Take your father's bull [a]and a second bull seven
years old, and pull down the altar of Baal which
belongs to your father, and cut down the [b,A]Asherah

5:31 [A]Ps 68:2; 92:9 [B]Ps 19:4-6; 89:36, 37 6:1 [A]Judg 2:11 [B]Num 22:4; 25:15-18; 31:1-3 6:2 [a]Lit *hand* [A]1 Sam 13:6; Heb 11:38 6:3 [a]Lit *go up* 6:4 [a]Lit *until your coming to* [A]Lev 26:16 [B]Deut 28:31 6:5 [A]Judg 7:12; 8:10 6:6 [A]Deut 28:43 6:8 [a]Lit *slaves* [A]Judg 2:1, 2 6:10 [a]Lit *listened to My voice* [A]2 Kin 17:35; Jer 10:2 6:11 [a]Or *terebinth* [A]Judg 2:1; 6:14; 13:3 [B]Josh 17:2; Judg 6:15 [C]Heb 11:32 6:13 [A]Judg 6:1; Ps 44:9 6:14 [a]Or *turned toward* [A]Heb 11:32-34 6:15 [a]Lit *with what* [A]Ex 3:11 [B]Judg 6:11 6:16 [a]Lit *smite* [A]Ex 3:12; Josh 1:5 6:17 [a]Lit *he* [A]Judg 6:37; Is 38:7, 8 6:19 [a]I.e. Approx one bu [b]Lit *and he put* [c]Or *terebinth* [A]Gen 18:6-8 6:21 [a]Or *departed* [A]Lev 9:24 6:22 [a]Lit *Gideon* [b]Heb *YHWH*, usually rendered *LORD* [A]Gen 32:30; Ex 33:20; Judg 13:21, 22 6:24 [a]Heb *Yahweh-shalom* [A]Judg 8:32 6:25 [a]Or *even* [b]I.e. wooden symbol of a female deity, also vv 26, 28, 30 [A]Ex 34:13

5:31 The intercessory prayer committed to God's will ends a song that has other aspects: blessing God (v. 2), praise (v. 3), affirming God's work in tribute (vv. 4, 20), and voicing God's curse (v. 23).

6:1 **Midian.** These wandering herdsmen from E of the Red Sea had been dealt a severe blow in Moses' time (Nu 31:1–18) and still resented the Israelites. They became the worst scourge yet to afflict Israel.

6:8 **the LORD sent a prophet.** He used prophets in isolated cases before Samuel, the band of prophets Samuel probably founded (1Sa 10:5), and later such prophets as Elijah, Elisha, and the writing prophets—major and minor. Here the prophet is sent to bring the divine curse because of their infidelity (v. 10).

6:11 **the angel.** This Angel (lit. "messenger") of the Lord is identified as "the LORD" Himself (vv. 14, 16, 23, 25, 27). Cf. Ge 16:7–14; 18:1; 32:24–30 for other appearances. *See note on Ex 3:2.* **Gideon was beating out wheat in the wine press . . . to save *it*.** This indicated a situation of serious distress; also it indicated a small amount of grain. This is clear because he is doing it rather than having cattle tread it. It is on bare ground or in the winepress rather than on a threshing floor made of wood, and is done remotely under a tree out of view. The fear of the Midianites caused this.

6:13 Gideon's language here indicates a weak theology. The very chastisements of God were proof of His care for and presence with Israel.

6:17 Like Moses (Ex 33), Gideon desired a sign; in both incidents revelation was so rare and wickedness so prevalent that they desired full assurance. God graciously gave it.

6:18–23 In the realization of the presence of God, the sensitive sinner is conscious of great guilt. Fire from God further filled Gideon with awe and even the fear of death. When he saw the Lord, he knew the Lord had also seen him in his fallenness. Thus he feared the death that sinners should die before Holy God. But God graciously promised life (v. 23). For a similar reaction to the presence of God, see Manoah in 13:22, 23 (cf. Eze 1:26–28; Is 6:1–9; Rev 1:17).

that is beside it; 26 and build an altar to the LORD your God on the top of this stronghold in an orderly manner, and take a second bull and offer a burnt offering with the wood of the Asherah which you shall cut down." 27 Then Gideon took ten men of his servants and did as the LORD had spoken to him; and because he was too afraid of his father's household and the men of the city to do it by day, he did it by night.

THE ALTAR OF BAAL DESTROYED

28 When the men of the city arose early in the morning, behold, the altar of Baal was torn down, and the Asherah which was beside it was cut down, and the second bull was offered on the altar which had been built. 29 They said to one another, "Who did this thing?" And when they searched about and inquired, they said, "Gideon the son of Joash did this thing." 30 Then the men of the city said to Joash, "Bring out your son, that he may die, for he has torn down the altar of Baal, and indeed, he has cut down the Asherah which was beside it." 31 But Joash said to all who stood against him, "Will you contend for Baal, or will you deliver him? Whoever will [a]plead for him shall be put to death by morning. If he is a god, let him contend for himself, because someone has torn down his altar." 32 Therefore on that day he named him [A]Jerubbaal, that is to say, "Let Baal contend against him," because he had torn down his altar.

33 Then all the Midianites and the Amalekites and the sons of the east assembled themselves; and they crossed over and camped in [A]the valley of Jezreel. 34 So [A]the Spirit of the LORD [a]came upon Gideon; and he [B]blew a trumpet, and the Abiezrites were called together to follow him. 35 He sent messengers throughout Manasseh, and they also were called together to follow him; and he sent messengers to Asher, [A]Zebulun, and Naphtali, and [B]they came up to meet them.

SIGN OF THE FLEECE

36 Then Gideon said to God, "[A]If You will deliver Israel [a]through me, as You have spoken, 37 behold, I will put a fleece of wool on the threshing floor. If there is dew on the fleece only, and it is dry on all the ground, then I will know that You will deliver Israel [a]through me, as You have spoken." 38 And it was so. When he arose early the next morning and squeezed the fleece, he drained the dew from the fleece, a bowl full of water. 39 Then Gideon said to God, "[A]Do not let Your anger burn against me that I may speak once more; please let me make a test once more with the fleece, let it now be dry only on the fleece, and let there be dew on all the ground." 40 God did so that night; for it was dry only on the fleece, and dew was on all the ground.

GIDEON'S 300 CHOSEN MEN

7 Then [A]Jerubbaal (that is, Gideon) and all the people who were with him, rose early and camped beside [a]the spring of Harod; and the camp of Midian was on the north side of [b]them by the hill of [B]Moreh in the valley.

2 The LORD said to Gideon, "The people who are with you are too many for Me to give Midian into their hands, [A]for Israel [a]would become boastful, saying, 'My own [b]power has delivered me.' 3 Now therefore [a]come, proclaim in the hearing of the people, saying, '[A]Whoever is afraid and trembling, let him return and depart from Mount Gilead.' " So 22,000 people returned, but 10,000 remained.

4 [A]Then the LORD said to Gideon, "The people are still too many; bring them down to the water and I will test them for you there. Therefore it shall be that he of whom I say to you, 'This one shall go with you,' he shall go with you; but everyone of whom I say to you, 'This one shall not go with you,' he shall not go." 5 So he brought the people down to the water. And the LORD said to Gideon, "You shall separate everyone who laps the water with his tongue as a dog laps, as well as everyone who kneels to drink." 6 Now the number of those who lapped, putting their hand to their mouth, was 300 men; but all the rest of the people kneeled to drink water. 7 The LORD said to Gideon, "I will deliver you [A]with the 300 men who lapped and will give the Midianites into your hands; so let all the *other* people go, each man to his [a]home." 8 So [a]the 300 men took the people's provisions and their trumpets into their hands. And [b]Gideon sent all the *other* men of Israel, each to his tent, but retained the 300 men; and the camp of Midian was below him in the valley.

9 Now the same night it came about that the LORD said to him, "Arise, go down against the camp, [A]for I

6:31 [a]Or *contend* 6:32 [A]Judg 7:1 6:33 [A]Josh 17:16 6:34 [a]Lit *clothed* [A]Judg 3:10 [B]Judg 3:27 6:35 [A]Judg 4:6, 10; 5:18 [B]Judg 7:3 6:36 [a]Lit *by my hand* [A]Judg 6:14, 16, 17 6:37 [a]Lit *by my hand* 6:39 [A]Gen 18:32 7:1 [a]Or *En-Harod* [b]Lit *him* [A]Judg 6:32 [B]Gen 12:6; Deut 11:30 7:2 [a]Lit *glorify itself against me* [b]Lit *hand* [A]Deut 8:17, 18 7:3 [a]Or *please* [A]Deut 20:8 7:4 [A]1 Sam 14:6 7:7 [a]Lit *place* [A]1 Sam 14:6 7:8 [a]Lit *they* [b]Lit *he* 7:9 [A]Josh 2:24; 10:8; 11:6

6:27 was . . . afraid. Very real human fear and wise precaution interplay with trust in an all-sufficient God.

6:32 Jerubbaal (lit. "let Baal contend") became a fitting and honorable second name for Gideon (7:1; 8:29; 9:1, 2). This was a bold rebuke to the nonexistent deity, who was utterly unable to respond.

6:36–40 Gideon's two requests for signs in the fleece should be viewed as weak faith; even Gideon recognized this when he said, "Do not let Your anger burn against me" (v. 39) since God had already specifically promised His presence and victory (vv. 12, 14, 16). But they were also legitimate requests for confirmation of victory against seemingly impossible odds (6:5; 7:2, 12). God nowhere reprimanded Gideon, but was very compassionate in giving what his inadequacy requested. In 7:10–15, God volunteered a sign to boost Gideon's faith. He should have believed God's promise in 7:9 but needed bolstering, so God graciously gave it without chastisement.

7:2 The people . . . are too many. Those of faith, though inadequate by human weakness, gain victory only through God's power (cf. 2Co 3:5; 4:7; 12:7–9). Three hundred men win against an incredible Midianite host (Jdg 7:7, 16–25). God gains the glory by making the outcome conspicuously His act, and no sinful pride is cultivated.

7:5 everyone who laps. Soldiers who lapped as a dog, scooping water with their hands as a dog uses its tongue, were chosen; while those who sank to their knees to drink were rejected. No reason for such distinction is given, so that it showed nothing about their ability as soldiers. It was merely a way to divide the crowd. Their abilities as soldiers had no bearing on the victory anyway since the enemy soldiers killed themselves and fled without engaging Gideon's men at all.

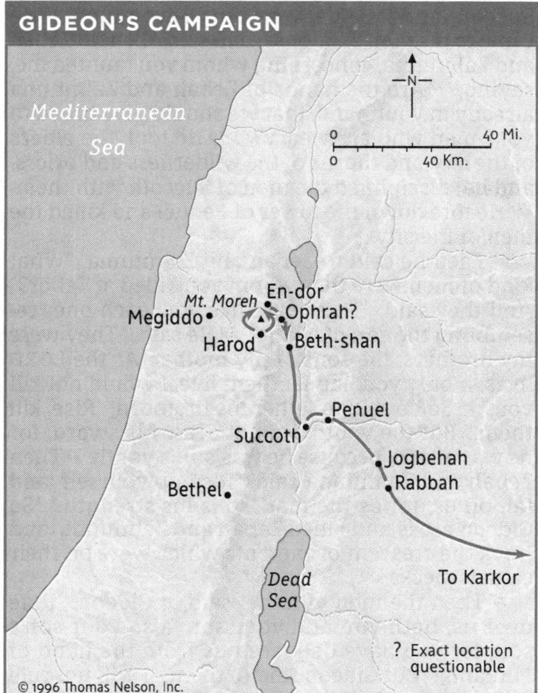

With a force of 300 Israelites, Gideon attacked the Midianites and Amalekites near Mt. Moreh. While in pursuit, he requested aid for his forces from Succoth and Penuel, but was denied. Nevertheless, Gideon's army was able to capture the remaining Midianite kings in Karkor.

have given it into your hands. 10 But if you are afraid to go down, go with Purah your servant down to the camp, 11 and you will hear what they say; and [A]afterward your hands will be strengthened that you may go down against the camp." So he went with Purah his servant down to the [a]outposts of the army that was in the camp. 12 Now the Midianites and the Amalekites and all the sons of the east were lying in the valley [A]as numerous as locusts; and their camels were without number, [B]as numerous as the sand on the seashore. 13 When Gideon came, behold, a man was relating a dream to his friend. And he said, "Behold, I [a]had a dream; [b]a loaf of barley bread was tumbling into the camp of Midian, and it came to the tent and struck it so that it fell, and turned it [c]upside down so that the tent lay flat." 14 His friend replied, "This is nothing less than the sword of Gideon the son of Joash, a man of Israel; God has given Midian and all the camp [A]into his hand."

15 When Gideon heard the account of the dream and its interpretation, he bowed in worship. He returned to the camp of Israel and said, "Arise, for the LORD has given the camp of Midian into your hands." 16 He divided the 300 men into three [a]companies, and he put trumpets and empty pitchers into the hands of all of them, with torches inside the pitchers. 17 He said to them, "Look at me and do likewise. And behold, when I come to the outskirts of the camp, [a]do as I do. 18 When I and all who are with me blow the trumpet, then you also blow the trumpets all around the camp and say, 'For the LORD and for Gideon.' "

CONFUSION OF THE ENEMY

19 So Gideon and the hundred men who were with him came to the outskirts of the camp at the beginning of the middle watch, when they had just posted the watch; and they blew the trumpets and smashed the pitchers that were in their hands. 20 When the three [a]companies blew the trumpets and broke the pitchers, they held the torches in their left hands and the trumpets in their right hands for blowing, and cried, "A sword for the LORD and for Gideon!" 21 Each stood in his place around the camp; and [A]all the [a]army ran, crying out as they fled. 22 When they blew 300 trumpets, the [A]LORD set the sword of one against another even throughout the whole [a]army; and the [a]army fled as far as Beth-shittah toward Zererah, as far as the edge of [B]Abel-meholah, by Tabbath. 23 The men of Israel were summoned from [A]Naphtali and Asher and all Manasseh, and they pursued Midian.

24 Gideon sent messengers throughout all the hill country of Ephraim, saying, "Come down [a]against Midian and [A]take the waters before them, as far as Beth-barah and the Jordan." So all the men of Ephraim were summoned and they took the waters as far as Beth-barah and the Jordan. 25 They captured the two leaders of Midian, [A]Oreb and Zeeb, and they killed Oreb at the rock of Oreb, and they killed Zeeb at the wine press of Zeeb, while they pursued Midian; and they brought the heads of Oreb and Zeeb to Gideon [B]from across the Jordan.

7:11 [a]Lit *extremity of the battle array* [A]Judg 7:15; 1 Sam 14:9, 10 7:12 [A]Judg 6:5; 8:10 [B]Josh 11:4 7:13 [a]Lit *dreamed* [b]Lit *and behold, a loaf* [c]Lit *upwards* 7:14 [A]Josh 2:9 7:16 [a]Lit *heads* 7:17 [a]Lit *it shall come about that just as I do, so you shall do* 7:20 [a]Lit *heads* 7:21 [a]Or *camp* [A]2 Kin 7:7 7:22 [a]Or *camp* [A]1 Sam 14:20 [B]1 Kin 4:12; 19:16 7:23 [A]Judg 6:35 7:24 [a]Lit *to meet* [A]Judg 3:28 7:25 [A]Ps 83:11; Is 10:26 [B]Judg 8:4

7:10 if you are afraid. God sensitively recognized Gideon's normal fear since he was the commander. God encouraged him to take his servant as protection. *See note on 6:36–40.*

7:15 Arise. God said this in 7:9. Infused with courage, Gideon is in step with the Lord.

7:16 Trumpets and torches at first concealed within clay pitchers were suddenly displayed at the most startling moment. The impression caused by blaring noise, the always terrible shouts of Israel (cf. Nu 23:21), and sudden lights surrounding the sleeping hosts and shattering the stillness conveyed one idea: Each light could mean a legion behind it, so that they believed an incredible host had moved in to catch the awaking army in a death trap.

7:19 beginning ... middle watch. About 10 p.m.

7:20 A sword for the LORD and for Gideon! Here was the power of God in harmony with the obedience of man. Such shouts reminded the enemies that the threat of the sword of Gideon and of God was for real. The impression was one of doom and terror.

7:22 the sword of one against another. Panic followed shock. Every soldier was on his own, in desperate retreat. In the darkness and crash of sounds the soldiers were unable to distinguish friend from enemy, and with their swords they slashed a path of escape through their own men.

ZEBAH AND ZALMUNNA ROUTED

8 Then the men of Ephraim said to him, "[A]What
is this thing you have done to us, not calling us
when you went to fight against Midian?" And they
contended with him vigorously. 2 But he said to
them, "What have I done now in comparison with
you? Is not the gleaning *of the grapes* of Ephraim
better than the vintage of Abiezer? 3 God has given
the leaders of Midian, Oreb and Zeeb into your
hands; and what was I able to do in comparison
with you?" Then their [a]anger toward him subsided
when he said [b]that.

4 Then Gideon and the 300 men who were with
him came [A]to the Jordan *and* crossed over, weary
yet pursuing. 5 He said to the men of [A]Succoth,
"Please give loaves of bread to the people who are
following me, for they are weary, and I am pursuing Zebah and Zalmunna, the kings of Midian."
6 The leaders of Succoth said, "[a,A]Are the hands of
Zebah and Zalmunna already in your hands, that
we should give bread to your army?" 7 Gideon said,
"[a]All right, [A]when the LORD has given Zebah and
Zalmunna into my hand, then I will [b]thrash your
[c]bodies with the thorns of the wilderness and with
briers." 8 He went up from there to [a,A]Penuel and
spoke similarly to them; and the men of Penuel
answered him just as the men of Succoth had answered. 9 So he spoke also to the men of Penuel,
saying, "When I return safely, [A]I will tear down
this tower."

10 Now Zebah and Zalmunna were in Karkor, and
their [a]armies with them, about 15,000 men, all who
were left of the entire [b]army of the sons of the east;
[A]for the fallen were 120,000 [c]swordsmen. 11 Gideon
went up by the way of those who lived in tents on
the east of Nobah and Jogbehah, and [a]attacked the
camp when the camp was [b]unsuspecting. 12 When
Zebah and Zalmunna fled, he pursued them and
captured the two kings of Midian, Zebah and Zalmunna, and routed the whole [a]army.

13 Then Gideon the son of Joash returned from
the battle [a]by the ascent of Heres. 14 And he captured a youth [a]from Succoth and questioned him.
Then *the youth* wrote down for him the princes of
Succoth and its elders, seventy-seven men. 15 He
came to the men of Succoth and said, "Behold Zebah
and Zalmunna, concerning whom you taunted me,
saying, '[a,A]Are the hands of Zebah and Zalmunna
already in your hand, that we should give bread to
your men who are weary?' " 16 He took the elders
of the city, and thorns of the wilderness and briers,
and he [a]disciplined the men of Succoth with them.
17 [A]He tore down the tower of Penuel and killed the
men of the city.

18 Then he said to Zebah and Zalmunna, "What
kind of men *were* they whom you killed at Tabor?"
And they said, "They were like you, each one [a]re-
sembling the son of a king." 19 He said, "They *were*
my brothers, the sons of my mother. *As* the LORD
lives, if only you had let them live, I would not kill
you." 20 So he said to Jether his firstborn, "Rise, kill
them." But the youth did not draw his sword, for
he was afraid, because he was still a youth. 21 Then
Zebah and Zalmunna said, "Rise up yourself, and
fall on us; for as the man, so is his strength." [A]So
Gideon arose and killed Zebah and Zalmunna, and
[B]took the crescent ornaments which were on their
camels' necks.

22 Then the men of Israel said to Gideon, "Rule
over us, both you and your son, also your son's
son, for you have delivered us from the hand of
Midian." 23 But Gideon said to them, "I will not rule
over you, nor shall my son rule over you; [A]the LORD
shall rule over you." 24 Yet Gideon said to them, "I
would [a]request of you, that each of you give me [b]an
earring from his spoil." (For they had gold earrings,
because they were [A]Ishmaelites.) 25 They said, "We
will surely give *them*." So they spread out a garment,
and every one of them threw an earring there from
his spoil. 26 The weight of the gold earrings that
he requested was 1,700 *shekels* of gold, besides the
crescent ornaments and the pendants and the purple robes which *were* on the kings of Midian, and
besides the neck bands that *were* on their camels'
necks. 27 Gideon made it into [A]an ephod, and placed
it in his city, Ophrah, and all Israel played the harlot
with it there, so that it became a snare to Gideon
and his household.

8:1 [A]Judg 12:1 8:3 [a]Lit *spirit* [b]Lit *this thing* 8:4 [A]Judg 7:25 8:5 [A]Gen 33:17 8:6 [a]Lit *Is the palm* [A]Judg 8:15 8:7 [a]Lit *For thus* [b]Or *trample* [c]Lit *flesh* [A]Judg 7:15 8:8 [a]In Gen 32:30, *Peniel* [A]Gen 32:31 8:9 [A]Judg 8:17 8:10 [a]Or *camps* [b]Or *camp* [c]Lit *men who drew sword* [A]Judg 6:5; 7:12; Is 9:4 8:11 [a]Lit *smote* [b]Or *secure* 8:12 [a]Or *camp* 8:13 [a]Or *from* 8:14 [a]Lit *of the men of* 8:15 [a]Lit *Is the palm* [A]Judg 8:6 8:16 [a]Lit *made the men...to know* 8:17 [A]Judg 8:9 8:18 [a]Lit *like the form of the sons* 8:21 [A]Ps 83:11 [B]Judg 8:26 8:23 [A]1 Sam 8:7; 10:19; 12:12; Ps 10:16 8:24 [a]Lit *request a request* [b]Or *a nose ring* [A]Gen 25:13-16 8:27 [A]Ex 28:6-35; Judg 17:5; 18:14-20

8:2 gleaning *of the grapes* of Ephraim. Ephraim resented being slighted in the call to battle but was placated by Gideon's compliment. His figures of speech implied that Ephraimite capital punishment of the two fleeing Midianite leaders (7:25) was "the vintage of Ephraim," to use an image drawn from their grape horticulture. It played a more strategic role than taking part in "the vintage of Abiezer," the suicide of the enemy under Gideon's leadership (cf. v. 3).

8:7 thorns. Gideon's threatened discipline of Succoth's leaders for refusing to help their brothers came due. He had them dragged under heavy weights over thorns and briers, which painfully tore their bodies. This was a cruel torture to which ancient captives were often subjected. He did it on his return, not wanting to delay the pursuit (v. 16).

8:9 tower. They probably had defiantly boasted of their strength and defensibility because of the tower. He kept his promise and more (v. 17).

8:20 Jether ... kill them. Gideon desired to place a great honor on his son by killing the enemies of Israel and of God.

8:21 killed Zebah and Zalmunna. The earlier Midianite scourge inflicted on Israel was the worst, so this victory lived long in their minds (cf. Ps 83:11).

8:22, 23 Rule over us. Israelites sinned by the misguided motive and request that Gideon reign as king. To his credit, the leader declined, insisting that God alone rule (cf. Ex 19:5, 6).

8:24 Ishmaelites. Synonymous with Midianites (cf. Ge 37:25, 28).

8:24–27 Gideon made ... an ephod. This was certainly a sad end to Gideon's influence as he, perhaps in an expression of pride, sought to lift himself up in the eyes of the people. Gideon intended nothing more than to make a breastpiece as David did (1Ch 15:27) to indicate civil, not priestly rule. It was never intended to set up idolatrous worship, but to be a symbol of civil power. That no evil was intended can be noted from the subduing of Midian (v. 28), quietness from wars (v. 28), and the fact that idolatry came after Gideon's death (v. 33) as well as the commendation of Gideon (v. 35).

8:26 The weight of the gold. The total was about 42 lbs.

FORTY YEARS OF PEACE

28 So Midian was subdued before the sons of Israel, and they did not lift up their heads anymore.
And the land was undisturbed for forty years in
the days of Gideon.

29 Then [A]Jerubbaal the son of Joash went and
lived in his own house. 30 Now Gideon had [A]seventy
sons who [a]were his direct descendants, for he had
many wives. 31 His concubine who was in Shechem
also bore him a son, and he [a]named him Abimelech.
32 And Gideon the son of Joash died at a ripe old age
and was buried in the tomb of his father Joash, in
Ophrah of the Abiezrites.

33 Then it came about, as soon as Gideon was dead,
[A]that the sons of Israel again played the harlot with
the Baals, and made [B]Baal-berith their god. 34 Thus the
sons of Israel [A]did not remember the LORD their God,
who had delivered them from the hands of all their
enemies on every side; 35 [A]nor did they show kindness to the household of Jerubbaal (*that is,* Gideon)
in accord with all the good that he had done to Israel.

ABIMELECH'S CONSPIRACY

9 And [A]Abimelech the son of Jerubbaal went to
Shechem to his mother's [a]relatives, and spoke
to them and to the whole clan of the household of
his mother's father, saying, 2 "Speak, now, in the
hearing of all the leaders of Shechem, 'Which is
better for you, that [A]seventy men, all the sons of
Jerubbaal, rule over you, or that one man rule over
you?' Also, remember that I am [B]your bone and
your flesh." 3 And his mother's [a]relatives spoke all
these words on his behalf in the hearing of all the
leaders of Shechem; and [b]they were inclined to follow Abimelech, for they said, "He is [A]our [c]relative."
4 They gave him seventy *pieces* of silver from the
house of [A]Baal-berith with which Abimelech hired
worthless and reckless fellows, and they followed
him. 5 Then he went to his father's house at Ophrah
and [A]killed his brothers the sons of Jerubbaal, [B]sev-
enty men, on one stone. But Jotham the youngest
son of Jerubbaal was left, for he hid himself. 6 All
the men of Shechem and all [a]Beth-millo assembled
together, and they went and made Abimelech king,
by the [b]oak of the pillar which was in Shechem.

7 Now when they told Jotham, he went and stood
on the top of [A]Mount Gerizim, and lifted his voice and
called out. Thus he said to them, "Listen to me, O men
of Shechem, that God may listen to you. 8 Once the
trees went forth to anoint a king over them, and they
said to the olive tree, 'Reign over us!' 9 But the olive
tree said to them, 'Shall I leave my fatness with [a]which
God and men are honored, and go to wave over the
trees?' 10 Then the trees said to the fig tree, 'You come,
reign over us!' 11 But the fig tree said to them, 'Shall
I leave my sweetness and my good [a]fruit, and go to
wave over the trees?' 12 Then the trees said to the vine,
'You come, reign over us!' 13 But the vine said to them,
'Shall I leave my new wine, which cheers God and
men, and go to wave over the trees?' 14 Finally all the
trees said to the bramble, 'You come, reign over us!'
15 The bramble said to the trees, 'If in [a]truth you are
anointing me as king over you, come and take refuge in my shade; but if not, may fire come out from
the bramble and consume the cedars of Lebanon.'

16 "Now therefore, if you have dealt in [a]truth and
integrity in making Abimelech king, and if you have
dealt well with [A]Jerubbaal and his house, and [b]have
dealt with him [c]as he deserved— 17 for my father
fought for you and [a]risked his life and delivered
you from the hand of Midian; 18 but you have risen
against my father's house today and have killed [A]his
sons, seventy men, on one stone, and have made
Abimelech, [B]the son of his maidservant, king over
the men of Shechem, because he is your [a]relative—
19 if then you have dealt in [a]truth and integrity with
Jerubbaal and his house this day, rejoice in Abimelech, and let him also rejoice in you. 20 But if not,
let fire come out from Abimelech and consume the
men of Shechem and [a]Beth-millo; and let fire come
out from the men of Shechem and from [a]Beth-millo,
and consume Abimelech." 21 Then Jotham escaped
and fled, and went to Beer and remained there because of Abimelech his brother.

SHECHEM AND ABIMELECH FALL

22 Now Abimelech ruled over Israel three years.
23 [A]Then God sent an evil spirit between Abimelech
and the men of Shechem; and the men of Shechem
[B]dealt treacherously with Abimelech, 24 [A]so that
the violence [a]done to the seventy sons of Jerubbaal might come, and [B]their blood might be laid on
Abimelech their brother, who killed them, and on
the men of Shechem, who strengthened his hands to
kill his brothers. 25 The men of Shechem set [a]men in
ambush against him on the tops of the mountains,
and they robbed all who might pass by them along
the road; and it was told to Abimelech.

26 Now Gaal the son of Ebed came with his [a]rela-
tives, and crossed over into Shechem; and the men

8:29 [A]Judg 7:1 8:30 [a]Lit *came from his loins* [A]Judg 9:2, 5 8:31 [a]Lit *appointed his name* 8:33 [A]Judg 2:11, 12 [B]Judg 9:4, 27, 46 8:34 [A]Deut 4:9; Judg 3:7 8:35 [A]Judg 9:16-18 9:1 [a]Lit *brothers* [A]Judg 8:31, 35 9:2 [A]Judg 8:30; 9:5, 18 [B]Gen 29:14 9:3 [a]Lit *brothers* [b]Lit *their hearts inclined after* [c]Lit *brother* [A]Gen 29:15 9:4 [A]Judg 8:33 9:5 [A]2 Kin 11:1, 2 [B]Judg 8:30; 9:2, 18 9:6 [a]Or *the house of Millo* [b]Or *terebinth* 9:7 [A]Deut 11:29, 30 9:9 [a]Lit *which by me* 9:11 [a]Or *produce* 9:15 [a]Or *sincerity* 9:16 [a]Or *sincerity* [b]Lit *if you have* [c]Lit *according to the dealing of his hands* [A]Judg 8:35 9:17 [a]Lit *cast his soul in front* 9:18 [a]Lit *brother* [A]Judg 8:30; 9:2, 5 [B]Judg 8:31 9:19 [a]Or *sincerity* 9:20 [a]Or *the house of Millo* 9:23 [A]1 Sam 16:14; Is 19:2, 14 [B]Is 33:1 9:24 [a]Lit *of the seventy* [A]Deut 27:25; Judg 9:56, 57 [B]Num 35:33 9:25 [a]Lit *liers-in-wait for* 9:26 [a]Lit *brothers*

8:30, 31 many wives. Gideon fell severely into the sin of polygamy, an iniquity tolerated by many but which never was God's blueprint for marriage (Ge 2:24). Abimelech, a son by yet another illicit relationship, grew up to be the wretched king in Jdg 9. Polygamy always resulted in trouble.

9:5 killed . . . brothers. This atrocity, common in ancient times, eliminated the greatest threat in the revolution—all the legitimate competitors.

9:6 Beth-millo. Lit. "house of the fortress." This was a section of Shechem, probably involving the tower stronghold of v. 46.

9:14 You come, reign over us! In Jotham's parable of trees asking for a king (vv. 7–15), the olive, fig, and vine decline. They do not represent specific men who declined; rather, they build the suspense and heighten the idea that the bramble (thornbush) is inferior and unsuitable. The bush represents Abimelech (vv. 6, 16).

9:23 God sent an evil spirit. In the course of God's providence, there appeared jealousy, distrust, and hate. God allowed it to work as punishment for the idolatry and mass murder.

9:26–45 A failed coup.

of Shechem put their trust in him. 27 They went out into the field and gathered *the grapes of* their vineyards and trod *them,* and held a [a]festival; and they went into the house of [A]their god, and ate and drank and cursed Abimelech. 28 Then Gaal the son of Ebed said, "Who is Abimelech, and who is Shechem, that we should serve him? Is he not the son of Jerubbaal, and *is* Zebul *not* his [a]lieutenant? Serve the men of [A]Hamor the father of Shechem; but why should we serve him? 29 [a,A]Would, therefore, that this people were under my authority! Then I would remove Abimelech." And he said to Abimelech, "Increase your army and come out."

30 When Zebul the ruler of the city heard the words of Gaal the son of Ebed, his anger burned. 31 He sent messengers to Abimelech [a]deceitfully, saying, "Behold, Gaal the son of Ebed and his [b]relatives have come to Shechem; and behold, they are [c]stirring up the city against you. 32 Now therefore, arise by night, you and the people who are with you, and lie in wait in the field. 33 In the morning, as soon as the sun is up, you shall rise early and rush upon the city; and behold, when he and the people who are with him come out against you, you shall [A]do to them [a]whatever you can."

34 So Abimelech and all the people who *were* with him arose by night and lay in wait against Shechem in four [a]companies. 35 Now Gaal the son of Ebed went out and stood in the entrance of the city gate; and Abimelech and the people who *were* with him arose from the ambush. 36 When Gaal saw the people, he said to Zebul, "[a]Look, people are coming down from the tops of the mountains." But Zebul said to him, "You are seeing the shadow of the mountains as *if they were* men." 37 Gaal spoke again and said, "Behold, people are coming down from [A]the [a]highest part of the land, and one [b]company comes by the way of [c]the diviners' [d]oak." 38 Then Zebul said to him, "Where is your [a]boasting now with which you said, 'Who is Abimelech that we should serve him?' Is this not the people whom you despised? Go out now and fight with them!" 39 So Gaal went out before the leaders of Shechem and fought with Abimelech. 40 Abimelech chased him, and he fled before him; and many fell wounded up to the entrance of the gate. 41 Then Abimelech remained at Arumah, but Zebul drove out Gaal and his [a]relatives so that they could not remain in Shechem.

42 Now it came about the next day, that the people went out to the field, and it was told to Abimelech. 43 So he took [a]his people and divided them into three [b]companies, and lay in wait in the field; when he looked and [c]saw the people coming out from the city, he arose against them and [d]slew them. 44 Then Abimelech and the [a]company who was with him dashed forward and stood in the entrance of the city gate; the other two [b]companies then dashed against all who *were* in the field and [c]slew them. 45 Abimelech fought against the city all that day, and he captured the city and killed the people who *were* in it; then he [A]razed the city and sowed it with salt.

46 When all the leaders of the tower of Shechem heard of *it,* they entered the inner chamber of the [a]temple of [A]El-berith. 47 It was told Abimelech that all the leaders of the tower of Shechem were gathered together. 48 So Abimelech went up to Mount [A]Zalmon, he and all the people who *were* with him; and Abimelech took [a]an axe in his hand and cut down a branch from the trees, and lifted it and laid *it* on his shoulder. Then he said to the people who *were* with him, "What you have seen me do, hurry *and* do [b]likewise." 49 All the people also cut down each one his branch and followed Abimelech, and put *them* on the inner chamber and set the inner chamber on fire over those *inside,* so that all the men of the tower of Shechem also died, about a thousand men and women.

50 Then Abimelech went to Thebez, and he camped against Thebez and captured it. 51 But there was a strong tower in the center of the city, and all the men and women with all the leaders of the city fled there and shut themselves in; and they went up on the roof of the tower. 52 So Abimelech came to the tower and fought against it, and approached the entrance of the tower to burn it with fire. 53 But [A]a certain woman threw an upper millstone on Abimelech's head, crushing his skull. 54 Then [A]he called quickly to the young man, his armor bearer, and said to him, "Draw your sword and kill me, so that it will not be said of me, 'A woman slew him.'" So [a]the young man pierced him through, and he died. 55 When the men of Israel saw that Abimelech was dead, each departed to his [a]home. 56 Thus [A]God repaid the wickedness of Abimelech, which he had done to his father in killing his seventy brothers. 57 Also God returned all the wickedness of the men of Shechem on their heads, and the curse of Jotham the son of Jerubbaal came [a]upon them.

OPPRESSION OF PHILISTINES AND AMMONITES

10 Now after Abimelech died, Tola the son of Puah, the son of Dodo, a man of Issachar, [A]arose to save Israel; and he lived in Shamir in the hill country of Ephraim. 2 He judged Israel twenty-three years. Then he died and was buried in Shamir.

3 After him, Jair the Gileadite arose and judged Israel twenty-two years. 4 He had thirty sons who

9:27 [a]Lit *rejoicing* [A]Judg 8:33; 9:46 9:28 [a]Lit *overseer* [A]Gen 34:2 9:29 [a]Lit *And who will give this people into my hand* [A]2 Sam 15:4 9:31 [a]Or *in Tormah* [b]Lit *brothers* [c]Lit *besieging* 9:33 [a]Lit *as your hand can find* [A]1 Sam 10:7 9:34 [a]Lit *heads* 9:36 [a]Lit *Behold* 9:37 [a]Or *center* [b]Lit *head* [c]Heb *Elommeonenim* [d]Or *terebinth* [A]Ezek 38:12 9:38 [a]Lit *mouth* 9:41 [a]Lit *brothers* 9:43 [a]Lit *the* [b]Lit *heads* [c]Lit *behold* [d]Lit *smote* 9:44 [a]Singular with Gr; Heb plural, *heads* [b]Lit *heads* [c]Lit *smote* 9:45 [A]2 Kin 3:25 9:46 [a]Lit *house* [A]Judg 8:33 9:48 [a]Lit *the axes* [b]Lit *like me* [A]Ps 68:14 9:53 [A]2 Sam 11:21 9:54 [a]Lit *his* [A]1 Sam 31:4 9:55 [a]Lit *place* 9:56 [A]Gen 9:5, 6; Ps 94:23 9:57 [a]Lit *to* 10:1 [A]Judg 2:16

9:37 diviners' oak. A tree regarded superstitiously where mystical ceremonies and soothsaying were done.

9:45 sowed it with salt. An act polluting soil and water, as well as symbolizing a verdict of permanent barrenness (Dt 29:23; Jer 17:6). Abimelech's intent finally was nullified when Jeroboam I rebuilt the city as his capital (1Ki 12:25), ca. 930–910 B.C.

9:57 That curse was pronounced in 9:20 for the pervasive idolatry.

10:3–5 Most likely, the judgeship of Jair

rode on thirty donkeys, and they had thirty cities [a]in the land of Gilead [A]that are called [b]Havvoth-jair to this day. 5 And Jair died and was buried in Kamon.

6 Then the sons of Israel again did evil in the sight of the LORD, [A]served the Baals and the Ashtaroth, the gods of Aram, the gods of Sidon, the gods of Moab, [B]the gods of the sons of Ammon, and the gods of the Philistines; thus [C]they forsook the LORD and did not serve Him. 7 The anger of the LORD burned against Israel, and He [A]sold them into the hands of the Philistines and into the hands of the sons of Ammon. 8 They [a]afflicted and crushed the sons of Israel [b]that year; for eighteen years they *afflicted* all the sons of Israel who were beyond the Jordan [c]in Gilead in the land of the Amorites. 9 The sons of Ammon crossed the Jordan to fight also against Judah, Benjamin, and the house of Ephraim, so that Israel was greatly distressed.

10 Then the [A]sons of Israel cried out to the LORD, saying, "We have sinned against You, for indeed, we have forsaken our God and served the Baals." 11 The LORD said to the sons of Israel, "*Did I* not *deliver you* [A]from the Egyptians, [B]the Amorites, [C]the sons of Ammon, and the Philistines? 12 Also when the Sidonians, the Amalekites and the Maonites [A]oppressed you, you cried out to Me, and I delivered you from their hands. 13 Yet [A]you have forsaken Me and served other gods; therefore I will no longer deliver you. 14 [A]Go and cry out to the gods which you have chosen; let them deliver you in the time of your distress." 15 The sons of Israel said to the LORD, "We have sinned, [A]do to us whatever seems good to You; only please deliver us this day." 16 [A]So they put away the foreign gods from among them and served the LORD; and [a,B]He could bear the misery of Israel no longer.

17 Then the sons of Ammon were summoned and they camped in Gilead. And the sons of Israel gathered together and camped in [A]Mizpah. 18 The people, the leaders of Gilead, said to one another, "Who is the man who will begin to fight against the sons of Ammon? He shall become head over all the inhabitants of Gilead."

JEPHTHAH THE NINTH JUDGE

11 Now [A]Jephthah the Gileadite was a [a]valiant warrior, but he was the son of a harlot. And Gilead [b]was the father of Jephthah. 2 Gilead's wife bore him sons; and when his wife's sons grew up, they drove Jephthah out and said to him, "You shall not have an inheritance in our father's house, for you are the son of another woman." 3 So Jephthah fled from his brothers and lived in the land of [A]Tob; and worthless fellows gathered themselves [a]about Jephthah, and they went out with him.

4 It came about after a while that [A]the sons of Ammon fought against Israel. 5 When the sons of Ammon fought against Israel, the elders of Gilead went to get Jephthah from the land of Tob; 6 and they said to Jephthah, "Come and be our chief that we may fight against the sons of Ammon." 7 Then Jephthah said to the elders of Gilead, "[A]Did you not hate me and drive me from my father's house? So why have you come to me now when you are in trouble?" 8 The elders of Gilead said to Jephthah, "For this reason we have now returned to you, that you may go with us and fight with the sons of Ammon and [A]become head over all the inhabitants of Gilead." 9 So Jephthah said to the elders of Gilead, "If you take me back to fight against the sons of Ammon and the LORD gives them up [a]to me, will I become your head?" 10 The elders of Gilead said to Jephthah, "[A]The LORD is [a]witness between us; surely we will do [b]as you have said." 11 Then Jephthah went with the elders of Gilead, and the people made him head and chief over them; and Jephthah spoke all his words before the LORD at [A]Mizpah.

12 Now Jephthah sent messengers to the king of the sons of Ammon, saying, "What is between you and me, that you have come to me to fight against my land?" 13 The king of the sons of Ammon said to the messengers of Jephthah, "Because Israel [A]took away my land when they came up from Egypt, from the Arnon as far as the [B]Jabbok and the Jordan; therefore, return them peaceably now." 14 But Jephthah sent messengers again to the king of the sons of Ammon, 15 and they said to him, "Thus says Jephthah, 'Israel did not take away the land of Moab nor the land of the sons of Ammon. 16 For when they came up from

10:4 [a]Lit *which are in* [b]I.e. the towns of Jair [A]Num 32:41 10:6 [A]Judg 2:13 [B]Judg 11:24 [C]Deut 31:16, 17; 32:15 10:7 [A]1 Sam 12:9 10:8 [a]Lit *shattered* [b]Lit *in that* [c]Lit *which is in* 10:10 [A]1 Sam 12:10 10:11 [A]Judg 2:12 [B]Num 21:21-25 [C]Judg 3:13 10:12 [A]Ps 106:42 10:13 [A]Jer 2:13 10:14 [A]Deut 32:37 10:15 [A]1 Sam 3:18 10:16 [a]Lit *His soul was short with the misery* [A]Josh 24:23 [B]Deut 32:36 10:17 [A]Judg 11:29 11:1 [a]Or *mighty man of valor* [b]Lit *begat* [A]Heb 11:32 11:3 [a]Lit *to* [A]2 Sam 10:6, 8 11:4 [A]Judg 10:9, 17 11:7 [A]Gen 26:27 11:8 [A]Judg 10:18 11:9 [a]Lit *before* 11:10 [a]Lit *hearer* [b]Lit *according to your word* [A]Gen 31:50; Jer 29:23; 42:5; Mic 1:2 11:11 [A]Judg 10:17; 11:29; 20:1; 1 Sam 10:17 11:13 [A]Num 21:24 [B]Gen 32:22

was the time period of Ruth.

10:10 **We have sinned.** Confession is followed by true repentance (vv. 15, 16).

10:13, 14 Here is the form of God's wrath, by which He abandons persistent, willful sinners to the consequences of their sins. This aspect of divine judgment is referred to in the case of Samson (16:20), as well as the warnings of Pr 1:20–31 and Ro 1:24–28. It is a pattern of rejection seen throughout history (cf. Ac 14:15, 16) even among the Jews (cf. Hos 4:17; Mt 15:14).

10:15 **do to us whatever seems good.** Genuine repentance acknowledges God's right to chasten, so His punishment is seen as just and He is thereby glorified. It also seeks the remediation that chastening brings, because genuine contrition pursues holiness.

11:1 **valiant warrior.** In a military situation, this means a strong, adept warrior, such as Gideon (6:12). In response to their repentance, God raised up Jephthah to lead the Israelites to freedom from the 18 years of oppression (v. 8).

11:3 **went out.** Such attacks would be against the Ammonites and other pagan peoples and brought fame to Jephthah.

11:11 **spoke … before the LORD.** Refers to confirming the agreement in a solemn public meeting with prayer invoking God as witness (v. 10).

11:13 **Israel took away my land.** The Ammonite ruler was claiming rights to the lands occupied by the Israelites. Jephthah's answer was direct: 1) those lands were not in the possession of Ammonites when Israel took them, but were Amorite lands; 2) Israel had been there 300 years in undisputed possession; 3) God had chosen to give them the lands, and thus they were entitled to them, just as the Ammonites felt they received their lands from their god (cf. v. 24).

11:15 **Israel did not take away the land.** These people initiated the hostility, and being at fault, invited loss of possession (vv. 16–22). This fit perfectly the will of God, who has ultimate rights (cf. Ge 1:1; Ps 24:1) to give the land to Israel.

Egypt, and Israel [A]went through the wilderness to
the [a]Red Sea and [B]came to Kadesh, 17 then Israel [A]sent
messengers to the king of Edom, saying, "Please let
us pass through your land," but the king of Edom
would not listen. [B]And they also sent to the king of
Moab, but he would not consent. So Israel remained
at Kadesh. 18 Then they went through the wilderness
and [A]around the land of Edom and the land of Moab,
and came to the east side of the land of Moab, and
they camped beyond the Arnon; but they [B]did not
enter the territory of Moab, for the Arnon *was* the
border of Moab. 19 And Israel sent [A]messengers to
Sihon king of the Amorites, the king of Heshbon, and
Israel said to him, "Please let us pass through your
land to our place." 20 But Sihon did not trust Israel to
pass through his territory; so Sihon gathered all his
people and camped in Jahaz and fought with Israel.
21 The LORD, the God of Israel, gave Sihon and all his
people into the hand of Israel, and they [a][A]defeated
them; so Israel possessed all the land of the Amorites,
the inhabitants of that country. 22 [A]So they possessed
all the territory of the Amorites, from the Arnon as
far as the Jabbok, and from the wilderness as far as
the Jordan. 23 Since now the LORD, the God of Israel,
drove out the Amorites from before His people Israel,
are you then to possess it? 24 Do you not possess what
[A]Chemosh your god gives you to possess? So whatever
the LORD our God has driven out before us, we will
possess it. 25 Now are you any better than [A]Balak the
son of Zippor, king of Moab? Did he ever strive with
Israel, or did he ever fight against them? 26 [A]While
Israel lived in Heshbon and its villages, and in Aroer
and its villages, and in all the cities that are on the
banks of the Arnon, three hundred years, why did you
not recover them within that time? 27 I therefore have
not sinned against you, but you are doing me wrong
by making war against me; [A]may the LORD, the Judge,
judge today between the sons of Israel and the sons
of Ammon.' " 28 But the king of the sons of Ammon
[a]disregarded the message which Jephthah sent him.

JEPHTHAH'S TRAGIC VOW

29 Now [A]the Spirit of the LORD came upon Jephthah, so that he passed through Gilead and Manasseh; then he passed through Mizpah of Gilead, and
from Mizpah of Gilead he went on to the sons of
Ammon. 30 Jephthah made a vow to the LORD and
said, "If You will indeed give the sons of Ammon into
my hand, 31 then it shall be that whatever comes out

THE GEOGRAPHY OF THE JUDGES

? Exact location questionable
Elon Name of Judge

Shamgar, Elon, Gideon, Jair, Tola, Abdon, Jephthah, Deborah, Ehud, Samson, Ibzan, Othniel

Mediterranean Sea; ASHER; NAPHTALI; MANASSEH; ZEBULUN; Kedesh Naphtali?; ISSACHAR; Ophrah?; Camon; Jordan River; MANASSEH; Shamir; Zaphon; Pirathon; GAD; Shiloh; EPHRAIM; DAN; BENJAMIN; Ashdod; Zorah; Bethlehem; Ashkelon; JUDAH; REUBEN; Hebron; Debir?; Gaza; Dead Sea; SIMEON

0 20 Mi.
0 20 Km.

© 1996 Thomas Nelson, Inc.

The Book of Judges lists a total of 12 judges (Barak served as a military leader under the judgeship of Deborah and was not technically a judge himself) who served in a variety of roles during a three-century era. While some of them are major figures about whom much is known, others are only minor figures, mentioned briefly without a geographical or tribal affiliation. The significance of the era of the judges is that no one tribe or region seemed to dominate in producing these leaders. God called and equipped the necessary persons from throughout the land to lead Israel during this turbulent period.

11:16 [a]Lit *Sea of Reeds* [A]Num 14:25; Deut 1:40 [B]Num 20:1, 4-21 11:17 [A]Num 20:14-21 [B]Josh 24:9 11:18 [A]Num 21:4; Deut 2:8 [B]Deut 2:9, 18, 19 11:19 [A]Num 21:21-32; Deut 2:26-36 11:21 [a]Lit *smote* [A]Num 21:24; Deut 2:32-34 11:22 [A]Deut 2:36, 37 11:24 [A]Num 21:29; 1 Kin 11:7 11:25 [A]Num 22:2; Josh 24:9; Mic 6:5 11:26 [A]Num 21:25, 26; Deut 2:36 11:27 [A]Gen 16:5; 18:25; 31:53; 1 Sam 24:12, 15 11:28 [a]Lit *did not listen to the words* 11:29 [A]Judg 3:10

11:26 three hundred years. With an early Exodus from Egypt (ca. 1445 B.C.), one can approximate the 480 years covered in Judges to 1Ki 6:1, Solomon's fourth year 967/966 B.C.: 38 from the Exodus to Heshbon; 300 from Heshbon to Jephthah in 11:26; possibly 7 more years for Jephthah; 40 for Samson, 20 for Eli, 20 for Samuel, 15–16 beyond Samuel for Saul, 40 for David, and 4 for Solomon, which totals about 480 years. It is quite possible that 300 has been rounded off.

11:29 the Spirit ... came upon Jephthah. That the Lord graciously empowered Jephthah for war on behalf of his people does not mean that all of the warrior's decisions were of God's wisdom. The rash vow (vv. 30, 31) is an example.

11:30 made a vow to the LORD. This was a custom among generals to promise the god of their worship something of great value as a reward for that god's giving them victory.

11:31 I will offer it. Some interpreters reason that Jephthah offered his daughter as a living sacrifice in perpetual virginity. With this idea, v. 31 is made to mean "shall be the LORD's" or "I will offer it up as a burnt offering." The view sees only perpetual virginity in vv. 37–40, and rejects his offering a human sacrifice as being against God's revealed will (Dt 12:31). On the other hand, since he was 1) beyond the Jordan, 2) far from the tabernacle, 3) a hypocrite in religious devotion, 4) familiar with human sacrifice among other nations, 5) influenced by such superstition, and 6) wanting victory badly, he likely meant a burnt offering. The translation in v. 31 is "and," not "or." His act came in an era of bizarre things, even inconsistency by leaders whom God otherwise empowered (cf. Gideon in 8:27).

of the doors of my house to meet me when I return in peace from the sons of Ammon, it shall be the LORD'S, and I will offer it up as a burnt offering." 32 So Jephthah crossed over to the sons of Ammon to fight against them; and the LORD gave them into his hand. 33 He struck them with a very great slaughter from Aroer [a]to the entrance of [A]Minnith, twenty cities, and as far as Abel-keramim. So the sons of Ammon were subdued before the sons of Israel.

34 When Jephthah came to his house at [A]Mizpah, behold, his daughter was coming out to meet him [B]with tambourines and with dancing. Now she was his one *and* only child; besides her he had no son or daughter. 35 When he saw her, he tore his clothes and said, "Alas, my daughter! You have brought me very low, and you are among those who trouble me; for I have [a]given my word to the LORD, and [A]I cannot take *it* back." 36 So she said to him, "My father, you have [a]given your word to the LORD; [A]do to me [b]as you have said, since the LORD has avenged you of your enemies, the sons of Ammon." 37 She said to her father, "Let this thing be done for me; let me alone two months, that I may [a]go to the mountains and weep because of [A]my virginity, I and my companions." 38 Then he said, "Go." So he sent her away for two months; and she left with her companions, and wept on the mountains because of her virginity. 39 At the end of two months she returned to her father, who did to her according to the vow which he had made; and she [a]had no relations with a man. Thus it became a custom in Israel, 40 that the daughters of Israel went yearly to [a]commemorate the daughter of Jephthah the Gileadite four days in the year.

JEPHTHAH AND HIS SUCCESSORS

12 Then the men of Ephraim were summoned, and they crossed [a]to Zaphon and [A]said to Jephthah, "Why did you cross over to fight against the sons of Ammon without calling us to go with you? We will burn your house down on you." 2 Jephthah said to them, "I and my people were at great strife with the sons of Ammon; when I called you, you did not deliver me from their hand. 3 When I saw that you would not deliver *me,* I [a,A]took my life in my hands and crossed over against the sons of Ammon, and the LORD gave them into my hand. Why then have you come up to me this day to fight against me?" 4 Then Jephthah gathered all the men of Gilead and fought Ephraim; and the men of Gilead [a]defeated Ephraim, because they said, "You are fugitives of Ephraim, O Gileadites, in the midst of Ephraim *and* in the midst of Manasseh." 5 The Gileadites [A]captured the fords of the Jordan opposite Ephraim. And it happened when *any of* the fugitives of Ephraim said, "Let me cross over," the men of Gilead would say to him, "Are you an Ephraimite?" If he said, "No," 6 then they would say to him, "Say now, 'Shibboleth.' " But he said, "Sibboleth," for he could not [a]pronounce it correctly. Then they seized him and slew him at the fords of the Jordan. Thus there fell at that time 42,000 of Ephraim.

7 Jephthah judged Israel six years. Then Jephthah the Gileadite died and was buried in *one of* the cities of Gilead.

8 Now Ibzan of Bethlehem judged Israel after him. 9 He had thirty sons, and thirty daughters *whom* he [a]gave in marriage outside *the family,* and he brought in thirty daughters from outside for his sons. And he judged Israel seven years. 10 Then Ibzan died and was buried in Bethlehem.

11 Now Elon the Zebulunite judged Israel after him; and he judged Israel ten years. 12 Then Elon the Zebulunite died and was buried at Aijalon in the land of Zebulun.

13 Now Abdon the son of Hillel the Pirathonite judged Israel after him. 14 He had forty sons and thirty grandsons who rode on seventy donkeys; and he judged Israel eight years. 15 Then Abdon the son of Hillel the Pirathonite died and was buried at Pirathon in the land of Ephraim, in the hill country of the Amalekites.

PHILISTINES OPPRESS AGAIN

13 Now the sons of Israel [A]again did evil in the sight of the LORD, so that the LORD gave them into the hands of the Philistines forty years.

2 There was a certain man of [A]Zorah, of the family of the Danites, whose name was Manoah; and his wife was barren and had borne no *children.* 3 [A]Then the angel of the LORD appeared to the woman and said to her, "Behold now, you are barren and have borne no *children,* but you shall conceive and give birth to a son. 4 Now therefore, be careful [A]not to drink wine or strong drink, nor eat any unclean thing. 5 [A]For behold, you shall conceive and give

11:33 [a]Lit *even until you are coming to* [A]Ezek 27:17 11:34 [A]Judg 10:17; 11:11 [B]Ex 15:20; 1 Sam 18:6; Jer 31:4 11:35 [a]Lit *opened my mouth* [A]Num 30:2; Eccl 5:4, 5 11:36 [a]Lit *opened your mouth* [b]Lit *according to what has proceeded from your mouth* [A]Num 30:2 11:37 [a]Lit *go and go down on* [A]Gen 30:23; Luke 1:25 11:39 [a]Lit *knew no man* 11:40 [a]Lit *recount;* ancient versions, *lament* 12:1 [a]Or *northward* [A]Judg 8:1 12:3 [a]Lit *put my soul in my palm* [A]1 Sam 19:5; 28:21; Job 13:14 12:4 [a]Lit *smote* 12:5 [A]Judg 3:28 12:6 [a]Lit *speak so* 12:9 [a]Lit *sent outside* 13:1 [A]Judg 2:11 13:2 [A]Josh 19:41 13:3 [A]Judg 6:11, 14; 13:6, 8, 10, 11; Luke 1:11-13 13:4 [A]Num 6:2, 3; Luke 1:15 13:5 [A]Luke 1:15

11:34 his daughter was coming out to meet him. She was thus to be the sacrificed pledge.

11:35 Alas. Here is indicated the pain felt by her father in having to take the life of his only daughter to satisfy his pious but unwise pledge.

12:1 Why did you ... fight ... without calling us ...? Ephraim's newest threat (cf. 8:1) was their jealousy of Jephthah's success and possibly a lust to share in his spoils. The threat was not only to burn the house, but to burn him.

12:4 fugitives. Here was a mockery referring to the Gileadites as low lifes, the outcasts of Ephraim. They retaliated with battle.

12:6 Shibboleth. The method used for discovering an Ephraimite was the way in which they pronounced this word. If they mispronounced it by an "s" rather than "sh" sound, it gave them away, being a unique indicator of their dialect.

12:9 thirty sons. Very large families suggest the father's marriage to several wives, a part of life tolerated but never matching God's blueprint of one wife at a time (Ge 2:24). To have many children had the lure of extending one's human power and influence.

13:3 the angel of the LORD. In this case, it was a pre-incarnate appearance of the Lord Himself (vv. 6–22), as elsewhere (*see note on 6:11*). *See note on Ex 3:2.*

13:5 Nazirite. The word is from the Heb. "to separate." For rigid Nazirite restrictions, such as here in Samson's case, *see note on Nu 6:2.* God gave 2 restrictions: no wine (v. 4) and no razor cutting the hair (v. 5). An additional restriction for a Nazirite was not to touch a dead body (Nu 6:6). Such outward actions indicated an inner dedication to God.

birth to a son, and no razor shall come upon his
head, for the boy shall be a [B]Nazirite to God from the
womb; and he shall begin to deliver Israel from the
hands of the Philistines." 6 Then the woman came
and told her husband, saying, "[A]A man of God came
to me and his appearance was like the appearance
of the angel of God, very awesome. And I did not
ask him where he *came* from, nor did he tell me
his name. 7 But he said to me, 'Behold, you shall
conceive and give birth to a son, and now you shall
not drink wine or strong drink nor eat any unclean
thing, for the boy shall be a Nazirite to God from
the womb to the day of his death.' "

8 Then Manoah entreated the LORD and said,
"O Lord, please let [A]the man of God whom You have
sent come to us again that he may teach us what to
do for the boy who is to be born." 9 God listened to
the voice of Manoah; and [A]the angel of God came
again to the woman as she was sitting in the field,
but Manoah her husband was not with her. 10 So the
woman ran quickly and told her [a]husband, "Behold,
[A]the man who [b]came the *other* day has appeared to
me." 11 Then Manoah arose and followed his wife,
and when he came to the man he said to him, "Are
you [A]the man who spoke to the woman?" And he
said, "I am." 12 Manoah said, "Now when your words
come *to pass,* what shall be the boy's mode of life
and his vocation?" 13 So [A]the angel of the LORD said
to Manoah, "[B]Let the woman pay attention [a]to all
that I said. 14 She should not eat anything that comes
from the [A]vine nor drink wine or strong drink, nor
eat any unclean thing; let her observe all that I
commanded."

15 Then Manoah said to [A]the angel of the LORD,
"Please let us detain you so that we may prepare a
young goat for you." 16 The angel of the LORD said
to Manoah, "Though you detain me, [A]I will not eat
your [a]food, but if you prepare a burnt offering,
then offer it to the LORD." For Manoah did not know
that he was the angel of the LORD. 17 Manoah said
to the angel of the LORD, "[A]What is your name, so
that when your words come *to pass,* we may honor
you?" 18 But the angel of the LORD said to him, "Why
do you ask my name, seeing it is [a,A]wonderful?"
19 So [A]Manoah took the young goat with the grain
offering and offered it on the rock to the LORD, and
He performed wonders while Manoah and his wife
looked on. 20 For it came about when the flame went
up from the altar toward heaven, that the angel of
the LORD ascended in the flame of the altar. When
Manoah and his wife saw *this,* they [A]fell on their
faces to the ground.

21 Now the angel of the LORD did not appear to
Manoah or his wife again. [A]Then Manoah knew that
he was the angel of the LORD. 22 So Manoah said to
his wife, "[A]We will surely die, for we have seen God."
23 But his wife said to him, "If the LORD had desired
to kill us, He would not have accepted a burnt offering and a grain offering from our hands, nor would
He have [A]shown us all these things, nor would He
have let us hear *things* like this at this time."

24 Then the woman gave birth to a son and named
him Samson; and the [A]child grew up and the LORD
blessed him. 25 And [A]the Spirit of the LORD began
to stir him in [a,B]Mahaneh-dan, between Zorah and
Eshtaol.

SAMSON'S MARRIAGE

14 Then Samson went down to Timnah and saw
a woman in Timnah, *one* of the daughters of
the Philistines. 2 So he came [a]back and told his father
and [b]mother, "I saw a woman in Timnah, *one* of the
daughters of the Philistines; now therefore, get her
for me as a wife." 3 Then his father and his mother
said to him, "Is there no woman among the daughters of your [a,A]relatives, or among all [b]our people,
that you go to [B]take a wife from the uncircumcised
Philistines?" But Samson said to his father, "Get her
for me, for she [c]looks good to me." 4 However, his
father and mother did not know that [A]it was of the
LORD, for He was seeking an occasion against the
Philistines. Now at that time the Philistines were
ruling over Israel.

5 Then Samson went down to Timnah with his
father and mother, and came as far as the vineyards
of Timnah; and behold, a young lion *came* roaring
toward him. 6 [A]The Spirit of the LORD [a]came upon
him mightily, so that [B]he tore him as one tears a
young goat though he had nothing in his hand; but
he did not tell his father or mother what he had done.
7 So he went down and talked to the woman; and she
[a]looked good to Samson. 8 When he returned later to

13:5 [B]Num 6:2-5 13:6 [A]Judg 6:11; 13:8, 10, 11 13:8 [A]Judg 13:3, 7 13:9 [A]Judg 13:8 13:10 [a]Lit *husband, and said to him* [b]Lit *came to me* [A]Judg 13:9 13:11 [A]Judg 13:8 13:13 [a]Lit *from* [A]Judg 13:11 [B]Judg 13:4 13:14 [A]Num 6:4 13:15 [A]Judg 13:3 13:16 [a]Lit *bread* [A]Judg 6:20 13:17 [A]Gen 32:29 13:18 [a]I.e. incomprehensible [A]Is 9:6 13:19 [A]Judg 6:20, 21 13:20 [A]Lev 9:24; 1 Chr 21:16; Ezek 1:28; Matt 17:6 13:21 [A]Judg 13:16 13:22 [A]Gen 32:30; Deut 5:26; Judg 6:22 13:23 [A]Ps 25:14 13:24 [A]1 Sam 3:19; Luke 1:80 13:25 [a]I.e. the camp of Dan [A]Judg 3:10 [B]Judg 18:11, 12 14:2 [a]Lit *up* [b]Lit *mother, saying,* 14:3 [a]Lit *brothers* [b]Lit *my* [c]Lit *is right in my eyes* [A]Gen 24:3, 4 [B]Ex 34:16; Deut 7:3 14:4 [A]Josh 11:20 14:6 [a]Lit *rushed upon* [A]Judg 3:10 [B]1 Sam 17:34-36 14:7 [a]Lit *was right in Samson's eyes*

13:16 offer it to the LORD. Manoah needed this explanation because he was going to offer this to Him, not as the Lord Himself, or even an angel, but just a human messenger. The instruction is intended to emphasize that this visitor is indeed the Lord.

13:17 What is Your name … ? This secret name is again indicative that the Angel is the Lord.

13:18 Why do you ask My name … ? That the Angel would not divulge His name reminds one of the Angel (God) whom Jacob encountered (Ge 32:24–30), who likewise did not give His name.

13:20 flame went up … toward heaven. This miraculous act points to divine acceptance of the offering.

13:22 We will surely die. This reaction of the fear of death is familiar with those who come into God's presence. Many did die when facing God, as the OT records. It is the terror in the heart of the sinner when in the presence of holy God. Cf. Ezekiel (Eze 1:28), Isaiah (Is 6:5), the 12 (Mk 4:35–41), Peter (Lk 5:8), and John (Rev 1:17, 18).

14:1–4 she looks good to me. The Philistines were not among the 7 nations of Canaan which Israel was specifically forbidden to marry. Nonetheless Samson's choice was seriously weak. Samson sins here, but God is sovereign and was able to turn the situation to please Him (v. 14). He was not at a loss, but used the opportunity to work against the wicked Philistines and provided gracious help to His people. He achieved destruction of these people, not by an army, but by the miraculous power of one man.

14:7 talked. Such conversation was not acceptable in the E, unless a couple was betrothed.

14:8 to take her. Usually a year until the wedding.

take her, he turned aside to look at the carcass of the
lion; and behold, a swarm of bees and honey were in
the body of the lion. 9 So he scraped [a]the honey into
his [b]hands and went on, eating as he went. When
he came to his father and mother, he gave *some* to
them and they ate *it;* but he did not tell them that he
had scraped the honey out of the body of the lion.
10 Then his father went down to the woman; and
Samson made a feast there, for the young men
customarily did this. 11 When they saw him, they
brought thirty companions to be with him.

SAMSON'S RIDDLE

12 Then Samson said to them, "Let me now [A]pro-
pound a riddle to you; if you will indeed tell it to me
within the seven days of the feast, and find it out,
then I will give you thirty linen wraps and thirty
[B]changes of clothes. 13 But if you are unable to tell
me, then you shall give me thirty linen wraps and
thirty changes of clothes." And they said to him,
"Propound your riddle, that we may hear it." 14 So
he said to them,

"Out of the eater came something to eat,
And out of the strong came
something sweet."

But they could not tell the riddle in three days.
15 Then it came about on the [a]fourth day that they
said to Samson's wife, "[A]Entice your husband, so that
he will tell us the riddle, [B]or we will burn you and
your father's house with fire. Have you invited us
to impoverish us? Is this not *so?*" 16 Samson's wife
wept before him and said, "[A]You only hate me, and
you do not love me; you have propounded a riddle
to the sons of my people, and have not told *it* to
me." And he said to her, "Behold, I have not told
it to my father or mother; so should I tell you?"
17 However she wept before him seven days while
their feast lasted. And on the seventh day he told
her because she pressed him so hard. She then told
the riddle to the sons of her people. 18 So the men
of the city said to him on the seventh day before
the sun went down,

"What is sweeter than honey?
And what is stronger than a lion?"

And he said to them,

"If you had not plowed with my heifer,
You would not have found out my riddle."

19 Then [A]the Spirit of the LORD [a]came upon him
mightily, and he went down to Ashkelon and killed
thirty of them and took their spoil and gave the
changes *of clothes* to those who told the riddle. And
his anger burned, and he went up to his father's
house. 20 But Samson's wife was [A]*given* to his companion who had been his [a]friend.

SAMSON BURNS PHILISTINE CROPS

15 But after a while, in the time of wheat harvest,
Samson visited his wife [A]with a young goat,
and said, "I will go in to my wife in *her* room." But
her father did not let him enter. 2 Her father said,
"I really thought that you hated her intensely; so I
[A]gave her to your companion. Is not her younger
sister [a]more beautiful than she? Please let her be
yours [b]instead." 3 Samson then said to them, "This
time I shall be blameless in regard to the Philistines
when I do them harm." 4 Samson went and caught
three hundred foxes, and took torches, and turned
the foxes tail to tail and put one torch in the middle between two tails. 5 When he had set fire to the
torches, he released [a]the foxes into the standing
grain of the Philistines, thus burning up both the
shocks and the standing grain, along with the vineyards *and* groves. 6 Then the Philistines said, "Who
did this?" And they said, "Samson, the son-in-law of
the Timnite, because [a]he took his wife and gave her
to his companion." So the Philistines came up and
[A]burned her and her father with fire. 7 Samson said
to them, "Since you act like this, I will surely take
revenge on you, but after that I will quit." 8 He struck
them [a]ruthlessly with a great slaughter; and he
went down and lived in the cleft of the rock of Etam.
9 Then the Philistines went up and camped in
Judah, and spread out in Lehi. 10 The men of Judah

14:9 [a]Lit *it* [b]Lit *palms* 14:12 [A]Ezek 17:2 [B]Gen 45:22; 2 Kin 5:22 14:15 [a]So with some ancient versions; Heb *seventh* [A]Judg 16:5 [B]Judg 15:6 14:16 [A]Judg 16:15 14:19 [a]Lit *rushed upon* [A]Judg 3:10; 13:25 14:20 [a]Or *best man* [A]Judg 15:2 15:1 [A]Gen 38:17 15:2 [a]Lit *better* [b]Lit *instead of her* [A]Judg 14:20 15:5 [a]Lit *them* 15:6 [a]I.e. the Timnite [A]Judg 14:15 15:8 [a]Lit *leg on thigh*

14:9 he scraped the honey into his hands. Some scholars suggest that Samson violated his Nazirite standard by coming in contact with a dead body (*see note on 13:5*). Others reason that Nu 6 specifies the body of a person, not an animal. Whether or not he sinned here, the context does show instances of him sinning.

14:10 feast. The wedding feast usually lasted a week.

14:16–18 Samson's wife wept. She cheated and manipulated, working against Samson's expectations that the men must come up with the answer. The men also cheated and threatened, having murder in their hearts (v. 15) and putting pressure on the woman.

14:19 his anger. God blesses the one who had been wronged. Samson's anger may be legitimate—righteous indignation against deceit (cf. Mk 3:5). The battle with the men at Ashkelon, about 23 mi. away, was a part of the war between Israel and Philistia.

14:20 Samson's wife was *given*. Another act of treachery was done. The Philistine father had no reason to assume that Samson would not be back, nor had Samson given word about not returning. He, as a Philistine, did not want his daughter marrying the enemy.

15:1 wheat harvest. Samson tactfully made his move when wheat harvest kept men busy. This was probably around May. A token of reconciliation was offered as he brought a young goat, showing the father and the daughter that they had nothing to fear.

15:2 I . . . thought. This flimsy excuse by the father was an effort to escape the trap he was in. He feared the Philistines if he turned on the new husband, yet feared Samson, so he offered his second daughter as a way out. This was insulting and unlawful (cf. Lv 18:18).

15:3 The cycle of retaliation began, and it ends in 16:30, 31.

15:4 caught three hundred foxes. Samson, insulted and provoked to fleshly resentment, took vengeance on the Philistines. It must have taken a while to catch so many foxes or jackals and to keep them penned and fed until the number reached 300. Apparently he tied them in pairs with a slow-burning torch, sending the pairs down the hills into fields thrashing with fire, igniting all the standing grain so dry at harvest. This was a loss of great proportion to the Philistine farmers.

15:6 the Philistines . . . burned her and her father. The general principle of reaping what is sown is apropos here (cf. Gal 6:7).

said, "Why have you come up against us?" And they
said, "We have come up to bind Samson in order
to do to him as he did to us." 11Then 3,000 men of
Judah went down to the cleft of the rock of Etam
and said to Samson, "Do you not know [A]that the
Philistines are rulers over us? What then is this
that you have done to us?" And he said to them,
"As they did to me, so I have done to them." 12They
said to him, "We have come down to bind you so
that we may give you into the hands of the Philistines." And Samson said to them, "Swear to me that
you will not [a]kill me." 13So they said to [a]him, "No,
but we will bind you fast and give you into their
hands; yet surely we will not kill you." Then they
bound him with two new ropes and brought him
up from the rock.

14When he came to Lehi, the Philistines shouted
as they met him. And [A]the Spirit of the LORD [a]came
upon him mightily so that the ropes that were on
his arms were as flax that is burned with fire, and
his bonds [b]dropped from his hands. 15He found a
fresh jawbone of a donkey, so he [a]reached out and
took it and [b]killed [A]a thousand men with it. 16Then
Samson said,

"With the jawbone of a donkey,
[a]Heaps upon heaps,
With the jawbone of a donkey
I have [b]killed a thousand men."

17When he had finished speaking, he threw the
jawbone from his hand; and he named that place
[a]Ramath-lehi. 18Then he became very thirsty, and
he [A]called to the LORD and said, "You have given
this great deliverance by the hand of Your servant,
and now [a]shall I die of thirst [b]and fall into the hands
of the uncircumcised?" 19But God split the hollow
place that is in Lehi so that water came out of it.
When he drank, [A]his [a]strength returned and he revived. Therefore he named it [b]En-hakkore, which is
in Lehi to this day. 20So [A]he judged Israel twenty
years in [B]the days of the Philistines.

SAMSON'S WEAKNESS

16 Now Samson went to [A]Gaza and saw a harlot
there, and went in to her. 2*When it was told* to
the Gazites, saying, "Samson has come here," they
[A]surrounded *the place* and lay in wait for him all
night at the gate of the city. And they kept silent all
night, saying, "*Let us wait* until the morning light,
then we will kill him." 3Now Samson lay until midnight, and at midnight he arose and took hold of the
doors of the city gate and the two posts and pulled
them up along with the bars; then he put them on
his shoulders and carried them up to the top of the
mountain which is opposite Hebron.

4After this it came about that he loved a woman
in the valley of Sorek, whose name was Delilah. 5The
[A]lords of the Philistines came up to her and said to
her, "[B]Entice him, and see where his great strength
lies and [a]how we may overpower him that we may
bind him to afflict him. Then we will each give you
eleven hundred *pieces* of silver." 6So Delilah said to
Samson, "Please tell me where your great strength
is and [a]how you may be bound to afflict you." 7Sam-
son said to her, "If they bind me with seven fresh
cords that have not been dried, then I will become
weak and be like any *other* man." 8Then the lords
of the Philistines brought up to her seven fresh
cords that had not been dried, and she bound him
with them. 9Now she had *men* lying in wait in an
inner room. And she said to him, "The Philistines
are upon you, Samson!" But he snapped the cords
as a string of tow snaps when it [a]touches fire. So
his strength was not discovered.

10Then Delilah said to Samson, "Behold, you have
deceived me and told me lies; now please tell me
[a]how you may be bound." 11He said to her, "If they
bind me tightly with new ropes [a]which have not
been used, then I will become weak and be like any
other man." 12So Delilah took new ropes and bound
him with them and said to him, "The Philistines are
upon you, Samson!" For the *men* were lying in wait
in the inner room. But he snapped [a]the ropes from
his arms like a thread.

13Then Delilah said to Samson, "Up to now you
have deceived me and told me lies; tell me [a]how you
may be bound." And he said to her, "If you weave the
seven locks of my [b]hair with the web [c][and fasten
it with a pin, then I will become weak and be like
any other man." 14So while he slept, Delilah took
the seven locks of his [a]hair and wove them into the
web]. And she fastened *it* with the pin and said to
him, "The Philistines are upon you, Samson!" But
he awoke from his sleep and pulled out the pin of
the loom and the web.

15:11 [A]Lev 26:25; Deut 28:43f; Judg 13:1; 14:4; Ps 106:40-42 15:12 [a]Lit *fall upon me yourselves* 15:13 [a]Lit *him, saying* 15:14 [a]Lit *rushed upon* [b]Lit *were melted* [A]Judg 14:19; 1 Sam 11:6 15:15 [a]Lit *stretched out his hand* [b]Lit *smote* [A]Lev 26:8; Josh 23:10 15:16 [a]Lit *Heap, two heaps;* Heb is same root as donkey [b]Lit *smitten* 15:17 [a]I.e. the high place of the jawbone 15:18 [a]Or *I shall…uncircumcised* [b]Or *or* [A]Judg 16:28 15:19 [a]Lit *spirit* [b]I.e. the spring of him who called [A]Is 40:29 15:20 [A]Judg 16:31; Heb 11:32 [B]Judg 13:1 16:1 [A]Josh 15:47 16:2 [A]1 Sam 23:26; Ps 118:10-12 16:5 [a]Lit *by what* [A]Josh 13:3 [B]Judg 14:15 16:6 [a]Lit *by what* 16:9 [a]Lit *smells* 16:10 [a]Lit *by what* 16:11 [a]Lit *with which work has not been done* 16:12 [a]Lit *them* 16:13 [a]Lit *by what* [b]Lit *head* [c]The passage in brackets is found in Gr but not in any Heb mss 16:14 [a]Lit *head*

15:15 killed a thousand men. Cf. 3:31. God gave miraculous power to Samson for destruction, but also to show fearful Israelites (v. 11) that He was with them, despite their lack of trust.

15:19 water came out. God worked a miracle of supplying a spring in response to Samson's prayerful cry in thirst. He called the place "the spring of him that called" (cf. Jer 33:3).

16:1–3 God was merciful in allowing Samson to be delivered from this iniquity, but chastening was only postponed. Sin blinds and later grinds (v. 21).

16:3 mountain … opposite Hebron. This place was about 38 mi. from Gaza.

16:4 loved … Delilah. His weakness for women of low character and Philistine loyalty reappeared (cf. Pr 6:27, 28). He erred continually by going to her daily (v. 16), allowing himself to be entrapped in her deceptions.

16:5 eleven hundred *pieces* of silver. Since there were 5 rulers of the Philistines, each giving that amount, this was a large sum.

16:7 Samson said. Samson played a lying game and gave away his manhood, here a little, there a little. He also played with giving away his secret—and finally gave it up, i.e., "told her all" (v. 17). He could be bought for a price, and Delilah paid it. Compare Esau selling his birthright (Ge 25:29–33) and Judas denying Jesus (Mt 26:14–16).

16:11 new ropes. Cf. 15:13.

DELILAH EXTRACTS HIS SECRET

15 Then she said to him, "[A]How can you say, 'I
love you,' when your heart is not with me? You
have deceived me these three times and have
not told me where your great strength is." 16 It
came about when she pressed him daily with her
words and urged him, that his soul was [a]annoyed
to death. 17 So he told her all *that was* in his heart
and said to her, "A razor has never come on my
head, for I have been a [A]Nazirite to God from my
mother's womb. If I am shaved, then my strength
will leave me and I will become weak and be like
any *other* man."

18 When Delilah saw that he had told her all *that
was* in his heart, she sent and called the lords of
the Philistines, saying, "Come up once more, for he
has told me all *that is* in his heart." Then the lords
of the Philistines came up to her and brought the
money in their hands. 19 She made him sleep on her
knees, and called for a man and had him shave off
the seven locks of his [a]hair. Then she began to afflict him, and his strength left him. 20 She said, "The
Philistines are upon you, Samson!" And he awoke
from his sleep and said, "I will go out as at other
times and shake myself free." But he did not know
that [A]the LORD had departed from him. 21 Then the
Philistines seized him and gouged out his eyes;
and they brought him down to Gaza and bound
him with bronze chains, and he was a grinder in
the prison. 22 However, the hair of his head began
to grow again after it was shaved off.

23 Now the lords of the Philistines assembled to
offer a great sacrifice to [A]Dagon their god, and to
rejoice, for they said,

> "Our god has given Samson our
> enemy into our hands."

24 When the people saw him, [A]they praised their
god, for they said,

> "Our god has given our enemy
> into our hands,
> Even the destroyer of our country,
> Who has slain many of us."

25 It so happened when [a]they were in high spirits,
that they said, "Call for Samson, that he may amuse
us." So they called for Samson from the prison, and
he [b]entertained them. And they made him stand
between the pillars. 26 Then Samson said to the boy
who was holding his hand, "Let me feel the pillars
on which the house rests, that I may lean against
them." 27 Now the house was full of men and women,
and all the lords of the Philistines were there. And
about 3,000 men and women were on the roof looking on while Samson was amusing *them*.

SAMSON IS AVENGED

28 [A]Then Samson called to the LORD and said,
"O Lord [a]GOD, please remember me and please
strengthen me just this time, O God, that I may at
once [B]be avenged of the Philistines for my two eyes."
29 Samson grasped the two middle pillars on which
the house rested, and braced himself against them,
the one with his right hand and the other with his
left. 30 And Samson said, "Let me die with the Philistines!" And he bent with [a]all his might so that the
house fell on the lords and all the people who were
in it. So the dead whom he killed at his death were
more than those whom he killed in his life. 31 Then
his brothers and all his father's household came
down, took him, brought him up and buried him
between Zorah and Eshtaol in the tomb of Manoah
his father. [A]Thus he had judged Israel twenty years.

MICAH'S IDOLATRY

17 Now there was a man of the hill country of
Ephraim whose name was Micah. 2 He said
to his mother, "The eleven hundred *pieces* of silver which were taken from you, about which you
uttered a curse [a]in my hearing, behold, the silver
is with me; I took it." And his mother said, "Blessed
be my son by the LORD." 3 He then returned the
eleven hundred *pieces* of silver to his mother, and
his mother said, "I wholly dedicate the silver from
my hand to the LORD for my son [A]to make a graven
image and a molten image; now therefore, I will
return [a]them to you." 4 So when he returned the
silver to his mother, his mother took two hundred
pieces of silver and gave them to the silversmith

16:15 [A]Judg 14:16 16:16 [a]Lit *impatient to the point of* 16:17 [A]Num 6:2, 5; Judg 13:5 16:19 [a]Lit *head* 16:20 [A]Num 14:42, 43; Josh 7:12; 1 Sam 16:14 16:23 [A]1 Sam 5:2 16:24 [A]1 Sam 31:9; 1 Chr 10:9; Ps 97:7 16:25 [a]Lit *their heart was pleasant* [b]Lit *made sport before them* 16:28 [a]Heb *YHWH*, usually rendered *LORD* [A]Judg 15:18 [B]Jer 15:15 16:30 [a]Lit *strength* 16:31 [A]Judg 15:20 17:2 [a]Lit *and also spoke it in my ears* 17:3 [a]Lit *it* [A]Ex 20:4, 23; 34:17

16:17 If I am shaved. His strength came from his unique relation to God, based on his Nazirite pledge. His long hair was only a sign of it. When Delilah became more important to him than God, his strength was removed.

16:20 he did not know that the LORD had departed from him. Here was the tragedy of the wrath of abandonment. His sin had caused him to forfeit the power of God's presence. This principle is seen in Ge 6:3; Pr 1:24–31; Mt 15:14; Ro 1:24–32. *See note on 10:13, 14.*

16:21 Gaza. The last town encountered in SW Canaan as a traveler went from Jerusalem toward Egypt, near the coast. It was nearly 40 mi. from Samson's birthplace, Zorah. There he was humiliated.

16:22 hair ... began to grow. His hair grew with his repentance, and his strength with his hair.

16:23 Dagon. He was a sea-god, an idol with the head of a man and the body of a fish.

16:24 they praised their god. It is tragic when a person's sin contributes to the unsaved community giving praise to a false god, for God alone is worthy of praise.

16:28 remember me. A prayer of repentance and trust pours from Samson.

16:29, 30 Some Philistine temples had roofs overlooking a courtyard, above wooden columns planted on stone foundations. The central pillars were set close to furnish extra support for the roof. Here the victory celebration and taunts flung at the prisoner below drew a big crowd. The full strength of Samson, renewed by God, enabled him to buckle the columns. As a result, the roof collapsed and the victory was Israel's, not Philistia's. He died for the cause of his country and his God. He was not committing suicide, but rather bringing God's judgment on His enemies and willing to leave his own life or death to God. He was the greatest champion of all Israel, yet a man of passion capable of severe sin. Still, he is in the list of the faithful (cf. Heb 11:32).

17:1 Chapters 17–21 give miscellaneous appendixes to illustrate the pervasively depraved conditions in the era of the judges.

who made [a]them into a graven image and a molten image, and [b]they were in the house of Micah.
5 And the man Micah had a [a,A]shrine and he made
an [B]ephod and [b,C]household idols and [c]consecrated
one of his sons, [D]that he might become his priest.
6 In those days [A]there was no king in Israel; [B]every
man did what was right in his own eyes.
7 Now there was a young man from [A]Bethlehem
in Judah, of the family of Judah, who was a Levite;
and he was [a]staying there. 8 Then the man departed
from the city, from Bethlehem in Judah, to [a]stay
wherever he might find *a place;* and as he made
his journey, he came to the [A]hill country of Ephraim
to the house of Micah. 9 Micah said to him, "Where
do you come from?" And he said to him, "I am a
Levite from Bethlehem in Judah, and I am going
to [a]stay wherever I may find *a place.*" 10 Micah then
said to him, "Dwell with me and be [A]a father and a
priest to me, and I will give you ten *pieces* of silver
a year, a suit of clothes, and your maintenance." So
the Levite went *in.* 11 The Levite agreed to live with
the man, and the young man became to him like
one of his sons. 12 So Micah [a]consecrated the Levite,
and the young man [A]became his priest and [b]lived
in the house of Micah. 13 Then Micah said, "Now I
know that the LORD will prosper me, seeing I have
a Levite as priest."

DANITES SEEK TERRITORY

18 [A]In those days there was no king of Israel;
and [B]in those days the tribe of the Danites
was seeking an inheritance for themselves to live
in, for until that day [a]an inheritance had not [b]been
allotted to them as a possession among the tribes
of Israel. 2 So the sons of Dan sent from their family
five men out of their whole number, [a]valiant men
from [A]Zorah and Eshtaol, to spy out the land and
to search it; and they said to them, "Go, search the
land." And they came to [B]the hill country of Ephraim,
to the house of Micah, and lodged there. 3 When they
were near the house of Micah, they recognized the
voice of the young man, the Levite; and they turned
aside there and said to him, "Who brought you here?
And what are you doing in this *place?* And what do
you have here?" 4 He said to them, "Thus and so has
Micah done to me, and he has hired me and [A]I have
become his priest." 5 They said to him, "Inquire of
God, please, that we may know whether our way on
which we are going will be prosperous." 6 The priest
said to them, "Go in peace; your way in which you
are going [a]has the LORD'S approval."
7 Then the five men departed and came to [A]Laish
and saw the people who were in it living in security, after the manner of the Sidonians, quiet and
secure; for there was no [a]ruler humiliating *them*
for anything in the land, and they were far from
the Sidonians and had no dealings with anyone.
8 When they came back to their brothers at Zorah
and Eshtaol, their brothers said to them, "What *do*
you *report?*" 9 They said, "Arise, and let us go up
against them; for we have seen the land, and behold, it is very good. And will you [a]sit still? Do not
delay to go, to enter, to possess the land. 10 When
you enter, you will come to a secure people with a
spacious land; for God has given it into your hand,
[A]a place where there is no lack of anything that is
on the earth."
11 Then from the family of the Danites, from Zorah and from Eshtaol, six hundred men armed with
weapons of war set out. 12 They went up and camped
at Kiriath-jearim in Judah. Therefore they called
that place [a,A]Mahaneh-dan to this day; behold, it is
[b]west of Kiriath-jearim. 13 They passed from there to
the hill country of Ephraim and came to the house
of Micah.

DANITES TAKE MICAH'S IDOLS

14 Then the five men who went to spy out the
country of Laish said to their kinsmen, "Do you
know that there are in these houses [A]an ephod and
[a]household idols and a graven image and a molten
image? Now therefore, consider what you should
do." 15 They turned aside there and came to the house
of the young man, the Levite, to the house of Micah,
and asked him of his welfare. 16 The six hundred
men armed with their weapons of war, who were of
the sons of Dan, stood by the entrance of the gate.
17 Now the five men who went to spy out the land
went up *and* entered there, *and* took [A]the graven
image and the ephod and [a]household idols and the
molten image, while the priest stood by the entrance
of the gate with the six hundred men armed with
weapons of war. 18 When these went into Micah's
house and took the graven image, the ephod and

17:4 [a]Lit *it* [b]Lit *it was* 17:5 [a]Lit *house of gods* [b]Heb *teraphim* [C]Lit *filled the hand of* [A]Judg 18:24 [B]Judg 8:27; 18:14 [C]Gen 31:19 [D]Num 3:10 17:6 [A]Judg 18:1; 19:1 [B]Deut 12:8; Judg 21:25 17:7 [a]Or *sojourning* [A]Judg 19:1; Ruth 1:1, 2; Mic 5:2; Matt 2:1 17:8 [a]Or *sojourn* [A]Josh 24:33 17:9 [a]Or *sojourn* 17:10 [A]Judg 18:19 17:12 [a]Lit *filled the hand of* [b]Lit *was* [A]Num 16:10; 18:1-7 18:1 [a]Lit *it* [b]Lit *fallen* [A]Judg 17:6; 19:1 [B]Josh 19:40-48 18:2 [a]Lit *men, sons of valor* [A]Judg 13:25 [B]Judg 17:1 18:4 [A]Judg 17:12 18:6 [a]Lit *is before the LORD* 18:7 [a]Lit *possessor of restraint* [A]Josh 19:47; Judg 18:29 18:9 [a]Lit *be* 18:10 [A]Deut 8:9 18:12 [a]I.e. the camp of Dan [b]Lit *behind* [A]Judg 13:25 18:14 [a]Heb *teraphim* [A]Judg 17:5 18:17 [a]Heb *teraphim* [A]Gen 31:19, 30; Is 41:29; Mic 5:13

17:5 Micah had a shrine. A counterfeit shrine and personal idols with a private priest is set up within the tribe of Ephraim (v. 1), whereas God's priests were of the tribe of Levi (cf. v. 13). The defection is one example of personal and family idolatry.

17:6 every man did … own eyes. This is the general characterization of the time, and of sinful behavior in all times. This attitude had been mentioned much earlier in Israel's history (cf. Dt 12:8; Jdg 21:25).

17:7–13 a Levite. He compromised in departing from one of the 48 cities God gave for Levite service to Israel (Jos 21). Then he sinned grossly by prostituting himself as a priest in a private idolatry.

18:2 On the migration by the tribe of Dan to a new territory, *see note on 1:34.* Dan was an example of tribal idolatry.

18:5 Inquire of God, please. The passage does not say if the Levite did in fact seek God's counsel before giving reassurance (v. 6); the Danites should have prayed to seek God's counsel before making this trip or consulting a disobedient priest as one would an oracle.

18:7 Laish. Known also as Leshem (cf. Jos 19:47), this was a secluded, rich land.

18:14–26 The Danites sinfully seized the idols of Micah by force, probably because they believed those false idols were the source of power to give them the land they had spied. The apostate Levite who had served Micah as priest, named Jonathan, sold out again to be a priest for the Danites (vv. 18–20, 30), who were not bothered by his defection, but rather believed in his spiritual power.

[a]household idols and the molten image, the priest said to them, "What are you doing?" 19 They said to him, "Be silent, [A]put your hand over your mouth and come with us, and be to us [B]a father and a priest. Is it better for you to be a priest to the house of one man, or to be priest to a tribe and a family in Israel?" 20 The priest's heart was glad, and he took the ephod and [a]household idols and the graven image and went among the people.

21 Then they turned and departed, and put the little ones and the livestock and the valuables in front of them. 22 When they had gone some distance from the house of Micah, the men who *were* in the houses near Micah's house assembled and overtook the sons of Dan. 23 They cried to the sons of Dan, who turned [a]around and said to Micah, "What is *the matter* with you, that you have assembled together?" 24 He said, "You have taken away my gods which I made, and the priest, and have gone away, and what do I have besides? So how can you say to me, 'What is *the matter* with you?' " 25 The sons of Dan said to him, "Do not let your voice be heard among us, or else [a]fierce men will fall upon you and you will [b]lose your life, with the lives of your household." 26 So the sons of Dan went on their way; and when Micah saw that they were too strong for him, he turned and went back to his house.

27 Then they took what Micah had made and the priest who had belonged to him, and came to [A]Laish, to a people quiet and secure, and struck them with the edge of the sword; and they burned the city with fire. 28 And there was no one to deliver *them,* because it was far from Sidon and they had no dealings with anyone, and it was in the valley which is near [A]Beth-rehob. And they rebuilt the city and lived in it. 29 [A]They called the name of the city Dan, after the name of Dan their father who was born in Israel; however, the name of the city formerly was Laish. 30 The sons of Dan set up for themselves [A]the graven image; and Jonathan, the son of [B]Gershom, the son of [a]Manasseh, [A]he and his sons were priests to the tribe of the Danites until the day of the captivity of the land. 31 So they set up for themselves Micah's graven image which he had made, all the time that the [A]house of God was at Shiloh.

A LEVITE'S CONCUBINE DEGRADED

19 Now it came about in those days, when [A]there was no king in Israel, that there was a certain Levite [a]staying in the remote part of the hill country of Ephraim, who took a concubine for himself from Bethlehem in Judah. 2 But his concubine played the harlot against him, and she went away from him to her father's house in Bethlehem in Judah, and was there for a period of four months. 3 Then her husband arose and went after her to [A]speak [a]tenderly to her in order to bring her back, [b]taking with him his servant and a pair of donkeys. So she brought him into her father's house, and when the girl's father saw him, he was glad to meet him. 4 His father-in-law, the girl's father, detained him; and he remained with him three days. So they ate and drank and lodged there. 5 Now on the fourth day they got up early in the morning, and he [a]prepared to go; and the girl's father said to his son-in-law, "[A]Sustain [b]yourself with a piece of bread, and afterward you may go." 6 So both of them sat down and ate and drank together; and the girl's father said to the man, "Please be willing to spend the night, and [A]let your heart be merry." 7 Then the man arose to go, but his father-in-law urged him so that he spent the night there again. 8 On the fifth day he arose to go early in the morning, and the girl's father said, "Please sustain [a]yourself, and wait until [b]afternoon"; so both of them ate. 9 When the man arose to go along with his concubine and servant, his father-in-law, the girl's father, said to him, "Behold now, the day has drawn [a]to a close; please spend the night. Lo, the day is [b]coming to an end; spend the night here that your heart may be merry. Then tomorrow you may arise early for your journey so that you may go [c]home."

10 But the man was not willing to spend the night, so he arose and departed and came to *a place* opposite [A]Jebus (that is, Jerusalem). And there were with him a pair of saddled donkeys; his concubine also was with him. 11 When they *were* near Jebus, the day was almost gone; and [A]the servant said to his master, "Please come, and let us turn aside into this city of the Jebusites and spend the night in it." 12 However, his master said to him, "We will not turn aside into the city of foreigners who are not of the sons of Israel; but we will go on as far as

18:18 [a]Heb *teraphim* 18:19 [A]Job 21:5; 29:9; 40:4 [B]Judg 17:10 18:20 [a]Heb *teraphim* 18:23 [a]Lit *their faces* 18:25 [a]Lit *bitter of soul* [b]Lit *gather* 18:27 [A]Josh 19:47; Judg 18:7 18:28 [A]2 Sam 10:6 18:29 [A]Josh 19:47 18:30 [a]Some ancient versions read *Moses* [A]Judg 17:3, 5 [B]Ex 2:22; 18:3 18:31 [A]Josh 18:1 19:1 [a]Or *sojourning* [A]Judg 18:1 19:3 [a]Lit *to her heart* [b]Lit *and* [A]Gen 34:3; 50:21 19:5 [a]Lit *arose* [b]Lit *your heart* [A]Gen 18:5; Judg 19:8 19:6 [A]Judg 16:25; 19:9, 22; Ruth 3:7; 1 Kin 21:7; Esth 1:10 19:8 [a]Lit *your heart* [b]Lit *the day declines* 19:9 [a]Lit *toward evening* [b]Lit *declining* [c]Lit *to your tent* 19:10 [A]1 Chr 11:4, 5 19:11 [A]Judg 19:19

18:29 name of the city Dan. This was in the northernmost extremity of the land of Canaan, hence the origin of the phrase, "from Dan to Beersheba," as indicating the land from N to S (cf. 20:1).

18:30 the son of Manasseh. Some manuscripts say "son of Manasseh," others "son of Moses," which may be more probable as Gershom was a son of Moses (Ex 2:22; 18:3). This idolatrous priestly service continued until the captivity. This is most likely 1) the captivity of Israel by Assyria in 722 B.C. (2Ki 15:29; 17:1–6), or possibly 2) the Philistine captivity of the ark from Shiloh (see Jdg 18:31) in 1Sa 4:11.

18:31 the house of God was at Shiloh. The ark of God was far away from them, so they justified their idolatry by their distance from the rest of Israel. This caused perpetual idolatry for many generations.

19:1–10 Here is an example of the kind of personal immorality that went on during this era.

19:1 concubine. Priests could marry (Lv 21:7, 13, 14). Though a concubine wife (usually a slave) was culturally legal, the practice was not acceptable to God (Ge 2:24).

19:2 played the harlot. She should have been killed as the law required and could have been if there was a devotion to holiness and obedience to Scripture (cf. Lv 20:10). A priest was not allowed to marry a harlot (Lv 21:14), so his ministry was greatly tainted. Yet, he made little of her sin and separation and sought her back sympathetically (v. 3).

19:10 Jebus. An early title for Jerusalem because of Jebusite control (Jdg 1:21) until David wrested it away to become his capital (2Sa 5:6–9). Another early name for the city was Salem (Ge 14:18; cf. Ps 76:2).

19:12 Gibeah. Jerusalem was still partially out of the control of Israelites. Gibeah was under Israelite control and safer.

Gibeah." 13 He said to his servant, "Come and let us
approach one of these places; and we will spend
the night in Gibeah or Ramah." 14 So they passed
along and went their way, and the sun set on them
near Gibeah which belongs to Benjamin. 15 They
turned aside there in order to enter *and* lodge in
Gibeah. When [a]they entered, [a]they sat down in the
open square of the city, for no one took them into
his house to spend the night.
16 Then behold, an old man was coming out of
the field from his work at evening. Now the man
was from [A]the hill country of Ephraim, and he was
[a]staying in Gibeah, but the men of the place [B]were
Benjamites. 17 And he lifted up his eyes and saw
the traveler in the open square of the city; and the
old man said, "Where are you going, and where do
you come from?" 18 He said to him, "We are passing
from Bethlehem in Judah to the remote part of the
hill country of Ephraim, *for* I am from there, and
I went to Bethlehem in Judah. But I am *now* going
to [a]my house, and no man will take me into his
house. 19 Yet there is both straw and fodder for our
donkeys, and also bread and wine for me, [a]your
maidservant, and [A]the young man who is with your
servants; there is no lack of anything." 20 The old
man said, "[A]Peace to you. Only let me *take care of*
all your needs; however, do not spend the night in
the open square." 21 [A]So he took him into his house
and gave the donkeys fodder, and they washed their
feet and ate and drank.
22 While they were [a]celebrating, behold, [A]the men
of the city, certain [b,B]worthless fellows, surrounded
the house, pounding the door; and they spoke to
the owner of the house, the old man, saying, "Bring
out the man who came into your house that we
may have [c]relations with him." 23 Then the man,
the owner of the house, went out to them and said
to them, "No, my fellows, please do not act so wickedly; since this man has come into my house, [A]do
not commit this act of folly. 24 [A]Here is my virgin
daughter and his concubine. Please let me bring
them out that you may ravish them and do to them
[a]whatever you wish. But do not commit such an act
of folly against this man." 25 But the men would not
listen to him. So the man seized his concubine and
brought *her* out to them; and they raped her and
abused her all night until morning, then let her
go at the approach of dawn. 26 [a]As the day began
to dawn, the woman came and fell down at the
doorway of the man's house where her master was,
until *full* daylight.
27 When her master arose in the morning and
opened the doors of the house and went out to go
on his way, then behold, his concubine was lying
at the doorway of the house with her hands on the
threshold. 28 He said to her, "Get up and let us go,"
[A]but there was no answer. Then he placed her on the
donkey; and the man arose and went to his [a]home.
29 When he entered his house, he took a knife and
laid hold of his concubine and [A]cut her in twelve
pieces, limb by limb, and sent her throughout the
territory of Israel. 30 All who saw *it* said, "Nothing
like this has *ever* happened or been seen from the
day when the sons of Israel came up from the land
of Egypt to this day. Consider it, [A]take counsel and
speak up!"

RESOLVE TO PUNISH THE GUILTY

20 Then all the sons of Israel from Dan to Beersheba, including the land of Gilead, came
out, and the congregation assembled as one man to
the LORD at [A]Mizpah. 2 The [a]chiefs of all the people,
even of all the tribes of Israel, took their stand in the
assembly of the people of God, 400,000 foot [b]soldiers
[A]who drew the sword. 3 (Now the sons of Benjamin
heard that the sons of Israel had gone up to Mizpah.)
And the sons of Israel said, "Tell *us*, how did this
wickedness take place?" 4 So the Levite, the husband
of the woman who was murdered, answered and
said, "I came with my concubine to spend the night
at Gibeah which belongs to Benjamin. 5 But the [A]men
of Gibeah rose up against me and surrounded the
house at night because of me. They intended to kill
me; instead, they [B]ravished my concubine so that

19:15 [a]So with Gr; M.T. *he* 19:16 [a]Or *sojourning* [A]Judg 19:1 [B]Judg 19:14 19:18 [a]Heb *the house of the LORD*, cf v 29 19:19 [a]I.e. my concubine [A]Judg 19:11 19:20 [A]Gen 43:23; Judg 6:23 19:21 [A]Gen 24:32, 33 19:22 [a]Lit *making their hearts merry* [b]Lit *sons of Belial* [c]Lit *intercourse* [A]Gen 19:4, 5; Ezek 16:46-48 [B]Deut 13:13; 1 Sam 2:12; 1 Kin 21:10; 2 Cor 6:15 19:23 [A]Gen 34:7; Deut 22:21; Judg 20:6; 2 Sam 13:12 19:24 [a]Lit *the good in your eyes* [A]Gen 19:8 19:26 [a]Lit *At the turning of the morning* 19:28 [a]Lit *place* [A]Judg 20:5 19:29 [A]1 Sam 11:7 19:30 [A]Judg 20:7; Prov 13:10 20:1 [A]1 Sam 7:5 20:2 [a]Lit *cornerstones* [b]Lit *men* [A]Judg 8:10 20:5 [A]Judg 19:22 [B]Judg 19:25f

19:15 People of the Benjamite town of Gibeah failed to extend the expected courtesy of a lodging. This opened the door to immorality.

19:18 going to my house. He was headed for Shiloh to return to priestly duty.

19:20 night in the open square. The old man knew the danger of such a place at night.

19:22 worthless fellows. Lit. "sons of Belial," i.e., base and perverse men, who desired to commit sodomy against the Levite. The phrase elsewhere is used for idolaters (Dt 13:13), neglecters of the poor (Dt 15:9), drunks (1Sa 1:16), immoral people (1Sa 2:12), and rebels against the civil authority (2Sa 20:1; Pr 19:28). "Belial" can be traced to the false god Baal, and is also a term for yoke (they cast off the yoke of decency), and a term for entangling or injuring. It is used in the NT of Satan (2Co 6:15).

19:24 let me bring them out. The host showed a disgraceful compromise in his exaggerated desire to extend hospitality to his male guest. He should have protected all in his house, and so should the Levite, even at the risk of their own lives in guarding the women. His sad estimate of women was demonstrated by his willingness to hand his daughter or the guest concubine over to indecent men. Lot's plunge from decency was similar (Ge 19). Here, repeated rape and finally murder were the pitiful sequel.

19:25 the man seized his concubine and brought *her* out to them. This is unthinkable weakness and cowardice for any man, especially a priest of God. Apparently he even slept through the night, or stayed in bed out of fear, since he didn't see her again until he awakened and prepared to leave (cf. v. 28).

19:29 cut her in twelve pieces. The Levite's bizarre butchery to divide the woman's body into 12 parts was his shocking summons for aroused Israelite redress. No doubt a message went with each part, and the fact that he "sent" assumes messengers (cf. 1Sa 11:7). As he calculated, many were incensed and desired to avenge the atrocity (cf. 20:30). Nothing could have aroused universal indignation and horror more than this radical summons from the Levite.

20:1 all the sons of Israel … came out. As a result of this horrible tragedy, a national assembly was convened with people coming from the N (Dan) and the S (Beersheba). **as one man to the LORD.** This indicated a humble attitude and desire to seek help from God for the nation.

she died. 6 And I [A]took hold of my concubine and
cut her in pieces and sent her throughout the land
of Israel's inheritance; for [B]they have committed a
lewd and disgraceful act in Israel. 7 Behold, all you
sons of Israel, [A]give your advice and counsel here."
8 Then all the people arose as one man, saying,
"Not one of us will go to his tent, nor will any of us
return to his house. 9 But now this is the thing which
we will do to Gibeah; *we will go up* against it by lot.
10 And we will take 10 men out of 100 throughout the
tribes of Israel, and 100 out of 1,000, and 1,000 out
of 10,000 to [a]supply food for the people, that when
they come to [b]Gibeah of Benjamin, they may [c]pun-
ish *them* for all the disgraceful acts that they have
committed in Israel." 11 Thus all the men of Israel
were gathered against the city, united as one man.
12 Then the tribes of Israel sent men through the
entire [a]tribe of Benjamin, saying, "What is this wickedness that has taken place among you? 13 Now
then, deliver up the men, the [a,A]worthless fellows
in Gibeah, that we may put them to death and [B]re-
move *this* wickedness from Israel." But the sons
of Benjamin would not listen to the voice of their
brothers, the sons of Israel. 14 The sons of Benjamin
gathered from the cities to Gibeah, to go out to battle
against the sons of Israel. 15 From the cities on that
day the [A]sons of Benjamin were [a]numbered, 26,000
men who draw the sword, besides the inhabitants
of Gibeah who were [a]numbered, 700 choice men.
16 Out of all these people 700 [A]choice men were
left-handed; each one could sling a stone at a hair
and not miss.
17 Then the men of Israel besides Benjamin were
[a]numbered, 400,000 men who draw the sword; all
these were men of war.

CIVIL WAR, BENJAMIN DEFEATED

18 Now the sons of Israel arose, went up to Bethel,
and [A]inquired of God and said, "Who shall go up first
for us to battle against the sons of Benjamin?" Then
the LORD said, "Judah *shall go up* first."
19 So the sons of Israel arose in the morning and
camped against Gibeah. 20 The men of Israel went
out to battle against Benjamin, and the men of
Israel arrayed for battle against them at Gibeah.
21 Then the sons of Benjamin came out of Gibeah
and [a,A]felled to the ground on that day 22,000 men
of Israel. 22 But the people, the men of Israel, encouraged themselves and arrayed for battle again
in the place where they had arrayed themselves the
first day. 23 [A]The sons of Israel went up and wept
before the LORD until evening, and [B]inquired of the
LORD, saying, "Shall we again draw near for battle
against the sons of my brother Benjamin?" And the
LORD said, "Go up against him."
24 Then the sons of Israel [a]came against the sons
of Benjamin the second day. 25 Benjamin went out
[a]against them from Gibeah the second day and
[b]felled to the ground again 18,000 men of the sons
of Israel; all these drew the sword. 26 Then [A]all the
sons of Israel and all the people went up and came
to Bethel and wept; thus they remained there before
the LORD and fasted that day until evening. And
they offered burnt offerings and peace offerings
before the LORD. 27 The sons of Israel [A]inquired of
the LORD (for the ark of the covenant of God *was*
there in those days, 28 and Phinehas the son of Eleazar, Aaron's son, stood before it to *minister* in
those days), saying, "Shall I yet again go out to battle
against the sons of my brother Benjamin, or shall I
cease?" And the LORD said, "Go up, [A]for tomorrow
I will deliver them into your hand."
29 [A]So Israel set men in ambush around Gibeah.
30 The sons of Israel went up against the sons of
Benjamin on the third day and arrayed themselves
against Gibeah as at other times. 31 [A]The sons of
Benjamin went out [a]against the people and were
drawn away from the city, and they began to strike
[b]and kill some of the people as at other times, on
the highways, one of which goes up to Bethel and
the other to Gibeah, *and* in the field, about thirty
men of Israel. 32 The sons of Benjamin said, "They
are struck down before us, as at the first." But the
sons of Israel said, "Let us flee that we may draw
them away from the city to the highways." 33 Then
all the men of Israel arose from their place and
arrayed themselves at Baal-tamar; [A]and the men
of Israel in ambush broke out of their place, even
out of Maareh-geba. 34 When ten thousand choice
men from all Israel came against Gibeah, the battle became [a]fierce; [A]but [b]Benjamin did not know
that [c]disaster was [d]close to them. 35 And the LORD
struck Benjamin before Israel, so that the sons of
Israel destroyed 25,100 men of Benjamin that day,
all [a]who draw the sword.
36 So the sons of Benjamin saw that they were
[a]defeated. [A]When the men of Israel gave [b]ground
to Benjamin because they relied on the men in
ambush whom they had set against Gibeah, 37 [A]the
men in ambush hurried and rushed against Gibeah;

20:6 [A]Judg 19:29 [B]Gen 34:7; Josh 7:15 20:7 [A]Judg 19:30 20:10 [a]Lit *take* [b]Heb *Geba* [c]Lit *do* 20:12 [a]Lit *tribes* 20:13 [a]Lit *sons of Belial* [A]2 Cor 6:15 [B]Deut 13:5; 17:12; 1 Cor 5:13 20:15 [a]Or *mustered* [A]Num 1:36, 37; 2:23; 26:41 20:16 [A]Judg 3:15; 1 Chr 12:2 20:17 [a]Or *mustered* 20:18 [A]Num 27:21; Judg 20:23, 27 20:21 [a]Lit *destroyed* [A]Judg 20:25 20:23 [A]Josh 7:6, 7 [B]Judg 20:18 20:24 [a]Lit *approached* 20:25 [a]Lit *to meet* [b]Lit *destroyed* 20:26 [A]Judg 20:23; 21:2 20:27 [A]Judg 20:18 20:28 [A]Judg 7:9 20:29 [A]Josh 8:4 20:31 [a]Lit *to meet* [b]Lit *slain ones* [A]Josh 8:16 20:33 [A]Josh 8:19 20:34 [a]Lit *heavy* [b]Lit *they* [c]Lit *evil* [d]Lit *touching* [A]Josh 8:14; Job 21:13 20:35 [a]Lit *these* 20:36 [a]Lit *smitten* [b]Lit *place* [A]Josh 8:15 20:37 [A]Josh 8:19

20:13 the sons of Benjamin would not listen. They hardened their hearts against the justice and decency of turning over the criminals. Even greatly outnumbered in war, they would not yield to what was right (cf. vv. 15–17). So civil war resulted.

20:18 inquired of God. The Lord gave His counsel from the location of the ark at Shiloh, probably through the Urim and Thummim (vv. 27, 28). The tribe of Judah was responsible to lead in battle since God had chosen a leadership role for that tribe (Ge 49:8–12; 1Ch 5:1, 2). *See note on Ex 28:30.*

20:22–25 Twice the Lord allowed great defeat and death to Israel to bring them to their spiritual senses regarding the cost of tolerating apostasy. Also, while they sought counsel, they placed too much reliance on their own prowess and on satisfying their own outrage. Finally, when desperate enough, they fasted and offered sacrifices (v. 26). The Lord then gave victory with a strategy similar to that at Ai (Jos 8).

20:32 Here was a battle strategy that lured the Benjamite army into a disastrous ambush (cf. vv. 36–46).

the men in ambush also deployed and struck all
the city with the edge of the sword. 38 Now the
appointed sign between the men of Israel and the
men in ambush was [A]that they would make a great
cloud of smoke rise from the city. 39 Then the men
of Israel turned in the battle, and Benjamin began
to strike [a]and kill about thirty men of Israel, [A]for
they said, "Surely they are [b]defeated before us, as
in the first battle." 40 But when the cloud began to
rise from the city in a column of smoke, Benjamin
looked [A]behind them; and behold, the whole city
was going up *in smoke* to heaven. 41 Then the men
of Israel turned, and the men of Benjamin were
terrified; for they saw that [a,A]disaster was [b]close
to them. 42 Therefore, they turned their backs before the men of Israel [A]toward the direction of the
wilderness, but the battle overtook them while
those who came out of the cities destroyed them
in the midst of them. 43 [A]They surrounded Benjamin, pursued them without rest *and* trod them
down opposite Gibeah toward the [a]east. 44 Thus
18,000 men of Benjamin fell; all these were valiant warriors. 45 [a]The rest turned and fled toward
the wilderness to the rock of [A]Rimmon, but they
[b]caught 5,000 of them on the highways and overtook them [c]at Gidom and [d]killed 2,000 of them.
46 So all of Benjamin who fell that day were 25,000
men who draw the sword; all these were valiant
warriors. 47 But 600 men turned and fled toward
the wilderness to the rock of Rimmon, and they
remained at the rock of Rimmon four months.
48 The men of Israel then turned back against the
sons of Benjamin and struck them with the edge
of the sword, both the entire city with the cattle
and all that they found; they also set on fire all the
cities which they found.

MOURNING LOST TRIBE

21 Now the men of Israel [A]had sworn in Mizpah,
saying, "None of us shall give his daughter to
Benjamin [a]in marriage." 2 [A]So the people came to
Bethel and sat there before God until evening, and
lifted up their voices and wept [a]bitterly. 3 They said,
"Why, O LORD, God of Israel, has this come about in
Israel, so that one tribe should be *missing* today in
Israel?" 4 It came about the next day that the people
arose early and built [A]an altar there and offered
burnt offerings and peace offerings.

5 Then the sons of Israel said, "Who is there
among all the tribes of Israel who did not come
up in the assembly to the LORD?" For [a]they had taken
a great oath concerning him [A]who did not come up
to the LORD at Mizpah, saying, "He shall surely be
put to death." 6 And the sons of Israel were sorry
for their brother Benjamin and said, "One tribe is
cut off from Israel today. 7 What shall we do for
wives for those who are left, since we have [A]sworn
by the LORD not to give them any of our daughters
in marriage?"

PROVISION FOR THEIR SURVIVAL

8 And they said, "What one is there of the tribes
of Israel who did not come up to the LORD at Mizpah?" And behold, no one had come to the camp
from Jabesh-gilead to the assembly. 9 For when
the people were [a]numbered, behold, not one of
the inhabitants of Jabesh-gilead was there. 10 And
the congregation sent 12,000 of the valiant warriors there, and commanded them, saying, "Go and
[A]strike the inhabitants of Jabesh-gilead with the
edge of the sword, with the women and the little
ones. 11 This is the thing that you shall do: you [A]shall
utterly destroy every man and every woman who
has [a]lain with a man." 12 And they found among the
inhabitants of Jabesh-gilead 400 young virgins who
had not known a man by lying with [a]him; and they
brought them to the camp at Shiloh, which is in the
land of Canaan.
13 Then the whole congregation sent *word* and
spoke to the sons of Benjamin who were [A]at the
rock of Rimmon, and [B]proclaimed peace to them.
14 Benjamin returned at that time, and they gave
them the women whom they had kept alive from
the women of Jabesh-gilead; yet they [a]were not
enough for them. 15 And the people were sorry for
Benjamin because the LORD had made a breach in
the tribes of Israel.
16 Then the elders of the congregation said,
"What shall we do for wives for those who are left,
since the women are destroyed out of Benjamin?"
17 They said, "*There must be* an inheritance for the
survivors of Benjamin, so that a tribe will not be
blotted out from Israel. 18 But we cannot give them
wives of our daughters." For the sons of Israel [A]had
sworn, saying, "Cursed is he who gives a wife to
Benjamin."

20:38 [A]Josh 8:20 20:39 [a]Lit *slain ones* [b]Lit *smitten* [A]Judg 20:32 20:40 [A]Josh 8:20 20:41 [a]Lit *evil* [b]Lit *touching* [A]Prov 5:22; 11:5, 6; 29:6 20:42 [A]Josh 8:15, 24 20:43 [a]Lit *sunrise* [A]Hos 9:9; 10:9 20:45 [a]So with Gr; Heb *And they* [b]Lit *gleaned* [c]Lit *as far as* [d]Lit *smote* [A]Judg 21:13 21:1 [a]Lit *for a wife* [A]Judg 21:7, 18 21:2 [a]Lit *with great weeping* [A]Judg 20:26 21:4 [A]Deut 12:5; 2 Sam 24:25 21:5 [a]Lit *there was a great oath* [A]Judg 5:23 21:7 [A]Judg 21:1 21:9 [a]Or *mustered* 21:10 [A]Num 31:17; Judg 5:23; 1 Sam 11:7 21:11 [a]Lit *known lying with* [A]Num 31:17 21:12 [a]Lit *a male* 21:13 [A]Judg 20:47 [B]Deut 20:10 21:14 [a]Lit *did not find it so* 21:18 [A]Judg 21:1

20:46 twenty-five thousand. A rounded number for the more exact 25,100 (cf. v. 35).

20:47 The number of Benjamites adds up to the 26,700 (v. 15) in a reasonable way: 18,000 killed (v. 44); 5,000 (v. 45); 2,000 (v. 45); 600 survived (v. 47); leaving an estimated 1,100 lost the first two days (v. 48).

21:1 sworn in Mizpah. The Israelites made an oath not to "give" their daughters to the 600 surviving Benjamites (20:47). But they realized that the latter would fade as a tribe unless they had wives (cf. 21:6, 7), since the Benjamite women had died in the total sack of Gibeah (20:37). Cf. v. 9.

21:8 No one had come from Jabesh-gilead, so the Israelites conquered Jabesh-gilead, which did not help against the Benjamites, and gave 400 virgins from there to the tribe (vv. 12–14).

21:8–16 Jabesh-gilead. Israelites placed such a premium on the unity of their tribes that they saw this city's non-cooperation in battle as worthy of widespread death. The passage does not give God's approval to this destruction of men, women, and children (vv. 10, 11). It is another of the bizarre actions of men when they do what is right in their own eyes, which is the point that both begins and ends this dark final section (17:6; 21:25).

21:16 wives for those who are left. Having recognized that the 200 others needed wives (vv. 17, 18), they decided to allow them to snatch brides on their own at a dance in Shiloh (vv. 16–22), not believing that this violated their oath of not directly "giving" their daughters.

19 So they said, "Behold, there is a feast of the
LORD from year to year in [A]Shiloh, which is on the
north side of Bethel, on the east side of the highway
that goes up from Bethel to Shechem, and on the
south side of Lebonah." 20 And they commanded the
sons of Benjamin, saying, "Go and lie in wait in the
vineyards, 21 and watch; and behold, if the daughters of Shiloh come out to [a,A]take part in the dances,
then you shall come out of the vineyards and each
of you shall catch his wife from the daughters of
Shiloh, and go to the land of Benjamin. 22 It shall
come about, when their fathers or their brothers
come to complain to us, that we shall say to them,
'Give them to us voluntarily, because we did not
take for each man *of Benjamin* [a]a wife in battle,
[b,A]nor did you give *them* to them, *else* you would
now be guilty.' " 23 The sons of Benjamin did so,
and took wives according to their number from
those who danced, whom they carried away. And
they went and returned to their inheritance and
[A]rebuilt the cities and lived in them. 24 The sons of
Israel departed from there at that time, every man
to his tribe and family, and each one of them went
out from there to his inheritance.
25 [A]In those days there was no king in Israel; everyone did what was right in his own eyes.

21:19 [A]Josh 18:1; Judg 18:31; 1 Sam 1:3 21:21 [a]Lit *dance* [A]Ex 15:20; Judg 11:34 21:22 [a]Lit *his* [b]Lit *because* [A]Judg 21:1, 18 21:23 [A]Judg 20:48 21:25 [A]Judg 17:6; 18:1; 19:1

21:25 Judges 17–21 vividly demonstrates how bizarre and deep sin can become when people throw off the authority of God as mediated through the king (cf. 17:6). This was the appropriate, but tragic, conclusion to a bleak period of Israelite history (cf. Dt 12:8).

THE BOOK OF RUTH

TITLE

Ancient versions and modern translations consistently entitle this book after Ruth the Moabitess heroine, who is mentioned by name 12 times (1:4 to 4:13). Only two OT books receive their names from women—Ruth and Esther. The OT does not again refer to Ruth, while the NT mentions her just once—in the context of Christ's genealogy (Mt 1:5; cf. Ru 4:18–22). "Ruth" most likely comes from a Moabite and/or Hebrew word meaning "friendship." Ruth arrived in Bethlehem as a foreigner (2:10), became a maidservant (2:13), married wealthy Boaz (4:13), and was included in the physical lineage of Christ (Mt 1:5).

AUTHOR AND DATE

Jewish tradition credits Samuel as the author, which is plausible since he did not die (1Sa 25:1) until after he had anointed David as God's chosen king (1Sa 16:6–13). However, neither internal features nor external testimony conclusively identify the writer. This exquisite story most likely appeared shortly before or during David's reign in Israel (1011–971 B.C.), since David is mentioned (4:17, 22) but not Solomon. Goethe reportedly labeled this piece of anonymous but unexcelled literature as "the loveliest, complete work on a small scale." What Venus is to statuary and the Mona Lisa is to paintings, Ruth is to literature.

BACKGROUND AND SETTING

Aside from Bethlehem (1:1), Moab (the perennial enemy of Israel, which was E of the Dead Sea), stands as the only other mentioned geographic/national entity (1:1, 2). This country originated when Lot fathered Moab by an incestuous union with his oldest daughter (Ge 19:37). Centuries later the Jews encountered opposition from Balak, king of Moab, through the prophet Balaam (Nu 22–25). For 18 years Moab oppressed Israel during the time of the judges (Jdg 3:12–30). Saul defeated the Moabites (1Sa 14:47) while David seemed to enjoy a peaceful relationship with them (1Sa 22:3, 4). Later, Moab again troubled Israel (2Ki 3:5–27; Ezr 9:1). Because of Moab's idolatrous worship of Chemosh (1Ki 11:7, 33; 2Ki 23:13) and its opposition to Israel, God cursed Moab (Is 15, 16; Jer 48; Eze 25:8–11; Am 2:1–3).

The story of Ruth occurred in the days "when the judges governed" Israel (1:1), ca. 1370 to 1041 B.C. (Jdg 2:16–19), and thus bridges time from the judges to Israel's monarchy. God used "a famine in the land" of Judah (1:1) to set in motion this beautiful drama, although the famine does not receive mention in Judges, which causes difficulty in dating the events of Ruth. However, by working backward in time from the well known date of David's reign (1011–971 B.C.), the time period of Ruth would most likely be during the judgeship of Jair, ca. 1126–1105 B.C. (Jdg 10:3–5).

Ruth covers about 11 or 12 years according to the following scenario: 1) 1:1–18, ten years in Moab (1:4); 2) 1:19–2:23, several months (mid-Apr. to mid-June) in Boaz's field (1:22; 2:23); 3) 3:1–18, one day in Bethlehem and one night at the threshing floor; and 4) 4:1–22, about one year in Bethlehem.

HISTORICAL AND THEOLOGICAL THEMES

All 85 verses of Ruth have been accepted as canonical by the Jews. Along with Song of Solomon, Esther, Ecclesiastes, and Lamentations, Ruth stands with the OT books of the Megilloth or "five scrolls." Rabbis read these books in the synagogue on 5 special occasions during the year—Ruth being read at Pentecost due to the harvest scenes of Ru 2, 3.

Genealogically, Ruth looks back almost 900 years to events in the time of Jacob (4:11) and forward about 100 years to the coming reign of David (4:17, 22). While Joshua and Judges emphasize the legacy of the nation and their land of promise, Ruth focuses on the lineage of David back to the patriarchal era.

At least 7 major theological themes emerge in Ruth. First, Ruth the Moabitess illustrates that God's redemptive plan extended beyond the Jews to Gentiles (2:12). Second, Ruth demonstrates that women are coheirs with men of God's salvation grace (cf. Gal 3:28). Third, Ruth portrays the virtuous woman of Pr 31:10 (cf. 3:11). Fourth, Ruth describes God's sovereign (1:6; 4:13) and providential care (2:3) of seemingly unimportant people at apparently insignificant times which later prove to be monumentally crucial to accomplishing God's will. Fifth, Ruth along with Tamar (Ge 38), Rahab (Jos 2), and Bathsheba (2Sa 11, 12) stand in the genealogy of the messianic line (4:17, 22; cf. Mt 1:5). Sixth, Boaz, as a type of Christ, becomes

Ruth's kinsman-redeemer (4:1–12). Finally, David's right (and thus Christ's right) to the throne of Israel is traced back to Judah (4:18–22; cf. Ge 49:8–12).

INTERPRETIVE CHALLENGES

Ruth should be understood as a true historical account. The reliable facts surrounding Ruth, in addition to its complete compatibility with Judges plus 1 and 2 Samuel, confirm Ruth's authenticity. However, some individual difficulties require careful attention. First, how could Ruth worship at the tabernacle then in Shiloh (1Sa 4:4), since Deuteronomy 23:3 expressly forbids Moabites from entering the assembly for 10 generations? Since the Jews entered the land ca. 1405 B.C. and Ruth was not born until ca. 1150 B.C., she then represented at least the 11th generation (probably later) if the time limitation ended at ten generations. If "ten generations" was an idiom meaning "forever" as Ne 13:1 implies, then Ruth would be like the foreigner of Is 56:1–8 who joined himself to the Lord (1:16), thus gaining entrance to the assembly.

Second, are there not immoral overtones to Boaz and Ruth spending the night together before marriage (3:3–18)? Ruth engaged in a common ancient Near Eastern custom by asking Boaz to take her for his wife, symbolically pictured by throwing a garment over the intended woman (3:9), just as Jehovah spread His garment over Israel (Eze 16:8). The text does not even hint at the slightest moral impropriety, noting that Ruth slept at his feet (3:14). Thus, Boaz became God's answer to his own earlier prayer for Ruth (2:12).

Third, would not the levirate principle of Dt 25:5, 6 lead to incest and/or polygamy if the nearest relative was already married? God would not design a good plan to involve the grossest of immoralities punishable by death. It is to be assumed that the implementation of Dt 25:5, 6 could involve only the nearest relative who was eligible for marriage as qualified by other stipulations of the law.

Fourth, was not marriage to a Moabitess strictly forbidden by the law? The nations or people to whom marriage was prohibited were those possessing the land that Israel would enter (Ex 34:16; Dt 7:1–3; Jos 23:12) which did not include Moab (cf. Dt 7:1). Further, Boaz married Ruth, a devout proselyte to Jehovah (1:16, 17), not a pagan worshiper of Chemosh—Moab's chief deity (cf. later problems in Ezr 9:1, 2 and Ne 13:23–25).

OUTLINE

I. Elimelech and Naomi's Ruin in Moab (1:1–5)

II. Naomi and Ruth Return to Bethlehem (1:6–22)

III. Boaz Receives Ruth in His Field (2:1–23)

IV. Ruth's Romance with Boaz (3:1–18)

V. Boaz Redeems Ruth (4:1–12)

VI. God Rewards Boaz and Ruth with a Son (4:13–17)

VII. David's Right to the Throne of Israel (4:18–22)

NAOMI WIDOWED

1 Now it came about in the days [A]when the judges
[a]governed, that there was [B]a famine in the land.
And a certain man [C]of Bethlehem in Judah went to
sojourn in the land of Moab [b]with his wife and his
two sons. 2 The name of the man *was* Elimelech, and
the name of his wife, Naomi; and the names of his
two sons *were* Mahlon and Chilion, Ephrathites of
Bethlehem in Judah. Now they [A]entered the land of
Moab and remained there. 3 Then Elimelech, Naomi's husband, died; and she was left with her two
sons. 4 They took for themselves Moabite women
as wives; the name of the one was Orpah and the
name of the other Ruth. And they lived there about
ten years. 5 Then [a]both Mahlon and Chilion also died,
and the woman was bereft of her two children and
her husband.

6 Then she arose with her daughters-in-law that
she might return from the land of Moab, for she
had heard in the land of Moab that the LORD had
[A]visited His people in [B]giving them food. 7 So she
departed from the place where she was, and her
two daughters-in-law with her; and they went on
the way to return to the land of Judah. 8 And Naomi
said to her two daughters-in-law, "Go, return each
of you to her mother's house. [A]May the LORD deal
kindly with you as you have dealt with the dead
and with me. 9 May the LORD grant that you may
find rest, each in the house of her husband." Then
she kissed them, and they lifted up their voices and
wept. 10 And they said to her, "*No,* but we will surely
return with you to your people." 11 But Naomi said,
"Return, my daughters. Why should you go with
me? Have I yet sons in my womb, that [A]they may be
your husbands? 12 Return, my daughters! Go, for I
am too old to have a husband. If I said I have hope,

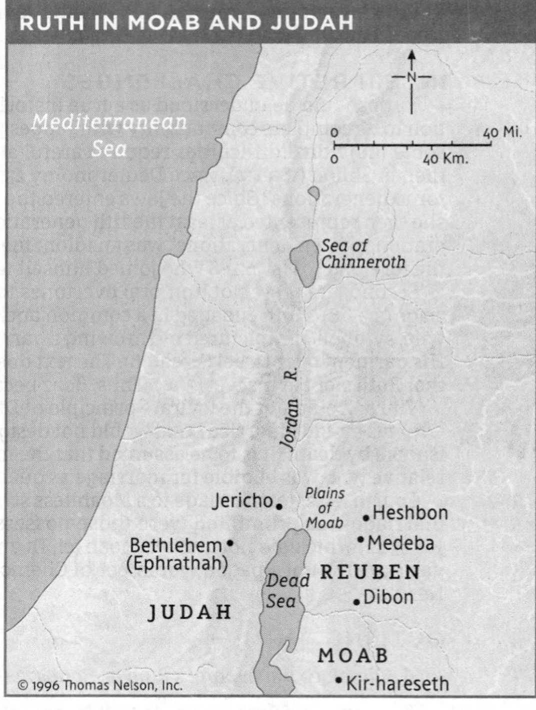

if I should even have a husband tonight and also
bear sons, 13 would you therefore wait until they
were grown? Would you therefore refrain from
marrying? No, my daughters; for it is [a]harder for
me than for you, for [A]the hand of the LORD has gone
forth against me."

1:1 [a]Or *judged* [b]Lit *he, and* [A]Judg 2:16-18 [B]Gen 12:10; 26:1; 2 Kin 8:1 [C]Judg 17:8; Mic 5:2 1:2 [A]Judg 3:30 1:5 [a]Lit *both of them* 1:6 [A]Ex 4:31; Jer 29:10; Zeph 2:7 [B]Ps 132:15; Matt 6:11 1:8 [A]2 Tim 1:16 1:11 [A]Gen 38:11; Deut 25:5 1:13 [a]Lit *more bitter* [A]Judg 2:15; Job 19:21; Ps 32:4

1:1–5 This introduction to Ruth sets in motion the following events, which culminate in Obed's birth and his relationship to the Davidic line of Christ. See Introduction: Background and Setting.

1:1 famine. This disaster sounds similar to the days of Abraham (Ge 12), Isaac (Ge 26), and Jacob (Ge 46). The text does not specify whether or not this famine was God's judgment (cf. 1Ki 17, 18, esp. 18:2). **Bethlehem in Judah.** Bethlehem ("house of bread") lies in the territory given to the tribe of Judah (Jos 15) about 6 mi. S of Jerusalem. Rachel, the wife of Jacob, was buried nearby (Ge 35:19; cf. 4:11). Bethlehem eventually received the title "city of David" (Lk 2:4, 11). Later, Mary delivered Christ (Lk 2:4–7; cf. Mic 5:2), and Herod slaughtered the infants here (Mt 2:16). This title (Jdg 17:7, 9; 19:1, 2, 18) serves to distinguish it from Bethlehem of Zebulun (Jos 19:15). **sojourn.** Elimelech intended to live temporarily in Moab as a resident alien until the famine passed. **Moab.** See Introduction: Background and Setting.

1:2 Elimelech. His name means "my God is king," signifying a devout commitment to the God of Israel. Most likely, he was a prominent man in the community whose brothers might have included the unnamed close relative and Boaz (cf. 4:3). **Naomi.** Her name means "pleasant." **Mahlon and Chilion.** Their names mean "sick" and "pining" respectively. **Ephrathites.** A title used of people who lived in the area anciently known as Ephrath (Ge 35:16, 19; 48:7) or Ephrathah (Ru 4:11; Mic 5:2), but later more prominently called Bethlehem (1:1). Jesse, father of David, is called "an Ephrathite of Bethlehem" (1Sa 17:12) and "Jesse the Bethlehemite" (1Sa 16:1, 18; 17:58).

1:4 Moabite women. See Introduction: Interpretive Challenges. **Orpah.** Her name means "stubborn." **Ruth.** Her name means "friendship." **about ten years.** This period would seem to include the entire time of Naomi's residency in Moab.

1:5 woman was bereft. Naomi, a widow in Moab whose two sons had died also, believed that the Lord had afflicted her with bitter days until she would die (1:13, 20, 21). No reason for the death of these 3 men in her life is given. Ruth married Mahlon, and Orpah united with Chilion (cf. 4:10).

1:6–22 The death of Elimelech and his two sons (1:3, 5) prepared the way for Naomi and Ruth to leave Orpah in Moab (1:6–14) and return together to Bethlehem (1:15–22).

1:6 the LORD had visited His people. Obviously the Lord had sent rain to break the famine. The sovereignty of Jehovah on behalf of Israel permeates the pages of Ruth in several ways: 1) actually for good (2:12; 4:12–14), 2) perceived by Naomi for bad (1:13, 21), and 3) in the context of prayer/blessing (1:8, 9, 17; 2:4, 12, 20; 3:10, 13; 4:11). The return of physical prosperity only shadowed the reality of a coming spiritual prosperity through the line of David in the person of Christ.

1:7 she departed. Naomi had friends (1:19), family (2:1), and prosperity (4:3) awaiting her in Bethlehem.

1:8–10 Naomi graciously encouraged her two daughters-in-law to return to their homes (1:8) and to remarry (1:9), but they emotionally insisted on going to Jerusalem (1:10).

1:11–13 Naomi selflessly reasoned a second time for their return, because she would be unable to provide them with new husbands (possibly in the spirit of a levirate marriage as described in Dt 25:5, 6). If Orpah and Ruth waited, they would most likely have become as old as Naomi was then before they could remarry (cf. Ge 38:11).

1:12 I am too old. Naomi was probably over 50.

1:13 the hand of the LORD. A figure of speech which describes the Lord's work. The Lord is spirit (Jn 4:24) and therefore does not have a literal hand.

RUTH'S LOYALTY

14 And they lifted up their voices and wept again;
and Orpah kissed her mother-in-law, but Ruth clung
to her.
15 Then she said, "Behold, your sister-in-law has
gone back to her people and her [A]gods; return after
your sister-in-law." 16 But Ruth said, "Do not urge
me to leave you *or* turn back from following you;
for where you go, I will go, and where you lodge,
I will lodge. Your people *shall be* my people, and
your God, my God. 17 Where you die, I will die, and
there I will be buried. Thus may [A]the LORD do to
me, and worse, if *anything but* death parts you and
me." 18 When [A]she saw that she was determined to
go with her, she [a]said no more to her.
19 So they both went until they came to Bethlehem. And when they had come to Bethlehem, [A]all the
city was stirred because of them, and [a]the women
said, "Is this Naomi?" 20 She said to them, "Do not
call me [a]Naomi; call me [b]Mara, for [c,A]the Almighty
has dealt very bitterly with me. 21 I went out full,
but [A]the LORD has brought me back empty. Why do
you call me Naomi, since the LORD has witnessed
against me and [a]the Almighty has afflicted me?"
22 So Naomi returned, and with her Ruth the Moabitess, her daughter-in-law, who returned from the
land of Moab. And they came to Bethlehem at [A]the
beginning of barley harvest.

RUTH GLEANS IN BOAZ' FIELD

2 Now Naomi had [a]a kinsman of her husband, a
[b]man of great wealth, of the family of [A]Elimelech,
whose name was Boaz. 2 And Ruth the Moabitess
said to Naomi, "Please let me go to the field and
[A]glean among the ears of grain after one in whose
sight I may find favor." And she said to her, "Go, my
daughter." 3 So she departed and went and gleaned
in the field after the reapers; and [a]she happened to
come to the portion of the field belonging to Boaz,
who was of the family of Elimelech. 4 Now behold,
Boaz came from Bethlehem and said to the reapers,
"[A]May the LORD be with you." And they said to him,
"May the LORD bless you." 5 Then Boaz said to his
servant who was [a]in charge of the reapers, "Whose
young woman is this?" 6 The servant [a]in charge
of the reapers replied, "She is the young Moabite
woman who returned with Naomi from the land of
Moab. 7 And she said, 'Please let me glean and gather
after the reapers among the sheaves.' Thus she came
and has remained from the morning until now;
she has been sitting in the house for a little while."
8 Then Boaz said to Ruth, "[a]Listen carefully, my
daughter. Do not go to glean in another field; furthermore, do not go on from this one, but stay here
with my maids. 9 Let your eyes be on the field which
they reap, and go after them. Indeed, I have commanded the servants not to touch you. When you are
thirsty, go to the [a]water jars and drink from what the
servants draw." 10 Then she [A]fell on her face, bowing
to the ground and said to him, "Why have I found
favor in your sight that you should take notice of
me, since I am a foreigner?" 11 Boaz replied to her,
"All that you have done for your mother-in-law after
the death of your husband has been fully reported to

1:15 [A]Josh 24:15; Judg 11:24 1:17 [A]1 Sam 3:17; 2 Kin 6:31 1:18 [a]Lit *ceased to speak* [A]Acts 21:14 1:19 [a]Lit *they* [A]Matt 21:10 1:20 [a]I.e. pleasant [b]I.e. bitter [c]Heb *Shaddai* [A]Ex 6:3; Job 6:4 1:21 [a]Heb *Shaddai* [A]Job 1:21 1:22 [A]Ex 9:31; Lev 23:10, 11 2:1 [a]Or *an acquaintance* [b]Or *mighty, valiant man* [A]Ruth 1:2 2:2 [A]Lev 19:9, 10; 23:22; Deut 24:19; Ruth 2:7 2:3 [a]Lit *her chance chanced upon* 2:4 [A]Judg 6:12; Ps 129:8; Luke 1:28; 2 Thess 3:16 2:5 [a]Lit *appointed over* 2:6 [a]Lit *who was appointed over* 2:8 [a]Lit *Have you not heard* 2:9 [a]Lit *vessels* 2:10 [A]1 Sam 25:23

1:14, 15 At the second plea to return, Orpah turned back. Naomi pleaded with Ruth a third time to return.

1:15 her gods. Refers to Chemosh the chief Moabite deity who required child sacrifice (2Ki 3:27) and other local deities.

1:16–18 Ruth recited her hallmark expression of loyalty to Naomi and commitment to the family she married into.

1:16 and your God, my God. This testimony evidenced Ruth's conversion from worshiping Chemosh to Jehovah of Israel (cf. 1Th 1:9, 10).

1:17 the LORD do to me. Ruth's vow bore further testimony to her conversion. She followed the path first blazed by Abraham (Jos 24:2).

1:19 they came to Bethlehem. A trip from Moab (at least 60–75 mi.) would have taken about 7–10 days. Having descended about 4,500 ft. from Moab into the Jordan Valley, they then ascended 3,750 ft. through the hills of Judea. **all the city.** Naomi had been well known in her prior residency (cf. Ephrathites of Bethlehem, 1:2). The question, "Is this Naomi?" most likely reflected the hard life of the last decade and the toll that it took on her appearance.

1:20, 21 Naomi ... Mara ... full ... empty. Naomi's outlook on life, although grounded in God's sovereignty, was not hopeful; thus she asked to be renamed "Mara," which means "bitter." Her experiences were not unlike Job's (Job 1, 2), but her perspective resembled that of Job's wife (Job 2:10). In reality, Naomi had 1) a full harvest prospect, 2) Ruth plus Boaz, and 3) the hope of God's future blessing.

1:22 Ruth the Moabitess. This title also appears at 2:2, 21; 4:5, 10. Ruth stands out as a foretaste of future Gentile conversions (cf. Ro 11). **at the beginning of barley harvest.** Normally the middle to the end of Apr.

2:1–23 Two widows, newly at home in Bethlehem after Naomi's 10-year absence, needed the basics of life. Ruth volunteered to go out and glean the fields for food (cf. Jas 1:27). In so doing, she unintentionally went to the field of Boaz, a close family relative, where she found great favor in his sight.

2:1 kinsman of her husband. Possibly as close as a brother of Elimelech (cf. 4:3), but if not, certainly within the tribe or clan. **a man of great wealth.** Lit. "a man of valor" (cf. Jdg 6:12; 11:1) who had unusual capacity to obtain and protect his property. **Boaz.** His name means "in him is strength." He had never married or was a widower (cf. 1Ch 2:11, 12; Mt 1:5; Lk 3:32).

2:2 glean. The Mosaic law commanded that the harvest should not be reaped to the corners nor the gleanings picked up (Lv 19:9, 10). Gleanings were stalks of grain left after the first cutting (cf. 2:3, 7, 8, 15, 17). These were dedicated to the needy, especially widows, orphans, and strangers (Lv 23:22; Dt 24:19–21).

2:3 she happened to come. Here was a classic example of God's providence at work. **portion of the field.** Possibly a large community field in which Boaz had a plot.

2:4–17 Note throughout how Boaz manifested the spirit of the law in going beyond what the Mosaic legislation required by 1) feeding Ruth (2:14), 2) letting Ruth glean among the sheaves (2:15), and 3) leaving extra grain for her to glean (2:16).

2:4 the LORD be with you. This unusual labor practice speaks to the exceptional godliness of Boaz and his workers.

2:7 sheaves. Bundles of grain stalks tied together for transport to the threshing floor.

2:7, 17 morning ... evening. Ruth proved to be diligent in her care for Naomi.

2:7 the house. Most likely a temporary shelter built with branches by the side of the field.

2:8 my daughter. Boaz was about 45–55 years old and a contemporary of Elimelech and Naomi. He would naturally see Ruth as a daughter (3:10, 11), much like Naomi did (cf. 2:2, 22; 3:1, 16, 18). Boaz contrasted himself with younger men (3:10). **my maids.** The ones who tied up the sheaves.

2:9 the servants. The ones who cut the grain with hand sickles (cf. 2:21).

2:10 a foreigner. Ruth remained ever mindful that she was an alien and, as such, must conduct herself humbly. Possibly she had knowledge of Dt 23:3, 4. She acknowledged the grace (lit. "favor") of Boaz.

2:11 fully reported to me. This speaks to both Naomi's quickness to speak kindly of Ruth and Boaz's network of influence in Bethlehem. Ruth remained true to her promise (1:16, 17).

me, and how you left your father and your mother
and the land of your birth, and came to a people
that you did not previously know. 12 [A]May the LORD
reward your work, and your wages be full from the
LORD, the God of Israel, [B]under whose wings you
have come to seek refuge." 13 Then she said, "I have
found favor in your sight, my lord, for you have
comforted me and indeed have spoken [a]kindly to
your maidservant, though I am not like one of your
maidservants."
14 At mealtime Boaz said to her, "[a]Come here,
that you may eat of the bread and dip your piece of
bread in the vinegar." So she sat beside the reapers;
and he [b]served her roasted grain, and she ate and
was satisfied [A]and had some left. 15 When she rose
to glean, Boaz commanded his servants, saying,
"Let her glean even among the sheaves, and do not
insult her. 16 Also you shall purposely pull out for
her *some grain* from the bundles and leave *it* that
she may glean, and do not rebuke her."
17 So she gleaned in the field until evening. Then
she beat out what she had gleaned, and it was about
an ephah of barley. 18 She took *it* up and went into
the city, and her mother-in-law saw what she had
gleaned. She also took *it* out and [A]gave [a]Naomi what
she had left after [b]she was satisfied. 19 Her mother-in-law then said to her, "Where did you glean
today and where did you work? May he who [A]took
notice of you be blessed." So she told her mother-in-law with whom she had worked and said, "The
name of the man with whom I worked today is
Boaz." 20 Naomi said to her daughter-in-law, "[A]May
he be blessed of the LORD who has not withdrawn
his kindness to the living and to the dead." Again
Naomi said to her, "The man is [a]our relative, he
is one of our [b]closest relatives." 21 Then Ruth the
Moabitess said, "[a]Furthermore, he said to me, 'You
should stay close to my servants until they have
finished all my harvest.'" 22 Naomi said to Ruth
her daughter-in-law, "It is good, my daughter, that
you go out with his maids, so that *others* do not fall
upon you in another field." 23 So she stayed close by
the maids of Boaz in order to glean until [A]the end
of the barley harvest and the wheat harvest. And
she lived with her mother-in-law.

BOAZ WILL REDEEM RUTH

3 Then Naomi her mother-in-law said to her, "My
daughter, shall I not seek [a]security for you, that it
may be well with you? 2 Now is not Boaz [A]our [a]kins-
man, with whose maids you were? Behold, he winnows barley at the threshing floor tonight. 3 Wash
yourself therefore, and anoint yourself and put on
your *best* clothes, and go down to the threshing
floor; *but* do not make yourself known to the man
until he has finished eating and drinking. 4 It shall be
when he lies down, that you shall [a]notice the place
where he lies, and you shall go and uncover his feet
and lie down; then he will tell you what you shall
do." 5 She said to her, "[A]All that you say I will do."
6 So she went down to the threshing floor and
did according to all that her mother-in-law had
commanded her. 7 When Boaz had eaten and drunk
and [A]his heart was merry, he went to lie down at
the end of the heap of grain; and she came secretly,
and uncovered his feet and lay down. 8 It happened
in the middle of the night that the man was startled and [a]bent forward; and behold, a woman was

2:12 [A]1 Sam 24:19 [B]Ruth 1:16; Ps 17:8; 36:7; 57:1; 61:4; 63:7; 91:4 2:13 [a]Lit *to the heart of your* 2:14 [a]Lit *Draw near* [b]Lit *held out to* [A]Ruth 2:18 2:18 [a]Lit *her* [b]Lit *her satiety* [A]Ruth 2:14 2:19 [A]Ps 41:1 2:20 [a]Lit *near to us* [b]Lit *redeemers* [A]2 Sam 2:5 2:21 [a]Lit *Also that* 2:23 [A]Deut 16:9 3:1 [a]Lit *rest* 3:2 [a]Or *acquaintance* [A]Deut 25:5-10 3:4 [a]Lit *know* 3:5 [A]Eph 6:1; Col 3:20 3:7 [A]Judg 19:6, 9; 2 Sam 13:28; 1 Kin 21:7; Esth 1:10 3:8 [a]Lit *twisted himself*

2:12 wings ... refuge. Scripture pictures God as catching Israel up on His wings in the Exodus (Ex 19:4; Dt 32:11). God is here portrayed as a mother bird sheltering the young and fragile with her wings (cf. Pss 17:8; 36:7; 57:1; 61:4; 63:7; 91:1, 4). Boaz blessed Ruth in light of her newfound commitment to and dependence on the Lord. Later, he would become God's answer to this prayer (cf. 3:9).

2:14 vinegar. Sour wine, mixed with a little oil, used to quench thirst.

2:15 among the sheaves. Boaz granted her request (2:7) to go beyond the letter of the law.

2:17 ephah. Over one-half bushel, weighing about 30 to 40 lbs.

2:18 what she had left. Not the gleaned grain, but rather the lunch ration which Ruth did not eat (cf. 2:14).

2:20 his kindness. Naomi began to understand God's sovereign working, covenant loyalty, lovingkindness, and mercy toward her because Ruth, without human direction (2:3), found the near relative Boaz. **one of our closest relatives.** The great kinsman-redeemer theme of Ruth begins here (cf. 3:9, 12; 4:1, 3, 6, 8, 14). A close relative could redeem 1) a family member sold into slavery (Lv 25:47–49), 2) land which needed to be sold under economic hardship (Lv 25:23–28), and/or 3) the family name by virtue of a levirate marriage (Dt 25:5–10). This earthly custom pictures the reality of God the Redeemer doing a greater work (Pss 19:14; 78:35; Is 41:14; 43:14) by reclaiming those who needed to be spiritually redeemed out of slavery to sin (Ps 107:2; Is 62:12). Thus, Boaz pictures Christ, who as a Brother (Heb 2:17), redeemed those who 1) were slaves to sin (Ro 6:15–18), 2) had lost all earthly possessions/privileges in the Fall (Ge 3:17–19), and 3) had been alienated by sin from God (2Co 5:18–21). Boaz stands in the direct line of Christ (Mt 1:5; Lk 3:32). This turn of events marks the point where Naomi's human emptiness (1:21) begins to be refilled by the Lord. Her night of earthly doubt has been broken by the dawning of new hope (cf. Ro 8:28–39).

2:22 do not fall upon you. Ruth the Moabitess would not be treated with such mercy and grace by strangers outside of the family.

2:23 the end of ... harvest. Barley harvest usually began about mid-Apr. and wheat harvest extended to mid-June—a period of intense labor for about two months. This generally coincided with the 7 weeks between Passover and the Feast of Weeks, i.e., Pentecost (cf. Lv 23:15, 16; Dt 16:9–12).

3:1–18 Encouraged by Ruth's days in Boaz's field, Naomi instructed Ruth in the way she should go to ensure a brighter future. Ruth carefully followed Naomi's directions to solicit redemption by Boaz, while the Lord had prepared Boaz to redeem Ruth. Only one potential obstacle remained, a relative nearer than Boaz.

3:1 security. Naomi felt responsible, just as she did in 1:9, for Ruth's future husband and home.

3:2 threshing floor. Usually a large, hard area of earth or stone on the downwind (E) side of the village where threshing took place (loosening the grain from the straw and winnowing). **tonight.** Winnowing (tossing grain into the air to finish separating the grain from the chaff) normally occurred in late afternoon when the Mediterranean winds prevailed. Sifting and bagging the grain would have carried over past dark, and Boaz may have remained all night to guard the grain from theft.

3:3, 4 Naomi instructed Ruth 1) to put on her best appearance and 2) to propose marriage to Boaz by utilizing an ancient Near Eastern custom. Since Boaz was a generation older than Ruth (2:8), this overture would indicate Ruth's desire to marry Boaz, which the older, gracious Boaz would not have initiated with a younger woman.

3:7 his heart was merry. Using the same language of 3:1 ("security" ... "be well"), Boaz is described as having a sense of well-being, which is most readily explained by the full harvest in contrast to previous years of famine (cf. Jdg 18:20; 1Ki 21:7).

lying at his feet. 9 He said, "Who are you?" And
she answered, "I am Ruth your maid. So spread
your covering over your maid, for you are a [a]close
relative." 10 Then he said, "[A]May you be blessed of
the LORD, my daughter. You have shown your last
kindness to be better than the first by not going
after young men, whether poor or rich. 11 Now, my
daughter, do not fear. I will do for you whatever
you [a]ask, for all my people in the [b]city know that
you are [A]a woman of excellence. 12 Now it is true I
am a [a]close relative; however, there is a [a]relative
closer than I. 13 Remain this night, and when morning comes, [A]if he will [a]redeem you, good; let him
redeem you. But if he does not wish to [a]redeem
you, then I will redeem you, [B]as the LORD lives. Lie
down until morning."
14 So she lay at his feet until morning and rose
before one could recognize another; and he said,
"[A]Let it not be known that the woman came to the
threshing floor." 15 Again he said, "Give me the cloak
that is on you and hold it." So she held it, and he
measured six *measures* of barley and laid *it* on her.
Then [a]she went into the city. 16 When she came to
her mother-in-law, she said, "[a]How did it go, my
daughter?" And she told her all that the man had
done for her. 17 She said, "These six *measures* of
barley he gave to me, for he said, 'Do not go to
your mother-in-law empty-handed.' " 18 Then she
said, "Wait, my daughter, until you know how the
matter [a]turns out; for the man will not rest until he
has [b]settled it today."

THE MARRIAGE OF RUTH

4 Now Boaz went up to the gate and sat down
there, and behold, [A]the [a]close relative of whom
Boaz spoke was passing by, so he said, "Turn aside,
[b]friend, sit down here." And he turned aside and
sat down. 2 He took ten men of the [A]elders of the
city and said, "Sit down here." So they sat down.
3 Then he said to the [a]closest relative, "Naomi, who
has come back from the land of Moab, has to sell
the piece of land [A]which belonged to our brother
Elimelech. 4 So I thought to [a]inform you, saying,
'[A]Buy *it* before those who are sitting *here*, and before the elders of my people. If you will redeem *it*,
redeem *it*; but if [b]not, tell me that I may know; for
[B]there is no one but you to redeem *it*, and I am after
you.' " And he said, "I will redeem *it*." 5 Then Boaz
said, "On the day you buy the field from the hand
of Naomi, you must also acquire Ruth the Moabitess, the widow of the deceased, in order [A]to raise
up the name of the deceased on his inheritance."

3:9 [a]Or *redeemer* 3:10 [A]Ruth 2:20 3:11 [a]Lit *say* [b]Lit *gate* [A]Prov 12:4; 31:10 3:12 [a]Or *redeemer* 3:13 [a]Or *act as close relative to* [A]Deut 25:5; Matt 22:24 [B]Judg 8:19; Jer 4:2; 12:16 3:14 [A]Rom 14:16; 2 Cor 8:21 3:15 [a]So with many mss; M.T. *he* 3:16 [a]Lit *Who are you?* 3:18 [a]Lit *falls* [b]Lit *finished the matter* 4:1 [a]Or *redeemer* [b]Lit *a certain one* [A]Ruth 3:12 4:2 [A]1 Kin 21:8; Prov 31:23 4:3 [a]Lit *redeemer* [A]Lev 25:25 4:4 [a]Lit *uncover your ear* [b]Lit *no one will redeem* [A]Jer 32:7f [B]Lev 25:25 4:5 [A]Gen 38:8; Deut 25:5f; Matt 22:24

3:9 spread your covering over your maid. Ruth righteously appealed to Boaz, using the language of Boaz's earlier prayer (2:12), to marry her according to the levirate custom (Dt 25:5–10). See Introduction: Interpretive Challenges.

3:10 kindness. Ruth's loyalty to Naomi, the Lord, and even Boaz is commended by Boaz. **after young men.** Ruth demonstrated moral excellence in that 1) she did not engage in immorality, 2) she did not remarry outside the family, and 3) she had appealed for levirate redemption to an older, godly man.

3:11 excellence. In all respects, Ruth personifies excellence (cf. Pr 31:10). This same language has been used of Boaz ("a man of great wealth" or more likely "a man of valor" in 2:1), thus making them the perfectly matched couple for an exemplary marriage.

3:12 a relative closer than I. Boaz righteously deferred to someone else who was nearer in relationship to Elimelech. The nearer relative may have been Boaz's older brother (cf. 4:3), or Boaz may have been his cousin. The fact that the neighbor women said, "A son has been born to Naomi" at Obed's birth would suggest the brother or cousin relationship to Elimelech (4:17).

3:13 I will redeem you. Boaz willingly accepted Ruth's proposal, if the nearer relative was unable or unwilling to exercise his levirate duty. **as the LORD lives.** The most solemn, binding oath an Israelite could vow.

3:14 lay at his feet. According to the text, no immorality occurred. Boaz even insisted on no appearance of evil.

3:15 six *measures*. The Hebrew text gives no standard of measurement, but some translations use the word *ephah*. However, 6 ephahs would weigh about 200 lbs., far too much for Ruth to carry home in her shawl. Therefore, deemed most reasonable is 6 seahs (60–80 lbs.), which would have been twice the amount Ruth had previously gleaned (see 2:17).

3:18 today. Naomi knew that Boaz was a man of integrity and would fulfill his promise with a sense of urgency. They needed to wait on the Lord to work through Boaz.

4:1–22 God's divine plan fully blossomed as Boaz redeemed Naomi's land and Ruth's hand in marriage. Naomi, once empty (1:21), is full; Ruth, once a widow (1:5), is married; most importantly, the Lord has prepared Christ's line of descent in David, through Boaz and Obed, back to Judah (Ge 49:10) to fulfill the proper messianic lineage.

4:1 went up. Apparently the threshing floor was below the level of the gate. Compare Ru 3:3, "go down to the threshing floor." **the gate.** The normal public place to transact business in ancient times (cf. 2Sa 15:2; Job 29:7; La 5:14). **friend.** The Heb. text is not clear whether Boaz called him directly by name (which is then not mentioned by the author) or addressed him indirectly.

4:2 ten men. This number apparently comprised a quorum to officially transact business, although only two or three witnesses were needed for judicial proceedings (cf. Dt 17:6; 19:15).

4:3 Naomi ... has to sell. As a widow, she needed the money for living expenses, knowing that the land would ultimately be returned at Jubilee (Lv 25:28). **our brother Elimelech.** Boaz and the unnamed relative were most likely either brothers or cousins.

4:4 Buy *it*. As authorized by the Mosaic law (Lv 25:23–28).

4:5 you must also acquire. Both redeeming Ruth and the land would not have been required by the letter of the levirate law (Dt 25:5, 6). Perhaps this exemplified Boaz's desire to obey the spirit of the law (*see note on 2:4–17*) or maybe redemption of land and marriage had been combined by local tradition. The levirate principle appears first in Scripture at Ge 38:8 (cf. Mt 22:23–28).

KINSMAN-REDEEMER

OT Qualification	Christ's Fulfillment
1. Blood Relationship	Gal 4:4, 5; Heb 2:16, 17
2. Necessary Resources	1Co 6:20; 1Pe 1:18, 19
3. Willingness to Buy	Jn 10:15–18; 1Jn 3:16

6 [A]The [a]closest relative said, "I cannot redeem *it*
for myself, because I would [b]jeopardize my own
inheritance. Redeem *it* for yourself; you *may have*
my right of redemption, for I cannot redeem *it*."
7 Now this was [A]*the custom* in former times in Israel concerning the redemption and the exchange
of land to confirm any matter: a man removed his
sandal and gave it to another; and this was the
manner of attestation in Israel. 8 So the [a]closest
relative said to Boaz, "Buy *it* for yourself." And he
removed his sandal. 9 Then Boaz said to the elders
and all the people, "You are witnesses today that
I have bought from the hand of Naomi all that
belonged to Elimelech and all that belonged to
Chilion and Mahlon. 10 Moreover, I have acquired
Ruth the Moabitess, the widow of Mahlon, to be
my wife in order to raise up the name of the deceased on his inheritance, so [A]that the name of the
deceased will not be cut off from his brothers or
from the [a]court of his *birth* place; you are witnesses
today." 11 All the people who were in the [a]court,
and the elders, said, "*We are* witnesses. May the
LORD make the woman who is coming into your
home [A]like Rachel and Leah, both of whom built
the house of Israel; and may you achieve [b]wealth
in Ephrathah and [c]become famous in Bethlehem.
12 Moreover, may your house be like the house of
[A]Perez whom Tamar bore to Judah, through the
[a]offspring which the LORD will give you by this
young woman."
13 So Boaz took Ruth, and she became his wife,
and he went in to her. And [A]the LORD [a]enabled her
to conceive, and she gave birth to a son. 14 Then
the [A]women said to Naomi, "Blessed is the LORD
who has not left you without a [a]redeemer today,
and may his name [b]become famous in Israel.

4:6 [a]Lit *redeemer* [b]Lit *ruin* [A]Lev 25:25 4:7 [A]Deut 25:8-10 4:8 [a]Lit *redeemer* 4:10 [a]Lit *gate* [A]Deut 25:6 4:11 [a]Lit *gate* [b]Or *power* [c]Lit *call the name in* [A]Gen 29:25-30 4:12 [a]Lit *seed* [A]Gen 38:29; 46:12; Ruth 4:18 4:13 [a]Lit *gave her conception* [A]Gen 29:31; 33:5 4:14 [a]Or *closest relative* [b]Lit *be called in* [A]Luke 1:58

4:6 I would jeopardize my own inheritance. He was unwilling to have the family portfolio split between his existing children and the potential offspring of a union with Ruth. **Redeem *it* for yourself.** The closer relative relinquished his legal right to the land and Ruth. This cleared the way for Boaz to redeem both.

4:7 removed his sandal. The Scripture writer explained to his own generation what had been a custom in former generations. This kind of tradition appears in Dt 25:5–10 and apparently continued at least to the time of Amos (2:6; 8:6). The closer relative legally transferred his right to the property as symbolized by the sandal, most likely that of the nearer relative.

4:9 I have bought. Boaz exercised his legal option to redeem both the land and Ruth before appropriate witnesses.

4:10 the widow of Mahlon. Only here is Ruth's former husband identified (cf. 1:5 note). Therefore, it can also be assumed that Chilion married Orpah. **I have acquired Ruth ... to be my wife.** Boaz exercised the spirit of the law and became Ruth's kinsman-redeemer (Dt 25:5, 6). **the name of the deceased.** Perpetuation of the family name (1Sa 24:21) was an important feature that the levirate process provided (cf. Dt 25:6).

4:11 *We are* witnesses. This affirmation signaled the strong approval of the city. **like Rachel and Leah.** Rachel, the most beloved wife of Jacob, was buried nearby (Ge 35:19); Leah was the mother of Judah (by Jacob), their namesake descendant (Ge 29:35). This remembrance went back almost 900 years to ca. 1915 B.C. **Ephrathah ... Bethlehem.** The ancient name of Bethlehem (Ge 35:19; 48:7). *See note on 1:2.* Micah later prophetically wrote that this city would be the birthplace of Messiah (5:2).

4:12 Perez ... Tamar ... Judah. Read Ge 38:1–30 for the background to these 3. Tamar, the widow of Judah's first son, Er, when denied a levirate marriage to Judah's remaining son, Shelah (38:14), took matters into her own hands and immorally consorted with her father-in-law Judah (38:18). Perez, the firstborn of twins by Tamar, became the main ancestor of the Ephrathites and Bethlehemites (1Ch 2:3–5, 19, 50, 51; 4:4). *See note on 4:18.* **offspring.** The firstborn son would be considered the son of Mahlon. Additional sons would legally be the offspring of Boaz (Dt 25:6).

4:13 he went in to her. OT euphemism for sexual intercourse. **the LORD enabled her to conceive.** As with Rachel (Ge 30:22) and Leah (Ge 29:31), so also with Ruth (cf. Ps 127:3).

4:14 the LORD ... has not left you. In contrast to Naomi's worst moments of despair (1:20, 21). **a redeemer ... his name.** Refers to Obed, not Boaz (cf. 4:11), who cared for Naomi in her latter years.

RUTH: THE PROVERBS 31 WIFE

The "virtuous" wife of Proverbs 31:10 is personified by "virtuous" Ruth of whom the same Heb. word is used (3:11). With amazing parallel, they share at least 8 character traits (see below). One wonders (in concert with Jewish tradition) if King Lemuel's mother might not have been Bathsheba, who orally passed the family heritage of Ruth's spotless reputation along to David's son Solomon. Lemuel, which means "devoted to God," could have been a family name for Solomon (cf. Jedediah, 2Sa 12:25), who then could have penned Pr 31:10–31 with Ruth in mind. Each woman was:

1. Devoted to her family (Ru 1:15–18 // Pr 31:10–12, 23)
2. Delighting in her work (Ru 2:2 // Pr 31:13)
3. Diligent in her labor (Ru 2:7, 17, 23 // Pr 31:14–18, 19–21, 24, 27)
4. Dedicated to godly speech (Ru 2:10, 13 // Pr 31:26)
5. Dependent on God (Ru 2:12 // Pr 31:25b, 30)
6. Dressed with care (Ru 3:3 // Pr 31:22, 25a)
7. Discreet with men (Ru 3:6–13 // Pr 31:11, 12, 23)
8. Delivering blessings (Ru 4:14, 15 // Pr 31:28, 29, 31)

15 May he also be to you a restorer of life and a
sustainer of your old age; for your daughter-in-law,
who loves you [a,A]and is better to you than seven
sons, has given birth to him."

THE LINE OF DAVID BEGAN HERE

16 Then Naomi took the child [a]and laid him in her
lap, and became his nurse. 17 The neighbor women
gave him a name, saying, "A son has been born to
Naomi!" So they named him Obed. He is the father
of Jesse, the father of David.
18 Now these are the generations of Perez: [A]to
Perez [a]was born Hezron, 19 and to Hezron was
born Ram, and to Ram, Amminadab, 20 and to
Amminadab was born Nahshon, and to Nahshon,
Salmon, 21 and to Salmon was born Boaz, and to
Boaz, Obed, 22 and to Obed was born Jesse, and
to Jesse, David.

4:15 [a]Lit *who* [A]Ruth 1:16, 17; 2:11, 12 4:16 [a]I.e. as her own 4:18 [a]Lit *begot,* and so through v 22 [A]Matt 1:3-6

4:15 better ... than seven sons. Seven represented the number of perfection and thus 7 sons would make the complete family (cf. 1Sa 2:5). However, Ruth exceeded this standard all by herself.

4:16 became his nurse. This expresses the natural affection of a godly grandmother for her God-given grandson.

4:17 The neighbor women gave him a name. Here is the only place in the OT where a child was named by someone other than the immediate family. Obed means "servant." A son has been born to Naomi! Ruth vicariously bore the son that would restore the family name of Naomi's deceased son Mahlon (cf. 4:1). Obed ... Jesse ... David. This complete genealogy appears identically in 4 other biblical texts (Ru 4:21, 22; 1Ch 2:12–15; Mt 1:5, 6; Lk 3:31, 32). Boaz and Ruth were the great-grandparents of David.

4:18–22 Perez ... David. This representative genealogy, which spans 9 centuries from Perez (ca. 1885 B.C.) to David (ca. 1040 B.C.), specifically names 10 generations. The first 5 (Perez to Nashon) cover the patriarchal times to the Exodus and wilderness wanderings. Salmon to David covers Joshua's lifetime and the judges to the monarchy. This genealogical compression by omission does not signal faulty records, because in Jewish thinking, "son" could mean "descendant" (cf. Mt 1:1). The purpose of a family record was not necessarily to include every generation, but rather to establish incontestable succession by way of the more notable ancestors.

4:18 Perez. *See note on v. 12.* Although this genealogy only goes back to Perez, it conclusively establishes that David's lineage extends further back through Judah (Ge 49:8–12), Jacob (Ge 28:10–17), and Isaac (Ge 26:24) to Abraham (Ge 12:1–3).

4:18, 19 Hezron. Cf. Ge 46:12.

4:19 Ram. Listed as Arni in some Gr. texts of Lk 3:33.

4:19, 20 Amminadab. The father-in-law of Aaron (Ex 6:23), who appears in 1Ch 2:10, and is cited in Mt 1:4 and Lk 3:33. Some Gr. mss. also include Admin between Ram and Amminadab in Lk 3:33.

4:20 Nahshon. The leader of Judah in the Exodus (Nu 1:7; 2:3; 7:12, 17; 10:14).

4:20, 21 Salmon. The husband of Rahab the harlot (cf. Mt 1:5).

4:21 to Salmon was born Boaz. Since Mt 1:5 lists Rahab the harlot, who lived ca. 1425–1350 B.C., as Salmon's wife, it thus indicates that some generations have been selectively omitted between Salmon and Boaz (ca. 1160–1090 B.C.).

4:22 David. Looking back at Ruth from a NT perspective, latent messianic implications become more apparent (cf. Mt 1:1). The fruit which is promised later on in the Davidic Covenant (2Sa 7:1–17) finds its seedbed here. The hope of a messianic king and kingdom (2Sa 7:12–14) will be fulfilled in the Lord Jesus Christ (Rev 19, 20) through the lineage of David's grandfather Obed, who was born to Boaz and Ruth the Moabitess.

THE FIRST AND SECOND BOOKS OF SAMUEL

TITLE

First and Second Samuel were considered as one book in the earliest Hebrew manuscripts, and were later divided into the two books by the translators of the Greek version, the Septuagint (LXX), a division followed by the Latin Vulgate (Vg.), English translations, and modern Hebrew Bibles. The earliest Hebrew manuscripts entitled the one book "Samuel" after the man God used to establish the kingship in Israel. Later Hebrew texts and the English versions call the divided book "1 and 2 Samuel." The LXX designated them "The First and Second Books of Kingdoms" and the Vg., "First and Second Kings," with our 1 and 2 Kings being "Third and Fourth Kings."

AUTHOR AND DATE

Jewish tradition ascribed the writing of "Samuel" to Samuel himself or to Samuel, Nathan, and Gad (based on 1Ch 29:29). But Samuel cannot be the writer because his death is recorded in 1Sa 25:1, before the events associated with David's reign even took place. Further, Nathan and Gad were prophets of the Lord during David's lifetime and would not have been alive when the book of Samuel was written. Though the written records of these 3 prophets could have been used for information in the writing of 1 and 2 Samuel, the human author of these books is unknown. The work comes to the reader as an anonymous writing, i.e., the human author speaks for the Lord and gives the divine interpretation of the events narrated.

The books of Samuel contain no clear indication of the date of composition. That the author wrote after the division of the kingdom between Israel and Judah in 931 B.C. is clear, due to the many references to Israel and Judah as distinct entities (1Sa 11:8; 17:52; 18:16; 2Sa 5:5; 11:11; 12:8; 19:42–43; 24:1, 9). Also, the statement concerning Ziklag's belonging "to the kings of Judah to this day" in 1Sa 27:6 gives clear evidence of a post-Solomonic date of writing. There is no such clarity concerning how late the date of writing could be. However, 1 and 2 Samuel are included in the Former Prophets in the Hebrew canon, along with Joshua, Judges, and 1 and 2 Kings. If the Former Prophets were composed as a unit, then Samuel would have been written during the Babylonian captivity (ca. 560–540 B.C.), since 2 Kings concludes during the exile (2Ki 25:27–30). However, since Samuel has a different literary style than Kings, it was most likely penned before the Exile during the period of the divided kingdom (ca. 931–722 B.C.) and later made an integral part of the Former Prophets.

BACKGROUND AND SETTING

The majority of the action recorded in 1 and 2 Samuel took place in and around the central highlands in the land of Israel. The nation of Israel was largely concentrated in an area that ran about 90 mi. from the hill country of Ephraim in the N (1Sa 1:1; 9:4) to the hill country of Judah in the S (Jos 20:7; 21:11) and between 15 to 35 mi. E to W. This central spine ranges in height from 1,500 ft. to 3,300 ft. above sea level. The major cities of 1 and 2 Samuel are to be found in these central highlands: Shiloh, the residence of Eli and the tabernacle; Ramah, the hometown of Samuel; Gibeah, the headquarters of Saul; Bethlehem, the birthplace of David; Hebron, David's capital when he ruled over Judah; and Jerusalem, the ultimate "city of David."

The events of 1 and 2 Samuel took place between the years ca. 1105 B.C., the birth of Samuel (1Sa 1:1–28), to ca. 971 B.C., the last words of David (2Sa 23:1–7). Thus, the books span about 135 years of history. During those years, Israel was transformed from a loosely knit group of tribes under "judges" to a united nation under the reign of a centralized monarchy. They look primarily at Samuel (ca. 1105–1030 B.C.), Saul who reigned ca. 1052–1011 B.C., and David who was king of the united monarchy ca. 1011–971 B.C.

HISTORICAL AND THEOLOGICAL THEMES

As 1 Samuel begins, Israel was at a low point spiritually. The priesthood was corrupt (1Sa 2:12–17, 22–26), the ark of the covenant was not at the tabernacle (1Sa 4:3–7:2), idolatry was practiced (1Sa 7:3, 4), and the judges were dishonest (1Sa 8:2, 3). Through the influence of godly Samuel (1Sa 12:23) and David (1Sa 13:14), these conditions were reversed. Second Samuel concludes with the anger of the Lord being withdrawn from Israel (2Sa 24:25).

During the years narrated in 1 and 2 Samuel, the great empires of the ancient world were in a state of weakness. Neither Egypt nor the Mesopotamian powers, Babylon and Assyria, were threats to Israel at that time. The two nations most hostile to the Israelites were the Philistines (1Sa 4; 7; 13; 14; 17; 23; 31; 2Sa 5) to the W and the Ammonites (1Sa 11; 2Sa 10–12) to the E. The major contingent of the Philistines had migrated from the Aegean Islands and Asia Minor in the 12th century B.C. After being denied access to Egypt, they settled among other preexisting Philistines along the Mediterranean coast of Canaan. The Philistines controlled the use of iron, which gave them a decided military and economic advantage over Israel (1Sa 13:19–22). The Ammonites were descendants of Lot (Ge 19:38) who lived on the Transjordan Plateau. David conquered the Philistines (2Sa 8:1) and the Ammonites (2Sa 12:29–31), along with other nations that surrounded Israel (2Sa 8:2–14).

There are four predominant theological themes in 1 and 2 Samuel. The first is the Davidic Covenant. The books are literarily framed by two references to the "anointed" king in the prayer of Hannah (1Sa 2:10) and the song of David (2Sa 22:51). This is a reference to the Messiah, the King who will triumph over the nations who are opposed to God (see Ge 49:8–12; Nu 24:7–9, 17–19). According to the Lord's promise, this Messiah will come through the line of David and establish David's throne forever (2Sa 7:12–16). The events of David's life recorded in Samuel foreshadow the actions of David's greater Son (i.e., Christ) in the future.

A second theme is the sovereignty of God, clearly seen in these books. One example is the birth of Samuel in response to Hannah's prayer (1Sa 9:17; 16:12, 13). Also, in relation to David, it is particularly evident that nothing can frustrate God's plan to have him rule over Israel (1Sa 24:20).

Third, the work of the Holy Spirit in empowering men for divinely appointed tasks is evident. The Spirit of the Lord came upon both Saul and David after their anointing as king (1Sa 10:10; 16:13). The power of the Holy Spirit brought forth prophecy (1Sa 10:6) and victory in battle (1Sa 11:6).

Fourth, the books of Samuel demonstrate the personal and national effects of sin. The sins of Eli and his sons resulted in their deaths (1Sa 2:12–17, 22–25; 3:10–14; 4:17, 18). The lack of reverence for the ark of the covenant led to the death of a number of Israelites (1Sa 6:19; 2Sa 6:6, 7). Saul's disobedience resulted in the Lord's judgment, and he was rejected as king over Israel (1Sa 13:9, 13, 14; 15:8, 9, 20–23). Although David was forgiven for his sin of adultery and murder after his confession (2Sa 12:13), he still suffered the inevitable and devastating consequences of his sin (2Sa 12:14).

INTERPRETIVE CHALLENGES

The books of Samuel contain a number of interpretive issues that have been widely discussed: 1) Which of the ancient mss. is closest to the original autograph? The standard Hebrew (Masoretic) text has been relatively poorly preserved, and the LXX often differs from it. Thus, the exact reading of the original autograph of the text is in places hard to determine (see 1Sa 13:1). The Masoretic text will be assumed to represent the original text unless there is a grammatical or contextual impossibility. This accounts for many of the numerical discrepancies. 2) Is Samuel ambivalent to the establishment of the human kingship in Israel? It is claimed that while 1Sa 9–11 presents a positive view of the kingship, 1Sa 8 and 12 are strongly anti-monarchial. It is preferable, however, to see the book as presenting a balanced perspective of the human kingship. While the desire of Israel for a king was acceptable (Dt 17:15), their reason for wanting a king showed a lack of faith in the Lord (*see notes on 1Sa 8:5, 20*). 3) How does one explain the bizarre behavior of the prophets? It is commonly held that 1 and 2 Samuel present the prophets as ecstatic speakers with bizarre behavior just like the pagan prophets of the other nations. But there is nothing in the text which is inconsistent with seeing the prophets as communicators of divine revelation, at times prophesying with musical accompaniment (*see notes on 1Sa 10:5; 19:23, 24*). 4) How did the Holy Spirit minister before Pentecost? The ministry of the Holy Spirit in 1Sa 10:6, 10; 11:6; 16:13, 14; 19:20, 23; 2Sa 23:2 was not describing salvation in the NT sense, but an empowering by the Lord for His service (see also Jdg 3:10; 6:34; 11:29; 13:25; 14:6, 19; 15:14). 5) What was the identity of the "distressing spirit"? Is it a personal being, i.e., a demon, or a spirit of discontent created by God in the heart (cf. Jdg 9:23)? Traditionally, it has been viewed as a demon (*see note on 1Sa 16:14*). 6) How did Samuel appear in 1Sa 28:3–5? It seems best to understand the appearance of Samuel as the Lord allowing the dead Samuel to speak with Saul. 7) What is the identity of David's seed in 2Sa 7:12–15? It is usually taken as Solomon. However, the NT refers the words to Jesus, God's Son in Heb 1:5 (*see notes on 2Sa 7:12–15*).

OUTLINE

I. Samuel: Prophet and Judge to Israel (1:1–7:17)
- A. Samuel the Prophet (1:1–4:1a)
  1. The birth of Samuel (1:1–28)
  2. The prayer of Hannah (2:1–10)
  3. The growth of Samuel (2:11–26)
  4. The oracle against Eli's house (2:27–36)
  5. The Word of the Lord through Samuel (3:1–4:1a)
- B. Samuel the Judge (4:1b–7:17)
  1. The saga of the ark (4:1b–7:1)
  2. Israel's victory over the Philistines and the judgeship of Samuel (7:2–17)

II. Saul: First King Over Israel (8:1–15:35)
- A. The Rise of Saul to the Kingship (8:1–12:25)
  - 1. The demand of Israel for a king (8:1–22)
  - 2. The process of Saul becoming king (9:1–11:13)
  - 3. The exhortation of Samuel to Israel concerning the king (11:14–12:25)
- B. The Decline of Saul in the Kingship (13:1–15:35)
  - 1. The rebuke of Saul (13:1–15)
  - 2. The wars of Saul (13:16–14:52)
  - 3. The rejection of Saul (15:1–35)

III. David and Saul: Transfer of the Kingship in Israel (16:1–31:13)
- A. The Introduction of David (16:1–17:58)
  - 1. The anointing of David (16:1–13)
  - 2. David in the court of Saul (16:14–23)
  - 3. David, the warrior of the Lord (17:1–58)
- B. David Driven from the Court of Saul (18:1–20:42)
  - 1. The anger and fear of Saul toward David (18:1–30)
  - 2. The defense of David by Jonathan and Michal (19:1–20:42)
- C. David's Flight from Saul's Pursuit (21:1–28:2)
  - 1. Saul's killing of the priests at Nob (21:1–22:23)
  - 2. Saul's life spared twice by David (23:1–26:25)
  - 3. David's despair and Philistine refuge (27:1–28:2)
- D. The Death of Saul (28:3–31:13)
  - 1. Saul's final night (28:3–25)
  - 2. David's dismissal by the Philistines (29:1–11)
  - 3. David's destruction of the Amalekites (30:1–31)
  - 4. Saul's final day (31:1–13)

ELKANAH AND HIS WIVES

1 Now there was a certain man from [A]Ra-
mathaim-zophim from the [B]hill country of
Ephraim, and his name was [C]Elkanah the son of
Jeroham, the son of Elihu, the son of Tohu, the son
of Zuph, an Ephraimite. 2 He had [A]two wives: the
name of one was [B]Hannah and the name of the
other Peninnah; and Peninnah had children, but
Hannah had no children.
3 Now this man would go up from his city [A]yearly
[B]to worship and to sacrifice to the LORD of hosts in
[C]Shiloh. And the two sons of Eli, Hophni and Phinehas, were priests to the LORD there. 4 When the
day came that Elkanah sacrificed, he [A]would give
portions to Peninnah his wife and to all her sons
and her daughters; 5 but to Hannah he would give
a double portion, for he loved Hannah, [A]but the
LORD had closed her womb. 6 Her rival, however,
[A]would provoke her bitterly to irritate her, because
the LORD had closed her womb. 7 It happened year
after year, as often as she went up to the house of
the LORD, she would provoke her; so she wept and
would not eat. 8 Then Elkanah her husband said to
her, "Hannah, why do you weep and why do you not
eat and why is your heart sad? [A]Am I not better to
you than ten sons?"
9 Then Hannah rose after eating and drinking in
Shiloh. Now Eli the priest was sitting on the seat
by the doorpost of [A]the temple of the LORD. 10 She,
[a]greatly distressed, prayed to the LORD and wept
bitterly. 11 She [A]made a vow and said, "O LORD of
hosts, if You will indeed [B]look on the affliction of
Your maidservant and remember me, and not forget
Your maidservant, but will give Your maidservant a
[a]son, then I will give him to the LORD all the days of
his life, and [C]a razor shall never come on his head."
12 Now it came about, as she [a]continued praying
before the LORD, that Eli was watching her mouth.
13 As for Hannah, [A]she was speaking in her heart,
only her lips were moving, but her voice was not
heard. So Eli thought she was drunk. 14 Then Eli said
to her, "[A]How long will you make yourself drunk?
Put away your wine from you." 15 But Hannah replied, "No, my lord, I am a woman [a]oppressed in
spirit; I have drunk neither wine nor strong drink,
but I [A]have poured out my soul before the LORD.
16 Do not [a]consider your maidservant as a worthless
woman, for I have spoken until now out of my great
concern and [b]provocation." 17 Then Eli answered
and said, "[A]Go in peace; and may the God of Israel
[B]grant your petition that you have asked of Him."
18 She said, "[A]Let your maidservant find favor in
your sight." So the woman went her way and ate,
and [B]her face was no longer *sad.*

SAMUEL IS BORN TO HANNAH

19 Then they arose early in the morning and worshiped before the LORD, and returned again to their

1:1 [A]1 Sam 1:19 [B]Josh 17:17, 18; 24:33 [C]1 Chr 6:22-28, 33-38 1:2 [A]Deut 21:15-17 [B]Luke 2:36 1:3 [A]Ex 34:23; 1 Sam 1:21; Luke 2:41 [B]Ex 23:14; Deut 12:5-7; 16:16 [C]Josh 18:1 1:4 [A]Deut 12:17, 18 1:5 [A]Gen 16:1; 30:1 1:6 [A]Job 24:21 1:8 [A]Ruth 4:15 1:9 [A]1 Sam 3:3 1:10 [a]Lit *bitter of soul* 1:11 [a]Lit *seed of men* [A]Num 30:6-11 [B]Gen 29:32 [C]Num 6:5; Judg 13:5 1:12 [a]Lit *multiplied* 1:13 [A]Gen 24:42-45 1:14 [A]Acts 2:4, 13 1:15 [a]Lit *severe* [A]Job 30:16; Ps 42:4; 62:8; Lam 2:19 1:16 [a]Lit *give* [b]Lit *my provocation* 1:17 [A]Judg 18:6; 1 Sam 25:35; 2 Kin 5:19; Mark 5:34; Luke 7:50 [B]Ps 20:3-5 1:18 [A]Gen 33:15; Ruth 2:13 [B]Rom 15:13

1:1–7:17 This first major division of the book begins and ends in Samuel's home town of Ramah (1:1; 7:17). The focus of these chapters is on the life and ministry of Samuel. First Samuel 1:1–4:1a concentrates on Samuel as a prophet of the Lord (see the concluding statement of 4:1a, "the word of Samuel came to all Israel"). The text in 4:1b–7:17 emphasizes Samuel as judge (see 7:17, "there he judged Israel").

1:1 a certain man. This verse resembles the introduction to the birth of Samson in Jdg 13:2. The strong comparison highlights similarities between Samson and Samuel: both men were judges over Israel, fighters of the Philistines, and lifelong Nazirites. **Ramathaim-zophim.** Possibly meaning "two heights," the name occurs only here in the OT. Elsewhere, the town is simply called Ramah. It was located about 5 mi. N of Jerusalem. **Elkanah.** Meaning "God has created," he was the father of Samuel. **Zuph.** "Zuph" is both a place (9:5) and a personal name (1Ch 6:35), as here. **Ephraimite.** First Chronicles 6:27 identifies Elkanah as a member of the Kohathite branch of the tribe of Levi. The Levites lived among the other tribes (Jos 21:20–22). Ephraim was the tribal area where this Levite lived.

1:2 two wives. Although polygamy was not God's intention for mankind (Ge 2:24), it was tolerated, but never endorsed in Israel (see Dt 21:15–17). Elkanah probably married Peninnah because Hannah was barren. **Hannah.** Meaning "grace," she was probably Elkanah's first wife. **Peninnah.** Meaning "ruby," she was Elkanah's second wife and the first bearer of his children.

1:3 This man would go up … yearly. All Israelite men were required to attend 3 annual feasts at the central sanctuary (Dt 16:1–17). Elkanah regularly attended these festivals with his wives. The festival referred to here was probably the Feast of Tabernacles (Sept./Oct.) because of the feasting mentioned in 1:9. **the LORD of hosts.** This is the first OT occurrence of "hosts" being added to the divine name. "Hosts" can refer to human armies (Ex 7:4), celestial bodies (Dt 4:19), or heavenly creatures (Jos 5:14). This title emphasizes the Lord as sovereign over all of the powers in heaven and on earth, especially over the armies of Israel. **Shiloh.** Located about 20 mi. N of Jerusalem in Ephraim, the tabernacle and ark of the covenant resided here (Jos 18:1; Jdg 18:31). **Eli.** Meaning "exalted is the Lord." He was the High Priest at Shiloh. **Hophni and Phinehas.** Each of Eli's two priestly sons had an Egyptian name: Hophni ("tadpole") and Phinehas ("nubian").

1:4 sacrificed. A peace offering since the worshipers ate a portion of the offering (see Lv 7:11–18).

1:5 the LORD had closed her womb. Hannah's barrenness was the result of divine providence like Sarah's (Ge 16:2) and Rachel's (Ge 30:2).

1:6 her rival. The other wife was an adversary. **would provoke her.** Lit. "to thunder against" her; see 2:10 for the same word.

1:7 would not eat. Hannah fasted because of the provocation of Peninnah. She did not eat of the peace offerings.

1:8 your heart sad. The idiom used reflects anger, not sadness (see Dt 15:10 for the same idiom).

1:9 temple. Actually, the tabernacle. The mention of sleeping quarters (3:2, 3) and doors (3:15) implies that at this time the tabernacle was part of a larger, more permanent building complex.

1:11 vow. Hannah pledged to give the Lord her son in return for God's favor in giving her that son. A married woman's vow could be confirmed or nullified by her husband according to Nu 30:6–15. **Your maidservant.** A humble, submissive way of referring to herself in the presence of her superior, sovereign God. **remember me.** Hannah requested special attention and care from the Lord. **all the days of his life.** A contrast to the normal Nazirite vow, which was only for a specified period of time (see Nu 6:4, 5, 8). **a razor.** Though not specified as such in this chapter, the Nazirite vow is certainly presupposed. The nonshaving of the hair on one's head is one of the 3 requirements of the vow (Nu 6:5). This expression was used elsewhere only of the Nazirite Samson (Jdg 13:5; 16:17).

1:13 drunk. Public prayer in Israel was usually audible. However, Hannah was praying silently, leaving Eli to surmise that she was drunk.

1:16 worthless woman. Lit. "daughter of Belial." Cf. 2:12.

house in [A]Ramah. And Elkanah [a]had relations with
Hannah his wife, and [B]the LORD remembered her.
20 It came about [a]in due time, after Hannah had
conceived, that she gave birth to a son; and she
named him Samuel, *saying,* "[A]Because I have asked
him of the LORD."
21 Then the man Elkanah [A]went up with all his
household to offer to the LORD the yearly sacrifice
and *pay* his vow. 22 But Hannah did not go up, for
she said to her husband, "*I will not go up* until
the child is weaned; then I will [A]bring him, that
he may appear before the LORD and [B]stay there
forever." 23 [A]Elkanah her husband said to her, "Do
what seems best [a]to you. Remain until you have
weaned him; only [B]may the LORD confirm His
word." So the woman remained and nursed her
son until she weaned him. 24 Now when she had
weaned him, [A]she took him up with her, with a
three-year-old bull and one ephah of flour and
a jug of wine, and brought him to [B]the house of
the LORD in Shiloh, although the child was young.
25 Then [A]they slaughtered the bull, and [B]brought
the boy to Eli. 26 She said, "Oh, my lord! [A]As your
soul lives, my lord, I am the woman who stood here
beside you, praying to the LORD. 27 [A]For this boy
I prayed, and the LORD has given me my petition
which I asked of Him. 28 [A]So I have also [a]dedi-
cated him to the LORD; as long as he lives he is
[a]dedicated to the LORD." And [B]he worshiped the
LORD there.

HANNAH'S SONG OF THANKSGIVING

2 Then Hannah [A]prayed and said,

"My heart exults in the LORD;
[B]My [a]horn is exalted in the LORD,
My mouth [b]speaks boldly
against my enemies,
Because [C]I rejoice in Your salvation.
2 "[A]There is no one holy like the LORD,
Indeed, [B]there is no one besides You,
[C]Nor is there any rock like our God.
3 "[a]Boast no more so very proudly,
[A]Do not let arrogance come
out of your mouth;
[B]For the LORD is a God of knowledge,
[C]And with Him actions are weighed.
4 "[A]The bows of the mighty are shattered,
[B]But the feeble gird on strength.
5 "Those who were full hire
themselves out for bread,
But those who were hungry
cease *to hunger.*
[A]Even the barren gives birth to seven,
But [B]she who has many
children languishes.
6 "[A]The LORD kills and makes alive;
[B]He brings down to [a]Sheol and raises up.
7 "[A]The LORD makes poor and rich;
[B]He brings low, He also exalts.
8 "[A]He raises the poor from the dust,
[B]He lifts the needy from the ash heap
[C]To make them sit with nobles,
And inherit a seat of honor;
[D]For the pillars of the earth are the LORD'S,
And He set the world on them.
9 "[A]He keeps the feet of His godly ones,
[B]But the wicked ones are
silenced in darkness;
[C]For not by might shall a man prevail.
10 "[A]Those who contend with the
LORD will be shattered;

1:19 [a]Lit *knew* [A]1 Sam 1:1; 2:11 [B]Gen 21:1; 30:22 1:20 [a]Lit *at the circuit of the days* [A]Gen 41:51, 52; Ex 2:10, 22; Matt 1:21 1:21 [A]Deut 12:11; 1 Sam 1:3 1:22 [A]Luke 2:22 [B]1 Sam 1:11, 28 1:23 [a]Lit *in your eyes* [A]Num 30:7, 10, 11 [B]1 Sam 1:17 1:24 [A]Num 15:9, 10; Deut 12:5, 6 [B]Josh 18:1; 1 Sam 4:3, 4 1:25 [A]Lev 1:5 [B]Luke 2:22 1:26 [A]2 Kin 2:2, 4, 6; 4:30 1:27 [A]1 Sam 1:11-13; Ps 6:9; 66:19, 20 1:28 [a]Lit *lent* [A]1 Sam 1:11, 22 [B]Gen 24:26, 52 2:1 [a]I.e. strength [b]Lit *is enlarged* [A]1 Sam 2:1-10; Luke 1:46-55 [B]Deut 33:17; Job 16:15; Ps 75:10; 89:17, 24; 92:10; 112:9 [C]Ps 9:14; 13:5; 35:9; Is 12:2, 3 2:2 [A]Ex 15:11; Lev 19:2; Ps 86:8 [B]2 Sam 22:32 [C]Deut 32:30, 31 2:3 [a]Lit *Talk much* [A]Prov 8:13 [B]1 Sam 16:7; 1 Kin 8:39 [C]Prov 16:2; 24:12 2:4 [A]Ps 37:15; 46:9 [B]Ps 18:39; Heb 11:32-34 2:5 [A]Ruth 4:15; Ps 113:9 [B]Jer 15:9 2:6 [a]I.e. the nether world [A]Deut 32:39; 2 Kin 5:7; Rev 1:18 [B]Is 26:19 2:7 [A]Deut 8:17, 18 [B]Job 5:11; Ps 75:7; James 4:10 2:8 [A]Job 42:10-12; Ps 75:7; 113:7 [B]2 Sam 7:8; Dan 2:48; James 2:5 [C]Job 36:7; Ps 113:8 [D]Job 38:4-6; Ps 75:3; 104:5 2:9 [A]Ps 91:11, 12; 121:3; Prov 3:26; 1 Pet 1:5 [B]Matt 8:12 [C]Ps 33:16, 17 2:10 [A]Ex 15:6; Ps 2:9

1:20 Samuel. The name lit. meant "name of God," but sounded like "heard by God." For Hannah the assonance was most important, because God had heard her prayer.

1:21 his vow. Elkanah supported and joined with his wife in her vow to the Lord. With the birth of Samuel he brought his votive offering to the Lord (Lv 7:16).

1:22 weaned. As was customary in the ancient world, Samuel was probably breast fed for two to three years. Then he was left to serve the Lord at the tabernacle for the rest of his life.

1:23 His word. Probably an earlier word of the Lord not recorded in the text.

1:24 bull … flour … wine. According to Nu 15:8–10, a bull, flour, and wine were to be sacrificed in fulfillment of a vow. Hannah brought all 3 in larger measure than required. An ephah was about .75 bu.

1:26 As your soul lives. Lit. "by the light of your soul," a common oath formula.

1:27, 28 asked … dedicated. These terms are from the same Heb. root used 4 times in these two verses. Twice in v. 27 it has the usual meaning of "asked." Twice in v. 28 it bears the derived meaning "lent on request." The son Hannah requested God had given, and she gives her gift back to the Giver.

2:1–10 In contrast to the prayer that came from her bitterness (1:10), Hannah prayed from joy in these verses. The prominent idea in Hannah's prayer is that the Lord is a righteous judge. He had brought down the proud (Peninnah) and exalted the humble (Hannah). The prayer has four sections: 1) Hannah prays to the Lord for His salvation (vv. 1, 2); 2) Hannah warned the proud of the Lord's humbling (vv. 3–8d); 3) Hannah affirmed the Lord's faithful care for His saints (vv. 8e–9b); 4) Hannah petitioned the Lord to judge the world and to prosper His anointed king (vv. 9c–10e). This prayer has a number of striking verbal similarities with David's song of 2Sa 22:2–51: "horn" (2:1; 22:3), "rock" (2:2; 22:2, 3), salvation/deliverance (2:1, 2; 22:2, 3), grave/Sheol (2:6; 22:6), "thunder" (2:10; 22:14), "king" (2:10; 22:51), and "anointed" (2:10; 22:51).

2:1 horn. A symbol of strength, power (see Dt 33:17).

2:2 rock. A metaphor for God that emphasized His strength and the security of those who trust in Him (see Dt 32:4; Ps 18:1, 2).

2:3 proudly … arrogance. The majestic and powerful God humbles all those who vaunt themselves against Him. The idea of God's humbling of the very proud is shown throughout 1, 2 Samuel, toward Peninnah, Eli's sons, the Philistines, Goliath, Saul, Nabal, Absalom, Shimei, Sheba, and even David.

2:4–7 Seven contrasts are found in these 4 verses: 1) mighty and weak; 2) full and hungry; 3) barren and fertile; 4) dead and alive; 5) sick and well; 6) poor and rich; and 7) humbled and exalted.

2:5 gives birth to seven. This is not a personal testimony since Hannah bore only 6 children (2:21). "Seven" here is a general reference to women whom God blesses.

2:8 pillars of the earth. A figure of speech which pictures the earth's stability (cf. Pss 75:3; 82:5; 104:5).

2:10 The LORD will judge the ends of the earth. The Lord will impose His righteous rule upon all the nations and peoples (see Is 2:2–4).

[B]Against them He will thunder
in the heavens,
[C]The LORD will judge the ends of the earth;
[D]And He will give strength to His king,
[E]And will exalt the [a]horn of His anointed."

11 Then Elkanah went to his home at [A]Ramah. [B]But
the boy ministered to the LORD before Eli the priest.

THE SIN OF ELI'S SONS

12 Now the sons of Eli were [a,A]worthless men; they
did not know the LORD 13 [A]and the custom of the
priests with the people. When any man was offering
a sacrifice, the priest's servant would come while
the meat was boiling, with a three-pronged fork in
his hand. 14 Then he would thrust it into the pan, or
kettle, or caldron, or pot; all that the fork brought up
the priest would take for himself. Thus they did in
Shiloh to all the Israelites who came there. 15 Also,
before [A]they burned the fat, the priest's servant
would come and say to the man who was sacrificing, "Give the priest meat for roasting, as he will
not take boiled meat from you, only raw." 16 If the
man said to him, "They must surely [a]burn the fat
[b]first, and then take as much as [c]you desire," then
he would say, "No, but you shall give *it to me* now;
and if not, I will take it by force." 17 Thus the sin of
the young men was very great before the LORD, for
the men [A]despised the offering of the LORD.

SAMUEL BEFORE THE LORD AS A BOY

18 Now [A]Samuel was ministering before the LORD,
as a boy [a,B]wearing a linen ephod. 19 And his mother
would make him a little [A]robe and bring it to him
from year to year when she would come up with
her husband to offer [B]the yearly sacrifice. 20 Then
Eli would [A]bless Elkanah and his wife and say, "May
the LORD give you [a]children from this woman in
place of [b]the one she [B]dedicated to the LORD." And
they went to their own [c]home.

21 [A]The LORD visited Hannah; and she conceived
and gave birth to three sons and two daughters. And
[B]the boy Samuel grew before the LORD.

ELI REBUKES HIS SONS

22 Now Eli was very old; and he heard [A]all that
his sons were doing to all Israel, and how they lay
with [B]the women who served at the doorway of the
tent of meeting. 23 He said to them, "Why do you do
such things, the evil things that I hear from all these

2:10 [a]I.e. strength [B]1 Sam 7:10; 2 Sam 22:14; Ps 18:13, 14 [C]Ps 96:13; 98:9; Matt 25:31, 32 [D]Ps 21:1, 7 [E]Ps 89:24 2:11 [A]1 Sam 1:1, 19 [B]1 Sam 1:28; 2:18; 3:1 2:12 [a]Lit *sons of Belial* [A]Jer 2:8; 9:3, 6; 2 Cor 6:15 2:13 [A]Lev 7:29-34 2:15 [A]Lev 3:3-5, 16 2:16 [a]Lit *offer up in smoke* [b]Lit *like the day* [c]Lit *your soul* 2:17 [A]Mal 2:7-9 2:18 [a]Lit *girded with* [A]1 Sam 2:11; 3:1 [B]1 Sam 2:28; 22:18; 2 Sam 6:14; 1 Chr 15:27 2:19 [A]Ex 28:31 [B]1 Sam 1:3, 21 2:20 [a]Lit *seed* [b]Lit *the one asked for which was lent* [c]Lit *place* [A]Luke 2:34 [B]1 Sam 1:11, 27, 28 2:21 [A]Gen 21:1 [B]Judg 13:24; 1 Sam 2:26; 3:19-21; Luke 1:80; 2:40 2:22 [A]1 Sam 2:13-17 [B]Ex 38:8

His king. Moses had already predicted the coming of a king who would exercise God's rule over all the nations of the earth (Ge 49:8–12; Nu 24:7–9, 17–19). It was this future, victorious king whom Hannah anticipated and Saul and David prefigured. **His anointed.** Previously in the OT, both the tabernacle and its utensils along with the priests (Aaron and his sons) had been anointed with oil. This pictured their consecrated and holy status before the Lord (Ex 30:26–30). In Samuel, first Saul (10:1), and then David (16:13; 2Sa 2:4; 5:3) were anointed as they were inaugurated for the kingship. From this point in the OT, it is usually the king who is referred as "the anointed (of the Lord)" (12:3; 24:6; 26:9, 11, 16; 2Sa 1:14, 16; 19:21). The kings of Israel, particularly David, foreshadowed the Lord's ultimate anointed king. The English word "Messiah" represents the Heb. word used here meaning "anointed." Thus, this ultimate King who would rule over the nations of the earth came to be referred to as "the Messiah," as here and 2:35; cf. 2Sa 22:51.

2:11 ministered to the LORD. As a Levite, the boy Samuel performed services that assisted Eli, the High Priest.

2:12 worthless. "Sons of Belial" was a Heb. way of saying base or wicked men. See 2Co 6:15, where it is used as a name for Satan. Eli had falsely considered Hannah a wicked woman (1:16). Eli's sons were, in fact, wicked men. **they did not know the LORD.** Eli's sons had no personal experience of, nor fellowship with, the Lord. The boy Samuel came to "know the LORD" when the Lord revealed Himself to him (see 3:7).

2:13 the custom of the priests. Not content with the specified portions of the sacrifices given to the priests (Dt 18:3), Eli's sons would take for themselves whatever meat a 3-pronged fork would collect from a boiling pot.

2:15 before they burned the fat. The law mandated that the fat of the sacrificial animal was to be burned on the altar to the Lord (Lv 7:31). In contrast, Eli's sons demanded raw meat, including the fat, from the worshipers.

2:18 Now Samuel. The faithful ministry of Samuel before the Lord was in sharp contrast to the disobedience of Eli's sons. **linen ephod.** A close fitting, sleeveless outer vest extending to the hips and worn by priests, especially when officiating before the altar (Ex 28:6–14).

2:19 little robe. A sleeveless garment reaching to the knees, worn under the ephod (Ex 28:31).

2:20 May the LORD give you children. Eli's blessing was a reminder of Hannah's faithfulness to her vow to the Lord. By providing Hannah with additional children, the Lord continued to be gracious to her.

2:22 lay with the women. Eli's sons included in their vile behavior having sexual relationships with the women who served at the tabernacle (see Ex 38:8). Such religious prostitution was common among Israel's Canaanite neighbors.

people? 24 No, my sons; for the report is not good
[A]which I hear [a]the LORD'S people circulating. 25 If
one man sins against another, [A]God will mediate
for him; but [B]if a man sins against the LORD, who
can intercede for him?" But they would not listen
to the voice of their father, for the [C]LORD desired
to put them to death.
26 Now the boy [A]Samuel [a]was growing in stature
and in favor both with the LORD and with men.
27 Then [A]a man of God came to Eli and said to
him, "Thus says the LORD, '[B]Did I *not* indeed reveal
Myself to the house of your father when they were
in Egypt *in bondage* to Pharaoh's house? 28 [A]Did I
not choose them from all the tribes of Israel to be
My priests, to go up to My altar, to burn incense,
to carry an ephod before Me; and did I *not* [B]give to
the house of your father all the fire *offerings* of the
sons of Israel? 29 Why do you [A]kick at My sacrifice
and at My offering [B]which I have commanded *in
My* [C]dwelling, and [D]honor your sons above Me, by
making yourselves fat with the [a]choicest of every
offering of My people Israel?' 30 Therefore the LORD
God of Israel declares, '[A]I did indeed say that your
house and the house of your father should walk before Me forever'; but now the LORD declares, 'Far be
it from Me—for [B]those who honor Me I will honor,
and those [C]who despise Me will be lightly esteemed.
31 Behold, [A]the days are coming when I will break
your [a]strength and the [a]strength of your father's
house so that there will not be an old man in your
house. 32 You will see [A]the distress of *My* dwelling,
in *spite of* all the good that [a]I do for Israel; and an
[B]old man will not be in your house forever. 33 Yet I
will not cut off every man of yours from My altar
[a]so that your eyes will fail *from weeping* and your
soul grieve, and all the increase of your house will
die [b]in the prime of life. 34 This will be [A]the sign to
you which will come concerning your two sons,
Hophni and Phinehas: [B]on the same day both of
them will die. 35 But [A]I will raise up for Myself a
faithful priest who will do according to what is
in My heart and in My soul; and [B]I will build him
an enduring house, and he will walk before [C]My
anointed always. 36 Everyone who is left in your
house will come and bow down to him for a [a]piece
of silver or a loaf of bread and say, "Please [b]assign
me to one of the priest's offices so that I may eat a
piece of bread." ' "

THE PROPHETIC CALL TO SAMUEL

3 Now [A]the boy Samuel was ministering to the
LORD before Eli. And [B]word from the LORD was
rare in those days, [a]visions were infrequent.
2 It happened at that time as Eli was lying down
in his place (now [A]his eyesight had begun to grow
dim *and* he could not see *well),* 3 and [A]the lamp of
God had not yet gone out, and Samuel was lying
down in the temple of the LORD where the ark of
God *was,* 4 that the LORD called Samuel; and he said,
"[A]Here I am." 5 Then he ran to Eli and said, "Here I

2:24 [a]Or *making the LORD'S people transgress* [A]1 Kin 15:26 2:25 [A]Deut 1:17 [B]Num 15:30; 1 Sam 3:14; Heb 10:26, 27 [C]Josh 11:20 2:26 [a]Lit *was going on both great and good* [A]1 Sam 2:21; Luke 2:52 2:27 [A]Deut 33:1; Judg 13:6 [B]Ex 4:14-16; 12:1, 43 2:28 [A]Ex 28:1-4; 30:7, 8; Lev 8:7, 8 [B]Lev 7:35, 36 2:29 [a]Or *first* [A]1 Sam 2:13-17 [B]Deut 12:5-9 [C]Ps 26:8 [D]Matt 10:37 2:30 [A]Ex 29:9; Num 25:13 [B]Ps 50:23 [C]Mal 2:9 2:31 [a]Or *arm* [A]1 Sam 4:11-18; 22:17-20 2:32 [a]Lit *He does* [A]1 Kin 2:26, 27 [B]Zech 8:4 2:33 [a]Lit *to waste away your eyes and to grieve your soul* [b]Lit *as men* 2:34 [A]1 Sam 10:7-9; 1 Kin 13:3 [B]1 Sam 4:11, 17 2:35 [A]1 Sam 3:1; 7:9; 9:12, 13 [B]1 Sam 8:3-5; 25:28; 2 Sam 7:11, 27; 1 Kin 11:38 [C]1 Sam 10:9, 10; 12:3; 16:13 2:36 [a]Or *payment* [b]Lit *attach* 3:1 [a]Lit *no vision spread abroad* [A]1 Sam 2:11, 18 [B]Ps 74:9; Ezek 7:26; Amos 8:11, 12 3:2 [A]Gen 27:1; 48:10; 1 Sam 4:15 3:3 [A]Ex 25:31-37; Lev 24:2, 3 3:4 [A]Is 6:8

2:25 who can intercede. Eli's point to his sons was that if God would surely judge when one sinned against another man, how much more would He bring judgment against those who sinned against Him. **the LORD desired to put them to death.** Because Eli's sons had persisted in their evil ways, God had already determined to judge them. This divine, judicial hardening, the result of defiant refusal to repent in the past, was the reason Hophni and Phinehas refused to heed Eli's warnings.

2:26 growing in stature and in favor. In contrast to the apostate sons of Eli, Samuel was maturing both spiritually and socially (cf. Lk 2:52).

2:27 man of God. Usually used as a synonym for "prophet" (see 9:9, 10). **house of your father ... in Egypt.** Although Eli's genealogy was not recorded in the OT, he was a descendant of Aaron. The Lord had revealed Himself to Aaron in Egypt before the Exodus (see Ex 4:4–16). Aaron had been divinely chosen to serve the Lord as the first in a long line of priests (Ex 28:1–4).

2:28 to be My priests. The chief duties of the priests were: 1) to place the offerings upon the altar; 2) to burn the incense in the holy place; and 3) to wear the linen ephod (see v. 18).

2:29 My offering. In recognition of their service to God and His people, the priests were allocated specific parts of the offering which were brought to the sanctuary (see Lv 2:3, 10; 7:31–36). **honor.** By condoning the sin of Hophni and Phinehas, Eli had shown preference for his sons above the Lord. Therefore, Eli was unworthy of the Lord's blessing.

2:30 I did indeed say. The Lord had promised that Aaron's descendants would always be priests (Ex 29:9), and He had confirmed that promise by oath (Nu 25:13). Because of flagrant disobedience, the house of Eli would forfeit their priesthood. Although the Aaronic priesthood was perpetual, priests could forfeit their position by their sin.

2:31 there will not be an old man in your house. The judgment of untimely death followed the descendants of Eli. Eli's sons died in the flower of their manhood (4:11). Later, Saul massacred the priests at Nob (22:16–19). Ultimately, Solomon removed Abiathar from the priesthood (1Ki 2:26, 27) and the priestly line of Eleazar prevailed, as God promised (cf. Nu 25:10–13).

2:32 the distress of *My* dwelling. This probably referred to the desecration of the tabernacle, where the Lord dwelt, at Shiloh by the Philistines (see Jer 7:12–14).

2:34 the sign to you. The death of Eli's two sons on the same day validated the prophecy (cf. 4:11, 17).

2:35 I will raise up for Myself a faithful priest. Although some have identified this priest as Samuel and others Christ, it is better to view the prophecy as fulfilled in the accession of Zadok and his family to the priestly office in the time of Solomon (see 1Ki 1:7, 8; 2:26, 27, 35). This reestablished the office of High Priest in the line of Eleazar and Phinehas (cf. Nu 25:10–13). **I will build him an enduring house.** The sons of Zadok will also serve in the millennial temple (see Eze 44:15; 48:11). **My anointed.** This refers to the Messiah who will defeat God's enemies and establish His rule in the Millennium (see v. 10).

2:36 a piece of bread. The judgment corresponded to the sin. Those who had gorged themselves on the sacrifices (vv. 12–17) were reduced to begging for a morsel of food.

3:1 the boy Samuel. Samuel was no longer a child (2:21, 26). While Jewish historian Josephus suggested he was 12 years of age, he was probably a teenager at this time. The same Heb. term translated here "boy" was used of David when he slew Goliath (17:33). **word from the LORD was rare.** The time of the judges was a period of extremely limited prophetic activity. The few visions that God did give were not widely known. **visions.** A divine revelation mediated through an auditory or visual encounter.

3:3 the lamp of God had not yet gone out. The golden lampstand, located in the Holy Place of the tabernacle, was filled with olive oil and lit at twilight (Ex 30:8). The lamp was kept burning from evening until morning (Ex 27:20, 21). Just before dawn, while the golden lampstand was still burning, Samuel was called to his prophetic ministry. **ark of God.** See Ex 25:10–22.

am, for you called me." But he said, "I did not call, lie down again." So he went and lay down. 6 The LORD called yet again, "Samuel!" So Samuel arose and went to Eli and said, "Here I am, for you called me." But he [a]answered, "I did not call, my son, lie down again." 7 [A]Now Samuel did not yet know the LORD, nor had the word of the LORD yet been revealed to him. 8 So the LORD called Samuel again for the third time. And he arose and went to Eli and said, "Here I am, for you called me." Then Eli discerned that the LORD was calling the boy. 9 And Eli said to Samuel, "Go lie down, and it shall be if He calls you, that you shall say, 'Speak, LORD, for Your servant is listening.' " So Samuel went and lay down in his place.

10 Then the LORD came and stood and called as at other times, "Samuel! Samuel!" And Samuel said, "Speak, for Your servant is listening." 11 The LORD said to Samuel, "Behold, [A]I am about to do a thing in Israel at which both ears of everyone who hears it will tingle. 12 In that day [A]I will carry out against Eli all that I have spoken concerning his house, from beginning to end. 13 For [A]I have told him that I am about to judge his house forever for [B]the iniquity which he knew, because [C]his sons brought a curse on themselves and [D]he did not rebuke them. 14 Therefore I have sworn to the house of Eli that [A]the iniquity of Eli's house shall not be atoned for by sacrifice or offering forever."

15 So Samuel lay down until morning. Then he [A]opened the doors of the house of the LORD. But Samuel was afraid to tell [B]the vision to Eli. 16 Then Eli called Samuel and said, "Samuel, my son." And he said, "Here I am." 17 He said, "What is the word that He spoke to you? Please do not hide it from me. [A]May God do so to you, and more also, if you hide anything from me of all the words that He spoke to you." 18 So Samuel told him everything and hid nothing from him. And he said, "[A]It is the LORD; let Him do what seems good to Him."

19 Thus [A]Samuel grew and [B]the LORD was with him and [C]let none of his words [a]fail. 20 All Israel [A]from Dan even to Beersheba knew that Samuel was confirmed as a prophet of the LORD. 21 And [A]the LORD appeared again at Shiloh, [B]because the LORD revealed Himself to Samuel at Shiloh by the word of the LORD.

PHILISTINES TAKE THE ARK IN VICTORY

4 Thus the word of Samuel came to all Israel. Now Israel went out to meet the Philistines in battle and camped beside [A]Ebenezer while the Philistines camped in [B]Aphek. 2 The Philistines drew up in battle array to meet Israel. When the battle spread, Israel was [a]defeated before the Philistines who killed about four thousand men on the battlefield. 3 When the people came into the camp, the elders of Israel said, "[A]Why has the LORD defeated us today before the Philistines? [B]Let us take to ourselves from Shiloh the ark of the covenant of the LORD, that [a]it may come among us and deliver us from the power of

3:6 [a]Lit *said* 3:7 [A]Acts 19:2; 1 Cor 13:11 3:11 [A]2 Kin 21:12; Jer 19:3 3:12 [A]1 Sam 2:27-36 3:13 [A]1 Sam 2:29-31 [B]1 Sam 2:22 [C]1 Sam 2:12, 17, 22 [D]Deut 17:12; 21:18 3:14 [A]Lev 15:31; Is 22:14 3:15 [A]1 Chr 15:23 [B]1 Sam 3:10 3:17 [A]2 Sam 3:35 3:18 [A]Ex 34:5-7; Lev 10:3; Job 2:10; Is 39:8 3:19 [a]Lit *fall to the ground* [A]1 Sam 2:21 [B]Gen 21:22; 28:15; 39:2 [C]1 Sam 9:6 3:20 [A]Judg 20:1 3:21 [A]Gen 12:7 [B]1 Sam 3:10 4:1 [A]1 Sam 7:12 [B]Josh 12:18; 1 Sam 29:1 4:2 [a]Lit *smitten* 4:3 [a]Or *he* [A]Josh 7:7, 8 [B]Num 10:35; Josh 6:6

3:7 Samuel did not yet know the LORD. Samuel had not yet encountered the Lord in a personal way, nor had he received God's Word by divine revelation (see 2:12).

3:8 Then Eli discerned. Eli was slow to recognize that God was calling Samuel. This indicates that Eli's spiritual perception was not what it should have been as the priest and judge of Israel (see also 1:12–16).

3:10 is listening. "To hear with interest," or "to hear so as to obey."

3:11 ears … will tingle. A message of impending destruction, here of Eli's house (see 2Ki 21:12; Jer 19:3).

3:12 all that I have spoken. See 2:27–36. The repetition of the oracle against Eli to Samuel confirmed the word spoken by the man of God.

3:13 brought a curse on themselves. LXX reads "his sons blasphemed God." Cursing God was an offense worthy of death (see Lv 24:11–16, 23). **did not rebuke them.** Eli was implicated in the sins of his sons because he did not intervene with judgment. If his sons were blaspheming God, they should have been stoned (see Lv 24:15, 16).

3:14 not be atoned for … forever. Eli's family was apparently guilty of presumptuous sin. For such defiant sin, there was no atonement and the death penalty could be immediately applied (see Nu 15:30, 31).

3:15 the doors of the house of the LORD. The doors of the tabernacle compound (see 1:9).

3:17 God do so to you, and more also. This is an oath of imprecation. Eli called down God's judgment on Samuel if he refused to tell everything he knew.

3:18 let Him do what seems good to Him. Eli resigned himself to divine sovereignty, without reluctance.

3:19 the LORD was with him. The Lord's presence was with Samuel, as it would be later with David (16:18; 18:12). The Lord's presence validated His choice of a man for His service. **let none of his words fail.** Everything Samuel said with divine authorization came true. This fulfillment of Samuel's word proved that he was a true prophet of God (see Dt 18:21, 22).

3:20 Dan even to Beersheba. The traditional limits of the land of Israel from the N to the S. **prophet of the LORD.** Samuel's status as a spokesman of God's message was acknowledged by all throughout Israel.

4:1 the word of Samuel came to all Israel. The text of 1:1–3:21 climaxes with the establishment of Samuel as God's spokesman/representative. Observe that "the word of the LORD" (3:21) has become equivalent to "the word of Samuel." **Philistines.** From the period of the judges through the end of David's reign, the Philistines ("Sea Peoples") were an ever-present enemy of Israel. They were non-Semitic immigrants (see Ge 10:14; 1Ch 1:12; Jer 47:4, 5; Am 9:7) who settled along the coastal regions of southern Canaan, organizing their power in five chief cities: Ashdod, Ashkelon, Ekron, Gath, and Gaza (1Sa 6:17; Jdg 3:13). The introduction of the Philistines into the narrative provides a link between the judgeship of Samuel and the judgeship which Samson was not able to complete (Jdg 13–16). **Ebenezer.** The location of this site has not been specifically identified. Opposite Aphek in Israelite territory, it is possibly modern Izbet Sarteh on the road to Shiloh. When translated it means "stone of help," and its mention here (and 5:1) and again in 7:12 of another location mark this section as a literary unit. **Aphek.** This site is located near the source of the Yarkon River, at the southern end of the coastal plain of Sharon, approximately 5 mi. E of the Mediterranean. This city marked the northeastern edge of Philistine territory.

4:3 Why has the LORD defeated us … ? The question of the elders reflected their knowledge that the Lord both fought their battles (2:10; 17:47) and allowed their defeat. To be defeated clearly meant that God was not "among" them (Nu 14:42; Dt 1:42). Instead of inquiring of the Lord for direction, they proceeded to take the matter into their own hands. **Let us take … the ark.** The ark symbolized the presence and power of the Lord. Yet, Israel treated it like a good-luck charm, which would ensure them victory over the Philistines. Knowing that victory or defeat depended upon the Lord's presence, they confused the symbol of His presence with His actual presence. In this way, their understanding of God resembled that of the Philistines (4:8).

our enemies." 4So the people sent to Shiloh, and
from there they carried the ark of the covenant of
the LORD of hosts [A]who sits *above* the cherubim;
and the two sons of Eli, Hophni and Phinehas, *were*
there with the ark of the covenant of God.
5As the ark of the covenant of the LORD came
into the camp, [A]all Israel shouted with a great shout,
so that the earth resounded. 6When the Philistines
heard the noise of the shout, they said, "What *does*
the noise of this great shout in the camp of the Hebrews *mean?*" Then they understood that the ark of
the LORD had come into the camp. 7The Philistines
were afraid, for they said, "God has come into the
camp." And they said, "[A]Woe to us! For nothing like
this has happened before. 8Woe to us! Who shall
deliver us from the hand of these mighty gods?
These are the gods who smote the Egyptians with
all *kinds of* plagues in the wilderness. 9[A]Take courage and be men, O Philistines, or you will become
slaves to the Hebrews, [B]as they have been slaves to
you; therefore, be men and fight."
10So the Philistines fought and [A]Israel was [a]de-
feated, and [B]every man fled to his tent; and the
slaughter was very great, for there fell of Israel
thirty thousand foot soldiers. 11And the ark of God
was taken; and [A]the two sons of Eli, Hophni and
Phinehas, died.
12Now a man of Benjamin ran from the battle line
and came to Shiloh the same day with [A]his clothes
torn and [a]dust on his head. 13When he came, behold,
[A]Eli was sitting on *his* seat [a]by the road eagerly
watching, because his heart was trembling for the
ark of God. So the man came to tell *it* in the city, and
all the city cried out. 14When Eli heard the noise
of the outcry, he said, "What *does* the noise of this
commotion *mean?*" Then the man came hurriedly
and told Eli. 15Now Eli was ninety-eight years old,
and [A]his eyes were set so that he could not see.
16The man said to Eli, "I am the one who came from
the battle line. Indeed, I escaped from the battle
line today." And he said, "[A]How did things go, my
son?" 17Then the one who brought the news replied,

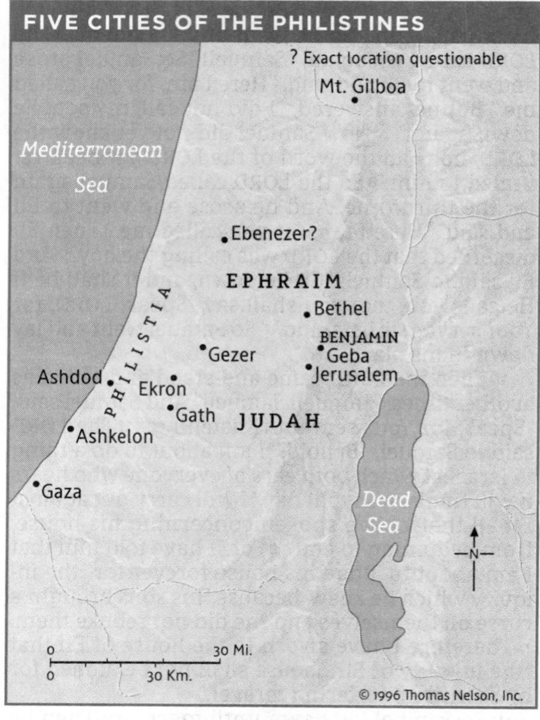

"Israel has fled before the Philistines and there
has also been a great slaughter among the people,
and your two sons also, Hophni and Phinehas, are
dead, and the ark of God has been taken." 18When
he mentioned the ark of God, [a,A]Eli fell off the seat
backward beside the gate, and his neck was broken
and he died, for [b]he was old and heavy. Thus he
judged Israel forty years.
19Now his daughter-in-law, Phinehas's wife, was
pregnant and about to give birth; and when she
heard the news that the ark of God was taken and
that her father-in-law and her husband had died,

4:4 [A]Ex 25:22; 2 Sam 6:2; Ps 80:1 4:5 [A]Josh 6:5, 20 4:7 [A]Ex 15:14 4:9 [A]1 Cor 16:13 [B]Judg 13:1; 1 Sam 14:21 4:10 [a]Lit *smitten* [A]Deut 28:15, 25; 1 Sam 4:2 [B]2 Sam 18:17; 19:8; 2 Kin 14:12; 2 Chr 25:22 4:11 [A]1 Sam 2:34; Ps 78:56-64 4:12 [a]Lit *ground* [A]Josh 7:6; 2 Sam 1:2; 15:32; Neh 9:1; Job 2:12 4:13 [a]Gr version reads *beside the gate watching the road* [A]1 Sam 1:9; 4:18 4:15 [A]1 Sam 3:2; 1 Kin 14:4 4:16 [A]2 Sam 1:4 4:18 [a]Lit *he* [b]Lit *the man* [A]1 Sam 4:13

4:4 sits *above* the cherubim. A repeated phrase used to describe the Lord (see 2Sa 6:2; 2Ki 19:15; 1Ch 13:6; Pss 80:1; 99:1; Is 37:16). It spoke of His sovereign majesty. **Hophni and Phinehas.** These were the two wicked sons of Eli (2:12–17, 27–36), of whom it was said that they "did not know the LORD" (2:12). The fact that they were mentioned together recalls the prophecy that they would die together (2:34).

4:6 Hebrews. In Ge 14:13, the name "Hebrew" was applied to Abram. Consequently, the name came to refer to the physical descendants of Abraham. It was used to distinguish them as a class of people distinct from the foreigners around them. It means that Abram was a descendant of Eber in the line of Shem (Ge 10:25; 11:14–16).

4:7 God has come into the camp. The idol, to the Philistine, was thought to be the actual dwelling place of his deity. Hence, when Israel brought the ark into the camp, the Philistines concluded that God was present, an exclamation that reflected a knowledge of God's power.

4:8 the gods who smote the Egyptians. Evidently, the news of God's victory over the Egyptians was common knowledge to the Philistines.

4:9 slaves ... as they have been slaves to you. Israel's failure to uproot all the inhabitants of Canaan (see Jdg 1:28) caused them to fall under the judgment of God. As a consequence of this judgment, Israel was enslaved to Philistine oppression (see Jdg 10, 13–16). The Philistines feared that they would become servants of the Hebrews.

4:11 the ark of God was taken. In spite of their hopes to manipulate God into giving them the victory, Israel was defeated and the ark fell into the hands of the Philistines. The view of having the ark of God being equivalent to having control of God, possessed both by Israel and then the Philistines, is to be contrasted with the power and providence of God in the remaining narrative. **Hophni and Phinehas, died.** In fulfillment of 2:34 and 3:12, Eli's sons died together.

4:12 his clothes torn and dust on his head. The actions of the man of Benjamin were considered to be universal signs of both mourning for the dead and of national calamity (cf. 2Sa 15:32).

4:13 his heart was trembling for the ark of God. Eli's concern for the ark stands in stark contrast to his earlier actions of honoring his two sons over honoring the Lord (2:29, 30; cf. 4:17, 18).

4:18 Eli ... died. As was the case with Hophni and Phinehas, Eli died. Thus, in fulfillment of the word of the Lord, all of the priestly line through Eli had been wiped out (2:29–34). *See note on 2:31.* **he judged Israel forty years.** Over that time Eli fulfilled the office of both priest and judge in Israel.

she kneeled down and gave birth, for her pains came upon her. 20And about the time of her death the women who stood by her said to her, "[A]Do not be afraid, for you have given birth to a son." But she did not answer or pay attention. 21And she called the boy [a]Ichabod, saying, "[A]The glory has departed from Israel," because [B]the ark of God was taken and because of her father-in-law and her husband. 22She said, "The glory has departed from Israel, for the ark of God was taken."

CAPTURE OF THE ARK PROVOKES GOD

5 Now the Philistines took the ark of God and [A]brought it from Ebenezer to [B]Ashdod. 2Then the Philistines took the ark of God and brought it to [A]the house of Dagon and set it by Dagon. 3When the Ashdodites arose early the next morning, behold, [A]Dagon had fallen on his face to the ground before the ark of the LORD. So they took Dagon and [B]set him in his place again. 4But when they arose early the next morning, behold, [A]Dagon had fallen on his face to the ground before the ark of the LORD. And the head of Dagon and both the palms of his hands *were* cut off on the threshold; [a]only the trunk of Dagon was left to him. 5Therefore neither the priests of Dagon nor all who enter Dagon's house [A]tread on the threshold of Dagon in Ashdod to this day.

6Now [A]the hand of the LORD was heavy on the Ashdodites, and [B]He ravaged them and smote them with [C]tumors, both Ashdod and its territories. 7When the men of Ashdod saw that it was so, they said, "The ark of the God of Israel must not remain with us, for His hand is severe on us and on Dagon our god." 8So they sent and [A]gathered all the lords of the Philistines to them and said, "What shall we do with the ark of the God of Israel?" And they said, "Let the ark of the God of Israel be brought around to Gath." And they brought the ark of the God of Israel *around*. 9After they had brought it around, [A]the hand of the LORD was against the city with very great confusion; and He smote the men of the city, both young and old, so that [B]tumors broke out on them. 10So they sent the ark of God to Ekron. And as the ark of God came to Ekron the Ekronites cried out, saying, "They have brought the ark of the God of Israel around to [a]us, to kill [a]us and [b]our people." 11They [A]sent therefore and gathered all the lords of the Philistines and said, "Send away the ark of the God of Israel, and let it return to its own place, so that it will not kill [a]us and [b]our people." For there was a deadly confusion throughout the city; [B]the hand of God was very heavy there. 12And the men who did not die were smitten with tumors and [A]the cry of the city went up to heaven.

THE ARK RETURNED TO ISRAEL

6 Now the ark of the LORD had been in the [a]country of the Philistines seven months. 2And [A]the Philistines called for the priests and the diviners, saying, "What shall we do with the ark of the LORD? Tell us [a]how we shall send it to its place."

4:20 [A]Gen 35:16-19 4:21 [a]I.e. No glory [A]Ps 26:8; Jer 2:11 [B]1 Sam 4:11 5:1 [A]1 Sam 4:1; 7:12 [B]Josh 13:3 5:2 [A]Judg 16:23-30; 1 Chr 10:8-10 5:3 [A]Is 19:1; 46:1, 2 [B]Is 46:7 5:4 [a]So with ancient versions; Heb *only Dagon* [A]Ezek 6:4, 6; Mic 1:7 5:5 [A]Zeph 1:9 5:6 [A]Ex 9:3; 1 Sam 5:7, 11; Ps 32:4; 145:20; 147:6; Acts 13:11 [B]1 Sam 6:5 [C]Deut 28:27; Ps 78:66 5:8 [A]1 Sam 5:11; 29:6-11 5:9 [A]Deut 2:15; 1 Sam 5:11; 7:13; 12:15 [B]1 Sam 5:6 5:10 [a]Lit *me* [b]Lit *my* 5:11 [a]Lit *me* [b]Lit *my* [A]1 Sam 5:8 [B]1 Sam 5:6, 9 5:12 [A]Ex 12:30; Is 15:3 6:1 [a]Lit *field* 6:2 [a]Or *with what* [A]Gen 41:8; Ex 7:11; Is 2:6

4:21 Ichabod ... The glory has departed. Due primarily to the loss of the ark, the symbol of God's presence, Phinehas' wife names her child Ichabod, meaning either "Where is the glory?" or "no glory." To the Hebrew, "glory" was often used to refer to God's presence; hence, the text means "Where is God?" The word "departed" carries the idea of having gone into exile. Thus, to the people of Israel, the capturing of the ark was a symbol that God had gone into exile. Although this was the mindset of Israel, the text narrative will reveal that God was present, even when He disciplined His people. *See note on Eze 10:18, 19.*

5:1 Ashdod. One of the 5 chief Philistine cities, inland from the coast (3 mi.) and approximately 33 mi. W of Jerusalem.

5:2 Dagon. Ancient literature identifies this deity as a fish god, whose image had the lower body of a fish and the upper body of a man. Dagon seems to have been the leader of the Philistine pantheon (Jdg 16:23) and is noted to be the father of Baal. The placing of the ark of God in the temple of Dagon was supposed to be a sign of Dagon's power and Yahweh's inferiority, a visual representation that the god of the Philistines was victorious over the God of the Hebrews. In addition, the textual connection of Dagon reinforces the affinity between the events written here and those in the life of Samson (cf. Jdg 13–16).

5:3 fallen on his face. Ironically, God Himself overturned the supposed supremacy of Dagon by having Dagon fallen over, as if paying homage to the Lord.

5:4 head ... hands *were* cut off. The first display of God's authority over Dagon was not perceived. God's second display of authority, the cutting off of Dagon's head and hands, was a common sign that the enemy was dead (Jdg 7:25; 8:6; 1Sa 17:54; 31:9; 2Sa 4:12), and was to be understood as God's divine judgment on the false idol.

5:5 tread on the threshold. Because the head and hands of Dagon fell on the threshold, superstition developed that it was cursed; therefore, the Philistines would not tread on it. **to this day.** This phrase supports the claim that the writer was living at a time removed from the actual event itself (see Introduction: Author and Date). This phrase and phrases equivalent to it are found throughout 1, 2 Samuel (6:18; 26:6; 30:25; 2Sa 4:3; 6:8; 18:18).

5:6 the hand of the LORD was heavy. In contrast to the hands of Dagon being cut off, symbolizing his helplessness against the power of Yahweh, the Lord was pictured to be actively involved in judging the Philistines. The imagery of God's hand is found throughout the ark narrative (4:8; 5:6, 7, 9, 11; 6:3, 5, 9). **tumors.** It has been suggested that this word refers to the sores or boils caused by an epidemic of the bubonic plague carried by rats (6:4, 5). The spread of the disease and its deadly effect (5:6, 9, 12; 6:11, 17) make this a likely view.

5:8 lords of the Philistines. Refers to those men who ruled the chief Philistine cities as kings (*see note on 4:1*). **Gath.** Another main Philistine city, located about 12 mi. E of Ashdod (cf. 5:1).

5:10 Ekron. With judgment on Gath, the Philistines sent the ark away to the next main city to see if God was behind their calamity. Located about 6 mi. N of Gath, it was the closest major Philistine city to Israel's border. **the ark ... to kill us.** The cry of the Ekronites was an admission that the Philistines had gotten the message that God was the source of their troubles. It is curious that the Philistines knew of God's power to smite the Egyptians (4:8), yet they proudly believed themselves stronger than Egypt. The severity of the plagues grew increasingly worse in vv. 6–12, corresponding with the failure of the Philistines to humble themselves before God. Their actions were very similar to those of the Egyptians (Ex 5–14).

6:2 the priests and the diviners. These men of the Philistines, specifically identified in Scripture as having notable fame (Is 2:6), were summoned to figure out how to appease God so that He would stop the plague. **send it to its place.** The Philistines understood that they had offended God. Their diviners decided to rightfully appease His wrath by sending the ark back to Israel.

3 They said, “If you send away the ark of the God of
Israel, [A]do not send it empty; but you shall surely
[B]return to Him a guilt offering. Then you will be
healed and it will be known to you why His hand
is not removed from you.” 4 Then they said, “What
shall be the guilt offering which we shall return to
Him?” And they said, “Five golden [A]tumors and five
golden mice [B]*according to* the number of the lords
of the Philistines, for one plague was on all of [a]you
and on your lords. 5 So you shall make likenesses
of your tumors and likenesses of your mice that
ravage the land, and [A]you shall give glory to the
God of Israel; perhaps [B]He will ease His hand from
you, [C]your gods, and your land. 6 Why then do you
harden your hearts [A]as the Egyptians and Pharaoh
hardened their hearts? When He had severely dealt
with them, [B]did they not allow [a]the people to go, and
they departed? 7 Now therefore, take and [A]prepare
a new cart and two milch cows on which there
[B]has never been a yoke; and hitch the cows to the
cart and take their calves home, away from them.
8 Take the ark of the LORD and place it on the cart;
and put [A]the articles of gold which you return to
Him as [B]a guilt offering in a box by its side. Then
send it away that it may go. 9 Watch, if it goes up
by the way of its own territory to [A]Beth-shemesh,
then He has done us this great evil. But if not, then
[B]we will know that it was not His hand that struck
us; it happened to us by chance.”

10 Then the men did so, and took two milch cows
and hitched them to the cart, and shut up their
calves at home. 11 They put the ark of the LORD on
the cart, and the box with the golden mice and the
likenesses of their tumors. 12 And the cows took the
straight way in the [a]direction of [A]Beth-shemesh;
they went along [B]the highway, lowing as they went,
and did not turn aside to the right or to the left.
And the lords of the Philistines followed them to
the border of Beth-shemesh.

13 Now *the people of* Beth-shemesh were reaping their wheat harvest in the valley, and they
raised their eyes and saw the ark and were glad to
see *it*. 14 The cart came into the field of Joshua the
Beth-shemite and stood there where there *was* a
large stone; and they split the wood of the cart and
[A]offered the cows as a burnt offering to the LORD.
15 [A]The Levites took down the ark of the LORD and
the box that was with it, in which were the articles
of gold, and put them on the large stone; and the
men of Beth-shemesh offered burnt offerings and
sacrificed sacrifices that day to the LORD. 16 When
the [A]five lords of the Philistines saw it, they returned
to Ekron that day.

17 [A]These are the golden tumors which the Philistines returned for a guilt offering to the LORD: one
for Ashdod, one for Gaza, one for Ashkelon, one for
Gath, one for Ekron; 18 and the golden mice, *according* to the number of all the cities of the Philistines
belonging to the five lords, [A]both of fortified cities
and of country villages. [B]The large [a]stone on which
they set the ark of the LORD *is a witness* to this day
in the field of Joshua the Beth-shemite.

19 [A]He struck down some of the men of
Beth-shemesh because they had looked into the

6:3 [A]Ex 23:15; Deut 16:16 [B]Lev 5:15, 16 6:4 [a]Lit *them* [A]1 Sam 5:6, 9, 12; 6:17 [B]Josh 13:3; Judg 3:3; 1 Sam 6:17, 18 6:5 [A]Josh 7:19; 1 Chr 16:28, 29; Is 42:12; Jer 13:16; John 9:24; Rev 14:7 [B]1 Sam 5:6, 11 [C]1 Sam 5:3, 4, 7 6:6 [a]Lit *them* [A]Ex 7:13; 8:15, 32; 9:34; 14:17 [B]Ex 12:31 6:7 [A]2 Sam 6:3 [B]Num 19:2; Deut 21:3, 4 6:8 [A]1 Sam 6:4, 5 [B]1 Sam 6:3 6:9 [A]Josh 15:10; 21:16 [B]1 Sam 6:3 6:12 [a]Lit *way* [A]1 Sam 6:9 [B]Num 20:19 6:14 [A]2 Sam 24:22; 1 Kin 19:21 6:15 [A]Josh 3:3 6:16 [A]Josh 13:3; Judg 3:3 6:17 [A]1 Sam 6:4 6:18 [a]So some mss and versions; Heb *Abel* [A]Deut 3:5 [B]1 Sam 6:14, 15 6:19 [A]Ex 19:21; Num 4:5, 15, 20; 2 Sam 6:7

6:3 guilt offering. The purpose behind this offering was to both acknowledge and compensate for their trespass of dishonoring the God of Israel. These pagans recognized their sin and the need for manifest repentance, which they did according to their religious tradition by means of votive trespass or guilt offerings.

6:4 Five golden tumors and five golden mice. It was their custom to make models of their sores (and the mice which brought the plague), in hopes that the deity would recognize that they knew why he was angry and remove the evil which had fallen upon them. The context of v. 17 suggests that the items were in the writer's presence at the time the account was recorded. The number 5 represents each of the Philistine cities and lords affected by God's judgment.

6:5 give glory to the God of Israel … He will ease His hand. While sympathetic magic was the Philistine custom, this statement expressly affirms the intention behind the offerings: They were to halt the dishonor, confess their sin, and give glory to the God of Israel by acknowledging who it was that they had offended and who was the supreme Deity.

6:6 Why then do you harden your hearts … ? The diviners correlate the Philistines' actions of not recognizing God with those of Pharaoh and the Egyptians. This is the same word "harden" that was used in Ex 7:14; 8:15, 32. It is an interesting correlation, because the dominant purpose in Ex 5–14 is that the Egyptians might "know that I am the LORD" (Ex 7:5).

6:7 on which … never been a yoke. To know without a doubt that the God of Israel was behind all of their troubles, the diviners devised a plan that would reveal whether God was the One responsible. Using cows which had "never been yoked" meant using animals that were untrained to pull a cart and probably would not go anywhere. **take their calves … away from them.** The second element in their plan was to use nursing cows taken away from their calves. For the cows unnaturally to head off in the opposite direction from their calves would be a clear sign that the cause of their judgment was supernatural.

6:9 Beth-shemesh. Named "house of the sun" and located in the Sorek Valley, this was a Levitical city about 15 mi. W of Jerusalem. Originally designated for the descendants of Aaron (Jos 21:16), it was chosen to be the destination of the cows pulling the cart.

6:12 lowing as they went. With the moaning from instinctive unwillingness to leave their calves behind, the cows went straight to Beth-shemesh, not turning to the right or left, leaving the inescapable conclusion that God had judged them.

6:13 reaping their wheat harvest. Sometime in June. These harvests were accomplished with the whole city participating.

6:14 Joshua the Beth-shemite. The cows stopped in the field of Joshua, where there was a large stone which was verifiable to the writer at the time the account was written. **burnt offering.** Because the cows and cart were used for sacred purposes, they could not be used for normal everyday purposes. Therefore, the men of Beth-shemesh sacrificed the cows using the cart for the fire.

6:15 Levites. The men of Beth-shemesh, being Levites, were qualified to move the ark. **put them on the large stone.** The stone mentioned was used as a pedestal for both the items of gold and the ark. At the time the account was written, it stood as a witness that God had returned to the land.

6:16 five lords of the Philistines. The lords of the Philistines, upon seeing that the ark arrived safely, returned to Ekron.

6:19 looked into the ark. This action on the part of the men of Beth-shemesh constituted the sin of presumption. This is first addressed in Nu 4:20 and is mentioned again in 2Sa 6:6, 7. **fifty thousand and seventy men.** Some debate whether this figure is too large. However, retaining the larger number is more consistent with the context of "a great slaughter," and the reference to 30,000 in 4:10 (cf. 11:8). However, a scribal error could have occurred, in which case the number would omit the 50,000 and likely be "seventy," as in Josephus.

ark of the LORD. He struck down of all the people,
50,070 men, and the people mourned because the
LORD had struck the people with a great slaughter.
20 The men of Beth-shemesh said, "[A]Who is able to
stand before the LORD, this holy God? And to whom
shall He go up from us?" 21 So they sent messengers
to the inhabitants of [A]Kiriath-jearim, saying, "The
Philistines have brought back the ark of the LORD;
come down and take it up to you."

DELIVERANCE FROM THE PHILISTINES

7 And the men of Kiriath-jearim came and took the
ark of the LORD and [A]brought it into the house
of Abinadab on the hill, and consecrated Eleazar
his son to keep the ark of the LORD. 2 From the day
that the ark remained at Kiriath-jearim, the time
was long, for it was twenty years; and all the house
of Israel lamented after the LORD.

3 Then Samuel spoke to all the house of Israel,
saying, "[A]If you return to the LORD with all your
heart, [B]remove the foreign gods and the [C]Ashtaroth
from among you and [D]direct your hearts to the LORD
and [E]serve Him alone; and He will deliver you from
the hand of the Philistines." 4 So the sons of Israel
removed the Baals and the Ashtaroth and served
the LORD alone.

5 Then Samuel said, "Gather all Israel to [A]Mizpah
and [B]I will pray to the LORD for you." 6 They gathered
to Mizpah, and drew water and [A]poured it out before
the LORD, and [B]fasted on that day and said there,
"[C]We have sinned against the LORD." And Samuel
judged the sons of Israel at Mizpah.

7 Now when the Philistines heard that the sons of
Israel had gathered to Mizpah, the lords of the Philistines went up against Israel. And when the sons of
Israel heard it, [A]they were afraid of the Philistines.
8 Then the sons of Israel said to Samuel, "[A]Do not
cease to cry to the LORD our God for us, that He may
save us from the hand of the Philistines." 9 Samuel
took [A]a suckling lamb and offered it for a whole
burnt offering to the LORD; and Samuel cried to
the LORD for Israel and [B]the LORD answered him.
10 Now Samuel was offering up the burnt offering,
and the Philistines drew near to battle against Israel. But [A]the LORD thundered with a great [a]thunder
on that day against the Philistines and [B]confused
them, so that they were [b]routed before Israel. 11 The
men of Israel went out of Mizpah and pursued the

6:20 [A]Lev 11:44, 45; 2 Sam 6:9; Mal 3:2; Rev 6:17 6:21 [A]Josh 9:17; 15:9, 60; 1 Chr 13:5, 6 7:1 [A]2 Sam 6:3, 4 7:3 [A]1 Kin 8:48; Is 55:7; Hos 6:1; Joel 2:12-14 [B]Gen 35:2; Josh 24:14, 23; Judg 10:16 [C]Judg 2:13; 1 Sam 31:10 [D]Deut 13:4; 2 Chr 19:3 [E]Deut 6:13; 10:20; 13:4; Josh 24:14; Matt 4:10; Luke 4:8 7:5 [A]Judg 10:17; 20:1 [B]1 Sam 8:6; 12:17-19 7:6 [A]1 Sam 1:15; Ps 62:8; Lam 2:19 [B]Lev 16:29; Neh 9:1 [C]Judg 10:10; 1 Kin 8:47; Ps 106:6 7:7 [A]1 Sam 13:6; 17:11 7:8 [A]1 Sam 12:19-24; Is 37:4 7:9 [A]Lev 22:27 [B]Ps 99:6; Jer 15:1 7:10 [a]Lit *voice* [b]Lit *smitten* [A]1 Sam 2:10; 2 Sam 22:14, 15; Ps 29:3, 4 [B]Josh 10:10; Ps 18:14

6:20 Who is able to stand before . . . God? This question climaxes the narrative of the ark. No one is able to stand against God's judgment. This applied to the people outside the covenant as well as those under the covenant. Presumption before God is unacceptable. **to whom shall He go.** The expression was used to denote the desire to take the ark away from them.

6:21 Kiriath-jearim. A city located approximately 10 mi. NE of Beth-shemesh. It would remain the resting place of the ark until David brought it to Jerusalem (2Sa 6:1–19). This location had long been associated with Baal worship (cf. Jos 15:9, 60; 18:14).

7:2 twenty years. Coupled with v. 3, the 20 years designated the period Israel neglected God and chased after foreign gods. After those 20 years, Israel returned to the Lord.

7:3 direct your hearts to the LORD . . . and He will deliver you. This statement recalls the cycle in the book of Judges: apostasy, oppression, repentance, and deliverance. It previews the contents of this chapter.

7:4 the Baals and the Ashtaroth. Most dominant of the Canaanite pantheon, these deities were the fertility gods which plagued Israel. "Baal" and "Ashtaroth" are plurals of majesty, which signify their supreme authority over other Canaanite deities. Ashtaroth represented the female goddess, while Baal represented the male sky god who fertilized the land.

7:5 Mizpah. This city was located 8 mi. NE of Kiriath-jearim in Benjamin. It became one of the cities of Samuel's circuit (v. 16). **I will pray.** Samuel was a man of prayer (7:8, 9; 8:6; 12:19, 23; 15:11).

7:6 drew water and poured it out before the LORD. The pouring out of water before the Lord was a sign of repentance. This act is repeated in 2Sa 23:16. **We have sinned against the LORD.** The symbol of Samuel pouring out the water and the acknowledgment of the people reveal a situation where true repentance had taken place. The condition of the heart superseded the importance or righteousness of the ritual. **Samuel judged.** At this point Samuel is introduced as the judge of Israel. His judgeship encompassed both domestic leadership and the conduct of war. The word links the text back to the last comment about Eli who judged 40 years (4:18). Samuel is shown to be the one taking over Eli's judgeship. He served as the last judge before the first king (cf. 1Sa 8:5).

7:7 Israel . . . afraid of the Philistines. When Israel heard that the Philistines had come up against them for war, they were afraid.

7:10 the LORD thundered . . . against the Philistines. In a literal manner, the Lord did to His enemies what was said by Hannah in her prayer (2:10).

7:11 Beth-car. The location is unknown.

CAPTURE AND RETURN OF THE ARK

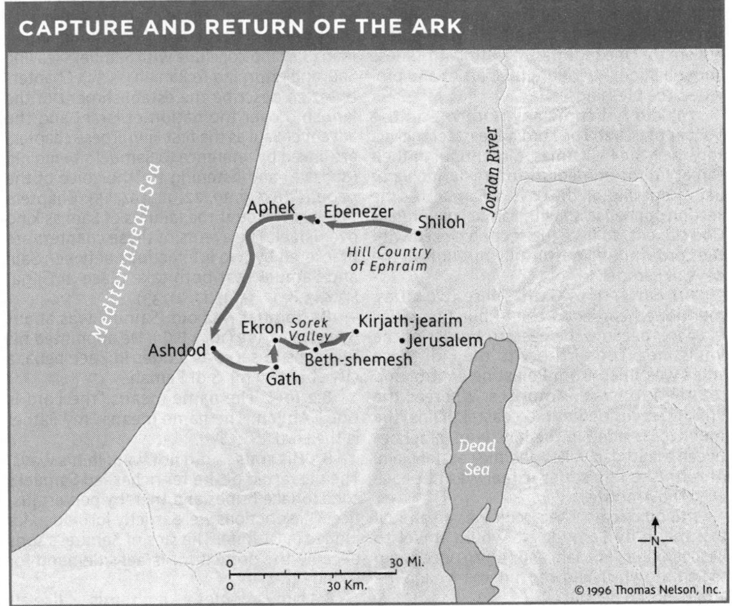

Philistines, and struck them down as far as below
Beth-car.
12 Then Samuel [A]took a stone and set it between
Mizpah and Shen, and named it [a]Ebenezer, saying,
"Thus far the LORD has helped us." 13 [A]So the Philistines were subdued and [B]they did not come anymore within the border of Israel. And the hand of
the LORD was against the Philistines all the days of
Samuel. 14 The cities which the Philistines had taken
from Israel were restored to Israel, from Ekron even
to Gath; and Israel delivered their territory from the
hand of the Philistines. So there was peace between
Israel and [A]the Amorites.

SAMUEL'S MINISTRY

15 Now Samuel [A]judged Israel all the days of his
life. 16 He used to go annually on circuit to [A]Bethel
and [B]Gilgal and [C]Mizpah, and he judged Israel in
all these places. 17 Then his return *was* to [A]Ramah,
for his house *was* there, and there he judged Israel;
and he [B]built there an altar to the LORD.

ISRAEL DEMANDS A KING

8 And it came about when Samuel was old that
[A]he appointed his sons judges over Israel. 2 Now
the name of his firstborn was Joel, and the name of
his second, Abijah; *they* were judging in [A]Beersheba.
3 His sons, however, did not walk in his ways, but
turned aside after dishonest gain and [A]took bribes
and perverted justice.
4 Then all the elders of Israel gathered together
and came to Samuel at [A]Ramah; 5 and they said to
him, "Behold, you have grown old, and your sons do
not walk in your ways. Now [A]appoint a king for us
to judge us like all the nations." 6 But the thing was
[a,A]displeasing in the sight of Samuel when they said,
"Give us a king to judge us." And [B]Samuel prayed to
the LORD. 7 The LORD said to Samuel, "Listen to the
voice of the people in regard to all that they say to
you, for [A]they have not rejected you, but they have
rejected Me from being king over them. 8 Like all
the deeds which they have done since the day that
I brought them up from Egypt even to this day—in
that they have forsaken Me and served other gods—
so they are doing to you also. 9 Now then, listen to
their voice; [A]however, you shall solemnly [a]warn
them and tell them of [B]the [b]procedure of the king
who will reign over them."

WARNING CONCERNING A KING

10 So Samuel spoke all the words of the LORD to [A]the
people who had asked of him a king. 11 He said, "[A]This
will be the [a]procedure of the king who will reign
over you: [B]he will take your sons and place *them* for
himself in his chariots and among his horsemen and
[C]they will run before his chariots. 12 [A]He will appoint
for himself commanders of thousands and of fifties,
and *some* to [a]do his plowing and to reap his harvest
and to make his weapons of war and equipment for
his chariots. 13 He will also take your daughters for

7:12 [a]I.e. The stone of help [A]Gen 35:14; Josh 4:9; 24:26 [B]Josh 5:9, 10 [C]1 Sam 7:5 7:13 [A]Judg 13:1-15 [B]1 Sam 13:5 7:14 [A]Num 13:29; Josh 10:5-10 7:15 [A]1 Sam 7:6 7:16 [A]Gen 28:19; 35:6 7:17 [A]1 Sam 1:1, 19; 2:11 [B]Judg 21:4 8:1 [A]Deut 16:18, 19 8:2 [A]Gen 22:19; 1 Kin 19:3; Amos 5:5 8:3 [A]Ex 23:6, 8; Deut 16:19 8:4 [A]1 Sam 7:17 8:5 [A]Deut 17:14, 15 8:6 [a]Or *evil* [A]1 Sam 12:17 [B]1 Sam 15:11 8:7 [A]Ex 16:8; 1 Sam 10:19 8:9 [a]Lit *testify to* [b]Lit *custom* [A]Ezek 3:18 [B]1 Sam 8:11-18; 10:25 8:10 [A]1 Sam 8:4 8:11 [a]Lit *custom* [A]Deut 17:14-20; 1 Sam 10:25 [B]1 Sam 14:52 [C]2 Sam 15:1 8:12 [a]Lit *plow his plowing* [A]Num 31:14; 1 Sam 22:7

7:12 Ebenezer. A different location from the one mentioned in 4:1 and 5:1. The name functions as the literary knot for the two ends of this unit (*see note on 4:1*). **Thus far the LORD has helped us.** This expression means that the Lord was the One responsible for getting Israel to this point. He was Israel's Sovereign One in times of both faithfulness and rebellion. He fought the battles and provided the blessings.

7:13 did not come anymore within the border of Israel. The Lord gave Israel the victory over the Philistines, discontinuing their threat for the immediate future during Samuel's judgeship. **all the days of Samuel.** As the section opened in 4:1 with Samuel pictured as God's agent, so here the section closed with the Lord working powerfully through all the days of Samuel.

7:14 Ekron … to Gath. These two cities, mentioned earlier as chief Philistine cities (5:8, 10), became the eastern border of the Philistines. The territory to the E of these cities was freed from Philistine control and returned to Israel. **Amorites.** Whereas the Philistines resided in the coastal plains, the Amorites resided in the hills W of Israel between the Jordan Valley and the coastal plain. As with the Philistines, Israel was at peace with the Amorites.

7:16 on circuit. The circuit was an annual trip made by Samuel; he would travel to Bethel, Gilgal, Mizpah, and return once again to Ramah, which allowed him to manage the affairs of the people.

7:17 Ramah. The first major division of the book (1:1–7:17) ends with Samuel returning to Ramah to judge the people.

8:1–15:35 This division of the book concentrates on the interaction between Israel, Samuel, and Saul. These chapters begin with the elders of Israel coming to Samuel at Ramah (8:4) and conclude with Samuel's leaving Saul and returning to Ramah (15:34). Chapters 8:1–12:25 describe the establishment of the kingship over the nation of Israel and the advent of Saul as the first king. These chapters are linked by reference to Samuel's being old (8:1; 12:2) and listening to "the voice of the people" (8:7, 9, 19, 22; 12:1, 14, 15). Chapters 13:1–15:35 recount the failures of Saul as king over Israel. The events of these chapters are bracketed by two interactions between Saul and Samuel that both take place in Gilgal (13:4, 7, 8, 12, 15; 15:12, 21, 33).

8:1 Samuel was old. Samuel was about 60 years of age (1043 B.C.). He appointed his two sons to serve as judges in Beersheba, a city about 57 mi. S of Ramah.

8:2 Joel. The name means "the Lord is God." **Abijah.** The name means "my Father is the Lord."

8:3 His sons … did not walk in his ways. The perverted desire for riches led Samuel's sons to take bribes and thereby pervert justice. These actions were strictly forbidden for judges in Dt 16:19. The sins of Samuel's sons became the pretext for Israel's demand for a king (vv. 4, 5).

8:5 Now appoint a king for us … like all the nations. When Israel entered the land, they encountered Canaanite city-states that were led by kings (see Jos 12:7–24). Additionally, during the period of the judges, Israel was enslaved by nations that were led by kings (Jdg 3:8, 12; 4:2; 8:5; 11:12). However, at the time of the judges there was no king in Israel (Jdg 17:6; 18:1; 19:1; 21:25). As Israel lived in the land surrounded by nations that had kings, the desire arose for a king in Israel also. According to Dt 17:14, God knew this would be their desire, and He would allow it to occur. However, v. 20 revealed a motive which was definitely counter to the Lord's will. *See note on 8:20.*

8:7 Listen to the voice of the people. The Lord had predicted that there would be kings over Israel (Ge 35:11; 36:31; 49:10; Nu 24:7–9, 17; Dt 17:14; 28:36). Here, the Lord told Samuel to obey the request of the people and give them a king. **they have not rejected you, but … Me.** The nature of this rejection of the Lord by Israel is explained in vv. 19, 20.

8:9 you shall solemnly warn them. Samuel obeyed the Lord by describing the behavior of a human king in vv. 10–18. A king would: 1) draft young men and women for his service (vv. 11–13); 2) tax the people's crops and flocks (vv. 14, 15, 17a); 3) appropriate the best of their animals and servants (v. 16); and 4) place limitations on their personal freedom (v. 17b).

8:10 who had asked of him a king. Just as Hannah asked for a son (1:20), Israel asked for a king. *See note on 9:2.*

perfumers and cooks and bakers. 14 [A]He will take
the best of your fields and your vineyards and your
olive groves and give *them* to his servants. 15 He will
take a tenth of your seed and of your vineyards and
give to his officers and to his servants. 16 He will also
take your male servants and your female servants
and your best young men and your donkeys and
[a]use *them* for his work. 17 He will take a tenth of your
flocks, and you yourselves will become his servants.
18 Then [A]you will cry out in that day because of your
king whom you have chosen for yourselves, but [B]the
LORD will not answer you in that day."
19 Nevertheless, the people [A]refused to listen to
the voice of Samuel, and they said, "No, but there
shall be a king over us, 20 [A]that we also may be like
all the nations, that our king may judge us and go
out before us and fight our battles." 21 Now after
Samuel had heard all the words of the people, [A]he
repeated them in the LORD'S hearing. 22 The LORD
said to Samuel, "[A]Listen to their voice and [a]appoint
them a king." So Samuel said to the men of Israel,
"Go every man to his city."

SAUL'S SEARCH

9 Now there was a man of Benjamin whose name
was [A]Kish the son of Abiel, the son of Zeror, the
son of Becorath, the son of Aphiah, the son of a Benjamite, a mighty man of [a]valor. 2 He had a son whose
name was Saul, a [A]choice and handsome *man,* and
there was not a more handsome person than he
among the sons of Israel; [B]from his shoulders and
up he was taller than any of the people.
3 Now the donkeys of Kish, Saul's father, were
lost. So Kish said to his son Saul, "Take now with
you one of the servants, and arise, go search for
the donkeys." 4 He passed through [A]the hill country
of Ephraim and passed through the land of [B]Shali-
shah, but they did not find *them.* Then they passed
through the land of [C]Shaalim, but *they were* not
there. Then he passed through the land of the Benjamites, but they did not find *them.*
5 When they came to the land of [A]Zuph, Saul said
to his servant who was with him, "Come, and let us
return, [B]or else my father will cease *to be concerned*
about the donkeys and will become anxious for us."
6 He said to him, "Behold now, there is [A]a man of
God in this city, and the man is held in honor; [B]all
that he says surely comes true. Now let us go there,
[C]perhaps he can tell us about our journey on which
we have set out." 7 Then Saul said to his servant, "But
behold, if we go, what shall we bring the man? For
the bread is gone from our sack and there is [A]no
present to bring to the man of God. What do we
have?" 8 The servant answered Saul again and said,
"Behold, I have in my hand a fourth of a shekel of
silver; I will give *it* to the man of God and he will
[A]tell us our way." 9 (Formerly in Israel, when a man
went to inquire of God, he used to say, "Come, and
let us go to the seer"; for *he who is called* a prophet
now was formerly called [A]a seer.) 10 Then Saul said
to his servant, "Well said; come, let us go." So they
went to the city where the man of God was.
11 As they went up the slope to the city, [A]they
found young women going out to draw water and
said to them, "Is the seer here?" 12 They answered
them and said, "He is; [a]see, *he is* ahead of you. Hurry
now, for he has come into the city today, for [A]the
people have a sacrifice on [B]the high place today. 13 As
soon as you enter the city you will find him before
he goes up to the high place to eat, for the people
will not eat until he comes, because [A]he must bless
the sacrifice; afterward those who are invited will
eat. Now therefore, go up for you will find him at
once." 14 So they went up to the city. As they came
into the city, behold, Samuel was coming out toward
them to go up to the high place.

8:14 [A]1 Kin 21:7; Ezek 46:18 8:16 [a]Lit *make* 8:18 [A]Is 8:21 [B]Prov 1:25-28; Is 1:15; Mic 3:4 8:19 [A]Is 66:4; Jer 44:16 8:20 [A]1 Sam 8:5 8:21 [A]Judg 11:11 8:22 [a]Lit *cause a king to reign for them* [A]1 Sam 8:7 9:1 [a]Or *wealth* or *influence* [A]1 Sam 14:51; 1 Chr 8:33; 9:36-39 9:2 [A]1 Sam 10:24 [B]1 Sam 10:23 9:4 [A]Josh 24:33 [B]2 Kin 4:42 [C]Josh 19:42 9:5 [A]1 Sam 1:1 [B]1 Sam 10:2 9:6 [A]Deut 33:1; 1 Kin 13:1; 2 Kin 5:8 [B]1 Sam 3:19 [C]Gen 24:42 9:7 [A]1 Kin 14:3; 2 Kin 5:15; 8:8, 9; Ezek 13:19 9:8 [A]1 Sam 9:6 9:9 [A]2 Sam 24:11; 2 Kin 17:13; 1 Chr 9:22; 26:28; 29:29; Is 30:10; Amos 7:12 9:11 [A]Gen 24:11, 15; 29:8, 9; Ex 2:16 9:12 [a]Or *behold* [A]Gen 31:54; Num 28:11-15; 1 Kin 3:2 [B]1 Sam 7:17; 10:5 9:13 [A]Luke 9:16; John 6:11

8:18 you will cry out … because of your king whom you have chosen. Samuel warned the people that they would live to regret their decision for a king and would later cry out for freedom from his rule (1Ki 12:4). **the LORD will not answer you.** In contrast to the Lord's response to Israel during the period of the judges (Jdg 2:18), the Lord would not be moved to pity and therefore would refuse to deliver the people out of the hand of their king who oppressed them.

8:19 there shall be a king over us. In spite of Samuel's warnings, the people demanded a king.

8:20 fight our battles. Up until this point, the Lord Himself had fought the battles for Israel and given continual victory (Jos 10:14; 1Sa 7:10). Israel no longer wanted the Lord to be their warrior; replacing Him with a human king was their desire. It was in this way that Israel rejected the Lord (see v. 7). The problem was not in having a king; rather the reason the people wanted a king was so that they would be like other nations. They also foolishly assumed there would be some greater power in a king leading them in battle.

9:1 a mighty man of valor. I.e., "a man of wealth," confirmed by the reference to donkeys and servants in v. 3 (cf. Boaz in Ru 2:1).

9:2 Saul. Son of Kish, a Benjamite, he was Israel's first king. The Heb. root for "Saul" means "asked (of God)." In 8:10, the people "asked … [for] a king." Although God appointed Saul, he was really the people's choice, given by the Lord in answer to their request. The Lord's choice would be from the tribe of Judah (cf. Ge 49:10). **a choice and handsome *man*.** Emphasis was placed on the external appearance of leaders (cf. David in 16:18).

9:3 the donkeys … were lost. "Lost donkeys" meant "lost wealth." Kish had servants who could have gone looking, but Saul was chosen to oversee this important task.

9:4 Shalishah … Shaalim. The locations are geographically unknown.

9:6 a man of God. A description of the prophet and judge, Samuel. "Man of God" referred to a prophet (see 2:27). *See note on Dt 33:1.*

9:7 no present to bring. A gift expressed gratitude and thankfulness for the service of the "man of God." Gifts were offered to prophets in 1Ki 14:3; 2Ki 4:42; 5:15, 16; 8:8, 9.

9:8 a fourth of a shekel. About one-tenth of an ounce.

9:9 a prophet now was formerly called a seer. Due to the God-given ability to know or "see" the future, the "seer" was so named in close relationship with what he did. The person called a prophet, by the time this book was written, had been termed a seer in the earlier time of Saul.

9:12 high place. This is essentially Canaanite in background (cf. Dt 12:2–5). Before the temple was built, the high place was used for worship and sacrifice because it provided the best vantage point for the participation of the people in worship and allowed them to visually see the sacrifice being made for them.

9:13 he must bless the sacrifice. The sacrifice was offered to the Lord as an act of worship by the "man of God."

GOD'S CHOICE FOR KING

15 Now a day before Saul's coming, [A]the LORD had
[a]revealed *this* to Samuel saying, 16 "About this time tomorrow I will send you a man from the land of Benjamin, and [A]you shall anoint him to be prince over
My people Israel; and he will deliver My people from
the hand of the Philistines. For [B]I have regarded My
people, because their cry has come to Me." 17 When
Samuel saw Saul, the LORD [a]said to him, "[A]Behold,
the man of whom I spoke to you! This one shall rule
over My people." 18 Then Saul approached Samuel in
the gate and said, "Please tell me where the seer's
house is." 19 Samuel answered Saul and said, "I am
the seer. Go up before me to the high place, for you
shall eat with me today; and in the morning I will
let you go, and will tell you all that is on your mind.
20 [A]As for your donkeys which were lost three days
ago, do not set your mind on them, for they have
been found. And [B]for whom is all that is desirable
in Israel? Is it not for you and for all your father's
household?" 21 Saul replied, "[A]Am I not a Benjamite,
of [B]the smallest of the tribes of Israel, and my family
the least of all the families of the [a]tribe of Benjamin?
Why then do you speak to me in this way?"
22 Then Samuel took Saul and his servant and
brought them into the hall and gave them a place
at the head of those who were invited, who were
about thirty men. 23 Samuel said to the cook, "[a]Bring
the portion that I gave you, concerning which I said
to you, 'Set it [b]aside.' " 24 Then the cook [A]took up the
leg with what was on it and set *it* before Saul. And
Samuel said, "Here is what has been reserved! Set
it before you *and* eat, because it has been kept for
you until the appointed time, [a]since I said I have
invited the people." So Saul ate with Samuel that day.
25 When they came down from the high place into
the city, *Samuel* spoke with Saul [A]on the [a]roof. 26 And
they arose early; and at daybreak Samuel called to
Saul on the roof, saying, "Get up, that I may send
you away." So Saul arose, and both he and Samuel
went out into the street. 27 As they were going down
to the edge of the city, Samuel said to Saul, "Say to
the servant that he might go ahead of us and pass
on, but you remain standing now, that I may proclaim the word of God to you."

SAUL AMONG PROPHETS

10 Then [A]Samuel took the flask of oil, poured it on
his head, [B]kissed him and said, "Has not [C]the
LORD anointed you a ruler over [D]His inheritance?
2 When you go from me today, then you will find
two men close to [A]Rachel's tomb in the territory of
Benjamin at Zelzah; and they will say to you, '[B]The
donkeys which you went to look for have been found.
Now behold, your father has [a]ceased to be concerned
about the donkeys and is anxious for you, saying,
"What shall I do about my son?" ' 3 Then you will go
on further from there, and you will come as far as
the [a,A]oak of Tabor, and there three men going up
[B]to God at Bethel will meet you, one carrying three
young goats, another carrying three loaves of bread,
and another carrying a jug of wine; 4 and they will
greet you and give you two *loaves* of bread, which
you will accept from their hand. 5 Afterward you will
come to [a,A]the hill of God where the Philistine garrison is; and it shall be as soon as you have come there
to the city, that you will meet [B]a group of prophets
coming down from the high place with harp, tambourine, flute, and a lyre before them, and [C]they will
be prophesying. 6 Then [A]the Spirit of the LORD will
come upon you mightily, and [B]you shall prophesy
with them and be changed into another man. 7 It shall
be when these signs come to you, [A]do for yourself
what [a]the occasion requires, for [B]God is with you.

9:15 [a]Lit *uncovered the ear* [A]1 Sam 15:1; Acts 13:21 9:16 [A]1 Sam 10:1 [B]Ex 3:7, 9 9:17 [a]Lit *answered* [A]1 Sam 16:12 9:20 [A]1 Sam 9:3 [B]1 Sam 8:5; 12:13 9:21 [a]So some ancient versions; Heb *tribes* [A]1 Sam 15:17 [B]Judg 20:46-48 9:23 [a]Lit *Give* [b]Lit *with you* 9:24 [a]Lit *saying* [A]Ex 29:22, 27; Lev 7:32, 33; Num 18:18 9:25 [a]Gr adds *and they spread a bed for Saul on the roof and he slept* [A]Deut 22:8; Luke 5:19; Acts 10:9 10:1 [A]Ex 30:23-33; 1 Sam 16:13; 2 Kin 9:3, 6 [B]Ps 2:12 [C]1 Sam 16:13; 26:9; 2 Sam 1:14 [D]Deut 32:9; Ps 78:71 10:2 [a]Lit *abandoned the matter of* [A]Gen 35:16-20; 48:7 [B]1 Sam 9:3-5 10:3 [a]Or *terebinth* [A]Gen 35:8 [B]Gen 28:19; 35:1, 3, 7 10:5 [a]Or *Gibeath-haelohim* [A]1 Sam 13:2, 3 [B]1 Sam 19:20; 2 Kin 2:3, 5, 15 [C]2 Kin 3:15; 1 Chr 25:1-6; 1 Cor 14:1 10:6 [A]Num 11:25, 29; Judg 14:6 [B]1 Sam 10:10; 19:23, 24 10:7 [a]Lit *your hand finds* [A]Eccl 9:10 [B]Josh 1:5; Judg 6:12; Heb 13:5

9:16 anoint him. This represents a setting apart for service to the Lord, which occurs in 10:1. *See note on 2:10.* **prince.** Lit. "one given prominence, one placed in front." The title referred to "one designated to rule" (cf. 1Ki 1:35; 2Ch 11:22). **their cry has come to Me.** The people had been crying out for deliverance from the Philistines, their longstanding rivals, just as they did for liberation from Egypt (cf. Ex 2:25; 3:9).

9:17 This one shall rule over My people. God identified Saul to Samuel, assuring there was no mistaking whom God was choosing to be king.

9:18 tell me where the seer's house is. A reference to Samuel's house.

9:20 all that is desirable in Israel. Saul was to become the focus of Israel's hope for military victories over her enemies (cf. 8:19, 20).

9:21 a Benjamite ... the least of all the families. Saul's humility and timidity was expressed by his proper assessment of his tribe and a humble estimation of his family.

9:22 the hall. The place where those who were invited ate with Samuel after the offering of the sacrifice on the high place (cf. vv. 12, 13).

9:24 the leg ... kept for you. Samuel was following Lv 7:28–36. Samuel received the leg, the portion of the sacrifice reserved for the priest. Samuel's giving of this choice piece of meat to Saul was a distinct honor and reflected Saul's new status as the designated king.

9:25 on the roof. The roof of Samuel's house provided a place for Saul and his servant to sleep for the night.

9:27 the word of God. Special revelation from God, given to Samuel and intended for Saul. *See note on 3:1.*

10:1 the LORD anointed you a ruler. The Lord chose Saul to be the leader of Israel and communicated His choice through the private anointing by Samuel, signifying a setting aside for God's service (see 2:10). **His inheritance.** The inheritance was God's nation, Israel, in the sense that she uniquely belonged to Him (Dt 4:20; 9:26).

10:2 Zelzah. Only mentioned here. Probably near Ramah, located between Bethel and Bethlehem, where Rachel died (Ge 35:19; 48:7).

10:3 Tabor. This is not the far-distant Mt. Tabor, but a location unknown, probably near Bethel.

10:5 the Philistine garrison. Most likely the garrison in Geba in Benjamin, about 5 mi. N of Jerusalem. **prophesying.** The prophet, as God's messenger, declared the Word of the Lord (2Sa 7:5; 12:1), sometimes accompanied by music (1Ch 25:1). Here, "prophesying" connotes praising God and instructing the people with musical accompaniment.

10:6 the Spirit of the LORD will come upon you. The Holy Spirit would enable Saul to declare the Word of the Lord with the prophets. **changed into another man.** With this empowerment by the Holy Spirit, Saul would emerge another man (cf. 10:9), equipped in the manner of Gideon and Jepthah for deeds of valor (cf. v. 9; Jdg 6:34; 11:29).

10:7 signs. The 3 signs of vv. 2–6: 1) the report of the found donkeys; 2) the encounter of the 3 men going to Bethel; and 3) the encounter with the prophets. **do ... what the occasion requires.** Saul was to do what his hand found to do (Ecc 9:10).

8 And [A]you shall go down before me to Gilgal; and behold, I will come down to you to offer burnt offerings and [B]sacrifice peace offerings. [C]You shall wait seven days until I come to you and show you what you should do."

9 Then it happened when he turned his back to leave Samuel, God [A]changed [a]his heart; and all those signs came about on that day. 10 [A]When they came to [a]the hill there, behold, a group of prophets met him; and the Spirit of God came upon him mightily, so that he prophesied among them. 11 It came about, when all who knew him previously saw that he prophesied now with the prophets, that the people said to one another, "What has happened to the son of Kish? [A]Is Saul also among the prophets?" 12 A man there said, "Now, who is their father?" Therefore it became a proverb: "[A]Is Saul also among the prophets?" 13 When he had finished prophesying, he came to the high place.

14 Now [A]Saul's uncle said to him and his servant, "Where did you go?" And he said, "[B]To look for the donkeys. When we saw that they could not be found, we went to Samuel." 15 Saul's uncle said, "Please tell me what Samuel said to you." 16 So Saul said to his uncle, "[A]He told us plainly that the donkeys had been found." But he did not tell him about the matter of the kingdom which Samuel had mentioned.

SAUL PUBLICLY CHOSEN KING

17 Thereafter Samuel called the [A]people together to the LORD at Mizpah; 18 and he said to the sons of Israel, "[A]Thus says the LORD, the God of Israel, 'I brought Israel up from Egypt, and I delivered you from the hand of the Egyptians and from the [a]power of all the kingdoms that were oppressing you.' 19 But you [A]have today rejected your God, who delivers you from all your calamities and your distresses; yet you have [a]said, 'No, but set a king over us!' Now therefore, [B]present yourselves before the LORD by your tribes and by your clans."

20 Thus Samuel brought all the tribes of Israel near, and the tribe of Benjamin was taken by lot. 21 Then he brought the tribe of Benjamin near by its families, and the Matrite family was taken. And Saul the son of Kish was taken; but when they looked for him, he could not be found. 22 Therefore [A]they inquired further of the LORD, "Has the man come here yet?" So the LORD said, "Behold, he is hiding himself by the baggage." 23 So they ran and took him from there, and when he stood among the people, [A]he was taller than any of the people from his shoulders upward. 24 Samuel said to all the people, "Do you see him [A]whom the LORD has chosen? Surely there is no one like him among all the people." So all the people shouted and said, "[a,B]*Long* live the king!"

25 Then Samuel told the people [A]the ordinances of the kingdom, and wrote *them* in the book and [B]placed *it* before the LORD. And Samuel sent all the people away, each one to his house. 26 Saul also went [A]to his house at Gibeah; and the valiant *men* whose hearts God had touched went with him. 27 But certain [a,A]worthless men said, "How can this one deliver us?" And they despised him and [B]did not bring him any present. But he kept silent.

SAUL DEFEATS THE AMMONITES

11 Now [A]Nahash the Ammonite came up and [a]besieged [B]Jabesh-gilead; and all the men of Jabesh said to Nahash, "Make [C]a covenant with us and we will serve you." 2 But Nahash the Ammonite said to them, "I will make *it* with you on this condition, [A]that I will gouge out the right eye of every one of you, thus I will make it [B]a reproach on all Israel." 3 [A]The elders of Jabesh said to him, "Let us alone for seven days, that we may send messengers throughout the territory of Israel. Then, if there is no one to deliver us, we will come out to you."

10:8 [A]1 Sam 11:14; 13:8 [B]1 Sam 11:15 [C]1 Sam 13:8 10:9 [a]Lit *for him another heart* [A]1 Sam 10:6 10:10 [a]Or *Gibeath* [A]1 Sam 10:5, 6; 19:20 10:11 [A]1 Sam 19:24; Amos 7:14, 15; Matt 13:54-57; John 7:15 10:12 [A]1 Sam 19:23, 24 10:14 [A]1 Sam 14:50 [B]1 Sam 9:3-6 10:16 [A]1 Sam 9:20 10:17 [A]Judg 20:1; 1 Sam 7:5 10:18 [a]Lit *hand* [A]Judg 6:8, 9 10:19 [a]So with several mss and versions; M.T. *said to Him* [A]1 Sam 8:6, 7; 12:12 [B]Josh 7:14-18; 24:1; Prov 16:33 10:22 [A]1 Sam 23:2, 4 10:23 [A]1 Sam 9:2 10:24 [a]Lit *May the king live* [A]Deut 17:15; 2 Sam 21:6 [B]1 Kin 1:25, 34, 39 10:25 [A]Deut 17:14-20; 1 Sam 8:11-18 [B]Deut 31:26 10:26 [A]1 Sam 11:4; 15:34 10:27 [a]Lit *sons of Belial*, cf 2 Cor 6:15 [A]Deut 13:13; 1 Sam 25:17 [B]1 Kin 10:25; 2 Chr 17:5 11:1 [a]Lit *camped against* [A]1 Sam 12:12 [B]Judg 21:8; 1 Sam 31:11 [C]Gen 26:28; 1 Kin 20:34; Job 41:4; Ezek 17:13 11:2 [A]Num 16:14 [B]1 Sam 17:26; Ps 44:13 11:3 [A]1 Sam 8:4

10:8 Gilgal. The town where Saul eventually would be declared king by Samuel (11:14, 15), offer sacrifice before the Lord without the prophet Samuel (13:12), and where Samuel slew king Agag (15:33). Gilgal was to the E of Jericho, but W of the Jordan River. **burnt offerings and ... peace offerings.** *See notes on Lv 1:3–17; 3:1–17.* **seven days.** The appointed time Saul was to wait for Samuel to come and tell him what to do (see 13:8).

10:9 God changed his heart. Lit. "God changed him for another heart," i.e., God prepared Saul for the kingship by having the Holy Spirit come upon him (cf. v. 6).

10:12 who is their father? A question asked to find out the identity of the leader of the prophetic band that now included Saul. **a proverb.** A saying of common occurrence.

10:16 the matter of the kingdom. The information Samuel gave Saul about becoming king he did not tell his uncle. This might reflect Saul's humility (cf. v. 22).

10:17 Samuel called the people. The Lord's choice of Saul was made public at Mizpah, the place of the spiritual revival before Israel's victory over the Philistines (7:5–8).

10:18, 19 the LORD, the God of Israel ... delivered you. Despite the past faithfulness of God to His people, they still desired a human king to deliver them from the hands of their enemies.

10:20, 21 taken. Probably Saul was selected by the casting of lots (cf. Lv 16:8–10; Jos 7:15–18). *See note on Pr 16:33.*

10:22 hiding ... by the baggage. Overwhelmed, Saul had hidden himself in the military supplies.

10:23 taller ... from his shoulders upward. Saul's physical stature was impressive; being head and shoulders above the rest gave Saul a kingly presence.

10:25 the ordinances of the kingdom. Samuel reminded the people of the regulations governing the conduct of kings according to Dt 17:14–20.

10:26 whose hearts God had touched. Valiant men who were eager to affirm God's choice of Saul and, in response to a divine impulse, joined him.

10:27 worthless men. Lit. "sons of Belial" (*see note on 2:12*). Those who did not recognize Saul with the respect befitting a king.

11:1 Nahash the Ammonite. Nahash, meaning "snake," was king of the Ammonites, the descendants of Lot (cf. Ge 19:36–38) who lived E of the Jordan. **Jabesh-gilead.** A town E of the Jordan River, about 22 mi. S of the Sea of Galilee, in the tribal territory of Manasseh (cf. Jdg 21:8–14).

11:2 gouge out the right eye. This barbarous mutilation was a common punishment of usurpers in the ancient Near East which would disable the warriors' depth-perception and peripheral vision, rendering them useless in battle.

11:3 seven days. The elders at Jabesh were hoping for deliverance from the Israelites W of the Jordan.

4 Then the messengers came [A]to Gibeah of Saul and
spoke these words in the hearing of the people,
and all the people [B]lifted up their voices and wept.
5 Now behold, Saul was coming from the field
[A]behind the oxen, and [a]he said, "What is *the matter*
with the people that they weep?" So they related
to him the words of the men of Jabesh. 6 Then [A]the
Spirit of God came upon Saul mightily when he
heard these words, and [a]he became very angry. 7 He
took a yoke of oxen and [A]cut them in pieces, and sent
them throughout the territory of Israel by the hand
of messengers, saying, "[B]Whoever does not come
out after Saul and after Samuel, so shall it be done
to his oxen." Then the dread of the LORD fell on the
people, and they came out [C]as one man. 8 He [a]num-
bered them in [A]Bezek; and the [B]sons of Israel were
300,000, and the men of Judah 30,000. 9 They said
to the messengers who had come, "Thus you shall
say to the men of Jabesh-gilead, 'Tomorrow, by the
time the sun is hot, you will have deliverance.' " So
the messengers went and told the men of Jabesh;
and they were glad. 10 Then the men of Jabesh said,
"[A]Tomorrow we will come out to you, and you may
do to us whatever seems good [a]to you." 11 The next
morning Saul put the people [A]in three companies;
and they came into the midst of the camp at the
morning watch and struck down the Ammonites
until the heat of the day. Those who survived were
scattered, so that no two of them were left together.
12 Then the people said to Samuel, "[A]Who is he
that said, 'Shall Saul reign over us?' [a,B]Bring the men,
that we may put them to death." 13 But Saul said,
"[A]Not a man shall be put to death this day, for today
[B]the LORD has accomplished deliverance in Israel."
14 Then Samuel said to the people, "Come and let
us go to [A]Gilgal and [B]renew the kingdom there." 15 So
all the people went to Gilgal, and there they made
Saul king [A]before the LORD in Gilgal. There they
also [B]offered sacrifices of peace offerings before
the LORD; and there Saul and all the men of Israel
rejoiced greatly.

SAMUEL ADDRESSES ISRAEL

12 Then Samuel said to all Israel, "Behold, [A]I have
listened to your voice in all that you said to
me and I [B]have [a]appointed a king over you. 2 Now,
[A]here is the king walking before you, but [B]I am old
and gray, and behold [C]my sons are with you. And [D]I
have walked before you from my youth even to this
day. 3 Here I am; bear witness against me before the
LORD and [A]His anointed. [B]Whose ox have I taken,
or whose donkey have I taken, or whom have I defrauded? Whom have I oppressed, or [C]from whose
hand have I taken a bribe to blind my eyes with it?
I will restore *it* to you." 4 They said, "You have not
defrauded us or oppressed us or taken anything
from any man's hand." 5 He said to them, "The LORD
is witness against you, and His anointed is witness
this day that [A]you have found nothing [B]in my hand."
And they said, "*He is* witness."
6 Then Samuel said to the people, "It is the LORD
who [a,A]appointed Moses and Aaron and who brought
your fathers up from the land of Egypt. 7 So now,
take your stand, [A]that I may plead with you before the LORD concerning all the righteous acts of
the LORD which He did for you and your fathers.
8 [A]When Jacob went into Egypt and [B]your fathers
cried out to the LORD, then [C]the LORD sent Moses
and Aaron [a,D]who brought your fathers out of Egypt
and settled them in this place. 9 But [A]they forgot the
LORD their God, so [B]He sold them into the hand of
Sisera, captain of the army of Hazor, and [C]into the
hand of the Philistines and [D]into the hand of the
king of Moab, and they fought against them. 10 [A]They
cried out to the LORD and said, 'We have sinned because we have forsaken the LORD and have served
[B]the Baals and the Ashtaroth; but [C]now deliver us
from the hands of our enemies, and we will serve

11:4 [A]1 Sam 10:26; 15:34 [B]Gen 27:38; Judg 2:4; 20:23, 26; 21:2; 1 Sam 30:4 11:5 [a]Lit *Saul* [A]1 Kin 19:19 11:6 [a]Lit *his anger burned exceedingly* [A]Judg 3:10; 6:34; 11:29; 13:25; 14:6; 1 Sam 10:10; 16:13 11:7 [A]Judg 19:29 [B]Judg 21:5, 8 [C]Judg 20:1 11:8 [a]Lit *mustered* [A]Judg 1:5 [B]Judg 20:2 11:10 [a]Lit *in your sight* [A]1 Sam 11:3 11:11 [A]Judg 7:16, 20 11:12 [a]Lit *Give* [A]1 Sam 10:27 [B]Luke 19:27 11:13 [A]1 Sam 10:27; 2 Sam 19:22 [B]Ex 14:13, 30; 1 Sam 19:5 11:14 [A]1 Sam 7:16; 10:8 [B]1 Sam 10:25 11:15 [A]1 Sam 10:17 [B]1 Sam 10:8 12:1 [a]Lit *made* [A]1 Sam 8:7, 9, 22 [B]1 Sam 10:24; 11:14, 15 12:2 [A]1 Sam 8:20 [B]1 Sam 8:1, 5 [C]1 Sam 8:3, 5 [D]1 Sam 3:10, 19, 20 12:3 [A]1 Sam 10:1; 24:6; 2 Sam 1:14 [B]Ex 20:17; Num 16:15; Acts 20:33 [C]Ex 23:8; Deut 16:19 12:5 [A]Acts 23:9; 24:20 [B]Ex 22:4 12:6 [a]Lit *made* [A]Ex 6:26; Mic 6:4 12:7 [A]Ezek 20:35; Mic 6:1-5 12:8 [a]Lit *and they brought* [A]Gen 46:5, 6 [B]Ex 2:23-25 [C]Ex 3:10; 4:14-16 [D]1 Sam 10:18 12:9 [A]Deut 32:18; Judg 3:7 [B]Judg 4:2 [C]Judg 3:31; 10:7; 13:1 [D]Judg 3:12-30 12:10 [A]Judg 10:10 [B]Judg 2:13; 3:7 [C]Judg 10:15, 16

11:4 Gibeah of Saul. Saul's home and the first capital city of the monarchy, about 3 mi. N of Jerusalem (cf. 10:26).

11:5 from the field. Saul continued to work as a farmer while waiting for the time to answer Israel's expectations of him as the king.

11:6 the Spirit of God came upon Saul. To fill him with divine indignation and to empower him to deliver the citizens of Jabesh-gilead (cf. 10:6).

11:7 cut them in pieces. Saul divided the oxen in sections to be taken throughout Israel to rouse the people for battle (see a similar action in Jdg 19:29; 20:6).

11:8 Bezek. A city 13 mi. N of Shechem and 17 mi. W of Jabesh-gilead. **sons of Israel … men of Judah.** This distinction made between Israel and Judah before the kingdom was divided indicates the book was written after 931 B.C. when the kingdom had been divided. See Introduction: Author and Date.

11:11 three companies. A military strategy of dividing up forces, it lessened the possibility of losing everyone to a sneak attack while giving greater military options. **at the morning watch.** The last of the 3 watches (2:00–6:00 a.m.), this surprise attack was before dawn, before the Ammonites were prepared for battle.

11:13 the LORD has accomplished deliverance in Israel. Saul recognized the deliverance of the Lord and refused to kill those who had rebelled against his kingship (10:27).

11:14 Gilgal. *See note on 10:8.* **renew the kingdom.** The reaffirmation of Saul's kingship by public acclamation.

11:15 they made Saul king before the LORD. All the people came to crown Saul king that day. The process of entering the kingship was the same for both Saul and David: 1) commissioned by the Lord (9:1–10:16; 16:1–13); 2) confirmed by military victory (10:17–11:11; 16:14-2Sa 1:27); and 3) crowned (11:12–15; 2Sa 2:4; 5:3). **peace offerings.** Sacrifices of thanksgiving (cf. Lv 7:13). **rejoiced greatly.** Along with the victory over the Ammonites, there was a great celebration over the nation being united.

12:1 I have listened to your voice. Samuel had obeyed the will of the Lord and the people and set the king of God's choice over them, though he had personal reservations concerning the monarchy.

12:3 Here I am. These familiar words for Samuel throughout his entire life (cf. 3:4, 5, 6, 8, 16) emphasized his availability to God and the people. **witness.** Samuel requested the people to "bear witness against" any covenant stipulations that he had violated.

12:7 I may plead with you before the LORD. Despite the nation being unified under the new king, Samuel still wanted to rebuke the nation for ignoring and rejecting what God had done without a king.

You.' 11 Then the LORD sent [A]Jerubbaal and [a,B]Bedan and [C]Jephthah and [D]Samuel, and delivered you from the hands of your enemies all around, so that you lived in security.

THE KING CONFIRMED

12 When you saw [A]that Nahash the king of the sons of Ammon came against you, you said to me, '[B]No, but a king shall reign over us,' [C]although the LORD your God *was* your king. 13 Now therefore, [A]here is the king whom you have chosen, [B]whom you have asked for, and behold, the LORD has set a king over you. 14 [A]If you will fear the LORD and serve Him, and listen to His voice and not rebel against the [a]command of the LORD, then both you and also the king who reigns over you will follow the LORD your God. 15 [A]If you will not listen to the voice of the LORD, but rebel against the [a]command of the LORD, then [B]the hand of the LORD will be against you, [C]*as it was* against your fathers. 16 Even now, [A]take your stand and see this great thing which the LORD will do before your eyes. 17 [A]Is it not the wheat harvest today? [B]I will call to the LORD, that He may send [a]thunder and rain. Then you will know and see that [C]your wickedness is great which you have done in the sight of the LORD by asking for yourselves a king." 18 So Samuel called to the LORD, and the LORD sent [a]thunder and rain that day; and [A]all the people greatly feared the LORD and Samuel.

19 Then all the people said to Samuel, "[A]Pray for your servants to the LORD your God, so that we may not die, for we have added to all our sins [B]*this* evil by asking for ourselves a king." 20 Samuel said to the people, "Do not fear. You have committed all this evil, yet [A]do not turn aside from following the LORD, but serve the LORD with all your heart. 21 You must not turn aside, for *then you would go* after [A]futile things which can not profit or deliver, because they are futile. 22 For [A]the LORD will not abandon His people [B]on account of His great name, because the LORD [C]has been pleased to make you a people for Himself. 23 Moreover, as for me, [A]far be it from me that I should sin against the LORD by ceasing to pray for you; but [B]I will instruct you in the good and right way. 24 [A]Only [a]fear the LORD and serve Him in truth with all your heart; for consider [B]what great things He has done for you. 25 [A]But if you still do wickedly, [B]both you and your king [C]will be swept away."

WAR WITH THE PHILISTINES

13 Saul was [a]*thirty* years old when he began to reign, and he reigned [b]*forty* two years over Israel.

2 Now Saul chose for himself 3,000 men of Israel, of which 2,000 were with Saul in [A]Michmash and in the hill country of Bethel, while 1,000 were with Jonathan at [B]Gibeah of Benjamin. But he sent away the rest of the people, each to his tent. 3 Jonathan smote [A]the garrison of the Philistines that was in [B]Geba, and the Philistines heard of *it*. Then Saul [C]blew the trumpet throughout the land, saying, "Let the Hebrews hear." 4 All Israel heard [a]the news that Saul had smitten the garrison of the Philistines, and also that Israel [A]had become odious to the Philistines. The people were then summoned [b]to Saul at Gilgal.

5 Now the Philistines assembled to fight with Israel, 30,000 chariots and 6,000 horsemen, and [A]people like the sand which is on the seashore in abundance; and they came up and camped in Michmash, east of [B]Beth-aven. 6 When the men of Israel

12:11 [a]Gr and Syr read *Barak* [A]Judg 6:31, 32; 7:1 [B]Judg 4:6; 11:1 [C]Judg 11:29 [D]1 Sam 3:20 12:12 [A]1 Sam 11:1, 2 [B]1 Sam 8:6, 19 [C]Judg 8:23; 1 Sam 8:7 12:13 [A]1 Sam 10:24 [B]1 Sam 8:5; 12:17, 19; Hos 13:11 12:14 [a]Lit *mouth* [A]Josh 24:14 12:15 [a]Lit *mouth* [A]Lev 26:14, 15; Josh 24:20; Is 1:20 [B]1 Sam 5:9 [C]1 Sam 12:9 12:16 [A]Ex 14:13, 31 12:17 [a]Lit *sounds* [A]Prov 26:1 [B]1 Sam 7:9, 10; James 5:16ff [C]1 Sam 8:7 12:18 [a]Lit *sounds* [A]Ex 14:31 12:19 [A]Ex 9:28; 1 Sam 12:23; Jer 15:1; 1 John 5:16 [B]1 Sam 12:17, 20 12:20 [A]Deut 11:16 12:21 [A]Deut 11:16; Is 41:29; Hab 2:18 12:22 [A]Deut 31:6; 1 Kin 6:13 [B]Ex 32:12; Num 14:13; Josh 7:9; Ps 106:8; Jer 14:21 [C]Deut 7:6-11; 1 Pet 2:9 12:23 [A]Rom 1:9; 1 Cor 9:16; Col 1:9; 1 Thess 3:10; 2 Tim 1:3 [B]1 Kin 8:36; Ps 34:11; Prov 4:11 12:24 [a]Or *reverence* [A]Eccl 12:13 [B]Deut 10:21; Is 5:12 12:25 [A]Is 1:20; 3:11 [B]Josh 24:20 [C]1 Sam 31:1-5; Hos 10:3 13:1 [a]As in some mss of the LXX; Heb omits *thirty* [b]See Acts 13:21; Heb omits *forty* 13:2 [A]1 Sam 13:5; 14:31 [B]1 Sam 10:26 13:3 [A]1 Sam 10:5 [B]1 Sam 13:16; 14:5 [C]Judg 3:27; 6:34 13:4 [a]Lit *saying* [b]Lit *after* [A]Gen 34:30; Ex 5:21; 2 Sam 10:6 13:5 [A]Josh 11:4 [B]Josh 18:12; 1 Sam 14:23

12:11 the LORD sent . . . and delivered you. It was the Lord who delivered them through the hands of the judges, not themselves.

12:12 When you saw that Nahash the king of the sons of Ammon came against you. According to the DSS and Josephus, Nahash was campaigning over a large area. It was that Ammonite threat that seemingly provoked Israel to demand a human king (8:1–20). **the LORD your God *was* your king.** The clearest indictment of Israel for choosing a mere man to fight for her instead of the Lord God (cf. 8:20).

12:13 the king whom you have chosen . . . asked for. The Lord gave them their request (cf. Ps 106:15).

12:14 fear the LORD. A reminder of Jos 24:14. Israel was to stand in awe of the Lord and submit to Him (cf. Dt 10:12). **you and . . . the king . . . follow the LORD.** Both the people and the king were given the same command. The standard was the same, obedience to God's commands.

12:15 rebel. "Disobey, not heed, forsake." Echoing the promises of Dt 28, there would be blessings for obeying and curses for disobeying the commands of the Lord.

12:16 this great thing. Though rain during the wheat harvest (late May to early June) was unusual, the Lord sent the rain and thunder to authenticate Samuel's words to the people.

12:19 Pray for your servants. The people's response to the power of God was their recognition of their sinful motives in asking for a king. They needed Samuel's prayers to intercede for them.

12:20 serve the LORD with all your heart. An often-expressed covenant requirement (Dt 10:12, 13; 11:13, 14).

12:21 futile things. "Vain things," i.e., idols.

13:1 *thirty* years . . . *forty* two years. The original numbers have not been preserved in this text. It lit. reads, "Saul was one year old when he became king and ruled two years over Israel." Ac 13:21 states that Saul ruled Israel 40 years. His age at his accession is recorded nowhere in Scripture. Probably the best reconstruction of vv. 1, 2 is "Saul was one and (perhaps) thirty years old when he began to reign, and when he had reigned two years over Israel, then Saul chose for himself three thousand men of Israel..."

13:2 Michmash. This area was located about 7 mi. NE of Jerusalem. **Jonathan.** "The Lord has given." Saul's firstborn son and heir apparent to the throne was evidently old enough to serve as a commander in Israel's army at this time, much like David when he slew Goliath (1Sa 17:32–37). **Gibeah of Benjamin.** This city was located 3 mi. N of Jerusalem. It was called Gibeah of Saul in 11:4.

13:3 Geba. This outpost was located about 5 mi. NNE of Jerusalem, 1 1/2 mi. SW of Michmash. **blew the trumpet.** Saul used the trumpet to summon additional troops for battle.

13:4 odious. Israel could expect retaliation from the Philistines for Jonathan's raid. **Gilgal.** This is the town of Saul's confirmation as king by Samuel and the people (11:14, 15). Saul chose Gilgal because of Samuel's word in 10:8.

13:5 thirty thousand chariots. This is probably a scribal error, since the number is too large for the corresponding horsemen. Three thousand is more reasonable and is found in some OT manuscripts. **Michmash.** *See note on 13:2.* **Beth-aven.** Lit. "house of nothingness." It was less than one mi. SW of Michmash.

saw that they were in a strait (for the people were
hard-pressed), then [A]the people hid themselves in
caves, in thickets, in cliffs, in cellars, and in pits.
7 Also *some of* the Hebrews crossed the Jordan
into the land of [A]Gad and Gilead. But as for Saul,
he *was* still in Gilgal, and all the people followed
him trembling.
8 Now [A]he waited seven days, according to the
appointed time set by Samuel, but Samuel did not
come to Gilgal; and the people were scattering from
him. 9 So Saul said, "Bring to me the burnt offering
and the peace offerings." And [A]he offered the burnt
offering. 10 As soon as he finished offering the burnt
offering, behold, Samuel came; and [A]Saul went out
to meet him *and* to [a]greet him. 11 But Samuel said,
"What have you done?" And Saul said, "Because I
saw that the people were scattering from me, and
that you did not come within the appointed days,
and that [A]the Philistines were assembling at Michmash, 12 therefore I said, 'Now the Philistines will
come down against me at Gilgal, and I have not
asked the favor of the LORD.' So I forced myself and
offered the burnt offering." 13 Samuel said to Saul,
"[A]You have acted foolishly; [B]you have not kept the
commandment of the LORD your God, which He
commanded you, for now the LORD would have established your kingdom [a]over Israel [C]forever. 14 But
[A]now your kingdom shall not endure. [B]The LORD has
sought out for Himself a man after His own heart,
and the LORD has appointed him as ruler over His
people, because you have not kept what the LORD
commanded you."
15 Then Samuel arose and went up from Gilgal
to [A]Gibeah of Benjamin. And Saul [a]numbered the
people who were present with him, [B]about six hundred men. 16 Now Saul and his son Jonathan and the
people who were present with them were staying
in [A]Geba of Benjamin while the Philistines camped
at Michmash. 17 And [A]the [a]raiders came from the
camp of the Philistines in three [b]companies: one
[c]company turned [d]toward [B]Ophrah, to the land of
Shual, 18 and another [a]company turned [b]toward
[A]Beth-horon, and another [a]company turned [b]toward
the border which overlooks the valley of [B]Zeboim
toward the wilderness.
19 Now [A]no blacksmith could be found in all the
land of Israel, for the Philistines said, "Otherwise
the Hebrews will make [a,B]swords or spears." 20 So all
Israel went down to the Philistines, each to sharpen
his plowshare, his mattock, his axe, and his hoe.
21 The charge was [a]two-thirds of a shekel for the
plowshares, the mattocks, the forks, and the axes,
and to fix the hoes. 22 So it came about on the day
of battle that [A]neither sword nor spear was found
in the hands of any of the people who *were* with
Saul and Jonathan, but they were found with Saul
and his son Jonathan. 23 And [A]the garrison of the
Philistines went out to [B]the pass of Michmash.

JONATHAN'S VICTORY

14 Now the day came that Jonathan, the son of
Saul, said to the young man who was carrying his armor, "Come and let us cross over to
the Philistines' garrison that is on the other side."
But he did not tell his father. 2 Saul was staying
in the outskirts of [A]Gibeah under the pomegranate tree which is in [B]Migron. And the people who
were with him *were* [C]about six hundred men, 3 and
Ahijah, the [A]son of Ahitub, [B]Ichabod's brother, the
son of Phinehas, the son of Eli, the priest of the
LORD at [C]Shiloh, [D]was [a]wearing an ephod. And
the people did not know that Jonathan had gone.

13:6 [A]Judg 6:2 13:7 [A]Num 32:33 13:8 [A]1 Sam 10:8 13:9 [A]Deut 12:5-14; 2 Sam 24:25; 1 Kin 3:4 13:10 [a]Lit *bless* [A]1 Sam 15:13 13:11 [A]1 Sam 13:2, 5, 16, 23 13:13 [a]Lit *to* [A]2 Chr 16:9 [B]1 Sam 15:11, 22, 28 [C]1 Sam 1:22 13:14 [A]1 Sam 15:28 [B]Acts 7:46; 13:22 13:15 [a]Lit *mustered* [A]1 Sam 13:2 [B]1 Sam 13:2, 6, 7; 14:2 13:16 [A]1 Sam 13:2, 3 13:17 [a]Lit *destroyers* [b]Lit *heads* [c]Lit *head* [d]Lit *toward the direction of* [A]1 Sam 14:15 [B]Josh 18:23 13:18 [a]Lit *head* [b]Lit *the direction of* [A]Josh 16:3; 18:13, 14 [B]Neh 11:34 13:19 [a]Lit *sword or spear* [A]Judg 5:8; 2 Kin 24:14; Jer 24:1; 29:2 [B]Judg 5:8 13:21 [a]Heb *pim* 13:22 [A]Judg 5:8 13:23 [A]1 Sam 14:1; 2 Sam 23:14 [B]1 Sam 14:4, 5; Is 10:28 14:2 [A]1 Sam 13:15, 16 [B]Is 10:28 [C]1 Sam 13:15 14:3 [a]Lit *carrying* [A]1 Sam 22:9-12, 20 [B]1 Sam 4:21 [C]1 Sam 1:3 [D]1 Sam 2:28

13:7 Gad and Gilead. Areas E of the Jordan River. **all the people followed him trembling.** The people were in fear over probable Philistine retaliation.

13:8 seven days ... the appointed time set by Samuel. This is a direct reference to Samuel's word in 10:8. Saul was commanded to wait 7 days to meet Samuel in Gilgal. **the people were scattering.** Saul's men were deserting him because of anxiety and fear over the coming battle.

13:9 he offered the burnt offering. Saul's sin was not specifically that he made a sacrifice (cf. 2Sa 24:25; 1Ki 8:62–64), but that he did not wait for priestly assistance from Samuel. See 10:8. He wished to rule as an autocrat, who possessed absolute power in civil and sacred matters. Samuel had wanted the 7 days as a test of Saul's character and obedience to God, but Saul failed it by invading the priestly office himself.

13:11 Because I saw. Saul reacted disobediently based upon what he saw and not by faith. He feared losing his men and did not properly consider what God would have him do.

13:13 you have not kept the commandment. Saul's disobedience was a direct violation of the command from Samuel in 10:8. **your kingdom ... forever.** How could this be in light of God's promise to Judah (Ge 49:10)? This would correct the potential contradiction of Saul being from Benjamin, not Judah.

13:14 a man after His own heart. Instead of Saul, God was going to choose one whose heart was like His own, i.e., one who had a will to obey God. Paul quotes this passage in Ac 13:22 of David (cf. 16:7). **ruler.** Someone else, namely David, had already been chosen to be God's leader over His people.

13:15 from Gilgal to Gibeah. This was about a 10 mi. trip westward. Samuel left Saul, realizing that Saul's kingship was doomed. **six hundred men.** This indicates the mass departure of the Israelites (v. 6) and gives a perspective on what Saul saw (v. 5).

13:17 raiders ... in three companies. Lit. these were "destroyers" in the Philistine army, divided into 3 groups.

13:19 no blacksmith. The Philistines had superior iron and metal-working craftsmen until David's time (cf. 1Ch 22:3), accounting for their formidable military force.

13:20 mattock. A pickax to work the ground by hand.

13:21 The Philistines charged a high price to sharpen instruments potentially that could be used against them.

13:22 neither sword nor spear. The Philistines had a distinct military advantage over Israel since they had a monopoly on iron weapons.

13:23 the pass of Michmash. Some of the Philistines had moved out to a pass leading to Michmash.

14:1 the other side. Jonathan and his armor bearer left the Israelite camp to approach the Philistine outpost.

14:2 pomegranate tree. These trees are common to Israel's landscape, normally growing as low shrubs with spreading branches. This may have been a particularly large one.

14:3 Ahijah. "Brother of the Lord." He was the great-grandson of Eli the High Priest, another house which had been rejected of the Lord (2:22–36). **wearing an ephod.** The ephod was a white garment worn by the priests that was attached to the body by a belt. A breastpiece worn over the ephod had pouches that were used by the priests to carry certain devices used in determining the will of God, i.e., the Urim and Thummim, or sacred

4 [A]Between the passes by which Jonathan sought to
cross over to the Philistines' garrison, there was a
sharp crag on the one side and a sharp crag on the
other side, and the name of the one was Bozez, and
the name of the other Seneh. 5 The one crag rose on
the north opposite Michmash, and the other on the
south opposite Geba.
6 Then Jonathan said to the young man who was
carrying his armor, "Come and let us cross over to
the garrison of [A]these uncircumcised; perhaps the
LORD will work for us, for [B]the LORD is not restrained
to save by many or by few." 7 His armor bearer said
to him, "Do all that is in your heart; turn yourself,
and here I am with you according to your [a]desire."
8 Then Jonathan said, "[A]Behold, we will cross over to
the men and reveal ourselves to them. 9 If they [a]say
to us, 'Wait until we come to you'; then we will stand
in our place and not go up to them. 10 But if they [a]say,
'Come up to us,' then we will go up, for the LORD has
given them into our hands; and [A]this shall be the sign
to us." 11 When both of them revealed themselves to
the garrison of the Philistines, the Philistines said,
"Behold, [A]Hebrews are coming out of the holes where
they have hidden themselves." 12 So the men of the
garrison [a]hailed Jonathan and his armor bearer and
said, "Come up to us and [A]we will tell you something."
And Jonathan said to his armor bearer, "Come up after me, for [B]the LORD has given them into the hands
of Israel." 13 Then Jonathan climbed up on his hands
and feet, with his armor bearer behind him; and they
fell before Jonathan, and his armor bearer put some
to death after him. 14 That first slaughter which Jonathan and his armor bearer made was about twenty
men within about half a furrow in an acre of land.
15 And there was a trembling in the camp, in the field,
and among all the people. Even the garrison and [A]the
raiders trembled, and [B]the earth quaked so [C]that it
became a [a]great trembling.
16 Now Saul's watchmen in Gibeah of Benjamin
looked, and behold, the multitude melted away; and
they went here and *there*. 17 Saul said to the people
who *were* with him, "[a]Number now and see who has
gone from us." And when they had [a]numbered, behold, Jonathan and his armor bearer were not *there*.
18 Then Saul said to Ahijah, "[A]Bring the ark of God
here." For the ark of God was at that time with the
sons of Israel. 19 [A]While Saul talked to the priest, the
commotion in the camp of the Philistines continued
and increased; so Saul said to the priest, "Withdraw
your hand." 20 Then Saul and all the people who *were*
with him rallied and came to the battle; and behold,
[A]every man's sword was against his fellow, *and*
there was very great confusion. 21 Now the Hebrews
who were with the Philistines previously, who went
up with them all around in the camp, even [A]they
also *turned* to be with the Israelites who *were* with
Saul and Jonathan. 22 When all the [A]men of Israel
who had hidden themselves in the hill country of
Ephraim heard that the Philistines had fled, even
they also pursued them closely in the battle. 23 So
[A]the LORD delivered Israel that day, and the battle
[a]spread beyond [B]Beth-aven.

SAUL'S FOOLISH ORDER

24 Now the men of Israel were hard-pressed on
that day, for Saul had [A]put the people under oath,
saying, "Cursed be the man who eats food [a]before
evening, and until I have avenged myself on my enemies." So none of the people tasted food. 25 All *the*
people of the land entered the forest, and there was
honey on the ground. 26 When the people entered
the forest, behold, [A]*there was* a flow of honey; but
no man put his hand to his mouth, for the people
feared the oath. 27 But Jonathan had not heard when
his father put the people under oath; therefore, [A]he
put out the end of the staff that *was* in his hand and
dipped it in the honeycomb, and put his hand to
his mouth, and [B]his eyes brightened. 28 Then one of
the people said, "Your father strictly put the people
under oath, saying, 'Cursed be the man who eats
food today.' " And the people were weary. 29 Then
Jonathan said, "[A]My father has troubled the land.

14:4 [A]1 Sam 13:23 14:6 [A]1 Sam 17:26, 36; Jer 9:25, 26 [B]Judg 7:4, 7; 1 Sam 17:46, 47; Ps 115:3; 135:6; Zech 4:6; Matt 19:26 14:7 [a]Lit *heart* 14:8 [A]Judg 7:9-14 14:9 [a]Lit *say thus* 14:10 [a]Lit *say thus* [A]Gen 24:14; Judg 6:36 14:11 [A]1 Sam 13:6; 14:22 14:12 [a]Lit *answered* [A]1 Sam 17:43, 44 [B]2 Sam 5:24 14:15 [a]Lit *trembling of God* [A]1 Sam 13:17, 18 [B]1 Sam 7:10 [C]Gen 35:5; 2 Kin 7:6 14:17 [a]Lit *muster(ed)* 14:18 [A]1 Sam 23:9; 30:7 14:19 [A]Num 27:21 14:20 [A]Judg 7:22; 2 Chr 20:23 14:21 [A]1 Sam 29:4 14:22 [A]1 Sam 13:6 14:23 [a]Lit *passed over* [A]Ex 14:30; 1 Sam 10:19; 14:23; 1 Chr 11:14; 2 Chr 32:22; Ps 44:7 [B]1 Sam 13:5 14:24 [a]Lit *until* [A]Josh 6:26 14:26 [A]Matt 3:4 14:27 [A]1 Sam 14:43 [B]1 Sam 30:12 14:29 [A]Josh 7:25; 1 Kin 18:18

lots. *See note on Ex 28:5–13*. Apparently, Saul chose not to use it for seeking the Lord's will.

14:4 **Bozez . . . Seneh.** Hebrew terms. Bozez may mean "slippery." Seneh means "thorny."

14:6 **uncircumcised.** This was a derogatory term used by the Israelites to describe the Philistines. **by many or by few.** Jonathan demonstrated the great faith that should have been demonstrated by the king (cf. 13:11).

14:10 **the sign to us.** This was an unusual manner for determining the will of the Lord, but not without similar precedent, e.g., Gideon's fleece (Jdg 6:36–40). Jonathan was allowed to determine the will of God by the reaction of his enemies.

14:11 **Hebrews.** The oldest term used by Gentile nations to refer to the people of Israel. **the holes where they have hidden.** Many of the Israelites were hiding in fear over the battle. Apparently they thought Jonathan and his armor bearer were Israelite deserters coming to the Philistine side.

14:15 **the earth quaked.** The earthquake affirms the fact that divine intervention aided Jonathan and his armor bearer in their raid. The earthquake caused a panic among the Philistines. God would have intervened on Saul's behalf in such a manner had he chosen to be faithfully patient (cf. 13:9).

14:18 **ark of God.** The LXX reads "ephod" instead of "ark," and this seems more likely since the ark was at Kiriath-jearim and the language of 14:19 better fits the ephod (v. 3) than the ark.

14:19 **Withdraw your hand.** Saul, in a hurry, ordered the priest to stop the inquiry into the will of the Lord.

14:21 **Hebrews.** This is a reference to Israelite deserters or mercenaries.

14:22 **the hill country of Ephraim.** A large and partially wooded area N and W of Michmash.

14:23 **So the LORD delivered Israel.** The writer uses similar language to that of the Exodus. In spite of their disobedient king, God was faithful to deliver Israel from her enemies. **Beth-aven.** *See note on 13:2.*

14:24 **were hard-pressed.** Saul's inept leadership failed to provide for the physical needs of his men, leaving them weak and fatigued. **Cursed.** Saul's first foolish oath pronounced a curse upon anyone tasting food until the battle was over. The scene fits chronologically after Jonathan's departure.

14:25 **honey on the ground.** This was a reference to honeycombs found in the forest (v. 27).

14:27 **Jonathan had not heard.** Jonathan apparently had departed before Saul made his oath.

14:29 **My father has troubled the land.** Jonathan saw the foolishness of Saul's oath and how it actually hurt Israel's cause instead of helping it.

See now, how my eyes have brightened because I
tasted a little of this honey. 30 How much more, if
only the people had eaten freely today of the spoil
of their enemies which they found! For now the
slaughter among the Philistines has not been great."
31 They struck among the Philistines that day
from [A]Michmash to [B]Aijalon. And the people were
very weary. 32 [A]The people [a]rushed greedily upon
the spoil, and took sheep and oxen and calves, and
slew *them* on the ground; and the people ate *them*
[B]with the blood. 33 Then they told Saul, saying, "Behold, the people are [A]sinning against the LORD by
eating with the blood." And he said, "You have acted
treacherously; roll a great stone to me today." 34 Saul
said, "Disperse yourselves among the people and
say to them, 'Each one of you bring me his ox or
his sheep, and slaughter *it* here and eat; and do not
sin against the LORD by eating with the blood.' "
So all the people that night brought each one his
ox [a]with him and slaughtered *it* there. 35 And [A]Saul
built an altar to the LORD; it was the first altar that
he built to the LORD.
36 Then Saul said, "Let us go down after the Philistines by night and take spoil among them until the
morning light, and let us not leave a man of them."
And they said, "Do whatever seems good [a]to you."
So [A]the priest said, "Let us draw near to God here."
37 Saul [A]inquired of God, "Shall I go down after the
Philistines? Will You give them into the hand of
Israel?" But [B]He did not answer him on that day.
38 Saul said, "[A]Draw near here, all you [a]chiefs of
the people, and investigate and see how this sin
has happened today. 39 For [A]as the LORD lives, who
delivers Israel, though it is in Jonathan my son, he
shall surely die." But not one of all the people answered him. 40 Then he said to all Israel, "You shall
be on one side and I and Jonathan my son will be
on the other side." And the people said to Saul, "Do
what seems good [a]to you." 41 Therefore, Saul said
to the LORD, the God of Israel, "[A]Give a perfect *lot*."
And Jonathan and Saul were taken, but the people
escaped. 42 Saul said, "Cast *lots* between me and
Jonathan my son." And Jonathan was taken.
43 Then Saul said to Jonathan, "[A]Tell me what you
have done." So Jonathan told him and said, "[B]I indeed tasted a little honey with the end of the staff
that was in my hand. Here I am, I must die!" 44 Saul
said, "[A]May God do [a]this *to me* and more also, for
[B]you shall surely die, Jonathan." 45 But the people
said to Saul, "Must Jonathan die, who has [a]brought
about this great deliverance in Israel? Far from it!
As the LORD lives, [A]not one hair of his head shall
fall to the ground, for [B]he has worked with God
this day." So the people [b]rescued Jonathan and he
did not die. 46 Then Saul went up from [a]pursuing
the Philistines, and the Philistines went to their
own place.

CONSTANT WARFARE

47 Now when Saul had taken the kingdom over
Israel, he fought against all his enemies on every
side, against Moab, [A]the sons of Ammon, Edom, [B]the
kings of Zobah, and [C]the Philistines; and wherever
he turned, he [a]inflicted punishment. 48 He acted
valiantly and [a,A]defeated the Amalekites, and delivered Israel from the hands of [b]those who plundered them.
49 Now [A]the sons of Saul were Jonathan and Ishvi
and Malchi-shua; and the names of his two daughters *were these:* the name of the firstborn [B]Merab
and the name of the younger [C]Michal. 50 The name
of Saul's wife was Ahinoam the daughter of Ahimaaz. And [A]the name of the captain of his army was
Abner the son of Ner, Saul's uncle. 51 [A]Kish *was* the
father of Saul, and Ner the father of Abner *was* the
son of Abiel.
52 Now the war against the Philistines was severe all the days of Saul; and when Saul saw any
mighty man or any valiant man, he [a,A]attached him
to [b]his staff.

14:31 [A]1 Sam 14:5 [B]Josh 10:12 14:32 [a]Lit *did with regard to the spoil* [A]1 Sam 15:19 [B]Gen 9:4; Lev 3:17; 17:10-14; 19:26; Deut 12:16, 23; Acts 15:20 14:33 [A]Lev 7:26, 27; 19:26; Deut 12:16, 23-25; 15:23 14:34 [a]Lit *in his hand* 14:35 [A]1 Sam 7:12, 17; 2 Sam 24:25; James 4:8 14:36 [a]Lit *in your eyes* [A]1 Sam 14:3, 18, 19 14:37 [A]1 Sam 10:22 [B]1 Sam 28:6 14:38 [a]Lit *corners* [A]Josh 7:11, 12; 1 Sam 10:19, 20 14:39 [A]1 Sam 14:24, 44; 2 Sam 12:5 14:40 [a]Lit *in your eyes* 14:41 [A]Acts 1:24 14:43 [A]Josh 7:19 [B]1 Sam 14:27 14:44 [a]Lit *thus* [A]Ruth 1:17; 1 Sam 25:22 [B]1 Sam 14:39 14:45 [a]Lit *worked* [b]Lit *ransomed* [A]2 Sam 14:11; 1 Kin 1:52; Luke 21:18; Acts 27:34 [B]2 Cor 6:1 14:46 [a]Lit *after* 14:47 [a]Or *condemned* [A]1 Sam 11:1-13 [B]2 Sam 8:3-10 [C]1 Sam 14:52 14:48 [a]Lit *smote* [b]Lit *its plunderers* [A]1 Sam 15:3, 7 14:49 [A]1 Sam 31:2; 1 Chr 8:33; 10:2 [B]1 Sam 18:17-19 [C]1 Sam 18:20, 27; 19:12; 2 Sam 6:20-23 14:50 [A]2 Sam 2:8 14:51 [A]1 Sam 9:1, 21 14:52 [a]Lit *gathered* [b]Lit *himself* [A]1 Sam 8:11

14:31 Aijalon. This area is located 15 mi. W of Michmash. This would have been a normal path back to the land of the Philistines.

14:32 ate *them* with the blood. The people were so severely hungry because of the oath (v. 24) that they disobeyed the law by eating the meat raw and not draining the blood (cf. Lv 17:10–14).

14:35 the first altar. The first and only altar built by Saul mentioned in Scripture.

14:36 Let us draw near to God. Ahijah the priest requested that they first seek the Lord regarding their course of action.

14:37 Saul inquired of God. At the request of Ahijah, Saul inquired of the Lord regarding his battle plan. **He did not answer him.** Because of the sin that Saul had caused in his army, God did not answer his inquiry. This would not be the last time that the Lord would refuse to respond to sinful Saul (cf. 28:6).

14:39 as the LORD lives. As an encore to his previous oath, Saul followed with another foolish oath, unknowingly jeopardizing his own son's life.

14:41 taken. The practice of casting lots was used to distinguish one person or group from another. Jonathan was indicated as the guilty party, though he acted innocently (v. 27).

14:44 God do this ... and more also. Saul, proud and concerned with his own authority and honor, was intent on fulfilling his vow.

14:45 worked with God this day. Jonathan, in stark contrast to his father the king, understood the sufficiency of God for the task and obediently relied on Him for the victory.

14:46 the Philistines went to their own place. The Philistines were left to continue their retreat unhindered.

14:47, 48 Saul's military accomplishments were significant and expanded Israel's borders in all directions: to the S (Edom), E (Ammon and Moab), N (Zobah), and W (Philistia). The defeat of the Amalekites is recorded in chap. 15.

14:49–51 Saul's children, Jonathan and Michal, would both play significant roles in the life of the next king, David. Nothing further is known of Saul's wife or other children mentioned here.

14:50 Abner. A cousin of Saul who commanded his army (cf. 1Sa 17:55, 57; 20:25; 26:14, 15).

14:52 war ... severe. The Philistines' opposition to Israel was persistent and continual to the very last day of Saul's life (1Sa 31:1–3). **mighty man ... valiant man.** Saul looked for the good warriors and attached them to his personal force. David was one such man, who would also continue this practice under his rule (2Sa 23:8–39).

SAUL'S DISOBEDIENCE

15 Then Samuel said to Saul, "[A]The LORD sent
me to anoint you as king over His people,
over Israel; now therefore, listen to the [a]words
of the LORD. 2 Thus says the LORD of hosts, 'I will
[a]punish Amalek [A]*for* what he did to Israel, how
he set himself against him on the way while he
was coming up from Egypt. 3 Now go and strike
Amalek and [A]utterly destroy all that he has, and
do not spare him; but [B]put to death both man and
woman, child and infant, ox and sheep, camel
and donkey.' "
4 Then Saul summoned the people and [a]num-
bered them in [A]Telaim, 200,000 foot soldiers and
10,000 men of Judah. 5 Saul came to the city of
Amalek and set an ambush in the valley. 6 Saul
said to [A]the Kenites, "Go, depart, go down from
among the Amalekites, so that I do not destroy
you with them; for [B]you showed kindness to all the
sons of Israel when they came up from Egypt." So
the Kenites departed from among the Amalekites.
7 So [A]Saul [a]defeated the Amalekites, from [B]Havi-
lah as you go to [C]Shur, which is [b]east of Egypt.
8 He captured [A]Agag the king of the Amalekites
alive, and [B]utterly destroyed all the people with
the edge of the sword. 9 But Saul and the people
[A]spared Agag and the best of the sheep, the oxen,
the fatlings, the lambs, and all that was good, and
were not willing to destroy them utterly; but everything despised and worthless, that they utterly
destroyed.

SAMUEL REBUKES SAUL

10 Then the word of the LORD came to Samuel,
saying, 11 "[A]I regret that I have made Saul king, for
[B]he has turned back from [a]following Me and has
not carried out My commands." And Samuel was
distressed and [C]cried out to the LORD all night.
12 Samuel rose early in the morning to meet Saul;
and it was told Samuel, saying, "Saul came to
[A]Carmel, and behold, he set up a monument for
himself, then turned and proceeded on [a]down to
[B]Gilgal." 13 Samuel came to Saul, and Saul said to
him, "[A]Blessed are you of the LORD! I have carried
out the command of the LORD." 14 But Samuel said,
"[A]What then is this [a]bleating of the sheep in my
ears, and the [a]lowing of the oxen which I hear?"
15 Saul said, "They have brought them from the
Amalekites, for [A]the people spared the best of the
sheep and oxen, to sacrifice to the LORD your God;
but the rest we have utterly destroyed." 16 Then
Samuel said to Saul, "Wait, and let me tell you
what the LORD said to me last night." And he said
to him, "Speak!"
17 Samuel said, "Is it not true, [A]though you were
little in your own eyes, you were *made* the head
of the tribes of Israel? And the LORD anointed
you king over Israel, 18 and the LORD sent you on
a [a]mission, and said, '[A]Go and utterly destroy the
sinners, the Amalekites, and fight against them
until they are exterminated.' 19 Why then did you
not obey the voice of the LORD, [A]but rushed upon
the spoil and did what was evil in the sight of
the LORD?"
20 Then Saul said to Samuel, "[A]I did obey the voice
of the LORD, and went on the [a]mission on which
the LORD sent me, and have brought back Agag
the king of Amalek, and have utterly destroyed the
Amalekites. 21 But [A]the people took *some* of the spoil,
sheep and oxen, the choicest of the things devoted

15:1 [a]Lit *sound of the words* [A]1 Sam 9:16; 10:1 15:2 [a]Or *visit* [A]Ex 17:8-16; Num 24:20; Deut 25:17-19 15:3 [A]Num 24:20; Deut 20:16-18; Josh 6:17-21 [B]1 Sam 22:19 15:4 [a]Lit *mustered* [A]Josh 15:24 15:6 [A]Num 24:21; Judg 1:16; 4:11 [B]Ex 18:9, 10; Num 10:29-32 15:7 [a]Lit *smote* [b]Lit *before* [A]1 Sam 14:48 [B]Gen 25:18 [C]Gen 16:7; Ex 15:22; 1 Sam 27:8 15:8 [A]Num 24:7; 1 Sam 15:20; Esth 3:1 [B]1 Sam 27:8, 9; 30:1; 2 Sam 8:12 15:9 [A]1 Sam 15:3, 15, 19 15:11 [a]Lit *after* [A]Gen 6:6, 7; Ex 32:14; 1 Sam 15:35; 2 Sam 24:16 [B]Josh 22:16; 1 Sam 13:13; 1 Kin 9:6, 7 [C]Ex 32:11-13; Luke 6:12 15:12 [a]Lit *and went down* [A]Josh 15:55; 1 Sam 25:2 [B]1 Sam 13:12, 15 15:13 [A]Gen 14:19; Judg 17:2; Ruth 3:10; 2 Sam 2:5 15:14 [a]Lit *sound* [A]Ex 32:21-24 15:15 [A]Gen 3:12, 13; Ex 32:22, 23; 1 Sam 15:9, 21 15:17 [A]1 Sam 9:21; 10:22 15:18 [a]Lit *way* [A]1 Sam 15:3 15:19 [A]1 Sam 14:32 15:20 [a]Lit *way* [A]1 Sam 15:13 15:21 [A]Ex 32:22, 23; 1 Sam 15:15

15:2 Amalek. The Amalekites, a nomadic people of the desert and descendants of Esau (Ge 36:12), became a marked people when they attacked Israel in the wilderness after leaving Egypt (*see notes on Ex 17:8–16*; cf. Nu 24:20; Dt 25:17–19; Jdg 6:3–5).

15:3 utterly destroy. God gave Saul an opportunity to redeem himself with obedience. The judgment was to be a complete and total annihilation of anything that breathed. God's judgment was severe on those who would destroy His people. It was equally severe to those who disobeyed (cf. Achan in Jos 7:10–26).

15:4 Telaim. The precise location of this area is unknown, but it may be a reference to Telem found in Jos 15:24.

15:5 the city of Amalek. This was possibly modern-day Tel Masos located about 7 mi. ESE of Beersheba.

15:6 the Kenites. Moses' father-in-law was a Kenite (cf. Jdg 1:16), a people friendly to the Israelites.

15:7 from Havilah … to Shur. Saul's victory was extensive, covering much of the Amalekite territory. However, the Amalekites were not completely destroyed (cf. 27:8; 30:1).

15:8 Agag. Another example of Saul's incomplete obedience, in the case of Agag, is recorded because it had such far-reaching implications. Over 5 centuries later an Agagite named Haman attempted to exterminate the Jewish race from his power base in Persia (cf. Est 3:1ff.). **all the people.** The Israelites killed everyone they came across, except for the king.

15:9 Saul and the people spared. Motivated by covetousness, both Saul and the people greedily spared the choice spoil of the land, disobeying God's Word and demonstrating their faithlessness.

15:11 Samuel was distressed. Samuel's role as priest over the people gave him great concern over the poor performance of the king, who was like the kings of other nations (1Sa 6:19, 20) i.e., self-centered, self-willed, and utterly disobedient to the things of God.

15:12 Carmel. This is not Mt. Carmel of Elijah fame (1Ki 18:20ff.), but a Carmel located 7 mi. S of Hebron. **monument for himself.** Saul, apparently taking credit for the victory, established a monument to himself (cf. Absalom in 2Sa 18:18). This foolish act of contemptible pride was Saul's expression of self-worship rather than true worship of God and another evidence of his spiritual weakness. **Gilgal.** The site of Samuel's first confrontation with Saul (13:7b–15) became the site of this pronouncement of judgment.

15:13 I have carried out the command of the LORD. Saul, either ignorantly or deceitfully, maintained that he did what was commanded (15:20).

15:15 the people spared the best … to sacrifice. Saul began to place blame on others, making room for his own excuses just as he had done earlier (cf. 13:11, 12). Then he tried to justify his sin by saying that the animals would be used to sacrifice to the God of Samuel. Saul's blatant disobedience at least pained his conscience so that he could not claim God as his God.

15:17 little in your own eyes. Saul's status before he became king was as a humble and lowly Benjamite (cf. 9:21).

15:19 rushed upon the spoil. Saul and the people greedily took the spoil like a bird of prey diving on its victim.

15:20, 21 I did obey the voice of the LORD. Instead of confessing his sin and repenting, Saul continued to justify himself.

to destruction, to sacrifice to the LORD your God at
Gilgal." 22 Samuel said,

"[A]Has the LORD as much delight in
burnt offerings and sacrifices
As in obeying the voice of the LORD?
Behold, [B]to obey is better than sacrifice,
And to heed than the fat of rams.
23 "For rebellion is as the sin of [A]divination,
And insubordination is as
[B]iniquity and idolatry.
Because you have rejected the
word of the LORD,
[C]He has also rejected you from *being* king."

24 Then Saul said to Samuel, "[A]I have sinned; [B]I have
indeed transgressed the [a]command of the LORD and
your words, because I feared the people and listened
to their voice. 25 Now therefore, [A]please pardon my sin
and return with me, that I may worship the LORD."
26 But Samuel said to Saul, "I will not return with you;
for [A]you have rejected the word of the LORD, and the
LORD has rejected you from being king over Israel."
27 As Samuel turned to go, [A]*Saul* seized the edge of
his robe, and it tore. 28 So Samuel said to him, "[A]The
LORD has torn the kingdom of Israel from you today and has given it to your neighbor, who is better
than you. 29 Also the [a,A]Glory of Israel [B]will not lie or
change His mind; for He is not a man that He should
change His mind." 30 Then he said, "I have sinned;
[A]*but* please honor me now before the elders of my
people and before Israel, and go back with me, [B]that I
may worship the LORD your God." 31 So Samuel went
back following Saul, and Saul worshiped the LORD.
32 Then Samuel said, "Bring me Agag, the king of
the Amalekites." And Agag came to him [a]cheerfully.
And Agag said, "Surely the bitterness of death is
past." 33 But Samuel said, "[A]As your sword has made
women childless, so shall your mother be childless
among women." And Samuel hewed Agag to pieces
before the LORD at Gilgal.

15:22 [A]Ps 40:6-8; 51:16, 17; Is 1:11-15; Mic 6:6-8; Heb 10:6-9 [B]Jer 7:22, 23; Hos 6:6; Matt 12:7; Mark 12:33 15:23 [A]Deut 18:10 [B]Gen 31:19, 34 [C]1 Sam 13:14 15:24 [a]Lit *mouth* [A]Num 22:34; 2 Sam 12:13; Ps 51:4 [B]Prov 29:25; Is 51:12, 13 15:25 [A]Ex 10:17 15:26 [A]1 Sam 13:14; 16:1 15:27 [A]1 Kin 11:30, 31 15:28 [A]1 Sam 28:17, 18; 1 Kin 11:31 15:29 [a]Or *Eminence* [A]1 Chr 29:11 [B]Num 23:19; Ezek 24:14; Titus 1:2 15:30 [A]John 5:44; 12:43 [B]Is 29:13 15:32 [a]Or *in bonds* 15:33 [A]Gen 9:6; Judg 1:7; Matt 7:2

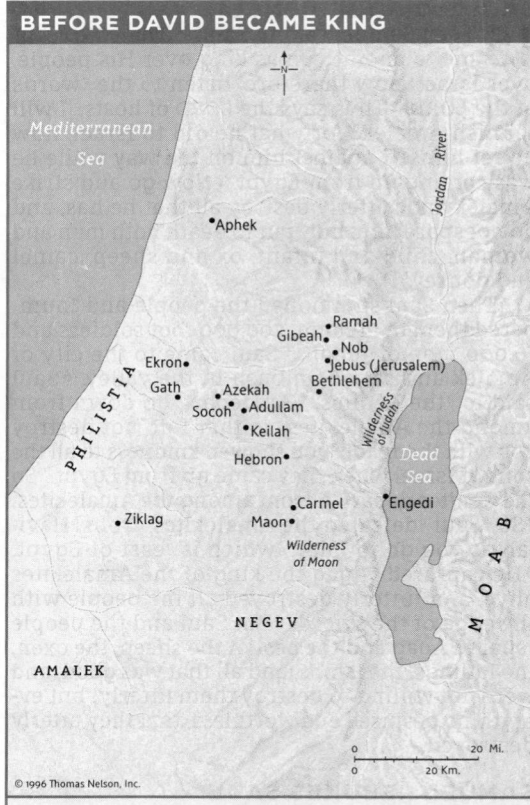

BEFORE DAVID BECAME KING

Near Socoh David defeated the giant Goliath (1Sa 17). Once Saul's wrath was kindled against the shepherd-soldier, David fled Saul's presence.

His journey went first to Nob, where he deceived the priest Ahimelech into giving him bread and Goliath's sword. He then sought refuge with the Philistine king Achish in Gath.

The suspicions of the Philistines forced David to continue his flight, now to the cave of Adullam, where he was joined by his family. After taking his family to the safety of Moab, he established camp at an unspecified stronghold (1Sa 22:4).

Saul's pursuit, however, would not allow David to remain in one place. Other stops included Keilah, Engedi, and finally Ziklag, David's camp until he moved to Hebron and became king of Judah.

15:22 to obey is better than sacrifice. This is an essential OT truth. Samuel stated that God desires heart obedience over the ritual sacrifice of animals (cf. Ps 51:16, 17; Is 1:10–17). The sacrificial system was never intended to function in place of living an obedient life, but was rather to be an expression of it (cf. Hos 6:6; Am 5:21–27; Mic 6:6–8).

15:23 rebellion ... insubordination. Saul needed to see that his real worship was indicated by his behavior and not by his sacrifices. He demonstrated himself to be an idolater whose idol was himself. He had failed the conditions (12:13–15) which would have brought blessing on the nation. His disobedience here was on the same level as witchcraft and idolatry, sins worthy of death. **Because you have rejected ... He has also rejected.** A universal principle is given here that those who continually reject God will one day be rejected by Him. The sins of Saul caused God to immediately depose Saul and his descendants forever from the throne of Israel.

15:24 I have sinned. This overdue confession appears to be generated more by a concern over consequences (regret) than by sorrow over having offended holy God (repentance). He bypasses his personal responsibility by shifting blame to the people.

15:25 return with me. Saul was concerned about having Samuel's visible presence as a show of support in front of the people (cf. 15:30).

15:28 torn the kingdom. Saul's judgment was a settled matter on the day of his disobedience with the Amalekites. Samuel used the illustration as it vividly portrayed how God would take the kingdom from Saul as he had just torn Samuel's robe. **your neighbor.** This was a reference to David (cf. 28:17).

15:29 the Glory of Israel. This was a unique title of God. **will not lie or change His mind.** Samuel emphasized God's attribute of immutability in regard to the judgment upon Saul.

15:30 honor me. Saul was still thinking of himself and how he could best salvage the situation for self-gain.

15:31 Samuel went back. Samuel agreed to follow Saul, perhaps seeing this as the wisest course of action for the nation at that time.

15:33 hewed Agag to pieces. This was an act of divine judgment to show the holy wrath of God against wanton sin. Sadly, the Israelites did not exterminate the wicked Amalekites, so they came back later to raid the southern territory and take women and children captive, including David's family (see 1Sa 30).

34 Then Samuel went to [A]Ramah, but Saul went up
to his house at [B]Gibeah of Saul. 35 [A]Samuel did not
see Saul again until the day of his death; for Samuel
[B]grieved over Saul. And the LORD regretted that He
had made Saul king over Israel.

SAMUEL GOES TO BETHLEHEM

16 Now the LORD said to Samuel, "[A]How long
will you grieve over Saul, since [B]I have rejected him from being king over Israel? [C]Fill your
horn with oil and go; I will send you to [D]Jesse the
Bethlehemite, for I have [E]selected a king for Myself
among his sons." 2 But Samuel said, "How can I go?
When Saul hears *of it,* he will kill me." And the LORD
said, "[A]Take a heifer with you and say, 'I have come
to sacrifice to the LORD.' 3 You shall invite Jesse to
the sacrifice, and [A]I will show you what you shall
do; and [B]you shall anoint for Me the one whom I
[a]designate to you." 4 So Samuel did what the LORD
said, and came to [A]Bethlehem. And the elders of the
city came trembling to meet him and said, "[B]Do you
come in peace?" 5 He said, "In peace; I have come to
sacrifice to the LORD. [A]Consecrate yourselves and
come with me to the sacrifice." He also consecrated
Jesse and his sons and invited them to the sacrifice.
6 When they entered, he looked at [A]Eliab and
thought, "Surely the LORD'S anointed is before Him."
7 But the LORD said to Samuel, "Do not look at his
appearance or at the height of his stature, because
I have rejected him; for [a]God *sees* not as man sees,
for man looks at the outward appearance, [A]but the
LORD looks at the heart." 8 Then Jesse called [A]Abina-
dab and made him pass before Samuel. And he said,
"The LORD has not chosen this one either." 9 Next
Jesse made [a,A]Shammah pass by. And he said, "The
LORD has not chosen this one either." 10 Thus Jesse
made seven of his sons pass before Samuel. But
Samuel said to Jesse, "The LORD has not chosen
these." 11 And Samuel said to Jesse, "Are these all
the children?" And he said, "[A]There remains yet the
youngest, and behold, he is tending the sheep." Then
Samuel said to Jesse, "Send and [a]bring him; for we
will not sit down until he comes here."

DAVID ANOINTED

12 So he sent and brought him in. Now he was
ruddy, with [A]beautiful eyes and a handsome appearance. And the LORD said, "[B]Arise, anoint him;
for this is he." 13 Then Samuel took the horn of oil
and [A]anointed him in the midst of his brothers;
and [B]the Spirit of the LORD came mightily upon
David from that day forward. And Samuel arose
and went to Ramah.
14 [A]Now the Spirit of the LORD departed from Saul,
and [B]an evil spirit from the LORD terrorized him.
15 Saul's servants then said to him, "Behold now, an

15:34 [A]1 Sam 7:17 [B]1 Sam 11:4 15:35 [A]1 Sam 19:24 [B]1 Sam 16:1 16:1 [A]1 Sam 15:35 [B]1 Sam 13:13, 14; 15:23 [C]1 Sam 9:16; 10:1; 2 Kin 9:1 [D]Ruth 4:17-22 [E]Ps 78:70, 71; Acts 13:22 16:2 [A]1 Sam 20:29 16:3 [a]Lit *say to you* [A]Ex 4:15; Acts 9:6 [B]Deut 17:14, 15; 1 Sam 9:16 16:4 [A]Gen 48:7; Luke 2:4 [B]1 Kin 2:13; 2 Kin 9:22; 1 Chr 12:17, 18 16:5 [A]Gen 35:2; Ex 19:10 16:6 [A]1 Sam 17:13 16:7 [a]So with Gr; Heb He does *not* see *what man sees* [A]1 Sam 2:3; 1 Kin 8:39; 1 Chr 28:9; Luke 16:15 16:8 [A]1 Sam 17:13 16:9 [a]In 2 Sam 13:3, *Shimeah;* in 1 Chr 2:13, *Shimea* [A]1 Sam 17:13 16:11 [a]Lit *take* [A]1 Sam 17:12; 2 Sam 13:3 16:12 [A]Gen 39:6; Ex 2:2; Acts 7:20 [B]1 Sam 9:17 16:13 [A]1 Sam 10:1 [B]Num 27:18; 1 Sam 10:6, 9, 10 16:14 [A]Judg 16:20; 1 Sam 11:6; 18:12; 28:15 [B]Judg 9:23; 1 Sam 16:15, 16; 18:10; 19:9; 1 Kin 22:19-22

15:35 Samuel did not see Saul again ... grieved. Samuel never went to visit the rejected King Saul again in his life (cf. 1Sa 28:11–19). On at least one further occasion, Saul sought Samuel (cf. 19:24).

16:1–31:13 The third major division of Samuel recounts the steady demise of Saul and the selection and preparation of David for the kingship. Chapter 16 begins with Samuel mourning for Saul as one would mourn for the dead. The death of Saul (31:1–13) concludes this last division of the book.

16:1 Jesse the Bethlehemite. God's new king of Israel (and ultimately the Messiah; Ge 3:15; Nu 24:17; 1Sa 2:10; Ps 2) would come from the tribe of Judah (Jesse; cf. Ru 4:12, 22; Ge 49:10) and from Bethlehem of Judah (cf. Mic 5:2; Mt 2:2–6). **I have selected ... Myself.** The king was chosen and provided by God (Dt 17:15), who orders all things according to the counsel of His own will (Is 40:14), not according to human desires (8:5, 6; 2Sa 2:8, 9).

16:2 Saul ... will kill me. Saul's unbalanced emotional state was already known in Israel. It is ironic that Samuel's initial reaction to the word of the Lord was fear of Saul instead of rejoicing at God's provision to Israel (and ultimately to all the nations; e.g., 1Ki 8:41–43). The route from Ramah to Bethlehem would take Samuel through Gibeah of Saul (cf. 10:26; 11:14). **I have come to sacrifice.** The place of sacrifice could be in any town until the establishment of the house of God in Jerusalem (Dt 12:11).

16:3 anoint. David's first anointing was performed by Samuel, symbolizing God's recognition/ordination (cf. 2:10). The following two anointings (2Sa 2:7; 5:3) were to establish David as king publicly for the benefit of Judah and Israel respectively.

16:4 the elders of the city came trembling. The elders, and no doubt all Israel, had heard of Samuel's execution of Agag (15:33). Israel still closely associated the "seer," or prophet, with the not-so-distant past office of "judge."

16:5 Consecrate yourselves. Worship of Yahweh was always preceded by cleansing or washing, both of the outward garments and the inner man (Ex 19:10, 14; 1Jn 1:9).

16:6 Eliab. Lit. "My God is Father." Since Eliab was the first of Jesse's sons to catch Samuel's eye, he must have been an impressive young man by outward appearance.

16:7 his appearance ... height of his stature. Samuel needed to be reminded that God's anointed was not chosen because of physical attributes. This was initially a difficult concept for Samuel as he was accustomed to a king whose only positive attributes were physical. **the LORD looks at the heart.** The Hebrew concept of "heart" embodies emotions, will, intellect, and desires. The life of the man will reflect his heart (cf. Mt 12:34, 35).

16:8 Abinadab. Lit. "My Father is noble." Samuel, now more sensitive to the leading of God's Spirit, quickly discerned that Abinadab was not God's anointed.

16:9 Shammah. Lit. "Yahweh hears (or heard)." See 16:8.

16:10 seven ... sons. With David, Jesse had 8 sons. The fact that 1Ch 2:13 indicates 7 sons must mean that one of the 8 died afterward, and this is not considered in the Chronicles account.

16:11 the youngest ... tending the sheep. God's favor/choice often fell on the younger and the least (cf. Jacob, Joseph, Gideon). David, although the youngest, was the firstborn over Israel (Ps 89:27), whose humble beginnings as a shepherd, and later rule as king, typify Jesus: the ultimate Shepherd and King of Israel.

16:12 ruddy ... beautiful eyes ... handsome. God's chosen king was handsome to look at, although that was not the reason for his selection by God. His appearance was perhaps enhanced by a genuine faith and joy in Yahweh. See also 17:42.

16:13 anointed him in the midst of his brothers. David's first anointing is before his family/house. His second anointing would be before the assembly of his tribe, Judah; and his third anointing would be before the nation Israel. (*See note on 16:3.*) **the Spirit of the LORD came ... upon David.** This familiar OT expression relates to empowerment for some God-given task (cf. 10:6, 11; 11:6; 19:20, 23; 2Sa 23:2; 2Ch 20:14; Is 11:2; 61:1; Eze 11:5; 37:1). David's anointing was an external symbol of an inward work of God. The operation of the Holy Spirit in this case was not for regeneration, but for empowerment to perform his (David's) role in God's program for Israel (cf. Saul, 10:6). After David sinned with Bathsheba (2Sa 11, 12), he prayed, "Do not take Your Holy Spirit from me" (Ps 51:11).

16:14 the Spirit of the LORD departed from Saul. When David's ascent to the throne began, Saul's slow and painful descent began also (cf. 18:12). Without God's empowering Holy Spirit, Saul was effectively no longer

evil spirit from God is terrorizing you. 16 Let our lord
now command your servants who are before you.
Let them seek a man who is a skillful player on the
harp; and it shall come about when the evil spirit
from God is on you, that [A]he shall play *the harp* with
his hand, and you will be well." 17 So Saul said to his
servants, "Provide for me now a man who can play
well and bring *him* to me." 18 Then one of the young
men said, "Behold, I have seen a son of Jesse the
Bethlehemite who is a skillful musician, [A]a mighty
man of valor, a warrior, one prudent in speech,
and a handsome man; and [B]the LORD is with him."
19 So Saul sent messengers to Jesse and said, "Send
me your son David who is with the flock." 20 Jesse
[A]took a donkey *loaded with* bread and a jug of wine
and a young goat, and sent *them* to Saul by David
his son. 21 Then David came to Saul and [a,A]attended
him; and [b]Saul loved him greatly, and he became
his armor bearer. 22 Saul sent to Jesse, saying, "Let
David now stand before me, for he has found favor
in my sight." 23 So it came about whenever [A]the *evil*
spirit from God came to Saul, David would take the
harp and play *it* with his hand; and Saul would be
refreshed and be well, and the evil spirit would
depart from him.

GOLIATH'S CHALLENGE

17 Now [A]the Philistines gathered their armies for
battle; and they were gathered at Socoh which
belongs to Judah, and they camped between [B]Socoh
and [C]Azekah, in [D]Ephes-dammim. 2 Saul and the men
of Israel were gathered and camped in [A]the valley of
Elah, and drew up in battle array to encounter the
Philistines. 3 The Philistines stood on the mountain
on one side while Israel stood on the mountain on
the other side, with the valley between them. 4 Then
a champion came out from the armies of the Philistines named [A]Goliath, from [B]Gath, whose height
was six [a]cubits and a span. 5 *He had* a bronze helmet
on his head, and he was clothed with scale-armor
[a]which weighed five thousand shekels of bronze.
6 *He* also *had* bronze [a]greaves on his legs and a
[A]bronze javelin *slung* between his shoulders. 7 [A]The
shaft of his spear was like a weaver's beam, and the
head of his spear *weighed* six hundred shekels of
iron; [B]his shield-carrier also walked before him. 8 He
stood and shouted to the ranks of Israel and said to
them, "Why do you come out to draw up in battle
array? Am I not the Philistine and you [A]servants
of Saul? Choose a man for yourselves and let him
come down to me. 9 [A]If he is able to fight with me
and [a]kill me, then we will become your servants;
but if I prevail against him and [a]kill him, then you
shall become our servants and serve us." 10 Again
the Philistine said, "[A]I defy the ranks of Israel this
day; give me a man that we may fight together."
11 When Saul and all Israel heard these words of the
Philistine, they were dismayed and greatly afraid.
12 Now David was [A]the son of [a]the [B]Ephrathite of
Bethlehem in Judah, whose name was Jesse, and [C]he
had eight sons. And [b]Jesse was old in the days of Saul,
advanced *in years* among men. 13 The three older sons

16:16 [A]1 Sam 18:10; 19:9; 2 Kin 3:15 16:18 [A]1 Sam 17:32-36 [B]1 Sam 3:19 16:20 [A]1 Sam 10:4, 27; Prov 18:16 16:21 [a]Lit *stood before him* [b]Lit *he* [A]Gen 41:46; Prov 22:29 16:23 [A]1 Sam 16:14-16 17:1 [A]1 Sam 13:5 [B]Josh 15:35; 2 Chr 28:18 [C]Josh 10:10 [D]1 Chr 11:13 17:2 [A]1 Sam 21:9 17:4 [a]I.e. One cubit equals approx 18 in. [A]2 Sam 21:19 [B]Josh 11:22 17:5 [a]Lit *and the weight of the armor* was 17:6 [a]Or *shin guards* [A]1 Sam 17:45 17:7 [A]2 Sam 21:19; 1 Chr 11:23 [B]1 Sam 17:41 17:8 [A]1 Sam 8:17 17:9 [a]Lit *smite* [A]2 Sam 2:12-16 17:10 [A]1 Sam 17:26, 36, 45; 2 Sam 21:21 17:12 [a]Lit *this* [b]Lit *the man* [A]Ruth 4:22; 1 Sam 16:18 [B]Gen 35:19 [C]1 Sam 16:10, 11; 1 Chr 2:13-15

king over Israel (15:28), although his physical removal from the throne, and his death, happened many years later. **an evil spirit.** God, in His sovereignty, allowed an evil spirit to torment Saul (cf. Jdg 9:23; 1Ki 22:19–23; Job 1:6–12) for His purpose of establishing the throne of David. This spirit, a messenger from Satan, is to be distinguished from a troubled emotional state brought on by indwelling sin, or the harmful consequences of the sinful acts of others (e.g., spirit of jealousy, Nu 5:14). This demon spirit attacked Saul from without, for there is no evidence that the demon indwelt Saul. **terrorized him.** Saul, whose inward constitution was already prone to questionable judgment and the fear of men, began to experience God's judgment in the form of severe bouts of depression, anger, and delusion, initiated and aggravated by the evil spirit assigned to him. There are several NT occasions where God turned people over to demons or Satan for judgment (see Ac 5:1–3; 1Co 5:1–7; 1Ti 1:18–20). He also used Satan or demons for the strengthening of the saints. See Job 1:1–2:6; Mt 4:1ff.; Lk 22:31, 32; 2Co 12:7–10.

16:16 he shall play . . . you will be well. God used the evil which had befallen Saul to introduce David into the court of the king and to the watching eyes of Israel.

16:18 a skillful musician . . . . handsome man. The writer of Samuel introduces David the sweet psalmist of Israel (2Sa 23:1) before introducing David the warrior. Later proven so skillful in the art of war and killing, David was also a tender musician of exceptional skill and reputation. **the LORD is with him.** The saints of God, OT and NT, are recognized by their fruit (2:26; Lk 2:40). God's approval of David was already recognized by certain people in Israel.

16:19 Send me your son David. Verbal link with 16:1, "I have selected a king for Myself among his (Jesse's) sons." David's lineage was of importance to Saul in the near future when he arranged a marriage between Michal, his daughter, and David. **with the flock.** David's lowly, humble occupation is emphasized. He gave evidence of that humility and patience as he returned faithfully to his duty following Samuel's anointing.

16:21 Saul loved him greatly. Saul loved David for his abilities, but later grew to jealously hate him because he knew he was blessed by the Lord (cf. 18:29). **his armor bearer.** David was most likely one of many such young men assigned to Saul's barracks.

17:1 Socoh . . . Azekah . . . Ephes-dammim. Following the anointing of David and his installation into the court of the king, there is this update on the situation of Israel in regards to Israel's enemies. Socoh and Azekah were towns of Judah (Jos 15:20, 35; Jer 34:7) approximately 15 mi. W and 17 mi. NW (respectively) of Bethlehem. Ephes-dammim (1Ch 11:12, 13; cf. 2Sa 23:9), the camp of the Philistines, probably lay one mi. to the S of Azekah.

17:2 valley of Elah. Where the camp of Israel was, approximately 3 mi. E of Ephes-dammim.

17:4–7 On human terms alone, Goliath was invincible. However, David counted on the Lord being with him and making the difference (17:34–37).

17:4 champion. Lit. "the man between two." An appropriate appellation as Goliath stood between the two armies of the Philistines and Israel, and offered his challenge to a "duel" of hand-to-hand combat, the outcome of which would settle the battle for both sides. **Gath.** One of the 5 chief Philistine cities, located 5 mi. W of Azekah. **six cubits and a span.** One cubit measures approximately 18 in. and one span about 9 in., making Goliath about 9 ft. 9 in. in height (cf. "Egyptian," 1Ch 11:23, and "Og of Bashan," Dt 3:11).

17:5 five thousand shekels. 125 lbs.

17:7 six hundred shekels. 15 lbs.

17:11 Saul . . . dismayed and greatly afraid. Saul and Israel had proven themselves to be greatly concerned with outward appearances (10:23, 24; 15:30) and able to be influenced by the fear of men (12:12; 15:24). It is only natural that Goliath would be their worst nightmare come true.

17:12 Ephrathite. Ephrath(ah), another name for Bethlehem in Judah (cf. Ru 4:11; Mic 5:2).

of Jesse had [a]gone after Saul to the battle. And [A]the names of his three sons who went to the battle were Eliab the firstborn, and the second to him Abinadab, and the third Shammah. 14 [A]David was the youngest. Now the three oldest followed Saul, 15 [A]but David went back and forth from Saul [B]to tend his father's flock at Bethlehem. 16 The Philistine came [a]forward morning and evening for forty days and took his stand.

17 Then Jesse said to David his son, "[A]Take now for your brothers an ephah of this roasted grain and these ten loaves and run to the camp to your brothers. 18 [A]Bring also these ten cuts of cheese to the commander of *their* thousand, [B]and look into the welfare of your brothers, and bring back [a]news of them. 19 For Saul and they and all the men of Israel are in the valley of Elah, fighting with the Philistines."

DAVID ACCEPTS THE CHALLENGE

20 So David arose early in the morning and left the flock with a keeper and took *the supplies* and went as Jesse had commanded him. And he came to the [A]circle of the camp while the army was going out in battle array shouting the war cry. 21 Israel and the Philistines drew up in battle array, army against army. 22 Then David left his [A]baggage in the [a]care of the baggage keeper, and ran to the battle line and entered in order to greet his brothers. 23 As he was talking with them, behold, the champion, the Philistine from Gath named Goliath, was coming up from the army of the Philistines, and he spoke [A]these same words; and David heard *them*.

24 When all the men of Israel saw the man, they fled from him and were greatly afraid. 25 The men of Israel said, "Have you seen this man who is coming up? Surely he is coming up to defy Israel. And it will be that the king will enrich the man who kills him with great riches and [A]will give him his daughter and make his father's house [a]free in Israel."

26 Then David spoke to the men who were standing by him, saying, "What will be done for the man who kills this Philistine and takes away [A]the reproach from Israel? For who is this [B]uncircumcised Philistine, that he should [C]taunt the armies of [D]the living God?" 27 The people [a]answered him in accord with this word, saying, "[A]Thus it will be done for the man who kills him."

28 Now Eliab his oldest brother heard when he spoke to the men; and [A]Eliab's anger burned against David and he said, "Why have you come down? And with whom have you left those few sheep in the wilderness? I know your insolence and the wickedness of your heart; for you have come down in order to see the battle." 29 But David said, "What have I done now? Was it not just a [a]question?" 30 Then he turned [a]away from him to another and [A]said the same thing; and the people answered the same thing as [b]before.

DAVID KILLS GOLIATH

31 When the words which David spoke were heard, they told *them* [a]to Saul, and he sent for him. 32 David said to Saul, "[A]Let no man's heart fail on account of him; [B]your servant will go and fight with this Philistine." 33 Then Saul said to David, "[A]You are not able to go against this Philistine to fight with him; for you are *but* a youth while he has been a warrior from his youth." 34 But David said to Saul, "Your servant was tending his father's sheep. When a lion or a bear came and took a lamb from the flock, 35 I went out after him and [a]attacked him, and [A]rescued *it* from his mouth; and when he rose up against me, I seized *him* by his beard and [a]struck him and killed him. 36 Your servant has [a]killed both the lion and the bear; and this uncircumcised Philistine will be like one of them, since he has taunted the armies of the living God." 37 And David said, "[A]The LORD who delivered me from the paw of the lion and from the paw of the bear, He will deliver me from the hand of this Philistine." And Saul said to David, "[B]Go, and may the LORD be with you." 38 Then Saul clothed David with his garments and put a bronze helmet on his head, and he clothed him with armor. 39 David girded his sword over his armor and tried to walk, for he had not tested *them*. So David said to Saul, "I cannot go with these, for I have not tested *them*." And David took them [a]off. 40 He took his stick in his hand and

17:13 [a]Lit *gone; they went* [A]1 Sam 16:6, 8, 9 17:14 [A]1 Sam 16:11 17:15 [A]1 Sam 16:21-23 [B]1 Sam 16:11, 19 17:16 [a]Lit *near* 17:17 [A]1 Sam 25:18 17:18 [a]Lit *their pledge* [A]1 Sam 16:20 [B]Gen 37:13, 14 17:20 [A]1 Sam 26:5, 7 17:22 [a]Lit *hand* [A]Judg 18:21; Is 10:28 17:23 [A]1 Sam 17:8-10 17:25 [a]I.e. free from taxes and public service [A]Josh 15:16 17:26 [A]1 Sam 11:2 [B]1 Sam 14:6; 17:36; Jer 9:25, 26 [C]1 Sam 17:10 [D]Deut 5:26; 2 Kin 19:4; Jer 10:10 17:27 [a]Lit *said to* [A]1 Sam 17:25 17:28 [A]Gen 37:4, 8-36; Prov 18:19; Matt 10:36 17:29 [a]Lit *word* 17:30 [a]Lit *from beside him* [b]Lit *the former word* [A]1 Sam 17:26, 27 17:31 [a]Lit *before* 17:32 [A]Deut 20:1-4 [B]1 Sam 16:18 17:33 [A]Num 13:31 17:35 [a]Lit *smote* [A]Amos 3:12 17:36 [a]Lit *smitten* 17:37 [A]2 Cor 1:10; 2 Tim 4:17, 18 [B]1 Sam 20:13; 1 Chr 22:11, 16 17:39 [a]Lit *off from himself*

17:15 David went back and forth from Saul. David's duties were divided between his billet with Saul as one of many armor bearers (16:21), and tending his father's sheep in Bethlehem. Doubtless, David learned important lessons regarding the weight of responsibility during this time, lessons that were later put to use in ruling over Israel.

17:17 ephah. About .75 of a bu.

17:23 these same words. Goliath continued to offer the challenge of 17:10, as he had been doing for 40 mornings and evenings (17:16).

17:25 great riches … his daughter. The reward of a daughter in marriage for a great victory over an enemy of Israel was not unusual (cf. Jos 15:13–17).

17:26 the reproach from Israel. David knew that although Goliath's challenge had been issued to (any) individual of the camp of Israel, Goliath's defiant attitude was a reproach to all Israel.

17:28 Eliab's anger. Eliab, perhaps still feeling the sting/rejection of having his "little" brother chosen over him by God/Samuel (16:6, 7), expressed his jealousy in anger (cf. Ge 37:4, 5, 8, 11).

17:32 Let no man's heart fail. Joshua and Caleb exhorted Israel in the same fashion regarding the giant Anakim 400 years prior (cf. Nu 13:30; 14:8, 9). The heathens' hearts fail at the name of the Lord God of Israel (cf. Rahab, Jos 2:11).

17:33 You are not able. David's faith, like that of Joshua and Caleb, was met with disbelief on the part of Saul. By all outward appearances, Saul was absolutely correct in his assessment, but he failed to consider the Lord's presence in David's life.

17:36 the lion and the bear. Just as David tended his flock of sheep and protected them from the lion and bear, his new responsibility as shepherd over Israel required him to eliminate the threat of Goliath.

17:37 The LORD … He will deliver me. Just as Jonathan believed earlier (14:6). David had a wholehearted faith in the God of Israel. **the LORD be with you.** One of the first explicit indications in the text that Saul knew that the Lord was with David (cf. 15:28).

17:40 stick … stones … sling. The tools of the shepherd proved to be appropriate weapons also for Israel's shepherd. One of David's honorable and chief men of battle, Benaiah, the son of Jehoiada, slew a formidable Egyptian warrior (2Sa 23:20, 21) with a staff like the one David carried toward Goliath.

chose for himself five smooth stones from the brook,
and put them in the shepherd's bag which he had,
even in *his* pouch, and [A]his sling was in his hand;
and he approached the Philistine.
41 Then the Philistine came on and approached
David, with the shield-bearer in front of him.
42 When the Philistine looked and saw David, [A]he
disdained him; for he was *but* a youth, and [B]ruddy,
with a handsome appearance. 43 The Philistine said
to David, "[A]Am I a dog, that you come to me with
sticks?" And [B]the Philistine cursed David by his
gods. 44 The Philistine also said to David, "Come to
me, and I will give your flesh [A]to the birds of the
sky and the beasts of the field." 45 Then David said
to the Philistine, "You come to me with a sword, a
spear, and a javelin, [A]but I come to you in the name
of the LORD of hosts, the God of the armies of Israel,
whom you have taunted. 46 This day the LORD will
deliver you up into my hands, and I will strike you
down and remove your head from you. And I will
give the [A]dead bodies of the army of the Philistines
this day to the birds of the sky and the wild beasts
of the earth, [B]that all the earth may know that there
is a God in Israel, 47 and that all this assembly may
know that [A]the LORD does not deliver by sword or
by spear; [B]for the battle is the LORD'S and He will
give you into our hands."
48 Then it happened when the Philistine rose and
came and drew near to meet David, that [A]David ran
quickly toward the battle line to meet the Philistine.
49 And David put his hand into his bag and took from
it a stone and slung *it*, and struck the Philistine on
his forehead. And the stone sank into his forehead,
so that he fell on his face to the ground.
50 Thus David prevailed over the Philistine with
a sling and a stone, and he struck the Philistine and
killed him; but there was no sword in David's hand.
51 Then David ran and stood over the Philistine
and [A]took his sword and drew it out of its sheath
and killed him, and cut off his head with it. [B]When
the Philistines saw that their champion was dead,
they fled. 52 The men of Israel and Judah arose and
shouted and pursued the Philistines [a]as far as the
valley, and to the gates of [A]Ekron. And the slain
Philistines [b]lay along the way to [B]Shaaraim, even
to Gath and Ekron. 53 The sons of Israel returned
from chasing the Philistines and plundered their
camps. 54 Then David took the Philistine's head and
brought it to Jerusalem, but he put his weapons
in his tent.
55 Now when Saul saw David going out against
the Philistine, he said to Abner the commander of
the army, "Abner, whose son is [A]this young man?"
And Abner said, "By your life, O king, I do not know."
56 The king said, "You inquire whose son the youth
is." 57 So when David returned from killing the Philistine, Abner took him and [A]brought him before
Saul with the Philistine's head in his hand. 58 Saul
said to him, "Whose son are you, young man?" And
David answered, "[A]*I am* the son of your servant
Jesse the Bethlehemite."

JONATHAN AND DAVID

18 Now it came about when he had finished
speaking to Saul, that [A]the soul of Jonathan
was knit to the soul of David, and [B]Jonathan loved
him as himself. 2 Saul took him that day and [A]did not
let him return to his father's house. 3 Then [A]Jonathan
made a covenant with David because he loved him
as himself. 4 [A]Jonathan stripped himself of the robe
that was on him and gave it to David, with his armor, including his sword and his bow and his belt.
5 So David went out wherever Saul sent him, *and*
[a]prospered; and Saul set him over the men of war.

17:40 [A]Judg 20:16 17:42 [A]Ps 123:4; Prov 16:18 [B]1 Sam 16:12 17:43 [A]1 Sam 24:14; 2 Sam 3:8; 2 Kin 8:13 [B]1 Kin 20:10 17:44 [A]1 Sam 17:46 17:45 [A]2 Sam 22:35; 2 Chr 32:8; Ps 124:8; Heb 11:32-34 17:46 [A]Deut 28:26 [B]Josh 4:24; 1 Kin 8:43; 18:36; 2 Kin 19:19; Is 37:20 17:47 [A]1 Sam 14:6; 2 Chr 14:11; 20:15; Ps 44:6; Hos 1:7; Zech 4:6 [B]2 Chr 20:15 17:48 [A]Ps 27:3 17:51 [A]1 Sam 21:9; 2 Sam 23:21 [B]Heb 11:34 17:52 [a]Lit *until your coming to* [b]Lit *fell* [A]Josh 15:11 [B]Josh 15:36 17:55 [A]1 Sam 16:12, 21, 22 17:57 [A]1 Sam 17:54 17:58 [A]1 Sam 17:12 18:1 [A]Gen 44:30 [B]Deut 13:6; 1 Sam 20:17; 2 Sam 1:26 18:2 [A]1 Sam 17:15 18:3 [A]1 Sam 20:8-17 18:4 [A]Gen 41:42; 1 Sam 17:38; Esth 6:8 18:5 [a]Or *acted wisely*

17:43 dog. Goliath uttered a statement of ironic truth about himself of which even he was unaware. As a wild dog can be a threat to the flock and must be chased away or killed, so must Goliath.

17:45 in the name of the LORD of hosts. Goliath came out to battle in his own name; David came to battle in the name of the Lord of all the hosts (armies). Cf. Dt 20:1–5.

17:46 all the earth may know. David fought in the name of the Lord and for the glory of the Lord, whose name and glory will extend to the uttermost parts of the earth, to all nations (cf. Jos 4:24; 2Sa 22:50; Ps 2).

17:47 the battle is the LORD's. Cf. Dt 31:6; Jdg 7:18. David fully understood the chief issue, i.e., the Philistines were in effect challenging the Lord by confronting the Lord's people.

17:48 David ran. David, unencumbered by armor or fear and emboldened by faith in God, ran to meet Goliath.

17:50 no sword. Iron weapons were scarce in Israel (13:9).

17:51 cut off his head. David completed his promise given to Goliath in v. 46a. The Philistines would later do the same with Saul's head (1Sa 31:9). **fled.** David's exclamation that there is a God in Israel (v. 46) was proven before the Philistines, who were no strangers to the wrath of Yahweh (1Sa 5–7). They wisely fled in terror, but did not honor the terms of Goliath if he lost (17:6–9).

17:54 to Jerusalem. The Jebusites, who were the inhabitants of Jerusalem, were a stubborn, resistant people (cf. Jos 15:63; Jdg 1:21; 19:10, 11), particularly to the tribe of Judah. They doubtless began to feel some anxiety concerning the victory of this Bethlehemite. The head of Goliath was a constant warning to them over the ensuing days as to their future (cf. 2Sa 5:6–10).

17:55 Abner. *See note on 14:50.* **whose son.** David's lineage was of the utmost importance to Saul at this point, since the victor over Goliath would marry into his family (cf. 17:25; 18:18).

18:1 Jonathan loved him. Jonathan loved David with a loyalty and devotion indicative of covenantal love (18:3). Hiram of Tyre had much the same covenantal love for David (cf. 2Sa 5:11; 1Ki 5:1; 9:11). David's later reign from Jerusalem is marked by loyalty to his covenant with Jonathan (2Sa 9:1).

18:2 did not let him return. Saul's interest in keeping David in his household was more self-serving than a token of generous hospitality. Saul was aware of his promise of wife and wealth (17:25), and, no doubt, the stirrings of anxiety/fear were in his heart toward David, who appeared as a threat. Saul preferred to have him in the court to keep a watchful eye on the young upstart.

18:3 covenant. See v. 1. Further mention of this honorable relationship is made in: 19:1; 20:8, 13–17, 42; 22:8; 23:18.

18:4 robe ... belt. Jonathan willingly and subserviently relinquished the outer garments and instruments that signified his position as prince of Israel and heir to the throne. Jonathan, a godly worshiper of Yahweh, quickly discerned that David was God's anointed and, without reservation, offered the robe of succession to the true king of Israel.

And it was pleasing in the sight of all the people
and also in the sight of Saul's servants.
6 It happened as they were coming, when David
returned from killing the Philistine, that [A]the women
came out of all the cities of Israel, singing and dancing, to meet King Saul, with tambourines, with joy
and with [a]musical instruments. 7 The women [A]sang
as they [a]played, and said,

"[B]Saul has slain his thousands,
[C]And David his ten thousands."

8 Then Saul became very angry, for this saying [a]dis-
pleased him; and he said, "They have ascribed to
David ten thousands, but to me they have ascribed
thousands. Now [A]what more can he have but the
kingdom?" 9 Saul looked at David with suspicion
from that day on.

SAUL TURNS AGAINST DAVID

10 Now it came about on the next day that [A]an evil
spirit from God came mightily upon Saul, and [B]he
raved in the midst of the house, while David was
playing *the harp* with his hand, [a,C]as usual; and [b,D]a
spear *was* in Saul's hand. 11 [A]Saul hurled the spear
for he thought, "I will [a]pin David to the wall." But
David [b]escaped from his presence twice.
12 Now [A]Saul was afraid of David, [B]for the LORD
was with him but [C]had departed from Saul. 13 Therefore Saul removed him from [a]his presence and appointed him as his commander of a thousand; and
[A]he went out and came in before the people. 14 David
was [a]prospering in all his ways for [A]the LORD *was*
with him. 15 When Saul saw that he was [a]prosper-
ing greatly, he dreaded him. 16 But [A]all Israel and
Judah loved David, and he went out and came in
before them.
17 Then Saul said to David, "[A]Here is my older
daughter Merab; I will give her to you as a wife,
only be a valiant man for me and fight [B]the LORD'S
battles." For Saul thought, "My hand shall not be
against him, but [C]let the hand of the Philistines be
against him." 18 But David said to Saul, "[A]Who am I,
and what is my life *or* my father's family in Israel,
that I should be the king's son-in-law?" 19 So it came
about at the time when Merab, Saul's daughter,
should have been given to David, that she was given
to [A]Adriel [B]the Meholathite for a wife.

DAVID MARRIES SAUL'S DAUGHTER

20 Now [A]Michal, Saul's daughter, loved David.
When they told Saul, the thing was agreeable [a]to
him. 21 Saul thought, "I will give her to him that
she may become a snare to him, and [A]that the hand
of the Philistines may be against him." Therefore
Saul said to David, "[B]For a second time you may be
my son-in-law today." 22 Then Saul commanded his
servants, "Speak to David secretly, saying, 'Behold,
the king delights in you, and all his servants love
you; now therefore, become the king's son-in-law.' "
23 So Saul's servants spoke these words [a]to David.
But David said, "Is it trivial in your sight to become
the king's son-in-law, [A]since I am a poor man and
lightly esteemed?" 24 The servants of Saul reported
to him [a]according to these words *which* David spoke.
25 Saul then said, "Thus you shall say to David, 'The
king does not desire any [A]dowry except a hundred
foreskins of the Philistines, [B]to take vengeance on
the king's enemies.' " Now [C]Saul planned to make
David fall by the hand of the Philistines. 26 When

18:6 [a]I.e. triangles; or three-stringed instruments [A]Ex 15:20, 21; Judg 11:34; Ps 68:25; 149:3 18:7 [a]Or *danced* [A]Ex 15:21; 1 Sam 21:11; 29:5 [B]1 Sam 21:11 [C]2 Sam 18:3 18:8 [a]Lit *was evil in his eyes* [A]1 Sam 15:28 18:10 [a]Lit *day by day* [b]Lit *the* [A]1 Sam 16:14 [B]1 Sam 19:23, 24 [C]1 Sam 16:23 [D]1 Sam 19:9 18:11 [a]Lit *strike David and the wall* [b]Lit *turned about* [A]1 Sam 19:10; 20:33 18:12 [A]1 Sam 18:15, 29 [B]1 Sam 16:13, 18 [C]1 Sam 16:14; 28:15 18:13 [a]Lit *with him* [A]Num 27:17; 1 Sam 18:16; 2 Sam 5:2 18:14 [a]Or *acting wisely* [A]Gen 39:2, 3, 23; Josh 6:27; 1 Sam 16:18 18:15 [a]Or *acting very wisely* 18:16 [A]1 Sam 18:5 18:17 [A]1 Sam 17:25 [B]Num 21:14; 1 Sam 17:36, 47; 25:28 [C]1 Sam 18:21, 25 18:18 [A]1 Sam 9:21; 18:23; 2 Sam 7:18 18:19 [A]2 Sam 21:8 [B]Judg 7:22; 1 Kin 19:16 18:20 [a]Lit *in his sight* [A]1 Sam 18:28 18:21 [A]1 Sam 18:17 [B]1 Sam 18:26 18:23 [a]Lit *in the ears of* [A]Gen 29:20; 34:12 18:24 [a]Lit *by saying according* 18:25 [A]Gen 34:12; Ex 22:17 [B]1 Sam 14:24 [C]1 Sam 18:17

18:7 David his ten thousands. This is a song that Saul grew to hate (cf. 21:11; 28:5) because it exalted David over him.

18:8 the kingdom. Saul's jealousy and malice toward David were now explicit. By his own statement, Saul acknowledged that David was the rightful heir to the throne and the one of whom Samuel spoke in Gilgal (15:28).

18:10 an evil spirit. The painful descent and eventual demise of Saul was marked by the persistent vexing of this spirit. See 16:14. **raved.** This means to speak before people, not predict the future. Saul's speeches in the midst of the house were the ravings of one troubled by an evil spirit like other false prophets (cf. 1Ki 22:19–23).

18:11 David escaped … twice. As Saul's behavior was becoming increasingly violent, he made more than one attempt on David's life with the javelin. It was evident that God was with David, as it would be no small feat to dodge a javelin cast by such an experienced warrior as Saul.

18:12 Saul was afraid of David. Saul, faced with the same conclusion reached by Jonathan in vv. 1–4, reacted with fear. Saul, a man who viewed life from a human perspective rather than a divine one, could view David only as a personal threat, rather than a blessing to Israel.

18:13 commander of a thousand. Saul gave David a military commission, intended as kind of an honorable exile. But this duty only served to give David opportunity to display his remarkable quality of character and strengthen his hold on the people's affections.

18:16 loved David. The writer of Samuel, inspired by the Holy Spirit, offers an editorial comment full of truth.

18:17 Merab. Lit. "compensation" or "substitute" (cf. 14:49). Saul's later retraction of the betrothal to Merab (v. 19) was similar to Laban's trickery with Jacob and Rachel (Ge 29:25). **fight the LORD's battles.** A phrase Saul knew would appeal to David. Saul made the offer out of a treacherous heart, desiring evil and calamity for David. Notice the similarity between Saul's treachery and that of David with Uriah (2Sa 11:15).

18:18 son-in-law. The familial lineage was crucial when marrying into the king's family. David asked, "Who am I … *or* my father's family in Israel, that I should be the king's son-in-law?" Saul had asked of David's lineage 3 times previously (17:55, 56, 58).

18:19 Adriel the Meholathite. Merab married this man and bore children, 5 of whom were sons later executed by David as punishment for Saul's disregard of Joshua's covenant with the Gibeonites (2Sa 21:8; cf. Jos 9:20).

18:20 Michal. Lit. "Who is like God?" Michal sincerely loved David and perhaps was aware, as Jonathan, of his certain ascent (and right) to the throne. Ironically, Saul offered her to David, not from a benevolent heart, but as a "snare" (v. 21).

18:25 dowry. Lit. "price." Saul resorted to the same treachery in his offer of betrothal to Merab, plotting to eliminate David by placing him in jeopardy with the Philistines. David, already having proved himself wise in many things (16:18), was aware, to some extent, of Saul's intent and acted obediently, valiantly, and wisely.

18:25, 27 foreskins. Such mutilations of the bodies of slain enemies were commonly practiced in ancient warfare. The number indicated the extent of the victory. Saul's intent was to expose David to deadly danger by engaging in such an extensive and hazardous task.

his servants told David these words, [a]it pleased
David to become the king's son-in-law. [b,A]Before the
days had expired 27 David rose up and went, [A]he
and his men, and struck down two hundred men
among the Philistines. Then [B]David brought their
foreskins, and they gave them in full number to the
king, that he might become the king's son-in-law.
So Saul gave him Michal his daughter for a wife.
28 When Saul saw and knew that the LORD was with
David, and *that* Michal, Saul's daughter, loved him,
29 then Saul was even more afraid of David. Thus
Saul was David's enemy continually.

30 Then the commanders of the Philistines [A]went
out *to battle,* and it happened as often as they went
out, that David [B]behaved himself more wisely than
all the servants of Saul. So his name was highly
esteemed.

DAVID PROTECTED FROM SAUL

19 Now Saul told Jonathan his son and all his
servants [A]to put David to death. But [B]Jonathan,
Saul's son, greatly delighted in David. 2 So Jonathan
told David saying, "Saul my father is seeking to put
you to death. Now therefore, please be on guard in
the morning, and stay in a secret place and hide
yourself. 3 I will go out and stand beside my father
in the field where you are, and I will speak with
my father about you; [A]if I [a]find out anything, then
I will tell you." 4 Then Jonathan [A]spoke well of David to Saul his father and said to him, "[B]Do not let
the king sin against his servant David, since he has
not sinned against you, and since his deeds *have
been* very [a]beneficial to you. 5 For [A]he took his life
in his hand and struck the Philistine, and [B]the LORD
brought about a great deliverance for all Israel; you
saw *it* and rejoiced. [C]Why then will you sin against
innocent blood by putting David to death without
a cause?" 6 Saul listened to the voice of Jonathan,
and Saul vowed, "As the LORD lives, he shall not
be put to death." 7 Then Jonathan called David, and
Jonathan told him all these words. And Jonathan
brought David to Saul, and he was in his presence
as [A]formerly.

8 When there was war again, David went out and
fought with the Philistines and [a]defeated them with
great slaughter, so that they fled before him. 9 Now
there was [A]an evil spirit from the LORD on Saul as
he was sitting in his house [B]with his spear in his
hand, [C]and David was playing *the harp* with *his*
hand. 10 [A]Saul tried to [a]pin David to the wall with the
spear, but he slipped away out of Saul's presence,
so that he [b]stuck the spear into the wall. And David
fled and escaped that night.

11 Then [A]Saul sent messengers to David's house
to watch him, in order to put him to death in the
morning. But Michal, David's wife, told him, saying,
"If you do not save your life tonight, tomorrow you
will be put to death." 12 [A]So Michal let David down
through a window, and he went out and fled and
escaped. 13 Michal took [A]the [a]household idol and
laid *it* on the bed, and put a quilt of goats' *hair* at
its head, and covered *it* with clothes. 14 When Saul
sent messengers to take David, she said, "[A]He is sick."
15 Then Saul sent messengers to see David, saying,
"Bring him up to me on [a]his bed, that I may put him
to death." 16 When the messengers entered, behold,
the [a]household idol *was* on the bed with the quilt
of goats' *hair* at its head. 17 So Saul said to Michal,
"Why have you deceived me like this and let my
enemy go, so that he has escaped?" And Michal said
to Saul, "He said to me, 'Let me go! [A]Why should I
put you to death?' "

18 Now David fled and escaped and came [A]to Samuel at Ramah, and told him all that Saul had done to
him. And he and Samuel went and stayed in [B]Nai-
oth. 19 It was told Saul, saying, "Behold, David is at

18:26 [a]Lit *it was agreeable in the sight of* [b]Lit *And the days had not expired* [A]1 Sam 18:21 18:27 [A]1 Sam 18:17 [B]2 Sam 3:14 18:30 [A]2 Sam 11:1 [B]1 Sam 18:5 19:1 [A]1 Sam 18:8, 9 [B]1 Sam 18:1-3 19:3 [a]Lit *see* [A]1 Sam 20:9, 13 19:4 [a]Lit *good* [A]1 Sam 20:32; Prov 31:8, 9 [B]Gen 42:22; Prov 17:13; Jer 18:20 19:5 [A]Judg 9:17; 1 Sam 17:49, 50; 28:21; Ps 119:109 [B]1 Sam 11:13; 1 Chr 11:14 [C]Deut 19:10-13; 1 Sam 20:32; Ps 94:21; Matt 27:4 19:7 [A]1 Sam 16:21; 18:2, 10, 13 19:8 [a]Lit *smote* 19:9 [A]1 Sam 16:14; 18:10, 11 [B]1 Sam 18:10 [C]1 Sam 16:16 19:10 [a]Lit *strike David and the wall* [b]Lit *struck* [A]1 Sam 18:11; 20:33; Prov 1:16 19:11 [A]Judg 16:2; Ps 59: title 19:12 [A]Josh 2:15; Acts 9:25; 2 Cor 11:33 19:13 [a]Heb *teraphim* [A]Gen 31:19; Judg 18:14, 17 19:14 [A]Josh 2:5 19:15 [a]Lit *the* 19:16 [a]Heb *teraphim* 19:17 [A]2 Sam 2:22 19:18 [A]1 Sam 7:17 [B]1 Sam 19:22, 23

18:27 his men. Cf. 22:2; 25:12, 13; 2Sa 23:8–39.

18:29 Saul was David's enemy. All of Saul's plans came to naught. Saul asked for 100 Philistine foreskins; David brought 200. Saul offered Michal as a "snare"; Michal loved David as did Saul's own son, Jonathan. There remained nothing else for Saul to contrive except open hatred toward David.

19:1 put David to death. Saul no longer tried to disguise or cover his evil intent toward David, but ironically made known his intent to those who held David in the highest esteem (cf. 16:18; 18:1–4). God, in His mercy, made sure that David had sympathetic ears within Saul's court to inform him of Saul's evil plans (e.g., 19:7; 20:2).

19:4 Jonathan spoke well of David. Jonathan attempted to persuade his father with calm reason. Jonathan's reason was tempered by a godly attitude centered on a remembrance of the Torah (14:6; cf. Nu 11:23; 14:9) and a covenantal loyalty toward and faithfulness for David.

19:4, 5 he has not sinned. Jonathan reminded Saul that David had done nothing to deserve death; in fact, he was worthy of honor for his good works toward the king and Israel. Jonathan knew that the spilling of innocent blood would affect all Israel, not just the house of Saul (Dt 21:8, 9).

19:6 he shall not be put to death. Saul temporarily responded to reason and conviction in his heart. His mental capacity was so unbalanced, however, that this response would not last for long.

19:9 an evil spirit. Jealousy, rage, and anger once again dominated Saul, who was enraged by David's success against the Philistines. See 16:14; 18:10.

19:10 pin David ... with the spear. Saul's already diminished capacity for reason was once again completely clouded by anger, and he responded toward David with murderous intent (cf. 18:10, 11).

19:11 Michal ... told him. Michal, far from being a "snare" (18:21) to David, was instrumental in saving his life. Michal, at this time in her relationship with David, displayed a covenantal love and faithfulness similar to that of Jonathan. See the title of Ps 59.

19:13 household idol. Heb. *teraphim.* The writer of Samuel draws a parallel between David/Michal/Saul and Jacob/Rachel/Laban (*see note on 18:17*), in that both Rachel and Michal employed the use of household gods ("teraphim") in trickery and out of loyalty for their husbands rather than their fathers (cf. Ge 31:30–35).

19:17 He said to me. Michal lied in telling Saul the exact opposite of what she said to David (v. 11).

19:18 Ramah. With the mention of Samuel's birthplace, the author establishes a verbal link with 1:1, and also reminds the reader of Saul's first encounter with Samuel the seer in Zuph (Ramathaim-zophim). **Naioth.** Perhaps dwellings or quarters within the town limits of Ramah, where Samuel and his company of prophet-disciples met for training, prayer, and fellowship (cf. Elisha at Gilgal, 2Ki 6:1, 2).

Naioth in Ramah." 20 Then [A]Saul sent messengers to
take David, but when they saw [B]the company of the
prophets prophesying, with Samuel standing *and*
presiding over them, the Spirit of God came upon
the messengers of Saul; and [C]they also prophesied.
21 When it was told Saul, he sent other messengers,
and they also prophesied. So Saul sent messengers
again the third time, and they also prophesied.
22 Then he himself went to Ramah and came as far
as the large well that is in Secu; and he asked and
said, "Where are Samuel and David?" And *someone*
said, "Behold, they are at Naioth in Ramah." 23 He
[a]proceeded there to Naioth in Ramah; and [A]the Spirit
of God came upon him also, so that he went along
prophesying continually until he came to Naioth in
Ramah. 24 He also stripped off his clothes, and he too
prophesied before Samuel and [a]lay down [b,A]naked
all that day and all that night. Therefore they say,
"[B]Is Saul also among the prophets?"

DAVID AND JONATHAN COVENANT

20 Then David fled from Naioth in Ramah, and
came and [A]said [a]to Jonathan, "What have
I done? What is my iniquity? And what is my sin
before your father, that he is seeking my life?" 2 He
said to him, "Far from it, you shall not die. Behold,
my father does nothing either great or small [a]with-
out disclosing it to me. So why should my father
hide this thing from me? It is not so!" 3 Yet David
[A]vowed again, [a]saying, "Your father knows well that
I have found favor in your sight, and he has said, 'Do
not let Jonathan know this, or he will be grieved.' But
truly [B]as the LORD lives and as your soul lives, there
is [b]hardly a step between me and death." 4 Then Jonathan said to David, "Whatever [a]you say, I will do for
you." 5 So David said to Jonathan, "Behold, tomorrow
is [A]the new moon, and I ought [B]to sit down to eat
with the king. But let me go, [C]that I may hide myself
in the field until the third evening. 6 If your father
misses me at all, then say, 'David earnestly asked
leave of me to run to [A]Bethlehem his city, because
it is [B]the yearly sacrifice there for the whole family.'
7 If he [a]says, 'It is good,' your servant *will be* safe;
but if he is very angry, [A]know that he has decided
on evil. 8 Therefore deal kindly with your servant,
for [A]you have brought your servant into a covenant
of the LORD with you. But [B]if there is iniquity in me,
put me to death yourself; for why then should you

19:20 [A]1 Sam 19:11, 14; John 7:32 [B]1 Sam 10:5, 6, 10 [C]Num 11:25; Joel 2:28 19:23 [a]Lit *went* [A]1 Sam 10:10 19:24 [a]Lit *fell* [b]I.e. without outward garments [A]2 Sam 6:20; Is 20:2; Mic 1:8 [B]1 Sam 10:10-12 20:1 [a]Lit *before* [A]1 Sam 24:9 20:2 [a]Lit *and he does not uncover my ear* 20:3 [a]Lit *and said* [b]Lit *about* [A]Deut 6:13 [B]1 Sam 25:26; 2 Kin 2:6 20:4 [a]Lit *your soul says* 20:5 [A]Num 10:10; 28:11-15; Amos 8:5 [B]1 Sam 20:24, 27 [C]1 Sam 19:2 20:6 [A]1 Sam 17:58 [B]Deut 12:5; 1 Sam 9:12 20:7 [a]Lit *says thus* [A]1 Sam 25:17 20:8 [A]1 Sam 18:3; 23:18 [B]2 Sam 14:32

19:20 company of the prophets prophesying. These prophets were declaring the Word of God, probably with musical accompaniment. Saul's messengers could not fulfill their task of taking David captive because they were irresistibly led to join the prophets and speak for and praise God.

19:22 large well ... in Secu. The exact location is unknown; the probable location was approximately two mi. N of Ramah.

19:23 the Spirit of God came upon him. This was the last time the Spirit of the Lord would rest on Saul. God turned Saul's heart to prophesy and not to harm David. *See note on 16:13.*

19:24 stripped off his clothes. Saul removed his armor and royal garments (cf. Jonathan, 18:4), prompted by the Spirit of God, thus signifying God's rejection of Saul as king over Israel. **lay down naked.** Without the royal garments, Saul was figuratively "naked," perhaps so overwhelmed by the Spirit of God as to be in a deep sleep. Other than Saul's utter despair and pitiful state at the home of the witch at En-dor (28:20) and his end at Mt. Gilboa (31:4–6), this episode represents one of the severest humblings in Saul's life. **Is Saul also among the prophets?** This is a final editorial comment tying together the Spirit of God's presence at Saul's inauguration (10:10, 11), and the final departure of the same at his rejection (19:24).

20:1 Naioth in Ramah. *See note on 19:18.*

20:2 why should my father hide this thing from me? Although Jonathan expressed his certainty that Saul was not seeking David's life, he may have been unaware of the most recent attempts on David's life (19:9–24) and was trusting in his father's oath not to harm David (19:6). Jonathan expected to be informed by Saul of any change in his plans.

20:5 the new moon. The first day of the month, referred to as "the New Moon," was celebrated with a sacrificial meal (cf. 2Ki 4:23; Is 1:13; Am 8:5) and served both as a religious and civil festival (Nu 10:10; 28:11–15). **hide ... in the field.** As in 19:2, 3, David hid from Saul in a secret place.

20:6 the yearly sacrifice. Apparently, David's family held an annual family reunion that coincided with one of the monthly New Moon celebrations (cf. vv. 28, 29).

20:8 covenant. Cf. 18:1, 3. Jonathan and David had solemnly pledged their friendship and loyalty to each other before the Lord. Their covenant is further amplified in vv. 13–17, 42; 23:17, 18. **put me to death yourself.** As his covenant friend, David asked Jonathan to kill him, if he was deserving of death because of his possible sin.

OVERVIEW OF SAUL'S LIFE

Passage	Saul's Sinful Choice	Consequence
1 Sam. 13:5–23	He assumed a priestly role and offered sacrifices before battle.	The prophet Samuel announced God's choice of a new king.
14:1–52	He made a foolish oath.	The people turned against him.
15:1–9	He disobeyed God's instructions by not completely destroying Agag.	Samuel announced God's utter rejection of him as king.
18:10–16	He personally tried to kill David.	He was overcome by fear and an evil spirit.
19:1–7	He ordered the murder of David.	He became paranoid.
19:8–10	He again tried to kill David.	He was tormented by an evil spirit.
19:11–24	He continued his murderous campaign against David.	He became consumed by jealousy and fear.
20:1–42	He tried to get his son Jonathan to assist in killing David.	He became violent toward his own son.
22:6–23	He ordered Doeg to kill the priests of Nob.	He slipped further into madness and depravity.
28:7–25	He visited a medium.	He became terrified of his future death.
31:4	He committed suicide.	A man with great potential died in great shame.

bring me to your father?" 9 Jonathan said, "Far be
it from you! For if I should indeed learn that evil
has been decided by my father to come upon you,
then would I not tell you about it?" 10 Then David
said to Jonathan, "Who will tell me [a]if your father
answers you harshly?" 11 Jonathan said to David,
"Come, and let us go out into the field." So both of
them went out to the field.

12 Then Jonathan said to David, "The LORD, the
God of Israel, *be witness!* When I have sounded out
my father about this time tomorrow, *or* the third
day, behold, if there is good *feeling* toward David,
shall I not then send to you and [a]make it known to
you? 13 If it please my father *to do* you harm, [A]may
the LORD do so to Jonathan and more also, if I do
not [a]make it known to you and send you away, that
you may go in safety. And [B]may the LORD be with
you as He has been with my father. 14 If I am still
alive, will you not show me the lovingkindness of
the LORD, that I may not die? 15 [A]You shall not cut
off your lovingkindness from my house forever,
not even when the LORD cuts off every one of the
enemies of David from the face of the earth." 16 So
Jonathan made a *covenant* with the house of David,
saying, "[A]May the LORD require *it* at the hands of
David's enemies." 17 Jonathan made David vow again
because of his love for him, because [A]he loved him
as he loved his own life.

18 Then Jonathan said to him, "[A]Tomorrow is the
new moon, and you will be missed because your seat
will be empty. 19 When you have stayed for three
days, you shall go down quickly and come to the
place where you hid yourself on that eventful day,
and you shall remain by the stone Ezel. 20 I will shoot
three arrows to the side, as though I shot at a target.
21 And behold, I will send the lad, *saying,* 'Go, find
the arrows.' If I specifically say to the lad, 'Behold,
the arrows are on this side of you, get them,' then
come; for there is safety for you and [a]no harm, as
the LORD lives. 22 But if I [a]say to the youth, '[A]Behold,
the arrows are beyond you,' go, for the LORD has
sent you away. 23 [A]As for the [a]agreement of which
you and I have spoken, behold, [B]the LORD is between
you and me forever."

24 So David hid in the field; and when the new
moon came, the king sat down to eat food. 25 The
king sat on his seat as usual, the seat by the wall;
then Jonathan rose up and Abner sat down by
Saul's side, but [A]David's place was empty. 26 Nevertheless Saul did not speak anything that day,
for he thought, "It is an accident, [A]he is not clean,
surely *he is* not clean." 27 It came about the next
day, the second *day* of the new moon, that David's place was empty; so Saul said to Jonathan
his son, "Why has the son of Jesse not come to
the meal, either yesterday or today?" 28 Jonathan
then answered Saul, "[A]David earnestly asked leave
of me *to go* to Bethlehem, 29 for he said, 'Please
[a]let me go, since our family has a sacrifice in the
city, and my brother has commanded me to attend. And now, if I have found favor in your sight,
please let me get away that I may see my brothers.' For this reason he has not come to the king's
table."

SAUL IS ANGRY WITH JONATHAN

30 Then Saul's anger burned against Jonathan and
he said to him, "You son of a perverse, rebellious
woman! Do I not know that you are choosing the
son of Jesse to your own shame and to the shame
of your mother's nakedness? 31 For [a]as long as the
son of Jesse lives on the earth, neither you nor your
kingdom will be established. Therefore now, send
and bring him to me, for [A]he [b]must surely die."
32 But Jonathan answered Saul his father and said
to him, "[A]Why should he be put to death? What has
he done?" 33 Then [A]Saul hurled his spear at him to
strike him down; [B]so Jonathan knew that his father
had decided to put David to death. 34 Then Jonathan
arose from the table in fierce anger, and did not
eat food on the second day of the new moon, for
he was grieved over David because his father had
dishonored him.

35 Now it came about in the morning that Jonathan went out into the field for the appointment
with David, and a little lad *was* with him. 36 He
said to his lad, "[A]Run, find now the arrows which
I am about to shoot." As the lad was running, he
shot [a]an arrow past him. 37 When the lad reached
the place of the arrow which Jonathan had shot,
Jonathan called after the lad and said, "[A]Is not the
arrow beyond you?" 38 And Jonathan called after the
lad, "Hurry, be quick, do not stay!" And Jonathan's
lad picked up the arrow and came to his master.

20:10 [a]Lit *or what* 20:12 [a]Lit *uncover your ear* 20:13 [a]Lit *uncover your ear* [A]Ruth 1:17; 1 Sam 3:17 [B]Josh 1:5; 1 Sam 17:37; 18:12; 1 Chr 22:11, 16 20:15 [A]2 Sam 9:1, 3 20:16 [A]Deut 23:21; 1 Sam 25:22 20:17 [A]1 Sam 18:1 20:18 [A]1 Sam 20:5, 25 20:21 [a]Lit *there is nothing* 20:22 [a]Lit *say thus* [A]1 Sam 20:37 20:23 [a]Lit *word* [A]1 Sam 20:14, 15 [B]Gen 31:49, 53; 1 Sam 20:42 20:25 [A]1 Sam 20:18 20:26 [A]Lev 7:20, 21; 15:5; 1 Sam 16:5 20:28 [A]1 Sam 20:6 20:29 [a]Lit *send me away* 20:31 [a]Lit *all the days which* [b]Lit *is a son of death* [A]2 Sam 12:5 20:32 [A]Gen 31:36; 1 Sam 19:5; Prov 31:9; Matt 27:23 20:33 [A]1 Sam 18:11; 19:10 [B]1 Sam 20:7 20:36 [a]Lit *the* [A]1 Sam 20:20, 21 20:37 [A]1 Sam 20:22

20:14 the lovingkindness of the LORD. Jonathan acknowledged that David would one day be Israel's king. With that in mind, Jonathan requested protection for him and his family when David took the throne.

20:16 the house of David. This covenant was not only binding on Jonathan and David, but also upon the descendants of each. See 2Sa 9:1–8 for the account of David's kindness to a descendant of Jonathan in fulfillment of this covenant. **David's enemies.** Jonathan perceived that among David's adversaries who would be cut off when he became king was his own father, Saul (cf. 18:29; 19:17).

20:17 vow. In response to Jonathan's words, David solemnly pledged to fulfill the covenant between himself and Jonathan. **loved him as ... his own life.** A deep concern and affection was the basis of the covenantal relationship between Jonathan and David. This is the affection commanded by God when He said, "Love your neighbor as yourself" (Lv 19:18; Mt 22:39).

20:19 stone Ezel. Ezel may mean "departure stone." The location of this stone is unknown, but it was a well-known landmark in the field where David was hiding.

20:25 Abner. Saul's cousin and commander of his army (*see note on 14:50*).

20:26 not clean. At first, Saul did not question David's absence at the feast, assuming that he was ritually unclean and thus could not participate in the meal (cf. Lv 7:20, 21; 15:16).

20:30 son of a perverse, rebellious woman! With a vile epithet, Saul was cursing Jonathan, not Jonathan's mother, for having sided with David to his own shame and the shame of the mother who birthed him.

39 But the lad was not aware of anything; only Jonathan and David knew about the matter. 40 Then
Jonathan gave his weapons to his lad and said to
him, "Go, bring *them* to the city." 41 When the lad
was gone, David rose from the south side and fell
on his face to the ground, and [A]bowed three times.
And they kissed each other and wept together,
but [B]David *wept* the more. 42 Jonathan said to David, "[A]Go in safety, inasmuch as we have sworn to
each other in the name of the LORD, saying, '[B]The
LORD will be between me and you, and between
my [a]descendants and your [a]descendants forever.' "
[b]Then he rose and departed, while Jonathan went
into the city.

DAVID TAKES CONSECRATED BREAD

21 Then David came to [A]Nob to Ahimelech the
priest; and Ahimelech [B]came trembling to
meet David and said to him, "Why are you alone
and no one with you?" 2 David said to Ahimelech
the priest, "The king has commissioned me with
a matter and has said to me, '[A]Let no one know
anything about the matter on which I am sending you and with which I have commissioned
you; and I have directed the young men to a certain place.' 3 Now therefore, what [a]do you have on
hand? Give [b]me five loaves of bread, or whatever
can be found." 4 The priest answered David and
said, "There is no ordinary bread [a]on hand, but
there is [A]consecrated bread; if only the young
men have [B]kept themselves from women." 5 David answered the priest and said to him, "[A]Surely
women have been kept from us as previously
when I set out and the [B]vessels of the young men
were holy, though it was an ordinary journey; how
much more then today will [a]their vessels *be holy?*"
6 So [A]the priest gave him consecrated *bread;* for
there was no bread there but the [B]bread of the
Presence which was removed from before the
LORD, in order to put hot bread *in its place* when
it was taken away.
7 Now one of the servants of Saul was there
that day, detained before the LORD; and his name
was [A]Doeg the Edomite, the [B]chief of Saul's shepherds.
8 David said to Ahimelech, "Now is there not a
spear or a sword [a]on hand? For I brought neither
my sword nor my weapons [b]with me, because the
king's matter was urgent." 9 Then the priest said,
"[A]The sword of Goliath the Philistine, whom you
[a]killed [B]in the valley of Elah, behold, it is wrapped
in a cloth behind the ephod; if you would take it
for yourself, take *it.* For there is no other except it
here." And David said, "There is none like it; give
it to me."
10 Then David arose and fled that day from Saul,
and went to [A]Achish king of Gath. 11 But the [A]ser-
vants of Achish said to him, "Is this not David the
king of the land? [B]Did they not sing of this one as
they danced, saying,

'Saul has slain his thousands,
And David his ten thousands'?"

12 David [A]took these words [a]to heart and greatly
feared Achish king of Gath. 13 So he [A]disguised his
sanity before them, and acted insanely in their
hands, and scribbled on the doors of the gate, and
let his saliva run down into his beard. 14 Then Achish
said to his servants, "Behold, you see the man behaving as a madman. Why do you bring him to me?
15 Do I lack madmen, that you have brought this one
to act the madman in my presence? Shall this one
come into my house?"

20:41 [A]Gen 42:6 [B]1 Sam 18:3 20:42 [a]Lit *seed* [b]Ch 21:1 in Heb [A]1 Sam 20:22 [B]1 Sam 20:15, 16, 23 21:1 [A]1 Sam 22:19; Neh 11:32; Is 10:32 [B]1 Sam 16:4 21:2 [A]Ps 141:3 21:3 [a]Lit *is under your hand?* [b]Lit *in my hand* 21:4 [a]Lit *under my hand* [A]Ex 25:30; Lev 24:5-9; Matt 12:4 [B]Ex 19:15 21:5 [a]Lit *it* be holy *in the vessel* [A]Ex 19:14, 15 [B]1 Thess 4:4 21:6 [A]Matt 12:3, 4; Luke 6:3, 4 [B]Lev 24:5-9 21:7 [A]1 Sam 14:47; 22:9; Ps 52: title [B]1 Chr 27:29, 31 21:8 [a]Lit *under your hand* [b]Lit *in my hand* 21:9 [a]Lit *smote* [A]1 Sam 17:51, 54 [B]1 Sam 17:2 21:10 [A]Ps 34: title 21:11 [A]Ps 56: title [B]1 Sam 18:7; 29:5 21:12 [a]Lit *in his* [A]Luke 2:19 21:13 [A]Ps 34: title

20:41 bowed three times. David's bowing down more than once acknowledged Jonathan as the prince, and expressed humble affection for him.

20:42 sworn. *See note on 20:17.* **the city.** I.e., Gibeah, the home of Saul. From this point until Saul's death, David was an outcast from the royal court.

21:1 Nob. "The city of the priests" (22:19). The priests dwelt on Mt. Scopus, about one mi. NE of Jerusalem. David went there for necessary supplies and for comfort and counsel. **Ahimelech.** A great grandson of Eli (1:9), who is possibly the brother of Ahijah (14:3; 22:11), or Ahimelech may be another name for Ahijah. Not only is there a rejected king on the throne (15:26–29) but also a disqualified priest (2:30–36). *See note on Mk 2:26.*

21:2 The king has commissioned me. David, fearing someone might tell Saul where he was, deceived Ahimelech the priest into thinking that he was on official business for the king. He supposed, as many do, that it is excusable to lie for the purpose of saving one's life. But what is essentially sinful can never, because of circumstances, change its immoral character (cf. Ps 119:29). David's lying led tragically to the deaths of the priests (22:9–18).

21:4 consecrated bread. Consecrated bread was set apart for use in the tabernacle to be eaten only by the priests (Ex 25:30; Lv 24:5–9). Ahimelech sought the Lord and received approval (22:10) when he recognized that his spiritual obligation to preserve David's life superseded the ceremonial regulation concerning who could eat the consecrated bread (see Mt 12:3, 4; Mk 2:25, 26). **kept themselves from women.** Though this was not a spiritual mission or religious journey, David and his men were ceremonially clean (see Ex 19:15).

21:5 their vessels. A euphemism for the bodies of the young men, as in 1Th 4:4.

21:6 consecrated *bread*. Since that bread was no longer on the Lord's table, having been replaced by hot bread, it was to be eaten by the priests and in these exigencies, by David under the law of necessity and mercy. *See note on 21:4.* The removal of the old bread and the replacing with new was done on the Sabbath (Lv 24:8).

21:7 Doeg the Edomite. The head shepherd of Saul's herd, who witnessed the encounter between David and Ahimelech and told Saul (cf. 22:9, 10), had embraced the Hebrew religion and was at the tabernacle, perhaps detained because it was the Sabbath and he could not travel.

21:9 The sword of Goliath. The sword which David had used to behead Goliath in the valley of Elah (17:51) was kept in the place for storing the sacred vestments ("the ephod") deposited there as a memorial to divine goodness in the deliverance of Israel. **the ephod.** *See notes on 2:18, 28; 14:3.*

21:10 Achish king of Gath. One of the kings or lords of the Philistines. *See notes on 4:1; 5:8* for Gath. This seemed to be a dangerous place to go, since David was their greatest enemy and carried Goliath's sword into the giant's hometown.

21:13 disguised his sanity. David feared for his life, lacked trust in God to deliver him, and feigned insanity to persuade Achish to send him away. See the titles of Pss 34, 56. Drooling in one's beard was considered in the East an intolerable indignity, as was spitting in another's beard.

THE PRIESTS SLAIN AT NOB

22 So David departed from there and [A]escaped to
[B]the cave of Adullam; and when his brothers
and all his father's household heard *of it,* they went
down there to him. 2 Everyone who was in distress,
and everyone who [a]was in debt, and everyone who
was [b]discontented gathered to him; and he became
captain over them. Now there were [A]about four
hundred men with him.
3 And David went from there to Mizpah of Moab;
and he said to the king of Moab, "Please let my father and my mother come *and stay* with you until I know what God will do for me." 4 Then he left
them with the king of Moab; and they stayed with
him all the time that David was in the stronghold.
5 [A]The prophet Gad said to David, "Do not stay in
the stronghold; depart, and go into the land of Judah." So David departed and went into the forest
of Hereth.
6 Then Saul heard that David and the men who
were with him had been discovered. Now [A]Saul
was sitting in Gibeah, under the tamarisk tree on
the height with his spear in his hand, and all his
servants were standing around him. 7 Saul said to
his servants who stood around him, "Hear now,
O Benjamites! Will the son of Jesse also give to all
of you fields and vineyards? [A]Will he make you all
commanders of thousands and commanders of
hundreds? 8 For all of you have conspired against
me so that there is no one who [a]discloses to me
[A]when my son makes *a covenant* with the son of
Jesse, and there is none of you [B]who is sorry for me
or [a]discloses to me that my son has stirred up my
servant against me to lie in ambush, as *it is* this
day." 9 Then [A]Doeg the Edomite, who was [a]stand-
ing by the servants of Saul, said, "[B]I saw the son
of Jesse coming to Nob, to [C]Ahimelech the son of
Ahitub. 10 [A]He inquired of the LORD for him, [B]gave
him provisions, and [C]gave him the sword of Goliath
the Philistine."
11 Then the king sent someone to summon Ahimelech the priest, the son of Ahitub, and all his father's
household, the priests who were in Nob; and all of
them came to the king. 12 Saul said, "Listen now, son
of Ahitub." And he [a]answered, "Here I am, my lord."
13 Saul then said to him, "Why have you and the son
of Jesse conspired against me, in that you have
given him bread and a sword and have inquired of
God for him, so that he would rise up against me
[A]by lying in ambush as *it is* this day?"
14 [A]Then Ahimelech answered the king and said,
"And who among all your servants is as faithful as
David, even the king's son-in-law, who [a]is captain over
your guard, and is honored in your house? 15 Did I *just*
begin [A]to inquire of God for him today? Far be it from
me! [B]Do not let the king impute anything to his servant *or* to any of the household of my father, for your
servant knows nothing [a]at all of this whole affair."
16 But the king said, "You shall surely die, Ahimelech,
you and all your father's household!" 17 And [A]the king
said to the [a]guards who were attending him, "Turn
around and put the priests of the LORD to death,
because their hand also is with David and because
they knew that he was fleeing and did not [b]reveal it
to me." But the [B]servants of the king were not willing to put forth their hands to [c]attack the priests of
the LORD. 18 Then the king said to Doeg, "You turn
around and [a]attack the priests." And Doeg the Edomite turned around and [b]attacked the priests, and [A]he
killed that day eighty-five men [B]who wore the linen
ephod. 19 And [A]he struck Nob the city of the priests
with the edge of the sword, both men and women,
children and infants; also oxen, donkeys, and sheep
he struck with the edge of the sword.
20 But [A]one son of Ahimelech the son of Ahitub,
named Abiathar, [B]escaped and fled after David.

22:1 [A]Ps 57: title [B]Josh 12:15; 15:35; 2 Sam 23:13; Ps 142: title 22:2 [a]Lit *had a creditor* [b]Lit *bitter of soul* [A]1 Sam 23:13; 25:13 22:5 [A]2 Sam 24:11; 1 Chr 21:9; 29:29; 2 Chr 29:25 22:6 [A]Judg 4:5; 1 Sam 14:2 22:7 [A]1 Sam 8:12; 1 Chr 12:16-18 22:8 [a]Lit *uncovers my ear* [A]1 Sam 18:3; 20:16 [B]1 Sam 23:21 22:9 [a]Or *set over* [A]Ps 52: title [B]1 Sam 21:1 [C]1 Sam 14:3; 21:1 22:10 [A]Num 27:21; 1 Sam 10:22 [B]1 Sam 21:6 [C]1 Sam 21:9 22:12 [a]Lit *said* 22:13 [A]1 Sam 22:8 22:14 [a]So with Gr; Heb *turns aside to* [A]1 Sam 19:4, 5; 20:32 22:15 [a]Lit *small or great* [A]2 Sam 5:19, 23 [B]2 Sam 19:18, 19 22:17 [a]Lit *runners* [b]Lit *uncover my ear* [c]Lit *fall upon* [A]2 Kin 10:25 [B]Ex 1:17 22:18 [a]Lit *smite* [b]Lit *smote* [A]1 Sam 2:31 [B]1 Sam 2:18 22:19 [A]1 Sam 15:3 22:20 [A]1 Sam 23:6, 9; 30:7; 1 Kin 2:26, 27 [B]1 Sam 23:6

22:1 cave of Adullam. A cave near Adullam was David's refuge. Adullam, which may mean "refuge," was located in the western foothills of Judah (Jos 15:33), about 17 mi. SW of Jerusalem and 10 mi. SE of Gath. See titles of Pss 57,142, which could possibly refer to 1Sa 24:3. **brothers and all his father's household.** David's family members went down from Bethlehem to join David in Adullam, a journey of about 12 mi.

22:2 captain over . . . four hundred men. David became the leader of a formidable force of men united by adverse circumstances. This personal army would soon grow to 600 (23:13).

22:3 Mizpah of Moab. Mizpah means "watch tower," or "place that overlooks." Located on one of the heights of the tableland E of the Dead Sea, this site cannot be exactly identified. **king of Moab.** This ruler was probably a mutual enemy of King Saul. David had Moabite blood from his great-grandmother Ruth, and thus sought refuge for his father and mother in Moab (see Ru 1:4–18; 4:13–22).

22:5 prophet Gad. As the prophet Samuel had helped and advised Saul, so now Gad performed the same functions for David (cf. 2 Sam 24:11, where Gad is called "David's seer"). **forest of Hereth.** Location in Judah unknown.

22:6 tamarisk tree. Possibly located on a hill outside Gibeah which had been given over to pagan worship (cf. Eze 16:24, 25, 31, 39). **spear.** A reminder of the threat that Saul was to friend and foe alike (cf. 18:10, 11; 19:9, 10; 20:3).

22:7 Benjamites. Saul asked those of his own tribe whether associating themselves with David would provide for them more possessions and privileges than they already had from Saul.

22:8 my son makes *a covenant*. *See note on 20:8.*

22:8–13 to lie in ambush. Saul insinuated that David was plotting his death. This was not true, as David would later spare Saul's life (24:1–22).

22:9, 10 Doeg the Edomite. *See note on 21:7* and the title of Ps 52.

22:13 conspired against me. Saul insisted falsely that Ahimelech was in league with his enemy David.

22:14 captain over your guard. Ahimelech responded to Saul by defending David's character as loyal to Saul.

22:16–19 This fulfills the curse on Eli's house (*see note on 1Sa 2:31*), with the exception of Abiathar, who was later dismissed from the priesthood by Solomon (1Ki 2:26–29).

22:17 not willing . . . to attack the priests. Although Saul condemned Ahimelech and the priests to death, his servants knew better than to raise their weapons against the priests of the Lord.

22:18 linen ephod. *See notes on 2:18; 14:3.*

22:19 Nob the city of the priests. *See note on 21:1.* What Saul failed to do righteously to the Amalekites (15:3, 8, 9), he unrighteously did to the citizens of Nob.

22:20 Abiathar. Lit. "The father is excellent." A son of Ahimelech (cf. 21:1) who escaped the slaughter and joined David's company, he performed priestly functions for David for the rest of David's life (cf. 23:6, 9; 30:7; 2Sa 8:17). *See note on 22:16–19.*

21 Abiathar told David that Saul had killed the priests
of the LORD. 22 Then David said to Abiathar, "I knew
on that day, when [A]Doeg the Edomite was there, that
he would surely tell Saul. I have brought about *the
death* of every person in your father's household.
23 Stay with me; do not be afraid, for [A]he who seeks
my life seeks your life, for you are [a]safe with me."

DAVID DELIVERS KEILAH

23 Then they told David, saying, "Behold, the
Philistines are fighting against [A]Keilah and
are plundering the threshing floors." 2 So David [A]in-
quired of the LORD, saying, "Shall I go and [a]attack
these Philistines?" And the LORD said to David, "Go
and [a]attack the Philistines and deliver Keilah." 3 But
David's men said to him, "Behold, we are afraid here
in Judah. How much more then if we go to Keilah
against the ranks of the Philistines?" 4 Then David
inquired of the LORD once more. And the LORD
answered him and said, "Arise, go down to Keilah,
for [A]I will give the Philistines into your hand." 5 So
David and his men went to Keilah and fought with
the Philistines; and he led away their livestock and
struck them with a great slaughter. Thus David delivered the inhabitants of Keilah.
6 Now it came about, when Abiathar the son of
Ahimelech [A]fled to David at Keilah, *that* he came
down *with* an ephod in his hand. 7 When it was
told Saul that David had come to Keilah, Saul said,
"God has [a]delivered him into my hand, for he shut
himself in by entering a city with double gates and
bars." 8 So Saul summoned all the people for war, to
go down to Keilah to besiege David and his men.
9 Now David knew that Saul was plotting evil against
him; so he said to [A]Abiathar the priest, "[B]Bring the
ephod here." 10 Then David said, "O LORD God of Israel, Your servant has heard for certain that Saul is
seeking to come to Keilah to destroy the city on my
account. 11 Will the men of Keilah surrender me into
his hand? Will Saul come down just as Your servant
has heard? O LORD God of Israel, I pray, tell Your
servant." And the LORD said, "He will come down."
12 Then David said, "Will the men of Keilah surrender me and my men into the hand of Saul?" And
the LORD said, "[A]They will surrender you." 13 Then
David and his men, [A]about six hundred, arose and
departed from Keilah, and they went [B]wherever
they could go. When it was told Saul that David
had escaped from Keilah, he [a]gave up the pursuit.
14 David stayed in the wilderness in the strongholds,
and remained in the hill country in the wilderness
of [A]Ziph. And Saul sought him every day, but [B]God
did not deliver him into his hand.

SAUL PURSUES DAVID

15 Now David [a]became aware that Saul had come
out to seek his life while David was in the wilderness
of Ziph at Horesh. 16 And Jonathan, Saul's son, arose
and went to David at Horesh, and [a,A]encouraged him
in God. 17 Thus he said to him, "[A]Do not be afraid, because the hand of Saul my father will not find you, and
you will be king over Israel and I will be next to you;
and [B]Saul my father knows that also." 18 So [A]the two of
them made a covenant before the LORD; and David
stayed at Horesh while Jonathan went to his house.
19 Then [A]Ziphites came up to Saul at Gibeah, saying, "Is David not hiding with us in the strongholds
at Horesh, on [B]the hill of Hachilah, which is on the
[a]south of [b]Jeshimon? 20 Now then, O king, come
down according to all the desire of your soul to [a]do
so; and [A]our part *shall be* to surrender him into the
king's hand." 21 Saul said, "May you be blessed of the
LORD, [A]for you have had compassion on me. 22 Go
now, make more sure, and investigate and see his
place where his [a]haunt is, *and* who has seen him
there; for I am told that he is very cunning. 23 So
look, and learn about all the hiding places where
he hides himself and return to me with certainty,
and I will go with you; and if he is in the land, I will
search him out among all the thousands of Judah."
24 Then they arose and went to Ziph before Saul.
Now David and his men were in the wilderness of
[A]Maon, in the Arabah to the [a]south of [b]Jeshimon.
25 When Saul and his men went to seek *him,* they told

22:22 [A]1 Sam 21:7 22:23 [a]Lit *a charge* [A]1 Kin 2:26 23:1 [A]Josh 15:44; Neh 3:17, 18 23:2 [a]Lit *smite* [A]1 Sam 23:4, 6, 9-12; 2 Sam 5:19, 23 23:4 [A]Josh 8:7; Judg 7:7 23:6 [A]1 Sam 22:20 23:7 [a]Lit *alienated* 23:9 [A]1 Sam 22:20 [B]1 Sam 23:6; 30:7 23:12 [A]Judg 15:10-13; 1 Sam 23:20 23:13 [a]Lit *ceased going out* [A]1 Sam 22:2; 25:13 [B]2 Sam 15:20 23:14 [A]Josh 15:55; 2 Chr 11:8 [B]Ps 32:7 23:15 [a]Lit *saw* 23:16 [a]Lit *strengthened his hand* [A]1 Sam 30:6; Neh 2:18 23:17 [A]Ps 27:1, 3; 118:6; Is 54:17; Heb 13:6 [B]1 Sam 20:31; 24:20 23:18 [A]1 Sam 18:3; 20:12-17, 42; 2 Sam 9:1; 21:7 23:19 [a]Lit *right side* [b]Or *the desert* [A]1 Sam 26:1; Ps 54: title [B]1 Sam 26:3 23:20 [a]Lit *come down* [A]1 Sam 23:12 23:21 [A]1 Sam 22:8 23:22 [a]Lit *foot* 23:24 [a]Lit *right side* [b]Or *the desert* [A]Josh 15:55; 1 Sam 25:2

22:22 I have brought about. David recognized his responsibility for causing the deaths of the priests' families and animals, acknowledging the devastating consequences of his lie to Ahimelech (cf. 21:1, 2).

23:1 Keilah. A city located in the western foothills of Judah (see Jos 15:44), about 18 mi. SW of Jerusalem and 3 mi. SE of Adullam.

23:2 inquired of the LORD. Such inquiries were made using the sacred lots, the Urim and Thummim, stored in the priestly ephod which Abiathar had brought to David (v. 6). *See note on Ex 28:30.*

23:7 gates and bars. Lit. "two doors and a bar." Keilah perhaps had only one gateway in its wall. Its two reinforced wooden doors had hinged posts at the sides of the entrance, meeting in the center and secured with a heavy bar spanning the entrance horizontally. Since there was only this one way in and out of the city, Saul believed he had David trapped.

23:11 surrender me. David inquired of the Lord again, using the ephod with the Urim and Thummim by which God revealed His will. David wanted to know whether the men of Keilah would be disloyal and surrender him into the hands of Saul. The Lord answered in the affirmative in v. 12.

23:13 men, about six hundred. *See note on 22:2* when David had only 400 men.

23:14 wilderness . . . strongholds. The wilderness of Judah is the barren desert area between the hill country and the Dead Sea. Many ravines and caves are found in this rugged region which David used as a place of refuge from Saul. The title of Ps 63 may refer to this incident or to 2Sa 15:23–28. **wilderness of Ziph.** The wilderness surrounding Ziph, 4 mi. S of Hebron. **God did not deliver him.** God sovereignly protected David from Saul for the fulfilling of His own divine purposes (cf. Is 46:9–11).

23:16, 17 encouraged him in God. Jonathan encouraged David by reminding him of the Lord's promise to him and concern for him, by emphatically assuring him that the Lord would make him the next king over Israel, as Saul well knew (see 20:30, 31).

23:18 covenant. *See notes on 18:3; 20:8.*

23:19 hill of Hachilah. Location unknown, somewhere between Ziph and the Dead Sea. See the title of Ps 54. **Jeshimon.** Another name for the wilderness of Judea.

23:24 wilderness of Maon. The barren territory in the vicinity of Maon (see Jos 15:48, 55), about 5 mi. S of Ziph.

23:25 the rock. A landmark in the wilderness of Maon, soon to be given a name (v. 28).

David, and he came down to the rock and stayed in
the wilderness of Maon. And when Saul heard *it,* he
pursued David in the wilderness of Maon. 26 Saul
went on one side of the mountain, and David and his
men on the other side of the mountain; and David
was hurrying to get away from Saul, for Saul and
his men [A]were surrounding David and his men to
seize them. 27 But a messenger came to Saul, saying,
"Hurry and come, for the Philistines have made a
raid on the land." 28 So Saul returned from pursuing
David and went to meet the Philistines; therefore
they called that place [a]the Rock of Escape. 29 [a]David
went up from there and stayed in the strongholds
of [A]Engedi.

DAVID SPARES SAUL'S LIFE

24 Now [A]when Saul returned from pursuing
the Philistines, [B]he was told, saying, "Behold,
David is in the wilderness of Engedi." 2 Then [A]Saul
took three thousand chosen men from all Israel and
went to seek David and his men in front of the Rocks
of the Wild Goats. 3 He came to the sheepfolds on
the way, where there *was* a cave; and Saul [A]went in
to [a]relieve himself. Now [B]David and his men were
sitting in the inner recesses of the cave. 4 The men
of David said to him, "Behold, [A]*this is* the day of
which the LORD said to you, 'Behold; [B]I am about
to give your enemy into your hand, and you shall
do to him as it seems good [a]to you.' " Then David
arose and cut off the edge of Saul's robe secretly.
5 It came about afterward that [A]David's [a]conscience
bothered him because he had cut off the edge of
Saul's *robe.* 6 So he said to his men, "[A]Far be it from
me because of the LORD that I should do this thing
to my lord, the LORD'S anointed, to stretch out my
hand against him, since he is the LORD'S anointed."
7 David [a]persuaded his men with *these* words and
did not allow them to rise up against Saul. And Saul
arose, [b]left the cave, and went on *his* way.
8 Now afterward David arose and went out of
the cave and called after Saul, saying, "My lord the
king!" And when Saul looked behind him, [A]David
bowed with his face to the ground and prostrated
himself. 9 David said to Saul, "Why do you listen to
the words of men, saying, 'Behold, David seeks [a]to
harm you'? 10 [A]Behold, this day your eyes have seen
that the LORD had given you today into my hand in
the cave, and [B]some said to kill you, but *my eye* had
pity on you; and I said, 'I will not stretch out my
hand against my lord, for he is the LORD'S anointed.'
11 Now, [A]my father, see! Indeed, see the edge of your
robe in my hand! For in that I cut off the edge of
your robe and did not kill you, know and perceive
that there is no evil or [a]rebellion in my hands, and I
have not sinned against you, though you [B]are lying
in wait for my life to take it. 12 [A]May the LORD judge
between [a]you and me, and may the LORD avenge me
on you; but my hand shall not be against you. 13 As
the proverb of the ancients says, '[A]Out of the wicked
comes forth wickedness'; but my hand shall not be
against you. 14 After whom has the king of Israel
come out? Whom are you pursuing? [A]A dead dog,
[B]a single flea? 15 [A]The LORD therefore be judge and
decide between [a]you and me; and may He see and
[B]plead my cause and [b]deliver me from your hand."
16 When David had finished speaking these words
to Saul, Saul said, "[A]Is this your voice, my son David?"
Then Saul lifted up his voice and wept. 17 [A]He said to
David, "You are more righteous than I; for [B]you have
dealt well with me, while I have dealt wickedly with
you. 18 You have declared today that you have done
good to me, that [A]the LORD delivered me into your
hand and *yet* you did not kill me. 19 For if a man [A]finds
his enemy, will he let him go away [a]safely? May the

23:26 [A]Ps 17:9 23:28 [a]Heb *Sela-hammahlekoth* 23:29 [a]Ch 24:1 in Heb [A]Josh 15:62; 2 Chr 20:2 24:1 [A]1 Sam 23:28, 29 [B]1 Sam 23:19 24:2 [A]1 Sam 26:2 24:3 [a]Lit *cover his feet* [A]Judg 3:24 [B]Ps 57: title; 142: title 24:4 [a]Lit *in your sight* [A]1 Sam 23:17; 25:28-30 [B]1 Sam 26:8, 11 24:5 [a]Lit *heart struck* [A]2 Sam 24:10 24:6 [A]1 Sam 26:11 24:7 [a]Lit *tore apart* [b]Lit *from* 24:8 [A]1 Sam 25:23, 24; 1 Kin 1:31 24:9 [a]Lit *your hurt* 24:10 [A]Ps 7:3, 4 [B]1 Sam 24:4 24:11 [a]Lit *transgression* [A]2 Kin 5:13 [B]1 Sam 23:14, 23; 26:20 24:12 [a]Lit *me and you* [A]Gen 16:5; 31:53; Judg 11:27; 1 Sam 26:10, 23 24:13 [A]Matt 7:16-20 24:14 [A]2 Sam 9:8 [B]1 Sam 26:20 24:15 [a]Lit *me and you* [b]Lit *vindicate* [A]1 Sam 24:12 [B]Ps 35:1; 43:1; 119:154; Mic 7:9 24:16 [A]1 Sam 26:17 24:17 [A]1 Sam 26:21 [B]Matt 5:44 24:18 [A]1 Sam 26:23 24:19 [a]Lit *on a good road* [A]1 Sam 23:17

23:26 surrounding David. Saul probably divided his forces into two groups and so surrounded David.

23:27 Philistines have made a raid on the land. Providentially, a messenger came to Saul telling him that the Philistines were invading the land so that he had no choice but to withdraw and postpone his pursuit of David.

23:28 the Rock of Escape. The timely retreat of Saul's men from David's men led to this name.

23:29 Engedi. An oasis on the western shore of the Dead Sea 14 mi. E of Ziph, where there is a fresh water spring and lush vineyards (SS 1:14), standing in stark contrast to the surrounding wilderness. The limestone that dominates this region is permeated with caves, which provided good hiding places for David.

24:2 three thousand chosen men. See 26:2. These were the most skilled soldiers. **Rocks of the Wild Goats.** The location of this cave is unknown, although "wild goats" stresses the inaccessibility of the cave (cf. Job 39:1). See the titles of Pss 57,142, which could also possibly refer to 1Sa 22:1.

24:3 to relieve himself. Lit. "to cover his feet." This is a euphemism for having a bowel movement, as the person would crouch with his inner garment dropped to his feet.

24:4 the day of which the LORD said to you. David's men perhaps believed that God had providentially placed Saul in the same cave where they were hiding so David could kill the king. However, nothing revelatory had previously been said by the Lord that indicated He wanted David to lift a hand against Saul.

24:5 David's conscience bothered him. David was able to cut off a piece of Saul's robe undetected. However, touching Saul's clothing was tantamount to touching his person, and David's conscience troubled him on this account.

24:6 LORD's anointed. David recognized that the Lord Himself had placed Saul into the kingship. Thus the judgment and removal of Saul had to be left to the Lord.

24:11 no evil or rebellion. If David were a wicked rebel against the rule of Saul, as Saul had said (22:8, 13), he would have killed Saul when given this opportunity. The corner of the robe was proof to Saul that David was not his enemy.

24:12 May the LORD judge. David called for the Lord Himself, the only fair and impartial Judge (cf. Jdg 11:27), to decide the fate of David and Saul (also v. 15).

24:13 proverb. A traditional pithy statement that evil deeds are perpetrated only by evil men. A similar point is made by Jesus in Mt 7:16, 20.

24:14 A dead dog, a single flea? David hereby expresses his lowliness and entire committal of his cause to God, who alone is the Judge and to whom alone belongs vengeance.

24:17 You are more righteous than I. Upon hearing David's testimony, Saul was moved with emotion and acknowledged that David was more righteous than he was. His testimony to David's righteousness recognized David's right to the kingship.

LORD therefore reward you with good in return for
what you have done to me this day. 20 Now, behold,
[A]I know that you will surely be king, and that [B]the
kingdom of Israel will be established in your hand.
21 So now [A]swear to me by the LORD that you will not
cut off my [a]descendants after me and that you will
not destroy my name from my father's household."
22 David swore to Saul. And Saul went to his home,
but David and his men went up to [A]the stronghold.

SAMUEL'S DEATH

25 [A]Then Samuel died; and all Israel gathered
together and [B]mourned for him, and [C]buried
him at his house in Ramah. And David arose and
went down to the [D]wilderness of Paran.

NABAL AND ABIGAIL

2 Now *there was* a man in [A]Maon whose business
was in [B]Carmel; and the man was very [a]rich, and he
had three thousand sheep and a thousand goats.
And it came about while [C]he was shearing his sheep
in Carmel 3 (now the man's name was Nabal, and
his [A]wife's name was Abigail. And the woman was
[a]intelligent and beautiful in appearance, but the
man was harsh and evil in *his* dealings, and he was
[B]a Calebite), 4 that David heard in the wilderness
that Nabal was shearing his sheep. 5 So David sent
ten young men; and David said to the young men,
"Go up to Carmel, [a]visit Nabal and greet him in my
name; 6 and thus you shall say, '[a]Have a long life,
[A]peace be to you, and peace be to your house, and
peace be to all that you have. 7 Now I have heard
[A]that you have shearers; now your shepherds have
been with us and we have not insulted them, [B]nor
have they missed anything all the days they were
in Carmel. 8 Ask your young men and they will tell
you. Therefore let *my* young men find favor in your
eyes, for we have come on [A]a [a]festive day. Please
give whatever you find at hand to your servants
and to your son David.' "
9 When David's young men came, they spoke to
Nabal according to all these words in David's name;
then they waited. 10 But Nabal answered David's
servants and said, "[A]Who is David? And who is the
son of Jesse? There are many servants today who
are each breaking away from his master. 11 Shall I
then [A]take my bread and my water and my meat
that I have slaughtered for my shearers, and give
it to men [a]whose origin I do not know?" 12 So David's young men retraced their way and went back;
and they came and told him according to all these
words. 13 David said to his men, "Each *of you* gird
on his sword." So each man girded on his sword.
And David also girded on his sword, and about
[A]four hundred men went up behind David while
two hundred [B]stayed with the baggage.
14 But one of the young men told Abigail, Nabal's
wife, saying, "Behold, David sent messengers from
the wilderness to [a,A]greet our master, and he scorned
them. 15 Yet the men were very good to us, and we
were not [A]insulted, nor did we miss anything [a]as
long as we went about with them, while we were in
the fields. 16 [A]They were a wall to us both by night
and by day, all the time we were with them tending
the sheep. 17 Now therefore, know and [a]consider
what you should do, for evil is plotted against our
master and against all his household; and he is such
a [b]worthless man that no one can speak to him."

ABIGAIL INTERCEDES

18 Then Abigail hurried and [A]took two hundred
loaves of bread and two jugs of wine and five sheep
already prepared and five measures of roasted grain
and a hundred clusters of raisins and two hundred
cakes of figs, and loaded *them* on donkeys. 19 She
said to her young men, "[A]Go on before me; behold,

24:20 [A]1 Sam 23:17 [B]1 Sam 13:14 24:21 [a]Lit *seed* [A]Gen 21:23; 1 Sam 20:14-17; 2 Sam 21:6-8 24:22 [A]1 Sam 23:29 25:1 [A]1 Sam 28:3 [B]Num 20:29; Deut 34:8 [C]2 Kin 21:18; 2 Chr 33:20 [D]Gen 21:21; Num 10:12; 13:3 25:2 [a]Lit *great* [A]1 Sam 23:24 [B]Josh 15:55 [C]Gen 38:13; 2 Sam 13:23 25:3 [a]Lit *of good understanding* [A]Prov 31:10 [B]Josh 15:13; 1 Sam 30:14 25:5 [a]Lit *go into* 25:6 [a]Lit *To life* [A]1 Chr 12:18; Ps 122:7; Luke 10:5 25:7 [A]2 Sam 13:23, 24 [B]1 Sam 25:15, 21 25:8 [a]Lit *good* [A]Neh 8:10-12; Esth 9:19, 22 25:10 [A]Judg 9:28 25:11 [a]Lit *from where they are* [A]Judg 8:6, 15 25:13 [A]1 Sam 23:13 [B]1 Sam 30:24 25:14 [a]Lit *bless* [A]1 Sam 13:10; 15:13 25:15 [a]Lit *all the days* [A]1 Sam 25:7, 21 25:16 [A]Ex 14:22; Job 1:10 25:17 [a]Lit *see* [b]Lit *son of Belial* 25:18 [A]2 Sam 16:1; 1 Chr 12:40 25:19 [A]Gen 32:16, 20

24:20 you will surely be king. Saul emphatically acknowledged that David would be the ruler over the kingdom of Israel. Saul had already been told by Samuel that God would take the kingdom away from him and give it to a man after His own heart (13:14; 15:28). Jonathan had testified that Saul already knew that David would be king (23:17). However, this recognition did not mean that Saul was ready to give up the kingdom.

24:22 David swore to Saul. By solemn oath, David agreed to preserve Saul's family and family name. While most of Saul's family was later slain (2Sa 21:8, 9), this pledge was fulfilled in the life of Mephibosheth (*see note on 2Sa 21:7*).

25:1 all Israel ... mourned for him. The death of Samuel, the last of the judges, brought Israel to the end of an era. So widespread was Samuel's influence among the people that all Israel gathered to lament his death. **wilderness of Paran.** A desert area in the NE region of the Sinai peninsula.

25:2 Carmel. "Vineyard land," "garden spot." About 7 mi. S of Hebron and one mi. N of Maon. This was the same spot where Saul erected a monument in his own honor (15:12).

25:3 Nabal. "Fool." An appropriate name in view of his foolish behavior (v. 25). **Abigail.** "My father is joy." The wife of Nabal who was intelligent and beautiful in contrast to her evil husband. **a Calebite.** Nabal was a descendant of Caleb and lived in Caleb's tribal holdings (Jos 14:13; 15:13), but did not possess the spiritual qualities of his illustrious forefather.

25:4, 5 shearing his sheep. While hiding out in the wilderness, David and his men took the job of protecting the flocks of Nabal (vv. 7, 15, 16). Upon hearing that Nabal was shearing his sheep, David sent 10 of his men to collect their rightful compensation for the good they had done (v. 8).

25:8 a festive day. A special day of rejoicing over the abundance of sheared wool from the sheep (cf. v. 11).

25:10, 11 This pretended ignorance of David was surely a sham. The knowledge of the young king-elect was widespread. Nabal pretended not to know to excuse his unwillingness to do what was right.

25:14 scorned. David sent his messengers to "greet" (lit. "bless") Nabal, but David's men were viciously rebuffed by Nabal. This term emphasized the wickedness of Nabal's action.

25:15, 16 The testimony of one of Nabal's men affirmed the value of David's protection. It was like a fortress "wall" enclosing a city, providing total security.

25:17 no one can speak to him. Nabal was a "son of Belial," a worthless fellow (*see note on 2:12*). Nabal's situation was the product of his own wickedness. His unwillingness to seek the counsel of others ultimately led to his demise.

25:18 five measures. Slightly more than one bu.

25:19 did not tell her husband. Abigail knew that Nabal would disagree with her actions, but knowing the Lord's choice of David (v. 28), she recognized the consequences involved in Nabal's cursing of David. By her actions, she chose to obey God rather than man (see Ac 5:29), as a wife may sometimes need to do.

I am coming after you." But she did not tell her
husband Nabal. 20 It came about as she was riding
on her donkey and coming down by the hidden
part of the mountain, that behold, David and his
men were coming down toward her; so she met
them. 21 Now David had said, "Surely in vain I have
guarded all that this *man* has in the wilderness, so
that nothing was missed of all that belonged to him;
and he has [A]returned me evil for good. 22 [A]May God
do so to the enemies of David, and more also, [B]if by
morning I leave *as much as* one [a]male of any who
belong to him."

23 When Abigail saw David, she hurried and dismounted from her donkey, and fell on her face before David [A]and bowed herself to the ground. 24 She
fell at his feet and said, "On me [a]alone, my lord, be
the blame. And please let your maidservant speak
[b]to you, and listen to the words of your maidservant. 25 Please do not let my lord [a]pay attention to
this [b]worthless man, Nabal, for as his name is, so
is he. [C]Nabal is his name and folly is with him; but
I your maidservant did not see the young men of
my lord whom you sent.

26 "Now therefore, my lord, as the LORD lives, and
as your soul lives, since the LORD has restrained
you from [a]shedding blood, and [A]from [b]avenging
yourself by your own hand, now then [B]let your
enemies and those who seek evil against my lord,
be as Nabal. 27 Now let [A]this [a]gift which your maidservant has brought to my lord be given to the
young men who [b]accompany my lord. 28 Please
forgive [A]the transgression of your maidservant;
for [B]the LORD will certainly make for my lord an
enduring house, because my lord is [C]fighting the
battles of the LORD, and [D]evil will not be found
in you all your days. 29 Should anyone rise up to
pursue you and to seek your [a]life, then the [a]life of
my lord shall be bound in the bundle of the living with the LORD your God; but the [a]lives of your
enemies [A]He will sling out [b]as from the hollow of
a sling. 30 And when the LORD does for my lord
according to all the good that He has spoken concerning you, and [A]appoints you ruler over Israel,
31 this will not [a]cause grief or a troubled heart to
my lord, both by having shed blood without cause
and by my lord having [b]avenged himself. [A]When
the LORD deals well with my lord, then remember
your maidservant."

32 Then David said to Abigail, "[A]Blessed be the
LORD God of Israel, who sent you this day to meet
me, 33 and blessed be your discernment, and blessed
be you, [A]who have kept me this day from [a]bloodshed
and from [b]avenging myself by my own hand. 34 Nevertheless, as the LORD God of Israel lives, [A]who has
restrained me from harming you, unless you had
come quickly to meet me, surely there would not
have been left to Nabal until the morning light *as
much as* one [a]male." 35 So David received from her
hand what she had brought him and said to her,
"[A]Go up to your house in peace. See, I have listened
to [a]you and [b,B]granted your request."

36 Then Abigail came to Nabal, and behold, he was
holding [A]a feast in his house, like the feast of a king.
And Nabal's heart was merry within him, [B]for he
was very drunk; so [C]she did not tell him anything
[a]at all until the morning light. 37 But in the morning,
when the wine had gone out of Nabal, his wife told
him these things, and his heart died within him so
that he became *as* a stone. 38 About ten days later,
[A]the LORD struck Nabal and he died.

DAVID MARRIES ABIGAIL

39 When David heard that Nabal was dead, he
said, "Blessed be the LORD, who has [A]pleaded the
cause of my reproach from the hand of Nabal and
[B]has kept back His servant from evil. The LORD has
also returned the evildoing of Nabal on his own
head." Then David sent [a,C]a proposal to Abigail, to
take her as his wife. 40 When the servants of David came to Abigail at Carmel, they spoke to her,
saying, "David has sent us to you to take you as
his wife." 41 She arose [A]and bowed with her face to
the ground and said, "Behold, your maidservant
is a maid [B]to wash the feet of my lord's servants."
42 Then [A]Abigail quickly arose, and rode on a donkey, with her five maidens who [a]attended her; and
she followed the messengers of David and became
his wife.

43 David had also taken Ahinoam of [A]Jezreel, and
[B]they both became his wives.

25:21 [A]Ps 109:5; Prov 17:13 25:22 [a]Lit *who urinates against the wall* [A]1 Sam 3:17; 20:13 [B]1 Kin 14:10 25:23 [A]1 Sam 20:41 25:24 [a]Lit *even me* [b]Lit *in your ears* 25:25 [a]Lit *set his heart to* [b]Lit *man of Belial* [C]I.e. Fool 25:26 [a]Lit *coming in with blood* [b]Lit *saving* [A]Heb 10:30 [B]2 Sam 18:32 25:27 [a]Lit *blessing* [b]Lit *walk at the feet of* [A]Gen 33:11; 1 Sam 30:26 25:28 [A]1 Sam 25:24 [B]1 Sam 22:14; 2 Sam 7:11, 16 [C]1 Sam 18:17 [D]1 Sam 24:11; Ps 7:3 25:29 [a]Lit *soul* [b]Lit *in the midst* [A]Jer 10:18 25:30 [A]1 Sam 13:14 25:31 [a]Lit *become staggering to you or a stumbling of the heart* [b]Lit *saved* [A]Gen 40:14; 1 Sam 25:30 25:32 [A]Ex 18:10; 1 Kin 1:48; Ps 41:13; 72:18; 106:48; Luke 1:68 25:33 [a]Lit *coming in with blood* [b]Lit *saving* [A]1 Sam 25:26 25:34 [a]Lit *who urinates against the wall* [A]1 Sam 25:26 25:35 [a]Lit *your voice* [b]Lit *lifted up your face* [A]1 Sam 20:42; 2 Kin 5:19 [B]Gen 19:21 25:36 [a]Lit *small or large* [A]2 Sam 13:28 [B]Prov 20:1; Is 5:11; Hos 4:11 [C]1 Sam 25:19 25:38 [A]1 Sam 26:10; 2 Sam 6:7; Ps 104:29 25:39 [a]Lit *and spoke* [A]1 Sam 24:15; Prov 22:23 [B]1 Sam 25:26, 34 [C]Song 8:8 25:41 [A]1 Sam 25:23 [B]Mark 1:7 25:42 [a]Lit *walked at her feet* [A]Gen 24:61-67 25:43 [A]Josh 15:56 [B]1 Sam 27:3; 30:5

25:22 May God do so. A strong oath of self-imprecation. David swore that he would kill every male in Nabal's household by daybreak.

25:25 this worthless man. I.e., "troublemaker." **as his name is, so is he.** A name was not simply a label of distinguishing one thing from another, but a profound insight into the character of the one named. "Fool" has the connotation of one who is "morally deficient."

25:28 an enduring house. Abigail's perceptive insight fit an essential feature of the Davidic Covenant (see 2Sa 7:11–16). **fighting the battles of the LORD.** Unlike the king previously desired by the people (8:20), David was a man who fought the Lord's battles. He was truly God's king.

25:29 bound in the bundle of the living. A metaphor that reflects the custom of binding valuables in a bundle to protect them from injury. The point here was that God cared for His own as a man would his valuable treasure. David, she said, enjoyed the protection of divine providence which destined him for great things. On the other hand, God would fling his enemies away like a stone in a sling-shot.

25:30 ruler over Israel. Abigail was certain that David would exercise effective rule over Israel after Saul's death. In the meantime, however, she did not want him to do anything to jeopardize his future, endanger his throne, or violate God's will by seeking personal vengeance in anger (vv. 26, 33–34).

25:37, 38 heart died ... became *as* a stone. Intoxicated, Nabal apparently suffered a stroke and became paralyzed until he died.

25:43 Ahinoam of Jezreel. David's third wife, joining Michal and Abigail. For Jezreel, *see note on 29:1.*

44 Now Saul had given [A]Michal his daughter, David's wife, to Palti the son of Laish, who was from
[B]Gallim.

DAVID AGAIN SPARES SAUL

26 Then the Ziphites came to Saul at Gibeah, saying, "[A]Is not David hiding on the hill of Hachilah, *which is* before [a]Jeshimon?" 2 So Saul arose
and went down to the wilderness of Ziph, having
with him [A]three thousand chosen men of Israel, to
search for David in the wilderness of Ziph. 3 Saul
camped in the hill of Hachilah, which is before [a]Je-
shimon, [A]beside the road, and David was staying in
the wilderness. When [B]he saw that Saul came after
him into the wilderness, 4 David sent out spies, and
he knew that Saul was definitely coming. 5 David
then arose and came to the place where Saul had
camped. And David saw the place where Saul lay,
and [A]Abner the son of Ner, the commander of his
army; and Saul was lying in the circle of the camp,
and the people were camped around him.
6 Then David said to Ahimelech [A]the Hittite and to
[B]Abishai the son of Zeruiah, Joab's brother, saying,
"Who [C]will go down with me to Saul in the camp?"
And Abishai said, "I will go down with you." 7 So
David and Abishai came to the people by night,
and behold, Saul lay sleeping inside the circle of
the camp with his spear stuck in the ground at his
head; and Abner and the people were lying around
him. 8 Then Abishai said to David, "Today God has
delivered your enemy into your hand; now therefore, please let me strike him with the spear [a]to
the ground with one stroke, and I will not [b]strike
him the second time." 9 But David said to Abishai,
"Do not destroy him, for [A]who can stretch out his
hand against the LORD'S anointed and be without
guilt?" 10 David also said, "As the LORD lives, [A]surely
the LORD will strike him, or [B]his day will come that
he dies, or [C]he will go down into battle and perish.
11 [A]The LORD forbid that I should stretch out my
hand against the LORD'S anointed; but now please
take the spear that is at his head and the jug of
water, and let us go." 12 So David took the spear and
the jug of water from *beside* Saul's head, and they
went away, but no one saw or knew *it,* nor did any
awake, for they were all asleep, because [A]a sound
sleep from the LORD had fallen on them.
13 Then David crossed over to the other side and
stood on top of the mountain at a distance *with*
a large area between them. 14 David called to the
people and to Abner the son of Ner, saying, "Will
you not answer, Abner?" Then Abner replied, "Who
are you who calls to the king?" 15 So David said to
Abner, "Are you not a man? And who is like you in
Israel? Why then have you not guarded your lord
the king? For one of the people came to destroy the
king your lord. 16 This thing that you have done is
not good. As the LORD lives, *all* of you [a,A]must surely
die, because you did not guard your lord, the LORD'S
anointed. And now, see where the king's spear is
and the jug of water that was at his head."
17 Then Saul recognized David's voice and said,
"[A]Is this your voice, my son David?" And David
said, "It is my voice, my lord the king." 18 He also
said, "[A]Why then is my lord pursuing his servant?
For what have I done? Or what evil is in my hand?
19 Now therefore, please let my lord the king listen
to the words of his servant. If [A]the LORD has stirred
you up against me, [B]let Him [a]accept an offering;
but [C]if it is [b]men, cursed are they before the LORD,
for [D]they have driven me out today so that I would
have no attachment with the inheritance of the
LORD, saying, 'Go, serve other gods.' 20 Now then,
do not let my blood fall to the ground away from
the presence of the LORD; for the king of Israel has
come out to search for [A]a single flea, just as one
hunts a partridge in the mountains."
21 Then Saul said, "[A]I have sinned. Return, my
son David, for I will not harm you again because
my life was precious in your sight this day. Behold,
I have played the fool and have committed a serious error." 22 David replied, "Behold the spear of

25:44 [A]1 Sam 18:27; 2 Sam 3:14 [B]Is 10:30 26:1 [a]Or *the desert* [A]1 Sam 23:19; Ps 54: title 26:2 [A]1 Sam 13:2; 24:2 26:3 [a]Or *the desert* [A]1 Sam 24:3 [B]1 Sam 23:15 26:5 [A]1 Sam 14:50, 51; 17:55 26:6 [A]Gen 23:3; 26:34; Josh 3:10; 1 Kin 10:29; 2 Kin 7:6 [B]1 Chr 2:16 [C]Judg 7:10, 11 26:8 [a]Lit *even into* [b]Lit *repeat with respect to him* 26:9 [A]1 Sam 24:6, 7; 2 Sam 1:14, 16 26:10 [A]Deut 32:35; 1 Sam 25:26, 38; Rom 12:19; Heb 10:30 [B]Gen 47:29; Deut 31:14; Ps 37:13 [C]1 Sam 31:6 26:11 [A]1 Sam 24:6, 12; Rom 12:17, 19; 1 Pet 3:9 26:12 [A]Gen 2:21; 15:12; Is 29:10 26:16 [a]Lit *are surely sons of death* [A]1 Sam 20:31 26:17 [A]1 Sam 24:16 26:18 [A]1 Sam 24:9, 11-14 26:19 [a]Lit *smell* [b]Lit *sons of men* [A]2 Sam 16:11 [B]Gen 8:21 [C]1 Sam 24:9 [D]Josh 22:25-27 26:20 [A]1 Sam 24:14 26:21 [A]Ex 9:27; 1 Sam 15:24, 30; 24:17

25:44 Palti ... from Gallim. Palti means "my deliverance." The location of Gallim is unknown, but was probably a few mi. N of Jerusalem. See 2Sa 3:13–16 for Michal's return to David.

26:1 hill of Hachilah ... Jeshimon. *See notes on 23:19.*

26:2 three thousand chosen men. See 24:2.

26:5 Saul lay. Saul was sleeping in an apparently invulnerable place. He had his commander beside him, inside the camp, surrounded by his entire army. **Abner.** *See note on 14:50.*

26:6 Ahimelech the Hittite. Mentioned only here, he was one of the many mercenaries who formed a part of David's army. **Abishai the son of Zeruiah, Joab's brother.** *See note on 2Sa 2:18.* He joined with Ahimelech in going down with David into the camp of Saul.

26:9 the LORD's anointed. *See note on 24:6.*

26:10 As the LORD lives. An oath usually associated with life-or-death matters. The sovereign God would decide when, where, and how Saul would perish, not David.

26:12 spear and the jug. Like the corner of Saul's robe (24:4), these were taken as proof that David had Saul's life in his hand (cf. v. 16). **a sound sleep from the LORD.** As with Adam in Ge 2:21 and Abraham in Ge 15:12, the Lord caused Saul to be unaware of what was taking place around him.

26:19 If the LORD ... if it is men. David set forth two possibilities for why Saul was pursuing him. First, David had sinned against the Lord. If that was the case, he was willing to offer a sacrifice for atonement. Second, evil men had caused Saul's hostility toward David. If that were the case, these men should be judged. **the inheritance of the LORD.** I.e., the land of Israel (cf. 2Sa 20:19; 21:3). **Go, serve other gods.** David's exile from the land was virtually equivalent to forcing him to abandon the worship of the Lord, for there were no sanctuaries to the Lord outside of Israelite territory.

26:20 flea ... partridge. The flea represents something that was worthless and the partridge something that was impossible to catch. Saul was wasting his time with his pursuit of David.

26:21 I have sinned. As in 24:17, Saul confessed his sin and wrongdoing. Although Saul may have been sincere, he could not be trusted and David wisely did not accept his invitation to return with him. **I have played the fool.** Saul had been foolish in his actions toward David, as had Nabal.

the king! Now let one of the young men come over
and take it. 23 [A]The LORD will repay each man *for*
his righteousness and his faithfulness; for the LORD
delivered you into *my* hand today, but [B]I refused to
stretch out my hand against the LORD'S anointed.
24 Now behold, as your life was [A]highly valued in my
sight this day, so may my life be highly valued in the
sight of the LORD, and may He [B]deliver me from all
distress." 25 Then Saul said to David, "[A]Blessed are
you, my son David; you will both accomplish much
and surely prevail." So [B]David went on his way, and
Saul returned to his place.

DAVID FLEES TO THE PHILISTINES

27 Then David said [a]to himself, "Now I will perish one day by the hand of Saul. [A]There is
nothing better for me than [b]to escape into the land
of the Philistines. Saul then will despair of searching
for me anymore in all the territory of Israel, and
I will escape from his hand." 2 So David arose and
crossed over, he and [A]the six hundred men who
were with him, to [B]Achish the son of Maoch, king
of Gath. 3 And David lived with Achish at Gath, he
and his men, [A]each with his household, *even* David
with [B]his two wives, Ahinoam the Jezreelitess, and
Abigail the Carmelitess, Nabal's [a]widow. 4 Now it
was told Saul that David had fled to Gath, so he no
longer searched for him.
5 Then David said to Achish, "If now I have found
favor in your sight, let them give me a place in one
of the cities in the country, that I may live there; for
why should your servant live in the royal city with
you?" 6 So Achish gave him Ziklag that day; therefore
[A]Ziklag has belonged to the kings of Judah to this day.
7 The number of days that David lived in the country of the Philistines was [A]a year and four months.
8 Now David and his men went up and raided [A]the
Geshurites and the Girzites and [B]the Amalekites; for
they were the inhabitants of the land from ancient
times, as you come to [C]Shur even as far as the land
of Egypt. 9 David [a]attacked the land and did not
leave a man or a woman alive, and he [A]took away
the sheep, the cattle, the donkeys, the camels, and
the clothing. Then he returned and came to Achish.
10 Now Achish said, "Where have you [A]made a raid
today?" And David said, "Against the [a]Negev of Judah and against the [a]Negev of [B]the Jerahmeelites
and against the [a]Negev of [C]the Kenites." 11 David did
not leave a man or a woman alive to bring to Gath,
saying, "Otherwise they will tell about us, saying,
'So has David done and so *has been* his practice
all the time he has lived in the country of the Philistines.'" 12 So Achish believed David, saying, "He
has surely made himself odious among his people
Israel; therefore he will become my servant forever."

SAUL AND THE SPIRIT MEDIUM

28 Now it came about in those days that [A]the
Philistines gathered their armed camps for
war, to fight against Israel. And Achish said to David, "Know assuredly that you will go out with me
in the camp, you and your men." 2 David said to
Achish, "Very well, you shall know what your servant can do." So Achish said to David, "Very well, I
will make you [a]my bodyguard [A]for life."
3 Now [A]Samuel was dead, and all Israel had lamented him and buried him [B]in Ramah, his own city.
And Saul had removed from the land those who [C]were

26:23 [A]1 Sam 24:19; Ps 7:8; 18:20; 62:12 [B]1 Sam 24:12 26:24 [A]1 Sam 18:30 [B]Ps 54:7 26:25 [A]1 Sam 24:19 [B]1 Sam 24:22 27:1 [a]Lit *in his heart* [b]Lit *that I should surely escape* [A]1 Sam 26:19 27:2 [A]1 Sam 25:13 [B]1 Sam 21:10; 1 Kin 2:39 27:3 [a]Lit *wife* [A]1 Sam 30:3; 2 Sam 2:3 [B]1 Sam 25:42, 43 27:6 [A]Josh 15:31; 19:5; Neh 11:28 27:7 [A]1 Sam 29:3 27:8 [A]Josh 13:2, 13 [B]Ex 17:8; 1 Sam 15:7, 8 [C]Ex 15:22 27:9 [a]Lit *smote* [A]1 Sam 15:3; Job 1:3 27:10 [a]I.e. South country [A]1 Sam 23:27 [B]1 Sam 30:29; 1 Chr 2:9, 25 [C]Judg 1:16; 4:11 28:1 [A]1 Sam 29:1 28:2 [a]Lit *keeper of my head* [A]1 Sam 1:22, 28 28:3 [A]1 Sam 25:1 [B]1 Sam 7:17 [C]Lev 19:31; 20:27; Deut 18:10; 1 Sam 15:23

26:25 surely prevail. Saul recognized the certain success of David's future as Israel's king (cf. 24:20).

27:1 by the hand of Saul. In direct contrast to Saul's word that David would prevail (26:25), David thought that Saul would ultimately kill him. This anxious thinking and the fear that fell upon him explain David's actions in this chapter. God had told him to stay in Judah (22:5), but he was afraid and sought protection again among the Philistine enemies of Israel (cf. 21:10–15).

27:3 two wives. His third wife, Michal, had been temporarily given to another man by Saul (cf. 25:44).

27:4 no longer searched for him. Saul was no longer able to pursue David since he was out of the land of Israel.

27:5 the royal city. I.e., Gath. David requested a city of his own in the country so that he could be free from the constant surveillance to which he was exposed in Gath, and so that he could avoid the pagan influence of that Philistine city.

27:6 Ziklag. This was a city located about 13 mi. NW of Beersheba that had been an Israelite possession (Jos 15:31; 19:5), but was then under Philistine control. **to this day.** Ziklag became a part of Judah and was still so at the time of the writing of Samuel, which is clearly in the post-Solomonic, divided kingdom era. See Introduction: Author and Date.

27:7 a year and four months. For 16 months David was able to deceive Achish concerning his actions. He remained there until after Saul's death when he moved to Hebron (2Sa 1:1; 2:1, 2).

27:8 Geshurites ... Girzites ... Amalekites. These peoples lived in southern Canaan and northern Sinai. **Shur ... Egypt.** *See note on 15:7.*

27:9 did not leave a man or a woman alive. David left no survivors from his raids in order that Achish might not learn the true nature of his desert exploits (see v. 11).

27:10 Judah ... Jerahmeelites ... Kenites. The regions S of the hill country centering around Beersheba. This region was far enough away from Gath so that Achish would be ignorant of David's movements. David implied to Achish that the hostility of Judah toward David was increasing, while in fact he was gaining the appreciation and loyalty of Judah toward himself by raiding their wilderness neighbors. Achish thought David was more securely his servant as his own people turned against him (vv. 2–4), but just the opposite was true.

28:1 Know assuredly. The kindness showed to David and his men by Achish in Gath was not without expectation of reciprocation. This phrase seems to presuppose an understanding of this expectation.

28:2 what your servant can do. Being a man of honor, David would not fail to help those who had shown him kindness. David was drawing attention to the fact that he had proven himself as a valiant and successful warrior and was assuring Achish of his fidelity and ability. **bodyguard.** In light of David's victory over Goliath (17:49–54) and imagined bad reputation among the Israelites, Achish was expressing considerable trust in David's loyalty and ability, for "bodyguard" lit. means "keeper of my head."

28:3–13 Having deprived himself of every legitimate means of spiritual input as a result of his own disobedience and rebellion, Saul walked in foolishness again by seeking out the very resource (a medium) he had previously removed from the land. Saul swore to the medium an oath of safety by the very God that he was disobeying even then. Yet the inexorable curiosity of Saul to consult Samuel, in spite of Samuel's death, was satisfied by the medium's willingness to "bring up" Samuel.

28:3 mediums and spiritists. By divine law, they were banned from Israel (Dt 18:11), and Israel was not to be defiled by them

mediums and spiritists. 4 So the Philistines gathered
together and came and camped [A]in Shunem; and Saul
gathered all Israel together and they camped in [B]Gil-
boa. 5 When Saul saw the camp of the Philistines, he
was afraid and his heart trembled greatly. 6 [A]When
Saul inquired of the LORD, [B]the LORD did not answer
him, either by [C]dreams or by [D]Urim or by prophets.
7 Then Saul said to his servants, "Seek for me a woman
who is a medium, that I may go to her and inquire of
her." And his servants said to him, "Behold, [A]there is
a woman who is a medium at [B]En-dor."
8 Then Saul [A]disguised himself by putting on
other clothes, and went, he and two men with him,
and they came to the woman by night; and he said,
"[B]Conjure up for me, please, and [C]bring up for me
whom I shall [a]name to you." 9 But the woman said
to him, "Behold, you know [A]what Saul has done,
how he has cut off those who are mediums and
spiritists from the land. Why are you then laying a
snare for my life to bring about my death?" 10 Saul
vowed to her by the LORD, saying, "As the LORD
lives, no punishment shall come upon you for this
thing." 11 Then the woman said, "Whom shall I bring
up for you?" And he said, "Bring up Samuel for me."
12 When the woman saw Samuel, she cried out with
a loud voice; and the woman spoke to Saul, saying,
"Why have you deceived me? For you are Saul." 13 The
king said to her, "Do not be afraid; but what do you
see?" And the woman said to Saul, "I see a [a]divine
being coming up out of the earth." 14 He said to her,
"What is his form?" And she said, "An old man is
coming up, and [A]he is wrapped with a robe." And
Saul knew that it was Samuel, and [B]he bowed with
his face to the ground and did homage.
15 Then Samuel said to Saul, "Why have you disturbed me by bringing me up?" And Saul answered,
"I am greatly distressed; for the Philistines are waging war against me, and [A]God has departed from me
and [B]no longer answers me, either through prophets
or by dreams; therefore I have called you, that you
may make known to me what I should do." 16 Samuel
said, "Why then do you ask me, since the LORD has
departed from you and has become your adversary?
17 The LORD has done [a]accordingly [A]as He spoke
through me; for the LORD has torn the kingdom
out of your hand and given it to your neighbor, to
David. 18 As [A]you did not [a]obey the LORD and did not
execute His fierce wrath on Amalek, so the LORD has
done this thing to you this day. 19 Moreover the LORD
will also give over Israel along with you into the
hands of the Philistines, therefore tomorrow [A]you
and your sons will be with me. Indeed the LORD
will give over the army of Israel into the hands of
the Philistines!"

28:4 [A]Josh 19:18; 1 Sam 28:4; 1 Kin 1:3; 2 Kin 4:8 [B]1 Sam 31:1 28:6 [A]1 Chr 10:13, 14 [B]1 Sam 14:37; Prov 1:24-31 [C]Num 12:6; Joel 2:28 [D]Ex 28:30; Num 27:21 28:7 [A]Acts 16:16 [B]Josh 17:11; Ps 83:10 28:8 [a]Lit *say* [A]2 Chr 18:29; 35:22 [B]1 Chr 10:13; Is 8:19 [C]Deut 18:10, 11 28:9 [A]1 Sam 28:3 28:13 [a]Or *god* 28:14 [A]1 Sam 15:27 [B]1 Sam 24:8 28:15 [A]1 Sam 16:14; 18:12 [B]1 Sam 28:6 28:17 [a]Lit *for himself* [A]1 Sam 15:28 28:18 [a]Lit *listen to the voice of* [A]1 Sam 15:20, 26; 1 Kin 20:42 28:19 [A]1 Sam 31:2; Job 3:17-19

(Lv 19:31). Turning to them was tantamount to playing the harlot and would result in God setting His face against the person and cutting him off from among His people (Lv 20:6). Mediums and spiritists were to be put to death by stoning (Lv 20:27). Even Saul understood this and had previously dealt with the issue (see v. 9).

28:4 Shunem. Situated SW of the hill of Moreh and 16 mi. SW of the Sea of Galilee; the Philistines designated it as their campsite. **Gilboa.** The mountain range beginning 5 mi. S of Shunem and extending southward along the eastern edge of the plain of Jezreel. *See note on 31:1.*

28:5 his heart trembled greatly. Saul had hidden himself when he was chosen by lot to be king (10:22). When the Spirit of the Lord came upon him, he was changed (10:6), but after the Spirit had departed (16:14), he was afraid and dismayed by Goliath (17:11, 24). He feared at Gilgal when faced by the overwhelming size of the Philistine army (13:11, 12). Saul was also afraid of David because he knew that the Lord was with David (18:12, 29). But Saul was to fear God (12:24), not people.

28:6 dreams … Urim … prophets. These were the 3 basic ways through which God revealed His Word and His will. Dreams and visions were the common manner through which the Lord revealed Himself and His will during the time of Moses (Nu 12:6). The Urim was used by the priest as a means of inquiring of the Lord (Nu 27:21). It was originally put in the breastpiece of judgment with the Thummim and worn over Aaron's heart when he went in before the Lord (*see note on Ex 28:30*). Somehow, unknown to us, God revealed His will by it. Prophets were formerly called seers (9:9) and were used as a reference for inquiring of the Lord. God also used prophets to declare His Word when people were not interested in it (Am 7:12, 13). Since Saul had rejected the Lord, God had rejected him (15:23). Saul appears to have had no court prophet in the manner that Gad and Nathan were to David (22:5; 2Sa 12); and, by this time, the ephod with the Urim was in David's possession by virtue of Abiathar the priest (23:6).

28:7 Seek for me .… medium. In Saul's desperation, he sought the very source that he had formerly removed from the land (28:3). In spite of the ban, Saul's servant knew exactly where to find a medium. **En-dor.** Located about 3.5 mi. NW of Shunem between Mt. Tabor and the Hill of Moreh. Saul risked his life by venturing into the Philistine-held territory to seek out the counsel of the medium; thus he went in disguise by night (v. 8).

28:10 vowed to her by the LORD. Though blatantly walking in disobedience to God, it is ironic that Saul would swear by the very existence of the Lord as a means of assuring his credibility to the medium. Even more, Saul swore that no punishment would come upon her when the Levitical law required her to be stoned to death (Lv 20:27).

28:12 the woman saw Samuel. Though questions have arisen as to the nature of Samuel's appearance, the text clearly indicates that Samuel, not an apparition, was evident to the eyes of the medium. God miraculously permitted the actual spirit of Samuel to speak (vv. 16–19). Because she understood her inability to raise the dead in this manner, she immediately knew 1) that it must have been by the power of God and 2) that her disguised inquirer must be Saul.

28:13 divine being coming up out of the earth. The word translated "divine being" is actually the Heb. word meaning "God, gods, angel, ruler, or judge." It can also be used to designate a likeness to one of these. From the medium's perspective, Samuel appeared to be "like a divine being" ascending out of the earth. There is no other such miracle as this in all of Scripture.

28:14 old man … with a robe. Obviously age and clothing do not exist in the realm of the spirits of those who have died, but God miraculously gave such appearances so that Saul was able to perceive that the spirit was Samuel. The question arises whether all believers will remain in the form they were in when they died. Samuel may have been as such simply for the benefit of Saul, or he might be in this state until he receives his resurrection body. Since Scripture teaches that the resurrection of OT saints is yet future (see Dan 12:1, 2), Samuel must have temporarily been in this condition solely for the benefit of Saul.

28:15 disturbed me. Samuel's comment expresses agitation caused by Saul's efforts to contact him since living humanity was not allowed to seek out discussions with the dead (Dt 18:11; Lv 20:6). Witchcraft puts the seeker in contact with demons impersonating those who are being sought, since the dead person cannot ordinarily be contacted, except in this unique case.

28:16, 18 your adversary. See 15:26–35.

28:19 will be with me. This could mean with him in "the abode of the righteous." There is no doubt that Samuel meant this to serve as a premonition of Saul's soon death.

20 Then Saul immediately fell full length upon the
ground and was very afraid because of the words of
Samuel; also there was no strength in him, for he had
eaten no [a]food all day and all night. 21 The woman
came to Saul and saw that he was terrified, and said to
him, "Behold, your maidservant has [a]obeyed you, and
[A]I have [b]taken my life in my hand and have listened
to your words which you spoke to me. 22 So now also,
please listen to the voice of your maidservant, and let
me set a piece of bread before you that *you may* eat
and have strength when you go on *your* way." 23 But
he refused and said, "[A]I will not eat." [B]However, his
servants together with the woman urged him, and he
listened to [a]them. So he arose from the ground and sat
on [C]the bed. 24 The woman had a [A]fattened calf in the
house, and she quickly slaughtered it; and she [B]took
flour, kneaded it and baked unleavened bread from
it. 25 She brought *it* before Saul and his servants, and
they ate. Then they arose and went away that night.

THE PHILISTINES MISTRUST DAVID

29 Now [A]the Philistines gathered together all
their armies to [B]Aphek, while the Israelites
were camping by the spring which is in [C]Jezreel.
2 And the lords of the Philistines were proceeding on by hundreds and by thousands, and [A]David
and his men were proceeding on in the rear with
Achish. 3 Then the commanders of the Philistines
said, "What *are* these Hebrews *doing here?*" And
Achish said to the commanders of the Philistines,
"Is this not David, the servant of Saul the king of
Israel, [A]who has been with me these days, or *rather*
these years, and [B]I have found no fault in him from
the day he [a]deserted *to me* to this day?" 4 But the
commanders of the Philistines were angry with him,
and the commanders of the Philistines said to him,
"Make the man go back, that he may return [A]to his
place where you have assigned him, and do not let
him go down to battle with us, [B]or in the battle he
may become an adversary to us. For with what could
this *man* make himself acceptable to his lord? *Would
it* not *be* with the heads of [a]these men? 5 Is this not
David, [A]of whom they sing in the dances, saying,

'Saul has slain his thousands,
And David his ten thousands'?"

6 Then Achish called David and said to him, "*As*
the LORD lives, you *have been* upright, and [A]your
going out and your coming in with me in the army
are pleasing in my sight; [B]for I have not found evil in
you from the day of your coming to me to this day.
Nevertheless, you are not pleasing in the sight of the
lords. 7 Now therefore return and go in peace, that
you may not displease the lords of the Philistines."
8 David said to Achish, "[A]But what have I done? And
what have you found in your servant from the day
when I came before you to this day, that I may not go
and fight against the enemies of my lord the king?"
9 But Achish replied to David, "I know that you are
pleasing in my sight, [A]like an angel of God; nevertheless [B]the commanders of the Philistines have
said, 'He must not go up with us to the battle.' 10 Now
then arise early in the morning [A]with the servants
of your lord who have come with you, and as soon
as you have arisen early in the morning and have
light, depart." 11 So David arose early, he and his men,
to depart in the morning to return to the land of the
Philistines. And the Philistines went up to Jezreel.

DAVID'S VICTORY OVER THE AMALEKITES

30 Then it happened when David and his men
came to [A]Ziklag on the third day, that [B]the

28:20 [a]Lit *bread* 28:21 [a]Lit *listened to your voice* [b]Lit *put* [A]Judg 12:3; 1 Sam 19:5; Job 13:14 28:23 [a]Lit *their voices* [A]1 Kin 21:4 [B]2 Kin 5:13 [C]Esth 1:6; Ezek 23:41 28:24 [A]Gen 18:7; Luke 15:23, 27, 30 [B]Gen 18:6 29:1 [A]1 Sam 28:1 [B]Josh 12:18; 19:30; 1 Sam 4:1; 1 Kin 20:30 [C]1 Kin 21:1; 2 Kin 9:30 29:2 [A]1 Sam 28:1, 2 29:3 [a]Lit *fell* [A]1 Sam 27:7 [B]1 Sam 27:1-6; 1 Chr 12:19, 20; Dan 6:5 29:4 [a]Lit *those* [A]1 Sam 27:6 [B]1 Sam 14:21 29:5 [A]1 Sam 18:7; 21:11 29:6 [A]2 Sam 3:25; 2 Kin 19:27; Is 37:28 [B]1 Sam 27:8-12; 29:3 29:8 [A]1 Sam 27:10-12 29:9 [A]2 Sam 14:17, 20; 19:27 [B]1 Sam 29:4 29:10 [A]1 Chr 12:19, 22 30:1 [A]1 Sam 29:4, 11 [B]1 Sam 15:7; 27:8-10

28:20 no strength in him. Already afraid with a heart that "trembled greatly" because of the Philistines (v. 5), Saul's fear was so heightened by the words of Samuel that he was completely deprived of strength and vigor, which was reinforced by a lack of nourishment. The woman met his physical needs, and he returned to his camp to await his doom (vv. 21–25).

29:1 gathered ... camping. The Philistines were assembling for battle while the Israelites were still camping by the spring. This picks up the story line originally started in 28:1, but which was sidelined to communicate Saul's encounter with the medium. **Aphek.** Located about 24 mi. N of Gath (cf. 4:1). **Jezreel.** Only a few mi. S of Shunem, and 40 mi. NE of Aphek, Jezreel was N of Mt. Gilboa.

29:3 no fault. David had proven himself as an honorable and righteous man before Achish, who knew that he could trust David.

29:4 he may become an adversary. The Philistine lords were not as willing as Achish to give favor and trust to David. Being very shrewd in their estimation of potential hazards, they realized that he might be feigning loyalty to the Philistines in order to seize a strategic moment in the battle when he could betray and fight against them.

29:5 David, of whom they sing. The fame of David had spread throughout the land. The Philistine lords were no stranger to the skill and the victories that God had given to mighty David.

29:6 *As the LORD lives.* When seeking the highest standard by which to assure David of his credibility, Achish swore by the existence of David's God. It is evident that the pagan world knows of God, but the irony is that their knowledge does not necessarily lead to repentance.

29:8 the enemies of my lord the king. David's fidelity to Achish seemed to be at its climax in this expression of loyalty. David appears to have been fully prepared to do battle on behalf of Achish against his enemies, namely Israel. In light of David's former refusal to stretch out his hand against the Lord's anointed (24:6, 10; 26:9, 11, 21), David might have been capitulating and compromising. He did not inquire of the Lord before going to live with Achish, nor did he inquire of the Lord as to whether he should go out to battle with Achish. On the other hand, it could be that while David gave the appearance of loyalty, he actually believed the Philistines would not let him go out to battle, just as it actually happened (cf. 27:8–12). The providence of God kept David from fighting against the Lord's anointed and his own countrymen.

29:9 an angel of God. The degree to which Achish praised David has led some to believe that his eulogy was merely a formal attempt at flattery.

29:11 Jezreel. This was used to designate both a city about 56 mi. N of Jerusalem as well as the plain of Jezreel, which served as a major battlefield for many nations. The city was situated in the territory of Issachar (Jos 19:18). It was bounded on the N and S by Megiddo and Beth-shean (1Ki 4:12) and on the W and E by Mt. Carmel and Mt. Gilboa.

30:1 Ziklag. Serving as a temporary place of residence for David and his 600 men, Ziklag was located in the Negev and given to David

Amalekites had made a raid on the [a]Negev and on
[C]Ziklag, and had [b]overthrown Ziklag and burned it
with fire; 2 and they took captive the women *and*
all who were in it, both small and great, [a,A]without
killing anyone, and carried *them* off and went their
way. 3 When David and his men came to the city,
behold, it was burned with fire, and their wives
and their sons and their daughters had been taken
captive. 4 Then David and the people who were with
him [A]lifted their voices and wept until there was no
strength in them to weep. 5 Now [A]David's two wives
had been taken captive, Ahinoam the Jezreelitess
and Abigail the [a]widow of Nabal the Carmelite.
6 Moreover David was greatly distressed because
[A]the people spoke of stoning him, for all the people
were [a]embittered, each one because of his sons and
his daughters. But [B]David strengthened himself in
the LORD his God.

7 Then [A]David said to [B]Abiathar the priest, the
son of Ahimelech, "Please bring me the ephod."
So Abiathar brought the ephod to David. 8 [A]David
inquired of the LORD, saying, "[B]Shall I pursue this
band? Shall I overtake them?" And He said to him,
"Pursue, for you will surely overtake them, [C]and you
will surely rescue *all*." 9 So David went, [A]he and the
six hundred men who were with him, and came to
the brook Besor, *where* those left behind remained.
10 But David pursued, he and four hundred men, for
[A]two hundred who were too exhausted to cross the
brook Besor remained *behind*.

11 Now they found an Egyptian in the field and
brought him to David, and gave him bread and he
ate, and they provided him water to drink. 12 They
gave him a piece of fig cake and two clusters of
raisins, and he ate; [A]then his spirit [a]revived. For he
had not eaten bread or drunk water for three days
and three nights. 13 David said to him, "To whom
do you belong? And where are you from?" And he
said, "I am a young man of Egypt, a servant of an
Amalekite; and my master left me behind when I
fell sick three days ago. 14 We made a raid on [A]the
[a]Negev of the Cherethites, and on that which belongs to Judah, and on [B]the [a]Negev of Caleb, and
[C]we burned Ziklag with fire." 15 Then David said to
him, "Will you bring me down to this band?" And
he said, "Swear to me by God that you will not kill
me or deliver me into the hands of my master, and
I will bring you down to this band."

16 When he had brought him down, behold, they
were [a]spread over all the land, [A]eating and drinking
and [b]dancing because of [B]all the great spoil that
they had taken from the land of the Philistines and
from the land of Judah. 17 David [a]slaughtered them
[A]from the twilight [b]until the evening of [c]the next
day; and not a man of them escaped, except four
hundred young men who rode on [B]camels and fled.
18 So David [A]recovered all that the Amalekites had
taken, and [a]rescued his two wives. 19 But nothing of
theirs was missing, whether small or great, sons or
daughters, spoil or anything that they had taken for
themselves; [A]David brought *it* all back. 20 So David
had [a]captured all the sheep and the cattle *which*
the people drove ahead of [b]the *other* livestock, and
they said, "[A]This is David's spoil."

THE SPOILS ARE DIVIDED

21 When [A]David came to the two hundred men
who were too exhausted to follow David, who had
also been left at the brook Besor, and they went out
to meet David and to meet the people who were with
him, then David approached the people and greeted
them. 22 Then all the wicked and worthless men
among those who went with David said, "Because
they did not go with [a]us, we will not give them any

30:1 [a]I.e. South country [b]Lit *smote* [C]1 Sam 27:6, 8 30:2 [a]Lit *they did not kill* [A]1 Sam 27:11 30:4 [A]Num 14:1 30:5 [a]Lit *wife* [A]1 Sam 25:42, 43; 2 Sam 2:2 30:6 [a]Lit *bitter in soul* [A]Ex 17:4; John 8:59 [B]1 Sam 23:16; Ps 18:2; 27:14; 31:24; 71:4, 5; Rom 4:20 30:7 [A]1 Sam 23:6, 9 [B]1 Sam 22:20-23 30:8 [A]1 Sam 23:2, 4; Ps 50:15; 91:15 [B]Ex 15:9 [C]1 Sam 30:18 30:9 [A]1 Sam 27:2 30:10 [A]1 Sam 30:9, 21 30:12 [a]Lit *returned to him* [A]Judg 15:19 30:14 [a]I.e. South country [A]1 Sam 30:1, 16; 2 Sam 8:18; 1 Kin 1:38, 44; Ezek 25:16; Zeph 2:5 [B]Josh 14:13; 15:13; 21:12 [C]1 Sam 30:1 30:16 [a]Lit *left* [b]Lit *keeping a pilgrim-feast* [A]Luke 12:19; 17:27f [B]1 Sam 30:14 30:17 [a]Lit *smote* [b]Lit *even until* [c]Lit *their* [A]1 Sam 11:11 [B]Judg 7:12; 1 Sam 15:3 30:18 [a]Lit *David rescued* [A]Gen 14:16 30:19 [A]1 Sam 30:8 30:20 [a]Lit *taken* [b]Lit *those livestock* [A]1 Sam 30:26-31 30:21 [A]1 Sam 30:10 30:22 [a]Lit *me*

by Achish the king of Gath (27:6). David used it as the base from which he would make raids on the neighboring tribes (27:8–11). **Amalekites.** Reaping the consequences of Saul's failure to utterly destroy the Amalekites (1Sa 15) and David's raids against them (27:8), David and his men were the victims of a successful raid in which the Amalekites took all of their wives and livestock captive before burning Ziklag, their city.

30:6 distressed ... embittered. Arriving home to the reality of their great tragedy caused David immense distress and provoked the wickedness of his men to entertain the treasonous idea of stoning him. Having not inquired of the Lord before his departure to support Achish in battle, David was in need of God's getting his attention. **strengthened himself in the LORD his God.** This was the key to David being a man after God's heart (cf. 1Sa 13:14; Ac 13:22).

30:7 Abiathar brought the ephod. Serving as a source through which one could make direct and specific inquiry into the will of God, the High Priest's ephod, which contained the Urim and Thummim, was sought by David. The distress of the moment drew his focus away from the treasonous thoughts of his men and back to God in his desperation to know what God would have him do.

30:9, 10 brook Besor. David most likely encountered the brook about 13 mi. S of Ziklag. It consisted of seasonal rivers from the area of Beersheba which ran NW and emptied into the Mediterranean. Likely, this was during the latter rains (Jan.-Apr.) and the brook was filled with a rampaging runoff that would account for the soldiers who were unable to cross over.

30:14 Negev of the Cherethites. Benaiah the son of Jehoiada was over the Cherethites and the Pelethites (2Sa 8:18), who are almost always mentioned together. They fled Jerusalem as allies with David (2Sa 15:18), and pursued Sheba the son of Bichri with Joab (2Sa 20:7). They were hand-picked by David to be present at Solomon's anointing as king. The Cherethites appear to have come from Crete, and to have been a part of the king's bodyguard (2Sa 23:20, 23). **Negev of Caleb.** Caleb, the son of Jephunneh, was one of 12 spies chosen to check out the Land, and one of only 2 spies who gave a favorable report (Nu 13:6–30). This was the land assigned to his family (Jos 14:13, 14).

30:16 all the great spoil. The Amalekites had not only what they took from Ziklag, but much more plunder from all their raids. After David conquered the Amalekites (vv. 17, 18) he returned what belonged to Ziklag (vv. 19, 26) and spread the rest all over Judah (vv. 26–31).

30:17 four hundred young men. It is obvious from Moses' encounter (Ex 17:8–16), Saul's failure (1Sa 15), and Mordecai's opposition (Est 3:1, 10–13) that the Amalekites were wicked people who hated God's people and died hard.

30:19 nothing ... was missing. In spite of David's previous failures, God showed Himself to be more than gracious and abundant in His stewardship of the wives, children, livestock, and possessions of David and his men.

30:22 worthless men. From the beginning of David's flight from Saul, he became captain of those who were in distress, discontent, and in debt (22:2), the least likely to exercise kindness and grace to others. This same expression

of the spoil that we have recovered, except to every
man his wife and his children, that they may lead
them away and depart." 23 Then David said, "You
must not do so, my brothers, with what the LORD
has given us, who has kept us and delivered into
our hand the band that came against us. 24 And who
will listen to you in this matter? For [A]as his share is
who goes down to the battle, so shall his share be
who stays by the baggage; they shall share alike."
25 So it has been from that day forward, that he made
it a statute and an ordinance for Israel to this day.

26 Now when David came to Ziklag, he sent *some*
of the spoil to the elders of Judah, to his friends,
saying, "Behold, [A]a [a]gift for you from the spoil of
[B]the enemies of the LORD: 27 to those who were in
[A]Bethel, and to those who were in [B]Ramoth of the
[a]Negev, and to those who were in [C]Jattir, 28 and to
those who were in [A]Aroer, and to those who were
in Siphmoth, and to those who were in [B]Eshtemoa,
29 and to those who were in Racal, and to those
who were in the cities of [A]the Jerahmeelites, and to
those who were in the cities of [B]the Kenites, 30 and to
those who were in [A]Hormah, and to those who were
in [B]Bor-ashan, and to those who were in Athach,
31 and to those who were in [A]Hebron, and to all the
places where David himself and his men were accustomed to [B]go."

SAUL AND HIS SONS SLAIN

31 [A]Now the Philistines were fighting against
Israel, and the men of Israel fled from before
the Philistines and fell slain [B]on Mount Gilboa. 2 The
Philistines overtook Saul and his sons; and the Philistines [a]killed [A]Jonathan and Abinadab and Malchi-shua the sons of Saul. 3 [A]The battle went heavily
against Saul, and the archers [a]hit him; and he was
badly wounded by the archers. 4 [A]Then Saul said to
his armor bearer, "Draw your sword and pierce me
through with it, otherwise [B]these uncircumcised
will come and pierce me through and make sport
of me." But his armor bearer would not, for he was
greatly afraid. [C]So Saul took his sword and fell on
it. 5 When his armor bearer saw that Saul was dead,
he also fell on his sword and died with him. 6 Thus
Saul died with his three sons, his armor bearer, and
all his men on that day together.

7 When the men of Israel who were on the other
side of the valley, with those who were beyond the
Jordan, saw that the men of Israel had fled and
that Saul and his sons were dead, they abandoned
the cities and fled; then the Philistines came and
lived in them.

8 It came about on the [a]next day when the Philistines came to strip the slain, that they found Saul
and his three sons fallen on Mount Gilboa. 9 They
cut off his head and stripped off his weapons, and
sent *them* [a]throughout the land of the Philistines, [A]to
carry the good news [B]to the house of their idols and
to the people. 10 They put his weapons in the [a]temple
of [A]Ashtaroth, and [B]they fastened his body to the
wall of [C]Beth-shan. 11 Now when [A]the inhabitants of
Jabesh-gilead heard [a]what the Philistines had done

30:24 [A]Num 31:27; Josh 22:8 30:26 [a]Lit *blessing* [A]1 Sam 25:27 [B]1 Sam 18:17; 25:28 30:27 [a]I.e. South country [A]Gen 12:8; Josh 7:2; 8:9; 16:1 [B]Josh 19:8 [C]Josh 15:48; 21:14 30:28 [A]Josh 13:16; 1 Chr 11:44 [B]Josh 15:50 30:29 [A]1 Sam 27:10 [B]Judg 1:16; 1 Sam 15:6 30:30 [A]Num 14:45; 21:3; Josh 12:14; 15:30; 19:4; Judg 1:17 [B]Josh 15:42; 19:7 30:31 [A]Num 13:22; Josh 14:13-15; 21:11-13; 2 Sam 2:1 [B]1 Sam 23:22 31:1 [A]1 Chr 10:1-12 [B]1 Sam 28:4 31:2 [a]Lit *smote* [A]1 Chr 8:33f 31:3 [a]Lit *found* [A]2 Sam 1:6 31:4 [A]Judg 9:54; 1 Chr 10:4 [B]Judg 14:3; 1 Sam 14:6; 17:26, 36 [C]2 Sam 1:6, 10 31:8 [a]Lit *morrow* 31:9 [a]Lit *into...around* [A]2 Sam 1:20 [B]Judg 16:23, 24 31:10 [a]Lit *house* [A]Judg 2:13; 1 Sam 7:3 [B]1 Sam 31:12; 2 Sam 21:12 [C]Josh 17:11 31:11 [a]Lit *about him what* [A]1 Sam 11:1-13

was used of the sons of Eli (2:12), of those who doubted Saul's ability as king (10:27), of Nabal the fool by his servant (25:17), of Nabal the fool by his wife (25:25), of David when he was cursed by Shimei (2Sa 16:7), of Sheba the son of Bichri who led a revolt against David (2Sa 20:1), and of those who would be thrust away like thorns by David (2Sa 23:6).

30:25 a statute and an ordinance. In spite of the opposition David received from the worthless men among him, he legislated his practice of kindness and equity into law for the people.

30:26–31 Being no stranger to adversity and a life lived on the run, David realized the important role that so many others had played in his safety and welfare. Being the recipient of such kindness, David missed no opportunity to reciprocate kindness and generosity. It would be presumptuous to think that David was merely paying off debts or buying support; rather he was giving back as he had received, expressing his debt of gratitude for the kindness and support shown him. *See note on 30:16.*

31:1–13 See 2Sa 1:4–12; 1Ch 10:1–12.

31:1 Mount Gilboa. Formerly the site of the Israeli camp, it was turned into the sight of the Israeli massacre. Saul and his sons lost their lives on Mt. Gilboa. *See note on 28:4.*

31:2 Jonathan and Abinadab and Malchi-shua. Three of the 4 sons of Saul were killed the same day in battle. The fourth son, Esh-baal, would later be referred to as Ish-bosheth, meaning "man of shame," an appropriate designation in light of his apparent absence from the battlefield (cf. 2Sa 2:8ff.). Jonathan, Ishvi, and Malchi-shua were named as Saul's sons in 14:49, but Jonathan, Abinadab, and Malchi-shua are named here; Ishvi and Abinadab are thus one and the same. First Chronicles 8:33 and 9:39 are the only verses naming all 4 sons.

31:4 these uncircumcised. A common term of derision used among Israelites to designate non-Israelites. Circumcision was given as the sign of the Abrahamic Covenant in Ge 17:10–14. *See note on 14:6.* **make sport.** Having engaged in several battles against the Philistines, Saul had succeeded in provoking their hatred and resentment. As the king, Saul had certainly received especially cruel treatment from the hands of his enemies, who would have likely made sport of him and tortured him before his death. **Saul took his sword and fell on it.** Though Saul's suicide is considered by some to be an act of heroism, Saul should have found his strength and courage in God as David did in 23:16 and 30:6 to fight to the end or to surrender. Saul's suicide is the ultimate expression of his faithlessness towards God at this moment in his life.

31:6 all his men. The question is whether "all" was used in a qualified sense or in an absolute sense. In consideration of the context, the meaning was most likely intended to be qualified, not absolute. It is not necessary to conclude that every single one of Saul's 3,000 men died that day and that none escaped. Where such a meaning is intended, the text usually provides more reinforcement, as in Jos 8:22 where the author specifically states, "and they slew them until no one was left of those who survived or escaped." In fact, Abner, the general of Saul's army, survived (2Sa 2:8). "All" here means those who were personally assigned to Saul's special guard (cf. 31:7).

31:9 cut off his head. There is a parallelism between the death of Saul and the death of Goliath. The giant champion of the Philistines had his head cut off by David, and the Philistines fled (17:51). The Philistines had taken revenge and done likewise to the giant champion of Israel, King Saul, who was "taller than any of the people from his shoulders upward" (10:23).

31:10 Ashtaroth. These were the fertility goddesses of the Canaanites, to whom the Philistines gave homage by placing the weapons of their defeated foe in the temple of Ashtaroth. As the sword of Goliath was put in the house of the Lord behind the ephod (1Sa 21:9), so the weapons of Saul were taken by the Philistines and put in the temple of Ashtaroth. Military victory was attributed to the gods, since the belief was that military encounters were battles between the deities of rival nations. **Beth-shan.** Located in the Jordan Valley about 16 mi. S of the Sea of Galilee.

31:11 Jabesh-gilead. Located E of the Jordan, its people stayed out of the war against Benjamin and suffered severe consequences

to Saul, 12 [A]all the valiant men rose and walked all night, and took the body of Saul and the bodies of his sons from the wall of Beth-shan, and they came to Jabesh and [B]burned them there. 13 They took their bones and [A]buried them under [B]the tamarisk tree at Jabesh, and [C]fasted seven days.

31:12 [A]2 Sam 2:4-7 [B]2 Chr 16:14 31:13 [A]2 Sam 21:12-14 [B]1 Sam 22:6 [C]2 Sam 1:12

as a result (Jdg 21). The men of Jabesh-gilead showed kindness and respect to Saul, a Benjamite, by rescuing his body from the wall of Beth-shan because Saul and his sons had saved Jabesh-gilead from the Ammonites (11:9–12) just after he had been chosen as king of Israel. By this act, they honored Saul for his faithfulness to them.

31:12 bodies ... burned. In light of Saul's head having been cut off and the mutilation that had taken place, it is thought that the citizens of Jabesh-gilead burned his body to hide the damage.

31:13 bones ... buried. It was considered disrespectful not to bury the dead. Abraham went to great lengths to bury Sarah (Ge 23:4–15), and Jacob made Joseph swear that he would not bury him in Egypt (Ge 47:29, 30). fasted seven days. In relation to death, fasting was often associated with mourning in the Hebrew culture. It was a sign of respect, seriousness, and grief. First Samuel began with the ark of the covenant being captured by the Philistines (1Sa 4:11), and in the end Israel's king had been killed by them. Second Samuel will recount how God vindicated His honor by David's defeating the Philistines (2Sa 5:17–25), establishing an uncontested kingdom (1Ki 2:12), and safely bringing the ark to Jerusalem, the city of God (2Sa 6:16–19).

David's Triumphs and Troubles

David's Triumphs In 2 Samuel	
David's Wise Actions	**David's Victories**
· David prayed for guidance (2:1). · David punished the assassins of his enemy Ish-bosheth (4:12). · David prayed for God's deliverance (5:19). · David brought the ark to Jerusalem (6:12). · David offered sacrifices to God and blessed the people (6:18). · David praised God for His goodness (7:18–24; 22:1–4). · David confessed his sins (12:13; 24:10).	· The Judeans anointed David king (2:4). · The Israelites anointed David king (5:3). · David conquered Jerusalem (5:6, 7). · God promised David an eternal dynasty (7:16). · David's army defeated the Philistines (8:1). · David's army defeated the Moabites (8:2). · David's army defeated the Arameans (8:6). · David's army defeated the Ammonites (11:1).
David's Troubles In 2 Samuel	
David's Unwise Actions	**David's Reverses**
· David seduced Bathsheba (11:4). · David ordered the murder of Uriah (11:15, 17). · David failed to forgive Absalom or instruct him (13:39; 14:24). · David ordered that a census be taken of the Israelites (24:2).	· Bathsheba became pregnant (11:5). · David and Bathsheba's child died (12:18). · Amnon seduced Tamar (13:14). · Absalom murdered Amnon (13:29). · Absalom usurped the throne (16:15). · A plague ravaged the Israelites (24:15).

THE SECOND BOOK OF SAMUEL

INTRODUCTION

See 1 Samuel for the Introductory Discussion.

OUTLINE

I. The Reign of David as King over Israel (1:1–20:26)

A. David's Accession to Kingship over Judah (1:1–3:5)
   1. The deaths of Saul and Jonathan (1:1–27)
   2. David anointed by Judah (2:1–7)
   3. David's victories over the house of Saul (2:8–3:1)
   4. David's wives/sons in Hebron (3:2–5)

B. David's Accession to Kingship over Israel (3:6–5:16)
   1. The deaths of Abner and Ish-bosheth (3:6–4:12)
   2. David anointed by all Israel (5:1–5)
   3. David's conquest of Jerusalem (5:6–12)
   4. David's wives/sons in Jerusalem (5:13–16)

C. David's Triumphal Reign (5:17–8:18)
   1. David's victories over the Philistines (5:17–25)
   2. David's spiritual victories (6:1–7:29)
   3. David's victories over the Philistines, Moabites, Arameans, and Edomites (8:1–18)

D. David's Troubled Reign (9:1–20:26)
   1. David's kindness to Mephibosheth (9:1–13)
   2. David's sins of adultery and murder (10:1–12:31)
   3. David's family troubles (13:1–14:33)
      a. The rape of Tamar (13:1–22)
      b. The murder of Amnon (13:23–39)
      c. The recall and return of Absalom (14:1–33)
   4. The rebellions against David (15:1–20:26)
      a. The rebellion of Absalom (15:1–19:43)
      b. The rebellion of Sheba (20:1–26)

II. Epilogue (21:1–24:25)

A. The Lord's Judgment against Israel (21:1–14)
B. David's Heroes (21:15–22)
C. David's Song of Praise (22:1–51)
D. David's Last Words (23:1–7)
E. David's Mighty Men (23:8–39)
F. The Lord's Judgment against David (24:1–25)

DAVID LEARNS OF SAUL'S DEATH

1 Now it came about after [A]the death of Saul, when
David had returned from [B]the slaughter of the
Amalekites, that David remained two days in Ziklag.
2 On the third day, behold, [A]a man came out of the
camp from Saul, [B]with his clothes torn and [a]dust
on his head. And it came about when he came to
David that [C]he fell to the ground and prostrated
himself. 3 Then David said to him, "From where do
you come?" And he said to him, "I have escaped
from the camp of Israel." 4 David said to him, "[A]How
did things go? Please tell me." And he said, "The
people have fled from the battle, and also many of
the people have fallen and are dead; and Saul and
Jonathan his son are dead also." 5 So David said to
the young man who told him, "How do you know
that Saul and his son Jonathan are dead?" 6 The
young man who told him said, "By chance I happened to be on [A]Mount Gilboa, and behold, [B]Saul
was leaning on his spear. And behold, the chariots
and the horsemen pursued him closely. 7 When he
looked behind him, he saw me and called to me.
And I said, 'Here I am.' 8 He said to me, 'Who are
you?' And I [a]answered him, '[A]I am an Amalekite.'
9 Then he said to me, 'Please stand beside me and kill
me, for agony has seized me because my [a]life still
lingers in me.' 10 So I stood beside him [A]and killed
him, because I knew that he could not live after he
had fallen. And [B]I took the crown which *was* on his
head and the bracelet which *was* on his arm, and
I have brought them here to my lord."
11 Then [A]David took hold of his clothes and tore
them, and *so* also *did* all the men who *were* with
him. 12 They mourned and wept and [A]fasted until
evening for Saul and his son Jonathan and for the
people of the LORD and the house of Israel, because
they had fallen by the sword. 13 David said to the
young man who told him, "Where are you from?"
And he [a]answered, "[A]I am the son of an alien, an
Amalekite." 14 Then David said to him, "How is it you
were not afraid [A]to stretch out your hand to destroy
the LORD'S anointed?" 15 And David called one of the
young men and said, "Go, [a]cut him down." [A]So he
struck him and he died. 16 David said to him, "[A]Your
blood is on your head, for [B]your mouth has testified against you, saying, 'I have killed the LORD'S
anointed.' "

DAVID'S DIRGE FOR SAUL AND JONATHAN

17 Then David [A]chanted with this lament over Saul
and Jonathan his son, 18 and he told *them* to teach
the sons of Judah *the song of* the bow; behold, it is
written in [A]the book of Jashar.

1:1 [A]1 Sam 31:6 [B]1 Sam 30:1, 17, 26 1:2 [a]Lit *ground* [A]2 Sam 4:10 [B]1 Sam 4:12 [C]1 Sam 25:23 1:4 [A]1 Sam 4:16 1:6 [A]1 Sam 28:4; 31:1-6; 1 Chr 10:4-10 [B]1 Sam 31:2-4 1:8 [a]Lit *said to* [A]1 Sam 15:3; 30:1, 13, 17 1:9 [a]Lit *whole life is still in me* 1:10 [A]Judg 9:54 [B]2 Kin 11:12 1:11 [A]Gen 37:29, 34; Josh 7:6; 2 Chr 34:27; Ezra 9:3 1:12 [A]2 Sam 3:35 1:13 [a]Lit *said* [A]2 Sam 1:8 1:14 [A]1 Sam 24:6; 26:9, 11, 16 1:15 [a]Lit *fall upon him* [A]2 Sam 4:10, 12 1:16 [A]1 Sam 26:9; 2 Sam 3:28, 29; 1 Kin 2:32 [B]2 Sam 1:10; Luke 19:22 1:17 [A]2 Chr 35:25 1:18 [A]Josh 10:13

1:1–3:5 David ascends to the kingship of Judah.

1:1 the death of Saul. Second Samuel 1:1–14 begins where 1Sa 31:1–13 ends, with the death of Saul (cf. 1Ch 10:1–12). **Amalekites.** The mention of these people serves as a reminder of David's obedience to the Lord (1Sa 30:1–31) and Saul's disobedience (1Sa 15:1–33). *See notes on Ex 17:8–16.* **Ziklag.** *See notes on 1Sa 27:6; 30:1.* This town was not so completely sacked and destroyed that David and his 600 men with their families could not stay there.

1:2 clothes torn and dust on his head. This was a common cultural sign of anguish and mourning over a death. Cf. 15:32; 1Sa 4:12.

1:4–12 See 1Sa 31:1–13; 1Ch 10:1–12.

1:6 chariots and the horsemen. Chariots and horsemen were a symbol of power and strength (cf. Ex 14:9; 1Sa 8:11; 13:5; 2Sa 8:4; 1Ki 4:26; 9:19; 10:26; 1Ch 19:6; 2Ch 1:14; 9:25; 12:3; 16:8; Da 11:40). The Philistines were in pursuit of Saul with an abundant number of warriors, making Saul's escape hopeless.

1:8 Amalekite. The man claiming to have killed Saul was from among the people whom David recently slaughtered (v. 1), whom God wanted eliminated (Ex 17:14; 1Sa 15:3), and who would plague Israel for generations (Ex 17:16) due to Saul's disobedience (1Sa 15:9–11).

1:10 killed him. The Amalekite claimed responsibility for Saul's death, saying that Saul was still alive when he found him. However, 1Sa 31:3–6 makes it clear that Saul died by falling on his own sword, not by the hand of the Amalekite. Thus, this man, who may have witnessed Saul's suicide, claimed to have killed Saul when in reality he had only reached his body before the Philistines and had fabricated the story to ingratiate himself with the new king by killing his enemy and by bringing Saul's crown and bracelet to David. The crown and bracelet in the hands of the Amalekite show that he was the first to pass by the body of Saul.

1:12 mourned and wept and fasted. David demonstrates genuine, heartfelt grief for the death of Saul and Jonathan by mourning and weeping, as well as fasting, which were common ways to demonstrate grief (cf. Est 4:3; Joel 2:12).

1:14 the LORD's anointed. Despite Saul's many attempts on David's life, David would not allow himself to see Saul as just a mere man or human monarch; he remained "the LORD's anointed," who occupied a sacred role before God (cf. 1Sa 24:1–15; 26:1–20).

1:15 cut him down. This most certainly came as a great surprise to the Amalekite, for he intended to win the favor of David by saying he had killed Saul. This story is very similar to that of the men who later killed Ish-bosheth, thinking they would be able to endear themselves to David (4:5–12).

1:16 Your blood is on your head. David executed the Amalekite on the basis of his own testimony, not on the basis of the truthfulness of his story.

1:17 lament. David chose to have both Saul and his noble son Jonathan remembered through this lament, which would be taught to all Israel as a national war song.

1:18 *the song of* the bow. This was the title of the poem in which the word "bow" may have been chosen with reference to Jonathan, whose bow is mentioned in v. 22. **book of Jashar.** A poetic collection of Israel's wars in which Israel's events and great men were commemorated (cf. Jos 10:13).

PLOT DEVELOPMENT OF 2 SAMUEL

Time period	Theme	Biblical References
7 years in Hebron	David's Political Triumphs	1:1—5:25
33 years in Jerusalem	David's Spiritual Triumphs	6:1—7:29
	David's Military Triumphs	8:1—10:19
	David's Transgressions	11:1–27
	Troubles in David's House	12:1—13:36
	Troubles in David's Kingdom	13:37—24:25

19 "[a]Your beauty, O Israel, is slain
on your high places!
[A]How have the mighty fallen!
20 "[A]Tell *it* not in Gath,
Proclaim it not in the streets of Ashkelon,
Or [B]the daughters of the
Philistines will rejoice,
The daughters of [C]the
uncircumcised will exult.
21 "[A]O mountains of Gilboa,
[B]Let not dew or rain be on you,
nor fields of offerings;
For there the shield of the
mighty was defiled,
The shield of Saul, not
[C]anointed with oil.
22 "[A]From the blood of the slain, from
the fat of the mighty,
[B]The bow of Jonathan did not turn back,
And the sword of Saul did
not return empty.
23 "Saul and Jonathan, beloved and
pleasant in their life,
And in their death they were not parted;
[A]They were swifter than eagles,
[B]They were stronger than lions.
24 "O daughters of Israel, weep over Saul,
Who clothed you luxuriously in scarlet,
Who put ornaments of gold
on your apparel.
25 "[A]How have the mighty fallen in
the midst of the battle!
Jonathan is slain on your high places.
26 "I am distressed for you, my
brother Jonathan;
You have been very pleasant to me.
[A]Your love to me was more wonderful
Than the love of women.
27 "[A]How have the mighty fallen,
And [B]the weapons of war perished!"

DAVID MADE KING OVER JUDAH

2 Then it came about afterwards that [A]David
inquired of the LORD, saying, "Shall I go up
to one of the cities of Judah?" And the LORD said
to him, "Go up." So David said, "Where shall I go
up?" And He said, "[B]To Hebron." 2 So David went
up there, and [A]his two wives also, Ahinoam the
Jezreelitess and Abigail the [a]widow of Nabal the
Carmelite. 3 And [A]David brought up his men who
were with him, each with his household; and they
lived in the cities of Hebron. 4 Then the men of
Judah came and there [A]anointed David king over
the house of Judah.
And they told David, saying, "It was [B]the men
of Jabesh-gilead who buried Saul." 5 David sent
messengers to the men of Jabesh-gilead, and said
to them, "[A]May you be blessed of the LORD because
you have [a]shown this kindness to Saul your lord,
and have buried him. 6 Now [A]may the LORD [a]show
lovingkindness and truth to you; and I also will
[a]show this goodness to you, because you have
done this thing. 7 Now therefore, let your hands
be strong and be [a]valiant; for Saul your lord is dead,
and also the house of Judah has anointed me king
over them."

1:19 [a]Lit *The* [A]2 Sam 1:25, 27 1:20 [A]1 Sam 31:8-13; Mic 1:10 [B]Ex 15:20, 21; 1 Sam 18:6 [C]1 Sam 14:6 1:21 [A]1 Sam 31:1 [B]Ezek 31:15 [C]Is 21:5 1:22 [A]Deut 32:42; Is 34:6 [B]1 Sam 18:4 1:23 [A]Jer 4:13 [B]Judg 14:18 1:25 [A]2 Sam 1:19, 27 1:26 [A]1 Sam 18:1-4 1:27 [A]2 Sam 1:19, 25 [B]Is 13:5 2:1 [A]1 Sam 23:2, 4, 9-12 [B]Josh 14:13; 1 Sam 30:31 2:2 [a]Lit *wife* [A]1 Sam 25:42, 43 2:3 [A]1 Sam 30:9; 1 Chr 12:1 2:4 [A]1 Sam 16:13; 2 Sam 5:3, 5 [B]1 Sam 31:11-13 2:5 [a]Lit *done* [A]1 Sam 23:21; Ps 115:15 2:6 [a]Lit *do* [A]Ex 34:6; 2 Tim 1:16 2:7 [a]Lit *sons of valor*

1:19 Your beauty, O Israel. Lit. the gazelle or antelope of Israel, the chosen symbol of youthful elegance and symmetry, most likely referring to Jonathan. Thus, the song began and ended with Saul's noble son (vv. 25, 26). **high places.** These were open-air worship sites generally established at high elevations. In this case the high place was Mt. Gilboa, where Saul had died. **How have the mighty fallen!** They were not only Israel's slain "beauty," but Saul and Jonathan were mighty men who had fallen in battle. This phrase is repeated as a refrain in vv. 25 and 27.

1:20 Gath … Ashkelon. Two chief cities which together could represent all of the Philistine territory. Gath was situated in the eastern part of the Philistine territory, while Ashkelon was in the W by the sea. David did not want the Philistines to rejoice at the calamities of Israel as Israel had rejoiced at the defeat of the Philistines (1Sa 18:7).

1:21 not dew or rain. David spoke a curse, seeking the absence of dew or rain upon the mountain where Saul and Jonathan died. **not anointed with oil.** It was necessary in those times to anoint a shield with oil (cf. Is 21:5) to prevent the leather from being hard and cracked. But there on Mt. Gilboa lay the shield of Saul dried out, a symbol of defeat and death.

1:22 bow … sword. These two weapons were used by Saul and Jonathan with much power, accuracy, and effectiveness. It was also with the bow that Jonathan helped David escape Saul's wrath (1Sa 20:35–42).

1:23 beloved. This generous commendation, including Saul who was seeking to kill David, showed David's gracious, forgiving attitude—a model of gracious love (cf. Mt 5:43–48).

1:26 more wonderful than the love of women. The bond between David and Jonathan was strong. However, this does not mean that their friendship was necessarily superior to the bond of love between a man and a woman. The commitment shared between the two of them was a noble, loyal, and selfless devotion (cf. 1Sa 18:3), which neither of them had ever felt for a woman. Unlike love between a man and a woman in which a sexual element is part of the strong attraction, this love between these two men had no such sexual feature, yet was compellingly strong.

1:27 weapons of war. A figurative expression referring to Saul and Jonathan.

2:1 David inquired of the LORD. After the death of Saul, David could move about the land freely as the Lord directed him. A contrast can be seen between Saul, who had inquired of the Lord and the Lord would not answer (cf. 1Sa 28:6) and David, who also inquired of the Lord and the Lord gave him direction. **cities of Judah.** David sought guidance from the Lord as to where to start his reign. David first asked if he should begin in the southern area of Judah. The Lord responded affirmatively, and thus David sought for a more precise destination. The nucleus of David's future government would come from the cities of Judah. **Hebron.** With the highest elevation of any town in Judah, the city was strategically chosen to be the initial location of David's rule over Israel. Hebron is located 20 mi. SSW of Jerusalem. Abraham had located there long before (Ge 13:18), and later Hebron had been given to Caleb (Jos 14:13, 14; Jdg 1:20) when Israel occupied the land after the wilderness wanderings.

2:2 Ahinoam … Abigail. Abigail became David's wife after the death of Nabal (cf. 1Sa 25:40–44).

2:4 anointed David king. David had already been privately anointed king by Samuel (cf. 1Sa 16:3). This anointing recognized his rule in the southern area of Judah. Later he would be anointed as king over all Israel (cf. 2Sa 5:3). **men of Jabesh-gilead.** Jabesh, a city of Israel E of the Jordan, demonstrated its loyalty to Saul by giving him a proper burial (cf. 1Sa 31:11–13).

2:7 Saul your lord is dead. David referred to Saul as "your lord" so as not to antagonize the men of Jabesh-gilead. He sought to win Israel over to his side, not force them into submission.

ISH-BOSHETH MADE KING OVER ISRAEL

8 But [A]Abner the son of Ner, commander of Saul's
army, had taken [a]Ish-bosheth the son of Saul and
brought him over to [B]Mahanaim. 9 He made him
king over [A]Gilead, over the [B]Ashurites, over [C]Jez-
reel, over Ephraim, and over Benjamin, even over
all Israel. 10 Ish-bosheth, Saul's son, was forty years
old when he became king over Israel, and he was
king for two years. The house of Judah, however,
followed David. 11 [A]The [a]time that David was king
in Hebron over the house of Judah was seven years
and six months.

CIVIL WAR

12 Now Abner the son of Ner, went out from Mahanaim to [A]Gibeon with the servants of Ish-bosheth
the son of Saul. 13 And [A]Joab the son of Zeruiah and
the servants of David went out and met [a]them by
the pool of Gibeon; and they sat down, [b]one on the
one side of the pool and [b]the other on the other
side of the pool. 14 Then Abner said to Joab, "Now
let the young men arise and [a,A]hold a contest before us." And Joab said, "Let them arise." 15 So they
arose and went over by count, twelve for Benjamin
and Ish-bosheth the son of Saul, and twelve of the
servants of David. 16 Each one of them seized his
[a]opponent by the head and *thrust* his sword in his
[b]opponent's side; so they fell down together. Therefore that place was called [c]Helkath-hazzurim, which
is in Gibeon. 17 That day the battle was very severe,
and [A]Abner and the men of Israel were beaten before the servants of David.
18 Now [A]the three sons of Zeruiah were there,
Joab and Abishai and Asahel; and Asahel *was* [B]*as*
[a]swift-footed as one of the gazelles which is in
the field. 19 Asahel pursued Abner and did not
[a]turn to the right or to the left from following
Abner. 20 Then Abner looked behind him and said,
"Is that you, Asahel?" And he answered, "It is I."
21 So Abner said to him, "[a]Turn to your right or to
your left, and take hold of one of the young men
for yourself, and take for yourself his spoil." But
Asahel was not willing to turn aside from following him. 22 Abner repeated again to Asahel, "Turn
[a]aside from following me. Why should I strike you
to the ground? [A]How then could I lift up my face
to your brother Joab?" 23 However, he refused to
turn aside; therefore Abner struck him in the belly
with the butt end of the spear, so that the spear
came out at his back. And he fell there and died
on the spot. And it came about that all who came
to the place where [A]Asahel had fallen and died,
stood still.
24 But Joab and Abishai pursued Abner, and when
the sun was going down, they came to the hill of
Ammah, which is in front of Giah by the way of
the wilderness of Gibeon. 25 The sons of Benjamin
gathered together behind Abner and became one
band, and they stood on the top of a certain hill.
26 Then Abner called to Joab and said, "Shall the
sword devour forever? Do you not know that it
will be bitter in the end? How long will you [a]refrain
from telling the people to turn back from following
their brothers?" 27 Joab said, "As God lives, if you
had not spoken, surely then the people would have
gone away in the morning, each from following his
brother." 28 So Joab blew the trumpet; and all the
people halted and pursued Israel no longer, [A]nor
did they continue to fight anymore. 29 Abner and his

2:8 [a]I.e. man of shame; cf 1 Chr 8:33, *Eshbaal* [A]1 Sam 14:50 [B]Gen 32:2; 2 Sam 17:24 2:9 [A]Josh 22:9 [B]Judg 1:32 [C]1 Sam 29:1 2:11 [a]Lit *number of days* [A]2 Sam 5:5 2:12 [A]Josh 10:12; 18:25 2:13 [a]Lit *them together* [b]Lit *these* [A]2 Sam 8:16; 1 Chr 2:16; 11:6 2:14 [a]Lit *make sport* [A]2 Sam 2:16, 17 2:16 [a]Lit *fellow* [b]Lit *fellow's* [c]I.e. the field of sword-edges 2:17 [A]2 Sam 3:1 2:18 [a]Lit *light in his feet* [A]1 Chr 2:16 [B]1 Chr 12:8; Hab 3:19 2:19 [a]Lit *turn to go to* 2:21 [a]Lit *Turn for yourself* 2:22 [a]Lit *aside for yourself* [A]2 Sam 3:27 2:23 [A]2 Sam 20:12 2:26 [a]Lit *not tell the people* 2:28 [A]2 Sam 3:1

2:8 Abner. Abner, cousin of Saul and general of his army (1Sa 14:50, 51), did not desire to follow the Lord's new anointed king, but placed Ish-bosheth on the throne, causing tension between Judah and the rest of the tribes in Israel. **Ish-bosheth.** His name means "man of shame." Saul's only surviving son was placed as king over the northern tribes of Israel and the eastern ones across the Jordan. **Mahanaim.** A town in Gilead to the E of the Jordan River. Ish-bosheth established himself there and reigned for two years in this city. This was the same city where Jacob saw the angels while on his way to Penuel (Ge 32:2). It was appointed to be a Levitical city from the territory of Gad (Jos 21:28; 1Ch 6:80). It later became the haven for David while fleeing from Absalom (17:24, 27; 19:32; 1Ki 2:8), because likely it was well fortified (cf. 18:24).

2:9 king over Gilead ... all Israel. Ish-bosheth's power seemed more solidified in the land of Gilead (E of the Jordan) than in the rest of Israel.

2:10 The house of Judah. A natural opposition arose between the tribe of Judah and the rest of Israel since Judah was under the reign of David, while the rest of Israel recognized the reign of Ish-bosheth.

2:11 seven years and six months. Several years passed before Ish-bosheth assumed the throne of Israel, so that Ish-bosheth's two-year reign came at the end of David's 7-year and 6-month reign over Judah. It must have taken Ish-bosheth about 5 years to regain the northern territory from the Philistines.

2:12 Gibeon. During the time of Joshua, Gibeon was a very important city (Jos 10:2). Its people probably had sided with David because Saul had broken a treaty with the Gibeonites and acted treacherously toward them (21:1).

2:13 Joab the son of Zeruiah. Joab was the leader of David's army and thus led the men against Abner. Although Ish-bosheth and David sat on the thrones of their respective territories, Joab and Abner truly had wielded the power and control by leading the military forces. Zeruiah was the sister of David (cf. 1Ch 2:16).

2:14 the young men ... hold a contest. Rather than all-out war, Abner proposed a representative contest between champions on behalf of the opposing armies. Because all 24 of the contestants lay fallen and dying in combat (vv. 15, 16), the contest settled nothing, but excited passions so that a battle between the two armies ensued (v. 17).

2:18 Abishai. Brother of Joab, he was an aide to David throughout his rise to power. Abishai was with David in the camp of Saul when David had opportunity to kill Saul and encouraged the murder of Saul, which David would not allow (cf. 1Sa 26:6–9). **Asahel.** Another brother of Joab, Asahel was single-minded with dogged determination; though he was extremely fleet-footed, his determination would prove to be fatal (v. 23).

2:21 take for yourself his spoil. To gain the armor or spoil of the enemy general, Abner, who was fleeing the defeat, would be to possess the greatest trophy. Asahel was ambitious to get it, while Abner kept warning him and suggested he take the spoil of some other soldier for his trophy, since he was not able to defeat Abner.

2:22 How then could I lift up my face to your brother Joab? Abner sought to spare Asahel so as to avoid unnecessary vengeance from Joab or David. Abner tried to give Asahel reasons to stop his pursuit, but Asahel was determined. Abner did not wish to strike down Asahel, but Asahel refused to listen, so he was forced to stop his effort with a fatal stab by the butt end of his spear.

2:26 Shall the sword devour forever? As Abner had earlier proposed that the hostilities begin, he now proposed that they cease.

2:29 Arabah. The central valley region marked by Mt. Hermon to the north and the Red Sea to the south. **Mahanaim.** See note on 2:8.

men then went through the Arabah all that night;
so they crossed the Jordan, walked all morning, and
came to [A]Mahanaim.
30 Then Joab returned from following Abner;
when he had gathered all the people together, [a]nine-
teen of David's servants besides Asahel were missing. 31 But the servants of David had struck down
many of Benjamin and Abner's men, *so that* three
hundred and sixty men died. 32 And they took up
Asahel and buried him [A]in his father's tomb which
was in Bethlehem. Then Joab and his men went all
night until the day [a]dawned at Hebron.

THE HOUSE OF DAVID STRENGTHENED

3 Now [A]there was a long war between the house
of Saul and the house of David; and David grew
steadily stronger, but the house of Saul grew weaker
continually.
2 [A]Sons were born to David at Hebron: his firstborn was Amnon, by [B]Ahinoam the Jezreelitess;
3 and his second, Chileab, by Abigail the [a]widow of
Nabal the Carmelite; and the third, Absalom the son
of [A]Maacah, the daughter of Talmai, king of [B]Geshur;
4 and the fourth, [A]Adonijah the son of Haggith; and
the fifth, Shephatiah the son of Abital; 5 and the
sixth, Ithream, by David's wife Eglah. These were
born to David at Hebron.

ABNER JOINS DAVID

6 It came about while there was war between the
house of Saul and the house of David that [A]Abner
was making himself strong in the house of Saul.
7 Now Saul had a concubine whose name was [A]Riz-
pah, the daughter of Aiah; and [a]Ish-bosheth said
to Abner, "Why have you gone in to my father's
concubine?" 8 Then Abner was very angry over the
words of Ish-bosheth and said, "[A]Am I a dog's head
that belongs to Judah? Today I show kindness to the
house of Saul your father, to his brothers and to his
friends, and have not delivered you into the hands
of David; and yet today you charge me with a guilt
concerning the woman. 9 [A]May God do so to Abner,
and more also, if [B]as the LORD has sworn to David,
I do not accomplish this for him, 10 [A]to transfer the
kingdom from the house of Saul and to establish the
throne of David over Israel and over Judah, [B]from
Dan even to Beersheba." 11 And he could no longer
answer Abner a word, because he was afraid of him.
12 Then Abner sent messengers to David in his
place, saying, "Whose is the land? Make your covenant with me, and behold, my hand shall be with
you to bring all Israel over to you." 13 He said, "Good!
I will make a covenant with you, but I demand one
thing of you, [a]namely, [A]you shall not see my face
unless you [B]first bring Michal, Saul's daughter, when
you come to see [b]me." 14 So David sent messengers

2:29 [A]2 Sam 2:8 2:30 [a]Lit *nineteen men* 2:32 [a]Lit *lighted on them* [A]Gen 47:29, 30; Judg 8:32 3:1 [A]1 Kin 14:30; Ps 46:9 3:2 [A]1 Chr 3:1-3 [B]1 Sam 25:42, 43 3:3 [a]Lit *wife* [A]1 Sam 27:8; 1 Chr 3:2 [B]2 Sam 14:32; 15:8 3:4 [A]1 Kin 1:5 3:6 [A]2 Sam 2:8, 9 3:7 [a]So some ancient mss and versions; M.T. *he* [A]2 Sam 21:8-11 3:8 [A]1 Sam 24:14; 2 Sam 9:8 3:9 [A]1 Kin 19:2 [B]1 Sam 15:28 3:10 [A]1 Sam 15:28 [B]1 Sam 3:20 3:13 [a]Lit *saying* [b]Lit *my face* [A]Gen 43:3 [B]1 Sam 18:20; 19:11

3:1 a long war. The conflict between Ish-bosheth and David did not end in quick victory. There was a gradual transfer of power from the house of Saul to the house of David (v. 10) that lasted at least through the two-year reign of Ish-bosheth and maybe longer.

3:2–5 See 1Ch 3:1–4.

3:2 Amnon. He raped and defiled his half-sister Tamar and later, by the command of Absalom, was killed for his crime (13:1–39).

3:3 Chileab. He apparently died before he was able to enter into position to contend for the throne, for nothing more is said about him. This child was born to David by the wife whom David had taken upon the death of Nabal (see 1Sa 25:3). **Absalom.** Lit. "My Divine Father Is Peace" or "Divine Father of Peace." Absalom was the son of Maacah who was a Geshurite princess from a region in Syria, not Israel. David may have married her as part of a diplomatic agreement made with Talmai, the Geshurite king, to give David an ally N of Ish-bosheth. Later Absalom, in fear of his life, fled to Geshur (13:37, 38).

3:4 Adonijah. He was a prominent figure in the contention for David's throne at the end of his reign (1Ki 1, 2), but was assassinated, allowing the throne to be given to Solomon (1Ki 2:25). Haggith was probably married to David after his accession to the throne. **Shephatiah ... Abital.** Shephatiah means "The Lord Judges." Abital means "My Divine Father Is Dew" or "My Divine Father of Dew."

3:5 Eglah. Eglah is called "David's wife." This may be because she is the last of the list and serves to draw emphasis to David's polygamy. The inclusion of these sons indicates all who would have been in contention for the throne. **born to David.** More children were born to David when he moved to Jerusalem (5:14).

3:6–5:16 David assumed the kingdom of all Israel by a similar progression of events as those which led to his assuming the throne of Judah. In both cases, a man comes seeking David's favor (Amalekite, 1:1–13; Abner, 3:6–21). Both of these men are executed for their deeds (Amalekite, 1:14–16; Abner, 3:22–32). In both cases, this is followed by a lament of David (1:17–27; 3:33–39). Close to the middle of both accounts is a brief look at the anointing of David as king (over Judah, 2:1–7; over Israel, 5:1–5). After this, David and his men are successful in defeating their enemies (2:8–3:1; 5:6–12). Each section concludes with a list of the children born to David (Hebron, 3:2–5; Jerusalem, 5:13–16).

3:6 Abner was making himself strong. Abner was the military leader of the country and the one who had put Ish-bosheth on the throne and whose power held him there. As time passed, Abner began to make his own move to take the throne.

3:7 Rizpah. By taking Rizpah, the concubine of Saul, Abner made a clear statement to the people that he would take the place of Saul as king over Israel. Going in to the king's concubine was a statement of power and rightful claim to the throne (cf. 16:21, 22 in regard to Absalom). Ish-bosheth reacted strongly against Abner, so Abner resented his reaction as an indignity and, compelled by revenge, determined to transfer all the weight of his influence and power to David's side (vv. 9, 10).

3:8 dog's head. This was another way to ask, "Am I a contemptible traitor allied with Judah?" This was a common expression to show disdain (1Sa 17:43). Abner used this opportunity to condemn Ish-bosheth by reminding him that he would not have been in power had Abner himself not placed him there.

3:9 as the LORD has sworn to David. Abner seemed to demonstrate the knowledge that David was to be the next king of Israel as God had sworn to David (1Sa 13:14; 15:28; 24:20).

3:10 transfer the kingdom. Part of Saul's kingdom had already been transferred to David, namely Judah; however, Abner vowed to complete the process by helping David obtain the rest of the kingdom. **Dan even to Beersheba.** This was an expression meaning the whole country (cf. Jdg 20:1), i.e., from Dan in the N to Beersheba in the S.

3:12 Whose is the land? Though Abner's language (vv. 9, 10) implied the conviction that in supporting Ish-bosheth he had been going against God's purpose of conferring the sovereignty of the kingdom on David, this acknowledgment was no justification of his motives. He selfishly wanted to be on the winning side and to be honored as the one who brought all the people under David's rule.

3:13 Michal, Saul's daughter. David requested Michal for two reasons. One, it would right the wrong Saul had committed toward David by having given Michal, who was David's wife and who loved him (1Sa 18:20, 28), to another man (1Sa 25:44). Two, it would serve to strengthen David's claim to the throne of all Israel by inclining some of Saul's house to be favorable to his cause.

3:14 a hundred foreskins of the Philistines. David reminded Ish-bosheth that he had not only paid the dowry to Saul for his daughter, 100 foreskins of the Philistines, but to Ish-bosheth, Saul's son, saying, "Give me my wife Michal, to whom I was betrothed [A]for a hundred foreskins of the Philistines." 15 Ish-bosheth sent and took her from *her* husband, from [a]Paltiel the son of Laish. 16 But her husband went with her, weeping as he went, and followed her as far as [A]Bahurim. Then Abner said to him, "Go, return." So he returned.

17 Now Abner had [a]consultation with [A]the elders of Israel, saying, "In times past you were seeking for David to be king over you. 18 Now then, do *it!* For the LORD has spoken of David, saying, '[A]By the hand of My servant David [a]I will save My people Israel from the hand of the Philistines and from the hand of all their enemies.' " 19 Abner also spoke in the hearing of Benjamin; and in addition Abner went to speak in the hearing of David in Hebron all that seemed good to Israel and to [A]the whole house of Benjamin.

20 Then Abner and twenty men with him came to David at Hebron. And David made a feast for Abner and the men who were with him. 21 Abner said to David, "Let me arise and go and [A]gather all Israel to my lord the king, that they may make a covenant with you, and that [B]you may be king over all that your soul desires." So David sent Abner away, and he went in peace.

22 And behold, [A]the servants of David and Joab came from a raid and brought much spoil with them; but Abner was not with David in Hebron, for he had sent him away, and he had gone in peace. 23 When Joab and all the army that was with him arrived, they told Joab, saying, "Abner the son of Ner came to the king, and he has sent him away, and he has gone in peace." 24 Then Joab came to the king and said, "What have you done? Behold, Abner came to you; why then have you sent him away and he is already gone? 25 You know Abner the son of Ner, that he came to deceive you and to learn of [A]your going out and coming in and to find out all that you are doing."

JOAB MURDERS ABNER

26 When Joab came out from David, he sent messengers after Abner, and they brought him back from the well of Sirah; but David did not know *it.* 27 So when Abner returned to Hebron, Joab took him aside into the middle of the gate to speak with him privately, and there [A]he struck him in the belly so that he died on account of the blood of Asahel his brother. 28 Afterward when David heard it, he said, "I and my kingdom are innocent before the LORD forever of the blood of Abner the son of Ner. 29 [A]May it [a]fall on the head of Joab and on all his father's house; and may there not fail from the house of Joab [B]one who has a discharge, or who is a leper, or who takes hold of a distaff, or who falls by the sword, or who lacks bread." 30 So Joab and Abishai his brother killed Abner [A]because he had put their brother Asahel to death in the battle at Gibeon.

DAVID MOURNS ABNER

31 Then David said to Joab and to all the people who were with him, "[A]Tear your clothes and gird on sackcloth and lament before Abner." And King David walked behind the bier. 32 Thus they buried Abner in Hebron; and the king lifted up his voice and wept at [A]the grave of Abner, and all the people wept. 33 [A]The king chanted a *lament* for Abner and said,

"Should Abner die as a fool dies?
34 "Your hands were not bound, nor
your feet put in fetters;
As one falls before the [a]wicked,
you have fallen."

And all the people wept again over him. 35 Then all the people came [A]to [a]persuade David to eat bread while it was still day; but David vowed, saying, "[B]May God do so to me, and more also, if I taste bread or anything else [C]before the sun goes down."

3:14 [A]1 Sam 18:25, 27 3:15 [a]In 1 Sam 25:44, *Palti* 3:16 [A]2 Sam 16:5; 19:16 3:17 [a]Lit *a word* [A]1 Sam 8:4 3:18 [a]So many ancient mss and versions; M.T. *he* [A]1 Sam 9:16; 15:28 3:19 [A]1 Sam 10:20, 21; 1 Chr 12:29 3:21 [A]2 Sam 3:10, 12 [B]1 Kin 11:37 3:22 [A]1 Sam 27:8 3:25 [A]Deut 28:6; 1 Sam 29:6; Is 37:28 3:27 [A]2 Sam 2:23; 20:9, 10; 1 Kin 2:5 3:29 [a]Lit *whirl* [A]Deut 21:6-9; 1 Kin 2:31-33 [B]Lev 13:46 3:30 [A]2 Sam 2:23 3:31 [A]Gen 37:34; Judg 11:35 3:32 [A]Job 31:28, 29; Prov 24:17 3:33 [A]2 Sam 1:17; 2 Chr 35:25 3:34 [a]Lit *sons of wickedness* 3:35 [a]Lit *cause* [A]2 Sam 12:17 [B]1 Sam 3:17 [C]2 Sam 1:12

had delivered double the asking price (1Sa 18:25–27). Thus, Michal rightfully belonged to David.

3:16 Bahurim. Located just E of Jerusalem, it became the final location where Paltiel (cf. 1Sa 25:44) would see Michal. This was also the town of Shimei, the man who cursed David during his flight from Jerusalem before Absalom (16:5). David's soldiers also found refuge in a well at Bahurim while being pursued by Absalom's men (17:18).

3:17 elders of Israel. These men were the recognized leaders of the people serving as Ish-bosheth's advisers who would have been consulted when important decisions needed to be made (cf. 19:7).

3:18 My servant David. David is called "the Lord's servant" more than 30 times in the OT. Abner's words to the elders of Israel clearly recognized David as the servant of the Lord, thus having the right to the throne according to God's sovereign will.

3:19 Benjamin. Abner gave special attention to the tribe of Benjamin, for they were Saul's and Ish-bosheth's kinsmen (see 1Sa 9:1, 2).

3:21 covenant with you. This covenant moved beyond the personal agreement made between Abner and David and was operative on the national level, uniting both N and S. **in peace.** The repetition of this phrase in vv. 22, 23 serves to emphasize the fact that David sought to ensure peace with Abner. This also accentuates the fact that David was not involved in Abner's death (vv. 26–30).

3:25 Abner . . . came to deceive you. It is ironic that Joab accused Abner of deception in spying on David in v. 25 when in v. 26 he deceived David by not telling him of his request to have Abner returned to Hebron. Joab used this deception to slay Abner out of personal vengeance for the death of his brother Asahel (v. 27; see 2:19–23).

3:26 well of Sirah. The only mention of this location is found here. The town was located about 2.5 mi. NW of Hebron.

3:27 in the belly. Abner died in a similar manner to Joab's brother Asahel, the man he had killed (2:23). However, Abner struck Asahel during battle (cf. 2:18–23) in self-defense, while Joab murdered Abner to avenge the death of Asahel.

3:28 the blood of Abner. Since life is in the blood (cf. Ge 9:4; Lv 17:11, 14; Dt 12:23), this expression refers to the life of Abner. David made it clear he had nothing to do with the murder of Abner, and David sought the Lord's help to punish Joab for his evil deed (v. 39).

3:31 lament. Joab was instructed to lament the death of Abner, as was the custom for commemorating the death of an individual. To further demonstrate David's condemnation of the killing of Abner, he instructed "all the people" to mourn the death of Abner, including Joab and his men (vv. 32–34).

3:35–39 David's feelings and conduct in response to Abner's death tended not only to remove all suspicion of guilt from him, but even turned the tide of public opinion in his favor and paved the way for his reigning over all the tribes much more honorably than by the negotiations of Abner (3:17–19).

36 Now all the people took note *of it,* and it [a]pleased
them, just as everything the king did [b]pleased all the
people. 37 So all the people and all Israel understood
that day that it had not been *the will* of the king to
put Abner the son of Ner to death. 38 Then the king
said to his servants, "Do you not know that a prince
and a great man has fallen this day in Israel? 39 I am
[A]weak today, though anointed king; and these men
[B]the sons of Zeruiah are too difficult for me. [C]May
the LORD repay the evildoer according to his evil."

ISH-BOSHETH MURDERED

4 Now when [a]Ish-bosheth, Saul's son, heard that
[A]Abner had died in Hebron, [b,B]he lost courage,
and all Israel was disturbed. 2 Saul's son *had* two
men who were commanders of bands: the name
of the one was Baanah and the name of the other
Rechab, sons of Rimmon the Beerothite, of the sons
of Benjamin (for [A]Beeroth is also considered [B]*part*
of Benjamin, 3 and the Beerothites fled to [A]Gittaim
and have been aliens there until this day).
4 Now [A]Jonathan, Saul's son, had a son crippled
in his feet. He was five years old when the [B]report
of Saul and Jonathan came from Jezreel, and his
nurse took him up and fled. And it happened that
in her hurry to flee, he fell and became lame. And
his name was [a,C]Mephibosheth.
5 So the sons of Rimmon the Beerothite, Rechab
and Baanah, departed and came to the house of
[A]Ish-bosheth in the heat of the day while he was
taking his midday rest. 6 [a]They came to the middle
of the house as [b]if to get wheat, and [A]they struck him
in the belly; and Rechab and Baanah his brother escaped. 7 Now when they came into the house, as he
was lying on his bed in his bedroom, they struck him
and killed him and beheaded him. And they took his
head and [a,A]traveled by way of the Arabah all night.
8 Then they brought the head of Ish-bosheth to David
at Hebron and said to the king, "Behold, the head of
Ish-bosheth [A]the son of Saul, your enemy, who sought
your life; thus the LORD has given my lord the king
vengeance this day on Saul and his [a]descendants."
9 David answered Rechab and Baanah his brother,
sons of Rimmon the Beerothite, and said to them,
"As the LORD lives, [A]who has redeemed my life from
all distress, 10 [A]when one told me, saying, 'Behold,
Saul is dead,' and [a]thought he was bringing good
news, I seized him and killed him in Ziklag, which
was the reward I gave him for *his* news. 11 How much
more, when wicked men have killed a righteous man
in his own house on his bed, shall I not now [A]require
his blood from your hand and [a]destroy you from the
earth?" 12 Then [A]David commanded the young men,
and they killed them and cut off their hands and
feet and hung them up beside the pool in Hebron.
But they took the head of Ish-bosheth [B]and buried
it in the grave of Abner in Hebron.

DAVID KING OVER ALL ISRAEL

5 [A]Then all the tribes of Israel came to David at
Hebron and [a]said, "Behold, we are [B]your bone
and your flesh. 2 Previously, when Saul was king
over us, [A]you were the one who led Israel out and
in. And the LORD said to you, '[B]You will shepherd My
people Israel, and you will be [C]a ruler over Israel.' "
3 So all the elders of Israel came to the king at Hebron, and King David [A]made a covenant with them
before the LORD at Hebron; then [B]they anointed
David king over Israel. 4 David was [A]thirty years old
when he became king, *and* [B]he reigned forty years.

3:36 [a]Lit *was good in their eyes* [b]Lit *was good in the eyes of all* 3:39 [A]1 Chr 29:1; 2 Chr 13:7 [B]2 Sam 19:5-7 [C]1 Kin 2:32-34 4:1 [a]So some ancient mss; M.T. *he* [b]Lit *his hands dropped* [A]2 Sam 3:27 [B]Ezra 4:4 4:2 [A]Josh 9:17 [B]Josh 18:25 4:3 [A]Neh 11:33 4:4 [a]I.e. Merib-baal [A]2 Sam 9:3, 6 [B]1 Sam 31:1-4 [C]1 Chr 8:34; 9:40 4:5 [A]2 Sam 2:8 4:6 [a]Lit *And here* [b]Lit *takers of wheat* [A]2 Sam 2:23 4:7 [a]Lit *went* [A]2 Sam 2:29 4:8 [a]Lit *seed* [A]1 Sam 24:4; 25:29 4:9 [A]Gen 48:16; 1 Kin 1:29; Ps 31:7 4:10 [a]Lit *he was as a bearer of good news in his own eyes* [A]2 Sam 1:2, 4, 15 4:11 [a]Lit *burn* [A]Gen 9:5; Ps 9:12 4:12 [A]2 Sam 1:15 [B]2 Sam 3:32 5:1 [a]Lit *said, saying* [A]1 Chr 11:1-3 [B]2 Sam 19:13 5:2 [A]1 Sam 18:5, 13, 16 [B]Gen 49:24; 2 Sam 7:7 [C]1 Sam 25:30 5:3 [A]2 Sam 3:21 [B]1 Sam 16:13; 2 Sam 2:4 5:4 [A]Gen 41:46; Num 4:3; Luke 3:23 [B]1 Kin 2:11; 1 Chr 26:31

3:39 weak … difficult. David had not yet solidified his power enough to exact his own judgment without jeopardizing his command. He was still "weak" and needed time to consolidate his authority. Once that was accomplished, he no longer needed to fear the strength of Joab and Abishai, who were Zeruiah's sons (2:18).

4:1 lost courage. Lit. "his hands became weak or limp" (cf. 2Ch 15:7). Ish-bosheth and all of Israel realized that Abner had been the source of strength and stability for Israel. With Abner dead, Israel was troubled because Ish-bosheth no longer had a leader for the army which secured him in power.

4:2 sons of Benjamin. It is stressed that these men were of the tribe of Benjamin (vv. 2, 3), perhaps to show the friction within the house of Saul and his son Ish-bosheth, and how the grab for power began once Abner was gone.

4:2, 3 Beeroth … Gittaim. Beeroth was a Canaanite town belonging to the tribe of Benjamin. Gittaim was also a village of the tribe of Benjamin.

4:4 Mephibosheth. He may be introduced here to demonstrate that his youth and physical handicap disqualified him from being considered for ruling Israel. He would have been only 12 years old at the time of Ish-bosheth's death. For the history of this man, see 9:6–13; 16:1–4; 19:24–30; 21:7.

4:5, 6 It was the custom to secure wheat for the soldiers under their command (v. 2) along with some pay. Under the pretense of that normal routine, they came and killed the king.

4:7 the Arabah. To avoid easy detection, the men traveled by way of the Arabah (cf. 2:29), i.e., the Jordan Valley. This plain extended about 30 mi. from Mahanaim to Hebron.

4:8 the LORD has given … vengeance. The murderers of Ish-bosheth came to David and proclaimed that the Lord had avenged David. However, as happened earlier to the Amalekite (1:2–15), the men were very surprised at the response of David. David did not see their deed as the Lord's vengeance, but as murder of an innocent man.

4:9 the LORD … has redeemed my life from all distress. A striking contrast is shown between David and the two murderers who claimed they were performing the Lord's work by killing Ish-bosheth. However, David praised the Lord for His providential work through Ish-bosheth's life and proclaimed the Lord's deliverance; thus, David condemned the murderers of Ish-bosheth and had them executed as he had done to the man who claimed to kill Saul (1:15, 16).

5:1–3 See 1Ch 11:1–3.

5:1, 2 all the tribes of Israel. The term "all" is used 3 times (vv. 1, 3, 5) to emphasize that the kingdom established under King David was truly a united monarchy. The "elders" of Israel (v. 3), representing the "tribes" (v. 1), came to David at Hebron with the express purpose of submitting to his rule. Three reasons were given by the Israelites for wanting to make David king: 1) he was an Israelite brother (cf. Dt 17:15); 2) he was Israel's best warrior and commander; and 3) he had been chosen by the Lord to be the king of Israel.

5:3 King David made a covenant. David bound himself formally to certain obligations toward the Israelites, including their rights and responsibilities to one another and to the Lord (cf. 2Ki 11:17). As good as this covenant was, it did not end the underlying sense of separate identity felt by Israel and Judah as

5 At Hebron [A]he reigned over Judah seven years and
six months, and in Jerusalem he reigned thirty-three
years over all Israel and Judah.
6 [A]Now the king and his men went to [B]Jerusalem
against the Jebusites, the inhabitants of the land,
and they said to [a]David, "You shall not come in here,
but the blind and lame will turn you away"; [b]think-
ing, "David cannot enter here." 7 Nevertheless, David
captured the stronghold of Zion, that is [A]the city of
David. 8 David said on that day, "Whoever would
strike the Jebusites, let him reach the lame and the
blind, who are hated by David's soul, through the
water tunnel." Therefore they say, "The blind or the
lame shall not come into the house." 9 So David lived
in the stronghold and called it [A]the city of David.
And David built all around from the [a,B]Millo and
inward. 10 [A]David became greater and greater, for
the LORD God of hosts was with him.
11 [A]Then Hiram king of Tyre sent messengers to
David with cedar trees and carpenters and stonemasons; and [B]they built a house for David. 12 And
David realized that the LORD had established him
as king over Israel, and that He had exalted his
kingdom for the sake of His people Israel.
13 Meanwhile [A]David took more concubines and
wives from Jerusalem, after he came from Hebron;
and more sons and daughters were born to David.
14 Now [A]these are the names of those who were
born to him in Jerusalem: Shammua, Shobab, Nathan, Solomon, 15 Ibhar, Elishua, Nepheg, Japhia,
16 Elishama, Eliada and Eliphelet.

WAR WITH THE PHILISTINES

17 When the Philistines heard that they had
anointed David king over Israel, [A]all the Philistines
went up to seek out David; and when David heard

5:5 [A]2 Sam 2:11; 1 Chr 3:4; 29:27 5:6 [a]Lit *David, saying* [b]Lit *saying* [A]1 Chr 11:4-9 [B]Josh 15:63; 18:28; Judg 1:21 5:7 [A]2 Sam 6:12, 16; 1 Kin 2:10; 9:24 5:9 [a]I.e. citadel [A]2 Sam 5:7 [B]1 Kin 9:15, 24 5:10 [A]2 Sam 3:1 5:11 [A]1 Kin 5:1, 10, 18; 1 Chr 14:1 [B]Ps 30: title 5:13 [A]Deut 17:17; 1 Chr 3:9 5:14 [A]1 Chr 3:5-8 5:17 [A]1 Sam 29:1

the revolt of Sheba (20:1) and the dissolution of the united kingdom under Rehoboam (1Ki 12:16) would later demonstrate. **they anointed David.** David's third anointing (2:4; 1Sa 16:13) resulted in the unification of the 12 tribes under his kingship.

5:5 Israel and Judah. The united kingdom was still known by its two component parts.

5:6–10 See 1Ch 11:4–9.

5:6 Jerusalem. This city is mentioned in the Bible more than any other (from Ge 14:18 to Rev 21:10). The city was located in the territory of Benjamin, near the northern border of Judah and was excellently fortified because of its elevation and the surrounding deep valleys, which made it naturally defensible on 3 sides. In addition, it had a good water supply, the Gihon spring, and was close to travel routes for trade. The city had earlier been conquered by Judah (Jdg 1:8), but neither Judah nor Benjamin had been successful in permanently dislodging the Jebusite inhabitants (Jos 15:33; Jdg 1:21). By taking Jerusalem, David was able to eliminate the foreign wedge between the northern and southern tribes and to establish his capital. **Jebusites.** A people of Canaanite descent (Ge 10:16–18). Since the earlier inhabitants of Jerusalem were Amorites (Jos 10:5), it seems that the Jebusites took control of Jerusalem after the time of the Israelite conquest. **the blind and lame.** The Jebusites taunted the Israelites and mocked the power of David by boasting that the blind and the lame could defend Jerusalem against him.

5:7 stronghold of Zion. This is the first occurrence of "Zion" in the Bible and the only one in 1 and 2 Samuel. Referring here to the Jebusite citadel on the southeastern hill, the name was also later used of the temple mount (Is 10:12) and of the entire city of Jerusalem (Is 28:16). **city of David.** Both Bethlehem, David's birthplace (Lk 2:4), and Jerusalem, David's place of reign, were called by this title.

5:8 water tunnel. A tunnel that channeled the city's water supply from the Gihon spring outside the city walls on the E side into the citadel.

5:9 Millo. Lit. "filling." Stone-filled terraces were built to serve as part of Jerusalem's northern defenses, since the city was most open to attack from that direction.

5:11–16 See 1Ch 14:1–7.

5:11 Hiram king of Tyre. Tyre was a Phoenician port city about 35 mi. N of Mt. Carmel and 25 mi. S of Sidon. During the latter part of David's reign and much of Solomon's, the friendly Hiram traded building materials for agricultural products. He also provided craftsmen to build David's palace, indicating how the long war had brought the nation to a low place where there were few good artisans. Psalm 30 could possibly refer to the dedication of this house or to the temporary shelter for the ark in Jerusalem (6:17).

5:12 the LORD had established him as king. Witnessing God's evident blessing on his life, David recognized the Lord's role in establishing his kingship.

5:13 more concubines and wives. The multiplication of David's wives and concubines was in direct violation of Dt 17:17. These marriages probably (cf. 2Sa 3:3) reflected David's involvement in international treaties and alliances that were sealed by the marriage of a king's daughter to the other participants in the treaty. This cultural institution accounted for some of David's and many of Solomon's wives (see 1Ki 11:1–3). In each case of polygamy in Scripture, the law of God was violated and the consequences were negative, if not disastrous.

5:17–8:18 This section is bracketed by the descriptions of David's military victories (5:17–25; 8:1–14). In between (6:1–7:29), David's concern for the ark of the covenant and a suitable building to house it are recounted.

5:17–23 See 1Ch 14:8–17.

5:17 Philistines. The Philistines had remained quiet neighbors during the long civil war between the house of Saul and David, but, jealous of the king who has consolidated the nation, they resolved to attack before his government was fully established. Realizing

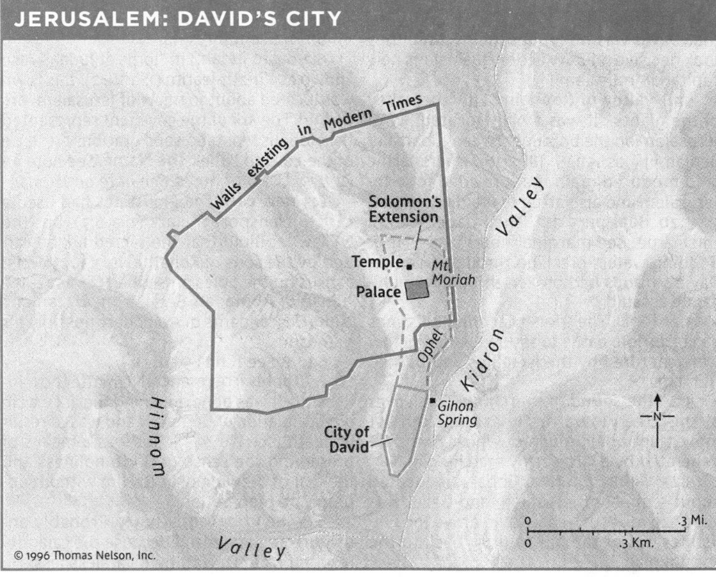

of it, he went down to the [B]stronghold. 18 Now the
Philistines came and spread themselves out in [A]the
valley of Rephaim. 19 Then [A]David inquired of the
LORD, saying, "Shall I go up against the Philistines?
Will You give them into my hand?" And [B]the LORD
said to David, "Go up, for I will certainly give the
Philistines into your hand." 20 So David came to
[A]Baal-perazim and [a]defeated them there; and he
said, "The LORD has broken through my enemies
before me like the breakthrough of waters." Therefore he named that place [b]Baal-perazim. 21 They
abandoned their idols there, so [A]David and his men
carried them away.

22 Now [A]the Philistines came up once again and
spread themselves out in the valley of Rephaim.
23 When [A]David inquired of the LORD, He said, "You
shall not go *directly* up; circle around behind them
and come at them in front of the [a]balsam trees. 24 It
shall be, when [A]you hear the sound of marching
in the tops of the [a]balsam trees, then you shall act
promptly, for then [B]the LORD will have gone out
before you to strike the army of the Philistines."
25 Then David did so, just as the LORD had commanded him, and struck down the Philistines from
[a,A]Geba [b]as far as [B]Gezer.

PERIL IN MOVING THE ARK

6 [A]Now David again gathered all the chosen men
of Israel, thirty thousand. 2 And David arose
and went with all the people who were with him
to [a,A]Baale-judah, to bring up from there the ark of
God which is called by the [B]Name, the very name
of the LORD of hosts who [C]is [b]enthroned *above* the
cherubim. 3 They [a]placed the ark of God on [A]a new
cart that they might bring it from the house of
Abinadab which was on the hill; and Uzzah and
Ahio, the sons of Abinadab, were leading the new
cart. 4 So [A]they brought it with the ark of God from
the house of Abinadab, which was on the hill; and
Ahio was walking ahead of the ark. 5 Meanwhile,
David and all the house of Israel [A]were celebrating
before the LORD [B]with all kinds of *instruments made*
of [a]fir wood, and with lyres, harps, tambourines,
castanets and cymbals.

6 But when they came to the [A]threshing floor
of Nacon, Uzzah [B]reached out toward the ark of
God and took hold of it, for the oxen nearly upset *it.* 7 And the anger of the LORD burned against
Uzzah, and [A]God struck him down there for [a]his
irreverence; and he died there by the ark of God.
8 David became angry because [a]of the LORD'S outburst against Uzzah, and that place is called [b]Pe-
rez-uzzah to this day. 9 So [A]David was afraid of the
LORD that day; and he said, "How can the ark of
the LORD come to me?" 10 And David was unwilling
to move the ark of the LORD into the city of David
with him; but David took it aside to the house of
[A]Obed-edom the Gittite. 11 Thus the ark of the LORD
remained in the house of Obed-edom the Gittite
three months, and the LORD [A]blessed Obed-edom
and all his household.

THE ARK IS BROUGHT TO JERUSALEM

12 Now it was told King David, saying, "The LORD
has blessed the house of Obed-edom and all that belongs to him, on account of the ark of God." [A]David
went and brought up the ark of God from the house
of Obed-edom into [B]the city of David with gladness.
13 And so it was, that when the [A]bearers of the ark of
the LORD had gone six paces, he sacrificed an [B]ox and

5:17 [B]2 Sam 23:14; 1 Chr 11:16 5:18 [A]Gen 14:5; Josh 15:8; 17:15; 18:16 5:19 [A]1 Sam 23:2 [B]2 Sam 2:1 5:20 [a]Lit *David smote* [b]I.e. the master of breakthrough [A]1 Chr 14:11; Is 28:21 5:21 [A]1 Chr 14:12 5:22 [A]2 Sam 5:18 5:23 [a]Or *baka-shrubs* [A]2 Sam 5:19 5:24 [a]Or *baka-shrubs* [A]2 Kin 7:6 [B]Judg 4:14 5:25 [a]In 1 Chr 14:16, *Gibeon* [b]Lit *until you are coming to* [A]Is 28:21 [B]Josh 12:12; 21:21 6:1 [A]1 Chr 13:5-14 6:2 [a]I.e. Kiriath-jearim [b]Lit *sitting* [A]Josh 15:9, 10; 1 Sam 7:1 [B]Lev 24:16 [C]Ex 25:22 6:3 [a]Lit *caused to ride* [A]Num 7:4-9; 1 Sam 6:7 6:4 [A]1 Sam 7:1; 1 Chr 13:7 6:5 [a]Or *cypress* [A]1 Sam 18:6, 7 [B]1 Chr 13:8 6:6 [A]1 Chr 13:9 [B]Num 4:15, 19, 20 6:7 [a]Lit *the* [A]1 Sam 6:19 6:8 [a]Lit *the LORD broke through a breakthrough* [b]I.e. the breakthrough of Uzzah 6:9 [A]Ps 119:120; Luke 5:8 6:10 [A]1 Chr 26:4-8 6:11 [A]Gen 30:27; 39:5 6:12 [A]1 Chr 15:25-16:3 [B]1 Kin 8:1 6:13 [A]Num 4:15; Josh 3:3; 1 Chr 15:2, 15 [B]1 Kin 8:5

that David was no longer their vassal, they took decisive military action against his new capital of Jerusalem.

5:18 valley of Rephaim. Lit. "the valley of the giants." It was a plain located SW of Jerusalem on the border between Judah and Benjamin (Jos 15:1, 8; 18:11, 16), where fertile land produced grain that provided food for Jerusalem and also attracted raiding armies.

5:20 Baal-perazim. The image seen in this name (see marginal note) was that of flooding waters breaking through a dam as David's troops had broken through the Philistine assault.

5:21 idols. The idols that the Philistines had taken into battle to assure them of victory were captured by the Israelites and burned (1Ch 14:12).

5:24 the sound of marching. The leaves of this tree would rustle at the slightest movement of air, much of which would be generated by a large army marching.

5:25 Geba ... Gezer. Geba was located about 5 mi. N of Jerusalem and Gezer was about 20 mi. W of Geba. David drove the Philistines out of the hill country back to the coastal plain.

6:1–11 See 1Ch 13:1–14.

6:2 Baale-judah. Lit. "lords of Judah." Also known as Kiriath-jearim (1Sa 7:1, 2), this town was located about 10 mi. W of Jerusalem. **ark of God.** The ark of the covenant represented the glorious reputation and gracious presence of the Lord to Israel. **the Name.** *See note on Dt 12:5.* **LORD of hosts.** *See note on 1Sa 1:3.*

6:3 new cart. The Philistines had used a cart to transport the ark (1Sa 6:7). But the OT law required that the sacred ark be carried by the sons of Kohath (Nu 3:30, 31; 4:15; 7:9), using the poles prescribed (Ex 25:12–15). **house of Abinadab.** See 1Sa 7:1. **Uzzah and Ahio.** Descendants of Abinadab, possibly his grandsons.

6:6–8 See 1Ch 13:9–12.

6:7 for his irreverence. No matter how innocently it was done, touching the ark was in direct violation of God's law and was to result in death (see Nu 4:15). This was a means of preserving the sense of God's holiness and the fear of drawing near to Him without appropriate preparation.

6:8 David became angry. Probably anger directed at himself because the calamity resulted from David's own carelessness. He was confused as to whether to carry on the transportation of the ark to Jerusalem (v. 9) and would not move it, fearing more death and calamity might come on him or the people (v. 10). It is likely that he waited to see the wrath of God subside before moving the ark.

6:10 Obed-edom the Gittite. Lit. "servant of Edom." The term "Gittite" can refer to someone from the Philistine city of Gath, but here it is better to see the term related to Gath-rimmon, one of the Levitical cities (cf. Jos 21:24, 25). Obed-edom is referred to as a Levite in Chronicles (1Ch 15:17–25; 16:5, 38; 26:4, 5, 8, 15; 2Ch 25:24).

6:12–19 See 1Ch 15:25–16:3.

6:12 blessed ... on account of the ark. During the 3 months when the ark remained with Obed-edom, the Lord blessed his family. In the same way God had blessed Obed-edom, David was confident that with the presence of the ark, the Lord would bless his house in ways that would last forever (7:29).

6:13 bearers of the ark. In David's second attempt to bring the ark to Jerusalem, it was transported in the manner prescribed by OT law. *See note on v. 3.* **six paces.** I.e., after the first 6 steps, not after every 6 steps.

a fatling. 14 And [A]David was dancing before the LORD
with all *his* might, and David was [a,B]wearing a linen
ephod. 15 So David and all the house of Israel were
bringing up the ark of the LORD with shouting and
the sound of the trumpet.
16 Then it happened *as* the ark of the LORD came
into the city of David that [A]Michal the daughter of
Saul looked out of the window and saw King David leaping and dancing before the LORD; and she
despised him in her heart.
17 So they brought in the ark of the LORD and
set it [A]in its place inside the tent which David had
pitched for it; and [B]David offered burnt offerings
and peace offerings before the LORD. 18 When David
had finished offering the burnt offering and the
peace offering, [A]he blessed the people in the name
of the LORD of hosts. 19 Further, he distributed to
all the people, to all the multitude of Israel, both to
men and women, a cake of bread and one of dates
and one of raisins to each one. Then all the people
departed each to his house.
20 But when David returned to bless his household, Michal the daughter of Saul came out to
meet David and said, "How the king of Israel distinguished himself today! [A]He uncovered himself
today in the eyes of his servants' maids as one of
the [B]foolish ones shamelessly uncovers himself!"
21 So David said to Michal, "[A]*It was* before the LORD,
who chose me above your father and above all his
house, to appoint me ruler over the people of the
LORD, over Israel; therefore I will celebrate before
the LORD. 22 I will be more lightly esteemed than
this and will be humble in my own eyes, but with
the maids of whom you have spoken, with them I
will be distinguished." 23 Michal the daughter of
Saul had no child to the day of her death.

DAVID PLANS TO BUILD A TEMPLE

7 [A]Now it came about when the king lived in his
house, and the LORD had given him rest on every side from all his enemies, 2 that the king said to
[A]Nathan the prophet, "See now, I dwell in [B]a house
of cedar, but the ark of God [C]dwells within tent curtains." 3 Nathan said to the king, "[A]Go, do all that is
in your mind, for the LORD is with you."
4 But in the same night the word of the LORD came
to Nathan, saying, 5 "Go and say to My servant David, 'Thus says the LORD, "[A]Are you the one who
should build Me a house to dwell in? 6 For [A]I have
not dwelt in a house since the day I brought up the
sons of Israel from Egypt, even to this day; but I have
been moving about [B]in a tent, even in a [a]tabernacle.
7 [A]Wherever I have gone with all the sons of Israel, did
I speak a word with one of the tribes of Israel, [B]which
I commanded to shepherd My people Israel, saying,
'Why have you not built Me a house of cedar?' " '

GOD'S COVENANT WITH DAVID

8 Now therefore, thus you shall say to My servant
David, 'Thus says the LORD of hosts, "[A]I took you

6:14 [a]Lit *girded with* [A]Ex 15:20, 21; Judg 11:34 [B]Ex 19:6; 1 Sam 2:18, 28 6:16 [A]2 Sam 3:14 6:17 [A]1 Chr 15:1; 2 Chr 1:4 [B]1 Kin 8:62-65 6:18 [A]1 Kin 8:14, 15 6:20 [A]2 Sam 6:14, 16; Eccl 7:17 [B]Judg 9:4 6:21 [A]1 Sam 13:14; 15:28 7:1 [A]1 Chr 17:1-27 7:2 [A]2 Sam 7:17; 12:1; 1 Kin 1:22; 1 Chr 29:29; 2 Chr 9:29 [B]2 Sam 5:11 [C]Ex 26:1 7:3 [A]1 Kin 8:17, 18; 1 Chr 22:7 7:5 [A]1 Kin 5:3, 4; 8:19 7:6 [a]Lit *dwelling place* [A]Josh 18:1; 1 Kin 8:16 [B]Ex 40:18, 34 7:7 [A]Lev 26:11, 12 [B]2 Sam 5:2 7:8 [A]1 Sam 16:11, 12; Ps 78:70, 71

6:14 David was dancing before the LORD. Cf. Ps 150:4. The Hebrews, like other ancient and modern people, had their physical expressions of religious joys as they praised God. **linen ephod.** See 1Sa 2:18.

6:16 Michal ... despised him. Michal's contempt for David is explained by her sarcastic remark in v. 20. She considered David's unbridled, joyful dancing as conduct unbefitting for the dignity and gravity of a king because it exposed him in some ways.

6:17 tent. David had made a tent for the ark of the covenant until a permanent building for it could be built. Psalm 30 could refer possibly to this tent or to David's own home (5:11, 12).

6:20 bless his household. David desired the same inevitable success from the Lord as experienced in the household of Obed-edom (see v. 11). The attitude of Michal aborted the blessing at that time, but the Lord would bless David's house in the future (7:29). **uncovered.** A derogatory reference to the priestly attire that David wore (v. 14) in place of his royal garments.

6:21 before the LORD. David's actions were for the delight of the Lord, not for the maidens.

6:22 humble in my own eyes. David viewed himself with humility. It is the humble whom the Lord will exalt (cf. 1Sa 7:7, 8).

6:23 Michal ... had no child. Whether David ceased to have marital relations with Michal or the Lord disciplined Michal for her contempt of David, Michal bore no children. In OT times, it was a reproach to be childless (1Sa 1:5, 6). Michal's childlessness prevented her from providing a successor to David's throne from the family of Saul (cf. 1Sa 15:22–28).

7:1–17 See 1Ch 17:1–15. These verses record the establishment of the Davidic Covenant, God's unconditional promise to David and his posterity. While not called a covenant here, it is later (23:5). This promise is an important key to understanding God's irrevocable pledge of a king from the line of David to rule forever (v. 16). It has been estimated that over 40 individual biblical passages are directly related to these verses (cf. Pss 89; 110; 132); thus, this text is a major highlight in the OT. The ultimate fulfillment comes at Christ's second advent when He sets up His millennial kingdom on earth (cf. Eze 37; Zec 14; Rev 19). This is the fourth of 5 irrevocable, unconditional covenants made by God. The first 3 include: 1) the Noahic Covenant (Ge 9:8–17); 2) the Abrahamic Covenant (Ge 15:12–21); and 3) the Levitic or Priestly Covenant (Nu 3:1–18; 18:1–20; 25:10–13). The New Covenant, which actually provided redemption, was revealed later through Jeremiah (Jer 31:31–34) and accomplished by the death and resurrection of Jesus Christ. *See note on Mt 26:28.*

7:1 lived in his house. See 5:11. David's palace was built with help from Hiram of Tyre. Since Hiram did not become king of Tyre until around 980 B.C., the events narrated in this chapter occurred in the last decade of David's reign. **rest ... from all his enemies.** David had conquered all the nations that were around Israel. See 8:1–14 for the details which occur prior to 2Sa 7.

7:2 Nathan. Mentioned here for the first time, Nathan played a significant role in chap. 12 (confronting David's sin with Bathsheba) and 1Ki 1 (upsetting Adonijah's plot to usurp the throne from Solomon). **within tent curtains.** *See note on 6:17.*

7:3 Go, do. Nathan the prophet encouraged David to pursue the noble project he had in mind and assured him of the Lord's blessing. However, neither David nor Nathan had consulted the Lord.

7:4–16 The Lord revealed His will to Nathan in this matter, to redirect the best human thoughts of the king.

7:5 Are you the one who should build Me a house ... ? Verses 5–7 are framed by two questions asked by the Lord, both of which pertain to building a temple for Him. The first question, asking if David was the one who should build the temple, expected a negative answer (see 1Ch 17:4). According to 1Ch 22:8; 28:3, David was not chosen by God to build the temple because he was a warrior who had shed much blood.

7:7 Why have you not built Me a house ... ? The second question, asking if the Lord had ever commanded any leader to build a temple for His ark, also expected a negative answer. So, contrary to Nathan's and David's intentions and assumptions, God did not want a house at that time and did not want David to build one.

7:8–16 a great name. These verses state the promises the Lord gave to David. Verses 8–11a give the promises to be realized during David's lifetime. Verses 11b–16 state the promises that would be fulfilled after

from the pasture, from following the sheep, [B]to be
ruler over My people Israel. 9 [A]I have been with you
wherever you have gone and [B]have cut off all your
enemies from before you; and I will make you a
great name, like the names of the great men who
are on the earth. 10 I will also appoint a place for
My people Israel and [A]will plant them, that they
may live in their own place and not be disturbed
again, [B]nor will the [a]wicked afflict them any more
as formerly, 11 even [A]from the day that I commanded
judges to be over My people Israel; and [B]I will give
you rest from all your enemies. The LORD also declares to you that [C]the LORD will make a house for
you. 12 [A]When your days are complete and you [B]lie
down with your fathers, [C]I will raise up your [a]de-
scendant after you, who will come forth from [b]you,
and I will establish his kingdom. 13 [A]He shall build a
house for My name, and [B]I will establish the throne
of his kingdom forever. 14 [A]I will be a father to him
and he will be a son to Me; [B]when he commits iniquity, I will correct him with the rod of men and the
strokes of the sons of men, 15 but My lovingkindness
shall not depart from him, [A]as I took *it* away from
Saul, whom I removed from before you. 16 [A]Your
house and your kingdom shall endure before [a]Me
forever; your throne shall be established forever." ' "
17 In accordance with all these words and all this
vision, so Nathan spoke to David.

DAVID'S PRAYER

18 Then David the king went in and sat before
the LORD, and he said, "[A]Who am I, O Lord [a]GOD,
and what is my house, that You have brought me
this far? 19 And yet this was insignificant in Your
eyes, O Lord GOD, [A]for You have spoken also of
the house of Your servant concerning the distant
future. And [B]this is the [a]custom of man, O Lord
GOD. 20 Again what more can David say to You?

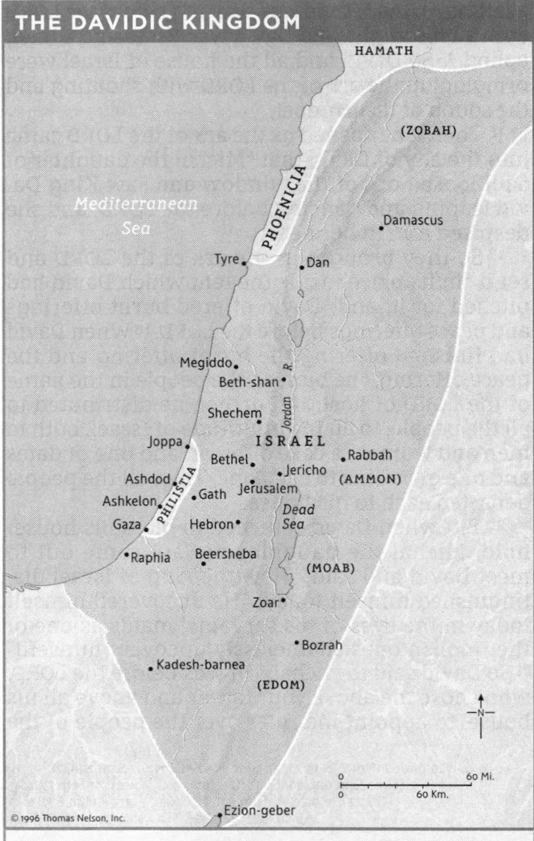

David's military exploits successfully incorporated into the Israelite kingdom the powers of Edom, Moab, Ammon, and Zobah.

7:8 [B]2 Sam 6:21 7:9 [A]1 Sam 5:10 [B]Ps 18:37-42 7:10 [a]Lit *sons of wickedness* [A]Ex 15:17; Is 5:2, 7 [B]Ps 89:22, 23; Is 60:18 7:11 [A]Judg 2:14-16; 1 Sam 12:9-11 [B]2 Sam 7:1 [C]1 Sam 25:28; 2 Sam 7:27 7:12 [a]Lit *seed* [b]Lit *your bowels* [A]1 Kin 2:1 [B]Deut 31:16; Acts 13:36 [C]1 Kin 8:20; Ps 132:11 7:13 [A]1 Kin 6:12; 8:19 [B]Is 9:7; 49:8 7:14 [A]Ps 89:26, 27; 2 Cor 6:18; Heb 1:5 [B]1 Kin 11:34; Ps 89:30-33 7:15 [A]1 Sam 15:23; 16:14 7:16 [a]So with Gr and some ancient mss; M.T. *you* [A]2 Sam 7:13; Ps 89:36, 37 7:18 [a]Heb *YHWH*, usually rendered *LORD*, and so through out the ch [A]Ex 3:11; 1 Sam 18:18 7:19 [a]Or *law* [A]2 Sam 7:11-16; 1 Chr 17:17 [B]Is 55:8, 9

David's death. During David's lifetime, the Lord: 1) gave David "a great name" (*see note on Ge 12:2*); 2) appointed a place for Israel; and 3) gave David "rest" from all his enemies. After David's death, the Lord gave David: 1) a son to sit on his national throne, whom the Lord would oversee as a father with necessary chastening, discipline, and mercy (Solomon); and 2) a Son who would rule a kingdom that will be established forever (Messiah). This prophecy referred in its immediacy to Solomon and to the temporal kingdom of David's family in the land. But in a larger and more sublime sense, it refers to David's greater Son of another nature, Jesus Christ (cf. Heb 1:8).

7:11 the LORD will make a house for you. Although David desired to build the Lord a "house," i.e., a temple, instead it would be the Lord who would build David a "house," i.e., a dynasty.

7:12 your descendant. According to the rest of Scripture, it was the coming Messiah who would establish David's kingdom forever (see Is 9:6, 7; Lk 1:32, 33).

7:14 a father . . . son. These words are directly related to Jesus the Messiah in Heb 1:5. In Semitic thought, since the son had the full character of the father, the future seed (or foremost Descendant) of David would have the same essence of God. That Jesus Christ was God incarnate is the central theme of John's gospel (see Introduction to John). **when he commits iniquity.** As a human father disciplines his sons, so the Lord would discipline David's descendants, if they committed iniquity. This has reference to the intermediary seed until Messiah's arrival (any king of David's line from Solomon on). However, the ultimate Seed of David will not be a sinner like David and his descendants were, as recorded in Samuel and Kings (see 2Co 5:21). Significantly, Chronicles, focusing more directly on the Messiah, does not include this statement in its record of Nathan's words (1Ch 17:13).

7:15 This is an expression of the unconditional character of the Davidic Covenant. The Messiah will come to His glorious, eternal Kingdom and that promise will not change.

7:16 Your house . . . your kingdom . . . your throne. Lk 1:32b, 33 indicates that these 3 terms are fulfilled in Jesus, "...and the Lord God will give Him the throne of His father David; and He will reign over the house of Jacob forever, and His kingdom will have no end." **forever.** This word conveys the idea of 1) an indeterminately long time or 2) into eternity future. It does not mean that there cannot be interruptions, but rather that the outcome is guaranteed. Christ's Davidic reign will conclude human history.

7:18–29 See 1Ch 17:16–27. David prayed with awe and thanksgiving over God's sovereign claim to bestow the divine blessing on his seed and nation.

7:18 sat before the LORD. I.e., before the ark of the covenant in the temporary tent. **Who am I . . . ?** David was overwhelmed by the Lord's promise that He would bring His kingdom through David's seed. In vv. 18–29, David referred to himself 10 times as "Your servant" (vv. 19, 20, 21, 25, 26, 27, 28, 29), acknowledging his God-given title, "My servant David" (v. 5).

7:19 the distant future. David recognized that the Lord had spoken about the distant future, not only about his immediate

For [A]You know Your servant, O Lord GOD! 21 [A]For
the sake of Your word, and according to Your own
heart, You have done all this greatness to let Your
servant know. 22 For this reason [A]You are great,
O Lord GOD; for [B]there is none like You, and there
is no God besides You, [C]according to all that we
have heard with our ears. 23 And [A]what one nation on the earth is like Your people Israel, whom
God went to redeem for Himself as a people and
to make a name for Himself, and [B]to do a great
thing for You and awesome things for Your land,
before [C]Your people whom [D]You have redeemed
for Yourself from Egypt, *from* nations and their
gods? 24 For [A]You have established for Yourself
Your people Israel as Your own people forever,
and [B]You, O LORD, have become their God. 25 Now
therefore, O LORD God, the word that You have
spoken concerning Your servant and his house,
confirm *it* forever, and do as You have spoken,
26 [A]that Your name may be magnified forever,
by saying, 'The LORD of hosts is God over Israel'; and may the house of Your servant David
be established before You. 27 For You, O LORD of
hosts, the God of Israel, have [a]made a revelation
to Your servant, saying, '[A]I will build you a house';
therefore Your servant has found [b]courage to pray
this prayer to You. 28 Now, O Lord GOD, You are
God, and [A]Your words are truth, and You have
[a]promised this good thing to Your servant. 29 Now
therefore, may it please You to bless the house of
Your servant, that it may continue forever before
You. For You, O Lord GOD, have spoken; and [A]with
Your blessing may the house of Your servant be
blessed forever."

DAVID'S TRIUMPHS

8 [A]Now after this it came about that David [a]de-
feated the Philistines and subdued them; and
David took [b]control of the chief city from the hand
of the Philistines.
2 [A]He [a]defeated [B]Moab, and measured them with
the line, making them lie down on the ground; and
he measured two lines to put to death and one full
line to keep alive. And [C]the Moabites became servants to David, [D]bringing tribute.
3 Then David [a]defeated [A]Hadadezer, the son of Rehob king of Zobah, as [B]he went to restore his [b]rule at
the [c]River. 4 David captured from him 1,700 horsemen
and 20,000 foot soldiers; and David [A]hamstrung the
chariot horses, but reserved *enough* of them for 100
chariots. 5 When [A]the Arameans of Damascus came to
help Hadadezer, king of Zobah, David [a]killed 22,000
Arameans. 6 Then David put garrisons among the
Arameans of Damascus, and [A]the Arameans became
servants to David, bringing tribute. And [B]the LORD
helped David wherever he went. 7 David took the
shields of gold which were [a]carried by the servants
of Hadadezer and brought them to Jerusalem. 8 From
[a]Betah and from [A]Berothai, cities of Hadadezer, King
David took a very large amount of bronze.
9 Now when Toi king of [A]Hamath heard that David
had [a]defeated all the army of Hadadezer, 10 Toi sent
[a]Joram his son to King David to [b]greet him and bless
him, because he had fought against Hadadezer and
[c]defeated him; for Hadadezer [d]had been at war with
Toi. And [e]*Joram* brought with him articles of silver,
of gold and of bronze. 11 King David also [A]dedicated
these to the LORD, with the silver and gold that he
had dedicated from all the nations which he had

7:20 [A]1 Sam 16:7; John 21:17 7:21 [A]1 Chr 17:19; Eph 4:32 7:22 [A]Deut 3:24; Ps 48:1; 86:10 [B]Ex 15:11; 1 Sam 2:2 [C]Ex 10:2; Ps 44:1 7:23 [A]Deut 4:32-38 [B]Deut 10:21 [C]Deut 15:15 [D]Deut 9:26 7:24 [A]Deut 32:6 [B]Gen 17:7, 8; Ex 6:7 7:26 [A]Ps 72:18, 19; Matt 6:9 7:27 [a]Lit *uncovered the ear of* [b]Lit *his heart* [A]2 Sam 7:13 7:28 [a]Or *spoken* [A]Ex 34:6; John 17:17 7:29 [A]Num 6:24-26 8:1 [a]Lit *smote* [b]Lit *the bridle of the mother city* [A]1 Chr 18 8:2 [a]Lit *smote* [A]Num 24:17 [B]1 Sam 22:3, 4 [C]2 Sam 8:6; 1 Kin 4:21 [D]2 Kin 3:4; 17:3 8:3 [a]Lit *smote* [b]Lit *hand* [c]I.e. Euphrates [A]1 Sam 14:47; 2 Sam 10:16, 19 [B]2 Sam 10:15-19 8:4 [A]Josh 11:6, 9 8:5 [a]Lit *smote* [A]1 Kin 11:23-25 8:6 [A]2 Sam 8:2 [B]2 Sam 3:18 8:7 [a]Lit *on* 8:8 [a]In 1 Chr 18:8, *Tibhath* [A]Ezek 47:16 8:9 [a]Lit *smitten* [A]1 Kin 8:65; 2 Chr 8:4 8:10 [a]In 1 Chr 18:10, *Hadoram* [b]Lit *ask him of his welfare* [c]Lit *smitten* [d]Lit *was a man of wars* [e]Lit *there were in his hand* 8:11 [A]1 Kin 7:51

descendant, Solomon. **the custom of man.** Lit. "and this is the law of man." The idea is that God's covenant promise is for an eternal kingdom, whereby the whole world of man shall be blessed, through the coming seed of David. The Davidic Covenant is thus a grant, conferring powers, rights, and privileges to David and his seed for the benefit of mankind, a promise that left David speechless (vv. 20–22).

7:23 Your people … Your land. David is remembering aspects of the Abrahamic Covenant (cf. Ge 12, 15, 17). **Israel.** In vv. 18–21, David praised the Lord for His favor to him. In vv. 22–24, David praised the Lord for the favor shown to the nation of Israel (cf. Dt 7:6–11).

7:25 the word … You have spoken. In vv. 25–29, David prayed for the fulfillment of the divine promise spoken to him.

7:26–29 Your words are truth. David's prayer indicated that he fully accepted by faith the extraordinary, irrevocable promises God made to David as king and to Israel as a nation.

8:1–14 These verses outline the expansion of David's kingdom under the hand of the Lord (vv. 6, 14). Israel's major enemies were all defeated as David's kingdom extended N, S, E, and W. See 1Ch 18:1–13. This conquering occurred before the event of chap. 7 (see 7:1).

8:1 Philistines … subdued. David's first priority was to deal with the Philistines to the W, whom he quickly defeated and subjugated (see 5:25). **chief city.** Probably a reference to the "chief city" of the Philistines, Gath (cf. 1Ch 18:1). He defeated his enemies to the W.

8:2 Moab. David also defeated the Moabites who dwelt in Transjordan, E of the Dead Sea. This represented a change from the good relationship David once enjoyed with the Moabite royalty (cf. 1Sa 22:3, 4). He defeated his enemies to the E. **measured two lines.** This could mean that David spared the young Moabites (whose height was approximately one cord) and executed the adults (whose height was two cords) or that one out of 3 rows of soldiers was arbitrarily chosen to be spared from execution. Such was a common practice of eastern kings in dealing with deadly enemies.

8:3–8 He defeated his enemies to the N. David had already defeated the Amalekites to the S (1Sa 30:16, 17).

8:3 Hadadezer. Lit. "Hadad (the personal name of the Canaanite storm god) is my help." Psalm 60 was written to commemorate this battle. **Zobah.** An Aramaean kingdom N of Damascus (cf. 1Sa 14:47). **River.** I.e., the most southwesterly point of the Euphrates River around the city of Tiphsah.

8:4 captured … 1,700 horsemen. The reading of "7,000" in 1Ch 18:4 is preferable. *See note there.* **hamstrung the chariot horses.** Hamstringing the horses disabled them from military action by cutting the back sinews of the hind legs (Jos 11:6).

8:5 Arameans. I.e., Syrians, who were peoples located around the city of Damascus as well as in the area of Zobah.

8:7 shields of gold. Ceremonial or decorative insignias that were not used in battle, but for decoration.

8:8 bronze. First Chronicles 18:8 notes 3 towns belonging to Hadadezer which yielded bronze that was later used in the construction of the temple.

8:9 Toi king of Hamath. Hamath was another Aramaean territory located about 100 mi. N of Damascus. The king, Toi, was thankful to see his enemy Zobah crushed and desired to establish good relations with David. So he gave David gifts to indicate that he voluntarily submitted to him as his vassal.

subdued: 12 from [a]Aram and [A]Moab and [B]the sons of
Ammon and [C]the Philistines and [D]Amalek, and from
the spoil of Hadadezer, son of Rehob, king of Zobah.
13 So [A]David made a name *for himself* when he returned from [a]killing 18,000 [b]Arameans in [B]the Valley
of Salt. 14 He put garrisons in Edom. In all Edom he put
garrisons, and [A]all the Edomites became servants to
David. And [B]the LORD helped David wherever he went.
15 So David reigned over all Israel; and David
[a]administered justice and righteousness for all his
people. 16 [A]Joab the son of Zeruiah *was* over the
army, and [B]Jehoshaphat the son of Ahilud *was* [C]re-
corder. 17 [A]Zadok the son of Ahitub and Ahimelech
the son of Abiathar *were* [B]priests, and Seraiah *was*
[C]secretary. 18 [A]Benaiah the son of Jehoiada [a]was over
the [B]Cherethites and the Pelethites; and David's sons
were [b,C]chief ministers.

DAVID'S KINDNESS TO MEPHIBOSHETH

9 Then David said, "Is there yet [a]anyone left of the
house of Saul, [A]that I may show him kindness
for Jonathan's sake?" 2 Now there was a servant of
the house of Saul whose name was Ziba, and they
called him to David; and the king said to him, "Are
you [A]Ziba?" And he said, "*I am* your servant." 3 The
king said, "Is there not yet anyone of the house of
Saul to whom I may show the [A]kindness of God?" And
Ziba said to the king, "[B]There is still a son of Jonathan
who is crippled in both feet." 4 So the king said to him,
"Where is he?" And Ziba said to the king, "Behold,
he is [A]in the house of Machir the son of Ammiel in
Lo-debar." 5 Then King David sent and brought him
from the house of Machir the son of Ammiel, from
Lo-debar. 6 [A]Mephibosheth, the son of Jonathan the
son of Saul, came to David and [B]fell on his face and
prostrated himself. And David said, "Mephibosheth."
And he said, "Here is your servant!" 7 David said to
him, "Do not fear, for [A]I will surely show kindness to
you for the sake of your father Jonathan, and [B]will
restore to you all the [a]land of your [b]grandfather Saul;
and [C]you shall [c]eat at my table regularly." 8 Again he
prostrated himself and said, "What is your servant,
that you should regard [A]a dead dog like me?"
9 Then the king called Saul's servant Ziba and
said to him, "[A]All that belonged to Saul and to all
his house I have given to your master's [a]grandson.
10 You and your sons and your servants shall cultivate the land for him, and you shall bring in *the*
produce so that your master's grandson may have
food; nevertheless [A]Mephibosheth your master's
grandson [B]shall [a]eat at my table regularly." Now
Ziba had fifteen sons and twenty servants. 11 Then
Ziba said to the king, "According [A]to all that my lord
the king commands his servant so your servant will
do." So Mephibosheth ate at [a]David's table as one of
the king's sons. 12 Mephibosheth had a young son
whose name was Mica. And all who lived in the
house of Ziba were servants to Mephibosheth. 13 So
Mephibosheth lived in Jerusalem, for [A]he ate at the
king's table regularly. Now [B]he was lame in both feet.

8:12 [a]Some mss read *Edom* [A]2 Sam 8:2 [B]2 Sam 10:14 [C]2 Sam 5:17-25 [D]1 Sam 27:8; 30:17-20 8:13 [a]Lit *smiting* [b]Some mss read *Edom* [A]2 Sam 7:9 [B]2 Kin 14:7 8:14 [A]Gen 27:37-40; Num 24:17, 18 [B]2 Sam 8:6 8:15 [a]Lit *was doing* 8:16 [A]1 Chr 11:6 [B]1 Kin 4:3 [C]2 Kin 18:18, 37 8:17 [A]1 Chr 6:4-8 [B]1 Chr 16:39, 40 [C]2 Kin 18:18 8:18 [a]Lit *and the Cherethites* [b]Lit *priests* [A]1 Kin 4:4 [B]1 Sam 30:14; 2 Sam 15:18; 20:7, 23; 1 Kin 1:38, 44 [C]1 Chr 18:17 9:1 [a]Lit *he who is* [A]1 Sam 20:14-17, 42 9:2 [A]2 Sam 16:1-4; 19:17, 29 9:3 [A]1 Sam 20:14 [B]2 Sam 4:4 9:4 [A]2 Sam 17:27-29 9:6 [A]2 Sam 16:4; 19:24-30 [B]1 Sam 25:23 9:7 [a]Lit *field* [b]Lit *father* [c]Lit *eat bread* [A]2 Sam 9:1, 3 [B]2 Sam 12:8 [C]2 Sam 19:28; 1 Kin 2:7; 2 Kin 25:29 9:8 [A]2 Sam 16:9; 1 Sam 24:14 9:9 [a]Lit *son* [A]2 Sam 16:4; 19:29 9:10 [a]Lit *eat bread* [A]2 Sam 9:7, 11, 13 [B]2 Sam 19:28; 1 Kin 2:7 9:11 [a]Lit *my* [A]2 Sam 16:1-4; 19:24-30 9:13 [A]2 Sam 9:7, 11 [B]2 Sam 9:3

8:12 Aram. See marginal reading of "Edom," which is preferred. These were David's enemies to the S.

8:13 a name. The Lord began to fulfill His promise of giving David a great name (see 7:9). **Arameans.** There is an alternate ms. reading that makes this a reference to David's defeat of the Edomites, not the Arameans. This reading is supported by Ps 60 and 1Ch 18:12. **Valley of Salt.** An area S of the Dead Sea.

8:15–18 See 1Ch 18:14–17. This is the record of the cabinet under David's rule.

8:15 justice and righteousness. David ruled his kingdom in a righteous manner, and in the future the "Messiah" will rule in a similar fashion (Is 9:7; Jer 23:5; 33:15).

8:16 Joab. David's general (2:13; 1Sa 26:6). **Jehoshaphat … recorder.** The keeper of state records, and possibly the royal herald (1Ki 4:3).

8:17 Zadok the son of Ahitub. Zadok, meaning "righteous," was a Levitical priest descended from Aaron through Eleazar (1Ch 6:3–8, 50–53), who, along with his house, was the fulfillment of the oracle by the man of God in 1Sa 2:35. Future sons of Zadok will be priests in the millennial kingdom of Messiah (Eze 44:15). Later, he became the only High Priest in Solomon's reign, fulfilling God's promise to Phinehas (cf. Nu 25:10–13). **Ahimelech the son of Abiathar.** Abiathar was actually the son of Ahimelech (1 Sa 22:20). This apparent error (cf. 1Ch 18:16; 24:3, 6, 31) can be explained by two possibilities: 1) a scribal error reversed the relationship or, more likely, 2) Abiathar named a son Ahimelech and shared the priesthood with him. Abiathar was David's priest along with Zadok (15:24, 35; 19:11). Abiathar traced his lineage through Eli (1Ki 2:27) to Ithamar (1Ch 24:3). With Abiathar's removal (1Ki 2:26, 27), God's curse on Eli was completed (1Sa 2:33), and God's promise to Phinehas of Eleazar's line was fulfilled (cf. Nu 25:10–13; 1Sa 2:35). **Seraiah *was* secretary.** His name means "The Lord prevails," and he served as the official secretary of David.

8:18 Benaiah. His name means "The Lord builds," and he served as the commander of David's personal bodyguard. He later became the commander-in-chief of Solomon's army (1Ki 2:34, 35; 4:4), after he killed Joab, David's general (cf. 1Ki 2:28–35). **Cherethites and the Pelethites.** *See note on 1Sa 30:14.* **chief ministers.** Though the Heb. text referred to the sons of David as priests, the LXX referred to them as "princes of the court." The latter reading is supported by 1Ch 18:17, which refers to David's sons as "chiefs at the king's side."

9:1–20:26 These chapters begin with "the house of Saul" (9:1) and end with "Sheba …. Benjamite" (20:1). As with Saul, David is shown to be a failed king, albeit a repentant failure. It was only the grace and mercy of the Lord and His irrevocable covenant that kept David from being removed from the kingship, as Saul had been (cf. 7:15). The emphasis in this section is upon the troubles of David, troubles brought on by his own sin.

9:1 show him kindness for Jonathan's sake. David continued to display loving loyalty toward Jonathan (1Sa 20:42) by ministering to the physical needs of his crippled son, Mephibosheth (cf. 4:4).

9:2 Ziba. A former servant of Saul, who is first mentioned here.

9:4 Machir the son of Ammiel. A man of wealth (see 17:27–29). **Lo-debar.** A city located in Gilead, E of the Jordan, about 10 mi. S of the Sea of Galilee.

9:6 Mephibosheth. *See note on 4:4.*

9:7 restore … the land of your grandfather Saul. The estate belonging to Saul was probably quite substantial. **eat at my table.** David desired to honor Mephibosheth by bringing him into the royal palace and providing for his daily needs (see 2Ki 25:29).

9:8 dead dog. A "dead dog" was considered contemptible and useless. Mephibosheth saw himself as such in that he knew that he had not merited David's kindness and that there was no way for him to repay it. David's offer was an extraordinary expression of grace and beauty to his covenant with Jonathan (cf. 1Sa 18:3; 20:15, 42).

9:10 fifteen sons and twenty servants. This number shows the power and influence of Ziba. It also shows that the land given by David was substantial.

9:12 Mica. The descendants of Mica, the son of Mephibosheth, are listed in 1Ch 8:35–38; 9:41–44.

AMMON AND ARAM DEFEATED

10 [A]Now it happened afterwards that [B]the king
of the Ammonites died, and Hanun his son
became king in his place. 2 Then David said, "I will
show kindness to Hanun the son of [A]Nahash, just
as his father showed kindness to me." So David sent
[a]some of his servants to console him concerning his
father. But when David's servants came to the land
of the Ammonites, 3 the princes of the Ammonites
said to Hanun their lord, "[a]Do you think that David is
honoring your father because he has sent consolers
to you? [A]Has David not sent his servants to you in
order to search the city, to spy it out and overthrow
it?" 4 So Hanun took David's servants and [A]shaved
off half of their beards, and [B]cut off their garments
in the middle as far as their hips, and sent them
away. 5 When they told *it* to David, he sent to meet
them, for the men were greatly humiliated. And the
king said, "[a]Stay at Jericho until your beards grow,
and *then* return."
6 Now when the sons of Ammon saw that [A]they
had become odious to David, the sons of Ammon
sent and [B]hired the Arameans of [C]Beth-rehob and
the [D]Arameans of Zobah, 20,000 foot soldiers, and
the king of [E]Maacah with 1,000 men, and the men
of Tob with 12,000 men. 7 When David heard *of it,*
he sent Joab and all the army, the mighty men.
8 The sons of Ammon came out and drew up in
battle array [A]at the entrance of the [a]city, while the
Arameans of Zobah and of Rehob and the men of
[B]Tob and Maacah *were* by themselves in the field.
9 Now when Joab saw that [a]the battle was set
against him in front and in the rear, he selected
from all the choice men of Israel, and arrayed *them*
against the Arameans. 10 But the remainder of the
people he placed in the hand of Abishai his brother,
and he arrayed *them* against the sons of Ammon.
11 He said, "If the Arameans are too strong for me,
then you shall help me, but if the sons of Ammon
are too strong for you, then I will come to help you.
12 [A]Be strong, and let us show ourselves courageous
for the sake of our people and for the cities of our
God; and [B]may the LORD do what is good in His
sight." 13 So Joab and the people who were with him
drew near to the battle against the Arameans, and
[A]they fled before him. 14 When the sons of Ammon
saw that the Arameans fled, they *also* fled before
Abishai and entered the city. [A]Then Joab returned
from *fighting* against the sons of Ammon and came
to Jerusalem.
15 When the Arameans saw that they had been
[a]defeated by Israel, they gathered themselves together. 16 [A]And Hadadezer sent and brought out the
Arameans who were beyond the [a]River, and they
came to Helam; and [B]Shobach the commander of
the army of Hadadezer [b]led them. 17 Now when it
was told David, he gathered all Israel together and
crossed the Jordan, and came to Helam. And the
Arameans arrayed themselves to meet David and
fought against him. 18 But the Arameans fled before Israel, and David killed [A]700 charioteers of the
Arameans and 40,000 horsemen and struck down
Shobach the commander of their army, and he died
there. 19 When all the kings, servants of Hadadezer,
saw that they were [a]defeated by Israel, [A]they made
peace with Israel and served them. So the Arameans feared to help the sons of Ammon anymore.

BATHSHEBA, DAVID'S GREAT SIN

11 [A]Then it happened [a,B]in the spring, at the time
when kings go out *to battle,* that David sent
Joab and his servants with him and all Israel, and
they destroyed the sons of Ammon and [C]besieged
Rabbah. But David stayed at Jerusalem.

10:1 [A]1 Chr 19:1-19 [B]1 Sam 11:1 10:2 [a]Lit *by the hand of* [A]1 Sam 11:1 10:3 [a]Lit *In your eyes is David honoring* [A]Gen 42:9, 16 10:4 [A]Is 15:2; Jer 41:5 [B]Is 20:4 10:5 [a]Lit *Return to* 10:6 [A]Gen 34:30; 1 Sam 27:12 [B]2 Sam 8:3, 5; 2 Kin 7:6 [C]Judg 18:28 [D]2 Sam 8:3 [E]Deut 3:14 10:8 [a]Lit *gate* [A]1 Chr 19:9 [B]Judg 11:3, 5 10:9 [a]Lit *the faces of the battle were against* 10:12 [A]Deut 31:6; Josh 1:6; 1 Cor 16:13 [B]1 Sam 3:18 10:13 [A]1 Kin 20:13-21 10:14 [A]2 Sam 11:1 10:15 [a]Lit *smitten before* 10:16 [a]I.e. Euphrates [b]Lit *before* [A]2 Sam 8:3-8 [B]1 Chr 19:16 10:18 [A]1 Chr 19:18 10:19 [a]Lit *smitten before* [A]2 Sam 8:6 11:1 [a]Lit *at the return of the year* [A]1 Chr 20:1 [B]2 Sam 10:14; 1 Kin 20:22, 26 [C]2 Sam 12:26-29; Jer 49:2, 3; Amos 1:14

10:1–19 See 1Ch 19:1–19.

10:1 **king of the Ammonites.** I.e., Nahash (*see note on 1Sa 11:1*).

10:2 **show kindness to Hanun.** Since Nahash was an enemy of Saul, he was viewed as a friend and supporter of David. It was implied that David and Nahash had entered into a covenant relationship, on the basis of which David desired to communicate his continuing loyalty to Nahash's son, Hanun.

10:3 **the city.** I.e., Rabbah (*see note on 11:1*).

10:4 **shaved off half of their beards.** Forced shaving was considered an insult and a sign of submission (cf. Is 7:20). **cut off their garments ... as far as their hips.** To those who wore long garments in that time, exposure of the buttocks was a shameful practice inflicted on prisoners of war (cf. Is 20:4). Perhaps this was partly the concern of Michal in regard to David's dancing (see 6:14, 20).

10:5 **Jericho.** The first place W of the Jordan River that would have been reached by the servants of David as they returned from Rabbah.

10:6 **Beth-rehob.** An Aramaean district located SW of Zobah (cf. Nu 13:21; Jdg 18:28). **Zobah.** *See note on "Zobah" on 8:3.* **Maacah.** The region N of Lake Huleh N of Galilee (Dt 3:14; Jos 13:11–13). **Tob.** A city E of the Jordan River, located 45 mi. NE of Rabbah (Jdg 11:3, 5).

10:6–11 The Ammonite army was in the city ready for defense, while the Aramean mercenaries were at some distance, encamped in the fields around the city. Joab divided his forces to deal with both. *See note on 1Sa 11:1.*

10:12 **Be strong ... courageous ... may the LORD do what is good in His sight.** Finding himself fighting on two fronts, Joab urged the army to "be strong" and recognize that the outcome of the battle depended ultimately upon the Lord (cf. 15:26). It was a just and necessary war forced on Israel, so they could hope for God's blessing—and they received it (vv. 13, 14).

10:14 **Then Joab returned.** He did not attempt to siege and capture the city of Rabbah at this time because the time was unseasonable (*see note on 11:1*). Cf. 12:26–29.

10:16 **Hadadezer.** *See note on 8:3.* **Helam.** The place of battle, about 7 mi. N of Tob.

10:18 **charioteers ... horsemen.** *See note on 1Ch 19:18.*

10:19 **made peace with Israel.** All the petty kingdoms of Aram became subject to Israel and feared to aid Ammon against Israel.

11:1 **the spring ... when kings go out *to battle.*** In the Near East, kings normally went out to battle in the spring of the year because of the good weather and the abundance of food available along the way. *See note on 10:14.* **David sent Joab.** David dispatched Joab, his army commander, with his mercenary soldiers and the army of Israel to continue the battle against Ammon begun the previous year (10:14). **Rabbah.** The capital of the Ammonites, about 24 mi. E of the Jordan River opposite Jericho. The previous year, Abishai had defeated the Ammonite army in the open country, after which the remaining Ammonites fled behind the walls of the city of Rabbah for protection (10:14). Joab returned the next year to besiege the city. **But David stayed at Jerusalem.** Staying home in such situations was not David's usual practice (5:2; 8:1–14; 10:17; but cf. 18:3; 21:17); this explicit remark implies criticism of David for remaining behind, as well as setting the stage for his devastating iniquity.

2 Now when evening came David arose from his
bed and walked around on [A]the roof of the king's
house, and from the roof he saw a woman bathing;
and the woman was very beautiful in appearance.
3 So David sent and inquired about the woman. And
one said, "Is this not [A]Bathsheba, the daughter of
Eliam, the wife of [B]Uriah the Hittite?" 4 David sent
messengers and took her, and when she came to
him, [A]he lay with her; [B]and when she had purified
herself from her uncleanness, she returned to her
house. 5 The woman conceived; and she sent and
told David, and said, "[A]I am pregnant."

6 Then David sent to Joab, *saying,* "Send me Uriah
the Hittite." So Joab sent Uriah to David. 7 When
Uriah came to him, [A]David asked concerning the
welfare of Joab and [a]the people and the state of the
war. 8 Then David said to Uriah, "Go down to your
house, and [A]wash your feet." And Uriah went out of
the king's house, and a present from the king [a]was
sent out after him. 9 But Uriah slept [A]at the door of
the king's house with all the servants of his lord,
and did not go down to his house. 10 Now when they
told David, saying, "Uriah did not go down to his
house," David said to Uriah, "Have you not come
from a journey? Why did you not go down to your
house?" 11 Uriah said to David, "[A]The ark and Israel
and Judah are staying in [a]temporary shelters, and
my lord Joab and [B]the servants of my lord are camping in the open field. Shall I then go to my house to
eat and to drink and to lie with my wife? By your
life and the life of your soul, I will not do this thing."
12 Then David said to Uriah, "[A]Stay here today also,
and tomorrow I will let you go." So Uriah remained
in Jerusalem that day and the [a]next. 13 Now David
called him, and he ate and drank before him, and
he [A]made him drunk; and in the evening he went
out to lie on his bed [B]with his lord's servants, but
he did not go down to his house.

14 Now in the morning David [A]wrote a letter to
Joab and sent *it* by the hand of Uriah. 15 [A]He had written in the letter, saying, "[a]Place Uriah in the front
line of the [b]fiercest battle and withdraw from him,
[B]so that he may be struck down and die." 16 So it was
as Joab kept watch on the city, that he put Uriah at
the place where he knew there *were* valiant men.
17 The men of the city went out and fought against
Joab, and some of the people among David's servants fell; and [A]Uriah the Hittite also died. 18 Then
Joab sent and reported to David all the events of the
war. 19 He charged the messenger, saying, "When
you have finished telling all the events of the war to
the king, 20 and if it happens that the king's wrath
rises and he says to you, 'Why did you go so near to
the city to fight? Did you not know that they would
shoot from the wall? 21 Who [A]struck down Abimelech the son of Jerubbesheth? Did not a woman
throw an upper millstone on him from the wall so
that he died at Thebez? Why did you go so near the
wall?'—then you shall say, 'Your servant Uriah the
Hittite is dead also.' "

22 So the messenger departed and came and reported to David all that Joab had sent him *to tell.*
23 The messenger said to David, "The men prevailed
against us and came out against us in the field, but
we [a]pressed them as far as the entrance of the gate.
24 Moreover, the archers shot at your servants from
the wall; so some of the king's servants are dead,
and your servant Uriah the Hittite is also dead."
25 Then David said to the messenger, "Thus you shall
say to Joab, 'Do not let this thing [a]displease you, for

11:2 [A]Deut 22:8; 1 Sam 9:25; Matt 24:17; Acts 10:9 11:3 [A]1 Chr 3:5 [B]2 Sam 23:39 11:4 [A]Ps 51: title; James 1:14, 15 [B]Lev 12:2-5; 15:18-28; 18:19 11:5 [A]Lev 20:10; Deut 22:22 11:7 [a]Lit *welfare of* [A]Gen 37:14; 1 Sam 17:22 11:8 [a]Lit *went out* [A]Gen 43:24; Luke 7:44 11:9 [A]1 Kin 14:27, 28 11:11 [a]Or *booths* [A]2 Sam 7:2, 6 [B]2 Sam 20:6 11:12 [a]Lit *morrow* [A]Job 20:12-14 11:13 [A]Prov 20:1; 23:29-35 [B]2 Sam 11:9 11:14 [A]1 Kin 21:8-10 11:15 [a]Lit *Give* [b]Lit *strong* [A]Eccl 8:11; Jer 17:9 [B]2 Sam 12:9 11:17 [A]2 Sam 11:21 11:21 [A]Judg 9:50-54 11:23 [a]Lit *were upon* 11:25 [a]Lit *be evil in your sight*

11:2 walked around on the roof. The higher elevation of the palace roof allowed David to see into the courtyard of the nearby house. That same roof would later become the scene of other sinful immoralities (see 16:22).

11:3 Bathsheba. Not until 12:24 is her name used again. Rather, to intensify the sin of adultery, it is emphasized that she was the wife of Uriah (vv. 3, 26; 12:10, 15). Even the NT says "the wife of Uriah" (Mt 1:6). Cf. Ex 20:17. **Eliam.** The father of Bathsheba was one of David's mighty men (23:34). Since Eliam was the son of Ahithophel, Bathsheba was Ahithophel's granddaughter (cf. 15:12; 16:15). This could explain why Ahithophel, one of David's counselors (15:12), later gave his allegiance to Absalom in his revolt against David. **Uriah.** Also one of David's mighty men (23:39). Although a Hittite (cf. Ge 15:20; Ex 3:8, 17), Uriah bore a Heb. name meaning "the Lord is my light," indicating he was a worshiper of the one true God.

11:4 she came ... he lay. These terms are euphemistic references to sexual intercourse (cf. Ge 19:34), indicating that both Bathsheba and David were guilty of adultery. **her uncleanness.** Her recent days had involved menstruation and the required ceremonial purification (Lv 15:19–30). They were followed by adulterous intercourse. The fact that she had just experienced menstruation makes it plain that Bathsheba was not pregnant by Uriah when she came to lie with David.

11:5 I am pregnant. The only words of Bathsheba recorded concerning this incident acknowledge the resultant condition of her sin, which became evident by her pregnancy and was punishable by death (Lv 20:10; Dt 22:22).

11:6, 7 This inane conversation was a ploy to get Uriah to come home and sleep with his wife, so it would appear that he had fathered the child, thus sparing David the public shame and Bathsheba possible death.

11:8 wash your feet. Since this washing was done before going to bed, the idiom means to go home and go to bed. To a soldier coming from the battlefield, it said boldly, "enjoy your wife sexually." Hopefully, David's tryst with Bathsheba would be masked by Uriah's union. **a present.** This was designed to help Uriah and Bathsheba enjoy their evening together.

11:9 Uriah slept. Wanting to be a loyal example to his soldiers who were still in the field, Uriah did not take advantage of the king's less-than-honorable offer (v. 11).

11:11 The ark. The ark of the covenant was residing in either the tent in Jerusalem (6:17) or in a tent with the army of Israel on the battlefield (1Sa 4:6; 14:18).

11:13 made him drunk. Failing in his first attempt to cover up his sin, David tried unsuccessfully to make Uriah drunk so he would lose his resolve and self-discipline and return to his home and his wife's bed.

11:15 he may ... die. Failing twice to cover up his sin with Bathsheba, the frustrated and panicked David plotted the murder of Uriah by taking advantage of Uriah's unswerving loyalty to him as king, even having Uriah deliver his own death warrant. Thus David engaged in another crime deserving of capital punishment (Lv 24:17). This is graphic proof of the extremes people go to in pursuit of sin and in the absence of restraining grace.

11:18–24 Joab sent ... Uriah ... is dead. He sent a messenger with a veiled message to tell David his wish had been carried out. Joab must have known the reason behind this otherwise stupid military deployment.

11:25 *so* encourage him. David hypocritically expressed indifference to those who died, and he consoled Joab, authorizing him to continue the attack against Rabbah.

the sword devours one as well as another; make
your battle against the city stronger and overthrow
it'; and *so* encourage him."
26 Now when the wife of Uriah heard that Uriah
her husband was dead, [A]she mourned for her husband. 27 When the *time of* mourning was over, David sent and [a]brought her to his house and [A]she
became his wife; then she bore him a son. But [B]the
thing that David had done was evil in the sight of
the LORD.

NATHAN REBUKES DAVID

12 Then the LORD sent [A]Nathan to David. And
[B]he came to him and [a]said,

"There were two men in one city, the
one rich and the other poor.
2 "The rich man had a great
many flocks and herds.
3 "But the poor man had nothing
except [A]one little ewe lamb
Which he bought and nourished;
And it grew up together with
him and his children.
It would eat of his [a]bread and drink
of his cup and lie in his bosom,
And was like a daughter to him.
4 "Now a traveler came to
the rich man,
And he [a]was unwilling to take from
his own flock or his own herd,
To prepare for the wayfarer
who had come to him;
Rather he took the poor man's ewe
lamb and prepared it for the
man who had come to him."

5 Then David's anger burned greatly against the
man, and he said to Nathan, "As the LORD lives,
surely the man who has done this [a,A]deserves to die.
6 He must make restitution for the lamb [A]fourfold,
because he did this thing and had no compassion."
7 Nathan then said to David, "[A]You are the man!
Thus says the LORD God of Israel, '[B]It is I who
anointed you king over Israel and it is I who delivered you from the hand of Saul. 8 I also gave you
[A]your master's house and your master's wives into
your [a]care, and I gave you the house of Israel and
Judah; and if *that had been* too little, I would have
added to you many more things like these! 9 Why
[A]have you despised the word of the LORD by doing
evil in His sight? [B]You have struck down Uriah the
Hittite with the sword, [C]have taken his wife to be
your wife, and have killed him with the sword of
the sons of Ammon. 10 Now therefore, [A]the sword
shall never depart from your house, because you
have despised Me and have taken the wife of Uriah
the Hittite to be your wife.' 11 Thus says the LORD,
'Behold, I will raise up evil against you from your
own household; [A]I will even take your wives before
your eyes and give *them* to your companion, and he
will lie with your wives in [a]broad daylight. 12 Indeed
[A]you did it secretly, but [B]I will do this thing before
all Israel, and [a]under the sun.' " 13 Then David said
to Nathan, "[A]I have sinned against the LORD." And
Nathan said to David, "The LORD also has [a,B]taken

11:26 [A]Gen 50:10; Deut 34:8; 1 Sam 31:13 11:27 [a]Lit *gathered* [A]2 Sam 12:9 [B]Ps 51:4, 5 12:1 [a]Lit *said to him* [A]2 Sam 7:2, 4, 17 [B]Ps 51: title 12:3 [a]Lit *morsel* [A]2 Sam 11:3 12:4 [a]Lit *spared* 12:5 [a]Lit *is a son of death* [A]1 Sam 26:16 12:6 [A]Ex 22:1; Luke 19:8 12:7 [A]1 Kin 20:42 [B]1 Sam 16:13 12:8 [a]Lit *bosom* [A]2 Sam 9:7 12:9 [A]1 Sam 15:23, 26 [B]2 Sam 11:14-17 [C]2 Sam 11:27 12:10 [A]2 Sam 13:28; 18:14; 1 Kin 2:25 12:11 [a]Lit *the sight of this sun* [A]Deut 28:30; 2 Sam 16:21, 22 12:12 [a]Lit *before* [A]2 Sam 11:4-15 [B]2 Sam 16:22 12:13 [a]Lit *caused your sin to pass away* [A]1 Sam 15:24, 30; 2 Sam 24:10; Luke 18:13 [B]Lev 20:10; 24:17; Prov 28:13; Mic 7:18

11:26, 27 *time of* **mourning was over.** The customary period of mourning was probably 7 days (Ge 50:10; 1Sa 31:13). Significantly, the text makes no mention of mourning by David.

11:27 evil in the sight of the LORD. This sinful act would bring forth evil consequences.

12:1–14 Psalm 51 records David's words of repentance after being confronted by Nathan over his sin with Bathsheba (cf. Ps 32, where David expresses his agony after Nathan's confrontation).

12:1 the LORD sent Nathan. The word "Lord" is conspicuously absent from the narrative of chap. 11 until v. 27, but then the Lord became actively involved by confronting David with his sin. As Joab had sent a messenger to David (11:18, 19), so the Lord now sent His messenger to David.

12:1–4 two men … rich … poor. To understand this parable, it is necessary only to recognize that the rich man represented David, the poor man, Uriah, and the ewe lamb, Bathsheba.

12:5 deserves to die. According to Ex 22:1, the penalty for stealing and slaughtering an ox or a sheep was not death, but restitution. However, in the parable, the stealing and slaughtering of the lamb represented the adultery with Bathsheba and the murder of Uriah by David. According to the Mosaic law, both adultery (Lv 20:10) and murder (Lv 24:17) required punishment by death. In pronouncing this judgment on the rich man in the story, David unwittingly condemned himself to death.

12:6 fourfold. Exodus 22:1 demanded a 4-fold restitution for the stealing of sheep. There is an allusion here to the subsequent death of 4 of David's sons: Bathsheba's first son (v. 18), Amnon (13:28, 29), Absalom (16:14, 15), and Adonijah (1Ki 2:25).

12:7 anointed. Earlier, the prophet Samuel's confrontation with the sinful Saul emphasized the same point (1Sa 15:17).

12:8 your master's wives. This phraseology means nothing more than that God in His providence had given David, as king, everything that was Saul's. There is no evidence that he ever married any of Saul's wives, though the harem of eastern kings passed to their successors. Ahinoam, the wife of David (2:2; 3:2; 1Sa 25:43; 27:3; 30:5), is always referred to as the Jezreelitess, whereas Ahinoam, the wife of Saul, is distinguished clearly from her by being called "the daughter of Ahimaaz" (1Sa 14:50).

12:9 despised. To despise the word of the Lord was to break His commands and thus incur punishment (cf. Nu 15:31). In summarizing David's violations, his guilt is divinely affirmed.

12:10 the sword shall never depart from your house. David's tragic punishment was a lingering one. Since Uriah was killed by violence, the house of David would be continually plagued by violence. These words anticipated the violent deaths of Amnon (13:28, 29), Absalom (18:14, 15), and Adonijah (1Ki 2:24, 25).

12:11 evil … from your own household. David had done evil to another man's family (11:27). Therefore, he would receive evil in his own family, such as Amnon's rape of Tamar (13:1–14), Absalom's murder of Amnon (13:28, 29), and Absalom's rebellion against David (15:1–12). **lie with your wives in broad daylight.** This prediction was fulfilled by Absalom's public appropriation of David's royal concubines during his rebellion (16:21, 22).

12:13 I have sinned against the LORD. David did not attempt to rationalize or justify his sin. When confronted with the facts, David's confession was immediate. The fuller confessions of David are found in Pss 32 and 51. **The LORD also has taken away your sin.** The Lord graciously forgave David's sin, but the inevitable temporal consequences of sin were experienced by him. Forgiveness does not always remove the consequences of sin in this life, only in the life to come. **you shall not die.** Although the sins of David legally demanded

away your sin; you shall not die. 14 However, because by this deed you have [A]given occasion to the
enemies of the LORD to blaspheme, the child also
that is born to you shall surely die." 15 So Nathan
went to his house.

LOSS OF A CHILD

Then the LORD struck the child that Uriah's [a]widow
bore to David, so that he was *very* sick. 16 David therefore inquired of God for the child; and David [A]fasted
and went and [B]lay all night on the ground. 17 [A]The
elders of his household stood beside him in order to
raise him up from the ground, but he was unwilling
and would not eat food with them. 18 Then it happened
on the seventh day that the child died. And the servants of David were afraid to tell him that the child
was dead, for they said, "Behold, while the child was
still alive, we spoke to him and he did not listen to
our voice. How then can we tell him that the child is
dead, since he might do *himself* harm!" 19 But when
David saw that his servants were whispering together,
David perceived that the child was dead; so David
said to his servants, "Is the child dead?" And they
said, "He is dead." 20 So David arose from the ground,
[A]washed, anointed *himself,* and changed his clothes;
and he came into the house of the LORD and [B]wor-
shiped. Then he came to his own house, and when
he requested, they set food before him and he ate.
21 Then his servants said to him, "What is this
thing that you have done? [a]While the child was
alive, you fasted and wept; but when the child died,
you arose and ate food." 22 He said, "While the child
was *still* alive, [A]I fasted and wept; for I said, '[B]Who
knows, the LORD may be gracious to me, that the
child may live.' 23 But now he has died; why should
I fast? Can I bring him back again? [A]I will go to him,
but [B]he will not return to me."

SOLOMON BORN

24 Then David comforted his wife Bathsheba, and
went in to her and lay with her; and she gave birth
to a son, and [a,A]he named him Solomon. Now the
LORD loved him 25 and sent *word* through Nathan
the prophet, and he named him [a]Jedidiah for the
LORD'S sake.

WAR AGAIN

26 [A]Now Joab fought against [B]Rabbah of the sons
of Ammon and captured the royal city. 27 Joab sent
messengers to David and said, "I have fought
against Rabbah, I have even captured the city of
waters. 28 Now therefore, gather the rest of the people together and camp against the city and capture
it, or I will capture the city myself and it will be
named after me." 29 So David gathered all the people
and went to Rabbah, fought against it and captured
it. 30 Then [A]he took the crown of [a]their king from
his head; and its weight *was* a talent of gold, and
in it [b]*was* a precious stone; and it was *placed* on
David's head. And he brought out the spoil of the
city in great amounts. 31 He also brought out the
people who were in it, and [A]set *them* under saws,
sharp iron instruments, and iron axes, and made
them pass through the brickkiln. And thus he did
to all the cities of the sons of Ammon. Then David
and all the people returned *to* Jerusalem.

AMNON AND TAMAR

13 Now it was after this that [A]Absalom the son
of David had a beautiful sister whose name
was [B]Tamar, and [C]Amnon the son of David loved
her. 2 Amnon was so frustrated because of his sister
Tamar that he made himself ill, for she was a virgin,
and it seemed [a]hard to Amnon to do anything to her.
3 But Amnon had a friend whose name was Jonadab,
the son of [a,A]Shimeah, David's brother; and Jonadab
was a very shrewd man. 4 He said to him, "O son of
the king, why are you so depressed morning after
morning? Will you not tell me?" Then Amnon said
to him, "I am in love with Tamar, the sister of my
brother Absalom." 5 Jonadab then said to him, "Lie
down on your bed and pretend to be ill; when your

12:14 [A]Is 52:5; Rom 2:24 12:15 [a]Lit *wife* 12:16 [A]Neh 1:4 [B]2 Sam 13:31 12:17 [A]Gen 24:2 12:20 [A]Ruth 3:3; Matt 6:17 [B]Ps 95:6-8; 103:1, 8-17; Prov 3:7 12:21 [a]Lit *On account of* 12:22 [A]Is 38:1-3 [B]Jon 3:9 12:23 [A]Gen 37:35 [B]Job 7:8-10 12:24 [a]Some mss read *she* [A]1 Chr 22:9; Matt 1:6 12:25 [a]I.e. beloved of the LORD 12:26 [A]1 Chr 20:1-3 [B]Deut 3:11 12:30 [a]Or *Malcam;* cf Zeph 1:5 [b]Or were *precious stones* [A]1 Chr 20:2 12:31 [A]1 Chr 20:3; Heb 11:37 13:1 [A]2 Sam 3:2, 3; 1 Chr 3:2 [B]1 Chr 3:9 [C]2 Sam 3:2 13:2 [a]Lit *hard in Amnon's eyes* 13:3 [a]In 1 Sam 16:9, *Shammah;* in 1 Chr 2:13, *Shimea* [A]1 Sam 16:9

his death (see v. 5), the Lord graciously released David from the required death penalty. There are events in the OT record where God required death and others where He showed grace and spared the sinner. This is consistent with justice and grace. Those who perished are illustrations of what all sinners deserve. Those who were spared are proofs and examples of God's grace.

12:14 the enemies of the LORD. Because of God's reputation among those who opposed Him, David's sin had to be judged. The judgment would begin with the death of Bathsheba's baby son.

12:23 I will go to him. I.e., David would someday join his son after his own death (cf. 1Sa 28:19). Here is the confidence that there is a future reunion after death, which includes infants who have died being reunited with saints who die (*see note on Mt 19:14;* cf. Mk 10:13–16).

12:24 Solomon. Either "(God is) peace" or "His replacement." Both were true of this child.

12:25 Jedidiah. "Beloved of the Lord" was Nathan's name for Solomon, who was loved in the sense of being chosen by the Lord to be the successor to David's throne, a remarkable instance of God's goodness and grace considering the sinful nature of the marriage.

12:29–31 See 1Ch 20:1–3.

12:29 David … captured it. David completed what Joab had begun by capturing the city of Rabbah.

12:30 a talent of gold. About 75 lbs.

12:31 set *them* under. David imposed hard labor on the Ammonites. But these verses can also be translated with the sense that the Ammonites were cut with saws, indicating that David imposed cruel death on the captives in accordance with Ammonite ways (cf. 1Sa 11:2; Am 1:13).

13:1, 2 Tamar. "Palm tree." She was David's daughter by Maacah, the daughter of Talmai, King of Geshur (3:3), Absalom's (David's third son) full sister and half-sister of Amnon, David's first son by Ahinoam (3:2). Amnon's love for her was not filial, but lustful, as became clear in the story. Unmarried daughters were kept in seclusion from men, so that none could see them alone. Amnon had seen Tamar because of their family relationship and had conceived a violent passion for her. This was forbidden by God (see Lv 18:11), yet with the example of Abraham (Ge 20:12) and the common practice among the surrounding nations of marrying half-sisters, he felt justified and wanted his passion fulfilled with Tamar.

13:3 Jonadab. The son of David's brother, called Shammah in 1Sa 16:9; 17:3 and Shimea in 1Ch 2:13. Jonadab was Amnon's cousin and counselor who gave Amnon the plan by which he was able to rape Tamar.

father comes to see you, say to him, 'Please let my
sister Tamar come and give me *some* food to eat,
and let her prepare the food in my sight, that I may
see *it* and eat from her hand.' " 6 So Amnon lay down
and pretended to be ill; when the king came to see
him, Amnon said to the king, "Please let my sister
Tamar come and [A]make me a couple of cakes in my
sight, that I may eat from her hand."
7 Then David sent to the house for Tamar, saying,
"Go now to your brother Amnon's house, and prepare food for him." 8 So Tamar went to her brother
Amnon's house, and he was lying down. And she
took dough, kneaded *it*, made cakes in his sight,
and baked the cakes. 9 She took the pan and [a]dished
them out before him, but he refused to eat. And
Amnon said, "[A]Have everyone go out from me."
So everyone went out from him. 10 Then Amnon
said to Tamar, "Bring the food into the [a]bedroom,
that I may eat from your hand." So Tamar took the
cakes which she had made and brought them into
the bedroom to her brother Amnon. 11 When she
brought *them* to him to eat, he [A]took hold of her
and said to her, "Come, lie with me, my sister." 12 But
she answered him, "No, my brother, do not violate
me, for [A]such a thing is not done in Israel; do not
do this [B]disgraceful thing! 13 As for me, where could
I [a]get rid of my reproach? And as for you, you will
be like one of the [b]fools in Israel. Now therefore,
please speak to the king, for [A]he will not withhold
me from you." 14 However, he would not listen to
[a]her; since he was stronger than she, he [A]violated
her and lay with her.
15 Then Amnon hated her with a very great hatred; for the hatred with which he hated her was
greater than the love with which he had loved her.
And Amnon said to her, "Get up, go away!" 16 But she
said to him, "No, because this wrong in sending me
away is greater than the other that you have done to
me!" Yet he would not listen to her. 17 Then he called
his young man who attended him and said, "Now
throw this woman out of my *presence*, and lock the
door behind her." 18 Now she had on [A]a [a]long-sleeved
garment; for in this manner the virgin daughters
of the king dressed themselves in robes. Then his
attendant took her out and locked the door behind
her. 19 [A]Tamar put [a]ashes on her head and [B]tore her
[b]long-sleeved garment which *was* on her; and [C]she
put her hand on her head and went away, crying
aloud as she went.
20 Then Absalom her brother said to her, "Has
Amnon your brother been with you? But now keep
silent, my sister, he is your brother; do not take
this matter to heart." So Tamar remained and was
desolate in her brother Absalom's house. 21 Now
when King David heard of all these matters, he
was very angry. 22 But Absalom did not speak to
Amnon [A]either good or bad; for [B]Absalom hated
Amnon because he had violated his sister Tamar.
23 Now it came about after two full years that
Absalom [A]had sheepshearers in Baal-hazor, which
is near Ephraim, and Absalom invited all the king's
sons.

ABSALOM AVENGES TAMAR

24 Absalom came to the king and said, "Behold
now, your servant has sheepshearers; please let
the king and his servants go with your servant."
25 But the king said to Absalom, "No, my son, we
should not all go, for we will be burdensome to
you." Although he [a]urged him, he would not go, but

13:6 [A]Gen 18:6 13:9 [a]Lit *poured* [A]Gen 45:1 13:10 [a]Or *inner room* 13:11 [A]Gen 39:12 13:12 [A]Lev 20:17 [B]Judg 19:23; 20:6 13:13 [a]Lit *cause to go* [b]Or *disgraceful ones* [A]Gen 20:12 13:14 [a]Lit *her voice* [A]Lev 18:9; Deut 22:25; 27:22; 2 Sam 12:11 13:18 [a]Lit *a varicolored tunic* [A]Gen 37:3, 23 13:19 [a]Or *dust* [b]Lit *varicolored tunic* [A]1 Sam 4:12; Esth 4:1 [B]Gen 37:29; 2 Sam 1:11 [C]Jer 2:37 13:22 [A]Gen 31:24 [B]Lev 19:17; 1 John 2:9, 11; 3:10, 12, 15 13:23 [A]1 Sam 25:7 13:25 [a]Lit *broke through*

13:12, 13 this disgraceful thing! Lit. "a wicked thing." Tamar appealed to Amnon with 4 reasons that he should not rape her. First, it was an utterly deplored act in Israel because it violated the law of God (see Lv 18:11), and Tamar knew that such action could bring disharmony and bloodshed to the king's family, as it did. **my reproach.** Second, as a fornicator, Tamar would be scorned as an object of reproach. Even though resistant to the evil crime perpetuated against her, Tamar would bear the stigma of one defiled. **like one of the fools in Israel.** Third, Amnon would be regarded by the people as a wicked fool, a God-rejecting man without principles who offended ordinary standards of morality, thereby jeopardizing Amnon's right to the throne. **the king ... will not withhold me from you.** Fourth, Tamar appealed to Amnon to fulfill his physical desire for her through marriage. She surely knew that such a marriage between half-siblings was not allowed by the Mosaic law (Lv 18:9, 11; 20:17; Dt 27:22), but in the desperation of the moment, Tamar was seeking to escape the immediate situation.

13:14 violated. A euphemism for "raped."

13:15 hated her. Amnon's "love" (v. 1) was nothing but sensual desire that, once gratified, turned to hatred. His sudden revulsion was the result of her unwilling resistance, the atrocity of what he had done, feelings of remorse, and dread of exposure and punishment. All of these rendered her intolerably undesirable to him.

13:15–17 Amnon's sending Tamar away was a greater wrong than the rape itself because it would inevitably have been supposed that she had been guilty of some shameful conduct, i.e., that the seduction had come from her.

13:18 long-sleeved garment. See Ge 37:33. A garment which identified the wearer's special position. For Tamar, the robe identified her as a virgin daughter of the king. The tearing of this garment symbolized her loss of this special position (v. 19).

13:19 put ashes ... tore her long-sleeved garment ... put her hand ... went away, crying aloud. The ashes were a sign of mourning. The torn garment symbolized the ruin of her life. The hand on the head was emblematic of exile and banishment. The crying showed that she viewed herself as good as dead.

13:20 do not take this matter to heart. Absalom told his sister not to pay undue attention or worry about the consequences of the rape. Absalom minimized the significance of what had taken place only for the moment, while already beginning to plot his revenge in using this crime as reason to do what he wanted to do anyway—remove Amnon from the line of succession to the throne (note also v. 32, where Jonadab knew of Absalom's plans). **desolate.** She remained unmarried and childless. Her full brother was her natural protector and the children of polygamists lived by themselves in different family units.

13:21 David ... was very angry. Fury and indignation were David's reactions to the report of the rape (Ge 34:7). Because he did not punish Amnon for his crime, he abdicated his responsibility both as king and as father. The lack of justice in the land would come back to haunt David in a future day (15:4).

13:22 Absalom hated Amnon. As Amnon hated Tamar (v. 15), Absalom loathed his half-brother, Amnon.

13:23–27 Baal-hazor. The Benjamite village of Hazor (Ne 11:33), located about 12 mi. NE of Jerusalem, was the place for a sheep-shearing feast put on by Absalom, to which he invited all his brothers and half-brothers, as well as King David and his royal court (v. 24). David declined, but encouraged Absalom to hold the feast for "the king's sons" as a means to unity and harmony (vv. 25–27). With David's denial

blessed him. 26 Then [A]Absalom said, "If not, please
let my brother Amnon go with us." And the king
said to him, "Why should he go with you?" 27 But
when Absalom [a]urged him, he let Amnon and all
the king's sons go with him.
28 Absalom commanded his servants, saying, "See
now, [A]when Amnon's heart is merry with wine, and
when I say to you, 'Strike Amnon,' then put him to
death. Do not fear; have not I myself commanded
you? Be courageous and be [a]valiant." 29 The servants of Absalom did to Amnon just as Absalom
had commanded. Then all the king's sons arose
and each mounted [A]his mule and fled.
30 Now it was while they were on the way that the
report came to David, saying, "Absalom has struck
down all the king's sons, and not one of them is
left." 31 Then the king arose, [A]tore his clothes and
[B]lay on the ground; and all his servants were standing by with clothes torn. 32 [A]Jonadab, the son of
Shimeah, David's brother, [a]responded, "Do not let
my lord [b]suppose they have put to death all the
young men, the king's sons, for Amnon alone is
dead; because by the [c]intent of Absalom this has
been determined since the day that he violated
his sister Tamar. 33 Now therefore, do not let my
lord the king [A]take the report to [a]heart, namely, 'all
the king's sons are dead,' for only Amnon is dead."
34 Now [A]Absalom had fled. And [B]the young man
who was the watchman raised his eyes and looked,
and behold, many people were coming from the
road behind him by the side of the mountain. 35 Jonadab said to the king, "Behold, the king's sons have
come; according to your servant's word, so it happened." 36 As soon as he had finished speaking, behold, the king's sons came and lifted their voices
and wept; and also the king and all his servants
wept [a]very bitterly.
37 Now [A]Absalom fled and went to [B]Talmai the
son of Ammihud, the king of [C]Geshur. And *David*
mourned for his son every day. 38 [A]So Absalom had
fled and gone to Geshur, and was there three years.
39 *The heart of* King David longed to go out to Absalom; for [A]he was comforted concerning Amnon,
since he was dead.

THE WOMAN OF TEKOA

14 Now Joab the son of Zeruiah perceived that
[A]the king's heart *was inclined* toward Absalom. 2 So Joab sent to [A]Tekoa and [a]brought a wise
woman from there and said to her, "Please pretend
to be a mourner, and put on mourning garments
now, and do not [B]anoint yourself with oil, but be
like a woman who has been mourning for the dead
many days; 3 then go to the king and speak to him in
this manner." So Joab put [A]the words in her mouth.
4 Now when the woman of Tekoa [a]spoke to the
king, she fell on her face to the ground and [A]pros-
trated herself and said, "[B]Help, O king." 5 The king
said to her, "What is your trouble?" And she [a]an-
swered, "Truly I am a widow, for my husband is
dead. 6 Your maidservant had two sons, but the
two of them struggled together in the field, and
there was no [a]one to separate them, so one struck
the other and killed him. 7 Now behold, [A]the whole
family has risen against your maidservant, and they
say, 'Hand over the one who struck his brother, that
we may put him to death for the life of his brother
whom he killed, [B]and destroy the heir also.' Thus
they will extinguish my coal which is left, so as to
[a]leave my husband neither name nor remnant on
the face of the earth."
8 Then the king said to the woman, "Go to your
house, and I will give orders concerning you." 9 The
woman of Tekoa said to the king, "O my lord, the
king, [A]the iniquity is on me and my father's house,
but [B]the king and his throne are guiltless." 10 So the
king said, "Whoever speaks to you, bring him to me,
and he will not touch you anymore." 11 Then she said,

13:26 [A]2 Sam 3:27; 11:13-15 13:27 [a]Lit *broke through* 13:28 [a]Lit *sons of valor* [A]Judg 19:6, 9, 22; 1 Sam 25:36-38 13:29 [A]2 Sam 18:9; 1 Kin 1:33, 38 13:31 [A]2 Sam 1:11 [B]2 Sam 12:16 13:32 [a]Lit *answered and said* [b]Lit *say* [c]Lit *mouth* [A]2 Sam 13:3-5 13:33 [a]Lit *his heart* [A]2 Sam 19:19 13:34 [A]2 Sam 13:37, 38 [B]2 Sam 18:24 13:36 [a]Lit *with a very great weeping* 13:37 [A]2 Sam 13:34 [B]2 Sam 3:3 [C]2 Sam 14:23, 32 13:38 [A]2 Sam 13:34 13:39 [A]2 Sam 12:19-23 14:1 [A]2 Sam 13:39 14:2 [a]Lit *took* [A]2 Sam 23:26; 2 Chr 11:6; Amos 1:1 [B]2 Sam 12:20 14:3 [A]2 Sam 14:19 14:4 [a]Many mss and ancient versions read *came* [A]1 Sam 25:23 [B]2 Kin 6:26-28 14:5 [a]Lit *said* 14:6 [a]Lit *deliverer between* 14:7 [a]Lit *set* [A]Num 35:19; Deut 19:12, 13 [B]Matt 21:38 14:9 [A]Gen 43:9; 1 Sam 25:24 [B]1 Kin 2:33

of the invitation, Absalom requested that Amnon go as his representative. Although David had reservations concerning Absalom's intent, he allowed all his sons to go.

13:28, 29 put him to death. Absalom murdered Amnon through his servants (cf. 11:15–17), just as David had killed Uriah through others (11:14–17). Though rape was punishable by death, personal vengeance such as this was unacceptable to God. Due course of law was to be carried out.

13:29 his mule. Mules were ridden by the royal family in David's kingdom (18:9; 1Ki 1:33, 38, 44).

13:30 all the king's sons. This exaggeration plunged everyone into grief (v. 31) until it was corrected *(v. 32).*

13:32 Jonadab … responded. Jonadab knew of Absalom's plot to kill Amnon (see v. 20) for the rape of Tamar. Death was prescribed in Lv 18:11, 29 ("cut off" means to execute). *See note on vv. 28, 29.*

13:34, 37 Absalom fled. The law regarding premeditated murder, as most would view Absalom's act, gave him no hope of returning (see Num 35:21). The cities of refuge would afford him no sanctuary, so he left his father's kingdom to live in Geshur, E of the Sea of Galilee, under the protection of the king who was the grandfather of both Tamar and Absalom *(see note on 13:1, 2).*

13:39 longed to go. David gradually accepted the fact of Amnon's death and desired to see Absalom again, but took no action to bring him back.

14:1 David was strongly attached to Absalom, and, having gotten over the death of Amnon, he desired the fellowship of his exiled son, 3 years absent. But the fear of public opinion made him hesitant to pardon his son. Joab, perceiving this struggle between parental affection and royal duty, devised a plan involving a wise country woman and a story told to the king.

14:2 Tekoa. A town about 10 mi. S of Jerusalem (cf. Am 1:1).

14:2, 3 Joab put the words in her mouth. Joab used a story, as Nathan had (12:1–12), to show David the error of his ways and to encourage him to call Absalom back to Jerusalem.

14:7 leave my husband neither name nor remnant. The story the woman told involved one brother killing another (v. 6). If the death penalty for murder was invoked (cf. Ex 21:12; Lv 24:17), there would be no living heir in the family, leaving that family with no future, a situation the law sought to avoid (Dt 25:5–10). This would extinguish the last "coal" of hope for a future for her line. Cf. 21:17; Ps 132:17, where the lamp refers to posterity.

14:9 the iniquity is on me. The woman was willing to receive whatever blame might arise from the sparing of her guilty son.

14:11 avenger of blood. This is a specific term identifying the nearest relative of the deceased who would seek to put to death the murderer (Nu 35:6–28; Dt 19:1–13; Mt 27:25). **not one hair.** This is an expression meaning that no harm will come to the son of the widow in the story.

"Please let the king remember the LORD your God,
[A]*so that* the avenger of blood will not continue to
destroy, otherwise they will destroy my son." And
he said, "[B]As the LORD lives, not one hair of your
son shall fall to the ground."
12 Then the woman said, "Please let your maidservant speak a word to my lord the king." And he
said, "Speak." 13 The woman said, "[A]Why then have
you planned such a thing against the people of
God? For in speaking this word the king is as one
who is guilty, *in that* the king does not bring back
[B]his banished one. 14 For [A]we will surely die and
are [B]like water spilled on the ground which cannot be gathered up again. Yet God does not take
away life, but plans [a]ways so that [C]the banished one
will not be cast out from him. 15 Now [a]the reason I
have come to speak this word to my lord the king
is that the people have made me afraid; so your
maidservant said, 'Let me now speak to the king,
perhaps the king will perform the [b]request of his
maidservant. 16 For the king will hear [a]and deliver
his maidservant from the [b]hand of the man who
would destroy [c]both me and my son from [A]the inheritance of God.' 17 Then your maidservant said,
'Please let the word of my lord the king be [a]com-
forting, for as [A]the angel of God, so is my lord the
king to discern good and evil. And may the LORD
your God be with you.' "
18 Then the king answered and said to the woman,
"Please do not hide anything from me that I am
about to ask you." And the woman said, "Let my lord
the king please speak." 19 So the king said, "Is the
hand of Joab with you in all this?" And the woman
replied, "As your soul lives, my lord the king, no one
can turn to the right or to the left from anything
that my lord the king has spoken. Indeed, it was
[A]your servant Joab who commanded me, and it was
he who put all these words in the mouth of your
maidservant; 20 in order to change the appearance
of things your servant Joab has done this thing.
But my lord is wise, [A]like the wisdom of the angel
of God, to know all that is in the earth."

ABSALOM IS RECALLED

21 Then the king said to Joab, "Behold now, [A]I will
surely do this thing; go therefore, bring back the
young man Absalom." 22 Joab fell on his face to the
ground, prostrated himself and blessed the king;
then Joab said, "Today your servant knows that I
have found favor in your sight, O my lord, the king,
in that the king has performed the [a]request of his
servant." 23 So Joab arose and went to [A]Geshur and
brought Absalom to Jerusalem. 24 However the king
said, "Let him turn to [A]his own house, and let him
not see my face." So Absalom turned to his own
house and did not see the king's face.
25 Now in all Israel was no one as handsome as
Absalom, so highly praised; [A]from the sole of his
foot to the crown of his head there was no defect
in him. 26 When he [A]cut the hair of his head (and
it was at the end of every year that he cut *it,* for
it was heavy on him so he cut it), he weighed the
hair of his head at 200 shekels by the king's weight.
27 [A]To Absalom there were born three sons, and
one daughter whose name was [B]Tamar; she was a
woman of beautiful appearance.
28 Now Absalom lived two full years in Jerusalem,
[A]and did not see the king's face. 29 Then Absalom sent
for Joab, to send him to the king, but he would not
come to him. So he sent again a second time, but he
would not come. 30 Therefore he said to his servants,
"See, [A]Joab's [a]field is next to mine, and he has barley
there; go and set it on fire." So Absalom's servants
set the [a]field on fire. 31 Then Joab arose, came to Absalom at his house and said to him, "Why have your
servants set my [a]field on fire?" 32 Absalom [a]answered
Joab, "Behold, I sent for you, saying, 'Come here,
that I may send you to the king, to say, "Why have
I come from Geshur? It would be better for me still
to be there." ' Now therefore, let me see the king's
face, [A]and if there is iniquity in me, let him put me
to death." 33 So when Joab came to the king and told
him, he called for Absalom. Thus he came to the king
and prostrated himself on his face to the ground
before the king, and [A]the king kissed Absalom.

14:11 [A]Num 35:19, 21; Deut 19:4-10 [B]1 Sam 14:45; 1 Kin 1:52; Matt 10:30 14:13 [A]2 Sam 12:7; 1 Kin 20:40-42 [B]2 Sam 13:37, 38 14:14 [a]Lit *devices* [A]Job 30:23; 34:15; Heb 9:27 [B]Ps 58:7 [C]Num 35:15, 25, 28 14:15 [a]Lit *that* [b]Lit *word* 14:16 [a]Lit *to* [b]Lit *palm* [c]Lit *together* [A]Deut 32:9; 1 Sam 26:19 14:17 [a]Lit *for rest* [A]1 Sam 29:9; 2 Sam 14:20; 19:27 14:19 [A]2 Sam 14:3 14:20 [A]2 Sam 14:17; 19:27 14:21 [A]2 Sam 14:11 14:22 [a]Lit *word* 14:23 [A]Deut 3:14; 2 Sam 13:37, 38 14:24 [A]2 Sam 13:20 14:25 [A]Deut 28:35; Job 2:7; Is 1:6 14:26 [A]Ezek 44:20 14:27 [A]2 Sam 18:18 [B]2 Sam 13:1 14:28 [A]2 Sam 14:24 14:30 [a]Lit *portion* [A]Judg 15:3-5 14:31 [a]Lit *portion* 14:32 [a]Lit *said to* [A]1 Sam 20:8; Prov 28:13 14:33 [A]Gen 33:4; Luke 15:20

14:13 against the people of God. The woman asserted that by allowing Absalom to remain in exile, David had jeopardized the future welfare of Israel. If he would be so generous to a son he did not know in a family he did not know, would he not forgive his own son?

14:14 like water spilled on the ground. I.e., death is irreversible. **God does not take away life.** The woman stated that since God acts according to the dictates of mercy, as in David's own experience (12:13), David was obligated to do likewise.

14:15, 16 the people ... the man who would destroy both me and my son. Those who were seeking to kill the son of the woman were like the people David feared who resented what Absalom had done and would have stood against a pardon for him.

14:18–20 David gets the intent of the story and discerns the source as Joab.

14:22 Joab's motives were selfish, in that he sought to ingratiate himself further with David for greater influence and power.

14:23 Geshur. *See note on 13:34, 37.*

14:24 let him not see my face. Absalom returned to Jerusalem, but the estrangement with his father continued.

14:25 handsome. As with Saul before him (1Sa 9:1, 2), Absalom looked like a king. His extraordinary popularity arose from his appearance.

14:26 hair of his head. At his annual haircut, it was determined that Absalom's head produced approximately 5 lbs. of hair that had to be cut off.

14:27 three sons. *See note on 18:18.* **daughter ... Tamar.** Absalom named his daughter after his sister Tamar.

14:28 two full years. Whatever were David's errors in recalling Absalom, he displayed great restraint in wanting to stay apart from Absalom to lead his son through a time of repentance and a real restoration. Rather than produce repentance, however, Absalom's non-access to the royal court and all its amenities frustrated him so that he sent for Joab to intercede (v. 29).

14:30–32 set the field on fire. This was an act of aggression by Absalom to force Joab to act in his behalf with David, his father. Such a crime was serious, as it destroyed the livelihood of the owner and workers. It reveals that Absalom's heart was not repentant and submissive, but manipulative. He wanted an ultimatum delivered to David: accept me or kill me!

14:33 the king kissed Absalom. The kiss signified David's forgiveness and Absalom's reconciliation with the family.

ABSALOM'S CONSPIRACY

15 Now it came about after this that [A]Absalom provided for himself a chariot and horses and fifty men as runners before him. 2 Absalom used to rise early and [A]stand beside the way to the gate; and when any man had a suit to come to the king for judgment, Absalom would call to him and say, "From what city are you?" And he would say, "Your servant is from one of the tribes of Israel." 3 Then Absalom would say to him, "See, [A]your [a]claims are good and right, but no man listens to you on the part of the king." 4 Moreover, Absalom would say, "[A]Oh that one would appoint me judge in the land, then every man who has any suit or cause could come to me and I would give him justice." 5 And when a man came near to prostrate himself before him, he would put out his hand and take hold of him and [A]kiss him. 6 In this manner Absalom dealt with all Israel who came to the king for judgment; [A]so Absalom stole away the hearts of the men of Israel.

7 Now it came about at the end of [a]forty years that Absalom said to the king, "Please let me go and pay my vow which I have vowed to the LORD, in [A]Hebron. 8 For your servant [A]vowed a vow while I was living at Geshur in Aram, saying, '[B]If the LORD shall indeed bring me back to Jerusalem, then I will serve the LORD.' " 9 The king said to him, "Go in peace." So he arose and went to Hebron. 10 But Absalom sent spies throughout all the tribes of Israel, saying, "As soon as you hear the sound of the trumpet, then you shall say, '[A]Absalom is king in Hebron.' " 11 Then two hundred men went with Absalom from Jerusalem, [A]who were invited and [B]went [a]innocently, and they did not know anything. 12 And Absalom sent for [A]Ahithophel the Gilonite, David's counselor, from his city [B]Giloh, while he was offering the sacrifices. And the conspiracy was strong, for [C]the people increased continually with Absalom.

DAVID FLEES JERUSALEM

13 Then a messenger came to David, saying, "[A]The hearts of the men of Israel are [a]with Absalom." 14 David said to all his servants who were with him at Jerusalem, "[A]Arise and let us flee, for *otherwise* none of us will escape from Absalom. Go in haste, or he will overtake us quickly and bring down calamity on us and strike the city with the edge of the sword." 15 Then the king's servants said to the king, "Behold, your servants *are ready to do* whatever my lord the king chooses." 16 So the king went out and all his household [a]with him. But [A]the king left ten concubines to keep the house. 17 The king went out and all the people [a]with him, and they stopped at the last house. 18 Now all his servants passed on beside him, [A]all the Cherethites, all the Pelethites and all the Gittites, [B]six hundred men who had come [a]with him from Gath, passed on before the king.

19 Then the king said to [A]Ittai the Gittite, "Why will you also go with us? Return and remain with the king, for you are a foreigner and also an exile; *return* to your own place. 20 You came *only* yesterday, and shall I today make you wander with us, while [A]I go where I will? Return and take back your brothers; [B]mercy and [a]truth be with you." 21 But Ittai answered the king and said, "As the LORD lives, and as my lord the king lives, surely [A]wherever my lord the king may be, whether for death or for life, there also your servant will be." 22 Therefore David said to Ittai, "Go and pass over." So Ittai the Gittite passed over with all his men and all the little ones who *were* with him. 23 While all the country was weeping with a loud voice, all the people passed over. The king also passed over [A]the brook Kidron,

15:1 [A]1 Kin 1:5 15:2 [A]Ruth 4:1; 2 Sam 19:8 15:3 [a]Lit *words* [A]Prov 12:2 15:4 [A]Judg 9:29 15:5 [A]2 Sam 14:33; 20:9 15:6 [A]Rom 16:18 15:7 [a]Some ancient versions render *four* [A]2 Sam 3:2, 3 15:8 [A]2 Sam 13:37, 38 [B]Gen 28:20, 21 15:10 [A]1 Kin 1:34; 2 Kin 9:13 15:11 [a]Lit *in their integrity* [A]1 Sam 9:13 [B]1 Sam 22:15 15:12 [A]2 Sam 15:31 [B]Josh 15:51 [C]Ps 3:1 15:13 [a]Lit *after* [A]Judg 9:3; 2 Sam 15:6 15:14 [A]2 Sam 12:11; Ps 3: title 15:16 [a]Lit *at his feet* [A]2 Sam 16:21, 22 15:17 [a]Lit *at his feet* 15:18 [a]Lit *at his feet* [A]2 Sam 8:18 [B]1 Sam 23:13; 25:13; 30:1, 9 15:19 [A]2 Sam 18:2 15:20 [a]Or *faithfulness* [A]1 Sam 23:13 [B]2 Sam 2:6 15:21 [A]Ruth 1:16, 17; Prov 17:17 15:23 [A]1 Kin 15:13; 2 Chr 29:16

15:1 chariot and horses and fifty men. After the reconciliation, Absalom possessed the symbols of royalty (see 1Sa 8:11).

15:1–6 stole away the hearts. Public hearings were always conducted early in the morning in a court held outside by the city gates. Absalom positioned himself there to win favor. Because King David was busy with other matters or with wars, and was also aging, many matters were left unresolved, building a deep feeling of resentment among the people. Absalom used that situation to undermine his father, by gratifying all he could with a favorable settlement and showing them all warm cordiality. Thus, he won the people to himself, without them knowing his wicked ambition.

15:7 forty years. See the marginal reference. The better reading is "four" because the number "forty" could refer neither to the age of Absalom since he was born at Hebron after David had begun to rule (3:2–5), nor the time of David's reign, since he ruled only 40 years total (5:4, 5). The 4-year period began either with Absalom's return from Geshur (14:23) or with his reconciliation with David (14:33).

15:7–9 Hebron. The city of Absalom's birth (3:2, 3), and the place where David was first anointed king over Judah (2:4) and over all Israel (5:3). Absalom said he had made a vow while in Geshur (*see note on 13:34, 37*) that if he was restored to Jerusalem, he would offer a sacrifice of thanksgiving in Hebron, where sacrifices were often made before the temple was built. David, who always encouraged such religious devotion, gave his consent.

15:10–12 Absalom formed a conspiracy, which included taking some of the leading men to create the impression that the king supported this action, and was in his old age sharing the kingdom. All of this was a subtle disguise so Absalom could have freedom to plan his revolution. Absalom was able to do this against his father not merely because of his cleverness, but also because of the laxness of his father (see 1Ki 1:6).

15:12 Ahithophel. A counselor of David who was considered a man who "inquired of the word of God" (16:23). This man was the father of Eliam (23:34) and the grandfather of Bathsheba (11:3; 23:24–39), who may have been looking for revenge on David. **Giloh.** A town in the hill country of Judah (Jos 15:48, 51), probably located a few mi. S of Hebron.

15:13–17 David's escape from Absalom is remembered in Ps 3. Because he wanted to preserve the city he had beautified, and not have a war there, and since he felt that he could find greater support in the country, David left the city with all his household and personal guards.

15:18 Cherethites ... Pelethites. Foreign mercenary soldiers of King David. *See note on 1Sa 30:14.* **Gittites.** Mercenary soldiers from Gath, i.e., Philistines.

15:19–22 Ittai. The commander of the Gittites, who had only recently joined David. In spite of David's words, he displayed his loyalty by going into exile with him. Ittai's later appointment as commander of one-third of the army (18:2, 5, 12) was David's way of expressing appreciation for his loyalty.

15:23–28 Psalm 63 has this occasion in view or possibly 1Sa 23:14.

15:23 brook Kidron. This familiar valley, running N/S along the eastern side of Jerusalem, separates the city from the Mt. of Olives.

and all the people passed over toward [B]the way of the wilderness.

24 Now behold, [A]Zadok also *came,* and all the Levites with him [B]carrying the ark of the covenant of God. And they set down the ark of God, and [C]Abiathar came up until all the people had finished passing from the city. 25 The king said to Zadok, "Return the ark of God to the city. If I find favor in the sight of the LORD, then [A]He will bring me back again and show me both it and [B]His habitation. 26 But if He should say thus, '[A]I have no delight in you,' behold, here I am, [B]let Him do to me as seems good [a]to Him." 27 The king said also to Zadok the priest, "Are you *not* [A]a seer? Return to the city in peace and your [B]two sons with you, your son Ahimaaz and Jonathan the son of Abiathar. 28 See, I am going to wait [A]at the fords of the wilderness until word comes from you to inform me." 29 Therefore Zadok and Abiathar returned the ark of God to Jerusalem and remained there.

30 And David went up the ascent of the *Mount of* Olives, and wept as he went, and [A]his head was covered and he walked [B]barefoot. Then all the people who were with him each covered his head and went up weeping as they went. 31 Now someone told David, saying, "[A]Ahithophel is among the conspirators with Absalom." And David said, "O LORD, I pray, [B]make the counsel of Ahithophel foolishness."

32 It happened as David was coming to the summit, where God was worshiped, that behold, Hushai the [A]Archite met him with his [a]coat torn and [b]dust on his head. 33 David said to him, "If you pass over with me, then you will be [A]a burden to me. 34 But if you return to the city, and [A]say to Absalom, 'I will be your servant, O king; as I have been your father's servant in time past, so I will now be your servant,' then you can thwart the counsel of Ahithophel for me. 35 Are not Zadok and Abiathar the priests with you there? So it shall be that [A]whatever you hear from the king's house, you shall report to Zadok and Abiathar the priests. 36 Behold [A]their two sons are with them there, Ahimaaz, Zadok's son and Jonathan, Abiathar's son; and [B]by them you shall send me everything that you hear." 37 So Hushai, [A]David's friend, came into the city, and [B]Absalom came into Jerusalem.

ZIBA, A FALSE SERVANT

16 Now when David had passed [A]a little beyond the summit, behold, [B]Ziba the servant of Mephibosheth met him [C]with a couple of saddled donkeys, and on them *were* two hundred loaves of bread, a hundred clusters of raisins, a hundred summer fruits, and a jug of wine. 2 The king said to Ziba, "Why do you have these?" And Ziba said, "[A]The donkeys are for the king's household to ride, and the bread and summer fruit for the young men to eat, and the wine, [B]for whoever is faint in the wilderness to drink." 3 Then the king said, "And where is [A]your master's son?" And [B]Ziba said to the king, "Behold, he is staying in Jerusalem, for he said, 'Today the house of Israel will restore the kingdom of my father to me.' " 4 So the king said to Ziba, "Behold, all that belongs to Mephibosheth is yours." And Ziba said, "I prostrate myself; let me find favor in your sight, O my lord, the king!"

DAVID IS CURSED

5 When King David came to [A]Bahurim, behold, there came out from there a man of the family of the house of Saul [B]whose name was Shimei, the son of Gera; he came out [C]cursing continually as he came. 6 He threw stones at David and at all the servants of King David; and all the people and all the mighty men were at his right hand and at his left. 7 Thus Shimei said when he cursed, "Get out, get out, [A]you man of bloodshed, and worthless fellow! 8 [A]The LORD has returned upon you all [B]the bloodshed of the house of Saul, in whose place you have reigned; and the LORD has given the kingdom into the hand of your son Absalom. And behold, you are *taken* in your own evil, for you are a man of bloodshed!"

9 Then [A]Abishai the son of Zeruiah said to the king, "Why should [B]this dead dog [C]curse my lord the king? Let me go over now and [a]cut off his head."

15:23 [B]2 Sam 15:28; 16:2 15:24 [A]2 Sam 8:17; 20:25 [B]Num 4:15; 1 Sam 4:4, 5 [C]1 Sam 22:20 15:25 [A]Ps 43:3 [B]Ex 15:13; Jer 25:30 15:26 [a]Lit *in His sight* [A]2 Sam 11:27; 1 Chr 21:7 [B]1 Sam 3:18 15:27 [A]1 Sam 9:6-9 [B]2 Sam 17:17 15:28 [A]Josh 5:10; 2 Sam 17:16 15:30 [A]Esth 6:12; Ezek 24:17, 23 [B]Is 20:2-4 15:31 [A]2 Sam 15:12 [B]2 Sam 16:23; 17:14, 23 15:32 [a]Or *tunic* [b]Lit *ground* [A]Josh 16:2 15:33 [A]2 Sam 19:35 15:34 [A]2 Sam 16:19 15:35 [A]2 Sam 17:15, 16 15:36 [A]2 Sam 15:27 [B]2 Sam 17:17 15:37 [A]2 Sam 16:16; 1 Chr 27:33 [B]2 Sam 16:15 16:1 [A]2 Sam 15:32 [B]2 Sam 9:2-13 [C]1 Sam 25:18 16:2 [A]Judg 10:4 [B]2 Sam 17:29 16:3 [A]2 Sam 9:9, 10 [B]2 Sam 19:26, 27 16:5 [A]2 Sam 3:16; 17:18 [B]2 Sam 19:16-23; 1 Kin 2:8, 9, 44 [C]Ex 22:28; 1 Sam 17:43 16:7 [A]2 Sam 12:9 16:8 [A]2 Sam 21:1-9 [B]2 Sam 1:16; 3:28, 29; 4:11, 12 16:9 [a]Lit *take off* [A]1 Sam 26:8; 2 Sam 19:21; Luke 9:54 [B]2 Sam 9:8 [C]Ex 22:28

15:24–29 Zadok … Abiathar. *See notes on 8:17.* They brought the ark to comfort David with assurance of God's blessing, but he saw that as placing more confidence in the symbol than in God and sent it back. David knew the possession of the ark did not guarantee God's blessing (cf. 1Sa 4:3).

15:28 fords of the wilderness. Probably the region along the western bank of the Jordan River (see 17:16; Jos 5:10).

15:30 *Mount of* Olives. The hill to the E of the city of Jerusalem was the location for David's contrition and remorse over his sins and their results. This was the location from which Jesus ascended to heaven (Ac 1:9–12).

15:32 summit. This was the place from which David could look toward the city to the W. **Hushai the Archite.** Hushai was of the clan of the Archites who lived in Ephraim on the border with Manasseh (Jos 16:2) and served as an official counselor to David (v. 37; 1Ch 27:33). David persuaded Hushai to return to Jerusalem and attach himself to Absalom as a counselor. His mission was to contradict the advice of Ahithophel (17:5–14) and to communicate Absalom's plans to David (17:21; 18:19).

16:1 Ziba. *See note on 9:2.* **Mephibosheth.** Saul's grandson by Jonathan (*see note on 4:4*).

16:3 where is your master's son? According to 9:9, 10, Ziba was able to garner such food and drink. His master had been Saul before his death and was then Mephibosheth. **restore the kingdom of my father.** Ziba, evidently trying to commend himself in the eyes of David by bringing these gifts, accused his master of disloyalty to the king and participation in Absalom's conspiracy for the purpose of bringing down the whole Davidic house. Thus the house of Saul would retake the throne, and he would be king. This was a false accusation (see 19:24, 25), but it was convincing to David, who believed the story and made a severe and rash decision that inflicted injury on a true friend, Mephibosheth.

16:5 Bahurim. *See note on 3:16.*

16:5–8 Shimei. Shimei was a distant relative of Saul, from the tribe of Benjamin, who cursed David as a "man of bloodshed" (vv. 7, 8) and a "worthless fellow" (*see note on 1Sa 2:12*). He could possibly be the Cush of Ps 7. Shimei declared that the loss of David's throne was God's retribution on his past sins (v. 8), and David accepted his curse as from the Lord (v. 11). It could be that Shimei was accusing David of the murders of Abner (3:27–39), Ish-bosheth (4:1–12), and Uriah (11:15–27).

16:9 Abishai. *See note on 2:18.* **dead dog.** I.e., worthless and despised (cf. 9:8).

10 But the king said, "[A]What have I to do with you,
O sons of Zeruiah? [B]If he curses, and if the LORD has
told him, 'Curse David,' [C]then who shall say, 'Why
have you done so?' " 11 Then David said to Abishai
and to all his servants, "Behold, [A]my son who came
out from [a]me seeks my life; how much more now
this Benjamite? Let him alone and let him curse,
[B]for the LORD has told him. 12 Perhaps the LORD
will look on my affliction and [a,A]return good to me
instead of his cursing this day." 13 So David and his
men went on the way; and Shimei went along on
the hillside parallel with him and as he went he
cursed and cast stones and threw dust at him. 14 The
king and all the people who were with him arrived
weary and he refreshed himself there.

ABSALOM ENTERS JERUSALEM

15 [A]Then Absalom and all the people, the men of
Israel, entered Jerusalem, and Ahithophel with him.
16 Now it came about when [A]Hushai the Archite,
David's friend, came to Absalom, that [B]Hushai said
to Absalom, "[C]*Long* live the king! *Long* live the king!"
17 Absalom said to Hushai, "Is this your [a]loyalty to
your friend? [A]Why did you not go with your friend?"
18 Then Hushai said to Absalom, "No! For whom the
LORD, this people, and all the men of Israel have
chosen, his I will be, and with him I will remain.
19 Besides, [A]whom should I serve? *Should I* not *serve*
in the presence of his son? As I have served in your
father's presence, so I will be in your presence."
20 Then Absalom said to Ahithophel, "Give your
advice. What shall we do?" 21 Ahithophel said to Absalom, "[A]Go in to your father's concubines, whom
he has left to keep the house; then all Israel will
hear that you have made yourself odious to your
father. The hands of all who are with you will also be
strengthened." 22 So they pitched a tent for Absalom
on the roof, [A]and Absalom went in to his father's
concubines [B]in the sight of all Israel. 23 [A]The advice
of Ahithophel, which he [a]gave in those days, *was*
as if one inquired of the word of God; [B]so was all
the advice of Ahithophel *regarded* by both David
and Absalom.

HUSHAI'S COUNSEL

17 Furthermore, Ahithophel said to Absalom,
"Please let me choose 12,000 men that I may
arise and pursue David tonight. 2 [A]I will come upon
him while he is weary and [a]exhausted and terrify
him, so that all the people who are with him will
flee. Then [B]I will strike down the king alone, 3 and
I will bring back all the people to you. [a]The return
of everyone depends on the man you seek; *then* all
the people will be at [A]peace." 4 So the [a]plan pleased
Absalom and all the elders of Israel.
5 Then Absalom said, "Now call [A]Hushai the
Archite also, and let us hear what [a]he has to say."
6 When Hushai had come to Absalom, Absalom said
to [a]him, "Ahithophel has spoken [b]thus. Shall we
[c]carry out his plan? If not, you speak." 7 So Hushai
said to Absalom, "[A]This time the advice that Ahithophel has [a]given is not good." 8 Moreover, Hushai
said, "You know your father and his men, that they
are mighty men and they are [a]fierce, [A]like a bear
robbed of her cubs in the field. And your father is
an [b]expert in warfare, and will not spend the night
with the people. 9 Behold, he has now hidden himself in one of the [a]caves or in another place; and it
will be [b]when he falls on them at the first attack,
that whoever hears *it* will say, 'There has been a
slaughter among the people who follow Absalom.'
10 And even the one who is valiant, whose heart is
like the heart of a lion, [A]will completely [a]lose heart;
for all Israel knows that your father is a mighty man
and those who are with him are valiant men. 11 But
I counsel that all Israel be surely gathered to you,
[A]from Dan even to Beersheba, [B]as the sand that is by
the sea in abundance, and that [a]you personally go
into battle. 12 So we shall come to him in one of the
places where he can be found, and we will [a]fall on
him [A]as the dew falls on the ground; and of him and
of all the men who are with him, not even one will
be left. 13 If he withdraws into a city, then all Israel
shall bring ropes to that city, and we will [A]drag it
into the [a]valley until not even a small stone is found
there." 14 Then Absalom and all the men of Israel
said, "The counsel of Hushai the Archite is better

16:10 [A]2 Sam 3:39; 19:22 [B]John 18:11 [C]Rom 9:20 16:11 [a]Lit *my body* [A]2 Sam 12:11 [B]Gen 45:5; 1 Sam 26:19 16:12 [a]Lit *the LORD will return* [A]Deut 23:5; Rom 8:28 16:15 [A]2 Sam 15:12, 37 16:16 [A]2 Sam 15:37 [B]2 Sam 15:34 [C]1 Sam 10:24; 2 Kin 11:12 16:17 [a]Or *kindness* [A]2 Sam 19:25 16:19 [A]2 Sam 15:34 16:21 [A]2 Sam 15:16; 20:3 16:22 [A]2 Sam 15:16; 20:3 [B]2 Sam 12:11, 12 16:23 [a]Lit *advised* [A]2 Sam 17:14, 23 [B]2 Sam 15:12 17:2 [a]Lit *slack of hands* [A]2 Sam 16:14 [B]1 Kin 22:31 17:3 [a]Lit *Like the return of the whole is the man whom you seek* [A]Jer 6:14 17:4 [a]Lit *word was pleasing in the sight of* 17:5 [a]Lit *is in his mouth—even he* [A]2 Sam 15:32-34 17:6 [a]Lit *him, saying* [b]Lit *according to this word* [c]Lit *do his word* 17:7 [a]Lit *advised* [A]2 Sam 16:21 17:8 [a]Lit *bitter of soul* [b]Lit *man of war* [A]Hos 13:8 17:9 [a]Lit *pits* [b]Lit *according to a falling among them* 17:10 [a]Lit *melt* [A]Josh 2:9-11 17:11 [a]Lit *your face go* [A]1 Sam 3:20 [B]Gen 22:17; 1 Sam 13:5 17:12 [a]Lit *settle down* [A]Ps 110:3; Mic 5:7 17:13 [a]Or *wadi* [A]Mic 1:6

16:10–14 The patience and restraint of David on this occasion was amazingly different from his violent reaction to the slanderous words of Nabal (1Sa 25:2ff.). On that occasion, he was eager to kill the man until placated by the wisdom of Abigail. He was a broken man at this later time and knew that while the rancor of Shimei was uncalled for, his accusations were true. He was penitent.

16:15 Ahithophel. *See note on 15:12.*

16:15–23 Absalom set up his royal court in Jerusalem.

16:16 Hushai. *See note on 15:32.*

16:21, 22 your father's concubines. David had left behind in Jerusalem 10 concubines to take care of the palace (15:16). In the Near East, possession of the harem came with the throne. Ahithophel advised Absalom to have sexual relations with David's concubines and thereby assert his right to his father's throne. On the roof of the palace in the most public place (cf. 11:2), a tent was set up for this scandalous event, thereby fulfilling the judgment announced by Nathan in 12:11, 12.

17:1–4 Ahithophel's second piece of advice to Absalom was that he immediately pursue and kill David to remove any possibility of his reclaiming the throne, which would incline David's followers to return and submit to Absalom.

17:4 all the elders of Israel. The same prominent tribal leaders who had accepted David's kingship in 5:3 had been won over as participants in Absalom's rebellion.

17:7–13 Providentially, the Lord took control of the situation through the counsel of Hushai (*see note on 15:32*) who advised Absalom in such a way as to give David time to prepare for war with Absalom. Hushai's plan seemed best to the elders. It had two features: 1) the need for an army larger than 12,000 (v. 1), so that Absalom would not lose, and 2) the king leading the army into battle (an appeal to Absalom's arrogance).

17:11 Dan even to Beersheba. *See note on 3:10.*

17:13 ropes. In besieging the town, hooks attached to ropes were cast over the protective wall and, with a large number of men pulling, the walls were pulled down.

17:14 the LORD had ordained. The text notes that Ahithophel's advice was rejected by Absalom because the Lord had determined

than the counsel of Ahithophel." For [A]the LORD had
ordained to thwart the good counsel of Ahithophel,
so that the LORD might bring calamity on Absalom.

HUSHAI'S WARNING SAVES DAVID

15 Then [A]Hushai said to Zadok and to Abiathar the
priests, "[a]This is what Ahithophel counseled Absalom and the elders of Israel, and [a]this is what I have
counseled. 16 Now therefore, send quickly and tell
David, saying, '[A]Do not spend the night at the fords
of the wilderness, but by all means cross over, or else
the king and all the people who are with him will be
[a]destroyed.' " 17 [A]Now Jonathan and Ahimaaz were
staying at [B]En-rogel, and a maidservant would go
and tell them, and they would go and tell King David,
for they could not be seen entering the city. 18 But
a lad did see them and told Absalom; so the two of
them departed quickly and came to the house of a
man [A]in Bahurim, who had a well in his courtyard,
and they went down [a]into it. 19 And [A]the woman [a]took
a covering and spread it over the well's mouth and
scattered grain on it, so that nothing was known.
20 Then Absalom's servants came to the woman at
the house and said, "Where are Ahimaaz and Jonathan?" And [A]the woman said to them, "They have
crossed the brook of water." And when they searched
and could not find *them,* they returned to Jerusalem.
21 It came about after they had departed that
they came up out of the well and went and told
King David; and they said to David, "[A]Arise and
cross over the water quickly for thus Ahithophel
has counseled against you." 22 Then David and all
the people who *were* with him arose and crossed
the Jordan; and by [a]dawn not even one remained
who had not crossed the Jordan.
23 Now when Ahithophel saw that his counsel was
not [a]followed, he [b]saddled *his* donkey and arose and
went to his home, to [A]his city, and [c,B]set his house
in order, and [C]strangled himself; thus he died and
was buried in the grave of his father.
24 Then David came to [A]Mahanaim. And Absalom
crossed the Jordan, he and all the men of Israel
with him. 25 Absalom set [A]Amasa over the army
in place of Joab. Now Amasa was the son of a man
whose name was [a]Ithra the Israelite, who went in to
Abigail the daughter of [B]Nahash, sister of Zeruiah,
Joab's mother. 26 And Israel and Absalom camped
in the land of Gilead.
27 Now when David had come to Mahanaim, Shobi
[A]the son of Nahash from [B]Rabbah of the sons of
Ammon, [C]Machir the son of Ammiel from Lo-debar,
and [D]Barzillai the Gileadite from Rogelim, 28 brought
[A]beds, basins, pottery, wheat, barley, flour, parched
grain, beans, lentils, parched *seeds,* 29 honey, curds,
sheep, and cheese of the herd, for David and for the
people who *were* with him, [A]to eat; for they said,
"The people are hungry and weary and thirsty in
the wilderness."

ABSALOM SLAIN

18 Then David [a]numbered the people who were
with him and [A]set over them commanders of
thousands and commanders of hundreds. 2 David
sent the people out, [A]one third under the [a]command
of Joab, one third under the [a]command of Abishai
the son of Zeruiah, Joab's brother, and one third under the [a]command of [B]Ittai the Gittite. And the king
said to the people, "I myself will surely go out with
you also." 3 But the people said, "[A]You should not go
out; for if we indeed flee, they will not care about us;
even if half of us die, they will not care about us. But
[a]you are worth ten thousand of us; therefore now it
is better that you *be ready* to help us from the city."
4 Then the king said to them, "Whatever seems best
to you I will do." So [A]the king stood beside the gate,
and all the people went out by hundreds and thousands. 5 The king charged Joab and Abishai and Ittai,
saying, "*Deal* gently for my sake with the young man
Absalom." And [A]all the people heard when the king
charged all the commanders concerning Absalom.

17:14 [A]2 Sam 15:31, 34; Ps 9:15, 16 17:15 [a]Lit *Thus and thus* [A]2 Sam 15:35, 36 17:16 [a]Lit *swallowed up* [A]2 Sam 15:28 17:17 [A]2 Sam 15:27, 36 [B]Josh 15:7; 18:16 17:18 [a]Lit *there* [A]2 Sam 3:16; 16:5 17:19 [a]Lit *took and spread the covering* [A]Josh 2:4-6 17:20 [A]Lev 19:11; Josh 2:3-5; 1 Sam 19:12-17 17:21 [A]2 Sam 17:15, 16 17:22 [a]Lit *the light of the morning* 17:23 [a]Lit *done* [b]Lit *bound* [c]Lit *gave charge to* [A]2 Sam 15:12 [B]2 Kin 20:1 [C]Matt 27:5 17:24 [A]Gen 32:2, 10; 2 Sam 2:8 17:25 [a]In 1 Chr 2:17, *Jether the Ishmaelite* [A]2 Sam 19:13; 20:9-12; 1 Kin 2:5, 32 [B]1 Chr 2:16 17:27 [A]1 Sam 11:1; 2 Sam 10:1, 2 [B]2 Sam 12:26, 29 [C]2 Sam 9:4 [D]2 Sam 19:31-39; 1 Kin 2:7 17:28 [A]Prov 11:25; Matt 5:7 17:29 [A]2 Sam 16:2, 14; Prov 21:26; Eccl 11:1; Rom 12:13 18:1 [a]Lit *mustered* [A]Ex 18:25; Num 31:14; 1 Sam 22:7 18:2 [a]Lit *hand* [A]Judg 7:16; 1 Sam 11:11 [B]2 Sam 15:19-22 18:3 [a]So with some ancient versions; M.T. *for now there are ten thousand like us* [A]2 Sam 21:17 18:4 [A]2 Sam 18:24 18:5 [A]2 Sam 18:12

to defeat the rebellion of Absalom, as prayed for by David (15:31). God's providence was controlling all the intrigues among the usurper's counselors.

17:16 cross over. Crossing over from the W side to the E side of the Jordan River was the means of protecting David and his people from the immediate onslaught if Ahithophel's plan was followed.

17:17 Jonathan and Ahimaaz. Jonathan was the son of the priest Abiathar and Ahimaaz the son of the priest Zadok (15:27). They were designated to take information from Hushai in Jerusalem to David by the Jordan River. **En-rogel.** A spring in the Kidron Valley on the border between Benjamin and Judah (Jos 15:1, 7; 18:11, 16) less than a mi. SE of Jerusalem.

17:18 Bahurim. *See note on 3:16.*

17:19 well's mouth. Using an empty cistern as a place for a covering of dry grain was a common practice.

17:23 strangled himself. When Ahithophel saw that his counsel to Absalom had not been followed, he took his own life. He probably foresaw Absalom's defeat and knew that he would then be accountable to David for his disloyalty.

17:24 Mahanaim. *See note on 2:8.*

17:25 Amasa. Absalom appointed Amasa as commander of the army of Israel, replacing Joab who had accompanied David on his flight from Jerusalem. Amasa was the son of Abigail, either David's sister or his half-sister (1Ch 2:17), making him David's nephew. His mother was also the sister of Zeruiah, the mother of Joab. Therefore, Amasa was a cousin of Absalom, Joab, and Abishai. Under his lead, the armies crossed the Jordan (v. 24) into Gilead, the high-eastern area. Sufficient time had passed for building the large army Hushai suggested, and so David had readied himself for the war (*see note on 17:7–13*).

17:27 Shobi. A son of Nahash and brother of Hanun, kings of the Ammonites (10:1, 2). **Machir.** *See note on 9:4.* **Barzillai.** An aged, wealthy benefactor of David from Gilead, on the east side of the Jordan (see 19:31–39; 1Ki 2:7).

18:2 A 3-pronged attack was a customary military strategy (see Jdg 7:16; 1Sa 11:11; 13:17).

18:3 You should not go out. David desired to lead his men into the battle; however, the people recognized that the death of David would mean sure defeat and Absalom would then be secure in the kingship. The people's words echo what Ahithophel had earlier pointed out to Absalom (17:2, 3). So David was persuaded to remain at Mahanaim.

18:5 *Deal* gently. David ordered his 3 commanders not to harm Absalom. The 4 uses of "the young man Absalom" (vv. 5, 12, 29, 32) imply that David sentimentally viewed Absalom as a youthful rebel who could be forgiven.

6 Then the people went out into the field against Israel, and the battle took place in [A]the forest of Ephraim.
7 The people of Israel were [a]defeated there before the
servants of David, and the slaughter there that day was
great, 20,000 men. 8 For the battle there was spread
over the whole countryside, and the forest devoured
more people that day than the sword devoured.
9 Now Absalom happened to meet the servants of
David. For Absalom was riding on *his* mule, and the
mule went under the thick branches of a great oak.
And [A]his head caught fast in the oak, so he was [a]left
hanging between heaven and earth, while the mule
that was under him kept going. 10 When a certain
man saw *it,* he told Joab and said, "Behold, I saw
Absalom hanging in an oak." 11 Then Joab said to
the man who had told him, "Now behold, you saw
him! Why then did you not strike him there to the
ground? And I would have given you ten *pieces* of
silver and a belt." 12 The man said to Joab, "Even if
I should receive a thousand *pieces of* silver in my
hand, I would not put out my hand against the king's
son; for [A]in our hearing the king charged you and
Abishai and Ittai, saying, '[a]Protect for me the young
man Absalom!' 13 Otherwise, if I had dealt treacherously against his life (and [A]there is nothing hidden
from the king), then you yourself would have stood
aloof." 14 Then Joab said, "I will not [a]waste time here
with you." [A]So he took three spears in his hand and
thrust them through the heart of Absalom while
he was yet alive in the [b]midst of the oak. 15 And
ten young men who carried Joab's armor gathered
around and struck Absalom and killed him.
16 Then [A]Joab blew the trumpet, and the people
returned from pursuing Israel, for Joab restrained
the people. 17 They took Absalom and cast him into
[a]a deep pit in the forest and [A]erected over him a very
great heap of stones. And [B]all Israel fled, each to his
tent. 18 Now Absalom in his lifetime had taken and
[A]set up for himself a pillar which is in [B]the King's
Valley, for he said, "[C]I have no son [a]to preserve my
name." So he named the pillar after his own name,
and it is called Absalom's Monument to this day.

DAVID IS GRIEF-STRICKEN

19 Then [A]Ahimaaz the son of Zadok said, "Please
let me run and bring the king news [B]that the LORD
has [a]freed him from the hand of his enemies." 20 But
Joab said to him, "You are not the man to carry
news this day, but you shall carry news another
day; however, you shall carry no news today because the king's son is dead." 21 Then Joab said to
the Cushite, "Go, tell the king what you have seen."
So the Cushite bowed to Joab and ran. 22 Now Ahimaaz the son of Zadok said once more to Joab, "But
whatever happens, please let me also run after the
Cushite." And Joab said, "Why would you run, my
son, since [A]you will have no reward for going?"
23 "But whatever happens," *he said,* "I will run." So
he said to him, "Run." Then Ahimaaz ran by way of
the plain and passed up the Cushite.
24 Now [A]David was sitting between the two gates;
and [B]the watchman went up to the roof of the gate
by the wall, and raised his eyes and looked, and behold, a man running by himself. 25 The watchman
called and told the king. And the king said, "If he is
by himself there is good news in his mouth." And he
came nearer and nearer. 26 Then the watchman saw
another man running; and the watchman called to
the gatekeeper and said, "Behold, *another* man running by himself." And the king said, "This one also is
bringing good news." 27 The watchman said, "I [a]think
the running of the first one [A]is like the running of
Ahimaaz the son of Zadok." And the king said, "[B]This
is a good man and comes with good news."
28 Ahimaaz called and said to the king, "[a]All is
well." And [A]he prostrated himself before the king
with his face to the ground. And he said, "[B]Blessed
is the LORD your God, who has delivered up the men
who lifted their hands against my lord the king."
29 The king said, "[A]Is it well with the young man
Absalom?" And Ahimaaz answered, "When Joab
sent the king's servant, and your servant, I saw
a great tumult, but [B]I did not know what *it was.*"
30 Then the king said, "Turn aside and stand here."
So he turned aside and stood still.

18:6 [A]Josh 17:15, 18; 2 Sam 17:26 18:7 [a]Lit *smitten* 18:9 [a]Lit *placed* [A]2 Sam 14:26 18:12 [a]So with some mss and the ancient versions; M.T. *Take care whoever* you are *of* [A]2 Sam 18:5 18:13 [A]2 Sam 14:19, 20 18:14 [a]Lit *tarry thus* [b]Lit *heart* [A]2 Sam 14:30 18:16 [A]2 Sam 2:28; 20:22 18:17 [a]Lit *the great* [A]Deut 21:20, 21; Josh 7:26; 8:29 [B]2 Sam 19:8; 20:1, 22 18:18 [a]Lit *for the sake of remembering* [A]1 Sam 15:12 [B]Gen 14:17 [C]2 Sam 14:27 18:19 [a]Lit *vindicated* [A]2 Sam 15:36 [B]2 Sam 18:31 18:22 [A]2 Sam 18:29 18:24 [A]2 Sam 19:8 [B]2 Sam 13:34; 2 Kin 9:17 18:27 [a]Lit *see* [A]2 Kin 9:20 [B]1 Kin 1:42 18:28 [a]Lit *Peace* [A]1 Sam 25:23; 2 Sam 14:4 [B]1 Sam 17:46 18:29 [A]2 Sam 20:9; 2 Kin 4:26 [B]2 Sam 18:22

18:6 the forest of Ephraim. A dense forest existed E of the Jordan River and N of the Jabbok River in Gilead, where the battle was waged.

18:8 the forest devoured more. Amazingly, because of the density of the trees and the rugged nature of the terrain, the pursuit through the forest resulted in more deaths than the actual combat (see v. 9).

18:9 mule. *See note on 13:29.* **his head caught fast in the oak.** Either Absalom's neck was caught in a fork formed by two of the branches *growing out* from a large oak tree or his hair was caught in a tangle of thick branches. The terminology and context (cf. 14:26) favor the latter view.

18:10 a certain man. One of David's soldiers, who refused to disobey the order of the king recorded in v. 5 to treat Absalom "gently," had done nothing for the suspended prince.

18:11, 12 ten ... thousand. Four ounces and 25 pounds respectively.

18:14 alive. The spears of Joab killed Absalom while Joab's armor-bearers struck him to make sure that he was dead (v. 15). In this action, Joab disobeyed the explicit order of David (v. 5).

18:16 blew the trumpet. Joab recalled his soldiers from the battle (cf. 2:28).

18:17 a very great heap of stones. Absalom was buried in a deep pit that was covered over with stones, perhaps symbolic of stoning, which was the legal penalty due to a rebel son (Dt 21:20, 21). A heap of stones often showed that the one buried was a criminal or enemy (Jos 7:26; 8:29).

18:18 set up for himself a pillar. Absalom had memorialized himself by erecting a monument in his own honor (cf. Saul's action in 1Sa 15:12). There is today a monument, a tomb in that area, called Absalom's tomb (perhaps on the same site) on which orthodox Jews spit when passing by. **King's Valley.** Traditionally, the Kidron Valley immediately E of the city of Jerusalem. **no son.** According to 14:27, Absalom had 3 sons, unnamed in the text, all of whom had died before him.

18:19 Ahimaaz. *See note on 17:17.*

18:21 Cushite. Cush was the area S of Egypt.

18:27 good man ... good news. David believed that the choice of the messenger was indicative of the content of the message.

18:29 I did not know. Ahimaaz concealed his knowledge of Absalom's death as Joab requested (v. 20).

31Behold, the Cushite arrived, and the Cushite
said, "Let my lord the king receive good news, for
[A]the LORD has [a]freed you this day from the hand
of all those who rose up against you." 32Then the
king said to the Cushite, "[A]Is it well with the young
man Absalom?" And the Cushite answered, "[B]Let
the enemies of my lord the king, and all who rise
up against you for evil, be as that young man!"
33[a]The king was deeply moved and went up to
the chamber over the gate and wept. And thus he
said as he walked, "[A]O my son Absalom, my son,
my son Absalom! [B]Would I had died instead of you,
O Absalom, my son, my son!"

JOAB REPROVES DAVID'S LAMENT

19 Then it was told Joab, "Behold, [A]the king is
weeping and mourns for Absalom." 2The [a]vic-
tory that day was turned to mourning for all the
people, for the people heard *it* said that day, "The
king is grieved for his son." 3So the people went
by stealth into the city that day, as people who are
humiliated steal away when they flee in battle. 4The
king [A]covered his face and [a]cried out with a loud
voice, "[B]O my son Absalom, O Absalom, my son, my
son!" 5Then Joab came into the house to the king and
said, "Today you have covered with shame the faces
of all your servants, who today have saved your life
and the lives of your sons and daughters, the lives
of your wives, and the lives of your concubines, 6by
loving those who hate you, and by hating those who
love you. For you have shown today that [a]princes
and servants are nothing to you; for I know this day
that if Absalom were alive and all of us were dead
today, then [b]you would be pleased. 7Now therefore
arise, go out and speak [a]kindly to your servants, for I
swear by the LORD, if you do not go out, surely [A]not
a man will pass the night with you, and this will be
worse for you than all the evil that has come upon
you from your youth until now."

DAVID RESTORED AS KING

8So the king arose and sat in the gate. When
they told all the people, saying, "Behold, the king
is [A]sitting in the gate," then all the people came
before the king.
Now [B]Israel had fled, each to his tent. 9All the
people were quarreling throughout all the tribes
of Israel, saying, "[A]The king delivered us from the
[a]hand of our enemies and [B]saved us from the [a]hand
of the Philistines, but now [C]he has fled out of the
land from Absalom. 10However, Absalom, whom
we anointed over us, has died in battle. Now then,
why are you silent about bringing the king back?"
11Then King David sent to [A]Zadok and Abiathar
the priests, saying, "Speak to the elders of Judah,
saying, 'Why are you the last to bring the king back
to his house, since the word of all Israel has come to
the king, *even* to his house? 12You are my brothers;
[A]you are my bone and my flesh. Why then should
you be the last to bring back the king?' 13Say to
[A]Amasa, 'Are you not my bone and my flesh? [B]May
God do so to me, and more also, if you will not be
[C]commander of the army before me continually [D]in
place of Joab.' " 14Thus he turned the hearts of all the
men of Judah [A]as one man, so that they sent *word* to
the king, *saying,* "Return, you and all your servants."
15The king then returned and came as far as the
Jordan. And Judah came to [A]Gilgal in order to go to
meet the king, to bring the king across the Jordan.
16Then [A]Shimei the son of Gera, the Benjamite
who was from Bahurim, hurried and came down
with the men of Judah to meet King David. 17There
were a thousand men of Benjamin with him, with
[A]Ziba the servant of the house of Saul, and his fifteen sons and his twenty servants with him; and
they rushed to the Jordan before the king. 18Then
they kept crossing the ford to bring over the king's
household, and to do what was good in his sight.
And Shimei the son of Gera fell down before the king

18:31 [a]Lit *vindicated* [A]Judg 5:31; 2 Sam 18:19 18:32 [A]2 Sam 18:29 [B]1 Sam 25:26 18:33 [a]Ch 19:1 in Heb [A]2 Sam 19:4 [B]Ex 32:32; Rom 9:3 19:1 [A]2 Sam 18:5, 14 19:2 [a]Lit *salvation* 19:4 [a]Lit *the king cried* [A]2 Sam 15:30 [B]2 Sam 18:33 19:6 [a]Or *commanders* [b]Lit *it would be right in your eyes* 19:7 [a]Lit *to the heart* [A]Prov 14:28 19:8 [A]2 Sam 15:2; 18:24 [B]2 Sam 18:17 19:9 [a]Lit *palm* [A]2 Sam 8:1-14 [B]2 Sam 5:20; 8:1 [C]2 Sam 15:14 19:11 [A]2 Sam 15:29 19:12 [A]2 Sam 5:1 19:13 [A]2 Sam 17:25 [B]1 Kin 19:2 [C]2 Sam 8:16 [D]2 Sam 3:27-39; 19:5-7 19:14 [A]Judg 20:1 19:15 [A]Josh 5:9; 1 Sam 11:14, 15 19:16 [A]2 Sam 16:5-13; 1 Kin 2:8 19:17 [A]2 Sam 16:1-4; 19:26, 27

18:32 as that young man. The Cushite's reply was not so much indirect as culturally phrased (cf. 1Sa 25:26).

18:33 my son. Repeated 5 times in this verse, David lamented the death of Absalom, his son (cf. 19:5). In spite of all the harm that Absalom had caused, David was preoccupied with his personal loss in a melancholy way that seems to be consistent with his weakness as a father. It was an unwarranted zeal for such a worthless son, and a warning about the pitiful results of sin.

19:3 the people went by stealth. Because of David's excessive grief, his soldiers returned from battle not as rejoicing victors, but as if they had been humiliated by defeat.

19:5 covered with shame ... your servants. Joab sternly rebuked David for being so absorbed in his personal trauma and failing to appreciate the victory that his men had won for him.

19:7 not a man will pass the night with you. Joab, who was the esteemed general of the army, was a dangerous person because of that power. He was also dangerous to David because he had disobeyed his command to spare Absalom, and killed him with no remorse. When he warned David that he would be in deep trouble if he did not immediately express appreciation to his men for their victory, David knew he could be in serious danger.

19:8 sat in the gate. It was at the gate of Mahanaim that David had reviewed his troops as they had marched out to battle (18:4). David's sitting in the gate represented a return to his exercise of kingly authority.

19:9 quarreling. An argument arose in Israel concerning whether David should be returned to the kingship. David's past military victories over the Philistines and the failure of Absalom argued for David's return. Therefore, David's supporters insisted on knowing why their fellow Israelites remained quiet about returning David to his rightful place on the throne in Jerusalem.

19:11 elders of Judah. Through the priests who had stayed in Jerusalem during the rebellion, David appealed to the leaders of his own tribe to take the initiative in restoring him to the throne in Jerusalem (see 2:4; 1Sa 30:26). Though this appeal produced the desired result, it also led to tribal jealousies (vv. 40–43).

19:13 Amasa. *See note on 17:25.* **commander of the army ... in place of Joab.** David appointed Amasa commander of his army, hoping to secure the allegiance of those who had followed Amasa when he led Absalom's forces, especially those of Judah. This appointment did persuade the tribe of Judah to support David's return to the kingship (v. 14) and secured the animosity of Joab against Amasa for taking his position (cf. 20:8–10).

19:15 Gilgal. *See note on 1Sa 10:8.*

19:16 Shimei. *See note on 16:5–8.* Shimei confessed his sin of cursing David and his life was spared, temporarily, for on his deathbed David ordered that Shimei be punished for his crime (1Ki 2:8, 9, 36–46).

as he was about to cross the Jordan. 19 So he said to
the king, "[A]Let not my lord consider me guilty, nor
remember what your servant did wrong on the day
when my lord the king came out from Jerusalem,
so that the king would [a]take *it* to heart. 20 For your
servant knows that I have sinned; therefore behold, I
have come today, [A]the first of all the house of Joseph
to go down to meet my lord the king." 21 But Abishai
the son of Zeruiah said, "[A]Should not Shimei be put
to death for this, [B]because he cursed the LORD'S
anointed?" 22 David then said, "[A]What have I to do
with you, O sons of Zeruiah, that you should this day
be an adversary to me? [B]Should any man be put to
death in Israel today? For do I not know that I am
king over Israel today?" 23 The king said to Shimei,
"[A]You shall not die." Thus the king swore to him.
24 Then [A]Mephibosheth the [a]son of Saul came
down to meet the king; and [B]he had neither [b]cared
for his feet, nor [b]trimmed his mustache, nor [C]washed
his clothes, from the day the king departed until the
day he came *home* in peace. 25 It was when he came
from Jerusalem to meet the king, that the king said
to him, "[A]Why did you not go with me, Mephibosheth?" 26 So he answered, "O my lord, the king, my
servant deceived me; for your servant said, 'I will
saddle a donkey for myself that I may ride on it and
go with the king,' [A]because your servant is lame.
27 Moreover, [A]he has slandered your servant to my
lord the king; but my lord the king is [B]like the angel
of God, therefore do what is good in your sight. 28 For
[A]all my father's household was nothing but dead
men before my lord the king; [B]yet you set your servant among those who ate at your own table. What
right do I have yet that I should [a]complain anymore
to the king?" 29 So the king said to him, "Why do you
still speak of your affairs? I have [a]decided, 'You and
Ziba shall divide the land.' " 30 Mephibosheth said to
the king, "Let him even take it all, since my lord the
king has come safely to his own house."
31 Now [A]Barzillai the Gileadite had come down from
Rogelim; and he went on to the Jordan with the king
to [a]escort him over the Jordan. 32 Now Barzillai was
very old, being eighty years old; and he had [a,A]sus-
tained the king while he stayed at Mahanaim, for he
was a very great man. 33 The king said to Barzillai,
"You cross over with me and I will [a]sustain you in
Jerusalem with me." 34 But Barzillai said to the king,
"[A]How long [a]have I yet to live, that I should go up with
the king to Jerusalem? 35 I am [a]now [A]eighty years old.
Can I distinguish between good and bad? Or can your
servant taste what I eat or what I drink? Or can I hear
anymore [B]the voice of singing men and women? [C]Why
then should your servant be an added burden to my
lord the king? 36 Your servant would merely cross
over the Jordan with the king. Why should the king
compensate me *with* this reward? 37 Please let your
servant return, that I may die in my own city near the
grave of my father and my mother. However, here is
your servant [A]Chimham, let him cross over with my
lord the king, and do for him what is good in your
sight." 38 The king answered, "Chimham shall cross
over with me, and I will do for him what is good in
your sight; and whatever you [a]require of me, I will
do for you." 39 All the people crossed over the Jordan
and the king crossed too. The king then [A]kissed Barzillai and blessed him, and he returned to his place.
40 Now the king went on to Gilgal, and Chimham
went on with him; and all the people of Judah and
also [A]half the people of Israel [a]accompanied the king.
41 And behold, all the men of Israel came to the king
and said to the king, "[A]Why had our brothers [B]the
men of Judah stolen you away, and brought the king
and his household and all David's men with him over
the Jordan?" 42 Then all the men of Judah answered
the men of Israel, "Because [A]the king is a close relative to [a]us. Why then [b]are you angry about this matter? Have we eaten at all at the king's *expense*, or has
[c]anything been taken for us?" 43 But the men of Israel
answered the men of Judah and said, "[a,A]We have
ten parts in the king, therefore [a]we also have more
claim on David than you. Why then did you treat us
with contempt? Was it not [a]our advice first to bring
back [a]our king?" Yet the words of the men of Judah
were harsher than the words of the men of Israel.

19:19 [a]Lit *set* [A]1 Sam 22:15; 2 Sam 16:6-8 19:20 [A]2 Sam 16:5 19:21 [A]2 Sam 16:7, 8 [B]Ex 22:28 19:22 [A]2 Sam 3:39; 16:9, 10 [B]1 Sam 11:13 19:23 [A]1 Kin 2:8 19:24 [a]I.e. grandson [b]Lit *done* [A]2 Sam 9:6-10 [B]2 Sam 12:20 [C]Ex 19:10 19:25 [A]2 Sam 16:17 19:26 [A]2 Sam 9:3 19:27 [A]2 Sam 16:3, 4 [B]2 Sam 14:17, 20 19:28 [a]Lit *cry out* [A]2 Sam 21:6-9 [B]2 Sam 9:7, 10, 13 19:29 [a]Lit *said* 19:31 [a]Lit *send* [A]2 Sam 17:27-29; 1 Kin 2:7 19:32 [a]Or *provided food for* [A]2 Sam 17:27-29 19:33 [a]Or *provide food for* 19:34 [a]Lit *are the days of the years of my life* [A]Gen 47:8 19:35 [a]Lit *today* [A]Ps 90:10 [B]Eccl 2:8; Is 5:11, 12 [C]2 Sam 15:33 19:37 [A]2 Sam 19:40; 1 Kin 2:7; Jer 41:17 19:38 [a]Lit *choose* 19:39 [A]Gen 31:55; Ruth 1:14; 2 Sam 14:33 19:40 [a]Lit *crossed over with* [A]2 Sam 19:9, 10 19:41 [A]Judg 8:1; 12:1 [B]2 Sam 19:11, 12 19:42 [a]Lit *me* [b]Lit *is it hot to you* [C]Or *a gift* [A]2 Sam 19:12 19:43 [a]Singular in Heb [A]2 Sam 5:1; 1 Kin 11:30, 31

19:20 house of Joseph. A reference to Ephraim, the descendant of Joseph, a large tribe of Israel which was representative of the 10 northern tribes. Here, even Shimei's tribe Benjamin was included.

19:24–30 Mephibosheth. *See note on 4:4.* Mephibosheth also met David, exhibiting the traditional marks of mourning, and explained that he had not followed David into exile because he had been deceived by his servant Ziba (see 16:1–4). He came to David with great humility, generosity of spirit, *and gratitude, recognizing all the good* the king had done for him before the evil deception (v. 28).

19:29 divide the land. David had previously given the estate of Saul to Mephibosheth to be farmed under him by Ziba (9:9, 10). Then when David was deceived, he gave it all to Ziba (16:4). Now David decided to divide Saul's estate between Ziba and Mephibosheth since he was either uncertain of the truth of Mephibosheth's story or who was guilty of what, and was too distracted to inquire fully into the matter. It was, in any case, a poor decision to divide the estate between the noble-hearted son of Jonathan and a lying deceiver. Mephibosheth was unselfish and suggested that his disloyal servant take it all—it was enough for him that David was back.

19:31–39 Barzillai. *See note on 17:27.* David *offered* to let Barzillai live in Jerusalem as his guest, but Barzillai preferred to live out his last years in his own house.

19:37 Chimham. Probably a son of Barzillai (see 1Ki 2:7). It is probable that David gave a part of his personal estate in Bethlehem to this man and his descendants (see Jer 41:17).

19:41 stolen you away. Because only the troops of Judah had escorted David as he crossed over the Jordan River, the 10 northern tribes complained to David that the men of Judah had "kidnapped" him from them.

19:42 a close relative. The men of Judah answered the men of Israel by stating that David was a member of their tribe. Nor had they taken advantage of their relationship to the king, as had some from the northern tribes.

19:43 ten parts. The men of Israel replied to the men of Judah that they had a greater right to David, since there were 10 northern tribes in contrast to the one tribe of Judah. Contrast the "ten parts" here with the "no portion" in 20:1. **treat us with contempt.** The Israel-Judah hostility evidenced here led to the rebellion of Sheba (20:1–22) and eventually to the division of the united kingdom (1Ki 12:1–24).

SHEBA'S REVOLT

20 Now [A]a worthless fellow happened to be
there whose name was Sheba, the son of [B]Bich-
ri, a Benjamite; and he blew the trumpet and said,

"[C]We have no portion in David,
Nor do we have inheritance
in [D]the son of Jesse;
[E]Every man to his tents, O Israel!"

2 So all the men of Israel [a]withdrew from following
David *and* followed Sheba the son of Bichri; but the
men of Judah [b]remained steadfast to their king,
from the Jordan even to Jerusalem.
3 Then David came to his house at Jerusalem, and
[A]the king took the ten women, the concubines whom
he had left to keep the house, and placed them under
guard and provided them with sustenance, but did
not go in to them. So they were shut up until the
day of their death, living as widows.
4 Then the king said to [A]Amasa, "Call out the men
of Judah for me within three days, and be present
here yourself." 5 So Amasa went to call out *the men
of* Judah, but he [A]delayed longer than the set time
which he had appointed him. 6 And David said to
[A]Abishai, "Now Sheba the son of Bichri will do us
more harm than Absalom; [B]take your lord's servants
and pursue him, so that he does not find for himself
fortified cities and escape from our sight." 7 So Joab's
men went out after him, [A]along with the Cherethites
and the Pelethites and all the mighty men; and they
went out from Jerusalem to pursue Sheba the son
of Bichri. 8 When they were at the large stone which
is in [A]Gibeon, Amasa came [a]to meet them. Now
Joab was [b]dressed in his military attire, and over
it was a belt with a sword in its sheath fastened at
his waist; and as he went forward, it fell out. 9 Joab
said to Amasa, "Is it well with you, my brother?"
And [A]Joab took Amasa by the beard with his right
hand to kiss him.

AMASA MURDERED

10 But Amasa was not on guard against the sword
which was in Joab's hand so [A]he struck him in the
belly with it and poured out his inward parts on the
ground, and did not *strike* him again, and he died.
Then Joab and Abishai his brother pursued Sheba
the son of Bichri. 11 Now there stood by him one of
Joab's young men, and said, "Whoever favors Joab
and whoever is for David, [A]*let him* follow Joab." 12 But
Amasa lay wallowing in *his* blood in the middle of
the highway. And when the man saw that all the
people stood still, he [a]removed Amasa from the
highway into the field and threw a garment over
him when he saw that everyone who came by him
stood still.

REVOLT PUT DOWN

13 As soon as he was removed from the highway,
all the men passed on after Joab to pursue Sheba
the son of Bichri.
14 Now he went through all the tribes of Israel
to Abel, even Beth-maacah, and all the Berites;
and they were gathered together and also went
after him. 15 They came and besieged him in [A]Abel
Beth-maacah, and [B]they [a]cast up a siege ramp
against the city, and it stood by the rampart; and
all the people who were with Joab were wreaking
destruction in order to topple the wall. 16 Then [A]a
wise woman called from the city, "Hear, hear! Please
tell Joab, 'Come here that I may speak with you.' "
17 So he approached her, and the woman said, "Are

20:1 [A]2 Sam 16:7 [B]Gen 46:21 [C]2 Sam 19:43; 1 Kin 12:16 [D]1 Sam 22:7-9 [E]1 Sam 13:2; 2 Sam 18:17; 2 Chr 10:16 20:2 [a]Lit *went up* [b]Lit *clung to* 20:3 [A]2 Sam 15:16; 16:21, 22 20:4 [A]2 Sam 17:25; 19:13 20:5 [A]1 Sam 13:8 20:6 [A]2 Sam 21:17 [B]2 Sam 11:11; 1 Kin 1:33 20:7 [A]2 Sam 8:18; 1 Kin 1:38 20:8 [a]Lit *before* [b]Lit *girded with military garment as clothing* [A]2 Sam 2:13; 3:30 20:9 [A]Matt 26:49 20:10 [A]2 Sam 2:23; 3:27; 1 Kin 2:5 20:11 [A]2 Sam 20:13 20:12 [a]Lit *caused to turn* 20:15 [a]Lit *poured out* [A]1 Kin 15:20; 2 Kin 15:29 [B]2 Kin 19:32; Ezek 4:2 20:16 [A]2 Sam 14:2

20:1 worthless fellow. *See note on 1Sa 2:12.* **Sheba.** Though nothing is known of this man, he must have been a person of considerable power and influence to raise so sudden and extensive a sedition. He belonged to Saul's tribe, where adherents of Saul's dynasty were still many, and he could see the disgust of the 10 tribes for Judah's presumption in the restoration. He sought to overturn David's authority in Israel. **no portion … inheritance.** Sheba's declaration that the northern tribes had no part in David's realm was similar to words later used in 1Ki 12:16 when Israel seceded from the united kingdom under Jeroboam.

20:2 Israel withdrew from following David. Once the 10 tribes withdrew, Judah was left alone to escort the king to Jerusalem. It seems that the disloyalty of the N continued as long as Sheba lived.

20:3 the concubines. When David returned to Jerusalem, he confined his concubines to a life of abstinence because of their sexual relations with Absalom (16:21, 22).

20:4 Amasa. Amasa was Absalom's general (*see note on 17:25*), whom David promised would be commander of his army after Absalom's death (*see note on 19:13*). Amasa was installed publicly because David thought it would be seen favorably by the 10 tribes. He was told to assemble an army in 3 days to end the insurrection started by Sheba, but could not in such a brief time.

20:6 Abishai. *See note on 2:18.* When Amasa failed to follow David's orders, David did not reinstate Joab, his former general who had Absalom killed against David's orders (see 18:5–15), but appointed Joab's brother Abishai as commander of his forces. **your lord's servants.** Called "Joab's men" in v. 7. Abishai was to take the army of Joab to pursue the rebel leader. Joab went also, determined to take vengeance on his rival Amasa.

20:7 the Cherethites and the Pelethites. *See note on 1Sa 30:14.* **mighty men.** Those men are listed in 23:8–39.

20:8 Gibeon. *See note on 2:12.* **Amasa came to meet them.** Having collected some forces, he marched rapidly and came first to Gibeon, thus assuming the role of commander. It is possible that Joab purposely let the sword fall from its sheath as he approached Amasa, in order that stooping as if to pick up the accidentally fallen weapon, he might salute the new general with his sword already in hand, without generating any suspicion of his intent. He used this ploy to gain the position to stab the new commander, whom he considered as usurping his post.

20:9 my brother. *See note on 17:25.* **by the beard.** Joab, present with his men, seized Amasa by his beard with his right hand apparently to give the kiss of greeting. Instead, with his left hand, he thrust his sword into Amasa's stomach (cf. 3:27).

20:11 one of Joab's young men. Joab was reinstated as commander of David's army by his troops. It is a striking illustration of Joab's influence over the army that he could murder the commander whom David had chosen, a killing right before their eyes, and they would follow him unanimously as their leader in pursuit of Sheba.

20:14 Abel, even Beth-maacah. I.e., Abel Beth-maacah. About 25 mi. N of the Sea of Galilee, 4 mi. W of the city of Dan.

20:16–19 This woman (probably a prominent judge in the city) was making an appeal based on the laws of warfare in Dt 20:10 that required the assaulting army to offer peace before making war. She pleaded for Joab to ask the city if they wanted peace and thus avert war (v. 18).

you Joab?" And he answered, "I am." Then she said to him, "Listen to the words of your maidservant." And he answered, "I am listening." 18 Then she spoke, saying, "Formerly they used to say, 'They will surely ask *advice* at Abel,' and thus they ended *the dispute*. 19 I am of those who are peaceable *and* faithful in Israel. [A]You are seeking to destroy a city, even a mother in Israel. Why would you swallow up [B]the inheritance of the LORD?" 20 Joab replied, "Far be it, far be it from me that I should swallow up or destroy! 21 Such is not the case. But a man from [A]the hill country of Ephraim, [B]Sheba the son of Bichri by name, has lifted up his hand against King David. Only hand him over, and I will depart from the city." And the woman said to Joab, "Behold, his head will be thrown to you over the wall." 22 Then the woman [A]wisely came to all the people. And they cut off the head of Sheba the son of Bichri and threw it to Joab. So [B]he blew the trumpet, and they were dispersed from the city, each to his tent. Joab also returned to the king at Jerusalem.

23 [A]Now Joab was over the whole army of Israel, and Benaiah the son of Jehoiada was over the Cherethites and the Pelethites; 24 and Adoram was over the forced labor, and [A]Jehoshaphat the son of Ahilud was the recorder; 25 and Sheva was scribe, and Zadok and [A]Abiathar were priests; 26 and Ira the Jairite was also a priest to David.

GIBEONITE REVENGE

21 Now there was [A]a famine in the days of David for three years, year after year; and [B]David sought the presence of the LORD. And the LORD said, "It is for Saul and his bloody house, because he put the Gibeonites to death." 2 So the king called the Gibeonites and spoke to them (now the Gibeonites were not of the sons of Israel but of the remnant of the Amorites, and [A]the sons of Israel [a]made a covenant with them, but Saul had sought to [b]kill them in his zeal for the sons of Israel and Judah). 3 Thus David said to the Gibeonites, "What should I do for you? And how can I make atonement that you may bless [A]the inheritance of the LORD?" 4 Then the Gibeonites said to him, "[A]We have no *concern* of silver or gold with Saul or his house, nor is it for us to put any man to death in Israel." And he said, "I will do for you whatever you say." 5 So they said to the king, "[A]The man who consumed us and who planned [a]to exterminate us from remaining within any border of Israel, 6 let seven men from his sons be given to us, and we will [a]hang them [A]before the LORD in Gibeah of Saul, [B]the chosen of the LORD." And the king said, "I will give *them*."

7 But the king spared [A]Mephibosheth, the son of Jonathan the son of Saul, [B]because of the oath of the LORD which was between them, between David and Saul's son Jonathan. 8 So the king took the two sons of [A]Rizpah the daughter of Aiah, Armoni and Mephibosheth whom she had borne to Saul, and the five sons of [a,B]Merab the daughter of Saul, whom she had borne to Adriel the son of Barzillai the [C]Meholathite. 9 Then he gave them into the hands of the Gibeonites, and they [a]hanged them in the mountain before the LORD, so that the seven of them fell together; and they were put to death in the first days of harvest at [A]the beginning of barley harvest.

20:19 [A]Deut 20:10 [B]1 Sam 26:19; 2 Sam 14:16; 21:3 20:21 [A]Josh 24:33 [B]2 Sam 20:2 20:22 [A]2 Sam 20:16; Eccl 9:13-16 [B]2 Sam 20:1 20:23 [A]2 Sam 8:16-18; 1 Kin 4:3-6 20:24 [A]1 Kin 4:3 20:25 [A]1 Kin 4:4 21:1 [A]Gen 12:10; 26:1; 42:5 [B]Num 27:21 21:2 [a]Lit *had sworn to* [b]Lit *smite* [A]Josh 9:3, 15-20 21:3 [A]1 Sam 26:19; 2 Sam 20:19 21:4 [A]Num 35:31, 32 21:5 [a]Lit *against us that we should be exterminated* [A]2 Sam 21:1 21:6 [a]Lit *expose them* [A]Num 25:4 [B]1 Sam 10:24 21:7 [A]2 Sam 4:4; 9:10 [B]1 Sam 18:3; 20:12-17; 23:18; 2 Sam 9:1-7 21:8 [a]So Gr and Heb mss [A]2 Sam 3:7 [B]1 Sam 18:19 [C]1 Kin 19:16 21:9 [a]Lit *exposed them* [A]Ex 9:31, 32

20:19 a mother in Israel. This is a reference to a specially honored city or a recognized capital of the region. **the inheritance of the LORD.** This refers to the land of Israel (see 1Sa 10:1).

20:20, 21 The ruthless general was a patriot at heart, who on taking the leader of the insurrection, was ready to end further bloodshed. The woman eagerly responded with the promise of Sheba's head.

20:21 hill country of Ephraim. A large, partially forested plateau that extended into the tribal territory of Benjamin from the N.

20:22 David could not get rid of Joab, though he hated him. He had to ignore the murder of Amasa and recognize Joab as army commander.

20:23–26 Cf. a similar list in 8:15–18.

20:24 Adoram. Rendered "Adoniram" in 1Ki 4:6; 5:14. He was in charge of the "forced labor," a term used to describe the hard labor imposed on subjugated peoples (Ex 1:11; Jos 16:10; Jdg 1:28). Adoram oversaw the forced labor on such projects as the building of highways, temples, and houses.

20:25 Sheva. He replaced Seraiah (8:17) as David's secretary.

20:26 Ira. He was David's royal adviser.

21:1–24:25 This is the final division of 2 Samuel. Like the book of Judges (Jdg 17:1–21:25), it concludes with this epilogue that contains material, not necessarily chronological, that further describes David's reign. There is a striking literary arrangement of the sections in this division of the book. The first and last sections (21:1–14; 24:1–25) are narratives that describe two occurrences of the Lord's anger against Israel. The second and fifth sections (21:15–22; 23:8–39) are accounts of David's warriors. The third and fourth sections (22:1–51; 23:1–7) record two of David's songs.

21:1–14 This event occurred after the display of David's kindness to Mephibosheth (v. 7; cf. 9:1–13) and before Shimei's cursing of David (cf. 16:7, 8).

21:1 a famine. When Israel experienced 3 years of famine, David recognized it as divine discipline (cf. Dt 28:47, 48) and sought God for the reason.

21:1, 2 Saul and his bloody house. By divine revelation David learned that the famine was a result of sin committed by Saul; namely that he had slain the Gibeonites. There is no further reference to this event. Saul was probably trying to do as God commanded and rid the land of the remnant of heathen in order that Israel might prosper (v. 2). But in his zeal he had committed a serious sin; he had broken a covenant that had been made 400 years before between Joshua and the Gibeonites, who were in the land when Israel took possession of it. They deceived Joshua into making the covenant, but it was, nevertheless, a covenant (see Jos 9:3–27). Covenant keeping was no small matter to God (see Jos 9:20).

21:2 Gibeonites ... Amorites. Names sometimes used to designate all the pre-Israelite inhabitants of Canaan (Ge 15:16; Jos 24:18; Jdg 6:10). More precisely, the Gibeonites were called Hivites (Jos 9:7; 11:19).

21:3 the inheritance of the LORD. *See note on 20:19.*

21:6 seven ... from his sons. "Seven" symbolized completeness, not necessarily the number of Gibeonites slain by Saul. "Sons" could be either sons or grandsons. **Gibeah of Saul.** *See note on 1Sa 11:4.*

21:7 the oath of the LORD ... between David and ... Jonathan. Because Mephibosheth was the son of Jonathan, he was spared in accordance with the covenant between David and Jonathan (1Sa 20:14, 15) and also between David and Saul (*see note on 1Sa 24:22*).

21:8 Rizpah. Saul's concubine (see 3:7). **Mephibosheth.** A son of Saul, different from the son of Jonathan with the same name. **Merab.** Merab was the mother of these 5 sons. She was the wife of Adriel (1Sa 18:19). **Barzillai the Meholathite.** A different man than Barzillai the Gileadite (17:27; 19:31).

21:9 before the LORD. These pagans were not bound by the law of Dt 21:22, 23, which forbade leaving a dead body hanging over night. Their intention was to let the bodies

10 [A]And Rizpah the daughter of Aiah took sackcloth and spread it for herself on the rock, from
the beginning of harvest until [a]it rained on them
from the sky; and [B]she [b]allowed neither the birds
of the sky to rest on them by day nor the beasts of
the field by night. 11 When it was told David what
Rizpah the daughter of Aiah, the concubine of Saul,
had done, 12 then David went and took [A]the bones
of Saul and the bones of Jonathan his son from the
men of Jabesh-gilead, who had stolen them from the
open square of [B]Beth-shan, [C]where the Philistines
had hanged them on the day [D]the Philistines struck
down Saul in Gilboa. 13 He brought up the bones
of Saul and the bones of Jonathan his son from
there, and they gathered the bones of those who
had been [a]hanged. 14 They buried the bones of Saul
and Jonathan his son in the country of Benjamin in
[A]Zela, in the grave of Kish his father; thus they did
all that the king commanded, and after that [B]God
was moved by prayer for the land.
15 Now when [A]the Philistines were at war again
with Israel, David went down and his servants with
him; and as they fought against the Philistines,
David became weary. 16 Then Ishbi-benob, who was
[A]among the descendants of the [a]giant, the weight of
whose spear was three hundred *shekels* of bronze
in weight, [b]was girded with a new *sword,* and he
[c]intended to kill David. 17 But [A]Abishai the son of
Zeruiah helped him, and struck the Philistine and
killed him. Then the men of David swore to him,
saying, "[B]You shall not go out again with us to battle,
so that you do not extinguish [C]the lamp of Israel."
18 [A]Now it came about after this that there was
war again with the Philistines at Gob; then [B]Sibbecai
the Hushathite struck down Saph, who was among
the descendants of the [a]giant. 19 There was war with
the Philistines again at Gob, and Elhanan the son of
Jaare-oregim the Bethlehemite [a]killed [b]Goliath the
Gittite, [A]the shaft of whose spear was like a weaver's
beam. 20 There was war at Gath again, where there
was a man of *great* stature who had six fingers on
each hand and six toes on each foot, twenty-four in
number; and he also had been born [A]to the [a]giant.
21 When he defied Israel, Jonathan the son of Shimei,
David's brother, struck him down. 22 [A]These four
were born to the [a]giant in Gath, and they fell by
the hand of David and by the hand of his servants.

DAVID'S PSALM OF DELIVERANCE

22 [A]And David spoke [B]the words of this song to
the LORD in the day that the LORD delivered
him from the [a]hand of all his enemies and from the
[a]hand of Saul. 2 He said,

"[A]The LORD is my [a]rock and my
fortress and my deliverer;

21:10 [a]Lit *water was poured* [b]Lit *gave* [A]Deut 21:23 [B]1 Sam 17:44, 46 21:12 [A]1 Sam 31:11-13 [B]Josh 17:11 [C]1 Sam 31:10 [D]1 Sam 31:3, 4 21:13 [a]Lit *exposed* 21:14 [A]Josh 18:28 [B]Josh 7:26; 2 Sam 24:25 21:15 [A]2 Sam 5:17-25 21:16 [a]Heb *Raphah* [b]Lit *and he was* [c]Lit *said* [A]Num 13:22, 28; Josh 15:14; 2 Sam 21:18-22 21:17 [A]2 Sam 20:6-10 [B]2 Sam 18:3 [C]2 Sam 22:29; 1 Kin 11:36 21:18 [a]Heb *Raphah* [A]1 Chr 20:4-8 [B]1 Chr 11:29; 27:11 21:19 [a]Lit *smote* [b]In 1 Chr 20:5, *Lahmi, the brother of Goliath* [A]1 Sam 17:7 21:20 [a]Heb *Raphah* [A]2 Sam 21:16, 18 21:22 [a]Heb *Raphah* [A]1 Chr 20:8 22:1 [a]Lit *palm* [A]Ps 18:2-50 [B]Ex 15:1; Deut 31:30 22:2 [a]Lit *crag* [A]1 Sam 23:25; 24:2; Ps 31:3; 71:3

hang until God signaled He was satisfied and sent rain to end the famine. Such a heathen practice, designed to propitiate their gods, was a superstition of these Gibeonites. God, in His providence, allowed this memorable retaliation as a lesson about keeping covenants and promises. **the beginning of barley harvest.** April (see Ru 1:22).

21:10 sackcloth … spread. Rizpah erected a tent nearby to keep watch over the bodies, to scare away birds and beasts. It was considered a disgrace for the bodies of the slain to become food for the birds and beasts (cf. Dt 28:26; 1Sa 17:44, 46; Rev 19:17, 18). **rained on them.** An unseasonably late spring or early summer shower. Possibly, the rain that ended the drought.

21:11–14 Finally, after the rain had come, David, encouraged by the example of the woman's devotion to her dead family members, ordered the remains of Saul and Jonathan transferred from their obscure grave in Jabesh-gilead (cf. 1Sa 31:11, 12), along with the 7 sons' bones, to the honorable family grave in Zela (cf. Jos 18:28; 1Sa 10:2, "Zelzah"). This location is unknown.

21:14 God was moved by prayer. The famine ended and God restored the land to prosperity.

21:15–22 This section describes the defeat of 4 Philistine giants at the hands of David and his men. Though these events cannot be located chronologically with any certainty, the narratives of victory provide a fitting preface to David's song of praise, which magnifies God's deliverance (22:1–51). See 1Ch 20:4–8.

21:16 the giant. The Heb. term used in vv. 16, 18, 20, 22 is "rapha." This was not the name of an individual, but a term used collectively for the "Rephaim" who inhabited the land of Canaan and were noted for their inordinate size (cf. Ge 15:19–21; Nu 13:33; Dt 2:11; 3:11, 13). The term "Rephaim" was used of the people called the "Anakim" (Dt 2:10, 11, 20, 21), distinguished for their size and strength. According to Jos 11:21, 22, the "Anakim" were driven from the hill country of Israel and Judah, but remained in the Philistine cities of Gaza, Gath, and Ashdod. Though the Philistines had succumbed to the power of Israel's army, the appearance of some great champion revived their courage and invited their hope for victory against the Israelite invaders. **three hundred *shekels*.** Approximately 7.5 lbs. **a new *sword*.** Lit. "a new thing." The weapon was not specified.

21:17 Abishai. *See note on 2:18.* **lamp of Israel.** David, who with God's help brought the light of prosperity and well-being to the whole land of Israel, was the symbol of Israel's hope and promise of security. Continued blessing resided in David and his house.

21:18 Gob. Near Gezer (cf. 1Ch 20:4), about 22 mi. W of Jerusalem.

21:19 Elhanan … killed Goliath. The minor scribal omission of "the brother of" (in the Heb.) belongs in this verse, based on 1Ch 20:5 which includes them, and because clearly the Scripture says that David killed Goliath as recorded in 1Sa 17:50. There has probably been a scribal error in the text which should read, "Elhanan … killed *the brother of* Goliath." A second possible solution is that Elhanan and David may be different names for the same person, just as Solomon had another name (cf. 12:24, 25). A third solution is, perhaps, that there were two giants named Goliath.

21:20 Gath. About 12 mi. S of Geza and 26 mi. SW of Jerusalem.

21:21 Jonathan. David's nephew, the son of Shimeah, also called Shammah in 1Sa 16:9, different from the son of Saul.

22:1–51 David's song of praise here is almost identical to Ps 18. This song also has many verbal links to Hannah's prayer (*see note on 1Sa 2:1–10*) and together with it forms the framework for the books of Samuel. This song focuses on the Lord's deliverance of David from all his enemies, in response to which David praised the Lord, his deliverer (vv. 2–4). The major part of the song (vv. 5–46) states the reason for this praise of the Lord. David first describes how the Lord had delivered him from his enemies (vv. 5–20), then declares why the Lord had delivered him from his enemies (vv. 21–28), then states the extent of the Lord's deliverance from his enemies (vv. 29–46). The song concludes with David's resolve to praise his delivering Lord, even among the Gentiles (vv. 47–51). *See notes on Ps 18:1–50* for a more detailed explanation.

22:1 all his enemies. Cf. 7:1, 9, 11. David composed this song toward the end of his life when the Lord had given him a settled kingdom and the promise of the Messianic seed embodied in the Davidic Covenant.

22:2–4 This introduction contains the sum and substance of the whole psalm, as David extols God as his defense, refuge, and deliverer in the many experiences of his agitated life.

22:2 rock. *See notes on 1Sa 2:2; Dt 32:4.*

3 [a][A]My God, my rock, in whom I take refuge,
My [B]shield and [C]the horn of my salvation,
my stronghold and [D]my refuge;
My savior, You save me from violence.
4 "I call upon the LORD, [A]who is
worthy to be praised,
And I am saved from my enemies.
5 "For [A]the waves of death encompassed me;
[B]The torrents of [a]destruction
[b]overwhelmed me;
6 [A]The cords of [a]Sheol surrounded me;
The snares of death confronted me.
7 "[A]In my distress I called upon the LORD,
Yes, I [a]cried to my God;
And from His temple He heard my voice,
And my cry for help *came* into His ears.
8 "Then [A]the earth shook and quaked,
[B]The foundations of heaven were trembling
And were shaken, because He was angry.
9 "Smoke went up [a]out of His nostrils,
[A]Fire from His mouth devoured;
[B]Coals were kindled by it.
10 "He bowed the heavens also,
and came down
With [A]thick darkness under His feet.
11 "[A]And He rode on a cherub and flew;
And He [a]appeared on [B]the
wings of the wind.
12 "[A]And He made darkness
[a]canopies around Him,
A mass of waters, thick clouds of the sky.
13 "From the brightness before Him
[A]Coals of fire were kindled.
14 "[A]The LORD thundered from heaven,
And the Most High uttered His voice.
15 "[A]And He sent out arrows,
and scattered them,
Lightning, and [a]routed them.
16 "Then the channels of the sea appeared,
The foundations of the world
were [a]laid bare
By the rebuke of the LORD,
[A]At the blast of the breath of His nostrils.
17 "[A]He sent from on high, He took me;
[B]He drew me out of many waters.
18 "He delivered me from my strong enemy,
From those who hated me, for
they were too strong for me.
19 "They confronted me in the
day of my calamity,
[A]But the LORD was my support.
20 "[A]He also brought me forth
into a broad place;
He rescued me, [B]because He
delighted in me.
21 "[A]The LORD has rewarded me
according to my righteousness;
[B]According to the cleanness of my
hands He has recompensed me.
22 "[A]For I have kept the ways of the LORD,
And have not acted wickedly
against my God.
23 "[A]For all His ordinances *were* before me,
And *as for* His statutes, I did
not depart from [a]them.
24 "[A]I was also [a]blameless toward Him,
And I kept myself from my iniquity.
25 "[A]Therefore the LORD has recompensed
me according to my righteousness,
According to my cleanness
before His eyes.
26 "[A]With the [a]kind You show Yourself [a]kind,
With the [b]blameless You show
Yourself [b]blameless;
27 [A]With the pure You show Yourself pure,
[B]And with the perverted You
show Yourself [a]astute.
28 "[A]And You save an afflicted people;
[B]But Your eyes are on the haughty
whom You abase.
29 "[A]For You are my lamp, O LORD;
And the LORD illumines my darkness.

22:3 [a]Lit *God of my rock* [A]Deut 32:4, 37; 1 Sam 2:2 [B]Gen 15:1; Deut 33:29 [C]Luke 1:69 [D]Ps 9:9 22:4 [A]Ps 48:1; 96:4 22:5 [a]Heb *Belial* [b]Or *terrified* [A]Ps 93:4; Jon 2:3 [B]Ps 69:14, 15 22:6 [a]I.e. the nether world [A]Ps 116:3 22:7 [a]Or *called* [A]Ps 116:4; 120:1 22:8 [A]Judg 5:4; Ps 97:4 [B]Job 26:11 22:9 [a]Or *in His wrath* [A]Ps 97:3; Heb 12:29 [B]2 Sam 22:13 22:10 [A]Ex 19:16; 1 Kin 8:12; Ps 97:2; Nah 1:3 22:11 [a]Many mss read *sped* [A]2 Sam 6:2 [B]Ps 104:3 22:12 [a]Or *pavilions* [A]Job 36:29 22:13 [A]2 Sam 22:9 22:14 [A]Job 37:2-5; Ps 29:3 22:15 [a]Lit *confused* [A]Deut 32:23; Josh 10:10; 1 Sam 7:10 22:16 [a]Or *uncovered* [A]Ex 15:8; Nah 1:4 22:17 [A]Ps 144:7 [B]Ex 2:10 22:19 [A]Ps 23:4 22:20 [A]Ps 31:8; 118:5 [B]2 Sam 15:26 22:21 [A]1 Sam 26:23; 1 Kin 8:32 [B]Ps 24:4 22:22 [A]Gen 18:19; Ps 128:1; Prov 8:32 22:23 [a]Lit *it* [A]Deut 6:6-9; Ps 119:30, 102 22:24 [a]Lit *complete; or having integrity* [A]Gen 6:9; 7:1; Eph 1:4; Col 1:21, 22 22:25 [A]2 Sam 22:21 22:26 [a]Or *loyal* [b]Lit *complete; or having integrity* [A]Matt 5:7 22:27 [a]Lit *twisted* [A]Matt 5:8; 1 John 3:3 [B]Lev 26:23, 24; Rom 1:28 22:28 [A]Ex 3:7, 8; Ps 72:12, 13 [B]Is 2:11, 12, 17; 5:15 22:29 [A]2 Sam 21:17; 1 Kin 11:36; Ps 27:1

22:3 shield. See Ge 15:1; Dt 33:29. **horn.** *See note on 1Sa 2:1.* **stronghold.** A secure, lofty retreat that the enemy finds inaccessible. As such, the Lord is the refuge of His chosen one, secure from all hostile attacks.

22:5–7 David described how he cried to the Lord in the midst of his distress.

22:5, 6 death. Pictured as violent floods of water like waves ready to break over him and traps set by a hunter to snare him, David faced the reality of imminent death *in his personal experience, most frequently* when pursued by Saul, but also in Absalom's conspiracy and in certain wars (see 21:16).

22:7 distress. The particular trouble David was referring to was the potential of his imminent death (vv. 5, 6). **His temple.** God's heavenly dwelling place (cf. Pss 11:4; 29:9).

22:8–16 In reaffirming the great majesty of God, David described His coming in power from heaven to earth (cf. Ex 19:16–20; Eze 1:4–28; Hab 3:3–15).

22:14 The LORD thundered. *See note on 1Sa 7:10.*

22:17–20 In personalizing what he just said in vv. 8–16, David explained how God reached down from heaven to save him on the earth.

22:20 He delighted in me. This expression that the Lord was "pleased" with David (cf. 15:26) provided a transition to vv. 21–28, where David described the basis of God's saving deliverance.

22:21–25 David was not claiming to be righteous or sinless in any absolute sense. Rather, David believed God, was considered righteous by faith, and desired to please the Lord and be obedient to His commands. Thus he was blameless when compared with his enemies.

22:26–28 David stated the basic principles that the Lord follows in delivering or judging people.

22:28 afflicted … haughty. For the idea that the Lord saves the humble, but brings low the proud, see also 1Sa 2:4–7.

22:29–46 Empowered by God (vv. 29–37), David was able to gain total victory over his enemies (vv. 38–43), both in Israel and throughout the nations (vv. 44–46).

22:29 my lamp. David as the "lamp" of Israel (*see note on 21:17*) reflected the light of the glory of God, who was the "Lamp" of David himself.

30 "[A]For by You I can [a]run upon a troop;
By my God I can leap over a wall.
31 "[A]As for God, His way is [a]blameless;
[B]The word of the LORD is tested;
[C]He is a shield to all who
take refuge in Him.
32 "[A]For who is God, besides the LORD?
[B]And who is a rock, besides our God?
33 "[A]God is my strong fortress;
And He [a]sets the [b]blameless in [c]His way.
34 "[A]He makes [a]my feet like hinds' *feet,*
[B]And sets me on my high places.
35 "[A]He trains my hands for battle,
[B]So that my arms can bend
a bow of bronze.
36 "You have also given me [A]the
shield of Your salvation,
And Your [a]help makes me great.
37 "[A]You enlarge my steps under me,
And my [a]feet have not slipped.
38 "I pursued my enemies and
[A]destroyed them,
And I did not turn back until
they were consumed.
39 "And I have devoured them and shattered
them, so that they did not rise;
And [A]they fell under my feet.
40 "For You have girded me with
strength for battle;
You have [a]subdued under me [A]those
who rose up against me.
41 "You have also [A]made my enemies
turn *their* backs to me,
And I [a]destroyed those who hated me.
42 "[A]They looked, but there was none to save;
[B]*Even* to the LORD, but He did
not answer them.
43 "[A]Then I pulverized them as
the dust of the earth;
[B]I crushed *and* stamped them as
the mire of the streets.
44 "[A]You have also delivered me from
the contentions of my people;
[B]You have kept me as head of the nations;
[C]A people whom I have not
known serve me.
45 "[A]Foreigners pretend obedience to me;
As soon as they hear, they obey me.
46 "Foreigners [a]lose heart,
[A]And [b]come trembling out
of their [c]fortresses.
47 "The LORD lives, and blessed be my rock;
And exalted be [a,A]God, the
rock of my salvation,
48 [A]The God who executes vengeance for me,
[B]And brings down peoples under me,
49 Who also brings me out from my enemies;
You even lift me above [A]those
who rise up against me;
[B]You rescue me from the violent man.
50 "[A]Therefore I will give thanks to You,
O LORD, among the nations,
And I will sing praises to Your name.
51 "[A]*He* is a tower of [a]deliverance to His king,
And [B]shows lovingkindness to His anointed,
[C]To David and his [b]descendants forever."

DAVID'S LAST SONG

23 Now these are the last words of David.

David the son of Jesse declares,
[A]The man who was raised on high declares,
[B]The anointed of the God of Jacob,
And the sweet psalmist of Israel,
2 "[A]The Spirit of the LORD spoke by me,
And His word was on my tongue.
3 "The God of Israel said,
[A]The Rock of Israel spoke to me,
'[B]He who rules over men righteously,
[C]Who rules in the fear of God,
4 [A]Is as the light of the morning
when the sun rises,
A morning without clouds,
When the tender grass *springs*
out of the earth,
Through sunshine after rain.'
5 "Truly is not my house so with God?
For [A]He has made an everlasting
covenant with me,
Ordered in all things, and secured;
For all my salvation and all *my* desire,
Will He not indeed make *it* grow?

22:30 [a]Or *crush a troop* [A]2 Sam 5:6-8 22:31 [a]Lit *complete;* or *having integrity* [A]Deut 32:4; Matt 5:48 [B]Ps 12:6; 119:140; Prov 30:5 [C]2 Sam 22:3; Ps 84:9 22:32 [A]1 Sam 2:2 [B]2 Sam 22:2 22:33 [a]Or *sets free* [b]Lit *complete;* or *having integrity* [c]Another reading is *my* [A]2 Sam 22:2; Ps 31:3, 4 22:34 [a]Another reading is *His* [A]2 Sam 2:18; Hab 3:19 [B]Deut 32:13 22:35 [A]Ps 144:1 [B]Job 20:24 22:36 [a]Lit *answering* [A]Eph 6:16, 17 22:37 [a]Lit *ankles* [A]2 Sam 22:20; Prov 4:12 22:38 [A]Ex 15:9 22:39 [A]Mal 4:3 22:40 [a]Lit *caused to bow down* [A]Ps 44:5 22:41 [a]Or *silenced* [A]Ex 23:27; Josh 10:24 22:42 [A]Is 17:7, 8 [B]1 Sam 28:6; Is 1:15 22:43 [A]2 Kin 13:7 [B]Is 10:6; Mic 7:10 22:44 [A]2 Sam 3:1; 19:9, 14 [B]2 Sam 8:1-14 [C]Is 55:5 22:45 [A]Ps 66:3; 81:15 22:46 [a]Lit *languish* [b]Lit *gird themselves* [c]Lit *fastnesses* [A]1 Sam 14:11; Mic 7:17 22:47 [a]Lit *the God of the rock* [A]2 Sam 22:3; Ps 89:26 22:48 [A]1 Sam 24:12; 25:39; 2 Sam 4:8; Ps 94:1 [B]Ps 144:2 22:49 [A]Ps 44:5 [B]Ps 140:1, 4, 11 22:50 [A]Rom 15:9 22:51 [a]I.e. victories; lit *salvation* [b]Lit *seed* [A]Ps 144:10 [B]Ps 89:24 [C]2 Sam 7:12-16 23:1 [A]2 Sam 7:8, 9; Ps 78:70, 71 [B]1 Sam 16:12, 13; Ps 89:20 23:2 [A]Matt 22:43; 2 Pet 1:21 23:3 [A]2 Sam 22:2, 3, 32 [B]Ps 72:1-3; Is 11:1-5 [C]2 Chr 19:7, 9 23:4 [A]Judg 5:31; Ps 72:6 23:5 [A]2 Sam 7:12-16; Ps 89:29; Is 55:3

22:50 Paul quotes this in Ro 15:9.

22:51 His king … His anointed. These terms are singular and thus do not seem to refer to David and his descendants. Rather they refer to the promised "descendant," the Messiah of 7:12. The deliverance and ultimate triumph of David foreshadow that of the coming Messiah. At the end of his life, David looked back in faith at God's promises and forward in hope to their fulfillment in the coming of a future "king," the "anointed one" (*see notes on 1Sa 2:10*).

23:1–7 last words. This is David's final literary legacy to Israel, not his final oral speech (see 1Ki 2:1–10).

23:1 declares. "Declares as an oracle" (cf. Nu 24:3, 15; 1Sa 2:30; Pr 30:1). David realized that the psalms he wrote, as directed by the Holy Spirit, were the very Word of God.

23:2 Spirit. God's Holy Spirit is the divine instrument of revelation and inspiration (cf. Zec 7:12; 2Ti 3:16, 17; 2Pe 1:19–21).

23:3, 4 He who rules. These words begin the record of direct speech from God, whose ideal king must exercise His authority with justice, in complete submission to divine sovereignty. Such a king is like the helpful rays of sun at dawn and the life-giving showers which nourish the earth. This ideal king was identified in the OT as the coming Messiah (cf. Is 9:6, 7).

23:5 is not my house so with God? In response to God's standard for His ideal king, David confessed that his house had not always ruled over God's people in righteousness and in the fear of God, and thus were not the fulfillment of 7:12–16. Further, none of

6 "[A]But the worthless, every one of them
will be thrust away like thorns,
Because they cannot be taken in hand;
7 But the man who touches them
Must be [a]armed with iron and
the shaft of a spear,
And [A]they will be completely burned
with fire in *their* [b]place."

HIS MIGHTY MEN

8 [A]These are the names of the mighty men whom
David had: Josheb-basshebeth a Tahchemonite, chief
of the [a]captains, he was *called* Adino the Eznite,
because of eight hundred slain *by him* at one time;
9 and after him was Eleazar the son of [A]Dodo the
[B]Ahohite, one of the three mighty men with David when they [a]defied the Philistines who were
gathered there to battle and the men of Israel had
[b]withdrawn. 10 [A]He arose and struck the Philistines
until his hand was weary and [a]clung to the sword,
and [B]the LORD brought about a great [b]victory that
day; and the people returned after him only to strip
the slain.

11 Now after him was Shammah the son of Agee a
[A]Hararite. And the Philistines were gathered [a]into a
troop where there was a plot of ground full of lentils,
and the people fled from the Philistines. 12 But he
took his stand in the midst of the plot, defended it
and struck the Philistines; and [A]the LORD brought
about a great [a]victory.

13 Then three of the thirty chief men went down
and came to David in the harvest time to the [A]cave
of Adullam, while the troop of the Philistines was
camping in [B]the valley of Rephaim. 14 David was
then [A]in the stronghold, while the garrison of the
Philistines was then in Bethlehem. 15 [A]David had a
craving and said, "Oh that someone would give me
water to drink from the well of Bethlehem which
is by the gate!" 16 [A]So the three mighty men broke
through the camp of the Philistines, and drew water
from the well of Bethlehem which was by the gate,
and took *it* and brought *it* to David. Nevertheless he
would not drink it, but [B]poured it out to the LORD;
17 and he said, "Be it far from me, O LORD, that I
should do this. [A]*Shall I drink* the blood of the men
who went in *jeopardy* of their lives?" Therefore he
would not drink it. These things the three mighty
men did.

18 [A]Abishai, the brother of Joab, the son of Zeruiah,
was [B]chief of the [a]thirty. And he swung his spear
against three hundred [b]and killed *them*, and had a
name as well as the three. 19 He was most honored
of the thirty, therefore he became their commander;
however, he did not attain to the three.

20 Then [A]Benaiah the son of Jehoiada, the son of
a valiant man of [B]Kabzeel, who had done mighty
deeds, [a]killed the [b]two *sons of* Ariel of Moab. He
also went down and killed a lion in the middle of
a pit on a snowy day. 21 He [a]killed an Egyptian, [b]an
impressive man. Now the Egyptian *had* a spear
in his hand, but he went down to him with a club
and snatched the spear from the Egyptian's hand
and killed him with his own spear. 22 These *things*
[A]Benaiah the son of Jehoiada did, and had a name
as well as the three mighty men. 23 He was honored
among the thirty, but he did not attain to the three.
And David appointed him over his guard.

24 [A]Asahel the brother of Joab was among the
thirty; Elhanan the son of Dodo of Bethlehem,
25 [A]Shammah the [B]Harodite, Elika the Harodite,
26 Helez the Paltite, Ira the son of Ikkesh the [A]Te-
koite, 27 Abiezer the [A]Anathothite, Mebunnai the
Hushathite, 28 Zalmon the Ahohite, Maharai the
[A]Netophathite, 29 [A]Heleb the son of Baanah the Netophathite, Ittai the son of Ribai of [B]Gibeah of the
sons of Benjamin, 30 Benaiah a [A]Pirathonite, Hiddai
of the brooks of [B]Gaash, 31 Abi-albon the Arbathite,
Azmaveth the [A]Barhumite, 32 Eliahba the [A]Shaal-
bonite, the sons of Jashen, Jonathan, 33 [A]Shammah
the Hararite, Ahiam the son of Sharar the Ararite,
34 Eliphelet the son of Ahasbai, the son of [A]the Maacathite, [B]Eliam the son of [C]Ahithophel the Gilonite,
35 [A]Hezro the [B]Carmelite, Paarai the Arbite, 36 Igal the
son of Nathan of [A]Zobah, Bani the Gadite, 37 Zelek the

23:6 [A]Matt 13:41 23:7 [a]Lit *filled* [b]Lit *sitting* [A]Matt 3:10; 13:30; Heb 6:8 23:8 [a]Or *three* [A]1 Chr 11:11-47 23:9 [a]Lit *reproached* [b]Lit *gone up* [A]1 Chr 27:4 [B]1 Chr 8:4 23:10 [a]Lit *his hand clung* [b]Lit *salvation* [A]1 Chr 11:13 [B]1 Sam 11:13; 19:5 23:11 [a]Possibly, at Lehi [A]2 Sam 23:33 23:12 [a]Lit *salvation* [A]2 Sam 23:10 23:13 [A]1 Sam 22:1 [B]2 Sam 5:18 23:14 [A]1 Sam 22:4, 5 23:15 [A]1 Chr 11:17 23:16 [A]1 Chr 11:18 [B]Gen 35:14 23:17 [A]Lev 17:10 23:18 [a]So two Heb mss and Syriac; M.T. *three* [b]Lit *slain ones* [A]2 Sam 10:10, 14; 18:2 [B]1 Chr 11:20, 21 23:20 [a]Lit *smote* [b]Or *two lion-like heroes* [A]2 Sam 8:18; 20:23 [B]Josh 15:21 23:21 [a]Lit *smote* [b]Lit *a man of appearance* 23:22 [A]2 Sam 23:20 23:24 [A]2 Sam 2:18; 1 Chr 27:7 23:25 [A]1 Chr 11:27 [B]Judg 7:1 23:26 [A]2 Sam 14:2 23:27 [A]Josh 21:18 23:28 [A]2 Kin 25:23 23:29 [A]1 Chr 11:30 [B]Josh 18:28 23:30 [A]Judg 12:13, 15 [B]Josh 24:30 23:31 [A]2 Sam 3:16 23:32 [A]Josh 19:42 23:33 [A]2 Sam 23:11 23:34 [A]2 Sam 10:6, 8; 20:14 [B]2 Sam 11:3 [C]2 Sam 15:12 23:35 [A]1 Chr 11:37 [B]Josh 15:55 23:36 [A]2 Sam 8:3

the kings of David's line (according to 1 and 2 Kings) met God's standard of righteous obedience. **everlasting covenant.** The promise given by the Lord to David recorded in 7:12–16 is here referred to as a "covenant," a binding agreement from the Lord that He will fulfill. In spite of the fact that David and his own household had failed (chaps. 9–20), David rightly believed that the Lord would not fail, but would be faithful to His promise of hope for the future in the descendant of David, the Eternal King, the anointed one (*see note on 7:12*), who would establish a kingdom of righteousness and peace forever.

23:6 worthless. Lit. "Belial" (*see note on 1Sa 2:12*). The wicked enemies of God will be cast aside in judgment when the Messiah, the fulfillment of the Davidic Covenant, establishes His rule upon the earth (cf. Is 63:1–6).

23:8–39 This fifth inset recalls David's mighty men. See 1Ch 11:10–41.

23:8 the mighty men. David's bravest warriors and most outstanding soldiers are memorialized. This list appears in 1Ch 11:11–41, with slight variations. According to 1Ch 11:10, these men helped David to become king. The listing of these men is presented in 3 sets: first, "the three" (vv. 8–12); second, two more honored other than "the thirty," but not attaining to "the three" (vv. 18–23); third, "the thirty" which is actually 32 (vv. 24–39). This list is expanded by 16 names in 1Ch 11:41–47. **eight hundred.** Probably a textual error. 1Ch 11:11 has "three hundred," the likely number.

23:13–17 three of the thirty. Three of the soldiers mentioned in vv. 34–39.

23:13 cave of Adullam. *See note on 1Sa 22:1.* **valley of Rephaim.** *See note on 5:18.*

23:14 stronghold. *See note on 22:3.*

23:16 poured it out to the LORD. Because David's men brought him water from Bethlehem's well at the risk of their own lives, he considered it as "blood" and refused to drink it. Instead, he poured it out on the ground as a sacrifice to the Lord (cf. Ge 35:14; Ex 30:9; Lv 23:13, 18, 37).

23:18 Abishai. *See note on 2:18.*

23:20 Benaiah. *See note on 8:18.*

23:24 Asahel. *See note on 2:18.*

23:24–39 thirty. A technical term for a small military contingent, named "the thirty" since it usually consisted of around 30 men, whereas 32 men are listed here, counting Joab.

Ammonite, Naharai the [A]Beerothite, armor bearers of Joab the son of Zeruiah, 38 Ira the [A]Ithrite, Gareb the Ithrite, 39 [A]Uriah the Hittite; thirty-seven in all.

THE CENSUS TAKEN

24 [A]Now [B]again the anger of the LORD burned against Israel, and it incited David against them to say, "[C]Go, number Israel and Judah." 2 The king said to Joab the commander of the army who was with him, "Go about now through all the tribes of Israel, [A]from Dan to Beersheba, and [a]register the people, that I may know the number of the people." 3 But Joab said to the king, "[A]Now may the LORD your God add to the people a hundred times as many as they are, while the eyes of my lord the king *still* see; but why does my lord the king delight in this thing?" 4 Nevertheless, the king's word prevailed against Joab and against the commanders of the army. So Joab and the commanders of the army went out from the presence of the king to [a]register the people of Israel. 5 They crossed the Jordan and camped in [A]Aroer, on the right side of the city that is in the middle of the valley of Gad and toward [B]Jazer. 6 Then they came to Gilead and to [a]the land of Tahtim-hodshi, and they came to Dan-jaan and around to [A]Sidon, 7 and came to the [A]fortress of Tyre and to all the cities of the [B]Hivites and of the Canaanites, and they went out to the south of Judah, *to* [C]Beersheba. 8 So when they had gone about through the whole land, they came to Jerusalem at the end of nine months and twenty days. 9 And Joab gave [A]the number of the [a]registration of the people to the king; and there were in Israel [B]eight hundred thousand valiant men who drew the sword, and the men of Judah were five hundred thousand men.

10 Now [A]David's heart [a]troubled him after he had numbered the people. So David said to the LORD, "[B]I have sinned greatly in what I have done. But now, O LORD, please [b]take away the iniquity of Your servant, for [C]I have acted very foolishly." 11 When David arose in the morning, the word of the LORD came to [A]the prophet Gad, David's [B]seer, saying, 12 "Go and speak to David, 'Thus the LORD says, "I am offering you three things; choose for yourself one of them, which I will do to you." ' " 13 So Gad came to David and told him, and said to him, "Shall [A]seven years of famine come to you in your land? Or will you flee three months before your foes while they pursue you? Or shall there be three days' pestilence in your land? Now consider and see what answer I shall return to Him who sent me." 14 Then David said to Gad, "I am in great distress. Let us now fall into the hand of the LORD [A]for His mercies are great, but do not let me fall into the hand of man."

23:37 [A]2 Sam 4:2 23:38 [A]1 Chr 2:53 23:39 [A]2 Sam 11:3, 6 24:1 [A]1 Chr 21:1 [B]2 Sam 21:1, 2 [C]1 Chr 27:23, 24 24:2 [a]Lit *muster* [A]Judg 20:1; 2 Sam 3:10 24:3 [A]Deut 1:11 24:4 [a]Lit *muster* 24:5 [A]Deut 2:36; Josh 13:9, 16 [B]Num 21:32; 32:35 24:6 [a]Or *Kadesh in the land of the Hittite* [A]Josh 19:28; Judg 1:31 24:7 [A]Josh 19:29 [B]Josh 11:3; Judg 3:3 [C]Gen 21:22-33 24:9 [a]Lit *muster* [A]Num 1:44-46 [B]1 Chr 21:5 24:10 [a]Lit *smote* [b]Lit *cause to pass away* [A]1 Sam 24:5 [B]2 Sam 12:13 [C]1 Sam 13:13; 2 Chr 16:9 24:11 [A]1 Sam 22:5; 1 Chr 29:29 [B]1 Sam 9:9 24:13 [A]1 Chr 21:12; Ezek 14:21 24:14 [A]Ps 51:1; 130:4, 7

23:39 Uriah. Here is inserted a mention of one of David's great soldiers, a reminder of David's great sin (11:1–27), and a preparation for David's further failure recorded in 24:1–10. **thirty-seven.** The 3 (vv. 8–12) with Abishai (vv. 18–19) and Benaiah (vv. 20–23) plus the 32 men of "the thirty" (vv. 24–39).

24:1–17 *See notes on 1Ch 21:1–16.*

24:1 again. A second outbreak of the divine wrath occurred after the 3-year famine recorded in 21:1. **against Israel.** The inciting of David to conduct a census was a punishment on Israel from the Lord for some unspecified sins. Perhaps sins of pride and ambition had led him to increase the size of his army unnecessarily and place heavy burdens of support on the people. Whatever the sin, it is clear God was dissatisfied with David's motives, goals, and actions and brought judgment. **it incited David.** *See note on 1Ch 21:1.* **number Israel and Judah.** A census was usually for military purposes, which seems to be the case here (see v. 9). Numbering the potential army of Israel had been done in the past (Nu 1:1, 2; 26:1–4). However, this census of Israel's potential army did not have the sanction of the Lord and proceeded from wrong motives. David either wanted to glory in the size of his fighting force or take more territory than what the Lord had granted him. He shifted his trust from God to military power (this is a constant theme in the Psalms; cf. 20:7; 25:2; 44:6).

24:2 from Dan to Beersheba. A proverbial statement for all the land of Israel from N to S.

24:3 but why . . . ? Although Joab protested the plan, he was overruled by David with no reason for the census being stated by David.

24:5 Aroer. The census began about 14 mi. E of the Dead Sea on the northern bank of the Arnon River, in the southeastern corner of Israel, and continued in a counterclockwise direction through the land. **Jazer.** A town in the territory of Gad about 6 mi. W of Rabbah. Jazer was close to the border of the Ammonite territory.

24:6 Gilead. The Transjordan territory N of Gad. **Dan-jaan.** Either a village near the town of Dan or a fuller name for Dan itself. Dan is 25 mi. N of the Sea of Galilee.

24:7 Tyre. The census takers seem to have gone N from Dan and then W towards Sidon before turning S toward Tyre, a city on the coast of the Mediterranean Sea ruled by David's friend Hiram (*see note on 5:11*), but remaining in Israelite territory. **Beersheba.** A major settlement in the S of the land of Israel located about 45 mi. SW of Jerusalem.

24:9 eight hundred thousand . . . five hundred thousand. First Chronicles 21:5 has "one million one hundred thousand" and "four hundred and seventy thousand," respectively. A solution can be found in seeing the 1 Chronicles figure including all the available men of military age, whether battle seasoned or not. But the 2 Samuel figure could be 800,000 battle-seasoned soldiers with the additional 300,000 being of military age who were in reserve but never fought, or it could be the 288,000 in the standing army (1Ch 27:1–15) rounded off to 300,000. Either of these two contingents would make up the 1.1 million number of 1Ch 21. As far as Judah was concerned, the number in 2 Samuel is 30,000 more than the 1 Chronicles figure. First Chronicles makes it clear that the numbering was not completed by Joab, because he didn't get to the census regarding Benjamin (or Levi) before David came under conviction about completing it all. Joab was glad to stop when he saw the king's changed heart. Because of the procedure selected (*see note on 24:5*) the numbering of Benjamin would have been last, so their number was not included. In the record of 2 Samuel the figure for Judah included the already-known number of 30,000 troops from Benjamin, hence the total of 500,000. The Benjamites remained loyal to David and Judah.

24:10 David's heart troubled him. Although God's prohibition is not clear in the text, it was clear to David. **sinned greatly . . . acted very foolishly.** David recognized the enormity of his willful rebellion against God. David's insight saw the seriousness of his error in relying on numerical strength instead of on the Lord, who can deliver by many or few (see 1Sa 14:6).

24:11 Gad. *See note on 1Sa 22:5.*

24:13 famine . . . foes . . . pestilence. David was given a choice of 3 possible punishments for his sin of numbering the people: 1) 7 years of famine in Israel (*see note on 1Ch 21:12*); 2) 3 months of fleeing from his enemies; or 3) 3 days of pestilence in the land. Implicit in the threat of pursuit by "foes" was death by the sword. Famine, sword, and plague were OT punishments of the Lord against His sinful people (Lv 26:23–26; Dt 28:21–26; Jer 14:12).

24:14 fall into the hand of the LORD. David knew that the Lord would be more merciful than his enemies, so he took the third option.

PESTILENCE SENT

15 So [A]the LORD [a]sent a pestilence upon Israel
from the morning until the appointed time, and
seventy thousand men of the people [B]from Dan to
Beersheba died. 16 [A]When the angel stretched out
his hand toward Jerusalem to destroy it, [B]the LORD
relented from the calamity and said to the angel
who destroyed the people, "It is enough! Now relax
your hand!" And the angel of the LORD was by the
threshing floor of Araunah the Jebusite. 17 Then David spoke to the LORD when he saw the angel who
was striking down the people, and said, "Behold,
[A]it is I who have sinned, and it is I who have done
wrong; but [B]these sheep, what have they done?
Please let Your hand be against me and against
my father's house."

DAVID BUILDS AN ALTAR

18 So Gad came to David that day and said to him,
"[A]Go up, erect an altar to the LORD on the threshing
floor of [a]Araunah the Jebusite." 19 David went up
according to the word of Gad, just as the LORD had
commanded. 20 Araunah looked down and saw the
king and his servants crossing over toward him; and
Araunah went out and bowed his face to the ground
before the king. 21 Then Araunah said, "Why has my
lord the king come to his servant?" And David said,
"To buy the threshing floor from you, in order to
build an altar to the LORD, [A]that the plague may be
held back from the people." 22 Araunah said to David,
"Let my lord the king take and offer up what is good
in his sight. Look, [A]the oxen for the burnt offering,
the threshing sledges and the yokes of the oxen for
the wood. 23 Everything, O king, Araunah gives to
the king." And Araunah said to the king, "May the
LORD your God [A]accept you." 24 However, the king
said to Araunah, "No, but I will surely buy *it* from
you for a price, for [A]I will not offer burnt offerings
to the LORD my God [a]which cost me nothing." So
[B]David bought the threshing floor and the oxen for
fifty shekels of silver. 25 David built there an altar
to the LORD and offered burnt offerings and peace
offerings. [A]Thus the LORD was moved by prayer for
the land, and the plague was held back from Israel.

24:15 [a]Lit *gave* [A]1 Chr 21:14; 27:24 [B]2 Sam 24:2 24:16 [A]Ex 12:23; 2 Kin 19:35; Acts 12:23 [B]Ex 32:14; 1 Sam 15:11 24:17 [A]2 Sam 24:10 [B]2 Sam 7:8; Ps 74:1 24:18 [a]In 2 Chr 3:1, *Ornan* [A]1 Chr 21:18 24:21 [A]Num 16:44-50 24:22 [A]1 Sam 6:14; 1 Kin 19:21 24:23 [A]Ezek 20:40, 41 24:24 [a]Lit *gratuitously* [A]Mal 1:13, 14 [B]1 Chr 21:24, 25 24:25 [A]2 Sam 21:14

24:16 relented. Or "repented, grieved," an expression of God's deep sorrow concerning man's sin and evil (see 1Sa 15:11, 29). **Araunah the Jebusite.** Araunah (or Ornan) was a pre-Israelite inhabitant of Jerusalem. He owned a threshing floor N of the citadel of Jerusalem and outside its fortified area.

24:17 let Your hand be against me. Rather than witness the further destruction of his people, David called down the wrath upon himself and his own family (cf. Ex 32:32).

24:18–25 See 1Ch 21:18–27.

24:18 altar. At this time, the altar associated with the tabernacle of Moses was located at Gibeon (1Ch 21:29; 2Ch 1:2–6). David was instructed by Gad to build another altar to the Lord at the place where the plague had stopped. This indicated where the Lord's choice was for the building of His temple.

24:24 cost me nothing. Sacrifice is an essential part of worship and service to God (see Mal 1:6–10; 2Co 8:1–5). **fifty shekels.** A little more than a pound of silver. First Chronicles 21:25 says David paid 600 shekels of gold. How is this discrepancy resolved? In the initial transaction, David either bought or leased the small threshing floor (usually 30 or 40 ft. square) and purchased the oxen. Fifty shekels of silver was appropriate. After that, 1Ch 21:25 says he bought "the site," costing 180 times as much, and referring to the entire area of Mt. Moriah.

24:25 the plague was held back. This indicates that judgment is not the final action of the Lord toward either Israel or the house of David. God will fulfill the Abrahamic and Davidic Covenants (cf. Eze 37).

THE FIRST AND SECOND BOOKS OF THE KINGS

TITLE

First and Second Kings were originally one book, called in the Hebrew text, "Kings," from the first word in 1:1. The Greek translation of the OT, the Septuagint (LXX), divided the book in two, and this was followed by the Latin Vulgate (Vg.) version and English translations. The division was for the convenience of copying this lengthy book on scrolls and codexes and was not based on features of content. Modern Hebrew Bibles title the books "Kings A" and "Kings B." The LXX and Vg. connected Kings with the books of Samuel, so that the titles in the LXX are "The Third and Fourth Books of Kingdoms" and in the Vg. "Third and Fourth Kings." The books of 1 and 2 Samuel and 1 and 2 Kings combined are a chronicle of the entire history of Judah's and Israel's kingship from Saul to Zedekiah. First and Second Chronicles provide only the history of Judah's monarchy.

AUTHOR AND DATE

Jewish tradition proposed that Jeremiah wrote Kings, though this is unlikely because the final event recorded in the book (see 2Ki 25:27–30) occurred in Babylon in 561 B.C. Jeremiah never went to Babylon, but to Egypt (Jer 43:1–7), and would have been at least 86 years old by 561 B.C. Actually, the identity of the unnamed author remains unknown. Since the ministry of prophets is emphasized in Kings, it seems that the author was most likely an unnamed prophet of the Lord who lived in exile with Israel in Babylon.

Kings was written between 561–538 B.C. Since the last narrated event (2Ki 25:27–30) sets the earliest possible date of completion and because there is no record of the end of the Babylonian captivity in Kings, the release from exile (538 B.C.) identifies the latest possible writing date. This date is sometimes challenged on the basis of "to this day" statements in 1Ki 8:8; 9:13, 20, 21; 10:12; 12:19; 2Ki 2:22; 8:22; 10:27; 14:7; 16:6; 17:23, 34, 41; 21:15. However, it is best to understand these statements as those of the sources used by the author, rather than statements of the author himself.

It is clear that the author used a variety of sources in compiling this book, including "the book of the acts of Solomon" (1Ki 11:41), "the Chronicles of the Kings of Israel" (1Ki 14:19; 15:31; 16:5, 14, 20, 27; 22:39; 2Ki 1:18; 10:34; 13:8, 12; 14:15, 28; 15:11, 15, 21, 26, 31), and "the Chronicles of the Kings of Judah" (1Ki 14:29; 15:7, 23; 22:45; 2Ki 8:23; 12:19; 14:18; 15:6, 36; 16:19; 20:20; 21:17, 25; 23:28; 24:5). Further, Is 36:1–39:8 provided information used in 2Ki 18:9–20:19, and Jer 52:31–34 seems to be the source for 2Ki 25:27–29. This explanation posits a single inspired author, living in Babylon during the Exile, using these pre-Exilic source materials at his disposal.

BACKGROUND AND SETTING

A distinction must be made between the setting of the books' sources and that of the books' author. The source material was written by participants in and eyewitnesses of the events. It was reliable information, which was historically accurate concerning the sons of Israel, from the death of David and the accession of Solomon (971 B.C.) to the destruction of the temple and Jerusalem by the Babylonians (586 B.C.). Thus, Kings traces the histories of two sets of kings and two nations of disobedient people, Israel and Judah, both of whom were growing indifferent to God's law and His prophets and were headed for captivity.

The book of Kings is not only accurate history, but interpreted history. The author, an exile in Babylon, wished to communicate the lessons of Israel's history to the exiles. Specifically, he taught the exilic community why the Lord's judgment of exile had come. The writer established early in his narrative that the Lord required obedience by the kings to the Mosaic law, if their kingdom was to receive His blessing; disobedience would bring exile (1Ki 9:3–9). The sad reality that history revealed was that all the kings of Israel and the majority of the kings of Judah "did evil in the sight of the Lord." These evil kings were apostates, who led their people to sin by not confronting idolatry, but sanctioning it. Because of the kings' failure, the Lord sent His prophets to confront both the monarchs and the people with their sin and their need to return to Him. Because the message of the prophets was rejected, the prophets foretold that the nation(s) would be carried into exile (2Ki 17:13–23; 21:10–15). Like every prophecy uttered by the prophets in Kings, this word from the Lord came to pass (2Ki 17:5, 6; 25:1–11). Therefore, Kings interpreted the people's experience of exile and helped them to see why they had suffered God's punishment for idolatry. It also explained that just as God had shown mercy to Ahab (1Ki 21:27–29) and Jehoiachin (2Ki 25:27–30), so He was willing to show them mercy.

The predominant geographical setting of Kings is the whole land of Israel, from Dan to Beersheba (1Ki 4:25), including Transjordan. Four invading nations played a dominant role in the affairs of Israel and Judah from 971 to 561 B.C. In the tenth century B.C., Egypt impacted Israel's history during the reigns of Solomon and Rehoboam (1Ki 3:1; 11:14–22, 40; 12:2; 14:25–27). Syria (Aram) posed a great threat to Israel's security during the ninth century B.C., ca. 890–800 B.C. (1Ki 15:9–22; 20:1–34; 22:1–4, 29–40; 2Ki 6:8–7:20; 8:7–15; 10:32, 33; 12:17, 18; 13:22–25). The years from ca. 800 to 750 B.C. were a half-century of peace and prosperity for Israel and Judah, because Assyria neutralized Syria and did not threaten to the south. This changed during the kingship of Tiglath-Pileser III (2Ki 15:19, 20, 29). From the mid-eighth century to the late seventh century B.C., Assyria terrorized Israel, finally conquering and destroying Israel (the northern kingdom) in 722 B.C. (2Ki 17:4–6) and besieging Jerusalem in 701 B.C. (2Ki 18:17–19:37). From 612 to 539 B.C., Babylon was the dominant power in the ancient world. Babylon invaded Judah (the southern kingdom) 3 times, with the destruction of Jerusalem and the temple occurring in 586 B.C. during that third assault (2Ki 24:1–25:21).

HISTORICAL AND THEOLOGICAL THEMES

Kings concentrates, then, on the history of the sons of Israel from 971 to 561 B.C. First Kings 1:1–11:43 deals with Solomon's accession and reign (971–931 B.C.). The two divided kingdoms of Israel and Judah (931–722 B.C.) are covered in 1Ki 12:1; 2Ki 17:41. The author arranged the material in a distinctive way in that the narration follows the kings in both the N and the S. For each reign described, there is the following literary framework. Every king is introduced with: 1) his name and relation to his predecessor; 2) his date of accession in relationship to the year of the contemporary ruler in the other kingdom; 3) his age on coming to the throne (for kings of Judah only); 4) his length of reign; 5) his place of reign; 6) his mother's name (for Judah only); and 7) spiritual appraisal of his reign. This introduction is followed by a narration of the events that occurred during the reign of each king. The details of this narration vary widely. Each reign is concluded with: 1) a citation of sources; 2) additional historical notes; 3) notice of death; 4) notice of burial; 5) the name of the successor; and 6) in a few instances, an added postscript (e.g., 1Ki 15:32; 2Ki 10:36). Second Kings 18:1–25:21 deals with the time when Judah survived alone (722–586 B.C.). Two concluding paragraphs speak of events after the Babylonian exile (2Ki 25:22–26, 27–30).

Three theological themes are stressed in Kings. First, the Lord judged Israel and Judah because of their disobedience to His law (2Ki 17:7–23). This unfaithfulness on the part of the people was furthered by the apostasy of the evil kings who led them into idolatry (2Ki 17:21, 22; 21:11), so the Lord exercised His righteous wrath against His rebellious people. Second, the word of the true prophets came to pass (1Ki 13:2, 3; 22:15–28; 2Ki 23:16; 24:2). This confirmed that the Lord did keep His Word, even His warnings of judgment. Third, the Lord remembered His promise to David (1Ki 11:12–13, 34–36; 15:4; 2Ki 8:19). Even though the kings of the Davidic line proved themselves to be disobedient to the Lord, He did not bring David's family to an end as He did the families of Jeroboam I, Omri, and Jehu in Israel. Even as the book closes, the line of David still exists (2Ki 25:27–30), so there is hope for the coming "seed" of David (see 2Sa 7:12–16). The Lord is thus seen as faithful, and His Word is trustworthy.

INTERPRETIVE CHALLENGES

The major interpretive challenge in Kings concerns the chronology of the kings of Israel and Judah. Though abundant chronological data is presented in the book of Kings, this data is difficult to interpret for two reasons. First, there seems to be internal inconsistency in the information given. For instance, 1Ki 16:23 states that Omri, king of Israel, began to reign in the 31st year of Asa, king of Judah, and that he reigned 12 years. But according to 1Ki 16:29, Omri was succeeded by his son Ahab in the 38th year of Asa, giving Omri a reign of only 7 years, not 12 (for resolution, *see note on 1Ki 16:23*). Second, from extrabiblical sources (Greek, Assyrian, and Babylonian), correlated with astronomical data, a reliable series of dates can be calculated from 892 to 566 B.C. Since Ahab and Jehu, kings of Israel, are believed to be mentioned in Assyrian records, 853 B.C. can be fixed as the year of Ahab's death and 841 B.C. as the year Jehu began to reign. With these fixed dates, it is possible to work backward and forward to determine that the date of the division of Israel from Judah was ca. 931 B.C., the fall of Samaria 722 B.C., and the fall of Jerusalem 586 B.C. But when the total years of royal reigns in Kings are added, the number for Israel is 241 years (not the 210 years of 931 to 722 B.C.) and Judah 393 years (not the 346 years of 931 to 586 B.C.). It is recognized that in both kingdoms there were some co-regencies, i.e., a period of rulership when two kings, usually father and son, ruled at the same time, so the overlapping years were counted twice in the total for both kings. Further, different methods of reckoning the years of a king's rule and even different calendars were used at differing times in the two kingdoms, resulting in the seeming internal inconsistencies. The general accuracy of the chronology in Kings can be demonstrated and confirmed.

A second major interpretive challenge deals with Solomon's relationship to the Abrahamic and Davidic Covenants. First Kings 4:20, 21 has been interpreted by some as the fulfillment of the promises given to Abraham (cf. Ge 15:18–21; 22:17). However, according to Nu 34:6, the western border of the land promised to Abraham was the Mediterranean Sea. In 1Ki 5:1ff., Hiram is seen as the independent king of Tyre (along the Mediterranean), dealing with Solomon as an equal. Solomon's empire was not the fulfillment of the land promise given to Abraham by the Lord, although a great portion of that land was under Solomon's control. Further, the statements of Solomon in 1Ki 5:5 and 8:20 are his claims to be the promised seed of the Davidic Covenant (cf. 2Sa 7:12–16). The author of Kings holds out the possibility that Solomon's temple was the fulfillment of the Lord's promise to David. However, while the conditions for the fulfillment of the promise to David are reiterated to Solomon (1Ki 6:12), it is clear that Solomon did not meet these conditions (1Ki 11:9–13). In fact, none of the historical kings in the house of David met the condition of complete obedience that was to be the sign of the Promised One. According to Kings, the fulfillment of the Abrahamic and Davidic Covenants did not take place in Israel's past, thus laying the foundation for the latter prophets (Isaiah, Jeremiah, Ezekiel, and the Twelve) who would point Israel to a future hope under Messiah when the Covenants would be fulfilled (see Is 9:6, 7).

OUTLINE

Since the division of 1 and 2 Kings arbitrarily takes place in the middle of the narrative concerning King Ahaziah in Israel, the following outline is for both 1 and 2 Kings.

OUTLINE

I. The United Kingdom: The Reign of Solomon (1Ki 1:1–11:43)

- A. The Rise of Solomon (1Ki 1:1–2:46)
- B. The Beginning of Solomon's Wisdom and Wealth (1Ki 3:1–4:34)
- C. The Preparations for the Building of the Temple (1Ki 5:1–18)
- D. The Building of the Temple and Solomon's House (1Ki 6:1–9:9)
- E. The Further Building Projects of Solomon (1Ki 9:10–28)
- F. The Culmination of Solomon's Wisdom and Wealth (1Ki 10:1–29)
- G. The Decline of Solomon (1Ki 11:1–43)

II. The Divided Kingdom: The Kings of Israel and Judah (1Ki 12:1–2Ki 17:41)

- A. The Rise of Idolatry: Jeroboam of Israel/Rehoboam of Judah (1Ki 12:1–14:31)
- B. Kings of Judah/Israel (1Ki 15:1–16:22)
- C. The Dynasty of Omri and Its Influence: The Rise and Fall of Baal Worship in Israel and Judah (1Ki 16:23–2Ki 13:25)
  1. The introduction of Baal worship (1Ki 16:23–34)
  2. The opposition of Elijah to Baal worship (1Ki 17:1–2Ki 1:18)
  3. The influence of Elisha concerning the true God (2Ki 2:1–9:13)
  4. The overthrow of Baal worship in Israel (2Ki 9:14–10:36)
  5. The overthrow of Baal worship in Judah (2Ki 11:1–12:21)
  6. The death of Elisha (2Ki 13:1–25)
- D. Kings of Judah/Israel (2Ki 14:1–15:38)
- E. The Defeat and Exile of Israel by Assyria (2Ki 16:1–17:41)

III. The Surviving Kingdom: The Kings of Judah (2Ki 18:1–25:21)

- A. Hezekiah's Righteous Reign (2Ki 18:1–20:21)
- B. Manasseh's and Amon's Wicked Reigns (2Ki 21:1–26)
- C. Josiah's Righteous Reign (2Ki 22:1–23:30)
- D. The Defeat and Exile of Judah by Babylon (2Ki 23:31–25:21)

IV. Epilogue: The People's Continued Rebellion and the Lord's Continued Mercy (2Ki 25:22–30)

DAVID IN OLD AGE

1 Now King David was old, advanced in age; and they covered him with clothes, but he could not keep warm. 2 So his servants said to him, "Let them seek a young virgin for my lord the king, and let her [a]attend the king and become his nurse; and let her lie in your bosom, that my lord the king may keep warm." 3 So they searched for a beautiful girl throughout all the territory of Israel, and found Abishag the [A]Shunammite, and brought her to the king. 4 The girl was very beautiful; and she became the king's nurse and served him, but the king did not [a]cohabit with her.

5 Now [A]Adonijah the son of Haggith exalted himself, saying, "I will be king." So [B]he prepared for himself chariots and horsemen with fifty men to run before him. 6 His father had never [a]crossed him at any time by asking, "Why have you done so?" And he was also a very handsome man, and [b,A]he was born after Absalom. 7 [a]He had conferred with [A]Joab the son of Zeruiah and with [B]Abiathar the priest; and following [C]Adonijah they helped him. 8 But [A]Zadok the priest, [B]Benaiah the son of Jehoiada, [C]Nathan the prophet, [D]Shimei, Rei, and [E]the mighty men who belonged to David, were not with Adonijah.

9 Adonijah sacrificed sheep and oxen and fatlings by the [a]stone of Zoheleth, which is beside [A]En-rogel; and he invited all his brothers, the king's sons, and all the men of Judah, the king's servants. 10 But he did not invite Nathan the prophet, Benaiah, the mighty men, and [A]Solomon his brother.

NATHAN AND BATHSHEBA

11 Then Nathan spoke to [A]Bathsheba the mother of Solomon, saying, "Have you not heard that Adonijah the son of Haggith has become king, and David our lord does not know *it?* 12 So now come, please let me [A]give you counsel and save your life and the life of your son Solomon. 13 Go [a]at once to King David and say to him, 'Have you not, my lord, O king, sworn to your maidservant, saying, "[A]Surely Solomon your son shall be king after me, and he shall sit on my throne"? Why then has Adonijah become king?' 14 Behold, while you are still there speaking with the king, I will come in after you and confirm your words."

15 So Bathsheba went in to the king in the bedroom. Now [A]the king was very old, and Abishag the Shunammite was ministering to the king. 16 Then Bathsheba bowed and prostrated herself [a]before the king. And the king said, "What [b]do you wish?" 17 She said to him, "My lord, you swore to your maidservant by the LORD your God, *saying,* '[A]Surely your son Solomon shall be king after me and he shall sit on my throne.' 18 Now, behold, Adonijah is king; and now, my lord the king, you do not know *it.* 19 [A]He has sacrificed oxen and fatlings and sheep in abundance, and has invited all the sons of the king and Abiathar the priest and Joab the commander of the army, but he has not invited Solomon your servant. 20 As for you now, my lord the king, the eyes of all Israel are on you, to tell them who shall sit on the throne of my lord the king after him. 21 Otherwise it will come about, [A]as soon as my lord the king sleeps with his fathers, that I and my son Solomon will be considered [a]offenders."

1:2 [a]Lit *stand before* 1:3 [A]Josh 19:18; 1 Sam 28:4 1:4 [a]Lit *know her* 1:5 [A]2 Sam 3:4 [B]2 Sam 15:1 1:6 [a]Lit *pained him* [b]Lit *she gave him birth* [A]2 Sam 3:3, 4 1:7 [a]Lit *his words were* [A]1 Chr 11:6 [B]1 Sam 22:20, 23; 2 Sam 20:25 [C]1 Kin 2:22 1:8 [A]2 Sam 20:25; 1 Chr 16:39 [B]2 Sam 8:18 [C]2 Sam 12:1 [D]1 Kin 4:18 [E]2 Sam 23:8-39 1:9 [a]Or *Gliding* or *Serpent Stone* [A]Josh 15:7; 18:16; 2 Sam 17:17 1:10 [A]2 Sam 12:24 1:11 [A]2 Sam 12:24 1:12 [A]Prov 15:22 1:13 [a]Lit *and enter* [A]1 Kin 1:30; 1 Chr 22:9-13 1:15 [A]1 Kin 1:1 1:16 [a]Lit *to* [b]Lit *to you* 1:17 [A]1 Kin 1:13 1:19 [A]1 Kin 1:9 1:21 [a]Lit *sinners* [A]Deut 31:16; 2 Sam 7:12; 1 Kin 2:10

1:1–11:43 The first division of Kings chronicles the reign of Solomon. The literary structure is centered around the building activities of Solomon (6:1–9:9) and climaxes with the failure of Solomon to follow the Lord wholeheartedly (11:1–43).

1:1 advanced in age. David was 70 years old (cf. 2Sa 5:4, 5).

1:2 the king may keep warm. In his old age, circulatory problems plagued King David so he had trouble keeping warm. The royal staff proposed a solution that a young virgin nurse watch over him and, at night, warm him with her body heat. This was in harmony with the medical customs of that day; both the Jewish historian Josephus (first century A.D.) and the Greek physician Galen (second century A.D.) record such a practice.

1:3 Abishag the Shunammite. Abishag was a very beautiful teenager from the town of Shunem, in the territory of Issachar located 3 mi. N of Jezreel (Jos 19:18; 1Sa 28:4; 2Ki 4:8). Though from the same town, she is not to be identified with the Shulammite in the Song of Solomon (6:13).

1:4 the king did not cohabit with her. Although apparently joining David's harem (cf. 2:17, 22–24), Abishag remained a virgin.

1:5 Adonijah. Adonijah was the fourth son of David (2Sa 3:4) and probably the oldest living son, since Amnon (2Sa 13:28, 29) and Absalom (2Sa 18:14, 15) had been killed, and Chileab apparently died in his youth, since there is no mention of him beyond his birth. As David's oldest surviving heir, Adonijah attempted to claim the kingship. **chariots and horsemen.** Like Absalom (2Sa 15:1), Adonijah sought to confirm and support his claim to kingship by raising a small army.

1:7 Joab. David's nephew (1Ch 2:16), the commander of the army of Israel (2Sa 8:16) and a faithful supporter of David's kingship (2Sa 18:2; 20:22). He was guilty of the illegal killings of Abner and Amasa (2:5; cf. 2Sa 3:39; 20:10). Adonijah wanted his support in his bid for the throne. **Abiathar.** One of the two High Priests serving concurrently during David's reign (2Sa 8:17), whose influence Adonijah sought.

1:8 Zadok. The other High Priest serving during David's reign (2Sa 8:17), whose descendants will serve the millennial temple (see Eze 44:15). He had been High Priest in the tabernacle at Gibeon under Saul (1Ch 16:39). **Benaiah.** The commander of the Cherethites and Pelethites (v. 44), David's official guards distinguished for bravery (see 2Sa 23:20). *See note on 1Sa 30:14.* He was regarded by Joab as a rival. **Nathan.** The most influential prophet during David's reign (2Sa 7:1–17; 12:1–15, 25). **Shimei.** Cf. 4:18. A different individual than the Shimei referred to in 2:8, 36–46; 2Sa 16:5–8. **the mighty men.** See 2Sa 23:8–39.

1:9 Zoheleth. Or "Serpent Stone," a standard landmark identified with a previous Jebusite snake worship location. **En-rogel.** Lit. "the spring of the fuller." Typically identified as being located at the N/W confluence of the Kidron and Hinnom Valleys. Here Adonijah held a political event to court popularity and secure his claim to the throne.

1:11–27 The revolt of Adonijah was defeated by Nathan, who knew the Lord's will (see 2Sa 7:12; 1Ch 22:9) and acted quickly, by having Bathsheba go to David first to report what was happening, after which he would follow (v. 23).

1:11 Bathsheba the mother of Solomon. The mothers of the kings of the Davidic line are continually noted (2:13, 19; 14:21; 15:2; 2Ki 8:26; 12:1; 14:2; 15:2, 33; 18:2; 21:1, 19; 22:1; 23:31, 36; 24:8). The queen mother held an influential position in the royal court. For the story of how David sinfully took her, see 2Sa 11.

1:12 save … the life of your son. If Adonijah had become king, the lives of Bathsheba and Solomon would have been in jeopardy, because often in the ancient Near East potential claimants to the throne and their families were put to death (cf. 15:29; 16:11; 2Ki 10:11).

1:13 Have you not … sworn. This oath was given privately (unrecorded in Scripture) by David, perhaps to both Nathan and Bathsheba. Solomon's choice by the Lord was implicit in his name Jedidiah, meaning "beloved of the LORD" (2Sa 12:24, 25) and explicit in David's declaration to Solomon (1Ch 22:6–13). Cf. vv. 17, 20, 35.

22 Behold, while she was still speaking with the
king, Nathan the prophet came in. 23 They told the
king, saying, "Here is Nathan the prophet." And
when he came in before the king, he prostrated
himself [a]before the king with his face to the ground.
24 Then Nathan said, "My lord the king, have you
said, 'Adonijah shall be king after me, and he shall
sit on my throne'? 25 [A]For he has gone down today
and has sacrificed oxen and fatlings and sheep
in abundance, and has invited all the king's sons
and the commanders of the army and Abiathar the
priest, and behold, they are eating and drinking before him; and they say, '[B]*Long* live King Adonijah!'
26 [A]But me, *even* me your servant, and Zadok the
priest and Benaiah the son of Jehoiada and your
servant Solomon, he has not invited. 27 Has this
thing been done by my lord the king, and you have
not shown to your [a]servants who should sit on the
throne of my lord the king after him?"
28 Then King David said, "Call Bathsheba to me."
And she came into the king's presence and stood
before the king. 29 The king vowed and said, "[A]As
the LORD lives, who has redeemed my life from all
distress, 30 surely as [A]I vowed to you by the LORD
the God of Israel, saying, 'Your son Solomon shall
be king after me, and he shall sit on my throne
in my place'; I will indeed do so this day." 31 Then
Bathsheba bowed with her face to the ground, and
prostrated herself [a]before the king and said, "[A]May
my lord King David live forever."
32 Then King David said, "Call to me [A]Zadok the
priest, Nathan the prophet, and Benaiah the son of
Jehoiada." And they came into the king's presence.
33 The king said to them, "Take with you [A]the servants
of your lord, and have my son Solomon ride on my
own mule, and bring him down to [B]Gihon. 34 Let Zadok the priest and Nathan the prophet [A]anoint him
there as king over Israel, and [B]blow the trumpet and
say, '[C]*Long* live King Solomon!' 35 Then you shall come
up after him, and he shall come and sit on my throne
and be king in my place; for I have appointed him to
be ruler over Israel and Judah." 36 Benaiah the son of
Jehoiada answered the king and said, "Amen! Thus
may the LORD, the God of my lord the king, say. 37 [A]As
the LORD has been with my lord the king, so may
He be with Solomon, and [B]make his throne greater
than the throne of my lord King David!"

SOLOMON ANOINTED KING

38 So [A]Zadok the priest, Nathan the prophet, Benaiah the son of Jehoiada, [B]the Cherethites, and
the Pelethites went down and had Solomon ride
on King David's mule, and brought him to [C]Gihon.
39 Zadok the priest then [A]took the horn of oil from
the tent and [B]anointed Solomon. Then they [C]blew the
trumpet, and all the people said, "[D]*Long* live King
Solomon!" 40 All the people went up after him, and
the people [a]were playing on flutes and rejoicing
with great joy, so that the earth [b]shook at their noise.
41 Now Adonijah and all the guests who *were* with
him heard *it* as they finished eating. When Joab
heard the sound of the trumpet, he said, "Why [a]is
the city making such an uproar?" 42 While he was
still speaking, behold, [A]Jonathan the son of Abiathar
the priest came. Then Adonijah said, "Come in, for
[B]you are a valiant man and bring good news." 43 But
Jonathan replied to Adonijah, "No! Our lord King
David has made Solomon king. 44 The king has also
sent with him Zadok the priest, Nathan the prophet,
Benaiah the son of Jehoiada, the Cherethites, and
the Pelethites; and they have made him ride on the
king's mule. 45 Zadok the priest and Nathan the prophet
have anointed him king in Gihon, and they have
come up from there rejoicing, [A]so that the city is in
an uproar. This is the noise which you have heard.
46 Besides, [A]Solomon has even taken his seat on the
throne of the kingdom. 47 Moreover, the king's servants came to bless our lord King David, saying,
'May [A]your God make the name of Solomon better
than your name and his throne greater than your
throne!' And [B]the king bowed himself on the bed.
48 The king has also said thus, 'Blessed be the LORD,
the God of Israel, who [A]has granted one to sit on
my throne today while my own eyes see *it*.' "
49 Then all the guests of Adonijah were terrified;
and they arose and each went on his way. 50 And

1:23 [a]Lit *to* 1:25 [A]1 Kin 1:9 [B]1 Sam 10:24 1:26 [A]1 Kin 1:8, 10 1:27 [a]Some mss read *servant* 1:29 [A]2 Sam 4:9 1:30 [A]1 Kin 1:13, 17 1:31 [a]Lit *to* [A]Dan 2:4; 3:9 1:32 [A]1 Kin 1:8 1:33 [A]2 Sam 20:6, 7 [B]2 Chr 32:30; 33:14 1:34 [A]1 Sam 10:1; 16:3, 12; 2 Sam 5:3; 1 Kin 19:16; 2 Kin 9:3 [B]2 Sam 15:10 [C]1 Kin 1:25 1:37 [A]Josh 1:5, 17; 1 Sam 20:13 [B]1 Kin 1:47 1:38 [A]1 Kin 1:8 [B]2 Sam 8:18 [C]1 Kin 1:33 1:39 [A]Ex 30:23-32; Ps 89:20 [B]1 Chr 29:22 [C]1 Kin 1:34 [D]1 Sam 10:24 1:40 [a]Lit *fluting* [b]Lit *was split* 1:41 [a]Lit *is the sound of the city an uproar* 1:42 [A]2 Sam 15:27, 36; 17:17 [B]2 Sam 18:27 1:45 [A]1 Kin 1:40 1:46 [A]1 Chr 29:23 1:47 [A]1 Kin 1:37 [B]Gen 47:31 1:48 [A]2 Sam 7:12; 1 Kin 3:6

1:28–53 See 1Ch 29:21–25.

1:29 The king vowed. David swore another oath to carry out his earlier commitment to make Solomon king, and he made good on it that very day.

1:33 my own mule. The riding of David's royal mule showed Israel that Solomon was David's chosen successor (see 2Sa 13:29). **Gihon.** This spring, which was Jerusalem's main water supply, was located about one-half mi. N of En-rogel (v. 9) and hidden from it by an intervening hill. Thus, the sound of Solomon's anointing ceremony could have been heard without being seen by Adonijah's party.

1:34 anoint him there as king. Saul and David had been anointed by Samuel, the Lord's priest and prophet (1Sa 10:1; 16:13); Solomon was also to be recognized by priest and prophet. The participation of the prophet Nathan gave Solomon's coronation evidence of the Lord's blessing. Throughout the book of Kings, God identified His chosen kings through prophets (11:37; 15:28, 29; 16:12; 2Ki 9:3). **blow the trumpet.** The blowing of the trumpet signaled a public assembly where the people corporately recognized Solomon's new status as co-regent with and successor to David (vv. 39, 40).

1:35 Israel and Judah. The two major geographical components of David's and Solomon's kingdoms. Even while still unified these two separate entities, that would later divide (12:20), were clearly identifiable.

1:39 tent. This was the tent David set up in Jerusalem (2Sa 6:17; 1Ch 15:1) to house the ark of the covenant, not the tabernacle of Moses (see 3:4).

1:41–49 Adonijah ... heard *it*. The loud shouts hailing Solomon as king reached the ears of those at Adonijah's feast at En-rogel nearby. A messenger came with the full report of the coronation of Solomon, so that the cause of Adonijah was lost and the party ended with the people leaving in fear.

1:42 Jonathan. The son of Abiathar the priest was an experienced messenger (2Sa 15:36; 17:17).

1:50 horns of the altar. Cf. 2:28. The "horns" were corner projections on the altar of burnt offering on which the priests smeared the blood of the sacrifices (Ex 27:2; 29:12). By taking hold of the horns, Adonijah sought to place himself under the protection of God (see Ex 21:13, 14).

Adonijah was afraid of Solomon, and he arose, went
and [A]took hold of the horns of the altar. 51 Now it was
told Solomon, saying, "Behold, Adonijah is afraid
of King Solomon, for behold, he has taken hold of
the horns of the altar, saying, 'Let King Solomon
swear to me today that he will not put his servant
to death with the sword.' " 52 Solomon said, "If he is
a worthy man, [A]not one of his hairs will fall to the
ground; but if wickedness is found in him, he will
die." 53 So King Solomon sent, and they brought him
down from the altar. And he came and prostrated
himself [a]before King Solomon, and Solomon said
to him, "Go to your house."

DAVID'S CHARGE TO SOLOMON

2 As David's [a,A]time to die drew near, he charged
Solomon his son, saying, 2 "[A]I am going the way
of all the earth. [B]Be strong, therefore, and [a]show
yourself a man. 3 Keep the charge of the LORD your
God, to walk in His ways, to keep His statutes, His
commandments, His ordinances, and His testimonies, [A]according to what is written in the Law of
Moses, that [B]you may succeed in all that you do
and wherever you turn, 4 so that [A]the LORD may
carry out His promise which He spoke concerning
me, saying, '[B]If your sons are careful of their way,
[C]to walk before Me in [a]truth with all their heart and
with all their soul, [b,D]you shall not lack a man on the
throne of Israel.'
5 "Now you also know what Joab the [A]son of Zeruiah did to me, what he did to the two commanders
of the armies of Israel, to [B]Abner the son of Ner,
and to [C]Amasa the son of Jether, whom he killed;
he also [a]shed the blood of war in peace. And he put
the blood of war on his belt [b]about his waist, and on
his sandals [c]on his feet. 6 [A]So act according to your
wisdom, and do not let his gray hair go down to
[a]Sheol in peace. 7 But [A]show kindness to the sons of
Barzillai the Gileadite, and [B]let them be among those
who eat at your table; [C]for they [a]assisted me when
I fled from Absalom your brother. 8 Behold, [A]there
is with you Shimei the son of Gera the Benjamite,
of Bahurim; now it was he who cursed me with a
[a]violent curse on the day I went to Mahanaim. But
when [B]he came down to me at the Jordan, I swore
to him by the LORD, saying, 'I will not put you to
death with the sword.' 9 Now therefore, do not let
him go unpunished, [A]for you are a wise man; and
you will know what you ought to do to him, and you
will bring his gray hair down to [a]Sheol with blood."

DEATH OF DAVID

10 Then [A]David slept with his fathers and was
buried in [B]the city of David. 11 [A]The days that David
reigned over Israel *were* forty years: [B]seven years
he reigned in Hebron and thirty-three years he
reigned in Jerusalem. 12 And [A]Solomon sat on the
throne of David his father, and his kingdom was
firmly established.
13 Now Adonijah the son of Haggith came to
Bathsheba the mother of Solomon. And she said,
"[A]Do you come peacefully?" And he said, "Peacefully." 14 Then he said, "I have something *to say* to
you." And she said, "Speak." 15 So he said, "You know
that [A]the kingdom was mine and [B]that all Israel
[a]expected me to be king; [C]however, the kingdom
has turned about and become my brother's, [D]for
it was his from the LORD. 16 Now I am making one
request of you; do not [a]refuse me." And she said
to him, "Speak." 17 Then he said, "Please speak to
Solomon the king, for he will not [a]refuse you, that
he may give me [A]Abishag the Shunammite as a
wife." 18 Bathsheba said, "Very well; I will speak to
the king for you."

1:50 [A]Ex 27:2; 30:10; 1 Kin 2:28 1:52 [A]1 Sam 14:45; 2 Sam 14:11; Acts 27:34 1:53 [a]Lit *to* 2:1 [a]Lit *days* [A]Gen 47:29; Deut 31:14 2:2 [a]Lit *become a man* [A]Josh 23:14 [B]Deut 31:7, 23; Josh 1:6, 7 2:3 [A]Deut 17:18-20 [B]1 Chr 22:12, 13 2:4 [a]Or *faithfulness* [b]Lit *there shall not be cast off to you a man from before Me* [A]2 Sam 7:25 [B]Ps 132:12 [C]2 Kin 20:3 [D]2 Sam 7:12, 13; 1 Kin 8:25; 9:5 2:5 [a]Lit *made* [b]Lit *that was about* [c]Lit *that were on* [A]2 Sam 2:13, 18 [B]2 Sam 3:27; 1 Kin 2:32 [C]2 Sam 20:10 2:6 [a]I.e. the nether world [A]1 Kin 2:9 2:7 [a]Lit *came near to* [A]2 Sam 19:31-38 [B]2 Sam 9:7, 10 [C]2 Sam 17:27-29 2:8 [a]Or *grievous* [A]2 Sam 16:5-8 [B]2 Sam 19:18-23 2:9 [a]I.e. the nether world [A]1 Kin 2:6 2:10 [A]Acts 2:29; 13:36 [B]2 Sam 5:7; 1 Kin 3:1 2:11 [A]2 Sam 5:4, 5; 1 Chr 3:4; 29:26, 27 [B]2 Sam 5:5 2:12 [A]1 Chr 29:23; 2 Chr 1:1 2:13 [A]1 Sam 16:4 2:15 [a]Lit *set their faces on me* [A]2 Sam 3:3, 4; 1 Kin 2:22 [B]1 Kin 1:5-25 [C]1 Kin 1:38-50 [D]1 Chr 22:9, 10; 28:5-7 2:16 [a]Lit *turn away my face* 2:17 [a]Lit *turn away your face* [A]1 Kin 1:3, 4

2:1 he charged Solomon. Leaders typically exhorted their successors, e.g., Moses (Dt 31:7, 8), Joshua (Jos 23:1–6), and Samuel (1Sa 12:1–25). So also David gave Solomon a final exhortation.

2:2 the way of all the earth. An expression for death (Jos 23:14; cf. Gen 3:19). **Be strong … show yourself a man.** An expression of encouragement (Dt 31:7, 23; Jos 1:6, 7, 9, 18; 1Sa 4:9) with which David sought to prepare Solomon for the difficult tasks and the battles in his future.

2:3 Keep the charge of the LORD your God. David admonished Solomon to obey the Mosaic law so he could have a successful kingship (cf. Dt 17:18–20).

2:4 His promise. The unconditional Davidic Covenant was made by God with David in 2Sa 7:4–17 and confirmed to Solomon in 1Ki 9:5, promising the perpetuation of the Davidic dynasty over Israel. **If your sons are careful of their way.** David declared that the king's obedience to the law of Moses was a necessary condition for the fulfillment of the divine promise. The book of Kings demonstrates that none of the descendants of David remained faithful to God's law; none of them met the conditions for the fulfillment of the divine promise. Rather, David's words provided a basis for explaining the Exile. Thus, the ultimate and final King of Israel would appear at a later, undesignated time.

2:5 Abner … Amasa. These were victims of Joab's jealousy and vengeance, who were killed after warfare had ceased (2Sa 3:27; 20:10), thus bringing Joab's punishment as a murderer (Dt 19:11–13).

2:7 sons of Barzillai. David told Solomon to repay Barzillai's kindness to David (2Sa 17:27–29) by showing similar kindness to Barzillai's sons. **eat at your table.** A position of honor that could include a royal stipend (2Sa 9:7; 1Ki 18:19; 2Ki 25:29).

2:8 Shimei. He had angrily stoned and vehemently cursed David when David was escaping from Absalom (2Sa 16:5–13). Shimei's actions were worthy of death (Ex 22:28), and David counseled Solomon through subtle means to arrange for his just punishment (vv. 36–46).

2:10–12 See 2Sa 5:5; 1Ch 29:26–28.

2:10 the city of David. I.e., Jerusalem (cf. 8:1).

2:11 forty years. David ruled from ca. 1011–971 B.C., probably with Solomon as co-regent during his final year (cf. 11:41).

2:12 firmly established. Solomon's succession enjoyed the Lord's approval, and Solomon experienced unchallenged authority, prosperity, and renown (v. 46).

2:15 all Israel expected me to be king. A reference to Adonijah's perceived right to the kingship as the oldest surviving son according to ancient Near East custom.

2:17 give me Abishag. In the ancient Near East, possession of the royal harem was a sign of kingship (cf. 2Sa 3:8; 12:8; 16:20–22). Adonijah's request for Abishag was an attempt to support his claim to the kingship and perhaps generate a revolt to usurp the throne. Bathsheba didn't see the treachery (vv. 18–21).

ADONIJAH EXECUTED

19 So Bathsheba went to King Solomon to speak to him for Adonijah. And the king arose to meet her, bowed before her, and sat on his throne; then he [A]had a throne set for the king's mother, and [B]she sat on his right. 20 Then she said, "I am making one small request of you; [A]do not [a]refuse me." And the king said to her, "Ask, my mother, for I will not [b]refuse you." 21 So she said, "[A]Let Abishag the Shunammite be given to Adonijah your brother as a wife." 22 King Solomon answered and said to his mother, "And why are you asking Abishag the Shunammite for Adonijah? [A]Ask for him also the kingdom—[B]for he is my older brother—even for him, for [C]Abiathar the priest, and for Joab the son of Zeruiah!" 23 Then King Solomon swore by the LORD, saying, "May God do so to me and more also, if Adonijah has [A]not spoken this word against his own [a]life. 24 Now therefore, as the LORD lives, who has established me and set me on the throne of David my father and [A]who has made me a house as He promised, surely Adonijah shall be put to death today." 25 So King Solomon [A]sent Benaiah the son of Jehoiada; and he fell upon him so that he died.

26 Then to Abiathar the priest the king said, "[A]Go to Anathoth to your own field, [B]for you [a]deserve to die; but I will not put you to death at this time, because [C]you carried the ark of the Lord [b]GOD before my father David, and because [D]you were afflicted in everything with which my father was afflicted." 27 So Solomon dismissed Abiathar from being priest to the LORD, in order to fulfill [A]the word of the LORD, which He had spoken concerning the house of Eli in Shiloh.

JOAB EXECUTED

28 Now the news came to Joab, [A]for Joab had followed Adonijah, [B]although he had not followed Absalom. And Joab fled to the tent of the LORD and [C]took hold of the horns of the altar. 29 It was told King Solomon that Joab had fled to the tent of the LORD, and behold, he is beside the altar. Then Solomon [A]sent Benaiah the son of Jehoiada, saying, "[B]Go, fall upon him." 30 So Benaiah came to the tent of the LORD and said to him, "Thus the king has said, 'Come out.' " But he said, "No, for I will die here." And Benaiah brought the king word again, saying, "Thus spoke Joab, and thus he answered me." 31 The king said to him, "[A]Do as he has spoken and fall upon him and bury him, [B]that you may remove from me and from my father's house the blood which Joab shed without cause. 32 [A]The LORD will return his blood on his own head, [B]because he fell upon two men more righteous and better than he and killed them with the sword, while my father David did not know *it:* [C]Abner the son of Ner, commander of the army of Israel, and [D]Amasa the son of Jether, commander of the army of Judah. 33 [A]So shall their blood return on the head of Joab and on the head of his [a]descendants forever; but to David and his [a]descendants and his house and his throne, may there be peace from the LORD forever." 34 Then [A]Benaiah the son of Jehoiada went up and fell upon him and put him to death, and he was buried at his own house [B]in the wilderness. 35 [A]The king appointed Benaiah the son of Jehoiada over the army in his place, and the king appointed [B]Zadok the priest [C]in the place of Abiathar.

SHIMEI EXECUTED

36 Now the king sent and called for [A]Shimei and said to him, "Build for yourself a house in Jerusalem and live there, and do not go out from there to any place. 37 For on the day you go out and [A]cross over the [a]brook Kidron, you will know for certain that you shall surely die; [B]your blood shall be on your own head." 38 Shimei then said to the king, "The word is good. As my lord the king has said, so your servant will do." So Shimei lived in Jerusalem many days.

39 But it came about at the end of three years, that two of the servants of Shimei ran away [A]to Achish son of Maacah, king of Gath. And they told Shimei, saying, "Behold, your servants are in Gath." 40 Then Shimei arose and saddled his donkey, and went to Gath to Achish to look for his servants. And Shimei went and brought his servants from Gath. 41 It was told Solomon that Shimei had gone from Jerusalem to Gath, and had returned. 42 So the king

2:19 [A]1 Kin 15:13 [B]Ps 45:9 2:20 [a]Lit *turn away my face* [b]Lit *turn away your face* [A]1 Kin 2:16 2:21 [A]1 Kin 1:3, 4 2:22 [A]2 Sam 12:8 [B]1 Kin 1:6; 2:15; 1 Chr 3:2, 5 [C]1 Kin 1:7 2:23 [a]Lit *soul* [A]Ruth 1:17 2:24 [A]2 Sam 7:11, 13; 1 Chr 22:10 2:25 [A]2 Sam 8:18 2:26 [a]Lit *are a man of death* [b]Heb *YHWH*, usually rendered *LORD* [A]Josh 21:18; Jer 1:1 [B]1 Sam 26:16 [C]1 Sam 23:6; 2 Sam 15:24-29 [D]1 Sam 22:20-23; 23:8, 9 2:27 [A]1 Sam 2:27-36 2:28 [A]1 Kin 1:7 [B]2 Sam 17:25; 18:2 [C]1 Kin 1:50 2:29 [A]1 Kin 2:25 [B]Ex 21:14 2:31 [A]Ex 21:14 [B]Num 35:33; Deut 19:13; 21:8, 9 2:32 [A]Gen 9:6; Judg 9:24, 57; Ps 7:16 [B]2 Chr 21:13, 14 [C]2 Sam 3:27 [D]2 Sam 20:9, 10 2:33 [a]Lit *seed* [A]2 Sam 3:29 2:34 [A]1 Kin 2:25 [B]Josh 15:61; Matt 3:1 2:35 [A]1 Kin 4:4 [B]1 Chr 6:53; 24:3; 29:22 [C]1 Kin 2:27 2:36 [A]2 Sam 16:5; 1 Kin 2:8 2:37 [a]Or *wadi* [A]2 Sam 15:23; 2 Kin 23:6; John 18:1 [B]Josh 2:19; 2 Sam 1:16; Ezek 18:13 2:39 [A]1 Sam 27:2

2:22 Ask for him also the kingdom. Solomon recognized Adonijah's request as the prelude to his usurping of the throne. Because Adonijah's request violated the terms of loyalty Solomon had previously specified (1:52), he pronounced a formal, legal death sentence on Adonijah (vv. 23, 24).

2:24 as He promised. Solomon viewed himself as the fulfillment of the Lord's promise to David in 2Sa 7:12–16 (see also 5:5; 8:18–21). The ultimate fulfillment will be the Messiah, Jesus, who will return to Israel and set up His kingdom (see Is 9:6, 7).

2:26 Anathoth. A priestly town, 3 mi. NE of Jerusalem (cf. Jer 1:1). There Abiathar, the disloyal High Priest (1:7), lived in banishment.

2:27 fulfill the word of the LORD. Solomon's removal of Abiathar from the office of priest fulfilled God's prophecy that Eli's line of priests would be cut off (1Sa 2:30–35). This reestablished the line of Eleazar/Phinehas in Zadok (2:35), as promised by God (cf. Nu 25:10–13).

2:28 Joab fled to the tent. Cf. 1:50. He knew he would have been killed already if he had not been so popular with the army. The altar provided no real sanctuary to the rebel and murderer (cf. Ex 21:14).

2:31 fall upon him. Like Adonijah (1:50), Joab sought asylum at the altar (2:28). The protection of the Lord at the altar applied only to accidental crimes, not premeditated murder (Ex 21:14), so Solomon ordered Benaiah to administer the violent death sought by David (2:6).

2:33 peace ... forever. This pledge is ultimately to be fulfilled in the Messiah's kingdom (see Is 2:2–4; 9:6, 7).

2:34 wilderness. The tomb of Joab's father was near Bethlehem (2Sa 2:32). Joab's house was probably on the edge of the Judean wilderness, E of Bethlehem.

2:36 do not go out. Shimei had not provoked Solomon directly as Adonijah had. Therefore, Solomon determined to keep Shimei under close watch by confining him to Jerusalem.

2:39 Gath. A major Philistine city about 30 mi. SW of Jerusalem.

sent and called for Shimei and said to him, "Did I
not make you swear by the LORD and solemnly
warn you, saying, 'You will know for certain that
on the day you depart and go anywhere, you shall
surely die'? And you said to me, 'The word which I
have heard is good.' 43 Why then have you not kept
the oath of the LORD, and the command which I
[a]have laid on you?" 44 The king also said to Shimei,
"[A]You know all the evil which [a]you acknowledge
in your heart, which you did to my father David;
therefore [B]the LORD shall return your evil on your
own head. 45 But King Solomon shall be blessed,
and [A]the throne of David shall be established before the LORD forever." 46 [A]So the king commanded
Benaiah the son of Jehoiada, and he went out and
fell upon him so that he died.

[B]Thus the kingdom was established in the hands
of Solomon.

SOLOMON'S RULE CONSOLIDATED

3 Then [A]Solomon [a]formed a marriage alliance
with Pharaoh king of Egypt, and took Pharaoh's
daughter [B]and brought her to the city of David [C]un-
til he had finished building his own house and the
house of the LORD and [D]the wall around Jerusalem. 2 [A]The people were still sacrificing on the high
places, because there was no house built for the
name of the LORD until those days.

3 Now [A]Solomon loved the LORD, [B]walking in the
statutes of his father David, except he sacrificed
and burned incense on the high places. 4 [A]The king
went to [B]Gibeon to sacrifice there, [C]for that was
the great high place; Solomon offered a thousand
burnt offerings on that altar. 5 [A]In Gibeon the LORD
appeared to Solomon [B]in a dream at night; and God
said, "[C]Ask what *you wish* Me to give you."

SOLOMON'S PRAYER

6 Then Solomon said, "[A]You have shown great
lovingkindness to Your servant David my father,
[B]according as he walked before You in [a]truth and
righteousness and uprightness of heart toward
You; and [C]You have [b]reserved for him this great
lovingkindness, that You have given him a son to
sit on his throne, as *it is* this day. 7 Now, O LORD my
God, [A]You have made Your servant king in place of
my father David, yet [B]I am but a little child; [C]I do not
know how to go out or come in. 8 [A]Your servant is
in the midst of Your people which You have chosen,
[B]a great people who are too many to be numbered
or counted. 9 So [A]give Your servant [a]an understanding heart to judge Your people [B]to discern between
good and evil. For who is able to judge this [b]great
people of Yours?"

GOD'S ANSWER

10 [a]It was pleasing in the sight of the Lord that
Solomon had asked this thing. 11 God said to him,
"Because you have asked this thing and have [A]not
asked for yourself [a]long life, nor have asked riches
for yourself, nor have you asked for the life of
your enemies, but have asked for yourself [b]dis-
cernment to understand justice, 12 behold, [A]I have
done according to your words. Behold, [B]I have
given you a wise and discerning heart, so that
there has been no one like you before you, nor
shall one like you arise after you. 13 [A]I have also
given you what you have not asked, both [B]riches
and honor, so that there will not be any among the
kings like you all your days. 14 [A]If you walk in My
ways, keeping My statutes and commandments,
as your father David walked, then I will [B]prolong
your days."

2:43 [a]Lit *commanded* 2:44 [a]Lit *your heart acknowledges* [A]2 Sam 16:5-13 [B]1 Sam 25:39; 2 Kin 11:1, 12-16; Ps 7:16 2:45 [A]2 Sam 7:13; Prov 25:5 2:46 [A]1 Kin 2:25, 34 [B]1 Kin 2:12; 2 Chr 1:1 3:1 [a]Lit *made himself a son-in-law of Pharaoh* [A]1 Kin 7:8; 9:16, 24; 2 Chr 8:11 [B]1 Kin 9:24 [C]1 Kin 7:1; 9:10 [D]1 Kin 9:15 3:2 [A]Lev 17:3-5; Deut 12:2, 13, 14; 1 Kin 22:43 3:3 [A]Deut 6:5; 10:12, 13; 11:13; 30:16; Ps 31:23; 145:20; 1 Cor 8:3 [B]1 Kin 2:3; 9:4; 11:4, 6, 38 3:4 [A]2 Chr 1:3 [B]Josh 18:21-25 [C]1 Chr 16:39; 21:29 3:5 [A]1 Kin 9:2; 11:9 [B]Num 12:6; Matt 1:20; 2:13 [C]John 15:7 3:6 [a]Or *faithfulness* [b]Lit *kept* [A]2 Sam 7:8-17; 2 Chr 1:8 [B]1 Kin 9:4 [C]1 Kin 1:48 3:7 [A]1 Chr 22:9-13 [B]1 Chr 29:1; Jer 1:6, 7 [C]Num 27:17 3:8 [A]Ex 19:6; Deut 7:6 [B]Gen 15:5; 22:17 3:9 [a]Lit *a hearing* [b]Lit *heavy* [A]2 Chr 1:10; Ps 72:1, 2; Prov 2:3-9; James 1:5 [B]2 Sam 14:17; Heb 5:14 3:10 [a]Lit *the thing* 3:11 [a]Lit *many days* [b]Lit *hearing* [A]James 4:3 3:12 [A]1 John 5:14, 15 [B]1 Kin 4:29-31; 5:12; 10:23, 24; Eccl 1:16 3:13 [A]1 Kin 4:21-24; 10:23, 27; Matt 6:33; Eph 3:20 [B]Prov 3:16 3:14 [A]1 Kin 3:6 [B]Ps 91:16; Prov 3:2

2:45 throne of David. In contrast to Shimei's curse (2Sa 16:5–8), the Lord's blessing was to come through the ruler of David's, not Saul's, line (cf. 2Sa 7:12, 13, 16).

2:46 With the death of Shimei, all the rival factions were eliminated.

3:1 a marriage alliance with Pharaoh. The Pharaoh was probably Siamun, the next-to-last ruler of the weak 21st dynasty. Solomon's treaty with Pharaoh signified that he held a high standing in the world of his day. Pharaoh's daughter was the most politically significant of Solomon's 700 wives (cf. 7:8; 9:16; 11:1).

3:2 the high places. The open-air, hilltop worship centers which the Israelites inherited from the Canaanites had been rededicated to the Lord; the use of pagan altars had been forbidden (Nu 33:52; Dt 7:5; 12:3). After the building of the temple, worship at the high places was condemned (11:7, 8; 12:31; 2Ki 16:17–20; 21:3; 23:26). **no house … for the name of the LORD.** "Name" represented the character and presence of the Lord (cf. Ex 3:13, 14). He had promised to choose one place "to establish His name there for His dwelling" (Dt 12:5). The temple at Jerusalem was to be that place (cf. 5:3, 5; 8:16, 17, 18, 19, 20, 29, 43, 44, 48; 9:3, 7). In the ancient Near East, to identify a temple with a god's name meant that the god owned the place and dwelt there.

3:3 except. Solomon's failure in completely following the Lord was exhibited in his continual worship at the high places.

3:4–15 See 2Ch 1:7–13.

3:4 Gibeon. A town about 7 mi. NW of Jerusalem, where the tabernacle of Moses and the original bronze altar were located (1Ch 21:29; 2Ch 1:2–6).

3:5 dream. God often gave revelation in dreams (Ge 26:24; 28:12; 46:2; Da 2:7; 7:1; Mt 1:20; 2:12, 19, 22). However, this dream was unique, a two-way conversation between the Lord and Solomon.

3:6 great lovingkindness. This term implies covenant faithfulness. Solomon viewed his succession to David as evidence of the Lord's faithfulness to His promises to David.

3:7 little child. Since Solomon was probably only about 20 years of age, he readily admitted his lack of qualification and experience to be king (cf. 1Ch 22:5; 29:1). *See note on Nu 27:15–17.*

3:8 a great people. Based on the census, which recorded 800,000 men of fighting age in Israel and 500,000 in Judah (2Sa 24:9), the total population was over 4 million, approximately double what it had been at the time of the Conquest (see Nu 26:1–65).

3:9 an understanding heart. Humbly admitting his need, Solomon sought "a listening heart" to govern God's people with wisdom.

3:10 pleasing in the sight of the Lord. The Lord was delighted that Solomon had not asked for personal benefits, e.g., long life, wealth, or the death of his enemies.

3:12 no one like you. Solomon was one of a kind in judicial insight, as illustrated in vv. 16–27.

3:14 prolong your days. In contrast to riches and honor that were already his, a long life was dependent on Solomon's future obedience to the Lord's commands. Because of his disobedience, Solomon died before reaching 70 years of age (cf. Ps 90:10).

15 Then [A]Solomon awoke, and behold, it was a dream. And he came to Jerusalem and stood before the ark of the covenant of the Lord, and offered burnt offerings and made peace offerings, and [B]made a feast for all his servants.

SOLOMON WISELY JUDGES

16 Then two women who were harlots came to the king and stood before him. 17 The one woman said, "Oh, my lord, [a]this woman and I live in the same house; and I gave birth to a child while she *was* in the house. 18 It happened on the third day after I gave birth, that this woman also gave birth to a child, and we were together. There was no stranger with us in the house, only the two of us in the house. 19 This woman's son died in the night, because she lay on it. 20 So she arose in the middle of the night and took my son from beside me while your maidservant slept, and laid him in her bosom, and laid her dead son in my bosom. 21 When I rose in the morning to nurse my son, behold, he was dead; but when I looked at him carefully in the morning, behold, he was not my son, whom I had borne." 22 Then the other woman said, "No! For the living one is my son, and the dead one is your son." But [a]the first woman said, "No! For the dead one is your son, and the living one is my son." Thus they spoke before the king.

23 Then the king said, "[a]The one says, 'This is my son who is living, and your son is the dead one'; and [a]the other says, 'No! For your son is the dead one, and my son is the living one.' " 24 The king said, "Get me a sword." So they brought a sword before the king. 25 The king said, "Divide the living child in two, and give half to the one and half to the other." 26 Then the woman whose child *was* the living one spoke to the king, for [a,A]she was deeply stirred over her son and said, "Oh, my lord, give her the living child, and by no means kill him." But the other said, "He shall be neither mine nor yours; divide *him!*" 27 Then the king said, "Give [a]the first woman the living child, and by no means kill him. She is his mother." 28 When all Israel heard of the judgment which the king had [a]handed down, they feared the king, for [A]they saw that the wisdom of God was in him to [b]administer justice.

SOLOMON'S OFFICIALS

4 Now King Solomon was king over all Israel. 2 These were his officials: Azariah the son of Zadok *was* [A]the priest; 3 Elihoreph and Ahijah, the sons of Shisha *were* secretaries; [A]Jehoshaphat the son of Ahilud *was* the recorder; 4 and [A]Benaiah the son of Jehoiada *was* over the army; and Zadok and [B]Abiathar *were* priests; 5 and Azariah the son of Nathan *was* over [A]the deputies; and Zabud the son of Nathan, a priest, *was* the king's friend; 6 and Ahishar was over the household; and Adoniram the son of Abda *was* over the men subject to forced labor.

7 Solomon had twelve deputies over all Israel, who [a]provided for the king and his household; each man had to [b]provide for a month in the year. 8 These are their names: Ben-hur, in the [A]hill country of Ephraim; 9 Ben-deker in Makaz and [A]Shaalbim and [B]Beth-shemesh and Elonbeth-hanan; 10 Ben-hesed, in Arubboth ([A]Socoh *was* his and all the land of [B]Hepher); 11 Ben-abinadab, *in* all [a]the [A]height of Dor (Taphath the daughter of Solomon was his wife); 12 Baana the son of Ahilud, *in* [A]Taanach and Megiddo, and all [B]Beth-shean which is beside [C]Zarethan below Jezreel, from Beth-shean to [D]Abel-meholah as far as the other side of [E]Jokmeam; 13 Ben-geber, in [A]Ramoth-gilead ([B]the towns of Jair, the son of Manasseh, which are in Gilead were his: [C]the region of Argob, which is in Bashan, sixty great cities with walls and bronze bars *were* his); 14 Ahinadab the son of Iddo, *in* [A]Mahanaim; 15 [A]Ahimaaz, in Naphtali (he also married Basemath the daughter of Solomon); 16 Baana the son of [A]Hushai, in Asher and [a]Bealoth; 17 Jehoshaphat the son of Paruah, in Issachar; 18 [A]Shimei the son of Ela, in Benjamin; 19 Geber the son of Uri, in the land of Gilead, [A]the country of Sihon king of the Amorites and of Og king of Bashan; and *he was* the only deputy who *was* in the land.

SOLOMON'S POWER, WEALTH AND WISDOM

20 [A]Judah and Israel *were* as numerous as the sand that is on the [a]seashore in abundance; *they* were eating and drinking and rejoicing.

3:15 [A]Gen 41:7 [B]1 Kin 8:65 3:17 [a]Lit *I and this woman* 3:22 [a]Lit *this one was saying* 3:23 [a]Lit *this one* 3:26 [a]Lit *her compassion grew warm* [A]Gen 43:30; Is 49:15; Jer 31:20; Hos 11:8 3:27 [a]Lit *her the living child* 3:28 [a]Lit *judged* [b]Lit *do* [A]1 Kin 3:9, 11, 12; Dan 1:17; Col 2:2, 3 4:2 [A]1 Chr 6:10 4:3 [A]2 Sam 8:16 4:4 [A]1 Kin 2:35 [B]1 Kin 2:27 4:5 [A]1 Kin 4:7 4:7 [a]Lit *nourished* [b]Lit *nourish* 4:8 [A]Josh 24:33 4:9 [A]Judg 1:35 [B]Josh 21:16 4:10 [A]Josh 15:35 [B]Josh 12:17 4:11 [a]Or *Naphoth-dor* [A]Josh 11:1, 2 4:12 [A]Judg 5:19 [B]Josh 17:11 [C]Josh 3:16 [D]1 Kin 19:16 [E]1 Chr 6:68 4:13 [A]1 Kin 22:3-15 [B]Num 32:41 [C]Deut 3:4 4:14 [A]Josh 13:26 4:15 [A]2 Sam 15:27 4:16 [a]Or *in Aloth* [A]2 Sam 15:32 4:18 [A]1 Kin 1:8 4:19 [A]Deut 3:8-10 4:20 [a]Lit *sea* [A]Gen 22:17; 32:12; 1 Kin 3:8

3:16–27 harlots came to the king. Here is an illustration of how wisely Solomon ruled. In Israel, the king was the ultimate "judge" of the land, and any citizen, even the basest prostitute, could petition him for a verdict (2Sa 14:2–21; 15:1–4; 2Ki 8:1–6).

3:25 half . . . half. In ordering his servants to cut the child in two, he knew the liar would not object, but out of maternal compassion the real mother would (cf. Ex 21:35).

3:28 feared the king. Israel was in awe of and willing to submit to the rule of Solomon because of his wisdom from God.

4:1 all Israel. Solomon was in firm control of all of the people. Israel's squabbling factions had fallen in line behind the king.

4:2 Azariah the son of Zadok. Actually, he was the son of Ahimaaz and the grandson of Zadok, as "son of" can mean "descendant of" (cf. 1Ch 6:8, 9). In David's roster of officials, the army commander came first (2Sa 8:16; 20:23). Under Solomon, the priest and other officials preceded the military leader.

4:3 secretaries. Probably they prepared royal edicts and kept official records. **recorder.** Likely, he maintained the records of all important daily affairs in the kingdom.

4:4 priests. Zadok and Abiathar had served together as High Priests under David (2Sa 8:17; 20:25). Although Abiathar had been removed from priestly service and exiled (2:26–27, 35), he maintained his priestly title until his death.

4:5 Nathan. Whether this is the prophet Nathan (*see note on 1:8*) or another person by that name is uncertain, but it could be that Solomon was honoring the sons of the prophet.

4:6 over the household. One who managed Solomon's properties, both lands and buildings (cf. 16:9; 18:3; 2Ki 18:18, 37; 19:2). **over the men subject to forced labor.** One who oversaw the conscripted workers of Solomon (cf. 5:13–18).

4:7 twelve deputies. Solomon divided the land into 12 geographical districts (different from the tribal boundaries), each supervised by a deputy. Each month a different deputy collected provisions in his district to supply the king and his staff.

4:20 numerous as the sand . . . on the seashore. A clear allusion to the Lord's promise

21 [a,A]Now Solomon ruled over all the kingdoms
[B]from the [b]River *to* the land of the Philistines and
to the border of Egypt; [C]*they* brought tribute and
served Solomon all the days of his life.
22 Solomon's [a]provision for one day was thirty
[b]kors of fine flour and sixty [b]kors of meal, 23 ten fat
oxen, twenty [a]pasture-fed oxen, a hundred sheep
besides deer, gazelles, roebucks, and fattened fowl.
24 For he had dominion over everything [a]west of
the [b]River, from Tiphsah even to [A]Gaza, [B]over all the
kings [a]west of the [b]River; and [C]he had peace on all
sides around about him. 25 [A]So Judah and Israel lived
in safety, every man under his vine and his fig tree,
[B]from Dan even to Beersheba, all the days of Solomon. 26 [A]Solomon had [a]40,000 stalls of horses for
his chariots, and 12,000 horsemen. 27 Those deputies
[a]provided for King Solomon and all who came to
King Solomon's table, each in his month; they left
nothing lacking. 28 They also brought barley and
straw for the horses and [A]swift steeds to the place
where it should be, each according to his charge.
29 Now [A]God gave Solomon wisdom and very great
discernment and breadth of [a]mind, [B]like the sand that
is on the seashore. 30 Solomon's wisdom surpassed
the wisdom of all [A]the sons of the east and [B]all the
wisdom of Egypt. 31 For [A]he was wiser than all men,
than [B]Ethan the Ezrahite, Heman, [C]Calcol and [a]Darda,
the sons of Mahol; and his [b]fame was *known* in all the
surrounding nations. 32 [A]He also spoke 3,000 proverbs,
and his songs were 1,005. 33 He spoke of trees, from
the cedar that is in Lebanon even to the hyssop that
grows on the wall; he spoke also of animals and birds
and creeping things and fish. 34 [a]Men [A]came from
all peoples to hear the wisdom of Solomon, from all
the kings of the earth who had heard of his wisdom.

4:21 [a]Ch 5:1 in Heb [b]I.e. Euphrates [A]2 Chr 9:26 [B]Gen 15:18; Josh 1:4 [C]2 Sam 8:2, 6
4:22 [a]Lit *bread* [b]I.e. One kor equals approx 10 bu 4:23 [a]Lit *oxen of the pasture*
4:24 [a]Lit *beyond* [b]I.e. Euphrates [A]Judg 1:18 [B]Ps 72:11 [C]1 Chr 22:9 4:25 [A]Jer 23:6; Mic 4:4; Zech 3:10 [B]1 Sam 3:20 4:26 [a]One ms reads *4000,* cf 2 Chr 9:25 [A]1 Kin 10:26; 2 Chr 1:14 4:27 [a]Or *nourished* 4:28 [A]Esth 8:10, 14; Mic 1:13
4:29 [a]Lit *heart* [A]1 Kin 3:12 [B]1 Kin 4:20 4:30 [A]Gen 29:1; Judg 6:33 [B]Is 19:11; Acts 7:22 4:31 [a]In 1 Chr 2:6, *Dara* [b]Lit *name* [A]1 Kin 3:12 [B]1 Chr 15:19; Ps 89: title [C]1 Chr 2:6 4:32 [A]Prov 1:1; 10:1; 25:1; Eccl 12:9; Song 1:1 4:34 [a]Lit *they* [A]1 Kin 10:1; 2 Chr 9:23

SOLOMON'S ADMINISTRATIVE DISTRICTS

© 1996 Thomas Nelson, Inc.

The growth and extension of Israel's borders under Solomon's leadership required extensive military expenditures. Coupled with this were ambitious building and commercial projects throughout his expanding kingdom. As a result, Solomon faced an urgent need for ever-increasing revenues.

To address this need, Solomon divided Israel into twelve districts and appointed governors over each district. These governors were responsible for levying and collecting taxes to provide for the needs of Jerusalem and the royal palace. The increasingly heavy taxes upon Israel created major dissension because the region of Judah was exempted. Furthermore, the divisions of the districts violated the old tribal boundaries.

to Abraham in Ge 22:17. The early years of Solomon's reign, characterized by population growth, peace, and prosperity, were a foreshadowing of the blessings that will prevail in Israel when the Abrahamic Covenant is fulfilled.

4:21 all the kingdoms. The borders of the kingdoms which Solomon influenced echoed the Lord's promise to Abram in Ge 15:18. However, Solomon's reign was not the fulfillment of the Abrahamic Covenant for 3 reasons: 1) Israel still only lived in the land "from Dan even to Beersheba" (v. 25). Abraham's descendants did not inhabit all the land promised to Abraham. 2) The non-Israelite kingdoms did not lose their identity and independence, but rather recognized *Solomon's authority* and brought him tribute without surrendering title to their lands. 3) According to Nu 34:6, the Mediterranean Sea is to be the western border of the Land of Promise, indicating that Tyre was to be a part of the Promised Land. However, Hiram king of Tyre was a sovereign who entered into a bilateral or parity treaty (between equals) with Solomon (5:1–12).

4:22 provision. I.e., the daily provisions for Solomon's palace.

4:24 Tiphsah ... Gaza. Tiphsah was located on the W bank of the Euphrates and Gaza on the southwestern Mediterranean coast. These towns represented the NE and SW points of Solomon's influence.

4:26 had 40,000 stalls. Though the Heb. text reads 40,000, this was probably a copyist's error in transcribing the text, and it should read 4,000 as in 2Ch 9:25.

4:30 the east ... Egypt. The men to the East of Israel in Mesopotamia and Arabia (cf. Job 1:3) and in Egypt were known for their wisdom. Egypt had been renowned for learning and science, as well as culture. Solomon's wisdom was superior to all at home or abroad (v. 31).

4:31 sons of Mahol. This probably meant "singers," a guild of musicians who created sacred songs.

4:32 proverbs ... songs. Hundreds of Solomon's proverbs have been preserved in the book of Proverbs (see Introduction to Proverbs). One of his songs is the Song of Solomon.

4:33 trees ... animals ... birds. Solomon described and taught about all kinds of plant and animal life, e.g., Pr 6:6–8; 28:15; 30:19.

4:34 Men came from all peoples. Solomon acquired an international reputation for his wisdom. Many important visitors came from faraway places to learn from Solomon's wisdom (cf. 10:1–13).

ALLIANCE WITH KING HIRAM

5 [a,A]Now Hiram king of Tyre sent his servants to
Solomon, when he heard that they had anointed
him king in place of his father, for [B]Hiram had [b]al-
ways been a friend of David. 2 Then [A]Solomon sent
word to Hiram, saying, 3 "You know that [A]David my
father was unable to build a house for the name of
the LORD his God because of the wars which surrounded him, until the LORD put them under the
soles of his feet. 4 But now [A]the LORD my God has
given me rest on every side; there is neither adversary nor [a]misfortune. 5 Behold, [A]I [a]intend to build a
house for the name of the LORD my God, as the LORD
spoke to David my father, saying, 'Your son, whom
I will set on your throne in your place, he will build
the house for My name.' 6 Now therefore, command
that they cut for me [A]cedars from Lebanon, and my
servants will be with your servants; and I will give
you wages for your servants according to all that
you say, for you know that there is no one among
us who knows how to cut timber like the Sidonians."
7 When Hiram heard the words of Solomon, he rejoiced greatly and said, "Blessed be the LORD today,
who has given to David a wise son over this great
people." 8 So Hiram sent *word* to Solomon, saying,
"I have heard *the message* which you have sent me;
I will do [a]what you desire concerning the cedar and
cypress timber. 9 My servants will bring *them* down
from Lebanon to the sea; and I will make them into
rafts *to go* by sea [A]to the place where you [a]direct

5:1 [a]Ch 5:15 in Heb [b]Lit *all the day* [A]2 Chr 2:3 [B]2 Sam 5:11; 1 Chr 14:1 5:2 [A]2 Chr 2:3 5:3 [A]2 Sam 7:5; 1 Chr 28:2, 3 5:4 [a]Lit *evil occurrence* [A]1 Kin 4:24; 1 Chr 22:9 5:5 [a]Lit *say* [A]2 Sam 7:12, 13; 1 Chr 17:12; 22:10; 28:6; 2 Chr 2:4 5:6 [A]2 Chr 2:8 5:8 [a]Lit *all your pleasure* 5:9 [a]Lit *send* [A]2 Chr 2:16

5:1–16 See 2Ch 2:1–18.

5:1 **Hiram king of Tyre.** Tyre was an important port city on the Mediterranean Sea N of Israel. Two towering mountain ranges ran within Lebanon's borders, and on their slopes grew thick forests of cedars. Hiram I ruled there ca. 978–944 B.C. He had earlier provided building materials and workers for David to build his palace (2Sa 5:11). Solomon maintained the friendly relations with Hiram established by David. They were beneficial to both as Israel exchanged wheat and oil for timber (see vv. 9–11).

5:4 **rest.** The guarantee of peace with the peoples surrounding Israel allowed Solomon to build the temple (cf. 4:24).

5:5 **the name.** "Name" represents the character and nature of the person indicated. *See note on 3:2.* **Your son.** Solomon claimed to be the promised offspring of David, the fulfillment of the Lord's promise to David in 2Sa 7:12, 13. However, Solomon's later disobedience proved that he was not the ultimate, promised offspring (11:9–13).

5:6 **cedars from Lebanon.** The cedars of Lebanon symbolized majesty and might (Ps 92:12; Eze 31:3). Because it was durable, resistant to rot and worms, closely-grained, and could be polished to a fine shine, its wood was regarded as the best timber for building. The logs were tied together and floated down the Mediterranean to Joppa (see v. 9; 2Ch 2:16), from where they could be transported to Jerusalem, 35 mi. inland. **Sidonians.** These are the inhabitants of the city of Sidon, located on the Mediterranean Sea about 22 mi. N of Tyre. Here, the term probably referred, in a general sense, to the Phoenicians, who were skilled craftsmen.

5:7 **Blessed be the LORD.** Perhaps Hiram was a worshiper of the true God, but it is equally possible that he was only acknowledging Jehovah as the God of the Hebrews (cf. 2Ch 2:16). **a wise son.** Hiram recognized Solomon's wisdom in seeking to honor his father David's desires.

5:9 **food to my household.** Tyre's rocky terrain grew great trees, but little good food. Hiram asked Solomon for food for his court in exchange for his lumber.

THE PLAN OF SOLOMON'S TEMPLE

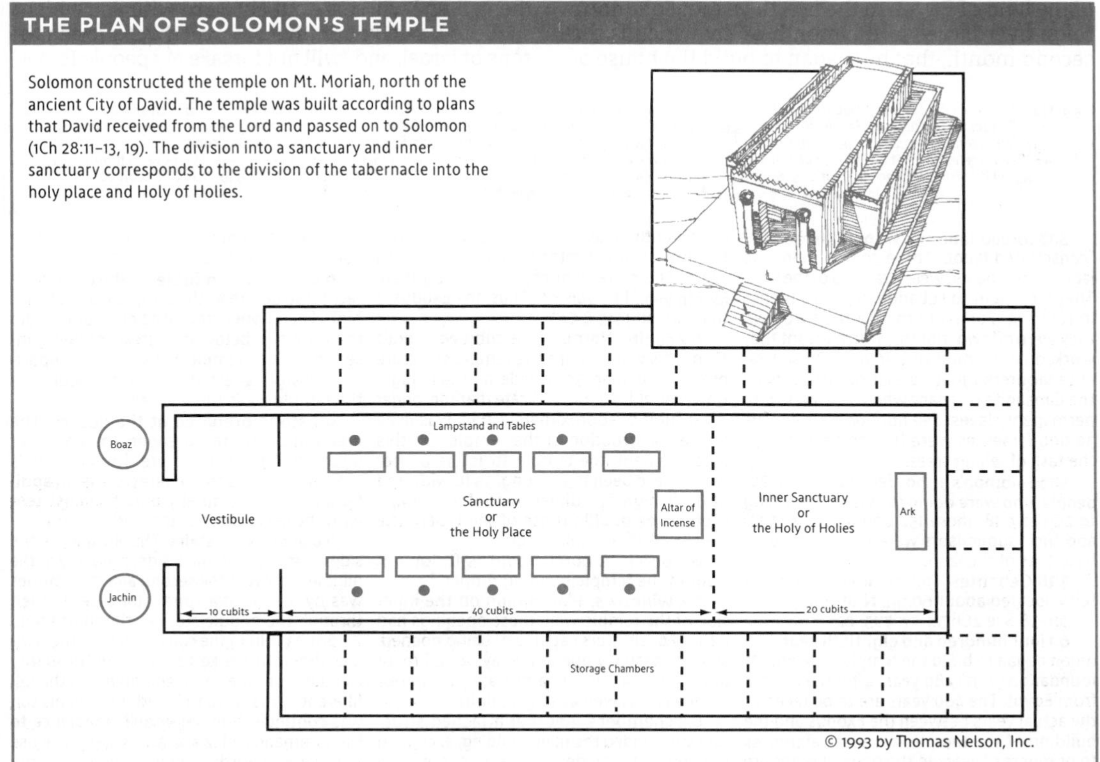

Solomon constructed the temple on Mt. Moriah, north of the ancient City of David. The temple was built according to plans that David received from the Lord and passed on to Solomon (1Ch 28:11–13, 19). The division into a sanctuary and inner sanctuary corresponds to the division of the tabernacle into the holy place and Holy of Holies.

me, and I will have them broken up there, and you
shall carry *them* away. Then [B]you shall accomplish
my desire by giving food to my household." 10 So
[a]Hiram [b]gave Solomon [c]as much as he desired of
the cedar and cypress timber. 11 [A]Solomon then gave
Hiram 20,000 [a]kors of wheat as food for his household, and twenty [a]kors of beaten oil; thus Solomon
would give Hiram year by year. 12 [A]The LORD gave
wisdom to Solomon, just as He [a]promised him; and
there was peace between Hiram and Solomon, and
the two of them made a covenant.

CONSCRIPTION OF LABORERS

13 Now [A]King Solomon [a]levied forced laborers
from all Israel; and the forced laborers [b]numbered
30,000 men. 14 He sent them to Lebanon, 10,000 a
month in relays; they were in Lebanon a month
and two months at home. And [A]Adoniram *was* over
the forced laborers. 15 Now [A]Solomon had 70,000
[a]transporters, and 80,000 hewers *of stone* in the
mountains, 16 [A]besides Solomon's 3,300 chief deputies who *were* over the [a]project *and* who ruled over
the people who were doing the work. 17 Then [A]the
king commanded, and they quarried great stones,
costly stones, to lay the foundation of the house with
cut stones. 18 So Solomon's builders and [a]Hiram's
builders and [A]the Gebalites [b]cut them, and prepared
the timbers and the stones to build the house.

THE BUILDING OF THE TEMPLE

6 [A]Now it came about in the four hundred and
eightieth year after the sons of Israel came out
of the land of Egypt, in the fourth year of Solomon's
reign over Israel, in the month of Ziv which is the
second month, that he [a]began to build the house of
the LORD. 2 As for the house which King Solomon
built for the LORD, its length *was* sixty [a]cubits and its
width twenty *cubits* and its height thirty cubits. 3 The
porch in front of the nave of the house *was* twenty
cubits [a]in length, [b]corresponding to the width of the
house, *and* its [c]depth along the front of the house *was*
ten cubits. 4 Also for the house [A]he made windows
with *artistic* frames. 5 [A]Against the wall of the house
he built stories encompassing the walls of the house
around both the nave and the [B]inner sanctuary; thus
he made [C]side chambers all around. 6 The lowest
story *was* five cubits wide, and the middle *was* six
cubits wide, and the third *was* seven cubits wide;
for on the outside he [a]made offsets *in the wall* of the
house all around in order that *the beams* would not
[b]be inserted in the walls of the house.

7 [A]The house, while it was being built, was built
of stone [a]prepared at the quarry, and there was
neither hammer nor axe nor any iron tool heard
in the house while it was being built.

8 The doorway for the [a]lowest side chamber *was*
on the right side of the house; and they would go up
by winding stairs to the middle *story*, and from the
middle to the third. 9 So [A]he built the house and finished it; and he covered the house with beams and
[a]planks of cedar. 10 He also built the stories against
the whole house, each five [a]cubits high; and they
[b]were fastened to the house with timbers of cedar.

11 Now the word of the LORD came to Solomon saying, 12 "*Concerning* this house which you are building,
[A]if you will walk in My statutes and execute My ordinances and keep all My commandments by walking in
them, then I will carry out My word with you which I
spoke to David your father. 13 [A]I will dwell among the
sons of Israel, and [B]will not forsake My people Israel."

5:9 [B]Ezra 3:7; Ezek 27:17 5:10 [a]Heb *Hirom* [b]Lit *was giving* [c]Lit *all his desire* 5:11 [a]I.e. One kor equals approx 10 bu [A]2 Chr 2:10 5:12 [a]Lit *spoke to* [A]1 Kin 3:12 5:13 [a]Lit *raised up* [b]Lit *was* [A]1 Kin 4:6; 9:15 5:14 [A]1 Kin 4:6; 12:18 5:15 [a]Or *burden bearers* [A]1 Kin 9:20-22; 2 Chr 2:17, 18 5:16 [a]Lit *work* [A]1 Kin 9:23 5:17 [A]1 Kin 6:7; 1 Chr 22:2 5:18 [a]Heb *Hirom's* [b]Or *chiseled* [A]Josh 13:5; Ezek 27:9 6:1 [a]Lit *built* [A]2 Chr 3:1, 2 6:2 [a]I.e. One cubit equals approx 18 in. 6:3 [a]Lit *in its length* [b]Lit *on the face of* [c]Lit *width* 6:4 [A]Ezek 40:16; 41:16 6:5 [A]Ezek 41:6 [B]1 Kin 6:16, 19, 20 [C]Ezek 41:5 6:6 [a]Lit *gave* [b]Lit *take hold* 6:7 [a]Lit *finished* [A]Ex 20:25; Deut 27:5, 6 6:8 [a]So with Gr and versions; M.T. *middle* 6:9 [a]Lit *rows* [A]1 Kin 6:14, 38 6:10 [a]I.e. One cubit equals approx 18 in. [b]Lit *took hold* 6:12 [A]2 Sam 7:5-16; 1 Kin 9:4 6:13 [A]Ex 25:8; 29:45; Lev 26:11 [B]Deut 31:6; Josh 1:5; Heb 13:5

5:13 forced laborers from all Israel. Lit. "conscripted labor." These 30,000 men who labored in Lebanon were Israelites of the land. They were sent to Lebanon, 10,000 a month in rotation. For every month they worked, they were off two months, which meant they worked only 4 months per year. These Israelite laborers must be distinguished from the Canaanite remnant who were made into permanent slaves. *See note on 9:21, 22.* The 30,000 Israelites were free and performed the task of felling trees.

5:16 Solomon's 3,300. *See note on 2Ch 2:2.* **people who were doing the work.** According to 2Ch 2:17, 18, these 150,000 laborers (5:15) and their supervisors were non-Israelite inhabitants of the land.

5:18 Gebalites. Inhabitants of Gebal, a town located about 60 mi. N of Tyre.

6:1–38 See 2Ch 3:1–17; 7:15–22.

6:1 four hundred and eightieth year. Solomon began to build the temple by laying its foundation (v. 37) 480 years after the Exodus from Egypt. The 480 years are to be taken as the actual years between the Exodus and the building of the temple, because references to numbers of years in the book of Kings are consistently taken in a literal fashion. Also, the literal interpretation correlates with Jephthah's statement recorded in Jdg 11:26. **fourth year.** I.e., 966 B.C. Thus, the Exodus is to be dated 1445 B.C.

6:2 cubits. Normally the cubit was about 18 in. This would make the temple structure proper 90 ft. long, 30 ft. wide, and 45 ft. high. However, 2Ch 3:3 may indicate that the longer royal cubit of approximately 21 in. was used in the construction of the temple. On this measurement, the temple structure proper would have been 105 ft. long, 35 ft. wide and 52 1/2 ft. high. The dimensions of the temple seem to be double those of the tabernacle (see Ex 26:15–30; 36:20–34).

6:3 porch. A porch about 15 ft. long in front of the temple building proper.

6:4 windows. Placed high on the inner side of the temple wall, these openings had lattices or shutters capable of being opened, shut, or partially opened. They served to let out the vapors of the lamps and the smoke of incense, as well as to give light.

6:5 chambers. Another attached structure surrounded the main building, excluding the porch. It provided rooms off of the main hall to house temple personnel and to store equipment and treasure (cf. 7:51).

6:6 lowest … middle … third. This attached structure to the temple was 3 stories high. Each upper story was one cubit wider than the one below it. Instead of being inserted into the temple walls, beams supporting the stories rested on recessed ledges in the temple walls themselves.

6:7 stone prepared at the quarry. The erection of the temple went much faster by utilizing pre-cut and pre-fitted materials moved on rollers to the temple site. In addition, the relative quiet would be consistent with the sacredness of the undertaking.

6:8 doorway … stairs. The entrance to the side rooms was on the S side, probably in the middle. Access to the second and third stories was by means of a spiral staircase that led through the middle story to the third floor.

6:11–13 During the construction of the temple, the Lord spoke to Solomon, probably through a prophet, and reiterated that the fulfillment of His Word to David through his son was contingent on Solomon's obedience to His commands (cf. 2:3, 4; 3:14; 9:4–8). The use of the same words, "I will dwell among the

14 [A]So Solomon built the house and finished it.
15 Then he [A]built the walls of the house on the inside
with boards of cedar; from the floor of the house to
the [a]ceiling he overlaid *the walls* on the inside with
wood, and he overlaid the floor of the house with
boards of cypress. 16 [A]He built twenty cubits on the
rear part of the house with boards of cedar from
the floor to the [a]ceiling; he built *them* for it on the
inside as an inner sanctuary, *even* as [B]the most holy
place. 17 The house, that is, the nave in front of *the*
inner sanctuary, was forty [a]cubits *long.* 18 There was
cedar on the house within, carved *in the shape* of
[A]gourds and open flowers; all was cedar, there was
no stone seen. 19 Then he prepared an inner sanctuary within the house in order to place there the ark
of the covenant of the LORD. 20 [a]The inner sanctuary
was twenty cubits in length, twenty cubits in width,
and twenty cubits in height, and he overlaid it with
pure gold. He also overlaid the altar with cedar. 21 So
Solomon overlaid the inside of the house with pure
gold. And he drew chains of gold across the front
of the inner sanctuary, and he overlaid it with gold.
22 He overlaid the whole house with gold, until all
the house was finished. Also [A]the whole altar which
was by the inner sanctuary he overlaid with gold.
23 [A]Also in the inner sanctuary he made two cherubim of olive wood, each ten cubits high. 24 Five
cubits *was* the one wing of the cherub and five
cubits the other wing of the cherub; from the end
of one wing to the end of the other wing *were* ten
cubits. 25 The other cherub *was* ten cubits; both
the cherubim were of the same measure and the
same form. 26 The height of the one cherub *was* ten
cubits, and so *was* the other cherub. 27 He placed
the cherubim in the midst of the inner house, and
[A]the wings of the cherubim were spread out, so
that the wing of the one was touching the *one* wall,
and the wing of the other cherub was touching the
other wall. So their wings were touching each other
in the center of the house. 28 He also overlaid the
cherubim with gold.
29 Then he carved all the walls of the house round
about with carved engravings of cherubim, palm
trees, and open flowers, inner and outer *sanctuar-*
ies. 30 He overlaid the floor of the house with gold,
inner and outer *sanctuaries.*
31 For the entrance of the inner sanctuary he made
doors of olive wood, the lintel *and* five-sided doorposts. 32 So *he made* two doors of olive wood, and
he carved on them carvings of cherubim, palm
trees, and open flowers, and overlaid them with
gold; and he spread the gold on the cherubim and
on the palm trees.
33 So also he made for the entrance of the nave
four-sided doorposts of olive wood 34 and [A]two doors
of cypress wood; the two leaves of the one door
turned on pivots, and the two [a]leaves of the other
door turned on pivots. 35 He carved *on it* cherubim,
palm trees, and open flowers; and he overlaid *them*
with gold evenly applied on the engraved work.
36 [A]He built the inner court with three rows of cut
stone and a row of cedar beams.
37 [A]In the fourth year the foundation of the house
of the LORD was laid, in the month of Ziv. 38 In the
eleventh year, in the month of Bul, which is the
eighth month, the house was finished throughout
all its parts and according to all its plans. So he was
seven years in building it.

SOLOMON'S PALACE

7 Now [A]Solomon was building his own house
thirteen years, and he finished all his house.
2 [A]He built the house of the forest of Lebanon; its
length was 100 [a]cubits and its width 50 cubits and
its height 30 cubits, on four rows of cedar pillars
with cedar beams on the pillars. 3 It was paneled

6:14 [A]1 Kin 6:9, 38 6:15 [a]Lit *walls of ceiling* [A]1 Kin 7:7 6:16 [a]Lit *walls* [A]2 Chr 3:8 [B]Ex 26:33, 34; Lev 16:2; 1 Kin 8:6; Heb 9:3 6:17 [a]I.e. One cubit equals approx 18 in. 6:18 [A]1 Kin 7:24 6:20 [a]Lit *before* 6:22 [A]Ex 30:1, 3, 6 6:23 [A]Ex 37:7-9; 2 Chr 3:10-12 6:27 [A]Ex 25:20; 37:9; 1 Kin 8:7 6:34 [a]So with Gr; M.T. *curtains* [A]Ezek 41:23-25 6:36 [A]1 Kin 7:12; Jer 36:10 6:37 [A]1 Kin 6:1 7:1 [A]1 Kin 3:1; 9:10; 2 Chr 8:1 7:2 [a]I.e. One cubit equals approx 18 in. [A]1 Kin 10:17, 21; 2 Chr 9:16

sons of Israel," in v. 13 as in Ex 29:45, implied that Solomon's temple was the legitimate successor to the tabernacle. The Lord forewarned Solomon and Israel that the temple was no guarantee of His presence; only their continued obedience would assure that.

6:16 the most holy place. This inner sanctuary, partitioned off from the main hall by cedar planks, was a perfect cube about 30 ft. on a side (v. 20) and was the most sacred area of the temple. The Most Holy Place is *further described in vv. 19–28.* The tabernacle also had a "most holy place" (Ex 26:33, 34).

6:17 the nave. This was the Holy Place, just outside the Most Holy Place, 60 ft. long, 30 ft. wide and 45 ft. high, that housed the altar of incense, the golden tables of the bread of the Presence, and the golden lampstands (7:48, 49).

6:19 the ark of the covenant of the LORD. The ark was a rectangular box made of acacia wood. The ark was made at Sinai by Bezalel according to the pattern given to Moses (Ex 25:10–22; 37:1–9). The ark served as the receptacle for the two tablets of the Ten Commandments (Ex 25:16, 21; 40:20; Dt 10:1–5) and the place in the inner sanctuary where the presence of the Lord met Israel (Ex 25:22).

6:20 overlaid it with pure gold. Cf. vv. 21, 22, 28, 30, 32, 35. Gold was beaten into fine sheets, and then hammered to fit over the beautifully embellished wood (vv. 18, 29), then attached to every surface in the temple proper, both in the Holy Place and in the Most Holy Place, so that no wood or stone was visible (v. 22).

6:23 cherubim. These two sculptured winged creatures, with human faces overlaid with gold (cf. Ge 3:24; Eze 41:18, 19), stood as guards on either side of the ark (see 2Ch 3:10–13) and are not to be confused with the cherubim on the mercy seat (see Ex 25:17–22). The cherubim represented angelic beings who were guardians of God's presence and stood on either side of the ark (8:6, 7) in the Most Holy Place. They were 15 ft. tall and 15 ft. between wing tips (v. 24–26). *See note on Ex 25:18.*

6:29 palm trees. An image reminiscent of the Garden of Eden in Ge 2. The palm tree represented the tree of life from the Garden.

6:31–35 There was distinct and magnificent separation by doors between the inner court of the temple (v. 36) and the Holy Place, as well as between the Holy Place and the Most Holy Place.

6:36 the inner court. This walled-in, open space that surrounded the temple was also called "the court of the priests" (2Ch 4:9) or the "upper court" (Jer 36:10). The wall of that court had a layer of wood between each of the 3 courses of stone. The alternation of timber beams with masonry was common in Mediterranean construction.

6:37 fourth year . . . month of Ziv. Cf. 6:1.

6:38 seven years. From foundation to finishing, the temple took 7 years and 6 months to build. *See note on 2Ch 5:1.*

7:1 thirteen years. Having built the house for the Lord, Solomon then built one for himself. Solomon's "house" was a complex of structures that took almost twice as long to build as the temple. The time involved was probably because there was not the same preparation for building or urgency as for the national place of worship. The temple and Solomon's house together took 20 years to complete (cf. 9:10).

7:2–5 the house of the forest of Lebanon. As a part of the palace complex, Solomon also built this large rectangular building, 150 ft.

with cedar above the side chambers which were
on the 45 pillars, 15 in each row. 4 *There were artistic window* frames in three rows, and window was
opposite window in three ranks. 5 All the doorways
and doorposts *had* squared *artistic* frames, and
window was opposite window in three ranks.
6 Then he made [A]the hall of pillars; its length
was 50 cubits and its width 30 cubits, and a porch
was in front of them and pillars and a [B]threshold
in front of them.
7 He made the hall of the [A]throne where he was
to judge, the hall of judgment, and [B]it was paneled
with cedar from floor to floor.
8 His house where he was to live, the other court
inward from the hall, was of the same workmanship.
[A]He also made a house like this hall for Pharaoh's
daughter, [B]whom Solomon had married.
9 All these were of costly stones, of stone cut according to measure, sawed with saws, inside and
outside; even from the foundation to the coping,
and so on the outside to the great court.
10 The foundation was of costly stones, *even* large
stones, stones of ten cubits and stones of eight cubits. 11 And above were costly stones, stone cut according to measure, and cedar. 12 So [A]the great court
all around *had* three rows of cut stone and a row of
cedar beams even as the inner court of the house
of the LORD, and [B]the porch of the house.

HIRAM'S WORK IN THE TEMPLE

13 Now [A]King Solomon sent and brought Hiram
from Tyre. 14 [A]He was a widow's son from the tribe
of Naphtali, and his father was a man of Tyre, a
worker in bronze; and [B]he was filled with wisdom
and understanding and skill for doing any work
in bronze. So he came to King Solomon and [C]per-
formed all his work.
15 He fashioned [A]the two pillars of bronze; [B]eigh-
teen cubits was the height of one pillar, and a line
of twelve cubits [a]measured the circumference of
both. 16 He also made two capitals of molten bronze
to set on the tops of the pillars; the height of the
one capital was five [a]cubits and the height of the
other capital was five cubits. 17 *There were* nets of
network and twisted threads of chainwork for the
capitals which were on the top of the pillars; seven
for the one capital and seven for the other capital.
18 So he made the pillars, and two rows around on
the one network to cover the capitals which were on
the top of the pomegranates; and so he did for the
other capital. 19 The capitals which *were* on the top
of the pillars in the porch were of lily design, four
cubits. 20 *There were* capitals on the two pillars, even
above *and* close to the [a]rounded projection which
was beside the network; and [A]the pomegranates
numbered two hundred in rows around [b]both capitals. 21 [A]Thus he set up the pillars at the [B]porch of
the nave; and he set up the right pillar and named
it [a]Jachin, and he set up the left pillar and named
it [b]Boaz. 22 On the top of the pillars was lily design.
So the work of the pillars was finished.
23 [A]Now he made the sea of [B]cast *metal* ten cubits
from brim to brim, circular in form, and its height
was five cubits, and [a]thirty cubits in circumference.
24 Under its brim [A]gourds went around encircling
it ten to a cubit, [B]completely surrounding the sea;
the gourds were in two rows, cast [a]with the rest.
25 [A]It stood on twelve oxen, three facing north,
three facing west, three facing south, and three
facing east; and the sea *was set* on top of them,
and all their rear parts *turned* inward. 26 It was a
handbreadth thick, and its brim was made like the
brim of a cup, *as* a lily blossom; it could hold two
thousand baths.

7:6 [A]1 Kin 7:12 [B]Ezek 41:25, 26 7:7 [A]Ps 122:5; Prov 20:8 [B]1 Kin 6:15, 16 7:8 [A]1 Kin 9:24; 2 Chr 8:11 [B]1 Kin 3:1 7:12 [A]1 Kin 6:36 [B]1 Kin 7:6 7:13 [A]2 Chr 2:13, 14; 4:11 7:14 [A]2 Chr 2:14 [B]Ex 28:3; 31:3-5; 35:31; 36:1 [C]2 Chr 4:11-16 7:15 [a]Lit *went around the other pillar* [A]2 Kin 25:17; 2 Chr 3:15; 4:12; Jer 52:21 [B]1 Kin 7:41 7:16 [a]I.e. One cubit equals approx 18 in. 7:20 [a]Lit *belly* [b]Lit *on the other capital* [A]1 Kin 7:42; 2 Chr 3:16; 4:13; Jer 52:23 7:21 [a]I.e. he shall establish [b]I.e. in it is strength [A]2 Chr 3:17 [B]1 Kin 6:3 7:23 [a]Lit *a line of 30 cubits went around it* [A]2 Chr 4:2 [B]2 Kin 16:17; 25:13 7:24 [a]Lit *in its casting* [A]1 Kin 6:18 [B]2 Chr 4:3 7:25 [A]2 Chr 4:4, 5; Jer 52:20

long, 75 ft. wide and 45 ft. high. It was built of a "forest" of cedar pillars from Lebanon. Three rows of cedar columns supported trimmed cedar beams and a cedar roof.

7:6 the hall of pillars. This colonnade was probably an entry hall or waiting area for the Hall of Judgment, which was probably used for the transaction of public business.

7:7 the hall of judgment. The place where Solomon would publicly hear petitions from Israelites and render judgments was added to the grand palace site.

7:8 house … court … house. Behind the Hall of Judgment was an open court. Within this court, Solomon built his own personal residence, a palace for his harem, and royal apartments for the Egyptian princess he had married.

7:9–12 A fortune was spent on building, adjacent to the temple, the whole palace with its 3 parts: 1) the king's home, 2) the courtyard in the middle, and 3) the house of the women on the other side.

7:13 Hiram. Although having the same Heb. name, this individual was distinct from the King of Tyre (5:1). Hiram had a Tyrian father, but his mother was of the tribe of Naphtali. Second Chronicles 2:14 states that Hiram's mother came from the tribe of Dan. Probably one verse refers to her place of birth and the other to her place of residence. Or, if her parents were originally from the two tribes, then he could legitimately claim either. The description of Hiram's skills in v. 14 is exactly the same as that of Bezalel who made the tabernacle (Ex 31:3; 36:1). Hiram made the pillars (vv. 14–22). *See note on 2Ch 2:13, 14.*

7:15 two pillars. One bronze pillar was on each side of the temple's entrance (v. 21). Each pillar was 27 ft. high and 18 ft. around. *See note on 2Ch 3:15.*

7:16 capitals. These distinctively treated upper ends of the bronze pillars added 7.5 ft. to the height of each pillar.

7:18 pomegranates. One of the fruits of the Promised Land (Nu 13:23; Dt 8:8), these were popular decorative motifs used on the hem of Aaron's priestly garment (Ex 28:33, 34).

7:21 Jachin … Boaz. See marginal note for the meanings. It is likely that each name recalls promises given to the Davidic house, and that they perpetually reminded the worshipers of God's grace in providing the Davidic monarchy as well as each king's need to depend on God for his success. *See note on 2Ch 3:17.* They were also symbolic of the strength and stability of God's promise of a kingdom forever, even though the temple would come down (see Jer 52:17).

7:23 the sea. A huge circular bronze basin corresponding to the laver of the tabernacle. According to v. 26, this great basin's capacity was about 12,000 gal. (*see note on 2Ch 4:5*). The sea stood in the courtyard on the temple's SE side and provided the priests water to wash themselves and their sacrifices (2Ch 4:6). It probably also supplied water for the 10 movable basins (vv. 38, 39). *See note on 2Ch 4:2.*

7:25 twelve oxen. Hiram arranged 3 oxen facing in each of the 4 directions of the compass to support the sea. *See note on 2Ch 4:4.*

7:26 two thousand baths. *See note on 2Ch 4:5.*

27 Then [A]he made the ten stands of bronze; the
length of each stand was four cubits and its width
four cubits and its height three cubits. 28 This was
the design of the stands: they had borders, even
borders between the [a]frames, 29 and on the borders
which were between the [a]frames *were* lions, oxen
and cherubim; and on the [a]frames there *was* a pedestal above, and beneath the lions and oxen *were*
wreaths of hanging work. 30 Now each stand had
four bronze wheels with bronze axles, and its four
feet had supports; beneath the basin *were* cast supports with wreaths at each side. 31 Its opening inside
the crown at the top *was* a cubit, and its opening
was round like the design of a pedestal, a cubit and a
half; and also on its opening *there were* engravings,
and their borders were square, not round. 32 The four
wheels *were* underneath the borders, and the axles
of the wheels *were* on the stand. And the height of
a wheel *was* a cubit and a half. 33 The workmanship
of the wheels *was* like the workmanship of a chariot
wheel. Their axles, their rims, their spokes, and their
hubs *were* all cast. 34 Now *there were* four supports
at the four corners of each stand; its supports *were*
part of the stand itself. 35 On the top of the stand
there was a circular form half a [a]cubit high, and on
the top of the stand its [b]stays and its borders *were*
part of it. 36 He engraved on the plates of its stays
and on its borders, cherubim, lions and palm trees,
according to the clear space on each, with wreaths
all around. 37 [A]He made the ten stands like this: all of
them had one casting, one measure and one form.
38 [A]He made ten basins of bronze, one basin held
forty baths; each basin *was* four cubits, *and* on each
of the ten stands *was* one basin. 39 Then he set the
stands, five on the right side of the house and five
on the left side of the house; and he set the sea *of
cast metal* on the right side of the house eastward
toward the south.
40 Now Hiram made the basins and the shovels
and the bowls. So Hiram finished doing all the work
which he performed for King Solomon *in* the house
of the LORD: 41 the two pillars and the *two* bowls of
the capitals which *were* on the top of the [A]two pillars, and the two networks to cover the two bowls
of the capitals which *were* on the top of the pillars;
42 and the [A]four hundred pomegranates for the two
networks, two rows of pomegranates for each network to cover the two bowls of the capitals which
were on the tops of the pillars; 43 and the ten stands
with the ten basins on the stands; 44 and [A]the one sea
and the twelve oxen under the sea; 45 and [A]the pails
and the shovels and the bowls; even all these utensils
which Hiram made for King Solomon *in* the house
of the LORD *were* of polished bronze. 46 [A]In the plain
of the Jordan the king cast them, in the clay ground
between [B]Succoth and [C]Zarethan. 47 Solomon left all
the utensils *unweighed,* because *they were* too many;
[A]the weight of the bronze could not be ascertained.
48 Solomon made all the furniture which *was in*
the house of the LORD: [A]the golden altar and the
golden table on which *was* the [B]bread of the Presence; 49 and the lampstands, five on the right side
and five on the left, in front of the inner sanctuary,
of pure gold; and [A]the flowers and the lamps and
the tongs, of gold; 50 and the cups and the snuffers
and the bowls and the spoons and the [A]firepans, of
pure gold; and the hinges both for the doors of the
inner house, the most holy place, *and* for the doors
of the house, *that is,* of the nave, of gold.
51 [A]Thus all the work that King Solomon performed *in* the house of the LORD was finished.
And [B]Solomon brought in the things dedicated by
his father David, the silver and the gold and the
utensils, *and* he put them in the treasuries of the
house of the LORD.

THE ARK BROUGHT INTO THE TEMPLE

8 [A]Then Solomon assembled the elders of Israel
and all [B]the heads of the tribes, the leaders of
the fathers' *households* of the sons of Israel, to King
Solomon in Jerusalem, [C]to bring up the ark of the
covenant of the LORD from [D]the city of David, which
is Zion. 2 All the men of Israel assembled themselves
to King Solomon at [A]the feast, in the month Ethanim,

7:27 [A]1 Kin 7:38; 2 Kin 25:13; 2 Chr 4:14 7:28 [a]Or *crossbars* 7:29 [a]Or *crossbars* 7:35 [a]I.e. One cubit equals approx 18 in. [b]Lit *hands* 7:37 [A]2 Chr 4:14 7:38 [A]Ex 30:18; 2 Chr 4:6 7:41 [A]1 Kin 7:17, 18 7:42 [A]1 Kin 7:20 7:44 [A]1 Kin 7:23, 25 7:45 [A]Ex 27:3; 2 Chr 4:16 7:46 [A]2 Chr 4:17 [B]Gen 33:17; Josh 13:27 [C]Josh 3:16 7:47 [A]1 Chr 22:3, 14 7:48 [A]Ex 30:1-3; 37:10-29; 2 Chr 4:8 [B]Ex 25:30 7:49 [A]Ex 25:31-38 7:50 [A]Ex 27:3; 2 Kin 25:15 7:51 [A]2 Chr 5:1 [B]2 Sam 8:11; 1 Chr 18:11; 2 Chr 5:1 8:1 [A]2 Chr 5:2-10 [B]Num 1:4; 7:2 [C]2 Sam 6:12-17; 1 Chr 15:25-29 [D]2 Sam 5:7 8:2 [A]Lev 23:34; 1 Kin 8:65; 2 Chr 7:8-10

7:27–37 stands. Hiram made 10 movable stands of bronze 6 ft. square and 4.5 ft. high. Each consisted of 4 upright corner poles joined together by square panels. For mobility, the stands rode on 4 wheels of bronze (v. 30).

7:38 basins. Hiram made 10 bronze basins as water containers for the stands. Each measured 6 ft. across and held about 240 gal. of water.

7:40 the shovels and the bowls. Shovels were used to scoop up the ashes that were then emptied into the bowls for disposal. The same tools served the same purpose in the tabernacle (Ex 27:3).

7:45 polished bronze. I.e., bronze polished to a high shine.

7:46 between Succoth and Zarethan. Succoth was located on the E side of the Jordan River just N of the Jabbok River (Ge 33:17; Jos 13:27; Jdg 8:4, 5). Zarethan was nearby. This location was conducive to good metallurgy, because it abounded in clay suitable for molds and lay close to a source of charcoal for heat, namely the forests across the Jordan.

7:48 the golden altar. The altar of incense stood in front of the Most Holy Place (cf. Ex 30:1–4). **the golden table.** The table on which the bread of the Presence was placed, which the Law required to be continually in God's presence (Ex 25:30).

7:49 lampstands. Ten golden lampstands standing directly in front of the Most Holy Place, 5 on either side of the doors, provided a corridor of light.

7:51 dedicated by . . . David. Solomon deposited that which David had dedicated to the Lord (2Sa 8:7–12) in the side rooms of the temple.

8:1–21 See 2Ch 5:2–6:11.

8:1 elders . . . heads. The "elders" of Israel were respected men who were in charge of local government and justice throughout Israel (Ex 18:13–26; Nu 11:16–30; 1Sa 8:1–9). They advised the king on important matters of state (1Sa 15:30; 2Sa 17:5; 1Ki 12:6–11). The "heads" of the tribes or "leaders" were the oldest living males within each extended family unit. They were the ones responsible for learning the law and leading their families to obey it.

8:2 seventh month. Solomon finished building the temple in the eighth month of the previous year (6:38; see 2Ch 5:1); all its detail signifying the magnificence and beauty of God's nature and His transcendent, uncommon glory. The celebration, then, did not take place until 11 months later. Apparently Solomon intentionally scheduled the dedication of the temple to coincide with the Feast of Booths or Tabernacles held in the seventh

which is the seventh month. 3 Then all the elders of
Israel came, and [A]the priests took up the ark. 4 They
brought up the ark of the LORD and [A]the tent of
meeting and all the holy utensils, which were in the
tent, and the priests and the Levites brought them
up. 5 And King Solomon and all the congregation
of Israel, who were assembled to him, [A]were with
him before the ark, sacrificing [a]so many sheep and
oxen they could not be counted or numbered. 6 Then
[A]the priests brought the ark of the covenant of the
LORD [B]to its place, into the inner sanctuary of the
house, to the most holy place, [C]under the wings of
the cherubim. 7 For the cherubim spread *their* wings
over the place of the ark, and the cherubim made a
covering over the ark and its poles from above. 8 But
[A]the poles were so long that the ends of the poles
could be seen from the holy place before the inner
sanctuary, but they could not be seen outside; they
are there to this day. 9 [A]There was nothing in the ark
except the two tablets of stone which Moses put
there at Horeb, where [B]the LORD made a covenant
with the sons of Israel, when they came out of the
land of Egypt. 10 It happened that when the priests
came from the holy place, [A]the cloud filled the house
of the LORD, 11 so that the priests could not stand to
minister because of the cloud, for the glory of the
LORD filled the house of the LORD.

SOLOMON ADDRESSES THE PEOPLE

12 [A]Then Solomon said,

"The LORD has said that [B]He would
dwell in the thick cloud.
13 "[A]I have surely built You a lofty house,
[B]A place for Your dwelling forever."

14 Then the king [a]faced about and [A]blessed all the
assembly of Israel, while all the assembly of Israel
was standing. 15 He said, "[A]Blessed be the LORD,
the God of Israel, [B]who spoke with His mouth to
my father David and has fulfilled *it* with His hand,
saying, 16 '[A]Since the day that I brought My people
Israel from Egypt, I did not choose a city out of all
the tribes of Israel *in which* to build a house that
[B]My name might be there, but [C]I chose David to be
over My people Israel.' 17 [A]Now it was [a]in the heart
of my father David to build a house for the name
of the LORD, the God of Israel. 18 But the LORD said
to my father David, 'Because it was [a]in your heart
to build a house for My name, you did well that it
was [a]in your heart. 19 [A]Nevertheless you shall not
build the house, but your son who [a]will be born to
you, he will build the house for My name.' 20 Now
the LORD has fulfilled His word which He spoke;
for [A]I have risen in place of my father David and
sit on the throne of Israel, as the LORD [a]promised,
and have built the house for the name of the LORD,
the God of Israel. 21 There I have set a place for the
ark, [A]in which is the covenant of the LORD, which
He made with our fathers when He brought them
from the land of Egypt."

THE PRAYER OF DEDICATION

22 Then [A]Solomon stood before the altar of the
LORD in the presence of all the assembly of Israel
and [B]spread out his hands toward heaven. 23 He
said, "O LORD, the God of Israel, [A]there is no God
like You in heaven above or on earth beneath, [B]keep-
ing covenant and *showing* lovingkindness to Your
servants who walk before You with all their heart,
24 who have kept with Your servant, my father David,

8:3 [A]Num 7:9; Deut 31:9; Josh 3:3, 6 8:4 [A]1 Kin 3:4; 2 Chr 1:3 8:5 [a]Lit *sheep and oxen...numbered for multitude* [A]2 Sam 6:13; 2 Chr 1:6 8:6 [A]1 Kin 8:3 [B]1 Kin 6:19 [C]1 Kin 6:27 8:8 [A]Ex 25:13-15; 37:4, 5 8:9 [A]Ex 25:16, 21; Deut 10:2-5; Heb 9:4 [B]Ex 24:7, 8; 40:20; Deut 4:13 8:10 [A]Ex 40:34, 35; 2 Chr 7:1, 2 8:12 [A]2 Chr 6:1 [B]Lev 16:2; Ps 18:11; 97:2 8:13 [A]2 Sam 7:13 [B]Ex 15:17; Ps 132:14 8:14 [a]Lit *turned his face about* [A]2 Sam 6:18; 1 Kin 8:55 8:15 [A]1 Chr 29:10, 20; Neh 9:5; Luke 1:68 [B]2 Sam 7:12, 13; 1 Chr 22:10 8:16 [A]2 Sam 7:4, 5; 1 Chr 17:3-10; 2 Chr 6:5 [B]Deut 12:5, 11 [C]1 Sam 16:1; 2 Sam 7:8 8:17 [a]Lit *with* [A]2 Sam 7:2, 3; 1 Chr 17:1, 2 8:18 [a]Lit *with* 8:19 [a]Lit *will come forth from your loins* [A]2 Sam 7:5, 12, 13; 1 Kin 5:3, 5; 1 Chr 17:11, 12; 22:8-10 8:20 [a]Lit *spoke* [A]1 Chr 28:5, 6 8:21 [A]Deut 31:26; 1 Kin 8:9 8:22 [A]1 Kin 8:54; 2 Chr 6:12 [B]Ex 9:33; Ezra 9:5 8:23 [A]1 Sam 2:2; 2 Sam 7:22 [B]Deut 7:9; Neh 1:5; 9:32; Dan 9:4

month, when there would be a general assembly of the people in Jerusalem. That was also a Jubilee year, so it was especially appropriate (Lv 23:33–36, 39–43; Dt 16:13–15).

8:4–6 brought up the ark. The ark of the covenant was transported by the priests and the Levites from the tent that David had made for it in Jerusalem (2Sa 6:17). They also brought to the temple the tabernacle and all its furnishings which had been located at Gibeon (2Ch 1:2–6). The ark was placed into the Most Holy Place (v. 6).

8:7, 8 poles. God had originally commanded that poles be used to carry the ark (Ex 25:13–15). They were left protruding to serve as a guide so the High Priest could be guided by them when he entered the dark inner sanctuary.

8:8 to this day. The phrase is used from the perspective of one who lived and wrote before the destruction of the temple in 586 B.C. The writer of 1 Kings incorporated such sources into his book (cf. 9:13, 21; 10:12; 12:19).

8:9 two tablets of stone. At this time the ark of the covenant contained only the two tablets inscribed with the Ten Commandments. The pot of manna (Ex 16:33) and Aaron's rod that budded (Nu 17:10) were no longer in the ark. See Heb 9:4.

8:10 the cloud. The cloud was "the glory of the LORD" (v. 11), the visible symbol of God's presence. It signaled the Lord's approval of this new temple. A similar manifestation took place when the tabernacle was dedicated (Ex 40:34, 35). *See note on Lv 9:23.*

8:12–21 See 2Ch 6:1–11.

8:12, 13 Solomon's solemn declaration was addressed to the Lord. Solomon recognized the thick darkness as the manifestation of the Lord's gracious presence among His people (cf. Ex 19:9; 20:21; Lv 16:2) and affirmed that he had built the temple so that the Lord could dwell there in the glory of thick darkness.

8:14–21 Solomon turned around from addressing the Lord and spoke to the assembly of Israel gathered at the temple. Solomon, in vv. 15–19, rehearsed the story of 2Sa 7:12–16 and claimed that he, having built the temple, had become the fulfillment of God's promise to his father David (vv. 20, 21). However, Solomon's claim was premature because the Lord later appeared to him declaring the necessity of obedience for the establishment of Solomon's throne (9:4–9), an obedience which would be lacking in Solomon (11:6, 9, 10).

8:22–53 *See note on 2Ch 6:12–40.* Solomon then moved to the altar of burnt offering to offer a lengthy prayer of consecration to the Lord. First, he affirmed that no god could compare to Israel's God, the Lord (vv. 23, 24). Second, he asked the Lord for His continued presence and protection (vv. 25–30). Third, he listed 7 typical Israelite prayers that would require the Lord's response (vv. 31–54). These supplications recalled the detailed list of curses that Dt 28:15–68 ascribed for the breaking of the law. Specifically, Solomon prayed that the Lord would judge between the wicked and the righteous (vv. 31, 32); the Lord would forgive the sins that had caused defeat in battle (vv. 33, 34); the Lord would forgive the sins that had brought on drought (vv. 35, 36); the Lord would forgive the sins that had resulted in national calamities (vv. 37–40); the Lord would show mercy to God-fearing foreigners (vv. 41–43); the Lord would give victory in battle (vv. 44, 45); and the Lord would bring restoration after captivity (vv. 46–54).

8:22 spread out his hands. The spreading of open hands toward heaven was a normal posture of individual prayer (Ex 9:29; Is 1:15).

that which You have [a]promised him; indeed, You
have spoken with Your mouth and have fulfilled it
with Your hand as it is this day. 25 Now therefore,
O LORD, the God of Israel, keep with Your servant
David my father that which You have [a]promised
him, saying, '[b,A]You shall not lack a man to sit on
the throne of Israel, if only your sons take heed to
their way to walk before Me as you have walked.'
26 Now therefore, O God of Israel, let Your word, I
pray, be confirmed [A]which You have spoken to Your
servant, my father David.

27 "But will God indeed dwell on the earth? Behold,
[A]heaven and the [a]highest heaven cannot contain
You, how much less this house which I have built!
28 Yet have regard to the [A]prayer of Your servant
and to his supplication, O LORD my God, to listen to
the cry and to the prayer which Your servant prays
before You today; 29 [A]that Your eyes may be open
toward this house night and day, toward [B]the place
of which You have said, 'My name shall be there,' to
listen to the prayer which Your servant shall pray
toward this place. 30 [A]Listen to the supplication of
Your servant and of Your people Israel, [B]when they
pray toward this place; hear in heaven Your dwelling place; hear and [C]forgive.

31 "[A]If a man sins against his neighbor and is
made to take an oath, and he comes *and* takes an
oath before Your altar in this house, 32 then hear
in heaven and act and judge Your servants, [A]condemning the wicked by bringing his way on his
own head and justifying the righteous by giving
him according to his righteousness.

33 "[A]When Your people Israel are [a]defeated before
an enemy, because they have sinned against You, [B]if
they turn to You again and confess Your name and
pray and make supplication to You in this house,
34 then hear in heaven, and forgive the sin of Your
people Israel, and bring them back to the land which
You gave to their fathers.

35 "[A]When the heavens are shut up and there is no
rain, because they have sinned against You, and they
pray toward this place and confess Your name and
turn from their sin when You afflict them, 36 then
hear in heaven and forgive the sin of Your servants
and of Your people Israel, [A]indeed, teach them the
good way in which they should walk. And [B]send rain
on Your land, which You have given Your people
for an inheritance.

37 "[A]If there is famine in the land, if there is pestilence, if there is blight *or* mildew, locust *or* grasshopper, if their enemy besieges them in the land
of their [a]cities, whatever plague, whatever sickness
there is, 38 whatever prayer or supplication is made
by any man *or* by all Your people Israel, [a]each knowing the [b]affliction of his own heart, and spreading
his [c]hands toward this house; 39 then hear in heaven
Your dwelling place, and forgive and act and render to each according to all his ways, [A]whose heart
You know, for [B]You alone know the hearts of all the
sons of men, 40 that they may [a]fear You all the days
that they live [b]in the land which You have given to
our fathers.

41 "Also concerning the foreigner who is not of
Your people Israel, when he comes from a far country for Your name's sake 42 (for they will hear of Your
great name [A]and Your mighty hand, and of Your outstretched arm); when he comes and prays toward
this house, 43 hear in heaven Your dwelling place,
and do according to all for which the foreigner calls
to You, in order [A]that all the peoples of the earth
may know Your name, to [a]fear You, as *do* Your people Israel, and that they may know that [b]this house
which I have built is called by Your name.

44 "When Your people go out to battle against
[a]their enemy, by whatever way You shall send them,
and [A]they pray to the LORD [b]toward the city which
You have chosen and the house which I have built
for Your name, 45 then hear in heaven their prayer
and their supplication, and maintain their [a]cause.

46 "When they sin against You (for [A]there is no
man who does not sin) and You are angry with them
and deliver them to an enemy, so that [a]they take
them away captive [B]to the land of the enemy, far off
or near; 47 [A]if they [a]take thought in the land where
they have been taken captive, and repent and make
supplication to You in the land of those who have
taken them captive, saying, '[B]We have sinned and
have committed iniquity, we have acted wickedly';
48 [A]if they return to You with all their heart and with
all their soul in the land of their enemies who have
taken them captive, and [B]pray to You toward their
land which You have given to their fathers, the city
which You have chosen, and the house which I have
built for Your name; 49 then hear their prayer and
their supplication in heaven Your dwelling place,
and maintain their [a]cause, 50 and forgive Your people
who have sinned against You and all their transgressions which they have transgressed against You,
and [A]make them *objects of* compassion before those
who have taken them captive, that they may have
compassion on them 51 ([A]for they are Your people
and Your inheritance which You have brought forth
from Egypt, [B]from the midst of the iron furnace),
52 [A]that Your eyes may be open to the supplication of
Your servant and to the supplication of Your people
Israel, to listen to them whenever they call to You.

8:24 [a]Lit *spoken to* 8:25 [a]Lit *spoken to* [b]Lit *There shall not be cut off to you a man from before Me* [A]1 Kin 2:4 8:26 [A]2 Sam 7:25 8:27 [a]Lit *heaven of heavens* [A]2 Chr 2:6; Ps 139:7-16; Is 66:1; Jer 23:24; Acts 7:49 8:28 [A]Phil 4:6 8:29 [A]2 Chr 7:15; Neh 1:6 [B]Deut 12:11 8:30 [A]Neh 1:6 [B]Dan 6:10 [C]Ex 34:6, 7; Ps 85:2; Dan 9:9; 1 John 1:9 8:31 [A]Ex 22:8-11 8:32 [A]Deut 25:1 8:33 [a]Lit *smitten* [A]Lev 26:17, 25; Deut 28:25, 48 [B]Lev 26:40-42 8:35 [A]Lev 26:19; Deut 11:16, 17; 2 Sam 24:10-13 8:36 [A]1 Sam 12:23; Ps 5:8; 25:4, 5; 27:11; 86:11; 119:133; Jer 6:16 [B]1 Kin 18:1, 41-45; Jer 14:22 8:37 [a]Lit *gates* [A]Lev 26:16, 25, 26; Deut 28:21-23, 38-42 8:38 [a]Lit *who shall know each* [b]Lit *plague* [c]Lit *palms* 8:39 [A]1 Sam 2:3; 16:7 [B]1 Chr 28:9; Ps 11:4; Jer 17:10; John 2:24, 25; Acts 1:24 8:40 [a]Or *revere* [b]Lit *on the face of the land* 8:42 [A]Ex 13:3; Deut 3:24 8:43 [a]Or *reverence* [b]Lit *Your name is called upon this house which I have built* [A]Josh 4:23, 24; 1 Sam 17:46; Ps 67:2 8:44 [a]Lit *his* [b]Lit *in the way of* [A]2 Chr 14:11 8:45 [a]Lit *right* or *justice* 8:46 [a]Lit *their captors take them captive* [A]Ps 130:3, 4; 143:2; Prov 20:9; Eccl 7:20; Rom 3:23; 1 John 1:8-10 [B]Lev 26:34-39; 2 Kin 17:6, 18; 25:21 8:47 [a]Lit *return to their heart* [A]Lev 26:40-42; Neh 9:2 [B]Ezra 9:6, 7; Neh 1:6; Ps 106:6; Dan 9:5 8:48 [A]Deut 4:29; 1 Sam 7:3, 4; Neh 1:9 [B]Dan 6:10; Jon 2:4 8:49 [a]Lit *judgment* 8:50 [A]2 Chr 30:9; Ps 106:46; Acts 7:10 8:51 [A]Ex 32:11, 12; Deut 9:26-29 [B]Deut 4:20; Jer 11:4 8:52 [A]1 Kin 8:29

8:27 heaven … cannot contain You. Solomon confessed that even though the Lord had chosen to dwell among His people in the cloud at the temple, He far transcended containment by anything in all creation.

53 For You have separated them from all the peoples of the earth as Your inheritance, [A]as You spoke
through Moses Your servant, when You brought our
fathers forth from Egypt, O Lord [a]GOD."

SOLOMON'S BENEDICTION

54 [A]When Solomon had finished praying this entire prayer and supplication to the LORD, [B]he arose
from before the altar of the LORD, from kneeling on
his knees with his [a]hands spread toward heaven.
55 And he stood and [A]blessed all the assembly of
Israel with a loud voice, saying:
56 "Blessed be the LORD, who has given rest to His
people Israel, [A]according to all that He [a]promised; [B]not
one word has [b]failed of all His good [c]promise, which
He [a]promised through Moses His servant. 57 May the
LORD our God be with us, as He was with our fathers;
[A]may He not leave us or forsake us, 58 that [A]He may
incline our hearts to Himself, to walk in all His ways
and to keep His commandments and His statutes and
His ordinances, which He commanded our fathers.
59 And may these words of mine, with which I have
made supplication before the LORD, be near to the
LORD our God day and night, that He may maintain
the [a]cause of His servant and the [a]cause of His people
Israel, [b]as each day requires, 60 so [A]that all the peoples
of the earth may know that [B]the LORD is God; there
is no one else. 61 [A]Let your heart therefore be [a]wholly
devoted to the LORD our God, to walk in His statutes
and to keep His commandments, as at this day."

DEDICATORY SACRIFICES

62 [A]Now the king and all Israel with him [B]offered
sacrifice before the LORD. 63 Solomon offered for the
sacrifice of peace offerings, which he offered to the
LORD, 22,000 oxen and 120,000 sheep. [A]So the king
and all the sons of Israel dedicated the house of the
LORD. 64 On the same day the king consecrated the
middle of the court that *was* before the house of the
LORD, because there he [a]offered the burnt offering
and the grain offering and the fat of the peace offerings; for [A]the bronze altar that *was* before the
LORD *was* too small to hold the burnt offering and
the grain offering and the fat of the peace offerings.
65 So [A]Solomon observed the feast at that time,
and all Israel with him, a great assembly [B]from the
entrance of Hamath [C]to the brook of Egypt, before
the LORD our God, for seven days and seven *more*
days, *even* fourteen days. 66 On the eighth day he
sent the people away and they blessed the king.
Then they went to their tents joyful and glad of heart
for all the goodness that the LORD had [a]shown to
David His servant and to Israel His people.

GOD'S PROMISE AND WARNING

9 [A]Now it came about when Solomon had finished
building the house of the LORD, and [B]the king's
house, and [C]all [a]that Solomon desired to do, 2 that
[A]the LORD appeared to Solomon a second time, as
He had appeared to him at Gibeon. 3 The LORD said
to him, "[A]I have heard your prayer and your supplication, which you have made before Me; I have
consecrated this house which you have built [B]by
putting My name there forever, and [C]My eyes and My
heart will be there perpetually. 4 As for you, [A]if you
will walk before Me as your father David walked, in
integrity of heart and uprightness, doing according
to all that I have commanded you *and* will keep My
statutes and My ordinances, 5 then [A]I will establish
the throne of your kingdom over Israel forever, just
as I [a]promised to your father David, saying, '[b]You
shall not lack a man on the throne of Israel.'

8:53 [a]Heb *YHWH*, usually rendered *LORD* [A]Ex 19:5, 6; Deut 9:26-29 8:54 [a]Lit *palms* [A]2 Chr 7:1 [B]2 Chr 6:13 8:55 [A]Num 6:23-26; 2 Sam 6:18; 1 Kin 8:14 8:56 [a]Lit *spoke* [b]Lit *fallen* [c]Lit *word* [A]Deut 12:10 [B]Josh 21:45; 23:14, 15 8:57 [A]Deut 31:6, 17; Josh 1:5; 1 Sam 12:22; Rom 8:31; Heb 13:5 8:58 [A]Ps 119:36; Jer 31:33 8:59 [a]Lit *judgment* [b]Lit *the thing of a day in its day* 8:60 [A]Josh 4:24; 1 Sam 17:46; 1 Kin 8:43; 2 Kin 19:19 [B]Deut 4:35; 1 Kin 18:39; Jer 10:10-12 8:61 [a]Lit *complete with* [A]Deut 18:13; 1 Kin 11:4; 2 Kin 20:3 8:62 [A]2 Chr 7:4-10 [B]2 Sam 6:17-19; Ezra 6:16, 17 8:63 [A]Ezra 6:15-18; Neh 12:27 8:64 [a]Lit *made* [A]2 Chr 4:1 8:65 [A]Lev 23:34-42; 1 Kin 8:2 [B]Num 34:8; Josh 13:5; Judg 3:3; 2 Kin 14:25 [C]Gen 15:18; Ex 23:31; Num 34:5; Josh 13:3 8:66 [a]Lit *done* 9:1 [a]Lit *Solomon's desire which he was pleased to do* [A]2 Chr 7:11 [B]1 Kin 7:1, 2 [C]2 Chr 8:6 9:2 [A]1 Kin 3:5; 11:9; 2 Chr 1:7 9:3 [A]2 Kin 20:5; Ps 10:17; 34:17 [B]1 Kin 8:29 [C]Deut 11:12; 2 Chr 6:40 9:4 [A]1 Kin 3:6, 14; 11:4, 6, 8; 2 Kin 20:3; Ps 128:1 9:5 [a]Lit *spoke* [b]Lit *There shall not be cut off to you a man* [A]2 Sam 7:12, 16; 1 Kin 2:4; 6:12; 1 Chr 22:10

8:54–61 Solomon arose to pronounce a benediction on the people. His words were substantially a brief recapitulation of the preceding prayer in which he affirmed the faithfulness of the Lord to Israel (v. 56) and exhorted Israel to faithfulness to the Lord (vv. 57–61).

8:62–66 See 2Ch 7:1–10.

8:62 offered sacrifice. To complete the temple's dedication, Solomon led the people in offering peace offerings to the Lord (cf. Lv 3:1–17; 7:11–21), in which they consumed 22,000 bulls and 120,000 sheep (v. 63). Although the number of sacrifices offered seems high, it was in keeping with the magnitude of this event. Obviously, the single bronze altar could not accommodate such an enormous number of sacrifices. Solomon first had to consecrate the entire middle courtyard, the one directly in front of the temple (v. 64). After consecrating the court, Solomon probably had a series of auxiliary altars set up in the court to accommodate all the peace offerings.

8:65 the entrance of Hamath to the brook of Egypt. "The entrance of Hamath" was located about 20 mi. S of Kadesh on the Orontes River and was the northern boundary of the land promised to Israel (Nu 34:7–9; Jos 13:5). "The brook of Egypt" is to be equated with Wadi El-Armish in the northeastern Sinai, the southern boundary of the land promised to Israel. These locations show that people from all over Israel attended the dedication of the temple.

9:1–9 See 2Ch 7:11–22.

9:1, 2 finished ... the king's house. According to 6:1, Solomon began building the temple in Apr./May 966 B.C. The temple was completed in Oct./Nov. 959 B.C. (6:38). The temple dedication and Solomon's prayer to the Lord occurred 11 months after the completion of the temple in Sep./Oct. 958 B.C. The Lord did not appear to Solomon this second time (cf. 3:5–14) until Solomon had completed the building of his own palace in 946 B.C. (cf. 7:1). Thus, the Lord's response came approximately 12 years after Solomon's prayer and supplication to the Lord recorded in 8:22–53.

9:3 consecrated. The Lord made the temple holy by being present in the cloud (cf. 8:10). As proof of the temple's consecration, the Lord told Solomon that He had put His name there (cf. 3:2). **forever.** God was not saying He will dwell in that building forever, since in less than 400 years it was destroyed by the Babylonians (cf. vv. 7–9). He was saying that Jerusalem and the temple mount are to be His earthly throne as long as the earth remains, through the millennial kingdom (see Is 2:1–4; Zec 14:16). Even during the New Heaven and New Earth, the eternal state, there will be the heavenly Jerusalem, where God will eternally dwell (see Rev 21:1, 2). **eyes ... heart.** These symbolized, respectively, the Lord's constant attention toward and deep affection for Israel. By implication, He promised them access to His presence and answers to their prayers.

9:4–9 See 2Ch 7:17–22.

9:4 if you will walk. The Lord reiterated to Solomon the importance of obedience to the Mosaic statutes in order to experience the blessings of the Davidic Covenant (cf. 2:3, 4).

6 "[A]But if you or your sons indeed turn away from following Me, and do not keep My commandments and My statutes which I have set before you, and go and serve other gods and worship them, 7 [A]then I will cut off Israel from the land which I have given them, and [B]the house which I have consecrated for My name, I will [a]cast out of My sight. So [C]Israel will become a proverb and a byword among all peoples. 8 And this house will become [a,A]a heap of ruins; everyone who passes by will be astonished and hiss and say, '[B]Why has the LORD done thus to this land and to this house?' 9 And they will say, '[A]Because they forsook the LORD their God, who brought their fathers out of the land of Egypt, and adopted other gods and worshiped them and served them, therefore the LORD has brought all this adversity on them.' "

CITIES GIVEN TO HIRAM

10 [A]It came about [B]at the end of twenty years in which Solomon had built the two houses, the house of the LORD and the king's house 11 (Hiram king of Tyre had supplied Solomon with cedar and cypress timber and gold according to all his desire), then King Solomon gave Hiram twenty cities in the land of Galilee. 12 So Hiram came out from Tyre to see the cities which Solomon had given him, and they [a]did not please him. 13 He said, "What are these cities which you have given me, my brother?" So [a]they were called the land of [b,A]Cabul to this day. 14 [A]And Hiram sent to the king 120 talents of gold.

15 Now this is the account of the forced labor which King Solomon [A]levied to build the house of the LORD, his own house, the [a,B]Millo, the wall of Jerusalem, [C]Hazor, [D]Megiddo, and [E]Gezer. 16 *For* Pharaoh king of Egypt had gone up and captured Gezer and burned it with fire, and killed the [A]Canaanites who lived in the city, and had [B]given it *as* a dowry to his daughter, Solomon's wife. 17 So Solomon rebuilt Gezer and the lower [A]Beth-horon 18 and [A]Baalath and Tamar in the wilderness, in the land *of Judah,* 19 and all the storage cities which Solomon had, even [A]the cities for [a]his chariots and the cities for [a,B]his horsemen, and [b,C]all that it pleased Solomon to build in Jerusalem, in Lebanon, and in all the land [c]under his rule. 20 *As for* all the people who were left of the Amorites, the Hittites, the Perizzites, the Hivites and the Jebusites, who were not of the sons of Israel, 21 [A]their descendants who were left after them in the land [B]whom the sons of Israel were unable to destroy utterly, [C]from them Solomon levied [D]forced laborers, even to this day. 22 But Solomon [A]did not make slaves of the sons of Israel; for they were men of war, his servants, his princes, his captains, his chariot commanders, and his horsemen.

23 These *were* the [a,A]chief officers who *were* over Solomon's work, five hundred and fifty, [B]who ruled over the people doing the work.

24 As soon as [A]Pharaoh's daughter came up from the city of David to her house which *Solomon* had built for her, [B]then he built the Millo.

25 Now [A]three times in a year Solomon offered burnt offerings and peace offerings on the altar which he built to the LORD, burning incense with them *on the altar* which *was* before the LORD. So he finished the house.

26 King Solomon also built a [A]fleet of ships in [B]Ezion-geber, which is near Eloth on the shore of the [a]Red Sea, in the land of Edom. 27 [A]And Hiram sent his servants with the fleet, sailors who knew the sea, along with the servants of Solomon.

9:6 [A]2 Sam 7:14-16; 1 Chr 28:9; Ps 89:30ff 9:7 [a]Lit *send* [A]Lev 18:24-29; Deut 4:26; 2 Kin 17:23 [B]Jer 7:4-14 [C]Deut 28:37; Ps 44:14; Jer 24:9 9:8 [a]Heb *high* [A]2 Kin 25:9; 2 Chr 36:19 [B]Deut 29:24-26; 2 Chr 7:21; Jer 22:8, 9, 28 9:9 [A]Deut 29:25-28; Jer 2:10-13 9:10 [A]2 Chr 8:1 [B]1 Kin 6:37, 38; 7:1; 9:1 9:12 [a]Lit *were not right in his sight* 9:13 [a]Lit *he called them* [b]I.e. as good as nothing [A]Josh 19:27 9:14 [A]1 Kin 9:11 9:15 [a]I.e. citadel [A]1 Kin 5:13 [B]2 Sam 5:9; 1 Kin 9:24 [C]Josh 11:1; 19:36 [D]Josh 17:11 [E]Judg 1:29 9:16 [A]Josh 16:10 [B]1 Kin 3:1; 7:8 9:17 [A]Josh 10:10; 16:3; 21:22; 2 Chr 8:5 9:18 [A]Josh 19:44 9:19 [a]Lit *the* [b]Lit *the desire of Solomon which he desired to build in Jerusalem* [c]Lit *of* [A]1 Kin 10:26; 2 Chr 1:14 [B]1 Kin 4:26 [C]1 Kin 9:1 9:21 [A]Judg 1:21-29; 3:1 [B]Josh 15:63; 17:12, 13 [C]Judg 1:28, 35 [D]Gen 9:25, 26; Ezra 2:55, 58 9:22 [A]Lev 25:39 9:23 [a]Or *officers of the deputies* [A]2 Chr 8:10 [B]1 Kin 5:16 9:24 [A]1 Kin 3:1; 7:8 [B]2 Sam 5:9; 1 Kin 9:15; 11:27; 2 Chr 32:5 9:25 [A]Ex 23:14-17; Deut 16:16 9:26 [a]Lit *Sea of Reeds* [A]1 Kin 22:48 [B]Num 33:35; Deut 2:8; 1 Kin 22:48 9:27 [A]1 Kin 5:6, 9; 10:11

9:6 if you … turn. If Israel ("you" is pl.) abandoned the Lord to worship other gods, God would expel Israel from the Land and destroy the temple (v. 7).

9:9 this adversity. The destruction of Jerusalem and exile from the land (v. 8) were predicted by Moses in Dt 29:24–28. The devastation of the temple, which came in 586 B.C., graphically demonstrated the Lord's anger against Israel's sin, particularly the sin of idolatry.

9:10–28 See 2Ch 8:1–18.

9:10 at the end of twenty years. The completion of the building of the temple (7 years) and the building of Solomon's palace (13 years) would be ca. 946 B.C. (*see note on 9:1, 2*).

9:11 Solomon gave Hiram twenty cities. Solomon sold these 20 cities in Galilee to Hiram in exchange for the gold (about 4.5 tons) mentioned in v. 14. Probably these cities lay along the border between Tyre and Israel, just outside the territory of Asher. Later, Hiram gave the towns back to Solomon. *See note on 2Ch 8:2.*

9:13 to this day. *See note on 8:8.*

9:15 the Millo. A landfill in the depression between the city of David and the temple and palace complex to the N (see 2Sa 5:9). **Hazor.** Ten mi. N of the Sea of Galilee, Hazor protected Israel's northeastern entrance from Syria and Mesopotamia. **Megiddo.** Megiddo guarded a crucial pass in the Carmel mountains, which linked the valley of Jezreel and the international coastal highway to Egypt. **Gezer.** Twenty mi. W of Jerusalem, Gezer lay in the coastal plain at the intersection of the coastal highway and the main road to Jerusalem.

9:17 lower Beth-horon. About 12 mi. NW of Jerusalem along a road connecting Gibeon with the western lowlands and providing a western approach to Jerusalem. *See note on 2Ch 8:5.*

9:18 Baalath. The designation of several cities in Canaan. *See note on 2Ch 8:6.* **Tamar.** This city was located 16 mi. SW of the Dead Sea on the southeastern boundary of the Land (cf. Eze 47:19; 48:28).

9:19 storage cities. Cities whose primary purpose was to store food (2Ch 17:12; 32:28). **cities for his chariots.** Solomon built military outposts for his chariots and horses. To defend his kingdom, these garrisons were probably located along key roads throughout the nation. All the cities listed in vv. 15–19 met this requirement.

9:20–23 See 2Ch 8:7–10.

9:21, 22 forced laborers. I.e., "conscripted slave labor." *See note on 5:13.* Only resident aliens permanently became part of this force since the law did not allow Israelites to make fellow-Israelites slaves against their will (Ex 21:2–11; Lv 25:44–46; Dt 15:12–18). Additionally, v. 22 adds that he did not move someone from an established post, even for a specific project.

9:21 to this day. *See note on 8:8.*

9:25 Solomon offered. Once the temple had been built, Solomon's practice of sacrificing to God at the various high places ceased (cf. 3:2–4). He kept Israel's 3 great annual feasts, Passover, Weeks, and Booths (Dt 16:1–17), at the temple in Jerusalem.

9:26 Ezion-geber. Solomon's port located on the modern Gulf of Aqabah.

28 They went to [A]Ophir and took four hundred and
twenty talents of gold from there, and brought *it*
to King Solomon.

THE QUEEN OF SHEBA

10 [A]Now when the [A]queen of [B]Sheba heard about
the fame of Solomon concerning the name
of the LORD, she came [C]to test him with difficult
questions. 2 So she came to Jerusalem with a very
large retinue, with camels [A]carrying spices and very
much gold and precious stones. When she came to
Solomon, she spoke with him about all that was in
her heart. 3 Solomon [a]answered all her questions;
nothing was hidden from the king which he did
not [b]explain to her. 4 When the queen of Sheba perceived all the wisdom of Solomon, the house that
he had built, 5 the food of his table, the seating of
his servants, the attendance of his waiters and their
attire, his cupbearers, and [a]his stairway by which
he went up to the house of the LORD, there was no
more spirit in her. 6 Then she said to the king, "It was
a true report which I heard in my own land about
your words and your wisdom. 7 Nevertheless I did
not believe the [a]reports, until I came and my eyes
had seen it. And behold, the half was not told me.
You exceed *in* wisdom and prosperity the report
which I heard. 8 How [A]blessed are your men, how
blessed are these your servants who stand before
you continually *and* hear your wisdom. 9 [A]Blessed
be the LORD your God who delighted in you to set
you on the throne of Israel; [B]because the LORD loved
Israel forever, therefore He made you king, [C]to do
justice and righteousness." 10 [A]She gave the king a
hundred and twenty talents of gold, and a very great
amount of spices and precious stones. Never again
did such abundance of spices come in as that which
the queen of Sheba gave King Solomon.
11 [A]Also the ships of Hiram, which brought gold
from Ophir, brought in from Ophir a very great
number of almug trees and precious stones. 12 [A]The
king made of the almug trees supports for the house
of the LORD and for the king's house, also lyres and
harps for the singers; such almug trees have not
come in *again* nor have they been seen to this day.
13 King Solomon gave to the queen of Sheba all
her desire which she requested, besides what he
gave her according to [a]his royal bounty. Then she
turned and went to her own land [b]together with
her servants.

WEALTH, SPLENDOR AND WISDOM

14 [A]Now the weight of gold which came in to Solomon in one year was 666 talents of gold, 15 besides
that from the traders and the [a]wares of the merchants and all the kings of the [A]Arabs and the governors of the country. 16 [A]King Solomon made 200
large shields of beaten gold, [a]using 600 *shekels of*
gold on each large shield. 17 *He made* [A]300 shields
of beaten gold, [a]using three minas of gold on each
shield, and [B]the king put them in the house of the
forest of Lebanon. 18 Moreover, the king made a great
throne of [A]ivory and overlaid it with refined gold.
19 *There were* six steps to the throne and a round top
to the throne at its rear, and [a]arms [b]on each side of
the seat, and two lions standing beside the [a]arms.
20 Twelve lions were standing there on the six steps
on the one side and on the other; nothing like *it* was
made for any other kingdom. 21 All King Solomon's
drinking vessels *were* of gold, and all the vessels of
the house of the forest of Lebanon *were* of pure gold.
None was of silver; it was not considered [a]valuable
in the days of Solomon. 22 For [A]the king had at sea
the ships of Tarshish with the ships of Hiram; once
every three years the ships of Tarshish came bringing gold and silver, ivory and apes and peacocks.
23 [A]So King Solomon became greater than all the
kings of the earth in riches and in wisdom. 24 All
the earth was seeking the presence of Solomon, [A]to
hear his wisdom which God had put in his heart.
25 [A]They brought every man his gift, articles of silver

9:28 [A]1 Chr 29:4; 2 Chr 8:18 10:1 [A]2 Chr 9:1; Matt 12:42; Luke 11:31 [B]Gen 10:7, 28; Ps 72:10, 15 [C]Judg 14:12-14; Ps 49:4 10:2 [A]1 Kin 10:10 10:3 [a]Lit *told her all her words* [b]Lit *tell her* 10:5 [a]Or *his burnt offering which he offered* 10:7 [a]Lit *words* 10:8 [A]Prov 8:34 10:9 [A]1 Kin 5:7 [B]1 Chr 17:22; 2 Chr 2:11 [C]2 Sam 8:15; 23:3; Ps 72:2 10:10 [A]1 Kin 10:2 10:11 [A]1 Kin 9:27, 28; Job 22:24 10:12 [A]2 Chr 9:11 10:13 [a]Lit *the hand of King Solomon* [b]Lit *she and* 10:14 [A]2 Chr 9:13-28 10:15 [a]Or *traffic* [A]2 Chr 9:14 10:16 [a]Lit *he brought up* [A]1 Kin 14:26-28; 2 Chr 12:9, 10 10:17 [a]Lit *he brought up* [A]1 Kin 14:26 [B]1 Kin 7:2 10:18 [A]1 Kin 10:22; 2 Chr 9:17; Ps 45:8 10:19 [a]Lit *hands* [b]Lit *on this side and on this at the place of the seat* 10:21 [a]Lit *anything* 10:22 [A]1 Kin 9:26-28; 22:48; 2 Chr 20:36 10:23 [A]1 Kin 3:12, 13; 4:30 10:24 [A]1 Kin 3:9, 12, 28 10:25 [A]Ps 68:29

9:28 Ophir. The location of Ophir is unknown. It has been suggested it was located on the southwestern Arabian peninsula. First Kings 10:11, 12 possibly suggests that Ophir was close to or a part of the kingdom of Sheba. **four hundred and twenty talents.** This was about 16 tons of gold. Second Chronicles 8:18 has 450 talents (*see note on 2Ch 8:18*).

10:1–29 See 2Ch 9:1–28.

10:1 Sheba. Sheba was located in southwestern Arabia, about 1,200 mi. from Jerusalem. **concerning the name of the LORD.** The primary motive for the queen's visit was to verify Solomon's reputation for wisdom and devotion to the Lord. **difficult questions.** Riddles designed to stump the hearer (cf. Jdg 14:12).

10:5 no more spirit in her. Lit. the experience "left her breathless."

10:9 the LORD your God. The queen was willing to credit Solomon's God with giving him wisdom that resulted in just and righteous decisions. Though she recognized the Lord as Israel's national God, there was no confession that Solomon's God had become her God to the exclusion of all others. There is no record that she made any offerings to God at the temple.

10:10 a hundred and twenty talents. About 4.5 tons (cf. 9:28).

10:11 almug trees. Probably the strong, long-lasting sandalwood, which is black on the outside and ruby red inside.

10:12 to this day. *See note on 8:8.*

10:14 weight ... was 666 talents. About 25 tons of gold.

10:15 Gold also came to Solomon from tolls and tariffs from traders, revenues from loyal administrators, and taxes from Arabian kings who used caravan routes under Solomon's control.

10:16, 17 shields. From his gold revenues, Solomon made 200 large shields, containing about 7.5 pounds of gold each, and 300 small shields, having 3.75 pounds of gold each, that were ornamental in design and restricted to ceremonial use.

10:21 house of the forest of Lebanon. *See note on 7:2–5.* **silver.** To show the wealth of Solomon's kingdom, the writer explains that gold was so plentiful that the value of silver dropped to nothing.

10:22 ships of Tarshish. These were large, all-weather cargo vessels designed to make long ocean voyages.

10:25 silver and gold ... horses. The wisdom God had given to Solomon (v. 24) caused many rulers, like the queen of Sheba (vv. 1–13), to bring presents to Solomon as they sought to buy his wisdom to be applied in their own nations. These gifts led Solomon to multiply for himself horses, as well as silver and gold, precisely that which God's king was warned against in Dt 17:16, 17. Solomon became ensnared by the blessings of his own wisdom and disobeyed God's commands.

and gold, garments, weapons, spices, horses, and
mules, so much year by year.
26 [A]Now Solomon gathered chariots and horsemen; and he had 1,400 chariots and 12,000 horsemen, and he [a]stationed them in the [B]chariot cities
and with the king in Jerusalem. 27 [A]The king made
silver *as common* as stones in Jerusalem, and he
made cedars as plentiful as sycamore trees that are
in the [a]lowland. 28 [A]Also Solomon's import of horses
was from Egypt and Kue, *and* the king's merchants
procured *them* from Kue for a price. 29 A chariot
[a]was imported from Egypt for 600 *shekels* of silver,
and a horse for 150; and [b]by the same means they
exported them [A]to all the kings of the Hittites and
to the kings of the Arameans.

SOLOMON TURNS FROM GOD

11 Now [A]King Solomon loved many foreign
women along with the daughter of Pharaoh:
Moabite, Ammonite, Edomite, Sidonian, and Hittite women, 2 from the nations concerning which
the LORD had said to the sons of Israel, "[A]You shall
not [a]associate with them, nor shall they [a]associate
with you, *for* they will surely turn your heart away
after their gods." Solomon held fast to these in love.
3 [A]He had seven hundred wives, princesses, and
three hundred concubines, and his wives turned
his heart away. 4 For when Solomon was old, his
wives turned his heart away after other gods; and
[A]his heart was not [a]wholly devoted to the LORD his
God, as the heart of David his father *had been.* 5 For
Solomon went after [A]Ashtoreth the goddess of the
Sidonians and after [a,B]Milcom the detestable idol of
the Ammonites. 6 Solomon did what was evil in the
sight of the LORD, and did not follow the LORD fully,
as David his father *had done.* 7 Then Solomon built
a high place for [A]Chemosh the detestable idol of
Moab, on the mountain which is [a]east of Jerusalem,
and for [B]Molech the detestable idol of the sons of
Ammon. 8 Thus also he did for all his foreign wives,
who burned incense and sacrificed to their gods.
9 Now [A]the LORD was angry with Solomon [B]be-
cause his heart was turned away from the LORD,
the God of Israel, [C]who had appeared to him twice,
10 and [A]had commanded him concerning this thing,
that he should not go after other gods; but he did
not observe what the LORD had commanded. 11 So
the LORD said to Solomon, "Because [a]you have
done this, and you have not kept My covenant
and My statutes, which I have commanded you,
[A]I will surely tear the kingdom from you, and will
give it to your servant. 12 Nevertheless I will not
do it in your days for the sake of your father David, *but* I will tear it out of the hand of your son.

10:26 [a]So with ancient versions; Heb *led* [A]1 Kin 4:26; 2 Chr 1:14-17; 9:25 [B]1 Kin 9:19 10:27 [a]Heb *Shephelah* [A]Deut 17:17; 2 Chr 1:15 10:28 [A]Deut 17:16; 2 Chr 1:16; 9:28 10:29 [a]Lit *came up and went out from* [b]Lit *in like manner by their hand* [A]2 Kin 7:6, 7 11:1 [A]Deut 17:17; Neh 13:23-27 11:2 [a]Lit *go among* [A]Ex 23:31-33; 34:12-16; Deut 7:3 11:3 [A]2 Sam 5:13-16 11:4 [a]Lit *complete with* [A]1 Kin 9:4 11:5 [a]In Jer 49:1, 3, *Malcam* [A]Judg 2:13; 10:6; 1 Sam 7:3, 4 [B]1 Kin 11:7 11:7 [a]Lit *before* [A]Num 21:29; Judg 11:24; 2 Kin 23:13 [B]Lev 20:2-5; 2 Kin 23:10; Acts 7:43 11:9 [A]Ps 90:7 [B]1 Kin 11:2, 4 [C]1 Kin 3:5; 9:2 11:10 [A]1 Kin 6:12; 9:6, 7 11:11 [a]Lit *this is with you* [A]1 Sam 2:30; 1 Kin 11:29-31; 12:15, 16, 20; 2 Kin 17:15, 21

10:28 Kue. Kue was in Cilicia, an area S of the Taurus Mountains in Asia Minor. In antiquity, Cilicia was fabled for breeding and selling the best horses.

10:29 chariot . . . for 600 *shekels*. About 15 lbs. of silver. **horse for 150.** About 3.75 lbs. of silver. **Hittites.** The majority of Hittites lived in Anatolia (Asia Minor). From ca. 1720–1200 B.C. a unified kingdom ruled over the Hittites. These kings spread the influence of the Hittites throughout the ancient Near East; the Hittite empire reached the peak of its power ca. 1380–1350 B.C. When the Hittite empire collapsed, ca. 1200 B.C., many Hittite city-states developed, each with its own king. These rulers were called "the kings of the Hittites" and were scattered in Solomon's day throughout Anatolia and northern Aram (Syria). **Arameans.** The geographical area within the bounds set by the Taurus Mountains in the N, the western bend of the Euphrates River and the edge of the desert in the E, the Litani River to the S and the Mediterranean Sea to the W, had as its major city, Damascus. Later known by the Gr. term "Syria," the land was known in OT times as Aram.

11:1–6 loved many foreign women. Many of Solomon's marriages were for the purpose of ratifying treaties with other nations, a common practice in the ancient Near East. The practice of multiplying royal wives, prohibited in Dt 17:17 because the practice would turn the king's heart away from the Lord, proved to be accurate in the experience of Solomon. His love for his wives (vv. 1, 2) led him to abandon his loyalty to the Lord and worship other gods (vv. 3–6). No sadder picture can be imagined than the ugly apostasy of his later years (over 50), which can be traced back to his sins with foreign wives. Polygamy was tolerated among the ancient Hebrews, though most in the East had only one wife. A number of wives was seen as a sign of wealth and importance. The king desired to have a larger harem than any of his subjects, and Solomon resorted to this form of state magnificence. But it was a sin directly violating God's law, and the very result which that law was designed to prevent happened.

11:1 Moabite. Descendants of Lot (Ge 19:37) who lived in the land E of the Dead Sea between the Arnon River to the N and the Zered Brook to the S. **Ammonite.** Descendants of Lot (Ge 19:38) who were located in the area of the Transjordan beginning about 25 mi. E of the Jordan River. **Edomite.** Descendants of Esau (Ge 36:1) who were located in the area S of Moab, to the SE of the Dead Sea. **Sidonian.** *See note on 5:6.* **Hittite.** *See note on 10:29.*

11:4 as . . . David. Cf. v. 6. David is consistently presented in Kings as the standard by which other kings were to act and be judged (3:14; 9:4; 14:8; 15:3; 2Ki 8:19; 22:2). This was not because David had not sinned (cf. 2Sa 11, 12), but rather because he repented appropriately from his sin (Pss 32; 51), and because sin did not continue as the pattern of his life.

11:5 Ashtoreth. A deliberate distortion of the Canaanite "ashtart," re-vocalized based on the Heb. word for "shame." She was the goddess of love and fertility, especially worshiped at Tyre and Sidon. **Milcom.** Another name for Molech (v. 7), the national god of the Ammonites. His name seems to mean "the one who rules." The worship of Molech was associated with the sacrifice of children in the fire (Lv 18:21; 20:2, 3, 4, 5; Jer 32:35).

11:6 evil in the sight of the LORD. The particular evil of Solomon was his tolerance of and personal practice of idolatry. These same words were used throughout the book of Kings to describe the rulers who promoted and practiced idolatry (15:26, 34; 16:19, 25, 30; 22:52; 2Ki 3:2; 8:18, 27; 13:2, 11; 14:24; 15:9, 18, 24, 28; 17:2; 21:2, 20; 23:32, 37; 24:9, 19). Solomon became an open idolater, worshiping images of wood and stone in the sight of the temple which, in his early years, he had erected to the one true God.

11:7 Chemosh. The god of the Moabites, to whom the sacrifice of children as a burnt offering was customary (2Ki 3:27). **mountain . . . east of Jerusalem.** Probably, the Mt. of Olives. This is the area called Tophet in Jer 7:30–34 and the mount of corruption in 2Ki 23:13.

11:9, 10 appeared to him twice. Once was at Gibeon (3:5), the next at Jerusalem (9:2). On both occasions, God had warned Solomon, so he had no excuses.

11:11 not kept My covenant. Solomon failed to obey the commandments to honor God (Ex 20:3–6), which were part of the Mosaic Covenant. Obedience to that Covenant was necessary for receiving the blessings of the Davidic Covenant (see 2:3, 4). **tear the kingdom from you.** The Lord's tearing of the kingdom from Solomon was announced in Ahijah's symbolic action of tearing his garment in vv. 29–39. The tearing of the robe, picturing the loss of the kingdom, recalls the interaction between Samuel and Saul (1Sa 15:27, 28), when the Lord took the kingdom away from Saul because of his disobedience. The great gifts to Solomon followed by his great abuse warranted such a judgment.

11:12 not do it in your days. The Lord's great love for David caused Him to temper His judgment with mercy by not disrupting

13 However, [A]I will not tear away all the kingdom,
but [B]I will give one tribe to your son for the sake
of My servant David and [C]for the sake of Jerusalem
which I have chosen."

GOD RAISES ADVERSARIES

14 Then the LORD raised up an adversary to Solomon, Hadad the Edomite; he was of the [a]royal line
in Edom. 15 For it came about, [A]when David was in
Edom, and Joab the commander of the army had
gone up to bury the slain, and had [B]struck down
every male in Edom 16 (for Joab and all Israel stayed
there six months, until he had cut off every male in
Edom), 17 that Hadad fled [a]to Egypt, he and certain
Edomites of his father's servants with him, while
Hadad *was* a young boy. 18 They arose from Midian and came to [A]Paran; and they took men with
them from Paran and came to Egypt, to Pharaoh
king of Egypt, who gave him a house and assigned
him food and gave him land. 19 Now Hadad found
great favor [a]before Pharaoh, so that he gave him
in marriage the sister of his own wife, the sister
of Tahpenes the queen. 20 The sister of Tahpenes
bore his son Genubath, whom Tahpenes weaned in
Pharaoh's house; and Genubath was in Pharaoh's
house among the sons of Pharaoh. 21 But [A]when
Hadad heard in Egypt that David slept with his
fathers and that Joab the commander of the army
was dead, Hadad said to Pharaoh, "Send me away,
that I may go to my own country." 22 Then Pharaoh
said to him, "But what have you lacked with me, that
behold, you are seeking to go to your own country?"
And he answered, "Nothing; nevertheless you must
surely [a]let me go."

23 [A]God also raised up *another* adversary to him,
Rezon the son of Eliada, who had fled from his lord
[B]Hadadezer king of Zobah. 24 He gathered men to
himself and became leader of a marauding band,
[A]after David slew them of *Zobah;* and they went to
Damascus and stayed [a]there, and reigned in Damascus. 25 So he was an adversary to Israel all the
days of Solomon, along with the evil that Hadad
did; and he abhorred Israel and reigned over Aram.

26 Then [A]Jeroboam the son of Nebat, an Ephraimite of Zeredah, Solomon's servant, whose mother's
name was Zeruah, a widow, [B]also [a]rebelled against
the king. 27 Now this was the reason why he [a]rebelled
against the king: [A]Solomon built the [b]Millo, *and*
closed up the breach of the city of his father David.
28 Now the man Jeroboam was a valiant warrior,
and when [A]Solomon saw that the young man was
[a]industrious, he appointed him over all the [b]forced
labor of the house of Joseph. 29 It came about at that
time, when Jeroboam went out of Jerusalem, that
[A]the prophet Ahijah the Shilonite found him on the
road. Now [a]Ahijah had clothed himself with a new
cloak; and both of them were alone in the field.
30 Then [A]Ahijah took hold of the new cloak which
was on him and tore it into twelve pieces. 31 He said
to Jeroboam, "Take for yourself ten pieces; for thus
says the LORD, the God of Israel, 'Behold, [A]I will tear
the kingdom out of the hand of Solomon and give
you ten tribes 32 ([A]but he will have one tribe, for the
sake of My servant David and for the sake of Jerusalem, [B]the city which I have chosen from all the
tribes of Israel), 33 because they have forsaken Me,
and [A]have worshiped Ashtoreth the goddess of the
Sidonians, [B]Chemosh the god of Moab, and Milcom
the god of the sons of Ammon; and they have not
walked in My ways, doing what is right in My sight
and *observing* My statutes and My ordinances, as
his father David *did.* 34 Nevertheless I will not take
the whole kingdom out of his hand, but I will make
him [a]ruler all the days of his life, for the sake of
My servant David whom I chose, who observed
My commandments and My statutes; 35 but [A]I will
take the kingdom from his son's hand and give it
to you, *even* ten tribes. 36 But [A]to his son I will give
one tribe, [B]that My servant David may have a lamp
always before Me in Jerusalem, [A]the city where I
have chosen for Myself to put My name. 37 I will
take you, and you shall reign over whatever [a]you

11:13 [A]2 Sam 7:15; 1 Chr 17:13; Ps 89:33 [B]1 Kin 11:32, 36; 12:20 [C]1 Kin 8:29 **11:14** [a]Lit *king's seed* **11:15** [A]2 Sam 8:14; 1 Chr 18:12, 13 [B]Deut 20:13 **11:17** [a]Lit *to go into* **11:18** [A]Num 10:12; Deut 1:1 **11:19** [a]Lit *in the sight of* **11:21** [A]1 Kin 2:10 **11:22** [a]Lit *send me away* **11:23** [A]1 Kin 11:14 [B]2 Sam 8:3; 10:16 **11:24** [a]Lit *in it* [A]2 Sam 10:8, 18 **11:26** [a]Lit *lifted up a hand* [A]1 Kin 11:11, 28; 12:2, 20; 2 Chr 13:6 [B]2 Sam 20:21 **11:27** [a]Lit *lifted up a hand* [b]I.e. citadel [A]1 Kin 9:15, 24 **11:28** [a]Lit *a doer of work* [b]Lit *burden* [A]Prov 22:29 **11:29** [a]Lit *he* [A]1 Kin 12:15; 14:2; 2 Chr 9:29 **11:30** [A]1 Sam 15:27, 28 **11:31** [A]1 Kin 11:11, 12 **11:32** [A]1 Kin 11:13; 12:21 [B]1 Kin 11:13; 14:21 **11:33** [A]1 Sam 7:3; 1 Kin 11:5-8 [B]Num 21:29; Jer 48:7, 13 **11:34** [a]Or *prince* **11:35** [A]1 Kin 11:12; 12:16, 17 **11:36** [A]1 Kin 11:13 [B]1 Kin 15:4; 2 Kin 8:19; Ps 132:17 **11:37** [a]Lit *your soul desires*

the kingdom in Solomon's lifetime (cf. v. 34). This showed that Solomon's disobedience did not annul the Davidic Covenant; the Lord's commitment to fulfill His Word to David remained firm (cf. 2Sa 7:12–16).

11:13 one tribe. The one tribe that remained loyal to the Davidic dynasty was Judah (cf. 12:20). **for the sake of Jerusalem.** The Lord had chosen Jerusalem as the place where His name would dwell forever (9:3). Therefore, Jerusalem and the temple would remain so that the divine promise might stand.

11:14–18 Hadad the Edomite. Even though Hadad belonged to the royal family that ruled Edom, he escaped death at the hands of David's army when he was a child, and he fled to Egypt (cf. 2Sa 8:13, 14; 1Ch 18:12, 13).

11:18 Midian. The land directly E of Edom, to which Hadad first fled on his way to Egypt. **Paran.** A wilderness SE of Kadesh in the central area of the Sinai peninsula (cf. Nu 12:16; 13:3).

11:21 Send me away. Like Moses (Ex 2:10), Hadad's son grew up in Pharaoh's household. As did Moses (Ex 5:1), Hadad requested that Pharaoh allow him to leave Egypt. Hearing of the deaths of David and Joab, he renounced his easy position and possessions in Egypt to return to Edom in order to regain his throne. His activities gave great trouble to Israel (v. 25).

11:23–25 Rezon. After David conquered Zobar (2Sa 8:3–8), Rezon and his men took Damascus and established the strong dynasty of Syrian kings that severely troubled Israel in the ninth century B.C. (cf. 15:18; 20:1).

11:26 Jeroboam the son of Nebat. In contrast to Hadad and Rezon, who were external adversaries of Solomon, God raised up Jeroboam from a town in Ephraim as an internal adversary. Jeroboam was from Ephraim, the leading tribe of Israel's northern 10 tribes. He was a young man of talent and energy who, having been appointed by Solomon as leader over the building works around Jerusalem, rose to public notice.

11:28 forced labor. *See note on 5:13.*

11:29 Ahijah the Shilonite. Ahijah was a prophet of the Lord who lived in Shiloh, a town in Ephraim about 20 mi. N of Jerusalem. *See note on 1Sa 1:3.*

11:30–32 Here is a monumental prophecy that because of Solomon's sins the kingdom would be divided and Jeroboam would rule in the northern area (cf. vv. 35–37).

11:33 *See notes on 11:5, 7.*

11:36 a lamp always before Me. A lighted lamp represented the life of an individual (Job 18:6; Ps 132:17). God promised that from the tribe of Judah David would continue to have descendants ruling in Jerusalem (cf. 2Sa 21:17; 1Ki 15:4; 2Ki 8:19).

desire, and you shall be king over Israel. 38 Then
it will be, that if you listen to all that I command
you and walk in My ways, and do what is right in
My sight by observing My statutes and My commandments, as My servant David did, then [A]I will
be with you and [B]build you an enduring house as I
built for David, and I will give Israel to you. 39 Thus
I will afflict the [a]descendants of David for this, but
not always.' " 40 Solomon sought therefore to put
Jeroboam to death; but Jeroboam arose and fled
to Egypt to [A]Shishak king of Egypt, and he was in
Egypt until the death of Solomon.

THE DEATH OF SOLOMON

41 [A]Now the rest of the acts of Solomon and
whatever he did, and his wisdom, are they not
written in the book of the acts of Solomon? 42 Thus
[A]the time that Solomon reigned in Jerusalem over
all Israel was forty years. 43 And Solomon [A]slept
with his fathers and was buried in the city of his
father David, and his son [B]Rehoboam reigned in
his place.

KING REHOBOAM ACTS FOOLISHLY

12 [A]Then Rehoboam went to Shechem, for all Israel had come to [B]Shechem to make him king.
2 Now [A]when Jeroboam the son of Nebat heard *of
it,* [a]he was living in Egypt (for he was yet in Egypt,
where he had fled from the presence of King Solomon). 3 Then they sent and called him, and Jeroboam
and all the assembly of Israel came and spoke to
Rehoboam, saying, 4 "[A]Your father made our yoke
hard; now therefore lighten the hard service of
your father and his heavy yoke which he put on
us, and we will serve you." 5 Then he said to them,
"[A]Depart [a]for three days, then return to me." So the
people departed.

6 King Rehoboam [A]consulted with the elders
who had [a]served his father Solomon while he was
still alive, saying, "How do you counsel *me* to answer this people?" 7 Then they spoke to him, saying,
"[A]If you will be a servant to this people today, and
will serve them and [a]grant them their petition,
and speak good words to them, then they will be
your servants forever." 8 But he forsook the counsel of the elders which they had given him, and
consulted with the young men who grew up with
him [a]and served him. 9 So he said to them, "What
counsel do you give that we may answer this people who have spoken to me, saying, 'Lighten the
yoke which your father put on us'?" 10 The young
men who grew up with him spoke to him, saying,
"Thus you shall say to this people who spoke to
you, saying, 'Your father made our yoke heavy,
now you make it lighter for us!' But you shall speak
to them, 'My little finger is thicker than my father's loins! 11 Whereas my father loaded you with
a heavy yoke, I will add to your yoke; my father
disciplined you with whips, but I will discipline
you with scorpions.' "
12 Then Jeroboam and all the people came to Rehoboam on the third day as the king had [a]directed,
saying, "[A]Return to me on the third day." 13 The king
answered the people harshly, for he forsook the
advice of the elders which they had [a]given him,
14 and he spoke to them according to the advice
of the young men, saying, "[A]My father made your
yoke heavy, but I will add to your yoke; my father
disciplined you with whips, but I will discipline you
with scorpions." 15 So the king did not listen to the
people; [A]for it was a turn *of events* from the LORD,
[B]that He might establish His word, which the LORD
spoke through Ahijah the Shilonite to Jeroboam the
son of Nebat.

11:38 [A]Deut 31:8; Josh 1:5 [B]2 Sam 7:11, 27 11:39 [a]Lit *seed* 11:40 [A]1 Kin 14:25; 2 Chr 12:2-9 11:41 [A]2 Chr 9:29 11:42 [A]2 Chr 9:30 11:43 [A]1 Kin 2:10; 2 Chr 9:31 [B]1 Kin 14:21; Matt 1:7 12:1 [A]2 Chr 10:1 [B]Judg 9:6 12:2 [a]Lit *Jeroboam* [A]1 Kin 11:26, 40 12:4 [A]1 Sam 8:11-18; 1 Kin 4:7, 21-25; 9:15 12:5 [a]Lit *yet three* [A]1 Kin 12:12 12:6 [a]Lit *stood before* [A]1 Kin 4:1-6; Job 12:12; 32:7 12:7 [a]Lit *answer them* [A]2 Chr 10:7; Prov 15:1 12:8 [a]Lit *who stood before* 12:12 [a]Lit *spoken* [A]1 Kin 12:5 12:13 [a]Lit *advised* 12:14 [A]Ex 1:13, 14; 5:5-9, 16-18 12:15 [A]Deut 2:30; Judg 14:4; 1 Kin 12:24; 2 Chr 10:15 [B]1 Kin 11:11, 31

11:38 if you listen to all that I command you. The Lord gave to Jeroboam the same promise that He had made to David—an enduring royal dynasty over Israel, the 10 northern tribes, if he obeyed God's law. The Lord imposed on Jeroboam the same conditions for his kingship that He had imposed on David (2:3, 4; 3:14).

11:39 but not always. This statement implied that the kingdom's division was not to be permanent and that David's house would ultimately rule all the tribes of Israel again (cf. Eze 37:15–28).

11:40 put Jeroboam to death. Though the prophecy was private (v. 29), the king heard about it and Jeroboam became a marked man, guilty in Solomon's eyes of rebellion and worthy of the death penalty. **Shishak.** Shishak was the founder of the 22nd dynasty in Egypt. He reigned ca. 945–924 B.C. He invaded Judah during the reign of Rehoboam (14:25, 26).

11:42 forty years. 971–931 B.C.

12:1–2Ki 17:41 The division of Solomon's kingdom had been predicted by the Lord to Solomon (11:11–13) and through Ahijah to Jeroboam (11:29–37). This section of the books of Kings shows how the Word of the Lord through the prophet was fulfilled and narrates the history of the divided kingdom, Israel (the northern kingdom) and Judah (the southern kingdom), from 931–722 B.C.

12:1–14:31 This section describes the disruption of the Kingdom (12:1–24) plus the establishment and royal sanctioning of idolatry in Israel (12:25–14:20) and Judah (14:21–31). The reigns of Solomon's son, Rehoboam, in the S (ca. 931–913 B.C.) and Solomon's servant, Jeroboam, in the N (ca. 931–910 B.C.) are discussed. See 2Ch 10:1–12:16.

12:1 Shechem. A city located in the hill country of northern Ephraim, 30 mi. N of Jerusalem. Shechem had a long and important history as a political and religious center (cf. Ge 12:6; Jos 8:30–35; 24:1–28, 32). **all Israel.** The representatives of the 10 northern tribes assembled to accept Rehoboam as king (cf. 2Sa 5:3).

12:2 heard *of it*. Jeroboam, in Egypt (11:40), learned about the death of Solomon (11:43).

12:3 Jeroboam ... spoke. The 10 northern tribes summoned Jeroboam from Egypt to become their representative and spokesman in their dealings with Rehoboam.

12:4 yoke. The hardships that resulted from Solomon's policy of compulsory labor service (cf. 5:13; 9:22; 11:28) and excessive taxes (cf. 4:7) came because the splendor of his courts, the magnitude of his wealth, and the profits of his enterprises were not enough to sustain his demands.

12:6, 7 the elders. These were older, experienced counselors and administrators who had served Solomon. They counseled Rehoboam to give concessions to the 10 tribes.

12:8–10 the young men. The contemporaries of Rehoboam, about forty years of age (cf. 14:21), who were acquainted only with the royal court life of Solomon, recommended that Rehoboam be even harsher on the 10 tribes than was Solomon.

12:10 My little finger ... my father's loins! A proverbial manner of saying he was going to come at them with greater force than Solomon had exhibited (vv. 11–14).

12:15 from the LORD. God sovereignly used the foolishness of Rehoboam to fulfill Ahijah's prophecy (11:29–39).

THE KINGDOM DIVIDED; JEROBOAM RULES ISRAEL

16 When all Israel *saw* that the king did not listen to them, the people answered the king, saying,

"What portion do we have in David?
We have no inheritance in
the son of Jesse;
[A]To your tents, O Israel!
Now look after your own house, David!"

So Israel departed to their tents. 17 But [A]as for the
sons of Israel who lived in the cities of Judah, Rehoboam reigned over them. 18 Then King Rehoboam
sent [A]Adoram, who was over the forced labor, and
all Israel stoned him [a]to death. And King Rehoboam
made haste to mount his chariot to flee to Jerusalem. 19 [A]So Israel has been in rebellion against the
house of David to this day.
20 It came about when all Israel heard that Jeroboam had returned, that they sent and called him
to the assembly and made him king over all Israel.
[A]None but the tribe of Judah followed the house
of David.
21 [A]Now when Rehoboam had come to Jerusalem, he assembled all the house of Judah and the
tribe of Benjamin, 180,000 chosen men who were
warriors, to fight against the house of Israel to

12:16 [A]2 Sam 20:1 12:17 [A]1 Kin 11:13, 36 12:18 [a]Lit *with stones that he died* [A]2 Sam 20:24; 1 Kin 4:6; 5:14 12:19 [A]2 Kin 17:21 12:20 [A]1 Kin 11:13, 32, 36 12:21 [A]2 Chr 11:1

12:16 David. These words of Israel (v. 16) expressed deliberate, willful rebellion against the dynasty of David (cf. v. 19). Defiantly, the Israelites quoted the rallying cry used in Sheba's failed rebellion against David (2Sa 20:1). The northern tribes declared that they had no legal tie with David and went their way.

12:17 the sons of Israel. People from the northern tribes who had migrated S and settled in Judah.

12:18 Adoram. Sending the chief of taxation and forced labor (Adoniram in 4:6; 5:14) to negotiate with the northern tribes was foolish (cf. v. 4).

12:19 to this day. *See note on 8:8.*

12:20–24 The kingdom was divided at that point. Israel (the northern 10 tribes) had its own king.

12:21 the tribe of Benjamin. The tribe of Benjamin had split loyalty and land during the divided-kingdom era. According to v. 20, only the tribe of Judah remained completely loyal to the house of David, but in vv. 21, 23 it is said that Benjamin was associated with "all

THE KINGS OF THE DIVIDED KINGDOM

Judah		Israel	
Rehoboam	931–913	Jeroboam I	931–910
Abijah (Abijam)	913–911	Nadab	910–909
Asa	911–870	Baasha	909–886
		Elah	886–885
		Zimri	885
		Tibni	885–880
Jehoshaphat	873–848	Omri	885–874
		Ahab	874–853
		Ahaziah	853–852
Jehoram (Joram)	853–841	Joram (Jehoram)	852–841
Ahaziah	841	Jehu	841–814
Athaliah (queen)	841–835		
Joash (Jehoash)	835–796		
		Jehoahaz	814–798
Amaziah	796–767	Jehoash (Joash)	798–782
Azariah (Uzziah)	790–739	Jeroboam II	793–753
Jotham	750–731	Zechariah	753
		Shallum	752
Ahaz	735–715	Menahem	752–742
		Pekahiah	742–740
Hezekiah	715–686	Pekah	752–732
		Hoshea	732–722
Manasseh	695–642		
Amon	642–640		
Josiah	640–609		
Jehoahaz	609		
Jehoiakim	609–597		
Jehoiachin	597		
Zedekiah	597–586		

restore the kingdom to Rehoboam the son of Solomon. 22 But the word of God came to [A]Shemaiah the man of God, saying, 23 "Speak to Rehoboam the son of Solomon, king of Judah, and to all the house of Judah and Benjamin and to the [A]rest of the people, saying, 24 'Thus says the LORD, "You must not go up and fight against your [a]relatives the sons of Israel; return every man to his house, [A]for this thing has come from Me." ' " So they listened to the word of the LORD, and returned and went *their way* according to the word of the LORD.

JEROBOAM'S IDOLATRY

25 Then [A]Jeroboam built Shechem in the hill country of Ephraim, and lived [a]there. And he went out from there and built [B]Penuel. 26 Jeroboam said in his heart, "Now the kingdom will return to the house of David. 27 [A]If this people go up to offer sacrifices in the house of the LORD at Jerusalem, then the heart of this people will return to their lord, *even* to Rehoboam king of Judah; and they will kill me and return to Rehoboam king of Judah." 28 So the king [a]consulted, and [A]made two golden [B]calves, and he said to them, "It is too much for you to go up to Jerusalem; [C]behold your gods, O Israel, that brought you up from the land of Egypt." 29 He set [A]one in [B]Bethel, and the other he put in [C]Dan. 30 Now [A]this thing became a sin, for the people went *to worship* before the one as far as Dan. 31 And [A]he made houses on high places, and [B]made priests from among [a]all the people who were not of the sons of Levi. 32 Jeroboam [a]instituted a feast in the eighth month on the fifteenth day of the month, [A]like the feast which is in Judah, and he [b]went up to the altar; thus he did in Bethel, sacrificing to the calves which he had made. And he stationed in Bethel [B]the priests of the high places which he had made. 33 Then he [a]went up to the altar which he had made in Bethel on the fifteenth day in the eighth month, even in the month which he had [b,A]devised [c]in his own heart; and he [b]instituted a feast for the sons of Israel and [a]went up to the altar [B]to burn [d]incense.

JEROBOAM WARNED, STRICKEN

13 Now behold, there came [A]a man of God from Judah to Bethel by the word of the LORD, while Jeroboam was standing by the altar [B]to burn incense. 2 [A]He cried against the altar by the word of the LORD, and said, "O altar, altar, thus says the LORD, 'Behold, a son shall be born to the house of David, [B]Josiah by name; and on you he shall sacrifice the priests of the high places who burn incense on you, and human bones shall be burned on you.' " 3 Then he gave a [a]sign the same day, saying, "[A]This is the [a]sign which the LORD has spoken, 'Behold, the altar shall be split apart and the [b]ashes which are on it

12:22 [A]2 Chr 11:2; 12:5-7 12:23 [A]1 Kin 12:17 12:24 [a]Lit *brothers* [A]1 Kin 12:15 12:25 [a]Lit *in it* [A]Gen 12:6; Judg 9:45-49 [B]Gen 32:30, 31; Judg 8:8, 17 12:27 [A]Deut 12:5-7, 14 12:28 [a]Lit *took counsel* [A]2 Kin 10:29; 17:16; Hos 8:4-7 [B]Hos 10:5 [C]Ex 32:4, 8 12:29 [A]Hos 10:5 [B]Gen 28:19 [C]Judg 18:26-31 12:30 [A]1 Kin 13:34; 2 Kin 17:21 12:31 [a]Or *extremities of* [A]1 Kin 13:32 [B]1 Kin 13:33; 2 Kin 17:32; 2 Chr 11:15; 13:9 12:32 [a]Lit *made* [b]Or *offered upon* [A]Lev 23:33, 34; Num 29:12; 1 Kin 8:2, 5 [B]Amos 7:10-13 12:33 [a]Or *offered upon* [b]Lit *made* [c]Lit *from* [d]Or *sacrifices* [A]Num 15:39 [B]1 Kin 13:1 13:1 [A]1 Kin 12:22; 2 Kin 23:17 [B]1 Kin 12:33 13:2 [A]1 Kin 13:32 [B]2 Kin 23:15, 16 13:3 [a]Lit *wonder* [b]Lit *ashes of fat* [A]Ex 4:1-5; Judg 6:17; Is 38:7; John 2:18; 1 Cor 1:22

the house of Judah," the emphasis being on the tribe of Judah. Certain towns of northern Benjamin, most notably Bethel (v. 29), were included in the northern kingdom. Simeon, the tribe originally given land in the southern section of Judah's territory (Jos 19:1–9), had apparently migrated N and was counted with the 10 northern tribes (cf. 1Ch 12:23–25; 2Ch 15:9; 34:6). Thus, the 10 northern tribes were Reuben, Simeon, Zebulun, Issachar, Dan, Gad, Asher, Naphtali, Manasseh, and Ephraim. The southern kingdom was the tribe of Judah only. The 12th tribe, Benjamin, was split between the two kingdoms. The tribe of Levi, originally scattered throughout both kingdoms (Jos 21:1–42), resided in Judah during the divided kingdom (see 2Ch 11:13–16).

12:22 the man of God. Cf. 17:24. A common OT expression designating a man with a message from God who would speak authoritatively on the Lord's behalf (cf. Deut 33:1; 2Ti 3:17). *See note on Dt 33:1.*

12:24 this thing has come from Me. Through the prophet Shemaiah, the Lord commanded Rehoboam and his army not to invade Israel. God, in judgment, had ordained the N-S split (v. 15; 11:29–39), so to attack Israel was to oppose God Himself.

12:25 Shechem. Cf. v. 1. Jeroboam fortified the city of Shechem and made it into his royal residence. Cf. Jdg 9:1–47. **Penuel.** Jeroboam also fortified Penuel, a city about 10 mi. E of the Jordan River on the River Jabbok, asserting his sovereignty over the Israelites E of the Jordan.

12:26 return to the house of David. The Lord had ordained a political, not a religious, division of Solomon's kingdom. The Lord had promised Jeroboam political control of the 10 northern tribes (11:31, 35, 37). However, Jeroboam was to religiously follow the Mosaic law, which demanded that he follow the Lord's sacrificial system at the temple in Jerusalem (11:38). Having received the kingdom from God, he should have relied on divine protection, but he did not. Seeking to keep his subjects from being influenced by Rehoboam when they went to Jerusalem to worship, he set up worship in the north (vv. 27, 28).

12:28 two golden calves. These two calves, probably made of wood overlaid with gold, were presented to Israel as pedestals on which the Lord supposedly sat or stood. He publicly presented them with the very words with which idolatrous Israel had welcomed Aaron's golden calf. He repeated Aaron's destructive sin of trying to make an earthly image of God. *See note on Ex 32:4.*

12:29 Bethel ... Dan. Bethel was located about 11 mi. N of Jerusalem within the territory of Benjamin (Jos 18:11–13, 22). It lay at the southern end of Jeroboam's kingdom on the main N-S road to Jerusalem. Israel had long revered Bethel as a sacred place because Jacob had worshiped there (Ge 28:10–22; 35:1–15). Dan was located in the northernmost part of Jeroboam's kingdom, about 25 mi. N of the Sea of Galilee. A paganized worship of the Lord was practiced at Dan during the period of the judges (Jdg 18:30, 31).

12:30 this thing became a sin. Jeroboam's policy promoted gross and flagrant violation of the second commandment (Ex 20:4–6) and led to violation of the first commandment (Ex 20:3).

12:31 high places. Jeroboam built minor sanctuaries on high places throughout the land of Israel. Over the centuries these high places became the breeding ground of Israel's idolatrous apostasy (cf. Hos 5:1). *See note on 3:2.* **priests.** Jeroboam appointed priests to run his sanctuaries from all his tribes. His action blatantly violated the stipulation that only Aaron's descendants were to hold that office in Israel (Nu 3:10).

12:32 instituted a feast. Jeroboam instituted a religious festival to compete with the Feast of Booths held at the temple in Jerusalem and scheduled it for the 15th day of the 8th month (Oct./Nov.), exactly one month after its divinely ordained Judean counterpart (Ex 34:22, 23; Lv 23:33–36, 39, 40).

13:1 man of God. *See note on 12:22.*

13:2 Josiah. He ruled Judah about 300 years later ca. 640–609 B.C. (cf. 2Ki 22:1–23:30). **sacrifice the priests of the high places.** The prophet predicted that Josiah would slaughter the illegitimate priests of the high places of his day who made offerings on the altar at Bethel. This prophecy was realized in 2Ki 23:15–20, executing the divine judgment on the non-Levitical priesthood established by Jeroboam (12:31, 32).

13:3 sign. An immediate "wonder" that served to authenticate the reliability of the long-term prediction (cf. Dt 18:21, 22), this sign came to pass in v. 5. **the ashes ... shall be poured out.** Proper ritual required the disposal of sacrificial ashes in a special "clean" place (Lv 4:12; 6:10, 11). Contact with the ground would render the ashes "unclean" and nullify the procedure.

shall be poured out.' " 4 Now when the king heard
the saying of the man of God, which he cried against
the altar in Bethel, Jeroboam stretched out his hand
from the altar, saying, "Seize him." But his hand
which he stretched out against him dried up, so that
he could not draw it back to himself. 5 The altar also
was split apart and the [a]ashes were poured out from
the altar, according to the [b]sign which the man of
God had given by the word of the LORD. 6 The king
said to the man of God, "Please [a,A]entreat the LORD
your God, and pray for me, that my hand may be
restored to me." So [B]the man of God [b]entreated the
LORD, and the king's hand was restored to him, and
it became as it was before. 7 Then the king said to
the man of God, "Come home with me and refresh
yourself, and [A]I will give you a reward." 8 But the
man of God said to the king, "[A]If you were to give
me half your house I would not go with you, nor
would I eat bread or drink water in this place. 9 For
so [a]it was commanded me by the word of the LORD,
saying, 'You shall eat no bread, nor drink water, nor
return by the way which you came.' " 10 So he went
another way and did not return by the way which
he came to Bethel.

THE DISOBEDIENT PROPHET

11 Now [A]an old prophet was living in Bethel; and
his [a]sons came and told him all the deeds which the
man of God had done that day in Bethel; the words
which he had spoken to the king, these also they
related to their father. 12 Their father said to them,
"[a]Which way did he go?" Now his sons [b]had seen
the way which the man of God who came from Judah had gone. 13 Then he said to his sons, "Saddle
the donkey for me." So they saddled the donkey for
him and he rode away on it. 14 So he went after the
man of God and found him sitting under [a]an oak;
and he said to him, "Are you the man of God who
came from Judah?" And he said, "I am." 15 Then he
said to him, "Come home with me and eat bread."
16 He said, "[A]I cannot return with you, nor go with
you, nor will I eat bread or drink water with you
in this place. 17 For a command *came* to me [A]by the
word of the LORD, 'You shall eat no bread, nor drink
water there; do not return by going the way which
you came.' " 18 He said to him, "[A]I also am a prophet
like you, and [B]an angel spoke to me by the word of
the LORD, saying, 'Bring him back with you to your
house, that he may eat bread and drink water.' " *But*
[C]he lied to him. 19 So he went back with him, and ate
bread in his house and drank water.

20 Now it came about, as they were sitting down
at the table, that the word of the LORD came to the
prophet who had brought him back; 21 and he cried
to the man of God who came from Judah, saying,
"Thus says the LORD, 'Because you have [a]disobeyed
the [b]command of the LORD, and have not observed
the commandment which the LORD your God commanded you, 22 but have returned and eaten bread
and drunk water in the place of which He said to
you, "Eat no bread and drink no water"; your body
shall not come to the grave of your fathers.' " 23 It
came about after he had eaten bread and after he
had drunk, that he saddled the donkey for him, for
the prophet whom he had brought back. 24 Now
when he had gone, [A]a lion met him on the way and
killed him, and his body was thrown on the road,
with the donkey standing beside it; the lion also
was standing beside the body. 25 And behold, men
passed by and saw the body thrown on the road,
and the lion standing beside the body; so they came
and told *it* in the city where [A]the old prophet lived.

26 Now when the prophet who brought him back
from the way heard *it,* he said, "It is the man of God,
who [a]disobeyed the [b]command of the LORD; therefore the LORD has given him to the lion, which has
torn him and killed him, according to the word of the
LORD which He spoke to him." 27 Then he spoke to his
sons, saying, "Saddle the donkey for me." And they
saddled *it.* 28 He went and found his body thrown on
the road with the donkey and the lion standing beside
the body; the lion had not eaten the body nor torn
the donkey. 29 So the prophet took up the body of the
man of God and laid it on the donkey and brought
it back, and he came to the city of the old prophet to
mourn and to bury him. 30 He laid his body in his own
grave, and they mourned over him, *saying,* "[A]Alas,
my brother!" 31 After he had buried him, he spoke to
his sons, saying, "When I die, bury me in the grave in
which the man of God is buried; [A]lay my bones beside

13:5 [a]Lit *ashes of fat* [b]Lit *wonder* 13:6 [a]Lit *soften the face of* [b]Lit *softened the face of* [A]Ex 8:8, 28; 9:28; 10:17; Acts 8:24; James 5:16 [B]Luke 6:27, 28 13:7 [A]1 Sam 9:7, 8; 2 Kin 5:15 13:8 [A]Num 22:18; 24:13; 1 Kin 13:16, 17 13:9 [a]Lit *he commanded me* 13:11 [a]Lit *son* [A]1 Kin 13:25; 2 Kin 23:18 13:12 [a]Lit *Where is the way he went* [b]Some ancient versions read *showed him* 13:14 [a]Or *a terebinth* 13:16 [A]1 Kin 13:8, 9 13:17 [A]1 Kin 20:35 13:18 [A]Matt 7:15; 1 John 4:1 [B]Gal 1:8 [C]Prov 12:19, 22; 19:5; Jer 29:31, 32; Ezek 13:8, 9; 1 Tim 4:1, 2 13:21 [a]Lit *rebelled* against [b]Lit *mouth* 13:24 [A]1 Kin 20:36 13:25 [A]1 Kin 13:11 13:26 [a]Lit *rebelled* against [b]Lit *mouth* 13:30 [A]Jer 22:18 13:31 [A]Ruth 1:17; 2 Kin 23:17, 18

13:9 commanded me by the word of the LORD. The prophet's divine commission expressly forbade receiving any hospitality at Bethel. It even required him to return home by a different route from the one by which he came, lest he should be recognized. The prophet's own conduct was to symbolize the Lord's total rejection of Israel's false worship and the recognition that all the people had become apostates.

13:11 an old prophet. Here was a spokesman for the Lord who had compromised his ministry by his willingness to live at the very center of the false system of worship without speaking out against it.

13:18 he lied to him. Why the old prophet deceived the man of God the text does not state. It may be that his own sons were worshipers at Bethel or perhaps priests, and this man wanted to gain favor with the king by showing up the man of God as an imposter who acted contrary to his own claim to have heard from God. Accustomed to receiving direct revelations, the Judean prophet should have regarded the supposed angelic message with suspicion and sought divine verification of this revised order.

13:20 the word of the LORD. The lie arose from his own imagination (cf. Jer 23:16; Eze 13:2, 7), but the true prophecy came from the Lord (cf. Ex 4:16; Dt 18:18; Jer 1:9).

13:22 your body shall not come to the grave of your fathers. Israelites buried their dead with the bones of ancestors in a common grave (Jdg 8:32; 2Sa 2:32). The lack of such a burial was considered in Israel a severe punishment and disgrace. *See note on Ecc 6:3–6.*

13:24 donkey . . . lion. Both the donkey and the lion acted unnaturally: the donkey did not run and the lion did not attack the donkey or disturb the man's body. Unlike the disobedient prophet, the beasts bent their wills to God's sovereignty.

his bones. 32 [A]For the thing shall surely come to pass
which he cried by the word of the LORD against the
altar in Bethel and [B]against all the houses of the high
places which are in the cities of [C]Samaria."
33 After this event Jeroboam did not return from
his evil way, but [A]again he made priests of the high
places from among [a]all the people; [B]any who would,
he ordained, to be priests of the high places. 34 [a,A]This
event became sin to the house of Jeroboam, [B]even
to blot *it* out and destroy *it* from off the face of the
earth.

AHIJAH PROPHESIES AGAINST THE KING

14 At that time Abijah the son of Jeroboam became sick. 2 Jeroboam said to his wife, "Arise
now, and [A]disguise yourself so that they will not
know that you are the wife of Jeroboam, and go to
[B]Shiloh; behold, Ahijah the prophet is there, who
[C]spoke concerning me *that I would be* king over this
people. 3 [A]Take ten loaves with you, *some* cakes and
a jar of honey, and go to him. He will tell you what
will happen to the boy."
4 Jeroboam's wife did so, and arose and went to
[A]Shiloh, and came to the house of [B]Ahijah. Now Ahijah could not see, [C]for his eyes were [a]dim because of
his age. 5 Now the LORD had said to Ahijah, "Behold,
the wife of Jeroboam is coming to [a]inquire of you
concerning her son, for he is sick. You shall say thus
and thus to her, for it will be when she arrives that
[A]she will pretend to be another woman."
6 When Ahijah heard the sound of her feet coming
in the doorway, he said, "Come in, wife of Jeroboam,
why do you pretend to be another woman? For I am
sent to you *with* a harsh *message*. 7 Go, say to Jeroboam, 'Thus says the LORD God of Israel, "[A]Because
I exalted you from among the people and made you
leader over My people Israel, 8 and [A]tore the kingdom away from the house of David and gave it to
you—[B]yet you have not been like My servant David,
who kept My commandments and who followed
Me with all his heart, [C]to do only that which was
right in My sight; 9 you also have done more evil
than all who were before you, and [A]have gone and
made for yourself other gods and [B]molten images
to provoke Me to anger, and have [C]cast Me behind
your back— 10 therefore behold, I am bringing calamity on the house of Jeroboam, and [A]will cut off
from Jeroboam [a]every male person, [B]both bond and
free in Israel, and I [C]will make a clean sweep of the
house of Jeroboam, as one sweeps away dung until
it is all gone. 11 [A]Anyone belonging to Jeroboam who
dies in the city the dogs will eat. And he who dies
in the field the birds of the heavens will eat; for
the LORD has spoken *it*." ' 12 Now you, arise, go to
your house. [A]When your feet enter the city the child
will die. 13 All Israel shall mourn for him and bury
him, for [a]he alone of Jeroboam's *family* will come
to the grave, because in him [A]something good was
found toward the LORD God of Israel in the house
of Jeroboam. 14 Moreover, [A]the LORD will raise up
for Himself a king over Israel who will cut off the
house of Jeroboam this day [a]and from now on.
15 "For the LORD will strike Israel, as a reed is
shaken in the water; and [A]He will uproot Israel from
[B]this good land which He gave to their fathers, and
[C]will scatter them beyond the *Euphrates* River, [D]be-
cause they have made their [a]Asherim, provoking the
LORD to anger. 16 He will give up Israel [A]on account
of the sins of Jeroboam, which he [a]committed and
with which he made Israel to sin."
17 Then Jeroboam's wife arose and departed and
came to [A]Tirzah. [B]As she was entering the threshold of the house, the child died. 18 [A]All Israel buried
him and mourned for him, according to the word
of the LORD which He spoke through His servant
Ahijah the prophet.
19 Now the rest of the acts of Jeroboam, [A]how he
made war and how he reigned, behold, they are
written in the Book of the Chronicles of the Kings

13:32 [A]1 Kin 13:2 [B]Lev 26:30; 1 Kin 12:31 [C]1 Kin 16:24; John 4:5; Acts 8:14 13:33 [a]Or *extremities of* [A]1 Kin 12:31, 32 [B]Judg 17:5 13:34 [a]Lit *by this thing he became* [A]1 Kin 12:30; 2 Kin 17:21 [B]1 Kin 14:10; 15:29, 30 14:2 [A]1 Sam 28:8; 2 Sam 14:2; 2 Chr 18:29 [B]Josh 18:1 [C]1 Kin 11:29-31 14:3 [A]1 Sam 9:7, 8; 1 Kin 13:7; 2 Kin 4:42 14:4 [a]Lit *set* [A]1 Kin 14:2 [B]1 Kin 11:29 [C]1 Sam 3:2; 4:15 14:5 [a]Lit *seek a word from* [A]2 Sam 14:2 14:7 [A]2 Sam 12:7; 1 Kin 11:28-31; 16:2 14:8 [A]1 Kin 11:31 [B]1 Kin 11:33, 38 [C]1 Kin 15:5 14:9 [A]1 Kin 12:28; 2 Chr 11:15 [B]Ex 34:17 [C]Neh 9:26; Ps 50:17; Ezek 23:35 14:10 [a]Lit *him who urinates against the wall* [A]1 Kin 21:21; 2 Kin 9:8 [B]Deut 32:36; 2 Kin 14:26 [C]1 Kin 15:29 14:11 [A]1 Kin 16:4; 21:24 14:12 [A]1 Kin 14:17 14:13 [a]Lit *the one* [A]2 Chr 19:3 14:14 [a]Lit *and what even now?* [A]1 Kin 15:27-29 14:15 [a]I.e. wooden symbols of a female deity [A]Deut 29:28; 2 Kin 17:6; Ps 52:5 [B]Josh 23:15, 16 [C]2 Kin 15:29 [D]Ex 34:13, 14; Deut 12:3, 4 14:16 [a]Lit *sinned* [A]1 Kin 12:30; 13:34; 15:30, 34; 16:2 14:17 [A]1 Kin 15:21, 33; 16:6-9, 15, 23; Song 6:4 [B]1 Kin 14:12 14:18 [A]1 Kin 14:13 14:19 [A]1 Kin 14:30; 2 Chr 13:2-20

13:32 shall surely come to pass. The old prophet instructed his sons to bury him beside the Judean prophet (v. 31). The old prophet was finally willing to identify himself with the message that the man of God from Judah had given against worship at Bethel.

13:33 again he made priests. Unlike the old prophet, Jeroboam did not change his evil ways, but continued appointing priests outside the tribe of Levi to serve the high places (12:30–32).

14:1 At that time. Probably indicating a time shortly after the incident recorded in chap. 13. **Abijah.** Meaning "my father is the Lord," Jeroboam's son's name implies that his father desired to be regarded as a worshiper of the Lord at the time of his son's birth. Abijah was referred to as a "child" (vv. 12, 17), a term which can be used from childhood through young adulthood. Of all of Jeroboam's family, Abijah was the most responsive to the Lord (v. 13). Jeroboam's son, Abijah, should not be confused with Rehoboam's son of the same name (*see note on 15:1–8*).

14:2 disguise yourself. Probably for the avoidance of recognition by the people. Jeroboam did not want his subjects to know that he was consulting a prophet of the Lord. **Shiloh.** *See note on 11:29.*

14:3 Take ten loaves. A simple ordinary food gift added to the disguise (cf. 1Sa 9:7, 8; 2Ki 8:8). Ten loaves of bread, some cakes, and a jar of honey reflected the means of a common person, not royalty.

14:9 more evil. Jeroboam had not only failed to live up to the standard of David, but his wickedness had surpassed even that of Saul and Solomon. He had installed a paganized system of worship for the entire population of the northern kingdom (cf. 16:25, 30; 2Ki 21:11).

14:11 dogs … birds. The covenant curse of Dt 28:26 was applied to Jeroboam's male descendants.

14:13 the grave. *See note on 13:22.*

14:14 a king. I.e., Baasha (15:27–30).

14:15 Ahijah announced God's stern judgment on Israel for joining Jeroboam's apostasy. Struck by the Lord, Israel would sway like a reed in a rushing river, a biblical metaphor for political instability (cf. Mt 11:7; Lk 7:24). One day, the Lord would uproot Israel from Palestinian soil and scatter it in exile E of the Euphrates. The fulfillment of this prophecy is recorded in 2Ki 17:23.

14:17 Tirzah. Jeroboam had apparently moved his capital from Shechem to Tirzah (cf. 12:25), located in the tribal region of Manasseh, about 7 mi. NE of Shechem and 35 mi. N of Jerusalem. Tirzah was famous for its beauty (SS 6:4).

of Israel. 20 The time that Jeroboam reigned *was*
twenty-two years; and he slept with his fathers,
and Nadab his son reigned in his place.

REHOBOAM MISLEADS JUDAH

21 [A]Now Rehoboam the son of Solomon reigned
in Judah. Rehoboam was forty-one years old when
he became king, and he reigned seventeen years in
Jerusalem, [B]the city which the LORD had chosen from
all the tribes of Israel to put His name there. And
his mother's name was Naamah the Ammonitess.
22 [A]Judah did evil in the sight of the LORD, and they
[B]provoked Him to jealousy more than all that their
fathers had done, with [a]the sins which they [b]commit-
ted. 23 For they also built for themselves [A]high places
and *sacred* [B]pillars and [a,C]Asherim on every high hill
and [D]beneath every luxuriant tree. 24 There were also
[A]male cult prostitutes in the land. They did according
to all the abominations of the nations which the LORD
dispossessed before the sons of Israel.
25 [A]Now it happened in the fifth year of King Rehoboam, that Shishak the king of Egypt came up
against Jerusalem. 26 He took away the treasures
of the house of the LORD and the treasures of the
king's house, and [A]he took everything, [a,B]even taking
all the shields of gold which Solomon had made.
27 So King Rehoboam made shields of bronze in
their place, and [A]committed them to the [a]care of
the commanders of the [b]guard who guarded the
doorway of the king's house. 28 Then it happened
as often as the king entered the house of the LORD,
that the [a]guards would carry them and would bring
them back into the [a]guards' room.
29 [A]Now the rest of the acts of Rehoboam and all
that he did, are they not written in the Book of the
Chronicles of the Kings of Judah? 30 [A]There was
war between Rehoboam and Jeroboam continually.
31 And Rehoboam slept with his fathers and was
buried with his fathers in the city of David; and [A]his
mother's name was Naamah the Ammonitess. And
Abijam his son became king in his place.

ABIJAM REIGNS OVER JUDAH

15 [A]Now in the eighteenth year of King Jeroboam,
the son of Nebat, Abijam became king over
Judah. 2 He reigned three years in Jerusalem; and
his mother's name was [a,A]Maacah the daughter of
[b,B]Abishalom. 3 He walked in all the sins of his father
which he had committed before him; and [A]his heart
was not [a]wholly devoted to the LORD his God, like
the heart of his father David. 4 But for David's sake
the LORD his God gave him a [A]lamp in Jerusalem, to
raise up his son after him and to establish Jerusalem;
5 [A]because David did what was right in the sight of the
LORD, and had not turned aside from anything that
He commanded him all the days of his life, [B]except
in the case of Uriah the Hittite. 6 [A]There was war between Rehoboam and Jeroboam all the days of his life.
7 Now [A]the rest of the acts of Abijam and all that
he did, are they not written in the Book of the Chronicles of the Kings of Judah? [B]And there was war
between Abijam and Jeroboam.

ASA SUCCEEDS ABIJAM

8 [A]And Abijam slept with his fathers and they
buried him in the city of David; and Asa his son
became king in his place.
9 So in the twentieth year of Jeroboam the king
of Israel, Asa began to reign as king of Judah. 10 He
reigned forty-one years in Jerusalem; and [A]his mother's name was Maacah the daughter of Abishalom.
11 [A]Asa did what was right in the sight of the LORD,
like David his father. 12 [A]He also put away the male cult
prostitutes from the land and [B]removed all the idols
which his fathers had made. 13 [a,A]He also removed Maacah his mother from *being* queen mother, because
she had made a horrid image [b]as an Asherah; and
Asa cut down her horrid image and [B]burned *it* at the

14:21 [A]2 Chr 12:13 [B]1 Kin 11:32, 36 14:22 [a]Lit *their* [b]Lit *sinned* [A]2 Chr 12:1, 14 [B]Deut 32:21; Ps 78:58; 1 Cor 10:22 14:23 [a]I.e. wooden symbols of a female deity [A]Deut 12:2; Ezek 16:24 [B]Deut 16:22 [C]1 Kin 14:15 [D]2 Kin 17:10; Is 57:5; Jer 2:20 14:24 [A]Gen 19:5; Deut 23:17; 1 Kin 15:12; 22:46; 2 Kin 23:7 14:25 [A]1 Kin 11:40; 2 Chr 12:2, 9 14:26 [a]Lit *and he took away* [A]1 Kin 15:18; 2 Chr 12:9 [B]1 Kin 10:17; 2 Chr 9:15, 16 14:27 [a]Lit *hand* [b]Lit *runner* [A]1 Sam 8:11; 22:17 14:28 [a]Lit *runners* 14:29 [A]2 Chr 12:15, 16 14:30 [A]1 Kin 12:21; 15:6 14:31 [A]1 Kin 14:21 15:1 [A]2 Chr 13:1 15:2 [a]In 2 Chr 13:2, *Micaiah, the daughter of Uriel* [b]In 2 Chr 11:20, *Absalom* [A]2 Chr 13:2 [B]2 Chr 11:21 15:3 [a]Lit *complete with* [A]1 Kin 11:4; Ps 119:80 15:4 [A]2 Sam 21:17; 1 Kin 11:36; 2 Chr 21:7 15:5 [A]1 Kin 9:4; 14:8; Luke 1:6 [B]2 Sam 11:3f, 15-17; 12:9, 10 15:6 [A]1 Kin 14:30; 2 Chr 12:15-13:20 15:7 [A]2 Chr 13:2, 21, 22 [B]2 Chr 13:3-20 15:8 [A]2 Chr 14:1 15:10 [A]1 Kin 15:2 15:11 [A]2 Chr 14:2 15:12 [A]Deut 23:17; 1 Kin 14:24; 22:46 [B]1 Kin 11:7, 8; 14:23; 2 Chr 14:2-5 15:13 [a]Lit *also Maacah his mother and he removed her* [b]Or *for Asherah* [A]2 Chr 15:16-18 [B]Ex 32:20

14:20 twenty-two years. 931–910 B.C.

14:21 seventeen years. 931–913 B.C.

14:22–24 Judah outdid her ancestors in evil, provoking the Lord to jealous anger (v. 22). Signs of idolatrous practice were everywhere (vv. 23, 24). She even practiced sacred prostitution to promote fertility (v. 24). Judah had begun the downward slide toward doom that Israel was in.

14:25 fifth year. 927/926 B.C. **Shishak.** *See note on 11:40.*

14:27 shields of bronze. These bronze shields replaced Solomon's gold shields, which were used as a ransom paid to Shishak. The bronze shields illustrate the sharp decline from the reign of Solomon to Rehoboam.

14:30 war … continually. Many border skirmishes erupted as the armies in the N/S maneuvered for tactical advantage and control of territory (14:19; 15:6). A major battle ultimately erupted during the reign of Abijam (cf. 2Ch 13:1–20).

15:1–16:22 Having documented the establishment of idolatry in both Israel and Judah (12:1–14:31), the text moves to a quick survey of the kings of Judah and Israel from 913 to 885 B.C. The author notes that the high places remained in Judah (15:14), and the sins of Jeroboam continued in Israel (15:26, 34; 16:13, 19).

15:1–8 Abijam. He was at first called Abijah in 2Ch 13:1, 2. Since Abijam means "father of the sea," and Abijah, "my father is the Lord," he may have had his name changed because of his sin. *See notes on 2Ch 13:1–22.*

15:2 three years. 913–911 B.C. Parts of years were considered as whole years in this reckoning (cf. v. 9).

15:3 his heart was not wholly devoted. Cf. 11:4, where the same statement was made concerning Solomon. Cf. v. 14.

15:4 a lamp. *See note on 11:36.*

15:5 what was right in the sight of the LORD. This commendation is frequently used in speaking of kings of Judah and means only that they did or did not do what was generally acceptable to God, e.g., v. 11.

15:7 war. See 14:30; 2Ch 13:1–20.

15:9–24 Asa. He was the first of the religiously good kings of Judah (cf. v. 11). *See notes on 2Ch 14:1–16:14.*

15:10 forty-one years. 911–870 B.C.

15:11–15 Asa did 4 good things: 1) he removed the sacred prostitutes (v. 12); 2) he rid the land of all the idols made by his predecessors (v. 12); 3) he removed the corrupt queen mother and burned the idol she had made; and 4) he placed "dedicated things," items that he and his father had dedicated to the Lord, back in the temple (v. 15). Though he never engaged in idolatry, Asa's failure was his toleration of "the high places" (v. 14).

15:13 horrid image. This term is derived from the verb "to shudder" (Job 9:6). "Horrible, repulsive thing" suggests a shocking,

brook Kidron. 14 [A]But the high places were not taken
away; nevertheless [B]the heart of Asa was [a]wholly
devoted to the LORD all his days. 15 [A]He brought into
the house of the LORD the dedicated things of his
father and his own dedicated things: silver and gold
and utensils.
16 [A]Now there was war between Asa and Baasha king of Israel all their days. 17 [A]Baasha king of
Israel went up against Judah and [a,B]fortified Ramah [C]in order to prevent *anyone* from going out
or coming in to Asa king of Judah. 18 Then [A]Asa
took all the silver and the gold which were left in
the treasuries of the house of the LORD and the
treasuries of the king's house, and delivered them
into the hand of his servants. And [B]King Asa sent
them to Ben-hadad the son of Tabrimmon, the son
of Hezion, king of Aram, who lived in [C]Damascus,
saying, 19 "*Let there be* a [A]treaty between [a]you and
me, *as* between my father and your father. Behold, I
have sent you a present of silver and gold; go, break
your treaty with Baasha king of Israel so that he
will withdraw from me." 20 So Ben-hadad listened
to King Asa and sent the commanders of his armies
against the cities of Israel, and [a]conquered [A]Ijon,
[B]Dan, [C]Abel-beth-maacah and all [D]Chinneroth, besides all the land of Naphtali. 21 When Baasha heard
of it, [A]he ceased [a]fortifying Ramah and remained
in [B]Tirzah. 22 Then King Asa made a proclamation
to all Judah—none was exempt—and they carried
away the stones of Ramah and its timber with which
Baasha had built. And King Asa built with them
[A]Geba of Benjamin and Mizpah.

JEHOSHAPHAT SUCCEEDS ASA

23 [A]Now the rest of all the acts of Asa and all his
might and all that he did and the cities which he
built, are they not written in the Book of the Chronicles of the Kings of Judah? But in the time of his
old age he was diseased in his feet. 24 And Asa slept
with his fathers and was buried with his fathers in
the city of David his father; and [A]Jehoshaphat his
son reigned in his place.

NADAB, THEN BAASHA, RULES OVER ISRAEL

25 Now [A]Nadab the son of Jeroboam became king
over Israel in the second year of Asa king of Judah,
and he reigned over Israel two years. 26 He did evil
in the sight of the LORD, and [A]walked in the way of
his father and [B]in his sin which he made Israel sin.
27 Then [A]Baasha the son of Ahijah of the house of
Issachar conspired against him, and Baasha struck
him down at [B]Gibbethon, which belonged to the
Philistines, while Nadab and all Israel were laying
siege to Gibbethon.
28 So Baasha killed him in the third year of Asa
king of Judah and reigned in his place. 29 It came
about as soon as he was king, he struck down all
the household of Jeroboam. He did not leave to Jeroboam [a]any persons alive, until he had destroyed
them, [A]according to the word of the LORD, which
He spoke by His servant Ahijah the Shilonite, 30 *and*
because of the sins of Jeroboam which he sinned,
and [A]which he made Israel sin, because of his provocation with which he provoked the LORD God of
Israel to anger.
31 [A]Now the rest of the acts of Nadab and all that
he did, are they not written in the Book of the Chronicles of the Kings of Israel?

WAR WITH JUDAH

32 [A]There was war between Asa and Baasha king
of Israel all their days.
33 In the third year of Asa king of Judah, Baasha
the son of Ahijah became king over all Israel at Tirzah, *and reigned* twenty-four years. 34 He did evil
in the sight of the LORD, and [A]walked in the way of
Jeroboam and in his sin which he made Israel sin.

15:14 [a]Lit *complete with* [A]1 Kin 22:43; 2 Kin 12:3 [B]1 Kin 8:61; 15:3 15:15 [A]1 Kin 7:51 15:16 [A]1 Kin 15:32 15:17 [a]Lit *built* [A]2 Chr 16:1-6 [B]Josh 18:25; 1 Kin 15:21, 22 [C]1 Kin 12:26-29 15:18 [A]1 Kin 14:26; 15:15 [B]2 Kin 12:17, 18; 2 Chr 16:2 [C]Gen 14:15; 1 Kin 11:23, 24 15:19 [a]Lit *me and you* [A]2 Chr 16:7 15:20 [a]Lit *smote* [A]2 Kin 15:29 [B]Judg 18:29; 1 Kin 12:29 [C]2 Sam 20:15; 2 Kin 15:29 [D]Josh 11:2; 12:3 15:21 [a]Lit *building* [A]1 Kin 15:17 [B]1 Kin 14:17; 16:15-18 15:22 [A]Josh 18:24; 21:17 15:23 [A]2 Chr 16:11-14 15:24 [A]1 Kin 22:41-44; 2 Chr 17:1; Matt 1:8 15:25 [A]1 Kin 14:20 15:26 [A]1 Kin 12:28-33; 13:33, 34 [B]1 Kin 14:16; 15:30, 34 15:27 [A]1 Kin 14:14 [B]Josh 19:44; 21:23; 1 Kin 16:15 15:29 [a]Lit *any breath* [A]1 Kin 14:9-16 15:30 [A]1 Kin 15:26 15:31 [A]1 Kin 14:19 15:32 [A]1 Kin 15:16 15:34 [A]1 Kin 15:26

perhaps even a sexually explicit, idol. Asa removed his mother ("grandmother" in some translations), Maacah, the official queen mother, because of her association with this idol. **brook Kidron.** A seasonal river that ran through the Kidron Valley that marks the eastern boundary of Jerusalem.

15:16 Baasha. Asa, who ruled Judah (ca. 911–870 B.C.), enjoyed 10 years of peace after Jeroboam's defeat by Abijam (2Ch 13:19, 20) until Baasha began attacking. *See notes on 15:27–16:7; 2Ch 16:1–6.*

15:17 Ramah. A strategic town in Benjamin, located about 5 mi. N of Jerusalem along the main N-S highway, built by Baasha, king of Israel, to effectively blockade the city of Jerusalem.

15:18 Ben-hadad. Ben-hadad I, the grandson of Hezion (probably Rezon; *see note on 11:23–25*, ca. 940–915 B.C.) and the son of Tabrimmon (ca. 912–890 B.C.). He was the powerful ruler of the Syrian kingdom (Aramea; *see note on 10:29*), centered in Damascus. The majority of historians think that Ben-hadad reigned ca. 900–860 B.C. and was succeeded by a son or grandson, Ben-hadad II, who ruled ca. 860–841 B.C. (cf. 20:34). Asa sent a sizable gift to influence Ben-hadad I to break his treaty with Israel, enter instead a treaty with Judah, and invade Israel from the N.

15:20 Ijon ... Naphtali. The army of Ben-hadad I invaded Israel and took cities in the land N of the Sea of Galilee, a conquest giving Syria control of the trade routes to the Mediterranean coast and Israel's fertile Jezreel Valley, and also making Syria a great military threat to Israel. Baasha gave up fortifying Ramah and went to live in Tirzah, the capital of the northern kingdom.

15:22 Geba ... Mizpah. With the threat to Judah from Israel removed, Asa conscripted a Judean labor force to fortify Geba, about 6 mi. NE of Jerusalem, and Mizpah, about 7 mi. N of Jerusalem, using the very building material for those fortifications that Baasha had used at Ramah.

15:25 Nadab ... two years. 910–909 B.C.

15:27–16:7 Baasha. *See note on 15:16.*

15:27 Gibbethon. This city, located about 32 mi. W of Jerusalem, within the territory of Dan, was given to the Levites (Jos 19:44) but controlled by the Philistines, on whose border it lay.

15:29 he struck down all the household of Jeroboam. Baasha, the northern king, in a vicious practice too common in the ancient Near East, annihilated all of Jeroboam's family. This act fulfilled Ahijah's prophecy against Jeroboam (cf. 14:9–11). However, Baasha went beyond the words of the prophecy, since 14:10 specified judgment only on every male, while Baasha killed all men, women, and children.

15:30 This epitaph for wicked Jeroboam of Israel follows through the history of the northern kingdom relentlessly as the standard of sin by which judgment fell on the successive kings (see 15:34; 16:2, 19, 31; 22:52; 2Ki 3:3; 10:29, 31; 13:2, 11; 14:24; 15:9, 18, 24, 28).

15:33 twenty-four years. 909–886 B.C.

PROPHECY AGAINST BAASHA

16 Now the word of the LORD came to [A]Jehu the
son of [B]Hanani against Baasha, saying, 2 "Inasmuch as I [A]exalted you from the dust and made you
leader over My people Israel, and [B]you have walked
in the way of Jeroboam and have made My people
Israel sin, provoking Me to anger with their sins,
3 behold, [A]I will consume [B]Baasha and his house, and
[C]I will make your house like the house of Jeroboam
the son of Nebat. 4 [A]Anyone of Baasha who dies in
the city the dogs will eat, and anyone of his who
dies in the field the birds of the heavens will eat."
5 [A]Now the rest of the acts of Baasha and what he
did and his might, are they not written in the Book
of the Chronicles of the Kings of Israel?

THE ISRAELITE KINGS

6 And Baasha slept with his fathers and was buried in [A]Tirzah, and Elah his son became king in his
place. 7 Moreover, the word of the LORD through [A]the
prophet Jehu the son of Hanani also came against Baasha and his household, both because of all the evil
which he did in the sight of the LORD, provoking Him
to anger with [B]the work of his hands, in being like
the house of Jeroboam, and because [C]he struck [a]it.
8 In the twenty-sixth year of Asa king of Judah,
Elah the son of Baasha became king over Israel at
Tirzah, *and reigned* two years. 9 His servant [A]Zimri,
commander of half his chariots, conspired against
him. Now he *was* at Tirzah drinking himself drunk
in the house of Arza, [B]who *was* over the household
at Tirzah. 10 Then Zimri went in and struck him and
put him to death in the twenty-seventh year of Asa
king of Judah, and became king in his place. 11 It
came about when he became king, as soon as he
sat on his throne, that [A]he [a]killed all the household
of Baasha; he did not leave [b]a single male, neither
of his [c]relatives nor of his friends.
12 Thus Zimri destroyed all the household of Baasha, [A]according to the word of the LORD, which He
spoke against Baasha through [B]Jehu the prophet,
13 for all the sins of Baasha and the sins of Elah his
son, which they sinned and which they made Israel
sin, [A]provoking the LORD God of Israel to anger with
their [a]idols. 14 [A]Now the rest of the acts of Elah and
all that he did, are they not written in the Book of
the Chronicles of the Kings of Israel?
15 In the twenty-seventh year of Asa king of Judah,
Zimri reigned seven days at Tirzah. Now the people
were camped against [A]Gibbethon, which belonged
to the Philistines. 16 The people who were camped
heard [a]it said, "Zimri has conspired and has also
struck down the king." Therefore all Israel made
Omri, the commander of the army, king over Israel
that day in the camp. 17 Then Omri and all Israel with
him went up from Gibbethon and besieged Tirzah.
18 When Zimri saw that the city was taken, he went
into the citadel of the king's house and burned the
king's house over him with fire, and [A]died, 19 because
of his sins which he sinned, doing evil in the sight of
the LORD, [A]walking in the way of Jeroboam, and in
his sin which he did, making Israel sin. 20 [A]Now the
rest of the acts of Zimri and his conspiracy which
he [a]carried out, are they not written in the Book of
the Chronicles of the Kings of Israel?
21 Then the people of Israel were divided into two
parts: half of the people followed Tibni the son of
Ginath, to make him king; the *other* half followed
Omri. 22 But the people who followed Omri prevailed over the people who followed Tibni the son
of Ginath. And Tibni died and Omri became king.
23 In the thirty-first year of Asa king of Judah, Omri
became king over Israel *and reigned* twelve years;
he reigned six years at [A]Tirzah. 24 He bought the
hill [a]Samaria from Shemer for two talents of silver;
and he built on the hill, and named the city which
he built [a,A]Samaria, after the name of Shemer, the
owner of the hill.
25 [A]Omri did evil in the sight of the LORD, and
[B]acted more wickedly than all who *were* before him.

16:1 [A]1 Kin 16:7; 2 Chr 19:2; 20:34 [B]2 Chr 16:7-10 16:2 [A]1 Sam 2:8; 1 Kin 14:7 [B]1 Kin 15:34 16:3 [A]1 Kin 14:10; 21:21 [B]1 Kin 16:11 [C]1 Kin 15:29 16:4 [A]1 Kin 14:11; 21:24 16:5 [A]1 Kin 14:19; 15:31 16:6 [A]1 Kin 14:17; 15:21 16:7 [a]Or *him* [A]1 Kin 16:1 [B]Ps 115:4; Is 2:8 [C]1 Kin 14:14; 15:27, 29 16:9 [A]2 Kin 9:30-33 [B]Gen 24:2; 39:4; 1 Kin 18:3 16:11 [a]Lit *smote* [b]Lit *him who urinates against the wall* [c]Lit *redeemers* [A]1 Kin 15:29; 16:3 16:12 [A]1 Kin 16:3 [B]2 Chr 19:2; 20:34 16:13 [a]Lit *vanities* [A]Deut 32:21; 1 Kin 15:30 16:14 [A]1 Kin 16:5 16:15 [A]1 Kin 15:27 16:16 [a]Lit *saying* 16:18 [A]1 Sam 31:4, 5; 2 Sam 17:23 16:19 [A]1 Kin 12:28; 14:16; 15:26 16:20 [a]Lit *conspired* [A]1 Kin 16:5, 14, 27 16:23 [A]1 Kin 15:21 16:24 [a]Heb *Shomeron* [A]1 Kin 16:28, 29, 32 16:25 [A]Mic 6:16 [B]1 Kin 14:9; 16:30-33

16:1 Jehu the son of Hanani. Cf. v. 7. This Hanani may have been the prophet who warned Judah's King Asa (2Ch 16:7–9). Jehu, like Ahijah before him (14:7–16), delivered the Lord's message of judgment to the king of Israel. The pattern emerges in the book of Kings that the Lord used His prophets as a legitimate means by which to confront the sin of Israel's kings.

16:2–4 Baasha had angered the Lord by following the sinful paths of Jeroboam. Appropriately, he faced the same humiliating judgment Jeroboam had (14:10, 11). Though he waded through slaughter to his throne, he owed it to the permission of God, by whom all kings reign. His judgment was that no long line of heirs would succeed him; instead, his family would be totally annihilated and their corpses shamefully scavenged by hungry dogs and birds.

16:8–14 Elah … two years. Ca. 886–885 B.C.

16:11 relatives. I.e., "relatives able to redeem." Cf. Ru 2:1. Zimri not only killed Elah and his immediate sons, but all of the extended relatives of Baasha who could help his family.

16:15 seven days. Zimri's reign (885 B.C.) was the shortest of any king of Israel. **Gibbethon.** *See note on 15:27.*

16:16 Omri. When the soldiers of Israel in the field heard of Elah's death, they immediately acclaimed Omri, the commander of Israel's army, as the new king.

16:21 Tibni. The death of Zimri (vv. 17, 18) automatically placed the kingdom in Omri's hands. Half of the population, including the army, sided with Omri, but the other half backed Tibni. Nothing further is known of Tibni, but he was strong enough to rival Omri for about 4 years (cf. v. 15 with v. 23).

16:21–28 Omri. Ruled the northern kingdom ca. 885–874 B.C.

16:23–2Ki 13:25 This section is strategic in the book(s) of Kings and contains over one-third of the total narrative of the book(s). The coming of the dynasty of Omri to the kingship of Israel brought with it the introduction of Baal worship with official sanction in Israel (16:31, 32). Through intermarriage with the house of Omri, Baal worship penetrated into Judah and corrupted the line of David (2Ki 8:18, 27), initiating a gigantic struggle before Baalism was officially eradicated in both Israel and Judah (2Ki 9:14–12:21).

16:23 twelve years. Omri ruled 12 years (ca. 885–874 B.C.), from Asa's 27th year (16:15) to Asa's 38th year (v. 29). This notice of his beginning to reign in Asa's 31st year must be a reference to his sole rule.

16:24 Samaria. The hill of Samaria, named after its owner, Shemer, was located 7 mi. NW of Shechem and stood 300 ft. high. Though ringed by other mountains, it stood by itself so that attackers had to charge uphill from every side. This new capital amounted to the northern equivalent of Jerusalem. Its central location gave Israelites easy access to it.

26 For he [A]walked in all the way of Jeroboam the son
of Nebat and in his sins which he made Israel sin,
provoking the LORD God of Israel with their [a]idols.
27 Now the rest of the acts of Omri which he did and
his might which he [a]showed, are they not written
in the Book of the Chronicles of the Kings of Israel?
28 So Omri slept with his fathers and was buried in
Samaria; and Ahab his son became king in his place.

29 Now Ahab the son of Omri became king over
Israel in the thirty-eighth year of Asa king of Judah,
and Ahab the son of Omri reigned over Israel in
Samaria twenty-two years. 30 Ahab the son of Omri
did evil in the sight of the LORD [A]more than all who
were before him.

31 It came about, as though it had been a trivial
thing for him to walk in the sins of Jeroboam the
son of Nebat, that [A]he married Jezebel the daughter of Ethbaal king of the [B]Sidonians, and went to
serve Baal and worshiped him. 32 So he erected an
altar for Baal in [A]the house of Baal which he built
in Samaria. 33 Ahab also made [A]the [a]Asherah. Thus
[B]Ahab did more to provoke the LORD God of Israel
than all the kings of Israel who were before him.
34 [A]In his days Hiel the Bethelite built Jericho; he
laid its foundations with the *loss of* Abiram his
firstborn, and set up its gates with the *loss of* his
youngest son Segub, according to the word of the
LORD, which He spoke by Joshua the son of Nun.

ELIJAH PREDICTS DROUGHT

17 Now Elijah the Tishbite, who was of [a,A]the settlers of Gilead, said to Ahab, "[B]As the LORD,
the God of Israel lives, before whom I stand, surely
[C]there shall be neither dew nor rain these years,
except by my word." 2 The word of the LORD came
to him, saying, 3 "Go away from here and turn eastward, and hide yourself by the brook Cherith, which
is [a]east of the Jordan. 4 It shall be that you will drink
of the brook, and [A]I have commanded the ravens to
provide for you there." 5 So he went and did according to the word of the LORD, for he went and lived
by the brook Cherith, which is [a]east of the Jordan.
6 The ravens brought him bread and meat in the
morning and bread and meat in the evening, and
he would drink from the brook. 7 It happened after
a while that the brook dried up, because there was
no rain in the land.

8 Then the word of the LORD came to him, saying,
9 "Arise, go to [A]Zarephath, which belongs to Sidon,
and stay there; behold, [B]I have commanded a widow
there to provide for you." 10 So he arose and went to
Zarephath, and when he came to the gate of the city,
behold, a widow was there gathering sticks; and [A]he
called to her and said, "Please get me a little water
in a [a]jar, that I may drink." 11 As she was going to
get *it,* he called to her and said, "Please bring me a
piece of bread in your hand." 12 But she said, "[A]As
the LORD your God lives, [B]I have no [a]bread, only a
handful of flour in the [b]bowl and a little oil in the
jar; and behold, I am gathering [c]a few sticks that
I may go in and prepare for me and my son, that
we may eat it and [C]die." 13 Then Elijah said to her,
"Do not fear; go, do as you have said, but make me
a little bread cake from [a]it first and bring *it* out to
me, and afterward you may make *one* for yourself
and for your son. 14 For thus says the LORD God of
Israel, 'The [a]bowl of flour shall not be exhausted,
nor shall the jar of oil [b]be empty, until the day that
the LORD sends rain on the face of the earth.' " 15 So
she went and did according to the word of Elijah,
and she and he and her household ate for *many*
days. 16 The [a]bowl of flour was not exhausted nor
did the jar of oil [b]become empty, according to the
word of the LORD which He spoke through Elijah.

16:26 [a]Lit *vanities* [A]1 Kin 16:19 16:27 [a]Lit *did* 16:30 [A]1 Kin 14:9; 16:25 16:31 [A]Deut 7:1-5 [B]Judg 18:7; 1 Kin 11:1-5; 2 Kin 10:18; 17:16 16:32 [A]2 Kin 10:21, 26, 27 16:33 [a]I.e. wooden symbol of a female deity [A]2 Kin 13:6 [B]1 Kin 14:9; 16:29, 30; 21:25 16:34 [A]Josh 6:26 17:1 [a]Or *Tishbe in Gilead* [A]Judg 12:4 [B]1 Kin 18:10; 22:14; 2 Kin 3:14; 5:20 [C]1 Kin 18:1; Luke 4:25; James 5:17 17:3 [a]Lit *before* 17:4 [A]1 Kin 17:9 17:5 [a]Lit *before* 17:9 [A]Obad 20; Luke 4:26 [B]1 Kin 17:4 17:10 [a]Or *vessel* [A]Gen 24:17; John 4:7 17:12 [a]Lit *cake* [b]Lit *pitcher* [c]Lit *two* [A]1 Kin 17:1 [B]2 Kin 4:2-7 [C]Gen 21:15, 16 17:13 [a]Lit *there* 17:14 [a]Lit *pitcher* [b]Lit *lack* 17:16 [a]Lit *pitcher* [b]Lit *lack*

16:29–22:40 **Ahab ... twenty-two years.** Ca. 874–853 B.C.; *see notes on 2Ch 18:1–34.*

16:30 **evil ... more than all who were before him.** With Ahab, Israel's spiritual decay reached its lowest point. He was even worse than his father, Omri, who was more wicked than all before him (v. 25). Ahab's evil consisted of perpetuating all the sins of Jeroboam and promoting the worship of Baal in Israel (vv. 31, 32). Of all Israel's kings, Ahab outraged the Lord most (v. 33).

16:31 **Jezebel.** The wretched wife of Ahab became symbolic of the evil of false religion (cf. Rev 2:20). **Ethbaal.** His name meant "Baal is alive." The father of Jezebel was the king of Phoenicia (including Tyre and Sidon) who had murdered his predecessor and, according to Josephus, was a priest of the gods Melqart and Astarte.

16:31, 32 **Baal.** Meaning "lord, husband, owner," Baal was the predominant god in Canaanite religion. He was the storm god who provided the rain necessary for the fertility of the land. The worship of Baal was widespread among the Canaanites with many local manifestations under various other titles, the Tyrians calling him Baal Melqart. The worship of Baal had infiltrated Israel long before the time of Ahab (Jdg 2:11, 13; 3:7; 10:6, 10; 1Sa 12:10). However, Ahab gave it official sanction in Samaria through building a temple for Baal (see 2Ki 3:2). As David had captured Jerusalem and his son Solomon had built a temple for the Lord there, so Omri established Samaria and his son Ahab built a temple for Baal there.

16:34 **Hiel the Bethelite built Jericho.** The re-fortification of Jericho was forbidden by God, who had supernaturally destroyed it. But Joshua predicted that a man and his sons would violate God's restriction (*see note on Jos 6:26*). Two of Hiel's sons died when they sought to assist him to fortify the city.

17:1 **Elijah.** His name means "the Lord is God." The prophet Elijah's ministry corresponded to his name: He was sent by God to confront Baalism and to declare to Israel that the Lord was God and there was no other. **Tishbite.** Elijah lived in a town called Tishbe, E of the Jordan River in the vicinity of the Jabbok River. **neither dew nor rain.** The autumn and spring rains and summer dew were necessities for the crops of Israel. The Lord had threatened to withhold these from the land if His people turned from Him to serve other gods (Lv 26:18, 19; Dt 11:16, 17; 28:23, 24). Elijah had prayed for the drought (cf. Jas 5:17) and God answered. It lasted 3 years and 6 months according to James (5:17). The drought proved that Baal, the god of the rains and fertility, was impotent before the Lord.

17:3 **brook Cherith.** Probably this was a seasonal brook that flowed during the rainy season but dried up when the weather turned hot. It was located E of the Jordan River.

17:6 **ravens brought.** God's supernatural provision, much like the manna and quail during Israel's wilderness wanderings (Ex 16:13–36).

17:9 **Zarephath.** A town on the Mediterranean coast about 7 mi. S of Sidon. Elijah was sent to live there, in a territory controlled by Ahab's father-in-law, Ethbaal. In this way, he showed the power of God in the very area where the impotent Baal was worshiped, as He provided miraculously for the widow in the famine (vv. 10–16).

ELIJAH RAISES THE WIDOW'S SON

17 Now it came about after these things that the
son of the woman, the mistress of the house, became
sick; and his sickness was so severe that there was no
breath left in him. 18 So she said to Elijah, "[A]What do I
have to do with you, O [B]man of God? [a]You have come
to me to bring my iniquity to remembrance and to
put my son to death!" 19 He said to her, "Give me your
son." Then he took him from her bosom and carried
him up to the upper room where he was living, and
laid him on his own bed. 20 He called to the LORD
and said, "O LORD my God, have You also brought
calamity to the widow with whom I am [a]staying, by
causing her son to die?" 21 [A]Then he stretched himself
upon the child three times, and called to the LORD
and said, "O LORD my God, I pray You, let this child's
life return [a]to him." 22 The LORD heard the voice of
Elijah, [A]and the life of the child returned [a]to him and
he revived. 23 Elijah took the child and brought him
down from the upper room into the house and gave
him to his mother; and Elijah said, "See, your son
is alive." 24 Then the woman said to Elijah, "[A]Now I
know that you are a man of God and that the word
of the LORD in your mouth is truth."

OBADIAH MEETS ELIJAH

18 Now it happened [A]*after* many days that the
word of the LORD came to Elijah in the third
year, saying, "Go, show yourself to Ahab, and [B]I will
send rain on the face of the earth." 2 So Elijah went to
show himself to Ahab. Now the famine *was* severe
in Samaria. 3 Ahab called Obadiah [A]who *was* over
the household. (Now Obadiah [a,B]feared the LORD
greatly; 4 for [A]when Jezebel [a]destroyed the prophets
of the LORD, Obadiah took a hundred prophets and
hid them by fifties in a cave, and [B]provided them
with bread and water.) 5 Then Ahab said to Obadiah,
"Go through the land to all the springs of water and
to all the valleys; perhaps we will find grass and
keep the horses and mules alive, and not [a]have to
kill some of the cattle." 6 So they divided the land
between them to [a]survey it; Ahab went one way by
himself and Obadiah went another way by himself.
7 Now as Obadiah was on the way, behold, Elijah
[a]met him, [A]and he recognized him and fell on his face
and said, "Is this you, Elijah my master?" 8 He said to
him, "It is I. Go, say to your master, 'Behold, Elijah *is*
here.' " 9 He said, "What [a]sin have I committed, that
you are giving your servant into the hand of Ahab
to put me to death? 10 [A]As the LORD your God lives,
there is no nation or kingdom where my master has
not sent to search for you; and when they said, 'He is
not *here,*' he made the kingdom or nation swear that
they could not find you. 11 And now you are saying,
'Go, say to your master, "Behold, Elijah *is here.*" ' 12 It
will come about when I leave you [A]that the Spirit
of the LORD will carry you where I do not know;
so when I come and tell Ahab and he cannot find
you, he will kill me, although *I* your servant have
[a]feared the LORD from my youth. 13 [A]Has it not been
told to my master what I did when Jezebel killed the
prophets of the LORD, that I hid [a]a hundred prophets
of the LORD by fifties in a cave, and provided them
with bread and water? 14 And now you are saying,
'Go, say to your master, "Behold, Elijah *is here*" '; he
will then kill me." 15 Elijah said, "[A]As the LORD of
hosts lives, before whom I stand, I will surely show
myself to him today." 16 So Obadiah went to meet
Ahab and told him; and Ahab went to meet Elijah.
17 When Ahab saw Elijah, [A]Ahab said to him, "Is this
you, you troubler of Israel?" 18 He said, "I have not
troubled Israel, but you and your father's house *have*,

17:18 [a]Or *Have you come...death?* [A]2 Sam 16:10; 2 Kin 3:13; Luke 4:34; John 2:4 [B]1 Kin 12:22 17:20 [a]Lit *sojourning* 17:21 [a]Lit *upon his inward part* [A]2 Kin 4:34, 35; Acts 20:10 17:22 [a]Lit *upon his inward part* [A]Luke 7:14; Heb 11:35 17:24 [A]John 2:11; 3:2; 16:30 18:1 [A]1 Kin 17:1; Luke 4:25; James 5:17 [B]Deut 28:12 18:3 [a]Or *revered* [A]1 Kin 16:9 [B]Neh 7:2; Job 28:28 18:4 [a]Lit *cut off* [A]1 Kin 18:13 [B]Matt 10:40-42 18:5 [a]Lit *cut off* 18:6 [a]Lit *pass through* 18:7 [a]Lit *to meet* [A]2 Kin 1:6-8 18:9 [a]Lit *have I sinned* 18:10 [A]1 Kin 17:1 18:12 [a]Or *revered* [A]2 Kin 2:16; Ezek 3:12, 14; Acts 8:39 18:13 [a]Lit *a hundred men of the prophets* [A]1 Kin 18:4 18:15 [A]1 Kin 17:1 18:17 [A]Josh 7:25; 1 Kin 21:20

17:23 your son is alive. Canaanite myths claimed that Baal could revive the dead, but here it was the Lord, not Baal, who gave back the boy's life. This conclusively demonstrated that the Lord was the only true God and Elijah was His prophet (v. 24).

17:24 a man of God. *See note on 12:22.* A man of God has a true word from God.

18:1 third year. Cf. Jas 5:17.

18:2 famine. This was to give Ahab opportunity to repent. He was the cause of national judgment in the famine. If he repented, rain would come.

18:3 Obadiah. His name means "servant of the Lord." He was the manager of Ahab's royal palace and a devout worshiper of the Lord, who had demonstrated his devotion to the Lord by protecting 100 of the Lord's prophets from death by Jezebel (vv. 4, 13) which had put him on tenuous ground with Ahab.

18:12 the Spirit of the LORD will carry you. The servant had been asked to tell Ahab that Elijah was present to speak with him (vv. 7, 18), but he was afraid because Ahab was seeking Elijah so intensely. Since Elijah had disappeared from sight earlier (17:5), Obadiah was afraid that the Holy Spirit would carry Elijah away again (cf. 2Ki 2:16) and the irrational Ahab would kill him for the false report of Elijah's presence.

18:17 troubler. Such was one who brought misfortune on a community by breaking an oath or by making a foolish one (Jos 6:18; 7:25).

18:18 Baals. These were the local idols of Baal (cf. Jdg 2:11). The prophet boldly told Ahab that the calamity of drought and famine was traceable directly to his and his family's patronage and practice of idolatry.

RESUSCITATIONS FROM THE DEAD	
1. Widow of Zarephath's son, raised by Elijah	1Ki 17:22
2. Shunammite woman's son, raised by Elisha	2Ki 4:34, 35
3. Man raised when he came into contact with the bones of Elisha	2Ki 13:20, 21
4. Widow of Nain's son, raised by Jesus	Lk 7:14, 15
5. Jairus' daughter, raised by Jesus	Lk 8:52–56
6. Lazarus of Bethany, brother of Mary and Martha, raised by Jesus	Jn 11
7. Dorcas, raised by Peter	Ac 9:40
8. Eutychus, raised by Paul	Ac 20:9–12

because [A]you have forsaken the commandments of
the LORD and [B]you have followed the Baals. 19 Now
then send *and* gather to me all Israel at [A]Mount Carmel, [B]*together* with 450 prophets of Baal and 400
prophets of [C]the Asherah, who eat at Jezebel's table."

GOD OR BAAL ON MOUNT CARMEL

20 So Ahab sent *a message* among all the sons of
Israel and brought the prophets together at Mount
Carmel. 21 Elijah came near to all the people and said,
"[A]How long *will* you [a]hesitate between two opinions?
[B]If the LORD is God, follow Him; but if Baal, follow
him." But the people did not answer him a word.
22 Then Elijah said to the people, "I [A]alone am left a
prophet of the LORD, but Baal's prophets are [B]450
men. 23 Now let them give us two oxen; and let them
choose one ox for themselves and cut it up, and
place it on the wood, but put no fire *under it;* and
I will prepare the other ox and lay it on the wood,
and I will not put a fire *under it.* 24 Then you call on
the name of your god, and I will call on the name of
the LORD, and [A]the God who answers by fire, He is
God." And all the people said, "[a]That is a good idea."
25 So Elijah said to the prophets of Baal, "Choose one
ox for yourselves and prepare it first for you are many,
and call on the name of your god, but put no fire
under it." 26 Then they took the ox which [a]was given
them and they prepared it and called on the name of
Baal from morning until noon saying, "O Baal, answer
us." But there was [A]no voice and no one answered.
And they [b]leaped about the altar which [c]they made.
27 It came about at noon, that Elijah mocked them
and said, "Call out with a loud voice, for he is a god;
either he is occupied or gone aside, or is on a journey,
or perhaps he is asleep and needs to be awakened."
28 So they cried with a loud voice and [A]cut themselves
according to their custom with swords and lances
until the blood gushed out on them. 29 When midday
was past, they [a]raved [A]until the time of the offering
of the *evening* sacrifice; but there was no voice, no
one answered, and no [b]one paid attention.
30 Then Elijah said to all the people, "Come near
to me." So all the people came near to him. And
[A]he repaired the altar of the LORD which had been
torn down. 31 Elijah took twelve stones according

18:18 [A]1 Kin 9:9; 2 Chr 15:2 [B]1 Kin 16:31; 21:25, 26 18:19 [A]Josh 19:26; 2 Kin 2:25 [B]1 Kin 18:22 [C]1 Kin 16:33 18:21 [a]Lit *limp on the two divided opinions* [A]2 Kin 17:41; Matt 6:24 [B]Josh 24:15 18:22 [A]1 Kin 19:10, 14 [B]1 Kin 18:19 18:24 [a]Lit *The matter is good* [A]1 Kin 18:38 18:26 [a]Lit *he gave* [b]Lit *limped;* i.e. a type of ceremonial dance [c]So some mss and the ancient versions; M.T. *he* [A]Ps 115:4, 5; Jer 10:5 18:28 [A]Lev 19:28; Deut 14:1 18:29 [a]Lit *prophesied* [b]Lit *attentiveness* [A]Ex 29:39, 41 18:30 [A]1 Kin 19:10, 14; 2 Chr 33:16

ELIJAH AND ELISHA

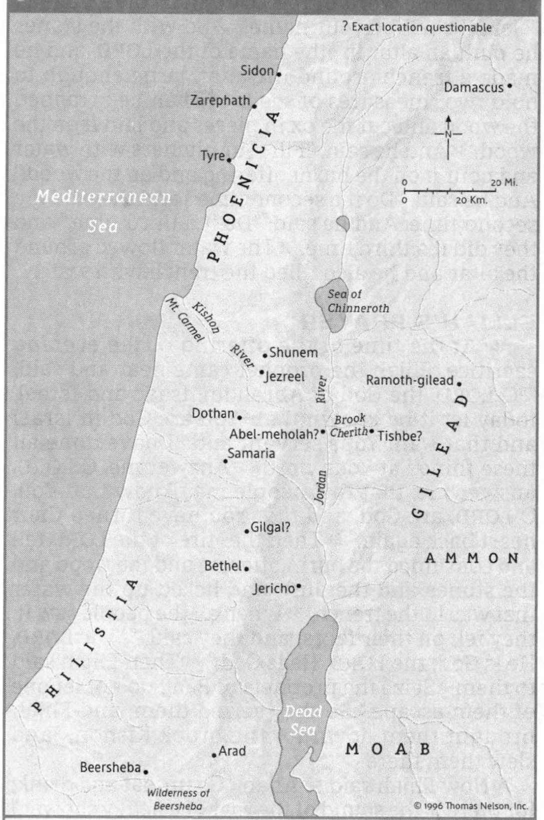

Elijah's victory on Mt. Carmel ended with the slaying of 450 prophets of Baal (1Ki 18:20–40). His ministry spanned Canaan from the Brook Cherith near his birthplace (17:1–7) to Zarephath where he performed the miracle that sustained the widow and her son, and to as far south as Mt. Horeb (not shown). In Samaria Elijah denounced King Ahab's injustice against Naboth of Jezreel (21:17–29). Near Jericho Elijah separated the waters of the Jordan River to cross over and subsequently was carried to heaven in a chariot of fire (2Ki 2:1–12).

Elisha healed Naaman of leprosy in the Jordan River (5:1–19) and led the blinded Syrians to their defeat at Samaria (6:8–23). In Damascus, Elisha prophesied the death of Ben-Hadad and the succession of Hazael as king of Syria.

18:19 Mount Carmel. The Carmel range of mountains, rising to 1,800 ft. at its highest point, extends about 30 mi. to the SE from the shores of the Mediterranean Sea into the S of the Jezreel Valley. A series of rounded peaks and valleys, it became a symbol of beauty and fruitfulness because of its lush tree cover (SS 7:5; Is 35:2). It is not known at exactly what point along this ridge the contest between Elijah and the prophets of Baal took place. The queen cared for 850 false prophets who were associated with her.

18:21 hesitate between two opinions. Lit. "limp along on or between two twigs." Israel had not totally rejected the Lord, but was seeking to combine worship of Him with the worship of Baal. The issue posed by Elijah was that Israel had to choose who was God, the Lord or Baal, and then serve God wholeheartedly. Rather than decide by his message, Elijah sought a visible sign from heaven.

18:24 the God who answers by fire. Since Baal's followers believed that he controlled the thunder, lightning, and storms, and the Lord's followers declared the same (Pss 18:14; 29:3–9; 104:3), this would prove to be a fair test to show who was God.

18:27 mocked. The myths surrounding Baal portrayed him as musing on actions to take, fighting a war, traveling, and even dying and coming back to life. Elijah's sarcastic advice to the prophets of Baal played on these beliefs.

18:28 the blood gushed out. Self-laceration was practiced to rouse a god's pity and response in the ancient world, but was prohibited by the OT law (Lv 19:28; Dt 14:1).

18:29 no ... no ... no. This 3-fold declaration emphasized the complete lack of response on the part of Baal. The fact that there was no response indicated Baal's impotence and nonexistence (Jer 10:5).

18:31 twelve stones. The 12 stones represented the 12 tribes, since this contest had significance for both Judah and Israel. Although the tribes had been divided into two nations,

to the number of the tribes of the sons of Jacob, to whom the word of the LORD had come, saying, "[A]Israel shall be your name." 32 So with the stones he built an altar in [A]the name of the LORD, and he made a trench around the altar, large enough to hold two [a]measures of seed. 33 [A]Then he arranged the wood and cut the ox in pieces and laid *it* on the wood. 34 And he said, "Fill four pitchers with water and pour *it* on the burnt offering and on the wood." And he said, "Do it a second time," and they did it a second time. And he said, "Do it a third time," and they did it a third time. 35 The water flowed around the altar and he also filled the trench with water.

ELIJAH'S PRAYER

36 [A]At the time of the offering of the *evening* sacrifice, Elijah the prophet came near and said, "[B]O LORD, the God of Abraham, Isaac and Israel, today let it be known that [C]You are God in Israel and that I am Your servant and [D]I have done all these things at Your word. 37 Answer me, O LORD, answer me, that this people may know that You, O LORD, are God, and *that* You have turned their heart back again." 38 Then the [A]fire of the LORD fell and consumed the burnt offering and the wood and the stones and the dust, and licked up the water that was in the trench. 39 When all the people saw it, they fell on their faces; and they said, "[A]The LORD, He is God; the LORD, He is God." 40 Then Elijah said to them, "Seize the prophets of Baal; do not let one of them escape." So they seized them; and Elijah brought them down to [A]the brook Kishon, [B]and slew them there.

41 Now Elijah said to Ahab, "Go up, eat and drink; for there is the sound of the roar of a *heavy* shower." 42 So Ahab went up to eat and drink. But Elijah went up to the top of [A]Carmel; and he [B]crouched down on the earth and put his face between his knees. 43 He said to his servant, "Go up now, look toward the sea." So he went up and looked and said, "There is nothing." And he said, "Go back" seven times. 44 It came about at the seventh *time,* that he said, "Behold, [A]a cloud as small as a man's hand is coming up from the sea." And he said, "Go up, say to Ahab, '[a]Prepare *your chariot* and go down, so that the *heavy* shower does not stop you.'" 45 In a little while the sky grew black with clouds and wind, and there was a heavy shower. And Ahab rode and went to [A]Jezreel. 46 Then [A]the hand of the LORD was on Elijah, and [B]he girded up his loins and [a]outran Ahab [b]to Jezreel.

ELIJAH FLEES FROM JEZEBEL

19 Now Ahab told Jezebel all that Elijah had done, and [a,A]how he had killed all the prophets with the sword. 2 Then Jezebel sent a messenger to Elijah, saying, "[A]So may the gods do to me and even more, if I do not make your [a]life as the [a]life of one of them by tomorrow about this time." 3 And he [a]was afraid and arose and ran for his [b]life and came to [A]Beersheba, which belongs to Judah, and left his servant there. 4 But he himself went a day's journey into the wilderness, and came and sat down under a [a]juniper tree; and [A]he requested for himself that he might die, and said, "It is enough; now, O LORD, take my [b]life, for I am not better than my fathers." 5 He lay down and slept under a [a]juniper tree; and behold, there was [A]an angel touching him, and he said to him, "Arise, eat." 6 Then he looked and behold, there was at his head a bread cake *baked on* hot stones, and a jar of water. So he ate and drank and lay down again. 7 The angel of the LORD came again a second time and touched him and said, "Arise, eat, because the journey is too great for you." 8 So he arose and ate and drank, and went in the strength of that food [A]forty days and forty nights to [B]Horeb, the mountain of God.

18:31 [A]Gen 32:28; 35:10; 2 Kin 17:34 18:32 [a]Heb *seahs;* i.e. one seah equals approx 11 qts [A]Col 3:17 18:33 [A]Gen 22:9; Lev 1:7, 8 18:36 [A]1 Kin 18:29 [B]Gen 28:13; Ex 3:6; 4:5; Matt 22:32 [C]1 Kin 8:43 [D]Num 16:28-32 18:38 [A]Gen 15:17; Lev 9:24; 10:1, 2; Judg 6:21; 2 Kin 1:12; 1 Chr 21:26; 2 Chr 7:1; Job 1:16 18:39 [A]1 Kin 18:21, 24 18:40 [A]Judg 4:7; 5:21 [B]Deut 13:5; 18:20; 2 Kin 10:24, 25 18:42 [A]1 Kin 18:19, 20 [B]James 5:18 18:44 [a]Lit *Tie, harness* [A]Luke 12:54 18:45 [A]Josh 17:16; Judg 6:33 18:46 [a]Lit *ran before* [b]Lit *until you are coming to* [A]2 Kin 3:15; Is 8:11; Ezek 3:14 [B]2 Kin 4:29; Jer 1:17; 1 Pet 1:13 19:1 [a]Lit *all* about *how* [A]1 Kin 18:40 19:2 [a]Lit *soul* [A]Ruth 1:17; 1 Kin 20:10; 2 Kin 6:31 19:3 [a]Reading of many mss; Heb text may read *saw* [b]Lit *soul* [A]Gen 21:31 19:4 [a]Or *broom-tree* [b]Lit *soul* [A]Num 11:15; Jer 20:14-18; Jon 4:3, 8 19:5 [a]Or *broom-tree* [A]Gen 28:12 19:8 [A]Ex 24:18; 34:28; Deut 9:9-11, 18; Matt 4:2 [B]Ex 3:1; 4:27

they were still one people in the Lord's plans, with the same covenants and a single destiny.

18:32 two measures. This was about 4 gal. or a third of a bu. of seed.

18:36 the *evening* sacrifice. This sacrifice was offered around 3:00 p.m. (Ex 29:38–41; Nu 28:3–8).

18:40 Seize the prophets. Taking advantage of the excited feelings of the people over the manifestation of Jehovah as the true God, Elijah called on them to seize the priestly imposters and fill the river with their blood, the river that was dried up by their idolatry. **brook Kishon.** This river, which drains the Jezreel Valley from E to the NW, was in the valley N of Mt. Carmel. **slew them.** The killing of the 450 prophets of Baal (18:19) fulfilled the law's demands that false prophets be executed (Dt 13:1–5) and that those embracing idolatry or inciting others to practice it were worthy of death (Dt 13:13–18; 17:2–7). Further, these deaths were just retribution for Jezebel's killing of the Lord's prophets (vv. 4, 13).

18:41 eat and drink. Elijah instructed Ahab to celebrate the end of the drought.

18:42 crouched down. Elijah's actions expressed his and Israel's humble submission to God. Elijah prayed for rain this time (cf. 17:1; Jas 5:17), and God again answered (cf. Jas 5:18). Since the Lord's curse was lifted, the rains would be coming.

18:45 Jezreel. A town located in the tribal allotment of Issachar at the eastern end of the Jezreel Valley, N of Mt. Gilboa, about 55 mi. N of Jerusalem. Jezreel was Ahab's winter capital (see 21:1), situated between 15 to 25 mi. E of the Carmel Range.

18:46 outran. It was customary in the ancient Near East for kings to have runners before their chariots. The prophet showed Ahab his loyalty by rendering to him that service. Empowered by God, Elijah ran on foot ahead of Ahab's chariot the 15 to 25 mi. from Mt. Carmel to Jezreel.

19:3 he was afraid. His hope shattered, Elijah fled as a prophet, broken by Jezebel's threats (v. 2), her unrepentant Baalism, and her continuing power over Israel. Elijah expected Jezebel to surrender; when she did not capitulate, he became a discouraged man (vv. 4, 10, 14). **Beersheba.** A city located 100 mi. S of Jezreel (18:45, 46) in the Negev, it marked the southern boundary of the population of Judah.

19:4 juniper tree. A desert bush that grew to a height of 10 ft. It had slender branches featuring small leaves and fragrant blossoms. **take my life.** Since Israelites believed that suicide was an affront to the Lord, it was not an option, whatever the distress. So Elijah asked the Lord for death (cf. Jon 4:3, 8) because he viewed the situation as hopeless. Job (Job 6:8, 9), Moses (Nu 11:10–15), and Jeremiah (Jer 20:14–18) had also reacted in similar fashion during their ministries.

19:6 cake ... and ... water. As at Cherith and Zarephath (17:6, 19), God provided food and drink for Elijah in the midst of his distress and the surrounding famine.

19:8 forty days. Elijah's trip took over double the time it should have taken. Therefore, the period had symbolic meaning as well as showing literal time. As the people of Israel

ELIJAH AT HOREB

9 Then he came there to a cave and lodged there;
and behold, [A]the word of the LORD *came* to him, and
He said to him, "What are you doing here, Elijah?"
10 He said, "[A]I have been very zealous for the LORD,
the God of hosts; for the sons of Israel have forsaken
Your covenant, [B]torn down Your altars and killed
Your prophets with the sword. And [C]I alone am left;
and they seek my life, to take it away."
11 So He said, "[A]Go forth and stand on the mountain before the LORD." And behold, the LORD was
passing by! And [B]a great and strong wind was rending the mountains and breaking in pieces the rocks
before the LORD; *but* the LORD *was* not in the wind.
And after the wind an earthquake, *but* the LORD
was not in the earthquake. 12 After the earthquake
a fire, *but* the LORD *was* not in the fire; and after
the fire [A]a sound of a gentle blowing. 13 When Elijah
heard *it,* [A]he wrapped his face in his mantle and
went out and stood in the entrance of the cave.
And behold, [B]a voice *came* to him and said, "What
are you doing here, Elijah?" 14 Then he said, "[A]I have
been very zealous for the LORD, the God of hosts;
for the sons of Israel have forsaken Your covenant,
torn down Your altars and killed Your prophets with
the sword. And I alone am left; and they seek my
life, to take it away."
15 The LORD said to him, "Go, return on your way
to the wilderness of Damascus, and when you have
arrived, [A]you shall anoint Hazael king over Aram;
16 and [A]Jehu the son of Nimshi you shall anoint
king over Israel; and [B]Elisha the son of Shaphat of
Abel-meholah you shall anoint as prophet in your
place. 17 It shall come about, the [A]one who escapes
from the sword of Hazael, Jehu [B]shall put to death,
and the one who escapes from the sword of Jehu,
Elisha shall put to death. 18 [A]Yet I will leave 7,000
in Israel, all the knees that have not bowed to Baal
and every mouth that has not [B]kissed him."
19 So he departed from there and found Elisha the
son of Shaphat, while he was plowing with twelve
pairs *of oxen* before him, and he with the twelfth.
And Elijah passed over to him and threw [A]his mantle on him. 20 He left the oxen and ran after Elijah
and said, "Please [A]let me kiss my father and my
mother, then I will follow you." And he said to him,
"Go back again, for what have I done to you?" 21 So
he returned from following him, and took the pair
of oxen and sacrificed them and [A]boiled their flesh
with the implements of the oxen, and gave *it* to the
people and they ate. Then he arose and followed
Elijah and ministered to him.

WAR WITH ARAM

20 Now [A]Ben-hadad king of Aram gathered all
his army, [B]and there *were* thirty-two kings
with him, and horses and chariots. And he went
up and [C]besieged Samaria and fought against it.
2 Then he sent messengers to the city to Ahab king
of Israel and said to him, "Thus says Ben-hadad,
3 'Your silver and your gold are mine; your most
beautiful wives and children are also mine.' " 4 The
king of Israel replied, "It is according to your word,
my lord, O king; I am yours, and all that I have."
5 Then the messengers returned and said, "Thus says
[a]Ben-hadad, 'Surely, I sent to you saying, "You shall
give me your silver and your gold and your wives
and your children," 6 but about this time tomorrow
I will send my servants to you, and they will search
your house and the houses of your servants; and
[a]whatever is desirable in your eyes, they will [b]take
in their hand and carry away.' "

19:9 [A]Ex 33:21, 22 19:10 [A]Ex 20:5; 34:14 [B]Rom 11:3, 4 [C]1 Kin 18:22 19:11 [A]Ex 19:20; 24:12, 18 [B]Ezek 1:4 19:12 [A]Job 4:16; Zech 4:6 19:13 [A]Ex 3:6 [B]1 Kin 19:9 19:14 [A]1 Kin 19:10 19:15 [A]2 Kin 8:8-15 19:16 [A]2 Kin 9:1-10 [B]1 Kin 19:19-21; 2 Kin 2:9, 15 19:17 [A]2 Kin 8:12; 13:3, 22 [B]2 Kin 9:14-10:25 19:18 [A]Rom 11:4 [B]Hos 13:2 19:19 [A]1 Sam 28:14; 2 Kin 2:8, 13, 14 19:20 [A]Matt 8:21, 22; Luke 9:61, 62; Acts 20:37 19:21 [A]2 Sam 24:22 20:1 [A]1 Kin 15:18, 20; 2 Kin 6:24 [B]1 Kin 22:31 [C]1 Kin 16:24; 2 Kin 6:24 20:5 [a]Lit *Ben-hadad, saying* 20:6 [a]Lit *all the desire of your eyes* [b]Lit *put*

had a notable spiritual failure and so wandered 40 years in the wilderness (Nu 14:26–35), so a discouraged Elijah was to spend 40 days in the desert. As Moses had spent 40 days on the mountain without bread and water, sustained only by God as he awaited a new phase of service (Ex 34:28), so Elijah was to spend 40 days depending on God's enablement as he prepared for a new commission from the Lord. As Moses had seen the presence of God (Ex 33:12–23), so Elijah experienced a manifestation of God. **Horeb.** An alternate name for Mt. Sinai, located about 200 mi. S of Beersheba.

19:10, 14 Elijah viewed the Israelites as rebels against the Mosaic Covenant, a rebellion that his ministry had been unable to arrest (see v. 3). Paul used this incident as an illustration in Ro 11:3.

19:11 the LORD was passing by. The 3 phenomena, wind, earthquake, and fire, announced the imminent arrival of the Lord (cf. Ex 19:16–19; Ps 18:7–15; Hab 3:3–6). The Lord's self-revelation to Elijah came in a faint, whispering voice (v. 12). The lesson for Elijah was that Almighty God was quietly, sometimes imperceptibly, doing His work in Israel (v. 18).

19:15 the wilderness of Damascus. The Syrian Desert S and E of the city of Damascus, the city located to the NE of Israel.

19:15–17 The Lord instructed Elijah to anoint Hazael of Aram (see 2Ki 8:8), Jehu (see 2Ki 9:2), and Elisha (v. 19) for the purpose of commissioning them to destroy Baal worship in Israel. Through these 3 men, the Lord completed the execution of Baal worshipers that Elijah had begun. Actually, Elijah commissioned only the last of these 3 men directly—the other two were indirectly commissioned through Elisha. Elisha was involved in Hazael's becoming Syria's king (2Ki 8:7–14), and one of Elisha's associates anointed Jehu (2Ki 9:1–3). By the time the last of these men died (2Ki 13:24), Baalism had been officially barred from Israel.

19:16 Abel-meholah. The hometown of Elisha was located in the Jordan Valley, 10 mi. S of Beth-shanon, in the tribal allotment of Manasseh.

19:18 Paul used God's response to Elijah as an illustration in Ro 11:4. **kissed him.** Kissing the image or symbol of Baal was apparently a common act in worship (cf. Hos 13:2).

19:19 Elisha. This name means "my God is salvation" and belonged to Elisha, the successor to Elijah (see 2Ki 2:9–15). **Shaphat.** Elisha's father, whose name meant "he judges." **twelve pairs *of oxen*.** It was a common practice for several teams of oxen, each with its own plow and driver, to work together in a row. After letting the others pass, Elijah threw his mantle around the last man, Elisha, thus designating him as his successor.

19:20 Go back again. Elijah instructed Elisha to go, but to keep in mind the solemn call of God and not to allow any earthly affection to detain his obedience.

19:21 sacrificed. The slaughter of the oxen was a farewell feast for family and friends, indicating that Elisha was making a decisive break. He followed Elijah and became his servant (lit. "aide," the same term used for Joshua's relationship with Moses in Ex 24:13; 33:11). Just as Elijah resembled Moses, so Elisha resembled Joshua.

20:1 Ben-hadad. This was likely Ben-hadad II of Syria (*see note on 15:18*), who marched on the capital of Israel and demanded surrender by Ahab (vv. 2–6). **thirty-two kings.** These were probably rulers of client city-states in the land of Syria (*see notes on 10:29*).

7 Then the king of Israel called all the elders of the land and said, "Please observe and [A]see how this man is looking for trouble; for he sent to me for my wives and my children and my silver and my gold, and I did not refuse him." 8 All the elders and all the people said to him, "Do not listen or consent." 9 So he said to the messengers of Ben-hadad, "Tell my lord the king, 'All that you sent for to your servant at the first I will do, but this thing I cannot do.' " And the messengers departed and brought him word again. 10 Ben-hadad sent to him and said, "May [A]the gods do so to me and more also, if the dust of Samaria will suffice for handfuls for all the people who [a]follow me." 11 Then the king of Israel replied, "Tell *him,* '[A]Let not him who girds on *his armor* boast like him who takes *it* off.' " 12 When *Ben-hadad* heard this message, as [A]he was drinking [a]with the kings in the [b]temporary shelters, he said to his servants, "Station *yourselves.*" So they stationed *themselves* against the city.

AHAB VICTORIOUS

13 Now behold, a prophet approached Ahab king of Israel and said, "Thus says the LORD, 'Have you seen all this great multitude? Behold, [A]I will deliver them into your hand today, and [B]you shall know that I am the LORD.' " 14 Ahab said, "By whom?" So he said, "Thus says the LORD, 'By the young men of the rulers of the provinces.' " Then he said, "Who shall [a]begin the battle?" And he [b]answered, "You." 15 Then he mustered the young men of the rulers of the provinces, and there were 232; and after them he mustered all the people, *even* all the sons of Israel, 7,000.

16 They went out at noon, while [A]Ben-hadad was drinking himself drunk in the [a]temporary shelters [b]with the thirty-two kings who helped him. 17 The young men of the rulers of the provinces went out first; and Ben-hadad sent out and they told him, saying, "Men have come out from Samaria." 18 [A]Then he said, "If they have come out for peace, take them alive; or if they have come out for war, take them alive."

19 So these went out from the city, the young men of the rulers of the provinces, and the army which followed them. 20 They [a]killed each his man; and the Arameans fled and Israel pursued them, and Ben-hadad king of Aram escaped on a horse with horsemen. 21 The king of Israel went out and [a]struck the horses and chariots, and [a]killed the Arameans with a great slaughter.

22 Then [A]the prophet came near to the king of Israel and said to him, "Go, strengthen yourself and observe and see what you have to do; for [B]at the turn of the year the king of Aram will come up against you."

23 Now the servants of the king of Aram said to him, "[A]Their gods are gods of the mountains, therefore they were stronger than we; but rather let us fight against them in the plain, *and* surely we will be stronger than they. 24 Do this thing: remove the kings, each from his place, and put captains in their place, 25 and [a]muster an army like the army that you have lost, horse for horse, and chariot for chariot. Then we will fight against them in the plain, and surely we will be stronger than they." And he listened to their voice and did so.

ANOTHER ARAMEAN WAR

26 [A]At the turn of the year, Ben-hadad mustered the Arameans and went up to [B]Aphek to fight against Israel. 27 The sons of Israel were mustered and were provisioned and went to meet them; and the sons of Israel camped before them like two little flocks of goats, [A]but the Arameans filled the country. 28 Then [A]a man of God came near and spoke to the king of Israel and said, "Thus says the LORD, 'Because the Arameans have said, "[B]The LORD is a god of *the* mountains, but He is not a god of *the* valleys," therefore [C]I will give all this great multitude into your hand, and you shall know that I am the LORD.' " 29 So they camped one over against the other seven days. And on the seventh day the battle was joined, and the sons of Israel [a]killed *of* the Arameans 100,000 foot soldiers in one day. 30 But the rest fled to [A]Aphek into the city, and the wall fell on 27,000 men who were left. And Ben-hadad fled and came into the city [B]into an inner chamber.

20:7 [A]2 Kin 5:7 20:10 [a]Lit *are at my feet* [A]1 Kin 19:2; 2 Kin 6:31 20:11 [A]Prov 27:1 20:12 [a]Lit *he and* [b]Or *booths* [A]1 Kin 16:9; Prov 31:4, 5 20:13 [A]1 Kin 20:28 [B]1 Kin 18:36 20:14 [a]Lit *bind* [b]Lit *said* 20:16 [a]Or *booths* [b]Lit *he and the 32 kings* [A]1 Kin 16:9; 20:12; Prov 20:1 20:18 [A]2 Kin 14:8-12 20:20 [a]Lit *smote* 20:21 [a]Lit *smote* 20:22 [A]1 Kin 20:13 [B]2 Sam 11:1; 1 Kin 20:26 20:23 [A]1 Kin 14:23; Jer 16:19-21; Rom 1:21-23 20:25 [a]Lit *number* 20:26 [A]1 Kin 20:22 [B]2 Kin 13:17 20:27 [A]Judg 6:3-5; 1 Sam 13:5-8 20:28 [A]1 Kin 17:18 [B]1 Kin 20:23 [C]1 Kin 20:13 20:29 [a]Lit *smote* 20:30 [A]1 Kin 20:26 [B]1 Kin 22:25; 2 Chr 18:24

20:9 I will do .... cannot do. Ahab was willing to give tribute to Ben-hadad as his vassal (vv. 2–4), but he refused to allow the Syrian king to plunder his palace (vv. 5–8).

20:10, 11 Ben-hadad boasted that his army would level the hill of Samaria to dust (v. 10). Ahab replied that Ben-hadad should not boast of the outcome of the battle before it began (v. 11).

20:13 I will deliver them into your hand today. These were the words of assurance given before battles when the Lord was about to fight on Israel's side (Jos 6:2, 16; 8:1, 18; Jdg 7:2; 18:10; 1Sa 23:4; 24:4). Further, the victory would show Ahab that the Lord was in every respect the mighty God He claimed to be. Though the people and king of Israel had dishonored God, He would not utterly cast them off (vv. 14, 15).

20:17–21 The battle strategy was to send out the young leaders who could perhaps draw near to the Syrians without arousing too much alarm and then, at a given signal, initiate a charge joined by Ahab's main striking force that would catch the drunken Syrians off guard and throw them into confusion. The glorious victory, won so easily and with such a small force, was granted so that Ahab and the people would know that God was sovereign.

20:22 the turn of the year. Spring was the usual time for battles in the ancient Near East (*see note on 2Sa 11:1*), and a prophet warned Ahab that Ben-hadad would retaliate in the following year.

20:23 gods of the mountains. The advisors of Ben-hadad believed that Israel had won the previous battle because it occurred in mountainous terrain, the area they believed was ruled by Israel's "gods." They counseled Ben-hadad to strengthen his army and fight Israel again, only on level ground (v. 25). Obviously, this attitude insulted Israel's God, the Lord, who is sovereign over the whole earth (cf. 2Ki 19:16–19). That blasphemous depreciation of the Lord's power meant certain defeat for the Syrians (v. 28).

20:26 Aphek. Though several towns in Israel bore the name Aphek, the one mentioned here probably lay about 3 mi. E of the Sea of Galilee, N of the Yarmuk River.

20:27 like two little flocks of goats. Compared to the massive herd of Arameans covering the land, Israel looked like two little goat flocks. Goats were never seen in large flocks or scattered like sheep; hence the description of the two compact, small divisions.

20:28 man of God. *See note on 12:22.*

20:30 inner chamber. Lit. "a room in a room," a safe, well-hidden place.

31 [A]His servants said to him, "Behold now, we
have heard that the kings of the house of Israel
are merciful kings, please let us [B]put sackcloth on
our loins and ropes on our heads, and go out to
the king of Israel; perhaps he will save your [a]life."
32 So [A]they girded sackcloth on their loins and *put*
ropes on their heads, and came to the king of Israel
and said, "[B]Your servant Ben-hadad says, 'Please
let me live.' " And he said, "Is he still alive? He is
my brother." 33 Now the men [a]took this as an omen,
and quickly [b]catching his word said, "Your brother
Ben-hadad." Then he said, "Go, bring him." Then
Ben-hadad came out to him, and he [c]took him up
into the chariot. 34 *Ben-hadad* said to him, "[A]The
cities which my father took from your father I will
restore, and you shall make streets for yourself in
Damascus, as my father made in Samaria." *Ahab
said,* "And I will let you go with this covenant." So
he made a covenant with him and let him go.
35 Now a certain man of [A]the sons of the prophets
said to [a]another [B]by the word of the LORD, "Please
strike me." But the man refused to strike him. 36 Then
he said to him, "Because you have not listened to
the voice of the LORD, behold, as soon as you have
departed from me, [A]a lion will [a]kill you." And as
soon as he had departed from him a lion found
him and [b]killed him. 37 Then he found another man
and said, "Please [a]strike me." And the man [b]struck
him, [c]wounding him. 38 So the prophet departed
and waited for the king by the way, and [A]disguised
himself with a bandage over his eyes. 39 As the king
passed by, he cried to the king and said, "Your servant went out into the midst of the battle; and behold, a man turned aside and brought a man to
me and said, 'Guard this man; if for any reason he
is missing, [A]then your life shall be for his life, or
else you shall pay a talent of silver.' 40 While your
servant was busy here and there, he was gone."
And the king of Israel said to him, "So shall your
judgment be; you yourself have decided *it.*" 41 Then
he hastily took the bandage away from his eyes, and
the king of Israel recognized him that he was of the
prophets. 42 He said to him, "Thus says the LORD,
'Because you have let go out of *your* hand the man
whom I had devoted to destruction, therefore [A]your
[a]life shall go for his [a]life, and your people for his
people.' " 43 So [A]the king of Israel went to his house
sullen and vexed, and came to Samaria.

AHAB COVETS NABOTH'S VINEYARD

21 Now it came about after these things that
Naboth the Jezreelite had a vineyard which
was in [A]Jezreel beside the palace of Ahab king of
Samaria. 2 Ahab spoke to Naboth, saying, "[A]Give me
your vineyard, that I may have it for a vegetable garden because it is close beside my house, and I will
give you a better vineyard than it in its place; if [a]you
like, I will give you the price of [b]it in money." 3 But
Naboth said to Ahab, "The LORD forbid me [A]that
I should give you the inheritance of my fathers."
4 [A]So Ahab came into his house sullen and vexed
because of the word which Naboth the Jezreelite
had spoken to him; for he said, "I will not give you
the inheritance of my fathers." And he lay down on
his bed and turned away his face and ate no [a]food.
5 But Jezebel his wife came to him and said to
him, "How is it that your spirit is so sullen that you
are not eating [a]food?" 6 So he said to her, "Because I
spoke to Naboth the Jezreelite and said to him, 'Give
me your vineyard for money; or else, if it pleases
you, I will give you a vineyard in its place.' But he
said, 'I will not give you my vineyard.' " 7 Jezebel his
wife said to him, "[A]Do you now [a]reign over Israel?
Arise, eat bread, and let your heart be joyful; I will
give you the vineyard of Naboth the Jezreelite."
8 [A]So she wrote letters in Ahab's name and sealed
them with his seal, and sent letters to [B]the elders
and to the nobles who were living with Naboth

20:31 [a]Lit *soul* [A]1 Kin 20:23-26 [B]Gen 37:34; 2 Sam 3:31 20:32 [A]1 Kin 20:31 [B]1 Kin 20:3-6 20:33 [a]Lit *divined* [b]Lit *caught from him* [c]Lit *caused him to come up* 20:34 [A]1 Kin 15:20 20:35 [a]Lit *his neighbor* [A]2 Kin 2:3-7 [B]1 Kin 13:17, 18 20:36 [a]Lit *smite* [b]Lit *smote* [A]1 Kin 13:24 20:37 [a]Lit *smite* [b]Lit *smote* [c]Lit *striking and wounding* 20:38 [A]1 Kin 14:2 20:39 [A]2 Kin 10:24 20:42 [a]Lit *soul* [A]1 Kin 20:39 20:43 [A]1 Kin 21:4
21:1 [A]Judg 6:33; 1 Kin 18:45, 46 21:2 [a]Lit *it is good in your eyes* [b]Lit *this* [A]1 Sam 8:14 21:3 [A]Lev 25:23; Num 36:7; Ezek 46:18
21:4 [a]Lit *bread* [A]1 Kin 20:43 21:5 [a]Lit *bread* 21:7 [a]Lit *exercise kingship* [A]1 Sam 8:14 21:8 [A]Esth 3:12; 8:8, 10 [B]1 Kin 20:7

20:31 sackcloth … and ropes. Sackcloth traditionally symbolized mourning and penitence. Ropes around the heads were symbols of surrender.

20:34 streets. Lit. "outside places." Bazaars were set up in a foreign land (cf. Ne 13:16), a lucrative market for Israelite goods.

20:35 sons of the prophets. An association of prophets that met and possibly lived together for study, encouragement, and service (*see note on 1Sa 10:5*).

20:35, 36 The prophet needed to be wounded as if in battle to carry out the drama. The refusal to do as the prophet said was wrong, as it was a withholding of necessary aid to a prophet of God in the discharge of his duty. It was severely punished as a warning to others (cf. 13:2–24).

20:39–43 The prophet illustrated that, just as a soldier pays dearly for losing a prisoner in war, Ahab will pay for letting Ben-hadad, the idolatrous enemy of God, live.

20:39 a talent of silver. This was about 75 lbs. of silver, more than a common soldier could afford and for which debt he would face death.

20:40 your judgment. This "judicial parable" was designed to trap Ahab into announcing the punishment for his own crime (see 2Sa 12:1–12). Unknowingly, Ahab declared his own judgment (v. 42).

20:42 destruction. By declaring the battles to be holy war (vv. 13, 22, 28), the Lord had put Ben-hadad and the Syrians under the ban, a reference to something belonging to the Lord and destined to be destroyed (Dt 7:2; 20:16). By freeing Ben-hadad, Ahab had disobeyed the law and would suffer the ban in place of Ben-hadad.

20:43 sullen and vexed. Ahab was resentful and angry because of the Lord's reaction to his actions (cf. 21:4).

21:1 Jezreel. *See note on 18:45.* Ahab had built a second palace in Jezreel, where he lived when not in the capital at Samaria.

21:2 Give me your vineyard. In Canaanite culture, since land was simply a commodity to be traded and sold for profit, Ahab's offer to Naboth of an exchange of property or offer of purchase was a common transaction in the Near East.

21:3 The LORD forbid. Naboth's words implied that trading or selling his property would be a disregard of the law and thus displeasing in God's eyes (cf. 1Sa 24:6; 26:11; 2Sa 23:17). The reason was that the vineyard was his ancestral property. The Lord, the owner of all of the land of Israel, had forbidden Israelite families to surrender ownership of family lands permanently (Lv 25:23–28; Nu 36:7–9). Out of loyalty to God, Naboth declined Ahab's offer.

21:7 Do you now reign over Israel? Jezebel was sarcastically rebuking Ahab for not exercising absolute royal power in the matter.

21:8 she wrote letters. Written by the royal scribe, ancient letters were mainly in the form of a scroll sealed in clay or wax with the sender's personal sign. The seal made the

in his city. 9 Now she wrote in the letters, saying,
"Proclaim a fast and seat Naboth at the head of
the people; 10 and seat two [A]worthless men before
him, and let them testify against him, saying, '[B]You
cursed God and the king.' Then take him out and
[C]stone him [a]to death."

JEZEBEL'S PLOT

11 So the men of his city, the elders and the nobles
who lived in his city, did as Jezebel had sent *word*
to them, just as it was written in the letters which
she had sent them. 12 They [A]proclaimed a fast and
seated Naboth at the head of the people. 13 Then the
two worthless men came in and sat before him;
and the worthless men testified against him, even
against Naboth, before the people, saying, "Naboth
cursed God and the king." [A]So they took him outside the city and stoned him [a]to death with stones.
14 Then they sent *word* to Jezebel, saying, "Naboth
has been stoned and is dead."

15 When Jezebel heard that Naboth had been
stoned and was dead, Jezebel said to Ahab, "Arise,
take possession of the vineyard of Naboth, the Jezreelite, which he refused to give you for money; for
Naboth is not alive, but dead." 16 When Ahab heard
that Naboth was dead, Ahab arose to go down to
the vineyard of Naboth the Jezreelite, to take possession of it.

17 Then the word of the LORD came to Elijah the
Tishbite, saying, 18 "Arise, go down to meet Ahab
king of Israel, [A]who is in Samaria; behold, he is in
the vineyard of Naboth where he has gone down
to take possession of it. 19 You shall speak to him,
saying, 'Thus says the LORD, "[A]Have you murdered
and also taken possession?" ' And you shall speak
to him, saying, 'Thus says the LORD, "[B]In the place
where the dogs licked up the blood of Naboth the
dogs will lick up your blood, even yours." ' "

20 Ahab said to Elijah, "[A]Have you found me, O my
enemy?" And he [a]answered, "I have found *you*, [B]be-
cause you have sold yourself to do evil in the sight
of the LORD. 21 Behold, I will bring evil upon you,
and [A]will utterly sweep you away, and will cut off
from Ahab every male, both bond and free in Israel;
22 and [A]I will make your house [B]like the house of Jeroboam the son of Nebat, and like the house of Baasha
the son of Ahijah, because of the provocation with
which you have provoked *Me* to anger, and *because*
you [C]have made Israel sin. 23 Of Jezebel also has the
LORD spoken, saying, '[A]The dogs will eat Jezebel in
the [a]district of Jezreel.' 24 [A]The one belonging to Ahab,
who dies in the city, the dogs will eat, and the one
who dies in the field the birds of heaven will eat."

25 [A]Surely there was no one like Ahab who sold
himself to do evil in the sight of the LORD, [a]because
Jezebel his wife incited him. 26 [A]He acted very abominably in following idols, [B]according to all that the
Amorites had done, whom the LORD cast out before
the sons of Israel.

27 It came about when Ahab heard these words, that
[A]he tore his clothes and put [a]on sackcloth and fasted,
and he lay in sackcloth and went about [b]despondently.
28 Then the word of the LORD came to Elijah the Tishbite, saying, 29 "Do you see how Ahab has humbled
himself before Me? Because he has humbled himself
before Me, I will not bring the evil in his days, *but* I
will bring the evil upon his house [A]in his son's days."

AHAB'S THIRD CAMPAIGN AGAINST ARAM

22 Three [a]years passed without war between Aram
and Israel. 2 [A]In the third year [B]Jehoshaphat the
king of Judah came down to the king of Israel. 3 Now
the king of Israel said to his servants, "Do you know
that [A]Ramoth-gilead belongs to us, and we [a]are still
doing nothing to take it out of the hand of the king

21:10 [a]Lit *so that he dies* [A]1 Sam 2:12; 2 Sam 20:1 [B]Ex 22:28; Lev 24:15, 16; Acts 6:11 [C]Lev 24:14 21:12 [A]Is 58:4 21:13 [a]Lit *with stones so that he died* [A]2 Kin 9:26; 2 Chr 24:21; Acts 7:58, 59; Heb 11:37 21:18 [A]1 Kin 16:29 21:19 [A]2 Sam 12:9 [B]1 Kin 22:38; 2 Kin 9:26 21:20 [a]Lit *said* [A]1 Kin 18:17 [B]1 Kin 21:25; 2 Kin 17:17; Rom 7:14 21:21 [A]1 Kin 14:10; 2 Kin 9:8 21:22 [A]1 Kin 15:29 [B]1 Kin 16:3, 11 [C]1 Kin 12:30; 13:34; 14:16 21:23 [a]Lit *portion;* some mss read *rampart* [A]2 Kin 9:10, 30-37 21:24 [A]1 Kin 14:11; 16:4 21:25 [a]Or *whom Jezebel his wife incited* [A]1 Kin 16:30-33; 21:20 21:26 [A]1 Kin 15:12; 2 Kin 17:12 [B]Gen 15:16; Lev 18:25-30; 2 Kin 21:11 21:27 [a]Lit *sackcloth on his flesh* [b]Or *softly* [A]Gen 37:34; 2 Sam 3:31; 2 Kin 6:30 21:29 [A]2 Kin 9:25-37 22:1 [a]Lit *they sat for three years* 22:2 [A]2 Chr 18:2 [B]1 Kin 15:24 22:3 [a]Lit *are silent so as not* [A]Deut 4:43; Josh 21:38; 1 Kin 4:13

contents of the letters a royal mandate and implied that disobedience would certainly lead to some kind of punishment.

21:9 Proclaim a fast. To call an assembly for solemn fasting implied that a disaster threatened the people that could be averted only if they would humble themselves before the Lord and remove any person whose sin had brought God's judgment upon them (cf. Jdg 20:26; 1Sa 7:5, 6; 2Ch 20:2–4).

21:10 two … men. The Mosaic law required two witnesses in capital cases (Nu 35:30; Dt 17:6; 19:5). **worthless men.** Lit. "sons of Belial." These were utterly wicked men. *See note on 1Sa 2:12.* **cursed God and the king.** The penalty for cursing God and the king was death (Ex 22:28).

21:13 outside the city. They hypocritically climaxed their violent murder by killing the innocent Naboth in a place that was in accordance with the Mosaic law (Lv 24:14; Nu 15:35, 36). He was stoned to death in the open fields and his sons were killed with him (2Ki 9:26), eliminating all possible heirs.

21:19 Elijah's first announcement of judgment applied to Ahab personally. He said that the dogs would lick Ahab's blood in the same place that Naboth died, outside the city of Jezreel. This prophecy was not fulfilled because of his repentance (vv. 27–29), but was partially fulfilled in the licking of Ahab's blood by dogs at the pool in Samaria (22:37, 38).

21:21–24 Elijah's second announcement of judgment applied to Ahab and his house. The judgment was virtually identical with one made to Jeroboam (14:10, 11) and similar to the one made to Baasha (16:3, 4).

21:23 Of Jezebel. Jezebel was singled out for judgment because of her initiative in driving Ahab in the promotion of Baalism (v. 25). Elijah's prophecy concerning her was literally fulfilled in 2Ki 9:10, 30–37.

21:27 tore his clothes. The tearing of garments was a common expression of grief, terror, or repentance in the face of great personal or national calamity (Nu 14:6; Jos 7:6; Jdg 11:35; 2Sa 1:2; 3:31).

21:29 his son's days. Since Ahab had truly humbled himself before the Lord, he did not see the disaster forecast for him (v. 19). Instead, God postponed it until the reign of his son, Joram, ca. 852–841 B.C. (2Ki 9:25, 26). Joram died in the field of Naboth (cf. v. 19).

22:1 Three years. Israel had peace for 3 years following the two years of war with Syria described in 20:1–34. During this peace, Ben-hadad, Ahab, and 10 other kings formed a coalition to repel an Assyrian invasion. Assyrian records described the major battle fought at Qarqar on the Orontes River in 853 B.C. Though Assyria claimed victory, later events show that they were stopped from further advance southward at that time. With the Assyrian threat neutralized, Ahab turned his attention to the unfinished conflict with Syria.

22:2 Jehoshaphat. The king of Judah, ca. 873–848, whose reign is described in vv. 41–50. *See notes on 2Ch 17:1–21:3.*

22:3 Ramoth-gilead. Ramoth-gilead was a Levitical city E of the Jordan River in Gilead, on the N border of Gad, the home of Jephthah (Jdg 11:34), and a key administrative center in

of Aram?" 4 And he said to Jehoshaphat, "Will you go
with me to battle at Ramoth-gilead?" And Jehoshaphat
said to the king of Israel, "[A]I am as you are, my people
as your people, my horses as your horses."
5 Moreover, Jehoshaphat said to the king of Israel,
"Please inquire [a]first for the word of the LORD."
6 Then [A]the king of Israel gathered the prophets together, about four hundred men, and said to them,
"Shall I go against Ramoth-gilead to battle or shall
I refrain?" And they said, "Go up, for the Lord will
give *it* into the hand of the king." 7 But [A]Jehoshaphat
said, "Is there not yet a prophet of the LORD here
that we may inquire of him?" 8 The king of Israel said
to Jehoshaphat, "There is yet one man by whom we
may inquire of the LORD, but I hate him, because
he does not prophesy good concerning me, but
evil. *He is* Micaiah son of Imlah." But Jehoshaphat
said, "Let not the king say so." 9 Then the king of
Israel called an officer and said, "[a]Bring quickly
Micaiah son of Imlah." 10 Now the king of Israel and
Jehoshaphat king of Judah were sitting each on his
throne, arrayed in *their* robes, at the threshing floor
at the entrance of the gate of Samaria; and [A]all the
prophets were prophesying before them. 11 Then
Zedekiah the son of Chenaanah made [A]horns of iron
for himself and said, "Thus says the LORD, '[B]With
these you will gore the Arameans until they are
consumed.' " 12 All the prophets were prophesying
thus, saying, "Go up to Ramoth-gilead and prosper,
for the LORD will give *it* into the hand of the king."

MICAIAH PREDICTS DEFEAT

13 Then the messenger who went to summon Micaiah spoke to him saying, "Behold now, the words of the
prophets are uniformly favorable to the king. Please
let your word be like the word of one of them, and
speak favorably." 14 But Micaiah said, "[A]As the LORD
lives, what [B]the LORD says to me, that I shall speak."
15 When he came to the king, the king said to him,
"Micaiah, shall we go to Ramoth-gilead to battle, or
shall we refrain?" And he [a]answered him, "[A]Go up
and succeed, and the LORD will give *it* into the hand
of the king." 16 Then the king said to him, "How many
times must I adjure you to speak to me nothing but
the truth in the name of the LORD?" 17 So he said,

"I saw all Israel
Scattered on the mountains,
[A]Like sheep which have no shepherd.
And the LORD said,
'These have no master.
Let each of them return to
his house in peace.' "

18 Then the king of Israel said to Jehoshaphat, "[A]Did
I not tell you that he would not prophesy good concerning me, but evil?"
19 [a]Micaiah said, "Therefore, hear the word of the
LORD. [A]I saw the LORD sitting on His throne, and [B]all
the host of heaven standing by Him on His right and
on His left. 20 The LORD said, 'Who will entice Ahab
to go up and fall at Ramoth-gilead?' And one said
this while another said that. 21 Then a spirit came
forward and stood before the LORD and said, 'I will
entice him.' 22 The LORD said to him, 'How?' And he
said, 'I will go out and [A]be a deceiving spirit in the
mouth of all his prophets.' Then He said, 'You are
to entice *him* and also prevail. Go and do so.' 23 Now
therefore, behold, [A]the LORD has put a deceiving
spirit in the mouth of all these your prophets; and
the LORD has proclaimed disaster against you."
24 Then [A]Zedekiah the son of Chenaanah came
near and struck Micaiah on the cheek and said,
"[B]How did the Spirit of the LORD pass from me to
speak to you?" 25 Micaiah said, "Behold, you shall
see on that day when you [A]enter an inner room
to hide yourself." 26 Then the king of Israel said,
"Take Micaiah and return him to Amon the governor of the city and to Joash the king's son; 27 and
say, 'Thus says the king, "[A]Put this man in prison
and feed him [a]sparingly with bread and water until
I return safely." ' " 28 Micaiah said, "[A]If you indeed
return safely the LORD has not spoken by me." And
he said, "[B]Listen, all you people."

22:4 [A]2 Kin 3:7 22:5 [a]Lit *as the day* 22:6 [A]1 Kin 18:19 22:7 [A]2 Kin 3:11 22:9 [a]Lit *Hasten Micaiah* 22:10 [A]1 Kin 22:6 22:11 [A]Zech 1:18-21 [B]Deut 33:17 22:14 [A]1 Kin 18:10, 15 [B]Num 22:18; 24:13 22:15 [a]Lit *said to* [A]1 Kin 22:12 22:17 [A]Num 27:17; 1 Kin 22:34-36; 2 Chr 18:16; Matt 9:36; Mark 6:34 22:18 [A]1 Kin 22:8 22:19 [a]Lit *he* [A]Is 6:1; Ezek 1:26-28; Dan 7:9, 10 [B]Job 1:6; 2:1; Ps 103:20, 21; Dan 7:10; Matt 18:10; Heb 1:7, 14 22:22 [A]Judg 9:23; 1 Sam 16:14; 18:10; 19:9; Ezek 14:9; 2 Thess 2:11 22:23 [A]Ezek 14:9 22:24 [A]1 Kin 22:11; Matt 5:39; Acts 23:2, 3 [B]2 Chr 18:23 22:25 [A]1 Kin 20:30 22:27 [a]Lit *with bread of affliction and water of affliction* [A]2 Chr 16:10; 18:25-27 22:28 [A]Deut 18:22 [B]Mic 1:2

Solomon's kingdom (4:13). It seems to have been one of the cities that Ben-hadad should have returned to Israel (20:34).

22:5 inquire first for the word of the LORD. Jehoshaphat was willing to help Ahab fight Syria (v. 4), but reminded Ahab of the need to seek the will of the Lord before going into battle (cf. 1Sa 23:1–5, 9–13; 2Sa 2:1; 5:19–25; 2Ki 3:11–20).

22:6 prophets. These 400 prophets of Ahab were not true prophets of the Lord. They worshiped at Bethel in the golden-calf center set up by Jeroboam (12:28, 29) and were supported by Ahab, whose religious policy also permitted Baal worship. Their words were designed to please Ahab (v. 8), so they refused to begin with the authoritative "thus says the Lord" and did not use the covenant name for Israel's God, "Lord."

22:7 a prophet of the LORD. Jehoshaphat recognized that the 400 prophets were not true prophets of the Lord, and wished to hear from a true prophet.

22:8 Micaiah. His name means "Who is like the Lord?"

22:10 throne. A portable, high-backed chair made of wood with armrests and separate footstool.

22:11 Zedekiah. He was the spokesman for the false prophets. In contrast to v. 6, he used the introductory formula and God's covenant name.

22:15 Go up and succeed. Micaiah sarcastically repeated the message of the false prophets as he had been encouraged to do (v. 13). Ahab clearly sensed the sarcasm and demanded that Micaiah tell him the truth (v. 16).

22:17 sheep which have no shepherd. The image of the king as a shepherd and his people as the sheep was a familiar one (Nu 27:16, 17; Zec 13:7). Micaiah's point was that Israel's shepherd, King Ahab, would be killed and his army scattered.

22:22 a deceiving spirit. This must be Satan, whom the Lord allowed to speak through 400 demons who indwelt the 400 false prophets.

22:24 struck ... on the cheek. This was a rebuke by the leader of the false prophets (v. 6) for the perceived insolence of Micaiah and his claim to truly speak for God. It was followed by a sarcastic question asking if the prophet could tell which direction the spirit in Zedekiah had gone.

22:28 If you indeed return. In accordance with Dt 18:21, 22, Micaiah declared to Ahab that if he lived to return from the battle, then he had uttered a false prophecy.

DEFEAT AND DEATH OF AHAB

29 So [A]the king of Israel and Jehoshaphat king of Judah went up against Ramoth-gilead. 30 The king of Israel said to Jehoshaphat, "[A]I will disguise myself and go into the battle, but you put on your robes." So the king of Israel disguised himself and went into the battle. 31 Now [A]the king of Aram had commanded the thirty-two captains of his chariots, saying, "Do not fight with small or great, but with the king of Israel alone." 32 So when the captains of the chariots saw Jehoshaphat, they said, "Surely it is the king of Israel," and they turned aside to fight against him, and Jehoshaphat cried out. 33 When the captains of the chariots saw that it was not the king of Israel, they turned back from pursuing him.

34 Now a certain man drew his bow at random and struck the king of Israel [a]in a joint of the armor. So he said to the driver of his chariot, "Turn [b]around and take me out of the [c]fight; [A]for I am severely wounded." 35 The battle [a]raged that day, and the king was propped up in his chariot in front of the Arameans, and died at evening, and the blood from the wound ran into the bottom of the chariot. 36 [A]Then a cry passed throughout the army close to sunset, saying, "Every man to his city and every man to his [a]country."

37 So the king died and was brought to Samaria, and they buried the king in Samaria. 38 They washed the chariot by the pool of Samaria, and the dogs licked up his blood (now the harlots bathed themselves *there*), [A]according to the word of the LORD which He spoke. 39 Now the rest of the acts of Ahab and all that he did and [A]the ivory house which he built and all the cities which he built, are they not written in the Book of the Chronicles of the Kings of Israel? 40 So Ahab slept with his fathers, and Ahaziah his son became king in his place.

THE NEW RULERS

41 [A]Now Jehoshaphat the son of Asa became king over Judah in the fourth year of Ahab king of Israel. 42 Jehoshaphat was thirty-five years old when he became king, and he reigned twenty-five years in Jerusalem. And his mother's name was Azubah the daughter of Shilhi. 43 [A]He walked in all the way of Asa his father; he did not turn aside from it, doing right in the sight of the LORD. [B]However, the high places were not taken away; the people still sacrificed and burnt incense on the high places. 44 [A]Jehoshaphat also made peace with the king of Israel.

45 Now the rest of the acts of Jehoshaphat, and his might which he showed and how he warred, are they not written [A]in the Book of the Chronicles of the Kings of Judah? 46 The remnant of [A]the sodomites who remained in the days of his father Asa, he [a]expelled from the land.

47 Now [A]there was no king in Edom; a deputy was king. 48 Jehoshaphat made [A]ships of Tarshish to go to [B]Ophir for gold, but [C]they did not go for the ships were broken at [D]Ezion-geber. 49 Then Ahaziah the son of Ahab said to Jehoshaphat, "Let my servants go with your servants in the ships." But Jehoshaphat was not willing. 50 [A]And Jehoshaphat slept with his fathers and was buried with his fathers in the city of his father David, and Jehoram his son became king in his place.

51 Ahaziah the son of Ahab [A]became king over Israel in Samaria in the seventeenth year of Jehoshaphat king of Judah, and he reigned two years over Israel. 52 He did evil in the sight of the LORD and [A]walked in the way of his father and in the way of his mother and in the way of Jeroboam the son of Nebat, who caused Israel to sin. 53 [A]So he served Baal and worshiped him and provoked the LORD God of Israel to anger, according to all that his father had done.

22:29 [A]1 Kin 22:3, 4 22:30 [A]2 Chr 35:22 22:31 [A]1 Kin 20:1, 16, 24; 2 Chr 18:30 22:34 [a]Lit *between the scale-armor and the breastplate* [b]Lit *your hand* [c]Lit *camp* [A]2 Chr 35:23 22:35 [a]Lit *went up* 22:36 [a]Lit *land* [A]2 Kin 14:12 22:38 [A]1 Kin 21:19 22:39 [A]Amos 3:15 22:41 [A]2 Chr 20:31 22:43 [A]2 Chr 17:3 [B]1 Kin 15:14; 2 Kin 12:3 22:44 [A]1 Kin 22:2; 2 Kin 8:16, 18; 2 Chr 19:2 22:45 [A]2 Chr 20:34 22:46 [a]Lit *consumed* [A]Gen 19:5; Deut 23:17; 1 Kin 14:24; 15:12; Jude 7 22:47 [A]2 Sam 8:14; 2 Kin 3:9 22:48 [A]1 Kin 10:22; 2 Chr 20:36 [B]1 Kin 9:28 [C]2 Chr 20:37 [D]1 Kin 9:26 22:50 [A]2 Chr 21:1 22:51 [A]1 Kin 22:40 22:52 [A]1 Kin 15:26; 21:25 22:53 [A]Judg 2:11; 1 Kin 16:30-32

22:30 disguise myself. Rejecting the prophecy, but fearing it also, Ahab decided not to wear his official robe, but the clothes of an ordinary soldier.

22:31 with the king of Israel alone. The very Syrian king, Ben-hadad, whose life Ahab had spared (20:34), ungratefully singled him out for death.

22:32 Jehoshaphat cried out. According to 2Ch 18:31, this was a prayer for the Lord's deliverance. Jehoshaphat's cry showed the Syrians that he was not Ahab.

22:34 at random. The Syrian bowman shot at an Israelite soldier, not knowing that it was the disguised Ahab. The arrow found a small groove between the breastpiece and the flexible scale armor that covered the lower abdomen and thighs. Instantly, Ahab slumped in his chariot, mortally wounded in the stomach and bleeding to death.

22:38 now the harlots bathed. The Heb. text may read "where" or "while." In either case, the point is the same: Ahab, the spiritual harlot (i.e., idolater), was associated with the physical harlots at his death. **according to the word of the LORD.** Ahab's death fulfilled the prophecies spoken by Elijah (21:19) and Micaiah (v. 17).

22:39 the ivory house. Ahab's palace at Samaria had internal walled panels that were made of inlaid ivory, indicative of his kingdom's economic prosperity. **cities which he built.** Archeological excavations show that Ahab strengthened the fortifications of Samaria, Megiddo, and Hazor.

22:41 fourth year. A reference to the beginning of Jehoshaphat's reign, after being co-regent with his father Asa, in 870 B.C.

22:42 twenty-five years. 873–848 B.C.

22:43 doing right. Jehoshaphat faithfully followed in his father Asa's footsteps, doing what pleased the Lord. His only major fault, like that of his father, was his failure to close down the high places.

22:44 made peace. In 2Ch 19:2, Jehu the prophet rebuked Jehoshaphat for this alliance.

22:45 warred. See 2Ki 3:7–27; 2Ch 17:11; 20:1–30.

22:47–49 Jehoshaphat controlled Edom, which gave him access to Ezion-geber. He sought to emulate Solomon's fleet and wealth (9:26–28), but was unsuccessful. According to 2Ch 20:36, 37, the Lord destroyed his fleet because of Jehoshaphat's alliance to build it with Ahaziah, king of Israel. First Kings 22:49 apparently refers to a subsequent attempt by Ahaziah to continue the joint venture after the disaster.

22:51–2Ki 1:18 Ahaziah ... two years. 853–852 B.C.

22:53 he served Baal. Ahaziah continued the official promotion of Baal worship (cf. 16:31, 32). First Kings ends at this point in the middle of Ahaziah's reign which is picked up in 2Ki 1:1–18. The explanation for this unusual break is found in Introduction: Title.

The Kings of Israel and Judah

KING	SCRIPTURE
United Kingdom	
Saul	1 Samuel 9:1–31:13; 1 Chronicles 10:1–14
David	2 Samuel; 1 Kings 1:1–2:9; 1 Chronicles 11:1–29:30
Solomon	1 Kings 2:10–11:43; 2 Chronicles 1:1–9:31
Northern Kingdom (Israel)	
Jeroboam I	1 Kings 12:25–14:20
Nadab	1 Kings 15:25–31
Baasha	1 Kings 15:32–16:7
Elah	1 Kings 16:8–14
Zimri	1 Kings 16:15–20
Tibni	1 Kings 16:21, 22
Omri	1 Kings 16:21–28
Ahab	1 Kings 16:29–22:40
Ahaziah	1 Kings 22:51–53; 2 Kings 1:1–18
Jehoram (Joram)	2 Kings 2:1–8:15
Jehu	2 Kings 9:1–10:36
Jehoahaz	2 Kings 13:1–9
Jehoash (Joash)	2 Kings 13:10–25
Jeroboam II	2 Kings 14:23–29
Zechariah	2 Kings 15:8–12
Shallum	2 Kings 15:13–15
Menahem	2 Kings 15:16–22
Pekahiah	2 Kings 15:23–26
Pekah	2 Kings 15:27–31
Hoshea	2 Kings 17:1–41
Southern Kingdom (Judah)	
Rehoboam	1 Kings 12:1–14:31; 2 Chronicles 10:1–12:16
Abijam (Abijah)	1 Kings 15:1–8; 2 Chronicles 13:1–22
Asa	1 Kings 15:9–24; 2 Chronicles 14:1–16:14
Jehoshaphat	1 Kings 22:41–50; 2 Chronicles 17:1–20:37
Joram (Jehoram)	2 Kings 8:16–24; 2 Chronicles 21:1–20
Ahaziah	2 Kings 8:25–29; 2 Chronicles 22:1–9
Athaliah (queen)	2 Kings 11:1–16; 2 Chronicles 22:1–23:21
Joash (Jehoash)	2 Kings 11:17–12:21; 2 Chronicles 23:16–24:27
Amaziah	2 Kings 14:1–22; 2 Chronicles 25:1–28
Uzziah (Azariah)	2 Kings 15:1–7; 2 Chronicles 26:1–23
Jotham	2 Kings 15:32–38; 2 Chronicles 27:1–9
Ahaz	2 Kings 16:1–20; 2 Chronicles 28:1–27
Hezekiah	2 Kings 18:1–20:21; 2 Chronicles 29:1–32:33
Manasseh	2 Kings 21:1–18; 2 Chronicles 33:1–20
Amon	2 Kings 21:19–26; 2 Chronicles 33:21–25
Josiah	2 Kings 22:1–23:30; 2 Chronicles 34:1–35:27
Jehoahaz	2 Kings 23:31–33; 2 Chronicles 36:1–4
Jehoiakim	2 Kings 23:34–24:7; 2 Chronicles 36:5–8
Jehoiachin	2 Kings 24:8–16; 2 Chronicles 36:9, 10
Zedekiah	2 Kings 24:18–25:21; 2 Chronicles 36:11–21

THE SECOND BOOK OF THE KINGS

AHAZIAH'S MESSENGERS MEET ELIJAH

1 Now [A]Moab rebelled against Israel after the
death of Ahab. 2 And Ahaziah fell through the
lattice in his upper chamber which *was* in Samaria,
and became ill. So he sent messengers and said to
them, "Go, [A]inquire of Baal-zebub, the god of Ekron,
[B]whether I will recover from this sickness." 3 But
the angel of the LORD said to [A]Elijah the Tishbite,
"Arise, go up to meet the messengers of the king
of Samaria and say to them, 'Is it because there is
no God in Israel *that* you are going to inquire of
[B]Baal-zebub, the god of Ekron?' 4 Now therefore thus
says the LORD, '[a,A]You shall not come down from the
bed where you have gone up, but you shall surely
die.' " Then Elijah departed.
5 When the messengers returned to him he said to
them, "[a]Why have you returned?" 6 They said to him,
"A man came up to meet us and said to us, 'Go, return to the king who sent you and say to him, "Thus
says the LORD, 'Is it because there is no God in Israel
that you are sending [A]to inquire of Baal-zebub, the
god of Ekron? Therefore [a]you shall not come down
from the bed where you have gone up, but shall
surely die.' " ' " 7 He said to them, "What kind of man
was he who came up to meet you and spoke these
words to you?" 8 They [a]answered him, "[A]*He was* a
hairy man with a leather girdle [b]bound about his
loins." And he said, "It is Elijah the Tishbite."
9 Then *the king* [A]sent to him a captain of fifty with
his fifty. And he went up to him, and behold, he was
sitting on the top of the hill. And he said to him,
"O man of God, the king says, 'Come down.' " 10 Elijah
replied to the captain of fifty, "If I am a man of God,
[A]let fire come down from heaven and consume you
and your fifty." [B]Then fire came down from heaven
and consumed him and his fifty.
11 So he again sent to him another captain of fifty
with his fifty. And he said to him, "O man of God,
thus says the king, 'Come down quickly.' " 12 Elijah
replied to them, "If I am a man of God, let fire come
down from heaven and consume you and your fifty."
Then the fire of God came down from heaven and
consumed him and his fifty.
13 So he [A]again sent the captain of a third fifty with
his fifty. When the third captain of fifty went up, he
came and bowed down on his knees before Elijah,
and begged him and said to him, "O man of God,
please let my life and the lives of these fifty servants
of yours be precious in your sight. 14 Behold fire
came down from heaven and consumed the first two
captains of fifty with their fifties; but now let my [a]life

1:1 [A]2 Sam 8:2; 2 Kin 3:5 1:2 [A]2 Kin 1:3, 6, 16; Matt 10:25; Mark 3:22 [B]2 Kin 8:7-10 1:3 [A]1 Kin 17:1; 21:17 [B]2 Kin 1:2 1:4 [a]Lit *The bed where you went up, you shall not come down from it* [A]2 Kin 1:6, 16 1:5 [a]Lit *What is this that you have returned?* 1:6 [a]V 4, note 1 [A]2 Kin 1:2 1:8 [a]Lit *said* [b]Or *girt* [A]Zech 13:4; Matt 3:4; Mark 1:6 1:9 [A]2 Kin 6:13, 14 1:10 [A]1 Kin 18:36-38; Luke 9:54 [B]Job 1:16 1:13 [A]Is 1:5; Jer 5:3 1:14 [a]Lit *soul*

1:1 Moab rebelled. *See note on Ge 19:37, 38;* Introduction to Ruth: Background and Setting; cf. 3:4–27.

1:2 Ahaziah. This king of the northern kingdom of Israel is not to be confused with Ahaziah of Judah (8:25–9:29). **lattice in his upper chamber.** Ahaziah's rooftop room was enclosed with crossbars of interwoven reed or wood strips, which shut out direct sunlight while letting in cool breezes. It was not sturdy enough to keep Ahaziah from falling to the ground below (for unexplained reasons). This took place ca. 852 B.C. **Baal-zebub.** This was a local expression of the Baal cult at Ekron (*see note on 1Ki 16:31, 32*). Baal-zebub meant "lord of the flies," suggesting that he was the storm god who controlled diseases brought by flies. On the other hand, the name may have been the sarcastic Israelite parody of Baal-zebul, meaning "prince Baal" or "exalted lord," a common title for Baal in extrabiblical Canaanite texts. The NT preserved the name in the form Beelzebul, a name for Satan, the prince of the demons (Mt 10:25; 12:24; Mk 3:22; Lk 11:15). **Ekron.** The northernmost of the major Philistine cities, located about 22 mi. W of Jerusalem (*see note on 1Sa 5:10*).

1:3 the angel of the LORD. Although some interpret this as a reference to the preincarnate Christ (e.g., Ge 16:7–14; Jdg 2:1–4; *see note on Ex 3:2*), probably here the reference is to an angelic messenger, like the one sent earlier by the Lord to Elijah (cf. 19:35; 1Ki 19:7). The Lord's messenger was in contrast to the messengers of the wicked king (vv. 2, 3, 5). **Elijah.** The record of this unusual prophet to Israel begins in 1Ki 17:1 and extends to 2Ki 2:11 (*see note on 1Ki 17:1*).

1:4 you shall surely die. The Lord's punishment on Ahaziah for consulting a false god instead of the true God was that he would fail to recover from his injuries. This was a merciful application of the Mosaic Law (cf. Ex 22:20), which demanded death. Cf. vv. 16, 17.

1:8 a hairy man. Lit. "possessor of hair." This has been interpreted in two ways: 1) Elijah was physically hairy; or 2) Elijah wore a garment made of hair. The language supports the second viewpoint that Elijah wore a coarse wool garment girded at the waist with a leather belt. Zechariah 13:4 describes such a garment as belonging to prophets (cf. Mt 7:15). Further, the NT describes John the Baptist, who came in the spirit and likeness of Elijah, as clothed in camel's hair (Mt 3:4).

1:9 O man of God. A technical title for a man who spoke for God. *See notes on Dt 33:1; 1Ki 12:22; 1Ti 6:11.*

1:10–12 fire came down from heaven. This was the proof that Elijah was a prophet of the Lord and entitled to respect. Additionally, it was an indication that Elijah was like Moses, who also was validated as the Lord's prophet by fire from heaven (Nu 16:35).

be precious in your sight." 15 [A]The angel of the LORD
said to Elijah, "Go down with him; [B]do not be afraid
of him." So he arose and went down with him to the
king. 16 Then he said to him, "Thus says the LORD,
'Because you have sent messengers [A]to inquire of
Baal-zebub, the god of Ekron—is it because there is
no God in Israel to inquire of His word?—therefore
[a]you shall not come down from the bed where you
have gone up, but shall surely die.' "

JEHORAM REIGNS OVER ISRAEL

17 So Ahaziah died according to the word of the
LORD which Elijah had spoken. And because he had
no son, Jehoram became king in his place [A]in the
second year of Jehoram the son of Jehoshaphat,
king of Judah. 18 Now the rest of the acts of Ahaziah
which he did, are they not written in the Book of
the Chronicles of the Kings of Israel?

ELIJAH TAKEN TO HEAVEN

2 And it came about when the LORD was about to
[A]take up Elijah by a [a]whirlwind to heaven, that
Elijah went with [B]Elisha from [C]Gilgal. 2 Elijah said
to Elisha, "[A]Stay here please, for the LORD has sent
me as far as [B]Bethel." But Elisha said, "[C]As the LORD
lives and as you yourself live, I will not leave you."
So they went down to Bethel. 3 Then [A]the sons of the
prophets who *were at* Bethel came out to Elisha and
said to him, "Do you know that the LORD will take
away your master from over [a]you today?" And he
said, "Yes, I know; be still."

4 Elijah said to him, "Elisha, please [A]stay here, for
the LORD has sent me to [B]Jericho." But he said, "[A]As
the LORD lives, and as you yourself live, I will not
leave you." So they came to Jericho. 5 [A]The sons of
the prophets who *were* at Jericho approached Elisha
and said to him, "[B]Do you know that the LORD will
take away your master from over [a]you today?" And
he [b]answered, "Yes, I know; be still." 6 Then Elijah
said to him, "Please [A]stay here, for the LORD has
sent me to [B]the Jordan." And he said, "As the LORD
lives, and as you yourself live, I will not leave you."
So the two of them went on.

7 Now [A]fifty men of the sons of the prophets went
and stood opposite *them* at a distance, while the two
of them stood by the Jordan. 8 Elijah [A]took his mantle
and folded it together and [B]struck the waters, and
they were divided here and there, so that the two
of them crossed over on dry ground.

9 When they had crossed over, Elijah said to Elisha, "Ask what I shall do for you before I am taken
from you." And Elisha said, "Please, let a [A]double
portion of your spirit be upon me." 10 He said, "You
have asked a hard thing. *Nevertheless,* if you [A]see
me when I am taken from you, it shall be so for you;
but if not, it shall not be *so.*" 11 As they were going
along and talking, behold, *there appeared* [A]a chariot of fire and horses of fire which separated the
two of them. And Elijah went up by a [a]whirlwind to
heaven. 12 Elisha saw *it* and cried out, "[A]My father,
my father, the [a]chariots of Israel and its horsemen!"
And he saw [b]Elijah no more. Then [B]he took hold of

1:15 [A]2 Kin 1:3 [B]Is 51:12; Jer 1:17; Ezek 2:6 1:16 [a]V 4, note 1 [A]2 Kin 1:3 1:17 [A]2 Kin 3:1; 8:16 2:1 [a]Or *windstorm* [A]Gen 5:24; Heb 11:5 [B]1 Kin 19:16-21 [C]Josh 4:19 2:2 [A]Ruth 1:15 [B]1 Kin 12:28, 29 [C]1 Sam 1:26; 2 Kin 2:4, 6 2:3 [a]Lit *your head* [A]2 Kin 4:1, 38; 5:22 2:4 [A]2 Kin 2:2 [B]Josh 6:26 2:5 [a]Lit *your head* [b]Lit *said* [A]2 Kin 2:3 [B]2 Kin 2:3 2:6 [A]2 Kin 2:2 [B]Josh 3:8, 15-17 2:7 [A]2 Kin 2:15, 16 2:8 [A]1 Kin 19:13, 19 [B]Ex 14:21, 22; 2 Kin 2:14 2:9 [A]Num 11:17-25; Deut 21:17 2:10 [A]Acts 1:10 2:11 [a]Or *windstorm* [A]2 Kin 6:17 2:12 [a]Lit *chariot* [b]Lit *him* [A]2 Kin 13:14 [B]Gen 37:34; Job 1:20

1:15 angel of the LORD. *See note on 1:3.*

1:16 Baal-zebub. *See note on 1:2.*

1:17 Jehoram ... Jehoram. The first Jehoram mentioned here was, like Ahaziah (1Ki 22:51), a son of Ahab (3:1), who ruled over the northern kingdom of Israel for 12 years, ca. 852–841 B.C. (*see note on 3:1*). The second Jehoram mentioned was the son and successor to Jehoshaphat, who ruled in the southern kingdom of Judah, ca. 853–841 B.C. (cf. 8:16–24). **second year.** Ca. 852 B.C. This was the second year of Jehoram of Judah's co-regency with Jehoshaphat his father (*see notes on 3:1; 8:17; 2Ch 21:4–20*).

2:1 by a whirlwind. Lit. "in the whirlwind." This was a reference to the specific storm with lightning and thunder in which Elijah was taken to heaven (v. 11). The Lord's presence was connected with a whirlwind in Job 38:1; 40:6; Jer 23:19; 25:32; 30:23; Zec 9:14. **Elisha.** The record of this prophet, who was the successor to Elijah, begins in 1Ki 19:16 and extends to his death in 2Ki 13:20 (*see note on 1Ki 19:16*). **Gilgal.** Although some take this to be the Gilgal located W of the Jordan River near Jericho (cf. Jos 4:19; 5:9), the close affinity to Bethel (v. 2) and its distance from Jericho (v. 4) seem to indicate that the Gilgal mentioned here was located in the hill country of Ephraim about 7 mi. N of Bethel.

2:2 Bethel. A town in Benjamin about 8 mi. N of Jerusalem, where one of Israel's false worship centers was located (*see note on 1Ki 12:29*).

2:3 the sons of the prophets. *See note on 1Ki 20:35.* **take away.** The same term was used of Enoch's translation to heaven in Ge 5:24. The question from the sons of the prophets implied that the Lord had revealed Elijah's imminent departure to them. Elisha's response that he didn't need to hear about it ("be still") explicitly stated that Elijah's departure had been revealed by the Lord to him also (cf. v. 5). **from over you.** I.e., from supervising you, an allusion to the habit of students sitting beneath the feet of their master, elevated on a platform. Elisha would soon change from being Elijah's assistant to serving as the leader among the prophets.

2:4 Jericho. A city about 14 mi. SE of Bethel in the Jordan River Valley (cf. Jos 2:1; 6:1), to which Elisha accompanied Elijah (cf. v. 6).

2:8 waters ... were divided. Elijah rolled up his cloak into a kind of rod and struck the water of the Jordan River. Immediately, the water parted, leaving a dry path through the riverbed for the two prophets to cross. Elijah's act recalled Moses' parting of the Red Sea with his rod (Ex 14:21, 22) and the parting of the Jordan when Israel crossed over into the land (Jos 3:14–17). The crossing put Elijah on the Jordan's E bank, the area where Moses' life came to an end (Dt 34:1–6).

2:9 a double portion. In Israel, the firstborn son inherited a double share of his father's possessions and with it the right of succession (Dt 21:17). "A double portion of your spirit" was not merely Elisha's request to succeed Elijah in his prophetic ministry, since the Lord had already revealed this succession in 1Ki 19:16–21. Nor was it Elisha's desire for ministry superior to Elijah's, though Elisha did, in fact, do twice as many recorded miracles as Elijah. Apparently, Elisha was asking to succeed Elijah in the prophetic office, as God had promised, with spiritual power beyond his own capabilities to meet the responsibilities of his position as Elijah's successor. He desired that Elijah's mighty power might continue to live through him.

2:10 a hard thing. Since only God can give spiritual power, Elijah did not have the ability to grant Elisha's request. Elijah told Elisha that if Elisha saw his departure, it would be the sign that God Himself would grant Elisha's request.

2:11 chariot of fire and horses of fire. The horse-drawn chariot was the fastest means of transport and the mightiest means of warfare in that day. Thus, the chariot and horses symbolized God's powerful protection, which was the true safety of Israel (v. 12). As earthly kingdoms are dependent for their defense on such military force as represented by horses and chariots, one single prophet had done more by God's power to preserve his nation than all their military preparations.

2:12 My father. The sons of the prophet recognized the leader of their company as their spiritual father. This title of respect for a person of authority (Ge 45:8; Jdg 17:10) was later used for Elisha (6:21; 13:14).

his own clothes and tore them in two pieces. 13 He
also took up the mantle of Elijah that fell from him
and returned and stood by the bank of the Jordan.
14 He took the mantle of Elijah that fell from him
and struck the waters and said, "Where is the LORD,
the God of Elijah?" And when he also had [A]struck
the waters, they were divided here and there; and
Elisha crossed over.

ELISHA SUCCEEDS ELIJAH

15 Now when [A]the sons of the prophets who *were*
at Jericho opposite *him* saw him, they said, "The
spirit of Elijah rests on Elisha." And they came to
meet him and bowed themselves to the ground
before him. 16 They said to him, "Behold now, there
are with your servants fifty strong men, please let
them go and search for your master; perhaps [A]the
Spirit of the LORD has taken him up and cast him on
some mountain or into some valley." And he said,
"You shall not send." 17 But when [A]they urged him
until he was ashamed, he said, "Send." They sent
therefore fifty men; and they searched three days
but did not find him. 18 They returned to him while
he was staying at Jericho; and he said to them, "Did
I not say to you, 'Do not go'?"
19 Then the men of the city said to Elisha, "Behold
now, the situation of this city is pleasant, as my lord
sees; but the water is bad and the land [a]is unfruitful." 20 He said, "Bring me a new jar, and put salt [a]in
it." So they brought *it* to him. 21 He went out to the
spring of water and [A]threw salt [a]in it and said, "Thus
says the LORD, 'I have [b]purified these waters; there
shall not be from there death or [c]unfruitfulness any
longer.'" 22 So the waters have been [a]purified to this
day, according to the word of Elisha which he spoke.
23 Then he went up from there to Bethel; and as
he was going up by the way, young lads came out
from the city and [A]mocked him and said to him, "Go
up, you baldhead; go up, you baldhead!" 24 When he
looked behind him and saw them, he [A]cursed them
in the name of the LORD. Then two female bears
came out of the woods and tore up forty-two lads
of [a]their number. 25 He went from there to [A]Mount
Carmel, and from there he returned to Samaria.

JEHORAM MEETS MOAB REBELLION

3 Now Jehoram the son of Ahab became king
over Israel at Samaria [A]in the eighteenth year
of Jehoshaphat king of Judah, and reigned twelve
years. 2 He did evil in the sight of the LORD, though
not like his father and his mother; for [A]he put away
the *sacred* pillar of Baal [B]which his father had made.
3 Nevertheless, [A]he clung to the sins of Jeroboam the
son of Nebat, [B]which he made Israel sin; he did not
depart from them.
4 Now Mesha king of Moab was a sheep breeder,
and [A]used to pay the king of Israel 100,000 lambs
and the wool of 100,000 rams. 5 But [A]when Ahab
died, the king of Moab rebelled against the king of
Israel. 6 And King Jehoram went out of Samaria [a]at

2:14 [A]2 Kin 2:8 2:15 [A]2 Kin 2:7 2:16 [A]1 Kin 18:12; Acts 8:39 2:17 [A]2 Kin 8:11 2:19 [a]Lit *causes barrenness* 2:20 [a]Lit *there* 2:21 [a]Lit *there* [b]Lit *healed* [c]Lit *barrenness* [A]Ex 15:25, 26; 2 Kin 4:41; 6:6 2:22 [a]Lit *healed* 2:23 [A]2 Chr 36:16; Ps 31:17, 18 2:24 [a]Lit *them* [A]Neh 13:25-27 2:25 [A]1 Kin 18:19, 20; 2 Kin 4:25 3:1 [A]2 Kin 1:17 3:2 [A]Ex 23:24; 2 Kin 10:18, 26-28 [B]1 Kin 16:31, 32 3:3 [A]1 Kin 12:28-32 [B]1 Kin 14:9, 16 3:4 [A]2 Sam 8:2; Is 16:1, 2 3:5 [A]2 Kin 1:1 3:6 [a]Lit *in that day*

2:13 the mantle of Elijah. Elijah's cloak (*see note on 1:8*), picked up by Elisha, authenticated him as Elijah's legitimate spiritual successor.

2:14 waters ... were divided. Elisha repeated the action of Elijah (v. 8) in using the cloak to immediately part the waters of the Jordan River, allowing Elisha to recross on dry land. This confirmed that Elisha had received from God the same great power as his master, Elijah.

2:15 bowed ... to the ground. This action symbolized the submission of the prophets to the preeminence of Elisha as the prophet in Israel.

2:16 They knew that when souls went into God's presence at death, bodies remained on earth. Out of sensitivity to the body of Elijah, they wanted to retrieve it for appropriate care. Elisha knew Elijah's body would not be left behind, because he had seen his bodily ascension (v. 11) while the others had not, so he said, "No."

2:17 ashamed. In 8:11 and Jdg 3:25, this term was used for the feeling of embarrassment under the unrelenting pressure of their request. But with shame for his own failure to believe what he had seen, Elisha was also embarrassed for the prophets, knowing the futile outcome of their search (v. 18). Cf. 1Ki 18:12.

2:20, 21 jar ... salt. Salt purifies water, but the small amount used there could not clean the whole water supply. Rather, the use of salt from a new jar symbolized the cleansing of the waters that God would miraculously do. The healing of Jericho's water, through Elisha, freed the city from Joshua's curse, making it habitable for humans once again (cf. Jos 6:26; 1Ki 16:34).

2:23 young lads. These were not children, but infidels and idolatrous young men in their late teens or twenties (cf. Ge 22:12; 37:2; 1Ki 20:14, 15). **baldhead.** Baldness was regarded as a disgrace (cf. Is 3:17, 24). The baldness of Elisha referred to here may be: 1) natural loss of hair; 2) a shaved head denoting his separation to the prophetic office; or more likely, 3) an epithet of scorn and contempt, Elisha not being literally bald. These youths were sarcastically taunting and insulting the Lord's prophet by telling him to repeat Elijah's translation ("go up").

2:24 cursed. Because these young people of about 20 years of age or older (the same term is used of Solomon in 1Ki 3:7) so despised the prophet of the Lord, Elisha called upon the Lord to deal with the rebels as He saw fit. The Lord's punishment was the mauling of 42 youths by two female bears. The penalty was clearly justified, for to ridicule Elisha was to ridicule the Lord Himself. The gravity of the penalty mirrored the gravity of the crime. The appalling judgment was God's warning to any and all who attempted to interfere with the newly invested prophet's ministry.

2:25 Mount Carmel. For the location, *see note on 1Ki 18:19.* Elisha associated his prophetic ministry with Elijah's stand against Baalism. **Samaria.** The capital city of the northern kingdom, located in central Israel (cf. 1Ki 16:24).

3:1 Jehoram. *See note on 1:17.* He was Ahaziah's brother (1Ki 22:51). **eighteenth year.** Ca. 852 B.C. This was Jehoshaphat of Judah's 18th year of rule after the death of his father Asa in 870 B.C. Jehoshaphat was co-regent with Asa from 873–870 B.C. Jehoshaphat's son Jehoram was co-regent with his father from 853–848 B.C. (*see notes on 1:17; 8:17*). **twelve years.** 852–841 B.C.

3:2 pillar of Baal. This was probably an image of the god Baal that King Ahab had made and placed in the temple he built to Baal (1Ki 16:32, 33). This image was only put in storage, not permanently destroyed, because it reappeared at the end of Jehoram's reign (10:26, 27).

3:3 Jeroboam. Ca. 931–910 B.C. *See notes on 1Ki 11:26–14:20; 2Ch 9:29–13:20.*

3:4 Mesha king of Moab. According to the Moabite Stone (discovered at Dihon, Moab, in A.D. 1868 and dated to ca. 840–820 B.C.), Moab, which is located E of the Dead Sea between the Arnon River and the Brook Zered, had been Israel's vassal since Omri (ca. 880 B.C.). Moab's king, Mesha, was a sheep breeder (cf. Am 1:1) who supplied the king of Israel with lambs and wool. This was Moab's annual tribute to the Israelite king.

3:5 Moab rebelled. Mesha used Ahab's death as an opportunity to cast off the political domination of Israel with its heavy economic burden. Moab's rebellion took place in 853 B.C. during the reign of Ahaziah (1:1). Jehoram determined to put down Moab's rebellion upon his accession to Israel's throne in 852 B.C. He mobilized Israel for war (v. 6) and asked Jehoshaphat of Judah to join him in the battle (v. 7).

that time and mustered all Israel. 7 Then he went
and sent *word* to Jehoshaphat the king of Judah,
saying, "The king of Moab has rebelled against me.
Will you go with me to fight against Moab?" And he
said, "I will go up; [A]I am as you are, my people as
your people, my horses as your horses." 8 He said,
"Which way shall we go up?" And he [a]answered,
"The way of the wilderness of Edom."

9 So [A]the king of Israel went with [B]the king of
Judah and [C]the king of Edom; and they made a
circuit of seven days' journey, and there was no
water for the army or for the cattle that followed
them. 10 Then the king of Israel said, "Alas! For the
LORD has called these three kings to give them
into the hand of Moab." 11 But Jehoshaphat said,
"[A]Is there not a prophet of the LORD here, that we
may inquire of the LORD by him?" And one of the
king of Israel's servants answered and said, "[B]Eli-
sha the son of Shaphat is here, [C]who used to pour
water on the hands of Elijah." 12 Jehoshaphat said,
"The word of the LORD is with him." So the king of
Israel and Jehoshaphat and the king of Edom went
down to him.

13 Now Elisha said to the king of Israel, "What do
I have to do with you? [A]Go to the prophets of your
father and to the prophets of your mother." And
the king of Israel said to him, "No, for the LORD has
called these three kings *together* to give them into
the hand of Moab." 14 Elisha said, "[A]As the LORD of
hosts lives, before whom I stand, were it not that
I regard the presence of Jehoshaphat the king of
Judah, I would not look at you nor see you. 15 But
now [A]bring me a minstrel." And it came about, when
the minstrel played, that [B]the hand of the LORD
came upon him. 16 He said, "Thus says the LORD,
'Make this valley full of trenches.' 17 For thus says
the LORD, 'You shall not see wind nor shall you see
rain; yet that valley [A]shall be filled with water, so
that you shall drink, both you and your cattle and
your beasts. 18 This is but a [A]slight thing in the sight
of the LORD; He will also give the Moabites into
your hand. 19 [A]Then you shall strike every fortified
city and every choice city, and fell every good tree
and stop all springs of water, and mar every good
piece of land with stones.' " 20 It happened in the
morning [A]about the time of offering the sacrifice,
that behold, water came by the way of Edom, and
the country was filled with water.

21 Now all the Moabites heard that the kings had
come up to fight against them. And all who were
able to [a]put on armor and older were summoned
and stood on the border. 22 They rose early in the
morning, and the sun shone on the water, and the
Moabites saw the water opposite *them* as red as
blood. 23 Then they said, "This is blood; the kings
have surely fought together, and they have slain one
another. Now therefore, Moab, to the spoil!" 24 But
when they came to the camp of Israel, the Israelites arose and struck the Moabites, so that they fled
before them; and they went forward [a]into the land,
[b]slaughtering the Moabites. 25 [A]Thus they destroyed
the cities; and each one threw a stone on every piece
of good land and filled it. So they stopped all the
springs of water and felled all the good trees, until
in [B]Kir-hareseth *only* they left its stones; however,
the slingers went about *it* and struck it. 26 When the
king of Moab saw that the battle was too fierce for
him, he took with him 700 men who drew swords,
to break through to the king of Edom; but they could
not. 27 Then he took his oldest son who was to reign
in his place, and [A]offered him as a burnt offering
on the wall. And there came great wrath against
Israel, and they departed from him and returned
to their own land.

3:7 [A]1 Kin 22:4 3:8 [a]Lit *said* 3:9 [A]2 Kin 3:1 [B]2 Kin 3:7 [C]1 Kin 22:47 3:11 [A]1 Kin 22:7 [B]2 Kin 2:25 [C]1 Kin 19:21; John 13:4, 5, 13, 14 3:13 [A]1 Kin 18:19; 22:6-11, 22-25 3:14 [A]1 Kin 17:1; 2 Kin 5:16 3:15 [A]1 Sam 16:23; 1 Chr 25:1 [B]1 Kin 18:46; Ezek 1:3 3:17 [A]Ps 107:35 3:18 [A]Jer 32:17, 27; Mark 10:27; Luke 1:37 3:19 [A]2 Kin 3:25 3:20 [A]Ex 29:39, 40 3:21 [a]Lit *gird themselves with a belt* 3:24 [a]Lit *into it* [b]Lit *smiting* 3:25 [A]2 Kin 3:19 [B]Is 16:7; Jer 48:31, 36 3:27 [A]Amos 2:1; Mic 6:7

3:8 the wilderness of Edom. This was the long and circuitous route by the lower bend of the Dead Sea, the arid land in the great depression S of the sea known as the Arabah, or an area of marshes on Edom's western side. According to the Moabite Stone (*see note on 3:4*), Mesha's army firmly controlled the northern approach into Moab. Therefore, an attack from the S had a much better chance of success. It was the most defenseless position and Mesha could not enlist help from the forces of Edom (v. 9).

3:11 pour water on the hands. Probably derived from the custom of washing hands before and after meals. The idiom meant that Elisha had personally served Elijah. Jehoshaphat recognized that Elisha was a true prophet of the Lord (v. 12).

3:13 What do I have to do with you? A Heb. idiom that expressed the completely different perspective of two individuals (cf. 2Sa 16:10). Elisha sarcastically ordered Jehoram to consult the prophets of his father Ahab, prophets of the northern kingdom's deviant religion (1Ki 22:6, 10–12), and the prophets of his mother Jezebel, the prophets of Baal and Asherah (1Ki 18:19).

3:14 regard the presence. Elisha agreed to seek word from the Lord because of his great respect for Jehoshaphat, the king of Judah, who did what was right in the eyes of the Lord (1Ki 22:43).

3:15 a minstrel. The music was used to accompany praise and prayer, which calmed the mind of the prophet that he might clearly hear the word of the Lord. Music often accompanied prophecies in the OT (cf. 1Ch 25:1).

3:16 this valley. Probably the NE area of the Arabah, W of the highlands of Moab and SE of the Dead Sea (see v. 8).

3:20 offering the sacrifice. This was offered daily (see Ex 29:38–41). **water came by the way of Edom.** Divinely created flash floods from the mountains of Edom caused water to flow in the direction of the Dead Sea. This water was caught in the canals that had been built in the valley (v. 16).

3:22 water ... red as blood. As the Moabites looked down at the unfamiliar water in the ditches dug in the valley below them, the combination of the sun's rays and the red sandstone terrain gave the water a reddish color, like pools of blood. Unaccustomed to water being in those places and having heard no storm (see v. 17), the Moabites thought that the coalition of kings had slaughtered each other (v. 23) and so went after the spoils. The coalition army led by Israel defeated the Moabites, who had been delivered into their hands by the Lord (see vv. 18, 24).

3:25 Kir-hareseth. The coalition army invaded Moab and besieged its capital city, Kir-hareseth, located about 11 mi. E of the Dead Sea and about 20 mi. NE of the Arabah.

3:27 his oldest son ... offered him. In desperate hope for intervention by his idol god, Mesha sacrificed his oldest son to the Moabite god Chemosh. This was done in plain view of everyone inside and outside the city in an attempt to induce Chemosh to deliver the Moabites from disastrous defeat. **great wrath against Israel.** It seems best to understand that the king's sacrifice inspired the Moabites to hate Israel more and fight more intensely. This fierceness perhaps led Israel to believe that Chemosh was fighting for the Moabites. Thus, the indignation or fury came from the Moabites.

THE WIDOW'S OIL

4 Now a certain woman of the wives of [A]the sons of the prophets cried out to [a]Elisha, "Your servant my husband is dead, and you know that your servant feared the LORD; and [B]the creditor has come to take my two children to be his slaves." 2 Elisha said to her, "What shall I do for you? Tell me, what do you have in the house?" And she said, "Your maidservant has nothing in the house except [A]a jar of oil." 3 Then he said, "Go, borrow vessels at large for yourself from all your neighbors, *even* empty vessels; do not get a few. 4 And you shall go in and shut the door behind you and your sons, and pour out into all these vessels, and you shall set aside what is full." 5 So she went from him and shut the door behind her and her sons; they were bringing *the vessels* to her and she poured. 6 When [A]the vessels were full, she said to her son, "Bring me another vessel." And he said to her, "There is not one vessel more." And the oil stopped. 7 Then she came and told [A]the man of God. And he said, "Go, sell the oil and pay your debt, and you *and* your sons can live on the rest."

THE SHUNAMMITE WOMAN

8 Now there came a day when Elisha passed over to [A]Shunem, where there was a [a]prominent woman, and she persuaded him to eat [b]food. And so it was, as often as he passed by, he turned in there to eat [b]food. 9 She said to her husband, "Behold now, I perceive that this is a holy [A]man of God passing by us continually. 10 Please, let us [A]make a little walled upper chamber and let us set a bed for him there, and a table and a chair and a lampstand; and it shall be, when he comes to us, *that* he can turn in there."

11 [a]One day he came there and turned in to the upper chamber and [b]rested. 12 Then he said to [A]Gehazi his servant, "Call this Shunammite." And when he had called her, she stood before him. 13 He said to him, "Say now to her, 'Behold, you have been [a]careful for us with all this [b]care; what can I do for you? Would you be spoken for to the king or to the captain of the army?' " And she [c]answered, "I live among my own people." 14 So he said, "What then is to be done for her?" And Gehazi [a]answered, "Truly she has no son and her husband is old." 15 He said, "Call her." When he had called her, she stood in the doorway. 16 Then he said, "[A]At this season [a]next year you will embrace a son." And she said, "No, my lord, O man of God, [B]do not lie to your maidservant."

17 The woman conceived and bore a son at that season [a]the next year, as Elisha had said to her.

THE SHUNAMMITE'S SON

18 When the child was grown, the day came that he went out to his father to the reapers. 19 He said to his father, "My head, my head." And he said to his servant, "Carry him to his mother." 20 When he had taken him and brought him to his mother, he sat on her [a]lap until noon, and *then* died. 21 She went up and [A]laid him on the bed of [B]the man of God, and shut *the door* behind him and went out. 22 Then she called to her husband and said, "Please send me one of the servants and one of the donkeys, that I may run to the man of God and return." 23 He said, "Why will you go to him today? It is neither [A]new moon nor sabbath." And she said, "*It will be* well." 24 Then she saddled a donkey and said to her servant, "Drive and go forward; do not slow down [a]the pace for me unless I tell you." 25 So she went and came to the man of God to [A]Mount Carmel.

When the man of God saw her at a distance, he said to Gehazi his servant, "Behold, [a]there is the Shunammite. 26 Please run now to meet her and say to her, 'Is it well with you? Is it well with your

4:1 [a]Lit *Elisha, saying* [A]2 Kin 2:3 [B]Lev 25:39-41, 48; 1 Sam 22:2; Neh 5:2-5 4:2 [A]1 Kin 17:12 4:6 [A]Matt 14:20 4:7 [A]1 Kin 12:22 4:8 [a]Lit *great* [b]Lit *bread* [A]Josh 19:18 4:9 [A]2 Kin 4:7 4:10 [A]Matt 10:41, 42; 25:40; Rom 12:13 4:11 [a]Lit *Now a day came that* [b]Lit *lay there* 4:12 [A]2 Kin 4:29-31; 5:20-27; 8:4, 5 4:13 [a]Lit *fearful* [b]Lit *fear* [c]Lit *said* 4:14 [a]Lit *said* 4:16 [a]Lit *when the time revives* [A]Gen 18:14 [B]2 Kin 4:28 4:17 [a]Lit *when the time revived* 4:20 [a]Lit *knees* 4:21 [A]2 Kin 4:32 [B]2 Kin 4:7 4:23 [A]Num 10:10; 28:11; 1 Chr 23:31 4:24 [a]Lit *riding* 4:25 [a]Lit *this Shunammite* [A]2 Kin 2:25

4:1 the sons of the prophets. *See note on 1Ki 20:35.* **my two children to be his slaves.** According to the Mosaic law, creditors could enslave debtors and their children to work off a debt when they could not pay (Ex 21:2–4; Dt 15:12–18). The period of servitude could last until the next year of Jubilee (Lv 25:39, 40). Rich people and creditors, however, were not to take advantage of the destitute (see Dt 15:1–18).

4:2 jar of oil. A flask of oil used to anoint the body.

4:4 shut the door behind you. Since the widow's need was private, the provision was to be private also. Further, the absence of Elisha demonstrated that the miracle happened only by God's power. God's power multiplied "little" into "much," filling all the vessels to meet the widow's need (cf. 1Ki 17:7–16).

4:8 Shunem. A town in the territory of Issachar near Jezreel (Jos 19:18), on the slopes of Mt. Moreh, overlooking the eastern end of the Jezreel Valley (*see note on 1Ki 1:3*). **a prominent woman.** The woman was "great" in wealth and in social prominence.

4:9 man of God. *See note on 1:9.* The woman recognized Elisha as a prophet uniquely separated unto God. Elisha's holiness prompted the woman to ask her husband that a separate, small, walled upper room be provided for the prophet (v. 10). The woman must have feared the "holy" Elisha coming into contact with their "profane" room (cf. Lv 10:10).

4:12 Gehazi. Elisha's personal servant who was prominent here and in 5:20–27. Probably Gehazi is the unnamed servant in v. 43; the term "servant" used there was used in 1Ki 19:21 of Elisha's relationship to Elijah. Throughout this narrative, Elisha contacted the Shunammite woman through Gehazi (vv. 11–13, 15, 25, 29). Gehazi was involved in this ministry so that he might have opportunity to mature in his service to the Lord.

4:13 I live among my own people. This reply expressed her contentment, since she wanted nothing.

4:14 no son and her husband is old. This remark implied two things: 1) she suffered the shame of being a barren woman (cf. Ge 16:1; 18:10–15; 25:21; 30:1, 2; 1Sa 1:6); and 2) her husband might die without an heir to carry on his name (Dt 25:5–10).

4:16 No, my lord. In response to Elisha's announcement that she would have a son, the woman asked Elisha not to build up her hopes if she would be disappointed later. Her reply indicated that she felt having a son was impossible. **man of God.** *See note on 1:9.*

4:17 conceived … bore. This was like Abraham and Sarah (Ge 21:1, 2).

4:19 My head, my head. The child probably suffered sunstroke. The cries of the boy, the part affected, and the season of the year ("reapers") lead to that conclusion. Sunstroke could be fatal, as in this case (v. 20).

4:23 neither new moon nor sabbath. The first day of the month and the seventh day of the week were both marked with special religious observances and rest from work (cf. Nu 28:9–15). The husband implied that only on such dates would a person visit a prophet. She apparently concealed the death of the child from him ("*It will be* well") to spare him unnecessary grief, in light of the power of the man of God whom she believed might do a miracle for the boy.

4:25 Mount Carmel. *See note on 1Ki 18:19.* The distance from Shunem was about 15 to 25 mi.

4:26 It is well. She withheld the real sorrow of her son's death, waiting to tell the prophet Elisha directly.

husband? Is it well with the child?' " And she [a]an-
swered, "It is well." 27 When she came to the man
of God [A]to the hill, she caught hold of his feet. And
Gehazi came near to push her away; but the man
of God said, "Let her alone, for her soul is [a]troubled
within her; and the LORD has hidden it from me and
has not told me." 28 Then she said, "Did I ask for a son
from my lord? Did I not say, '[A]Do not deceive me'?"
29 Then he said to Gehazi, "[A]Gird up your loins and
[B]take my staff in your hand, and go your way; if you
meet any man, do not [C]salute him, and if anyone sa-
lutes you, do not answer him; and [D]lay my staff on the
lad's face." 30 The mother of the lad said, "[A]As the LORD
lives and as you yourself live, I will not leave you." And
he arose and followed her. 31 Then Gehazi passed on
before them and laid the staff on the lad's face, but
there was no sound or [a]response. So he returned to
meet him and told [b]him, "The lad [A]has not awakened."
32 When Elisha came into the house, behold the lad
was dead and laid on his bed. 33 So he entered and
[A]shut the door behind them both and prayed to the
LORD. 34 And [A]he went up and lay on the child, and
put his mouth on his mouth and his eyes on his eyes
and his hands on his hands, and he stretched himself
on him; and the flesh of the child became warm.
35 Then he returned and walked in the house once
back and forth, and went up and [A]stretched himself
on him; and the lad sneezed seven times and the lad
opened his eyes. 36 He called Gehazi and said, "Call
this Shunammite." So he called her. And when she
came in to him, he said, "Take up your son." 37 Then
she went in and fell at his feet and bowed herself to
the ground, and [A]she took up her son and went out.

THE POISONOUS STEW

38 When Elisha returned to [A]Gilgal, *there was* [B]a
famine in the land. [a]As [C]the sons of the prophets
[D]were sitting before him, he said to his servant,
"[E]Put on the large pot and boil stew for the sons of
the prophets." 39 Then one went out into the field
to gather herbs, and found a wild vine and gathered from it his lap full of wild gourds, and came
and sliced them into the pot of stew, for they did
not know *what they were.* 40 So they poured *it* out
for the men to eat. And as they were eating of the
stew, they cried out and said, "O man of God, there
is [A]death in the pot." And they were unable to eat.
41 But he said, "Now bring meal." [A]He threw it into
the pot and said, "Pour *it* out for the people that
they may eat." Then there was no harm in the pot.
42 Now a man came from Baal-shalishah, and
brought the man of God bread of the first fruits,
twenty loaves of barley and fresh ears of grain in
his sack. And he said, "[A]Give *them* to the people that
they may eat." 43 His attendant said, "What, [A]will I
set this before a hundred men?" But he said, "Give
them to the people that they may eat, for thus says
the LORD, 'They shall eat and have *some* left over.' "
44 So he set *it* before them, and they ate and [A]had
some left over, according to the word of the LORD.

NAAMAN IS HEALED

5 Now [A]Naaman, captain of the army of the king
of Aram, was a great man [a]with his master, and
highly respected, because by him the LORD had
given victory to Aram. The man was also a valiant
warrior, *but he was* a leper. 2 Now the Arameans had
gone out [A]in bands and had taken captive a little girl
from the land of Israel; and she [a]waited on Naaman's
wife. 3 She said to her mistress, "I wish that my master were [a]with the prophet who is in Samaria! Then
he would cure him of his leprosy." 4 [a]Naaman went
in and told his master, saying, "Thus and thus spoke
the girl who is from the land of Israel." 5 Then the
king of Aram said, "Go [a]now, and I will send a letter
to the king of Israel." He departed and [A]took with

4:26 [a]Lit *said* 4:27 [a]Lit *bitter* [A]2 Kin 4:25 4:28 [A]2 Kin 4:16 4:29 [A]1 Kin 18:46; 2 Kin 9:1 [B]Ex 4:17; 2 Kin 2:14 [C]Luke 10:4 [D]Ex 7:19, 20; 14:16 4:30 [A]2 Kin 2:2, 4 4:31 [a]Lit *attentiveness* [b]Lit *him, saying* [A]John 11:11 4:33 [A]2 Kin 4:4; Matt 6:6; Luke 8:51 4:34 [A]1 Kin 17:21-23 4:35 [A]1 Kin 17:21 4:37 [A]Heb 11:35 4:38 [a]Lit *And* [A]2 Kin 2:1 [B]2 Kin 8:1 [C]2 Kin 2:3 [D]Luke 10:39; Acts 22:3 [E]Ezek 11:3, 7, 11; 24:3 4:40 [A]Ex 10:17 4:41 [A]Ex 15:25; 2 Kin 2:21 4:42 [A]Matt 14:16-21; 15:32-38 4:43 [A]Luke 9:13; John 6:9 4:44 [A]Matt 14:20; 15:37; John 6:13 5:1 [a]Lit *before* [A]Luke 4:27 5:2 [a]Lit *was before* [A]2 Kin 6:23; 13:20 5:3 [a]Lit *before* 5:4 [a]Lit *He* 5:5 [a]Lit *enter* [A]1 Sam 9:7; 2 Kin 4:42

4:27 of his feet. The grasping of the feet was a sign of humiliation and veneration.

4:28 See v. 16.

4:29 lay my staff on the lad's face. Elisha sent Gehazi ahead because he was younger and, therefore, faster. He may have expected the Lord to restore the child's life when his staff was placed upon him, viewing that staff as representative of his own presence and a symbol of divine power (cf. 2:8).

4:34 stretched himself on him. Like Elijah (see 1Ki 17:17–24), Elisha demonstrated the Lord's power over death by raising their son from the dead. Also like Elijah, part of the restoration process involved lying on top of the boy's body.

4:38 Gilgal. *See note on 2:1.* This was about 40 mi. S of Shunem. **sons of the prophets.** *See note on 1Ki 20:35.*

4:39 wild gourds. Probably a kind of wild cucumber that can be fatally poisonous if eaten in large quantities.

4:41 meal. The meal itself did not make the noxious stew edible, but a miraculous cure was accomplished through the meal. Like Elijah (cf. 1Ki 17:14–16), Elisha used meal to demonstrate the concern of God for man.

4:42 Baal-shalishah. The exact location is uncertain. **bread of the first fruits.** Normally, the firstfruits were reserved for God (Lv 23:20) and the Levitical priests (Nu 18:13; Dt 18:4, 5). Though the religion in the northern kingdom was apostate, the man who brought the loaves to Elisha was a representative of godly religion in Israel.

4:43, 44 The multiplication of the loaves in accordance with the Word of the Lord through His prophet anticipated the messianic ministry of Jesus Himself (cf. Mt 14:16–20; 15:36, 37; Jn 6:11–13).

5:1 Naaman. A common name in ancient Aram, or Syria, meaning "gracious, fair." Four phrases describe the importance of Naaman: 1) he was the supreme commander of the army of Aram as indicated by the term "captain," used of an army's highest ranking officer (Ge 21:22; 1Sa 12:9; 1Ch 27:34); 2) he was "a great man," a man of high social standing and prominence; 3) he was "highly respected," a man highly regarded by the king of Syria because of the military victories he had won; and 4) he was "a valiant warrior," a term used in the OT for both a man of great wealth (Ru 2:1) and a courageous warrior (Jdg 6:12; 11:1). Severely mitigating against all of this was the fact that he suffered from leprosy, a serious skin disease (cf. v. 27; *see notes on Lv 13, 14*). **king of Aram.** Either Ben-hadad I or, more likely, Ben-hadad II. *See note on 1Ki 15:18.* **by him the LORD had given victory to Aram.** Naaman's military success was attributable to the God of Israel, who is sovereign over all the nations (cf. Is 10:13; Am 9:7).

5:2 bands. Naaman led the Syrian army in quick penetrations across Israel's border (cf. 1Sa 30:8, 15). On one of his raids, he captured a young Israelite girl used as a servant, who ultimately told him of Elisha.

5:3 the prophet … in Samaria. Elisha maintained a residence in the city of Samaria (6:32).

5:5 king of Israel. Jehoram. *See note on 1:17.* **ten talents of silver and six thousand**

him ten talents of silver and six thousand *shekels*
of gold and ten [B]changes of clothes.
6 He brought the letter to the king of Israel, saying, "And now as this letter comes to you, behold,
I have sent Naaman my servant to you, that you
may cure him of his leprosy." 7 When the king of
Israel read the letter, [A]he tore his clothes and said,
"[B]Am I God, to kill and to make alive, that this man
is sending *word* to me to cure a man of his leprosy?
But [C]consider now, and see how he is seeking [a]a
quarrel against me."
8 It happened when Elisha [A]the man of God heard
that the king of Israel had torn his clothes, that he
sent *word* to the king, saying, "Why have you torn
your clothes? Now let him come to me, and he shall
know that there is a prophet in Israel." 9 So Naaman
came with his horses and his chariots and stood at
the doorway of the house of Elisha. 10 Elisha sent
a messenger to him, saying, "[A]Go and wash in the
Jordan seven times, and your flesh will be restored
to you and *you will* be clean." 11 But Naaman was furious and went away and said, "Behold, I [a]thought,
'He will surely come out to me and stand and call
on the name of the LORD his God, and wave his
hand over the place and cure the leper.' 12 Are not
[a]Abanah and Pharpar, the rivers of Damascus, better than all the waters of Israel? Could I not wash
in them and be clean?" So he turned and [A]went
away in a rage. 13 [A]Then his servants came near
and spoke to him and said, "[B]My father, had the
prophet told you *to do some* great thing, would
you not have done *it?* How much more *then,* when
he says to you, 'Wash, and be clean'?" 14 So he went
down and dipped *himself* seven times in the Jordan, according to the word of the man of God; and
[A]his flesh was restored like the flesh of a little child
and [B]he was clean.

GEHAZI'S GREED

15 When he returned to the man of God [a]with all
his company, and came and stood before him, he
said, "Behold now, [A]I know that there is no God in
all the earth, but in Israel; so please [B]take a [b]present
from your servant now." 16 But he said, "[A]As the
LORD lives, before whom I stand, [B]I will take nothing." And he urged him to take *it,* but he refused.
17 Naaman said, "If not, please let your servant at
least be given two mules' load of [A]earth; for your
servant will no longer offer burnt offering nor will
he sacrifice to other gods, but to the LORD. 18 In this
matter may the LORD pardon your servant: when my
master goes into the house of Rimmon to worship
there, and [A]he leans on my hand and I bow myself
in the house of Rimmon, when I bow myself in the
house of Rimmon, the LORD pardon your servant
in this matter." 19 He said to him, "[A]Go in peace." So
he departed from him some distance.
20 But [A]Gehazi, the servant of Elisha the man of
God, [a]thought, "Behold, my master has spared this
Naaman the Aramean, [b]by not receiving from his
hands what he brought. [B]As the LORD lives, I will
run after him and take something from him." 21 So
Gehazi pursued Naaman. When Naaman saw one
running after him, he came down from the chariot
to meet him and said, "Is all well?" 22 He said, "[A]All
is well. My master has sent me, saying, 'Behold, just
now two young men of the sons of the prophets
have come to me from [B]the hill country of Ephraim.
Please give them a talent of silver and [C]two changes
of clothes.' " 23 Naaman said, "[A]Be pleased to take two

5:5 [B]Judg 14:12; 2 Kin 5:22, 23 5:7 [a]Lit *an occasion* [A]Gen 37:29 [B]Gen 30:2; 1 Sam 2:6 [C]1 Kin 20:7; Luke 11:54 5:8 [A]1 Kin 12:22 5:10 [A]John 9:7 5:11 [a]Lit *said* 5:12 [a]Another reading is *Amanah* [A]Prov 14:17; 16:32; 19:11 5:13 [A]1 Sam 28:23 [B]2 Kin 2:12; 6:21; 8:9 5:14 [A]2 Kin 5:10; Job 33:25 [B]Luke 4:27; 5:13 5:15 [a]Lit *he and* [b]Lit *blessing* [A]Josh 2:11; 1 Sam 17:46, 47; 2 Kin 5:8 [B]1 Sam 25:27 5:16 [A]2 Kin 3:14 [B]Gen 14:22, 23; 2 Kin 5:20, 26 5:17 [A]Ex 20:24 5:18 [A]2 Kin 7:2, 17 5:19 [A]Ex 4:18; 1 Sam 1:17; Mark 5:34 5:20 [a]Lit *said* [b]Lit *from* [A]2 Kin 4:12, 31, 36 [B]Ex 20:7; 2 Kin 6:31 5:22 [A]2 Kin 4:26 [B]Josh 24:33 [C]2 Kin 5:5 5:23 [A]2 Kin 6:3

***shekels* of gold.** About 750 lbs. of silver and 150 lbs. of gold.

5:7 tore his clothes. This action was a sign of distress and grief (cf. 1Ki 21:27). Jehoram thought that Ben-hadad expected him to cure Naaman's leprosy. Since Jehoram knew that this was impossible, he thought he was doomed to have a major battle with the Syrians. When Elisha heard of Jehoram's distress, he told the king to send Naaman to him for healing (v. 8).

5:11 surely come out to me. Because of his personal greatness (v. 1), his huge gift (v. 5), and diplomatic letter (v. 6), Naaman expected personal attention to his need. However, Elisha did not even go out to meet him. Instead, he sent his instructions for healing through a messenger (v. 10). Naaman was angry because he anticipated a personal cleansing ceremony from the prophet himself.

5:12 Abanah ... Pharpar. The Abanah River (modern Barada) began in the Lebanon mountains and flowed to Damascus, its clear water producing orchards and gardens. The Pharpar River flowed E from Mt. Hermon to the S of Damascus. If Naaman needed to wash in a river, those two rivers were superior to the muddy Jordan. However, it was obedience to God's Word that was the issue, not the quality of the water.

5:13 My father. The title "father" was not usually employed by servants to their masters. The use of the term here may indicate something of the warmness that the servants felt for Naaman (cf. 2:12). His servants pointed out to Naaman that he had been willing to do anything, no matter how hard, to be cured. He should be even more willing, therefore, to do something as easy as washing in a muddy river.

5:14 flesh of a little child. This description indicates that ancient leprosy was a disease of the skin, distinct from modern leprosy, a disease primarily of the nerves.

5:15 there is no God ... but in Israel. Upon his healing, Naaman returned from the Jordan River to Elisha's house in Samaria (about 25 mi.) to give confession of his new belief. Naaman confessed that there was only one God, Israel's God, the Lord. In saying this, Naaman put to shame the Israelites who continued to blasphemously believe that both the Lord and Baal were gods (cf. 1Ki 18:21).

5:16 he refused. To show that he was not driven by the mercenary motives of pagan priests and prophets, Elisha, though accepting gifts on other occasions (cf. 4:42), declined them here so the Syrians would see the honor of God only.

5:17 two mules' load of earth. In the ancient Near East it was thought that a god could be worshiped only on the soil of the nation to which he was bound. Therefore, Naaman wanted a load of Israelite soil on which to make burnt offerings and sacrifices to the Lord when he returned to Damascus. This request confirmed how Naaman had changed—whereas he had previously disparaged Israel's river, now he wanted to take a pile of Israel's soil to Damascus.

5:18 Rimmon. The Heb. term "Rimmon" (lit. "pomegranate") is a parody of the Syrian deity, Hadad, whom the Assyrians named "Rananu" (lit. "the thunderer"). Hadad was the storm god, usually identified with the Canaanite god, Baal. As an aide to Syria's king, Naaman's duty demanded that he accompany the king to religious services at the temple of Rimmon in Damascus. Naaman requested that the Lord forgive this outward compromise of his true faith in and commitment to the Lord.

5:22 My master has sent me. A lie for selfish gain revealed the sad state of Gehazi's character. Another lie followed to cover up (v. 25).

5:23 two talents of silver. About 150 lbs. of silver.

talents." And he urged him, and bound two talents of silver in two bags with two changes of clothes and gave them to two of his servants; and they carried *them* before him. 24 When he came to the [a]hill, he took them from their hand and [A]deposited them in the house, and he sent the men away, and they departed. 25 But he went in and stood before his master. And Elisha said to him, "Where have you been, Gehazi?" And he said, "[A]Your servant went nowhere."

26 Then he said to him, "Did not my heart go *with you,* when the man turned from his chariot to meet you? [A]Is it a time to receive money and to receive clothes and olive groves and vineyards and sheep and oxen and male and female servants? 27 Therefore, the leprosy of Naaman shall cling to you and to your [a]descendants forever." So he went out from his presence [A]a leper *as white* as snow.

THE AXE HEAD RECOVERED

6 Now [A]the sons of the prophets said to Elisha, "Behold now, the place before you where we are living is too limited for us. 2 Please let us go to the Jordan and each of us take from there a beam, and let us make a place there for ourselves where we may live." So he said, "Go." 3 Then one said, "Please be willing to go with your servants." And he [a]answered, "I shall go." 4 So he went with them; and when they came to the Jordan, they cut down trees. 5 But as one was felling a beam, [a]the axe head fell into the water; and he cried out and said, "Alas, my master! For it was borrowed." 6 Then the man of God said, "Where did it fall?" And when he showed him the place, [A]he cut off a stick and threw *it* in there, and made the iron float. 7 He said, "Take it up for yourself." So he put out his hand and took it.

THE ARAMEANS PLOT TO CAPTURE ELISHA

8 Now the king of Aram was warring against Israel; and he [a]counseled with his servants saying, "In such and such a place shall be my camp." 9 [A]The man of God sent *word* to the king of Israel saying, "Beware that you do not pass this place, for the Arameans are coming down there." 10 The king of Israel sent to the place about which the man of God had told him; thus he warned him, so that he guarded himself there, [a]more than once or twice.

11 Now the heart of the king of Aram was enraged over this thing; and he called his servants and said to them, "Will you tell me which of us is for the king of Israel?" 12 One of his servants said, "No, my lord, O king; but Elisha, the prophet who is in Israel, tells the king of Israel the words that you speak in your bedroom." 13 So he said, "Go and see where he is, that I may send and take him." And it was told him, saying, "Behold, he is in [A]Dothan." 14 He sent horses and chariots and a great army there, and they came by night and surrounded the city.

15 Now when the attendant of the man of God had risen early and gone out, behold, an army with horses and chariots was circling the city. And his servant said to him, "Alas, my master! [a]What shall we do?" 16 So he [a]answered, "[A]Do not fear, for [B]those who are with us are more than those who are with them." 17 Then Elisha prayed and said, "[A]O LORD, I pray, open his eyes that he may see." And the LORD opened the servant's eyes and he saw; and behold, the mountain was full of [B]horses and chariots of fire

5:24 [a]Lit *Ophel* [A]Josh 7:1, 11, 12, 21; 1 Kin 21:16 5:25 [A]2 Kin 5:22 5:26 [A]2 Kin 5:16 5:27 [a]Lit *seed* [A]Ex 4:6; Num 12:10 6:1 [A]2 Kin 2:3 6:3 [a]Lit *said* 6:5 [a]Lit *as for the iron, it fell* 6:6 [A]Ex 15:25; 2 Kin 2:21; 4:41 6:8 [a]Lit *took counsel* 6:9 [A]2 Kin 4:1, 7; 6:12 6:10 [a]Lit *not once or twice* 6:13 [A]Gen 37:17 6:15 [a]Lit *How* 6:16 [a]Lit *said* [A]Ex 14:13 [B]2 Chr 32:7, 8; Rom 8:31 6:17 [A]2 Kin 6:20 [B]2 Kin 2:11; Ps 68:17; Zech 6:1-7

5:26 Did not my heart go with you . . . ? Elisha knew Gehazi lied. Though his body did not move, Elisha's mind had seen all that had transpired between Gehazi and Naaman.

5:27 leprosy . . . shall cling to you. Gehazi's greed had cast a shadow over the integrity of Elisha's prophetic office. This made him no better in the people's thinking than Israel's false prophets, who prophesied for material gain, the very thing he wanted to avoid (vv. 15, 16). Gehazi's act betrayed a lack of faith in the Lord's ability to provide. As a result, Elisha condemned Gehazi and his descendants to suffer Naaman's skin disease forever. The punishment was a twist for Gehazi, who had gone to "take something" from Naaman (v. 20), but what he received was Naaman's disease.

6:1 place . . . where we are living. The sons of the prophets, those specially instructed by Elisha, lived together in a communal setting. The word translated "live" can also be understood as "sit before." The term is used this way of David sitting before the Lord in worship (2Sa 7:18) and the elders sitting before Ezekiel to hear his advice (Eze 8:1; 14:1). The "place" here refers to a dormitory where Elisha instructed the sons of the prophets. The growing number of men who wished to be taught led to the need for a larger building.

6:4 Jordan . . . trees. The Jordan Valley had mostly smaller kinds of trees, e.g., willow, tamarisk, and acacia that did not give heavy lumber. The resulting structure would be a humble, simple building.

6:5 axe head . . . borrowed. Iron was expensive and relatively rare in Israel at that time and the student-prophet was very poor. The axe head was loaned to the prophet since he could not have afforded it on his own and would have had no means to reimburse the owner for it.

6:6 made the iron float. Elisha threw a stick in the river at the exact spot where the axe head entered, and the stick caused the heavy iron object to float to the surface. Through this miracle, the Lord again provided for one who was faithful to Him.

6:8 king of Aram. Either Ben-hadad I or, more likely, Ben-hadad II (v. 24). *See note on 1Ki 15:18.* **warring.** The king of Aram, or Syria, was probably sending raiding parties (v. 23) to pillage and plunder Israelite towns.

6:9 The man of God. I.e., Elisha (v. 12). *See note on Dt 33:1.* **king of Israel.** I.e., Jehoram. *See note on 1:17.*

6:9, 10 do not pass this place. Elisha, receiving supernatural revelation, continually identified to Jehoram the Israelite towns which the king of Aram, or Syria, planned to attack. Jehoram then took the proper precautions and appropriately fortified those towns so as to frustrate the Syrian plan.

6:11 which of us. The Syrian king was sure someone in his household was revealing his plans to Israel.

6:13 take him. The king of Syria's plan was to capture Elisha, who knew all his secrets (v. 12), so that no matter how great Elisha's knowledge might be, he would not be free to inform Israel's king. **Dothan.** A town in the hill country of Manasseh located about 10 mi. N of Samaria and 12 mi. S of Jezreel. Dothan commanded a key mountain pass along a main road that connected Damascus and Egypt (cf. Ge 37:17).

6:14 a great army. In contrast to the smaller raiding parties (vv. 8, 23), the king of Syria sent a sizable force, including horses and chariots, to take Elisha prisoner. Arriving at Dothan, the army encircled the town.

6:16 those who are with us. Elisha was referring to God's heavenly army or "host" (cf. Jos 5:13–15; 2Ch 32:7, 8; Dan 10:20; 12:1).

6:17 open his eyes. Elisha asked the Lord to enable his servant to see this heavenly host. The Lord gave his servant the ability to see the normally unseen world of God's heavenly armies, here waiting to do battle with the Syrians (cf. Ge 32:1, 2).

all around Elisha. 18 When they came down to him,
Elisha prayed to the LORD and said, "Strike this [a]peo-
ple with blindness, I pray." So He [A]struck them with
blindness according to the word of Elisha. 19 Then
Elisha said to them, "This is not the way, nor is this
the city; follow me and I will bring you to the man
whom you seek." And he brought them to Samaria.
20 When they had come into Samaria, Elisha said,
"O [A]LORD, open the eyes of these *men,* that they
may see." So the LORD opened their eyes and they
saw; and behold, they were in the midst of Samaria.
21 Then the king of Israel when he saw them, said
to Elisha, "[A]My father, shall I [a]kill them? Shall I [a]kill
them?" 22 He [a]answered, "You shall not [b]kill *them.*
Would you [b,A]kill those you have taken captive with
your sword and with your bow? [B]Set bread and water before them, that they may eat and drink and
go to their master." 23 So he prepared a great feast
for them; and when they had eaten and drunk he
sent them away, and they went to their master. And
[A]the marauding bands of Arameans did not come
again into the land of Israel.

THE SIEGE OF SAMARIA—CANNIBALISM

24 Now it came about after this, that [A]Ben-hadad
king of Aram gathered all his army and went up
and besieged Samaria. 25 There was a great [A]fam-
ine in Samaria; and behold, they besieged it, until
a donkey's head was sold for eighty *shekels* of silver,
and a fourth of a [a]kab of dove's dung for five *shekels*
of silver. 26 As the king of Israel was passing by on
the wall a woman cried out to him, saying, "Help,
my lord, O king!" 27 He said, "[a]If the LORD does not
help you, from where shall I help you? From the
threshing floor, or from the wine press?" 28 And the
king said to her, "[A]What [a]is the matter with you?"
And she [b]answered, "This woman said to me, 'Give
your son that we may eat him today, and we will eat
my son tomorrow.' 29 [A]So we boiled my son and ate
him; and I said to her on the next day, 'Give your son,
that we may eat him'; but she has hidden her son."
30 When the king heard the words of the woman,
[A]he tore his clothes—now he was passing by on the
wall—and the people looked, and behold, he had
sackcloth [a]beneath on his [b]body. 31 Then he said,
"May [A]God do so to me and more also, if the head of
Elisha the son of Shaphat [a]remains on him today."
32 Now Elisha was sitting in his house, and [A]the
elders were sitting with him. And *the king* sent a
man from his presence; but before the messenger
came to him, he said to the elders, "Do you [B]see how
this son of a murderer has sent to take away my
head? Look, when the messenger comes, shut the
door and [a]hold the door shut against him. Is not the
sound of his master's feet behind him?" 33 While he
was still talking with them, behold, the messenger
came down to him and he said, "[A]Behold, this evil
is from the LORD; why should I wait for the LORD
any longer?"

6:18 [a]Lit *nation* [A]Gen 19:11 6:20 [A]2 Kin 6:17 6:21 [a]Lit *smite* [A]2 Kin 2:12; 5:13; 8:9 6:22 [a]Lit *said* [b]Lit *smite* [A]Deut 20:11-16; 2 Chr 28:8-15 [B]Rom 12:20 6:23 [A]2 Kin 5:2; 24:2 6:24 [A]1 Kin 20:1 6:25 [a]I.e. One kab equals approx 2 qts [A]Lev 26:26 6:27 [a]Lit *No, let the LORD help you* 6:28 [a]Lit *to you* [b]Lit *said* [A]Judg 18:23 6:29 [A]Lev 26:27-29; Deut 28:52, 53, 57; Lam 4:10 6:30 [a]Lit *within* [b]Lit *flesh* [A]1 Kin 21:27 6:31 [a]Lit *stands* [A]Ruth 1:17; 1 Kin 19:2 6:32 [a]Lit *press him with the door* [A]Ezek 8:1; 14:1; 20:1 [B]1 Kin 18:4, 13, 14; 21:10, 13 6:33 [A]Is 8:21

6:18 blindness. This word occurs only here and in Ge 19:11. The term is related to "light" and seems to mean "a dazzling from bright light" (note the "chariots of fire" in v. 17). Both biblical uses of the term involve a miraculous act with angelic presence, and both are used in the context of deliverance from danger.

6:19 follow me … to the man whom you seek. By going to Samaria himself, Elisha did not lie, but did truly lead the Syrian army to where he ultimately would be found.

6:20 in … Samaria. God delivered a sizable portion of the Syrian army into the hands of the king of Israel without bloodshed. The Syrians discovered they were surrounded and captives of Israel.

6:21 My father. *See note on 5:13.* By using this expression, which conveyed the respect a child had for his father, King Jehoram of Israel acknowledged the authority of Elisha.

6:22 You shall not kill *them*. Elisha, bearing divinely delegated authority, prohibited the execution of the captives. It was uncommon and unusually cruel to put war captives to death in cold blood, even when taken by the point of a sword, but especially by the miraculous power of God. Kindness would testify to the goodness of God and likely stall future opposition from the Aramean, or Syrian, raiders. These kind deeds gained a moral conquest (v. 23).

6:23 a great feast. In the ancient Near East, a common meal could signify the making of a covenant between two parties (cf. Lv 7:15–18).

6:24 Ben-hadad. *See note on 1Ki 15:18.* This same Ben-hadad had laid siege to Samaria earlier (1Ki 20:1), which was the result of Ahab's foolish and misplaced kindness (1Ki 20:42). **all his army.** In contrast to the smaller raiding parties (vv. 8, 23) and the larger force seeking Elisha's capture (v. 14), Ben-hadad gathered his entire army, marched to Samaria, and besieged the capital.

6:25 a donkey's head … eighty *shekels* of silver. The siege resulted in a terrible famine gripping the city of Samaria. This ignominious body part of an unclean animal (Lv 11:2–7; Dt 14:4–8) sold at an overvalued price of about two lbs. of silver. **dove's dung … five *shekels* of silver.** "Dove's dung" was either a nickname for some small pea or root, or literal dung to be used as fuel or food in the desperate situation. Approximately one pt. cost about two oz. of silver.

6:26 Help, my lord, O king! The woman asked King Jehoram to render a legal decision in her dispute with another woman (*see note on 1Ki 3:16–27*).

6:28, 29 Give your son that we may eat him. The curses of the Mosaic Covenant, especially for the sin of apostasy, predicted this sort of pagan cannibalism (Lv 26:29; Dt 28:52–57). The way in which the woman presented her case without feeling added to the horror of it.

6:30 tore his clothes. A sign of distress and grief (*see note on 1Ki 21:27*). **sackcloth … on his body.** A coarse cloth, made from goat's hair, worn as a sign of mourning (cf. Ge 37:34). He was not truly humbled for his sins and the nation's, or he would not have called for vengeance on Elisha.

6:31 the head of Elisha. Jehoram swore an oath to have Elisha killed. The reason Jehoram desired the death of Elisha could have been: 1) the king viewed the siege as the work of the Lord (v. 33), so he assumed that the Lord's representative, the prophet, with whom the kings of Israel were in conflict, was involved as well; or 2) the king remembered when Elijah had ended a famine (1Ki 18:41–46); or 3) Jehoram thought that Elisha's clemency to the Syrian army (v. 22) had somehow led to and added intensity to the present siege; or 4) because Elisha had miracle power, he should have ended the famine. But, most likely, the reason he wanted Elisha dead was because he expected that his mourning, perhaps counseled by the prophet as an act of true repentance (which it was not; *see note on v. 30*), would result in the end of the siege. When it did not, he sought the prophet's head.

6:32 the elders were sitting with him. The elders were the leading citizens of Samaria, whose gathering indicated the high regard in which Elisha was held by the prominent of Samarian society. **son of a murderer.** This phrase can mean both that: 1) Jehoram was the son of Ahab, who was guilty of murder (1Ki 21:1–16); and that 2) he had the character of a murderer.

6:33 why should I wait for the LORD any longer? Jehoram rightly viewed the Lord as the instigator of the siege and famine in Samaria and declared that he saw no hope that the Lord would reverse this situation.

ELISHA PROMISES FOOD

7 Then Elisha said, "Listen to the word of the LORD; thus says the LORD, '[A]Tomorrow about this time a [a]measure of fine flour will be *sold* for a shekel, and two measures of barley for a shekel, in the gate of Samaria.' " 2 [A]The royal officer on whose hand the king was leaning answered the man of God and said, "Behold, [B]if the LORD should make windows in heaven, could this thing be?" Then he said, "Behold, you will see it with your own eyes, but you will not eat [a]of it."

FOUR LEPERS RELATE ARAMEANS' FLIGHT

3 Now there were four [A]leprous men at the entrance of the gate; and they said to one another, "Why do we sit here until we die? 4 If we say, 'We will enter the city,' then the famine is in the city and we will die there; and if we sit here, we die also. Now therefore come, and let us [a]go over to [A]the camp of the Arameans. If they spare us, we will live; and if they kill us, we will but die." 5 They arose at twilight to go to the camp of the Arameans; when they came to the outskirts of the camp of the Arameans, behold, there was no one there. 6 For [A]the Lord had caused the army of the Arameans to hear a sound of chariots and a sound of horses, *even* the sound of a great army, so that they said to one another, "Behold, the king of Israel has hired against us [B]the kings of the Hittites and [C]the kings of the Egyptians, to come upon us." 7 Therefore they [A]arose and fled in the twilight, and left their tents and their horses and their donkeys, *even* the camp just as it was, and fled for their life. 8 When these lepers came to the outskirts of the camp, they entered one tent and ate and drank, and [A]carried from there silver and gold and clothes, and went and hid *them;* and they returned and entered another tent and carried from there *also,* and went and hid *them.*

9 Then they said to one another, "We are not doing right. This day is a day of good news, but we are keeping silent; if we wait until morning light, punishment will [a]overtake us. Now therefore come, let us go and tell the king's household." 10 So they came and called to the gatekeepers of the city, and they told them, saying, "We came to the camp of the Arameans, and behold, there was no one there, nor the voice of man, only the horses tied and the donkeys tied, and the tents just as they were." 11 The gatekeepers called and told *it* within the king's household. 12 Then the king arose in the night and said to his servants, "I will now tell you what the Arameans have done to us. They know that [A]we are hungry; therefore they have gone from the camp [B]to hide themselves in the field, saying, 'When they come out of the city, we will capture them alive and get into the city.' " 13 One of his servants said, "Please, let some *men* take five of the horses which remain, which are left [a]in the city. Behold, they *will be in any case* like all the multitude of Israel who are left in it; behold, they *will be in any case* like all the multitude of Israel who have already perished, so let us send and see." 14 They took therefore two chariots with horses, and the king sent after the army of the Arameans, saying, "Go and see."

THE PROMISE FULFILLED

15 They went after them to the Jordan, and behold, all the way was full of clothes and equipment which the Arameans had thrown away in their haste. Then the messengers returned and told the king.

16 So the people went out and plundered the camp of the Arameans. Then a [a]measure of fine flour *was sold* for a shekel and two [a]measures of barley for a shekel, [A]according to the word of the LORD. 17 Now the king appointed [A]the royal officer on whose hand he leaned [a]to have charge of the gate; but the people trampled on him at the gate, and he died just as the man of God had said, [B]who spoke when the king came down to him. 18 It happened just as the man of God had spoken to the king, saying, "[A]Two [a]measures of barley for a shekel and a [a]measure of

7:1 [a]Heb *seah* [A]2 Kin 7:18 7:2 [a]Lit *from there* [A]2 Kin 5:18; 7:17, 19 [B]Gen 7:11; Mal 3:10 7:3 [A]Lev 13:45, 46; Num 5:2-4; 12:10-14 7:4 [a]Lit *fall* [A]2 Kin 6:24 7:6 [A]2 Sam 5:24 [B]1 Kin 10:29 [C]2 Chr 12:2, 3; Is 31:1; 36:9 7:7 [A]Ps 48:4-6; Prov 28:1 7:8 [A]Josh 7:21 7:9 [a]Lit *find* 7:12 [A]2 Kin 6:25-29 [B]Josh 8:4-12 7:13 [a]Lit *in it* 7:16 [a]Heb *seah;* i.e. one seah equals approx 11 qts [A]2 Kin 7:1 7:17 [a]Lit *over the gate* [A]2 Kin 7:2 [B]2 Kin 6:32 7:18 [a]Heb *seah;* i.e. one seah equals approx 11 qts [A]2 Kin 7:1

7:1 a measure … for a shekel. About 7 quarts of flour would sell for about two-fifths of an ounce of silver. **two measures … for a shekel.** About 13–14 quarts of barley would also sell for about two-fifths of an ounce of silver. These prices, when compared to those in 6:25, indicated that the next day the famine in Samaria would end. **in the gate.** In ancient Israel, the city gate was the marketplace where business was transacted (cf. Ru 4:1; 2Sa 15:1–5). Normal trade at the city gate of Samaria implied that the siege would be lifted.

7:2 officer on whose hand the king was leaning. For "officer" *see note on 9:25.* The king depended upon this officer as his chief adviser. **you will see … but … not eat.** The royal official questioned the Lord's ability to provide food within the day. For that offense against God, Elisha predicted that the officer would witness the promised miracle, but he would not eat any of it. How this prophecy was fulfilled is described in vv. 16, 17.

7:3 leprous men. The account of these lepers is used to tell of the siege's end and the provisions for Samaria (vv. 3–11). **at the entrance of the gate.** In the area immediately outside the city gate, 4 lepers lived, shut out of Samaria because of their disease (Lv 13:46; Nu 5:3). The lepers knew that living in Samaria, whether just outside or inside the gate, offered them nothing but death.

7:5 the outskirts of the camp of the Arameans. Lit. "the edge of the camp." The normal meaning of this phrase would refer to the back edge of the army camp, the farthest point from the wall of Samaria.

7:6 the Hittites and … Egyptians. Sometime before the arrival of the lepers, the Lord had made the Syrians hear the terrifying sound of a huge army approaching. They thought the Israelite king had hired two massive foreign armies to attack them. The Hittites were descendants of the once-great Hittite empire who lived in small groups across northern Syria (*see note on 1Ki 10:29*). Egypt was in decline at this time, but its army would still have represented a great danger to the Syrians.

7:9 punishment. The lepers did not fear that the Syrians would return, but that the Lord would punish them for their sin of not telling the Israelite king of their discovery.

7:12 what the Arameans have done to us. Jehoram greeted the report from the lepers with great suspicion. He thought that the Arameans, or Syrians, were feigning the pull back to appear defeated, in order to lure the Israelites out of Samaria for a surprise attack on them to gain entrance into the city. However, vv. 13–15 describe how the leper's report was confirmed.

7:16–20 By repeating words from vv. 1, 2 and by explicit statements ("according to the word of the LORD," v. 16; "just as the man of God had said/spoken," vv. 17, 18), the text emphasizes that Elisha's prophecy in 7:2 literally came to pass.

fine flour for a shekel, will be *sold* tomorrow about
this time at the gate of Samaria." 19 Then the royal
officer answered the man of God and said, "Now behold, [A]if the LORD should make windows in heaven,
could such a thing be?" And he said, "Behold, you
will see it with your own eyes, but you will not eat
[a]of it." 20 And so it happened to him, for the people
trampled on him at the gate and he died.

JEHORAM RESTORES THE SHUNAMMITE'S LAND

8 Now [A]Elisha spoke to the woman whose son
he had restored to life, saying, "Arise and go
[a]with your household, and sojourn wherever you
can sojourn; for the [B]LORD has called for a famine,
and [C]it will even come on the land for seven years."
2 So the woman arose and did according to the word
of the man of God, and she went with her household
and sojourned in the land of the Philistines seven
years. 3 At the end of seven years, the woman returned from the land of the Philistines; and she went
out to [a]appeal to the king for her house and for her
field. 4 Now the king was talking with [A]Gehazi, the
servant of the man of God, saying, "Please relate to
me all the great things that Elisha has done." 5 As
he was relating to the king [A]how he had restored
to life the one who was dead, behold, the woman
whose son he had restored to life [a]appealed to the
king for her house and for her field. And Gehazi said,
"My lord, O king, this is the woman and this is her
son, whom Elisha restored to life." 6 When the king
asked the woman, she related *it* to him. So the king
appointed for her a certain officer, saying, "Restore
all that was hers and all the produce of the field
from the day that she left the land even until now."

ELISHA PREDICTS EVIL FROM HAZAEL

7 Then Elisha came to [A]Damascus. Now [B]Ben-ha-
dad king of Aram was sick, and it was told him,
saying, "[C]The man of God has come here." 8 The king
said to [A]Hazael, "[B]Take a gift in your hand and go
to meet the man of God, and [C]inquire of the LORD
by him, saying, 'Will I recover from this sickness?' "
9 So Hazael went to meet him and took a gift in his
hand, even every kind of good thing of Damascus,
forty camels' loads; and he came and stood before
him and said, "[A]Your son Ben-hadad king of Aram
has sent me to you, saying, 'Will I recover from this
sickness?' " 10 Then Elisha said to him, "[A]Go, say to
him, 'You will surely recover,' but the [B]LORD has
shown me that he will certainly die." 11 He [a]fixed his
gaze steadily *on him* [A]until he was ashamed, and
[B]the man of God wept. 12 Hazael said, "Why does my
lord weep?" Then he [a]answered, "Because [A]I know
the evil that you will do to the sons of Israel: their
strongholds you will set on fire, and their young
men you will kill with the sword, and their little
ones you [B]will dash in pieces, and their women with
child you will rip up." 13 Then Hazael said, "But what
is your servant, [A]*who is but* a dog, that he should do
this great thing?" And Elisha [a]answered, "[B]The LORD
has shown me that you will be king over Aram."

7:19 [a]Lit *from there* [A]2 Kin 7:2 8:1 [a]Lit *you and your* [A]2 Kin 4:18, 31-35 [B]Ps 105:16; Hag 1:11 [C]Gen 41:27, 54 8:3 [a]Lit *cry out* 8:4 [A]2 Kin 4:12; 5:20-27 8:5 [a]Lit *cried out* [A]2 Kin 4:35 8:7 [A]1 Kin 11:24 [B]2 Kin 6:24 [C]2 Kin 5:20 8:8 [A]1 Kin 19:15, 17 [B]1 Kin 14:3 [C]2 Kin 1:2 8:9 [A]2 Kin 5:13 8:10 [A]2 Kin 8:14 [B]2 Kin 8:15 8:11 [a]Lit *made his face stand fast and he set* [A]2 Kin 2:17 [B]Luke 19:41 8:12 [a]Lit *said* [A]2 Kin 10:32, 33; 12:17; 13:3, 7 [B]2 Kin 15:16; Nah 3:10 8:13 [a]Lit *said* [A]1 Sam 17:43; 2 Sam 9:8 [B]1 Kin 19:15

8:1–6 The chronological question of when the events recounted in these verses took place in Elisha's ministry has been much debated. Interpreters hold to one of 3 positions: 1) The encounter between the Shunammite woman, the king of Israel, and Gehazi took place toward the end of the reign of Jehoram in Israel. However, this would mean Gehazi was in the presence of the king (vv. 4, 5), although afflicted with leprosy (5:27), and King Jehoram was asking what great things Elisha had done after personally witnessing the events recorded in 6:8–7:19. 2) Because the king of Israel did not know Elisha's exploits, some interpreters place the final encounter during the early reign of Jehu. However, there are still the issues of Gehazi's leprosy and Jehu's being well acquainted with the prophecy of Elijah (9:36, 37; 10:17) that predicted Elisha's ministry (1Ki 19:15–18). 3) The best explanation is that the record is out of chronological sequence, being thematically tied to the subject of famine in 6:24–7:20, but having occurred earlier in the reign of King Jehoram of Israel, before the events recorded in 5:1–7:20.

8:1 a famine … for seven years. Seven-year famines were known in the ancient Near East (cf. Ge 41:29–32). Since the Shunammite woman would have been only a resident alien in a foreign land, her return within 7 years may have aided her legal claim to her property (cf. Ex 21:2; 23:10, 11; Lv 25:1–7; Dt 15:1–6).

8:2 land of the Philistines. The area located SW of Israel along the Mediterranean Sea coastal plain between the Jarkon River in the N and the Besor Brook in the S. The fact that the famine was localized in Israel demonstrated that this was a curse, a punishment for apostasy (cf. Dt 28:38–40), because of Israel's disobedience of the Mosaic Covenant.

8:3 appeal to the king. The Shunammite woman made a legal appeal to the king to support her ownership claim. In Israel, the king was the final arbiter of such disputes (*see note on 1Ki 3:16–27*). Providentially, the widow arrived just as Gehazi was describing how Elisha had raised her son from the dead (v. 5).

8:6 Restore all … and all the produce. The king's judgment was to return to the woman everything she owned, including the land's earnings during her absence.

8:7 Elisha came to Damascus. It was unusual for a prophet to visit foreign capitals, but not unknown (cf. Jon 3:3). Elisha went to Damascus, the capital of Syria, to carry out one of the 3 commands God had given to Elijah at Horeb (1Ki 19:15, 16). **Ben-hadad.** *See note on 1Ki 15:18.* Ben-hadad died ca. 841 B.C., the same year as Jehoram of Israel (3:1), Jehoram of Judah (8:17), and Ahaziah of Judah (8:25, 26). **man of God.** *See note on Dt 33:1.*

8:8 Hazael. His name means "God sees" or "whom God beholds." Hazael was a servant of Ben-hadad and not a member of the royal family. Assyrian records called Hazael the "son of a nobody" and his lineage was not recorded because he was a commoner.

8:9 every … good thing of Damascus. The city of Damascus was a trade center between Egypt, Asia Minor, and Mesopotamia. It had within it the finest merchandise of the ancient Near East. Ben-hadad evidently thought that an impressive gift would influence Elisha's prediction. **Your son.** Ben-hadad approached Elisha with the humble respect of a son for his father (cf. 5:13; 6:21).

8:10 recover … die. Ben-hadad wanted to know whether or not he would recover from his present illness. In response, Elisha affirmed two interrelated things: 1) Ben-hadad would be restored to health; his present sickness would not be the means of his death. 2) Ben-hadad would surely die by some other means.

8:11 he was ashamed. With a fixed gaze, Elisha stared at Hazael because it had been revealed to him what Hazael would do, including the murder of Ben-hadad (v. 15). Hazael was embarrassed, knowing that Elisha knew of his plan to assassinate the Syrian king.

8:12 the evil. Elisha mourned, knowing the atrocities that Hazael would bring on Israel. The harsh actions mentioned here were common in ancient wars (Ps 137:9; Is 13:16; Hos 10:14; 13:16; Am 1:13; Na 3:10). Hazael did prove to be a constant foe of Israel (9:14–16; 10:32; 12:17, 18; 13:3, 22).

8:13 your servant … dog. To call oneself a dog was an expression of humility (*see note on 2Sa 9:8*). Hazael sought to deny that he would ever have the power to commit such

[14]So he departed from Elisha and returned to his
master, who said to him, "What did Elisha say to
you?" And he [a]answered, "He told me that [A]you
would surely recover." [15]On the following day, he
took the cover and dipped it in water and spread
it on his face, [A]so that he died. And Hazael became
king in his place.

ANOTHER JEHORAM REIGNS IN JUDAH

[16]Now in the fifth year of [A]Joram the son of Ahab
king of Israel, Jehoshaphat being then the king of
Judah, Jehoram the son of Jehoshaphat king of Judah became king. [17]He was [A]thirty-two years old
when he became king, and he reigned eight years
in Jerusalem. [18]He walked in the way of the kings of
Israel, just as the house of Ahab had done, for [A]the
daughter of Ahab became his wife; and he did evil
in the sight of the LORD. [19]However, the LORD was
not willing to destroy Judah, for the sake of David
His servant, [A]since He had [a]promised him to give
a [b]lamp to him through his sons always.
[20]In his days [A]Edom revolted from under the
hand of Judah, and made a king over themselves.
[21]Then Joram crossed over to Zair, and all his chariots with him. And he arose by night and struck
the Edomites who had surrounded him and the
captains of the chariots; [A]but *his* [a]army fled to their
tents. [22][A]So Edom revolted [a]against Judah to this
day. Then [B]Libnah revolted at the same time. [23]The
rest of the acts of Joram and all that he did, are
they not written in the Book of the Chronicles of
the Kings of Judah?

AHAZIAH SUCCEEDS JEHORAM IN JUDAH

[24]So Joram slept with his fathers and [A]was buried
with his fathers in the city of David; and [B]Ahaziah
his son became king in his place.
[25][A]In the twelfth year of Joram the son of Ahab
king of Israel, Ahaziah the son of Jehoram king of Judah began to reign. [26][A]Ahaziah *was* twenty-two years
old when he became king, and he reigned one year in
Jerusalem. And his mother's name *was* Athaliah the
granddaughter of Omri king of Israel. [27][A]He walked
in the way of the house of Ahab and did evil in the
sight of the LORD, like the house of Ahab *had done,*
because he was a son-in-law of the house of Ahab.
[28]Then he went with Joram the son of Ahab to
war against [A]Hazael king of Aram at [B]Ramoth-gile-
ad, and the Arameans [a]wounded Joram. [29]So [A]King
Joram returned to be healed in Jezreel of the wounds
which the Arameans had [a]inflicted on him at [B]Ra-
mah when he fought against Hazael king of Aram.
Then [C]Ahaziah the son of Jehoram king of Judah
went down to see Joram the son of Ahab in Jezreel
because he was sick.

JEHU REIGNS OVER ISRAEL

9 Now Elisha the prophet called one of [A]the sons
of the prophets and said to him, "[B]Gird up your
loins, and [C]take this flask of oil in your hand and go
to [D]Ramoth-gilead. [2]When you arrive there, [a]search
out [A]Jehu the son of Jehoshaphat the son of Nimshi,
and go in and [b,B]bid him arise from among his brothers, and bring him to an inner room. [3]Then take the
flask of oil and pour it on his head and say, 'Thus

8:14 [a]Lit *said* [A]2 Kin 8:10 8:15 [A]2 Kin 8:10 8:16 [A]2 Kin 1:17; 3:1 8:17 [A]2 Chr 21:5-10 8:18 [A]2 Kin 8:27 8:19 [a]Lit *said* [b]I.e. descendant on the throne [A]2 Sam 7:12-15; 1 Kin 11:36 8:20 [A]1 Kin 22:47; 2 Kin 3:9, 26, 27; 8:22 8:21 [a]Lit *the people* [A]2 Sam 18:17; 19:8 8:22 [a]Lit *from under the hand of* [A]Gen 27:40 [B]Josh 21:13; 2 Kin 19:8 8:24 [A]2 Chr 21:20 [B]2 Chr 21:1, 7 8:25 [A]2 Chr 22:1-6 8:26 [A]2 Chr 22:2 8:27 [A]2 Chr 22:3 8:28 [a]Lit *smote* [A]2 Kin 8:15 [B]1 Kin 22:3, 29 8:29 [a]Lit *struck* [A]2 Kin 9:15 [B]2 Kin 8:28; 2 Chr 22:5, 6 [C]2 Kin 9:16 9:1 [A]2 Kin 2:3 [B]2 Kin 4:29 [C]1 Sam 10:1; 16:1; 1 Kin 1:39 [D]2 Kin 8:28, 29 9:2 [a]Lit *and look there for* [b]Lit *cause him to* [A]1 Kin 19:16, 17; 2 Kin 9:14, 20 [B]2 Kin 9:5, 11

atrocities. He was trying to convince Elisha that he had no plan to take over the kingship of Syria. **you will be king over Aram.** In response to Hazael's feigned self-deprecation, Elisha affirmed that the Lord willed that Hazael be king over Aram, or Syria (cf. 1Ki 19:15).

8:15 he died. Hazael took a bed furnishing, soaked it, and killed Ben-hadad by suffocation. **Hazael became king.** Upon Ben-hadad's death, Hazael took the kingship of Syria and ruled ca. 841–801 B.C., during the reigns of Jehoram, Jehu, and Jehoahaz in Israel and Ahaziah, Athaliah, and Joash in Judah.

8:16 fifth year. Ca. 848 B.C., the year Jehoshaphat of Judah died. **Joram.** An alternate name for the king referred to as Jehoram previously (1:17; 3:1, 6). *See notes on 2Ch 21:4–20.*

8:17 eight years. 848–841 B.C. *See notes on 2Ch 21:4–20.* Jehoram of Judah served as co-regent with his father Jehoshaphat for the final 4 years of his reign, 853–848 B.C. Joram (Jehoram) became king of Israel during the second year of this co-regency, 852 B.C. (*see notes on 1:17; 3:1*). Jehoram of Judah ruled alone for 8 years after his father's death, until 841 B.C. (cf. 2Ch 21:15). Most likely, Obadiah prophesied during his reign.

8:18 as the house of Ahab. Jehoram officially sanctioned Baal worship in Judah as Ahab had in Israel (1Ki 16:31–33). **the daughter of Ahab.** Jehoram was married to Athaliah, the daughter of Ahab and Jezebel (v. 26). Just as Jezebel incited Ahab to do evil in the sight of the Lord (1Ki 21:25), so Athaliah influenced Jehoram. Athaliah's wicked actions are recorded in 11:1–16; 2Ch 22:10–23:15.

8:19 a lamp ... always. *See note on 1Ki 11:36.*

8:20 Edom revolted. Edom had been a vassal of the united kingdom, and of the southern kingdom of Judah since David's reign (2Sa 8:13, 14).

8:21 Zair. The exact location is unknown.

8:22 Edom revolted ... to this day. During the reign of Jehoram, Edom defeated the Judean army, took some border lands, and became independent of Judah's rule. The continuing sovereignty of Edom proved that not one of the future kings of Judah recorded in 2 Kings was the anticipated Messiah because He would possess Edom (cf. Nu 24:18). **Libnah.** A town located in the Shephelah on the border with Philistia, about 20 mi. SW of Jerusalem (Jos 15:42; 21:13). The revolt of Libnah was probably connected with that of the Philistines and Arabians recounted in 2Ch 21:16, 17.

8:25–29 The reign of Ahaziah (ca. 841 B.C.) is not to be confused with that of Israel's King Ahaziah (1Ki 22:51–2Ki 1:8). *See notes on 2Ki 9:27; 2Ch 22:1–9.*

8:26 Athaliah. *See note on v. 18.*

8:27 like the house of Ahab. Like his father, Jehoram, Ahaziah continued the official sanctioning of Baal worship in Judah (*see note on v. 18*).

8:28 Ramoth-gilead. *See note on 1Ki 22:3.*

8:29 went down to see Joram. Ahaziah's travel to visit the recuperating Joram (also called Jehoram) king of Israel placed him in Jezreel (W of the Jordan, SW of the Sea of Galilee) during Jehu's purge of the house of Omri (see 9:21–29).

9:2 Jehu. The Lord had previously told Elijah that Jehu would become king over Israel and kill those involved in the worship of Baal (cf. 1Ki 19:17). The fulfillment of the prophecy is recorded from 9:1–10:31. **inner room.** A private room that could be closed off to the public. Elisha commissioned one of the younger prophets to anoint Jehu alone behind closed doors. The rite was to be a secret affair without Elisha present so that Jehoram would not suspect that a coup was coming.

9:3 anointed you king over Israel. The anointing with olive oil by a prophet of the Lord confirmed that God Himself had earlier chosen that man to be king (cf. 1Sa 10:1; 16:13). This action of anointing by a commissioned prophet indicated divine investiture with God's sovereign power to Jehu. **flee and do**

says the LORD, “[A]I have anointed you king over Israel.” ’ Then open the door and flee and do not wait.”
4 So [A]the young man, the servant of the prophet,
went to Ramoth-gilead. 5 When he came, behold, the
captains of the army were sitting, and he said, “I
have a word for you, O captain.” And Jehu said, “[a]For
which *one* of us?” And he said, “For you, O captain.”
6 He arose and went into the house, and he poured
the oil on his head and said to him, “Thus says the
LORD, the God of Israel, ‘[A]I have anointed you king
over the people of the LORD, *even* over Israel. 7 You
shall strike the house of Ahab your master, [A]that I
may avenge [B]the blood of My servants the prophets,
and the blood of all the servants of the LORD, [C]at
the hand of Jezebel. 8 For the whole house of Ahab
shall perish, and [A]I will cut off from Ahab [B]every
male person [C]both bond and free in Israel. 9 [A]I will
make the house of Ahab like the house of Jeroboam
the son of Nebat, and [B]like the house of Baasha the
son of Ahijah. 10 [A]The dogs shall eat Jezebel in the
territory of Jezreel, and none shall bury *her*.’ ” Then
he opened the door and fled.
11 Now Jehu came out to the servants of his master,
and one said to him, “[A]Is all well? Why did this [B]mad
fellow come to you?” And he said to them, “You know
very well the man and his talk.” 12 They said, “It is a
lie, tell us now.” And he said, “Thus and thus he said
to me, ‘Thus says the LORD, “I have anointed you king
over Israel.” ’ ” 13 Then [A]they hurried and each man
took his garment and placed it under him on the bare
steps, and [B]blew the trumpet, saying, “Jehu is king!”

JEHORAM (JORAM) IS ASSASSINATED

14 So Jehu the son of Jehoshaphat the son of Nimshi conspired against Joram. [A]Now Joram [a]with all
Israel was [b]defending Ramoth-gilead against Hazael
king of Aram, 15 but [A]King [a]Joram had returned to
Jezreel to be healed of the wounds which the Arameans had [b]inflicted on him when he fought with
Hazael king of Aram. So Jehu said, “If this is your
mind, *then* let no one escape *or* [c]leave the city to go
tell *it* in Jezreel.” 16 Then Jehu rode in a chariot and
went to Jezreel, for Joram was lying there. [A]Ahaziah
king of Judah had come down to see Joram.
17 Now the watchman was standing on the tower
in Jezreel and he saw the [a]company of Jehu as he
came, and said, “I see a [a]company.” And Joram said,
“Take a horseman and send him to meet them and
let him say, ‘Is it peace?’ ” 18 So a horseman went
to meet him and said, “Thus says the king, ‘Is it
peace?’ ” And Jehu said, “[A]What have you to do with
peace? Turn behind me.” And the watchman [a]re-
ported, “The messenger came to them, but he did
not return.” 19 Then he sent out a second horseman,
who came to them and said, “Thus says the king, ‘Is
it peace?’ ” And Jehu [a]answered, “What have you to
do with peace? Turn behind me.” 20 The watchman
[a]reported, “He came even to them, and he did not
return; and [A]the driving is like the driving of [B]Jehu
the son of Nimshi, for he drives furiously.”
21 Then [a]Joram said, “[b]Get ready.” And they made
his chariot ready. [a,A]Joram king of Israel and Ahaziah king of Judah went out, each in his chariot,
and they went out to meet Jehu and found him in
the [c,B]property of Naboth the Jezreelite. 22 When [a]Jo-
ram saw Jehu, he said, “Is it peace, Jehu?” And he
[b]answered, “What peace, [A]so long as the harlotries
of your mother Jezebel and her witchcrafts are so
many?” 23 So [a]Joram [b]reined about and fled and
said to Ahaziah, “[A]*There is* treachery, O Ahaziah!”
24 And [A]Jehu [a]drew his bow with his full strength
and [b]shot [c]Joram between his arms; and the arrow
went [d]through his heart and he sank in his chariot.
25 Then *Jehu* said to Bidkar his officer, “Take *him* up

9:3 [A]2 Chr 22:7 9:4 [A]2 Kin 9:1 9:5 [a]Lit *To whom of us all?* 9:6 [A]1 Sam 2:7, 8; 1 Kin 19:16; 2 Kin 9:3; 2 Chr 22:7 9:7 [A]Deut 32:35, 43 [B]1 Kin 18:4; 21:15, 21, 25 [C]2 Kin 9:32-37 9:8 [A]1 Kin 21:21; 2 Kin 10:17 [B]1 Sam 25:22 [C]Deut 32:36; 2 Kin 14:26 9:9 [A]1 Kin 14:10, 11; 15:29 [B]1 Kin 16:3-5, 11, 12 9:10 [A]1 Kin 21:23; 2 Kin 9:35, 36 9:11 [A]2 Kin 9:17, 19, 22 [B]Jer 29:26; Hos 9:7; Mark 3:21 9:13 [A]Matt 21:7, 8; Mark 11:7, 8 [B]2 Sam 15:10; 1 Kin 1:34, 39 9:14 [a]Lit *he and* [b]Lit *keeping* [A]1 Kin 22:3; 2 Kin 8:28 9:15 [a]Heb *Jehoram* [b]Lit *struck* [c]Lit *go out from* [A]2 Kin 8:29 9:16 [A]2 Kin 8:29 9:17 [a]Lit *multitude* 9:18 [a]Lit *told, saying* [A]2 Kin 9:19, 22 9:19 [a]Lit *said* 9:20 [a]Lit *told, saying* [A]2 Sam 18:27 [B]1 Kin 19:17 9:21 [a]Heb *Jehoram* [b]Lit *Yoke the chariot* [c]Lit *portion* [A]2 Chr 22:7 [B]1 Kin 21:1-7, 15-19; 2 Kin 9:26 9:22 [a]Heb *Jehoram* [b]Lit *said* [A]1 Kin 16:30-33; 18:19; 2 Chr 21:13 9:23 [a]Heb *Jehoram* [b]Lit *turned his hands* [A]2 Kin 11:14 9:24 [a]Lit *filled his hand with the bow* [b]Lit *smote* [c]Heb *Jehoram* [d]Lit *out at* [A]1 Kin 22:34

not wait. The need for haste by the young prophet underscored the danger of the assignment. A prophet in the midst of Israel's army camp would alert the pro-Jehoram elements to the possibility of the coup.

9:7 avenge the blood. Jehu was to be the Lord's avenger (cf. Nu 35:12) for the murders of the Lord's prophets (1Ki 18:4) and of people like Naboth who served the Lord (1Ki 21:1–16).

9:9 like the house of Jeroboam … Baasha. God would thoroughly annihilate Ahab's line in the same way as Jeroboam's dynasty and Baasha's dynasty had previously ended violently (1Ki 15:27–30; 16:8–13).

9:10 dogs shall eat. Dogs were considered scavengers in the ancient Near East, and they would devour the corpse of Jezebel. **Jezreel.** Formerly the area of Naboth's vineyard (1Ki 21:1–16). **none shall bury *her*.** In Israel, the failure to be buried indicated disgrace (*see note on 1Ki 13:22*).

9:11 this mad fellow. The soldier demonstrated his disdain for Elisha's servant (vv. 1, 4) by referring to him as crazy or demented. In Jer 29:26 and Hos 9:7 this same term was used as a derogatory term for prophets whose messages were considered crazy. Jehu's response referred to the prophet's "babble," not his behavior.

9:12 Thus and thus. This refers to the repeating of the prophecy in vv. 4–10.

9:13 blew the trumpet. Having laid their cloaks under Jehu's feet with the steps of the house serving as a makeshift throne, the officers blew trumpets acclaiming Jehu as king. A trumpet often heralded such a public proclamation and assembly, including the appointment of a king (cf. 11:14; 2Sa 15:10; 1Ki 1:34).

9:15 let no one … go tell *it* in Jezreel. For Jehu to succeed in his revolt and to avoid a civil conflict, it was important to take Joram totally by surprise. Therefore, Jehu ordered the city of Ramoth-gilead where he had been anointed (vv. 2, 3) to be sealed lest someone loyal to Joram escape and notify the king.

9:16 to Jezreel. From Ramoth-gilead, Jezreel was straight W across the Jordan, N of Mt. Gilboa.

9:21 Naboth the Jezreelite. Providentially, the kings of Israel and Judah met Jehu at the very place where Ahab and Jezebel had Naboth killed (1Ki 21:1–16). The alarmed king, aware by then of impending disaster, summoned his forces and, accompanied by Ahaziah, met Jehu as Jehu's men ascended the slope up to the city from the northern side.

9:22 What peace. Joram wished to know if Jehu's coming meant peace, apparently unsure of Jehu's rebellious plans. Jehu replied that there could be no true peace in Israel because of Jezebel's influence. "Harlotries," a common biblical metaphor for idolatry, and "witchcrafts," i.e., seeking information from demonic forces, described the nature of Jezebel's influence. Idolatry had lured Israel into demonic practices.

9:25 Bidkar his officer. "Officer" originally referred to the third man in a chariot, besides the driver and a warrior; it was his task to hold the shield and arms of the warrior. The term was eventually applied to a high-ranking official (cf. 7:2). Jehu and Bidkar either rode

and [A]cast him into the [a]property of the field of Naboth the Jezreelite, for I remember when [b]you and
I were riding together after Ahab his father, that
the [B]LORD laid this [C]oracle against him: 26 'Surely
[A]I have seen yesterday the blood of Naboth and the
blood of his sons,' says the LORD, 'and [B]I will repay
you in this [a]property,' says the LORD. Now then,
take and cast him into the [a]property, according to
the word of the LORD."

JEHU ASSASSINATES AHAZIAH

27 [A]When Ahaziah the king of Judah saw *this,*
he fled by the way of the garden house. And Jehu
pursued him and said, "[a]Shoot him too, in the chariot." *So they shot him* at the ascent of Gur, which is
at [B]Ibleam. But he fled to Megiddo and died there.
28 [A]Then his servants carried him in a chariot to
Jerusalem and buried him in his grave with his
fathers in the city of David.
29 Now in [A]the eleventh year of Joram, the son of
Ahab, Ahaziah became king over Judah.
30 When Jehu came to Jezreel, Jezebel heard *of
it,* and [A]she painted her eyes and adorned her head
and looked out the window. 31 As Jehu entered the
gate, she said, "[A]Is it [a]well, Zimri, [b]your master's
murderer?" 32 Then he lifted up his face to the window and said, "Who is on my side? Who?" And two
or three officials looked down at him.

JEZEBEL IS SLAIN

33 He said, "Throw her down." So they threw her
down, and some of her blood was sprinkled on the
wall and on the horses, and he trampled her under
foot. 34 When he came in, he ate and drank; and he
said, "See now to [A]this cursed woman and bury
her, for [B]she is a king's daughter." 35 They went to
bury her, but they found nothing more of her than
the skull and the feet and the palms of her hands.
36 Therefore they returned and told him. And he
said, "This is the word of the LORD, which He spoke
by His servant Elijah the Tishbite, saying, '[A]In the
[a]property of Jezreel the dogs shall eat the flesh of
Jezebel; 37 and [A]the corpse of Jezebel will be as dung
on the face of the field in the [a]property of Jezreel,
so they cannot say, "This is Jezebel." ' "

JUDGMENT UPON AHAB'S HOUSE

10 Now Ahab had seventy sons in [A]Samaria.
And Jehu wrote letters and sent *them* to
Samaria, to the rulers of Jezreel, the elders, and
to the guardians of *the children of* Ahab, saying,
2 "Now, [A]when this letter comes to you, since your
master's sons are with you, [a]as well as the chariots
and horses and a fortified city and the weapons,
3 select the best and [a]fittest of your master's sons,
and set *him* on his father's throne, and fight for
your master's house." 4 But they feared greatly and
said, "Behold, [A]the two kings did not stand before
him; how then can we stand?" 5 And the one who
was over the household, and he who *was* over the
city, the elders, and the guardians of *the children,*
sent *word* to Jehu, saying, "[A]We are your servants,
all that you say to us we will do, we will not make
any man king; do what is good in your sight." 6 Then
he wrote a letter to them a second time saying, "If
you are on my side, and you will listen to my voice,
take the heads of the men, your master's sons, and
come to me at Jezreel tomorrow about this time."

9:25 [a]Lit *portion* [b]Lit *I and you* [A]1 Kin 21:1 [B]1 Kin 21:19, 24-29 [C]Is 13:1 9:26 [a]Lit *portion* [A]1 Kin 21:13, 19 [B]2 Kin 9:21, 25 9:27 [a]Lit *smite* [A]2 Chr 22:7, 9 [B]Josh 17:11; Judg 1:27 9:28 [A]2 Kin 23:30 9:29 [A]2 Kin 8:25 9:30 [A]Jer 4:30; Ezek 23:40 9:31 [a]Lit *peace* [b]Lit *his* [A]1 Kin 16:9-20; 2 Kin 9:18-22 9:34 [A]1 Kin 21:25 [B]1 Kin 16:31 9:36 [a]Lit *portion* [A]1 Kin 21:23 9:37 [a]Lit *portion* [A]Jer 8:1-3 10:1 [A]1 Kin 16:24-29 10:2 [a]Lit *and with you the* [A]2 Kin 5:6 10:3 [a]Lit *most upright* 10:4 [A]2 Kin 9:24, 27 10:5 [A]Josh 9:8, 11; 1 Kin 20:4, 32; 2 Kin 18:14

together in one chariot as part of the chariot team or were in different chariots behind Ahab when Elijah gave his prediction to Ahab recorded in 1Ki 21:17–24. **the LORD laid this oracle against him.** The term "oracle" referred to a prophetic oracle, the prophetic utterance of Elijah recorded in 1Ki 21:19, 20–24. Jehu viewed himself as God's avenging agent fulfilling Elijah's prediction.

9:26 Naboth ... sons. Although their deaths are not expressly mentioned in the record concerning Naboth, they are plainly implied in the confiscation of his property (see 1Ki 21:16).

9:27 Ahaziah the king of Judah ... died. Jehu and his men pursued Ahaziah and wounded him at the ascent of Gur by Ibleam. According to 2Ch 22:9, Ahaziah reached Samaria, where he hid for a while. Ahaziah then fled N to Megiddo, about 12 mi. N of Samaria, where he died.

9:29 eleventh year. Ca. 841 B.C. Cf. 8:25, "twelfth year." In 8:25, the non-accession-year system of dating was used, so that Joram's accession year was counted as the first year of his reign (*see note on 12:6*). Here, the accession-year dating system was used, where Joram's accession year and his second year were counted as the first year of his reign.

9:30 painted her eyes. The painting of the eyelids with a black powder mixed with oil and applied with a brush darkened them to give an enlarged effect. Jezebel's appearance at the window gave the air of a royal audience to awe Jehu.

9:31 Zimri. In referring to Jehu by that name, Jezebel sarcastically alluded to the previous purge of Zimri (1Ki 16:9–15). Since Zimri died 7 days after beginning to reign, Jezebel was implying that the same fate awaited Jehu.

9:32 officials. Some of Jezebel's own officials threw her out of a second-story window, after which Jehu drove his horses and chariots over her body.

9:34 a king's daughter. Jehu recognized Jezebel's royalty, while denying that she deserved to be the queen of Israel.

9:36 This is the word of the LORD. Where and how Jezebel died fulfilled Elijah's prophetic oracle (1Ki 21:23).

10:1 seventy sons. These were the male descendants of Ahab, both sons and grandsons. Ahab had a number of wives (1Ki 20:5) and therefore many descendants. Since these living relatives could avenge a dead kinsman by killing the person responsible for his death (cf. Nu 35:12), Jehu's life was in jeopardy while Ahab's male descendants survived. **Samaria.** Ahab's surviving family members were living in the capital city of the northern kingdom, located about 25 mi. S of Jezreel. **rulers ... elders ... guardians.** Jehu sent the same message (vv. 2, 3) in a number of letters to: 1) the royal officials, who had probably fled from Jezreel to Samaria; 2) the leaders of the tribes of Israel; and 3) those appointed as the custodians and educators of the royal children.

10:3 fight for your master's house. Realizing potential conflict existed between himself and Ahab's family, Jehu was demanding that Ahab's appointed officials either fight to continue the royal line of Ahab or select a new king from Ahab's descendants who would fight Jehu in battle to decide which family would rule Israel (cf. 1Sa 17:8, 9; 2Sa 2:9).

10:5 one who *was* over the household ... city. These two officials were the palace administrator and the city governor, probably the commander of the city's fighting force. **We are your servants.** These officials and leaders transferred their allegiance from the house of Omri to Jehu.

10:6 the heads of the men. As a tangible sign of their surrender, Jehu required the officials to decapitate all of Ahab's male descendants and bring their heads to Jehu at Jezreel by the next day.

Now the king's sons, seventy persons, *were* with
the great men of the city, *who* were rearing them.
7 When the letter came to them, they took the king's
sons and [A]slaughtered *them,* seventy persons, and
put their heads in baskets, and sent *them* to him
at Jezreel. 8 When the messenger came and told
him, saying, "They have brought the heads of the
king's sons," he said, "Put them in two heaps at
the entrance of the gate until morning." 9 Now
in the morning he went out and stood and said to
all the people, "You are [a]innocent; behold, [A]I conspired against my master and killed him, but [B]who
[b]killed all these? 10 Know then that [A]there shall fall
to the earth nothing of the word of the LORD, which
the LORD spoke concerning the house of Ahab,
for the LORD has done [B]what He spoke [a]through His
servant Elijah." 11 So Jehu [a]killed all who remained
of the house of Ahab in [A]Jezreel, and all his great
men and his acquaintances and his priests, until
he left him without a survivor.
12 Then he arose and departed and went to Samaria. On the way while he was at [a]Beth-eked of the
shepherds, 13 [A]Jehu [a]met the [b]relatives of Ahaziah
king of Judah and said, "Who are you?" And they
[c]answered, "We are the [b]relatives of Ahaziah; and
we have come down [d]to greet the sons of the king
and the sons of the queen mother." 14 He said, "Take
them alive." So they took them alive and killed them
at the pit of Beth-eked, forty-two men; and he left
none of them.
15 Now when he had departed from there, he
[a]met [A]Jehonadab the son of [B]Rechab *coming* to
meet him; and he [b]greeted him and said to him, "Is
your heart right, as my heart is with your heart?"
And Jehonadab [c]answered, "It is." *Jehu said,* "If
it is, [C]give *me* your hand." And he gave him his
hand, and he took him up to him into the chariot.
16 He said, "Come with me and [A]see my zeal for the
LORD." So [a]he made him ride in his chariot. 17 When
he came to Samaria, [A]he [a]killed all who remained
to Ahab in Samaria, until he had destroyed him,
[B]according to the word of the LORD which He spoke
to Elijah.

JEHU DESTROYS BAAL WORSHIPERS

18 Then Jehu gathered all the people and said to
them, "[A]Ahab served Baal a little; Jehu will serve
him much. 19 Now, [A]summon all the prophets of
Baal, all his worshipers and all his priests; let no
one be missing, for I have a great sacrifice for Baal;
whoever is missing shall not live." But Jehu did it in
[a]cunning, so that he might destroy the worshipers
of Baal. 20 And Jehu said, "[A]Sanctify a solemn assembly for Baal." And [B]they proclaimed *it.* 21 Then Jehu
sent [a]throughout Israel and all the worshipers of
Baal came, so that there was not a man left who did
not come. And when they went into [A]the house of
Baal, the house of Baal was filled from one end to
the other. 22 He said to the one who *was* [a]in charge
of the wardrobe, "Bring out garments for all the
worshipers of Baal." So he brought out garments
for them. 23 Jehu went into the house of Baal with
Jehonadab the son of Rechab; and he said to the
worshipers of Baal, "Search and see that there is
here with you none of the servants of the LORD, but
only the worshipers of Baal." 24 Then they went in
to offer sacrifices and burnt offerings.
Now Jehu had stationed for himself eighty men
outside, and he had said, "[A]The one who permits
any of the men whom I bring into your hands to
escape [a]shall give up his life in exchange."
25 Then it came about, as soon as he had finished
offering the burnt offering, that Jehu said to the
[a,A]guard and to the royal officers, "[B]Go in, [b]kill them;
let none come out." And they [c]killed them with the
edge of the sword; and the [a]guard and the royal
officers threw *them* out, and went to the [d]inner
room of the house of Baal. 26 They brought out the
sacred [A]pillars of the house of Baal and burned
them. 27 They also broke down the *sacred* pillar of
Baal and broke down the house of Baal, and [A]made
it a latrine to this day.

10:7 [A]Judg 9:5; 2 Kin 11:1 10:9 [a]Lit *just* [b]Lit *smote* [A]2 Kin 9:14-24 [B]2 Kin 10:6 10:10 [a]Lit *by the hand of* [A]2 Kin 9:7-10 [B]1 Kin 21:19-29 10:11 [a]Lit *smote* [A]Hos 1:4 10:12 [a]I.e. house of binding 10:13 [a]Lit *found* [b]Lit *brothers* [c]Lit *said* [A]2 Kin 8:24, 29; 2 Chr 21:17; 22:8 10:13 [d]Lit *about the welfare of* 10:15 [a]Lit *found* [b]Lit *blessed* [c]Lit *said* [A]Jer 35:6-19 [B]1 Chr 2:55 [C]Ezra 10:19; Ezek 17:18 10:16 [a]Lit *they* [A]1 Kin 19:10 10:17 [a]Lit *smote* [A]2 Kin 9:8 [B]2 Kin 10:10 10:18 [A]1 Kin 16:31, 32 10:19 [a]Lit *insidiousness* [A]1 Kin 18:19; 22:6 10:20 [A]Joel 1:14 [B]Ex 32:4-6 10:21 [a]Lit *in all* [A]1 Kin 16:32; 2 Kin 11:18 10:22 [a]Lit *over the* 10:24 [a]Lit *his soul for his soul* [A]1 Kin 20:30-42 10:25 [a]Lit *runners* [b]Lit *smite* [c]Lit *smote* [d]Lit *city* [A]1 Sam 22:17 [B]1 Kin 18:40 10:26 [A]1 Kin 14:23; 2 Kin 3:2 10:27 [A]Ezra 6:11; Dan 2:5; 3:29

10:7 heads in baskets. Out of fear, the officials obeyed Jehu by decapitating Ahab's male descendants. However, they did not personally go to Jehu in Jezreel, probably fearing that a similar fate would await them.

10:8 two heaps. The practice of piling the heads of conquered subjects at the city gate was common in the ancient Near East, especially by the Assyrians. The practice was designed to dissuade rebellion.

10:9 I conspired ... killed. Jehu is referring to his murder of Joram (9:14–24).

10:10 word of the LORD. God had prophesied through Elijah the destruction of Ahab's house (1Ki 21:17–24).

10:11 Jehu killed all. Jehu went beyond God's mandate and executed all of Ahab's officials, a deed for which God later judged Jehu's house (cf. Hos 1:4).

10:13 relatives of Ahaziah. Since the brothers of Ahaziah, the slain king of Judah (9:27–29), had been previously killed by the Philistines (2Ch 21:17), these must have been relatives of Ahaziah in a broader sense, like nephews and cousins.

10:14 This slaughter by Jehu was because these people might have stimulated and strengthened those who were still loyal to the family of Ahab.

10:15 Jehonadab the son of Rechab. This man was a faithful follower of the Lord and a strict observer of the Mosaic law, leading a life of austerity and abstinence. According to Jer 35:1–16, the Rechabites did not plant fields or drink wine. They shook hands, indicating a pledge of support for Jehu from this influential man.

10:18, 19 Ahab served Baal a little; Jehu will serve him much. Though it was in fact a ruse (v. 19), Jehu promised to outdo Ahab's devotion to Baal. The people of Samaria might have thought that Jehu was seeking a military, not a religious, reformation. If so, Jehu was seeking Baal's blessing on his reign as king (v. 20).

10:21 house of Baal. The idolatrous worship center that Ahab had built in Samaria (1Ki 16:32). All the worshipers could fit into that one edifice because the number of Baal devotees had been reduced by the influence of Elijah and Elisha and by the neglect and discontinuance of Baal worship under Joram.

10:26 *sacred* pillars. These were wooden idols distinct from the main image "pillar" of Baal (v. 27).

10:27 a latrine. Lit. "place of dung." This desecration of the site discouraged any rebuilding of the temple of Baal.

28 Thus Jehu eradicated Baal out of Israel. 29 However, [A]*as for* the sins of Jeroboam the son of Nebat,
which he made Israel sin, from these Jehu did not
depart, *even* the [B]golden calves that *were* at Bethel
and that *were* at Dan. 30 The LORD said to Jehu,
"Because you have done well in executing what
is right in My eyes, *and* have done to the house of
Ahab according to all that *was* in My heart, [A]your
sons of the fourth generation shall sit on the throne
of Israel." 31 But Jehu [a,A]was not careful to walk in
the law of the LORD, the God of Israel, with all his
heart; [B]he did not depart from the sins of Jeroboam,
which he made Israel sin.
32 In those days the [A]LORD began to cut off *portions* [a]from Israel; and [B]Hazael [b]defeated them
throughout the territory of Israel: 33 from the Jordan eastward, all the land of Gilead, the Gadites and
the Reubenites and the Manassites, from [A]Aroer,
which is by the valley of the Arnon, even [B]Gilead
and Bashan.

JEHOAHAZ SUCCEEDS JEHU

34 Now the rest of the acts of Jehu and all that he
did and all his might, are they not written in the
Book of the Chronicles of the Kings of Israel? 35 And
Jehu slept with his fathers, and they buried him in
Samaria. And Jehoahaz his son became king in his
place. 36 Now the [a]time which Jehu reigned over
Israel in Samaria *was* twenty-eight years.

ATHALIAH QUEEN OF JUDAH

11 [A]When Athaliah the mother of Ahaziah saw that
her son was dead, she rose and destroyed all
the royal [a]offspring. 2 But Jehosheba, the daughter
of King Joram, sister of Ahaziah, [A]took Joash the son
of Ahaziah and stole him from among the king's
sons who were being put to death, and placed him
and his nurse in the bedroom. So they hid him from
Athaliah, and he was not put to death. 3 So he was
hidden with her in the house of the LORD six years,
while Athaliah was reigning over the land.
4 [A]Now in the seventh year Jehoiada sent and
brought the captains of hundreds of [B]the Carites
and of the [a]guard, and brought them to him in the
house of the LORD. Then he made a covenant with
them and put them under oath in the house of the
LORD, and showed them the king's son. 5 He commanded them, saying, "This is the thing that you
shall do: [A]one third of you, who come in on the
sabbath and keep watch over the king's house 6 (one
third also *shall be* at the gate Sur, and one third at
the gate behind the [a]guards), [b]shall keep watch over
the house for defense. 7 Two parts of you, *even* all
who go out on the sabbath, shall also keep watch
over the house of the LORD for the king. 8 Then you
shall surround the king, each with his weapons
in his hand; and whoever comes within the ranks
shall be put to death. And [A]be with the king when
he goes out and when he comes in."
9 So the captains of hundreds [A]did according to
all that Jehoiada the priest commanded. And each
one of them took his men who were to come in on
the sabbath, with those who were to go out on the
sabbath, and came to Jehoiada the priest. 10 [A]The
priest gave to the captains of hundreds the spears
and shields that *had been* King David's, which *were*

10:29 [A]1 Kin 12:28-30; 13:33, 34 [B]1 Kin 12:29 10:30 [A]2 Kin 15:12 10:31 [a]Lit *did not watch* [A]Prov 4:23 [B]2 Kin 10:29 10:32 [a]Lit *in* [b]Lit *smote* [A]2 Kin 13:25; 14:25 [B]1 Kin 19:17; 2 Kin 8:12; 13:22 10:33 [A]Deut 2:36 [B]Amos 1:3-5 10:36 [a]Lit *days* 11:1 [a]Lit *seed* [A]2 Chr 22:10-12 11:2 [A]2 Kin 11:21; 12:1 11:4 [a]Lit *runners* [A]2 Chr 23:1-21 [B]2 Sam 20:23; 2 Kin 11:19 11:5 [A]1 Chr 9:25 11:6 [a]Lit *runners* [b]Lit *and shall* 11:8 [A]Num 27:16, 17 11:9 [A]2 Chr 23:8 11:10 [A]2 Sam 8:7; 1 Chr 18:7

10:28 eradicated Baal out of Israel. Jehu rid the northern kingdom of royally sanctioned Baal worship. It was done, however, not from spiritual and godly motives, but because Jehu believed that Baalism was inextricably bound to the dynasty and influence of Ahab. By its extermination, he thought he would kill all the last vestiges of Ahab loyalists and incur the support of those in the land who worshiped the true God. Jehonadab didn't know of that motive, so he concurred with what Jehu did.

10:29 the sins of Jeroboam. However, Jehu did continue to officially sanction other idolatry introduced into the northern kingdom by Jeroboam I (cf. 1Ki 12:28–33).

10:33 from the Jordan eastward. Because Jehu failed to keep the Lord's law wholeheartedly (v. 31), the Lord punished him by giving Israel's land E of the Jordan River to Syria. This lost region was the homeland of the tribes of Gad, Reuben, and half of Manasseh (Nu 32:1–42).

10:36 twenty-eight years. 841–814 B.C.

11:1 Athaliah. A granddaughter of Omri (8:26) and daughter of Ahab and Jezebel. She was zealous to rule after the death of her son, Ahaziah (9:27) and was dedicated to seeing the worship of Baal officially sanctioned in Judah (*see note on 8:18*). She reigned for 6 years (v. 3) ca. 841–835 B.C. *See note on 2Ch 22:10–23:21.* **destroyed all the royal offspring.** The previous deaths of Jehoram's brothers (2Ch 21:4) and Ahaziah's brothers and relatives (10:12–14; 2Ch 21:17) left only her grandchildren for Athaliah to put to death to destroy the Davidic line. Though the Lord had promised that the house of David would rule over Israel and Judah forever (2Sa 7:16), Athaliah's purge brought the house of David to the brink of extinction.

11:2 Jehosheba. She was probably the daughter of Jehoram by a wife other than Athaliah, and so a half-sister of Ahaziah, who was married to the High Priest, Jehoiad (2Ch 22:11). **Joash.** The grandson of Athaliah who escaped her purge. **bedroom.** Lit. "the room of the beds." It was either the palace storeroom where servants kept the bedding or a room in the living quarters of the temple priests.

11:3 in the house of the LORD. The temple in Jerusalem. **six years.** 841–835 B.C.

11:4 seventh year. The beginning of Athaliah's 7th year of reign, 835 B.C. **Jehoiada.** The High Priest during Athaliah's reign (*see note on 2Ch 24:15, 16*). He was the husband of Jehosheba (v. 2; 2Ch 22:11). **captains of hundreds.** These were the commanders of each 100 soldier unit; 2Ch 23:1, 2 names 5 of these commanders. The bodyguards were "Carites" associated with the Pelethites (2Sa 20:23), who were mercenary soldiers serving as royal bodyguards. The escorts, lit. "runners," were probably another unit of royal bodyguards who provided palace security (see 1Ki 14:27). Jehoiada received an agreement of support from the royal guards, sealed with an oath of allegiance, and then presented Joash to them. The military leaders supported the plan to dispose of Athaliah and make Joash king.

11:5–8 Jehoiada outlined his plan to crown Joash as the king. On a selected Sabbath, the royal guards coming on duty, including priests and Levites (2Ch 23:4), would guard the palace as usual. They would especially make sure that no word concerning the coup in the temple courtyard reached Athaliah and those loyal to her. The companies going off duty would not return to their quarters as usual, but would instead report to the temple to form a tight security ring around the young potential king. The successful accomplishment of Jehoiada's plan is recorded in vv. 9–12.

11:6 the gate Sur. The exact location of this gate is unknown. Verse 19 implies that this gate connected the temple with the palace.

11:10 spears and shields. These were probably part of the plunder David captured from King Hadadezer of Zobah (2Sa 8:3–12). Dedicated to the Lord by David (2Sa 8:7, 11), these articles were stored in the temple. Since the soldiers were already armed, these additional ancient weapons symbolically reassured the soldiers that the temple authorities approved of their actions.

in the house of the LORD. 11The [a]guards stood each
with his weapons in his hand, from the right [b]side
of the house to the left [b]side of the house, by the
altar and by the house, around the king. 12Then he
brought the king's son out and [A]put the crown on
him and *gave him* [B]the testimony; and they made
him king and anointed him, and they clapped their
hands and said, "[C]*Long* live the king!"
13[A]When Athaliah heard the noise of the guard
and of the people, she came to the people in the
house of the LORD. 14She looked and behold, the king
was standing [A]by the pillar, according to the custom, with the captains and the [a]trumpeters beside
the king; and [B]all the people of the land rejoiced
and blew trumpets. Then Athaliah [C]tore her clothes
and cried, "[D]Treason! Treason!" 15And Jehoiada the
priest commanded the captains of hundreds who
were appointed over the army and said to them,
"Bring her out [a]between the ranks, and whoever
follows her put to death with the sword." For the
priest said, "Let her not be put to death in the house
of the LORD." 16So they [a]seized her, and when she
arrived at the horses' entrance of the king's house,
she was [A]put to death there.
17Then [A]Jehoiada made a covenant between
the LORD and the king and the people, that they
would be the LORD'S people, also [B]between the
king and the people. 18All the people of the land
went to [A]the house of Baal, and tore it down; [B]his
altars and his images they broke in pieces thoroughly, and [C]killed Mattan the priest of Baal before
the altars. And the priest appointed [a]officers over
the house of the LORD. 19He took the captains of
hundreds and the [A]Carites and the [a]guards and all
the people of the land; and they brought the king
down from the house of the LORD, and came by
the way of [B]the gate of the [a]guards to the king's
house. And he sat on the throne of the kings. 20So
[A]all the people of the land rejoiced and the city was
quiet. For they had put Athaliah to death with the
sword at the king's house.
21[a,A]Jehoash was seven years old when he became king.

JOASH (JEHOASH) REIGNS OVER JUDAH

12 In the seventh year of Jehu, [A]Jehoash became
king, and he reigned forty years in Jerusalem;
and his mother's name was Zibiah of Beersheba.
2Jehoash did right in the sight of the LORD all his
days in which Jehoiada the priest instructed him.
3Only [A]the high places were not taken away; the
people still sacrificed and burned incense on the
high places.

THE TEMPLE TO BE REPAIRED

4Then Jehoash said to the priests, "All the
money of the sacred things [A]which is brought
into the house of the LORD, in current money, *both*
[B]the money of each man's assessment *and* all the
money [a]which any man's heart prompts him to
bring into the house of the LORD, 5let the priests
take it for themselves, each from his acquaintance;
and they shall repair the [a]damages of the house
wherever any damage may be found."
6But it came about that in the twenty-third year
of King Jehoash [A]the priests had not repaired the
damages of the house. 7Then King Jehoash called

11:11 [a]Lit *runners* [b]Lit *shoulder* 11:12 [A]2 Sam 1:10 [B]Ex 25:16; 31:18 [C]1 Sam 10:24 11:13 [A]2 Chr 23:12 11:14 [a]Lit *trumpets* [A]2 Kin 23:3; 2 Chr 34:31 [B]1 Kin 1:39, 40 [C]Gen 37:29; 44:13 [D]2 Kin 9:23 11:15 [a]Lit *from within* 11:16 [a]Lit *placed hands to her* [A]Gen 9:6; Lev 24:17 11:17 [A]Josh 24:25; 2 Chr 15:12-14; 34:31 [B]1 Sam 10:25; 2 Sam 5:3 11:18 [a]Lit *offices* [A]2 Kin 10:26, 27 [B]Deut 12:2, 3 [C]1 Kin 18:40 11:19 [a]Lit *runners* [A]2 Kin 11:4 [B]2 Kin 11:6 11:20 [A]Prov 11:10 11:21 [a]Ch 12:1 in Heb [A]2 Chr 24:1-14 12:1 [A]2 Chr 24:1 12:3 [A]2 Kin 14:4; 15:35 12:4 [a]Lit *which it comes into…to bring* [A]2 Kin 22:4 [B]Ex 30:13-16; 35:5, 22, 29; 1 Chr 29:3-9 12:5 [a]Lit *breaches*, and so through v 12 12:6 [A]2 Chr 24:5

11:12 the testimony. This was a copy of the whole law (Ps 119:88). According to Dt 17:18–20, a copy of the law was to be kept with the king always so that it became his guide for life. **anointed.** A priest or prophet customarily anointed kings, as here (1Sa 10:1; 16:13; 1Ki 1:39; 2Ki 9:6).

11:14 pillar. Either one of the two pillars, Jachin or Boaz, on the temple's front porch (1Ki 7:21), or a raised platform in the court of the temple (cf. 2Ch 6:13). **people of the land.** Probably Jehoiada chose to stage his coup on the Sabbath during one of the major religious festivals, when those from Judah who were loyal to the Lord would be in Jerusalem.

11:16 king's house, she was put to death. Execution was not appropriate in the temple area since it was a place of worship (cf. 2Ch 24:20–22). Thus, the soldiers seized Athaliah and put her to death at one of the entrances to the palace grounds.

11:17 a covenant. The renewal of the agreement between the people and the Lord and between the house of David and the people was appropriate because of the disruption under Athaliah. A similar ceremony was held later, during the reign of Josiah (23:1–3). *See notes on Ex 24:4–8.*

11:18 the house of Baal. A temple that had been built in Jerusalem and used by Athaliah to promote the worship of Baal in Judah. As Jezebel had promoted Baalism in Israel, her daughter Athaliah had sought its sanction in Judah. During Athaliah's reign as queen, Baalism gained its strongest foothold in Judah. This purge of Baalism in Judah paralleled the earlier purge of Baalism led by Jehu in the northern kingdom (10:18–29).

11:21 Jehoash. Jehoash and Joash are variants of the same name, meaning "The Lord gave." *See notes on 2Ch 24:1–27.*

12:1 seventh year. 835 B.C. Jehu of Israel began his reign in 841 B.C. (*see notes on 9:29; 10:36*). **forty years.** 835–796 B.C.

12:2 all his days…Jehoiada…instructed him. Joash did what pleased the Lord while Jehoida served as his parental guardian and tutor. After Jehoida died, Joash turned away from the Lord (*see note on 2Ch 24:17, 18a*).

12:3 the high places. *See note on 1Ki 3:2.* As with most kings of Judah, Joash failed to remove these places of worship where, contrary to the Mosaic law, the people sacrificed and burned incense to the Lord (cf. Dt 12:2–7, 13, 14).

12:4–16 See 2Ch 24:5–14.

12:4 the sacred things. Lit. "holy gifts." These offerings were given to the priests and used to support the temple. These 3 main offerings were the half a shekel assessed from every male 20 years old and above whenever a census was taken (Ex 30:11–16), the payments of personal vows (Lv 27:1–8), and voluntary offerings (Lv 22:18–23; Dt 16:10).

12:5 his acquaintance. This person would be a friend of the priest who either gave offerings or collected the offerings for the priest. However, some interpret the Heb. term to mean "treasurer." This understanding views the individual as a member of the temple personnel who assisted the priests with the valuation of sacrifices and offerings brought to the temple. **repair the damages of the house.** During the reign of Athaliah, the temple had suffered major damages and temple articles had been taken for use in the temple of Baal (2Ch 24:7). Joash ordered the priests to channel the temple offerings to fund the needed repairs. This was to be in addition to the normal temple expenses.

12:6 twenty-third year. Ca. 813 B.C. Judah seems to have used the non-accession-year system during the reigns of Athaliah and Joash (*see note on 13:1*), which did not count the first year of the reign but began with the second. This is how we count ages today, starting with the beginning of the second year as one. Joash was 29 years of age.

12:7, 8 The plan of Joash did not work. Either the revenue from these sources was

for Jehoiada the priest, and for the *other* priests and
said to them, "Why do you not repair the damages of
the house? Now therefore take no *more* money from
your acquaintances, but pay it for the damages of
the house." 8 So the priests agreed that they would
take no *more* money from the people, nor repair
the damages of the house.
9 But [A]Jehoiada the priest took a chest and bored
a hole in its lid and put it beside the altar, on the
right side as one comes into the house of the
LORD; and the priests who guarded the threshold
put in it all the money which was brought into the
house of the LORD. 10 When they saw that there
was much money in the chest, [A]the king's scribe
and the high priest came up and tied *it* in bags
and counted the money which was found in the
house of the LORD. 11 They gave the money which
was weighed out into the hands of those who did
the work, who had the oversight of the house of
the LORD; and they [a]paid it out to the carpenters
and the builders who worked on the house of the
LORD; 12 and [A]to the masons and the stonecutters,
and for buying timber and hewn stone to repair
the damages to the house of the LORD, and for all
that was [a]laid out for the house to repair it. 13 But
[A]there were not made for the house of the LORD
[B]silver cups, snuffers, bowls, trumpets, any vessels
of gold, or vessels of silver from the money which
was brought into the house of the LORD; 14 for they
gave that to those who did the work, and with
it they repaired the house of the LORD. 15 Moreover, [A]they did not require an accounting from
the men into whose hand they gave the money
to pay to those who did the work, for they dealt
faithfully. 16 The [A]money from the guilt offerings
and [B]the money from the sin offerings was not
brought into the house of the LORD; [C]it was for
the priests.
17 Then [A]Hazael king of Aram went up and fought
against Gath and captured it, and [B]Hazael set his
face to go up to Jerusalem. 18 [A]Jehoash king of Judah took all the sacred things that Jehoshaphat and
Jehoram and Ahaziah, his fathers, kings of Judah,
had dedicated, and [B]his own sacred things and all
the gold that was found among the treasuries of
the house of the LORD and of the king's house, and
sent *them* to Hazael king of Aram. Then he went
away from Jerusalem.

JOASH (JEHOASH) SUCCEEDED BY AMAZIAH IN JUDAH

19 Now the rest of the acts of Joash and all that he
did, are they not written in the Book of the Chronicles of the Kings of Judah? 20 [A]His servants arose
and made a conspiracy and [B]struck down Joash at
[C]the house of Millo *as he was* going down to Silla.
21 For Jozacar the son of Shimeath and Jehozabad
the son of [A]Shomer, his servants, struck *him* and
he died; and they buried him with his fathers in
the city of David, and [B]Amaziah his son became
king in his place.

KINGS OF ISRAEL: JEHOAHAZ AND JEHOASH

13 In the twenty-third year of Joash the son of
Ahaziah, king of Judah, Jehoahaz the son of
Jehu became king over Israel at Samaria, *and he
reigned* seventeen years. 2 He did evil in the sight
of the LORD, and followed the sins of Jeroboam
the son of Nebat, [A]with which he made Israel sin;

12:9 [A]Mark 12:41; Luke 21:1 12:10 [A]2 Sam 8:17; 2 Kin 19:2; 22:3, 4, 12 12:11 [a]Lit *brought* 12:12 [a]Lit *went out* [A]2 Kin 22:5, 6 12:13 [A]2 Chr 24:14 [B]1 Kin 7:48, 50 12:15 [A]2 Kin 22:7; 1 Cor 4:2; 2 Cor 8:20 12:16 [A]Lev 5:15-18 [B]Lev 4:24, 29 [C]Lev 7:7; Num 18:19 12:17 [A]1 Kin 19:17; 2 Kin 8:12; 10:32, 33 [B]2 Chr 24:23, 24 12:18 [A]1 Kin 14:26; 15:18; 2 Kin 16:8; 18:15, 16 [B]2 Kin 12:4 12:20 [A]2 Chr 24:25-27 [B]2 Kin 14:5 [C]Judg 9:6; 2 Sam 5:9; 1 Kin 11:27 12:21 [A]2 Chr 24:26 [B]2 Kin 14:1 13:2 [A]1 Kin 12:26-33

inadequate to support the priests and Levites and also to pay for the temple repairs, or the priests for some unknown reason would not fund the temple repairs. Therefore, the priests no longer received the offerings from the people, nor did they fund the temple repairs from the income they had already received.

12:9–16 Joash instituted a new plan. First, a single collection box was to receive all incoming offerings. When the chest was full, only the royal secretary and High Priest would be authorized to empty it. Second, from the funds thus generated, men were hired to supervise and pay the carpenters, builders, masons, and stonecutters who worked on the temple repairs. The men involved were so trustworthy that no accounting was taken of them (v. 15).

12:9 priests who guarded the threshold. These were priests who normally screened the people to keep unclean worshipers from entering the temple (25:18; Jer 52:24). These priests took the offerings from the worshipers, who then personally watched the priests drop them into the chest.

12:16 money from the guilt offerings and … sin offerings. The income from these offerings was distinct from the income mentioned in v. 4 and so was not used in the repair of the temple, but remained the property of the priests (see Lv 4:1–6:7). The temple repairs did not deprive the priests of their income (Lv 7:7).

12:17 Hazael. *See notes on 8:8–15.* **Gath.** One of the 5 major Philistine cities (1Sa 5:8), located about 25 mi. SW of Jerusalem. Gath had previously belonged to Judah (2Ch 11:8).

12:18 all the sacred things. When Joash's army was defeated by Hazael and his leading men killed (2Ch 24:23, 24), he averted further attacks against Jerusalem by sending tribute to the king of Syria. This tribute included gifts donated to the temple in Jerusalem by kings of Judah (cf. 1Ki 15:15, 18).

12:19 acts of Joash. A more complete account of the reign of Joash is found in 2Ch 22:10–24:27.

12:20 a conspiracy. Some of the officials of Joash conspired against him because he had killed the High Priest Zechariah, the son of the priest Jehoiada (2Ch 24:20–22). **house of Millo.** Probably a house built on a landfill N of David's city of Jerusalem and S of the temple mount. Cf. 2Ch 24:25. **Silla.** Possibly a ramp that descended from the landfill to the Kidron Valley.

12:21 Amaziah. See 14:1–22 for the reign of Amaziah.

13:1 twenty-third year. 814 B.C. Joash of Judah began his reign in 835 B.C. (*see note on 12:1*) and Jehu of Israel died in 814 B.C. (*see note on 10:36*). Thus the 23rd year of Joash of Judah was calculated according to the non-accession-year system (*see notes on 12:6; 13:10*). **seventeen years.** 814–798 B.C., i.e., part of 17 calendar years, with the actual reign counted as 16 years.

13:2 Jeroboam. For his sins, *see notes on 1Ki 12:25–32.* This description of Jeroboam as one who "made Israel sin" occurs in 13:6, 11; 1Ki 14:16; 15:30; 16:31; 2Ki 3:3; 10:29, 31; 14:24; 15:9, 18, 24, 28; 17:21, 22.

13:2–7 The record of the reign of Jehoahaz, the king of Israel, has literary and verbal similarities to the book of Judges: 1) Jehoahaz did evil in the sight of the Lord (v. 2; cf. Jdg 2:11–13; 3:7); 2) the anger of the Lord was aroused against Israel and He delivered them over to their enemies (v. 3; cf. Jdg 2:14, 15; 3:8); 3) Jehoahaz cried out to the Lord who saw their oppression (v. 4; cf. Jdg 2:18; 3:9); 4) the Lord raised up a deliverer for Israel who rescued them out of the hand of their enemies (v. 5; cf. Jdg 2:16, 18; 3:9); and 5) Israel continued in her evil ways with the result of further oppression (vv. 6, 7; cf. Jdg 2:19; 3:12–14).

he did not turn from them. 3 [A]So the anger of the
LORD was kindled against Israel, and He gave them
continually into the hand of [B]Hazael king of Aram,
and into the hand of [C]Ben-hadad the son of Hazael.
4 Then [A]Jehoahaz entreated the favor of the LORD,
and the LORD listened to him; for [B]He saw the oppression of Israel, how the king of Aram oppressed
them. 5 The LORD gave Israel a [a,A]deliverer, so that
they [b]escaped from under the hand of the Arameans; and the sons of Israel lived in their tents as
formerly. 6 Nevertheless they did not turn away
from the sins of the house of Jeroboam, [A]with which
he made Israel sin, but walked in [a]them; and [B]the
Asherah also remained standing in Samaria. 7 For
he left to Jehoahaz of the [a]army not more than fifty
horsemen and ten chariots and 10,000 footmen, for
the king of Aram had destroyed them and [A]made
them like the dust at threshing. 8 Now the rest of the
acts of Jehoahaz, and all that he did and his might,
are they not written in the Book of the Chronicles
of the Kings of Israel? 9 And Jehoahaz slept with his
fathers, and they buried him in Samaria; and Joash
his son became king in his place.
10 In the thirty-seventh year of Joash king of Judah, Jehoash the son of Jehoahaz became king over
Israel in Samaria, *and reigned* sixteen years. 11 He
did evil in the sight of the LORD; he did not turn
away from all the sins of Jeroboam the son of Nebat, with which he made Israel sin, but he walked
in [a]them. 12 [A]Now the rest of the acts of Joash and
all that he did and his might with which he fought
against Amaziah king of Judah, are they not written
in the Book of the Chronicles of the Kings of Israel?
13 So Joash slept with his fathers, and Jeroboam sat
on his throne; and Joash was buried in Samaria with
the kings of Israel.

DEATH OF ELISHA

14 When Elisha [a]became sick with the illness of
which he was to die, Joash the king of Israel came
down to him and wept over [b]him and said, "[A]My
father, my father, the chariots of Israel and its horsemen!" 15 Elisha said to him, "Take a bow and arrows."
So he [a]took a bow and arrows. 16 Then he said to the
king of Israel, "Put your hand on the bow." And he
put his hand *on it,* then Elisha laid his hands on the
king's hands. 17 He said, "Open the window toward
the east," and he opened *it.* Then Elisha said, "Shoot!"
And he shot. And he said, "The LORD'S arrow of
victory, even the arrow of victory over Aram; for
you will [a]defeat the Arameans at [A]Aphek until you
have [b]destroyed *them.*" 18 Then he said, "Take the
arrows," and he took them. And he said to the king
of Israel, "Strike the ground," and he struck *it* three
times and [a]stopped. 19 So [A]the man of God was angry
with him and said, "You should have struck five or
six times, then you would have struck Aram until
you would have [a]destroyed *it.* But now you shall
strike Aram [B]*only* three times."
20 Elisha died, and they buried him. Now [A]the
bands of the Moabites would invade the land in the
spring of the year. 21 As they were burying a man,
behold, they saw a marauding band; and they cast
the man into the grave of Elisha. And when the
man [a]touched the bones of Elisha he [A]revived and
stood up on his feet.

13:3 [A]Judg 2:14 [B]2 Kin 12:17 [C]2 Kin 13:24, 25 13:4 [A]Num 21:7-9 [B]Ex 3:7, 9; 2 Kin 14:26 13:5 [a]Or *savior* [b]Lit *went out* [A]2 Kin 13:25; 14:25, 27; Neh 9:27 13:6 [a]Lit *it* [A]2 Kin 13:2 [B]1 Kin 16:33 13:7 [a]Lit *people* [A]Amos 1:3 13:11 [a]Lit *it* 13:12 [A]2 Kin 13:14-19; 14:8-15 13:14 [a]Lit *was sick with his sickness* [b]Lit *his face* [A]2 Kin 2:12 13:15 [a]Lit *took to himself* 13:17 [a]Lit *smite* [b]Lit *made an end of* [A]1 Kin 20:26 13:18 [a]Lit *stood* 13:19 [a]Lit *made an end of* [A]2 Kin 5:20 [B]2 Kin 13:25 13:20 [A]2 Kin 3:7; 24:2 13:21 [a]Lit *went and touched* [A]Matt 27:52

13:3 Hazael. *See notes on 8:8–15.* **Ben-hadad.** Either Ben-hadad II or, more likely, III (*see note on 1Ki 15:18*). His reign as king of Syria began ca. 801 B.C. The length of his rule is unknown.

13:5 a deliverer. The deliverer was not specifically named. This deliverer was: 1) the Assyrian king Adad-Nirari III (ca. 810–783 B.C.), whose attack on the Syrians or Arameans, enabled the Israelites to break Syria's control over Israelite territory (see v. 25; 14:25); or 2) Elisha, who as the leader of Israel's military successes (see v. 14; cf. 6:13, 16–23) commissioned Joash to defeat the Syrians (vv. 15–19); or 3) Jeroboam II (ca. 793–753 B.C.), who was able to extend Israel's boundaries back into Syrian territory (14:25–27).

13:6 sins . . . of Jeroboam. *See note on v. 2.* **Asherah.** This idol representing Asherah, a Canaanite goddess and a consort of Baal, had been set up by Ahab (1Ki 16:33) and had escaped destruction by Jehu when he purged Baal worship from Samaria (10:27, 28). Along with the other idolatrous religion of Jeroboam II, there were still remnants of Baal worship in the northern kingdom.

13:7 the army. Syria was able to dominate Israel militarily because the Lord had left Jehoahaz only a small army with very few chariots. **dust at threshing.** The army of Israel was so inconsequential, particularly when compared to the armies of Syria and Assyria, that it was likened to the dust left over after grain had been winnowed at a threshing floor.

13:10 thirty-seventh year. Ca. 798 B.C. Joash of Judah began his reign in 835 B.C. (*see note on 12:1*). There is a change here to the accession-year system of dating for the reign of Joash of Judah (*see note on 13:1*). This explains how Jehoahaz of Israel could reign 16 years with only a 15-year advance on Joash of Judah's regnal years (cf. v. 1). **Jehoash.** This king of Israel had the same name as his contemporary, the king of Judah (*see note on 11:21*). **sixteen years.** 798–782 B.C.

13:12 fought against Amaziah. *See notes on 14:8–14.*

13:14 Elisha. The last previous reference to Elisha the prophet was in 9:1 when Jehu was anointed king of Israel. Since Jehu and Jehoahaz reigned from 841–798 B.C. (*see notes on 10:36; 13:1*), nothing was recorded for over 40 years of Elisha's life. Elisha began ministering with Elijah during the kingship of Ahab ca. 874–853 B.C. (1Ki 19:19–21) and so must have been over 70 years of age when these final events of his life took place. **My father.** Jehoash humbly voiced his great respect for Elisha and his dependence upon his counsel (*see note on 2:12*). **the chariots of Israel and its horsemen.** Jehoash acknowledged through this metaphor that the Lord, through Elisha, was the real strength and power of Israel against all her adversaries (*see note on 2:11*).

13:16 Elisha laid his hands on the king's hands. This symbolic act indicated that Jehoash would exert power against the Syrians that came from the Lord through His prophet.

13:17 window toward the east. This window opened toward the E to the Transjordan region controlled by Syria (10:32, 33). **The LORD's arrow of victory.** When Jehoash obeyed Elisha by shooting an arrow out the window, the prophet interpreted the meaning of the action. The shot symbolized the Lord's deliverance for Israel through the defeat of the Syrian army by Jehoash (cf. v. 5). **Aphek.** *See note on 1Ki 20:26.*

13:19 three times. Further, Elisha commanded Jehoash to shoot the remaining arrows into the ground (v. 18). Jehoash shot only 3 arrows into the ground instead of emptying the entire quiver. Because of his lack of faith, Jehoash would win only 3 victories over the Syrians instead of completely destroying them. The account of these victories is given in v. 25.

13:20 spring. The prophet, who was Israel's defense (v. 14), was dead, and it was the season for war campaigns to begin after the rains of winter.

13:21 he revived. A dead man returned to life after touching Elisha's bones. This miracle

22 Now [A]Hazael king of Aram had oppressed Israel all the days of Jehoahaz. 23 But the [A]LORD was
gracious to them and [B]had compassion on them
and turned to them because of [C]His covenant with
Abraham, Isaac, and Jacob, and would not destroy
them or cast them from His presence until now.
24 When Hazael king of Aram died, Ben-hadad
his son became king in his place. 25 Then [A]Jehoash
the son of Jehoahaz took again from the hand of
Ben-hadad the son of Hazael the cities which he had
taken in war from the hand of Jehoahaz his father.
[B]Three times Joash [a]defeated him and recovered
the cities of Israel.

AMAZIAH REIGNS OVER JUDAH

14 [A]In the second year of Joash son of Joahaz king
of Israel, [B]Amaziah the son of Joash king of
Judah became king. 2 He was twenty-five years old
when he became king, and he reigned twenty-nine
years in Jerusalem. And his mother's name was
Jehoaddin of Jerusalem. 3 He did right in the sight
of the LORD, yet not like David his father; he did
according to all that Joash his father had done.
4 Only [A]the high places were not taken away; [B]the
people still sacrificed and burned incense on the
high places. 5 Now it came about, as soon as the
kingdom was firmly in his hand, that he [a,A]killed
his servants who had slain the king his father. 6 But
the sons of the [a]slayers he did not put to death, according to what is written in the book of the Law
of Moses, as the LORD commanded, saying, "[A]The
fathers shall not be put to death for the sons, nor
the sons be put to death for the fathers; but [B]each
shall be put to death for his own sin."
7 He [a]killed *of* Edom in [A]the Valley of Salt 10,000
and took [B]Sela by war, and named it [C]Joktheel to
this day.
8 [A]Then Amaziah sent messengers to Jehoash, the
son of Jehoahaz son of Jehu, king of Israel, saying,
"[B]Come, let us face each other." 9 Jehoash king of
Israel sent to Amaziah king of Judah, saying, "[A]The
thorn bush which was in Lebanon sent to the cedar
which was in Lebanon, saying, 'Give your daughter
to my son in marriage.' But there passed by a wild
beast that was in Lebanon, and trampled the thorn
bush. 10 [A]You have indeed [a]defeated Edom, and [B]your
heart has [b]become proud. Enjoy your glory and stay
at home; for why should you provoke trouble so
that you, even you, would fall, and Judah with you?"
11 But Amaziah would not listen. So Jehoash king
of Israel went up; and he and Amaziah king of Judah
faced each other at [A]Beth-shemesh, which belongs
to Judah. 12 Judah was defeated [a]by Israel, and [A]they
fled each to his tent. 13 Then Jehoash king of Israel
captured Amaziah king of Judah, the son of Jehoash the son of Ahaziah, at Beth-shemesh, and came

13:22 [A]2 Kin 8:12, 13 13:23 [A]2 Kin 14:27 [B]1 Kin 8:28 [C]Gen 13:16, 17; 17:2-5 13:25 [a]Lit *smote* [A]2 Kin 10:32, 33; 14:25 [B]2 Kin 13:18, 19 14:1 [A]2 Chr 25:1 [B]2 Kin 13:10 14:4 [A]2 Kin 12:3 [B]2 Kin 16:4 14:5 [a]Lit *smote* [A]2 Kin 12:20 14:6 [a]Lit *smiters* [A]Deut 24:16 [B]Jer 31:30; Ezek 18:4, 20 14:7 [a]Lit *smote* [A]2 Sam 8:13; 1 Chr 18:12; 2 Chr 25:11 [B]Is 16:1 [C]Josh 15:38 14:8 [A]2 Chr 25:17-24 [B]2 Sam 2:14-17 14:9 [A]Judg 9:8-15 14:10 [a]Lit *smitten* [b]Lit *lifted you up* [A]2 Kin 14:7 [B]Deut 8:14; 2 Chr 26:16 14:11 [A]Josh 19:38 14:12 [a]Lit *before* [A]2 Sam 18:17

was a sign that God's power continued to work in relationship to Elisha even after his death. What God had promised to Jehoash through Elisha when he was alive would surely come to pass after the prophet's death (cf. vv. 19, 25) in the defeat of the enemy, the recovery of the cities that had been taken, and their restoration to the kingdom of Israel (vv. 22–25).

13:22 *See note on 8:12.*

13:23 His covenant with Abraham, Isaac, and Jacob. During the wicked reign of Jehoahaz (vv. 2–7), the Lord was very patient and did not bring the ultimate military defeat that would lead to exile for Israel. This was because of His agreement with the patriarchs to give their descendants the land (Ge 15:18–21; 26:2–5; 28:13–15). It was God's promise, not the Israelites' goodness, that motivated God to be merciful and compassionate toward Israel.

14:1–15:38 This section quickly surveys the kings and selected events of the northern and southern kingdoms from 796 to 735 B.C. In contrast to the previous 19 chapters (1Ki 17:1–2Ki 13:25), which narrated 90 years of history (885–796 B.C.) with a concentration on the ministries of Elijah and Elisha during the final 65 years of that period (860–796 B.C.), 62 years are covered in these two chapters. The previous section concluded with a shadow of hope: officially sanctioned Baal worship had been eradicated in both Israel (10:18–28) and Judah (11:17, 18); the temple of the Lord in Jerusalem had been repaired (12:9–15); and the Syrian threat to Israel had been overcome (13:25). However, this section emphasizes that the fundamental problems still remained: the false religion established by Jeroboam I continued in Israel even with the change of royal families (14:24–15:9, 18, 24, 28), and the high places were not removed in Judah even though there were only good kings there during those years (14:4; 15:4, 35).

14:1 second year. 796 B.C. **Amaziah.** *See notes on 2Ch 25:1–28.*

14:2 twenty-nine years. 796–767 B.C.

14:3 not like David. David set a high standard of unswerving devotion to the Lord for the kings of Judah who were his descendants to follow (cf. 1Ki 11:4, 6; 15:3). Amaziah did not follow the Lord completely, as David had, because he, like his father Joash, did not remove the high places (v. 4) where, in disregard for Mosaic law, the people worshiped the Lord (Dt 12:2–7, 13, 14). Further, according to 2Ch 25:14–16, Amaziah embraced the false gods of the Edomites.

14:5, 6 When firmly in control of the kingdom, Amaziah took revenge on Jozachar and Jehozabad, the officials who assassinated his father Joash (12:20, 21). However, he spared the lives of their sons, in obedience to the Mosaic law that children were not to die for their fathers' sins (Dt 24:16; cf. Eze 18:1–20).

14:7 For an elaboration of Amaziah's war with Edom, *see the notes on 2Ch 25:5–16.* Edom had revolted in Joram's reign (see 8:20), so the king wanted them subjugated again. **the Valley of Salt.** Probably a marshy plain at the S end of the Dead Sea (*see note on 2Sa 8:13*). **Sela ... Joktheel.** Sela (meaning "rock" in Heb.) is best identified as Petra (meaning "rock" in Gr.), a city carved out of sheer mountain walls located about 50 mi. S of the Dead Sea, though some prefer to place it in northern Edom near Bozra on the King's Highway (Jdg 1:36). Renaming a captured city, as Amaziah did with the name Joktheel, implied his control over it.

14:8 Jehoash ... of Israel. *See notes on 13:10–23.* **face each other.** Amaziah's challenge to Jehoash constituted a declaration of war. Amaziah, emboldened by his victory over Edom (v. 10), thought he could defeat the stronger army of Israel (cf. 13:25). He was probably also upset by the refusal of Jehoash to establish a marriage alliance with him (v. 9).

14:9 thorn bush ... cedar. In this parable (cf. Jdg 9:8–15), the thorn bush (Amaziah), an irritating and worthless plant, sought to become the equal of the majestic cedar (Jehoash), but a wild animal crushed the bush. Jehoash counseled Amaziah that he was overestimating his power and prominence and should not go to war with Israel lest he be crushed (v. 10).

14:11 Beth-shemesh. A town about 15 mi. W of Jerusalem, where the armies of Israel and Judah faced each other in battle.

14:13 Jehoash ... captured Amaziah. Winning the battle, Jehoash also captured Amaziah. Jehoash probably took Amaziah back to Samaria as a hostage (v. 14). The king of Judah was forced to stay in Samaria until the death of Jehoash in 782 B.C. (v. 17). **Gate of Ephraim ... Corner Gate.** The Corner Gate (cf. Jer 31:38; Zec 14:10) was at the NW corner of the wall around Jerusalem. The Ephraim Gate was in Jerusalem's northern wall facing

to Jerusalem and tore down the wall of Jerusalem from [A]the Gate of Ephraim to [B]the Corner Gate, 400 [a]cubits. 14 [A]He took all the gold and silver and all the utensils which were found in the house of the LORD, and in the treasuries of the king's house, the hostages also, and returned to Samaria.

JEROBOAM II SUCCEEDS JEHOASH IN ISRAEL

15 [A]Now the rest of the acts of Jehoash which he did, and his might and how he fought with Amaziah king of Judah, are they not written in the Book of the Chronicles of the Kings of Israel? 16 So Jehoash slept with his fathers and was buried in Samaria with the kings of Israel; and Jeroboam his son became king in his place.

AZARIAH (UZZIAH) SUCCEEDS AMAZIAH IN JUDAH

17 [A]Amaziah the son of Joash king of Judah lived fifteen years after the death of Jehoash son of Jehoahaz king of Israel. 18 Now the rest of the acts of Amaziah, are they not written in the Book of the Chronicles of the Kings of Judah? 19 They conspired against him in Jerusalem, and he fled to [A]Lachish; but they sent after him to Lachish and killed him there. 20 Then they brought him on horses and he was buried at Jerusalem with his fathers in the city of David. 21 All the people of Judah took [a]Azariah, who *was* sixteen years old, and made him king in the place of his father Amaziah. 22 [A]He built Elath and restored it to Judah after the king slept with his fathers.

23 In the fifteenth year of Amaziah the son of Joash king of Judah, Jeroboam the son of Joash king of Israel became king in Samaria, *and reigned* forty-one years. 24 He did evil in the sight of the LORD; he did not depart from all the sins of Jeroboam the son of Nebat, which he made Israel sin. 25 [A]He restored the border of Israel from [B]the entrance of Hamath as far as [C]the Sea of the Arabah, according to the word of the LORD, the God of Israel, which He spoke [a]through His servant [D]Jonah the son of Amittai, the prophet, who was of [E]Gath-hepher. 26 For the [A]LORD saw the affliction of Israel, *which was* very bitter; for [B]there was neither bond nor free, nor was there any helper for Israel. 27 The [A]LORD did not say that He would blot out the name of Israel from under heaven, but He saved them by the hand of Jeroboam the son of Joash.

ZECHARIAH REIGNS OVER ISRAEL

28 Now the rest of the acts of Jeroboam and all that he did and his might, how he fought and how he recovered for Israel, [A]Damascus and [B]Hamath, *which had belonged* to Judah, are they not written in the Book of the Chronicles of the Kings of Israel? 29 And Jeroboam slept with his fathers, even with the kings of Israel, and Zechariah his son became king in his place.

14:13 [a]I.e. One cubit equals approx 18 in. [A]Neh 8:16; 12:39 [B]2 Chr 25:23 14:14 [A]1 Kin 14:26; 2 Kin 12:18 14:15 [A]2 Kin 13:12, 13 14:17 [A]2 Chr 25:25-28 14:19 [A]Josh 10:31; 2 Kin 18:14, 17 14:21 [a]In 2 Chr 26:1, *Uzziah* 14:22 [A]1 Kin 9:26; 2 Kin 16:6; 2 Chr 8:17 14:25 [a]Lit *by* [A]2 Kin 10:32; 13:25 [B]1 Kin 8:65 [C]Deut 3:17 [D]Jon 1:1; Matt 12:39, 40 [E]Josh 19:13 14:26 [A]2 Kin 13:4 [B]Deut 32:36 14:27 [A]2 Kin 13:23 14:28 [A]1 Kin 11:24 [B]2 Chr 8:3

Ephraim, 600 ft. E of the Corner Gate. This northwestern section of the wall of Jerusalem, torn down by Jehoash, was the point where Jerusalem was most vulnerable.

14:14 He took. Jehoash plundered both the temple at Jerusalem and the palace of Amaziah. The value of the plundered articles was probably not great, because Jehoash of Judah had previously sent the temple and palace treasures to pay tribute to Hazael of Damascus (12:17, 18). Jehoash probably took hostages from Jerusalem to Samaria to secure additional payments of tribute in view of the small war booty.

14:17 fifteen years. 782–767 B.C.

14:18 the acts of Amaziah. His apostasy (2Ch 25:27), his disastrous war with Israel, the ruinous condition of Jerusalem, the plunder of the temple, and the loss of hostages lost him the respect of his people who rebelled and killed him.

14:19 Lachish. A town about 25 mi. SW of Jerusalem to which Amaziah fled seeking to escape death.

14:21 sixteen years old. Azariah, a.k.a. Uzziah (*see note on 15:1*) had actually begun to reign at the age of 16 in 790 B.C. when his father Amaziah was taken prisoner to Samaria (v. 13). When Amaziah returned to Judah, Azariah ruled with him as co-regent from 782–767 B.C. (v. 17). In 767 B.C. when Amaziah was killed (v. 19), Azariah began his sole rule (15:1). *See notes on 2Ch 26:1–23.*

14:22 Elath. Elath was located on the northern coast of the Gulf of Aqabah and was closely associated with Ezion-geber, a seaport of Solomon (1Ki 9:26). Azariah's restoration of Elath to Judah marked the first significant act of his sole rule; his further successes are summarized in 2Ch 26:6–15.

14:23 fifteenth year. Ca. 782 B.C. This marked the beginning of the sole reign of Jeroboam II. Since his son Zechariah succeeded him in 753 B.C. (see 15:8), Jeroboam II must have had a co-regency with his father Jehoash for 11 years, making a total reign of 41 years (793–753 B.C.), longer than any other king in the northern kingdom. **Jeroboam.** This was Jeroboam II, who like the other kings of Israel, followed the false religion of Jeroboam I. During the reign of Jeroboam II, the prophets Hosea (Hos 1:1) and Amos (Am 1:1) ministered to the northern kingdom. These prophets showed that Jeroboam II's reign was a time of great prosperity and greater spiritual apostasy in Israel.

14:25 restored the border of Israel. Jeroboam II's greatest accomplishment was the restoration of Israel's boundaries to approximately their extent in Solomon's time, excluding the territory belonging to Judah. The northern boundary was the entrance of Hamath, the same as Solomon's (cf. 1Ki 8:65) and the southern boundary was the Sea of the Arabah, the Dead Sea (Jos 3:16; 12:3). Jeroboam II took Hamath, a major city located on the Orontes River, about 160 mi. N of the Sea of Galilee. He also controlled Damascus, indicating that the Transjordan territory S to Moab was also under his authority. These victories of Jeroboam II were accomplished because the Syrians had been weakened by attacks from the Assyrians, while Assyria herself was weak at this time, suffering from threats on her northern border, internal dissension, and a series of weak kings. **Jonah.** The territorial extension of Jeroboam II was in accordance with the will of the Lord as revealed through the prophet Jonah. This was the same Jonah who traveled to Nineveh with God's message of repentance for the Assyrians (see Introduction to Jonah). **Gath-hepher.** A town located in the tribal area of Zebulun, about 14 mi. W of the Sea of Galilee (Jos 19:13).

14:25, 26 The explanation for Jonah's prophecy is given here. The Lord Himself had personally witnessed the heavy, bitter affliction borne by all in Israel with no human help available (v. 26). Further, the Lord had not decreed Israel's final doom (v. 27). To "blot out their name from under heaven" meant to annihilate Israel totally, leaving no trace or memory of her (Dt 9:14; 29:20). Thus, moved with compassion, the Lord Himself used Jeroboam II's reign to rescue His suffering people. However, as the books of Hosea and Amos show, Israel did not respond to God's grace with repentance.

14:28 Without devotion to the Lord, Jeroboam, by might and clever leadership, brought Israel more prosperity than the country had known since Solomon. The people rested in their prosperity rather than God's power. Material blessing was no sign of God's blessing, since they had no commitment to Him.

SERIES OF KINGS: AZARIAH (UZZIAH) OVER JUDAH

15 [A]In the twenty-seventh year of Jeroboam king of Israel, Azariah son of Amaziah king of Judah became king. 2 He was [A]sixteen years old when he became king, and he reigned fifty-two years in Jerusalem; and his mother's name was [a]Jecoliah of Jerusalem. 3 He did right in the sight of the LORD, according to all that his father Amaziah had done. 4 Only [A]the high places were not taken away; the people still sacrificed and burned incense on the high places. 5 [A]The LORD struck the king, so that he was a leper to the day of his death. And he [B]lived in a separate house, [a]while Jotham the king's son was over the household, judging the people of the land. 6 Now the rest of the acts of Azariah and all that he did, are they not written in the Book of the Chronicles of the Kings of Judah? 7 And Azariah slept with his fathers, and they buried him with his fathers in the city of David, and Jotham his son became king in his place.

ZECHARIAH OVER ISRAEL

8 [A]In the thirty-eighth year of Azariah king of Judah, Zechariah the son of Jeroboam became king over Israel in Samaria *for* six months. 9 He did evil in the sight of the LORD, as his fathers had done; he did not depart from the sins of Jeroboam the son of Nebat, which he made Israel sin. 10 Then Shallum the son of Jabesh conspired against him and [A]struck him before the people and [a]killed him, and reigned in his place. 11 Now the rest of the acts of Zechariah, behold they are written in the Book of the Chronicles of the Kings of Israel. 12 This is [A]the word of the LORD which He spoke to Jehu, saying, "Your sons to the fourth generation shall sit on the throne of Israel." And so it was.

13 Shallum son of Jabesh became king in the [A]thirty-ninth year of Uzziah king of Judah, and he reigned one month in [B]Samaria. 14 Then Menahem son of Gadi went up from [A]Tirzah and came to Samaria, and struck Shallum son of Jabesh in Samaria, and killed him and became king in his place. 15 Now the rest of the acts of Shallum and his conspiracy which he made, behold they are written in the Book of the Chronicles of the Kings of Israel. 16 Then Menahem struck Tiphsah and all who were in it and its borders from Tirzah, because they did not open *to him;* therefore he struck *it* and ripped up [A]all its women who were with child.

MENAHEM OVER ISRAEL

17 In the [A]thirty-ninth year of Azariah king of Judah, Menahem son of Gadi became king over Israel *and reigned* ten years in Samaria. 18 He did evil in the sight of the LORD; he did not depart all his days from the sins of Jeroboam the son of Nebat, which he made Israel sin.

19 [A]Pul, king of Assyria, came against the land, and Menahem gave Pul a thousand talents of silver so that his hand might be with him to [B]strengthen the kingdom [a]under his rule. 20 Then Menahem exacted the money from Israel, even from all the mighty men of wealth, from each man fifty shekels of silver to pay the king of Assyria. So the king of Assyria returned and did not remain there in the land. 21 Now the rest of the acts of Menahem and all that he did, are they not written in the Book of the Chronicles of the Kings of Israel? 22 And Menahem slept with his fathers, and Pekahiah his son became king in his place.

PEKAHIAH OVER ISRAEL

23 In [A]the fiftieth year of Azariah king of Judah, Pekahiah son of Menahem became king over Israel in

15:1 [A]2 Kin 14:17 15:2 [a]In 2 Chr 26:3, *Jechiliah* [A]2 Chr 26:3, 4 15:4 [A]2 Kin 12:3 15:5 [a]Lit *and* [A]2 Chr 26:21-23 [B]Lev 13:46; Num 12:14 15:8 [A]2 Kin 15:1 15:10 [a]Lit *smote* [A]Amos 7:9 15:12 [A]2 Kin 10:30 15:13 [A]2 Kin 15:1, 8 [B]1 Kin 16:24 15:14 [A]1 Kin 14:17 15:16 [A]2 Kin 8:12; Hos 13:16 15:17 [A]2 Kin 15:1, 8, 13 15:19 [a]Lit *in his hand* [A]1 Chr 5:25, 26 [B]2 Kin 14:5 15:23 [A]2 Kin 15:1, 8, 13, 17

15:1 **twenty-seventh year.** 767 B.C. This included the 11 years of Jeroboam II's co-regency with Jehoash (*see note on 14:23*). **Azariah.** The name means "The Lord has helped" (14:21; 15:6, 7, 8, 17, 23, 27; 1Ch 3:12). He was also called Uzziah, meaning "The Lord is my strength" (15:13, 30, 32, 34; 2Ch 26:1–23; Is 1:1; 6:1; Hos 1:1; Am 1:1; Zec 14:5). Isaiah the prophet began his public ministry during Azariah's reign (Is 1:1).

15:2 **fifty-two years.** 790–739 B.C. Azariah was 16 when he began his co-regency with his father Amaziah. Azariah's sole rule began in 767 B.C. (*see note on v. 8*).

15:4 Cf. 12:3; 14:4.

15:5 **leper.** Azariah suffered from leprosy as punishment for usurping the priestly function of burning incense on the altar in the temple (*see notes on 2Ch 26:16–18, 19, 20*). The disease eventually killed him (*see note on Is 6:1*). **separate house.** Lit. "in a house of freedom." Azariah was relieved of all royal responsibilities. His son Jotham served as co-regent until Azariah's death (750–739 B.C.; *see notes on 15:2, 32*). As co-regent, Jotham specifically supervised the palace and governed the nation.

15:8 **thirty-eighth year.** 753 B.C., making Azariah's co-reign with his father Amaziah (*see notes on 14:21; 15:2*) begin in 792–791 B.C. (accession year) or 790 B.C. (non-accession year). **Zechariah.** Zechariah was the fourth and final generation of the dynasty of Jehu (ca. 753/752 B.C.). His death fulfilled the prophecy given by the Lord (cf. 15:12; 10:30).

15:10 **Shallum.** Shallum killed Zechariah and replaced him as king of Israel. Assyrian records call Shallum "the son of nobody," indicating that he was not from the royal family.

15:13 **thirty-ninth year.** 752 B.C. Zechariah's reign spanned the last months of Azariah's 38th year (v. 8) and the first months of the following year.

15:14 **Menahem.** Menahem had probably been a military commander under Zechariah. **Tirzah.** The former capital of the northern kingdom (1Ki 14:17; 15:21, 33), located about 9 mi. E of Samaria. Menahem was probably stationed with his troops at Tirzah.

15:16 **Tiphsah.** Since Tiphsah was located on the Euphrates River about 325 mi. N of Samaria (1Ki 4:24), a majority of interpreters translate this term "Tappuah," a town 14 mi. SW of Tirzah (Jos 17:8). **ripped up.** The ripping open of pregnant women was a barbarous practice and elsewhere associated only with foreign armies (8:12; Hos 13:16; Am 1:13). Menahem probably did this as a visible reminder of the city's failure to "open" up, or surrender, to his demands.

15:17 **thirty-ninth year.** 752 B.C. **ten years.** 752–742 B.C. With Menahem, the northern kingdom changed from the non-accession to the accession-year system of computing reigns.

15:19 **Pul.** Assyrian kings frequently had two names, a throne name for Assyria and another for Babylon. Pul was the Babylonian throne name of the Assyrian king Tiglath-pileser III (cf. 1Ch 5:26) who reigned ca. 745–727 B.C.

15:19, 20 Tiglath-pileser III invaded Israel in 743 B.C. Menahem paid tribute of 1,000 talents of silver (ca. 37 tons) raised from the wealthy men of Israel. Each of 60,000 men paid 20 oz. of silver to raise the required 37 tons of silver. For his tribute, Tiglath-pileser III supported Menahem's claim to the throne of Israel and withdrew his army. By this action, Menahem became a vassal of the Assyrian king.

15:23 **fiftieth year.** 742 B.C. **two years.** 742–740 B.C.

Samaria, *and reigned* two years. 24 He did evil in the
sight of the LORD; he did not depart from the sins of
Jeroboam son of Nebat, which he made Israel sin.
25 Then Pekah son of Remaliah, his officer, conspired
against him and struck him in Samaria, in [A]the castle
of the king's house with Argob and Arieh; and with him
were fifty men of the Gileadites, and he killed him and
became king in his place. 26 Now the rest of the acts of
Pekahiah and all that he did, behold they are written
in the Book of the Chronicles of the Kings of Israel.

PEKAH OVER ISRAEL

27 In [A]the fifty-second year of Azariah king of
Judah, [B]Pekah son of Remaliah became king over
Israel in Samaria, *and reigned* twenty years. 28 He
did evil in the sight of the LORD; he did not depart
from the sins of Jeroboam son of Nebat, which he
made Israel sin.
29 In the days of Pekah king of Israel, [a,A]Tig-
lath-pileser king of Assyria came and [b]captured
Ijon and Abel-beth-maacah and Janoah and Kedesh
and Hazor and Gilead and Galilee, all the land of
Naphtali; and [B]he carried them captive to Assyria.
30 And Hoshea the son of Elah made a conspiracy
against Pekah the son of Remaliah, and struck him
and put him to death and became king in his place,
in the twentieth year of Jotham the son of Uzziah.
31 Now the rest of the acts of Pekah and all that he

15:25 [A]1 Kin 16:18 15:27 [A]2 Kin 15:23 [B]2 Chr 28:6; Is 7:1 15:29 [a]In 1 Chr 5:6, 26, *Tilgath-pilneser* [b]Lit *took* [A]2 Kin 15:19 [B]2 Kin 17:6

15:24 sins of Jeroboam. *See notes on 13:2; 1Ki 12:25–32.*

15:25 Pekah. *See note on 15:27.* Pekah was one of Pekahiah's military officers, probably commanding Gilead, since 50 Gileadites accompanied him when he assassinated Pekahiah. Argob and Arieh were either Pekahiah's sons or loyal military officers. Pekah probably represented the anti-Assyrian faction in Israel (cf. 16:5).

15:27 fifty-second year. 740 B.C. **twenty years.** On the basis of Assyrian records, it can be determined that Tilgath-pileser III deposed Pekah as king of Israel in 732 B.C., evidently using Hoshea as his instrument. Therefore, Pekah reigned ca. 752–732 B.C., using the accession-year system of dating (that is, counting the first year as one). For an explanation of this dating system see 1 Kings Introduction: Interpretive Challenges. This included the years 752–740 B.C., when Pekah ruled in Gilead while Menahem (vv. 17–22) and Pekahiah (vv. 23–26) reigned in Samaria (the Jordan River being the boundary of the split kingdom). Verse 25 seems to indicate that Pekah had an alliance with Menahem and Pekahiah, ruling Gilead for them.

15:29 Ijon . . . Naphtali. The areas of Galilee and Gilead are described here. When Pekah and Rezin, the king of Syria, sought to have Judah join their anti-Assyrian alliance, another invasion by Assyria was provoked (cf. 16:5–9) in 733/732 B.C. Tiglath-pileser III took Galilee and Gilead and converted them into 3 Assyrian provinces governed by royal appointees. He also was involved in replacing Pekah with Hoshea as king over the remaining area of Israel (*see note on 15:27*).

15:30 twentieth year. Jotham of Judah began his reign in 750 B.C. (*see note on 15:32*).

THE ASSYRIAN EMPIRE (650 B.C.)

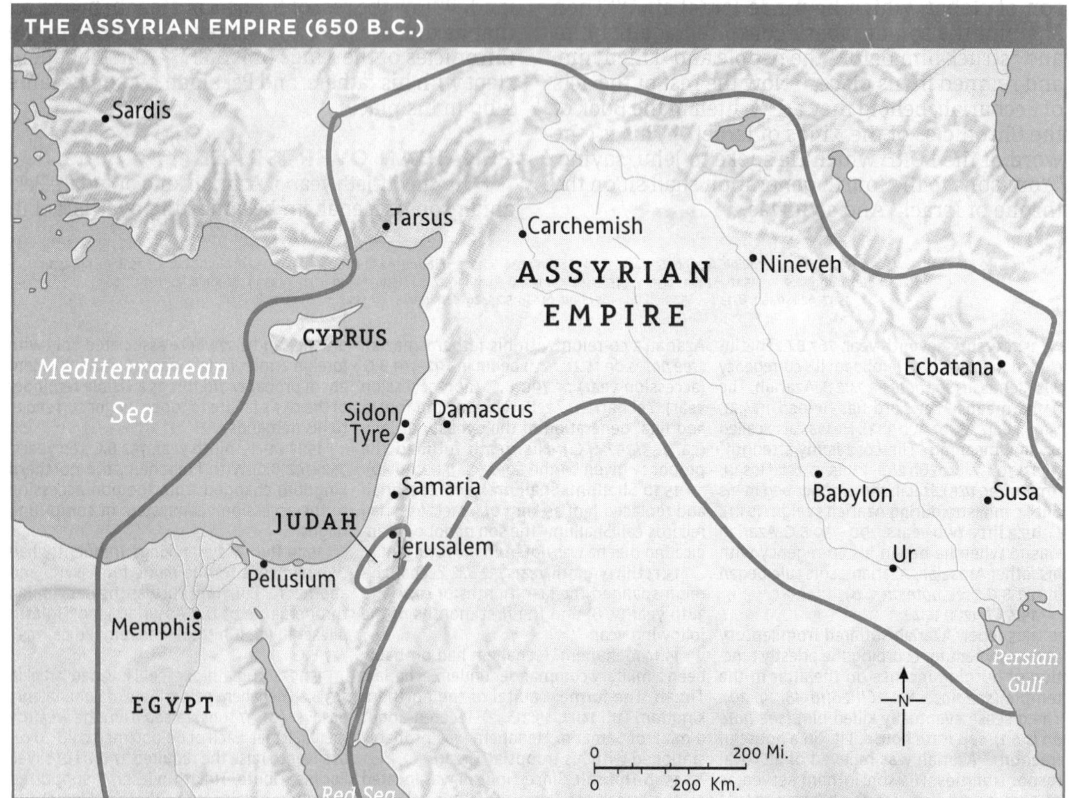

By 650 B.C. the Assyrian Empire, whose capital was Nineveh, stretched from the Persian Gulf in the east through the fertile crescent into Palestine and beyond, embracing for a short time all of Egypt in the southwest. Judah paid tribute to Assyria during the reign of Manasseh, even though it was technically a free zone.

did, behold, they are written in the Book of the
Chronicles of the Kings of Israel.

JOTHAM OVER JUDAH

32 In the second year of Pekah the son of Remaliah
king of Israel, Jotham the son of [a]Uzziah king of Judah became king. 33 [A]He was twenty-five years old
when he became king, and he reigned sixteen years
in Jerusalem; and his mother's name *was* Jerusha
the daughter of Zadok. 34 [A]He did what was right in
the sight of the LORD; he did according to all that his
father Uzziah had done. 35 Only [A]the high places were
not taken away; the people still sacrificed and burned
incense on the high places. [B]He built the upper gate
of the house of the LORD. 36 Now the rest of the acts
of Jotham and all that he did, are they not written
in the Book of the Chronicles of the Kings of Judah?
37 In those days [A]the LORD began to send Rezin king
of Aram and Pekah the son of Remaliah against
Judah. 38 And Jotham slept with his fathers, and he
was buried with his fathers in the city of David his
father; and Ahaz his son became king in his place.

AHAZ REIGNS OVER JUDAH

16 In the seventeenth year of Pekah the son of
Remaliah, [A]Ahaz the son of Jotham, king of
Judah, became king. 2 [A]Ahaz *was* twenty years old
when he became king, and he reigned sixteen years
in Jerusalem; and he did not do what was right in
the sight of the LORD his God, as his father David
had done. 3 But he walked in the way of the kings
of Israel, [A]and even made his son pass through the
fire, [B]according to the abominations of the nations
whom the LORD had [a]driven out from before the
sons of Israel. 4 He [A]sacrificed and burned incense
on the high places and on the hills and under every green tree.
5 Then [A]Rezin king of Aram and Pekah son of
Remaliah, king of Israel, came up to Jerusalem to
wage war; and they besieged Ahaz, [B]but could not
[a]overcome him. 6 At that time Rezin king of Aram
recovered [A]Elath for Aram, and cleared the Judeans
out of [a]Elath entirely; and the [b]Arameans came to
Elath and have lived there to this day.

AHAZ SEEKS HELP OF ARAM

7 [A]So Ahaz sent messengers to [B]Tiglath-pileser
king of Assyria, saying, "I am your servant and
your son; come up and deliver me from the [a]hand
of the king of Aram and from the [a]hand of the king
of Israel, who are rising up against me." 8 [A]Ahaz took
the silver and gold that was found in the house of
the LORD and in the treasuries of the king's house,
and sent a present to the king of Assyria. 9 [A]So the
king of Assyria listened to him; and the king of Assyria went up against Damascus and [B]captured it,

15:32 [a]I.e. Azariah 15:33 [A]2 Chr 27:1 15:34 [A]2 Kin 15:3, 4; 2 Chr 26:4, 5 15:35 [A]2 Kin 12:3 [B]2 Chr 23:20; 27:3 15:37 [A]2 Kin 16:5; Is 7:1 16:1 [A]2 Chr 28:1 16:2 [A]2 Chr 28:1-4 16:3 [a]Or *dispossessed* [A]Lev 18:21; 2 Kin 17:17; 21:6 [B]Deut 12:31; 2 Kin 21:2, 11 16:4 [A]Deut 12:2; 2 Kin 14:4 16:5 [a]Lit *fight* [A]2 Kin 15:37; Is 7:1 [B]2 Chr 28:5, 6 16:6 [a]Heb *Eloth* [b]So with some ancient versions; Heb *Edomites* [A]2 Kin 14:22; 2 Chr 26:2 16:7 [a]Lit *palm* [A]2 Chr 28:16 [B]2 Kin 15:29 16:8 [A]2 Kin 12:17, 18; 18:15 16:9 [A]2 Chr 28:21 [B]Amos 1:3-5

His 20th year was 732 B.C., according to the non-accession-year system. Assyrian records confirm that Hoshea began to rule Israel in 732 B.C. (*see notes on v. 27; 2Ch 27:1–9*).

15:32 second year. 750 B.C., the year of Pekah's second year of rule in Gilead, according to the accession-year system (*see note on 15:27*).

15:33 sixteen years. 750–735 B.C. According to v. 30, Jotham reigned until 731 B.C. Jotham was probably replaced as a functioning king of Judah by a pro-Assyrian faction who established Ahaz as ruler (*see notes on 15:1, 2*) while leaving Jotham as a powerless co-regent. Isaiah (Is 1:1) and Micah (Mic 1:1) the prophets ministered to Judah during Jotham's reign.

15:35 the upper gate. Probably the upper Benjamin Gate, which stood along the N side of the temple complex facing the territory of Benjamin (cf. Jer 20:2; Eze 9:2; Zec 14:10). Other accomplishments of Jotham are noted in 2Ch 27:3–6.

15:37 Rezin ... Pekah. *See notes on 16:5–9.*

16:1–17:41 At this point the narrative turns to the defeat and exile of Israel by Assyria. In 17:7–23, the prophetic writer states the reasons why Israel was punished by the Lord. A major reason was the sinful religion established by Jeroboam I (17:21–23), which was followed by every king in Israel. Ominously, the section begins with the narrative concerning Ahaz of Judah who "walked in the way of the kings of Israel" (16:3). The kind of punishment that came upon Israel would come later upon Judah for the same reason (17:19, 20).

16:1 seventeenth year. 735 B.C., since Pekah's reign began in 752 B.C. (*see note on 15:27*). Although Jotham, the father of Ahaz, was still alive (*see note on 15:30*), Ahaz exercised the sovereign authority in Judah from 735 B.C. to Jotham's death in ca. 731 B.C. Isaiah (Is 1:1–7:1) and Micah (Mic 1:1) the prophets continued to minister to Judah during the reign of Ahaz. *See notes on 2Ch 28:1–27.*

16:2 sixteen years. 731–715 B.C. The principle of "dual dating" was followed here. See 1 Kings Introduction: Interpretive Challenges for an explanation of this principle. In 16:1 and 17:1, Ahaz was recognized as king in the year he came to the throne as a co-regent, but the year of his official accession was determined as the year when he began to reign alone. Ahaz shared royal power with Azariah (to 739 B.C.) and Jotham from 744 to 735 B.C. (*see note on 17:1*); he exercised total authority as co-regent with Jotham from 735–731 B.C. (*see note on 16:1*); he was sole king from 731 to 729 B.C. and was co-regent with his son Hezekiah from 729 to 715 B.C. (*see note on 18:1*).

16:3 walked in the way of the kings of Israel. This does not necessarily mean that Ahaz participated in the calf worship introduced by Jeroboam I at Bethel and Dan, but that he increasingly brought pagan, idolatrous practices into the worship of the Lord in Jerusalem. These are specified in vv. 10–16 and parallel those of Jeroboam I in the northern kingdom. This included idols to Baal (2Ch 28:2). **made his son pass through the fire.** As a part of the ritual worship of Molech, the god of the Moabites, children were sacrificed by fire (cf. 3:27). This horrific practice was continually condemned in the OT (Lv 18:21; 20:2–5; Dt 18:10; Jer 7:31; 19:5; 32:35). **the abominations of the nations.** *See note on Dt 18:9–12.*

16:4 the high places. Ahaz was the first king in the line of David since Solomon who was said to have personally worshiped at the high places. While all the other kings of Judah had tolerated the high places, Ahaz actively participated in the immoral Canaanite practices that were performed at the "high places" on hilltops under large trees (cf. Hos 4:13).

16:5 Rezin ... Pekah. The kings of Syria and Israel wanted to overthrow Ahaz in order to force Judah into their anti-Assyrian coalition. The two kings with their armies besieged Jerusalem, seeking to replace Ahaz with their own king (cf. Is 7:1–6). The Lord delivered Judah and Ahaz from this threat because of His promise to David (cf. Is 7:7–16).

16:6 Elath. The Syrians did displace Judah from Elath (*see note on 14:22*). Later this important port town on the Gulf of Aqabah was captured by the Edomites.

16:7 Tiglath-pileser. *See notes on 15:19, 29.* **your servant and your son.** Ahaz willingly became a vassal of the Assyrian king in exchange for his military intervention. This was a pledge that Judah would serve Assyria from this point on. In support of his pledge, Ahaz sent Tiglath-pileser III silver and gold from the temple and from the palace treasuries (v. 8). Evidently the prosperous reigns of Azariah and Jotham had replenished the treasures plundered by Jehoash of Israel 50 years earlier during Amaziah's reign (14:14).

16:9 the king of Assyria listened to him. According to Assyrian records, in 733 B.C. Tiglath-pileser III's army marched against and carried *the people of* it away into exile to [C]Kir, and put Rezin to death.

DAMASCUS FALLS

10 Now King Ahaz went to Damascus to meet [A]Tiglath-pileser king of Assyria, and saw the altar which *was* at Damascus; and King Ahaz sent to [B]Urijah the priest the [a]pattern of the altar and its model, according to all its workmanship. 11 So Urijah the priest built an altar; according to all that King Ahaz had sent from Damascus, thus Urijah the priest made *it*, [a]before the coming of King Ahaz from Damascus. 12 When the king came from Damascus, the king saw the altar; then [A]the king approached the altar and [a]went up to it, 13 and [a]burned his burnt offering and his meal offering, and poured his drink offering and sprinkled the blood of his peace offerings on the altar. 14 [A]The bronze altar, which *was* before the LORD, [a]he brought from the front of the house, from between [B]*his* altar and the house of the LORD, and he put it on the north side of *his* altar. 15 Then King Ahaz [a]commanded Urijah the priest, saying, "Upon the great altar [b]burn [A]the morning burnt offering and the evening meal offering and the king's burnt offering and his meal offering, with the burnt offering of all the people of the land and their meal offering and their drink offerings; and sprinkle on it all the blood of the burnt offering and all the blood of the sacrifice. But [B]the bronze altar shall be for me to inquire *by*." 16 So Urijah the priest did according to all that King Ahaz commanded.

17 Then King Ahaz [A]cut off the borders of the stands, and removed the laver from them; he also [B]took down the sea from the bronze oxen which were under it and put it on a pavement of stone. 18 The covered way for the sabbath which they had built in the house, and the outer entry of the king, he removed from the house of the LORD because of the king of Assyria.

HEZEKIAH REIGNS OVER JUDAH

19 Now the rest of the acts of Ahaz which he did, are they not written [A]in the Book of the Chronicles of the Kings of Judah? 20 So [A]Ahaz slept with his fathers, and [B]was buried with his fathers in the city of David; and his son Hezekiah reigned in his place.

HOSHEA REIGNS OVER ISRAEL

17 In the twelfth year of Ahaz king of Judah, [A]Hoshea the son of Elah became king over Israel in Samaria, *and reigned* nine years. 2 He did evil in the sight of the LORD, only not as the kings of Israel who were before him. 3 [A]Shalmaneser king of Assyria came up [B]against him, and Hoshea became his servant and paid him tribute. 4 But the king of Assyria found conspiracy in Hoshea, who had sent messengers to So king of Egypt and had offered no tribute to the king of Assyria, as *he had done* year by year; so the king of Assyria shut him up and bound him in prison.

5 Then the king of Assyria invaded the whole land and went up to [A]Samaria and besieged it three years.

16:9 [C]Is 22:6; Amos 9:7 16:10 [a]Lit *likeness* [A]2 Kin 15:29 [B]Is 8:2 16:11 [a]Lit *until* 16:12 [a]Or *offered on it* [A]2 Chr 26:16, 19 16:13 [a]Lit *offered in smoke* 16:14 [a]Lit *he also* [A]Ex 27:1, 2; 40:6, 29; 2 Chr 4:1 [B]2 Kin 16:11 16:15 [a]Lit *commanded him, Urijah* [b]Lit *offer in smoke* [A]Ex 29:39-41 [B]2 Kin 16:14 16:17 [A]1 Kin 7:27, 28, 38 [B]1 Kin 7:23, 25 16:19 [A]2 Chr 28:26 16:20 [A]Is 14:28 [B]2 Chr 28:27 17:1 [A]2 Kin 15:30 17:3 [A]Hos 10:14 [B]2 Kin 18:9-12 17:5 [A]Hos 13:16

Damascus, the Syrian capital, laid siege for two years, and captured it. The victorious Assyrian king executed Rezin and deported his subjects to Kir, whose location is unknown.

16:10 the altar. When Ahaz traveled to Damascus to meet Tiglath-pileser III, he saw a large altar (v. 15) which was most likely Assyrian. Ahaz sent a sketch of this altar to Urijah the High Priest in Jerusalem and Urijah built an altar just like it. The serious iniquity in this was meddling with and changing, according to personal taste, the furnishings of the temple, the design for which had been given by God (Ex 25:40; 26:30; 27:1–8; 1Ch 28:19). This was like building an idol in the temple, done to please the pagan Assyrian king, whom Ahaz served instead of God.

16:12, 13 offerings. As did Solomon and Jeroboam before him (1Ki 8:63; 12:32), Ahaz dedicated the new altar by offering sacrifices.

16:14–16 bronze altar. Feeling confident about his alterations in the temple, Ahaz moved the old bronze altar dedicated by Solomon (1Ki 8:22, 54, 64), which stood in front of the temple between the new altar and the temple itself (v. 14). Ahaz had the bronze altar moved to a spot N of the new altar, thereby relegating it to a place of secondary importance. All offerings from then on were to be given on the altar dedicated by Ahaz, while Ahaz reserved the bronze altar for his personal use in seeking guidance (v. 15). The term "inquire" probably referred here to pagan divination through religious rituals. Dt 18:9–14 expressly forbade such divination in Israel.

16:17, 18 Ahaz made further changes in the temple at Jerusalem. First, he removed the side panels ("borders") and "laver" from the portable stands (cf. 1Ki 7:27–29, 38, 39). Second, he removed the large ornate reservoir called "the sea" from atop the 12 bronze bulls to a new stone base (cf. 1Ki 7:23–26). Third, he removed the "covered way," probably some sort of canopy used by the king on the Sabbath. Fourth, he removed "the outer entry," probably a special entrance to the temple used by the king on Sabbaths and feast days (cf. 1Ki 10:5).

16:18 because of the king of Assyria. Both items mentioned here were moved from the temple in hope that if the king of Assyria laid siege to Jerusalem, Ahaz could secure the entrance of the temple from him.

16:20 Hezekiah. For his reign, see 18:1–20:21.

17:1 twelfth year. 732 B.C. This date for the accession of Hoshea as king of Israel is well established according to biblical and extra-biblical data (*see note on 15:27*). Therefore, Ahaz of Judah must have become co-regent with his father Jotham, who was himself co-regent with his father, Azariah, at that time (*see notes on 15:30, 33*), in 744 B.C. (*see note on 16:2*). **nine years.** 732–722 B.C. according to the accession-year system. Hoshea was imprisoned (v. 4) during the siege of Samaria by Assyria in 724–722 B.C. (v. 5).

17:2 He did evil. Though Hoshea was characterized as a wicked king, it is not stated that he promoted the religious practices of Jeroboam I. In this way, he was some improvement on the kings of Israel who had gone before him. However, this slight improvement did not offset the centuries of sin by Israel's kings nor divert her inevitable doom.

17:3 Shalmaneser. Shalmaneser V succeeded his father Tiglath-pileser III as king of Assyria and reigned from 727–722 B.C. During the siege of Samaria, when the Assyrians began the destruction and captivity of the northern kingdom, Shalmaneser V died and was succeeded by Sargon II (see Is 20:1), who completed the siege, captured the city, destroyed the nation of Israel, and exiled the inhabitants (v. 6). Sargon II reigned as king from 722–705 B.C. *See note on Hos 10:14.*

17:4 So king of Egypt. Instead of paying his yearly tribute owed as a vassal of Assyria, Hoshea tried to make a treaty with Osorkon IV (ca. 727–716 B.C.), king of Egypt. This was foolish because Assyria was powerful. It was also against God's will, which forbade such alliances with pagan rulers (cf. Dt 7:2). This rebellion led to Israel's destruction (vv. 5, 6).

17:5 Samaria ... besieged. In 724 B.C., Shalmaneser V invaded Israel and quickly conquered the land and captured Hoshea. However, the capital city of Samaria resisted the Assyrian invaders until 722 B.C. Like all major cities, Samaria had an internal water supply and plenty of stored food that allowed her to endure the siege for 3 years.

ISRAEL CAPTIVE

6 In the ninth year of Hoshea, [A]the king of Assyria
captured Samaria and [B]carried Israel away into exile
to Assyria, and [C]settled them in Halah and Habor, *on*
the river of [D]Gozan, and [E]in the cities of the Medes.

WHY ISRAEL FELL

7 Now [A]*this* came about because the sons of Israel
had sinned against the LORD their God, [B]who had
brought them up from the land of Egypt from under
the hand of Pharaoh, king of Egypt, [C]and they had
[a]feared other gods 8 and [A]walked in the [a]customs of
the nations whom the LORD had driven out before
the sons of Israel, and *in the customs* [B]of the kings
of Israel which they had [b]introduced. 9 The sons
of Israel [a]did things secretly which were not right
against the LORD their God. Moreover, they built
for themselves high places in all their towns, from
[A]watchtower to fortified city. 10 [A]They set for themselves *sacred* pillars and [a,B]Asherim on every high
hill and under every green tree, 11 and there they
burned incense on all the high places as the nations
did which the LORD had carried away to exile before
them; and they did evil things provoking the LORD.
12 They served idols, [A]concerning which the LORD
had said to them, "You shall not do this thing." 13 Yet
the [A]LORD warned Israel and Judah [B]through all His
prophets *and* [C]every seer, saying, "[D]Turn from your
evil ways and keep My commandments, My statutes
according to all the law which I commanded your
fathers, and which I sent to you through My servants
the prophets." 14 However, they did not listen, but
[A]stiffened their neck [a]like their fathers, who did not
believe in the LORD their God. 15 [A]They rejected His
statutes and [B]His covenant which He made with their
fathers and His warnings with which He warned
them. And [C]they followed vanity and [D]became vain,
and *went* after the nations which surrounded them,
concerning which the [E]LORD had commanded them
not to do like them. 16 They forsook all the commandments of the LORD their God and made for
themselves molten images, *even* [A]two calves, and
[B]made an [a]Asherah and [C]worshiped all the host of
heaven and [D]served Baal. 17 Then [A]they made their
sons and their daughters pass through the fire, and
[B]practiced divination and enchantments, and [C]sold
themselves to do evil in the sight of the LORD, provoking Him. 18 So the LORD was very angry with
Israel and [A]removed them from His [a]sight; [B]none
was left except the tribe of Judah.

19 Also [A]Judah did not keep the commandments
of the LORD their God, but [B]walked in the [a]customs
[b]which Israel had [c]introduced. 20 The LORD rejected
all the [a]descendants of Israel and afflicted them and
[A]gave them into the hand of plunderers, until He
had cast them [b]out of His sight.

21 When [A]He had torn Israel from the house of
David, [B]they made Jeroboam the son of Nebat king.
Then [C]Jeroboam drove Israel away from follow-
ing the LORD and made them [a]commit a great sin.

17:6 [A]Hos 13:16 [B]Deut 28:64; 29:27, 28 [C]2 Kin 18:11; 1 Chr 5:26 [D]Is 37:12 [E]Is 13:17; 21:2 17:7 [a]Lit *revered,* and so throughout the ch [A]Josh 23:16 [B]Ex 14:15-30 [C]Judg 6:10 17:8 [a]Lit *statutes* [b]Lit *made* [A]Lev 18:3; Deut 18:9 [B]2 Kin 16:3; 17:19 17:9 [a]Or *uttered words which* [A]2 Kin 18:8 17:10 [a]I.e. wooden symbols of a female deity [A]Ex 34:12-14 [B]1 Kin 14:23; Mic 5:14 17:12 [A]Ex 20:4 17:13 [A]Neh 9:29, 30 [B]2 Kin 17:23 [C]1 Sam 9:9 [D]Jer 7:3-7; 18:11; Ezek 18:31 17:14 [a]Lit *like the neck of* [A]Ex 32:9; 33:3; Acts 7:51 17:15 [A]Jer 8:9 [B]Ex 24:6-8; Deut 29:25 [C]Deut 32:21 [D]Jer 2:5; Rom 1:21-23 [E]Deut 12:30, 31 17:16 [a]I.e. a wooden symbol of a female deity [A]1 Kin 12:28 [B]1 Kin 14:15, 23 [C]Deut 4:19; 2 Kin 21:3 [D]1 Kin 16:31 17:17 [A]2 Kin 16:3 [B]Lev 19:26; Deut 18:10-12 [C]1 Kin 21:20 17:18 [a]Lit *face* [A]2 Kin 17:6 [B]1 Kin 11:13, 32, 36 17:19 [a]Lit *statutes* [b]Lit *of Israel which they* [c]Lit *made* [A]1 Kin 14:22, 23 [B]2 Kin 16:3 17:20 [a]Lit *seed* [b]Lit *from His face* [A]2 Kin 15:29 17:21 [a]Lit *sin* [A]1 Kin 11:11, 31 [B]1 Kin 12:20 [C]1 Kin 12:28-33

17:6 king of Assyria. Sargon II (*see note on 17:3*). **carried Israel away.** The capture of Samaria marked the end of the northern kingdom. According to Assyrian records, the Assyrians deported 27,290 inhabitants of Israel to distant locations. The relocation of populations was characteristic of Assyrian policy during that era. The Israelites were resettled in the upper Tigris-Euphrates Valley and never returned to the Promised Land. "Halah" was a city NE of Nineveh. The "Habor" River was a northern tributary of the Euphrates. The "cities of the Medes" were NE of Nineveh. Samaria was resettled with foreigners (v. 24). God did what He said He would do in Dt 28. The Jews were carried as far E as Susa, where the book of Esther later took place.

17:7–23 In these verses, the writer departs from quoting his written sources and gives his own explanation for the captivity of Israel. Judah is included, though her captivity did not occur until 605/604–586 B.C. at the hands of the Babylonians. Her sins were the same. Here is a very full and impressive vindication of God's action in punishing His privileged but rebellious and apostate people. In v. 7, he begins by stating that the Israelites had sinned against the Lord who had redeemed them from Egypt. Gross perversion of the worship of God and national propensity to idolatry finally exhausted divine patience. The idolatry of Israel is described in vv. 7–12. In response to Israel's actions, the Lord sent His prophets to Israel and Judah with a message of repentance (v. 13). However, the people failed to respond to the prophets' messages, because, like their fathers, they did not have faith in the Lord (v. 14). Their lack of faith resulted in disobedience to the Lord's commands and the further pursuit of idolatry (vv. 15–17). The idolatry of Israel (and Judah) brought forth the anger of the Lord, which resulted in exile (v. 18). The "great sin" of both Israel and Judah was their continual following of the sinful pattern of Jeroboam I, departing from the Lord and practicing idolatry, thus bringing down the judgment of captivity predicted by the prophets (vv. 19–23).

17:7 feared other gods. The primary cause of Israel's exile was the worship of other gods. The fear of the Lord led to listening to His Word and obeying His ordinances and statutes (Dt 4:10; 5:29; 6:24), but the fear of the gods of Canaan led Israel to obey the laws of the Canaanite gods (v. 8). The result of this obedience to false gods is recorded in vv. 9–12, 16, 17.

17:8 walked in the customs of the nations. This was expressly forbidden in Lv 18:3; 20:23.

17:9 built … high places. In addition to their private sins ("secret"), judgment came for public wickedness and idolatry. These were not the high places utilized by Israel for worshiping God before the building of the temple (*see note on 1Ki 3:2*). In direct disobedience to Dt 12:1–4, the Israelites built new raised altars in the Canaanite pattern after the temple was constructed. These "high places" were in all the habitations of Israel, from small fortified structures to large garrison cities, i.e., from the smallest to largest towns. The altars were on wooded hills with images representing the false gods (v. 10; cf. Dt 16:21, 22).

17:13 Turn from your evil ways. The prophets continually called the people to repentance (cf. Jer 7:3, 5; 18:11; Eze 33:11).

17:14 stiffened their neck. A stubborn refusal to respond (*see note on Dt 9:6*; cf. Ex 32:9; 33:3, 5; 34:9; Ac 7:51).

17:16 molten images, *even* two calves. Worship of these idols was instituted by Jeroboam (see 1Ki 12:25–33). **an Asherah.** Built by Rehoboam (see 1Ki 14:15, 23). **the host of heaven.** In the ancient Near East, the sun, moon, and stars were deified and worshiped. This astral worship entered Israel and Judah (21:5; 23:4, 5; Eze 8:15, 16; Am 5:26). The worship of the heavenly bodies was prohibited by the Mosaic law (Dt 4:19; 17:3).

17:17 pass through the fire. *See notes on 3:27; 16:3.* **divination and enchantments.** *See note on Dt 18:9–12.* Isaiah prophesied of the devastation these practices would produce (8:19–22).

17:19 Judah followed Israel into sin and judgment.

17:21 He had torn Israel. *See notes on 1Ki 11:11–13, 29–39.*

22 The sons of Israel walked in all the sins of Jeroboam which he did; they did not depart from them
23 [A]until the LORD removed Israel from His sight, [B]as
He spoke through all His servants the prophets. [A]So
Israel was carried away into exile from their own
land to Assyria until this day.

CITIES OF ISRAEL FILLED WITH STRANGERS

24 [A]The king of Assyria brought *men* from Babylon
and from Cuthah and from [a,B]Avva and from [C]Hamath
and Sepharvaim, and settled *them* in the cities of Samaria in place of the sons of Israel. So they possessed
Samaria and lived in its cities. 25 At the beginning of
their living there, they [A]did not fear the LORD; therefore the LORD sent lions among them which killed
some of them. 26 So they spoke to the king of Assyria,
saying, "The nations whom you have carried away
into exile in the cities of Samaria do not know the
custom of the god of the land; so he has sent lions
among them, and behold, they kill them because
they do not know the custom of the god of the land."
27 Then the king of Assyria commanded, saying,
"Take there one of the priests whom you carried
away into [a]exile and let [b]him go and live there; and
let him teach them the custom of the god of the land."
28 So one of the priests whom they had carried away
into exile from Samaria came and lived at Bethel,
and taught them how they should fear the LORD.
29 But every nation still made gods of its own and
put them [A]in the houses of the high places which the
people of Samaria had made, every nation in their
cities in which they lived. 30 [A]The men of Babylon
made Succoth-benoth, the men of Cuth made Nergal,
the men of Hamath made Ashima, 31 and the Av-
vites made Nibhaz and Tartak; and [A]the Sepharvites
burned their children in the fire to [B]Adrammelech
and Anammelech the gods of [C]Sepharvaim. 32 [A]They
also feared the LORD and [a,B]appointed from among
themselves priests of the high places, who acted for
them in the houses of the high places. 33 They feared
the LORD and served their own gods according to
the custom of the nations from among whom they
had been carried away into exile.
34 To this day they do according to the earlier customs: they do not fear the LORD, nor do they [a]follow
their statutes or their ordinances or the law, or the
commandments which the LORD commanded the
sons of Jacob, [A]whom He named Israel; 35 with whom
the LORD made a covenant and commanded them,
saying, "[A]You shall not fear other gods, nor [B]bow
down yourselves to them nor [C]serve them nor sacrifice to them. 36 But the LORD, [A]who brought you up
from the land of Egypt with great power and with
[B]an outstretched arm, [C]Him you shall fear, and to Him
you shall bow yourselves down, and to Him you shall
sacrifice. 37 The statutes and the ordinances and the
law and the commandment which He wrote for you,
[A]you shall observe to do forever; and you shall not
fear other gods. 38 The covenant that I have made
with you, [A]you shall not forget, nor shall you fear
other gods. 39 But the LORD your God you shall fear;
and He will deliver you from the hand of all your enemies." 40 However, they did not listen, but they did
according to their earlier custom. 41 [A]So while these
nations feared the LORD, they also served their [a]idols;
their children likewise and their grandchildren, as
their fathers did, so they do to this day.

HEZEKIAH REIGNS OVER JUDAH

18 Now it came about [A]in the third year of
Hoshea, the son of Elah king of Israel, that

17:23 [A]2 Kin 17:6 [B]2 Kin 17:13 17:24 [a]In 2 Kin 18:34, *Ivvah* [A]Ezra 4:2, 10 [B]2 Kin 18:34 [C]1 Kin 8:65 17:25 [A]2 Kin 17:32-41 17:27 [a]Lit *exile from there* [b]Lit *them* 17:29 [A]1 Kin 12:31; 13:32 17:30 [A]2 Kin 17:24 17:31 [A]2 Kin 17:17 [B]2 Kin 19:37 [C]2 Kin 17:24 17:32 [a]Lit *made for themselves from among* [A]Zeph 1:5 [B]1 Kin 12:31 17:34 [a]Lit *do according to* [A]Gen 32:28; 35:10 17:35 [A]Judg 6:10 [B]Ex 20:5 [C]Deut 5:9 17:36 [A]Ex 14:15-30 [B]Ex 6:6; 9:15 [C]Lev 19:32; Deut 6:13 17:37 [A]Deut 5:32 17:38 [A]Deut 4:23; 6:12 17:41 [a]Or *graven images* [A]Zeph 1:5; Matt 6:24 18:1 [A]2 Kin 16:2; 17:1

17:22 the sins of Jeroboam. *See notes on 1Ki 12:25–32.* The sins of that king put in motion an unbroken pattern of idolatrous iniquity. *See note on 13:2.*

17:23 until this day. The exiles of Israel never returned en masse as did Judah (*see note on 1Ch 9:1*).

17:24 Samaria. After its conquest by the Assyrians, the central hill and coastal plain region of the former northern kingdom of Israel became an Assyrian province, all of which was called "Samaria" after the ancient capital city (cf. vv. 28, 29). The Assyrian king, Sargon II, settled alien people, who came from widely scattered areas also conquered by Assyria, into the abandoned Israelite towns. Babylon and Cuthah were located in southern Mesopotamia. Hamath was a town on the Orontes River in Syria. The exact location of Avva and Sepharvaim are unknown. These people, who intermarried with the Jews who escaped exile, became the Samaritans—a mixed Jew and Gentile people, later hated by NT Jews (cf. Mt 10:5; Jn 4:9; *see notes on Lk 10:29–36*).

17:25 lions among them. Lions were employed occasionally as instruments of punishment by God (cf. 1Ki 13:24; 20:36).

17:26 the custom of the god. The newcomers interpreted the lions as a punishment from the God of Israel, whom they viewed as a deity who needed to be placated. Since they did not know how to appease Him, they appealed for help to Sargon II.

17:27, 28 one of the priests. In response, the Assyrian king ordered an Israelite priest back to Samaria from exile to teach the people what the God of the land required in worship.

17:29–32 Though they had been taught the proper way to worship God, these people all placed God alongside their other gods in an eclectic kind of worship that was blasphemy to the one true and living God.

17:30 Succoth-benoth. Lit. "tents of the daughters," probably indicating some deity worshiped by sexual orgies. **Nergal.** Perhaps the Assyrian god of war. **Ashima.** An idol in the form of a bald he-goat.

17:31 Nibhaz. A dog-like idol. **Tartak.** Either a donkey or a celestial body, Saturn. **Adrammelech.** Perhaps the same as Molech, worshiped in the form of the sun, a mule or a peacock. **Anammelech.** A rabbit or a goat idol.

17:33 served their own gods. The religion of the Samaritans was syncretistic; it combined elements of the worship of the Lord with the worship practices of the gods which the Assyrian settlers had brought with them (*see note on v. 24*).

17:34–41 Having shown how the Samaritan people and their religion came into being (vv. 24–33), the writer of Kings shows how the syncretistic worship of the Samaritans continued for generations, even to his own day (cf. v. 41; during the Babylonian exile). The religion of the Samaritans was, at its foundation, no different from Jeroboam I's deviant religion.

18:1–25:21 With the fall of Samaria, the northern kingdom of Israel came to an end (17:5, 6; 18:9–12). This last major division of the books of Kings narrates the events in the surviving southern kingdom of Judah from 722 B.C. to its captivity and destruction in 586 B.C. These chapters are dominated by the accounts of two good kings, Hezekiah (18:1–20:21) and Josiah (22:1–23:30). However, the reforms of these two godly kings did not reverse the effects of the two worst kings of Judah, Ahaz (16:1–20) and Manasseh (21:1–18). The result of Judah's apostasy was exile, just as it was for Israel (23:31–25:21). The books of Kings begin with the building of the temple (1Ki 5:1–6:38) and end with its destruction (25:8, 9, 13–17), chronicling the sad journey from the establishment of true worship to the destruction of apostasy.

18:1 third year. Ca. 729 B.C. Hoshea began

[B]Hezekiah the son of Ahaz king of Judah became king. 2 He was [A]twenty-five years old when he became king, and he reigned twenty-nine years in Jerusalem; and his mother's name was Abi the daughter of Zechariah. 3 [A]He did right in the sight of the LORD, according to all that his father David had done. 4 [A]He removed the high places and broke down the *sacred* pillars and cut down the [a]Asherah. He also broke in pieces [B]the bronze serpent that Moses had made, for until those days the sons of Israel burned incense to it; and it was called [b]Nehushtan. 5 [A]He trusted in the LORD, the God of Israel; [B]so that after him there was none like him among all the kings of Judah, nor *among those* who were before him. 6 For he [A]clung to the LORD; he did not depart from following Him, but kept His commandments, which the LORD had commanded Moses.

HEZEKIAH VICTORIOUS

7 [A]And the LORD was with him; wherever he went he prospered. And [B]he rebelled against the king of Assyria and did not serve him. 8 [A]He [a]defeated the Philistines as far as Gaza and its territory, from [B]watchtower to fortified city.

9 Now in the fourth year of King Hezekiah, which was the seventh year of Hoshea son of Elah king of Israel, [A]Shalmaneser king of Assyria came up against Samaria and besieged it. 10 At the end of three years they captured it; in the sixth year of Hezekiah, which was [A]the ninth year of Hoshea king of Israel, Samaria was captured. 11 Then the king of Assyria carried Israel away into exile to Assyria, and put them in [A]Halah and on the Habor, the river of Gozan, and in the cities of the Medes, 12 because they [A]did not obey the voice of the LORD their God, but transgressed His covenant, *even* all that Moses the servant of the LORD commanded; they would neither listen nor do *it*.

INVASION OF JUDAH

13 [A]Now in the fourteenth year of King Hezekiah, Sennacherib king of Assyria came up against all the fortified cities of Judah and seized them. 14 Then Hezekiah king of Judah sent to the king of Assyria at Lachish, saying, "[A]I have done wrong. [a]Withdraw from me; whatever you [b]impose on me I will bear." So the king of Assyria [c]required of Hezekiah king of Judah three hundred talents of silver and thirty talents of gold. 15 [A]Hezekiah gave *him* all the silver which was found in the house of the LORD, and in the treasuries of the king's house. 16 At that time Hezekiah cut off *the gold from* the doors of the temple of the LORD, and *from* the doorposts which Hezekiah king of Judah had overlaid, and gave it to the king of Assyria.

17 Then the king of Assyria sent [A]Tartan and Rab-saris and Rabshakeh from Lachish to King Hezekiah with a large army to Jerusalem. So they went up and came to Jerusalem. And when they went up, they came and stood by the [B]conduit of the upper pool, which is on the highway of the [a]fuller's

18:1 [B]2 Chr 28:27 18:2 [A]2 Chr 29:1, 2 18:3 [A]2 Kin 20:3; 2 Chr 31:20 18:4 [a]I.e. a wooden symbol of a female deity [b]I.e. a piece of bronze [A]2 Kin 18:22; 2 Chr 31:1 [B]Num 21:8, 9 18:5 [A]2 Kin 19:10 [B]2 Kin 23:25 18:6 [A]Deut 10:20; Josh 23:8 18:7 [A]Gen 39:2, 3; 1 Sam 18:14 [B]2 Kin 16:7 18:8 [a]Lit *smote* [A]2 Chr 28:18; Is 14:29 [B]2 Kin 17:9 18:9 [A]2 Kin 17:3-7 18:10 [A]2 Kin 17:6 18:11 [A]1 Chr 5:26 18:12 [A]1 Kin 9:6; Dan 9:6, 10 18:13 [A]2 Chr 32:1; Is 36:1-39:8 18:14 [a]Lit *Return* [b]Lit *give* [c]Lit *put on* [A]2 Kin 18:7 18:15 [A]1 Kin 15:18, 19; 2 Kin 12:18; 16:8 18:17 [a]I.e. launderer's [A]Is 20:1 [B]2 Kin 20:20; Is 7:3

to reign in 732 B.C. (*see notes on 15:27; 17:1*). Hezekiah was co-regent with Ahaz to 715 B.C. (*see note on 16:2*). *See notes on 2Ch 29:1–32:32.* With this verse, the writer returned from his digression summarizing the causes of captivity to the historical record of the kings of the southern kingdom, Judah.

18:2 **twenty-nine years.** 715–686 B.C. He reigned by himself for 20 years (715–695 B.C.), and with his son, Manasseh, for 9 years (695–686 B.C.). The 29 years given here indicate only those years after his co-regency with Ahaz was over, when he was the actual sovereign. During Hezekiah's reign, the prophets Isaiah (19:2; Is 1:1; 37:21) and Micah (Mic 1:1) continued to minister in Judah.

18:4 **removed the high places.** Hezekiah was the first king of Judah to totally eradicate the high places, i.e., the worship centers built contrary to the Mosaic law (cf. Dt 12:2–7, 13, 14). ***sacred* pillars ... Asherah.** Hezekiah destroyed the idols used in the worship of Baal and Asherah. **the bronze serpent.** Hezekiah broke the Nehushtan into pieces, i.e., the bronze snake made by Moses in the wilderness (*see notes on Nu 21:4–9*), because Judah had come to worship it as an idol, perhaps influenced by Canaanite religion, which regarded snakes as fertility symbols.

18:5 **He trusted in the LORD, the God of Israel.** The most noble quality of Hezekiah (in dramatic contrast to his father, Ahaz) was that he relied on the Lord as his exclusive hope in every situation. What distinguished him from all other kings of Judah (after the division of the kingdom) was his firm trust in the Lord during a severe national crisis (18:17–19:34). Despite troublesome events, Hezekiah clung tightly to the Lord, faithfully following Him and obeying His commands (v. 6). As a result, the Lord was with him and gave him success (v. 7).

18:7 **he rebelled against ... Assyria.** Before he became king, his father had submitted to Assyria. Courageously, Hezekiah broke that control by Assyria and asserted independence (cf. Dt 7:2).

18:8 **Gaza.** The southernmost city of the Philistines, located about 55 mi. SW of Jerusalem. Since Assyria had controlled Philistia, Hezekiah's invasion defied Assyrian rule and brought the threat of retaliation.

18:9–12 These verses flash back to the time just before Israel's destruction and captivity to give a summary of the fall of Samaria (more fully narrated in 17:5–23) as a graphic reminder of the Assyrian power and the threat they still were to Judah. This review sets the scene for the siege of Jerusalem with its reminder of Israel's apostasy against which Hezekiah's faith in the Lord was a bright contrast.

18:13–20:19 This narrative, with a few omissions and additions, is found in Is 36:1–39:8. *See Isaiah notes* for amplification.

18:13 **fourteenth year.** 701 B.C. Hezekiah began his sole rule in 715 B.C. (*see notes on 18:1, 2*). This date for the siege of Jerusalem is confirmed in Assyrian sources. **Sennacherib.** He succeeded Sargon II as king of Assyria in 705 B.C. and ruled until 681 B.C. Hezekiah had rebelled against him (v. 7), probably by withholding tribute when he invaded Philistia. **fortified cities.** *See note on Is 36:1.*

18:14–16 Hezekiah sought to rectify the situation with Sennacherib by admitting his error in rebelling and paying the tribute the Assyrian king demanded. Sennacherib asked for about 11 tons of silver and one ton of gold. To pay, Hezekiah emptied the temple and palace treasuries and stripped the layers of gold off the doors and doorposts of the temple.

18:17–24 The tribute did not satisfy Sennacherib, who sent messengers to demand Hezekiah's complete surrender.

18:17 **Tartan.** General of the Assyrian army (cf. Is 20:1). **Rab-saris.** A high official in the palace. **Rabshakeh.** The word is not a proper noun, but means "commander." He was the spokesman for Sennacherib, who represented the king against Jerusalem on this occasion. **Lachish.** *See note on 14:19.* Sennacherib's conquest of this city was in its closing phase when he sent the messengers. **large army.** This was a token force of the main army (19:35) with which Sennacherib hoped to bluff Judah into submitting. **conduit of the upper pool.** Isaiah had met Ahaz at the same spot to try, unsuccessfully, to dissuade him from trusting in foreign powers (Is 7:3). It was probably located on the higher ground NW of Jerusalem on the main N-S highway

field. 18 When they called to the king, [A]Eliakim the
son of Hilkiah, who was over the household, and
[B]Shebnah the scribe and Joah the son of Asaph the
recorder, came out to them.
19 Then Rabshakeh said to them, "Say now to Hezekiah, 'Thus says the great king, the king of Assyria,
"[A]What is this confidence that you [a]have? 20 You say
(but *they are* [a]only empty words), '*I have* counsel
and strength for the war.' Now on whom do you rely,
[A]that you have rebelled against me? 21 Now behold,
you [a,A]rely on the staff of this crushed reed, *even* on
Egypt; on which if a man leans, it will go into his
[b]hand and pierce it. So is Pharaoh king of Egypt to
all who rely on him. 22 But if you say to me, 'We trust
in the LORD our God,' is it not He whose high places
and [A]whose altars Hezekiah has taken away, and has
said to Judah and to Jerusalem, 'You shall worship
before this altar in Jerusalem'? 23 Now therefore,
[a]come, make a bargain with my master the king of
Assyria, and I will give you two thousand horses,
if you are able on your part to set riders on them.
24 How then can you [a]repulse one [b]official of the
least of my master's servants, and [c]rely on Egypt
for chariots and for horsemen? 25 Have I now come
up [a]without the LORD'S approval against this place
to destroy it? The LORD said to me, 'Go up against
this land and destroy it.' " ' "
26 Then Eliakim the son of Hilkiah, and Shebnah
and Joah, said to Rabshakeh, "Speak now to your
servants in Aramaic, for we [a]understand *it;* and
do not speak with us in [b,A]Judean in the hearing of
the people who are on the wall." 27 But Rabshakeh
said to them, "Has my master sent me only to your
master and to you to speak these words, *and* not
to the men who sit on the wall, *doomed* to eat their
own dung and drink their own urine with you?"
28 Then Rabshakeh stood and cried with a loud
voice in Judean, [a]saying, "Hear the word of the great
king, the king of Assyria. 29 Thus says the king, '[A]Do
not let Hezekiah deceive you, for he will not be able
to deliver you from [a]my hand; 30 nor let Hezekiah
make you trust in the LORD, saying, "The LORD will
surely deliver us, and this city will not be given into
the hand of the king of Assyria." 31 Do not listen to

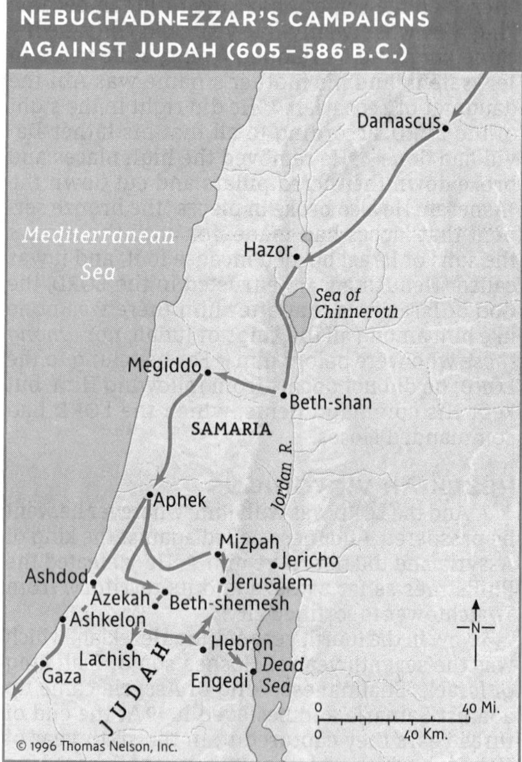

Nebuchadnezzar became king of Babylon in 605 B.C. and conducted several campaigns in Palestine. He squelched Jehoiakim's rebellion in about 602 B.C., deported Jehoiachin in 597 B.C., and destroyed Jerusalem in 586 B.C.

Hezekiah, for thus says the king of Assyria, "[a]Make
your peace with me and come out to me, and eat
[A]each of his vine and each of his fig tree and drink
each of the waters of his own cistern, 32 until I come
and take you away [A]to a land like your own land,
a land of grain and new wine, a land of bread and
vineyards, a land of olive trees and honey, that you

18:18 [A]2 Kin 19:2; Is 22:20 [B]Is 22:15 18:19 [a]Lit *trust* [A]2 Chr 32:10 18:20 [a]Lit *a word of the lips* [A]2 Kin 18:7 18:21 [a]Lit *rely for yourself* [b]Lit *palm* [A]Is 30:2, 3, 7; Ezek 29:6, 7 18:22 [A]2 Kin 18:4; 2 Chr 31:1 18:23 [a]Lit *please exchange pledges* 18:24 [a]Lit *turn away the face of* [b]Or *governor* [c]Lit *rely for yourself* 18:25 [a]Lit *without the LORD* 18:26 [a]Lit *hear* [b]I.e. Hebrew [A]Ezra 4:7; Dan 2:4 18:28 [a]Lit *and spoke, saying,* 18:29 [a]Heb *his* [A]2 Chr 32:15 18:31 [a]Lit *Make with me a blessing* [A]1 Kin 4:20, 25 18:32 [A]Deut 8:7-9; 11:12

between Judah and Samaria. **fuller's.** The word means "launderer" and indicates the field where such activity was done, being near the water supply.

18:18 Eliakim ... Shebnah. Eliakim was the palace administrator and Shebnah, the secretary. *See notes on Is 22:19–22.* **Joah ... the recorder.** The position was that of an intermediary between the king and the people (cf. 2Sa 8:16).

18:19–25 The Rabshakeh's logic was twofold: 1) Egypt would be unable to deliver Jerusalem (vv. 20, 21, 23, 24); and 2) the Lord had called on the Assyrians to destroy Judah (vv. 22, 25).

18:19 great king. Cf. v. 28. The self-appropriated title of Assyrian kings. In contrast, Rabshakeh rudely omitted any title for Hezekiah (vv. 19, 22, 29, 30, 31, 32).

18:20 empty words. *See note on Is 36:5.* **on whom do you rely ... ?** The implication was that Assyria was so strong, there was none stronger.

18:21 crushed reed ... Egypt. The Assyrian's advice strongly resembled that of Isaiah (Is 19:14–16; 30:7; 31:3). Egypt was not strong and could not be counted on for help.

18:22 He whose high places and whose altars. The Rabshakeh mistakenly thought Hezekiah's reforms in removing idols from all over the land and reestablishing central worship in Jerusalem (18:4; 2Ch 31:1) had removed opportunities to worship the Lord, and thus cut back on honoring Judah's God, thereby displeasing Him and forfeiting His help in war. **this altar.** That all worship should center in Solomon's temple was utterly foreign to the polytheistic Assyrians.

18:23, 24 *See note on Is 36:8, 9.*

18:25 The LORD said. *See note on Is 36:10.*

18:26 Aramaic ... Judean. *See note on Is 36:11.*

18:27 men ... on the wall. *See note on Is 36:12.*

18:28–32 The Rabshakeh spoke longer and louder in Heb. suggesting that Hezekiah could not save the city, but the great king of Assyria would fill the people with abundance if they would promise to surrender to his sovereign control, give tribute to him, and be willing to go into a rich and beneficial exile (vv. 31, 32).

18:32 take you away. *See note on Is 36:17.*

18:32–35 *See note on Is 36:18–20.*

may live and not die." But do not listen to Hezekiah
when he misleads you, saying, "The LORD will deliver us." 33 [A]Has any one of the gods of the nations
delivered his land from the hand of the king of
Assyria? 34 [A]Where are the gods of Hamath and
[B]Arpad? Where are the gods of Sepharvaim, Hena
and [a,C]Ivvah? Have they delivered Samaria from
my hand? 35 Who among all the gods of the lands
[a]have delivered their land from my hand, [A]that the
LORD should deliver Jerusalem from my hand?' "
36 But the people were silent and answered him
not a word, for the king's commandment was, "Do
not answer him." 37 Then [A]Eliakim the son of Hilkiah,
who was over the household, and Shebna the scribe
and Joah the son of Asaph, the recorder, came to
Hezekiah [B]with their clothes torn and told him the
words of Rabshakeh.

ISAIAH ENCOURAGES HEZEKIAH

19 [A]And when King Hezekiah heard *it,* he [B]tore
his clothes, [C]covered himself with sackcloth
and entered the house of the LORD. 2 Then he sent
Eliakim who was over the household with Shebna
the scribe and the elders of the priests, [A]covered
with sackcloth, to [B]Isaiah the prophet the son of
Amoz. 3 They said to him, "Thus says Hezekiah, 'This
day is a day of distress, rebuke, and rejection; for
children have come to birth and there is no strength
to *deliver.* 4 [A]Perhaps the LORD your God will hear
all the words of Rabshakeh, whom his master the
king of Assyria has sent [B]to reproach the living
God, and will rebuke the words which the LORD
your God has heard. Therefore, offer a prayer for
[C]the remnant that is left.' " 5 So the servants of King
Hezekiah came to Isaiah. 6 Isaiah said to them, "Thus
you shall say to your master, 'Thus says the LORD,
"Do not be afraid because of the words that you
have heard, with which the [A]servants of the king of
Assyria [B]have blasphemed Me. 7 Behold, I will put
a spirit in him so that [A]he will hear a rumor and
return to his own land. And [B]I will make him fall
by the sword in his own land." ' "

SENNACHERIB DEFIES GOD

8 Then Rabshakeh returned and found the king of
Assyria fighting against [A]Libnah, for he had heard
that [a]the king had left [B]Lachish. 9 When he heard
them say concerning Tirhakah king of [a]Cush, "Behold, he has come out to fight against you," he sent
messengers again to Hezekiah saying, 10 "Thus you
shall say to Hezekiah king of [a]Judah, 'Do not [A]let your
God in whom you trust deceive you saying, "[B]Jeru-
salem will not be given into the hand of the king of
Assyria." 11 Behold, you have heard what the kings of
Assyria have done to all the lands, destroying them
completely. So will you be [a]spared? 12 [A]Did the gods
of [a]those nations which my fathers destroyed deliver
them, *even* [B]Gozan and [C]Haran and Rezeph and [D]the
sons of Eden who *were* in Telassar? 13 [A]Where is the
king of Hamath, the king of Arpad, the king of the
city of Sepharvaim, and *of* Hena and Ivvah?' "

HEZEKIAH'S PRAYER

14 Then [A]Hezekiah took the [a]letter from the hand
of the messengers and read it, and he went up to
the house of the LORD and [b]spread it out before the
LORD. 15 Hezekiah prayed before the LORD and said,
"O LORD, the God of Israel, [A]who are [a]enthroned
above the cherubim, [B]You are the God, You alone,
of all the kingdoms of the earth. You have made
heaven and earth. 16 [A]Incline Your ear, O LORD, and
hear; [B]open Your eyes, O LORD, and see; and listen to
the words of Sennacherib, which he has sent [C]to reproach the living God. 17 Truly, O LORD, the kings of
Assyria have devastated the nations and their lands
18 and have cast their gods into the fire, [A]for they
were not gods but the work of men's hands, wood
and stone. So they have destroyed them. 19 Now,
O LORD our God, I pray, deliver us from his hand
[A]that all the kingdoms of the earth may know that
You alone, O [B]LORD, are God."

GOD'S ANSWER THROUGH ISAIAH

20 Then Isaiah the son of Amoz sent to Hezekiah
saying, "Thus says the LORD, the God of Israel,

18:33 [A]2 Kin 19:12; Is 10:10, 11 18:34 [a]In 2 Kin 17:24, *Avva* [A]2 Kin 19:13 [B]Is 10:9 [C]2 Kin 17:24 18:35 [a]Lit *who have* [A]Ps 2:1-3; 59:7 18:37 [A]2 Kin 18:26 [B]2 Kin 6:30 19:1 [A]2 Chr 32:20-22; Is 37:1 [B]2 Kin 18:37 [C]1 Kin 21:27 19:2 [A]2 Sam 3:31 [B]Is 1:1; 2:1 19:4 [A]Josh 14:12; 2 Sam 16:12 [B]2 Kin 18:35 [C]Is 1:9 19:6 [A]2 Kin 18:17 [B]2 Kin 18:22-25, 30, 35 19:7 [A]2 Kin 7:6 [B]2 Kin 19:37 19:8 [a]Lit *he* [A]Josh 10:29 [B]2 Kin 18:14 19:9 [a]Or *Ethiopia* 19:10 [a]Lit *Judah, saying,* [A]2 Kin 18:5 [B]2 Kin 18:30 19:11 [a]Lit *delivered* 19:12 [a]Lit *the* [A]2 Kin 18:33 [B]2 Kin 17:6 [C]Gen 11:31 [D]Is 37:12 19:13 [A]2 Kin 18:34 19:14 [a]Lit *letters...read them* [b]Lit *Hezekiah spread* [A]Is 37:14 19:15 [a]Lit *seated* [A]Ex 25:22; Is 37:14 [B]2 Kin 5:15 19:16 [A]Ps 31:2; Is 37:17 [B]1 Kin 8:29; 2 Chr 6:40 [C]2 Kin 19:4 19:18 [A]Is 44:9-20; Acts 17:29 19:19 [A]1 Kin 8:42, 43 [B]2 Kin 19:15

18:36 were silent. *See note on Is 36:21.*

18:37 clothes torn. *See note on Is 36:22.*

19:1 tore ... sackcloth. *See note on 6:30.* A reaction that symbolized Hezekiah's grief, repentance, and contrition. The nation had to repent and the king had to lead the way. house of the LORD. *See note on Is 37:1.*

19:2 elders of the priests. *See note on Is 37:2.* Isaiah the prophet. The first reference in 1, 2 Kings to one of the Lord's greatest prophets (cf. Is 1:1). He had already been ministering for 40 years since the days of Uzziah (Is 6:1), also called Azariah (14:21).

19:3 come to birth ... no strength. *See note on Is 37:3.*

19:4 reproach the living God. *See note on Is 37:4.* remnant that is left. *See note on Is 37:4.*

19:6 Do not be afraid. Sennacherib had blasphemed the Lord by equating Him with other gods. The Lord would personally demonstrate to the Assyrian king His superiority over all other so-called deities.

19:7 spirit. The Lord promised to incline Sennacherib's attitude in such a way that he would leave Jerusalem unharmed and return home. How the Lord did that is recorded in vv. 35–37.

19:8 Libnah. *See note on Is 37:8.*

19:9 Tirhakah king of Cush. *See note on Is 37:9.*

19:9–13 The king of Assyria sent messengers to summarize the arguments given in the Rabshakeh's ultimatum of 18:19–25.

19:10 deceive. The accusation of deception was first against Hezekiah (18:29), then against the Lord.

19:11–13 The threat repeated the thrust of 18:33–35.

19:12, 13 The conquered cities mentioned here lay between the Tigris and Euphrates Rivers in Mesopotamia, and were cities of Syria that had recently fallen to Sennacherib and the Assyrians.

19:14 house of the LORD. Godly Hezekiah returned to the house of the Lord (cf. v. 1) as he should have, in contrast to Ahaz who in a similar crisis refused even to ask a sign from the Lord (Is 7:11, 12).

19:15 are enthroned ... made heaven and earth. *See note on Is 37:16.*

19:16 hear ... see ... listen. *See note on Is 37:17.*

19:17, 18 *See note on Is 37:18, 19.*

19:19 You alone. *See note on Is 37:20.*

19:20 Isaiah the son of Amoz. *See note on Is 37:21.*

'Because you have prayed to Me about Sennacherib king of Assyria, [A]I have heard *you*.' [21]This is the word that the LORD has spoken against him:

'She has despised you and mocked you,
[A]The virgin daughter of Zion;
She [B]has shaken *her* head behind you,
The daughter of Jerusalem!
22 'Whom have you [A]reproached
and [B]blasphemed?
And against whom have you
raised *your* voice,
And [a]haughtily lifted up your eyes?
Against the [C]Holy One of Israel!
23 '[A]Through your messengers you
have reproached the Lord,
And you have said, "With
my many chariots
I came up to the heights of the mountains,
To the remotest parts of Lebanon;
And I [a]cut down its tall cedars
and its choice cypresses.
And I [a]entered its farthest lodging
place, its [B]thickest forest.
24 "I dug *wells* and drank foreign waters,
And with the sole of my feet I [a,A]dried up
All the rivers of [b]Egypt."

25 '[A]Have you not heard?
Long ago I did it;
From ancient times I planned it.
[B]Now I have brought it to pass,
That you should turn fortified
cities into ruinous heaps.
26 'Therefore their inhabitants
were short of strength,
They were dismayed and put to shame;
They were [A]as the vegetation of the
field and as the green herb,
As grass on the housetops is
scorched before it is grown up.
27 'But [A]I know your sitting down,
And your going out and your coming in,
And your raging against Me.
28 'Because of your raging against Me,
And because your [a]arrogance
has come up to My ears,
Therefore I [A]will put My hook in your nose,
And My bridle in your lips,
And [B]I will turn you back by the
way which you came.

[29]'Then this shall be [A]the sign for you: [a]you will eat
this year what grows of itself, in the second year what
springs from the same, and in the third year sow, reap,
plant vineyards, and eat their fruit. [30][A]The surviving
remnant of the house of Judah will again take root
downward and bear fruit upward. [31]For out of Jerusalem will go forth a remnant, and [A]out of Mount Zion
[a]survivors. [B]The zeal of [b]the LORD will perform this.
[32]'Therefore thus says the LORD concerning the
king of Assyria, "[A]He will not come to this city or
shoot an arrow there; and he will not come before
it with a shield or throw up a siege ramp against
it. [33][A]By the way that he came, by the same he will
return, and he shall not come to this city," ' declares
the LORD. [34]'[A]For I will defend this city to save it for
My own sake and [B]for My servant David's sake.' "
[35][A]Then it happened that night that the angel of
the LORD went out and struck 185,000 in the camp
of the Assyrians; and when [a]men rose early in the
morning, behold, all of them were [b]dead. [36]So [A]Sen-
nacherib king of Assyria departed and returned
home, and lived at [B]Nineveh. [37]It came about as he
was worshiping in the house of Nisroch his god, that
[a,A]Adrammelech and Sharezer killed him with the
sword; and they escaped into [B]the land of Ararat.
And [C]Esarhaddon his son became king in his place.

HEZEKIAH'S ILLNESS AND RECOVERY

20 [A]In those days Hezekiah became [a]mortally
ill. And Isaiah the prophet the son of Amoz

19:20 [A]2 Kin 20:5 19:21 [A]Jer 14:17; Lam 2:13 [B]Ps 109:25; Matt 27:39 19:22 [a]Lit *on high* [A]2 Kin 19:4 [B]2 Kin 19:6 [C]Is 5:24; 30:11-15 19:23 [a]So with some ancient versions; M.T. *will cut...will enter* [A]2 Kin 18:17 [B]2 Chr 26:10; Is 10:18 19:24 [a]So with some ancient versions; M.T. *will dry up* [b]Lit *the besieged place* [A]Is 19:6 19:25 [A]Is 45:7 [B]Is 10:5 19:26 [A]Ps 129:6 19:27 [A]Ps 139:1 19:28 [a]Lit *complacency* [A]Ezek 19:9; 29:4 [B]2 Kin 19:33, 36 19:29 [a]Lit *eating* [A]Ex 3:12; 2 Kin 20:8, 9 19:30 [A]2 Kin 19:4; 2 Chr 32:22, 23 19:31 [a]Lit *those who escape* [b]Some ancient mss read *the LORD of hosts* [A]Is 10:20 [B]Is 9:7 19:32 [A]Is 8:7-10 19:33 [A]2 Kin 19:28 19:34 [A]2 Kin 20:6; Is 31:5 [B]1 Kin 11:12, 13 19:35 [a]Lit *they* [b]Lit *dead bodies* [A]2 Sam 24:16; 2 Chr 32:21 19:36 [A]2 Kin 19:7, 28, 33 [B]Jon 1:2 19:37 [a]Some ancient mss read *Adrammelech and Sharezer his sons smote him* [A]2 Kin 19:17, 31 [B]Gen 8:4; Jer 51:27 [C]Ezra 4:2 20:1 [a]Lit *sick to the point of death* [A]2 Chr 32:24; Is 38:1-22

19:21 mocked you. *See note on Is 37:22.*

19:22 you reproached and blasphemed. The Lord had heard Sennacherib's reproach against Him (v. 16).

19:23, 24 *See note on Is 37:24, 25.*

19:25–28 I have brought it to pass. *See notes on Is 37:26–29.*

19:29 sign. The two years in which they were sustained by the growth of the crops were the two in which Sennacherib ravaged them. He left immediately after the deliverance (v. 36), so in the third year the people remaining could plant again.

19:30, 31 remnant ... remnant. From the remnant of survivors in Jerusalem came descendants who covered the land once again (cf. Is 1:9, 27; 3:10; 4:3; 6:13; 8:16, 17; 10:20, 22; 11:12, 16; 26:1–4, 8; 27:12; 28:5; 37:4).

19:31 zeal of the LORD. The same confirmation of God's promise in 19:7 assured the future establishment of the messianic kingdom. Deliverance from Sennacherib in Hezekiah's day was a down payment on the literal, final restoration of Israel at Christ's second coming.

19:32 will not come ... throw up a siege ramp. *See note on Is 37:33.*

19:33 he will return. *See note on Is 37:34.*

19:34 for My own sake. Since Sennacherib had directly challenged the Lord's faithfulness to His Word (v. 10), the faithfulness of God was at stake in this contest with the Assyrians (cf. Eze 36:22, 23). **for My servant David's sake.** God pledged to perpetuate David's line on his throne (2Sa 7:16; cf. Is 9:6, 7; 11:1; 55:3).

19:35 the angel of the LORD. For identification, *see note on Ex 3:2.* For the angel as an agent of destruction, see Ge 19:15; 2Sa 24:16.

19:35–37 struck. *See notes on Is 37:36–38.*

20:1 In those days ... mortally ill. The date of Hezekiah's sickness poses 3 reasonable possibilities: 1) since Hezekiah would be given 15 years of life and delivered from the Assyrians (v. 6), the sickness occurred ca. 701 B.C.; 2) since Berodach-baladan (v. 12) died in 703 B.C., the sickness occurred shortly before and was followed by the embassy from Babylon that saw the temple treasures (vv. 12–19); or 3) since Berodach-baladan's greatest power was ca. 721–710 B.C., Hezekiah's sickness occurred during those years. The first or second possibility is most likely. **Set your house in order.** An instruction telling Hezekiah to make his final will known to his family (cf. 2Sa 17:23). **you shall die and not live.** The prediction sounded final, but Hezekiah knew God was willing to hear his appeal (cf. Ex 32:7–14).

came to him and said to him, "Thus says the LORD,
'[B]Set your house in order, for you shall die and not
live.' " 2 Then he turned his face to the wall and
prayed to the LORD, saying, 3 "[A]Remember now,
O LORD, I beseech You, [B]how I have walked before
You in truth and with a whole heart and have done
what is good in Your sight." And [C]Hezekiah wept
[a]bitterly. 4 Before Isaiah had gone out of the middle
court, the word of the LORD came to him, saying,
5 "Return and say to [A]Hezekiah the leader of My
people, 'Thus says the LORD, the God of your father
David, "[B]I have heard your prayer, [C]I have seen your
tears; behold, I will heal you. On the third day you
shall go up to the house of the LORD. 6 I will add
fifteen years to your [a]life, and I will deliver you and
this city from the hand of the king of Assyria; and
[A]I will defend this city for My own sake and for My
servant David's sake." ' " 7 Then Isaiah said, "Take a
cake of figs." And they took and laid *it* on the boil,
and he recovered.

8 Now Hezekiah said to Isaiah, "What will be the
sign that the LORD will heal me, and that I shall go
up to the house of the LORD the third day?" 9 Isaiah
said, "[A]This shall be the sign to you from the LORD,
that the LORD will do the thing that He has spoken:
shall the shadow go forward ten steps or go back ten
steps?" 10 So Hezekiah [a]answered, "It is easy for the
shadow to decline ten steps; no, but let the shadow
turn backward ten steps." 11 Isaiah the prophet cried
to the LORD, and [A]He brought the shadow on the
[a]stairway back ten steps by which it had gone down
on the [a]stairway of Ahaz.

HEZEKIAH SHOWS BABYLON HIS TREASURES

12 [A]At that time [a]Berodach-baladan a son of Bal-
adan, king of Babylon, sent letters and a present to
Hezekiah, for he heard that Hezekiah had been sick.
13 Hezekiah listened to them, and showed them [A]all
his treasure house, the silver and the gold and the
spices and the precious oil and the house of his armor and all that was found in his treasuries. There
was nothing in his house nor in all his dominion
that Hezekiah did not show them. 14 Then Isaiah the
prophet came to King Hezekiah and said to him,
"What did these men say, and from where have
they come to you?" And Hezekiah said, "They have
come from a far country, from Babylon." 15 He said,
"What have they seen in your house?" So Hezekiah
[a]answered, "They have seen all that is in my house;
there is nothing among my treasuries that I have
not shown them."

16 Then Isaiah said to Hezekiah, "Hear the word
of the LORD. 17 'Behold, the days are coming when
[A]all that is in your house, and all that your fathers
have laid up in store to this day will be carried
to Babylon; nothing shall be left,' says the LORD.
18 'Some [A]of your sons who shall issue from you,
whom you will beget, will be taken away; and they
will become [B]officials in the palace of the king of
Babylon.' " 19 Then Hezekiah said to Isaiah, "The
word of the LORD which you have spoken is [A]good."
For he [a]thought, "Is it not so, if there will be peace
and truth in my days?"

20 [A]Now the rest of the acts of Hezekiah and all his
might, and how he [B]made the pool and the conduit
and brought water into the city, are they not written
in the Book of the Chronicles of the Kings of Judah?
21 [A]So Hezekiah slept with his fathers, and Manasseh
his son became king in his place.

MANASSEH SUCCEEDS HEZEKIAH

21 [A]Manasseh was twelve years old when he became king, and he reigned fifty-five years in
Jerusalem; and his mother's name was Hephzibah.
2 [A]He did evil in the sight of the LORD, [B]according to

20:1 [B]2 Sam 17:23 20:3 [a]Lit *great weeping* [A]Neh 5:19; 13:14, 22, 31 [B]2 Kin 18:3-6 [C]2 Sam 12:21, 22 20:5 [A]1 Sam 9:16; 10:1 [B]2 Kin 19:20 [C]Ps 39:12 20:6 [a]Lit *days* [A]2 Kin 19:34 20:9 [A]Is 38:7 20:10 [a]Lit *said* 20:11 [a]Lit *steps* [A]Josh 10:12-14; Is 38:8 20:12 [a]Many mss and ancient versions read *Merodach-baladan;* cf Is 39:1 [A]2 Chr 32:31; Is 39:1-8 20:13 [A]2 Chr 32:27 20:15 [a]Lit *said* 20:17 [A]2 Kin 24:13; 25:13-15; 2 Chr 36:10; Jer 52:17-19 20:18 [A]2 Kin 24:12; 2 Chr 33:11 [B]Dan 1:3-7 20:19 [a]Lit *said* [A]1 Sam 3:18 20:20 [A]2 Chr 32:32 [B]Neh 3:16 20:21 [A]2 Chr 32:33 21:1 [A]2 Chr 33:1-9 21:2 [A]Jer 15:4 [B]2 Kin 16:3

20:2, 3 prayed ... wept bitterly. Hezekiah reminded the Lord in prayer of his piety and devotion to God. He did not specifically ask to be healed. Based on the interpretation of the date from v. 1, Hezekiah wept because: 1) he thought his death would give Sennacherib cause for boasting; or 2) his son Manasseh was too young to become king.

20:3 whole heart. *See note on Is 38:3.*

20:6 fifteen years. The Lord's immediate (v. 4) response granted the king's request. Having to reverse a prophecy so quickly did not alarm Isaiah as it did Jonah later on (Jon 4:2, 3). Isaiah resembled Nathan in this respect (2Sa 7:3–6). **I will deliver ... this city.** *See note on Is 38:6.*

20:8–11 sign ... back ten steps. Here is the first biblical mention of any means of marking time. Hezekiah requested this sign to confirm the Lord's promise of healing.

20:12 At that time. Just after Hezekiah's sickness and recovery. **Berodach-baladan.** Berodach-baladan (see marginal note), ruler of the city of Babylon, defied Assyria repeatedly between 721 and 710 B.C. He apparently approached Hezekiah (ca. 703 B.C.) for help against Sargon, king of Assyria, though interest in the reversal of the sundial (2Ch 32:31) and Hezekiah's recovery may have been part of his motivation.

20:13 Hezekiah listened. The text does not say whether it was because of flattery or out of a desire for help against the Assyrian threat. Cf. "pleased" in Is 39:2.

20:13, 14 treasure house ... treasuries. *See notes on Is 39:2, 3.*

20:16, 17 word of the LORD ... carried to Babylon. Isaiah predicted the Babylonian captivity that would come over a century later (586 B.C.), another prophecy historically fulfilled in all of its expected detail.

20:17 nothing shall be left. Hezekiah's sin of parading his wealth before the visitors backfired, though this sin was only symptomatic of the ultimate reason for the captivity. The major cause was the corrupt leadership of Manasseh, Hezekiah's son (21:11–15).

20:18 sons who shall issue from you. Hezekiah's sons had to go into captivity. See 24:12–16; 2Ch 33:11; Da 1:3, 4, 6 for the prophecy's fulfillment.

20:19 word of the LORD ... good. A surprising response to the negative prophecy of vv. 16–18. It acknowledged Isaiah as God's faithful messenger, and God's goodness in not destroying Jerusalem during Hezekiah's lifetime. **peace and truth in my days.** Hezekiah might have reacted selfishly, or perhaps he looked for a bright spot to lighten the gloomy fate of his descendants.

20:20 conduit. *See note on 2Ch 32:30.*

21:1 twelve years old. Manasseh began to reign as co-regent alongside his father, Hezekiah, in 695 B.C. Since the years of the subsequent royal reigns in Judah total 10 years longer than the actual historical period and the dates of the later kings synchronize well with history, it is best to assume a 10 year co-regency in Manasseh's long reign. Hezekiah groomed his son as a youth to succeed him as king; however, Manasseh turned out to be the worst king in Judah's history. **fifty-five years.** 695–642 B.C. *See notes on 2Ch 33:1–20.*

21:2 the abominations of the nations. The detestable practices of the Canaanites were enumerated in Dt 18:9–12. Israel's re-

the abominations of the nations whom the LORD
dispossessed before the sons of Israel. 3 For [A]he
rebuilt the high places which Hezekiah his father
had destroyed; and [B]he erected altars for Baal and
made an [a]Asherah, as Ahab king of Israel had done,
and [C]worshiped all the host of heaven and served
them. 4 [A]He built altars in the house of the LORD, of
which the LORD had said, "[B]In Jerusalem I will put
My name." 5 For he built altars for [A]all the host of
heaven in [B]the two courts of the house of the LORD.
6 [A]He made his son pass through the fire, [B]practiced
witchcraft and used divination, and dealt with mediums and spiritists. He did much evil in the sight
of the LORD provoking *Him to anger.* 7 Then [A]he set
the carved image of Asherah that he had made, in
the house of which the LORD said to David and to
his son Solomon, "[B]In this house and in Jerusalem,
which I have chosen from all the tribes of Israel,
I will put My name forever. 8 And I [A]will not make
the feet of Israel wander anymore from the land
which I gave their fathers, if only they will observe
to do according to all that I have commanded them,
and according to all the law that My servant Moses
commanded them." 9 But they did not listen, and
Manasseh [A]seduced them to do evil more than the
nations whom the LORD destroyed before the sons
of Israel.

THE KING'S IDOLATRIES REBUKED

10 Now the LORD spoke through His servants the
prophets, saying, 11 "[A]Because Manasseh king of
Judah has done these abominations, [B]having done
wickedly more than all the Amorites did who *were*
before him, and [C]has also made Judah sin [D]with
his idols; 12 therefore thus says the LORD, the God
of Israel, 'Behold, I am bringing *such* calamity on
Jerusalem and Judah, that whoever hears of it, [A]both
his ears will tingle. 13 [A]I will stretch over Jerusalem
the line of Samaria and the plummet of the house
of Ahab, and I will wipe Jerusalem as one wipes
a dish, wiping it and turning it upside down. 14 I
will abandon the remnant of My inheritance and
deliver them into the hand of their enemies, and
they will become as plunder and spoil to all their
enemies; 15 because they have done evil in My sight,
and have been provoking Me to anger since the day
their fathers came from Egypt, even to this day.' "

16 [A]Moreover, Manasseh shed very much innocent
blood until he had filled Jerusalem from one end
to another; besides his sin [B]with which he made
Judah sin, in doing evil in the sight of the LORD.
17 [A]Now the rest of the acts of Manasseh and all that
he did and his sin which he [a]committed, are they not
written in the Book of the Chronicles of the Kings
of Judah? 18 [A]And Manasseh slept with his fathers
and was buried in the garden of his own house,
[B]in the garden of Uzza, and Amon his son became
king in his place.

AMON SUCCEEDS MANASSEH

19 [A]Amon was twenty-two years old when he became king, and he reigned two years in Jerusalem;
and his mother's name *was* Meshullemeth the daughter of Haruz of Jotbah. 20 He did evil in the sight of
the LORD, [A]as Manasseh his father had done. 21 For
he walked in all the way that his father had walked,
and served the idols that his father had served and
worshiped them. 22 So [A]he forsook the LORD, the God
of his fathers, and did not walk in the way of the
LORD. 23 [A]The servants of Amon conspired against
him and killed the king in his own house. 24 Then [A]the
people of the land [a]killed all those who had conspired

21:3 [a]I.e. a wooden symbol of a female deity [A]2 Kin 18:4 [B]1 Kin 16:31-33 [C]Deut 17:2-5; 2 Kin 17:16; 23:5 21:4 [A]2 Kin 16:10-16 [B]2 Sam 7:13; 1 Kin 8:29 21:5 [A]2 Kin 23:4, 5 [B]1 Kin 7:12; 2 Kin 23:12 21:6 [A]Lev 18:21; 2 Kin 16:3; 17:17 [B]Lev 19:26, 31; Deut 18:10-14 21:7 [A]Deut 16:21; 2 Kin 23:6 [B]1 Kin 8:29; 9:3; 2 Chr 7:12, 16 21:8 [A]2 Sam 7:10; 2 Kin 18:11, 12 21:9 [A]Prov 29:12 21:11 [A]2 Kin 21:2; 24:3, 4 [B]Gen 15:16; 1 Kin 21:26 [C]2 Kin 21:16 [D]2 Kin 21:21 21:12 [A]1 Sam 3:11; Jer 19:3 21:13 [A]Is 34:11; Amos 7:7, 8 21:16 [A]2 Kin 24:4 [B]2 Kin 21:11 21:17 [a]Lit *sinned* [A]2 Chr 33:11-19 21:18 [A]2 Chr 33:20 [B]2 Kin 21:26 21:19 [A]2 Chr 33:21-23 21:20 [A]2 Kin 21:2-6, 11, 16 21:22 [A]2 Kin 22:17; 1 Chr 28:9 21:23 [A]2 Kin 12:20; 14:19 21:24 [a]Lit *smote* [A]2 Kin 14:5

production of these abominable practices of the nations that preceded her in the land was forbidden in Dt 12:29–31. The idolatry of Manasseh is detailed in vv. 3–9 (cf. 17:7–12, 15–17).

21:3 high places ... altars ... Asherah. Manasseh reversed the reforms of Hezekiah (cf. 18:4), reestablishing the worship of Baal as an official state-sanctioned religion in Judah, just as Ahab had done in Israel (cf. 1Ki 16:30–33). **host of heaven.** *See note on 17:16.* The worship of the sun, moon, and stars was prohibited in Dt 4:19; 17:2–5.

21:4 altars in the house of the LORD. These altars were dedicated to "the host of heaven" (v. 5).

21:6 made his son pass through the fire. *See note on 16:3.* **witchcraft ... divination ... mediums and spiritists.** The king was engaged in every form of occultism, including black magic, fortune-telling, demon contacts, and wizards. All this was in direct violation of God's law (Lv 19:31; Dt 18:9–12).

21:7 set ... put. Manasseh provoked the Lord by "setting" an idol of a Canaanite goddess in the temple where the Lord had "set" His name (see 1Ki 8:29; 9:3; 2Ch 7:12, 16). Asherah (cf. 23:4; 2Ch 15:16) was believed to be the mother of 70 deities, including Baal.

21:8, 9 This alludes to the promise of 2Sa 7:10. From the very start of their time in Canaan, the people were called to this obedience, but because the people of Judah did not follow carefully the stipulations of the Mosaic law, they were again led into idolatry by Manasseh. Their idolatry even exceeded the idolatry of the Canaanites from whom they took the land.

21:10 the prophets. Through his spokesman, the Lord announced Judah's judgment. In vv. 11–15, the prophetic message to Judah is summarized.

21:11 Amorites. A general designation of the original inhabitants of Canaan (cf. Ge 15:16; Jos 24:8).

21:13 the plummet. These were weighted lines dropped from walls to see whether they were structurally straight (cf. Is 28:17; Am 7:7, 8). Walls out of line were torn down. The Lord had measured Jerusalem by the standard of His Word and had determined that the fate of Samaria (Israel) was also to befall Jerusalem. **wipe Jerusalem.** As one would wipe food off a dish, the Lord would wipe Jerusalem clean off the earth, i.e., obliterate her, and leave her turned upside down, empty, and useless.

21:14 abandon. The Lord was going to abandon His people into the hands of enemies who would plunder them (cf. Jer 12:7). **remnant.** Judah, the only remaining group of the chosen people.

21:15 provoking Me to anger. The history of God's people Israel was a history of disobedience toward the Lord. With the reign of Manasseh, the sin of God's people climaxed, God's patience was withdrawn, and the judgment of exile became inevitable (cf. 24:1–4).

21:16 very much innocent blood. The reference here is ambiguous and several interpretations have been offered: 1) child sacrifice (cf. v. 6); 2) oppression and persecution of the weak (Jer 7:6; 22:3, 17; Eze 22:6–31); or 3) the martyrdom of God's prophets (cf. v. 10). A combination of all 3 is most likely. Jewish and Christian tradition alike report that Manasseh had Isaiah sawn in two inside a hollow log (cf. Heb 11:37).

21:19 two years. 642–640 B.C. Amon continued the idolatrous practices of his father, abandoning the Lord completely (vv. 20–22). *See note on 2Ch 33:21–25.*

21:24 the people of the land. Probably a group of Judah's national leaders who killed

against King Amon, and the people of the land made
Josiah his son king in his place. 25 Now the rest of
the acts of Amon which he did, are they not written
in the Book of the Chronicles of the Kings of Judah?
26 He was buried in his grave [A]in the garden of Uzza,
and Josiah his son became king in his place.

JOSIAH SUCCEEDS AMON

22 [A]Josiah was eight years old when he became
king, and he reigned thirty-one years in Jerusalem; and his mother's name *was* Jedidah the
daughter of Adaiah of [B]Bozkath. 2 He did right in
the sight of the LORD and walked in all the way of
his father David, nor did he [A]turn aside to the right
or to the left.

3 Now [A]in the eighteenth year of King Josiah, the
king sent Shaphan, the son of Azaliah the son of
Meshullam the scribe, to the house of the LORD
saying, 4 "[A]Go up to Hilkiah the high priest that he
may [a]count the money brought in to the house of the
LORD which the doorkeepers have gathered from
the people. 5 [A]Let them deliver it into the hand of the
workmen who have the oversight of the house of the
LORD, and let them give it to the workmen who are
in the house of the LORD to repair the [a]damages of
the house, 6 to the carpenters and the builders and
the masons and for buying timber and hewn stone
to repair the house. 7 Only [A]no accounting shall be
made with them for the money delivered into their
hands, for they deal faithfully."

THE LOST BOOK

8 Then Hilkiah the high priest said to Shaphan
the scribe, "[A]I have found the book of the law in the
house of the LORD." And Hilkiah gave the book to
Shaphan who read it. 9 Shaphan the scribe came to
the king and brought back word to the king and said,
"Your servants have emptied out the money that
was found in the house, and have delivered it into
the hand of the workmen who have the oversight
of the house of the LORD." 10 Moreover, Shaphan
the scribe told the king saying, "Hilkiah the priest
has given me a book." And Shaphan read it in the
presence of the king.

11 When the king heard the words of the book
of the law, [A]he tore his clothes. 12 Then the king
commanded Hilkiah the priest, [A]Ahikam the son of
Shaphan, [a,B]Achbor the son of Micaiah, Shaphan the
scribe, and Asaiah the king's servant saying, 13 "Go,
inquire of the LORD for me and the people and all
Judah concerning the words of this book that has
been found, for [A]great is the wrath of the LORD that
burns against us, because our fathers have not listened to the words of this book, to do according to
all that is written concerning us."

HULDAH PREDICTS

14 So Hilkiah the priest, Ahikam, Achbor, Shaphan,
and Asaiah went to Huldah the prophetess, the wife
of Shallum the son of [a,A]Tikvah, the son of Harhas,
keeper of the wardrobe (now she lived in Jerusalem
in the [B]Second Quarter); and they spoke to her. 15 She
said to them, "Thus says the LORD God of Israel, 'Tell
the man who sent you to me, 16 thus says the LORD,
"Behold, I [A]bring evil on this place and on its inhabitants, *even* all the words of the book which the king of
Judah has read. 17 [A]Because they have forsaken Me and
have burned incense to other gods that they might

21:26 [A]2 Kin 21:18 22:1 [A]2 Chr 34:1 [B]Josh 15:39 22:2 [A]Deut 5:32; Josh 1:7 22:3 [A]2 Chr 34:8 22:4 [a]Or *total* [A]2 Kin 12:4, 9, 10 22:5 [a]Lit *breach* [A]2 Kin 12:11-14 22:7 [A]2 Kin 12:15; 1 Cor 4:2 22:8 [A]Deut 31:24-26; 2 Chr 34:14, 15 22:11 [A]Gen 37:34; Josh 7:6 22:12 [a]In 2 Chr 34:20, *Abdon, son of Micah* [A]2 Kin 25:22; Jer 26:24 [B]2 Chr 34:20 22:13 [A]Deut 29:23-28; 31:17, 18 22:14 [a]In 2 Chr 34:22, *Tokhath, son of Hasrah* [A]2 Chr 34:22 [B]Zeph 1:10 22:16 [A]Deut 29:27; Dan 9:11-14 22:17 [A]Deut 29:25, 26; 2 Kin 21:22

the assassins of Amon and installed his son Josiah on the throne. Apparently, they desired to maintain the Davidic dynasty (cf. 2Ki 11:14–18).

22:1 **thirty-one years.** 640–609 B.C. During Josiah's reign, power in the ancient Near East passed from Assyria to Babylon. Nineveh, the capital of Assyria, was destroyed by the Babylonians in 612 B.C. and the whole Assyrian empire fell in 609 B.C. Josiah was the last good king of the Davidic line prior to the Babylonian exile. Jeremiah (Jer 1:2), possibly Habakkuk, and Zephaniah (Zep 1:1) were prophets to Judah during the reign of Josiah. *See notes on 2Ch 34:1–35:27.*

22:2 **nor did he turn aside.** Josiah had complete devotion to God's approved course of conduct for his life (cf. 23:25). He obeyed the Mosaic stipulations as he came to know them, following the example of David, who set the pattern for the rulers of God's people (Dt 17:11, 20; Jos 1:7).

22:3 **eighteenth year.** 622 B.C., when Josiah was 26 years of age.

22:4 **Hilkiah.** The High Priest was the father of Azariah and the grandfather of Seraiah, the High Priest who would be executed at the time of the exile by the Babylonians (cf. 25:8–20).

22:4–7 **the doorkeepers.** *See note on 12:9.* Josiah used the same procedure as King Joash had for collecting funds to repair the temple after its abuse in the days of Manasseh and Amon.

22:8 **the book of the law.** A scroll containing the Torah (the Pentateuch), the revelation of God through Moses to Israel (*see notes on 23:2; Dt 28:61*). Manasseh may have destroyed all the copies of God's law that were not hidden. This could have been the official copy laid beside the ark of the covenant in the Most Holy Place (Dt 31:25, 26). It may have been removed from its place under Ahaz, Manasseh, or Amon (cf. 2Ch 35:3), but was found during repair work.

22:9, 10 Some believe that Shaphan must have read Dt 28–30, in which are recorded a renewal of the national covenant and a listing of the terrible threats and curses against all who violate the law of God.

22:11 **tore his clothes.** Josiah's reaction at the reading of the law was one of immediate contrition, expressed by the common sign of lamentation and grief (see 18:37; 19:1). Josiah's grief sprang from Judah's guilt and God's punishment (v. 13).

22:14 **Huldah.** This prophetess is otherwise unknown in the OT. She was held in some regard for her prophetic gift, though why she was consulted and not another prophet like Jeremiah or Zephaniah (*see note on 22:1*) is unexplained. Rarely did God speak to the nation through a woman (cf. Miriam, Ex 15; Deborah, Jdg 5), and never did a woman have an ongoing prophetic ministry identified in Scripture. No woman was inspired to author any of Scripture's 66 books. **the wardrobe.** Likely, these were the royal garments or those used by the priests. **the Second Quarter.** This district of Jerusalem was called "second" because it comprised the city's first major expansion. It was probably located on the western hill of Jerusalem, an area enclosed by the city wall and built during the reign of Hezekiah. The expansion of the city during Hezekiah's reign was perhaps to accommodate Jewish refugees who had escaped from the Assyrian invasion of Israel.

22:15–20 Huldah gave God's message to Josiah through his messengers. First, the Lord confirmed to Josiah that He was surely going to bring His judgment upon Jerusalem because of her idolatry (vv. 15–17). Second, the Lord's personal word to Josiah was that he would die "in peace" (v. 20), meaning that he would escape the horrors in store for Jerusalem. This promise was based on Josiah's response of tenderness and humility before the Lord when he heard the scroll describing Judah's future devastation (vv. 18, 19).

provoke Me to anger with all the work of their hands,
therefore My wrath burns against this place, and it
shall not be quenched." ' 18 But to [A]the king of Judah
who sent you to inquire of the LORD thus shall you say
to him, 'Thus says the LORD God of Israel, "*Regarding*
the words which you have heard, 19 [A]because your
heart was tender and [B]you humbled yourself before
the LORD when you heard what I spoke against this
place and against its inhabitants that they should become [C]a desolation and a [D]curse, and you have [E]torn
your clothes and wept before Me, I truly have heard
you," declares the LORD. 20 "Therefore, behold, I will
gather you to your fathers, and [A]you will be gathered
to your grave in peace, and your eyes will not see all
the evil which I will bring on this place." ' " So they
brought back word to the king.

JOSIAH'S COVENANT

23 [A]Then the king sent, and they gathered to him
all the elders of Judah and of Jerusalem. 2 The
king went up to the house of the LORD and all the
men of Judah and all the inhabitants of Jerusalem
with him, and the priests and the prophets and all
the people, both small and great; and [A]he read in
their hearing all the words of the book of the covenant [B]which was found in the house of the LORD.
3 [A]The king stood by the pillar and made a covenant
before the LORD, [B]to walk after the LORD, and to keep
His commandments and His testimonies and His
statutes with all *his* heart and all *his* soul, to carry out
the words of this covenant that were written in this
book. And all the people [a]entered into the covenant.

REFORMS UNDER JOSIAH

4 Then the king commanded Hilkiah the high priest
and [A]the priests of the second order and the [a]door-
keepers, [B]to bring out of the temple of the LORD all
the vessels that were made for Baal, for [b]Asherah, and
for all the host of heaven; and [C]he burned them outside Jerusalem in the fields of the Kidron, and carried
their ashes to Bethel. 5 He did away with the idolatrous
priests whom the kings of Judah had appointed to
burn incense in the high places in the cities of Judah
and in the surrounding area of Jerusalem, also those
who burned incense to Baal, to the sun and to the
moon and to the constellations and to all the [A]host of
heaven. 6 He brought out the Asherah from the house
of the LORD outside Jerusalem to the brook Kidron,
and burned it at the brook Kidron, and [A]ground *it* to
dust, and [B]threw its dust on the graves of the [a]common
people. 7 He also broke down the houses of the [A]*male*
cult prostitutes which *were* in the house of the LORD,
where [B]the women were weaving [a]hangings for the
Asherah. 8 Then he brought all the priests from the
cities of Judah, and defiled the high places where the
priests had burned incense, from [A]Geba to Beersheba;
and he broke down the high places of the gates which
were at the entrance of the gate of Joshua the governor
of the city, which *were* on one's left at the city gate.
9 Nevertheless [A]the priests of the high places did not
go up to the altar of the LORD in Jerusalem, but they
ate unleavened bread among their brothers. 10 [A]He
also defiled [a]Topheth, which is in the valley of the son
of Hinnom, [B]that no man might make his son or his
daughter pass through the fire for [C]Molech. 11 He did
away with the horses which the kings of Judah had
given to the [A]sun, at the entrance of the house of the
LORD, by the chamber of Nathan-melech the official,
which *was* in the precincts; and he burned the chariots
of the sun with fire. 12 [A]The altars which *were* on the
roof, the upper chamber of Ahaz, which the kings of
Judah had made, and [B]the altars which Manasseh had
made in the two courts of the house of the LORD, the
king broke down; and he [a]smashed them there and

22:18 [A]2 Chr 34:26 22:19 [A]1 Sam 24:5; Ps 51:17 [B]Ex 10:3; 1 Kin 21:29 [C]Lev 26:31 [D]Jer 26:6 [E]2 Kin 22:11 22:20 [A]2 Kin 23:30 23:1 [A]2 Chr 34:29-32 23:2 [A]Deut 31:10-13 [B]2 Kin 22:8 23:3 [a]Lit *took a stand in* [A]2 Kin 11:14, 17 [B]Deut 13:4 23:4 [a]Lit *keepers of the threshold* [b]I.e. a wooden symbol of a female deity, and so throughout the ch [A]2 Kin 25:18; Jer 52:24 [B]2 Kin 21:3, 7; 2 Chr 33:3 [C]2 Kin 23:15 23:5 [A]2 Kin 21:3 23:6 [a]Lit *sons of the people* [A]2 Kin 23:15 [B]2 Chr 34:4 23:7 [a]Or *tents;* lit *houses* [A]1 Kin 14:24; 15:12 [B]Ex 35:25, 26; Ezek 16:16 23:8 [A]Josh 21:17; 1 Kin 15:22 23:9 [A]Ezek 44:10-14 23:10 [a]I.e. place of burning [A]Is 30:33; Jer 7:31, 32; 19:4-6 [B]Lev 18:21 [C]1 Kin 11:7 23:11 [A]Deut 4:19; Job 31:26; Ezek 8:16 23:12 [a]Or *ran from there* [A]Jer 19:13; Zeph 1:5 [B]2 Kin 21:5; 2 Chr 33:5

22:20 **in peace.** His heart was at peace with God and he never lived to see Jerusalem destroyed, but he did die in battle (2Ch 35:23).

23:2 **book of the covenant.** Although this designation was used in Ex 24:7 with reference to the contents of Ex 20:22–23:33, it seems here to refer to a larger writing. Since the larger part of the Pentateuch focused on the Mosaic Covenant, these 5 books came to be called thusly. Since all the men of Judah and all the inhabitants of Jerusalem were assembled together by Josiah, it seems best to view this as the reading of the whole written law found in Ge 1 through Dt 34 (*see notes on Dt 31:9, 11*).

23:3 **pillar.** *See note on 11:14.* **a covenant ... this covenant.** Josiah made a public, binding agreement to completely obey the Lord by doing all that was commanded in the Book of the Covenant that the people had just heard read to them. Following Josiah's example, all the people promised to keep the stipulations of the Mosaic Covenant. *See notes on 11:17; Ex 24:4–8.*

23:4 **Asherah.** *See note on 21:7.* **the fields of the Kidron.** Josiah burned everything in the temple that was devoted to idolatry. This was done in the lower portion of the Kidron Valley, E of the city of Jerusalem (cf. v. 6). **ashes to Bethel.** Located about 10 mi. N of Jerusalem, Bethel was one of the two original places where Jeroboam I established an apostate worship center (1Ki 12:28–33). Bethel was located just N of the border of Judah in the former northern kingdom, which was then the Assyrian province of Samaria. With a decline in Assyrian power, Josiah was able to exert his religious influence in the N. He used the ashes of the burned articles of idolatry to desecrate Jeroboam's religious center (cf. vv. 15–20).

23:5 **constellations.** Cf. 21:3. The astrologers were also removed. See Is 47:13.

23:6 **Asherah.** The idol of Asherah (*see note on 21:7*). **graves of the common people.** The Kidron Valley contained a burial ground for the common people (cf. Jer 26:23). Scattering ashes from the object of idolatry is said in 2Ch 34:4 to have been on the graves of those who sacrificed to that idol. The "common people" had followed their leaders to apostasy, defilement, and damnation—all symbolized by the act of scattering the ashes.

23:7 **houses.** Tents (called "Succoth-benoth" in 17:30) used by women who were devoted to Asherah, in which they made hangings and committed sexual sins.

23:8 **Geba to Beersheba.** Geba was located about 7 mi. NE of Jerusalem at the far N of Judah and Beersheba was located ca. 45 mi. S of Jerusalem at the southern end of Judah. Thus, this phrase was an idiomatic way of saying "throughout all of Judah."

23:10 **Topheth.** Meaning "a drum" and identifying the area in the Valley of Hinnom where child sacrifice occurred (cf. Is 30:33; Jer 7:31, 32; 19:5, 6). Perhaps called "drum" because drums were beaten to drown out the cries of the children being sacrificed.

23:11 **horses ... given to the sun.** The horses and the chariots of the sun were probably thought to symbolize the sun blazing a trail across the sky and were a part of worshiping the sun. Recently, a religious shrine with horse figurines has been found in Jerusalem (cf. Eze 8:16).

23:12 **on the roof.** Altars were erected on the flat roofs of houses so people could worship

[C]threw their dust into the brook Kidron. 13 The high
places which *were* before Jerusalem, which *were* on
the right of [A]the mount of destruction which Solomon the king of Israel had built for [B]Ashtoreth the
abomination of the Sidonians, and for [C]Chemosh the
abomination of Moab, and for Milcom the abomination of the sons of Ammon, the king defiled. 14 [A]He
broke in pieces the *sacred* pillars and cut down the
Asherim and [B]filled their places with human bones.
15 Furthermore, [A]the altar that *was* at Bethel *and*
the [B]high place which Jeroboam the son of Nebat, who
made Israel sin, had made, even that altar and the
high place he broke down. Then he [a,C]demolished its
stones, ground them to dust, and burned the Asherah.
16 Now when Josiah turned, he saw the graves that
were there on the mountain, and he sent and took
the bones from the graves and burned *them* on the
altar and defiled it [A]according to the word of the LORD
which the man of God proclaimed, who proclaimed
these things. 17 Then he said, "What is this monument
that I see?" And the men of the city told him, "[A]It is
the grave of the man of God who came from Judah
and proclaimed these things which you have done
against the altar of Bethel." 18 He said, "Let him alone;
let no one disturb his bones." So they [a]left his bones
undisturbed [A]with the bones of the prophet who came
from Samaria. 19 Josiah also removed all the houses of
the high places which *were* [A]in the cities of Samaria,
which the kings of Israel had made provoking [a]the
LORD; and he did to them [b]just as he had done in
Bethel. 20 All the priests of the high places who *were*
there [A]he slaughtered on the altars and burned human bones on them; then he returned to Jerusalem.

PASSOVER REINSTITUTED

21 Then the king commanded all the people saying, "[A]Celebrate the Passover to the LORD your
God [B]as it is written in this book of the covenant."
22 [A]Surely such a Passover had not been celebrated
from the days of the judges who judged Israel, nor
in all the days of the kings of Israel and of the kings
of Judah. 23 But in the eighteenth year of King Josiah, this Passover was observed to the LORD in
Jerusalem.
24 Moreover, Josiah [a]removed [A]the mediums and
the spiritists and the [B]teraphim and [C]the idols and
all the abominations that were seen in the land of
Judah and in Jerusalem, [D]that he might [b]confirm the
words of the law which were written [E]in the book
that Hilkiah the priest found in the house of the
LORD. 25 Before him there was no king [A]like him who
turned to the LORD with all his heart and with all
his soul and with all his might, according to all the
law of Moses; nor did any like him arise after him.
26 However, the LORD did not turn from the
fierceness of His great wrath with which His anger burned against Judah, [A]because of all the prov-
ocations with which Manasseh had provoked Him.
27 The LORD said, "I will remove Judah also from My
sight, [A]as I have removed Israel. And [B]I will cast off
Jerusalem, this city which I have chosen, and the
[a]temple of which I said, 'My name shall be there.' "

JEHOAHAZ SUCCEEDS JOSIAH

28 Now the rest of the acts of Josiah and all that he
did, are they not written in the Book of the Chronicles of the Kings of Judah? 29 [A]In his days [B]Pharaoh
Neco king of Egypt went up to the king of Assyria to
the river Euphrates. And King Josiah went to meet
him, and when *Pharaoh Neco* saw him he killed
him at [C]Megiddo. 30 [A]His servants drove [a]his body
in a chariot from Megiddo, and brought him to
Jerusalem and buried him in his own tomb. [B]Then
the people of the land took Jehoahaz the son of

23:12 [C]2 Kin 23:4, 6 23:13 [A]1 Kin 11:7 [B]1 Kin 11:5 [C]Num 21:29 23:14 [A]Deut 7:5, 25 [B]2 Kin 23:16 23:15 [a]So the Gr; Heb *burned the high place* [A]1 Kin 13:1 [B]1 Kin 12:28-33 [C]2 Kin 23:6 23:16 [A]1 Kin 13:2 23:17 [A]1 Kin 13:1, 30, 31 23:18 [a]Lit *let his bones escape with* [A]1 Kin 13:11, 31 23:19 [a]So with ancient versions [b]Lit *according to all the acts* [A]2 Chr 34:6, 7 23:20 [A]2 Kin 10:25; 11:18 23:21 [A]2 Chr 35:1-17 [B]Num 9:2-4; Deut 16:2-8 23:22 [A]2 Chr 35:18, 19 23:24 [a]Lit *consumed* [b]Or *perform* [A]Lev 19:31; 2 Kin 21:6 [B]Gen 31:19 mg [C]2 Kin 21:11, 21 [D]Deut 18:10-22 [E]2 Kin 22:8 23:25 [A]2 Kin 18:5 23:26 [A]2 Kin 21:11-13; Jer 15:4 23:27 [a]Lit *house* [A]2 Kin 18:11 [B]2 Kin 21:13, 14 23:29 [A]2 Chr 35:20-24 [B]Jer 46:2 [C]Judg 5:19 23:30 [a]Lit *him, dead* [A]2 Kin 9:28 [B]2 Chr 36:1-4

the "host of heaven" by burning incense (Jer 19:13; Zep 1:5).

23:13 Solomon . . . had built. Solomon had built high places E of Jerusalem on the Mt. of Olives, renamed after the desecration, to be used in worship of foreign gods, e.g., the fertility goddess Ashtoreth from Sidon, the Moabite god Chemosh, and the Ammonite god Molech (1Ki 11:7). These altars existed for over 300 years before Josiah finally destroyed them. The placing of human bones defiled them and, thus, rendered these sites unclean and unsuitable as places of worship.

23:15 the altar . . . at Bethel. Josiah reduced the altar that Jeroboam I had built at Bethel to dust and ashes (see 1Ki 12:28–33).

23:16 graves. Seeing graves nearby, perhaps where idolatrous priests were buried, Josiah had their bones removed and burned on the altar at Bethel to defile it. This action fulfilled a prophecy given about the altar approximately 300 years before (1Ki 13:2).

23:17, 18 See 1Ki 13:1–32, especially vv. 31, 32.

23:18 Samaria. The former northern kingdom of Israel had become known as Samaria, so named as an Assyrian province (*see note on 17:24*).

23:19 cities of Samaria. The desecration of the high place at Bethel was only the beginning of Josiah's desecration of all the high places in the Assyrian province of Samaria.

23:20 All the priests . . . he slaughtered. These non-Levitical priests, who led apostate worship in the former northern kingdom, were idolaters who seduced God's people into idolatry. They were put to death in accordance with the statutes of Dt 13:6–18; 17:2–7, and their graves were doubly defiled with burned bones.

23:21, 22 such a Passover. Judah's celebration of this Passover (see Dt 16:2–8) more closely conformed to the instructions given in the Mosaic law than any in the previous 400 years of Israel's history. Though the Passover was observed by Hezekiah (2Ch 30), no observance had been in exact conformity to God's law since the judges. Further details of this Passover observance are found in 2Ch 35:1–19.

23:23 eighteenth year. Ca. 622 B.C. All the reforms of Josiah described took place in the same year (cf. 22:3).

23:24 the book . . . found. See 22:8.

23:25 no king like him. Of all the kings in David's line, including David himself, no king more closely approximated the royal ideal of Dt 17:14–20 than Josiah (cf. Mt 22:37). Yet, even Josiah fell short of complete obedience because he had multiple wives (cf. vv. 31, 36; *see note on Ge 2:24*). However, even this righteous king could not turn away the Lord's wrath because of Manasseh's sin (vv. 26, 27). See chaps. 17, 18.

23:29 Neco. Pharaoh Neco II (609–594 B.C.) was an ally of Assyria against the growing power of Babylon. For some unstated reason, Josiah was determined to stop Neco and his army from joining the Assyrian army at the Euphrates River to fight Babylon. **Megiddo.** The well-fortified stronghold overlooking the Jezreel Valley about 65 mi. N of Jerusalem. Megiddo guarded a strategic pass on the route between Egypt and Mesopotamia. Josiah's death is explained in more detail in 2Ch 35:20–27.

Josiah and anointed him and made him king in
place of his father.
31 [A]Jehoahaz was twenty-three years old when
he became king, and he reigned three months in
Jerusalem; and his mother's name was [B]Hamutal
the daughter of Jeremiah of Libnah. 32 He did evil
in the sight of the LORD, [A]according to all that his
fathers had done. 33 [A]Pharaoh Neco imprisoned him
at [B]Riblah in the land of [C]Hamath, that he might
not reign in Jerusalem; and he imposed on the
land a fine of one hundred talents of silver and a
talent of gold.

JEHOIAKIM MADE KING BY PHARAOH

34 Pharaoh Neco made [A]Eliakim the son of Josiah
king in the place of Josiah his father, and [B]changed
his name to Jehoiakim. But he took Jehoahaz away
and [a,C]brought *him* to Egypt, and he died there. 35 So
Jehoiakim [A]gave the silver and gold to Pharaoh, but
he taxed the land in order to give the money at the
[a]command of Pharaoh. He exacted the silver and
gold from the people of the land, each according to
his valuation, to give it to Pharaoh Neco.
36 [A]Jehoiakim was twenty-five years old when
he became king, and he reigned eleven years in
Jerusalem; and his mother's name *was* Zebidah
the daughter of Pedaiah of Rumah. 37 He did evil
in the sight of the LORD, [A]according to all that his
fathers had done.

BABYLON CONTROLS JEHOIAKIM

24 [A]In his days Nebuchadnezzar king of Babylon
came up, and Jehoiakim became his servant
for three years; then he turned and rebelled against
him. 2 The LORD sent against him [A]bands of Chaldeans, [B]bands of Arameans, [C]bands of Moabites,
and bands of Ammonites. So He sent them against
Judah to destroy it, [D]according to the word of the
LORD which He had spoken through His servants
the prophets. 3 [A]Surely at the [a]command of the LORD
it came upon Judah, to remove *them* from His sight
[B]because of the sins of Manasseh, according to all
that he had done, 4 and [A]also for the innocent blood
which he shed, for he filled Jerusalem with innocent blood; and the LORD would not forgive. 5 Now
the rest of the acts of Jehoiakim and all that he did,
are they not written in the Book of the Chronicles
of the Kings of Judah?

JEHOIACHIN REIGNS

6 So [A]Jehoiakim slept with his fathers, and Jehoiachin his son became king in his place. 7 [A]The king
of Egypt did not come out of his land again, [B]for
the king of Babylon had taken all that belonged to
the king of Egypt from [C]the brook of Egypt to the
river Euphrates.
8 [A]Jehoiachin was [B]eighteen years old when he
became king, and he reigned three months in Jerusalem; and his mother's name *was* Nehushta the
daughter of Elnathan of Jerusalem. 9 He did evil
in the sight of the LORD, [A]according to all that his
father had done.

DEPORTATION TO BABYLON

10 At that time the servants of Nebuchadnezzar
king of Babylon went up to Jerusalem, and the city
came under siege. 11 And Nebuchadnezzar the king
of Babylon came to the city, while his servants were
besieging it. 12 [A]Jehoiachin the king of Judah went out
to the king of Babylon, he and his mother and his servants and his captains and his officials. So [B]the king
of Babylon took him captive in the eighth year of his

23:31 [A]1 Chr 3:15; Jer 22:11 [B]2 Kin 24:18 23:32 [A]2 Kin 21:2-7 23:33 [A]2 Kin 23:29 [B]2 Kin 25:6 [C]1 Kin 8:65 23:34 [a]So with Gr; Heb *he came* [A]1 Chr 3:15 [B]2 Kin 24:17; 2 Chr 36:4 [C]Jer 22:11, 12; Ezek 19:3, 4 23:35 [a]Lit *mouth* [A]2 Kin 23:33 23:36 [A]2 Chr 36:5; Jer 22:18, 19; 26:1 23:37 [A]2 Kin 23:32 24:1 [A]2 Chr 36:6; Jer 25:1; Dan 1:1, 2 24:2 [A]Jer 35:11f [B]2 Kin 6:23 [C]2 Kin 13:20 [D]2 Kin 23:27 24:3 [a]Lit *mouth* [A]2 Kin 18:25 [B]2 Kin 23:26 24:4 [A]2 Kin 21:16 24:6 [A]Jer 22:18, 19 24:7 [A]Jer 37:5-7 [B]Jer 46:2 [C]Gen 15:18 24:8 [A]1 Chr 3:16 [B]2 Chr 36:9 24:9 [A]2 Kin 21:2-7 24:12 [A]Jer 22:24-30; 24:1; 29:1, 2 [B]2 Chr 36:10

23:31 three months. Jehoahaz reigned during 609 B.C., became a prisoner of Pharaoh Neco II, and ultimately died in Egypt. *See note on 2Ch 36:1–4.*

23:33 Riblah in the land of Hamath. Jehoahaz was in prison at Pharaoh Neco II's military headquarters located on the Orontes River in the N Lebanon Valley (*see note on 25:6*). **silver ... gold.** The tax imposed on Judah, whose king was imprisoned, was 750 lbs. of silver and 7.5 lbs. of gold.

23:34 Eliakim ... Jehoiakim. In 609 B.C., Pharaoh Neco II placed Jehoahaz's older brother on the throne of Judah. Neco changed his name from Eliakim, meaning "God has established," to Jehoiakim, "the Lord has established." The naming of a person was regarded in the ancient Near East as a sign of authority; so by naming Jehoiakim, Neco demonstrated that he was the lord who controlled Judah. As a vassal of Egypt, Judah risked attack by Egypt's enemy Babylon. *See note on 2Ch 36:5–8.*

23:35 Jehoiakim taxed his people severely to pay tribute to Egypt, though he still had enough to build a magnificent palace for himself (see Jer 22:13, 14).

23:36 eleven years. 609–597 B.C.

24:1 Nebuchadnezzar. Nebuchadnezzar II was the son of Nabopolassar, king of Babylon from 626–605 B.C. As crown prince, Nebuchadnezzar had led his father's army against Pharaoh Neco and the Egyptians at Carchemish on the Euphrates River in northern Syria (605 B.C.). By defeating the Egyptians, Babylon was established as the strongest nation in the ancient Near East. Egypt and its vassals, including Judah, became vassals of Babylon with this victory. Nebuchadnezzar followed up his victory at Carchemish by invading the land of Judah. Later, in 605 B.C., Nebuchadnezzar took some captives to Babylon, including Daniel and his friends (cf. Da 1:1–3). Toward the end of 605 B.C., Nabopolassar died and Nebuchadnezzar succeeded him as king of Babylon, 3 years after Jehoiakim had taken the throne in Judah (Jer 25:1). Nebuchadnezzar reigned from 605–562 B.C. **three years.** Nebuchadnezzar returned to the W in 604 B.C. and took tribute from all of the kings of the W, including Jehoiakim of Judah. Jehoiakim submitted to Babylonian rule from 604–602 B.C. In 602 B.C., Jehoiakim rebelled against Babylon, disregarding the advice of the prophet Jeremiah (Jer 27:9–11).

24:2 the LORD sent ... bands. As punishment for Jehoiakim's disobedience of the Lord's Word through His prophet Jeremiah, the Lord sent Babylonian troops, along with the troops of other loyal nations, to inflict military defeats upon Judah.

24:4 innocent blood. *See note on 21:16.*

24:7 king of Egypt. In 601 B.C., Nebuchadnezzar again marched W against Egypt and was turned back by strong Egyptian resistance. However Egypt, though able to defend its own land, was not able to be aggressive and recover its conquered lands or provide any help for its allies, including Judah.

24:8 eighteen. This reading is preferred over the "eight" of 2Ch 36:9 (*see note*). **three months.** Having regrouped, Nebuchadnezzar invaded Judah for a second time in the spring of 597 B.C. Before he could enter Jerusalem, Jehoiakim died and was succeeded as king of Judah by his son, Jehoiachin. Jehoiachin ruled for a short time in 597 B.C. *See note on 2Ch 36:9, 10.*

24:10–12 The Babylonian siege of Jerusalem was begun by the troops of Nebuchadnezzar. Later, Nebuchadnezzar himself went to Jerusalem and it was to the king himself that Jehoiachin surrendered (v. 12).

24:12 eighth year. 597 B.C. For the first time, the books of Kings dated an event in Israelite history by a non-Israelite king. This

reign. 13 [A]He carried out from there all the treasures of
the house of the LORD, and the treasures of the king's
house, and [B]cut in pieces all the vessels of gold [C]which
Solomon king of Israel had made in the temple of the
LORD, just as the LORD had said. 14 Then [A]he led away
into exile all Jerusalem and all the captains and all
the mighty men of valor, [B]ten thousand captives, and
[C]all the craftsmen and the smiths. None remained
[D]except the poorest people of the land.
15 So [A]he led Jehoiachin away into exile to Babylon;
also the king's mother and the king's wives and his
officials and the leading men of the land, he led away
into exile from Jerusalem to Babylon. 16 All the men
of valor, [A]seven thousand, and the craftsmen and the
smiths, one thousand, all strong and fit for war, and
these the king of Babylon brought into exile to Babylon.

ZEDEKIAH MADE KING

17 [A]Then the king of Babylon made [a]his uncle Mattaniah king in his place, and changed his name to
Zedekiah.
18 [A]Zedekiah was twenty-one years old when
he became king, and he reigned eleven years in
Jerusalem; and his mother's name was [B]Hamutal
the daughter of Jeremiah of Libnah. 19 He did evil
in the sight of the LORD, [A]according to all that Jehoiakim had done. 20 For [A]through the anger of the
LORD *this* came about in Jerusalem and Judah until
He cast them out from His presence. And [B]Zedekiah
rebelled against the king of Babylon.

NEBUCHADNEZZAR BESIEGES JERUSALEM

25 [A]Now in the ninth year of his reign, on the
tenth day of the tenth month, [B]Nebuchad-
nezzar king of Babylon came, he and all his army,
against Jerusalem, camped against it and [C]built a
siege wall all around [a]it. 2 So the city was under
siege until the eleventh year of King Zedekiah.
3 On the ninth day of the *fourth* month [A]the famine
was so severe in the city that there was no food for
the people of the land. 4 [A]Then the city was broken
into, and all the men of war *fled* by night by way of
the gate between the two walls beside [B]the king's
garden, though the Chaldeans were all around
the city. And [a]they went by way of the Arabah.

24:13 [A]2 Kin 20:17; Is 39:6 [B]2 Kin 25:13-15 [C]1 Kin 7:48-50 24:14 [A]Jer 24:1 [B]2 Kin 24:16; Jer 52:28 [C]Jer 24:1; 29:2 [D]2 Kin 25:12 24:15 [A]2 Chr 36:10; Jer 22:24-28; Ezek 17:12 24:16 [A]2 Kin 24:14 24:17 [a]I.e. Jehoiachin's uncle [A]2 Chr 36:10-13; Jer 37:1 24:18 [A]Jer 27:1; 28:1; 52:1 [B]2 Kin 23:31 24:19 [A]2 Kin 23:37 24:20 [A]Deut 4:24; 29:27; 2 Kin 23:26 [B]2 Chr 36:13; Ezek 17:15 25:1 [a]Lit *against it* [A]2 Chr 36:17-20; Jer 39:1-7 [B]Jer 21:2; 34:1, 2; Ezek 24:2 [C]Ezek 21:22 25:3 [A]2 Kin 6:24, 25; Lam 4:9, 10 25:4 [a]So some ancient mss and versions; M.T. *he* [A]Ezek 33:21 [B]Neh 3:15

indicated that Judah's exile was imminent and the land would be in the hands of Gentiles.

24:13 Nebuchadnezzar plundered the treasures of the temple and king's palace, just as the Lord had said he would (cf. 20:16–18).

24:14–16 In 597 B.C., Nebuchadnezzar took an additional 10,000 Judeans as captives to Babylon, in particular the leaders of the nation. This included the leaders of the military and those whose skills would support the military. Included in this deportation was the prophet Ezekiel (*see notes on Eze 1:1–3*). Only the lower classes remained behind in Jerusalem. The Babylonian policy of captivity was different from that of the Assyrians, who took most of the people into exile and resettled the land of Israel with foreigners (17:24). The Babylonians took only the leaders and the strong, while leaving the weak and poor, elevating those left to leadership and thereby earning their loyalty. Those taken to Babylon were allowed to work and live in the mainstream of society. This kept the captive Jews together, so it would be possible for them to return, as recorded in Ezra.

THE (MEDO-) BABYLONIAN EMPIRE (560 B.C.)

In 605 B.C. Nebuchadnezzar successfully concluded a two-year siege of Carchemish, and most of the Assyrian Empire rapidly became the Babylonian Empire. In 586 B.C. Nebuchadnezzar conquered all of Judah, besieging and destroying Jerusalem and the Jewish temple. At its zenith in 560 B.C., Babylon ruled the entire fertile crescent and Arabia as well, although Egypt regained its autonomy.

24:17 Mattaniah ... Zedekiah. Mattaniah was a son of Josiah and an uncle of Jehoiachin (cf. 1Ch 3:15; Jer 1:3). Mattaniah's name, meaning "gift of the Lord," was changed to Zedekiah, "righteousness of the Lord." Nebuchadnezzar's changing of Zedekiah's name demonstrated his authority as lord over him (*see note on 23:34*). *See notes on 2Ch 36:11–21.*

24:18 eleven years. Zedekiah ruled in Jerusalem, under Babylonian sovereignty, from 597–586 B.C.

24:20 Zedekiah rebelled. In 588 B.C., Apries (also called Hophra), the grandson of Neco, became Pharaoh over Egypt. He appears to have influenced Zedekiah to revolt against Babylon (cf. Eze 17:15–18).

25:1 ninth year. Responding to Zedekiah's rebellion (24:20), Nebuchadnezzar sent his whole army to lay siege against the city of Jerusalem. The siege began in the ninth year of Zedekiah's reign, Jan., 588 B.C. The "siege wall" was comprised of either wood towers higher than the walls of the city or a dirt rampart encircling the city.

25:2 eleventh year. Jerusalem withstood the siege until the 11th year of Zedekiah, July, 586 B.C. Hezekiah's tunnel guaranteed the city an uninterrupted supply of fresh water (20:20) and an Egyptian foray into Judah gave the city a temporary reprieve from the siege (Jer 37:5).

25:3 famine. After a siege of 2 1/2 years, the food supply in Jerusalem ran out (Jer 38:2, 3).

25:4 the city was broken into. The two walls near the king's garden were probably

5 But the army of the Chaldeans pursued the king
and overtook him in the plains of Jericho and all his
army was scattered from him. 6 Then [A]they captured
the king and [B]brought him to the king of Babylon
at [C]Riblah, and [a]he passed sentence on him. 7 [A]They
slaughtered the sons of Zedekiah before his eyes,
then [B]put out the eyes of Zedekiah and bound him
with bronze fetters and brought him to Babylon.

JERUSALEM BURNED AND PLUNDERED

8 [A]Now on the seventh day of the [B]fifth month,
which was the nineteenth year of King Nebuchadnezzar, king of Babylon, Nebuzaradan the captain of
the guard, a servant of the king of Babylon, came to
Jerusalem. 9 [A]He burned the house of the LORD, [B]the
king's house, and all the houses of Jerusalem; even
every great house he burned with fire. 10 So all the
army of the Chaldeans who *were with* the captain
of the guard [A]broke down the walls around Jerusalem. 11 Then [A]the rest of the people who were left in
the city and the deserters who had deserted to the
king of Babylon and the rest of the people, Nebuzaradan the captain of the guard carried away into
exile. 12 But the captain of the guard left some of [A]the
poorest of the land to be vinedressers and plowmen.
13 [A]Now the bronze pillars which were in the house
of the LORD, and the stands and [B]the bronze sea
which were in the house of the LORD, the Chaldeans
broke in pieces and carried the [a]bronze to Babylon.
14 [A]They took away the pots, the shovels, the snuffers,
the spoons, and all the bronze vessels which were
used in *temple* service. 15 The captain of the guard
also took away the firepans and the basins, what
was fine gold and what was fine silver. 16 The two
pillars, the one sea, and the stands which Solomon
had made for the house of the LORD—[A]the bronze of
all these vessels was beyond weight. 17 [A]The height
of the one pillar was eighteen [a]cubits, and a bronze
capital was on it; the height of the capital was three
[a]cubits, with a network and pomegranates on the
capital all around, all of bronze. And the second
pillar was like these with network.

25:6 [a]Lit *they spoke judgment with him* [A]Jer 34:21, 22 [B]Jer 32:4 [C]2 Kin 23:33 25:7 [A]Jer 39:6, 7 [B]Ezek 12:13 25:8 [A]Jer 52:12 [B]Jer 39:8-12 25:9 [A]1 Kin 9:8; 2 Chr 36:19; Ps 74:3-7 [B]Amos 2:5 25:10 [A]2 Kin 14:13; Neh 1:3 25:11 [A]2 Chr 36:20 25:12 [A]2 Kin 24:14; Jer 40:7 25:13 [a]Lit *bronze of them* [A]1 Kin 7:15-22; 2 Kin 20:17; 2 Chr 3:15-17; 36:18 [B]1 Kin 7:23-26; 2 Chr 4:2-4 25:14 [A]Ex 27:3; 1 Kin 7:47-50; 2 Chr 4:16 25:16 [A]1 Kin 7:47 25:17 [a]I.e. One cubit equals approx 18 in. [A]1 Kin 7:15-22

located at the extreme SE corner of the city, giving direct access to the Kidron Valley. This gave Zedekiah and his soldiers an opportunity to flee for their lives to the E.

25:5 plains of Jericho. Zedekiah fled toward the Jordan Rift Valley. Babylonian pursuers caught him in the Jordan Valley S of Jericho, about 20 mi. E of Jerusalem.

25:6 Riblah. Located on the Orontes River about 180 mi. N of Jerusalem, Riblah was Nebuchadnezzar's military headquarters for his invasion of Judah. This location was ideally situated as a field headquarters for military forces because ample provisions could be found nearby (cf. 23:33). The captured traitor Zedekiah was brought to Nebuchadnezzar at Riblah, where he was blinded after witnessing the death of his sons. The execution of the royal heirs ensured the impossibility of a future claim to the throne or rebellion from his descendants. The blinding made his own future rebellion or retaliation impossible. Jeremiah had warned Zedekiah that he would see Nebuchadnezzar (*see notes on Jer 32:2–5; 34:3*), while Ezekiel had said he would not see Babylon (*see note on Eze 12:10–13*). Both prophecies were accurately fulfilled.

25:8 seventh day. *See note on Jer 52:12.* This was Aug., 586 B.C., one month after the Babylonian breakthrough of Jerusalem's walls (vv. 2–4). **Nebuzaradan.** He was the commander of Nebuchadnezzar's own imperial guard, sent by the king to oversee the destruction of Jerusalem. The dismantling and destruction of Jerusalem was accomplished by the Babylonians in an orderly progression.

25:9 First, Jerusalem's most important buildings were burned.

25:10 Second, the Babylonian army tore down Jerusalem's outer walls, the city's main defense.

25:11, 12 Third, Nebuzaradan organized and led a forced march of remaining Judeans into exile in Babylon. The exiles included survivors from Jerusalem and those who had surrendered to the Babylonians before the capture of the city. Only poor, unskilled laborers were left behind to tend the vineyards and farm the fields.

25:13–17 Fourth, the items made with precious metals in the temple were carried away to Babylon. *See notes on 1Ki 7:15–49.*

25:17 three cubits. *See note on Jer 52:22.*

25:18–21 Fifth, Nebuzaradan took Jerusalem's remaining leaders to Riblah, where Nebuchadnezzar had them executed. This insured that they would never lead another rebellion against Babylon.

SECOND KINGS, JEREMIAH, AND LAMENTATIONS COMPARED

	2 Kings 25 (See also 2Ch 36:11–21)	Jeremiah	Lamentations
1. The siege of Jerusalem	1, 2	39:1–3; 52:4, 5	2:20–22; 3:5, 7
2. The famine in the city	3	37:21; 52:6	1:11, 19; 2:11, 12; 2:19, 20; 4:4, 5, 9, 10; 5:9, 10
3. The flight of the army and the king	4–7	39:4–7; 52:8–11	1:3, 6; 2:2; 4:19, 20
4. The burning of the palace, temple, and city	8, 9	39:8; 52:13	2:3–5; 4:11; 5:18
5. The breaching of the city walls	10	33:4, 5; 52:7	2:7–9
6. The exile of the populace	11, 12	28:3, 4, 14; 39:9, 10	1:1, 4, 5, 18; 2:9, 14; 3:2, 19; 4:22; 5:2
7. The looting of the temple	13–15	51:51	1:10; 2:6, 7
8. The execution of the leaders	18–21	39:6	1:15; 2:2, 20
9. The vassal status of Judah	22–25	40:9	1:1; 5:8, 9
10. The collapse of the expected foreign help	24:7	27:1–11; 37:5–10	4:17; 5:6

[18] Then the captain of the guard took [A]Seraiah the chief priest and [B]Zephaniah the second priest, with the three [a]officers of the temple. [19] From the city he took one official who was overseer of the men of war, and [A]five [a]of the king's advisers who were found in the city; and the [b]scribe of the captain of the army who mustered the people of the land; and sixty men of the people of the land who were found in the city. [20] Nebuzaradan the captain of the guard took them and brought them to the king of Babylon at [A]Riblah. [21] Then the king of Babylon struck them down and put them to death at Riblah in the land of Hamath. [A]So Judah was led away into exile from its land.

GEDALIAH MADE GOVERNOR

[22] Now *as for* the people who were left in the land of Judah, whom Nebuchadnezzar king of Babylon had left, he appointed [A]Gedaliah the son of Ahikam, the son of Shaphan over them. [23] [A]When all the captains of the forces, they and *their* men, heard that the king of Babylon had appointed Gedaliah *governor,* they came to Gedaliah to [B]Mizpah, namely, Ishmael the son of Nethaniah, and Johanan the son of Kareah, and Seraiah the son of Tanhumeth the Netophathite, and Jaazaniah the son of the Maacathite, they and their men. [24] Gedaliah swore to them and their men and said to them, "Do not be afraid of the servants of the Chaldeans; live in the land and serve the king of Babylon, and it will be well with you."

[25] [A]But it came about in the seventh month, that Ishmael the son of Nethaniah, the son of Elishama, of the royal [a]family, came [b]with ten men and struck Gedaliah down so that he died along with the Jews and the Chaldeans who were with him at Mizpah. [26] [A]Then all the people, both small and great, and the captains of the forces arose and went to Egypt; for they were afraid of the Chaldeans.

[27] [A]Now it came about in the thirty-seventh year of [B]the exile of Jehoiachin king of Judah, in the twelfth month, on the twenty-seventh *day* of the month, that Evil-merodach king of Babylon, in the year that he became king, [a,C]released Jehoiachin king of Judah from prison; [28] and he [A]spoke kindly to him and set his throne above the throne of the kings who *were* with him in Babylon. [29] [a]Jehoiachin changed his prison clothes and [b,A]had his meals in [c]the king's presence regularly all the days of his life; [30] and for his [A]allowance, a regular allowance was given him by the king, a portion for each day, all the days of his life.

25:18 [a]Lit *keepers of the door* [A]1 Chr 6:14; Ezra 7:1 [B]Jer 21:1; 29:25, 29 25:19 [a]Lit *men of those seeing the king's face* [b]Or *scribe, a captain* [A]Esth 1:14 25:20 [A]2 Kin 23:33 25:21 [A]Deut 28:64; 2 Kin 23:27 25:22 [A]Jer 39:14; 40:7-9 25:23 [A]Jer 40:7-9 [B]Josh 18:26 25:25 [a]Lit *seed* [b]Lit *and ten men with him* [A]Jer 41:1, 2 25:26 [A]Jer 43:4-7 25:27 [a]Lit *lifted up the head of* [A]Jer 52:31-34 [B]2 Kin 24:12, 15 [C]Gen 40:13, 20 25:28 [A]Dan 2:37; 5:18, 19 25:29 [a]Lit *he* [b]Lit *ate bread* [c]Lit *his presence* [A]2 Sam 9:7 25:30 [A]Neh 11:23; 12:47

25:18 Seraiah. Seraiah was the grandson of Hilkiah (22:4, 8; 1Ch 6:13, 14) and an ancestor of Ezra (Ezr 7:1). Even though Seraiah was executed, his sons were deported (1Ch 6:15).

25:21 Judah ... led away into exile. Exile was the ultimate curse brought upon Judah because of her disobedience to the Mosaic Covenant (cf. Lv 26:33; Dt 28:36, 64). The book of Lamentations records the sorrow of Jeremiah over this destruction of Jerusalem.

25:22–30 The books of Kings conclude with this brief epilogue. Despite the punishment of the Lord experienced by Israel and Judah, the people were still rebellious (vv. 22–26). However, due to the Lord's mercy, the house of David endured (vv. 27–30). The books of Kings end with a note of hope.

25:22 Gedaliah. In an attempt to maintain political stability, Nebuchadnezzar appointed a governor from an important Judean family. A more detailed account of Gedaliah's activities is found in Jer 40:7–41:18. Gedaliah's grandfather, Shaphan, was Josiah's secretary, who had implemented that king's reforms (22:3). His father, Ahikam, was part of Josiah's delegation sent to Huldah (22:14) and a supporter of the prophet Jeremiah (Jer 26:24).

25:23 Mizpah. Located about 8 mi. N of Jerusalem, Mizpah became the new center of Judah. Mizpah might have been one of the few towns left standing after the Babylonian invasion.

25:24 swore. As governor, Gedaliah pledged to the remaining people that loyalty to the Babylonians would ensure their safety.

25:25 seventh month. October, 586 B.C., two months after the destruction of Jerusalem (cf. v. 8). Ishmael. Elishama, Ishmael's grandfather, was a secretary under Jehoiakim (Jer 36:12; 41:1). Ishmael probably assassinated Gedaliah because he wished to reestablish the kingship in Judah with himself as king, since he was of royal blood (cf. Jer 41:1).

25:26 went to Egypt. Fearing reprisals from the Babylonians, the people fled to Egypt.

25:27 thirty-seventh year. March, 561 B.C. Jehoiachin was about 55 years old (cf. 24:8). Evil-merodach. The son and successor of Nebuchadnezzar, he ruled as king of Babylon from 562–560 B.C. To gain favor with the Jews, the king released Jehoiachin from his imprisonment and gave him special privileges.

25:28–30 spoke kindly to him. This good word from the king of Babylon to the surviving representative of the house of David served as a concluding reminder of God's good Word to David. Through the curse of exile, the dynasty of David had survived. There was still hope that God's good Word to David concerning the seed who will build God's temple and establish God's eternal kingdom would be fulfilled (cf. 2Sa 7:12–16). The book of 2 Kings opened with Elijah being carried away to heaven, the destination of all those faithful to God. The book ends with Israel, and then Judah, being carried away to pagan lands as a result of failing to be faithful to God.

THE FIRST AND SECOND BOOKS OF THE

CHRONICLES

TITLE

The original title in the Hebrew Bible read "The annals (i.e., events or happenings) of the days." First and Second Chronicles were comprised of one book until later divided into separate books in the Greek OT translation, the Septuagint (LXX), ca. 200 B.C. The title also changed at that time to the inaccurate title, "the things omitted," i.e., reflecting material not in 1, 2 Samuel and 1, 2 Kings. The English title "Chronicles" originated with Jerome's Latin Vulgate translation (ca. 400 A.D.), which used the fuller title "The Chronicles of the Entire Sacred History."

AUTHOR AND DATE

Neither 1 nor 2 Chronicles contains direct statements regarding the human author, though Jewish tradition strongly favors Ezra the priest (cf. Ezr 7:1–6) as "the chronicler." These records were most likely recorded ca. 450–430 B.C. The genealogical record in 1Ch 1–9 supports a date after 450 B.C. for the writing. The NT does not directly quote either 1 or 2 Chronicles.

BACKGROUND AND SETTING

The immediate historical backdrop encompassed the Jews' three-phase return to the Promised Land from the Babylonian exile: 1) Zerubbabel in Ezr 1–6 (ca. 538 B.C.); 2) Ezra in Ezr 7–10 (ca. 458 B.C.); and 3) Nehemiah in Ne 1–13 (ca. 445 B.C.). Previous history looks back to the Babylonian deportation/Exile (ca. 605–538 B.C.) as predicted/reported by 2 Kings, Jeremiah, Ezekiel, Daniel, and Habakkuk. The prophets of this restoration era were Haggai, Zechariah, and Malachi.

The Jews had returned from their 70 years of captivity (ca. 538 B.C.) to a land that was markedly different from the one once ruled by King David (ca. 1011–971 B.C.) and King Solomon (971–931 B.C.): 1) there was no Hebrew king, but rather a Persian governor (Ezr 5:3; 6:6); 2) there was no security for Jerusalem, so Nehemiah had to rebuild the wall (Ne 1–7); 3) there was no temple, so Zerubbabel had to reconstruct a pitiful semblance of the Solomonic temple's former glory (Ezr 3); 4) the Jews no longer dominated the region, but rather were on the defensive (Ezr 4; Ne 4); 5) they enjoyed few divine blessings beyond the fact of their return; 6) they possessed little of the kingdom's former wealth; and 7) God's divine presence no longer resided in Jerusalem, having departed ca. 597–591 B.C. (Eze 8–11).

To put it mildly, their future looked bleak compared to their majestic past, especially the time of David and Solomon. The return could best be described as bittersweet, i.e., bitter because their present poverty brought hurtful memories about what was forfeited by God's judgment on their ancestors' sin, but sweet because at least they were back in the Land God had given Abraham 17 centuries earlier (Ge 12:1–3). The chronicler's selective genealogy and history of Israel, stretching from Adam (1Ch 1:1) to the return from Babylon (2Ch 26:23), was intended to remind the Jews of God's promises and intentions about: 1) the Land; 2) the nation; 3) the Davidic king; 4) the Levitical priests; 5) the temple; and 6) true worship, none of which had been abrogated because of the Babylonian captivity. All of this was to remind them of their spiritual heritage during the difficult times they faced, and to encourage them to be faithful to God.

HISTORICAL AND THEOLOGICAL THEMES

First and Second Chronicles, as named by Jerome, recreate an OT history in miniature, with particular emphases on the Davidic Covenant and temple worship. In terms of literary parallel, 1 Chronicles is the partner of 2 Samuel, in that both detail the reign of King David. First Chronicles opens with Adam (1:1) and closes with the death of David (29:26–30) in 971 B.C. Second Chronicles begins with Solomon (1:1) and covers the same historical period as 1 and 2 Kings, while focusing exclusively on the kings of the southern kingdom of Judah, thus excluding the history of the northern 10 tribes and their rulers, because of their complete wickedness and false worship. It ranges from the reign of Solomon (1:1) in 971 B.C. to the return from Babylon in 538 B.C. (36:23). Over 55 percent of the material in Chronicles is unique, i.e., not found in 2 Samuel or 1 and 2 Kings. The "chronicler" tended to omit what was negative or in opposition to the Davidic kingship; on the other hand, he tended to make unique contributions in validating temple worship and the line of David. Whereas 2Ki 25 ends dismally with the deportation of Judah to Babylon, 2Ch 36:22–23 concludes hopefully with the Jews' release from Persia and return to Jerusalem.

These two books were written to the repatriated Jewish exiles as a chronicle of God's intention of future blessing, in spite of the nation's past moral/spiritual failure for which the people paid dearly under God's wrath. First and Second Chronicles could be briefly summarized as follows:

I. A Selected Genealogical History of Israel (1Ch 1–9)

II. Israel's United Kingdom Under Saul (1Ch 10), David (1Ch 11–29), and Solomon (2Ch 1–9)

III. Judah's Monarchy in the Divided Kingdom (2Ch 10–36:21)

IV. Judah's Release From Their Seventy Year Captivity (2Ch 36:22, 23).

The historical themes are inextricably linked with the theological in that God's divine purposes for Israel have been and will be played out on the stage of human history. These two books are designed to assure the returning Jews that, in spite of their checkered past and present plight, God will be true to His covenant promises. They have been returned by God to the Land first given to Abraham as a race of people whose ethnic identity (Jewish) was not obliterated by the deportation and whose national identity (Israel) has been preserved (Ge 12:1–3; 15:5), although they are still under God's judgment as prescribed by the Mosaic legislation (Dt 28:15–68). The priestly line of Eleazar's son Phinehas and the Levitical line were still intact so that temple worship could continue in the hopes that God's presence would one day return (Nu 25:10–13; Mal 3:1). The Davidic promise of a king was still valid, although future in its fulfillment (2Sa 7:8–17; 1Ch 17:7–15). Their individual hope of eternal life and restoration of God's blessings forever rested in the New Covenant (Jer 31:31–34).

Two basic principles enumerated in these two books prevail throughout the OT, namely, obedience brings blessing, disobedience brings judgment. In the Chronicles, when the king obeyed and trusted the Lord, God blessed and protected. But when the king disobeyed and/or put his trust in something or someone other than the Lord, God withdrew His blessing and protection. Three basic failures by the kings of Judah brought God's wrath: 1) personal sin; 2) false worship/idolatry; and/or 3) trust in man rather than God.

INTERPRETIVE CHALLENGES

First and Second Chronicles present a combination of selective genealogical and historical records and no insurmountable challenges within the two books are encountered. A few issues arise, such as: 1) Who wrote 1 and 2 Chronicles? Does the overlap of 2Ch 36:22–23 with Ezr 1:1–3 point to Ezra as author? 2) Does the use of multiple sources taint the inerrancy doctrine of Scripture? 3) How does one explain the variations in the genealogies of 1Ch 1–9 from other OT genealogies? 4) Are the curses of Dt 28 still in force, even though the 70 year captivity has concluded? 5) How does one explain the few variations in numbers when comparing Chronicles with parallel passages in Samuel and Kings? These will be dealt with in the notes at the appropriate places.

OUTLINE

I. Selective Genealogy (1:1–9:34)
- A. Adam to Before David (1:1–2:55)
- B. David to the Captivity (3:1–24)
- C. Twelve Tribes (4:1–9:1)
- D. Jerusalem Dwellers (9:2–34)

II. David's Ascent (9:35–12:40)
- A. Saul's Heritage and Death (9:35–10:14)
- B. David's Anointing (11:1–3)
- C. Jerusalem's Conquest (11:4–9)
- D. David's Men (11:10–12:40)

III. David's Reign (13:1–29:30)
- A. The Ark of the Covenant (13:1–16:43)
- B. The Davidic Covenant (17:1–27)
- C. Selected Military History (18:1–21:30)
- D. Temple-Building Preparations (22:1–29:20)
- E. Transition to Solomon (29:21–30)

GENEALOGY FROM ADAM

1 [A]Adam, Seth, Enosh, 2 Kenan, Mahalalel, Jared,
3 Enoch, Methuselah, Lamech, 4 Noah, Shem, Ham
and Japheth.
5 [A]The sons of Japheth *were* Gomer, Magog, Madai,
Javan, Tubal, Meshech and Tiras. 6 The sons of Gomer *were* Ashkenaz, [a]Diphath, and Togarmah. 7 The
sons of Javan *were* Elishah, Tarshish, Kittim and
[a]Rodanim.
8 The sons of Ham *were* Cush, Mizraim, Put, and
Canaan. 9 The sons of Cush *were* Seba, Havilah,
Sabta, Raama and Sabteca; and the sons of Raamah
were Sheba and Dedan. 10 Cush [a]became the father of
Nimrod; he began to be a mighty one in the earth.
11 [A]Mizraim became the father of the people of
Lud, Anam, Lehab, Naphtuh, 12 Pathrus, Casluh, from
which the [a]Philistines came, and Caphtor.
13 Canaan became the father of Sidon, his firstborn, Heth, 14 and the Jebusites, the Amorites, the
Girgashites, 15 the Hivites, the Arkites, the Sinites,
16 the Arvadites, the Zemarites and the Hamathites.
17 [A]The sons of Shem *were* Elam, Asshur, Arpachshad, Lud, Aram, Uz, Hul, Gether and [a]Meshech.
18 Arpachshad became the father of Shelah and Shelah became the father of Eber. 19 Two sons were born
to Eber, the name of the one was Peleg, for in his
days the earth was divided, and his brother's name
was Joktan. 20 Joktan became the father of Almodad,
Sheleph, Hazarmaveth, Jerah, 21 Hadoram, Uzal,
Diklah, 22 [a]Ebal, Abimael, Sheba, 23 Ophir, Havilah
and Jobab; all these *were* the sons of Joktan.
24 [A]Shem, Arpachshad, Shelah, 25 Eber, Peleg, Reu,
26 Serug, Nahor, Terah, 27 Abram, that is Abraham.

DESCENDANTS OF ABRAHAM

28 The sons of Abraham *were* Isaac and Ishmael.
29 [A]These are their genealogies: the firstborn of Ishmael *was* Nebaioth, then Kedar, Adbeel, Mibsam,
30 Mishma, Dumah, Massa, Hadad, Tema, 31 Jetur,
Naphish and Kedemah; these *were* the sons of Ishmael. 32 [A]The sons of Keturah, Abraham's concubine,
whom she bore, *were* Zimran, Jokshan, Medan, Midian, Ishbak and Shuah. And the sons of Jokshan
were Sheba and Dedan. 33 The sons of Midian were
Ephah, Epher, Hanoch, Abida and Eldaah. All these
were the sons of Keturah.
34 [A]Abraham became the father of Isaac. The sons
of Isaac *were* [B]Esau and Israel. 35 [A]The sons of Esau
were Eliphaz, Reuel, Jeush, Jalam and Korah. 36 The
sons of Eliphaz *were* Teman, Omar, [a]Zephi, Gatam,
Kenaz, Timna and Amalek. 37 The sons of Reuel *were*
Nahath, Zerah, Shammah and Mizzah. 38 [A]The sons
of Seir *were* Lotan, Shobal, Zibeon, Anah, Dishon,
Ezer and Dishan. 39 The sons of Lotan *were* Hori and
[a]Homam; and Lotan's sister *was* Timna. 40 The sons
of Shobal *were* [a]Alian, Manahath, Ebal, [b]Shephi and
Onam. And the sons of Zibeon *were* Aiah and Anah.
41 The [a]son of Anah *was* Dishon. And the sons of
Dishon *were* [b]Hamran, Eshban, Ithran and Cheran.
42 The sons of Ezer *were* Bilhan, Zaavan and [a]Jaakan.
The sons of Dishan *were* Uz and Aran.
43 [A]Now these are the kings who reigned in the
land of Edom before any king of the sons of Israel
reigned. Bela was the son of Beor, and the name
of his city was Dinhabah. 44 When Bela died, Jobab
the son of Zerah of [A]Bozrah became king in his
place. 45 When Jobab died, Husham of the land of
[A]the Temanites became king in his place. 46 When
Husham died, Hadad the son of Bedad, who [a]de-
feated Midian in the field of Moab, became king
in his place; and the name of his city *was* Avith.
47 When Hadad died, Samlah of Masrekah became
king in his place. 48 When Samlah died, Shaul of
Rehoboth by the River became king in his place.
49 When Shaul died, Baal-hanan the son of Achbor
became king in his place. 50 When Baal-hanan died,
[a]Hadad became king in his place; and the name of
his city was [b]Pai, and his wife's name was Mehetabel,

1:1 [A]Gen 4:25-5:32 1:5 [A]Gen 10:2-4 1:6 [a]In Gen 10:3, *Riphath* 1:7 [a]In Gen 10:4, *Dodanim* 1:10 [a]Lit *begot,* and so throughout the ch 1:11 [A]Gen 10:13-18 1:12 [a]Or *people of Pelisht* 1:17 [a]In Gen 10:23, *Mash* [A]Gen 10:22-29 1:22 [a]In Gen 10:28, *Obal* 1:24 [A]Gen 11:10-26; Luke 3:34-36 1:29 [A]Gen 25:13-16 1:32 [A]Gen 25:1-4 1:34 [A]1 Chr 1:28 [B]Gen 25:25, 26; 32:28 1:35 [A]Gen 36:4-10 1:36 [a]In Gen 36:11, *Zepho* 1:38 [A]Gen 36:20-28 1:39 [a]In Gen 36:22, *Hemam* 1:40 [a]In Gen 36:23, *Alvan* [b]In Gen 36:23, *Shepho* 1:41 [a]Lit *sons* [b]In Gen 36:26, *Hemdan* 1:42 [a]Or *Akan,* as in Gen 36:27 1:43 [A]Gen 36:31-43 1:44 [A]Is 34:6 1:45 [A]Job 2:11 1:46 [a]Lit *smote* 1:50 [a]In Gen 36:39, *Hadar* [b]In Gen 36:39, *Pau*

1:1–9:44 This abbreviated genealogy summarizes the divinely selected course of redemptive history: 1) from Adam to Noah (1:1–4; Ge 1–6); 2) from Noah's son Shem to Abraham (1:4–27; Ge 7–11); 3) from Abraham to Jacob (1:28–34; Ge 12–25); 4) from Jacob to the 12 tribes (1:34–2:2; Ge 25–50); and 5) from the 12 tribes to those who had returned to Jerusalem after the 70-year captivity (2:3–9:44; Ex 1:1–2Ch 36:23). This genealogical listing is unique to the purposes of "the chronicler" and is not intended to necessarily be an exact duplication of any other list(s) in Scripture.

1:19 **days ... divided.** Peleg, which means "divided," apparently lived when the Lord divided, or scattered, the human race because of Babel (cf. Ge 11:1–9).

1:28–31 These 12 sons of Ishmael developed 12 tribes and settled the great northern desert of Arabia and became Arab peoples.

1:43 **kings ... Edom.** Esau's children settled in Edom, E and S of Israel, and are included among the Arab nations.

A SHORT HARMONY OF SAMUEL, KINGS, AND CHRONICLES

1. Selected Genealogies	----	1Ch 1–9
2. Samuel's Judgeship	1Sa 1–8	----
3. Saul's Reign	1Sa 9–31	1Ch 10
4. David's Reign	2Sa 1–24	1Ch 11–29
5. Solomon's Reign	1Ki 1–11	2Ch 1–9
6. Divided Kingdom Pt. 1	1Ki 12–2Ki 17	2Ch 10–27 (to the Assyrian exile)
7. Divided Kingdom Pt. 2	2Ki 18–25	2Ch 28–36:21 (to the Babylonian exile)
8. Return from Babylon	----	2Ch 36:22, 23

the daughter of Matred, the daughter of Mezahab.
51 Then Hadad died.
Now the chiefs of Edom were: chief Timna, chief
[a]Aliah, chief Jetheth, 52 chief Oholibamah, chief Elah,
chief Pinon, 53 chief Kenaz, chief Teman, chief Mibzar, 54 chief Magdiel, chief Iram. These *were* the
chiefs of Edom.

GENEALOGY: TWELVE SONS OF JACOB (ISRAEL)

2 [A]These are the sons of Israel: Reuben, Simeon,
Levi, Judah, Issachar, Zebulun, 2 Dan, Joseph,
Benjamin, Naphtali, Gad and Asher.
3 [A]The sons of Judah *were* Er, Onan and Shelah;
these three were born to him by Bath-shua the Ca-
naanitess. And Er, Judah's firstborn, was wicked
in the sight of the LORD, so He put him to death.
4 [A]Tamar his daughter-in-law bore him Perez and
Zerah. Judah had five sons in all.
5 The sons of Perez *were* Hezron and Hamul. 6 The
sons of Zerah *were* [a]Zimri, Ethan, Heman, Calcol
and [b]Dara; five of them in all. 7 The [a]son of Carmi
was [b,A]Achar, the troubler of Israel, who violated the
ban. 8 The [a]son of Ethan *was* Azariah.

GENEALOGY OF DAVID

9 Now the sons of Hezron, who were born to him
were Jerahmeel, Ram and Chelubai. 10 Ram [a]became
the father of Amminadab, and Amminadab became
the father of Nahshon, leader of the sons of Judah;
11 Nahshon became the father of Salma, Salma became the father of Boaz, 12 Boaz became the father
of Obed, and Obed became the father of Jesse; 13 and
Jesse became the father of Eliab his firstborn, then
Abinadab the second, [a]Shimea the third, 14 Nethanel
the fourth, Raddai the fifth, 15 Ozem the sixth, David the seventh; 16 and their sisters *were* Zeruiah
and Abigail. And the three sons of Zeruiah *were*
[a]Abshai, Joab and Asahel. 17 Abigail bore Amasa,
and the father of Amasa was [a]Jether the Ishmaelite.
18 Now Caleb the son of Hezron had sons by Azubah *his* wife, and by Jerioth; and these were her
sons: Jesher, Shobab, and Ardon. 19 When Azubah
died, Caleb married Ephrath, who bore him Hur.
20 Hur became the father of Uri, and Uri became
the father of Bezalel.
21 Afterward Hezron went in to the daughter of
Machir the father of Gilead, whom he married when
he was sixty years old; and she bore him Segub.
22 Segub became the father of Jair, who had twenty-three cities in the land of Gilead. 23 But Geshur
and Aram took [a]the towns of Jair from them, with
Kenath and its villages, *even* sixty cities. All these
were the sons of Machir, the father of Gilead. 24 After the death of Hezron in Caleb-ephrathah, Abijah,
Hezron's wife, bore him Ashhur the father of Tekoa.
25 Now the sons of Jerahmeel the firstborn of Hezron *were* Ram the firstborn, then Bunah, Oren, Ozem
and Ahijah. 26 Jerahmeel had another wife, whose
name was Atarah; she was the mother of Onam.
27 The sons of Ram, the firstborn of Jerahmeel, were
Maaz, Jamin and Eker. 28 The sons of Onam were
Shammai and Jada. And the sons of Shammai *were*
Nadab and Abishur. 29 The name of Abishur's wife
was Abihail, and she bore him Ahban and Molid.
30 The sons of Nadab *were* Seled and Appaim, and
Seled died without sons. 31 The [a]son of Appaim *was*
Ishi. And the [a]son of Ishi *was* Sheshan. And the
[a]son of Sheshan *was* Ahlai. 32 The sons of Jada the
brother of Shammai *were* Jether and Jonathan, and
Jether died without sons. 33 The sons of Jonathan
were Peleth and Zaza. These were the sons of Jerahmeel. 34 Now Sheshan had no sons, only daughters.
And Sheshan had an Egyptian servant whose name
was Jarha. 35 Sheshan gave his daughter to Jarha
his servant in marriage, and she bore him Attai.
36 Attai became the father of Nathan, and Nathan
became the father of Zabad, 37 and Zabad became
the father of Ephlal, and Ephlal became the father
of Obed, 38 and Obed became the father of Jehu, and
Jehu became the father of Azariah, 39 and Azariah
became the father of Helez, and Helez became the
father of Eleasah, 40 and Eleasah became the father
of Sismai, and Sismai became the father of Shallum,
41 and Shallum became the father of Jekamiah, and
Jekamiah became the father of Elishama.
42 Now the sons of Caleb, the brother of Jerahmeel, *were* Mesha his firstborn, who was the father of Ziph; and [a]his son was Mareshah, the father
of Hebron. 43 The sons of Hebron *were* Korah and
Tappuah and Rekem and Shema. 44 Shema became
the father of Raham, the father of Jorkeam; and Rekem became the father of Shammai. 45 The son of
Shammai was Maon, and Maon *was* the father of
Bethzur. 46 Ephah, Caleb's concubine, bore Haran,
Moza and Gazez; and Haran became the father of
Gazez. 47 The sons of Jahdai *were* Regem, Jotham,
Geshan, Pelet, Ephah and Shaaph. 48 Maacah, Caleb's
concubine, bore Sheber and Tirhanah. 49 She also
bore Shaaph the father of Madmannah, Sheva the
father of Machbena and the father of Gibea; and
the daughter of Caleb *was* Achsah. 50 These were
the sons of Caleb.
The [a]sons of Hur, the firstborn of Ephrathah,
were Shobal the father of Kiriath-jearim, 51 Salma
the father of Bethlehem *and* Hareph the father of

1:51 [a]In Gen 36:40, *Alvah* 2:1 [A]Gen 35:22-26; 46:8-25 2:3 [A]Gen 38:2-10 2:4 [A]Gen 38:13-30 2:6 [a]In Josh 7:1, *Zabdi* [b]In 1 Kin 4:31, *Darda* 2:7 [a]Lit *sons* [b]In Josh 7:18, *Achan* [A]Josh 7:1 2:8 [a]Lit *sons* 2:10 [a]Lit *begot*, and so throughout the ch 2:13 [a]In 1 Sam 16:9, *Shammah*; in 2 Sam 13:3, *Shimeah* 2:16 [a]In 2 Sam 2:18, *Abishai* 2:17 [a]In 2 Sam 17:25, *Ithra the Israelite* 2:23 [a]Or *Havvoth-jair* 2:31 [a]Lit *sons* 2:42 [a]Lit *the sons of* 2:50 [a]Lit *son*

2:1–7:40 These genealogies reflect the lineage of Jacob/Israel through his 12 sons. The tribe of Judah leads the list, indicating its importance, no doubt because of the Davidic heritage. After Judah, Levi receives the most attention, indicating the importance of their priestly role. Joseph (2:2) is later enumerated in terms of his sons Manasseh and Ephraim. Dan and Zebulun are not mentioned here, although they both are identified in the millennial distribution of land (cf. Eze 48:1, 2, 26, 27). The exact reason for these omissions is unknown. Benjamin is given additional attention in 8:1–40. The tribes are mentioned as follows: 1) Judah (2:3–4:23); 2) Simeon (4:24–43); 3) Reuben (5:1–10); 4) Gad (5:11–22); 5) Manasseh-East (5:23–26); 6) Levi (6:1–81); 7) Issachar (7:1–5); 8) Benjamin (7:6–12); 9) Naphtali (7:13); 10) Manasseh-West (7:14–19); 11) Ephraim (7:20–29); and 12) Asher (7:30–40).

2:7 Achar. This is a variant spelling of Achan, who in Jos 7:1–26 disobeyed the Lord by taking goods from under God's Jericho ban.

Beth-gader. 52 Shobal the father of Kiriath-jearim had sons: Haroeh, half of the Manahathites, 53 and the families of Kiriath-jearim: the Ithrites, the Puthites, the Shumathites and the Mishraites; from these came the Zorathites and the Eshtaolites. 54 The sons of Salma *were* Bethlehem and the Netophathites, Atroth-beth-joab and half of the Manahathites, the Zorites. 55 The families of scribes who lived at Jabez *were* the Tirathites, the Shimeathites *and* the Sucathites. Those are the Kenites who came from Hammath, the father of the house of Rechab.

FAMILY OF DAVID

3 [A]Now these were the sons of David who were born to him in Hebron: the firstborn *was* Amnon, by Ahinoam the Jezreelitess; the second *was* Daniel, by Abigail the Carmelitess; 2 the third *was* Absalom the son of Maacah, the daughter of Talmai king of Geshur; the fourth *was* Adonijah the son of Haggith; 3 the fifth *was* Shephatiah, by Abital; the sixth *was* Ithream, by his wife Eglah. 4 Six were born to him in Hebron, and [A]there he reigned seven years and six months. And in Jerusalem he reigned thirty-three years. 5 [A]These were born to him in Jerusalem: Shimea, Shobab, Nathan and [B]Solomon, four, by [C]Bath-shua the daughter of Ammiel; 6 and Ibhar, Elishama, Eliphelet, 7 Nogah, Nepheg and Japhia, 8 Elishama, Eliada and Eliphelet, nine. 9 All *these were* the sons of David, besides the sons of the concubines; and [A]Tamar *was* their sister.

10 Now Solomon's son *was* Rehoboam, Abijah *was* his son, Asa his son, Jehoshaphat his son, 11 Joram his son, Ahaziah his son, Joash his son, 12 Amaziah his son, Azariah his son, Jotham his son, 13 Ahaz his son, Hezekiah his son, Manasseh his son, 14 Amon his son, Josiah his son. 15 The sons of Josiah *were* Johanan the firstborn, and the second *was* Jehoiakim, the third Zedekiah, the fourth Shallum. 16 The sons of Jehoiakim *were* Jeconiah his son, Zedekiah his son. 17 The sons of Jeconiah, the prisoner, *were* Shealtiel his son, 18 and Malchiram, Pedaiah, Shenazzar, Jekamiah, Hoshama and Nedabiah. 19 The sons of Pedaiah *were* Zerubbabel and Shimei. And the [a]sons of Zerubbabel *were* Meshullam and Hananiah, and Shelomith *was* their sister; 20 and Hashubah, Ohel, Berechiah, Hasadiah and Jushab-hesed, five. 21 The [a]sons of Hananiah *were* Pelatiah and Jeshaiah, the sons of Rephaiah, the sons of Arnan, the sons of Obadiah, the sons of Shecaniah. 22 The [a]descendants of Shecaniah *were* Shemaiah, and the sons of Shemaiah: Hattush, Igal, Bariah, Neariah and Shaphat, six. 23 The [a]sons of Neariah *were* Elioenai, Hizkiah and Azrikam, three. 24 The sons of Elioenai *were* Hodaviah, Eliashib, Pelaiah, Akkub, Johanan, Delaiah and Anani, seven.

LINE OF HUR, ASHER

4 [A]The sons of Judah *were* Perez, Hezron, Carmi, Hur and Shobal. 2 Reaiah the son of Shobal [a]became the father of Jahath, and Jahath became the father of Ahumai and Lahad. These *were* the families of the Zorathites. 3 These *were* the [a]sons of Etam: Jezreel, Ishma and Idbash; and the name of their sister *was* Hazzelelponi. 4 Penuel *was* the father of Gedor, and Ezer the father of Hushah. These *were* the sons of Hur, the firstborn of Ephrathah, the father of Bethlehem. 5 Ashhur, the father of Tekoa, had two wives, Helah and Naarah. 6 Naarah bore him Ahuzzam, Hepher, Temeni and Haahashtari. These were the sons of Naarah. 7 The sons of Helah *were* Zereth, [a]Izhar and Ethnan. 8 Koz became the father of Anub and Zobebah, and the families of Aharhel the son of Harum. 9 Jabez was more honorable than his brothers, and his mother named him Jabez saying, "Because I bore *him* with pain." 10 Now Jabez called on the God of Israel, saying, "Oh that You would bless me indeed and enlarge my border, and that Your hand might be with me, and that You would keep *me* from harm that *it* may not pain me!" And God granted him what he requested.

11 Chelub the brother of Shuhah became the father of Mehir, who was the father of Eshton. 12 Eshton became the father of Beth-rapha and Paseah, and Tehinnah the father of [a]Ir-nahash. These are the men of Recah.

13 Now the sons of Kenaz *were* Othniel and Seraiah. And the sons of Othniel *were* Hathath and Meonothai. 14 Meonothai became the father of Ophrah, and Seraiah became the father of Joab the father of [a]Ge-harashim, for they were craftsmen. 15 The sons of Caleb the son of Jephunneh *were* Iru, Elah and Naam; and the [a]son of Elah *was* [b]Kenaz. 16 The sons of Jehallelel *were* Ziph and Ziphah, Tiria and Asarel. 17 The [a]sons of Ezrah *were* Jether, Mered, Epher and Jalon. ([b]And these are the sons of Bithia the daughter of Pharaoh, whom Mered took) and she conceived *and bore* Miriam, Shammai and Ishbah the father of Eshtemoa. 18 His Jewish wife bore Jered the father of Gedor, and Heber the father of Soco, and Jekuthiel the father of Zanoah. 19 The sons of the wife of Hodiah, the sister of Naham, *were* the [a]fathers of Keilah the Garmite and Eshtemoa the Maacathite. 20 The sons of Shimon *were* Amnon and Rinnah, Benhanan and Tilon. And the sons of Ishi *were* Zoheth and Ben-zoheth. 21 The sons of Shelah the son of Judah

3:1 [A]2 Sam 3:2-5 3:4 [A]2 Sam 2:11; 5:4, 5; 1 Kin 2:11; 1 Chr 29:27 3:5 [A]2 Sam 5:14-16; 1 Chr 14:4-7 [B]2 Sam 12:24, 25 [C]2 Sam 11:3 3:9 [A]2 Sam 13:1 3:19 [a]Lit *son* 3:21 [a]Lit *son* 3:22 [a]Lit *sons* 3:23 [a]Lit *son* 4:1 [A]1 Chr 2:3 4:2 [a]Lit *begot,* and so throughout the ch 4:3 [a]So with some ancient versions; Heb *father* 4:7 [a]Another reading is *Zohar* 4:12 [a]Or *the city of Nahash* 4:14 [a]Or *valley of craftsmen* 4:15 [a]Lit *sons* [b]Lit *and Kenaz* 4:17 [a]Lit *son* [b]In the Heb the words in ( ) are at the end of v 18 4:19 [a]Lit *father*

3:1–4 See 2Sa 3:2–5.

3:1 David. The chief reason for such detailed genealogies is that they affirm the line of Christ from Adam (Lk 3:38) through Abraham and David (Mt 1:1), thus emphasizing the kingdom intentions of God in Christ.

3:5–8 See 2Sa 5:14–16 and 1Ch 14:4–7.

3:10–16 Rehoboam ... Zedekiah. The reigns of these descendants of David are delineated in 2Ch 10:1–36:21.

3:16 Jeconiah. God's curse resulting in no royal descendants from the line of Jeconiah (a.k.a. Jehoiachin), as given by Jeremiah (Jer 22:30), was enforced by God. Even though Jeconiah was in the line of Christ, the Messiah was not a physical child of that line, thus affirming the curse, yet sustaining the legality of His kingship through Joseph, who was in David's line. His blood birthright came through Mary, who traced her line to David through his son Nathan, not Solomon (cf. Lk 3:31).

were Er the father of Lecah and Laadah the father
of Mareshah, and the families of the house of the
linen workers at Beth-ashbea; 22 and Jokim, the
men of Cozeba, Joash, Saraph, who ruled in Moab,
and Jashubi-lehem. And the [a]records are ancient.
23 These were the potters and the inhabitants of
Netaim and Gederah; they lived there with the
king for his work.

DESCENDANTS OF SIMEON

24 The sons of Simeon *were* [a]Nemuel and Jamin,
[b]Jarib, [c]Zerah, Shaul; 25 Shallum his son, Mibsam his
son, Mishma his son. 26 The sons of Mishma *were*
Hammuel his son, Zaccur his son, Shimei his son.
27 Now Shimei had sixteen sons and six daughters;
but his brothers did not have many sons, nor did all
their family multiply like the sons of Judah. 28 They
lived at Beersheba, Moladah and Hazar-shual, 29 at
Bilhah, Ezem, Tolad, 30 Bethuel, Hormah, Ziklag,
31 Beth-marcaboth, Hazar-susim, Beth-biri and Shaaraim. These *were* their cities until the reign of
David. 32 Their villages *were* Etam, Ain, Rimmon,
Tochen and Ashan, five cities; 33 and all their villages that *were* around the same cities as far as
[a]Baal. These *were* their settlements, and they have
their genealogy.

34 Meshobab and Jamlech and Joshah the son
of Amaziah, 35 and Joel and Jehu the son of Josh-
ibiah, the son of Seraiah, the son of Asiel, 36 and
Elioenai, Jaakobah, Jeshohaiah, Asaiah, Adiel,
Jesimiel, Benaiah, 37 Ziza the son of Shiphi, the
son of Allon, the son of Jedaiah, the son of Shimri,
the son of Shemaiah; 38 these mentioned by name
were leaders in their families; and their fathers'
houses increased greatly. 39 They went to the entrance of Gedor, even to the east side of the valley,
to seek pasture for their flocks. 40 They found
rich and good pasture, and [A]the land was broad
and quiet and peaceful; for those who lived there
formerly *were* Hamites. 41 [A]These, recorded by
name, came in the days of Hezekiah king of Judah, and [a]attacked their tents and the Meunites
who were found there, and destroyed them utterly to this day, and lived in their place, because
there was pasture there for their flocks. 42 From
them, from the sons of Simeon, five hundred
men went to [A]Mount Seir, with Pelatiah, Neariah,
Rephaiah and Uzziel, the sons of Ishi, as their
leaders. 43 [A]They [a]destroyed the remnant of the
Amalekites who escaped, and have lived there to
this day.

GENEALOGY FROM REUBEN

5 Now the sons of Reuben the firstborn of Israel
(for [A]he was the firstborn, but because [B]he defiled his father's bed, [C]his birthright was given to
the sons of Joseph the son of Israel; so that he is not
enrolled in the genealogy according to the birthright. 2 [A]Though Judah prevailed over his brothers,
and [B]from him *came* the leader, yet the birthright
belonged to Joseph), 3 [A]the sons of Reuben the firstborn of Israel *were* Hanoch and Pallu, Hezron and
Carmi. 4 The sons of Joel *were* Shemaiah his son,
Gog his son, [A]Shimei his son, 5 Micah his son, Reaiah his son, Baal his son, 6 Beerah his son, whom
[a]Tilgath-pilneser king of Assyria carried away into
exile; he was leader of the Reubenites. 7 His [a]kinsmen
by their families, [A]in the genealogy of their generations, *were* Jeiel the chief, then Zechariah 8 and Bela
the son of Azaz, the son of Shema, the son of Joel,
who lived in [A]Aroer, even to Nebo and Baal-meon.
9 To the east he settled as far as the entrance of the
wilderness from the river Euphrates, [A]because their
cattle had increased in the land of Gilead. 10 In the
days of Saul [A]they made war with the Hagrites, who
fell by their hand, so that they [a]occupied their tents
throughout [b]all the land east of Gilead.

11 Now the sons of Gad lived opposite them in
the land of [A]Bashan as far as [B]Salecah. 12 Joel *was*
the chief and Shapham the second, then Janai and
Shaphat in Bashan. 13 Their [a]kinsmen of their fathers'
households *were* Michael, Meshullam, Sheba, Jorai,
Jacan, Zia and Eber, seven. 14 These *were* the sons of
Abihail, the son of Huri, the son of Jaroah, the son
of Gilead, the son of Michael, the son of Jeshishai,
the son of Jahdo, the son of Buz; 15 Ahi the son of
Abdiel, the son of Guni, *was* head of their fathers'
households. 16 They lived in Gilead, in Bashan and
in its towns, and in all the pasture lands of [A]Sharon,
as far as their [a]borders. 17 All of these were enrolled
in the genealogies in the days of [A]Jotham king of
Judah and in the days of [B]Jeroboam king of Israel.

18 The sons of Reuben and the Gadites and the
half-tribe of Manasseh, *consisting* of valiant men,
men who bore shield and sword and shot with bow
and *were* skillful in battle, *were* 44,760, who [A]went to
war. 19 They made war against [A]the Hagrites, [B]Jetur,
Naphish and Nodab. 20 They were helped against
them, and the Hagrites and all who *were* with them
were given into their hand; for [A]they cried out to
God in the battle, and He answered their prayers
because [B]they trusted in Him. 21 They took away their
cattle: their 50,000 camels, 250,000 sheep, 2,000

4:22 [a]Lit *words* 4:24 [a]In Gen 46:10 and Ex 6:15, *Jemuel* [b]In Num 26:12, *Jachin* [c]In Gen 46:10 and Ex 6:15, *Zohar* 4:33 [a]In Josh 19:8, *Baalath* 4:40 [A]Judg 18:7-10 4:41 [a]Lit *smote* [A]1 Chr 4:33-38 4:42 [A]Gen 36:8, 9 4:43 [a]Lit *smote* [A]1 Sam 15:7, 8; 30:17 5:1 [A]Gen 29:32; 1 Chr 2:1 [B]Gen 35:22; 49:4 [C]Gen 48:15-22 5:2 [A]Gen 49:8-10; Ps 60:7; 108:8 [B]Mic 5:2; Matt 2:6 5:3 [A]Gen 46:9; Ex 6:14; Num 26:5-9 5:4 [A]1 Chr 5:8 5:6 [a]In 2 Kin 15:29, *Tiglath-pileser* 5:7 [a]Lit *brothers* [A]1 Chr 5:17 5:8 [A]Num 32:34; Josh 12:2 5:9 [A]Josh 22:8, 9 5:10 [a]Lit *dwelt in* [b]Lit *all the face of the east* [A]1 Chr 5:18-21 5:11 [A]Josh 13:11 [B]Deut 3:10 5:13 [a]Lit *brother* 5:16 [a]Lit *goings out* [A]1 Chr 27:29; Song 2:1; Is 35:2; 65:10 5:17 [A]2 Kin 15:5, 32 [B]2 Kin 14:16, 28 5:18 [A]Num 1:3 5:19 [A]1 Chr 5:10 [B]Gen 25:15; 1 Chr 1:31 5:20 [A]2 Chr 14:11-13 [B]Ps 9:10; 20:7, 8; 22:4, 5

3:22 six Only 5 sons are named, so the number includes their father Shemaiah.

4:41 Hezekiah. He ruled Judah ca. 715–686 B.C.

4:43 Amalekites. Longstanding enemies of Israel whom God purposed to exterminate. Another branch of the Amalekite family tree had appeared in Persia, represented by Haman, who attempted to exterminate the Jews (Est 3:1ff.).

5:2 Judah prevailed. In accordance with Jacob's blessing (Ge 49:10), the king of Israel is to come from Judah. This prophecy had historical reference to the Davidic Covenant (cf. 2Sa 7; 1Ch 17) with full messianic implications.

5:6 Tilgath-pilneser. The king of Assyria (ca. 745–727 B.C.) who threatened Judah and made Ahaz pay a tribute (cf. 2Ki 16:7–20; 2Ch 28:16–21).

donkeys; and 100,000 [a]men. 22 For many fell slain, because [A]the war *was* of God. And [B]they settled in their place until the [C]exile.

23 Now the sons of the half-tribe of Manasseh lived in the land; from Bashan to Baal-hermon and [A]Senir and Mount Hermon they were numerous. 24 These were the heads of their fathers' households, even Epher, Ishi, Eliel, Azriel, Jeremiah, Hodaviah and Jahdiel, mighty men of valor, famous men, heads of their fathers' households.

25 But they [A]acted treacherously against the God of their fathers and [B]played the harlot [C]after the gods of the peoples of the land, whom God had destroyed before them. 26 So the God of Israel stirred up the spirit of [A]Pul, king of Assyria, even the spirit of [a]Tilgath-pilneser king of Assyria, and he [B]carried them away into exile, namely the Reubenites, the Gadites and the half-tribe of Manasseh, and brought them to Halah, Habor, Hara and to the river of Gozan, to this day.

GENEALOGY: THE PRIESTLY LINE

6 [a,A]The sons of Levi *were* [b]Gershon, Kohath and Merari. 2 The sons of Kohath *were* Amram, Izhar, Hebron and Uzziel. 3 The children of Amram *were* Aaron, Moses and Miriam. And the sons of Aaron *were* Nadab, Abihu, Eleazar and Ithamar. 4 Eleazar [a]became the father of Phinehas, *and* Phinehas became the father of Abishua, 5 and Abishua became the father of Bukki, and Bukki became the father of Uzzi, 6 and Uzzi became the father of Zerahiah, and Zerahiah became the father of Meraioth, 7 Meraioth became the father of Amariah, and Amariah became the father of Ahitub, 8 and [A]Ahitub became the father of Zadok, and Zadok [B]became the father of Ahimaaz, 9 and Ahimaaz became the father of Azariah, and Azariah became the father of Johanan, 10 and Johanan became the father of Azariah ([A]it was he who served as the priest in the house [B]which Solomon built in Jerusalem), 11 and [A]Azariah became the father of Amariah, and Amariah became the father of Ahitub, 12 and Ahitub became the father of Zadok, and Zadok became the father of [a]Shallum, 13 and Shallum became the father of Hilkiah, and Hilkiah became the father of Azariah, 14 and Azariah became the father of [A]Seraiah, and Seraiah became the father of Jehozadak; 15 and Jehozadak went *along* when the LORD carried Judah and Jerusalem away into exile [a]by Nebuchadnezzar.

16 [a,A]The sons of Levi *were* [b]Gershom, Kohath and Merari. 17 These are the names of the sons of Gershom: Libni and Shimei. 18 The sons of Kohath *were* Amram, Izhar, Hebron and Uzziel. 19 The sons of [A]Merari *were* Mahli and Mushi. And these are the families of the Levites according to their fathers' *households.* 20 Of Gershom: Libni his son, Jahath his son, Zimmah his son, 21 Joah his son, Iddo his son, Zerah his son, Jeatherai his son. 22 The sons of Kohath *were* Amminadab his son, Korah his son, Assir his son, 23 Elkanah his son, Ebiasaph his son and Assir his son, 24 Tahath his son, Uriel his son, Uzziah his son and Shaul his son. 25 The sons of Elkanah *were* Amasai and Ahimoth. 26 *As for* Elkanah, the sons of Elkanah *were* Zophai his son and Nahath his son, 27 Eliab his son, Jeroham his son, Elkanah his son. 28 The sons of Samuel *were* [A]Joel the firstborn, and Abijah the second. 29 The sons of Merari *were* Mahli, Libni his son, Shimei his son, Uzzah his son, 30 Shimea his son, Haggiah his son, Asaiah his son.

31 [A]Now these are those whom David appointed over the service of song in the house of the LORD, [B]after the ark rested *there.* 32 They ministered with song before the tabernacle of the tent of meeting, until Solomon had built the house of the LORD in Jerusalem; and they [a]served in their office according to their order. 33 These are those who [a]served with their sons: From the sons of the Kohathites *were* Heman the singer, the son of Joel, the son of Samuel, 34 the son of Elkanah, the son of Jeroham, the son of Eliel, the son of Toah, 35 the son of Zuph, the son of Elkanah, the son of Mahath, the son of Amasai, 36 the son of Elkanah, the son of Joel, the son of Azariah, the son of Zephaniah, 37 the son of Tahath, the son of Assir, the son of Ebiasaph, the son of Korah, 38 the son of Izhar, the son of Kohath, the son of Levi, the son of Israel. 39 *Heman's* brother Asaph stood at his right hand, even Asaph the son of Berechiah, the son of Shimea, 40 the son of Michael, the son of Baaseiah, the son of Malchijah, 41 the son of Ethni, the son of Zerah, the son of Adaiah, 42 the son of Ethan, the son of Zimmah, the son of Shimei, 43 the son of Jahath, the son of Gershom, the son of Levi. 44 On the left hand *were* their [a]kinsmen the sons of Merari: Ethan the son of Kishi, the son of

5:21 [a]Lit *souls of men* 5:22 [A]Josh 23:10; 2 Chr 32:8; Rom 8:31 [B]1 Chr 4:41 [C]2 Kin 15:29; 17:6 5:23 [A]Deut 3:9 5:25 [A]Deut 32:15-18 [B]Ex 34:15 [C]2 Kin 17:7 5:26 [a]In 2 Kin 15:29, *Tiglath-pileser* [A]2 Kin 15:19, 29; 2 Chr 28:20 [B]2 Kin 17:6 6:1 [a]Ch 5:27 in Heb [b]In v 16, *Gershom* [A]Gen 46:11; Ex 6:16-25 6:4 [a]Lit *begot,* and so throughout the ch 6:8 [A]2 Sam 8:17 [B]2 Sam 15:27 6:10 [A]2 Chr 26:17 [B]1 Kin 6:1; 2 Chr 3:1 6:11 [A]Ezra 7:3 6:12 [a]In ch 9:11, *Meshullam* 6:14 [A]Neh 11:11 6:15 [a]Lit *by the hand of* 6:16 [a]Ch 6:1 in Heb [b]In v 1, *Gershon* [A]Gen 46:11; Ex 6:16 6:19 [A]Num 3:33; 1 Chr 23:21 6:28 [A]1 Sam 8:2; 1 Chr 6:33 6:31 [A]1 Chr 15:16-22, 27; 16:4-6 [B]2 Sam 6:17; 1 Kin 8:4; 1 Chr 15:25-16:1 6:32 [a]Lit *stood over* 6:33 [a]Lit *stood* 6:44 [a]Lit *brothers*

5:22 the exile. The Assyrian deportation of 722 B.C. is meant (cf. 5:26).

6:1–15 This section lists the High Priestly lineage from Levi (6:1) through Aaron (6:3), through Eleazar (6:3, 4), and through Phinehas (6:4), with whom God covenanted for a perpetual priesthood (Nu 25:11–13).

6:8 Zadok. By the time of David's reign, the High Priestly line had wrongly been shifted to the sons of Ithamar as represented by Abiathar. When Abiathar sided with Adonijah rather than Solomon, Zadok became the ruling High Priest (1Ki 2:26, 27) and restored the high-priesthood to the Levitical line through Phinehas (cf. Nu 25:10–13).

6:13 Hilkiah. The High Priest who rediscovered the law in Josiah's reign ca. 622 B.C. (2Ki 22:8–13; 2Ch 34:14–21).

6:14 Seraiah. The High Priest who was executed by the Babylonians after their occupation of Jerusalem ca. 586 B.C. (2Ki 25:18–21). **Jehozadak.** (a.k.a. Jozadak.) The father of Jeshua, the first High Priest in the return (cf. Ezr 3:2; 5:2).

6:16–30 The sons of Levi (6:16–19) and their families (6:20–30) are given here.

6:27, 28 Samuel, a Levite, by exceptional, divine direction, offered priestly sacrifices (cf. 1Sa 7:9; 10:8; 11:14, 15). The fact that Elkanah was from Ephraim (1Sa 1:1) indicates where he lived, not his family history (Nu 35:6–8).

6:31–48 The Levitical musicians are listed as they relate to: 1) Kohath and Heman (6:33–38); 2) Gershon and Asaph (6:39–43); and 3) Merari and Ethan (6:44–47).

Abdi, the son of Malluch, 45 the son of Hashabiah,
the son of Amaziah, the son of Hilkiah, 46 the son
of Amzi, the son of Bani, the son of Shemer, 47 the
son of Mahli, the son of Mushi, the son of Merari,
the son of Levi. 48 Their [a]kinsmen the Levites were
[b]appointed for all the service of the tabernacle of
the house of God.

49 But Aaron and his sons [a,A]offered on the altar
of burnt offering and [B]on the altar of incense, for
all the work of the most holy place, and [C]to make
atonement for Israel, according to all that Moses the
servant of God had commanded. 50 [A]These are the
sons of Aaron: Eleazar his son, Phinehas his son,
Abishua his son, 51 Bukki his son, Uzzi his son, Zerahiah his son, 52 Meraioth his son, Amariah his son,
Ahitub his son, 53 Zadok his son, Ahimaaz his son.

54 Now these are their settlements according to
their camps within their borders. To the sons of
Aaron of the families of the Kohathites (for theirs
was the [A]*first* lot), 55 to them they gave [A]Hebron in
the land of Judah and its pasture lands around it;
56 [A]but the fields of the city and its villages, they
gave to Caleb the son of Jephunneh. 57 [A]To the sons
of Aaron they gave the *following* cities of refuge:
Hebron, Libnah also with its pasture lands, Jattir,
Eshtemoa with its pasture lands, 58 [a]Hilen with its
pasture lands, Debir with its pasture lands, 59 [a]Ashan
with its pasture lands and Beth-shemesh with its
pasture lands; 60 and from the tribe of Benjamin:
Geba with its pasture lands, [a]Allemeth with its pasture lands, and Anathoth with its pasture lands. All
their cities throughout their families were thirteen
cities.

61 [A]Then to the rest of the sons of Kohath *were
given* by lot, from the family of the tribe, from the
half-tribe, the half of Manasseh, ten cities. 62 To the
sons of Gershom, according to their families, *were
given* from the tribe of Issachar and from the tribe
of Asher, the tribe of Naphtali, and the tribe of Manasseh, thirteen cities in Bashan. 63 [A]To the sons of
Merari *were given* by lot, according to their families, from the tribe of Reuben, the tribe of Gad and
the tribe of Zebulun, twelve cities. 64 [A]So the sons
of Israel gave to the Levites the cities with their
pasture lands. 65 They gave by lot from the tribe of
the sons of Judah, the tribe of the sons of Simeon
and the tribe of the sons of Benjamin, [A]these cities
which are mentioned by name.

66 [A]Now some of the families of the sons of Kohath had cities of their territory from the tribe of
Ephraim. 67 They gave to them the *following* cities of
refuge: Shechem in the hill country of Ephraim with
its pasture lands, Gezer also with its pasture lands,
68 Jokmeam with its pasture lands, Beth-horon with
its pasture lands, 69 Aijalon with its pasture lands
and Gath-rimmon with its pasture lands; 70 and from
the half-tribe of Manasseh: Aner with its pasture
lands and Bileam with its pasture lands, for the
rest of the family of the sons of Kohath.

71 To the sons of Gershom *were given,* from the
family of the half-tribe of Manasseh: Golan in Bashan with its pasture lands and Ashtaroth with its
pasture lands; 72 and from the tribe of Issachar:
Kedesh with its pasture lands, Daberath with its
pasture lands 73 and Ramoth with its pasture lands,
Anem with its pasture lands; 74 and from the tribe
of Asher: Mashal with its pasture lands, Abdon with
its pasture lands, 75 Hukok with its pasture lands
and Rehob with its pasture lands; 76 and from the
tribe of Naphtali: Kedesh in Galilee with its pasture
lands, Hammon with its pasture lands and Kiriathaim with its pasture lands.

77 To the rest of *the Levites,* the sons of Merari,
were given, from the tribe of Zebulun: Rimmono
with its pasture lands, Tabor with its pasture lands;
78 and beyond the Jordan at Jericho, on the east side
of the Jordan, *were given them,* from the tribe of
Reuben: Bezer in the wilderness with its pasture
lands, Jahzah with its pasture lands, 79 Kedemoth
with its pasture lands and Mephaath with its pasture lands; 80 and from the tribe of Gad: Ramoth in
Gilead with its pasture lands, Mahanaim with its
pasture lands, 81 Heshbon with its pasture lands
and Jazer with its pasture lands.

GENEALOGY FROM ISSACHAR

7 Now the sons of Issachar *were* four: Tola, [a]Puah,
[b]Jashub and Shimron. 2 The sons of Tola *were*
Uzzi, Rephaiah, Jeriel, Jahmai, Ibsam and Samuel,
heads of their fathers' households. *The sons* of Tola
were mighty men of valor in their generations;
[A]their number in the days of David was 22,600. 3 The
[a]son of Uzzi *was* Izrahiah. And the sons of Izrahiah
were Michael, Obadiah, Joel, Isshiah; all five of them
were [A]chief men. 4 With them by their generations
according to their fathers' households were 36,000
[a]troops of the army for war, for they had many wives
and sons. 5 Their [a]relatives among all the families
of Issachar *were* mighty men of valor, enrolled by
genealogy, in all 87,000.

DESCENDANTS OF BENJAMIN

6 [A]*The sons of* Benjamin *were* three: Bela and
Becher and Jediael. 7 The sons of Bela were five:
Ezbon, Uzzi, Uzziel, Jerimoth and Iri. They *were*
heads of fathers' households, mighty men of valor,
and were 22,034 enrolled by genealogy. 8 The sons
of Becher *were* Zemirah, Joash, Eliezer, Elioenai,
Omri, Jeremoth, Abijah, Anathoth and Alemeth. All
these *were* the sons of Becher. 9 They were enrolled

6:48 [a]Lit *brothers* [b]Lit *given* 6:49 [a]Lit *offered up in smoke* [A]Ex 27:1-8 [B]Ex 30:1-7 [C]Ex 30:10-16 6:50 [A]1 Chr 6:4-8; Ezra 7:5 6:54 [A]Josh 21:4, 10 6:55 [A]Josh 14:13; 21:11f 6:56 [A]Josh 15:13 6:57 [A]Josh 21:13, 19 6:58 [a]In Josh 21:15, *Holon* 6:59 [a]In Josh 21:16, *Ain* 6:60 [a]In Josh 21:18, *Almon* 6:61 [A]Josh 21:5; 1 Chr 6:66-70 6:63 [A]Josh 21:7, 34-40 6:64 [A]Num 35:1-8; Josh 21:3, 41, 42 6:65 [A]1 Chr 6:57-60 6:66 [A]Josh 21:20-26 7:1 [a]In Gen 46:13, *Puvvah;* in Num 26:23, *Puvah* [b]In Gen 46:13, *Iob* 7:2 [A]2 Sam 24:1-9 7:3 [a]Lit *sons* [A]1 Chr 5:24 7:4 [a]Or *bands* 7:5 [a]Lit *brothers,* and so throughout the ch 7:6 [A]1 Chr 8:1-40

6:49–53 This is a repeat of the High Priestly line enumerated in 6:4–8 through Zadok. This repeated genealogy could possibly point to the Zadokian high-priesthood for the temple in the Millennium (cf. Eze 40:46; 43:19; 44:15; 48:11).

6:54–81 This section rehearses the 48 cities given to the Levites instead of a section of land (cf. Nu 35:1–8; Jos 21:1–42) which signals God's intention for the Jewish nation to have a priesthood and future in the land first given to Abraham (cf. Ge 12:1–3).

by genealogy, according to their generations, heads
of their fathers' households, 20,200 mighty men of
valor. 10 The [a]son of Jediael *was* Bilhan. And the sons
of Bilhan *were* Jeush, Benjamin, Ehud, Chenaanah,
Zethan, Tarshish and Ahishahar. 11 All these *were*
sons of Jediael, according to the heads of their fathers' households, 17,200 mighty men of valor, who
were [a]ready to go out with the army to war. 12 [a]Shup-
pim and [b]Huppim *were* the sons of [c]Ir; Hushim *was*
the [d]son of [e]Aher.

SONS OF NAPHTALI

13 The sons of Naphtali *were* [a]Jahziel, Guni, Jezer,
and [b]Shallum, the sons of Bilhah.

DESCENDANTS OF MANASSEH

14 The sons of Manasseh *were* Asriel, whom his
Aramean concubine bore; she bore Machir the father of Gilead. 15 Machir took a wife for Huppim
and Shuppim, [a]whose sister's name was Maacah.
And the name of the second was Zelophehad, and
Zelophehad had daughters. 16 Maacah the wife of
Machir bore a son, and she named him Peresh;
and the name of his brother *was* Sheresh, and his
sons *were* Ulam and Rakem. 17 The [a]son of Ulam
was Bedan. These *were* the sons of Gilead the son
of Machir, the son of Manasseh. 18 His sister Ham-
molecheth bore Ishhod and [a]Abiezer and Mahlah.
19 The sons of Shemida were Ahian and Shechem
and Likhi and Aniam.

DESCENDANTS OF EPHRAIM

20 [A]The sons of Ephraim *were* Shuthelah and [a]Be-
red his son, Tahath his son, Eleadah his son, Tahath
his son, 21 Zabad his son, Shuthelah his son, and Ezer
and Elead whom the men of Gath who were born
in the land killed, because they came down to take
their livestock. 22 Their father Ephraim [A]mourned
many days, and his relatives [B]came to comfort him.
23 Then he went in to his wife, and she conceived
and bore a son, and he named him [a]Beriah, because misfortune had come upon his house. 24 His
daughter was Sheerah, [A]who built lower and upper
Beth-horon, also Uzzen-sheerah. 25 Rephah was his
son *along* with Resheph, Telah his son, Tahan his
son, 26 Ladan his son, Ammihud his son, Elishama
his son, 27 [a]Non his son and [A]Joshua his son.

28 [A]Their possessions and settlements *were* Bethel
with its towns, and to the east [a]Naaran, and to the
west Gezer with its towns, and Shechem with its
towns as far as [b]Ayyah with its towns, 29 and along
the borders of the sons of Manasseh, Beth-shean
with its towns, Taanach with its towns, Megiddo
with its towns, Dor with its towns. In these lived
the [A]sons of Joseph the son of Israel.

DESCENDANTS OF ASHER

30 [A]The sons of Asher *were* Imnah, Ishvah, Ishvi
and Beriah, and Serah their sister. 31 The sons of Beriah *were* Heber and Malchiel, who was the father
of Birzaith. 32 Heber [a]became the father of Japhlet,
[b]Shomer and Hotham, and Shua their sister. 33 The
sons of Japhlet *were* Pasach, Bimhal and Ashvath.
These were the sons of Japhlet. 34 The sons of [a]She-
mer *were* Ahi and Rohgah, Jehubbah and Aram.
35 The [a]sons of his brother Helem *were* Zophah,
Imna, Shelesh and Amal. 36 The sons of Zophah *were*
Suah, Harnepher, Shual, Beri and Imrah, 37 Bezer,
Hod, Shamma, Shilshah, Ithran and Beera. 38 The
sons of Jether *were* Jephunneh, Pispa and Ara. 39 The
sons of Ulla *were* Arah, Hanniel and Rizia. 40 All
these *were* the sons of Asher, heads of the fathers'
houses, choice and mighty men of valor, heads of
the princes. And the number of them enrolled by
genealogy for service in war was 26,000 men.

GENEALOGY FROM BENJAMIN

8 And [A]Benjamin [a]became the father of Bela his
firstborn, Ashbel the second, [B]Aharah the third,
2 Nohah the fourth and Rapha the fifth. 3 Bela had
sons: [a]Addar, Gera, Abihud, 4 Abishua, Naaman, Ahoah,
5 Gera, Shephuphan and Huram. 6 These are the sons
of Ehud: these are the heads of fathers' *households* of
the inhabitants of Geba, and they carried them into
exile to Manahath, 7 namely, Naaman, Ahijah and
Gera—he carried them into exile; and he became the
father of Uzza and Ahihud. 8 Shaharaim became the
father of children in the [a]country of Moab after he had
[b]sent away Hushim and Baara his wives. 9 By Hodesh
his wife he became the father of Jobab, Zibia, Mesha,
Malcam, 10 Jeuz, Sachia, Mirmah. These were his sons,
heads of fathers' *households*. 11 By Hushim he became
the father of Abitub and Elpaal. 12 The sons of Elpaal
were Eber, Misham, and Shemed, who built Ono and
Lod, with its towns; 13 and Beriah and Shema, who were
heads of fathers' *households* of the inhabitants of Aijalon, who put to flight the inhabitants of Gath; 14 and
[a]Ahio, Shashak and Jeremoth. 15 Zebadiah, Arad, Eder,
16 Michael, Ishpah and Joha *were* the sons of Beriah.
17 Zebadiah, Meshullam, Hizki, Heber, 18 Ishmerai, Iz-
liah and Jobab *were* the sons of Elpaal. 19 Jakim, Zichri,
Zabdi, 20 Elienai, Zillethai, Eliel, 21 Adaiah, Beraiah and
Shimrath *were* the sons of [a]Shimei. 22 Ishpan, Eber,
Eliel, 23 Abdon, Zichri, Hanan, 24 Hananiah, Elam, An-
thothijah, 25 Iphdeiah and Penuel *were* the sons of Shashak. 26 Shamsherai, Shehariah, Athaliah, 27 Jaareshiah,
Elijah and Zichri *were* the sons of Jeroham. 28 These
were heads of the fathers' *households* according to
their generations, chief men [a]who lived in Jerusalem.

29 [A]Now in Gibeon, *Jeiel,* the father of Gibeon lived,
and his wife's name was Maacah; 30 and his firstborn

7:10 [a]Lit *sons* 7:11 [a]Lit *going out* 7:12 [a]In Num 26:39, *Shephupham* [b]In Num 26:39, *Hupham* [c]In v 7, *Iri* [d]Lit *sons* [e]In Num 26:38, *Ahiram* 7:13 [a]In Gen 46:24, *Jahzeel* [b]In Gen 46:24 and Num 26:49, *Shillem* 7:15 [a]Lit *and his* 7:17 [a]Lit *sons* 7:18 [a]In Num 26:30, *Iezer* 7:20 [a]In Num 26:35, *Becher* [A]Num 26:35, 36 7:22 [A]Gen 37:34 [B]Job 2:11; John 11:19 7:23 [a]I.e. on misfortune 7:24 [A]Josh 16:3, 5; 2 Chr 8:5 7:27 [a]In Ex 33:11, *Nun* [A]Ex 17:9-14; 24:13 7:28 [a]In Josh 16:7, *Naarah* [b]Many mss read *Azzah* [A]Josh 16:2 7:29 [A]Judg 1:22-29 7:30 [A]Gen 46:17; Num 26:44-46 7:32 [a]Lit *begot* [b]In v 34, *Shemer* 7:34 [a]In v 32, *Shomer* 7:35 [a]Lit *son* 8:1 [a]Lit *begot,* and so throughout the ch [A]Gen 46:21; 1 Chr 7:6-12 [B]1 Chr 7:12 8:3 [a]In Gen 46:21 and Num 26:40, *Ard* 8:8 [a]Lit *field* [b]Lit *sent them away* 8:14 [a]Or *his brothers* 8:21 [a]In v 13, *Shema* 8:28 [a]Lit *these* 8:29 [A]1 Chr 9:35-38

8:1–40 This section enlarges on the genealogy of Benjamin in 7:6–12, most likely because of that tribe's important relationship with Judah in the southern kingdom. Thus these two tribes taken in captivity together and the Levites make up the returning remnant in 538 B.C.

son *was* Abdon, then Zur, Kish, Baal, Nadab, 31 Gedor,
Ahio and [a]Zecher. 32 Mikloth became the father of
[a]Shimeah. And they also lived with their [b]relatives
in Jerusalem opposite their *other* [b]relatives.

GENEALOGY FROM KING SAUL

33 [A]Ner became the father of Kish, and Kish
became the father of Saul, and Saul became the
father of Jonathan, Malchi-shua, [a]Abinadab and
[b]Eshbaal. 34 The son of Jonathan *was* [a]Merib-baal,
and Merib-baal became the father of Micah. 35 The
sons of Micah *were* Pithon, Melech, [a]Tarea and Ahaz.
36 Ahaz became the father of [a]Jehoaddah, and Jeho-
addah became the father of Alemeth, Azmaveth and
Zimri; and Zimri became the father of Moza. 37 Moza
became the father of Binea; [a]Raphah *was* his son, Eleasah his son, Azel his son. 38 Azel had six sons, and
these *were* their names: Azrikam, Bocheru, Ishmael,
Sheariah, Obadiah and Hanan. All these *were* the
sons of Azel. 39 The sons of Eshek his brother *were*
Ulam his firstborn, Jeush the second and Eliphelet
the third. 40 The sons of Ulam were mighty men of
valor, archers, and had many sons and grandsons,
150 *of them*. All these *were* of the sons of Benjamin.

PEOPLE OF JERUSALEM

9 So all Israel was enrolled by genealogies; and
behold, they are written in the Book of the Kings

8:31 [a]In ch 9:37, *Zechariah* 8:32 [a]In ch 9:38, *Shimeam* [b]Lit *brothers* 8:33 [a]1 Sam 14:49, *Ishvi* [b]In 2 Sam 2:8, *Ish-bosheth* [A]1 Chr 9:39-44 8:34 [a]In 2 Sam 4:4, *Mephibosheth* 8:35 [a]In 9:41, *Tahrea* 8:36 [a]In 9:42, *Jarah* 8:37 [a]In 9:43, *Rephaiah*

9:1 all Israel. Even though the northern kingdom of Israel never returned from dispersion in 722 B.C., many from the 10 tribes which made up that kingdom migrated S after the division in 931 B.C. The result was that Judah, the southern kingdom, had people from all tribes, so that when returning from captivity "all Israel" was truly represented.

THE CHRONICLES' SOURCES

The inspiration of Scripture (2Ti 3:16) was sometimes accomplished through direct revelation from God without a human writer, e.g., the Mosaic law. At other times, God used human sources, as mentioned in Lk 1:1–4. Such was the experience of the chronicler as evidenced by the many contributing sources. Whether the material came through direct revelation or by existing resources, God's inspiration through the Holy Spirit prevented the original human authors of Scripture from any error (2Pe 1:19–21). Although relatively few scribal errors have been made in copying Scripture, they can be identified and corrected. Thus, the original, inerrant content of the Bible has been preserved.

1. Book of the Kings of Israel/Judah (1Ch 9:1; 2Ch 16:11; 20:34; 25:26; 27:7; 28:26; 32:32; 35:27; 36:8)
2. The Chronicles of David (1Ch 27:24)
3. The Chronicles of Samuel (1Ch 29:29)
4. The Chronicles of Nathan (1Ch 29:29; 2Ch 9:29)
5. The Chronicles of Gad (1Ch 29:29)
6. Prophecy of Ahijah the Shilonite (2Ch 9:29)
7. Visions of Iddo (2Ch 9:29)
8. Records of Shemaiah (2Ch 12:15)
9. Records of Iddo (2Ch 12:15)
10. Treatise of Iddo (2Ch 13:22)
11. Annals of Jehu (2Ch 20:34)
12. Treatise of the Book of the Kings (2Ch 24:27)
13. Acts of Uzziah by Isaiah (2Ch 26:22)
14. Letters/Message of Sennacherib (2Ch 32:10–17)
15. Vision of Isaiah (2Ch 32:32)
16. Words of the Seers (2Ch 33:18)
17. Records of Hozai (2Ch 33:19)
18. Written instructions of David and Solomon (2Ch 35:4)
19. The Lamentations (2Ch 35:25)

of Israel. And [A]Judah was carried away into exile
to Babylon for their unfaithfulness.
2 [A]Now the first who lived in their possessions in
their cities *were* Israel, the priests, the Levites and
[B]the [a]temple servants. 3 Some of the sons of Judah,
of the sons of Benjamin and of the sons of Ephraim
and Manasseh lived in [A]Jerusalem: 4 Uthai the son
of Ammihud, the son of Omri, the son of Imri, the
son of Bani, from the sons of Perez the [A]son of Judah. 5 From the Shilonites *were* Asaiah the firstborn
and his sons. 6 From the sons of Zerah *were* Jeuel
and their [a]relatives, 690 *of them.* 7 From the sons of
Benjamin *were* Sallu the son of Meshullam, the son
of Hodaviah, the son of Hassenuah, 8 and Ibneiah
the son of Jeroham, and Elah the son of Uzzi, the
son of Michri, and Meshullam the son of Shephatiah, the son of Reuel, the son of Ibnijah; 9 and their
relatives according to their generations, [A]956. All
these *were* heads of fathers' *households* according
to their fathers' houses.
10 [A]From the priests *were* Jedaiah, Jehoiarib,
Jachin, 11 and [a]Azariah the son of Hilkiah, the son
of Meshullam, the son of Zadok, the son of Meraioth,
the son of Ahitub, [A]the chief officer of the house of
God; 12 and Adaiah the son of Jeroham, the son of
Pashhur, the son of Malchijah, and Maasai the son
of Adiel, the son of Jahzerah, the son of Meshullam,
the son of Meshillemith, the son of Immer; 13 and
their relatives, heads of their fathers' households,
1,760 very able men for the work of the service of
the house of God.
14 [A]Of the Levites *were* Shemaiah the son of Hasshub, the son of Azrikam, the son of Hashabiah, of
the sons of Merari; 15 and Bakbakkar, Heresh and
Galal and Mattaniah the son of Mica, the son of
[a]Zichri, the son of Asaph, 16 and [a]Obadiah the son
of [b]Shemaiah, the son of Galal, the son of Jeduthun,
and Berechiah the son of Asa, the son of Elkanah,
who lived in the villages of the Netophathites.
17 Now the gatekeepers *were* [a]Shallum and Akkub
and Talmon and Ahiman and their relatives (Shallum the chief 18 *being stationed* until now at [A]the
king's gate to the east). These *were* the gatekeepers
for the camp of the sons of Levi. 19 Shallum the son
of Kore, the son of [a]Ebiasaph, the son of Korah, and
his relatives of his father's house, the Korahites,
were over the work of the service, keepers of the
thresholds of the tent; and their fathers had been
over the camp of the LORD, keepers of the entrance.
20 [A]Phinehas the son of Eleazar was ruler over them
previously, *and* the LORD was with him. 21 [A]Zecha-
riah the son of Meshelemiah was gatekeeper of the
entrance of the tent of meeting. 22 All these who
were chosen to be gatekeepers at the thresholds
were 212. These were enrolled by genealogy in their
villages, [A]whom David and Samuel the seer appointed [B]in their office of trust. 23 So they and their
sons [a]had charge of the gates of the house of the
LORD, *even* the house of the tent, as guards. 24 The
gatekeepers were [a]on the four sides, to the east,
west, north and south. 25 Their relatives in their
villages [A]*were* to come in every seven days from
time to time *to be* with [a]them; 26 for the four chief
gatekeepers who *were* Levites, were in an office
of trust, and were over the chambers and over the
treasuries in the house of God. 27 They spent the
night around the house of God, [A]because the watch
was [a]committed to them; and they *were* [b]in charge
of opening *it* morning by morning.
28 Now some of them [a]had charge of the utensils of service, for [b]they counted them when they
brought them in and when they took them out.
29 Some of them also were appointed over the furniture and over all the utensils of the sanctuary and
[A]over the fine flour and the wine and the oil and the
frankincense and the spices. 30 Some of [A]the sons of
the priests prepared the mixing of the spices. 31 Mattithiah, one of the Levites, who was the firstborn of
Shallum the Korahite, had [A]the [a]responsibility over
the things which were baked in pans. 32 Some of
their relatives of the sons of the Kohathites [A]*were*
over the showbread to prepare it every sabbath.
33 Now these are [A]the singers, heads of fathers'
households of the Levites, *who lived* in the chambers *of the temple* free *from other service;* for they
were [a]engaged [B]in their work day and night. 34 These
were heads of fathers' *households* of the Levites
according to their generations, chief men, [a]who
lived in Jerusalem.

ANCESTRY AND DESCENDANTS OF SAUL

35 [A]In Gibeon Jeiel the father of Gibeon lived, and
his wife's name was Maacah, 36 and his firstborn
son *was* Abdon, then Zur, Kish, Baal, Ner, Nadab,
37 Gedor, Ahio, Zechariah and Mikloth. 38 Mikloth
became the father of Shimeam. And they also lived
with their relatives in Jerusalem opposite their *other*
relatives. 39 [A]Ner became the father of Kish, and
Kish became the father of Saul, and Saul became
the father of Jonathan, Malchi-shua, Abinadab and
Eshbaal. 40 The son of Jonathan *was* Merib-baal; and
Merib-baal became the father of Micah. 41 The sons
of Micah *were* Pithon, Melech, Tahrea [A]*and Ahaz.*
42 Ahaz became the father of Jarah, and Jarah became the father of Alemeth, Azmaveth and Zimri;
and Zimri became the father of Moza, 43 and Moza
became the father of Binea and Rephaiah his son,

9:1 [A]1 Chr 5:25, 26 9:2 [a]Heb *Nethinim* [A]Ezra 2:70; Neh 7:73; 11:3-22 [B]Ezra 2:43, 58; 8:20 9:3 [A]Neh 11:1 9:4 [A]Gen 46:12; Num 26:20 9:6 [a]Lit *brothers,* and so throughout the ch 9:9 [A]Neh 11:8 9:10 [A]Neh 11:10-14 9:11 [a]In Neh 11:11, *Seraiah* [A]Jer 20:1 9:14 [A]Neh 11:15-19 9:15 [a]In Neh 11:17, *Zabdi* 9:16 [a]In Neh 11:17, *Abda* [b]In Neh 11:17, *Shammua* 9:17 [a]In v 21, *Meshelemiah;* in 26:14, *Shelemiah;* in Neh 12:25, *Meshullam* 9:18 [A]Ezek 44:1; 46:1, 2 9:19 [a]In Ex 6:24, *Abiasaph* 9:20 [A]Num 25:7-13 9:21 [A]1 Chr 26:2, 14 9:22 [A]1 Chr 26:1 [B]2 Chr 31:15, 18 9:23 [a]Lit were *over the gates* 9:24 [a]Lit *to the four winds* 9:25 [a]Lit *these* [A]2 Kin 11:5, 7; 2 Chr 23:8 9:27 [a]Lit *on them* [b]Lit *over the opening* [A]1 Chr 23:30-32 9:28 [a]Lit *were over the* [b]Lit *by count they brought them in and by count they took them out* 9:29 [A]1 Chr 23:29 9:30 [A]Ex 30:23-25 9:31 [a]Lit *office of trust* [A]1 Chr 9:22 9:32 [A]Lev 24:5-8 9:33 [a]Lit *over them in the work* [A]1 Chr 6:31-47; 25:1 [B]Ps 134:1 9:34 [a]Lit *these* 9:35 [A]1 Chr 8:29-32 9:39 [A]1 Chr 8:33-38 9:41 [A]1 Chr 8:35-37

9:2 first who lived. This chapter has genealogies of returning 1) Israelites (9:3–9); 2) priests (9:10–13); and 3) Levites (9:14–34). **temple servants.** These temple servants (Ezr 8:20) were possibly descendants of the Gibeonites (cf. Jos 9:3, 4, 23).

9:35–44 This section records Saul's lineage as a transition to the main theme of the rest of the book, which is the kingship of David (ca. 1011 B.C.).

Eleasah his son, Azel his son. 44 Azel had six sons whose names are these: Azrikam, Bocheru and Ishmael and Sheariah and Obadiah and Hanan. These were the sons of Azel.

DEFEAT AND DEATH OF SAUL AND HIS SONS

10 [A]Now the Philistines fought against Israel; and the men of Israel fled before the Philistines and fell slain on Mount Gilboa. 2 The Philistines closely pursued Saul and his sons, and the Philistines struck down Jonathan, [a,A]Abinadab and Malchi-shua, the sons of Saul. 3 The battle became heavy against Saul, and the archers [a]overtook him; and he was wounded by the archers. 4 Then Saul said to his armor bearer, "Draw your sword and thrust me through with it, otherwise these uncircumcised will come and abuse me." But his armor bearer would not, for he was greatly afraid. [A]Therefore Saul took his sword and fell on it. 5 When his armor bearer saw that Saul was dead, he likewise fell on his sword and died. 6 [A]Thus Saul died with his three sons, and all *those* of his house died together.

7 When all the men of Israel who were in the valley saw that they had fled, and that Saul and his sons were dead, they forsook their cities and fled; and the Philistines came and lived in them.

8 It came about the next day, when the Philistines came to strip the slain, that they found Saul and his sons fallen on Mount Gilboa. 9 [A]So they stripped him and took his head and his armor and sent *messengers* around the land of the Philistines to carry the good news to their idols and to the people. 10 They put his armor in the house of their gods and fastened his head in the house of Dagon.

JABESH-GILEAD'S TRIBUTE TO SAUL

11 When all Jabesh-gilead heard all that the Philistines had done to Saul, 12 [A]all the valiant men arose and took away the body of Saul and the bodies of his sons and brought them to Jabesh, and they buried their bones under the oak in Jabesh, and fasted seven days.

13 [A]So Saul died for his trespass which he committed against the LORD, because of the word of the LORD which he did not keep; and also [B]because he asked counsel of a medium, making inquiry *of it,* 14 and did not inquire of the LORD. Therefore He killed him and [A]turned the kingdom to David the son of Jesse.

DAVID MADE KING OVER ALL ISRAEL

11 [A]Then all Israel gathered to David at Hebron [a]and said, "Behold, we are your bone and your flesh. 2 In times past, even when Saul was king, you *were* the one who led out and brought in Israel; and the LORD your God said to you, '[A]You shall shepherd My people Israel, and you shall be prince over My people Israel.' " 3 So all the elders of Israel came to the king at Hebron, and David made a covenant with them in Hebron before the LORD; and [A]they anointed David king over Israel, [B]according to the word of the LORD through Samuel.

JERUSALEM, CAPITAL CITY

4 Then David and all Israel went to Jerusalem ([A]that is, Jebus); and the Jebusites, the inhabitants of the land, *were* there. 5 The inhabitants of Jebus said to David, "You shall not enter here." Nevertheless David captured the stronghold of Zion (that is, the city of David). 6 Now David had said, "Whoever strikes down a Jebusite first shall be chief and commander." [A]Joab the son of Zeruiah went up first, so he became chief. 7 Then David dwelt in the stronghold; therefore it was called the city of David. 8 He [a]built the city all around, from the [b]Millo even to the surrounding area; and Joab [c]repaired the rest of the city. 9 [A]David became greater and greater, for the LORD of hosts *was* with him.

DAVID'S MIGHTY MEN

10 [A]Now these are the heads of the mighty men whom David had, who gave him strong support in his kingdom, together with all Israel, to make him king, [B]according to the word of the LORD concerning Israel. 11 These *constitute* the list of the mighty men whom David had: [A]Jashobeam, the son of a Hachmonite, [B]the chief of the thirty; he lifted up his spear against three hundred [a]whom he killed at one time.

12 After him was Eleazar the son of [A]Dodo, the Ahohite, who *was* [a]one of the three mighty men. 13 He was with David at [a]Pasdammim [A]when the Philistines were gathered together there to battle, and there was a plot of ground full of barley; and the people fled before the Philistines. 14 They took their stand in the midst of the plot and defended it, and struck down the Philistines; and the LORD saved them by a great [a]victory.

15 Now three of the thirty chief men went down to the rock to David, into the cave of Adullam, while

10:1 [A]1 Sam 31:1-13 10:2 [a]In 1 Sam 14:49, *Ishvi* [A]1 Sam 31:2 10:3 [a]Lit *found him* 10:4 [A]1 Sam 31:4 10:6 [A]1 Sam 31:6 10:9 [A]1 Sam 31:9 10:12 [A]1 Sam 31:12f 10:13 [A]1 Sam 13:13, 14; 15:23 [B]Lev 19:31; 20:6; 1 Sam 28:7 10:14 [A]1 Sam 15:28; 1 Chr 12:23 11:1 [a]Lit *saying* [A]2 Sam 5:1, 3, 6-10 11:2 [A]2 Sam 5:2; 7:7 11:3 [A]2 Sam 2:4; 5:3, 5 [B]1 Sam 16:1, 3, 12, 13 11:4 [A]Josh 15:8, 63; Judg 1:21 11:6 [A]2 Sam 8:16 11:8 [a]Or *fortified* [b]I.e. citadel [c]Lit *revived* 11:9 [A]2 Sam 3:1 11:10 [A]2 Sam 23:8-39 [B]1 Chr 11:3 11:11 [a]Lit *slain ones* [A]2 Sam 23:8 [B]1 Chr 12:18 11:12 [a]Lit *among* [A]1 Chr 27:4 11:13 [a]In 1 Sam 17:1, *Ephesdammim* [A]2 Sam 23:11, 12 11:14 [a]Or *salvation*

10:1–12 *See notes on 1Sa 31:1–13* (cf. 2Sa 1:4–12).

10:13, 14 This summary is unique to 1Ch and provides the proper transition from Saul's kingship to David's reign.

10:14 He killed him. Though Saul killed himself (v. 4), God took responsibility for Saul's death, which was fully deserved for consulting a medium, an activity punishable by death (cf. Lv 20:6). This demonstrates that human behavior is under the ultimate control of God, who achieves His purpose through the actions of people.

11:1–29:30 This section selectively recounts the reign of David with a heavy emphasis on the placement of the ark in Jerusalem and preparation to build the temple.

11:1–3 *See notes on 2Sa 5:1–3.*

11:4–9 *See notes on 2Sa 5:6–10.*

11:10–41 *See notes on 2Sa 23:8–39.*

11:11 Jashobeam … Hachmonite. In 27:2, he is called the son of Zabdiel, so Hachmon may be, strictly speaking, his grandfather (27:32). For a variation in name and number (300), *see note on 2Sa 23:8*. A copyist's error would best account for 800 being reported in 2Sa 23:8.

[A]the army of the Philistines was camping in the valley of Rephaim. 16 David was then in the stronghold,
while [A]the garrison of the Philistines *was* then in
Bethlehem. 17 David had a craving and said, "Oh
that someone would give me water to drink from
the well of Bethlehem, which is by the gate!" 18 So
the three broke through the camp of the Philistines
and drew water from the well of Bethlehem which
was by the gate, and took *it* and brought *it* to David;
nevertheless David would not drink it, but poured
it out to the LORD; 19 and he said, "Be it far from me
before my God that I should do this. Shall I drink the
blood of these men *who went* [a]at the risk of their
lives? For at the risk of their lives they brought it."
Therefore he would not drink it. These things the
three mighty men did.

20 As for [a]Abshai the brother of Joab, he was chief
of the [b]thirty, and he swung his spear against three
hundred [c]and killed them; and he had a name as
well as the [b]thirty. 21 Of the three in the second *rank*
he was the most honored and became their commander; however, he did not attain to the *first* three.

22 [A]Benaiah the son of Jehoiada, the son of a valiant man of Kabzeel, mighty in deeds, struck down
the [a]two *sons of* Ariel of Moab. He also went down
and [b]killed a lion inside a pit on a snowy day. 23 He
[a]killed an Egyptian, a man of *great* stature five [b]cu-
bits tall. Now in the Egyptian's hand *was* [A]a spear
like a weaver's beam, but he went down to him with
a club and snatched the spear from the Egyptian's
hand and [a]killed him with his own spear. 24 These
things Benaiah the son of Jehoiada did, and had a
name as well as the three mighty men. 25 Behold,
he was honored among the thirty, but he did not
attain to the three; and David appointed him over
his guard.

26 Now the mighty men of the armies *were* Asahel the brother of Joab, Elhanan the son of Dodo
of Bethlehem, 27 [a]Shammoth the Harorite, Helez the
[b]Pelonite, 28 Ira the son of Ikkesh the Tekoite, Abiezer
the Anathothite, 29 [a]Sibbecai the Hushathite, [b]Ilai
the Ahohite, 30 Maharai the Netophathite, [a]Heled
the son of Baanah the Netophathite, 31 Ithai the son
of Ribai of Gibeah of the sons of Benjamin, Benaiah
the Pirathonite, 32 [a]Hurai of the brooks of Gaash,
[b]Abiel the Arbathite, 33 Azmaveth the Baharumite,
Eliahba the Shaalbonite, 34 the sons of [a]Hashem the
Gizonite, Jonathan the son of Shagee the Hararite,
35 Ahiam the son of [a]Sacar the Hararite, [b]Eliphal
the son of Ur, 36 Hepher the Mecherathite, Ahijah
the Pelonite, 37 Hezro the Carmelite, [a]Naarai the
son of Ezbai, 38 Joel the brother of Nathan, Mibhar
the son of Hagri, 39 Zelek the Ammonite, Naharai
the Berothite, the armor bearer of Joab the son of
Zeruiah, 40 Ira the Ithrite, Gareb the Ithrite, 41 Uriah
the Hittite, Zabad the son of Ahlai, 42 Adina the son
of Shiza the Reubenite, a chief of the Reubenites,
and thirty with him, 43 Hanan the son of Maacah and
Joshaphat the Mithnite, 44 Uzzia the Ashterathite,
Shama and Jeiel the sons of Hotham the Aroerite,
45 Jediael the son of Shimri and Joha his brother, the
Tizite, 46 Eliel the Mahavite and Jeribai and Josha-
viah, the sons of Elnaam, and Ithmah the Moabite,
47 Eliel and Obed and Jaasiel the Mezobaite.

DAVID'S SUPPORTERS IN ZIKLAG

12 [A]Now these are the ones who came to David
at Ziklag, while he was still restricted because
of Saul the son of Kish; and they were among the
mighty men who helped *him* in war. 2 They were
equipped with bows, [A]using both the right hand
and the left *to sling* stones and *to shoot* arrows from
the bow; [B]*they were* Saul's kinsmen from Benjamin.
3 The chief was Ahiezer, then Joash, the sons of She-
maah the Gibeathite; and Jeziel and Pelet, the sons
of Azmaveth, and Beracah and Jehu the Anathothite,
4 and Ishmaiah the Gibeonite, a mighty man among
the thirty, and over the thirty. [a]Then Jeremiah, Jahaziel, Johanan, Jozabad the Gederathite, 5 [a]Eluzai,
Jerimoth, Bealiah, Shemariah, Shephatiah the Haru-
phite, 6 Elkanah, Isshiah, Azarel, Joezer, Jashobeam,
the Korahites, 7 and Joelah and Zebadiah, the sons
of Jeroham of Gedor.

8 From the Gadites there [a]came over to David in
the stronghold in the wilderness, mighty men of
valor, men trained for war, who could handle shield
and spear, and whose faces were like the faces of
lions, and [A]*they were* as swift as the gazelles on the
mountains. 9 Ezer *was* the first, Obadiah the second,
Eliab the third, 10 Mishmannah the fourth, Jeremiah
the fifth, 11 Attai the sixth, Eliel the seventh, 12 Johanan the eighth, Elzabad the ninth, 13 Jeremiah the
tenth, Machbannai the eleventh. 14 These of the sons
of Gad were [a]captains of the army; [A]he who was
least was equal to a hundred and the greatest to a
thousand. 15 [A]These are the ones who crossed the
Jordan in the first month when it was overflowing
all its banks and they put to flight all those in the
valleys, both to the east and to the west.

16 Then some of the sons of Benjamin and Judah came to the stronghold to David. 17 David went
out to meet them, and said to them, "If you come

11:15 [A]1 Chr 14:9 11:16 [A]1 Sam 10:5 11:19 [a]Lit *with their souls* 11:20 [a]In 2 Sam 23:18, *Abishai* [b]So Syriac; M.T. *three* [c]Lit *slain ones* 11:22 [a]Or *two lion-like heroes* of [b]Lit *smote* [A]2 Sam 8:18 11:23 [a]Lit *smote* [b]I.e. One cubit equals approx 18 in. [A]1 Sam 17:7 11:27 [a]In 2 Sam 23:25, *Shammah the Harodite* [b]In 2 Sam 23:26, *Paltite* 11:29 [a]In 2 Sam 23:27, *Mebunnai* [b]In 2 Sam 23:28, *Zalmon* 11:30 [a]In 2 Sam 23:29, *Heleb* 11:32 [a]In 2 Sam 23:30, *Hiddai* [b]In 2 Sam 23:31, *Abi-albon* 11:34 [a]In 2 Sam 23:32, *Jashen* 11:35 [a]In 2 Sam 23:33, *Sharar* [b]In 2 Sam 23:34, *Eliphelet the son of Ahasbai* 11:37 [a]In 2 Sam 23:35, *Paarai the Arbite* 12:1 [A]1 Sam 27:2-6 12:2 [A]Judg 3:15; 20:16 [B]1 Chr 12:29 12:4 [a]In Heb the beginning of v 5, making 41 vv in ch 12:5 [a]V 6 in Heb 12:8 [a]Lit *separated themselves* [A]2 Sam 2:18 12:14 [a]Or *chiefs* [A]Deut 32:30 12:15 [A]Josh 3:15; 4:18

11:41–47 This adds new material to 2Sa 23.

12:1–40 These events predate those of 11:1–47. They are divided between David's time at Ziklag (12:1–22) and Hebron (12:23–40). They summarize the narrative covered in 1Sa 27–2Sa 5.

12:1 **Ziklag.** Located in the S near the Edomite border. The territory was ruled by the Philistines, who made David a ruler over it during the latter period of Saul's reign when he was pursuing David (1Sa 27:6, 7). This was prior to David's taking the rule over all Israel (cf. v. 38).

12:1–14 Men from Benjamin (12:2, 3, 16–18), Gad (12:8–15), Judah (12:16–18), and Manasseh (12:19–22) came to help David conquer enemies on both sides of the Jordan (v. 15).

12:15 **first month.** Mar./Apr. when the Jordan River was at flood stage due to melting snow in the N. The Gadites would be crossing from E to W.

peacefully to me to help me, my heart shall be united
with you; but if to betray me to my adversaries,
since there is no [a]wrong in my hands, may the God
of our fathers look on *it* and decide.” 18 Then [A]the
Spirit [a]came upon [B]Amasai, who was the chief of
the thirty, *and he said,*

“*We* are yours, O David,
And with you, O son of Jesse!
[C]Peace, peace to you,
And peace to him who helps you;
Indeed, your God helps you!”

Then David received them and made them [b]cap-
tains of the band.
19 [A]From Manasseh also some defected to David
when he was about to go to battle with the Philistines against Saul. But they did not help them, for
the lords of the Philistines after consultation sent
him away, saying, “At *the cost of* our heads he may
defect to his master Saul.” 20 As he went to Ziklag
there defected to him from Manasseh: Adnah, Jozabad, Jediael, Michael, Jozabad, Elihu and Zillethai,
[a]captains of thousands who belonged to Manasseh.
21 They helped David against [A]the band of raiders,
for they were all mighty men of valor, and were
captains in the army. 22 For day by day *men* came
to David to help him, until there was a great army
[A]like the army of God.

SUPPORTERS GATHERED AT HEBRON

23 Now these are the numbers of the [a]divisions
equipped for war, [A]who came to David at Hebron,
[B]to turn the kingdom of Saul to him, [C]according to
the [b]word of the LORD. 24 The sons of Judah who
bore shield and spear *were* 6,800, equipped for
war. 25 Of the sons of Simeon, mighty men of valor
for war, 7,100. 26 Of the sons of Levi 4,600. 27 Now
Jehoiada was the leader of *the house of* Aaron, and
with him were 3,700, 28 also [A]Zadok, a young man
mighty of valor, and of his father’s house twenty-two captains. 29 Of the sons of Benjamin, [A]Saul’s
kinsmen, 3,000; for until now [B]the greatest part
of them had kept their allegiance to the house of
Saul. 30 Of the sons of Ephraim 20,800, mighty men
of valor, famous men in their fathers’ households.
31 Of the half-tribe of Manasseh 18,000, who were
designated by name to come and make David king.
32 Of the sons of Issachar, [A]men who understood the
times, with knowledge of what Israel should do,
their chiefs *were* two hundred; and all their kinsmen
were at their command. 33 Of Zebulun, there were
50,000 who went out in the army, who could draw
up in battle formation with all kinds of weapons of
war and helped *David* [a]with [A]an undivided heart.
34 Of Naphtali *there were* 1,000 captains, and with
them 37,000 with shield and spear. 35 Of the Danites
who could draw up in battle formation, *there were*
28,600. 36 Of Asher *there were* 40,000 who went out
in the army to draw up in battle formation. 37 From
the other side of the Jordan, of the Reubenites and
the Gadites and of the half-tribe of Manasseh, *there
were* 120,000 with all *kinds* of weapons of war for
the battle.
38 All these, being men of war who could draw up
in battle formation, came to Hebron with [A]a perfect
heart to make David king over all Israel; and all the
rest also of Israel were of one mind to make David
king. 39 They were there with David three days, eating and drinking, for their kinsmen had prepared
for them. 40 Moreover those who were near to them,
even as far as Issachar and Zebulun and Naphtali,
[A]brought food on donkeys, camels, mules and on
oxen, great quantities of flour cakes, fig cakes and
bunches of raisins, wine, oil, oxen and sheep. There
was joy indeed in Israel.

PERIL IN TRANSPORTING THE ARK

13 Then David consulted with the captains of the
thousands and the hundreds, even with every
leader. 2 David said to all the assembly of Israel, “If
it seems good to you, and if it is from the LORD our
God, let us send everywhere to our kinsmen who
remain in all the land of Israel, also to the priests
and Levites who are with them in their cities with
pasture lands, that they may meet with us; 3 and
let us bring back the ark of our God to us, [A]for we
did not seek it in the days of Saul.” 4 Then all the
assembly said that they would do so, for the thing
was right in the eyes of all the people.
5 [A]So David assembled all Israel together, from
the Shihor of Egypt even to the entrance of Hamath, [B]to bring the ark of God from Kiriath-jearim.
6 [A]David and all Israel went up to [B]Baalah, *that is,*
to Kiriath-jearim, which belongs to Judah, to bring
up from there the ark of God, the LORD [C]who is

12:17 [a]Lit *violence* 12:18 [a]Lit *clothed* [b]Or *chiefs* [A]Judg 3:10; 6:34 [B]1 Chr 2:17 [C]1 Sam 25:5, 6 12:19 [A]1 Sam 29:2-9 12:20 [a]Or *chiefs* 12:21 [A]1 Sam 30:1 12:22 [A]Gen 32:2; Josh 5:13-15 12:23 [a]Lit *heads* [b]Lit *mouth* [A]2 Sam 2:3, 4 [B]1 Chr 10:14 [C]1 Chr 11:10 12:28 [A]2 Sam 8:17; 1 Chr 6:8, 53 12:29 [A]1 Chr 12:2 [B]2 Sam 2:8, 9 12:32 [A]Esth 1:13 12:33 [a]Lit *not of double heart* [A]Ps 12:2 12:38 [A]2 Sam 5:1-3; 1 Chr 12:33 12:40 [A]1 Sam 25:18 13:3 [A]1 Sam 7:1, 2 13:5 [A]2 Sam 6:1; 1 Kin 8:65; 1 Chr 15:3 [B]1 Sam 6:21; 7:1 13:6 [A]2 Sam 6:2-11 [B]Josh 15:9 [C]Ex 25:22; 2 Kin 19:15

12:18 the Spirit. A temporary empowerment by the Holy Spirit to assure David that the Benjamites and Judahites were loyal to him and that the cause was blessed by God.

12:19, 20 First Samuel 29 provides the background.

12:21, 22 First Samuel 30 provides the background.

12:23–37 This recounts the period of David’s 7-year, 6-month reign in Hebron until he was crowned king of the entire nation and was ready to relocate in Jerusalem (2Sa 2–5). This narrative comes full circle back to 1Ch 11:1ff.

12:38–40 This feast was associated with the king’s coronation in 2Sa 5.

13:1–16:43 This section recounts the ark of the covenant being brought from Kiriath-jearim (v. 5) to Jerusalem.

13:1–14 *See notes on 2Sa 6:1–11.* First Chronicles 13:1–6 adds new material to the narrative.

13:3 the ark of our God. Not only had the ark been stolen and profaned by the Philistines (1Sa 5–6), but when it was returned, Saul neglected to seek God’s instruction for it. Scripture records only one occasion when Saul sought God’s ark after its return (cf. 1Sa 14:18).

13:5 Shihor. The “river of Egypt” was a small stream flowing into the Mediterranean, which forms the southern boundary of Israel (cf. Jos 13:3). It is also called the “brook of Egypt” (Jos 15:4, 47; Nu 34:5; 2Ch 7:8). **Hamath.** On the northern boundary of Israel’s territory. **Kiriath-jearim.** A location approximately 10 mi. W of Jerusalem that the Canaanites called Baalah (cf. 13:6). The ark of God had resided here for the previous 20 years (cf. 1Sa 7:1, 2).

enthroned *above* the cherubim, where His name
is called. 7 They [a]carried the ark of God on a new
cart from [A]the house of Abinadab, and Uzza and
Ahio drove the cart. 8 David and all Israel were celebrating before God with all *their* might, [A]even with
songs and with lyres, harps, tambourines, cymbals
and with trumpets.
9 When they came to [A]the threshing floor of
Chidon, Uzza put out his hand to hold the ark,
because the oxen nearly upset *it*. 10 The anger
of the LORD burned against Uzza, so He struck
him down [A]because he put out his hand to the
ark; [B]and he died there before God. 11 Then David
became angry because [a]of the LORD'S outburst
against Uzza; and he called that place [b]Perez-uzza
to this day. 12 David was afraid of God that day,
saying, "How can I bring the ark of God *home* to
me?" 13 So David did not take the ark with him
to the city of David, but took it aside [A]to the house
of Obed-edom the Gittite. 14 Thus the ark of God
remained with the family of Obed-edom in his
house three months; and [A]the LORD blessed the
family of Obed-edom with all that he had.

DAVID'S FAMILY ENLARGED

14 [A]Now Hiram king of Tyre sent messengers to
David with cedar trees, masons and carpenters, to build a house for him. 2 And David realized
that the LORD had established him as king over
Israel, *and* that his kingdom was highly exalted,
for the sake of His people Israel.
3 Then David took more wives at Jerusalem, and
David [a]became the father of more sons and daughters. 4 [A]These are the names of the children [a]born
to him in Jerusalem: Shammua, Shobab, Nathan,
Solomon, 5 Ibhar, Elishua, Elpelet, 6 Nogah, Nepheg,
Japhia, 7 Elishama, Beeliada and Eliphelet.

PHILISTINES DEFEATED

8 When the Philistines heard that David had been
anointed king over all Israel, all the Philistines went
up in search of David; and David heard of it and
went out against them. 9 Now the Philistines had
come and [A]made a raid in the valley of Rephaim.
10 David inquired of God, saying, "Shall I go up
against the Philistines? And will You give them
into my hand?" Then the LORD said to him, "Go up,
for I will give them into your hand." 11 So they came
up to Baal-perazim, and David [a]defeated them there;
and David said, "God has broken through my enemies by my hand, like the breakthrough of waters."
Therefore they named that place [b]Baal-perazim.
12 They abandoned their gods there; so David gave
the order and they were burned with fire.
13 The Philistines made [A]yet another raid in the
valley. 14 David inquired again of God, and God
said to him, "You shall not go up after them; circle
around [a]behind them and come at them in front of
the [b]balsam trees. 15 It shall be when you hear the
sound of marching in the tops of the balsam trees,
then you shall go out to battle, for God will have
gone out before you to strike the army of the Philistines." 16 David did just as God had commanded him,
and they struck down the army of the Philistines
from [a]Gibeon even as far as Gezer. 17 Then the fame
of David went out into all the lands; and [A]the LORD
brought the fear of him on all the nations.

PLANS TO MOVE THE ARK TO JERUSALEM

15 Now *David* built houses for himself in the
city of David; and he prepared a place for
the ark of God and [A]pitched a tent for it. 2 Then
David said, "[A]No one is to carry the ark of God but
the Levites; for the LORD chose them to carry the
ark of God and to minister to Him forever." 3 And
[A]David assembled all Israel at Jerusalem to bring
up the ark of the LORD [B]to its place which he had
prepared for it. 4 David gathered together the sons
of Aaron and [A]the Levites: 5 of the sons of Kohath,
Uriel the chief, and 120 of his [a]relatives; 6 of the sons
of Merari, Asaiah the chief, and 220 of his relatives;
7 of the sons of Gershom, Joel the chief, and 130 of
his relatives; 8 of the sons of Elizaphan, Shemaiah
the chief, and 200 of his relatives; 9 of the sons of
Hebron, Eliel the chief, and 80 of his relatives; 10
of the sons of Uzziel, Amminadab the chief, and
112 of his relatives.
11 Then David called for [A]Zadok and [B]Abiathar
the priests, and for the Levites, for Uriel, Asaiah,

13:7 [a]Lit *caused to ride* [A]1 Sam 7:1 13:8 [A]1 Chr 15:16 13:9 [A]2 Sam 6:6 13:10 [A]1 Chr 15:13, 15 [B]Lev 10:2 13:11 [a]Lit *the LORD had broken through a breakthrough* [b]I.e. the breakthrough of Uzza 13:13 [A]1 Chr 15:25 13:14 [A]1 Chr 26:4, 5 14:1 [A]2 Sam 5:11 14:3 [a]Lit *begot* 14:4 [a]Lit *were to* [A]1 Chr 3:5-8 14:9 [A]1 Chr 11:15; 14:13 14:11 [a]Lit *smote* [b]I.e. the master of breakthrough 14:13 [A]1 Chr 14:9 14:14 [a]Lit *from upon* [b]Or *baka shrubs* 14:16 [a]In 2 Sam 5:25, *Geba* 14:17 [A]Ex 15:14-16; Deut 2:25 15:1 [A]1 Chr 15:3; 16:1; 17:1-5 15:2 [A]Num 4:15; Deut 10:8 15:3 [A]1 Kin 8:1; 1 Chr 13:5 [B]Ex 40:20f; 2 Sam 6:12, 17; 1 Chr 15:1, 12 15:4 [A]1 Chr 6:16-30; 12:26 15:5 [a]Lit *brothers;* i.e. fellow tribesmen, and so throughout the ch 15:11 [A]1 Chr 12:28 [B]1 Sam 22:20-23; 1 Kin 2:26, 35

13:7–14 *See notes on 2Sa 6:1–11.* The violation of divine directives (Nu 4:1–49) for moving the ark proved fatal to Uzza(h) (vv. 7–10).

14:1–7 *See notes on 2Sa 5:11–13.* The events of this chapter took place before those of 1Ch 13.

14:3–7 This is a repeat of 1Ch 3:5–9.

14:8–17 The Philistines desired to ruin David before the throne was consolidated. Their plan was to kill David, but God gave him victory over the Philistines (unlike Saul) and thus declared both to the Philistines and Israel His support of Israel's new king. For details, *see notes on 2Sa 5:17–23.*

14:12 gods ... burned. Second Samuel 5:21 reports that the idols were carried away, presenting an apparent contradiction. Most likely the idols were first carried away and then burned later, according to the Mosaic law (cf. Dt 7:5, 25).

15:1–29 The chronicler picks up the narrative concerning the ark where it left off at 1Ch 13:14, as David brings the ark from Obed-edom.

15:1 *David built houses for himself.* He was able by the alliance and help of Hiram (18:1) to build a palace for himself and separate houses for his wives and their children. While the ark remained near Jerusalem at the home of Obed-edom for 3 months (13:13, 14), David constructed a new tabernacle in Jerusalem to fulfill God's Word in Dt 12:5–7 of a permanent residency.

15:2 carry the ark. After a lapse of 3 months (13:14), David followed the Mosaic directives for moving the ark (cf. Nu 4:1–49; Dt 10:8; 18:5). These directions had been violated when the ark was moved from Kiriath-jearim to Obed-edom, and it cost Uzza(h) his life (cf. 13:6–11).

15:4–7 Kohath ... Merari ... Gershom. David conducted the ark's relocation with the same families as had Moses (cf. Nu 4). In the restoration from Babylon, these identical 3 divisions of Levi participated (cf. 1Ch 6:1–48).

15:11 Zadok ... Abiathar. These two High Priests, heads of the two priestly houses of Eleazar and Ithamar, were colleagues in the high-priesthood (2Sa 20:25). They served the Lord simultaneously in David's reign. Zadok attended the tabernacle in Gibeon (1Ch 16:39),

Joel, Shemaiah, Eliel and Amminadab, 12 and said to
them, "You are the heads of the fathers' *households*
of the Levites; [A]consecrate yourselves both you and
your relatives, that you may bring up the ark of the
LORD God of Israel [B]to *the place* that I have prepared
for it. 13 [A]Because you did not *carry it* at the first,
the LORD our God made an outburst on us, for we
did not seek Him according to the ordinance." 14 [A]So
the priests and the Levites consecrated themselves
to bring up the ark of the LORD God of Israel. 15 The
sons of [A]the Levites carried the ark of God on their
shoulders with the poles thereon, as Moses had
commanded according to the word of the LORD.
16 Then David spoke to the chiefs of the Levites [A]to
appoint their relatives the singers, with instruments
of music, harps, lyres, loud-sounding cymbals, to raise
sounds of joy. 17 So [A]the Levites appointed Heman the
son of Joel, and from his relatives, Asaph the son of
Berechiah; and from the sons of Merari their relatives,
Ethan the son of Kushaiah, 18 and with them their
relatives of the second rank, Zechariah, [a]Ben, Jaaziel,
Shemiramoth, Jehiel, Unni, Eliab, Benaiah, Maaseiah,
Mattithiah, Eliphelehu, Mikneiah, Obed-edom and
Jeiel, the gatekeepers. 19 So the singers, Heman, Asaph
and Ethan *were appointed* to sound aloud cymbals of
bronze; 20 and Zechariah, Aziel, Shemiramoth, Jehiel,
Unni, Eliab, Maaseiah and Benaiah, with [a]harps *tuned*
to [A]alamoth; 21 and Mattithiah, Eliphelehu, Mikneiah,
Obed-edom, Jeiel and Azaziah, to lead with [a]lyres
tuned to [A]the sheminith. 22 Chenaniah, chief of the Levites, was *in charge of* the singing; he gave instruction
in singing because he was skillful. 23 Berechiah and
Elkanah were gatekeepers for the ark. 24 Shebaniah,
Joshaphat, Nethanel, Amasai, Zechariah, Benaiah and
Eliezer, the priests, [A]blew the trumpets before the ark
of God. Obed-edom and Jehiah also *were* gatekeepers
for the ark.
25 [A]So *it was* David, with the elders of Israel and
the captains over thousands, who went to bring
up the ark of the covenant of the LORD from [B]the
house of Obed-edom with joy. 26 Because God was
helping the Levites who were carrying the ark of the
covenant of the LORD, they sacrificed [A]seven bulls
and seven rams. 27 Now David was clothed with a
robe of fine linen with all the Levites who were carrying the ark, and the singers and Chenaniah the
leader of the singing *with* the singers. [A]David also
wore an ephod of linen. 28 Thus all Israel brought
up the ark of the covenant of the LORD with shouting, and with sound of the horn, with trumpets,
with loud-sounding cymbals, with harps and lyres.
29 It happened when the ark of the covenant of
the LORD came to the city of David, that [A]Michal
the daughter of Saul looked out of the window and
saw King David leaping and celebrating; and she
despised him in her heart.

A TENT FOR THE ARK

16 And they brought in the ark of God and
[A]placed it inside the tent which David had
pitched for it, and they offered burnt offerings and
peace offerings before God. 2 When David had finished offering the burnt offering and the peace
offerings, he blessed the people in the name of the
LORD. 3 He distributed to everyone of Israel, both
man and woman, to everyone a loaf of bread and
a portion *of meat* and a raisin cake.
4 He appointed some of the Levites *as* ministers before the ark of the LORD, even to celebrate and to thank
and praise the LORD God of Israel: 5 Asaph the chief,
and second to him Zechariah, *then* [a]Jeiel, Shemiramoth, Jehiel, Mattithiah, Eliab, Benaiah, Obed-edom
and Jeiel, with musical instruments, harps, lyres; also
Asaph *played* loud-sounding cymbals, 6 and Benaiah
and Jahaziel the priests *blew* trumpets continually
before the ark of the covenant of God.
7 Then on that day David [A]first assigned [a]Asaph
and his [b]relatives to give thanks to the LORD.

PSALM OF THANKSGIVING

8 [A]Oh give thanks to the LORD,
call upon His name;
[B]Make known His deeds among the peoples.
9 Sing to Him, sing praises to Him;
[a]Speak of all His [b]wonders.
10 [a]Glory in His holy name;
Let the heart of those who
seek the LORD be glad.
11 [A]Seek the LORD and His strength;
Seek His face continually.
12 [A]Remember His wonderful deeds
which He has done,
[B]His marvels and the judgments
from His mouth,
13 O seed of Israel His servant,
Sons of Jacob, His chosen ones!
14 He is the LORD our God;
[A]His judgments are in all the earth.
15 Remember His covenant forever,
The word which He commanded
to a thousand generations,
16 [A]*The covenant* which He made
with Abraham,
And His oath to Isaac.
17 [A]He also confirmed it to Jacob for a statute,
To Israel as an everlasting covenant,

15:12 [A]Ex 19:14, 15; 2 Chr 35:6 [B]1 Chr 15:1, 3 15:13 [A]2 Sam 6:3; 1 Chr 13:7 15:14 [A]1 Chr 15:12 15:15 [A]Ex 25:14; Num 4:5f 15:16 [A]1 Chr 13:8; 25:1 15:17 [A]1 Chr 25:1 15:18 [a]Omitted in Gr and many mss 15:20 [a]Or *harps of maiden-like tone* [A]Ps 46: title 15:21 [a]Or *octave harps* [A]Ps 6: title 15:24 [A]1 Chr 15:28; 16:6 15:25 [A]2 Sam 6:12, 15 [B]1 Chr 13:13 15:26 [A]Num 23:1-4, 29 15:27 [A]2 Sam 6:14 15:29 [A]2 Sam 3:13f; 6:16 16:1 [A]1 Chr 15:1 16:5 [a]In 1 Chr 15:18, *Jaaziel* 16:7 [a]Lit *by the hand of Asaph* [b]Lit *brothers* [A]2 Sam 22:1; 23:1 16:8 [A]1 Chr 16:8-36; Ps 105:1-15 [B]1 Kin 8:43; 2 Kin 19:19 16:9 [a]Or *Meditate on* [b]I.e. wonderful acts 16:10 [a]Or *Boast* 16:11 [A]Ps 24:6 16:12 [A]Ps 103:2 [B]Ps 78:43-68 16:14 [A]Ps 48:10 16:16 [A]Gen 12:7; 17:2; 22:16-18; 26:3 16:17 [A]Gen 35:11, 12

while Abiathar served the temporary place of the ark in Jerusalem. Ultimately, Zadok prevailed (cf. 1Ki 2:26, 27).

15:12 consecrate yourselves. This was a special sanctification required on all special occasions, demanding complete cleanliness.

15:13 an outburst. God's anger broke out when the ark had been improperly handled and transported by Uzza(h) (2Sa 6:6–8; 1Ch 13:9–12).

15:16–24 Eminent Levites were instructed to train the musicians and singers for the solemn procession.

15:25–16:3 *See notes on 2Sa 6:12–19.*

16:4–6 Levites … ministers. As soon as the ark was placed into its tent, the Levites began their duties.

16:7–22 *See notes on Ps 105:1–15.*

18 Saying, "[A]To you I will give
the land of Canaan,
As the portion of your inheritance."
19 [A]When they were only a few in number,
Very few, and strangers in it,
20 And they wandered about
from nation to nation,
And from *one* kingdom to another people,
21 He permitted no man to oppress them,
And [A]He reproved kings for
their sakes, *saying,*
22 "Do not touch My anointed ones,
And [A]do My prophets no harm."
23 [A]Sing to the LORD, all the earth;
Proclaim good tidings of His
salvation from day to day.
24 Tell of His glory among the nations,
His wonderful deeds among all the peoples.
25 For [A]great is the LORD, and
greatly to be praised;
He also is [B]to be feared above all gods.
26 For all the gods of the peoples are [a,A]idols,
[B]But the LORD made the heavens.
27 Splendor and majesty are before Him,
Strength and joy are in His place.
28 Ascribe to the LORD, O families
of the peoples,
Ascribe to the LORD glory and strength.
29 Ascribe to the LORD the
glory due His name;
Bring an [a]offering, and come before Him;
[A]Worship the LORD in [b]holy array.
30 Tremble before Him, all the earth;
Indeed, the world is firmly
established, it will not be moved.
31 [A]Let the heavens be glad, and
let the earth rejoice;
And let them say among the
nations, "[B]The LORD reigns."
32 [A]Let the sea [a]roar, and [b]all it contains;
Let the field exult, and all that is in it.
33 Then the trees of the forest will
sing for joy before the LORD;
For He is coming to judge the earth.
34 [A]O give thanks to the LORD, for *He is* good;
For His lovingkindness is everlasting.
35 [A]Then say, "Save us, O God of our salvation,
And gather us and deliver
us from the nations,
To give thanks to Your holy name,
And [a]glory in Your praise."
36 [A]Blessed be the LORD, the God of Israel,
From everlasting even to everlasting.

Then all the people [B]said, "Amen," and praised the
LORD.

WORSHIP BEFORE THE ARK

37 So he left Asaph and his [a]relatives there [A]before
the ark of the covenant of the LORD to minister before
the ark continually, [B]as every day's work required;
38 and [A]Obed-edom with [a]his 68 relatives; Obed-edom,
also the son of Jeduthun, and [B]Hosah as gatekeepers.
39 *He left* [A]Zadok the priest and his [a]relatives the priests
[B]before the [b]tabernacle of the LORD in the high place
which *was* at Gibeon, 40 to offer burnt offerings to the
LORD on the altar of burnt offering continually morning and evening, [A]even according to all that is written
in the law of the LORD, which He commanded Israel.
41 With them *were* [A]Heman and Jeduthun, and [B]the rest
who were chosen, who were designated by name, to
[C]give thanks to the LORD, because His lovingkindness
is everlasting. 42 And with them *were* Heman and
Jeduthun *with* trumpets and cymbals for those who
should sound aloud, and *with* instruments *for* [A]the
songs of God, and the sons of Jeduthun for the gate.
43 [A]Then all the people departed each to his house,
and David returned to bless his household.

GOD'S COVENANT WITH DAVID

17 [A]And it came about, when David dwelt in his
house, that David said to Nathan the prophet,
"Behold, I am dwelling in a house of cedar, but the
ark of the covenant of the LORD is under curtains."
2 Then Nathan said to David, "Do all that is in your
heart, for God is with you."
3 It came about the same night that the word of
God came to Nathan, saying, 4 "Go and tell David My
servant, 'Thus says the LORD, "[A]You shall not build
a house for Me to dwell in; 5 for I have not dwelt in a
house since the day that I brought up Israel to this
day, [A]but I have [a]gone from tent to tent and from *one*
dwelling place *to another.* 6 In all places where I have
walked with all Israel, have I spoken a word [A]with
any of the judges of Israel, whom I commanded to
shepherd My people, saying, 'Why have you not built
for Me a house of cedar?' " ' 7 Now, therefore, thus shall
you say to My servant David, 'Thus says the LORD of
hosts, "I took you from the pasture, from following
the sheep, to be leader over My people Israel. 8 I have
been with you wherever you have gone, and have cut
off all your enemies from before you; and I will make
you a name like the name of the great ones who are in
the earth. 9 I will appoint a place for My people Israel,
and will plant them, so that they may dwell in their
own place and not be moved again; and the [a]wicked
will not waste them anymore as formerly, 10 even

16:18 [A]Gen 13:15 16:19 [A]Gen 34:30; Deut 7:7 16:21 [A]Gen 12:17; 20:3; Ex 7:15-18 16:22 [A]Gen 20:7 16:23 [A]Ps 96:1-13 16:25 [A]Ps 144:3-6 [B]Ps 89:7 16:26 [a]Or *non-existent things* [A]Lev 19:4 [B]Ps 102:25 16:29 [a]Or *a grain offering* [b]Or *the splendor of holiness* [A]Ps 29:2 16:31 [A]Is 44:23; 49:13 [B]Ps 93:1; 96:10 16:32 [a]Or *thunder* [b]Lit *its fullness* [A]Ps 98:7 16:34 [A]2 Chr 5:13; 7:3; Ezra 3:11; Ps 106:1; 136:1; Jer 33:11 16:35 [a]Lit *boast* [A]Ps 106:47, 48 16:36 [A]1 Kin 8:15, 56; Ps 72:18 [B]Deut 27:15; Neh 8:6 16:37 [a]Lit *brothers* [A]1 Chr 16:4, 5 [B]2 Chr 8:14; Ezra 3:4 16:38 [a]Lit *their brothers, 68* [A]1 Chr 13:14 [B]1 Chr 26:10 16:39 [a]Lit *brothers* [b]Lit *dwelling place* [A]1 Chr 15:11 [B]1 Kin 3:4 16:40 [A]Ex 29:38-42; Num 28:3, 4 16:41 [A]1 Chr 6:33 [B]1 Chr 25:1-6 [C]2 Chr 5:13 16:42 [A]1 Chr 25:7; 2 Chr 7:6; 29:27 16:43 [A]2 Sam 6:19 17:1 [A]2 Sam 7:1-29 17:4 [A]1 Chr 28:2, 3 17:5 [a]Lit *been* [A]Ex 40:2, 3; 2 Sam 7:6 17:6 [A]2 Sam 7:7 17:9 [a]Lit *sons of wickedness*

16:23–33 *See notes on Ps 96:1–13.*

16:34–36 *See notes on Ps 106:1, 47, 48.*

16:37–42 **continually ... every day's work.** The ministry was established with continuity.

16:39 **Gibeon.** Located 6 mi. NW of Jerusalem.

17:1–27 This section recounts God's bestowing the Davidic Covenant. For a full explanation, *see notes on 2Sa 7.*

17:1, 10 Second Samuel 7:1, 11 adds that God had and would give David rest from all of his enemies.

17:5 Second Samuel 7:14–17 adds new material.

from the day that I commanded judges *to be* over
My people Israel. And I will subdue all your enemies.
Moreover, I tell you that the LORD will build a
house for you. 11 When your days are fulfilled that
you must go *to be* with your fathers, that I will set
up *one of* your [a]descendants after you, who will be
of your sons; and I will establish his kingdom. 12 He
shall build for Me a house, and I will establish his
throne forever. 13 [A]I will be his father and he shall be
My son; and I will not take My lovingkindness away
from him, [B]as I took it from him who was before
you. 14 But I will settle him in My house and in My
kingdom forever, and his throne shall be established
forever."'" 15 According to all these words and according to all this vision, so Nathan spoke to David.

DAVID'S PRAYER IN RESPONSE

16 Then David the king went in and sat before the
LORD and said, "[A]Who am I, O LORD God, and what
is my house that You have brought me this far?
17 This was a small thing in Your eyes, O God; but
You have spoken of Your servant's house for a great
while to come, and have regarded me according to
the standard of a man of high degree, O LORD God.
18 What more can David still *say* to You concerning
the honor *bestowed* on Your servant? For You know
Your servant. 19 O LORD, [A]for Your servant's sake,
and according to Your own heart, You have wrought
all this greatness, to make known all these great
things. 20 O LORD, there is none like You, nor is there
any God besides You, according to all that we have
heard with our ears. 21 And what one nation in the
earth is like Your people Israel, whom God went to
redeem for Himself *as* a people, to make You a name
by great and terrible things, in driving out nations
from before Your people, whom You redeemed out of
Egypt? 22 [A]For Your people Israel You made Your own
people forever, and You, O LORD, became their God.
23 "Now, O LORD, let the word that You have spoken
concerning Your servant and concerning his house be
established forever, and do as You have spoken. 24 Let
Your name be established and magnified forever,
saying, 'The LORD of hosts is the God of Israel, *even*
a God to Israel; and the house of David Your servant
is established before You.' 25 For You, O my God, have
revealed to Your servant that You will build for him
a house; therefore Your servant has found *courage*
to pray before You. 26 Now, O LORD, You are God, and
have [a]promised this good thing to Your servant. 27 And
now it has pleased You to bless the house of Your
servant, that it may [a]continue forever before You; for
You, O LORD, have blessed, and it is blessed forever."

DAVID'S KINGDOM STRENGTHENED

18 Now after this [A]it came about that David [a]de-
feated the Philistines and subdued them and
took Gath and its towns from the hand of the Philistines. 2 He defeated Moab, and the Moabites became
servants to David, bringing tribute.
3 David also defeated Hadadezer king of Zobah
as far as Hamath, as he went to establish his [a]rule
to the Euphrates River. 4 David took from him 1,000
chariots and 7,000 horsemen and 20,000 foot soldiers, and David hamstrung all the chariot horses,
but reserved *enough* of them for 100 chariots.
5 When the Arameans of [a]Damascus came to help
Hadadezer king [A]of Zobah, David [b]killed 22,000 men
of the Arameans. 6 Then David put *garrisons* among
the Arameans of [a]Damascus; and the Arameans
became servants to David, bringing tribute. And
the LORD helped David wherever he went. 7 David
took the shields of gold which were [a]carried by the
servants of Hadadezer and brought them to Jerusalem. 8 Also from [a]Tibhath and from Cun, cities
of Hadadezer, David took a very large amount of
bronze, with which [A]Solomon made the bronze sea
and the pillars and the bronze utensils.
9 Now when [a]Tou king of Hamath heard that David had [b]defeated all the army of Hadadezer king
of Zobah, 10 he sent [a]Hadoram his son to King David to [b]greet him and to bless him, because he had
fought against Hadadezer and had [c]defeated him;
for Hadadezer had been at war with Tou. And *Hadoram brought* all kinds of articles of gold and silver and bronze. 11 King David also dedicated these
to the LORD with the silver and the gold which he

17:11 [a]Lit *seed* 17:13 [A]2 Cor 6:18; Heb 1:5 [B]1 Chr 10:14 17:16 [A]2 Sam 7:18 17:19 [A]2 Sam 7:21; Is 37:35 17:22 [A]Ex 19:5, 6 17:26 [a]Lit *said* 17:27 [a]Lit *be* 18:1 [a]Lit *smote*, and so in vv 1-3 [A]2 Sam 8:1-18 18:3 [a]Lit *hand* 18:5 [a]Heb *Darmeseq* [b]Lit *smote* [A]1 Chr 19:6 18:6 [a]Heb *Darmeseq* 18:7 [a]Lit *on* 18:8 [a]In 2 Sam 8:8, *Betah* [A]1 Kin 7:40-47; 2 Chr 4:11-18 18:9 [a]In 2 Sam 8:9, *Toi* [b]Lit *smitten* 18:10 [a]In 2 Sam 8:10, *Joram* [b]Lit *ask him of his welfare* [c]Lit *smitten*

18:1–21:30 This section selectively recounts David's military exploits.

18:1–11 *See notes on 2Sa 8:1–12.*

18:2 Second Samuel 8:2 adds details to the judgment of Moab.

18:4 The numbers here are correct; the number in 2Sa 8:4 for the horsemen is 1,700, which would not seem as consistent with the other numbers, so the 1,700 probably resulted from a copyist's error.

18:11 Second Samuel 8:12 adds new material.

THE DAVIDIC COVENANT IN CHRONICLES

For an exposition of the details and significance of the Davidic Covenant, see the notes on 2 Samuel 7.

1. 1Ch 17:7–27	God to Nathan to David
2. 1Ch 22:6–16	David to Solomon
3. 1Ch 28:6, 7	David to Solomon
4. 2Ch 6:8, 9, 16, 17	Solomon to the nation
5. 2Ch 7:17, 18	God to Solomon
6. 2Ch 13:4, 5	Abijah to Jeroboam
7. 2Ch 21:7	Chronicle's commentary

had carried away from all the nations: from Edom,
Moab, the sons of Ammon, the Philistines, and from
Amalek.
12 Moreover Abishai the son of Zeruiah [a]defeated
18,000 Edomites in the Valley of Salt. 13 Then he put
garrisons in Edom, and all the Edomites became
servants to David. And the LORD helped David wherever he went.
14 So David reigned over all Israel; and he [a]admin-
istered justice and righteousness for all his people.
15 [A]Joab the son of Zeruiah *was* over the army, and
Jehoshaphat the son of Ahilud *was* recorder; 16 and
Zadok the son of Ahitub and Abimelech the son
of Abiathar *were* priests, and Shavsha *was* secretary; 17 and Benaiah the son of Jehoiada *was* over
the Cherethites and the Pelethites, and the sons of
David *were* chiefs at the king's side.

DAVID'S MESSENGERS ABUSED

19 [A]Now it came about after this, that Nahash
the king of the sons of Ammon died, and his
son became king in his place. 2 Then David said, "I
will show kindness to Hanun the son of Nahash,
because his father showed kindness to me." So David sent messengers to console him concerning his
father. And David's servants came into the land of
the sons of Ammon to Hanun to console him. 3 But
the princes of the sons of Ammon said to Hanun,
"[a]Do you think that David is honoring your father,
in that he has sent comforters to you? Have not his
servants come to you to search and to overthrow
and to spy out the land?" 4 So Hanun took David's
servants and shaved them and cut off their garments in the middle as far as their hips, and sent
them away. 5 Then *certain persons* went and told
David about the men. And he sent to meet them,
for the men were greatly humiliated. And the king
said, "[a]Stay at Jericho until your beards grow, and
then return."
6 When the sons of Ammon saw that they had
made themselves odious to David, Hanun and the
sons of Ammon sent 1,000 talents of silver to hire
for themselves chariots and horsemen from Mesopotamia, from Aram-maacah and [A]from Zobah.
7 So they hired for themselves 32,000 chariots, and
the king of Maacah and his people, who came and
camped before [A]Medeba. And the sons of Ammon
gathered together from their cities and came to
battle. 8 When David heard *of it,* he sent Joab and
all the army, the mighty men. 9 The sons of Ammon
came out and drew up in battle array at the entrance
of the city, and the kings who had come were by
themselves in the field.

AMMON AND ARAM DEFEATED

10 Now when Joab saw that the [a]battle was set
against him in front and in the rear, he selected
from all the choice men of Israel and they arrayed
themselves against the Arameans. 11 But the remainder of the people he placed in the hand of [a]Abshai
his brother; and they arrayed themselves against
the sons of Ammon. 12 He said, "If the Arameans
are too strong for me, then you shall help me; but
if the sons of Ammon are too strong for you, then
I will help you. 13 Be strong, and let us show ourselves courageous for the sake of our people and
for the cities of our God; and may the LORD do what
is good in His sight." 14 So Joab and the people who
were with him drew near to the battle against the
Arameans, and they fled before him. 15 When the
sons of Ammon saw that the Arameans fled, they
also fled before Abshai his brother and entered the
city. Then Joab came to Jerusalem.
16 When the Arameans saw that they had been
[a]defeated by Israel, they sent messengers and
brought out the Arameans who were beyond the
[b]River, with Shophach the commander of the army
of Hadadezer [c]leading them. 17 When it was told
David, he gathered all Israel together and crossed
the Jordan, and came upon them and drew up in
formation against them. And when David drew up
in battle array against the Arameans, they fought
against him. 18 The Arameans fled before Israel, and
David killed of the Arameans 7,000 charioteers and
40,000 foot soldiers, and put to death Shophach the
commander of the army. 19 So when the servants of
Hadadezer saw that they were [a]defeated by Israel,
they made peace with David and served him. Thus
the Arameans were not willing to help the sons of
Ammon anymore.

WAR WITH PHILISTINE GIANTS

20 [A]Then it happened [a]in the spring, at the time
when kings go out *to battle,* that Joab led
out the army and ravaged the land of the sons of
Ammon, and came and besieged Rabbah. But David
stayed at Jerusalem. And [B]Joab struck Rabbah and
overthrew it. 2 [A]David took the crown of [a]their king
from his head, and he found it to weigh a talent of
gold, and there was a precious stone in it; and it
was placed on David's head. And he brought out the
spoil of the city, a very great amount. 3 He brought
out the people who *were* in it, [A]and cut *them* with
saws and with sharp instruments and with axes.
And thus David did to all the cities of the sons of
Ammon. Then David and all the people returned
to Jerusalem.

18:12 [a]Lit *smote* 18:14 [a]Lit *was doing* 18:15 [A]1 Chr 11:6 19:1 [A]2 Sam 10:1-19 19:3 [a]Lit *In your eyes is David honoring your father because* 19:5 [a]Lit *Return to* 19:6 [A]1 Chr 18:5, 9 19:7 [A]Num 21:30; Josh 13:9, 16 19:10 [a]Lit *the face of the battle* 19:11 [a]In 2 Sam 10:10, *Abishai* 19:16 [a]Lit *smitten before* [b]I.e. Euphrates [c]Lit *before* 19:19 [a]Lit *smitten before* 20:1 [a]Lit *at the return of the year* [A]2 Sam 11:1 [B]2 Sam 12:26 20:2 [a]In Zeph 1:5, *Malcam* [A]2 Sam 12:30, 31 20:3 [A]2 Sam 12:31

18:12 Second Samuel 8:13 adds that David was involved.

18:14–17 *See notes on 2Sa 8:15–18.*

19:1–19 *See notes on 2Sa 10:1–19.*

19:18 killed ... 7,000. Second Samuel 10:18 erroneously has 700; this is apparently a discrepancy due to copyist error. **foot soldiers.** This is likely more correct than "horsemen" in 2Sa 10:18.

20:1–3 *See notes on 2Sa 11:1; 12:29–31.* The chronicler was not inspired by God to mention David's sin with Bathsheba and subsequent sins recorded in 2Sa 11:2–12:23. The adultery and murder occurred at this time, while David stayed in Jerusalem instead of going to battle. The story was likely omitted because the book was written to focus on God's permanent interest in His people, Israel, and the perpetuity of David's kingdom.

4 [A]Now it came about after this, that war [a]broke
out at [b]Gezer with the Philistines; then Sibbecai the
Hushathite [c]killed Sippai, one of the descendants
of the [d]giants, and they were subdued. 5 And there
was war with the Philistines again, and Elhanan the
son of [A]Jair [a]killed Lahmi the brother of Goliath the
Gittite, the [B]shaft of whose spear *was* like a weaver's
beam. 6 Again there was war at Gath, where there
was a man of *great* stature who had twenty-four
fingers and toes, six *fingers on each hand* and six
toes on each foot; and he also was descended from
the giants. 7 When he taunted Israel, Jonathan the
son of Shimea, David's brother, [a]killed him. 8 These
were descended from the giants in Gath, and they
fell by the hand of David and by the hand of his
servants.

CENSUS BRINGS PESTILENCE

21 [A]Then Satan stood up against Israel and moved
David to number Israel. 2 So David said to Joab
and to the princes of the people, "[A]Go, number Israel
from Beersheba even to Dan, and bring me *word*
that I may know their number." 3 Joab said, "[A]May
the LORD add to His people a hundred times as
many as they are! But, my lord the king, are they
not all my lord's servants? Why does my lord seek
this thing? Why should he be a cause of guilt to
Israel?" 4 Nevertheless, the king's word prevailed
against Joab. Therefore, Joab departed and went
throughout all Israel, and came to Jerusalem. 5 Joab
gave the number of the [a]census of *all* the people
to David. And [A]all Israel were 1,100,000 men who
drew the sword; and Judah *was* 470,000 men who
drew the sword. 6 [A]But he did not [a]number Levi and
Benjamin among them, for the king's [b]command
was abhorrent to Joab.
7 [a]God was displeased with this thing, so He struck
Israel. 8 David said to God, "I have sinned greatly,
in that I have done this thing. [A]But now, please take
away the iniquity of Your servant, for I have done
very foolishly."
9 The LORD spoke to [A]Gad, David's [B]seer, saying,
10 "Go and speak to David, saying, 'Thus says the
LORD, "I [a]offer you three things; choose for yourself one of them, which I will do to you." ' " 11 So Gad
came to David and said to him, "Thus says the LORD,
'Take for yourself 12 [A]either three years of famine,
or three months to be swept away before your foes,
while the sword of your enemies overtakes *you,*
or else three days of the sword of the LORD, even
pestilence in the land, and the angel of the LORD
destroying throughout all the territory of Israel.'
Now, therefore, consider what answer I shall return
to Him who sent me." 13 David said to Gad, "I am in
great distress; please let me fall into the hand of
the LORD, [A]for His mercies are very great. But do
not let me fall into the hand of man."
14 [A]So the LORD [a]sent a pestilence on Israel;
70,000 men of Israel fell. 15 And God sent an angel
to Jerusalem to destroy it; but as he was about to
destroy *it,* the LORD saw and [A]was sorry over the
calamity, and said to the destroying angel, "It is
enough; now relax your hand." And the angel of
the LORD was standing by the threshing floor of
[a]Ornan the Jebusite. 16 Then David lifted up his eyes
and saw the angel of the LORD standing between
earth and heaven, with his drawn sword in his hand
stretched out over Jerusalem. Then David and the
elders, [A]covered with sackcloth, fell on their faces.
17 David said to God, "Is it not I who [a]commanded
to count the people? Indeed, I am the one who has
sinned and done very wickedly, [A]but these sheep,
what have they done? O LORD my God, please let
Your hand be against me and my father's household, but not against Your people that they should
be plagued."

20:4 [a]Lit *stood up* [b]In 2 Sam 21:18, *Gob* [c]Lit *smote* [d]Heb *Raphah,* and so in vv 6, 8 [A]2 Sam 21:18-22 20:5 [a]Lit *smote* [A]2 Sam 21:19 [B]1 Sam 17:7; 1 Chr 11:23 20:7 [a]Lit *smote* 21:1 [A]2 Sam 24:1-25 21:2 [A]1 Chr 27:23, 24 21:3 [A]Deut 1:11 21:5 [a]Lit *muster* [A]2 Sam 24:9 21:6 [a]Lit *muster* [b]Lit *word* [A]1 Chr 27:24 21:7 [a]Lit *it was evil in the sight of God* 21:8 [A]2 Sam 12:13 21:9 [A]2 Sam 24:11; 1 Chr 29:29 [B]1 Sam 9:9 21:10 [a]Lit *stretch out to* 21:12 [A]2 Sam 24:13 21:13 [A]Ps 51:1; 130:4, 7 21:14 [a]Lit *gave* [A]1 Chr 27:24 21:15 [a]In 2 Sam 24:16, *Araunah* [A]Ex 32:14; 1 Sam 15:11; Jon 3:10 21:16 [A]1 Kin 21:27 21:17 [a]Lit *said* [A]2 Sam 7:8; Ps 74:1

20:4–8 *See notes on 2Sa 21:15–22.* The chronicler chose not to write of some of the darker days in David's reign, especially the revolt of David's son Absalom, for the same reason the iniquity of the king with Bathsheba was left out.

21:1 There is approximately a 20-year gap between 20:8 and 21:1, ca. 995–975 B.C.

21:1–27 For the explanation of this section, *see notes on 2Sa 24:1–25.*

21:1 **Satan ... moved.** Second Samuel 24:1 reports that "the anger of the LORD burned against Israel," and this "incited" David to take the census. This apparent discrepancy is resolved by understanding that God sovereignly and permissively uses Satan to achieve His purposes. God uses Satan to judge sinners (cf. Mk 4:15; 2Co 4:4), to refine saints (cf. Job 1:8–2:10; Lk 22:31, 32), to discipline those in the church (cf. 1Co 5:1–5; 1Ti 1:20), and to further purify obedient believers (cf. 2Co 12:7–10). Neither God nor Satan forced David to sin (cf. Jas 1:13–15), but God allowed Satan to tempt David, and he chose to sin. The sin surfaced his proud heart and God dealt with him for it. **number Israel.** David's census brought tragedy because, unlike the census in Moses' time (Nu 1, 2) which God had commanded, this census by David was to gratify his pride in the great strength of his army and consequent military power. He was also putting more trust in his forces than in his God. He was taking credit for his victories by the building of his great army. This angered God, who moved Satan to bring the sin to a head.

21:3, 4 **a cause of guilt to Israel.** Joab knew David was operating on a sinful motive, but the king's arrogance led him to ignore the warning.

21:5 **all Israel ... 1,100,000 men.** Second Samuel 24:9 reports 800,000 and 500,000 respectively. For the resolution of this discrepancy, *see note on 2Sa 24:9.*

21:6 **he did not number Levi and Benjamin.** Levites were not soldiers (v. 5) and were not numbered in the Mosaic census (Nu 1:47–53). Benjamin had already been numbered (7:6–11) and the register preserved in the archives of that tribe. From the course followed in the census (2Sa 24:4–8), it appears Judah and Benjamin were last to be visited. Before the census could be finished in Judah and begin in Benjamin, David recognized his sin and called for it to stop (cf. 27:24).

21:7 **He struck Israel.** David's sin dramatically affected the entire kingdom in experiencing God's wrath.

21:12 "Three years" here is correct; "7 years" in 2Sa 24:13 is most likely a copyist's error, since it seems 3 years, 3 months, 3 days is the intent.

21:15 **Ornan.** This is a Heb. name. He is called Araunah in 2Sa 24:18, a Jebusite or Canaanite equivalent. He had been converted to worship the true God.

21:16 This additional detail does not appear in the Heb. of 2Sa 24. The "angel of the LORD" was the executioner poised to destroy Jerusalem, whose menacing destruction was halted (v. 27) because David and the leaders repented as indicated by the "sackcloth" and falling "on their faces."

DAVID'S ALTAR

18 [A]Then the angel of the LORD [a]commanded
Gad to say to David, that David should go up and
build an altar to the LORD on the threshing floor
of Ornan the Jebusite. 19 So David went up at the
word of Gad, which he spoke in the name of the
LORD. 20 Now Ornan turned back and saw the
angel, and his four sons *who were* with him hid
themselves. And Ornan was threshing wheat.
21 As David came to Ornan, Ornan looked and saw
David, and went out from the threshing floor and
prostrated himself [a]before David with his face to
the ground. 22 Then David said to Ornan, "Give
me the [a]site of *this* threshing floor, that I may
build on it an altar to the LORD; for the full price
you shall give it to me, that the plague may be
restrained from the people." 23 Ornan said to David, "Take *it* for yourself; and let my lord the king
do what is good in his sight. See, I will give the
oxen for burnt offerings and the threshing sledges
for wood and the wheat for the grain offering; I
will give *it* all." 24 But King David said to Ornan,
"No, but I will surely buy *it* for the full price; for
I will not take what is yours for the LORD, or offer a burnt offering [a]which costs me nothing."
25 So [A]David gave Ornan 600 shekels of gold by
weight for the [a]site. 26 Then David built an altar
to the LORD there and offered burnt offerings
and peace offerings. And he called to the LORD
and [A]He answered him with fire from heaven
on the altar of burnt offering. 27 The LORD commanded the angel, and he put his sword back in its
sheath.

28 At that time, when David saw that the LORD
had answered him on the threshing floor of Ornan
the Jebusite, he offered sacrifice there. 29 [A]For the
tabernacle of the LORD, which Moses had made
in the wilderness, and the altar of burnt offering *were* in the high place at Gibeon at that time.
30 But David could not go before it to inquire of
God, for he was terrified by the sword of the angel of the LORD.

21:18 [a]Lit *said to* [A]2 Chr 3:1; [A]2 Sam 24:24 21:21 [a]Lit *to* 21:22 [a]Lit *place* 21:24 [a]Lit *gratuitously* 21:25 [a]Lit *place* 21:26 [A]Lev 9:24; Judg 6:21 21:29 [A]1 Kin 3:4; 1 Chr 16:39

21:20, 21 This additional detail does not appear in the Heb. of 2Sa 24. "Threshing wheat" was done by spreading the grain out on a high level area and driving back and forth over it with a heavy sled and rollers pulled by oxen. One would drive the oxen while others raked the chaff away from the kernels.

21:25 gave ... 600 shekels. The 50 shekels reported in 2Sa 24:24 was for the instruments and oxen alone, while the price here includes the whole property, Mt. Moriah, on which the future temple stood. The threshing floor of Ornan is today believed to be the very flat rock under the Moslem mosque, the Dome of the Rock, inside the temple ground in Jerusalem.

21:28–30 This also is new data not included in 2Sa 24.

21:29 high place ... Gibeon. The ark of the covenant resided at Jerusalem in a tent (1Ch 15) awaiting the building of the temple on Ornan's threshing floor, while the Mosaic tabernacle and altar remained in Gibeon until the temple was completed (cf. 1Ki 8:4).

21:30 the sword. Cf. 21:12, 16, 27. David continued to remain at the threshing floor and offer sacrifices because the Lord had appeared to him there (2Ch 3:1) and thus hallowed the place, and because he feared a menacing angel at Gibeon, the center of worship.

TEMPLE DUTIES		
Administrative Duties	Supervisors	1 Chronicles 23:4, 5
	Baliffs	1 Chronicles 23:4, 5
	Judges	1 Chronicles 23:4, 5
	Public administrators	1 Chronicles 26:29, 30
Ministerial Duties	Priests	1 Chronicles 24:1, 2
	Prophets	1 Chronicles 25:1
	Assistants for sacrifices	1 Chronicles 23:29–31
	Assistants for purification ceremonies	1 Chronicles 23:27, 28
Service Duties	Bakers of the Bread of the Presence	1 Chronicles 23:29
	Those who checked the weights and measures	1 Chronicles 23:29
	Custodians	1 Chronicles 23:28
Financial Duties	Those who cared for the treasury	1 Chronicles 26:20
	Those who cared for dedicated items	1 Chronicles 26:26–28
Artistic Duties	Musicians	1 Chronicles 25:6
	Singers	1 Chronicles 25:7
Protective Duties	Temple guards	1 Chronicles 23:5
	Guards for the gates and storehouses	1 Chronicles 26:12–18
Individual Assignments	Recording secretary	1 Chronicles 24:6
	Chaplain to the king	1 Chronicles 25:4
	Private prophet to the king	1 Chronicles 25:2
	Captain of the guard	1 Chronicles 26:1
	Chief officer of the treasury	1 Chronicles 26:23, 24

DAVID PREPARES FOR TEMPLE BUILDING

22 Then David said, "[A]This is the house of the LORD God, and this is the altar of burnt offering for Israel."

2 So David [a]gave orders to gather [A]the foreigners who were in the land of Israel, and [B]he set stonecutters to hew out stones to build the house of God. 3 David [A]prepared large quantities of iron [a]to make the nails for the doors of the gates and for the clamps, and more [B]bronze than could be weighed; 4 and timbers of cedar logs beyond number, for [A]the Sidonians and Tyrians brought large quantities of cedar timber to David. 5 David said, "My son [A]Solomon is young and inexperienced, and the house that is to be built for the LORD shall be exceedingly magnificent, famous and glorious throughout all lands. *Therefore* now I will make preparation for it." So David made ample preparations before his death.

SOLOMON CHARGED WITH THE TASK

6 Then [A]he called for his son Solomon, and charged him to build a house for the LORD God of Israel. 7 David said to Solomon, "[A]My son, [a]I had intended to build a house to the name of the LORD my God. 8 But the word of the LORD came to me, saying, '[A]You have shed much blood and have [a]waged great wars; you shall not build a house to My name, because you have shed *so* much blood on the earth before Me. 9 Behold, a son will be born to you, who shall be a man of rest; and [A]I will give him rest from all his enemies on every side; for [B]his name shall be [a]Solomon, and I will give peace and quiet to Israel in his days. 10 [A]He shall build a house for My name, and he shall be My son and I will be his father; and I will establish the throne of his kingdom over Israel forever.' 11 Now, my son, [A]the LORD be with you that you may be successful, and build the house of the LORD your God just as He has spoken concerning you. 12 [A]Only the LORD give you discretion and understanding, and give you charge over Israel, so that you may [B]keep the law of the LORD your God. 13 [A]Then you will prosper, if you are careful to observe the statutes and the ordinances which the LORD commanded Moses concerning Israel. [B]Be strong and courageous, do not fear nor be dismayed. 14 Now behold, [a]with great pains I have prepared for the house of the LORD [A]100,000 talents of gold and 1,000,000 talents of silver, and [B]bronze and iron beyond weight, for [b]they are in great quantity; also timber and stone I have prepared, and you may add to them. 15 Moreover, there are many workmen with you, stonecutters and masons of stone and carpenters, and all men who are skillful in every kind of work. 16 Of the gold, the silver and the bronze and the iron there is no limit. Arise and work, and may [A]the LORD be with you."

17 [A]David also commanded all the leaders of Israel to help his son Solomon, *saying,* 18 "Is not the LORD your God with you? And [A]has He not given you rest on every side? For He has given the inhabitants of the land into my hand, and the land is subdued before the LORD and before His people. 19 Now [A]set your heart and your soul to seek the LORD your God; arise, therefore, and build the sanctuary of the LORD God, [B]so that you may bring the ark of the covenant of the LORD and the holy vessels of God into the house that is to be built [C]for the name of the LORD."

22:1 [A]1 Chr 21:18-28; 2 Chr 3:1 22:2 [a]Lit *said to* [A]1 Kin 9:20, 21; 2 Chr 2:17 [B]1 Kin 5:17, 18 22:3 [a]Lit *for* [A]1 Chr 29:2, 7 [B]1 Chr 22:14 22:4 [A]1 Kin 5:6-10 22:5 [A]1 Kin 3:7; 1 Chr 29:1 22:6 [A]1 Kin 2:1 22:7 [a]Lit *as for me, it was in my heart* [A]2 Sam 7:2, 3; 1 Chr 17:1 22:8 [a]Lit *made* [A]1 Chr 28:3 22:9 [a]I.e. peaceful [A]1 Kin 4:20, 25 [B]2 Sam 12:24, 25 22:10 [A]2 Sam 7:13, 14; 1 Chr 17:12 22:11 [A]1 Chr 22:16 22:12 [A]1 Kin 3:9-12; 2 Chr 1:10 [B]1 Kin 2:3 22:13 [A]1 Chr 28:7 [B]Josh 1:6-9 22:14 [a]Lit *in my affliction* [b]Lit *it is* [A]1 Chr 29:4 [B]1 Chr 22:3 22:16 [A]1 Chr 22:11 22:17 [A]1 Chr 28:1-6 22:18 [A]1 Chr 22:9; 23:25 22:19 [A]1 Chr 28:9 [B]1 Kin 8:6, 21; 2 Chr 5:7 [C]1 Chr 22:7

22:1–29:20 This section recounts David's preparations for Solomon to build the temple. General preparation and various charges are discussed in 22:1–19. The division of labor unfolds in 23:1–27:33. Solomon's final commission comes in 28:1–29:20.

22:1–19 David gives 3 charges to: 1) the workman (vv. 2–5); 2) Solomon (vv. 6–16); and 3) the leaders (vv. 17–19).

22:1 house. The land David had just purchased (21:22–30), he dedicated for the Jerusalem temple to be built by Solomon (v. 6; 28:9, 10).

22:2 foreigners. These were non-Israelite artisans made up of descendants of the Canaanites (2Ch 8:7–10) and war captives (2Ch 2:7), for whom the Mosaic legislation provided compassion and protection (cf. Ex 22:21; 23:9; Lv 19:33; Dt 24:14, 15) and from whom service was exacted. Only here were the laborers called "foreigners" (cf. 1Ki 5:13–18).

22:3 iron … bronze. David would have acquired the iron technology from the Philistines (1Sa 13:19–21) and the bronze would have come from spoils of war (cf. 18:8).

22:4 cedar. This came from Lebanon, the heavily wooded and mountainous country N of Israel, and was provided by the residents of Sidon and Tyre, most likely under the leadership of David's friend, King Hiram (cf. 14:1; 1Ki 5:1).

22:5 young. Solomon was born early in David's reign (ca. 1000–990 B.C.) and was at this time 20 to 30 years of age. The magnificent and complex challenge of building such a monumental edifice with all its elements required an experienced leader for preparation. **magnificent.** David understood that the temple needed to reflect on earth something of God's heavenly majesty, so he devoted himself to the collection of the plans and materials, tapping the vast amount of spoils from people he had conquered and cities he had sacked (vv. 14–16).

22:6–16 Here is David's careful instruction to Solomon for the building which David could not do because he had killed so many in his battles (v. 8). Cf. 1Ki 5:3.

22:8–10 David reflects on the covenant God had made with him (cf. 2Sa 7; 1Ch 17), which included 1) the divine mandate that Solomon build the temple and 2) overtones of the messianic reign.

22:11–13 David's spiritual charge to Solomon resembles the Lord's exhortation to Joshua (cf. Jos 1:6–9). Solomon asked God for and received the very "discretion and understanding" his father, David, desired for him (cf. 1Ki 3:3–14; 2Ch 1:7–12). He learned the value of such spiritual counsel and passed it on in Ecc 12:1, 13.

22:14 prepared … 100,000 talents of gold. Assuming a talent weighed about 75 lbs., this would be approximately 3,750 tons, a staggering amount of gold. **and 1,000,000 talents of silver.** This would be approximately 37,500 tons of silver.

22:17–19 Knowing that Solomon was young and inexperienced (22:5) and that he could not undertake this colossal project alone, David wisely enlisted the loyalty and help of his leaders to transfer their allegiance to Solomon who would carry out the divine will and the last wishes of his father. The Lord undertook to make Solomon the wisest man on earth (cf. 1Ki 3:3–14).

SOLOMON REIGNS

23 [A]Now when David [a]reached old age, [B]he made his son Solomon king over Israel. 2 And he gathered together all the leaders of Israel with the priests and the Levites.

OFFICES OF THE LEVITES

3 [A]The Levites were numbered from thirty years old and upward, and [B]their number by [a]census of men was 38,000. 4 Of these, 24,000 were [A]to oversee the work of the house of the LORD; and 6,000 *were* [B]officers and judges, 5 and 4,000 *were* gatekeepers, and [A]4,000 *were* praising the LORD with the instruments which [a]David made for giving praise. 6 David divided them into divisions [A]according to the sons of Levi: Gershon, Kohath, and Merari.

GERSHONITES

7 Of the Gershonites *were* [a]Ladan and Shimei. 8 The sons of Ladan *were* Jehiel the first and Zetham and Joel, three. 9 The sons of Shimei *were* Shelomoth and Haziel and Haran, three. These were the heads of the fathers' *households* of Ladan. 10 The sons of Shimei *were* Jahath, [a]Zina, Jeush and Beriah. These four *were* the sons of Shimei. 11 Jahath was the first and Zizah the second; but Jeush and Beriah did not have many sons, so they became a father's household, one [a]class.

KOHATHITES

12 The sons of Kohath were four: Amram, Izhar, Hebron and Uzziel. 13 [A]The sons of Amram were Aaron and Moses. And [B]Aaron was set apart to sanctify him as most holy, he and his sons forever, [C]to burn incense before the LORD, to minister to Him and to bless in His name forever. 14 But *as for* [A]Moses the man of God, his sons were named among the tribe of Levi. 15 The sons of Moses *were* Gershom and Eliezer. 16 The [a]son of Gershom *was* [b]Shebuel the chief. 17 The [a]son of Eliezer was Rehabiah the chief; and Eliezer had no other sons, but the sons of Rehabiah were very many. 18 The [a]son of Izhar was [b]Shelomith the chief. 19 The sons of Hebron *were* Jeriah the first, Amariah the second, Jahaziel the third and Jekameam the fourth. 20 The sons of Uzziel *were* Micah the first and Isshiah the second.

MERARITES

21 The sons of Merari were Mahli and Mushi. The sons of Mahli *were* Eleazar and Kish. 22 Eleazar died and had no sons, but daughters only, so their brothers, the sons of Kish, took them *as wives*. 23 The sons of Mushi *were* three: Mahli, Eder and Jeremoth.

DUTIES REVISED

24 [A]These were the sons of Levi according to their fathers' households, *even* the heads of the fathers' *households* of those of them who were [a]counted, in the number of names by their [b]census, doing the work for the service of the house of the LORD, [B]from twenty years old and upward. 25 For David said, "The LORD God of Israel [A]has given rest to His people, and He dwells in Jerusalem forever. 26 Also, [A]the Levites will no longer need to carry the tabernacle and all its utensils for its service." 27 For by the last words of David the sons of Levi *were* numbered from twenty years old and upward. 28 For their office is [a]to assist the sons of Aaron with the service of the house of the LORD, in the courts and in the chambers and in the purifying of all holy things, even the work of the service of the house of God, 29 [A]and with the showbread, and [B]the fine flour for a grain offering, and unleavened wafers, or [C]*what is baked in* the pan or [D]what is well-mixed, and [E]all measures of volume and size. 30 They are to stand every morning to thank and to praise the LORD, and likewise at evening, 31 and to offer all burnt offerings to the LORD, [A]on the sabbaths, the new moons and [B]the fixed festivals in the number *set* by the ordinance concerning them, continually before the LORD. 32 Thus [A]they are to keep charge of the tent of meeting, and charge of the holy place, and [B]charge of the sons of Aaron their [a]relatives, for the service of the house of the LORD.

DIVISIONS OF LEVITES

24 Now the divisions of the [a]descendants of Aaron *were these:* [A]the sons of Aaron *were*

23:1 [a]Lit *became old and sated with days* [A]1 Chr 29:28 [B]1 Kin 1:1-40; 2:12; 1 Chr 28:5; 29:22 23:3 [a]Lit *their heads* [A]Num 4:3-49 [B]Num 4:48; 1 Chr 23:24 23:4 [A]Ezra 3:8, 9 [B]1 Chr 26:29 23:5 [a]Lit *I made* [A]1 Chr 15:16 23:6 [A]1 Chr 6:1 23:7 [a]In Ex 6:17, *Libni* 23:10 [a]In v 11, *Zizah* 23:11 [a]Lit *mustering* 23:13 [A]Ex 6:20 [B]Ex 28:1 [C]Ex 30:6-10 23:14 [A]Deut 33:1; Ps 90: title 23:16 [a]Lit *sons* [b]In ch 24:20, *Shubael* 23:17 [a]Lit *sons...were* 23:18 [a]Lit *sons* [b]In ch 24:22, *Shelomoth* 23:24 [a]Lit *mustered* [b]Lit *heads* [A]Num 10:17, 21 [B]1 Chr 23:3 23:25 [A]1 Chr 22:18 23:26 [A]Num 4:5, 15; 7:9; Deut 10:8 23:28 [a]Lit *at the hand of* 23:29 [A]Lev 24:5-9 [B]Lev 6:20 [C]1 Chr 9:31 [D]Lev 6:21 [E]Lev 19:35, 36 23:31 [A]Is 1:13, 14 [B]Lev 23:2-4 23:32 [a]Lit *brothers* [A]Num 1:53; 1 Chr 9:27 [B]Num 3:6-9, 38 24:1 [a]Lit *sons* [A]Ex 6:23

23:1–27:34 This labor-intensive project needed more than building materials. David marshaled his human resources and announced their division of labor as follows: 1) the Levites (23:1–32); 2) the priests (24:1–31); 3) the singers (25:1–31); 4) the gatekeepers (26:1–19); 5) the administrators (26:20–32); 6) the army (27:1–24); and 7) the leaders (27:25–34). Remember, the original readers of Chronicles were the Jews, who returned from exile in Babylon and were rebuilding the destroyed temple. This would remind them of what their fathers' sin forfeited, and how inferior their new temple was.

23:1 he made. For fuller narrative of Solomon's coronation and the attempts to seize his throne, see 28, 29; 1Ki 1:1–2:9.

23:3 thirty years old and upward. Numbers 4:3 establishes the age of recognized priests from 30 to 50 years of age. A 5-year apprenticeship began at 25 (cf. Nu 8:24), and in some cases 20 (1Ch 23:24, 27). This number, 38,000, is 4 times greater than the early census in Moses' time (cf. Nu 4, 26).

23:4 oversee. The duties of these Levites are discussed in 1Ch 24. **officers and judges.** This particular function is covered in 1Ch 26:20–32.

23:5 gatekeepers. First Chronicles 26:1–19 gives information on them. **praising.** First Chronicles 25 identifies and describes these musicians. **which David made.** David, a gifted musician, was not only the maker, but the inventor of musical instruments (cf. Am 6:5).

23:6 divisions. The Levites were divided among the 3 groups with distinct duties, just as they were in Moses' day (Nu 3:14–37) and in Ezra's day (1Ch 6:16–30). The family of Gershon (23:7–11), Kohath (23:12–20), and Merari (23:21–23) are each discussed.

23:24, 27 twenty years. *See note on 23:3.*

23:25–32 The duties of the nonpriestly Levites are enumerated in their duties to provide the temple service in support of the priests who descended from Levi, through Kohath, through Aaron, through Eleazar and Ithamar (cf. 1Ch 6:1–3). The original duties of the 3 families are given specifically in Nu 3:25, 31, 36, 37.

24:1–31 The divisions and duties of the priests are outlined. Temple worship was carefully structured, without hindering the Holy Spirit or true worship (cf. 1Co 14:40).

24:1 Nadab, Abihu. Consult Lv 10:1–3 for their disgrace and demise. **Eleazar.** The line

Nadab, Abihu, Eleazar and Ithamar. 2 [A]But Nadab
and Abihu died before their father and had no [a]sons.
So Eleazar and Ithamar served as priests. 3 David,
with [A]Zadok of the sons of Eleazar and Ahimelech
of the sons of Ithamar, divided them according to
their offices [a]for their ministry. 4 Since more chief
men were found from the [a]descendants of Eleazar
than the [a]descendants of Ithamar, they divided them
thus: *there were* sixteen heads of fathers' households
of the [a]descendants of Eleazar and eight of the [a]de-
scendants of Ithamar, according to their fathers'
households. 5 [A]Thus they were divided by lot, the
one as the other; for they were officers of the sanctuary and officers of God, both from the [a]descen-
dants of Eleazar and the [a]descendants of Ithamar.
6 Shemaiah, the son of Nethanel the scribe, from the
Levites, recorded them in the presence of the king,
the princes, Zadok the priest, [A]Ahimelech the son of
Abiathar, and the heads of the fathers' *households*
of the priests and of the Levites; one father's household taken for Eleazar and one taken for Ithamar.
7 Now the first lot came out for Jehoiarib, the second for Jedaiah, 8 the third for Harim, the fourth for
Seorim, 9 the fifth for Malchijah, the sixth for Mijamin, 10 the seventh for Hakkoz, the eighth for [A]Abi-
jah, 11 the ninth for Jeshua, the tenth for Shecaniah,
12 the eleventh for Eliashib, the twelfth for Jakim,
13 the thirteenth for Huppah, the fourteenth for Je-
shebeab, 14 the fifteenth for Bilgah, the sixteenth for
Immer, 15 the seventeenth for Hezir, the eighteenth
for Happizzez, 16 the nineteenth for Pethahiah, the
twentieth for Jehezkel, 17 the twenty-first for Jachin,
the twenty-second for Gamul, 18 the twenty-third for
Delaiah, the twenty-fourth for Maaziah. 19 [A]These
were their offices for their ministry when *they* came
in to the house of the LORD according to the ordinance *given* to them through Aaron their father,
just as the LORD God of Israel had commanded him.
20 Now for the rest of the sons of Levi: of the sons
of Amram, [a]Shubael; of the sons of Shubael, Jehdeiah. 21 Of Rehabiah: of the sons of Rehabiah, Isshiah
the first. 22 Of the Izharites, [a]Shelomoth; of the sons
of Shelomoth, Jahath. 23 The sons [A]*of Hebron:* Jeriah
the first, Amariah the second, Jahaziel the third,
Jekameam the fourth. 24 *Of* the sons of Uzziel, Micah; of the sons of Micah, Shamir. 25 The brother of
Micah, Isshiah; of the sons of Isshiah, Zechariah.
26 The sons of Merari, Mahli and Mushi; the sons
of Jaaziah, Beno. 27 The sons of Merari: by Jaaziah
were Beno, Shoham, Zaccur and Ibri. 28 By Mahli:
Eleazar, who had no sons. 29 By Kish: the sons of
Kish, Jerahmeel. 30 The sons of Mushi: Mahli, Eder
and Jerimoth. These *were* the sons of the Levites
according to their fathers' households. 31 [A]These also
cast lots just as their [a]relatives the sons of Aaron
in the presence of David the king, [B]Zadok, Ahimelech, and the heads of the fathers' *households* of
the priests and of the Levites—the head of fathers'
households as well as those of his younger brother.

NUMBER AND SERVICES OF MUSICIANS

25 Moreover, David and the commanders of the
army set apart for the service *some* of the
sons of [A]Asaph and of Heman and of Jeduthun, who
were to [B]prophesy with lyres, [C]harps and cymbals;
and the number of [a]those who performed their
service was: 2 Of the sons of Asaph: Zaccur, Joseph,
Nethaniah and [a]Asharelah; the sons of Asaph *were*
under the [b]direction of Asaph, who prophesied under the [b]direction of the king. 3 [A]Of Jeduthun, the
sons of Jeduthun: Gedaliah, [a]Zeri, Jeshaiah, [b]Shimei,
Hashabiah and Mattithiah, six, under the [c]direction
of their father Jeduthun with the harp, who prophesied in giving thanks and praising the LORD. 4 Of
Heman, the sons of Heman: Bukkiah, Mattaniah,
[a]Uzziel, [b]Shebuel and Jerimoth, Hananiah, Hanani,
Eliathah, Giddalti and Romamti-ezer, Joshbekashah,
Mallothi, Hothir, Mahazioth. 5 All these *were* the sons
of Heman [A]the king's seer to [a]exalt him according to
the words of God, for God gave fourteen sons and
three daughters to Heman. 6 All these were under
the [a]direction of their father to sing in the house of
the LORD, [A]with cymbals, harps and lyres, for the
service of the house of God. [B]Asaph, Jeduthun and
Heman *were* under the [a]direction of the king. 7 Their

24:2 [a]Or *children* [A]Lev 10:2 24:3 [a]Lit *in their service* [A]1 Chr 6:8 24:4 [a]Lit *sons* 24:5 [a]Lit *sons* [A]1 Chr 24:31 24:6 [A]1 Chr 18:16 24:10 [A]Neh 12:4; Luke 1:5 24:19 [A]1 Chr 9:25 24:20 [a]In 23:16, *Shebuel* 24:22 [a]In 23:18, *Shelomith* 24:23 [A]1 Chr 23:19 24:31 [a]Lit *brothers* [A]1 Chr 24:5, 6 [B]1 Chr 24:6 25:1 [a]Lit *workmen according to their service* [A]1 Chr 6:33, 39 [B]2 Kin 3:15 [C]1 Chr 15:16 25:2 [a]In v 14, *Jesharelah* [b]Lit *hand(s)* 25:3 [a]In v 11, *Izri* [b]So with mss and ancient versions, cf v 17 [c]Lit *hands* [A]1 Chr 16:41, 42 25:4 [a]In v 18, *Azarel* [b]In v 20, *Shubael* 25:5 [a]Lit *lift up the horn* [A]2 Sam 24:11; 1 Chr 21:9 25:6 [a]Lit *hands* [A]1 Chr 15:16 [B]1 Chr 15:19

of the High Priest would be through Eleazar's offspring in accord with the priestly covenant made by God with Phinehas (Nu 25:11–13).

24:3 **Zadok.** *See notes on 1Ch 6:8, 49–53.* **Ahimelech.** This was the son of Abiathar whom Solomon released from his duties for siding with Adonijah (cf. 1Ki 1, 2) and the grandson of another Ahimelech, who was a priest killed by Saul (1Sa 22:11–18). Second Samuel 8:17 confirms the Zadok and Ahimelech high-priestly combination, one at Jerusalem where the ark was kept and the other at Gibeon serving the tabernacle. *See note on 1Ch 15:11.*

24:4–19 Priesthood duties were divided up in David's day into 24 divisions, 16 of Eleazar and 8 of Ithamar. The reasons Eleazar's family had twice as many divisions were that: 1) he had received the birthright since his older brothers, Nadab and Abihu, had been killed (Lv 10); 2) he had more descendants; and 3) his descendants had more leadership ability. These divisions each served for either 1) two-week periods annually or, more likely, 2) a one-month period every two years (cf. 27:1–15). These divisions appear again in Ne 10:2–8; 12:1–7; 12:12–21. These divisions extended even into the time of Christ (cf. Lk 1:5–9). The rest of the time they ministered to people in their own hometowns.

24:5 **divided by lot.** The ancient method of discerning God's will (cf. Pr 16:33; Ac. 1:26) was used to sort out all the duties, so that all cause for pride or jealousy was mitigated (cf. v. 31; 26:13).

24:10 **Abijah.** The division of Zacharias, John the Baptist's father (cf. Lk 1:5).

25:1–31 David, the sweet psalmist of Israel (2Sa 23:1), established music as a central feature in the worship of God.

25:1 **the commanders of the army.** David relied on his mighty men for help (cf. 11:10). **Asaph . . . Heman . . . Jeduthun.** David's 3 chief ministers of music (cf. 6:31–48). **prophesy.** This is not necessarily to be taken in a revelatory sense, but rather in the sense of proclamation and exhortation through the lyrics of their music (cf. 25:2, 3). Prophesying is not necessarily predicting the future or even speaking direct revelation. It is proclaiming truth (v. 5) to people (cf. 1Co 14:3), and music is a vehicle for such proclamation in praise (v. 3). David and the leaders selected those most capable (v. 7) of leading the people to worship God through their music.

25:5 **seer.** A term used to describe a prophet in that he knew and understood the ways and will of God.

number who were trained in singing to the LORD,
with their [a]relatives, all who were skillful, *was* [A]288.

DIVISIONS OF MUSICIANS

8 [A]They cast lots for their duties, all alike, the small
as well as the great, the teacher *as well* as the pupil.
9 Now the first lot came out for Asaph to Joseph,
the second for Gedaliah, he with his relatives and
sons *were* twelve; 10 the third to Zaccur, his sons
and his relatives, twelve; 11 the fourth to [a]Izri, his
sons and his relatives, twelve; 12 the fifth to Nethaniah, his sons and his relatives, twelve; 13 the sixth
to Bukkiah, his sons and his relatives, twelve; 14 the
seventh to [a]Jesharelah, his sons and his relatives,
twelve; 15 the eighth to Jeshaiah, his sons and his relatives, twelve; 16 the ninth to Mattaniah, his sons and
his relatives, twelve; 17 the tenth to Shimei, his sons
and his relatives, twelve; 18 the eleventh to Azarel,
his sons and his relatives, twelve; 19 the twelfth to
Hashabiah, his sons and his relatives, twelve; 20 for
the thirteenth, Shubael, his sons and his relatives,
twelve; 21 for the fourteenth, Mattithiah, his sons
and his relatives, twelve; 22 for the fifteenth to Jeremoth, his sons and his relatives, twelve; 23 for the
sixteenth to Hananiah, his sons and his relatives,
twelve; 24 for the seventeenth to Joshbekashah, his
sons and his relatives, twelve; 25 for the eighteenth
to Hanani, his sons and his relatives, twelve; 26 for
the nineteenth to Mallothi, his sons and his relatives,
twelve; 27 for the twentieth to Eliathah, his sons
and his relatives, twelve; 28 for the twenty-first to
Hothir, his sons and his relatives, twelve; 29 for the
twenty-second to Giddalti, his sons and his relatives,
twelve; 30 for the twenty-third to Mahazioth, his sons
and his relatives, twelve; 31 for the twenty-fourth to
Romamti-ezer, his sons and his relatives, twelve.

DIVISIONS OF THE GATEKEEPERS

26 For the divisions of the gatekeepers *there*
were of the Korahites, [a]Meshelemiah the son
of Kore, of the sons of [b]Asaph. 2 Meshelemiah had
sons: Zechariah the firstborn, Jediael the second,
Zebadiah the third, Jathniel the fourth, 3 Elam the
fifth, Johanan the sixth, Eliehoenai the seventh.
4 [A]Obed-edom had sons: Shemaiah the firstborn, Jehozabad the second, Joah the third, Sacar the fourth,
Nethanel the fifth, 5 Ammiel the sixth, Issachar the
seventh *and* Peullethai the eighth; God had indeed
blessed him. 6 Also to his son Shemaiah sons were
born who ruled over the house of their father, for
they were mighty men of valor. 7 The sons of Shemaiah *were* Othni, Rephael, Obed and Elzabad, whose
brothers, Elihu and Semachiah, were valiant men.
8 All these *were* of the sons of Obed-edom; they and
their sons and their [a]relatives *were* able men with
strength for the service, 62 from Obed-edom. 9 Meshelemiah had sons and relatives, 18 valiant men.
10 Also [A]Hosah, *one* of the sons of Merari had sons:
Shimri the first (although he was not the firstborn,
his father made him first), 11 Hilkiah the second,
Tebaliah the third, Zechariah the fourth; all the
sons and relatives of Hosah *were* 13.
12 To these divisions of the gatekeepers, the chief
men, *were given* duties like their relatives to minister in the house of the LORD. 13 [A]They cast lots,
the small and the great alike, according to their
fathers' households, for every gate. 14 The lot to the
east fell to [a]Shelemiah. Then they cast lots *for* his
son Zechariah, a counselor with insight, and his
lot came out to the north. 15 For Obed-edom *it fell*
to the south, and to his sons went the storehouse.
16 For Shuppim and Hosah *it was* to the west, by
the gate of Shallecheth, on the ascending highway.
Guard corresponded to guard. 17 On the east there
were six Levites, on the north four daily, on the
south four daily, and at the storehouse two by two.
18 At the [a,A]Parbar on the west *there were* four at the
highway and two at the Parbar. 19 These were the
divisions of the gatekeepers of the sons of Korah
and of the sons of Merari.

KEEPERS OF THE TREASURE

20 [a]The Levites, their relatives, [b]had [A]charge of the
treasures of the house of God and of the treasures
of the dedicated gifts. 21 The sons of Ladan, the sons
of the Gershonites belonging to Ladan, *namely,* the
Jehielites, *were* the heads of the fathers' *households,*
belonging to Ladan the Gershonite.
22 The sons of Jehieli, Zetham and Joel his brother,
[a]had charge of the treasures of the house of the
LORD. 23 As for the Amramites, the Izharites, the
Hebronites and the Uzzielites, 24 Shebuel the son
of Gershom, the son of Moses, was officer over the
treasures. 25 His relatives by Eliezer *were* Rehabiah
his son, Jeshaiah his son, Joram his son, Zichri his
son and Shelomoth his son. 26 This Shelomoth and
his relatives [a]had charge of all the treasures of the
dedicated gifts [A]which King David and the heads of

25:7 [a]Lit *brothers,* and so throughout the ch [A]1 Chr 23:5 25:8 [A]1 Chr 26:13 25:11 [a]In v 3, *Zeri* 25:14 [a]In v 2, *Asherelah* 26:1 [a]In v 14, *Shelemiah* [b]In 9:19, *Ebiasaph* 26:4 [A]2 Sam 6:11; 1 Chr 13:14 26:8 [a]Lit *brothers,* and so throughout the ch 26:10 [A]1 Chr 16:38 26:13 [A]1 Chr 24:5, 31; 25:8 26:14 [a]In 9:17, *Shallum* 26:18 [a]Possibly *court* or *colonnade* [A]2 Kin 23:11 26:20 [a]So Gr; Heb *As for the Levites, Ahijah had* [b]Lit *were over* [A]1 Chr 26:22, 24, 26; 28:12; Ezra 2:69 26:22 [a]Lit *were over* 26:26 [a]Lit *were over* [A]2 Sam 8:11

25:9–31 The musicians were divided up into 24 divisions (corresponding to that of the priests [24:4–18]) of 12 musicians each, for a total of 288. These would give leadership to the 4,000 instrumentalists (23:5).

26:1–19 Cf. 1Ch 9:17–27 for another discussion of the temple gatekeepers or guards as we would call them. They had other duties, such as checking out equipment and utensils; storing, ordering and maintaining food for the priests and sacrifices; caring for the temple furniture; mixing the incense daily burned; and accounting for gifts brought. Their "duties" (v. 12) are given in 1Ch 9:17–27.

26:14 east. The gate assignments were based on 4 geographical points. Cf. also N (26:14), S (26:15), and W (26:16).

26:16 gate of Shallecheth. A gate assumed to be on the west side, but other details are unknown.

26:18 Parbar. Probably a courtyard, extending westward. Verses 17, 18 indicate a total of 24 guards posted at all points of entrance and exit.

26:20–32 This section lists miscellaneous administrative posts handled by the Levites, by those in Jerusalem (26:20–28), and by those outside (26:29–32).

26:20 treasures. The Levites watched over the store of valuables given to the Lord. This is a general reference to all the precious things committed to their trust, including contributions from David and the people, as well as war spoils given by triumphant soldiers (vv. 26, 27).

the fathers' *households,* the commanders of thousands and hundreds, and the commanders of the
army, had dedicated. 27 They dedicated [a]part of the
spoil won in battles to repair the house of the LORD.
28 And all that Samuel the seer had dedicated and
Saul the son of Kish, Abner the son of Ner and Joab
the son of Zeruiah, everyone who had dedicated
anything, all of this was [a]in the care of [b]Shelomoth
and his relatives.

OUTSIDE DUTIES

29 As for the Izharites, Chenaniah and his sons
[A]were *assigned* to outside duties for Israel, as [B]offi-
cers and judges. 30 As for the Hebronites, [A]Hashabiah
and his relatives, 1,700 capable men, had charge of
the affairs of Israel [a]west of the Jordan, for all the
work of the LORD and the service of the king. 31 As
for the Hebronites, [A]Jerijah the chief [a](these Hebronites were investigated according to their genealogies and fathers' *households,* in the fortieth year of
David's reign, and men of outstanding capability
were found among them at [B]Jazer of Gilead) 32 and
his relatives, capable men, *were* 2,700 in number,
heads of fathers' *households.* And King David made
them overseers of the Reubenites, the Gadites and
the half-tribe of the Manassites [A]concerning [a]all the
affairs of God and of the king.

COMMANDERS OF THE ARMY

27 Now *this is* the enumeration of the sons of
Israel, the heads of fathers' *households,* the
commanders of thousands and of hundreds, and
their officers who served the king in all the affairs
of the divisions which came in and went out month
by month throughout all the months of the year,
each division *numbering* 24,000:
2 Jashobeam the son of Zabdiel [a,A]had charge of
the first division for the first month; and in his
division *were* 24,000. 3 *He was* from the sons of
Perez, *and was* chief of all the commanders of the
army for the first month. 4 Dodai the Ahohite and
his division had charge of the division for the second month, Mikloth *being* the chief officer; and in
his division *were* 24,000. 5 The third commander of
the army for the third month *was* Benaiah, the son
of Jehoiada the priest, *as* chief; and in his division
were 24,000. 6 This Benaiah *was* the mighty man of
the thirty, and had charge of thirty; and over his
division was Ammizabad his son. 7 The fourth for
the fourth month *was* Asahel the brother of Joab,
and Zebadiah his son after him; and in his division
were 24,000. 8 The fifth for the fifth month *was* the
commander Shamhuth the Izrahite; and in his division *were* 24,000. 9 The sixth for the sixth month *was*
Ira the son of Ikkesh the Tekoite; and in his division
were 24,000. 10 The seventh for the seventh month
was Helez the Pelonite of the sons of Ephraim; and
in his division *were* 24,000. 11 The eighth for the
eighth month *was* Sibbecai the Hushathite of the Zerahites; and in his division *were* 24,000. 12 The ninth
for the ninth month *was* Abiezer the Anathothite
of the Benjamites; and in his division *were* 24,000.
13 The tenth for the tenth month *was* Maharai the
Netophathite of the Zerahites; and in his division
were 24,000. 14 The eleventh for the eleventh month
was Benaiah the Pirathonite of the sons of Ephraim;
and in his division *were* 24,000. 15 The twelfth for
the twelfth month *was* Heldai the Netophathite of
Othniel; and in his division *were* 24,000.

CHIEF OFFICERS OF THE TRIBES

16 Now in charge of the tribes of Israel: chief officer for the Reubenites was Eliezer the son of Zichri;
for the Simeonites, Shephatiah the son of Maacah;
17 for Levi, Hashabiah the son of Kemuel; for Aaron,
Zadok; 18 for Judah, Elihu, *one* of David's brothers;
for Issachar, Omri the son of Michael; 19 for Zebulun,
Ishmaiah the son of Obadiah; for Naphtali, Jeremoth the son of Azriel; 20 for the sons of Ephraim,
Hoshea the son of Azaziah; for the half-tribe of Manasseh, Joel the son of Pedaiah; 21 for the half-tribe
of Manasseh in Gilead, Iddo the son of Zechariah;
for Benjamin, Jaasiel the son of Abner; 22 for Dan,
Azarel the son of Jeroham. [A]These *were* the princes
of the tribes of Israel. 23 But David did not [a]count
those twenty years of age and under, [A]because the
LORD had said He would multiply Israel [B]as the
stars of heaven. 24 Joab the son of Zeruiah had begun to count *them,* but did not finish; and because
of [A]this, wrath came upon Israel, and the number
was not included in the account of the chronicles
of King David.

VARIOUS OVERSEERS

25 Now Azmaveth the son of Adiel had charge of the
king's storehouses. And Jonathan the son of Uzziah
had charge of the storehouses in the country, in the
cities, in the villages and in the towers. 26 Ezri the
son of Chelub had charge of the [a]agricultural workers who tilled the soil. 27 Shimei the Ramathite had

26:27 [a]Heb *from the battles and from the spoil* 26:28 [a]Lit *under the hand* [b]Heb *Shelomith* 26:29 [A]Neh 11:16 [B]1 Chr 23:4 26:30 [a]Lit *beyond the Jordan westward* [A]1 Chr 27:17 26:31 [a]Heb *according to the Hebronites...father's households* [A]1 Chr 23:19 [B]1 Chr 6:81 26:32 [a]Lit *every matter of God and matter of the king* [A]2 Chr 19:11 27:2 [a]Lit *was over,* and so throughout the ch [A]2 Sam 23:8-30; 1 Chr 11:11-31 27:22 [A]1 Chr 28:1 27:23 [a]Lit *take their number from* [A]1 Chr 21:2-5 [B]Gen 15:5; 22:17; 26:4 27:24 [A]2 Sam 24:12-15; 1 Chr 21:1-7 27:26 [a]Lit *doers of the work of the field for the tilling of...*

26:29–32 officers and judges. There were 6,000 magistrates exercising judicial functions throughout the Land.

26:31 fortieth year. The last year of David's reign (ca. 971 B.C.).

27:1–34 First Chronicles 23–26 discusses spiritual leadership, while here the chronicler focuses on the civil aspects of David's kingdom.

27:1–15 This section enumerates the standing army of Israel (288,000 men), which had responsibility to guard the nation and temple. They were divided into 12 divisions, each of which served for one month during the year. When full war occurred, a larger force could be called into action (cf. 21:5).

27:16–22 While 12 officers are named, the tribes of Asher and Gad are not mentioned for unknown reasons.

27:23, 24 Here is further comment on the sinful census detailed in 1Ch 21:1–30. David didn't try to number all Israelites because they were too many (cf. Ge 28:14). Nor did he finish the census, being interrupted by guilt and judgment.

27:24 the chronicles of King David. Daily records were kept of the king's reign. None was kept of this calamity because the record was too painful.

27:25–31 A summary of officials who looked over David's various agricultural assets.

charge of the vineyards; and Zabdi the Shiphmite had
charge of the [a]produce of the vineyards *stored* in the
wine cellars. 28 Baal-hanan the Gederite had charge
of the olive and [A]sycamore trees in the [a]Shephelah;
and Joash had charge of the stores of oil. 29 Shitrai the
Sharonite had charge of the cattle which were grazing
in [A]Sharon; and Shaphat the son of Adlai had charge
of the cattle in the valleys. 30 Obil the Ishmaelite had
charge of the camels; and Jehdeiah the Meronothite
had charge of the donkeys. 31 Jaziz the [A]Hagrite had
charge of the flocks. All these were [a]overseers of the
property which belonged to King David.

COUNSELORS

32 Also Jonathan, David's uncle, *was* a counselor, a
man of understanding, and a scribe; and Jehiel the
son of Hachmoni [a]tutored the king's sons. 33 [A]Ahith-
ophel *was* counselor to the king; and [B]Hushai the
Archite *was* the king's friend. 34 Jehoiada the son
of [A]Benaiah, and [B]Abiathar [a]succeeded Ahithophel;
and Joab was the [C]commander of the king's army.

DAVID'S ADDRESS ABOUT THE TEMPLE

28 Now [A]David assembled at Jerusalem all the
officials of Israel, the princes of the tribes,
and the commanders of the divisions that served
the king, and the commanders of thousands, and
the commanders of hundreds, and the overseers of
all the property and livestock belonging to the king
and his sons, with the officials and [B]the mighty men,
even all the valiant men. 2 Then King David rose to
his feet and said, "Listen to me, my brethren and my
people; I [A]*had* [a]intended to build a [b]permanent home
for the ark of the covenant of the LORD and for [B]the
footstool of our God. So I had made preparations to
build *it*. 3 But God said to me, '[A]You shall not build a
house for My name because you are a man of war
and have shed blood.' 4 Yet, the LORD, the God of
Israel, [A]chose me from all the house of my father
to be king over Israel [B]forever. For [C]He has chosen
Judah to be a leader; and [D]in the house of Judah, my
father's house, and among the sons of my father He
took pleasure in me to make *me* king over all Israel.
5 [A]Of all my sons (for the LORD has given me many
sons), [B]He has chosen my son Solomon to sit on the
throne of the kingdom of the LORD over Israel. 6 He
said to me, 'Your son [A]Solomon is the one who shall
build My house and My courts; for I have chosen him
to be a son to Me, and I will be a father to him. 7 I
will establish his kingdom forever [A]if he resolutely
performs My commandments and My ordinances,
as [a]is done now.' 8 So now, in the sight of all Israel,
the assembly of the LORD, and in the hearing of our
God, observe and seek after all the commandments of
the LORD your God so that you may possess the good
land and bequeath *it* to your sons after you forever.
9 "As for you, my son Solomon, know the God of
your father, and [A]serve Him with [a]a whole heart and
a willing [b]mind; [B]for the LORD searches all hearts,
and understands every intent of the thoughts. [C]If
you seek Him, He will let you find Him; but if you
forsake Him, He will reject you forever. 10 Consider
now, for the LORD has chosen you to build a house
for the sanctuary; [A]be courageous and act."
11 Then David gave to his son Solomon [A]the plan
of [B]the porch *of the temple*, its buildings, its storehouses, its upper rooms, its inner rooms and [C]the
room for the mercy seat; 12 and the plan of all that
he had in [a]mind, for the courts of the house of the
LORD, and for all the surrounding rooms, for [A]the
storehouses of the house of God and for the storehouses of the dedicated things; 13 also for [A]the divisions of the priests and [B]the Levites and for all
the work of the service of the house of the LORD
and for all the utensils of service in the house of
the LORD; 14 for the golden *utensils*, the weight of
gold for all utensils for every kind of service; for the
silver utensils, the weight *of silver* for all utensils
for every kind of service; 15 and the weight *of gold*
for the [A]golden lampstands and their golden lamps,
with the weight of each lampstand and its lamps;
and *the weight of silver* for the silver lampstands,
with the weight of each lampstand and its lamps
according to the use of each lampstand; 16 and the
gold by weight for the tables of showbread, for
each table; and silver for the silver tables; 17 and
the forks, the basins, and the pitchers of pure gold;
and for the golden bowls with the weight for each
bowl; and for the silver bowls with the weight for
each bowl; 18 and for [A]the altar of incense refined
gold by weight; and gold for the model of the chariot, *even* [B]the cherubim that spread out *their wings*
and covered the ark of the covenant of the LORD.

27:27 [a]Lit *what was in the vineyards of the storehouses of wine* 27:28 [a]Or *lowlands* [A]1 Kin 10:27; 2 Chr 1:15 27:29 [A]1 Chr 5:16 27:31 [a]Or *rulers* [A]1 Chr 5:10 27:32 [a]Lit *was with* 27:33 [A]2 Sam 15:12 [B]2 Sam 15:32, 37 27:34 [a]Lit *after* [A]1 Chr 27:5 [B]1 Kin 1:7 [C]1 Chr 11:6 28:1 [A]1 Chr 23:2; 27:1-31 [B]1 Chr 11:10-47 28:2 [a]Lit *in my heart* [b]Lit *house of rest* [A]1 Chr 17:1, 2 [B]Ps 132:7; Is 66:1 28:3 [A]1 Chr 22:8 28:4 [A]1 Sam 16:6-13 [B]1 Chr 17:23, 27 [C]Gen 49:8-10; 1 Chr 5:2 [D]1 Sam 16:1 28:5 [A]1 Chr 3:1-9; 14:3-7 [B]1 Chr 22:9, 10 28:6 [A]2 Sam 7:13, 14 28:7 [a]Lit *at this day* [A]1 Chr 22:13 28:9 [a]Or *the same* [b]Lit *soul* [A]1 Kin 8:61; 1 Chr 29:17-19 [B]1 Sam 16:7 [C]2 Chr 15:2; Jer 29:13 28:10 [A]1 Chr 22:13 28:11 [A]Ex 25:40; 1 Chr 28:12, 19 [B]1 Kin 6:3 [C]Ex 25:17-22 28:12 [a]Lit *the spirit with him* [A]1 Chr 26:20, 28 28:13 [A]1 Chr 24:1 [B]1 Chr 23:6 28:15 [A]Ex 25:31-39 28:18 [A]Ex 30:1-10 [B]Ex 25:18-22

27:32–34 A summary of those whose duties kept them in close contact with the king (cf. 18:14–17), perhaps like a cabinet. When David's son, Absalom, rebelled against him, Ahithophel betrayed David and joined the revolution. Hushai pretended loyalty to Absalom, and his advice caused Absalom's death (cf. 2Sa 15:31–17:23).

28:1–29:20 A record is given of David's last assembly in which the king charged Solomon and the people to build the temple for God's glory. These final chapters present the transition from David to Solomon. The chronicler does not mention Adonijah's conspiracy (1Ki 1:5–9) or David's weakness (1Ki 1:1–4), but looks at the positive contribution of the Davidic kingdom.

28:2–8 For the assembly's sake, David testified to the Davidic Covenant originally given by God to him in 2Sa 7 (cf. 17:7–27; 22:6–16). David makes it clear that Solomon was God's choice (v. 5) as had been frequently intimated (cf. 2Sa 12:24, 25; 1Ki 1:13), just as the coming Christ will be God's chosen Son to ultimately fulfill the kingdom promise.

28:8 Cf. Dt 5:29, 33; 6:1–3.

28:9–21 David turns his words to Solomon with 4 perspectives: 1) spiritual devotion (28:9, 10); 2) architectural execution (28:11–19); 3) divine intervention (28:20); and 4) human participation (28:21).

28:9, 10 Cf. notes on 22:11–13, 17–19.

28:18 **the chariot.** Using the imagery of Ps 18:10, the cherubim are depicted as the vehicle in which God moves.

19 “All *this,*” *said David,* “the LORD made me understand in writing by His hand upon me, [A]all the
[a]details of this pattern.”
20 Then David said to his son Solomon, “[A]Be
strong and courageous, and act; do not fear nor
be dismayed, for the LORD God, my God, is with
you. [B]He will not fail you nor forsake you until all
the work for the service of the house of the LORD
is finished. 21 Now behold, [A]*there are* the divisions
of the priests and the Levites for all the service of
the house of God, and [B]every willing man of any
skill will be with you in all the work for all kinds of
service. The officials also and all the people will be
entirely at your command.”

OFFERINGS FOR THE TEMPLE

29 Then King David said to the entire assembly, “My son Solomon, whom alone God has
chosen, [A]is still young and inexperienced and the
work is great; for [B]the [a]temple is not for man, but
for the LORD God. 2 Now [A]with all my ability I have
provided for the house of my God the gold for the
things of gold, and the silver for the *things of* silver,
and the bronze for the *things of* bronze, the iron for
the *things of* iron, and wood for the *things of* wood,
onyx stones and inlaid *stones,* stones of antimony
and stones of various colors, and all kinds of precious stones and alabaster in abundance. 3 Moreover,
in my delight in the house of my God, the treasure
I have of gold and silver, I give to the house of my
God, over and above all that I have already provided for the holy [a]temple, 4 *namely,* [A]3,000 talents
of gold, of [B]the gold of Ophir, and 7,000 talents of
refined silver, to overlay the walls of the [a]buildings;
5 of gold for the *things of* gold and of silver for the
things of silver, that is, for all the work [a]done by
the craftsmen. Who then is willing [b]to consecrate
himself this day to the LORD?”
6 Then [A]the rulers of the fathers’ *households,* and
the princes of the tribes of Israel, and the commanders of thousands and of hundreds, with [B]the
overseers over the king’s work, offered willingly;
7 and for the service for the house of God they gave
5,000 talents and 10,000 [A]darics of gold, and 10,000
talents of silver, and 18,000 talents of brass, and
100,000 talents of iron. 8 [a]Whoever possessed *pre-*
cious stones gave them to the treasury of the house
of the LORD, [b]in care of [A]Jehiel the Gershonite. 9 Then
the people rejoiced because they had offered so willingly, for they made their offering to the LORD [A]with
a whole heart, and King David also rejoiced greatly.

DAVID’S PRAYER

10 So David blessed the LORD in the sight of all
the assembly; and David said, “Blessed are You,
O LORD God of Israel our father, forever and ever.
11 [A]Yours, O LORD, is the greatness and the power
and the glory and the victory and the majesty, indeed everything that is in the heavens and the
earth; Yours is the dominion, O LORD, and You exalt
Yourself as head over all. 12 [A]Both riches and honor
come from You, and You rule over all, and [B]in Your
hand is power and might; and it lies in Your hand
to make great and to strengthen everyone. 13 Now
therefore, our God, we thank You, and praise Your
glorious name.
14 “But who am I and who are my people that we
should [a]be able to offer as generously as this? For
all things come from You, and from Your hand we
have given You. 15 For [A]we are sojourners before You,
and tenants, as all our fathers were; [B]our days on
the earth are like a shadow, and there is no hope.
16 O LORD our God, all this abundance that we have
provided to build You a house for Your holy name, it
is from Your hand, and all is Yours. 17 Since I know,
O my God, that [A]You try the heart and [B]delight in
uprightness, I, in the integrity of my heart, have
willingly offered all these *things;* so now with joy I
have seen Your people, who are present here, make
their offerings willingly to You. 18 O LORD, the God
of Abraham, Isaac and Israel, our fathers, preserve
this forever in the [a]intentions of the heart of Your

28:19 [a]Lit *works* [A]1 Chr 28:11, 12 28:20 [A]1 Chr 22:13 [B]Josh 1:5; Heb 13:5 28:21 [A]1 Chr 28:13 [B]Ex 35:25-35; 36:1, 2 29:1 [a]Lit *palace* [A]1 Chr 22:5 [B]1 Chr 29:19 29:2 [A]1 Chr 22:3-5 29:3 [a]Lit *house* 29:4 [a]Lit *houses* [A]1 Chr 22:14 [B]1 Kin 9:28 29:5 [a]Lit *by the hand of the craftsmen* [b]Lit *to fill his hand* 29:6 [A]1 Chr 27:1; 28:1 [B]1 Chr 27:25-31 29:7 [A]Ezra 2:69; Neh 7:70 29:8 [a]Lit *Those with whom were found* [b]Lit *under the hand of* [A]1 Chr 23:8 29:9 [A]1 Kin 8:61; 2 Cor 9:7 29:11 [A]Matt 6:13; Rev 5:13 29:12 [A]2 Chr 1:12 [B]2 Chr 20:6 29:14 [a]Lit *retain strength* 29:15 [A]Lev 25:23 [B]Job 14:2, 10-12 29:17 [A]1 Chr 28:9 [B]Ps 15:2 29:18 [a]Lit *intent of the thoughts of the heart*

28:19 in writing. David wrote down the plans under the Holy Spirit’s divine inspiration (non-canonical, written revelation). This divine privilege was much like that of Moses for the tabernacle (Ex 25:9, 40; 27:8; Heb 8:5).

28:20, 21 Solomon’s associates in the building project were God, the owner and general contractor (28:20), plus the human workforce (28:21).

29:1–5 David called for consecrated giving to the project (cf. 28:1), based on the example of his generosity (vv. 3, 4). David gave his personal fortune to the temple building, a fortune almost immeasurable.

29:1 young and inexperienced. *See notes on 1Ch 22:5.*

29:4 *namely,* 3,000 talents. Assuming a talent weighed about 75 lbs., this amounts to almost 112 tons of gold, plus the 7,000 talents of silver which would be 260 tons. The total worth of such precious metals has been estimated in the billions of dollars. **gold of Ophir.** This was held to be the purest and finest in the world (cf. Job 22:24; 28:16; Is 13:12).

29:6–9 willingly. Here is the key to all free-will giving, i.e., giving what one desires to give. Tithes were required for taxation, to fund the theocracy, similar to taxation today. The law required that to be paid. This, however, is the voluntary giving from the heart to the Lord. The NT speaks of this (cf. Lk 6:38; 2Co 9:1–8) and never demands that a tithe be given to God, but that taxes be paid to one’s government (cf. Ro 13:6, 7). Paying taxes and giving God whatever one is willing to give, based on devotion to Him and His glory, is biblical giving.

29:7 gave 5,000 talents. Assuming a talent weighed about 75 lbs., this amounts to 187 tons of gold. **darics.** A Persian coin, familiar to Jews from the captivity, possibly named after Darius I (cf. Ezr 8:27). The readers of this material in Ezra’s day would know it as a contemporary measurement. **and 10,000 talents.** This amounts to 375 tons of silver. **and 18,000 talents.** This amounts to almost 675 tons of bronze. **and 100,000 talents.** This amounts to 3,750 tons of iron. The sum of all this is staggering, and has been estimated into the billions of dollars.

29:10–15 David responds to the phenomenal offering expressing amazing sacrifices of wealth with praise in which he acknowledges that all things belong to and come from God. He concludes that God is everything and that man is nothing, much like Ps 8. This magnificent prayer of thanks gives God all credit, even for the people’s generosity (v. 14).

29:16–20 David leads in a prayer of commitment.

29:17 try the heart. Opportunities for giving to God are tests of the character of a believer’s devotion to the Lord. The king acknowledges that the attitude of one’s heart is

people, and direct their heart to You; 19 and [A]give
to my son Solomon a perfect heart to keep Your
commandments, Your testimonies and Your statutes, and to do *them* all, and [B]to build the [a]temple,
for which I have made provision."
20 Then David said to all the assembly, "Now bless
the LORD your God." And [A]all the assembly blessed
the LORD, the God of their fathers, and [B]bowed low
and did homage to the LORD and to the king.

SACRIFICES

21 On the next day [A]they [a]made sacrifices to the
LORD and offered burnt offerings to the LORD, 1,000
bulls, 1,000 rams *and* 1,000 lambs, with their drink
offerings and sacrifices in abundance for all Israel.
22 So they ate and drank that day before the LORD
with great gladness.

SOLOMON AGAIN MADE KING

And they made Solomon the son of David king
[A]a second time, and they [B]anointed *him* as ruler for
the LORD and Zadok as priest. 23 Then [A]Solomon sat
on the throne of the LORD as king instead of David
his father; and he prospered, and all Israel obeyed
him. 24 All the officials, the mighty men, and also all
the sons of King David [a]pledged allegiance to King
Solomon. 25 [A]The LORD highly exalted Solomon in
the sight of all Israel, and [B]bestowed on him royal
majesty which had not been on any king before
him in Israel.
26 Now [A]David the son of Jesse reigned over all
Israel. 27 [A]The period which he reigned over Israel
was forty years; he reigned in Hebron seven years
and [a]in Jerusalem thirty-three *years*.

DEATH OF DAVID

28 Then he died in [A]a [a]ripe old age, [B]full of days,
riches and honor; and his son Solomon reigned in
his place. 29 Now the acts of King David, from first
to last, are written in the chronicles of [A]Samuel the
seer, in the chronicles of [B]Nathan the prophet and in
the chronicles of [C]Gad the seer, 30 with all his reign,
his power, and the circumstances which came on
him, on Israel, and on all the kingdoms of the lands.

29:19 [a]Lit *palace* [A]1 Chr 28:9; Ps 72:1 [B]1 Chr 29:1, 2 29:20 [A]Josh 22:33 [B]Ex 4:31 29:21 [a]Lit *sacrificed* [A]1 Kin 8:62, 63 29:22 [A]1 Chr 23:1 [B]1 Kin 1:33-39 29:23 [A]1 Kin 2:12 29:24 [a]Lit *put a hand under Solomon* 29:25 [A]2 Chr 1:1 [B]1 Kin 3:13; 2 Chr 1:12 29:26 [A]1 Chr 18:14 29:27 [a]Lit *he reigned in* [A]2 Sam 5:4, 5; 1 Kin 2:11; 1 Chr 3:4 29:28 [a]Lit *good* [A]Gen 15:15; Acts 13:36 [B]1 Chr 23:1 29:29 [A]1 Sam 9:9 [B]2 Sam 7:2-4; 12:1-7 [C]1 Sam 22:5

significantly more important than the amount of offering in one's hand.

29:20 **bowed ... did homage.** The ultimate physical expression of an inward submission to God in all things.

29:21–30 The chronicler records in selective fashion the final days of David and the enthronement of Solomon. For a more complete treatment see 1Ki 1:1–53.

29:22 **a second time.** This most likely refers to a public ceremony subsequent to the private one of 1Ki 1:35–39 in response to Adonijah's conspiracy. David's High Priest Zadok had been loyal to both father and son (1Ki 1:32–40; 2:27–29), so he continued on as High Priest during Solomon's reign.

29:26–28 Cf. 1Ki 2:10–12.

29:27 **forty years.** Ca. 1011–971 B.C.

29:29 **Samuel.** This most likely refers to the canonical book of 1 and 2 Samuel. **seer ... prophet ... seer.** All 3 are different, but synonymous, Heb. terms referring to the prophetic office from the perspectives of: 1) to understand; 2) to proclaim; and 3) to understand respectively. **Nathan ... Gad.** These are noncanonical, but reliable, historical records that the chronicler utilized. God's Spirit protected the record from error in the original writing (2Ti 3:16, 17; 2Pe 1:20, 21).

THE SECOND
BOOK OF THE

CHRONICLES

INTRODUCTION

See 1 Chronicles for the Introductory Discussion.

OUTLINE

I. The Reign of Solomon (1:1–9:31)

A. Coronation and Beginnings (1:1–17)
B. Temple Building (2:1–7:22)
C. Wealth/Achievements (8:1–9:28)
D. Death (9:29–31)

II. The Reign of the Kings of Judah (10:1–36:21)

A. Rehoboam (10:1–12:16)
B. Abijah (13:1–22)
C. Asa (14:1–16:14)
D. Jehoshaphat (17:1–21:3)
E. Jehoram (21:4–20)
F. Ahaziah (22:1–9)
G. Athaliah (22:10–23:21)
H. Joash (24:1–27)
I. Amaziah (25:1–28)
J. Uzziah (26:1–23)
K. Jotham (27:1–9)
L. Ahaz (28:1–27)
M. Hezekiah (29:1–32:33)
N. Manasseh (33:1–20)
O. Amon (33:21–25)
P. Josiah (34:1–35:27)
Q. Jehoahaz (36:1–4)
R. Jehoiakim (36:5–8)
S. Jehoiachin (36:9, 10)
T. Zedekiah (36:11–21)

III. The Return Proclamation of Cyrus (36:22, 23)

SOLOMON WORSHIPS AT GIBEON

1 Now [A]Solomon the son of David established himself securely over his kingdom, and the LORD his
God *was* with him and [B]exalted him greatly.
2 Solomon spoke to all Israel, [A]to the commanders
of thousands and of hundreds and to the judges
and to every leader in all Israel, the heads of the
fathers' *households.* 3 Then Solomon and all the
assembly with him went to [A]the high place which
was at Gibeon, [B]for God's tent of meeting was there,
which Moses the servant of the LORD had made in
the wilderness. 4 However, David had brought up
[A]the ark of God from Kiriath-jearim [a]to [B]the place
he had prepared for it, for he had pitched a tent
for it in Jerusalem. 5 Now [A]the bronze altar, which
Bezalel the son of Uri, the son of Hur, had made,
[a]was there before the tabernacle of the LORD, and
Solomon and the assembly sought it out. 6 Solomon
went up there before the LORD to the bronze altar
which *was* at the tent of meeting, and [A]offered a
thousand burnt offerings on it.
7 [A]In that night God appeared to Solomon and
said to him, "Ask what I shall give you."

SOLOMON'S PRAYER FOR WISDOM

8 Solomon said to God, "You have dealt with my
father David with great lovingkindness, and [A]have
made me king in his place. 9 Now, O LORD God, [A]Your
[a]promise to my father David is fulfilled, for You
have made me king over [B]a people as numerous as
the dust of the earth. 10 [A]Give me now wisdom and
knowledge, [B]that I may go out and come in before
this people, for who can rule this great people of
Yours?" 11 [A]God said to Solomon, "Because [a]you had
this in mind, and did not ask for riches, wealth or
honor, or the life of those who hate you, nor have
you even asked for long life, but you have asked
for yourself wisdom and knowledge that you may
rule My people over whom I have made you king,
12 wisdom and knowledge have been granted to you.
And [A]I will give you riches and wealth and honor,
[a]such as none of the kings who were before you has
possessed nor those who will [b]come after you." 13 [A]So
Solomon went [a]from the high place which was at
Gibeon, from the tent of meeting, to Jerusalem, and
he reigned over Israel.

SOLOMON'S WEALTH

14 [A]Solomon amassed chariots and horsemen. [B]He
had 1,400 chariots and 12,000 horsemen, and he stationed them in [C]the chariot cities and with the king
at Jerusalem. 15 [A]The king made [B]silver and gold as
plentiful in Jerusalem as stones, and he made cedars
as plentiful as sycamores in the [a]lowland. 16 Solomon's [A]horses were imported from Egypt and from
Kue; the king's traders procured them from Kue
for a price. 17 They [a]imported chariots from Egypt
for 600 *shekels* of silver apiece and horses for 150

1:1 [A]1 Kin 2:12, 46 [B]1 Chr 29:25 1:2 [A]1 Chr 28:1 1:3 [A]1 Kin 3:4 [B]Ex 36:8 1:4 [a]Lit *where David had prepared for it* [A]1 Chr 15:25-28 [B]2 Chr 6:2 1:5 [a]Lit *he put* [A]Ex 31:9; 38:1-7 1:6 [A]1 Kin 3:4 1:7 [A]1 Kin 3:5-14 1:8 [A]1 Chr 28:5 1:9 [a]Lit *word* [A]2 Sam 7:12-16 [B]Gen 13:16; 22:17; 28:14 1:10 [A]1 Kin 3:9 [B]Num 27:17; 2 Sam 5:2 1:11 [a]Lit *this was in your heart* [A]1 Kin 3:11 1:12 [a]Lit *which was not so to the kings who were before you* [b]Lit *be* [A]1 Chr 29:25; 2 Chr 9:22 1:13 [a]Lit *to* [A]2 Chr 1:3 1:14 [A]1 Kin 10:26-29 [B]1 Kin 4:26 [C]1 Kin 9:19 1:15 [a]Heb *shephelah* [A]1 Kin 10:27 [B]Deut 17:17 1:16 [A]Deut 17:16 1:17 [a]Lit *brought up and brought out*

1:1–9:31 This section continues from 1 Chronicles and covers the rule of Solomon (ca. 971–931 B.C.; cf. 1Ki 3–11). The major theme is Solomon's building God's temple in Jerusalem for the purpose of centralizing and unifying the nation in the worship of God.

1:3 Gibeon. *See notes on 1Ch 16:39 and 21:29.* The tabernacle remained at Gibeon while the ark resided in Jerusalem, waiting for the temple to be built. **tent of meeting.** Built in the days of Moses, this tent was where God met with the people (cf. Ex 25:22; 29:42, 43; 40:34–38). The center of worship was there until the temple was built (cf. v. 6).

1:4 Kiriath-jearim. *See note on 1Ch 13:5.*

1:5 Bezalel. The Spirit-enabled craftsman who built the bronze altar for the tabernacle (cf. Ex 31:1–11; 38:1, 2).

1:7–13 The account is paralleled in 1Ki 3:5–15. Every king of Israel needed to heed God's instructions recorded in Dt 17:14–20.

1:9 Your promise. A reference to the Davidic Covenant in 2Sa 7; 1Ch 17.

1:10 Solomon had agreed with his father (cf. 1Ch 22:5 and 29:1) on his need for wisdom, and that is what he sought from God (cf. 1Ki 3:3–15; Pr 3:15; Jas 1:5).

1:14–17 1Ki 10:14–29 and 2Ch 9:13–28 also extol Solomon's wealth.

1:14 chariot cities. Gezer, Hazor, and Megiddo were among the chief cities.

1:16 Kue. Possibly Cilicia.

1:17 chariots . . . for 600 *shekels*. Assuming a shekel weighs .4 oz., this represents 15 lbs. of silver for one chariot. **horses for 150 apiece.** Assuming the weight is in shekels,

THE SPREAD OF SOLOMON'S FAME

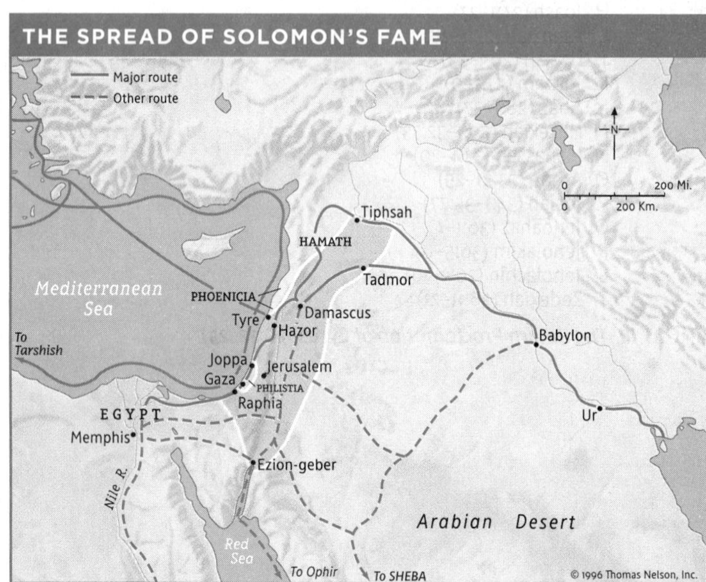

Solomon's influence in economic and political affairs was enhanced by the transportation and trade routes that intersected his kingdom. That Solomon acquired much through trade is suggested by the response of the queen of Sheba on her visit to Solomon, and by the mention of traders and merchants (9:14) in the account of his wealth. Solomon may have fortified Tadmor (8:4) in order to have a safe and direct trade route from Asia Minor to Damascus.

apiece, and [b]by the same means they [c]exported them to all the kings of the Hittites and the kings of Aram.

SOLOMON WILL BUILD A TEMPLE AND PALACE

2 [a,A]Now Solomon [b]decided to build a house for the name of the LORD and a [c]royal palace for himself. 2 [a]So [A]Solomon [b]assigned 70,000 men to carry loads and 80,000 men to quarry *stone* in the mountains and 3,600 to supervise them.

3 [A]Then Solomon sent *word* to [a]Huram the king of Tyre, saying, "[B]As you dealt with David my father and sent him cedars to build him a house to dwell in, so do for me. 4 Behold, I am about to build a house for the name of the LORD my God, dedicating it to Him, [A]to burn fragrant incense before Him and *to set out* [B]the showbread continually, and to offer [C]burnt offerings morning and evening, [D]on sabbaths and on new moons and on the appointed feasts of the LORD our God, this *being required* forever in Israel. 5 The house which I am about to build *will be* great, for [A]greater is our God than all the gods. 6 But [A]who is able to build a house for Him, for the heavens and the highest heavens cannot contain Him? So who am I, that I should build a house for Him, except to [a]burn *incense* before Him? 7 Now [A]send me a skilled man to work in gold, silver, brass and iron, and in purple, crimson and violet *fabrics,* and who knows how to make engravings, to *work* with the skilled men [a,B]whom I have in Judah and Jerusalem, whom David my father provided. 8 [A]Send me also cedar, cypress and algum timber from Lebanon, for I know that your servants know how to cut timber of Lebanon; and indeed [B]my servants *will work* with your servants, 9 to prepare timber in abundance for me, for the house which I am about to build *will be* great and wonderful. 10 Now behold, [A]I will give to your servants, the woodsmen who cut the timber, 20,000 [a]kors of crushed wheat and 20,000 [a]kors of barley, and 20,000 baths of wine and 20,000 baths of oil."

HURAM TO ASSIST

11 Then Huram, king of Tyre, [a]answered in a letter sent to Solomon: "[A]Because the LORD loves His people, He has made you king over them." 12 Then Huram [a]continued, "Blessed be [A]the LORD, the God of Israel, who has made heaven and earth, who has given King David a wise son, [b]endowed with discretion and understanding, [B]who will build a house for the LORD and a [c]royal palace for himself.

13 "Now I am sending Huram-abi, a skilled man, [a]endowed with understanding, 14 [A]the son of a [a]Danite woman and [b]a Tyrian father, who knows how to work in gold, silver, bronze, iron, stone and wood, *and* in purple, violet, linen and crimson fabrics, and *who knows how* to make all kinds of engravings and to [c]execute any design which may be assigned to him, *to work* with your skilled men and with [d]those of my lord David your father. 15 Now then, let my lord send to his servants wheat and barley, oil and wine, of [A]which he has spoken. 16 [A]We will cut whatever timber you need from Lebanon and bring it to you on rafts by sea to Joppa, so that you may carry it up to Jerusalem."

17 Solomon numbered all the aliens who *were* in the land of Israel, [A]following the [a]census which his father David had [b]taken; and 153,600 were found. 18 [A]He appointed 70,000 of them to carry loads and 80,000 to quarry *stones* in the mountains and 3,600 supervisors to make the people work.

THE TEMPLE CONSTRUCTION IN JERUSALEM

3 [A]Then Solomon began to build the house of the LORD in Jerusalem on Mount Moriah, where

1:17 [b]Lit *and in like manner by their hand* [c]Lit *brought out* 2:1 [a]Ch 1:18 in Heb [b]Lit *said* [c]Lit *house for his royalty* [A]1 Kin 5:5 2:2 [a]Ch 2:1 in Heb [b]Lit *numbered* [A]1 Kin 5:15, 16; 2 Chr 2:18 2:3 [a]In 1 Kin 5:18, *Hiram* [A]1 Kin 5:2-11 [B]1 Chr 14:1 2:4 [A]Ex 30:7 [B]Ex 25:30 [C]Ex 29:38-42 [D]Num 28:9, 10 2:5 [A]Ex 15:11; 1 Chr 16:25 2:6 [a]Lit *offer up in smoke* [A]1 Kin 8:27; 2 Chr 6:18 2:7 [a]Lit *who are with me* [A]Ex 31:3-5; 2 Chr 2:13, 14 [B]1 Chr 22:15 2:8 [A]1 Kin 5:6 [B]2 Chr 9:10, 11 2:10 [a]I.e. One kor equals approx 10 bu [A]1 Kin 5:11 2:11 [a]Lit *said...and he sent* [A]1 Kin 10:9; 2 Chr 9:8 2:12 [a]Lit *said* [b]Lit *knowing discretion* [c]Lit *house for his royalty* [A]Ps 33:6; 102:25 [B]2 Chr 2:1 2:13 [a]Lit *knowing understanding* 2:14 [a]Lit *a woman of the daughters of Dan* [b]Lit *whose father is a Tyrian man* [c]Lit *devise any device* [d]Lit *skilled men* [A]1 Kin 7:14 2:15 [A]2 Chr 2:10 2:16 [A]1 Kin 5:8, 9 2:17 [a]Lit *numbering* [b]Lit *numbered of them* [A]1 Chr 22:2 2:18 [A]2 Chr 2:2 3:1 [A]1 Kin 6:1

this would be about 3.75 lbs. of silver. Deuteronomy 17:16 warned against the king's amassing horses. **the Hittites.** People, once expelled from Israel, who lived N of Israel and NW of Syria.

2:1–18 This section reports how Solomon selected men to gather building materials for the temple. This was in addition to the massive supplies stockpiled by David (cf. 1Ch 22, 29). This section parallels 1Ki 5:1–16.

2:1 house for the name of the LORD. God's covenant name, Yahweh or Jehovah (cf. Ex 3:14), is in mind. David wanted to do this, but was not allowed to do any more than plan and prepare (1Ch 23–26; 28:11–13), purchase the land (2Sa 24:18–25; 1Ch 22), and gather the materials (1Ch 22:14–16). **royal palace.** See 1Ki 7:1–12 for details (cf. 2Ch 7:11; 8:1).

2:2 These numbers are repeated in 2:17, 18. First Kings 5:16 records 3,300 overseers, compared to 3,600 in 2:18. If, however, the additional supervisors (250 in 2Ch 8:10, but 550 in 1Ki 9:23) are added, then both 1 Kings and 2 Chronicles agree that a total of 3,850 men worked. David had done similarly at an earlier date (1Ch 22:2).

2:3–10 Compare with the contents of 1Ki 5:3–6. The differences can be accounted for in much the same way as in the Gospels, by combining the narratives of 1Ki 5:3–6 and 2Ch 2:3–10 to complete the entire correspondence.

2:7 send me a skilled man. The Israelites were familiar with agriculture, but not metalworking. They needed experts for that.

2:8 algum. A coniferous tree native to Lebanon. Some identify it as sandalwood, a smooth, expensive red wood that could be polished to a high gloss.

2:10 This listing of goods is more complete than that of 1Ki 5:11. Lebanon traded with Israel regularly for food. **give ... 20,000 kors.** A kor is the same as a homer and could have measured as much as 7.5 bu., making this amount about 150,000 bu. **and 20,000 baths.** A bath measured about 6 gal. This would be about 120,000 gal. The 20 kors of "beaten oil" in 1Ki 5:11 is most likely not a scribal error but rather a finer grade of oil.

2:11–16 Compare with the context of 1Ki 5:7–9.

2:12 God ... who has made heaven and earth. This was the common identification of the true God when pagans spoke of or were told of Him (cf. 2Ch 36:23; Ezr 1:2; 5:11, 12; 6:10; 7:12, 21, 23; Jer 10:11, 12; Ac 4:24; 14:15; 17:24–26; Col 1:16, 17; Rev 11:1, 6).

2:13, 14 Huram-abi. First Kings 7:14 states that his mother was of the tribe of Naphtali, not Dan, as reported here. This is resolved if she was of Naphtali by birth, but living in the territory of Dan. Or, if his parents were originally from the two tribes, then he could legitimately claim either. He was the parallel to Bezalel, who constructed the tabernacle. *See note on 2Ch 1:5.*

2:16 Joppa. A major coastal port of Israel. Later, Jonah would sail from Joppa (Jon 1:3), and much later Peter would be there to receive God's call in a vision (Ac 10:5ff.).

2:17, 18 *See note on 2Ch 2:2.*

3:1–17 Cf. 1Ki 6:1–38; 7:15–22 for amplification and additional material on the building of the temple.

3:1 threshing floor. *See notes on Ge 22:1–18; 2Sa 24:18–25; 1Ch 21:20–30.*

the LORD had appeared to his father David, at the
place that David had prepared [B]on the threshing
floor of [a]Ornan the Jebusite. 2 He began to build on
the second *day* in the second month [a]of the fourth
year of his reign.

DIMENSIONS AND MATERIALS OF THE TEMPLE

3 Now these are the [a]foundations which [A]Solomon
laid for building the house of God. The length in
[b]cubits, according to the old standard *was* sixty
cubits, and the width twenty cubits. 4 The porch
which was in front of the house [A]was as long as the
width of the house, twenty cubits, and the height
120; and inside he overlaid it with pure gold. 5 He
overlaid [A]the [a]main room with cypress wood and
overlaid it with fine gold, and [b]ornamented it with
palm trees and chains. 6 Further, he [a]adorned the
house with precious stones; and the gold was gold
from [b]Parvaim. 7 [A]He also overlaid the house with
gold—the beams, the thresholds and its walls and
its doors; and he [B]carved cherubim on the walls.
8 Now he made [A]the [a]room of the holy of holies:
its length across the width of the house *was* twenty
cubits, and its width *was* twenty cubits; and he
overlaid it with fine gold, *amounting* to 600 talents.
9 The weight of the nails was fifty shekels of gold.
He also overlaid [A]the upper rooms with gold.
10 [A]Then he made two [a]sculptured cherubim in the
room of the holy of holies and overlaid them with
gold. 11 The wingspan of the cherubim *was* twenty
cubits; the wing of one, of five cubits, touched the
wall of the house, and *its* other wing, of five cubits, touched the wing of the other cherub. 12 The
wing of the other cherub, of five cubits, touched the
wall of the house; and *its* other wing of five cubits
was attached to the wing of the [a]first cherub. 13 The
wings of these cherubim extended twenty cubits,
and they stood on their feet [a]facing the *main* room.
14 [A]He made the veil of violet, purple, crimson and
fine linen, and he worked cherubim on it.
15 [A]He also made two pillars for the front of the
house, thirty-five cubits [a]high, and the capital on
the top of each *was* five cubits. 16 He made chains
in the inner sanctuary and placed *them* on the tops
of the pillars; and he made one hundred pomegranates and placed *them* on the chains. 17 [A]He erected
the pillars in front of the temple, one on the right
and the other on the left, and named the one on the
right Jachin and the one on the left Boaz.

FURNISHINGS OF THE TEMPLE

4 Then [A]he made a bronze altar, twenty cubits in
length and twenty cubits in width and ten cubits
in height. 2 [A]Also he made the cast *metal* sea, ten
cubits from brim to brim, circular in form, and its
height *was* five cubits and [a]its circumference thirty
cubits. 3 Now figures like oxen *were* under it *and* all
around it, ten cubits, entirely encircling the sea. The
oxen *were* in two rows, cast [a]in one piece. 4 It stood
on twelve oxen, three facing the north, three facing
west, three facing south and three facing east; and
the sea *was set* on top of them and all their hind-
quarters turned inwards. 5 It was a handbreadth
thick, and its brim was made like the brim of a cup,
like a lily blossom; it [A]could hold 3,000 baths. 6 [A]He
also made ten basins in which to wash, and he set
five on the right side and five on the left [a]to rinse
things for the burnt offering; but the sea *was* for
the priests to wash in.
7 Then [A]he made the ten golden lampstands in
the way prescribed for them and he set them in the
temple, five on the right side and five on the left.
8 He also made [A]ten tables and placed them in the

3:1 [a]In 2 Sam 24:18, *Araunah* [B]1 Chr 21:18 3:2 [a]Lit *in* 3:3 [a]Lit *founding of Solomon to build* [b]I.e. One cubit equals approx 18 in. [A]1 Kin 6:2 3:4 [A]1 Kin 6:3 3:5 [a]Lit *great house* [b]Lit *put on it palm trees* [A]1 Kin 6:17 3:6 [a]Lit *overlaid...for beauty* [b]Or *country of gold* 3:7 [A]1 Kin 6:20-22 [B]1 Kin 6:29-35 3:8 [a]Lit *house* [A]Ex 26:33; 1 Kin 6:16 3:9 [A]1 Chr 28:11 3:10 [a]Lit *cherubim of sculptured work* [A]Ex 25:18-20; 1 Kin 6:23-28 3:12 [a]Lit *other* 3:13 [a]Lit *and their faces to* 3:14 [A]Ex 26:31 3:15 [a]Lit *long* [A]1 Kin 7:15-20 3:17 [A]1 Kin 7:21 4:1 [A]Ex 27:1, 2; 2 Kin 16:14 4:2 [a]Lit *a line of 30 cubits encircling it round about* [A]1 Kin 7:23-26 4:3 [a]Lit *in its casting* 4:5 [A]1 Kin 7:26 4:6 [a]Lit *in which to* [A]Ex 30:17-21; 1 Kin 7:38, 40 4:7 [A]Ex 25:31-40; 1 Kin 7:49 4:8 [A]1 Kin 7:48

3:2 second month … fourth year. Ca. Apr.–May, 966 B.C. (cf. 1Ki 6:1). The project took 7 years, 6 months to complete ca. Oct.–Nov. 959 B.C. (cf. 1Ki 6:37, 38).

3:3 cubits … old standard. About 18 in. or possibly the royal cubit of 21 in. (cf. Eze 40:5).

3:6 Parvaim. An unknown location.

3:8 gold … 600 talents. Equal to almost 23 tons of gold.

3:9 fifty shekels. Equal to 1.25 lbs. Most likely, this small amount gilded only the spike heads.

3:10–13 two sculptured cherubim. *See note on 1Ki 6:23.* This free-standing set of cherubim was in addition to the more diminutive set on the ark itself.

3:14 veil. Cf. Ex 26:31–35 on the veil of the tabernacle. The veil separated the Holy Place from the Holy of Holies, which was entered once annually by the High Priest on the Day of Atonement (cf. Lv 16). This highly limited access to the presence of God was eliminated by the death of Christ, when the veil in Herod's temple was torn in two from top to bottom (Mt 27:51). It signified that believers had immediate, full access to God's presence through their Mediator and High Priest Jesus Christ, who was the perfect, once-for-all sacrifice (cf. Heb 3:14–16; 9:19–22).

3:15 thirty-five cubits. First Kings 7:15, 2Ki 25:17, and Jer 52:21 uniformly describe these cast-bronze pillars as 18 cubits high (about 27 ft.). Most likely this is accounted for because the chronicler gave the combined height of both as they were lying in their molds (cf. v. 17).

3:17 Jachin … Boaz. Most likely these were so named because of the names' meaning rather than in honor of particular people. Jachin means "He shall establish" and Boaz means "In it is strength" (cf. 1Ki 7:21).

4:1–5:1 See 1Ki 7:23–51 for amplification and additional details.

4:1 bronze altar. This is the main altar on which sacrifices were offered (cf. the millennial temple altar, Eze 43:13–17). For comparison to the tabernacle's altar, see Ex 27:1–8; 38:1–7. If the cubit of 18 in. was used rather than the royal cubit of 21 in., it would make the altar 30 ft. by 30 ft. by 15 ft. high.

4:2 made the … sea. This large laver was used for ritual cleansing (cf. Ex 30:17–21 as it relates to the tabernacle). In Ezekiel's millennial temple, the laver will apparently be replaced by the waters that flow through the temple (Eze 47:1–12).

4:3 oxen. First Kings 7:24 reports "gourds," which is the more likely translation. These were also around the laver, which was set on top of the 12 oxen.

4:4 twelve oxen. Very likely the 12 oxen represent the 12 tribes who were similarly arrayed around the tabernacle as they set out on their journey in the wilderness (cf. Nu 2:1–34).

4:5 could hold 3,000 baths. A bath equaled almost 6 gal. First Kings 7:26 reads 2,000 baths. This discrepancy has been reconciled by accounting here not only for the water the basin held, but also the water source that was necessary to keep it flowing as a fountain.

4:6 ten basins. There were no such corresponding basins in the tabernacle.

4:7, 8 ten golden lampstands … ten tables. The tabernacle had one of each. Everything was large because of the crowds of thousands that came on a daily basis and for special occasions.

temple, five on the right side and five on the left. And he made one hundred golden bowls. 9 Then he made [A]the court of the priests and [B]the great court and doors for the court, and overlaid their doors with bronze. 10 [A]He set the sea on the right [a]side *of the house* toward the southeast.

11 [A]Huram also made the pails, the shovels and the bowls. So Huram finished doing the work which he performed for King Solomon in the house of God: 12 the two pillars, the bowls and the two capitals on top of the pillars, and the two networks to cover the two bowls of the capitals which were on top of the pillars, 13 and [A]the four hundred pomegranates for the two networks, two rows of pomegranates for each network to cover the two bowls of the capitals which were on the pillars. 14 [A]He also made the stands and he made the basins on the stands, 15 *and* the one sea with the twelve oxen under it. 16 The pails, the shovels, the forks and all its utensils, [A]Huram-abi made of polished bronze for King Solomon for the house of the LORD. 17 On the plain of the Jordan the king cast them in the clay ground between Succoth and Zeredah. 18 [A]Thus Solomon made all these utensils in great quantities, for the weight of the bronze could not be found out.

19 Solomon also made all the things that *were* in the house of God: even the golden altar, [A]the tables with the bread of the Presence on them, 20 the lampstands with their lamps of pure gold, [A]to burn in front of the inner sanctuary in the way prescribed; 21 the flowers, the lamps, and the tongs of gold, of purest gold; 22 and the snuffers, the bowls, the spoons and the firepans of pure gold; and the entrance of the house, its inner doors for the holy of holies and the doors of the house, *that is,* of the nave, of gold.

THE ARK IS BROUGHT INTO THE TEMPLE

5 [A]Thus all the work that Solomon performed for the house of the LORD was finished. And Solomon brought in the [a,B]things that David his father had dedicated, even the silver and the gold and all the utensils, *and* put *them* in the treasuries of the house of God.

2 [A]Then Solomon assembled to Jerusalem the elders of Israel and all the heads of the tribes, the leaders of the fathers' *households* of the sons of Israel, [B]to bring up the ark of the covenant of the LORD out of the city of David, which is Zion. 3 [A]All the men of Israel assembled themselves to the king at [B]the feast, that is *in* the seventh month. 4 Then all the elders of Israel came, and [A]the Levites took up the ark. 5 They brought up the ark and the tent of meeting and all the holy utensils which *were* in the tent; the Levitical priests brought them up. 6 And King Solomon and all the congregation of Israel who were assembled with him before the ark, were sacrificing [a]so many sheep and oxen that they could not be counted or numbered. 7 Then the priests brought the ark of the covenant of the LORD to its place, into the inner sanctuary of the house, to the holy of holies, under the wings of the cherubim. 8 For the cherubim spread their wings over the place of the ark, so that the cherubim made a covering over the ark and its [a]poles. 9 The poles were so long that [A]the ends of the poles of the ark could be seen in front of the inner sanctuary, but they could not be seen outside; and [a]they are there to this day. 10 [A]There was nothing in the ark except the two tablets which Moses put *there* at Horeb, where the LORD made a covenant with the sons of Israel, when they came out of Egypt.

THE GLORY OF GOD FILLS THE TEMPLE

11 When the priests came forth from the holy place (for all the priests who were present had sanctified themselves, without regard [A]to divisions), 12 and all the Levitical singers, [A]Asaph, Heman, Jeduthun, and their sons and kinsmen, clothed in fine linen, [B]with cymbals, harps and lyres, standing east of the altar, and with them one hundred and twenty priests [C]blowing trumpets 13 in unison when the trumpeters and the singers were to make themselves heard with one voice to praise and to glorify the LORD, and when they lifted up their voice [A]accompanied by trumpets and cymbals and instruments of music, and when they praised the LORD *saying,* "[B]*He* indeed is good for His lovingkindness is everlasting," then the house, the house of the LORD, was filled with a cloud, 14 so that the priests could not stand to minister because of the cloud, for [A]the glory of the LORD filled the house of God.

4:9 [A]1 Kin 6:36 [B]2 Kin 21:5 4:10 [a]Lit *shoulder* [A]1 Kin 7:39 4:11 [A]1 Kin 7:40-51 4:13 [A]1 Kin 7:20 4:14 [A]1 Kin 7:27-43 4:16 [A]1 Kin 7:14; 2 Chr 2:13 4:18 [A]1 Kin 7:47 4:19 [A]2 Chr 4:8 4:20 [A]Ex 25:31-37; 2 Chr 5:7 5:1 [a]Lit *dedicated things of David,* [A]1 Kin 7:51 [B]2 Sam 8:11; 1 Chr 18:11 5:2 [A]1 Kin 8:1-9 [B]2 Sam 6:12-15; 1 Chr 15:25-28; 2 Chr 1:4 5:3 [A]1 Kin 8:2 [B]2 Chr 7:8-10 5:4 [A]Josh 3:6; 2 Chr 5:7 5:6 [a]Lit *sheep...numbered for multitude* 5:8 [a]Lit *poles above* 5:9 [a]Lit *it is* [A]1 Kin 8:8, 9 5:10 [A]Deut 10:2-5; Heb 9:4 5:11 [A]1 Chr 24:1-5 5:12 [A]1 Chr 25:1-4 [B]1 Chr 13:8; 15:16, 24 [C]2 Chr 7:6 5:13 [A]1 Chr 16:42 [B]1 Chr 16:34; 2 Chr 7:3; Ezra 3:11; Ps 100:5; Jer 33:11 5:14 [A]Ex 40:35; 1 Kin 8:11

4:11–5:1 *See notes on 1Ki 7:40–51.* All these details emphasize the great care and concern for worship, and served as a manual for the new temple being built by Zerubbabel after the Jews returned from Babylon.

4:11 Huram. *See note on 2:13, 14.* He led the actual work which Solomon directed.

5:1 The temple took 7 years, 6 months to build and was completed in Solomon's 11th year (959 B.C.) in the eighth month (cf. 1Ki 6:38). Since it was dedicated in the seventh month (5:3), its dedication occurred 11 months later to coincide with the Feast of Booths, or Tabernacles. *See note on 1Ki 8:2.* Why is there so much emphasis in the OT on the temple? 1) It was the center of worship that called people to correct belief through the generations. 2) It was the symbol of God's presence with His people. 3) It was the symbol of forgiveness and grace, reminding the people of the seriousness of sin and the availability of mercy. 4) It prepared the people for the true Lamb of God, Jesus Christ, who would take away sin. 5) It was a place of prayer. Cf. 7:12–17.

5:2–10 *See notes on 1Ki 8:1–9.*

5:2 The ark was in Jerusalem in a temporary tent (2Sa 6:17), not the original tabernacle, which was still at Gibeon (1Ch 16:39).

5:11 the holy place. This was to be the last time anyone but the High Priest went in, and then only once a year. It took several priests to place the ark in its new home.

5:12 Asaph, Heman, Jeduthun. *See notes on 1Ch 25.*

5:13, 14 the glory of the LORD. The Lord's presence indwelt the temple and the first service of worship was held. In the same manner He descended on the tabernacle (Ex 40:34–38). He will do likewise on the millennial temple (Eze 43:1–5). His glory is representative of His person (cf. Ex 33), and entering the temple signified His presence.

SOLOMON'S DEDICATION

6 [A]Then Solomon said,

"The LORD has said that He would
dwell in the thick cloud.
2 "I have built You a lofty house,
And a place for Your dwelling forever."

3 Then the king [a]faced about and blessed all the
assembly of Israel, while all the assembly of Israel
was standing. 4 He said, "Blessed be the LORD, the
God of Israel, who spoke with His mouth to my father David and has fulfilled *it* with His hands, saying, 5 'Since the day that I brought My people from
the land of Egypt, I did not choose a city out of all
the tribes of Israel *in which* to build a house that My
name might be there, nor did I choose any man for
a leader over My people Israel; 6 but [A]I have chosen
Jerusalem that My name might be there, and I [B]have
chosen David to be over My people Israel.' 7 [A]Now
it was [a]in the heart of my father David to build a
house for the name of the LORD, the God of Israel.
8 But the LORD said to my father David, 'Because it
was [a]in your heart to build a house for My name,
you did well that it was [a]in your heart. 9 Nevertheless you shall not build the house, but your son who
[a]will be born to you, he shall build the house for
My name.' 10 Now the LORD has fulfilled His word
which He spoke; for I have risen in the place of my
father David and sit on the throne of Israel, as the
LORD [a]promised, and have built the house for the
name of the LORD, the God of Israel. 11 There I have
set the ark [A]in which is the covenant of the LORD,
which He made with the sons of Israel."

SOLOMON'S PRAYER OF DEDICATION

12 Then he stood before the altar of the LORD in
the presence of all the assembly of Israel and spread
out his hands. 13 [A]Now Solomon had made a bronze
platform, five cubits long, five cubits wide and three
cubits high, and had set it in the midst of the court;
and he stood on it, [B]knelt on his knees in the presence of all the assembly of Israel and spread out
his hands toward heaven. 14 He said, "O LORD, the
God of Israel, [A]there is no god like You in heaven or
on earth, [B]keeping covenant and *showing* lovingkindness to Your servants who walk before You with
all their heart; 15 [A]who has kept with Your servant
David, my father, that which You have [a]promised
him; indeed You have spoken with Your mouth and
have fulfilled it with Your hand, as it is this day.
16 Now therefore, O LORD, the God of Israel, keep
with Your servant David, my father, that which You
have [a]promised him, saying, '[b,A]You shall not lack a
man to sit on the throne of Israel, if only your sons
take heed to their way, to walk in My law as you
have walked before Me.' 17 Now therefore, O LORD,
the God of Israel, let Your word be confirmed which
You have spoken to Your servant David.
18 "But [A]will God indeed dwell with mankind on
the earth? Behold, [B]heaven and the [a]highest heaven
cannot contain You; how much less this house which
I have built. 19 Yet have regard to the prayer of Your
servant and to his supplication, O LORD my God,
to listen to the cry and to the prayer which Your
servant prays before You; 20 that Your [A]eye may
be open toward this house day and night, toward
[B]the place of which You have said that *You would*
put Your name there, to listen to the prayer which
Your servant shall pray toward this place. 21 Listen
to the supplications of Your servant and of Your
people Israel when they pray toward this place;
hear from Your dwelling place, from heaven; [A]hear
and forgive.
22 "If a man sins against his neighbor and is made
to take an oath, and he comes *and* takes an oath
before Your altar in this house, 23 then hear from
heaven and act and judge Your servants, [a,A]pun-
ishing the wicked by bringing his way on his own
head and justifying the righteous by giving him
according to his righteousness.
24 "If Your people Israel [a]are defeated before an
enemy because [A]they have sinned against You, and
they return *to You* and confess Your name, and pray
and make supplication before You in this house,
25 then hear from heaven and forgive the sin of
Your people Israel, and bring them back to the land
which You have given to them and to their fathers.
26 "When the [A]heavens are shut up and there is no
rain because they have sinned against You, and they
pray toward this place and confess Your name, and
turn from their sin when You afflict them; 27 then
hear in heaven and forgive the sin of Your servants
and Your people Israel, indeed, [A]teach them the good
way in which they should walk. And send rain on
Your land which You have given to Your people for
an inheritance.
28 "If there is [A]famine in the land, if there is pestilence, if there is blight or mildew, if there is locust
or grasshopper, if their enemies besiege them in the
land of their [a]cities, whatever plague or whatever
sickness *there is*, 29 whatever prayer or supplication
is made by any man or by all Your people Israel,
[a]each knowing his own affliction and his own pain,
and spreading his hands toward this house, 30 then
hear from heaven Your dwelling place, and forgive,
and render to each according to all his ways, whose
heart You know [A]for You alone know the hearts of

6:1 [A]1 Kin 8:12-50 6:3 [a]Lit *turned his face about* 6:6 [A]2 Chr 12:13 [B]1 Chr 28:4 6:7 [a]Lit *with* [A]1 Kin 5:3; 1 Chr 28:2 6:8 [a]Lit *with* 6:9 [a]Lit *will come forth from your loins* 6:10 [a]Lit *spoke* 6:11 [A]2 Chr 5:7, 10 6:13 [A]Neh 8:4 [B]1 Kin 8:54 6:14 [A]Ex 15:11; Deut 3:24 [B]Deut 7:9 6:15 [a]Lit *spoken to* [A]1 Chr 22:9, 10 6:16 [a]Lit *spoken to* [b]Lit *There shall not be cut off to you a man from before Me* [A]1 Kin 2:4; 2 Chr 7:18 6:18 [a]Lit *heaven of heavens* [A]Ps 113:5, 6 [B]2 Chr 2:6; Is 66:1; Acts 7:49 6:20 [A]Ps 33:18; 34:15 [B]Deut 12:11 6:21 [A]Is 43:25; 44:22; Mic 7:18 6:23 [a]Lit *returning* [A]Is 3:11; Rom 2:8, 9 6:24 [a]Lit *smitten* [A]Ps 51:4 6:26 [A]1 Kin 17:1 6:27 [A]Ps 94:12 6:28 [a]Lit *gates* [A]2 Chr 20:9 6:29 [a]Lit *whoever shall know* 6:30 [A]1 Sam 16:7; 1 Chr 28:9

6:1–11 *See notes on 1Ki 8:12–21.*

6:11 the covenant of the LORD. The Mosaic law written on tablets of stone (cf. 5:10).

6:12–40 *See note on 1Ki 8:22–53.* As Solomon led his people in prayer, he asked God to help them in many situations: 1) crime (vv. 22, 23); 2) enemy attacks (vv. 24, 25); 3) drought (vv. 26, 27); 4) famine (vv. 28–31); 5) foreigners (vv. 32, 33); 6) war (vv. 34, 35); and 7) sin (vv. 36–39).

6:13 knelt. Solomon, in an unusually humbling act for a king, acknowledged God's sovereignty.

6:18 Solomon marveled that God would condescend to live there. Cf. Jn 1:14; Col 2:9.

the sons of men, 31 that they may [a]fear You, to walk
in Your ways [b]as long as they live in the land which
You have given to our fathers.
32 "Also concerning [A]the foreigner who is not from
Your people Israel, when he comes from a far country
for Your great name's sake and Your mighty hand and
Your outstretched arm, when they come and pray toward this house, 33 then hear from heaven, from Your
dwelling place, and do according to all for which the
foreigner calls to You, in order that all the peoples of
the earth may know Your name, and [a]fear You as *do*
Your people Israel, and that they may know that [b]this
house which I have built is [A]called by Your name.
34 "When Your people go out to battle against their
enemies, by whatever way You shall send them,
and they pray to You toward this city which You
have chosen and the house which I have built for
Your name, 35 then hear from heaven their prayer
and their supplication, and maintain their cause.
36 "When they sin against You ([A]for there is no
man who does not sin) and You are angry with them
and deliver them to an enemy, so that [a]they take
them away captive to a land far off or near, 37 if they
[a]take thought in the land where they are taken captive, and repent and make supplication to You in the
land of their captivity, saying, 'We have sinned, we
have committed iniquity and have acted wickedly';
38 [A]if they return to You with all their heart and with
all their soul in the land of their captivity, where
they have been taken captive, and pray toward their
land which You have given to their fathers and the
city which You have chosen, and toward the house
which I have built for Your name, 39 then hear from
heaven, from Your dwelling place, their prayer and
supplications, and maintain their cause and forgive
Your people who have sinned against You.
40 "Now, O my God, I pray, [A]let Your eyes be open and
[B]Your ears attentive to the prayer *offered* in this place.
41 "[A]Now therefore arise, O LORD God, to Your
resting place, You and the ark of Your might; let
Your priests, O LORD God, be clothed with salvation
and let Your godly ones rejoice in what is good.
42 "O LORD God, do not turn away the face of Your
anointed; [A]remember *Your* lovingkindness to Your
servant David."

THE SHEKINAH GLORY

7 [A]Now when Solomon had finished praying, [B]fire
came down from heaven and consumed the
burnt offering and the sacrifices, and the glory of
the LORD filled the house. 2 [A]The priests could not
enter into the house of the LORD because the glory
of the LORD filled the LORD'S house. 3 All the sons of
Israel, seeing the fire come down and the glory of
the LORD upon the house, bowed down on the pavement with their faces to the ground, and they worshiped and gave praise to the LORD, *saying,* "[A]Truly
He is good, truly His lovingkindness is everlasting."

SACRIFICES OFFERED

4 [A]Then the king and all the people offered sacrifice before the LORD. 5 King Solomon offered a
sacrifice of 22,000 oxen and 120,000 sheep. Thus the
king and all the people dedicated the house of God.
6 The priests stood at their posts, and [A]the Levites
also, with the instruments of music to the LORD,
which King David had made for giving praise to
the LORD—"for His lovingkindness is everlasting"—
whenever [a]he gave praise by their [b]means, while
[B]the priests on the other side blew trumpets; and
all Israel was standing.
7 [A]Then Solomon consecrated the middle of the
court that *was* before the house of the LORD, for
there he offered the burnt offerings and the fat
of the peace offerings because the bronze altar
which Solomon had made was not able to contain
the burnt offering, the grain offering and the fat.

THE FEAST OF DEDICATION

8 So [A]Solomon observed the feast at that time for
seven days, and all Israel with him, a very great
assembly *who came* from the entrance of Hamath
to the [B]brook of Egypt. 9 On the eighth day they
held [A]a solemn assembly, for the dedication of the
altar they observed seven days and the feast seven
days. 10 Then on the twenty-third day of the seventh
month he sent the people to their tents, rejoicing
and happy of heart because of the goodness that
the LORD had shown to David and to Solomon and
to His people Israel.

GOD'S PROMISE AND WARNING

11 [A]Thus Solomon finished the house of the LORD
and the king's palace, and successfully completed
all that [a]he had planned on doing in the house of
the LORD and in his palace.
12 Then the LORD appeared to Solomon at night
and said to him, "I have heard your prayer and [A]have
chosen this place for Myself as a house of sacrifice.
13 [A]If I shut up the heavens so that there is no rain,

6:31 [a]Or *reverence* [b]Lit *all the days that they live on the face of the land* 6:32 [A]Is 56:3-8 6:33 [a]Or *reverence* [b]Lit *Your name is called upon this house* [A]2 Chr 7:14 6:36 [a]Lit *their captors take them captive* [A]Job 15:14-16; James 3:2; 1 John 1:8-10 6:37 [a]Lit *return to their heart* 6:38 [A]Jer 29:12, 13 6:40 [A]2 Chr 7:15; Neh 1:6, 11 [B]Ps 17:1 6:41 [A]Ps 132:8, 9 6:42 [A]Ps 89:24, 28; 132:10-12; Is 55:3 7:1 [A]1 Kin 8:54 [B]Lev 9:23f; 1 Kin 18:24, 38 7:2 [A]2 Chr 5:14 7:3 [A]2 Chr 5:13; 20:21 7:4 [A]1 Kin 8:62, 63 7:6 [a]Lit *David* [b]Lit *hand* [A]1 Chr 15:16-21 [B]2 Chr 5:12 7:7 [A]1 Kin 8:64-66 7:8 [A]1 Kin 8:65 [B]Gen 15:18 7:9 [A]Lev 23:36 7:11 [a]Lit *came upon the heart of Solomon to do* [A]1 Kin 9:1-9 7:12 [A]Deut 12:5, 11 7:13 [A]2 Chr 6:26-28

6:41, 42 *See notes on Ps 132:8–10; 1Ki 8:54–61.*

7:1–3 **fire came down.** This also occurred when the tabernacle was dedicated (Lv 9:23, 24). This was the genuine dedication, because only God can truly sanctify.

7:4, 5 *See note on 1Ki 8:62.*

7:8–10 Solomon's celebration included the special assembly to dedicate the altar on the 8th–14th of the 7th month (Sept.–Oct.) which included the Day of Atonement. It was immediately followed by the Feast of Booths, or Tabernacles (15th–21st) and a special assembly on the 8th day, i.e., 22nd day of the month.

7:8 **Hamath ... brook of Egypt.** Lit. from the northern boundary to the southern boundary.

7:11, 12 *See note on 1Ki 9:1, 2.* Perhaps years had passed since the dedication of the temple in chap. 6 during which he had also built "the king's palace" (cf. 8:1). After all that time, God confirmed that He had heard Solomon's prayer (v. 12).

7:13–16 This section is almost all unique to 2 Chronicles (cf. 1Ki 9:3), and features the conditions for national forgiveness of Israel's sins: 1) humility; 2) prayer; 3) longing for God; and 4) repentance.

or if I command the locust to devour the land, or if I
send pestilence among My people, 14 [A]and My people
[a]who are called by My name humble themselves and
pray and seek My face and turn from their wicked
ways, then I will hear from heaven, will forgive
their sin and will heal their land. 15 [A]Now My eyes
will be open and My ears attentive to the [a]prayer
offered in this place. 16 For [A]now I have chosen and
consecrated this house that My name may be there
forever, and My eyes and My heart will be there
perpetually. 17 As for you, if you walk before Me as
your father David walked, even to do according to
all that I have commanded you, and will keep My
statutes and My ordinances, 18 then I will establish
your royal throne as I covenanted with your father
David, saying, '[a,A]You shall not lack a man *to be*
ruler in Israel.'

19 "[A]But if you turn away and forsake My statutes
and My commandments which I have set before
you, and go and serve other gods and worship
them, 20 [A]then I will uproot you from My land which
I have given [a]you, and this house which I have
consecrated for My name I will cast out of My sight
and I will make it [B]a proverb and a byword among
all peoples. 21 As for this house, which was exalted,
everyone who passes by it will be astonished and
say, '[A]Why has the LORD done thus to this land and
to this house?' 22 And they will say, 'Because [A]they
forsook the LORD, the God of their fathers who
brought them from the land of Egypt, and they
adopted other gods and worshiped them and served
them; therefore He has brought all this adversity
on them.' "

SOLOMON'S ACTIVITIES AND ACCOMPLISHMENTS

8 [A]Now it came about at the end of the twenty
years in which Solomon had built the house
of the LORD and his own house 2 that he built the
cities which Huram had given to [a]him, and settled
the sons of Israel there.

3 Then Solomon went to Hamath-zobah and captured it. 4 He built Tadmor in the wilderness and all
the storage cities which he had built in Hamath. 5 He
also built upper [A]Beth-horon and lower Beth-horon,
[B]fortified cities *with* walls, gates and bars; 6 and Baalath and all the storage cities that Solomon had,
and all the cities for [a]his chariots and cities for [a]his
horsemen, and all that it pleased Solomon to build
in Jerusalem, in Lebanon, and in all the land [b]un-
der his rule.

7 [A]All of the people who were left of the Hittites,
the Amorites, the Perizzites, the Hivites and the
Jebusites, who were not of Israel, 8 *namely,* from
their descendants who were left after them in the
land whom the sons of Israel had not destroyed,
[A]them Solomon raised as forced laborers to this
day. 9 But Solomon did not make slaves for his work
from the sons of Israel; they were men of war, his
chief captains and commanders of his chariots and
his horsemen. 10 These were the chief [a]officers of
King Solomon, two hundred and fifty who ruled
over the people.

11 [A]Then Solomon brought Pharaoh's daughter up
from the city of David to the house which he had
built for her, for he said, "My wife shall not dwell in
the house of David king of Israel, because [a]the places
are holy where the ark of the LORD has entered."

12 Then Solomon offered burnt offerings to the
LORD on [A]the altar of the LORD which he had built
before the porch; 13 and [A]*did so* according to the
daily rule, offering *them* up [B]according to the commandment of Moses, for [C]the sabbaths, [D]the new
moons and the [E]three annual feasts—the Feast of
Unleavened Bread, the Feast of Weeks and the Feast
of Booths.

14 Now according to the ordinance of his father
David, he appointed [A]the divisions of the priests
for their service, and [B]the Levites for their duties of
praise and ministering before the priests according to the daily rule, and [C]the gatekeepers by their
divisions at every gate; for [D]David the man of God

7:14 [a]Lit *over whom My name is called* [A]2 Chr 6:37-39; James 4:10 7:15 [a]Lit *prayer of this place* [A]2 Chr 6:20, 40 7:16 [A]2 Chr 7:12 7:18 [a]Lit *There shall not be cut off to you a man* [A]1 Kin 2:4; 2 Chr 6:16 7:19 [A]Lev 26:14, 33; Deut 28:15 7:20 [a]Ancient versions and Heb read *them* [A]Deut 29:28; 1 Kin 14:15 [B]Deut 28:37 7:21 [A]Deut 29:24-27 7:22 [A]Judg 2:13 8:1 [A]1 Kin 9:10-28 8:2 [a]Lit *Solomon* 8:5 [A]1 Chr 7:24 [B]2 Chr 14:7 8:6 [a]Lit *the* [b]Lit *of* 8:7 [A]Gen 15:18-21; 1 Kin 9:20 8:8 [A]1 Kin 4:6; 9:21 8:10 [a]Or *deputies* 8:11 [a]Lit *they are* [A]1 Kin 3:1; 7:8 8:12 [A]2 Chr 4:1 8:13 [A]Ex 29:38-42 [B]Num 28:3 [C]Num 28:9, 10 [D]Num 28:11 [E]Ex 23:14-17; 34:22, 23; Deut 16:16 8:14 [A]1 Chr 24:1 [B]1 Chr 25:1 [C]1 Chr 26:1 [D]Neh 12:24, 36

7:17–22 *See notes on 1Ki 9:4–9.*

7:17, 18 if ... then. If there was obedience on the part of the nation, the kingdom would be established, and they would have "a man *to be* ruler." Their disobedience was legendary and so was the destruction of their kingdom and their dispersion. When Israel is saved (cf. Zec 12:14; Ro 11:25–27), then their King Messiah will set up this glorious kingdom (Rev 20:1ff.).

8:1 twenty years. Ca. 946 B.C., 24 years after Solomon's reign began.

8:2 Cf. 1Ki 9:10–14. Though these cities were within the boundaries of the Promised Land, they had never been conquered, so Solomon gave Huram the right to settle them. Huram, however, returned the Galilean cities which Solomon had given him because they were unacceptably poor. Solomon apparently then improved them and settled Israelites there.

8:3–6 Here are additional military campaigns and building projects not mentioned in 1Ki 9. He was building storage places for his commercial enterprises and fortifying his borders to secure his kingdom from invasion.

8:3 Hamath-zobah. A city located in Syria, N of Damascus and in close proximity to but S of Hamath.

8:4 Tadmor. A city 150 mi. NE of Damascus. **Hamath.** A city N of Damascus.

8:5 Beth-horon. Two cities NW of Jerusalem. Upper Beth-horon is at 2,022 ft., 11 mi. NW of Jerusalem. Lower Beth-horon is at 1,210 ft., 13 mi. NW of Jerusalem. They were both on a strategic road that connected Jerusalem with Joppa on the coast.

8:6 Baalath. A city originally in Danite territory (Jos 19:44) ca. 30 mi. W of Jerusalem.

8:10 two hundred and fifty. *See note on 2Ch 2:2.*

8:11 Pharaoh's daughter. Cf. 1Ki 9:24. First Kings 3:1 mentions the marriage and the fact that Solomon brought her to Jerusalem until he could build a house for her. Until that palace was built, Solomon lived in David's palace, but did not allow her to do so, because she was a heathen and because the ark of God had once been in David's house. He surely knew his marriage to this pagan did not please God (cf. Dt 7:3, 4). Eventually his pagan wives caused tragic consequences (1Ki 11:1–11).

8:12–15 This section expands on 1Ki 9:25, and indicates that Solomon was, in spite of his disobedience in marriage, still faithful to the religious practices required in the temple.

8:13 three ... feasts. These were prescribed in the Mosaic legislation: 1) Unleavened Bread, or Passover; 2) Weeks, or Pentecost; and 3) Booths, or Tabernacles (cf. Ex 23:14–17; Dt 16:1–17).

had so commanded. 15 And they did not depart from the commandment of the king to the priests and Levites in any manner or concerning the storehouses.

16 Thus all the work of Solomon was carried out [a]from the day of the foundation of the house of the LORD, and until it was finished. So the house of the LORD was completed.

17 Then Solomon went to [A]Ezion-geber and to [B]Eloth on the seashore in the land of Edom. 18 And Huram by his servants sent him ships and servants who knew the sea; and they went with Solomon's servants to Ophir, and [A]took from there four hundred and fifty talents of gold and brought them to King Solomon.

VISIT OF THE QUEEN OF SHEBA

9 [A]Now when the queen of Sheba heard of the fame of Solomon, she came to Jerusalem to test Solomon with difficult questions. She had a very large retinue, with camels carrying spices and a large amount of gold and precious stones; and when she came to Solomon, she spoke with him about all that was on her heart. 2 Solomon [a]answered all her questions; nothing was hidden from Solomon which he did not [b]explain to her. 3 When the queen of Sheba had seen the wisdom of Solomon, the house which he had built, 4 the food at his table, the seating of his servants, the attendance of his ministers and their attire, his cupbearers and their attire, and [a]his stairway by which he went up to the house of the LORD, she was breathless. 5 Then she said to the king, "It was a true report which I heard in my own land about your words and your wisdom. 6 Nevertheless I did not believe their reports until I came and my eyes had seen it. And behold, the half of the greatness of your wisdom was not told me. You surpass the report that I heard. 7 How [a]blessed are your men, how [a]blessed are these your servants who stand before you continually and hear your wisdom. 8 Blessed be the LORD your God who delighted in you, [A]setting you on His throne as king for the LORD your God; [B]because your God loved Israel establishing them forever, therefore He made you king over them, to do justice and righteousness." 9 Then she gave the king one hundred and twenty talents of gold and a very great *amount of* spices and precious stones; there had never been spice like that which the queen of Sheba gave to King Solomon.

10 The servants of Huram and the servants of Solomon [A]who brought gold from Ophir, also brought algum trees and precious stones. 11 From the algum trees the king made steps for the house of the LORD and for the king's palace, and lyres and harps for the singers; and none like that was seen before in the land of Judah.

12 King Solomon gave to the queen of Sheba all her desire which she requested besides *a return for* what she had brought to the king. Then she turned and went to her own land with her servants.

SOLOMON'S WEALTH AND POWER

13 [A]Now the weight of gold which came to Solomon in one year was 666 talents of gold, 14 besides that which the traders and merchants brought; and all [A]the kings of Arabia and the governors of the country brought gold and silver to Solomon. 15 King Solomon made 200 large shields of beaten gold, [a]using 600 *shekels of* beaten gold on each large shield. 16 *He made* 300 shields of beaten gold, [a]using three hundred shekels of gold on each shield, and the king put them in the house of the forest of Lebanon.

17 Moreover, the king made a great throne of ivory and overlaid it with pure gold. 18 *There were* six steps to the throne and a footstool in gold attached to the throne, and [a]arms [b]on each side of the seat, and two lions standing beside the [a]arms. 19 Twelve lions were standing there on the six steps on the one side and on the other; nothing like *it* was made for any *other* kingdom. 20 All King Solomon's drinking vessels *were* of gold, and all the vessels of the house of the forest of Lebanon *were* of pure gold; silver was not considered [a]valuable in the days of Solomon. 21 [A]For the king had ships which went to Tarshish with the servants of Huram; once every three years the ships of Tarshish came bringing gold and silver, ivory and apes and peacocks.

22 [A]So King Solomon became greater than all the kings of the earth in riches and wisdom. 23 And all the kings of the earth were seeking the presence of Solomon, to hear his wisdom which God had put in his heart. 24 [A]They brought every man his gift, articles of silver and gold, garments, weapons, spices, horses and mules, so much year by year.

25 Now Solomon had [A]4,000 stalls for horses and chariots and 12,000 horsemen, and he stationed them in the chariot cities and with the king in Jerusalem. 26 [A]He was the ruler over all the kings from the Euphrates River even to the land of the Philistines, and as far as the border of Egypt. 27 [A]The king made

8:16 [a]So ancient versions; M.T. *as far as* 8:17 [A]1 Kin 9:26 [B]2 Kin 14:22 8:18 [A]2 Chr 9:10, 13 9:1 [A]1 Kin 10:1-13; Matt 12:42; Luke 11:31 9:2 [a]Lit *told her all her words* [b]Lit *tell* 9:4 [a]*Or his burnt offering which he offered* 9:7 [a]Or *happy* 9:8 [A]1 Chr 28:5; 29:23 [B]Deut 7:8; 2 Chr 2:11 9:10 [A]1 Kin 10:11; 2 Chr 8:18 9:13 [A]1 Kin 10:14-28 9:14 [A]Ps 68:29; 72:10 9:15 [a]Lit *he brought up* 9:16 [a]Lit *he brought up* 9:18 [a]Lit *hands* [b]Lit *on this side and on this at the place of the seat* 9:20 [a]Lit *anything* 9:21 [A]2 Chr 20:36, 37 9:22 [A]1 Kin 3:13; 2 Chr 1:12 9:24 [A]Ps 72:10 9:25 [A]Deut 17:16; 1 Kin 4:26; 10:26; 2 Chr 1:14 9:26 [A]Gen 15:18; 1 Kin 4:21, 24 9:27 [A]2 Chr 1:15-17

8:17, 18 *See notes on 1Ki 9:26–28.* These two ports where Solomon had received ships were located on the eastern gulf of the Red Sea, called Aqabah. Solomon was cultivating peace and commerce plus using Hiram's sailors to teach his people how to sail.

8:18 four hundred and fifty talents. First Kings 9:28 reports 420 talents, probably accounted for by a scribal error in transmission. This was about 17 tons of gold.

9:1–28 *See notes on 1Ki 10:1–29.*

9:8 His throne. The thought that Solomon sat on God's throne is not included in the queen of Sheba's words in 1Ki 10:9. The blessing of God on Israel and on Solomon was to last as long as he followed the Lord as David had (2Ch 7:17–21).

9:16 shekels. "Bekah," not shekel, is the correct unit of weight. Since one mina equals 50 shekels and one shekel equals two bekahs, then the 3 minas in 1Ki 10:17 equals the 300 bekahs here and both texts agree. This would represent a little less than 4 lbs.

9:18 footstool in gold. The chronicler adds this detail, which is absent in 1Ki 10:19.

9:25 had 4,000 stalls. This reading is preferable to "40,000" in 1Ki 4:26 (cf. margin).

silver *as common* as stones in Jerusalem, and he
made cedars as plentiful as sycamore trees that are
in the [a]lowland. 28 [A]And they were bringing horses
for Solomon from Egypt and from all countries.
29 [A]Now the rest of the acts of Solomon, from
first to last, [B]are they not written in the [a]records of
Nathan the prophet, and in the prophecy of Ahijah
the Shilonite, and in the visions of [b]Iddo the seer
concerning Jeroboam the son of Nebat? 30 [A]Solomon
reigned forty years in Jerusalem over all Israel.

DEATH OF SOLOMON

31 And Solomon slept with his fathers and was
buried in [A]the city of his father David; and his son
Rehoboam reigned in his place.

REHOBOAM'S REIGN OF FOLLY

10 [A]Then Rehoboam went to Shechem, for all
Israel had come to Shechem to make him
king. 2 When Jeroboam the son of Nebat heard *of*
it (for [A]he was in Egypt where he had fled from the
presence of King Solomon), Jeroboam returned
from Egypt. 3 So they sent and summoned him.
When Jeroboam and all Israel came, they spoke to
Rehoboam, saying, 4 "Your father made our [A]yoke
hard; now therefore lighten the hard service of
your father and his heavy yoke which he put on us,
and we will serve you." 5 He said to them, "Return
to me again in three days." So the people departed.
6 Then King Rehoboam [A]consulted with the elders
who had [a]served his father Solomon while he was
still alive, saying, "How do you counsel *me* to answer this people?" 7 They spoke to him, saying, "If
you will be kind to this people and please them and
[A]speak good words to them, then they will be your
servants forever." 8 But he [A]forsook the counsel of
the elders which they had given him, and consulted
with the young men who grew up with him [a]and
served him. 9 So he said to them, "What counsel do
you give that we may answer this people, who have
spoken to me, saying, 'Lighten the yoke which your
father put on us'?" 10 The young men who grew up
with him spoke to him, saying, "Thus you shall say
to the people who spoke to you, saying, 'Your father
made our yoke heavy, but you make it lighter for
us.' Thus you shall say to them, 'My little finger is
thicker than my father's loins! 11 Whereas my father
loaded you with a heavy yoke, I will add to your
yoke; my father disciplined you with whips, but I
will discipline you with scorpions.' "
12 So Jeroboam and all the people came to Rehoboam on the third day as the king had [a]directed,
saying, "Return to me on the third day." 13 The king
answered them harshly, and King Rehoboam forsook the counsel of the elders. 14 He spoke to them
according to the advice of the young men, saying,
"[a]My father made your yoke heavy, but I will add to
it; my father disciplined you with whips, but I *will*
discipline you with scorpions." 15 So the king did not
listen to the people, [A]for it was a turn *of events* from
God [B]that the LORD might establish His word, which
He spoke through Ahijah the Shilonite to Jeroboam
the son of Nebat.
16 When all Israel *saw* that the king did not listen to them the people answered the king, saying,

"[A]What portion do we have in David?
We have no inheritance in
the son of Jesse.
Every man to your tents, O Israel;
Now look after your own house, David."

[B]So all Israel departed to their tents. 17 But as for the
sons of Israel who lived in the cities of Judah, Rehoboam reigned over them. 18 Then King Rehoboam
sent Hadoram, who was [A]over the forced labor,
and the sons of Israel stoned him [a]to death. And
King Rehoboam made haste to mount his chariot to
flee to Jerusalem. 19 So [A]Israel has been in rebellion
against the house of David to this day.

REHOBOAM REIGNS OVER JUDAH AND BUILDS CITIES

11 [A]Now when Rehoboam had come to Jerusalem,
he assembled the house of Judah and Benjamin,
180,000 chosen men who were warriors, to fight
against Israel to restore the kingdom to Rehoboam.
2 But the word of the LORD came to [A]Shemaiah the
man of God, saying, 3 "Speak to Rehoboam the son
of Solomon, king of Judah, and to all Israel in Judah

9:27 [a]Heb *shephelah* 9:28 [A]2 Chr 1:16 9:29 [a]Lit *words* [b]Heb *Jedo* [A]1 Kin 11:41-43 [B]1 Chr 29:29 9:30 [A]1 Kin 11:42, 43 9:31 [A]1 Kin 2:10 10:1 [A]1 Kin 12:1-20 10:2 [A]1 Kin 11:40 10:4 [A]1 Kin 5:13-16 10:6 [a]Lit *stood before* [A]Job 8:8, 9; 32:7 10:7 [A]Prov 15:1 10:8 [a]Lit *who stood before* [A]2 Sam 17:14; Prov 13:20 10:12 [a]Lit *spoken* 10:14 [a]Many mss read *I have made* 10:15 [A]2 Chr 25:16-20 [B]1 Kin 11:29-39 10:16 [A]2 Sam 20:1 [B]2 Chr 10:19 10:18 [a]Lit *with stones that he died* [A]1 Kin 4:6; 5:14 10:19 [A]1 Kin 12:19 11:1 [A]1 Kin 12:21-24 11:2 [A]2 Chr 12:5-7, 15

9:29–31 See 1Ki 11:41–43.

9:29 First Kings 11:41 reports that Solomon's deeds were written in "the book of the acts of Solomon." For the rest of the record of Solomon's life, read 1Ki 10:26–11:43. In later years, he turned away from God and, due to the influence of his wives, he led the nation into idolatry. This split the kingdom and sowed the seeds that led to its defeat and dispersion. The Chronicles do not record this sad end to Solomon's life because the focus is on encouraging the returning Jews from Babylon with God's pledge to them for a glorious future in the Davidic Covenant.

10:1–36:21 This section records all 20 of the Judean rulers in the divided kingdom from Solomon's son Rehoboam (ca. 931 B.C.) to Zedekiah (ca. 586 B.C.) when the people were taken captive to Babylon. The righteous kings and the revivals under them are presented, as well as the wicked kings and their disastrous influence. The northern kingdom is absent since Chronicles focuses on the Davidic line.

10:1–12:16 The reign of Rehoboam (ca. 931–913 B.C.). Cf. 1Ki 12–14.

10:1–11:4 For details on this chapter, *see notes on 1Ki 12:1–24*. Rehoboam followed foolish and bad advice from novices rather than the good counsel of wise, seasoned men. The result was the division of the nation. Amazingly, with all the strength of Solomon's reign, unity was fragile, and one fool in the place of leadership ended it. Rehoboam tried to unite the people by force, but was not allowed to by God (11:1–4).

10:2 Jeroboam. He became the first king of the northern kingdom of Israel (ca. 931–910 B.C.). His story leading to his return from Egypt is told in 1Ki 11:26–40.

10:16–19 Here is recorded the beginning of the divided kingdom. Ten tribes followed Jeroboam and were called Israel. The other two tribes, Benjamin and Judah, stayed loyal to David's line, accepted Rehoboam's rule, and were called Judah. However, Benjamin at times demonstrated split loyalties (*see note on 1Ki 12:21*).

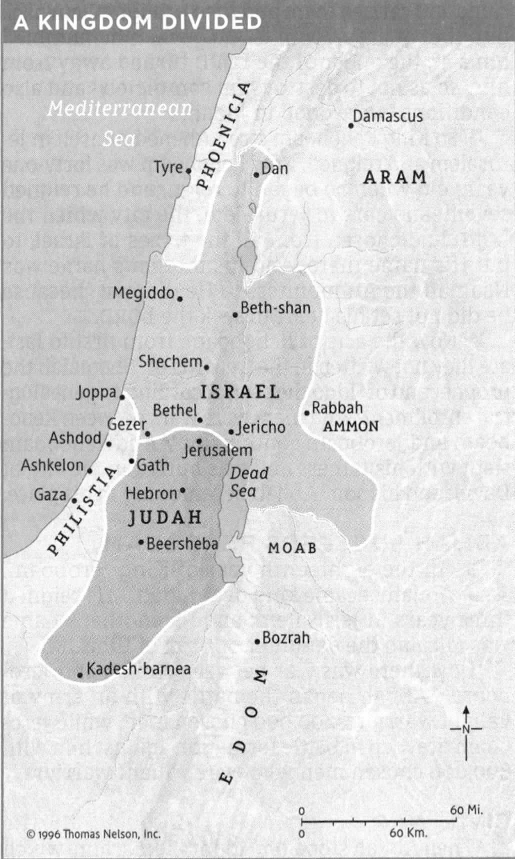

The glory of the united kingdom faded after the death of Solomon. Bitter feelings had been aroused by some of the harsh policies of Solomon's rule. The system of forced labor for building projects (1Ki 5:13) and the administrative districts which cut across old tribal boundaries (1Ki 4:7–19) were not popular with the people.

When Solomon's son Rehoboam ascended the throne, he inherited the tension between north and south that had to be addressed if the kingdom was to remain united. At Shechem the people, with Jeroboam as their leader, asked for change. Rehoboam's harsh rejection of their demands led to the people's rebellious response: "To your tents, O Israel! Now look after your own house, David!" The kingdom split, Rehoboam reigned over Judah in the south, and Jeroboam became king of Israel in the north.

and Benjamin, saying, 4 'Thus says the LORD, "You
shall not go up or fight against [A]your [a]relatives;
return every man to his house, [B]for this thing is
from Me." ' " So they listened to the words of the
LORD and returned from going against Jeroboam.
5 Rehoboam lived in Jerusalem and [A]built cities
for defense in Judah. 6 Thus he built Bethlehem,
Etam, Tekoa, 7 Beth-zur, Soco, Adullam, 8 Gath, Mareshah, Ziph, 9 Adoraim, Lachish, Azekah, 10 Zorah,
Aijalon and Hebron, which are fortified cities in
Judah and in Benjamin. 11 He also strengthened
the fortresses and put officers in them and stores
of food, oil and wine. 12 *He put* shields and spears
in every city and strengthened them greatly. So he
held Judah and Benjamin.
13 Moreover, the priests and the Levites who were
in all Israel stood with him from all their districts.

JEROBOAM APPOINTS FALSE PRIESTS

14 For [A]the Levites left their pasture lands and their
property and came to Judah and Jerusalem, for [B]Jero-
boam and his sons had excluded them from serving
as priests to the LORD. 15 [A]He set up priests of his own
for the high places, for the satyrs and for the calves
which he had made. 16 [A]Those from all the tribes of
Israel who set their hearts on seeking the LORD God
of Israel [a]followed them to Jerusalem, to sacrifice to
the LORD God of their fathers. 17 [A]They strengthened
the kingdom of Judah and supported Rehoboam the
son of Solomon for three years, for they walked in
the way of David and Solomon for three years.

REHOBOAM'S FAMILY

18 Then Rehoboam took as a wife Mahalath the
daughter of Jerimoth the son of David *and of* Abihail
the daughter of [A]Eliab the son of Jesse, 19 and she
bore him sons: Jeush, Shemariah and Zaham. 20 After her he took [A]Maacah the daughter of [a]Absalom,
and she bore him Abijah, Attai, Ziza and Shelomith.
21 Rehoboam loved Maacah the daughter of Absalom
more than all his *other* wives and concubines. For
[A]he had taken eighteen wives and sixty concubines
and fathered twenty-eight sons and sixty daughters.
22 [A]Rehoboam appointed Abijah the son of Maacah
as head and leader among his brothers, for he *intended* to make him king. 23 He acted wisely and
distributed [a]some of his sons through all the territories of Judah and Benjamin to all the fortified
cities, and he gave them food in abundance. And
he sought many wives *for them*.

11:4 [a]Lit *brothers* [A]2 Chr 28:8-11 [B]2 Chr 10:15 11:5 [A]2 Chr 8:2-6; 11:23 11:14 [A]Num 35:2-5 [B]1 Kin 12:28-33; 2 Chr 13:9 11:15 [A]1 Kin 12:31; 13:33 11:16 [a]Lit *came after* [A]2 Chr 15:9 11:17 [A]2 Chr 12:1 11:18 [A]1 Sam 16:6 11:20 [a]In 1 Kin 15:2, *Abishalom* [A]1 Kin 15:2; 2 Chr 13:2 11:21 [A]Deut 17:17 11:22 [A]Deut 21:15-17 11:23 [a]Lit *from all*

11:6 built. To be understood as built further/strengthened/fortified (cf. 11:11, 12).

11:13, 14 The priests and Levites from all the northern 10 tribes were rejected by Israel's king, Jeroboam (ca. 931–910 B.C.), who saw them as a threat because of their loyalty to Jerusalem and the temple. He appointed his own idol priests and all true priests moved S and found refuge in Judah with Rehoboam.

11:15 He set up. This is in reference to Jeroboam (cf. 1Ki 12:25–33), who established idolatry in the N. "Satyrs" is another term for idols (cf. Lv 17:7).

11:16, 17 God's blessing rested on Rehoboam for 3 years because the people's commitment to the ways of God was patterned after David and Solomon.

11:18–23 A summary of Rehoboam's life is given with special emphasis on succession to the throne. This is not a commendation of polygamy or concubinage, which violated God's law for marriage (cf. Ge 2:24, 25) and resulted in severe trouble and disaffection toward God. Never is polygamy commended in Scripture, and usually its tragic results are recorded.

11:21 The chronicler did not include the similar summary of Solomon's wives (cf. 1Ki 11:3), but clearly Rehoboam learned this disastrous marital style from his father Solomon. Even David was a polygamist. Polygamy was often practiced by the kings to secure alliances with nearby nations.

SHISHAK OF EGYPT INVADES JUDAH

12 [A]When the kingdom of Rehoboam was established and strong, [B]he and all Israel with him
forsook the law of the LORD. 2 [A]And it came about in
King Rehoboam's fifth year, because they had been
unfaithful to the LORD, that [B]Shishak king of Egypt
came up against Jerusalem 3 with 1,200 chariots
and 60,000 horsemen. And the people who came
with him from Egypt were without number: [A]the
Lubim, the Sukkiim and the Ethiopians. 4 He captured [A]the fortified cities of Judah and came as far
as Jerusalem. 5 Then [A]Shemaiah the prophet came to
Rehoboam and the princes of Judah who had gathered at Jerusalem because of Shishak, and he said to
them, "Thus says the LORD, '[B]You have forsaken Me,
so I also have forsaken you [a]to Shishak.' " 6 So the
princes of Israel and the king humbled themselves
and said, "The [A]LORD is righteous."

7 When the LORD saw that they humbled themselves, the word of the LORD came to Shemaiah, saying, "[A]They have humbled themselves *so* I will not
destroy them, but I will grant them some *measure*
of deliverance, and [B]My wrath shall not be poured
out on Jerusalem by means of Shishak. 8 But they
will become his slaves so [A]that they may learn *the*
difference between My service and the service of
the kingdoms of the countries."

PLUNDER IMPOVERISHES JUDAH

9 [A]So Shishak king of Egypt came up against Jerusalem, and took the treasures of the house of the
LORD and the treasures of the king's palace. He took
everything; [B]he even took the golden shields which
Solomon had made. 10 Then King Rehoboam made
shields of bronze in their place and committed them
to the [a]care of the commanders of the [b]guard who
guarded the door of the king's house. 11 As often as
the king entered the house of the LORD, the [a]guards
came and carried them and *then* brought them back
into the [a]guards' room. 12 And [A]when he humbled
himself, the anger of the LORD turned away from
him, so as not to destroy *him* completely; and also
conditions [B]were good in Judah.

13 [A]So King Rehoboam strengthened himself in Jerusalem and reigned. Now Rehoboam was forty-one
years old when he began to reign, and he reigned
seventeen years in Jerusalem, the city which the
LORD had chosen from all the tribes of Israel, to
put His name there. And his mother's name was
Naamah the Ammonitess. 14 He did evil [A]because
he did not set his heart to seek the LORD.

15 [A]Now the acts of Rehoboam, from first to last,
are they not written in the [a]records of [B]Shemaiah the
prophet and of [C]Iddo the seer, according to genealogical enrollment? And *there were* wars between Rehoboam and Jeroboam continually. 16 And Rehoboam
slept with his fathers and was buried in the city of
David; and his son [A]Abijah became king in his place.

ABIJAH SUCCEEDS REHOBOAM

13 [A]In the eighteenth year of King Jeroboam,
Abijah became king over Judah. 2 He reigned
three years in Jerusalem; and his mother's name
was Micaiah the daughter of Uriel of Gibeah.

[A]Now there was war between Abijah and Jeroboam. 3 Abijah began the battle with an army of
valiant warriors, 400,000 chosen men, while Jeroboam drew up in battle formation against him with
800,000 chosen men *who were* valiant warriors.

CIVIL WAR

4 Then Abijah stood on Mount [A]Zemaraim, which
is in the hill country of Ephraim, and said, "Listen
to me, Jeroboam and all Israel: 5 Do you not know
that [A]the LORD God of Israel gave the rule over Israel forever to David [a]and his sons by [B]a covenant

12:1 [A]2 Chr 11:17; 12:13 [B]2 Chr 26:13-16 12:2 [A]1 Kin 14:25 [B]1 Kin 11:40 12:3 [A]2 Chr 16:8; Nah 3:9 12:4 [A]2 Chr 11:5-12 12:5 [a]Lit *in the hand of* [A]2 Chr 11:2 [B]Deut 28:15; 2 Chr 15:2 12:6 [A]Ex 9:27; Dan 9:14 12:7 [A]1 Kin 21:29 [B]2 Chr 34:25-27; Ps 78:38 12:8 [A]Deut 28:47, 48 12:9 [A]1 Kin 14:26-28 [B]1 Kin 10:16, 17; 2 Chr 9:15, 16 12:10 [a]Lit *hands* [b]Lit *runners* 12:11 [a]Lit *runners* 12:12 [A]2 Chr 12:6, 7 [B]2 Chr 19:3 12:13 [A]1 Kin 14:21 12:14 [A]2 Chr 19:3 12:15 [a]Lit *words* [A]1 Kin 14:29 [B]2 Chr 12:5 [C]2 Chr 9:29 12:16 [A]2 Chr 11:20 13:1 [A]1 Kin 15:1, 2 13:2 [A]1 Kin 15:7 13:4 [A]Josh 18:22 13:5 [a]Lit *to him and to his sons* [A]2 Sam 7:12-16 [B]Lev 2:13; Num 18:19

12:1, 2 fifth year. Ca. 926 B.C. Presumably, Rehoboam's 3 years of blessing preceded a fourth year of spiritual rebellion, which God judged in his fifth year with judgment at the hand of the Egyptians.

12:2–5 Shishak. He ruled over Egypt ca. 945–924 B.C. An Egyptian record of this invasion written on stone has been found, recording that Shishak's army penetrated all the way N to the Sea of Galilee. He wanted to restore Egypt's once-great power, but was unable to conquer both Israel and Judah. However, he was able to destroy cities in Judah and gain some control of trade routes. Judah came under Egyptian control.

12:6, 7 humbled themselves. In the face of the Egyptian conqueror, the leaders responded to the Word of God through the prophet (v. 5) and repented, so that God would end His wrath worked through Shishak.

12:8 But. A fitting punishment arose to remind the Jews of their heritage in relationship to Egypt. This was the first major military encounter with Egypt since the Exodus had ended hundreds of years of slavery there. A taste of being enslaved again to a people from whom God had given liberation was bitter. The message was crystal clear—if the Jews would forsake the true worship of God, they would also lose His protective hand of blessing. It was much better to serve God than to have to serve "kingdoms of the countries."

12:9 against Jerusalem. After the parenthetical section (vv. 5–8) describing the state of the beleaguered court, the historian returns to discuss the attack on Jerusalem and the pillage of the temple and palace.

12:9–16 *See notes on 1Ki 14:25–30.*

12:10, 11 bronze. The pure gold was replaced by bronze, which was carefully guarded.

12:12 Cf. 12:7. God preserved Judah because of her repentance.

12:13 Ca. 931–913 B.C. By the general revival of true worship, Rehoboam's reign acquired new life and continued many years after the departure of Shishak. Sadly he faltered (v. 14), probably due largely to his heathen mother (v. 13).

12:16 Abijah. Cf. 11:20, 22. In 1Ki 15:3, he is called a great sinner. But consistent with his pattern, the writer of the Chronicles highlights the little good he did to indicate that he was still in line with God's covenant promise to David.

13:1–22 In the succession of Judah's kings, the reign of Abijah/Abijam is next (ca. 913–911 B.C.; cf. 1Ki 15:1–8). The disobedient nature of Abijah's reign is mentioned in 1Ki 15:3, as is his faithless treaty with Syria (2Ch 16:3).

13:3 *See notes on 1Ki 15:1–8.* These numbers are large, but not surprising, given the immense number of capable men who could fight, as counted in David's census (cf. 1Ch 21:5). Both armies were set for civil war.

13:4 Mount Zemaraim. The exact location is unknown, but it is likely near Bethel (Jos 18:22) inside Israel's territory.

13:5 covenant of salt. Salt is associated elsewhere with the Mosaic Covenant sacrifices (Lv 2:13), the Priestly Covenant (Nu 18:19), and the New Covenant symbolic sacrifices

of salt? 6 Yet [A]Jeroboam the son of Nebat, the servant of Solomon the son of David, rose up and rebelled against his [a]master, 7 and worthless men
gathered about him, scoundrels, who proved too
strong for Rehoboam, the son of Solomon, when
[a,A]he was young and timid and could not hold his
own against them.
8 "So now you intend to resist the kingdom of the
LORD [a]through the sons of David, [b]being a great multitude and *having* with you [A]the golden calves which
Jeroboam made for gods for you. 9 [A]Have you not
driven out the priests of the LORD, the sons of Aaron
and the Levites, and made for yourselves priests
like the peoples of *other* lands? Whoever comes [B]to
consecrate himself with a young bull and seven
rams, even he may become a priest of *what are* [C]no
gods. 10 But as for us, the LORD is our God, and we
have not forsaken Him; and the sons of Aaron are
ministering to the LORD as priests, and the Levites
[a]attend to their work. 11 Every morning and evening
[A]they [a]burn to the LORD burnt offerings and fragrant
incense, and [B]the showbread is *set* on the clean table,
and the golden lampstand with its lamps is *ready* to
light every evening; for we keep the charge of the
LORD our God, but you have forsaken Him. 12 Now
behold, God is with us at *our* head and [A]His priests
with the signal trumpets to sound the alarm against
you. O sons of Israel, do not fight against the LORD
God of your fathers, for you will not succeed."
13 But Jeroboam [A]had set an ambush to come
from the rear, so that *Israel* was in front of Judah
and the ambush was behind them. 14 When Judah
turned around, behold, [a]they were attacked both
front and rear; so [A]they cried to the LORD, and the
priests blew the trumpets. 15 Then the men of Judah
raised a war cry, and when the men of Judah raised
the war cry, then it was that God [a,A]routed Jeroboam
and all Israel before Abijah and Judah. 16 When the
sons of Israel fled before Judah, [A]God gave them
into their hand. 17 Abijah and his people defeated
them with a great slaughter, so that 500,000 chosen
men of Israel fell slain. 18 Thus the sons of Israel
were subdued at that time, and the sons of Judah
[a]conquered [A]because they trusted in the LORD, the
God of their fathers. 19 Abijah pursued Jeroboam
and captured from him *several* cities, Bethel with
its villages, Jeshanah with its villages and [a]Ephron
with its villages.

DEATH OF JEROBOAM

20 Jeroboam did not again recover strength in
the days of Abijah; and the [A]LORD struck him and
[B]he died.
21 But Abijah became powerful; and took fourteen
wives to himself, and became the father of twenty-two sons and sixteen daughters. 22 Now the rest
of the acts of Abijah, and his ways and his words
are written in [A]the [a]treatise of [B]the prophet Iddo.

ASA SUCCEEDS ABIJAH IN JUDAH

14 [a,A]So Abijah slept with his fathers, and they
buried him in the city of David, and his son
Asa became king in his place. The land was undisturbed for ten years during his days.
2 [a]Asa did good and right in the sight of the LORD
his God, 3 for he removed [A]the foreign altars and
[B]high places, tore down the *sacred* pillars, cut down
the [a,C]Asherim, 4 and commanded Judah to seek
the LORD God of their fathers and to observe the
law and the commandment. 5 He also removed the
high places and the [A]incense altars from all the
cities of Judah. And the kingdom was undisturbed
under him. 6 [A]He built fortified cities in Judah, since
the land was undisturbed, and [a]there was no one
at war with him during those years, [B]because the
LORD had given him rest. 7 For he said to Judah,
"[A]Let us build these cities and surround *them* with
walls and towers, gates and bars. The land is still
[a]ours because we have sought the LORD our God;
we have sought Him, and He has given us rest on
every side." So they built and prospered. 8 Now Asa
had an army of [A]300,000 from Judah, bearing large

13:6 [a]Or *lord* [A]1 Kin 11:26 13:7 [a]Lit *Rehoboam* [A]2 Chr 12:13 13:8 [a]Lit *in the hands of* [b]Lit *and you are a* [A]1 Kin 12:28; 2 Chr 11:15 13:9 [A]2 Chr 11:14, 15 [B]Ex 29:29-33 [C]Jer 2:11; 5:7 13:10 [a]Lit *in the work* 13:11 [a]Lit *offer up in smoke* [A]Ex 29:38; 2 Chr 2:4 [B]Ex 25:30-39; Lev 24:5-9 13:12 [A]Num 10:8, 9 13:13 [A]Josh 8:4-9 13:14 [a]Lit *the battle was before and behind them* [A]2 Chr 14:11 13:15 [a]Lit *smote* [A]2 Chr 14:12 13:16 [A]2 Chr 16:8 13:18 [a]Lit *were strong* [A]2 Chr 14:11 13:19 [a]Another reading is *Ephrain* 13:20 [A]1 Sam 25:38 [B]1 Kin 14:20 13:22 [a]Heb *midrash* [A]2 Chr 24:27 [B]2 Chr 9:29 14:1 [a]Ch 13:23 in Heb [A]1 Kin 15:8 14:2 [a]Ch 14:1 in Heb 14:3 [a]I.e. wooden symbols of a female deity [A]Deut 7:5 [B]1 Kin 15:12-14 [C]Ex 34:13 14:5 [A]2 Chr 34:4, 7 14:6 [a]Lit *there was not with him war* [A]2 Chr 11:5 [B]2 Chr 15:15 14:7 [a]Lit *before us* [A]2 Chr 8:5 14:8 [A]2 Chr 13:3

in the millennial kingdom (Eze 43:24). The preservative quality of salt represents the fidelity or loyalty intended in keeping the covenant. Here it would refer to God's irrevocable pledge and intended loyalty in fulfilling the Davidic Covenant and God's desire for the loyalty of David's lineage to Him if the people are to enjoy the blessings of the covenant.

13:6 For the story of Jeroboam, read 1Ki 11:26–40 and 2Ch 10. He was the first king of the northern kingdom called Israel.

13:7 **young.** He was 41 (cf. 2Ch 12:13).

13:8 **kingdom of the LORD.** Abijah reminds all that the Davidic Covenant is God's expressed will concerning who would rule on His behalf in the earthly kingdom. Thus Judah is God's nation, since the king is in the line of David. **golden calves.** Cf. 1Ki 12:25–33; 2Ch 11:15. Israel was full of idols and false priests, having driven out all the Levitical priests and, with them, the true worship of God.

13:10–12 Abijah confessed a national commitment to pure worship and thus confidence in God's favor in battle.

13:15 **God routed Jeroboam and all Israel.** At the time of certain defeat, with 400,000 troops behind and the same number in front, Judah was saved by divine intervention. What God did is unknown, but the army of Israel began to flee (v. 16), and the soldiers of Judah massacred 500,000 of them in an unimaginable blood bath (v. 17).

13:17 Before the battle, Jeroboam outnumbered Abijah two to one (13:3). After the fray, in which the Lord intervened on behalf of Judah, Abijah outnumbered Jeroboam 4 to 3.

13:19 **Bethel.** Located 12 mi. N of Jerusalem. Although their exact locations are unknown, Jeshanah and Ephron are believed to be in the vicinity of Bethel.

13:20 **he died.** Again God acted, in a manner not described, to end the life of this wicked ruler (ca. 910 B.C.).

14:1–16:14 The reign of Asa (ca. 911–870 B.C.). Cf. 1Ki 15:9–24.

14:1, 2 First Kings 15:11 says that Asa did as his forefather David had done—honoring God while building the kingdom (vv. 6–8). Times of peace were used for strengthening.

14:3–5 He removed elements of false worship that had accumulated over the years of Solomon, Rehoboam, and Abijah (cf. 1Ki 15:12, 13). Apparently, he did not remove all the high places or, once removed, they reappeared (cf. 15:17; 1Ki 15:14). His son Jehoshaphat later had to remove them (cf. 2Ch 17:6), although not completely (cf. 20:33). This was done in an effort to comply with Dt 12:2, 3.

14:8 Asa had an army of 580,000 compared to Abijah's 400,000 (2Ch 13:3).

shields and spears, and 280,000 from Benjamin,
bearing shields and wielding bows; all of them
were valiant warriors.
9 Now Zerah the Ethiopian [A]came out against
them with an army of a million men and 300 chariots, and he came to [B]Mareshah. 10 So Asa went
out [a]to meet him, and they drew up in battle formation in the valley of Zephathah at Mareshah.
11 Then Asa [A]called to the LORD his God and said,
"LORD, there is no one besides You to help *in the
battle* between the powerful and those who have
no strength; so help us, O LORD our God, [B]for we
trust in You, and in Your name have come against
this multitude. O LORD, You are our God; let not
man prevail against You." 12 So [A]the LORD [a]routed
the Ethiopians before Asa and before Judah, and
the Ethiopians fled. 13 Asa and the people who *were*
with him pursued them as far as [A]Gerar; and so
many Ethiopians fell that [a]they could not recover,
for they were shattered before the LORD and before
His army. And they carried away very much plunder. 14 They [a]destroyed all the cities around Gerar,
[A]for the dread of the LORD had fallen on them; and
they despoiled all the cities, for there was much
plunder in them. 15 They also struck down [a]those
who owned livestock, and they carried away large
numbers of sheep and camels. Then they returned
to Jerusalem.

THE PROPHET AZARIAH WARNS ASA

15 Now [A]the Spirit of God came on Azariah the
son of Oded, 2 and he went out [a]to meet Asa
and said to him, "Listen to me, Asa, and all Judah
and Benjamin: [A]the LORD is with you when you are
with Him. And [B]if you seek Him, He will let you find
Him; but if you forsake Him, He will forsake you.
3 [A]For many days Israel was without the true God
and without [B]a teaching priest and without law.
4 But [A]in their distress they turned to the LORD God
of Israel, and they sought Him, and He let them find
Him. 5 [A]In those times there was no peace to him
who went out or to him who came in, for many disturbances [a]afflicted all the inhabitants of the lands.
6 [A]Nation was crushed by nation, and city by city,
for God troubled them with every kind of distress.
7 But you, [A]be strong and do not [a]lose courage, for
there is [B]reward for your work."

ASA'S REFORMS

8 Now when Asa heard these words and the
[a]prophecy which Azariah the son of Oded the
prophet spoke, he took courage and removed the
abominable idols from all the land of Judah and
Benjamin and from [A]the cities which he had captured in the hill country of Ephraim. [B]He then restored the altar of the LORD which was in front of
the porch of the LORD. 9 He gathered all Judah and
Benjamin and those from Ephraim, Manasseh and
Simeon [A]who resided with them, for many defected
to him from Israel when they saw that the LORD
his God was with him. 10 So they assembled at Jerusalem in the third month of the fifteenth year of
Asa's reign. 11 [A]They sacrificed to the LORD that day
700 oxen and 7,000 sheep from the spoil they had
brought. 12 [A]They entered into the covenant to seek
the LORD God of their fathers with all their heart
and soul; 13 and whoever would not seek the LORD
God of Israel [A]should be put to death, whether small
or great, man or woman. 14 Moreover, they made an
oath to the LORD with a loud voice, with shouting,
with trumpets and with horns. 15 All Judah rejoiced
concerning the oath, for they had sworn with their
whole heart and had sought Him [a]earnestly, and
He let them find Him. So [A]the LORD gave them rest
on every side.
16 [A]He also removed Maacah, the mother of King
Asa, from the *position of* queen mother, because she
had made a horrid image [a]as [B]an Asherah, and [C]Asa
cut down her horrid image, crushed *it* and burned
it at the brook Kidron. 17 But the high places were
not removed from Israel; nevertheless Asa's heart
was blameless all his days. 18 He brought into the
house of God the dedicated things of his father
and his own dedicated things: silver and gold and
utensils. 19 And there was no more war until the
thirty-fifth year of Asa's reign.

14:9 [A]2 Chr 12:2, 3; 16:8 [B]2 Chr 11:8 14:10 [a]Lit *before him* 14:11 [A]2 Chr 13:14 [B]2 Chr 13:18 14:12 [a]Lit *struck* [A]2 Chr 13:15 14:13 [a]Or *there was none left alive* [A]Gen 10:19 14:14 [a]Lit *smote* [A]2 Chr 17:10 14:15 [a]Lit *tents of livestock* 15:1 [A]2 Chr 20:14; 24:20 15:2 [a]Lit *before Asa* [A]2 Chr 20:17 [B]2 Chr 15:4, 15 15:3 [A]1 Kin 12:28-33 [B]Lev 10:8-11; 2 Chr 17:9 15:4 [A]Deut 4:29 15:5 [a]Lit *were on* [A]Judg 5:6 15:6 [A]Matt 24:7 15:7 [a]Lit *let your hands drop* [A]Josh 1:7, 9 [B]Ps 58:11 15:8 [a]With several ancient versions; Heb *the prophecy, Oded the prophet* [A]2 Chr 13:19 [B]2 Chr 4:1; 8:12 15:9 [A]2 Chr 11:16 15:11 [A]2 Chr 14:13-15 15:12 [A]2 Chr 23:16 15:13 [A]Ex 22:20; Deut 13:6-9 15:15 [a]Lit *with their whole desire* [A]2 Chr 14:7 15:16 [a]Or for *Asherah* [A]1 Kin 15:13-15 [B]Ex 34:13 [C]2 Chr 14:2-5

14:9–15 A major threat developed from Zerah, the Ethiopian, probably on behalf of the Egyptian Pharaoh, who was attempting to regain control as Shishak had during the days of Rehoboam (cf. 2Ch 12:7, 8), ca. 901–900 B.C.

14:9 Mareshah. Located about 8 mi. SE of Gath and 25 mi. SW of Jerusalem. Rehoboam had earlier reinforced this city (2Ch 11:8).

14:11 Asa's appeal to God centered on God's omnipotence and reputation.

14:13–15 plunder. It appears that this great horde was a nomadic people who moved with all their possessions and had set up their camp near Gerar. The spoils of Judah's victory were immense.

14:13 Gerar. Approximately 8 mi. S of Gaza on the Mediterranean coast. Egypt does not appear on the scene again for over 150 years (cf. 2Ki 17:4).

15:1 Spirit of God. An act of the Holy Spirit, common in the OT enabling servants of God to speak or act uniquely for Him. Azariah. This man was a prophet mentioned only here, who met Asa as he returned from the victory and spoke to him before all his army.

15:2 The spiritual truth here is basic, namely that God is present and powerful in defense of His obedient people. Cf. Dt 20:1; 1Ch 28:9; Is 55:6, 7; Jer 29:12–14; Jas 4:8. While good Asa ruled for 41 years, 8 wicked kings ruled in Israel, including Jeroboam, who along with the others, was a negative illustration of this truth (cf. 12:1ff.).

15:8 porch. This refers to the area outside the Holy Place, where the altar of the burnt offering was located.

15:9 Ephraim, Manasseh and Simeon. This indicates that not all the people in the 10 tribes which constituted the apostate northern kingdom of Israel had abandoned God. Many migrated S into Judah, so that all tribes were represented in the mix of Jews in Judah.

15:10 fifteenth year. Ca. 897 B.C. in May/June. The Feast of Weeks would have been the occasion.

15:11–15 The assembled worshipers entered into a renewed promise to obey (cf. Ex 24:1ff.) and to rigorously enforce the laws which made idolatry punishable by death (cf. Dt 17:2–5). This was inaugurated with the sacrifices of animals taken in spoil from the Ethiopians (14:15).

15:16–18 *See note on 1Ki 15:11–15.*

15:19 thirty-fifth year. Ca. 875 B.C.

ASA WARS AGAINST BAASHA

16 In the thirty-sixth year of Asa's reign [A]Ba-
asha king of Israel came up against Judah
and [a]fortified Ramah in order to prevent *anyone*
from going out or coming in to Asa king of Judah.
2 Then Asa brought out silver and gold from the
treasuries of the house of the LORD and the king's
house, and sent them to Ben-hadad king of Aram,
who lived in Damascus, saying, 3 "*Let there be* a
treaty between [a]you and me, *as* between my father and your father. Behold, I have sent you silver
and gold; go, break your treaty with Baasha king
of Israel so that he will withdraw from me." 4 So
Ben-hadad listened to King Asa and sent the commanders of his armies against the cities of Israel,
and they [a]conquered Ijon, Dan, Abel-maim and all
[A]the [b]store cities of Naphtali. 5 When Baasha heard
of it, he ceased [a]fortifying Ramah and stopped his
work. 6 Then King Asa brought all Judah, and they
carried away the stones of Ramah and its timber
with which Baasha had been building, and with
them he [a]fortified Geba and Mizpah.

ASA IMPRISONS THE PROPHET

7 At that time [A]Hanani the seer came to Asa king
of Judah and said to him, "[B]Because you have relied on the king of Aram and have not relied on
the LORD your God, therefore the army of the king
of Aram has escaped out of your hand. 8 Were not
[A]the Ethiopians and the Lubim [B]an immense army
with very many chariots and horsemen? Yet [C]be-
cause you relied on the LORD, He delivered them
into your hand. 9 For [A]the eyes of the LORD move to
and fro throughout the earth that He may strongly
support those [B]whose heart is completely His. You
have acted foolishly in this. Indeed, from now on
you will surely have wars." 10 Then Asa was angry
with the seer and put him in [a]prison, for he was
enraged at him for this. And Asa oppressed some
of the people at the same time.

11 [A]Now, the acts of Asa from first to last, behold,
they are written in the Book of the Kings of Judah
and Israel. 12 In the thirty-ninth year of his reign Asa
became diseased in his feet. His disease was severe,
yet even in his disease he [A]did not seek the LORD, but
the physicians. 13 So Asa slept with his fathers, [a]hav-
ing died in the forty-first year of his reign. 14 They
buried him in his own tomb which he had cut out
for himself in the city of David, and they laid him
in the resting place which he had filled [A]with spices
of various kinds blended by the perfumers' art; and
[B]they made a very great fire for him.

JEHOSHAPHAT SUCCEEDS ASA

17 [A]Jehoshaphat his son then became king in
his place, and made his position over Israel
firm. 2 He placed troops in all [A]the fortified cities
of Judah, and set garrisons in the land of Judah
and in the cities of Ephraim [B]which Asa his father
had captured.

HIS GOOD REIGN

3 The LORD was with Jehoshaphat because he
[a]followed the example of his father David's earlier
days and did not seek the Baals, 4 but sought the God
of his father, [a]followed His commandments, [A]and
did not act as Israel did. 5 So the LORD established
the kingdom in his [a]control, and all Judah brought
tribute to Jehoshaphat, and [A]he had great riches
and honor. 6 [a]He took great pride in the ways of the
LORD and again [A]removed the high places and the
Asherim from Judah.

16:1 [a]Lit *built* [A]1 Kin 15:17-22 16:3 [a]Lit *me and you* 16:4 [a]Lit *smote* [b]Lit *storage places of the cities* [A]Ex 1:11 16:5 [a]Lit *building* 16:6 [a]Lit *built* 16:7 [A]1 Kin 16:1; 2 Chr 19:2 [B]2 Chr 14:11; 32:7, 8 16:8 [A]2 Chr 14:9 [B]2 Chr 12:3 [C]2 Chr 13:16, 18 16:9 [A]Prov 15:3; Jer 16:17; Zech 4:10 [B]2 Chr 15:17 16:10 [a]Lit *the house of the stocks* 16:11 [A]1 Kin 15:23, 24 16:12 [A]Jer 17:5 16:13 [a]Lit *and* 16:14 [A]Gen 50:2; John 19:39, 40 [B]2 Chr 21:19 17:1 [A]1 Kin 15:24 17:2 [A]2 Chr 11:5 [B]2 Chr 15:8 17:3 [a]Lit *walked in the earlier ways of his father* 17:4 [a]Lit *walked in* [A]1 Kin 12:28 17:5 [a]Lit *hand* [A]2 Chr 18:1 17:6 [a]Lit *his heart was high* [A]2 Chr 15:17

16:1 thirty-sixth year. Since Baasha (ca. 909–886 B.C.) died in the 26th year of Asa's reign (cf. 1Ki 15:33), this could not mean that they were at war 10 years later. However, if the time reference was to the 35th year since the kingdom was divided, then the year is ca. 896 B.C. in the 14th year of Baasha's reign and the 16th of Asa's reign. This manner of reckoning was generally followed in the book of the record of the kings of Judah and Israel, the public annals of that time, from which the inspired writer drew his account (cf. v. 11). This could be a cause for the defections of people from Israel to Judah as described in 2Ch 15:9. Cf. 1Ki 15:16, 17. **Ramah.** This frontier town was on the high road about 6 mi. N of Jerusalem. Because of the topography and fortification of that city, this would effectively block all traffic into Jerusalem from the N. Cf. 1Ki 15:16–22.

16:2–6 Asa sinfully resorted to trusting in a pagan king, Ben-hadad, for protection against the king of Israel in contrast to 1) Abijah (13:2–20) and 2) even earlier to his own battle against the Ethiopians (14:9–15), when they both trusted wholly in the Lord. *See note on 1Ki 15:18.*

16:3 my father … your father. A previously unmentioned treaty between Abijah (ca. 913–911 B.C.) and Tabrimmon (ca. 912–890 B.C.).

16:4 Ijon … cities. Along with the other cities mentioned, these were located N and E of the Sea of Galilee.

16:6 Geba … Mizpah. Located two mi. NNE and two miles E of Ramah respectively.

16:7 Hanani. God used this prophet to rebuke Asa 1) for his wicked appropriation of temple treasures devoted to God to purchase power, and 2) for his faithless dependence on a pagan king instead of the Lord, in contrast to before when opposed by Egypt (2Ch 14:9–15). **army of the king of Aram has escaped.** Asa forfeited by this sin the opportunity of gaining victory not only over Israel, but also Aram, or Syria. This could have been a greater victory than over the Ethiopians, which would have deprived Syria of any future successful attacks on Judah. Though God had delivered them when they were outnumbered (13:3ff.; 14:9ff.), the king showed his own spiritual decline both in lack of trust and in his treatment of the prophet of God who spoke truth (v. 10).

16:9 strongly support … heart is completely His. *See note on 15:2.* **you will surely have wars.** Divine judgment on the king's faithlessness.

16:10–12 During Asa's last 6 years, he uncharacteristically exhibited the ungodly behavior of: 1) anger at truth (v. 10); 2) oppression of God's prophet and people (v. 10); and 3) seeking man not God (v. 12).

16:12 thirty-ninth year. Ca. 872 B.C. He died as a result of what may have been severe gangrene.

16:13 forty-first year. Ca. 870 B.C.

16:14 great fire. Due to the longevity of his reign and his notable accomplishments, Asa was honored by the people in their memorial of his death. Cremation was rarely used by the Hebrews (cf. 21:19; 1Sa 31:13; Am 6:10). Later, Jehoram was not honored by fire (21:19) because of his shameful reign.

17:1–21:3 The reign of Jehoshaphat (ca. 873–848 B.C.). Cf. 1Ki 15:24; 22:1–50.

17:1, 2 Jehoshaphat prepared the nation militarily for any aggression, particularly from the northern kingdom of Israel.

17:3 the Baals. This is a general term used for idols. Cf. Jdg 2:11–13.

17:3–9 Jehoshaphat made three strategic moves, spiritually speaking: 1) he obeyed the Lord (17:3–6); 2) he removed false worship from the land (17:6); and 3) he sent out teachers who taught the people the law of the Lord (17:7–9).

7 Then in the third year of his reign he sent his
officials, Ben-hail, Obadiah, Zechariah, Nethanel and
Micaiah, [A]to teach in the cities of Judah; 8 and with
them [A]the Levites, Shemaiah, Nethaniah, Zebadiah,
Asahel, Shemiramoth, Jehonathan, Adonijah, Tobijah and Tobadonijah, the Levites; and with them
Elishama and Jehoram, the priests. 9 They taught
in Judah, *having* [A]the book of the law of the LORD
with them; and they went throughout all the cities
of Judah and taught among the people.
10 Now [A]the dread of the LORD was on all the kingdoms of the lands which *were* around Judah, so
that they did not make war against Jehoshaphat.
11 Some of the Philistines [A]brought gifts and silver
as tribute to Jehoshaphat; the Arabians also brought
him flocks, 7,700 rams and 7,700 male goats. 12 So
Jehoshaphat grew greater and greater, and he built
fortresses and store cities in Judah. 13 He had large
supplies in the cities of Judah, and warriors, valiant
men, in Jerusalem. 14 This was their muster according to their fathers' households: of Judah, commanders of thousands, Adnah *was* the commander, and
with him 300,000 valiant warriors; 15 and next to him
was Johanan the commander, and with him 280,000;
16 and next to him Amasiah the son of Zichri, [A]who
volunteered for the LORD, and with him 200,000
valiant warriors; 17 and of Benjamin, Eliada a valiant
warrior, and with him 200,000 armed with bow and
shield; 18 and next to him Jehozabad, and with him
180,000 equipped for war. 19 These are they who
served the king, apart from [A]those whom the king
put in the fortified cities through all Judah.

JEHOSHAPHAT ALLIES WITH AHAB

18 Now [A]Jehoshaphat had great riches and
honor; and he allied himself by marriage with
Ahab. 2 [A]Some years later he went down to *visit* Ahab
at Samaria. And Ahab slaughtered many sheep and
oxen for him and the people who were with him, and
induced him to go up against Ramoth-gilead. 3 Ahab
king of Israel said to Jehoshaphat king of Judah,
"Will you go with me *against* Ramoth-gilead?" And
he said to him, "I am as you are, and my people as
your people, and *we will be* with you in the battle."
4 Moreover, Jehoshaphat said to the king of Israel, "Please inquire [a]first for the word of the LORD."
5 Then the king of Israel assembled the prophets, four
hundred men, and said to them, "Shall we go against
Ramoth-gilead to battle, or shall I refrain?" And they
said, "Go up, for God will give *it* into the hand of
the king." 6 But Jehoshaphat said, "Is there not yet
a prophet of the LORD here that we may inquire of
him?" 7 The king of Israel said to Jehoshaphat, "There
is yet one man by whom we may inquire of the LORD,
but I hate him, for he never prophesies good concerning me but always evil. He is Micaiah, son of
Imla." But Jehoshaphat said, "Let not the king say so."

AHAB'S FALSE PROPHETS ASSURE VICTORY

8 Then the king of Israel called an officer and said,
"[a]Bring quickly Micaiah, Imla's son." 9 Now the king
of Israel and Jehoshaphat the king of Judah were
sitting each on his throne, arrayed in *their* robes,
and *they* were sitting [A]at the threshing floor at the
entrance of the gate of Samaria; and all the prophets
were prophesying before them. 10 Zedekiah the son
of Chenaanah made horns of iron for himself and
said, "Thus says the LORD, 'With these you shall gore
the Arameans until they are consumed.' " 11 All the
prophets were prophesying thus, saying, "Go up to
Ramoth-gilead and succeed, for the LORD will give
it into the hand of the king."

MICAIAH BRINGS WORD FROM GOD

12 Then the messenger who went to summon
Micaiah spoke to him saying, "Behold, the words of
the prophets are uniformly favorable to the king. So
please let your word be like one of them and speak
favorably." 13 But Micaiah said, "As the LORD lives,
[A]what my God says, that I will speak."
14 When he came to the king, the king said to him,
"Micaiah, shall we go to Ramoth-gilead to battle,
or shall I refrain?" He said, "Go up and succeed, for
they will be given into your hand." 15 Then the king
said to him, "How many times must I adjure you to
speak to me nothing but the truth in the name of
the LORD?" 16 So he said,

"I saw all Israel
Scattered on the mountains,
[A]Like sheep which have no shepherd;
And the LORD said,
'These have no master.
Let each of them return to
his house in peace.' "

17 Then the king of Israel said to Jehoshaphat, "Did
I not tell you that he would not prophesy good concerning me, but evil?"

17:7 [A]2 Chr 15:3; 35:3 17:8 [A]2 Chr 19:8 17:9 [A]Deut 6:4-9 17:10 [A]2 Chr 14:14 17:11 [A]2 Chr 9:14; 26:8 17:16 [A]Judg 5:2, 9; 1 Chr 29:9 17:19 [A]2 Chr 17:2 18:1 [A]2 Chr 17:5 18:2 [A]1 Kin 22:2-35 18:4 [a]Lit *as the day* 18:8 [a]Lit *Hasten* 18:9 [A]Ruth 4:1 18:13 [A]Num 22:18-20, 35 18:16 [A]Num 27:17; 1 Kin 22:17; Ezek 34:5; 35:4-8; Matt 9:36; Mark 6:34

17:10, 11 Jehoshaphat's spiritual strategy accomplished its intended purpose, i.e., invoking God's blessing and protection, much like it did with Abijah (13:2–20) and Asa (14:9–15). It should be noted that the Jews needed animals for extensive sacrificial uses, as much as for food and clothing.

17:12, 13 These verses indicate the massive wealth that developed under divine blessing (cf. 18:1), as well as formidable military power (vv. 14–19).

18:1–34 *See notes on 1Ki 22:1–39.* Ahab was king in Israel. Jehoshaphat arranged for his son (cf. 21:6) to marry Athaliah, daughter of wicked Ahab, then made a military alliance with him. This folly had tragic results: 1) Jehoshaphat drew God's wrath (19:2); 2) after Jehoshaphat died and Athaliah became queen, she seized the throne and almost killed all of David's descendants (22:10ff.); and 3) she brought the wicked idols of Israel into Judah, which eventually led to the nation's destruction and captivity in Babylon. Jehoshaphat had a tendency to rely on other kings as evidenced by this unique report of a marriage alliance with Ahab (v. 1). See also 2Ch 20:35–37 concerning an alliance with Ahaziah (ca. 853–852 B.C.).

18:5 Evil kings had false prophets who told them what they wanted to hear (cf. Is 30:10, 11; Jer 14:13–16; 23:16, 21, 30–36). The true prophet spoke God's Word and was arrested (v. 26).

18 Micaiah said, "Therefore, hear the word of the
LORD. [A]I saw the LORD sitting on His throne, and all
the host of heaven standing on His right and on His
left. 19 The LORD said, 'Who will entice Ahab king of
Israel to go up and fall at Ramoth-gilead?' And one
said this while another said that. 20 Then a [A]spirit
came forward and stood before the LORD and said,
'I will entice him.' And the LORD said to him, 'How?'
21 He said, 'I will go and be [A]a deceiving spirit in the
mouth of all his prophets.' Then He said, 'You are to
entice *him* and prevail also. Go and do so.' 22 Now
therefore, behold, [A]the LORD has put a deceiving
spirit in the mouth of these your prophets, for the
LORD has proclaimed disaster against you."
23 Then Zedekiah the son of Chenaanah came near
and [A]struck Micaiah on the cheek and said, "[a]How
did the Spirit of the LORD pass from me to speak to
you?" 24 Micaiah said, "Behold, you will see on that
day when you enter an inner room to hide yourself."
25 Then the king of Israel said, "[A]Take Micaiah and
return him to Amon [B]the governor of the city and to
Joash the king's son; 26 and say, 'Thus says the king,
"[A]Put this *man* in prison and feed him [a]sparingly with
bread and water until I return safely." ' " 27 Micaiah
said, "If you indeed return safely, the LORD has not
spoken by me." And he said, "[A]Listen, all you people."

AHAB'S DEFEAT AND DEATH

28 So the king of Israel and Jehoshaphat king of
Judah went up against Ramoth-gilead. 29 The king
of Israel said to Jehoshaphat, "I will disguise myself and go into battle, but you put on your robes."
So the king of Israel disguised himself, and they
went into battle. 30 Now the king of Aram had commanded the captains of his chariots, saying, "Do
not fight with small or great, but with the king of
Israel alone." 31 So when the captains of the chariots saw Jehoshaphat, they said, "It is the king of
Israel," and they turned aside to fight against him.
But Jehoshaphat [A]cried out, and the LORD helped
him, and God diverted them from him. 32 When the
captains of the chariots saw that it was not the king
of Israel, they turned back from pursuing him. 33 A
certain man drew his bow at random and struck
the king of Israel [a]in a joint of the armor. So he said
to the driver of the chariot, "Turn [b]around and take
me out of the [c]fight, for I am severely wounded."
34 The battle raged that day, and the king of Israel
propped himself up in his chariot in front of the
Arameans until the evening; and at sunset he died.

JEHU REBUKES JEHOSHAPHAT

19 Then Jehoshaphat the king of Judah returned
in safety to his house in Jerusalem. 2 [A]Jehu
the son of Hanani the seer went out to meet him
and said to King Jehoshaphat, "[B]Should you help
the wicked and love those who hate the LORD and
[a,C]so *bring* wrath on yourself from the LORD? 3 But
[a,A]there is *some* good in you, for [B]you have removed
the [b]Asheroth from the land and you [C]have set your
heart to seek God."
4 So Jehoshaphat lived in Jerusalem and went out
again among the people from Beersheba to the hill
country of Ephraim and [A]brought them back to the
LORD, the God of their fathers.

REFORMS INSTITUTED

5 He appointed [A]judges in the land in all the fortified cities of Judah, city by city. 6 He said to the
judges, "Consider what you are doing, for [A]you do
not judge for man but for the LORD who is with you
[a]when you render judgment. 7 Now then let the fear
of the LORD be upon you; [a]be very careful what you
do, for [b]the LORD our God will [A]have no part in unrighteousness [B]or partiality or the taking of a bribe."
8 In Jerusalem also Jehoshaphat appointed some
[A]of the Levites and priests, and some of the heads of
the fathers' *households* of Israel, for the judgment
of the LORD and to judge [a]disputes among the inhabitants of Jerusalem. 9 Then he charged them
saying, "Thus you shall do in the fear of the LORD,
faithfully and wholeheartedly. 10 [A]Whenever any
dispute comes to you from your brethren who live
in their cities, between blood and blood, between
law and commandment, statutes and ordinances,
you shall warn them so that they may not be guilty
before the LORD, and [B]wrath may *not* come on you
and your brethren. Thus you shall do and you will
not be guilty. 11 Behold, Amariah the chief priest will
be over you in [a,A]all that pertains to the LORD, and
Zebadiah the son of Ishmael, the ruler of the house
of Judah, in [a]all that pertains to the king. Also the
Levites shall be officers before you. [b,B]Act resolutely,
and the LORD be with the upright."

JUDAH INVADED

20 Now it came about after this that the sons of
Moab and the sons of Ammon, together with
some of the [a,A]Meunites, came to make war against
Jehoshaphat. 2 Then some came and reported to
Jehoshaphat, saying, "A great multitude is coming

18:18 [A]Is 6:1-5; Dan 7:9, 10 18:20 [A]Job 1:6; 2 Thess 2:9 18:21 [A]John 8:44 18:22 [A]Is 19:14; Ezek 14:9 18:23 [a]Lit *Which way* [A]Jer 20:2; Mark 14:65; Acts 23:2 18:25 [A]2 Chr 18:8 [B]2 Chr 34:8 18:26 [a]Lit *with bread of affliction and water of affliction* [A]2 Chr 16:10 18:27 [A]Mic 1:2 18:31 [A]2 Chr 13:14, 15 18:33 [a]Lit *between the scale-armor and the breastplate* [b]Lit *your hand* [c]Lit *camp* 19:2 [a]Lit *by this* [A]1 Kin 16:1; 2 Chr 20:34 [B]2 Chr 18:1, 3 [C]2 Chr 24:18 19:3 [a]Lit *good things are found* [b]I.e. wooden pillars [A]2 Chr 12:12 [B]2 Chr 17:6 [C]2 Chr 12:14 19:4 [A]2 Chr 15:8-13 19:5 [A]Deut 16:18-20 19:6 [a]Lit *in the word of judgment* [A]Lev 19:15; Deut 1:17 19:7 [a]Lit *be careful and do* [b]Lit *there is not with the LORD our God* [A]Gen 18:25; Deut 32:4 [B]Deut 10:17, 18 19:8 [a]So the versions; Heb reads *disputes. And they returned to Jerusalem,* or *And they lived in Jerusalem* [A]2 Chr 17:8, 9 19:10 [A]Deut 17:8 [B]2 Chr 19:2 19:11 [a]Lit *every matter of* [b]Lit *Be strong and do* [A]2 Chr 19:8 [B]1 Chr 28:20 20:1 [a]So with Gr; Heb *Ammonites* [A]1 Chr 4:41; 2 Chr 26:7

19:1–3 Having faced possible death that was diverted by God (18:31), Jehoshaphat was rebuked because of his alliances. The prophet condemned the king's alliance with God's enemy, Ahab (1Ki 22:2), yet there was mercy mingled with wrath because of the king's concern personally and nationally for the true worship of God.

19:2 Hanani. This same prophet had earlier given Jehoshaphat's father, Asa, a similar warning (2Ch 16:7–9).

19:4–11 Jehoshaphat put God's kingdom in greater spiritual order than at any time since Solomon. To ensure this order, he set "judges" (v. 5) in place and gave them principles to rule by: 1) accountability to God (v. 6); 2) integrity and honesty (v. 7); 3) loyalty to God (v. 9); 4) concern for righteousness (v. 10); and 5) courage (v. 11). All are essentials to spiritual leadership.

20:1, 2 The offspring of Lot, i.e., Moab and Ammon, located E of the Jordan, and those from Edom to the S (the offspring of Esau), had intentions of dethroning Jehoshaphat. They

against you from beyond the sea, out of [a]Aram and behold, they are in [A]Hazazon-tamar (that is Engedi)." 3 Jehoshaphat was afraid and [a,A]turned his attention to seek the LORD, and [B]proclaimed a fast throughout all Judah. 4 So Judah gathered together to [A]seek help from the LORD; they even came from all the cities of Judah to seek the LORD.

JEHOSHAPHAT'S PRAYER

5 Then Jehoshaphat stood in the assembly of Judah and Jerusalem, in the house of the LORD before the new court, 6 and he said, "O LORD, the God of our fathers, [A]are You not God in the heavens? And [B]are You not ruler over all the kingdoms of the nations? Power and might are in Your hand so that no one can stand against You. 7 Did You not, O our God, drive out the inhabitants of this land before Your people Israel and [A]give it to the descendants of [B]Abraham Your friend forever? 8 They have lived in it, and have built You a sanctuary there for Your name, saying, 9 '[A]Should evil come upon us, the sword, *or* judgment, or pestilence, or famine, we will stand before this house and before You (for [B]Your name is in this house) and cry to You in our distress, and You will hear and deliver *us.*' 10 Now behold, [A]the sons of Ammon and Moab and [a]Mount Seir, [B]whom You did not let Israel invade when they came out of the land of Egypt (they turned aside from them and did not destroy them), 11 see *how* they are rewarding us by [A]coming to drive us out from Your possession which You have given us as an inheritance. 12 O our God, [A]will You not judge them? For we are powerless before this great multitude who are coming against us; nor do we know what to do, but [B]our eyes are on You."

13 All Judah was standing before the LORD, with their infants, their wives and their children.

JAHAZIEL ANSWERS THE PRAYER

14 Then in the midst of the assembly [A]the Spirit of the LORD came upon Jahaziel the son of Zechariah, the son of Benaiah, the son of Jeiel, the son of Mattaniah, the Levite of the sons of Asaph; 15 and he said, "Listen, all Judah and the inhabitants of Jerusalem and King Jehoshaphat: thus says the LORD to you, '[A]Do not fear or be dismayed because of this great multitude, for [B]the battle is not yours but God's. 16 Tomorrow go down against them. Behold, they will come up by the ascent of Ziz, and you will find them at the end of the valley in front of the wilderness of Jeruel. 17 You *need* not fight in this *battle;* station yourselves, [A]stand and see the salvation of the LORD on your behalf, O Judah and Jerusalem.' Do not fear or be dismayed; tomorrow go out to face them, [B]for the LORD is with you."

18 Jehoshaphat [A]bowed his head with *his* face to the ground, and all Judah and the inhabitants of Jerusalem fell down before the LORD, worshiping the LORD. 19 The Levites, from the sons of the Kohathites and of the sons of the Korahites, stood up to praise the LORD God of Israel, with a very loud voice.

ENEMIES DESTROY THEMSELVES

20 They rose early in the morning and went out to the wilderness of Tekoa; and when they went out, Jehoshaphat stood and said, "Listen to me, O Judah and inhabitants of Jerusalem, [A]put your trust in the LORD your God and you will be established. Put your trust in His prophets and succeed." 21 When he had consulted with the people, he appointed those who sang to the LORD and those who [A]praised *Him* in holy attire, as they went out before the army and said, "[B]Give thanks to the LORD, for His lovingkindness is everlasting." 22 When they began singing and praising, the LORD [A]set ambushes against the sons of [B]Ammon, Moab and Mount Seir, who had come against Judah; so they were [a]routed. 23 For the sons of Ammon and Moab rose up against the inhabitants of Mount Seir destroying *them* completely; and when they had finished with the inhabitants of Seir, [A]they helped to destroy one another.

24 When Judah came to the lookout of the wilderness, they looked toward the multitude, and behold, they *were* corpses lying on the ground, and no one had escaped. 25 When Jehoshaphat and his people came to take their spoil, they found much among them, *including* goods, [a]garments and valuable things which they took for themselves, more than they could carry. And they were three days taking the spoil because there was so much.

20:2 [a]Another reading is *Edom* [A]Gen 14:7 20:3 [a]Lit *set his face* [A]2 Chr 19:3 [B]1 Sam 7:6; Ezra 8:21 20:4 [A]Joel 1:14 20:6 [A]Deut 4:39 [B]1 Chr 29:11 20:7 [A]Is 41:8 [B]James 2:23 20:9 [A]2 Chr 6:28-30 [B]2 Chr 6:20 20:10 [a]I.e. Edom [A]2 Chr 20:1, 22 [B]Num 20:17-21 20:11 [A]Ps 83:12 20:12 [A]Judg 11:27 [B]Ps 25:15; 121:1, 2 20:14 [A]2 Chr 15:1; 24:20 20:15 [A]Ex 14:13; Deut 20:1-4; 2 Chr 32:7, 8 [B]1 Sam 17:47 20:17 [A]Ex 14:13 [B]2 Chr 15:2 20:18 [A]Ex 4:31 20:20 [A]Is 7:9 20:21 [A]1 Chr 16:29; Ps 29:2 [B]1 Chr 16:34 20:22 [a]Lit *struck down* [A]2 Chr 13:13 [B]2 Chr 20:10 20:23 [A]Judg 7:22; 1 Sam 14:20 20:25 [a]So several ancient mss; others read *corpses*

had come around the S end of the Dead Sea as far N as Engedi, at the middle of the western shore. This was a common route for enemies since they were invisible to the people on the other side of the mountains to the W.

20:3, 4 Jehoshaphat made the appropriate spiritual response, i.e., the king and the nation appealed to God in prayer and fasting. The fast was national, including even the children (v. 13). Cf. Joel 2:12–17; Jon 3:7.

20:5–12 Jehoshaphat stood in the redecorated center court praying for the nation, appealing to the promises, the glory, and the reputation of God which were at stake since He was identified with Judah. In his prayer he acknowledged God's sovereignty (v. 6), God's covenant (v. 7), God's presence (vv. 8, 9), God's goodness (v. 10), God's possession (v. 11), and their utter dependence on Him (v. 12).

20:10 **Mount Seir.** A prominent landmark in Edom.

20:14–17 The Lord responded immediately, sending a message of confidence through the prophet Jahaziel.

20:16 **ascent of Ziz ... wilderness of Jeruel.** These areas lie between Engedi on the Dead Sea and Tekoa, which is 10 mi. S of Jerusalem and 17 mi. NW of Engedi. This is the pass that leads from the valley of the Dead Sea toward Jerusalem.

20:18–21 Here was the praise of faith. They were confident enough in God's promise of victory to begin the praise before the battle was won. So great was their trust that the choir marched in front of the army, singing psalms.

20:21 **in holy attire.** This refers to the manner in which the Levite singers were clothed in symbolic sacred clothing (cf. 1Ch 16:29) in honor of the Lord's holiness.

20:22–24 Similar to God's intervention in Gideon's day (Jdg 7:15–23), God caused confusion among the enemy, who mistakenly turned upon themselves and slaughtered each other. Some think this may have been done by angels who appeared and set off this uncontrolled and deadly panic. The destruction was complete before Jehoshaphat and his army ever met the enemy (v. 24).

20:25–28 They went back just as they had gone out—with music (cf. vv. 21, 22).

TRIUMPHANT RETURN TO JERUSALEM

26 Then on the fourth day they assembled in the
valley of Beracah, for there they blessed the LORD.
Therefore they have named that place "The Valley
of [a]Beracah" until today. 27 Every man of Judah and
Jerusalem returned with Jehoshaphat at their head,
returning to Jerusalem with joy, [A]for the LORD had
made them to rejoice over their enemies. 28 They
came to Jerusalem with harps, lyres and trumpets
to the house of the LORD. 29 And [A]the dread of God
was on all the kingdoms of the lands when they
heard that the LORD had fought against the enemies
of Israel. 30 So the kingdom of Jehoshaphat was at
peace, [A]for his God gave him rest on all sides.
31 [A]Now Jehoshaphat reigned over Judah. He *was*
thirty-five years old when he became king, and he
reigned in Jerusalem twenty-five years. And his
mother's name *was* Azubah the daughter of Shilhi.
32 He walked in the way of his father Asa and did not
depart from it, doing right in the sight of the LORD.
33 [A]The high places, however, were not removed;
[B]the people had not yet directed their hearts to the
God of their fathers.
34 Now the rest of the acts of Jehoshaphat, first
[a]to last, behold, they are written in the annals of
[A]Jehu the son of Hanani, which is [b]recorded in the
Book of the Kings of Israel.

ALLIANCE DISPLEASES GOD

35 [A]After this Jehoshaphat king of Judah allied
himself with Ahaziah king of Israel. He acted wickedly [a]in so doing. 36 So he allied himself with him
to make ships to go [A]to Tarshish, and they made
the ships in Ezion-geber. 37 Then Eliezer the son of
Dodavahu of Mareshah prophesied against Jehoshaphat saying, "Because you have allied yourself with
Ahaziah, the LORD has destroyed your works." So
the ships were broken and could not go to Tarshish.

JEHORAM SUCCEEDS JEHOSHAPHAT IN JUDAH

21 [A]Then Jehoshaphat slept with his fathers and
was buried with his fathers in the city of David, and Jehoram his son became king in his place.
2 He had brothers, the sons of Jehoshaphat: Azariah,
Jehiel, Zechariah, [a]Azaryahu, Michael and Shephatiah. All these *were* the sons of Jehoshaphat king [A]of
Israel. 3 Their father gave them many gifts of silver,
gold and precious things, [A]with fortified cities in
Judah, but he gave the kingdom to Jehoram because
he was the firstborn.
4 Now when Jehoram had [a]taken over the kingdom
of his father and made himself [b]secure, he [A]killed all
his brothers with the sword, and some of the rulers
of Israel also. 5 [A]Jehoram *was* thirty-two years old
when he became king, and he reigned eight years
in Jerusalem. 6 [A]He walked in the way of the kings
of Israel, just as the house of Ahab did ([B]for Ahab's
daughter was his wife), and he did evil in the sight
of the LORD. 7 Yet the LORD was not willing to destroy the house of David because of the covenant
which He had made with David, [A]and since He had
promised to give a lamp to him and his sons forever.

REVOLT AGAINST JUDAH

8 In his days [A]Edom revolted [a]against the rule of
Judah and set up a king over themselves. 9 Then
Jehoram crossed over with his commanders and
all his chariots with him. And he arose by night
and struck down the Edomites who were surrounding him and the commanders of the chariots. 10 So
Edom revolted [a]against Judah to this day. Then Libnah revolted at the same time [b]against his rule, because he had forsaken the LORD God of his fathers.
11 Moreover, [A]he made high places in the mountains
of Judah, and caused the inhabitants of Jerusalem
[B]to play the harlot and led Judah astray.
12 Then a letter came to him from Elijah the prophet
saying, "Thus says the LORD God of your father David, 'Because [A]you have not walked in the ways of
Jehoshaphat your father [B]and the ways of Asa king
of Judah, 13 but [A]have walked in the way of the kings
of Israel, and have caused Judah and the inhabitants
of Jerusalem to play the harlot [B]as the house of Ahab
played the harlot, and you [C]have also killed your
brothers, [a]your own family, who were better than
you, 14 behold, the LORD is going to strike your people, your sons, your wives and all your possessions
with a great [a]calamity; 15 and [A]you will suffer [a]severe
sickness, a disease of your bowels, until your bowels
come out because of the sickness, day by day.' "
16 Then [A]the LORD stirred up against Jehoram the
spirit of the Philistines and [B]the Arabs who [a]bor-
dered the Ethiopians; 17 and they came against Judah

20:26 [a]I.e. blessing 20:27 [A]Neh 12:43 20:29 [A]2 Chr 14:14; 17:10 20:30 [A]2 Chr 14:6, 7; 15:15 20:31 [A]1 Kin 22:41-43 20:33 [A]2 Chr 17:6 [B]2 Chr 19:3 20:34 [a]Lit *and* [b]Lit *taken up* [A]2 Chr 19:2 20:35 [a]Lit *to do* [A]1 Kin 22:48, 49 20:36 [A]2 Chr 9:21 21:1 [A]1 Kin 22:50 21:2 [a]Or *Azariah* [A]2 Chr 12:6; 23:2 21:3 [A]2 Chr 11:5 21:4 [a]Lit *risen up* [b]Lit *strong* [A]Gen 4:8; Judg 9:5 21:5 [A]2 Kin 8:17-22 21:6 [A]1 Kin 12:28-30 [B]2 Chr 18:1 21:7 [A]2 Sam 7:12-17; 1 Kin 11:13, 36 21:8 [a]Lit *from under the hand of* [A]2 Chr 20:22, 23; 21:10 21:10 [a]Lit *from under the hand of* [b]Lit *from under his hand* 21:11 [A]1 Kin 11:7 [B]Lev 20:5 21:12 [A]2 Chr 17:3, 4 [B]2 Chr 14:2-5 21:13 [a]Lit *your father's house* [A]2 Chr 21:6 [B]1 Kin 16:31-33 [C]2 Chr 21:4 21:14 [a]Lit *blow* 21:15 [a]Lit *in many sicknesses* [A]2 Chr 21:18, 19 21:16 [a]Lit *were at the hand of* [A]2 Chr 33:11 [B]2 Chr 17:11; 22:1

20:29 This is the second time in Jehoshaphat's reign that fear came on the nations (cf. 2Ch 17:10), which was similar to that when Israel came out of Egypt (Ex 23:27; Nu 22:3; Jos 2:9–11; 9:9, 10).

20:31–21:3 *See notes on 1Ki 22:41–49.*

21:2–5 When the co-regency with his father ended at his father's death, Jehoram killed all who might have threatened his throne.

21:4–20 The reign of Jehoram (ca. 853–841 B.C.). Cf. 2Ki 8:16–24. Most likely, Obadiah prophesied during his reign.

21:4–10 *See notes on 2Ki 8:16–22.*

21:11 **led Judah astray.** Undoubtedly he was influenced by his marriage to Ahab's daughter (cf. v. 6) and was influenced in the alliance just like his father (2Ch 18:1). They had not learned from Solomon's sinful example (cf. 1Ki 11:3, 4). His wicked wife, Athaliah, later became ruler over Judah and tried to wipe out David's royal line (2Ch 22:10).

21:12–15 Elijah, best known for his confrontations with Israel's Ahab and Jezebel (1Ki 17–2Ki 2:11), confronted prophetically Jehoram's sins of idolatry and murder (21:13). The consequences from God's judgment extended beyond himself to his family and the nation (21:14, 15). This event undoubtedly occurred in the early years of Jehoram's co-regency with his father Jehoshaphat and shortly before Elijah's departure to heaven, ca. 848 B.C. (cf. 2Ki 2:11, 12).

21:16–20 The consequences of his sin were far-reaching. He suffered military losses, his country was ravaged, his capital taken, his palace plundered, his wives taken, all his children killed but the youngest, he died with a painful disease, and was buried without honor (21:16–22:1).

and invaded it, and carried away all the possessions
found in the king's house together with his sons
and his wives, so that no son was left to him except
[a,A]Jehoahaz, the youngest of his sons.
18 So after all this the LORD smote him [A]in his
bowels with an incurable sickness. 19 Now it came
about in the course of time, at the end of two years,
that his bowels came out because of his sickness
and he died in great pain. And his people made
no fire for him like [A]the fire for his fathers. 20 He
was thirty-two years old when he became king,
and he reigned in Jerusalem eight years; and he
departed [a,A]with no one's regret, and they buried
him in the city of David, [B]but not in the tombs of
the kings.

AHAZIAH SUCCEEDS JEHORAM IN JUDAH

22 [A]Then the inhabitants of Jerusalem made
[a]Ahaziah, his youngest son, king in his place,
for the band of men who came with [B]the Arabs
to the camp had slain all the older *sons*. So Ahaziah the son of Jehoram king of Judah began to
reign. 2 Ahaziah *was* [a]twenty-two years old when
he became king, and he reigned one year in Jerusalem. And his mother's name was Athaliah, the
[b]granddaughter of Omri. 3 He also walked in the
ways of the house of Ahab, for his mother was
his counselor to do wickedly. 4 He did evil in the
sight of the LORD like the house of Ahab, for they
were his counselors after the death of his father,
to [A]his destruction.

AHAZIAH ALLIES WITH JEHORAM OF ISRAEL

5 He also walked according to their counsel, and
went with Jehoram the son of Ahab king of Israel
to wage war against Hazael king of Aram at Ramoth-gilead. But the [a,A]Arameans [b]wounded [c]Jo-
ram. 6 So he returned to be healed in Jezreel of the
wounds [a]which they had inflicted on him at Ramah,
when he fought against Hazael king of Aram. And
[b]Ahaziah, the son of Jehoram king of Judah, went
down to see Jehoram the son of Ahab in Jezreel,
because he was sick.
7 Now [A]the destruction of Ahaziah was from God,
in that [a]he went to Joram. For when he came, [B]he
went out with Jehoram against Jehu the son of Nimshi, [C]whom the LORD had anointed to cut off the
house of Ahab.

JEHU MURDERS PRINCES OF JUDAH

8 [A]It came about when Jehu was executing judgment on the house of Ahab, he found the princes
of Judah and the sons of Ahaziah's brothers ministering to Ahaziah, and slew them. 9 [A]He also sought
Ahaziah, and they caught him while he was hiding
in Samaria; they brought him to Jehu, put him to
death [B]and buried him. For they said, "He is the son
of Jehoshaphat, [C]who sought the LORD with all his
heart." So there was no one of the house of Ahaziah
to retain the power of the kingdom.
10 [A]Now when Athaliah the mother of Ahaziah
saw that her son was dead, she rose and destroyed
all the royal [a]offspring of the house of Judah. 11 But
Jehoshabeath the king's daughter took Joash the son
of Ahaziah, and stole him from among the king's
sons who were being put to death, and placed him
and his nurse in the bedroom. So Jehoshabeath, the
daughter of King Jehoram, the wife of Jehoiada the
priest (for she was the sister of Ahaziah), hid him
from Athaliah so that she would not put him to
death. 12 He was hidden with them in the house of
God six years while Athaliah reigned over the land.

JEHOIADA SETS JOASH ON THE THRONE OF JUDAH

23 [A]Now in the seventh year Jehoiada strengthened himself, and took captains of hundreds:
Azariah the son of Jeroham, Ishmael the son of Johanan, Azariah the son of Obed, Maaseiah the son
of Adaiah, and Elishaphat the son of Zichri, *and
they entered* into a covenant with him. 2 They went
throughout Judah and gathered the Levites from
all the cities of Judah, and the heads of the fathers'
households of [A]Israel, and they came to Jerusalem.
3 Then all the assembly made a covenant with the
king in the house of God. And [a]Jehoiada said to them,
"Behold, the king's son shall reign, [A]as the LORD has
spoken concerning the sons of David. 4 This is the
thing which you shall do: one third of you, of the
priests and Levites [A]who come in on the sabbath,
shall be gatekeepers, 5 and one third *shall be* at the
king's house, and a third at the Gate of the Foundation; and all the people *shall be* in the courts of the
house of the LORD. 6 But let no one enter the house
of the LORD except the priests and [A]the ministering
Levites; they may enter, for they are holy. And let all
the people keep the charge of the LORD. 7 The Levites
will surround the king, each man with his weapons
in his hand; and whoever enters the house, let him

21:17 [a]In 2 Chr 22:1, *Ahaziah* [A]2 Chr 25:23 21:18 [A]2 Chr 21:15 21:19 [A]2 Chr 16:14 21:20 [a]Lit *without desire* [A]Jer 22:18, 28 [B]2 Chr 24:25; 28:27 22:1 [a]In 2 Chr 21:17, *Jehoahaz* [A]2 Kin 8:24-29 [B]2 Chr 21:16 22:2 [a]So some versions and 2 Kin 8:26; Heb *42 years* [b]Lit *daughter* 22:4 [A]Prov 13:20 22:5 [a]Heb *archers* [b]Lit *smote* [c]I.e. Jehoram [A]2 Kin 8:28 22:6 [a]Lit *with which...smitten* [b]So with 2 Kin 8:29; Heb *Azariah* 22:7 [a]Lit *to go* [A]2 Chr 10:15 [B]2 Kin 9:21 [C]2 Kin 9:6, 7 22:8 [A]2 Kin 10:11-14 22:9 [A]2 Kin 9:27 [B]2 Kin 9:28 [C]2 Chr 17:4 22:10 [a]Lit *seed* [A]2 Kin 11:1-3 23:1 [A]2 Kin 11:4-20 23:2 [A]2 Chr 11:13-17; 21:2 23:3 [a]Lit *he* [A]2 Sam 7:12; 2 Chr 21:7 23:4 [A]1 Chr 9:25 23:6 [A]1 Chr 23:28-32

21:20 eight years. These were the years of his exclusive reign, not including his coregency with his father.

22:1–9 The reign of Ahaziah (ca. 841 B.C.). Cf. 2Ki 8:25–29; 9:21–29.

22:1–6 *See notes on 2Ki 8:25–29.*

22:2 twenty-two. Some versions read "forty-two" here, a copyist's error easily made due to the small stroke that differentiates two Heb. letters. The reading from 2Ki 8:26 of "twenty-two" should be followed.

22:3 his mother was his counselor ... wickedly. Athaliah and the rest of Ahab's house who were in the young king's life taught him wickedness and led him to moral corruption, idolatry, and folly in being induced to war with the Arameans, or Syrians (vv. 5, 6).

22:7–9 *See notes on 2Ki 8:28–9:29.*

22:10–23:21 The reign of Athaliah (ca. 841–835 B.C.). Cf. 2Ki 11:1–20.

23:3 as the LORD has spoken. This is one of the most dramatic moments in messianic history. The human offspring of David have been reduced to one—Joash. If he had died, there would have been no human heir to the Davidic throne, and it would have meant the destruction of the line of the Messiah. However, God remedied the situation by providentially protecting Joash (22:10–12) and eliminating Athaliah (23:12–21).

be killed. Thus be with the king when he comes in and when he goes out."

8 So the Levites and all Judah did according to all that Jehoiada the priest commanded. And each one of them took his men who were to come in on the sabbath, with those who were to go out on the sabbath, for Jehoiada the priest did not dismiss *any of* [A]the divisions. 9 Then Jehoiada the priest gave to the captains of hundreds the spears and the large and small shields which had been King David's, which were in the house of God. 10 He stationed all the people, each man with his weapon in his hand, from the right [a]side of the house to the left [a]side of the house, by the altar and by the house, around the king. 11 Then they brought out the king's son and put the crown on him, and *gave him* [A]the testimony and made him king. And Jehoiada and his sons anointed him and said, "[B]*Long* live the king!"

ATHALIAH MURDERED

12 When Athaliah heard the noise of the people running and praising the king, she came into the house of the LORD to the people. 13 She looked, and behold, the king was standing by his pillar at the entrance, and the captains and the [a]trumpeters *were* beside the king. And all the people of the land rejoiced and blew trumpets, the singers with *their* musical instruments [b]leading the praise. Then Athaliah tore her clothes and said, "Treason! Treason!" 14 Jehoiada the priest brought out the captains of hundreds who were appointed over the army and said to them, "Bring her out [a]between the ranks; and whoever follows her, put to death with the sword." For the priest said, "Let her not be put to death in the house of the LORD." 15 So they [a]seized her, and when she arrived at the entrance of [A]the Horse Gate of the king's house, they [B]put her to death there.

REFORMS CARRIED OUT

16 Then [A]Jehoiada made a covenant between himself and all the people and the king, that they would be the LORD'S people. 17 And all the people went to the house of Baal and tore it down, and they broke in pieces his altars and his images, and [A]killed Mattan the priest of Baal before the altars. 18 Moreover, Jehoiada placed the offices of the house of the LORD under the [a]authority of [A]the Levitical priests, [B]whom David had assigned over the house of the LORD, to offer the burnt offerings of the LORD, as it is written in the law of Moses—[C]with rejoicing and singing according to the [b]order of David. 19 He stationed [A]the gatekeepers of the house of the LORD, so that no one would enter *who was* in any way unclean. 20 [A]He took the captains of hundreds, the nobles, the rulers of the people and all the people of the land, and brought the king down from the house of the LORD, and came through the upper gate to the king's house. And they placed the king upon the royal throne. 21 So [A]all of the people of the land rejoiced and the city was quiet. For they had put Athaliah to death with the sword.

YOUNG JOASH INFLUENCED BY JEHOIADA

24 [A]Joash *was* seven years old when he became king, and he reigned forty years in Jerusalem; and his mother's name *was* Zibiah from Beersheba. 2 [A]Joash did what was right in the sight of the LORD all the days of Jehoiada the priest. 3 Jehoiada took two wives for him, and he became the father of sons and daughters.

FAITHLESS PRIESTS

4 Now it came about after this that Joash [a]decided [A]to restore the house of the LORD. 5 He gathered the priests and Levites and said to them, "Go out to the cities of Judah and collect money from all [A]Israel to [a]repair the house of your God [b]annually, and you shall do the matter quickly." But the Levites did not act quickly. 6 So the king summoned Jehoiada the chief *priest* and said to him, "Why have you not required the Levites to bring in from Judah and from Jerusalem [A]the levy *fixed by* Moses the servant of the LORD on the congregation of Israel [B]for the tent of the testimony?" 7 For [A]the sons of the wicked Athaliah had broken into the house of God and even [a]used the holy things of the house of the LORD for the Baals.

TEMPLE REPAIRED

8 So the king commanded, and [A]they made a chest and set it outside by the gate of the house of the LORD. 9 [A]They made a proclamation in Judah and Jerusalem to bring to the LORD [B]the levy *fixed by* Moses the servant of God on Israel in the wilderness. 10 All the officers and all the people rejoiced and brought in their levies and [a]dropped *them* into the chest until they had finished. 11 It came about whenever the chest was brought in to the king's officer by the Levites, and when [A]they saw that there was much money, then the king's scribe and the chief priest's officer would come, empty the chest, take it, and return it to its place. Thus they did daily and collected much money. 12 The king and Jehoiada gave it to those who did the work of the service of the house of the LORD; and they hired masons and carpenters to restore the house of the LORD, and also workers in iron and bronze to [a]repair the house of the LORD. 13 So the workmen labored, and the repair work progressed in their hands, and they [a]restored the house of God [b]according to its specifications and strengthened it. 14 When they had finished,

23:8 [A]1 Chr 24:1 23:10 [a]Lit *shoulder* 23:11 [A]Ex 25:16, 21 [B]1 Sam 10:24 23:13 [a]Lit *trumpets* [b]Lit *and leading for praising* 23:14 [a]Lit *from within* 23:15 [a]Lit *placed hands to her* [A]Neh 3:28; Jer 31:40 [B]2 Chr 22:10 23:16 [A]2 Kin 11:17 23:17 [A]Deut 13:6-9; 1 Kin 18:40 23:18 [a]Lit *hand* [b]Lit *hands of* [A]2 Chr 5:5 [B]1 Chr 23:6, 25-31 [C]1 Chr 25:1 23:19 [A]1 Chr 9:22 23:20 [A]2 Kin 11:19 23:21 [A]2 Kin 11:20 24:1 [A]2 Kin 11:21; 12:1-15 24:2 [A]2 Chr 26:4, 5 24:4 [a]Lit *was with a heart* [A]2 Chr 24:7 24:5 [a]Lit *to strengthen* [b]Lit *from year to year* [A]2 Chr 21:2 24:6 [A]Ex 30:12-16 [B]Num 1:50 24:7 [a]Lit *made* [A]2 Chr 21:17 24:8 [A]2 Kin 12:9 24:9 [A]2 Chr 36:22 [B]2 Chr 24:6 24:10 [a]Lit *threw* 24:11 [A]2 Kin 12:10 24:12 [a]Lit *to strengthen* 24:13 [a]Lit *set up* [b]Lit *upon its proportion*

23:11 testimony. The usual meaning is a copy of the law (cf. Dt 17:18; Job 31:35, 36).

24:1–27 The reign of Joash (ca. 835–796 B.C.). Cf. 2Ki 11:17–12:21. Most likely, Joel prophesied during his reign, and his prophecy provides much helpful background to the time.

24:1–14 *See notes on 2Ki 11:17–12:16.*

they brought the rest of the money before the king
and Jehoiada; and it was made into utensils for the
house of the LORD, utensils for the service and the
burnt offering, and pans and utensils of gold and
silver. And they offered burnt offerings in the house
of the LORD continually all the days of Jehoiada.
15 Now when Jehoiada [a]reached a ripe old age he
died; he was one hundred and thirty years old at
his death. 16 They buried him [A]in the city of David
among the kings, because he had done well in [B]Is-
rael and [a]to God and His house.
17 But after the death of Jehoiada the officials of Judah came and bowed down to the king, and the king
listened to them. 18 They abandoned [A]the house of the
LORD, the God of their fathers, and [B]served the [a]Ashe-
rim and the idols; so [C]wrath came upon Judah and
Jerusalem for this their guilt. 19 Yet [A]He sent prophets
to them to bring them back to the LORD; though they
testified against them, they would not listen.

JOASH MURDERS SON OF JEHOIADA

20 [A]Then the Spirit of God [a]came on Zechariah the
son of Jehoiada the priest; and he stood above the
people and said to them, "Thus God has said, '[B]Why
do you transgress the commandments of the LORD
and do not prosper? [C]Because you have forsaken
the LORD, He has also forsaken you.' " 21 So [A]they
conspired against him and at the command of the
king they stoned him [a]to death in the court of the
house of the LORD. 22 Thus Joash the king did not
remember the kindness which his father Jehoiada
had shown him, but he murdered his son. And as
he died he said, "May [A]the LORD see and [a]avenge!"

ARAM INVADES AND DEFEATS JUDAH

23 Now it happened at the turn of the year that
[A]the army of the Arameans came up against him;
and they came to Judah and Jerusalem, destroyed
all the officials of the people from among the people, and sent all their spoil to the king of Damascus.
24 Indeed the army of the Arameans came with a
small number of men; yet [A]the LORD delivered a
very great army into their hands, [B]because they had
forsaken the LORD, the God of their fathers. Thus
they executed judgment on Joash.
25 [A]When they had departed from him (for they
left him very sick), his own servants conspired
against him because of the blood of the [a]son of
Jehoiada the priest, and murdered him on his bed.
So he died, and they buried him in the city of David,
but they did not bury him in the tombs of the kings.
26 Now these are those who conspired against him:
Zabad the son of Shimeath the Ammonitess, and
Jehozabad the son of Shimrith the Moabitess. 27 As
to his sons and the many [a]oracles against him and
[A]the [b]rebuilding of the house of God, behold, they
are written in the [c,B]treatise of the Book of the Kings.
Then Amaziah his son became king in his place.

AMAZIAH SUCCEEDS JOASH IN JUDAH

25 [A]Amaziah was twenty-five years old when
he became king, and he reigned twenty-nine
years in Jerusalem. And his mother's name was
Jehoaddan of Jerusalem. 2 He did right in the sight
of the LORD, [A]yet not with a whole heart. 3 Now [A]it
came about as soon as the kingdom was [a]firmly in
his grasp, that he killed his servants who had slain
his father the king. 4 However, he did not put their
children to death, but *did* as it is written in the law
in the book of Moses, which the LORD commanded,
saying, "[A]Fathers shall not be put to death for sons,
nor sons be put to death for fathers, but each shall
be put to death for his own sin."

AMAZIAH DEFEATS EDOMITES

5 Moreover, Amaziah assembled Judah and appointed them according to *their* fathers' households
under commanders of thousands and commanders
of hundreds throughout Judah and Benjamin; and
he [a]took a census of those [A]from twenty years old
and upward and found them to be [B]300,000 choice
men, *able* to go to war *and* handle spear and shield.

24:15 [a]Lit *became old and satisfied with days* 24:16 [a]Lit *with* [A]2 Chr 21:20 [B]2 Chr 21:2 24:18 [a]I.e. wooden symbols of a female deity [A]2 Chr 24:4 [B]Ex 34:12-14 [C]Josh 22:20 24:19 [A]Jer 7:25 24:20 [a]Lit *clothed* [A]2 Chr 20:14 [B]Num 14:41 [C]2 Chr 15:2 24:21 [a]Lit *with stones* [A]Neh 9:26; Matt 23:34, 35 24:22 [a]Lit *seek*, or *require* [A]Gen 9:5 24:23 [A]2 Kin 12:17 24:24 [A]2 Chr 16:7, 8 [B]2 Chr 24:20 24:25 [a]So some ancient versions; Heb *sons* [A]2 Kin 12:20, 21 24:27 [a]Or *burdens upon* [b]Lit *founding* [c]Heb *midrash* [A]2 Chr 24:12 [B]2 Chr 13:22 25:1 [A]2 Kin 14:1-6 25:2 [A]2 Chr 25:14 25:3 [a]Lit *firm upon him* [A]2 Kin 14:5 25:4 [A]Deut 24:16 25:5 [a]Lit *mustered* [A]Num 1:3 [B]2 Chr 26:13

24:15, 16 Jehoiada. This man was the High Priest of Athaliah's and Joash's reigns (cf. 2Ch 23:1–24:16), who championed God's cause of righteousness during days of evil by: 1) leading the fight against idols; 2) permitting the coup against Athaliah; and 3) granting the throne to Joash to bring about the subsequent revival.

24:17, 18a After Jehoiada's death, the leaders of Judah convinced King Joash that they needed to return to idolatry. With the death of the old priest came the turning point in the reign of Joash. He "listened" means Joash gave consent for the idol worship, and thus it began.

24:18b, 19 God's righteousness judged the evil of Judah, while at the same time His mercy sent prophets to preach the truth of repentance.

24:20–22 The specific example of Zechariah, son of Jehoiada (not to be confused with Zechariah, son of Berechiah [Zec 1:1; Mt 23:35]) is alluded to by NT writers in such texts as Ac 7:51, 52; Heb 11:37. This priest told the people that faithfulness to the Lord is the condition for blessing (cf. 12:5; 15:2). The conspiracy against this man who spoke the truth was with the king's full authority, and he bore the greatest guilt for the murder (v. 22). *See note on Mt 23:35.*

24:22 did not remember. Cf. 22:11, where Jehoiada's wife preserved Joash from certain death as an infant, or 2Ch 23:1–24:1, where Jehoiada devised a plan to dethrone Athaliah and crown Joash king, or 2Ch 24:2, where Jehoiada is acknowledged as the voice of righteousness for Joash. Yet, Joash willfully ignored all that. Zechariah died pronouncing the just doom that would eventually come.

24:23–25 As Zechariah had prayed (24:22), so God repaid Joash's apostasy with defeat by Syria and death at the hands of his own people.

24:24 small number. As the Lord had previously given victory to Judah's smaller army because of their faithfulness (2Ch 13:2–20; 14:9–15), He gave Judah defeat at the hands of a lesser force because of their wickedness.

24:25 Unlike righteous Asa (2Ch 16:13, 14), but like unrighteous Jehoram (2Ch 21:18–20), Joash died an ignominious death and received burial without honor.

24:26, 27 *See notes on 2Ki 12:19–21.*

25:1–28 The reign of Amaziah (ca. 796–767 B.C.). Cf. 2Ki 14:1–20.

25:1–4 *See notes on 2Ki 14:1–6.*

25:4 Cf. Eze 18.

25:5–16 This section is an elaboration of 2Ki 14:7.

25:5–13 Amaziah gathered his army, which was small compared to the army of Jehoshaphat, which was over 1,000,000 (cf. 17:14–19). This shows how the southern kingdom had declined in 80 years.

6 He hired also 100,000 valiant warriors out of Israel
for one hundred talents of silver. 7 But [A]a man of God
came to him saying, "O king, do not let the army of
Israel go with you, for the LORD is not with Israel
nor with any of the sons of Ephraim. 8 But if you do
go, do *it,* be strong for the battle; *yet* God will [a]bring
you down before the enemy, [A]for God has power to
help and to [a]bring down." 9 Amaziah said to the man
of God, "But what *shall we* do for the hundred talents
which I have given to the troops of Israel?" And the
man of God answered, "[A]The LORD has much more
to give you than this." 10 Then Amaziah [a]dismissed
them, the troops which came to him from Ephraim,
to go home; so their anger burned against Judah
and they returned [b]home in fierce anger.

11 Now Amaziah strengthened himself and led
his people forth, and went to [A]the Valley of Salt and
struck down 10,000 of the sons of Seir. 12 The sons of
Judah also captured 10,000 alive and brought them
to the top of the cliff and threw them down from
the top of the cliff, so that they were all dashed to
pieces. 13 But the [a]troops whom Amaziah sent back
from going with him to battle, raided the cities
of Judah, from Samaria to Beth-horon, and struck
down 3,000 of them and plundered much spoil.

AMAZIAH REBUKED FOR IDOLATRY

14 Now after Amaziah came from slaughtering the
Edomites, [A]he brought the gods of the sons of Seir,
set them up as his gods, bowed down before them
and burned incense to them. 15 Then the anger of the
LORD burned against Amaziah, and He sent him a
prophet who said to him, "Why have you sought the
gods of the people [A]who have not delivered their own
people from your hand?" 16 As he was talking with
him, [a]the king said to him, "Have we appointed you
a royal counselor? Stop! Why should you be struck
down?" Then the prophet stopped and said, "I know
that God has planned to destroy you, because you
have done this and have not listened to my counsel."

AMAZIAH DEFEATED BY JOASH OF ISRAEL

17 [A]Then Amaziah king of Judah took counsel and
sent to Joash the son of Jehoahaz the son of Jehu,
the king of Israel, saying, "Come, let us face each
other." 18 Joash the king of Israel sent to Amaziah
king of Judah, saying, "[A]The thorn bush which was
in Lebanon sent to the cedar which was in Lebanon,
saying, 'Give your daughter to my son in marriage.'
But there passed by a wild beast that was in Lebanon
and trampled the thorn bush. 19 You said, 'Behold,
you have [a]defeated Edom.' And [A]your heart has
[b]become proud in boasting. Now stay at home; for
why should you provoke trouble so that you, even
you, would fall and Judah with you?"

20 But Amaziah would not listen, for it was from
God, that He might deliver them into the hand *of Joash*
because they had sought the gods of Edom. 21 So Joash
king of Israel went up, and he and Amaziah king of
Judah faced each other at Beth-shemesh, which belonged to Judah. 22 Judah was defeated [a]by Israel, and
they fled each to his tent. 23 Then Joash king of Israel
captured Amaziah king of Judah, the son of Joash the
son of [A]Jehoahaz, at Beth-shemesh, and brought him
to Jerusalem and tore down the wall of Jerusalem
from the Gate of Ephraim to the Corner Gate, 400
[a]cubits. 24 *He took* all the gold and silver and all the
utensils which were found in the house of God with
[A]Obed-edom, and the treasures of the king's house,
the hostages also, and returned to Samaria.

25 [A]And Amaziah, the son of Joash king of Judah,
lived fifteen years after the death of Joash, son of
Jehoahaz, king of Israel. 26 Now the rest of the acts
of Amaziah, from first to last, behold, are they not
written in the Book of the Kings of Judah and Israel?
27 From the time that Amaziah turned away from
following the LORD they conspired against him in
Jerusalem, and he fled to Lachish; but they sent
after him to Lachish and killed him there. 28 Then
they brought him on horses and buried him with
his fathers in the city of Judah.

UZZIAH SUCCEEDS AMAZIAH IN JUDAH

26 And all the people of Judah took [a]Uzziah, who
was sixteen years old, and made him king
in the place of his father Amaziah. 2 He built Eloth
and restored it to Judah after the king slept with
his fathers. 3 Uzziah was [A]sixteen years old when
he became king, and he reigned fifty-two years in
Jerusalem; and his mother's name was [a]Jechiliah

25:7 [A]2 Kin 4:9 25:8 [a]Lit *cause to stumble* [A]2 Chr 14:11; 20:6 25:9 [A]Deut 8:18; Prov 10:22 25:10 [a]Lit *separated* [b]Lit *to their own place* 25:11 [A]2 Kin 14:7 25:13 [a]Lit *sons of the troops* 25:14 [A]2 Chr 28:23 25:15 [A]2 Chr 25:11, 12 25:16 [a]Lit *he* 25:17 [A]2 Kin 14:8-14 25:18 [A]Judg 9:8-15 25:19 [a]Lit *smitten* [b]Lit *lifted you up to boast* [A]2 Chr 26:16; 32:25 25:22 [a]Lit *before* 25:23 [a]I.e. One cubit equals approx 18 in. [A]2 Chr 21:17; 22:1 25:24 [A]1 Chr 26:15 25:25 [A]2 Kin 14:17-22 26:1 [a]In 2 Kin 14:21, *Azariah* 26:3 [a]In 2 Kin 15:2, *Jecoliah* [A]2 Kin 15:2, 3

25:6 one hundred talents. If a talent weighs 75 lbs., this represents almost 4 tons of silver. This wealth was paid to the king of Israel, Jehoahaz, who ordered the mercenaries of Israel to aid Amaziah against Edom.

25:7 man of God. This is a technical term used about 70 times in the OT, always referring to one who spoke for God. He warned Amaziah not to make idolatrous Israel his ally because the Lord was not with Ephraim, i.e., Israel, the capital of idolatry. *See note on Dt 33:1.*

25:8 God has power. *See note on 2Ch 24:24.* The man of God reminded the king sarcastically that he would need to be strong, since God wouldn't help.

25:9, 10 The man of God told Amaziah to cut his losses and trust the Lord. The king obeyed and sent the Israelite mercenaries home in anger.

25:11 Valley of Salt. Most likely this is located at the southern end of the Dead Sea, where David had several centuries before been victorious (cf. 1Ch 18:12, 13). **Seir.** Another name for Edom.

25:12 cliff. This mode of execution was common among pagan nations (cf. Ps 137:9).

25:13 Samaria. This was the well-known town of Israel from which they launched their attacks. **Beth-horon.** *See note on 2Ch 8:5.*

25:14–16 Amaziah did the unthinkable from both a biblical and political perspective—he embraced the false gods of the people whom he had just defeated. Perhaps he did this because he was seduced by the wicked pleasures of idolatry and because he thought it would help him in assuring no future threat from Edom. However, it only brought destruction to the king, who just wanted to silence the voice of God.

25:17–28 *See notes on 2Ki 14:8–19.*

26:1–23 The reign of Uzziah, a.k.a. Azariah (ca. 790–739 B.C.). Cf. 2Ki 14:21, 22; 15:1–7. Hosea (Hos 1:1), Amos (Am 1:1), Jonah, and Isaiah (Is 6) ministered during his reign.

26:1–4 *See notes on 2Ki 14:21, 22; 15:1–4.*

of Jerusalem. 4 He did right in the sight of the LORD
according to all that his father Amaziah had done.
5 [A]He continued to seek God in the days of Zechariah, [B]who had understanding [a]through the vision
of God; and [b,C]as long as he sought the LORD, God
prospered him.

UZZIAH SUCCEEDS IN WAR

6 Now he went out and [A]warred against the Philistines, and broke down the wall of Gath and the
wall of Jabneh and the wall of Ashdod; and he built
cities in *the area of* Ashdod and among the Philistines. 7 [A]God helped him against the Philistines, and
against the Arabians who lived in Gur-baal, and the
Meunites. 8 The Ammonites also gave [A]tribute to Uzziah, and his [a]fame extended to the border of Egypt,
for he became very strong. 9 Moreover, Uzziah built
towers in Jerusalem at [A]the Corner Gate and at the
[B]Valley Gate and at the corner buttress and fortified
them. 10 He built towers in the wilderness and [A]hewed
many cisterns, for he had much livestock, both in the
[a]lowland and in the plain. *He also had* plowmen and
vinedressers in the hill country and the fertile fields,
for he loved the soil. 11 Moreover, Uzziah had an army
ready for battle, which [a]entered combat by divisions
according to the number of their muster, [b]prepared
by Jeiel the scribe and Maaseiah the official, under
the direction of Hananiah, one of the king's officers.
12 The total number of the heads of the [a]households,
of valiant warriors, was 2,600. 13 Under their direction
was an [a]elite army of [A]307,500, who could wage war
with great power, to help the king against the enemy.
14 Moreover, Uzziah prepared [a]for all the army shields,
spears, helmets, body armor, bows and sling stones.
15 In Jerusalem he made engines *of war* invented by
skillful men to be on the towers and on the corners
for the purpose of shooting arrows and great stones.
Hence his [a]fame spread afar, for he was marvelously
helped until he *was* strong.

PRIDE IS UZZIAH'S UNDOING

16 But [A]when he became strong, his heart was so
[a]proud that he acted corruptly, and he was unfaithful
to the LORD his God, for [B]he entered the temple of
the LORD to burn incense on the altar of incense.
17 Then [A]Azariah the priest entered after him and
with him eighty priests of the LORD, valiant men.
18 [A]They opposed Uzziah the king and said to him,
"[B]It is not for you, Uzziah, to burn incense to the
LORD, [C]but for the priests, the sons of Aaron who
are consecrated to burn incense. Get out of the
sanctuary, for you have been unfaithful and will
have no honor from the LORD God." 19 But Uzziah,
with a censer in his hand for burning incense,
was enraged; and while he was enraged with the
priests, [A]the leprosy broke out on his forehead before the priests in the house of the LORD, beside
the altar of incense. 20 Azariah the chief priest and
all the priests looked at him, and behold, he *was*
leprous on his forehead; and they hurried him out
of there, and he himself also hastened to get out
because the LORD had smitten him. 21 [A]King Uzziah
was a leper to the day of his death; and he lived in
[B]a separate house, being a leper, for he was cut off
from the house of the LORD. And Jotham his son
was over the king's house judging the people of
the land.

22 Now the rest of the acts of Uzziah, first to last,
the prophet [A]Isaiah, the son of Amoz, has written.
23 So Uzziah slept with his fathers, and they buried
him with his fathers [A]in the field of the grave which
belonged to the kings, for they said, "He is a leper."
And Jotham his son became king in his place.

JOTHAM SUCCEEDS UZZIAH IN JUDAH

27 [A]Jotham was twenty-five years old when he
became king, and he reigned sixteen years
in Jerusalem. And his mother's name was Jerushah
the daughter of Zadok. 2 He did right in the sight of
the LORD, according to all that his father Uzziah had
done; [A]however he did not enter the temple of the
LORD. But the people continued acting corruptly.
3 He built the upper gate of the house of the LORD,
and he built extensively the wall of [A]Ophel. 4 Moreover, he built [A]cities in the hill country of Judah, and
he built fortresses and towers on the wooded *hills*.

26:5 [a]Many mss read *in the fear of God* [b]Lit *in the days of his seeking* [A]2 Chr 24:2 [B]Dan 1:17 [C]2 Chr 15:2 26:6 [A]Is 14:29 26:7 [A]2 Chr 21:16 26:8 [a]Lit *name went to the entering of Egypt* [A]2 Chr 17:11 26:9 [A]2 Chr 25:23 [B]Neh 2:13, 15; 3:13 26:10 [a]Heb *shephelah* [A]Gen 26:18-21 26:11 [a]Lit *goes out to* [b]Lit *by the hand of* 26:12 [a]Lit *fathers* 26:13 [a]Lit *powerful* [A]2 Chr 25:5 26:14 [a]Lit *for them, for all* 26:15 [a]Lit *name* 26:16 [a]Lit *lifted up* [A]Deut 32:15; 2 Chr 25:19 [B]1 Kin 13:1-4 26:17 [A]1 Chr 6:10 26:18 [A]2 Chr 19:2 [B]Num 3:10; 16:39, 40 [C]Ex 30:7, 8 26:19 [A]2 Kin 5:25-27 26:21 [A]2 Kin 15:5-7 [B]Lev 13:46 26:22 [A]Is 1:1 26:23 [A]2 Chr 21:20; 28:27; Is 6:1 27:1 [A]2 Kin 15:33-35 27:2 [A]2 Chr 26:16 27:3 [A]2 Chr 33:14; Neh 3:26 27:4 [A]2 Chr 11:5

26:5 Zechariah. An otherwise unknown prophet during Uzziah's reign, not the priestly spokesman of 24:20, nor the prophet Zechariah who wrote the prophetic book to Judah ca. 520 B.C. **sought ... prospered.** This summarizes a major theme in 2 Chronicles.

26:6–15 A summary of Uzziah's prosperity in the realm of: 1) conquering the Philistines (26:6–8); 2) domestic affairs (26:9, 10); and 3) military might (26:11–15).

26:6–8 A description of Judah's military success to the W, E, and S. Israel to the N is not mentioned.

26:6 Gath ... Jabneh ... Ashdod. Key Philistine cities to the SW of Jerusalem.

26:7 Arabians ... Gur-baal. Most likely a nomadic group who lived in an area whose location is unknown. **Meunites.** A nomadic people living in Edom (cf. 2Ch 20:1).

26:8 Ammonites. Offspring of Lot who lived E of the Jordan.

26:9 Corner Gate. Located in the NW section of Jerusalem. **Valley Gate.** Located in the SW section of Jerusalem. **corner buttress.** Located in the E section of Jerusalem.

26:11–15 With over 300,000 in the army and the development of new weapons, he posed a threat to would-be assailants and thus secured the nation in peace.

26:16–18 Uzziah attempted to usurp the role of the priest, which is forbidden in the Levitical code (cf. Nu 3:10; 18:7). Proverbs 16:18 indicates that pride precipitates a fall, and it did in his case. Even the king could not live above God's law.

26:19, 20 God judged the king's refusal to heed the law but was merciful in that He did not kill Uzziah. With leprosy, Uzziah had to submit to the priests in a new way according to the laws of leprosy (cf. Lv 13, 14), and endure isolation the rest of his life from the temple as well.

26:21–23 *See notes on 2Ki 15:5.*

26:22 Not the canonical book of Isaiah, but rather a reference to some other volume that the prophet wrote.

26:23 It was in that very year that Isaiah had his vision of God's glory (cf. Is 6:1ff.).

27:1–9 The reign of Jotham (ca. 750–731 B.C.). Cf. 2Ki 15:32–38. Isaiah (Is 1:1) and Hosea (Hos 1:1) continued to minister during his reign, plus Micah (Mic 1:1) prophesied during that time also.

27:1–4, 7–9 *See notes on 2Ki 15:33–37.*

27:3 wall of Ophel. Located on the S side of Jerusalem.

5 He fought also with the king of the Ammonites and
prevailed over them so that the Ammonites gave
him during that year one hundred talents of silver,
ten thousand [a]kors of wheat and ten thousand of
barley. The Ammonites also paid him this *amount*
in the second and in the third year. 6 [A]So Jotham
became mighty because he ordered his ways before the LORD his God. 7 [A]Now the rest of the acts
of Jotham, even all his wars and his acts, behold,
they are written in the Book of the Kings of Israel
and Judah. 8 He was [A]twenty-five years old when
he became king, and he reigned sixteen years in
Jerusalem. 9 And Jotham slept with his fathers, and
they buried him in the city of David; and Ahaz his
son became king in his place.

AHAZ SUCCEEDS JOTHAM IN JUDAH

28 [A]Ahaz *was* twenty years old when he became king, and he reigned sixteen years in
Jerusalem; and [B]he did not do right in the sight of
the LORD as David his father *had done.* 2 [A]But he
walked in the ways of the kings of Israel; he also
[B]made molten images for the Baals. 3 Moreover, [A]he
burned incense in the valley of Ben-hinnom and
[B]burned his sons in fire, [C]according to the abominations of the nations whom the LORD had driven
out before the sons of Israel. 4 He sacrificed and
[A]burned incense on the high places, on the hills
and under every green tree.

JUDAH IS INVADED

5 Wherefore, [A]the LORD his God delivered him into
the hand of the king of Aram; and they [a]defeated
him and carried away from him a great number of
captives and brought *them* to Damascus. And he
was also delivered into the hand of the king of Israel, who [b]inflicted him with heavy casualties. 6 For
[A]Pekah the son of Remaliah slew in Judah 120,000
in one day, all valiant men, because they had forsaken the LORD God of their fathers. 7 And Zichri, a
mighty man of Ephraim, slew Maaseiah the king's
son and Azrikam the ruler of the house and Elkanah
the second to the king.
8 [A]The sons of Israel carried away captive of [B]their
brethren 200,000 women, sons and daughters; and
they [a]took also a great deal of spoil from them, and
brought the spoil to Samaria. 9 But a prophet of the
LORD was there, whose name *was* Oded; and [A]he
went out to meet the army which came to Samaria
and said to them, "Behold, because the LORD, the
God of your fathers, [B]was angry with Judah, He has
delivered them into your hand, and you have slain
them in a rage [C]*which* has even reached heaven.
10 Now you are proposing to [A]subjugate for yourselves the people of Judah and Jerusalem for male
and female slaves. Surely, *do* you not *have* transgressions of your own against the LORD your God?
11 Now therefore, listen to me and return the captives
[A]whom you captured from your brothers, [B]for the
burning anger of the LORD is against you." 12 Then
some of the heads of the sons of Ephraim—Azariah
the son of Johanan, Berechiah the son of Meshillemoth, Jehizkiah the son of Shallum, and Amasa
the son of Hadlai—arose against those who were
coming from the battle, 13 and said to them, "You
must not bring the captives in here, for you are
proposing *to bring* upon us guilt against the LORD
adding to our sins and our guilt; for our guilt is great
so that *His* burning anger is against Israel." 14 So the
armed men left the captives and the spoil before the
officers and all the assembly. 15 Then [A]the men who
were designated by name arose, took the captives,
and they clothed all their naked ones from the spoil;
and they gave them clothes and sandals, fed them
and [B]gave them drink, anointed them *with oil,* led
all their feeble ones on donkeys, and brought them
to Jericho, [C]the city of palm trees, to their brothers;
then they returned to Samaria.

COMPROMISE WITH ASSYRIA

16 [A]At that time King Ahaz sent to the [a]kings of
Assyria for help. 17 [A]For again the Edomites had
come and attacked Judah and carried away captives.
18 [A]The Philistines also had invaded the cities of the
[a]lowland and of the Negev of Judah, and had taken
Beth-shemesh, Aijalon, Gederoth, and Soco with
its villages, Timnah with its villages, and Gimzo
with its villages, and they settled there. 19 For the
LORD humbled Judah because of Ahaz king of [A]Is-
rael, for he had brought about a lack of restraint

27:5 [a]I.e. One kor equals approx 10 bu 27:6 [A]2 Chr 26:5 27:7 [A]2 Kin 15:36 27:8 [A]2 Chr 27:1 28:1 [A]2 Kin 16:2-4 [B]2 Chr 27:2 28:2 [A]2 Chr 22:3 [B]Ex 34:17 28:3 [A]Josh 15:8 [B]Lev 18:21; 2 Chr 33:6 [C]2 Chr 33:2 28:4 [A]2 Chr 28:25 28:5 [a]Lit *smote* [b]Lit *smote him with a great smiting* [A]2 Kin 16:5; 2 Chr 24:24; Is 7:1 28:6 [A]2 Kin 16:5 28:8 [a]Lit *plundered* [A]Deut 28:25, 41 [B]2 Chr 11:4 28:9 [A]2 Chr 25:15 [B]Is 47:6 [C]Ezra 9:6; Rev 18:5 28:10 [A]Lev 25:39 28:11 [A]2 Chr 28:8 [B]James 2:13 28:15 [A]2 Chr 28:12 [B]2 Kin 6:22; Prov 25:21, 22 [C]Deut 34:3 28:16 [a]Ancient versions read *king* [A]2 Kin 16:7 28:17 [A]Obad 10, 14 28:18 [a]Heb *shephelah* [A]Ezek 16:57 28:19 [A]2 Chr 21:2

27:5 Ammonites. *See note on 2Ch 26:8.* Jotham repelled the invasion, pursuing the enemy into their own land and imposing a yearly tribute, which they paid for two years until Rezin, king of Syria, and Pekah, king of Israel, revolted and attacked. Jotham was too distracted to bother with the Ammonites (cf. 2Ki 15:37). one hundred talents. If a talent is about 75 lbs., this represents almost 4 tons of silver. ten thousand kors. If a kor is 7.5 bu., this represents 75,000 bu.

27:6 His one failure was in not removing the idolatrous high places and stopping idol worship by the people (cf. v. 2; 2Ki 15:35).

28:1–27 The reign of Ahaz (ca. 735–715 B.C.). Cf. 2Ki 16:1–20. Isaiah (Is 1:1), Hosea (Hos 1:1), and Micah (Mic 1:1) all continued to minister during his reign. Second Kings 17:1–9 reports that it was after the 12th year of Ahaz, when Hosea was king in Israel, that the Assyrians took Israel into captivity (722 B.C.).

28:1–5a *See notes on 2Ki 16:1–6.*

28:2 Baals. *See note on 17:3.*

28:5b-8 Ahaz's gross disobedience earned him God's wrath, by which both Aram, or Syria, and Israel defeated his army, as they had in Jotham's day (cf. 2Ki 15:37). This was likely a continuation of the same campaign against Judah begun earlier.

28:5, 6 Damascus. The capital city of Aram, or Syria, NE of Judah. Pekah. King of Israel (ca. 752–732 B.C.).

28:8 Samaria. The capital city of the northern kingdom of Israel.

28:9 Oded. An otherwise unknown prophet, with the same name as an earlier Oded (cf. 15:1, 8). The prophet said that Israel had won the victory because God was judging Judah. But he protested the viciousness of the killing and the effort to enslave them (v. 10) and warned them of God's wrath for such action (v. 11). Amazingly the apostate and hostile Israelites complied with the prophet's warning (vv. 12–15).

28:16 kings of Assyria. Most likely sing. "king," as per marginal note, who was Tilgath-pilneser, or Tiglath-pileser (ca. 745–727 B.C.).

28:18 cities … lowland. To the SW of Jerusalem.

in Judah and was very unfaithful to the LORD. 20 So
[A]Tilgath-pilneser king of Assyria came against him
and afflicted him instead of strengthening him.
21 [A]Although Ahaz took a portion out of the house
of the LORD and out of the palace of the king and
of the princes, and gave *it* to the king of Assyria, it
did not help him.

22 Now in the time of his distress this same King
Ahaz [A]became yet more unfaithful to the LORD.
23 [A]For he sacrificed to the gods of Damascus which
had [a]defeated him, and said, "[B]Because the gods of
the kings of Aram helped them, I will sacrifice to
them that they may help me." But they became the
[b]downfall of him and all Israel. 24 Moreover, when
Ahaz gathered together the utensils of the house
of God, he [A]cut the utensils of the house of God in
pieces; and he [B]closed the doors of the house of the
LORD and [C]made altars for himself in every corner
of Jerusalem. 25 In every city of Judah he made high
places to burn incense to other gods, and provoked
the LORD, the God of his fathers, to anger. 26 [A]Now
the rest of his acts and all his ways, from first to last,
behold, they are written in the Book of the Kings of
Judah and Israel. 27 [A]So Ahaz slept with his fathers,
and they buried him in the city, in Jerusalem, for
they did not bring him into the tombs of the kings
of [B]Israel; and Hezekiah his son reigned in his place.

HEZEKIAH SUCCEEDS AHAZ IN JUDAH

29 [A]Hezekiah became king *when he was* twenty-five years old; and he reigned twenty-nine
years in Jerusalem. And his mother's name *was*
Abijah, the daughter of Zechariah. 2 [A]He did right
in the sight of the LORD, according to all that his
father David had done.

3 In the first year of his reign, in the first month,
he [A]opened the doors of the house of the LORD and
repaired them. 4 He brought in the priests and the
Levites and gathered them into the square on the
east.

REFORMS BEGUN

5 Then he said to them, "Listen to me, O Levites.
[A]Consecrate yourselves now, and consecrate the
house of the LORD, the God of your fathers, and
carry the uncleanness out from the holy place. 6 For
our fathers have been unfaithful and have done
evil in the sight of the LORD our God, and have
forsaken Him and [A]turned their faces away from
the dwelling place of the LORD, and have [a]turned
their backs. 7 They have also [A]shut the doors of the
porch and put out the lamps, and have not burned
incense or offered burnt offerings in the holy place
to the God of Israel. 8 Therefore [A]the wrath of the
LORD was against Judah and Jerusalem, and He
has made them an object of terror, of horror, and
of [B]hissing, as you see with your own eyes. 9 For
behold, [A]our fathers have fallen by the sword, and
our sons and our daughters and our wives are in
captivity for this. 10 Now it is in my heart [A]to make
a covenant with the LORD God of Israel, that His
burning anger may turn away from us. 11 My sons,
do not be negligent now, for [A]the LORD has chosen
you to stand before Him, to minister to Him, and
to be His ministers and burn incense."

12 Then the Levites arose: [A]Mahath, the son of
Amasai and Joel the son of Azariah, from the sons
of [B]the Kohathites; and from the sons of Merari, Kish
the son of Abdi and Azariah the son of Jehallelel; and
from the Gershonites, Joah the son of Zimmah and
Eden the son of Joah; 13 and from the sons of Elizaphan, Shimri and [a]Jeiel; and from the sons of Asaph,
Zechariah and Mattaniah; 14 and from the sons of
Heman, [a]Jehiel and Shimei; and from the sons of
Jeduthun, Shemaiah and Uzziel. 15 They assembled
their brothers, [A]consecrated themselves, and went
in [B]to cleanse the house of the LORD, according to
the commandment of the king [C]by the words of the
LORD. 16 So the priests went in to the inner part of
the house of the LORD to cleanse *it,* and every unclean thing which they found in the temple of the
LORD they brought out to the court of the house
of the LORD. Then the Levites received *it* to carry
out to [A]the Kidron [a]valley. 17 Now they began [a]the
consecration [A]on the first *day* of the first month,
and on the eighth day of the month they entered
the porch of the LORD. Then they consecrated the
house of the LORD in eight days, and finished on the
sixteenth day of the first month. 18 Then they went
in to King Hezekiah and said, "We have cleansed
the whole house of the LORD, the altar of burnt
offering with all of its utensils, and the table of

28:20 [A]1 Chr 5:26 28:21 [A]2 Kin 16:8, 9 28:22 [A]Is 1:5; Jer 5:3; Rev 16:11 28:23 [a]Lit *smitten* [b]Lit *stumbling* [A]2 Chr 25:14 [B]Jer 44:17, 18 28:24 [A]2 Kin 16:17 [B]2 Chr 29:7 [C]2 Chr 30:14; 33:3-5 28:26 [A]2 Kin 16:19, 20 28:27 [A]2 Kin 16:20; 2 Chr 24:25; Is 14:28 [B]2 Chr 21:2 29:1 [A]2 Kin 18:1-3 29:2 [A]2 Chr 28:1; 34:2 29:3 [A]2 Chr 28:24; 29:7 29:5 [A]2 Chr 29:15, 34; 35:6 29:6 [a]Lit *given* [A]Ezek 8:16 29:7 [A]2 Chr 28:24 29:8 [A]2 Chr 24:20 [B]Jer 25:9, 18 29:9 [A]2 Chr 28:5-8, 17 29:10 [A]2 Chr 23:16 29:11 [A]Num 3:6; 8:6 29:12 [A]2 Chr 31:13 [B]Num 3:19, 20 29:13 [a]Or *Jeuel* 29:14 [a]Or *Jehuel,* 1 Chr 15:18, 20 29:15 [A]2 Chr 29:5 [B]1 Chr 23:28 [C]2 Chr 30:12 29:16 [a]Or *wadi* [A]2 Chr 15:16 29:17 [a]Lit *to consecrate* [A]2 Chr 29:3

28:20, 21 Tilgath-pilneser. *See note on 2Ch 28:16.* In spite of temporary relief by the conquest of Damascus and slaughter of Rezin (2Ki 16:9), little benefit came from this king to Ahaz because he allied with Assyria.

28:22–27 Ahaz surrendered himself to idolatry with the ignorance of a wicked pagan and a ruthless defiance of God that ruined him and his nation. He was justly dishonored in his burial (v. 27).

29:1–32:33 The reign of Hezekiah (ca. 715–686 B.C.). Cf. 2Ki 18:1–20:21; Is 36–39. Second Kings 18:5 notes that Hezekiah's trust in the Lord had not been equaled by any king who preceded him nor by any who followed (cf. 2Ch 31:21). Isaiah (Is 1:1), Hosea (Hos 1:1), and Micah (Mic 1:1) prophesied during his reign.

29:1, 2 *See notes on 2Ki 18:1, 2.*

29:3 first year … first month. Hezekiah addressed the spiritual problems first, which reflected his life priorities. Hezekiah correctly diagnosed Judah's ills—she had abandoned the true worship of God. So the king stepped in to reverse the policy of his father (28:22–25) and to repair the temple and return proper temple worship as God had prescribed in His Word (vv. 3–7). He knew such a revival of devotion to God would turn God's wrath away from Judah (v. 10).

29:12–14 Fourteen leaders undertook to collect and prepare for the cleansing of the temple.

29:12 Kohathites … Merari … Gershonites. The 3 familial lines of Levi (cf. 1Ch 6:1).

29:13, 14 Elizaphan. An important leader among the Kohathites (cf. Nu 3:30; 1Ch 15:8). Asaph … Heman … Jeduthun. The 3 lines of Levitical musicians (cf. 1Ch 25:1).

29:15–19 to cleanse. Beginning with the outer courts and working for 8 days, they then went inside. But as the Levites were not allowed within the walls of the holy places, the priests had to bring out all the debris to be carted off. This took 8 more days.

29:16 Kidron valley. To the E of Jerusalem, between the temple and the Mt. of Olives.

showbread with all of its utensils. 19 Moreover, [A]all
the utensils which King Ahaz had discarded during
his reign in his unfaithfulness, we have prepared
and consecrated; and behold, they are before the
altar of the LORD."

HEZEKIAH RESTORES TEMPLE WORSHIP

20 Then King Hezekiah arose early and assembled
the princes of the city and went up to the house of
the LORD. 21 They brought seven bulls, seven rams,
seven lambs and seven male goats [A]for a sin offering
for the kingdom, the sanctuary, and Judah. And he
ordered the priests, the sons of Aaron, to offer *them*
on the altar of the LORD. 22 So they slaughtered the
bulls, and the priests took the blood and sprinkled
it on the altar. They also slaughtered the rams and
sprinkled the blood on the altar; they slaughtered
the lambs also and [A]sprinkled the blood on the altar. 23 Then they brought the male goats of the sin
offering before the king and the assembly, and [A]they
laid their hands on them. 24 The priests slaughtered
them and purged the altar with their blood [A]to atone
for all Israel, for the king ordered the burnt offering
and the sin offering for all Israel.
25 [A]He then stationed the Levites in the house of
the LORD with cymbals, with harps and with lyres,
[B]according to the command of David and of [C]Gad
the king's seer, and of [D]Nathan the prophet; for the
command was from the LORD through His prophets.
26 The Levites stood with [A]the *musical* instruments
of David, and [B]the priests with the trumpets. 27 Then
Hezekiah gave the order to offer the burnt offering
on the altar. When the burnt offering began, [A]the
song to the LORD also began with the trumpets,
[a]*accompanied* by the instruments of David, king
of Israel. 28 While the whole assembly worshiped,
the singers also sang and the trumpets sounded; all
this *continued* until the burnt offering was finished.
29 Now at the completion of the burnt offerings,
[A]the king and all who were present with him bowed
down and worshiped. 30 Moreover, King Hezekiah
and the officials ordered the Levites to sing praises
to the LORD with the words of David and Asaph
the seer. [A]So they sang praises with joy, and bowed
down and worshiped.
31 Then Hezekiah said, "[A]Now *that* you have [a]con-
secrated yourselves to the LORD, come near and
bring sacrifices and thank offerings to the house
of the LORD." And the assembly brought sacrifices
and thank offerings, and [B]all those who were [b]will-
ing *brought* burnt offerings. 32 The number of the
burnt offerings which the assembly brought was
70 bulls, 100 rams, and 200 lambs; all these were
for a burnt offering to the LORD. 33 The consecrated
things were 600 bulls and 3,000 sheep. 34 But the
priests were too few, so that they were unable to skin
all the burnt offerings; [A]therefore their brothers the
Levites helped them until the work was completed
and until the *other* priests had consecrated themselves. For [B]the Levites were more [a]conscientious
to consecrate themselves than the priests. 35 There
were also [a,A]many burnt offerings with [B]the fat of the
peace offerings and with [C]the libations for the burnt
offerings. Thus the service of the house of the LORD
was established *again*. 36 Then Hezekiah and all the
people rejoiced over what God had prepared for the
people, because the thing came about suddenly.

ALL ISRAEL INVITED TO THE PASSOVER

30 Now Hezekiah sent to all Israel and Judah
and wrote letters also to Ephraim and Manasseh, that they should come to the house of the
LORD at Jerusalem to [a]celebrate the Passover to the
LORD God of Israel. 2 For the king and his princes
and all the assembly in Jerusalem had decided [A]to
celebrate the Passover in the second month, 3 since
they could not celebrate it [A]at that time, because the
priests had not consecrated themselves in sufficient
numbers, nor had the people been gathered to Jerusalem. 4 Thus the thing was right in the sight of the
king and [a]all the assembly. 5 So they established a
decree to circulate a [a]proclamation throughout all
Israel [A]from Beersheba even to Dan, that they should
come to celebrate the Passover to the LORD God of
Israel at Jerusalem. For they had not celebrated *it*
in great numbers as it was [b]prescribed. 6 [A]The [a]cou-
riers went throughout all Israel and Judah with the
letters from the hand of the king and his princes,
even according to the command of the king, saying, "O sons of Israel, return to the LORD God of

29:19 [A]2 Chr 28:24 29:21 [A]Lev 4:3-14 29:22 [A]Lev 4:18 29:23 [A]Lev 4:15 29:24 [A]Lev 4:26 29:25 [A]1 Chr 25:6 [B]2 Chr 8:14 [C]2 Sam 24:11 [D]2 Sam 7:2 29:26 [A]1 Chr 23:5 [B]2 Chr 5:12 29:27 [a]Lit *and according to the authority of the instruments* [A]2 Chr 23:18 29:29 [A]2 Chr 20:18 29:30 [A]Ps 100:1; 106:12 29:31 [a]Lit *filled your hands* [b]Lit *willing of heart* [A]2 Chr 13:9 [B]Ex 35:5, 22 29:34 [a]Lit *upright of heart* [A]2 Chr 35:11 [B]2 Chr 30:3 29:35 [a]Lit *the burnt offerings to an abundance* [A]2 Chr 29:32 [B]Lev 3:16 [C]Num 15:5-10 30:1 [a]Lit *do*, so in vv 2, 3, 5, 13, 21, 23 30:2 [A]Num 9:10, 11; 2 Chr 30:13, 15 30:3 [A]2 Chr 29:17, 34 30:4 [a]Lit *in the sight of all* 30:5 [a]Lit *voice* [b]Lit *written* [A]Judg 20:1 30:6 [a]Lit *runners* [A]Esth 8:14; Job 9:25; Jer 51:31

29:20–36 Hezekiah restored true temple worship as practiced in the time of David and Solomon, producing great joy (v. 36).

29:26 instruments of David. The instruments David had made for the temple (cf. 1Ch 23:5).

29:34 Levites were more conscientious . . . than the priests. Perhaps the priests had become used to participating in all the idol sacrifices they had instituted (cf. 28:25).

30:1–27 Hezekiah reached back to restore the Passover (Ex 12:1–20; Lv 23:1–8) which apparently had not been properly and regularly observed in some time, perhaps since the division of the kingdom 215 years earlier (v. 5). The Passover would later be revived again by Josiah (2Ch 35:1–9) and Zerubbabel (Ezr 6:19–22). It celebrated God's forgiveness and redemption of His believing people.

30:1 Israel. These would be the remnant of the northern 10 tribes (vv. 6, 25) left in the land or escaped from the enemy after the northern kingdom was taken captive following the invasion by Assyria in 722 B.C. (2Ki 17:1–9). Ephraim and Manasseh were the leading tribes.

30:2 second month. This call to Passover was to unite the nation again in worship. Normally the Passover would be in the first month (Mar./Apr.). The rule of exception for individuals who were unclean or absent (Nu 9:9–11) was applied to the whole nation.

30:5 Beersheba even to Dan. These two cities were at the extreme ends of the country, so this expression was a way of saying, "from S to N."

30:6 return. The nation was required by law to annually celebrate 3 feasts in Jerusalem: 1) Passover; 2) Weeks, or Pentecost; and 3) Booths, or Tabernacles (cf. Ex 23; Lv 23; Nu 28, 29; Dt 16). God would have returned to bless the people of the northern apostate and idolatrous kingdom of Israel if they had returned to Him. Cf. 15:2; 20:20; 26:5; 31:21, where this recurring theme is affirmed.

Abraham, Isaac and Israel, that He may return to those of you who escaped *and* are left from [B]the [b]hand of the kings of Assyria. 7 [A]Do not be like your fathers and your brothers, who were unfaithful to the LORD God of their fathers, so that [B]He made them a horror, as you see. 8 Now do not [A]stiffen your neck like your fathers, but [a]yield to the LORD and enter His sanctuary which He has consecrated forever, and serve the LORD your God, [B]that His burning anger may turn away from you. 9 For [A]if you return to the LORD, your brothers and your sons *will find* compassion before those who led them captive and will return to this land. [B]For the LORD your God is gracious and compassionate, and will not turn *His* face away from you if you return to Him."

10 So the [a]couriers passed from city to city through the country of Ephraim and Manasseh, and as far as Zebulun, but [A]they laughed them to scorn and mocked them. 11 Nevertheless [A]some men of Asher, Manasseh and Zebulun humbled themselves and came to Jerusalem. 12 The [A]hand of God was also on Judah to give them one heart to do what the king and the princes commanded by the word of the LORD.

PASSOVER REINSTITUTED

13 Now many people were gathered at Jerusalem to celebrate the Feast of Unleavened Bread [A]in the second month, a very large assembly. 14 They arose and removed the altars which *were* in Jerusalem; they also [A]removed all the incense altars and [B]cast *them* into the brook Kidron. 15 Then [A]they slaughtered the Passover *lambs* on the fourteenth of the second month. And [B]the priests and Levites were ashamed of themselves, and consecrated themselves and brought burnt offerings to the house of the LORD. 16 [A]They stood at their stations after their custom, according to the law of Moses the man of God; the priests sprinkled the blood *which they received* from the hand of the Levites. 17 For *there were* many in the assembly who had not consecrated themselves; therefore, [A]the Levites *were* over the slaughter of the Passover *lambs* for everyone who *was* unclean, in order to consecrate *them* to the LORD. 18 For a multitude of the people, [A]*even* many from Ephraim and Manasseh, Issachar and Zebulun, had not purified themselves, [B]yet they ate the Passover [C]otherwise than [a]prescribed. For Hezekiah prayed for them, saying, "May the good LORD pardon 19 [A]everyone who prepares his heart to seek God, the LORD God of his fathers, though not according to the purification *rules* of the sanctuary." 20 So the LORD heard Hezekiah and [A]healed the people. 21 The sons of Israel present in Jerusalem [A]celebrated the Feast of Unleavened Bread *for* seven days with great joy, and the Levites and the priests praised the LORD day after day with loud instruments to the LORD. 22 Then Hezekiah [A]spoke [a]encouragingly to all the Levites who showed good insight *in the things* of the LORD. So they ate for the appointed seven days, sacrificing peace offerings and [B]giving thanks to the LORD God of their fathers.

23 Then the whole assembly [A]decided to celebrate *the feast* another seven days, so they celebrated the seven days with joy. 24 For [A]Hezekiah king of Judah had contributed to the assembly 1,000 bulls and 7,000 sheep, and the princes had contributed to the assembly 1,000 bulls and 10,000 sheep; and [B]a large number of priests consecrated themselves. 25 All the assembly of Judah rejoiced, with the priests and the Levites and [A]all the assembly that came from Israel, both the sojourners who came from the land of Israel and those living in Judah. 26 So there was great joy in Jerusalem, because there was nothing like this in Jerusalem [A]since the days of Solomon the son of David, king of Israel. 27 Then [A]the Levitical priests arose and [B]blessed the people; and their voice was heard and their prayer came to [C]His holy dwelling place, to heaven.

IDOLS ARE DESTROYED

31 Now when all this was finished, all Israel who were present went out to the cities of Judah, [A]broke the pillars in pieces, cut down the [a]Asherim and pulled down the high places and the altars throughout all Judah and Benjamin, as well as in Ephraim and Manasseh, [b]until they had destroyed them all. Then all the sons of Israel returned to their cities, each to his possession.

30:6 [b]Lit *palm* [B]2 Chr 28:20 30:7 [A]Ezek 20:13 [B]2 Chr 29:8 30:8 [a]Lit *give a hand* [A]Ex 32:9 [B]2 Chr 29:10 30:9 [A]Deut 30:2 [B]Ex 34:6, 7; Mic 7:18 30:10 [a]Lit *runners* [A]2 Chr 36:16 30:11 [A]2 Chr 30:18, 21, 25 30:12 [A]2 Cor 3:5; Phil 2:13; Heb 13:20, 21 30:13 [A]2 Chr 30:2 30:14 [A]2 Chr 28:24 [B]2 Chr 29:16 30:15 [A]2 Chr 30:2, 3 [B]2 Chr 29:34 30:16 [A]2 Chr 35:10, 15 30:17 [A]2 Chr 29:34 30:18 [a]Lit *written* [A]2 Chr 30:11, 25 [B]Num 9:10 [C]Ex 12:43-49 30:19 [A]2 Chr 19:3 30:20 [A]James 5:16 30:21 [A]Ex 12:15; 13:6 30:22 [a]Lit *to the heart of* [A]2 Chr 32:6 [B]Ezra 10:11 30:23 [A]1 Kin 8:65 30:24 [A]2 Chr 35:7, 8 [B]2 Chr 29:34; 30:3 30:25 [A]2 Chr 30:11, 18 30:26 [A]2 Chr 7:8-10 30:27 [A]2 Chr 23:18 [B]Num 6:23 [C]Deut 26:15; Ps 68:5 31:1 [a]I.e. wooden symbols of a female deity [b]Lit *even to completion* [A]2 Kin 18:4

30:8 stiffen your neck. This is the same kind of language used by Stephen in Ac 7:51–53, which in effect says, "Don't be obstinate."

30:9 Not all the people of Israel had been taken captive in the invasion of the Assyrians during Hezekiah's reign (cf. 2Ki 17:5–23; 18:9–12).

30:10 Scorn was the response of these tribes, showing their wickedness even after judgment on them had begun. Note v. 18 for the additional brazen sin of these tribes.

30:13 second month. Normally, Passover, including the Feast of Unleavened Bread, was held in the first month; however, at this special time it was better to be one month late, than not at all.

30:14 These altars had been erected to idols by Ahaz. See 2Ch 28:25; 29:16. Hezekiah was able to cleanse the city of idols and altars, something his predecessors failed to do.

30:18–20 The attitude of the heart was to prevail over their outward activity (cf. 1Sa 15:22; Jer 7:22, 23; Hos 6:6). Hezekiah reminded them that God forgives even the most heinous sins, and He did (v. 20).

30:23 This speaks to the authenticity of revival in that the people knew how sinful they had been and how desperately in need of cleansing they actually were. They doubled the time for the feast which pointed to God's salvation and deliverance of the faithful.

30:26 nothing like this. A telling statement about the spiritual degeneracy of the divided kingdom since the time of Solomon over 215 years earlier.

31:1 Judah and Benjamin … Ephraim and Manasseh. The first two referred to the southern kingdom; the last two represented the northern kingdom. The Passover had been a real revival and they carried the conviction of it back to their homes to destroy all the idolatry. So the reign of idolatry ended, and the worship of God was restored. The people went home in hope of divine blessing and a future of peace and prosperity.

2 And Hezekiah appointed [A]the divisions of the priests and the Levites by their divisions, each according to his service, *both* the priests and the Levites, [B]for burnt offerings and for peace offerings, to minister and to give thanks and to praise in the gates of the camp of the LORD.

REFORMS CONTINUED

3 *He* also *appointed* [A]the king's portion of his goods for the burnt offerings, *namely,* for the morning and evening burnt offerings, and the burnt offerings for the sabbaths and for the new moons and for the fixed festivals, [B]as it is written in the law of the LORD. 4 Also he [a]commanded the people who lived in Jerusalem to give [A]the portion due to the priests and the Levites, that they might devote themselves to [B]the law of the LORD. 5 As soon as the [a]order spread, the sons of Israel provided in abundance the first fruits of grain, new wine, oil, honey and of all the produce of the field; and they brought in abundantly [A]the tithe of all. 6 The sons of Israel and Judah who lived in the cities of Judah also brought in the tithe of oxen and sheep, and [A]the tithe of [a]sacred gifts which were consecrated to the LORD their God, and placed *them* in heaps. 7 In the third month they began to [a]make the heaps, and finished *them* by the seventh month. 8 When Hezekiah and the rulers came and saw the heaps, they blessed the LORD and [A]His people Israel. 9 Then Hezekiah questioned the priests and the Levites concerning the heaps. 10 Azariah the chief priest [A]of the house of Zadok said to [a]him, "[B]Since the contributions began to be brought into the house of the LORD, we have had enough to eat with plenty left over, for the LORD has blessed His people, and this great quantity is left over."

11 Then Hezekiah commanded *them* to prepare [A]rooms in the house of the LORD, and they prepared *them.* 12 They faithfully brought in the contributions and the tithes and the consecrated things; and Conaniah the Levite *was* the officer in charge [A]of them and his brother Shimei *was* second. 13 Jehiel, Azaziah, Nahath, Asahel, Jerimoth, Jozabad, Eliel, Ismachiah, Mahath and Benaiah *were* overseers [a]under the authority of Conaniah and Shimei his brother by the appointment of King Hezekiah, and [A]Azariah *was* the *chief* officer of the house of God. 14 Kore the son of Imnah the Levite, the keeper of the eastern *gate, was* over the freewill offerings of God, to apportion the contributions for the LORD and the most holy things. 15 [a]Under his authority *were* [A]Eden, Miniamin, Jeshua, Shemaiah, Amariah and Shecaniah in [B]the cities of the priests, to distribute faithfully *their portions* to their brothers by divisions, whether great or small, 16 without regard to their genealogical enrollment, to the males from [a,A]thirty years old and upward—everyone who entered the house of the LORD [B]for his daily obligations—for their work in their duties according to their divisions; 17 as well as the priests who were enrolled genealogically according to their fathers' households, and the Levites [A]from twenty years old and upwards, by their duties *and* their divisions. 18 The genealogical enrollment *included* [a]all their little children, their wives, their sons and their daughters, for the whole assembly, for they consecrated themselves [b]faithfully in holiness. 19 Also for the sons of Aaron the priests *who were* in [A]the pasture lands of their cities, or in each and every city, [B]*there were* men who were designated by name to distribute portions to every male among the priests and to everyone genealogically enrolled among the Levites.

20 Thus Hezekiah did throughout all Judah; and [A]he did what *was* good, right and true before the LORD his God. 21 Every work which he began in the service of the house of God in law and in commandment, seeking his God, he did with all his heart and [A]prospered.

SENNACHERIB INVADES JUDAH

32 After these [a]acts of faithfulness [A]Sennacherib king of Assyria came and invaded Judah and besieged the fortified cities, and [b]thought to break into them for himself. 2 Now when Hezekiah saw that Sennacherib had come and that [a]he intended to make war on Jerusalem, 3 he decided with his officers and his warriors to cut off the *supply of* water from the springs which *were* outside the city, and they helped him. 4 So many people assembled [A]and stopped up all the springs and [B]the stream which flowed [a]through the region, saying, "Why should the

31:2 [A]1 Chr 24:1 [B]1 Chr 23:28-31 31:3 [A]2 Chr 35:7 [B]Num 28:1-29:40 31:4 [a]Lit *said to* [A]Num 18:8 [B]Mal 2:7 31:5 [a]Lit *word* [A]Neh 13:12 31:6 [a]Lit *consecrated things* [A]Lev 27:30; Deut 14:28 31:7 [a]Lit *found* 31:8 [A]Deut 33:29; Ps 33:12; 144:15 31:10 [a]Lit *him, and he said* [A]1 Chr 6:8, 9 [B]Mal 3:10 31:11 [A]1 Kin 6:5, 8 31:12 [A]2 Chr 35:9 31:13 [a]Lit *from the hand of* [A]2 Chr 31:10 31:15 [a]Lit *under his hand* [A]2 Chr 29:12 [B]Josh 21:9-19 31:16 [a]Heb *three* [A]1 Chr 23:3 [B]Ezra 3:4 31:17 [A]1 Chr 23:24 31:18 [a]Lit *with all* [b]Lit *in their faithfulness* 31:19 [A]Lev 25:34; Num 35:2-5 [B]2 Chr 31:12-15 31:20 [A]2 Kin 20:3; 22:2 31:21 [A]Deut 29:9; Prov 3:9, 10 32:1 [a]Lit *things and this faithfulness* [b]Lit *said* [A]2 Kin 18:13-19, 37; Is 36:1-37:38 32:2 [a]Lit *his face for war against* 32:4 [a]Lit *in the midst of the land* [A]2 Kin 20:20 [B]2 Chr 32:30

31:2–19 divisions of the priests and the Levites. The priestly service had not been supported by the government during the reign of the wicked kings, so Hezekiah restored that support as God originally ordained it (cf. 1Ch 24:1ff.; 2Ch 8:12–14).

31:6 tithe. Since the priests and Levites served the nation, they were to be supported by the people through the taxation of the tithe. According to Lv 27:30–33 and Nu 18:21, 24, the people were to give the tenth (tithe) to supply all the needs of the Levites. Malachi 3:8 says they were robbing God when they did not give the tithe. Deuteronomy 12:6, 7 called for a second tithe that was to support the nation's devotion to the temple by being used for the national festivals at the temple in Jerusalem. This was called the festival tithe. Deuteronomy 14:28, 29 called for a third tithe every 3 years for the poor. The sum of this tax plan totaled about 23 percent annually.

31:7 third … seventh month. From the time of the Feast of Weeks, or Pentecost, in May/June until the Feast of Booths, or Tabernacles, in Sept./Oct.

31:11 rooms. These were stone houses, granaries, and cellars to replace the old decayed ones. In these places the Levites stored the tithes (v. 12).

31:17 twenty years old. *See notes on 1Ch 23:3.* Cf. Nu 4:3; 28:24.

31:19 pasture lands. This refers to the 48 Levitical cities (cf. Jos 21:1–42). The tithes-taxes collected from everyone were used not only for festivals at the temple, but also for regular daily support of the priests living and leading throughout the Land (*see note on v. 6*).

31:20, 21 *See notes on 2Ki 18:5–7.*

32:1–23 Hezekiah's dealings with Sennacherib, king of Assyria (ca. 705–681 B.C.). *See notes on 2Ki 18:13–19:37; Is 36, 37.* The Assyrian king came because Hezekiah, determined to recover the independence of his nation, refused to pay the tribute his father had bound him to pay to Assyria. Sennacherib retaliated, and Hezekiah fortified the city (v. 5) and trusted God (vv. 8, 11), who delivered them (vv. 21, 22) and was glorified (v. 23).

kings of Assyria come and find abundant water?"
5 And he took courage and [A]rebuilt all the wall that
had been broken down and [a]erected towers on it,
and *built* [B]another outside wall and strengthened
the [C]Millo *in* the city of David, and made weapons
and shields in great number. 6 He appointed military officers over the people and gathered them
to him in the square at the city gate, and [A]spoke
[a]encouragingly to them, saying, 7 "[A]Be strong and
courageous, do not fear or be dismayed because of
the king of Assyria nor because of all the horde that
is with him; [B]for the one with us is greater than the
one with him. 8 With him is *only* [A]an arm of flesh,
but [B]with us is the LORD our God to help us and
to fight our battles." And the people relied on the
words of Hezekiah king of Judah.

SENNACHERIB UNDERMINES HEZEKIAH

9 After this [A]Sennacherib king of Assyria sent
his servants to Jerusalem while he *was* [a]besieging
Lachish with all his forces with him, against Hezekiah king of Judah and against all Judah who *were*
at Jerusalem, saying, 10 "Thus says Sennacherib
king of Assyria, 'On what are you trusting that you
are remaining in Jerusalem under siege? 11 Is not
Hezekiah misleading you to give yourselves over
to die by hunger and by thirst, saying, "The LORD
our God will deliver us from the [a]hand of the king
of Assyria"? 12 [A]Has not the same Hezekiah taken
away His high places and His altars, and said to
Judah and [a]Jerusalem, "You shall worship before
one altar, and on it you shall [b]burn incense"? 13 Do
you not know what I and my fathers have done
to all the peoples of the lands? [A]Were the gods of
the nations of the lands able at all to deliver their
land from my hand? 14 [A]Who *was there* among all
the gods of those nations which my fathers utterly
destroyed who could deliver his people out of my
hand, that your God should be able to deliver you
from my hand? 15 Now therefore, do not let Hezekiah
deceive you or mislead you like this, and do not
believe him, for [A]no god of any nation or kingdom
was able to deliver his people from my hand or
from the hand of my fathers. How much less will
your God deliver you from my hand?' "
16 His servants spoke further against the LORD
God and against His servant Hezekiah. 17 He also
wrote letters to insult the LORD God of Israel, and
to speak against Him, saying, "[A]As the gods of the
nations of the lands [a]have not delivered their people
from my hand, so the God of Hezekiah will not deliver His people from my hand." 18 [A]They called this
out with a loud voice in the language of Judah to
the people of Jerusalem who were on the wall, to
frighten and terrify them, so that they might take
the city. 19 They spoke [a]of the God of Jerusalem as
of [A]the gods of the peoples of the earth, the work
of men's hands.

HEZEKIAH'S PRAYER IS ANSWERED

20 But King Hezekiah and Isaiah the prophet,
the son of Amoz, prayed about this and cried out
to heaven. 21 And the LORD sent an angel who destroyed every mighty warrior, commander and
officer in the camp of the king of Assyria. So he
returned [a]in shame to his own land. And when he
had entered the temple of his god, some of his own
children killed him there with the sword. 22 So the
LORD [A]saved Hezekiah and the inhabitants of Jerusalem from the hand of Sennacherib the king of
Assyria and from the hand of all *others*, and [a]guided
them on every side. 23 And [A]many were bringing
gifts to the LORD at Jerusalem and choice presents
to Hezekiah king of Judah, so that [B]he was exalted
in the sight of all nations thereafter.
24 [A]In those days Hezekiah became [a]mortally ill;
and he prayed to the LORD, and [b]the LORD spoke
to him and gave him a sign. 25 But Hezekiah gave
no return for the benefit [a]he received, [A]because his
heart was [b]proud; [B]therefore wrath came on him
and on Judah and Jerusalem. 26 However, [A]Heze-
kiah [a]humbled the pride of his heart, both he and
the inhabitants of Jerusalem, so that the wrath
of the LORD did not come on them in the days of
Hezekiah.
27 Now Hezekiah had immense riches and honor;
and he made for himself treasuries for silver, gold,
precious stones, spices, shields and all kinds of valuable articles, 28 storehouses also for the produce of
grain, wine and oil, pens for all kinds of cattle and
[a]sheepfolds for the flocks. 29 He made cities for himself and acquired flocks and herds in abundance,
for [A]God had given him very great [a]wealth. 30 It was
Hezekiah who [A]stopped the upper outlet of the waters of [B]Gihon and directed them to the west side
of the city of David. And Hezekiah prospered in all
that he did. 31 Even *in the matter of* [A]the envoys of
the rulers of Babylon, who sent to him to inquire
of [B]the wonder that had happened in the land, God
left him *alone only* [C]to test him, that He might know
all that was in his heart.

32:5 [a]Lit *raised on the towers* [A]2 Chr 25:23 [B]2 Kin 25:4 [C]1 Kin 9:24 32:6 [a]Lit *upon their hearts* [A]2 Chr 30:22 32:7 [A]1 Chr 22:13 [B]2 Kin 6:16 32:8 [A]Jer 17:5 [B]2 Chr 20:17 32:9 [a]Lit *against* [A]2 Kin 18:17 32:11 [a]Lit *palm* 32:12 [a]Lit *Jerusalem, saying,* [b]Lit *offer up in smoke* [A]2 Chr 31:1 32:13 [A]2 Kin 18:33-35 32:14 [A]Is 10:9-11 32:15 [A]Ex 5:2; Is 36:18-20; Dan 3:15 32:17 [a]Lit *who have* [A]2 Chr 32:14 32:18 [A]2 Kin 18:28 32:19 [a]Lit *to* [A]Ps 115:4-8 32:21 [a]Lit *in shame of face* 32:22 [a]Another reading is *gave them rest* [A]Is 31:5 32:23 [A]2 Sam 8:10 [B]2 Chr 1:1 32:24 [a]Lit *sick to the point of death* [b]Lit *He* [A]2 Kin 20:1-11; Is 38:1-8 32:25 [a]Lit *to him* [b]Lit *high* [A]2 Chr 26:16; 32:31 [B]2 Chr 24:18 32:26 [a]Lit *humbled himself in* [A]Jer 26:18, 19 32:28 [a]So ancient versions; Heb *flocks for the sheepfolds* 32:29 [a]Lit *possessions, property* [A]1 Chr 29:12 32:30 [A]2 Kin 20:20 [B]1 Kin 1:33 32:31 [A]2 Kin 20:12; Is 39:1 [B]2 Chr 32:24; Is 38:7, 8 [C]Deut 8:16

32:24–26 *See notes on 2Ki 20:1–11 and Is 38.*

32:27–31 *See notes on 2Ki 20:12–20 and Is 39.*

32:30 A 1,700 ft. long tunnel cut through solid rock (below Jerusalem) redirected water from the spring Gihon outside of Jerusalem (to the E) toward the S of Jerusalem into the pool of Siloam within the city to provide water in time of siege. The tunnel was a remarkable feat of engineering and boring skill, often 60 ft. below the ground and large enough to walk through. It was discovered in 1838, but not until 1909 was it cleared of the debris left by the destruction of Jerusalem back in 586 B.C. This may not have been the first water shaft, since David may have entered Jerusalem 300 years earlier through a water shaft (cf. 2Sa 5:6–8).

32:31 **Babylon.** This empire was gradually gaining power as Assyria declined due to internal strife and weak kings. Assyria was crushed in 612 B.C. and Babylon, under Nebuchadnezzar, became the world ruler (cf. 2Ki 20:14).

32 Now the rest of the acts of Hezekiah and his
deeds of devotion, behold, they are written in the
vision of Isaiah the prophet, the son of Amoz, in the
Book of the Kings of Judah and Israel. 33 So Hezekiah slept with his fathers, and they buried him in
the [a]upper section of the tombs of the sons of David; and all Judah and the inhabitants of Jerusalem
[A]honored him at his death. And his son Manasseh
became king in his place.

MANASSEH SUCCEEDS HEZEKIAH IN JUDAH

33 [A]Manasseh was twelve years old when he became king, and he reigned fifty-five years in
Jerusalem. 2 [A]He did evil in the sight of the LORD according to the abominations of the nations whom the
LORD dispossessed before the sons of Israel. 3 For [A]he
rebuilt the high places which Hezekiah his father had
broken down; [B]he also erected altars for the Baals and
made [a]Asherim, and worshiped all the host of heaven
and served them. 4 [A]He built altars in the house of the
LORD of which the LORD had said, "My name shall be
[B]in Jerusalem forever." 5 For he built altars for all the
host of heaven in [A]the two courts of the house of the
LORD. 6 [A]He made his sons pass through the fire in the
valley of Ben-hinnom; and he practiced witchcraft,
used divination, practiced sorcery and [B]dealt with
mediums and spiritists. He did much evil in the sight
of the LORD, provoking Him *to anger.* 7 Then he put
[A]the carved image of the idol which he had made in
the house of God, of which God had said to David and
to Solomon his son, "[B]In this house and in Jerusalem,
which I have chosen from all the tribes of Israel, I will
put My name forever; 8 and I will not again remove the
foot of Israel from the land [A]which I have appointed
for your fathers, if only they will observe to do all that
I have commanded them according to all the law, the
statutes and the ordinances *given* through Moses."
9 Thus Manasseh misled Judah and the inhabitants
of Jerusalem to do more evil than the nations whom
the LORD destroyed before the sons of Israel.

MANASSEH'S IDOLATRY REBUKED

10 The LORD spoke to Manasseh and his people,
but [A]they paid no attention. 11 [A]Therefore the LORD
brought the commanders of the army of the king of
Assyria against them, and they captured Manasseh
with [a]hooks, [B]bound him with bronze *chains* and
took him to Babylon. 12 When [A]he was in distress, he
entreated the LORD his God and [B]humbled himself
greatly before the God of his fathers. 13 When he
prayed to Him, [A]He was moved by his entreaty and
heard his supplication, and brought him again to
Jerusalem to his kingdom. Then Manasseh [B]knew
that the LORD *was* God.
14 Now after this he built the outer wall of the
city of David on the west side of [A]Gihon, in the valley, even to the entrance of the [B]Fish Gate; and he
encircled the [C]Ophel *with it* and made it very high.
Then he put army commanders in all the fortified
cities of Judah. 15 He also [A]removed the foreign gods
and the idol from the house of the LORD, as well as
all the altars which he had built on the mountain
of the house of the LORD and in Jerusalem, and he
threw *them* outside the city. 16 He set up the altar of
the LORD and sacrificed [A]peace offerings and thank
offerings on it; and he ordered Judah to serve the
LORD God of Israel. 17 Nevertheless [A]the people still
sacrificed in the high places, *although* only to the
LORD their God.
18 Now the rest of the acts of Manasseh even [A]his
prayer to his God, and the words of [B]the seers who
spoke to him in the name of the LORD God of Israel,
behold, they are among the records of the kings
of [C]Israel. 19 His prayer also and [A]*how God* was entreated by him, and all his sin, his unfaithfulness,
and [B]the sites on which he built high places and
erected the Asherim and the carved images, before
he humbled himself, behold, they are written in the
records of the [a]Hozai. 20 So Manasseh slept with his
fathers, and they buried him in his own house. And
Amon his son became king in his place.

AMON BECOMES KING IN JUDAH

21 [A]Amon *was* twenty-two years old when he became king, and he reigned two years in Jerusalem.
22 He did evil in the sight of the LORD as Manasseh his father [A]had done, and Amon sacrificed to
all [B]the carved images which his father Manasseh
had made, and he served them. 23 Moreover, he did

32:33 [a]Or *ascent to* [A]Ps 112:6; Prov 10:7 33:1 [A]2 Kin 21:1-9 33:2 [A]2 Chr 28:3; Jer 15:4 33:3 [a]I.e. wooden symbols of a female deity [A]2 Chr 31:1 [B]Deut 16:21; 2 Kin 23:5, 6 33:4 [A]2 Chr 28:24 [B]2 Sam 7:13; 2 Chr 7:16 33:5 [A]2 Chr 4:9 33:6 [A]2 Chr 28:3 [B]Lev 19:31; 20:27 33:7 [A]2 Chr 33:15 [B]1 Kin 9:3-5; 2 Chr 7:16; 33:4 33:8 [A]2 Sam 7:10 33:10 [A]Neh 9:29; Jer 25:4 33:11 [a]I.e. thongs put through the nose [A]Deut 28:36 [B]2 Chr 36:6 33:12 [A]Ps 118:5; 120:1; 130:1, 2 [B]2 Chr 32:26 33:13 [A]1 Chr 5:20; Ezra 8:23 [B]Dan 4:32 33:14 [A]1 Kin 1:33 [B]Neh 3:3 [C]2 Chr 27:3 33:15 [A]2 Chr 33:3-7 33:16 [A]Lev 7:11-18 33:17 [A]2 Chr 32:12 33:18 [A]2 Chr 33:12, 13 [B]2 Chr 33:10 [C]2 Chr 21:2 33:19 [a]Gr reads *seers* [A]2 Chr 33:13 [B]2 Chr 33:3 33:21 [A]2 Kin 21:19-24 33:22 [A]2 Chr 33:2-7 [B]2 Chr 34:3, 4

32:32 Isaiah. Cf. Is 1:1.

33:1–20 The reign of Manasseh (ca. 695–642 B.C.). Cf. 2Ki 21:1–18.

33:1–10 *See notes on 2Ki 21:1–10.*

33:6 Ben-hinnom. This valley to the S and E of the temple was where the worship of Molech involved burning children to death (Ps 106:37). This was forbidden in Lv 18:21; 20:2–5; Deut 18:10. Such horrible practices appeared in Israel from the time of Ahaz (cf. 28:3).

33:11–17 God's retribution was swift. Manasseh apparently repented, but the spiritual damage was not easily reversed.

33:11 king of Assyria. Most likely Ashurbanipal (ca. 669–633 B.C.). Between 652 and 648 B.C., Babylon rebelled against Assyria. The city of Babylon was defeated temporarily, but Assyria may have felt Manasseh supported Babylon's rebellion, so he was taken to trial in Babylon.

33:12, 13 Manasseh. This king was very wicked and idolatrous, a murderer of his children, and a desecrater of the temple. God graciously forgave this "chief of sinners" (cf. 1Ti 1:15) when he repented. He did what he could to reverse the effect of his life (vv. 15–17). Although the people worshiped God and not idols, they were doing it in the wrong place and wrong way. God had commanded them to offer sacrifices only in certain places (Dt 12:13, 14) to keep them from corrupting the prescribed forms and to protect them from pagan religious influence. Disobedience to God's requirements in this matter surely contributed to the decline under the next king, Amon (vv. 21–25), whose corruption his successor, Josiah, had to eliminate (34:3–7).

33:14 A wall running from S of the temple and Ophel (W of the Kidron Valley) SE/NW reaching to the Fish Gate, NW of the temple.

33:18–20 See 2Ki 21:17, 18.

33:21–25 The reign of Amon (ca. 642–640 B.C.). Cf. 2Ki 21:19–26. *See notes on 2Ki 21:19–24.*

not humble himself before the LORD [A]as his father Manasseh had [a]done, but Amon multiplied guilt. 24 Finally [A]his servants conspired against him and put him to death in his own house. 25 But the people of the land [a]killed all the conspirators against King Amon, and the people of the land made Josiah his son king in his place.

JOSIAH SUCCEEDS AMON IN JUDAH

34 [A]Josiah *was* eight years old when he became king, and he reigned thirty-one years in Jerusalem. 2 [A]He did right in the sight of the LORD, and walked in the ways of his father David and did not turn aside to the right or to the left. 3 For in the eighth year of his reign while he was still a youth, he began to [A]seek the God of his father David; and in the twelfth year he began [B]to purge Judah and Jerusalem of the high places, the Asherim, the carved images and the molten images. 4 They tore down the altars of the Baals in his presence, and [A]the incense altars that were high above them he chopped down; also the Asherim, the carved images and the molten images he broke in pieces and [B]ground to powder and scattered *it* on the graves of those who had sacrificed to them. 5 Then [A]he burned the bones of the priests on their altars and purged Judah and Jerusalem. 6 [A]In the cities of Manasseh, Ephraim, Simeon, even as far as Naphtali, in their surrounding ruins, 7 he also tore down the altars and [A]beat the Asherim and the carved images into powder, and chopped down all the incense altars throughout the land of Israel. Then he returned to Jerusalem.

JOSIAH REPAIRS THE TEMPLE

8 [A]Now in the eighteenth year of his reign, when he had purged the land and the house, he sent Shaphan the son of Azaliah, and Maaseiah [B]an official of the city, and Joah the son of Joahaz the recorder, to repair the house of the LORD his God. 9 They came to [A]Hilkiah the high priest and delivered the money that was brought into the house of God, which the Levites, the [a]doorkeepers, had collected [b]from [B]Manasseh and Ephraim, and from all the remnant of Israel, and from all Judah and Benjamin and the inhabitants of Jerusalem. 10 Then they gave *it* into the hands of the workmen who had the oversight of the house of the LORD, and the workmen who were working in the house of the LORD [a]used it to restore and repair the house. 11 They in turn gave *it* to the carpenters and to the builders to buy quarried stone and timber for couplings and to make beams for the houses [A]which the kings of Judah had let go to ruin. 12 [A]The men did the work faithfully with foremen over them to supervise: Jahath and Obadiah, the Levites of the sons of Merari, Zechariah and Meshullam of the sons of the Kohathites, and [B]the Levites, all who were skillful with musical instruments. 13 *They were* also over [A]the burden bearers, and supervised all the workmen from job to job; and *some* of the Levites *were* scribes and officials and gatekeepers.

HILKIAH DISCOVERS LOST BOOK OF THE LAW

14 When they were bringing out the money which had been brought into the house of the LORD, [A]Hilkiah the priest found the book of the law of the LORD *given* by Moses. 15 Hilkiah responded and said to Shaphan the scribe, "I have found the book of the law in the house of the LORD." And Hilkiah gave the book to Shaphan. 16 Then Shaphan brought the book to the king and [a]reported further word to the king, saying, "Everything that was [b]entrusted to your servants they are doing. 17 They have also emptied out the money which was found in the house of the LORD, and have delivered it into the hands of the supervisors and the workmen." 18 Moreover, Shaphan the scribe told the king saying, "Hilkiah the priest gave me a book." And Shaphan read from it in the presence of the king.

19 When the king heard [A]the words of the law, [B]he tore his clothes. 20 Then the king commanded Hilkiah, Ahikam the son of Shaphan, [a]Abdon the son of Micah, Shaphan the scribe, and Asaiah the king's servant, saying, 21 "Go, inquire of the LORD for me and for those who are left in Israel and in Judah, concerning the words of the book which has been found; for [A]great is the wrath of the LORD which is poured out on us because our fathers have not observed the word of the LORD, to do according to all that is written in this book."

HULDAH, THE PROPHETESS, SPEAKS

22 So Hilkiah and *those* whom the king [a]had told went to Huldah the prophetess, the wife of Shallum the son of [b]Tokhath, the son of Hasrah, the keeper of the wardrobe (now she lived in Jerusalem in the Second Quarter); and they spoke to her regarding this. 23 She said to them, "Thus says the LORD, the God of Israel, 'Tell the man who sent you to Me, 24 thus says the LORD, "Behold, [A]I am bringing evil on this place and on its inhabitants, *even* all [B]the curses written in the book which they have read in the presence of the king of Judah. 25 [A]Because they have forsaken Me and have burned incense

33:23 [a]Lit *humbled himself* [A]2 Chr 33:12, 19 33:24 [A]2 Chr 25:27 33:25 [a]Lit *smote* 34:1 [A]2 Kin 22:1, 2; Jer 1:2; 3:6 34:2 [A]2 Chr 29:2 34:3 [A]2 Chr 15:2; Prov 8:17 [B]1 Kin 13:2; 2 Chr 33:22 34:4 [A]2 Kin 23:4, 5, 11 [B]Ex 32:20 34:5 [A]1 Kin 13:2; 2 Kin 23:20 34:6 [A]2 Kin 23:15, 19 34:7 [A]2 Chr 31:1 34:8 [A]2 Kin 22:3-20 [B]2 Chr 18:25 34:9 [a]Lit *guardians of the threshold* [b]Lit *from the hand of* [A]2 Chr 35:8 [B]2 Chr 30:10, 18 34:10 [a]Lit *gave* 34:11 [A]2 Chr 33:4-7 34:12 [A]2 Kin 12:15 [B]1 Chr 25:1 34:13 [A]Neh 4:10 34:14 [A]2 Chr 34:9 34:16 [a]Lit *returned* [b]Lit *given into the hand of* 34:19 [A]Deut 28:3-68 [B]Josh 7:6 34:20 [a]In 2 Kin 22:12, *Achbor, son of Micaiah* 34:21 [A]2 Chr 29:8 34:22 [a]So with Gr [b]In 2 Kin 22:14 *Tikvah, son of Harhas* 34:24 [A]2 Chr 36:14-20 [B]Deut 28:15-68 34:25 [A]2 Chr 33:3

34:1–35:27 The reign of Josiah (ca. 640–609 B.C.). Cf. 2Ki 22:1–23:30. Jeremiah prophesied during this reign (2Ch 35:24; Jer 1:2) as did Habakkuk, Zephaniah (Zep 1:1), and Nahum.

34:1, 2 *See notes on 2Ki 22:1, 2.* At the age of 16, Josiah began to cultivate a love for God in his heart, and by age 20 his character was strong enough in devotion to Him that he went into action to purge his nation.

34:3–7 *See notes on 2Ki 23:4–20.*

34:8 **repair the house of the LORD.** During the 55-year reign of Manasseh (33:1) and the two-year reign of Amon (33:21), the work of Hezekiah on the temple restoration was undone, which called for another extensive enterprise to "restore and repair" it (vv. 9–13).

34:8–13 *See notes on 2Ki 22:3–7.*

34:8–33 *See notes on 2Ki 22:8–23:20.*

to other gods, that they might provoke Me to anger with all the works of their hands; therefore My
wrath will be poured out on this place and it shall
not be quenched." ' 26 But to the king of Judah who
sent you to inquire of the LORD, thus you will say
to him, 'Thus says the LORD God of Israel *regarding* the words which you have heard, 27 "[A]Because
your heart was tender and you humbled yourself
before God when you heard His words against this
place and against its inhabitants, and *because* you
humbled yourself before Me, tore your clothes and
wept before Me, I truly have heard you," declares the
LORD. 28 "Behold, I will gather you to your fathers
and you shall be gathered to your grave in peace,
so your eyes will not see all the evil which I will
bring on this place and on its inhabitants." ' " And
they brought back word to the king.

29 [A]Then the king sent and gathered all the elders
of Judah and Jerusalem. 30 The king went up to the
house of the LORD and [A]all the men of Judah, the
inhabitants of Jerusalem, the priests, the Levites
and all the people, from the greatest to the least;
and he read in their hearing all the words of the
book of the covenant which was found in the house
of the LORD.

JOSIAH'S GOOD REIGN

31 Then the king [A]stood in his place and [B]made a
covenant before the LORD to walk after the LORD,
and to keep His commandments and His testimonies
and His statutes with all his heart and with all his
soul, to perform the words of the covenant written
in this book. 32 Moreover, he made all who were present in Jerusalem and Benjamin to stand *with him*.
So the inhabitants of Jerusalem did according to the
covenant of God, the God of their fathers. 33 Josiah
[A]removed all the abominations from all the lands
belonging to the sons of Israel, and made all who
were present in Israel to serve the LORD their God.
Throughout his [a]lifetime they did not turn from
following the LORD God of their fathers.

THE PASSOVER OBSERVED AGAIN

35 Then Josiah [A]celebrated the Passover to the
LORD in Jerusalem, and [B]they slaughtered
the Passover *animals* on the fourteenth *day* of the
first month. 2 He set the priests in their offices and
[A]encouraged them in the service of the house of
the LORD. 3 He also said to [A]the Levites who taught
all Israel *and* who were holy to the LORD, "Put the
holy ark in the house which Solomon the son of David king of Israel built; [B]it will be a burden on *your*
shoulders no longer. Now serve the LORD your God
and His people Israel. 4 [A]Prepare *yourselves* by your
fathers' households in your divisions, according to
the writing of David king of Israel and [B]according to
the writing of his son Solomon. 5 Moreover, [A]stand
in the holy place according to the sections of the
fathers' households of your brethren the [a]lay people,
and according to the Levites, by division of a father's
household. 6 Now [A]slaughter the Passover *animals*,
[B]sanctify yourselves and prepare for your brethren
to do according to the word of the LORD by Moses."

7 Josiah contributed to the lay people, to all who
were present, flocks of lambs and young goats, all
for the Passover offerings, numbering 30,000 plus
3,000 bulls; these were from the king's possessions.
8 His officers also contributed a freewill offering to
the people, the priests and the Levites. Hilkiah and
Zechariah and Jehiel, [A]the officials of the house of
God, gave to the priests for the Passover offerings
2,600 *from the flocks* and 300 bulls. 9 [A]Conaniah
also, and Shemaiah and Nethanel, his brothers, and
Hashabiah and Jeiel and Jozabad, the officers of the
Levites, contributed to the Levites for the Passover
offerings 5,000 *from the flocks* and 500 bulls.

10 So the service was prepared, and [A]the priests
stood at their stations and the Levites by their divisions according to the king's command. 11 [a,A]They
slaughtered the Passover *animals*, and while [B]the
priests sprinkled [b]the blood *received* from their
hand, [C]the Levites skinned *them*. 12 Then they removed the burnt offerings that *they* might give
them to the sections of the fathers' households of the
lay people to present to the LORD, as it is written in
the book of Moses. *They did* this also with the bulls.
13 So [A]they roasted the Passover *animals* on the fire
according to the ordinance, and they boiled [B]the
holy things in pots, in kettles, in pans, and carried
them speedily to all the lay people. 14 Afterwards
they prepared for themselves and for the priests,
because the priests, the sons of Aaron, *were* offering
the burnt offerings and the fat until night; therefore
the Levites prepared for themselves and for the
priests, the sons of Aaron. 15 The singers, the sons of
Asaph, *were* also at their stations [A]according to the
command of David, Asaph, Heman, and Jeduthun
the king's seer; and [B]the gatekeepers at each gate

34:27 [A]2 Kin 22:19; 2 Chr 12:7; 32:26 34:29 [A]2 Kin 23:1-3 34:30 [A]Neh 8:1-3 34:31 [A]2 Kin 11:14; 23:3; 2 Chr 30:16 [B]2 Chr 23:16; 29:10 34:33 [a]Lit *days* [A]2 Chr 34:3-7 35:1 [A]2 Kin 23:21 [B]Ex 12:6; Num 9:3 35:2 [A]2 Chr 29:11 35:3 [A]2 Chr 17:8, 9; Neh 8:7 [B]1 Chr 23:26 35:4 [A]1 Chr 9:10-13 [B]2 Chr 8:14 35:5 [a]Lit *sons of the people*, and so throughout the ch [A]Ezra 6:18 35:6 [A]2 Chr 35:1 [B]2 Chr 29:5 35:8 [A]2 Chr 31:13 35:9 [A]2 Chr 31:12 35:10 [A]2 Chr 35:5 35:11 [a]I.e. the Levites [b]So with Gr [A]2 Chr 35:1, 6 [B]2 Chr 29:22 [C]2 Chr 29:34 35:13 [A]Ex 12:8, 9 [B]Lev 6:28 35:15 [A]1 Chr 25:1 [B]1 Chr 26:12-19

34:33 Throughout his lifetime. This noble king had a life-long influence by the power of his godly life and firm devotion to God and His Word. The strength of his character held the nation together serving the Lord. It started because as a young man he "began to seek ... God" (cf. v. 3).

35:1–19 The chronicler, probably Ezra, gave much more attention to this Passover celebration than does 2Ki 23:21–23.

35:1, 2 Obviously, the temple's contents had been disturbed and the sacrifices/festivals interrupted by lack of attention, idolatrous practices, and foreign intervention. As Hezekiah had restored the Passover in his time (30:1ff.), so did Josiah. This was the central feast in devotion to the Lord (Ex 12, 13).

35:3 the holy ark. The ark of the covenant which was to remain in the Most Holy Place had been removed, probably by Manasseh, who set a carved image in its place (cf. 33:7). The law for the carrying of the ark during the tabernacle days, when it was portable, called for poles to be placed through rings on the sides, and Levites (Kohathites) to carry it by the poles without touching it (cf. Ex 25:14, 15). Uzza(h) died for touching the ark while he was improperly transporting the ark on a cart (1Ch 13:6–10). Now that the temple was built and the ark had a permanent place, it no longer needed to be transported in the old way.

35:6 Moses. *See notes on Ex 12, 13.* The prescribed pattern for the Passover in the temple was followed (vv. 7–17).

did not have to depart from their service, because
the Levites their brethren prepared for them.
16 So all the service of the LORD was prepared
on that day to celebrate the Passover, and to offer
burnt offerings on the altar of the LORD according
to the command of King Josiah. 17 Thus [A]the sons of
Israel who were present celebrated the Passover at
that time, and the Feast of Unleavened Bread seven
days. 18 [A]There had not been celebrated a Passover
like it in Israel since the days of Samuel the prophet;
nor had any of the kings of Israel celebrated such a
Passover as Josiah did with the priests, the Levites,
all Judah and Israel who were present, and the inhabitants of Jerusalem. 19 In the eighteenth year of
Josiah's reign this Passover was celebrated.

JOSIAH DIES IN BATTLE

20 [A]After all this, when Josiah had set the [a]temple
in order, Neco king of Egypt came up to make war
at [B]Carchemish on the Euphrates, and Josiah went
out to engage him. 21 But [a]Neco sent messengers to
him, saying, "[A]What have we to do with each other,
O King of Judah? *I am* not *coming* against you today
but against the house with which I am at war, and
God has ordered me to hurry. Stop for your own sake
from *interfering with* God who is with me, so that
He will not destroy you." 22 However, Josiah would
not turn [a]away from him, but [A]disguised himself
in order to make war with him; nor did he listen
to the words of Neco [B]from the mouth of God, but
came to make war on the plain of [C]Megiddo. 23 The
archers shot King Josiah, and the king said to his
servants, "Take me away, for I am badly wounded."
24 So his servants took him out of the chariot and
carried him in the second chariot which he had, and
brought him to Jerusalem [a]where he died and was
buried in the tombs of his fathers. [A]All Judah and
Jerusalem mourned for Josiah. 25 Then [A]Jeremiah
chanted a lament for Josiah. And all the male and
female singers speak about Josiah in their lamentations to this day. And they made them an ordinance
in Israel; behold, they are also written in the Lamentations. 26 Now the rest of the acts of Josiah and
his deeds of devotion as written in the law of the
LORD, 27 and his acts, first to last, behold, they are
written in the Book of the Kings of Israel and Judah.

JEHOAHAZ, JEHOIAKIM, THEN JEHOIACHIN RULE

36 [A]Then the people of the land took [a,B]Joahaz the
son of Josiah, and made him king in place of
his father in Jerusalem. 2 Joahaz was twenty-three
years old when he became king, and he reigned
three months in Jerusalem. 3 Then the king of Egypt
deposed him at Jerusalem, and imposed on the
land a fine of one hundred talents of silver and one
talent of gold. 4 The king of Egypt made Eliakim
his brother king over Judah and Jerusalem, and
changed his name to Jehoiakim. But [A]Neco took
Joahaz his brother and brought him to Egypt.
5 [A]Jehoiakim was twenty-five years old when he
became king, and he reigned eleven years in Jerusalem; and he did evil in the sight of the LORD his
God. 6 Nebuchadnezzar king of Babylon came up
[A]against him and [B]bound him with bronze *chains*
to take him to Babylon. 7 [A]Nebuchadnezzar also
brought *some* of the articles of the house of the
LORD to Babylon and put them in his temple at
Babylon. 8 [A]Now the rest of the acts of Jehoiakim
and [a]the abominations which he did, and what was
found against him, behold, they are written in the
Book of the Kings of Israel and Judah. And Jehoiachin his son became king in his place.
9 [A]Jehoiachin was eight years old when he became
king, and he reigned three months and ten days in
Jerusalem, and he did evil in the sight of the LORD.

CAPTIVITY IN BABYLON BEGUN

10 [A]At the turn of the year King Nebuchadnezzar
sent and brought him to Babylon with the valuable
articles of the house of the LORD, and he made his
kinsman [B]Zedekiah king over Judah and Jerusalem.

35:17 [A]Ex 12:1-20; 2 Chr 30:21 35:18 [A]2 Kin 23:21; 2 Chr 30:5 35:20 [a]Lit *house* [A]2 Kin 23:29, 30 [B]Is 10:9; Jer 46:2 35:21 [a]Lit *he* [A]2 Chr 25:19 35:22 [a]Lit *his face* [A]2 Chr 18:29 [B]2 Chr 35:21 [C]Judg 5:19 35:24 [a]Lit *and* [A]Zech 12:11 35:25 [A]Jer 22:10; Lam 4:20 36:1 [a]I.e. short form of Jehoahaz [A]2 Kin 23:30-34 [B]Jer 22:11 36:4 [A]Jer 22:10-12 36:5 [A]2 Kin 23:36, 37; Jer 22:13-19; 26:1; 35:1 36:6 [A]2 Kin 24:1; Jer 25:1-9 [B]2 Chr 33:11 36:7 [A]2 Kin 24:13 36:8 [a]Lit *his* [A]2 Kin 24:5 36:9 [A]2 Kin 24:8-17 36:10 [A]2 Sam 11:1; Jer 22:25; 24:1; 29:1; Ezek 17:12 [B]Jer 37:1

35:18 not .... Passover like it. Hezekiah's Passover (cf. 2Ch 30) differed. It was not celebrated strictly according to Mosaic law in that: 1) it was celebrated in the second month (2Ch 30:2); 2) not all the people were purified (2Ch 30:18); and 3) not all of the people came (2Ch 30:10).

35:18, 19 since ... Samuel. Ca. 1100–1015 B.C. It had been over 400 years, since before all the kings of Israel and Judah.

35:20–27 The details of Josiah's tragic death are given. When compared with the account in 2Ki 23:28–30, the events become clearer. Toward the end of Josiah's reign, the Egyptian Pharaoh Neco (ca. 609–594 B.C.) set out on a military expedition to aid the king of Assyria in a war at Carchemish, Assyria's latest capital, 250 mi. NE of Damascus on the bank of the Euphrates River. Fearing such an alliance would present future danger to Israel, Josiah decided to intercept Pharaoh Neco's army and fight to protect his nation. Coming from Egypt, likely by ship to Acco, a northern seaport in Israel, and by land up the coastal plain of Israel, the Egyptian army had landed and proceeded E to the plain of Megiddo (v. 22), i.e., Jezreel on the plain of Esdraelon. This was the most direct way to Carchemish. There Josiah met him for battle and was wounded by an arrow. He made it back to Jerusalem (60 mi. S), where he died.

35:21 God has ordered me. He is referring to the true God; whether he had a true revelation or not is unknown. Josiah had no way to know either, and it is apparent he did not believe that Neco spoke the Word of God. There is no reason to assume his death was punishment for refusing to believe. He probably thought Neco was lying and, once victorious with Assyria over Babylon, they would together be back to assault Israel.

35:25 There is no record of Jeremiah's elegy. The people continued to mourn the loss of Josiah up to the writing of the Chronicles in 450–430 B.C., nearly 200 years after the event. In fact, the location of the battle, the town of Hadadrimmon in the plain of Megiddo, was part of a proverb lamenting Josiah's death even in Zechariah's day (Zec 12:11), 90 years later.

36:1–4 The reign of Joahaz (ca. 609 B.C.). Cf. 2Ki 23:31–33. Jeremiah continued to prophesy during this reign (Jer 1:3).

36:5–8 The reign of Jehoiakim, a.k.a. Eliakim (ca. 609–597 B.C.; cf. 2Ki 23:34–24:7). *See notes on 2Ki 23:34–24:7.* Daniel was taken captive to Babylon in 605 B.C. Jeremiah prophesied during this reign (Jer 1:3), and Habakkuk likely appeared on the scene at this time of kingly abominations.

36:9, 10 The reign of Jehoiachin (ca. 597 B.C.). Cf. 2Ki 24:8–16. *See notes on 2Ki 24:8–16.* Ezekiel was taken captive to Babylon in 597 B.C. Jeremiah prophesied during this reign.

36:9 eight years old. Eighteen years old is preferable, as stated in 2Ki 24:8, because

ZEDEKIAH RULES IN JUDAH

11 [A]Zedekiah was twenty-one years old when he became king, and he reigned eleven years in Jerusalem. 12 He did evil in the sight of the LORD his God; [A]he did not humble himself [B]before Jeremiah the prophet [a]who spoke for the LORD. 13 [A]He also rebelled against King Nebuchadnezzar who had made him swear *allegiance* by God. But [B]he stiffened his neck and hardened his heart against turning to the LORD God of Israel. 14 Furthermore, all the officials of the priests and the people were very unfaithful *following* all the abominations of the nations; and they defiled the house of the LORD which He had sanctified in Jerusalem.

15 The LORD, the God of their fathers, [A]sent *word* to them again and again by His messengers, because He had compassion on His people and on His dwelling place; 16 but they *continually* [A]mocked the messengers of God, [B]despised His words and scoffed at His prophets, [C]until the wrath of the LORD arose against His people, until there was no remedy. 17 [A]Therefore He brought up against them the king of the Chaldeans who slew their young men with the sword in the house of their sanctuary, and had no compassion on young man or virgin, old man or infirm; He gave *them* all into his hand. 18 [A]All the articles of the house of God, great and small, and the treasures of the house of the LORD, and the treasures of the king and of his officers, he brought *them* all to Babylon. 19 Then [A]they burned the house of God and broke down the wall of Jerusalem, and burned all its fortified buildings with fire and destroyed all its valuable articles. 20 Those who had escaped from the sword he [A]carried away to Babylon; and [B]they were servants to him and to his sons until the rule of the kingdom of Persia, 21 [A]to fulfill the word of the LORD by the mouth of Jeremiah, until [B]the land had enjoyed its sabbaths. [C]All the days of its desolation it kept sabbath [a,D]until seventy years were complete.

CYRUS PERMITS RETURN

22 [A]Now in the first year of Cyrus king of Persia—in order to fulfill the word of the LORD [B]by the mouth of Jeremiah—the LORD [C]stirred up the spirit of Cyrus king of Persia, so that he sent a proclamation throughout his kingdom, and also *put it* in writing, saying, 23 "Thus says Cyrus king of Persia, 'The LORD, the God of heaven, has given me all the kingdoms of the earth, and He has appointed me to build Him a house in Jerusalem, which is in Judah. Whoever there is among you of all His people, may the LORD his God be with him, and let him go up!' "

36:11 [A]2 Kin 24:18-20; Jer 27:1; 28:1; 52:1 36:12 [a]Lit *from the mouth of the LORD* [A]2 Chr 33:23 [B]Jer 21:3-7 36:13 [A]Jer 52:3; Ezek 17:15 [B]2 Chr 30:8 36:15 [A]Jer 7:13; 25:3 36:16 [A]2 Chr 30:10; Jer 5:12, 13 [B]Prov 1:24-32 [C]Ezra 5:12 36:17 [A]2 Kin 25:1-7; Jer 21:1-10 36:18 [A]2 Chr 36:7, 10 36:19 [A]1 Kin 9:8; 2 Kin 25:9; Jer 52:13 36:20 [A]2 Kin 25:11 [B]Jer 27:7 36:21 [a]Lit *to fulfill seventy years* [A]Jer 29:10 [B]Lev 26:34 [C]Lev 25:4 [D]Jer 25:11 36:22 [A]Ezra 1:1-3 [B]Jer 25:12; 29:10 [C]Is 44:28

of the full development of his wickedness (see Ezekiel's description of him in 19:5–9).

36:11–21 The reign of Zedekiah, a.k.a. Mattaniah (ca. 597–586 B.C.). Cf. 2Ki 24:17–25:21; Jer 52:4–27. Jeremiah prophesied during this reign (Jer 1:3) and wrote Lamentations to mourn the destruction of Jerusalem and the temple in 586 B.C. Ezekiel received his commission during this reign (Eze 1:1) and prophesied from 592 B.C. to his death in 560 B.C.

36:11–20 *See notes on 2Ki 24:17–25:21.*

36:20 *See notes on 2Ki 25:22–30* for the fate of those who remained behind in Jerusalem.

36:21 **sabbaths.** This suggests that the every seventh year Sabbath which God required for the land (Lv 25:1–7) had not been kept for 490 years dating back to the days of Eli, ca. 1107–1067 B.C. (cf. 1Sa 1–4). Leviticus 26:27–46 warns of God's judgment in general if this law were to be violated. Jeremiah 25:1–11 applied this judgment to Judah from 605 B.C. at the time of the first Babylonian deportation until 536 B.C. when the first Jews returned to Jerusalem and started to rebuild the temple (cf. Ezr 3:8).

36:22, 23 *See notes on Ezr 1:1–3.* The chronicler ended with a ray of hope because the 70 years were completed (cf. Da 9:1, 2) and Abraham's offspring were returning to the Land to rebuild the temple.

THE BOOK OF EZRA

TITLE

Even though Ezra's name does not enter the account of Judah's post-Exilic return to Jerusalem until 7:1, the book bears his name ("Jehovah helps") as a title. This is because both Jewish and Christian tradition attribute authorship to this famous scribe-priest. New Testament writers do not quote the book of Ezra.

AUTHOR AND DATE

Ezra is most likely the author of both Ezra and Nehemiah, which might have originally been one book. Ezra 4:8–6:18 and 7:12–26 are written in Aramaic. Although Ezra never states his authorship, internal arguments favor him strongly. After his arrival in Jerusalem (ca. 458 B.C.), he changed from writing in the third person to writing in the first person. In the earlier section it is likely that he had used the third person because he was quoting his memoirs. Ezra is believed to possibly be the author of the books of the Chronicles. It would have been natural for the same author to continue the OT narrative by showing how God fulfilled His promise by returning His people to the land after 70 years of captivity. There is also a strong priestly tone in Chronicles, and Ezra was a priestly descendant of Aaron (cf. 7:1–5). The concluding verses of 2 Chronicles (36:22, 23) are virtually identical to the beginning verses of Ezra (1:1–3a), affirming his authorship of both.

Ezra was a scribe who had access to the myriad of administrative documents found in Ezra and Nehemiah, especially those in the book of Ezra. Very few people would have been allowed access to the royal archives of the Persian Empire, but Ezra proved to be the exception (cf. Ezr 1:2–4; 4:9–22; 5:7–17; 6:3–12). His role as a scribe of the law is spelled out in 7:10: "For Ezra had set his heart to study the law of the LORD, and to practice *it,* and to teach *His* statutes and ordinances in Israel." He was a strong and godly man who lived at the time of Nehemiah (cf. Ne 8:1–9; 12:36). Tradition says he was founder of the Great Synagogue, where the complete OT canon was first formally recognized.

Ezra led the second return from Persia (ca. 458 B.C.), so the completed book was written sometime in the next several decades (ca. 457–444 B.C.).

BACKGROUND AND SETTING

God had originally brought Israel out of the slave markets of Egypt in the Exodus (ca. 1445 B.C.). Hundreds of years later, before the events of Ezra, God told His people that if they chose to break their covenant with Him, He would again allow other nations to take them into slavery (Jer 2:14–25). In spite of God's repeated warnings from the mouths of His prophets, Israel and Judah chose to reject their Lord and to participate in the worship of foreign gods, in addition to committing the abominable practices which accompanied idolatry (cf. 2Ki 17:7–18; Jer 2:7–13). True to His promise, God brought the Assyrians and Babylonians to issue His chastisement upon wayward Israel and Judah.

In 722 B.C. the Assyrians deported the 10 northern tribes and scattered them all over their empire (cf. 2Ki 17:24–41; Is. 7:8). Several centuries later, in 605–586 B.C., God used the Babylonians to sack and nearly depopulate Jerusalem. Because Judah persisted in her unfaithfulness to the covenant, God chastened His people with 70 years of captivity (Jer 25:11), from which they returned to Jerusalem as reported by Ezra and Nehemiah. Cyrus, the Persian, overthrew Babylon in 539 B.C., and the book of Ezra begins with the decree of Cyrus one year later for the Jews to return to Jerusalem (ca. 538 B.C.), and it chronicles the reestablishment of Judah's national calendar of feasts and sacrifices, including the rebuilding of the second temple (begun in 536 B.C. and completed in 516 B.C.).

As there had been 3 waves of deportation from Israel into Babylon (605 B.C., 597 B.C., and 586 B.C.), so there were actually 3 returns to Jerusalem over a 9-decade span. Zerubbabel first returned in 538 B.C. He was followed by Ezra, who led the second return in 458 B.C. Nehemiah did likewise 13 years later, in 445 B.C. Complete uncontested political autonomy, however, never returned. The prophets Haggai and Zechariah preached during Zerubbabel's time, about 520 B.C. and following.

HISTORICAL AND THEOLOGICAL THEMES

The Jews' return from the Babylonian captivity seemed like a second Exodus, sovereignly patterned in some ways after Israel's first redemption from Egyptian bondage. The return trip from Babylon involved activities similar to those of the original Exodus: 1) the rebuilding of the temple and the city walls; 2) the reinstitution of the law, which made Zerubbabel, Ezra, and Nehemiah collectively seem like a second Moses; 3) the challenge of the local enemies; and 4) the temptation to intermarry with non-Jews, resulting in idolatry. Other parallels between the original Exodus and the return from Babylon must have seemed to the returnees as though they had been given a fresh start by God.

In his account of the return, Ezra drew upon a collection of Persian administrative documents to which he had access as a scribe. The presence of actual royal administrative documents carries a powerful message when accompanied by the resounding line "the hand of the LORD my God *was* upon him/me" (7:6, 28). The decrees, proclamations, letters, lists, genealogies, and memoranda, many of them written by the Persian administration, attest to the sovereign hand of God in Israel's restoration. The primary message of the book is that God orchestrated the past grim situation (captivity) and would continue to work through a pagan king and his successors to give Judah hope for the future (return). God's administration overrides that of any of the kings of this world, and thus the book of Ezra is a message of God's continuing covenant grace to Israel.

Another prominent theme which surfaces in Ezra is opposition from the local Samaritan residents whose ancestors had been imported from Assyria (4:2; cf. Jn 4:4–42). For reasons of spiritual sabotage, Israel's enemies requested to participate in rebuilding the temple (4:1, 2). After being shunned, the enemies hired counselors against the Jews (cf. 4:4, 5). But the Lord, through the preaching of Haggai and Zechariah, rekindled the spirit of the people and their leaders to build, with the words "... take courage ... and work; for I am with you" (Hag 2:4; cf. Ezr 4:24–5:2). The reconstruction resumed (ca. 520 B.C.) and the temple was soon finished, dedicated, and back in service to God (ca. 516 B.C.).

INTERPRETIVE CHALLENGES

First, how do the post-Exilic historical books of 1 and 2 Chronicles, Ezra, Nehemiah, and Esther relate to the post-Exilic prophets Haggai, Zechariah, and Malachi? For the chronology of Ezra, Nehemiah, and Esther, *see the notes on Ezr 6:22–7:1*. The two books of Chronicles were written by Ezra as a reminder of the promised Davidic kingship, the Aaronic priesthood, and appropriate temple worship. Haggai and Zechariah prophesied in the period of Ezr 4–6 when temple construction was resumed. Malachi wrote during Nehemiah's revisit to Persia (cf. Ne 13:6).

Second, what purpose does the book serve? Ezra historically reports the first two of three post-Exilic returns to Jerusalem from the Babylonian captivity. The first return (chaps. 1–6) was under Zerubbabel (ca. 538 B.C.) and the second (chaps. 7–10) was led by Ezra himself (ca. 458 B.C.). Spiritually, Ezra reestablished the importance of the Aaronic priesthood by tracing his ancestry to Eleazar, Phinehas, and Zadok (cf. Ezr 7:1–5). He reported on the rebuilding of the second temple (chaps. 3–6). How he dealt with the gross sin of intermarriage with foreigners is presented in chaps. 9, 10. Most importantly, he reports how the sovereign hand of God moved kings and overcame varied opposition to reestablish Israel as Abraham's seed, nationally and individually, in the land promised to Abraham, David, and Jeremiah.

Third, the temple was built during the reign of Cyrus. Mention of Ahasuerus (4:6) and Artaxerxes (4:7–23) might lead one to conclude that the temple could also have been built during their reigns. Such a conclusion, however, violates history. Ezra was not writing about the construction accomplishments of Ahasuerus or Artaxerxes, but rather he continued to chronicle their oppositions after the temple was built, which continued even to Ezra's day. It is apparent, then, that Ezr 4:1–5 and 4:24–5:2 deal with rebuilding the temple under Zerubbabel, while 4:6–23 is a parenthesis recounting the history of opposition in the times of Ezra and Nehemiah.

Fourth, the interpreter must decide where Esther fits in to the time of Ezra. A careful examination indicates it took place between the events of chaps. 6 and 7. *See notes on Esther.*

Fifth, how does divorce in Ezr 10 correlate with the fact that God hates divorce (Mal 2:16)? Ezra does not establish the norm, but rather deals with a special case in history. It seems to have been decided (Ezr 10:3) on the principle that the lesser wrong (divorce) would be preferable to the greater wrong of the Jewish race being polluted by intermarriage, so that the nation and the messianic line of David would not be ended by being mingled with Gentiles. To solve the problem this way magnifies the mercy of God in that the only other solution would have been to kill all of those involved (husband, wives, and children) by stoning, as was done during the first Exodus at Shittim (Nu 25:1–9).

OUTLINE

I. The First Return under Zerubbabel (1:1–6:22)

- A. Cyrus' Decree to Return (1:1–4)
- B. Treasures to Rebuild the Temple (1:5–11)
- C. Those Who Returned (2:1–70)
- D. Construction of the Second Temple (3:1–6:22)
  1. Building begins (3:1–13)
  2. Opposition surfaces (4:1–5)
  3. Excursus on future opposition (4:6–23)

4. Construction renewed (4:24–5:2)
5. Opposition renewed (5:3–6:12)
6. Temple completed and dedicated (6:13–22)

II. The Second Return under Ezra (7:1–10:44)

A. Ezra Arrives (7:1–8:36)
B. Ezra Leads Revival (9:1–10:44)

CYRUS'S PROCLAMATION

1 [A]Now in the first year of Cyrus king of Persia,
in order to fulfill the word of the LORD by the
mouth of Jeremiah, the LORD stirred up the spirit
of Cyrus king of Persia, so that he [B]sent a proclamation throughout all his kingdom, and also *put*
it in writing, saying:
2 "Thus says Cyrus king of Persia, 'The LORD, the
God of heaven, has given me all the kingdoms of
the earth and [A]He has appointed me to build Him
a house in Jerusalem, which is in Judah. 3 Whoever
there is among you of all His people, may his God
be with him! Let him go up to Jerusalem which is
in Judah and rebuild the house of the LORD, the
God of Israel; [A]He is the God who is in Jerusalem.
4 Every survivor, at whatever place he may [a]live,
let the men of [b]that place support him with silver
and gold, with goods and cattle, together with a
freewill offering for the house of God which is in
Jerusalem.' "

HOLY VESSELS RESTORED

5 Then the heads of fathers' *households* of Judah
and Benjamin and the priests and the Levites arose,
[A]even everyone whose spirit God had stirred to go up
and rebuild the house of the LORD which is in Jerusalem. 6 All those about them [a,A]encouraged them with
articles of silver, with gold, with goods, with cattle
and with valuables, aside from all that was given as
a freewill offering. 7 [A]Also King Cyrus brought out
the articles of the house of the LORD, [B]which Nebuchadnezzar had carried away from Jerusalem and put
in the house of his gods; 8 and Cyrus, king of Persia,
had them brought out by the hand of Mithredath the
treasurer, and he counted them out to [A]Sheshbazzar,
the prince of Judah. 9 Now this *was* their number: 30
[A]gold dishes, 1,000 silver dishes, 29 [a]duplicates; 10 30
gold bowls, 410 silver bowls of a second *kind and* 1,000
other articles. 11 All the articles of gold and silver *numbered* 5,400. Sheshbazzar brought them all up with
the exiles who went up from Babylon to Jerusalem.

1:1 [A]2 Chr 36:22; Jer 25:12; 29:10 [B]Ezra 5:13 1:2 [A]Is 44:28; 45:1, 12, 13 1:3 [A]1 Kin 8:23; 18:39; Is 37:16; Dan 6:26 1:4 [a]Or *reside as an alien* [b]Lit *his* 1:5 [A]Ezra 1:1, 2 1:6 [a]Lit *strengthened their hands* [A]Neh 6:9; Is 35:3 1:7 [A]Ezra 5:14; 6:5 [B]2 Kin 24:13; 2 Chr 36:7 1:8 [A]Ezra 5:14 1:9 [a]Heb obscure; other possible meanings are *knives, censers* [A]Ezra 8:27

1:1–3a These verses are almost identical to 2Ch 36:22, 23. The pre-Exilic history of 1 and 2 Chronicles gave the post-Exilic returnees direction regarding the Davidic kingship, the Aaronic priesthood, and temple worship. This book continues the story.

1:1 **first year.** Ca. 538 B.C. **Cyrus king of Persia.** Ca. 550–530 B.C. The Lord had prophesied through Isaiah, who said of Cyrus, "*He is* My shepherd," and declares of Jerusalem, "She will be built," and to the temple, "Your foundation will be laid" (Is 44:28). The historian Josephus records an account of the day when Daniel read Isaiah's prophecy to Cyrus, and in response he was moved to declare the proclamation of 1:2–4 (538 B.C.). **by the mouth of Jeremiah.** Jeremiah had prophesied the return of the exiles after a 70-year captivity in Babylon (Jer 25:11; 29:10–14; cf. Da 9:2). This was no isolated event, but rather an outworking of the covenant promises made to Abraham in Ge 12:1–3. **the LORD stirred up.** A strong expression of the fact that God sovereignly works in the lives of kings to effect His purposes (Pr 21:1; Da 2:21; 4:17). **sent a proclamation.** This was the most common form of spoken, public communication, usually from the central administration. The king would dispatch a herald, perhaps with a written document, into the city. In order to address the people, he would either go to the city gate, where people often congregated for social discourse, or gather the people together in a square, occasionally by the blowing of a horn. The herald would then make the proclamation to the people. A document called the Cyrus Cylinder, recovered in reasonably good condition by archeologists, commissions people from many lands to return to their cities to rebuild the temples to their gods, apparently as some sort of general policy of Cyrus. Whether or not this document was an extension of the proclamation made to the exiles in this passage must remain a matter of speculation (cf. 6:2–5). ***put it* in writing.** Proclamations were oral statements, usually made by a herald, which were often written down for recordkeeping.

1:2–4 It is possible that Daniel played a part in the Jews' receiving such favorable treatment (cf. Da 6:25–28). According to the Jewish historian Josephus, he was Cyrus' prime minister who shared Isaiah's prophecies with Cyrus (Is 44:28; 46:1–4). The existence of such documents, written over a century before Cyrus was born, led him to acknowledge that all his power came from the God of Israel and prompted him to fulfill the prophecy.

1:2 **LORD, the God of heaven.** The God of Israel was recognized as the utmost divine authority (cf. 5:12; 6:9, 10; 7:12, 21, 23), who sovereignly dispenses authority to human monarchs. **a house.** This refers to the second temple, which would be built after the return to the land by Zerubbabel.

1:5 **whose spirit God had stirred.** The primary underlying message of Ezra and Nehemiah is that the sovereign hand of God is at work in perfect keeping with His plan at His appointed times. The 70 years of captivity were complete, so God stirred up not only the spirit of Cyrus to make the decree, but His own people to go and build up Jerusalem and the temple (cf. 1:1).

1:6 **All those about them.** A basic similarity to the Exodus is seen throughout Ezra and Nehemiah. One can hear faint echoes of the Egyptians supplying treasures in order to provide splendor for the tabernacle (cf. Ex 11:2; 12:35, 36). Here other nations around Israel are called to contribute. They were assisted by some of their captive countrymen, who had been born in Babylon and chose to remain, and perhaps by some Babylonians and Assyrians who were favorably disposed to Cyrus and/or the Jews.

1:7 **the articles of the house of the LORD.** Cf. Ezr 6:5. These were the vessels which Nebuchadnezzar removed when he sacked the temple (ca. 605–586 B.C.; 2Ki 24:13; 25:14, 15; Da 1:2). God had preserved them (2Ch 36:7) with the Babylonians (cf. Da 5:1–4) for the return as prophesied by Jeremiah (Jer 27:22).

1:8 **Sheshbazzar, the prince of Judah.** Cf. 1:11; 5:14, 16. Nothing is said about this man biblically except in Ezra. Most likely, he was a political appointee of Cyrus to oversee Judah. He is not to be confused with Zerubbabel, who was the leader recognized by the Jews (cf. 2:2; 3:2, 8; 4:2, 3; 5:2) and by God (cf. Hag 1, 2; Zec 4). While Zerubbabel did not serve as king, he was in the Davidic line of Messiah (cf. Hag 2:23; Mt 1:12).

1:9–11 The 2,499 articles counted in vv. 9, 10 are only representative of the total of 5,400 mentioned in v. 11.

1:11 **exiles.** Those whom Nebuchadnezzar had taken into Babylonian captivity from Jerusalem, whose return probably occurred early in the reign of Cyrus (ca. 538/537 B.C.). **Babylon to Jerusalem.** A journey taking 3–5 months (cf. Ezr 7:8, 9).

POST-EXILIC RETURNS TO JERUSALEM

Sequence	Date	Scripture	Jewish Leader	Persian Ruler
First	538 B.C.	Ezra 1–6	Zerubbabel, Jeshua	Cyrus
Second	458 B.C.	Ezra 7–10	Ezra	Artaxerxes
Third	445 B.C.	Nehemiah 1–13	Nehemiah	Artaxerxes

NUMBER OF THOSE RETURNING

2 [A]Now these are the [a]people of the province who came up out of the captivity of the exiles whom Nebuchadnezzar the king of Babylon had carried away to Babylon, and returned to Jerusalem and Judah, each to his city. 2 [a]These came with Zerubbabel, Jeshua, Nehemiah, [b]Seraiah, [c]Reelaiah, Mordecai, Bilshan, [d]Mispar, Bigvai, [e]Rehum *and* Baanah.

The number of the men of the people of Israel: 3 the sons of Parosh, 2,172; 4 the sons of Shephatiah, 372; 5 the sons of [A]Arah, 775; 6 the sons of [A]Pahath-moab of the sons of Jeshua *and* Joab, 2,812; 7 the sons of Elam, 1,254; 8 the sons of Zattu, 945; 9 the sons of Zaccai, 760; 10 the sons of [a]Bani, 642; 11 the sons of Bebai, 623; 12 the sons of Azgad, 1,222; 13 the sons of [A]Adonikam, 666; 14 the sons of Bigvai, 2,056; 15 the sons of Adin, 454; 16 the sons of Ater of Hezekiah, 98; 17 the sons of Bezai, 323; 18 the sons of [a]Jorah, 112; 19 the sons of Hashum, 223; 20 the sons of [a]Gibbar, 95; 21 the [a]men of [A]Bethlehem, 123; 22 the men of Netophah, 56; 23 the men of Anathoth, 128; 24 the sons of [a]Azmaveth, 42; 25 the sons of [a]Kiriath-arim, Chephirah and Beeroth, 743; 26 the sons of [A]Ramah and Geba, 621; 27 the men of Michmas, 122; 28 the men of Bethel and Ai, 223; 29 the sons of Nebo, 52; 30 the sons of Magbish, 156; 31 the sons of the other Elam, 1,254; 32 the sons of Harim, 320; 33 the sons of Lod, Hadid and Ono, 725; 34 the [a]men of [A]Jericho, 345; 35 the sons of Senaah, 3,630.

PRIESTS RETURNING

36 [A]The priests: the sons of Jedaiah of the house of Jeshua, 973; 37 the sons of [A]Immer, 1,052; 38 [A]the sons of Pashhur, 1,247; 39 the sons of [A]Harim, 1,017.

LEVITES RETURNING

40 The Levites: the sons of Jeshua and Kadmiel, of the sons of [a]Hodaviah, 74. 41 The singers: the sons of Asaph, 128. 42 The sons of the gatekeepers: the sons of Shallum, the sons of Ater, the sons of Talmon, the sons of Akkub, the sons of Hatita, the sons of Shobai, in all 139.

43 The [A]temple servants: the sons of Ziha, the sons of Hasupha, the sons of Tabbaoth, 44 the sons of Keros, the sons of [a]Siaha, the sons of Padon, 45 the sons of Lebanah, the sons of Hagabah, the sons of Akkub, 46 the sons of Hagab, the sons of Shalmai, the sons of Hanan, 47 the sons of Giddel, the sons of Gahar, the sons of Reaiah, 48 the sons of Rezin, the sons of Nekoda, the sons of Gazzam, 49 the sons of Uzza, the sons of Paseah, the sons of Besai, 50 the sons of Asnah, the sons of Meunim, the sons of [a]Nephisim, 51 the sons of Bakbuk, the sons of Hakupha, the sons of Harhur, 52 the sons of [a]Bazluth, the sons of Mehida, the sons of Harsha, 53 the sons of Barkos, the sons of Sisera, the sons of Temah, 54 the sons of Neziah, the sons of Hatipha.

55 The sons of [A]Solomon's servants: the sons of Sotai, the sons of [a]Hassophereth, the sons of [b]Peruda, 56 the sons of Jaalah, the sons of Darkon, the sons of Giddel, 57 the sons of Shephatiah, the sons of Hattil, the sons of Pochereth-hazzebaim, the sons of [a]Ami.

58 All the [A]temple servants and the sons of [B]Solomon's servants were 392.

59 Now these are those who came up from Tel-melah, Tel-harsha, Cherub, [a]Addan *and* Immer, but they were not able to [b]give evidence of their fathers' households and their [c]descendants, whether they were of Israel: 60 the sons of Delaiah, the sons of Tobiah, the sons of Nekoda, 652.

PRIESTS REMOVED

61 Of the sons of the priests: the sons of [a]Habaiah, the sons of Hakkoz, the sons of [A]Barzillai, who took a wife from the daughters of Barzillai the Gileadite, and he was called by their name. 62 These searched *among* their ancestral registration, but they could not be located; [A]therefore they were considered unclean *and excluded* from the priesthood. 63 The [a]governor said to them [A]that they should not eat from the most holy things until a priest stood up with [B]Urim and Thummim.

64 The whole assembly [a]numbered 42,360, 65 besides their male and female servants [a]who numbered 7,337; and they had 200 [A]singing men and

2:1 [a]Lit *sons* [A]2 Kin 24:14-16; 25:11; 2 Chr 36:20; Neh 7:6-73 2:2 [a]Lit *who* [b]In Neh 7:7, *Azariah* [c]In Neh 7:7, *Raamiah* [d]In Neh 7:7, *Mispereth* [e]In Neh 7:7, *Nehum* 2:5 [A]Neh 7:10 2:6 [A]Neh 7:11 2:10 [a]In Neh 7:15, *Binnui* 2:13 [A]Ezra 8:13 2:18 [a]In Neh 7:24, *Hariph* 2:20 [a]In Neh 7:25, *Gibeon* 2:21 [a]Lit *sons* [A]Gen 35:19; Matt 2:6 2:24 [a]In Neh 7:28, *Beth-azmaveth* 2:25 [a]In Neh 7:29, *Kiriath-jearim* 2:26 [A]Josh 18:25 2:34 [a]Lit *sons* [A]1 Kin 16:34; 2 Chr 28:15 2:36 [A]1 Chr 24:7-18 2:37 [A]1 Chr 24:14 2:38 [A]1 Chr 9:12 2:39 [A]1 Chr 24:8 2:40 [a]In Ezra 3:9, *Judah;* in Neh 7:43, *Hodevah* 2:43 [A]1 Chr 9:2 2:44 [a]In Neh 7:47, *Sia* 2:50 [a]In Neh 7:52, *Nephushesim* 2:52 [a]In Neh 7:54, *Bazlith* 2:55 [a]In Neh 7:57, *Sophereth* [b]In Neh 7:57, *Perida* [A]1 Kin 9:21 2:57 [a]In Neh 7:59, *Amon* 2:58 [A]1 Chr 9:2 [B]1 Kin 9:21 2:59 [a]In Neh 7:61, *Addon* [b]Lit *tell* [c]Lit *seed* 2:61 [a]In Neh 7:63, *Hobaiah* [A]2 Sam 17:27; 1 Kin 2:7 2:62 [A]Num 16:39, 40 2:63 [a]Heb *Tirshatha,* a Persian title [A]Lev 2:3, 10 [B]Ex 28:30; Num 27:21 2:64 [a]Lit *together was* 2:65 [a]Lit *they were* [A]2 Chr 35:25

2:1–70 This list is given almost identically in Ne 7:6–73 (*see notes there*).

2:1 the province. This refers to Judah, reduced from an illustrious, independent, and powerful kingdom to an obscure, servile province of the Persian Empire. The returning Jews were still considered subjects of Cyrus living in a Persian province.

2:2 Zerubbabel. This man was the rightful leader of Judah in that he was of the lineage of David through Jehoiachin (cf. 1Ch 3:17). He did not serve as king (cf. the curse on Jehoiachin's line, Jer 22:24–30), but was still in the messianic line because the curse was bypassed (cf. Mt 1:12; Lk 3:27). The curse of the messianic line for Christ was bypassed in Luke's genealogy by tracing the lineage through David's son Nathan. His name means "offspring of Babylon," indicating his place of birth. He, rather than Cyrus' political appointee Sheshbazzar (cf. 1:11), led Judah according to God's will. **Jeshua.** The High Priest of the first return whose name means "Jehovah saves." He is called Joshua in Hag 1:1 and Zec 3:1. His father Jozadak (Ezr 3:2) had been exiled (cf. 1Ch 6:15). He came from the lineage of Levi, Aaron, Eleazar, and Phinehas; thus he was legitimately in the line of the High Priest (cf. Nu 25:10–13). **Nehemiah … Mordecai.** These are not the same men in Nehemiah or Esther.

2:3–20 Various Jewish families are listed.

2:21–35 These were people from various Judean cities.

2:36–42 Priests and Levites. See Ne 12:1–9 for additional details.

2:43–54 temple servants. These were descendants of the Gibeonites who performed servile duties at the temple.

2:55–58 Here are descendants of Solomon's servants.

2:59–62 Those whose genealogical information could not be verified.

2:63 Urim and Thummim. *See note on Ex 28:30.* These objects, kept in the breastpiece of the High Priest, were used to determine God's will.

2:64, 65 This gross amount is 12,000 more than the particular numbers given in the catalogue, when added together. Reckoning up the smaller numbers, we will find they amount to 29,818 in this chapter, and to 31,089 in the parallel chapter of Nehemiah. Ezra also mentions 494 persons omitted by

women. 66 Their horses were 736; their mules, 245;
67 their camels, 435; *their* donkeys, 6,720.
68 Some of the heads of fathers' *households,* when
they arrived at the house of the LORD which is in Jerusalem, offered willingly for the house of God to [a]restore
it on its foundation. 69 According to their ability they
gave [A]to the treasury for the work 61,000 gold drachmas and 5,000 silver minas and 100 priestly [a]garments.
70 [A]Now the priests and the Levites, some of the
people, the singers, the gatekeepers and the temple
servants lived in their cities, and all Israel in their
cities.

ALTAR AND SACRIFICES RESTORED

3 Now when the seventh month came, and [A]the
sons of Israel *were* in the cities, the people gathered together as one man to Jerusalem. 2 Then [A]Jeshua
the son of Jozadak and his brothers the priests, and
[B]Zerubbabel the son [C]of Shealtiel and his brothers
arose and [D]built the altar of the God of Israel to offer

2:68 [a]Lit *establish* 2:69 [a]Or *tunics* [A]Ezra 8:25-34 2:70 [A]1 Chr 9:2; Neh 11:3 3:1 [A]Neh 7:73; 8:1 3:2 [A]Neh 12:1, 8 [B]Ezra 2:2; Hag 1:1; 2:2 [C]1 Chr 3:17 [D]Ex 27:1

Nehemiah, and Nehemiah mentions 1,765 not noticed by Ezra. If, therefore, Ezra's surplus is added to the sum in Nehemiah, and Nehemiah's surplus to the number in Ezra, they will both become 31,583. Subtracting this from 42,360, there is a deficiency of 10,777. These are omitted because they did not belong to Judah and Benjamin, or to the priests, but to the other tribes. The servants and singers, male and female, are reckoned separately (v. 65), so that putting all these items together, the number of all who went with Zerubbabel amounted to 50,000 with 8,000 beasts of burden.

2:69 drachmas ... minas. "Drachma" probably refers to a Persian coin, the daric, named after Darius I. This would have amounted to approximately 1,100 lbs. of gold. A mina weighed about 1.2 lbs., so this would represent 3 tons of silver (cf. 1Ch 29:7).

2:70 temple servants. *See note on vv. 43–54.*

3:1–13 The worship and regular calendar resumed. The altar was probably rebuilt in 537 B.C.

3:1 After their arrival, they were occupied with their own dwellings in and around Jerusalem. After that work was done, they turned to building the altar of burnt offering in time for the feasts, resolved to celebrate as if the temple had been completed. The month (ca. Sept.–Oct. 537 B.C.) of the Feasts of Trumpets, Atonement, and Booths, or Tabernacles (cf. v. 4) was the seventh month. Such an assembly had not convened for 70 years. They obeyed according to Lv 23:24–44. Over 90 years later, Nehemiah and Ezra would lead a similar celebration (cf. Ne 8:13–18).

3:2 Jeshua ... and Zerubbabel. The recognized spiritual and civil leaders, respectively. *See notes on 2:2.* **as it is written in the law of Moses.** The burnt offerings were in accord with Lv 1:3–17.

THE RETURN FROM EXILE

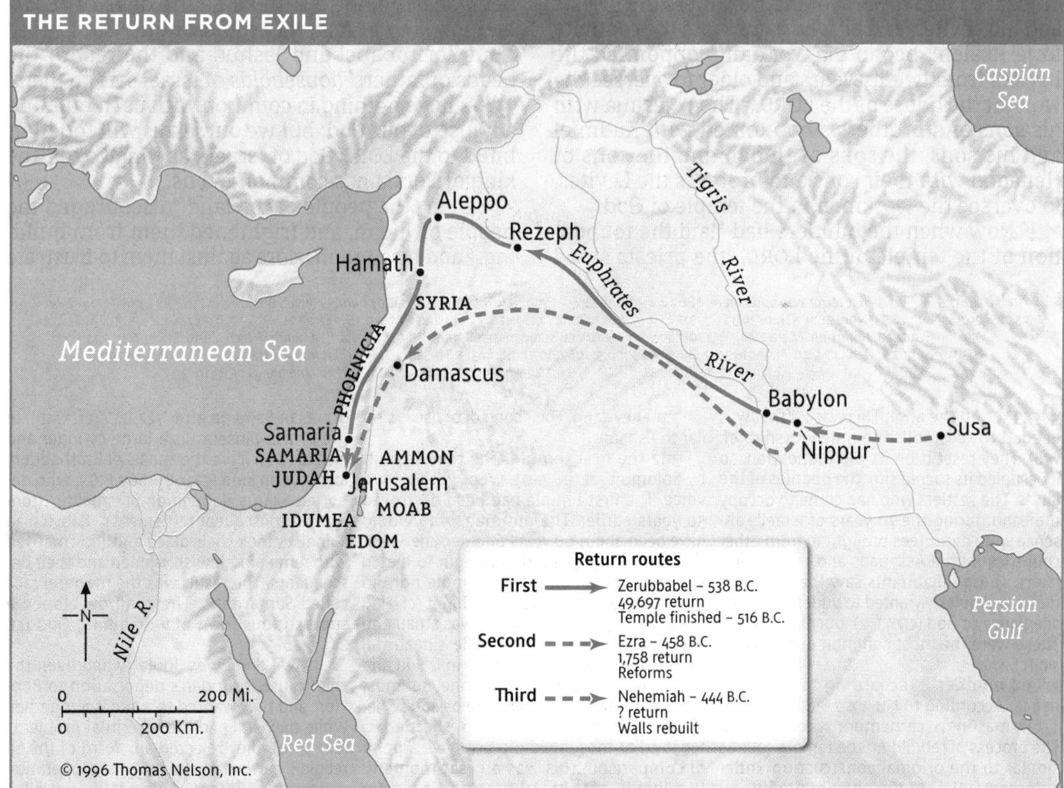

Restoration of the Jewish exiles began under Cyrus (559–530 B.C.), who allowed them to return to Judah with the captured temple treasures. The temple was consecrated in 516 B.C. by official permission of Darius I (522–486).

Ezra won the approval of Artaxerxes I (465–424 B.C.) to return with additional exiles and to promote obedience to the law; Nehemiah, to rebuild the walls of Jerusalem.

Babylon and its vicinity long retained a large and prosperous Jewish community, as clay tablets from the Murashu archives at Nippur testify.

burnt offerings on it, [E]as it is written in the law of Moses, the man of God. 3 So they set up the altar on its foundation, for [a,A]they were terrified because of the peoples of the lands; and they [B]offered burnt offerings on it to the LORD, burnt offerings morning and evening. 4 They celebrated the [A]Feast of [a]Booths, [B]as it is written, and *offered* [b]the fixed number of burnt offerings daily, [C]according to the ordinance, as each day required; 5 and afterward *there was* a [A]continual burnt offering, also [B]for the new moons and [C]for all the fixed festivals of the LORD that were consecrated, and from everyone who offered a freewill offering to the LORD. 6 From the first day of the seventh month they began to offer burnt offerings to the LORD, but the foundation of the temple of the LORD had not been laid. 7 Then they gave money to the masons and carpenters, and [A]food, drink and oil to the Sidonians and to the Tyrians, [B]to bring cedar wood from Lebanon to the sea at [C]Joppa, according to the permission they had [a]from [D]Cyrus king of Persia.

TEMPLE RESTORATION BEGUN

8 Now in the second year of their coming to the house of God at Jerusalem in the second month, [A]Zerubbabel the son of Shealtiel and Jeshua the son of Jozadak and the rest of their brothers the priests and the Levites, and all who came from the captivity to Jerusalem, began *the work* and [B]appointed the Levites from twenty years and older to oversee the work of the house of the LORD. 9 Then [A]Jeshua *with* his sons and brothers stood united *with* Kadmiel and his sons, the sons of [a]Judah *and* the sons of Henadad *with* their sons and brothers the Levites, to oversee the workmen in the temple of God.

10 Now when the builders had [A]laid the foundation of the temple of the LORD, [a]the priests stood in their apparel with trumpets, and the Levites, the sons of Asaph, with cymbals, to praise the LORD [B]according to the [b]directions of King David of Israel. 11 [A]They sang, praising and giving thanks to the LORD, *saying,* "[B]For He is good, for His lovingkindness is upon Israel forever." And all the people shouted with a great shout when they praised the LORD because the foundation of the house of the LORD was laid. 12 Yet many of the priests and Levites and heads of fathers' *households,* [A]the old men who had seen the first [a]temple, wept with a loud voice when the foundation of this house was laid before their eyes, while many shouted aloud for joy, 13 so that the people could not distinguish the sound of the shout of joy from the sound of the weeping of the people, for the people shouted with a loud shout, and the sound was heard far away.

ADVERSARIES HINDER THE WORK

4 Now when [A]the enemies of Judah and Benjamin heard that [B]the people of the exile were building a temple to the LORD God of Israel, 2 they approached Zerubbabel and the heads of fathers' *households,* and said to them, "Let us build with you, for we, like you, seek your God; [A]and we have been sacrificing to Him since the days of [B]Esarhaddon king of Assyria, who brought us up here." 3 But Zerubbabel and Jeshua and the rest of the heads of fathers' *households* of Israel said to them, "[A]You have nothing in common with us in building a house to our God; but we ourselves will together build to the LORD God of Israel, [B]as King Cyrus, the king of Persia has commanded us."

4 Then [A]the people of the land [a]discouraged the people of Judah, and frightened them from building, 5 and hired counselors against them to frustrate

3:2 [E]Deut 12:5, 6 3:3 [a]Lit *terror* was *upon them* [A]Ezra 4:4 [B]Num 28:2 3:4 [a]Or *Tabernacles* [b]Lit *by number* [A]Neh 8:14; Zech 14:16 [B]Ex 23:16 [C]Num 29:12 3:5 [A]Ex 29:38; Num 28:3 [B]Num 28:11 [C]Num 29:39 3:7 [a]Lit *of* [A]2 Chr 2:10; Acts 12:20 [B]2 Chr 2:16 [C]Acts 9:36 [D]Ezra 1:2; 6:3 3:8 [A]Ezra 3:2; 4:3 [B]1 Chr 23:4, 24 3:9 [a]In Ezra 2:40, *Hodaviah* [A]Ezra 2:40 3:10 [a]So with the Gr and some mss; M.T. *they set the priests* [b]Lit *hands* [A]Zech 4:6-10 [B]1 Chr 6:31; 25:1 3:11 [A]2 Chr 7:3; Neh 12:24, 40 [B]1 Chr 16:34; 2 Chr 5:13; Ps 100:5; 106:1; 107:1; 118:1; 131:1; Jer 33:11 3:12 [a]Lit *house* [A]Hag 2:3 4:1 [A]Ezra 4:7-10 [B]Ezra 1:11 4:2 [A]2 Kin 17:32 [B]2 Kin 19:37 4:3 [A]Neh 2:20 [B]Ezra 1:1, 2 4:4 [a]Lit *weakened the hands of* [A]Ezra 3:3

3:3 set up the altar. This was all that was needed to reestablish temple worship (cf. v. 6). They reset it on its old foundation, so it occupied its sacred site. **the peoples of the lands.** The settlers who had come to occupy the Land during the 70 years of Israel's absence were deportees brought in from other countries by the Assyrians and the Babylonians. These inhabitants saw the Jews as a threat and quickly wanted to undermine their allegiance to God (cf. 4:1, 2). **burnt offerings.** These were the most common offerings for sin (cf. v. 2).

3:4 number ... according to the ordinance. According to Nu 29:12–38.

3:7 masons ... carpenters ... cedar wood. The process of rebuilding the temple sounds similar to the original construction under Solomon (1Ki 5, 6; 1Ch 22; 2Ch 2). **Sidonians ... Joppa.** The materials were shipped from the Phoenician ports of Sidon and Tyre S to Joppa, the main seaport, about 35 mi. from Jerusalem. **permission they had from Cyrus.** Cf. 1:2–4.

3:8 second year ... second month. Ca. Apr./May 536 B.C. This officially ended the 70 year captivity that began in 605 B.C.

3:11 They sang. Their song of praise is similar to Ps 136:1.

3:12 the first temple. The temple built by Solomon (cf. 1Ki 5–7). **wept with a loud voice.** The first temple had been destroyed 50 years earlier. The old men, who would have been about 60 years or older, knew that this second temple did not begin to match the splendor of Solomon's temple nor did the presence of God reside within it (cf. Hag 2:1–4; Zec 4:9, 10). The nation was small and weak, the temple smaller and less beautiful by far. There were no riches as in David and Solomon's days. The ark was gone. But most disappointing was the absence of God's Shekinah glory. Thus the weeping. **shouted ... for joy.** For those who did not have a point of comparison, this was a great moment. Possibly Ps 126 was written and sung for this occasion.

4:1 the enemies. Cf. 5:3–17. These were Israel's enemies in the region, who resisted their reestablishment.

4:2 we have been sacrificing to Him. This false claim represented the syncretistic worship of the Samaritans, whose ancestry came from intermarriage with foreign immigrants in Samaria after 722 B.C. (cf. v. 10). In the British Museum is a large cylinder and inscribed on it are the annals of Esarhaddon, an Assyrian king (ca. 681–669 B.C.), who deported a large population of Israelites from Israel. A consequent settlement of Babylonian colonists took their place and intermarried with remaining Jewish women and their descendants. The result was the mongrel race called Samaritans. They had developed a superstitious form of worshiping God (cf. 2Ki 17:26–34).

4:3 we ourselves. Idolatry had been the chief cause for Judah's deportation to Babylon, and they wanted to avoid it altogether. While they still had their spiritual problems (Ezr 9, 10), they rejected any form of mixed religion, particularly this offer of cooperation which had sabotage as its goal (cf. vv. 4, 5). **King Cyrus ... commanded us.** Cf. Ezr 1:2–4 (ca. 538 B.C.). This note gave authority to their refusal.

4:5 frustrate. This caused a 16-year delay (ca. 536–520 B.C.). As a result, the people took more interest in their personal affairs than spiritual matters (cf. Hag 1:2–6). **Darius.** Darius ruled Persia ca. 521–486 B.C.

their counsel all the days of Cyrus king of Persia,
even until the reign of Darius king of Persia.
6 Now in the reign of [a,A]Ahasuerus, in the beginning of his reign, they wrote an accusation against
the inhabitants of Judah and Jerusalem.
7 And in the days of [a]Artaxerxes, Bishlam, Mithredath, Tabeel and the rest of his colleagues wrote
to Artaxerxes king of Persia; and the [b]text of the
letter was written in Aramaic and translated [A]*from*
Aramaic.

THE LETTER TO KING ARTAXERXES

8 [a]Rehum the commander and Shimshai the
scribe wrote a letter against Jerusalem to King
Artaxerxes, as follows— 9 then *wrote* Rehum the
commander and Shimshai the scribe and [A]the rest
of their colleagues, the judges and [B]the lesser governors, the officials, the secretaries, the men of
Erech, the Babylonians, the men of Susa, that is,
the Elamites, 10 and the rest of the nations which
the great and honorable [a]Osnappar deported and
settled in the city of Samaria, and in the rest of the
region beyond the [b]River. [A]Now 11 this is the copy
of the letter which they sent to him:
"To King Artaxerxes: Your servants, the men in
the region beyond the River, and now 12 let it be
known to the king that the Jews who came up from
you have come to us at Jerusalem; they are rebuilding [A]the rebellious and evil city and [B]are finishing
the walls and repairing the foundations. 13 Now let
it be known to the king, that if that city is rebuilt
and the walls are finished, [A]they will not pay tribute,
custom or toll, and it will damage the revenue of the
kings. 14 Now because we [a]are in the service of the
palace, and it is not fitting for us to see the king's
dishonor, therefore we have sent and informed the
king, 15 so that a search may be made in the record
books of your fathers. And you will discover in the
record books and learn that that city is a rebellious
city and damaging to kings and provinces, and that
they have incited revolt within it in past days; therefore that city was laid waste. 16 We inform the king
that if that city is rebuilt and the walls finished, as
a result you will have no possession in *the province*
beyond the River."

THE KING REPLIES AND WORK STOPS

17 *Then* the king sent an answer to Rehum the
commander, to Shimshai the scribe, and to the rest
of their colleagues who live in Samaria and in the
rest of *the provinces* beyond the River: "Peace. And
now 18 the document which you sent to us has been
[a,A]translated and read before me. 19 A decree has been
[a]issued by me, and a search has been made and it has
been discovered that that city has risen up against
the kings in past days, that rebellion and revolt have
been perpetrated in it, 20 [A]that mighty kings have
[a]ruled over Jerusalem, governing all *the provinces*
[B]beyond the River, and that [C]tribute, custom and toll
were paid to them. 21 So, now issue a decree to make
these men stop *work,* that this city may not be rebuilt
until a decree is issued by me. 22 Beware of being
negligent in carrying out this *matter;* why should
damage increase to the detriment of the kings?"
23 Then as soon as the copy of King Artaxerxes'
document was read before Rehum and Shimshai
the scribe and their colleagues, they went in haste
to Jerusalem to the Jews and stopped them by force
of arms.
24 Then work on the house of God in Jerusalem
ceased, and it was stopped until the second year of
the reign of Darius king of Persia.

4:6 [a]Or *Xerxes;* Heb *Ahash-verosh* [A]Esth 1:1; Dan 9:1 4:7 [a]Heb *Artah-shashta* [b]Lit *writing* [A]2 Kin 18:26; Dan 2:4 4:8 [a]Ch 4:8-6:18 is in Aram 4:9 [A]2 Kin 17:24 [B]Ezra 5:6; 6:6 4:10 [a]I.e. probably Ashurbanipal [b]I.e. Euphrates River, and so throughout the ch [A]Ezra 4:11, 17; 7:12 4:12 [A]2 Chr 36:13 [B]Ezra 5:3, 9 4:13 [A]Ezra 4:20; 7:24 4:14 [a]Lit *eat the salt* 4:18 [a]Lit *plainly read before* [A]Neh 8:8 4:19 [a]Lit *put* forth 4:20 [a]Lit *been* [A]1 Kin 4:21; 1 Chr 18:3 [B]Gen 15:18; Josh 1:4 [C]Ezra 4:13; 7:24

4:6–23 This section represents later opposition which Ezra chose to put here as a parenthetical continuation of the theme "opposition to resettling and rebuilding Judah" (see Introduction: Interpretive Challenges). He first referred to the opposition from Israel's enemies under King Ahasuerus (a regal title) or Xerxes (ca. 486–464 B.C.), who ruled at the time of Esther (4:6). Ezr 4:7–23 then recounts opposition in Nehemiah's day under Artaxerxes I (ca. 464–423 B.C.) expressed in a detailed letter of accusation against the Jews (vv. 7–16). It was successful in stopping the work, as the king's reply indicates (vv. 17–23). Most likely, this opposition is that also spoken of in Ne 1:3. All this was the ongoing occurrence of severe animosity between the Israelites and Samaritans, which was later aggravated when the Samaritans built a rival temple on Mt. Gerizim (cf. Jn 4:9). The opposition to Zerubbabel picks up again at 4:24–5:2 during the reign of Darius I, who actually reigned before either Ahasuerus or Artaxerxes.

4:6 they wrote an accusation. The word translated "accusation" means "a complaint." Satan, meaning "legal adversary" or "opponent," is a related term.

4:7, 8 letter ... letter. Two different words are used here. The first is an official document as opposed to a simple letter. The second is the generic term for letter. The context verifies the choices of two different terms, since two different letters are indicated.

4:8–6:18 Since this section contains predominantly correspondence, it is written in Aramaic (also 7:12–26) rather than Hebrew, generally reflecting the diplomatic language of the day (cf. 2Ki 18:26; Is 36:11).

4:10 Osnapper. Most likely another name for the Assyrian king Ashurbanipal, ca. 669–633 B.C. settled ... city of Samaria. The race of Samaritans resulted from the intermarriage of these immigrants with the poor people who were not taken captive to Nineveh (*see note on v. 2* and 2Ki 17:24–41).

4:11 Artaxerxes. *See note on vv. 6–23.* beyond the River. West of the Euphrates River.

4:12 Jews. This name was generally used after the Captivity because the exiles who returned were mainly of Judah. Most of the people of the 10 northern tribes were dispersed, and the largest number of returnees came from the two southern tribes.

4:13, 14 This accusation is full of hypocrisy. They did not relish paying taxes either, but they did hate the Jews.

4:15 the record books. An administrative document called a "memorandum" kept on file in the royal archives. city was laid waste. A reference to Jerusalem's destruction by the Babylonian king Nebuchadnezzar (ca. 586 B.C.).

4:19 A decree has been issued by me. This was no simple routine order given to one person, but rather a major edict to a large group of people.

4:21 now issue a decree. No small order for one or two workers, but rather the efforts of 50,000 were called to a halt. The king was commissioning a decree of great significance. The original language calls for the difference. This decree would not lose its authority until the king established a new decree.

4:23 document. Another official document, as opposed to a generic letter, came from Artaxerxes, a transfer of authority to the regional leaders to establish the decree. Without the king's official administrative correspondence, the decree could not be established.

4:24 ceased ... stopped. For 16 years, from 536 B.C. to 520 B.C., work on rebuilding was halted.

TEMPLE WORK RESUMED

5 When the prophets, [A]Haggai the prophet and
[B]Zechariah the son of Iddo, prophesied to the
Jews who were in Judah and Jerusalem in the name
of the God of Israel, who was over them, 2 then [A]Ze-
rubbabel the son of Shealtiel and Jeshua the son
of Jozadak arose and began to rebuild the house
of God which is in Jerusalem; and [B]the prophets of
God were with them supporting them.
3 At that time [A]Tattenai, the governor of *the province* beyond the [a]River, and Shethar-bozenai and
their colleagues came to them and spoke to them
thus, "[B]Who issued you a decree to rebuild this [b]tem-
ple and to finish this structure?" 4 [A]Then we told
them accordingly what the names of the men were
who were reconstructing this building. 5 But [A]the
eye of their God was on the elders of the Jews, and
they did not stop them until a report could come
to Darius, and then a written reply be returned
concerning it.

ADVERSARIES WRITE TO DARIUS

6 *This is* the copy of the letter which [A]Tattenai,
the governor of *the province* beyond the River,
and Shethar-bozenai and his colleagues [B]the officials, who were beyond the River, sent to Darius
the king. 7 They sent a report to him in which it
was written thus: "To Darius the king, all peace.
8 Let it be known to the king that we have gone to
the province of Judah, to the house of the great
God, which is being built with huge stones, and
[a]beams are being laid in the walls; and this work
is going on with great care and is succeeding in
their hands. 9 Then we asked those elders and said
to them thus, 'Who issued you a decree to rebuild
this temple and to finish this structure?' 10 We also
asked them their names so as to inform you, and
that we might write down the names of the men
who were at their head. 11 Thus they [a]answered us,
saying, 'We are the servants of the God of heaven
and earth and are rebuilding the temple that was
built many years ago, [A]which a great king of Israel
built and finished. 12 But [A]because our fathers had
provoked the God of heaven to wrath, [B]He gave them
into the hand of Nebuchadnezzar king of Babylon,
the Chaldean, *who* destroyed this temple and deported the people to Babylon. 13 However, [A]in the
first year of Cyrus king of Babylon, King Cyrus [B]is-
sued a decree to rebuild this house of God. 14 Also
[A]the gold and silver utensils of the house of God
which Nebuchadnezzar had taken from the temple
[a]in Jerusalem, and brought them to the temple of
Babylon, these King Cyrus took from the temple of
Babylon and they were given to one [B]whose name
was Sheshbazzar, whom he had appointed governor. 15 He said to him, "Take these utensils, go *and*
deposit them in the temple [a]in Jerusalem and let
the house of God be rebuilt in its place." 16 Then
that Sheshbazzar came *and* [A]laid the foundations
of the house of God [a]in Jerusalem; and from then
until now it has been under construction and it is
[B]not *yet* completed.' 17 Now if it pleases the king, [A]let
a search be conducted in the king's treasure house,
which is there in Babylon, if it be that a decree was
issued by King Cyrus to rebuild this house of God at
Jerusalem; and let the king send to us his decision
concerning this *matter*."

DARIUS FINDS CYRUS'S DECREE

6 Then King Darius issued a decree, and [A]search
was made in the [a]archives, where the treasures
were stored in Babylon. 2 In [a]Ecbatana in the fortress, which is [A]in the province of Media, a scroll
was found and there was written in it as follows:

5:1 [A]Hag 1:1 [B]Zech 1:1 5:2 [A]Ezra 3:2; Hag 1:12; Zech 4:6-9 [B]Ezra 6:14; Hag 2:4; Zech 3:1 5:3 [a]I.e. Euphrates River, and so throughout the ch [b]Lit *house,* and so in vv 9, 11, 12 [A]Ezra 6:6, 13 [B]Ezra 1:3; 5:9 5:4 [A]Ezra 5:10 5:5 [A]Ezra 7:6, 28 5:6 [A]Ezra 5:3 [B]Ezra 4:9 5:8 [a]Lit *timber is* 5:11 [a]Lit *returned us the word* [A]1 Kin 6:1, 38 5:12 [A]2 Chr 36:16, 17 [B]2 Kin 25:8-11; Jer 52:12-15 5:13 [A]Ezra 1:1 [B]Ezra 1:1-4 5:14 [a]Lit *that was in* [A]Ezra 1:7; 6:5; Dan 5:2 [B]Ezra 1:8; 5:16 5:15 [a]Lit *that is in* 5:16 [a]Lit *that is in* [A]Ezra 3:8, 10 [B]Ezra 6:15 5:17 [A]Ezra 6:1, 2 6:1 [a]Lit *house of the books* [A]Ezra 5:17 6:2 [a]Aram *Achmetha* [A]2 Kin 17:6

5:1 Haggai … and Zechariah. The book of Haggai is styled as a "royal administrative correspondence" (cf. Hag 1:13) sent from the Sovereign King of the Universe through the "messenger of the LORD," Haggai (Hag 1:13). Part of its message is addressed specifically to Zerubbabel, the political leader, and Joshua, the religious leader, telling them to "take courage … and work" on the temple because God was with them (Hag 2:4). These two prophets gave severe reproaches and threats if the people did not return to the building and promised national prosperity if they did. Not long after the exiles heard this message, the temple work began afresh after a 16-year hiatus. *See notes on Haggai and Zechariah.*

5:2 prophets of God. These would be in addition to Haggai and Zechariah.

5:3 Tattenai. Most likely a Persian official. **Who issued you a decree … ?** In other words, "Who gave you royal permission to build?" Cf. Ezr 5:9.

5:5 But the eye of their God was on the elders. God's hand of protection which led this endeavor allowed the work to continue while official communication was going on with Darius, the Persian king *(see note on 4:5).*

5:8 huge stones, and beams. This technique of using beams and stone blocks was a well known form of wall construction. The reason for mentioning it here was it seemed to be a preparation for conflict, or battle. Including this piece of information served as a threat to the Persian official who wanted no such conflict.

5:11 they answered us. They sent back a report (official document for the archives). **a great king of Israel.** Solomon built the first temple (ca. 966–960 B.C.; 1Ki 5–7).

5:12 gave them into the hand of Nebuchadnezzar. The expression is used commonly in royal administrative correspondence when a more powerful administrator, such as a king, relinquishes some of his authority to an underling and yet keeps the lower administrative official completely under his command. The point here is that God, as King of the universe, satisfied His wrath by relinquishing the authority for this administrative action to Nebuchadnezzar. The greatest king the ancient Near East has ever known was merely a petty official in the administration of the sovereign Lord.

5:13 Cyrus … decree. Cf. Ezr 1:2–4.

5:14, 16 Sheshbazzar … laid the foundations. This seems to contradict the statement in Ezr 3:8–10 that Zerubbabel, Jeshua, and the Jewish workmen laid the foundation, but it actually does not, since Sheshbazzar was the political appointee of the Persian king over the Jews and thus is given official credit for work actually done by them. *See note on 1:8.*

6:1 King Darius issued a decree. Rather than a public edict, this was a simple order issued to a small group of officials.

6:1, 2 Babylon … Ecbatana. Ecbatana was one of the Persian capitals, 300 mi. NE of Babylon in the foothills, where Cyrus and others had their summer homes.

6:2 there was written. A particular kind of document called a memorandum (Ezr 4:15; Mal 3:16). Administrative officials often kept these documents of administrative decisions made, or issues remaining to be settled, to retain the details of administrative action for future reference.

"Memorandum— 3 [A]In the first year of King Cyrus,
Cyrus the king issued a decree: '*Concerning* the
house of God at Jerusalem, let the [a]temple, the place
where sacrifices are offered, be rebuilt and let its
foundations be [b]retained, its height being 60 cubits and its width 60 cubits; 4 [A]with three layers of
huge stones and [a]one layer of timbers. And let the
cost be paid from the [b]royal treasury. 5 Also let [A]the
gold and silver utensils of the house of God, which
Nebuchadnezzar took from the temple in Jerusalem
and brought to Babylon, be returned and [a]brought
to their places in the temple in Jerusalem; and you
shall put *them* in the house of God.'
6 "Now *therefore,* [A]Tattenai, governor of *the province* beyond the [a]River, Shethar-bozenai and [b]your
colleagues, the officials of *the provinces* beyond the
[a]River, [c]keep away from there. 7 Leave this work on
the house of God alone; let the governor of the Jews
and the elders of the Jews rebuild this house of God
on its site. 8 Moreover, [A]I issue a decree concerning
what you are to do for these elders of Judah in the
rebuilding of this house of God: the full cost is to
be paid to these people from the royal treasury out
of the taxes of *the provinces* beyond the River, and
that without delay. 9 Whatever is needed, both young
bulls, rams, and lambs for a burnt offering to the God
of heaven, and wheat, salt, wine and anointing oil,
as the priests in Jerusalem request, *it* is to be given
to them daily without fail, 10 that they may offer [a]ac-
ceptable sacrifices to the God of heaven and [A]pray
for the life of the king and his sons. 11 And I issued a
decree that [A]any man who violates this edict, a timber shall be drawn from his house and he shall be
impaled on it and [B]his house shall be made a refuse
heap on account of this. 12 May the God who [A]has
caused His name to dwell there overthrow any king
or people who [a]attempts to change *it,* so as to destroy
this house of God in Jerusalem. I, Darius, have issued
this decree, let *it* be carried out with all diligence!"

THE TEMPLE COMPLETED AND DEDICATED

13 Then [A]Tattenai, the governor of *the province* beyond the River, Shethar-bozenai and their colleagues
carried out *the decree* with all diligence, just as King
Darius had sent. 14 And [A]the elders of the Jews [a]were
successful in building through the prophesying of
Haggai the prophet and Zechariah the son of Iddo.
And [b]they finished building according to the command of the God of Israel and the decree [B]of Cyrus,
[C]Darius, and [D]Artaxerxes king of Persia. 15 This [a]tem-
ple was completed [b]on the third day of the [A]month
Adar; it was the sixth year of the reign of King Darius.
16 And the sons of Israel, the priests, the Levites
and the rest of the [a]exiles, [A]celebrated the dedication of this house of God with joy. 17 They offered
for the dedication of this temple of God 100 bulls,
200 rams, 400 lambs, and as a sin offering for all
Israel [A]12 male goats, corresponding to the number
of the tribes of Israel. 18 Then they appointed the
priests to [A]their divisions and the Levites in [B]their
orders for the service of God [a]in Jerusalem, [C]as it
is written in the book of Moses.

THE PASSOVER OBSERVED

19 [A]The exiles observed the Passover on [B]the fourteenth of the first month. 20 [A]For the priests and the
Levites had purified themselves together; all of them
were pure. Then [B]they slaughtered the Passover *lamb*
for all the exiles, both for their brothers the priests
and for themselves. 21 The sons of Israel who returned
from exile and [A]all those who had separated themselves from [B]the impurity of the nations of the land
to *join* them, to seek the LORD God of Israel, ate *the
Passover.* 22 And [A]they observed the Feast of Unleavened Bread seven days with joy, for the LORD had
caused them to rejoice, and [B]had turned the heart of
[C]the king of Assyria toward them to [a]encourage them
in the work of the house of God, the God of Israel.

6:3 [a]Lit *house* [b]Or *fixed, laid* [A]Ezra 1:1; 5:13 6:4 [a]So Gr; Aram *a layer of new timber* [b]Lit *king's house* [A]1 Kin 6:36 6:5 [a]Lit *go* [A]Ezra 1:7; 5:14 6:6 [a]I.e. Euphrates River, and so throughout the ch [b]Aram *their* [c]Lit *be distant* [A]Ezra 5:3; 6:13 6:8 [A]Ezra 6:4; 7:14-22 6:10 [a]Lit *pleasing; or sweet-smelling sacrifices* [A]Ezra 7:23; Jer 29:7; 1 Tim 2:1, 2 6:11 [A]Ezra 7:26 [B]Dan 2:5; 3:29 6:12 [a]Lit *sends his hand* [A]Deut 12:5, 11; 1 Kin 9:3 6:13 [A]Ezra 6:6 6:14 [a]Lit *were building and succeeding* [b]Lit *built and finished* [A]Ezra 5:1, 2 [B]Ezra 1:1; 5:13 [C]Ezra 4:24; 6:12 [D]Ezra 7:1 6:15 [a]Lit *house* [b]Lit *until* [A]Esth 3:7 6:16 [a]Lit *sons of the captivity* [A]1 Kin 8:63; 2 Chr 7:5 6:17 [A]Ezra 8:35 6:18 [a]Lit *which is in* [A]1 Chr 24:1; 2 Chr 35:5 [B]1 Chr 23:6 [C]Num 3:6; 8:9 6:19 [A]Ezra 1:11 [B]Ex 12:6 6:20 [A]2 Chr 29:34; 30:15 [B]2 Chr 35:11 6:21 [A]Neh 9:2; 10:28 [B]Ezra 9:11 6:22 [a]Lit *strengthen their hands* [A]Ex 12:15 [B]Ezra 7:27; Prov 21:1 [C]Ezra 1:1; 6:1

6:3 first year. Ca. 538 B.C. (cf. 1:2–4). **being 60 cubits … 60 cubits.** These dimensions exceed those of Solomon's temple (cf. 1Ki 6:2).

6:5 Nebuchadnezzar took. *See note on 1:7.*

6:6, 7 God so favored the Jews (cf. 5:5) that, through Darius, He forbade the officials from interfering with the building project.

6:8–10 Not only could the officials not hinder the building, but they also had to help finance it by giving the Jews some of their portion of taxes collected for the Persian king. The Jews could draw from the provincial treasury.

6:10 pray for the life of the king and his sons. This was essentially the same self-serving motive that prompted Cyrus to decree that all captured peoples should return to their countries, rebuild the temples that Nebuchadnezzar and others had destroyed, and placate the offended deities. He wanted all the gods on his side, including Israel's God.

6:11 drawn … impaled … made a refuse heap. Typical punishment for a serious infraction (cf. Rev 22:18, 19). This was specifically directed at the hostile Samaritans.

6:14 successful. Cf. Hag 1:7–11. **the command of the God of Israel … the decree of Cyrus.** This is not the normal term for command, but it is the same word translated "decree" or "administrative order" throughout the book. The message here is powerful. It was the decree from God, the Sovereign of the universe, which gave administrative authority to rebuild the temple. The decrees (same word) of 3 of the greatest monarchs in the history of the ancient Near East were only a secondary issue. God rules the universe and He raises up kings, then pulls them from their thrones when they have served His administration. **Artaxerxes.** Although he did not contribute to the project under Zerubbabel, he did under Ezra (cf. 7:11–26).

6:15 Adar … sixth year. The 12th month (Feb./Mar.) in 516 B.C.

6:18 divisions. Cf. 1Ch 24, where the priestly divisions are delineated. Although David arranged the priests and Levites in order according to families, it was Moses who assigned their rights, privileges, and duties (*see notes on Nu 3, 4*). **the book of Moses.** I.e., the Pentateuch.

6:19 Passover. Cf. Lv 23:4–8. Other notable Passovers include Hezekiah's (2Ch 30:1–22) and Josiah's (2Ch 35:1–19). **first month.** Mar./Apr.

6:21 the impurity of the nations. These were proselytes to Judaism, who had confessed their spiritual uncleanness before the Lord, been circumcised, and renounced idolatry to keep the Passover (v. 22).

6:22 turned the heart of the king of Assyria toward them. By turning the heart of the king in their favor in allowing them to complete the rebuilding, God encouraged His people. They understood the verse, "The king's heart is … in the hand of the LORD" (Pr 21:1) better through this ordeal. The title "King of Assyria" was held by every king who succeeded the great Neo-Assyrian Empire regardless of what country they may have come from.

6:22–7:1 The book of Esther fits in this 59-year gap between the completion of the

EZRA JOURNEYS FROM BABYLON TO JERUSALEM

7 [A]Now after these things, in the reign of [B]Arta-
xerxes king of Persia, *there went up* Ezra son
of Seraiah, son of Azariah, son of Hilkiah, 2 son
of Shallum, son of Zadok, son of Ahitub, 3 son of
Amariah, son of Azariah, son of Meraioth, 4 son of
Zerahiah, son of Uzzi, son of Bukki, 5 son of Abishua,
son of Phinehas, son of Eleazar, son of Aaron the
chief priest. 6 This Ezra went up from Babylon, and
he was a [A]scribe skilled in the law of Moses, which
the LORD God of Israel had given; and the king
granted him all [a]he requested [B]because the hand
of the LORD his God *was* upon him. 7 [A]Some of the
sons of Israel and some of the priests, the Levites,
the singers, the gatekeepers and the temple servants went up to Jerusalem in the seventh year of
King Artaxerxes.

8 He came to Jerusalem in the fifth month, which
was in the seventh year of the king. 9 For on the first
of the first month [a]he began to go up from Babylon;
and on the first of the fifth month he came to Jerusalem, [A]because the good hand of his God *was*
upon him. 10 For Ezra had set his heart to [a]study the
law of the LORD and to practice *it,* and [A]to teach *His*
statutes and ordinances in Israel.

KING'S DECREE ON BEHALF OF EZRA

11 Now this is the copy of the decree which King Artaxerxes gave to Ezra the priest, the scribe, [a]learned
in the words of the commandments of the LORD and
His statutes to Israel: 12 "[a]Artaxerxes, [A]king of kings,
to Ezra the priest, the scribe of the law of the God of
heaven, perfect *peace.* And now 13 [A]I have issued a decree that any of the people of Israel and their priests
and the Levites in my kingdom who are willing to go
to Jerusalem, may go with you. 14 Forasmuch as you
are sent [a]by the king and his [A]seven counselors to
inquire concerning Judah and Jerusalem according
to the law of your God which is in your hand, 15 and
to bring the silver and gold, which the king and his
counselors have freely offered to the God of Israel,
[A]whose dwelling is in Jerusalem, 16 with [A]all the silver and gold which you find in the whole province
of Babylon, along [B]with the freewill offering of the
people and of the priests, who [C]offered willingly for
the house of their God which is in Jerusalem; 17 with
this money, therefore, you shall diligently buy bulls,
rams and lambs, [A]with their grain offerings and their
drink offerings and [B]offer them on the altar of the
house of your God which is in Jerusalem. 18 Whatever
seems good to you and to your brothers to do with
the rest of the silver and gold, you may do according

7:1 [A]1 Chr 6:4-14 [B]Ezra 7:12, 21; Neh 2:1 7:6 [a]Lit *his request* [A]Ezra 7:11, 12, 21 [B]Ezra 7:9, 28; 8:22 7:7 [A]Ezra 8:1-20 7:9 [a]Lit *was the foundation* [A]Ezra 7:6; Neh 2:8 7:10 [a]Lit *seek* [A]Deut 33:10; Ezra 7:25; Neh 8:1 7:11 [a]Lit *the scribe of* 7:12 [a]Ch 7:12-26 is in Aram [A]Ezek 26:7; Dan 2:37 7:13 [A]Ezra 6:1 7:14 [a]Lit *from before* [A]Ezra 7:15, 28; 8:25 7:15 [A]2 Chr 6:2; Ezra 6:12; Ps 135:21 7:16 [A]Ezra 8:25 [B]Ezra 1:4, 6 [C]1 Chr 29:6 7:17 [A]Num 15:4-13 [B]Deut 12:5-11

temple (ca. 516 B.C.) under Zerubbabel (Ezr 1–6) and the second return (ca. 458 B.C.) under Ezra (Ezr 7–10). Ezra 4:6 provides a glimpse into this period also.

7:1–10:44 This section covers the return of the second group to Judah, led by Ezra (ca. 458 B.C.).

7:1 **Artaxerxes.** King of Persia from 464–423 B.C. **Ezra.** See Introduction: Author and Date. **son of.** Ezra traced his lineage back through such notable High Priests as Zadok (1Ki 2:35), Phinehas (Nu 25:10–13), and Eleazar (Nu 3:4).

7:6 **a scribe skilled in the law.** Ezra's role as a scribe was critical to reinstate the nation since the leaders had to go back to the law and interpret it. This was no small task because many aspects of life had changed in the intervening 1,000 years since the law was first given. Tradition says Ezra had the law memorized and could write it from recall. **the hand of the LORD his God *was* upon him.** This refrain occurs throughout the books of Ezra and Nehemiah. Its resounding presence assures the reader that it was not by the shrewd leadership skills of a few men that Judah, with its temple and walls, was rebuilt in the midst of a powerful Medo-Persian Empire. Rather it was the sovereign hand of the wise and powerful King of the universe that allowed this to happen.

7:7 **temple servants.** *See note on 2:43–54.* **seventh year.** Ca. 458 B.C.

7:8, 9 The 4-month journey from Babylon to Jerusalem, covering almost 1,000 mi., started in Mar./Apr. and ended in Jul./Aug.

7:10 **study ... practice ... teach.** The pattern of Ezra's preparation is exemplary. He studied before he attempted to live a life of obedience, and he studied and practiced the law in his own life before he opened his mouth to teach that law. But the success of Ezra's leadership did not come from his strength alone, but most significantly because "the good hand of his God *was* upon him" (7:9).

7:11 **copy of the decree.** The original was usually kept for a record. The letter was addressed to Ezra because the decree recorded therein was the critical administrative document. Decrees were commonly embedded in letters. The letter in essence authorized the document into Ezra's hands so that he could carry it and read it to its intended audience.

7:12–26 This is a remarkable decree that evidences God's sovereign rule over earthly kings and His intent to keep the Abrahamic, Davidic, and New Covenants with Israel. This section is in Aramaic, as was 4:8–6:18.

7:12 **king of kings.** Though it was true that Artaxerxes ruled over other kings, Jesus Christ is the ultimate King of Kings (cf. Rev 19:16), who alone can genuinely make that claim since He will rule over all kings in His coming kingdom (cf. Rev 11:15).

7:14 **seven counselors.** This number was according to the Persian tradition (cf. Est 1:14).

7:17 **therefore.** The royal decree protocol recorded in the opening words of 7:13–16 leads up to the section introduced by this word.

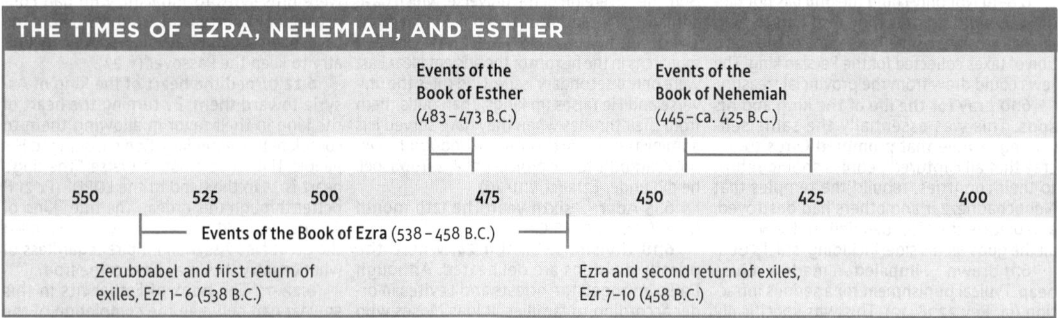

to the will of your God. 19 Also the utensils which are
given to you for the service of the house of your God,
deliver in full before the God of Jerusalem. 20 The rest
of the needs for the house of your God, for which
you may have occasion to provide, [A]provide *for it*
from the royal treasury.
21 "I, even I, King Artaxerxes, issue a decree to all
the treasurers who are *in the provinces* beyond the
[a]River, that whatever Ezra the priest, [A]the scribe of
the law of the God of heaven, may require of you,
it shall be done diligently, 22 *even* up to 100 talents
of silver, 100 [a]kors of wheat, 100 baths of wine, 100
baths of oil, and salt [b]as needed. 23 Whatever is [a]com-
manded by the God of heaven, let it be done with
zeal for the house of the God of heaven, [A]so that
there will not be wrath against the kingdom of the
king and his sons. 24 We also inform you that [A]it is
not allowed to [a]impose tax, tribute or toll [B]*on* any of
the priests, Levites, singers, doorkeepers, Nethinim
or servants of this house of God.
25 "You, Ezra, according to the wisdom of your
God which is in your hand, [A]appoint magistrates
and judges that they may judge all the people who
are in *the province* beyond the River, *even* all those
who know the laws of your God; and you may [B]teach
anyone who is ignorant *of them.* 26 [A]Whoever will
not observe the law of your God and the law of the
king, let judgment be executed upon him strictly,
whether for death or for [a]banishment or for confiscation of goods or for imprisonment."

THE KING'S KINDNESS

27 Blessed be the LORD, the God of our fathers,
[A]who has put *such a thing* as this in the king's heart,
to adorn the house of the LORD which is in Jerusalem,
28 and [A]has extended lovingkindness to me before
the king and his counselors and before all the king's
mighty princes. Thus I was strengthened according
to [B]the hand of the LORD my God upon me, and I
gathered [a]leading men from Israel to go up with me.

PEOPLE WHO WENT WITH EZRA

8 Now these are the heads of their fathers' *house-*
holds and the genealogical enrollment of those
who went up with me from Babylon in the reign of
King Artaxerxes: 2 of the sons of Phinehas, Gershom;
of the sons of Ithamar, Daniel; of the sons of David,
[A]Hattush; 3 of the sons of Shecaniah *who was* of the
sons of [A]Parosh, Zechariah and with him 150 males
who were in the genealogical list; 4 of the sons of
Pahath-moab, Eliehoenai the son of Zerahiah and
200 males with him; 5 of the sons of Zattu, Shecaniah, the son of Jahaziel and 300 males with him;
6 and of the sons of [A]Adin, Ebed the son of Jonathan
and 50 males with him; 7 and of the sons of Elam,
Jeshaiah the son of Athaliah and 70 males with him;
8 and of the sons of Shephatiah, Zebadiah the son
of Michael and 80 males with him; 9 of the sons of
Joab, Obadiah the son of Jehiel and 218 males with
him; 10 and of the sons of Bani, Shelomith, the son
of Josiphiah and 160 males with him; 11 and of the
sons of Bebai, Zechariah the son of Bebai and 28
males with him; 12 and of the sons of Azgad, Johanan
the son of Hakkatan and 110 males with him; 13 and
of the sons of Adonikam, the last ones, these being
their names, Eliphelet, Jeuel and Shemaiah, and 60
males with them; 14 and of the sons of Bigvai, Uthai
and [a]Zabbud, and 70 males with [b]them.

EZRA SENDS FOR LEVITES

15 Now I assembled them at [A]the river that runs to
Ahava, where we camped for three days; and when
I observed the people and the priests, I [B]did not find
any Levites there. 16 So I sent for Eliezer, Ariel, Shemaiah, Elnathan, Jarib, Elnathan, Nathan, Zechariah
and Meshullam, [a]leading men, and for Joiarib and
Elnathan, teachers. 17 I sent them to Iddo the [a]leading
man at the place Casiphia; and I [b]told them what to
say to [c]Iddo *and* his brothers, [A]the temple servants
at the place Casiphia, *that is,* to bring ministers to us
for the house of our God. 18 [A]According to the good
hand of our God upon us they brought us a [B]man
of insight of the sons of Mahli, the son of Levi, the
son of Israel, namely Sherebiah, and his sons and
brothers, 18 men; 19 and Hashabiah and [a]Jeshaiah of
the sons of Merari, with his brothers and their sons,
20 men; 20 and 220 of [A]the temple servants, whom
David and the princes had given for the service of
the Levites, all of them designated by name.

PROTECTION OF GOD INVOKED

21 Then I proclaimed [A]a fast there at [B]the river of
Ahava, that we might [C]humble ourselves before our
God to seek from Him a [a]safe journey for us, our little

7:20 [A]Ezra 6:4 7:21 [a]I.e. Euphrates River, and so throughout the ch [A]Ezra 7:6 7:22 [a]I.e. One kor equals approx ten bu [b]Lit *without prescription* 7:23 [a]Lit *from the decree of* [A]Ezra 6:10 7:24 [a]Lit *throw on them* [A]Ezra 4:13, 20 [B]Ezra 7:7 7:25 [A]Ex 18:21; Deut 16:18 [B]Ezra 7:10; Mal 2:7; Col 1:28 7:26 [a]Lit *rooting out* [A]Ezra 6:11, 12 7:27 [A]Ezra 6:22 7:28 [a]Lit *heads* [A]Ezra 9:9 [B]Ezra 5:5 8:2 [A]1 Chr 3:22 8:3 [A]Ezra 2:3 8:6 [A]Ezra 2:15; Neh 7:20; 10:16 8:14 [a]Or *Zakkur* [b]Or *him* 8:15 [A]Ezra 8:21, 31 [B]Ezra 7:7; 8:2 8:16 [a]Lit *heads* 8:17 [a]Lit *head* [b]Lit *put words in their mouth to say* [c]So Gr; Heb *Iddo his brother* [A]Ezra 2:43 8:18 [A]Ezra 7:6, 28 [B]2 Chr 30:22 8:19 [a]So Gr; Heb *with him Jeshaiah* 8:20 [A]Ezra 2:43; 7:7 8:21 [a]Lit *straight way* [A]1 Sam 7:6; 2 Chr 20:3 [B]Ezra 8:15, 31 [C]Lev 16:29; 23:29; Is 58:3, 5

7:22 up to 100 talents. Approaching 4 tons in weight. **to … 100 kors.** Approximately 750 bushels. **to … 100 baths.** Six hundred gallons.

7:25 You, Ezra. The letter in which the decree was embedded was written to Ezra. The king turned to him in a demonstration of administrative trust and granted him permission to appoint magistrates and judges for the region. The effect of this decision would be to offer a measure of local autonomy to the Jews.

8:1–14 from Babylon. The list that follows no doubt includes those who lived in the surrounding areas. The total number of males in this section is 1,496 plus the men named, so with the addition of the women and children the number easily approaches 7,000 to 8,000. Just as these had not gone with the first group of returnees, so many Jews remained in Babylon after this group had departed. During the 70 years, many of the exiles had settled into a comfortable lifestyle. No small conflict arose between those who returned and those who stayed in Babylon.

8:15 river … Ahava. An unknown location where a canal/river flowed into the Euphrates. This was in Babylon and chosen for the place where the returning Jews would render vows for several days in preparation to leave. **not find any Levites.** There were no Levites who chose to return, so Ezra pursued such needed men by sending a command to Iddo, who was chief of the temple servants. Iddo's influence brought 38 Levites and 220 temple servants (vv. 16–20).

8:21–23 I proclaimed a fast. They would soon begin the long journey. Such travel was dangerous, for the roads were frequented by

ones, and all our possessions. 22 For I was ashamed to
request from the king troops and horsemen to [a]pro-
tect us from the enemy on the way, because we had
said to the king, "[A]The hand of our God is [b]favorably
disposed to all those who seek Him, but [B]His power
and His anger are against all those who [C]forsake
Him." 23 So we fasted and sought our God concerning this *matter,* and He [a,A]listened to our entreaty.
24 Then I set apart twelve of the leading priests,
[A]Sherebiah, Hashabiah, and with them ten of their
brothers; 25 and I [A]weighed out to them [B]the silver,
the gold and the utensils, the offering for the house
of our God which the king and [C]his counselors and
his princes and all Israel present *there* had offered.
26 [A]Thus I weighed into their hands 650 talents of
silver, and silver utensils *worth* 100 talents, *and* 100
gold talents, 27 and 20 gold bowls *worth* 1,000 darics,
and two utensils of fine shiny bronze, precious as
gold. 28 Then I said to them, "[A]You are holy to the
LORD, and the [B]utensils are holy; and the silver and
the gold are a freewill offering to the LORD God of
your fathers. 29 Watch and keep *them* [A]until you
weigh *them* before the leading priests, the Levites
and the heads of the fathers' *households* of Israel
at Jerusalem, *in* the chambers of the house of the
LORD." 30 So the priests and the Levites [A]accepted
the weighed out silver and gold and the utensils,
to bring *them* to Jerusalem to the house of our God.
31 Then we journeyed from [A]the river Ahava on
[B]the twelfth of the first month to go to Jerusalem;
and [C]the hand of our God was over us, and He delivered us from the hand of the enemy and the ambushes by the way. 32 [A]Thus we came to Jerusalem
and remained there three days.

TREASURE PLACED IN THE TEMPLE

33 On the fourth day the silver and the gold and
the utensils [A]were weighed out in the house of our
God into the hand of [B]Meremoth the son of Uriah
the priest, and with him *was* Eleazar the son of
Phinehas; and with them *were* the Levites, Jozabad
the son of Jeshua and Noadiah the son of Binnui.
34 Everything *was* numbered and weighed, and all
the weight was recorded at that time.
35 [A]The exiles who had come from the captivity offered burnt offerings to the God of Israel: [B]12 bulls for
all Israel, 96 rams, 77 lambs, 12 male goats for a sin offering, all as a burnt offering to the LORD. 36 Then [A]they
delivered the king's edicts to [B]the king's satraps and
to the governors *in the provinces* beyond the [a]River,
and they supported the people and the house of God.

MIXED MARRIAGES

9 Now when these things had been completed,
the princes approached me, saying, "The people of Israel and the priests and the Levites have
not [A]separated themselves from the peoples of the
lands, [B]according to their abominations, *those* of the
Canaanites, the Hittites, the Perizzites, the Jebusites,
the Ammonites, the Moabites, the Egyptians and
the Amorites. 2 For [A]they have taken some of their
daughters *as wives* for themselves and for their
sons, so that [B]the holy [a]race has [C]intermingled with
the peoples of the lands; indeed, the hands of the
princes and the rulers have been foremost in this
unfaithfulness." 3 When I heard about this matter,
I [A]tore my garment and my robe, and pulled some
of the hair from my head and my beard, and [B]sat
down appalled. 4 Then [A]everyone who trembled at
the words of the God of Israel on account of the
unfaithfulness of the exiles gathered to me, and I
sat appalled until [B]the evening offering.

PRAYER OF CONFESSION

5 But at the evening offering I arose from my
[a]humiliation, even with my garment and my robe
torn, and I fell on my knees and [A]stretched out my
[b]hands to the LORD my God; 6 and I said, "O my

8:22 [a]Lit *help* [b]Lit *upon all…for good* [A]Ezra 7:6, 9, 28 [B]Josh 22:16 [C]2 Chr 15:2 8:23 [a]Lit *was entreated by us* [A]1 Chr 5:20; 2 Chr 33:13 8:24 [A]Ezra 8:18, 19 8:25 [A]Ezra 8:33 [B]Ezra 7:15, 16 [C]Ezra 7:14 8:26 [A]Ezra 1:9-11 8:28 [A]Lev 21:6-8 [B]Lev 22:2, 3 8:29 [A]Ezra 8:33, 34 8:30 [A]Ezra 1:9 8:31 [A]Ezra 8:15, 21 [B]Ezra 7:9 [C]Ezra 8:22 8:32 [A]Neh 2:11 8:33 [A]Ezra 8:30 [B]Neh 3:4, 21 8:35 [A]Ezra 2:1 [B]Ezra 6:17 8:36 [a]I.e. Euphrates River [A]Ezra 7:21-24 [B]Ezra 4:7; 5:6 9:1 [A]Ezra 6:21; Neh 9:2 [B]Lev 18:24-30 9:2 [a]Lit *seed* [A]Deut 7:3; Ezra 10:2, 18 [B]Ex 22:31; Deut 14:2; 2 Cor 6:14 [C]Neh 13:3 9:3 [A]2 Kin 18:37 [B]Neh 1:4 9:4 [A]Ezra 10:3; Is 66:2 [B]Ex 29:39 9:5 [a]Or *fasting* [b]Lit *palms* [A]Ex 9:29

thieves who robbed for survival. Even messengers traveled with caravans to ensure their safety. Ezra and the people did not want to confuse the king regarding their trust in God's protection so they entreated Him for safety with a prayerful fast. God honored their prayer of faith with His protection.

8:26 weighed … 650 talents. Over 25 tons. ***worth* 100 talents.** Almost 4 tons.

8:27 bowls *worth* 1,000 darics. About 20 lbs. *See note on 2:69.*

8:31 Ahava. *See note on v. 15.* **first month.** *See note on 7:8, 9.* The 12-day delay occurred because of a 3-day delay searching for more Levites (8:15) and the fast which sought God's protection (8:21).

8:36 they delivered the king's edicts. The plural "edicts" may account for a change of terminology. This would include the decrees plus other edicts in the official correspondence Artaxerxes gave to Ezra to deliver, to support the Jews and their building of the temple.

9:1 when these things had been completed. This refers to the implementation of the different trusts and duties committed to him. **priests … Levites.** As was the case before the Assyrian and Babylonian deportations, the spiritual leadership defaulted along with the people (cf. Is 24:2; Jer 5:30, 31; 6:13–15; Hos 4:9; Mal 2:1–9; 2Ti 4:2–4). **abominations.** The reason for this exclusiveness was to keep the people pure. In the first settlement, Israel was warned not to make covenants with the nations, which would result in intermarriages and inevitably the worship of foreign gods (Ex 34:10–17; Dt 7:1–5). To a great extent, the continual violation of this precipitated the 70-year exile from which they had just returned. Ezra found out it had happened again and called for immediate repentance. Nehemiah (Ne 13:23–27) and Malachi (Mal 2:14–16) later encountered the same sin. It is unthinkable that the Jews would so quickly go down the same disastrous path of idolatry. Neither wrath from God in the exile to Babylon, nor grace from God in the return was enough to keep them from defecting again. **Canaanites … Amorites.** *See notes on Joshua 3:10.*

9:2 holy race. The seed of Abraham that God had set apart (cf. Ge 13:15, 16; 17:4–14) was not to be mixed with other nations; and if so, it violated God's covenant (cf. Dt 7:2, 3). This marriage with Gentile women would bring idolatry into the next generation for certain, so Ezra reacted strongly.

9:3 tore … pulled … sat. An outward expression of a grieving, disturbed spirit over sin (cf. 2Ch 34:27) characterized Ezra as he saw the people returning to their old ways which would bring judgment again.

9:4 trembled at the words. In contrast to those who participated in the intermarriage, there were those who saw it as an abomination. They greatly feared the Lord's judgment on them again (cf. Is 66:2, 5) and sat with Ezra until the gathering of the people for the evening sacrifice, when there was surely public prayer and confession as Ezra fasted, lamented, and prayed (v. 5) in an effort to lead the leaders and people to repent.

9:5–15 Ezra's priestly prayer of intercession and confession is like Daniel's (Da 9:1–20) and Nehemiah's (Ne 1:4–11), in that he used plural

God, I am ashamed and embarrassed to lift up my
face to You, my God, for our iniquities have [a]risen
above our heads and our [A]guilt has grown even to
the heavens. 7 [A]Since the days of our fathers to this
day we *have been* in great guilt, and on account of
our iniquities we, our kings *and* our priests have
been given into the hand of the kings of the lands,
to the sword, to captivity and to plunder and to
[a,B]open shame, as *it is* this day. 8 But now for a brief
moment grace has been *shown* from the LORD our
God, [A]to leave us an escaped remnant and to give
us a [B]peg in His holy place, that our God may [C]en-
lighten our eyes and grant us a little reviving in our
bondage. 9 [A]For we are slaves; yet in our bondage
our God has not forsaken us, but [B]has extended
lovingkindness to us in the sight of the kings of
Persia, to give us reviving to raise up the house of
our God, to restore its ruins and to give us a wall
in Judah and Jerusalem.
10 "Now, our God, what shall we say after this? For
we have forsaken Your commandments, 11 which You
have commanded by Your servants the prophets,
saying, 'The land which you are entering to possess is an unclean land with the uncleanness of
the peoples of the lands, with their abominations
which have filled it from end to end *and* [A]with their
impurity. 12 So now do not [A]give your daughters to
their sons nor take their daughters to your sons,
and [B]never seek their peace or their prosperity, that
you may be strong and eat the good *things* of the
land and [C]leave *it* as an inheritance to your sons
forever.' 13 After all that has come upon us for our
evil deeds and [A]our great guilt, since You our God
have requited *us* less than our iniquities *deserve,*
and have given us [B]an escaped remnant as this,
14 [A]shall we again break Your commandments and
intermarry with the peoples [a]who commit these
abominations? [B]Would You not be angry with us [b]to
the point of destruction, until there is no remnant
nor any who escape? 15 O LORD God of Israel, [A]You
are righteous, for we have been left an escaped
remnant, as *it is* this day; behold, we are before
You in [B]our guilt, for [C]no one can stand before You
because of this."

RECONCILIATION WITH GOD

10 Now [A]while Ezra was praying and making
confession, weeping and prostrating himself
[B]before the house of God, a very large assembly,
men, women and children, gathered to him from
Israel; for the people wept bitterly. 2 Shecaniah the
son of Jehiel, one of the sons of Elam, said to Ezra,
"[A]We have been unfaithful to our God and have [a]mar-
ried foreign women from the peoples of the land;
yet now there is hope for Israel in spite of this. 3 So
now [A]let us make a covenant with our God to put
away all the wives and [a,B]their children, according
to the counsel of [b]my lord and of [C]those who tremble at the commandment of our God; and let it be
done [D]according to the law. 4 Arise! For *this* matter
is [a]your responsibility, but we will be with you; [A]be
courageous and act."
5 Then Ezra rose and [A]made the leading priests,
the Levites and all Israel, take oath that they would
do according to this [a]proposal; so they took the
oath. 6 Then Ezra [A]rose from before the house of
God and went into the chamber of Jehohanan the
son of Eliashib. Although he went there, [B]he did not
eat bread nor drink water, for he was mourning
over the unfaithfulness of the exiles. 7 They made a
proclamation throughout Judah and Jerusalem to all
the exiles, that they should assemble at Jerusalem,

9:6 [a]Lit *multiplied over the head* [A]2 Chr 28:9; Ezra 9:13, 15; Rev 18:5 9:7 [a]Lit *shame of faces* [A]2 Chr 29:6; Ps 106:6 [B]Dan 9:7 9:8 [A]Ezra 9:13-15 [B]Is 22:23 [C]Ps 13:3 9:9 [A]Neh 9:36 [B]Ezra 7:28 9:11 [A]Ezra 6:21 9:12 [A]Ex 34:15, 16; Deut 7:3; Ezra 9:2 [B]Deut 23:6 [C]Prov 13:22 9:13 [A]Ezra 9:6, 7 [B]Ezra 9:8 9:14 [a]Lit *of these abominations* [b]Lit *to destroy* [A]Ezra 9:2 [B]Deut 9:8, 14 9:15 [A]Neh 9:33; Dan 9:7 [B]Ezra 9:6 [C]Job 9:2; Ps 130:3 10:1 [A]Dan 9:4, 20 [B]2 Chr 20:9 10:2 [a]Lit *given dwelling to* [A]Ezra 9:2; Neh 13:27 10:3 [a]Lit *that which is born of them* [b]Or *the Lord* [A]2 Chr 34:31 [B]Ezra 10:44 [C]Ezra 9:4 [D]Deut 7:2, 3 10:4 [a]Lit *upon you* [A]1 Chr 28:10 10:5 [a]Lit *word, thing* [A]Neh 5:12; 13:25 10:6 [A]Ezra 10:1 [B]Deut 9:18

pronouns that identified himself with the people's sin, even though he did not participate in it. The use of "we," "our" and "us" demonstrates Ezra's understanding that the sin of the few is sufficient to contaminate the many.

9:8 a peg in His holy place. A figure of speech that indicated permanence and prominence.

9:8, 9 grace … lovingkindness. God had been true to His character and His covenant (cf. La 3:22–23) in restoring Israel, Jerusalem, and the temple.

9:9 a wall. As a people scattered all over the Fertile Crescent, the Jews were vulnerable to the nations. Together in Judah, with God as protector, they were safe. The wall does not exclude the walls of Jerusalem yet to be built, but it speaks more broadly of God's provision for protection.

9:10–12 Your commandments. This is not a quotation of any single text of Scripture, but rather a summation of God's commands on the subject (cf. Ex 34:15–17; Dt 7:1–6).

9:13, 14 Cf. a similar situation in the first Exodus, when the Israelites engaged in idolatry and immorality led by Aaron, who was then confronted by Moses (Ex 32:1–35).

9:14 no remnant. Ezra feared that this sin would provoke the ultimate judgment of God and the abrogation of God's unconditional covenants. While God would judge sin, the coming of Messiah and Paul's insights on God's continued faithfulness in His promise to the Jews (Ro 9–11) assures that God's calling of Israel as a beloved people and nation is irrevocable (Ro 11:25–29).

9:15 no one can stand before You. All were reckoned guilty and had no right to stand in God's presence, yet they came penitently seeking the grace of forgiveness.

10:1 praying and making confession, weeping and prostrating. Ezra's contrite spirit before the people was evident and they joined him. These extreme expressions of contrition demonstrated the seriousness of the sin and the genuineness of their repentance.

10:2 Shecaniah. This leader, not involved in the mixed marriages since his name does not appear in the list in vv. 18–44 (though his father and 5 paternal uncles do appear in v. 26), was bold and chose to obey God rather than please his relatives. **hope for Israel in spite of this.** This hope is centered in God's covenant love and forgiveness of truly repentant sinners.

10:3 make a covenant. Shecaniah calls for the people and leaders to accomplish the specific action of divorcing the wives and children and acknowledges that Ezra has counseled a course of action consistent with Scripture (cf. 2Ch 29:10). **those who tremble.** Cf. Is 66:2, 5. This refers to those who take the Word of God seriously, especially His judgment on their sin. **according to the law.** They wanted to get in line with God's law as revealed in Dt 7:2, 3.

10:4 your responsibility. Ezra is acknowledged as the chief spiritual leader with appropriate divine authority and human responsibility to take on the execution of this formidable task of dealing with divorces for so many (cf. vv. 18–44).

10:5 take oath. The oath in relation to the covenant specified in 10:3. Cf. Ne 10:28–39 for the content of a later oath under similar conditions.

10:7 They made a proclamation. A proclamation was delivered orally by a herald. It often had the force of law as did this one. Not participating in the assembly, as some

8 and that whoever would not come within three
days, according to the counsel of the leaders and
the elders, all his possessions should be forfeited
and he himself excluded from the assembly of
the exiles.
9 So all the men of Judah and Benjamin assembled at Jerusalem within the three days. It was the
ninth month on the twentieth of the month, and
all the people sat in the open square *before* the
house of God, [A]trembling because of this matter
and the heavy rain. 10 Then Ezra the priest stood
up and said to them, "You have been unfaithful
and have married foreign wives adding to the
guilt of Israel. 11 Now therefore, [A]make confession to the LORD God of your fathers and [B]do His
will; and [C]separate yourselves from the peoples
of the land and from the foreign wives." 12 Then
all the assembly replied with a loud voice, "That's
right! As you have said, so it is [a]our duty to do.
13 But there are many people; it is the rainy season and we are not able to stand in the open. Nor
can the task *be done* in one or two days, for we
have transgressed greatly in this matter. 14 Let
our leaders [a]represent the whole assembly and
let all those in our cities who have married foreign wives come at appointed times, together
with the elders and judges of each city, until the
[A]fierce anger of our God on account of this matter
is turned away from us." 15 Only Jonathan the son
of Asahel and Jahzeiah the son of Tikvah [a]opposed
this, with Meshullam and Shabbethai the Levite
supporting them.
16 But the exiles did so. And [a]Ezra the priest selected men *who were* heads of fathers' *households*
for *each of* their father's households, all of them
by name. So they [b]convened on the first day of the
tenth month to investigate the matter. 17 They finished *investigating* all the men who had married
foreign wives by the first day of the first month.

LIST OF OFFENDERS

18 Among the sons of the priests who had married
foreign wives were found of the sons of [A]Jeshua the
son of Jozadak, and his brothers: Maaseiah, Eliezer,
Jarib and Gedaliah. 19 They [a]pledged to put away
their wives, and being guilty, [A]*they offered* a ram
of the flock for their offense. 20 Of the sons of Immer *there were* Hanani and Zebadiah; 21 and of the
sons of Harim: Maaseiah, Elijah, Shemaiah, Jehiel
and Uzziah; 22 and of the sons of Pashhur: Elioenai,
Maaseiah, Ishmael, Nethanel, Jozabad and Elasah.
23 Of Levites *there were* Jozabad, Shimei, Kelaiah
(that is, Kelita), Pethahiah, Judah and Eliezer.
24 Of the singers *there was* Eliashib; and of the
gatekeepers: Shallum, Telem and Uri.
25 Of Israel, of the sons of [A]Parosh *there were* Ra-
miah, Izziah, Malchijah, Mijamin, Eleazar, Malchijah
and Benaiah; 26 and of the sons of Elam: Mattaniah,
Zechariah, Jehiel, Abdi, Jeremoth and Elijah; 27 and
of the sons of [A]Zattu: Elioenai, Eliashib, Mattaniah,
Jeremoth, Zabad and Aziza; 28 and of the sons of Bebai: Jehohanan, Hananiah, Zabbai *and* Athlai; 29 and
of the sons of Bani: Meshullam, Malluch and Adaiah,
Jashub, Sheal *and* Jeremoth; 30 and of the sons of
Pahath-moab: Adna, Chelal, Benaiah, Maaseiah, Mattaniah, Bezalel, Binnui and Manasseh; 31 and *of* the
sons of Harim: Eliezer, Isshijah, [A]Malchijah, Shemaiah, Shimeon, 32 Benjamin, Malluch *and* Shemariah;
33 of the sons of Hashum: Mattenai, Mattattah, Zabad,
Eliphelet, Jeremai, Manasseh *and* Shimei; 34 of the
sons of Bani: Maadai, Amram, Uel, 35 Benaiah, Bedeiah,
Cheluhi, 36 Vaniah, Meremoth, Eliashib, 37 Mattaniah,
Mattenai, Jaasu, 38 Bani, Binnui, Shimei, 39 Shelemiah,
Nathan, Adaiah, 40 Machnadebai, Shashai, Sharai,
41 Azarel, Shelemiah, Shemariah, 42 Shallum, Amariah
and Joseph. 43 Of the sons of [A]Nebo *there were* Jeiel,
Mattithiah, Zabad, Zebina, Jaddai, Joel *and* Benaiah.
44 All these had married [A]foreign wives, and some of
them had wives *by whom* they had children.

10:9 [A]1 Sam 12:18; Ezra 9:4; 10:3 10:11 [A]Lev 26:40; Prov 28:13 [B]Rom 12:2 [C]Ezra 10:3 10:12 [a]Lit *upon us* 10:14 [a]Lit *stand for* [A]2 Kin 23:26; 2 Chr 28:11-13; 29:10; 30:8 10:15 [a]Lit *stood against* 10:16 [a]Heb reads *there were set apart Ezra the priest, men...* [b]Lit *sat*
10:18 [A]Ezra 5:2; Hag 1:1, 12; 2:4; Zech 3:1; 6:11 10:19 [a]Lit *gave their hand* [A]Lev 5:15; 6:6 10:25 [A]Ezra 2:3; 8:3; Neh 7:8
10:27 [A]Ezra 2:8; Neh 7:13 10:31 [A]Neh 3:11 10:43 [A]Num 32:38; Ezra 2:29 10:44 [A]1 Kin 11:1-3; Ezra 10:3

might have been tempted to do, meant not just losing your property, but being ostracized from Israel.

10:8 three days. The message had to go out, and the people were required to respond within 72 hours. Since only the territories of Judah and Benjamin were involved, the greatest distance would have been no more than 40–50 mi.

10:9 all the men. Serious consequences highlighted the gravity of the situation, and thus everyone came. **ninth month.** Dec./Jan., the time of the heaviest rains and coldest weather, especially in Jerusalem, which is over 2,500 ft. in elevation.

10:11 confession ... separate. Here are the two essential elements of repentance—agreeing with God and taking righteous action to separate from sin.

10:12–14 all ... many people. This demonstrates how widespread this sin was among the people. With the heavy rain and the large number of people to be processed, the whole operation could go long, so the people made an administrative suggestion for dealing with the magnitude of the problem. For each unlawful marriage, a questioning or court session could be locally conducted. All of these details had to be treated with great care; thus, delegating the court process was a suggestion much like Jethro's back in the wilderness (cf. Ex 18).

10:15 opposed this. It is unclear whether these 4 opposed the delay in dealing with the situation or whether they opposed dealing with the sin at all. It was, however, a good plan and brought about a reasonably fast resolution.

10:16, 17 tenth month ... first month. It took 3 months to rectify the situation in all cases, after which the people were prepared to celebrate Passover with a clear conscience.

10:18 the sons of Jeshua the son of Jozadak, and his brothers. At the head of the list of those who had intermarried were the descendants and other relatives of the High Priest who first returned with Zerubbabel and led in the temple reconstruction. They set the example for all the people in giving the appropriate trespass offering (v. 19).

10:18–44 Given the fact that it took 3 months to resolve the situation, this list of 113 men could represent only those in leadership (cf. "many people," 10:13). There were apparently more violators among the people. Even though the problem was dealt with directly, it would eventually reappear (cf. Ne 9, 10, 13).

10:44 An appropriate provision was doubtlessly made for the divorced wives and the children.

THE BOOK OF NEHEMIAH

TITLE

Nehemiah ("Jehovah comforts") is a famous cupbearer, who never appears in Scripture outside of this book. As with the books of Ezra and Esther, named after his contemporaries (see Introductions to Ezra and Esther), the book recounts selected events of his leadership and was titled after him. Both the Greek Septuagint (LXX) and the Latin Vulgate named this book "Second Ezra." Even though the two books of Ezra and Nehemiah are separate in most English Bibles, they may have once been joined together in a single unit as currently in the Hebrew texts. New Testament writers do not quote Nehemiah.

AUTHOR AND DATE

Though much of this book was clearly drawn from Nehemiah's personal diaries and written from his first person perspective (1:1–7:5; 12:27–43; 13:4–31), both Jewish and Christian traditions recognize Ezra as the author. This is based on external evidence that Ezra and Nehemiah were originally one book as reflected in the LXX and Vulgate; it is also based on internal evidence such as the recurrent "hand of the Lord" theme which dominates both Ezra and Nehemiah and the author's role as a priest-scribe. As a scribe, he had access to the royal archives of Persia, which accounts for the myriad of administrative documents found recorded in the two books, especially in the book of Ezra. Very few people would have been allowed access to the royal archives of the Persian Empire, but Ezra proved to be the exception (cf. Ezr 1:2–4; 4:9–22; 5:7–17; 6:3–12).

The events in Nehemiah 1 commence late in the year 446 B.C., the 20th year of the Persian king, Artaxerxes (464–423 B.C.). The book follows chronologically from Nehemiah's first term as governor of Jerusalem ca. 445–433 B.C. (Ne 1–12) to his second term, possibly beginning ca. 424 B.C. (Ne 13). Nehemiah was written by Ezra sometime during or after Nehemiah's second term, but no later than 400 B.C.

BACKGROUND AND SETTING

True to God's promise of judgment, He brought the Assyrians and Babylonians to deliver His chastisement upon wayward Judah and Israel. In 722 B.C. the Assyrians deported the 10 northern tribes and scattered them all over the then known world (2Ki 17). Several centuries later, ca. 605–586 B.C., God used the Babylonians to sack, destroy, and nearly depopulate Jerusalem (2Ki 25) because Judah had persisted in her unfaithfulness to the covenant. God chastened His people with 70 years of captivity in Babylon (Jer 25:11).

During the Jews' captivity, world empire leadership changed hands from the Babylonians to the Persians (ca. 539 B.C.; Da 5), after which Daniel received most of his prophetic revelation (cf. Da 6, 9–12). The book of Ezra begins with the decree of Cyrus, a Persian king, to return God's people to Jerusalem to rebuild God's house (ca. 539 B.C.), and chronicles the reestablishment of Judah's national calendar of feasts and sacrifices. Zerubbabel and Joshua led the first return (Ezr 1–6) and rebuilt the temple. Esther gives a glimpse of the Jews left in Persia (ca. 483–473 B.C.) when Haman attempted to eliminate the Jewish race. Ezra 7–10 recounts the second return led by Ezra in 458 B.C. Nehemiah chronicles the third return to rebuild the wall around Jerusalem (ca. 445 B.C.).

At that time in Judah's history, the Persian Empire dominated the entire Near Eastern world. Its administration of Judah, although done with a loose hand, was mindful of disruptions or any signs of rebellion from its vassals. Rebuilding the walls of conquered cities posed the most glaring threat to the Persian central administration. Only a close confidant of the king himself could be trusted for such an operation. At the most critical juncture in Judah's revitalization, God raised up Nehemiah to exercise one of the most trusted roles in the empire, the King's cupbearer and confidant. Life under the Persian king Artaxerxes (ca. 464–423 B.C.) had its advantages for Nehemiah. Much like Joseph, Esther, and Daniel, he had attained a significant role in the palace which then ruled the ancient world, a position from which God could use him to lead the rebuilding of Jerusalem's walls in spite of its implications for Persian control of that city.

Several other historical notes are of interest. First, Esther was Artaxerxes' stepmother (*see note on Est 1:9*) and could have easily influenced him to look favorably upon the Jews, especially Nehemiah. Second, Daniel's prophetic 70 weeks began with the decree to rebuild the city issued by Artaxerxes in 445 B.C. (cf. chaps. 1, 2; *see notes on Da 9:24–26*). Third, the Elephantine papyri (Egyptian documents), dated to the late 5th century B.C., support the account of Nehemiah by mentioning Sanballat the governor of Samaria (2:19), Jehohanan (6:18; 12:23), and Nehemiah's being replaced as governor of Jerusalem by Bigvai (ca. 410 B.C.; Ne 10:16). Finally, Nehemiah and Malachi represent the last of the OT canonical writings, both in terms of the time the events occurred (chap. 13; Mal 1–4) and the time when they were recorded by Ezra. Thus the next messages from God for Israel do not come until over 400 years of silence had passed, after which the births of John the Baptist and Jesus Christ were announced (Mt 1; Lk 1, 2).

With the full OT revelation of Israel's history prior to Christ's incarnation being completed, the Jews had not yet experienced the fullness of God's various covenants and promises to them. While there was a Jewish remnant, as promised to Abraham (cf. Ge 15:5), it does not appear to be even as large as at the time of the Exodus (Nu 1:46). The Jews neither possessed the Land (Ge 15:7) nor did they rule as a sovereign nation (Ge 12:2). The Davidic throne was unoccupied (cf. 2Sa 7:16), although the High Priest was of the line of Eleazar and Phinehas (cf. Nu 25:10–13). God's promise to consummate the New Covenant of redemption awaited the birth, crucifixion, and resurrection of Messiah (cf. Heb 7–10).

HISTORICAL AND THEOLOGICAL THEMES

Careful attention to the reading of God's Word in order to perform His will is a constant theme. The spiritual revival came in response to Ezra's reading of "the book of the law of Moses" (8:1). After the reading, Ezra and some of the priests carefully explained its meaning to the people in attendance (8:8). The next day, Ezra met with some of the fathers of the households, the priests, and Levites, in order to "gain insight into the words of the law" (8:13). The sacrificial system was carried on with careful attention to perform it "as it is written in the law" (10:34, 36). So deep was their concern to abide by God's revealed will that they took "a curse and an oath to walk in God's law ...." (10:29). When the marriage reforms were carried out, they acted in accordance with that which "they read aloud from the book of Moses" (13:1).

A second major theme, the obedience of Nehemiah, is explicitly referred to throughout the book due to the fact that the book is based on the memoirs or first-person accounts of Nehemiah. God worked through the obedience of Nehemiah; however, He also worked through the wrongly motivated, wicked hearts of His enemies. Nehemiah's enemies failed, not so much as a result of the success of Nehemiah's strategies, but because "God had frustrated their plan" (4:15). God used the opposition of Judah's enemies to drive His people to their knees in the same way that He used the favor of Cyrus to return His people to the land, to fund their building project, and to even protect the reconstruction of Jerusalem's walls. Not surprisingly, Nehemiah acknowledged the true motive of his strategy to repopulate Jerusalem: "my God put it into my heart" (7:5). It was He who accomplished it.

Another theme in Nehemiah, as in Ezra, is opposition. Judah's enemies started rumors that God's people had revolted against Persia. The goal was to intimidate Judah into forestalling reconstruction of the walls. In spite of opposition from without and heartbreaking corruption and dissension from within, Judah completed the walls of Jerusalem in only 52 days (6:15), experienced revival after the reading of the law by Ezra (8:1ff.), and celebrated the Feast of Tabernacles (8:14ff.; ca. 445 B.C.).

The book's detailed insight into the personal thoughts, motives, and disappointments of Nehemiah makes it easy for the reader to primarily identify with him rather than "the sovereign hand of God" theme and the primary message of His control and intervention into the affairs of His people and their enemies. But the exemplary behavior of the famous cupbearer is eclipsed by God who orchestrated the reconstruction of the walls in spite of much opposition and many setbacks; the "good hand of God" theme carries through the book of Nehemiah (1:10; 2:8, 18).

INTERPRETIVE CHALLENGES

The reader must recognize that the time line of chapters 1–12 encompassed about one year (445 B.C.), followed by a long gap of time (over 20 years) after Ne 12 and before Ne 13 (*see "Time Line of Nehemiah"*). Also, it must be recognized that Nehemiah actually served two governorships in Jerusalem, the first from 445–433 B.C. (cf. Ne 5:14; 13:6) and the second beginning possibly in 424 B.C. and extending to no longer than 410 B.C.

OUTLINE

I. Nehemiah's First Term as Governor (1:1–12:47)

- A. Nehemiah's Return and Reconstruction (1:1–7:73a)
  1. Nehemiah goes to Jerusalem (1:1–2:20)
  2. Nehemiah and the people rebuild the walls (3:1–7:3)
  3. Nehemiah recalls the first return under Zerubbabel (7:4–73a)
- B. Ezra's Revival and Renewal (7:73b–10:39)
  1. Ezra expounds the law (7:73b–8:12)
  2. The people worship and repent (8:13–9:37)
  3. Ezra and the priests renew the covenant (9:38–10:39)
- C. Nehemiah's Resettlement and Rejoicing (11:1–12:47)
  1. Jerusalem is resettled (11:1–12:26)
  2. The people dedicate the walls (12:27–47)

II. Nehemiah's Second Term as Governor (13:1–31)

NEHEMIAH'S GRIEF FOR THE EXILES

1 The words of [A]Nehemiah the son of Hacaliah.
Now it happened in [B]the month Chislev, [C]*in* the
twentieth year, while I was in [D]Susa the [a]capitol,
2 that [A]Hanani, one of my brothers, and [a]some men
from Judah came; and I asked them concerning
the Jews who had escaped *and* had survived the
captivity, and about Jerusalem. 3 They said to me,
"The remnant there in the [A]province who survived
the captivity are in great distress and [B]reproach,
and [B]the wall of Jerusalem is broken down and [C]its
gates are burned with fire."
4 When I heard these words, [A]I sat down and
wept and mourned for days; and I was fasting
and praying before [B]the God of heaven. 5 I said,
"I beseech You, O LORD God of heaven, [A]the great
and awesome God, [B]who preserves the covenant
and lovingkindness for those who love Him and
keep His commandments, 6 [A]let Your ear now be
attentive and Your eyes open to hear the prayer
of Your servant which I am praying before You
now, day and night, on behalf of the sons of Israel
Your servants, [B]confessing the sins of the sons of
Israel which we have sinned against You; [C]I and my
father's house have sinned. 7 [A]We have acted very
corruptly against You and have not kept the commandments, nor the statutes, nor the ordinances
[B]which You commanded Your servant Moses. 8 Remember the word which You commanded Your
servant Moses, saying, '[A]If you are unfaithful I will
scatter you among the peoples; 9 [A]but *if* you return
to Me and keep My commandments and do them,
though those of you who have been scattered were
in the most remote part of the heavens, I [B]will gather
them from there and will bring them [C]to the place
where I have chosen to cause My name to dwell.'
10 [A]They are Your servants and Your people whom
You redeemed by Your great power and by Your

1:1 [a]Or *palace* or *citadel* [A]Neh 10:1 [B]Zech 7:1 [C]Neh 2:1 [D]Esth 1:2; Dan 8:2 1:2 [a]Lit *he and some* [A]Neh 7:2 1:3 [A]Neh 7:6 [B]Neh 2:17 [C]Neh 2:3 1:4 [A]Ezra 9:3; 10:1 [B]Neh 2:4 1:5 [A]Neh 4:14; 9:32; Dan 9:4 [B]Ex 20:6; Ps 89:2, 3 1:6 [A]Dan 9:17 [B]Ezra 10:1; Dan 9:20 [C]2 Chr 29:6 1:7 [A]Dan 9:5 [B]Deut 28:14 1:8 [A]Lev 26:33 1:9 [A]Deut 30:2, 3 [B]Deut 30:4 [C]Deut 12:5 1:10 [A]Ex 32:11; Deut 9:29

1:1–7:73a Nehemiah returns to Jerusalem and successfully leads a 52 day "rebuilding of the wall" project (cf. 6:15).

1:1–2:20 This section details how Nehemiah became the governor of Judah (cf. 5:14; 8:9; 10:1; 12:26).

1:1 The words of Nehemiah. The personal records of this famous royal cupbearer, whose name means "Jehovah comforts" (cf. 3:16; 7:7; 8:9; 10:1; 12:26, 47), contribute greatly to this book. Unlike Esther and Mordecai, named after Mesopotamian deities Ishtar and Marduk, Nehemiah was given a Heb. name. **Hacaliah.** Nehemiah's father is mentioned again in Ne 10:1, but nowhere else in the OT. **Chislev.** This is in Nov./Dec. 446 B.C., 4 months before Nisan (Mar./Apr.), when Nehemiah came before the king to get permission to go to Jerusalem (2:1). **twentieth year.** The 20th year (ca. 446/445 B.C.) in the reign of Persian king Artaxerxes (ca. 464–423 B.C.; cf. 2:1). **Susa.** Also known as Shushan, this city was situated E of Babylon, about 150 mi. N of the Persian Gulf. Susa was one of the Medo-Persian strongholds, a wintering city for many officials, and the setting of Esther.

1:2 Hanani. Apparently a sibling of Nehemiah (cf. 7:2), he had gone to Jerusalem in the second return under Ezra's leadership (ca. 458 B.C.). **Jews ... Jerusalem.** Nehemiah was deeply concerned about the people and the city, especially during the previous 13 years, since the second return under Ezra (458 B.C.).

1:3 wall of Jerusalem ... gates. The opposition had successfully thwarted the Jews' attempts to reestablish Jerusalem as a distinctively Jewish city capable of withstanding its enemies' assaults, which could possibly lead to another destruction of the newly rebuilt temple (ca. 516 B.C.; cf. Ezr 4:7–23).

1:4 sat down and wept and mourned for days. Although Nehemiah was neither a prophet nor a priest, he had a deep sense of Jerusalem's significance to God and was greatly distressed that affairs there had not advanced the cause and glory of God.

1:5–11 This prayer represents one of the Scripture's most moving confessions and intercessions before God (cf. Ezr 9:6–15; Da 9:4–19).

1:5 preserves the covenant and lovingkindness for those who love Him. After 70 years of captivity in Babylon, God kept His promise to restore His people to the Promised Land. The promise appeared to be failing, and Nehemiah appealed to God's character and covenant as the basis by which He must intervene and accomplish His pledges to His people.

1:6 we have sinned against You. Nehemiah may have believed that the sins of the returnees (cf. Ezr 9, 10) had prompted God to change His mind and withhold His favor from the Jews.

1:7 commandments ... statutes ... ordinances. Those which are recorded in Exodus, Leviticus, Numbers, and Deuteronomy.

1:8 Remember. Not a reminder to God as if He had forgotten, but a plea to activate His Word.

1:8, 9 the word ... Moses. This represents a summary of various Mosaic writings. On "scatter" (v. 8) see Dt 4:25–28; 28:63–65. On "gather" see Dt 4:29–31; 30:1–5.

1:10 redeemed by Your great power and by Your strong hand. His allusion to the Exodus redemption recalled the faithful and strong hand of God which had brought Israel out of bondage once before and grounded his confidence in God's power as the basis of his appeal for a second deliverance that will be as successful as the first.

TIME LINE OF NEHEMIAH

Reference	Date		Event
1:1, 4	Nov./Dec.	446 B.C. (Kislev)	Nehemiah hears of problems and prays.
2:1–6	Mar./Apr.	445 B.C. (Nisan)	Nehemiah is dispatched to Jerusalem.
3:1; 6:15	July/Aug.	445 B.C. (Ab)	Nehemiah starts the wall.
6:15	Aug./Sept.	445 B.C. (Elul)	Nehemiah completes the wall.
7:73b	Sept./Oct.	445 B.C. (Tishri)	Day of Trumpets celebrated (implied).
8:13–15	Sept./Oct.	445 B.C. (Tishri)	Feast of Booths celebrated.
9:1	Sept./Oct.	445 B.C. (Tishri)	Time of confession.
12:27	Sept./Oct.	445 B.C. (Tishri)	Wall dedicated.
13:6		445–433 B.C.	Nehemiah's first term as governor (Ne 1–12).
13:6		433–424 B.C. (?)	Nehemiah returns to Persia.
No ref.		433–? B.C.	Malachi prophesies in Jerusalem during Nehemiah's absence.
13:1, 4, 7		424–? B.C.	Nehemiah returns and serves a second term as governor (Ne 13).

strong hand. 11 O Lord, I beseech You, [A]may Your ear be attentive to the prayer of Your servant and the prayer of Your servants who delight to [a]revere Your name, and make Your servant successful today and grant him compassion before this man."

Now I was the [B]cupbearer to the king.

NEHEMIAH'S PRAYER ANSWERED

2 And it came about in the month Nisan, [A]in the twentieth year of King [B]Artaxerxes, that wine *was* before him, and [C]I took up the wine and gave it to the king. Now I had not been sad in his presence. 2 So the king said to me, "Why is your face sad though you are not sick? [A]This is nothing but sadness of heart." Then I was very much afraid. 3 I said to the king, "[A]Let the king live forever. Why should my face not be sad [B]when the city, the place of my fathers' tombs, lies desolate and its gates have been consumed by fire?" 4 Then the king said to me, "What would you request?" [A]So I prayed to the God of heaven. 5 I said to the king, "If it please the king, and if your servant has found favor before you, send me to Judah, to the city of my fathers' tombs, that I may rebuild it." 6 Then the king said to me, the queen sitting beside him, "How long will your journey be, and when will you return?" So it pleased the king to send me, and [A]I gave him a definite time. 7 And I said to the king, "If it please the king, let letters be given me [A]for the governors *of the provinces* beyond the River, that they may allow me to pass through until I come to Judah, 8 and a letter to Asaph the keeper of the king's [A]forest, that he may give me timber to make beams for the gates of [B]the fortress which is by the [a]temple, for the wall of the city and for the house to which I will go." And the king granted *them* to me because [C]the good hand of my God *was* on me.

9 Then I came to [A]the governors *of the provinces* beyond the River and gave them the king's letters. Now [B]the king had sent with me officers of the army and horsemen. 10 When [A]Sanballat the Horonite and Tobiah the Ammonite [a]official heard *about it,* it was very displeasing to them that someone had come to seek the welfare of the sons of Israel.

1:11 [a]Or *fear* [A]Neh 1:6 [B]Gen 40:21; Neh 2:1 2:1 [A]Neh 1:1 [B]Ezra 7:1 [C]Neh 1:11 2:2 [A]Prov 15:13 2:3 [A]Dan 2:4 [B]2 Kin 25:8-10; 2 Chr 36:19; Neh 1:3; Jer 52:12-14 2:4 [A]Neh 1:4 2:6 [A]Neh 13:6 2:7 [A]Ezra 7:21; 8:36 2:8 [a]Lit *house* [A]Eccl 2:5, 6 [B]Neh 7:2 [C]Ezra 7:6; Neh 2:18 2:9 [A]Neh 2:7 [B]Ezra 8:22 2:10 [a]Lit *servant* [A]Neh 2:19; 4:1

1:11 who delight to revere Your name. Nehemiah alluded to the fact that Israel was the place which God had chosen for His name to dwell (1:9); the people desired to fear His name and, thus, were praying for God's intervention. **before this man.** The reference to King Artaxerxes anticipated the discussion in 2:1ff. **cupbearer to the king.** As an escort of the monarch at meals, the cupbearer had a unique advantage to petition the king. Not only did the king owe him his life, since the cupbearer tested all the king's beverages for possible poison, thus putting his own life at risk, but he also became a close confidant. God sovereignly used this relationship between a Gentile and Jew to deliver His people, such as He did with Joseph, Daniel, Esther, and Mordecai.

2:1 Nisan. Mar./Apr. 445 B.C. **twentieth year.** *See note on 1:1.* **that wine *was* before him.** Since the act of tasting wine to ensure it was not dangerous to the king strengthened the trust between king and cupbearer, this was the appropriate time for Nehemiah to win Artaxerxes' attention and approval. Not surprisingly, kings often developed so much trust in their cupbearers that the latter became counselors to the kings. **Now I had not been sad.** Sadness was a dangerous emotion to express in the king's presence. The king wanted his subjects to be happy, since this reflected the well-being brought about by his administrative prowess.

2:2 very much afraid. He feared that either his countenance, his explanation, or his request would anger the king and thus lead to his death (cf. Est 4:11 with 5:1–3).

2:3 tombs ... gates. Nehemiah's deep concern and sadness over the condition of Jerusalem and his people was expressed in his reference to tombs and gates. A tomb was a place to show respect for dead community members who birthed the living generation and passed on their spiritual values to them. Tombs were also the place where the present generation hoped to be honored by burial at death. Gates were emblematic of the life of the city, since the people gathered for judicial procedure or basic social interaction near the gates. The burned gates represented the death of social life, i.e., the end of a community of people.

2:4 What would you request? The king rightly interpreted Nehemiah's sad countenance as a desire to take action on behalf of his people and homeland. His immediate response to the king's question illustrates how continual his prayer life was (cf. 1:6). **God of heaven.** *See note on Ezr 1:2.*

2:5 that I may rebuild it. The request undeniably referred to the city walls, for there could be no permanence without walls, but it also may have included political and administrative rebuilding as well.

2:6 the queen. Since Esther was the queen of the previous king Ahasuerus (Xerxes) ca. 486–464 B.C. and the stepmother of Artaxerxes, it could be that she had previously influenced the present king and queen to be favorably disposed to the Jews. **return.** This presupposes that Nehemiah was being dispatched on his desired mission and upon its completion would return to Persia (cf. Ne 13:6).

2:7 let letters be given me. Official letters transferred a portion of the king's authority to Nehemiah. In this context, he needed to pass through the lands of Judah's enemies who could harm him or prevent him from rebuilding Jerusalem. The roads upon which messengers, ambassadors, and envoys of all sorts traveled had stations where such letters could be inspected for passage. Three months of travel from Susa to Jerusalem was long, dangerous, and ridden with protocol where letters were required for passage. The danger associated with the passage, but particularly the administrative authority which Nehemiah carried in the letters, led Artaxerxes to send captains of the army and horsemen with Nehemiah for protection (2:9). *See notes on Ezr 1:11; 7:8, 9.*

2:8 and a letter to Asaph the keeper of the king's forest. Lumber was a very precious commodity. This is illustrated in a document from one ancient city in Mesopotamia in which a forest official is taken to court for cutting down a tree. Forests were carefully guarded, and written permission from the king would assure Nehemiah of the lumber he would need to build the citadel, wall reinforcements, and his own residence from which he would administrate the reconstruction. **fortress.** This edifice located next to the temple on the NW side was a fortified building for the purpose of guarding the temple. It was subsequently rebuilt by Herod and named Antonia. **the good hand of my God *was* on me.** This refrain is common to both Ezra and Nehemiah. It is a frequent reminder in these inspired books that God works through His servants to accomplish His will (cf. Ezr 1:5; 7:6).

2:9–3:1 The journey from Persia to Jerusalem and the preparation period was to be 3–4 months (cf. 2:1 with 6:15).

2:9 I came to the governors. Nehemiah's encroachment upon their provincial control posed a tremendous threat to these officials. If handled improperly, disregard for the other local officials would have put Nehemiah's life and the lives of those in Jerusalem in jeopardy. To prevent such a reaction, God had moved the Persian king to dispatch royal army captains and horsemen to accompany Nehemiah and to guard against such attacks.

2:10 Sanballat ... Tobiah. These men were probably also behind the opposition described in Ezr 4:7–23 which stopped the work in Jerusalem. Sanballat served as governor of Samaria (Horonaim being a town in Moab, he was probably a Moabite) and Tobiah of the region E of the Jordan. These district magistrates were leaders of Samaritan factions (see chap. 6) to the N and E. They had lost any recourse to prevent Judah from rebuilding since God's people were authorized to fortify their settlement against attack from enemies such as these two officials. To

NEHEMIAH INSPECTS JERUSALEM'S WALLS

[11] So I [A]came to Jerusalem and was there three days. [12] And I arose in the night, I and a few men with me. I did not tell anyone what my God was putting into my [a]mind to do for Jerusalem and there was no animal with me except the animal on which I was riding. [13] So I went out at night by [A]the Valley Gate in the direction of the Dragon's Well and *on* to the [a]Refuse Gate, inspecting the walls of Jerusalem [B]which were broken down and its [C]gates which were consumed by fire. [14] Then I passed on to [A]the Fountain Gate and [B]the King's Pool, but there was no place for [a]my mount to pass. [15] So I went up at night by the [A]ravine and inspected the wall. Then I entered the Valley Gate again and returned. [16] The officials did not know where I had gone or what I had done; nor had I as yet told the Jews, the priests, the nobles, the officials or the rest who did the work.

[17] Then I said to them, "You see the bad situation we are in, that [A]Jerusalem is desolate and its gates burned by fire. Come, let us rebuild the wall of Jerusalem so that we will no longer be a reproach." [18] I told them how the hand of my God had been favorable to me and also about the king's words which he had spoken to me. Then they said, "Let us arise and build." [A]So they put their hands to the good *work.* [19] But when Sanballat the Horonite and Tobiah the Ammonite [a]official, and [A]Geshem the Arab heard *it,* [B]they mocked us and despised us and said, "What is this thing you are doing? [A]Are you rebelling against the king?" [20] So I answered them and said to them, "[A]The God of heaven will give us success; therefore we His servants will arise and build, [B]but you have no portion, right or memorial in Jerusalem."

BUILDERS OF THE WALLS

3 Then [A]Eliashib the high priest arose with his brothers the priests and built [B]the Sheep Gate; they consecrated it and [C]hung its doors. They consecrated [a]the wall to [D]the Tower of the Hundred *and* [E]the Tower of Hananel. [2] Next to him [A]the men of Jericho built, and next to [a]them Zaccur the son of Imri built.

[3] Now the sons of Hassenaah built [A]the Fish Gate; they laid its beams and hung its doors with its bolts and bars. [4] Next to them Meremoth the son of Uriah the son of Hakkoz made repairs. And next to him Meshullam the son of Berechiah the son of Meshezabel made repairs. And next to [a]him Zadok the son of Baana *also* made repairs. [5] Moreover, next to [a]him the Tekoites made repairs, but their nobles did not [b]support the work of their masters.

[6] Joiada the son of Paseah and Meshullam the son of Besodeiah repaired [A]the Old Gate; they laid its beams and hung its doors with its bolts and its bars. [7] Next to them Melatiah the Gibeonite and Jadon the

2:11 [A]Ezra 8:32 2:12 [a]Lit *heart* 2:13 [a]Lit *Gate of Ash-heaps* [A]Neh 3:13 [B]Neh 1:3 [C]Neh 2:3, 17 2:14 [a]Lit *the animal under me* [A]Neh 3:15 [B]2 Kin 20:20 2:15 [A]John 18:1 2:17 [A]Neh 1:3 2:18 [A]2 Sam 2:7 2:19 [a]Lit *servant* [A]Neh 6:6 [B]Neh 4:1 2:20 [A]Ezra 4:3 [B]Neh 2:4; Acts 8:21 3:1 [a]Lit *it* [A]Neh 3:20; 13:28 [B]Neh 3:32; 12:39 [C]Neh 6:1; 7:1 [D]Neh 12:39 [E]Jer 31:38 3:2 [a]Lit *him* [A]Neh 7:36 3:3 [A]Neh 12:39 3:4 [a]Lit *them* 3:5 [a]Lit *them* [b]Lit *bring their neck to* 3:6 [A]Neh 12:39

overtly attack or oppose the Jews would be to oppose the Persian king.

2:11–16 Nehemiah spent 3 days discerning what course to follow before informing anyone of his plan; then, he wisely viewed the terrain in secret and surveyed the southern end of the city, noting the broken and burnt conditions of the walls and gates.

2:13, 15 Valley Gate. Nehemiah began and ended his trip at the same spot (cf. 3:13) on the W side.

2:13 Dragon's Well. The exact location is unknown, although it is somewhere in the southern section of Jerusalem. **Refuse Gate.** A.k.a. Dung Gate. At the southern tip of the city (cf. 3:13; 12:31) a common sewer ran to the Kidron Brook into the Valley of Hinnom.

2:14 Fountain Gate. The exact location is unknown, although it was somewhere in the southern section of Jerusalem, probably on the E side. **King's Pool.** Possibly the pool of Siloam (cf. 3:15).

2:15 the ravine. The Kidron Valley, running N and S to the E of the temple mount.

2:17 we will no longer be a reproach. The destruction of the city by Nebuchadnezzar brought great reproach upon Israel, but particularly upon their God. Nehemiah assured the Jews (v. 20) that because God would prosper them in this endeavor for His glory, they should move ahead.

2:18 The sight of Nehemiah's credentials and his motivating message revived their drooping spirits to begin the building despite the bitter taunts of influential men (vv. 19, 20).

2:19 Sanballat . . . Tobiah. *See note on 2:10.* **Geshem the Arab.** This ruler most likely officiated to the S of Jerusalem.

2:20 God of heaven. Cf. Ne 1:5 and *see note on Ezr 1:2.* Not only did Nehemiah have the king's permission and was not rebelling, but he had God's protection. Those enemies who tried to intimidate against the work had neither, since they were not commissioned by God or the king.

3:1–7:3 A detailed account of rebuilding the wall is given.

3:1 Eliashib the high priest. The grandson of Jeshua the High Priest in Zerubbabel's era (cf. Ne 12:10). **built.** On the fourth of Ab, (Jul./Aug.) 445 B.C. (cf. 6:15). **Sheep Gate.** This is located in the NE section of Jerusalem (cf. 3:32; 12:39). The narrative moves around the perimeter of Jerusalem in a counterclockwise direction. **Tower of the Hundred . . . Tower of Hananel.** This northern section of Jerusalem opened up to the central Benjamin plateau where enemy forces could attack most easily from the N. The rest of the perimeter of the city was protected by the natural valley topography.

3:3 Fish Gate. So named because merchants sold fish on the northern side of Jerusalem. Men of Tyre and other coastal towns routinely brought fish to sell (cf. 12:39; 13:16).

3:5 nobles did not support the work of their masters. One explanation, beyond just the laziness of the rich, is that these nobles had been pledged to Tobiah for personal gain (6:17–19).

3:6 Old Gate. Believed to be in the NW corner of Jerusalem (cf. 12:39).

SEVEN ATTEMPTS TO STOP NEHEMIAH'S WORK	
1. 2:19	Sanballat, Tobiah, and Geshem mocked Nehemiah.
2. 4:1–3	Sanballat and Tobiah mocked Nehemiah.
3. 4:7–23	The enemy threatened a military attack.
4. 6:1–4	Sanballat and Geshem attempted to lure Nehemiah outside of Jerusalem to Ono.
5. 6:5–9	Sanballat threatened Nehemiah with false charges.
6. 6:10–14	Shemaiah, Noadiah, and others were paid to prophesy falsely and discredit Nehemiah.
7. 6:17–19	Tobiah had spies in Jerusalem and wrote Nehemiah letters in order to frighten him.

Meronothite, the men of Gibeon and of Mizpah, [a]also made repairs for the official seat of the [A]governor *of the province* beyond the River. 8 Next to him Uzziel the son of Harhaiah of the [A]goldsmiths made repairs. And next to him Hananiah, one of the perfumers, made repairs, and they restored Jerusalem as far as [B]the Broad Wall. 9 Next to them Rephaiah the son of Hur, [A]the official of half the district of Jerusalem, made repairs. 10 Next to them Jedaiah the son of Harumaph made repairs opposite his house. And next to him Hattush the son of Hashabneiah made repairs. 11 Malchijah the son of Harim and Hasshub the son of Pahath-moab repaired another section and [A]the Tower of Furnaces. 12 Next to him Shallum the son of Hallohesh, [A]the official of half the district of Jerusalem, made repairs, he and his daughters.

13 Hanun and the inhabitants of Zanoah repaired [A]the Valley Gate. They built it and hung its doors with its bolts and its bars, and a thousand cubits of the wall to the [a]Refuse Gate.

14 Malchijah the son of Rechab, the official of the district of [A]Beth-haccherem repaired the [a,B]Refuse Gate. He built it and hung its doors with its bolts and its bars.

15 Shallum the son of Col-hozeh, the official of the district of Mizpah, [A]repaired the Fountain Gate. He built it, covered it and hung its doors with its bolts and its bars, and the wall of the Pool of Shelah at [B]the king's garden as far as [C]the steps that descend from the city of David. 16 After him Nehemiah the son of Azbuk, [A]official of half the district of Beth-zur, made repairs as far as *a point* opposite the tombs of David, and as far as [B]the artificial pool and the house of the mighty men. 17 After him the Levites carried out repairs *under* Rehum the son of Bani. Next to him Hashabiah, the official of half the district of Keilah, carried out repairs for his district. 18 After him their brothers carried out repairs *under* Bavvai the son of Henadad, official of *the other* half of the district of Keilah. 19 Next to him Ezer the son of Jeshua, [A]the official of Mizpah, repaired [a]another section in front of the ascent of the armory [B]at the Angle. 20 After him Baruch the son of Zabbai zealously repaired another section, from the Angle to the doorway of the house of [A]Eliashib the high priest. 21 After him Meremoth the son of Uriah the son of Hakkoz repaired another section, from the doorway of Eliashib's house even as far as the end of [a]his house. 22 After him the priests, [A]the men of the [a]valley, carried out repairs. 23 After [a]them Benjamin and Hasshub carried out repairs in front of their house. After [a]them Azariah the son of Maaseiah, son of Ananiah, carried out repairs beside his house. 24 After him Binnui the son of Henadad repaired another section, from the house of Azariah as far as [A]the Angle and as far as the corner. 25 Palal the son of Uzai *made repairs* in front of the Angle and the tower projecting from the upper house of the king, which is by [A]the court of the guard. After him Pedaiah the son of Parosh *made repairs*. 26 [A]The temple servants living in [B]Ophel *made repairs* as far as the front of [C]the Water Gate toward the east and the projecting tower. 27 After [a]them [A]the Tekoites repaired another section in front of the great projecting tower and as far as the wall of Ophel.

28 Above [A]the Horse Gate the priests carried out repairs, each in front of his house. 29 After [a]them Zadok the son of Immer carried out repairs in front of his house. And after him Shemaiah the son of Shecaniah, the keeper of the East Gate, carried out repairs. 30 After him Hananiah the son of Shelemiah, and Hanun the sixth son of Zalaph, repaired another section. After him Meshullam the son of Berechiah carried out repairs in front of his own [a]quarters. 31 After him Malchijah, [a]one of [A]the goldsmiths, carried out repairs as far as the house of the temple servants and of the merchants, in front of the [b]Inspection Gate and as far as the upper room of the corner. 32 Between the upper room of the corner and [A]the Sheep Gate the goldsmiths and the merchants carried out repairs.

WORK IS RIDICULED

4 [a]Now it came about that when [A]Sanballat heard that we were rebuilding the wall, he became furious and very angry and mocked the Jews. 2 He spoke in the presence of his brothers and [A]the [a]wealthy *men* of Samaria and said, "What are these feeble Jews doing? Are they going to restore *it* for themselves? Can they offer sacrifices? Can they finish in a day? Can they revive the stones from the [b,B]dusty rubble even the burned ones?" 3 Now Tobiah the Ammonite *was* near him and he said, "Even what they are building—[A]if a fox should [a]jump on *it,* he would break their stone wall down!"

3:7 [a]Or *which was under the jurisdiction of the governor* of the province *beyond the River, also made repairs* [A]Neh 2:7 3:8 [A]Neh 3:31, 32 [B]Neh 12:38 3:9 [A]Neh 3:12, 17 3:11 [A]Neh 12:38 3:12 [A]Neh 3:9 3:13 [a]Lit *Gate of Ash-heaps* [A]Neh 2:13 3:14 [a]Lit *Gate of Ash-heaps* [A]Jer 6:1 [B]Neh 2:13 3:15 [A]Neh 2:17 [B]2 Kin 25:4 [C]Neh 12:37 3:16 [A]Neh 3:9, 12, 17 [B]2 Kin 20:20; Is 7:3 3:19 [a]Lit *a second measure,* and so in vv 20, 21, 24, 30 [A]Neh 3:15 [B]2 Chr 26:9 3:20 [A]Neh 3:1 3:21 [a]Lit *Eliashib's* 3:22 [a]Lit *circle;* i.e. lower Jordan valley [A]Neh 12:28 3:23 [a]Lit *him* 3:24 [A]Neh 3:19 3:25 [A]Jer 32:2 3:26 [A]Neh 7:46 [B]Neh 11:21 [C]Neh 8:1 3:27 [a]Lit *him* [A]Neh 3:5 3:28 [A]2 Kin 11:16; 2 Chr 23:15; Jer 31:40 3:29 [a]Lit *him* 3:30 [a]Or *cell* 3:31 [a]Lit *son of* [b]Or *Mustering* [A]Neh 3:8, 32 3:32 [A]Neh 3:1; 12:39 4:1 [a]Ch 3:33 in Heb [A]Neh 2:10 4:2 [a]Or *army* [b]Lit *heaps of dust* [A]Ezra 4:9, 10 [B]Neh 4:10 4:3 [a]Lit *go up* [A]Lam 5:18

3:8 Broad Wall. On the western side of the northern sector (cf. 12:38).

3:11 Tower of Furnaces. On the western side of Jerusalem (cf. 12:38).

3:13 Valley Gate. *See note on 2:13, 15.* **Refuse Gate.** *See note on 2:13.*

3:15 Pool of Shelah. *See note on 2:14.* **king's garden.** In the SE sector.

3:16 tombs of David. Cf. 2:5. Presumably in the SE sector. **house of the mighty men.** This location is probably associated with David's mighty men (cf. 2Sa 23:8–39).

3:19 the armory. Located on the eastern side of Jerusalem.

3:26 Ophel. An area S of the temple mount, near the Water Gate, where the temple servants lived (cf. 2Ch 27:3; 33:14; Ne 11:21). **Water Gate.** Near the Gihon Spring on the E side of Jerusalem (cf. 8:16; 12:37).

3:28 Horse Gate. In the NE sector.

3:29 East Gate. Possibly located to the E of the temple mount.

3:31 Inspection Gate. In the NE sector.

3:32 Sheep Gate. Having traveled around Jerusalem in a counterclockwise direction, the narrative ends where it began (cf. 3:1; 12:39).

4:1–23 This section describes the intimidation and opposition to the project.

4:2 the wealthy *men* of Samaria. While it is a possibility that his intentions were to provoke the Samaritans to action, which would have brought the Persian overlord down on Samaria swiftly, harassment and mockery (v. 3) became the primary strategy to prevent the reconstruction of the walls.

4 [A]Hear, O our God, how we are despised! [B]Return
their reproach on their own heads and give them up
for plunder in a land of captivity. 5 Do not [a,A]forgive
their iniquity and let not their sin be blotted out
before You, for they have [b]demoralized the builders.
6 So we built the wall and the whole wall was
joined together to half its *height,* for the people
had a [a]mind to work.
7 [a]Now when Sanballat, Tobiah, the Arabs, the
Ammonites and the Ashdodites heard that the [b]re-
pair of the walls of Jerusalem went on, *and* that the
breaches began to be closed, they were very angry.
8 All of them [A]conspired together to come *and* fight
against Jerusalem and to cause a disturbance in it.

DISCOURAGEMENT OVERCOME

9 But we prayed to our God, and because of them
we [A]set up a guard against them day and night.
10 Thus [a]in Judah it was said,

"The strength of the burden
bearers is failing,
Yet there is much [b]rubbish;
And we ourselves are unable
To rebuild the wall."

11 Our enemies said, "They will not know or see until
we come among them, kill them and put a stop to
the work." 12 When the Jews who lived near them
came and told us ten times, "[a]They will come up
against us from every place where you may turn,"
13 then I stationed *men* in the lowest parts of the
space behind the wall, the [a]exposed places, and I
[A]stationed the people in families with their swords,
spears and bows. 14 When I saw *their fear,* I rose and
spoke to the nobles, the officials and the rest of the
people: "[A]Do not be afraid of them; remember the
Lord who is great and awesome, and [B]fight for your
brothers, your sons, your daughters, your wives
and your houses."

15 When our enemies heard that it was known to
us, and that [A]God had frustrated their plan, then
all of us returned to the wall, each one to his work.
16 From that day on, half of my servants carried on
the work while half of them held the spears, the
shields, the bows and the breastplates; and the captains *were* behind the whole house of Judah. 17 Those
who were rebuilding the wall and those who carried
burdens took *their* load with one hand doing the
work and the other holding a weapon. 18 As for the
builders, each *wore* his sword girded at his side as
he built, while [a]the trumpeter *stood* near me. 19 I
said to the nobles, the officials and the rest of the
people, "The work is great and extensive, and we
are separated on the wall far from one another. 20 At
whatever place you hear the sound of the trumpet,
[a]rally to us there. [A]Our God will fight for us."
21 So we carried on the work with half of them
holding spears from [a]dawn until the stars [b]ap-
peared. 22 At that time I also said to the people,
"Let each man with his servant spend the night
within Jerusalem so that they may be a guard for
us by night and a laborer by day." 23 So neither I, my
brothers, my servants, nor the men of the guard
who followed me, none of us removed our clothes,
each *took* his weapon *even to* the water.

USURY ABOLISHED

5 Now [A]there was a great outcry of the people
and of their wives against their [B]Jewish brothers. 2 For there were those who said, "We, our sons
and our daughters are many; therefore let us [A]get
grain that we may eat and live." 3 There were others who said, "We are mortgaging our fields, our
vineyards and our houses that we might get grain
because of the famine." 4 Also there were those who
said, "We have borrowed money [A]for the king's tax
on our fields and our vineyards. 5 Now [A]our flesh
is like the flesh of our brothers, our children like
their children. Yet behold, [B]we are forcing our sons

4:4 [A]Ps 123:3, 4 [B]Ps 79:12 4:5 [a]Lit *cover* [b]Lit *offended against* [A]Ps 69:27, 28; Jer 18:23 4:6 [a]Lit *heart* 4:7 [a]Ch 4:1 in Heb [b]Lit *healing* 4:8 [A]Ps 83:3 4:9 [A]Neh 4:11 4:10 [a]Lit *Judah said* [b]Lit *dust* 4:12 [a]So Gr; Heb omits *they...up* 4:13 [a]Lit *bare* [A]Neh 4:17, 18 4:14 [A]Num 14:9; Deut 1:29, 30 [B]2 Sam 10:12 4:15 [A]2 Sam 17:14 4:18 [a]Lit *he who sounded the trumpet* 4:20 [a]Lit *assemble yourselves* [A]Ex 14:14; Deut 1:30 4:21 [a]Lit *rising of the dawn* [b]Lit *came out* 5:1 [A]Lev 25:35 [B]Deut 15:7 5:2 [A]Hag 1:6 5:4 [A]Ezra 4:13; 7:24 5:5 [A]Gen 37:27 [B]Lev 25:39

4:4, 5 Nehemiah's dependence on his sovereign God is never more evident than in his prayer (cf. 1:5–11; 2:4).

4:7, 8 the Ashdodites. Added to the list of enemies already given are the dwellers of Ashdod, one of the former Philistine cities to the W of Jerusalem. Apparently they came to the point where they were at least contemplating a full-scale attack on Jerusalem because of the rapid progress of the wall.

4:9 The Jews exhibited a balance between faith in God and readiness, employing some of the wall builders as guards.

4:10 much rubbish. Lit. "dust," the term refers to the rubble or ruins of the prior destruction (586 B.C.), which they had to clear away before they could make significant progress on the rebuilding of the walls.

4:11, 12 Part of the strategy of the enemy coalition was to frighten and intimidate the Jews by making them think their army would soon surprise them with a massive force that would quickly engulf them.

4:13–15 stationed *men*. Nehemiah and the others had received word that Sanballat had mustered the army of Samaria (4:2). In fact, God made sure the strategy was known by letting the nearby Jews know, so they would report it to Judah's leaders. Though vigilant, armed, and ready, Nehemiah and those he led consistently gave God the glory for their victories and construction successes.

4:16–18a The threats cut the work force in half, and even those who worked carried weapons in case of attack (cf. v. 21).

4:18b–20 trumpet. Among other functions, trumpets were used to sound an alarm in the event of danger or to summon soldiers to battle. Nehemiah kept a trumpeter at his side always, so that the alarm could be sounded immediately. His plan also included perpetual diligence (vv. 22, 23).

5:1–13 Enemy opposition and difficult times in general had precipitated economic conditions which had a devastating effect on Judah's fragile life. The effect of this extortion on the morale of the returnees was worse than the enemy opposition.

5:1–5 Jewish brothers. Perhaps this refers again to the nobles who would not work and had alliances with the enemies (*see note on 3:5*). The people were fatigued with hard labor, drained by the relentless harassment of enemies, poor and lacking the necessities of life, lacking tax money and borrowing for it, and working on the wall in the city rather than getting food from the country. On top of this came complaints against the terrible exploitation and extortion by the rich Jews who would not help, but forced people to sell their homes and children, while having no ability to redeem them back. Under normal conditions, the law offered the hope of releasing these young people through the remission of debts which occurred every 7 years or in the 50th year of Jubilee (Lv 25). The custom of redemption made it possible to "buy back" the enslaved individual at almost any time, but the desperate financial situation of those times made that appear impossible.

and our daughters to be slaves, and some of our
daughters are forced into bondage *already,* and
[a]we are helpless because our fields and vineyards
belong to others."
6 Then I was very [A]angry when I had heard their
outcry and these words. 7 I consulted with myself
and contended with the nobles and the rulers and
said to them, "[A]You are exacting usury, each from
his brother!" Therefore, I held a great assembly
against them. 8 I said to them, "We according to our
ability [A]have [a]redeemed our Jewish brothers who
were sold to the nations; now would you even sell
your brothers that they may be sold to us?" Then
they were silent and could not find a word *to say.*
9 Again I said, "The thing which you are doing is
not good; should you not walk in the fear of our
God because of [A]the reproach of the nations, our
enemies? 10 And likewise I, my brothers and my
servants are lending them money and grain. Please,
let us leave off this usury. 11 Please, give back to them
this very day their fields, their vineyards, their olive
groves and their houses, also the hundredth *part*
of the money and of the grain, the new wine and
the oil that you are exacting from them." 12 Then
they said, "We [A]will give *it* back and [B]will require
nothing from them; we will do exactly as you say."
So I called the priests and [C]took an oath from them
that they would do according to this [a]promise. 13 I
[A]also shook out the [a]front of my garment and said,
"Thus may God shake out every man from his house
and from his possessions who does not fulfill this
[b]promise; even thus may he be shaken out and emptied." And [B]all the assembly said, "Amen!" And they
praised the LORD. Then the people did according
to this [b]promise.

NEHEMIAH'S EXAMPLE

14 Moreover, from the day that I was appointed
to be their governor in the land of Judah, from [A]the
twentieth year to the [B]thirty-second year of King
Artaxerxes, *for* twelve years, neither I nor my [a]kins-
men have eaten the governor's food *allowance.*
15 But the former governors who were before me
[a]laid burdens on the people and took from them
bread and wine besides forty shekels of silver; even
their servants domineered the people. But I did not
do so [A]because of the fear of God. 16 I also [a]applied
myself to the work on this wall; we did not buy any
land, and all my servants were gathered there for
the work. 17 Moreover, [A]*there were* at my table one
hundred and fifty Jews and officials, besides those
who came to us from the nations that were around
us. 18 Now [A]that which was prepared for each day
was one ox *and* six choice sheep, also birds were
prepared for me; and once in ten days all sorts of
wine *were furnished* in abundance. Yet for all this
[B]I did not demand the governor's food *allowance,*
because the servitude was heavy on this people.
19 [A]Remember me, O my God, for good, *according
to* all that I have done for this people.

THE ENEMY'S PLOT

6 Now when it was reported to Sanballat, Tobiah,
to Geshem the Arab and to the rest of our enemies that I had rebuilt the wall, and *that* no breach
remained in it, [A]although at that time I had not set

5:5 [a]Lit *there is not the power in our hands* 5:6 [A]Ex 11:8 5:7 [A]Ex 22:25; Lev 25:36; Deut 23:19, 20 5:8 [a]Lit *bought* [A]Lev 25:48 5:9 [A]Neh 4:4 5:12 [a]Lit *word* [A]2 Chr 28:15 [B]Neh 10:31 [C]Ezra 10:5 5:13 [a]Lit *bosom* [b]Lit *word* [A]Acts 18:6 [B]Neh 8:6 5:14 [a]Lit *brothers* [A]Neh 1:1 [B]Neh 13:6 5:15 [a]Lit *made heavy* [A]Neh 5:9; Job 31:23 5:16 [a]Or *held fast* 5:17 [A]1 Kin 18:19 5:18 [A]1 Kin 4:22, 23 [B]2 Thess 3:8 5:19 [A]Neh 13:14, 22, 31 6:1 [A]Neh 3:1, 3

5:7 I ... contended with the nobles and the rulers. The commitment of the nobles and rulers to the reconstruction project was negligible (cf. 3:5), while their loyalty to Tobiah and others in opposition added to their opportunistic attitudes, placing them close to the status of opposition. They had become the enemy from within. **exacting usury.** Usury can refer to normal interest, or it can signify excessive interest. According to Mosaic law, the Jews were forbidden to take interest from their brothers on the loan of money, food, or anything else. If the person was destitute, they should consider it a gift. If they could pay it back later, it was to be without interest (see Lv 25:36, 37; Dt 23:19, 20). Such generosity marked the godly (see Ps 15:5; Jer 15:10; cf. Pr 28:8). Interest could be taken from foreigners (Dt 23:20). Interest loans were known to exceed 50 percent at times in ancient nations. Such usury took advantage of people's desperation and was virtually impossible to repay, consuming their entire family assets and reducing the debtors to permanent slavery. *See notes on Dt 23:19, 20; 24:10–13.*

5:8 We ... have redeemed. Nehemiah denounced with just severity the evil conduct of selling a brother by means of usury. He contrasted it with his own action of redeeming with his own money some of the Jewish exiles, who through debt had lost their freedom in Babylon.

5:10 likewise I. Nehemiah set the example again by making loans, but not in exacting usury.

5:11 give back to them. To remedy the evil that they had brought, those guilty of usury were to return the property they had confiscated from those who couldn't pay the loans back, as well as returning the interest they had charged *(see notes on Lk 19:2–10).*

5:12 an oath. The consciences of the guilty were struck by Nehemiah's words, so that their fear, shame, and contrition caused them to pledge the release of their loans and restore property and interest, including setting slaves free. This cancellation of debt had a profoundly unifying effect on both sides of the indebtedness. The proceedings were formally consummated with the people binding themselves by a solemn oath from the priests (with them as administrators) that they would be faithful to the pledge.

5:13 shook out the front. This curse rite from the governor, Nehemiah, called down God's wrath upon anyone who would not follow through with his commitment to release debts. The people agreed and did as they had promised.

5:14 twentieth year. *See note on 1:1.* **thirty-second year.** The year Nehemiah returned to Artaxerxes in Persia (ca. 433 B.C.; cf. 13:6). **eaten the governor's food *allowance.*** This refers to the provisions from the Persian administration, but from which he had chosen not to partake because it would have to come from taxing his poverty-stricken people (v. 15). The statement is testimony to the wealth of Nehemiah gained as the king's cupbearer in Persia. Verses 17, 18 record that he supported 150 men with abundant provisions who ruled with him (and their families), indicating the personal wealth he had brought from Babylon.

5:15 forty shekels. Approximately one lb. of silver. **because of the fear of God.** Nehemiah would not exact usury from his fellow countrymen as his predecessors had, because he viewed it as an act of disobedience toward God.

5:16 we did not buy any land. Even though the time to purchase property from those forced to sell couldn't have been better, Nehemiah maintained a consistent personal policy not to take advantage of another's distress. He worked on the wall rather than spending his time building personal wealth.

5:18 governor's food *allowance.* *See note on 5:14.* In the ancient Near East, it was customary to calculate the expense of a king's establishment, not by the quantity of money, but by the quantity of his provisions (cf. 1Ki 4:22; 18:19; Ecc 5:11).

5:19 Remember me. The first of 4 such prayers (cf. 13:14, 22, 31).

6:1 Sanballat, Tobiah ... Geshem. *See notes on 2:10, 19.*

up the doors in the gates, 2 then Sanballat and Geshem sent *a message* to me, saying, "Come, let us
meet together at [a]Chephirim in the plain of [A]Ono."
But they were planning to [b]harm me. 3 So I sent
messengers to them, saying, "I am doing a great
work and I cannot come down. Why should the
work stop while I leave it and come down to you?"
4 They sent *messages* to me four times in this manner, and I answered them in the same way. 5 Then
Sanballat sent his servant to me in the same manner
a fifth time with an open letter in his hand. 6 In it
was written, "It is reported among the nations, and
[a]Gashmu says, that [A]you and the Jews are planning
to rebel; therefore you are rebuilding the wall. And
you are to be their king, according to these reports.
7 You have also appointed prophets to proclaim in
Jerusalem concerning [a]you, 'A king is in Judah!' And
now it will be reported to the king according to these
reports. So come now, let us take counsel together."
8 Then I sent *a message* to him saying, "Such things
as you are saying have not been done, but you are
[A]inventing them [a]in your own mind." 9 For all of
them were *trying* to frighten us, [a]thinking, "[b]They
will become discouraged with the work and it will
not be done." But now, [A]*O God,* strengthen my hands.

10 When I entered the house of Shemaiah the son
of Delaiah, son of Mehetabel, [A]who was [a]confined at
home, he said, "Let us meet together in the house of
God, within the temple, and let us close the doors
of the temple, for they are coming to kill you, and
they are coming to kill you at night." 11 But I said,
"[A]Should a man like me flee? And could one such
as I go into the temple [a]to save his life? I will not
go in." 12 Then I perceived [a]that surely God had not
sent him, but he uttered *his* prophecy against me
because Tobiah and Sanballat had hired him. 13 He
was hired for this reason, [A]that I might become
frightened and act accordingly and sin, so that they
might have an evil report in order that they could
reproach me. 14 [A]Remember, O my God, Tobiah and
Sanballat according to these works of theirs, and
also Noadiah [B]the prophetess and the rest of the
prophets who were *trying* to frighten me.

THE WALL IS FINISHED

15 So [A]the wall was completed on the twenty-fifth
of *the month* Elul, in fifty-two days. 16 [A]When all our
enemies heard *of it,* and all the nations surrounding
us saw *it,* they [a]lost their confidence; for [B]they recognized that this work had been accomplished [b]with

6:2 [a]Another reading is, one of *the villages* [b]Lit *do evil to me* [A]1 Chr 8:12 6:6 [a]In v 1 and elsewhere, *Geshem* [A]Neh 2:19 6:7 [a]Lit *you, saying* 6:8 [a]Lit *from your heart* [A]Job 13:4; Ps 52:2 6:9 [a]Lit *saying,* [b]Lit *Their hands will drop from* [A]Ps 138:3 6:10 [a]Lit *shut up* [A]Jer 36:5 6:11 [a]Lit *and live* [A]Prov 28:1 6:12 [a]Lit *and behold God* 6:13 [A]Neh 6:6 6:14 [A]Neh 13:29 [B]Ezek 13:17 6:15 [A]Neh 4:1, 2 6:16 [a]Lit *fell exceedingly in their own eyes* [b]Lit *from our God* [A]Neh 2:10; 4:1, 7 [B]Ex 14:25

6:2 sent *a message* to me. This suggests either a letter or an oral message delivered by messenger to Nehemiah. Satisfied that they could not prevent Nehemiah's project from succeeding by open military engagement (*see note on 4:13–15*), they decided to overcome him by deception. **plain of Ono.** Located S of Joppa on the western extremity of Judah along the seacoast.

6:3 So I sent messengers. Because he knew they were luring him into a trap, he sent representatives, who themselves might have been killed or imprisoned for ransom.

6:5 open letter. Official letters were typically rolled up and sealed with an official signet by the letter's sender or one of his assisting officials. An open or unsealed letter was not only a sign of disrespect and open criticism, but also suggested the information therein was public knowledge. The goal of this document was to intimidate Nehemiah into stopping the work.

6:6 It is reported among the nations. The letter suggested that Nehemiah's intent to revolt was common knowledge which would get back to the king of Persia if he didn't come to the requested conference. **you and the Jews are planning to rebel.** This information would have brought Persian troops against the Jews had it been true. Even though Judah had a reputation for breaking its allegiances with its overlord kings, on this occasion that was not the case. **rebuilding the wall ... be their king.** Artaxerxes had commissioned the rebuilding of the wall based on his relationship of trust with Nehemiah. Once the project was accomplished, the king expected Nehemiah to return to Susa. Allegations that Nehemiah was fortifying the city so that he might be made king would seriously violate the Persian king's trust, if not create a war. The plot was an attempt to intimidate Nehemiah with the idea that a wedge was to be driven between Nehemiah and Artaxerxes so that Nehemiah would come to the meeting with those enemies—a meeting that would have featured his death.

6:7 appointed prophets to proclaim. If there were such prophets, Sanballat actually hired them to feed incorrect information generating the false rumor (cf. 6:10–14). By dispatching such prophets to make public proclamations that Nehemiah had made himself king, the Persian imperial rule would have appeared to be supplanted.

6:10 Shemaiah. When the open letter failed to intimidate Nehemiah into stopping the work and coming to a meeting, his enemies decided to try intimidation from within. They hired a false prophet (v. 12), Shemaiah, to lure Nehemiah into the Holy Place in the temple for refuge from a murder plot. To enter and shut himself in the Holy Place would have been a desecration of the house of God and would have caused people to question his reverence for God. Shemaiah was the son of a priest who was an intimate friend of Nehemiah. This plan would give them grounds to raise an evil report against Nehemiah, who was not a priest and had no right to go into the Holy Place (cf. 6:13). It could also make the people question his courage (v. 11). Other disloyal Jews included: 1) the nobles (3:5; 6:17); 2) Jews who lived near Sanballat (4:12); 3) Noadiah (6:14); 4) Meshullam (6:17–19); 5) Eliashib (13:4, 7); and 6) the High Priest's grandson (13:28). **the house of God.** This is a frequently used name for the temple (cf. 8:16; 10:32–39; 11:11, 16, 22; 12:40; 13:4, 7, 9, 11, 14).

6:15 Elul. Aug./Sept., 445 B.C. Knowing that the project lasted 52 days, it commenced on the fourth of Ab (Jul./Aug.) 445 B.C.

6:16 this work had been accomplished with the help of our God. While modern readers might be tempted to exalt the leadership qualities which brought the work to

NEHEMIAH'S EXAMPLE OF SERVANTHOOD

A Servant . . .	because God . . .
prays for his people (1:4)	**preserves** His covenant (1:5).
plans for his people (2:6–8)	**places** ideas in his mind (2:12).
pleads for unity among his people (5:10, 11)	is **pleased** with unity (5:9, 13).
perceives falsehood and remains faithful (6:2, 8, 12)	**proclaims** His name among the nations (6:16).

the help of our God. 17Also in those days many letters went from the nobles of Judah to Tobiah, and Tobiah's *letters* came to them. 18For many in Judah were bound by oath to him because he was the son-in-law of Shecaniah the son of Arah, and his son Jehohanan had married the daughter of Meshullam the son of Berechiah. 19Moreover, they were speaking about his good deeds in my presence and reported my words to him. Then Tobiah sent letters to frighten me.

CENSUS OF FIRST RETURNED EXILES

7 Now when [A]the wall was rebuilt and I had set up the doors, and the gatekeepers and the singers and the Levites were appointed, 2then I put [A]Hanani my brother, and [B]Hananiah the commander of [C]the fortress, in charge of Jerusalem, for he was [D]a faithful man and feared God more than many. 3Then I said to them, "Do not let the gates of Jerusalem be opened until the sun is hot, and while they are standing *guard,* let them shut and bolt the doors. Also appoint guards from the inhabitants of Jerusalem, each at his post, and each in front of his own house." 4Now the city was large and spacious, but the people in it were few and the houses were not built.

5[A]Then my God put it into my heart to assemble the nobles, the officials and the people to be enrolled by genealogies. Then I found the book of the genealogy of those who came up first [a]in which I found the following record:

6[A]These are the [a]people of the province who came up from the captivity of the exiles whom Nebuchadnezzar the king of Babylon had carried away, and who returned to Jerusalem and Judah, each to his city, 7who came with Zerubbabel, Jeshua, Nehemiah, [a]Azariah, [b]Raamiah, Nahamani, Mordecai, Bilshan, [c]Mispereth, Bigvai, [d]Nehum, Baanah.

The number of men of the people of Israel: 8the sons of Parosh, 2,172; 9the sons of Shephatiah, 372; 10the sons of Arah, 652; 11the sons of Pahath-moab of the sons of Jeshua and Joab, 2,818; 12the sons of Elam, 1,254; 13the sons of Zattu, 845; 14the sons of Zaccai, 760; 15the sons of [a]Binnui, 648; 16the sons of Bebai, 628; 17the sons of Azgad, 2,322; 18the sons of Adonikam, 667; 19the sons of Bigvai, 2,067; 20the sons of Adin, 655; 21the sons of Ater, of Hezekiah, 98; 22the sons of Hashum, 328; 23the sons of Bezai, 324; 24the sons of [a]Hariph, 112; 25the sons of [a]Gibeon, 95; 26the men of Bethlehem and Netophah, 188; 27the men of Anathoth, 128; 28the men of [a]Beth-azmaveth, 42; 29the men of [a]Kiriath-jearim, Chephirah and Beeroth, 743; 30the men of Ramah and Geba, 621; 31the men of Michmas, 122; 32the men of Bethel and Ai, 123; 33the men of the other Nebo, 52; 34the sons of the other Elam, 1,254; 35the sons of Harim, 320; 36the [a]men of Jericho, 345; 37the sons of Lod, Hadid and Ono, 721; 38the sons of Senaah, 3,930.

39The priests: the sons of Jedaiah of the house of Jeshua, 973; 40the sons of Immer, 1,052; 41the sons of Pashhur, 1,247; 42the sons of Harim, 1,017.

43The Levites: the sons of Jeshua, of Kadmiel, of the sons of [a]Hodevah, 74. 44The singers: the sons of Asaph, 148. 45The gatekeepers: the sons of Shallum, the sons of Ater, the sons of Talmon, the sons of Akkub, the sons of Hatita, the sons of Shobai, 138.

46The temple servants: the sons of Ziha, the sons of Hasupha, the sons of Tabbaoth, 47the sons of Keros, the sons of [a]Sia, the sons of Padon, 48the sons of Lebana, the sons of Hagaba, the sons of Shalmai, 49the sons of Hanan, the sons of Giddel, the sons of Gahar, 50the sons of Reaiah, the sons of Rezin, the sons of Nekoda, 51the sons of Gazzam, the sons of Uzza, the sons of Paseah, 52the sons of Besai, the sons of Meunim, the sons of [a]Nephushesim, 53the sons of Bakbuk, the sons of Hakupha, the sons of Harhur, 54the sons of [a]Bazlith, the sons of Mehida, the sons of Harsha, 55the sons of Barkos, the sons of Sisera, the sons of Temah, 56the sons of Neziah, the sons of Hatipha.

57The sons of Solomon's servants: the sons of Sotai, the sons of [a]Sophereth, the sons of [b]Perida, 58the sons of Jaala, the sons of Darkon, the sons of Giddel, 59the sons of Shephatiah, the sons of Hattil, the sons of Pochereth-hazzebaim, the sons of [a]Amon.

60All the temple servants and the sons of Solomon's servants *were* 392.

61These *were* they who came up from Tel-melah, Tel-harsha, Cherub, [a]Addon and Immer; but they could not show their fathers' houses or their [b]descendants, whether they were of Israel: 62the sons of

7:1 [A]Neh 6:1, 15 7:2 [A]Neh 1:2 [B]Neh 10:23 [C]Neh 2:8 [D]Neh 13:13 7:5 [a]Lit *and I found written in it* [A]Prov 2:6; 3:6 7:6 [a]Lit *sons* [A]Ezra 2:1-70 7:7 [a]In Ezra 2:2, *Seraiah* [b]In Ezra 2:2, *Reelaiah* [c]In Ezra 2:2, *Mispar* [d]In Ezra 2:2, *Rehum* 7:15 [a]In Ezra 2:10, *Bani* 7:24 [a]In Ezra 2:18, *Jorah* 7:25 [a]In Ezra 2:20, *Gibbar* 7:28 [a]In Ezra 2:24, *Azmaveth* 7:29 [a]In Ezra 2:25, *Kiriath-arim* 7:36 [a]Lit *sons* 7:43 [a]In Ezra 2:40, *Hodaviah* 7:47 [a]In Ezra 2:44, *Siaha* 7:52 [a]In Ezra 2:50, *Nephisim* 7:54 [a]In Ezra 2:52, *Bazluth* 7:57 [a]In Ezra 2:55, *Hassophereth* [b]In Ezra 2:55, *Peruda* 7:59 [a]In Ezra 2:57, *Ami* 7:61 [a]In Ezra 2:59, *Addan* [b]Lit *seed*

completion, Nehemiah's conclusion was seen through the eyes of his enemies, i.e., God works through faithful people, but it is God who works. This is a change from the attitudes indicated in 4:1 and 5:9.

6:17–19 many letters went from the nobles of Judah to Tobiah. Nehemiah added a footnote that in the days of building the wall, the nobles of Judah who refused to work (3:5) were in alliance and correspondence with Tobiah because, although his ancestors were Ammonites (2:19), he had married into a respectable Jewish family. Shemaiah was from the family of Arah (Ezr 2:5); his son Jehohanan was the son-in-law of Meshullam who shared in the work of building (3:4, 30). According to 13:4, the High Priest, Eliashib, was related to Tobiah (which is a Jewish name). The meddling of these nobles, by trying to play both sides through reports to Tobiah and to Nehemiah (v. 19), only widened the breach as Tobiah escalated efforts to frighten the governor.

7:2 Hanani. Cf. 1:2. **the fortress.** *See note on 2:8.*

7:3 In the ancient Near East, it was customary to open the city gates at sunrise and close them at sunset. Nehemiah recommended that this not be done, because of the hostility of the enemies. Rather the gates were to be kept shut until well into the heat of the morning when everyone was up and active. When the gates were shut, they were to be guarded by sentinels at watch stations and in front of their own vulnerable homes (v. 4).

7:5a my God put it into my heart. Throughout the book, Nehemiah claimed the hand of God was at work in all circumstances (cf. 2:8, 18; 6:16).

7:5b, 6 I found the book of genealogy. Nehemiah discovered a record of the people made by Ezra in Babylon before the first group returned, a listing of the people who had come with Zerubbabel.

7:6–73a Nehemiah gave the list of those in the first return from Persia to Jerusalem under Zerubbabel in 538 B.C. *See notes on Ezr 2:1–70.* Minor discrepancies are possibly due to Ezra listing those who intended to depart, while Nehemiah listed those who actually arrived; or some other unknown reason.

Delaiah, the sons of Tobiah, the sons of Nekoda, 642.
63 Of the priests: the sons of [a]Hobaiah, the sons of
Hakkoz, the sons of Barzillai, who took a wife of the
daughters of Barzillai, the Gileadite, and was named
after them. 64 These searched *among* their ancestral
registration, but it could not be located; therefore
they were considered unclean *and excluded* from
the priesthood. 65 [A]The [a]governor said to them that
they should not eat from the most holy things until
a priest arose with [B]Urim and Thummim.

TOTAL OF PEOPLE AND GIFTS

66 The whole assembly together *was* 42,360, 67 besides their male and their female servants, [a]of whom
there were 7,337; and they had 245 male and female
singers. 68 [a,A]Their horses were 736; their mules, 245;
69 *their* camels, 435; *their* donkeys, 6,720.
70 Some from among the heads of fathers' *households* gave to the work. The [a,A]governor gave to the
treasury 1,000 gold drachmas, 50 basins, 530 priests'
garments. 71 Some of the heads of fathers' *households* gave into the treasury of the work 20,000 gold
drachmas and 2,200 silver minas. 72 That which the
rest of the people gave was 20,000 gold drachmas
and 2,000 silver minas and 67 priests' garments.
73 Now [A]the priests, the Levites, the gatekeepers,
the singers, some of the people, the temple servants
and all Israel, lived in their cities.
[B]And when the seventh month came, the sons of
Israel *were* in their cities.

EZRA READS THE LAW

8 And all the people gathered as one man at the
square which was in front of [A]the Water Gate,
and they [a]asked [B]Ezra the scribe to bring [C]the book
of the law of Moses which the LORD had [b]given
to Israel. 2 Then [A]Ezra the priest brought the law
before the assembly of men, women and all who
could listen with understanding, on [B]the first day
of the seventh month. 3 He read from it before the
square which was in front of [A]the Water Gate from
[a]early morning until midday, in the presence of men
and women, those who could understand; and all
the people were attentive to the book of the law.
4 Ezra the scribe stood at a wooden podium which
they had made for the purpose. And beside him
stood Mattithiah, Shema, Anaiah, Uriah, Hilkiah,
and Maaseiah on his right hand; and Pedaiah, Mishael, Malchijah, Hashum, Hashbaddanah, Zechariah
and Meshullam on his left hand. 5 Ezra opened [A]the
book in the sight of all the people for he was standing above all the people; and when he opened it,
all the people [B]stood up. 6 Then Ezra blessed the
LORD the great God. And all the people answered,
"[A]Amen, Amen!" while lifting up their hands; then
[B]they bowed low and worshiped the LORD with *their*
faces to the ground. 7 Also Jeshua, Bani, Sherebiah,
Jamin, Akkub, Shabbethai, Hodiah, Maaseiah, Kelita, Azariah, Jozabad, Hanan, Pelaiah, the Levites,
explained the law to the people while the people
remained in their place. 8 They read from the book,
from the law of God, [a]translating to give the sense
so that they understood the reading.

"THIS DAY IS HOLY"

9 Then Nehemiah, who was the [a,A]governor, and
Ezra [B]the priest *and* scribe, and the Levites who
taught the people said to all the people, "[C]This day is
holy to the LORD your God; [D]do not mourn or weep."
For all the people were weeping when they heard
the words of the law. 10 Then he said to them, "Go,
eat of the fat, drink of the sweet, and [A]send portions

7:63 [a]In Ezra 2:61, *Habaiah* 7:65 [a]Heb *Tirshatha*, a Persian title [A]Neh 8:9; 10:1 [B]Ex 28:30; Deut 33:8 7:67 [a]Lit *these* 7:68 [a]So with some ancient mss and Gr [A]Ezra 2:66 7:70 [a]Heb *Tirshatha*, a Persian title [A]Neh 7:65; 8:9 7:73 [A]1 Chr 9:2 [B]Ezra 3:1 8:1 [a]Lit *said to* [b]Lit *commanded* [A]Neh 3:26 [B]Ezra 7:6 [C]2 Chr 34:15 8:2 [A]Deut 31:9-11; Neh 8:9 [B]Lev 23:24 8:3 [a]Lit *the light* [A]Neh 8:1 8:5 [A]Neh 8:3 [B]Judg 3:20; 1 Kin 8:12-14 8:6 [A]Neh 5:13 [B]Ex 4:31 8:8 [a]Or *explaining* 8:9 [a]Heb *Tirshatha*, a Persian title [A]Neh 7:65, 70 [B]Neh 12:26 [C]Neh 8:2 [D]Deut 12:7, 12 8:10 [A]Deut 26:11-13

7:65 arose with Urim and Thummim. One of the methods used to discern the will of God on a specific matter. *See note on Ex 28:30.*

7:73b–10:39 God gave revival under Ezra's spiritual leadership.

7:73b–8:12 The revival began with an exposition of God's Word.

7:73b seventh month. The month of Tishri (Sept./Oct.), 445 B.C., less than one week after completing the walls (cf. 6:15). The Feast of Booths, or Tabernacles, usually began on the fifteenth day (cf. 6:14 with Lv 23:33–44), but here it began on the second (cf. 8:13), and it was a feast to which the whole nation was called. Usually the Feast of Trumpets occurred on the first day (cf. Lev 23:23–25).

8:1, 2 the book of the law. In response to the people's request, Ezra brought the law of the Lord, which he had set his heart to study, practice, and teach to the people (cf. Ezr 7:10). At this time, the law was a scroll, as opposed to a text consisting of bound pages. Such a reading was required every 7 years at the Feast of Booths, or Tabernacles (cf. Dt 31:10–13), even though it had been neglected since the Babylonian captivity until this occasion.

8:1 Water Gate. *See note on 3:26.* **Ezra.** This is the first mention of Ezra in the book of Nehemiah, though he had been ministering in Jerusalem since 458 B.C. (cf. Ezr 7:1–10:44).

8:3 read ... understand. Here is the general summary of the event of reading and explaining the Scripture from daybreak to noon, a period of at least 6 hours (more detail is added in vv. 4–8).

8:4 podium ... beside him. The platform was big enough to hold 14 people for the long hours of reading and explaining (v. 8). The men, probably priests, stood with Ezra to show agreement.

8:5 stood up. In respect at the reading of God's Word, as though they were in the presence of God Himself, the people stood for all the hours of the exposition.

8:6 blessed the LORD. A praise befitting the reading. In a synagogue, the reading is preceded by a benediction. The response of "Amen, Amen" was an affirmation of what Ezra prayed.

8:7, 8 Some of the Levites assisted Ezra with the people's understanding of the Scripture by reading and explaining it.

8:8 give the sense. This may have involved translation for people who were only Aramaic speakers in exile, but more likely it means "to break down" the text into its parts so that the people could understand it. This was an exposition or explanation of the meaning and not just translation. **so that they understood the reading.** In this act of instruction, Ezra's personal commitment to study the law, practice it in his own life, and then teach it (Ezr 7:10) was reflected.

8:9 governor. *See note on 5:14.* **Ezra the priest.** Cf. Ezr 7:11, 12, 21; 10:10, 16. **weeping when they heard the words of the law.** When they heard and understood God's law, they understood their violations of it. Not tears of joy, but penitent sorrow (8:10) came forth as they were grieved by conviction (8:11) over the distressing manifestations of sin in transgressing the Lord's commands and the consequent punishments they had suffered in their captivity.

8:10–12 the joy of the LORD is your strength. The event called for a holy day of worship to prepare them for the hard days ahead (cf. 12:43), so they were encouraged to rejoice. The words they had heard did remind them that God punishes sin, but also that God blesses obedience. That was reason to celebrate. They had not been utterly destroyed as a nation, in spite of their sin, and were, by God's grace, on the brink of a new beginning. That called for celebration.

to him who has nothing prepared; for this day is
holy to our Lord. Do not be grieved, for the joy of
the LORD is your strength." 11 So the Levites calmed
all the people, saying, "Be still, for the day is holy;
do not be grieved." 12 All the people went away to
eat, to drink, [A]to send portions and to [a]celebrate a
great festival, [B]because they understood the words
which had been made known to them.

FEAST OF BOOTHS RESTORED

13 Then on the second day the heads of fathers'
households of all the people, the priests and the
Levites were gathered to Ezra the scribe that they
might gain insight into the words of the law. 14 They
found written in the law how the LORD had commanded through Moses that the sons of Israel
[A]should live in booths during the feast of the seventh month. 15 [a,A]So they proclaimed and circulated
a proclamation in all their cities and [B]in Jerusalem, saying, "[C]Go out to the hills, and bring olive
branches and [b]wild olive branches, myrtle branches,
palm branches and branches of *other* leafy trees,
to make booths, as it is written." 16 So the people
went out and brought *them* and made booths for
themselves, each [A]on his roof, and in their courts
and in the courts of the house of God, and in the
square at [B]the Water Gate and in the square at [C]the
Gate of Ephraim. 17 The entire assembly of those
who had returned from the captivity made booths
and lived in [a]them. The sons of Israel [A]had indeed
not done so from the days of Joshua the son of Nun
to that day. And [B]there was great rejoicing. 18 [A]He
read from the book of the law of God daily, from
the first day to the last day. And they [B]celebrated
the feast seven days, and on [C]the eighth day *there
was* a solemn assembly according to the ordinance.

THE PEOPLE CONFESS THEIR SIN

9 Now on the twenty-fourth day of [A]this month
the sons of Israel assembled [B]with fasting, in
sackcloth and with [C]dirt upon them. 2 The [a,A]descen-
dants of Israel separated themselves from all foreigners, and stood and [B]confessed their sins and
the iniquities of their fathers. 3 While [A]they stood
in their place, they read from the book of the law
of the LORD their God for a fourth of the day; and
for *another* fourth they confessed and worshiped
the LORD their God. 4 [A]Now on the Levites' platform
stood Jeshua, Bani, Kadmiel, Shebaniah, Bunni,
Sherebiah, Bani *and* Chenani, and they cried with
a loud voice to the LORD their God.
5 Then the Levites, Jeshua, Kadmiel, Bani, Hashabneiah, Sherebiah, Hodiah, Shebaniah *and* Pethahiah, said, "Arise, bless the LORD your God forever
and ever!

O may Your glorious name be blessed
And exalted above all blessing
  and praise!
6 "[A]You alone are the LORD.
[B]You have made the heavens,
The heaven of heavens with
  all their host,
The earth and all that is on it,
The seas and all that is in them.
[C]You give life to all of them
And the heavenly host bows
  down before You.
7 "You are the LORD God,
[A]Who chose Abram
And brought him out from
  [B]Ur of the Chaldees,
And [C]gave him the name Abraham.

8:12 [a]Lit *make a great rejoicing* [A]Neh 8:10 [B]Neh 8:7, 8 8:14 [A]Lev 23:34, 40, 42 8:15 [a]Lit *And that they will cause to be heard* [b]Lit *oil tree,* species unknown [A]Lev 23:4 [B]Deut 16:16 [C]Lev 23:40 8:16 [A]Jer 32:29 [B]Neh 8:1 [C]2 Kin 14:13; Neh 12:39 8:17 [a]Lit *the booths* [A]2 Chr 7:8; 8:13 [B]2 Chr 30:21 8:18 [A]Deut 31:11 [B]Lev 23:36 [C]Num 29:35 9:1 [A]Neh 8:2 [B]Ezra 8:23 [C]1 Sam 4:12 9:2 [a]Lit *seed* [A]Ezra 10:11; Neh 13:3 [B]Prov 28:13; Jer 3:13 9:3 [A]Neh 8:4 9:4 [A]Neh 8:7 9:6 [A]Deut 6:4; 2 Kin 19:15 [B]Gen 1:1 [C]Col 1:16f 9:7 [A]Gen 12:1 [B]Gen 11:31 [C]Gen 17:5

8:13–9:37 The Jews celebrated the Feast of Booths, or Tabernacles, and confessed their history of sins.

8:13 might gain insight into the words of the law. The smaller group that gathered to Ezra consisted of those who had teaching responsibilities: the heads of the fathers' houses to their families, and the priests and Levites to the general population in the community (Mal 2:6, 7).

8:14 Cf. Ex 23:16; Lv 23:33–44; Nu 29:12–38; Dt 16:13–17 for details on the Feast of Booths, or Tabernacles.

8:15, 16 they proclaimed and circulated a proclamation. Proclamations such as this carried the authority of the administration represented by leaders such as Nehemiah, who was the governor, and Ezra, the priest and scribe (8:9), who had been used to reestablish the city, its worship, and its social life. The people responded to their directive.

8:16 Water Gate. *See notes on 3:26; 12:37.* **Gate of Ephraim.** This is believed to have been near the Old Gate (cf. 3:6; 12:39).

8:17 from the days of Joshua ... great rejoicing. The Feast of Booths, or Tabernacles, had been celebrated since Joshua (2Ch 7:8–10; Ezr 3:4), but not with such joy.

8:18 This was more than was required and arose from the exuberant zeal of the people.

9:1 this month. Tishri (Sept./Oct.), 445 B.C. (cf. 7:73b; 8:2). **with fasting, in sackcloth and with dirt.** The outward demonstration of deep mourning and heaviness of heart for their iniquity seems to have been done in the spirit of the Day of Atonement which was normally observed on the tenth day of the seventh month (cf. Lv 16:1–34; 23:26–32).

9:2 separated themselves from all foreigners. This call for divorcing all lawful wives taken from among the heathen was needed, since the last time, prompted 13 years before by Ezra (*see notes on Ezr 10*), had only been partially successful. Many had escaped the required action of divorce and kept their pagan wives. Perhaps new defaulters had appeared also, and were confronted for the first time with this necessary action of divorce. Nehemiah's efforts were successful in removing this evil mixture.

9:3 they stood ... read ... confessed and worshiped. The succession of events helped to reestablish the essential commitment of Israel to God and His law. They read for 3 hours about the sins of their fathers and for 3 more hours confessed that they had been partakers of similar evil deeds. In response to all of this, they worshiped.

9:4–37 This long confession of sin in the context of the recitation of God's mighty redemptive acts on Israel's behalf is an expression of worship (v. 3) that recalls some of the psalms in their theme and worshipful purpose. This season of national humiliation centered on adoring God for His great mercy in the forgiveness of their multiplied iniquities, in delivering them from judgment, protecting them, and blessing them graciously. Apparently, this great prayer of worship offered to God was recited by a group of Levites (vv. 4, 5) indicating it had been prepared and adopted beforehand, probably by Ezra. This prayer initiated the 3 hours of confession and worship (v. 3), which led to a national promise of obedience to God in the future (v. 38).

9:6 have made the heavens. The recitation was ordered historically, although themes of promise and judgment are traced through Israel's history with God. The first feature is the celebration of God's greatness as Creator (cf. Ge 1, 2). **the heavenly host bows down before You.** The praise which Israel offered on earth was also echoed in the heavens by angelic hosts.

8 "You found [A]his heart faithful before You,
And made a covenant with him
To give *him* the land of the Canaanite,
Of the Hittite and the Amorite,
Of the Perizzite, the Jebusite
and the Girgashite—
To give *it* to his [a]descendants.
And You [B]have fulfilled Your promise,
For You are righteous.

9 "[A]You saw the affliction of our
fathers in Egypt,
And [B]heard their cry by the [a]Red Sea.
10 "Then You performed [A]signs and
wonders against Pharaoh,
Against all his servants and all
the people of his land;
For You knew that [B]they acted
arrogantly toward them,
And [C]made a name for Yourself
as *it is* this day.
11 "[A]You divided the sea before them,
So they passed through the midst
of the sea on dry ground;
And [B]their pursuers You
hurled into the depths,
Like a stone into [a]raging waters.
12 "And with a pillar of cloud
[A]You led them by day,
And with a pillar of fire by night
To light for them the way
In which they were to go.
13 "Then [A]You came down on Mount Sinai,
And [B]spoke with them from heaven;
You gave them [C]just ordinances
and true laws,
Good statutes and commandments.
14 "So You made known to them
[A]Your holy sabbath,
And laid down for them
commandments, statutes and law,
Through Your servant Moses.
15 "You [A]provided bread from heaven
for them for their hunger,
You [B]brought forth water from a
rock for them for their thirst,
And You [C]told them to enter
in order to possess
The land which You [a]swore to give them.

16 "But they, our fathers, [A]acted arrogantly;
They [a,B]became stubborn and would
not listen to Your commandments.
17 "They refused to listen,
And [A]did not remember Your
wondrous deeds which You had
performed among them;
So they became stubborn and
[B]appointed a leader to return
to their slavery [a]in Egypt.
But You are a God [C]of forgiveness,
Gracious and compassionate,
Slow to anger and abounding
in lovingkindness;
And You did not forsake them.
18 "Even when they [A]made for themselves
A calf of molten metal
And said, 'This is your God
Who brought you up from Egypt,'
And committed great [a]blasphemies,
19 [A]You, in Your great compassion,
Did not forsake them in the wilderness;
[B]The pillar of cloud did not
leave them by day,
To guide them on their way,
Nor the pillar of fire by night, to light for
them the way in which they were to go.
20 "[A]You gave Your good Spirit to instruct them,
Your manna You did not withhold
from their mouth,
And You gave them water for their thirst.
21 "Indeed, [A]forty years You provided
for them in the wilderness *and*
they were not in want;
Their clothes did not wear out,
nor did their feet swell.
22 "You also gave them kingdoms
and peoples,
And allotted *them* to them as a [a]boundary.
[A]They took possession of the land of
Sihon [b]the king of Heshbon
And the land of Og the king of Bashan.

9:8 [a]Lit *seed* [A]Gen 15:6, 18-21 [B]Josh 21:43-45 9:9 [a]Lit *Sea of Reeds* [A]Ex 3:7 [B]Ex 14:10-14, 31 9:10 [A]Ex 7:8-12:32 [B]Ex 5:2 [C]Ex 9:16 9:11 [a]Lit *strong, mighty* [A]Ex 14:21 [B]Ex 15:1, 5, 10 9:12 [A]Ex 13:21, 22 9:13 [A]Ex 19:11, 18-20 [B]Ex 20:1 [C]Ps 19:7-9 9:14 [A]Ex 16:23; 20:8 9:15 [a]Lit *lifted up Your hand* [A]Ex 16:4, 14, 15 [B]Ex 17:6; Num 20:7-13 [C]Deut 1:8, 21 9:16 [a]Lit *stiffened their neck;* so also v 17 [A]Neh 9:10 [B]Deut 1:26-33; 31:27; Neh 9:29 9:17 [a]So Gr and some Heb mss; Heb reads *in their rebellion* [A]Ps 78:11, 42-55 [B]Num 14:4 [C]Ex 34:6, 7; Num 14:18 9:18 [a]Lit *acts of contempt* [A]Ex 32:4-8, 31 9:19 [A]Deut 8:2-4; Neh 9:27, 31 [B]Neh 9:12 9:20 [A]Num 11:17; Neh 9:30; Is 63:11-14 9:21 [A]Deut 2:7 9:22 [a]Lit *side, corner* [b]So the Gr and the Latin; Heb reads *and the land of the king of Heshbon* [A]Num 21:21-35

9:8 found his heart faithful before You. The Abrahamic Covenant (Ge 12:1–3; 15:4–7; 17:1–9) was based on God's faithfulness to His Word and given to a man who was faithful to Him. *See notes on Ge 15:6 and Ro 4,* where the faithful heart of Abraham is discussed. **a covenant with him to give *him* the land.** The covenant was a covenant of salvation, but also involved the Promised Land. The people, having just returned from captivity, understandably emphasized that feature of the covenant, since God had returned them to the land.

9:9–12 This section of the prayer of praise and confession recounts the Exodus (see Ex 2–15).

9:10 made a name for Yourself. God established His righteous reputation over the powers of Egypt by the miracles of immense power performed in Egypt.

9:13–19 The months at Sinai are remembered (see Ex 19–40).

9:17 they . . . appointed a leader. The Heb. of this statement is almost a repeat of Nu 14:4, which records the discontent of the people with God's plan and Moses' leadership.

9:19–21 This section remembers the 38 years of wandering in the wilderness (cf. Nu 9–19).

9:21 they were not in want. The same word is used in Ps 23:1, "I shall not want." Even during the long season of chastisement, God miraculously cared for their every need.

9:22–25 These verses encompass the period of possessing the Promised Land, as recorded in Nu 20–Jos 24.

9:22 gave them kingdoms and peoples. Canaan was comprised of a number of politically semiautonomous groups all loosely connected under the waning authority of Egypt. The Lord divided Canaan into tribal districts, thus apportioning the land for Israel's possession.

23 "You made their sons numerous
as [A]the stars of heaven,
And You brought them into the land
Which You had told their fathers
to enter and possess.
24 "[A]So their sons entered and
possessed the land.
And [B]You subdued before them
the inhabitants of the land,
the Canaanites,
And You gave them into their hand, with
their kings and the peoples of the land,
To do with them [a]as they desired.
25 "[A]They captured fortified cities
and a [a,B]fertile land.
They took possession of [C]houses
full of every good thing,
Hewn cisterns, vineyards, olive groves,
Fruit trees in abundance.
So they ate, were filled and [D]grew fat,
And [E]reveled in Your great goodness.

26 "[A]But they became disobedient
and rebelled against You,
And [B]cast Your law behind their backs
And [C]killed Your prophets who
had [D]admonished them
So that they might return to You,
And [E]they committed great [a]blasphemies.
27 "Therefore You [A]delivered them into
the hand of their oppressors
who oppressed them,
But when they cried to You [B]in
the time of their distress,
You heard from heaven, and according
to Your great compassion
You [C]gave them deliverers who
delivered them from the
hand of their oppressors.
28 "But [A]as soon as they had rest, they
did evil again before You;
Therefore You abandoned them
to the hand of their enemies, so
that they ruled over them.
When they cried again to You,
You heard from heaven,
And [B]many times You rescued them
according to Your compassion,
29 And [A]admonished them in order to
turn them back to Your law.
Yet [B]they acted arrogantly
and did not listen to Your
commandments but sinned
against Your ordinances,
By [C]which if a man observes
them he shall live.
And they [a,D]turned a stubborn
shoulder and stiffened their
neck, and would not listen.
30 "[A]However, You bore with them
for many years,
And [B]admonished them by [C]Your
Spirit through Your prophets,
Yet they would not give ear.
Therefore You gave them into the
hand of the peoples of the lands.
31 "Nevertheless, in Your great
compassion You [A]did not make an
end of them or forsake them,
For You are [B]a gracious and
compassionate God.

32 "Now therefore, our God, [A]the great, the
mighty, and the awesome God, who
keeps covenant and lovingkindness,
Do not let all the hardship seem
insignificant before You,
Which has come upon us, our kings, our
princes, our priests, our prophets,
our fathers and on all Your people,
[B]From the days of the kings of
Assyria to this day.
33 "However, [A]You are just in all
that has come upon us;
For You have dealt faithfully, but
we have acted wickedly.
34 "For our kings, our leaders,
our priests and our fathers
have not kept Your law
Or paid attention to Your
commandments and Your
[a]admonitions with which You
have [b]admonished them.
35 "But [A]they, in their own kingdom,
[B]With Your great goodness
which You gave them,
With the broad and rich land
which You set before them,
Did not serve You or turn
from their evil deeds.

9:23 [A]Gen 15:5; 22:17 9:24 [a]Lit *according to their desire* [A]Josh 11:23; 21:43 [B]Josh 18:1 9:25 [a]Lit *fat* [A]Deut 3:5 [B]Num 13:27 [C]Deut 6:11 [D]Deut 32:15 [E]1 Kin 8:66 9:26 [a]Lit *acts of contempt* [A]Judg 2:11 [B]1 Kin 14:9 [C]2 Chr 36:16 [D]Neh 9:30 [E]Neh 9:18 9:27 [A]Judg 2:14 [B]Deut 4:29 [C]Judg 2:16 9:28 [A]Judg 3:11 [B]Ps 106:43 9:29 [a]Lit *gave* [A]Neh 9:26, 30 [B]Neh 9:10, 16 [C]Lev 18:5 [D]Zech 7:11 9:30 [A]Ps 95:10; Acts 13:18 [B]2 Kin 17:13-18; 2 Chr 36:15, 16; Neh 9:26, 29 [C]Neh 9:20 9:31 [A]Jer 4:27 [B]Neh 9:17 9:32 [A]Neh 1:5 [B]2 Kin 15:19, 29; 2 Kin 17:3-6; Ezra 4:2, 10 9:33 [A]Gen 18:25; Jer 12:1 9:34 [a]Lit *testimonies* [b]Or *witnessed* 9:35 [A]Deut 28:47 [B]Neh 9:25

9:23 made their sons numerous. A nation of offspring was another aspect of the promise made to Abraham (Ge 12:1–3). God told Abraham that his descendants would be like the stars of heaven (Ge 15:5) and Ex 1:1–3 reminded Israel that their multiplication in Egypt was nothing short of miraculous.

9:24 subdued before them. Moses said in Ex 15:3, "The LORD is a warrior." As Israel's military leader and king, He led them into battle to defeat their enemies and take the land.

9:26–31 This section summarizes the period from the judges to the Assyrian deportation (722 B.C.) and Babylonian exile (586 B.C.). See 2Ki 17–25.

9:26 who had admonished them. God's prophets brought them to God's court to be judged by His law. This theme is repeated throughout the message (vv. 29, 30, 34).

9:32 Now therefore. Having reviewed the faithfulness of God to the Abrahamic Covenant (vv. 7, 8) throughout Israel's national history, the prayer picks up with the present time confessing their unfaithfulness to (vv. 33–35) and renewed commitment to the Mosaic Covenant (vv. 36–38). **kings of Assyria to this day.** This statement sweeps across a summary of Assyrian, Babylonian, and Persian domination of the nation for almost 4 centuries up to that time.

36 “Behold, [A]we are slaves today,
And as to the land which You gave to our
fathers to eat of its fruit and its bounty,
Behold, we are slaves in it.
37 “[A]Its abundant produce is for the kings
Whom You have set over us
because of our sins;
They also rule over our bodies
And over our cattle as they please,
So we are in great distress.

A COVENANT RESULTS

38 “[a]Now because of all this
[A]We are making an agreement in writing;
And on the [B]sealed document *are*
the names of our leaders, our
Levites *and* our priests.”

SIGNERS OF THE DOCUMENT

10 [a]Now on the [A]sealed document *were the*
names of: Nehemiah the [b]governor, the son
of Hacaliah, and Zedekiah, 2 Seraiah, Azariah, Jeremiah, 3 Pashhur, Amariah, Malchijah, 4 Hattush,
Shebaniah, Malluch, 5 Harim, Meremoth, Obadiah,
6 Daniel, Ginnethon, Baruch, 7 Meshullam, Abijah,
Mijamin, 8 Maaziah, Bilgai, Shemaiah. These *were*
the priests. 9 And the Levites: Jeshua the son of Az-
aniah, Binnui of the sons of Henadad, Kadmiel;
10 also their brothers Shebaniah, Hodiah, Kelita,
Pelaiah, Hanan, 11 Mica, Rehob, Hashabiah, 12 Zaccur, Sherebiah, Shebaniah, 13 Hodiah, Bani, Beninu.
14 The leaders of the people: Parosh, Pahath-moab,
Elam, Zattu, Bani, 15 Bunni, Azgad, Bebai, 16 Adonijah, Bigvai, Adin, 17 Ater, Hezekiah, Azzur, 18 Hodiah, Hashum, Bezai, 19 Hariph, Anathoth, Nebai,
20 Magpiash, Meshullam, Hezir, 21 Meshezabel, Zadok, Jaddua, 22 Pelatiah, Hanan, Anaiah, 23 Hoshea,
Hananiah, Hasshub, 24 Hallohesh, Pilha, Shobek,
25 Rehum, Hashabnah, Maaseiah, 26 Ahiah, Hanan,
Anan, 27 Malluch, Harim, Baanah.

OBLIGATIONS OF THE DOCUMENT

28 Now [A]the rest of the people, the priests, the
Levites, the gatekeepers, the singers, the temple servants and [B]all those who had separated themselves
from the peoples of the lands to the law of God, their
wives, their sons and their daughters, all those who
had knowledge and understanding, 29 are joining
with their [a]kinsmen, their nobles, and are [b,A]taking
on themselves a curse and an oath to walk in God’s
law, which was given through Moses, God’s servant,
and to keep and to observe all the commandments
of [c]GOD our Lord, and His ordinances and His statutes; 30 and [A]that we will not give our daughters
to the peoples of the land or take their daughters
for our sons. 31 As [A]for the peoples of the land who
bring wares or any grain on the sabbath day to sell,
we will not buy from them on the sabbath or a holy
day; and we will forego *the crops* the [B]seventh year
and the [C]exaction of every debt.
32 We also [a]placed ourselves under obligation to
contribute yearly [A]one third of a shekel for the service of the house of our God: 33 for the [A]showbread,
for the continual grain offering, for the continual
burnt offering, the sabbaths, the new moon, for the
appointed times, for the holy things and for the sin
offerings to make atonement for Israel, and all the
work of the house of our God.
34 Likewise [A]we cast lots [B]for the supply of wood
among the priests, the Levites and the people so
that they might bring it to the house of our God,
according to our fathers’ households, at fixed times
annually, to burn on the altar of the LORD our God,
as it is written in the law; 35 and that they might
bring the first fruits of our ground and [A]the first
fruits of all the fruit of every tree to the house of the

9:36 [A]Deut 28:48 9:37 [A]Deut 28:33 9:38 [a]Ch 10:1 in Heb [A]Neh 10:29 [B]Neh 10:1 10:1 [a]Ch 10:2 in Heb [b]Heb *Tirshatha,* a Persian title [A]Neh 9:38 10:28 [A]Ezra 2:36-58 [B]Neh 9:2 10:29 [a]Lit *brothers* [b]Lit *entering into a* [c]Heb *YHWH,* usually rendered *LORD* [A]Neh 5:12 10:30 [A]Ex 34:16; Deut 7:3 10:31 [A]Neh 13:15-22 [B]Ex 23:10, 11; Lev 25:1-7 [C]Deut 15:1, 2 10:32 [a]Lit *imposed commandments on us* [A]Ex 30:11-16; Matt 17:24 10:33 [A]Lev 24:5, 6; 2 Chr 2:4 10:34 [A]Neh 11:1 [B]Neh 13:31 10:35 [A]Ex 23:19; 34:26; Deut 26:2

9:36, 37 **in it … over us.** The praise prayer rejoices that the Jews have been returned to the land, but grieves that Gentiles still rule over them.

9:37 **abundant produce is for the kings.** Because God’s people continued in widespread sin, enemy kings enjoyed the bounty that would have been Israel’s.

9:38–10:39 The nation makes a new covenant with God to keep the Mosaic law. Though well intended, as they had been in Ex 24:1–8, their failure was forthcoming (*see note on 13:10–13*).

9:38 **because of all this.** The history of God’s faithfulness, in spite of Israel’s unfaithfulness, is the ground of a pledge and promise which the people make to obey God and not repeat the sins of their fathers. **We are making an agreement in writing.** An agreement, or covenant, was a binding contract between two parties. In short, it was a formalized relationship with commitments to loyalty. In this case, the nation initiated this covenant with God.

10:1–27 The list of sealed signatures on the covenant were from the leaders. Surprisingly, Ezra’s name is not listed.

10:28 **temple servants.** *See note on Ezr 2:43–54.* **who had separated themselves.** These are those who 1) had followed the demand of Ezra and Nehemiah to divorce pagan spouses or 2) had been left in the land but never joined themselves to any heathen, thus remaining separate. Intermarriage with the nations had previously precipitated an influence in Israel which had culminated in Babylonian slavery, thus playing a major role in Israel’s unfaithfulness to the covenant.

10:29 **a curse and an oath.** Covenants characteristically were ratified by an oath ceremony in which the parties swore to the terms of the covenant. A curse rite was often included wherein the slaughtering of an animal indicated similar consequences for the covenant breaker. Israel’s pledged adherence to the law was thus solemnly affirmed.

10:30 **not give our daughters … or take their daughters.** Parents controlled marriages, so this part of the covenant came from them. Again, it stressed the serious matter of marrying a heathen from an idolatrous people (see Ezr 10).

10:32–39 The remainder of the conditions the people made in their covenant involved matters of the temple.

10:32, 33 **We also placed ourselves under obligation.** What the people were committing themselves to do by covenant turned into law requiring a one-third shekel temple tax. The Mosaic ordinance required one-half of a shekel (see Ex 30:11–16), but the severe economic straits of the time led to the reduced amount. By the time of Christ, the people had returned to the Mosaic stipulation of one-half of a shekel. *See note on Mt 17:24.*

10:34 The carrying of the wood for the constantly burning altar (Lv 6:12 ff.) had formerly been the duty of the temple servants, but few of them had returned from Babylon (7:60) so more people were chosen to assist in this task.

10:35–39 Laws for all the offerings and tithes were reinstated so as not to “neglect the house of our God” (v. 39).

10:35–37 **first fruits … firstborn … firstborn.** These laws required the firstfruits of

LORD annually, 36 and [A]bring to the house of our God
the firstborn of our sons and of our cattle, and the
firstborn of our herds and our flocks as it is written
in the law, for the priests who are ministering in
the house of our God. 37 [A]We will also bring the first
of our [a]dough, our contributions, the fruit of every
tree, the new wine and the oil [B]to the priests at the
chambers of the house of our God, and the [C]tithe of
our ground to the Levites, for the Levites are they
who receive the tithes in all the rural towns. 38 [A]The
priest, the son of Aaron, shall be with the Levites
when the Levites receive tithes, and the Levites
shall bring up the tenth of the tithes to the house
of our God, to the chambers of [B]the storehouse.
39 For the sons of Israel and the sons of Levi shall
bring the [A]contribution of the grain, the new wine
and the oil to the chambers; there are the utensils
of the sanctuary, the priests who are ministering,
the gatekeepers and the singers. Thus [B]we will not
[a]neglect the house of our God.

TIME PASSES; HEADS OF PROVINCES

11 Now [A]the leaders of the people lived in Jerusalem, but the rest of the people [B]cast lots to
bring one out of ten to live in Jerusalem, [C]the holy
city, while nine-tenths *remained* in the *other* cities.
2 And the people blessed all the men who [A]volun-
teered to live in Jerusalem.
3 [A]Now these are the heads of the provinces who
lived in Jerusalem, but in the cities of Judah [B]each
lived on his own property in their cities—the [a]Is-
raelites, the priests, the Levites, the [b,C]temple servants and the [c,D]descendants of Solomon's servants.
4 Some of the sons of Judah and some of the sons
of Benjamin lived in Jerusalem. From the sons of
Judah: Athaiah the son of Uzziah, the son of Zechariah, the son of Amariah, the son of Shephatiah,
the son of Mahalalel, of the sons of Perez; 5 and
Maaseiah the son of Baruch, the son of Col-hozeh,
the son of Hazaiah, the son of Adaiah, the son of
Joiarib, the son of Zechariah, the son of the Shilonite. 6 All the sons of Perez who lived in Jerusalem
were 468 able men.
7 Now these are the sons of Benjamin: Sallu the
son of Meshullam, the son of Joed, the son of Pedaiah, the son of Kolaiah, the son of Maaseiah, the
son of Ithiel, the son of Jeshaiah; 8 and after him
Gabbai *and* Sallai, 928. 9 Joel the son of Zichri was
their overseer, and Judah the son of Hassenuah was
second [a]in command of the city.
10 From the priests: Jedaiah the son of Joiarib,
Jachin, 11 Seraiah the son of Hilkiah, the son of Meshullam, the son of Zadok, the son of Meraioth, the
son of Ahitub, the leader of the house of God, 12 and
their [a]kinsmen who performed the work of the [b]tem-
ple, 822; and Adaiah the son of Jeroham, the son
of Pelaliah, the son of Amzi, the son of Zechariah,
the son of Pashhur, the son of Malchijah, 13 and his
kinsmen, heads of fathers' *households,* 242; and
Amashsai the son of Azarel, the son of Ahzai, the
son of Meshillemoth, the son of Immer, 14 and their
brothers, valiant warriors, 128. And their overseer
was Zabdiel, the son of [a]Haggedolim.
15 Now from the Levites: Shemaiah the son of Hasshub, the son of Azrikam, the son of Hashabiah, the
son of Bunni; 16 and Shabbethai and Jozabad, from
the [a]leaders of the Levites, who were [b]in charge of
[A]the outside work of the house of God; 17 and Mattaniah the son of Mica, the son of [a]Zabdi, the son
of Asaph, who was the [b]leader in beginning the
thanksgiving at prayer, and Bakbukiah, the second
among his brethren; and [c]Abda the son of [d]Sham-
mua, the son of Galal, the son of Jeduthun. 18 All the
Levites in [A]the holy city *were* 284.
19 Also the gatekeepers, Akkub, Talmon and their
brethren who kept watch at the gates, *were* 172.

OUTSIDE JERUSALEM

20 The rest of Israel, of the priests *and* of the Levites, *were* in all the cities of Judah, each [A]on his
own inheritance. 21 But [A]the temple servants were
living in Ophel, and Ziha and Gishpa were [a]in charge
of the temple servants.
22 Now [A]the overseer of the Levites in Jerusalem
was Uzzi the son of Bani, the son of Hashabiah, the
son of Mattaniah, the son of Mica, from the sons of
Asaph, who were the singers for the [a]service of the
house of God. 23 [A]For *there was* a commandment
from the king concerning them and a firm regulation for the song leaders [B]day by day. 24 Pethahiah
the son of Meshezabel, of the sons [A]of Zerah the
son of Judah, was the [B]king's [a]representative in all
matters concerning the people.
25 Now as for the villages with their fields, some
of the sons of Judah lived in [A]Kiriath-arba and its
[a]towns, in [B]Dibon and its [a]towns, and in Jekabzeel
and its villages, 26 and in Jeshua, in Moladah and
Beth-pelet, 27 and in Hazar-shual, in Beersheba
and its towns, 28 and in Ziklag, in Meconah and
in its towns, 29 and in En-rimmon, in Zorah and in

10:36 [A]Ex 13:2 10:37 [a]Or *coarse meal* [A]Lev 23:17 [B]Neh 13:5, 9 [C]Lev 27:30; Num 18:21 10:38 [A]Num 18:26 [B]Neh 13:12, 13 10:39 [a]Lit *forsake* [A]Deut 12:6 [B]Neh 13:10, 11
11:1 [A]Neh 7:4 [B]Neh 10:34 [C]Neh 11:18; Is 48:2 11:2 [A]Judg 5:9 11:3 [a]Lit *Israel* [b]Heb *Nethinim* [c]Lit *sons* [A]1 Chr 9:2-34 [B]Neh 7:73; 11:20 [C]Ezra 2:43 [D]Neh 7:57
11:9 [a]Lit *over* 11:12 [a]Lit *brothers,* and so throughout the ch [b]Lit *house* 11:14 [a]Or *the great ones* 11:16 [a]Lit *heads* [b]Lit *over* [A]1 Chr 26:29 11:17 [a]In 1 Chr 9:15, *Zichri* [b]Lit *head* [c]In 1 Chr 9:16, *Obadiah* [d]In 1 Chr 9:16, *Shemaiah* 11:18 [A]Neh 11:1 11:20 [A]Neh 11:3 11:21 [a]Lit *over* [A]Neh 3:26 11:22 [a]Or *work* [A]Neh 11:9, 14
11:23 [A]Ezra 6:8; 7:20 [B]Neh 12:47 11:24 [a]Lit *hand* [A]Gen 38:30 [B]1 Chr 18:17 11:25 [a]Lit *daughters,* and so throughout the ch [A]Josh 14:15 [B]Josh 13:9, 17

the ground (see Ex 23:19; 34:26; Dt 26:2), the firstfruits of the trees (see Lv 19:24; Nu 18:13), the firstborn sons redeemed by the estimated price of the priest (see Nu 18:15), and the firstborn of the herds and flocks (see Ex 13:12; Nu 18:15, 17). All of this was kept at the storehouses near the temple and distributed for the support of the priests and Levites. The Levites then gave a tenth of what they received to the priests (cf. Nu 18:26).

11:1–13:31 Details of Nehemiah exercising his governorship are given in this section.

11:1–12:26 Jerusalem and Judah are resettled.

11:1 cast lots. A method of decision-making which God honored (Pr 16:33). Nehemiah redistributed the population so that one out of every 10 Jews lived in Jerusalem. The other 9 were free to reestablish their family heritage in the land.

11:3–24 The people who dwelt in Jerusalem are identified.

11:21 Ophel. *See note on 3:26.*

11:25–36 These are the places where 90 percent of the people dwelt outside of Jerusalem (cf. Ezr 2:21–23, 27, 34).

Jarmuth, 30 Zanoah, Adullam, and their villages,
Lachish and its fields, Azekah and its towns. So
they encamped from Beersheba as far as the valley
of Hinnom. 31 The sons of Benjamin also *lived* from
Geba *onward,* at Michmash and Aija, at Bethel and
its towns, 32 at Anathoth, Nob, Ananiah, 33 Hazor, Ramah, Gittaim, 34 Hadid, Zeboim, Neballat, 35 Lod and
Ono, the valley of craftsmen. 36 From the Levites,
some divisions in Judah belonged to Benjamin.

PRIESTS AND LEVITES WHO RETURNED TO JERUSALEM WITH ZERUBBABEL

12 Now these are [A]the priests and the Levites who
came up with Zerubbabel the son of Shealtiel, and Jeshua: Seraiah, Jeremiah, Ezra, 2 Amariah,
Malluch, Hattush, 3 Shecaniah, Rehum, Meremoth,
4 Iddo, Ginnethoi, Abijah, 5 Mijamin, Maadiah, Bilgah, 6 Shemaiah and Joiarib, Jedaiah, 7 Sallu, Amok,
Hilkiah and Jedaiah. These were the heads of the
priests and their [a]kinsmen in the days of Jeshua.
8 The Levites *were* Jeshua, Binnui, Kadmiel, Sherebiah, Judah, *and* Mattaniah *who was* [a]in charge
of the songs of thanksgiving, he and his brothers.
9 Also Bakbukiah and Unni, their brothers, stood
opposite them [A]in *their* service divisions. 10 Jeshua
[a]became the father of Joiakim, and Joiakim [a]became
the father of Eliashib, and Eliashib [a]became the father of Joiada, 11 and Joiada became the father of Jonathan, and Jonathan became the father of Jaddua.
12 Now in the days of Joiakim, the priests, the heads
of fathers' *households* were: of Seraiah, Meraiah; of
Jeremiah, Hananiah; 13 of Ezra, Meshullam; of Amariah, Jehohanan; 14 of [a]Malluchi, Jonathan; of Shebaniah, Joseph; 15 of Harim, Adna; of Meraioth, Helkai;
16 of Iddo, Zechariah; of Ginnethon, Meshullam; 17 of
Abijah, Zichri; of Miniamin, of Moadiah, Piltai; 18 of Bilgah, Shammua; of Shemaiah, Jehonathan; 19 of Joiarib,
Mattenai; of Jedaiah, Uzzi; 20 of Sallai, Kallai; of Amok,
Eber; 21 of Hilkiah, Hashabiah; of Jedaiah, Nethanel.

THE CHIEF LEVITES

22 As for the Levites, the heads of fathers' *households* were registered in the days of Eliashib, Joiada,
and Johanan and Jaddua; so *were* the priests in the
reign of Darius the Persian. 23 The sons of Levi, the
heads of fathers' *households,* were registered in the
Book of the Chronicles up to the days of Johanan
the son of Eliashib. 24 The heads of the Levites *were*
Hashabiah, Sherebiah and Jeshua the son of Kadmiel, with their brothers opposite them, [A]to praise
and give thanks, [a]as prescribed by David the man
of God, [B]division corresponding to division. 25 Mattaniah, Bakbukiah, Obadiah, Meshullam, Talmon
and Akkub *were* gatekeepers keeping watch at [A]the
storehouses of the gates. 26 These *served* in the days
of Joiakim the son of Jeshua, the son of Jozadak, and
in the days of [A]Nehemiah the governor and of Ezra
the priest *and* scribe.

DEDICATION OF THE WALL

27 Now at the dedication of the wall of Jerusalem
they sought out the Levites from all their places,
to bring them to Jerusalem so that they might celebrate the dedication with gladness, with hymns
of thanksgiving and with songs [A]*to the accompaniment* of cymbals, harps and lyres. 28 So the sons
of the singers were assembled from the district
around Jerusalem, and from [A]the villages of the
Netophathites, 29 from Beth-gilgal and from *their*
fields in Geba and Azmaveth, for the singers had
built themselves villages around Jerusalem. 30 The
priests and the Levites [A]purified themselves; they
also purified the people, the gates and the wall.

PROCEDURES FOR THE TEMPLE

31 Then I had the leaders of Judah come up on
top of the wall, and I appointed two great [a]choirs,
[b,A]the first proceeding to the right on top of the wall
toward [B]the Refuse Gate. 32 Hoshaiah and half of the
leaders of Judah followed them, 33 with Azariah,
Ezra, Meshullam, 34 Judah, Benjamin, Shemaiah,
Jeremiah, 35 and some of the sons of the priests
with trumpets; *and* Zechariah the son of Jonathan,
the son of Shemaiah, the son of Mattaniah, the son
of Micaiah, the son of Zaccur, the son of Asaph,
36 and his [a]kinsmen, Shemaiah, Azarel, Milalai, Gil-
alai, Maai, Nethanel, Judah *and* Hanani, [A]with the

12:1 [A]Ezra 2:1; 7:7 12:7 [a]Lit *brothers* 12:8 [a]Lit *over* 12:9 [A]Neh 12:24 12:10 [a]Lit *begot,* and so in vv 11, 12 12:14 [a]In Neh 12:2, *Malluch* 12:24 [a]Lit *in the commandment of* [A]Neh 11:17 [B]Neh 12:9 12:25 [A]1 Chr 26:15 12:26 [A]Neh 8:9 12:27 [A]1 Chr 15:16, 28 12:28 [A]1 Chr 9:16 12:30 [A]Neh 13:22, 30 12:31 [a]Lit *thanksgiving choirs* [b]Heb *and processions to the right* [A]Neh 12:38 [B]Neh 2:13 12:36 [a]Lit *brothers* [A]Neh 12:24

12:1–26 Originally there were 24 courses of priests, each course serving in the temple for a period of two weeks per year or for one month biannually (see 1Ch 24:1–20). Only four of those houses returned from Babylon (see 7:39–42; Ezr 2:36–39), but these were divided into 24 courses of which 22 are listed here. Perhaps two are omitted because their families had become extinct, because no sons were born since the time Zerubbabel originally named them. This then is a selective rather than exhaustive listing of priests and Levites from the time of Zerubbabel and Jeshua, recording the key priests and Levites through 3 generations of High Priests: 1) Jeshua who came in the initial return with Zerubbabel ca. 538 B.C. (vv. 1–11); 2) Joiakim, the son of Jeshua (vv. 12–21); 3) Eliashib (cf. 3:1) the son of Joiakim (vv. 22, 23); 4) a miscellaneous group who served in the days of Joiakim (vv. 24–26).

12:1 Zerubbabel . . . Jeshua. *See note on Ezr 2:2.*

12:10, 11 This record lists 6 generations of High Priests beginning with Jeshua. The Jonathan of v. 11 is the Johanan of v. 22.

12:12–21 Each of the 22 families in vv. 1–7 is repeated, except one (cf. Hattush; v. 2). Perhaps by the time of Joiakim's High-Priesthood, this family had become extinct, the fathers having no male offspring.

12:22 Darius the Persian. This refers to Darius II, ca. 423–404 B.C.

12:23 Book of the Chronicles. Lit. "were written on the scroll of the matters of the days." This involved precise genealogical records kept in the administrative archives of Judah.

12:27–13:3 The walls were dedicated.

12:27–43 the dedication of the wall. In the same manner marking the dedications of the temple in Solomon's day (2Ch 5–7) and the rebuilt temple several decades earlier (Ezr 6:16–18), the rebuilt walls were dedicated with the music of thanksgiving (most likely shortly after the events of Ne 9).

12:30 purified. See Lv 16:30 for the sense of moral purity in this symbolic act.

12:31–40 They probably assembled at the Valley Gate on the W. One of the choirs was led by Ezra (v. 36), the other accompanied by Nehemiah (v. 38). Moving in different directions (v. 38), they assembled together in the temple area (v. 40).

12:31 Refuse Gate. *See notes on 2:13; 3:13.*

12:36 the musical instruments of David.

musical instruments of David the man of God. And
Ezra the scribe went before them. 37 At [A]the Fountain
Gate they went directly up [B]the steps of the city of
David by the stairway of the wall above the house
of David to [C]the Water Gate on the east.
38 [A]The second [a]choir proceeded to the [b]left, while
I followed them with half of the people on the wall,
[B]above the Tower of Furnaces, to [C]the Broad Wall,
39 and above [A]the Gate of Ephraim, by [B]the Old Gate,
by the [C]Fish Gate, [D]the Tower of Hananel and the
Tower of the Hundred, as far as the Sheep Gate; and
they stopped at [E]the Gate of the Guard. 40 Then the
two choirs took their stand in the house of God. So
did I and half of the officials with me; 41 and the
priests, Eliakim, Maaseiah, Miniamin, Micaiah, Elioenai, Zechariah and Hananiah, with the trumpets;
42 and Maaseiah, Shemaiah, Eleazar, Uzzi, Jehohanan, Malchijah, Elam and Ezer. And the singers
[a]sang, with Jezrahiah *their* leader, 43 and on that day
they offered great sacrifices and rejoiced because
[A]God had given them great joy, even the women
and children rejoiced, so that the joy of Jerusalem
was heard from afar.
44 On that day [A]men were also appointed over
the chambers for the stores, the contributions, the
first fruits and the tithes, to gather into them from
the fields of the cities the portions required by the
law for the priests and Levites; for Judah rejoiced
over the priests and Levites who [a]served. 45 For they
performed the [a]worship of their God and the service
of purification, together with the singers and the
gatekeepers [A]in accordance with the command of
David *and* of his son Solomon. 46 For in the days
of David and [A]Asaph, in ancient times, *there were*
[a,B]leaders of the singers, songs of praise and hymns
of thanksgiving to God. 47 So all Israel in the days
of Zerubbabel and Nehemiah gave the portions
due the singers and the gatekeepers [A]as each day
required, and [B]set apart the consecrated *portion* for
the Levites, and the Levites set apart the consecrated
portion for the sons of Aaron.

FOREIGNERS EXCLUDED

13 On that day [A]they read aloud from the book
of Moses in the hearing of the people; and
there was found written in it that [B]no Ammonite
or Moabite should ever enter the assembly of God,
2 because they did not meet the sons of Israel with
bread and water, but [A]hired Balaam against them
to curse them. However, [B]our God turned the curse
into a blessing. 3 So when they heard the law, [A]they
excluded [B]all foreigners from Israel.

TOBIAH EXPELLED AND THE TEMPLE CLEANSED

4 Now prior to this, Eliashib the priest, [A]who was
appointed over the chambers of the house of our
God, being [a]related to [B]Tobiah, 5 had prepared a large
[a]room for him, where formerly they put the grain offerings, the frankincense, the utensils and the tithes
of grain, wine and oil [A]prescribed for the Levites,
the singers and the gatekeepers, and the [b]contribu-
tions for the priests. 6 But during all this *time* I was
not in Jerusalem, for in [A]the thirty-second year of
[B]Artaxerxes king of Babylon I had gone to the king.
After some time, however, I asked leave from the
king, 7 and I came to Jerusalem and [a]learned about
the evil that Eliashib had done for Tobiah, [A]by preparing a [b]room for him in the courts of the house of
God. 8 It was very displeasing to me, so I [A]threw all
of Tobiah's household goods out of the room. 9 Then
I gave an order and [A]they cleansed the rooms; and I
returned there the utensils of the house of God with
the grain offerings and the frankincense.

12:37 [A]Neh 2:14 [B]Neh 3:15 [C]Neh 3:26 12:38 [a]Lit *thanksgiving choir* [b]Lit *front* [A]Neh 12:31 [B]Neh 3:11 [C]Neh 3:8 12:39 [A]Neh 8:16 [B]Neh 3:6 [C]Neh 3:3 [D]Neh 3:1 [E]Neh 3:25 12:42 [a]Lit *caused their voices to be heard* 12:43 [A]Ps 9:2; 92:4 12:44 [a]Lit *stood* [A]Neh 13:4, 5, 12, 13 12:45 [a]Lit *service* [A]1 Chr 25:1 12:46 [a]Lit *heads* [A]2 Chr 29:30 [B]1 Chr 9:33 12:47 [A]Neh 11:23 [B]Num 18:21 13:1 [A]Neh 9:3 [B]Deut 23:3-5; Neh 13:23 13:2 [A]Num 22:3-11 [B]Deut 23:5 13:3 [A]Neh 9:2; 10:28 [B]Ex 12:38 13:4 [a]Lit *close to* [A]Neh 12:44 [B]Neh 2:10; 6:1, 17, 18 13:5 [a]Or *chamber* [b]Lit *heave offerings* [A]Num 18:21 13:6 [A]Neh 5:14 [B]Ezra 6:22 13:7 [a]Or *understood* [b]Or *chamber,* and so in vv 8, 9 [A]Neh 13:5 13:8 [A]John 2:13-16 13:9 [A]2 Chr 29:5, 15, 16

This phrase could refer to the same kind of instruments David's musicians used or the actual instruments constructed in David's time, now being used centuries later. Cf. 1Ch 15:16; 23:5; 2Ch 29:26; Ezr 3:10. **the man of God.** *See note on Dt 33:1*; cf. Ac 13:22.

12:37 Fountain Gate. *See note on 2:14.* **Water Gate.** *See notes on 3:26; 8:16.*

12:38 to the left. This second choir marched clockwise to the N (cf. 12:31). **Tower of Furnaces.** *See note on 3:11.*

12:39 Gate of Ephraim. *See note on 8:16.* **Old Gate.** *See note on 3:6.* **Fish Gate.** *See note on 3:3.* **Tower of Hananel.** *See note on 3:1.* **Tower of the Hundred.** *See note on 3:1.* **Sheep Gate.** *See notes on 3:1, 32.* **Gate of the Guard.** Located in the NE section of Jerusalem.

12:43 because God had given them great joy. The God of all joy (cf. 1Ch 12:40; Ne 8:10; Pss 16:11; 33:1; 43:4; Gal 5:22) activated their inner joy which brought corporate celebration. Though these may have been few and far between, moments like this characterized the life of obedience and blessing which God had set before Israel.

12:44–47 A listing of miscellaneous temple activities is given.

12:44 required by the law. Cf. Lv 7:34–36; Dt 18:1–5.

12:45 the command of David … Solomon. Cf. 1Ch 25, 26.

12:47 the sons of Aaron. The priests.

13:1–31 Nehemiah left Jerusalem in the 32nd year of Artaxerxes ca. 433 B.C. (cf. 5:14; 13:6) and returned to Persia as he promised (cf. 2:6). During his absence, the people returned to their former ways, led by the High Priest Eliashib (vv. 4, 5). Such a defection called for the needed reforms of vv. 1–3, 10–30. It was during Nehemiah's absence that Malachi also wrote his prophetic book indicting both priests and people for their sinful defection. Possibly having heard of Eliashib's evil, Nehemiah returned (vv. 4–7). Nehemiah 13 was the last portion of the OT to be written.

13:1, 2 On that day they read aloud from the book of Moses. Not surprisingly, as they read on the regular calendar cycle, they were confronted with areas in which their thinking and practice had wavered from the Scriptures, specifically with regard to the requirements of Dt 23:3–6.

13:2 Balaam. See Nu 22–24.

13:3 This was done in compliance with their recent pledge (cf. 10:26–29) before Nehemiah left for Persia.

13:4 Tobiah. *See note on 2:10.* Eliashib had allied with Israel's enemy for some personal gain and taken it to such an extreme as to desecrate the house of God.

13:6 I had gone to the king. Nehemiah returned to Persia as he promised (cf. 2:6) ca. 433 B.C., in the 32nd year of Artaxerxes (cf. 5:14). It is unknown exactly how long Nehemiah remained in Persia, perhaps until ca. 424 B.C., but in that interval the disobedience developed.

13:7–9 Nehemiah's response to the desecration of the temple was similar to Christ's almost 5 centuries later (cf. Mt 21:12, 13; Jn 2:13–17).

13:9 utensils of the house of God. In order to accommodate Tobiah, they had moved the utensils of the house of God from their rightful place and put idols in the temple courts.

TITHES RESTORED

10 I also [a]discovered that [A]the portions of the Levites had not been given *them,* so that the Levites
and the singers who performed the service had
[b]gone away, [B]each to his own field. 11 So I [a,A]repri-
manded the officials and said, "[B]Why is the house
of God forsaken?" Then I gathered them together
and restored them to their posts. 12 All Judah then
brought [A]the tithe of the grain, wine and oil into
the storehouses. 13 In charge of the storehouses I
appointed Shelemiah the priest, Zadok the scribe,
and Pedaiah of the Levites, and in addition to them
was Hanan the son of Zaccur, the son of Mattaniah;
for [A]they were considered reliable, and it was [a]their
task to distribute to their [b]kinsmen. 14 [A]Remember
me for this, O my God, and do not blot out my loyal
deeds which I have performed for the house of my
God and its services.

SABBATH RESTORED

15 In those days I saw in Judah some who were
treading wine presses [A]on the sabbath, and bringing
in sacks of grain and loading *them* on donkeys, as
well as wine, grapes, figs and all kinds of loads, [B]and
they brought *them* into Jerusalem on the sabbath
day. So [C]I admonished *them* on the day they sold
food. 16 Also men of Tyre were living [a]there *who*
imported fish and all kinds of merchandise, and
sold *them* to the sons of Judah on the sabbath, even
in Jerusalem. 17 Then [A]I [a]reprimanded the nobles of
Judah and said to them, "What is this evil thing you
are doing, [b]by profaning the sabbath day? 18 [A]Did not
your fathers do the same, so that our God brought on
us and on this city all this trouble? Yet you are adding to the wrath on Israel by profaning the sabbath."
19 [A]It came about that just as it grew dark at the
gates of Jerusalem before the sabbath, I commanded
that the doors should be shut [a]and that they should
not open them until after the sabbath. Then I stationed some of my servants at the gates *so that* no
load would enter on the sabbath day. 20 Once or
twice the traders and merchants of every kind of
merchandise spent the night outside Jerusalem.
21 Then [A]I [a]warned them and said to them, "Why do
you spend the night in front of the wall? If you do
so again, I will [b]use force against you." From that
time on they did not come on the sabbath. 22 And
I commanded the Levites that [A]they should purify
themselves and come as gatekeepers to sanctify
the sabbath day. *For* this also [B]remember me, O my
God, and have compassion on me according to the
greatness of Your lovingkindness.

MIXED MARRIAGES FORBIDDEN

23 In those days I also saw that the Jews had
[a,A]married women from [B]Ashdod, [C]Ammon *and*
Moab. 24 As for their children, half spoke in the language of Ashdod, and none of them was able to
speak the language of Judah, but [a]the language of
his own people. 25 So [A]I contended with them and
cursed them and [B]struck some of them and pulled
out their hair, and [C]made them swear by God, "You
shall not give your daughters to their sons, nor take
of their daughters for your sons or for yourselves.
26 [A]Did not Solomon king of Israel sin regarding
these things? [B]Yet among the many nations there
was no king like him, and [C]he was loved by his God,
and God made him king over all Israel; nevertheless
the foreign women caused even him to sin. 27 [a]Do
we then hear about you that you have committed
all this great evil [A]by acting unfaithfully against
our God by [b]marrying foreign women?" 28 Even one
of the sons of Joiada, the son of Eliashib the high
priest, was a son-in-law of [A]Sanballat the Horonite,
so I drove him away from me. 29 [A]Remember them,
O my God, [a]because they have defiled the priesthood
and the [B]covenant of the priesthood and the Levites.
30 [A]Thus I purified them from everything foreign
and appointed duties for the priests and the Levites,
each in his task, 31 and *I arranged* [A]for the supply
of wood at appointed times and for the first fruits.
[B]Remember me, O my God, for good.

13:10 [a]Or *knew* [b]Lit *fled* [A]Deut 12:19; Neh 10:37 [B]Neh 12:28, 29 13:11 [a]Or *contended with* [A]Neh 13:17, 25 [B]Neh 10:39 13:12 [A]Neh 10:37; 12:44; Mal 3:10 13:13 [a]Lit *on them to* [b]Lit *brothers* [A]Neh 7:2 13:14 [A]Neh 5:19; 13:22, 31 13:15 [A]Ex 20:8; 34:21; Deut 5:12-14; Jer 17:22 [B]Neh 10:31; Jer 17:21 [C]Neh 9:29; 13:21 13:16 [a]Lit *in it* 13:17 [a]Or *contended with* [b]Lit *and* [A]Neh 13:11, 25 13:18 [A]Ezra 9:13; Jer 17:21 13:19 [a]Lit *and commanded* [A]Lev 23:32 13:21 [a]Lit *witnessed against* [b]Lit *send a hand against* [A]Neh 13:15 13:22 [A]1 Chr 15:12; Neh 12:30 [B]Neh 13:14, 31 13:23 [a]Lit *given dwelling to* [A]Ex 34:11-16; Deut 7:1-5; Ezra 9:2; Neh 10:30 [B]Neh 4:7 [C]Ezra 9:1; Neh 13:1 13:24 [a]Lit *according to the tongue of people and people* 13:25 [A]Neh 13:11, 17 [B]Deut 25:2 [C]Neh 10:29, 30 13:26 [A]1 Kin 11:1 [B]1 Kin 3:13; 2 Chr 1:12 [C]2 Sam 12:24, 25 13:27 [a]Or *Is it reported* [b]Lit *giving dwelling to* [A]Ezra 10:2; Neh 13:23 13:28 [A]Neh 2:10, 19; 4:1 13:29 [a]Lit *for the defilings of* [A]Neh 6:14 [B]Num 25:13 13:30 [A]Neh 10:30 13:31 [A]Neh 10:34 [B]Neh 13:14, 22

13:10–13 In Nehemiah's absence, the Jews violated their previous covenant with God regarding offerings (cf. 10:35–39) as reported by Mal 1:6–14 and 3:8–12. In his presence, it was immediately restored (*see notes on 9:38–10:39*).

13:10 gone away, each to his own field. By neglecting the tithe, the people failed to support the Levites. Consequently, they had to abandon their responsibilities in the house of God and perform field labor in order to survive.

13:14 Remember me. This refrain is used 3 times here, once after each rebuke (cf. 13:22, 31).

13:15–17 They went against their previous agreement by violating the Sabbath (cf. 10:31).

13:16 Tyre. A Phoenician coastal town 20 mi. S of Sidon.

13:18 Jeremiah had rebuked their fathers for the same things (see Jer 17:21ff.). By such acts their fathers had brought the misery of exile and oppression, and they were doing the same—increasing God's wrath against them.

13:19–22 Nehemiah had to force compliance with threats.

13:23–29 Both the priests and the people had married pagans of the land in violation of the Mosaic law (cf. Ex 34:15, 16; Dt 7:3), the earlier reforms of Ezra (cf. Ezr 9, 10), and their own covenant (cf. 10:30). Malachi spoke against this sin (Mal 2:10–16).

13:23 Ashdod. *See note on 4:7.* **Ammon** ***and*** **Moab.** Neighboring countries E of the Jordan whose beginnings were by Lot's incestuous relationship with his two daughters (cf. Ge 19:30–38).

13:28 Even the grandson of the High Priest (cf. 12:10) sinfully married a daughter of Sanballat (*see note on 2:10*).

13:29, 30 Malachi 2:1–8 recognizes the uncleanness within the priesthood.

13:31 Remember me. Nehemiah prayed this for the third time (cf. 13:14, 22), desiring God's blessing on his obedient efforts.

THE
BOOK OF

ESTHER

TITLE

"Esther" serves as the title without variation through the ages. This book and the book of Ruth are the only OT books named after women. Like Song of Solomon, Obadiah, and Nahum, the NT does not quote or allude to Esther.

"Hadassah" (2:7), meaning "myrtle," was the Heb. name of Esther, which came either from the Persian word "star" or possibly from the name of the Babylonian love goddess, Ishtar. As the orphaned daughter of her father Abihail, Esther grew up in Persia with her older cousin, Mordecai, who raised her as if she were his own daughter (2:7, 15).

AUTHOR AND DATE

The author remains unknown, although Mordecai, Ezra, and Nehemiah have been suggested. Whoever penned Esther possessed a detailed knowledge of Persian customs, etiquette, and history, plus particular familiarity with the palace at Shushan (1:5–7). He also exhibited intimate knowledge of the Hebrew calendar and customs, while additionally showing a strong sense of Jewish nationalism. Possibly a Persian Jew, who later moved back to Israel, wrote Esther.

Esther appears as the 17th book in the literary chronology of the OT and closes the OT historical section. Only Ezr 7–10, Nehemiah, and Malachi report later OT history than Esther. The account in Esther ends in 473 B.C. before Ahasuerus died by assassination (ca. 465 B.C.). Esther 10:2 speaks as though Ahasuerus' reign has been completed, so the earliest possible writing date would be after his reign around mid-fifth century B.C. The latest reasonable date would be prior to 331 B.C. when Greece conquered Persia.

BACKGROUND AND SETTING

Esther occurred during the Persian period of world history, ca. 539 B.C. (Da 5:30, 31) to ca. 331 B.C. (Da 8:1–27). Ahasuerus ruled from ca. 486 to 465 B.C.; Esther covers the 483–473 B.C. portion of his reign. The name Ahasuerus represents the Heb. transliteration of the Persian name "Khshayarsha," while "Xerxes" represents his Gr. name.

The events of Esther occurred during the wider time span between the first return of the Jews after the 70-year captivity in Babylon (Da 9:1–19) under Zerubbabel ca. 538 B.C. (Ezr 1–6) and the second return led by Ezra ca. 458 B.C. (Ezr 7–10). Nehemiah's journey (the third return) from Susa to Jerusalem (Ne 1–2) occurred later (ca. 445 B.C.).

Esther and Exodus both chronicle how vigorously foreign powers tried to eliminate the Jewish race and how God sovereignly preserved His people in accordance with His covenant promise to Abraham ca. 2100–2075 B.C. (Ge 12:1–3; 17:1–8). As a result of God's prevailing, Est 9, 10 records the beginning of Purim—a new annual festival in the 12th month (Feb.-Mar.) to celebrate the nation's survival. Purim became one of two festivals given outside of the Mosaic legislation to still be celebrated in Israel (Hanukkah, or the Festival of Lights, is the other, cf. Jn 10:22).

HISTORICAL AND THEOLOGICAL THEMES

All 167 verses of Esther have ultimately been accepted as canonical, although the absence of God's name anywhere has caused some to unnecessarily doubt its authenticity. The Greek Septuagint (LXX) added an extra 107 apocryphal verses which supposedly compensated for this lack. Along with Song of Solomon, Ruth, Ecclesiastes, and Lamentations, Esther stands with the OT books of the Megilloth, or "5 scrolls." Rabbis read these books in the synagogue on 5 special occasions during the year—Esther being read at Purim (cf. 9:20–32).

The historical genesis for the drama played out between Mordecai (a Benjamite descendant of Saul—2:5) and Haman (an Agagite—3:1, 10; 8:3, 5; 9:24) goes back almost 1,000 years when the Jews exited from Egypt (ca. 1445 B.C.) and were attacked by the Amalekites (Ex 17:8–16), whose lineage began with Amalek, grandson of Esau (Ge 36:12). God pronounced His curse on the Amalekites, which resulted in their total elimination as a people (Ex 17:14; Dt 25:17–19). Although Saul (ca. 1030 B.C.) received orders to kill all the Amalekites, including their king Agag (1Sa 15:2, 3), he disobeyed (1Sa 15:7–9) and incurred God's displeasure (1Sa 15:11,

26; 28:18). Samuel finally hacked Agag into pieces (1Sa 15:32, 33). Because of his lineage from Agag, Haman carried deep hostility toward the Jews.

The time of Esther arrived 550 years after the death of Agag, but in spite of such passage of time, neither Haman the Agagite nor Mordecai the Benjamite had forgotten the tribal feud that still smoldered in their souls. This explains why Mordecai refused to bow down to Haman (3:2, 3) and why Haman so viciously attempted to exterminate the Jewish race (3:5, 6, 13). As expected, God's prophecy to extinguish the Amalekites (Ex 17:14; Dt 25:17–19) and God's promise to preserve the Jews (Ge 17:1–8) prevailed.

Because of God's faithfulness to save His people, the festival of Purim (named after the Akkadian word for "lot"—3:7; 9:26), an annual, two-day holiday of feasting, rejoicing, sending food to one another, and giving gifts to the poor (9:21, 22), was decreed to be celebrated in every generation, by every family, in every province and city (9:27, 28). Esther later added a new feature of fasting with lamentation (9:31). Purim is not biblically mentioned again, although it has been celebrated throughout the centuries in Israel.

Esther could be compared to a chess game. God and Satan (as invisible players) moved real kings, queens, and nobles. When Satan put Haman into place, it was as if he announced "Check." God then positioned Esther and Mordecai in order to put Satan into "Checkmate!" Ever since the fall of man (Ge 3:1–19), Satan has attempted to spiritually sever God's relationship with His human creation and disrupt God's covenant promises with Israel. For example, Christ's line through the tribe of Judah had been murderously reduced to Joash alone, who was rescued and preserved (2Ch 22:10–12). Later, Herod slaughtered the infants of Bethlehem, thinking Christ was among them (Mt 2:16). Satan tempted Christ to denounce God and worship him (Mt 4:9). Peter, at Satan's insistence, tried to block Christ's journey to Calvary (Mt 16:22). Finally, Satan entered into Judas who then betrayed Christ to the Jews and Romans (Lk 22:3–6). While God was not mentioned in Esther, He was everywhere apparent as the One who opposed and foiled Satan's diabolical schemes by providential intervention.

In Esther, all of God's unconditional covenant promises to Abraham (Ge 17:1–8) and to David (2Sa 7:8–16) were jeopardized. However, God's love for Israel is nowhere more apparent than in this dramatic rescue of His people from pending elimination. "Behold, He who keeps Israel will neither slumber nor sleep" (Ps 121:4).

INTERPRETIVE CHALLENGES

The most obvious question raised by Esther comes from the fact that God is nowhere mentioned, as in Song of Solomon. Nor does the writer or any participant refer to the law of God, the Levitical sacrifices, worship, or prayer. The skeptic might ask, "Why would God never be mentioned when the Persian king receives over 175 references? Since God's sovereignty prevailed to save the Jews, why does He then not receive appropriate recognition?"

It seems satisfying to respond that if God desired to be mentioned, He could just as sovereignly have moved the author to write of Him as He acted to save Israel. This situation seems to be more of a problem at the human level than the divine, because Esther is the classic illustration of God's providence as He, the unseen power, controls everything for His purpose. There are no miracles in Esther, but the preservation of Israel through providential control of every event and person reveals the omniscience and omnipotence of Jehovah. Whether He is named is not the issue. He is clearly the main character in the drama.

Second, "Why were Mordecai and Esther so secular in their lifestyles?" Esther (2:6–20) does not seem to have the zeal for holiness like Daniel (Da 1:8–20). Mordecai kept his and Esther's Jewish heritage secret, unlike Daniel (Da 6:5). The law of God was absent in contrast to Ezra (Ezr 7:10). Nehemiah had a heart for Jerusalem that seemingly eluded the affections of Esther and Mordecai (Ne 1:1–2:5).

The following observations help to shed some light on these issues. First, this short book does not record everything. Perhaps Mordecai and Esther actually possessed a deeper faith than becomes apparent here (cf. 4:16). Second, even godly Nehemiah did not mention his God when talking to King Artaxerxes (Ne 2:1–8). Third, the Jewish festivals which provided structure for worship had been lost long before Esther, e.g., Passover (2Ki 23:22) and Booths (Ne 8:17). Fourth, possibly the anti-Jewish letter written by the Samaritans to Ahasuerus several years earlier had frightened them (ca. 486 B.C.; Ezr 4:6). Fifth, the evil intentions of Haman did not just first surface when Mordecai refused to bow down (3:1, 2). Most likely they were long before shared by others which would have intimidated the Jewish population. Sixth, Esther did identify with her Jewish heritage at a most appropriate time (7:3, 4). And yet, the nagging question of why Esther and Mordecai did not seem to have the same kind of open devotion to God as did Daniel remains. Further, Nehemiah's prayer (Ne 1:5–11, esp. v. 7) seems to indicate a spiritual lethargy among the Jewish exiles in Susa. So this issue must ultimately be resolved by God since He alone knows human hearts.

OUTLINE

I. Esther Replaces Vashti (1:1–2:18)
- A. Vashti's Insubordination (1:1–22)
- B. Esther's Coronation (2:1–18)

II. Mordecai Overcomes Haman (2:19–7:10)
- A. Mordecai's Loyalty (2:19–23)
- B. Haman's Promotion and Decree (3:1–15)
- C. Esther's Intervention (4:1–5:14)

- D. Mordecai's Recognition (6:1–13)
- E. Haman's Fall (6:14–7:10)

III. Israel Survives Haman's Genocide Attempt (8:1–10:3)

- A. Esther and Mordecai's Advocacy (8:1–17)
- B. The Jews' Victory (9:1–19)
- C. Purim's Beginning (9:20–32)
- D. Mordecai's Fame (10:1–3)

THE BANQUETS OF THE KING

1 Now it took place in the days of [A]Ahasuerus, the
Ahasuerus who reigned [B]from India to [a]Ethiopia
over [C]127 provinces, 2 in those days as King Ahasuerus
[A]sat on his royal throne which *was* at the citadel in
[B]Susa, 3 in the third year of his reign [A]he gave a banquet for all his princes and attendants, the army *officers* of Persia and Media, the nobles and the princes
of his provinces being in his presence. 4 [a]And he displayed the riches of his royal glory and the splendor
of his great majesty for many days, 180 days.
5 When these days were completed, the king gave
a banquet lasting seven days for all the people who
were present at the citadel in Susa, from the greatest
to the least, in the court of [A]the garden of the king's
palace. 6 *There were hangings of* fine white and violet linen held by cords of fine purple linen on silver
rings and marble columns, *and* [A]couches of gold and
silver on a mosaic pavement of porphyry, marble,
mother-of-pearl and precious stones. 7 Drinks were
served in golden vessels of various kinds, and the
royal wine was plentiful [A]according to the king's
[a]bounty. 8 The drinking was *done* according to the
law, there was no compulsion, for so the king had
given orders to each official of his household that he
should do according to the desires of each person.
9 Queen Vashti also gave a banquet for the women
in the [a]palace which belonged to King Ahasuerus.

QUEEN VASHTI'S REFUSAL

10 On the seventh day, when the heart of the king
was [A]merry with wine, he commanded Mehuman,
Biztha, Harbona, Bigtha, Abagtha, Zethar and Carkas,
the seven eunuchs who served in the presence of King
Ahasuerus, 11 to bring Queen Vashti before the king
with *her* royal [A]crown in order to display her beauty
to the people and the princes, for she was beautiful.
12 But Queen Vashti refused to come at the king's
command delivered by the eunuchs. Then the king
became very angry and his wrath burned within him.
13 Then the king said to [A]the wise men [B]who understood the times—for it was the custom of the
king so *to speak* before all who knew law and justice 14 and were close to him: Carshena, Shethar,
Admatha, Tarshish, Meres, Marsena and Memucan,
the seven princes of Persia and Media [A]who [a]had
access to the king's presence and sat in the first
place in the kingdom— 15 "According to law, what
is to be done with Queen Vashti, because she did
not [a]obey the command of King Ahasuerus *delivered* by the eunuchs?" 16 In the presence of the king
and the princes, Memucan said, "Queen Vashti has
wronged not only the king but *also* all the princes
and all the peoples who are in all the provinces
of King Ahasuerus. 17 For the queen's conduct will
[a]become known to all the women causing them [b]to
look with contempt on their husbands by saying,
'King Ahasuerus commanded Queen Vashti to be
brought in to his presence, but she did not come.'
18 This day the ladies of Persia and Media who have
heard of the queen's conduct will speak in *the same
way* to all the king's princes, and there will be plenty
of contempt and anger. 19 If it pleases the king, let
a royal [a]edict be issued by him and let it be written
in the laws of Persia and Media so [A]that it cannot
[b]be repealed, that Vashti may no longer come into
the presence of King Ahasuerus, and let the king
give her royal position to [c]another who is more
worthy than she. 20 When the king's edict which
he will make is heard throughout all his kingdom,

1:1 [a]Lit *Cush* [A]Ezra 4:6; Dan 9:1 [B]Esth 8:9 [C]Esth 9:30 1:2 [A]1 Kin 1:46 [B]Neh 1:1; Dan 8:2 1:3 [A]Esth 2:18 1:4 [a]Lit *When* 1:5 [A]Esth 7:7, 8 1:6 [A]Ezek 23:41; Amos 6:4 1:7 [a]Lit *hand* [A]Esth 2:18 1:9 [a]Lit *royal house* 1:10 [A]Judg 16:25 1:11 [A]Esth 2:17; 6:8 1:13 [A]Jer 10:7; Dan 2:2 [B]1 Chr 12:32 1:14 [a]Lit *saw the face of the king* [A]2 Kin 25:19; Matt 18:10 1:15 [a]Lit *do* 1:17 [a]Lit *go forth* [b]Lit *to despise...in their eyes* 1:19 [a]Lit *word go forth from* [b]Lit *pass away* [c]Lit *her neighbor* [A]Esth 8:8; Dan 6:8

1:1 Ahasuerus. See Introduction: Background and Setting. **reigned ... over 127 provinces.** The kingdom comprised 20 regions (3:12; 8:9; 9:3) which were further divided into provinces ruled over by governors (3:12). **India to Ethiopia.** Ethiopia, not Asia Minor, is mentioned as representing the western edge of the kingdom to avoid any remembrance of the king's previous defeat by the Greeks ca. 481–479 B.C. (cf. 8:9). This description also avoided any confusion with the Ahasuerus of Da 9:1.

1:2 the citadel in Susa. Susa, the winter residence, was one of 4 capital cities; the other 3 included Babylon, Ecbatana (Ezr 6:2), and Persepolis. The citadel refers to the fortified palace complex built above the city for protection.

1:3 the third year. Ca. 483 B.C. This probably included the planning phase for Ahasuerus' later campaign against Greece in which the king suffered a humiliating defeat (ca. 481–479 B.C.). **Persia and Media.** Cyrus the Persian inherited Media and thus the name Media became just as prominent as Persia (ca. 550 B.C.).

1:9 Queen Vashti. Greek literature records her name as Amestris. She gave birth (ca. 483 B.C.) to Ahasuerus' third son, Artaxerxes, who later succeeded his father Ahasuerus on the throne (Ezr 7:1).

1:12 Vashti refused. Her reason is not recorded, although suggestions have included that 1) her appearance would have involved lewd behavior before drunken men, or 2) that she was still pregnant with Artaxerxes.

1:14 the seven princes. These highest ranking officials (cf. Ezr 7:14) were perhaps equivalent to the magi of Da 1:20.

1:19 cannot be repealed. The irrevocable nature of Persian law (cf. Da 6:8, 12, 15) played an important role in how the rest of Esther concluded (cf. 8:8).

THE HISTORICAL CHRONOLOGY FOR ESTHER

The events described in Esther took place during the reign of Ahasuerus (Xerxes I, 486–465 B.C.). This chart places Esther within that broader context.

Date	Events	Reference
486	Ahasuerus succeeds Darius I	
483–480	Vashti dethroned; Esther chosen to be queen; Ahasuerus begins campaign against the Greeks	1:3—2:17
479–475	Failure of the campaign against the Greeks; Haman's growing hatred of Mordecai	2:18—3:6
474–473	Haman's decree, Esther's plan; deliverance of the people; The Feast of Purim; Mordecai's advancement	3:7—10:3

[a]great as it is, then [A]all women will give honor to
their husbands, great and small."
21 *This* word pleased the king and the princes, and
the king did [a]as Memucan proposed. 22 So he sent
letters to all the king's provinces, [A]to each province
according to its script and to every people according
to their language, that every man should [B]be the
master in his own house and the one who speaks
in the language of his own people.

VASHTI'S SUCCESSOR SOUGHT

2 After these things [A]when the anger of King Ahasuerus had subsided, he remembered Vashti
and what she had done and [B]what had been decreed against her. 2 Then the king's attendants, who
served him, said, "[A]Let beautiful young virgins be
sought for the king. 3 Let the king appoint overseers
in [A]all the provinces of his kingdom that they may
gather every beautiful young virgin to the citadel
of Susa, to the harem, into the custody of [B]Hegai,
the king's eunuch, who is in charge of the women;
and [C]let their cosmetics be given *them.* 4 Then let
the young lady who pleases the king be queen in
place of Vashti." And the matter pleased the king,
and he did accordingly.
5 *Now* there was at the citadel in Susa a Jew whose
name was [A]Mordecai, the son of Jair, the son of Shimei,
the son of Kish, a Benjamite, 6 [A]who had been taken
into exile from Jerusalem with the captives who had
been exiled with Jeconiah king of Judah, whom Nebuchadnezzar the king of Babylon had exiled. 7 He was
bringing up Hadassah, that is [A]Esther, his uncle's
daughter, for she had no father or mother. Now the
young lady was beautiful of form and [a]face, and when

1:20 [a]Lit *for great is it* [A]Eph 5:22; Col 3:18 1:21 [a]Lit *according to the word of* 1:22 [A]Esth 3:12; 8:9 [B]Eph 5:22-24 2:1 [A]Esth 7:10 [B]Esth 1:19, 20 2:2 [A]1 Kin 1:2 2:3 [A]Esth 1:1, 2 [B]Esth 2:8, 15 [C]Esth 2:9, 12 2:5 [A]Esth 3:2 2:6 [A]2 Kin 24:14, 15; 2 Chr 36:10 2:7 [a]Lit *good of appearance* [A]Esth 2:15

1:22 letters. The efficient Persian communication network (a rapid relay by horses) played an important role in speedily publishing kingdom edicts (cf. 3:12–14; 8:9, 10, 14; 9:20, 30).

2:1 After these things. Most likely during the latter portion of the king's ill-fated war with Greece (ca. 481–479 B.C.). **he remembered Vashti.** The king was legally unable to restore Vashti (cf. 1:19–22), so the counselors proposed a new plan with promise.

2:5 Mordecai. See Introduction: Historical and Theological Themes. He was among the fourth generation of deported Jews. **Kish.** Mordecai's great grandfather who actually experienced the Babylonian deportation. After Babylon fell to Medo-Persia (ca. 539 B.C.), Jews were moved to other parts of the new kingdom. Kish represents a Benjamite family name that could be traced back (ca. 1100 B.C.) to Saul's father (1Sa 9:1).

2:6 Jeconiah. Former king of Judah (also known as Jehoiachin and Coniah) who was deported ca. 597 B.C. (cf. 2Ki 24:14, 15; 2Ch 36:9, 10). Due to his disobedience, the Lord removed his descendants from the line of David to Christ (Jer 22:24–30). The family of Mordecai and Esther were part of the good figs in Jer 24:1–7.

2:7 Esther. See Introduction: Title.

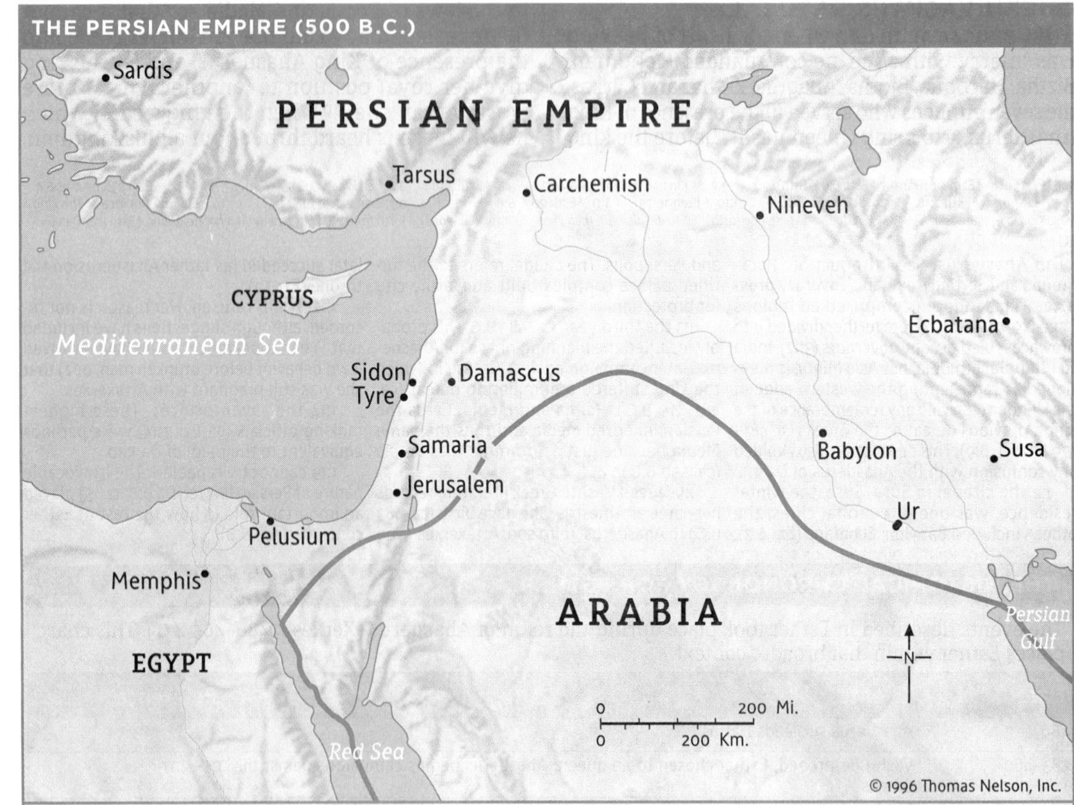

By Esther's time the Persian Empire stretched from India in the east through Asia Minor to Greece in the west, and included Egypt and some of coastal Africa to the south.

her father and her mother died, Mordecai took her
as his own daughter.

ESTHER FINDS FAVOR

8 So it came about when the command and decree of the king were heard and [A]many young ladies were gathered to the citadel of Susa into the
custody of [B]Hegai, that Esther was taken to the
king's [a]palace into the custody of Hegai, who was in
charge of the women. 9 Now the young lady pleased
him and found favor with him. So he quickly provided her with her [A]cosmetics and [a]food, gave her
seven choice maids from the king's palace and
transferred her and her maids to the best place
in the harem. 10 [A]Esther did not make known her
people or her kindred, for Mordecai had instructed
her that she should not make *them* known. 11 Every
day Mordecai walked back and forth in front of the
court of the harem to learn how Esther was and
how she fared.

12 Now when the turn of each young lady came to
go in to King Ahasuerus, after the end of her twelve
months under the regulations for the women—for
the days of their beautification were completed
as follows: six months with oil of myrrh and six
months with spices and the cosmetics for women—
13 the young lady would go in to the king in this
way: anything that she [a]desired was given her to
take with her from the harem to the king's palace.
14 In the evening she would go in and in the morning she would return to the second harem, to the
[a]custody of Shaashgaz, the king's eunuch who was
in charge of the concubines. She would not again
go in to the king unless the king delighted in her
and she was summoned by name.

15 Now when the turn of Esther, [A]the daughter of
Abihail the uncle of Mordecai who had taken her
as his daughter, came to go in to the king, she did
not request anything except what [B]Hegai, the king's
eunuch who was in charge of the women, [a]advised.
And Esther found favor in the eyes of all who saw
her. 16 So Esther was taken to King Ahasuerus to his
royal palace in the tenth month which is the month
Tebeth, in the seventh year of his reign.

ESTHER BECOMES QUEEN

17 The king loved Esther more than all the women,
and she found favor and kindness with him more
than all the virgins, so that [A]he set the royal crown
on her head and made her queen instead of Vashti.
18 Then [A]the king gave a great banquet, Esther's
banquet, for all his princes and his servants; he
also made a holiday for the provinces and gave
gifts [B]according to the king's bounty.

19 [A]When the virgins were gathered together the
second time, then Mordecai [B]was sitting at the king's
gate. 20 [A]Esther had not yet made known her kindred
or her people, even as Mordecai had commanded
her; for Esther did [a]what Mordecai told her as she
had done [B]when under his care.

MORDECAI SAVES THE KING

21 In those days, while Mordecai was sitting at the
king's gate, [A]Bigthan and Teresh, two of the king's
officials from those who guarded the door, became
angry and sought to [a]lay hands on King Ahasuerus.
22 But the [a]plot became known to Mordecai and [A]he
told Queen Esther, and Esther [b]informed the king in
Mordecai's name. 23 Now when the plot was investigated and found *to be so,* they were both hanged
on a [a]gallows; and it was written in [A]the Book of
the Chronicles in the king's presence.

HAMAN'S PLOT AGAINST THE JEWS

3 After these events King Ahasuerus [A]promoted
Haman, the son of Hammedatha [B]the Agagite,
and [A]advanced him and [a]established his authority
over all the princes who *were* with him. 2 All the
king's servants who were at the king's gate bowed
down [a]and paid homage to Haman; for so the king
had commanded concerning him. But [A]Mordecai
neither bowed down nor paid homage. 3 Then the
king's servants who were at [A]the king's gate said to
Mordecai, "[B]Why are you transgressing the king's
command?" 4 Now it was when they had spoken
daily to him and he would not listen to them, that
they told Haman to see whether Mordecai's reason
would stand; for he had told them that he was a
Jew. 5 When Haman saw that [A]Mordecai neither

2:8 [a]Lit *house* [A]Esth 2:3 [B]Esth 2:3, 15 2:9 [a]Lit *portions* [A]Esth 2:3, 12 2:10 [A]Esth 2:20 2:13 [a]Lit *said* 2:14 [a]Lit *hand* 2:15 [a]Lit *said* [A]Esth 2:7; 9:29 [B]Esth 2:3, 8 2:17 [A]Esth 1:11 2:18 [A]Esth 1:3 [B]Esth 1:7 2:19 [A]Esth 2:3, 4 [B]Esth 2:21; 3:2 2:20 [a]Lit *the word of Mordecai* [A]Esth 2:10 [B]Esth 2:7 2:21 [a]Lit *send a hand against* [A]Esth 6:2 2:22 [a]Lit *matter,* so also v 23 [b]Lit *told* [A]Esth 6:1, 2 2:23 [a]Lit *tree* [A]Esth 10:2 3:1 [a]Lit *set his seat* [A]Esth 5:11 [B]Esth 3:10; 8:3 3:2 [a]Lit *and prostrated themselves before* [A]Esth 2:19; 5:9 3:3 [A]Esth 2:19 [B]Esth 3:2 3:5 [A]Esth 5:9

2:8 Esther was taken. It is impossible to tell if Esther went voluntarily or against her will.

2:9 pleased him. That she pleased Hegai points to God's providential control.

2:10 not make *them* known. Possibly because of the hostile letter mentioned in Ezr 4:6 or the anti-Semitic sentiments of Haman and other like-minded people.

2:14 the second harem. The place of concubines.

2:15 found favor. According to the Lord's providential plan.

2:16 Tebeth. The tenth month corresponding to Dec./Jan. **the seventh year.** Ca. 479–478 B.C. Four years had elapsed since Vashti's fall from favor.

2:18 a holiday. Probably refers to a remission of taxes and/or release from military service.

2:19 the second time. Perhaps the king intended to add the second best to his concubine collection.

2:21 the king's gate. Indicates the strong possibility that Mordecai held a position of prominence (cf. 3:2; Da 2:49). **became angry.** Perhaps in revenge over the loss of Vashti.

2:23 hanged on a gallows. The Persian execution consisted of being impaled (cf. Ezr 6:11). It is likely that they were the inventors of crucifixion. **Book of the Chronicles.** The king would 5 years later (Ahasuerus' 12th year) read these Persian records as the turning point in Esther (6:1, 2).

3:1 After these events. Sometime between the seventh (2:16) and twelfth year (3:7) of the king's reign. **Haman ... the Agagite.** See Introduction: Historical and Theological Themes.

3:2 neither bowed down. There is a question as to whether Esther and Mordecai were inclined to obey the Mosaic law. This refusal may be more likely grounded in the family feud between the Benjamites and the Agagites (see Introduction: Historical and Theological Themes) than Mordecai's allegiance to the second commandment (Ex 20:4–6).

3:4 he was a Jew. It seems evident from Haman's fury and attempted genocide that there were strong anti-Semitic attitudes in Susa, which seems to explain Mordecai's reluctance to reveal his true ethnic background.

bowed down nor paid homage to him, Haman was
filled with rage. 6 But he [a]disdained to [b]lay hands
on Mordecai alone, for they had told him *who* the
people of Mordecai *were;* therefore Haman [A]sought
to destroy all the Jews, the people of Mordecai, who
were throughout the whole kingdom of Ahasuerus.
7 In the first month, which is the month Nisan, in
the twelfth year of King Ahasuerus, [a]Pur, that is the
lot, was [A]cast before Haman from day to day and
from month *to month,* [b]until the twelfth month,
that is [B]the month Adar. 8 Then Haman said to King
Ahasuerus, "There is a certain people scattered and
dispersed among the peoples in all the provinces
of your kingdom; [A]their laws are different from
those of all *other* people and they do not observe
the king's laws, so it is not in the king's interest to
let them remain. 9 If it is pleasing to the king, let it
be [a]decreed that they be destroyed, and I will pay
ten thousand talents of silver into the hands of those
who carry on the *king's* business, to put into the
king's treasuries." 10 Then [A]the king took his signet
ring from his hand and gave it to Haman, the son of
Hammedatha [B]the Agagite, [C]the enemy of the Jews.
11 The king said to Haman, "The silver is [a]yours, and
the people *also,* to do with them as you please."
12 [A]Then the king's scribes were summoned on the
thirteenth day of the first month, and it was written
just as Haman commanded to [B]the king's satraps, to
the governors who were over each province and to
the princes of each people, each province according
to its script, each people according to its language,
being written [C]in the name of King Ahasuerus and
sealed with the king's signet ring. 13 Letters were
sent by [A]couriers to all the king's provinces [B]to destroy, to kill and to annihilate all the Jews, both
young and old, women and children, [C]in one day,
the thirteenth *day* of the twelfth month, which is
the month Adar, and to [D]seize their possessions as
plunder. 14 [A]A copy of the edict to be [a]issued as law
in every province was published to all the peoples
so that they should be ready for this day. 15 The
couriers went out impelled by the king's command
while the decree was [a]issued at the citadel in Susa;
and while the king and Haman sat down to drink,
[A]the city of Susa was in confusion.

ESTHER LEARNS OF HAMAN'S PLOT

4 When Mordecai learned [A]all that had been done,
[a]he tore his clothes, put on sackcloth and ashes,
and went out into the midst of the city and wailed
loudly and bitterly. 2 He went as far as the king's gate,
for no one was to enter the king's gate clothed in sackcloth. 3 In each and every province where the command and decree of the king came, there was great
mourning among the Jews, with [A]fasting, weeping
and wailing; and many lay on sackcloth and ashes.
4 Then Esther's maidens and her eunuchs came
and told her, and the queen writhed in great anguish. And she sent garments to clothe Mordecai
that he might remove his sackcloth from him, but
he did not accept *them.* 5 Then Esther summoned
Hathach from the king's eunuchs, whom [a]the king
had appointed to attend her, and ordered him *to go*
to Mordecai to learn what this *was* and why it *was.*
6 So Hathach went out to Mordecai to the city square
in front of the king's gate. 7 Mordecai told him all
that had happened to him, and [A]the exact amount
of money that Haman had promised to pay to the
king's treasuries for the destruction of the Jews. 8 He
also gave him [A]a copy of the text of the edict which
had been issued in Susa for their destruction, that
he might show Esther and inform her, and to order
her to go in to the king to implore his favor and to
plead with him for her people.
9 Hathach came back and related Mordecai's
words to Esther. 10 Then Esther spoke to Hathach
and ordered him *to reply* to Mordecai: 11 "All the
king's servants and the people of the king's provinces know that for any man or woman who [A]comes
to the king to the inner court who is not summoned,
[B]he has but one law, that he be put to death, unless
the king holds out [C]to him the golden scepter so

3:6 [a]Lit *despised in his eyes* [b]Lit *send a hand against* [A]Ps 83:4 3:7 [a]Lit *he cast Pur…before* [b]Gr *and the lot fell on the thirteenth day of* [A]Esth 9:24-26 [B]Ezra 6:15 3:8 [A]Ezra 4:12-15; Acts 16:20, 21 3:9 [a]Lit *written* 3:10 [A]Gen 41:42; Esth 8:2 [B]Esth 3:1 [C]Esth 7:6 3:11 [a]Lit *given to you* 3:12 [A]Esth 8:9 [B]Ezra 8:36 [C]1 Kin 21:8; Esth 8:8, 10 3:13 [A]2 Chr 30:6; Esth 8:10, 14 [B]Esth 7:4 [C]Esth 8:12 [D]Esth 8:11; 9:10 3:14 [a]Lit *given* [A]Esth 8:13, 14 3:15 [a]Lit *given* [A]Esth 8:15 4:1 [a]Lit *Mordecai* [A]2 Sam 1:11; Esth 3:8-10; Jon 3:5, 6 4:3 [A]Esth 4:16 4:5 [a]Lit *he* 4:7 [A]Esth 3:9 4:8 [A]Esth 3:14 4:11 [A]Esth 5:1; 6:4 [B]Dan 2:9 [C]Esth 5:2; 8:4

3:6 the people of Mordecai. Haman was being satanically used to target the entire Jewish race in an unsuccessful attempt to change the course of redemptive history and God's plans for Israel.

3:7 Nisan. The time period Mar./Apr. Ironically, the Jews should have been celebrating the Passover to remind them of a former deliverance. **twelfth year.** Ca. 474 B.C. **Pur … lot.** A lot would be like modern dice which were cast to determine future decisions (cf. the Hebrew lot, 1Ch 26:14; Ne 10:34; Jon 1:7). Proverbs 16:33 states that God providentially controlled the outcome of the lot. **Adar.** Feb./Mar. There would have been an 11 month interval between Haman's decree and its expected fulfillment.

3:8 a certain people. Haman never divulged their identity.

3:9 ten thousand talents. The exact dollar amount is uncertain, but reportedly it would have weighed 375 tons and equaled almost 70 percent of the king's annual revenue. Since this sum would have been derived from the plunder of the Jews, it indicates that they had grown prosperous.

3:10, 11 The king would have easily been eager to eliminate any rebellion against his authority (cf. 3:8), although he did not seem to be interested in the money.

3:10 the enemy of the Jews. Cf. 7:6; 8:1; 9:10, 24.

3:12 sealed … king's signet ring. This would be equivalent to the king's signature. The date has been calculated by historians to be Apr. 7, 474 B.C.

3:13 to destroy. An ambitious plot to annihilate the Jews in just one day. Historians have calculated the date to be Mar. 7, 473 B.C. The king had unwittingly approved this provision which would kill his own queen.

3:14 as law. It would be irrevocable (cf. 1:19; 8:5–8).

3:15 in confusion. No specific reason is stated. Most likely even this pagan population was puzzled at the extreme and deadly racism of the king and Haman.

4:1 sackcloth and ashes. An outward sign of inward distress and humiliation (cf. Jer 6:26; Da 9:3; Mt 11:21). Mordecai realized that he had prompted this genocidal retaliation by Haman.

4:4 she sent garments. Mordecai could then enter the king's gate (cf. 4:2) and talk with Esther directly (cf. Ne 2:2).

4:5 Hathach. A trusted eunuch who knew of Esther's Jewish background.

4:7, 8 That Mordecai possessed this specific knowledge and a copy of the edict further evidences his prominent position in Persia.

4:11 golden scepter. In order to protect the king's life from would-be assassins, this practice prevailed. Seemingly, the king would extend the

that he may live. And I have not been summoned to come to the king for these thirty days." 12 They related Esther's words to Mordecai.

13 Then Mordecai told *them* to reply to Esther, "Do not imagine that you in the king's palace can escape any more than all the Jews. 14 For if you remain silent at this time, relief and [A]deliverance will arise for the Jews from another place and you and your father's house will perish. And who knows whether you have not attained royalty for such a time as this?"

ESTHER PLANS TO INTERCEDE

15 Then Esther told *them* to reply to Mordecai, 16 "Go, assemble all the Jews who are found in Susa, and fast for me; [A]do not eat or drink for [B]three days, night or day. I and my maidens also will fast in the same way. And thus I will go in to the king, which is not according to the law; and if I perish, I perish." 17 So Mordecai went away and did just as Esther had commanded him.

ESTHER PLANS A BANQUET

5 Now it came about [A]on the third day that Esther put on her royal robes and stood [B]in the inner court of the king's palace in front of the king's [a]rooms, and the king was sitting on his royal throne in the [b]throne room, opposite the entrance to the palace. 2 When the king saw Esther the queen standing in the court, [A]she obtained favor in his sight; and [B]the king extended to Esther the golden scepter which *was* in his hand. So Esther came near and touched the top of the scepter. 3 Then the king said to her, "What is *troubling* you, Queen Esther? And what is your request? [A]Even to half of the kingdom it shall be given to you." 4 Esther said, "If it pleases the king, may the king and Haman come this day to the banquet that I have prepared for him."

5 Then the king said, "[A]Bring Haman quickly that we may do [a]as Esther desires." So the king and Haman came to the banquet which Esther had prepared. 6 [a]As they drank their wine at the banquet, [A]the king said to Esther, "[B]What is your petition, for it shall be granted to you. And what is your request? Even to half of the kingdom it shall be done." 7 So Esther replied, "My petition and my request is: 8 [A]if I have found favor in the sight of the king, and if it pleases the king to grant my petition and do [a]what I request, may the king and Haman come to [B]the banquet which I will prepare for them, and tomorrow I will do [b]as the king says."

HAMAN'S PRIDE

9 Then Haman went out that day glad and pleased of heart; but when Haman saw Mordecai [A]in the king's gate and [B]that he did not stand up or [a]tremble before him, Haman was filled with anger against Mordecai. 10 Haman controlled himself, however, went to his house and [a]sent for his friends and his wife [A]Zeresh. 11 Then Haman recounted to them the glory of his riches, and the [a,A]number of his sons, and every *instance* where the king had magnified him and how he had [b,B]promoted him above the princes and servants of the king. 12 Haman also said, "Even Esther the queen let no one but me come with the king to the banquet which she had prepared; and [A]tomorrow also I am [a]invited by her with the king. 13 Yet all of this [a]does not satisfy me every time I see Mordecai the Jew sitting at [A]the king's gate." 14 Then Zeresh his wife and all his friends said to him, "[A]Have a [a]gallows fifty cubits high made and in the morning ask the king to have Mordecai hanged on it; then go joyfully with the king to the banquet." And the [b]advice pleased Haman, so he had the gallows made.

THE KING PLANS TO HONOR MORDECAI

6 During that night [a]the king [A]could not sleep so he gave an order to bring [B]the book of records, the chronicles, and they were read before the king. 2 It was found written what [A]Mordecai had reported concerning Bigthana and Teresh, two of the king's eunuchs who were doorkeepers, that they had sought to lay hands on King Ahasuerus. 3 The king said, "What honor or dignity has been bestowed on Mordecai for this?" Then the king's servants who attended him said, "Nothing has been done for him."

4:14 [A]Lev 26:42; 2 Kin 13:5 4:16 [A]Joel 1:14; 2:12 [B]Esth 5:1 5:1 [a]Lit *house* [b]Lit *royal house* [A]Esth 4:16 [B]Esth 4:11; 6:4 5:2 [A]Esth 2:9 [B]Esth 4:11; 8:4 5:3 [A]Esth 7:2; Mark 6:23 5:5 [a]Lit *the word of Esther* [A]Esth 6:14 5:6 [a]Lit *at the banquet of wine* [A]Esth 7:2 [B]Esth 5:3 5:8 [a]Lit *my request* [b]Lit *according to the word of the king* [A]Esth 7:3; 8:5 [B]Esth 6:14 5:9 [a]Or *move for* [A]Esth 2:19 [B]Esth 3:5 5:10 [a]Lit *sent and brought* [A]Esth 6:13 5:11 [a]Lit *multitude* [b]Lit *lifted* [A]Esth 9:7-10 [B]Esth 3:1 5:12 [a]Lit *summoned to her* [A]Esth 5:8 5:13 [a]Lit *is not suitable to me* [A]Esth 5:9 5:14 [a]Lit *tree* [b]Lit *thing* [A]Esth 6:4; 7:9, 10 6:1 [a]Lit *the king's sleep fled* [A]Dan 6:18 [B]Esth 2:23; 10:2 6:2 [A]Esth 2:21, 22

scepter (a sign of kingly authority) only to those whom he knew and from whom he welcomed a visit (cf. 5:2; 8:4). **these thirty days.** Perhaps Esther feared she had lost favor with the king since he had not summoned her recently.

4:14 relief and deliverance. Mordecai exhibited a healthy faith in God's sovereign power to preserve His people. He may have remembered the Lord's promise to Abraham (cf. Ge 12:3; 17:1–8). **you ... will perish.** Mordecai indicated that Esther would not escape the sentence or be overlooked because of her prominence (cf. 4:13). **such a time as this.** Mordecai indirectly appealed to God's providential timing.

4:16 fast. The text does not mention prayer being included such as was Daniel's practice (Da 9:3), though it surely was. **perish.** Esther's heroic willingness to die for the sake of her fellow Jews is commendable.

5:2 she obtained favor. This actually means that Esther first found favor with the God of Israel (cf. Pr 21:1).

5:3 what is your request? Esther deferred her real wish until 7:2, 3.

5:3, 6 Even to half of the kingdom. Royal hyperbole that was not intended to be taken at face value (cf. Mk 6:22, 23).

5:4 the banquet. The first of two (cf. 5:4–8; 6:14–7:1) that Esther prepared. God would providentially intervene between the two (6:1, 2).

5:11 the number of his sons. At least 10 sons were fathered by Haman (cf. 9:13), who personified sinful pride (cf. Pr 16:18; 1Co 10:12; Gal 6:3).

5:13 does not satisfy me. Haman expressed raging fixation on killing Mordecai.

5:14 gallows. A stake on which a human would be impaled to death and/or displayed after death (cf. 2:23). **fifty cubits.** Approximately 75 ft. or almost 8 stories high. Perhaps the gallows involved displaying a shorter stake atop a building or wall to attain this height.

6:1 the book. Five years (cf. 2:16 with 3:7) had intervened since Mordecai's loyal, but as yet unrewarded, act (cf. 2:23). At exactly the proper moment, God providentially intervened so that the king suffered insomnia, called for the book of records, read of Mordecai's unrewarded deeds 5 years past, and then desired to reward him (cf. Da 6:18).

4 So the king said, "Who is in the court?" Now Haman
had just [A]entered the outer court of the king's palace
in order to speak to the king about [B]hanging Mordecai on the gallows which he had prepared for him.
5 The king's servants said to him, "Behold, Haman is
standing in the court." And the king said, "Let him
come in." 6 So Haman came in and the king said to
him, "What is to be done for the man [A]whom the
king desires to honor?" And Haman said [a]to himself,
"Whom would the king desire to honor more than
me?" 7 Then Haman said to the king, "For the man
whom the king desires to honor, 8 let them bring a
royal robe which the king has worn, and [A]the horse
on which the king has ridden, and on whose head
[B]a royal crown has been placed; 9 and let the robe
and the horse be handed over to one of the king's
most noble princes and let them array the man
whom the king desires to honor and lead him on
horseback through the city square, [A]and proclaim
before him, 'Thus it shall be done to the man whom
the king desires to honor.' "

HAMAN MUST HONOR MORDECAI

10 Then the king said to Haman, "Take quickly
the robes and the horse as you have said, and do
so for Mordecai the Jew, who is sitting at the king's
gate; do not fall short in anything of all that you
have said." 11 So Haman took the robe and the horse,
and arrayed Mordecai, and led him *on horseback*
through the city square, and proclaimed before
him, "Thus it shall be done to the man whom the
king desires to honor."

12 Then Mordecai returned to the king's gate. But
Haman hurried home, mourning, [A]with *his* head
covered. 13 Haman recounted [A]to Zeresh his wife
and all his friends everything that had happened
to him. Then his wise men and Zeresh his wife said
to him, "If Mordecai, before whom you have begun
to fall, is [a]of Jewish origin, you will not overcome
him, but will surely fall before him."

14 While they were still talking with him, the king's
eunuchs arrived and hastily [A]brought Haman to the
banquet which Esther had prepared.

ESTHER'S PLEA

7 Now the king and Haman came to drink *wine*
with Esther the queen. 2 And the king said to
Esther on the second day also [a]as they drank their
wine at the banquet, "[A]What is your petition, Queen
Esther? It shall be granted you. And what is your request? [B]Even to half of the kingdom it shall be done."
3 Then Queen Esther replied, "[A]If I have found favor
in your sight, O king, and if it pleases the king, let
my life be given me as my petition, and my people
as my request; 4 for [A]we have been sold, I and my
people, to be destroyed, [B]to be killed and to be annihilated. Now if we had only been sold as slaves,
men and women, I would have remained silent,
for the [a]trouble would not be commensurate with
the [b]annoyance to the king." 5 Then King Ahasuerus
[a]asked Queen Esther, "Who is he, and where is he,
[b]who would presume to do thus?" 6 Esther said, "[A]A
foe and an enemy is this wicked Haman!" Then Haman became terrified before the king and queen.

HAMAN IS HANGED

7 The king arose [A]in his anger from [a]drinking
wine *and went* into [B]the palace garden; but Haman
stayed to beg for his life from Queen Esther, for he
saw that harm had been determined against him
by the king. 8 Now when the king returned from
the palace garden into the [a]place where they were
drinking wine, Haman was falling on [A]the couch
where Esther was. Then the king said, "Will he even
assault the queen with me in the house?" As the
word went out of the king's mouth, they covered
Haman's face. 9 Then Harbonah, one of the eunuchs
who *were* before the king said, "Behold indeed, [A]the
gallows standing at Haman's house fifty cubits high,
which Haman made for Mordecai [B]who spoke good

6:4 [A]Esth 4:11 [B]Esth 5:14 6:6 [a]Lit *in his heart* [A]Esth 6:7, 9, 11 6:8 [A]1 Kin 1:33 [B]Esth 1:11; 2:17 6:9 [A]Gen 41:43 6:12 [A]2 Sam 15:30 6:13 [a]Lit *from the seed of the Jews* [A]Esth 5:10 6:14 [A]Esth 5:8 7:2 [a]Lit *at the banquet of wine* [A]Esth 5:6; 9:12 [B]Esth 5:3 7:3 [A]Esth 5:8; 8:5 7:4 [a]Or *enemy could not compensate for the loss* [b]Or *damage* [A]Esth 3:9 [B]Esth 3:13 7:5 [a]Lit *said and said to* [b]Lit *whose heart has been filled* 7:6 [A]Esth 3:10 7:7 [a]Lit *the banquet of wine* [A]Esth 1:12 [B]Esth 1:5 7:8 [a]Lit *house of the banquet of wine* [A]Esth 1:6 7:9 [A]Esth 5:14 [B]Esth 2:22

6:4 Who is in the court? The drama intensified as Haman arrived at just the wrong time and for just the wrong reason.

6:6, 7 Haman ironically defined the honor to be given to Mordecai at Haman's expense. To his potential wealth from the Jewish plunder, he thought public acclaim would be added.

6:8 royal robe ... royal crown. An honor which involved being treated as though the recipient were the king himself (cf. 8:15). This is reminiscent of Joseph in Egypt (Ge 41:39–45). History affirms that horses were adorned with the royal crown.

6:9 the city square. Whereas Mordecai had been there the day before in sackcloth and ashes (4:1, 6), he arrived with royal honor.

6:10 Mordecai the Jew. Cf. 8:7; 9:29, 31; 10:3. Why the king did not remember Haman's edict against the Jews remains unknown.

6:12 mourning. Deservedly, Haman has inherited Mordecai's distress (cf. 4:1, 2). What a difference a day makes! His imagined honors had quickly turned to unimaginable humiliation. ***his* head covered.** An extreme sign of shame (cf. 2Sa 15:30; Jer 14:3, 4).

6:13 you have begun to fall. Neither divine prophecy (Ex 17:14) nor biblical history (1Sa 15:8, 9) stood in Haman's favor. Haman's entourage seemed to have some knowledge of this biblical history.

6:14 Haman to the banquet. Like a lamb led to slaughter, Haman was escorted off to his just due.

7:2 second day. The first-day reference point included the first banquet. This refers to the second banquet on the second day (cf. 5:8). **what is your request?** This was the third time that the king inquired (cf. 5:3, 6).

7:3 my people. This plea paralleled God's message through Moses to Pharaoh, "Let My people go," almost 1,000 years earlier (Ex 7:16).

7:4 sold. Refers back to Haman's bribe (cf. 3:9; 4:7). **destroyed ... killed ... annihilated.** Esther recounted the exact language of Haman's decree (cf. 3:13).

7:6 this wicked Haman. Similar to Nathan's famous accusation against King David, "You are the man" (2Sa 12:7). Haman's honor had quickly turned to humiliation, and then to horror.

7:8 assault the queen. Blinded by anger, Ahasuerus interpreted Haman's plea to be an act of violence against Esther rather than a plea for mercy.

7:9 Harbonah. Cf. 1:10. **Behold.** Because the place prepared by Haman for Mordecai's execution towered above the city, it became the obvious spot for Haman's death. **Mordecai who spoke good.** Haman heard the third capital offense charged against him. One, he manipulated the king in planning to kill the queen's people. Two, he was perceived to accost the queen. Three, he planned to execute a man whom the king had just greatly honored for extreme loyalty to the kingdom.

on behalf of the king!" And the king said, "Hang him on it." 10 [A]So they hanged Haman on the [a]gallows which he had prepared for Mordecai, [B]and the king's anger subsided.

MORDECAI PROMOTED

8 On that day King Ahasuerus gave the house of Haman, [A]the enemy of the Jews, to Queen Esther; and Mordecai came before the king, for Esther had disclosed [B]what he was to her. 2 [A]The king took off his signet ring which he had taken away from Haman, and gave it to Mordecai. And Esther set Mordecai over the house of Haman.

3 Then Esther spoke again to the king, fell at his feet, wept and implored him to avert the evil *scheme* of Haman the Agagite and his plot which he had devised against the Jews. 4 [A]The king extended the golden scepter to Esther. So Esther arose and stood before the king. 5 Then she said, "[A]If it pleases the king and if I have found favor before him and the matter *seems* proper to the king and I am pleasing in his sight, let it be written to revoke the [B]letters devised by Haman, the son of Hammedatha the Agagite, which he wrote to destroy the Jews who are in all the king's provinces. 6 For [A]how can I endure to see the calamity which will befall my people, and how can I endure to see the destruction of my kindred?" 7 So King Ahasuerus said to Queen Esther and to Mordecai the Jew, "Behold, [A]I have given the house of Haman to Esther, and him they have hanged on the gallows because he had stretched out his hands against the Jews.

THE KING'S DECREE AVENGES THE JEWS

8 Now you write to the Jews [a]as you see fit, in the king's name, and [A]seal *it* with the king's signet ring; for a decree which is written in the name of the king and sealed with the king's signet ring [B]may not be revoked."

9 [A]So the king's scribes were called at that time in the third month (that is, the month Sivan), on the twenty-third [a]day; and it was written according to all that Mordecai commanded to the Jews, the satraps, the governors and the princes of the provinces which *extended* [B]from India to [b]Ethiopia, 127 provinces, to [C]every province according to its script, and to every people according to their language as well as to the Jews according to their script and their language. 10 He wrote in the name of King Ahasuerus, and sealed it with the king's signet ring, and sent letters by couriers on [A]horses, riding on steeds sired by the royal stud. 11 [a]In them the king granted the Jews who were in each and every city *the right* [A]to assemble and to defend their lives, [B]to destroy, to kill and to annihilate the entire army of any people or province which might attack them, including children and women, and [C]to plunder their spoil, 12 on [A]one day in all the provinces of King Ahasuerus, the thirteenth *day* of the twelfth month (that is, the month Adar). 13 [A]A copy of the edict to be [a]issued as law in each and every province was published to all the peoples, so that the Jews would be ready for this day to avenge themselves on their enemies. 14 The couriers, hastened and impelled by the king's command, went out, riding on the royal steeds; and the decree was given out at the citadel in Susa.

15 Then Mordecai went out from the presence of the king [A]in royal robes of [a]blue and white, with a large crown of gold and [B]a garment of fine linen and purple; and [C]the city of Susa shouted and rejoiced. 16 For the Jews there was [A]light and gladness and joy and honor. 17 In each and every province and in each and every city, wherever the king's commandment and his decree arrived, there was gladness and joy for the Jews, a feast and a [a,A]holiday. And [B]many among the peoples of the land became Jews, for the dread of the Jews had fallen on them.

THE JEWS DESTROY THEIR ENEMIES

9 Now [A]in the twelfth month (that is, the month Adar), on [B]the thirteenth [a]day [C]when the king's command and edict [b]were about to be executed, on the day when the enemies of the Jews hoped to gain the mastery over them, it was turned to the contrary so that the Jews themselves gained the mastery over those who hated them. 2 [A]The Jews assembled in their cities throughout all the provinces of King Ahasuerus to lay hands on those who sought their harm; and no one could stand before them, [B]for the dread of them had fallen on all the peoples.

7:10 [a]Lit *tree* [A]Ps 7:16; 94:23 [B]Esth 7:7, 8 8:1 [A]Esth 7:6 [B]Esth 2:7, 15 8:2 [A]Esth 3:10 8:4 [A]Esth 4:11; 5:2 8:5 [A]Esth 5:8; 7:3 [B]Esth 3:13 8:6 [A]Esth 7:4; 9:1 8:7 [A]Esth 8:1 8:8 [a]Lit *according to the good in your eyes* [A]Esth 3:12; 8:10 [B]Esth 1:19 8:9 [a]Lit *in it* [b]Lit *Cush* [A]Esth 3:12 [B]Esth 1:1 [C]Esth 1:22; 3:12 8:10 [A]1 Kin 4:28 8:11 [a]Lit *Which* [A]Esth 9:2 [B]Esth 3:13 [C]Esth 9:10 8:12 [A]Esth 3:13; 9:1 8:13 [a]Lit *given* [A]Esth 3:14 8:15 [a]Or *violet* [A]Esth 5:11 [B]Gen 41:42 [C]Esth 3:15 8:16 [A]Ps 97:11; 112:4 8:17 [a]Lit *good day* [A]Esth 9:19 [B]Esth 9:27 9:1 [a]Lit *day in it* [b]Lit *drew near* [A]Esth 8:12 [B]Esth 9:17 [C]Esth 3:13 9:2 [A]Esth 8:11; 9:15-18 [B]Esth 8:17

7:10 they hanged Haman. The ultimate expression of justice (cf. Ps 9:15, 16).

8:1 the house of Haman. Property of a traitor by Persian custom returned to the king. In this case, he gave it to his queen, Esther, who put Mordecai over it (8:2). The outcome for Haman's wife Zeresh and his wise men is unknown (5:14; 6:12, 13). Haman's 10 sons later died (9:7–10).

8:5 to revoke. This proved to be impossible in light of the inflexible nature of the king's edicts (1:19). However, a counter-decree was possible (cf. 8:8, 11, 12).

8:9 Sivan. Refers to the period May/June. It had been two months and 10 days since Haman's decree (cf. 3:12); 8 months and 20 days remained until both decrees became simultaneously effective (cf. 3:13).

8:11 the king granted. Just as the king had permitted Haman, so he allowed the Jews to defend themselves and to plunder their spoil (cf. 9:10, 15, 16).

8:15 Mordecai went out. This second reward exceeded the first (cf. 6:6–9). Blue and white were the royal colors of the Persian Empire.

8:17 many ... peoples ... Jews. The population realized that the God of the Jews greatly exceeded anything that the pantheon of Persian deities could offer (cf. Ex 15:14–16; Ps 105:38; Ac 5:11), especially in contrast to their recent defeat by the Greeks.

9:1 twelfth month. During the period Feb.–Mar. Here is a powerful statement with regard to God's providential preservation of the Jewish race in harmony with God's unconditional promise to Abraham (Ge 17:1–8). This providential deliverance stands in contrast to God's miraculous deliverance of the Jews from Egypt; yet in both cases the same end had been accomplished by the supernatural power of God.

3 Even all the princes of the provinces, [A]the satraps,
the governors and those who were doing the king's
business [a]assisted the Jews, because the dread of
Mordecai had fallen on them. 4 Indeed, Mordecai
was great in the king's house, and his fame spread
throughout all the provinces; for the man Mordecai [A]became greater and greater. 5 Thus [A]the Jews
struck all their enemies with [a]the sword, killing
and destroying; and they did what they pleased to
those who hated them. 6 At the citadel in Susa the
Jews killed and destroyed five hundred men, 7 and
Parshandatha, Dalphon, Aspatha, 8 Poratha, Adalia,
Aridatha, 9 Parmashta, Arisai, Aridai and Vaizatha,
10 [A]the ten sons of Haman the son of Hammedatha,
the Jews' enemy; but [B]they did not lay their hands
on the plunder.

11 On that day the number of those who were
killed at the citadel in Susa [a]was reported to the
king. 12 The king said to Queen Esther, "The Jews
have killed and destroyed five hundred men and
the ten sons of Haman at the citadel in Susa. What
then have they done in the rest of the king's provinces! [A]Now what is your petition? It shall even be
granted you. And what is your further request? It
shall also be done." 13 Then said Esther, "If it pleases
the king, [A]let tomorrow also be granted to the Jews
who are in Susa to do according to the edict of
today; and let Haman's ten sons be hanged on the
gallows." 14 So the king commanded that it should
be done so; and an edict was issued in Susa, and
Haman's ten sons were hanged. 15 The Jews who
were in Susa assembled also on the fourteenth
day of the month Adar and killed [A]three hundred
men in Susa, but [B]they did not lay their hands on
the plunder.

16 Now [A]the rest of the Jews who *were* in the
king's provinces [B]assembled, to defend their lives
and [a]rid themselves of their enemies, and kill
75,000 of those who hated them; but they did not
lay their hands on the plunder. 17 *This was done* on
[A]the thirteenth day of the month Adar, and [B]on the
fourteenth [a]day they rested and made it a day of
feasting and rejoicing.

18 But the Jews who were in Susa [A]assembled
on the thirteenth and [B]the fourteenth [a]of the same
month, and they rested on the fifteenth [a]day and
made it a day of feasting and rejoicing. 19 Therefore
the Jews of the rural areas, who live in [A]the rural
towns, make the fourteenth day of the month Adar
a [a,B]holiday for rejoicing and feasting and [C]sending
portions *of food* to one another.

THE FEAST OF PURIM INSTITUTED

20 Then Mordecai recorded these events, and
he sent letters to all the Jews who were in all the
provinces of King Ahasuerus, both near and far,
21 obliging them to celebrate the fourteenth day of
the month Adar, and the fifteenth day [a]of the same
month, annually, 22 because on those days the Jews
[a]rid themselves of their enemies, and *it was a* month
which was [A]turned for them from sorrow into gladness and from mourning into a [b]holiday; that they
should make them days of feasting and rejoicing
and [B]sending portions *of food* to one another and
gifts to the poor.

23 Thus the Jews undertook what they had started
to do, and what Mordecai had written to them. 24 For
Haman the son of Hammedatha, the Agagite, the
adversary of all the Jews, had schemed against the
Jews to destroy them and [A]had cast Pur, that is the
lot, to disturb them and destroy them. 25 But [A]when
it came [a]to the king's attention, he commanded by
letter [B]that his wicked scheme which he had [b]de-
vised against the Jews, [C]should return on his own
head and that he and his sons should be hanged
on the [c]gallows. 26 Therefore they called these days
Purim after the name of Pur. [a]And [A]because of the
instructions in this letter, both what they had seen
in this regard and what had happened to them,
27 the Jews established and [a]made a custom for
themselves and for their [b]descendants and for [A]all
those who allied themselves with them, so that
[c]they would not fail [B]to celebrate these two days
according to their [d]regulation and according to their
appointed time annually. 28 So these days were to
be remembered and celebrated throughout every
generation, every family, every province and every
city; and these days of Purim were not to [a]fail from
among the Jews, or their memory [b]fade from their
[c]descendants.

29 Then Queen Esther, [A]daughter of Abihail,
with Mordecai the Jew, wrote with full authority

9:3 [a]Lit *lifted up* [A]Ezra 8:36 9:4 [A]2 Sam 3:1; 1 Chr 11:9 9:5 [a]Lit *the stroke of* [A]Esth 3:13 9:10 [A]Esth 5:11 [B]Esth 8:11 9:11 [a]Lit *came* 9:12 [A]Esth 5:6; 7:2 9:13 [A]Esth 8:11; 9:15 9:15 [A]Esth 9:12 [B]Esth 9:10 9:16 [a]Lit *have rest from* [A]Esth 9:2 [B]Lev 26:7, 8; Esth 8:11 9:17 [a]Lit *in it* [A]Esth 9:1 [B]Esth 9:21 9:18 [a]Lit *in it* [A]Esth 8:11; 9:2 [B]Esth 9:21 9:19 [a]Lit *rejoicing and feasting and a good day and sending* [A]Deut 3:5; Zech 2:4 [B]Esth 9:22 [C]Neh 8:10 9:21 [a]Lit *in it* 9:22 [a]Lit *had rest from* [b]Lit *good day* [A]Ps 30:11 [B]Neh 8:12 9:24 [A]Esth 3:7 9:25 [a]Lit *before the king, he* [b]Lit *schemed* [c]Lit *tree* [A]Esth 7:4-10 [B]Esth 3:6-15 [C]Ps 7:16 9:26 [a]Lit *Therefore because of all the words* [A]Esth 9:20 9:27 [a]Lit *received* [b]Lit *seed* [c]Lit *it should not pass away* [d]Lit *writing* [A]Esth 8:17 [B]Esth 9:20, 21 9:28 [a]Lit *pass away* [b]Lit *end* [c]Lit *seed* 9:29 [A]Esth 2:15

9:3 the dread of Mordecai. Pragmatically, the nation had a change of heart toward the Jews, knowing that the king, the queen, and Mordecai were the ranking royal officials of the land. To be pro-Jewish would put one in favor with the king and his court and put one on the side of God, the ultimate King (cf. Rev 19:16).

9:6, 7 Five hundred men died in Susa.

9:10 did not lay their hands. Unlike Saul, who did take the plunder (cf. 1Sa 15:3 with 15:9), the Jews focused only on the mission at hand, i.e., to preserve the Jewish race (cf. vv. 15, 16), even though the king's edict permitted this (8:11).

9:12 further request? Even this pagan king served the cause of utterly blotting out the Amalekites in accord with God's original decree (Ex 17:14) by allowing for a second day of killing in Susa to eliminate all Jewish enemies.

9:13 be hanged. I.e., be publicly displayed.

9:15, 16 Over 1,500 years earlier God had promised to curse those who curse Abraham's descendants (Ge 12:3).

9:15 fourteenth day. Another 300 men died the second day of killing in Susa, bringing the total dead in Susa to 810.

9:16 kill. Outside of Susa, only one day of killing occurred in which 75,000 enemies died.

9:18, 19 This section recounted why Purim would be celebrated for two days rather than one.

9:20–25 A brief summary of God's providential intervention on behalf of the Jews.

9:26 Purim. The first and last biblically revealed, non-Mosaic festival with perpetual significance.

9:29 second letter. An additional letter (cf. v. 20 for the first letter), which added "fasting" and "lamentations" to the prescribed activity of Purim.

to confirm [B]this second letter about Purim. 30 He
sent letters to all the Jews, [A]to the 127 provinces
of the kingdom of Ahasuerus, *namely,* words of
peace and truth, 31 to establish these days of Purim at their appointed times, just as Mordecai
the Jew and Queen Esther had established for
them, and just as they had established for themselves and for their [a]descendants with [b]instruc-
tions [A]for their times of fasting and their lamentations. 32 The command of Esther established
these [a]customs for [A]Purim, and it was written in
the book.

MORDECAI'S GREATNESS

10 Now King Ahasuerus laid a tribute on the land
and on the [A]coastlands of the sea. 2 And all
the [a]accomplishments of his authority and strength,
and the full account of the greatness of Mordecai [A]to
which the king [b]advanced him, are they not written
in [B]the Book of the Chronicles of the Kings of Media
and Persia? 3 For Mordecai the Jew was [A]second *only*
to King Ahasuerus, and great among the Jews and
in favor with his many kinsmen, [B]one who sought
the good of his people and one who spoke for the
welfare of his whole nation.

9:29 [B]Esth 9:20, 21 9:30 [A]Esth 1:1 9:31 [a]Lit *seed* [b]Lit *words* [A]Esth 4:3 9:32 [a]Lit *words* [A]Esth 9:26 10:1 [A]Is 11:11; 24:15 10:2 [a]Lit *doings* [b]Lit *made him great* [A]Esth 8:15; 9:4 [B]Esth 2:23 10:3 [A]Gen 41:43, 44 [B]Neh 2:10

9:32 **written in the book.** This could be the chronicle referred to in 10:2, or another archival type document. It certainly does not hint that Esther wrote this canonical book.

10:1–3 Apparently a postscript.

10:3 **Mordecai … was second.** Mordecai joined the top echelon of Jewish international statesmen like Joseph, who ranked second in the Egyptian dynasty (Ge 41:37–45), and Daniel, who succeeded in both the Babylonian (Da 2:46–49; 5:29) and Medo-Persian Empires (Da 6:28). **spoke for the welfare.** Less than 10 years later (ca. 465 B.C.), Ahasuerus was assassinated. There are no further details concerning Esther and Mordecai. What Mordecai did for less than a decade on behalf of Israel, Jesus Christ will do for all eternity as the Prince of Peace (Is 9:6, 7; Zec 9:9, 10)

THE BOOK OF JOB

TITLE

As with other books of the Bible, Job bears the name of the narrative's primary character. This name might have been derived from the Hebrew word for "persecution," thus meaning "persecuted one," or from an Arabic word meaning "repent," thus bearing the name "repentant one." The author recounts an era in the life of Job, in which he was tested and the character of God was revealed. New Testament writers directly quote Job two times (Ro 11:35; 1Co 3:19), plus Eze 14:14, 20 and Jas 5:11 show Job was a real person.

AUTHOR AND DATE

The book does not name its author. Job is an unlikely candidate because the book's message rests on Job's ignorance of the events that occurred in heaven as they related to his ordeal. One Talmudic tradition suggests Moses as author since the land of Uz (1:1) was adjacent to Midian where Moses lived for 40 years, and he could have obtained a record of the story there. Solomon is also a good possibility due to the similarity of content with parts of the book of Ecclesiastes, as well as the fact that Solomon wrote the other Wisdom books (except Psalms, and he did author Pss 72; 127). Though he lived long after Job, Solomon could have written about events that occurred long before his own time, in much the same manner as Moses was inspired to write about Adam and Eve. Elihu, Isaiah, Hezekiah, Jeremiah, and Ezra have also been suggested as possible authors, but without support.

The date of the book's writing may be much later than the events recorded therein. This conclusion is based on: 1) Job's age (42:16); 2) his life span of nearly 200 years (42:16), which fits the patriarchal period (Abraham lived 175 years; Ge 25:7); 3) the social unit being the patriarchal family; 4) the Chaldeans who murdered Job's servants (1:17) were nomads and had not yet become city dwellers; 5) Job's wealth being measured in livestock rather than gold and silver (1:3; 42:12); 6) Job's priestly functions within his family (1:4, 5); and 7) a basic silence on matters such as the covenant of Abraham, Israel, the Exodus, and the law of Moses. The events of Job's odyssey appear to be patriarchal. Job, on the other hand, seemed to know about Adam (31:33) and the Noahic flood (12:15). These cultural/historical features found in the book appear to place the events chronologically at a time probably after Babel (Ge 11:1–9) but before or contemporaneous with Abraham (Ge 11:27ff.).

BACKGROUND AND SETTING

This book begins with a scene in heaven that explains everything to the reader (1:6–2:10). Job was suffering because God was contesting with Satan. Job never knew that, nor did any of his friends, so they all struggled to explain suffering from the perspective of their ignorance, until finally Job rested in nothing but faith in God's goodness and the hope of His redemption. That God vindicated his trust is the culminating message of the book. When there are no rational or, even, theological explanations for disaster and pain, trust God.

HISTORICAL AND THEOLOGICAL THEMES

The occasion and events that follow Job's sufferings present significant questions for the faith of believers in all ages. Why does Job serve God? Job is heralded for his righteousness, being compared with Noah and Daniel (Eze 14:14–20), and for his spiritual endurance (Jas 5:11). Several other questions are alluded to throughout Job's ordeal, for instance, "Why do the righteous suffer?" Though an answer to that question may seem important, the book does not set forth such an answer. Job never knew the reasons for his suffering and neither did his friends. The righteous sufferer does not appear to learn about any of the heavenly court debates between God and Satan that precipitated his pain. In fact, when finally confronted by the Lord of the universe, Job put his hand over his mouth and said nothing. Job's silent response in no way trivialized the intense pain and loss he had endured. It merely underscored the importance of trusting God's purposes in the midst of suffering because suffering, like all other human experiences, is directed by perfect divine wisdom. In the end, the lesson learned was that one may never know the specific reason for his suffering; but one must trust in Sovereign God. That is the real answer to suffering.

The book treats two major themes and many other minor ones, both in the narrative framework of the prologue (chaps. 1, 2) and epilogue (42:7–17), and in the poetic account of Job's torment that lies in between (3:1–42:6). A key to understanding the first theme of the book is to notice the debate between God and Satan in heaven and how it connects with the 3 cycles of earthly debates between Job and his friends. God wanted to prove the character of believers to Satan and to all demons, angels, and people. The accusations are by Satan, who indicted God's claims of Job's righteousness as being untested, if not questionable. Satan accused the righteous of being faithful to God only for what they could get. Since Job did not serve God with pure motives, according to Satan, the whole relationship between him and God was a sham. Satan's confidence that he could turn Job against God came, no doubt, from the fact that he had led the holy angels to rebel with him (*see note on Rev 12:4*). Satan thought he could destroy Job's faith in God by inflicting suffering on him, thus showing in principle that saving faith could be shattered. God released Satan to make his point if he could, but he failed, as true faith in God proved unbreakable. Even Job's wife told him to curse God (2:9), but he refused; his faith in God never failed (see 13:15). Satan tried to do the same to Peter (see Lk 22:31–34) and was unsuccessful in destroying Peter's faith (see Jn 21:15–19). When Satan has unleashed all that he can do to destroy saving faith, it stands firm (cf. Ro 8:31–39). In the end, God proved His point with Satan that saving faith can't be destroyed no matter how much trouble a saint suffers, or how incomprehensible and undeserved it seems.

A second and related theme concerns proving the character of God to men. Does this sort of ordeal, in which God and His opponent Satan square off, with righteous Job as the test case, suggest that God is lacking in compassion and mercy toward Job? Not at all. As James says, "You have heard of the endurance of Job and have seen the outcome of the Lord's dealings, that the Lord is full of compassion and *is* merciful" (Jas 5:11). It was to prove the very opposite (42:10–17). Job says, "Shall we indeed accept good from God and not accept adversity?" (2:10). God's servant does not deny that he has suffered. He does deny that his suffering is a result of sin. Nor does he understand why he suffers. Job simply commits his ordeal with a devout heart of worship and humility (42:5, 6) to a sovereign and perfectly wise Creator—and that was what God wanted him to learn in this conflict with Satan. In the end, God flooded Job with more blessings than he had ever known.

The major reality of the book is the inscrutable mystery of innocent suffering. God ordains that His children walk in sorrow and pain, sometimes because of sin (cf. Nu 12:10–12), sometimes for chastening (cf. Heb 12:5–12), sometimes for strengthening (cf. 2Co 12:7–10; 1Pe 5:10), and sometimes to give opportunity to reveal His comfort and grace (2Co 1:3–7). But there are times when the compelling issue in the suffering of the saints is unknowable because it is for a heavenly purpose that those on earth can't discern (cf. Ex 4:11; Jn 9:1–3).

Job and his friends wanted to analyze the suffering and look for causes and solutions. Using all of their sound theology and insight into the situation, they searched for answers, but found only useless and wrong ideas, for which God rebuked them in the end (42:7). They couldn't know why Job suffered because what happened in heaven between God and Satan was unknown to them. They thought they knew all the answers, but they only intensified the dilemma by their insistent ignorance.

By spreading out some of the elements of this great theme, we can see the following truths in Job's experience:

I. There are matters going on in heaven with God that believers know nothing about; yet, they affect their lives;

II. Even the best effort at explaining the issues of life can be useless;

III. God's people do suffer. Bad things happen all the time to good people, so one cannot judge a person's spirituality by his painful circumstances or successes;

IV. Even though God seems far away, perseverance in faith is a most noble virtue since God is good and one can safely leave his life in His hands;

V. The believer in the midst of suffering should not abandon God, but draw near to Him, so out of the fellowship can come the comfort—without the explanation; and

VI. Suffering may be intense, but it will ultimately end for the righteous and God will bless abundantly.

INTERPRETIVE CHALLENGES

The most critical interpretive challenge involves the book's primary message. Although often thought to be the pressing issue of the book, the question of why Job suffers is never revealed to Job, though the reader knows that it involves God's proving a point to Satan—a matter which completely transcends Job's ability to understand. James' commentary on Job's case (5:11) draws the conclusion that it was to show God's compassion and mercy, but without apology it offers no explanation for Job's specific ordeal. Readers find themselves putting their proverbial hands over their mouths, with no right to question or accuse the all-wise and all-powerful Creator, who will do as He pleases, and in so doing, both proves His points in the spiritual realm to angels and demons and defines His compassion and mercy. Engaging in "theodicy," i.e., man's attempt to defend God's involvement in calamity and suffering, is shown to be appropriate in these circumstances, though in the end, it is apparent that God does not need nor want a human advocate. The book of Job poignantly illustrates Dt 29:29, "The secret things belong to the LORD our God ..."

The nature of Job's guilt and innocence raises perplexing questions. God declared Job perfect, upright,

God-fearing, and shunning evil (1:1). But Job's comforters raised a critical question based on Job's ordeal: had not Job sinned? On several occasions Job readily admitted to having sinned (7:21; 13:26). But Job questioned the extent of his sin as compared to the severity of his suffering. God rebuked Job in the end for his demands to be vindicated of the comforters' accusations (chaps. 38–41). But He also declared that what Job said was correct and what the comforters said was wrong (42:7).

Another challenge comes in keeping separate the preunderstandings that Job and his comforters brought to Job's ordeal. At the outset, all agreed that God punishes evil, rewards obedience, and no exceptions are possible. Job, due to his suffering innocently, was forced to conclude that exceptions are possible in that the righteous also suffer. He also observed that the wicked prosper. These are more than small exceptions to the rule, thus forcing Job to rethink his simple understanding about God's sovereign interaction with His people. The type of wisdom Job comes to embrace was not dependent merely on the promise of reward or punishment. The long, peevish, disputes between Job and his accusers were attempts to reconcile the perceived inequities of God's retribution in Job's experiences. Such an empirical method is dangerous. In the end, God offered no explanation to Job, but rather called all parties to a deeper level of trust in the Creator, who rules over a sin-confused world with power and authority directed by perfect wisdom and mercy. *See notes on Ps 73.*

Understanding this book requires 1) understanding the nature of wisdom, particularly the difference between man's wisdom and God's, and 2) admitting that Job and his friends lacked the divine wisdom to interpret Job's circumstances accurately, though his friends kept trying while Job learned to be content in God's sovereignty and mercy. The turning point or resolution for this matter is found in Job 28 where the character of divine wisdom is explained: divine wisdom is rare and priceless; man cannot hope to purchase it; and God possesses it all. We may not know what is going on in heaven or what God's purposes are, but we must trust Him. Because of this, the matter of believers suffering takes a back seat to the matter of divine wisdom.

OUTLINE

I. The Dilemma (1:1–2:13)
- A. Introduction of Job (1:1–5)
- B. Divine Debates with Satan (1:6–2:10)
- C. Arrival of Friends (2:11–13)

II. The Debates (3:1–37:24)
- A. The First Cycle (3:1–14:22)
  1. Job's first speech expresses despair (3:1–26)
  2. Eliphaz's first speech kindly protests and urges humility and repentance (4:1–5:27)
  3. Job's reply to Eliphaz expresses anguish and questions the trials, asking for sympathy in his pain (6:1–7:21)
  4. Bildad's first speech accuses Job of impugning God (8:1–22)
  5. Job's response to Bildad admits he is not perfect, but may protest what seems unfair (9:1–10:22)
  6. Zophar's first speech tells Job to get right with God (11:1–20)
  7. Job's response to Zophar tells his friends they are wrong and only God knows and will, hopefully, speak to him (12:1–14:22)
- B. The Second Cycle (15:1–21:34)
  1. Eliphaz's second speech accuses Job of presumption and disregarding the wisdom of the ancients (15:1–35)
  2. Job's response to Eliphaz appeals to God against his unjust accusers (16:1–17:16)
  3. Bildad's second speech tells Job he is suffering just what he deserves (18:1–21)
  4. Job's response to Bildad cries out to God for pity (19:1–29)
  5. Zophar's second speech accuses Job of rejecting God by questioning His justice (20:1–29)
  6. Job's response to Zophar says he is out of touch with reality (21:1–34)
- C. The Third Cycle (22:1–26:14)
  1. Eliphaz's third speech denounces Job's criticism of God's justice (22:1–30)
  2. Job's response to Eliphaz is that God knows he is without guilt, and yet in His providence and refining purpose He permits temporary success for the wicked (23:1–24:25)
  3. Bildad's third speech scoffs at Job's direct appeal to God (25:1–6)
  4. Job's response to Bildad is that God is indeed perfectly wise and absolutely sovereign, but not simplistic as they thought (26:1–14)
- D. The Final Defense of Job (27:1–31:40)
  1. Job's first monologue affirms his righteousness and that man can't discover God's wisdom (27:1–28:28)
  2. Job's second monologue remembers his past, describes his present, defends his innocence, and asks for God to defend him (29:1–31:40)
- E. The Speeches of Elihu (32:1–37:24)
  1. Elihu enters into the debate to break the impasse (32:1–22)
  2. Elihu charges Job with presumption in criticizing God, not recognizing that God may have a loving purpose, even in allowing Job to suffer (33:1–33)

3. Elihu declares that Job has impugned God's integrity by claiming that it does not pay to lead a godly life (34:1–37)
4. Elihu urges Job to wait patiently for the Lord (35:1–16)
5. Elihu believes that God is disciplining Job (36:1–21)
6. Elihu argues that human observers can hardly expect to understand adequately God's dealings in administering justice and mercy (36:22–37:24)

III. The Deliverance (38:1–42:17)

A. God Interrogates Job (38:1–41:34)
   1. God's first response to Job (38:1–40:2)
   2. Job's answer to God (40:3–5)
   3. God's second response to Job (40:6–41:34)

B. Job Confesses, Worships, and Is Vindicated (42:1–17)
   1. Job passes judgment upon himself (42:1–6)
   2. God rebukes Eliphaz, Bildad, and Zophar (42:7–9)
   3. God restores Job's family, wealth, and long life (42:10–17)

JOB'S CHARACTER AND WEALTH

1 There was a man in the [A]land of Uz whose name
was [B]Job; and that man was [C]blameless, upright,
[D]fearing God and [E]turning away from evil. 2 [A]Seven
sons and three daughters were born to him. 3 [A]His
possessions also were 7,000 sheep, 3,000 camels, 500
yoke of oxen, 500 female donkeys, and very many
servants; and that man was [B]the greatest of all the
[a]men of the east. 4 His sons used to go and hold a
feast in the house of each one on his day, and they
would send and invite their three sisters to eat and
drink with them. 5 When the days of feasting had
completed their cycle, Job would send and consecrate
them, rising up early in the morning and offering
[A]burnt offerings *according to* the number of them
all; for Job said, "[B]Perhaps my sons have sinned and
[C]cursed God in their hearts." Thus Job did continually.

6 [A]Now there was a day when the [B]sons of God came
to present themselves before the LORD, and [a]Satan
also came among them. 7 The LORD said to Satan,
"From where do you come?" Then Satan answered
the LORD and said, "[A]From roaming about on the
earth and walking around on it." 8 The LORD said to
Satan, "Have you [a]considered [A]My servant Job? For
there is no one like him on the earth, [B]a blameless and
upright man, [b]fearing God and turning away from

1:1 [A]Jer 25:20; Lam 4:21 [B]Ezek 14:14, 20; James 5:11 [C]Gen 6:9; 17:1; Deut 18:13 [D]Gen 22:12; 42:18; Ex 18:21; Prov 8:13 [E]Job 28:28 1:2 [A]Job 42:13 1:3 [a]Lit *sons* [A]Job 42:12 [B]Job 29:25 1:5 [A]Gen 8:20; Job 42:8 [B]Job 8:4 [C]1 Kin 21:10, 13 1:6 [a]I.e. the adversary, and so throughout chs 1 and 2 [A]Job 2:1 [B]Job 38:7 1:7 [A]1 Pet 5:8 1:8 [a]Lit *set your heart to* [b]Or *revering* [A]Num 12:7; Josh 1:2, 7; Job 42:7, 8 [B]Job 1:1

1:1–2:13 This section identifies the main persons and sets the stage for the drama to follow.

1:1 Uz. Job's home was a walled city with gates (29:7, 8), where he held a position of great respect. The city was in the land of Uz in northern Arabia, adjacent to Midian, where Moses lived for 40 years (Ex 2:15). **Job.** The story begins on earth with Job as the central figure. He was a rich man with 7 sons and 3 daughters, in his middle years with a grown family, but still young enough to father 10 more children (see 42:13). He was good, a family man, rich, and widely known. **blameless, upright, fearing God ... turning away from evil.** Cf. 1:8. Job was not perfect or without sin (cf. 6:24; 7:21; 9:20); however, it appears from the language that he had put his trust in God for redemption and faithfully lived a God-honoring, sincere life of integrity and consistency personally, maritally (2:10), and parentally (1:4, 5).

1:3 sheep ... camels ... oxen ... female donkeys. As typically in the ancient Near East, Job's wealth was not measured in money or land holdings, but in his numerous livestock, like the patriarchs (cf. Ge 13:1–7). **greatest ... of the east.** A major claim by any standard. Solomon held a similar reputation, "Solomon's wisdom surpassed the wisdom of all the sons of the east" (1Ki 4:30). The "east" denotes those living E of Canaan, as the people of the northern Arabian desert did (cf. Jdg 6:3; Eze 25:4).

1:4 on his day. Of the week (7 sons). This reference to the main meal of each day of the week, which moved from house to house, implies the love and harmony of the family members. The sisters are especially noted to show these were cared for with love.

1:5 send and consecrate. At the end of every week, Job would offer up as many burnt offerings as he had sons (see Lv 1:4), officiating as family priest weekly ("continually") in a time before the Aaronic priesthood was established. These offerings were to cover any sin that his children may have committed that week, indicating the depth of his spiritual devotion. This record is included to demonstrate the righteousness and virtue of Job and his family, which made his suffering all the more amazing. **burnt offerings.** This kind of offering was known as early as Noah (Ge 8:20).

1:6 sons of God. Job's life is about to be caught up in heavenly strategies as the scene moves from earth to heaven, where God is holding council with His heavenly court. Neither Job nor his friends ever knew about this. The angelic host (cf. 38:7; Pss 29:1; 89:7; Da 3:25) came to God's throne to render account of their ministry throughout the earth and heaven (cf. 1Ki 22:19–22). Like a Judas among the apostles, Satan was with the angels. **Satan.** Emboldened by the success he had with the unfallen Adam in paradise (Ge 3:6–12, 17–19), he was confident that the fear of God in Job, one of a fallen race, would not stand his tests. And he had fallen himself (see Is 14:12). As opposed to a personal name, Satan as a title means "adversary," in either a personal or judicial sense. This demon is the ultimate spiritual adversary of all time and has been accusing the righteous throughout the ages (see Rev 12:10). In a courtroom setting, the adversary usually stood to the right of the accused. This location is reported when Satan in heaven accused Joshua the High Priest (Zec 3:1). That he is still unsuccessful is the thesis of Ro 8:31–39.

1:7 The LORD said. Lest there be any question about God's role in this ordeal, it was He who initiated the dialogue. The adversary was not presiding. If anything, Satan raised the penetrating question that might well be asked by anyone, perhaps even Job himself: does Job serve God with pure motives, or is he in it only as long as the blessings flow?

1:7, 8 roaming about on the earth. The picture is of haste. No angel, fallen or holy, is an omnipresent creature, but they move rapidly. In Satan's case, as prince of this world (Jn 12:31; 14:30; 16:11) and ruler of demons (Mt 9:34; 12:24), the earth is his domain, where he prowls like a "roaring lion, seeking someone to devour" (1Pe 5:8). God gave him Job to test.

BIOGRAPHICAL SKETCH OF JOB
1. A spiritually mature man (1:1, 8; 2:3)
2. Father of many children (1:2; 42:13)
3. Owner of many herds (1:3; 42:12)
4. A wealthy and influential man (1:3b)
5. A priest to his family (1:5)
6. A loving, wise husband (2:9)
7. A man of prominence in community affairs (29:7–11)
8. A man of benevolence (29:12–17; 31:32)
9. A wise leader (29:21–24)
10. Grower of crops (31:38–40)

evil." 9 Then [A]Satan answered the [a]LORD, "Does Job
fear God for nothing? 10 [A]Have You not made a hedge
about him and his house and all that he has, on every
side? [B]You have blessed the work of his hands, and
his [C]possessions have increased in the land. 11 [A]But
put forth Your hand now and [B]touch all that he has;
he will surely curse You to Your face." 12 Then the
LORD said to Satan, "Behold, all that he has is in your
[a]power, only do not put forth your hand on him." So
Satan departed from the presence of the LORD.

SATAN ALLOWED TO TEST JOB

13 Now on the day when his sons and his daughters were eating and drinking wine in their oldest
brother's house, 14 a messenger came to Job and
said, "The oxen were plowing and the [a]donkeys
feeding beside them, 15 and [a]the [A]Sabeans [b]attacked
and took them. They also [c]slew the servants with
the edge of the sword, and [d]I alone have escaped to
tell you." 16 While he was still speaking, another also
came and said, "[A]The fire of God fell from heaven
and burned up the sheep and the servants and consumed them, and I alone have escaped to tell you."
17 While he was still speaking, another also came
and said, "The [A]Chaldeans formed three bands
and made a raid on the camels and took them and
[a]slew the servants with the edge of the sword, and
I alone have escaped to tell you." 18 While he was
still speaking, another also came and said, "Your
sons and your daughters were eating and drinking
wine in their oldest brother's house, 19 and behold,
a great wind came from across the wilderness and
struck the four corners of the house, and it fell on
the young people and they died, and I alone have
escaped to tell you."

20 Then Job arose and [A]tore his robe and shaved
his head, and he fell to the ground and worshiped.
21 He said,

> "[A]Naked I came from my mother's womb,
> And naked I shall return there.
> The [B]LORD gave and the LORD
> has taken away.
> Blessed be the name of the LORD."

22 [A]Through all this Job did not sin nor did he
[a]blame God.

JOB LOSES HIS HEALTH

2 [A]Again there was a day when the sons of God
came to present themselves before the LORD, and
Satan also came among them to present himself before the LORD. 2 The LORD said to Satan, "Where have
you come from?" Then Satan answered the LORD and
said, "From roaming about on the earth and walking around on it." 3 The LORD said to Satan, "Have
you [a]considered My servant Job? For there is no one
like him on the earth, a blameless and upright man
[b]fearing God and turning away from evil. And he
still [A]holds fast his integrity, although you incited Me
against him to [c]ruin him without cause." 4 Satan answered the LORD and said, "Skin for skin! Yes, all that a
man has he will give for his life. 5 [A]However, put forth
Your hand now, and [B]touch his bone and his flesh; he
will curse You to Your face." 6 So the LORD said to Satan, "Behold, he is in your [a]power, only spare his life."

1:9 [a]Lit *LORD and said* [A]Rev 12:9f 1:10 [A]Job 29:2-6; Ps 34:7 [B]Job 31:25 [C]Job 1:3; 31:25 1:11 [A]Job 2:5 [B]Job 19:21 1:12 [a]Lit *hand* 1:14 [a]Lit *female donkeys* 1:15 [a]Lit *Sheba* [b]Lit *fell upon* [c]Lit *smote* [d]Lit *only I alone,* and so also vv 16, 17, 19 [A]Gen 10:7; Job 6:19 1:16 [A]Gen 19:24; Lev 10:2; Num 11:1-3 1:17 [a]Lit *smote* [A]Gen 11:28, 31 1:20 [A]Gen 37:29, 34; Josh 7:6 1:21 [A]Eccl 5:15 [B]1 Sam 2:7, 8; Job 2:10 1:22 [a]Lit *ascribe unseemliness to* [A]Job 2:10 2:1 [A]Job 1:6-8 2:3 [a]Lit *set your heart to* [b]Or *revering* [c]Lit *swallow him up* [A]Job 27:5, 6 2:5 [A]Job 1:11 [B]Job 19:20 2:6 [a]Lit *hand*

1:9–11 Satan asserted that true believers are only faithful as long as they prosper. Take away their prosperity, he claims, and they will reject God. He wanted to prove that salvation is not permanent, that saving faith can be broken and those who were God's could become his. That is the first of the two great themes of this book (see Introduction: Historical and Theological Themes). Satan repeated this affront with Jesus (see Mt 4), Peter (see Lk 22:31), and Paul (see 2Co 12:7). The OT has many promises from God in which He pledges to sustain the faith of His children. Cf. Pss 37:23, 28; 97:10; 121:4–7. For NT texts, cf. Lk 22:31, 32; Jude 24.

1:12 **power.** God allowed Satan to test Job's faith by attacking "all that he has." With God's sovereign permission, Satan was allowed to move on Job, except that he could not attack Job physically.

1:13–19 With 4 rapid-fire disasters, Satan destroyed or removed Job's livestock, servants, and children. Only the 4 messengers survived.

1:15 **Sabeans.** Lit. "Sheba," part of Arabia. These people were terrorizing robbers, who had descended from Ham (Ge 10:6, 7) and/or Shem (Ge 10:28).

1:16 **fire of God . . . heaven.** This probably refers to severe lightning.

1:17 **Chaldeans.** A semi-nomadic people of the Arabian desert, experienced in marauding and war (cf. Hab 1:6–8).

1:19 **great wind.** Most likely a tornado-type wind. Cf. Is 21:1; Hos 13:15.

1:20, 21 **worshiped.** He heard the other messages calmly, but on hearing about the death of his children, he expressed all the symbols of grief (cf. Ge 37:34; Jer 41:5; Mic 1:16), but also worshiped God in the expression of v. 21. Instead of cursing, he blessed the name of Jehovah. Job's submissive response disproved the adversary's accusations (1:9–11). So far, Job was what God claimed him to be, a true believer with faith that cannot be broken (v. 8).

1:22 **did not sin nor did he blame God.** Better, "sin by charging God with wrong." Hasty words against God in the midst of grief are foolish and wicked. Christians are to submit to trials and still worship God, not because they see the reasons for them, but because God wills them and has His own reasons which believers are to trust.

2:1–3a The scene changes again to the heavenly court, where the angels came before the Lord and Satan was also present, having been again searching the earth for victims to assault. *See notes on 1:6–8.*

2:3 **he still holds fast his integrity.** God affirmed that Job had won round one. **without cause.** God uses the same expression the adversary used in Job 1: "for nothing" (1:9) and "without cause" (2:3). The message behind God's turn of words is that the adversary is the guilty party in this case, not Job who had suffered all the disaster without any personal cause. He had done nothing to incur the pain and loss, though it was massive. The issue was purely a matter of conflict between God and Satan. This is a crucial statement, because when Job's friends tried to explain why all the disasters had befallen him, they always put the blame on Job. Grasping this assessment from God—that Job had not been punished for something, but suffered for nothing related to him personally—is a crucial key to the story. Sometimes suffering is caused by divine purposes unknowable to us (see Introduction: Historical and Theological Themes).

2:4, 5 **Skin for skin!** Satan contended that what he had done to Job so far was just touching the skin, scratching the surface. Job endured the loss of all that he had, even the lives of his children, but would not endure the loss of his own well-being. If God allowed Satan to make the disaster a personal matter of his own physical body, the Adversary contended, Job's faith would fail.

2:6 **spare his life.** The Lord sovereignly limited the Adversary, although death seemed preferable. Job believed that to be the case (cf. 7:15), as did his wife (2:9).

7 Then Satan went out from the presence of the
LORD and smote Job with [A]sore boils from the sole
of his foot to the crown of his head. 8 And he took
a potsherd to scrape himself while [A]he was sitting
among the ashes.
9 Then his wife said to him, "Do you still hold
fast your integrity? Curse God and die!" 10 But he
said to her, "You speak as one of the foolish women
speaks. [A]Shall we indeed accept good from God
and not accept adversity?" [B]In all this Job did not
sin with his lips.
11 Now when Job's three friends heard of all this
adversity that had come upon him, they came each
one from his own place, Eliphaz the [A]Temanite,
Bildad the [B]Shuhite and Zophar the Naamathite;
and they made an appointment together to come
to [C]sympathize with him and comfort him. 12 When
they lifted up their eyes at a distance and did not
recognize him, they raised their voices and wept.
And each of them [A]tore his robe and they [B]threw
dust over their heads toward the sky. 13 [A]Then they
sat down on the ground with him for seven days
and seven nights with no one speaking a word to
him, for they saw that *his* pain was very great.

JOB'S LAMENT

3 Afterward Job opened his mouth and cursed
[a]the day of his *birth*. 2 And Job [a]said,

3 "[A]Let the day perish on which
I was to be born,
And the night *which* said, 'A
[a]boy is conceived.'
4 "May that day be darkness;
Let not God above care for it,
Nor light shine on it.
5 "Let [A]darkness and black
gloom claim it;
Let a cloud settle on it;
Let the blackness of the day terrify it.
6 "*As for* that night, let darkness seize it;
Let it not rejoice among the
days of the year;
Let it not come into the
number of the months.
7 "Behold, let that night be barren;
Let no joyful shout enter it.
8 "Let those curse it who curse the day,
Who are [a]prepared to [A]rouse Leviathan.

2:7 [A]Deut 28:35; Job 7:5; 13:28; 30:17, 18, 30 2:8 [A]Job 42:6; Jer 6:26; Ezek 27:30; Jon 3:6 2:10 [A]Job 1:21 [B]Job 1:22; Ps 39:1; James 1:12 2:11 [A]Gen 36:11; Job 6:19; Jer 49:7 [B]Gen 25:2 [C]Job 42:11; Rom 12:15 2:12 [A]Job 1:20 [B]Josh 7:6; Neh 9:1; Lam 2:10; Ezek 27:30 2:13 [A]Gen 50:10; Ezek 3:15
3:1 [a]Lit *his day* 3:2 [a]Lit *answered and said* 3:3 [a]Lit *man-child* [A]Jer 20:14-18 3:5 [A]Jer 13:16 3:8 [a]Or *skillful* [A]Job 41:1, 25

2:7 Satan ... smote Job. This appears to be an exceptional case with no other exact parallel in Scripture. In the gospels, demons caused physical problems when they dwelled within people (cf. Luke 13:11, 16), but that is not the case here. God's permissive will operated for purposes Job can't know; God was hidden from him along with the reasons for his suffering. **sore boils.** Although the nature of Job's affliction cannot be diagnosed exactly, it produced extreme physical trauma (cf. 2:13; 3:24; 7:5, 14; 13:28; 16:8; 19:17; 30:17, 30; 33:21). One cannot fully understand Job's conversations throughout the book without considering the extraordinary physical distress he endured in a day without medicine or pain relief. His boils would have been similar to those of the Egyptians (Ex 9:8–11) and Hezekiah (2Ki 20:7).

2:8 potsherd ... ashes. Suffering terribly, Job took himself to where the lepers go: the ash heap outside the city, where he scraped at his sores with a piece of broken pottery, perhaps breaking them open to release the infection.

2:9 your integrity. Through all this, Job's faith remained strong in the confusion, so that his wife could not accuse him of insincerity as Satan had. Her argument in effect was "let go of your piety and curse God; then He will end your life for blaspheming," (i.e., death under these conditions would be preferable to living). She added temptation to affliction because she advised him to sin.

2:10 foolish. Not meaning silly or ridiculous, but acting as one who rejects God or God's revealed will. The word is used of the unwise in the Psalms (14:1; 53:1) and in Proverbs (30:22). She is not seen nor heard of again in this book, except indirectly in 42:13–15. **accept.** Job lived out and explained the text of Dt 29:29. His words and deeds demonstrated his confidence in God and vindicated God's confidence in him.

2:11–13 Here is one of the most moving scenes in the whole story, as Job's friends came to comfort and commiserate with him in his pain. They expressed all the traditional gestures of grief.

2:11 Temanite. Most likely Teman was a city of Edom (cf. Ge 36:4, 11; Jer 49:7, 20; Eze 25:13; Am 1:12; Ob 8, 9). **Shuhite.** The Shuhites were descendants of Abraham through Keturah (Ge 25:2, 6). **Naamathite.** A resident of an unknown location probably in Edom or Arabia, although some have suggested Naamah on the Edomite border (cf. Jos 15:41).

2:13 *his* pain was very great. The expression actually meant that his disease produced pain that was still increasing. The agony was so great, his friends were speechless for a week.

3:1–42:6 This whole section is poetry—a dramatic poem of speeches attempting to understand Job's suffering.

3:1–37:24 This section covers the cycles of speeches between Job and his well-meaning friends, including Elihu (chaps. 32–37).

3:1–14:22 The first cycle of speeches given by Job and his 3 friends begins. Job was the first to break the week-long silence with a lament (3:1–26).

3:1–10 Job began his first speech by cursing the day of his birth, which should have been a day of great rejoicing, and welcomed the day he would finally die. In short, Job says "I wish I'd never been born." See 3; 6, 7; 9, 10; 12–14; 16, 17; 19; 21; 23, 24; 26; 40:3–5; 42:1–6 for Job's speeches.

3:1 cursed the day of his *birth*. Job was in deep pain and despair. What God was allowing hurt desperately, but while Job did not curse God (cf. 2:8), he did curse his birth (vv. 10, 11). He wished he had never been conceived (v. 3) or born because the joys of his life were not worth all the pain. He felt it would have been better to have never lived than to suffer like that; better to have never had wealth than to lose it; better to have never had children than to have them all killed. He never wanted his birthday remembered, and wished it had been obliterated from the calendar (vv. 4–7).

3:8 who curse ... Leviathan. Those who pronounce the most powerful curses, even to arousing the destructive sea monster (*see note on 41:1*; cf. Pss 74:14; 104:26; Is 27:1).

THE SCRIPT	
1. Job	Job 3; 6–7; 9–10; 12–14; 16–17; 19; 21; 23–24; 26–31; 40:3–5; 42:1–6
2. Eliphaz	Job 4–5; 15; 22
3. Bildad	Job 8; 18; 25
4. Zophar	Job 11; 20
5. Elihu	Job 32–37
6. God	Job 38:1–40:2; 40:6–41:34

9 "Let the stars of its twilight be darkened;
Let it wait for light but have none,
And let it not see the [a]breaking dawn;
10 Because it did not shut the opening
of my *mother's* womb,
Or hide trouble from my eyes.

11 "[A]Why did I not die [a]at birth,
Come forth from the womb and expire?
12 "Why did the knees receive me,
And why the breasts, that I should suck?
13 "For now I [A]would have lain
down and been quiet;
I would have slept then, I
would have been at rest,
14 With [A]kings and *with*
[B]counselors of the earth,
Who rebuilt [C]ruins for themselves;
15 Or with [A]princes [B]who had gold,
Who were filling their houses *with* silver.
16 "Or like a miscarriage which is
[a]discarded, I would not be,
As infants that never saw light.
17 "There the wicked cease from raging,
And there the [a]weary are at [A]rest.
18 "The prisoners are at ease together;
They do not hear the voice
of the taskmaster.
19 "The small and the great are there,
And the slave is free from his master.

20 "Why is [A]light given to him who suffers,
And life to the bitter of soul,
21 Who [a,A]long for death, but there is none,
And dig for it more than for
[B]hidden treasures,
22 Who rejoice greatly,
And exult when they find the grave?
23 "*Why is light given* to a man
[A]whose way is hidden,
And whom [B]God has hedged in?
24 "For [A]my groaning comes at
the sight of my food,
And [B]my cries pour out like water.
25 "For [a,A]what I fear comes upon me,
And what I dread befalls me.
26 "I [A]am not at ease, nor am I quiet,
And I am not at rest, but turmoil comes."

ELIPHAZ: INNOCENT DO NOT SUFFER

4 Then Eliphaz the Temanite [a]answered,

2 "If one ventures a word with you,
will you become impatient?
But [A]who can refrain [a]from speaking?
3 "Behold [A]you have admonished many,
And you have strengthened weak hands.
4 "Your words have [a]helped the
tottering to stand,
And you have strengthened [b]feeble knees.
5 "But now it has come to you,
and you [A]are impatient;
It [B]touches you, and you are dismayed.
6 "Is not your [a,A]fear *of God* [B]your confidence,
And the integrity of your ways your hope?

7 "Remember now, [A]who *ever*
perished being innocent?
Or where were the upright destroyed?
8 "According to what I have seen,
[A]those who plow iniquity
And those who sow trouble harvest it.
9 "By [A]the breath of God they perish,
And [B]by the [a]blast of His anger
they come to an end.
10 "The [A]roaring of the lion and the
voice of the *fierce* lion,
And the teeth of the young
lions are broken.
11 "The [A]lion perishes for lack of prey,
And the [B]whelps of the
lioness are scattered.

3:9 [a]Lit *eyelids* 3:11 [a]Lit *from the womb* [A]Job 10:18, 19 3:13 [A]Job 3:13-19; 7:8-10, 21; 10:21, 22; 14:10-15, 20-22; 16:22; 17:13-16; 19:25-27; 21:13, 23-26; 24:19, 20; 26:5, 6; 34:22 3:14 [A]Job 12:18 [B]Job 12:17 [C]Job 15:28; Is 58:12 3:15 [A]Job 12:21 [B]Job 27:16, 17 3:16 [a]Lit *hidden* 3:17 [a]Lit *weary of strength* [A]Job 17:16 3:20 [A]Jer 20:18 3:21 [a]Lit *wait* [A]Rev 9:6 [B]Prov 2:4 3:23 [A]Job 19:6, 8, 12 [B]Job 19:8; Ps 88:8; Lam 3:7 3:24 [A]Job 6:7; 33:20 [B]Job 30:16; Ps 42:4 3:25 [a]Lit *the fear I fear and* [A]Job 9:28; 30:15 3:26 [A]Job 7:13, 14 4:1 [a]Lit *answered and said* 4:2 [a]Lit *in words* [A]Job 32:18-20 4:3 [A]Job 4:3, 4; 29:15, 16, 21, 25 4:4 [a]Lit *caused* [b]Lit *bowing* 4:5 [A]Job 6:14 [B]Job 19:21 4:6 [a]Or *reverence* [A]Job 1:1 [B]Prov 3:26 4:7 [A]Job 8:20; 36:6, 7; Ps 37:25 4:8 [A]Job 15:31, 35; Prov 22:8; Hos 10:13; Gal 6:7 4:9 [a]Lit *wind* [A]Job 15:30; Is 11:4; 30:33; 2 Thess 2:8 [B]Job 40:11-13 4:10 [A]Job 5:15; Ps 58:6 4:11 [A]Job 29:17; Ps 34:10 [B]Job 5:4; 20:10; 27:14

3:11–26 Job left the matter of never having been born (vv. 1–10) and moved to a desire to have been stillborn (vv. 11–19), then to a desire for the "light" of life to be extinguished in death (vv. 20–23). There is no hint that Job wanted to take his own life, for there was nothing stopping him. Job still trusted God for His sovereign hand in the matter of death, but he did consider the many ways in which death would be a perceived improvement to the present situation, because of the pain.

3:23 hedged in. Satan spoke of a hedge of protection and blessing (1:10), whereas Job spoke of this hedge as a prison of living death.

3:24 groaning ... cries. These destroyed any appetite he might have had.

3:25, 26 what I fear. Not a particular thing but a generic classification of suffering. The very worst fear that anyone could have was coming to pass in Job's life, and he is experiencing severe anxiety, fearing more.

4:1–5:27 Eliphaz. Eliphaz's first speech. See chaps. 15 and 22 for Eliphaz's other speeches. He spoke profoundly and gently, but knew nothing of the scene in heaven that had produced the suffering of Job.

4:2–6 Job's friend finally spoke after 7 days of silence and began kindly by acknowledging that Job was recognized for being a wise man. Unfortunately, with the opening of their mouths for the first speech, all the wisdom of their silence departed.

4:7 who *ever* perished being innocent? Eliphaz, recognizing Job's "fear *of God*" and "integrity" (v. 6), was likely encouraging Job at the outset by saying he wouldn't die because he was innocent of any deadly iniquity, but must be guilty of some serious sin because he was reaping such anger from God. This was a moral universe and moral order was at work, he thought. He had oversimplified God's pattern of retribution. This simple axiom, "the righteous will prosper and the wicked will suffer," does not always hold up in human experience. It is true that plowing and sowing iniquity reap judgment, so Eliphaz was partially right (cf. Gal 6:7–9; 1Pe 3:12), but not everything we reap in life is the result of something we have sown (*see notes on 2Co 12:7–10*). Eliphaz was replacing theology with simplistic logic. To say that wherever there is suffering, it is the result of sowing sin is wrong (cf. Ex 4:11; Jn 9:1–3).

4:10, 11 Wanting to demonstrate that wicked men experience calamities in spite of their strength and resources, Eliphaz illustrated his point by the destruction that comes on lions in spite of their prowess. Five Heb. words were used here for lion, emphasizing the various characters of wicked people, all of whom can be broken and perish.

12 "Now a word [A]was brought
to me stealthily,
And my ear received a [B]whisper of it.
13 "Amid disquieting [A]thoughts from
the visions of the night,
When deep sleep falls on men,
14 Dread came upon me, and trembling,
And made [a]all my bones shake.
15 "Then a [a]spirit passed by my face;
The hair of my flesh bristled up.
16 "It stood still, but I could not
discern its appearance;
A form *was* before my eyes;
There was silence, then I heard a voice:
17 'Can [A]mankind be just [a]before God?
Can a man be pure [a]before his [B]Maker?
18 '[A]He puts no trust even in His servants;
And against His angels
He charges error.
19 'How much more those who
dwell in [A]houses of clay,
Whose [B]foundation is in the dust,
Who are crushed before the moth!
20 '[A]Between morning and evening
they are broken in pieces;
Unobserved, they [B]perish forever.
21 'Is not their [A]tent-cord plucked
up within them?
They die, yet [B]without wisdom.'

GOD IS JUST

5 "Call now, is there anyone who
will answer you?
And to which of the [A]holy
ones will you turn?
2 "For [A]anger slays the foolish man,
And jealousy kills the simple.
3 "I have seen the [A]foolish taking root,
And I [B]cursed his abode immediately.
4 "His [A]sons are far from safety,
They are even [a]oppressed in the gate,
And there is no deliverer.
5 "[a]His harvest the hungry devour
And take it to a *place of* thorns,
And the [b,A]schemer is eager
for their wealth.
6 "For [A]affliction does not come
from the dust,
Nor does trouble sprout from the ground,
7 For [A]man is born for trouble,
As sparks fly upward.

8 "But as for me, I would [A]seek God,
And I would place my cause before God;
9 Who [A]does great and unsearchable things,
[a]Wonders without number.
10 "He [A]gives rain on the earth
And sends water on the fields,
11 So that [A]He sets on high
those who are lowly,
And those who mourn are lifted to safety.
12 "He [A]frustrates the plotting of the shrewd,
So that their hands cannot attain success.
13 "He [A]captures the wise by their
own shrewdness,
And the advice of the cunning
is quickly thwarted.
14 "By day they [A]meet with darkness,
And grope at noon as in the night.
15 "But He saves from [A]the sword
of their mouth,
And [B]the poor from the
hand of the mighty.
16 "So the helpless has hope,
And [A]unrighteousness must
shut its mouth.

17 "Behold, how [A]happy is the man
whom God reproves,
So do not despise the [B]discipline
of [a]the Almighty.
18 "For [A]He inflicts pain, and [a]gives relief;
He wounds, and His hands *also* heal.
19 "[a]From six troubles [A]He will deliver you,
Even in seven [B]evil will not touch you.
20 "In [A]famine He will redeem
you from death,
And [B]in war from the power of the sword.

4:12 [A]Job 4:12-17; 33:15-18 [B]Job 26:14 4:13 [A]Job 33:15 4:14 [a]Lit *the multitude of* 4:15 [a]Or *breath passed over* 4:17 [a]Lit *from* [A]Job 9:2; 25:4 [B]Job 31:15; 32:22; 35:10; 36:3 4:18 [A]Job 15:15 4:19 [A]Job 10:9; 33:6 [B]Gen 2:7; 3:19; Job 22:16 4:20 [A]Job 14:2 [B]Job 14:20; 20:7 4:21 [A]Job 8:22 [B]Job 18:21; 36:12 5:1 [A]Job 15:15 5:2 [A]Prov 12:16; 27:3 5:3 [A]Jer 12:2 [B]Job 24:18; 31:30 5:4 [a]Lit *crushed* [A]Job 4:11 5:5 [a]Lit *Whose* [b]Ancient versions read *thirsty* [A]Job 18:8-10; 22:10 5:6 [A]Job 15:35 5:7 [A]Job 14:1 5:8 [A]Job 13:2, 3; Ps 50:15 5:9 [a]Or *Miracles* [A]Job 9:10; 37:14, 16; 42:3 5:10 [A]Job 36:27-29; 37:6-11; 38:26 5:11 [A]Job 22:29; 36:7 5:12 [A]Ps 33:10 5:13 [A]Job 37:24; 1 Cor 3:19 5:14 [A]Job 12:25; 15:30; 18:18; 20:26; 24:13 5:15 [A]Job 4:10, 11; Ps 35:10 [B]Job 29:17; 34:28; 36:6, 15; 38:15 5:16 [A]Ps 107:42 5:17 [a]Heb *Shaddai,* and so throughout ch 6 [A]Ps 94:12 [B]Job 36:15, 16; Prov 3:11; Heb 12:5-11; James 1:12 5:18 [a]Lit *binds* [A]Deut 32:39; 1 Sam 2:6; Is 30:26; Hos 6:1 5:19 [a]Lit *In* [A]Ps 34:19 [B]Ps 91:10 5:20 [A]Ps 33:19; 37:19 [B]Ps 144:10

4:12–16 a word was brought to me stealthily. Eliphaz spoke of a mysterious messenger in a vision, eerie fantasy, or a dream. He claimed to have had divine revelation to bolster his viewpoint.

4:17 Here is the conclusion of Eliphaz's revelation—that Job suffered because he was not holy enough, not righteous enough.

4:17–21 This is the content of the message which is, in effect, that God judges sin and sinners among men (described in v. 19 as "houses of clay") as He did among angels (v. 18; cf. Rev 12:3, 4).

5:1 holy ones. Angelic beings (cf. 4:18) are in view. Job was told that not even the angels could help him. He must recognize his mortality and sin if he would be healed.

5:2–6 Job was told not to be a fool or simpleton, but to recognize that sin is judged, wrath kills, envy slays, foolishness is cursed (vv. 2–5), and this wasn't merely a physical matter (v. 6), but came from man's sin. Sin is inevitable in man; so is trouble (v. 7).

5:7 sparks. Lit. "the sons of Resheph," an expression which describes all sorts of fire-like movement (cf. Dt 32:24; Ps 78:48; SS 8:6).

5:8 Job's solution was to go to God and repent, his friend thought.

5:9–16 The whole of Eliphaz's argument is based on the moral perfection of God, so he extolled God's greatness and goodness.

5:13 Paul used this line from Eliphaz in 1Co 3:19 to prove the foolishness of man's wisdom before God.

5:17 happy is the man whom God reproves. Eliphaz put a positive spin on his advice by telling Job that enviable or desirable is the situation of the one God cares enough to chasten. "If only Job admitted his sin, he could be happy again" was the advice.

5:18–27 The language of this section promising blessing for penitence was strongly reminiscent of Lv 26, which elaborated the blessing of a faithful covenant

21 "You will be [A]hidden from the
scourge of the tongue,
[B]And you will not be afraid of
violence when it comes.
22 "You will [A]laugh at violence and famine,
[B]And you will not be afraid of [a]wild beasts.
23 "For you will be in league with
the stones of the field,
And [A]the beasts of the field will
be at peace with you.
24 "You will know that your [A]tent is secure,
For you will visit your abode
and fear no loss.
25 "You will know also that your
[a,A]descendants will be many,
And [B]your offspring as the
grass of the earth.
26 "You will [A]come to the grave in full vigor,
Like the stacking of grain in its season.
27 "Behold this; we have investigated
it, *and* so it is.
Hear it, and know for yourself."

JOB'S FRIENDS ARE NO HELP

6 Then Job [a]answered,

2 "[A]Oh that my grief were actually weighed
And laid in the balances together
with my calamity!
3 "For then it would be [A]heavier
than the sand of the seas;
Therefore my words have been rash.
4 "For the [A]arrows of the Almighty
are within me,
[a]Their [B]poison my spirit drinks;
The [C]terrors of God are
arrayed against me.
5 "Does the [A]wild donkey bray over *his* grass,
Or does the ox low over his fodder?
6 "Can something tasteless be
eaten without salt,
Or is there any taste in the
[a]white of an egg?
7 "My soul [A]refuses to touch *them;*
They are like loathsome food to me.

5:21 [A]Job 5:15; Ps 31:20 [B]Ps 91:5, 6 5:22 [a]Lit *beasts of the earth* [A]Job 8:21 [B]Ps 91:13; Ezek 34:25; Hos 2:18 5:23 [A]Is 11:6-9; 65:25 5:24 [A]Job 8:6 5:25 [a]Lit *seed* [A]Ps 112:2 [B]Is 44:3, 4; 48:19 5:26 [A]Job 42:17 6:1 [a]Lit *answered and said* 6:2 [A]Job 31:6 6:3 [A]Job 23:2 6:4 [a]Lit *Whose* [A]Job 16:13; Ps 38:2 [B]Job 20:16; 21:20 [C]Job 30:15 6:5 [A]Job 39:5-8 6:6 [a]Heb *hallamuth,* meaning uncertain. Perhaps the juice of a plant 6:7 [A]Job 3:24; 33:20

relationship with God. If Job confessed, he would have prosperity, security, a family, and a rich life.

5:23 in league … at peace. Even the created order will be in harmony with the man whose relationship with God is corrected through God's disciplinary process.

6:1–7:21 Job's response to Eliphaz was recorded. On top of his physical misery and his tempting wife, he had to respond to ignorance and insensitivity from his friend, by expressing his frustration.

6:2, 3 The heaviness of his burden caused the rashness of his words.

6:4 the arrows of the Almighty … terrors of God. Here are figures of speech picturing the trials as coming from God, indicating that Job believed these were God's judgments.

6:5–7 These are all illustrations of the fact that Job complained because he had reason. Even animals expect palatable food.

JOB'S LIVING DEATH
1. Painful boils from head to toe (2:7, 13; 30:17)
2. Severe itching/irritation (2:7, 8)
3. Great grief (2:13)
4. Lost appetite (3:24; 6:6, 7)
5. Agonizing discomfort (3:24)
6. Insomnia (7:4)
7. Worm and dust infested flesh (7:5)
8. Continual oozing of boils (7:5)
9. Hallucinations (7:14)
10. Decaying skin (13:28)
11. Shriveled up (16:8; 17:7; 19:20)
12. Severe halitosis (19:17)
13. Teeth fell out (19:20)
14. Relentless pain (30:17)
15. Skin turned black (30:30)
16. Raging fever (30:30)
17. Dramatic weight loss (33:21)

8 “Oh that my request might come to pass,
And that God would grant my longing!
9 “Would that God were [A]willing to crush me,
That He would loose His
hand and cut me off!
10 “But it is still my consolation,
And I rejoice in unsparing pain,
That I [A]have not [a]denied the
words of the Holy One.
11 “What is my strength, that I should wait?
And what is my end, that I
should [a,A]endure?
12 “Is my strength the strength of stones,
Or is my flesh bronze?
13 “Is it that my [A]help is not within me,
And that [a,B]deliverance is driven from me?

14 “For the [A]despairing man *there should*
be kindness from his friend;
So that he does not [B]forsake the
[a]fear of the Almighty.
15 “My brothers have acted
[A]deceitfully like a [a]wadi,
Like the torrents of [a]wadis which vanish,
16 Which are turbid because of ice
And into which the snow [a]melts.
17 “When [A]they become waterless,
they [a]are silent,
When it is hot, they vanish
from their place.
18 “The [a]paths of their course wind along,
They go up into nothing and perish.
19 “The caravans of [A]Tema looked,
The travelers of [B]Sheba hoped for them.
20 “They [A]were [a]disappointed
for they had trusted,
They came there and were confounded.
21 “Indeed, you have now become such,
[A]You see a terror and are afraid.
22 “Have I said, ‘Give me *something,*’
Or, ‘Offer a bribe for me
from your wealth,’
23 Or, ‘Deliver me from the hand
of the adversary,’
Or, ‘Redeem me from the
hand of the tyrants’?
24 “Teach me, and [A]I will be silent;
And show me how I have erred.
25 “How painful are honest words!
But what does your argument prove?
26 “Do you intend to reprove *my* words,
When the [A]words of one in despair
belong to the wind?
27 “You would even [A]cast *lots*
for [B]the orphans
And [C]barter over your friend.
28 “Now please look at me,
And *see* if I [A]lie to your face.
29 “Desist now, let there be no injustice;
Even desist, [A]my righteousness is yet in it.
30 “Is there injustice on my tongue?
Cannot [A]my palate discern [a]calamities?

JOB’S LIFE SEEMS FUTILE

7 “[a]Is not man [A]forced to labor on earth,
And *are not* his days like the
days of [B]a hired man?
2 “As a slave who pants for the shade,
And as a hired man who eagerly
waits for his wages,
3 So am I allotted months of vanity,
And [A]nights of trouble are
appointed me.
4 “When I [A]lie down I say,
‘When shall I arise?’
But the night continues,
And I am [a]continually tossing until dawn.
5 “My [A]flesh is clothed with worms
and a crust of dirt,
My skin hardens and runs.
6 “My days are [A]swifter than a
weaver’s shuttle,
And come to an end [B]without hope.

6:9 [A]Num 11:15; 1 Kin 19:4; Job 7:16; 9:21; 10:1 6:10 [a]Lit *hidden* [A]Job 22:22; 23:11, 12 6:11 [a]Lit *prolong my soul* [A]Job 21:4 6:13 [a]So ancient versions [A]Job 26:2 [B]Job 26:3 6:14 [a]Or *reverence* [A]Job 4:5 [B]Job 1:5; 15:4 6:15 [a]Or *brooks* [A]Jer 15:18 6:16 [a]Lit *hides itself* 6:17 [a]Or *cease* [A]Job 24:19 6:18 [a]Or *caravans turn from their course, they go up into the waste and perish* 6:19 [A]Gen 25:15; Is 21:14; Jer 25:23 [B]Job 1:15 6:20 [a]Lit *ashamed* [A]Jer 14:3 6:21 [A]Ps 38:11 6:24 [A]Ps 39:1 6:26 [A]Job 8:2; 15:2; 16:3 6:27 [A]Joel 3:3; Nah 3:10 [B]Job 22:9; 24:3, 9 [C]2 Pet 2:3 6:28 [A]Job 27:4; 33:3; 36:4 6:29 [A]Job 13:18; 19:6; 23:10; 27:5, 6; 34:5; 42:1-6 6:30 [a]Or *words* [A]Job 12:11 7:1 [a]Lit *Has not man compulsory labor* [A]Job 5:7; 10:17; 14:1, 14 [B]Job 14:6 7:3 [A]Job 16:7 7:4 [a]Lit *sated with* [A]Deut 28:67; Job 7:13, 14 7:5 [A]Job 2:7; 17:14 7:6 [A]Job 9:25 [B]Job 13:15; 14:19; 17:15, 16; 19:10

6:8, 9 my request. Job’s request was that God would finish whatever process He began. Death was desirable for no other reason than it would be relief from the inevitable course of events (see chap. 3).

6:9 cut me off. This is a metaphor from a weaver, who cuts off the excess thread on the loom (cf. Is 38:12).

6:10 the words of the Holy One. Job had not been avoiding the revelation of God that he had received. The commands of the Holy One were precious to him and he had lived by them. This was confusing to him, as he couldn’t find any sinful source for his suffering. He would rejoice in his pain if he knew it would soon lead to death, but he couldn’t see any hope for death or deliverance in himself (vv. 11–13).

6:14 kindness ... So that ... forsake. Job rebuked his friends with sage words. Even if a man has forsaken God (which he hadn’t), should not his friends still show kindness to him? How can Eliphaz be so unkind as to continually indict him?

6:15–23 Job described his friends as being about as useful with their counsel as a dry riverbed in summer. “You are no help,” he said (v. 21), “although all I asked for was a little sympathy, not some great gift or deliverance” (vv. 22, 23).

6:19 Tema ... Sheba. Tema in the N, named for the son of Ishmael (Ge 25:15; Is 21:14), and Sheba in the S (Jer 6:20) were part of the Arabian desert, where water was precious.

6:24–30 Teach me ... show me how I have erred. Job was not admitting to having sinned. Rather he said to his accusers, “If I’ve sinned, show me where.” The sufferer indicted his friends for their insensitivity, and while not claiming sinlessness, he was convinced there was no sin in his life that led directly to such suffering.

7:1–21 After having directed his words at his friends in chap. 6, Job then directed them at God. Throughout this section he used words and arguments that sounded much like Solomon in Ecclesiastes, i.e., “labor, vanity, trouble, and breath.”

7:1–10 forced to labor. He felt like a slave under tyranny of his master, longing for relief and reward (vv. 1, 2); he was sleepless (vv. 3, 4); he was loathsome because of worms and scabs, dried filth, and new running sores (v. 5); he was like a weaver’s shuttle, tossed back and forth (v. 6); he was like a breath or cloud that comes and goes on its way to death (vv. 7–10). In this discourse, Job attempted to reconcile in his own mind what God was doing.

7 "Remember that my life [A]is *but* breath;
My eye will [B]not again see good.
8 "The [A]eye of him who sees me
will behold me no longer;
Your eyes *will be* on me, but [B]I will not be.
9 "When a [A]cloud vanishes, it is gone,
So [B]he who goes down to [C]Sheol
does not come up.
10 "He will not return again to his house,
Nor will [A]his place know him anymore.

11 "Therefore [A]I will not restrain my mouth;
I will speak in the anguish of my spirit,
I will complain in the
bitterness of my soul.
12 "Am I the sea, or [A]the sea monster,
That You set a guard over me?
13 "If I say, '[A]My bed will comfort me,
My couch will [a]ease my complaint,'
14 Then You frighten me with dreams
And terrify me by visions;
15 So that my soul would choose suffocation,
Death rather than my [a]pains.
16 "I [a,A]waste away; I will not live forever.
Leave me alone, [B]for my days
are *but* a breath.
17 "[A]What is man that You magnify him,
And that You [a]are concerned about him,
18 That [A]You examine him every morning
And try him every moment?
19 "[a,A]Will You never turn Your
gaze away from me,
Nor let me alone until I
swallow my spittle?
20 "[A]Have I sinned? What have I done to You,
O [B]watcher of men?
Why have You set me as Your target,
So that I am a burden to myself?
21 "Why then [A]do You not pardon
my transgression
And take away my iniquity?
For now I will [B]lie down in the dust;
And You will seek me, [C]but I will not be."

BILDAD SAYS GOD REWARDS THE GOOD

8 Then Bildad the Shuhite [a]answered,

2 "How long will you say these things,
And the [A]words of your mouth
be a mighty wind?
3 "Does [A]God pervert justice?
Or does [a]the Almighty pervert
what is right?
4 "[A]If your sons sinned against Him,
Then He delivered them into the
[a]power of their transgression.
5 "If you would [A]seek God
And implore the compassion
of [a]the Almighty,
6 If you are pure and upright,
Surely now [A]He would rouse
Himself for you
And restore your righteous [a,B]estate.
7 "Though your beginning was insignificant,
Yet your [A]end will increase greatly.

8 "Please [A]inquire of past generations,
And consider the things searched
out by their fathers.
9 "For we are *only* of yesterday
and know nothing,
Because [A]our days on earth
are as a shadow.
10 "Will they not teach you *and* tell you,
And bring forth words from their minds?

11 "Can the papyrus grow up
without a marsh?
Can the rushes grow without water?

7:7 [A]Job 7:16; Ps 78:39; James 4:14 [B]Job 9:25 7:8 [A]Job 8:18; 20:9 [B]Job 7:21 7:9 [A]Job 30:15 [B]Job 3:13-19 [C]2 Sam 12:23; Job 11:8; 14:13; 17:13, 16 7:10 [A]Job 8:18; 20:9; 27:21, 23 7:11 [A]Job 10:1; 21:4; 23:2; Ps 40:9 7:12 [A]Ezek 32:2, 3 7:13 [a]Lit *bear* [A]Job 7:4; Ps 6:6 7:15 [a]Lit *bones* 7:16 [a]Or *loathe* [A]Job 6:9; 9:21; 10:1 [B]Job 7:7 7:17 [a]Lit *set Your heart on* [A]Job 22:2; Ps 8:4; 144:3; Heb 2:6 7:18 [A]Job 14:3 7:19 [a]Lit *How long will You not* [A]Job 9:18; 10:20; 14:6 7:20 [A]Job 35:3, 6 [B]Ps 36:6 7:21 [A]Job 9:28; 10:14 [B]Job 10:9 [C]Job 7:8 8:1 [a]Lit *answered and said* 8:2 [A]Job 6:26 8:3 [a]Heb *Shaddai* [A]Gen 18:25; Deut 32:4; 2 Chr 19:7; Job 34:10, 12; 36:23; 37:23; Rom 3:5 8:4 [a]Lit *hand* [A]Job 1:5, 18, 19 8:5 [a]Heb *Shaddai* [A]Job 5:17-27 8:6 [a]Lit *place* [A]Job 22:27; 34:28; Ps 7:6 [B]Job 5:24 8:7 [A]Job 42:12 8:8 [A]Deut 4:32; 32:7; Job 15:18; 20:4 8:9 [A]Job 14:2

7:11 Therefore. On the basis of all he had said in vv. 1–10, he felt he had a right to express his complaint.

7:12 sea, or the sea monster. The sea and the whale are two threatening forces that must be watched or curbed due to their destructive force. Job was not like that.

7:13, 14 Even when he slept, he had terrifying dreams so that he longed for death (vv. 15, 16).

7:17, 18 Why is he so important, Job wonders, that God would spend all this attention on him? Why did God cause all this misery to one so insignificant as he?

7:19 until I swallow my spittle. This strange statement was an Arabic proverb, indicating a brief moment. Job was asking for a moment "to catch his breath," or in the case of the proverb, "swallow my spittle."

7:21 not pardon my transgression. Job conceded the argument of Eliphaz that he must have sinned, not because he was convinced, but because he seemed to find no other explanation (cf. 6:24).

8:1–22 The second friendly accuser, Bildad, now offered his wisdom to Job. Bildad, also absolutely certain that Job had sinned and should repent, was ruthless in the charges he raised against God's servant. See Job 18; 25 for Bildad's other speeches.

8:2–7 Bildad accused Job of defending his innocence with a lot of hot air and reasoned that Job's circumstances were God's judgment on his sins and those of his family. Again, this is logical, based on the principle that God punishes sin, but it failed to account for the mystery of the heavenly debate between God and Satan (see chaps. 1, 2). He was sure something was wrong in Job's relationship with God, thus his call for repentance, with the confidence that when Job repented he would be blessed (vv. 6, 7).

8:3 Almighty pervert what is right. Bildad took Job's claims for innocence and applied them to his simplistic notion of retribution. He concluded that Job was accusing God of injustice when God must be meting out justice to Job. Job tried to avoid outright accusations of this sort, but the evidence led Bildad to this conclusion because he had no knowledge of the heavenly facts.

8:7 In fact, this was Job's outcome (cf. 42:10–17), not because Job repented of some specific sin, but because he humbled himself before the sovereign, inscrutable will of God.

8:8–10 Here Bildad appealed to past authorities, godly ancestors who taught the same principle—that where there is suffering, there must be sin. So he had history as a witness to his misjudgment.

8:11–19 He further supported his simple logic of cause and effect by illustrations from nature. Again he accused Job of sin, but surely he had forgotten God as well (v. 13).

12 "While it is still green *and* not cut down,
Yet it withers before any *other* [a]plant.
13 "So are the paths of [A]all who forget God;
And the [B]hope of the godless will perish,
14 Whose confidence is fragile,
And whose trust a [A]spider's [a]web.
15 "He [a]trusts in his [A]house, but
it does not stand;
He holds fast to it, but it does not endure.
16 "He [a,A]thrives before the sun,
And his [B]shoots spread out over his garden.
17 "His roots wrap around a rock pile,
He [a]grasps a house of stones.
18 "If he is [a]removed from [A]his place,
Then it will deny him, *saying,*
'[B]I never saw you.'
19 "Behold, [A]this is the joy of His way;
And out of the dust others will spring.
20 "Lo, [A]God will not reject *a man of* integrity,
Nor [B]will He [a]support the evildoers.
21 "He will yet fill [A]your mouth with laughter
And your lips with shouting.
22 "Those who hate you will be
[A]clothed with shame,
And the [B]tent of the wicked
will be no longer."

JOB SAYS THERE IS NO ARBITRATOR BETWEEN GOD AND MAN

9 Then Job [a]answered,

2 "In truth I know that this is so;
But how can a [A]man be in the
right [a]before God?
3 "If one wished to [A]dispute with Him,
He could not answer Him once
in a thousand *times.*
4 "[A]Wise in heart and [B]mighty in strength,
Who has [a,C]defied Him [b]without harm?
5 "[A]*It is God* who removes the
mountains, they know not *how,*
When He overturns them in His anger;
6 Who [A]shakes the earth out of its place,
And its [B]pillars tremble;
7 Who commands the [A]sun [a]not to shine,
And sets a seal upon the stars;
8 Who alone [A]stretches out the heavens
And [a,B]tramples down the waves of the sea;
9 Who makes the [A]Bear, Orion
and the Pleiades,
And the [B]chambers of the south;
10 Who [A]does great things, [a]unfathomable,
And wondrous works without number.
11 "Were He to pass by me, [A]I
would not see Him;
Were He to move past *me,* I
would not perceive Him.
12 "Were He to snatch away, who
could [A]restrain Him?
Who could say to Him, '[B]What
are You doing?'

13 "God will not turn back His anger;
Beneath Him crouch the
helpers of [A]Rahab.
14 "How then can [A]I [a]answer Him,
And choose my words [b]before Him?
15 "For [A]though I were right, I
could not [a]answer;
I would have to [B]implore the
mercy of my judge.
16 "If I called and He answered me,
I could not believe that He was
listening to my voice.
17 "For He [A]bruises me with a tempest
And multiplies my wounds without cause.
18 "He will [A]not allow me to get my breath,
But saturates me with [B]bitterness.
19 "If *it is a matter* of power, [A]behold,
He is the strong one!
And if *it is a matter* of justice,
who can summon [a]Him?

8:12 [a]Lit *reed* 8:13 [A]Ps 9:17 [B]Job 11:20; 13:16; 15:34; 20:5; 27:8 8:14 [a]Lit *house* [A]Is 59:5, 6 8:15 [a]Lit *leans on* [A]Job 8:22; 27:18; Ps 49:11 8:16 [a]Lit *is lush* [A]Ps 37:35; Jer 11:16 [B]Ps 80:11 8:17 [a]Heb *sees* 8:18 [a]Lit *swallowed up* [A]Job 7:10 [B]Job 7:8 8:19 [A]Job 20:5 8:20 [a]Lit *strengthen the hand of* [A]Job 4:7 [B]Job 21:30 8:21 [A]Job 5:22; Ps 126:1, 2 8:22 [A]Ps 132:18 [B]Job 8:15; 15:34; 18:14; 21:28 9:1 [a]Lit *answered and said* 9:2 [a]Lit *with* [A]Job 4:17; 25:4 9:3 [A]Job 10:2; 13:19; 23:6; 40:2 9:4 [a]Lit *stiffened his neck against* [b]Lit *and remained safe* [A]Job 11:6; 12:13; 28:23; 38:36, 37 [B]Job 9:19; 23:6 [C]2 Chr 13:12; Prov 29:1 9:5 [A]Job 9:5-10; 26:6-14; 41:11 9:6 [A]Is 2:19, 21; 13:13; Hag 2:6 [B]Ps 75:3 9:7 [a]Lit *and it does not shine* [A]Is 13:10; Ezek 32:7, 8 9:8 [a]Lit *treads upon the heights of* [A]Gen 1:1; Job 37:18; Ps 104:2; Is 40:22 [B]Job 38:16; Ps 77:19 9:9 [A]Job 38:31, 32; Amos 5:8 [B]Job 37:9 9:10 [a]Lit *until there is no searching out* [A]Job 5:9 9:11 [A]Job 23:8, 9; 35:14 9:12 [A]Job 10:7; 11:10 [B]Is 45:9 9:13 [A]Job 26:12; Ps 89:10; Is 30:7; 51:9 9:14 [a]Or *plead my case* [b]Lit *with* [A]Job 9:3, 32 9:15 [a]Or *plead my case* [A]Job 9:20, 21; 10:15 [B]Job 8:5 9:17 [A]Job 16:12, 14; 30:22 9:18 [A]Job 7:19; 10:20 [B]Job 13:26; 27:2 9:19 [a]So with Gr; Heb *me* [A]Job 9:4

8:20 God will not reject *a man of* integrity. This comment contains a veiled offer of hope. Job could laugh again, but he must take steps to become blameless. But Bildad, like Job, was unaware of the dialogue between the Sovereign Judge and the Accuser in the opening chapters of the book and unaware that God had already pronounced Job "blameless" twice to heavenly beings (1:8; 2:3), as had the writer (1:1). Cf. Pss 1:6; 126:2; 132:18.

9:1–10:22 Job, in a mood of deep despair, responded to Bildad's accusations with arguments surrounding God's nature, also raised by Bildad, and started to rationalize something about which he would later admit he knew dangerously little. Job concluded that God is holy, wise, and strong (vv. 4–10); but he wondered if He is fair (v. 22) and why He wouldn't make Himself known to him. Before the mighty God, Job felt only despair. If God is not fair, all is hopeless, he thought.

9:3 dispute with Him. Job referred to disputing one's innocence or guilt before God as a useless endeavor. Psalm 130:3 illustrates the point, "If You … should mark iniquities [keep records of sin], … who could stand [innocently in judgment]?"

9:6 pillars tremble. In the figurative language of the day, this phrase described the supporting power that secured the position of the earth in the universe.

9:9 Bear, Orion … Pleiades. Three stellar constellations (cf. Job 38:31, 32). **the chambers of the south.** These were other constellations in the southern hemisphere, unseen by those who could see and name the 3 in the northern skies.

9:13 the helpers of Rahab. This is symbolic of the ancient mythological sea monster (cf. 3:8; 7:12). God smiting the proud was a poetic way of saying that if the mythical monster of the sea (a metaphor for powerful, evil, chaotic forces) could not stand before God's anger, how could Job hope to? In a battle in God's court, he would lose. God is too strong (vv. 14–19).

9:15, 20 though I were right. He means here, not sinless, but having spiritual integrity, i.e., a pure heart to love, serve, and obey God. He was affirming again that his suffering was not due to sins he was not willing to confess. Even at that, God found something to condemn him for, he felt, making it hopeless, then, to contend with God.

20 "[A]Though I am righteous, my
mouth will [B]condemn me;
Though I am guiltless, He
will declare me guilty.
21 "I am [A]guiltless;
I do not take notice of myself;
I [B]despise my life.
22 "It is *all* one; therefore I say,
'He [A]destroys the guiltless and the wicked.'
23 "If the scourge kills suddenly,
He [A]mocks the despair of the innocent.
24 "The earth [A]is given into the
hand of the wicked;
He [B]covers the faces of its judges.
If *it is* not *He,* then who is it?

25 "Now [A]my days are swifter than a runner;
They flee away, [B]they see no good.
26 "They slip by like [A]reed boats,
Like an [B]eagle that swoops on [a]its prey.
27 "Though I say, 'I will forget [A]my complaint,
I will leave off my *sad* countenance
and be cheerful,'
28 I am [A]afraid of all my pains,
I know that [B]You will not acquit me.
29 "I am accounted [A]wicked,
Why then should I toil in vain?
30 "If I should [A]wash myself with snow
And cleanse [B]my hands with lye,
31 Yet You would plunge me into the pit,
And my own clothes would abhor me.
32 "For [A]*He is* not a man as I am
that [B]I may answer Him,
That we may go to [a]court together.
33 "There is no [A]umpire between us,
Who may lay his hand upon us both.
34 "Let Him [A]remove His rod from me,
And let not dread of Him terrify me.
35 "*Then* I [A]would speak and not fear Him;
But I am not like that in myself.

JOB DESPAIRS OF GOD'S DEALINGS

10 "[a,A]I loathe my own life;
I will give full vent to [B]my complaint;
I will speak in the bitterness of my soul.
2 "I will say to God, '[A]Do not condemn me;
Let me know why You contend with me.
3 'Is it [a]right for You indeed to [A]oppress,
To reject [B]the labor of Your hands,
And [b]to look favorably on [C]the
schemes of the wicked?
4 'Have You eyes of flesh?
Or do You [A]see as a man sees?
5 'Are Your days as the days of a mortal,
Or [A]Your years as man's years,
6 That [A]You should seek for my guilt
And search after my sin?
7 'According to Your knowledge
[A]I am indeed not guilty,
Yet there is [B]no deliverance
from Your hand.

8 '[A]Your hands fashioned and
made me [a]altogether,
[B]And would You destroy me?
9 'Remember now, that You have
made me as [A]clay;
And would You [B]turn me into dust again?
10 'Did You not pour me out like milk
And curdle me like cheese;
11 Clothe me with skin and flesh,
And knit me together with
bones and sinews?
12 'You have [A]granted me life
and lovingkindness;
And Your care has preserved my spirit.
13 'Yet [A]these things You have
concealed in Your heart;
I know that this is within You:
14 If I sin, then You would [A]take note of me,
And [B]would not acquit me of my guilt.

9:20 [A]Job 9:15 [B]Job 9:29; 15:6 9:21 [A]Job 1:1; 12:4; 13:18 [B]Job 7:16 9:22 [A]Job 10:7, 8 9:23 [A]Job 24:12 9:24 [A]Job 10:3; 12:6; 16:11 [B]Job 12:17 9:25 [A]Job 7:6 [B]Job 7:7 9:26 [a]Lit *food* [A]Is 18:2 [B]Job 39:29; Hab 1:8 9:27 [A]Job 7:11 9:28 [A]Job 3:25 [B]Job 7:21; 10:14 9:29 [A]Job 10:2; Ps 37:33 9:30 [A]Jer 2:22 [B]Job 31:7 9:32 [a]Lit *judgment* [A]Eccl 6:10 [B]Job 9:3; Rom 9:20 9:33 [A]1 Sam 2:25; Job 9:19; Is 1:18 9:34 [A]Job 13:21 9:35 [A]Job 13:22 10:1 [a]Lit *My soul loathes* [A]Job 7:16 [B]Job 7:11 10:2 [A]Job 9:29 10:3 [a]Lit *good* [b]Lit *You shine forth* [A]Job 9:22-24; 16:11; 19:6; 27:2 [B]Job 10:8; 14:15; Ps 138:8; Is 64:8 [C]Job 21:16; 22:18 10:4 [A]1 Sam 16:7; Job 28:24; 34:21 10:5 [A]Job 36:26 10:6 [A]Job 14:16 10:7 [A]Job 9:21; 13:18 [B]Job 9:12; 23:13; 27:22 10:8 [a]Lit *together round about* [A]Job 10:3; Ps 119:73 [B]Job 9:22 10:9 [A]Job 4:19; 33:6 [B]Job 7:21 10:12 [A]Job 33:4 10:13 [A]Job 23:13 10:14 [A]Job 7:20 [B]Job 7:21; 9:28

9:24 covers the faces of its judges. Job here indicted God for the inequities of His world. He accused God of treating all the same way, unfairly (vv. 21–23), and of even covering the eyes of earthly judges so that they would not see injustice. These are the charges that bring about God's rebuke of Job (chaps. 38–41) and for which he eventually repented (42:1–6).

9:25, 26 Couriers running with messages, ships cutting swiftly, and eagles swooping rapidly convey the blur of painful, meaningless days of despair that move by.

9:27, 28 Job said if he promised to change to a happy mood, he would break that promise and God would add that to His list of accusations.

9:29, 30 "God seems to have found me guilty," Job concluded, "so why struggle? Even if I make every effort to clean every aspect of my life, You will still punish me." This was deep despair and hopelessness.

9:32 That we may go to court together. Job acknowledged that, as a mere man, he had no right to call on God to declare his innocence or to contend with God over his innocence. Job was not arguing that he was sinless, but he didn't believe he had sinned to the extent that he deserved his severe suffering. Job held on to the same simplistic system of retribution as that of his accusers, which said that suffering was always caused by sin. And he knew he was not sinless, but he couldn't identify any unconfessed or unrepented sins. "Where is mercy?" he wondered.

9:33–35 no umpire between us. A court official who sees both sides clearly, as well as the source of disagreement, so as to bring resolution was not found. Where was an advocate, an arbitrator, an umpire, or a referee? Was there no one to remove God's rod and call for justice?

10:2 condemn me. Not the condemnation of Job's soul, but Job's physical suffering as a punishment. He held nothing back in his misery (v. 1), but asked God to show him why all this had happened.

10:3 the labor of Your hands. This is a biblical expression identifying what someone produces, in this case man, as created by God (cf. 14:15; Ps 102:25; Heb 1:10).

10:4–7 see as a man sees. Because he believed he was innocent, Job facetiously, somewhat sarcastically, asked if God was as limited in His ability to discern Job's spiritual condition as were Job's friends. He concluded by affirming that God did know he was innocent and that there was no higher court of appeal (v. 7).

10:8–12 Again he returned to the question "Why was I born?" The answer that God had created him is given in magnificent language, indicating that life begins at conception.

10:13–16 Job wondered if God had planned in His divine purpose not to be merciful to him.

15 'If [A]I am wicked, woe to me!
And [B]if I am righteous, I dare
not lift up my head.
I am sated with disgrace and
[a]conscious of my misery.
16 'Should *my head* be lifted up, [A]You
would hunt me like a lion;
And again You would show
Your [B]power against me.
17 'You renew [A]Your witnesses against me
And increase Your anger toward me;
[a,B]Hardship after hardship is with me.

18 '[A]Why then have You brought
me out of the womb?
Would that I had died and
no eye had seen me!
19 'I should have been as though
I had not been,
Carried from womb to tomb.'
20 "Would He not let [A]my few days alone?
[a,B]Withdraw from me that I may
have a little cheer
21 Before I go—[A]and I shall not return—
[B]To the land of darkness
and [C]deep shadow,
22 The land of utter gloom as darkness *itself,*
Of deep shadow without order,
And which shines as the darkness."

ZOPHAR REBUKES JOB

11 Then Zophar the Naamathite [a]answered,

2 "Shall a multitude of words
go unanswered,
And a [A]talkative man be acquitted?
3 "Shall your boasts silence men?
And shall you [A]scoff and none rebuke?
4 "For [A]you have said, 'My teaching is pure,
And [B]I am innocent in your eyes.'
5 "But would that God might speak,
And open His lips against you,
6 And show you the secrets of wisdom!
For sound wisdom [a,A]has two sides.
Know then that God [b]forgets a
part of [B]your iniquity.

7 "[A]Can you discover the depths of God?
Can you discover the limits
of the Almighty?
8 "*They are* [A]high as [a]the heavens,
what can you do?
Deeper than [b,B]Sheol, what
can you know?
9 "Its measure is longer than the earth
And broader than the sea.
10 "If He passes by or shuts up,
Or calls an assembly, [A]who
can restrain Him?
11 "For [A]He knows false men,
And He [B]sees iniquity [a]without
investigating.
12 "[a,A]An idiot will become intelligent
When the [b]foal of a [B]wild
donkey is born a man.

13 "[A]If you would [B]direct your heart right
And [C]spread out your hand to Him,
14 If iniquity is in your hand,
[A]put it far away,
And do not let wickedness
dwell in your tents;

10:15 [a]Lit *see* [A]Job 10:7; Is 3:11 [B]Job 6:29 10:16 [A]Is 38:13; Lam 3:10; Hos 13:7 [B]Job 5:9 10:17 [a]Lit *Changes and warfare are with me* [A]Ruth 1:21; Job 16:8 [B]Job 7:1 10:18 [A]Job 3:11-13 10:20 [a]Lit *Put* [A]Job 14:1 [B]Job 7:16, 19 10:21 [A]2 Sam 12:23; Job 3:13-19; 16:22 [B]Ps 88:12 [C]Job 10:22; 34:22; 38:17; Ps 23:4 11:1 [a]Lit *answered and said* 11:2 [A]Job 8:2; 15:2; 18:2 11:3 [A]Job 17:2; 21:3 11:4 [A]Job 6:10 [B]Job 10:7 11:6 [a]Lit *is double* [b]Lit *causes to be forgotten for you* [A]Job 9:4 [B]Job 15:5; 22:5 11:7 [A]Job 33:12, 13; 36:26; 37:5, 23; Rom 11:33 11:8 [a]Lit *the heights of heaven* [b]I.e. the nether world [A]Job 22:12; 35:5 [B]Job 26:6; 38:17 11:10 [A]Job 9:12 11:11 [a]Or *even He does not consider* [A]Job 34:21-23 [B]Job 24:23; 28:24; 31:4 11:12 [a]Lit *A hollow man* [b]Lit *donkey* [A]Ps 39:5, 11; 62:9; 144:4; Eccl 1:2; 11:10 [B]Job 39:5 11:13 [A]Job 5:17-27; 11:13-20 [B]1 Sam 7:3; Ps 78:8 [C]Job 22:27; Ps 88:9; 143:6 11:14 [A]Job 22:23

10:17 renew Your witnesses. Job said God seemed to be sending people to accuse him. With each witness came another wave of condemnation and increased suffering.

10:18 brought me out of the womb? Job returned to the question of why God allowed him to be born. This time he was not just lamenting the day of his birth, but he was asking God for the reason He allowed it to occur.

10:20–22 "Since I was destined to these ills from my birth, at least give me a little breathing room during the brief days left to me, before I die," he said. Death was gloomily described as "darkness."

11:1–20 Zophar the Naamathite now stepped in to interrogate Job. He was quite close to his friends and chose to pound Job with the same law of retaliation. Job must repent, he said, not understanding the reality. He was indignant at Job's protests of innocence. See Job 20 for Zophar's other speech.

11:2, 3 a talkative man be acquitted? The allegations against Job moved to a new level. Not only was Job guilty and unrepentant, he was also an empty talker. In fact, Job's long-winded defense of his innocence and God's apparent injustice were sin worthy of rebuke, in Zophar's mind.

11:4 innocent in your eyes. Job never claimed sinlessness; in fact, he acknowledged that he had sinned (Job 7:21; 13:26). But he still maintained his innocence of any great transgression or attitude of unrepentance, affirming his sincerity and integrity as a man of faith and obedience to God. This claim infuriated Zophar, and he wished God Himself would confirm the accusations of Job's friends (v. 5).

11:6 secrets of wisdom. Job would have been much wiser if he had only known the unknowable secrets of God; in this case the scene in heaven between God and Satan would have clarified everything. But Job couldn't know the secret wisdom of God (vv. 7–9). Zophar should have applied his point to himself. If God's wisdom was so deep, high, long, and broad, how was it that he could understand it and have all the answers? Like his friends, Zophar thought he understood God and reverted to the same law of retaliation, the sowing and reaping principle, to again indict Job. He implied that Job was wicked (vv. 10, 11) and thought he was wise, though actually he was out of control as if he were a "wild donkey" man (v. 12).

11:13, 14 Zophar set out 4 steps of Job's repentance: 1) devote your heart to God; 2) stretch your hands to Him in prayer for forgiveness; 3) put your sin far away; and 4) don't allow any sin in your tent. If Job did these things, he would be blessed (vv. 15–19). If Job didn't repent, he would die (v. 20). Zophar was right that the life of faith in God is based on penitence and obedience. He was right that God blesses His people with hope, security, and peace. But, like his friends, he was wrong in not understanding that God allows unpredictable and seemingly unfair suffering for reasons not known to us. He was wrong in presuming that the answer for Job was repentance.

11:13–20 Zophar started out this section speaking directly to Job, "If you would …." and concluded speaking proverbially, "But the eyes of the wicked …." In so doing Zophar avoided directly calling Job wicked, but succeeded with even greater force by being indirect. In the end, he told Job that his sin would bring about his death.

15 Then, indeed, you could [A]lift up your
face without *moral* defect,
And you would be steadfast
and [B]not fear.
16 "For you would [A]forget *your* trouble,
As [B]waters that have passed by,
you would remember *it.*
17 "Your [a]life would be [b,A]brighter
than noonday;
Darkness would be like the morning.
18 "Then you would trust, because
there is hope;
And you would look around
and rest securely.
19 "You would [A]lie down and none
would disturb *you,*
And many would [B]entreat your [a]favor.
20 "But the [A]eyes of the wicked will fail,
And [a]there will [B]be no
escape for them;
And their [C]hope is [b,D]to
breathe their last."

JOB CHIDES HIS ACCUSERS

12 Then Job [a]responded,

2 "Truly then [A]you are the people,
And with you wisdom will die!
3 "But [A]I have intelligence as well as you;
I am not inferior to you.
And [a]who does not know
such things as these?
4 "I am a [A]joke to [a]my friends,
The one who called on God
and He answered him;
The just *and* [B]blameless *man* is a joke.
5 "[a]He who is at ease holds
calamity in contempt,
As prepared for those whose feet slip.
6 "The [A]tents of the destroyers prosper,
And those who provoke
God [B]are secure,
[a]Whom God brings [C]into their power.
7 "But now ask the beasts, and
let them teach you;
And the birds of the heavens,
and let them tell you.
8 "Or speak to the earth, and let it teach you;
And let the fish of the sea declare to you.
9 "Who among all these does not know
That [A]the hand of the LORD has done this,
10 [A]In whose hand is the life of
every living thing,
And [B]the breath of all mankind?
11 "Does not [A]the ear test words,
As the palate [a]tastes its food?
12 "Wisdom is with [A]aged men,
With [a]long life is understanding.

JOB SPEAKS OF THE POWER OF GOD

13 "With Him are [A]wisdom and [A]might;
To Him belong counsel and
[B]understanding.
14 "Behold, He [A]tears down, and
it cannot be rebuilt;
He [a,B]imprisons a man, and
[b]there can be no release.
15 "Behold, He [A]restrains the
waters, and they dry up;
And He [B]sends them out, and
they [a]inundate the earth.
16 "With Him are strength and
sound wisdom,
The [A]misled and the misleader
belong to Him.
17 "He makes [A]counselors walk [a]barefoot
And makes fools of [B]judges.
18 "He [A]loosens the [a]bond of kings
And binds their loins with a girdle.
19 "He makes priests walk [a]barefoot
And overthrows [A]the secure ones.
20 "He deprives the trusted ones of speech
And [A]takes away the discernment
of the elders.
21 "He [A]pours contempt on nobles
And [B]loosens the belt of the strong.

11:15 [A]Job 22:26 [B]Ps 27:3; 46:2 11:16 [A]Is 65:16 [B]Job 22:11 11:17 [a]Lit *duration of life* [b]Lit *above noonday* [A]Job 22:26 11:19 [a]Lit *face* [A]Lev 26:6; Is 17:2; Mic 4:4; Zeph 3:13 [B]Is 45:14 11:20 [a]Lit *escape has perished from them* [b]Lit *the expiring of the soul* [A]Deut 28:65; Job 17:5 [B]Job 27:22; 34:22 [C]Job 8:13 [D]Job 6:9 12:1 [a]Lit *answered and said* 12:2 [A]Job 17:10 12:3 [a]Lit *with whom is there not like these?* [A]Job 13:2 12:4 [a]Lit *his* [A]Job 17:6; 30:1, 9, 10; 34:7 [B]Job 6:29 12:5 [a]Lit *Contempt for calamity is the thought of him who is at ease* 12:6 [a]Or *He who brings God into his hand* [A]Job 9:24; 21:7-9 [B]Job 24:23 [C]Job 22:18 12:9 [A]Is 41:20 12:10 [A]Acts 17:28 [B]Job 27:3; 33:4 12:11 [a]Lit *tastes food for itself* [A]Job 34:3 12:12 [a]Lit *length of days* [A]Job 15:10; 32:7 12:13 [A]Job 9:4 [B]Job 11:6; 26:12; 32:8; 36:5; 38:36 12:14 [a]Lit *shuts against* [b]Lit *it is not opened* [A]Job 19:10; Is 25:2 [B]Job 37:7 12:15 [a]Lit *overturn* [A]Deut 11:17; 1 Kin 8:35; 17:1 [B]Gen 7:11-24 12:16 [A]Job 13:7, 9 12:17 [a]Or *stripped* [A]Job 3:14 [B]Job 9:24 12:18 [a]Or *discipline* [A]Ps 116:16 12:19 [a]Or *stripped* [A]Job 24:22; 34:24-28; 35:9 12:20 [A]Job 17:4; 32:9 12:21 [A]Job 34:19; Ps 107:40 [B]Job 12:18

12:1–14:22 Job responded in his defense with strong words, completing the first cycle of speeches.

12:2–4 **you are the people ... with you wisdom will die!** Job responded with cutting sarcasm directed at his know-it-all friends (v. 2) and then reminded them that he understood the principles of which they had spoken (v. 3), but they were irrelevant to his situation. On top of that, he despaired at the pain of becoming a derision to his friends, though he was innocent (v. 4).

12:4 **The just *and* blameless.** If this sounds like presumption, one only needs to recall that this was God's pronouncement on Job (1:8; 2:3).

12:5 **holds calamity in contempt.** When all was at ease with Job's friends, they didn't need him, and even mocked him.

12:6 **God brings.** Job refuted the simplistic idea that the righteous always prosper and the wicked always suffer, by reminding them that God allows thieves and sinners to be prosperous and secure. So, why not believe He may also allow the righteous to suffer?

12:7–10 All these elements (animals, birds, earth, and fish) of creation are called as illustrations that the violent prosper and live securely (v. 6). God made it so that the more vicious survive.

12:12 **Wisdom is with aged men.** The questioning force of the preceding verse may carry over to make this a question also. "Shouldn't aged men be wise?" If this is true, then v. 12 is stinging sarcasm against Job's aged friends who gave unwise advice (cf. 15:10), and heard and spoke only what suited them (v. 11).

12:13–13:3 This section gives vivid definition to the wisdom, power, and sovereignty of God (v. 13). Job, despite his questions about his suffering, affirms that God's power is visible in nature, human society, religious matters, and national and international affairs. Job, however, expressed this in terms of fatalistic despair. Job knew all this and it didn't help (13:1, 2); so he didn't want to argue with them anymore—he wanted to take his case before God (v. 3).

22 "He [A]reveals mysteries from the darkness
And brings the deep darkness into light.
23 "He [A]makes the nations great,
then destroys them;
He [a]enlarges the nations, then
leads them away.
24 "He [A]deprives of intelligence the
chiefs of the earth's people
And makes them wander in
a pathless waste.
25 "They [A]grope in darkness with no light,
And He makes them [B]stagger
like a drunken man.

JOB SAYS HIS FRIENDS' PROVERBS ARE ASHES

13 "[A]Behold, my eye has seen all *this*,
My ear has heard and understood it.
2 "[A]What you know I also know;
I am not inferior to you.

3 "But [A]I would speak to [a]the Almighty,
And I desire to [B]argue with God.
4 "But you [A]smear with lies;
You are all [B]worthless physicians.
5 "O that you would [A]be completely silent,
And that it would become
your wisdom!
6 "Please hear my argument
And listen to the contentions
of my lips.
7 "Will you [A]speak what is unjust for God,
And speak what is deceitful for Him?
8 "Will you [A]show partiality for Him?
Will you contend for God?
9 "Will it be well when He examines you?
Or [A]will you deceive Him as
one deceives a man?
10 "He will surely reprove you
If you secretly [A]show partiality.
11 "Will not [A]His [a]majesty terrify you,
And the dread of Him fall on you?
12 "Your memorable sayings are
proverbs of ashes,
Your defenses are defenses of clay.

JOB IS SURE HE WILL BE VINDICATED

13 "[A]Be silent before me so that I may speak;
Then let come on me what may.
14 "Why should I take my flesh in my teeth
And [A]put my life in my [a]hands?
15 "[A]Though He slay me,
I will hope in Him.
Nevertheless I [B]will argue my
ways [a]before Him.
16 "This also will be my [A]salvation,
For [B]a godless man may not
come before His presence.
17 "Listen carefully to my speech,
And let my declaration *fill* your ears.
18 "Behold now, I have [A]prepared my case;
I know that [B]I will be vindicated.
19 "[A]Who will contend with me?
For then I would be silent and [B]die.

20 "Only two things do not do to me,
Then I will not hide from Your face:
21 [A]Remove Your [a]hand from me,
And let not the dread of You terrify me.
22 "Then call, and [A]I will answer;
Or let me speak, then reply to me.
23 "[A]How many are my iniquities and sins?
Make known to me my
[a]rebellion and my sin.
24 "Why do You [A]hide Your face
And consider me [B]Your enemy?
25 "Will You cause a [A]driven leaf to tremble?
Or will You pursue the dry [B]chaff?
26 "For You write [A]bitter things against me
And [B]make me to inherit the
iniquities of my youth.
27 "You [A]put my feet in the stocks
And watch all my paths;
You [a]set a limit for the soles of my feet,

12:22 [A]Dan 2:22; 1 Cor 4:5 12:23 [a]Or *spreads out* [A]Is 9:3; 26:15 12:24 [A]Job 12:20 12:25 [A]Job 5:14 [B]Is 24:20 13:1 [A]Job 12:9 13:2 [A]Job 12:3 13:3 [a]Heb *Shaddai* [A]Job 13:22; 23:4 [B]Job 13:15 13:4 [A]Ps 119:69 [B]Jer 23:32 13:5 [A]Job 13:13; 21:5; Prov 17:28 13:7 [A]Job 27:4 13:8 [A]Lev 19:15; Prov 24:23 13:9 [A]Job 12:16 13:10 [A]Job 13:8; 32:21; 34:19 13:11 [a]Lit *exaltation* [A]Job 31:23 13:13 [A]Job 13:5 13:14 [a]Lit *palm* [A]Ps 119:109 13:15 [a]Lit *to His face* [A]Job 7:6 [B]Job 27:5 13:16 [A]Job 23:7; Is 12:1, 2 [B]Job 34:21-23 13:18 [A]Job 23:4 [B]Job 9:21; 10:7; 12:4 13:19 [A]Is 50:8 [B]Job 7:21; 10:8 13:21 [a]Lit *palm* [A]Job 9:34; Ps 39:10 13:22 [A]Job 9:16; 14:15 13:23 [a]Or *transgression* [A]Job 7:21 13:24 [A]Ps 13:1; 44:24; 88:14; Is 8:17 [B]Job 19:11; 33:10; Lam 2:5 13:25 [A]Lev 26:36 [B]Job 21:18 13:26 [A]Job 9:18 [B]Ps 25:7 13:27 [a]Lit *carve for* [A]Job 33:11

13:4–19 Job addressed his ineffective counselors.

13:4, 5 Job couldn't hold back from a blistering denunciation of his useless counselors, telling them that their silence would be true wisdom (cf. v. 13).

13:7 unjust for God ... deceitful for Him. He accused them of using lies and fallacies to vindicate God, when they asserted that Job was a sinner because he was a sufferer.

13:8 Will you contend for God? "Are you wise enough to argue in God's defense?" he asked. To think that is very brash and really mocks God by misrepresenting Him (v. 9) and should lead to fear of chastening (vv. 10, 11).

13:12 ashes ... clay. Ineffective and worthless.

13:14 A proverb meaning "Why should I anxiously desire to save my life?" Like an animal who holds its prey in its mouth to preserve it or a man who holds in his hand what he wants to secure, Job could try to preserve his life, but that was not his motive.

13:15 Though He slay me, I will hope in Him. Job assured his accusers that his convictions were not self-serving, because he was ready to die trusting God. But still he would defend his innocence before God, and was confident that he was truly saved and not a hypocrite (v. 16).

13:17–19 declaration ... case ... vindicated ... contend. The language of a courtroom came out strongly. Job could not just be silent and die (v. 19). He finished strongly before turning to God in prayer (13:20–14:22).

13:20–14:22 Job turned to reason with God (v. 3) and pleaded his case.

13:20–22 Job asked God to end his pain and stop frightening him with such terrors (cf. v. 24), then speak to him. He was concerned with his misery, but even more with his relation to the God he loved and worshiped.

13:23 How many are my iniquities and sins? Job wanted to know how many so that he could determine if his measure of suffering matched the severity of his sin, and he could then repent for sins he was unaware of.

13:26 write bitter things against me. This is a judicial phrase referencing the writing down of a sentence against a criminal, used figuratively for the extreme suffering as if it were a divine sentence as just punishment for extreme sin. Job felt God might be punishing him for sins committed years earlier in his youth.

13:27 watch all my paths. In another context these words would speak of protec-

28 While [a]I am decaying like a [A]rotten thing,
Like a garment that is moth-eaten.

JOB SPEAKS OF THE FINALITY OF DEATH

14 "[A]Man, who is born of woman,
Is [a]short-lived and [B]full of turmoil.
2 "[A]Like a flower he comes forth and withers.
He also flees like [B]a shadow
and does not remain.
3 "You also [A]open Your eyes on him
And [B]bring [a]him into judgment
with Yourself.
4 "[A]Who can make the clean out of the unclean?
No one!
5 "Since his days are determined,
The [A]number of his months is with You;
And his limits You have [a]set
so that he cannot pass.
6 "[A]Turn Your gaze from him that he may [a]rest,
Until he [b]fulfills his day like a hired man.

7 "For there is hope for a tree,
When it is cut down, that it
will sprout again,
And its shoots will not [a]fail.
8 "Though its roots grow old in the ground
And its stump dies in the dry soil,
9 At the scent of water it will flourish
And put forth sprigs like a plant.
10 "But [A]man dies and lies prostrate.
Man [B]expires, and where is he?
11 "*As* [A]water [a]evaporates from the sea,
And a river becomes parched and dried up,
12 So [A]man lies down and does not rise.
Until the heavens are no longer,
[a]He will not awake nor be
aroused out of [b]his sleep.

13 "Oh that You would hide me in [a]Sheol,
That You would conceal me [A]until
Your wrath returns *to You,*
That You would set a limit for
me and remember me!
14 "If a man dies, will he live *again?*
All the days of my struggle I will wait
Until my change comes.
15 "You will call, and I will answer You;
You will long for [A]the work of Your hands.
16 "For now You [A]number my steps,
You do not [B]observe my sin.
17 "My transgression is [A]sealed up in a bag,
And You [a]wrap up my iniquity.

18 "But the falling mountain [a]crumbles away,
And the rock moves from its place;
19 Water wears away stones,
Its torrents wash away the
dust of the earth;
So You [A]destroy man's hope.
20 "You forever overpower him
and he [A]departs;
You change his appearance
and send him away.
21 "His sons achieve honor, but
[A]he does not know *it;*
Or they become insignificant, but
he does not perceive it.
22 "But his [a]body pains him,
And he mourns only for himself."

ELIPHAZ SAYS JOB PRESUMES MUCH

15 Then Eliphaz the Temanite [a]responded,

2 "Should a wise man answer
with windy knowledge
[A]And fill [a]himself with the east wind?
3 "Should he argue with useless talk,
Or with words which are not profitable?
4 "Indeed, you do away with [a]reverence
And hinder meditation before God.
5 "For [A]your guilt teaches your mouth,
And you choose the language of [B]the crafty.
6 "Your [A]own mouth condemns you, and not I;
And your own lips testify against you.

7 "Were you the first man to be born,
Or [A]were you brought forth before the hills?

13:28 [a]Lit *he is* [A]Job 2:7 14:1 [a]Lit *short of days* [A]Job 5:7 [B]Eccl 2:23 14:2 [A]Ps 90:5, 6; 103:15; Is 40:6, 7; James 1:10; 1 Pet 1:24 [B]Job 8:9 14:3 [a]So with some ancient versions; M.T. *me* [A]Ps 8:4; 144:3 [B]Ps 143:2 14:4 [A]Job 15:14; 25:4; Ps 51:5 14:5 [a]Lit *made* [A]Job 21:21 14:6 [a]Lit *cease* [b]Lit *makes acceptable* [A]Job 7:19; Ps 39:13 14:7 [a]Or *cease* 14:10 [A]Job 3:13; 14:10-15 [B]Job 13:9 14:11 [a]Lit *disappears* [A]Is 19:5 14:12 [a]Lit *They* [b]Lit *their* [A]Job 3:13 14:13 [a]I.e. the nether world [A]Is 26:20 14:15 [A]Job 10:3 14:16 [A]Job 31:4; 34:21; Ps 139:1-3; Prov 5:21 [B]Job 10:6 14:17 [a]Lit *plaster;* or *glue together* [A]Deut 32:32-34 14:18 [a]Lit *withers* 14:19 [A]Job 7:6 14:20 [A]Job 4:20; 20:7 14:21 [A]Eccl 9:5 14:22 [a]Lit *flesh* 15:1 [a]Lit *answered and said* 15:2 [a]Lit *his belly* [A]Job 6:26 15:4 [a]Lit *fear* 15:5 [A]Job 22:5 [B]Job 5:12, 13 15:6 [A]Job 18:7 15:7 [A]Job 38:4, 21; Prov 8:25

tion, but here, Job questioned whether or not God had held him on too tight a leash. The comment amounts to saying that God is being overly rigorous toward Job's sin, as compared to others.

13:28 This general comment on the plight of man should not be separated from 14:1ff., which it introduces.

14:1–12 Job embraced the fact of God's control over the issues of this life, but challenged their meaning. Life is short (vv. 1, 2), all are sinners (v. 4), and days are limited (v. 5), then comes death (vv. 7–12). In light of this, Job asked God for a little grace instead of such intense judgment (v. 3), and a little rest from all the pain (v. 6), and suggested that a tree has more hope than he did (v. 7).

14:13–17 Job asked to die and remain in the grave until God's anger was over, then be raised to life again when God called him back (vv. 13–15). If he were dead, God wouldn't be watching every step, counting every sin (v. 16); it would all be hidden (v. 17). Here was the hope of resurrection for those who trusted God. Job had hope that if he died, he would live again (v. 14).

14:18–22 Job returned to his complaint before God, and reverted to a hopeless mood, speaking about death as inevitable (vv. 18–20) and causing separation (v. 21). He was painfully sad to think of it (v. 22).

15:1–21:34 The second cycle of speeches given by Job and his 3 friends. Job's resistance to their viewpoint and his appeals energized them to greater intensity in their confrontation.

15:1–35 Eliphaz returns for his second session (see Job 4, 5).

15:1–6 He began by accusing Job of sinning by attacking God with his complaints. He felt Job was guilty of empty words and had not exhibited godly fear and righteous prayer (v. 4), but rather was sinning in his prayer (vv. 5, 6).

15:7–13 Eliphaz condemned Job for rejecting the conventional wisdom, as if he had more insight than other men (vv. 7–9) and could reject the wisdom of the aged (v. 10) and the kindness of God (v. 11).

8 "Do you hear the [A]secret counsel of God,
And limit wisdom to yourself?
9 "[A]What do you know that we do not know?
What do you understand that [a]we do not?
10 "Both the [A]gray-haired and the
aged are among us,
Older than your father.
11 "Are [A]the consolations of God
too small for you,
Even the [B]word *spoken* gently with you?
12 "Why does your [A]heart carry you away?
And why do your eyes flash,
13 That you should turn your
spirit against God
And allow *such* words to go
out of your mouth?
14 "What is man, that [A]he should be pure,
Or [B]he who is born of a woman,
that he should be righteous?
15 "Behold, He puts no trust in His [A]holy ones,
And the [B]heavens are not
pure in His sight;
16 How much less one who is
[A]detestable and corrupt,
Man, who [B]drinks iniquity like water!

WHAT ELIPHAZ HAS SEEN OF LIFE

17 "I will tell you, listen to me;
And what I have seen I will also declare;
18 What wise men have told,
And have not concealed
from [A]their fathers,
19 To whom alone the land was given,
And no alien passed among them.
20 "The wicked man writhes [A]in
pain all *his* days,
And [a]numbered are the years
[B]stored up for the ruthless.
21 "[a]Sounds of [A]terror are in his ears;
[B]While at peace the destroyer
comes upon him.
22 "He does not believe that he will
[A]return from darkness,
And he is destined for [B]the sword.
23 "He wanders about for food,
saying, 'Where is it?'
He knows that a day of
[A]darkness is [a]at hand.
24 "Distress and anguish terrify him,
They overpower him like a king
ready for the attack,
25 Because he has stretched out
his hand against God
And conducts himself [A]arrogantly
against [a]the Almighty.
26 "He rushes [a]headlong at Him
With [b]his massive shield.
27 "For he has [A]covered his face with his fat
And made his thighs heavy with flesh.
28 "He has [A]lived in desolate cities,
In houses no one would inhabit,
Which are destined to become [a]ruins.
29 "He [A]will not become rich, nor
will his wealth endure;
And his grain will not bend
down to the ground.
30 "He will [A]not [a]escape from darkness;
The [B]flame will wither his shoots,
And by [C]the breath of His
mouth he will go away.
31 "Let him not [A]trust in emptiness,
deceiving himself;
For emptiness will be his [a]reward.
32 "It will be accomplished [A]before his time,
And his palm [B]branch will not be green.
33 "He will drop off his unripe
grape like the vine,
And will [A]cast off his flower
like the olive tree.
34 "For the company of [A]the godless is barren,
And fire consumes [B]the tents
of [a]the corrupt.
35 "They [A]conceive [a]mischief and
bring forth iniquity,
And their [b]mind prepares deception."

JOB SAYS FRIENDS ARE SORRY COMFORTERS

16 Then Job [a]answered,

2 "I have heard many such things;
[a,A]Sorry comforters are you all.

15:8 [A]Job 29:4; Rom 11:34; 1 Cor 2:11 15:9 [a]Lit *is not within us?* [A]Job 12:3; 13:2 15:10 [A]Job 12:12; 32:6, 7 15:11 [A]Job 5:17-19; 36:15, 16 [B]Job 6:10; 23:12 15:12 [A]Job 11:13; 36:13 15:14 [A]Job 14:4; Prov 20:9; Eccl 7:20 [B]Job 25:4 15:15 [A]Job 5:1 [B]Job 25:5 15:16 [A]Ps 14:1 [B]Job 34:7; Prov 19:28 15:18 [A]Job 8:8; 20:4 15:20 [a]Lit *the number of years are* [A]Job 15:24 [B]Job 24:1; 27:13 15:21 [a]Lit *A sound of terrors is* [A]Job 15:24; 18:11; 20:25; 24:17; 27:20 [B]Job 20:21; 1 Thess 5:3 15:22 [A]Job 15:30 [B]Job 19:29; 27:14; 33:18; 36:12 15:23 [a]Lit *ready at his hand* [A]Job 15:22, 30 15:25 [a]Heb *Shaddai* [A]Job 36:9 15:26 [a]Lit *with a stiff neck* [b]Lit *the thick-bossed shields* 15:27 [A]Ps 73:7; 119:70 15:28 [a]Or *heaps* [A]Job 3:14; Is 5:8, 9 15:29 [A]Job 27:16, 17 15:30 [a]Lit *turn aside* [A]Job 5:14; 15:22 [B]Job 15:34; 20:26; 22:20; 31:12 [C]Job 4:9 15:31 [a]Lit *exchange* [A]Job 35:13; Is 59:4 15:32 [A]Job 22:16; Eccl 7:17 [B]Job 18:16 15:33 [A]Job 14:2 15:34 [a]Lit *a bribe* [A]Job 8:13 [B]Job 8:22 15:35 [a]Or *pain* [b]Lit *belly* [A]Ps 7:14; Is 59:4 16:1 [a]Lit *answered and said* 16:2 [a]Lit *Comforters of trouble* [A]Job 13:4; 21:34

15:14–16 A strong statement with regard to the sinfulness of man (cf. Ro 3:23), that attacked Job's claim to righteousness. Verse 15 refers to holy angels who fell and brought impurity into the heavens (cf. Rev 12:1–4). The truth is accurate, that all men are sinners—but irrelevant in Job's case, because his suffering was not due to any sin.

15:17–35 Eliphaz once again returned to the same perspective and indicted Job for sin because Job was suffering. To support his relentless point, he launched into a lengthy monologue about the wicked and their outcomes in life, including many parallels to the sufferings of Job. He had pain and didn't know when his life would end (v. 20). He suffered from fear, every sound alarmed him, and he thought his destroyer was near (vv. 21, 22). He worried about having food (v. 23). His suffering made him question God (vv. 24–26). Once well-nourished, housed, and rich (vv. 27–29), he would lose it all (vv. 30–33). Eliphaz concluded by calling Job a hypocrite (vv. 34, 35), saying that this was the reason things were going so badly.

16:1–17:16 Job responded with his second rebuttal.

16:2–5 **Sorry comforters are you all.** Job's friends had come to comfort him. In spite of 7 blissful days of silence at the outset, their mission had failed miserably, and their comfort had turned into more torment for Job. What started out as Eliphaz's sincere efforts to help Job understand his dilemma had turned into rancor and sarcasm. In the end, their haranguing had heightened the frustrations of all parties involved. If the matter were reversed and Job was comforter to his friends, he would never treat them as they have treated him. He would have strengthened and comforted them.

3 “Is there *no* limit to [A]windy words?
Or what plagues you that you answer?
4 “I too could speak like you,
If [a]I were in your place.
I could compose words against you
And [A]shake my head at you.
5 “I could strengthen you with my mouth,
And the solace of my lips
could lessen *your pain.*

JOB SAYS GOD SHATTERED HIM

6 “If I speak, [A]my pain is not lessened,
And if I hold back, what has left me?
7 “But now He has [A]exhausted me;
You have laid [B]waste all my company.
8 “You have shriveled me up,
[A]It has become a witness;
And my [B]leanness rises up against me,
It testifies to my face.
9 “His anger has [A]torn me and
[a]hunted me down,
He has [B]gnashed at me with His teeth;
My [C]adversary [b]glares at me.
10 “They have [A]gaped at me with their mouth,
They have [a,B]slapped me on the
cheek with contempt;
They have [C]massed themselves against me.
11 “God hands me over to ruffians
And tosses me into the
hands of the wicked.
12 “I was at ease, but [A]He shattered me,
And He has grasped me by the neck
and shaken me to pieces;
He has also set me up as His [B]target.
13 “His [A]arrows surround me.
Without mercy He splits my kidneys open;
He pours out [B]my gall on the ground.
14 “He [A]breaks through me with
breach after breach;
He [B]runs at me like a warrior.
15 “I have sewed [A]sackcloth over my skin
And [B]thrust my horn in the dust.
16 “My face is flushed from [A]weeping,
[B]And deep darkness is on my eyelids,
17 Although there is no [A]violence in my hands,
And [B]my prayer is pure.

18 “O earth, do not cover my blood,
And let there be no *resting* place for my cry.
19 “Even now, behold, [A]my witness is in heaven,
And my [a]advocate is [B]on high.
20 “My friends are my scoffers;
[A]My eye [a]weeps to God.
21 “O that a man might plead with God
As a man with his neighbor!
22 “For when a few years are past,
I shall go the way [A]of no return.

JOB SAYS HE HAS BECOME A BYWORD

17 “My spirit is broken, my days
are extinguished,
The [a,A]grave is *ready* for me.
2 “[A]Surely mockers are with me,
And my eye [a]gazes on their provocation.

3 “Lay down, now, a pledge [A]for
me with Yourself;
Who is there that will [a]be my guarantor?
4 “For You have [a,A]kept their heart
from understanding,
Therefore You will not exalt *them.*
5 “He who [A]informs against friends
for a share *of the spoil,*
The [B]eyes of his children also will languish.

6 “But He has made me a
[A]byword of the people,
And I am [a]one at whom men [B]spit.
7 “My eye has also grown [A]dim
because of grief,
And all my [B]members are as a shadow.
8 “The upright will be appalled at this,
And the [A]innocent will stir up
himself against the godless.
9 “Nevertheless [A]the righteous
will hold to his way,
And [B]he who has clean hands will
grow stronger and stronger.

16:3 [A]Job 6:26 16:4 [a]Lit *your soul were in place of my soul* [A]Ps 22:7; 109:25; Zeph 2:15; Matt 27:39 16:6 [A]Job 9:27, 28 16:7 [A]Job 7:3 [B]Job 16:20; 19:13-15 16:8 [A]Job 10:17 [B]Job 19:20; Ps 109:24 16:9 [a]Lit *borne a grudge against me* [b]Lit *sharpens his eyes* [A]Job 19:11; Hos 6:1 [B]Ps 35:16; Lam 2:16; Acts 7:54 [C]Job 13:24; 33:10 16:10 [a]Lit *struck* [A]Ps 22:13 [B]Is 50:6; Lam 3:30; Acts 23:2 [C]Job 30:12; Ps 35:15 16:12 [A]Job 9:17 [B]Job 7:20; Lam 3:12 16:13 [A]Job 6:4; 19:12; 25:3 [B]Job 20:25 16:14 [A]Job 9:17 [B]Joel 2:7 16:15 [A]Gen 37:34; Ps 69:11 [B]Ps 7:5 16:16 [A]Job 16:20 [B]Job 24:17 16:17 [A]Is 59:6; Jon 3:8 [B]Job 27:4 16:19 [a]Or *witness* [A]Gen 31:50; Job 19:25-27; Rom 1:9; Phil 1:8; 1 Thess 2:5 [B]Job 31:2 16:20 [a]Or *drips* [A]Job 17:7 16:22 [A]Job 3:13 17:1 [a]Lit *graves* [A]Ps 88:3, 4 17:2 [a]Lit *lodges* [A]Job 12:4; 17:6 17:3 [a]Lit *strike hands with me* [A]Ps 119:122; Is 38:14 17:4 [a]Lit *hidden* [A]Job 12:20 17:5 [A]Lev 19:13, 16 [B]Job 11:20 17:6 [a]Lit *a spitting to the faces* [A]Job 17:2 [B]Job 30:10 17:7 [A]Job 16:16 [B]Job 16:8 17:8 [A]Job 22:19 17:9 [A]Prov 4:18 [B]Job 22:30; 31:7

16:6–9, 12–14 These poignant thoughts from Job lamented his suffering as severe judgment from God, who had worn him out, withered his strength, and chewed him up by severe scrutiny (“glares”). Job refers to God as his “adversary,” who had shattered, shaken, shot at, and sliced him (vv. 12–14).

16:15–20 He had no one to turn to in his sorrow, except God (v. 19), who was silent and had not vindicated him.

16:21 a man might plead with God. The pleading would be for a verdict of innocent on behalf of a friend or neighbor in a court setting before the judge/king. God anticipated the need of an advocate, and He has provided One in the person of the Lord Jesus Christ (cf. 1Ti 2:5; 1Jn 2:1, 2).

17:2 mockers. The would-be counselors had become actual enemies and the provocation for Job’s tears (cf. 16:20).

17:3 pledge. He called on God to promise (by a symbolic handshake) that his case would be heard in the heavenly court.

17:4 not exalt *them*. The blindness of Job’s friends toward his innocence came from God, so Job asked that God would not let them succeed in their efforts against him.

17:5 informs against. This Heb. term came to mean “a prey,” so that Job was referring to someone who delivers up a friend as prey to some enemy.

17:6 a byword. This refers to shame, reproach, and a reputation that is extremely bad (cf. Dt 28:37; Ps 69:11). **spit.** The most disdainful act a person could commit to heap scorn and shame on someone as a wicked and unworthy person. Job’s friends were aiding him in getting such a reputation (vv. 7, 8).

17:9 Nevertheless the righteous will hold to his way. Job, and other righteous people who find themselves in a similar situation, must remain righteous. If they do, Job knew, the suffering would produce strength (cf. 2Co 12:7–10).

10 "But come again all of [a]you now,
For I [A]do not find a wise man among you.
11 "My [A]days are past, my plans
are torn apart,
Even the wishes of my heart.
12 "They make night into day, *saying,*
'The light is near,' in the
presence of darkness.
13 "If I look for [A]Sheol as my home,
I [a]make my bed in the darkness;
14 If I call to the [A]pit, 'You are my father';
To the [B]worm, 'my mother
and my sister';
15 Where now is [A]my hope?
And who regards my hope?
16 "[a]Will it go down with me to Sheol?
Shall we together [A]go down
into the dust?"

BILDAD SPEAKS OF THE WICKED

18 Then Bildad the Shuhite [a]responded,

2 "How long will you hunt for words?
Show understanding and
then we can talk.
3 "Why are we [A]regarded as beasts,
As stupid in your eyes?
4 "O [a]you who tear yourself in your anger—
For your sake is the earth
to be abandoned,
Or the rock to be moved from its place?

5 "Indeed, the [A]light of the wicked goes out,
And the [a]flame of his fire gives no light.
6 "The light in his tent is [A]darkened,
And his lamp goes out above him.
7 "His [a]vigorous stride is shortened,
And his [A]own scheme brings him down.
8 "For he is [A]thrown into the
net by his own feet,
And he steps on the webbing.
9 "A snare seizes *him* by the heel,
And a trap snaps shut on him.
10 "A noose for him is hidden in the ground,
And a trap for him on the path.
11 "All around [A]terrors frighten him,
And [B]harry him at every step.
12 "His strength is [A]famished,
And calamity is ready at his side.
13 "[a]His skin is devoured by disease,
The firstborn of death
[A]devours his [b]limbs.
14 "He is [A]torn from [a]the security of his tent,
And [b]they march him before
the king of [B]terrors.
15 "[a]There dwells in his tent nothing of his;
[A]Brimstone is scattered on his habitation.
16 "His [A]roots are dried below,
And his [B]branch is cut off above.
17 "[A]Memory of him perishes from the earth,
And he has no name abroad.
18 "[a]He is driven from light [A]into darkness,
And [B]chased from the inhabited world.
19 "He has no [A]offspring or posterity
among his people,
Nor any survivor where he sojourned.
20 "Those [a]in the west are
appalled at [A]his [b]fate,
And those [c]in the east are
seized with horror.
21 "Surely such are the [A]dwellings
of the wicked,
And this is the place of him
who does not know God."

JOB FEELS INSULTED

19 Then Job [a]responded,

2 "How long will you torment [a]me
And crush me with words?
3 "These ten times you have insulted me;
You are not ashamed to wrong me.
4 "Even if I have truly erred,
My error lodges with me.
5 "If indeed you [A]vaunt
yourselves against me
And prove my disgrace to me,
6 Know then that [A]God has wronged me
And has closed [B]His net around me.

EVERYTHING IS AGAINST HIM

7 "Behold, [A]I cry, 'Violence!'
but I get no answer;
I shout for help, but there is no justice.

17:10 [a]With some ancient mss and versions; M.T. *them* [A]Job 12:2 17:11 [A]Job 7:6 17:13 [a]Lit *spread out* [A]Job 3:13 17:14 [A]Job 7:5; 13:28; 30:30 [B]Job 21:26; 25:6 17:15 [A]Job 7:6 17:16 [a]So the Gr; Heb possibly *Let my* limbs *sink down to Sheol, since there is rest in the dust for all* [A]Job 3:17; 21:33 18:1 [a]Lit *answered and said* 18:3 [A]Ps 73:22 18:4 [a]Lit *he…tears himself…his* 18:5 [a]Lit *spark* [A]Job 21:17; Prov 13:9; 20:20; 24:20 18:6 [A]Job 12:25 18:7 [a]Lit *steps of his strength* [A]Job 15:6 18:8 [A]Job 22:10; Ps 9:15; 35:8; Is 24:17, 18 18:11 [A]Job 15:21 [B]Job 18:18; 20:8 18:12 [A]Is 8:21 18:13 [a]Heb *It eats parts of his skin* [b]Or *parts* [A]Zech 14:12 18:14 [a]Lit *his tent his trust* [b]Or *you or she shall march* [A]Job 8:22; 18:6 [B]Job 15:21 18:15 [a]A suggested reading is *Fire dwells in his tent* [A]Ps 11:6 18:16 [A]Is 5:24; Hos 9:16; Amos 2:9; Mal 4:1 [B]Job 15:30, 32 18:17 [A]Job 24:20; Ps 34:16; Prov 10:7 18:18 [a]Lit *They drive him…And chase him* [A]Job 5:14; Is 8:22 [B]Job 20:8; 27:21-23 18:19 [A]Job 27:14, 15; Is 14:22 18:20 [a]Lit *who come after* [b]Lit *day* [c]Lit *who have gone before* [A]Ps 37:13; Jer 50:27; Obad 12 18:21 [A]Job 21:28 19:1 [a]Lit *answered and said* 19:2 [a]Lit *my soul* 19:5 [A]Ps 35:26; 38:16; 55:12, 13 19:6 [A]Job 16:11; 27:2 [B]Job 18:8-10; Ps 66:11; Lam 1:13 19:7 [A]Job 9:24; 30:20, 24; Hab 1:2

17:10 Job was not unteachable. He invited his friends to speak again if they had something wise to say, for a change, but not to talk about his restoration because he was done (vv. 11–16).

17:15 Where now is my hope? Job's hope was in God alone.

17:16 Sheol. A reference to death, also used by our Lord in Mt 16:18.

18:1–21 Bildad, like his predecessor, ruthlessly attacked Job in his second speech (cf. chap. 8) by telling Job to stop complaining and to become sensible (v. 2). Next, he turned to scorn (vv. 3, 4). Then he turned to another long tale of the bad outcomes the wicked experience (vv. 5–21).

18:13 The firstborn of death. A poetical expression meaning the most deadly disease death ever produced.

18:14 the king of terrors. Death, with all its terrors to the ungodly, personified.

18:21 who does not know God. This describes "know" in a redemptive sense and is here applied to an unbeliever.

19:1–29 Job's response to Bildad's second speech was desperate.

19:1–5 He began with the anguished cry that his friends have become recalcitrant and relentless for mentors (vv. 2, 3), and they have had no effect on his dealing with the sin they imagine is present (v. 4).

19:5–7 Job confessed that if God sent him friends like Bildad, who needs enemies? He feared there was no justice.

8 "He has [A]walled up my way
so that I cannot pass,
And He has put [B]darkness on my paths.
9 "He has [A]stripped my honor from me
And removed the [B]crown from my head.
10 "He [A]breaks me down on every
side, and I am gone;
And He has uprooted my
[B]hope [C]like a tree.
11 "He has also [A]kindled His
anger against me
And [B]considered me as His enemy.
12 "His [A]troops come together,
And [B]build up their [a]way against me
And camp around my tent.

13 "He has [A]removed my brothers
far from me,
And my [B]acquaintances are
completely estranged from me.
14 "My relatives have failed,
And my [A]intimate friends
have forgotten me.
15 "Those who live in my house and my
maids consider me a stranger.
I am a foreigner in their sight.
16 "I call to my servant, but he
does not answer;
I have to implore him with my mouth.
17 "My breath is [a]offensive to my wife,
And I am loathsome to
my own brothers.
18 "Even young children despise me;
I rise up and they speak against me.
19 "All [a]my [A]associates abhor me,
And those I love have turned against me.
20 "My [A]bone clings to my skin and my flesh,
And I have escaped *only* by
the skin of my teeth.
21 "Pity me, pity me, O you my friends,
For the [A]hand of God has struck me.
22 "Why do you [A]persecute me as God *does,*
And are not satisfied with my flesh?

JOB SAYS, "MY REDEEMER LIVES"

23 "Oh that my words were written!
Oh that they were [A]inscribed in a book!
24 "That with an iron stylus and lead
They were engraved in the rock forever!
25 "As for me, I know that [A]my
[a]Redeemer lives,
And [b]at the last He will take
His stand on the [c]earth.
26 "Even after my skin [a]is destroyed,
Yet from my flesh I shall [A]see God;
27 Whom I [a]myself shall behold,
And whom my eyes will see
and not another.
My [b]heart [A]faints [c]within me!
28 "If you say, 'How shall we [A]persecute him?'
And '[a]What pretext for a case
against him can we find?'
29 "*Then* be afraid of [A]the sword
for yourselves,
For wrath *brings* the punishment
of the sword,
So that you may know [B]there
is judgment."

ZOPHAR SAYS, "THE TRIUMPH OF THE WICKED IS SHORT"

20 Then Zophar the Naamathite [a]answered,

2 "Therefore my disquieting thoughts
make me [a]respond,
Even because of my [b]inward agitation.
3 "I listened to [A]the reproof
which insults me,
And the spirit of my understanding
makes me answer.
4 "Do you know this from [A]of old,
From the establishment of man on earth,
5 That the [A]triumphing of the
wicked is short,
And [B]the joy of the godless momentary?
6 "Though his loftiness [a,A]reaches the heavens,
And his head touches the clouds,

19:8 [A]Job 3:23; Lam 3:7, 9 [B]Job 30:26 19:9 [A]Job 12:17, 19; Ps 89:44 [B]Job 16:15; Ps 89:39; Lam 5:16 19:10 [A]Job 12:14 [B]Job 7:6 [C]Job 24:20 19:11 [A]Job 16:9 [B]Job 13:24; 33:10 19:12 [a]I.e. siegework [A]Job 16:13 [B]Job 30:12 19:13 [A]Job 16:7; Ps 69:8 [B]Job 16:20; Ps 88:8, 18 19:14 [A]Job 19:19 19:17 [a]Lit *strange* 19:19 [a]Lit *the men of my council* [A]Ps 38:11; 55:12, 13 19:20 [A]Job 16:8; 33:21; Ps 102:5; Lam 4:8 19:21 [A]Job 1:11; Ps 38:2 19:22 [A]Job 13:24, 25; 16:11; 19:6; Ps 69:26 19:23 [A]Is 30:8; Jer 36:2 19:25 [a]Or *Vindicator, defender;* lit *kinsman* [b]Or *as the Last* [c]Lit *dust* [A]Job 16:19; Ps 78:35; Prov 23:11; Is 43:14; Jer 50:34 19:26 [a]Lit *which they have cut off* [A]Ps 17:15; Matt 5:8; 1 Cor 13:12; 1 John 3:2 19:27 [a]Or *on my side* [b]Lit *kidneys* [c]Lit *in my loins* [A]Ps 73:26 19:28 [a]Or *the root of the matter is found in him* [A]Job 19:22 19:29 [A]Job 15:22 [B]Job 22:4; Ps 1:5; 9:7; Eccl 12:14 20:1 [a]Lit *answered and said* 20:2 [a]Lit *return* [b]Lit *haste within me* 20:3 [A]Job 19:3 20:4 [A]Job 8:8 20:5 [A]Job 8:12, 13; Ps 37:35, 36 [B]Job 8:13 20:6 [a]Lit *goes up to* [A]Is 14:13, 14; Obad 3, 4

19:8–21 Job rehearsed his suffering. God had closed him in, stripped him, broken him, and turned against him (vv. 8–12). His family and friends had failed him (vv. 15–19), so that he was to be pitied because God had caused this to occur (vv. 21, 22).

19:12 build up their way against me. In the ancient world, conquering armies often had their own road crews level out the rough places so that their military forces could attack.

19:20 skin of my teeth. This was the origin of a common slang phrase, referring to skin that is thin and fragile. The idea is that he had escaped death by a very slim margin. The loss of all his family and the abuse of his friends were added to the terror of God-forsakenness which had gripped him.

19:23–29 At the point of Job's greatest despair, his faith appeared at its highest as he confidently affirmed that God was his Redeemer. He wanted that confidence in the record for all to know (vv. 23, 24). Job wished that the activities of his life were put into words and "engraved in the rock," so all would know that he had not sinned to the magnitude of his suffering. God granted his prayer. God was his Redeemer (cf. Ex 6:6; Pss 19:14; 72:14; Is 43:14; 47:4; 49:26; Jer 50:34), who would vindicate him in that last day of judgment on the earth when justice was finally done (cf. Jer 12:1–3; Jn 5:25, 29; Rev 20:11–15).

19:26, 27 Job had no hope left for this life, but was confident that "after" he was dead, his Redeemer would vindicate him in the glory of a physical ("from my flesh") resurrection in which he would enjoy perfect fellowship with the Redeemer. That Jesus Christ is that Redeemer is the clear message of the gospel. See Lk 2:38; Ro 3:24; Gal 3:13; Eph 1:7; Heb 9:12.

19:28, 29 Job warned his friends that their misjudgment of him and violence against him could bring punishment on them.

20:1–29 Zophar spoiled it all again for Job with his second and last speech (cf. 11:1–20), in which he admonished Job again to consider the fate of the wicked.

20:5, 6 wicked … godless … loftiness. The application of Zophar's words about this wicked, hypocritical, proud person were aimed at Job. He would, like others so wicked, suffer the consequences of his sins (vv. 7–29).

7 He [A]perishes forever like his refuse;
Those who have seen him
[B]will say, 'Where is he?'
8 "He flies away like a [A]dream, and
they cannot find him;
Even like a vision of the night
he is [B]chased away.
9 "The [A]eye which saw him sees him no longer,
And [B]his place no longer beholds him.
10 "His [A]sons [a]favor the poor,
And his hands [B]give back his wealth.
11 "His [A]bones are full of his youthful vigor,
But it lies down with him [a]in the dust.

12 "Though [A]evil is sweet in his mouth
And he hides it under his tongue,
13 *Though* he [a]desires it and will not let it go,
But holds it [A]in his [b]mouth,
14 *Yet* his food in his stomach is changed
To the [a]venom of cobras within him.
15 "He swallows riches,
But will [A]vomit them up;
God will expel them from his belly.
16 "He sucks [A]the poison of cobras;
The viper's tongue slays him.
17 "He does not look at [A]the streams,
The rivers flowing with honey and curds.
18 "He [A]returns what he has attained
And cannot swallow *it;*
As to the riches of his trading,
He cannot even enjoy *them.*
19 "For he has [A]oppressed *and*
forsaken the poor;
He has seized a house which
he has not built.

20 "Because he knew no quiet [a]within him,
He does [A]not retain anything he desires.
21 "Nothing remains [a]for him to devour,
Therefore [A]his prosperity
does not endure.
22 "In the fullness of his plenty
he will be cramped;
The [A]hand of everyone who suffers
will come *against* him.
23 "When he [A]fills his belly,
God will send His fierce anger on him
And will [B]rain *it* on him
[a]while he is eating.
24 "He may [A]flee from the iron weapon,
But the bronze bow will pierce him.
25 "It is drawn forth and comes
out of his back,
Even the glittering point from [A]his gall.
[B]Terrors come upon him,
26 Complete [A]darkness is held in
reserve for his treasures,
And unfanned [B]fire will devour him;
It will consume the survivor in his tent.
27 "The [A]heavens will reveal his iniquity,
And the earth will rise up against him.
28 "The [A]increase of his house will depart;
His possessions will flow away
[B]in the day of His anger.
29 "This is the wicked man's
[A]portion from God,
Even the heritage decreed to him by God."

JOB SAYS GOD WILL DEAL WITH THE WICKED

21 Then Job [a]answered,

2 "Listen carefully to my speech,
And let this be your *way of* consolation.
3 "Bear with me that I may speak;
Then after I have spoken, you may [A]mock.
4 "As for me, is [A]my complaint [a]to man?
And [B]why should [b]I not be impatient?
5 "Look at me, and be astonished,
And [A]put *your* hand over *your* mouth.
6 "Even when I remember, I am disturbed,
And [A]horror takes hold of my flesh.
7 "Why [A]do the wicked *still* live,
Continue on, also become very [B]powerful?
8 "Their [a,A]descendants are established
with them in their sight,
And their offspring before their eyes,
9 Their houses [A]are safe from fear,
And the rod of God is not on them.
10 "His ox mates [a]without fail;
His cow calves and does not abort.
11 "They send forth their little
ones like the flock,
And their children skip about.
12 "They [a]sing to the timbrel and harp
And rejoice at the sound of the flute.
13 "They [A]spend their days in prosperity,
And [a]suddenly they go down to [b]Sheol.

20:7 [A]Job 4:20; 14:20 [B]Job 7:10; 8:18 20:8 [A]Ps 73:20; 90:5 [B]Job 18:18; 27:21-23 20:9 [A]Job 7:8; 8:18 [B]Job 7:10 20:10 [a]Or *seek the favor of* [A]Job 5:4; 27:14 [B]Job 20:18; 27:16, 17 20:11 [a]Lit *on* [A]Job 21:23, 24 20:12 [A]Job 15:16 20:13 [a]Lit *has compassion on* [b]Lit *palate* [A]Num 11:18-20, 33; Job 20:23 20:14 [a]Lit *gall* 20:15 [A]Job 20:10, 20, 21 20:16 [A]Deut 32:24, 33 20:17 [A]Deut 32:13, 14; Job 29:6 20:18 [A]Job 20:10, 15 20:19 [A]Job 24:2-4; 35:9 20:20 [a]Lit *in his belly* [A]Eccl 5:13-15 20:21 [a]Or *of what he devours* [A]Job 15:29 20:22 [A]Job 5:5 20:23 [a]Or *as his food* [A]Job 20:13, 14 [B]Num 11:18-20, 33; Ps 78:30, 31 20:24 [A]Is 24:18; Amos 5:19 20:25 [A]Job 16:13 [B]Job 18:11, 14 20:26 [A]Job 18:18 [B]Job 15:30; Ps 21:9 20:27 [A]Deut 31:28; Is 26:21 20:28 [A]Deut 28:31 [B]Job 20:15; 21:30 20:29 [A]Job 27:13; 31:2, 3 21:1 [a]Lit *answered and said* 21:3 [A]Job 11:3; 17:2 21:4 [a]Or *against* [b]Lit *my spirit* [A]Job 7:11 [B]Job 6:11 21:5 [A]Judg 18:19; Job 13:5; 29:9; 40:4 21:6 [A]Ps 55:5 21:7 [A]Job 9:24; Ps 73:3; Jer 12:1; Hab 1:13 [B]Job 12:19 21:8 [a]Lit *seed* [A]Ps 17:14 21:9 [A]Job 12:6 21:10 [a]Lit *and does not fail* 21:12 [a]Lit *lifted up the voice* 21:13 [a]So with most versions; M.T. *are shattered by Sheol* [b]I.e. the nether world [A]Job 21:23; 36:11

20:11 The wicked die young.

20:12–22 Evil in a life takes away all the enjoyment, implying that Job had no joy because of sin, such as that in v. 19.

20:23–29 Zophar concluded that more than just losing the enjoyment of life by sin, the wicked fall under the fury of God determined for such wickedness.

21:1–34 Job's reply to Zophar's last speech, ending the second cycle of speeches, refuted the simplistic set of laws by which the mockers lived. He showed that the wicked prosper, and since it is clear that they do (they had argued that the wicked *only* suffer), then by inference, perhaps the righteous suffer. This presented serious problems for their supposed open-and-shut case against Job.

21:1–16 Job called for his friends to be quiet and to listen to some amazing and terrifying truth (vv. 1–6), namely that the wicked do prosper (vv. 7–13) though they deny God (vv. 14, 15), and they prosper not by their doing, but God's (v. 16).

14 "They say to God, '[A]Depart from us!
We do not even desire the
knowledge of Your ways.
15 '[a]Who is [b]the Almighty, that
we should serve Him,
And [A]what would we gain if
we entreat Him?'
16 "Behold, their prosperity is
not in their hand;
The [A]counsel of the wicked is far from me.

17 "How often is [A]the lamp of
the wicked put out,
Or does their [B]calamity fall on them?
Does [a]God apportion destruction
in His anger?
18 "Are they as [A]straw before the wind,
And like [B]chaff which the
storm carries away?
19 "*You say,* '[A]God stores away [a]a
man's iniquity for his sons.'
Let [b]God repay him so that
he may know *it.*
20 "Let his [A]own eyes see his decay,
And let him [B]drink of the
wrath of [a]the Almighty.
21 "For what does he care for his
household [a]after him,
When the number of his
months is cut off?
22 "Can anyone [A]teach God knowledge,
In that He [B]judges those on high?
23 "One [A]dies in his full strength,
Being wholly at ease and [a]satisfied;
24 His [a]sides are filled out with fat,
And the [A]marrow of his bones is moist,
25 While another dies with a bitter soul,
Never even [a]tasting *anything* good.
26 "Together they [A]lie down in the dust,
And [B]worms cover them.

27 "Behold, I know your thoughts,
And the plans by which you
would wrong me.
28 "For you say, 'Where is the house
of [A]the nobleman,
And where is the [B]tent, the dwelling
places of the wicked?'
29 "Have you not asked wayfaring men,
And do you not recognize their [a]witness?
30 "For the [A]wicked is reserved for
the day of calamity;
They will be led forth at [B]the day of fury.
31 "Who will [a]confront him with his actions,
And who will repay him for
what he has done?
32 "While he is carried to the grave,
Men will keep watch over *his* tomb.
33 "The [A]clods of the valley will
[a]gently cover him;
Moreover, [B]all men will [b]follow after him,
While countless ones *go* before him.
34 "How then will you vainly [A]comfort me,
For your answers remain
full of [a]falsehood?"

ELIPHAZ ACCUSES AND EXHORTS JOB

22 Then Eliphaz the Temanite [a]responded,

2 "Can a vigorous [A]man be of use to God,
Or a wise man be useful to himself?
3 "Is there any pleasure to [a]the
Almighty if you are righteous,
Or profit if you make your ways perfect?
4 "Is it because of your [a]reverence
that He reproves you,
That He [A]enters into judgment against you?
5 "Is not [A]your wickedness great,
And your iniquities without end?
6 "For you have [A]taken pledges of
your brothers without cause,
And [B]stripped [a]men naked.
7 "To the weary you have [A]given
no water to drink,
And from the hungry you
have [B]withheld bread.
8 "But the earth [A]belongs to
the [B]mighty man,
And [C]the honorable man dwells in it.
9 "You have sent [A]widows away empty,
And the [a]strength of the [B]orphans
has been crushed.

21:14 [A]Job 22:17 21:15 [a]Lit *What* [b]Heb *Shaddai* [A]Job 22:17; 34:9 21:16 [A]Job 22:18 21:17 [a]Lit *He* [A]Job 18:5, 6 [B]Job 31:2, 3 21:18 [A]Job 13:25; Ps 83:13 [B]Ps 1:4; 35:5; Is 17:13; Hos 13:3 21:19 [a]Lit *his* [b]Lit *Him* [A]Ex 20:5; Jer 31:29; Ezek 18:2 21:20 [a]Heb *Shaddai* [A]Num 14:28-32; Jer 31:30; Ezek 18:4 [B]Ps 60:3; Is 51:17; Jer 25:15; Rev 14:10 21:21 [a]I.e. after he dies 21:22 [A]Job 35:11; 36:22; Is 40:14; Rom 11:34 [B]Job 4:18; 15:15; Ps 82:1 21:23 [a]Or *quiet* [A]Job 20:11; 21:13 21:24 [a]So with Syr; Heb uncertain. Some render as, *his pails are full of milk* [A]Prov 3:8 21:25 [a]Lit *eating* 21:26 [A]Job 3:13; 20:11; Eccl 9:2 [B]Job 24:20; Is 14:11 21:28 [A]Job 1:3; 31:37 [B]Job 8:22; 18:21 21:29 [a]Lit *signs* 21:30 [A]Job 20:29; Prov 16:4; 2 Pet 2:9 [B]Job 21:17, 20; 40:11 21:31 [a]Lit *declare his way to his face* 21:33 [a]Lit *be sweet to him* [b]Lit *draw* [A]Job 3:22; 17:16 [B]Job 3:19; 24:24 21:34 [a]Or *faithlessness* [A]Job 16:2 22:1 [a]Lit *answered and said* 22:2 [A]Job 35:7; Luke 17:10 22:3 [a]Heb *Shaddai* 22:4 [a]Or *fear* [A]Job 14:3; 19:29 22:5 [A]Job 11:6; 15:5 22:6 [a]Lit *clothing of the naked* [A]Ex 22:26; Deut 24:6, 17; Job 24:3, 9; Ezek 18:16 [B]Job 31:19, 20 22:7 [A]Job 31:16, 17 [B]Job 31:31 22:8 [A]Job 9:24 [B]Job 12:19 [C]Is 3:3; 9:15 22:9 [a]Lit *arms* [A]Job 24:3, 21; 29:13; 31:16, 18 [B]Job 6:27

21:17–22 Playing off Bildad's sentiment (see 18:5, 6, 18, 19), this whole section repeats the assertions of Job's friends regarding the judgment of sinners. To refute that perspective, Job suggested that his friends were guilty of telling God how He must deal with people (v. 22).

21:23–26 Some of the wicked live and die in prosperity, but some don't, canceling the absolutist nature of his counselors' argument.

21:27, 28 Again Job referred to the statements of his friends, Zophar in this case (see 20:7), who were trying to prove their "sin equals suffering" idea.

21:29–33 Job knew they would not listen to him, so he suggested they ask travelers, any of whom would tell them that wicked people prosper sometimes in this life, but there will be a day of doom for them when they die.

21:34 The boastful words of the counselors were contradicted by facts.

22:1–31:40 The third cycle of speeches is given by Job and his friends, with Zophar abstaining.

22:1–30 Eliphaz's last speech got nasty with Job, as his frustration rose.

22:2–4, 12–14 This counselor repeated the emphasis on the almighty nature of God, saying that God was so lofty and transcendent that He had no direct concern at all with Job. God didn't care personally about his complaints and claims to righteousness. God was not involved in the trivia of his life.

22:5–11 This miserable comforter accused Job of wickedness that was great, naming various sins against humanity as the reasons for Job's trouble (vv. 10, 11).

10 "Therefore [A]snares surround you,
And sudden [B]dread terrifies you,
11 Or [A]darkness, so that you cannot see,
And an [B]abundance of water covers you.

12 "Is not God [A]*in* the height of heaven?
Look also at the [a]distant stars,
how high they are!
13 "You say, '[A]What does God know?
Can He judge through the thick darkness?
14 '[A]Clouds are a hiding place for
Him, so that He cannot see;
And He walks on the [a]vault of heaven.'
15 "Will you keep to the ancient path
Which [A]wicked men have trod,
16 Who were snatched away
[A]before their time,
Whose [B]foundations were
[a]washed away by a river?
17 "They [A]said to God, 'Depart from us!'
And 'What can [a]the Almighty do to them?'
18 "Yet He [A]filled their houses
with good *things;*
But [B]the counsel of the wicked
is far from me.
19 "The [A]righteous see and are glad,
And the innocent mock them,
20 *Saying,* 'Truly our adversaries are cut off,
And their [a]abundance [A]the
fire has consumed.'

21 "[a,A]Yield now and be at peace with Him;
Thereby good will come to you.
22 "Please receive [a,A]instruction
from His mouth
And establish His words in your heart.
23 "If you [A]return to [a]the Almighty,
you will be [b]restored;
If you [B]remove unrighteousness
far from your tent,
24 And [A]place *your* [a]gold in the dust,
And *the gold of* Ophir among
the stones of the brooks,
25 Then [a]the Almighty will be your [b]gold
And choice silver to you.
26 "For then you will [A]delight
in [a]the Almighty
And lift up your face to God.
27 "You will [A]pray to Him, and
[B]He will hear you;
And you will pay your vows.
28 "You will also decree a thing, and it
will be established for you;
And [A]light will shine on your ways.
29 "When [a]you are cast down, you
will speak with [b]confidence,
And the [c,A]humble person He will save.
30 "He will deliver one who is not innocent,
And he will be [A]delivered through
the cleanness of your hands."

JOB SAYS HE LONGS FOR GOD

23 Then Job [a]replied,

2 "Even today my [A]complaint is rebellion;
[a]His hand is [B]heavy despite my groaning.
3 "Oh that I knew where I might find Him,
That I might come to His seat!
4 "I would [A]present *my* case before Him
And fill my mouth with arguments.
5 "I would learn the words *which*
He would [a]answer,
And perceive what He would say to me.
6 "Would He contend with me by [A]the
greatness of *His* power?
No, surely He would pay attention to me.
7 "There the upright would
[A]reason with Him;
And I [a]would be [B]delivered
forever from my Judge.

8 "Behold, I go forward but He is not *there,*
And backward, but I [A]cannot
perceive Him;
9 When He acts on the left, I
cannot behold *Him;*
He turns on the right, I cannot see Him.
10 "But He knows the [a]way I take;
When He has [A]tried me, I shall
come forth as gold.

22:10 [A]Job 18:8 [B]Job 15:21 22:11 [A]Job 5:14 [B]Job 38:34; Ps 69:2; 124:5; Lam 3:54 22:12 [a]Lit *head, top-most* [A]Job 11:7-9 22:13 [A]Ps 10:11; 59:7; 64:5; 94:7; Is 29:15; Ezek 8:12 22:14 [a]Lit *circle* [A]Job 26:9 22:15 [A]Job 34:36 22:16 [a]Lit *poured out* [A]Job 15:32; 21:13, 18 [B]Job 14:19; Ps 90:5; Is 28:2; Matt 7:26, 27 22:17 [a]Heb *Shaddai* [A]Job 21:14, 15 22:18 [A]Job 12:6 [B]Job 21:16 22:19 [A]Ps 52:6; 58:10; 107:42 22:20 [a]Or *excess* [A]Job 15:30 22:21 [a]Or *Know intimately* [A]Ps 34:10 22:22 [a]Or *law* [A]Job 6:10; 23:12; Prov 2:6 22:23 [a]Heb *Shaddai* [b]Lit *built up* [A]Job 8:5; 11:13; Is 19:22; 31:6; Zech 1:3 [B]Job 11:14 22:24 [a]Lit *ore* [A]Job 31:24, 25 22:25 [a]Heb *Shaddai* [b]Lit *ore* 22:26 [a]Heb *Shaddai* [A]Job 27:10; Ps 37:4; Is 58:14 22:27 [A]Job 11:13; 33:26; Is 58:9 [B]Job 34:28 22:28 [A]Job 11:17; Ps 112:4 22:29 [a]Lit *they cast you down* [b]Lit *pride* [c]Lit *lowly of eyes* [A]Job 5:11; 36:7; Matt 23:12; James 4:6; 1 Pet 5:5 22:30 [A]Job 42:7, 8; Ps 18:20; 24:3, 4 23:1 [a]Lit *answered and said* 23:2 [a]So with Gr and Syr; M.T. *My* [A]Job 7:11 [B]Job 6:2, 3; Ps 32:4 23:4 [A]Job 13:18 23:5 [a]Lit *answer me* 23:6 [A]Job 9:4 23:7 [a]Or *bring forth my justice forever* [A]Job 13:3 [B]Job 13:16; 23:10 23:8 [A]Job 9:11; 35:14 23:10 [a]Lit *way with me* [A]Job 7:18; Ps 7:9; 11:5; 66:10; Zech 13:9; 1 Pet 1:7

22:15–19 Again, the fate of the wicked was expressed in the simplistic idea that all suffering comes from sin. Contrary to what Job had argued, the wicked characteristically die prematurely, and Job's claim that God prospered them (v. 18a) was counsel that Eliphaz rejected (vv. 18b–20).

22:21–30 Eliphaz painted a picture of the life of blessing in store for Job if only he would return to God and repent of his sin (v. 23), emphasizing again that he did not believe Job was innocent (v. 30). "Stop all the speeches and complaints, repent, and everything will be fine," he thought.

22:24 Ophir. A land with high quality gold, whose location is uncertain (cf. 28:16; Ge 10:29).

23:1–24:25 Job's reply to Eliphaz's third speech was not a rebuttal, but expressed Job's longing for fellowship with God, so he could experience God's love and goodness and hear from Him the meaning of all his suffering.

23:3 His seat. A place of judgment.

23:4 *my* case. Job's claim to innocence.

23:6, 7 contend. Engage in court debate over evidence, witnesses, etc. Job knew God was not going to enter a contest with him to determine, as in a court case, who was right. But he wanted God to at least listen to him, so confident was he that he could make his case, and be delivered by his just Judge (cf. 1:8; 2:3).

23:8–12 Even though Job couldn't sense God's presence, he believed He was present and affirmed his commitment to God's purpose in this test (v. 10) and his continued obedience to God's Word, which were the most important issues in his life (vv. 11, 12).

11 “My foot has [A]held fast to His path;
I have kept His way and not turned aside.
12 “I have not departed from the
command of His lips;
I have treasured the [A]words of His mouth
[a]more than my [b]necessary food.
13 “But He is unique and who can turn Him?
And *what* His soul desires, that He does.
14 “For He performs what is
appointed for me,
And many such *decrees* are with Him.
15 “Therefore, I would be dismayed
at His presence;
When I consider, I am terrified of Him.
16 “*It is* God *who* has made my [A]heart faint,
And the Almighty *who*
has dismayed me,
17 But I [A]am not silenced by the darkness,
Nor [B]deep gloom *which* covers me.

JOB SAYS GOD SEEMS TO IGNORE WRONGS

24 “[A]Why are [a]times not stored
up by the Almighty,
And why do those who know
Him not see [B]His days?
2 “[a]Some [A]remove the landmarks;
They seize and [b]devour flocks.
3 “They drive away the donkeys
of the [A]orphans;
They take the [B]widow’s ox for a pledge.
4 “They push [A]the needy aside
from the road;
The [B]poor of the land are made to
hide themselves altogether.
5 “Behold, as [A]wild donkeys
in the wilderness
They [B]go forth seeking food
in their activity,
As [a]bread for *their* children in the desert.
6 “They harvest their fodder in the field
And glean the vineyard of the wicked.
7 “[A]They spend the night naked,
without clothing,
And have no covering against the cold.
8 “They are wet with the mountain rains
And hug the rock for want of a shelter.
9 “[a]Others snatch the [A]orphan from the breast,
And against the poor they take a pledge.
10 “They cause *the poor* to go about
naked without clothing,
And they take away the sheaves
from the hungry.
11 “Within the walls they produce oil;
They tread wine presses but thirst.
12 “From the city men groan,
And the souls of the wounded cry out;
Yet God [A]does not pay attention to folly.

13 “[a]Others have been with those who
rebel against the light;
They do not want to know its ways
Nor abide in its paths.
14 “The murderer [A]arises at dawn;
He [B]kills the poor and the needy,
And at night he is as a thief.
15 “The eye of the [A]adulterer
waits for the twilight,
Saying, ‘No eye will see me.’
And he [a]disguises his face.
16 “In the dark they [A]dig into houses,
They [B]shut themselves up by day;
They do not know the light.
17 “For the morning is the same to
him as thick darkness,
For he is familiar with the
[A]terrors of thick darkness.

18 “They are [a,A]insignificant on the
surface of the water;
Their portion is [B]cursed on the earth.
They do not turn [b]toward the [C]vineyards.
19 “Drought and heat [a,A]consume
the snow waters,
So does [b,B]Sheol *those who* have sinned.
20 “A [a,A]mother will forget him;
The [B]worm feeds sweetly till he
is [C]no longer remembered.
And wickedness will be
broken [D]like a tree.

23:11 [A]Job 31:7; Ps 17:5; 44:18 23:12 [a]Or with some versions, *in my breast* [b]Lit *prescribed portion* [A]Job 6:10; 22:22 23:16 [A]Deut 20:3; Job 27:2; Jer 51:46 23:17 [A]Job 10:18, 19 [B]Job 19:8 24:1 [a]I.e. times of judgment [A]Acts 1:7 [B]Is 2:12; Jer 46:10; Obad 15; Zeph 1:7 24:2 [a]Lit *They* [b]Or *pasture* [A]Deut 19:14; 27:17; Prov 23:10 24:3 [A]Job 6:27 [B]Deut 24:17; Job 22:9 24:4 [A]Job 24:14; 29:16; 30:25; 31:19 [B]Job 29:12; Ps 41:1; Prov 14:31; 28:28; Amos 8:4 24:5 [a]Lit *his bread* [A]Job 39:5-8 [B]Ps 104:23 24:7 [A]Ex 22:26; Job 22:6 24:9 [a]Lit *They* [A]Job 6:27 24:12 [A]Job 9:23, 24 24:13 [a]Lit *They* 24:14 [A]Mic 2:1 [B]Ps 10:8 24:15 [a]Or *puts a covering on his face* [A]Prov 7:9 24:16 [A]Ex 22:2; Matt 6:19 [B]John 3:20 24:17 [A]Job 15:21 24:18 [a]Or *light or swift* [b]Lit *to the path of* [A]Job 22:11, 16; 27:20 [B]Job 5:3 [C]Job 24:6, 11 24:19 [a]Lit *seize* [b]I.e. nether world [A]Job 6:16, 17 [B]Job 21:13 24:20 [a]Lit *womb* [A]Is 49:15 [B]Job 21:26 [C]Job 18:17; Ps 34:16; Prov 10:7 [D]Job 19:10; Dan 4:14

23:14 He performs what is appointed for me. Job’s resignation to God’s sovereignty faltered at times in practice, but he returned to it repeatedly. It is the great lesson of the book: trust sovereign God when you can’t understand why things go badly in life.

24:1–25 Job had made the point that the unrighteous prosper in spite of their sin (chap. 21). Extending that theme, he listed the kinds of severe sins which go on in the world and God doesn’t seem to do anything to stop them (vv. 2–17), so that the wicked, in general, prosper and live long lives, seemingly unabated. These sins—oppressing the orphans, widows, and poor as well as committing murder, thievery, and adultery—are the very ones forbidden in other parts of the OT.

24:1 times not stored up. Job believed that God knew the appointed times for all activities under the sun (Ecc 3:1–8), but he bemoaned the fact that God did not inform man about them.

24:2 remove the landmarks. This ancient practice is addressed in Dt 19:14; Pr 22:28; 23:10, “Do not move the ancient boundary.” Corrupt landowners often did this to increase their holdings, particularly where the land was owned by bereaved widows. Taking advantage of widows will be treated by the ultimate court in heaven.

24:7 spend the night. It was common practice to take an outer garment as a pledge for money owed. But OT law forbade keeping the garment at night since its owner could get cold and sick (cf. 24:10).

24:12 Yet God does not pay attention to folly. This is a stinging accusation from Job. Human courts prosecuted offenders for most of these social crimes. Job, in essence, was saying “If human courts punish the wicked, then why doesn’t God?”

24:18–21 Again Job referred to the opinions of his counselors, saying that, if their view were correct, all the wicked should be experiencing punishment. But it is obvious they were not.

21 "He wrongs the [a]barren woman
And does no good for [A]the widow.
22 "But He drags off the valiant by [A]His power;
He rises, but [B]no one has assurance of life.
23 "He provides them [A]with security,
and they are supported;
And His [B]eyes are on their ways.
24 "They are exalted a [A]little while,
then they are gone;
Moreover, they are [B]brought low and
like everything gathered up;
Even like the heads of grain they are cut off.
25 "Now if it is not so, [A]who can prove me a liar,
And make my speech worthless?"

BILDAD SAYS MAN IS INFERIOR

25 Then Bildad the Shuhite [a]answered,

2 "[A]Dominion and awe [a]belong to Him
Who establishes peace in [B]His heights.
3 "Is there any number to [A]His troops?
And upon whom does His light not rise?
4 "How then can a man be [A]just with God?
Or how can he be [B]clean who
is born of woman?
5 "If even [A]the moon has no brightness
And the [B]stars are not pure in His sight,
6 How much less [A]man, *that* [B]maggot,
And the son of man, *that* worm!"

JOB REBUKES BILDAD

26 Then Job [a]responded,

2 "What a help you are to [a,A]the weak!
How you have saved the arm
[B]without strength!
3 "What counsel you have given
to *one* without wisdom!
What helpful insight you have
abundantly [a]provided!
4 "To whom have you uttered words?
And whose [a]spirit was
expressed through you?

THE GREATNESS OF GOD

5 "The [a,A]departed spirits tremble
Under the waters and their inhabitants.
6 "Naked is [a,A]Sheol before Him,
And [b,B]Abaddon has no covering.
7 "He [A]stretches out the north
over empty space
And hangs the earth on nothing.
8 "He [A]wraps up the waters in His clouds,
And the cloud does not burst under them.
9 "He [a,A]obscures the face of the [b]full moon
And spreads His cloud over it.
10 "He has inscribed a [A]circle on
the surface of the waters
At the [B]boundary of light and darkness.
11 "The pillars of heaven tremble
And are amazed at His rebuke.
12 "He [A]quieted the sea with His power,
And by His [B]understanding
He shattered [C]Rahab.
13 "By His breath the [A]heavens are [a]cleared;
His hand has pierced [B]the fleeing serpent.
14 "Behold, these are the fringes of His ways;
And how faint [A]a word we hear of Him!
But His mighty [B]thunder, who
can understand?"

JOB AFFIRMS HIS RIGHTEOUSNESS

27 Then Job [a]continued his [A]discourse and said,

2 "As God lives, [A]who has taken
away my right,
And the Almighty, [B]who has
embittered my soul,
3 For as long as [a]life is in me,
And the [b,A]breath of God is in my nostrils,

24:21 [a]Lit *barren who does not bear* [A]Job 22:9 24:22 [A]Job 9:4 [B]Job 18:20 24:23 [A]Job 12:6 [B]Job 10:4; 11:11 24:24 [A]Ps 37:10 [B]Job 14:21 24:25 [A]Job 6:28; 27:4 25:1 [a]Lit *answered and said* 25:2 [a]Lit *are with Him* [A]Job 9:4; 36:5, 22; 37:23; 42:2 [B]Job 16:19; 31:2 25:3 [A]Job 16:13 25:4 [A]Job 4:17; 9:2 [B]Job 14:4 25:5 [A]Job 31:26 [B]Job 15:15 25:6 [A]Job 7:17 [B]Job 17:14 26:1 [a]Lit *responded and said* 26:2 [a]Lit *no power* [A]Job 6:11, 12 [B]Ps 71:9 26:3 [a]Lit *made known* 26:4 [a]Lit *breath has gone forth* 26:5 [a]Or *shades;* Heb *Rephaim* [A]Job 3:13; Ps 88:10 26:6 [a]I.e. the nether world [b]I.e. place of destruction [A]Job 9:5-10; 26:6-14; 38:17; 41:11 [B]Job 28:22; 31:12 26:7 [A]Job 9:8 26:8 [A]Job 37:11; Prov 30:4 26:9 [a]Lit *covers* [b]Or *throne* [A]Job 22:14; Ps 97:2; 105:39 26:10 [A]Job 38:1-11; Prov 8:29 [B]Job 38:19, 20, 24 26:12 [A]Is 51:15; Jer 31:35 [B]Job 12:13 [C]Job 9:13 26:13 [a]Lit *made beautiful* [A]Job 9:8 [B]Is 27:1 26:14 [A]Job 4:12 [B]Job 36:29; 37:4, 5 27:1 [a]Or *again took up* [A]Job 13:12; 29:1 27:2 [A]Job 16:11; 34:5 [B]Job 9:18 27:3 [a]Lit *breath* [b]Or *spirit* [A]Job 32:8; 33:4

24:22–25 Job's view was that their punishment would come eventually ("exalted a little while"). Retribution needed the timing of God's wisdom, when He determined wrongs would be made right. Job was totally confident that his point could not be refuted.

25:1–6 Bildad made his third speech (the last speech for the three friends), and restated the same theory—that God was majestic and exalted (vv. 2, 3) and man was sinful, especially Job (vv. 4–6).

26:1–31:40 Job made his last speech in rebuttal to Eliphaz, Bildad, and Zophar.

26:1–4 Job responded to Bildad's lack of concern for him, showing that all his friend's theological and rational words missed the point of Job's need altogether and had been no help.

26:5–14 As before, in chaps. 9 and 12, Job showed that he was not inferior to his friends in describing God's greatness. He understood that as well as they did. He described it as manifested in the realm of the dead called Sheol and Abaddon, or place of destruction (vv. 5, 6), the earth and sky (v. 7), the waters above (vv. 8–10) and below (v. 12), and the stars (v. 13).

26:7 hangs the earth on nothing. A statement that is accurate, given in ancient time, before scientific verification. This indicates the divine authorship of Scripture.

26:10 a circle. This describes the earth as a circular globe, another scientifically accurate statement at a time when many thought the world was flat.

26:11 pillars of heaven. A figure of speech for the mountains that seem to hold up the sky (cf. Ps 104:32).

26:12 shattered Rahab. Cf. 7:12; 9:13; 26:13. "Rahab" seems to be widely used to describe various things that wreak havoc.

26:13 His breath. Cf. 33:4. The Holy Spirit, described here as God's "breath," worked mightily in creation (cf. Ge 1:2). **the fleeing serpent.** This is figurative language for the idea that God brought all constellations into subjection under His authority (cf. 26:12). "Serpent" could be translated "crooked" and refer to any wayward stars or planets being brought under control by His mighty power.

26:14 Behold, these are the fringes of His ways. Poetic language reminding his counselors that all that could be said and understood by man was only a glimpse of God's powerful hand.

27:1–12 Job turned from speaking about God (26:5–14) to defending his righteousness.

27:2 who has taken away my right. God did not speak to declare Job innocent. Cf. the treatment of Christ in Is 53:8 and Ac 8:33.

27:3–6 Job affirmed his true and steadfast devotion to righteous living, no matter

4 My lips certainly will not speak unjustly,
Nor will [A]my tongue mutter deceit.
5 "Far be it from me that I should
declare you right;
Till I die [A]I will not put away
my integrity from me.
6 "I [A]hold fast my righteousness
and will not let it go.
My heart does not reproach any of my days.

THE STATE OF THE GODLESS

7 "May my enemy be as the wicked
And [a]my opponent as the unjust.
8 "For what is [A]the hope of the
godless [a]when he is cut off,
When God requires [B]his [b]life?
9 "Will God [A]hear his cry
When [B]distress comes upon him?
10 "Will he take [A]delight in the Almighty?
Will he call on God at all times?
11 "I will instruct you in the [a]power of God;
What is with the Almighty
I will not conceal.
12 "Behold, all of you have seen *it;*
Why then do you [a]act foolishly?

13 "This is [A]the portion of a
wicked man from God,
And the inheritance *which* [B]tyrants
receive from the Almighty.
14 "Though his sons are many, [a]they
are destined [A]for the sword;
And his [B]descendants will not
be satisfied with bread.
15 "His survivors will be buried
because of the plague,
And [a]their [A]widows will not
be able to weep.
16 "Though he piles up silver like dust
And prepares garments as
plentiful as the clay,
17 He may prepare *it,* [A]but the
just will wear *it*
And the innocent will divide the silver.
18 "He has built his [A]house like
the [a]spider's web,
Or as a hut *which* the
watchman has made.
19 "He lies down rich, but never [a]again;
He opens his eyes, and [A]it is no longer.
20 "[A]Terrors overtake him like a flood;
A tempest steals him away [B]in the night.
21 "The east [A]wind carries him
away, and he is gone,
For it whirls him [B]away from his place.
22 "For it will hurl at him [A]without sparing;
He will surely try to [B]flee from its [a]power.
23 "*Men* will clap their hands at him
And will [A]hiss him from his place.

JOB TELLS OF EARTH'S TREASURES

28 "Surely there is a [a]mine for silver
And a place [b]where they refine gold.
2 "Iron is taken from the dust,
And copper is smelted from rock.
3 "*Man* puts an end to darkness,
And [A]to the farthest limit
he searches out
The rock in gloom and deep shadow.
4 "He [a]sinks a shaft far from [b]habitation,
Forgotten by the foot;
They hang and swing to and
fro far from men.
5 "The earth, from it comes food,
And underneath it is turned up as fire.
6 "Its rocks are the [a]source of sapphires,
And its dust *contains* gold.
7 "The path no bird of prey knows,
Nor has the falcon's eye caught sight of it.
8 "The [a]proud beasts have not trodden it,
Nor has the *fierce* lion passed over it.
9 "He puts his hand on the flint;
He overturns the mountains at the [a]base.
10 "He hews out channels through the rocks,
And his eye sees anything precious.
11 "He dams up the streams from [a]flowing,
And what is hidden he brings
out to the light.

27:4 [A]Job 6:28; 33:3 27:5 [A]Job 6:29 27:6 [A]Job 2:3; 13:18 27:7 [a]Lit *he who rises up against me* 27:8 [a]Or *though he gains* [b]Lit *soul* [A]Job 8:13; 11:20 [B]Job 12:10 27:9 [A]Job 35:12, 13; Ps 18:41; Prov 1:28; Is 1:15; Jer 14:12; Mic 3:4 [B]Prov 1:27 27:10 [A]Job 22:26, 27; Ps 37:4; Is 58:14 27:11 [a]Lit *hand* 27:12 [a]Or *speak vanity* 27:13 [A]Job 20:29 [B]Job 15:20 27:14 [a]Lit *the sword is for them* [A]Job 15:22; 18:19 [B]Job 20:10 27:15 [a]So ancient versions; Heb *his* [A]Ps 78:64 27:17 [A]Job 20:18-21 27:18 [a]So ancient versions; Heb *moth* [A]Job 8:15; 18:14 27:19 [a]So ancient versions; Heb *will be gathered* [A]Job 7:8, 21; 20:7 27:20 [A]Job 15:21 [B]Job 20:8; 34:20 27:21 [A]Job 21:18 [B]Job 7:10 27:22 [a]Lit *hand* [A]Jer 13:14; Ezek 5:11; 24:14 [B]Job 11:20 27:23 [A]Job 18:18; 20:8 28:1 [a]Or *source* [b]Lit *for gold they refine* 28:3 [A]Eccl 1:13 28:4 [a]Lit *breaks open* [b]Lit *sojourning* 28:6 [a]Or *place* 28:8 [a]Lit *sons of pride* 28:9 [a]Lit *roots* 28:11 [a]Lit *weeping*

what happened. He refused to live with a guilty conscience (v. 6b). This was no brash claim, because God had recognized Job's virtue (1:8; 2:3).

27:7 He could have been calling for God to judge his accusers as He judges the wicked.

27:8–10 Job reminded the friends that he would never be hypocritical because he understood the consequences.

27:11 I will instruct you in the power of God. Job had pinpointed the issue between him and his friends. They disagreed on the outworking of God's retribution. They agreed that God was powerful, wise, and sovereign. But because Job knew there was no cherished sin in his life that would bring upon him such intense suffering, Job was forced to conclude that the simplistic notion—that all suffering comes from sin and all righteousness is rewarded—was wrong. At the outset, Job himself probably believed as the comforters still did, but he had seen that his friends' limitation of God's action was drastically in need of revision; in fact, it was nonsense. Job's comments here introduced his exposition on wisdom which follows in Job 28.

27:13–23 Job wanted it made clear he was not denying that the wicked are punished with severe distress, so he agreed that they suffer greatly and affirmed so in this section.

27:18 house like … spider's web … hut. These are temporary dwellings which illustrate that the wicked will not live long.

27:23 clap their hands. A gesture of mocking.

28:1–28 Though Job had agreed that the wicked suffer (27:13–23), that explained nothing in his case, since he was righteous. So Job called on his friends to consider that maybe God's wisdom was beyond their comprehension. That is the theme of this chapter. The wisdom of God is not gained by natural or theoretical knowledge. What God does not reveal, we can't know.

28:1–11 References to mining silver, gold, iron, sapphires, and flint, as well as smelting copper. Tremendous effort is made by men who seek these precious things. Cf. Pr 2:1–9.

THE SEARCH FOR WISDOM IS HARDER

12 "But [A]where can wisdom be found?
And where is the place
of understanding?
13 "[A]Man does not know its value,
Nor is it found in the land of the living.
14 "The deep says, 'It is not in me';
And the sea says, 'It is not with me.'
15 "[A]Pure gold cannot be given
in exchange for it,
Nor can silver be weighed as its price.
16 "It cannot be valued in the gold of Ophir,
In precious onyx, or sapphire.
17 "[A]Gold or glass cannot equal it,
Nor can it be exchanged for
articles of fine gold.
18 "Coral and crystal are not to be mentioned;
And the acquisition of [A]wisdom
is above *that of* pearls.
19 "The topaz of Ethiopia cannot equal it,
Nor can it be valued in [A]pure gold.
20 "[A]Where then does wisdom come from?
And where is the place of understanding?
21 "Thus it is hidden from the
eyes of all living
And concealed from the birds of the sky.
22 "[a,A]Abaddon and Death say,
'With our ears we have heard
a report of it.'

23 "[A]God understands its way,
And He knows its place.
24 "For He [A]looks to the ends of the earth
And sees everything under the heavens.
25 "When He imparted [A]weight to the wind
And [B]meted out the waters by measure,
26 When He set a [A]limit for the rain
And a course for the [B]thunderbolt,
27 Then He saw it and declared it;
He established it and also searched it out.
28 "And to man He said, 'Behold, the [A]fear
of the Lord, that is wisdom;
And to depart from evil is understanding.' "

JOB'S PAST WAS GLORIOUS

29 And Job again took up his [A]discourse and
said,

2 "Oh that I were as in months gone by,
As in the days when God [A]watched over me;
3 When [A]His lamp shone over my head,
And [B]by His light I walked
through darkness;
4 As I was in [a]the prime of my days,
When the [b,A]friendship of God
was over my tent;
5 When [a]the Almighty was yet with me,
And my children were around me;
6 When my steps were bathed in [A]butter,
And the [B]rock poured out for
me streams of oil!
7 "When I went out to [A]the gate of the city,
When I [a]took my seat in the square,
8 The young men saw me and
hid themselves,
And the old men arose *and* stood.
9 "The princes [A]stopped talking
And [B]put *their* hands on their mouths;
10 The voice of the nobles was [a,A]hushed,
And their [B]tongue stuck to their palate.
11 "For when [A]the ear heard, it
called me blessed,
And when the eye saw, it
gave witness of me,
12 Because I delivered [A]the poor
who cried for help,
And the [B]orphan who had no helper.
13 "The blessing of the one [A]ready
to perish came upon me,
And I made the [B]widow's heart sing for joy.

28:12 [A]Job 28:23, 28; Eccl 7:24 28:13 [A]Matt 13:44-46 28:15 [A]Prov 3:13, 14; 8:10, 11; 16:16 28:17 [A]Prov 8:10; 16:16 28:18 [A]Prov 8:11 28:19 [A]Prov 8:19 28:20 [A]Job 28:23, 28 28:22 [a]I.e. Destruction [A]Job 26:6; Prov 8:32-36 28:23 [A]Job 9:4; Prov 8:22-36 28:24 [A]Ps 11:4; 33:13, 14; 66:7; Prov 15:3 28:25 [A]Ps 135:7 [B]Job 12:15; 38:8-11 28:26 [A]Job 37:6, 11, 12; 38:26-28 [B]Job 37:3; 38:25 28:28 [A]Ps 111:10; Prov 1:7; 9:10; Eccl 12:13 29:1 [A]Num 23:7; 24:3; Job 13:12; 27:1 29:2 [A]Jer 31:28 29:3 [A]Job 18:6 [B]Job 11:17 29:4 [a]Lit *the days of my autumn* [b]Lit *counsel* [A]Job 15:8; Ps 25:14; Prov 3:32 29:5 [a]Heb *Shaddai* 29:6 [A]Deut 32:14; Job 20:17 [B]Deut 32:13; Ps 81:16 29:7 [a]Lit *set up* [A]Job 31:21 29:9 [A]Job 29:21 [B]Job 21:5 29:10 [a]Lit *hidden* [A]Job 29:22 [B]Ps 137:6 29:11 [A]Job 4:3, 4 29:12 [A]Job 24:4, 9; 34:28; Ps 72:12; Prov 21:13 [B]Job 31:17, 21 29:13 [A]Job 31:19 [B]Job 22:9

28:12, 20 These verses sum up the message of the chapter with the point that no amount of effort, even as vigorous and demanding as mining, will yield God's wisdom. It can't be valued or found in the world (vv. 13, 14). It can't be bought for any price (vv. 15–19). The living can't find it (v. 21), and neither can the dead (v. 22; cf. 26:6).

28:16 **Ophir.** *See note on 22:24.*

28:23 **God understands its way ... knows its place.** These are perhaps the most important thoughts in the chapter for the debates. Job and his friends have probed God's wisdom for 3 court rounds and basically have arrived nowhere near the truth. Finally, Job made the point clearly that the divine wisdom necessary to explain his suffering was inaccessible to man. Only God knew all about it, because He knows everything (v. 24). True wisdom belongs to the One who is the Almighty Creator (vv. 25, 26). One can only know it if He declares it to him (cf. Dt 29:29).

28:28 **Behold, the fear of the Lord, that is wisdom.** Job had made the connection that the others would not. While the specific features of God's wisdom may not be revealed to us, the alpha and omega of wisdom is to revere God and avoid sin (cf. Ps 111:10; Pr 1:7; 9:10; Ecc 12:13, 14), leaving the unanswered questions to Him in trusting submission. All we can do is trust and obey (cf. Ecc 12:13), and that is enough wisdom (this is the wisdom of Pr 1:7–2:9). One may never know the reasons for life's sufferings.

29:1–25 Job did not change his mind about his sin, but continued to deny that he had earned this pain with his iniquity. The realities of his own words in chap. 28 had not yet fully taken over his mind, so he swung back to despair and rehearsed his life before the events of Job 1, 2, when he was so fulfilled because God was with him (v. 5). God still was with him, but it seemed as if He were gone.

29:5 **When the Almighty was yet with me.** Job felt abandoned by God. But God would demonstrate to Job, by addressing his criticisms, that God was with him all throughout this ordeal.

29:6 **butter ... oil.** He had the richest dairy products and best olive oil in abundance.

29:7 **gate ... my seat.** This was a place in society reserved for city leaders. Job had been one because he was a very wealthy and powerful man.

29:12, 13 **poor ... orphan ... one ready to perish ... widow's.** All over the ancient Near Eastern world, a man's virtue was measured by his treatment of the weakest and most vulnerable members of society. If he protected and provided for this group, he was respected as being a noble man. These things, which Job had done, his accusers said he must not have done or he wouldn't be suffering (see 22:1–11).

14 "I [A]put on righteousness, and it clothed me;
My justice was like a robe and a turban.
15 "I was [A]eyes to the blind
And feet to the lame.
16 "I was a father to [A]the needy,
And I investigated the case
which I did not know.
17 "I [A]broke the jaws of the wicked
And snatched the prey from his teeth.
18 "Then I [a]thought, 'I shall die [b]in my nest,
And I shall multiply *my* days as the sand.
19 'My [A]root is spread out to the waters,
And [B]dew lies all night on my branch.
20 'My glory is *ever* new with me,
And my [A]bow is renewed in my hand.'

21 "To me [A]they listened and waited,
And kept silent for my counsel.
22 "After my words they did not [A]speak again,
And [B]my speech dropped on them.
23 "They waited for me as for the rain,
And opened their mouth as
for the spring rain.
24 "I smiled on them when they
did not believe,
And the light of my face they
did not cast down.
25 "I chose a way for them and sat as [A]chief,
And dwelt as a king among the troops,
As one who [B]comforted the mourners.

JOB'S PRESENT STATE IS HUMILIATING

30 "But now those younger than I [A]mock me,
Whose fathers I disdained to put
with the dogs of my flock.
2 "Indeed, what *good was* the strength
of their hands to me?
Vigor had perished from them.
3 "From want and famine they are gaunt
Who gnaw the dry ground by night
in waste and desolation,
4 Who pluck [a]mallow by the bushes,
And whose food is the root
of the broom shrub.
5 "They are driven from the community;
They shout against them
as *against* a thief,
6 So that they dwell in dreadful [a]valleys,
In holes of the earth and of the rocks.
7 "Among the bushes they [a]cry out;
Under the nettles they are
gathered together.
8 "[a]Fools, even [b]those without a name,
They were scourged from the land.

9 "And now I have become their [a,A]taunt,
I have even become a [B]byword to them.
10 "They abhor me *and* stand aloof from me,
And they do not [a]refrain from
[A]spitting at my face.
11 "Because [a]He has loosed [b]His
[c]bowstring and [A]afflicted me,
They have cast off [B]the bridle before me.
12 "On the right hand their [a]brood arises;
They [A]thrust aside my feet [B]and build up
against me their ways of destruction.
13 "They [A]break up my path,
They profit [a]from my destruction;
No one restrains them.
14 "As *through* a wide breach they come,
[a]Amid the tempest they roll on.
15 "[A]Terrors are turned against me;
They pursue my [a]honor as the wind,
And my [b]prosperity has passed
away [B]like a cloud.

16 "And now [A]my soul is poured out [a]within me;
Days of affliction have seized me.
17 "At night it pierces [A]my bones [a]within me,
And my gnawing *pains* take no rest.
18 "By a great force my garment is [A]distorted;
It binds me about as the collar of my coat.
19 "He has cast me into the [A]mire,
And I have become like dust and ashes.
20 "I [A]cry out to You for help, but
You do not answer me;
I stand up, and You turn Your
attention against me.

29:14 [A]Job 27:5, 6; Ps 132:9; Is 59:17; 61:10; Eph 6:14 29:15 [A]Num 10:31 29:16 [A]Job 24:4; Prov 29:7 29:17 [A]Ps 3:7 29:18 [a]Lit *said* [b]Lit *with* 29:19 [A]Jer 17:8 [B]Hos 14:5 29:20 [A]Gen 49:24; Ps 18:34 29:21 [A]Job 4:3; 29:9 29:22 [A]Job 29:10 [B]Deut 32:2 29:25 [A]Job 1:3; 31:37 [B]Job 4:4; 16:5 30:1 [A]Job 12:4 30:4 [a]I.e. plant of the salt marshes 30:6 [a]Or *wadis* 30:7 [a]Or *bray* 30:8 [a]Lit *Sons of fools* [b]Lit *sons* 30:9 [a]Lit *song* [A]Job 12:4 [B]Job 17:6; Ps 69:11; Lam 3:14, 63 30:10 [a]Lit *withhold spit from my face* [A]Num 12:14; Deut 25:9; Job 17:6; Is 50:6; Matt 26:67 30:11 [a]Or *they* [b]Some mss read *my* [c]Or *cord* [A]Ruth 1:21; Ps 88:7 [B]Ps 32:9 30:12 [a]Possibly *sprout* or *offspring* [A]Ps 140:4, 5 [B]Job 19:12 30:13 [a]Lit *for* [A]Is 3:12 30:14 [a]Lit *Under* 30:15 [a]Or *nobility* [b]Or *welfare* [A]Job 3:25; 31:23; Ps 55:3-5 [B]Job 7:9; Hos 13:3 30:16 [a]Lit *upon* [A]1 Sam 1:15; Job 3:24; Ps 22:14; 42:4; Is 53:12 30:17 [a]Lit *from upon* [A]Job 30:30 30:18 [A]Job 2:7 30:19 [A]Ps 69:2, 14 30:20 [A]Job 19:7

29:15, 16 **blind ... lame ... needy.** Contrary to the accusations of the 3 friends, Job went beyond the standards of the day to care for the widow, the orphan, the poor, the disabled, and the abused.

29:16 **investigated the case.** Much oppression occurred in unjust courts, and there Job protected the weak.

29:18–20 Job had vigorous health like a widely rooted tree enjoying fresh dew, and he had expected to live a long life with his family ("nest").

29:21–25 Job reminded his friends that there had been a day when no one rejected his insights. He was the one sought for counsel.

29:24 **smiled.** This is likely a reference to saying something facetiously or jokingly. Job's word was so respected that they didn't believe his humor was humor, but took it seriously.

29:25 **as a king.** Job was not a king but some sort of high local official such as a mayor. Mayors, called "hazannu" in Job's day, performed all of the activities Job claimed in the previous section.

30:1–31 Job moved from the recollection of good days in the past (chap. 29) to lament his present losses.

30:2–8 Job described these mockers as dissipated vagabonds who, because of their uselessness and wickedness, were not welcome in society, so were driven out of the land. These base men had made Job the object of their sordid entertainment (vv. 9–15).

30:9 **I have become their taunt.** Job was the object of their jeering, whereas in former days he would not hire their fathers to tend his animals like sheepdogs (30:1).

30:16–19 Job's life ebbed away, suffering gripped him, his bones ached, gnawing pain never relented, his skin ("garment") was changed (v. 30), and he was reduced to mud, dust, and ashes.

30:20 This caused the most suffering of all—what seemed to be the cruel silence of God (v. 21).

21 "You have [a]become cruel to me;
With the might of Your hand
You [A]persecute me.
22 "You [A]lift me up to the wind
and cause me to ride;
And You dissolve me in a storm.
23 "For I know that You [A]will
bring me to death
And to the [B]house of meeting
for all living.

24 "Yet does not one in a heap of
ruins stretch out *his* hand,
Or in his disaster therefore
[A]cry out for help?
25 "Have I not [A]wept for the [a]one
whose life is hard?
Was not my soul grieved for [B]the needy?
26 "When I [A]expected good, then evil came;
When I waited for light, [B]then
darkness came.
27 "[a]I am seething [A]within and cannot relax;
Days of affliction confront me.
28 "I go about [a,A]mourning without comfort;
I stand up in the assembly
and [B]cry out for help.
29 "I have become a brother to [A]jackals
And a companion of ostriches.
30 "My [A]skin turns black [a]on me,
And my [B]bones burn with [b]fever.
31 "Therefore my [A]harp [a]is
turned to mourning,
And my flute to the sound
of those who weep.

JOB ASSERTS HIS INTEGRITY

31 "I have made a covenant with my [A]eyes;
How then could I gaze at a virgin?
2 "And what is [A]the portion of
God from above
Or the heritage of the Almighty
from on high?
3 "Is it not [A]calamity to the unjust
And disaster to [B]those who work iniquity?
4 "Does He not [A]see my ways
And [B]number all my steps?
5 "If I have [A]walked with falsehood,
And my foot has hastened after deceit,
6 Let Him [A]weigh me with
[a]accurate scales,
And let God know [B]my integrity.
7 "If my step has [A]turned from the way,
Or my heart [a]followed my eyes,
Or if any [B]spot has stuck to my hands,
8 Let me [A]sow and another eat,
And let my [a,B]crops be uprooted.

9 "If my heart has been [A]enticed
by a woman,
Or I have lurked at my
neighbor's doorway,
10 May my wife [A]grind for another,
And let [B]others [a]kneel down over her.
11 "For that would be a [A]lustful crime;
Moreover, it would be [B]an iniquity
punishable by judges.
12 "For it would be [A]fire that
consumes to [a,B]Abaddon,
And would [C]uproot all my [b]increase.

13 "If I have [A]despised the claim of
my male or female slaves
When they filed a complaint against me,
14 What then could I do when God arises?
And when He calls me to account,
what will I answer Him?
15 "Did not [A]He who made me in
the womb make him,
And the same one fashion
us in the womb?

16 "If I have kept [A]the poor from *their* desire,
Or have caused the eyes of
[B]the widow to fail,
17 Or have [A]eaten my morsel alone,
And [B]the orphan has not [a]shared it
18 (But from my youth he grew up
with me as with a father,
And from [a]infancy I guided her),
19 If I have seen anyone perish
[A]for lack of clothing,
Or that [B]the needy had no covering,

30:21 [a]Lit *turned to be* [A]Job 10:3; 16:9, 14; 19:6, 22 30:22 [A]Job 9:17; 27:21 30:23 [A]Job 9:22; 10:8 [B]Job 3:19; Eccl 12:5 30:24 [A]Job 19:7 30:25 [a]Lit *hard of day* [A]Ps 35:13, 14; Rom 12:15 [B]Job 24:4 30:26 [A]Job 3:25, 26; Jer 8:15 [B]Job 19:8 30:27 [a]Lit *My inward parts are boiling* [A]Lam 2:11 30:28 [a]Or *blackened, but not by the heat of the sun* [A]Job 30:31; Ps 38:6; 42:9; 43:2 [B]Job 19:7 30:29 [A]Ps 44:19; Mic 1:8 30:30 [a]Lit *from upon* [b]Lit *heat* [A]Job 2:7 [B]Ps 102:3 30:31 [a]Lit *becomes* [A]Is 24:8 31:1 [A]Matt 5:28 31:2 [A]Job 20:29 31:3 [A]Job 18:12; 21:30 [B]Job 34:22 31:4 [A]2 Chr 16:9; Job 24:23; 28:24; 34:21; 36:7; Prov 5:21; 15:3 [B]Job 14:16; 31:37 31:5 [A]Job 15:31; Mic 2:11 31:6 [a]Lit *just* [A]Job 6:2, 3 [B]Job 23:10; 27:5, 6 31:7 [a]Lit *walked after* [A]Job 23:11 [B]Job 9:30 31:8 [a]Or *offspring* [A]Lev 26:16; Job 20:18; Mic 6:15 [B]Job 31:12 31:9 [A]Job 24:15; 31:1 31:10 [a]I.e. sexual relations [A]Is 47:2 [B]Deut 28:30; Jer 8:10 31:11 [A]Lev 20:10; Deut 22:24 [B]Job 31:28 31:12 [a]I.e. place of destruction [b]Or *yield* [A]Job 15:30 [B]Job 26:6 [C]Job 20:28; 31:8 31:13 [A]Deut 24:14, 15 31:15 [A]Job 10:3 31:16 [A]Job 5:16; 20:19 [B]Ex 22:22-24; Job 22:9 31:17 [a]Lit *eaten from it* [A]Job 22:7 [B]Job 29:12 31:18 [a]Lit *my mother's womb* 31:19 [A]Job 22:6; 29:13 [B]Job 24:4

30:23 the house of meeting. The grave.

30:24–26 This seems to be saying that God must have some sympathy, if Job has (v. 25), so as not to destroy altogether what is already ruined. Job thought that and reached out for help in his misery and received only evil (v. 26).

30:30 My skin ... my bones. Job was describing the effect of his disease (see 2:7).

31:1–40 As Job became more forceful in his pursuit of being cleared of false accusations, he intensified the claim that he was innocent, comparatively speaking, and demanded justice. In situations where an individual was innocent, he would attest to it by taking an oath before the king or a deity. This procedure found among Job's neighboring nations was often protocol for court procedures. The repeated "If ... let" statements amount to the terms of the oath: "If" tells what Job might have done wrong; "let" describes a curse which could result. He accepted the curses (the "let" statements through the chapter) if he deserved them. This represented Job's last attempt to defend himself before both God and man. In terms of purity (v. 1), sin in general (vv. 2, 3), truth (v. 5), covetousness (v. 7), marital faithfulness (v. 9), equity (v. 13), compassion (vv. 16–21), materialism (vv. 24, 25), false religion (vv. 26, 27), love for enemies and strangers (vv. 29–32), secret sin (vv. 33, 34), and business relations (vv. 38–40) Job had no pattern of sin. He asked God to answer him (v. 35), and to explain why he suffered.

31:1 made a covenant with my eyes. He spoke here of purity toward women (cf. Pr 6:25; Mt 5:28).

20 If his loins have not [a]thanked me,
And if he has not been warmed
with the fleece of my sheep,
21 If I have lifted up my hand
against [A]the orphan,
Because I saw [a]I had support [B]in the gate,
22 Let my shoulder fall from the [a]socket,
And my [A]arm be broken off [b]at the elbow.
23 "For [A]calamity from God is a terror to me,
And because of [B]His [a]majesty
I can do nothing.

24 "If I have put my confidence *in* [A]gold,
And called fine gold my trust,
25 If I have [A]gloated because my
wealth was great,
And because my hand had
secured *so* much;
26 If I have [A]looked at the [a]sun when it shone
Or the moon going in splendor,
27 And my heart became secretly enticed,
And my hand [a]threw a kiss from my mouth,
28 That too would have been [A]an
iniquity *calling for* [a]judgment,
For I would have [B]denied God above.

29 "Have I [A]rejoiced at the
extinction of my enemy,
Or [a]exulted when evil befell him?
30 "[a]No, [A]I have not [b]allowed my mouth to sin
By asking for his life in [B]a curse.
31 "Have the men of my tent not said,
'Who can [a]find one who has not
been [A]satisfied with his meat'?
32 "The alien has not lodged outside,
For I have opened my doors
to the [a]traveler.
33 "Have I [A]covered my transgressions
like [a]Adam,
By hiding my iniquity in my bosom,
34 Because I [A]feared the great multitude,
And the contempt of families terrified me,
And kept silent and did not
go out of doors?
35 "Oh that I had one to hear me!
Behold, here is my [a]signature;
[A]Let the Almighty answer me!
And the indictment which my
[B]adversary has written,
36 Surely I would carry it on my shoulder,
I would bind it to myself like a crown.
37 "I would declare to Him [A]the
number of my steps;
Like [B]a prince I would approach Him.

38 "If my [A]land cries out against me,
And its furrows weep together;
39 If I have [A]eaten its [a]fruit without money,
Or have [B]caused [b]its owners
to lose their lives,
40 Let [A]briars [a]grow instead of wheat,
And stinkweed instead of barley."

The words of Job are ended.

ELIHU IN ANGER REBUKES JOB

32 Then these three men ceased answering
Job, because he was [A]righteous in his own
eyes. 2 But the anger of Elihu the son of Barachel
the [A]Buzite, of the family of Ram burned; against
Job his anger burned [B]because he justified himself
[a,C]before God. 3 And his anger burned against his
three friends because they had found no answer,
and yet had condemned Job. 4 Now Elihu had waited
[a]to speak to Job because they were years older than
he. 5 And when Elihu saw that there was no answer
in the mouth of the three men his anger burned.
6 So Elihu the son of Barachel the Buzite [a]spoke
out and said,

"I am young in years and you are [A]old;
Therefore I was shy and afraid
to tell you [b]what I think.
7 "I [a]thought [b,A]age should speak,
And [c]increased years should teach wisdom.
8 "But it is a spirit in man,
And the [A]breath of the Almighty
gives them [B]understanding.
9 "The [a]abundant *in years* may not be wise,
Nor may [A]elders understand justice.
10 "So I [a]say, 'Listen to me,
I too will tell [b]what I think.'

31:20 [a]Lit *blessed* 31:21 [a]Lit *my help* [A]Job 29:12; 31:17 [B]Job 29:7 31:22 [a]Lit *shoulder;* or *back* [b]Lit *from the bone of the upper arm* [A]Job 38:15 31:23 [a]Lit *exaltation* [A]Job 31:3 [B]Job 13:11 31:24 [A]Job 22:24; Mark 10:23-25 31:25 [A]Job 1:3, 10; Ps 62:10 31:26 [a]Lit *light* [A]Deut 4:19; 17:3; Ezek 8:16 31:27 [a]Lit *kissed my mouth* 31:28 [a]Lit *judges* [A]Deut 17:2-7; Job 31:11 [B]Josh 24:27; Is 59:13 31:29 [a]Lit *lifted myself up* [A]Prov 17:5; 24:17; Obad 12 31:30 [a]Lit *And* [b]Lit *given my palate* [A]Ps 7:4 [B]Job 5:3 31:31 [a]Lit *give* [A]Job 22:7 31:32 [a]M.T. *way* 31:33 [a]Or *mankind* [A]Gen 3:10; Prov 28:13 31:34 [A]Ex 23:2 31:35 [a]Lit *mark* [A]Job 19:7; 30:20, 24, 28; 35:14 [B]Job 27:7 31:37 [A]Job 31:4 [B]Job 1:3; 29:25 31:38 [A]Job 24:2 31:39 [a]Lit *strength* [b]Lit *the soul of its owners to expire* [A]Job 24:6, 10-12; James 5:4 [B]1 Kin 21:19 31:40 [a]Lit *come forth* [A]Job 32:13; Is 5:6 32:1 [A]Job 10:7; 13:18; 27:5, 6; 31:6 32:2 [a]Or *more than* [A]Gen 22:21 [B]Job 27:5, 6 [C]Job 30:21 32:4 [a]Lit *for Job with words;* or possibly *while they were speaking with Job* 32:6 [a]Lit *answered* [b]Lit *my knowledge* [A]Job 15:10 32:7 [a]Lit *said* [b]Lit *days* [c]Lit *many* [A]Job 8:8, 9 32:8 [A]Job 33:4 [B]Job 38:36 32:9 [a]Or *nobles* [A]Job 32:7 32:10 [a]Or *said* [b]Lit *my knowledge*

31:33 like Adam. Perhaps best taken "as mankind" (cf. Hos 6:7).

31:35 the indictment which my adversary has written. Job wished that God, the perfect Prosecutor who knows the allegations perfectly, had written a book that would have revealed God's will and wisdom and the reasons for Job's pain. This would have cleared him of all charges by his friends.

31:40 The words of Job are ended. The 3 cycles of speeches which began in Job 3:1 were finished and Job had the first and last word among his friends.

32:1–37:24 A new participant who had been there with the other 3 (vv. 3–5) entered the debate over Job's condition—the younger Elihu, who took a new approach to the issue of Job's suffering. Angry with the other 3, he had some new thoughts, but was very hard on Job. Elihu was angry, full of self-importance, and verbose, but his approach was refreshing after listening repetitiously to the others, though not really helpful to Job. Why was it necessary to record and read those 4 blustering speeches by this man? Because they happened as part of the story, while Job was still waiting for God to disclose Himself (chaps. 38–41).

32:2 Buzite. Elihu's ancestry was traced to the Arabian tribe of Buz (cf. Jer 25:23). The "family of Ram" is unknown.

32:6–8 Elihu may have called his words "what I think" (vv. 6, 10, 17), but he claimed it had come by inspiration from God (v. 8; cf. 33:6, 33).

11 "Behold, I waited for your words,
I listened to your reasonings,
While you [a]pondered what to say.
12 "I even paid close attention to you;
[a]Indeed, there was no one who refuted Job,
Not one of you who answered his words.
13 "Do not say,
'[A]We have found wisdom;
God will [a]rout him, not man.'
14 "For he has not arranged *his*
words against me,
Nor will I reply to him with
your [a]arguments.

15 "They are dismayed, they
no longer answer;
Words have [a]failed them.
16 "Shall I wait, because they do not speak,
Because they [a]stop *and* no
longer answer?
17 "I too will answer my share,
I also will tell my opinion.
18 "For I am full of words;
The spirit within me constrains me.
19 "Behold, my belly is like unvented wine,
Like new wineskins it is about to burst.
20 "Let me speak that I may get relief;
Let me open my lips and answer.
21 "Let me now [A]be partial to no one,
Nor flatter *any* man.
22 "For I do not know how to flatter,
Else my Maker would soon take me away.

ELIHU CLAIMS TO SPEAK FOR GOD

33 "However now, Job, please
[A]hear my speech,
And listen to all my words.
2 "Behold now, I open my mouth,
My tongue in my [a]mouth speaks.
3 "My words are *from* the
uprightness of my heart,
And my lips speak [A]knowledge sincerely.
4 "The [A]Spirit of God has made me,
And the [B]breath of [a]the
Almighty gives me life.
5 "[A]Refute me if you can;
Array yourselves before me,
take your stand.
6 "Behold, I belong to God like you;
I too have been [a]formed out of the [A]clay.
7 "Behold, [A]no fear of me should terrify you,
Nor should my pressure
weigh heavily on you.

8 "Surely you have spoken in my hearing,
And I have heard the sound of *your* words:
9 'I am [A]pure, [B]without transgression;
I am innocent and there [C]is no guilt in me.
10 'Behold, He [a]invents pretexts against me;
He [A]counts me as His enemy.
11 'He [A]puts my feet in the stocks;
He watches all my paths.'
12 "Behold, let me [a]tell you, [A]you
are not right in this,
For God is greater than man.

13 "Why do you [A]complain against Him
That He does not give an account
of all His doings?
14 "Indeed [A]God speaks once,
Or twice, *yet* no one notices it.
15 "In a [A]dream, a vision of the night,
When sound sleep falls on men,
While they slumber in their beds,
16 Then [A]He opens the ears of men,
And seals their instruction,
17 That He may turn man aside
from his conduct,
And [a]keep man from pride;
18 He [A]keeps back his soul from the pit,
And his life from [a]passing over [B]into Sheol.

19 "[a]Man is also chastened with
[A]pain on his bed,
And with unceasing complaint
in his bones;
20 So that his life [A]loathes bread,
And his soul favorite food.
21 "His [A]flesh wastes away from sight,
And his [B]bones which were
not seen stick out.
22 "Then [A]his soul draws near to the pit,
And his life to those who bring death.

23 "If there is an angel *as* [A]mediator for him,
One out of a thousand,
To remind a man what is [a]right for him,
24 Then let him be gracious to him, and say,
'Deliver him from [A]going down to the pit,
I have found a [B]ransom';

32:11 [a]Lit *searched out words* 32:12 [a]Lit *Behold* 32:13 [a]Lit *drive away* [A]Jer 9:23 32:14 [a]Lit *words* 32:15 [a]Lit *moved away from* 32:16 [a]Lit *stand* 32:21 [A]Lev 19:15; Job 13:8, 10; 34:19 33:1 [A]Job 13:6 33:2 [a]Lit *palate* 33:3 [A]Job 6:28; 27:4; 36:4 33:4 [a]Heb *Shaddai* [A]Gen 2:7; Job 10:3; 32:8 [B]Job 27:3 33:5 [A]Job 33:32 33:6 [a]Lit *cut out of* [A]Job 4:19 33:7 [A]Job 13:21 33:9 [A]Job 9:21; 10:7; 13:18; 16:17 [B]Job 7:21; 13:23; 14:17 [C]Job 10:14 33:10 [a]Lit *finds* [A]Job 13:24 33:11 [A]Job 13:27 33:12 [a]Lit *answer* [A]Eccl 7:20 33:13 [A]Job 40:2; Is 45:9 33:14 [A]Job 33:29; 40:5; Ps 62:11 33:15 [A]Job 4:12-17; 33:15-18 33:16 [A]Job 36:10, 15 33:17 [a]Lit *hide* 33:18 [a]M.T. *perishing by the sword* [A]Job 33:22, 24, 28, 30 [B]Job 15:22 33:19 [a]Lit *He* [A]Job 30:17 33:20 [A]Job 3:24; 6:7; Ps 107:18 33:21 [A]Job 16:8 [B]Job 19:20; Ps 22:17; 102:5 33:22 [A]Job 33:18, 28 33:23 [a]Lit *his uprightness* [A]Gen 40:8 33:24 [A]Job 33:18, 28; Is 38:17 [B]Job 36:18; Ps 49:7

33:1–33 The first of Elihu's challenges to Job began with proud claims (vv. 1–7), followed by references to Job's questions/complaints (vv. 8–11). Then came Elihu's answers (vv. 12–33).

33:13 Job had complained that God did not speak to him. Elihu reminded Job that God didn't have to defend His will and actions to anyone.

33:14–18 God does speak, he contended, in many ways such as dreams and visions to protect people from evil and deadly ways (vv. 17, 18).

33:18 the pit. A reference to the realm of the dead (cf. vv. 21, 24, 30).

33:19–28 Job has lamented that his suffering was not deserved. Elihu answered that complaint by saying he was God's messenger, a mediator to Job to show him that God doesn't act in a whimsical way, but allows suffering as chastening to bring a person to submit to Him as upright (v. 23) and to repent (v. 27) that his life may be spared (vv. 24, 28, 30). God allows suffering for spiritual benefit.

25 Let his flesh become fresher
than in youth,
Let him return to the days of
his youthful vigor;
26 Then he will [A]pray to God, and
He will accept him,
That [B]he may see His face with joy,
And He may restore His
righteousness to man.
27 "He will sing to men and say,
'I [A]have sinned and perverted
what is right,
And it is not [B]proper for me.
28 'He has redeemed my soul
from going to the pit,
And my life shall [A]see the light.'

29 "Behold, God does [A]all these
[a]oftentimes with men,
30 To [A]bring back his soul from the pit,
That he may be enlightened
with the light of life.
31 "Pay attention, O Job, listen to me;
Keep silent, and let me speak.
32 "*Then* if [a]you have anything
to say, answer me;
Speak, for I desire to justify you.
33 "If not, [A]listen to me;
Keep silent, and I will teach you wisdom."

ELIHU VINDICATES GOD'S JUSTICE

34 Then Elihu continued and said,

2 "Hear my words, you wise men,
And listen to me, you who know.
3 "For [A]the ear tests words
As the palate tastes food.
4 "Let us choose for ourselves what is right;
Let us know among ourselves
what is good.
5 "For Job has said, '[A]I am righteous,
But [B]God has taken away my right;
6 [a]Should I lie concerning my right?
My [b,A]wound is incurable, *though*
I am without transgression.'
7 "What man is like Job,
Who [A]drinks up derision like water,
8 Who goes [A]in company with
the workers of iniquity,
And walks with wicked men?
9 "For he has said, '[A]It profits a man nothing
When he [a]is pleased with God.'

10 "Therefore, listen to me, you
men of understanding.
Far be it from God to [A]do wickedness,
And from the Almighty to do wrong.
11 "For He pays a man according to [A]his work,
And makes [a]him find it
according to his way.
12 "Surely, [A]God will not act wickedly,
And the Almighty will not pervert justice.
13 "Who [A]gave Him authority over the earth?
And who [B]has laid *on Him*
the whole world?
14 "If He should [a]determine to do so,
If He should [A]gather to Himself
His spirit and His breath,
15 All [A]flesh would perish together,
And man would [B]return to dust.

16 "But if *you have* understanding, hear this;
Listen to the sound of my words.
17 "Shall [A]one who hates justice rule?
And [B]will you condemn the
righteous mighty One,
18 Who says to a king, 'Worthless one,'
To nobles, 'Wicked ones';
19 Who shows no [A]partiality to princes
Nor regards the rich above the poor,
For they all are the [B]work of His hands?
20 "In a moment they die, and [A]at midnight
People are shaken and pass away,
And [B]the mighty are taken
away without a hand.

21 "For [A]His eyes are upon the ways of a man,
And He sees all his steps.
22 "There is [A]no darkness or deep shadow
Where the workers of iniquity
may hide themselves.
23 "For He does not [A]*need to*
consider a man further,
That he should go before God in judgment.

33:26 [A]Job 22:27; 34:28; Ps 50:14, 15 [B]Job 22:26 33:27 [A]2 Sam 12:13; Luke 15:21 [B]Rom 6:21 33:28 [A]Job 22:28 33:29 [a]Lit *twice, three times* [A]Eph 1:11; Phil 2:13 33:30 [A]Job 33:18; Zech 9:11 33:32 [a]Lit *there are words* 33:33 [A]Ps 34:11 34:3 [A]Job 12:11 34:5 [A]Job 13:18; 33:9 [B]Job 27:2 34:6 [a]Or *Although I am right I am accounted a liar* [b]Lit *arrow* [A]Job 6:4 34:7 [A]Job 15:16 34:8 [A]Job 22:15 34:9 [a]Or *takes delight in God* [A]Job 21:15; 35:3; Ps 50:18 34:10 [A]Gen 18:25; Deut 32:4; Job 8:3; 34:12; Rom 9:14 34:11 [a]Lit *a man* [A]Job 34:25; Ps 62:12; Prov 24:12; Jer 32:19; Ezek 33:20; Matt 16:27; Rom 2:6; 2 Cor 5:10; Rev 22:12 34:12 [A]Job 34:10 34:13 [A]Job 38:4 [B]Job 38:5 34:14 [a]Lit *set His mind on Himself* [A]Job 12:10; Ps 104:29; Eccl 12:7 34:15 [A]Gen 7:21; Job 9:22 [B]Gen 3:19; Job 10:9 34:17 [A]2 Sam 23:3; Job 34:30 [B]Job 40:8 34:19 [A]Lev 19:15; Deut 10:17; 2 Chr 19:7; Acts 10:34; Rom 2:11; Gal 2:6; Eph 6:9; Col 3:25; 1 Pet 1:17 [B]Job 10:3 34:20 [A]Ex 12:29; Job 34:25; 36:20 [B]Job 12:19 34:21 [A]Job 24:23; 31:4; Prov 5:21; 15:3; Jer 16:17 34:22 [A]Ps 139:11, 12; Amos 9:2, 3 34:23 [A]Job 11:11

33:32 I desire to justify you. Elihu expressed he was on Job's side and wanted to see him vindicated in his claims to righteousness, so he gave opportunity for Job to dialogue with him as he spoke (v. 33).

34:1–37 Elihu addressed Job and his accusers. His approach was to quote Job directly (vv. 5–9), then respond to his complaints, but at times he misinterpreted Job's remarks, and at other times he put the words of the accusers in Job's mouth. The most obvious example of the latter wrongdoing was in saying that Job claimed to be sinlessly perfect (v. 6). Job never claimed that; in fact, Job acknowledged his sin (7:21; 13:26). Elihu didn't know it, but God had pronounced Job innocent (1:8; 2:3). In answer to Job's complaints that God seemed unjust, Elihu reminded Job that God was too holy to do anything wrong (v. 10), fair in dealing with people (vv. 11, 12), powerful (vv. 13, 14), just (vv. 17, 18), impartial (vv. 19, 20), omniscient (vv. 21, 22), the Judge of all (v. 23), and the Sovereign who does what He wills to prevent evil (vv. 24–30).

34:9 For he has said. Elihu was incorrect. He was putting words into Job's mouth that Job did not utter.

34:23 go before God in judgment. These words do not refer to the judgment of the last days, but rather to the general accountability toward God that man experiences on a daily basis. The point Elihu made was that God did not need to go through all of the trappings of the court to get to the sentence. God "knows their works" (34:25).

24 "He breaks in pieces [A]mighty
men without inquiry,
And sets others in their place.
25 "Therefore He [A]knows their works,
And [B]He overthrows *them* in the night,
And they are crushed.
26 "He [A]strikes them like the wicked
[a]In a public place,
27 Because they [A]turned aside
from following Him,
And [B]had no regard for any of His ways;
28 So that they caused [A]the cry of
the poor to come to Him,
And that He might [B]hear the
cry of the afflicted—
29 When He keeps quiet, who
then can condemn?
And when He hides His face,
who then can behold Him,
That is, in regard to both nation and man?—
30 "So that [A]godless men would not rule
Nor be snares of the people.

31 "For has anyone said to God,
'I have borne *chastisement;*
I will not offend *anymore;*
32 Teach me what I do not see;
If I have [A]done iniquity,
I will not do it again'?
33 "Shall He [A]recompense on your terms,
because you have rejected *it?*
For you must choose, and not I;
Therefore declare what you know.
34 "Men of understanding will say to me,
And a wise man who hears me,
35 'Job [A]speaks without knowledge,
And his words are without wisdom.
36 'Job ought to be tried [a]to the limit,
Because he answers [A]like wicked men.
37 'For he adds [A]rebellion to his sin;
He [B]claps his hands among us,
And multiplies his words against God.' "

ELIHU SHARPLY REPROVES JOB

35 Then Elihu continued and said,

2 "Do you think this is according to [A]justice?
Do you say, 'My righteousness
is more than God's'?
3 "For you say, '[A]What advantage
will it be to [a]You?
[B]What profit will I have, more
than if I had sinned?'
4 "I will answer you,
And your friends with you.
5 "[A]Look at the heavens and see;
And behold [B]the clouds—they
are higher than you.
6 "If you have sinned, [A]what do you
accomplish against Him?
And if your transgressions are
many, what do you do to Him?
7 "If you are righteous, [A]what
do you give to Him,
Or what does He receive
from your hand?
8 "Your wickedness is for a
man like yourself,
And your righteousness is
for a son of man.

9 "Because of the [A]multitude of
oppressions they cry out;
They cry for help because of
the arm [B]of the mighty.
10 "But [A]no one says, 'Where is
God my Maker,
Who [B]gives songs in the night,
11 Who [A]teaches us more than
the beasts of the earth
And makes us wiser than the
birds of the heavens?'
12 "There [A]they cry out, but He
does not answer
Because of the pride of evil men.
13 "Surely [A]God will not listen
to [a]an empty *cry,*
Nor will the Almighty regard it.
14 "How much less when [A]you say
you do not behold Him,
The [B]case is before Him, and
you must wait for Him!
15 "And now, because He has not
visited *in* His anger,
Nor has He acknowledged
[a]transgression well,
16 So Job opens his mouth [a]emptily;
He multiplies words [A]without knowledge."

34:24 [A]Job 12:19 34:25 [A]Job 34:11 [B]Job 34:20 34:26 [a]Lit *In the place of the ones seeing* [A]Ps 9:5; 11:5 34:27 [A]1 Sam 15:11 [B]Job 21:14 34:28 [A]Job 35:9; James 5:4 [B]Ex 22:23; Job 22:27 34:30 [A]Job 5:15; 20:5; 34:17; Prov 29:2-12 34:32 [A]Job 33:27 34:33 [A]Job 41:11 34:35 [A]Job 35:16; 38:2 34:36 [a]Or *to the end* [A]Job 22:15 34:37 [A]Job 23:2 [B]Job 27:23 35:2 [A]Job 27:2 35:3 [a]Or *you* [A]Job 34:9 [B]Job 9:30, 31 35:5 [A]Gen 15:5; Ps 8:3 [B]Job 22:12 35:6 [A]Job 7:20; Prov 8:36; Jer 7:19 35:7 [A]Job 22:2, 3; Prov 9:12; Luke 17:10; Rom 11:35 35:9 [A]Ex 2:23 [B]Job 12:19 35:10 [A]Job 21:14; 27:10; 36:13; Is 51:13 [B]Job 8:21; Ps 42:8; 77:6; 149:5; Acts 16:25 35:11 [A]Job 36:22; Ps 94:12; Jer 32:33 35:12 [A]Prov 1:28 35:13 [a]Or *falsehood* [A]Job 27:9; Prov 15:29; Is 1:15; Jer 11:11; Mic 3:4 35:14 [A]Job 9:11; 23:8, 9 [B]Job 31:35 35:15 [a]Or *arrogance* 35:16 [a]Lit *vainly* [A]Job 34:35; 38:2

34:31–33 God will not be regulated in His dealings by what men may think. He does not consult men. If He chooses to chasten He will decide when it is enough.

34:34–37 Apparently, Elihu was convinced Job hadn't had enough chastening because of how he answered his prosecutors. He continued to defend his innocence and speak to God.

35:1–16 Elihu again referred to Job's complaints, first of all his thinking that there appeared to be no advantage to being righteous (v. 3), which Job had said, as recorded in 21:15 and 34:9. The first part of his answer is that Job gained nothing by sinning or not sinning because God was so high that nothing men do affects Him (vv. 5–7). It only affects other men (v. 8). Job had also complained that God did not answer his prayers when he cried under this oppression (see 24:12; 30:20). Elihu coldly gave 3 reasons why Job's prayers had not been heard: pride (vv. 10, 12), wrong motives (v. 13), and lack of patient trust (v. 14). Again, all this theoretical talk missed Job's predicament completely because he was righteous. Elihu was no more help than the other counselors.

35:15, 16 Elihu suggested that although Job had suffered, his suffering was not the fullness of God's anger, or He would have punished Job more for the sinfulness of his

ELIHU SPEAKS OF GOD'S DEALINGS WITH MEN

36 Then Elihu continued and said,
2 "Wait for me a little, and I will show you
That there [a]is yet more to be
said in God's behalf.
3 "I will fetch my knowledge from afar,
And I will ascribe [A]righteousness
to my Maker.
4 "For truly [A]my words are not false;
One who is [B]perfect in
knowledge is with you.
5 "Behold, God is mighty but
does not [A]despise *any;*
He is [B]mighty in strength
of understanding.
6 "He does not [A]keep the wicked alive,
But gives justice to [B]the afflicted.
7 "He does not [A]withdraw His eyes
from the righteous;
But [B]with kings on the throne
He has seated them forever,
and they are exalted.
8 "And if they are bound in fetters,
And are caught in the
cords of [A]affliction,
9 Then He declares to them their work
And their transgressions, that they
have [A]magnified themselves.
10 "[A]He opens their ear to instruction,
And [B]commands that they
return from evil.
11 "If they hear and serve *Him,*
They will [A]end their days in prosperity
And their years in [B]pleasures.
12 "But if they do not hear, they shall
[a]perish [A]by the sword
And they will [B]die without knowledge.
13 "But the godless in heart lay up anger;
They do not cry for help
when He binds them.
14 "[a]They die in youth,
And their life *perishes* among
the [A]cult prostitutes.
15 "He delivers the afflicted in
[a]their [A]affliction,
And [B]opens their ear [b]in
time of oppression.
16 "Then indeed, He [A]enticed you
from the mouth of distress,
Instead of it, a broad place
with no constraint;
And that which was set on your
table was full of [a]fatness.

17 "But you were full of [A]judgment
on the wicked;
Judgment and justice take hold *of you.*
18 "*Beware* that [A]wrath does not
entice you to scoffing;
And do not let the greatness of
the [B]ransom turn you aside.
19 "Will your [a]riches keep you from distress,
Or all the forces of *your* strength?
20 "Do not long for [A]the night,
When people [a]vanish in their place.
21 "Be careful, do [A]not turn to evil,
For you have preferred this to [B]affliction.
22 "Behold, God is exalted in His power;
Who is a [A]teacher like Him?
23 "Who has appointed Him His way,
And who has said, '[A]You
have done wrong'?

24 "Remember that you should
[A]exalt His work,
Of which men have [B]sung.
25 "All men have seen it;
Man beholds from afar.
26 "Behold, God is [A]exalted, and
[B]we do not know *Him;*
The [C]number of His years is unsearchable.
27 "For [A]He draws up the drops of water,
They distill rain from [a]the [b]mist,
28 Which the clouds pour down,
They drip upon man abundantly.
29 "Can anyone understand the
[A]spreading of the clouds,
The [B]thundering of His [a]pavilion?

36:2 [a]Lit *are yet words for God* 36:3 [A]Job 8:3; 37:23 36:4 [A]Job 33:3 [B]Job 37:16 36:5 [A]Ps 22:24; 69:33; 102:17 [B]Job 12:13 36:6 [A]Job 8:22; 34:26 [B]Job 5:15 36:7 [A]Ps 33:18; 34:15 [B]Job 5:11; Ps 113:8 36:8 [A]Job 36:15, 21 36:9 [A]Job 15:25 36:10 [A]Job 33:16; 36:15 [B]2 Kin 17:13; Job 36:21; Jon 3:8 36:11 [A]1 Tim 4:8 [B]Ps 16:11 36:12 [a]Lit *pass away* [A]Job 15:22 [B]Job 4:21 36:14 [a]Or *Their soul dies* [A]Deut 23:17 36:15 [a]Lit *his* [b]Or *in adversity* [A]Job 36:8, 21 [B]Job 36:10 36:16 [a]Or *rich food* [A]Hos 2:14 36:17 [A]Job 22:5, 10, 11 36:18 [A]Jon 4:4, 9 [B]Job 33:24 36:19 [a]Or *cry* 36:20 [a]Lit *go up* [A]Job 34:20, 25 36:21 [A]Job 36:10; Ps 31:6; 66:18 [B]Job 36:8, 15; Heb 11:25 36:22 [A]Job 35:11 36:23 [A]Deut 32:4; Job 8:3 36:24 [A]Ps 92:5; Rev 15:3 [B]Ex 15:1; Judg 5:1; 1 Chr 16:9; Ps 59:16; 138:5 36:26 [A]Job 11:7-9; 37:23 [B]1 Cor 13:12 [C]Job 10:5; Ps 90:2; 102:24, 27; Heb 1:12 36:27 [a]Lit *its* [b]Or *flood* [A]Job 5:10; 36:26-29; 37:6, 11; 38:28; Ps 147:8 36:29 [a]Lit *booth* [A]Job 37:11, 16 [B]Job 26:14

speeches. He thought God had actually overlooked the folly of Job in his useless words.

36:1–37:24 Elihu had agreed with his 3 co-counselors that Job had sinned, if nowhere else, in the way he questioned God (33:12), by seeing his suffering as indicating God is unjust (34:34–37) and by feeling that righteousness had no reward (chap. 35). In this final answer to Job, he turned to focus mostly on God rather than the sufferer (v. 2).

36:4 One who is perfect in knowledge. Elihu made what appeared to be an outrageous claim in order to give credibility to his remarks.

36:5–12 Elihu began by repeating the thought that though God sends trouble, He is just and merciful (v. 6); He watches over the righteous (v. 7); He convicts them of sin (vv. 8, 9); He teaches them to turn from it (v. 10) and rewards their obedience (v. 11) or punishes their rebellion (vv. 12–14).

36:15 opens their ear in *time of* oppression. This was a new insight and perhaps the most helpful thing Elihu said. He went beyond all that had been said about God's using suffering to chasten and bring repentance. He was saying that God used suffering to open men's ears, to draw them to Himself. But as long as Job kept complaining, he was turning to iniquity rather than drawing near to God in his suffering (vv. 16–21).

36:22–37:24 Instead of complaining and questioning God, as Job had been doing, which was sin (as Job will later confess in 42:6), he needed to see God in his suffering and worship Him (33:24).

36:26 we do not know *Him.* Though one may have a personal knowledge of God in salvation, the fullness of His glory is beyond human comprehension.

36:27–37:4 Elihu gave a picture of God's power in the rain storm.

30 "Behold, He spreads His
[a]lightning about Him,
And He covers the depths of the sea.
31 "For by these He [A]judges peoples;
He [B]gives food in abundance.
32 "He covers *His* hands with the [a]lightning,
And [A]commands it to strike the mark.
33 "Its [A]noise declares [a]His presence;
The cattle also, concerning
what is coming up.

ELIHU SAYS GOD IS BACK OF THE STORM

37 "At this also my heart trembles,
And leaps from its place.
2 "Listen closely to the [A]thunder of His voice,
And the rumbling that goes
out from His mouth.
3 "Under the whole heaven He lets it loose,
And His [a]lightning to the
[A]ends of the earth.
4 "After it, a voice roars;
He thunders with His majestic voice,
And He does not restrain [a]the lightnings
when His voice is heard.
5 "God [A]thunders with His
voice wondrously,
Doing [B]great things which we
cannot comprehend.
6 "For to [A]the snow He says,
'Fall on the earth,'
And to the [a,B]downpour and
the rain, 'Be strong.'
7 "He [A]seals the hand of every man,
That [B]all men may know His work.
8 "Then the beast goes into its [A]lair
And remains in its [a]den.
9 "Out of the [a,A]south comes the storm,
And out of the [b]north the cold.
10 "From the breath of God [A]ice is made,
And the expanse of the waters is frozen.
11 "Also with moisture He [A]loads
the thick cloud;
He [B]disperses [C]the cloud of His [a]lightning.
12 "It changes direction, turning
around by His guidance,
That [a]it may do whatever
He [A]commands [b]it
On the [B]face of the inhabited earth.
13 "Whether for [a,A]correction,
or for [B]His world,
Or for [C]lovingkindness, He
causes it to [b]happen.

14 "Listen to this, O Job,
Stand and consider the wonders of God.
15 "Do you know how God establishes them,
And makes the [a]lightning of
His cloud to shine?
16 "Do you know about the layers
of the thick clouds,
The [A]wonders of one [B]perfect
in knowledge,
17 You whose garments are hot,
When the land is still because
of the south wind?
18 "Can you, with Him, [A]spread out the skies,
Strong as a molten mirror?
19 "Teach us what we shall say to Him;
We [A]cannot arrange *our case*
because of darkness.
20 "Shall it be told Him that I would speak?
[a]Or should a man say that he
would be swallowed up?

21 "Now [a]men do not see the light
which is bright in the skies;
But the wind has passed
and cleared them.
22 "Out of the north comes golden *splendor;*
Around God is awesome majesty.
23 "The Almighty—[A]we cannot find Him;
He is [B]exalted in power
And [C]He will not do violence [D]to justice
and abundant righteousness.
24 "Therefore men [A]fear Him;
He does not [B]regard any who
are wise of heart."

GOD SPEAKS NOW TO JOB

38 Then the LORD [A]answered Job out of the whirlwind and said,

36:30 [a]Lit *light* 36:31 [A]Job 37:13 [B]Ps 104:27; 136:25; Acts 14:17 36:32 [a]Lit *light* [A]Job 37:11, 12, 15 36:33 [a]Lit *concerning Him* [A]Job 37:2 37:2 [A]Job 36:33; 37:4, 5; Ps 29:3-9 37:3 [a]Lit *light* [A]Job 28:24; 37:11, 12; 38:13 37:4 [a]Lit *them* 37:5 [A]Job 26:14 [B]Job 5:9; 37:14, 16, 23 37:6 [a]Lit *shower of rain and shower of rains* [A]Job 38:22 [B]Job 36:27 37:7 [A]Job 12:14 [B]Ps 111:2 37:8 [a]Lit *dens* [A]Job 38:40; Ps 104:21, 22 37:9 [a]Lit *chamber* [b]Lit *scattering winds* [A]Job 9:9 37:10 [A]Job 38:29; Ps 147:17 37:11 [a]Lit *light* [A]Job 36:27 [B]Job 36:29 [C]Job 37:15 37:12 [a]Lit *they* [b]Lit *them* [A]Job 36:32; Ps 148:8 [B]Is 14:21; 27:6 37:13 [a]Lit *the rod* [b]Lit *be found* [A]Ex 9:18, 23; 1 Sam 12:18, 19 [B]Job 38:26, 27 [C]1 Kin 18:41-46 37:15 [a]Lit *light* 37:16 [A]Job 37:5, 14, 23 [B]Job 36:4 37:18 [A]Job 9:8; Ps 104:2; Is 44:24; 45:12; Jer 10:12; Zech 12:1 37:19 [A]Job 9:14; Rom 8:26 37:20 [a]Or *If a man speak, surely he shall be swallowed up* 37:21 [a]Lit *they* 37:23 [A]Job 11:7, 8; Rom 11:33; 1 Tim 6:16 [B]Job 9:4; 36:5 [C]Is 63:9; Lam 3:33; Ezek 18:23, 32; 33:11 [D]Job 8:3 37:24 [A]Matt 10:28 [B]Job 5:13; Matt 11:25; 1 Cor 1:26 38:1 [A]Job 40:6

36:31 judges … gives food. The rain storm can be a disaster of punishment from God or a source of abundant crops.

37:5–13 He described God's power expressed in the cold winter. The storms and the hard winters remind us of the world in which harsh things occur, but for God's good purposes of either "correction" or "lovingkindness" (37:13).

37:14–18 These words picture the scene in the sky when the storms and winters have passed, the sunlight breaks through, the warm wind blows, and the sky clears.

37:19, 20 In this passage Elihu reminded Job that since man can't explain the wonders of God's power and purpose, he ought to be silent and not contend with God. What a man has to say against God's plans is not worthy to utter and could bring judgment.

37:21–23 Elihu illustrated the folly of telling God what to do by describing staring into the golden sun on a brilliant day (vv. 21, 22). We can't confront God in His great glory; we are not even able to look at the sun He created (v. 21).

37:24 does not regard. God is the Righteous Judge who will not take a bribe or perform favors in judgment. Thus, in his concluding speech, Elihu had pointed both Job and the reader up to God, who was ready, at last, to speak (38:1).

38:1–40:2 God appeared and engaged in His first interrogation of Job, who had raised some accusations against Him. God had His day in court with Job.

38:1 the LORD. Yahweh, the covenant Lord, was the name used for God in the book's prologue, where the reader was introduced to Job and his relationship with God. However,

2 "Who is this that [A]darkens counsel
By words without knowledge?
3 "Now [A]gird up your loins like a man,
And [B]I will ask you, and
you instruct Me!
4 "Where were you [A]when I laid the
foundation of the earth?
Tell *Me,* if you [a]have understanding,
5 Who set its [A]measurements?
Since you know.
Or who stretched the line on it?
6 "On what [A]were its bases sunk?
Or who laid its cornerstone,
7 When the morning stars sang together
And all the [A]sons of God
shouted for joy?

8 "Or *who* [A]enclosed the sea with doors
When, bursting forth, it went
out from the womb;
9 When I made a cloud its garment
And thick darkness its swaddling band,
10 And I [a,A]placed boundaries on it
And set a bolt and doors,
11 And I said, 'Thus far you shall
come, but no farther;
And here shall your proud
waves stop'?

GOD'S MIGHTY POWER

12 "Have you [a]ever in your life
commanded the morning,
And caused the dawn to know its place,
13 That it might take hold of
[A]the ends of the earth,
And [B]the wicked be shaken out of it?
14 "It is changed like clay *under* the seal;
And they stand forth like a garment.
15 "[A]From the wicked their light is withheld,
And the [B]uplifted arm is broken.

16 "Have you entered into [A]the
springs of the sea
Or walked [a]in the recesses of the deep?
17 "Have the gates of death been
revealed to you,
Or have you seen the gates
of [A]deep darkness?
18 "Have you understood the
[a]expanse of [A]the earth?
Tell *Me,* if you know all this.

19 "Where is the way to the dwelling of light?
And darkness, where is its place,
20 That you may take it to [A]its territory
And that you may discern the
paths to its [a]home?
21 "You know, for [A]you were born then,
And the number of your days is great!
22 "Have you entered the
storehouses [A]of the snow,
Or have you seen the
storehouses of the [B]hail,
23 Which I have reserved for
the time of distress,
For the day of war and battle?
24 "Where is the way that [A]the
light is divided,
Or the east wind scattered on the earth?

25 "Who has cleft a channel for the flood,
Or a way for the thunderbolt,
26 To bring [A]rain on a land without [a]people,
On a desert without a man in it,
27 To [A]satisfy the waste and desolate land
And to make the [a]seeds of grass to sprout?
28 "Has [A]the rain a father?
Or who has begotten the drops of dew?
29 "From whose womb has come the [A]ice?
And the frost of heaven, who
has given it birth?

38:2 [A]Job 35:16; 42:3 38:3 [A]Job 40:7 [B]Job 42:4 38:4 [a]Lit *know understanding* [A]Job 15:7; Ps 104:5; Prov 8:29; 30:4 38:5 [A]Prov 8:29; Is 40:12 38:6 [A]Job 26:7 38:7 [A]Job 1:6 38:8 [A]Gen 1:9; Ps 104:6-9; Prov 8:29; Jer 5:22 38:10 [a]Lit *broke My decree on it* [A]Gen 1:9; Ps 33:7; 104:9; Prov 8:29; Jer 5:22 38:12 [a]Lit *from your days* 38:13 [A]Job 28:24; 37:3 [B]Job 34:25, 26; 36:6 38:15 [A]Job 5:14 [B]Num 15:30; Ps 10:15; 37:17 38:16 [a]Or *in search of* [A]Gen 7:11; 8:2; Prov 8:24, 28 38:17 [A]Job 10:21; 26:6; 34:22 38:18 [a]Or *width* [A]Job 28:24 38:20 [a]Lit *house* [A]Job 26:10 38:21 [A]Job 15:7 38:22 [A]Job 37:6 [B]Ex 9:18; Josh 10:11; Is 30:30; Ezek 13:11, 13; Rev 16:21 38:24 [A]Job 26:10 38:26 [a]Lit *man* [A]Job 36:27 38:27 [a]Or *growth* [A]Ps 104:13, 14; 107:35 38:28 [A]Job 36:27, 28; Ps 147:8; Jer 14:22 38:29 [A]Job 37:10; Ps 147:17

in chaps. 3–37, the name Yahweh is not used. God is called El Shaddai, God the Almighty. In this book that change becomes a way of illustrating that God has been detached and distant. The relationship is restored in rich terms as God reveals Himself to Job using His covenant name. **out of the whirlwind.** Job had repeatedly called God to court in order to verify his innocence. God finally came to interrogate Job on some of the comments he had made to his own accusers. God was about to be Job's vindicator, but He first brought Job to a right understanding of Himself.

38:2 Job's words had only further confused matters already confused by useless counselors.

38:3 I will ask you. God silenced Job's presumption in constantly wanting to ask the questions of God, by becoming Job's questioner. It must be noted that God never told Job about the reason for his pain, about the conflict between Himself and Satan, which was the reason for Job's suffering. He never gave Job any explanation at all about the circumstances of his trouble. He did one thing in all He said. He asked Job if he was as eternal, great, powerful, wise, and perfect as God. If not, Job would have been better off to be quiet and trust Him.

38:4–38 God asked Job if he participated in creation as He did. That was a crushing, humbling query with an obvious "no" answer.

38:4–7 Creation is spoken of using the language of building construction.

38:7 morning stars ... sons of God. The angelic realm, God's ministering spirits.

38:8–11 God's power over the sea by raising the continents is described, along with the thick clouds that draw up its water to carry rain to the land.

38:12, 13 The dawn rises, and as it spreads light over the earth, it exposes the wicked, like shaking the corners of a cloth exposes dirt.

38:14 clay *under* the seal. Documents written on clay tablets were signed using personal engraved seals upon which was written the bearer's name. The Heb. for "changed" is "turned." It conveys the idea that the earth is turned or rotated like a cylindrical seal rolled over the soft clay. Such rolling cylinder seals were found in Babylon. This speaks of the earth, rotating on its axis, an amazing statement that only God could reveal in ancient days. The dawn rolls across the earth as it rotates.

38:15 their light. The light of the wicked is darkness, because that is when they do their works. The dawn takes away their opportunity to do their deeds and stops their arm lifted and ready to harm. Was Job around when God created light? (v. 21).

38:22 storehouses. The storehouse of these elements is the clouds.

30 "Water [a]becomes hard like stone,
And the surface of the deep
is imprisoned.

31 "Can you bind the chains
of the [A]Pleiades,
Or loose the cords of Orion?
32 "Can you lead forth a [a]constellation
in its season,
And guide the Bear with her [b]satellites?
33 "Do you know the [A]ordinances
of the heavens,
Or fix their rule over the earth?

34 "Can you lift up your voice to the clouds,
So that an [A]abundance of
water will cover you?
35 "Can you [A]send forth lightnings
that they may go
And say to you, 'Here we are'?
36 "Who has [A]put wisdom in the
innermost being
Or given [B]understanding to the [a]mind?
37 "Who can count the clouds by wisdom,
Or [A]tip the water jars of the heavens,
38 When the dust hardens into a mass
And the clods stick together?

39 "Can you hunt the [A]prey for the lion,
Or satisfy the appetite of
the young lions,
40 When they [A]crouch in *their* dens
And lie in wait in *their* lair?
41 "Who prepares for [A]the raven
its nourishment
When its young cry to God
And wander about without food?

GOD SPEAKS OF NATURE AND ITS BEINGS

39 "Do you know the time the
[a,A]mountain goats give birth?
Do you observe the calving of the [B]deer?
2 "Can you count the months they fulfill,
Or do you know the time
they give birth?
3 "They kneel down, they bring
forth their young,
They get rid of their labor pains.
4 "Their offspring become strong, they
grow up in the open field;
They leave and do not return to them.

5 "Who sent out the [A]wild donkey free?
And who loosed the bonds
of the swift donkey,
6 To whom I gave [A]the
wilderness for a home
And the salt land for his dwelling place?
7 "He scorns the tumult of the city,
The shoutings of the driver
he does not hear.
8 "He explores the mountains for his pasture
And searches after every green thing.
9 "Will the [A]wild ox consent to serve you,
Or will he spend the night
at your manger?
10 "Can you bind the wild ox in
a furrow with [a]ropes,
Or will he harrow the valleys after you?
11 "Will you trust him because
his strength is great
And leave your labor to him?
12 "Will you have faith in him that
he will return your [a]grain
And gather *it from* your threshing floor?

13 "The ostriches' wings flap joyously
With the pinion and plumage of [a]love,
14 For she abandons her eggs to the earth
And warms them in the dust,
15 And she forgets that a foot
may crush [a]them,
Or that a wild beast may trample [a]them.
16 "She treats her young [A]cruelly,
as if *they* were not hers;
Though her labor be in vain,
she is [a]unconcerned;
17 Because God has made her forget wisdom,
And has not given her a share
of understanding.
18 "When she lifts herself [a]on high,
She laughs at the horse and his rider.

19 "Do you give the horse *his* might?
Do you clothe his neck with a mane?
20 "Do you make him [A]leap like the locust?
His majestic [B]snorting is terrible.
21 "[a]He paws in the valley, and
rejoices in *his* strength;
He [A]goes out to meet the weapons.
22 "He laughs at fear and is not dismayed;
And he does not turn back from the sword.
23 "The quiver rattles against him,
The flashing spear and javelin.

38:30 [a]Lit *hides itself* 38:31 [A]Job 9:9; Amos 5:8 38:32 [a]Heb *Mazzaroth* [b]Lit *sons* 38:33 [A]Ps 148:6; Jer 31:35, 36 38:34 [A]Job 22:11; 36:27, 28; 38:37 38:35 [A]Job 36:32; 37:3 38:36 [a]Or *rooster* [A]Job 9:4; Ps 51:6; Eccl 2:26 [B]Job 32:8 38:37 [A]Job 38:34 38:39 [A]Ps 104:21 38:40 [A]Job 37:8 38:41 [A]Ps 147:9; Matt 6:26; Luke 12:24 39:1 [a]Lit *goats of the rock* [A]Deut 14:5; 1 Sam 24:2; Ps 104:18 [B]Ps 29:9 39:5 [A]Job 6:5; 11:12; 24:5; Ps 104:11 39:6 [A]Job 24:5; Jer 2:24; Hos 8:9 39:9 [A]Num 23:22; Deut 33:17; Ps 22:21; 29:6; 92:10; Is 34:7 39:10 [a]Lit *his rope* 39:12 [a]Lit *seed* 39:13 [a]Or *a stork* 39:15 [a]Lit *it* 39:16 [a]Lit *without fear* [A]Lam 4:3 39:18 [a]Or *to flee* 39:20 [A]Joel 2:5 [B]Jer 8:16 39:21 [a]Lit *They paw* [A]Jer 8:6

38:31, 32 Pleiades ... Orion ... Bear. Stellar constellations (cf. Job 9:9) are in view.

38:33 ordinances of the heavens. The laws and powers that regulate all heavenly bodies.

38:36 wisdom ... understanding. This is at the heart of the real issue. The wisdom of God which created and sustains the universe is at work in Job's suffering also. See also 39:17.

38:39–39:30 God asked Job the humiliating questions about whether he could take care of the animal kingdom. Job must have been feeling less and less significant under the crushing indictment of such comparisons with God.

39:5 swift donkey. A species of donkey.

39:13–18 ostriches' wings. The silly ostrich that leaves her eggs on the ground lacks sense. God has not given her wisdom. She is almost a picture of Job, who is a mixture of foolishness and strength (v. 18).

39:19–25 Here is a magnificent, vivid picture of the warhorse.

24 "With shaking and rage he
[a]races over the ground,
And he does not stand still at
the voice of the trumpet.
25 "As often as the trumpet
sounds he says, 'Aha!'
And he scents the battle from afar,
And the thunder of the captains
and the war cry.

26 "Is it by your understanding
that the hawk soars,
Stretching his wings toward the south?
27 "Is it at your [a]command that
the eagle mounts up
And makes [A]his nest on high?
28 "On the cliff he dwells and lodges,
Upon the rocky crag, an inaccessible place.
29 "From there he [A]spies out food;
His eyes see *it* from afar.
30 "His young ones also suck up blood;
And [A]where the slain are, there is he."

JOB: WHAT CAN I SAY?

40 Then the LORD said to Job,

2 "Will the faultfinder [A]contend
with the Almighty?
Let him who [B]reproves God answer it."

3 Then Job answered the LORD and said,

4 "Behold, I am insignificant;
what can I reply to You?
I [A]lay my hand on my mouth.
5 "Once I have spoken, and [A]I will not answer;
Even twice, and I will add nothing more."

GOD QUESTIONS JOB

6 Then the [A]LORD answered Job out of the storm
and said,

7 "Now [A]gird up your loins like a man;
I will [B]ask you, and you instruct Me.
8 "Will you really [A]annul My judgment?
Will you [B]condemn Me [C]that
you may be justified?
9 "Or do you have an arm like God,
And can you [A]thunder with a voice like His?

10 "[A]Adorn yourself with eminence
and dignity,
And clothe yourself with
honor and majesty.
11 "Pour out [A]the overflowings of your anger,
And look on everyone who is
[B]proud, and make him low.
12 "Look on everyone who is proud,
and [A]humble him,
And [B]tread down the wicked
[a]where they stand.
13 "[A]Hide them in the dust together;
Bind [a]them in the hidden *place*.
14 "Then I will also [a]confess to you,
That your own right hand can save you.

GOD'S POWER SHOWN IN CREATURES

15 "Behold now, [a]Behemoth, which
[A]I made [b]as well as you;
He eats grass like an ox.
16 "Behold now, his strength in his loins
And his power in the muscles of his belly.
17 "He bends his tail like a cedar;
The sinews of his thighs are knit together.
18 "His bones are tubes of bronze;
His [a]limbs are like bars of iron.

19 "He is the [A]first of the ways of God;
Let his [B]maker bring near his sword.
20 "Surely the mountains [A]bring him food,
And all the beasts of the field [B]play there.
21 "Under the lotus plants he lies down,
In the covert of the reeds and the marsh.
22 "The lotus plants cover him with [a]shade;
The willows of the brook surround him.
23 "If a river [a]rages, he is not alarmed;
He is confident, though the [A]Jordan
rushes to his mouth.

39:24 [a]Or *swallows up* 39:27 [a]Lit *mouth* [A]Jer 49:16; Obad 4 39:29 [A]Job 9:26 39:30 [A]Matt 24:28; Luke 17:37 40:2 [A]Job 9:3; 10:2; 33:13; Is 45:9 [B]Job 13:3; 23:4; 31:35 40:4 [A]Job 21:5; 29:9 40:5 [A]Job 9:3, 15 40:6 [A]Job 38:1 40:7 [A]Job 38:3 [B]Job 38:3; 42:4 40:8 [A]Rom 3:4 [B]Job 10:3, 7; 16:11; 19:6; 27:2 [C]Job 13:18; 27:6 40:9 [A]Job 37:5; Ps 29:3 40:10 [A]Ps 93:1; 104:1 40:11 [A]Is 42:25; Nah 1:6, 8 [B]Is 2:12; Dan 4:37 40:12 [a]Lit *under them* [A]1 Sam 2:7; Is 2:12; 13:11; Dan 4:37 [B]Is 63:3 40:13 [a]Or *their faces* [A]Is 2:10-12 40:14 [a]Or *praise you* 40:15 [a]Or *the hippopotamus* [b]Lit *with* [A]Job 40:19 40:18 [a]Lit *bones* 40:19 [A]Job 41:33 [B]Job 40:15 40:20 [A]Ps 104:14 [B]Ps 104:26 40:22 [a]Lit *his shade* 40:23 [a]Or *oppresses* [A]Gen 13:10

40:2 God challenged Job to answer all the questions he had posed. God didn't need to know the answer, but Job needed to admit his weakness, inferiority, and inability to even try to figure out God's infinite mind. God's wisdom was so superior, His sovereign control of everything so complete, that this was all Job needed to know.

40:3–5 Job's first response to God was "I am guilty as charged. I will say no more." He knows he should not have found fault with the Almighty. He should not have insisted on his own understanding. He should not have thought God unjust. So he was reduced to silence at last.

40:6–41:34 As if the first was not enough, God's second interrogation of Job commenced along the very same lines, only focusing on two unique animals in God's creation: Behemoth (40:15–24) and Leviathan (41:1–34), two creatures powerful and fearful who embodied all that is overwhelming, uncontrollable, and terrorizing in this world. Man can't control them, but God can.

40:8–14 God unleashed another torrent of crushing rebukes to Job, in which He mocked Job's questionings of Him by telling the sufferer that if he really thought he knew what was best for him rather than God (v. 8), then he should take over being God! (vv. 9–14).

40:15–24 **Behemoth.** While this is a generic term used commonly in the OT for large cattle or land animals, the description in this passage suggests an extraordinary creature. The hippopotamus has been suggested by the details in the passage (vv. 19–24). However, the short tail of a hippo is hardly consistent with v. 17, where tail could be translated "trunk." It could refer to an elephant, who could be considered "first" or chief of God's creatures whom only He can control (v. 19). Some believe God is describing His most impressive creation of land animals, the dinosaur species, which fit all the characteristics.

40:23 God was not saying this creature lived in the Jordan River, but rather, recognizing that the Jordan was familiar to Job, used it to illustrate how much water this beast could ingest. He could swallow the Jordan! It was a word used to refer to something of enormous size and threatening power.

24 "Can anyone capture him
[a]when he is on watch,
With [b]barbs can anyone pierce *his* nose?

GOD'S POWER SHOWN IN CREATURES

41 "[a]Can you draw out [b,A]Leviathan
with a fishhook?
Or press down his tongue with a cord?
2 "Can you [A]put a [a]rope in his nose
Or pierce his jaw with a [b]hook?
3 "Will he make many supplications to you,
Or will he speak to you soft words?
4 "Will he make a covenant with you?
Will you take him for a
servant forever?
5 "Will you play with him as with a bird,
Or will you bind him for your maidens?
6 "Will the [a]traders bargain over him?
Will they divide him among
the merchants?
7 "Can you fill his skin with harpoons,
Or his head with fishing spears?
8 "Lay your hand on him;
Remember the battle; [a]you
will not do it again!
9 "[a]Behold, [b]your expectation is false;
Will [c]you be laid low even
at the sight of him?
10 "No one is so fierce that he
dares to [A]arouse him;
Who then is he that can
stand before Me?
11 "Who has [a,A]given to Me that
I should repay *him?*
Whatever is [B]under the whole
heaven is Mine.

12 "I will not keep silence
concerning his limbs,
Or his mighty strength, or
his [a]orderly frame.
13 "Who can [a]strip off his outer armor?
Who can come within his double [b]mail?
14 "Who can open the doors of his face?
Around his teeth there is terror.
15 "*His* [a]strong scales are *his* pride,
Shut up *as with* a tight seal.
16 "One is so near to another
That no air can come between them.
17 "They are joined one to another;
They clasp each other and
cannot be separated.
18 "His sneezes flash forth light,
And his eyes are like the
[A]eyelids of the morning.
19 "Out of his mouth go burning torches;
Sparks of fire leap forth.
20 "Out of his nostrils smoke goes forth
As *from* a boiling pot and *burning* rushes.
21 "His breath kindles coals,
And a flame goes forth from his mouth.
22 "In his neck lodges strength,
And dismay leaps before him.
23 "The folds of his flesh are joined together,
Firm on him and immovable.
24 "His heart is as hard as a stone,
Even as hard as a lower millstone.
25 "When he raises himself up,
the [a]mighty fear;
Because of the crashing they
are bewildered.
26 "The sword that reaches him cannot avail,
Nor the spear, the dart or the javelin.
27 "He regards iron as straw,
Bronze as rotten wood.
28 "The [a]arrow cannot make him flee;
Slingstones are turned into stubble for him.
29 "Clubs are regarded as stubble;
He laughs at the rattling of the javelin.
30 "His underparts are *like* sharp potsherds;
He [a]spreads out *like* a threshing
sledge on the mire.
31 "He makes the depths boil like a pot;
He makes the sea like a jar of ointment.
32 "Behind him he makes a wake to shine;
One would think the deep
to be gray-haired.
33 "[A]Nothing on [a]earth is like him,
One made without fear.
34 "[a]He looks on everything that is high;
He is king over all the [A]sons of pride."

JOB'S CONFESSION

42 Then Job answered the LORD and said,

2 "I know that [A]You can do all things,
And that no purpose of Yours
can be thwarted.

40:24 [a]Lit *in his eyes* [b]Lit *snares* 41:1 [a]Ch 40:25 in Heb [b]Or *the crocodile* [A]Job 3:8; Ps 74:14; 104:26; Is 27:1 41:2 [a]Lit *rope of rushes* [b]Or *thorn or ring* [A]2 Kin 19:28; Is 37:29 41:6 [a]Lit *partners* 41:8 [a]Lit *do not add* 41:9 [a]Ch 41:1 in Heb [b]Lit *his* [c]Lit *he* 41:10 [A]Job 3:8 41:11 [a]Lit *anticipated* [A]Rom 11:35 [B]Ex 19:5; Deut 10:14; Job 9:5-10; 26:6-14; 28:24; Ps 24:1; 50:12; 1 Cor 10:26 41:12 [a]Or *graceful* 41:13 [a]Lit *uncover the face of his garment* [b]So Gr; Heb *bridle* 41:15 [a]Lit *rows of shields* 41:18 [A]Job 3:9 41:25 [a]Or *gods* 41:28 [a]Lit *son of the bow* 41:30 [a]Or *moves across* 41:33 [a]Lit *dust* [A]Job 40:19 41:34 [a]Ch 41:26 in Heb [A]Job 28:8 42:2 [A]Gen 18:14; Matt 19:26

41:1 Leviathan. This term appears in 4 other OT texts (Job 3:8; Pss 74:14; 104:26; Is 27:1). In each case Leviathan refers to some mighty creature who can overwhelm man but who is no match for God. Since this creature lives in the sea among ships (Ps 104:26), some form of sea monster, possibly an ancient dinosaur, is in view. Some feel it was a crocodile, which had scaly hide (v. 15), terrible teeth (v. 14), and speed in the water (v. 32). But crocodiles are not sea creatures, and clearly this one was (v. 31). Some have thought it was a killer whale or a great white shark, because he is the ultimate killer beast over all other proud beasts (v. 34). It could also have been some sea-going dinosaur.

41:4 Will he make a covenant with you? "Will this monstrous creature need, for any reason, to come to terms with you, Job? Are you able to control him?" God asked.

41:10 Who then is he that can stand before Me? This was the essential question being asked in both the Behemoth and Leviathan passages. God created these awesome creatures, and His might is far greater than theirs. If Job couldn't stand against them, what was he doing contending with God? He would be better off to fight a dinosaur or a killer shark.

41:11 God did not need to buy anything; He already owned all things. Paul quoted this in Ro 11:35.

42:1–6 Job's confession and repentance took place finally. He still did not know why he suffered so profoundly, but he was done

3 'Who is this that [A]hides counsel
without knowledge?'
Therefore I have declared that
which I did not understand,
Things [B]too wonderful for me,
which I did not know.
4 'Hear, now, and I will speak;
I will [A]ask You, and You instruct me.'
5 "I have [A]heard of You by the
hearing of the ear;
But now my [B]eye sees You;
6 Therefore I retract,
And I repent in dust and ashes."

GOD DISPLEASED WITH JOB'S FRIENDS

7 It came about after the LORD had spoken these
words to Job, that the LORD said to Eliphaz the Temanite, "My wrath is kindled against you and against
your two friends, because you have not spoken of Me
what is right [A]as My servant Job has. 8 Now therefore,
take for yourselves [A]seven bulls and seven rams,
and go to My servant Job, and offer up a [B]burnt
offering for yourselves, and My servant Job will
[C]pray for you. [D]For I will [a]accept him so that I may
not do with you *according to your* folly, because you
have not spoken of Me what is right, as My servant
Job has." 9 So Eliphaz the Temanite and Bildad the
Shuhite *and* Zophar the Naamathite went and did
as the LORD told them; and the LORD [a]accepted Job.

GOD RESTORES JOB'S FORTUNES

10 The LORD [A]restored the fortunes of Job when
he prayed for his friends, and the LORD increased
all that Job had twofold. 11 Then all his [A]brothers and
all his sisters and all who had known him before
came to him, and they ate bread with him in his
house; and they [B]consoled him and comforted him
for all the adversities that the LORD had brought on
him. And each one gave him one [a]piece of money,
and each a ring of gold. 12 [A]The LORD blessed the
latter *days* of Job more than his beginning; [B]and
he had 14,000 sheep and 6,000 camels and 1,000
yoke of oxen and 1,000 female donkeys. 13 [A]He had
seven sons and three daughters. 14 He named the
first Jemimah, and the second Keziah, and the third
Keren-happuch. 15 In all the land no women were
found so fair as Job's daughters; and their father
gave them inheritance among their brothers. 16 After
this, Job lived 140 years, and saw his sons and his
grandsons, four generations. 17 [A]And Job died, an
old man and full of days.

42:3 [A]Job 38:2 [B]Ps 40:5; 131:1; 139:6 42:4 [A]Job 38:3; 40:7 42:5 [A]Job 26:14; Rom 10:17 [B]Is 6:5; Eph 1:17, 18 42:7 [A]Job 40:3-5; 42:1-6 42:8 [a]Lit *lift up his face* [A]Num 23:1 [B]Job 1:5 [C]Gen 20:17; James 5:16; 1 John 5:16 [D]Job 22:30 42:9 [a]Lit *lifted up the face of* 42:10 [A]Deut 30:3; Job 1:2, 3; Ps 14:7; 85:1-3; 126:1-6 42:11 [a]Heb *qesitah* [A]Job 19:13 [B]Job 2:11 42:12 [A]Job 1:10; 8:7; James 5:11 [B]Job 1:3 42:13 [A]Job 1:2 42:17 [A]Gen 15:15; 25:8; Job 5:26

complaining, questioning, and challenging God's wisdom and justice. He was reduced to such utter humility, crushed beneath the weight of God's greatness, that all he could do was repent for his insolence. Without answers to all of his questions, Job quietly bowed in humble submission before his Creator and admitted that God was sovereign (cf. Is 14:24; 46:8–11). Most importantly for the message of the book, Job was still diseased and without his children and possessions, and God had not changed anything (except for the humbling of the heart of His servant). Satan had been proven completely wrong in the charges he brought against Job and in thinking he could destroy true saving faith; Job's companions were completely wrong in the charges they brought against him; but most critically, Job himself was completely wrong in the charges he had raised against God. He expressed his own sorrowful regret that he had not just accepted God's will without such ignorant complaints and questions.

42:3, 4 Job twice alluded to statements God had made in His interrogation of Job. The first allusion "Who is this that hides counsel without knowledge?" (cf. 38:2) indicted Job's pride and presumption regarding God's counsel. The second, "I will ask You, and You instruct Me" (38:3; 40:7) expressed God's judicial authority to demand answers from His own accuser, Job. The two quotes manifested that Job understood the divine rebuke.

42:5 have heard … now my eye sees You. At last, Job said he understood God whom he had seen with the eyes of faith. He had never so well grasped the greatness, majesty, sovereignty, and independence of God as he did at that moment.

42:6 repent in dust and ashes. All that was left to do was repent! The ashes upon which the broken man sat had not changed, but the heart of God's suffering servant had. Job did not need to repent of some sins which Satan or his accusers had raised. But Job had exercised presumption and allegations of unfairness against his Lord and hated himself for this in a way that called for brokenness and contrition.

42:7–17 The text goes back to prose, from the poetry begun in 3:1.

42:7, 8 you have not spoken of Me what is right. God directly vindicated Job by saying that Job had spoken right about God in rejecting the error of his friends. They are then rebuked for those misrepresentations of insensitivity and arrogance. This does not mean that everything they said was incorrect, but they had made wrong statements about the character and works of God, and also had raised erroneous allegations against Job.

42:8 seven bulls and seven rams. This was the number of sacrifices specified in Nu 23:1 by Balaam the prophet, so perhaps, it was a traditional kind of burnt offering for sin.

42:8, 9 As God had been gracious to Job, so He was to Job's friends, by means of sacrifice and prayer. Here the book points to the need for a sacrifice for sin, fulfilled in the Lord Jesus Christ who gave Himself as an offering for sins and ever lives to intercede (cf. 1Ti 2:5). Even before the Levitical priesthood, family heads acted as priests, offering sacrifices and mediating through prayer.

42:13 seven sons … three daughters. While the animals are double the number of Job 1:3, why are not the children? It is obvious that Job still had 7 sons and 3 daughters waiting for him in the presence of God (42:17).

42:14 These names are representative of the joys of restoration. Jemimah means "day light," Keziah means "sweet smelling," and Keren-happuch describes a beautiful color ladies used to paint their eyelids.

42:15 gave them inheritance. This was unusual in the East. By Jewish law, daughters only received an inheritance when there were no sons (Nu 27:8). Job had plenty for all.

42:17 And Job died, an old man and full of days. These concluding words take the reader back to where the account began (1:1). Job died in prosperity and his days were counted as a blessing. In the words of Jas (5:11), we have seen the outcome of the Lord's dealings, that the Lord is "full of compassion and *is* merciful." But the "accuser of our brethren" (Rev 12:10) is still "roaming about on the earth" (Job 1:7), and God's servants are still learning to trust in the all-wise, all-powerful Judge of the universe for what they cannot understand.

THE BOOK OF

PSALMS

TITLE

The entire collection of Psalms is entitled "Praises" in the Hebrew text. Later, rabbis often designated it "The Book of Praises." The Septuagint (LXX), the Greek translation of the OT, labeled it "Psalms" (cf. "The Book of Psalms" in the NT: Lk 20:42; Ac 1:20). The Greek verb from which the noun "psalms" comes basically denotes the "plucking or twanging of strings," so that an association with musical accompaniment is implied. The English title derives from the Greek term and its background. The Psalms constituted Israel's ancient, God-breathed (2Ti 3:16) "hymnbook," which defined the proper spirit and content of worship.

There are 116 psalms that have superscriptions or "titles." The Hebrew text includes these titles with the verses themselves. When the titles are surveyed individually and studied as a general phenomenon, there are significant indications that they were appended to their respective psalms shortly after composition and that they contain reliable information (cf. Lk 20:42).

These titles convey various kinds of information such as authorship, dedication, historical occasion, liturgical assignment to a worship director, liturgical instructions (e.g., what kind of song it is, whether it is to have a musical accompaniment, and what tune to use), plus other technical instructions of uncertain meaning due to their great antiquity. One very tiny, attached Hebrew preposition shows up in the majority of the Psalm titles. It may convey different relationships, e.g., "of," "from," "by," "to," "for," "in reference to," "about." Sometimes it occurs more than once, even in short headings, usually supplying "of," or "by," person X ... "to," or "for," person Y information. However, this little preposition most frequently indicates the authorship of a psalm, whether "of" David, the accomplished psalmist of Israel, or "by" Moses, Solomon, Asaph, or the sons of Korah.

AUTHOR AND DATE

From the divine perspective, the Psalter points to God as its author. Approaching authorship from the human side one can identify a collection of more than 7 composers. King David wrote at least 73 of the 150 psalms; the sons of Korah accounted for 10 (Pss 42, 44–49, 84, 85, 87); and Asaph contributed 12 (Pss 50, 73–83). Other penmen included Solomon (Pss 72, 127), Moses (Ps 90), Heman (Ps 88), and Ethan (Ps 89). The remaining 50 psalms remain anonymous in their authorship, although Ezra is thought to be the author of some. The time range of the Psalms extends from Moses, ca. 1410 B.C. (Ps 90), to the late sixth or early fifth century B.C. post-Exilic period (Ps 126), which spans about 900 years of Jewish history.

BACKGROUND AND SETTING

The backdrop for the Psalms is twofold: 1) the acts of God in creation and history, and 2) the history of Israel. Historically, the psalms range in time from the origin of life to the post-Exilic joys of the Jews liberated from Babylon. Thematically, the psalms cover a wide spectrum of topics, ranging from heavenly worship to earthly war. The collected psalms comprise the largest book in the Bible and the most frequently quoted OT book in the NT. Psalm 117 represents the middle chapter (out of 1,189) in the Bible. Psalm 119 is the largest chapter in the entire Bible. Through the ages, the psalms have retained their original primary purpose, i.e., to engender the proper praise and worship of God.

HISTORICAL AND THEOLOGICAL THEMES

The basic theme of Psalms is living real life in the real world, where two dimensions operate simultaneously: 1) a horizontal or temporal reality, and 2) a vertical or transcendent reality. Without denying the pain of the earthly dimension, the people of God are to live joyfully and dependently on the Person and promises standing behind the heavenly/eternal dimension. All cycles of human troubles and triumphs provide occasions for expressing human complaints, confidence, prayers, or praise to Israel's sovereign Lord.

In view of this, Psalms presents a broad array of theology, practically couched in day-to-day reality. The sinfulness of man is documented concretely, not only through the behavioral patterns of the wicked, but also by the periodic stumblings of believers. The sovereignty of God is everywhere recognized, but not at the expense of genuine human responsibility. Life often seems to be out of control, and yet all events and situations are understood in the light of divine providence as being right on course according to

God's timetable. Assuring glimpses of a future "God's day" bolsters the call for perseverance to the end. This book of praise manifests a very practical theology.

A commonly misunderstood phenomenon in Psalms is the association that often develops between the "one" (the psalmist) and the "many" (the theocratic people). Virtually all of the cases of this occur in the psalms of King David. There was an inseparable relationship between the mediatorial ruler and his people; as life went for the king, so it went for the people. Furthermore, at times this union accounted for the psalmist's apparent connection with Christ in the messianic psalms (or messianic portions of certain psalms). The so-called imprecatory (curse pronouncing) psalms may be better understood with this perspective. As God's mediatorial representative on earth, David prayed for judgment on his enemies, since these enemies were not only hurting him, but were primarily hurting God's people. Ultimately, they challenged the King of Kings, the God of Israel.

INTERPRETIVE CHALLENGES

It is helpful to recognize certain recurring genres or literary types in the Psalter. Some of the most obvious are: 1) the wisdom type with instructions for right living; 2) lamentation patterns which deal with the pangs of life (usually arising from enemies without); 3) penitential psalms (mostly dealing with the "enemy" within, i.e., sin); 4) kingship emphases (universal or mediatorial; theocratic and/or messianic rule); and 5) thanksgiving psalms. A combination of style and subject matter help to identify such types when they appear.

The comprehensive literary characteristic of the psalms is that all of them are poetry par excellence. Unlike most English poetry, which is based on rhyme and meter, Hebrew poetry is essentially characterized by logical parallelisms. Some of the most important kinds of parallelisms are: 1) synonymous (the thought of the first line is restated with similar concepts in the second line, e.g., Ps 2:1); 2) antithetic (the thought of the second line is contrasted with the first, e.g., Ps 1:6); 3) climactic (the second and any subsequent lines pick up a crucial word, phrase, or concept and advance it in a stair-step fashion, e.g., Ps 29:1, 2); and 4) chiastic or introverted (the logical units are developed in an A.... B... B'... A' pattern, e.g., Ps 1:2).

On a larger scale, some psalms in their development from the first to the last verse employ an acrostic or alphabetical arrangement. Psalms 9, 10, 25, 34, 37, 111, 112, 119, and 145 are recognized as either complete or incomplete acrostics. In the Hebrew text, the first letter of the first word of every verse or section begins with a different Hebrew consonant, which advances in alphabetical order until the 22 consonants are exhausted. Such a literary vehicle undoubtedly aided in the memorization of the content and served to indicate that its particular subject matter had been covered from "A to Z." Psalm 119 stands out as the most complete example of this device, since the first letter of each of its 22, 8-verse stanzas moves completely through the Hebrew alphabet.

OUTLINE

The 150 canonical psalms were organized quite early into 5 "books." Each of these books ends with a doxology (Pss 41:13; 72:18–20; 89:52; 106:48; 150:6). Jewish tradition appealed to the number 5 and alleged that these divisions echoed the Pentateuch, i.e., the 5 books of Moses. It is true that there are clusters of psalms, such as 1) those drawn together by an association with an individual or group (e.g., "The sons of Korah," Pss 42–49; Asaph, Pss 73–83); 2) those dedicated to a particular function (e.g., "Songs of ascents," Pss 120–134); 3) those devoted explicitly to praise worship (Pss 146–150). But no one configuration key unlocks the "mystery" as to the organizing theme of this 5-book arrangement. Thus, there is no identifiable thematic structure to the entire collection of psalms. A brief introduction and outline for each psalm will be provided with the study notes for individual psalms.

The following expressions occur often in the Psalms:

Selah	May mean *Pause, Crescendo* or *Musical Interlude*
Maskil	Possibly, *Contemplative,* or *Didactic,* or *Skillful Psalm*
Mikhtam	Possibly, *Epigrammatic Poem,* or *Atonement Psalm*
Sheol	The nether world

BOOK 1

PSALM 1

THE RIGHTEOUS AND THE WICKED CONTRASTED.

1 How blessed is the man who [A]does not
walk in the [B]counsel of the wicked,
Nor stand in the [a,C]path of sinners,
Nor [D]sit in the seat of scoffers!
2 But his [A]delight is [B]in the law of the LORD,
And in His law he meditates
[C]day and [D]night.
3 He will be like [A]a tree *firmly*
planted by [a]streams of water,
Which yields its fruit in its season
And its [b]leaf does not wither;
And [c]in whatever he does, [B]he prospers.
4 The wicked are not so,
But they are like [A]chaff which
the wind drives away.
5 Therefore [A]the wicked will not
stand in the [B]judgment,
Nor sinners in [C]the assembly
of the righteous.
6 For the LORD [a,A]knows the
way of the righteous,
But the way of [B]the wicked will perish.

PSALM 2

THE REIGN OF THE LORD'S ANOINTED.

1 Why are [A]the [a]nations in an uproar
And the peoples [B]devising a vain thing?
2 The [A]kings of the earth take their stand
And the rulers take counsel together

1:1 [a]Or *way* [A]Prov 4:14 [B]Ps 5:9, 10; 10:2-11; 36:1-4 [C]Ps 17:4; 119:104 [D]Ps 26:4, 5; Jer 15:17 1:2 [A]Ps 119:14, 16, 35 [B]Josh 1:8 [C]Ps 25:5 [D]Ps 63:5, 6 1:3 [a]Or *canals* [b]Or *foliage* [c]Or *all that he does prospers* [A]Ps 92:12-14; Jer 17:8; Ezek 19:10 [B]Gen 39:2, 3, 23; Ps 128:2 1:4 [A]Job 21:18; Ps 35:5; Is 17:13 1:5 [A]Ps 5:5 [B]Ps 9:7, 8, 16 [C]Ps 89:5, 7 1:6 [a]Or *approves* or *has regard to* [A]Ps 37:18; Nah 1:7; John 10:14; 2 Tim 2:19 [B]Ps 9:5, 6; 11:6 2:1 [a]Or *Gentiles* [A]Ps 46:6; 83:2-5; Acts 4:25, 26 [B]Ps 21:11 2:2 [A]Ps 48:4-6

1:1–6 This wisdom psalm basically functions as an introduction to the entire book of Psalms. Its theme is as big as the whole Bible because it tells of people, paths, and ultimate destinations (for a significant parallel see Jer 17:5–8). By two cycles of contrast, Ps 1 separates all people into their respective spiritual categories:

I. By observation, all people are separated ethically (1:1–4)
   A. A Picture of the Godly (1:1–3)
   B. A Picture of the Ungodly (1:4)
II. By outcome, all people are separated judicially (1:5, 6)
   A. The Failure of Ungodly People (1:5)
   B. The Fruition of Lifestyles (1:6)
      1. Recognition of the godly (1:6a)
      2. Ruination of the ungodly (1:6b)

1:1 blessed. From the perspective of the individual, this is a deep-seated joy and contentment in God; from the perspective of the believing community, it refers to redemptive favor (cf. the blessings and cursings of Dt 27:11–28:6). **not walk ... Nor stand ... Nor sit.** The "beatitude" man (cf. Mt 5:3–11) is first described as one who avoids such associations as these which exemplify sin's sequential downward drag.

1:2 his delight ... in the law. Switching to a positive description, the spiritually "happy" man is characterized by the consistent contemplation and internalization of God's Word for ethical direction and obedience.

1:3 like a tree. Because of the mostly arid terrain of Israel, a lush tree served as a fitting symbol of blessing in the OT. **planted.** Lit. "transplanted." Trees do not plant themselves; neither do sinful people transport themselves into God's kingdom. Salvation is His marvelous work of grace (cf. Is 61:3; Mt 15:13). Yet, there is genuine responsibility in appropriating the abundant resources of God (cf. Jer 17:8), which lead to eventual productivity.

1:4 The wicked are not so. This is an abrupt contrast, lit. "Not so the wicked!" **chaff.** A frequent OT word picture from harvest time for what is unsubstantial, without value, and worthy only to be discarded.

1:5 Therefore ... not stand. "Therefore" introduces the strong conclusion that the ungodly will not be approved by God's judgment.

1:6 the LORD knows. This is far more than recognition; the Lord "knows" everything. In this context, the reference is to personal intimacy and involvement with His righteous ones (contra. Mt 7:23; cf. 2Ti 2:19). **the way of.** The repetition of this phrase picks up on the "path" imagery so characteristic of this psalm. It refers to one's total course of life, i.e., lifestyle. Here these two courses arrive at the ways of life and death, as in Dt 30:19; Jer 21:8; cf. Mt 7:13, 14. **will perish.** One day the wicked person's way will end in ruin; a new order is coming and it will be a righteous order. So Ps 1 begins with the "blessed" and ends with those who "perish" (cf. Pss 9:5, 6; 112:10).

2:1–12 Sometimes Ps 2 is said to share with Ps 1 in the role of introducing the Psalter (cf. "blessed" in 1:1 and 2:12). Also, it seems that, while the function of Ps 1 is to disclose the two different "ways" for individuals, Ps 2 follows up with its application to nations. This psalm is normally termed "royal" and has had a long history of messianic interpretation. Although it has no title, it seems to bear the imprint of David's hand. As such, it fluidly moves from the lesser David through the Davidic dynasty to the Greater David—Jesus Christ. Psalm 2 progressively shines its poetic spotlight on 4 vivid scenes relating to the mutiny of mankind against God:

I. Scene One: Human Rebellion (2:1–3)
II. Scene Two: Divine Reaction (2:4–6)
III. Scene Three: Divine Rule (2:7–9)
IV. Scene Four: Human Responsibility (2:10–12)

2:1 devising a vain thing. This is the irony of man's depravity—devising, conspiring, and scheming emptiness (cf. Ps 38:12; Pr 24:2; Is 59:3, 13).

2:2 Against ... against. The nations and peoples, led by their kings and rulers (v. 1), direct their hostility toward the Lord and His anointed one. The consecrated and commissioned

TYPES OF PSALMS

Type	Psalms	Act of Worship
Individual and Communal Lament	3–7; 12; 13; 22; 25–28; 35; 38–40; 42–44; 51; 54–57; 59–61; 63; 64; 69–71; 74; 79; 80; 83; 85; 86; 88; 90; 102; 109; 120; 123; 130; 140–143	Express need for God's deliverance
Thanksgiving	8; 18; 19; 29; 30; 32–34; 36; 40; 41; 66; 103–106; 111; 113; 116; 117; 124; 129; 135; 136; 138; 139; 146–148; 150	Make aware of God's blessings Express thanks
Enthronement	47; 93; 96–99	Describe God's sovereign rule
Pilgrimage	43; 46; 48; 76; 84; 87; 120–134	Establish a mood of worship
Royal	2; 18; 20; 21; 45; 72; 89; 101; 110; 132; 144	Portray Christ the sovereign ruler
Wisdom	1; 37; 119	Instruct as to God's will
Imprecatory	7; 35; 40; 55; 58; 59; 69; 79; 109; 137; 139; 144	Invoke God's wrath and judgment against His enemies

[B]Against the LORD and against
His [a,C]Anointed, saying,
3 "Let us [A]tear their fetters apart
And cast away their cords from us!"

4 He who [a]sits in the heavens [A]laughs,
The Lord [B]scoffs at them.
5 Then He will speak to them in His [A]anger
And [B]terrify them in His fury, saying,
6 "But as for Me, I have [a]installed [A]My King
Upon Zion, [B]My holy mountain."

7 "I will surely tell of the [a]decree of the LORD:
He said to Me, 'You are [A]My Son,
Today I have begotten You.
8 'Ask of Me, and [A]I will surely give [B]the
[a]nations as Your inheritance,
And the *very* [C]ends of the earth
as Your possession.
9 'You shall [a,A]break them with a [b]rod of iron,
You shall [B]shatter them like
[c]earthenware.' "

10 Now therefore, O kings,
[A]show discernment;
Take warning, O [a]judges of the earth.
11 [a]Worship the LORD with [b,A]reverence
And rejoice with [B]trembling.
12 [a]Do homage to [A]the Son, that
He not become angry, and
you perish *in* the way,
For [B]His wrath may [b]soon be kindled.
How blessed are all who
[C]take refuge in Him!

PSALM 3

MORNING PRAYER OF TRUST IN GOD.

A Psalm of David, when [†]he fled
from Absalom his son.

1 O LORD, how [A]my adversaries
have increased!
Many are rising up against me.
2 Many are saying [a]of my soul,
"There is no [b,A]deliverance for him in God."
[c]*Selah*

3 But You, O LORD, are [A]a shield about me,
My [B]glory, and the One who
[C]lifts my head.
4 I was crying to the LORD
with my voice,
And He [A]answered me from [B]His holy
[a]mountain. *Selah*
5 [a]I [A]lay down and slept;
I awoke, for the LORD sustains me.
6 I will [A]not be afraid of ten
thousands of people
Who have [B]set themselves
against me round about.

7 [A]Arise, O LORD; [B]save me, O my God!
For You [a]have [C]smitten all my
enemies on the [b]cheek;
You [c]have [D]shattered the
teeth of the wicked.
8 [a,A]Salvation belongs to the LORD;
Your [B]blessing [b]*be* upon Your people!
Selah

2:2 [a]Or *Messiah* [B]Ps 74:18, 23 [C]John 1:41 2:3 [A]Jer 5:5 2:4 [a]Or *is enthroned* [A]Ps 37:13 [B]Ps 59:8 2:5 [A]Ps 21:8, 9; 76:7 [B]Ps 78:49, 50 2:6 [a]Or *consecrated* [A]Ps 45:6 [B]Ps 48:1, 2 2:7 [a]Or *decree: The LORD said to Me* [A]Acts 13:33; Heb 1:5; 5:5 2:8 [a]Or *Gentiles* [A]Ps 21:1, 2 [B]Ps 22:27 [C]Ps 67:7 2:9 [a]Another reading is *rule* [b]Or *scepter or staff* [c]Lit *potter's ware* [A]Ps 89:23; 110:5, 6; Rev 2:26, 27; 12:5; 19:15 [B]Ps 28:5; 52:5; 72:4 2:10 [a]Or *leaders* [A]Prov 8:15; 27:11 2:11 [a]Or *Serve* [b]Or *fear* [A]Ps 5:7 [B]Ps 119:119, 120 2:12 [a]Lit *Kiss;* some ancient versions read *Do homage purely*, or, *Lay hold of instruction* [b]Or *quickly, suddenly, easily* [A]Ps 2:7 [B]Rev 6:16, 17 [C]Ps 5:11; 34:22 3:1 [†]2 Sam 15:13-17, 29 [A]2 Sam 15:12; Ps 69:4 3:2 [a]Or *to* [b]Or *salvation* [c]*Selah* may mean: *Pause, Crescendo* or *Musical interlude* [A]Ps 22:7, 8; 71:11 3:3 [A]Ps 5:12; 28:7 [B]Ps 62:7 [C]Ps 9:13; 27:6 3:4 [a]Or *hill* [A]Ps 4:3; 34:4 [B]Ps 2:6; 15:1; 43:3 3:5 [a]Or *As for me, I* [A]Lev 26:6; Ps 4:8; Prov 3:24 3:6 [A]Ps 23:4; 27:3 [B]Ps 118:10-13 3:7 [a]Or *smite* [b]Or *jaw* [c]Or *shatter* [A]Ps 7:6 [B]Ps 6:4; 22:21 [C]Job 16:10 [D]Ps 57:4; 58:6 3:8 [a]Or *Deliverance* [b]Or *is* [A]Ps 28:8; 35:3; Is 43:11 [B]Ps 29:11

mediatorial representative referred to David in a near sense and Messiah, i.e., Christ, in the ultimate sense (cf. Ac 4:25, 26).

2:3 their fetters … their cords. Mutinous mankind, instead of understanding that these are God's love-bonds (Hos 11:4), view them as yoke-bonds (Jer 5:5).

2:5 Then. After mocking them with the laughter of divine contempt, God speaks and acts from His perfectly balanced anger.

2:6 I have installed. Their puny challenge (v. 3) is answered by this powerful pronouncement. It's as good as done: his king will be enthroned on Jerusalem's most prominent hill.

2:7 I will … tell of the decree. The installed mediator now recites the Lord's previously issued enthronement ordinance. **You are My Son.** This recalls 2Sa 7:8–16 as the basis for the Davidic king. It is the first OT reference to the Father/Son relationship—the paternal/filial roles—in the Trinity. **Today I have begotten You.** Rather than a reference to origin (there is no procreation within the Trinity), this vividly conveys the essential oneness shared between the Father and the Son. This verse is quoted in the NT with reference to the birth of Jesus (Heb 1:5–6) and also to His resurrection (Ac 13:33–34) as the earthly affirmations.

2:9 You shall … You shall. The supreme sovereignty of "the King of kings" is pictured in its subjugating might. The shepherd's "rod" and the king's "scepter" are the same word in the original. Shepherding and kingly imagery often merged in ancient Near Eastern thought (cf. Mic 7:14).

2:10–12 The tone of these verses is surprising. Instead of immediate judgment, the Lord and His Anointed mercifully provide an opportunity for repentance. Five commands place responsibility on mutinous mankind.

2:12 Do homage to the Son. This symbolic act would indicate allegiance and submission (cf. 1Sa 10:1; 1Ki 19:18). The word for "Son" here is not the Heb. word for "son" that was used in v. 7, but rather its Aram. counterpart (cf. Da 7:13), which is a term that would especially be suitable for these commands being addressed to "nations" (v. 1). **perish *in* the way.** These words pick up the major burden of Ps 1.

3:1–8 This psalm intermingles both lament and confidence. In its sweeping scope, it becomes a pattern for praise, peace, and prayer amidst pressure. As it unfolds through 3 interrelated historical phenomena, David shares his theological "secret" of having assurance in the face of adversity.

I. The Psalmist's Predicament (3:1, 2)
II. The Psalmist's Peace (3:3–6)
III. The Psalmist's Prayer (3:7, 8)

3:Title The first of 73 psalms attributed to David by superscription. Further information connects its occasion with the Absalom episode (2Sa 15–18), although many of its features are more descriptive of persecution in general.

3:1, 2 increased … Many … Many. The psalmist begins on a low note with his multiplied miseries.

3:2, 3 no deliverance for him … But You …. shield about me. There is a strong contrast between the allegation and the psalmist's assurance. David's attitude and outlook embraces the theology that Paul summarized in Ro 8:31. Psalm 3 also introduces Divine Warrior language (cf. Ex 15 as a background).

3:5 I lay down and slept. Since God is known for His sustaining protection, David could relax in the most trying of circumstances.

3:7 Arise, O LORD. This is a battle cry for God to engage the enemy and defend His soldiers (cf. Nu 10:35; Ps 68:1).

3:8 Salvation belongs to the LORD. This is a broad-sweeping, all-inclusive deliverance, whether in the temporal or eternal realm.

PSALM 4

EVENING PRAYER OF TRUST IN GOD.

[†]For the choir director; on stringed
instruments. A Psalm of David.

1 [A]Answer me when [B]I call, O God
[a]of my righteousness!
You have [b,C]relieved me in my distress;
Be [D]gracious to me and [E]hear my prayer.

2 O sons of men, how long
will [A]my [a]honor become
[B]a reproach?
How long will you love
[C]what is worthless and
aim at [D]deception? [b]*Selah*
3 But know that the LORD
has [a,A]set apart the [B]godly
man for Himself;
The LORD [C]hears when I call to Him.

4 [a,A]Tremble, [b,B]and do not sin;
[c,C]Meditate in your heart upon
your bed, and be still. *Selah*
5 Offer [a]the [A]sacrifices
of righteousness,
And [B]trust in the LORD.

6 Many are saying, "[A]Who will
show us *any* good?"
[B]Lift up the light of
Your countenance upon
us, O LORD!
7 You have put [A]gladness
in my heart,
More than when their grain
and new wine abound.
8 In peace I will [a]both [A]lie
down and sleep,
For You alone, O LORD, make
me to [B]dwell in safety.

4:1 [†]I.e. Belonging to the choir director's anthology [a]I.e. who maintains my right [b]Lit *made room for* [A]Ps 3:4; 17:6 [B]Ps 18:6 [C]Ps 18:18, 19 [D]Ps 25:16 [E]Ps 17:6; 39:12 4:2 [a]Or *glory* [b]*Selah* may mean: *Pause, Crescendo* or *Musical interlude* [A]Ps 3:3 [B]Ps 69:7-10, 19, 20 [C]Ps 12:2; 31:6 [D]Ps 31:18 4:3 [a]Another reading is *dealt wonderfully with* [A]Ps 135:4 [B]Ps 31:23; 50:5; 79:2 [C]Ps 6:8, 9; 17:6 4:4 [a]I.e. with anger or fear [b]Or *but* [c]Lit *Speak* [A]Ps 99:1 [B]Ps 119:11; Eph 4:26 [C]Ps 77:6 4:5 [a]Or *righteous sacrifices* [A]Deut 33:19; Ps 51:19 [B]Ps 37:3, 5; 62:8 4:6 [A]Job 7:7; 9:25 [B]Num 6:26; Ps 80:3, 7, 19 4:7 [A]Ps 97:11, 12; Is 9:3; Acts 14:17 4:8 [a]Or *at the same time* [A]Job 11:19; Ps 3:5 [B]Lev 25:18; Deut 12:10; Ps 16:9

4:1–8 There are certain similarities between Pss 3 and 4. For example, the former is sometimes labeled a morning psalm (cf. 3:5), while the latter has been called an evening psalm (cf. 4:8). In both, David is besieged with suffering, injustice, and oppression. Additionally, Ps 4 also exhibits the changing attitudes of the worshiper in his most difficult circumstances. David's movement will be from anxiety to assurance as he travels down the road of prayer and trust in God. At the end of yet another day of pressure, pain, and persecution, David engages in 3 conversations which ultimately lead to a point of blessed relaxation:

I. Praying to God for Preservation (4:1)
II. Reasoning with His enemies about Repentance (4:2–5)
III. Praising God for True Perspective (4:6–8)

4:Title Psalm 4 introduces the first of 55 assignments to the master, director, or chief overseer of worship services in its title. Further instruction is given in the direction "on stringed instruments." The chief musician, therefore, was to lead the great choir and the string portion of the orchestra in this celebration of worship.

4:1 O God of my righteousness! The ultimate basis for divine intervention resides in God, not in the psalmist. On union with God's righteousness based on His mercy, see Jer 23:6 (cf. 1Co 1:30). **distress.** This is an important word for trying circumstances in the psalms. It pictures the psalmist's plight as being in straits, i.e., painfully restricted. Here his testimony to God's historical salvation, "You have relieved me," conveys the picture that his Lord had provided space or room for him.

4:2, 3 God's agenda for David (v. 3) is radically contrasted with that of his enemies (v. 2). The term for "godly" or "pious" in the OT is above all else indicating a person blessed by God's grace.

4:4 Tremble, and do not sin. In this context, the admonition means to tremble or shake in the fear of the Lord so as not to sin (cf. Is 32:10, 11; Hab 3:16).

4:5 trust. This command reflects the primary word group in the OT for faith-commitment.

4:6–8 The taunting skeptics are cut off by the testimony of the psalmist to his rest because of God's personal blessings.

4:8 dwell in safety. The word "safety" introduces a play on words by going back to the term "trust" in v. 5. David evidences a total confidence in God amidst his crisis.

HISTORICAL BACKGROUND TO PSALMS BY DAVID

Psalm	Historical Background	OT Text
Ps 3	when David fled from Absalom his son	2Sa 15:13–17
Ps 7	concerning the words of Cush a Benjamite	2Sa 16:5; 19:16
Ps 18	the day the Lord delivered David from his enemies/Saul	2Sa 22:1–51
Ps 30	at the dedication of the house of David	2Sa 5:11, 12; 6:17
Ps 34	when David pretended madness before Achish	1Sa 21:10–15
Ps 51	when Nathan confronted David over sin with Bathsheba	2Sa 12:1–14
Ps 52	when Doeg the Edomite warned Saul about David	1Sa 22:9, 10
Ps 54	when the Ziphites warned Saul about David	1Sa 23:19
Ps 56	when the Philistines captured David in Gath	1Sa 21:10, 11
Ps 57	when David fled from Saul into the cave	1Sa 22:1; 24:3
Ps 59	when Saul sent men to watch the house in order to kill David	1Sa 19:11
Ps 60	when David fought against Mesopotamia and Syria	2Sa 8:3, 13
Ps 63	when David was in the wilderness of Judea	1Sa 23:14; or 2Sa 15:23–28
Ps 142	when David was in a cave	1Sa 22:1; 24:3

PSALM 5

PRAYER FOR PROTECTION FROM THE WICKED.

For the choir director; for [†]flute accompaniment.
A Psalm of David.

1 [A]Give ear to my words, O LORD,
Consider my [a,B]groaning.
2 Heed [A]the sound of my cry for
help, [B]my King and my God,
For to You I pray.
3 In the morning, O LORD, [a]You
will hear my voice;
In the [A]morning I will order *my* [b]*prayer*
to You and *eagerly* [B]watch.

4 For You are not a God [A]who takes
pleasure in wickedness;
[B]No evil [a]dwells with You.
5 The [A]boastful shall not [B]stand
before Your eyes;
You [C]hate all who do iniquity.
6 You [A]destroy those who speak falsehood;
The LORD abhors [B]the man of
bloodshed and deceit.
7 But as for me, [A]by Your abundant
lovingkindness I will enter Your house,
[a]At Your holy temple I will [B]bow
in [C]reverence for You.

8 O LORD, [A]lead me [B]in Your righteousness
[C]because of [a]my foes;
Make Your way [b]straight before me.
9 There is [A]nothing [a]reliable in [b]what they say;
Their [B]inward part is destruction *itself.*
Their [C]throat is an open grave;
They [c]flatter with their tongue.
10 Hold them guilty, O God;
[A]By their own devices let them fall!
In the multitude of their
transgressions [B]thrust them out,
For they are [C]rebellious against You.

11 But let all who [A]take refuge in You [B]be glad,
Let them ever sing for joy;
And [a]may You [C]shelter them,
That those who [D]love Your
name may exult in You.
12 For it is You who [A]blesses the
righteous man, O LORD,
You [B]surround him with favor
as with a shield.

PSALM 6

PRAYER FOR MERCY IN TIME OF TROUBLE.

For the choir director; with stringed instruments,
[†]upon an eight-string lyre. A Psalm of David.

1 O LORD, [A]do not rebuke me in Your anger,
Nor chasten me in Your wrath.
2 Be gracious to me, O LORD,
for I *am* [A]pining away;
[B]Heal me, O LORD, for [C]my
bones are dismayed.

5:1 [†]Heb *Nehiloth* [a]Or *meditation* [A]Ps 54:2 [B]Ps 104:34 5:2 [A]Ps 140:6 [B]Ps 84:3 5:3 [a]Or *May You hear* [b]Or sacrifice [A]Ps 88:13 [B]Ps 130:5 5:4 [a]Lit *sojourns* [A]Ps 11:5; 34:16 [B]Ps 92:15 5:5 [A]Ps 73:3; 75:4 [B]Ps 1:5 [C]Ps 11:5; 45:7 5:6 [A]Ps 52:4, 5 [B]Ps 55:23 5:7 [a]Or *Toward* [A]Ps 69:13 [B]Ps 138:2 [C]Ps 115:11, 13 5:8 [a]Or *those who lie in wait for me* [b]Or *smooth* [A]Ps 31:3 [B]Ps 31:1 [C]Ps 27:11 5:9 [a]Or *true* [b]Lit *his mouth* [c]Or *make their tongue smooth* [A]Ps 52:3 [B]Ps 7:14 [C]Rom 3:13 5:10 [A]Ps 9:16 [B]Ps 36:12 [C]Ps 107:10, 11 5:11 [a]Or *You shelter* [A]Ps 2:12 [B]Ps 33:1; 64:10 [C]Ps 12:7 [D]Ps 69:36 5:12 [A]Ps 29:11 [B]Ps 32:7, 10 6:1 [†]Or *according to a lower octave* (Heb *Sheminith*) [A]Ps 38:1; 118:18 6:2 [A]Ps 102:4, 11 [B]Ps 41:4; 147:3; Hos 6:1 [C]Ps 22:14; 31:10

5:1–12 Psalm 5 is basically a lament with elements of declarations of innocence and confidence and prayers for protection. David was standing in the presence of the Lord when he put his enemies before his God. His prayers have two major concerns: "Help me and harm them!" Therefore, David releases his respective prayers for divine intervention and imprecation upon two rounds of contrast which differentiate the enemies of God from the children of God.

I. Round One: Theological Contrast of Retribution with Reconciliation (5:1–8)
   A. David's Prayer for Intervention Expressed (5:1–3)
   B. David's Prayer for Intervention Explained (5:4–8)
II. Round Two: Practical Contrast of the Wayward with the Worshipful (5:9–12)
   A. David's Prayer of Imprecation Expressed (5:10a-c)
   B. David's Prayer of Imprecation Explained (5:9, 10d–12)

5:Title Whereas the instructions to the worship leader in Ps 4 pertain to a stringed accompaniment, Ps 5 is to be celebrated in community worship with flute accompaniment (cf. 1Sa 10:5; 1Ki 1:40; Is 30:29).

5:1 **Give ear.** This command is built upon the word for "ear." It takes its place alongside of parallel requests that God would pay careful attention to the supplicant and his sufferings (Pss 17:1; 55:1, 2).

5:2 **my King and my God.** David may have been the anointed theocratic king on earth, but he fully understood that the ultimate King of all Israel and of the whole earth is God (for God's conditional allowance for mediatorial kingship, see 1Sa 8:19ff.).

5:3 **In the morning . . . In the morning.** These words have led many to label this a morning psalm (cf. Ps 3:5).

5:4–6 **not . . . No . . . not . . . hate . . . destroy . . . abhors.** These 3 negatively phrased descriptions follow 3 directly stated affirmations. This reveals God's perfect standard of justice both in principle and in practice.

5:7 **But as for me.** The psalmist starkly contrasts himself with his enemies. They are haughty; he is humble.

5:8, 9 To man's "hoof" problem, David exposes man's "mouth" problem, with special application to his slick-talking enemies. Proverbs is especially given to exposing the deadliness of mankind's spiritual "hoof" and "mouth" disease, i.e., one's walk and talk. Paul includes these assessments from Ps 5:9 in his list of 14 terrible indictments of all mankind in Ro 3:13.

5:8 **lead me . . . Make Your way straight.** Disciples are to walk in God's way(s), being obedient to His direction(s) for their lives, yet they are fully dependent upon His grace for responsible progress (cf. Ps 119:1–5, 26, 27, 30, 32, 33).

5:10–12 He prays for the just ends of the wicked according to God's revealed standard of justice (Dt 25:1), and contrastingly urges those who are regarded as righteous by the Lord's grace to joyfully celebrate His blessings.

6:1–10 This lament seems to be quite intensive, for apparently David is sleepless. His circumstances seem hopeless and helpless. The early Christian church regarded this psalm as the first among the "penitential psalms" (cf. Pss 32, 38, 51, 102, 130, 143). David's cries, coming up from the depths of his personal pit of persecution, indicate a radical change in his frame of mind as he addresses two different audiences.

I. Pouring out His Soul before God: A Defeatist Frame of Mind (6:1–7)
   A. A Tone of Helplessness (6:1–4)
   B. A Tone of Hopelessness (6:5–7)
II. Turning His Attention to His Enemies: A Defiant Frame of Mind (6:8–10)
   A. His Boldness about It (6:8a)
   B. His Basis for It (6:8b–10)

6:Title A new musical direction appears, lit. "upon an eight," indicating either "upon an eight-stringed lyre" or "upon the octave" (i.e., a lower bass melody to accompany these lyrics of intense lament).

6:1 **in Your anger . . . in Your wrath.** He does not ask for immunity from judgment, but for the tempering of God's discipline with mercy.

6:2, 7 **bones . . . eye.** Many assume that

3 And my [A]soul is greatly dismayed;
But You, O LORD—[B]how long?

4 Return, O LORD, [A]rescue my [a]soul;
Save me because of Your lovingkindness.
5 For [A]there is no [a]mention
of You in death;
In [b]Sheol who will give You thanks?

6 I am [A]weary with my sighing;
Every night I make my bed swim,
I dissolve my couch with [B]my tears.
7 My [A]eye has wasted away with grief;
It has become old because of
all my adversaries.

8 [A]Depart from me, all you who do iniquity,
For the LORD [B]has heard the
voice of my weeping.
9 The LORD [A]has heard my supplication,
The LORD [B]receives my prayer.
10 All my enemies will [A]be ashamed
and greatly dismayed;
They shall [a]turn back, they will
[B]suddenly be ashamed.

PSALM 7

THE LORD IMPLORED TO DEFEND THE PSALMIST AGAINST THE WICKED.

A [†]Shiggaion of David, which he sang to the LORD [*]concerning Cush, a Benjamite.

1 O LORD my God, [A]in You I
have taken refuge;
Save me from all those who
pursue me, and [B]deliver me,
2 Or he will tear [a]my soul [A]like a lion,
[b]Dragging me away, while there
is none to deliver.

3 O LORD my God, if I have done this,
If there is [A]injustice in my hands,
4 If I have [A]rewarded evil
to [a]my friend,
Or have [B]plundered [b]him who without
cause was my adversary,
5 Let the enemy pursue [a]my
soul and overtake [b]*it;*
And let him trample my life
down to the ground
And lay my glory in the dust. [c]*Selah*

6 [A]Arise, O LORD, in Your anger;
[B]Lift up Yourself against [C]the
rage of my adversaries,
And [D]arouse Yourself [a]for me; You
have appointed judgment.
7 Let the assembly of the [A]peoples
encompass You,
And over [a]them return on high.
8 The LORD [A]judges the peoples;
[a,B]Vindicate me, O LORD, according
to my righteousness and my
integrity that is in me.
9 O let [A]the evil of the wicked
come to an end, but
[B]establish the righteous;
For the righteous God [C]tries
the hearts and [a]minds.

6:3 [A]Ps 88:3; John 12:27 [B]Ps 90:13 6:4 [a]Or *life* [A]Ps 17:13 6:5 [a]Or *remembrance* [b]I.e. the nether world [A]Ps 30:9; 88:10-12; 115:17; Eccl 9:10; Is 38:18 6:6 [A]Ps 69:3 [B]Ps 42:3 6:7 [A]Job 17:7; Ps 31:9; 38:10 6:8 [A]Ps 119:115; Matt 7:23; Luke 13:27 [B]Ps 3:4; 28:6 6:9 [A]Ps 116:1 [B]Ps 66:19, 20 6:10 [a]Or *again be ashamed suddenly* [A]Ps 71:13, 24 [B]Ps 73:19 7:1 [†]I.e. Dithyrambic rhythm; or wild passionate song [*]Or *concerning the words of* [A]Ps 31:1; 71:1 [B]Ps 31:15 7:2 [a]Or *me* [b]Or *Rending it in pieces, while* [A]Ps 57:4; Is 38:13 7:3 [A]1 Sam 24:11 7:4 [a]Lit *him who was at peace with me* [b]Or *my adversary without cause* [A]Ps 109:4, 5 [B]1 Sam 24:7; 26:9 7:5 [a]Or *me* [b]Or me [c]*Selah* may mean: *Pause, Crescendo* or *Musical interlude* 7:6 [a]One ancient version reads *O my God* [A]Ps 3:7 [B]Ps 94:2 [C]Ps 138:7 [D]Ps 35:23; 44:23 7:7 [a]Lit *it* [A]Ps 22:27 7:8 [a]Lit *Judge* [A]Ps 96:13; 98:9 [B]Ps 18:20; 26:1; 35:24; 43:1 7:9 [a]Lit *kidneys,* figurative for inner man [A]Ps 34:21; 94:23 [B]Ps 37:23; 40:2 [C]Ps 11:4, 5; Jer 11:20; Rev 2:23

because the psalmist mentions bodily "parts" his affliction was a grave physical illness. Obviously, his circumstances would have had an effect on his physical dimension. However, in OT anthropology such references are picturesque metaphors for an affliction of his total being (cf. all the parallel, personal references, e.g., "me," "my soul," i.e., my being or person, "I," etc.).

6:3 **how long?** This is a common exclamation of intense lament (cf. Ps 90:13; Hab 2:6; Rev 6:10).

6:4 **rescue my soul … Your lovingkindness.** This introduces a new synonym for salvation, connoting an action of drawing off or out. He desires the Lord to graciously extricate him (cf. Job 36:15; Pss 18:19; 116:8).

6:5 **no mention of You.** There is much about "death" and "the grave," i.e., Sheol, in Psalms. Such language as that of v. 5 does not imply annihilation, but inability to participate temporally in public praise offerings (cf. Hezekiah's reasoning in Is 38:18).

6:6, 7 Sleep has eluded him because of his severe sorrow.

6:8–10 Out of his dire straits, boldness surprisingly breaks through as he addresses his enemies. This boldness also has only one basis, that the psalmist's confidence is wholly grounded upon his Lord's attention and ultimate intervention.

7:1–17 This psalm is basically a plea for divine vindication in the light of the oppressor's allegations and actions. David's confidence in the Divine Judge is the backbone of Ps 7 (cf. Abraham in Ge 18:25). As this truth grips him more and more, he will move from a tense anxiety to a transcendent assurance. This psalm follows David through 3 progressively calming stages of expression in response to the painfully false accusations that were being hurled against him.

I. Stage One: David's Concern as He Passionately Begs the Attention of the Divine Judge (7:1–5)
II. Stage Two: David's Court Appearance as He Painstakingly Argues His Case before the Divine Judge (7:6–16)
III. Stage Three: David's Composure as He Patiently Waits for the Verdict of the Divine Judge (7:17)

7:Title This title introduces one of the more enigmatic terms found in superscriptions of the psalms—"a Shiggaion (Heb.) of David." It is probably related to the idea of wondering, reeling, veering, or weaving. Consequently, the term may also indicate the song's irregularity in rhythm (cf. Hab 3:1). "He sang" also indicates that this was a vocal solo. The occasion, "concerning Cush, a Benjamite," cannot be readily identified from the historical books; however, whoever this was or whatever the name represented, some enemy had obviously been falsely charging David (cf. Shimei—2Sa 16:5; 19:16).

7:2 **tear my soul like a lion.** Often the psalmist's enemies are symbolized by vicious, attacking animals, with "the king of beasts" occurring frequently (Pss 10:9; 17:12; 22:13, 16, 21).

7:3–5 Such self-pronounced curses are powerful protestations of innocence (not sinlessness) in the context of being falsely charged (cf. the boldness of Job in 31:5ff.).

7:6 **Arise.** The battle cry relating back to Nu 10:35 recurs (cf. Pss 9:19; 10:12; 17:13; 44:26; 102:13).

7:8 **my righteousness … my integrity.** These are not declarations of sinlessness but of innocence in this "court case."

7:9 **the righteous God tries the hearts and minds.** The Just Judge has perfect insight (cf. God examining the heart and mind in Jer 17:10; also cf. Ac 1:24; 15:8).

10 My [A]shield is [a]with God,
Who [B]saves the upright in heart.
11 God is a [A]righteous judge,
And a God who has
[B]indignation every day.

12 If [a]a man [A]does not repent, He
will [B]sharpen His sword;
He has [C]bent His bow and [b]made it ready.
13 He has also prepared [a]for
Himself deadly weapons;
He makes His [A]arrows fiery shafts.
14 Behold, he travails with wickedness,
And he [A]conceives mischief and
brings forth falsehood.
15 He has dug a pit and hollowed it out,
And has [A]fallen into the hole
which he made.
16 His [A]mischief will return
upon his own head,
And his [B]violence will descend
upon [a]his own pate.

17 I will give thanks to the LORD
[A]according to His righteousness
And will [B]sing praise to the name
of the LORD Most High.

PSALM 8

THE LORD'S GLORY AND MAN'S DIGNITY.

For the choir director; on the Gittith.
A Psalm of David.

1 O LORD, our Lord,
How majestic is Your name
in all the earth,
Who have [a,A]displayed
Your splendor above
the heavens!
2 [A]From the mouth of infants
and nursing babes You have
established [a,B]strength
Because of Your adversaries,
To make [C]the enemy and the
revengeful cease.

3 When I [a,A]consider [B]Your
heavens, the work
of Your fingers,
The [C]moon and the stars, which
You have [b]ordained;
4 [A]What is man that You [a]take
thought of him,
And the son of man that
You care for him?
5 Yet You have made him a
[A]little lower than [a]God,
And [B]You crown him with
[C]glory and majesty!
6 You make him to [A]rule over the
works of Your hands;
You have [B]put all things
under his feet,
7 All sheep and oxen,
And also the [a]beasts
of the field,
8 The birds of the heavens and
the fish of the sea,
Whatever passes through
the paths of the seas.

9 [A]O LORD, our Lord,
How majestic is Your name
in all the earth!

7:10 [a]Lit *upon* [A]Ps 18:2, 30 [B]Ps 97:10, 11; 125:4 7:11 [A]Ps 50:6 [B]Ps 90:9 7:12 [a]Lit *he* [b]Lit *fixed it* [A]Ps 58:5 [B]Deut 32:41 [C]Ps 64:7 7:13 [a]Or *His deadly weapons* [A]Ps 18:14; 45:5 7:14 [A]Job 15:35; Is 59:4; James 1:15 7:15 [A]Job 4:8; Ps 57:6 7:16 [a]I.e. the crown of his own head [A]Esth 9:25; Ps 140:9 [B]Ps 140:11 7:17 [A]Ps 71:15, 16 [B]Ps 9:2; 66:1, 2, 4 8:1 [a]Or *set* [A]Ps 57:5, 11; 113:4; 148:13 8:2 [a]Or *a bulwark* [A]Matt 21:16; 1 Cor 1:27 [B]Ps 29:1; 118:14 [C]Ps 44:16 8:3 [a]Or *see* [b]Or *appointed, fixed* [A]Ps 111:2 [B]Ps 89:11; 144:5 [C]Ps 136:9 8:4 [a]Or *remember him* [A]Job 7:17; Ps 144:3; Heb 2:6-8 8:5 [a]Or *the angels;* Heb *Elohim* [A]Gen 1:26; Ps 82:6 [B]Ps 103:4 [C]Ps 21:5 8:6 [A]Gen 1:26, 28 [B]1 Cor 15:27; Eph 1:22; Heb 2:8 8:7 [a]Or *animals* 8:9 [A]Ps 8:1

7:11–13 This shows yet another blending of the Divine Warrior and Divine Judge themes.

7:14–16 Often the principle of exact retribution surfaces in the psalms (cf. the maxim of Pr 26:27 and the judgment of Hab 2:15–18).

8:1–9 The beginning and ending of the psalm suggest that it is essentially a hymn of praise. Yet, a major portion qualifies it as a so-called nature psalm, i.e., a psalm of creation. Furthermore, there is a significant focus on the created dignity of man. Through this vehicle, the important subject of Adamic theology comes to the forefront, making this psalm ultimately suitable to the important association of the "One," the Last Adam, i.e., Christ and the "many" (cf. Heb 2:6–8). Structurally, Ps 8's beginning and concluding bursts of praise are driven by David's contemplation of two pairs of radical contrasts.

I. Introductory Praise (8:1)
II. Two Pairs of Radical Contrasts (8:2–8)
  A. Between the Nature of "Infants" and Infidels (8:2)
  B. Between Unaided General Revelation and Unveiled Special Revelation (8:3–8)
III. Concluding Praise (8:9)

8:Title Another instrument is referenced in this title, most probably a guitar-like harp associated with Gath in Philistia.

8:1 **LORD … Lord.** Of these twin nouns of direct address to God, the first is His specially revealed name Yahweh (Ex 3:14) and the second puts an emphasis on His sovereignty. **Your name.** The name of God refers to the revealed Person of God, encompassing all of His attributes.

8:2 The introductory irony about infants sets the stage for a contrast between the dependent and the foolishly self-sufficient.

8:3 **Your heavens, the work of Your fingers.** The heavens are created by God (Pss 33:6, 9; 102:25; 136:5). The anthropomorphism "Your fingers" miniaturizes the magnitude of the universe in the presence of the Creator.

8:4–6 Quoted in the NT at 1Co 15:27, 28; Eph 1:22; Heb 2:5–10.

8:4 **What is man.** If the whole universe is diminutive in the sight of the Divine Creator, how much less is the significance of mankind! Even the word for "man" used in v. 4 alludes to his weakness (cf. Pss 9:19, 20; 90:3a; 103:15, etc.). **And the son of man.** This phrase also looks upon man as insignificant and transitory (e.g., Ps 90:3b). Yet, the Aram. counterpart of this phrase is found in Da 7:13, which has profound messianic overtones (cf. also Jesus' favorite self-designation in the NT, Son of Man).

8:5–8 These verses consistently emphasize the significance of man, who was created in the image and likeness of God to exercise dominion over the rest of creation (Ge 1:26–28).

PSALM 9

A PSALM OF THANKSGIVING FOR GOD'S JUSTICE.

For the choir director; on †Muth-labben.
A Psalm of David.

1 I will give thanks to the LORD
with all [A]my heart;
I will [B]tell of all Your [a]wonders.
2 I will be glad and [A]exult in You;
I will [B]sing praise to Your
name, O [C]Most High.

3 When my enemies turn back,
They stumble and [A]perish before You.
4 For You have [A]maintained [a]my just cause;
You have sat on the throne
[b,B]judging righteously.
5 You have [A]rebuked the nations, You
have destroyed the wicked;
You have [B]blotted out their
name forever and ever.
6 [a]The enemy has come to an
end in perpetual ruins,
And You have uprooted the cities;
The very [A]memory of
them has perished.

7 But the [A]LORD [a]abides forever;
He has established His
[B]throne for judgment,
8 And He will [A]judge the world
in righteousness;
He will execute judgment for
the peoples with equity.
9 [a]The LORD also will be a [A]stronghold
for the oppressed,
A stronghold in times of trouble;
10 And [a]those who [A]know Your name
will put their trust in You,

9:1 †I.e. "Death to the Son" [a]Or *miracles* [A]Ps 86:12 [B]Ps 26:7 9:2 [A]Ps 5:11; 104:34 [B]Ps 66:2, 4 [C]Ps 83:18; 92:1 9:3 [A]Ps 27:2 9:4 [a]Lit *my right and my cause* [b]Or *a righteous Judge* [A]Ps 140:12 [B]Ps 50:6 9:5 [A]Ps 119:21 [B]Ps 69:28; Prov 10:7 9:6 [a]Or *O enemy, desolations are finished forever; And their cities You have plucked up* [A]Ps 34:16 9:7 [a]Or *sits as king* [A]Ps 10:16 [B]Ps 89:14 9:8 [A]Ps 96:13; 98:9 9:9 [a]Or *Let the LORD also be* [A]Ps 32:7; 59:9, 16, 17 9:10 [a]Or *let those...name put* [A]Ps 91:14

9:1–20 Psalms 9 and 10 go together, so much so that early Gr. and Lat. vss. treat and number them as one. However, Pss 9 and 10 evidence two different forms: the first is an individual hymn, while the second is an individual lament.

In the first part (vv. 1–12) praise is prominent, and in the second part (vv. 13–20) prayer is prominent. Many subtle patterns weave the thoughts of its verses and lines together. Shifting back and forth between the individual and corporate perspectives is characteristic, as are introverted (i.e., chiastic) structures. Basically, David's hymn in Ps 9 ebbs and flows through two respective tides of prayer and praise.

I. First Tide: Divine Justice and Praise (9:1–12)
   A. Individual Praise and Divine Justice (9:1–4)
   B. Divine Justice and Corporate Praise (9:5–12)
II. Second Tide: Divine Justice and Prayer (9:13–20)
   A. Individual Prayer and Divine Justice (9:13–16)
   B. Divine Justice and Corporate Prayer (9:17–20)

9:Title The new element of this title lit. reads "Death to the Son." Many conjectures have arisen about this puzzling phrase, but it is safest to regard these words as designating a particular tune.

9:1, 2 **I will .... will .... will .... will.** These 4 "I wills" launch Ps 9 with David's dedication to exuberant worship of the Lord.

9:1 **Your wonders.** This especially references God's extraordinary interventions into history on behalf of His people (cf. the Exodus events).

9:4 **You have maintained my just cause.** This is exactly what God is known to do (cf. Dt 10:18; 1Ki 8:45, 49).

9:5–10 Verses 5 and 6 reveal the Just Judge's dealings with the godless, vv. 7, 8, His dealings with all men in general, and vv. 9, 10, His gracious dealings with dependent disciples.

MESSIANIC PROPHECIES IN THE PSALMS

Prophecy	Psalm	Fulfillment
1. God will announce Christ to be His Son	2:7	Mt 3:17; Ac 13:33; Heb 1:5
2. All things will be put under Christ's feet	8:6	1Co 15:27; Heb 2:8
3. Christ will be resurrected from the grave	16:10	Mk 16:6, 7; Ac 13:35
4. God will forsake Christ in His moment of agony	22:1	Mt 27:46; Mk 15:34
5. Christ will be scorned and ridiculed	22:7, 8	Mt 27:39–43; Lk 23:35
6. Christ's hands and feet will be pierced	22:16	Jn 20:25, 27; Ac 2:23
7. Others will gamble for Christ's clothes	22:18	Mt 27:35, 36
8. Not one of Christ's bones will be broken	34:20	Jn 19:32, 33, 36
9. Christ will be hated unjustly	35:19	Jn 15:25
10. Christ will come to do God's will	40:7, 8	Heb 10:7
11. Christ will be betrayed by a friend	41:9	Jn 13:18
12. Christ's throne will be eternal	45:6	Heb 1:8
13. Christ will ascend to heaven	68:18	Eph 4:8
14. Zeal for God's temple will consume Christ	69:9	Jn 2:17
15. Christ will be given vinegar and gall	69:21	Mt 27:34; Jn 19:28–30
16. Christ's betrayer will be replaced	109:8	Ac 1:20
17. Christ's enemies will bow down to Him	110:1	Ac 2:34, 35
18. Christ will be a priest like Melchizedek	110:4	Heb 5:6; 6:20; 7:17
19. Christ will be the chief cornerstone	118:22	Mt 21:42; Ac 4:11
20. Christ will come in the name of the Lord	118:26	Mt 21:9

For You, O LORD, have not [B]forsaken
those who seek You.

11 Sing praises to the LORD,
who [A]dwells in Zion;
[B]Declare among the peoples
His deeds.
12 For [A]He who [a]requires blood
remembers them;
He does not forget [B]the cry
of the afflicted.
13 Be gracious to me, O LORD;
See my affliction from those
[A]who hate me,
You who [B]lift me up from
the gates of death,
14 That I may tell of [A]all Your praises,
That in the gates of the
daughter of Zion
I may [B]rejoice in Your [a]salvation.
15 The nations have sunk down [A]in
the pit which they have made;
In the [B]net which they hid, their
own foot has been caught.
16 The LORD has [A]made
Himself known;
He has [B]executed judgment.
In the work of his own hands the wicked
is snared. *[a]Higgaion [b]Selah*

17 The wicked will [a,A]return to [b]Sheol,
Even all the nations who [B]forget God.
18 For the [A]needy will not
always be forgotten,
Nor the [B]hope of the afflicted
perish forever.
19 [A]Arise, O LORD, do not let man prevail;
Let the nations be [B]judged before You.
20 Put them [A]in fear, O LORD;
Let the nations know that they are
[B]but men. *Selah*

PSALM 10

A PRAYER FOR THE OVERTHROW OF THE WICKED.

1 Why [A]do You stand afar off, O LORD?
Why [B]do You hide [a]*Yourself*
in times of trouble?
2 In [A]pride the wicked [a]hotly
pursue the afflicted;
[b]Let them be [B]caught in the plots
which they have devised.

3 For the wicked [A]boasts of his [B]heart's desire,
And [a]the greedy man curses
and [C]spurns the LORD.
4 The wicked, in the haughtiness of his
countenance, [A]does not seek *Him.*
All his [a]thoughts are, "[B]There is no God."

5 His ways [a,A]prosper at all times;
Your judgments are on high,
[B]out of his sight;
As for all his adversaries,
he snorts at them.
6 He says to himself, "[A]I will not be moved;
[a]Throughout all generations [B]I
will not be in adversity."
7 His [A]mouth is full of curses and
deceit and [B]oppression;
[C]Under his tongue is mischief
and wickedness.
8 He sits in the [A]lurking places
of the villages;
In the hiding places he [B]kills the innocent;
His eyes [a]stealthily watch for
the [b,C]unfortunate.
9 He lurks in a hiding place as
[A]a lion in his [a]lair;
He [B]lurks to catch [C]the afflicted;
He catches the afflicted when he
draws him into his [D]net.

9:10 [B]Ps 37:28; 94:14 9:11 [A]Ps 76:2 [B]Ps 105:1; 107:22 9:12 [a]I.e. avenges bloodshed [A]Gen 9:5; Ps 72:14 [B]Ps 9:18 9:13 [A]Ps 38:19 [B]Ps 30:3; 86:13 9:14 [a]Or *deliverance* [A]Ps 106:2 [B]Ps 13:5; 20:5; 35:9; 51:12 9:15 [A]Ps 7:15, 16 [B]Ps 57:6 9:16 [a]Perhaps, resounding music or meditation [b]*Selah* may mean: *Pause, Crescendo* or *Musical interlude* [A]Ex 7:5 [B]Ps 9:4 9:17 [a]Or *turn* [b]I.e. the nether world [A]Ps 49:14 [B]Job 8:13; Ps 50:22 9:18 [A]Ps 9:12; 12:5 [B]Ps 62:5; 71:5; Prov 23:18 9:19 [A]Num 10:35 [B]Ps 9:5 9:20 [A]Ps 14:5 [B]Ps 62:9 10:1 [a]Or Your eyes [A]Ps 22:1 [B]Ps 13:1; 55:1 10:2 [a]Lit *burn* [b]Or *They will be caught* [A]Ps 73:6, 8 [B]Ps 7:16; 9:16 10:3 [a]Or *blesses the greedy man* [A]Ps 49:6; 94:3, 4 [B]Ps 112:10 [C]Ps 10:13 10:4 [a]Or *plots* [A]Ps 10:13; 36:2 [B]Ps 14:1; 36:1 10:5 [a]Lit *are strong* [A]Ps 52:7 [B]Ps 28:5 10:6 [a]Lit *To* [A]Ps 49:11; Eccl 8:11 [B]Rev 18:7 10:7 [A]Rom 3:14 [B]Ps 73:8 [C]Job 20:12; Ps 140:3 10:8 [a]Lit *lie in wait* [b]Or *poor* [A]Ps 11:2 [B]Ps 94:6 [C]Ps 72:12 10:9 [a]Or *thicket* [A]Ps 17:12 [B]Ps 59:3; Mic 7:2 [C]Ps 10:2 [D]Ps 140:5

9:11 the LORD, who dwells in Zion. There is a both/and tension running throughout the OT, i.e., God is enthroned in and above the heavens, and also, He symbolically dwells locally in His tabernacle (cf. 1Ki 8; Ps 11:4).

9:12, 18 the afflicted … the needy … the afflicted. These designations often stand for the individual psalmist and/or the corporate community of disciples he represents. The terms all point to those who are afflicted, vulnerable, and, therefore, totally dependent upon the Lord.

9:15, 16 The "boomerang" principle of exact retribution returns.

9:17–20 Prominent theological themes from Pss 1 and 2 also return as the psalmist draws this great hymn to a climax.

10:1–18 Whereas Ps 9 started out with praise, Ps 10 begins in despair. In Ps 9 the psalmist was confident of the sure coming of Divine justice; in Ps 10 injustice is rampant and God seems disinterested. However, the psalmist's walking more by sight than by faith will slowly turnaround as he shifts his focus from empirical observations to theological facts. This is not an easy turnaround, especially since he is surrounded by so many practical atheists (cf. vv. 4, 11, 13). But hope will begin to dawn for the helpless (e.g., v. 12). In view of such kinds of general observations, the psalmist's expressions in Ps 10 exemplify how true believers seem to live in two different worlds at the same time.

I. From His World of Hostility, Discouragement (10:1–11)
II. From His World of Hope, Encouragement (10:12–18)

10:1 Why …. Why … ? Two "whys" of lament boldly blurt out the psalmist's question: "God, why do You remain aloof?" (cf. Pss 13:1; 22:11; 38:21; 44:24; 71:12; 88:14).

10:3 curses … spurns. The wicked's *modus operandi* is the opposite of what God demands (Dt 25:1).

10:5 His ways prosper at all times. God seems to be rewarding the ruthless. The psalmist's questioning insinuation is, "Has God also abandoned His own standards for retribution and reward?" Cf. other why-do-the-wicked-prosper inquiries in Job 20:2ff.; Jer 12:1.

10:7–11 Evidences of "hoof" and "mouth" disease (walk/talk) return in application to the wicked. These are enhanced by a return also of the ungodly being described as stalking, rapacious beasts.

10 He [a]crouches, he [b]bows down,
And the [c]unfortunate fall [d]by
his mighty ones.
11 He [A]says to himself,
"God has forgotten;
He has hidden His face; He
will never see it."

12 Arise, O LORD; O God,
[A]lift up Your hand.
[B]Do not forget the afflicted.
13 Why has the wicked
[A]spurned God?
He has said to himself, "You
will not require *it*."
14 You have seen *it*, for You have
beheld [A]mischief and vexation
to [a]take it into Your hand.
The [b,B]unfortunate commits
himself to You;
You have been the [C]helper
of the orphan.
15 [A]Break the arm of the wicked
and the evildoer,
[a,B]Seek out his wickedness
until You find none.

16 The LORD is [A]King forever and ever;
[B]Nations have perished from His land.
17 O LORD, You have heard the
[A]desire of the [a]humble;
You will [B]strengthen their heart,
[C]You will incline Your ear
18 To [a]vindicate the [A]orphan
and the [B]oppressed,
So that man who is of the earth
will no longer cause [C]terror.

PSALM 11

THE LORD A REFUGE AND DEFENSE.

For the choir director.
A Psalm of David.

1 In the LORD I [A]take refuge;
How can you say to
my soul, "Flee *as* a bird
to your [B]mountain;
2 For, behold, the wicked
[A]bend the bow,
They [a,B]make ready their
arrow upon the string
To [C]shoot in darkness at the
upright in heart.
3 "If the [A]foundations
are destroyed,
What can the righteous do?"

4 The LORD is in His [A]holy
temple; the [a]LORD'S
[B]throne is in heaven;
His [C]eyes behold, His eyelids
test the sons of men.
5 The LORD [A]tests the righteous
and [B]the wicked,
And the one who loves
violence His soul hates.
6 Upon the wicked He will
[A]rain [a]snares;
[B]Fire and brimstone and
[C]burning wind will be the
portion of [D]their cup.
7 For the LORD is [A]righteous, [B]He
loves [a]righteousness;
The upright will [C]behold His face.

10:10 [a]Or *is crushed* [b]Or *is bowed down* [c]Or *poor* [d]Or *into his claws* 10:11 [A]Ps 10:4 10:12 [A]Ps 17:7; Mic 5:9 [B]Ps 9:12 10:13 [A]Ps 10:3 10:14 [a]Lit *put, give* [b]Or *poor* [A]Ps 10:7 [B]Ps 22:11 [C]Ps 68:5 10:15 [a]Or *May You seek* [A]Ps 37:17 [B]Ps 140:11 10:16 [A]Ps 29:10 [B]Deut 8:20 10:17 [a]Or *afflicted* [A]Ps 9:18 [B]1 Chr 29:18 [C]Ps 34:15 10:18 [a]Lit *judge* [A]Ps 146:9 [B]Ps 9:9; 74:21 [C]Is 29:20 11:1 [A]Ps 2:12 [B]Ps 121:1 11:2 [a]Or *fixed* [A]Ps 7:12; 37:14 [B]Ps 64:3 [C]Ps 64:4 11:3 [A]Ps 82:5; 87:1; 119:152 11:4 [a]Lit *LORD, His throne* [A]Ps 18:6; Mic 1:2; Hab 2:20 [B]Ps 103:19; Is 66:1; Matt 5:34; Rev 4:2 [C]Ps 33:18; 34:15, 16 11:5 [A]Gen 22:1; Ps 34:19; James 1:12 [B]Ps 5:5 11:6 [a]Or *coals of fire* [A]Ps 18:13, 14 [B]Gen 19:24; Ezek 38:22 [C]Jer 4:11, 12 [D]Ps 75:8 11:7 [a]Or *righteous deeds* [A]Ps 7:9, 11 [B]Ps 33:5; 45:7 [C]Ps 16:11; 17:15

10:12 Arise. The battle cry of Nu 10:35 also comes back again (cf. Pss 7:6; 9:19). **lift up Your hand.** This is an idiom for God's strength and power especially as it is used in the context of retaliation.

10:14 helper of the orphan. God is pictured as Helper or Advocate again, but this time in association with orphans. He is the Defender par excellence of the defenseless (on the imagery, cf. Ex 22:21ff.; Dt 10:18ff.; 1Sa 1:17; Jer 7:6).

10:15 Break the arm of the wicked. The "hand" of God (vv. 12, 14) is more than sufficiently strong to shatter the arm (another figure for power) of ungodly men.

10:16–18 The confident mood of this great climax outshines the psalm's introductory protestations. The psalmist's great Lord listens (v. 17) and acts (v. 18).

11:1–7 The panic that launched this psalm was not David's but that of his apparently well-meaning counselors. Their mood is panic, but David's is peace. In view of David's attitude, this psalm can be listed with the psalms of confidence (Pss 4, 16, 23, 27, 62, 125, 131). Also, the solidarity of the theocratic king and the theocratic people is obvious, as indicated by the shifts back and forth between sing. and pl. phrasings. The developing verses and lines of this psalm reveal that, although two different "voices" were speaking to David in yet another context of personal and national crisis, he had made up his mind to trust only in the Lord.

I. Introductory Affirmation (11:1a)
II. The Two Voices
   A. The Voice Urging Flight (11:1b–3)
   B. The Voice Urging Faith (11:4–7)

11:1 In the LORD I take refuge. God is the exclusive refuge for His persecuted children (cf. Pss 16:1; 36:7).

11:3 These are the words of a committed but confused saint. His philosophical problem is, "In view of the crumbling of the theocratic society, what can one righteous person, out of a shrinking remnant, do?"

11:4a in His holy temple … in heaven. This emphasizes the transcendent throne room of God, yet God has sovereign sway over all the affairs of earth (cf. Hab 2:20).

11:4b-5a His eyes behold, His eyelids test. His transcendence previously depicted does not negate His eminence here presented from the perspective of the divine scrutiny of all men, including the righteous (cf. Jer 6:27–30; 17:10).

11:5b-6 His soul hates. This is undiluted, perfect retribution.

11:7a For the LORD is righteous. He loves righteousness. He Himself is the perfect norm or standard for all spiritual integrity.

11:7b His face. Cf. Pss 17:15; 27:4; 63:2; 1Jn 3:2.

PSALM 12

GOD, A HELPER AGAINST THE TREACHEROUS.

For the choir director; [†]upon an eight-stringed lyre. A Psalm of David.

1 Help, LORD, for [A]the godly
man ceases to be,
For the faithful disappear from
among the sons of men.
2 They [A]speak [a]falsehood
to one another;
With [B]flattering [b]lips and with a
double heart they speak.
3 May the LORD cut off
all flattering lips,
The tongue that [A]speaks great things;
4 Who [A]have said, "With our
tongue we will prevail;
Our lips are [a]our own; who
is lord over us?"
5 "Because of the [A]devastation of
the afflicted, because of the
groaning of the needy,
Now [B]I will arise," says the LORD;
"I will [C]set him in the safety
for which he longs."

6 The [A]words of the LORD are pure words;
As silver [B]tried in a furnace on the
earth, refined seven times.
7 You, O LORD, will keep them;
You will [A]preserve him from
this generation forever.
8 The [A]wicked strut about on every side
When [a,B]vileness is exalted
among the sons of men.

PSALM 13

PRAYER FOR HELP IN TROUBLE.

For the choir director. A Psalm of David.

1 How long, O LORD? Will You
[A]forget me forever?
How long [B]will You hide Your face from me?
2 How long shall I [A]take counsel in my soul,
Having [B]sorrow in my heart all the day?
How long will my enemy be
exalted over me?

3 [A]Consider *and* answer me, O LORD my God;
[B]Enlighten my eyes, or I will
[C]sleep the *sleep of* death,
4 And my enemy will [A]say, "I
have overcome him,"
And [B]my adversaries will rejoice
when I am shaken.

5 But I have [A]trusted in Your
lovingkindness;
My heart shall [B]rejoice in Your salvation.
6 I will [A]sing to the LORD,
Because He has [B]dealt
bountifully with me.

PSALM 14

FOLLY AND WICKEDNESS OF MEN.

For the choir director. *A Psalm* of David.

1 The fool has [A]said in his heart,
"There is no God."
They are corrupt, they have
committed abominable [a]deeds;
There is [B]no one who does good.

12:1 [†]Or *according to a lower octave* (Heb *Sheminith*) [A]Is 57:1; Mic 7:2 12:2 [a]Or *emptiness* [b]Lit *lip* [A]Ps 10:7; 41:6 [B]Ps 28:3; 55:21; Jer 9:8; Rom 16:18 12:3 [A]Dan 7:8; Rev 13:5 12:4 [a]Lit *with us* [A]Ps 73:8, 9 12:5 [A]Ps 9:9; 10:18 [B]Is 33:10 [C]Ps 34:6; 35:10 12:6 [A]2 Sam 22:31; Ps 18:30; 19:8, 10; 119:140 [B]Prov 30:5 12:7 [A]Ps 37:28; 97:10 12:8 [a]Or *worthlessness* [A]Ps 55:10, 11 [B]Is 32:5 13:1 [A]Ps 44:24 [B]Job 13:24; Ps 89:46 13:2 [A]Ps 42:4 [B]Ps 42:9 13:3 [A]Ps 5:1 [B]1 Sam 14:29; Ezra 9:8; Job 33:30; Ps 18:28 [C]Jer 51:39 13:4 [A]Ps 12:4 [B]Ps 25:2; 38:16 13:5 [A]Ps 52:8 [B]Ps 9:14 13:6 [A]Ps 96:1, 2 [B]Ps 116:7; 119:17; 142:7 14:1 [a]Lit *doings* [A]Ps 10:4; 53:1 [B]Ps 14:1-3; 130:3; Rom 3:10-12

12:1–8 Men's words do hurt, but the Lord's words heal. These thoughts preoccupy David in Ps 12. The psalm begins and ends with the reality of the current reign of the wicked. Yet amidst this very black setting, the gemstone truth of v. 5 shines all the more brightly. These 8 verses are characterized by subtle repetitions and bold contrasts. In the development of Ps 12, David provides a model for passing a spiritual hearing test, in that genuine disciples listen to and properly respond to two radically different sources of speech.

I. Surviving the Propaganda of Depraved Speech (12:1–4)
   A. By Prayer (12:1, 2)
   B. By Petition (12:3, 4)
II. Security in the Protection of Divine Speech (12:5–8)
   A. Its Divine Promises (12:5)
   B. Its Divine Purity (12:6)
   C. Its Divine Perseverance (12:7, 8)

12:1 for the godly man ceases. His words and phraseology are deliberately hyperbolic, yet David's perception indeed was that the pious have perished!

12:2–4 These smooth-talking sinners verbally abuse the remnant (vv. 2, 3) and verbally defy their Sovereign (v. 4).

12:3a May the LORD cut off all flattering lips. Here is a call for death in the light of sin. On the obnoxious sin of lying lips, cf. Ps 5:9; Is 30:10; Da 11:32; Ro 3:13.

12:6 pure … refined. The Lord's perfect words present a most radical contrast with the profane words of arrogant sinners. The purity of God's Person assures the purity of His promises (cf. Ps 19:7–10).

12:7, 8 The hostile realities of v. 8 call for the heavenly resources of v. 7.

13:1–6 Psalm 13 launches with an explosion of 4 "How longs?" indicating another lament is about to begin. But David will shift radically from turmoil to tranquility in the space of 6 short verses through 3 levels of attitude.

I. Below "Sea Level" Expressions of Despair (13:1, 2)
II. "Sea Level" Expressions of Desires (13:3, 4)
III. "Mountaintop Level" Expressions of Delight (13:5, 6)

13:1, 2 These lines reintroduce the familiar triangle of the psalmist, his God, and his enemies. This 3-way relationship produces perplexity and pain. In view of God's apparent absence (v. 1), he seems left to his own resources which are unable to deal with the reality of his enemies (v. 2).

13:4b–5b rejoice … rejoice. Using the same verb, he deliberately contrasts his enemy's celebration with his own confidence in divine deliverance.

14:1–7 Psalm 14, a wisdom poem, along with its nearly identical twin Ps 53, contains profound deliberations on human depravity. David's representative desire for deliverance (v. 7) provides the chorus to his two preceding dirges on depravity.

I. The Dirges on Depravity (14:1–6)
   A. The First Dirge: In the Form of a Round, Addresses the Universality of Depravity (14:1–3)
   B. The Second Dirge: In the Form of a Ballad, Addresses the Futility of Depravity (14:4–6)
II. The Chorus on Deliverance (14:7)
   A. The Wish for It (14:7a)
   B. The Worship Attending It (14:7b-c)

14:1 The fool. In the Bible, this designation carries moral rather than intellectual meaning (Is 32:6).

14:1–3 The "alls" and "no ones" of these lines make the indictments universally applicable. No wonder Paul included these indictments in

2 The LORD has [A]looked down from
heaven upon the sons of men
To see if there are any who [a,B]understand,
Who [C]seek after God.
3 They have all [A]turned aside, together
they have become corrupt;
There is [B]no one who does
good, not even one.

4 Do all the workers of
wickedness [A]not know,
Who [B]eat up my people *as* they eat bread,
And [C]do not call upon the LORD?
5 There they are in great dread,
For God is with the [A]righteous generation.
6 You would put to shame the
counsel of the afflicted,
But the LORD is his [A]refuge.

7 Oh, that [A]the salvation of Israel
[a]would come out of Zion!
When the LORD [b,B]restores
His captive people,
Jacob will rejoice, Israel will be glad.

PSALM 15

DESCRIPTION OF A CITIZEN OF ZION.

A Psalm of David.

1 O LORD, who may [a]abide [A]in Your tent?
Who may dwell on Your [B]holy hill?
2 He who [A]walks with integrity,
and works righteousness,
And [B]speaks truth in his heart.
3 He [A]does not slander [a]with his tongue,
Nor [B]does evil to his neighbor,
Nor [C]takes up a reproach
against his friend;
4 In [a]whose eyes a reprobate is despised,
But [b]who [A]honors those
who fear the LORD;
He [B]swears to his own hurt
and does not change;
5 He [A]does not put out his
money [a]at interest,
Nor [B]does he take a bribe
against the innocent.
[C]He who does these things
will never be shaken.

PSALM 16

THE LORD THE PSALMIST'S PORTION IN LIFE AND DELIVERER IN DEATH.

A [†]Mikhtam of David.

1 [A]Preserve me, O God, for [B]I
take refuge in You.
2 [a]I said to the LORD, "You are [b]my Lord;
I [A]have no good besides You."
3 As for the [a,A]saints who are in the earth,
[b]They are the majestic ones [B]in
whom is all my delight.
4 The [a,A]sorrows of those who
have [b]bartered for another
god will be multiplied;
I shall not pour out their drink
offerings of [B]blood,
Nor will I [C]take their names upon my lips.

14:2 [a]Or *act wisely* [A]Ps 33:13, 14; 102:19 [B]Ps 92:6 [C]1 Chr 22:19 14:3 [A]Ps 58:3 [B]Ps 143:2 14:4 [A]Ps 82:5 [B]Ps 27:2; Jer 10:25; Mic 3:3 [C]Ps 79:6; Is 64:7 14:5 [A]Ps 73:15; 112:2 14:6 [A]Ps 9:9; 40:17; 46:1; 142:5 14:7 [a]Lit *would be* [b]Or *restores the fortunes of His people* [A]Ps 53:6 [B]Ps 85:1, 2 15:1 [a]Lit *sojourn* [A]Ps 27:5, 6; 61:4 [B]Ps 24:3 15:2 [A]Ps 24:4; Is 33:15 [B]Zech 8:16; Eph 4:25 15:3 [a]Lit *according to* [A]Ps 50:20 [B]Ps 28:3 [C]Ex 23:1 15:4 [a]Lit *his* [b]Lit *he* [A]Acts 28:10 [B]Judg 11:35 15:5 [a]I.e. to a fellow Israelite [A]Ex 22:25; Lev 25:36; Deut 23:20; Ezek 18:8 [B]Ex 23:8; Deut 16:19 [C]2 Pet 1:10 16:1 [†]Possibly *Epigrammatic Poem* or *Atonement Psalm* [A]Ps 17:8 [B]Ps 7:1 16:2 [a]Or O my soul, *you said* [b]Or *the Lord* [A]Ps 73:25 16:3 [a]Lit *holy ones;* i.e. the godly [b]Lit *And the majestic ones...delight* [A]Ps 101:6 [B]Ps 119:63 16:4 [a]I.e. sorrows due to idolatry [b]Or *hastened to* [A]Ps 32:10 [B]Ps 106:37, 38 [C]Ex 23:13; Josh 23:7

Ro 3:10–12. There is also a common scriptural association of doing with thinking.

14:4–6 The shift from third person affirmations about the wicked (vv. 4, 5) to the second person (v. 6a) intensifies this confrontation with divine judgment.

14:7 Zion. The place on earth where God was pleased to reveal His presence, protection, and power (cf. Pss 3:4; 20:2; 128:5; 132:13; 134:3).

15:1–5 Whereas Ps 14 focused on the way of the wicked, Ps 15 concentrates on the way of the righteous (cf. Ps 1). The saved sinner is described as exhibiting indications of ethical integrity. These characteristics alternate in triplets of positive and negative descriptions. The whole psalm unfolds through a question-and-answer vehicle, and indeed it may be regarded as the ultimate Q and A session. With its focus on moral responsibility, the psalm offers a sequence of responses to the question of acceptable worship.

I. A Two-Part Question (15:1)
II. A Twelve-Part Response (15:2–5b)
   A. Three Positively Phrased Ethical Characteristics (15:2)
      1. His lifestyle exhibits integrity
      2. His deeds exhibit justice
      3. His speech exhibits reliability
   B. Three Negatively Cast Ethical Characteristics (15:3)
      1. He does not tread over people with his tongue
      2. He does not harm his fellow man
      3. He does not dump reproach upon family or friend
   C. Three Positively Phrased Ethical Characteristics (15:4a-c)
      1. He views the reprobate as rejected
      2. He respects the people of God
      3. He holds himself accountable
   D. Three Negatively Cast Ethical Characteristics (15:4d–5b)
      1. He is not fickle
      2. He is not greedy
      3. He cannot be bought
III. A One-Part Guarantee (15:5c)

15:1 Your tent. Cf. Ps 61:4; for possible background see 2Sa 6:12–17.

15:2–5 Notice the focus on life-and-lip qualities.

15:4 despised ... honors. Whom God rejects, the psalmist rejects; whom God loves, he loves.

15:5 interest. Interest rates ran as high as 50 percent, but God's law put strict regulations on borrowing and lending (*see notes on Dt 23:19, 20; 24:10–13*). **He ... will never be shaken.** This is an important promise in the light of its usage in Psalms and Proverbs (cf. Pss 10:6; 13:4; 16:8; 46:5; 62:2, 6; Pr 10:30).

16:1–11 The only prayer of Ps 16 comes in the first line. The rest of the psalm consists of David's weaving together his personal testimonies of trust in the Lord. In view of this, David's opening prayer is bolstered by two cycles of testimony.

I. David's Introductory Prayer (16:1)
II. David's Testimony (16:2–11)
   A. His Testimony of Communion (16:2–4)
      1. Its divine dimension (16:2)
      2. Its human dimension (16:3, 4)
   B. His Testimony of Confidence (16:5–11)
      1. Its past and present dimensions (16:5–8)
      2. Its present and future dimensions (16:9–11)

16:Title A Mikhtam of David. Cf. Pss 56, 57, 58, 59, 60. In spite of many conjectures, this designation remains obscure.

16:1 Preserve me. This is a frequent request begging God to protect the psalmist (cf. Pss 17:8; 140:4; 141:9).

16:2 I have no good besides You. I.e., "My well-being is entirely dependent upon You."

16:4 He will have nothing to do with false

5 The LORD is the [A]portion of my
inheritance and my [B]cup;
You support my [C]lot.
6 The [A]lines have fallen to me
in pleasant places;
Indeed, my heritage is [B]beautiful to me.

7 I will bless the LORD who
has [A]counseled me;
Indeed, my [a,B]mind instructs
me in the night.
8 [A]I have [B]set the LORD continually before me;
Because He is [C]at my right hand,
[D]I will not be shaken.
9 Therefore [A]my heart is glad
and [B]my glory rejoices;
My flesh also will [C]dwell securely.
10 For You [A]will not abandon
my soul to [a]Sheol;
Nor will You [b,B]allow Your [c]Holy
One to [d]undergo decay.
11 You will make known to me [A]the path of life;
In [B]Your presence is fullness of joy;
In Your right hand there are
[C]pleasures forever.

PSALM 17

PRAYER FOR PROTECTION AGAINST OPPRESSORS.

A Prayer of David.

1 Hear a [A]just cause, O LORD,
[B]give heed to my cry;
[C]Give ear to my prayer, which is
not from [D]deceitful lips.
2 Let [A]my [a]judgment come forth
from Your presence;
Let Your eyes look with [B]equity.
3 You have [A]tried my heart;
You have visited *me* by night;
You have [B]tested me and
[C]You find [a]nothing;
I have [D]purposed that my mouth
will not transgress.
4 As for the deeds of men, [A]by
the word of Your lips
I have kept from the [B]paths of the violent.
5 My [A]steps have held fast to Your [a]paths.
My [B]feet have not slipped.

6 I have [A]called upon You, for You
will answer me, O God;
[B]Incline Your ear to me, hear my speech.
7 [A]Wondrously show Your lovingkindness,
O [B]Savior of those who take
refuge [a]at Your right hand
From those who rise up *against them.*
8 Keep me as [a]the [A]apple of the eye;
Hide me [B]in the shadow of Your wings
9 From the [A]wicked who despoil me,
My [B]deadly enemies who surround me.
10 They have [A]closed their [a]unfeeling *heart,*
With their mouth they [B]speak proudly.
11 They have now [A]surrounded
us in our steps;
They set their eyes [B]to cast *us*
down to the ground.
12 He is [A]like a lion that is eager to tear,
And as a young lion [B]lurking
in hiding places.

13 [A]Arise, O LORD, confront him,
[B]bring him low;
[C]Deliver my soul from the wicked
with [D]Your sword,

16:5 [A]Ps 73:26; 119:57; 142:5; Lam 3:24 [B]Ps 23:5 [C]Ps 125:3 mg 16:6 [A]Ps 78:55 [B]Jer 3:19 16:7 [a]Lit *kidneys,* figurative for inner man [A]Ps 73:24 [B]Ps 77:6 16:8 [A]Ps 16:8-11; Acts 2:25-28 [B]Ps 27:8; 123:1, 2 [C]Ps 73:23; 110:5; 121:5 [D]Ps 112:6 16:9 [A]Ps 4:7; 13:5 [B]Ps 30:12; 57:8; 108:1 [C]Ps 4:8 16:10 [a]I.e. the nether world [b]Lit *give* [c]Or *godly one* [d]Or *see corruption* or *the pit* [A]Ps 49:15; 86:13 [B]Acts 13:35 16:11 [A]Ps 139:24; Matt 7:14 [B]Ps 21:6; 43:4 [C]Job 36:11; Ps 36:7, 8; 46:4 17:1 [A]Ps 9:4 [B]Ps 61:1; 142:6 [C]Ps 88:2 [D]Is 29:13 17:2 [a]I.e. vindication [A]Ps 103:6 [B]Ps 98:9; 99:4 17:3 [a]Or *no evil device in me; My mouth* [A]Ps 26:1, 2 [B]Job 23:10; Ps 66:10; Zech 13:9; 1 Pet 1:7 [C]Jer 50:20 [D]Ps 39:1 17:4 [A]Ps 119:9, 101 [B]Ps 10:5-11 17:5 [a]Lit *tracks* [A]Job 23:11; Ps 44:18; 119:133 [B]Ps 18:36; 37:31 17:6 [A]Ps 86:7; 116:2 [B]Ps 88:2 17:7 [a]Or *from those who rise up...at Your right hand* [A]Ps 31:21 [B]Ps 20:6 17:8 [a]Lit *the pupil, the daughter of the eye* [A]Deut 32:10; Zech 2:8 [B]Ruth 2:12; Ps 36:7; 57:1; 61:4; 63:7; 91:1, 4 17:9 [A]Ps 31:20 [B]Ps 27:12 17:10 [a]Lit *fat* [A]Job 15:27; Ps 73:7 [B]1 Sam 2:3; Ps 31:18; 73:8 17:11 [A]Ps 88:17 [B]Ps 37:14 17:12 [A]Ps 7:2 [B]Ps 10:9 17:13 [A]Ps 3:7 [B]Ps 55:23 [C]Ps 22:20 [D]Ps 7:12

gods or the people pursuing them.

16:5, 6 These lines use OT metaphors to describe the blessing of God.

16:9 my glory. Starting back at v. 7, the psalmist referred to his core of being as "my mind," then "my heart," now "my glory," and next "My flesh" and "my soul." The anthropological terms stand for the whole person, so it is best to consider "my glory" as referring to that distinctive way in which man is created in the image of God, i.e., his intelligence and ability to speak.

16:10 These words expressed the confidence of the lesser David, but were applied messianically to the resurrection of the Greater David (the Lord Jesus Christ) both by Peter (Ac 2:25–28) and Paul (Ac 13:35).

17:1–15 This "prayer" of David brims with petitions, as many as seventeen of them depending upon the translation of certain Heb. verb forms. There are many literary parallels with Ps 16. Although the psalm shows indications of mixed forms, it is essentially a prayer for protection. David is fond of using themes and phrases from the Exodus narrative (cf. Ex 15; Dt 32). A logical chiastic development is detected in its verses, with the focus shifting from the psalmist (vv. 1–8) to his enemies (vv. 9–12), remaining on his enemies in vv. 13, 14, then shifting back to David (v. 15). Or viewing its development from another angle, David approaches the divine court with 3 clusters of appeals in seeking justice.

I. Appeals Dealing with Response and Recognition (17:1–5)
II. Appeals Dealing with Rescue and Relief (17:6–12)
   A. His Need for Rescue Is Presented (17:6–8)
   B. His Need for Relief Is Documented (17:9–12)
III. Appeals Dealing with Retribution and Rest (17:13–15)
   A. His Anticipation of Their Retribution (17:13, 14)
   B. His Assurance of His Own Rest (17:15)

17:Title This is the first psalm simply entitled "A Prayer" (cf. Pss 86, 90, 102, 142).

17:1, 2 The introductory language is that of the law court, and David stands before the ultimate Chief Justice to present his case.

17:3–5 His basic integrity (vv. 3, 4) especially in view of the present case, was, is, and shall be dependent upon the grace of God (v. 5).

17:8 the apple of the eye. An expression meaning the pupil of the human eye. As a person protects that vital organ of vision, so God protects His people.

17:10 They have closed their unfeeling *heart.* Lit. "They have closed their fat." This was a common OT idiom for insensitivity (cf. Dt 32:15; Job 15:27; Ps 73:7; Jer 5:28).

17:13 Divine Warrior language.

14 From men with [A]Your hand, O LORD,
From men [a]of the world, [B]whose
portion is in *this* life,
And whose belly You [C]fill
with Your treasure;
They are satisfied with children,
And leave their abundance to their babes.
15 As for me, I shall [A]behold Your
face in righteousness;
[B]I will be satisfied [a]with Your
[C]likeness when I awake.

PSALM 18

THE LORD PRAISED FOR GIVING DELIVERANCE.

For the choir director. A *Psalm* of David the servant of the LORD, [†]who spoke to the LORD the words of this song in the day that the LORD delivered him from the hand of all his enemies and from the hand of Saul. And he said,

1 "I love You, O LORD, [A]my strength."
2 The LORD is [A]my [a]rock and [B]my
fortress and my [C]deliverer,
My God, my rock, in whom I take refuge;
My [D]shield and the [E]horn of my
salvation, my [F]stronghold.
3 I call upon the LORD, who is
[A]worthy to be praised,
And I am [B]saved from my enemies.

4 The [A]cords of death encompassed me,
And the [B]torrents of [a]ungodliness
[b]terrified me.
5 The [A]cords of [a]Sheol surrounded me;
The snares of death confronted me.
6 In my [A]distress I called upon the LORD,
And cried to my God for help;
He heard my voice [B]out of His temple,
And my [C]cry for help before
Him came into His ears.

7 Then the [A]earth shook and quaked;
And the [B]foundations of the
mountains were trembling
And were shaken, because He was angry.
8 Smoke went up [a]out of His nostrils,
And [A]fire from His mouth devoured;
Coals were kindled by it.

17:14 [a]Or *whose portion in life is of the world* [A]Ps 17:7 [B]Ps 73:3-7; Luke 16:25 [C]Ps 49:6 17:15 [a]Or *with* beholding [A]Ps 11:7; 16:11; 140:13; 1 John 3:2 [B]Ps 4:6, 7 [C]Num 12:8 18:1 [†]2 Sam 22:1-51 [A]Ps 59:17 18:2 [a]Or *crag* [A]Deut 32:18; 1 Sam 2:2; Ps 18:31, 46; 28:1; 31:3; 42:9; 71:3; 78:15 [B]Ps 144:2 [C]Ps 19:14 [D]Ps 28:7; 33:20; 59:11; 84:9, 11; Prov 30:5 [E]Ps 75:10 [F]Ps 59:9 18:3 [A]Ps 48:1; 96:4; 145:3 [B]Ps 34:6 18:4 [a]Or *destruction;* Heb *Belial* [b]Or *were assailing* or *terrifying* [A]Ps 116:3 [B]Ps 69:2; 124:3, 4 18:5 [a]I.e. the nether world [A]Ps 116:3 18:6 [A]Ps 50:15; 120:1 [B]Ps 3:4 [C]Ps 34:15 18:7 [A]Judg 5:4; Ps 68:7, 8; Is 13:13; Hag 2:6 [B]Ps 114:4, 6 18:8 [a]Or *in His wrath* [A]Ps 50:3

17:14, 15 The common grace of God is overlooked by those who are satisfied with temporal prosperities (v. 14), but David brings back the proper perspective on true satisfaction in v. 15. Cf. Jesus' teaching on these vital issues in Mt 6:19–34.

18:1–50 Psalm 18 is clearly an individual psalm of thanksgiving, also bearing royal characteristics. Its poetry and themes resemble other ancient testimonies to God's great historical deliverances (e.g., Ex 15; Jdg 5). Between David's opening (vv. 1–3) and closing (vv. 46–50) praises to God, his life with the Lord is described in 3 stages.

I. Prelude: His Opening Praises (18:1–3)
II. The Stages of His Life (18:4–45)
  A. In the Pit of Peril (18:4–19)
    1. His desperation (18:4, 5)
    2. His defender (18:6–15)
    3. His deliverance (18:16–19)
  B. On a Course of Ethical Integrity (18:20–28)
    1. The principles of the Lord's direction (18:20–26)
    2. The privileges of the Lord's direction (18:27, 28)
  C. In the Turbulent Atmosphere of Leadership (18:29–45)
    1. Military leadership (18:29–42)
    2. Theocratic leadership (18:43–45)
III. Postscript: His Closing Praises (18:46–50)

18:Title This large psalm bears a large title. Although the title seems to refer to only one specific occasion (e.g., "in the day"), it does state that God's deliverance was "from the hand of all his enemies and from the hand of Saul." Therefore, it is preferable that the language of this superscription be understood to summarize the testimony of David's whole life in retrospect.

18:1 love. This is not the normal word for love that often bears covenant meaning (e.g., Dt 7:8; Ps 119:97), but it is a rare verb form of a word group that expresses tender intimacy. David's choice of words intended to express very strong devotion, like Peter's in Jn 21:15–17.

18:2 Military metaphors for the Divine Warrior multiply in this verse. Both defensively and offensively, the Lord was all David needed in life's tough battles.

18:4 cords of death. Cf. Jon 2:2–9.

18:7–15 This theophany, a vivid poetic picture of God's presence, rivals other biblical presentations (cf. Ex 19:16ff.; Dt 33:2ff.; Jdg 4, 5; Ps 68:7, 8; Mic 1:3, 4; Hab 3; Rev 19). His presence is largely described by various catastrophic responses by all creation.

IMAGES OF GOD IN THE PSALMS

Images of God as	Reference in Psalms
Shield	3:3; 28:7; 119:114
Rock	18:2; 42:9; 95:1
King	5:2; 44:4; 74:12
Shepherd	23:1; 80:1
Judge	7:11
Refuge	46:1; 62:7
Fortress	31:3; 71:3
Avenger	26:1
Creator	8:1, 6
Deliverer	37:39, 40
Healer	30:2
Protector	5:11
Provider	78:23–29
Redeemer	107:2

9 He [A]bowed the heavens also,
and came down
With thick [B]darkness under His feet.
10 He rode upon a [A]cherub and flew;
And He sped upon the [B]wings of the wind.
11 He made [A]darkness His hiding place,
[B]His [a]canopy around Him,
Darkness of waters, thick
clouds of the skies.
12 From the [A]brightness before Him
passed His thick clouds,
Hailstones and [B]coals of fire.
13 The LORD also [A]thundered in the heavens,
And the Most High uttered His voice,
Hailstones and coals of fire.
14 He [A]sent out His arrows,
and scattered them,
And lightning flashes in abundance,
and [a]routed them.
15 Then the [A]channels of water appeared,
And the foundations of the
world were [a]laid bare
At Your [B]rebuke, O LORD,
At the blast of the [C]breath of Your nostrils.

16 He [A]sent from on high, He took me;
He drew me out of [B]many waters.
17 He [A]delivered me from my strong enemy,
And from those who hated me, for
they were [B]too mighty for me.
18 They confronted me in [A]the
day of my calamity,
But [B]the LORD was my stay.
19 He brought me forth also
into a [A]broad place;
He rescued me, because [B]He
delighted in me.

20 The LORD has [A]rewarded me
according to my righteousness;
According to the [B]cleanness of my
hands He has recompensed me.
21 For I have [A]kept the ways of the LORD,
And have [B]not wickedly
departed from my God.
22 For all [A]His ordinances were before me,
And I did not put away His
[B]statutes from me.
23 I was also [a,A]blameless with Him,
And I [B]kept myself from my iniquity.
24 Therefore the LORD has [A]recompensed
me according to my righteousness,
According to the cleanness of
my hands in His eyes.

25 With [A]the kind You show Yourself kind;
With the [a]blameless [B]You show
Yourself blameless;
26 With the pure You show Yourself [A]pure,
And with the crooked [B]You
show Yourself [a]astute.
27 For You [A]save an afflicted people,
But [B]haughty eyes You abase.
28 For You [A]light my lamp;
The LORD my God [B]illumines
my darkness.
29 For by You I can [a,A]run upon a troop;
And by my God I can [B]leap over a wall.

30 As for God, His way is [a,A]blameless;
The [B]word of the LORD is tried;
He is a [C]shield to all who
take refuge in Him.
31 For [A]who is God, but the LORD?
And who is a [B]rock, except our God,
32 The God who [A]girds me with strength
And [a]makes my way [b,B]blameless?
33 He [A]makes my feet like hinds' *feet,*
And [B]sets me upon my high places.
34 He [A]trains my hands for battle,
So that my arms can [B]bend
a bow of bronze.
35 You have also given me [A]the
shield of Your salvation,
And Your [B]right hand upholds me;
And [C]Your [a]gentleness makes me great.
36 You [A]enlarge my steps under me,
And my [a,B]feet have not slipped.

37 I [A]pursued my enemies and
overtook them,
And I did not turn back [B]until
they were consumed.
38 I shattered them, so that they
were [A]not able to rise;
They fell [B]under my feet.
39 For You have [A]girded me with
strength for battle;
You have [a,B]subdued under me those
who rose up against me.

18:9 [A]Ps 144:5 [B]Ps 97:2 18:10 [A]Ps 80:1; 99:1 [B]Ps 104:3 18:11 [a]Or *pavilion* [A]Deut 4:11 [B]Ps 97:2 18:12 [A]Ps 104:2 [B]Ps 97:3; 140:10; Hab 3:4 18:13 [A]Ps 29:3; 104:7 18:14 [a]Lit *confused* [A]Ps 144:6; Hab 3:11 18:15 [a]Or *uncovered* [A]Ps 106:9 [B]Ps 76:6 [C]Ps 18:8 18:16 [A]Ps 144:7 [B]Ps 32:6 18:17 [A]Ps 59:1 [B]Ps 35:10; 142:6 18:18 [A]Ps 59:16 [B]Ps 16:8 18:19 [A]Ps 4:1; 31:8; 118:5 [B]Ps 37:23; 41:11 18:20 [A]1 Sam 24:19; Job 33:26; Ps 7:8 [B]Job 22:30; Ps 24:4 18:21 [A]Ps 37:34; 119:33; Prov 8:32 [B]2 Chr 34:33; Ps 119:102 18:22 [A]Ps 119:30 [B]Ps 119:83 18:23 [a]Lit *complete;* or *having integrity;* or *perfect* [A]Ps 18:32 [B]Ps 19:12, 13; 25:11; 66:18 18:24 [A]1 Sam 26:23; Ps 18:20 18:25 [a]V 23, note 1 [A]1 Kin 8:32; Ps 62:12; Matt 5:7 [B]Ps 18:30 18:26 [a]Lit *twisted* [A]Job 25:5; Hab 1:13 [B]Lev 26:23, 24, 27, 28; Prov 3:34 18:27 [A]Ps 72:12 [B]Ps 101:5; Prov 6:17 18:28 [A]1 Kin 15:4; Job 18:6; Ps 132:17 [B]Ps 27:1 18:29 [a]Or *crush a troop* [A]Ps 118:10-12 [B]Ps 18:33; 40:2 18:30 [a]V 23, note 1 [A]Deut 32:4; Ps 19:7; 145:17; Rev 15:3 [B]Ps 12:6 [C]Ps 17:7; 91:4 18:31 [A]Deut 32:39; 1 Sam 2:2; Ps 86:8-10; Is 45:5 [B]Deut 32:31; Ps 18:2; 62:2 18:32 [a]Or *has made* [b]Lit *complete;* or *having integrity* [A]Ps 18:39; Is 45:5 [B]Ps 18:23 18:33 [A]Hab 3:19 [B]Deut 32:13 18:34 [A]Ps 144:1 [B]Job 29:20 18:35 [a]Or *condescension* [A]Ps 33:20 [B]Ps 63:8; 119:117 [C]Ps 138:6 18:36 [a]Lit *ankles* [A]Ps 18:33 [B]Ps 66:9; Prov 4:12 18:37 [A]Ps 44:5 [B]Ps 37:20 18:38 [A]Ps 36:12 [B]Ps 47:3 18:39 [a]Lit *caused to bow down* [A]Ps 18:32 [B]Ps 18:47

18:16–19 His sheer power, exhibited so dramatically in vv. 7–15, is now amazingly attested as coming to rescue the psalmist personally.

18:20–24, 37, 38 These verses should not be taken out of context, making David look like an arrogant boaster. As in vv. 25–36 and 39–50, both David and the community, although responsible for living with integrity within the covenant relationship, are fully dependent on the resources of God to do so. Therefore, his "boasting" is biblical, since it is ultimately in the Lord (Jer 9:23, 24).

18:31 a rock. Cf. vv. 2, 46. Moses, at the beginning of his great song about the Lord in Dt 32, called God "The Rock" (v. 4). The Lord is indeed a massive, unshakable foundation and source of protection.

40 You have also made my enemies
[A]turn their backs to me,
And I [a,B]destroyed those who hated me.
41 They cried for help, but there
was [A]none to save,
Even to the LORD, but [B]He did
not answer them.
42 Then I beat them fine as the
[A]dust before the wind;
I emptied them out as the
mire of the streets.

43 You have delivered me from the
[A]contentions of the people;
You have placed me as [B]head of the nations;
A [C]people whom I have not
known serve me.
44 As soon as they hear, they obey me;
Foreigners [a,A]submit to me.
45 Foreigners [A]fade away,
And [B]come trembling out
of their [a]fortresses.

46 The LORD [A]lives, and blessed be [B]my rock;
And exalted be [C]the God of my salvation,
47 The God who [A]executes vengeance for me,
And [B]subdues peoples under me.
48 He [A]delivers me from my enemies;
Surely You [B]lift me above those
who rise up against me;
You rescue me from the [C]violent man.
49 Therefore I will [A]give thanks to You
among the nations, O LORD,
And I will [B]sing praises to Your name.
50 He gives great [a,A]deliverance to His king,
And shows lovingkindness to [B]His anointed,
To David and [C]his [b]descendants forever.

PSALM 19

THE WORKS AND THE WORD OF GOD.

For the choir director. A Psalm of David.

1 The [A]heavens are telling of
the glory of God;
And their [B]expanse is declaring
the work of His hands.
2 Day to [A]day pours forth speech,
And [B]night to night reveals knowledge.
3 There is no speech, nor are there words;
Their voice is not heard.
4 Their [a,A]line has gone out
through all the earth,
And their utterances to the
end of the world.
In them He has [B]placed a tent for the sun,
5 Which is as a bridegroom coming
out of his chamber;
It rejoices as a strong man
to run his course.
6 Its [A]rising is from [a]one end of the heavens,
And its circuit to the [b]other end of them;
And there is nothing hidden from its heat.

7 [A]The law of the LORD is [a,B]perfect,
[C]restoring the soul;
The testimony of the LORD is [D]sure,
making [E]wise the simple.
8 The precepts of the LORD are
[A]right, [B]rejoicing the heart;
The commandment of the LORD is
[C]pure, [D]enlightening the eyes.
9 The fear of the LORD is clean,
enduring forever;
The judgments of the LORD are [A]true;
they are [B]righteous altogether.

18:40 [a]Or *silenced* [A]Ps 21:12 [B]Ps 94:23 18:41 [A]Ps 50:22 [B]Job 27:9; Prov 1:28 18:42 [A]Ps 83:13 18:43 [A]2 Sam 3:1; 19:9; Ps 35:1 [B]2 Sam 8:1-18; Ps 89:27 [C]Is 55:5 18:44 [a]Lit *deceive me;* i.e. give feigned obedience [A]Ps 66:3 18:45 [a]Lit *fastnesses* [A]Ps 37:2 [B]Mic 7:17 18:46 [A]Job 19:25 [B]Ps 18:2 [C]Ps 51:14 18:47 [A]Ps 94:1 [B]Ps 18:43; 47:3; 144:2 18:48 [A]Ps 3:7 [B]Ps 27:6; 59:1 [C]Ps 11:5 18:49 [A]Rom 15:9 [B]Ps 108:1 18:50 [a]I.e. victories; lit *salvations* [b]Lit *seed* [A]Ps 21:1; 144:10 [B]Ps 28:8 [C]Ps 89:4 19:1 [A]Ps 8:1; 50:6; Rom 1:19, 20 [B]Gen 1:6, 7 19:2 [A]Ps 74:16 [B]Ps 139:12 19:4 [a]Another reading is *sound* [A]Rom 10:18 [B]Ps 104:2 19:6 [a]Lit *the* [b]Lit *the ends* [A]Ps 113:3; Eccl 1:5 19:7 [a]I.e. blameless [A]Ps 111:7 [B]Ps 119:160 [C]Ps 23:3 [D]Ps 93:5 [E]Ps 119:98-100 19:8 [A]Ps 119:128 [B]Ps 119:14 [C]Ps 12:6 [D]Ps 36:9 19:9 [A]Ps 119:142 [B]Ps 119:138

18:50 This concluding verse is another royal messianic affirmation of the Davidic Covenant in 2Sa 7.

19:1–14 Because of its two distinct parts and two different names for God, some have tried to argue that Ps 19 was really two compositions, one ancient and one more recent. However, the shorter form of the name "God" (cf. the longer form in Ge 1:1) speaks of His power, especially power exhibited as Creator, while "LORD" fits the relational focus. Consequently, David depicted the Lord God as author of both His world and Word in a unified hymn. God has revealed Himself to mankind through these two avenues. The human race stands accountable to Him because of His non-verbal and verbal communications. In the light of these intentions, Ps 19 eloquently summarizes two prominent vehicles of God's self-disclosure.

I. God's General Self-Disclosure in the World (19:1–6)
   A. The Publication of the Skies (19:1–4b)
   B. The Prominence of the Sun (19:4c–6)
II. God's Special Self-Disclosure in the Word (19:7–14)
   A. The Attributes of the Word (19:7–9)
   B. An Appreciation for the Word (19:10, 11)
   C. The Application of the Word (19:12–14)

19:1–6 The testimony of the universe comes forth consistently and clearly, but sinful mankind persistently resists it. For this reason, general revelation cannot convert sinners, but it does make them highly accountable (cf. Ro 1:18ff.). Salvation comes ultimately only through special revelation, i.e., as the Word of God is effectually applied by the Spirit of God.

19:1 heavens … expanse. Both are crucial elements of the creation in Ge 1 (cf. vv. 1, 8). **telling … declaring.** Both verbs emphasize the continuity of these respective disclosures. **work of His hands.** An anthropomorphism illustrating God's great power (cf. the "work of Your fingers" in Ps 8:3).

19:2, 3 speech … no speech. This is not a contradiction, but shows that the constant communication of the heavens is not with words of a literal nature.

19:4 The message of the created world extends to everywhere.

19:4c–6 Neither the sun nor the heavens are deified as was the case in many pagan religions. In the Bible, God is the Creator and Ruler over all creation.

19:7–14 The scene shifts from God's world to God's Word.

19:7, 8 Each of 4 parallel lines contains a word (a synonym) for God's Word; each describes what His Word is; and each pronounces what it effectually accomplishes.

19:7 law. This might better be translated, "His teaching," "a direction," or "instruction" (cf. Ps 1:2). **testimony.** This word for the Word derives from the root "to bear witness." It, so to speak, bears testimony to its Divine Author.

19:8 precepts. This synonym looks upon God's Word as orders, charges, statutes, etc. They are viewed as the Governor's governings. **commandment.** This word is related to the verb "to command" or "order." The Word is therefore also perceived as divine orders.

19:9 fear. This is not technically a word for the Word, but it does reflect the reality that Scripture is the manual for worship of God. **judgments.** This term looks upon God's Word as conveying His judicial decisions.

10 They are more desirable than [A]gold,
yes, than much fine gold;
[B]Sweeter also than honey and the
drippings of the honeycomb.
11 Moreover, by them [A]Your
servant is warned;
In keeping them there
is great [B]reward.
12 Who can [A]discern *his* errors?
[B]Acquit me of [C]hidden *faults.*
13 Also keep back Your servant
[A]from presumptuous *sins;*
Let them not [B]rule over me;
Then I will be [a,C]blameless,
And I shall be acquitted of
[D]great transgression.
14 Let the words of my mouth and
[A]the meditation of my heart
Be acceptable in Your sight,
O LORD, [B]my rock and my [C]Redeemer.

PSALM 20

PRAYER FOR VICTORY OVER ENEMIES.

For the choir director. A Psalm of David.

1 May the LORD answer you [A]in
the day of trouble!
May the [B]name of the [C]God of Jacob
set you *securely* on high!
2 May He send you help [A]from
the sanctuary
And [B]support you from Zion!
3 May He [A]remember all your
meal offerings
And [B]find your burnt offering
[a]acceptable! [b]*Selah*
4 May He grant you your [A]heart's desire
And [B]fulfill all your [a]counsel!
5 [a]We will [A]sing for joy over your [b]victory,
And in the name of our God we
will [B]set up our banners.
May the LORD [C]fulfill all your petitions.

6 Now [A]I know that the LORD
saves His anointed;
He will [B]answer him from
His holy heaven
With the [a,C]saving strength
of His right hand.
7 Some [a]*boast* in chariots and
some in [A]horses,
But [B]we [b]will boast in the name
of the LORD, our God.
8 They have [A]bowed down and fallen,
But we have [B]risen and stood upright.
9 [a,A]Save, O LORD;
May the [B]King answer us
in the day we call.

PSALM 21

PRAISE FOR DELIVERANCE.

For the choir director. A Psalm of David.

1 O LORD, in Your strength the
king will [A]be glad,
And in Your [a]salvation how
greatly he will rejoice!
2 You have [A]given him his heart's desire,
And You have not withheld the request of
his lips. [a]*Selah*
3 For You [A]meet him with the
blessings of good things;
You set a [B]crown of fine gold on his head.

19:10 [A]Ps 119:72, 127 [B]Ps 119:103 19:11 [A]Ps 17:4 [B]Ps 24:5, 6; Prov 29:18 19:12 [A]Ps 40:12; 139:6 [B]Ps 51:1, 2 [C]Ps 90:8; 139:23, 24 19:13 [a]Lit *complete* [A]Num 15:30 [B]Ps 119:133 [C]Ps 18:32 [D]Ps 25:11 19:14 [A]Ps 104:34 [B]Ps 18:2 [C]Ps 31:5; Is 47:4 20:1 [A]Ps 50:15 [B]Ps 91:14 [C]Ps 46:7, 11 20:2 [A]Ps 3:4 [B]Ps 110:2 20:3 [a]Lit *fat* [b]*Selah* may mean: *Pause, Crescendo* or *Musical interlude* [A]Acts 10:4 [B]Ps 51:19 20:4 [a]Or *purpose* [A]Ps 21:2 [B]Ps 145:19 20:5 [a]Or *Let us sing* [b]Or *salvation* [A]Ps 9:14 [B]Ps 60:4 [C]1 Sam 1:17 20:6 [a]Or *mighty deeds of the victory of His right hand* [A]Ps 41:11 [B]Is 58:9 [C]Ps 28:8 20:7 [a]Or praise *chariots,* or trust, or are strong *through* [b]Lit *make mention of;* or *praise the name* [A]Ps 33:17 [B]2 Chr 32:8 20:8 [A]Is 2:11, 17 [B]Ps 37:24; Mic 7:8 20:9 [a]Or *O LORD, save the king; answer us* [A]Ps 3:7 [B]Ps 17:6 21:1 [a]Or *victory* [A]Ps 59:16, 17 21:2 [a]*Selah* may mean: *Pause, Crescendo* or *Musical interlude* [A]Ps 20:4; 37:4 21:3 [A]Ps 59:10 [B]2 Sam 12:30

19:12, 13 The psalmist deals respectively with unintentional sins and high-handed infractions (cf. Lv 4:1ff.; Nu 15:22ff.). David's concerns reflect the attitude of a maturing disciple who, by God's grace and provisions, deals with his sins and does not deny them.

19:14 **Be acceptable.** Using a term often associated with God's acceptance of properly offered, literal sacrifices, he asks for grace and enablement as he lays his "lip-and-life" sacrifices on the "altar" (cf. Jos 1:8).

20:1–9 Psalms 20 and 21 are twin warfare events—Ps 20 is mostly ceremony before a battle, while Ps 21 is mostly celebration after a battle. In the theocracy, these were to be considered holy wars with the chain of command being as follows: the Lord is Commander-in-Chief over the anointed king-general and the theocratic people—soldiers. All holy convocations, both before and after battles, involved prayer and praise assemblies dedicated to God, who grants victories through the theocratic king-general. Psalm 20, in anticipation of a military campaign, commemorates a 3-phased ceremony regularly conducted by the people in the presence of the Commander-in-Chief on behalf of the king-general.

I. An Offering of Their Prayers (20:1–5)
II. A Confirmation of Their Confidence (20:6–8)
III. A Reaffirmation of Their Dependence (20:9)

20:1 **May the LORD answer you in the day of trouble!** This is the prayer of God's people for their king-general (cf. "His anointed," v. 6).

20:2 **from the sanctuary ... from Zion.** These are designations about the place of God's symbolic presence in the ark which David had recaptured and installed in a tabernacle on Mt. Zion. The people's wish was that the Lord Himself would uphold, support, and sustain the king-general with His extending, powerful presence throughout the military campaign.

20:5 **your victory.** Here, by contrast, God's salvation is victory in battle.

20:7 **Some *boast* in ...** Trust, boast, and praise must not be directed to the wrong objects but only to God Himself (cf., e.g., Dt 17:16; 20:1–4; Lv 26:7, 8; Ps 33:16, 17; Is 31:1–3; Jer 9:23, 24; Zec 4:6).

20:9 This verse could also be rendered: "Lord, grant victory to the king! Answer us when we call!"

21:1–13 The first part of Ps 21 is a thanksgiving for victory; the last part is an anticipation of future victories in the Lord through the king-general. Two scenarios of victory provide a context for praise and prayer to the Commander-in-Chief of Israel's king-general.

I. A Present-Past Scenario of Praise: Grounded upon Victories Accomplished in the Lord (21:1–6)
II. A Present-Future Scenario of Prayer and Praise: Grounded upon Victories Anticipated in the Lord (21:7–13)

21:2 Cf. Ps 20:4, the before; Ps 21:2, the after.

21:3 **You set a crown of fine gold on his head.** This is symbolic of superlative blessing (note the reversal in Eze 21:25–27).

4 He asked life of You,
You [A]gave it to him,
[B]Length of days forever and ever.
5 His [A]glory is great through
Your [a]salvation,
[B]Splendor and majesty You
place upon him.
6 For You make him [a]most
[A]blessed forever;
You make him joyful [B]with
gladness in Your presence.

7 For the king [A]trusts in the LORD,
And through the lovingkindness
of the Most High [B]he
will not be shaken.
8 Your hand will [A]find out
all your enemies;
Your right hand will find out
those who hate you.
9 You will make them [A]as a fiery oven
in the time [a]of your anger;
The LORD will [B]swallow them
up in His wrath,
And [C]fire will devour them.
10 Their [a]offspring You will
destroy from the earth,
And their [b,A]descendants from
among the sons of men.
11 Though they [a,A]intended
evil against You
And [B]devised a plot,
They will not succeed.
12 For You will [A]make them turn their back;
You will [a]aim [B]with Your
bowstrings at their faces.
13 Be exalted, O LORD, in Your strength;
We will [A]sing and praise Your power.

PSALM 22

A CRY OF ANGUISH AND A SONG OF PRAISE.

For the choir director; upon [†]Aijeleth Hashshahar. A Psalm of David.

1 [A]My God, my God, why have
You forsaken me?
[a,B]Far from my deliverance are the
words of my [b,C]groaning.
2 O my God, I [A]cry by day, but
You do not answer;
And by night, but [a]I have no rest.
3 Yet [A]You are holy,
O You who [a]are enthroned upon
[B]the praises of Israel.
4 In You our fathers [A]trusted;
They trusted and You [B]delivered them.
5 To You they cried out
and were delivered;
[A]In You they trusted and were
not [a]disappointed.

6 But I am a [A]worm and not a man,
A [B]reproach of men and
[C]despised by the people.
7 All who see me [a,A]sneer at me;
They [b]separate with the lip, they
[B]wag the head, *saying,*
8 "[a]Commit *yourself* to the LORD;
[A]let Him deliver him;
Let Him rescue him, because
He delights in him."

9 Yet You are He who [A]brought
me forth from the womb;
You made me trust *when* upon
my mother's breasts.

21:4 [A]Ps 61:6; 133:3 [B]Ps 91:16 21:5 [a]Or *victory* [A]Ps 9:14; 20:5 [B]Ps 8:5; 96:6 21:6 [a]Lit *blessings* [A]1 Chr 17:27 [B]Ps 43:4 21:7 [A]Ps 125:1 [B]Ps 112:6 21:8 [A]Is 10:10 21:9 [a]Or *of your presence* [A]Mal 4:1 [B]Lam 2:2 [C]Ps 50:3 21:10 [a]Lit *fruit* [b]Lit *seed* [A]Ps 37:28 21:11 [a]Lit *stretched out* [A]Ps 2:1-3 [B]Ps 10:2 21:12 [a]Lit *make ready* [A]Ps 18:40 [B]Ps 7:12, 13 21:13 [A]Ps 59:16; 81:1 22:1 [†]Lit *the hind of the morning* [a]Or Why are You so *far from helping me,* and from *the words of my groaning?* [b]Lit *roaring* [A]Matt 27:46; Mark 15:34 [B]Ps 10:1 [C]Job 3:24; Ps 6:6; 32:3; 38:8 22:2 [a]Lit *there is no silence for me* [A]Ps 42:3; 88:1 22:3 [a]Or *inhabit the praises* [A]Ps 99:9 [B]Deut 10:21; Ps 148:14 22:4 [A]Ps 78:53 [B]Ps 107:6 22:5 [a]Or *ashamed* [A]Is 49:23 22:6 [A]Job 25:6; Is 41:14 [B]Ps 31:11 [C]Is 49:7; 53:3 22:7 [a]Or *mock me* [b]I.e. make mouths at me [A]Ps 79:4; Is 53:3; Luke 23:35 [B]Matt 27:39; Mark 15:29 22:8 [a]Lit *Roll;* another reading is *He committed* himself [A]Ps 91:14; Matt 27:43 22:9 [A]Ps 71:5, 6

21:4 The first part of the verse most likely pertains to preservation of life in battle, and the second part to perpetuation of the dynasty (cf. 2Sa 7:13, 16, 29; Pss 89:4; 132:12).

21:5, 6 The King had given great prominence to the king-general.

21:7 **For the king.** The human responsibility dimension of the previous divine blessings is identified as the king-general's dependent trust in God. But the sovereign grace of God provides the ultimate basis for one not being moved or "shaken" (cf. Pss 15:5; 16:8; 17:5; Pr 10:30).

21:8 **Your ... you.** Without denying the mediatorship of the king-general, these delineations obviously put the spotlight upon the Commander-in-Chief.

22:1–31 This psalm presents the reader with a great contrast in mood. Lament characterizes the first 21 verses, while praise and thanksgiving describe the last 10 verses. Prayer accounts for this dramatic shift from lament to praise. It is the story of first being God-forsaken and then God-found and filled. It was applied immediately to David and ultimately to the Greater David, Messiah. The NT contains 15 messianic quotations of or allusions to this psalm, leading some in the early church to label it "the fifth gospel."

I. The Psalmist's Hopelessness (22:1–10)
   A. His Hopelessness and National History (22:1–5)
   B. His Hopelessness and Natal History (22:6–10)
II. The Psalmist's Prayer (22:11–21)
   A. A No-Help Outlook (22:11–18)
   B. A Divine-Help Outlook (22:19–21)
III. The Psalmist's Testimonies and Worship (22:22–31)
   A. An Individual Precipitation of Praise (22:22–25)
   B. A Corporate Perpetuation of Praise (22:26–31)

22:Title **Aijeleth Hashshahar.** This unique phrase in the superscription is probably best taken as a tune designation.

22:1 This heavy lament rivals Job 3; Ps 69; Jer 20:14–18. **My God, my God, why have You forsaken me?** The repeated noun of direct address to God reflects a personal molecule of hope in a seemingly hopeless situation. "Forsaken" is a strong expression for personal abandonment, intensely felt by David and supremely experienced by Christ on the cross (Mt 27:46).

22:2–5 The thrust of these verses is "even though You have not responded to me, You remain the Holy One of Israel who has demonstrated His gracious attention time and time again to Your people."

22:6–8 Reproach and ridicule were overwhelming the psalmist. For messianic applications, cf. Mt 27:39–44; Lk 23:35.

22:7 **They separate with the lip.** An idiom for sneering (cf. Job 16:10; Ps 35:21; Heb 5:5).

22:8 **Commit ... to the LORD.** Lit. "he rolled to the Lord." The idea is that he turned his burden over to the Lord (cf. Ps 37:5; Pr 16:3).

22:9, 10 The psalmist had a long history of reliance upon God.

10 Upon You I was cast [A]from [a]birth;
You have been my God from
my mother's womb.

11 [A]Be not far from me, for [a]trouble is near;
For there is [B]none to help.
12 Many [A]bulls have surrounded me;
Strong *bulls* of [B]Bashan have encircled me.
13 They [A]open wide their mouth at me,
As a ravening and a roaring [B]lion.
14 I am [A]poured out like water,
And all my [B]bones are out of joint;
My [C]heart is like wax;
It is melted within [a]me.
15 My [A]strength is dried up like a potsherd,
And [B]my tongue cleaves to my jaws;
And You [C]lay me [a]in the dust of death.
16 For [A]dogs have surrounded me;
[a]A band of evildoers has encompassed me;
[b]They [B]pierced my hands and my feet.
17 I can count all my bones.
[A]They look, they stare at me;
18 They [A]divide my garments among them,
And for my clothing they cast lots.

19 But You, O LORD, [A]be not far off;
O You my help, [B]hasten to my assistance.
20 Deliver my [a]soul from [A]the sword,
My [B]only *life* from the [b]power of the dog.
21 Save me from the [A]lion's mouth;
From the horns of the [B]wild
oxen You [C]answer me.

22 I will [A]tell of Your name to my brethren;
In the midst of the assembly
I will praise You.
23 [A]You who fear the LORD, praise Him;
All you [a]descendants of
Jacob, [B]glorify Him,
And [C]stand in awe of Him, all
you [a]descendants of Israel.

24 For He has [A]not despised nor abhorred
the affliction of the afflicted;
Nor has He [B]hidden His face from him;
But [C]when he cried to Him
for help, He heard.

25 From You *comes* [A]my praise
in the great assembly;
I shall [B]pay my vows before
those who fear Him.
26 The [a]afflicted will eat and [A]be satisfied;
Those who seek Him will [B]praise the LORD.
Let your [C]heart live forever!
27 All the [A]ends of the earth will
remember and turn to the LORD,
And all the [B]families of the nations
will worship before [a]You.
28 For the [A]kingdom is the LORD'S
And He [B]rules over the nations.
29 All the [a,A]prosperous of the earth
will eat and worship,
All those who [B]go down to the
dust will bow before Him,
Even he who [b,C]cannot keep his soul alive.
30 [a,A]Posterity will serve Him;
It will be told of the Lord to
[B]the *coming* generation.
31 They will come and [A]will declare
His righteousness
To a people [B]who will be born,
that He has performed *it.*

PSALM 23

THE LORD, THE PSALMIST'S SHEPHERD.

A Psalm of David.

1 The LORD is my [A]shepherd,
I [a]shall [B]not want.
2 He makes me lie down in [A]green pastures;
He [B]leads me beside [a,C]quiet waters.

22:10 [a]Lit a *womb* [A]Is 46:3; 49:1 22:11 [a]Or *distress* [A]Ps 71:12 [B]2 Kin 14:26; Ps 72:12; Is 63:5 22:12 [A]Ps 22:21; 68:30 [B]Deut 32:14; Amos 4:1 22:13 [A]Job 16:10; Ps 35:21; Lam 2:16; 3:46 [B]Ps 10:9; 17:12 22:14 [a]Lit *my inward parts* [A]Job 30:16 [B]Ps 31:10; Dan 5:6 [C]Josh 7:5; Job 23:16; Ps 73:26; Nah 2:10 22:15 [a]Lit *to* [A]Ps 38:10 [B]John 19:28 [C]Ps 104:29 22:16 [a]Or *An assembly* [b]Another reading is *Like a lion, my...* [A]Ps 59:6, 7 [B]Matt 27:35; John 20:25 22:17 [A]Luke 23:27, 35 22:18 [A]Matt 27:35; Mark 15:24; Luke 23:34; John 19:24 22:19 [A]Ps 22:11 [B]Ps 70:5 22:20 [a]Or *life* [b]Lit *paw* [A]Ps 37:14 [B]Ps 35:17 22:21 [A]Ps 22:13 [B]Ps 22:12 [C]Ps 34:4; 118:5; 120:1 22:22 [A]Ps 40:10; Heb 2:12 22:23 [a]Lit *seed* [A]Ps 135:19, 20 [B]Ps 86:12 [C]Ps 33:8 22:24 [A]Ps 69:33 [B]Ps 27:9; 69:17; 102:2 [C]Ps 31:22; Heb 5:7 22:25 [A]Ps 35:18; 40:9, 10 [B]Ps 61:8; Eccl 5:4 22:26 [a]Or *poor* [A]Ps 107:9 [B]Ps 40:16 [C]Ps 69:32 22:27 [a]Some versions read *Him* [A]Ps 2:8; 82:8 [B]Ps 86:9 22:28 [A]Ps 47:7; Obad 21; Zech 14:9; Matt 6:13 [B]Ps 47:8 22:29 [a]Lit *fat ones* [b]Or *did not* [A]Ps 17:10; 45:12; Hab 1:16 [B]Ps 28:1; Is 26:19 [C]Ps 89:48 22:30 [a]Lit *A seed* [A]Ps 102:28 [B]Ps 102:18 22:31 [A]Ps 40:9; 71:18 [B]Ps 78:6 23:1 [a]Or *do* [A]Ps 78:52; 80:1; Is 40:11; Jer 31:10; Ezek 34:11-13; John 10:11; 1 Pet 2:25 [B]Ps 34:9, 10; Phil 4:19 23:2 [a]Lit *waters of rest* [A]Ps 65:11-13; Ezek 34:14 [B]Rev 7:17 [C]Ps 36:8; 46:4

22:12, 13 This imagery of enemies as rapacious beasts returns (cf. vv. 16, 20, 21).

22:14, 15 These are graphic images showing that his vitality and courage had left him.

22:16 They pierced my hands and my feet. The Heb. text reads "like a lion," i.e., these vicious attacking enemies, like animals, have torn me. Likely, a messianic prediction with reference to crucifixion (cf. Is 53:5; Zec 12:10).

22:17 This is a graphic picture of emaciation and exhaustion (cf. Job 33:21; Ps 102:5).

22:18 They divide . . . they cast. All 4 gospel writers appeal to this imagery in describing Christ's crucifixion (Mt 27:35; Mk 15:24; Lk 23:34; Jn 19:24).

22:21 You answer me. A welcomed breaking of God's silence finally arrives. This is fully in keeping with His character (cf. Pss 20:6; 28:6; 31:22; 118:5).

22:22 The psalmist cannot contain himself; he must testify loudly in the great assembly of God's great mercies. His exuberance is meant to be contagious (cf. Heb 2:12).

22:27 His testimony expands by soliciting universal praises for universal divine blessings (cf. Pss 67:7; 98:3).

23:1–6 This psalm is probably the best-known passage of the OT. It is a testimony by David to the Lord's faithfulness throughout his life. As a hymn of confidence, it pictures the Lord as a disciple's Shepherd-King-Host. David, by using some common ancient Near Eastern images in Ps 23, progressively unveils his personal relationship with the Lord in 3 stages.

I. David's Exclamation: "The LORD Is My Shepherd" (23:1a)
II. David's Expectations (23:1b–5b)
   A. "I Shall Not Want" (23:1b–3)
   B. "I Fear No Evil" (23:4, 5b)
III. David's Exultation: "My Cup Overflows" (23:5c–6)

23:1 The LORD is my shepherd. Cf. Ge 48:15; 49:24; Dt 32:6–12; Pss 28:9; 74:1; 77:20; 78:52; 79:13; 80:1; 95:7; 100:3; Is 40:11; Jer 23:3; Eze 34; Hos 4:16; Mic 5:4; 7:14; Zec 9:16 on the image of the Lord as a Shepherd. This imagery was used commonly in kingly applications and is frequently applied to Jesus in the NT (e.g., Jn 10; Heb 13:20; 1Pe 2:25; 5:4).

23:2, 3 Four characterizing activities of the Lord as Shepherd (i.e., emphasizing His grace

3 He [A]restores my soul;
He [B]guides me in the [a,C]paths
of righteousness
For His name's sake.

4 Even though I [A]walk through the
[a]valley of the shadow of death,
I [B]fear no [b]evil, for [C]You are with me;
Your [D]rod and Your staff, they comfort me.
5 You [A]prepare a table before me in
the presence of my enemies;
You [a]have [B]anointed my head with oil;
My [C]cup overflows.
6 [a]Surely [A]goodness and lovingkindness
will follow me all the days of my life,
And I will [b,B]dwell in the house
of the LORD [c]forever.

PSALM 24

THE KING OF GLORY ENTERING ZION.

A Psalm of David.

1 The [A]earth is the LORD'S,
and [a]all it contains,
The [B]world, and those who dwell in it.
2 For He has [A]founded it upon the seas
And established it upon the rivers.
3 Who may [A]ascend into the
[B]hill of the LORD?
And who may stand in His holy [C]place?
4 He who has [A]clean hands
and a [B]pure heart,
Who has not [C]lifted up his
soul [a]to falsehood
And has not [D]sworn deceitfully.
5 He shall receive a [A]blessing from the LORD
And [a,B]righteousness from the
God of his salvation.
6 [a]This is the generation of
those who [A]seek Him,
Who seek Your face—*even* Jacob. [b]*Selah*

7 [A]Lift up your heads, O gates,
And be lifted up, O [a]ancient doors,
That the King of [B]glory may come in!
8 Who is the King of glory?
The LORD [A]strong and mighty,
The LORD [B]mighty in battle.
9 Lift up your heads, O gates,
And lift *them* up, O [a]ancient doors,
That the King of [A]glory may come in!
10 Who is this King of glory?
The LORD of [A]hosts,
He is the King of glory. *Selah*

PSALM 25

PRAYER FOR PROTECTION, GUIDANCE AND PARDON.

A Psalm of David.

1 To You, O LORD, I [A]lift up my soul.
2 O my God, in You [A]I trust,
Do not let me [B]be ashamed;
Do not let my [C]enemies exult over me.

23:3 [a]Lit *tracks* [A]Ps 19:7 [B]Ps 5:8; 31:3 [C]Ps 85:13; Prov 4:11; 8:20 23:4 [a]Or *valley of deep darkness* [b]Or *harm* [A]Job 10:21, 22; Ps 107:14 [B]Ps 3:6; 27:1 [C]Ps 16:8; Is 43:2 [D]Mic 7:14 23:5 [a]Or *anoint* [A]Ps 78:19 [B]Ps 92:10; Luke 7:46 [C]Ps 16:5 23:6 [a]Or *Only* [b]Another reading is *return to* [c]Lit *for length of days* [A]Ps 25:7, 10 [B]Ps 27:4-6 24:1 [a]Lit *its fullness* [A]1 Cor 10:26 [B]Ps 89:11 24:2 [A]Ps 104:3, 5; 136:6 24:3 [A]Ps 15:1 [B]Ps 2:6 [C]Ps 65:4 24:4 [a]Or *in vain* [A]Job 17:9; Ps 22:30; 26:6 [B]Ps 51:10; 73:1; Matt 5:8 [C]Ezek 18:15 [D]Ps 15:4 24:5 [a]I.e. as vindicated [A]Ps 115:13 [B]Ps 36:10 24:6 [a]Or *Such* [b]*Selah* may mean: *Pause, Crescendo* or *Musical interlude* [A]Ps 27:4, 8 24:7 [a]Lit *everlasting* [A]Ps 118:20; Is 26:2 [B]Ps 29:2, 9; 97:6; Acts 7:2; 1 Cor 2:8 24:8 [A]Deut 4:34; Ps 96:7 [B]Ex 15:3, 6; Ps 76:3-6 24:9 [a]Lit *everlasting* [A]Ps 26:8; 57:11 24:10 [A]Gen 32:2; Josh 5:14; 2 Sam 5:10; Neh 9:6 25:1 [A]Ps 86:4; 143:8 25:2 [A]Ps 31:1 [B]Ps 25:20; 31:1 [C]Ps 13:4; 41:11

and guidance) are followed by the ultimate basis for His goodness, i.e., "His name's sake" (cf. Pss 25:11; 31:3; 106:8; Is 43:25; 48:9; Eze 36:22–32).

23:4 the valley of the shadow of death. Phraseology used to convey a perilously threatening environment (cf. Job 10:21, 22; 38:17; Pss 44:19; 107:10; Jer 2:6; Lk. 1:79). **Your rod and Your staff.** The shepherd's club and crook are viewed as comforting instruments of protection and direction, respectively.

23:5, 6 The able Protector (v. 4) is also the abundant Provider.

23:5 You have anointed. The biblical imagery of anointing is frequently associated with blessing (Pss 45:7; 92:10; 104:15; 133:2; Ecc 9:8; Am 6:6; Lk 7:46).

23:6 And I will dwell. There is some question concerning the form in the Heb. text (cf. also Ps 27:4). Should it be rendered "I shall return" or "I shall dwell"? Whichever way it is taken, by the grace of his Lord, David is expecting ongoing opportunities of intimate fellowship.

24:1–10 The form of Ps 24 has been disputed. For example, it has been labeled by some as an entrance ceremony (cf. Ps 15), by others, a hymn of praise, and yet by others, a mixture of both elements. Its occasion has also been contended; however, the view that it might have been used at the time of the bringing of the ark to Jerusalem (2Sa 6:12–19; 1Ch 13) still has credible appeal. The early church designated it messianically as an ascension psalm (cf. v. 3). The movement of the psalm seems to follow the movement of the people. It traces the community's worship procession, both spatially and spiritually, through 3 progressive stages.

I. Stage One: Worship of the Creator through Contemplation (24:1, 2)
II. Stage Two: Worship of the Savior through Consecration (24:3–6)
   A. The Probing Questions Inviting Consecration (24:3)
   B. The Proper Qualities Indicating Consecration (24:4–6)
III. Stage Three: Worship of the King through Commemoration (24:7–10)

24:1 the LORD's. On His universal ownership, cf. Ex 19:5; Dt 10:14; Pss 50:12; 89:11; in the NT, cf. 1Co 3:21, 23.

24:2 This is a poetic, not a scientific, picture of creation (cf. Ge 1:9, 10; 7:11; 49:25; Ex 20:4; Dt 33:13; Job 26:10; Pss 74:13; 136:6; 2Pe 3:5).

24:3 In the liturgy, the questions were most likely asked by the priest. The worshipers would have then responded antiphonally with the "answers." On the form, cf. Ps 15 and Is 33:14–16.

24:4 These sample qualities do not signify sinless perfection, but rather basic integrity of inward motive and outward manner.

24:7–9 These are bold personifications indicating that the city gates need to stretch themselves to make way for the awesome entrance of the Great King. By so doing, they too participate in worshiping Him.

24:10 The LORD of hosts. The Divine Warrior possibly comes back into consideration; He, the Commander-in-Chief, is "the God of the armies" (cf. 1Sa 17:45).

25:1–22 David grapples with the heavy issues of life, avoiding denial and affirming dependence. He must trust God in the face of his troubles and troublemakers. These 22 verses follow an acrostic development. On a larger scale, the psalm develops chiastically: Verses 1–7 and 16–22 are parallel sections of prayers for protection and/or deliverance, while the core, vv. 8–15, contains affirmations about God and about His dealings with believers.

I. Prayers in Times of Trial (25:1–7)
II. Praise in Periods of Confidence (25:8–15)
III. Petition for Help in Trouble (25:16–22)

25:1 I lift up my soul. This is a vivid picture of David's dependence (cf. Pss 86:4; 143:8).

25:2, 3 ashamed. The important phenomenon of shame for the wicked and no shame

3 Indeed, [A]none of those who wait
for You will be ashamed;
[a]Those who [B]deal treacherously
without cause will be ashamed.

4 [A]Make me know Your ways, O LORD;
Teach me Your paths.
5 Lead me in [A]Your truth and teach me,
For You are the [B]God of my salvation;
For You I [C]wait all the day.
6 [A]Remember, O LORD, Your compassion
and Your lovingkindnesses,
For they have been [a,B]from of old.
7 Do not remember the [A]sins of my
youth or my transgressions;
[B]According to Your lovingkindness
remember me,
For Your [C]goodness' sake, O LORD.

8 [A]Good and [B]upright is the LORD;
Therefore He [C]instructs
sinners in the way.
9 He [A]leads the [a]humble in justice,
And He [B]teaches the [a]humble His way.
10 All the paths of the LORD are
[A]lovingkindness and truth
To [B]those who keep His covenant
and His testimonies.
11 For [A]Your name's sake, O LORD,
[B]Pardon my iniquity, for it is great.

12 Who is the man who [A]fears the LORD?
He will [B]instruct him in the
way he should choose.
13 His soul will [A]abide in [a]prosperity,
And his [b]descendants will
[B]inherit the [c]land.
14 The [a,A]secret of the LORD is for
those who fear Him,
[b]And He will [B]make them
know His covenant.
15 My [A]eyes are continually
toward the LORD,
For He will [a,B]pluck my feet out of the net.

16 [A]Turn to me and be gracious to me,
For I am [B]lonely and afflicted.
17 [a]The [A]troubles of my heart are enlarged;
Bring me [B]out of my distresses.
18 [A]Look upon my affliction
and my [a]trouble,
And [B]forgive all my sins.
19 Look upon my enemies, for
they [A]are many,
And they [B]hate me with violent hatred.
20 [A]Guard my soul and deliver me;
Do not let me [B]be ashamed, for
I take refuge in You.
21 Let [A]integrity and uprightness
preserve me,
For [B]I wait for You.
22 [A]Redeem Israel, O God,
Out of all his troubles.

PSALM 26

PROTESTATION OF INTEGRITY AND PRAYER FOR PROTECTION.

A Psalm of David.

1 [a,A]Vindicate me, O LORD, for I have
[B]walked in my integrity,
And I have [C]trusted in the LORD
[b,D]without wavering.

25:3 [a]Or *Let those...be ashamed* [A]Ps 37:9; 40:1; Is 49:23 [B]Ps 119:158; Is 21:2; Hab 1:13 25:4 [A]Ex 33:13; Ps 27:11; 86:11 25:5 [A]Ps 25:10; 43:3 [B]Ps 79:9 [C]Ps 40:1 25:6 [a]Or *everlasting* [A]Ps 98:3 [B]Ps 103:17 25:7 [A]Job 13:26; 20:11 [B]Ps 51:1 [C]Ps 31:19 25:8 [A]Ps 86:5 [B]Ps 92:15 [C]Ps 32:8 25:9 [a]Or *afflicted* [A]Ps 23:3 [B]Ps 27:11 25:10 [A]Ps 40:11 [B]Ps 103:18 25:11 [A]Ps 31:3; 79:9 [B]Ex 34:9 25:12 [A]Ps 31:19 [B]Ps 25:8; 37:23 25:13 [a]Lit *good* [b]Lit *seed* [c]Or *earth* [A]Prov 1:33; Jer 23:6 [B]Ps 37:11; 69:36; Matt 5:5 25:14 [a]Or *counsel* or *intimacy* [b]Or *And His covenant, to make them know it* [A]Prov 3:32; John 7:17 [B]Gen 17:1, 2 25:15 [a]Lit *bring out* [A]Ps 123:2; 141:8 [B]Ps 31:4; 124:7 25:16 [A]Ps 69:16 [B]Ps 143:4 25:17 [a]Some commentators read *Relieve the troubles of my heart* [A]Ps 40:12 [B]Ps 107:6 25:18 [a]Lit *toil* [A]2 Sam 16:12; Ps 31:7 [B]Ps 103:3 25:19 [A]Ps 3:1 [B]Ps 9:13 25:20 [A]Ps 86:2 [B]Ps 25:2 25:21 [A]Ps 41:12 [B]Ps 25:3 25:22 [A]Ps 130:8 26:1 [a]Lit *Judge* [b]Lit *I do not slide* [A]Ps 7:8 [B]2 Kin 20:3; Prov 20:7 [C]Ps 13:5; 28:7 [D]Heb 10:23

for the righteous returns (cf. a millennial expression of this great principle in Is 49:23).

25:4, 5 The noun and verb metaphors speak of direction for life's pathways (cf. the thrust of Ps 1).

25:6, 7 Remember . . . Do not remember . . . remember. These are not concerns about God forgetting something, but the psalmist's prayer reminds the readers about God's gracious covenant promises and provisions, all of which are grounded upon His "goodness' sake" (cf. v. 11, "Your name's sake").

25:8–10 More metaphors for life's paths are used for the purpose of begging divine direction (cf. vv. 4, 5). The last line of v. 10 emphasizes covenant responsibilities on the human side (cf. the divine side in vv. 6, 7).

25:11 Pardon my iniquity, for it is great. A maturing disciple develops an increasing sensitivity to sin which drives him more consistently to an appropriation of the promises of God's pardoning grace (cf. v. 18b).

25:12 Who . . . ? This interrogative device (cf. Pss 15, 24) serves as an introductory vehicle to the hallmarks of genuine discipleship.

25:14 The secret. This could well be rendered the "counsel" or intimate personal communion (cf. Job 29:4; Ps 55:14; Pr 3:32).

25:15 net. The snare of the hunter or fowler (cf. Ps 31:4).

25:16–21 Ten rapid-fire prayer requests, asking for relief and encouragement, lie at the heart of these 6 verses.

25:16 lonely and afflicted. These terms speak of isolation and humiliation.

25:22 The shift from the individual to the community is really not surprising, since the welfare of the theocratic people is inextricably connected to the covenant individual (cf. Ps 51:18, 19).

26:1–12 Psalms 26, 27, and 28 mention the house, or sanctuary, of the Lord because public worship is the central interest. The form of Ps 26 is mixed, i.e., containing elements of declarations of innocence, prayer, and confidence (cf. v. 1 as a paradigm). Structurally, 4 intermingling prayers and proofs reveal the psalmist's passion to worship the Lord in spirit and in truth.

I. His Situation (26:1)
   A. His Prayer for Justice (26:1a)
   B. His Proofs of Commitment (26:1b)
II. His Transparency (26:2–8)
   A. His Prayer for Scrutiny (26:2)
   B. His Proofs of Loyalty (26:3–8)
III. His Eschatological Outlook (26:9–11a)
   A. His Prayers for Final Favor (26:9)
   B. His Proofs of Measurable Difference (26:10–11a)
IV. His Confidence (26:11b–12)
   A. His Prayers Show Confidence in the Person of God (26:11b)
   B. His Proofs Show Confidence in the Provision of God (26:12)

26:1 Vindicate me. Lit. "Judge me!" This refers to exoneration of some false accusations and/or charges under the protection of the covenant stipulations of the theocratic law (cf. Pss 7:8; 35:24; 43:1). **my integrity.** Again, this is not a claim to perfection, but of innocence, particularly as viewed within the context of

2 [A]Examine me, O LORD, and try me;
[B]Test my [a]mind and my heart.
3 For Your [A]lovingkindness
is before my eyes,
And I have [B]walked in Your [a]truth.
4 I do not [A]sit with [a]deceitful men,
Nor will I go with [b,B]pretenders.
5 I [A]hate the assembly of evildoers,
And I will not sit with the wicked.
6 I shall [A]wash my hands in innocence,
And I will go about [B]Your altar, O LORD,
7 That I may proclaim with the
voice of [A]thanksgiving
And declare all Your [a]wonders.

8 O LORD, I [A]love the habitation
of Your house
And the place [a]where Your [B]glory dwells.
9 [A]Do not [a]take my soul away
along with sinners,
Nor my life with [B]men of bloodshed,
10 In whose hands is a [A]wicked scheme,
And whose right hand is full of [B]bribes.
11 But as for me, I shall [A]walk
in my integrity;
[B]Redeem me, and be gracious to me.
12 [A]My foot stands on a [B]level place;
In the [C]congregations I shall
bless the LORD.

PSALM 27

A PSALM OF FEARLESS TRUST IN GOD.

A Psalm of David.

1 The LORD is my [A]light and my [B]salvation;
Whom shall I fear?
The LORD is the [a,C]defense of my life;
[D]Whom shall I dread?
2 When evildoers came upon me
to [A]devour my flesh,
My adversaries and my enemies,
they [B]stumbled and fell.
3 Though a [A]host encamp against me,
My heart will not fear;
Though war arise against me,
In *spite of* this I [a]shall be [B]confident.

4 [A]One thing I have asked from the
LORD, that I shall seek:
That I may [B]dwell in the house of the
LORD all the days of my life,
To behold [C]the [a]beauty of the LORD
And to [b,D]meditate in His temple.
5 For in the [A]day of trouble He will
[B]conceal me in His [a]tabernacle;
In the secret place of His tent
He will [C]hide me;
He will [D]lift me up on a rock.
6 And now [A]my head will be lifted up
above my enemies around me,
And I will offer in His tent
[B]sacrifices [a]with shouts of joy;
I will [C]sing, yes, I will sing
praises to the LORD.

7 [A]Hear, O LORD, when I cry
with my voice,
And be gracious to me
and [B]answer me.
8 *When You said,* "[A]Seek My face,"
my heart said to You,
"Your face, O LORD, [B]I shall seek."
9 [A]Do not hide Your face from me,
Do not turn Your servant away in [B]anger;
You have been [C]my help;
[D]Do not abandon me nor [E]forsake me,
O God of my salvation!

26:2 [a]Lit *kidneys*, figurative for inner man [A]Ps 17:3; 139:23 [B]Ps 7:9 26:3 [a]Or *faithfulness* [A]Ps 48:9 [B]2 Kin 20:3; Ps 86:11 26:4 [a]Or *worthless men;* lit *men of falsehood* [b]Or *dissemblers, hypocrites* [A]Ps 1:1 [B]Ps 28:3 26:5 [A]Ps 31:6; 139:21 26:6 [A]Ps 73:13 [B]Ps 43:3, 4 26:7 [a]Or *miracles* [A]Ps 9:1 26:8 [a]Lit *of the tabernacle of Your glory* [A]Ps 27:4 [B]Ps 24:7 26:9 [a]Lit *gather* [A]Ps 28:3 [B]Ps 139:19 26:10 [A]Ps 37:7 [B]Ps 15:5 26:11 [A]Ps 26:1 [B]Ps 44:26; 69:18 26:12 [A]Ps 40:2 [B]Ps 27:11 [C]Ps 22:22 27:1 [a]Or *refuge* [A]Ps 18:28; Is 60:20; Mic 7:8 [B]Ex 15:2; Ps 62:7; 118:14; Is 33:2; Jon 2:9 [C]Ps 28:8 [D]Ps 118:6 27:2 [A]Ps 14:4 [B]Ps 9:3 27:3 [a]Lit *am confident* [A]Ps 3:6 [B]Job 4:6 27:4 [a]Lit *delightfulness* [b]Lit *inquire* [A]Ps 26:8 [B]Ps 23:6 [C]Ps 90:17 [D]Ps 18:6 27:5 [a]Or *shelter* [A]Ps 50:15 [B]Ps 31:20 [C]Ps 17:8 [D]Ps 40:2 27:6 [a]Lit *of shouts* [A]Ps 3:3 [B]Ps 107:22 [C]Ps 13:6 27:7 [A]Ps 4:3; 61:1 [B]Ps 13:3 27:8 [A]Ps 105:4; Amos 5:6 [B]Ps 34:4 27:9 [A]Ps 69:17 [B]Ps 6:1 [C]Ps 40:17 [D]Ps 94:14 [E]Ps 37:28

ungrounded "legal" charges (cf. Ps 7:8; Pr 10:9; 19:1; 20:7; 28:6). **without wavering.** Cf. Pss 18:36; 37:31; contra. Ps 73:18–20.

26:2 Examine ... try ... Test. These 3 invitations to divine scrutiny are essentially synonymous ways of testing, refining, and purifying (cf. Pss 11:4, 5; 12:6; 17:3; 66:10; Jer 17:9, 10).

26:4, 5 This language suggests that David is making a personal application of the characteristics of Ps 1:1.

26:6 Personal cleansing is a necessary prerequisite for acceptable worship (cf. Ps 24:3, 4).

26:7 That I may proclaim. The Heb. text reads "to hear the sound of praise and to proclaim ...," a reference to the enjoyment of and participation in public worship.

26:8 Your glory. God's "glory" most frequently refers to His self-manifestation, e.g., His attributes revealed and exhibited. *See note on Lv 9:23.*

26:9–11 This is another sharp contrast between the injurious and the innocent.

26:12 My foot stands. Cf. v. 1, "without wavering."

27:1–14 This psalm is characterized by strong contrasts such as lament and laud; persecution and praise; plus warfare and worship. In Ps 27, the psalmist, in the presence of his Lord, engages in 3 conversations which help him balance the ups and downs of real life.

I. He Converses with Himself about Privileges (27:1–6)
II. He Converses with the Lord about Problems (27:7–12)
III. He Converses with Himself about Perseverance (27:13, 14)

27:1 light. This important biblical word picture with exclusively positive connotations pictures the light of redemption in contrast to the darkness of condemnation (cf. Pss 18:28; 36:9; 43:3; Is 60:1, 19, 20; Mic 7:8; Jn 8:12; 12:46; 1Jn 1:5).

27:2 to devour my flesh. An allusion to the psalmist's enemies being like vicious beasts (cf. Pss 7:2; 14:4; 17:12; Job 19:22; Jer 30:16; 50:7). This wording was also employed to describe slander and defamation (cf. a close Aram. parallel in Da 3:8; 6:24). **they stumbled and fell.** This doublet conveys thorough defeat (cf. Is 3:8; 8:15; 31:3; Jer 46:6).

27:4 One thing. The primary issue in David's life was to live in God's presence and by His purpose (cf. Pss 15:1; 23:6; cf. Paul's "one thing" in Php 3:13).

27:5 His tabernacle. David portrays the privileges of divine protection as being hidden in God's "booth" or "shelter," a term in parallelism with "tabernacle" or "tent."

27:8, 9 Seek My face ... Your face ... Your face. God's "face" indicates His personal presence or simply His being (Pss 24:6; 105:4); and seeking His face is a primary characteristic of true believers who desire fellowship with God (cf. Dt 4:29; 2Ch 11:16; 20:4; Ps 40:16; Jer 50:4; Hos 3:5; Zec 8:22).

10 [a]For my father and [A]my mother
have forsaken me,
But [B]the LORD will take me up.

11 [A]Teach me Your way, O LORD,
And lead me in a [B]level path
Because of [a]my foes.
12 Do not deliver me over to the
[a,A]desire of my adversaries,
For [B]false witnesses have
risen against me,
And such as [C]breathe out violence.
13 [a]*I would have despaired* unless I
had believed that I would see
the [A]goodness of the LORD
In the [B]land of the living.
14 [A]Wait for the LORD;
Be [B]strong and let your
heart take courage;
Yes, wait for the LORD.

PSALM 28

A PRAYER FOR HELP, AND PRAISE FOR ITS ANSWER.

A Psalm of David.

1 To You, O LORD, I call;
My [A]rock, do not be deaf to me,
For if You [B]are silent to me,
I will become like those who
[C]go down to the pit.
2 Hear the [A]voice of my supplications
when I cry to You for help,
When I [B]lift up my hands [C]toward
[a]Your holy [D]sanctuary.
3 [A]Do not drag me away with the wicked
And with those who work iniquity,
Who [B]speak peace with their neighbors,
While evil is in their hearts.
4 Requite them [A]according to their
work and according to the
evil of their practices;
Requite them according to the
deeds of their hands;
Repay them their [a]recompense.
5 Because they [A]do not regard
the works of the LORD
Nor the deeds of His hands,
He will tear them down and
not build them up.

6 Blessed be the LORD,
Because He [A]has heard the voice
of my supplication.
7 The LORD is my [A]strength and my [B]shield;
My heart [C]trusts in Him, and I am helped;
Therefore [D]my heart exults,
And with [E]my song I shall thank Him.
8 The LORD is [a]their [A]strength,
And He is a [b,B]saving defense
to His anointed.
9 [A]Save Your people and bless
[B]Your inheritance;
Be their [C]shepherd also, and
[D]carry them forever.

PSALM 29

THE VOICE OF THE LORD IN THE STORM.

A Psalm of David.

1 [A]Ascribe to the LORD, O [a]sons
of the mighty,
Ascribe to the LORD glory and strength.

27:10 [a]Or *If my father...forsake me, Then the LORD* [A]Is 49:15 [B]Is 40:11 27:11 [a]Or *those who lie in wait for me* [A]Ps 25:4; 86:11 [B]Ps 5:8; 26:12 27:12 [a]Lit *soul* [A]Ps 41:2 [B]Deut 19:18; Ps 35:11; Matt 26:60 [C]Acts 9:1 27:13 [a]Or *Surely I believed* [A]Ps 31:19 [B]Job 28:13; Ps 52:5; 116:9; 142:5; Is 38:11; Jer 11:19; Ezek 26:20 27:14 [A]Ps 25:3; 37:34; 40:1; 62:5; 130:5; Prov 20:22; Is 25:9 [B]Ps 31:24 28:1 [A]Ps 18:2 [B]Ps 35:22; 39:12; 83:1 [C]Ps 88:4; 143:7; Prov 1:12 28:2 [a]Lit *the innermost place of Your sanctuary* [A]Ps 140:6 [B]Ps 134:2; 141:2; Lam 2:19; 1 Tim 2:8 [C]Ps 5:7; 138:2 [D]1 Kin 6:5 28:3 [A]Ps 26:9 [B]Ps 12:2; 55:21; 62:4; Jer 9:8 28:4 [a]Or *dealings* [A]Ps 62:12; 2 Tim 4:14; Rev 18:6; 22:12 28:5 [A]Is 5:12 28:6 [A]Ps 28:2 28:7 [A]Ps 18:2; 59:17 [B]Ps 3:3 [C]Ps 13:5; 112:7 [D]Ps 16:9 [E]Ps 40:3; 69:30 28:8 [a]A few mss and ancient versions read *the strength of His people* [b]Or *refuge of salvation* [A]Ps 20:6; 89:17 [B]Ps 27:1; 140:7 28:9 [A]Ps 106:47 [B]Deut 9:29; 32:9; 1 Kin 8:51; Ps 33:12; 106:40 [C]Ps 80:1 [D]Deut 1:31; Is 40:11; 46:3; 63:9 29:1 [a]Or *sons of gods* [A]1 Chr 16:28, 29; Ps 96:7-9

27:10 Even though those nearest and dearest to David might abandon him, his Lord would always be concerned about and care for him (cf. Dt 31:6, 8; Is 49:14, 15; Heb 13:5).

27:14 Wait ... wait. This particular word for waiting connotes either a tense or eager and patient anticipation of the Lord (cf. Pss 37:34; 40:1).

28:1–9 We encounter a radical shift from lamentation and prayer to thanksgiving. The psalmist, without regard for his unchanged circumstances, shows confidence in crisis. David, moving through two cycles of crisis and confidence, magnifies the justice of God.

- I. First Cycle: Individual in Outlook, and Terminates in Praise (28:1–7)
  - A. His Personal Crisis (28:1–5b)
  - B. His Personal Confidence (28:5c–7)
- II. Second Cycle: Corporate in Outlook, and Terminates in Prayer (28:8, 9)
  - A. His Reassurance in the Light of Corporate Confidence (28:8)
  - B. His Request in the Face of Corporate Crisis (28:9)

28:1 deaf ... silent. On the striking picture of God being deaf and dumb regarding his situation, cf. Pss 35:22; 83:1; 109:1; Is 57:11; 64:12; 65:6; Hab 1:13.

28:2 When I lift up my hands. On this symbolic "posture" representing the heart's attitude in dependent prayer, see Ex 9:29; 17:11, 12; Ps 63:4; 1Ti 2:8.

28:3–5 The iniquities of the psalmist's (really God's) enemies bring forth sharp imprecations.

28:6 Because He has heard the voice of my supplication. Contrast vv. 1, 2. Through faith, the psalmist will live his life as though God has already intervened.

28:8 His anointed. This is most likely a corporate reference to the people of God being anointed, not to an individual (cf. Hab 3:13).

28:9 Your inheritance. God amazingly considers His people a most precious possession (cf. Dt 7:6–16; 9:29; 1 Sam 10:1; Pss 33:12; 94:5; Eph 1:18).

29:1–11 This psalm has all the earmarks of the earliest Heb. poetry (cf. Ex 15; Jdg 5). As to its general form, it is a hymn. Many of its images appear in parallel literature, especially in referencing pagan gods by various "forces of nature." However, the Lord is the unique Creator and supreme Sovereign over all these phenomena. He alone is "the God of gods" (Da 11:36). In view of these realities, 3 representative realms of the supremacy of God bring forth praise to Yahweh (Jehovah) alone.

- I. The Lord's Supremacy over Heavenly Beings (29:1, 2)
- II. The Lord's Supremacy over the "Forces of Nature" (29:3–9)
- III. The Lord's Supremacy over Humanity (29:10, 11)

29:1 sons of the mighty. Lit "sons of God" (cf. Ps 89:6 in its context of vv. 5–10; cf. the plural form of "gods" in Ex 15:11). The reference here in Ps 29 is most likely to Yahweh's mighty angels.

2 Ascribe to the LORD the glory
[a]due to His name;
Worship the LORD [A]in [b]holy array.

3 The [A]voice of the LORD is upon the waters;
The God of glory [B]thunders,
The LORD is over [a,C]many waters.
4 The voice of the LORD is [A]powerful,
The voice of the LORD is majestic.
5 The voice of the LORD breaks the cedars;
Yes, the LORD breaks in pieces
[A]the cedars of Lebanon.
6 He makes Lebanon [A]skip like a calf,
And [B]Sirion like a young wild ox.
7 The voice of the LORD hews
out [a]flames of fire.
8 The voice of the LORD [a]shakes
the wilderness;
The LORD shakes the wilderness of [A]Kadesh.
9 The voice of the LORD makes
[A]the deer to calve
And strips the forests bare;
And [B]in His temple everything says, "Glory!"

10 The LORD sat *as King* at the [A]flood;
Yes, the LORD sits as [B]King forever.
11 [a]The LORD will give [A]strength to His people;
[b]The LORD will bless His people with [B]peace.

PSALM 30

THANKSGIVING FOR DELIVERANCE FROM DEATH.

A Psalm; a Song at the Dedication of the House.
A Psalm of David.

1 I will [A]extol You, O LORD, for
You have [B]lifted me up,
And have not let my [C]enemies
rejoice over me.
2 O LORD my God,
I [A]cried to You for help, and You [B]healed me.
3 O LORD, You have [A]brought up
my soul from [a]Sheol;
You have kept me alive, [b]that I
would not [B]go down to the pit.
4 [A]Sing praise to the LORD, you
[B]His godly ones,
And [C]give thanks to His holy [a,D]name.
5 For [A]His anger is but for a moment,
His [B]favor is for a lifetime;
Weeping may [C]last for the night,
But a shout of joy *comes* in the morning.

6 Now as for me, I said in my prosperity,
"I will [A]never be moved."
7 O LORD, by Your favor You have made
my mountain to stand strong;
You [A]hid Your face, I was dismayed.
8 To You, O LORD, I called,
And to the Lord I made supplication:
9 "What profit is there in my blood,
if I [A]go down to the pit?
Will the [B]dust praise You? Will it
declare Your faithfulness?

10 "[A]Hear, O LORD, and be gracious to me;
O LORD, be my [B]helper."
11 You have turned for me [A]my
mourning into dancing;
You have [B]loosed my sackcloth and
girded me with [C]gladness,
12 That *my* [a,A]soul may sing praise
to You and not be silent.
O LORD my God, I will [B]give
thanks to You forever.

29:2 [a]Lit *of His name* [b]Or *the majesty of holiness* [A]2 Chr 20:21; Ps 110:3 29:3 [a]Or *great* [A]Ps 104:7 [B]Job 37:4, 5; Ps 18:13 [C]Ps 18:16; 107:23 29:4 [A]Ps 68:33 29:5 [A]Judg 9:15; 1 Kin 5:6; Ps 104:16; Is 2:13; 14:8 29:6 [A]Ps 114:4, 6 [B]Deut 3:9 29:7 [a]I.e. lightning 29:8 [a]Or *causes...to whirl* [A]Num 13:26 29:9 [A]Job 39:1 [B]Ps 26:8 29:10 [A]Gen 6:17 [B]Ps 10:16 29:11 [a]Or *May the LORD give* [b]Or *May the LORD bless* [A]Ps 28:8; 68:35; Is 40:29 [B]Ps 37:11; 72:3 30:1 [A]Ps 118:28; 145:1 [B]Ps 3:3 [C]Ps 25:2; 35:19, 24 30:2 [A]Ps 88:13 [B]Ps 6:2; 103:3; Is 53:5 30:3 [a]I.e. the nether world [b]Some mss read *from among those who go down* [A]Ps 86:13 [B]Ps 28:1 30:4 [a]Lit *memorial* [A]Ps 149:1 [B]Ps 50:5 [C]Ps 97:12 [D]Ex 3:15; Ps 135:13; Hos 12:5 30:5 [A]Ps 103:9; Is 26:20; 54:7, 8 [B]Ps 118:1 [C]Ps 126:5; 2 Cor 4:17 30:6 [A]Ps 10:6; 62:2, 6 30:7 [A]Deut 31:17; Ps 104:29; 143:7 30:9 [A]Ps 28:1 [B]Ps 6:5 30:10 [A]Ps 4:1; 27:7 [B]Ps 27:9; 54:4 30:11 [A]Eccl 3:4; Jer 31:4, 13 [B]Is 20:2 [C]Ps 4:7 30:12 [a]Lit *glory* [A]Ps 16:9; 57:8; 108:1 [B]Ps 44:8

29:3–9 This is an awesome theophany, depicting dramatic movements in the powerful manifestations of the Lord God, which function to establish His supremacy as the only true God in comparison with any of the so-called gods of Israel's pagan neighbors.

29:3 The voice of the LORD. His voice is frequently associated with the thunder (cf., e.g., 1Sa 7:10; Job 37:4, 5; Ps 18:13; Is 30:30, 31).

29:5 the cedars … the cedars of Lebanon. These are the grandest of forest trees, and those of Lebanon were especially impressive.

29:6 Sirion. This is the Phoenician name for Mt. Hermon to the N of Dan (cf. Dt 3:9).

29:8 the wilderness of Kadesh. Kadesh-barnea is in the southern desert country. For its importance in the history of Israel, *see note on Nu 20:1.*

29:10 the flood. This refers to the universal flood of Ge 6–8 (esp., Ge 7:17).

30:1–12 A mixture of forms characterize Ps 30. David speaks out of a cycle of life (i.e., lamentation and laud), especially moving through prayer to praise. In spite of great variety, the psalm is bonded together by praise emphases (cf. vv. 4, 9, 12). The psalmist's beginning and ending pledges to praise provide structure for his prayers and testimonies.

I. His Beginning Pledge of Praise (30:1a)
II. His Look Back upon Historic Prayers and Testimonies (30:1b–9)
  A. His Individual Remembrance (30:1b–3)
  B. His Public Reminders (30:4, 5)
  C. His Individual Reflections (30:6–9)
III. His Look Ahead to Continuing Prayers and Testimonies (30:10–12a)
IV. His Concluding Pledge of Praise (30:12b)

30:Title The first and last parts of this title, i.e., "A Psalm … of David," are common notations in the superscriptions of many psalms. However, the middle words, "a Song at the Dedication of the House," were probably added later, although they could have referenced David's temporary tent for the ark erected on Mt. Zion (2Sa 6:17) or his own house (2Sa 5:11, 12).

30:2, 3 You healed me. God alone is the unique healer (cf. Ex 15:26; Dt 32:39; Ps 107:20). David is extolling God for bringing him back from a near-death experience.

30:5 This stark contrast constitutes one of the most worshipful testimonies from the Scriptures (cf. the principle in Is 54:7, 8; Jn 16:20–22; 2Co 4:17).

30:6 David recalls his previous independent attitude and arrogant talk. God had warned the nation and its leaders about such sinfully myopic outlooks (cf. Dt 8:11–20; note sample failures in Dt 32:15; 2Ch 32:25; Jer 22:21; Hos 13:6; Da 4:28–37). By the grace of God, David woke up to the fact that he was acting like his arrogant adversaries (cf. Ps 10:6).

30:8–10 A familiar argument for preservation of life (cf. Pss 6:5; 28:1; 88:10–12; 115:17; Is 38:18, 19).

30:12 *my* soul. Now with renewed perspective (contra. v. 6), he recognizes that all he is and has is due to God's unmerited grace (cf. v. 7a).

PSALM 31

A PSALM OF COMPLAINT AND OF PRAISE.

For the choir director. A Psalm of David.

1 [A]In You, O LORD, I have taken refuge;
Let me never [B]be ashamed;
[C]In Your righteousness deliver me.
2 [A]Incline Your ear to me, rescue me quickly;
Be to me a [B]rock of [a]strength,
A stronghold to save me.
3 For You are my [a]rock and [A]my fortress;
For [B]Your name's sake You will
lead me and guide me.
4 You will [A]pull me out of the net which
they have secretly laid for me,
For You are my [B]strength.
5 [A]Into Your hand I commit my spirit;
You have [B]ransomed me,
O LORD, [C]God of [a]truth.

6 I hate those who [A]regard [a]vain idols,
But I [B]trust in the LORD.
7 I will [A]rejoice and be glad in
Your lovingkindness,
Because You have [B]seen my affliction;
You have known the troubles of my soul,
8 And You have not [A]given me over
into the hand of the enemy;
You have set my feet in a large place.

9 Be gracious to me, O LORD,
for [A]I am in distress;
My [B]eye is wasted away from grief,
[C]my soul and my body *also.*
10 For my life is spent with [A]sorrow
And my years with sighing;
My [B]strength has failed
because of my iniquity,
And [C]my [a]body has wasted away.
11 Because of all my adversaries, I
have become a [A]reproach,
Especially to my [B]neighbors,
And an object of dread to
my acquaintances;
Those who see me in the
street flee from me.
12 I am [A]forgotten as a dead
man, out of mind;
I am like a broken vessel.
13 For I have heard the [a,A]slander of many,
[B]Terror is on every side;
While they [C]took counsel
together against me,
They [D]schemed to take away my life.

14 But as for me, I trust in You, O LORD,
I say, "[A]You are my God."
15 My [A]times are in Your hand;
[B]Deliver me from the hand of my enemies
and from those who persecute me.
16 Make Your [A]face to shine
upon Your servant;
[B]Save me in Your lovingkindness.
17 Let me not be [A]put to shame,
O LORD, for I call upon You;
Let the [B]wicked be put to shame,
let them [C]be silent in [a]Sheol.
18 Let the [A]lying lips be mute,
Which [B]speak arrogantly
against the righteous
With pride and contempt.

19 How great is Your [A]goodness,
Which You have stored up for
those who fear You,
Which You have wrought for those
who [B]take refuge in You,
[C]Before the sons of men!
20 You hide them in the [A]secret
place of Your presence from
the [B]conspiracies of man;
You keep them secretly in a [a]shelter
from the [C]strife of tongues.

31:1 [A]Ps 31:1-3; 71:1-3 [B]Ps 25:2 [C]Ps 143:1 31:2 [a]Or *refuge, protection* [A]Ps 17:6; 71:2; 86:1; 102:2 [B]Ps 18:2; 71:3 31:3 [a]Or *crag* [A]Ps 18:2 [B]Ps 23:3; 25:11 31:4 [A]Ps 25:15 [B]Ps 46:1 31:5 [a]Or *faithfulness* [A]Luke 23:46; Acts 7:59 [B]Ps 55:18; 71:23 [C]Deut 32:4; Ps 71:22 31:6 [a]Lit *empty vanities* [A]Jon 2:8 [B]Ps 52:8 31:7 [A]Ps 90:14 [B]Ps 10:14 31:8 [A]Deut 32:30; Ps 37:33 31:9 [A]Ps 66:14; 69:17 [B]Ps 6:7 [C]Ps 63:1 31:10 [a]Or *bones, substance* [A]Ps 13:2 [B]Ps 39:11 [C]Ps 32:3; 38:3; 102:3 31:11 [A]Ps 69:19 [B]Job 19:13; Ps 38:11; 88:8, 18 31:12 [A]Ps 88:5 31:13 [a]Lit *whispering* [A]Ps 50:20; Jer 20:10 [B]Lam 2:22 [C]Ps 62:4; Matt 27:1 [D]Ps 41:7 31:14 [A]Ps 140:6 31:15 [A]Job 14:5; 24:1 [B]Ps 143:9 31:16 [A]Num 6:25; Ps 4:6; 80:3 [B]Ps 6:4 31:17 [a]I.e. the nether world [A]Ps 25:2, 20 [B]Ps 25:3 [C]1 Sam 2:9; Ps 94:17; 115:17 31:18 [A]Ps 109:2; 120:2 [B]1 Sam 2:3; Ps 94:4; Jude 15 31:19 [A]Ps 65:4; 145:7; Is 64:4; Rom 2:4; 11:22 [B]Ps 5:11 [C]Ps 23:5 31:20 [a]Or *pavilion* [A]Ps 27:5 [B]Ps 37:12 [C]Job 5:21; Ps 31:13

31:1–24 This psalm contains more of David's problems, prayers, and praises. David will again walk a road that takes him from anguish to assurance. Within the two settings of Ps 31, the psalmist's testimonies passionately celebrate the sufficiencies of God.

I. The Originally Private Setting (31:1–18)
   A. His Testimony about Security and Salvation (31:1–5)
   B. His Testimony about Discernment and Deliverance (31:6–8)
   C. His Testimony about Reproach and Relief (31:9–18)
II. The Ultimately Public Setting (31:19–24)
   A. His Testimonies and Divine Exaltation (31:19–22)
   B. His Testimonies and Human Exhortation (31:23, 24)

31:2 **Incline Your ear to me.** This is a bold pay-attention-to-my-prayer demand (cf. Ps 102:2).

31:3 The language resembles that of Ps 23:1–3, except it now comes packaged in prayer requests.

31:5 **Into Your hand.** This is applied to both the lesser David and the Greater David (Lk 23:46); here it involves the common denominator of trust. This is a metaphor depicting God's power and control (cf. v. 15a; contra. vv. 8, 15b).

31:6 **I hate.** Cf. Ps 26:5 on the proper basis for such hatred (cf. Ps 139:21). **vain idols.** This is a common designation for false gods (cf. Dt 32:21; 1Ki 16:13; Jer 10:15; 14:22; 16:19; 18:15; Jon 2:8). On the "idiocy" of idolatry, see Hab 2:18–20.

31:9, 10 These terms quite frequently are employed metaphysically to convey the nonphysical impact of trials and tribulations.

31:11 He was a reproach to adversaries and personal acquaintances alike, a very painful alienation (cf. Ps 88:8, 18).

31:13 **Terror is on every side.** (cf. Jer 6:25; 20:3, 10; 46:5; 49:29; La 2:22). **They schemed.** On such wicked plotting, cf. Jer 11:19; 18:23.

31:16 This is a request for a personal application of the blessing of Nu 6:25 (cf. Pss 4:6; 67:1; 80:3, 7, 19; 119:135).

31:17 On their shame but not his, cf. Ps 25:2, 3, 20; Jer 17:18.

31:18, 20 His enemies exhibit signs of "mouth" disease.

31:19 **Your goodness.** As in the case of His other attributes, God being perfectly good is the ground for His doing good things (cf. Ps 119:68).

21 [A]Blessed be the LORD,
For He has made [B]marvelous His
lovingkindness to me in a besieged [C]city.
22 As for me, [A]I said in my alarm,
"I am [B]cut off from before Your eyes";
Nevertheless You [C]heard the
voice of my supplications
When I cried to You.

23 O love the LORD, all you [A]His godly ones!
The LORD [B]preserves the faithful
And fully [C]recompenses the proud doer.
24 [A]Be strong and let your heart take courage,
All you who [a]hope in the LORD.

PSALM 32

BLESSEDNESS OF FORGIVENESS AND OF TRUST IN GOD.

A Psalm of David. A [†]Maskil.

1 [A]How blessed is he whose
transgression is forgiven,
Whose sin is covered!
2 How blessed is the man to whom the
LORD [A]does not impute iniquity,
And in whose spirit there is [B]no deceit!

3 When [A]I kept silent *about my sin,*
[B]my [a]body wasted away
Through my [b,C]groaning all day long.
4 For day and night [A]Your hand
was heavy upon me;
My [a,B]vitality was drained away *as* with
the fever heat of summer. [b]*Selah*
5 I [A]acknowledged my sin to You,
And my iniquity I [B]did not hide;
I said, "[C]I will confess my
transgressions to the LORD";
And You [D]forgave the [a]guilt of my sin.
Selah
6 Therefore, let everyone who is godly pray to
You [a,A]in a time when You may be found;
Surely [B]in a flood of great waters
they will not reach him.
7 You are [A]my hiding place; You
[B]preserve me from trouble;
You surround me with [a,C]songs of
deliverance. *Selah*

8 I will [A]instruct you and teach you in
the way which you should go;
I will counsel you [B]with My eye upon you.
9 Do not be [A]as the horse or as the mule
which have no understanding,
Whose trappings include bit and
bridle to hold them in check,
Otherwise they will not come near to you.
10 Many are the [A]sorrows of the wicked,
But [B]he who trusts in the LORD,
lovingkindness shall surround him.
11 Be [A]glad in the LORD and rejoice,
you righteous ones;
And shout for joy, all you who
are [B]upright in heart.

PSALM 33

PRAISE TO THE CREATOR AND PRESERVER.

1 [A]Sing for joy in the LORD,
O you righteous ones;
Praise is [B]becoming to the upright.

31:21 [A]Ps 28:6 [B]Ps 17:7 [C]1 Sam 23:7; Ps 87:5 31:22 [A]Ps 116:11 [B]Ps 88:5; Is 38:11, 12; Lam 3:54 [C]Ps 18:6; 66:19; 145:19 31:23 [A]Ps 30:4; 37:28; 50:5 [B]Ps 145:20; Rev 2:10 [C]Deut 32:41; Ps 94:2 31:24 [a]Or *wait for* [A]Ps 27:14 32:1 [†]Possibly *Contemplative,* or *Didactic,* or *Skillful Psalm* [A]Ps 85:2; 103:3; Rom 4:7, 8 32:2 [A]2 Cor 5:19 [B]John 1:47 32:3 [a]Or *bones, substance* [b]Lit *roaring* [A]Ps 39:2, 3 [B]Ps 31:10 [C]Ps 38:8 32:4 [a]Lit *life juices were turned into the drought of summer* [b]*Selah* may mean: *Pause, Crescendo* or *Musical interlude* [A]1 Sam 5:6; Job 23:2; 33:7; Ps 38:2; 39:10 [B]Ps 22:15 32:5 [a]Or *iniquity* [A]Lev 26:40 [B]Job 31:33 [C]Ps 38:18; Prov 28:13; 1 John 1:9 [D]Ps 103:12 32:6 [a]Lit *in a time of finding out* [A]Ps 69:13; Is 55:6 [B]Ps 46:1-3; 69:1; 124:5; 144:7; Is 43:2 32:7 [a]Or *shouts* [A]Ps 9:9; 31:20; 91:1; 119:114 [B]Ps 121:7 [C]Ex 15:1; Judg 5:1; Ps 40:3 32:8 [A]Ps 25:8 [B]Ps 33:18 32:9 [A]Prov 26:3 32:10 [A]Ps 16:4; Prov 13:21; Rom 2:9 [B]Ps 5:11, 12; Prov 16:20 32:11 [A]Ps 64:10; 68:3; 97:12 [B]Ps 7:10; 64:10 33:1 [A]Ps 32:11; Phil 3:1; 4:4 [B]Ps 92:1; 147:1

31:23 love the LORD. Biblical love includes an attitudinal response and demonstrated obedience (cf. Dt 6:4, 5; 10:12; Jn 14:15, 21; 15:10; 2Jn 6). The assurance of both reward and retribution is a biblical maxim (e.g., Dt 7:9, 10).

31:24 Be strong … take courage. A sing. form of this pl. imperative was addressed to Joshua in 1:7. It is used nearly 20 times in the OT, particularly in anticipation of battle.

32:1–11 This psalm has been classified by the early church as one of 7 penitential psalms (cf. 6; 38; 51; 102; 130; 143). Among these, Pss 32 and 51 stand out as confessional giants. As historically related to the life of David and especially in connection with the Bathsheba episode (cf. 2Sa 11–12), Ps 51 would have preceded Ps 32. The overall thrust, intent, and development of Ps 32 may be summarized as follows: Life's most important lessons about sin, confession, and forgiveness are skillfully shared by David through two avenues of approach.

I. First Avenue: Remembering These Lessons (32:1–5)
   A. Lessons about Results (32:1, 2)
   B. Lessons about Resistance (32:3, 4)
   C. Lessons about Responses (32:5)
II. Second Avenue: Relaying These Lessons (32:6–11)
   A. Lessons about Responses (32:6, 7)
   B. Lessons about Resistance (32:8, 9)
   C. Lessons about Results (32:10, 11)

32:Title "A Maskil" in the heading introduces a new technical term. It could indicate that Ps 32 was a "*contemplative* poem," or a "psalm of *understanding,*" or a "*skillful* psalm."

32:1, 2 transgression … sin … iniquity. Three key OT words for sin occur, viewing it respectively as rebellion, failure, and perversion.

32:3, 4 These are vivid descriptions of the physical effects of his impenitent state.

32:5 David picks up the key terms that he had used to describe sin in vv. 1, 2, but now, in a context of personal confession, he identifies those heinous affronts to the person of God as his own. On the priority of confession, cf. Pr 28:13; 1Jn 1:8–10.

32:6 David slips right back into teaching mode in this verse, emphasizing that every person who knows the grace of God should not presume upon that grace by putting off confession.

32:8 instruct … teach … counsel. This terminology applies to biblical wisdom.

32:9 horse … mule. I.e., Don't be stubborn. Such animals are used as pointed illustrations of this sin (cf. Pr 26:3; Is 1:3; Jas 3:3).

33:1–22 This psalm is a general hymn of praise. Its two primary themes are: 1) Yahweh is the Lord of nature, and 2) He is Lord of history. In biblical thought, these realms are always related; the Creator sovereignly rules over His total creation, over all creatures throughout time.

I. A Praise Prelude (33:1–3)
II. The Rationale for Praise (33:4, 5)
   A. The Lord's Sovereign Power in Natural History (33:4)
   B. The Lord's Sovereign Providence over Human History (33:5)
III. The Response of Praise (33:6–19)
   A. The Creator's Sovereign Power (33:6–9)
   B. The Creator's Sovereign Providence (33:10–19)
IV. A Prayer Finale (33:20–22)

33:1 becoming. This means that praise to Him is proper, suitable, and fitting. On the propriety of praise, cf. Ps 147:1.

2 Give thanks to the LORD with the [A]lyre;
Sing praises to Him with a
[B]harp of ten strings.
3 Sing to Him a [A]new song;
Play skillfully with [B]a shout of joy.
4 For the word of the LORD [A]is upright,
And all His work is *done* [B]in faithfulness.
5 He [A]loves righteousness and justice;
The [B]earth is full of the
lovingkindness of the LORD.

6 By the [A]word of the LORD the
heavens were made,
And [B]by the breath of His
mouth [C]all their host.
7 He gathers the [A]waters of the
sea together [a]as a heap;
He lays up the deeps in storehouses.
8 Let [A]all the earth fear the LORD;
Let all the inhabitants of the
world [B]stand in awe of Him.
9 For [A]He spoke, and it was done;
He commanded, and it [a]stood fast.
10 The LORD [A]nullifies the
counsel of the nations;
He frustrates the plans of the peoples.
11 The [A]counsel of the LORD stands forever,
The [B]plans of His heart from
generation to generation.
12 Blessed is the [A]nation whose
God is the LORD,
The people whom He has [B]chosen
for His own inheritance.

13 The LORD [A]looks from heaven;
He [B]sees all the sons of men;
14 From [A]His dwelling place He looks out
On all the inhabitants of the earth,
15 He who [A]fashions [a]the hearts of them all,
He who [B]understands all their works.
16 [A]The king is not saved by a mighty army;
A warrior is not delivered
by great strength.
17 A [A]horse is a false hope for victory;
Nor does it deliver anyone
by its great strength.

18 Behold, [A]the eye of the LORD is
on those who fear Him,
On those who [a,B]hope for
His lovingkindness,
19 To [A]deliver their soul from death
And to keep them alive [B]in famine.
20 Our soul [A]waits for the LORD;
He is our [B]help and our shield.
21 For our [A]heart rejoices in Him,
Because we trust in His holy name.
22 Let Your lovingkindness,
O LORD, be upon us,
According as we have [a]hoped in You.

PSALM 34

THE LORD, A PROVIDER AND DELIVERER.

A Psalm of David when he [†]feigned madness before
[•]Abimelech, who drove him away and he departed.

1 I will [A]bless the LORD at all times;
His [B]praise shall continually
be in my mouth.
2 My soul will [A]make its boast in the LORD;
The [B]humble will hear it and rejoice.
3 O [A]magnify the LORD with me,
And let us [B]exalt His name together.

4 I [A]sought the LORD, and He answered me,
And [B]delivered me from all my fears.
5 They [A]looked to Him and were radiant,
And their faces will [B]never be ashamed.
6 This [a]poor man cried, and
[A]the LORD heard him
And saved him out of all his troubles.
7 The [A]angel of the LORD encamps
around those who fear Him,
And rescues them.

33:2 [A]Ps 71:22; 147:7 [B]Ps 144:9 33:3 [A]Ps 40:3; 96:1; 98:1; 144:9; Is 42:10; Rev 5:9 [B]Ps 98:4 33:4 [A]Ps 19:8 [B]Ps 119:90 33:5 [A]Ps 11:7; 37:28 [B]Ps 119:64 33:6 [A]Gen 1:6; Ps 148:5; Heb 11:3 [B]Ps 104:30 [C]Gen 2:1 33:7 [a]Some versions read *in a water skin;* i.e. container [A]Ex 15:8; Josh 3:16; Ps 78:13 33:8 [A]Ps 67:7 [B]Ps 96:9 33:9 [a]Or *stood forth* [A]Gen 1:3; Ps 148:5 33:10 [A]Ps 2:1-3; Is 8:10; 19:3 33:11 [A]Job 23:12; Prov 19:21 [B]Ps 40:5; 92:5; 139:17; Is 55:8 33:12 [A]Ps 144:15 [B]Ex 19:5; Deut 7:6; Ps 28:9 33:13 [A]Job 28:24; Ps 14:2 [B]Ps 11:4 33:14 [A]1 Kin 8:39, 43; Ps 102:19 33:15 [a]Or *their heart together* [A]Job 10:8; Ps 119:73 [B]2 Chr 16:9; Job 34:21; Jer 32:19 33:16 [A]Ps 44:6; 60:11 33:17 [A]Ps 20:7; 147:10; Prov 21:31 33:18 [a]Or *wait* [A]Job 36:7; Ps 32:8; 34:15; 1 Pet 3:12 [B]Ps 32:10; 147:11 33:19 [A]Ps 56:13; Acts 12:11 [B]Job 5:20; Ps 37:19 33:20 [A]Ps 62:1; 130:6; Is 8:17 [B]Ps 115:9 33:21 [A]Ps 13:5; 28:7; Zech 10:7; John 16:22 33:22 [a]Or *waited for* 34:1 [†]Or *changed his behavior* [•]Possibly a title of King Achish of Gath, see 1 Sam 21:10-15 [A]Eph 5:20; 1 Thess 5:18 [B]Ps 71:6 34:2 [A]Ps 44:8; Jer 9:24; 1 Cor 1:31 [B]Ps 69:32 34:3 [A]Ps 35:27; 69:30; Luke 1:46 [B]Ps 18:46 34:4 [A]2 Chr 15:2; Ps 9:10; Matt 7:7 [B]Ps 34:6, 17, 19 34:5 [A]Ps 36:9; Is 60:5 [B]Ps 25:3 34:6 [a]Or *afflicted* [A]Ps 34:4 34:7 [A]Ps 91:11; Dan 6:22

33:3 a new song. I.e., a new occasion and impulse for expressing fresh praise to God (cf. Pss 96:1; 98:1; 149:1).

33:6, 9 God's utterances created a universe out of nothing (cf. "God said" in Ge 1:3, 6, 9, 11, 14, 20, 24, 26).

33:6 host. This designation refers to stellar and planetary bodies (cf. Is 40:26; 45:12) and/or heaven's complement of angels (cf. Ps 103:20–22). The former emphasis is more prominent in the immediate context.

33:7 He lays up. On this picturesque language of God's "heaping up" waters as a "pile" of dirt or sand, cf. Ex 15:8; Jos 3:13–16; Ps 78:13.

33:10, 11 A sharp contrast is drawn between mankind's shaky plans and the Lord's sovereign plans.

33:15 He who fashions the hearts. This is the potter's word (cf. Ge 2:7); for the significance of this statement, see Is 29:15, 16.

33:16–19 On the teaching of these verses, cf. the maxim of Zec 4:6.

34:1–22 This acrostic psalm is quite similar to Ps 25, not just in form, but also in major themes (e.g., the emphasis on redemption that brings each psalm to a close in 25:22 and 34:22). Individual and corporate applications of the Lord's deliverance are found throughout. This psalm unfolds with a praise mode followed by teaching.

I. Personal Testimony (34:1–10)
II. Personal Teaching (34:11–22)

34:Title The historical occasion to which this heading alludes is found in 1Sa 21:10–15; however, there is nothing obvious in the context of Ps 34 to make such a specific connection. Abimelech, like Pharaoh, was a dynastic designation, not a proper name.

34:1–3 This is one of the greatest invitations in the Psalms to all the people to join together in praise.

34:2 This is proper boasting because of the only proper object, God Himself (cf. Jer 9:23, 24).

34:7 The angel of the LORD. A special manifestation of Yahweh Himself at strategic historical junctures (cf. Ge 16:7ff.; 18; 19; 31:11ff.; Jos 5; Jdg 6; 13). A strong case can be made that these were pre-incarnate

8 O [A]taste and see that the LORD is good;
How [B]blessed is the man who
takes refuge in Him!
9 O fear the LORD, you [A]His saints;
For to those who fear Him
there is [B]no want.
10 The young lions do lack and suffer hunger;
But they who seek the LORD shall [A]not
be in want of any good thing.
11 [A]Come, you children, listen to me;
[B]I will teach you [C]the fear of the LORD.
12 [A]Who is the man who desires life
And loves *length of* days that
he may [B]see good?
13 Keep [A]your tongue from evil
And your lips from speaking [B]deceit.
14 [A]Depart from evil and do good;
Seek peace and [B]pursue it.

15 The [A]eyes of the LORD are
toward the righteous
And His ears are *open* to their cry.
16 The [A]face of the LORD is against evildoers,
To [B]cut off the memory of
them from the earth.
17 *The righteous* [A]cry, and the LORD hears
And delivers them out of
all their troubles.
18 The LORD [A]is near to the [B]brokenhearted
And saves those who are
[a,C]crushed in spirit.

19 [A]Many are the [B]afflictions of the righteous,
But the LORD [C]delivers him
out of them all.
20 He keeps all his bones,
[A]Not one of them is broken.
21 [A]Evil shall slay the wicked,
And those who hate the righteous
will be [a]condemned.
22 The LORD [A]redeems the soul
of His servants,
And none of those who [B]take refuge
in Him will be [a]condemned.

PSALM 35

PRAYER FOR RESCUE FROM ENEMIES.

A Psalm of David.

1 Contend, O LORD, with those
who [A]contend with me;
Fight against those who
[B]fight against me.
2 Take hold of [a,A]buckler and shield
And rise up for [B]my help.
3 Draw also the spear and [a]the battle-axe
to meet those who pursue me;
Say to my soul, "I am [A]your salvation."
4 Let those be [A]ashamed and
dishonored who seek my [a]life;
Let those be [B]turned back and humiliated
who devise evil against me.
5 Let them be [A]like chaff before the wind,
With the angel of the LORD
driving *them* on.
6 Let their way be dark and [A]slippery,
With the angel of the LORD
pursuing them.
7 For [A]without cause they [B]hid
their net for me;
Without cause they dug a [a]pit for my soul.
8 Let [A]destruction come upon
him unawares,
And [B]let the net which he
hid catch himself;
Into that very [C]destruction let him fall.

9 And my soul shall [A]rejoice in the LORD;
It shall [B]exult in His salvation.

34:8 [A]Ps 119:103; Heb 6:5; 1 Pet 2:3 [B]Ps 2:12 34:9 [A]Ps 31:23 [B]Ps 23:1 34:10 [A]Ps 84:11 34:11 [A]Ps 66:16 [B]Ps 32:8 [C]Ps 111:10 34:12 [A]Ps 34:12-16; 1 Pet 3:10-12 [B]Eccl 3:13 34:13 [A]Ps 141:3; Prov 13:3; James 1:26 [B]1 Pet 2:22 34:14 [A]Ps 37:27; Is 1:16, 17 [B]Rom 14:19; Heb 12:14 34:15 [A]Job 36:7; Ps 33:18 34:16 [A]Lev 17:10; Jer 44:11; Amos 9:4 [B]Job 18:17; Ps 9:6; 109:15; Prov 10:7 34:17 [A]Ps 34:6; 145:19 34:18 [a]Or *contrite* [A]Ps 145:18 [B]Ps 147:3; Is 61:1 [C]Ps 51:17; Is 57:15 34:19 [A]Prov 24:16 [B]Ps 71:20; 2 Tim 3:11f [C]Ps 34:4, 6, 17 34:20 [A]John 19:33, 36 34:21 [a]Or *held guilty* [A]Ps 94:23; 140:11; Prov 24:16 34:22 [a]V 21, note 1 [A]1 Kin 1:29; Ps 71:23 [B]Ps 37:40 35:1 [A]Ps 18:43; Is 49:25 [B]Ps 56:2 35:2 [a]I.e. small shield [A]Ps 91:4 [B]Ps 44:26 35:3 [a]Or *close up the path against those* [A]Ps 62:2 35:4 [a]Or *soul* [A]Ps 70:2 [B]Ps 40:14; 129:5 35:5 [A]Job 21:18; Ps 83:13; Is 29:5 35:6 [A]Ps 73:18; Jer 23:12 35:7 [a]*Pit* has been transposed from line above [A]Ps 69:4; 109:3; 140:5 [B]Ps 9:15 35:8 [A]Ps 55:23; Is 47:11; 1 Thess 5:3 [B]Ps 9:15 [C]Ps 73:18 35:9 [A]Is 61:10 [B]Ps 9:14; 13:5; Luke 1:47

appearances of the Lord Jesus Christ. *See note on Ex 3:2.*

34:11 This solicitation to wisdom compares with Pr 1–9.

34:12–14 This introduces some crucial character qualities of God's true people; cf. Ps 15:1–5.

34:14 The pathway theme of Ps 1; here the emphasis is on leaving the evil and doing good (cf. Job 28:28; Pr 3:7; 16:6, 17; Is 1:16, 17; etc.).

34:18 brokenhearted ... crushed in spirit. These are graphic idioms that describe dependent disciples (cf. Pss 51:17; 147:3; Is 57:15; 61:1; 66:2; Mt 5:3).

34:19–22 The side-by-side realities of human persecution and divine preservation once again vividly depict real life in the real world.

35:1–28 Psalm 35, as to its form, is an individual lament. Its context of literal and legal warfare suggests a scenario of the theocratic king being accused, and about to be attacked, by a foreign power with whom he had previously entered into a covenant. David presents his "case" before the Divine Judge, moving from a complaint about the situation, to prayer about the situation, and finally, when the Lord would justly respond to the situation, praise for His righteous intervention. So, 3 cycles of exasperation and expectation in Ps 35 convey the psalmist's prayers about his opponents to God.

I. First Cycle: The Attacks He Was Experiencing (35:1–10)
II. Second Cycle: The Perjury He Was Experiencing (35:11–18)
   A. He Prays that God Would Examine the Evidence (35:11–16)
   B. He Prays that God Would Act without Delay (35:17)
   C. He Pledges Praise (35:18)
III. Third Cycle: The Mockery He Was Anticipating (35:19–28)
   A. He Prays for Judgment concerning Them (35:19–21)
   B. He Prays for Justice concerning Himself (35:22–26)
   C. He Pledges Praise (35:27, 28)

35:1 Contend ... Fight. The first bold prayer solicits the legal advocacy of God (cf. Pr 25:8, 9; Is 3:13), while the second asks the Divine Warrior to fight his battles for him (e.g., Ex 15:3; Dt 32:41ff.).

35:3 Say to my soul, "I am your salvation." David is longing for reassurance (cf. Ps 3:8a).

35:4–8 Cf. the imprecations of Pss 7, 69, 109.

35:7 without cause ... Without cause. This adds to his defense; all their attacks, from a covenant or legal standpoint, have been unjustified.

10 All my [A]bones will say, "LORD,
[B]who is like You,
Who delivers the afflicted from him
[C]who is too strong for him,
And [D]the afflicted and the needy
from him who robs him?"
11 [A]Malicious witnesses rise up;
They ask me of things that I do not know.
12 They [A]repay me evil for good,
To the bereavement of my soul.
13 But as for me, [A]when they were sick,
my [B]clothing was sackcloth;
I [C]humbled my soul with fasting,
And my [D]prayer kept returning
to my bosom.
14 I went about as though it were
my friend or brother;
I [A]bowed down [a]mourning, as one
who sorrows for a mother.
15 But [A]at my [a]stumbling they rejoiced
and gathered themselves together;
The [b,B]smiters whom I did not know
gathered together against me,
They [c,C]slandered me without ceasing.
16 Like godless jesters at a feast,
They [A]gnashed at me with their teeth.

17 Lord, [A]how long will You look on?
Rescue my soul [B]from their ravages,
My [C]only *life* from the lions.
18 I will [A]give You thanks in the
great congregation;
I will [B]praise You among a mighty throng.
19 [A]Do not let those who are wrongfully
[B]my enemies rejoice over me;
Nor let those [C]who hate me without
cause [a,D]wink maliciously.
20 For they do not speak peace,
But they devise [A]deceitful words against
those who are quiet in the land.
21 They [A]opened their mouth wide against me;
They said, "[B]Aha, aha, our
eyes have seen it!"

22 [A]You have seen it, O LORD,
[B]do not keep silent;
O Lord, [C]do not be far from me.
23 [A]Stir up Yourself, and awake to my right
And to my cause, my God and my Lord.
24 [A]Judge me, O LORD my God, according
to Your righteousness,
And [B]do not let them rejoice over me.
25 Do not let them say in their
heart, "[A]Aha, our desire!"
Do not let them say, "We have
[B]swallowed him up!"
26 Let [A]those be ashamed and humiliated
altogether who rejoice at my distress;
Let those be [B]clothed with shame
and dishonor who [C]magnify
themselves over me.

27 Let them [A]shout for joy and rejoice,
who favor [B]my vindication;
And [C]let them say continually,
"The LORD be magnified,
Who [D]delights in the prosperity
of His servant."
28 And [A]my tongue shall declare
Your righteousness
And Your praise all day long.

PSALM 36

WICKEDNESS OF MEN AND LOVINGKINDNESS OF GOD.

For the choir director. *A Psalm* of David
the servant of the LORD.

1 Transgression speaks to the
ungodly within [a]his heart;
There is [A]no fear of God before his eyes.

35:10 [A]Ps 51:8 [B]Ex 15:11; Ps 86:8; Mic 7:18 [C]Ps 18:17 [D]Ps 37:14; 109:16 35:11 [A]Ps 27:12 35:12 [A]Ps 38:20; 109:5; Jer 18:20; John 10:32 35:13 [A]Job 30:25 [B]Ps 69:11 [C]Ps 69:10 [D]Matt 10:13; Luke 10:6 35:14 [a]Or *dressed in black* [A]Ps 38:6 35:15 [a]Or *limping* [b]Or *smitten ones* [c]Lit *tore* [A]Obad 12 [B]Job 30:1, 8, 12 [C]Ps 7:2 35:16 [A]Job 16:9; Ps 37:12; Lam 2:16 35:17 [A]Ps 13:1; Hab 1:13 [B]Ps 35:7 [C]Ps 22:20, 21 35:18 [A]Ps 22:22 [B]Ps 22:25 35:19 [a]Or *wink the eye* [A]Ps 13:4; 30:1; 38:16 [B]Ps 38:19; 69:4 [C]John 15:25 [D]Prov 6:13; 10:10 35:20 [A]Ps 55:21; Jer 9:8; Mic 6:12 35:21 [A]Job 16:10; Ps 22:13 [B]Ps 40:15; 70:3 35:22 [A]Ex 3:7; Ps 10:14 [B]Ps 28:1 [C]Ps 10:1; 22:11; 38:21; 71:12 35:23 [A]Ps 7:6; 44:23; 59:4; 80:2 35:24 [A]Ps 9:4; 26:1; 43:1 [B]Ps 35:19 35:25 [A]Ps 35:21 [B]Ps 56:1; 124:3; Prov 1:12; Lam 2:16 35:26 [A]Ps 40:14 [B]Ps 109:29 [C]Job 19:5; Ps 38:16 35:27 [A]Ps 32:11 [B]Ps 9:4 [C]Ps 40:16; 70:4 [D]Ps 147:11; 149:4 35:28 [A]Ps 51:14; 71:15, 24 36:1 [a]Another reading is *my heart* [A]Rom 3:18

35:10 LORD, who is like You. This had become a canonized expression of awe at the uniqueness of Israel's great God (cf. Ex 15:11; Mic 7:18).

35:11–14 A strong contrast is drawn between the psalmist's attitude about the covenant agreement and that of his treaty partner.

35:16 On the painful maimings of mockery, cf. Job 16:9; Pss 37:12; 112:10; La 2:16.

35:17 how long . . . ? On laments, cf. Ps 13:1; Hab 1:2.

35:19 wrongfully. Cf. "without cause" twice in v. 7.

35:21 Aha, aha. This taunting chorus will return in v. 25.

35:21, 22 our eyes have seen it! You have seen it, O LORD. What David's enemy allegedly saw, the Lord has seen perfectly. David knew that his God would vindicate him based upon the true evidence, all in his favor.

35:23 to my cause. He brings back the advocacy theme of v. 1.

35:27 Cf. Ps 40:16. **His servant.** Besides being a polite third-person reference to the psalmist, the terminology was also used of an OT disciple regarding himself as bound to the Lord.

36:1–12 At least 3 themes may be detected in this psalm: 1) wisdom, vv. 1–4; 2) praise, vv. 5–9; and 3) prayer, vv. 10–12. Psalm 36 resembles Ps 14 in its description of human depravity; it also brings to mind David's personal confession found in Ps 32. Paul used Ps 36:1 to summarize his list of 14 indictments against the whole race in Ro 3:10–18. As to its overall structure, David's two different moods in Ps 36 exemplify his continuing quest for balance concerning the realities of human wickedness and divine benevolence.

I. Mood of Deliberation (36:1–9)
   A. His Deliberations on Human Infidelity (36:1–4)
   B. His Deliberations on Divine Fidelity (36:5–9)
II. Mood of Dependence (36:10–12)
   A. Implemented through Prayer (36:10, 11)
   B. Intimated through Perspective (36:12)

36:Title The term "servant," found in Ps 35:27, appears in this title. It carries an association with covenant relationship emphasizing submission to and service for God. For its application to David within the texts of Psalms, cf. 78:70; 89:3.

36:1 no fear. This is the opposite of the attitude which characterizes true disciples. The word here is actually "dread" or "terror" (cf. Dt 2:25; Ps 119:120; Is 2:10, 19, 21; etc.).

2 For [a]it [A]flatters him in his *own* eyes
Concerning the discovery of his
iniquity *and* the hatred *of it.*
3 The [A]words of his mouth are
wickedness and deceit;
He has [B]ceased to [a]be wise
and to do good.
4 He [A]plans wickedness upon his bed;
He sets himself on a [B]path
that is not good;
He [C]does not despise evil.

5 Your [A]lovingkindness, O LORD,
[a]extends to the heavens,
Your faithfulness *reaches* to the skies.
6 Your [A]righteousness is like the
[a]mountains of God;
Your [B]judgments are *like* a great deep.
O LORD, You [C]preserve man and beast.
7 How [A]precious is Your
lovingkindness, O God!
And the children of men [B]take refuge
in the shadow of Your wings.
8 They [A]drink their fill of the
[a]abundance of Your house;
And You give them to drink of
the [B]river of Your delights.
9 For with You is the [A]fountain of life;
In Your light we see light.

10 O continue Your lovingkindness
to [A]those who know You,
And Your [B]righteousness to
the upright in heart.
11 Let not the foot of pride come upon me,
And let not the hand of the
wicked drive me away.
12 There the doers of iniquity have fallen;
They have been thrust down
and [A]cannot rise.

PSALM 37

SECURITY OF THOSE WHO TRUST IN THE LORD, AND INSECURITY OF THE WICKED.

A Psalm of David.

1 [A]Do not fret because of evildoers,
Be not [B]envious toward wrongdoers.
2 For they will [A]wither quickly like the grass
And [B]fade like the green herb.
3 [A]Trust in the LORD and do good;
[B]Dwell in the land and
[a,C]cultivate faithfulness.
4 [A]Delight yourself in the LORD;
And He will [B]give you the
desires of your heart.
5 [A]Commit your way to the LORD,
Trust also in Him, and He will do it.
6 He will bring forth [A]your
righteousness as the light
And your judgment [B]as the noonday.

7 [a]Rest in the LORD and [A]wait
[b]patiently for Him;
[B]Do not fret because of him who
[C]prospers in his way,
Because of the man who carries
out wicked schemes.
8 Cease from anger and [A]forsake wrath;
Do not fret; *it leads* only to evildoing.
9 For [A]evildoers will be cut off,
But those who wait for the LORD,
they will [B]inherit the land.
10 Yet [A]a little while and the wicked
man will be no more;
And you will look carefully for [B]his
place and he will not be *there.*
11 But [A]the humble will inherit the land
And will delight themselves in
[B]abundant prosperity.

36:2 [a]Or *he flatters himself* [A]Deut 29:19; Ps 10:11; 49:18 36:3 [a]Or *understand to do good* [A]Ps 10:7; 12:2 [B]Ps 94:8; Jer 4:22 36:4 [A]Prov 4:16; Mic 2:1 [B]Is 65:2 [C]Ps 52:3; Rom 12:9 36:5 [a]Lit *is in* [A]Ps 57:10; 103:11; 108:4 36:6 [a]Or *mighty mountains* [A]Ps 71:19 [B]Job 11:8; Ps 77:19; Rom 11:33 [C]Neh 9:6; Ps 104:14, 15; 145:16 36:7 [A]Ps 40:5; 139:17 [B]Ruth 2:12; Ps 17:8; 57:1; 91:4 36:8 [a]Lit *fatness* [A]Ps 63:5; 65:4; Is 25:6; Jer 31:12-14 [B]Job 20:17; Ps 46:4; Rev 22:1 36:9 [A]Jer 2:13 36:10 [A]Jer 22:16 [B]Ps 24:5 36:12 [A]Ps 140:10; Is 26:14 37:1 [A]Prov 23:17; 24:19 [B]Ps 73:3; Prov 3:31 37:2 [A]Job 14:2; Ps 90:6; 92:7; James 1:11 [B]Ps 129:6 37:3 [a]Or *feed securely* or *feed on His faithfulness* [A]Ps 62:8 [B]Deut 30:20 [C]Is 40:11; Ezek 34:13, 14 37:4 [A]Job 22:26; Ps 94:19; Is 58:14 [B]Ps 21:2; 145:19; Matt 7:7, 8 37:5 [A]Ps 55:22; Prov 16:3; 1 Pet 5:7 37:6 [A]Ps 97:11; Is 58:8, 10; Mic 7:9 [B]Job 11:17 37:7 [a]Or *Be still* [b]Or *longingly* [A]Ps 40:1; 62:5; Lam 3:26 [B]Ps 37:1, 8 [C]Jer 12:1 37:8 [A]Eph 4:31; Col 3:8 37:9 [A]Ps 37:2, 22 [B]Ps 25:13; Prov 2:21; Is 57:13; 60:21; Matt 5:5 37:10 [A]Job 24:24 [B]Job 7:10; Ps 37:35, 36 37:11 [A]Matt 5:5 [B]Ps 72:7

36:2 I.e., he flatters himself so much that he is unable to understand enough to hate his own iniquity.

36:3, 4 Although Paul cites only Ps 36:1b in Ro 3, the same categories of characteristic sinfulness also show up in that context; cf. character: Ps 36:2 with Ro 3:10–12; communications: Ps 36:3a with Ro 3:13–14; and conduct: Ps 36:3b–4 with Ro 3:15–17.

36:5, 6 These attributes of God are immeasurable.

36:7 the shadow of Your wings. Although some would take this as referring to wings of the cherubim over the ark, it is probably more generally a reference to the protective care of a parent bird for its young (Dt 32:11; Pss 17:8; 91:4; Ru 2:12; cf. Jesus' allusion to the word picture in Mt 23:37).

36:9 In Your light we see light. It is likely that this phraseology bears both literal and figurative significance, i.e., God is the source of physical life and also of spiritual life. The Lord is the Source and Sustainer of all light and life.

36:11 the foot of pride. This is likely military imagery referring to the practice of a victorious king-general symbolically placing his foot upon the neck of a prostrated, defeated king-general.

36:12 Cf. Pss 14:5a; 18:38; Pr 24:16.

37:1–40 Psalm 37, an irregular acrostic, is a wisdom poem addressed to man, not God. Verses 12–24 sound very much like the maxims of Proverbs. The covenant promises of the "land" for Israel are prominent in its verses (cf. vv. 3, 9, 11, 22, 29, 34). Its basic theme deals with the age-old question "Why do the ungodly prosper while the godly painfully struggle through life?" An intricate arrangement puts forth David's answer. In Ps 37, David mixes and matches 6 thoughts in order to advance his major message on the eventual arrival of divine justice.

I. An Introductory Overview (37:1, 2)
II. An Initial Expansion (37:3–11)
III. Some Proverbial Perspectives (37:12–24)
IV. An Initial Testimony (37:25, 26)
V. A Final Expansion (cf. vv. 3–11) (37:27–34)
VI. A Final Testimony (cf. vv. 25, 26) (37:35–40)

37:2 Here-today-gone-tomorrow illustrations about the wicked characterize this psalm. On this theme, cf. Job 14:1, 2; Pss 90:5, 6; 103:15, 16; Is 40:6–8; Mt 6:30; Jas 1:10, 11; 1Jn 2:17.

37:7, 8 The message of "Relax! Don't react!" returns (cf. v. 1).

37:10 Yet a little while. Cf. similar terminology in Jer 51:33; Hos 1:4. The Lord's intervention is imminent.

12 The wicked [A]plots against the righteous
And [B]gnashes at him with his teeth.
13 The Lord [A]laughs at him,
For He sees [B]his day is coming.
14 The wicked have drawn the
sword and [A]bent their bow
To cast down the [B]afflicted
and the needy,
To [C]slay those who are
upright in conduct.
15 Their sword will enter their own heart,
And their [A]bows will be broken.

16 [A]Better is the little of the righteous
Than the abundance of many wicked.
17 For the [A]arms of the wicked
will be broken,
But the LORD [B]sustains the righteous.
18 The LORD [A]knows the days
of the [a]blameless,
And their [B]inheritance will be forever.
19 They will not be ashamed
in the time of evil,
And [A]in the days of famine they
will have abundance.
20 But the [A]wicked will perish;
And the enemies of the LORD will be
like the [a]glory of the pastures,
They vanish—[B]like smoke
they vanish away.
21 The wicked borrows and
does not pay back,
But the righteous [A]is gracious and gives.
22 For [A]those blessed by Him
will [B]inherit the land,
But those [C]cursed by Him will be cut off.

23 [A]The steps of a man are
established by the LORD,
And He [B]delights in his way.
24 When [A]he falls, he will not
be hurled headlong,
Because [B]the LORD is the One
[a]who holds his hand.
25 I have been young and now I am old,
Yet [A]I have not seen the
righteous forsaken
Or [B]his [a]descendants begging bread.
26 All day long [A]he is gracious and lends,
And [B]his [a]descendants are a blessing.

27 [A]Depart from evil and do good,
[a]So you will abide [B]forever.
28 For the LORD [A]loves [a]justice
And [B]does not forsake His godly ones;
They are [C]preserved forever,
But the [b,D]descendants of the
wicked will be cut off.
29 The righteous will [A]inherit the land
And [B]dwell in it forever.
30 The mouth of the righteous
[A]utters wisdom,
And his tongue [B]speaks justice.
31 The [A]law of his God is in his heart;
His [B]steps do not slip.
32 The [A]wicked spies upon the righteous
And [B]seeks to kill him.
33 The LORD will [A]not leave
him in his hand
Or [B]let him be condemned
when he is judged.
34 [A]Wait for the LORD and keep His way,
And He will exalt you to
inherit the land;
When the [B]wicked are cut
off, you will see it.

35 I have [A]seen a wicked, violent man
Spreading himself like a [B]luxuriant
[a]tree in its native soil.
36 Then [a]he passed away, and
lo, he [A]was no more;
I sought for him, but he
could not be found.
37 Mark the [a,A]blameless man, and
behold the [B]upright;
For the man of peace will
have a [b,C]posterity.
38 But transgressors will be
altogether [A]destroyed;
The [a]posterity of the wicked
will be [B]cut off.
39 But the [A]salvation of the righteous
is from the LORD;
He is their strength [B]in
time of trouble.
40 [A]The LORD helps them and
delivers them;
He [B]delivers them from the
wicked and saves them,
Because they [C]take refuge in Him.

37:12 [A]Ps 31:13, 20 [B]Ps 35:16 37:13 [A]Ps 2:4 [B]1 Sam 26:10; Job 18:20 37:14 [A]Ps 11:2; Lam 2:4 [B]Ps 35:10; 86:1 [C]Ps 11:2 37:15 [A]1 Sam 2:4; Ps 46:9 37:16 [A]Prov 15:16; 16:8 37:17 [A]Job 38:15; Ps 10:15; Ezek 30:21 [B]Ps 71:6; 145:14 37:18 [a]Lit *complete;* or *perfect* [A]Ps 1:6; 31:7 [B]Ps 37:27, 29 37:19 [A]Job 5:20; Ps 33:19 37:20 [a]I.e. flowers [A]Ps 73:27 [B]Ps 68:2; 102:3 37:21 [A]Ps 112:5, 9 37:22 [A]Prov 3:33 [B]Ps 37:9 [C]Job 5:3 37:23 [A]1 Sam 2:9; Ps 40:2; 66:9; 119:5 [B]Ps 147:11 37:24 [a]Or *who sustains him with His hand* [A]Ps 145:14; Prov 24:16; Mic 7:8 [B]Ps 147:6 37:25 [a]Lit *seed* [A]Ps 37:28; Is 41:17; Heb 13:5 [B]Ps 109:10 37:26 [a]Lit *seed* [A]Deut 15:8; Ps 37:21 [B]Ps 147:13 37:27 [a]Or *And dwell forever* [A]Ps 34:14 [B]Ps 37:18; 102:28 37:28 [a]Lit *judgment* [b]Lit *seed* [A]Ps 11:7; 33:5 [B]Ps 37:25 [C]Ps 31:23 [D]Ps 21:10; 37:9; Prov 2:22; Is 14:20 37:29 [A]Ps 37:9; Prov 2:21 [B]Ps 37:18 37:30 [A]Ps 49:3; Prov 10:13 [B]Ps 101:1; 119:13 37:31 [A]Deut 6:6; Ps 40:8; 119:11; Is 51:7; Jer 31:33 [B]Ps 26:1; 37:23 37:32 [A]Ps 10:8; 17:11 [B]Ps 37:14 37:33 [A]Ps 31:8; 2 Pet 2:9 [B]Ps 34:22; 109:31 37:34 [A]Ps 27:14; 37:9 [B]Ps 52:5, 6; 91:8 37:35 [a]Lit *native;* Heb obscure [A]Job 5:3; Jer 12:2 [B]Job 8:16 37:36 [a]Ancient versions read *I passed by* [A]Job 20:5; Ps 37:10 37:37 [a]Lit *complete;* or *perfect* [b]Lit *an end* [A]Ps 37:18 [B]Ps 7:10 [C]Is 57:1, 2 37:38 [a]Lit *end* [A]Ps 1:4-6; 37:20, 28 [B]Ps 37:9; 73:17 37:39 [A]Ps 3:8; 62:1 [B]Ps 9:9; 37:19 37:40 [A]Ps 54:4 [B]Ps 22:4; Is 31:5; Dan 3:17; 6:23 [C]1 Chr 5:20; Ps 34:22

37:17 **the arms of the wicked will be broken.** Their members will be shattered for grabbing and getting wealth (v. 16b). Cf. Job 38:15; Ps 10:15; Jer 48:25; Eze 30:21.

37:18 Cf. Ps 1:6.

37:21 The OT contains both precepts and proverbs about borrowing and lending; cf. Dt 15:6; 28:12, 44; Ps 112:1–6; Pr 22:7.

37:24 For corroborations of such divine comfort, cf. Ps 145:14; Pr 24:16; Mic 7:8.

37:31 **The law of his God is in his heart.** On God's internalized instruction, cf. Dt 6:6; Pss 40:8; 119 (throughout); Jer 31:33; Is 51:7.

37:38 **cut off.** On this truth of judgment, cf. vv. 9, 22, 28, 34, and Ps 109:13. For a positive presentation in reference to the faithful, cf. Pr 23:18; 24:14, 20.

37:39 **salvation ... from the LORD.** Since salvation belongs to Him (Ps 3:8), He is the perennial Source of it (cf. Ps 62:1, 2).

PSALM 38

PRAYER OF A SUFFERING PENITENT.

A Psalm of David, for a memorial.

1 O LORD, [A]rebuke me not in Your wrath,
And chasten me not in Your
burning anger.
2 For Your [A]arrows have sunk deep into me,
And [B]Your hand has pressed down on me.
3 There is [A]no soundness in my flesh
[B]because of Your indignation;
There is no health [C]in my bones
because of my sin.
4 For my [A]iniquities are
gone over my head;
As a heavy burden they weigh
too much for me.
5 My [a]wounds grow foul *and* fester
Because of [A]my folly.
6 I am bent over and [A]greatly bowed down;
I [B]go mourning all day long.
7 For my loins are filled with [A]burning,
And there is [B]no soundness in my flesh.
8 I am [A]benumbed and [a]badly crushed;
I [b,B]groan because of the
[c]agitation of my heart.

9 Lord, all [A]my desire is [a]before You;
And my [B]sighing is not hidden from You.
10 My heart throbs, [A]my strength fails me;
And the [B]light of my eyes, even
[a]that [b]has gone from me.
11 My [a,A]loved ones and my friends
stand aloof from my plague;
And my kinsmen [B]stand afar off.
12 Those who [A]seek my life
[B]lay snares *for me;*
And those who [C]seek to injure me
have [a]threatened destruction,
And they [D]devise treachery all day long.

13 But I, like a deaf man, do not hear;
And *I am* like a [A]mute man who
does not open his mouth.
14 Yes, I am like a man who does not hear,
And in whose mouth are no arguments.
15 For [A]I [a]hope in You, O LORD;
You [B]will answer, O Lord my God.
16 For I said, "May they not rejoice over me,
Who, when my foot slips, [A]would
magnify themselves against me."
17 For I am [A]ready to fall,
And [B]my [a]sorrow is continually
before me.
18 For I [a,A]confess my iniquity;
I am full of [B]anxiety because of my sin.
19 But my [A]enemies are vigorous
and [a]strong,
And many are those who
[B]hate me wrongfully.
20 And those who [A]repay evil for good,
They [B]oppose me, because I
follow what is good.
21 Do not forsake me, O LORD;
O my God, [A]do not be far from me!
22 Make [A]haste to help me,
O Lord, [B]my salvation!

PSALM 39

THE VANITY OF LIFE.

For the choir director, for [†]Jeduthun.
A Psalm of David.

1 I said, "I will [A]guard my ways
That I [B]may not sin with my tongue;
I will guard [C]my mouth as with a muzzle
While the wicked are in my presence."

38:1 [A]Ps 6:1 38:2 [A]Job 6:4 [B]Ps 32:4 38:3 [A]Is 1:6 [B]Ps 102:10 [C]Job 33:19; Ps 6:2; 31:10 38:4 [A]Ezra 9:6; Ps 40:12 38:5 [a]Or *stripes* [A]Ps 69:5 38:6 [A]Ps 35:14 [B]Job 30:28; Ps 42:9; 43:2 38:7 [A]Ps 102:3 [B]Ps 38:3 38:8 [a]Or *greatly* [b]Lit *roar* [c]Lit *growling* [A]Lam 1:13, 20f; 2:11; 5:17 [B]Job 3:24; Ps 22:1; 32:3 38:9 [a]Or known to You [A]Ps 10:17 [B]Ps 6:6; 102:5 38:10 [a]Lit *they have* [b]Lit *is not with me* [A]Ps 31:10 [B]Ps 6:7; 69:3; 88:9 38:11 [a]Or *lovers* [A]Ps 31:11; 88:18 [B]Luke 23:49 38:12 [a]Lit *spoken* [A]Ps 54:3 [B]Ps 140:5 [C]Ps 35:4 [D]Ps 35:20 38:13 [A]Ps 39:2, 9 38:15 [a]Or *wait for* [A]Ps 39:7 [B]Ps 17:6 38:16 [A]Ps 35:26 38:17 [a]Lit *pain* [A]Ps 35:15 [B]Ps 13:2 38:18 [a]Or *declare* [A]Ps 32:5 [B]2 Cor 7:9, 10 38:19 [a]Or *numerous* [A]Ps 18:17 [B]Ps 35:19 38:20 [A]Ps 35:12 [B]Ps 109:5; 1 John 3:12 38:21 [A]Ps 22:19; 35:22 38:22 [A]Ps 40:13, 17 [B]Ps 27:1 39:1 [†]1 Chr 16:41 [A]1 Kin 2:4; 2 Kin 10:31; Ps 119:9 [B]Job 2:10; Ps 34:13; James 3:5-12 [C]Ps 141:3; James 3:2

38:1–22 Prayers surround a core of intense lament (vv. 2–20). In many ways David's laments parallel those of Job. David's perspective is that his painful plight is due, at least in part, to his personal sin. Organizationally, David's opening and closing prayers in Ps 38 relate to two onslaughts by enemies.

I. Introductory Prayer (38:1, 2)
II. First Onslaught: The Enemy Within (38:3–10)
III. Second Onslaught: Enemies Without (38:11–20)
IV. Concluding Prayers (38:21, 22)

38:Title for a memorial. Lit. "To cause to remember" (cf. the title to Ps 70). The psalmist either 1) reminds God of his plight so that He might act, or 2) reminds himself and the community of his historic predicament so that both he and they would fervently pray in similar contexts of acute suffering.

38:1 Cf. Pss 6:1; 39:11; Jer 31:18.

38:2 Your arrows. The language relates to the Divine Warrior motif; on God as Archer, cf. Dt 32:23; Job 6:4; 16:13; Ps 7:12; La 3:12, 13; etc.

38:5 my folly. On culpable ethical folly, cf. Ps 69:5. David views this as the reason for the divine chastisements of v. 3ff.

38:11 loved ones … friends … kinsmen. Those near and dear to him had abandoned him to his adversity, adding insult to injury.

38:13, 14 The ultimate example of nonresponse to tauntings and torturings may be seen in the Suffering Servant of Is 53:7; cf. 1Pe 2:23.

38:19, 20 Although he had confessed personal sins, he remained legally innocent in comparison with his persecutors.

39:1–13 Psalm 39 is an exceptionally heavy lament, which compares with Job 7 and much of Ecclesiastes. It also carries on the here-today-gone-tomorrow emphasis of Ps 37 with a new twist, an application to *all* men, especially the psalmist. In this intense lament, David will break his initial silence with two rounds of requests and reflections about the brevity and burdens of life.

I. Introduction: David's Silence (39:1–3)
II. Round One: The Brevity and Burdens of Life (39:4–6)
   A. His Request for Perspective (39:4)
   B. His Reflections on Perspective (39:5, 6)
III. Round Two: The Brevity and Burdens of Life (39:7–13)
   A. His Reflection on Hope (39:7)
   B. His Requests and Reflections on Providence (39:8–11)
   C. His Requests for Relief (39:12, 13)

39:Title for Jeduthun. This is most likely a specifically designated worship director (cf. 1Ch 9:16; 16:37ff.; 25:1–3; Ne 11:17).

39:1 I will …. will. The form of these expressions intimate strong volitional commitments. **not sin with my tongue.** This sinning could have been in one or both of two ways: 1) directly, by criticizing God for not bringing retribution on the wicked, and 2) indirectly, by complaining in the hearing of the wicked.

2 I was [A]mute [a]and silent,
I [b]refrained *even* from good,
And my [c]sorrow grew worse.
3 My [A]heart was hot within me,
While I was musing the fire burned;
Then I spoke with my tongue:
4 "LORD, make me to know [A]my end
And what is the extent of my days;
Let me know how [B]transient I am.
5 "Behold, You have made [A]my
days *as* handbreadths,
And my [B]lifetime as nothing in Your sight;
Surely every man [a]at his best is [b]a mere
[C]breath. [c]*Selah*
6 "Surely every man [A]walks
about as [a]a phantom;
Surely they make an [B]uproar for nothing;
He [C]amasses *riches* and does not
know who will gather them.

7 "And now, Lord, for what do I wait?
My [A]hope is in You.
8 "[A]Deliver me from all my transgressions;
Make me not the [B]reproach of the foolish.
9 "I have become [A]mute, I do
not open my mouth,
Because it is [B]You who have done *it*.
10 "[A]Remove Your plague from me;
Because of [B]the opposition of
Your hand I am [a]perishing.
11 "With [A]reproofs You chasten
a man for iniquity;
You [B]consume as a moth what
is precious to him;
Surely [C]every man is a mere breath. *Selah*
12 "[A]Hear my prayer, O LORD, and
give ear to my cry;
Do not be silent [B]at my tears;
For I am [C]a stranger with You,
A [D]sojourner like all my fathers.
13 "[A]Turn Your gaze away from me,
that I may [a]smile *again*
Before I depart and am no more."

PSALM 40

GOD SUSTAINS HIS SERVANT.

For the choir director. A Psalm of David.

1 I [A]waited [a]patiently for the LORD;
And He inclined to me and [B]heard my cry.
2 He brought me up out of the [A]pit of
destruction, out of the [a]miry clay,
And [B]He set my feet upon a rock
[C]making my footsteps firm.
3 He put a [A]new song in my mouth,
a song of praise to our God;
Many will [B]see and fear
And will trust in the LORD.

4 How [A]blessed is the man who has
made the LORD his trust,
And [B]has not [a]turned to the proud, nor
to those who [C]lapse into falsehood.
5 Many, O LORD my God, are [A]the
wonders which You have done,
And Your [B]thoughts toward us;
There is none to compare with You.
If I would declare and speak of them,
They [C]would be too numerous to count.

39:2 [a]Lit *with silence* [b]Lit *kept silence* [c]Lit *pain* [A]Ps 38:13 39:3 [A]Ps 32:4; Jer 20:9; Luke 24:32 39:4 [A]Job 6:11; Ps 90:12; 119:84 [B]Ps 78:39; 103:14 39:5 [a]Lit *standing firm* [b]Or *altogether vanity* [c]*Selah* may mean: *Pause, Crescendo* or *Musical interlude* [A]Ps 89:47 [B]Ps 144:4 [C]Job 14:2; Ps 62:9; Eccl 6:12 39:6 [a]Lit *an image* [A]1 Cor 7:31; James 1:10, 11; 1 Pet 1:24 [B]Ps 127:2; Eccl 5:17 [C]Ps 49:10; Eccl 2:26; 5:14; Luke 12:20 39:7 [A]Ps 38:15 39:8 [A]Ps 51:9, 14; 79:9 [B]Ps 44:13; 79:4; 119:22 39:9 [A]Ps 39:2 [B]2 Sam 16:10; Job 2:10 39:10 [a]Or *wasting away* [A]Job 9:34; 13:21 [B]Ps 32:4 39:11 [A]Ezek 5:15; 2 Pet 2:16 [B]Job 13:28; Ps 90:7; Is 50:9 [C]Ps 39:5 39:12 [A]Ps 102:1; 143:1 [B]2 Kin 20:5; Ps 56:8 [C]Lev 25:23; 1 Chr 29:15; Ps 119:19; Heb 11:13; 1 Pet 2:11 [D]Gen 47:9 39:13 [a]Or *become cheerful* [A]Job 7:19; 10:20, 21; 14:6; Ps 102:24 40:1 [a]Or *intently* [A]Ps 25:5; 27:14; 37:7 [B]Ps 34:15 40:2 [a]Lit *mud of the mire* [A]Ps 69:2, 14; Jer 38:6 [B]Ps 27:5 [C]Ps 37:23 40:3 [A]Ps 32:7; 33:3 [B]Ps 52:6; 64:9 40:4 [a]Lit *regard* [A]Ps 34:8; 84:12 [B]Job 37:24 [C]Ps 125:5 40:5 [A]Job 5:9; Ps 136:4 [B]Ps 139:17; Is 55:8 [C]Ps 71:15; 139:18

39:2 His silence did not ease his pain; it seemed to make it all the worse.

39:3 Cf. Jeremiah's predicament in Jer 20:9. **Then I spoke with my tongue.** Contrast the silence of v. 1. Yet, he did not violate the conditions of his original commitment, since he did not vent before men, but unloaded his burdens before God (cf. vv. 4ff.)

39:4 For similar prayers about the brevity and burdens of life, cf. Job 6:11; 7:7; 14:13; 16:21, 22; Ps 90:12; Ecc 2:3.

39:5 **handbreadths.** He measures the length of his life with the smallest popular measuring unit of ancient times (1Ki 7:26); cf. "four fingers" (i.e., about 2.9 in.) in Jer 52:21. **And my lifetime as nothing in Your sight.** On "measuring" God's age, cf. Ps 90:2. **breath.** For the same Heb. word, cf. Ecc 1:2ff., "vanity" (a total of 31 occurrences of this term are in Ecc); Ps 144:4. On the concept in the NT, cf. Jas 4:14.

39:6 **Surely they make an uproar for nothing.** On the futility and irony of this phenomenon, cf. Job 27:16 in context; Ecc 2:18–23; Lk 12:16–20.

39:9 In this verse, the terminology of Pss 38:13; 39:2 reappears, accompanied by the theology of Job 42.

39:11 **as a moth.** The moth normally represented one of the most destructive creatures, but here the delicacy of the moth is intended (cf. Job 13:28; Is 50:9; 51:8; Mt 6:19ff.).

39:12 **stranger ... sojourner.** He considers himself to be a temporary guest and squatter in the presence of God; on the terminology, cf. Lv 25:23; Dt 24:19ff.; 1Ch 29:15; Ps 119:19; and for the concept in the NT, cf. Heb 11:13; 1Pe 2:11.

39:13 This stark request is parallel in its intention with v. 10.

40:1–17 Psalm 40 begins with a high-flight of thanksgiving and ends with a mixture of prayer and lament (cf. the movement of Ps 27). Furthermore, the last 5 verses of Ps 40 are nearly identical to Ps 70. Crucial associations surface throughout this psalm. The first is between the theocratic king as an individual and the community of the theocratic people. Beyond this, from the vantage point of NT revelation, an association with the Greater David is contained in seed form in vv. 6–8 (cf. Heb 10:5–7). Historical precedent and prayers for a present plight move the psalm along from beginning to end. Attitudinally, David understood the importance of what would be explicitly commanded through Paul in Ro 12:1, 2. These elements constitute only a part of the richness of Ps 40. The following notes will help to follow David's mental movements through these 17 verses: two situations constitute the framework for the psalmist's publicized expressions of worship in Ps 40.

I. Precedent from a Past Situation (40:1–10)
   A. The Merciful Rescue by God (40:1–3)
   B. The Multiple Resources in God (40:4, 5)
   C. The Motivational Responses to God (40:6–10)
II. Prayers for a Present Situation (40:11–17)

40:2 **the pit of destruction ... the miry clay.** The imagery describes his past hopeless and helpless situation; cf. the language of Ps 69:2, 14; Jer 38:6ff. God by His grace had taken him from no footing to sure footing.

40:3 **a new song.** *See note on Ps 33:3.*

40:3, 4 **trust in the LORD ... the LORD his trust.** The verb and the noun forms of this important Heb. root connote a faith of confident commitment, here in the right object, God alone (cf. the teaching of Jer 17:7). David's desire was always to make such commitment contagious.

40:5 Cf. the psalmist's pleasant "frustration" in Ps 139:12–18.

6 [a,A]Sacrifice and meal offering
You have not desired;
My ears You have [b]opened;
Burnt offering and sin offering
You have not required.
7 Then I said, "Behold, I come;
In the scroll of the book it
is [a]written of me.
8 "[A]I delight to do Your will, O my God;
[B]Your Law is within my heart."

9 I have [A]proclaimed glad tidings
of righteousness in the
great congregation;
Behold, I will [B]not restrain my lips,
O LORD, [C]You know.
10 I have [A]not hidden Your righteousness
within my heart;
I have [B]spoken of Your faithfulness
and Your salvation;
I have not concealed Your
lovingkindness and Your truth
from the great congregation.

11 You, O LORD, will not withhold
Your compassion from me;
[a]Your [A]lovingkindness and Your truth
will continually preserve me.
12 For evils beyond number
have [A]surrounded me;
My [B]iniquities have overtaken me,
so that I am not able to see;
They are [C]more numerous than
the hairs of my head,
And my [D]heart has [a]failed me.

13 [A]Be pleased, O LORD, to deliver me;
Make [B]haste, O LORD, to help me.
14 Let those be [A]ashamed and
humiliated together
Who [B]seek my [a]life to destroy it;
Let those be turned back
and dishonored
Who delight [b]in my hurt.
15 Let those [A]be [a]appalled
because of their shame
Who [B]say to me, "Aha, aha!"
16 [A]Let all who seek You rejoice
and be glad in You;
Let those who love Your salvation
[B]say continually,
"The LORD be magnified!"
17 Since [A]I am afflicted and needy,
[a,B]Let the Lord be mindful of me.
You are my help and my deliverer;
Do not delay, O my God.

PSALM 41

THE PSALMIST IN SICKNESS COMPLAINS OF ENEMIES AND FALSE FRIENDS.

For the choir director. A Psalm of David.

1 How blessed is he who
[A]considers the [a]helpless;
The LORD will deliver him
[B]in a day of [b]trouble.
2 The LORD will [A]protect him
and keep him alive,
And he shall [a]be called [B]blessed
upon the earth;
And [C]do not give him over to
the desire of his enemies.
3 The LORD will sustain him
upon his sickbed;
In his illness, You [a]restore him to health.

40:6 [a]I.e. Blood sacrifice [b]Lit *dug;* or possibly *pierced* [A]1 Sam 15:22; Ps 51:16; Is 1:11; Jer 6:20; 7:22, 23; Amos 5:22; Mic 6:6-8; Heb 10:5-7 40:7 [a]Or *prescribed for* 40:8 [A]John 4:34 [B]Ps 37:31; Jer 31:33; 2 Cor 3:3 40:9 [A]Ps 22:22, 25 [B]Ps 119:13 [C]Josh 22:22; Ps 139:4 40:10 [A]Acts 20:20, 27 [B]Ps 89:1 40:11 [a]Or *May...preserve* [A]Ps 43:3; 57:3; 61:7; Prov 20:28 40:12 [a]Lit *forsaken* [A]Ps 18:5; 116:3 [B]Ps 38:4; 65:3 [C]Ps 69:4 [D]Ps 73:26 40:13 [A]Ps 70:1 [B]Ps 22:19; 71:12 40:14 [a]Or *soul* [b]Or *to injure me* [A]Ps 35:4, 26; 70:2; 71:13 [B]Ps 63:9 40:15 [a]Or *desolated* [A]Ps 70:3 [B]Ps 35:21; 70:3 40:16 [A]Ps 70:4 [B]Ps 35:27 40:17 [a]Or *The Lord is mindful* [A]Ps 70:5; 86:1; 109:22 [B]Ps 40:5; 1 Pet 5:7 41:1 [a]Or *poor* [b]Or *evil* [A]Ps 82:3, 4; Prov 14:21 [B]Ps 27:5; 37:19 41:2 [a]Or *be blessed* [A]Ps 37:28 [B]Ps 37:22 [C]Ps 27:12 41:3 [a]Lit *turn all his bed*

40:6–8 The author of Hebrews dramatically applies these verses to the Greater David (10:5–7).

40:6 **Sacrifice and meal offering You have not desired.** He is not negating the commandment to offer sacrifices, but is emphasizing their being offered with the right attitude of heart (contra. Saul, 1Sa 15:22, 23; note the emphases on proper spiritual prerequisites for sacrifices in Pss 19:14; 50:7–15; 51:15–17; 69:30, 31; Is 1:10–15; Jer 7:21–26; Hos 6:6; Am 5:21–24; Mic 6:6–8; Mt 23:23). **My ears You have opened.** Lit. "ears" or "two ears You have dug for me." This pictures obedience and dedication.

40:7 **In the scroll of the book it is written of me.** Deuteronomy 17:14–20 would apply to the lesser David; cf. likely applications regarding the Greater David in passages like Lk 24:27; Jn 5:39, 46.

40:9 **glad tidings of righteousness.** This word for "good news" in Heb. (cf. the root in Is 40:9; 41:27; 52:7; 60:6; 61:1) is the precursor of the NT terminology for the "gospel" and "preaching the gospel," i.e., "announcing the good news." "Righteousness" is identified as God's righteousness in the next verse (v. 10).

40:10 David's spirit here was encountered previously in Ps 22:22, 23.

40:12 Cf. both external persecution and internal perversity in Ps 38.

40:13–17 *See notes on Ps 70.*

41:1–13 The words of this psalm are general and apply to anyone who might be considered "down." The most painful and specific factor addressed here is the insult which is being added to the psalmist's injury (cf. Pss 6, 38; and portions of Job and Jeremiah). While the form and structure of Ps 41 are quite complex, "blessed" serves as bookends in vv. 1, 13. Within these, other elements include 1) confidence (vv. 1b–3, 11, 12), 2) prayers (vv. 4, 10), and 3) lament (vv. 5–9), with moments of wisdom and praise. David's message in Ps 41 speaks of God's tender, loving care in the critical care unit of life.

I. Recognizes Human Compassion (41:1a)
II. Revels in God's Care for the Compassionate (41:1b–3)
III. Requests Grace, Health, and Forgiveness (41:4)
IV. Rehearses the Meanness that He Has Experienced (41:5–9)
V. Requests Grace, Health, and Retribution (41:10)
VI. Revels in God's Care for Him Personally (41:11, 12)
VII. Recognizes Divine Compassion (41:13)

41:1 **blessed.** On this "blessed," cf. Pss 1:1; 2:12.

41:2 **be called blessed upon the earth.** The verb "be ... blessed" is from the same Heb. root as the exclamatory description "blessed" of v. 1 (on other occurrences of the verb, cf. Pr 3:18; 31:28; SS 6:9).

41:3 **The LORD will sustain him upon his sickbed.** This pictures God as Physician dispensing His tender, loving care.

4 As for me, I said, "O LORD,
be gracious to me;
[A]Heal my soul, for [B]I have
sinned against You."
5 My enemies [A]speak evil against me,
"When will he die, and his name perish?"
6 And [a]when he comes to see *me*,
he [A]speaks [b]falsehood;
His heart gathers wickedness to itself;
When he goes outside, he tells it.
7 All who hate me whisper
together against me;
Against me they [A]devise my hurt, *saying*,
8 "A wicked thing is poured out [a]upon him,
That when he lies down, he
will [A]not rise up again."
9 Even my [A]close friend in whom I trusted,
Who ate my bread,
Has lifted up his heel against me.

10 But You, O LORD, be gracious
to me and [A]raise me up,
That I may repay them.
11 By this I know that [A]You are
pleased with me,
Because [B]my enemy does not
shout in triumph over me.
12 As for me, [A]You uphold me
in my integrity,
And You set me [B]in Your presence forever.

13 [A]Blessed be the LORD, the God of Israel,
From everlasting to everlasting.
Amen and Amen.

BOOK 2

PSALM 42

THIRSTING FOR GOD IN TROUBLE AND EXILE.

For the choir director. A [†]Maskil of the sons of Korah.

1 As the deer [a]pants for the water brooks,
So my soul [a,A]pants for You, O God.
2 My soul [A]thirsts for God, for the [B]living God;
When shall I come and
[a,C]appear before God?
3 My [A]tears have been my food day and night,
While *they* [B]say to me all day
long, "Where is your God?"
4 These things I remember and I
[A]pour out my soul within me.
For I [B]used to go along with the
throng *and* [a]lead them in
procession to the house of God,
With the voice of [C]joy and thanksgiving,
a multitude keeping festival.

5 [A]Why are you [a,B]in despair, O my soul?
And *why* have you become
[C]disturbed within me?
[b,D]Hope in God, for I shall [c]again praise [d]Him
For the [e,E]help of His presence.
6 O my God, my soul is [a]in despair within me;
Therefore I [A]remember You from
[B]the land of the Jordan
And the [b]peaks of [C]Hermon,
from Mount Mizar.

41:4 [A]Ps 6:2; 103:3; 147:3 [B]Ps 51:4 41:5 [A]Ps 38:12 41:6 [a]Or *if he* [b]Or *emptiness* [A]Ps 12:2; 62:4; Prov 26:24-26 41:7 [A]Ps 56:5 41:8 [a]Or *within* [A]Ps 71:10, 11 41:9 [A]2 Sam 15:12; Job 19:13, 19; Ps 55:12, 13, 20; Jer 20:10; Mic 7:5; Matt 26:23; Luke 22:21; John 13:18 41:10 [A]Ps 3:3 41:11 [A]Ps 37:23; 147:11 [B]Ps 25:2 41:12 [A]Ps 18:32; 37:17; 63:8 [B]Job 36:7; Ps 21:6 41:13 [A]Ps 72:18, 19; 89:52; 106:48; 150:6 42:1 [†]Possibly *Contemplative*, or *Didactic*, or *Skillful Psalm* [a]Lit *longs for* [A]Ps 119:131 42:2 [a]Some mss read *see the face of God* [A]Ps 63:1; 84:2; 143:6 [B]Josh 3:10; Ps 84:2; Jer 10:10; Dan 6:26; Matt 26:63; Rom 9:26; 1 Thess 1:9 [C]Ex 23:17; Ps 43:4; 84:7 42:3 [A]Ps 80:5; 102:9 [B]Ps 79:10; 115:2; Joel 2:17; Mic 7:10 42:4 [a]Or *move slowly with them* [A]1 Sam 1:15; Job 30:16; Ps 62:8; Lam 2:19 [B]Ps 55:14; 122:1; Is 30:29 [C]Ps 100:4 42:5 [a]Or *sunk down* [b]Or *Wait for* [c]Or *still* [d]Some ancient versions read *Him, the help of my countenance and my God* [e]Or *saving acts of* [A]Ps 42:11; 43:5 [B]Ps 38:6; Matt 26:38 [C]Ps 77:3 [D]Ps 71:14; Lam 3:24 [E]Ps 44:3 42:6 [a]Or *sunk down* [b]Lit *Hermons* [A]Ps 61:2 [B]2 Sam 17:22 [C]Deut 3:8

41:4 **for I have sinned against You.** The ancient Near Eastern association of sin and sickness returns (cf. Pss 31:10; 32:5; 38:3, 4, 18; 40:12; etc.). On the explicit combination of "sinning against," cf. Ps 51:4. This perspective of the psalmist does not negate the reference to his basic "integrity" in v. 12.

41:6 **And when he comes ... he goes outside.** This hypocritical "sick call" really adds insult to injury. The visitor lies to the sick one and gathers "information" for more slander.

41:9 **Even my close friend ... lifted up his heel against me.** David's close companion betrayed him; he kicked him while he was "down." The Greater David's experience and the employment of this reference in Jn 13:18 was to Judas (cf. Mt 26:21ff.).

41:13 **Blessed be.** The essence of the Heb. root of "amen" is "it is true," i.e., reliable, confirmed, verified. Note that Book I of the Psalms (Pss 1–41) closes with a doxology; cf. the endings of the other 4 books (Pss 72:18, 19; 89:52; 106:48; 150:6).

42:1–11 As in the case of Pss 9 and 10, Pss 42 and 43 were originally probably one. Some ancient manuscripts put them together; Ps 43 has no title, while the rest around it do. In form, Ps 42 may be considered an individual lament. This psalm also exemplifies a primary characteristic of Book II of the Psalms, the preference of the ascription "God" (or parallels to it) for the Deity. The occasion and situation of Ps 42 are historically unspecified; however, what is obvious is that the psalmist's situation was intense and greatly aggravated by his surrounding mockers. Consequently, Ps 42 is a dirge of two stanzas.

I. Stanza One: The Psalmist Sings of His Drought (42:1–5)
   A. The Content of This Stanza (42:1–4)
   B. The Chorus of This Dirge (cf. v. 11) (42:5)
II. Stanza Two: The Psalmist Sings of His Drowning (42:6–11)
   A. The Content of This Stanza (42:6–10)
   B. The Chorus of This Dirge (cf. v. 5) (42:11)

42:Title The references to "the choir director," i.e., the worship director, and Maskil, a "contemplation" or lesson (see marginal note; cf. Ps 32:1) are not new, but the reference to "the sons of Korah" is. On the ancestry of "the sons of Korah," cf. Nu 26:10ff.; 1Ch 6:16ff.; 2Ch 20:19. A total of 11 psalms are associated with this group, and 7 of them are found in Book II (Pss 42, 44, 45, 46, 47, 48, 49). These people are probably better regarded as the Levitical performers, rather than the authors of these psalms (i.e., "For the sons of Korah").

42:1 **As the deer pants ... my soul pants.** On this simile from nature, cf. Joel 1:20. In the psalmist's estimation, he is facing a severe divine drought.

42:2 **My soul thirsts for God.** On this desire for the water of God, cf. Ps 36:8, 9; Is 41:17; 55:1; Jer 2:13; 14:1–9; 17:13; Jn 4:10; 7:37, 38; Rev 7:17; 21:6; 22:1, 17.

42:4 **These things I remember and I pour out my soul.** Such language also characterizes Jeremiah's Lamentations, indicating a heavy dirge. On "pouring out one's soul" or "heart," cf. 1Sa 1:15; Ps 62:8; La 2:19. These are attempts at trying to unburden oneself from intolerable pain, grief, and agony.

42:5 **in despair ... disturbed.** In this active introspection the psalmist rebukes himself for his despondency.

42:6 **the land of the Jordan ... the peaks of Hermon ... Mount Mizar.** The Jordan and Mt. Hermon notations refer to a location in northern Israel, an area of headwaters which flow southward. These locations signal that a sharp contrast in the word pictures describing the psalmist's change in condition is imminent. He is about to move from drought to drowning (cf. vv. 7ff.). The location and significance of Mt. Mizar is not known.

7 Deep calls to deep at the sound
of Your waterfalls;
All Your [A]breakers and Your
waves have rolled over me.
8 The LORD will [A]command His
lovingkindness in the daytime;
And His song will be with
me [B]in the night,
A prayer to [C]the God of my life.

9 I will say to God [A]my rock, "Why
have You forgotten me?
Why do I go [B]mourning [a]because of
the [C]oppression of the enemy?"
10 As a shattering of my bones, my
adversaries revile me,
While they [A]say to me all day
long, "Where is your God?"
11 [A]Why are you [a]in despair, O my soul?
And why have you become
disturbed within me?
[b]Hope in God, for I shall yet praise Him,
The [c]help of my countenance and my God.

PSALM 43

PRAYER FOR DELIVERANCE.

1 [A]Vindicate me, O God, and [B]plead my
case against an ungodly nation;
[a]O deliver me from [C]the deceitful
and unjust man!
2 For You are the [A]God of my strength;
why have You [B]rejected me?
Why do I go [C]mourning [a]because of
the oppression of the enemy?

3 O send out Your [A]light and Your
truth, let them lead me;
Let them bring me to Your [B]holy hill
And to Your [C]dwelling places.
4 Then I will go to [A]the altar of God,
To God [a]my exceeding [B]joy;
And upon the [C]lyre I shall praise
You, O God, my God.

5 [A]Why are you [a]in despair, O my soul?
And why are you disturbed within me?
[b]Hope in God, for I shall
[c]again praise Him,
The [d]help of my countenance and my God.

PSALM 44

FORMER DELIVERANCES AND PRESENT TROUBLES.

For the choir director. A [†]Maskil
of the sons of Korah.

1 O God, we have heard with our ears,
Our [A]fathers have told us
The [B]work that You did in their days,
In the [C]days of old.
2 You with Your own hand
[A]drove out the nations;
Then You [B]planted them;
You [C]afflicted the peoples,
Then You [D]spread them abroad.

42:7 [A]Ps 69:1, 2; 88:7; Jon 2:3 42:8 [A]Ps 57:3; 133:3 [B]Job 35:10; Ps 16:7; 63:6; 77:6; 149:5 [C]Eccl 5:18; 8:15 42:9 [a]Or *while the enemy oppresses* [A]Ps 18:2 [B]Ps 38:6 [C]Ps 17:9 42:10 [A]Ps 42:3; Joel 2:17 42:11 [a]Or *sunk down* [b]Or *Wait for* [c]Or *saving acts of* [A]Ps 42:5; 43:5 43:1 [a]Or *May You* [A]Ps 26:1; 35:24 [B]1 Sam 24:15; Ps 35:1 [C]Ps 5:6; 38:12 43:2 [a]Or *while the enemy oppresses* [A]Ps 18:1; 28:7; 31:4 [B]Ps 44:9; 88:14 [C]Ps 42:9 43:3 [A]Ps 36:9 [B]Ps 2:6; 3:4; 42:4; 46:4 [C]Ps 84:1 43:4 [a]Lit *the gladness of my joy* [A]Ps 26:6 [B]Ps 21:6 [C]Ps 33:2; 49:4; 57:8; 71:22 43:5 [a]Or *sunk down* [b]Or *Wait for* [c]Or *still* [d]Or *saving acts of* [A]Ps 42:5, 11 44:1 [†]Possibly *Contemplative*, or *Didactic*, or *Skillful Psalm* [A]Ex 12:26, 27; Deut 6:20; Judg 6:13; Ps 78:3 [B]Ps 78:12 [C]Deut 32:7; Ps 77:5; Is 51:9; 63:9 44:2 [A]Josh 3:10; Neh 9:24; Ps 78:55; 80:8 [B]Ex 15:17; 2 Sam 7:10; Jer 24:6; Amos 9:15 [C]Ps 135:10-12 [D]Ps 80:9-11; Zech 2:6

42:7 Deep … Your waterfalls … Your waves. He alleges that God is ultimately responsible for the oceans of trial in which he seems to be drowning.

42:8 The LORD will command His lovingkindness. This statement of confidence interrupts his laments (cf. their continuance in vv. 9, 10), providing a few gracious gulps of divine "air" under the cascading inundations of his trials and tormentors.

43:1–5 Psalm 43 might be conceived of as an epilogue to Ps 42. The psalmist moves away from introspection toward invocation. However, as v. 5 will indicate, the psalmist's problems had not ended, at least not fully and finally. Nevertheless, spiritual progress is evident. By interrelating the psalmist's two modes of communication in Ps 43 and then by comparing them with the laments of Ps 42, one observes indications of that progress as *he continued to deal with his despondency.*

I. Prayers to God (43:1–4)
   A. Righting Wrongs (43:1, 2)
   B. Restoring "Rights" (i.e., proper or appropriate things) (43:3, 4)
II. "Pep-talks" to Oneself (43:5)
   A. Exhortation (43:5a-b)
   B. Encouragement (43:5c-d)

43:1 Vindicate me … plead my case. Lit. "Judge me, O God, and argue my case." This combination of legal terms demonstrates respectively that the psalmist was requesting God to be both his Divine Judge (cf. Jdg 11:27; 1Sa 24:12; Pss 7:8; 26:1) and Defense Attorney (cf. Ps 119:154; Pr 22:23; 23:11; Jer 50:34; La 3:58). On both concepts together, as here, cf. 1Sa 24:15; Ps 35:1, 24; Mic 7:9.

43:2 why …. Why … ? Since God was his refuge of strength, the psalmist questioned why this divine rejection and why his dejection?

43:3 Your light and Your truth, let them lead me. These are bold personifications for divine guidance. He desired that these "messenger-attributes" divinely direct (cf. such "leading" and "guiding" in Ge 24:48; Pss 78:14, 53, 72; 107:30; Is 57:18) so as to bring him successfully to his destination, i.e., Israel's designated place for worship.

43:5 Why … why … Hope. Cf. Ps 42:5, 11.

44:1–26 Psalm 44 is a national lament following some great but historically unidentifiable defeat in battle. Throughout this psalm there are subtle shifts between speakers of the first person plural (i.e., "We" and "us"; cf. vv. 1–3, 5, 7, 8, 9–14, 17–22) and the first person singular (i.e., "I" or "my"; cf. vv. 4, 6, 15–16). This may indicate that the psalm was originally sung antiphonally with alterations coming from both the beaten king-general and his defeated nation. The prayers of vv. 23–26 may have been offered in unison as a climax. By employing 3 historical centers in Ps 44, the psalmist tries to understand and deal with a national tragedy.

I. Focus on Past History: The Shock of This National Tragedy (44:1–8)
II. Focus on Current History: The Inscrutability of This National Tragedy (44:9–22)
III. Focus on Future History: A Prayer for an End to This National Tragedy (44:23–26)

44:Title The words of this title are the same as those in the title of Ps 42; however, in the Hebrew text their order is slightly different.

44:1 we have heard. There was a rich tradition about God's great acts which the nation's fathers had passed on. Indeed the rehearsal of holy history was commanded (cf. Ex 10:1, 2; 12:26ff.; 13:14ff.; Dt 6:20ff.; Jos 4:6ff.; Ps 78:3).

44:2 You planted. On the imagery of God's planting His people, cf. 2Sa 7:10; Is 5:1ff.; Jer 12:2; also cf. their being planted and taking root in Ps 80:8–11.

3 For by their own sword they
[A]did not possess the land,
And their own arm did not save them,
But Your right hand and Your [B]arm
and the [C]light of Your presence,
For You [D]favored them.

4 You are [A]my King, O God;
[B]Command [a]victories for Jacob.
5 Through You we will [A]push
back our adversaries;
Through Your name we will [B]trample
down those who rise up against us.
6 For I will [A]not trust in my bow,
Nor will my sword save me.
7 But You [A]have saved us from
our adversaries,
And You have [B]put to shame
those who hate us.
8 In God we have [A]boasted all day long,
And we will [B]give thanks to Your name
forever. [a]*Selah*

9 Yet You [A]have rejected *us* and
brought us to [B]dishonor,
And [C]do not go out with our armies.
10 You cause us to [A]turn back
from the adversary;
And those who hate us [B]have
taken spoil for themselves.
11 You give us as [A]sheep [a]to be eaten
And have [B]scattered us
among the nations.
12 You [A]sell Your people [a]cheaply,
And have not [b]profited by their sale.
13 You make us a [A]reproach
to our neighbors,
A scoffing and a [B]derision
to those around us.
14 You make us [A]a byword
among the nations,
A [a,B]laughingstock among the peoples.
15 All day long my dishonor is before me
And [a]my [A]humiliation has
overwhelmed me,

44:3 [A]Deut 8:17, 18; Josh 24:12 [B]Ps 77:15 [C]Ps 4:6; 89:15 [D]Deut 4:37; 7:7, 8; 10:15; Ps 106:4 44:4 [a]Lit *salvation* [A]Ps 74:12 [B]Ps 42:8 44:5 [A]Deut 33:17; Ps 60:12; Dan 8:4 [B]Ps 108:13; Zech 10:5 44:6 [A]1 Sam 17:47; Ps 33:16; Hos 1:7 44:7 [A]Ps 136:24 [B]Ps 53:5 44:8 [a]*Selah* may mean: *Pause, Crescendo* or *Musical interlude* [A]Ps 34:2 [B]Ps 30:12 44:9 [A]Ps 43:2; 60:1, 10; 74:1; 89:38; 108:11 [B]Ps 69:19 [C]Ps 60:10; 108:11 44:10 [A]Lev 26:17; Josh 7:8, 12; Ps 89:43 [B]Ps 89:41 44:11 [a]Lit *for food* [A]Ps 44:22; Rom 8:36 [B]Lev 26:33; Deut 4:27; 28:64; Ps 106:27; Ezek 20:23 44:12 [a]Lit *for no wealth* [b]Or *set a high price on them* [A]Deut 32:30; Judg 2:14; 3:8; Is 52:3, 4; Jer 15:13 44:13 [A]Deut 28:37; Ps 79:4; 89:41 [B]Ps 80:6; Ezek 23:32 44:14 [a]Lit *shaking of the head* [A]Job 17:6; Ps 69:11; Jer 24:9 [B]2 Kin 19:21; Ps 109:25 44:15 [a]Lit *the shame of my face has covered me* [A]2 Chr 32:21; Ps 69:7

44:3 they did not … But Your right hand. This is a brief historical summary of the theology of divine grace, intervention, and enablement (cf. Jos 24:17, 18).

44:4 Command victories for Jacob. If the division of the Heb. consonants is taken at a different point (as it is in some early versions), this line would better fit into the immediate context, reading: "You are my King, my God, who commands [or, orders] victories for Jacob." "Jacob," the original name of the ancient patriarch, is often used to designate the nation of Israel, especially in poetry.

44:5–8 Through You … For I will not trust in my bow … But You have saved us. The defeated king-general picks up the theology of v. 3 and adds his personal commitment to it.

44:9 Yet You … do not go out with our armies. The Lord God is viewed here as having resigned His commission as the nation's Divine Warrior.

44:11–16 You give … You sell. These are graphic descriptions of God superintending the defeat and utter humiliation of the nation.

ANOINTING OF THE HOLY SPIRIT IN THE OLD TESTAMENT

Old Testament Israel had mediators who stood between God and His people. To empower the OT mediators, the Holy Spirit gave special administrative ability to carry out the management of the nation and military skills which enabled them to defeat the theocracy's enemies. The Lord first anointed Moses with this ministry of the Spirit and then, in a truly dramatic scene, took some of this ministry of the Spirit and shared it with the 70 elders. Thus they were enabled to help Moses administer Israel (Nu 11:17–25).

Also Joshua (Dt 34:9), the judges (Jdg 3:10; 6:34), and the kings of united Israel and the southern kingdom were anointed with this special ministry of the Spirit. When the Spirit of the Lord came upon King Saul, for example, "God changed his heart" (1Sa 10:6–10). This does not mean that he was regenerated at this point in his life, but that he was given skills to be a king. Later the theocratic anointing was taken from Saul and given to David (1Sa 16:1–14). Saul, from that time on, became a totally incapable leader.

King David no doubt had this special ministry of the Spirit in mind in his prayer of repentance in Psalm 51. He was not afraid of losing his salvation when he prayed, "do not take Your Holy Spirit from me" (Ps 51:11), but rather was concerned that God would remove His spiritual wisdom and administrative skill from him. David had earlier seen such a tragedy in the life of Saul when that king of Israel lost the anointing of the Holy Spirit. David was thus pleading with God not to remove His hand of guidance.

King Solomon also perceived his youthful inabilities at the beginning of his reign and requested God to give him special wisdom in administering Israel. God was greatly pleased with this request and granted an extra measure to the young man (1Ki 3:7–12, 28; 4:29–34). Although the OT is silent in this regard about the kings who succeeded Solomon, the theocratic anointing of the Spirit likely came on all of the descendants of David in connection with the Davidic Covenant.

When the theocracy went out of existence as Judah was carried away into captivity, and the last Davidic king was disempowered, the theocratic anointing was no longer given (Eze 8–11). The kings of the northern tribes, on the other hand, being essentially apostate and not in the Davidic line, never had the benefit of this special ministry of the Spirit.

16 Because of the voice of him who
[A]reproaches and reviles,
Because of the presence of the
[B]enemy and the avenger.

17 All this has come upon us, but we
have [A]not forgotten You,
And we have not [B]dealt falsely
with Your covenant.
18 Our heart has not [A]turned back,
And our steps [B]have not
deviated from Your way,
19 Yet You have [A]crushed us in
a place of [B]jackals
And covered us with [C]the
shadow of death.

20 If we had [A]forgotten the name of our God
Or extended our [a]hands
to [B]a strange god,
21 Would not God [A]find this out?
For He knows the secrets of the heart.
22 But [A]for Your sake we are
killed all day long;
We are considered as [B]sheep
to be slaughtered.
23 [A]Arouse Yourself, why [B]do
You sleep, O Lord?
Awake, [C]do not reject us forever.
24 Why do You [A]hide Your face
And [B]forget our affliction
and our oppression?
25 For our [A]soul has sunk down into the dust;
Our body cleaves to the earth.
26 [A]Rise up, be our help,
And [B]redeem us for the sake of
Your lovingkindness.

PSALM 45

A SONG CELEBRATING THE KING'S MARRIAGE.

For the choir director; according to the [†]Shoshannim. A [•]Maskil of the sons of Korah. A Song of Love.

1 My heart [a]overflows with a good theme;
I [b]address my [c]verses to the [d]King;
My tongue is the pen of [A]a ready writer.
2 You are fairer than the sons of men;
[A]Grace is poured [a]upon Your lips;
Therefore God has [B]blessed You forever.

3 Gird [A]Your sword on *Your*
thigh, O [a,B]Mighty One,
In Your splendor and Your majesty!
4 And in Your majesty ride on victoriously,
For the cause of truth and
[A]meekness *and* righteousness;
Let Your [B]right hand teach
You [a]awesome things.
5 Your [A]arrows are sharp;
The [B]peoples fall under You;
Your arrows are [C]in the heart
of the King's enemies.

6 [A]Your throne, O God, is forever and ever;
A scepter of [B]uprightness is the
scepter of Your kingdom.
7 You have [A]loved righteousness
and hated wickedness;
Therefore God, Your God,
has [B]anointed You
With the oil of joy above Your fellows.
8 All Your garments are *fragrant with*
[A]myrrh and aloes *and* cassia;

44:16 [A]Ps 74:10 [B]Ps 8:2 44:17 [A]Ps 78:7; 119:61, 83, 109, 141, 153, 176 [B]Ps 78:57 44:18 [A]Ps 78:57 [B]Job 23:11; Ps 119:51, 157 44:19 [A]Ps 51:8; 94:5 [B]Job 30:29; Is 13:22; Jer 9:11 [C]Job 3:5; Ps 23:4 44:20 [a]Lit *palms* [A]Ps 78:11 [B]Deut 6:14; Ps 81:9 44:21 [A]Ps 139:1, 2; Jer 17:10 44:22 [A]Rom 8:36 [B]Is 53:7; Jer 12:3 44:23 [A]Ps 7:6 [B]Ps 78:65 [C]Ps 77:7 44:24 [A]Job 13:24; Ps 88:14 [B]Ps 42:9; Lam 5:20 44:25 [A]Ps 119:25 44:26 [A]Ps 35:2 [B]Ps 6:4; 25:22 45:1 [†]Or possibly *Lilies* [•]Possibly *Contemplative*, or *Didactic*, or *Skillful Psalm* [a]Lit *is astir* [b]Lit *am saying* [c]Lit *works* [d]Probably refers to Solomon as a type of Christ [A]Ezra 7:6 45:2 [a]Or *through* [A]Luke 4:22 [B]Ps 21:6 45:3 [a]Or *warrior* [A]Heb 4:12; Rev 1:16 [B]Is 9:6 45:4 [a]Or *fearful* [A]Zeph 2:3 [B]Ps 21:8 45:5 [A]Ps 18:14; 120:4; Is 5:28; 7:13 [B]Ps 92:9 [C]2 Sam 18:14 45:6 [A]Ps 93:2; Heb 1:8, 9 [B]Ps 98:9 45:7 [A]Ps 11:7; 33:5 [B]Ps 2:2 45:8 [A]Song 4:14; John 19:39

44:17–21 but we have not forgotten You ... If we had forgotten the name of our God. The nation's recent defeat was painfully perplexing in view of their basic loyalty to God.

44:22 But for Your sake. They had no specific answers; only this inescapable conclusion that, by God's sovereign will, they were allowed to be destroyed by their enemies. Cf. Paul's quote of this verse in Ro 8:36 and its general principle in Mt 5:10–12; 1Pe 3:13–17; 4:12–16.

44:23 Arouse ... Awake. Cf. Ps 35:23. God does not actually sleep. This is only in appearance to man's perception.

44:26 Rise up. Cf. Nu 10:35; Pss 3:7; 7:6. **redeem us for ... Your lovingkindness.** The psalm therefore comes full circle from the history of God's gracious redemption (vv. 1–3) to the hope for the same in the near future (v. 26).

45:1–17 Some portions of Ps 45 convey a secular emphasis, while others suggest a sacred extension. Upon the occasion of a royal wedding, the psalmist offers a 3-part song of celebration.

I. Poetic Preface (45:1)
II. Song of Celebration (45:2–16)
  A. The King-Groom (45:2–9)
    1. Endowments of the king-groom (45:2)
    2. Exploits of the king-groom (45:3–5)
    3. Elevation of the king-groom (45:6, 7)
    4. Eminence of the king-groom (45:8, 9)
  B. The Princess-Bride (45:10–15)
    1. A challenge to the princess-bride (45:10–12)
    2. The procession of the princess-bride (45:13–15)
  C. Future Children from This Union (45:16)
III. Poetic Postscript (45:17)

45:Title Two new notations are found, "according to the Shoshannim" and "A Song of Love." The first most likely had to do with the tune used in accompaniment with its words. The second notation referring to its content probably indicated that this psalm was a wedding song, and even more specifically, a royal wedding composition.

45:1 My heart overflows ... My tongue. The psalmist is overwhelmed with emotion upon the occasion of the king's marriage; consequently, he puts his stirred-up mind and feelings into words. In v. 2ff. his tongue is the brush that he uses to paint vivid word pictures.

45:2 You are fairer. I.e., you are "more beautiful than," or, "most handsome among" (cf. an ancient prerequisite for kingship; in the Bible note the comments, e.g., in 1Sa 9:2; 10:23; 16:12; 2Sa 14:25; 1Ki 1:6; SS 5:10; Is 33:17). **Grace is poured upon Your lips.** The implication is that God has anointed the king's words (cf. Ecc 10:12; Lk 4:22).

45:3–5 Gird Your sword. In these verses the psalmist wishes the king future victories in battle.

45:6, 7 Your throne, O God. Since this king-groom was likely a member of the Davidic dynasty (e.g., 2Sa 7), there was a near and immediate application (cf. 1Ch 28:5; 29:23). Through progressive revelation (i.e., Heb 1:8, 9), we learn of the ultimate application to "a greater than Solomon" who is God—the Lord Jesus Christ.

Out of ivory palaces [B]stringed
instruments have made You glad.
9 Kings' daughters are among
[A]Your noble ladies;
At Your [B]right hand stands the
queen in [C]gold from Ophir.

10 Listen, O daughter, give attention
and incline your ear:
[A]Forget your people and
your father's house;
11 Then the King will desire your beauty.
Because He is your [A]Lord,
[B]bow down to Him.
12 The daughter of [A]Tyre *will*
come with a gift;
The [B]rich among the people
will seek your favor.

13 The King's daughter is
all glorious within;
Her clothing is [A]interwoven with gold.
14 She will be [A]led to the King [B]in
embroidered work;
The [C]virgins, her companions
who follow her,
Will be brought to You.
15 They will be led forth with
gladness and rejoicing;
They will enter into the King's palace.

16 In place of your fathers will be your sons;
You shall make them princes
in all the earth.
17 I will cause [A]Your name to be
remembered in all generations;
Therefore the peoples [B]will give
You thanks forever and ever.

PSALM 46

GOD THE REFUGE OF HIS PEOPLE.

For the choir director. *A Psalm* of the sons
of Korah, [†]set to Alamoth. A Song.

1 God is our [A]refuge and strength,
[a]A very [B]present help [C]in [b]trouble.
2 Therefore we will [A]not fear, though
[B]the earth should change
And though [C]the mountains slip
into the heart of the [a]sea;
3 Though its [A]waters roar *and* foam,
Though the mountains quake at its
swelling pride. [a]*Selah*

4 There is a [A]river whose streams
make glad the [B]city of God,
The holy [C]dwelling places
of the Most High.
5 God is [A]in the midst of her, she
will not be moved;
God will [B]help her [a]when morning dawns.
6 The [a]nations [A]made an uproar,
the kingdoms tottered;
He [b,B]raised His voice, the earth [C]melted.
7 The LORD of hosts [A]is with us;
The God of Jacob is [B]our stronghold.
Selah

45:8 [B]Ps 150:4 45:9 [A]Song 6:8 [B]1 Kin 2:19 [C]1 Kin 9:28; Is 13:12 45:10 [A]Deut 21:13; Ruth 1:16, 17 45:11 [A]Gen 18:12; 1 Pet 3:6 [B]Eph 5:33 45:12 [A]Ps 87:4 [B]Ps 22:29; 68:29; 72:10, 11; Is 49:23 45:13 [A]Ex 39:2, 3 45:14 [A]Song 1:4 [B]Judg 5:30; Ezek 16:10 [C]Ps 45:9 45:17 [A]Mal 1:11 [B]Ps 138:4 46:1 [†]Possibly *for soprano voices* [a]Or *Abundantly available for help* [b]Or *tight places* [A]Ps 14:6; 62:7, 8 [B]Deut 4:7; Ps 145:18 [C]Ps 9:9 46:2 [a]Lit *seas* [A]Ps 23:4; 27:1 [B]Ps 82:5 [C]Ps 18:7 46:3 [a]*Selah* may mean: *Pause, Crescendo* or *Musical interlude* [A]Ps 93:3, 4; Jer 5:22 46:4 [A]Ps 36:8; 65:9; Is 8:6; Rev 22:1 [B]Ps 48:1; 87:3; 101:8; Is 60:14; Rev 3:12 [C]Ps 43:3 46:5 [a]Lit *at the turning of the morning* [A]Deut 23:14; Is 12:6; Ezek 43:7, 9; Hos 11:9; Joel 2:27; Zech 2:5 [B]Ps 37:40; Is 41:14; Luke 1:54 46:6 [a]Or *Gentiles* [b]Lit *gave forth* [A]Ps 2:1, 2 [B]Ps 18:13; 68:33; Jer 25:30; Joel 2:11; Amos 1:2 [C]Amos 9:5; Mic 1:4; Nah 1:5 46:7 [A]Num 14:9; 2 Chr 13:12 [B]Ps 9:9; 48:3

45:9 **Kings' daughters ... noble ladies ... the queen.** This court picture could refer to royal female guests, but also includes the other wives and concubines of the king-groom (cf. the situation with Solomon in 1Ki 11:1). Such polygamy, of course, was prohibited by God's Word; unfortunately, it was still common among the kings of Israel. **gold from Ophir.** Although its geographical location is not known, "Ophir" was well known as the location of the purest gold.

45:10–15 **O daughter.** The major emphasis of this portion is "Here comes the bride!" However, even in this section the focus still concentrates, according to ancient Near Eastern precedent, upon the royal groom.

45:16 **In place of your fathers will be your sons.** The loyal and joyful poet now speaks of the blessings of anticipated children from this union.

46:1–11 Psalm 46 was the scriptural catalyst for Martin Luther's great hymn, "A Mighty Fortress Is Our God." This psalm also launches a trilogy of psalms (i.e., 46, 47, 48); they are all songs of triumph. Furthermore, it has also been grouped among the so-called "songs of Zion" (cf. Pss 48, 76, 84, 87, 122). Psalm 46 extols the adequacy of God in facing threats from nature and the nations. God indeed protects (cf. vv. 1, 7, 11) His people upon the earth (cf. vv. 2, 6, 8, 9, 10). The major burden of Ps 46 is that God provides stability for His people who live in two exceedingly unstable environments.

I. The Unstable Environment of Nature (46:1–3)
   A. The Affirmation of His Stability (46:1)
   B. The Application of His Stability (46:2, 3)
II. The Unstable Environment of the Nations (46:4–11)
   A. The First Chorus (46:4–7)
   B. The Follow-Up Chorus (46:8–11)

46:Title The new element in this title is "Alamoth." The early Gr. translation (LXX) interprets this technical term as "hidden things." However, the Heb. word normally has to do with "girls" or "young maidens." Consequently, the most likely conjecture about this phrase is that it is a technical musical notation, possibly indicating a song which was to be sung with female voices at a higher range.

46:2 **though the earth should change.** I.e., "When earth changes and when mountains move (or) shake (or) totter (or) slip ...." (cf. the language of Is 24:19, 20; 54:10; Hag 2:6). These are poetic allusions to earthquakes. Since "the earth" and "mountains" are regarded by men as symbols of stability, when they "dance" great terror normally ensues. But when the most stable becomes unstable, there should be "no fear" because of the transcendent stability of God.

46:3 **Though its waters roar.** This is an illustration of powerfully surging and potentially destructive floods of waters. These will not erode God's protective fortifications.

46:4 **There is a river whose streams.** These words about refreshing waters contrast with those about the threatening torrents of v. 3. Cf. the garden of paradise concept often mentioned in ancient Near Eastern literature, but most importantly, cf. the biblical revelation, noting especially the "bookends" of Ge 2:10 and Rev 22:1, 2. **the city of God.** These words in their present setting refer to Jerusalem, God's chosen earthly residence (cf. Ps 48:1, 2; Is 60:14).

46:5, 6 **she will not be moved.** These verses pick up some of the key terms about moving, slipping, tottering, sliding, and roaring from vv. 1–3; however, here, because of the presence of God, the forces of nature and the nations are no longer a threat to the people of God who dwell with Him.

46:7 **The LORD of hosts is with us.** The precious personal presence (cf. "God with us" in Is 7:14; 8:8, 10) of the Divine Warrior (cf. "LORD of hosts" or "armies," e.g., Pss 24:10; 48:8; 59:5) secures the safety of His people.

8 Come, [A]behold the works of the LORD,
[a]Who has wrought [B]desolations
in the earth.
9 He [A]makes wars to cease to
the end of the earth;
He [B]breaks the bow and cuts
the spear in two;
He [C]burns the chariots with fire.
10 "[a]Cease *striving* and [A]know that I am God;
I will be [B]exalted among the [b]nations,
I will be exalted in the earth."
11 The LORD of hosts is with us;
The God of Jacob is our stronghold.
Selah

PSALM 47

GOD THE KING OF THE EARTH.

For the choir director. A Psalm
of the sons of Korah.

1 O [A]clap your hands, all peoples;
[B]Shout to God with the voice of [a]joy.
2 For the LORD Most High is to be [A]feared,
A [B]great King over all the earth.
3 He [A]subdues peoples under us
And nations under our feet.
4 He chooses our [A]inheritance for us,
The [B]glory of Jacob whom He loves.
[a]*Selah*
5 God has [A]ascended [a]with a shout,
The LORD, [a]with the [B]sound of a trumpet.
6 [A]Sing praises to God, sing praises;
Sing praises to [B]our King, sing praises.
7 For God is the [A]King of all the earth;
Sing praises [B]with a [a]skillful psalm.
8 God [A]reigns over the nations,
God [a]sits on [B]His holy throne.
9 The [a,A]princes of the people have
assembled themselves *as* the
[B]people of the God of Abraham,
For the [C]shields of the earth belong to God;
He [b]is [D]highly exalted.

PSALM 48

THE BEAUTY AND GLORY OF ZION.

A Song; a Psalm of the sons of Korah.

1 [A]Great is the LORD, and
greatly to be praised,
In the [B]city of our God, His
[C]holy mountain.
2 [A]Beautiful in elevation, [B]the
joy of the whole earth,
Is Mount Zion *in* the far north,
The [C]city of the great King.
3 God, in her palaces,
Has made Himself known
as a [A]stronghold.

46:8 [a]Or *Which He has wrought as desolations* [A]Ps 66:5 [B]Is 61:4; Jer 51:43 46:9 [A]Is 2:4; Mic 4:3 [B]1 Sam 2:4; Ps 76:3 [C]Is 9:5; Ezek 39:9 46:10 [a]Or *Let go, relax* [b]Or *Gentiles* [A]Ps 100:3 [B]Is 2:11, 17 47:1 [a]Or *a ringing cry* [A]Ps 98:8 [B]Ps 106:47 47:2 [A]Deut 7:21; Neh 1:5; Ps 66:3, 5; 68:35 [B]Mal 1:14 47:3 [A]Ps 18:47 47:4 [a]*Selah* may mean: *Pause, Crescendo* or *Musical interlude* [A]1 Pet 1:4 [B]Amos 6:8; 8:7; Nah 2:2 47:5 [a]Or *amid* [A]Ps 68:18 [B]Ps 98:6 47:6 [A]Ps 68:4 [B]Ps 89:18 47:7 [a]Heb *Maskil* [A]Zech 14:9 [B]1 Cor 14:15 47:8 [a]Or *has taken His seat* [A]1 Chr 16:31; Ps 22:28 [B]Ps 97:2 47:9 [a]Or *nobles* [b]Lit *has greatly exalted Himself* [A]Ps 72:11; 102:22; Is 49:7, 23 [B]Rom 4:11, 12 [C]Ps 89:18 [D]Ps 97:9 48:1 [A]1 Chr 16:25; Ps 96:4; 145:3 [B]Ps 46:4 [C]Ps 2:6; 87:1; Is 2:3; Mic 4:1; Zech 8:3 48:2 [A]Ps 50:2 [B]Lam 2:15 [C]Matt 5:35 48:3 [A]Ps 46:7

46:8 desolations. This word not only characterizes God's past exploits, but it is also employed in various "Day of the Lord" contexts (e.g., Is 13:9; Hos 5:9; Zep 2:15).

46:10 Cease *striving* and know that I am God. These twin commands to not panic and to recognize His sovereignty are probably directed to both His nation for comfort and all other nations for warning.

47:1–9 The main concepts of Ps 47 develop around key words and phrases, e.g., "peoples" and "nations" (vv. 1, 3, 8, 9); "earth" and "all the earth" (vv. 2, 7, 9); and "king" or "reigning (as king)" (vv. 2, 6, 7, 8). The major message of this psalm is that God is the unique Sovereign over all. Structurally, there are two choruses of worship in Ps 47 which celebrate this universal kingship of the Lord God Most High.

I. First Chorus: God as the Victorious King-Warrior (47:1–5)
 A. Its Call to Worship (47:1)
 B. Its Causes for Worship (47:2–5)
II. Second Chorus: God as the Sovereign King-Governor (47:6–9)
 A. Its Call to Worship (47:6)
 B. Its Causes for Worship (47:7–9b)
 C. Its Code of Worship (47:9c)

47:1 all peoples. The call to worship is universal.

47:3 He subdues. An axiomatic truth about the past, present, and future.

47:4 He chooses. Again, "He chooses" serves as a timeless truth. Cf. the election of Israel in Dt 7:6ff.; Ps 135:4. On the land of promise as "inheritance," cf. Dt 32:8, 9; Ps 105:11. *See notes on Eph 1:4; 1Pe 1:2* for a discussion of the doctrine of divine election. **The glory of Jacob whom He loves.** The "glory" or "pride" of Jacob also refers to the land of Canaan (cf. the term illustratively in Is 13:19; then in Is 60:15; Na 2:2; etc.). "Whom He loves" is signal terminology for God's special, elective, covenantal "love" (cf., e.g., Mal 1:2ff.). This special focus on God's covenant with Israel does not negate the bigger picture involving blessing to all nations sketched out in the original Abrahamic Covenant of Ge 12:1–3.

47:5 God has ascended with a shout. The imagery likely refers to God's presence, after having gone into battle with His people, now ascending victoriously to His immanent "residence" on Mt. Zion and to His transcendent residence in heaven. This procession with the ark of God was accompanied by great shouts and blasts of celebration in vv. 5, 6.

47:9 the shields of the earth. This imagery stands parallel with "the princes of the people." Illustratively, there may be a loose analogy to God's sovereignly appointed human governors (cf. Ro 13:1–7) as protectors for the masses.

48:1–14 In Ps 48, it often appears that Zion itself is the object of praise. While referring to Zion, this hymn of confidence (cf. Pss 46, 47) contains several checks and balances showing that it is ultimately God, who dwells in Zion, who is to be praised. Therefore, this perspective must be kept in mind as the lines of Ps 48 flow back and forth with respective emphases on the city and the great God of that city. This psalm, sung with orchestral accompaniment, therefore contrasts two different responses to the God of Zion and the Zion of God.

I. Introduction (48:1–3)
II. The Panic-Response of the Provokers of God (48:4–7)
 A. The Chronicling of It (48:4–6)
 B. The Cause of It (48:7)
III. The Praise-Response of the People of God (48:8–14)
 A. Their Celebration (48:8–13)
 B. Their Conclusion (48:14)

48:2 the joy of the whole earth. Cf. the judgment context of La 2:15. **the far north.** "North" is an interpretive translation of a word term that occurs as a Semitic place name, i.e., "Zaphon." In Canaanite mythology Zaphon was an ancient Near Eastern equivalent to Mt. Olympus, the dwelling place of pagan gods. If this was the psalmist's intention in Ps 48:2, the reference becomes a polemical description of the Lord; He is not only King of kings but also is God of all so-called gods. **The city of the great King.** Cf. Ps 47:2 and Mt 5:34, 35. God Himself has always been the King of kings.

48:3 God, in her palaces. Better, "God is in her citadels, or fortresses." The context points to the military connotation of this word.

4 For, lo, the [A]kings assembled themselves,
They passed by together.
5 They saw *it,* then they were amazed;
They were [A]terrified, they [a]fled in alarm.
6 [a]Panic seized them there,
Anguish, as of [A]a woman in childbirth.
7 With the [A]east wind
You [B]break the [C]ships of Tarshish.
8 As we have heard, so have we seen
In the city of the LORD of hosts,
in the city of our God;
God will [A]establish her forever. [a]*Selah*

9 We have thought on [A]Your
lovingkindness, O God,
In the midst of Your temple.
10 As is Your [A]name, O God,
So is Your [B]praise to the
ends of the earth;
Your [C]right hand is full
of righteousness.
11 Let Mount [A]Zion be glad,
Let the [A]daughters of Judah rejoice
Because of Your judgments.
12 Walk about Zion and go around her;
Count her [A]towers;
13 Consider her [A]ramparts;
Go through her palaces,
That you may [B]tell *it* to the
next generation.
14 For [a]such is God,
Our God forever and ever;
He will [A]guide us [b]until death.

PSALM 49

THE FOLLY OF TRUSTING IN RICHES.

For the choir director. A Psalm
of the sons of Korah.

1 [A]Hear this, all peoples;
Give ear, all [B]inhabitants of the world,
2 Both [A]low and high,
Rich and poor together.
3 My mouth will [A]speak wisdom,
And the meditation of my heart
will be [B]understanding.
4 I will incline my ear to [A]a proverb;
[B]I will [a]express my [C]riddle on the harp.

5 Why should I [A]fear in days of adversity,
When the iniquity of my
[a]foes surrounds me,
6 Even those who [A]trust in their wealth
And boast in the abundance
of their riches?
7 No man can by any means
[A]redeem *his* brother
Or give to God a [B]ransom for him—
8 For [A]the redemption of [a]his soul is costly,
And he should cease *trying* forever—
9 That he should [A]live on eternally,
That he should not [a,B]undergo decay.

10 For he sees *that even* [A]wise men die;
The [B]stupid and the senseless
alike perish
And [C]leave their wealth to others.

48:4 [A]2 Sam 10:6-19 48:5 [a]Lit *were hurried away* [A]Ex 15:15 48:6 [a]Lit *Trembling* [A]Is 13:8 48:7 [A]Jer 18:17 [B]1 Kin 22:48 [C]1 Kin 10:22; Ezek 27:25 48:8 [a]*Selah* may mean: *Pause, Crescendo* or *Musical interlude* [A]Ps 87:5 48:9 [A]Ps 26:3; 40:10 48:10 [A]Deut 28:58; Josh 7:9; Mal 1:11 [B]Ps 65:1, 2; 100:1 [C]Is 41:10 48:11 [A]Ps 97:8 48:12 [A]Neh 3:1, 11, 25-27 48:13 [A]Ps 122:7 [B]Ps 78:5-7 48:14 [a]Lit *this* [b]Lit *upon;* some mss and the Gr read *forever* [A]Ps 23:4; Is 58:11 49:1 [A]Ps 78:1; Is 1:2; Mic 1:2 [B]Ps 33:8 49:2 [A]Ps 62:9 49:3 [A]Ps 37:30 [B]Ps 119:130 49:4 [a]Lit *open up* [A]Ps 78:2 [B]2 Kin 3:15 [C]Num 12:8 49:5 [a]Lit *supplanters* [A]Ps 23:4; 27:1 49:6 [A]Job 31:24; Ps 52:7; Prov 11:28; Mark 10:24 49:7 [A]Matt 25:8, 9 [B]Job 36:18, 19 49:8 [a]Lit *their* [A]Matt 16:26 49:9 [a]Or *see corruption* or *the pit* [A]Ps 22:29 [B]Ps 16:10; 89:48 49:10 [A]Eccl 2:16 [B]Ps 92:6; 94:8 [C]Ps 39:6; Eccl 2:18, 21; Luke 12:20

48:4–7 This dramatic, poetic rapid-fire, historical rehearsal of events chronicles some serious threat to Jerusalem from a hostile coalition of forces. They had come arrogantly to destroy Jerusalem, the Zion of God; but the God of Zion surprisingly and powerfully devastated them.

48:7 **the ships of Tarshish.** A notable Mediterranean port of uncertain location (cf. Jon 1:3), possibly Spain.

48:8 **As we have heard, so have we seen.** Cf. the personal, individual testimony of Job (i.e., 42:5). The historical tradition of vv. 1–3 had been proven true once again in the events of vv. 4–7.

48:11 **the daughters of Judah.** This phrase would refer to the surrounding cities and villages.

48:14 **For such is God.** Other options for translating the Heb. text of this line are: 1) "For this God is our God," or 2) "For this is God, our God."

49:1–20 Psalm 49 deals with the most real thing about life—the certainty of death. One of its major lessons is that "you really can't take it with you." Containing these kinds of very practical lessons about life and death, it falls neatly into the category of a didactic or wisdom poem. At places it sounds very much like portions of Job, Proverbs, and Ecclesiastes. It contains warnings to the rich and famous and words of comfort for the poor. These timeless OT messages undergird many NT passages, such as the accounts about the rich fool in Lk 12:13–21 or the rich man and Lazarus in Lk 16. After a fairly lengthy introduction the body of the psalm falls into two parts as indicated by the climaxing refrain in vv. 12 and 20. The wisdom poet of Ps 49 developed his somber theme in two stages, focusing on death as the universal experience of all men.

I. Introduction (49:1–4)
II. Stage One: The Common Experience *of* Death (49:5–12)
   A. Applying His Teaching through an Important Reflection (49:5, 6)
   B. Explaining His Teaching through Important Reminders (49:7–12)
III. Stage Two: The Contrasting Experience *in* Death (49:13–20)
   A. The Assurance of This Contrasting Experience in Death (49:13–15)
   B. The Application of This Contrasting Experience in Death (49:16–20)

49:1 **all peoples ... all inhabitants.** The scope of his message is geographically universal.

49:2 **low and high ... Rich and poor.** Note the chiastic order (i.e., A-B-B-A) of these descriptives. The scope of his message is also socially universal.

49:3, 4 **wisdom ... understanding ... proverb ... riddle.** All these are wisdom terms (cf. respectively, Pr 1:20; 9:1; 14:1; 24:7; then Pr 2:3; 3:13; 5:1; 14:29; 18:2; 19:8; next Pr 1:6; Eze 17:2; and finally, Jdg 14:12ff.).

49:5 **the iniquity of my foes.** This indicates evil chasing him.

49:6 **those who trust in their wealth.** Mankind's propensity to trust in his own material goods is well attested in Scripture (e.g., Ps 52:7; Jer 17:5). Biblically this is exposed as the epitome of stupidity (cf., e.g., Pr 23:4, 5; Lk 12:16ff.).

49:7–9 **No man can.** No person, regardless of his means, is able to escape death; it is inevitable (Heb 9:27). This passage anticipates the second death of hell (cf. Rev 20:11–15), except for those who by faith have repented of their sin and embraced the only adequate ransom—the one paid by the Lord Jesus Christ with His death on the cross (cf. Mt 20:28; 1Pe 1:18, 19).

49:9b–10a **not undergo decay ... For he sees.** The irony is obvious; the wealthy person somehow hopes to get around death, yet he witnesses people constantly dying all around him, from the wise to the foolish.

11 Their [a,A]inner thought is *that*
their houses [B]are forever
And their dwelling places
to all generations;
They have [C]called their lands
after their own names.
12 But [A]man in *his* [a]pomp will not endure;
He is like the [b]beasts that [c]perish.

13 This is the [A]way of those
who are foolish,
And of those after them who [B]approve
their words. [a]*Selah*
14 As sheep they are appointed [A]for [a]Sheol;
Death shall be their shepherd;
And the [B]upright shall rule over
them in the morning,
And their form shall be for
[a]Sheol [C]to consume
[b]So that they have no habitation.
15 But God will [A]redeem my soul
from the [a]power of [b]Sheol,
For [B]He will receive me. *Selah*

16 Do not be afraid [A]when a
man becomes rich,
When the [a]glory of his house is increased;
17 For when he dies he will
[A]carry nothing away;
His [a]glory will not descend after him.
18 Though while he lives he
[A]congratulates [a]himself—
And though *men* praise you when
you do well for yourself—
19 [a]He shall [A]go to the generation
of his fathers;
They will never see [B]the light.
20 [A]Man in *his* [a]pomp, yet without
understanding,
Is [B]like the [b]beasts that [c]perish.

PSALM 50

GOD THE JUDGE OF THE RIGHTEOUS AND THE WICKED.

A Psalm of [†]Asaph.

1 [A]The Mighty One, God, the
LORD, has spoken,
And summoned the earth [B]from the
rising of the sun to its setting.
2 Out of Zion, [A]the perfection of beauty,
God [B]has shone forth.
3 May our God [A]come and not keep silence;
[B]Fire devours before Him,
And it is very [C]tempestuous around Him.
4 He [A]summons the heavens above,
And the earth, to judge His people:
5 "Gather My [A]godly ones to Me,
Those who have made a [B]covenant
with Me by [C]sacrifice."
6 And the [A]heavens declare
His righteousness,
For [B]God Himself is judge. [a]*Selah*

7 "[A]Hear, O My people, and I will speak;
O Israel, I will testify [a]against you;
I am God, [B]your God.

49:11 [a]Some versions read *graves are their houses* [A]Ps 64:6 [B]Ps 10:6 [C]Gen 4:17; Deut 3:14 49:12 [a]Lit *honor* [b]Or *animals* [c]Lit *are destroyed* [A]Ps 49:20 49:13 [a]*Selah* may mean: *Pause, Crescendo* or *Musical interlude* [A]Jer 17:11 [B]Ps 49:18 49:14 [a]I.e. the nether world [b]Lit *Away from his habitation* [A]Ps 9:17 [B]Dan 7:18; Mal 4:3; 1 Cor 6:2; Rev 2:26 [C]Job 24:19 49:15 [a]Lit *hand* [b]I.e. the nether world [A]Ps 16:10; 56:13; Hos 13:14 [B]Gen 5:24; Ps 16:11; 73:24 49:16 [a]Or *wealth* [A]Ps 37:7 49:17 [a]Or *wealth* [A]Ps 17:14; 1 Tim 6:7 49:18 [a]Lit *his soul* [A]Deut 29:19; Ps 10:3, 6; Luke 12:19 49:19 [a]Lit *You;* or *It* [A]Gen 15:15 [B]Job 33:30; Ps 56:13 49:20 [a]Lit *honor* [b]Or *animals* [c]Lit *are destroyed* [A]Ps 49:12 [B]Eccl 3:19 50:1 [†]1 Chr 15:17; 2 Chr 29:30 [A]Josh 22:22 [B]Ps 113:3 50:2 [A]Ps 48:2; Lam 2:15 [B]Deut 33:2; Ps 80:1; 94:1 50:3 [A]Ps 96:13 [B]Lev 10:2; Num 16:35; Ps 97:3; Dan 7:10 [C]Ps 18:12, 13 50:4 [A]Deut 4:26; 31:28; 32:1; Is 1:2 50:5 [A]Ps 30:4; 37:28; 52:9 [B]Ex 24:7; 2 Chr 6:11; Ps 25:10 [C]Ps 50:8 50:6 [a]*Selah* may mean: *Pause, Crescendo* or *Musical interlude* [A]Ps 89:5; 97:6 [B]Ps 75:7; 96:13 50:7 [a]Or *to* [A]Ps 49:1; 81:8 [B]Ex 20:2; Ps 48:14

49:12 But man ... will not endure. This refrain (cf. v. 20) is the main point of the psalm. Cf. this concept in Ecc 3:19. While man and beast both die, man's spirit lives on eternally but beasts have no life after death.

49:14 As sheep they are appointed for Sheol; Death shall be their shepherd. More irony; they are considered as sheep once noted for their grazing; now death shall graze on them. **the upright shall rule ... in the morning.** This harbinger of good news to come (cf. v. 15) interrupts this long series of confirmations of the condemnation of the self-reliant.

49:15 But God will redeem my soul ... He will receive me. This is one of the greatest affirmations of confidence in God in the Psalms. Although the faithless person cannot buy his way out of death (v. 7ff.), the faithful one is redeemed by the only Redeemer, God Himself. On the significance of the word "receive," cf. Ge 5:24; 2Ki 2:10; Ps 73:24; Heb 11:5. So in v. 15 the psalmist expresses his confidence in God that He would raise him to eternal life.

49:17 he will carry nothing away. An explicit you-can't-take-it-with-you attestation (cf. Job 1:21; Ecc 5:15; 1Ti 6:6, 7).

49:20 Man ... yet without understanding. The refrain is similar to that of v. 12.

50:1–23 God Himself is quoted throughout the psalm. Consequently, its form resembles the prophetic writings which specialized in delivering divine oracles. Its major burden is to delineate the nature of true worship (i.e., "worship in spirit and truth," cf. Jn 4:24). The psalmist skillfully develops this burden in a polemical fashion with its exposures of externalism and hypocrisy. The Lord God, the Supreme Judge, levels two felony charges against His professing people.

I. Introduction: The Supreme Judge Enters to Preside (50:1–6)
II. The Supreme Judge Levels Two Charges (50:7–21)
   A. First Charge: Ritualism (50:7–15)
   B. Second Charge: Rebellion (50:16–21)
III. The Supreme Judge Offers a Solution (50:22, 23)

50:Title This is the first psalm entitled "A Psalm of Asaph" (cf. Pss 73–83 in Book III of Psalms). For references to "Asaph," cf. 1Ch 6:39; 15:16ff.; 16:5ff.; 25:1ff.; 2Ch 5:12; 29:30; Ezr 2:41; Ne 12:46. Sometimes the simple "Asaph" may stand for the longer expression "the sons of Asaph." Each occasion needs to be examined to see what the relationship between a given psalm and "Asaph" might be, i.e., composed by, handed down by, sung by this special Levitical choir. Many older commentators feel that Ps 50 was authored by the original "Asaph."

50:1 The Mighty One, God, the LORD. The Divine Judge is introduced with three significant OT names. The first two are the short and longer forms of the most common word for "God" in the OT, and the third is the name for Israel's God par excellence, i.e., Yahweh (cf. its historical origin in Ex 3:14). **from the rising of the sun to its setting.** A common OT idiom conveying from E to W, i.e., all over the planet.

50:2, 3 God has shone forth. These verses utilize the language of theophany (cf. Ex 19:16–19).

50:4, 5 He summons the heavens ... the earth ... His people ... My godly ones. He summons the heavens and the earth as personified witnesses for these charges He is about to level concerning His professing people (cf., e.g., Dt 32:1ff.; Is 1:2ff.).

50:5 a covenant with Me by sacrifice. Such a ratification of covenant is serious, sacred business (cf. Ex 24:3–8). This reference to "sacrifice" will set the stage for His first felony charge in v. 7ff.

8 "I do [A]not reprove you for your sacrifices,
And your burnt offerings are
continually before Me.
9 "I shall take no [A]young bull out of your house
Nor male goats out of your folds.
10 "For [A]every beast of the forest is Mine,
The cattle on a thousand hills.
11 "I know every [A]bird of the mountains,
And everything that moves
in the field is [a]Mine.
12 "If I were hungry I would not tell you,
For the [A]world is Mine, and [a]all it contains.
13 "Shall I eat the flesh of [a,A]bulls
Or drink the blood of male goats?
14 "Offer to God [A]a sacrifice of thanksgiving
And [B]pay your vows to the Most High;
15 [A]Call upon Me in the day of trouble;
I shall [B]rescue you, and you
will [C]honor Me."

16 But to the wicked God says,
"What right have you to tell of My statutes
And to take [A]My covenant in your mouth?
17 "For you [A]hate discipline,
And you [B]cast My words behind you.
18 "When you see a thief, you [a,A]are
pleased with him,
And [b]you [B]associate with adulterers.
19 "You [a,A]let your mouth loose in evil
And your [B]tongue frames deceit.
20 "You sit and [A]speak against your brother;
You slander your own mother's son.
21 "These things you have done
and [A]I kept silence;
You thought that I was just like you;
I will [B]reprove you and state *the*
case in order before your eyes.

22 "Now consider this, you who [A]forget God,
Or I will [B]tear *you* in pieces, and
there will be none to deliver.
23 "He who [A]offers a sacrifice of
thanksgiving honors Me;
And to him who [a,B]orders *his* way *aright*
I shall [C]show the salvation of God."

PSALM 51

A CONTRITE SINNER'S PRAYER FOR PARDON.

For the choir director. A Psalm of David, when [†]Nathan the prophet came to him, after he had gone in to Bathsheba.

1 [A]Be gracious to me, O God, according
to Your lovingkindness;
According to the greatness of
[B]Your compassion [C]blot out
my transgressions.
2 [A]Wash me thoroughly from my iniquity
And [B]cleanse me from my sin.
3 For [a]I [A]know my transgressions,
And my sin is ever before me.
4 [A]Against You, You only, I have sinned
And done what is [B]evil in Your sight,
So that [C]You [a]are justified
[b]when You speak
And [c]blameless when You judge.

5 Behold, I was [A]brought forth in iniquity,
And in sin my mother conceived me.
6 Behold, You desire [A]truth in
the [a]innermost being,
And in the hidden part You will
[B]make me know wisdom.

50:8 [A]Ps 40:6; 51:16; Is 1:11; Hos 6:6 50:9 [A]Ps 69:31 50:10 [A]Ps 104:24 50:11 [a]Or *in My mind;* lit *with Me* [A]Matt 6:26 50:12 [a]Lit *its fullness* [A]Ex 19:5; Deut 10:14; Ps 24:1; 1 Cor 10:26 50:13 [a]Lit *strong ones* [A]Ps 50:9 50:14 [A]Ps 27:6; 69:30; 107:22; 116:17; Hos 14:2; Rom 12:1; Heb 13:15 [B]Num 30:2; Deut 23:21; Ps 22:25; 56:12; 61:8; 65:1; 76:11 50:15 [A]Ps 91:15; 107:6, 13; Zech 13:9 [B]Ps 81:7 [C]Ps 22:23 50:16 [A]Is 29:13 50:17 [A]Prov 5:12; 12:1; Rom 2:21, 22 [B]1 Kin 14:9; Neh 9:26 50:18 [a]Some ancient versions read *run together* [b]Lit *your part is with* [A]Rom 1:32 [B]1 Tim 5:22 50:19 [a]Lit *send* [A]Ps 10:7 [B]Ps 36:3; 52:2 50:20 [A]Job 19:18; Matt 10:21 50:21 [A]Eccl 8:11; Is 42:14; 57:11 [B]Ps 90:8 50:22 [A]Job 8:13; Ps 9:17 [B]Ps 7:2 50:23 [a]Lit *sets* [A]Ps 50:14 [B]Ps 85:13 [C]Ps 91:16 51:1 [†]2 Sam 12:1 [A]Ps 4:1; 109:26 [B]Ps 69:16; 106:45 [C]Ps 51:9; Is 43:25; 44:22; Acts 3:19; Col 2:14 51:2 [A]Ps 51:7; Is 1:16; 4:4; Jer 4:14; Acts 22:16; Rev 1:5 [B]Jer 33:8; Ezek 36:33; Heb 9:14; 1 John 1:7, 9 51:3 [a]Or *I myself know* [A]Is 59:12 51:4 [a]Or *may be in the right* [b]Many mss read *in Your words* [c]Lit *pure* [A]Gen 20:6; 39:9; 2 Sam 12:13; Ps 41:4 [B]Luke 15:21 [C]Rom 3:4 51:5 [A]Job 14:4; 15:14; Ps 58:3; Eph 2:3 51:6 [a]Or *inward parts* [A]Job 38:36; Ps 15:2 [B]Prov 2:6; Eccl 2:26; James 1:5

50:8 I do not reprove you for your sacrifices. The Divine Judge's condemnations are directed not at the act of sacrifice but at the people's attitude in sacrificing (cf. 1Sa 15:22; Pss 40:6–8; 51:17; 69:30; Is 1:12; Jer 7:21–26; Hos 6:6; Mic 6:6–8).

50:9–13 shall take no young bull out of your house. God refuses mere ritual; it is an abomination to Him. He, unlike the pagan deities, needs nothing; He created everything and owns everything.

50:14 Offer to God ... thanksgiving. Here is the sacrifice that always pleases Him (cf. Ps 51:17; Heb 13:15).

50:16–20 the wicked. Whereas the first charge dealt with a vertical relationship (cf. the first tablet of the Ten Commandments), this one in v. 16ff. focuses on evidences of horizontal violations of covenant (i.e., rebellion against God in the context of man to fellow man offenses; cf. the second half of the Ten Commandments).

50:21 I kept silence .... will reprove you. God's longsuffering grace must never be looked upon as laxity (cf. 2Pe 3:3–10) nor abused. His reckoning for rebellion will indeed be manifested.

50:22 Now consider this. Before destruction, mercifully comes an opportunity for deliberation and repentance.

50:23 He who offers ... thanksgiving honors Me. Cf. v. 14. This remains the remedy for mere ritualism. The conclusions of vv. 22 and 23 came in chiastic order, heightening the total impact of the psalm's two felony charges (i.e., the recounting of *ritualism,* vv. 7–15; the recounting of *rebellion,* vv. 16–21; the remedy of repentance for *rebellion,* v. 22; the remedy of repentance for *ritualism,* v. 23).

51:1–19 This is the classic passage in the OT on man's repentance and God's forgiveness of sin. Along with Ps 32, it was written by David after his affair with Bathsheba and his murder of Uriah, her husband (2Sa 11; 12). It is one of 7 poems called penitential psalms (6, 32, 38, 51, 102, 130, 143). To David's credit, he recognized fully how horrendous his sin was against God, blamed no one but himself, and begged for divine forgiveness.

I. Plea for Forgiveness (51:1, 2)
II. Proffer of Confession (51:3–6)
III. Prayer for Moral Cleanness (51:7–12)
IV. Promise of Renewed Service (51:13–17)
V. Petition for National Restoration (51:18, 19)

51:1 lovingkindness. Even though he had sinned horribly, David knew that forgiveness was available, based on God's covenant love.

51:4 Against You, You only. David realized what every believer seeking forgiveness must; even though he had tragically wronged Bathsheba and Uriah, his ultimate crime was against God and His holy law (cf. 2Sa 11:27). Romans 3:4 quotes Ps 51:4.

51:5 brought forth in iniquity. David also acknowledged that his sin was not God's fault in any way (vv. 4b, 6), nor was it some aberration. Rather, the source of David's sin was a fallen, sinful disposition, his since conception.

7 [a]Purify me [A]with hyssop, and
I shall be clean;
[b]Wash me, and I shall be
[B]whiter than snow.
8 [a]Make me to hear [A]joy and gladness,
Let the [B]bones which You
have broken rejoice.
9 [A]Hide Your face from my sins
And blot out all my iniquities.

10 [A]Create [a]in me a [B]clean heart, O God,
And renew [b]a [C]steadfast spirit within me.
11 [A]Do not cast me away from Your presence
And do not take Your [B]Holy
Spirit from me.
12 Restore to me the [A]joy of Your salvation
And sustain me with a [B]willing spirit.
13 *Then* I will [A]teach transgressors
Your ways,
And sinners will [a]be [B]converted to You.

14 Deliver me from [A]bloodguiltiness,
O God, [B]the God of my salvation;
Then my [C]tongue will joyfully
sing of Your righteousness.
15 O Lord, [a,A]open my lips,
That my mouth may [B]declare Your praise.
16 For You [A]do not delight in sacrifice,
otherwise I would give it;
You are not pleased with burnt offering.
17 The sacrifices of God are a [A]broken spirit;
A broken and a contrite heart,
O God, You will not despise.

18 [A]By Your favor do good to Zion;
[a,B]Build the walls of Jerusalem.
19 Then You will delight in
[a,A]righteous sacrifices,
In [B]burnt offering and whole
burnt offering;
Then [b]young bulls will be
offered on Your altar.

PSALM 52

FUTILITY OF BOASTFUL WICKEDNESS.

For the choir director. A [†]Maskil of David, [•]when Doeg the Edomite came and told Saul and said to him, "David has come to the house of Ahimelech."

1 Why do you [A]boast in evil,
O mighty man?
The [B]lovingkindness of God
endures all day long.
2 Your tongue devises [A]destruction,
Like a [B]sharp razor, [C]O worker of deceit.
3 You [A]love evil more than good,
[B]Falsehood more than speaking what is
right. [a]*Selah*
4 You love all words that devour,
O [A]deceitful tongue.

5 [a]But God will break you
down forever;
He will snatch you up and [A]tear
you away from *your* tent,
And [B]uproot you from the [C]land of the
living. *Selah*
6 The righteous will [A]see and fear,
And will [B]laugh at him, *saying,*
7 "Behold, the man who would not
make God his refuge,
But [A]trusted in the abundance
of his riches
And [B]was strong in [a]his *evil* desire."

8 But as for me, I am like a [A]green
olive tree in the house of God;
I [B]trust in the lovingkindness
of God forever and ever.
9 I will [A]give You thanks forever,
because You have done *it,*
And I will wait on Your name,
[B]for *it is* good, in the presence
of Your godly ones.

51:7 [a]Or *May You purify…that I may be clean* [b]Or *May You wash* [A]Ex 12:22; Lev 14:4; Num 19:18; Heb 9:19 [B]Is 1:18 51:8 [a]Or *May You make* [A]Is 35:10; Joel 1:16 [B]Ps 35:10 51:9 [A]Jer 16:17 51:10 [a]Lit *for* [b]Or *an upright* [A]Ezek 18:31; Eph 2:10 [B]Ps 24:4; Matt 5:8; Acts 15:9 [C]Ps 78:37 51:11 [A]2 Kin 13:23; 24:20; Jer 7:15 [B]Is 63:10, 11 51:12 [A]Ps 13:5 [B]Ps 110:3 51:13 [a]Or *turn back* [A]Acts 9:21, 22 [B]Ps 22:27 51:14 [A]2 Sam 12:9; Ps 26:9 [B]Ps 25:5 [C]Ps 35:28; 71:15 51:15 [a]Or *may You open* [A]Ex 4:15 [B]Ps 9:14 51:16 [A]1 Sam 15:22; Ps 40:6 51:17 [A]Ps 34:18 51:18 [a]Or *May You build* [A]Ps 69:35; Is 51:3 [B]Ps 102:16; 147:2 51:19 [a]Or *sacrifices of righteousness* [b]Lit *they will offer young bulls* [A]Ps 4:5 [B]Ps 66:13, 15 52:1 [†]Possibly *Contemplative*, or *Didactic*, or *Skillful Psalm* [•]1 Sam 22:9 [A]Ps 94:4 [B]Ps 52:8 52:2 [A]Ps 5:9 [B]Ps 57:4; 59:7 [C]Ps 101:7 52:3 [a]*Selah* may mean: *Pause, Crescendo* or *Musical interlude* [A]Ps 36:4 [B]Ps 58:3; Jer 9:5 52:4 [A]Ps 120:3 52:5 [a]Or *Also* [A]Is 22:18, 19 [B]Prov 2:22 [C]Ps 27:13 52:6 [A]Ps 37:34; 40:3 [B]Job 22:19 52:7 [a]Or *his destruction* [A]Ps 49:6 [B]Ps 10:6 52:8 [A]Ps 92:12; 128:3; Jer 11:16 [B]Ps 13:5 52:9 [A]Ps 30:12 [B]Ps 54:6

51:7 hyssop. Old Testament priests used hyssop, a leafy plant, to sprinkle blood or water on a person being ceremonially cleansed from defilements such as leprosy or touching a dead body (cf. Lv 14:6ff.; Nu 19:16–19). Here hyssop is a figure for David's longing to be spiritually cleansed from his moral defilement. In forgiveness, God washes away sin (cf. Ps 103:12; Is 1:16; Mic 7:19).

51:8 bones. A figure of speech for the framework of the entire person. He was experiencing personal collapse under guilt (cf. Ps 32:3, 4).

51:11 Your Holy Spirit from me. This is a reference to the special Holy Spirit anointing on theocratic mediators.

51:12 willing spirit. God is generous, willing, and eager to uphold the believer. This mention of spirit possibly refers to the Holy Spirit.

51:16 You do not delight in sacrifice. Ritual without genuine repentance is useless. However, with a right heart attitude, sacrifices were acceptable (see v. 19).

52:1–9 This psalm is a poetic lesson about the futility of evil, the final triumph of righteousness, and the sovereign control of God over the moral events of history. The event in David's life which motivated him to write this psalm is recorded in 1Sa 21, 22.

I. The Rashness of the Wicked (52:1–5)
II. The Reaction of the Righteous (52:6, 7)
III. The Rejoicing of the Godly (52:8, 9)

52:1 mighty man. A reference to Doeg, the chief of Saul's shepherds, who reported to Saul that the priests of Nob had aided David when he was a fugitive (cf. 1Sa 22:9, 18, 19).

52:5 God will break you down. Ultimately, the wicked are in the hands of a holy God (cf. Heb 9:27).

52:6 see and fear. God's punishment of the wicked serves as a reinforcement to the righteous to obey God. **will laugh at him.** In the end, the wicked become a laughingstock in a universe controlled by God.

52:8 green olive tree. The psalmist exults (through this simile) that the one who trusts in the mercy of God is productive and secure.

PSALM 53

FOLLY AND WICKEDNESS OF MEN.

For the choir director; according to †Mahalath. A •Maskil of David.

1 [A]The fool has said in his heart,
"There is no God,"
They are corrupt, and have committed abominable injustice;
[B]There is no one who does good.
2 God has looked down from heaven upon the sons of men
To see if there is [A]anyone who [a]understands,
Who [B]seeks after God.
3 [A]Every one of them has turned aside; together they have become corrupt;
There is no one who does good, not even one.

4 Have the workers of wickedness [A]no knowledge,
Who eat up My people *as though* they ate bread
And have not called upon God?
5 There they were in great [a]fear
[A]*where* no [a]fear had been;
For God [B]scattered the bones of [b]him who encamped against you;
You [C]put *them* to shame, because [D]God had rejected them.
6 Oh, that [A]the salvation of Israel [a]would come out of Zion!
When God [b]restores His captive people,
[c]Let Jacob rejoice, let Israel be glad.

PSALM 54

PRAYER FOR DEFENSE AGAINST ENEMIES.

For the choir director; on stringed instruments. A †Maskil of David, •when the Ziphites came and said to Saul, "Is not David hiding himself among us?"

1 Save me, O God, by [A]Your name,
And [a]vindicate me by [B]Your power.
2 [A]Hear my prayer, O God;
[B]Give ear to the words of my mouth.
3 For strangers have [A]risen against me
And [B]violent men have [C]sought my [a]life;
They have [D]not set God before them.
[b]*Selah*

4 Behold, [A]God is my helper;
The Lord is [a]the [B]sustainer of my soul.
5 [a]He will [A]recompense the evil to [b]my foes;
[c,B]Destroy them [c]in Your [d]faithfulness.

6 [a,A]Willingly I will sacrifice to You;
I will give [B]thanks to Your name,
O LORD, for it is good.
7 For [a]He has [A]delivered me from all [b]trouble,
And my eye has [B]looked *with satisfaction* upon my enemies.

PSALM 55

PRAYER FOR THE DESTRUCTION OF THE TREACHEROUS.

For the choir director; on stringed instruments. A †Maskil of David.

1 [A]Give ear to my prayer, O God;
And [B]do not hide Yourself from my supplication.

53:1 †I.e. sickness, a sad tone •Possibly *Contemplative*, or *Didactic*, or *Skillful Psalm* [A]Ps 10:4; 14:1-7; 53:1-6 [B]Rom 3:10 53:2 [a]Or *acts wisely* [A]Rom 3:11 [B]2 Chr 15:2 53:3 [A]Rom 3:12 53:4 [A]Jer 4:22 53:5 [a]Or *dread* [b]Or possibly *those* [A]Lev 26:17, 36; Prov 28:1 [B]Ps 141:7; Jer 8:1, 2; Ezek 6:5 [C]Ps 44:7 [D]2 Kin 17:20; Jer 6:30; Lam 5:22 53:6 [a]Lit *would be* [b]Or *restores the fortunes of His people* [c]Or *Jacob will rejoice, Israel will be glad* [A]Ps 14:7 54:1 †Possibly *Contemplative*, or *Didactic*, or *Skillful Psalm* •1 Sam 23:19; 26:1 [a]Lit *judge* [A]Ps 20:1 [B]2 Chr 20:6 54:2 [A]Ps 17:6; 55:1 [B]Ps 5:1 54:3 [a]Or *soul* [b]*Selah* may mean: *Pause, Crescendo* or *Musical interlude* [A]Ps 86:14 [B]Ps 18:48; 86:14; 140:1, 4, 11 [C]1 Sam 20:1; 25:29; Ps 40:14; 63:9; 70:2 [D]Ps 36:1 54:4 [a]Lit *as those who sustain* [A]Ps 30:10; 37:40; 118:7 [B]Ps 37:17, 24; 41:12; 51:12; 145:14; Is 41:10 54:5 [a]Lit *The evil will return* [b]Or *those who lie in wait for me* [c]Or *Put to silence* [d]Or *truth* [A]Ps 94:23 [B]Ps 143:12 [C]Ps 89:49; 96:13; Is 42:3 54:6 [a]Or *With a freewill offering* [A]Num 15:3; Ps 116:17 [B]Ps 50:14 54:7 [a]Or *it;* i.e. His name [b]Or *distress* [A]Ps 34:6 [B]Ps 59:10; 92:11; 112:8; 118:7 55:1 †Possibly *Contemplative*, or *Didactic*, or *Skillful Psalm* [A]Ps 54:2; 61:1; 86:6 [B]Ps 27:9

53:1–6 This psalm is nearly identical to Ps 14 (Ps 53:1–5a is from Ps 14:1–5a; Ps 53:6 is from Ps 4:7). The major difference is v. 5, in which the psalmist celebrates a military victory over an enemy. Apparently Ps 14 is here rephrased to apply to a specified war event, earning it a distinct place in the canon.

I. The Description of Those Who Reject God and His People (53:1–4)
II. The Danger to Those Who Reject God and His People (53:5)
III. The Deliverance of His People (53:6)

53:Title Mahalath. The name of a tune or an instrument.

53:1–4 *See notes on Ps 14.* Romans 3:10–12 quotes Ps 53:1–3.

53:2 God. The reference to "God" rather than "Lord" is another difference between Ps 14 and 53. "Elohim" is used 3 times in Ps 14, but 7 times in Ps 53.

53:5 in great fear. The verse describes a sudden reversal in the fortunes of war. The haughty enemy besieging Israel was suddenly terrified and utterly defeated. Historical examples of such unexpected terrors to Israel's enemy are recorded in 2Ch 20 and Is 37. **scattered the bones.** Perhaps nothing was more disgraceful to a nation at war than to have the bones of its dead army scattered over the land rather than buried.

54:1–7 This psalm apparently comes from the same period of David's life as does Ps 52. Even though David had recently rescued an Israelite border town from the Philistines, he was still considered a traitor to Saul (1Sa 23 and 26). In the wake of this emotional devastation, David prayed to God for vindication. The psalm provides encouragement to any believer who has been maligned.

I. The Prayer for Deliverance (54:1–3)
II. The Anticipation of Deliverance (54:4, 5)
III. The Thanksgiving for Deliverance (54:6, 7)

54:1 by Your name. In the ancient world, a person's name was essentially the person himself. Here, God's name includes His covenant protection. **vindicate.** David requests that God will execute justice for him, as in a court trial when a defendant is declared not guilty.

54:2 Give ear. An anthropomorphism meaning "listen," "pay attention."

54:3 strangers. Either non-Israelites or Israelites who had broken the covenant with God might be called strangers. Since in this case Saul and the Ziphites are the oppressors, the strangers are apostate Israelites (cf. 1Sa 23:19; 26:1).

54:5 in Your faithfulness. Since God is omniscient, He can execute perfect justice against the wicked.

54:7 looked *with satisfaction*. David anticipates with confidence that which he has seen in the past—the defeat of his enemies.

55:1–23 In this individual lament, David pours out his heart to his Lord because a former close friend has betrayed him (vv. 12–14). There is a strong possibility that this psalm was occasioned by the betrayal of Absalom and/or Ahithophel (cf. 2Sa 15–18). Most of the psalm

2 Give [A]heed to me and answer me;
I am restless in my [B]complaint
and [a,C]am surely distracted,
3 Because of the voice of the enemy,
Because of the [A]pressure of the wicked;
For they [B]bring down [a]trouble upon me
And in anger they [C]bear a grudge against me.

4 My [A]heart is in anguish within me,
And the terrors of [B]death
have fallen upon me.
5 Fear and [A]trembling come upon me,
And [a,B]horror has overwhelmed me.
6 I said, "Oh, that I had wings like a dove!
I would fly away and [a,A]be at rest.
7 "Behold, I would wander far away,
I would [A]lodge in the wilderness. [a]*Selah*
8 "I would hasten to my place of refuge
From the [A]stormy wind *and* tempest."

9 [a]Confuse, O Lord, [A]divide their tongues,
For I have seen [B]violence
and strife in the city.
10 Day and night they go around
her upon her walls,
And iniquity and mischief are in her midst.
11 [A]Destruction is in her midst;
[B]Oppression and deceit do not
depart from her [a]streets.

12 For it is [A]not an enemy who reproaches me,
Then I could bear *it;*
Nor is it one who hates me who [B]has
exalted himself against me,
Then I could hide myself from him.
13 But it is you, a man [a]my equal,
My [A]companion and my [b,B]familiar friend;
14 We who had sweet [a]fellowship together
[A]Walked in the house of God in the throng.
15 Let [a]death come [A]deceitfully upon them;
Let them [B]go down alive to [b]Sheol,
For evil is in their dwelling, in their midst.

16 As for me, I shall [A]call upon God,
And the LORD will save me.
17 [A]Evening and [B]morning and at [C]noon,
I will complain and murmur,
And He will hear my voice.
18 He will [A]redeem my soul in peace [a]from
the battle *which is* against me,
For they are [B]many *who strive* with me.
19 God will [A]hear and [a]answer them—
Even the one [B]who [b]sits enthroned from
of old— *Selah*
With whom there [c]is no change,
And who [C]do not fear God.
20 He has put forth his hands against
[A]those who were at peace with him;
He has [a,B]violated his covenant.
21 His [a]speech was [A]smoother than butter,
But his heart was war;
His words were [A]softer than oil,
Yet they were drawn [B]swords.

22 [A]Cast [a]your burden upon the LORD
and He will sustain you;
[B]He will never allow the
righteous to [b,C]be shaken.
23 But You, O God, will bring them down
to the [a,A]pit of destruction;
[B]Men of bloodshed and deceit will
[C]not live out half their days.
But I will [D]trust in You.

PSALM 56

SUPPLICATION FOR DELIVERANCE AND GRATEFUL TRUST IN GOD.

For the choir director; according to [†]Jonath elem rehokim. A •Mikhtam of David, *when the Philistines seized him in Gath.

1 Be gracious to me, O God, for man
has [a,A]trampled upon me;
[b]Fighting all day long he [B]oppresses me.

55:2 [a]Or *I must moan* [A]Ps 66:19; 86:6, 7 [B]1 Sam 1:16; Job 9:27; Ps 64:1; 77:3; 142:2 [C]Is 38:14; 59:11; Ezek 7:16 55:3 [a]Or *wickedness* [A]Ps 17:9 [B]2 Sam 16:7, 8 [C]Ps 71:11; 143:3 55:4 [A]Ps 38:8 [B]Ps 18:4, 5; 116:3 55:5 [a]Lit *shuddering* [A]Ps 119:120 [B]Job 21:6; Is 21:4; Ezek 7:18 55:6 [a]Lit *settle down* [A]Job 3:13 55:7 [a]*Selah* may mean: *Pause, Crescendo* or *Musical interlude* [A]1 Sam 23:14 55:8 [A]Is 4:6; 25:4; 29:6 55:9 [a]Lit *Swallow up* [A]Gen 11:9 [B]Ps 11:5; Jer 6:7 55:11 [a]Or *plaza* [A]Ps 5:9 [B]Ps 10:7; 17:9 55:12 [A]Ps 41:9 [B]Ps 35:26 55:13 [a]Lit *according to my valuation* [b]Or *acquaintance* [A]2 Sam 15:12 [B]Job 19:14; Ps 41:9 55:14 [a]Lit *counsel;* or *intimacy* [A]Ps 42:4 55:15 [a]Another reading is *desolations be upon them* [b]I.e. the nether world [A]Ps 64:7; Prov 6:15; Is 47:11; 1 Thess 5:3 [B]Num 16:30, 33 55:16 [A]Ps 57:2, 3 55:17 [A]Ps 141:2; Dan 6:10; Acts 3:1; 10:3, 30 [B]Ps 5:3; 88:13; 92:2 [C]Acts 10:9 55:18 [a]Or *so that none may approach me* [A]Ps 103:4 [B]Ps 56:2 55:19 [a]Or *afflict* [b]Or *abides from* [c]Lit *are no changes* [A]Ps 78:59 [B]Deut 33:27; Ps 90:2; 93:2 [C]Ps 36:1 55:20 [a]Lit *profaned* [A]Ps 7:4; 120:7 [B]Num 30:2; Ps 89:34 55:21 [a]Lit *mouth* [A]Ps 12:2; 28:3; Prov 5:3, 4 [B]Ps 57:4; 59:7 55:22 [a]Or *what He has given you* [b]Or *totter* [A]Ps 37:5; 1 Pet 5:7 [B]Ps 37:24 [C]Ps 15:5; 112:6 55:23 [a]Or *lowest pit* [A]Ps 73:18; Is 38:17; Ezek 28:8 [B]Ps 5:6 [C]Job 15:32; Prov 10:27 [D]Ps 25:2; 56:3 56:1 [†]Or *The silent dove of those who are far off,* or, *The dove of the distant terebinths* •Possibly *Epigrammatic Poem,* or *Atonement Psalm* *1 Sam 21:10, 11 [a]Or *snapped at* [b]Or *A fighting man* [A]Ps 57:3 [B]Ps 17:9

alternates between prayers for his enemy's ruin (vv. 9, 15, 19, 23) and praises for God's blessings (vv. 16, 18, 22). The high point of the psalm for Christians who have been "stabbed in the back" by a confidant is v. 22. Though despairing, David expresses ultimate confidence in God.

I. The Prayer of Distress (55:1–8)
II. The Prayer for Justice (55:9–15)
III. The Prayer of Assurance (55:16–23)

55:3 bring down trouble. The verb pictures something being tipped over, crashing down on the victim.

55:6 wings like a dove! David expresses his escapist feelings.

55:9 divide their tongues. Perhaps this is an allusion to the Tower of Babel, where God destroyed the force of the movement against Him by multiplying languages (cf. Ge 11:5–9).

55:15 go down alive to Sheol. Since God had done this once with the enemies of Moses (Nu 16:30), David asks Him to perform the same judgment on his enemies.

55:19 there is no change. David's enemies were too set in their ways and too secure to pay any attention to God.

55:20 violated his covenant. This enemy had broken a treaty in his treachery, even against his allies.

55:21 his heart was war. Though the traitor talked peace, his intention was war.

55:22 Cast your burden upon the LORD. The word for "burden" implies one's circumstances, one's lot. The psalmist promises that the Lord will uphold the believer in the struggles of life.

55:23 the pit of destruction. Compare the unusual death of Absalom (2Sa 18:9–15) and the suicide of Ahithophel (2Sa 17:23).

56:1–13 This psalm, apparently written when David had been endangered by the Philistines (1Sa 21:10–15), expresses the kind of confidence in the Lord that believers should exude when they find themselves in terrifying circumstances. David's natural reaction was to panic (vv. 3, 4, 11). But he demonstrates in this psalm that the believer can replace potential terror with the composure of trust.

I. Fear and Faith (56:1–4)
II. Destroyer and Deliverer (56:5–9)
III. Trust and Thanksgiving (56:10–13)

56:Title according to Jonath elem rehokim. Possibly a tune name which links Ps 56

2 My foes have [a,A]trampled
upon me all day long,
For [b]they are many who [B]fight
proudly against me.
3 [a]When I am [A]afraid,
[b]I will [B]put my trust in You.
4 [A]In God, whose word I praise,
In God I have put my trust;
I shall not be afraid.
[B]What can *mere* [a]man do to me?
5 All day long they [a,A]distort my words;
All their [b,B]thoughts are
against me for evil.
6 They [a,A]attack, they lurk,
They [B]watch my [b]steps,
As they have [C]waited *to take* my [c]life.
7 Because of wickedness,
[a,A]cast them forth,
In anger [B]put down the peoples, O God!

8 You [A]have taken account of
my wanderings;
Put my [B]tears in Your bottle.
Are *they* not in [C]Your book?
9 Then my enemies will [A]turn back
[B]in the day when I call;
This I know, [a]that [C]God is for me.
10 In God, *whose* word I praise,
In the LORD, *whose* word I praise,
11 In God I have put my [a]trust,
I shall not be afraid.
What can man do to me?
12 Your [A]vows are *binding* upon me, O God;
I will render thank offerings to You.
13 For You have [A]delivered my
soul from death,
[a]Indeed [B]my feet from stumbling,
So that I may [C]walk before God
In the [D]light of the [b]living.

PSALM 57

PRAYER FOR RESCUE FROM PERSECUTORS.

For the choir director; *set to* [†]Al-tashheth.
A •Mikhtam of David, *when he
fled from Saul in the cave.

1 Be gracious to me, O God,
be gracious to me,
For my soul [A]takes refuge in You;
And in the [B]shadow of Your
wings I will take refuge
Until destruction [C]passes by.
2 I will cry to God Most High,
To God who [A]accomplishes
all things for me.
3 He will [A]send from heaven and save me;
He reproaches him who [a,B]tramples upon
me. [b]*Selah*
God will send forth His
[C]lovingkindness and His [c]truth.

4 My soul is among [A]lions;
I must lie among those who
breathe forth fire,
Even the sons of men, whose
[B]teeth are spears and arrows
And their [C]tongue a sharp sword.
5 [A]Be exalted above the heavens, O God;
Let Your glory *be* above all the earth.
6 They have [a]prepared a [A]net for my steps;
My soul is [B]bowed down;
They [C]dug a pit before me;
They *themselves* have [D]fallen into the
midst of it. *Selah*

7 [A]My [B]heart is steadfast, O God,
my heart is steadfast;
I will sing, yes, I will sing praises!

56:2 [a]Or *snapped at* [b]Or *many are fighting* [A]Ps 35:25; 57:3; 124:3 [B]Ps 35:1 56:3 [a]Lit *In the day* [b]Or *I am one who puts* [A]Ps 55:4, 5 [B]Ps 11:1 56:4 [a]Lit *flesh* [A]Ps 56:10, 11 [B]Ps 118:6; Heb 13:6 56:5 [a]Or *trouble my affairs* [b]Or *purposes* [A]2 Pet 3:16 [B]Ps 41:7 56:6 [a]Or *stir up strife* [b]Lit *heels* [c]Lit *soul* [A]Ps 59:3; 140:2; Is 54:15 [B]Ps 17:11 [C]Ps 71:10 56:7 [a]Or *will they have escape?* [A]Ps 36:12; Prov 19:5; Ezek 17:15; Rom 2:3 [B]Ps 55:23 56:8 [A]Ps 139:3 [B]2 Kin 20:5; Ps 39:12 [C]Mal 3:16 56:9 [a]Or *because* [A]Ps 9:3 [B]Ps 102:2 [C]Ps 41:11; 118:6; Rom 8:31 56:11 [a]Or *trust without fear* 56:12 [A]Ps 50:14 56:13 [a]Or *have You not delivered* [b]Or *life* [A]Ps 33:19; 49:15; 86:13 [B]Ps 116:8 [C]Ps 116:9 [D]Job 33:30 57:1 [†]Lit *Do Not Destroy* •Possibly, *Epigrammatic Poem* or *Atonement Psalm* *1 Sam 22:1; 24:3 [A]Ps 2:12; 34:22 [B]Ruth 2:12; Ps 17:8; 36:7; 63:7; 91:4 [C]Is 26:20 57:2 [A]Ps 138:8 57:3 [a]Or *snaps at* [b]*Selah* may mean: *Pause, Crescendo* or *Musical interlude* [c]Or *faithfulness* [A]Ps 18:16; 144:5, 7 [B]Ps 56:2 [C]Ps 25:10; 40:11 57:4 [A]Ps 35:17; 58:6 [B]Prov 30:14 [C]Ps 55:21; 59:7; 64:3; Prov 12:18 57:5 [A]Ps 57:11; 108:5 57:6 [a]Or *spread* [A]Ps 10:9; 31:4; 35:7; 140:5 [B]Ps 145:14 [C]Ps 7:15 [D]Prov 26:27; 28:10; Eccl 10:8 57:7 [A]Ps 57:7-11; 108:1-5 [B]Ps 112:7

with Ps 55 (cf. Ps 55:6ff.). *See note on Ps 16:Title.*

56:3 I will put my trust in You. Confidence in the Lord is a purposeful decision, replacing an emotional reaction to one's circumstances.

56:5 All day. Anguish is intensified by unceasing harassment.

56:7 In anger. The anger of God is not an emotional loss of temper, but a judicial outrage resulting from God's holy nature reacting to wickedness and ungodliness.

56:8 my tears ... Your bottle. David asked God to keep a remembrance of all of his sufferings so that God would eventually vindicate him.

56:11 What can man do to me? No human has the power to overcome God's providential control.

56:12 vows. Confident that the Lord would deliver him, David had already vowed to present a thank offering to God (cf. Lv 7:12; Ps 50:14).

57:1–11 This is another lament expressing supreme confidence in the Lord in the midst of calamitous circumstances. Though David finds himself hiding from Saul (see Title), he knows that his real refuge is not in the walls of the cave (cf. 1Sa 22:1; 24:3), but in the shadow of God's wings.

I. The Plea for Protection (57:1–6)
II. The Proffering of Praise (57:7–11)

57:Title Al-tashheth. Possibly the opening words of a known song, implying that this psalm should be sung to the same tune. *See note on Ps 16:Title.*

57:1 the shadow of Your wings. Metaphorically, God cares for His own as a mother bird protects its young. Symbolically, there may be a reference here to the cherubim wings on the ark of the covenant where God was specifically present (cf. Ex 37:1–16; Pss 17:8; 36:7; 61:4; 63:7; 91:1, 4). **I will take refuge.** When life becomes bizarre, only one's relationship with his God calms the soul.

57:2 God Most High. God is transcendent, elevated far above His creation and all powerful. **accomplishes *all things* for me.** God's transcendence (v. 2a) never removes Him from intimate involvement in His peoples' lives.

57:4 lions. The wicked are pictured as menacing animals, ready to destroy their prey with their razor-edged teeth (cf. Pss 7:2; 10:9; 17:12; 22:13). **breathe forth fire.** The wicked are like a consuming fire.

57:5 Be exalted .... God. A truly godly person wants God's glory to be exhibited more than he wants his own personal problems to be solved.

57:6 a net .... pit. Set a trap, as a hunter might entangle an animal's feet with a net.

57:7–11 These verses were borrowed by David for Ps 108:1–5.

8 Awake, [A]my glory!
Awake, [B]harp and lyre!
I will awaken the dawn.
9 [A]I will give thanks to You, O Lord,
among the peoples;
I will sing praises to You
among the [a]nations.
10 For Your [A]lovingkindness is
great to the heavens
And Your [a]truth to the clouds.
11 [A]Be exalted above the heavens, O God;
Let Your glory *be* above all the earth.

PSALM 58

PRAYER FOR THE PUNISHMENT OF THE WICKED.

For the choir director; *set to* [†]Al-tashheth.
A •Mikhtam of David.

1 Do you indeed [a]speak
righteousness, O [b]gods?
Do you [A]judge [c]uprightly, O sons of men?
2 No, in heart you [A]work unrighteousness;
On earth you [B]weigh out the
violence of your hands.
3 The wicked are estranged
[A]from the womb;
These who speak lies [B]go
astray from [a]birth.
4 They have venom like the
[A]venom of a serpent;
Like a deaf cobra that stops up its ear,
5 So that it [A]does not hear the
voice of [a,B]charmers,
Or a skillful caster of spells.
6 O God, [A]shatter their teeth in their mouth;
Break out the fangs of the
young lions, O LORD.
7 Let them [A]flow away like
water that runs off;
When he [a,B]aims his arrows, let
them be as [b]headless shafts.
8 *Let them be* as a snail which [a]melts
away as it goes along,
Like the [A]miscarriages of a woman
which never see the sun.
9 Before your [A]pots can feel *the fire of* thorns
He will [B]sweep them away
with a whirlwind, the [a]green
and the burning alike.

10 The [A]righteous will rejoice when
he [B]sees the vengeance;
He will [C]wash his feet in the
blood of the wicked.
11 And men will say, "Surely there is
a [a,A]reward for the righteous;
Surely there is a God who
[B]judges [b]on earth!"

PSALM 59

PRAYER FOR DELIVERANCE FROM ENEMIES.

For the choir director; *set to* [†]Al-tashheth. A •Mikhtam of David, *when Saul sent *men* and they watched the house in order to kill him.

1 [A]Deliver me from my enemies, O my God;
[a,B]Set me *securely* on high away from
those who rise up against me.

57:8 [A]Ps 16:9; 30:12 [B]Ps 150:3 57:9 [a]Lit *peoples* [A]Ps 108:3 57:10 [a]Or *faithfulness* [A]Ps 36:5; 103:11; 108:4 57:11 [A]Ps 57:5; 108:5 58:1 [†]Lit *Do Not Destroy* •Possibly *Epigrammatic Poem* or *Atonement Psalm* [a]Another reading is *speak righteousness in silence* [b]Or *mighty ones or judges* [c]Or *uprightly the sons of men* [A]Ps 82:2 58:2 [A]Mal 3:15 [B]Ps 94:20; Is 10:1 58:3 [a]Lit *the womb* [A]Ps 51:5; Is 48:8 [B]Ps 53:3 58:4 [A]Deut 32:33; Ps 140:3 58:5 [a]Or *whisperers* [A]Jer 8:17 [B]Eccl 10:11 58:6 [A]Job 4:10; Ps 3:7 58:7 [a]Lit *bends* [b]Lit *though they were cut off* [A]Josh 2:11; 7:5; Ps 112:10; Is 13:7; Ezek 21:7 [B]Ps 64:3 58:8 [a]I.e. secretes slime [A]Job 3:16; Eccl 6:3 58:9 [a]Lit *living* [A]Ps 118:12; Eccl 7:6 [B]Job 27:21; Ps 83:15; Prov 10:25 58:10 [A]Job 22:19; Ps 32:11; 64:10; 107:42 [B]Deut 32:43; Ps 91:8; Jer 11:20; 20:12 [C]Ps 68:23 58:11 [a]Lit *fruit* [b]Or *in* [A]Ps 18:20; 19:11; Is 3:10; Luke 6:23, 35 [B]Ps 9:8; 67:4; 75:7; 94:2 59:1 [†]Lit *Do Not Destroy* •Possibly *Epigrammatic Poem* or *Atonement Psalm* *1 Sam 19:11 [a]Or *May You put me in an inaccessibly high place* [A]Ps 143:9 [B]Ps 20:1; 69:29

57:8 my glory! The mind, that rational, intellectual, emotional part of a person which interacts with and praises God. *See note on 16:9.* **I will awaken the dawn.** He cannot wait until morning to praise the Lord for all of His blessings. He must wake up the personified dawn so that he can praise the Lord.

57:9 the peoples … nations. References to Gentiles, nations which would not normally know Jehovah God.

57:10 to the heavens. David is thinking as broadly (v. 9) and as highly (vv. 10, 11) as he can. God's mercy, truth, and glory are immense and unfathomable (cf. Ro 11:33; Eph 3:17, 18).

58:1–11 As a lament against tyranny, the first half of the psalm rehearses a series of charges against wicked leaders and judges; and the second half is an imprecatory prayer that they be obliterated. In the end, the psalmist is certain that God will act with ultimate justice.

I. The Indictment of Unjust Leaders (58:1–5)
II. The Imprecation Against Unjust Leaders (58:6–11)

58:Title Al-tashheth. *See note on Ps 57:Title. See note on Ps 16:Title.*

58:1 O gods. The leaders were silent when they should have spoken up for righteousness.

58:2 weigh out. These wicked rulers meditate on the strategy for wicked schemes.

58:3 go astray from birth. All people are born totally depraved. Without being made new creatures in Christ by God's power, they are prevented by their wicked nature from pleasing God (cf. Ps 51:5; Ro 3:9–18; 2Co 5:17).

58:4 They have venom. The words and actions of these tyrants are like poisonous venom in a serpent's fangs. **deaf cobra.** Like a cobra which cannot hear its charmer are these stubborn rulers, who ignore all encouragements to righteousness.

58:6 shatter their teeth … fangs. The psalmist prays that the means of doing evil would be destroyed.

58:7 flow away like water. An imprecatory prayer that the tyrants would disappear like water seeping into sand in a dry wadi. **arrows … as headless shafts.** Apparently a prayer that the intentions of evil would be rendered as ineffective as broken arrows.

58:8 snail which melts away. A simile for that which is transitive, perhaps based facetiously on the idea that a snail depletes itself in its own trail as it moves along.

58:9 Before your pots … thorns. An obscure metaphor implying swiftness. The Lord will quickly destroy the wicked rulers.

58:10 wash his feet in the blood. The point of the figure is that the wicked will eventually be defeated and the righteous will share with the Lord in His victory.

58:11 God who judges on earth. In the end, the righteous will see that Jehovah is not indifferent to injustices.

59:1–17 This is another in a series of laments in which the psalmist pleads for God to defend him against his oppressors. The psalm is a mixture of prayers, unfavorable descriptions of the adversary, imprecations, and praise to God. Though written when David was king of Israel, the psalm recalls an earlier time of anguish when Saul sought to kill David (1Sa 19:11). Ultimately David's strong confidence in God's sovereignty transforms the lament into a song of assurance.

I. A Plea for God's Deliverance (59:1–15)
II. Praise for God's Defense (59:16, 17)

59:Title Al-tashheth. *See note on Ps 57:Title.* **Mikhtam.** *See note on Ps 16:Title.* **Saul sent *men* … to kill him.** The setting for the

2 Deliver me from [A]those who do iniquity
And save me from [B]men of bloodshed.
3 For behold, they [A]have [a]set an
ambush for my [b]life;
[c]Fierce men [d,A]launch an attack against me,
[B]Not for my transgression nor
for my sin, O LORD,
4 [a,A]For no guilt of *mine,* they run and
set themselves against me.
[B]Arouse Yourself to [b]help me, and see!
5 You, [A]O LORD God of hosts, the God of Israel,
Awake to [a,B]punish all the nations;
[C]Do not be gracious to any *who are*
treacherous in iniquity. [b]*Selah*
6 They [A]return at evening, they
howl like a [B]dog,
And go around the city.
7 Behold, they [A]belch forth with their mouth;
[B]Swords are in their lips,
For, *they say,* "[C]Who hears?"
8 But You, O LORD, [A]laugh at them;
You [B]scoff at all the nations.

9 *Because of* [a]his [A]strength I
will watch for You,
For God is my [B]stronghold.
10 [a]My God [A]in His lovingkindness
will meet me;
God will let me [B]look *triumphantly*
upon [b]my foes.
11 Do not slay them, [A]or my
people will forget;
[a,B]Scatter them by Your power,
and bring them down,
O Lord, [C]our shield.
12 [a]*On account of* the [A]sin of their mouth
and the words of their lips,
Let them even be [B]caught in their pride,
And on account of [C]curses and
[b]lies which they utter.
13 [a,A]Destroy *them* in wrath, [a]destroy
them that they may be no more;
That *men* may [B]know that
God [b]rules in Jacob
To the ends of the earth. *Selah*
14 They [A]return at evening,
they howl like a dog,
And go around the city.
15 They [A]wander about [a]for food
And [b]growl if they are not satisfied.

16 But as for me, I shall [A]sing of Your strength;
Yes, I shall [B]joyfully sing of Your
lovingkindness in the [C]morning,
For You have been my [D]stronghold
And a [E]refuge in the day of my distress.
17 [A]O my strength, I will sing praises to You;
For God is my [B]stronghold, the [a]God
who shows me lovingkindness.

PSALM 60

LAMENT OVER DEFEAT IN BATTLE, AND PRAYER FOR HELP.

For the choir director; according to [†]Shushan Eduth. A [•]Mikhtam of David, to teach; [*]when he struggled with Aram-naharaim and with Aram-zobah, and Joab returned, and smote twelve thousand of Edom in the Valley of Salt.

1 O God, [A]You have rejected us.
You have [a,B]broken us;
You have been [C]angry; O, [D]restore us.
2 You have made the [a,A]land quake,
You have split it open;
[B]Heal its breaches, for it totters.
3 You have [a,A]made Your people
experience hardship;
You have given us [b]wine to [B]drink
that makes us stagger.

59:2 [A]Ps 28:3; 36:12; 53:4; 92:7; 94:16 [B]Ps 26:9; 139:19; Prov 29:10 59:3 [a]Or *lain in wait* [b]Lit *soul* [c]Or *Strong* [d]Or *stir up strife* [A]Ps 56:6 [B]1 Sam 24:11; Ps 7:3, 4; 69:4 59:4 [a]Lit *Without guilt* [b]Lit *meet* [A]Ps 35:19 [B]Ps 7:6; 35:23 59:5 [a]Lit *visit* [b]*Selah* may mean: *Pause, Crescendo* or *Musical interlude* [A]Ps 69:6; 80:4; 84:8 [B]Ps 9:5; Is 26:14 [C]Is 2:9; Jer 18:23 59:6 [A]Ps 59:14 [B]Ps 22:16 59:7 [A]Ps 94:4; Prov 15:2, 28 [B]Ps 57:4; Prov 12:18 [C]Job 22:13; Ps 10:11; 73:11; 94:7 59:8 [A]Ps 37:13; Prov 1:26 [B]Ps 2:4 59:9 [a]Many mss and some ancient versions read *My strength* [A]Ps 18:17 [B]Ps 9:9; 62:2 59:10 [a]Many mss and some ancient versions read *The God of my lovingkindness* [b]Lit *those who lie in wait for me* [A]Ps 21:3 [B]Ps 54:7 59:11 [a]Or *Make them wander* [A]Deut 4:9; 6:12 [B]Ps 106:27; 144:6; Is 33:3 [C]Ps 84:9 59:12 [a]Or *The sin of their mouth is the word of their lips,* [b]Lit *lying* [A]Prov 12:13 [B]Zeph 3:11 [C]Ps 10:7 59:13 [a]Lit *Bring to an end* [b]Or *is Ruler* [A]Ps 104:35 [B]Ps 83:18 59:14 [A]Ps 59:6 59:15 [a]Or *to devour* [b]Another reading is *tarry all night* [A]Job 15:23 59:16 [A]Ps 21:13 [B]Ps 101:1 [C]Ps 5:3; 88:13 [D]Ps 59:9 [E]2 Sam 22:3; Ps 46:1 59:17 [a]Lit *God of my lovingkindness* [A]Ps 59:9 [B]Ps 59:10 60:1 [†]Lit *The lily of testimony* [•]Possibly, *Epigrammatic Poem* or *Atonement Psalm* [*]2 Sam 8:3, 13; 1 Chr 18:3, 12 [a]Or *broken out upon us* [A]Ps 44:9 [B]2 Sam 5:20 [C]Ps 79:5 [D]Ps 80:3 60:2 [a]Or *earth* [A]Ps 18:7 [B]2 Chr 7:14; Is 30:26 60:3 [a]Lit *caused Your people to see* [b]Lit *wine of staggering* [A]Ps 66:12; 71:20 [B]Ps 75:8; Is 51:17, 22; Jer 25:15

psalm is 1Sa 19:11. David's wife (Saul's daughter) helped David escape through a window in the middle of the night.

59:5 God of hosts. "Hosts" represent God's angels as His army.

59:6 howl like a dog. Dogs of the ancient world were often wild scavengers. Here, they serve as a simile for the messengers of Saul outside David's house setting an ambush.

59:7 belch … with their mouth. Pictures the coarse, uncouth character of Saul's henchmen (cf. v. 12). **Swords are in their lips.** Their conversation was dedicated to the assassination of David. *they say,* "Who hears?" A blasphemy implying that God either doesn't exist or doesn't know what happens in the affairs of mankind.

59:8 all the nations. Gentiles (*see note on Ps 57:9*). This phrase and "my people" in v. 11 imply that this psalm was written several years after the event when David was king and involved in international affairs. David wrote his psalms as a prophet under the superintendence of the Holy Spirit (2Sa 23:2).

59:11 my people will forget. The psalmist thinks that if the Lord were to destroy the wicked too quickly, the lesson of God's hatred of evil might not be impressed on the minds of the people.

60:1–12 This psalm is a national lament written after the unexpected military setback alluded to in 2Sa 8:13 and 1Ch 18:12. While David and the main part of his army were fighting in the northern part of the country, one of Israel's other neighboring enemies, Edom, successfully attacked the southern part of Judah. David ultimately prevailed in victory. The psalm expresses the feelings of a people shocked and confused by a tragedy which suggested that God had abandoned them. Verses 5–12 are essentially repeated in Ps 108:6–13.

I. The People's Contemplation of Abandonment (60:1–5)
II. The Lord's Control over the Nations (60:6–8)
III. The People's Confidence in God (60:9–12)

60:Title Joab … smote twelve thousand. The Lord soon rewarded their confidence in Him, enabling the armies of Israel to slaughter the Edomites.

60:2 land quake. Earthquake imagery is used to illustrate that what appears secure sometimes is not.

60:3 wine … that makes us stagger. This metaphor compares the impact of wine on the mind with the confusion which comes

4 You have given a [A]banner to
those who fear You,
That it may be displayed because of the
truth. [a]*Selah*
5 [A]That Your [B]beloved may
be delivered,
[C]Save with Your right hand,
and answer [a]us!

6 God has spoken in His [a,A]holiness:
"I will exult, I will portion
out [B]Shechem and measure
out the valley of [C]Succoth.
7 "[A]Gilead is Mine, and
Manasseh is Mine;
[B]Ephraim also is the
[a]helmet of My head;
Judah is My [b,C]scepter.
8 "[A]Moab is My washbowl;
Over [B]Edom I shall
throw My shoe;
Shout loud, O [C]Philistia,
because of Me!"

9 Who will bring me into
the besieged city?
Who [a]will lead me to Edom?
10 Have not You Yourself,
O God, [A]rejected us?
And [B]will You not go forth with
our armies, O God?
11 O give us help against the adversary,
For [A]deliverance [a]by man is in vain.
12 [a]Through God we shall [A]do valiantly,
And it is He who will [B]tread
down our adversaries.

PSALM 61

CONFIDENCE IN GOD'S PROTECTION.

For the choir director; on a stringed
instrument. *A Psalm* of David.

1 [A]Hear my cry, O God;
[B]Give heed to my prayer.
2 From the [A]end of the earth I call to
You when my heart is [B]faint;
Lead me to [C]the rock that is higher than I.
3 For You have been a [A]refuge for me,
A [B]tower of strength [a]against the enemy.
4 Let me [a,A]dwell in Your tent forever;
Let me [B]take refuge in the shelter of Your
wings. [b]*Selah*

5 For You have heard my [A]vows, O God;
You have given *me* the inheritance
of those who [B]fear Your name.
6 You will [a,A]prolong the king's [b]life;
His years will be as many generations.
7 He will [a]abide [A]before God forever;
Appoint [B]lovingkindness and truth
that they may preserve him.
8 So I will [A]sing praise to Your name forever,
That I may [B]pay my vows day by day.

PSALM 62

GOD ALONE A REFUGE FROM TREACHERY AND OPPRESSION.

For the choir director; [†]according
to Jeduthun. A Psalm of David.

1 [A]My soul *waits* in silence for God only;
From Him [B]is my salvation.

60:4 [a]*Selah* may mean: *Pause, Crescendo* or *Musical interlude* [A]Ps 20:5; Is 5:26; 11:12; 13:2 60:5 [a]Some authorities read *me* [A]Ps 60:5-12; 108:6-13 [B]Deut 33:12; Ps 127:2; Is 5:1; Jer 11:15 [C]Ps 17:7 60:6 [a]Or *sanctuary* [A]Ps 89:35 [B]Gen 12:6; 33:18; Josh 17:7 [C]Gen 33:17; Josh 13:27 60:7 [a]Lit *protection* [b]Or *lawgiver* [A]Josh 13:31 [B]Deut 33:17 [C]Gen 49:10 60:8 [A]2 Sam 8:2 [B]2 Sam 8:14 [C]2 Sam 8:1 60:9 [a]Or *has led* 60:10 [A]Ps 60:1; 108:11 [B]Josh 7:12; Ps 44:9 60:11 [a]Lit *of* [A]Ps 146:3 60:12 [a]Or *In* or *With* [A]Num 24:18; Ps 118:16 [B]Ps 44:5; Is 63:3 61:1 [A]Ps 64:1 [B]Ps 86:6 61:2 [A]Ps 42:6 [B]Ps 77:3 [C]Ps 18:2; 94:22 61:3 [a]Lit *from* [A]Ps 62:7 [B]Ps 59:9; Prov 18:10 61:4 [a]Or *sojourn* [b]*Selah* may mean: *Pause, Crescendo* or *Musical interlude* [A]Ps 23:6; 27:4 [B]Ps 17:8; 91:4 61:5 [A]Job 22:27; Ps 56:12 [B]Deut 28:58; Neh 1:11; Ps 86:11; 102:15; Is 59:19; Mal 2:5; 4:2 61:6 [a]Lit *add days to* [b]Lit *days* [A]Ps 21:4 61:7 [a]Or *sit enthroned* [A]Ps 41:12 [B]Ps 40:11 61:8 [A]Judg 5:3; Ps 30:4; 33:2; 71:22 [B]Ps 65:1; Is 19:21 62:1 [†]Cf 1 Chr 16:41; 25:1; Ps 39 and 77 titles [A]Ps 33:20 [B]Ps 37:39

from a bewildering event in life.

60:4 banner. God and His truth serve as a rallying point for the perplexed people.

60:5 beloved. Beloved refers to God's beloved people ruled over by David.

60:6 Shechem … Succoth. These are two territories on opposite sides of the Jordan, occupied by Israel. Jacob had settled in Succoth (E of the Jordan) when he returned from his sojourn with Laban (cf. Ge 33:17).

60:7 Gilead … Ephraim. All of these key geographical locations in Israel ultimately belonged to God, who was more interested in their welfare than anyone else. **helmet.** Ephraim was the primary source of defense to the N of Israel. **scepter.** Judah was the tribe which was to govern Israel, from which David and his descendants came.

60:8 Moab … Edom … Philistia. The 3 principal enemies surrounding Israel to the NE, SE, and W, respectively. **Moab is My washbowl.** The psalmist pictures Moab as a humble, menial servant to God, either being or bringing a washbasin for His use. **Over Edom … shoe.** The picture is that of a man entering his house and throwing his shoes to his servant. Edom, like Moab, was a servant under God's sovereign control. **Shout loud, O Philistia.** The difficult translation has two possibilities: 1) Philistia shouts its submission to God or 2) God shouts over Philistia in victory. Either one exalts God as victor/ruler.

60:12 Through God … valiantly. The nation relearned the truth that only God gives victory.

61:1–8 David may have written this wonderful psalm when his own son, Absalom, temporarily drove him away from his throne in Israel (2Sa 15–18). The psalm is rich in metaphors and references to God's covenants with Israel. David once again demonstrates a godly response to overwhelming and depressing developments in life.

I. The Cry for Help (61:1, 2)
II. The Confidence in God (61:3–7)
III. The Commitment to Loyalty (61:8)

61:2 From the end of the earth. David's absence from his homeland compounds his feelings of discouragement and exhaustion. The phrase also hints at feelings of estrangement from God. **my heart is faint.** David's hope and courage were failing. **the rock that is higher.** David expresses his disregard of personal autonomy and his reliance on his God in this metaphor for refuge.

61:3 tower of strength. One of 4 figures of speech in vv. 3, 4 for security; the strong towers stabilized the city walls and served as places of defense and refuge.

61:5 inheritance. Refers to the benefits, including life in the Promised Land (cf. Dt 28–30), of participating in a covenant with God.

61:6 prolong the king's life. In the immediate context, David prays for himself in his struggle with Absalom. Beyond this, here is a prayer for the continuity of the divinely established monarchy. Because he realized that one of his descendants would be the Messiah, David sometimes does not distinguish himself from the messianic dynasty.

61:7 forever. The Davidic Covenant guaranteed that on the basis of God's merciful and faithful dealings with David and the nation, David's descendants would rule on the throne of Israel forever (cf. 2Sa 7; Pss 40:11; 89:4, 33–37).

61:8 pay my vows day by day. As a regular means of expressing thanksgiving for prayers answered, the psalmist promised daily obedience to his Lord (cf. Ps 56:12).

62:1–12 Whether Absalom's rebellion is the

2 He only is my [A]rock and my salvation,
My [B]stronghold; I shall not
be greatly shaken.

3 How long will you assail a man,
That you may murder *him,* all of you,
Like a [A]leaning wall, like
a tottering fence?
4 They have counseled only to thrust
him down from his high position;
They [A]delight in falsehood;
They [B]bless with [a]their mouth,
But inwardly they curse. [b]*Selah*

5 My soul, [A]wait in silence for God only,
For my hope is from Him.
6 He only is [A]my rock and
my salvation,
My stronghold; I shall not be shaken.
7 On God my [A]salvation and
my glory *rest;*
The rock of my strength, my
[B]refuge is in God.
8 [A]Trust in Him at all times, O people;
[B]Pour out your heart before Him;
God is a refuge for us. *Selah*

9 Men of [A]low degree are only [B]vanity
and men of rank are a [C]lie;
In the [D]balances they go up;
They are together lighter than breath.
10 [A]Do not trust in oppression
And do not [a]vainly hope in [B]robbery;
If riches increase, [C]do not set
your heart *upon them.*

11 [a]Once God has [A]spoken;
[b]Twice I have heard this:
That [B]power belongs to God;
12 And lovingkindness [A]is Yours, O Lord,
For You [B]recompense a man
according to his work.

PSALM 63

THE THIRSTING SOUL SATISFIED IN GOD.

A Psalm of David, [†]when he was in the wilderness of Judah.

1 O God, [A]You are my God; I shall
seek You [a]earnestly;
My soul [B]thirsts for You, my
flesh [b]yearns for You,
In a [C]dry and weary land where
there is no water.
2 Thus I have [A]seen You in the sanctuary,
To see Your power and Your glory.
3 Because Your [A]lovingkindness
is better than life,
My lips will praise You.
4 So I will bless You [A]as long as I live;
I will [B]lift up my hands in Your name.
5 My soul is [A]satisfied as with
[a]marrow and fatness,
And my mouth offers [B]praises
with joyful lips.

6 When I remember You [A]on my bed,
I meditate on You in the [B]night watches,
7 For [A]You have been my help,
And in the [B]shadow of Your
wings I sing for joy.
8 My soul [A]clings [a]to You;
Your [B]right hand upholds me.

9 But those who [A]seek my [a]life to destroy it,
Will go into the [b,B]depths of the earth.

62:2 [A]Ps 89:26 [B]Ps 59:17; 62:6 62:3 [A]Is 30:13 62:4 [a]Lit *his* [b]*Selah* may mean: *Pause, Crescendo* or *Musical interlude* [A]Ps 4:2 [B]Ps 28:3; 55:21 62:5 [A]Ps 62:1 62:6 [A]Ps 62:2 62:7 [A]Ps 85:9; Jer 3:23 [B]Ps 46:1 62:8 [A]Ps 37:3, 5; 52:8; Is 26:4 [B]1 Sam 1:15; Ps 42:4; Lam 2:19 62:9 [A]Ps 49:2 [B]Job 7:16; Ps 39:5; Is 40:17 [C]Ps 116:11 [D]Is 40:15 62:10 [a]Lit *become vain in robbery* [A]Is 30:12 [B]Is 61:8; Ezek 22:29; Nah 3:1 [C]Job 31:25; Ps 49:6; 52:7; Mark 10:24; Luke 12:15; 1 Tim 6:10 62:11 [a]Or *One thing* [b]Or *These two things I have heard* [A]Job 33:14; 40:5 [B]Ps 59:17; Rev 19:1 62:12 [A]Ps 86:5; 103:8; 130:7 [B]Job 34:11; Ps 28:4; Jer 17:10; Matt 16:27; Rom 2:6; 1 Cor 3:8; Rev 2:23 63:1 [†]1 Sam 22:5; 23:14 [a]Lit *early* [b]Lit *faints* [A]Ps 118:28 [B]Ps 42:2; 84:2; Matt 5:6 [C]Ps 143:6 63:2 [A]Ps 27:4 63:3 [A]Ps 69:16 63:4 [A]Ps 104:33; 146:2 [B]Ps 28:2; 143:6 63:5 [a]Lit *fat* [A]Ps 36:8 [B]Ps 71:23 63:6 [A]Ps 4:4 [B]Ps 16:7; 42:8; 119:55 63:7 [A]Ps 27:9 [B]Ps 17:8 63:8 [a]Lit *after* [A]Num 32:12; Deut 1:36; Hos 6:3 [B]Ps 18:35; 41:12 63:9 [a]Lit *soul* [b]Lit *lowest places* [A]Ps 40:14 [B]Ps 55:15

setting or not (2Sa 15–18), David writes this psalm while facing treason from someone. David faces the problem of his adversaries forthrightly (vv. 3, 4), but his thoughts focus primarily on God (cf. Php 4:4–13).

I. Affirming God's Covenant Relationship (62:1, 2, 5, 6)
II. Confronting One's Treasonous Adversaries (62:3, 4)
III. Trusting God's Sovereignty (62:7–10)
IV. Praising God's Power and Mercy (62:11, 12)

62:Title according to Jeduthun. An official temple musician. *See note on Ps 39:Title.*

62:1 *waits* in silence for God. Silence indicates trust that is both patient and uncomplaining (cf. v. 5).

62:2 greatly shaken. Means "demoralized."

62:3 leaning wall ... tottering fence. A metaphor for imminent collapse. Some apply it to the victim, but as translated here it refers to the attacker.

62:6 I shall not be shaken. David demonstrates his increased confidence in the Lord.

62:9 low degree ... men of rank. All men, regardless of social status, are woefully inadequate objects of trust.

63:1–11 In deepest words of devotion, this psalm expresses David's intense love for his Lord. The psalm was written while David was in the Judean wilderness, either during his flight from Saul (1Sa 23), or more likely from Absalom (2Sa 15; cf. 63:11 "the king"). David writes from the perspective of these tenses:

I. Present—Seeking God's Presence (63:1–5)
II. Past—Remembering God's Power (63:6–8)
III. Future—Anticipating God's Judgment (63:9–11)

63:1 I shall seek You earnestly. Eagerness to be with the Lord in every situation is more in view than the time of day. **My soul thirsts.** David longs for God's presence like a wanderer in a desert longs for water. **In a dry and weary land.** David writes this psalm while hiding in the wilderness of Judea, but longing to be back worshiping in Jerusalem.

63:3 better than life. God's covenant love is more valuable to David than life itself (cf. Php 1:21; Ac 20:24).

63:4 lift up my hands. As an OT posture of prayer, the upheld hands pictured both the ascent of prayer and the readiness to receive every good gift which comes from God (cf. Jas 1:17). It was thus a posture of trust in God alone.

63:5 marrow and fatness. A metaphor comparing the spiritual and emotional satisfaction of the divine presence with the satisfaction of rich banquet food.

63:8 My soul clings to You. In response to God's repeated invitation to "hold fast" to Him (Dt 4:4; 10:20; 13:4), the psalmist clings to God. This signifies David's unfailing commitment to his Lord.

63:9 into the depths of the earth. A reference to the realm of the dead. *See note on Eph 4:9.*

10 [a]They will be [b,A]delivered over to
the power of the sword;
They will be a [c,B]prey for foxes.
11 But the [A]king will rejoice in God;
Everyone who [B]swears
by Him will glory,
For the [C]mouths of those who
speak lies will be stopped.

PSALM 64

PRAYER FOR DELIVERANCE FROM SECRET ENEMIES.

For the choir director. A Psalm of David.

1 Hear my voice, O God,
in [A]my [a]complaint;
[B]Preserve my life from
dread of the enemy.
2 Hide me from the [A]secret
counsel of evildoers,
From the tumult of [B]those
who do iniquity,
3 Who [A]have sharpened their
tongue like a sword.
They [B]aimed bitter speech *as* their arrow,
4 To [A]shoot [a]from concealment
at the blameless;
Suddenly they shoot at him,
and [B]do not fear.
5 They [a]hold fast to themselves
an evil purpose;
They [b]talk of [A]laying snares secretly;
They say, "[B]Who can see them?"
6 They [a]devise injustices, *saying,*
"We are [b]ready with a well-conceived plot";
For the [c,A]inward thought and the
heart of a man are [d]deep.
7 But [A]God [a]will shoot at them
with an arrow;
Suddenly [b]they will be wounded.
8 So [a]they [b]will [A]make him stumble;
[B]Their own tongue is against them;
All who see them will [C]shake the head.
9 Then all men [a]will [A]fear,
And they [b]will [B]declare the work of God,
And [c]will consider [d]what He has done.
10 The righteous man will be [A]glad in the
LORD and will [B]take refuge in Him;
And all the upright in heart will glory.

PSALM 65

GOD'S ABUNDANT FAVOR TO EARTH AND MAN.

For the choir director. A Psalm of David. A Song.

1 There will be silence [a]before You,
and praise in Zion, O God,
And to You the [A]vow will be performed.
2 O You who hear prayer,
To You [A]all [a]men come.
3 [a,A]Iniquities prevail against me;
As for our transgressions,
You [b,B]forgive them.
4 How [A]blessed is the one whom You
[B]choose and bring near *to You*
To dwell in Your courts.
We will be [C]satisfied with the
goodness of Your house,
Your holy temple.

5 By [A]awesome *deeds* You answer us in
righteousness, O [B]God of our salvation,
You who are the trust of all the [C]ends of
the earth and of the farthest [a,D]sea;

63:10 [a]Lit *They will pour him out* [b]Lit *poured out by* [c]Lit *portion* [A]Jer 18:21; Ezek 35:5 [B]Lam 5:18 63:11 [A]Ps 21:1 [B]Deut 6:13; Is 45:23; 65:16 [C]Job 5:16; Ps 107:42; Rom 3:19 64:1 [a]Or *concern* [A]Ps 55:2 [B]Ps 140:1 64:2 [A]Ps 56:6 [B]Ps 59:2 64:3 [A]Ps 140:3 [B]Ps 58:7 64:4 [a]Lit *in* [A]Ps 10:8; 11:2 [B]Ps 55:19 64:5 [a]Lit *make firm* [b]Lit *tell of* [A]Ps 140:5 [B]Job 22:13; Ps 10:11 64:6 [a]Or *search out* [b]Lit *complete* [c]Or *inward part* [d]Or *unsearchable* [A]Ps 49:11 64:7 [a]Or *shot* [b]Or *they were wounded;* lit *their wounds occurred* [A]Ps 7:12, 13 64:8 [a]Or *they make their tongue a stumbling for themselves* [b]Or *made* [A]Ps 9:3 [B]Prov 12:13; 18:7 [C]Ps 22:7; 44:14; Jer 18:16; 48:27; Lam 2:15 64:9 [a]Or *feared* [b]Or *declared* [c]Or *considered* [d]Lit *His work* [A]Ps 40:3 [B]Jer 51:10 64:10 [A]Job 22:19; Ps 32:11 [B]Ps 11:1; 25:20 65:1 [a]Lit *to* [A]Ps 116:18 65:2 [a]Lit *flesh* [A]Ps 86:9; 145:21; Is 66:23 65:3 [a]Lit *Words of iniquities* [b]Lit *cover over, atone for* [A]Ps 38:4; 40:12 [B]Ps 79:9 65:4 [A]Ps 33:12; 84:4 [B]Ps 4:3 [C]Ps 36:8 65:5 [a]Or *seas* [A]Ps 45:4; 66:3 [B]Ps 85:4 [C]Ps 22:27; 48:10 [D]Ps 107:23

63:10 **foxes.** Scavengers, feasting on unburied bodies (*see note on Ps 53:5*).

63:11 **who swears by Him.** The Mosaic Covenant instructed this practice expressing loyalty to the true God alone (cf. Dt 6:13; 10:20; 1Ki 8:31; Jer 12:16).

64:1–10 This psalm begins with a vivid description of the devious ways of the wicked, especially their speech (vv. 3–5, 8). Still, the psalmist does not fear that God will lose control of the situation. After seeing His justice at work, the righteous will be glad and trust all the more in Him (64:10).

I. The Malevolent Ingenuity of the Wicked (64:1–6)
II. The Memorable Reciprocation by the Lord (64:7–10)

64:1 **Preserve ... from dread.** The psalmist recognized that the fear of an enemy can be as destructive as an actual assault.

64:3 **sharpened their tongue.** Their intent was to slander with their speech (cf. Ps 59:7).

64:4 **from concealment.** Anonymously.

64:5 **Who can see them?** This was a question of brazen autonomy. They mock the omniscience of God (cf. Ps 59:7).

64:6 **inward thought ... heart ... deep.** The evil intent of the unrighteous flows from inward depravity.

64:7 **God will shoot ... arrow.** The arrows of God, as OT history demonstrates, include natural judgments such as deadly disease, defeat, and calamity.

64:8 **stumble ... own tongue.** God providentially steers the plots of the wicked to their own demise.

64:9 **will declare.** Believers should glorify God, not only for His love and mercy, but also for His marvelous acts of judgment on the wicked.

65:1–13 This is a praise psalm, full of hopeful, confident, even enthusiastic feelings in response to God's goodness with no complaints or curses. The setting is a celebration at the tabernacle, perhaps at Passover and the Feast of Unleavened Bread in the spring, or the Feast of Booths, or Tabernacles, in the fall.

I. Praise for Spiritual Blessings (65:1–5)
II. Praise for Natural Blessings (65:6–13)

65:1 **Zion.** Specifically the hill in Jerusalem where Israel worshiped Jehovah, but also synonymous with the Promised Land (cf. Ps 48:2; also Pss 3:4; 9:12; 24:3; 68:5; 87). **vow ... performed.** This is likely a reference to vows made by the farmers because of an abundant harvest (cf. Pss 56:12; 61:8).

65:2 **all men come.** Reference to the future millennial kingdom when all the world will worship the Lord (cf. Zec 14:16–19).

65:3 **forgive.** The word, found 3 times in the Psalms (78:38; 79:9), means to cover sin and its effects. In the OT, atonement was symbolized in sacrificial ritual (cf. Ex 30:10; Lv 16:10, 11), though actual forgiveness of sin was ultimately based on the death of Christ applied to the penitent sinner (cf. Heb 9).

65:5 **trust ... earth ... sea.** Unlike local heathen gods, Jehovah God is not just the

6 Who [A]establishes the mountains
by His strength,
Being [B]girded with might;
7 Who [A]stills the roaring of the seas,
The roaring of their waves,
And the [B]tumult of the peoples.
8 They who dwell in the [A]ends *of the earth* stand in awe of Your signs;
You make the [a]dawn and the
sunset shout for joy.

9 You visit the earth and [A]cause
it to overflow;
You greatly [B]enrich it;
The [a,C]stream of God is full of water;
You prepare their [D]grain, for thus
You prepare [b]the earth.
10 You water its furrows abundantly,
You [a]settle its ridges,
You soften it [A]with showers,
You bless its growth.
11 You have crowned the year
[a]with Your [b,A]bounty,
And Your [c]paths [B]drip *with* fatness.
12 [A]The pastures of the wilderness drip,
And the [B]hills gird themselves
with rejoicing.
13 The meadows are [A]clothed with flocks
And the valleys are [B]covered with grain;
They [C]shout for joy, yes, they sing.

PSALM 66

PRAISE FOR GOD'S MIGHTY DEEDS AND FOR HIS ANSWER TO PRAYER.

For the choir director. A Song. A Psalm.

1 [A]Shout joyfully to God, all the earth;
2 Sing the [A]glory of His name;
Make His [B]praise glorious.
3 Say to God, "How [A]awesome
are Your works!
Because of the greatness of Your
power Your enemies will [a,B]give
feigned obedience to You.
4 "[A]All the earth will worship You,
And will [B]sing praises to You;
They will sing praises to Your name."
[a]*Selah*

5 [A]Come and see the works of God,
Who is [B]awesome in *His* deeds
toward the sons of men.
6 He [A]turned the sea into dry land;
They passed through [B]the river on foot;
There let us [C]rejoice in Him!
7 He [A]rules by His might forever;
His [B]eyes keep watch on the nations;
Let not the rebellious [C]exalt themselves.
Selah

8 Bless our God, O peoples,
And [a,A]sound His praise abroad,
9 Who [a,A]keeps us in life
And [B]does not allow our feet to [b]slip.
10 For You have [A]tried us, O God;
You have [B]refined us as silver is refined.
11 You [A]brought us into the net;
You laid an oppressive burden
upon our loins.
12 You made men [A]ride over our heads;
We went through [B]fire and through water,
Yet You [C]brought us out into
a place of abundance.
13 I shall [A]come into Your house
with burnt offerings;
I shall [B]pay You my vows,
14 Which my lips uttered
And my mouth spoke when
I was [A]in distress.

65:6 [A]Ps 95:4 [B]Ps 93:1 65:7 [A]Ps 89:9; 93:3, 4; 107:29; Matt 8:26 [B]Ps 2:1; 74:23; Is 17:12, 13 65:8 [a]Lit *the outgoings of the morning and evening* [A]Ps 2:8; 139:9; Is 24:16 65:9 [a]Or *channel* [b]Lit *it* [A]Lev 26:4; Job 5:10; Ps 68:9; 104:13; 147:8; Jer 5:24 [B]Ps 104:24 [C]Ps 46:4 [D]Ps 104:14; 147:14 65:10 [a]Or *smooth* [A]Deut 32:2; Ps 72:6; 147:8 65:11 [a]Lit *of* [b]Or *goodness* [c]I.e. wagon tracks [A]Ps 104:28 [B]Job 36:28; Ps 147:14 65:12 [A]Job 38:26, 27; Joel 2:22 [B]Ps 98:8; Is 55:12 65:13 [A]Ps 144:13; Is 30:23 [B]Ps 72:16 [C]Ps 98:8; Is 44:23; 55:12 66:1 [A]Ps 81:1; 95:1; 98:4; 100:1 66:2 [A]Ps 79:9; Is 42:8 [B]Is 42:12 66:3 [a]Lit *deceive* [A]Ps 47:2; 65:5; 145:6 [B]Ps 18:44; 81:15 66:4 [a]*Selah* may mean: *Pause, Crescendo* or *Musical interlude* [A]Ps 22:27; 67:7; 86:9; 117:1; Zech 14:16 [B]Ps 67:4 66:5 [A]Ps 46:8 [B]Ps 106:22 66:6 [A]Ex 14:21; Ps 106:9 [B]Josh 3:16; Ps 114:3 [C]Ps 105:43 66:7 [A]Ps 145:13 [B]Ps 11:4 [C]Ps 140:8 66:8 [a]Lit *cause to hear the sound of His praise* [A]Ps 98:4 66:9 [a]Lit *puts our soul in life* [b]Or *dodder, stumble* [A]Ps 30:3 [B]Ps 121:3 66:10 [A]Job 23:10; Ps 7:9; 17:3; 26:2 [B]Is 48:10; Zech 13:9; Mal 3:3; 1 Pet 1:7 66:11 [A]Lam 1:13; Ezek 12:13 66:12 [A]Is 51:23 [B]Ps 78:21; Is 43:2 [C]Ps 18:19 66:13 [A]Ps 96:8; Jer 17:26 [B]Ps 22:25; 116:14; Eccl 5:4 66:14 [A]Ps 18:6

God of a single locality. The universal worship of the Lord is required of all men (cf. Ro 1:18–32) and will be a reality in the messianic era when the kingdom of God will cover the earth (cf. Is 2:1–4; Zec 14:9).

65:8 dawn … sunset. The nations who live in the E where the sun first makes its morning appearance, and those who live in the W where the sun disappears into darkness rejoice in the Lord.

65:11 paths drip *with* fatness. Like a farm wagon dropping its overflow along the cart path.

66:1–20 This joyful psalm begins with group praise and then focuses on the individual worship. The psalmist rehearses some of the major miracles in Israel's history and testifies that God has always been faithful in the midst of serious troubles.

I. Communal Hymn of Praise to God (66:1–12)
  A. For Future Glory (66:1–4)
  B. For Previous Faithfulness (66:5–7)
  C. For Continual Protection (66:8–12)
II. An Individual Hymn of Praise to God (66:13–20)
  A. Through Fulfilled Vows (66:13–15)
  B. For Answered Prayer (66:16–20)

66:1 Shout joyfully. A shout of loyalty and homage, as in 1Sa 10:24.

66:4 All the earth will worship You. This praise is not only an acknowledgment of God's universal Lordship, but also an intimation of the people's belief in a future worldwide kingdom where God will be worshiped (cf. Is 66:23; Zec 14:16; Php 2:10, 11).

66:6 sea … river. A reference to the crossing of the Red Sea and possibly the Jordan River. The OT writers considered the Red Sea crossing the ultimate demonstration of God's power, as well as His care for Israel.

66:9 feet to slip. God had prevented them from prematurely slipping into the realm of the dead.

66:10 refined us as silver. God had brought the nation through purifying trials.

66:11 brought us into the net. The psalmist speaks of a hunter's net or snare as a metaphor for some extremely difficult situations into which God had brought Israel.

66:12 ride over our heads. A picture of a hostile army riding in victory over Israel's defeated troops.

66:13 pay You my vows. Paying the vows is spelled out in the following verses as offering sacrifices of dedication which had been previously promised God (cf. Lv 1; 22:18, 21; Pss 56:12; 61:8; 65:1).

15 I shall [A]offer to You burnt
offerings of fat beasts,
With the smoke of [B]rams;
I shall make *an offering of* [a]bulls with
male goats. *Selah*

16 [A]Come *and* hear, all who [a]fear God,
And I will [B]tell of what He
has done for my soul.
17 I cried to Him with my mouth,
And [a]He was [A]extolled with my tongue.
18 If I [a,A]regard wickedness in my heart,
The [B]Lord [b]will not [c]hear;
19 But certainly [A]God has heard;
He has given heed to the
voice of my prayer.
20 [A]Blessed be God,
Who [B]has not turned away my prayer
Nor His lovingkindness from me.

PSALM 67

THE NATIONS EXHORTED TO PRAISE GOD.

For the choir director; with stringed instruments. A Psalm. A Song.

1 God be gracious to us and [A]bless us,
And [B]cause His face to shine [a]upon us—
[b]*Selah*
2 That [A]Your way may be
known on the earth,
[B]Your salvation among all nations.
3 Let the [A]peoples praise You, O God;
Let all the peoples praise You.
4 Let the [A]nations be glad and sing for joy;
For You will [B]judge the peoples
with uprightness
And [C]guide the nations on the earth.
Selah
5 Let the [A]peoples praise You, O God;
Let all the peoples praise You.
6 The [A]earth has yielded its produce;
God, our God, [B]blesses us.
7 God blesses us,
[a]That [A]all the ends of the
earth may fear Him.

PSALM 68

THE GOD OF SINAI AND OF THE SANCTUARY.

For the choir director. A Psalm of David. A Song.

1 [a]Let [A]God arise, [b]let His
enemies be scattered,
And [c]let those who hate Him
flee before Him.
2 As [A]smoke is driven away,
so drive *them* away;
As [B]wax melts before the fire,
So let the [C]wicked perish before God.
3 But let the [A]righteous be glad;
let them exult before God;
Yes, let them rejoice with gladness.
4 Sing to God, [A]sing praises to His name;
[a,B]Lift up *a song* for Him who [C]rides
through the deserts,
Whose [D]name is [b]the LORD,
and exult before Him.

5 A [A]father of the fatherless and a
[B]judge [a]for the widows,
Is God in His [C]holy habitation.
6 God [a,A]makes a home for the lonely;
He [B]leads out the prisoners into prosperity,
Only [C]the rebellious dwell
in a parched land.

7 O God, when You [A]went forth
before Your people,
When You [B]marched through the
wilderness, [a]*Selah*
8 The [A]earth quaked;
The [B]heavens also dropped *rain*
at the presence of God;
[a,C]Sinai itself *quaked* at the presence
of God, the God of Israel.

66:15 [a]Or *cattle* [A]Ps 51:19 [B]Num 6:14 66:16 [a]Or *revere* [A]Ps 34:11 [B]Ps 71:15, 24 66:17 [a]Or *praise was under my tongue* [A]Ps 30:1 66:18 [a]Or *had regarded* [b]Or *would* [c]Or *have heard* [A]Job 36:21; John 9:31 [B]Job 27:9; Ps 18:41; Prov 1:28; 28:9; Is 1:15; James 4:3 66:19 [A]Ps 18:6; 116:1, 2 66:20 [A]Ps 68:35 [B]Ps 22:24 67:1 [a]Lit *with* [b]*Selah* may mean: *Pause, Crescendo* or *Musical interlude* [A]Num 6:25 [B]Ps 4:6; 31:16; 80:3, 7, 19; 119:135 67:2 [A]Ps 98:2; Acts 18:25; Titus 2:11 [B]Is 52:10 67:3 [A]Ps 66:4 67:4 [A]Ps 100:1, 2 [B]Ps 9:8; 96:10, 13; 98:9 [C]Ps 47:8 67:5 [A]Ps 67:3 67:6 [A]Lev 26:4; Ps 85:12; Ezek 34:27; Zech 8:12 [B]Ps 29:11; 115:12 67:7 [a]Or *And let all...earth fear Him* [A]Ps 22:27; 33:8 68:1 [a]Or *God shall* [b]Or *His enemies shall* [c]Or *those who hate Him shall* [A]Num 10:35; Ps 12:5; 132:8 68:2 [A]Ps 37:20; Is 9:18; Hos 13:3 [B]Ps 22:14; 97:5; Mic 1:4 [C]Ps 9:3; 37:20; 80:16 68:3 [A]Ps 32:11; 64:10; 97:12 68:4 [a]Or *Cast up* a highway [b]Heb *YAH* [A]Ps 66:2 [B]Is 57:14; 62:10 [C]Deut 33:26; Ps 18:10; 68:33; Is 40:3 [D]Ex 6:3; Ps 83:18 68:5 [a]Lit *of* [A]Ps 10:14; 146:9 [B]Deut 10:18 [C]Deut 26:15 68:6 [a]Lit *makes the solitary to dwell in a house* [A]Ps 107:4-7; 113:9 [B]Ps 69:33; 102:20; 107:10, 14; 146:7; Acts 12:7; 16:26 [C]Ps 78:17; 107:34, 40 68:7 [a]*Selah* may mean: *Pause, Crescendo* or *Musical interlude* [A]Ex 13:21; Ps 78:14; Hab 3:13 [B]Judg 5:4; Ps 78:52 68:8 [a]Lit *This is Sinai* which [A]Ex 19:18; Judg 5:4; 2 Sam 22:8; Ps 77:18; Jer 10:10 [B]Judg 5:4; Ps 18:9; Is 45:8 [C]Ex 19:18; Judg 5:5

67:1–7 This brief psalm develops two optimistic themes: the need and result of God's mercy, and the future universal worship of God. The psalm reflects the promise to Abraham that God would bless his descendants, and in Abraham, "all the families of the earth" (Ge 12:1–3).

I. The Prayer for Divine Mercy (67:1, 2)
II. The Plea for Universal Worship (67:3–5)
III. The Prospect of Divine Blessings (67:6, 7)

67:1 face to shine. When a king smiled on a supplicant with pleasure, the petitioner was likely to receive his request (cf. Nu 6:24–26; Pss 31:16; 44:3; 80:3, 7, 19; 119:135; Pr 16:15).

67:3 peoples. A reference to the inclusion of the Gentile nations in the millennial kingdom (cf. Is 56:3–8; 60:1–14; Zec 14:16–19; Mt 8:11; 25:31–46; Rev 20:1–10).

68:1–35 This exuberant psalm includes prayer, praise, thanksgiving, historical reminder, and imprecation. It expresses a pride in Jehovah God for His care over His people and His majesty in the universe. The writing of this psalm may have come out of David's jubilant restoration of the ark of the covenant to Jerusalem (cf. 2Sa 6:12–15).

I. A Fanfare of Commendation (68:1–6)
II. A Reflection on Faithfulness (68:7–18)
III. An Acclamation of Majesty (68:19–31)
IV. An Invitation to Praise (68:32–35)

68:1 Let God arise. The first sentence in this psalm is essentially the same as Nu 10:35. It was perhaps a fanfare of words announcing the movement of the ark of the covenant (cf. vv. 24–27; also 2Sa 6:12–15).

68:4 name is the LORD. Other names for God in this psalm include God (Elohim, v. 1), Lord (Adonai, v. 11), Almighty (v. 14), Lord God (v. 18), God the Lord (v. 20), and King (v. 24).

68:6 home for the lonely. God cares for those who have lost families, especially the

9 You [A]shed abroad a plentiful rain, O God;
You confirmed Your inheritance
when it was [a]parched.
10 Your creatures settled in it;
You [A]provided in Your goodness
for the poor, O God.

11 The Lord gives the [a]command;
The [A]women who proclaim the
good tidings are a great host:
12 "[A]Kings of armies flee, they flee,
And she who remains at home
will [B]divide the spoil!"
13 [a]When you lie down [A]among
the [b]sheepfolds,
You are like the wings of a dove
covered with silver,
And its pinions with glistening gold.
14 When the Almighty [A]scattered
the kings [a]there,
It was snowing in [B]Zalmon.

15 A [a,A]mountain of God is the
mountain of Bashan;
A mountain *of many* peaks is
the mountain of Bashan.
16 Why do you look with envy,
O mountains with *many* peaks,
At the mountain which God has
[A]desired for His abode?
Surely [B]the LORD will dwell *there* forever.
17 The [A]chariots of God are [a]myriads,
[B]thousands upon thousands;
[b]The Lord is among them *as*
at Sinai, in holiness.
18 You have [A]ascended on high, You
have [B]led captive *Your* captives;
You have received gifts among men,
Even *among* the rebellious also, that
[a]the LORD God may dwell *there.*

19 Blessed be the Lord, who daily
[A]bears our burden,
[B]The God *who* is our salvation. *Selah*

20 God is to us a [A]God of deliverances;
And [B]to [a]GOD the Lord belong
escapes [b]from death.
21 Surely God will [A]shatter the
head of His enemies,
The hairy crown of him who goes
on in his guilty deeds.
22 The Lord [a]said, "[A]I will bring
them back from Bashan.
I will bring *them* back from
the depths of the sea;
23 That [a,A]your foot may shatter
them in blood,
The tongue of your [B]dogs *may have*
its portion from *your* enemies."

24 They have seen [A]Your
[a]procession, O God,
The [a]procession of my God, my
King, [b,B]into the sanctuary.
25 The [A]singers went on, the
musicians after *them,*
[a]In the midst of the [B]maidens
beating tambourines.
26 [A]Bless God in the congregations,
Even the LORD, *you who are* of
the [B]fountain of Israel.
27 There is [A]Benjamin, the
[a]youngest, [b]ruling them,
The princes of Judah *in* their throng,
The princes of [B]Zebulun, the
princes of Naphtali.

28 [a]Your God has [A]commanded your strength;
Show Yourself strong, O God, [B]who
have acted [b]on our behalf.
29 [a]Because of Your temple at Jerusalem
[A]Kings will bring gifts to You.
30 Rebuke the [A]beasts [a]in the reeds,
The herd of [B]bulls with the
calves of the peoples,
Trampling under foot the pieces of silver;
He has [C]scattered the peoples
who delight in war.

68:9 [a]Lit *weary* [A]Lev 26:4; Deut 11:11; Job 5:10; Ezek 34:26 68:10 [A]Ps 65:9; 74:19; 78:20; 107:9 68:11 [a]Lit *word* [A]Ex 15:20; 1 Sam 18:6 68:12 [A]Josh 10:16; Judg 5:19; Ps 135:11 [B]Judg 5:30; 1 Sam 30:24 68:13 [a]Lit *If* [b]Or *cooking stones* or *saddle bags* [A]Gen 49:14; Judg 5:16 68:14 [a]Lit *in it* [A]Josh 10:10 [B]Judg 9:48 68:15 [a]Or *mighty mountain is* [A]Ps 36:6 68:16 [A]Deut 12:5; Ps 87:1, 2; 132:13 [B]Ps 132:14 68:17 [a]Lit *twice ten thousand* [b]Another reading is *The Lord came from Sinai into the sanctuary* [A]2 Kin 6:17; Hab 3:8 [B]Deut 33:2; Dan 7:10 68:18 [a]Heb *YAH* [A]Ps 7:7; 47:5; Eph 4:8 [B]Judg 5:12 68:19 [A]Ps 55:22; Is 46:4 [B]Ps 65:5 68:20 [a]Heb *YHWH,* usually rendered *LORD* [b]I.e. in view of; lit *for* [A]Ps 106:43 [B]Deut 32:39; Ps 49:15; 56:13 68:21 [A]Ps 110:6; Hab 3:13 68:22 [a]Or *says* [A]Num 21:33; Amos 9:1-3 68:23 [a]Some versions render, you may *bathe your foot in blood* [A]Ps 58:10 [B]1 Kin 21:19; Jer 15:3 68:24 [a]Lit *goings* [b]Lit *in the sanctuary;* or *in holiness* [A]Ps 77:13 [B]Ps 63:2 68:25 [a]Or *The maidens in the midst* [A]1 Chr 13:8; 15:6; Ps 47:6 [B]Ex 15:20; Judg 11:34 68:26 [A]Ps 22:22, 23; 26:12 [B]Deut 33:28; Is 48:1 68:27 [a]Or *smallest* [b]Or *their ruler* [A]Judg 5:14; 1 Sam 9:21 [B]Judg 5:18 68:28 [a]Some mss read *Command, God* [b]Lit *for us* [A]Ps 29:11; 44:4 [B]Is 26:12 68:29 [a]Or *From Your temple* [A]1 Kin 10:10, 25; 2 Chr 32:23; Ps 45:12; 72:10; Is 18:7 68:30 [a]Lit *of* [A]Job 40:21; Ezek 29:3 [B]Ps 22:12 [C]Ps 18:14; 89:10

orphans and widows (v. 5; cf. Ex 22:22–24; Ps 10:14; Jas 1:27). **leads out the prisoners.** Speaks of God's liberating prisoners of war.

68:9 confirmed Your inheritance. God sustains His covenant people.

68:14 snowing in Zalmon. "Zalmon" means "black" or "dark mountain." The "snow" pictures the contrast of corpses or bones scattered over the mountain.

68:15 mountain of Bashan. A mountain across the Jordan to the E, here figuratively described as jealous of Mt. Zion (cf. v. 16), the place which had been chosen for the special presence of God (cf. Jer 22:20, 21).

68:17 Sinai, in holiness. God's presence had been with the armies in the same way it had been on Mt. Sinai at the giving of the law (cf. Ex 19).

68:18 ascended on high. Paul quotes this text in Eph 4:8 where he applies it to Christ's ascending to the heavens in triumph.

68:22 Bashan … sea. Whether the enemy tries to escape by land (Bashan) or by sea, God will bring them back to be destroyed by His people (cf. Am 9:2–4).

68:24 procession … sanctuary. A description of the celebration when the ark of the covenant, a symbol of God's presence, was brought to Mt. Zion (cf. 1Ch 15:16–28).

68:27 Benjamin … Naphtali. Representative tribes of Israel, two from the S (Benjamin and Judah) and two from the N (Zebulun and Naphtali).

68:29 Kings … gifts. This section of praise (vv. 28–35) looks forward to the Messiah's reign when the world will universally worship God in the temple in Jerusalem (cf. Is 2:2–4; 18:7; 45:14; 60:3–7; Eze 40–48; Hag 2:7; Zec 2:11–13; 6:15; 8:21, 22; 14:16–19).

68:30 pieces of silver. Tribute money, signifying subservience to God.

31 Envoys will come out of [A]Egypt;
[a,B]Ethiopia will quickly stretch
out her hands to God.

32 Sing to God, O [A]kingdoms of the earth,
[B]Sing praises to the Lord, *Selah*
33 To Him who [A]rides upon
the [a,B]highest heavens, which
are from ancient times;
Behold, [C]He [b]speaks forth with
His voice, a [D]mighty voice.
34 [A]Ascribe strength to God;
His majesty is over Israel
And [B]His strength is in the [a]skies.
35 [a]O God, *You are* [A]awesome
from Your [b]sanctuary.
The God of Israel Himself [B]gives
strength and power to the people.
[C]Blessed be God!

PSALM 69

A CRY OF DISTRESS AND IMPRECATION ON ADVERSARIES.

For the choir director; according to [†]Shoshannim. *A Psalm* of David.

1 Save me, O God,
For the [A]waters have [a]threatened my life.
2 I have sunk in deep [A]mire, and
there is no foothold;
I have come into deep waters, and
a [a,B]flood overflows me.
3 I am [A]weary with my crying;
my throat is parched;
My [B]eyes fail while I wait for my God.
4 Those [A]who hate me without a cause
are more than the hairs of my head;
Those who would [a]destroy
me [B]are powerful, being
wrongfully my enemies;
[C]What I did not steal, I then
have to restore.
5 O God, it is You who knows [A]my folly,
And [B]my wrongs are not
hidden from You.
6 May those who wait for You not
[A]be ashamed through me,
O Lord [a]GOD of hosts;
May those who seek You not
be dishonored through
me, O God of Israel,
7 Because [A]for Your sake I have
borne reproach;
[B]Dishonor has covered my face.
8 I have become [A]estranged
[a]from my brothers
And an alien to my mother's sons.
9 For [A]zeal for Your house
has consumed me,
And [B]the reproaches of those who
reproach You have fallen on me.
10 When I wept [A]in my soul with fasting,
It became my reproach.
11 When I made [A]sackcloth my clothing,
I became [B]a byword to them.
12 Those who [A]sit in the gate talk about me,
And I *am* the [a,B]song of the drunkards.

13 But as for me, my prayer is to You,
O LORD, [A]at an acceptable time;
O God, in the [B]greatness of
Your lovingkindness,
Answer me with [a]Your saving truth.
14 Deliver me from the [A]mire and
do not let me sink;
May I be [B]delivered from [a]my foes
and from the [b,A]deep waters.
15 May the [a,A]flood of water not overflow me
Nor the deep swallow me up,
Nor the [B]pit shut its mouth on me.

16 Answer me, O LORD, for [A]Your
lovingkindness is good;
[B]According to the greatness of Your
compassion, [C]turn to me,

68:31 [a]Lit *Cush* [A]Is 19:19, 21 [B]Is 45:14; Zeph 3:10 68:32 [A]Ps 102:22 [B]Ps 67:4 68:33 [a]Lit *heaven of heavens of old* [b]Lit *gives forth* [A]Deut 33:26; Ps 18:10; 104:3 [B]Deut 10:14; 1 Kin 8:27 [C]Ps 46:6 [D]Ps 29:4 68:34 [a]Lit *clouds* [A]Ps 29:1 [B]Ps 150:1 68:35 [a]Or *Awesome is God from your sanctuary* [b]Lit *holy places* [A]Deut 7:21; 10:17; Ps 47:2; 66:5 [B]Ps 29:11; Is 40:29 [C]Ps 66:20; 2 Cor 1:3 69:1 [†]Or possibly *Lilies* [a]Lit *come to the soul* [A]Job 22:11; Ps 32:6; 42:7; 69:14, 15; Jon 2:5 69:2 [a]Lit *flowing stream* [A]Ps 40:2 [B]Jon 2:3 69:3 [A]Ps 6:6 [B]Deut 28:32; Ps 38:10; 119:82, 123; Is 38:14 69:4 [a]Or *silence* [A]Ps 35:19; John 15:25 [B]Ps 35:19; 38:19; 59:3 [C]Ps 35:11; Jer 15:10 69:5 [A]Ps 38:5 [B]Ps 44:21 69:6 [a]Heb *YHWH*, usually rendered *LORD* [A]2 Sam 12:14 69:7 [A]Jer 15:15 [B]Ps 44:15; Is 50:6; Jer 51:51 69:8 [a]Lit *to* [A]Job 19:13-15; Ps 31:11; 38:11 69:9 [A]Ps 119:139; John 2:17 [B]Ps 89:41, 50; Rom 15:3 69:10 [A]Ps 35:13 69:11 [A]1 Kin 20:31; Ps 35:13 [B]1 Kin 9:7; Job 17:6; Ps 44:14; Jer 24:9 69:12 [a]Lit *songs* [A]Gen 19:1; Ruth 4:1 [B]Job 30:9 69:13 [a]Or *the faithfulness of Your salvation* [A]Ps 32:6; Is 49:8; 2 Cor 6:2 [B]Ps 51:1 69:14 [a]Lit *those who hate me* [b]Lit *deep places of water* [A]Ps 69:2 [B]Ps 144:7 69:15 [a]Lit *stream* [A]Ps 124:4, 5 [B]Num 16:33; Ps 28:1; 141:7 69:16 [A]Ps 63:3; 109:21 [B]Ps 51:1; 106:45 [C]Ps 25:16; 86:16

69:1–36 This psalm is a prayer of desperation. David realizes that because he is hated by others, he may shortly be killed. Though he begs for rescue, and calls down curses on his enemies, he concludes the psalm with a high note of praise, with inferences concerning the coming messianic kingdom when all enemies of God's people are dealt with swiftly and severely (cf. Rev 2:27). Much of this psalm was applied to Christ by the NT writers. This psalm expresses the feelings of any believer who is being horribly ridiculed, but it uniquely refers to Christ.

I. The Prayer of Desperation (69:1–28)
   A. The Description of His Situation (69:1–3)
   B. The Reason for His Situation (69:4–12)
   C. The Hope for His Situation (69:13–18)
   D. The Reproach of His Situation (69:19–21)
   E. The Revenge for His Situation (69:22–28)
II. The Promise of Salvation (69:29–36)

69:Title according to Shoshannim. The name of a tune. *See note on Ps 45:Title.*

69:4 hate me. Quoted in Jn 15:25.

69:6 be ashamed. The psalmist fears that his dismal situation may be a stumbling block to other believers.

69:8 alien … sons. Even his family rejected him (cf. Mt 12:46–50; Jn 7:3–5).

69:9 has consumed me. The psalmist has brought hatred and hostility on himself by his unyielding insistence that the behavior of the people measure up to their outward claim of devotion to God. Whenever God was dishonored he felt the pain, because he loved God so greatly. Jesus claimed for Himself this attitude, as indicated in Jn 2:17; Ro 15:3.

69:11 sackcloth. David's wearing of sackcloth, a symbol of grief, brought even more ridicule.

69:12 sit in the gate. The highest in society, those who sat in the gate of a city, were usually governmental officials. Even their city leaders were gossiping about the psalmist. **song of the drunkards.** The dregs of society, the drunkards, ridiculed David in their raucous songs.

69:15 pit shut its mouth. The "pit" was another word for Sheol, the realm of the dead. The psalmist felt that death was imminent.

17 And [A]do not hide Your face
from Your servant,
For I am [B]in distress; answer me quickly.
18 Oh draw near to my soul *and* [A]redeem it;
[B]Ransom me because of my enemies!
19 You know my [A]reproach and my
shame and my dishonor;
All my adversaries are [a]before You.

20 Reproach has [A]broken my
heart and I am so sick.
And [B]I looked for sympathy,
but there was none,
And for [C]comforters, but I found none.
21 They also gave me [a,A]gall [b]for my food
And for my thirst they [B]gave
me vinegar to drink.

22 May [A]their table before them
become a snare;
And [a,B]when they are in peace,
may it become a trap.
23 May their [A]eyes grow dim so
that they cannot see,
And make their [B]loins
shake continually.
24 [A]Pour out Your indignation on them,
And may Your burning anger
overtake them.
25 May their [a,A]camp be desolate;
May none dwell in their tents.
26 For they have [A]persecuted him whom
[B]You Yourself have smitten,
And they tell of the pain of those
whom [C]You have [a]wounded.
27 Add [A]iniquity to their iniquity,
And [B]may they not come into
[C]Your righteousness.
28 May they be [A]blotted out of
the [B]book of life
And may they not be [a,C]recorded
with the righteous.

29 But I am [A]afflicted and in pain;
[a]May Your salvation, O God, [B]set
me *securely* on high.
30 I will [A]praise the name of God with song
And [B]magnify Him with [C]thanksgiving.
31 And it will [A]please the LORD
better than an ox
Or a young bull with horns and hoofs.
32 The [A]humble [a]have seen
it and are glad;
You who seek God, [B]let
your heart [b]revive.
33 For [A]the LORD hears the needy
And [B]does not despise His
who are prisoners.

34 Let [A]heaven and earth praise Him,
The seas and [B]everything
that moves in them.
35 For God will [A]save Zion and
[B]build the cities of Judah,
That they may dwell there and [C]possess it.
36 The [a,A]descendants of His
servants will inherit it,
And those who love His name
[B]will dwell in it.

PSALM 70

PRAYER FOR HELP AGAINST PERSECUTORS.

For the choir director. *A Psalm* of David;
for a memorial.

1 [A]O God, *hasten* to deliver me;
O LORD, hasten to my help!
2 [A]Let those be ashamed and humiliated
Who seek my [a]life;
Let those be turned back and dishonored
Who delight [b]in my hurt.
3 [A]Let those be [a]turned back
because of their shame
Who say, "Aha, aha!"

4 Let all who seek You rejoice
and be glad in You;
And let those who love Your
salvation say continually,
"Let God be magnified."
5 But [A]I am afflicted and needy;
[B]Hasten to me, O God!
You are my help and my deliverer;
O LORD, do not delay.

69:17 [A]Ps 27:9; 102:2; 143:7 [B]Ps 31:9; 66:14 69:18 [A]2 Sam 4:9; Ps 26:11; 49:15 [B]Ps 119:134 69:19 [a]Or known *to You* [A]Ps 22:6; 31:11 69:20 [A]Jer 23:9 [B]Ps 142:4; Is 63:5 [C]Job 16:2 69:21 [a]Or *poison* [b]Or *in* [A]Deut 29:18 [B]Matt 27:34, 48; Mark 15:23, 36; Luke 23:36; John 19:28-30 69:22 [a]Lit *for those who are secure* [A]Rom 11:9, 10 [B]1 Thess 5:3 69:23 [A]Is 6:10 [B]Dan 5:6 69:24 [A]Ps 79:6; Jer 10:25; Ezek 20:8; Hos 5:10 69:25 [a]Lit *encampment* [A]Matt 23:38; Luke 13:35; Acts 1:20 69:26 [a]Lit *pierced* [A]2 Chr 28:9; Zech 1:15 [B]Is 53:4 [C]Ps 109:22 69:27 [A]Neh 4:5; Ps 109:14; Rom 1:28 [B]Is 26:10 [C]Ps 103:17 69:28 [a]Lit *written* [A]Ex 32:32, 33; Rev 3:5 [B]Phil 4:3; Rev 13:8; 17:8; 20:15 [C]Ps 87:6; Ezek 13:9; Luke 10:20; Heb 12:23 69:29 [a]Or *Your salvation, O God, will set...* [A]Ps 70:5 [B]Ps 20:1; 59:1 69:30 [A]Ps 28:7 [B]Ps 34:3 [C]Ps 50:14 69:31 [A]Ps 50:13, 14; 51:16 69:32 [a]Some mss and ancient versions read *will see* [b]Or *live* [A]Ps 34:2 [B]Ps 22:26 69:33 [A]Ps 12:5 [B]Ps 68:6 69:34 [A]Ps 96:11; 98:7; 148:1-13; Is 44:23; 49:13 [B]Is 55:12 69:35 [A]Ps 46:5; 51:18 [B]Ps 147:2; Is 44:26 [C]Obad 17 69:36 [a]Lit *seed* [A]Ps 25:13; 102:28 [B]Ps 37:29 70:1 [A]Ps 40:13-17; 70:1-5 70:2 [a]Or *soul* [b]Or *to injure me* [A]Ps 35:4, 26 70:3 [a]Some mss read *appalled* [A]Ps 40:15 70:5 [A]Ps 40:17 [B]Ps 141:1

69:21 gall ... vinegar. Gall was a poisonous herb. Here it serves as a metaphor for betrayal. Friends who should provide sustenance to the psalmist had turned against him. Gall in vinegar was actually offered to Christ while He was on the cross (Mt 27:34).

69:22 table ... become a snare. A snare was a trap for birds. The psalmist prays that the plots of the wicked against him would backfire and destroy them instead.

69:22, 23 Quoted in Ro 11:9, 10.

69:25 Quoted in Ac 1:20 with reference to Judas.

69:26 him whom You ... have smitten. Those hostile to the psalmist were ridiculing him as one suffering from God's chastisement. In its messianic application, the suffering of the Messiah was a part of God's plan from eternity past (cf. Is 53:10).

69:31 better than an ox ... bull. See Ps 51:16; also Heb 9:11, 12; 10:9–12. **horns and hoofs.** Implies a grown animal, one that would be especially valuable.

70:1–5 This prayer for deliverance from one's enemies is nearly identical to Ps 40:13–17. It substitutes "God" for "Lord" in vv. 1, 4, 5.

PSALM 71

PRAYER OF AN OLD MAN FOR DELIVERANCE.

1 [A]In You, O LORD, I have taken refuge;
Let me never be ashamed.
2 [A]In Your righteousness deliver
me and rescue me;
[B]Incline Your ear to me and save me.
3 [A]Be to me a rock of [B]habitation to
which I may continually come;
You have given [C]commandment
to save me,
For You are [D]my [a]rock and my fortress.
4 [A]Rescue me, O my God, out of
the hand of the wicked,
Out of the [a]grasp of the wrongdoer
and ruthless man,
5 For You are my [A]hope;
O Lord [a]GOD, *You are* my
[B]confidence from my youth.
6 [a]By You I have been [A]sustained
from *my* birth;
You are He who [B]took me from
my mother's womb;
My [C]praise is continually [b]of You.

7 I have become a [A]marvel to many,
For You are [B]my strong refuge.
8 My [A]mouth is filled with Your praise
And with [B]Your glory all day long.
9 Do not cast me off in the
[A]time of old age;
Do not forsake me when
my strength fails.
10 For my enemies have spoken
[a]against me;
And those who [A]watch for my [b]life
[B]have consulted together,
11 Saying, "[A]God has forsaken him;
Pursue and seize him, for there
is [B]no one to deliver."

12 O God, [A]do not be far from me;
O my God, [B]hasten to my help!
13 Let those who are adversaries of my
soul be [A]ashamed *and* consumed;
Let them be [B]covered with
reproach and dishonor,
who [C]seek [a]to injure me.
14 But as for me, I will [A]hope continually,
And will [a,B]praise You yet
more and more.
15 My [A]mouth shall tell of Your
righteousness
And of [B]Your salvation all day long;
For I [C]do not know the [a]sum *of them*.
16 I will come [A]with the mighty
deeds of the Lord [a]GOD;
I will [B]make mention of Your
righteousness, Yours alone.

17 O God, You [A]have taught me
from my youth,
And I still [B]declare Your
wondrous deeds.
18 And even when *I am* [A]old and gray,
O God, do not forsake me,
Until I [B]declare Your [a]strength
to *this* generation,
Your power to all who are to come.
19 [a]For Your [A]righteousness, O God,
reaches to the [b]heavens,
You who have [B]done great things;
O God, [C]who is like You?
20 You who have [A]shown [a]me many
troubles and distresses
Will [B]revive [a]me again,
And will bring [a]me up again [C]from
the depths of the earth.
21 May You increase my [A]greatness
And turn *to* [B]comfort me.

22 I will also praise You with [a,A]a harp,
Even Your [b]truth, O my God;
To You I will sing praises with the [B]lyre,
O [C]Holy One of Israel.
23 My lips will [A]shout for joy when
I sing praises to You;
And my [B]soul, which You have redeemed.
24 My [A]tongue also will utter Your
righteousness all day long;
For they are [B]ashamed, for they are
humiliated who seek [a]my hurt.

71:1 [A]Ps 25:2, 3; 31:1-3; 71:1-3 71:2 [A]Ps 31:1 [B]Ps 17:6 71:3 [a]Or *crag* [A]Ps 31:2, 3 [B]Deut 33:27; Ps 90:1; 91:9 [C]Ps 7:6; 42:8 [D]Ps 18:2 71:4 [a]Lit *palm* [A]Ps 140:1, 4 71:5 [a]Heb *YHWH*, usually rendered *LORD* [A]Ps 39:7; Jer 14:8; 17:7, 13, 17; 50:7 [B]Ps 22:9 71:6 [a]Lit *Upon You I have been supported* [b]Lit *in* [A]Ps 22:10; Is 46:3 [B]Job 10:18; Ps 22:9 [C]Ps 34:1 71:7 [A]Is 8:18; 1 Cor 4:9 [B]Ps 61:3 71:8 [A]Ps 35:28; 63:5 [B]Ps 96:6; 104:1 71:9 [A]Ps 71:18; 92:14; Is 46:4 71:10 [a]Lit *with reference to* [b]Lit *soul* [A]Ps 56:6 [B]Ps 31:13; 83:3; Matt 27:1 71:11 [A]Ps 3:2 [B]Ps 7:2 71:12 [A]Ps 10:1; 22:11; 35:22; 38:21 [B]Ps 38:22; 40:13; 70:1, 5 71:13 [a]Lit *my injury* [A]Ps 35:4, 26; 40:14 [B]Ps 109:29 [C]Esth 9:2; Ps 71:24 71:14 [a]Lit *add upon all Your praise* [A]Ps 130:7 [B]Ps 71:8 71:15 [a]Lit *numbers* [A]Ps 35:28 [B]Ps 96:2 [C]Ps 40:5 71:16 [a]Heb *YHWH*, usually rendered *LORD* [A]Ps 106:2 [B]Ps 51:14 71:17 [A]Deut 4:5; 6:7 [B]Ps 26:7; 40:5; 119:27 71:18 [a]Lit *arm* [A]Ps 71:9 [B]Ps 22:31; 78:4, 6 71:19 [a]Or *And* [b]Lit *height* [A]Ps 36:6; 57:10 [B]Ps 126:2; Luke 1:49 [C]Deut 3:24; Ps 35:10 71:20 [a]Another reading is *us* [A]Ps 60:3 [B]Ps 80:18; 85:6; 119:25; 138:7; Hos 6:1, 2 [C]Ps 86:13 71:21 [A]Ps 18:35 [B]Ps 23:4; 86:17; Is 12:1; 49:13 71:22 [a]Lit *an instrument of a harp* [b]Or *faithfulness* [A]Ps 33:2; 81:2; 92:1-3; 144:9 [B]Ps 33:2; 147:7 [C]2 Kin 19:22; Ps 78:41; 89:18; Is 1:4 71:23 [A]Ps 5:11; 32:11; 132:9, 16 [B]Ps 34:22; 55:18; 103:4 71:24 [a]Or *to injure me* [A]Ps 35:28 [B]Ps 71:13

71:1–24 One of the features of the psalms is that they meet the circumstances of life. This psalm to God expresses the concerns of old age. At a time in his life when he thinks he should be exempt from certain kinds of troubles, he once again is personally attacked. Though his enemies conclude that God has abandoned him, the psalmist is confident that God will remain faithful.

I. Confidence in God Stated (71:1–8)
II. Confidence in God Practiced in Prayer (71:9–13)
III. Confidence in God Vindicated (71:14–24)

71:3 continually. Psalm 71:1–3 is almost the same as Ps 31:1–3a. One difference, however, is the word "continually," which the elderly person writing this psalm wants to emphasize. God has "continually" been faithful (cf. vv. 6, 14).

71:7 a marvel. A reference to his trials. People are amazed at this person's life, some interpreting his trials as God's care, and others as God's punishment.

71:15 the sum *of them*. The blessings of God's salvation and righteousness are innumerable.

71:20 from the depths of the earth. Not actual resurrection, but rescue from near-death conditions and renewal of life's strength and meaning.

PSALM 72

THE REIGN OF THE RIGHTEOUS KING.

A Psalm of Solomon.

1 Give the king [A]Your judgments, O God,
And [B]Your righteousness to the king's son.
2 [a]May [b]he [A]judge Your people
with righteousness
And [c,B]Your afflicted with justice.
3 [a]Let the mountains bring
[b,A]peace to the people,
And the hills, in righteousness.
4 [a]May he [A]vindicate the [b]afflicted
of the people,
Save the children of the needy
And crush the oppressor.

5 [a]Let them fear You [A]while
the sun *endures,*
And [b]as long as the moon,
throughout all generations.
6 [a]May he come down [A]like rain
upon the mown grass,
Like [B]showers that water the earth.
7 In his days [a]may the
[A]righteous flourish,
And [B]abundance of peace till
the moon is no more.

8 May he also rule [A]from sea to sea
And from the River to the
ends of the earth.
9 [a]Let [A]the nomads of the desert
[B]bow before him,
And his enemies [C]lick the dust.
10 [a]Let the kings of [A]Tarshish and of
the [b,B]islands bring presents;
The kings of [C]Sheba and
[D]Seba [E]offer [c]gifts.
11 [a]And let all [A]kings bow down before him,
All [B]nations serve him.
12 For he will [A]deliver the needy
when he cries for help,
The [a]afflicted also, and him
who has no helper.
13 He will have [A]compassion on
the poor and needy,
And the [a]lives of the
needy he will save.
14 He will [a,A]rescue their [b]life from
oppression and violence,
And their blood will be
[B]precious in his sight;
15 So may he live, and may the [A]gold
of Sheba be given to him;
And let [a]them pray for
him continually;
Let [a]them bless him all day long.

16 May there be abundance
of grain in the earth on
top of the mountains;
Its fruit will wave like *the*
cedars of [A]Lebanon;
And may those from the city flourish
like [B]vegetation of the earth.
17 May his [A]name endure forever;
May his name [a]increase [b,B]as
long as the sun *shines;*
And let *men* [C]bless themselves by him;
[D]Let all nations call him blessed.

18 [A]Blessed be the LORD God,
the God of Israel,
Who alone [B]works wonders.
19 And blessed be His [A]glorious
name forever;
And may the whole [B]earth be
filled with His glory.
[C]Amen, and Amen.

20 The prayers of David the son
of Jesse are ended.

72:1 [A]1 Kin 3:9; 1 Chr 22:13 [B]Ps 24:5 72:2 [a]Or *He* will judge [b]Many of the pronouns in this Psalm may be rendered *He* since the typical reference is to the Messiah [c]Or *Your humble* [A]Is 9:7; 11:2-5; 32:1 [B]Ps 82:3 72:3 [a]Or *The mountains will bring* [b]Or *prosperity* [A]Is 2:4; 9:5, 6; Mic 4:3, 4; Zech 9:10 72:4 [a]Or *He will vindicate* [b]Or *humble* [A]Is 11:4 72:5 [a]Or *They will fear* [b]Lit *before the moon* [A]Ps 72:17; 89:36, 37 72:6 [a]Or *He will come down* [A]Deut 32:2; 2 Sam 23:4; Hos 6:3 [B]Ps 65:10 72:7 [a]Or *the righteous will flourish* [A]Ps 92:12 [B]Is 2:4 72:8 [A]Ex 23:31; Zech 9:10 72:9 [a]Or *The nomads...will bow* [A]Ps 74:14; Is 23:13 [B]Ps 22:29 [C]Is 49:23; Mic 7:17 72:10 [a]Or *The kings...will bring* [b]Or *coastlands* [c]Or *tribute* [A]2 Chr 9:21; Ps 48:7 [B]Ps 97:1; Is 42:4, 10; Zeph 2:11 [C]1 Kin 10:1; Job 6:19; Is 60:6 [D]Gen 10:7; Is 43:3 [E]Ps 45:12; 68:29 72:11 [a]Or *All kings will bow down* [A]Ps 138:4; Is 49:23 [B]Ps 86:9 72:12 [a]Or *humble* [A]Job 29:12; Ps 72:4 72:13 [a]Lit *souls* [A]Prov 19:17; 28:8 72:14 [a]Lit *redeem* [b]Lit *soul* [A]Ps 69:18 [B]1 Sam 26:21; Ps 116:15 72:15 [a]Lit *him* [A]Is 60:6 72:16 [A]Ps 104:16 [B]Job 5:25 72:17 [a]Or *sprout forth* [b]Lit *before the sun* [A]Ex 3:15; Ps 135:13 [B]Ps 89:36 [C]Gen 12:3; 22:18 [D]Luke 1:48 72:18 [A]1 Chr 29:10; Ps 41:13; 89:52; 106:48 [B]Ex 15:11; Job 5:9; Ps 77:14; 86:10; 136:4 72:19 [A]Neh 9:5; Ps 96:8 [B]Num 14:21 [C]Ps 41:13

72:1–20 This is a Coronation Psalm, dedicated to the prosperity of Solomon at the beginning of his reign (1Ki 2). No NT writer applies any of the psalm to Christ. Still, since the Davidic kings and the Messiah's rule occasionally merge into each other in the OT literature, the messianic inferences here ought not to be missed (vv. 7, 17; cf. Is 11:1–5; 60–62). This psalm describes a reign when God, the king, nature, all classes of society, and foreign nations all live together in harmony.

I. A Just Reign (72:1–4)
II. A Universal Reign (72:5–11)
III. A Compassionate Reign (72:12–14)
IV. A Prosperous Reign (72:15–17)
V. A Glorious Reign (72:18–20)

72:1 Your judgments. A prayer that the king would faithfully mediate God's justice on the nation (cf. Dt 17:18–20). **the king's son.** A reference primarily to Solomon, emphasizing his bond with the Davidic dynasty; but it also anticipates the Messiah's reign as the culmination of the Davidic Covenant (cf. 2Sa 7:12, 13; Ps 2:1–12).

72:3 mountains … peace. When the king rules with justice and compassion, the earth itself radiates well-being.

72:7 till the moon is no more. Primarily referring to the length of the Davidic dynasty, and possibly also specifically to the messianic reign (2Sa 7:16; Ps 89:3, 4, 29, 36, 37; Lk 1:30–33). Jeremiah also makes the same kind of observation (cf. Jer 33:23–26).

72:8 the River. Israel's boundaries were to extend to the River Euphrates (cf. Ex 23:31; 1Ki 4:21; Ps 89:25).

72:10 Tarshish … Seba. Countries near and far which brought tribute to Solomon (cf. 1Ki 4:21; 10:1, 23, 24; Is 60:4–7; Jer 6:20). Tarshish is probably in Spain; Sheba, a kingdom in southern Arabia (modern Yemen); and Seba, a N African nation.

72:20 are ended. Asaph's psalms immediately follow after this (Pss 73–83), though David did author some of the psalms included later in the collection (e.g., Pss 86, 101, 103). This closes Book II (Pss 42–72) of the Psalms.

BOOK 3

PSALM 73

THE END OF THE WICKED CONTRASTED WITH THAT OF THE RIGHTEOUS.

A Psalm of Asaph.

1 Surely God is [A]good to Israel,
To those who are [B]pure in heart!
2 But as for me, [A]my feet came
close to stumbling,
My steps [a]had almost slipped.
3 For I was [A]envious of the [a]arrogant
As I saw the [B]prosperity of the wicked.
4 For there are no pains in their death,
And their [a]body is fat.
5 They are [A]not [a]in trouble *as other* [b]men,
Nor are they [B]plagued [c]like mankind.
6 Therefore pride is [A]their necklace;
The [B]garment of violence covers them.
7 Their eye [a]bulges from [A]fatness;
The imaginations of *their* heart [b]run riot.
8 They [A]mock and [a]wickedly
speak of oppression;
They [B]speak from on high.
9 They have [A]set their mouth
[a]against the heavens,
And their tongue [b]parades
through the earth.

10 Therefore [a]his people return to this place,
And waters of [A]abundance
are [b]drunk by them.
11 They say, "[A]How does God know?
And is there knowledge [a]with
the Most High?"
12 Behold, [A]these are the wicked;
And always [B]at ease, they have
increased *in* wealth.
13 Surely [A]in vain I have [a]kept my heart pure
And [B]washed my hands in innocence;
14 For I have been stricken [A]all day long
And [a,B]chastened every morning.

15 If I had said, "I will speak thus,"
Behold, I would have betrayed the
[A]generation of Your children.
16 When I [A]pondered to understand this,
It was [a]troublesome in my sight
17 Until I came into the [a,A]sanctuary of God;
Then I perceived their [B]end.
18 Surely You set them in [A]slippery places;
You cast them down to [a,B]destruction.
19 How they are [a,A]destroyed in a moment!
They are utterly swept away
by [B]sudden terrors!
20 Like a [A]dream when one awakes,
O Lord, when [B]aroused, You
will [C]despise their [a]form.

21 When my [A]heart was embittered
And I was [B]pierced [a]within,
22 Then I was [A]senseless and ignorant;
I was *like* [a]a [B]beast [b]before You.
23 Nevertheless [A]I am continually with You;
You have taken hold of my right hand.
24 With Your counsel You will [A]guide me,
And afterward [B]receive me [a]to glory.

25 [A]Whom have I in heaven *but You?*
And [a]besides You, I desire
nothing on earth.
26 My [A]flesh and my heart may fail,
But God is the [a]strength of my heart
and my [B]portion forever.
27 For, behold, [A]those who are far
from You will [B]perish;
You have [a]destroyed all those
who [b,C]are unfaithful to You.

73:1 [A]Ps 86:5 [B]Ps 24:4; 51:10; Matt 5:8 73:2 [a]Lit *were caused to slip* [A]Ps 94:18 73:3 [a]Or *boasters* [A]Ps 37:1; Prov 23:17 [B]Job 21:7; Ps 37:7; Jer 12:1 73:4 [a]Or *belly* 73:5 [a]Lit *in the trouble of men* [b]Or *mortals* [c]Lit *with* [A]Job 21:9; Ps 73:12 [B]Ps 73:14 73:6 [A]Gen 41:42; Prov 1:9 [B]Ps 109:18 73:7 [a]Lit *goes forth* [b]Lit *overflow* [A]Job 15:27; Ps 17:10; Jer 5:28 73:8 [a]Or *they speak in wickedness; From on high they speak of oppression* [A]Ps 1:1 [B]Ps 17:10; 2 Pet 2:18; Jude 16 73:9 [a]Or *in* [b]Lit *walks* [A]Rev 13:6 73:10 [a]Or *His* [b]Lit *drained out* [A]Ps 23:5 73:11 [a]Lit *in* [A]Job 22:13 73:12 [A]Ps 49:6; 52:7 [B]Jer 49:31; Ezek 23:42 73:13 [a]Or *cleansed my heart* [A]Job 21:15; 34:9; 35:3 [B]Ps 26:6 73:14 [a]Lit *my chastening* [A]Ps 38:6 [B]Job 33:19; Ps 118:18 73:15 [A]Ps 14:5 73:16 [a]Lit *labor, trouble* [A]Eccl 8:17 73:17 [a]Lit *sanctuaries* [A]Ps 27:4; 77:13 [B]Ps 37:38 73:18 [a]Lit *ruins* [A]Ps 35:6 [B]Ps 35:8; 36:12 73:19 [a]Lit *become a desolation* [A]Num 16:21; Is 47:11 [B]Job 18:11 73:20 [a]Or *image* [A]Job 20:8 [B]Ps 78:65 [C]1 Sam 2:30 73:21 [a]Lit *in my kidneys* [A]Judg 10:16 [B]Acts 2:37 73:22 [a]Or *an animal* [b]Lit *with You* [A]Ps 49:10; 92:6 [B]Job 18:3; Ps 49:20; Eccl 3:18 73:23 [A]Ps 16:8 73:24 [a]Or *with honor* [A]Ps 32:8; 48:14; Is 58:11 [B]Gen 5:24; Ps 49:15 73:25 [a]Or *with* [A]Ps 16:2; Phil 3:8 73:26 [a]Lit *rock* [A]Ps 38:10; 40:12; 84:2; 119:81 [B]Ps 16:5 73:27 [a]Or *silenced* [b]Lit *go to a whoring from* [A]Ps 119:155 [B]Ps 37:20 [C]Ex 34:15; Num 15:39; Ps 106:39; Hos 4:12; 9:1

73:1–28 This psalm illustrates the results of allowing one's faith in God to be buried under self-pity. The psalmist became depressed when he contrasted the seeming prosperity of the wicked with the difficulties of living a righteous life. Beginning in v. 15, however, his attitude changes completely. He looks at life from the perspective of being under the control of a sovereign, holy God, and concludes that it is the wicked, not the righteous, who have blundered.

I. Perplexity Over the Prosperity of the Wicked (73:1–14)
   A. Their Prosperity (73:1–5)
   B. Their Pride (73:6–9)
   C. Their Presumption (73:10–14)
II. Proclamation of the Justice of God (73:15–28)
   A. His Perspective (73:15–17)
   B. His Judgments (73:18–20)
   C. His Guidance (73:21–28)

73:Title Asaph. Asaph was a Levite who led one of the temple choirs (1Ch 15:19; 25:1, 2). His name is identified with Ps 73–83, and also Ps 50 (*see note on 50:Title*). He either wrote these psalms, or his choir sang them, or later choirs in the tradition of Asaph sang them.

73:4 no pains in their death. The wicked seem to go through life in good health, and then die a painless death.

73:9 tongue parades through the earth. The insolent speech of the wicked can be heard anywhere one goes.

73:10 are drunk by them. Those who associate with the wicked person "drink in" everything he declares (cf. Ps 1).

73:11 is there knowledge with the Most High? The wicked insist on living as if God is not omniscient and does not know what happens on earth.

73:17 sanctuary of God. As the psalmist worshiped God at the worship center, he began to understand God's perspective on the fate of the wicked. This is the turning point of the psalm.

73:20 despise their form. The wicked are like a bad dream which one forgets as soon as he awakens. Their well-being is fleeting.

73:22 *like* a beast before You. The psalmist confesses his sin of evaluating life secularly and faithlessly.

73:27 perish … You have destroyed. The psalmist concludes that those who abandon God and attempt to live an autonomous life based on self-chosen idols will eventually endure eternal death.

28 But as for me, [A]the nearness
of God is my good;
I have made the Lord [a]GOD my [B]refuge,
That I may [C]tell of all Your works.

PSALM 74

AN APPEAL AGAINST THE DEVASTATION OF THE LAND BY THE ENEMY.

A [†]Maskil of Asaph.

1 O God, why have You [A]rejected *us* forever?
Why does Your anger [B]smoke against
the [C]sheep of Your [a]pasture?
2 Remember Your congregation, which
You have [A]purchased of old,
Which You have [B]redeemed to be
the [C]tribe of Your inheritance;
And this Mount [D]Zion, where You have dwelt.
3 [a]Turn Your footsteps toward
the [A]perpetual ruins;
The enemy [B]has damaged everything
within the sanctuary.
4 Your adversaries have [A]roared in the
midst of Your meeting place;
They have set up their [B]own
[a]standards [C]for signs.
5 It seems as if one had lifted up
His [a,A]axe in a [b]forest of trees.
6 And now [a]all its [A]carved work
They smash with hatchet and [b]hammers.
7 They have [a,A]burned Your
sanctuary [b]to the ground;
They have [B]defiled the dwelling
place of Your name.
8 They [A]said in their heart, "Let us
[a]completely [b]subdue them."
They have burned all the meeting
places of God in the land.

9 We do not see our [A]signs;
There is [B]no longer any prophet,
Nor is there any among us
who knows [C]how long.
10 How long, O God, will the
adversary [A]revile,
And the enemy [B]spurn Your name forever?
11 Why [A]do You withdraw Your hand,
even Your right hand?
From within Your bosom, [B]destroy *them!*

12 Yet God is [A]my king from of old,
Who works deeds of deliverance
in the midst of the earth.
13 [a]You [A]divided the sea by Your strength;
[a]You [B]broke the heads of the [C]sea
monsters [b]in the waters.
14 [a]You crushed the heads of [b,A]Leviathan;
[a]You gave him as food for the
[c]creatures [B]of the wilderness.
15 [a]You [A]broke open springs and torrents;
[a]You [B]dried up ever-flowing streams.
16 Yours is the day, Yours also is the night;
[a]You have [A]prepared the [b]light and the sun.
17 [a]You have [A]established all the
boundaries of the earth;
[a]You have [b]made [B]summer and winter.

18 Remember this, [a]O LORD, that
the enemy has [A]reviled,
And a [B]foolish people has
spurned Your name.
19 Do not deliver the soul of Your
[A]turtledove to the wild beast;
[B]Do not forget the life of Your
afflicted forever.
20 Consider the [A]covenant;
For the [B]dark places of the land are
full of the habitations of violence.

73:28 [a]Heb *YHWH*, usually rendered *LORD* [A]Ps 65:4; Heb 10:22; James 4:8 [B]Ps 14:6; 71:7 [C]Ps 40:5; 107:22; 118:17 74:1 [†]Possibly, *Contemplative*, or *Didactic*, or *Skillful Psalm* [a]Or *pasturing* [A]Ps 44:9; 77:7 [B]Deut 29:20; Ps 18:8; 89:46 [C]Ps 79:13; 95:7; 100:3 74:2 [A]Ex 15:16; Deut 32:6 [B]Ex 15:13; Ps 77:15; 106:10; Is 63:9 [C]Deut 32:9; Is 63:17; Jer 10:16; 51:19 [D]Ps 9:11; 68:16 74:3 [a]Lit *Lift up* [A]Is 61:4 [B]Ps 79:1 74:4 [a]Lit *signs* [A]Lam 2:7 [B]Num 2:2 [C]Ps 74:9 74:5 [a]Lit *axes* [b]Lit *thicket* [A]Jer 46:22 74:6 [a]Lit *altogether* [b]Or *axes* [A]1 Kin 6:18, 29, 32, 35 74:7 [a]Lit *set on fire* [b]Or *To the ground they...* [A]2 Kin 25:9 [B]Ps 89:39; Lam 2:2 74:8 [a]Lit *altogether* [b]Or *oppress* [A]Ps 83:4 74:9 [A]Ps 78:43 [B]1 Sam 3:1; Lam 2:9; Ezek 7:26; Amos 8:11 [C]Ps 6:3; 79:5; 80:4 74:10 [A]Ps 44:16; 79:12; 89:51 [B]Lev 24:16 74:11 [A]Lam 2:3 [B]Ps 59:13 74:12 [A]Ps 44:4 74:13 [a]Or *You Yourself* [b]Lit *on* [A]Ex 14:21; Ps 78:13 [B]Is 51:9 [C]Ps 148:7; Jer 51:34 74:14 [a]Or *You Yourself* [b]Or *sea monster* [c]Lit *people* [A]Job 41:1; Ps 104:26; Is 27:1 [B]Ps 72:9 74:15 [a]Or *You Yourself* [A]Ex 17:5, 6; Num 20:11; Ps 78:15; 105:41; 114:8; Is 48:21 [B]Ex 14:21, 22; Josh 2:10; 3:13; Ps 114:3 74:16 [a]Or *You Yourself* [b]Or *luminary* [A]Gen 1:14-18; Ps 104:19; 136:7, 8 74:17 [a]Or *You Yourself* [b]Or *formed* [A]Deut 32:8; Acts 17:26 [B]Gen 8:22; Ps 147:16-18 74:18 [a]Or *that the enemy has reviled the LORD* [A]Ps 74:10 [B]Deut 32:6; Ps 14:1; 39:8; 53:1 74:19 [A]Song 2:14 [B]Ps 9:18 74:20 [A]Gen 17:7; Ps 106:45 [B]Ps 88:6; 143:3

74:1–23 This community lament expresses the agony of the people in the midst of the most excruciating of circumstances. It was bad enough that Israel's enemies had destroyed the temple (cf. 2Ki 25). But even worse, it seemed to the psalmist that God had abandoned them. In this prayer he reminds God of His bond with Israel, His past supernatural deeds in the protection of Israel, and begs God to save His covenant nation now (cf. Ps 137 and Lamentations).

I. The Terror of Abandonment (74:1–11)
II. The Remembrance of Omnipotence (74:12–17)
III. The Plea for Help (74:18–23)

74:Title Asaph. If this psalm reflects the destruction of the temple by Nebuchadnezzar in 586 B.C., Asaph would have been dead by then. Thus this title may mean that this psalm was written by or sung by a later Asaph choir (*see notes on Pss 50, 73:Title*).

74:2 tribe of Your inheritance. The psalmist laments that even though God possessed Israel, He had not protected it.

74:3 Turn Your footsteps. An anthropomorphism meaning to hurry to come to examine the rubble.

74:4 their own standards for signs. The ravagers had set up their military and pagan religious banners in God's temple.

74:5 lifted up *His* axe. Like lumberjacks surrounded by trees, the enemy had furiously destroyed everything in sight in the temple of God.

74:8 the meeting places. God allowed only one sanctuary and during Josiah's revival, the high places had been destroyed (cf. 2Ki 22, 23). This may be a reference to the several rooms of the temple, or to nonsacrificial religious sites throughout the land.

74:9 signs. While hostile, pagan signs abounded (cf. v. 4), signs from God were nowhere to be seen (cf. 78:43; 86:17; 105:27) nor were prophets of God to be heard.

74:13 divided the sea. Most likely a reference to God's creation activity, rather than to the parting of the Red Sea (cf. Ge 1:6–8; Ex 14:26–31). **sea monsters.** This identifies whales, sharks, and other large sea creatures, including dinosaurs.

74:14 Leviathan. *See note on Job 41:1.*

74:15 broke open springs and torrents. This may be a reference to the universal flood (cf. Ge 7:11), or it may describe creation (Ge 1:6–8).

74:17 established all the boundaries. As Creator, God made day and night, the seasons (v. 16); He divided the land from the sea; and He even established national boundaries.

74:20 the covenant. The people had apostatized (cf. Ex 16:3–8). God, however, was still in an eternal covenant (the Abrahamic

21 Let not the [A]oppressed
return dishonored;
Let the [B]afflicted and needy
praise Your name.

22 Arise, O God, *and* [A]plead
Your own cause;
Remember [a]how the [B]foolish man
reproaches You all day long.
23 Do not forget the voice of
Your [A]adversaries,
The [B]uproar of those who rise against
You which ascends continually.

PSALM 75

GOD ABASES THE PROUD, BUT EXALTS THE RIGHTEOUS.

For the choir director; *set to* [†]Al-tashheth.
A Psalm of Asaph, a Song.

1 We [A]give thanks to You, O God,
we give thanks,
For Your name is [B]near;
Men declare [C]Your wondrous works.
2 "When I select an [A]appointed time,
It is I who [B]judge with equity.
3 "The [A]earth and all who dwell in it [a]melt;
It is I who have firmly set its [B]pillars.
[b]*Selah*
4 "I said to the boastful, 'Do not boast,'
And to the wicked, '[A]Do not
lift up the horn;
5 Do not lift up your horn on high,
[A]Do not speak with insolent [a]pride.' "

6 For not from the east, nor from the west,
Nor from the [a,A]desert *comes* exaltation;
7 But [A]God is the Judge;
He [B]puts down one and exalts another.
8 For a [A]cup is in the hand of the
LORD, and the wine foams;
It is [a,B]well mixed, and He pours out of this;
Surely all the wicked of the earth must
drain *and* [C]drink down its dregs.

9 But as for me, I will [A]declare *it* forever;
I will sing praises to the God of Jacob.
10 And all the [A]horns of the
wicked [a]He will cut off,
But [B]the horns of the righteous
will be lifted up.

PSALM 76

THE VICTORIOUS POWER OF THE GOD OF JACOB.

For the choir director; on stringed instruments.
A Psalm of Asaph, a Song.

1 God is [A]known in Judah;
His name is [B]great in Israel.
2 His [a,A]tabernacle is in [B]Salem;
His [C]dwelling place also is in Zion.
3 There He [A]broke the [a]flaming arrows,
The shield and the sword and the
[b]weapons of war. [c]*Selah*

4 You are resplendent,
[a]More majestic than the mountains of prey.
5 The [A]stouthearted were plundered,
[a]They sank into sleep;
And none of the [b]warriors
could use his hands.
6 At Your [A]rebuke, O God of Jacob,
Both [a,B]rider and horse were
cast into a dead sleep.
7 You, even You, are [A]to be feared;
And [B]who may stand in Your presence
when once [a]You are angry?

74:21 [A]Ps 103:6 [B]Ps 35:10; Is 41:17 74:22 [a]Lit *Your reproach from the foolish man* [A]Ps 43:1; Is 3:13; 43:26; Ezek 20:35 [B]Ps 14:1; 53:1; 74:18 74:23 [A]Ps 74:10 [B]Ps 65:7 75:1 [†]Lit *Do Not Destroy* [A]Ps 79:13 [B]Ps 145:18 [C]Ps 26:7; 44:1; 71:17 75:2 [A]Ps 102:13 [B]Ps 9:8; 67:4; Is 11:4 75:3 [a]Or *totter* [b]*Selah* may mean: *Pause, Crescendo* or *Musical interlude* [A]Ps 46:6; Is 24:19 [B]1 Sam 2:8 75:4 [A]Zech 1:21 75:5 [a]Lit *neck* [A]1 Sam 2:3; Ps 94:4 75:6 [a]Or *mountainous desert* [A]Ps 3:3 75:7 [A]Ps 50:6 [B]1 Sam 2:7; Ps 147:6; Dan 2:21 75:8 [a]Lit *full of mixture* [A]Job 21:20; Ps 11:6; 60:3; Jer 25:15 [B]Prov 23:30 [C]Obad 16 75:9 [A]Ps 22:22; 40:10 75:10 [a]Heb *I* [A]Ps 101:8; Jer 48:25 [B]1 Sam 2:1; Ps 89:17; 92:10; 148:14 76:1 [A]Ps 48:3 [B]Ps 99:3 76:2 [a]Lit *shelter* [A]Ps 27:5; Lam 2:6 [B]Gen 14:18 [C]Ps 9:11; 132:13; 135:21 76:3 [a]Lit *fiery shafts of the bow* [b]Lit *battle* [c]*Selah* may mean: *Pause, Crescendo* or *Musical interlude* [A]Ps 46:9 76:4 [a]Or *Majestic from the mountains* 76:5 [a]Lit *They slumbered their sleep* [b]Lit *men of might have found their hands* [A]Is 10:12; 46:12 76:6 [a]Lit *chariot* [A]Ps 80:16 [B]Ex 15:1, 21; Ps 78:53 76:7 [a]Lit *Your anger is* [A]1 Chr 16:25; Ps 89:7; 96:4 [B]Ezra 9:15; Ps 130:3; Nah 1:6; Mal 3:2; Rev 6:17

Covenant) with the nation (cf. Ge 17:1–8).

75:1–10 In this psalm, the believing community asserts that, in spite of physical, moral, and societal turmoil, God never loses control of the universe. He gives stability to earthly life, and He will judge the wicked at the appropriate time. Structurally, the psalm revolves around 3 metaphors: pillars of the earth (v. 3); horns (vv. 5, 6, 10); and God's cup of wrath (v. 8).

I. Divine Stability of the Universe (75:1–3)
II. Divine Justice over the World (75:4–10)

75:Title Al-tashheth *See note on Ps 57:Title.*

75:1 Your name is near. God's name represents His presence. The history of God's supernatural interventions on behalf of His people demonstrated that God was personally immanent. But OT saints did not have the fullness from permanent, personal indwelling of the Holy Spirit (cf. Jn 14:1, 16, 17; 1Co 3:16; 6:19).

75:3 I … firmly set its pillars. In uncertain times, God stabilizes societies through His common grace.

75:4 Do not lift up the horn. The horn symbolized an animal's or human's strength and majesty (cf. Dt 33:17; Am 6:13; Zec 1:18–21). Lifting up the horn apparently described a stubborn animal who kept itself from entering a yoke by holding its head up as high as possible. The phrase thus symbolized insolence or rebellion.

75:8 cup. The cup of wrath describes God's judgment which He forces down the throats of the wicked (cf. Job 21:20; Is 51:17; Jer 25:15–29; Mt 20:22; 26:39).

75:10 horns … cut off. To cut off the horns of the wicked would be to humble them (cf. v. 4).

76:1–12 This psalm teaches that God is willing to use His great power for His people. Some commentators, including the editors of the LXX, have suggested that this psalm was written to celebrate the destruction of Sennacherib's Assyrian army in 701 B.C., as well as the subsequent assassination of Sennacherib himself (vv. 5, 6; cf. 2Ki 18, 19; Is 36, 37). The psalm also includes eschatological overtones (especially vv. 8–12), when Jehovah will defeat His enemies and bring them into judgment.

I. God's Nearness to His People (76:1–3)
II. God's Deliverance of His People (76:4–9)
III. God's Majesty to His People (76:10–12)

76:Title Asaph. *See notes on Pss 50, 73, 74:Title.*

76:3 broke the … arrows … shield … sword. God destroyed the enemy's weapons.

76:4 mountains of prey. Probably a poetic description of the attackers.

76:5 use his hands. God had crippled the enemy soldiers.

8 You caused judgment to be
heard from heaven;
The earth [A]feared and was still
9 When God [A]arose to judgment,
To save all the humble of the earth.
Selah
10 For the [a,A]wrath of man shall praise You;
With a remnant of wrath You
will gird Yourself.

11 [A]Make vows to the LORD your
God and [B]fulfill *them;*
Let all who are around Him [C]bring
gifts to Him who is to be feared.
12 He will cut off the spirit of princes;
He is [a,A]feared by the kings of the earth.

PSALM 77

COMFORT IN TROUBLE FROM RECALLING GOD'S MIGHTY DEEDS.

For the choir director; [†]according
to Jeduthun. A Psalm of Asaph.

1 My voice *rises* to God, and
I will [A]cry aloud;
My voice *rises* to God, and
He will hear me.
2 In the [A]day of my trouble I
sought the Lord;
[B]In the night my [C]hand was stretched
out [a]without weariness;
My soul [D]refused to be comforted.
3 *When* I remember God, then
I am [A]disturbed;
When I [B]sigh, then [C]my spirit grows faint.
[a]*Selah*
4 You have held my eyelids *open;*
I am so troubled that I [A]cannot speak.
5 I have considered the [A]days of old,
The years of long ago.
6 I will remember my [A]song in the night;
I [B]will meditate with my heart,
And my spirit [a]ponders:
7 Will the Lord [A]reject forever?
And will He [B]never be
favorable again?
8 Has His [A]lovingkindness
ceased forever?
Has *His* [a,B]promise come to
an end [b]forever?
9 Has God [A]forgotten to be gracious,
Or has He in anger [a]withdrawn His
[B]compassion? *Selah*
10 Then I said, "[A]It is my [a]grief,
That the [B]right hand of the Most
High has changed."

11 I shall remember the [A]deeds of [a]the LORD;
Surely I will [A]remember Your
wonders of old.
12 I will [A]meditate on all Your work
And muse on Your deeds.
13 Your way, O God, is [A]holy;
[B]What god is great like our God?
14 You are the [A]God who works wonders;
You have [B]made known Your
strength among the peoples.
15 You have by Your [a]power
[A]redeemed Your people,
The sons of Jacob and [B]Joseph. *Selah*

16 The [A]waters saw You, O God;
The waters saw You, they
were in anguish;
The deeps also trembled.
17 The [A]clouds poured out water;
The skies [B]gave forth a sound;
Your [C]arrows [a]flashed here and there.
18 The [A]sound of Your thunder
was in the whirlwind;
The [B]lightnings lit up the world;
The [C]earth trembled and shook.
19 Your [A]way was in the sea
And Your paths in the mighty waters,
And Your footprints may not be known.
20 You [A]led Your people like a flock
By the hand of [B]Moses and Aaron.

76:8 [A]1 Chr 16:30; 2 Chr 20:29, 30; Ps 33:8 76:9 [A]Ps 9:7, 8; 74:22; 82:8 76:10 [a]Lit *wraths* [A]Ex 9:16; Rom 9:17 76:11 [A]Eccl 5:4-6 [B]Ps 50:14 [C]2 Chr 32:23; Ps 68:29 76:12 [a]Lit *awesome to* [A]Ps 47:2 77:1 [†]1 Chr 16:41 [A]Ps 3:4; 142:1 77:2 [a]Lit *and did not grow numb* [A]Ps 50:15; 86:7 [B]Ps 63:6; Is 26:9 [C]Job 11:13; Ps 88:9 [D]Gen 37:35 77:3 [a]*Selah* may mean: *Pause, Crescendo* or *Musical interlude* [A]Ps 42:5, 11; 43:5 [B]Ps 55:2; 142:2 [C]Ps 61:2; 143:4 77:4 [A]Ps 39:9 77:5 [A]Deut 32:7; Ps 44:1; 143:5; Is 51:9 77:6 [a]Lit *searched* [A]Ps 42:8 [B]Ps 4:4 77:7 [A]Ps 44:9 [B]Ps 85:1, 5 77:8 [a]Lit *word* [b]Lit *from generation to generation* [A]Ps 89:49 [B]2 Pet 3:9 77:9 [a]Lit *shut up* [A]Is 49:15 [B]Ps 25:6; 40:11; 51:1 77:10 [a]Or *infirmity, the years of the right hand of the Most High* [A]Ps 31:22; 73:14 [B]Ps 44:2, 3 77:11 [a]Heb *YAH* [A]Ps 105:5; 143:5 77:12 [A]Ps 145:5 77:13 [A]Ps 63:2; 73:17 [B]Ex 15:11; Ps 71:19; 86:8 77:14 [A]Ps 72:18 [B]Ps 106:8 77:15 [a]Lit *arm* [A]Ex 6:6; Deut 9:29; Ps 74:2; 78:42 [B]Ps 80:1 77:16 [A]Ex 14:21; Ps 114:3; Hab 3:8, 10 77:17 [a]Lit *went* [A]Judg 5:4 [B]Ps 68:33 [C]Ps 18:14 77:18 [A]Ps 18:13; 104:7 [B]Ps 97:4 [C]Judg 5:4; Ps 18:7 77:19 [A]Is 51:10; Hab 3:15 77:20 [A]Ex 13:21; 14:19; Ps 78:52; 80:1; Is 63:11-13 [B]Ex 6:26; Ps 105:26

76:10 wrath of man shall praise You. The railings against God and His people are turned into praise to God when God providentially brings the wicked down (cf. Is 36:4–20; Ac 2:23; Ro 8:28).

76:12 cut off the spirit of princes. God shatters the attitude of proud governmental leaders who rebel against Him.

77:1–20 This psalm illustrates one cure for depression. The psalmist does not explain the cause of his despair, but he was definitely locked into gloom. When he thought about God, it only caused him to complain bitterly. But beginning in v. 10, the psalmist's mood starts to change because he commits himself to focusing on God's goodness and past acts of deliverance. His lament then changes into a hymn of praise.

I. The Irritations of a Depressed Soul (77:1–9)
II. The Intention to Refocus the Mind (77:10–15)
III. The Illustrations of God's Past Blessings (77:16–20)

77:Title Jeduthun. *See note on Ps 39:Title.*

77:2 hand was stretched out. This was the posture for prayer. The psalmist prayed throughout the night.

77:4 held my eyelids *open*. The psalmist was so upset that he could neither sleep nor talk rationally.

77:6 my song in the night. The remembrance of happier times only deepened his depression. **spirit ponders.** His spirit continually meditated on possible solutions to his problems.

77:10 right hand of the Most High. The psalmist began to remember the times when God used His right hand (power) to strengthen and protect him.

77:16 waters ... were in anguish. A dramatic picture of God's parting the waters of the Red Sea (cf. v. 19; also Ex 14:21–31; 15:1–19).

77:17 Your arrows. A metaphor for lightning flashes.

PSALM 78

GOD'S GUIDANCE OF HIS PEOPLE IN SPITE OF THEIR UNFAITHFULNESS.

A [†]Maskil of Asaph.

1 [A]Listen, O my people, to my [a]instruction;
[B]Incline your ears to the
words of my mouth.
2 I will [A]open my mouth in a parable;
I will utter [B]dark sayings of old,
3 Which we have heard and known,
And [A]our fathers have told us.
4 We will [A]not conceal them
from their children,
But [B]tell to the generation to come
the praises of the LORD,
And His strength and His [C]wondrous
works that He has done.

5 For He established a [A]testimony in Jacob
And appointed a [B]law in Israel,
Which He [C]commanded our fathers
That they should [a,D]teach them
to their children,
6 [A]That the generation to come might know,
even [B]the children *yet* to be born,
That they may arise and [C]tell
them to their children,
7 That they should put their
confidence in God
And [A]not forget the works of God,
But [B]keep His commandments,
8 And [A]not be like their fathers,
A [B]stubborn and rebellious generation,
A generation that [C]did not
[a]prepare its heart
And whose spirit was not [D]faithful to God.

9 The sons of Ephraim [a]were [A]archers
equipped with bows,
Yet [B]they turned back in the day of battle.
10 They [A]did not keep the covenant of God
And refused to [B]walk in His law;
11 They [A]forgot His deeds
And His [a]miracles that He
had shown them.
12 [A]He wrought wonders before their fathers
In the land of Egypt, in the [B]field of Zoan.
13 He [A]divided the sea and caused
them to pass through,
And He made the waters
stand [B]up like a heap.
14 Then He led them with
the cloud by [A]day
And all the night with a [B]light of fire.
15 He [A]split the rocks in the wilderness
And gave *them* abundant drink
like the ocean depths.
16 He [A]brought forth streams
also from the rock
And caused waters to run
down like rivers.

17 Yet they still continued to
sin against Him,
To [A]rebel against the Most
High in the desert.
18 And in their heart they [A]put
God to the test
By asking [B]food according
to their desire.
19 Then they spoke against God;
They said, "[A]Can God prepare a
table in the wilderness?
20 "Behold, He [A]struck the rock so
that waters gushed out,
And streams were overflowing;
Can He give bread also?
Will He provide [a,B]meat for His people?"

21 Therefore the LORD heard and
[a]was [A]full of wrath;
And a fire was kindled against Jacob
And anger also mounted against Israel,
22 Because they [A]did not believe in God
And did not trust in His salvation.

78:1 [†]Possibly, *Contemplative*, or *Didactic*, or *Skillful Psalm* [a]Or *law, teaching* [A]Is 51:4 [B]Is 55:3 78:2 [A]Ps 49:4; Matt 13:35 [B]Prov 1:6 78:3 [A]Ps 44:1 78:4 [A]Ex 12:26; Deut 6:7; 11:19; Job 15:18; Ps 145:4; Is 38:19; Joel 1:3 [B]Ex 13:8, 14; Ps 22:30 [C]Job 37:16; Ps 26:7; 71:17 78:5 [a]Lit *make them known* [A]Ps 19:7; 81:5; Is 8:20 [B]Ps 147:19 [C]Deut 6:4-9 [D]Deut 4:9 78:6 [A]Ps 102:18 [B]Ps 22:31 [C]Deut 11:19 78:7 [A]Deut 4:9; 6:12; 8:14 [B]Deut 4:2; 5:1, 29; 27:1; Josh 22:5 78:8 [a]Or *put right* [A]2 Kin 17:14; 2 Chr 30:7; Ezek 20:18 [B]Ex 32:9; Deut 9:7, 24; 31:27; Judg 2:19; Is 30:9 [C]Job 11:13; Ps 78:37 [D]Ps 51:10 78:9 [a]Or *being* [A]1 Chr 12:2 [B]Judg 20:39; Ps 78:57 78:10 [A]Judg 2:20; 1 Kin 11:11; 2 Kin 17:15; 18:12 [B]Ps 119:1; Jer 32:23; 44:10, 23 78:11 [a]Or *wonderful works* [A]Ps 106:13 78:12 [A]Ex chs 7-12; Ps 106:22 [B]Num 13:22; Ps 78:43; Is 19:11; 30:4; Ezek 30:14 78:13 [A]Ex 14:21; Ps 74:13; 136:13 [B]Ex 15:8; Ps 33:7 78:14 [A]Ex 13:21; Ps 105:39 [B]Ex 14:24 78:15 [A]Ex 17:6; Num 20:11; Ps 105:41; 114:8; Is 48:21; 1 Cor 10:4 78:16 [A]Num 20:8, 10, 11 78:17 [A]Deut 9:22; Is 63:10; Heb 3:16 78:18 [A]Ex 17:6; Deut 6:16; Ps 78:41, 56; 95:9; 106:14; 1 Cor 10:9 [B]Num 11:4 78:19 [A]Ex 16:3; Num 11:4; 20:3; 21:5; Ps 23:5 78:20 [a]Lit *flesh* [A]Num 20:11; Ps 78:15, 16 [B]Num 11:18 78:21 [a]Or *became infuriated* [A]Num 11:1 78:22 [A]Deut 1:32; 9:23; Heb 3:18

78:1–72 This didactic psalm was written to teach the children how gracious God had been in the past in spite of their ancestors' rebellion and ingratitude. If the children learn well the theological interpretation of their nation's history, hopefully they would "not be like their fathers" (v. 8). The psalmist especially focuses on the history of the Exodus.

I. Exhortation on the Instruction of Children (78:1–11)
II. Lecture on the Graciousness of God (78:12–72)
  A. Rehearsal of Israel's History (78:12–39)
  B. Reiteration of Historical Lessons (78:40–72)

78:2 parable. The word is used here in the broader sense of a story with moral and spiritual applications. **dark sayings.** Puzzling, ambiguous information. The lessons of history are not easily discerned correctly. For an infallible interpretation of history, there must be a prophet. The specific puzzle in Israel's history is the nation's rebellious spirit in spite of God's grace.

78:9 sons of Ephraim. The act of treachery or apostasy of this largest of the northern tribes is not specifically identified in Israel's history.

78:12 field of Zoan. The regions of Zoan, an Egyptian city.

78:13 waters stand up like a heap. The parting of the Red Sea at the beginning of the Exodus, which allowed Israel to escape from the Egyptian armies, was always considered by the OT saints to be the most spectacular miracle of their history (cf. Ex 14).

78:15 split the rocks. Twice in the wilderness, when Israel desperately needed a great water supply, God brought water out of rocks (cf. Ex 17:6; Nu 20:11).

78:18 food according to their desire. Instead of being grateful for God's marvelous provisions of manna, the Israelites complained against God and Moses. God sent them meat, but also judged them (Nu 11).

78:19 prepare a table in the wilderness? The answer was "yes," but the question implied a sarcastic lack of faith.

23 Yet He commanded the clouds above
And [A]opened the doors of heaven;
24 He [A]rained down manna upon them to eat
And gave them [a,B]food from heaven.
25 Man did eat the bread of [a]angels;
He sent them [b]food [c,A]in abundance.
26 He [A]caused the east wind to
blow in the heavens
And by His [a]power He directed
the south wind.
27 When He rained [a]meat upon
them like the dust,
Even [A]winged fowl like the sand of the seas,
28 Then He let *them* fall in the
midst of [a]their camp,
Round about their dwellings.
29 So they [A]ate and were well filled,
And their desire He gave to them.
30 [a]Before they had satisfied their desire,
[A]While their food was in their mouths,
31 The [A]anger of God rose against them
And killed [a]some of their [B]stoutest ones,
And [b]subdued the choice men of Israel.
32 In spite of all this they [A]still sinned
And [B]did not believe in His
wonderful works.
33 So He brought [A]their days to
an end in [a]futility
And their years in sudden terror.

34 When He killed them, then
they [A]sought Him,
And returned and searched
[B]diligently for God;
35 And they remembered that
God was their [A]rock,
And the Most High God their [B]Redeemer.
36 But they [A]deceived Him with their mouth
And [B]lied to Him with their tongue.
37 For their heart was not
[A]steadfast toward Him,
Nor were they faithful in His covenant.
38 But He, being [A]compassionate, [a,B]forgave
their iniquity and did not destroy *them;*
And often He [b,C]restrained His anger
And did not arouse all His wrath.
39 Thus [A]He remembered that
they were but [B]flesh,
A [a,C]wind that passes and does not return.
40 How often they [A]rebelled against
Him in the wilderness
And [B]grieved Him in the [C]desert!
41 Again and again they [a,A]tempted God,
And pained the [B]Holy One of Israel.
42 They [A]did not remember [B]His [a]power,
The day when He [C]redeemed
them from the adversary,
43 When He performed His [A]signs in Egypt
And His [B]marvels in the field of Zoan,
44 And [A]turned their rivers to blood,
And their streams, they could not drink.
45 He sent among them swarms of
[A]flies which devoured them,
And [B]frogs which destroyed them.
46 He gave also their crops to
the [A]grasshopper
And the product of their labor to the [B]locust.
47 He [a]destroyed their vines with [A]hailstones
And their sycamore trees with frost.
48 He gave over their [A]cattle
also to the hailstones
And their herds to bolts of lightning.
49 He [A]sent upon them His burning anger,
Fury and indignation and trouble,
[a]A band of destroying angels.
50 He leveled a path for His anger;
He did not spare their soul from death,
But [A]gave over their life to the plague,
51 And [A]smote all the firstborn in Egypt,
The [B]first *issue* of their virility
in the tents of [C]Ham.
52 But He [A]led forth His own
people like sheep
And guided them in the
wilderness [B]like a flock;
53 He led them [A]safely, so that
they did not fear;
But [B]the sea engulfed their enemies.

54 So [A]He brought them to His holy [a]land,
To this [b,B]hill country [C]which His
right hand had gained.
55 He also [A]drove out the
nations before them
And [B]apportioned them for an
inheritance by measurement,
And made the tribes of Israel
dwell in their tents.

78:23 [A]Gen 7:11; Mal 3:10 78:24 [a]Lit *grain* [A]Ex 16:4 [B]Ps 105:40; John 6:31 78:25 [a]Lit *mighty ones* [b]Or *provision* [c]Lit *to satiation* [A]Ex 16:3 78:26 [a]Or *strength* [A]Num 11:31 78:27 [a]Lit *flesh* [A]Ex 16:13; Ps 105:40 78:28 [a]Lit *His* 78:29 [A]Num 11:19, 20 78:30 [a]Lit *They were not estranged from* [A]Num 11:33 78:31 [a]Lit *among their fat ones* [b]Lit *caused to bow down* [A]Num 11:33, 34; Job 20:23 [B]Is 10:16 78:32 [A]Num chs 14, 16, 17 [B]Num 14:11; Ps 78:11 78:33 [a]Lit *vanity, a mere breath* [A]Num 14:29, 35 78:34 [A]Num 21:7; Hos 5:15 [B]Ps 63:1 78:35 [A]Deut 32:4 [B]Ex 15:13; Deut 9:26; Ps 74:2; Is 41:14 78:36 [A]Ex 24:7, 8; Ezek 33:31 [B]Ex 32:7, 8; Is 57:11 78:37 [A]Ps 51:10; 78:8; Acts 8:21 78:38 [a]Lit *covered over, atoned for* [b]Lit *turned away* [A]Ex 34:6 [B]Num 14:18-20 [C]Is 48:9 78:39 [a]Or *breath* [A]Job 10:9; Ps 103:14 [B]Gen 6:3 [C]Job 7:7, 16; Ps 103:14; James 4:14 78:40 [A]Ps 95:8, 9; 106:43; 107:11; Heb 3:16 [B]Ps 95:10; Is 63:10; Eph 4:30 [C]Ps 106:14 78:41 [a]Or *put God to the test* [A]Num 14:22 [B]2 Kin 19:22; Ps 89:18 78:42 [a]Lit *hand* [A]Judg 8:34 [B]Ps 44:3 [C]Ps 106:10 78:43 [A]Ps 105:27 [B]Ex 4:21; 7:3 78:44 [A]Ex 7:20; Ps 105:29 78:45 [A]Ex 8:24; Ps 105:31 [B]Ex 8:6; Ps 105:30 78:46 [A]1 Kin 8:37; Ps 105:34 [B]Ex 10:14 78:47 [a]Lit *was killing* [A]Ex 9:23-25; Ps 105:32 78:48 [A]Ex 9:19 78:49 [a]Lit *A deputation of angels of evil* [A]Ex 15:7 78:50 [A]Ex 12:29, 30 78:51 [A]Ex 12:29; Ps 105:36; 135:8; 136:10 [B]Gen 49:3 [C]Ps 105:23, 27; 106:22 78:52 [A]Ex 15:22 [B]Ps 77:20 78:53 [A]Ex 14:19, 20 [B]Ex 14:27, 28; Ps 106:11 78:54 [a]Lit *border, territory* [b]Or *mountain* [A]Ex 15:17 [B]Ps 68:16; Is 11:9 [C]Ps 44:3 78:55 [A]Josh 11:16-23; Ps 44:2 [B]Josh 13:7; 23:4; Ps 105:11; 135:12

78:27 rained meat. A poetic description of the quail which dropped into Israel's camp in the wilderness (Nu 11:31–35).

78:41 pained the Holy One. The Israelites did this by doubting God's power.

78:42 did not remember His power. The generations of Israelites which left Egypt and eventually died in the wilderness were characterized by ignoring God's previous acts of power and faithfulness. The following verses (vv. 43–55) rehearse the plagues and miracles of the Exodus from Egypt, which marvelously demonstrated God's omnipotence and covenant love.

56 Yet they [a,A]tempted and [B]rebelled
against the Most High God
And did not keep His testimonies,
57 But turned back and [A]acted
treacherously like their fathers;
They [B]turned aside like a treacherous bow.
58 For they [A]provoked Him with
their [B]high places
And [C]aroused His jealousy with
their [D]graven images.
59 When God heard, He [a]was
filled with [A]wrath
And greatly [B]abhorred Israel;
60 So that He [A]abandoned the
[B]dwelling place at Shiloh,
The tent [a]which He had
pitched among men,
61 And gave up His [A]strength to captivity
And His glory [B]into the hand
of the adversary.
62 He also [A]delivered His
people to the sword,
And [a]was filled with wrath
at His inheritance.
63 [A]Fire devoured [a]His young men,
And [a]His [B]virgins had no wedding songs.
64 [a]His [A]priests fell by the sword,
And [a]His [B]widows could not weep.

65 Then the Lord [A]awoke as *if from* sleep,
Like a [B]warrior [a]overcome by wine.
66 He [a,A]drove His adversaries backward;
He put on them an everlasting reproach.
67 He also [A]rejected the tent of Joseph,
And did not choose the
tribe of Ephraim,
68 But chose the tribe of Judah,
Mount [A]Zion which He loved.
69 And He [A]built His sanctuary
like the heights,
Like the earth which He has
founded forever.
70 He also [A]chose David His servant
And took him from the sheepfolds;
71 From [a,A]the care of the [b]ewes [B]with
suckling lambs He brought him
To [C]shepherd Jacob His people,
And Israel [D]His inheritance.
72 So he shepherded them according
to the [A]integrity of his heart,
And guided them with his skillful hands.

PSALM 79

A LAMENT OVER THE DESTRUCTION OF JERUSALEM, AND PRAYER FOR HELP.

A Psalm of Asaph.

1 O God, the [A]nations have [a]invaded
[B]Your inheritance;
They have defiled Your [C]holy temple;
They have [D]laid Jerusalem in ruins.
2 They have given the [A]dead bodies
of Your servants for food to
the birds of the heavens,
The flesh of Your godly ones to
the beasts of the earth.
3 They have poured out their blood like
water round about Jerusalem;
And there was [A]no one to bury them.
4 We have become a [A]reproach
to our neighbors,
A scoffing and derision to those around us.
5 [A]How long, O LORD? Will You
be angry forever?
Will Your [B]jealousy [C]burn like fire?
6 [A]Pour out Your wrath upon the nations
which [B]do not know You,
And upon the kingdoms which [C]do
not call upon Your name.
7 For they have [A]devoured Jacob
And [B]laid waste his [a]habitation.

8 [A]Do not remember [a]the iniquities of
our forefathers against us;
Let Your compassion come
quickly to [B]meet us,
For we are [C]brought very low.

78:56 [a]Or *put to the test* [A]Ps 78:18 [B]Judg 2:11-13; Ps 78:40 78:57 [A]Ezek 20:27, 28 [B]Hos 7:16 78:58 [A]Deut 4:25; Judg 2:12; 1 Kin 14:9; Is 65:3 [B]Lev 26:30; 1 Kin 3:2; 2 Kin 16:4; Jer 17:3 [C]Deut 32:16, 21; 1 Kin 14:22 [D]Ex 20:4; Lev 26:1; Deut 4:25 78:59 [a]Or *became infuriated* [A]Deut 1:34; 9:19; Ps 106:40 [B]Lev 26:30; Deut 32:19; Amos 6:8 78:60 [a]Some ancient versions read *where He dwelt* [A]1 Sam 4:11; Ps 78:67; Jer 7:12, 14; 26:6 [B]Josh 18:1 78:61 [A]Ps 63:2; 132:8 [B]1 Sam 4:17 78:62 [a]Or *became infuriated* [A]Judg 20:21; 1 Sam 4:10 78:63 [a]Or *their* [A]Num 11:1; 21:28; Is 26:11; Jer 48:45 [B]Jer 7:34; 16:9; Lam 2:21 78:64 [a]Or *their* [A]1 Sam 4:17; 22:18 [B]Job 27:15; Ezek 24:23 78:65 [a]Or *sobered up from* [A]Ps 44:23; 73:20 [B]Is 42:13 78:66 [a]Lit *smote* [A]1 Sam 5:6 78:67 [A]Ps 78:60 78:68 [A]Ps 87:2; 132:13 78:69 [A]1 Kin 6:1-38 78:70 [A]1 Sam 16:11, 12 78:71 [a]Lit *following* [b]Lit *ewes which gave suck, He...* [A]2 Sam 7:8; Is 40:11 [B]Gen 33:13 [C]2 Sam 5:2; 1 Chr 11:2; Ps 28:9 [D]1 Sam 10:1 78:72 [A]1 Kin 9:4 79:1 [a]Lit *come into* [A]Lam 1:10 [B]Ps 74:2 [C]Ps 74:3, 7 [D]2 Kin 25:9, 10; 2 Chr 36:17-19; Jer 26:18; 52:12-14; Mic 3:12 79:2 [A]Deut 28:26; Jer 7:33; 16:4; 19:7; 34:20 79:3 [A]Jer 14:16; 16:4 79:4 [A]Ps 44:13; 80:6; Dan 9:16 79:5 [A]Ps 13:1; 74:1, 9, 10; 85:5; 89:46 [B]Deut 29:20; Ezek 36:5; 38:19 [C]Ps 89:46; Zeph 3:8 79:6 [A]Ps 69:24; Jer 10:25; Ezek 21:31; Zeph 3:8 [B]1 Thess 4:5; 2 Thess 1:8 [C]Ps 14:4; 53:4 79:7 [a]Lit *pasture* [A]Ps 53:4 [B]2 Chr 36:19; Jer 39:8 79:8 [a]Or our *former iniquities* [A]Ps 106:6; Is 64:9 [B]Ps 21:3 [C]Deut 28:43; Ps 116:6; 142:6; Is 26:5

78:57 treacherous bow. This is a useless bow.

78:60 dwelling place at Shiloh. Shiloh was an early location of Jehovah worship in the Promised Land. The capture and removal of the ark from Shiloh by the Philistines symbolized God's judgment (cf. Jos 18:1; 1Sa 1:9; 3:1; 4:1–22).

78:65 warrior ... wine. The picture is that of a furious, raging warrior entering the battle on Israel's side.

78:68 the tribe of Judah. Instead of the prestigious tribes, God chose Judah. In Judah was Mt. Zion where the central worship center of Jehovah was located. Also, David, their king, and his royal descendants were from this tribe.

79:1–13 The historical basis for this lament psalm was probably Nebuchadnezzar's destruction of the temple in 586 B.C. (cf. Ps 74; 2Ki 25:8–21; La 1–5). The psalm contains prayer for the nation's spiritual needs, curses against the enemies of God's people, and praises in anticipation of God's actions. The psalm helps the believer express his anguish in a disaster when it seems as though God is aloof.

I. The Lamentation Over the National Disaster (79:1–4)
II. The Supplication for Divine Intervention (79:5–13)
   A. The Prayer for Vindication (79:5–7)
   B. The Prayer for Forgiveness (79:8, 9)
   C. The Prayer for Reprisal (79:10–12)
   D. The Praise for Response (79:13)

79:1 nations. In this context, the word refers to heathen, pagan people. **inheritance.** The inheritance of God was national Israel, and specifically its capital city, Jerusalem, where the temple was located.

9 [A]Help us, O God of our salvation,
for the glory of [B]Your name;
And deliver us and [a,C]forgive our
sins [D]for Your name's sake.
10 [A]Why should the nations say,
"Where is their God?"
Let there be known among the
nations in our sight,
[B]Vengeance for the blood
of Your servants which
has been shed.
11 Let [A]the groaning of the prisoner
come before You;
According to the greatness of
Your [a]power preserve [b]those
who are [A]doomed to die.
12 And return to our neighbors
[A]sevenfold [B]into their bosom
[a]The [C]reproach with which they
have reproached You, O Lord.
13 So we Your people and the
[A]sheep of Your [a]pasture
Will [B]give thanks to You forever;
To all generations we will
[C]tell of Your praise.

PSALM 80

GOD IMPLORED TO RESCUE HIS PEOPLE FROM THEIR CALAMITIES.

For the choir director; *set to* [†]El Shoshannim;
[•]Eduth. A Psalm of Asaph.

1 Oh, give ear, [A]Shepherd of Israel,
You who lead [B]Joseph like a flock;
You who [C]are enthroned *above*
the cherubim, shine forth!
2 Before [A]Ephraim and
Benjamin and Manasseh,
[B]stir up Your power
And come to save us!
3 O God, [A]restore us
And [B]cause Your face to shine *upon*
us, [a]and we will be saved.
4 O [A]LORD God *of* hosts,
[B]How long will You [a]be angry with
the prayer of Your people?
5 You have fed them with the
[A]bread of tears,
And You have made them to drink
tears in [a]large measure.
6 You make us [a]an object of
contention [A]to our neighbors,
And our enemies laugh
among themselves.
7 O God *of* hosts, restore us
And cause Your face to shine *upon*
us, [a]and we will be saved.

8 You removed a [A]vine from Egypt;
You [B]drove out the [a]nations
and [C]planted it.
9 You [A]cleared *the ground* before it,
And it [B]took deep root and filled the land.
10 The mountains were covered
with its shadow,
And [a]the cedars of God with its [A]boughs.
11 It was sending out its
branches [A]to the sea
And its shoots to the River.
12 Why have You [A]broken down its [a]hedges,
So that all who pass *that*
way pick its *fruit?*
13 A boar from the forest [A]eats it away
And whatever moves in the
field feeds on it.

14 O God *of* hosts, [A]turn again
now, we beseech You;
[B]Look down from heaven and see,
and take care of this vine,
15 Even the [a,A]shoot which Your
right hand has planted,
And on the [b]son whom You have
[c]strengthened for Yourself.
16 It is [A]burned with fire, it is cut down;
They perish at the [B]rebuke of
Your countenance.

79:9 [a]Lit *cover over, atone for* [A]2 Chr 14:11 [B]Ps 31:3 [C]Ps 25:11; 65:3 [D]Jer 14:7 79:10 [A]Ps 42:10; 115:2 [B]Ps 94:1, 2 79:11 [a]Lit *arm* [b]Lit *the children of death* [A]Ps 102:20 79:12 [a]Lit *Their* [A]Gen 4:15; Lev 26:21, 28; Ps 12:6; 119:164; Prov 6:31; 24:16; Is 30:26 [B]Ps 35:13; Is 65:6, 7; Jer 32:18; Luke 6:38 [C]Ps 74:10, 18, 22 79:13 [a]Or *pasturing* [A]Ps 74:1; 95:7; 100:3 [B]Ps 44:8 [C]Ps 89:1; Is 43:21 80:1 [†]Possibly, *to the Lilies* [•]Lit *A testimony* [A]Ps 23:1 [B]Ps 77:15; 78:67; Amos 5:15 [C]Ex 25:22; 1 Sam 4:4; 2 Sam 6:2; Ps 99:1 80:2 [A]Num 2:18-24 [B]Ps 35:23 80:3 [a]Or *that we may* [A]Ps 60:1; 80:7, 19; 85:4; 126:1; Lam 5:21 [B]Num 6:25; Ps 4:6; 31:16 80:4 [a]Lit *smoke against* [A]Ps 59:5; 84:8 [B]Ps 79:5; 85:5 80:5 [a]Lit *a third part of a* [A]Ps 42:3; 102:9; Is 30:20 80:6 [a]Lit *a strife to* [A]Ps 44:13; 79:4 80:7 [a]Or *that we may* 80:8 [a]Or *Gentiles* [A]Ps 80:15; Is 5:1, 2, 7; Jer 2:21; 12:10; Ezek 17:6; 19:10 [B]Josh 13:6; 2 Chr 20:7; Ps 44:2; Acts 7:45 [C]Jer 11:17; 32:41; Ezek 17:23; Amos 9:15 80:9 [A]Ex 23:28; Josh 24:12; Is 5:2 [B]Hos 14:5 80:10 [a]Or *its boughs are like the cedars of God* [A]Gen 49:22 80:11 [A]Ps 72:8 80:12 [a]Or *walls, fences* [A]Ps 89:40; Is 5:5 80:13 [A]Jer 5:6 80:14 [A]Ps 90:13 [B]Ps 102:19; Is 63:15 80:15 [a]Or *root* [b]Or figuratively: *branch* [C]Or *secured* [A]Ps 80:8 80:16 [A]2 Chr 36:19; Ps 74:8; Jer 52:13 [B]Ps 39:11; 76:6

79:9 forgive. See Ps 65:3. **for Your name's sake.** A defeat of a nation was believed to be a defeat of its god. A mark of spiritual maturity is one's concern for the reputation of God.

79:10 Where is their God? The heathen were mocking Israel's God by saying that the destruction of the nation implied that its God was nonexistent.

79:11 doomed to die. A prayer for the preservation of the prisoners awaiting execution in the enemy's dungeon.

79:12 sevenfold into their bosom. A petition that God would restore His reputation by bringing a destruction of the enemies much worse than what had happened to Israel.

80:1–19 This psalm was probably written from Jerusalem in astonishment at the captivity of the 10 northern tribes in 722 B.C. The psalmist recognized that God's people had removed themselves through apostasy from the blessings of the Mosaic Covenant. So he begs God to act and to restore His people into covenant blessings (vv. 3, 7, 14, 19).

I. Prayer for Divine Restoration (80:1–3)
II. Despair over God's Anger (80:4–7)
III. Description of God's Vine (80:8–16a)
IV. Prayer for Divine Restoration (80:16b–19)

80:Title El Shoshannim. The name of a tune. *See note on Ps 45:Title.*

80:1 enthroned *above* the cherubim. A reference to the ark of the covenant, a symbol for God's presence. The images of two cherubim sat on top of the ark, facing each other (cf. Ex 37:1–9).

80:3 face to shine. *See note on Ps 67:1;* cf. 80:7, 19.

80:4 God of hosts. *See note on Ps 59:5;* cf. 80:7, 14.

80:8 vine from Egypt. The vine is a metaphor for Israel, whom God delivered out of Egypt and nurtured into a powerful nation (cf. Is 5:1–7; 27:2–6; Mt 21:33–40).

17 Let [A]Your hand be upon the
man of Your right hand,
Upon the son of man whom You
[B]made strong for Yourself.
18 Then we shall not [A]turn back from You;
[B]Revive us, and we will call upon Your name.
19 O LORD God of hosts, [A]restore us;
Cause Your face to shine *upon*
us, [a]and we will be saved.

PSALM 81

GOD'S GOODNESS AND ISRAEL'S WAYWARDNESS.

For the choir director; [†]on the Gittith.
A Psalm of Asaph.

1 [A]Sing for joy to God our [B]strength;
Shout [C]joyfully to the [D]God of Jacob.
2 Raise a song, strike [A]the timbrel,
The sweet sounding [B]lyre with the [C]harp.
3 Blow the trumpet at the [A]new moon,
At the full moon, on our [B]feast day.
4 For it is a statute for Israel,
An ordinance of the God of Jacob.
5 He established it for a testimony in Joseph
When he [a,A]went throughout
the land of Egypt.
I heard a [B]language that I did not know:

6 "I [a,A]relieved his shoulder of the burden,
His hands were freed from the [b]basket.
7 "You [A]called in trouble and I rescued you;
I [B]answered you in the hiding
place of thunder;
I proved you at the [C]waters of Meribah.
[a]*Selah*

8 "[A]Hear, O My people, and I
will [a]admonish you;
O Israel, if you [B]would listen to Me!
9 "Let there be no [A]strange god among you;
Nor shall you worship any foreign god.
10 "[A]I, the LORD, am your God,
Who brought you up from
the land of Egypt;
[B]Open your mouth wide and I will [C]fill it.

11 "But My people [A]did not listen to My voice,
And Israel did not [a]obey Me.
12 "So I [A]gave [a]them over to the
stubbornness of their heart,
To walk in their own devices.
13 "Oh that My people [A]would listen to Me,
That Israel would [B]walk in My ways!
14 "I would quickly [A]subdue their enemies
And [B]turn My hand against
their adversaries.
15 "[A]Those who hate the LORD would
[B]pretend obedience to Him,
And their time *of punishment*
would be forever.
16 "[a]But I would feed you with the
[b,A]finest of the wheat,
And with [B]honey from the rock
I would satisfy you."

PSALM 82

UNJUST JUDGMENTS REBUKED.

A Psalm of Asaph.

1 God takes His [A]stand in [a]His
own congregation;
He [B]judges in the midst of the [b,C]rulers.

80:17 [A]Ps 89:21 [B]Ps 80:15 80:18 [A]Is 50:5 [B]Ps 71:20 80:19 [a]Or *that we may* [A]Ps 80:3 81:1 [†]Or *according to* [A]Ps 51:14; 59:16; 95:1 [B]Ps 46:1 [C]Ps 66:1; 95:2; 98:4 [D]Ps 84:8 81:2 [A]Ex 15:20; Ps 149:3 [B]Ps 92:3; 98:5; 147:7 [C]Ps 108:2; 144:9 81:3 [A]Num 10:10 [B]Lev 23:24 81:5 [a]Lit *went out over* [A]Ex 11:4 [B]Deut 28:49; Ps 114:1; Jer 5:15 81:6 [a]Lit *removed his shoulder from* [b]Or *brick load* [A]Is 9:4; 10:27 81:7 [a]*Selah* may mean: *Pause, Crescendo* or *Musical interlude* [A]Ex 2:23; 14:10; Ps 50:15 [B]Ex 19:19; 20:18 [C]Ex 17:6, 7; Num 20:13; Ps 95:8 81:8 [a]Or *bear witness against* [A]Ps 50:7 [B]Ps 95:7 81:9 [A]Ex 20:3; Deut 5:7; 32:12; Ps 44:20; Is 43:12 81:10 [A]Ex 20:2; Deut 5:6 [B]Job 29:23 [C]Ps 37:4; 78:25; 107:9 81:11 [a]Lit *yield to* [A]Deut 32:15; Ps 106:25 81:12 [a]Lit *him* [A]Job 8:4; Acts 7:42; Rom 1:24, 26 81:13 [A]Deut 5:29; Ps 81:8; Is 48:18 [B]Ps 128:1; Is 42:24; Jer 7:23 81:14 [A]Ps 18:47; 47:3 [B]Amos 1:8 81:15 [A]Rom 1:30 [B]Ps 18:44; 66:3 81:16 [a]Lit *He would feed him* [b]Lit *fat* [A]Deut 32:14; Ps 147:14 [B]Deut 32:13 82:1 [a]Lit *the congregation of God* [b]Lit *gods* [A]Is 3:13 [B]2 Chr 19:6; Ps 58:11 [C]Ex 21:6; 22:8, 28

80:17 son of man. In this context, this phrase is primarily a reference to Israel. In a secondary sense, the "son of man" may allude to the Davidic dynasty and even extend to the Messiah, since He is so frequently called by that title in the NT.

81:1–16 This psalm was intended to be used in the celebration of one of the feasts of Israel, most likely the Feast of Booths, or Tabernacles. After the call to worship (vv. 1–5), the psalm presents a message from God in the first person (vv. 6–16). This oracle pleads with Israel to "listen" to Him (v. 13), so that He might pour out on the nation the blessings of the covenant.

I. A Call to Joyful Worship (81:1–5)
II. A Call to Godly Obedience (81:6–16)

81:Title on the Gittith. *See note on Ps 8:Title.*

81:2 harp. A musical instrument with a long and narrow neck resembling a guitar. This word is rendered as *lute* by some translations.

81:3 new moon … full moon. The seventh month of Israel's year (Tishri; Sept./Oct.) culminated the festival year with a succession of celebrations. The month began with the blowing of the trumpets, continued with the Day of Atonement on the tenth day, and celebrated the Feast of Booths, or Tabernacles, on the fifteenth day when the moon was full. The Feast of Tabernacles praised God for His care in the wilderness wanderings, and also pointed to the coming kingdom (Mt 17:1–4).

81:5 language … did not know. Either the psalmist heard a message, the meaning of which he did not grasp, in which case this message is presented as an oracle in the following verses; or, the psalmist is referring to the Egyptian language, which the Jews did not know.

81:6 hands … freed … basket. The Israelites in Egypt were forced to carry bricks and clay in baskets.

81:7 hiding place of thunder. Probably a reference to God's presence on Mt. Sinai at the giving of the law (cf. Ex 19:16ff.; 20:18ff.). **waters of Meribah.** Meribah, which means "strife" or "dispute," marked places where Israel tempted God (cf. Ex 17:1–7; Nu 20:1–13; Pss 95:8; 106:32).

81:14 quickly subdue their enemies. One of the blessings of obedience promised to Israel in the Mosaic Covenant was victory over its enemies (cf. Nu 33:52–56; Dt 6:16–19; 7:16–24).

81:16 honey from the rock. This phrase was first used by Moses in his song of praise (Dt 32:13). Though honey is sometimes found in the clefts of rocks, the intent of the figure here is more likely to valuable food provided from unlikely places.

82:1–8 This psalm, like Pss 2 and 58, focuses on the injustices of tyranny. The psalmist pictures God standing in the assembly of earthly leaders, to whom He has delegated authority, and condemning their injustices. The final prayer of the psalmist (v. 8) is that God Himself will take direct control of the affairs of this world.

I. The Assembly of World Leaders Before God (82:1)
II. The Evaluation of World Leaders by God (82:2–7)
III. The Replacement of World Leaders with God (82:8)

82:1 His own congregation. The scene opens with God having called the world

2 How long will you [A]judge unjustly
And [B]show partiality to the wicked? [a]*Selah*
3 [A]Vindicate the weak and fatherless;
Do justice to the afflicted and destitute.
4 [A]Rescue the weak and needy;
Deliver *them* out of the
hand of the wicked.

5 They [A]do not know nor do
they understand;
They [B]walk about in darkness;
All the [C]foundations of the
earth are shaken.
6 [a]I [A]said, "You are gods,
And all of you are [B]sons
of the Most High.
7 "Nevertheless [A]you will die like men
And fall like *any* [B]one of the princes."
8 [A]Arise, O God, [B]judge the earth!
For it is You who [C]possesses
all the nations.

PSALM 83

GOD IMPLORED TO CONFOUND HIS ENEMIES.

A Song, a Psalm of Asaph.

1 O God, [A]do not remain quiet;
[B]Do not be silent and, O God, do not be still.
2 For behold, Your enemies
[A]make an uproar,
And [B]those who hate You have
[a,C]exalted themselves.
3 They [A]make shrewd plans
against Your people,
And [a]conspire together against
[B]Your [b]treasured ones.
4 They have said, "Come, and [A]let us
wipe them out [a]as a nation,
That the [B]name of Israel be
remembered no more."
5 For they have [a,A]conspired
together with one mind;
Against You they make a covenant:
6 The tents of [A]Edom and the [B]Ishmaelites,
[C]Moab and the [D]Hagrites;
7 [A]Gebal and [B]Ammon and [C]Amalek,
[D]Philistia with the inhabitants of [E]Tyre;
8 [A]Assyria also has joined with them;
They have become [a]a help to the [B]children
of Lot. [b]*Selah*

9 Deal with them [A]as with Midian,
As [B]with Sisera *and* Jabin at
the torrent of Kishon,
10 Who were destroyed at En-dor,
Who [A]became as dung for the ground.
11 Make their nobles like [A]Oreb and Zeeb
And all their princes like
[B]Zebah and Zalmunna,

82:2 [a]*Selah* may mean: *Pause, Crescendo* or *Musical interlude* [A]Ps 58:1 [B]Deut 1:17; Prov 18:5 82:3 [A]Deut 24:17; Ps 10:18; Is 11:4; Jer 22:16 82:4 [A]Job 29:12 82:5 [A]Ps 14:4; Jer 4:22; Mic 3:1 [B]Prov 2:13; Is 59:9; Jer 23:12 [C]Ps 11:3 82:6 [a]Lit *I, on my part* [A]Ps 82:1; John 10:34 [B]Ps 89:26 82:7 [A]Job 21:32; Ps 49:12; Ezek 31:14 [B]Ps 83:11 82:8 [A]Ps 12:5 [B]Ps 58:11; 96:13 [C]Ps 2:8; Rev 11:15 83:1 [A]Ps 28:1; 35:22 [B]Ps 109:1 83:2 [a]Lit *lifted up the head* [A]Ps 2:1; Is 17:12 [B]Ps 81:15 [C]Judg 8:28; Zech 1:21 83:3 [a]Or *consult* [b]Or *hidden ones* [A]Ps 64:2; Is 29:15 [B]Ps 27:5; 31:20 83:4 [a]Lit *from* [A]Esth 3:6; Ps 74:8; Jer 48:2 [B]Ps 41:5; Jer 11:19 83:5 [a]Or *consulted* [A]Ps 2:2; Dan 6:7 83:6 [A]2 Chr 20:10; Ps 137:7 [B]Gen 25:12-16 [C]2 Chr 20:10 [D]1 Chr 5:10 83:7 [A]Josh 13:5; Ezek 27:9 [B]2 Chr 20:10 [C]1 Sam 15:2 [D]1 Sam 4:1; 29:1 [E]Ezek 27:3; Amos 1:9 83:8 [a]Lit *an arm* [b]*Selah* may mean: *Pause, Crescendo* or *Musical interlude* [A]2 Kin 15:19 [B]Deut 2:9 83:9 [A]Judg 7:1-24 [B]Judg 4:7, 15, 21-24 83:10 [A]Zeph 1:17 83:11 [A]Judg 7:25 [B]Judg 8:12, 21

leaders together. **midst of the rulers.** The best interpretation is that these are human leaders, such as judges, kings, legislators, and presidents (cf. Ex 22:8, 9, 28; Jdg 5:8, 9). God the Great Judge, presides over these lesser judges.

82:2–4 judge unjustly. God accuses the lesser human judges of social injustices which violate the Mosaic law (e.g., Dt 24).

82:5 darkness. Signifies both intellectual ignorance and moral iniquity. **foundations of the earth are shaken.** When leaders rule unjustly, the divinely established moral order which undergirds human existence is undermined.

82:6 I said. Kings and judges are set up ultimately by the decree of God (Ps 2:6). God, in effect, invests His authority in human leaders for the stability of the universe (cf. Ro 13:1–7). But God may revoke this authority (v. 7). **You are gods.** Jesus, in quoting this phrase in Jn 10:34, supported the interpretation that the "gods" were human beings. In a play on words, He claims that if human leaders can be called "gods," certainly the Messiah can be called God. **sons of the Most High.** Created by God for noble life.

82:7 die like men. In spite of being made in God's image, they were mortal and would die like human beings. **fall like … princes.** The unjust rulers would become vulnerable to the violent deaths which often accompanied tyranny.

82:8 You who possess all the nations. The psalmist prayerfully anticipates the future when God will set up His kingdom and restore order and perfect justice to a sin-cursed world (cf. Pss 96, 97; Is 11:1–5).

83:1–18 This psalm, a national lament which includes prayer and imprecations, may be best studied with a map since several individual national enemies of Israel are noted. Second Chronicles 20:1–30 may record the specific historical event prompting this psalm, though some Bible students believe that the nations mentioned are only symbolic of all of Israel's enemies. The psalmist begs God to rescue Israel from its enemies as He had done so many times in the past.

I. A Plea for Help (83:1)
II. A Protest Against Israel's Enemies (83:2–8)
III. A Petition for Divine Judgment (83:9–18)

83:2 Your enemies. Throughout this psalm, the hostile nations are described as God's enemies.

83:4 wipe them out. The hostile nations, under Satan's influence, repudiated God's promise to preserve forever the nation of Israel (cf. Ge 17:7, 8; Ps 89:34–37).

83:6 Edom … Hagrites. The list of nations represents Israel's enemies throughout its history. Edom descended from Esau and lived SE of Israel. The Ishmaelites, descendants from Abraham and Hagar, were Bedouin tribes. The Moabites descended from Lot (cf. v. 8) and were tribal people living E of the Jordan (cf. Jdg 11:17, 18; Is 15, 16). The Hagrites were a nomadic tribe living E of the Jordan (1Ch 5:10, 19, 20).

83:7 Gebal … Tyre. Gebal was probably a community S of the Dead Sea, near Petra in Edom. Ammon, a nation descending from Lot, was located E of the Jordan River. The Amalekites, nomads living SE of the Jordan River, were descendants of Esau (cf. Ge 36:12, 16; Ex 17:8–13; Nu 24:20; Jdg 6:3; 1Sa 15:1–8). Philistia was located SW of Israel (Jdg 14–16). Tyre was NW of Israel (cf. Eze 27).

83:8 Assyria. This dominant nation of the eighth century B.C. took captive the northern 10 tribes of Israel in 722 B.C. Assyria used smaller nations, like Moab and Ammon (the children of Lot; cf. Ge 19:36–38), to accomplish its military goals.

83:9 Midian … Jabin. The psalmist reminded God of famous past victories. Gideon had defeated the Midianites (Jdg 7:19–25). Barak and Deborah defeated Jabin and his army commander, Sisera, near the Brook Kishon (Jdg 4, 5).

83:11 Oreb … Zalmunna. These men were chiefs of the Midianites when they were defeated by Gideon (cf. Jdg 6–8).

12 Who said, "[A]Let us possess for ourselves
The [B]pastures of God."
13 O my God, make them like
the [a,A]whirling dust,
Like [B]chaff before the wind.
14 Like [A]fire that burns the forest
And like a flame that [B]sets the
mountains on fire,
15 So pursue them [A]with Your tempest
And terrify them with Your storm.
16 [A]Fill their faces with dishonor,
That they may seek Your name, O LORD.
17 Let them be [A]ashamed and
dismayed forever,
And let them be humiliated and perish,
18 That they may [A]know that [B]You
alone, whose name is the LORD,
Are the [C]Most High over all the earth.

PSALM 84

LONGING FOR THE TEMPLE WORSHIP.

For the choir director; [†]on the Gittith.
A Psalm of the sons of Korah.

1 How lovely are Your [A]dwelling places,
O LORD of hosts!
2 My [A]soul longed and even yearned
for the courts of the LORD;
My heart and my flesh sing for
joy to the [B]living God.
3 The bird also has found a house,
And the swallow a nest for herself,
where she may lay her young,
Even Your [A]altars, O LORD of hosts,
[B]My King and my God.
4 How [A]blessed are those who
dwell in Your house!
They are [B]ever praising You. [a]*Selah*
5 How blessed is the man whose
[A]strength is in You,
In [a]whose heart are the
[B]highways *to Zion!*
6 Passing through the valley of
[a]Baca they make it a [b]spring;
The [A]early rain also covers
it with blessings.
7 They [A]go from strength to strength,
[a]*Every one of them* [B]appears
before God in Zion.
8 O [A]LORD God of hosts,
hear my prayer;
Give ear, O [B]God of Jacob! *Selah*
9 Behold our [A]shield, O God,
And look upon the face
of [B]Your anointed.
10 For [A]a day in Your courts is better
than a thousand *outside.*
I would rather stand at the threshold
of the house of my God
Than dwell in the tents of wickedness.
11 For the LORD God is [A]a sun and [B]shield;
The LORD gives grace and [C]glory;
[D]No good thing does He withhold
[a]from those who walk [b]uprightly.
12 O LORD of hosts,
How [A]blessed is the man
who trusts in You!

83:12 [A]2 Chr 20:11 [B]Ps 132:13 83:13 [a]Or *tumbleweed* [A]Is 17:13 [B]Job 21:18; Ps 35:5; Is 40:24; Jer 13:24 83:14 [A]Is 9:18 [B]Ex 19:18; Deut 32:22 83:15 [A]Job 9:17; Ps 58:9 83:16 [A]Job 10:15; Ps 109:29; 132:18 83:17 [A]Ps 35:4; 70:2 83:18 [A]Ps 59:13 [B]Ps 86:10; Is 45:21 [C]Ps 9:2; 18:13; 97:9 84:1 [†]Or *according to* [A]Ps 43:3; 132:5 84:2 [A]Ps 42:1, 2; 63:1 [B]Ps 42:2 84:3 [A]Ps 43:4 [B]Ps 5:2 84:4 [a]*Selah* may mean: *Pause, Crescendo* or *Musical interlude* [A]Ps 65:4 [B]Ps 42:5, 11 84:5 [a]Lit *their* [A]Ps 81:1 [B]Ps 86:11; 122:1; Jer 31:6 84:6 [a]Probably, *Weeping;* or *Balsam trees* [b]Or *place of springs* [A]Ps 107:35; Joel 2:23 84:7 [a]Some ancient versions read *The God of gods will be seen in Zion* [A]Prov 4:18; Is 40:31; John 1:16; 2 Cor 3:18 [B]Ex 34:23; Deut 16:16; Ps 42:2 84:8 [A]Ps 59:5; 80:4; 84:1 [B]Ps 81:1 84:9 [A]Gen 15:1; Ps 3:3; 28:7; 59:11; 115:9-11 [B]1 Sam 16:6; 2 Sam 19:21; Ps 2:2; 132:17 84:10 [A]Ps 27:4 84:11 [a]Lit *with regard to* [b]Lit *with integrity* [A]Is 60:19, 20; Mal 4:2; Rev 21:23 [B]Gen 15:1 [C]Ps 85:9 [D]Ps 34:9, 10 84:12 [A]Ps 2:12; 40:4

83:13–15 The psalmist uses several dramatic similes in his prayer for the destruction of Israel's enemies.

83:18 know … Most High. The purpose of the maledictions against the hostile nations is neither personal nor national, but spiritual: that the nations may know and glorify God. **You alone … the LORD.** The Gentile nations need to know that the God of the Bible is the only God.

84:1–12 This psalm, like other psalms of ascent (Pss 120–134), expresses the joy of a pilgrim traveling up to Jerusalem, then up into the temple to celebrate one of the feasts. The pilgrim focuses his attention especially on the thought of being in the very presence of the Lord God. The NT believer-priest, in an even greater way, can come into the presence of the Lord (cf. Heb 4:16; 10:19–22).

I. The Expectation of Worshiping God (84:1–4)
II. The Expedition to Worship God (84:5–7)
III. The Elation at Worshiping God (84:8–12)

84:Title on the Gittith. *See note on Ps 8:Title.* **sons of Korah.** These descendants of Levi through Kohath were the gatekeepers and musicians in the temple at Jerusalem (1Ch 6:22; 9:17–32; 26:1; see all Pss 42–49; 84, 85; 87, 88).

84:1 lovely are Your dwelling places. The temple worship center was "lovely" because it enabled the OT saint to come into the presence of God (cf. Pss 27; 42:1, 2; 61:4; 63:1, 2). **LORD of hosts!** "Hosts" represent God's angelic armies, thus God's omnipotence over all powers in heaven and on earth (cf. vv. 3, 8, 12).

84:2 longed … yearned … sing for. The psalmist is consumed with his happy, but intense desire to worship God in the temple.

84:3 bird … swallow. The psalmist admires these birds who were able to build their nests in the temple courtyards, near the altars of God.

84:4 blessed. This word is used 3 times (vv. 4, 5, 12) to describe the happiness of those who, like the sons of Korah, "spent the night around the house of God" (1Ch 9:27).

84:6 valley of Baca. "Baca" can be translated as "weeping" or "balsam tree." The valley was an arid place on the way to Jerusalem. **they make it a spring.** The pilgrims traveling to a festival of worship at Jerusalem turn an arid valley into a place of joy.

84:7 from strength to strength. Anticipation of joyous worship of God in Jerusalem overcame the pilgrims' natural weariness in their difficult journey. **Zion.** *See note on Ps 87:2.*

84:9 Behold our shield. A metaphor for the king, who also would have participated in a festival at the temple (cf. Ps 47:9; Hos 4:18). **the face of Your anointed.** The king is regularly described as God's "anointed" (Pss 2:2; 18:50; 20:6; 28:8; 89:38, 51). The psalmist thus prays that God would look upon the king with favor, blessing his reign with prosperity.

84:10 stand at the threshold. One day standing at the door of the temple, or just being near even if not inside, was better than a thousand days fellowshiping with the wicked.

84:11 sun and shield. This pictures God's overall provision and protection.

PSALM 85

PRAYER FOR GOD'S MERCY UPON THE NATION.

For the choir director. A Psalm
of the sons of Korah.

1 O LORD, You showed [A]favor to Your land;
You [a,B]restored the captivity of Jacob.
2 You [A]forgave the iniquity of Your people;
You [B]covered all their sin. [a]*Selah*
3 You [A]withdrew all Your fury;
You [B]turned away from Your
burning anger.

4 [A]Restore us, O God of our salvation,
And [B]cause Your indignation
toward us to cease.
5 Will [A]You be angry with us forever?
Will You prolong Your anger
to [a]all generations?
6 Will You not Yourself [a,A]revive us again,
That Your people may [B]rejoice in You?
7 Show us Your lovingkindness, O LORD,
And [A]grant us Your salvation.

8 [a]I will hear what God the LORD will say;
For He will [A]speak peace to His
people, [b]to His godly ones;
But let them not [B]turn back to [c]folly.
9 Surely [A]His salvation is near to
those who [a]fear Him,
That [B]glory may dwell in our land.
10 [A]Lovingkindness and [a]truth
have met together;
[B]Righteousness and peace have
kissed each other.
11 [a]Truth [A]springs from the earth,
And righteousness looks
down from heaven.
12 Indeed, [A]the LORD will give what is good,
And our [B]land will yield its produce.
13 [A]Righteousness will go before Him
And will make His footsteps into a way.

PSALM 86

A PSALM OF SUPPLICATION AND TRUST.

A Prayer of David.

1 [A]Incline Your ear, O LORD, *and* answer me;
For I am [B]afflicted and needy.
2 [A]Preserve my [a]soul, for I am a [B]godly man;
O You my God, save Your servant
who [C]trusts in You.
3 Be [A]gracious to me, O Lord,
For [B]to You I cry all day long.
4 Make glad the soul of Your servant,
For to You, O Lord, [A]I lift up my soul.
5 For You, Lord, are [A]good, and
[B]ready to forgive,
And [C]abundant in lovingkindness
to all who call upon You.
6 [A]Give ear, O LORD, to my prayer;
And give heed to the voice
of my supplications!
7 In [A]the day of my trouble I
shall call upon You,
For [B]You will answer me.
8 There is [A]no one like You among
the gods, O Lord,
Nor are there any works [B]like Yours.

85:1 [a]Or *restore the fortunes* [A]Ps 77:7; 106:4 [B]Ezra 1:11; Ps 14:7; 126:1; Jer 30:18; Ezek 39:25; Hos 6:11; Joel 3:1 85:2 [a]*Selah* may mean: *Pause, Crescendo* or *Musical interlude* [A]Num 14:19; 1 Kin 8:34; Ps 78:38; 103:3; Jer 31:34 [B]Ps 32:1 85:3 [A]Ps 78:38; 106:23 [B]Ex 32:12; Deut 13:17; Ps 106:23; Jon 3:9 85:4 [A]Ps 80:3, 7 [B]Dan 9:16 85:5 [a]Lit *generation and generation* [A]Ps 74:1; 79:5; 80:4 85:6 [a]Or *bring to life* [A]Ps 71:20; 80:18 [B]Ps 33:1; 90:14; 149:2 85:7 [A]Ps 106:4 85:8 [a]Or *Let me hear* [b]Lit *even to* [c]Or *stupidity* [A]Ps 29:11; Hag 2:9; Zech 9:10 [B]Ps 78:57; 2 Pet 2:21 85:9 [a]Or *reverence* [A]Ps 34:18; Is 46:13 [B]Ps 84:11; Hag 2:7; Zech 2:5; John 1:14 85:10 [a]Or *faithfulness* [A]Ps 25:10; 89:14; Prov 3:3 [B]Ps 72:3; Is 32:17 85:11 [a]Or *Faithfulness* [A]Is 45:8 85:12 [A]Ps 84:11; James 1:17 [B]Lev 26:4; Ps 67:6; Ezek 34:27; Zech 8:12 85:13 [A]Ps 89:14 86:1 [A]Ps 17:6; 31:2; 71:2 [B]Ps 40:17; 70:5 86:2 [a]Or *life* [A]Ps 25:20 [B]Ps 4:3; 50:5 [C]Ps 25:2; 31:14; 56:4 86:3 [A]Ps 4:1; 57:1 [B]Ps 25:5; 88:9 86:4 [A]Ps 25:1; 143:8 86:5 [A]Ps 25:8 [B]Ps 130:4 [C]Ex 34:6; Neh 9:17; Ps 103:8; 145:8; Joel 2:13; Jon 4:2 86:6 [A]Ps 55:1 86:7 [A]Ps 50:15; 77:2 [B]Ps 17:6 86:8 [A]Ex 15:11; 2 Sam 7:22; 1 Kin 8:23; Ps 89:6; Jer 10:6 [B]Deut 3:24

85:1–13 The psalmist pledges that God will again demonstrate His covenant love to Israel. God has been merciful in the past; He is angry presently; but He will restore Israel in the future (cf. Dt 30; Hos 3:4, 5). Though God judges, He is faithful to His promises. The feelings expressed in this psalm may describe those of the Jews returning from exile in Babylon. Though they were grateful for restoration to their land, they were disappointed that the conditions did not measure up to the glory of the pre-Exilic life there (cf. Ezr 3:12, 13).

I. Review of God's Past Mercies (85:1–3)
II. Recognition of God's Present Anger (85:4–7)
III. Revelation of God's Future Salvation (85:8–13)

85:Title sons of Korah. *See note on Ps 84:Title.*

85:1 favor to Your land. In the past, God deemed His nation, Israel, to be acceptable.

85:3 Your burning anger. *See note on Ps 56:7.*

85:7 lovingkindness. The word means "loyal love" or "unfailing love," and specifies God's faithfulness to His people through His covenant relationship.

85:8 peace. Ultimately this comes in the Messiah's kingdom (cf. Mt 10:34; Lk 2:14).

85:9 salvation ... who fear Him. Only those who renounce their sinful autonomy and put their complete trust in the living God will participate in the blessings of salvation and the future kingdom (cf. Jn 3:3–5). glory may dwell in our land. The departure of the glory of God, which signified His presence, is described in Eze 10, 11. He withdrew His glory because of the apostasy of the nation immediately preceding the Babylonian Exile (cf. Eze 8–11). The return of the glory of the Lord in the future millennial temple is foretold in Eze 43:1–4 (cf. Pss 26:8; 63:2; Is 40:3–5; 60:1–3; 62:1–5). *See note on Lv 9:23.*

85:10 Lovingkindness ... truth ... Righteousness ... peace. These 4 spiritual qualities characterizing the atmosphere of the future kingdom of Christ will relate to each other in perfect harmony and will saturate kingdom life (cf. vv. 10, 13).

85:12 our land ... produce. Increase in the fertility and productivity of the land will also characterize the future kingdom of Christ (cf. Is 4:2; 30:23–26; 32:15; Jer 31:12; Eze 36:8–11; Am 9:13–15; Zec 8:11, 12).

86:1–17 This psalm is an individual lament (cf. Ps 56) in which David expresses his distress and overcomes that distress through praise and worship. There is a sense of urgency demonstrated by some 14 prayer requests. Undergirding the requests is the covenant relationship (vv. 2, 5, 13).

I. The Request for God's Attention (86:1–7)
II. The Testimony to God's Uniqueness (86:8–13)
III. The Plea for God's Deliverance (86:14–17)

86:2 I am a godly man. David, though recognizing his sinfulness (v. 1), insisted that by the grace of God he had not broken his covenant with the Lord.

86:4 soul ... soul. The psalmist requests that his inner person would be preserved according to the covenant agreements (cf. Dt 7, 8, 20).

86:8 among the gods. David is here contrasting the true God with the imaginary deities of the heathen nations (cf. v. 10; also Ex 15:11; Ps 89:6; Is 46:5–11).

9 [A]All nations whom You
have made shall come and
worship before You, O Lord,
And they shall glorify Your name.
10 For You are [A]great and [B]do
[a]wondrous deeds;
You alone [C]are God.

11 [A]Teach me Your way, O LORD;
I will walk in Your truth;
[B]Unite my heart to fear Your name.
12 I will [A]give thanks to You,
O Lord my God, with
all my heart,
And will glorify Your name forever.
13 For Your lovingkindness
toward me is great,
And You have [A]delivered my soul
from the [a]depths of [b]Sheol.

14 O God, arrogant men have
[A]risen up against me,
And [a]a band of violent men
have sought my [b]life,
And they have not set
You before them.
15 But You, O Lord, are a God
[A]merciful and gracious,
Slow to anger and abundant in
lovingkindness and [a]truth.
16 [A]Turn to me, and be
gracious to me;
Oh [B]grant Your strength
to Your servant,
And save the [C]son of
Your handmaid.
17 [A]Show me a sign for good,
That those who hate me may
[B]see *it* and be ashamed,
Because You, O LORD, [C]have helped
me and comforted me.

PSALM 87

THE PRIVILEGES OF CITIZENSHIP IN ZION.

A Psalm of the sons of Korah. A Song.

1 His [A]foundation is in
the holy mountains.
2 The LORD [A]loves the
gates of Zion
More than all the *other* dwelling
places of Jacob.
3 [A]Glorious things are spoken of you,
O [B]city of God. [a]*Selah*
4 "I shall mention [a,A]Rahab and Babylon
[b]among those who know Me;
Behold, Philistia and [B]Tyre
with [c,C]Ethiopia:
'This one was born there.' "
5 But of Zion it shall be said, "This one
and that one were born in her";
And the Most High Himself
will [A]establish her.
6 The LORD will count when He
[A]registers the peoples,
"This one was born there." *Selah*
7 Then those who [A]sing as
well as those who [a,B]play
the flutes *shall say,*
"All my [C]springs *of joy* are in you."

86:9 [A]Ps 22:27; 66:4; Is 66:23; Rev 15:4 86:10 [a]Or *miracles* [A]Ps 77:13 [B]Ex 15:11; Ps 72:18; 77:14; 136:4 [C]Deut 6:4; 32:39; Ps 83:18; Is 37:16; 44:6, 8; Mark 12:29; 1 Cor 8:4 86:11 [A]Ps 25:5 [B]Jer 32:39 86:12 [A]Ps 111:1 86:13 [a]Lit *lowest Sheol* [b]I.e. the nether world [A]Ps 30:3 86:14 [a]Or *an assembly* [b]Lit *soul* [A]Ps 54:3 86:15 [a]Or *faithfulness* [A]Ps 86:5 86:16 [A]Ps 25:16 [B]Ps 68:35 [C]Ps 116:16 86:17 [A]Judg 6:17; Ps 119:122 [B]Ps 112:10 [C]Ps 118:13 87:1 [A]Ps 78:69; Is 28:16 87:2 [A]Ps 78:67, 68 87:3 [a]*Selah* may mean: *Pause, Crescendo* or *Musical interlude* [A]Is 60:1 [B]Ps 46:4; 48:8 87:4 [a]I.e. Egypt [b]Or *as* [C]Lit *Cush* [A]Job 9:13; Ps 89:10; Is 19:23-25 [B]Ps 45:12 [C]Ps 68:31 87:5 [A]Ps 48:8 87:6 [A]Ps 69:28; Is 4:3; Ezek 13:9 87:7 [a]Or *dance* [A]Ps 68:25; 149:3 [B]2 Sam 6:14; Ps 30:11 [C]Ps 36:9

86:9 All nations … worship. The psalmists and prophets often look into the future messianic age when all the nations of the world will worship the Lord (cf. Ps 22:27; Is 2:3; Zec 8:21, 22; 14:16–19; Rev 15:4).

86:11 Unite my heart. The psalmist prays that he would have an undivided heart, single-heartedly loyal to his Lord (cf. Ro 7:15; Jas 1:8).

86:14 arrogant men. The arrogant (i.e., proud, insolent) are those who act independently from God, rebelling against Him and His people (cf. Ps 119:21, 51, 69, 78, 85, 122).

86:16 the son of Your handmaid. David asks for special favor from God just as a servant born in the household would receive more than a servant brought in from outside the household (cf. Ps 116:16).

86:17 a sign. A request for a favorable indication that would demonstrate that God was truly on David's side.

87:1–7 This psalm describes the Lord's love for Jerusalem and exalts this city as the religious center of the world in the coming messianic kingdom (cf. Ps 48). Though the nations of the world (even including some of Israel's former enemies) will worship the Lord then, Israel will still be the favored nation (cf. Is 2:2–4; 19:23–25; 45:22–25; 56:6–8; Zec 8:20–23; 14:16–19).

I. The Lord's Love for Zion (87:1–3)
II. The Lord's Favor of Israel (87:4–6)
III. The Musicians' Exultation over Jerusalem (87:7)

87:Title sons of Korah. *See note on Ps 84:Title.*

87:1 His foundation … holy mountains. "His foundation" means "His founded city," namely Jerusalem, located in the hill country of Judea.

87:2 gates of Zion. Zion is a poetic description of Jerusalem, seemingly used by the OT writers when special spiritual and religious significance was being attached to the city. Though God certainly loved other cities in Israel, He did not choose any of them to be His worship center (cf. Pss 122, 125, 132, 133). The gates represent the access of the potential worshiper into the city where he could come into a special worshiping relationship with God. **More than all the … dwelling places of Jacob.** The other cities in Israel were not chosen by God to be the place of His special dwelling.

87:3 O city of God. Jerusalem was God's city because there God met His people in praise and offerings.

87:4 Rahab and Babylon. Rahab was a monster of ancient pagan mythology and symbolized Egypt in the OT (cf. Ps 89:10; Is 30:7; 51:9). Two of the superpowers of the ancient world, fierce enemies of Israel, will one day worship the Lord in Zion (cf. Is 19:19–25). **Philistia … Tyre … Ethiopia.** Three more Gentile nations, ancient enemies of Israel, whose descendants will worship the Lord in Jerusalem (cf. Is 14:28–32; 18:1–7). This multinational worship is pictured as a great joy to the Lord Himself. **This one was born there.** To be born in Jerusalem will be noted as a special honor in the messianic kingdom (cf. vv. 5, 6; also Zec 8:20–23).

87:7 All my springs … are in you. "Springs" is a metaphor for the source of joyful blessings. Eternal salvation, including the death and resurrection of Christ, is rooted in Jerusalem. The prophets also tell of a literal fountain flowing from the temple in Jerusalem which will water the surrounding land (cf. Joel 3:18; Eze 47:1–12).

PSALM 88

A PETITION TO BE SAVED FROM DEATH.

A Song. A Psalm of the sons of Korah. For the choir director; according to Mahalath Leannoth. A [†]Maskil of Heman •the Ezrahite.

1 O LORD, the [A]God of my salvation,
I have [B]cried out by
day and in the night
before You.
2 Let my prayer [A]come before You;
[B]Incline Your ear to my cry!
3 For my [A]soul has [a]had
enough troubles,
And [B]my life has drawn
near to [b]Sheol.
4 I am reckoned among those
who [A]go down to the pit;
I have become like a man
[B]without strength,
5 [a]Forsaken [A]among the dead,
Like the slain who lie
in the grave,
Whom You remember no more,
And they are [B]cut off
from Your hand.
6 You have put me in [A]the lowest pit,
In [B]dark places, in the [C]depths.
7 Your wrath [A]has rested upon me,
And You have afflicted me
with [B]all Your waves. [a]*Selah*
8 You have removed [A]my
acquaintances far from me;
You have made me an [a,B]object
of loathing to them;
I am [C]shut up and cannot go out.
9 My [A]eye has wasted away
because of affliction;
I have [B]called upon You
every day, O LORD;
I have [C]spread out my [a]hands to You.

10 Will You perform wonders
for the dead?
Will [A]the [a]departed spirits
rise *and* praise You? *Selah*
11 Will Your lovingkindness be
declared in the grave,
Your faithfulness in [a]Abaddon?
12 Will Your wonders be made
known in the [A]darkness?
And Your [a]righteousness in the
land of forgetfulness?

13 But I, O LORD, have cried
out [A]to You for help,
And [B]in the morning my prayer
comes before You.
14 O LORD, why [A]do You
reject my soul?
Why do You [B]hide Your
face from me?
15 I was afflicted and [A]about to
die from my youth on;
I suffer [B]Your terrors;
I am [a]overcome.
16 Your [A]burning anger
has passed over me;
Your terrors have
[a,B]destroyed me.
17 They have [A]surrounded me
[B]like water all day long;
They have [C]encompassed
me altogether.
18 You have removed [A]lover and
friend far from me;
My acquaintances are *in* darkness.

88:1 [†]Possibly, *Contemplative,* or *Didactic,* or *Skillful Psalm* [•]1 Kin 4:31; 1 Chr 2:6; Ps 89: title [A]Ps 24:5; 27:9 [B]Ps 22:2; 86:3; Luke 18:7 88:2 [A]Ps 18:6 [B]Ps 31:2; 86:1 88:3 [a]Or *been satisfied with* [b]I.e. the nether world [A]Ps 107:26 [B]Ps 107:18; 116:3 88:4 [A]Ps 28:1; 143:7 [B]Job 29:12; Ps 22:11 88:5 [a]Lit *A freed one among the dead* [A]Ps 31:12 [B]Ps 31:22; Is 53:8 88:6 [A]Ps 86:13; Lam 3:55 [B]Ps 143:3 [C]Ps 69:15 88:7 [a]*Selah* may mean: *Pause, Crescendo* or *Musical interlude* [A]Ps 32:4; 39:10 [B]Ps 42:7 88:8 [a]Lit *abomination to them* [A]Job 19:13, 19; Ps 31:11; 142:4 [B]Job 30:10 [C]Ps 142:7; Jer 32:2; 36:5 88:9 [a]Lit *palms* [A]Ps 6:7; 31:9 [B]Ps 22:2; 86:3 [C]Job 11:13; Ps 143:6 88:10 [a]Or *ghosts, shades* [A]Ps 6:5; 30:9 88:11 [a]I.e. place of destruction 88:12 [a]I.e. faithfulness to His gracious promises [A]Job 10:21; Ps 88:6 88:13 [A]Ps 30:2 [B]Ps 5:3; 119:147 88:14 [A]Ps 43:2; 44:9 [B]Job 13:24; Ps 13:1; 44:24 88:15 [a]Or *embarrassed* [A]Prov 24:11 [B]Job 6:4; 31:23 88:16 [a]Or *silenced* [A]2 Chr 28:11; Is 13:13; Lam 1:12 [B]Lam 3:54; Ezek 37:11 88:17 [A]Ps 118:10-12 [B]Ps 124:4 [C]Ps 17:11; 22:12, 16 88:18 [A]Job 19:13; Ps 88:8; 31:11; 38:11

88:1–18 This lament is unusual in that it does not end on a happy note. The psalmist has been ill or injured since the days of his youth (v. 15) and bemoans God's failure to hear his prayer for good health. He assumes that God is angry with him, but like Job, he knows of no cause for that anger. But though he does not understand God's ways, the psalmist does turn to God, thus indicating an underlying trust.

I. Complaints Against God's Action (88:1–9)
II. Challenges to God's Wisdom (88:10–12)
III. Charges Against God's Conduct (88:13–18)

88:Title **sons of Korah.** *See note on Ps 84:Title.* **Mahalath Leannoth.** "Mahalath" is either the name of a tune or an instrument, possibly a reed pipe which was played on sad occasions. "Leannoth" may mean "to afflict" and describes the despair which permeates this psalm. **Maskil.** *See note on Ps 32:Title.* **Heman the Ezrahite.** Heman was a musician from the family of the Kohathites, who founded the Korahite choir (cf. 1Ch 6:33; 2Ch 5:12; 35:15). He may be the same person who was one of the wise men during Solomon's reign (1Ki 4:31). "Ezrahite" may mean "native born," or may be the name of a family clan (cf. 1Ch 2:6).

88:4 **go down to the pit.** "Pit" is one of several references to the grave in this psalm (cf. the dead, vv. 5, 10; Sheol, or the grave, vv. 3, 5, 11; Abaddon, v. 11).

88:5 **Forsaken among the dead.** Expresses the idea that death cuts off all ties to friends and family as well as to God.

88:7 **all Your waves.** Like the waves rolling onto the seashore, so God has directed trouble after trouble on the psalmist (cf. v. 17).

88:8 **removed my acquaintances.** The psalmist claims that the Lord has turned his friends against him. Some see this as a quarantine experience, as from leprosy (cf. v. 18; also Job 19:13–20).

88:9 **eye has wasted away.** This could be a description of the psalmist's tears, used as a figure for his entire collapse under this distress.

88:10 **wonders for the dead?** The psalmist reminds God, through a series of rhetorical questions, that the dead cannot testify to God's goodness.

88:14 **hide Your face.** That is, not answer prayer.

88:15 **die from my youth** The psalmist has had some serious illness or injury from the time of his youth.

88:18 **lover ... friend ... acquaintances.** *See note on v. 8.*

PSALM 89

THE LORD'S COVENANT WITH DAVID, AND ISRAEL'S AFFLICTIONS.

A [†]Maskil of •Ethan *the Ezrahite.

1 I will [A]sing of the lovingkindness
of the LORD forever;
To all generations I will [B]make known
Your [C]faithfulness with my mouth.
2 For I have said, "[A]Lovingkindness
will be built up forever;
In the heavens You will establish
Your [B]faithfulness."
3 "I have made a covenant with [A]My chosen;
I have [B]sworn to David My servant,
4 I will establish your [A]seed forever
And build up your [B]throne to all
generations." [a]*Selah*

5 The [A]heavens will praise Your
wonders, O LORD;
Your faithfulness also [B]in the
assembly of the [C]holy ones.
6 For [A]who in the skies is
comparable to the LORD?
Who among the [a,B]sons of the
mighty is like the LORD,
7 A God [A]greatly feared in the
council of the [B]holy ones,
And [C]awesome above all those
who are around Him?
8 O LORD God of hosts, [A]who is like
You, O mighty [a]LORD?
Your faithfulness also surrounds You.
9 You rule the swelling of the sea;
When its waves rise, You [A]still them.
10 You Yourself crushed [a,A]Rahab
like one who is slain;
You [B]scattered Your enemies
with [b]Your mighty arm.

11 The [A]heavens are Yours, the
earth also is Yours;
The [B]world and [a]all it contains,
You have founded them.
12 The [A]north and the south, You
have created them;
[B]Tabor and [C]Hermon [D]shout
for joy at Your name.
13 You have [a]a strong arm;
Your hand is mighty, Your
[A]right hand is exalted.
14 [A]Righteousness and justice are the
foundation of Your throne;
[B]Lovingkindness and
[a]truth go before You.
15 How blessed are the people who
know the [a,A]joyful sound!
O LORD, they walk in the [B]light
of Your countenance.
16 In [A]Your name they rejoice all the day,
And by Your righteousness
they are exalted.
17 For You are the glory
of [A]their strength,
And by Your favor [a]our [B]horn is exalted.
18 For our [A]shield belongs to the LORD,
[a]And our king to the [B]Holy One of Israel.

89:1 [†]Possibly, *Contemplative*, or *Didactic*, or *Skillful Psalm* •1 Kin 4:31 *Ps 88: title [A]Ps 59:16; 101:1 [B]Ps 40:10 [C]Ps 36:5; 88:11; 89:5, 8, 24, 33, 49; 92:2; 119:90; Is 25:1; Lam 3:23 89:2 [A]Ps 103:17 [B]Ps 36:5; 119:90 89:3 [A]1 Kin 8:16 [B]Ps 132:11 89:4 [a]*Selah* may mean: *Pause, Crescendo* or *Musical interlude* [A]2 Sam 7:16 [B]2 Sam 7:13; Is 9:7; Luke 1:33 89:5 [A]Ps 19:1; 97:6 [B]Ps 149:1 [C]Job 5:1 89:6 [a]Or *sons of gods* [A]Ps 86:8; 113:5 [B]Ps 29:1; 82:1 89:7 [A]Ps 47:2; 68:35; 76:7, 11 [B]Ps 89:5 [C]Ps 96:4 89:8 [a]Heb *YAH* [A]Ps 35:10; 71:19 89:9 [A]Ps 65:7; 107:29 89:10 [a]I.e. Egypt [b]Lit *the arm of Your might* [A]Ps 87:4; Is 30:7; 51:9 [B]Ps 18:14; 68:1; 144:6 89:11 [a]Lit *its fullness* [A]Gen 1:1; 1 Chr 29:11; Ps 96:5 [B]Ps 24:1 89:12 [A]Job 26:7 [B]Josh 19:22; Judg 4:6; Jer 46:18 [C]Deut 3:8; Josh 11:17; 12:1; Ps 133:3; Song 4:8 [D]Ps 98:8 89:13 [a]Lit *an arm with strength* [A]Ps 98:1; 118:16 89:14 [a]Or *faithfulness* [A]Ps 97:2 [B]Ps 85:13 89:15 [a]Or *blast of the trumpet, shout of joy* [A]Lev 23:24; Num 10:10; Ps 98:6 [B]Ps 4:6; 44:3; 67:1; 80:3; 90:8 89:16 [A]Ps 105:3 89:17 [a]Another reading is *You exalt our horn* [A]Ps 28:8 [B]Ps 75:10; 92:10; 148:14 89:18 [a]Or *Even to the Holy One of Israel our King* [A]Ps 47:9 [B]Ps 71:22; 78:41

89:1–52 This psalm describes the author's attempt to reconcile the seeming contradictions between his theology and the reality of his nation's conditions. Through the first 37 verses, he rehearses what he knows to be theologically accurate: God has sovereignly chosen Israel to be His nation, and David's descendants to rule. The last third of the psalm reflects the psalmist's chagrin that the nation had been ravaged and the Davidic monarchy had apparently come to a disgraceful end. To his credit, the psalmist refuses to explain away his theology, but instead keeps the tension, hopefully to be resolved at a later time with the promised reestablishment of an earthly kingdom under one of David's descendants (cf. Pss 110, 132).

I. God's Manifest Faithfulness to the Davidic Covenant (89:1–37)
   A. God's Covenant Love (89:1–4)
   B. God's Praiseworthiness (89:5–18)
   C. God's Covenant with David (89:19–37)
II. God's Apparent Neglect of the Davidic Covenant (89:38–52)
   A. The Psalmist's Lament (89:38–45)
   B. The Psalmist's Consternation (89:46–51)
   C. The Doxology (89:52)

89:Title Ethan the Ezrahite. Possibly the Levitical singer mentioned in 1Ch 6:42 and 15:17, 19 (*see note on Ps 88:Title*).

89:1 lovingkindness. *See note on Ps 85:7* (cf. vv. 2, 14, 24, 28, 33, 49).

89:2 You will establish … faithfulness. The psalmist exults that the Lord Himself will guarantee the eternality of the Davidic dynasty (cf. 2Sa 23:5).

89:3 covenant with My chosen. The Davidic Covenant, culminating in Messiah's reign, was established in 2Sa 7 (cf. 1Ki 8:23; 1Ch 17; 2Ch 21:7; Pss 110, 132). The covenant was in the form of a royal grant covenant as God, the Great King, chose David as His servant king. In this type of covenant, the person with whom the Lord established the covenant could violate the terms of the covenant and the Lord would still be obligated to maintain the covenant.

89:4 seed forever … throne. The covenant with David was extended to his descendants. The throne promise guaranteed that the rightful heir to the throne would always be a descendant of David (cf. vv. 29, 36; see also 2Sa 7:13, 16, 18; Lk 1:31–33). The genealogies of Jesus qualify Him for the throne (cf. Mt 1:1–17; Lk 3:23–38).

89:5 faithfulness. The word suggests constant and habitual actions, meaning here that God was reliable. For God to violate this consistency of actions would be to violate His very nature (cf. vv. 1, 2, 8, 24, 33, 49).

89:6 sons of the mighty. Lit. "sons of God," i.e., angels.

89:7 council of the holy ones. This pictures a gathering of the angels around their sovereign Lord.

89:10 Rahab. A figurative term for Egypt. *See note on Ps 87:4.*

89:12 Tabor and Hermon. Mountains in Israel pictured joining in praise with the rest of creation.

89:15 the joyful sound! Refers to a cheer, a shout of joyful homage to God (cf. Pss 33:3; 47:5; 95:1; 98:4; 100:1. *See note on Ps 66:1*).

89:17 our horn is exalted. *See note on Ps 75:4* (cf. v. 24).

89:18 shield belongs to the LORD. The "shield" was a metaphor for the king (*see note on Ps 84:9*).

19 [a]Once You spoke in vision to
Your godly [b]ones,
And said, "I have [c]given help
to one who is [A]mighty;
I have exalted one [B]chosen from the people.
20 "I have [A]found David My servant;
With My holy [B]oil I have anointed him,
21 With whom [A]My hand will be established;
My arm also will [B]strengthen him.
22 "The enemy will not [a]deceive him,
Nor the [b,A]son of wickedness afflict him.
23 "But I shall [A]crush his
adversaries before him,
And strike those who hate him.
24 "My [A]faithfulness and My
lovingkindness will be with him,
And in My name his [B]horn will be exalted.
25 "I shall also set his hand [A]on the sea
And his right hand on the rivers.
26 "He will cry to Me, 'You are [A]my Father,
My God, and the [B]rock of my salvation.'
27 "I also shall make him *My* [A]firstborn,
The [B]highest of the kings of the earth.
28 "My [A]lovingkindness I will
keep for him forever,
And My [B]covenant shall be
confirmed to him.
29 "So I will establish his [a,A]descendants forever
And his [B]throne [C]as the days of heaven.

30 "If his sons [A]forsake My law
And do not walk in My judgments,
31 If they [a]violate My statutes
And do not keep My commandments,
32 Then I will punish their
transgression with the [A]rod
And their iniquity with stripes.
33 "But I will not break off [A]My
lovingkindness from him,
Nor deal falsely in My faithfulness.
34 "My [A]covenant I will not [a]violate,
Nor will I [B]alter [b]the utterance of My lips.
35 "[a]Once I have [A]sworn by My holiness;
I will not lie to David.
36 "His [a,A]descendants shall endure forever
And his [B]throne [C]as the sun before Me.
37 "It shall be established forever
[A]like the moon,
And the [B]witness in the sky is faithful."
[a]*Selah*

38 But You have [A]cast off and [B]rejected,
You have been full of wrath
[a]against Your [C]anointed.
39 You have [A]spurned the covenant
of Your servant;
You have [B]profaned [C]his crown [a]in the dust.
40 You have [A]broken down all his walls;
You have [B]brought his
strongholds to ruin.
41 [A]All who pass along the way plunder him;
He has become a [B]reproach
to his neighbors.
42 You have [A]exalted the right
hand of his adversaries;
You have [B]made all his enemies rejoice.
43 You also turn back the edge of his sword
And have [A]not made him stand in battle.
44 You have made his [a,A]splendor to cease
And cast his throne to the ground.
45 You have [A]shortened the
days of his youth;
You have [B]covered him with shame.
Selah

89:19 [a]Or *At that time* [b]Some mss read *one* [C]Lit *placed help upon* [A]2 Sam 17:10 [B]1 Kin 11:34; Ps 78:70 89:20 [A]1 Sam 13:14; 16:1-12; Acts 13:22 [B]1 Sam 16:13 89:21 [A]Ps 18:35; 80:17 [B]Ps 18:32 89:22 [a]Or *exact usury from him* [b]Or *wicked man* [A]2 Sam 7:10; Ps 125:3 89:23 [A]2 Sam 7:9; Ps 18:40 89:24 [A]Ps 89:1 [B]Ps 132:17 89:25 [A]Ps 72:8 89:26 [A]2 Sam 7:14; 1 Chr 22:10; Jer 3:19 [B]2 Sam 22:47; Ps 95:1 89:27 [A]Ex 4:22; Ps 2:7; Jer 31:9; Col 1:15, 18 [B]Num 24:7; Ps 72:11; Rev 19:16 89:28 [A]Ps 89:33 [B]Ps 89:3, 34 89:29 [a]Lit *seed* [A]Ps 18:50; 89:4, 36 [B]1 Kin 2:4; Ps 89:4; 132:12; Is 9:7; Jer 33:17 [C]Deut 11:21 89:30 [A]2 Sam 7:14; Ps 119:53 89:31 [a]Lit *profane* 89:32 [A]Job 9:34; 21:9 89:33 [A]2 Sam 7:15 89:34 [a]Lit *profane* [b]Lit *that which goes forth* [A]Deut 7:9; Jer 33:20, 21 [B]Num 23:19 89:35 [a]Or *One thing* [A]Ps 60:6; Amos 4:2 89:36 [a]Lit *seed* [A]Ps 89:29; Luke 1:33 [B]Ps 72:5 [C]Ps 72:17 89:37 [a]*Selah* may mean: *Pause, Crescendo* or *Musical interlude* [A]Ps 72:5 [B]Job 16:19 89:38 [a]Lit *with* [A]Ps 44:9 [B]Deut 32:19; 1 Chr 28:9 [C]Ps 20:6; 89:20, 51 89:39 [a]Lit *to the ground* [A]Ps 78:59; Lam 2:7 [B]Ps 74:7 [C]Lam 5:16 89:40 [A]Ps 80:12 [B]Lam 2:2, 5 89:41 [A]Ps 80:12 [B]Ps 44:13; 69:9, 19; 79:4 89:42 [A]Ps 13:2 [B]Ps 80:6 89:43 [A]Ps 44:10 89:44 [a]Lit *clearness, luster* [A]Ezek 28:7 89:45 [A]Ps 102:23 [B]Ps 44:15; 71:13; 109:29

89:19 Your godly ones. The "godly ones" (cf. marginal note) were people like the prophet, Nathan, whom the Lord used to tell David about His covenant with David (2Sa 7:4ff.).

89:25 hand … sea … rivers. A reference to the promise of Ex 23:31 that the Lord would give Israel the land between the Red Sea and the Euphrates River.

89:27 *My* firstborn. The firstborn child was given a place of special honor and a double portion of the inheritance (Ge 27; 2Ki 2:9). However, in a royal grant covenant, a chosen person could be elevated to the level of firstborn sonship and thus have title to a perpetual gift involving dynastic succession (cf. Ps 2:7). Though not actually the first, Israel was considered the firstborn among nations (Ex 4:22); Ephraim the younger was treated as the firstborn (Ge 48:13–20); and David was the firstborn among kings. In this latter sense of prominent favor, Christ can be called the firstborn over all creation (Col 1:15), in that He is given the preeminence over all created beings.

89:32 rod … stripes. The rod was an instrument for inflicting wounds, and the stripes were marks left by such a flogging. God's warning reflects His knowledge of the evident potential for disobedience among the descendants of David (cf. 2Sa 7:14). In the lifetime of David's grandsons, for example, the kingdom was split with the 10 northern tribes leaving the rulership of the Davidic line (cf. Jer 31:31 and Eze 37:16, 17 for the future reunification of the 12 tribes).

89:33 My lovingkindness. Though the Lord might have to severely discipline David's descendants, He would never remove His covenant from this family (cf. 2Sa 7:15). Thus the covenant could be conditional in any one or more generations and yet be unconditional in its final outcome (cf. Eze 37:24–28).

89:37 witness in the sky is faithful. God's covenant with David regarding his descendants was as certain as the establishment of the sun (v. 36) and the moon in the heavens (cf. Jer 33:14–26). The promise involved a kingdom "in the earth" (Jer 33:15).

89:39 spurned the covenant. The Heb. word behind "spurned" is rare, and it may better be translated "disdained." It seemed to the psalmist that the condition of Israel indicated that God was neglecting His covenant with David (cf. Eze 37:1–14). **profaned his crown.** This depicts a serious insult to the dynasty because it is of divine origin.

89:40–45 The ruin is depicted in several images: left with broken hedges, thus defenseless; a stronghold whose ruins invite invaders; a weakling plundered by all his enemies; a soldier with a useless sword; and a youth prematurely old.

89:45 shortened the days of his youth. This is a figure for the relative brevity of the Davidic dynasty. The dynasty was cut off in its youth.

46 [A]How long, O LORD?
Will You hide Yourself forever?
Will Your [B]wrath burn like fire?
47 [A]Remember [a]what my span of life is;
For what [B]vanity [b]You have
created all the sons of men!
48 What man can live and not [A]see death?
Can he [B]deliver his soul from the [a]power
of [b]Sheol? *Selah*

49 Where are Your former
lovingkindnesses, O Lord,
Which You [A]swore to David
in Your faithfulness?
50 Remember, O Lord, the [A]reproach
of Your servants;
[a]How I bear in my bosom *the reproach*
of all the many peoples,
51 With which [A]Your enemies have
reproached, O LORD,
With which they have reproached
the footsteps of [B]Your anointed.

52 [A]Blessed be the LORD forever!
Amen and Amen.

BOOK 4

PSALM 90

GOD'S ETERNITY AND MAN'S TRANSITORINESS.

A Prayer of [†]Moses, the man of God.

1 Lord, You have been our [a,A]dwelling
place in all generations.
2 Before [A]the mountains
were born
[a]Or You [B]gave birth to the
earth and the world,
Even [C]from everlasting to
everlasting, You are God.

3 You [A]turn man back into dust
And say, "Return,
O children of men."
4 For [A]a thousand years
in Your sight
Are like [B]yesterday when
it passes by,
[a]Or *as* a [C]watch in the night.
5 You [A]have [a]swept them
away like a flood,
they [b,B]fall asleep;
In the morning they are like
[C]grass which [c]sprouts anew.
6 In the morning it [A]flourishes
and [a]sprouts anew;
Toward evening it [B]fades
and [C]withers away.

7 For we have been [A]consumed
by Your anger
And by Your wrath we have
been [a]dismayed.
8 You have [A]placed our
iniquities before You,
Our [B]secret *sins* in the light
of Your presence.
9 For [A]all our days have
declined in Your fury;
We have finished our
years like a [a]sigh.

89:46 [A]Ps 13:1; 44:24 [B]Ps 79:5; 80:4 89:47 [a]Lit *of what duration I am* [b]Or *have You…men?* [A]Job 7:7; 10:9; 14:1 [B]Ps 39:5; 62:9; Eccl 1:2; 2:11 89:48 [a]Lit *hand* [b]I.e. the nether world [A]Ps 22:29; 49:9 [B]Ps 49:15 89:49 [A]2 Sam 7:15; Jer 30:9; Ezek 34:23 89:50 [a]Lit *My bearing in my bosom* [A]Ps 69:9; 74:18, 22 89:51 [A]Ps 74:10, 18, 22 [B]Ps 89:38 89:52 [A]Ps 41:13; 72:19; 106:48 90:1 [†]Deut 33:1 [a]Or *hiding place;* some ancient mss read *place of refuge* [A]Deut 33:27; Ps 71:3; 91:1; Ezek 11:16 90:2 [a]Or *And* [A]Job 15:7; Prov 8:25 [B]Gen 1:1; Ps 102:25; 104:5 [C]Ps 93:2; 102:24, 27; Jer 10:10 90:3 [A]Gen 3:19; Job 34:14, 15; Ps 104:29 90:4 [a]Or *And* [A]2 Pet 3:8 [B]Ps 39:5 [C]Ex 14:24; Judg 7:19 90:5 [a]Or *flooded* [b]Lit *become asleep* [c]Or *passes away* [A]Job 22:16; 27:20 [B]Job 14:12; 20:8; Ps 76:5 [C]Ps 103:15; Is 40:6 90:6 [a]Or *passes away* [A]Job 14:2 [B]Ps 92:7; Matt 6:30 [C]James 1:11 90:7 [a]Or *terrified* [A]Ps 39:11 90:8 [A]Ps 50:21; Jer 16:17 [B]Ps 19:12; Eccl 12:14 90:9 [a]Or *whisper* [A]Ps 78:33

89:46 hide Yourself forever? By God's seeming refusal to answer prayer and restore the Davidic kingship, it seemed as though God was hiding Himself. Of course, the discipline of disobedient kings had been foretold (v. 32). According to the prophets, God would eventually restore Israel and the Davidic throne in an earthly kingdom (cf. Hos 3:4, 5). Never in the OT is there a sense that this Davidic promise would be fulfilled by Christ with a spiritual and heavenly reign.

89:47 The prosperity of the Davidic kingdom is linked to the welfare of all people (cf. Ps 72:17; Is 9:7; 11:1–10). If the kingdom fails, who can survive? (v. 48).

89:49–51 Here is a final plea for God to come to the help of His people, so as to avoid reproach (cf. Is 37:17–35).

89:52 Blessed be the LORD. This blessing, indicating returning confidence, closes not only Ps 89, but all of Book III (Pss 73–89) of the Psalms.

90:1–17 The thrust of this magnificent prayer is to ask God to have mercy on frail human beings living in a sin-cursed universe. Moses begins the psalm with a reflection on God's eternality, then expresses his somber thoughts about the sorrows and brevity of life in their relationship to God's anger, and concludes with a plea that God would enable His people to live a significant life. The psalm seems to have been composed as the older generation of Israelites who had left Egypt were dying off in the wilderness (Nu 14).

I. The Praise of God's Eternality (90:1, 2)
II. The Perception of Man's Frailty (90:3–12)
III. The Plea for God's Mercy (90:13–17)

90:Title Moses, the man of God. Moses the prophet (Dt 18:15–22) was unique in that the Lord knew him "face to face" (Dt 34:10–12). "Man of God" (Dt 33:1) is a technical term used over 70 times in the OT, always referring to one who spoke for God. It is used of Timothy in the NT (1Ti 6:11; 2Ti 3:17).

90:1 our dwelling place. God is our sanctuary for protection, sustenance, and stability (cf. Dt 33:27; Ps 91:9).

90:2 from everlasting to everlasting. God's nature is without beginning or end, free from all succession of time, and contains in itself the cause of time (cf. Ps 102:27; Is 41:4; 1Co 2:7; Eph 1:4; 1Ti 6:16; Rev 1:8).

90:3 You turn man back into dust. Though different from the "dust" of Ge 3:19, this phrase is no doubt a reference to that passage. Humanity lives under a sovereign decree of death and cannot escape it.

90:4 a watch in the night. A "watch" was a 4-hour period of time (cf. Ex 14:24; La 2:19; 2Pe 3:8).

90:5 like a flood. Humankind is snatched from the earth as though it were being swept away by floodwaters. **they fall asleep.** Humanity lives its existence as though asleep or in a coma. People are insensitive to the brevity of life and the reality of God's wrath.

90:7 consumed by Your anger. The physical bodies of the human race wear out by the effects of God's judgment on sin in the universe (cf. Dt 4:25–28; 11:16, 17). Death is by sin (Ro 5:12).

90:8 the light of Your presence. All sin is in clear view to the "face" of God.

90:9 like a sigh. After struggling through his life of afflictions and troubles, a man's

10 As for the days of our [a]life, [b]they
contain seventy years,
Or if due to strength, [A]eighty years,
Yet their pride is *but* [B]labor and sorrow;
For soon it is gone and we [C]fly away.
11 Who [a]understands the [A]power
of Your anger
And Your fury, according to the
[B]fear [b]that is due You?
12 So [A]teach us to number our days,
That we may [a,B]present to You
a heart of wisdom.

13 Do [A]return, O LORD; [B]how long *will it be?*
And [a]be [C]sorry for Your servants.
14 O [A]satisfy us in the morning with
Your lovingkindness,
That we may [B]sing for joy and
be glad all our days.
15 [A]Make us glad [a]according to the
days You have afflicted us,
And the [B]years we have seen [b]evil.
16 Let Your [A]work appear to Your servants
And Your [B]majesty [a]to their children.
17 Let the [A]favor of the Lord
our God be upon us;
And [a,B]confirm for us the
work of our hands;
Yes, [a]confirm the work of our hands.

PSALM 91

SECURITY OF THE ONE WHO TRUSTS IN THE LORD.

1 He who dwells in the [A]shelter
of the Most High
Will abide in the [B]shadow of the Almighty.
2 I will say to the LORD, "My
[A]refuge and my [B]fortress,
My God, in whom I [C]trust!"
3 For it is He who delivers you from
the [A]snare of the trapper
And from the deadly [B]pestilence.
4 He will [A]cover you with His pinions,
And [B]under His wings you
may seek refuge;
His [C]faithfulness is a
[D]shield and bulwark.

5 You [A]will not be afraid of
the [B]terror by night,
Or of the [C]arrow that flies by day;
6 Of the [A]pestilence that
[a]stalks in darkness,
Or of the [B]destruction that
lays waste at noon.
7 A thousand may fall at your side
And ten thousand at your right hand,
But [A]it shall not approach you.
8 You will only look on with your eyes
And [A]see the recompense of the wicked.
9 [a]For you have made the LORD, [A]my refuge,
Even the Most High, [B]your dwelling place.
10 [A]No evil will befall you,
Nor will any plague come near your [a]tent.

11 For He will give [A]His angels
charge concerning you,
To guard you in all your ways.
12 They will [A]bear you up in their hands,
That you do not strike your
foot against a stone.
13 You will [A]tread upon the lion and cobra,
The young lion and the [a]serpent
you will trample down.

90:10 [a]Lit *years* [b]Lit *in them are* [A]2 Kin 19:35 [B]Eccl 12:2-7; Jer 20:18 [C]Job 20:8; Ps 78:39 90:11 [a]Or *knows* [b]Lit *of You* [A]Ps 76:7 [B]Neh 5:9 90:12 [a]Or *gain, bring in* [A]Deut 32:29; Ps 39:4 [B]Prov 2:1-6 90:13 [a]Or *repent in regard to* [A]Ps 6:4; 80:14 [B]Ps 6:3; 74:10 [C]Ex 32:12; Deut 32:36; Ps 106:45; 135:14; Amos 7:3, 6; Jon 3:9 90:14 [A]Ps 36:8; 65:4; 103:5; Jer 31:14 [B]Ps 31:7; 85:6 90:15 [a]Or *as many days as* [b]Or *trouble* [A]Ps 86:4 [B]Deut 2:14-16; Ps 31:10 90:16 [a]Or *upon* [A]Deut 32:4; Ps 44:1; 77:12; 92:4; Hab 3:2 [B]1 Kin 8:11; Is 6:3 90:17 [a]Or *give permanence to* [A]Ps 27:4 [B]Ps 37:23; Is 26:12; 1 Cor 3:7 91:1 [A]Ps 27:5; 31:20; 32:7 [B]Ps 17:8; 121:5; Is 25:4; 32:2 91:2 [A]Ps 14:6; 91:9; 94:22; 142:5 [B]Ps 18:2; 31:3; Jer 16:19 [C]Ps 25:2; 56:4 91:3 [A]Ps 124:7; Prov 6:5 [B]1 Kin 8:37; 2 Chr 20:9; Ps 91:6 91:4 [A]Is 51:16 [B]Ps 17:8; 36:7; 57:1; 63:7 [C]Ps 40:11 [D]Ps 35:2 91:5 [A]Job 5:19-23; Ps 23:4; 27:1 [B]Song 3:8 [C]Ps 64:4 91:6 [a]Or *walks* [A]2 Kin 19:35; Ps 91:10 [B]Job 5:22 91:7 [A]Gen 7:23; Josh 14:10 91:8 [A]Ps 37:34; 58:10 91:9 [a]Or *For You O LORD are my Refuge; You have made the Most High your dwelling place* [A]Ps 91:2 [B]Ps 90:1 91:10 [a]Or *dwelling* [A]Prov 12:21 91:11 [A]Ps 34:7; Matt 4:6; Luke 4:10, 11; Heb 1:14 91:12 [A]Matt 4:6; Luke 4:11 91:13 [a]Or *dragon* [A]Judg 14:6; Dan 6:22; Luke 10:19

life ends with a moan of woe and weariness.

90:10 seventy years … eighty years. Though Moses lived to be 120 years old, and his "eye was not dim, nor his vigor abated" (Dt 34:7), human life was usually more brief and lived under the anger of God. Because of this certain and speedy end, life is sad.

90:11 Your fury … fear … due You? Instead of explaining away life's curses, a wise person will recognize God's wrath toward sin as the ultimate cause of all afflictions and consequently learn to fear God.

90:12 number our days. Evaluate the use of time in light of the brevity of life. **heart of wisdom.** Wisdom repudiates autonomy and focuses on the Lord's sovereignty and revelation.

90:14 Your lovingkindness. *See note on Ps 85:7.*

90:15 glad … afflicted us. A prayer that one's days of joy would equal his days of distress.

90:17 the favor of the Lord. The Lord's favor implies His delight and approval. **confirm the work of our hands.** By God's mercy and grace, one's life can have value, significance, and meaning (cf. 1Co 15:58).

91:1–16 This psalm describes God's ongoing sovereign protection of His people from the ever-present dangers and terrors which surround humanity. The original setting may be that of an army about to go to battle. Most of the terrors mentioned in this psalm are left undefined, no doubt intentionally, so that no kind of danger is omitted from application. Believers in every age can read this psalm to learn that nothing can harm a child of God unless the Lord permits it. However, in light of the many references in the Psalms to the future messianic kingdom (cf. especially Pss 96–100), this psalm must be read as being literally fulfilled then.

I. The Lord's Protection (91:1–13)
   A. The Confidence (91:1, 2)
   B. The Dangers (91:3–6)
   C. The Examples (91:7–13)
II. The Lord's Pledge (91:14–16)

91:1 shelter of the Most High. An intimate place of divine protection. The use of "Most High" for God emphasizes that no threat can ever overpower Him. **shadow of the Almighty.** In a land where the sun can be oppressive and dangerous, a "shadow" was understood as a metaphor for care and protection.

91:3 snare of the trapper. This metaphor represents any plots against the believer intended to endanger his life. **deadly pestilence.** The reference here and in v. 6 is specifically to dreaded diseases, plagues, and epidemics (cf. Jer 14:12; Eze 5:12; 14:19).

91:4 under His wings. Pictures the protection of a parent bird (*see note on Ps 57:1*).

91:8 only … with your eyes. The righteous are so safe in disaster all around them that they are only spectators.

91:11, 12 This promise of angelic protection was misquoted by Satan in his temptation of the Messiah (see Mt 4:6).

91:13 tread … lion and cobra. In general, a

14 "[A]Because he has loved Me,
therefore I will deliver him;
I will [B]set him *securely* on high,
because he has [C]known My name.
15 "He will [A]call upon Me, and I
will answer him;
I will be with him in [a]trouble;
I will rescue him and [B]honor him.
16 "With [a]a [A]long life I will satisfy him
And [b,B]let him see My salvation."

PSALM 92

PRAISE FOR THE LORD'S GOODNESS.

A Psalm, a Song for the Sabbath day.

1 It is [A]good to give thanks to the LORD
And to [B]sing praises to Your
name, O Most High;
2 To [A]declare Your lovingkindness
in the morning
And Your [B]faithfulness [a]by night,
3 [a]With the [A]ten-stringed lute
and [a]with the [A]harp,
[a]With resounding music [b]upon the [A]lyre.
4 For You, O LORD, have made me
glad by [a]what You [A]have done,
I will [B]sing for joy at the
[C]works of Your hands.

5 How [A]great are Your works, O LORD!
Your [a,B]thoughts are very [C]deep.
6 A [A]senseless man has no knowledge,
Nor does a [A]stupid man understand this:
7 That when the wicked
[A]sprouted up like grass
And all [B]who did iniquity flourished,
It *was only* that they might be
[C]destroyed forevermore.
8 But You, O LORD, are [A]on high forever.
9 For, behold, Your enemies, O LORD,
For, behold, [A]Your enemies will perish;
All who do iniquity will be [B]scattered.

10 But You have exalted my [A]horn
like *that of* the wild ox;
I have [a]been [B]anointed with fresh oil.
11 And my eye has [A]looked
exultantly upon [a]my foes,
My ears hear of the evildoers
who rise up against me.
12 The [A]righteous man will [a]flourish
like the palm tree,
He will grow like a [B]cedar in Lebanon.
13 [A]Planted in the house of the LORD,
They will flourish [B]in the courts of our God.
14 They will still [a,A]yield fruit in old age;
They shall be [b]full of sap and very green,
15 To [a]declare that [A]the LORD is upright;
He is my [B]rock, and there is [C]no
unrighteousness in Him.

PSALM 93

THE MAJESTY OF THE LORD.

1 [A]The LORD [a]reigns, He is
[B]clothed with majesty;
The LORD has [C]clothed and girded
Himself with strength;
Indeed, the [D]world is firmly
established, it will not be moved.
2 Your [A]throne is established from of old;
You [B]are from everlasting.

91:14 [A]Ps 145:20 [B]Ps 59:1 [C]Ps 9:10 91:15 [a]Or *distress* [A]Job 12:4; Ps 50:15 [B]1 Sam 2:30; John 12:26 91:16 [a]Lit *length of days* [b]Or *cause him to feast his eyes on* [A]Deut 6:2; Ps 21:4; Prov 3:1, 2 [B]Ps 50:23 92:1 [A]Ps 147:1 [B]Ps 135:3 92:2 [a]Lit *nights* [A]Ps 59:16 [B]Ps 89:1 92:3 [a]Lit *Upon* [b]Lit *by means of* [A]1 Sam 10:5; 1 Chr 13:8; Neh 12:27; Ps 33:2 92:4 [a]Lit *Your working* [A]Ps 40:5; 90:16 [B]Ps 106:47 [C]Ps 8:6; 111:7; 143:5 92:5 [a]Or *purposes* [A]Ps 40:5; 111:2; Rev 15:3 [B]Ps 33:11; 40:5; 139:17 [C]Ps 36:6; Rom 11:33 92:6 [A]Ps 49:10; 73:22; 94:8 92:7 [A]Job 12:6; Ps 90:5 [B]Ps 94:4 [C]Ps 37:38 92:8 [A]Ps 83:18; 93:4; 113:5 92:9 [A]Ps 37:20 [B]Ps 68:1; 89:10 92:10 [a]Or *become moist* [A]Ps 75:10; 89:17; 112:9 [B]Ps 23:5; 45:7 92:11 [a]Or *those who lie in wait for me* [A]Ps 54:7; 91:8 92:12 [a]Lit *sprout* [A]Num 24:6; Ps 1:3; 52:8; 72:7; Jer 17:8; Hos 14:5, 6 [B]Ps 104:16; Ezek 31:3 92:13 [A]Ps 80:15; Is 60:21 [B]Ps 100:4; 116:19 92:14 [a]Or *thrive in* [b]Lit *fat and* [A]Prov 11:30; Is 37:31; John 15:2; James 3:18 92:15 [a]Or *show forth* [A]Job 34:10; Ps 25:8 [B]Deut 32:4; Ps 18:2; 94:22 [C]Rom 9:14 93:1 [a]Or *has assumed kingship* [A]Ps 96:10; 97:1; 99:1 [B]Ps 104:1 [C]Ps 65:6; Is 51:9 [D]Ps 96:10 93:2 [A]Ps 45:6; Lam 5:19 [B]Ps 90:2

metaphor for God's protection from all deadly attacks (*see notes on Ps 58:4ff.*).

91:14 he has loved Me. God Himself is the speaker in this section (vv. 14–16) and He describes the blessing He gives to those who know and love Him. The word for "loved" means a "deep longing" for God, or a "clinging" to God.

91:16 long life. Long life was a specific promise to the OT saint for obedience to the law (e.g., Ex 20:12; Pr 3:2). The prophets also promise it to God's people in the future messianic kingdom (cf. Is 65:17–23).

92:1–15 This psalm expresses the exuberance of the psalmist as he recognizes that God is merciful in salvation, great in His works of creation, just in His dealings with the wicked, and faithful in prospering His children.

I. An Expression of Theistic Optimism (92:1–5)
II. An Observation Concerning Righteous Sovereignty (92:6–9)
III. A Testimony to God's Goodness (92:10–15)

92:Title for the Sabbath day. In the post-Exilic community, some psalms were sung throughout the week in connection with the morning and evening sacrifice; others were designated especially for Sabbath worship.

92:2 lovingkindness … faithfulness. These attributes are constant themes of the psalms (*see notes on Pss 85:7; 89:5;* see also Lk 10:2).

92:3 harp. *See note on Ps 81:2.*

92:10 my horn. *See note on Ps 75:4.* **anointed with fresh oil.** This figure is based on a practice of making an animal's horns gleam by rubbing oil on them. Thus God, in effect, had invigorated the psalmist (cf. Pss 23:5; 133:2).

92:11 my eye … upon my foes. God gratified the psalmist's desire by bringing his enemies to ruin.

92:12 flourish like the palm tree. The palm tree and the cedar symbolized permanence and strength (cf. v. 14). They are in contrast to the transience of the wicked, who are pictured as temporary as grass (v. 7). *See notes on Ps 1.*

92:13 Planted in the house of the LORD. A tree planted in the courtyard of the temple symbolized the thriving conditions of those who maintain a close relationship with the Lord (*see note on Ps 52:8*).

93:1–5 Psalms 93 and 95–100 (cf. Ps 47) are dedicated to celebrating God's sovereign kingship over the world. Psalm 93 glorifies God's eternal, universal kingdom which is providentially administered through His Son (Col 1:17). Nothing is more powerful than the Lord; nothing is more steadfast than His reign, nothing is more sure than His revelation.

I. The Lord's Universal Kingdom (93:1–4)
  A. Over the Earth (93:1, 2)
  B. Over the Sea (93:3, 4)
II. The Lord's Authoritative Revelation (93:5)

93:1 The LORD reigns. An exclamation of the Lord's universal reign over the earth from the time of creation (v. 2; cf. Pss 103:19;

3 The [A]floods have lifted up, O LORD,
The floods have lifted up their voice,
The floods lift up their pounding waves.
4 More than the sounds of many waters,
Than the mighty breakers of the sea,
The LORD [A]on high is mighty.
5 Your [A]testimonies are fully confirmed;
[B]Holiness befits Your house,
O LORD, [a]forevermore.

PSALM 94

THE LORD IMPLORED TO AVENGE HIS PEOPLE.

1 O LORD, God of [a,A]vengeance,
God of [a]vengeance, [b,B]shine forth!
2 [A]Rise up, O [B]Judge of the earth,
Render recompense [C]to the proud.
3 How long shall the wicked, O LORD,
How long shall the [A]wicked exult?
4 They pour forth *words,* they
[A]speak arrogantly;
All who do wickedness [B]vaunt themselves.
5 They [A]crush Your people, O LORD,
And [B]afflict Your heritage.
6 They [A]slay the widow and the [a]stranger
And murder the orphans.
7 [A]They have said, "[a]The LORD does not see,
Nor does the God of Jacob pay heed."

8 Pay heed, you [A]senseless among the people;
And when will you understand,
[A]stupid ones?
9 He who [A]planted the ear,
[a]does He not hear?
He who formed the eye, [a]does He not see?
10 He who [a,A]chastens the nations,
will He not rebuke,
Even He who [B]teaches man knowledge?
11 The LORD [A]knows the thoughts of man,
[a]That they are a *mere* breath.

12 Blessed is the man whom
[A]You chasten, O [a]LORD,
And [B]whom You teach out of Your law;
13 That You may grant him [A]relief
from the [B]days of adversity,
Until [C]a pit is dug for the wicked.
14 For [A]the LORD will not
abandon His people,
Nor will He [B]forsake His inheritance.
15 For [a,A]judgment [b]will again be righteous,
And all the upright in heart [c]will follow it.
16 Who will [A]stand up for me
against evildoers?
Who will take his stand for me [B]against
those who do wickedness?

17 If [A]the LORD had not been my help,
My soul would soon have dwelt
in *the abode of* silence.
18 If I should say, "[A]My foot has slipped,"
Your lovingkindness, O LORD,
will hold me up.
19 When my anxious thoughts
[a]multiply within me,
Your [A]consolations delight my soul.
20 Can a [a,A]throne of destruction
be allied with You,
One [B]which devises [b]mischief by decree?
21 They [A]band themselves together
against the [a]life of the righteous
And [B]condemn [b]the innocent to death.
22 But the LORD has been my [A]stronghold,
And my God the [B]rock of my refuge.
23 He has [A]brought back their
wickedness upon them
And will [a,B]destroy them in their evil;
The LORD our God will [a]destroy them.

93:3 [A]Ps 96:11; 98:7, 8 93:4 [A]Ps 65:7; 89:6, 9; 92:8 93:5 [a]Lit *for length of days* [A]Ps 19:7 [B]Ps 29:2; 96:9; 1 Cor 3:17 94:1 [a]Or *avenging acts* [b]Or *has shone forth* [A]Deut 32:35; Is 35:4; Nah 1:2; Rom 12:19 [B]Ps 50:2; 80:1 94:2 [A]Ps 7:6 [B]Gen 18:25 [C]Ps 31:23 94:3 [A]Job 20:5 94:4 [A]Ps 31:18; 75:5 [B]Ps 10:3; 52:1 94:5 [A]Is 3:15 [B]Ps 79:1 94:6 [a]Or *sojourner* [A]Is 10:2 94:7 [a]Heb *YAH* [A]Job 22:13; Ps 10:11 94:8 [A]Ps 92:6 94:9 [a]Or *can* [A]Ex 4:11; Prov 20:12 94:10 [a]Or *instructs* [A]Ps 44:2 [B]Job 35:11; Is 28:26 94:11 [a]Or *For* [A]Job 11:11; 1 Cor 3:20 94:12 [a]Heb *YAH* [A]Deut 8:5; Job 5:17; Ps 119:71; Prov 3:11, 12; Heb 12:5, 6 [B]Ps 119:171 94:13 [A]Job 34:29; Hab 3:16 [B]Ps 49:5 [C]Ps 9:15; 55:23 94:14 [A]1 Sam 12:22; Lam 3:31; Rom 11:2 [B]Ps 37:28 94:15 [a]I.e. administration of justice [b]Lit *will return to righteousness* [c]Lit *will be after it* [A]Ps 97:2; Is 42:3; Mic 7:9 94:16 [A]Num 10:35; Is 28:21; 33:10 [B]Ps 17:13; 59:2 94:17 [A]Ps 124:1, 2 94:18 [A]Ps 38:16; 73:2 94:19 [a]Or *are many* [A]Is 57:18; 66:13 94:20 [a]Or *tribunal* [b]Or *trouble, misfortune* [A]Amos 6:3 [B]Ps 50:16; 58:2 94:21 [a]Or *soul* [b]Lit *innocent blood* [A]Ps 56:6; 59:3 [B]Ex 23:7; Ps 106:38; Prov 17:15; Matt 27:4 94:22 [A]Ps 9:9; 59:9 [B]Ps 18:2; 71:7 94:23 [a]Or *silence* [A]Ps 7:16; 140:9, 11 [B]Gen 19:15

145:13) and forever.

93:3, 4 The sea with all its power is nothing in comparison to the power of God. The doubling and tripling of expressions throughout this psalm (vv. 1, 3, 4) are poetic means of generating literary energy and emphasis.

93:5 testimonies are fully confirmed. As God's rule over the earth is stable, so His revelation given through Scripture is trustworthy (cf. Ps 19:7).

94:1–23 The psalmist's urgent concern in this psalm is that the righteous are being oppressed, the wicked are prospering, and it does not look as though God cares. The psalmist thus pleads with God to punish the wicked (cf. Pss 73, 82).

I. Address to God (94:1, 2)
II. Arrogance of the Wicked (94:3–7)
III. Admonition to the Foolish (94:8–11)
IV. Assurance for the Righteous (94:12–15)
V. Advocacy from God (94:16–23)

94:1 God of vengeance. Vengeance from God is not in the sense of uncontrolled vindictiveness, but in the sense of just retribution by the eternal Judge for trespasses against His law. **shine forth!** Make an appearance; he may even be asking for a theophany (cf. Pss 50:2; 80:1).

94:7 The LORD does not see. An autonomous and atheistic attitude (*see note on Ps 59:7*).

94:11 thoughts of man ... *mere* breath. The wicked designs of the human mind amount to nothing (cf. Ps 92:5; 1Co 3:20).

94:12 Blessed. To be blessed was to be wise and prosperous in life, as a result of the instruction of God (cf. Ps 84:5, 12).

94:14 will not abandon His people. God has a permanent commitment to His people, Israel, established through a covenant based on His abiding love (Ge 15; Jer 12:15; Mic 7:18). This important truth serves as a doctrinal basis for Pss 93–100 and was intended to encourage the nation during difficult times. Paul refers to this in Ro 11:1 as he assures the future salvation of Israel.

94:17 soul ... dwelt in ... silence. "Silence" here is another term for Sheol, the realm of the dead (cf. Ps 31:17).

94:18 Your lovingkindness. *See note on Ps 85:7.*

94:20 throne of destruction. A reference to a corrupt judge or ruler. **devises mischief by decree?** Corrupt judges and rulers counter the very divine moral order of the universe by using law for wickedness rather than for good.

94:23 destroy them in their evil. Portrays destruction while they are sinning.

PSALM 95

PRAISE TO THE LORD, AND WARNING AGAINST UNBELIEF.

1 O come, let us [A]sing for joy to the LORD,
Let us shout joyfully to [B]the
rock of our salvation.
2 Let us [A]come before His presence
[B]with [a]thanksgiving,
Let us shout joyfully to Him
[C]with [b]psalms.
3 For the LORD is a [A]great God
And a great King [B]above all gods,
4 In whose hand are the
[A]depths of the earth,
The peaks of the mountains are His also.
5 [a]The sea is His, for it was He [A]who made it,
And His hands formed the dry land.

6 Come, let us [A]worship and bow down,
Let us [B]kneel before the LORD our [C]Maker.
7 For He is our God,
And [A]we are the people of His [a,B]pasture
and the sheep of His hand.
[C]Today, [b]if you would hear His voice,
8 Do not harden your hearts,
as at [a,A]Meribah,
As in the day of [b,B]Massah
in the wilderness,
9 "When your fathers [A]tested Me,
They tried Me, though they
had seen My work.
10 "For [A]forty years I loathed
that generation,
And said they are a people
who err in their heart,
And they do not know My ways.
11 "Therefore I [A]swore in My anger,
Truly they shall not enter into My [B]rest."

PSALM 96

A CALL TO WORSHIP THE LORD THE RIGHTEOUS JUDGE.

1 [A]Sing to the LORD a [B]new song;
Sing to the LORD, all the earth.
2 Sing to the LORD, bless His name;
[A]Proclaim good tidings of His
salvation from day to day.
3 Tell of [A]His glory among the nations,
His wonderful deeds among
all the peoples.
4 For [A]great is the LORD and
[B]greatly to be praised;
He is to be [C]feared [D]above all gods.
5 For [A]all the gods of the peoples are [a]idols,
But [B]the LORD made the heavens.
6 [A]Splendor and majesty are before Him,
Strength and beauty are in His sanctuary.

7 [a]Ascribe to the LORD, O [A]families
of the peoples,
[a,B]Ascribe to the LORD glory and strength.

95:1 [A]Ps 66:1; 81:1 [B]Ps 89:26 95:2 [a]Or *a song of thanksgiving* [b]Or *songs* (with instrumental accompaniment) [A]Mic 6:6 [B]Ps 100:4; 147:7; Jon 2:9 [C]Ps 81:2; Eph 5:19; James 5:13 95:3 [A]Ps 48:1; 135:5; 145:3 [B]Ps 96:4; 97:9 95:4 [A]Ps 135:6 95:5 [a]Lit *Who has the sea* [A]Gen 1:9, 10; Ps 146:6; Jon 1:9 95:6 [A]Ps 96:9; 99:5, 9 [B]2 Chr 6:13; Dan 6:10; Phil 2:10 [C]Ps 100:3; 149:2; Is 17:7; Hos 8:14 95:7 [a]Lit *pasturing* [b]Or *O that you would obey* [A]Ps 79:13 [B]Ps 74:1 [C]Heb 3:7-11, 15; 4:7 95:8 [a]Or *place of strife* [b]Or *temptation* [A]Ex 17:2-7; Num 20:13 [B]Ex 17:7; Deut 6:16 95:9 [A]Num 14:22; Ps 78:18; 1 Cor 10:9 95:10 [A]Acts 7:36; 13:18; Heb 3:10, 17 95:11 [A]Num 14:23, 28-30; Deut 1:35; Heb 4:3, 5 [B]Deut 12:9 96:1 [A]1 Chr 16:23-33 [B]Ps 40:3 96:2 [A]Ps 71:15 96:3 [A]Ps 145:12 96:4 [A]Ps 48:1; 145:3 [B]Ps 18:3 [C]Ps 89:7 [D]Ps 95:3 96:5 [a]Or *non-existent things* [A]1 Chr 16:26; Jer 10:11 [B]Ps 115:15; Is 42:5 96:6 [A]Ps 104:1 96:7 [a]Lit *Give* [A]Ps 22:27 [B]1 Chr 16:28, 29; Ps 29:1, 2

95:1–11 This psalm, with its references to the wilderness wanderings, may have been composed by David (Heb 4:7) for the Feast of the Booths, or Tabernacles (cf. Ps 81). During this feast, the people of Israel lived in booths, remembering God's provisions for them in the wilderness. After a call to worship (95:1–7a), a prophecy in the voice of the Holy Spirit Himself (cf. Heb 3:7) breaks in and reminds the people of the dangers of rebellion and tempting God. Verses 7b–11 are quoted verbatim in Heb 3:7–11 (cf. Heb 3:15; 4:3–7) with the warning that those vacillating Jews also were in danger of missing the promised "rest" (i.e., salvation).

I. Positive Call to Worship (95:1–7a)
II. Negative Warning of Wrath (95:7b–11)

95:1 rock of our salvation. This metaphor for God was especially appropriate in this psalm, which refers (vv. 8, 9) to the water that came from the rock in the wilderness (cf. Ex 17:1–7; Nu 20:1–13; 1Co 10:4).

95:3 a great King above all gods. This is a poetic way of denying the existence of other gods (cf. 96:5), which existed only as statues, not persons (cf. Jer 10:1–10).

95:4 depths of the earth. This refers to the depths of the seas, valleys, and caverns, and contrasts with the hills. The point (cf. v. 5) is that God was not a local god like the imaginary gods of the heathens, usually put up in high places, but the universal Creator and Ruler of the whole earth (*see note on Ps 65:5*).

95:8 at Meribah. Meribah (translated "rebellion") was the place in the wilderness where the Israelites rebelled against the Lord. Their complaint about lack of water demonstrated their lack of faith in the Lord (Ex 17:1–7; Nu 20:1–13; Ps 81:7).

95:9 tested Me. This is a reference to the same event (v. 8), also called "Massah" (translated "testing"), when God brought water out of the rock (Ex 17:7; cf. Dt 6:16; 9:22; 33:8). The writer to the Hebrews applies the principle of this event to his readers, suggesting that their inclination to doubt the Lord and return to Judaism was parallel with their fathers' inclination to doubt the Lord and go back to Egypt.

95:10 err in their heart. Their wanderings in the desert were the outworking of straying hearts.

95:11 My rest. The "rest" was originally the Promised Land (i.e., Canaan), where the people came at the end of Israel's 40-year journey in the wilderness. It was analogously applied in the book of Hebrews to salvation by grace (Heb 3:7–4:10; cf. Heb 2:3).

96:1–13 The substance of this psalm, and portions of Pss 97, 98, and 100 are found in 1Ch 16, which was used by David's direction in the dedication of the tabernacle on Mt. Zion. The psalm has importance beyond that historical occasion, however, because it anticipates kingdom praise for the Lord from all the nations of the world (vv. 3, 4, 7, 9–13; cf. Is 2:2–4; Zec 14:16–19), and even from nature itself. It also expresses the intense joy that will saturate the earth when the Messiah is ruling from Jerusalem (cf. Is 25:9; 40:9, 10).

I. The Proclamation of Praise (96:1–6)
  A. The Invitation to Praise (96:1–3)
  B. The Recipient of Praise (96:4–6)
II. The Exhortation to Worship (96:7–13)
  A. Worship from the Gentile Nations (96:7–10)
  B. Worship from Personified Nature (96:11–13)

96:1 a new song. This new song was intended for the future inauguration of the millennial rule of the Lord over the earth (cf. Pss 144:9; 149:1; Rev 5:9; 14:3).

96:2 Proclaim good tidings. Genuine praise includes a testimony to others of God's plan of redemption.

96:3 His glory ... nations. The glory of the Lord is more than just His majestic splendor. It includes all of the reasons for admiring and praising Him, such as His acts of creation (cf. Ps 19:2) and redemption (v. 2). **all the peoples.** *See note on Ps 67:3.*

96:4 feared above all gods. *See note on Ps 95:3.*

8 [a]Ascribe to the LORD the
[A]glory of His name;
Bring an [b,B]offering and come
into His courts.
9 [A]Worship the LORD in [a]holy attire;
[B]Tremble before Him, all the earth.
10 Say among the nations,
"[A]The LORD reigns;
Indeed, the [A]world is firmly
established, it will not be moved;
He will [B]judge the peoples with [a]equity."

11 Let the [A]heavens be glad, and
let the [B]earth rejoice;
Let [C]the sea [a]roar, and [b]all it contains;
12 Let the [A]field exult, and all that is in it.
Then all the [B]trees of the
forest will sing for joy
13 Before the LORD, [A]for He is coming,
For He is coming to judge the earth.
[B]He will judge the world
in righteousness
And the peoples in His faithfulness.

PSALM 97

THE LORD'S POWER AND DOMINION.

1 [A]The LORD [a]reigns, let the [B]earth rejoice;
Let the many [b,C]islands be glad.
2 [A]Clouds and thick darkness surround Him;
[B]Righteousness and justice are the
foundation of His throne.
3 [A]Fire goes before Him
And [B]burns up His adversaries
round about.
4 His [A]lightnings lit up the world;
The earth saw and [B]trembled.
5 The mountains [A]melted like wax
at the presence of the LORD,
At the presence of the [B]Lord
of the whole earth.
6 The [A]heavens declare
His righteousness,
And [B]all the peoples have
seen His glory.

7 Let all those be ashamed who
serve [A]graven images,
Who boast themselves of [B]idols;
[a,C]Worship Him, all you [b]gods.
8 Zion [a]heard *this* and [A]was glad,
And the daughters of
Judah have rejoiced
Because of Your judgments, O LORD.
9 For You are the LORD [A]Most
High over all the earth;
You are exalted far [B]above all [a]gods.

10 [A]Hate evil, you who love the LORD,
Who [B]preserves the souls
of His godly ones;
He [C]delivers them from the
hand of the wicked.
11 [A]Light is sown *like seed* for the righteous
And [B]gladness for the upright in heart.
12 Be [A]glad in the LORD, you righteous ones,
And [B]give thanks [a]to His holy name.

96:8 [a]Lit *Give* [b]Or *meal offering* [A]Ps 79:9; 115:1 [B]Ps 45:12; 72:10 96:9 [a]Or *the splendor of holiness* [A]1 Chr 16:29; 2 Chr 20:21; Ps 29:2; 110:3 [B]Ps 33:8; 114:7 96:10 [a]Or *uprightness* [A]Ps 93:1; 97:1 [B]Ps 9:8; 58:11; 67:4; 98:9 96:11 [a]Or *thunder* [b]Lit *its fullness* [A]Ps 69:34; Is 49:13 [B]Ps 97:1 [C]Ps 98:7 96:12 [A]Ps 65:13; Is 35:1; 55:12, 13 [B]Is 44:23 96:13 [A]Ps 98:9 [B]Rev 19:11 97:1 [a]Or *has assumed Kingship* [b]Or *coastlands* [A]Ps 96:10 [B]Ps 96:11 [C]Is 42:10, 12 97:2 [A]Ex 19:9; Deut 4:11; 1 Kin 8:12; Ps 18:11 [B]Ps 89:14 97:3 [A]Ps 18:8; 50:3; Dan 7:10; Hab 3:5 [B]Mal 4:1; Heb 12:29 97:4 [A]Ex 19:16; Ps 77:18 [B]Ps 96:9; 104:32 97:5 [A]Ps 46:6; Amos 9:5; Mic 1:4; Nah 1:5 [B]Josh 3:11 97:6 [A]Ps 19:1; 50:6 [B]Ps 98:2; Is 6:3; 40:5; 66:18 97:7 [a]Or *All the gods have worshiped Him* [b]Or *supernatural powers* [A]Ps 78:58; Is 42:17; 44:9, 11; Jer 10:14 [B]Ps 106:36; Jer 50:2; Hab 2:18 [C]Heb 1:6 97:8 [a]Or possibly *hears and is glad* [A]Ps 48:11; Zeph 3:14 97:9 [a]Or *supernatural powers* [A]Ps 83:18 [B]Ex 18:11; Ps 95:3; 96:4; 135:5 97:10 [A]Ps 34:14; Prov 8:13; Amos 5:15; Rom 12:9 [B]Ps 31:23; 145:20; Prov 2:8 [C]Ps 37:40; Jer 15:21; Dan 3:28 97:11 [A]Job 22:28; Ps 112:4; Prov 4:18 [B]Ps 64:10 97:12 [a]Lit *for the memory of His holiness* [A]Ps 32:11 [B]Ps 30:4

96:8 an offering. According to the psalmists and prophets, offerings and sacrifices will be presented to the Lord in the millennial kingdom (cf. Ps 45:12; Eze 40–46).

96:9 holy attire. That is, "worship the Lord because of the splendor of His holiness" (cf. Pss 29:2; 99; 110:3; also 1Ch 16:29). *See note on 2Ch 20:21.*

96:10 firmly established. Instead of the continuance of international chaos in human history, the world will be settled and efficiently managed by the Messiah in the millennial kingdom (cf. Ps 2; Mic 4:1–5). **judge the peoples with equity.** Not only will the Lord establish international peace and stability in the future messianic kingdom, but He will also rule the world with impeccable justice (cf. v. 13; Is 11:1–5).

96:11, 12 This is what even inanimate creation awaits (cf. Ro 8:19–22).

96:13 He is coming. The rule of the Lord described in this psalm is not the present universal kingdom (Ps 93), but one which will be established when Christ returns to earth.

97:1–12 The psalmist, though recognizing the Lord's universal rule at the present (v. 9), anticipates a new coming of the Lord to judge the earth. The imagery of the Lord's presence may, in fact, be the basis of some NT passages' descriptions of the second coming (cf. Mt 24; Rev 19). Special emphasis is also placed on the Lord's totally righteous judgments on the world in His kingdom, as well as His obliteration of false religions.

I. The Announcement of the Reign of the Lord (97:1, 2)
II. The Effect of the Reign of the Lord (97:3–12)
  A. On His Foes (97:3–9)
  B. On His Friends (97:10–12)

97:1 many islands. Refers to all the continents, as well as islands, of the world (cf. Is 42:10; Da 2:34, 35, 44; Zec 14:9).

97:2 Clouds and thick darkness. Such a description emphasizes the terrifying effect of the Lord's presence, both in the past (Ex 19:16–18), and in the future Day of the Lord (Joel 2:2; Zep 1:15; Mt 24:29, 30).

97:3 burns up His adversaries. The Lord will utterly destroy His enemies in the future Day of the Lord (cf. Zec 14:12).

97:4 His lightnings. This is perhaps a reference to the Lord's awesome and public coming to rule the world (Mt 24:26–30).

97:5 mountains melted. At the coming of the Lord, the mountains will fade away (cf. Is 40:3–5; Zec 14:4, 10).

97:6 heavens declare His righteousness. See the parallel description of Christ's coming in glory in Is 40:5 and Mt 24:29–31 (cf. Rev 19:11–15).

97:7 all you gods. No false gods or religions will be allowed in the messianic kingdom (cf. Zec 13:2, 3).

97:8 Zion. *See note on Ps 87:2.* **Because of Your judgments.** A major reason for joy and well-being in the messianic kingdom will be the perfectly righteous judgments of Christ on the peoples of the world (cf. vv. 1–3; also Ps 48:11; Is 11:1–5; Zec 8:3).

97:10 preserves the souls of His godly ones. Here the doctrine of eternal security is stated. Gratitude for such grace should motivate believers to holiness.

97:11 Light is sown. This is a poetic way of describing the ultimate triumph of righteousness and the righteous (cf. Is 58:8, 10; 60:19, 20; Mal 4:2).

PSALM 98

A CALL TO PRAISE THE LORD FOR HIS RIGHTEOUSNESS.

A Psalm.

1 O sing to the LORD a [A]new song,
For He has done [B]wonderful things,
His [C]right hand and His [D]holy arm
have [a]gained the victory for Him.
2 [A]The LORD has made known His salvation;
He has [B]revealed His [a]righteousness
in the sight of the nations.
3 He has [A]remembered His
lovingkindness and His faithfulness
to the house of Israel;
[B]All the ends of the earth have seen
the salvation of our God.

4 [A]Shout joyfully to the LORD, all the earth;
[B]Break forth and sing for joy
and sing praises.
5 Sing praises to the LORD with the [A]lyre,
With the lyre and the [a,B]sound of melody.
6 With [A]trumpets and the sound of the horn
[B]Shout joyfully before [C]the King, the LORD.

7 Let the [A]sea roar and [a]all it contains,
The [B]world and those who dwell in it.
8 Let the [A]rivers clap their hands,
Let the [B]mountains sing together for joy
9 Before the LORD, for He is coming
to [A]judge the earth;
He will judge the world
with righteousness
And [B]the peoples with [a]equity.

PSALM 99

PRAISE TO THE LORD FOR HIS FIDELITY TO ISRAEL.

1 [A]The LORD reigns, let the peoples tremble;
He [a,B]is enthroned *above* the
cherubim, let the earth shake!
2 The LORD [a]is [A]great in Zion,
And He is [B]exalted above all the peoples.
3 Let them praise Your [A]great
and awesome name;
[B]Holy is [a]He.
4 The [a]strength of the King [A]loves [b]justice;
You have established [c,B]equity;
You have [C]executed [b]justice and
righteousness in Jacob.
5 [a,A]Exalt the LORD our God
And [B]worship at His footstool;
[C]Holy is He.

6 [A]Moses and Aaron were
among His [B]priests,
And [A]Samuel was among those
who [C]called on His name;
They [D]called upon the LORD
and He answered them.
7 He [A]spoke to them in the pillar of cloud;
They [B]kept His testimonies
And the statute that He gave them.
8 O LORD our God, You [A]answered them;
You were a [B]forgiving God to them,
And *yet* an [C]avenger of their *evil* deeds.
9 Exalt the LORD our God
And worship at His holy hill,
For holy is the LORD our God.

98:1 [a]Or *accomplished salvation* [A]Ps 33:3 [B]Ps 40:5; 96:3 [C]Ex 15:6 [D]Is 52:10 98:2 [a]I.e. faithfulness to His gracious promises [A]Is 52:10 [B]Is 62:2; Rom 3:25 98:3 [A]Luke 1:54, 72 [B]Ps 22:27 98:4 [A]Ps 100:1 [B]Is 44:23 98:5 [a]Or *voice of song* (accompanied by music) [A]Ps 92:3 [B]Is 51:3 98:6 [A]Num 10:10; 2 Chr 15:14 [B]Ps 66:1 [C]Ps 47:7 98:7 [a]Lit *its fullness* [A]Ps 96:11 [B]Ps 24:1 98:8 [A]Ps 93:3; Is 55:12 [B]Ps 65:12; 89:12 98:9 [a]Or *uprightness* [A]Ps 96:13 [B]Ps 96:10 99:1 [a]Lit *sits* [A]Ps 97:1 [B]Ex 25:22; 1 Sam 4:4; Ps 80:1 99:2 [a]Or *in Zion is great* [A]Ps 48:1; Is 12:6 [B]Ps 97:9; 113:4 99:3 [a]Or *it* [A]Deut 28:58; Ps 76:1 [B]Lev 19:2; Josh 24:19; 1 Sam 2:2; Ps 22:3; Is 6:3 99:4 [a]Or *You have established in equity the strength of the King who loves justice* [b]Or *judgment* [c]Or *uprightness* [A]Ps 11:7; 33:5 [B]Ps 17:2; 98:9 [C]Ps 103:6; 146:7; Jer 23:5 99:5 [a]The verb is plural [A]Ps 34:3; 107:32; 118:28 [B]Ps 132:7 [C]Ps 99:3 99:6 [A]Jer 15:1 [B]Ex 24:6-8; 29:26; 40:23-27; Lev 8:1-30 [C]1 Sam 7:9; 12:18; Ps 22:4, 5 [D]Ex 15:25; 32:30-34 99:7 [A]Ex 33:9; Num 12:5 [B]Ps 105:28 99:8 [A]Ps 106:44 [B]Num 14:20; Ps 78:38 [C]Ex 32:28; Num 20:12; Ps 95:11; 107:12

98:1–9 Like the surrounding psalms, this psalm proclaims the excitement and joy of the whole earth over the rule of the Lord in the kingdom. This psalm is given over entirely to praise, with only a brief mention of the wicked.

I. Celebration of the Lord's Victorious Reign (98:1–6)
   A. Triumphs of the Lord (98:1–3)
   B. Praise to the Lord (98:4–6)
II. Exaltation of the Lord's Righteous Judgments (98:7–9)

98:1 a new song. *See note on Ps 96:1.* **right hand … holy arm.** These are symbols of power. **the victory.** The Lord is often pictured in the OT as a Divine Warrior (Ex 15:2, 3; Pss 18; 68:1–8; Is 59:15ff.). According to the prophets, Christ will begin His millennial reign following His victory over the nations of the world which will gather against Israel in the end times (cf. Zec 14:1–15; Rev 19:11–21).

98:2 the nations. *See notes on Pss 57:9; 67:3; 82:8.*

98:3 His lovingkindness and His faithfulness. *See notes on Pss 85:7 and 89:5.* **salvation.** These words are a metaphor for the Lord's establishment of His righteous kingdom on earth (cf. Is 46:13; 51:5–8).

98:4 Shout joyfully. A great cheer, greeting and welcoming a king (cf. Zec 9:9; Mt 21:4–9). **Break forth.** The idea is that of an eruption of praise which could not be contained (cf. Is 14:7; 44:23; 55:12).

98:5, 6 lyre … trumpets … horn. Instruments normally used in temple worship (cf. 1Ch 16:5, 6; 2Ch 5:12, 13; 29:25–30; Ezr 3:10–13).

98:8 rivers clap their hands. Different parts of nature are pictured as rejoicing in this universal scene of joy (cf. Is 35:1, 2; Ro 8:19–21).

98:9 He is coming. *See note on Ps 96:13.*

99:1–9 The theme of this psalm is summed up in its last phrase: "holy is the LORD our God" (v. 9). The psalmist encourages praise to the king for His holiness (vv. 3, 5, 9), which is the utter separateness of God's being from all other creatures and things, as well as His moral separateness from sin. The psalmist also exults in the truth that such a holy God has had an intimate saving relationship with Israel throughout her history (vv. 6–9).

I. Exaltation of the King's Holiness (99:1–5)
II. Examples of the King's Holiness (99:6–9)

99:1 *above* the cherubim. *See note on Ps 80:1*; cf. Ps 18:6–19; Eze 10:1ff.

99:2 Zion. *See note on Ps 87:2*; cf. Heb 12:22–24. **peoples.** *See notes on Pss 57:9 and 67:3.*

99:4 strength of the King loves justice. "Strength of the King" may be a kind of epithet for God; or (combining this phrase with v. 3) the psalmist may be saying that a holy name is the strength of a just king. **equity.** That is, fairness (cf. Is 11:1–5).

99:5 His footstool. In general, this is a metaphor for the temple in Jerusalem (cf. Is 60:13; La 2:1); but more specifically, for the ark of the covenant (1Ch 28:2). Footstools were included with the thrones of the kings of Israel (2Ch 9:18).

99:6 Moses … Aaron … Samuel. Using three of the nation's famous heroes for examples, the psalmist demonstrates that a holy God has had an enduring, intimate, and saving relationship with Israel.

99:7 pillar of cloud. This was a medium of divine direction (cf. Ex 13:21, 22; 33:9, 10; Nu 12:5; Dt 31:15ff.). **testimonies … statute.** Terms in Psalms for God's Word (see Ps 119).

99:9 His holy hill. This is the hill in Jerusalem where the temple was (cf. Pss 15:1; 24:3),

PSALM 100

ALL MEN EXHORTED TO PRAISE GOD.

A Psalm for [†]Thanksgiving.

1 [A]Shout joyfully to the
LORD, all the earth.
2 [A]Serve the LORD with gladness;
[B]Come before Him with joyful singing.
3 Know that [A]the LORD [a]Himself is God;
It is He who has [B]made us,
and [b]not we ourselves;
We are [C]His people and the
sheep of His pasture.

4 Enter His gates [A]with [a]thanksgiving
And His courts with praise.
Give thanks to Him, [B]bless His name.
5 For [A]the LORD is good;
[B]His lovingkindness is everlasting
And His [C]faithfulness to all generations.

PSALM 101

THE PSALMIST'S PROFESSION OF UPRIGHTNESS.

A Psalm of David.

1 I will [A]sing of lovingkindness and [a]justice,
To You, O LORD, I will sing praises.
2 I will [a,A]give heed to the [b]blameless way.
When will You come to me?
I will walk within my house in
the [c,B]integrity of my heart.
3 I will set no [A]worthless thing
before my eyes;
I hate the [a]work of those who [B]fall away;
It shall not fasten its grip on me.
4 A [A]perverse heart shall depart from me;
I will know no evil.
5 Whoever secretly [A]slanders his
neighbor, him I will [a]destroy;
No one who has a [B]haughty look and
an arrogant heart will I endure.

6 My eyes shall be upon the faithful of the
land, that they may dwell with me;
He who walks in a [a,A]blameless way is
the one who will minister to me.
7 He who [A]practices deceit shall
not dwell within my house;
He who speaks falsehood [B]shall not
[a]maintain his position before me.
8 [A]Every morning I will [a,B]destroy
all the wicked of the land,
So as to [C]cut off from the [D]city of the
LORD all those who do iniquity.

PSALM 102

PRAYER OF AN AFFLICTED MAN FOR MERCY ON HIMSELF AND ON ZION.

A Prayer of the Afflicted when he is faint and [†]pours out his complaint before the LORD.

1 [A]Hear my prayer, O LORD!
And let my cry for help [B]come to You.

100:1 [†]Or *thank offering* [A]Ps 95:1; 98:4, 6 100:2 [A]Deut 12:11, 12; 28:47 [B]Ps 95:2 100:3 [a]Or *He* [b]Some mss read *His we are* [A]Deut 4:35; 1 Kin 18:39; Ps 46:10 [B]Job 10:3, 8; Ps 95:6; 119:73 [C]Ps 74:1, 2; 95:7; Is 40:11; Ezek 34:30, 31 100:4 [a]Or *a thank offering* [A]Ps 95:2; 116:17 [B]Ps 96:2 100:5 [A]1 Chr 16:34; 2 Chr 5:13; 7:3; Ezra 3:11; Ps 25:8; 86:5; 106:1; 107:1; 118:1; Jer 33:11; Nah 1:7 [B]Ps 136:1 [C]Ps 119:90 101:1 [a]Or *judgment* [A]Ps 51:14; 89:1; 145:7 101:2 [a]Or *behave prudently in* [b]Or *way of integrity* [C]Or *blamelessness* [A]1 Sam 18:5, 14 [B]1 Kin 9:4 101:3 [a]Or *practice of apostasy* [A]Deut 15:9 [B]Josh 23:6; Ps 40:4 101:4 [A]Prov 11:20 101:5 [a]Or *silence* [A]Ps 50:20; Jer 9:4 [B]Ps 10:4; 18:27; Prov 6:17 101:6 [a]Or *way of integrity* [A]Ps 119:1 101:7 [a]Lit *be established before my eyes* [A]Ps 43:1; 52:2 [B]Ps 52:4, 5 101:8 [a]Or *silence* [A]Jer 21:12 [B]Ps 75:10 [C]Ps 118:10-12 [D]Ps 46:4; 48:2, 8 102:1 [†]Ps 142:2 [A]Ps 39:12; 61:1 [B]Ex 2:23; 1 Sam 9:16

and where it will be located in the future messianic kingdom (cf. Is 24:23).

100:1–5 This well-known psalm, emphasizing the universal nature of God's kingship, is a benediction to the series of psalms which are occupied with the Lord's kingdom rule (Pss 93, 95–100). Most of it is a call to praise and thanksgiving, while vv. 3 and 5 fix the reasons for that worship.

I. A Call to Praise the Lord (100:1–3)
II. A Call to Thank the Lord (100:4, 5)

100:1 **Shout joyfully.** *See note on Ps 66:1.*

100:3 **Know.** In the sense of experiencing and being completely assured of the truth. **the LORD Himself is God.** A confession that Israel's covenant God, Jehovah, is the only true God. **made us.** Though God's actual creation of every human being is understood here, this phrase seems to refer to God's making and blessing Israel as a nation (cf. Dt 32:6, 15; Ps 95:6; Is 29:22, 23; 44:2). **His people . . . His pasture.** The shepherd image is often ascribed to the king of Israel, as well as to the Lord (cf. Ps 78:70–72; Is 44:28; Jer 10:21; Zec 10:3; 11:4–17; also Pss 23:1; 28:9; 74:1; 77:20; 78:52, 53; 80:1; 95:7). The figure suggests intimate care (cf. Lk 15:3–6). According to the NT, the Lord is also the Shepherd of saints in the church age (Jn 10:16).

100:4 **His gates . . . courts.** The gates and courts were those of the temple.

100:5 **the LORD is good.** God is the source and perfect example of goodness. **His lovingkindness.** *See note on Ps 85:7.* **His faithfulness.** God's faithfulness in the sense of keeping His promises.

101:1–8 This Davidic psalm expresses the righteous commitments of the mediatorial king (David) to his eternal king (the Lord) in regard to 1) his own personal life and 2) the lives of those who inhabit the kingdom. Possibly, this psalm was used later at the coronations of future kings over Israel. Ultimately, only King Jesus would perfectly fulfill these holy resolutions (cf. Is 9:6, 7; 11:1–5).

I. Personal Life of the King (101:1–4)
II. Personal Outcome of Kingdom Inhabitants (101:5–8)
A. The Just (101:6)
B. The Unjust (101:5, 7, 8)

101:2 **blameless way.** As the king goes, so go his followers (cf. v. 6). **When will You come to me?** This is not an eschatological expectation, but rather a personal expression of David's need for God's immanent involvement in his earthly kingship. **my house.** The king first starts with his own personal life (cf. v. 7), and then looks beyond to his kingdom (cf. vv. 5, 8).

101:3, 4 Similar to the "blessed man" in Ps 1:1.

101:3 **my eyes.** The king desires to look at nothing but that which is righteous (cf. v. 6).

101:4 **evil.** The king will not engage in wickedness (cf. v. 8).

101:5 **slanders . . . haughty look . . . arrogant heart.** Neither character assassination nor pride will be tolerated in the kingdom.

101:6 **the faithful of the land.** Compare to "the wicked of the land" in v. 8.

101:7 **deceit . . . falsehood.** A premium is put on truth as foundational for a kingdom associated with the God of truth (cf. Jn 14:6).

101:8 **the land . . . the city of the LORD.** Israel and Jerusalem respectively.

102:1–28 The nonspecific superscription is unique to this psalm which highlights the thoughts of one who is afflicted (cf. Pss 22, 69, 79, 102, 130, 142), perhaps expressing exilic lament (cf. Pss 42, 43, 74, 79, 137). Like Job, whose troubles were not the result of God's judgment for personal sin, the psalmist cries out in pain. His only relief comes from refocusing on sovereign God and His eternal purposes. Messianic overtones are present as Heb 1:10–12 quotes Ps 102:25, 26.

I. A Plea for Immediate Divine Help (102:1–11)
II. A Perspective of God's Sovereignty and Eternality (102:12–22)
III. A Prayer for Longer Life (102:23–28)

102:1, 2 Frequently the Psalms begin with a cry for God's sovereign intervention when human resources have proved insufficient, e.g., Pss 77:1; 142:1.

2 [A]Do not hide Your face from me
in the day of my distress;
[B]Incline Your ear to me;
In the day when I call [A]answer me quickly.
3 For my days [A]have been
[a]consumed in smoke,
And my [B]bones have been
scorched like a hearth.
4 My heart [A]has been smitten like
[a]grass and has [B]withered away,
Indeed, I [C]forget to eat my bread.
5 Because of the [a]loudness of my groaning
My [A]bones [b]cling to my flesh.
6 I [a]resemble a [A]pelican of the wilderness;
I have become like an owl
of the waste places.
7 I [A]lie awake,
I have become like a lonely
bird on a housetop.

8 My enemies [A]have reproached
me all day long;
Those who [a,B]deride me [b]have
used my *name* as a [C]curse.
9 For I have eaten ashes like bread
And [A]mingled my drink with weeping
10 [A]Because of Your indignation
and Your wrath,
For You have [B]lifted me up
and cast me away.
11 My days are like a [a,A]lengthened shadow,
And [b]I [B]wither away like [c]grass.

12 But You, O LORD, [a,A]abide forever,
And Your [b,B]name to all generations.
13 You will [A]arise *and* have
[B]compassion on Zion;
For [C]it is time to be gracious to her,
For the [D]appointed time has come.
14 Surely Your servants [a]find
pleasure in her stones
And feel pity for her dust.
15 [a]So the [b,A]nations will fear the
name of the LORD
And [B]all the kings of the earth Your glory.
16 For the LORD has [A]built up Zion;
He has [B]appeared in His glory.
17 He has [A]regarded the prayer
of the [a]destitute
And has not despised their prayer.

18 [a]This will be [A]written for the
[B]generation to come,
[b]That [C]a people yet to be created
[c]may praise [d]the LORD.
19 For He [A]looked down from
His holy height;
[B]From heaven the LORD gazed
[a]upon the earth,
20 To hear the [A]groaning of the prisoner,
To [B]set free [a]those who were
doomed to death,
21 That *men* may [A]tell of the name
of the LORD in Zion
And His praise in Jerusalem,
22 When [A]the peoples are gathered together,
And the kingdoms, to serve the LORD.

23 He has weakened my strength in the way;
He has [A]shortened my days.
24 I say, "O my God, [A]do not take me
away in the [a]midst of my days,
Your [B]years are throughout
all generations.
25 "Of old You [A]founded the earth,
And the [B]heavens are the
work of Your hands.
26 "[a]Even they will [A]perish, but You endure;
And all of them will wear
out like a garment;
Like clothing You will change them
and they will be changed.

102:2 [A]Ps 69:17 [B]Ps 31:2 102:3 [a]Or *finished* [A]Ps 37:20; James 4:14 [B]Job 30:30; Lam 1:13 102:4 [a]Lit *herbage* [A]Ps 90:5, 6 [B]Ps 37:2; Is 40:7 [C]1 Sam 1:7; 2 Sam 12:17; Ezra 10:6; Job 33:20 102:5 [a]Lit *voice* [b]Lit *have cleaved* [A]Job 19:20; Lam 4:8 102:6 [a]Lit *have become similar to* [A]Is 34:11; Zeph 2:14 102:7 [A]Ps 77:4 102:8 [a]Or *made a fool of* [b]Lit *have sworn by me* [A]Ps 31:11 [B]Acts 26:11 [C]2 Sam 16:5; Is 65:15; Jer 29:22 102:9 [A]Ps 42:3; 80:5 102:10 [A]Ps 38:3 [B]Job 27:21; 30:22 102:11 [a]Lit *stretched out* [b]Or *as for me, I* [c]Lit *herbage* [A]Job 14:2; Ps 109:23 [B]Ps 102:4 102:12 [a]Or *sit enthroned* [b]Lit *memorial* [A]Ps 9:7; 10:16; Lam 5:19 [B]Ex 3:15; Ps 135:13 102:13 [A]Ps 12:5; 44:26 [B]Is 60:10; Zech 1:12 [C]Ps 119:126 [D]Ps 75:2; Dan 8:19 102:14 [a]Or *have found* 102:15 [a]Or *And* [b]Or *Gentiles, heathen* [A]1 Kin 8:43; Ps 67:7 [B]Ps 138:4 102:16 [A]Ps 147:2 [B]Is 60:1, 2 102:17 [a]Or *naked* [A]Neh 1:6; Ps 22:24 102:18 [a]Or *Let this be written* [b]Or *And* [c]Or *will* [d]Heb *YAH* [A]Deut 31:19; Rom 15:4; 1 Cor 10:11 [B]Ps 22:30; 48:13 [C]Ps 22:31; 78:6f 102:19 [a]Lit *toward* [A]Deut 26:15; Ps 14:2; 53:2 [B]Ps 33:13 102:20 [a]Lit *the sons of death* [A]Ps 79:11 [B]Ps 146:7 102:21 [A]Ps 22:22 102:22 [A]Ps 22:27; 86:9; Is 49:22, 23; 60:3; Zech 8:20-23 102:23 [A]Ps 39:5 102:24 [a]Lit *half* [A]Ps 39:13; Is 38:10 [B]Job 36:26; Ps 90:2; 102:12; Hab 1:12 102:25 [A]Gen 1:1; Neh 9:6; Heb 1:10-12 [B]Ps 96:5 102:26 [a]Lit *They themselves* [A]Is 34:4; 51:6; Matt 24:35; 2 Pet 3:10; Rev 20:11

102:2 Your face … Your ear. Anthropomorphic language (i.e., a figure of speech that attributes human features to God) which points to God's attention and response respectively.

102:3–5 bones … heart … bones. These terms describe the emotional and physical toll of the psalmist's ordeal.

102:6 pelican. Possibly a desert owl. The verse describes a desolate situation, extreme loneliness (cf. Is 34:8–15; Zep 2:13–15). **owl.** Owls were unclean animals, cf. Lv 11:16–18.

102:7 lonely bird. Feeling like a solitary bird, the psalmist expresses his perceived abandonment by both God and man.

102:10, 11 a lengthened shadow. The time of sunset is used to describe the psalmist's desperate sense that his life will end shortly because God has punished him by withdrawing His presence and strength.

102:12–22 The psalmist radically shifts his focus from earth to heaven—from his dilemma to God—and basks in the eternal nature of God and the eternal outworking of God's redemptive plan.

102:13–16 Zion. Earthly Zion or Jerusalem is in view (cf. vv. 16, 21, 22). Perhaps this points to the time of restoration after the Babylonian Exile (ca. 605–536 B.C.).

102:18 written. The psalmist had a sense of the perpetuation of his literary effort.

102:19 looked down … gazed. The transcendent omniscience of God is in view.

102:22 the peoples … the kingdoms. This will ultimately be fulfilled in Christ's messianic reign over the world (cf. Ps 2).

102:23, 24 The psalmist desires to live longer but acknowledges his mortality compared to God's eternality.

102:24 the midst of my days. Lit. at the halfway point of life.

102:25–27 Eternal God created the heavens and earth, which will one day perish (v. 26). Hebrews 1:10–12 applies this passage to the Lord Jesus Christ, who is superior to the angels because: 1) He is eternal, while they had a beginning; and 2) He created, but they were created. This passage clearly affirms the eternality and deity of Christ. The unchangeable God will outlast His creation, even into the new creation (cf. Mal 3:6; Jas 1:17; 2Pe 3; Rev 21, 22).

27 "But You are [a,A]the same,
And Your years will not come to an end.
28 "The [A]children of Your servants
will continue,
And their [a,B]descendants will be
established before You."

PSALM 103

PRAISE FOR THE LORD'S MERCIES.

A Psalm of David.

1 [A]Bless the LORD, O my soul,
And all that is within me,
bless His [B]holy name.
2 Bless the LORD, O my soul,
And [A]forget none of His benefits;
3 Who [A]pardons all your iniquities,
Who [B]heals all your diseases;
4 Who [A]redeems your life from the pit,
Who [B]crowns you with lovingkindness
and compassion;
5 Who [A]satisfies your [a]years with good things,
So that your youth is [B]renewed
like the eagle.

6 The LORD [A]performs [a]righteous deeds
And judgments for all who are [B]oppressed.
7 He [A]made known His ways to Moses,
His [B]acts to the sons of Israel.
8 The LORD is [A]compassionate
and gracious,
[B]Slow to anger and abounding
in lovingkindness.
9 He [A]will not always strive *with us,*
Nor will He [B]keep *His anger* forever.
10 He has [A]not dealt with us
according to our sins,
Nor rewarded us according
to our iniquities.
11 For as high [A]as the heavens
are above the earth,
So great is His lovingkindness
toward those who [a]fear Him.

102:27 [a]Lit *He* [A]Is 41:4; 43:10; Mal 3:6; James 1:17 102:28 [a]Lit *seed* [A]Ps 69:36 [B]Ps 89:4 103:1 [A]Ps 104:1, 35 [B]Ps 33:21; 105:3; 145:21; Ezek 36:21; 39:7 103:2 [A]Deut 6:12; 8:11 103:3 [A]Ex 34:7; Ps 86:5; 130:8; Is 43:25 [B]Ex 15:26; Ps 30:2; Jer 30:17 103:4 [A]Ps 49:15 [B]Ps 5:12 103:5 [a]Or *desire* [A]Ps 107:9; 145:16 [B]Is 40:31 103:6 [a]Or *deeds of vindication* [A]Ps 99:4; 146:7 [B]Ps 12:5 103:7 [A]Ex 33:13; Ps 99:7; 147:19 [B]Ps 78:11; 106:22 103:8 [A]Ex 34:6; Num 14:18; Neh 9:17; Ps 86:15; Jon 4:2; James 5:11 [B]Ps 145:8; Joel 2:13; Nah 1:3 103:9 [A]Ps 30:5; Is 57:16 [B]Jer 3:5, 12; Mic 7:18 103:10 [A]Ezra 9:13; Lam 3:22 103:11 [a]Or *revere* [A]Ps 36:5; 57:10

102:28 The realistic hope of one who perceives that though he is about to die, God's purposes on earth will be accomplished in future generations.

103:1–22 Psalms 103 and 104 appear as an intentional pair designed to promote the blessing and exaltation of God. This psalm represents a soliloquy in which David surveys God's goodness and encourages the angels and the works of God's creation to join him in divine praise.

I. A Call for Human Praise (103:1–19)
   A. Personally (103:1–5)
   B. Corporately (103:6–19)
II. A Call for Creation's Praise (103:20–22b)
   A. Angels (103:20–21)
   B. Works of Creation (103:22a-b)
III. A Refrain of Personal Praise (103:22c)

103:1 Bless the LORD. Cf. 103:2, 22; 104:1, 35

103:2 forget none of His benefits. These earthly gifts from God included: 1) forgiveness of sin (v. 3), 2) recovery from sickness (v. 3), 3) deliverance from death (v. 4), 4) abundant lovingkindness and mercy (v. 4), and 5) food to sustain life (v. 5).

103:3 diseases. This is not a promise, but rather a testimony which should be understood in the light of Dt 32:39.

103:5 youth is renewed like the eagle. The mysterious way of the long-lived eagle symbolized strength and speed (cf. Ex 19:4; Jer 48:40), which also characterizes human youth. As a general rule, a person blessed of God will grow weak and slow down less rapidly than otherwise (cf. Is 40:29–31, which uses the same language).

103:6–19 The psalmist rehearses the attributes of God with which He blesses the saints.

103:7, 8 His ways to Moses. Cf. Moses' request (Ex 33:13) with God's answer (Ex 34:6, 7).

103:9 not always strive. There will be a final day of accountability, both at death (Lk 16:19–31) and the Great White Throne (Rev 20:11–15). The Genesis flood served as a stark preview of this truth (cf. Ge 6:3).

103:10 not dealt. God's great mercy (v. 11) and irreversible, complete justification (v. 12) have redemptively accomplished for us, by the death of Christ (cf. 2Co 5:21; Php 3:9), what we ourselves could not do.

CHRIST IN THE PSALMS (LUKE 24:44)

Psalms	NT Quote	Significance
2:1–12	Ac 4:25, 26; 13:33; Heb 1:5; 5:5	Incarnation, Crucifixion, Resurrection
8:3–8	1Co 15:27, 28; Eph 1:22; Heb 2:5–10	Creation
16:8–11	Ac 2:24–31; 13:35–37	Death, Resurrection
22:1–31	Mt 27:35–46; Jn 19:23, 24; Heb 2:12; 5:5	Incarnation, Crucifixion, Resurrection
40:6–8	Heb 10:5–9	Incarnation
41:9	Jn 13:18, 21	Betrayal
45:6, 7	Heb 1:8, 9	Deity
68:18	Eph 4:8	Ascension, Enthronement
69:20, 21, 25	Mt 27:34, 48; Ac 1:15–20	Betrayal, Crucifixion
72:6–17	———	Millennial Kingship
78:1, 2, 15	Mt 13:35; 1Co 10:4	Theophany, Earthly teaching ministry
89:3–37	Ac 2:30	Millennial Kingship
102:25–27	Heb 1:10–12	Creation, Eternality
109:6–19	Ac 1:15–20	Betrayal
110:1–7	Mt 22:43–45; Ac 2:33–35; Heb 1:13; 5:6–10; 6:20; 7:24	Deity, Ascension, Heavenly Priesthood, Millennial Kingship
118:22, 23	Mt 21:42; Mk 12:10, 11; Lk 20:17; Ac 4:8–12; 1Pe 2:7	Rejection as Savior
132:12–18	Ac 2:30	Millennial Kingship

12 As far as the east is from the west,
So far has He [A]removed our
transgressions from us.
13 Just [A]as a father has compassion
on *his* children,
So the LORD has compassion
on those who [a]fear Him.
14 For [A]He Himself knows [a]our frame;
He [B]is mindful that we are *but* [C]dust.

15 As for man, his days are [A]like grass;
As a [B]flower of the field,
so he flourishes.
16 When the [A]wind has passed
over it, it is no more,
And its [B]place acknowledges
it no longer.
17 But the [A]lovingkindness of the LORD
is from everlasting to everlasting
on those who [a]fear Him,
And His [b]righteousness [B]to
children's children,
18 To [A]those who keep His covenant
And remember His precepts
to do them.

19 The LORD has established His
[A]throne in the heavens,
And His [a,B]sovereignty
rules over [b]all.
20 Bless the LORD, you [A]His angels,
[B]Mighty in strength, who
[C]perform His word,
[D]Obeying the voice of His word!
21 Bless the LORD, all you [A]His hosts,
You [B]who serve Him, doing His will.
22 Bless the LORD, [A]all you works of His,
In all places of His dominion;
Bless the LORD, O my soul!

PSALM 104

THE LORD'S CARE OVER ALL HIS WORKS.

1 [A]Bless the LORD, O my soul!
O LORD my God, You are very great;
You are [B]clothed with
splendor and majesty,
2 Covering Yourself with [A]light
as with a cloak,
[B]Stretching out heaven like a *tent* curtain.
3 [a]He [A]lays the beams of His upper
chambers in the waters;
[a]He makes the [B]clouds His chariot;
[a]He walks upon the [C]wings of the wind;
4 [a]He makes [b,A]the winds His messengers,
[C]Flaming [B]fire His ministers.

5 He [A]established the earth
upon its foundations,
So that it will not [a]totter forever and ever.
6 You [A]covered it with the deep
as with a garment;
The waters were standing
above the mountains.
7 At Your [A]rebuke they fled,
At the [B]sound of Your thunder
they hurried away.
8 The mountains rose; the
valleys sank down
To the [A]place which You
established for them.
9 You set a [A]boundary that they
may not pass over,
So that they will not return
to cover the earth.

10 [a]He sends forth [A]springs in the valleys;
They flow between the mountains;

103:12 [A]2 Sam 12:13; Is 38:17; 43:25; Zech 3:9; Heb 9:26 103:13 [a]Or *revere* [A]Mal 3:17 103:14 [a]I.e. what we are made of [A]Is 29:16 [B]Ps 78:39 [C]Gen 3:19; Eccl 12:7 103:15 [A]Ps 90:5; Is 40:6; 1 Pet 1:24 [B]Job 14:2; James 1:10, 11 103:16 [A]Is 40:7 [B]Job 7:10; 8:18; 20:9 103:17 [a]Or *revere* [b]I.e. faithfulness to His gracious promises [A]Ps 25:6 [B]Ex 20:6; Deut 5:10; Ps 105:8 103:18 [A]Deut 7:9; Ps 25:10 103:19 [a]Or *kingdom* [b]I.e. the universe [A]Ps 11:4 [B]Ps 47:2, 8; Dan 4:17, 25 103:20 [A]Ps 148:2 [B]Ps 29:1; 78:25 [C]Matt 6:10 [D]Ps 91:11; Heb 1:14 103:21 [A]1 Kin 22:19; Neh 9:6; Ps 148:2; Luke 2:13 [B]Ps 104:4 103:22 [A]Ps 145:10 104:1 [A]Ps 103:22 [B]Ps 93:1 104:2 [A]Dan 7:9 [B]Is 40:22 104:3 [a]Lit *The one who* [A]Amos 9:6 [B]Is 19:1 [C]Ps 18:10 104:4 [a]Lit *Who* [b]Or *His angels, spirits* [c]Or *His ministers flames of fire* [A]Ps 148:8; Heb 1:7 [B]2 Kin 2:11; 6:17 104:5 [a]Or *move out of place* [A]Job 38:4; Ps 24:2 104:6 [A]Gen 1:2 104:7 [A]Ps 18:15; 106:9; Is 50:2 [B]Ps 29:3; 77:18 104:8 [A]Ps 33:7 104:9 [A]Job 38:10, 11; Jer 5:22 104:10 [a]Lit *The one who sends* [A]Ps 107:35; Is 41:18

103:13 as a father. Unlike the pagan gods, who are apathetic or hostile.

103:14 dust. Physically speaking, as Adam was created of dust (Ge 2:7), so mankind at death decomposes back into dust (Ge 3:19).

103:15, 16 days ... like grass. Man's life is short and transitory (cf. Is 40:8).

103:17, 18 the lovingkindness of the LORD. Those who appeal to God's mercy by proper fear (v. 17) and obedience (v. 18) will overcome the shortness of physical life with eternal life. Lk 1:50 quotes Ps 103:17.

103:19 His throne in the heavens. From everlasting to everlasting God has always ruled over all things (cf. Pss 11:4; 47:1–9; 148:8–13). This universal kingdom is to be distinguished from God's mediatorial kingdom on earth.

103:20, 21 His angels ... His hosts. Unfallen, righteous angels who serve God night and day (cf. Ps 148:2; Rev 5:11–13).

103:22 works of His. Refers to God's creation, which is also to His praise (cf. Pss 148–150, also 1Ch 29:10–13).

104:1–35 In vivid poetic detail, the psalmist sings of the Lord's glory in creation (cf. Ge 1, 2; Job 38–41; Pss 19:1–6; 148:1–6; Pr 30:4; Is 40:1–6; Jn 1:1–3; Ro 1:18–25; Col 1:16, 17). He refers to the original creation (cf. 104:5) without forgetting the fall of man and the cursed earth (104:23, 29, 35). He alternates reciting God's greatness by 1) personal praise to the Creator (104:1, 2, 5–9, 20–30), and 2) declaring God's handiwork to his human audience (104:3, 4, 10–19, 31–35). The flow of the psalm loosely follows the order of creation as first reported in Ge 1:1–31 but closes (v. 35) with an allusion to the end time events recorded in Rev 20–22.

I. The Heavens and Earth Created (104:1–9)
II. The Needs of Creatures Met (104:10–18)
III. The Sun and Moon (104:19–23)
IV. The Sea and Its Inhabitants (104:24–26)
V. God's Providential Care (104:27–30)
VI. Benediction to the Creator (104:31–35)

104:1–9 This section approximates the first two days of creation (cf. Ge 1:1–8).

104:1 very great. The Creator is greater than His creation. Therefore, the Creator is to be worshiped, not the creation (cf. Ex 20:3, 4; Ro 1:29).

104:3 the waters. Refers to the original creation with the waters above the heaven (cf. Ge 1:7, 8).

104:4 winds ... Flaming fire. Hebrews 1:7 attributes these characteristics to angels describing their swiftness and destructiveness as God's instruments of judgment.

104:5 foundations. Cf. Job 38:4.

104:6–9 While this might sound like the worldwide flood of Ge 6–9, it continues to refer to the creation, especially Ge 1:9, 10 regarding the third day of creation.

104:10–18 With water (vv. 10–13), vegetation (v. 14), food-producing vines, trees, and grain (v. 15), trees (vv. 16, 17), and cliffs (v. 18), the Creator provides for the basic needs of

11 They [A]give drink to every
beast of the field;
The [B]wild donkeys quench their thirst.
12 [a]Beside them the birds of the
heavens [A]dwell;
They [b]lift up *their* voices
among the branches.
13 [a]He [A]waters the mountains from
His upper chambers;
[B]The earth is satisfied with the
fruit of His works.

14 [a]He causes the [A]grass to
grow for the [b]cattle,
And [B]vegetation for the [c]labor of man,
So that [d]he may bring forth
[e]food [C]from the earth,
15 And [A]wine which makes
man's heart glad,
[B]So that he may make *his*
face glisten with oil,
And [a]food which [C]sustains
man's heart.
16 The trees of the LORD [a]drink their fill,
The cedars of Lebanon
which He planted,
17 Where the [A]birds build their nests,
And the [B]stork, whose home
is the [a]fir trees.

18 The high mountains are for
the [A]wild goats;
The [B]cliffs are a refuge for
the [a,C]shephanim.
19 He made the moon [A]for the seasons;
The [B]sun knows the place of its setting.
20 You [A]appoint darkness and
it becomes night,
In which all the [B]beasts of the
forest [a]prowl about.
21 The [A]young lions roar after their prey
[a]And [B]seek their food from God.
22 *When* the sun rises they withdraw
And lie down in their [A]dens.
23 Man goes forth to [A]his work
And to his labor until evening.

24 O LORD, how [A]many are Your works!
[a]In [B]wisdom You have made them all;
The [C]earth is full of Your [b]possessions.
25 [a]There is the [A]sea, great and [b]broad,
In which are swarms without number,
Animals both small and great.
26 There the [A]ships move along,
And [a,B]Leviathan, which You
have formed to sport in it.

27 They all [A]wait for You
To [B]give them their food
in [a]due season.
28 You give to them, they gather *it* up;
You [A]open Your hand, they are
satisfied with good.
29 You [A]hide Your face, they are dismayed;
You [B]take away their [a]spirit, they expire
And [C]return to their dust.
30 You send forth Your [a,A]Spirit,
they are created;
And You renew the face of the ground.

31 Let the [A]glory of the LORD
endure forever;
Let the LORD [B]be glad in His works;
32 [a]He [A]looks at the earth,
and it [B]trembles;
He [C]touches the mountains,
and they smoke.
33 [a]I will sing to the LORD
[b,A]as long as I live;
[a]I will [B]sing praise to my God
[c]while I have my being.
34 Let my [A]meditation be pleasing to Him;
As for me, I shall [B]be glad in the LORD.
35 Let sinners be [A]consumed
from the earth
And let the [B]wicked be no more.
[C]Bless the LORD, O my soul.
[a,D]Praise [b]the LORD!

104:11 [A]Ps 104:13 [B]Job 39:5 104:12 [a]Or *Over,* Above [b]Lit *give forth* [A]Matt 8:20 104:13 [a]Lit *Who* [A]Ps 65:9; 147:8 [B]Jer 10:13 104:14 [a]Lit *Who* [b]Or *beasts* [c]Or *cultivation by* or *service of* [d]Or *He* [e]Lit *bread* [A]Job 38:27; Ps 147:8 [B]Gen 1:29 [C]Job 28:5 104:15 [a]Lit *bread* [A]Judg 9:13; Prov 31:6; Eccl 10:19 [B]Ps 23:5; 92:10; 141:5; Luke 7:46 [C]Gen 18:5; Judg 19:5, 8 104:16 [a]Lit *are satisfied* 104:17 [a]Or *cypress* [A]Ps 104:12 [B]Lev 11:19 104:18 [a]Small, shy, furry animals *(Hyrax syriacus)* found in the peninsula of the Sinai, northern Israel, and the region round the Dead Sea; KJV *coney,* orig NASB *rock badgers* [A]Job 39:1 [B]Prov 30:26 [C]Lev 11:5 104:19 [A]Gen 1:14 [B]Ps 19:6 104:20 [a]Lit *creep* [A]Ps 74:16; Is 45:7 [B]Ps 50:10; Is 56:9; Mic 5:8 104:21 [a]Lit *And to seek* [A]Job 38:39 [B]Ps 145:15; Joel 1:20 104:22 [A]Job 37:8 104:23 [A]Gen 3:19 104:24 [a]Or *With* [b]Or *creatures* [A]Ps 40:5 [B]Ps 136:5; Prov 3:19; Jer 10:12; 51:15 [C]Ps 65:9 104:25 [a]Or *This* [b]Or *broad of dimensions* (lit *hands*) [A]Ps 8:8; 69:34 104:26 [a]Or *a sea monster* [A]Ps 107:23; Ezek 27:9 [B]Job 41:1; Ps 74:14; Is 27:1 104:27 [a]Lit *its appointed time* [A]Ps 145:15 [B]Job 36:31; 38:41; Ps 136:25; 147:9 104:28 [A]Ps 145:16 104:29 [a]Or *breath* [A]Deut 31:17; Ps 30:7 [B]Job 34:14, 15; Ps 146:4; Eccl 12:7 [C]Gen 3:19; Job 10:9; Ps 90:3 104:30 [a]Or *breath* [A]Job 33:4; Ezek 37:9 104:31 [A]Ps 86:12; 111:10 [B]Gen 1:31 104:32 [a]Lit *The one who* [A]Judg 5:5; Ps 97:4, 5; 114:7 [B]Hab 3:10 [C]Ex 19:18; Ps 144:5 104:33 [a]Or *Let me sing* [b]Lit *in my lifetime* [c]Lit *while I still am* [A]Ps 63:4 [B]Ps 146:2 104:34 [A]Ps 19:14 [B]Ps 9:2 104:35 [a]Or *Hallelujah!* [b]Heb *YAH* [A]Ps 59:13 [B]Ps 37:10 [C]Ps 104:1 [D]Ps 105:45; 106:48

His creation. This corresponds to the third day of creation (cf. Ge 1:11–13).

104:13 upper chambers. Refers to rain clouds.

104:19–23 This section corresponds to the fourth day of creation in Ge 1:14–19. The work period of predators (the night) is contrasted with the work time of humans (the day).

104:24–26 This portion corresponds to the fifth day of creation in Ge 1:20–23.

104:26 Leviathan. This term appears in 4 other OT passages (Job 3:8; 41:1; Ps 74:14; Is 27:1). In each case, Leviathan refers to some mighty creature who can overwhelm man but who is no match for God. Some form of sea monster, probably a dinosaur, is in view. *See note on Job 41:1.*

104:27–30 All of creation waits upon God for His providential care. These verses allude to the sixth day of creation (cf. Ge 1:24–31).

104:30 Your Spirit. This most likely should be translated "Your breath," which corresponds to "the breath of life" in Ge 2:7.

104:31–35 The psalmist closes with a benediction to the Creator in which he prays that the ungodly might no longer spiritually pollute God's universe (104:35). This prayer anticipates the new heaven and new earth (cf. Rev 21, 22).

104:32 trembles ... smoke. Earthquakes and fires caused by lightning are in view.

104:35 sinners ... wicked. Although God has been merciful to let His fallen human creation live on (cf. Ge 3:1–24), those who bless and praise the Lord desire to see the day when 1) sinful men have been abolished from the earth (cf. Rev 20:11–15), and 2) the curse of the earth is reversed (cf. Rev 22:3).

PSALM 105

THE LORD'S WONDERFUL WORKS IN BEHALF OF ISRAEL.

1 Oh [A]give thanks to the LORD,
[B]call upon His name;
[C]Make known His deeds
among the peoples.
2 Sing to Him, [A]sing praises to Him;
[a,B]Speak of all His [b]wonders.
3 [a]Glory in His holy name;
Let the [A]heart of those who
seek the LORD be glad.
4 Seek the LORD and [A]His strength;
[B]Seek His face continually.
5 Remember His [a,A]wonders
which He has done,
His marvels and the [B]judgments
[b]uttered by His mouth,
6 O seed of [A]Abraham, His servant,
O sons of [B]Jacob, His [C]chosen ones!
7 He is the LORD our God;
His [A]judgments are in all the earth.

8 He has [A]remembered His
covenant forever,
The word which He commanded
to a [B]thousand generations,
9 *The* [A]*covenant* which He
made with Abraham,
And His [B]oath to Isaac.
10 Then He [A]confirmed it to
Jacob for a statute,
To Israel as an everlasting covenant,
11 Saying, "[A]To you I will give
the land of Canaan
As the [a,B]portion of your inheritance,"
12 When they were only a [A]few
men in number,
Very few, and [B]strangers in it.
13 And they wandered about
from nation to nation,
From *one* kingdom to another people.
14 He [A]permitted no man to oppress them,
And He [B]reproved kings for their sakes:
15 "[A]Do not touch My anointed ones,
And do My prophets no harm."

16 And He [A]called for a famine upon the land;
He [B]broke the whole staff of bread.
17 He [A]sent a man before them,
Joseph, *who* was [B]sold as a slave.
18 They afflicted his [A]feet with fetters,
[a]He himself was laid in irons;
19 Until the time that his [A]word came to pass,
The word of the LORD [a,B]tested him.
20 The [A]king sent and released him,
The ruler of peoples, and set him free.
21 He [A]made him lord of his house
And ruler over all his possessions,
22 To [a]imprison his princes [b,A]at will,
That he might teach his elders wisdom.
23 [A]Israel also came into Egypt;
Thus Jacob [B]sojourned in the land of Ham.
24 And He [A]caused His people
to be very fruitful,
And made them stronger than
their adversaries.

105:1 [A]1 Chr 16:8-22, 34; Ps 106:1; Is 12:4 [B]Ps 99:6 [C]Ps 145:12 105:2 [a]Or *Meditate on* [b]I.e. wonderful acts [A]Ps 96:1; 98:5 [B]Ps 77:12; 119:27; 145:5 105:3 [a]Or *Boast* [A]Ps 33:21 105:4 [A]Ps 63:2 [B]Ps 27:8 105:5 [a]I.e. wonderful acts [b]Lit *of His mouth* [A]Ps 40:5; 77:11 [B]Ps 119:13 105:6 [A]Ps 105:42 [B]Ps 135:4 [C]1 Chr 16:13; Ps 106:5; 135:4 105:7 [A]Is 26:9 105:8 [A]Ps 105:42; 106:45; Luke 1:72 [B]Deut 7:9 105:9 [A]Gen 12:7; 17:2, 8; 22:16-18; Gal 3:17 [B]Gen 26:3 105:10 [A]Gen 28:13-15 105:11 [a]Lit *measuring line* [A]Gen 13:15; 15:18 [B]Josh 23:4; Ps 78:55 105:12 [A]Gen 34:30; Deut 7:7 [B]Gen 23:4; Heb 11:9 105:14 [A]Gen 20:7; 35:5 [B]Gen 12:17; 20:3, 7 105:15 [A]Gen 26:11 105:16 [A]Gen 41:54 [B]Lev 26:26; Is 3:1; Ezek 4:16 105:17 [A]Gen 45:5 [B]Gen 37:28, 36; Acts 7:9 105:18 [a]Lit *His soul came into* [A]Gen 39:20; 40:15 105:19 [a]Or *refined* [A]Gen 40:20, 21 [B]Ps 66:10 105:20 [A]Gen 41:14 105:21 [A]Gen 41:40-44 105:22 [a]Lit *bind* [b]Lit *at his* [A]Gen 41:44 105:23 [A]Gen 46:6; Acts 7:15 [B]Acts 13:17 105:24 [A]Ex 1:7, 9

105:1–45 Just as Pss 103 and 104 were matched pairs; so are Pss 105 and 106, as they look at Israel's history from God's perspective and then Israel's vantage respectively. This psalm possibly originated by command of David to Asaph on the occasion when the ark of the covenant was first brought to Jerusalem (2Sa 6:12–19; 1Ch 16:1–7). Psalm 105:1–15 repeats 1Ch 16:8–22.

I. Rejoicing in God's Works for Israel (105:1–3)
II. Remembering God's Works for Israel (105:4–6)
III. Recounting the Work of God for Israel (105:7–45)
 A. Abraham to Joseph (105:7–25)
 B. Moses to Joshua (105:26–45)

105:1–5 Ten imperatives call Israel to a time of remembering, celebrating, and spreading the report abroad of the work of God on Israel's behalf as a result of God's covenant with Abraham.

105:6 seed of Abraham … sons of Jacob. Those who were to obey the commands of 105:1–5, i.e., the nation of Israel.

105:7–12 This section rehearses the Abrahamic Covenant.

105:8 a thousand generations. A reference to an exceedingly long time (a generation is normally 40 years) which would encompass the remainder of human history, i.e., forever (cf. Dt 7:9; 1Ch 16:15).

105:9, 10 The original covenant that God had made with Abraham. He later renewed it with Isaac and then Jacob (cf. Abraham—Ge 12:1–3; 13:14–18; 15:18–21; 17:1–21; 22:15–19; Isaac—26:23–25; and Jacob—35:9–12).

105:10 an everlasting covenant. From the time of the covenant until the end. Five OT covenants are spoken of as "everlasting": 1) the Noahic Covenant, Ge 9:16; 2) the Abrahamic Covenant, Ge 17:7, 13, 19; 3) the Priestly Covenant, Lv 24:8; 4) the Davidic Covenant, 2Sa 23:5; and 5) the New Covenant, Jer 32:40.

105:11 Saying. This probably has God's promise to Abraham at Ge 17:8 in view.

105:12 only a few. God promised Abraham that He would multiply his small number of descendants to be as numerous as the stars of heaven and the sand of the seashore (cf. Ge 13:16; 15:5; 17:2, 6; 22:17).

105:13 nation to nation. Abraham had migrated from Ur of the Chaldeans to Haran and finally to Canaan (Ge 11:31). Later, he visited Egypt (Ge 12:10–13:1).

105:14 He reproved. The Lord struck Pharaoh and his house with great plagues when Sarai was taken to his quarters (Ge 12:17). Abimelech, king of Gerar, was also rebuked by God (Ge 20:3–7).

105:15 Do not touch … no harm. No one passage in the OT records this exact statement. The psalmist most likely is summarizing several occasions, such as Ge 20:7; 26:11. **My anointed ones … My prophets.** With poetic parallelism, God's prophets are termed those whom He chose to represent Him on earth. In Ge 20:7, Abraham is called a prophet. This title could also apply to Isaac and Jacob.

105:16–25 The history recorded in Ge 37–50 is in view. Verses 16–22 refer to Joseph's experience in Egypt (cf. Ge 37–41), while v. 23 looks to Jacob's trek to Egypt that resulted in a 430-year stay (Ge 42–50; cf. Ge 15:13, 14; Ex 12:40). Verses 24, 25 give an overall summary of Israel's experience in Egypt (cf. Ex 1:7–14).

105:23 the land of Ham. Another name for the area in Egypt where part of the descendants of Ham, the youngest son of Noah, settled (cf. Ge 9:24; Ps 78:51).

105:23–25 God sovereignly used Egypt to judge Israel (cf. Ge 15:13).

25 He [A]turned their heart to hate His people,
To [B]deal craftily with His servants.
26 He [A]sent Moses His servant,
And [B]Aaron, whom He had chosen.
27 They [a,A]performed His wondrous
acts among them,
And miracles in the land of Ham.
28 He [A]sent darkness and made *it* dark;
And they did not [B]rebel against His words.
29 He [A]turned their waters into blood
And caused their fish to die.
30 Their land swarmed with [A]frogs
Even in the [B]chambers of their kings.
31 He spoke, and there came
a [A]swarm of flies
And [B]gnats in all their territory.
32 He [a]gave them [A]hail for rain,
And flaming fire in their land.
33 He [A]struck down their vines
also and their fig trees,
And shattered the trees of their territory.
34 He spoke, and [A]locusts came,
And young locusts, even without number,
35 And ate up all vegetation in their land,
And ate up the fruit of their ground.
36 He also [A]struck down all the
firstborn in their land,
The [B]first fruits of all their vigor.

37 Then He brought them out
with [A]silver and gold,
And among His tribes there was
not one who stumbled.
38 Egypt was [A]glad when they departed,
For the [B]dread of them had
fallen upon them.
39 He spread a [A]cloud for a [a]covering,
And [B]fire to illumine by night.
40 [a]They [A]asked, and He brought [B]quail,
And satisfied them with the
[b,C]bread of heaven.
41 He opened the [a]rock and
[A]water flowed out;
[b]It ran in the dry places *like* a river.
42 For He [A]remembered His holy word
With Abraham His servant;
43 And He brought forth
His people with joy,
His chosen ones with a joyful [A]shout.
44 He [A]gave them also the lands
of the [a]nations,
That they [B]might take possession of
the fruit of the peoples' labor,
45 So that they might [A]keep His statutes
And observe His laws,
[a]Praise [b]the LORD!

PSALM 106

ISRAEL'S REBELLIOUSNESS AND THE LORD'S DELIVERANCES.

1 [a]Praise [b]the LORD!
Oh [A]give thanks to the LORD,
for He [B]is good;
For [C]His lovingkindness is everlasting.
2 Who can speak of the [A]mighty
deeds of the LORD,
Or can show forth all His praise?
3 How blessed are those
who keep [a]justice,
[b]Who [A]practice righteousness at all times!

4 Remember me, O LORD, in *Your*
[A]favor [a]toward Your people;
Visit me with Your salvation,

105:25 [A]Ex 1:8; 4:21 [B]Ex 1:10; Acts 7:19 105:26 [A]Ex 3:10; 4:12 [B]Ex 4:14; Num 16:5; 17:5-8 105:27 [a]Lit *set the words of His signs* [A]Ps 78:43-51; 105:27-36 105:28 [A]Ex 10:21, 22 [B]Ps 99:7 105:29 [A]Ex 7:20, 21 105:30 [A]Ex 8:6 [B]Ex 8:3 105:31 [A]Ex 8:21 [B]Ex 8:16, 17 105:32 [a]Or *made their rain hail* [A]Ex 9:23-25 105:33 [A]Ps 78:47 105:34 [A]Ex 10:12-15 105:36 [A]Ex 12:29; 13:15; Ps 135:8; 136:10 [B]Gen 49:3 105:37 [A]Ex 12:35, 36 105:38 [A]Ex 12:33 [B]Ex 15:16 105:39 [a]Or *curtain* [A]Ex 13:21; Neh 9:12; Ps 78:14; Is 4:5 [B]Ex 40:38 105:40 [a]Or *One* [b]Or *food* [A]Ex 16:12; Ps 78:18 [B]Ex 16:13; Num 11:31; Ps 78:27 [C]Ex 16:15; Neh 9:15; Ps 78:24; John 6:31 105:41 [a]Or *boulder* [b]Lit *They went* [A]Ex 17:6; Num 20:11; Ps 78:15; 114:8; Is 48:21; 1 Cor 10:4 105:42 [A]Gen 15:13, 14; Ps 105:8 105:43 [A]Ex 15:1; Ps 106:12 105:44 [a]Or *Gentiles* [A]Josh 11:16-23; 13:7; Ps 78:55 [B]Deut 6:10, 11 105:45 [a]Or *Hallelujah!* [b]Heb *YAH* [A]Deut 4:1, 40 106:1 [a]Or *Hallelujah!* [b]Heb *YAH* [A]Ps 105:1; 107:1; 118:1; 136:1; Jer 33:11 [B]2 Chr 5:13; 7:3; Ezra 3:11; Ps 100:5 [C]1 Chr 16:34, 41 106:2 [A]Ps 145:4, 12; 150:2 106:3 [a]Or *judgment* [b]Many Heb mss read *The one who performs* [A]Ps 15:2 106:4 [a]Lit *of* [A]Ps 44:3; 119:132

105:26–36 God's deliverance of Israel from Egypt through the leadership of Moses and Aaron is rehearsed with a special emphasis on the 10 plagues, ending with the Passover (cf. Ex 5–12).

105:28 darkness. The ninth plague (cf. Ex 10:21–29).

105:29 waters into blood. The first plague (cf. Ex 7:14–25).

105:30 frogs. The second plague (cf. Ex 8:1–15).

105:31 swarm of flies ... gnats. The fourth and third plagues respectively (cf. Ex 8:16–32). The fifth plague of pestilence (Ex 9:1–7) and the sixth plague of boils (Ex 9:8–12) are not mentioned.

105:32, 33 hail ... flaming fire. The seventh plague (cf. Ex 9:13–35).

105:34, 35 locusts. The eighth plague (cf. Ex 10:1–20).

105:36 struck down ... the firstborn. The tenth and final plague, which was death to the firstborn of man and beast (cf. Ex 11:1–12:51).

105:37–41 The psalmist summarizes Israel's Exodus from Egypt. God provided for their financial and physical needs (cf. Ex 11:2, 3; 12:35 and Ex 15:26); protection by day and night (cf. Ex 14:19, 20); food needs (Ex 16:1–36); and water needs (cf. Ex 17:6; Nu 20:1–11).

105:42–45 The psalmist concludes with a summary that alludes to Joshua's leading the nation back into the Land, first promised to Abraham, (Jos 1–12) and then distributed to the 12 tribes of Israel (Jos 13–24). What God promised (cf. 105:7–12) He delivered.

105:42 He remembered. As promised in v. 8.

105:45 keep ... observe. This theme of obedience begins (1:6–9) and ends (24:14, 15, 16, 18, 21, 24) the book of Joshua.

106:1–48 Psalm 106 rehearses God's mercy during Israel's history in spite of Israel's sinfulness (cf. Ne 9:1–38; Ps 78; Is 63:7–64:12; Eze 20:1–44; Da 9:1–19; Ac 7:2–53; 1Co 10:1–13). The occasion for this psalm is most likely the repentance (v. 6) of post-Exilic Jews who had returned to Jerusalem (vv. 46, 47). Verses 1, 47, 48 seem to be borrowed from 1Ch 16:34–36, which was sung on the occasion of the ark's first being brought to Jerusalem by David (cf. 2Sa 6:12–19; 1Ch 16:1–7). True revival appears to be the psalmist's intention.

I. The Invocation (106:1–5)
II. The Identification with Israel's Sins (106:6)
III. The Confession of Israel's Sins (106:7–46)
  A. During Moses' Time (106:7–33)
  B. From Joshua to Jeremiah (106:34–46)
IV. The Plea for Salvation (106:47)
V. The Benediction (106:48)

106:1 good ... lovingkindness. These attributes of God are especially praiseworthy to the psalmist in light of Israel's historical sin pattern (cf. 106:6–46).

106:2, 3 Verse 2 asks the question answered in v. 3.

106:4, 5 The psalmist has the benefits of the Abrahamic Covenant in mind (*see note on Ps*

5 That I may see the [A]prosperity
of Your chosen ones,
That I may [B]rejoice in the
gladness of Your nation,
That I may [C]glory with Your [a]inheritance.

6 [A]We have sinned [a,B]like our fathers,
We have committed iniquity, we
have behaved wickedly.
7 Our fathers in Egypt did not
understand Your [a]wonders;
They [A]did not remember [b]Your
abundant kindnesses,
But [B]rebelled by the sea, at the [c]Red Sea.
8 Nevertheless He saved them
[A]for the sake of His name,
That He might [B]make
His power known.
9 Thus He [A]rebuked the [a]Red
Sea and it [B]dried up,
And He [C]led them through the deeps,
as through the wilderness.
10 So He [A]saved them from the [a]hand
of the one who hated *them,*
And [B]redeemed them from the
[a]hand of the enemy.
11 [A]The waters covered their adversaries;
Not one of them was left.
12 Then they [A]believed His words;
They [B]sang His praise.

13 They quickly [A]forgot His works;
They [B]did not wait for His counsel,
14 But [A]craved intensely in the wilderness,
And [a,B]tempted God in the desert.
15 So He [A]gave them their request,
But [B]sent a [a]wasting disease
among them.

16 When they became [A]envious
of Moses in the camp,
And of Aaron, the holy one of the LORD,
17 The [A]earth opened and
swallowed up Dathan,
And engulfed the [a]company of Abiram.
18 And a [A]fire blazed up in their [a]company;
The flame consumed the wicked.

19 They [A]made a calf in Horeb
And worshiped a molten image.
20 Thus they [A]exchanged their glory
For the image of an ox that eats grass.
21 They [A]forgot God their Savior,
Who had done [B]great things in Egypt,
22 [a,A]Wonders in the land of Ham
And awesome things by the [b]Red Sea.
23 Therefore [A]He said that He
would destroy them,
Had not [B]Moses His chosen one
stood in the breach before Him,
To turn away His wrath from
destroying *them.*
24 Then they [A]despised the [B]pleasant land;
They [C]did not believe in His word,
25 But [A]grumbled in their tents;
They did not listen to the
voice of the LORD.
26 Therefore He [a,A]swore to them
That He would cast them down
in the wilderness,

106:5 [a]I.e. people [A]Ps 1:3 [B]Ps 118:15 [C]Ps 105:3 106:6 [a]Lit *with* [A]1 Kin 8:47; Ezra 9:7; Neh 1:7; Jer 3:25; Dan 9:5 [B]2 Chr 30:7; Neh 9:2; Ps 78:8, 57; Zech 1:4 106:7 [a]I.e. wonderful acts [b]Lit *the multitude of Your lovingkindnesses* [c]Lit *Sea of Reeds* [A]Judg 3:7; Ps 78:11, 42 [B]Ex 14:11, 12; Ps 78:17 106:8 [A]Ezek 20:9 [B]Ex 9:16 106:9 [a]Lit *Sea of Reeds* [A]Ps 18:15; 78:13; Is 50:2; Nah 1:4 [B]Ex 14:21; Is 51:10 [C]Is 63:11-13 106:10 [a]Or *power* [A]Ex 14:30 [B]Ps 78:42; 107:2 106:11 [A]Ex 14:27, 28; 15:5; Ps 78:53 106:12 [A]Ex 14:31 [B]Ex 15:1-21; Ps 105:43 106:13 [A]Ex 15:24; 16:2; 17:2 [B]Ps 107:11 106:14 [a]Or *put God to the test* [A]Num 11:4; Ps 78:18; 1 Cor 10:6 [B]Ex 17:2; 1 Cor 10:9 106:15 [a]Or *leanness into their soul* [A]Num 11:31; Ps 78:29 [B]Is 10:16 106:16 [A]Num 16:1-3 106:17 [a]Or *assembly, band* [A]Num 16:32; Deut 11:6 106:18 [a]Or *assembly, band* [A]Num 16:35 106:19 [A]Ex 32:4; Deut 9:8; Acts 7:41 106:20 [A]Jer 2:11; Rom 1:23 106:21 [A]Ps 78:11; 106:7, 13 [B]Deut 10:21 106:22 [a]I.e. Wonderful acts [b]Lit *Sea of Reeds* [A]Ps 105:27 106:23 [A]Ex 32:10; Deut 9:14; Ezek 20:8, 13 [B]Ex 32:11-14; Deut 9:25-29 106:24 [A]Num 14:31 [B]Deut 8:7; Jer 3:19; Ezek 20:6 [C]Deut 1:32; 9:23; Heb 3:19 106:25 [A]Num 14:2; Deut 1:27 106:26 [a]Lit *lifted up His hand* [A]Num 14:28-35; Ps 95:11; Ezek 20:15; Heb 3:11

105:9, 10). He prays here for personal deliverance (v. 4) and later for national deliverance (v. 47).

106:6 We ... fathers. The psalmist acknowledges the perpetual sinfulness of Israel, including that of his own generation.

106:7–12 This section recalls the crossing of the Red Sea during the Exodus by the nation, when Pharaoh and his army were in pursuit (cf. Ex 14:1–31).

106:7 Red Sea. *See note on Ex 13:18.*

106:8 sake of His name. The glory and reputation of God provide the highest motive for His actions. This frequent OT phrase appears 6 other places in the Psalms (cf. Pss 23:3; 25:11; 31:3; 79:9; 109:21; 143:11).

106:9 He rebuked the Red Sea. This reliable historical account recalls a true supernatural miracle of God (cf. Ex 14:21, 22) just as He would later provide a way for the nation to cross the Jordan into the land (cf. Jos 3:14–17).

106:10 Quoted in Lk 1:71.

106:11 Not one of them was left. As recorded in Ex 14:28 (cf. Ps 78:53).

106:12 They sang His praise. The Song of Moses is in view (cf. Ex 15:1–21).

106:13–33 This section remembers the nation's wanderings in the wilderness (cf. Nu 14–Dt 34).

106:13–15 The Jews forgot what God had most recently done on their behalf, but 1) remembered the basics of life that Egypt provided, and 2) doubted that they would have water (cf. Ex 15:24) or food (cf. Ex 16:2, 3) in the future.

106:14 tempted God. According to Nu 14:22, the nation tempted, or tested, God at least 10 times (cf. Ex 5:21; 6:9; 14:11, 12; 15:24; 16:2, 3; 17:2, 3; 32:1–6; Nu 11:1–6; 12:1, 2; 14:2, 3).

106:16–18 Korah, who is not named here, led the rebellion that is recounted (cf. Nu 16:1–35). God's judgment concluded with fire which consumed 250 men (cf. Nu 16:35).

106:19–23 This section remembers when the nation convinced Aaron to make a golden calf for idol worship while Moses was on the mountain receiving the commandments of God (cf. Ex 32:1–14; Dt 9:7–21).

106:19 Horeb. Most likely another name for Mt. Sinai (cf. Ex 19:11). This special place, called "the mountain of God" (cf. Ex 3:1; 1Ki 19:8), is where Moses received the commandments of God (Dt 1:6; 5:2; 29:1; Mal 4:4).

106:21 God their Savior. This title, common in the pastoral epistles, is seldom used in the OT outside of Isaiah (19:20; 43:3, 11; 45:15, 21; 49:26; 60:16; 63:8). Here it refers to physical deliverance. It looks forward to Jesus Christ as spiritual redeemer (Lk 2:11).

106:22 Ham. Another name for the part of Egypt, which was settled by descendants of Ham, the youngest son of Noah (cf. Ge 9:24; 10:6–20).

106:23 Moses ... in the breach. Moses pleaded with God, based on the Abrahamic Covenant promises, not to destroy the nation in spite of their idolatry and immoral behavior (cf. Ex 32:11–14).

106:24–27 This portion recounts 1) the nation's rejection of Joshua's and Caleb's positive report from the Land, and 2) their desire to return to Egypt (cf. Nu 14:1–4). God responded with judgment (Nu 14:11–38).

106:24 the pleasant land. A term used of the Land God promised to Abraham for the nation Israel (cf. Jer 3:19, Zec 7:14).

27 And that He would [A]cast their
seed among the nations
And [B]scatter them in the lands.

28 They [A]joined themselves
also to [a]Baal-peor,
And ate [B]sacrifices offered to the dead.
29 Thus they [A]provoked *Him* to
anger with their deeds,
And the plague broke out among them.
30 Then Phinehas [A]stood up and interposed,
And so the [B]plague was stayed.
31 And it was [A]reckoned to him
for righteousness,
To all generations forever.

32 They also [A]provoked *Him* to wrath
at the waters of [a]Meribah,
So that it [B]went hard with
Moses on their account;
33 Because they [A]were rebellious
against [a]His Spirit,
He spoke rashly with his lips.

34 They [A]did not destroy the peoples,
As [B]the LORD commanded them,
35 But [A]they mingled with the nations
And learned their [a]practices,
36 And [A]served their idols,
[B]Which became a snare to them.
37 They even [A]sacrificed their sons and
their daughters to the [B]demons,
38 And shed [A]innocent blood,
The blood of their [B]sons and
their daughters,
Whom they sacrificed to the
idols of Canaan;
And the land was [C]polluted with the blood.
39 Thus they became [A]unclean
in their [a]practices,
And [B]played the harlot in their deeds.

40 Therefore the [A]anger of the LORD
was kindled against His people
And He [B]abhorred His [a,C]inheritance.
41 Then [A]He gave them into the
hand of the [a]nations,
And those who hated them
ruled over them.
42 Their enemies also [A]oppressed them,
And they were subdued under their [a]power.
43 Many times He would [A]deliver them;
They, however, were rebellious
in their [B]counsel,
And *so* [C]sank down in their iniquity.

44 Nevertheless He looked
upon their distress
When He [A]heard their cry;
45 And He [A]remembered His
covenant for their sake,
And [a,B]relented [C]according to the
greatness of His lovingkindness.
46 He also made them [A]*objects* of compassion
In the presence of all their captors.

47 [A]Save us, O LORD our God,
And [B]gather us from among the nations,
To give thanks to Your holy name
And [a,C]glory in Your praise.

106:27 [A]Deut 4:27 [B]Lev 26:33; Ps 44:11 106:28 [a]Or *Baal of Peor* [A]Num 25:3; Deut 4:3; Hos 9:10 [B]Num 25:2 106:29 [A]Num 25:4 106:30 [A]Num 25:7 [B]Num 25:8 106:31 [A]Gen 15:6; Num 25:11-13 106:32 [a]Lit *strife* [A]Num 20:2-13; Ps 81:7; 95:9 [B]Num 20:12 106:33 [a]Or *his spirit* [A]Num 20:3, 10; Ps 78:40; 107:11 106:34 [A]Judg 1:21, 27-36 [B]Deut 7:2, 16 106:35 [a]Lit *works* [A]Judg 3:5, 6 106:36 [A]Judg 2:12 [B]Deut 7:16 106:37 [A]Deut 12:31; 32:17; 2 Kin 16:3; 17:17; Ezek 16:20, 21; 1 Cor 10:20 [B]Lev 17:7 106:38 [A]Ps 94:21 [B]Deut 18:10 [C]Num 35:33; Is 24:5; Jer 3:1, 2 106:39 [a]Lit *works* [A]Lev 18:24; Ezek 20:18 [B]Lev 17:7; Num 15:39; Judg 2:17; Hos 4:12 106:40 [a]I.e. people [A]Judg 2:14; Ps 78:59 [B]Lev 26:30; Deut 32:19 [C]Deut 9:29; 32:9 106:41 [a]Or *Gentiles* [A]Judg 2:14; Neh 9:27 106:42 [a]Lit *hand* [A]Judg 4:3; 10:12 106:43 [A]Judg 2:16-18 [B]Ps 81:12 [C]Judg 6:6 106:44 [A]Judg 3:9; 6:7; 10:10 106:45 [a]Lit *was sorry* [A]Lev 26:42; Ps 105:8 [B]Judg 2:18 [C]Ps 69:16 106:46 [A]1 Kin 8:50; 2 Chr 30:9; Ezra 9:9; Neh 1:11; Jer 42:12 106:47 [a]Lit *boast* [A]1 Chr 16:35, 36 [B]Ps 147:2 [C]Ps 47:1

106:28–31 This scene recounts Israel's encounter with the prophet Balaam who, on behalf of Balak, King of Moab, tried to curse Israel but was prevented from doing so by God (cf. Nu 22–24; Dt 23:4; Jos 24:9, 10; Ne 13:2). Having failed, Balaam advised Balak to entice Israel with immorality and idolatry (cf. Nu 31:16 with 25:1; 2Pe 2:15; Jude 11; Rev 2:14). Israel sinned and God judged (Nu 25:1–13). Balaam was later slain by Israel (cf. Jos 13:22).

106:28 Baal-peor. Refers to Baal, a god of the Moabites, whose worship occurred at the location of the mountain called Peor (cf. Nu 23:28). sacrifices offered to the dead. This most likely refers to sacrifices made to lifeless idols (cf. 1Th 1:9). Israel should have been worshiping "the living God" (cf. Dt 5:26; 1Sa 17:26, 36; Pss 42:2; 84:2; Jer 10:3–10; Da 6:20, 26).

106:30 Phinehas. The son of Eleazar, son of Aaron (cf. Nu 25:7).

106:31 reckoned to him for righteousness. This was a just and rewardable action, evidencing faith in God. As with Abraham (cf. Ge 15:6 and Ro 4:3; Gal 3:6; Jas 2:23), so it was also with Phinehas. The everlasting covenant of perpetual priesthood through Aaron, from the house of Levi, was first made by God in Lv 24:8, 9 (cf. Jer 33:17–22; Mal 2:4–8). This covenant was reaffirmed in Nu 18:8, 19. In this text, the covenant is further specified to be through the line of faithful Phinehas.

106:32, 33 This scene looks back to Nu 20:1–13 when Moses, provoked by the continuing rebellion of Israel, nonetheless wrongly struck the rock in anger (cf. Ex 11:8; 16:20) and thus offended God (cf. Nu 20:12). As a result, both Aaron (cf. Nu 20:22–29) and Moses (Dt 34:1–8) died prematurely without entering the Promised Land.

106:32 the waters of Meribah. Cf. Nu 20:13.

106:33 His Spirit. This most likely refers to the Holy Spirit of God. The Spirit of God had an extensive ministry in the OT (cf. Ge 1:2; 6:3; 2Sa 23:2; Ne 9:30; Ps 139:7; Is 48:16; Eze 2:2; 3:12–14; 8:3; 11:1, 5, 24; Hag 2:5, Zec 7:12). Both Is 63:10, 11 and Ac 7:51 point to this particular event.

106:34–39 This section describes the general sins of Israel from the time they entered the Land (Jos 3, 4) until they were exiled to Assyria (2Ki 17) and Babylon (2Ki 24, 25). They failed to expel the heathen and sadly conformed to their idolatry.

106:36–38 idols ... demons ... idols. Demons impersonate idols and encourage idol worship (cf. Dt 32:17; 2Ch 33:5–7; 1Co 10:14–21; Rev 9:20). The sacrifice of children was not uncommon (cf. Dt 12:31; 2Ki 17:17; Eze 16:20, 21).

106:39 their practices ... deeds. God held Israel directly responsible for their sin without excuse.

106:40–43 From the time of the judges until the Assyrian and Babylonian exiles, God used the hand of His enemies to discipline Israel for their sin.

106:44–46 This emphasizes the unconditional nature of God's covenant with Abraham.

106:45 He remembered His covenant. This answers the psalmist's prayer of vv. 4, 5 with regard to the Abrahamic Covenant that 1) the descendants of Abraham would multiply, and 2) they would possess the land (*see note on Ps 105:9, 10*; cf. Lk 1:72–75). for their sake. A secondary complement to God, who was primarily acting for His name's sake (cf. v. 8).

106:47 The psalmist pleads, on behalf of the nation and in light of the Abrahamic Covenant, for the nation to be regathered in

48 [A]Blessed be the LORD, the God of Israel,
From everlasting even to everlasting.
And let all the people say, "Amen."
[a]Praise [b]the LORD!

BOOK 5

PSALM 107

THE LORD DELIVERS MEN FROM MANIFOLD TROUBLES.

1 Oh [A]give thanks to the LORD,
for [B]He is good,
For His lovingkindness is everlasting.
2 Let [A]the redeemed of the LORD say *so,*
Whom He has [B]redeemed from
the hand of the adversary
3 And [A]gathered from the lands,
From the east and from the west,
From the north and from the [a]south.

4 They [A]wandered in the wilderness
in a [a]desert region;
They did not find a way to
[b]an inhabited [B]city.
5 *They were* hungry [a]and thirsty;
Their [A]soul fainted within them.
6 Then they [A]cried out to the
LORD in their trouble;
He delivered them out of their distresses.
7 He led them also by a [a,A]straight way,
To go to [b,B]an inhabited city.
8 [A]Let them give thanks to the LORD
for His lovingkindness,
And for His [a]wonders to
the sons of men!
9 For He has [A]satisfied the [a]thirsty soul,
And the [B]hungry soul He has
filled with what is good.

10 There were those who [A]dwelt in darkness
and in the shadow of death,
[B]Prisoners in [a]misery and [b]chains,
11 Because they had [A]rebelled
against the words of God
And [B]spurned the [C]counsel
of the Most High.
12 Therefore He humbled their
heart with labor;
They stumbled and there
was [A]none to help.
13 Then they [A]cried out to the
LORD in their trouble;
He saved them out of their distresses.
14 He [A]brought them out of darkness
and the shadow of death
And [B]broke their bands apart.
15 [A]Let them give thanks to the LORD
for His lovingkindness,
And for His [a]wonders to the sons of men!
16 For He has [A]shattered gates of bronze
And cut bars of iron asunder.

17 Fools, because of [a]their rebellious way,
And [A]because of their iniquities,
were afflicted.
18 Their [A]soul abhorred all kinds of food,
And they [B]drew near to the [C]gates of death.
19 Then they cried out to the
LORD in their trouble;
He saved them out of their distresses.
20 He [A]sent His word and [B]healed them,
And [C]delivered *them* from
their [a]destructions.

106:48 [a]Or *Hallelujah!* [b]Heb *YAH* [A]Ps 41:13; 72:18; 89:52 107:1 [A]1 Chr 16:34; Ps 106:1; 118:1; 136:1; Jer 33:11 [B]2 Chr 5:13; 7:3; Ezra 3:11; Ps 100:5 107:2 [A]Is 35:9, 10; 62:12; 63:4 [B]Ps 78:42; 106:10 107:3 [a]Lit *sea* [A]Deut 30:3; Neh 1:9; Ps 106:47; Is 11:12; 43:5; 56:8; Ezek 11:17; 20:34 107:4 [a]Lit *waste* [b]Or *a habitable city;* lit *a city of habitation* [A]Num 14:33; 32:13; Deut 2:7; 32:10; Josh 5:6; 14:10 [B]Ps 107:7, 36 107:5 [a]Lit *also* [A]Ps 77:3 107:6 [A]Ps 50:15; 107:13, 19, 28 107:7 [a]Or *level* [b]Or *a habitable city;* lit *a city of habitation* [A]Ezra 8:21; Ps 5:8; Jer 31:9 [B]Ps 107:4, 36 107:8 [a]I.e. wonderful acts [A]Ps 107:15, 21, 31 107:9 [a]Or *parched* [A]Ps 22:26; 34:10; 63:5; 103:5 [B]Ps 146:7; Matt 5:6; Luke 1:53 107:10 [a]Lit *affliction* [b]Lit *irons* [A]Ps 143:3; Is 42:7; Mic 7:8; Luke 1:79 [B]Job 36:8; Ps 102:20 107:11 [A]Ps 78:40; 106:7; Lam 3:42 [B]Num 15:31; 2 Chr 36:16; Prov 1:25; Is 5:24 [C]Ps 73:24 107:12 [A]Ps 22:11; 72:12 107:13 [A]Ps 107:6 107:14 [A]Ps 86:13; 107:10 [B]Ps 116:16; Jer 2:20; 30:8; Nah 1:13; Luke 13:16; Acts 12:7 107:15 [a]I.e. wonderful acts [A]Ps 107:8, 21, 31 107:16 [A]Is 45:1, 2 107:17 [a]Lit *the way of their transgression* [A]Is 65:6, 7; Jer 30:14, 15; Lam 3:39; Ezek 24:23 107:18 [A]Job 33:20; Ps 102:4 [B]Job 33:22; Ps 88:3 [C]Job 38:17; Ps 9:13 107:20 [a]Or *pits* [A]Ps 147:15, 18; Matt 8:8 [B]2 Kin 20:5; Ps 30:2; 103:3; 147:3 [C]Job 33:28, 30; Ps 30:3; 49:15; 56:13; 103:4

Israel. He remembers what the men of Moses' day forgot, i.e., God as their Savior (cf. 106:21). Even though the tribes of Judah and Benjamin returned to Israel in Ezra and Nehemiah, this text looks ahead to the regathering of Israel at the time when the Lord Jesus Christ returns to rule over the promised Davidic (2Sa 7) millennial kingdom (Rev 20) on earth (cf. Eze 37:11–28; Hos 14:4–8; Joel 3:18–21; Am 9:7–15; Mic 7:14–20; Zep 3:8–20; Zec 12–14).

106:48 From everlasting even to everlasting. With the hopeful prayer of 106:47 on his lips, the psalmist closes the fourth book of the Psalms (Pss 90–106) with a grand benediction focusing on the eternal character of God, Israel's Savior (cf. 1Ch 16:36; Pss 41:13; 90:2).

107:1–43 The opening line of Pss 105–107, "Oh give thanks to the LORD," links together this trilogy of songs which praise God for His goodness and mercy to Israel. Most likely this psalm has a post-Exilic origin (cf. 107:3). The psalm develops two main themes: 1) praising God for His continual deliverance (107:4–32), and 2) remembering God's response to man's obedience/disobedience (107:33–42).

I. The Call to Praise (107:1–3)
II. The Cause of Rejoicing—Deliverance (107:4–32)
III. The Consequences of Obedience/Disobedience (107:33–42)
IV. The Commentary on Wisdom/Understanding (107:43)

107:1–3 All of those who have been delivered (redeemed) from the hand of Israel's enemy focus on God's goodness and everlasting mercy. They had been delivered through the centuries from Egypt to the S (cf. Ex 12–14), Syria and Assyria to the N (cf. 2Ki 19:29–37), the Philistines to the W (cf. 2Sa 8:1; 2Ki 18:8), and Babylon to the E (cf. Ezr 1). Compare the psalmist's prayer in 106:47 with v. 3.

107:4–32 This portion contains four pictures or actual situations which illustrate the disastrous end of sin in the nation: 1) wandering in the wilderness (vv. 4–9), 2) languishing in prison (vv. 10–16); 3) enduring sickness (vv. 17–22); and 4) tossing on a stormy sea (vv. 23–32). Each picture follows the same sequence of four events: 1) man's predicament (vv. 4, 5, 10–12, 17, 18, 23–27); 2) man's petition (vv. 6a, 13a, 19a, 28a); 3) God's pardon (vv. 6b, 7, 13b, 14, 19b, 20, 28b–30); and 4) man's praise (vv. 8, 9, 15, 16, 21, 22, 31, 32).

107:4–9 Possibly the psalmist looked back at the desert wanderings of ungrateful, faithless Israel after the miraculous Exodus (Nu 14–Jos 2).

107:10–16 Possibly the psalmist thought of the capture and imprisonment of King Zedekiah ca. 586 B.C. (cf. 2Ki 25:4–7; Jer 39:4–8; Jer 52:1–11).

107:17–22 Possibly the psalmist recalled the mass affliction and subsequent mass healing in Nu 21:4–9.

21 [A]Let them give thanks to the LORD
for His lovingkindness,
And for His [a]wonders to the sons of men!
22 Let them also offer [A]sacrifices
of thanksgiving,
And [B]tell of His works with joyful singing.

23 Those who [A]go down to the sea in ships,
Who do business on great waters;
24 They have seen the works of the LORD,
And His [a]wonders in the deep.
25 For He [A]spoke and raised
up a [B]stormy wind,
Which [C]lifted up the waves [a]of the sea.
26 They rose up to the heavens, they
went down to the depths;
Their soul [A]melted away in *their* misery.
27 They reeled and [A]staggered
like a drunken man,
And [a]were at their wits' end.
28 Then they cried to the LORD
in their trouble,
And He brought them out
of their distresses.
29 He [A]caused the storm to be still,
So that the waves [a]of the sea were hushed.
30 Then they were glad because
they were quiet,
So He guided them to their desired haven.
31 [A]Let them give thanks to the LORD
for His lovingkindness,
And for His [a,B]wonders to the sons of men!
32 Let them [A]extol Him also [B]in the
congregation of the people,
And [C]praise Him at the seat of the elders.

33 He [a,A]changes rivers into a [b]wilderness
And springs of water into
a thirsty ground;
34 A [A]fruitful land into a [B]salt waste,
Because of the wickedness of
those who dwell in it.
35 He [a,A]changes a [b]wilderness
into a pool of water
And a dry land into springs of water;
36 And there He makes the hungry to dwell,
So that they may establish
[a,A]an inhabited city,
37 And sow fields and [A]plant vineyards,
And [a]gather a fruitful harvest.
38 Also He blesses them and
they [A]multiply greatly,
And He [B]does not let their cattle decrease.

39 When they are [A]diminished
and [B]bowed down
Through oppression, misery and sorrow,
40 He [A]pours contempt upon [a]princes
And [B]makes them wander
[C]in a pathless waste.
41 But He [A]sets the needy [a]securely
on high away from affliction,
And [B]makes *his* families like a flock.
42 The [A]upright see it and are glad;
But all [B]unrighteousness shuts its mouth.
43 Who is [A]wise? Let him give
heed to these things,
And consider the [B]lovingkindnesses
of the LORD.

PSALM 108

GOD PRAISED AND SUPPLICATED TO GIVE VICTORY.

A Song, a Psalm of David.

1 [A]My heart is steadfast, O God;
I will sing, I will sing praises,
even with my [a]soul.
2 Awake, harp and lyre;
I will awaken the dawn!
3 I will give thanks to You, O LORD,
among the peoples,
And I will sing praises to You
among the nations.
4 For Your [A]lovingkindness is
great [B]above the heavens,
And Your truth *reaches* to the skies.
5 [A]Be exalted, O God, above the heavens,
And Your glory above all the earth.

107:21 [a]I.e. wonderful acts [A]Ps 107:8, 15, 31 107:22 [A]Lev 7:12; Ps 50:14; 116:17 [B]Ps 9:11; 73:28; 118:17 107:23 [A]Is 42:10; Jon 1:3 107:24 [a]I.e. wonderful acts 107:25 [a]Lit *of it* [A]Ps 105:31, 34 [B]Ps 148:8; Jon 1:4 [C]Ps 93:3, 4 107:26 [A]Ps 22:14; 119:28 107:27 [a]Lit *all their wisdom was swallowed up* [A]Job 12:25; Is 24:20 107:29 [a]Lit *of it* [A]Ps 65:7; 89:9; Matt 8:26; Luke 8:24 107:31 [a]I.e. wonderful acts [A]Ps 107:8, 15, 21 [B]Ps 78:4; 111:4 107:32 [A]Ps 34:3; 99:5; Is 25:1 [B]Ps 22:22, 25 [C]Ps 35:18 107:33 [a]Or *turns* [b]Or *desert* [A]1 Kin 17:1, 7; Ps 74:15; Is 42:15; 50:2 107:34 [A]Gen 13:10; 14:3; 19:24, 25; Deut 29:23 [B]Job 39:6; Jer 17:6 107:35 [a]Or *turns* [b]Or *desert* [A]Ps 105:41; 114:8; Is 35:6, 7; 41:18 107:36 [a]Or *a habitable city;* lit *a city of habitation* [A]Ps 107:4, 7 107:37 [a]Lit *acquire fruits of yield* [A]2 Kin 19:29; Is 65:21; Amos 9:14 107:38 [A]Gen 12:2; 17:20; Ex 1:7; Deut 1:10 [B]Deut 7:14 107:39 [A]2 Kin 10:32; Ezek 5:11; 29:15 [B]Ps 38:6; 44:25; 57:6 107:40 [a]Or *nobles* [A]Job 12:21 [B]Job 12:24 [C]Deut 32:10 107:41 [a]Lit *in an inaccessibly high place* [A]1 Sam 2:8; Ps 59:1; 113:7, 8 [B]Job 21:11; Ps 78:52; 113:9 107:42 [A]Job 22:19; Ps 52:6 [B]Job 5:16; Ps 63:11; Rom 3:19 107:43 [A]Ps 64:9; Jer 9:12; Hos 14:9 [B]Ps 107:1 108:1 [a]Lit *glory* [A]Ps 57:7-11; 108:1-5 108:4 [A]Num 14:18; Deut 7:9; Ps 36:5; 100:5; Mic 7:18-20 [B]Ps 113:4 108:5 [A]Ps 57:5

107:23–32 Possibly the psalmist had Jonah and the sailors bound for Tarshish in mind (cf. Jon 1).

107:33–42 This section contrasts God's blessing in response to man's obedience with God's judgment on man's sin. The psalmist makes his point with 4 illustrations: 1) descending from prosperity to poverty (vv. 33, 34); 2) being lifted up from barrenness to blessedness (vv. 35–38); 3) falling from the top to the bottom (vv. 39, 40); and 4) being elevated from low to high (vv. 41, 42).

107:33, 34 Perhaps the 3 years of drought from Ahab's and Jezebel's sins are in view (cf. 1Ki 17:1; 18:18).

107:35–38 Perhaps the time of Abraham (Ge 24:1, 34, 35) or Joshua (Jos 24:13) is in view.

107:39, 40 Perhaps the Assyrian Exile (2Ki 17:4–6) or the Babylonian Captivity (2Ki 24:14, 15) is in view.

107:41, 42 Perhaps the impoverished Jews in Egypt who were made rich with Egyptian gold and other treasures are in view (cf. Ex 1:13, 14 with 3:21, 22; 11:2; 12:35, 36).

107:43 Perhaps the psalmist has Pr 8:1–36, Ecc 12:13, 14, or Hos 14:9 in mind as he pens these concluding words.

108:1–13 David combines portions of his own previously written Pss 57 and 60 to make up this psalm commemorating God's victories (vv. 1–5 are from 57:7–11; vv. 6–13 are from 60:5–12). He deleted the laments that began each psalm (57:1–6 and 60:1–4) while combining his own words of exaltation and confidence in God with only slight word variation. No specific historical occasion behind this psalm is given. *See notes on Ps 57:7–11 and Ps 60:5–12.*

I. Personal Exaltation of God (108:1–5)
II. Personal Confidence in God (108:6–13)

6 [A]That Your beloved may be delivered,
Save with Your right hand, and answer me!

7 God has spoken in His [a]holiness:
"I will exult, I will portion out Shechem
And measure out the valley of Succoth.
8 "Gilead is Mine, Manasseh is Mine;
Ephraim also is the [a]helmet of My head;
[A]Judah is My [b]scepter.
9 "Moab is My washbowl;
Over Edom I shall throw My shoe;
Over Philistia I will shout aloud."

10 [A]Who will bring me into the besieged city?
Who [a]will lead me to Edom?
11 Have not You Yourself, O God, [A]rejected us?
And will You not go forth with
our armies, O God?
12 Oh give us help against the adversary,
For [A]deliverance [a]by man is in vain.
13 [a]Through God we will do valiantly,
And [A]it is He who shall tread
down our adversaries.

PSALM 109

VENGEANCE INVOKED UPON ADVERSARIES.

For the choir director. A Psalm of David.

1 O [A]God of my praise,
[B]Do not be silent!
2 For they have opened the [a]wicked and
[A]deceitful mouth against me;
They have spoken [b]against me
with a [B]lying tongue.
3 They have also surrounded me
with words of hatred,
And fought against me [A]without cause.
4 In return [A]for my love they
act as my accusers;
But [B]I am *in* prayer.
5 Thus they have [a,A]repaid me evil for good
And [B]hatred for my love.

6 Appoint a wicked man over him,
And let an [a,A]accuser stand
at his right hand.
7 When he is judged, let him
[A]come forth guilty,
And let his [B]prayer become sin.
8 Let [A]his days be few;
Let [B]another take his office.
9 Let his [A]children be fatherless
And his [B]wife a widow.
10 Let his [A]children wander about and beg;
And let them [B]seek *sustenance* [a]far
from their ruined homes.
11 Let [A]the creditor [a]seize all that he has,
And let [B]strangers plunder the
product of his labor.
12 Let there be none to [a,A]extend
lovingkindness to him,
Nor [B]any to be gracious to his
fatherless children.
13 Let his [A]posterity be [a]cut off;
In a following generation let
their [B]name be blotted out.

14 Let [A]the iniquity of his fathers be
remembered [a]before the LORD,
And do not let the sin of his
mother be [B]blotted out.
15 Let [A]them be before the LORD continually,
That He may [B]cut off their
memory from the earth;
16 Because he did not remember
to show lovingkindness,
But persecuted the [A]afflicted
and needy man,
And the [B]despondent in heart,
to [C]put *them* to death.

108:6 [A]Ps 60:5-12; 108:6-13 108:7 [a]Or *sanctuary* 108:8 [a]Lit *protection* [b]Or *lawgiver* [A]Gen 49:10 108:10 [a]Or *has led* [A]Ps 60:9 108:11 [A]Ps 44:9 108:12 [a]Lit *of* [A]Is 30:3 108:13 [a]Or *In* or *With* [A]Is 60:12; 63:1-4 109:1 [A]Deut 10:21 [B]Ps 28:1; 83:1 109:2 [a]Lit *wicked mouth and the deceitful* [b]Lit *with* [A]Ps 10:7; 52:4 [B]Ps 120:2 109:3 [A]Ps 35:7; 69:4; John 15:25 109:4 [A]Ps 38:20 [B]Ps 69:13; 141:5 109:5 [a]Lit *laid upon me* [A]Ps 35:12; 38:20 [B]John 7:7; 10:32 109:6 [a]Or *adversary, Satan* [A]Zech 3:1 109:7 [A]Ps 1:5 [B]Prov 28:9 109:8 [A]Ps 55:23 [B]Acts 1:20 109:9 [A]Ex 22:24 [B]Jer 18:21 109:10 [a]Or *out of their desolate places* [A]Gen 4:12; Job 30:5-8; Ps 59:15 [B]Ps 37:25 109:11 [a]Lit *ensnare, strike at* [A]Neh 5:7; Job 5:5; 20:15 [B]Is 1:7; Lam 5:2; Ezek 7:21 109:12 [a]Lit *continue* [A]Ezra 7:28; 9:9 [B]Job 5:4; Is 9:17 109:13 [a]Lit *for cutting off* [A]Job 18:19; Ps 21:10; 37:28 [B]Ps 9:5; Prov 10:7 109:14 [a]Lit *to* [A]Ex 20:5; Num 14:18; Is 65:6, 7; Jer 32:18 [B]Neh 4:5; Jer 18:23 109:15 [A]Ps 90:8; Jer 16:17 [B]Job 18:17; Ps 34:16 109:16 [A]Ps 37:14 [B]Ps 34:18 [C]Ps 37:32; 94:6

109:1–31 This imprecatory psalm of David cannot be conclusively connected by the psalm's general details with any particular incident/person in the king's life as chronicled in 1, 2Sa; 1Ki; and 1Ch David responds here to those who have launched a vicious verbal assault of false accusations against him (cf. 109:2, 3, 20). This psalm is considered messianic in nature, since Ac 1:20 quotes v. 8 in reference to Judas' punishment for betraying Christ (cf. Pss 41:9; 69:25). David reverses roles with his enemies by moving from being the accused in man's court to being the accuser/prosecutor before the bar of God.

I. The Plaintiff's Plea (109:1–5)
II. The Punishment Desired (109:6–20)
III. The Petition for Justice (109:21–29)
IV. The Praise of the Judge (109:30, 31)

109:1 O God of my praise. David begins and ends (cf. v. 30) with praise for the Chief Justice of the universe. At v. 21, David addresses the Judge as "O GOD, the Lord" and at v. 26 as "O LORD my God."

109:2–5 David's complaint was that the innocent were being accused by the guilty. He asserted that the charges were without cause (109:3). While Doeg the Edomite has been identified by some (cf. 1Sa 21, 22; Ps 52), the far more likely candidate would be Saul (cf. 1Sa 18–27). Eight of the 14 historical superscriptions in other psalms refer to the sufferings of David related to Saul's pursuits for the purpose of killing David (cf. Pss 18, 34, 54, 56, 57, 59, 63, 142).

109:2 In vv. 2–5, 20, 25, 27–29, David refers to a group of accusers, in contrast to vv. 6–19 where an individual is mentioned. Most likely, the individual is the group leader.

109:6–20 The Mosaic law had anticipated false accusations and malicious witnesses (cf. Dt 19:16–21) by decreeing that the false accuser was to be given the punishment intended for the accused. It would appear that David had this law in mind here and vv. 26–29. Thus, his imprecations are not malicious maledictions, but rather a call for justice according to the law. These severe words have respect not to the penitent, but to the impenitent and hard-hearted foes of God and His cause, whose inevitable fate is set.

109:8 The apostle Peter cited this verse as justification for replacing Judas the betrayer with another apostle (cf. Ac. 1:20).

17 He also loved cursing, so [A]it came to him;
And he did not delight in blessing,
so it was far from him.
18 But he [A]clothed himself with
cursing as with his garment,
And it [B]entered into [a]his body like water
And like oil into his bones.
19 Let it be to him as [A]a garment with
which he covers himself,
And for a belt with which he
constantly [B]girds himself.
20 [a]Let this be the [A]reward of my
accusers from the LORD,
And of those who [B]speak evil
against my soul.

21 But You, O [a]GOD, the Lord, deal *kindly*
with me [A]for Your name's sake;
Because [B]Your lovingkindness
is good, deliver me;
22 For [A]I am afflicted and needy,
And [a]my heart is [B]wounded within me.
23 I am passing [A]like a shadow
when it lengthens;
I am shaken off [B]like the locust.
24 My [A]knees [a]are weak from [B]fasting,
And my flesh has grown lean,
without fatness.
25 I also have become a [A]reproach to them;
When they see me, they [B]wag their head.

26 [A]Help me, O LORD my God;
Save me according to Your lovingkindness.
27 [a]And let them [A]know that
this is Your hand;
You, LORD, have done it.
28 [A]Let them curse, but You bless;
When they arise, they
shall be ashamed,
But Your [B]servant shall be glad.
29 [a]Let [A]my accusers be clothed
with dishonor,
And [b]let them [B]cover themselves with
their own shame as with a robe.

30 With my mouth I will give thanks
abundantly to the LORD;
And in the midst of many
[A]I will praise Him.
31 For He stands [A]at the right
hand of the needy,
To save him from those who
[B]judge his soul.

PSALM 110

THE LORD GIVES DOMINION TO THE KING.

A Psalm of David.

1 [A]The LORD says to my Lord:
"[B]Sit at My right hand
Until I make [C]Your enemies a
footstool for Your feet."
2 The LORD will stretch forth Your
strong [A]scepter from Zion, *saying,*
"[B]Rule in the midst of Your enemies."
3 Your [A]people [a]will volunteer freely
in the day of Your [b]power;
[B]In [c]holy array, from the
womb of the dawn,
[d]Your youth are to You *as* the [C]dew.

109:17 [A]Prov 14:14; Ezek 35:9; Matt 7:2 109:18 [a]Lit *his inward parts* [A]Ps 73:6; 109:29; Ezek 7:27 [B]Num 5:22 109:19 [A]Ps 73:6; 109:29; Ezek 7:27 [B]2 Sam 22:40; Ps 30:11; Is 11:5 109:20 [a]Lit *This is* [A]Ps 54:5; 94:23; Is 3:11; 2 Tim 4:14 [B]Ps 41:5; 71:10 109:21 [a]Heb *YHWH*, usually rendered *LORD* [A]Ps 23:3; 25:11; 79:9; 106:8; Ezek 36:22 [B]Ps 69:16 109:22 [a]Lit *one has pierced my heart within me* [A]Ps 40:17; 86:1 [B]Job 24:12; Ps 143:4; Prov 18:14 109:23 [A]Ps 102:11 [B]Ex 10:19; Job 39:20 109:24 [a]Or *totter* [A]Heb 12:12 [B]Ps 35:13 109:25 [A]Ps 22:6 [B]Ps 22:7; Jer 18:16; Lam 2:15; Matt 27:39; Mark 15:29 109:26 [A]Ps 119:86 109:27 [a]Or *That they may know* [A]Job 37:7 109:28 [A]2 Sam 16:11, 12 [B]Is 65:14 109:29 [a]Or *My accusers will be* [b]Or *they will cover* [A]Job 8:22; Ps 132:18 [B]Job 8:22; Ps 35:26 109:30 [A]Ps 22:22; 35:18; 111:1 109:31 [A]Ps 16:8; 73:23; 110:5; 121:5 [B]Ps 37:33 110:1 [A]Matt 22:44; Mark 12:36; Luke 20:42, 43; Acts 2:34, 35; Heb 1:13 [B]Matt 26:64; Eph 1:20; Col 3:1; Heb 1:3; 8:1; 10:12; 12:2 [C]1 Cor 15:25; Eph 1:22 110:2 [A]Ps 45:6; Jer 48:17; Ezek 19:14 [B]Ps 2:9; 72:8; Dan 7:13, 14 110:3 [a]Lit *will be freewill offerings* [b]Or *army* [c]Or *the splendor of holiness* [d]Or *The dew of Your youth is Yours* [A]Judg 5:2; Neh 11:2 [B]1 Chr 16:29; Ps 96:9 [C]2 Sam 17:12; Mic 5:7

109:21–29 David petitioned the court for justice by asking for deliverance for the judge's sake (109:21) and then for his own sake (vv. 22–25). Afterwards, he requested that his enemies be rightfully punished (vv. 26–29).

109:30, 31 David's praise for the Divine Magistrate (v. 30) was based on his confidence in the compassion and mercy of the judge (v. 31). Second Samuel 22 and Ps 18 record the general outcome to David's case, which was tried in God's courtroom.

110:1–7 This psalm contains one of the most exalted prophetic portions of Scripture presenting Jesus Christ as both a holy king and a royal High Priest—something that no human monarch of Israel ever experienced. It, along with Ps 118, is by far the most quoted psalm in the NT (Mt 22:44; 26:64; Mk 12:36; 14:62; Lk 20:42, 43; 22:69; Ac 2:34, 35; Heb 1:13; 5:6; 7:17, 21; 10:13). While portraying the perfect king, the perfect High Priest, and the perfect government, Ps 110 declares Christ's current role in heaven as the resurrected Savior (110:1) and His future role on earth as the reigning Monarch (110:2–7). This psalm is decidedly messianic and millennial in content. Jesus Christ (Mt 22:43, 44) verifies the Davidic authorship. The exact occasion of this psalm is unknown, but it could easily have been associated with God's declaration of the Davidic Covenant in 2Sa 7:4–17.

I. Christ the King (110:1–3)
II. Christ the High Priest (110:4–7)

110:1 **my Lord.** Refers to the divine/human King of Israel—the Lord Jesus Christ. Christ's humanity descended from David, which is demanded by the Davidic promise of 2Sa 7:12. Using this passage, Christ also declared His deity in the gospels (Mt 22:44; Mk 12:36; Lk 20:42–43) by arguing that only God could have been lord to King David. **My right hand.** God the Father invited God the Son in His ascension to sit at the place of honor in the heavenly throne room (cf. Ac. 2:22–36; Heb 10:10–12). **Your enemies a footstool.** Footstool was an ancient Near Eastern picture of absolute victory portraying the idea that one's enemy was now underfoot (cf. Pss 8:6, 7; 47:3; Is 66:1; 1Co 15:27). This anticipates Christ's Second Advent (cf. Rev 19:11–21) as a conquering king (cf. Heb 10:13).

110:2 **Your strong scepter.** From the human side, the ancestral staff of Judah is in view (cf. Ge 49:10). From the divine side, the rod of iron by which King Jesus will subdue the earth is intended (cf. Ps 2:9). **Zion.** God intends to install His ultimate earthly king in Jerusalem (the SW side is Zion; cf. Ps 132:13–18). The earthly Zion (cf. Ps 2:6; Is 59:20) is in view, not the heavenly Zion because 1) there are no enemies in heaven, and 2) none of the activities in vv. 5–7 will take place in heaven. **Rule.** Christ will rule on the earthly throne of His father David (cf. Lk 1:32), in fulfillment of Is 9:6 and Zec 14:9.

110:3 **volunteer.** The redeemed inhabitants of earth will willingly serve the King of kings and Lord of lords. **the day of Your power.** Refers to the power displayed during the millennial reign of Jesus Christ (cf. Zec 14:1–21; Rev 19:11–20:6). **holy array ... womb ... dew.** This seems to apply to the King and

4 [A]The LORD has sworn and will
[B]not [a]change His mind,
"You are a [C]priest forever
According to the order
of Melchizedek."
5 The Lord is [A]at Your right hand;
He [a]will [B]shatter kings in the
[C]day of His wrath.
6 He will [A]judge among the nations,
He [a]will fill *them* with [B]corpses,
He [b]will [C]shatter the [c]chief men
over a broad country.
7 He will [A]drink from the brook
by the wayside;
Therefore He will [B]lift up *His* head.

PSALM 111

THE LORD PRAISED FOR HIS GOODNESS.

1 [a]Praise [b]the LORD!
I [A]will give thanks to the LORD
with all *my* heart,
In the [B]company of the upright
and in the assembly.
2 [A]Great are the works of the LORD;
They are [a,B]studied by all
who delight in them.
3 [a,A]Splendid and majestic is His work,
And [B]His righteousness endures forever.
4 He has made His [a]wonders
[b]to be remembered;
The LORD is [A]gracious and
compassionate.
5 He has [A]given [a]food to those
who [b]fear Him;
He will [B]remember His
covenant forever.
6 He has made known to
His people the power
of His works,
In giving them the heritage
of the nations.
7 The works of His hands are
[a,A]truth and justice;
All His precepts [B]are [b]sure.
8 They are [A]upheld forever and ever;
They are performed in [a,B]truth
and uprightness.
9 He has sent [A]redemption
to His people;
He has [a]ordained His
covenant forever;
[B]Holy and [b]awesome is His name.
10 The [a,A]fear of the LORD is the
beginning of wisdom;
A [B]good understanding
have all those who [b]do
His commandments;
His [C]praise endures forever.

110:4 [a]Lit *be sorry* [A]Heb 7:21 [B]Num 23:19 [C]Zech 6:13; Heb 5:6, 10; 6:20; 7:17, 21 110:5 [a]Or *has shattered* [A]Ps 16:8; 109:31 [B]Ps 68:14; 76:12 [C]Ps 2:5, 12; Rom 2:5; Rev 6:17 110:6 [a]Or *has filled* [b]Or *has shattered* [c]Lit *head over* [A]Is 2:4; Joel 3:12; Mic 4:3 [B]Is 66:24 [C]Ps 68:21 110:7 [A]Judg 7:5, 6 [B]Ps 27:6 111:1 [a]Or *Hallelujah! I will* [b]Heb *YAH* [A]Ps 35:18; 138:1 [B]Ps 89:7; 149:1 111:2 [a]Lit *sought out* [A]Ps 92:5 [B]Ps 143:5 111:3 [a]Lit *Splendor and majesty* [A]Ps 96:6; 145:5 [B]Ps 112:3, 9; 119:142 111:4 [a]I.e. wonderful acts [b]Lit *a memorial* [A]Ps 86:5, 15; 103:8; 145:8 111:5 [a]Lit *prey* [b]Or *revere* [A]Matt 6:31-33 [B]Ps 105:8 111:7 [a]Or *faithfulness* [b]Or *trustworthy* [A]Rev 15:3 [B]Ps 19:7; 93:5 111:8 [a]Or *faithfulness* [A]Ps 119:160; Is 40:8; Matt 5:18 [B]Ps 19:9 111:9 [a]Lit *commanded* [b]I.e. inspiring reverence [A]Luke 1:68 [B]Ps 99:3; Luke 1:49 111:10 [a]Or *reverence for* [b]Lit *do* them [A]Job 28:28; Prov 1:7; 9:10; Eccl 12:13 [B]Ps 119:98; Prov 3:4 [C]Ps 145:2

to represent Him as in the constant vigor of youth, a period distinguished by strength and activity, or it may refer to His holiness, eternality and deity.

110:4 You are a priest. The first time in the history of Israel when a king simultaneously served as High Priest. Christ (a.k.a. "Branch," cf. Is 4:2; Jer 23:5, 6; Zec 3:8; 6:12, 13) will build the temple at which the world will worship God (cf. 2Sa 7:13; Is 2:2–4; Eze 40–48). **forever.** Christ represents the final and foremost High Priest in the history of Israel. **the order of Melchizedek.** This High Priest could not be of Aaron's lineage in that he would not be eternal, not be of Judah, not be a king, and not be of the New Covenant (Jer 31:31–33; Heb 8, 9). Melchizedek, which means "king of righteousness," served as the human priest/king of Salem in Ge 14:17–20 and provides a picture of the order of Christ's priesthood (cf. Heb 5:6; 7:17, 21). The sons of Zadok will serve with Christ in the Millennium as His human priestly associates (cf. Eze 44:15; 48:11).

110:5 Your right hand. The roles have here reversed—the Father now stands at the right hand of the Son. This pictures the Father supplying the needs of the Son (cf. Pss 16:8; 109:31; Is 41:13). The Father provides the defeat of His enemies on earth so that His Son can fulfill God's land and nation promises to Abraham (Ge 12:1, 2) and kingship promise to David (2Sa 7:12, 13, 16). **the day of His wrath.** This refers to the "Day of the Lord" (cf. v. 3 "the day of Your power"), which finds its global expression at the end of Daniel's 70th week (cf. Da 9:24–27). This term exclusively speaks of God's wrath, which will be poured out on an unrepentant world in order to set up Christ's 1,000-year (millennial) reign (cf. Joel 2:1, 11, 31; 3:14; Rev 6:16, 17; 14:19; 19:15).

110:6 judge . . . fill . . . shatter. Cf. Pss 2:8, 9; 50:1–6; Is 2:4; 9:6, 7; Da 2:44, 45; 7:26, 27; Joel 3:2, 12; Mic 4:3; Mt 25:32; Rev 6:15–17; 14:20; 16:14; 19:19–21.

110:7 He will drink. This pictures a refreshed conqueror who has kingly access to the whole world. This could anticipate the E-W flow of fresh water out of Jerusalem as recorded in Zec 14:8. **He will lift up.** The lifted head pictures Christ's strength in victory (cf. Pss 3:3; 27:6; 75:10). As Ps 22:28 reports, "For the kingdom is the LORD's and He rules over the nations" (cf. Zec 14:9).

111:1–10 Psalms 111 and 112 are alike in that 1) they both begin with, "Praise the LORD!" (as does Ps 113), and 2) they both are acrostics with 22 lines corresponding to the 22 letters of the Heb. alphabet. Psalm 111 exalts the works of God, while Ps 112 extols the man who fears God. The author(s) and occasion(s) are unknown.

I. A Word of Praise (111:1)
II. Words about God's Works (111:2–9)
III. A Word of Wisdom (111:10)

111:1 all *my* heart. Jesus might have had this passage in mind when He stated that the greatest commandment was, "You shall love the LORD your God with all your heart ...." (Mt 22:37).

111:2–9 God's work(s) are mentioned 5 times (vv. 2, 3, 4, 6, 7). Overall, the greater work of redemption seems to be in view (v. 9) without excluding lesser works of a temporal nature (vv. 5, 6).

111:5 food . . . His covenant. It is quite possible that the psalmist has alluded to God's faithfulness in providing food for Jacob through Joseph (Ge 37–50) in fulfillment of the Abrahamic Covenant to make the nation like the stars of the sky (Ge 15:5).

111:6 the heritage of the nations. It seems even more sure that the psalmist has the Abrahamic Covenant in view (cf. Ge 15:18–21; 17:1–8), specifically the Exodus (Ex–Dt) and the conquering/dividing of the land (Joshua). *See notes on Dt 7:1, 2.*

111:9 ordained His covenant forever. In light of vv. 5, 6 and Gal 3:6–9, this appears to look at the redemption aspects of the Abrahamic Covenant, which was declared frequently to be an "everlasting" or "forever" covenant (cf. Ge 17:7, 13, 19; 1Ch 16:15, 17; Ps 105:8, 10; Is 24:5).

111:10 The fear of the LORD. *See note on Pr 1:7.*

PSALM 112

PROSPERITY OF THE ONE WHO FEARS THE LORD.

1 [a]Praise [b]the LORD!
How [A]blessed is the man
who [c]fears the LORD,
Who greatly [B]delights in His
commandments.
2 His [a,A]descendants will be mighty [b]on earth;
The generation of the [B]upright
will be blessed.
3 [A]Wealth and riches are in his house,
And his righteousness endures forever.
4 Light arises in the darkness
[A]for the upright;
He is [B]gracious and compassionate
and righteous.
5 It is well with the man who [A]is
gracious and lends;
He will [a]maintain his cause in judgment.
6 For he will [A]never be shaken;
The [B]righteous will be [a]remembered forever.

7 He will not fear [A]evil tidings;
His [B]heart is steadfast,
[C]trusting in the LORD.
8 His [A]heart is upheld, he [B]will not fear,
Until he [C]looks *with satisfaction*
on his adversaries.
9 [a]He [A]has given freely to the poor,
His righteousness endures forever;
His [B]horn will be exalted in honor.

10 The [A]wicked will see it and be [a]vexed,
He will [B]gnash his teeth and [C]melt away;
The [D]desire of the wicked will perish.

PSALM 113

THE LORD EXALTS THE HUMBLE.

1 [a]Praise [b]the LORD!
[A]Praise, O [B]servants of the LORD,
Praise the name of the LORD.
2 [A]Blessed be the name of the LORD
From this time forth and forever.
3 [A]From the rising of the
sun to its setting
The [B]name of the LORD is
to be praised.
4 The LORD is [A]high above all nations;
His [B]glory is above the heavens.

5 [A]Who is like the LORD our God,
Who [B]is enthroned on high,
6 Who [a,A]humbles Himself to behold
The things that are in heaven
and in the earth?
7 He [A]raises the poor from the dust
And lifts the needy from the ash heap,
8 To make *them* [A]sit with [a]princes,
With the [a]princes of His people.
9 He [A]makes the barren woman
abide in the house
As a joyful mother of children.
[a]Praise [b]the LORD!

PSALM 114

GOD'S DELIVERANCE OF ISRAEL FROM EGYPT.

1 When Israel went forth [A]from Egypt,
The house of Jacob from a people
of [B]strange language,

112:1 [a]Or *Hallelujah! Blessed* [b]Heb *YAH* [c]Or *reveres* [A]Ps 128:1 [B]Ps 1:2; 119:14, 16 112:2 [a]Lit *seed* [b]Or *in the land* [A]Ps 102:28; 127:4 [B]Ps 128:4 112:3 [A]Prov 3:16; 8:18; Matt 6:33 112:4 [A]Job 11:17; Ps 97:11 [B]Ps 37:26 112:5 [a]Or *conduct his affairs with justice* [A]Ps 37:21 112:6 [a]Lit *for an eternal remembrance* [A]Ps 15:5; 55:22 [B]Prov 10:7 112:7 [A]Prov 1:33 [B]Ps 57:7; 108:1 [C]Ps 56:4 112:8 [A]Heb 13:9 [B]Ps 27:1; 56:11; Prov 1:33; 3:24; Is 12:2 [C]Ps 54:7; 59:10 112:9 [a]Lit *He has scattered, he has given to…* [A]2 Cor 9:9 [B]Ps 75:10; 89:17; 92:10; 148:14 112:10 [a]Or *angry* [A]Ps 86:17 [B]Ps 35:16; 37:12; Matt 8:12; 25:30; Luke 13:28 [C]Ps 58:7 [D]Job 8:13; Prov 10:28; 11:7 113:1 [a]Or *Hallelujah! Praise* [b]Heb *YAH* [A]Ps 135:1 [B]Ps 34:22; 69:36; 79:10; 90:13 113:2 [A]Ps 145:21; Dan 2:20 113:3 [A]Ps 50:1; Is 59:19; Mal 1:11 [B]Ps 18:3; 48:1, 10 113:4 [A]Ps 97:9; 99:2 [B]Ps 8:1; 57:11; 148:13 113:5 [A]Ex 15:11; Ps 35:10; 89:6 [B]Ps 103:19 113:6 [a]Or *looks far below in the heavens and on the earth?* [A]Ps 11:4; 138:6; Is 57:15 113:7 [A]1 Sam 2:8; Ps 107:41 113:8 [a]Or *nobles* [A]Job 36:7 113:9 [a]Or *Hallelujah!* [b]Heb *YAH* [A]1 Sam 2:5; Ps 68:6; Is 54:1 114:1 [A]Ex 12:51; 13:3 [B]Ps 81:5

112:1–10 *See note on Ps 111:1–10.*

I. The Blessing of Obedience (112:1–9)
II. The Emptiness of Sin (112:10)

112:1 who fears the LORD. This psalm begins where 111:10 ended and links the two together.

112:2–9 The desire of every human for prosperity can only come through obedience to the commands of God (cf. Ps 1:1–3).

112:9 His horn. Horns on an animal were an indication of strength and prosperity. This is applied figuratively to the righteous.

112:10 In utter contrast to the righteous man of vv. 2–9, the wicked man lives a worthless existence without strength (cf. Ps 1:4–6).

113:1–9 Psalms 113–118 comprise a rich 6-psalm praise to God commonly called the "Egyptian Hallel" ("hallel" meaning praise in Heb.). These were sung at Passover, Pentecost, and Tabernacles, but had the greatest significance at Passover, which celebrated the Jews' deliverance from Egypt (cf. Ex 12–14). Traditionally, Pss 113, 114 were sung before the Passover meal and Pss 115–118 afterwards. Psalm 118 would most likely be what Christ and the disciples sang before they left the Upper Room the night Christ was betrayed (cf. Mt 26:30; Mk 14:26). There are two other notable sets of praise in the Psalter: 1) The Great Hallel (Pss 120–136) and 2) The Final Hallel (Pss 145–150).

I. The Call to Praise (113:1–3)
II. The Cause for Praise (113:4–9)
  A. God's Transcendence (113:4, 5)
  B. God's Immanence (113:6–9)

113:1 servants. Refers to the redeemed, all of whom should serve God with obedience. **the name.** The name of God represents all His attributes.

113:2 this time … forever. Praise is to be rendered always (cf. Eph 5:20; 1Th 5:18).

113:3 rising … setting. From the first moment of consciousness in the morning to the last waking moment before sleep.

113:4, 5 Believers are to praise the only One worthy of praise for His transcendent sovereignty.

113:6–9 humbles. In appearance, God must figuratively lean over from the faraway heavens to examine the earth (cf. Is 40:12–17). In a far greater way Christ humbled Himself in the incarnation (cf. Php 2:5–11).

113:7, 8 the poor. This is borrowed almost exactly from Hannah's song in 1Sa 2:8. God is responsible for both the rich and the poor (Pr 22:2). God's compassion reaches out to the poor and needy (cf. Ps 72:12, 13). Ultimately, Christ came to save those who are poor in spirit (cf. Is 61:2; Lk 4:18).

113:9 the barren woman. Sarah (Ge 21:2), Rebekah (Ge 25:21), and Rachel (Ge 30:23) would be the most significant since the outcome of the Abrahamic Covenant depended on these childless women being blessed by God to be mothers.

114:1–8 *See note on Ps 113:1–9.* This psalm is the one most explicitly related to the Exodus (Ex 12–14). It recounts God's response to a captive nation (Israel in Egypt) in order to honor His promises in the Abrahamic Covenant (Ge 28:13–17) given to Jacob (cf. 114:1, "The house of Jacob"; 114:7, "the God of Jacob").

I. God Inhabits Israel (114:1, 2)
II. God Intimidates Nature (114:3–6)
III. God Invites Trembling (114:7, 8)

2 Judah became [A]His sanctuary,
Israel, [B]His dominion.

3 The [A]sea looked and fled;
The [B]Jordan turned back.
4 The mountains [A]skipped like rams,
The hills, like lambs.
5 What [A]ails you, O sea, that you flee?
O Jordan, that you turn back?
6 O mountains, that you skip like rams?
O hills, like lambs?

7 [A]Tremble, O earth, before the Lord,
Before the God of Jacob,
8 Who [A]turned the rock into a [B]pool of water,
The [C]flint into a fountain of water.

PSALM 115

HEATHEN IDOLS CONTRASTED WITH THE LORD.

1 [A]Not to us, O LORD, not to us,
But [B]to Your name give glory
Because of Your lovingkindness,
because of Your [a]truth.
2 [A]Why should the nations say,
"[B]Where, now, is their God?"
3 But our [A]God is in the heavens;
He [B]does whatever He pleases.
4 Their [A]idols are silver and gold,
The [B]work of man's hands.
5 They have mouths, but they [A]cannot speak;
They have eyes, but they cannot see;
6 They have ears, but they cannot hear;
They have noses, but they cannot smell;
7 [a]They have hands, but they cannot feel;
[b]They have feet, but they cannot walk;
They cannot make a sound
with their throat.
8 [A]Those who make them [a]will
become like them,
Everyone who trusts in them.

9 O [A]Israel, [B]trust in the LORD;
He is their [C]help and their shield.
10 O house of [A]Aaron, trust in the LORD;
He is their help and their shield.
11 You who [a,A]fear the LORD,
trust in the LORD;
He is their help and their shield.
12 The LORD [A]has been mindful
of us; He will bless *us;*
He will bless the house of Israel;
He will bless the house of Aaron.
13 He will [A]bless those who
[a]fear the LORD,
[B]The small together with the great.
14 May the LORD [A]give you increase,
You and your children.
15 May you be blessed of the LORD,
[A]Maker of heaven and earth.

16 The heavens are [A]the heavens
of the LORD,
But [B]the earth He has given
to the sons of men.
17 The [A]dead do not praise [a]the LORD,
Nor *do* any who go down into [B]silence;
18 But as for us, we will [A]bless [a]the LORD
From this time forth and forever.
[b]Praise [a]the LORD!

PSALM 116

THANKSGIVING FOR DELIVERANCE FROM DEATH.

1 [A]I love the LORD, because He [B]hears
My voice *and* my supplications.

114:2 [A]Ex 15:17; 29:45, 46; Ps 78:68, 69 [B]Ex 19:6 114:3 [A]Ex 14:21; Ps 77:16 [B]Josh 3:13, 16 114:4 [A]Ex 19:18; Judg 5:5; Ps 18:7; 29:6; Hab 3:6 114:5 [A]Hab 3:8 114:7 [A]Ps 96:9 114:8 [A]Ex 17:6; Num 20:11; Ps 78:15; 105:41 [B]Ps 107:35 [C]Deut 8:15 115:1 [a]Or *faithfulness* [A]Is 48:11; Ezek 36:22 [B]Ps 29:2; 96:8 115:2 [A]Ps 79:10 [B]Ps 42:3, 10 115:3 [A]Ps 103:19 [B]Ps 135:6; Dan 4:35 115:4 [A]Ps 115:4-8; 135:15-18; Jer 10:4 [B]Deut 4:28; 2 Kin 19:18; Is 37:19; 44:10, 20; Jer 10:3 115:5 [A]Jer 10:5 115:7 [a]Lit *Their hands* [b]Lit *Their feet* 115:8 [a]Or *are like them* [A]Ps 135:18; Is 44:9-11 115:9 [A]Ps 118:2; 135:19 [B]Ps 37:3; 62:8 [C]Ps 33:20 115:10 [A]Ps 118:3; 135:19 115:11 [a]Or *revere* [A]Ps 22:23; 103:11; 135:20 115:12 [A]Ps 98:3 115:13 [a]Or *revere* [A]Ps 103:11; 112:1; 128:1 [B]Rev 11:18; 19:5 115:14 [A]Deut 1:11 115:15 [A]Gen 1:1; Neh 9:6; Ps 96:5; 102:25; 121:2; 124:8; 134:3; 146:6; Acts 14:15; Rev 14:7 115:16 [A]Ps 89:11 [B]Ps 8:6 115:17 [a]Heb *YAH* [A]Ps 6:5; 88:10-12; Is 38:18 [B]Ps 31:17 115:18 [a]Heb *YAH* [b]Or *Hallelujah!* [A]Ps 113:2; Dan 2:20 116:1 [A]Ps 18:1 [B]Ps 6:8; 66:19; Is 37:17; Dan 9:18

114:2 Judah … Israel. Judah/Benjamin and the northern ten tribes respectively. **sanctuary … dominion.** God dwelt among the peoples as a pillar of cloud by day and a pillar of fire by night (cf. Ex 13:21, 22; 14:19).

114:3 The sea … Jordan. Two miracles of God, i.e., separating the waters began and ended the Exodus. On the way out of Egypt, God parted the Red Sea (Ex 14:15–31) and 40 years later He parted the Jordan River in order for the Jews to enter the Promised Land (Jos 3:1–17).

114:4 mountains … hills. Refers to the violent appearance of God to Israel at Sinai (cf. Ex 19:18; Jdg 5:4, 5; Ps 68:17, 18).

114:5, 6 In poetic imagery, God questioned why the most fixed of geographical features, i.e., water and mountains, could not resist His power and will.

114:7 Tremble. The only proper response of helpless nature before omnipotent God.

114:8 the rock. Refers to the first incident at Massah/Meribah (Ex 17:5, 6) and/or the second (Nu 20:8–11).

115:1–18 *See note on Ps 113:1–9.* This praise psalm appears to be antiphonal in nature, following this outline and pattern: 1) the people (vv. 1–8); 2) the priests (vv. 9–11); 3) the people (vv. 12, 13); 4) the priests (vv. 14, 15); and 5) the people (vv. 16–18). Verses 4–11 are very similar to Ps 135:15–20. It has been suggested that this psalm is post-Exilic (cf. v. 2) and could have first been sung at the dedication of the second temple (cf. Ezr 6:16).

115:1 to Your name give glory. God declared He would share His glory with no one (Is 42:8; 48:11).

115:2 Where … is their God? (cf. Pss 42:3, 10; 79:10; Joel 2:17; Mic 7:10). The Jews despised this Gentile taunt.

115:3 Israel's God is alive and rules the earth from His throne room above.

115:4–8 In contrast, Gentiles worship dead gods of their own making, fashioned in the image of the fallen creature (cf. Is 44:9–20; 46:5–7; Jer 10:3–16; Ro 1:21–25). The idol worshiper becomes like the idol—spiritually useless.

115:9–11 This 3-verse, priestly admonition (cf. 118:2–4; 135:19, 20) could apply to 3 different groups: 1) the nation Israel (115:9); 2) the Levitical priests from the house of Aaron (115:10); and 3) proselytes to Judaism who are God fearers (115:11). To all 3 groups, God is their help and shield.

115:16 the earth. Strong implications that planet earth alone is the dwelling place of life.

116:1–19 *See note on Ps 113:1–9.* This is an intensely personal "thank you" psalm to the Lord for saving the psalmist from death

2 Because He has [A]inclined His ear to me,
Therefore I shall call *upon*
Him as long as I live.
3 The [A]cords of death encompassed me
And the [a]terrors of [b]Sheol [c]came upon me;
I found distress and sorrow.
4 Then [A]I called upon the name of the LORD:
"O LORD, I beseech You, [a,B]save my life!"

5 [A]Gracious is the LORD, and [B]righteous;
Yes, our God is [C]compassionate.
6 The LORD preserves [A]the simple;
I was [B]brought low, and He saved me.
7 Return to your [A]rest, O my soul,
For the LORD has [B]dealt
bountifully with you.
8 For You have [A]rescued my
soul from death,
My eyes from tears,
My feet from stumbling.
9 I shall walk before the LORD
In the [a,A]land of the living.
10 I [A]believed when I said,
"I am [B]greatly afflicted."
11 I [A]said in my alarm,
"[B]All men are liars."

12 What shall I [A]render to the LORD
For all His [B]benefits [a]toward me?
13 I shall lift up the [A]cup of salvation
And [B]call upon the name of the LORD.
14 I shall [A]pay my vows to the LORD,
Oh *may it be* [B]in the presence
of all His people.
15 [A]Precious in the sight of the LORD
Is the death of His godly ones.
16 O LORD, [a]surely I am [A]Your servant,
I am Your servant, the [B]son
of Your handmaid,
You have [C]loosed my bonds.
17 To You I shall offer [A]a sacrifice
of thanksgiving,
And [B]call upon the name
of the LORD.
18 I shall [A]pay my vows to the LORD,
Oh *may it be* in the presence
of all His people,
19 In the [A]courts of the LORD'S house,
In the midst of you, O [B]Jerusalem.
[a]Praise [b]the LORD!

PSALM 117

A PSALM OF PRAISE.

1 [A]Praise the LORD, all nations;
Laud Him, all peoples!
2 For His [A]lovingkindness [a]is
great toward us,
And the [b,B]truth of the
LORD is everlasting.
[c]Praise [d]the LORD!

116:2 [A]Ps 17:6; 31:2; 40:1 116:3 [a]Lit *straits* [b]I.e. the nether world [c]Lit *found me* [A]Ps 18:4, 5 116:4 [a]Or *deliver my soul* [A]Ps 18:6; 118:5 [B]Ps 17:13; 22:20 116:5 [A]Ps 86:15; 103:8 [B]Ezra 9:15; Neh 9:8; Ps 119:137; 145:17; Jer 12:1; Dan 9:14 [C]Ex 34:6 116:6 [A]Ps 19:7; Prov 1:4 [B]Ps 79:8; 142:6 116:7 [A]Jer 6:16; Matt 11:29 [B]Ps 13:6; 142:7 116:8 [A]Ps 49:15; 56:13; 86:13 116:9 [a]Lit *lands* [A]Ps 27:13 116:10 [A]2 Cor 4:13 [B]Ps 88:7 116:11 [A]Ps 31:22 [B]Ps 62:9; Rom 3:4 116:12 [a]Lit *upon* [A]2 Chr 32:25; 1 Thess 3:9 [B]Ps 103:2 116:13 [A]Ps 16:5 [B]Ps 80:18; 105:1 116:14 [A]Ps 50:14; 116:18 [B]Ps 22:25 116:15 [A]Ps 72:14 116:16 [a]Or *because* [A]Ps 86:16; 119:125; 143:12 [B]Ps 86:16 [C]Ps 107:14 116:17 [A]Lev 7:12; Ps 50:14 [B]Ps 116:13 116:18 [A]Ps 116:14 116:19 [a]Or *Hallelujah!* [b]Heb *YAH* [A]Ps 92:13; 96:8; 135:2 [B]Ps 102:21 117:1 [A]Rom 15:11 117:2 [a]Lit *prevails over us* [b]Or *faithfulness* [c]Or *Hallelujah!* [d]Heb *YAH* [A]Ps 103:11 [B]Ps 100:5; 146:6

(116:3, 8). The occasion and author remain unknown, although the language used by Jonah in his prayer from the fish's stomach is remarkably similar. While this appears to deal with physical death, the same song could be sung by those who have been saved from spiritual death.

I. The Lord's Response to the Psalmist's Prayer for Deliverance from Death (116:1–11)
II. The Psalmist's Reaction to God's Deliverance of Him from Death (116:12–19)

116:3 **Sheol.** Another term for grave/death.

116:9 **I shall walk.** A vow of obedience.

116:10 **I believed.** Faith in God and His ability to deliver preceded the psalmist's prayer for deliverance. This verse is quoted by the apostle Paul in 2Co 4:13. It rehearses the principle of walking by faith, not by sight.

116:11 **All men are liars.** Either the psalmist is reacting to his false accusers or to men who say that they can deliver him but have not.

116:12 **What shall I render.** God needs nothing and puts no price on His free mercy and grace. The psalmist renders the only acceptable gift—obedience and thanksgiving.

116:13 **the cup of salvation.** This is the only place in the OT where this exact phrase is used. It probably has the meaning of the cup in Pss 16:5; 23:5; i.e., the redeemed life circumstances provided by God, in contrast to Ps 75:8, which speaks about the cup of God's wrath.

116:14 **I shall pay my vows.** Most likely this refers to the vows made during the time of duress (cf. 116:18, 19).

116:15, 16 The psalmist realized what a special blessing his deliverance ("loosed my bonds") was in light of v. 15. Therefore, he reemphasized his role as a servant of God following the example of his mother.

116:17–19 These verses parallel vv. 13, 14. Jonah made an almost identical statement (Jon 2:9).

116:17 **a sacrifice of thanksgiving.** Probably not a Mosaic sacrifice, but rather actual praise and thanksgiving rendered from the heart in the spirit of Pss 136 and 138 (cf. Pss 50:23; 100:4; 119:108).

116:19 **the LORD's house.** Refers to 1) the tabernacle in Jerusalem if written by David or before, or 2) the temple in Jerusalem if written by Solomon or later.

117:1, 2 *See note on Ps 113:1–9.* The seal of redemptive truth is bound up in this diminutive but seminal psalm—its profundity far outdistances its size. This pivotal psalm exhibits 3 distinguishing features: 1) it is the shortest psalm; 2) it is the shortest chapter in the Bible; and 3) it is the middle chapter of the Bible. That God looked redemptively beyond the borders of Israel in the OT is made clear here. The psalm looks back to God's intent for Adam and Eve in Eden (Ge 1, 2) and looks ahead to the ultimate fulfillment in the new heavens and earth (Rev 21, 22).

I. A Global Invitation (117:1)
II. A Grand Explanation (117:2)

117:1 **nations … peoples!** Paul quoted this verse in Ro 15:11 to make the point that from the very beginning of time God has pursued a worldwide redemptive purpose (cf. Ro 15:7–13). Other passages quoted by Paul in Ro 15 to make this point include: Dt 32:43, 2Sa 22:50, and Is 11:10. While not as obvious in the OT, the NT makes this point unmistakably clear (cf. Ac. 10:34, 35; Ro 1:16; 1Co 12:13; Gal 3:1–29, esp. 28; Col 3:11).

117:2 The reasons for such exalted praise as that commanded in v. 1 are: 1) because of God's redemptive kindness, and 2) because of God's eternal truth. Therefore, what God has promised, He will provide (cf. Jn 6:37–40).

PSALM 118

THANKSGIVING FOR THE LORD'S SAVING GOODNESS.

1 [A]Give thanks to the LORD, for [B]He is good;
For His lovingkindness is everlasting.
2 Oh let [A]Israel say,
"His lovingkindness is everlasting."
3 Oh let the [A]house of Aaron say,
"His lovingkindness is everlasting."
4 Oh let those [A]who [a]fear the LORD say,
"His lovingkindness is everlasting."

5 From *my* [A]distress I called upon [a]the LORD;
[a]The LORD answered me *and*
[B]*set me* in a large place.
6 The LORD is [A]for me; I will [B]not fear;
[C]What can man do to me?
7 The LORD is for me [A]among
those who help me;
Therefore I will [B]look *with satisfaction*
on those who hate me.
8 It is [A]better to take refuge in the LORD
Than to trust in man.
9 It is [A]better to take refuge in the LORD
Than to trust in princes.

10 All nations [A]surrounded me;
In the name of the LORD I will
surely [B]cut them off.
11 They [A]surrounded me, yes,
they surrounded me;
In the name of the LORD I will
surely cut them off.
12 They surrounded me [A]like bees;
They were extinguished as
a [B]fire of thorns;
In the name of the LORD I will
surely cut them off.
13 You [A]pushed me violently so
that I [a]was falling,
But the LORD [B]helped me.
14 [a,A]The LORD is my strength and song,
And He has become [B]my salvation.

15 The sound of [A]joyful shouting
and salvation is in the tents
of the righteous;
The [B]right hand of the LORD
does valiantly.
16 The [A]right hand of the LORD is exalted;
The right hand of the LORD does valiantly.
17 I [A]will not die, but live,
And [B]tell of the works of [a]the LORD.
18 [a]The LORD has [A]disciplined me severely,
But He has [B]not given me over to death.

19 [A]Open to me the gates of righteousness;
I shall enter through them, I shall
give thanks to [a]the LORD.
20 This is the gate of the LORD;
The [A]righteous will enter through it.
21 I shall give thanks to You, for
You have [A]answered me,
And You have [B]become my salvation.

22 The [A]stone which the builders rejected
Has become the chief corner *stone*.

118:1 [A]1 Chr 16:8, 34; Ps 106:1; 107:1; Jer 33:11 [B]2 Chr 5:13; 7:3; Ezra 3:11; Ps 100:5; 136:1-26 118:2 [A]Ps 115:9 118:3 [A]Ps 115:10 118:4 [a]Or *revere* [A]Ps 115:11 118:5 [a]Heb *YAH* [A]Ps 18:6; 86:7; 120:1 [B]Ps 18:19 118:6 [A]Job 19:27; Ps 56:9; Heb 13:6 [B]Ps 23:4; 27:1 [C]Ps 56:4, 11 118:7 [A]Ps 54:4 [B]Ps 54:7; 59:10 118:8 [A]2 Chr 32:7, 8; Ps 40:4; 108:12; Is 31:1, 3; 57:13; Jer 17:5 118:9 [A]Ps 146:3 118:10 [A]Ps 3:6; 88:17 [B]Ps 18:40 118:11 [A]Ps 88:17 118:12 [A]Deut 1:44 [B]Ps 58:9; Nah 1:10 118:13 [a]Or *fell* [A]Ps 140:4 [B]Ps 86:17 118:14 [a]Heb *YAH* [A]Ex 15:2; Is 12:2 [B]Ps 27:1 118:15 [A]Ps 68:3 [B]Ex 15:6; Ps 89:13; Luke 1:51 118:16 [A]Ex 15:6; Ps 89:13 118:17 [a]Heb *YAH* [A]Ps 6:5; 116:8, 9; Hab 1:12 [B]Ps 73:28; 107:22 118:18 [a]Heb *YAH* [A]Ps 73:14; Jer 31:18; 1 Cor 11:32; 2 Cor 6:9 [B]Ps 86:13 118:19 [a]Heb *YAH* [A]Is 26:2 118:20 [A]Ps 15:1, 2; 24:3-6; 140:13; Is 35:8; Rev 22:14 118:21 [A]Ps 116:1; 118:5 [B]Ps 118:14 118:22 [A]Matt 21:42; Mark 12:10, 11; Luke 20:17; Acts 4:11; Eph 2:20; 1 Pet 2:7

118:1–29 *See note on Ps 113:1–9.* This psalm, along with Ps 110, is intensely messianic and thus the most quoted by the NT (Mt 21:9, 42; 23:39; Mk 11:9, 10; 12:10, 11; Lk 13:35; 19:38; 20:17; Jn 12:13; Ac 4:11; Heb 13:6; 1Pe 2:7). Neither the author nor the specific circumstances of the psalm are identified. Two reasonable possibilities could be entertained: 1) it was written during Moses' day in the Exodus, or 2) it was written sometime after the Jews returned to Jerusalem from Exile. Probably it was the former, given 1) the nature of the Egyptian Hallel (esp. Ps 114); 2) its use by the Jewish community especially at Passover; 3) the close similarity to Moses' experience in the Exodus; 4) the striking similarity in language (Ps 118:14 with Ex 15:2; 118:15, 16 with Ex 15:6, 12; 118:28 with Ex 15:2); and 5) the particularly pointed messianic significance as it relates to the redemption provided by Christ our Passover (1Co 5:7). It seems reasonable to propose that Moses possibly wrote this beautiful psalm to look back in worship at the historical Passover and look ahead in wonder to the spiritual Passover in Christ.

I. Call to Worship (118:1–4)
II. Personal Praise (118:5–21)
III. Corporate Praise (118:22–24)
IV. Commitment to Worship (118:25–29)

118:1 Give thanks. Cf. Pss 105–107, 136. The psalm ends in v. 29 as it began here.

118:2–4 Israel ... Aaron ... those who fear the LORD. *See note on Ps 115:9–11.* The phrase "His lovingkindness is everlasting" is repeated in all 26 verses of Ps 136 (cf. 118:1, 29).

118:5–21 This section contains individual praise by the psalmist, possibly Moses.

118:5–9 The psalmist focuses intensely on the Lord.

118:6 Hebrews 13:6 quotes this verse; cf. Ps 56:4, 11.

118:10–14 It seems obvious that the leader of the nation is speaking here.

118:12 a fire of thorns. Dried thorns burn easily and quickly.

118:13 You pushed me. Refers to the psalmist's enemy.

118:14 These words are identical to Moses' words in Ex 15:2.

118:15–18 A declaration of victory.

118:15, 16 The right hand. Very similar to Moses' words in Ex 15:6, 12.

118:18 This possibly refers to the incident at Meribah where Moses struck the rock (cf. Nu 20:8–13).

118:19–21 The victory against overwhelming odds elicits from the psalmist a great desire to praise God.

118:19 gates of righteousness. Most likely a figurative reference, i.e., spiritual gates through which the righteous pass (cf. Ps 100:4), rather than to the gates of the temple, e.g., 1Ch 9:23.

118:20 the gate. This points to the entryway which leads to the presence of the Lord. Jesus may have had this psalm in mind when He taught about "the narrow gate" in Mt 7:13, 14.

118:21 my salvation. The Lord has delivered the psalmist from otherwise certain defeat and death (cf. 118:14, 15).

118:22–26 The NT quotes of vv. 22, 23 and vv. 25, 26 lend strong messianic significance here. If Moses is the author, then the NT writers use a perfect analogy in connecting this passage to Christ. For example, Moses said that God would raise up another prophet like himself (Dt 18:15). Peter identified this other prophet as the Lord Jesus Christ (cf. Ac 3:11–26). So Moses is a legitimate, biblically recognized type of Christ.

118:22 stone ... builders rejected ... chief corner *stone*. Peter identified the chief cornerstone in the NT as Christ (Ac 4:11; 1Pe 2:7). In the parable of the vineyard (Mt 21:42; Mk 12:10–11; Lk 20:17), the rejected son of the vineyard owner is likened to the rejected stone which

23 This is [a]the LORD'S doing;
It is marvelous in our eyes.
24 This is the day which the LORD has made;
Let us [A]rejoice and be glad in it.
25 O LORD, [A]do save, we beseech You;
O LORD, we beseech You, do
send [B]prosperity!
26 [A]Blessed is the one who comes
in the name of the LORD;
We have [B]blessed you from
the house of the LORD.
27 [A]The LORD is God, and He
has given us [B]light;
Bind the festival sacrifice with cords
[a]to the [C]horns of the altar.
28 [A]You are my God, and I give
thanks to You;
You are my God, [B]I extol You.
29 [A]Give thanks to the LORD, for He is good;
For His lovingkindness is everlasting.

PSALM 119

MEDITATIONS AND PRAYERS RELATING TO THE LAW OF GOD.

א ALEPH.
1 How blessed are those whose
way is [a,A]blameless,
Who [B]walk in the law of the LORD.
2 How blessed are those who
[A]observe His testimonies,
Who [B]seek Him [C]with all *their* heart.
3 They also [A]do no unrighteousness;
They walk in His ways.
4 You have [a,A]ordained Your precepts,
[b]That we should keep *them* diligently.
5 Oh that my [A]ways may be established
To [B]keep Your statutes!
6 Then I [A]shall not be ashamed
When I look [a]upon all Your
commandments.
7 I shall [A]give thanks to You with
uprightness of heart,
When I learn Your righteous judgments.
8 I shall keep Your statutes;
Do not [A]forsake me utterly!

ב BETH.
9 How can a young man keep his way pure?
By [A]keeping *it* according to Your word.
10 With [A]all my heart I have sought You;
Do not let me [B]wander from
Your commandments.
11 Your word I have [A]treasured in my heart,
That I may not sin against You.
12 Blessed are You, O LORD;
[A]Teach me Your statutes.
13 With my lips I have [A]told of
All the [B]ordinances of Your mouth.

118:23 [a]Lit *from the LORD* 118:24 [A]Ps 31:7 118:25 [A]Ps 106:47 [B]Ps 122:6, 7 118:26 [A]Matt 21:9; 23:39; Mark 11:9; Luke 13:35; 19:38; John 12:13 [B]Ps 129:8 118:27 [a]Lit *unto* [A]1 Kin 18:39 [B]Esth 8:16; Ps 18:28; 27:1; 1 Pet 2:9 [C]Ex 27:2 118:28 [A]Ps 63:1; 140:6 [B]Ex 15:2; Is 25:1 118:29 [A]Ps 118:1 119:1 [a]Lit *complete;* or *having integrity* [A]Ps 101:2, 6; Prov 11:20; 13:6 [B]Ps 128:1; Ezek 11:20; 18:17; Mic 4:2 119:2 [A]Ps 25:10; 99:7; 119:22, 168 [B]Deut 4:29; Ps 119:10 [C]Deut 6:5; 10:12; 11:13; 13:3; 30:2 119:3 [A]1 John 3:9; 5:18 119:4 [a]Lit *commanded* [b]Lit *To keep* [A]Deut 4:13; Neh 9:13 119:5 [A]Ps 40:2; Prov 4:26 [B]Deut 12:1; 2 Chr 7:17 119:6 [a]Lit *to* [A]Job 22:26; Ps 119:80 119:7 [A]Ps 119:62 119:8 [A]Ps 38:21; 71:9, 18 119:9 [A]1 Kin 2:4; 8:25; 2 Chr 6:16 119:10 [A]2 Chr 15:15; Ps 119:2, 145 [B]Ps 119:21, 118 119:11 [A]Ps 37:31; 40:8; Luke 2:19, 51 119:12 [A]Ps 119:26, 64, 108, 124, 135, 171 119:13 [A]Ps 40:9 [B]Ps 119:72

became the chief cornerstone. Christ was that rejected stone. Jewish leaders were pictured as builders of the nation. Now, this passage in v. 22 has a historical basis which is paralleled in its major features by analogy with the rejection of Christ who came to deliver/save the nation. Moses' experience, as a type of Christ, pictured Christ's rejection. On at least 3 occasions Moses ("stone") was rejected by the Jews ("builders") as their God sent the deliverer ("chief corner *stone*"). For examples see Ex 2:11–15, cf. Ac 7:35; Ex 14:10–14, 10; 16:1–3, 11, 12, 20.

118:24 the day. Probably refers to 1) the day of deliverance and/ or 2) the day the stone was made the chief cornerstone, which they now celebrate.

118:25 LORD, do save, we beseech. Transliterated from Heb., this becomes "Hosanna." These words were shouted by the crowd to Christ at the time of His triumphal entry to Jerusalem (Mt 21:9; Mk 11:9, 10; Jn 12:13). Days later they rejected Him because He did not provide military/political deliverance.

118:26 Blessed. Christ taught that the nation of Israel would not see Him again after His departure (ascension to heaven) until they could genuinely offer these words to Him at His second coming (cf. Mt 23:39; Lk 13:35). In this historical text, it could have easily been sung by the Jews of Moses' day, especially at the end of the 40 years but prior to Moses' death (cf. Dt 1–33). **the house of the LORD.** A phrase used in reference to the tabernacle of Moses (cf. Ex 23:19; 34:26; Dt 23:18) and later the temple (cf. 1Ki 6:1).

118:27 light. Similar to the Mosaic benediction of Nu 6:25. **the altar.** The altar of burnt offerings, which stood on the E in the court outside of the Holy Place (cf. Ex 27:1–8; 38:1–7).

118:28 This bears a striking resemblance to Ex 15:2.

118:29 A repetition of 118:1.

119:1–176 This longest of psalms and chapters in the Bible stands as the "Mt. Everest" of the Psalter. It joins Pss 1 and 19 in exalting God's Word. The author is unknown for certain, although David, Daniel, or Ezra have reasonably been suggested. The psalmist apparently wrote while under some sort of serious duress (cf. vv. 23, 42, 51, 61, 67, 71, 78, 86–87, 95, 110, 121, 134, 139, 143, 146, 153, 154, 157, 161, 169). This is an acrostic psalm (cf. Pss 9, 10, 25, 34, 37, 111, 112, 145) composed of 22 sections, each containing 8 lines. All 8 lines of the first section start with the first letter of the Heb. alphabet; thus the psalm continues until all 22 letters have been used in order. The 8 different terms referring to Scripture occurring throughout the psalm are: 1) law, 2) testimonies, 3) precepts, 4) statutes, 5) commandments, 6) judgments, 7) word, and 8) ordinances. From before sunrise to beyond sunset, the Word of God dominated the psalmist's life, e.g., 1) before dawn (v. 147), 2) daily (v. 97), 3) 7 times daily (v. 164), 4) nightly (vv. 55, 148), and 5) at midnight (v. 62). Other than the acrostic form, Ps 119 does not have an outline. Rather, there are many frequently recurring themes which will be delineated in the notes.

119:1, 2 blessed . . . blessed. Similar to Ps 1:1–3. Elsewhere, the psalmist declares that Scripture is more valuable than money (vv. 14, 72, 127, 162) and brings more pleasure than the sweetness of honey (v. 103; cf. Pr 13:13; 16:20; 19:16).

119:1 walk. A habitual pattern of living.

119:2 all *their* heart. "Heart" refers to intellect, volition, and emotion (cf. vv. 7, 10, 11, 32, 34, 36, 58, 69, 70, 80, 111, 112, 145, 161). Complete commitment or "all my heart" appears 6 times (vv. 2, 10, 34, 58, 69, 145).

119:4 keep . . . diligently. The psalmist passionately desired to obey God's Word (cf. vv. 4, 8, 30–32, 44, 45, 51, 55, 57, 59–61, 63, 67, 68, 74, 83, 87, 101, 102, 106, 110, 112, 129, 141, 157, 167, 168).

119:5, 6 Oh. It is hard at times to distinguish where the psalmist's testimony ends and prayer begins (cf. vv. 29, 36, 58, 133).

119:7 shall give thanks to You. The Scriptures provoke singing, thanksgiving, rejoicing, and praise (cf. vv. 13, 14, 54, 62, 108, 151, 152, 160, 164, 171, 172, 175). **righteous.** God's Word reflects the character of God, especially righteousness (cf. vv. 7, 62, 75, 106, 123, 138, 144, 160, 164, 172).

119:9–11 Internalizing the Word is a believer's best weapon to defend against encroaching sin.

119:12 Teach me. The student/psalmist invites the Divine Author to be his instructor (cf. vv. 26, 33, 64, 66, 68, 108, 124, 135) with the result that the psalmist did not turn aside from the Word (v. 102).

14 I have [A]rejoiced in the way
of Your testimonies,
[a]As much as in all riches.
15 I will [A]meditate on Your precepts
And [a]regard [B]Your ways.
16 I shall [a,A]delight in Your statutes;
I shall [B]not forget Your word.

ג GIMEL.

17 [A]Deal bountifully with Your servant,
That I may live and keep Your word.
18 Open my eyes, that I may behold
Wonderful things from Your law.
19 I am a [A]stranger in the earth;
Do not hide Your commandments from me.
20 My soul is crushed [a,A]with longing
After Your ordinances at all times.
21 You [A]rebuke the arrogant, [a]the [B]cursed,
Who [C]wander from Your commandments.
22 [A]Take away reproach and
contempt from me,
For I [B]observe Your testimonies.
23 Even though [A]princes sit
and talk against me,
Your servant [B]meditates on Your statutes.
24 Your testimonies also are my [A]delight;
They are [a]my counselors.

ד DALETH.

25 My [A]soul cleaves to the dust;
[B]Revive me [C]according to Your word.
26 I have told of my ways, and
You have answered me;
[A]Teach me Your statutes.
27 Make me understand the way
of Your precepts,
So I will [A]meditate on Your wonders.
28 My [A]soul [a]weeps because of grief;
[B]Strengthen me according to Your word.
29 Remove the false way from me,
And graciously grant me Your law.
30 I have chosen the faithful way;
I have [a]placed Your ordinances *before me.*
31 I [A]cling to Your testimonies;
O LORD, do not put me to shame!
32 I shall run the way of Your commandments,
For You will [A]enlarge my heart.

ה HE.

33 [A]Teach me, O LORD, the way of Your statutes,
And I shall observe it to the end.
34 [A]Give me understanding, that I
may [B]observe Your law
And keep it [C]with all *my* heart.
35 Make me walk in the [A]path of
Your commandments,
For I [B]delight in it.
36 [A]Incline my heart to Your testimonies
And not to [B]*dishonest* gain.
37 Turn away my [A]eyes from looking at vanity,
And [B]revive me in Your ways.
38 [A]Establish Your [a]word to Your servant,
[b]As that which produces reverence for You.
39 [A]Turn away my reproach which I dread,
For Your ordinances are good.
40 Behold, I [A]long for Your precepts;
Revive me through Your righteousness.

ו VAV.

41 May Your [A]lovingkindnesses
also come to me, O LORD,
Your salvation [B]according to Your [a]word;
42 So I will have an [A]answer for
him who [B]reproaches me,
For I trust in Your word.
43 And do not take the word of truth
utterly out of my mouth,
For I [a,A]wait for Your ordinances.

119:14 [a]Lit *As over all* [A]Ps 119:111, 162 119:15 [a]Or *look upon* [A]Ps 1:2; 119:23, 48, 78, 97, 148 [B]Ps 25:4; 27:11; Is 58:2 119:16 [a]Lit *delight myself* [A]Ps 1:2; 119:24, 35, 47, 70, 77, 92, 143, 174 [B]Ps 119:93 119:17 [A]Ps 13:6; 116:7 119:19 [A]Gen 47:9; Lev 25:23; 1 Chr 29:15; Ps 39:12; 119:54; Heb 11:13 119:20 [a]Lit *for* [A]Ps 42:1, 2; 63:1; 84:2; 119:40, 131 119:21 [a]Or *Cursed are those who wander...* [A]Ps 68:30 [B]Deut 27:26; Ps 37:22 [C]Ps 119:10, 118 119:22 [A]Ps 39:8; 119:39 [B]Ps 119:2 119:23 [A]Ps 119:161 [B]Ps 119:15 119:24 [a]Lit *the men of my counsel* [A]Ps 119:16 119:25 [A]Ps 44:25 [B]Ps 119:37, 40, 88, 93, 107, 149, 154, 156, 159; 143:11 [C]Ps 119:65 119:26 [A]Ps 25:4; 27:11; 86:11; 119:12 119:27 [A]Ps 105:2; 145:5 119:28 [a]Lit *drops* [A]Ps 22:14; 107:26 [B]Ps 20:2; 1 Pet 5:10 119:30 [a]Or *accounted Your ordinances worthy* 119:31 [A]Deut 11:22 119:32 [A]1 Kin 4:29; Is 60:5; 2 Cor 6:11, 13 119:33 [A]Ps 119:5, 12 119:34 [A]Ps 119:27, 73, 125, 144, 169 [B]1 Chr 22:12; Ezek 44:24 [C]Ps 119:2, 69 119:35 [A]Ps 25:4; Is 40:14 [B]Ps 112:1; 119:16 119:36 [A]1 Kin 8:58 [B]Ezek 33:31; Mark 7:21, 22; Luke 12:15; Heb 13:5 119:37 [A]Is 33:15 [B]Ps 71:20; 119:25 119:38 [a]Or *promise* [b]Lit *Which is for the fear of You* [A]2 Sam 7:25 119:39 [A]Ps 119:22 119:40 [A]Ps 119:20 119:41 [a]Or *promise* [A]Ps 119:77 [B]Ps 119:58, 76, 116, 170 119:42 [A]Prov 27:11 [B]Ps 102:8; 119:39 119:43 [a]Or *hope in* [A]Ps 119:49, 74, 81, 114, 147

119:14 all riches. Cf. vv. 72, 127.

119:15 meditate ... regard. The psalmist reflected frequently on the Scriptures (cf. vv. 23, 27, 48, 78, 97, 99, 148).

119:16 I shall delight. (cf. vv. 24, 35, 47, 70, 77, 92, 143, 174). **I shall not forget.** (cf. vv. 93, 176).

119:18 Open my eyes. Perhaps this is the supreme prayer that a student of Scripture could speak since it confesses the student's inadequacy and the Divine Author's sufficiency (cf. vv. 98, 99, 105, 130).

119:19 a stranger. As a citizen of God's kingdom, the psalmist was a mere sojourner in the kingdom of men.

119:20 crushed with longing. This expresses the psalmist's deep passion for the Word (cf. vv. 40, 131).

119:21 the arrogant, the cursed. The psalmist identified with God's rebuke of those who disobey His Word (cf. vv. 53, 104, 113, 115, 118, 126).

119:24 my counselors. The chief means of biblical counseling is the application of God's Word by God's Spirit to the heart of a believer (cf. vv. 98–100).

119:25 Revive me. Revival is greatly desired by the psalmist, who realizes that God and God's Word alone are sufficient (cf. vv. 37, 40, 50, 88, 93, 107, 149, 154, 156, 159).

119:27 Make me understand. Philip asked the Ethiopian eunuch who was reading Is 53, "Do you understand what you are reading?" (Ac 8:30). The psalmist understood God to be the best source of instruction (cf. vv. 34, 73, 100, 125, 144, 169).

119:28 weeps because of grief. Refers to grief or sorrow over sin.

119:29, 30 the false way ... the faithful way. The psalmist desired to emulate the true character of God in contrast to the lying ways of Satan (cf. v. 163).

119:32 run the way. Reflects the energetic response of the psalmist to God's Word.

119:37 looking at vanity. The psalmist desires to examine the things of greatest value, i.e., God's Word (cf. vv. 14, 72, 127).

119:39 good. The very attributes of God (cf. v. 68) become the characteristics of Scripture: 1) trustworthy (v. 42); 2) true (vv. 43, 142, 151, 160); 3) faithful (v. 86); 4) unchangeable (v. 89); 5) eternal (vv. 90, 152); 6) light (v. 105); and 7) pure (v. 140).

119:41 Your salvation. This reflects a repeated desire (cf. vv. 64, 76, 81, 88, 94, 109, 123, 134, 146, 149, 153, 154, 159, 166).

119:43 wait. The psalmist waits patiently for the working of God's Word (cf. vv. 49, 74, 81, 114, 147).

44 So I will [A]keep Your law continually,
Forever and ever.
45 And I will [A]walk [a]at liberty,
For I [B]seek Your precepts.
46 I will also speak of Your
testimonies [A]before kings
And shall not be ashamed.
47 I shall [a,A]delight in Your
commandments,
Which I [B]love.
48 And I shall lift up my hands to
Your commandments,
Which I [A]love;
And I will [B]meditate on Your statutes.

ז ZAYIN.

49 Remember the word to Your servant,
[a]In which You have made me hope.
50 This is my [A]comfort in my affliction,
That Your word has [a]revived me.
51 The arrogant [A]utterly deride me,
Yet I do not [B]turn aside from Your law.
52 I have [A]remembered Your ordinances
from [a]of old, O LORD,
And comfort myself.
53 Burning [A]indignation has seized
me because of the wicked,
Who [B]forsake Your law.
54 Your statutes are my songs
In the house of my [A]pilgrimage.
55 O LORD, I [A]remember Your
name [B]in the night,
And keep Your law.
56 This has become mine,
[a]That I [A]observe Your precepts.

ח HETH.

57 The LORD is my [A]portion;
I have [a]promised to [B]keep Your words.
58 I [A]sought Your favor [B]with all *my* heart;
[C]Be gracious to me [D]according
to Your [a]word.
59 I [A]considered my ways
And turned my feet to Your testimonies.
60 I hastened and did not delay
To keep Your commandments.
61 The [A]cords of the wicked
have encircled me,
But I have [B]not forgotten Your law.
62 At [A]midnight I shall rise to
give thanks to You
Because of Your [B]righteous ordinances.
63 I am a [A]companion of all
those who [a]fear You,
And of those who keep Your precepts.
64 [A]The earth is full of Your
lovingkindness, O LORD;
[B]Teach me Your statutes.

ט TETH.

65 You have dealt well with Your servant,
O LORD, according to Your word.
66 Teach me good [a,A]discernment
and knowledge,
For I believe in Your commandments.
67 [A]Before I was afflicted I went astray,
But now I keep Your word.
68 You are [A]good and [B]do good;
[C]Teach me Your statutes.
69 The arrogant [a]have [A]forged a lie against me;
With all *my* heart I will
[B]observe Your precepts.
70 Their heart is [a,A]covered with fat,
But I [B]delight in Your law.
71 It is [A]good for me that I was afflicted,
That I may learn Your statutes.
72 The [A]law of Your mouth is better to me
Than thousands of gold and silver *pieces*.

י YODH.

73 [A]Your hands made me and [a]fashioned me;
[B]Give me understanding, that I may
learn Your commandments.
74 May those who [a]fear You
[A]see me and be glad,
Because I [b,B]wait for Your word.
75 I know, O LORD, that Your
judgments are [A]righteous,
And that [B]in faithfulness You
have afflicted me.
76 O may Your lovingkindness [a]comfort me,
According to Your [b]word to Your servant.
77 May [A]Your compassion come
to me that I may live,
For Your law is my [B]delight.
78 May [A]the arrogant be ashamed, for
they subvert me [B]with a lie;
But I shall [C]meditate on Your precepts.

119:44 [A]Ps 119:33 119:45 [a]Lit *in a wide place* [A]Prov 4:12 [B]Ps 119:94, 155 119:46 [A]Matt 10:18; Acts 26:1, 2 119:47 [a]Lit *delight myself* [A]Ps 119:16 [B]Ps 119:97, 127, 159 119:48 [A]Ps 119:97, 127, 159 [B]Ps 119:15 119:49 [a]Lit *On* 119:50 [a]Or *preserved me alive* [A]Job 6:10; Rom 15:4 119:51 [A]Job 30:1; Jer 20:7 [B]Job 23:11; Ps 44:18; 119:157 119:52 [a]Or *everlasting* [A]Ps 103:18 119:53 [A]Ex 32:19; Ezra 9:3; Neh 13:25; Ps 119:158 [B]Ps 89:30 119:54 [A]Gen 47:9; Ps 119:19 119:55 [A]Ps 63:6 [B]Ps 42:8; 92:2; 119:62; Is 26:9; Acts 16:25 119:56 [a]Or *Because* [A]Ps 119:22, 69, 100 119:57 [a]Lit *said that I would keep* [A]Ps 16:5; Lam 3:24 [B]Deut 33:9 119:58 [a]Or *promise* [A]1 Kin 13:6 [B]Ps 119:2 [C]Ps 41:4; 56:1; 57:1 [D]Ps 119:41 119:59 [A]Mark 14:72; Luke 15:17 119:61 [A]Job 36:8; Ps 140:5 [B]Ps 119:83, 141, 153, 176 119:62 [A]Ps 119:55 [B]Ps 119:7 119:63 [a]Or *revere* [A]Ps 101:6 119:64 [A]Ps 33:5 [B]Ps 119:12 119:66 [a]Or *judgment* [A]Phil 1:9 119:67 [A]Ps 119:71, 75; Jer 31:18, 19; Heb 12:5-11 119:68 [A]Ps 86:5; 100:5; 106:1; 107:1; Matt 19:17 [B]Deut 8:16; 28:63; 30:5; Ps 125:4 [C]Ps 119:12 119:69 [a]Lit *besmear me with lies* [A]Job 13:4; Ps 109:2 [B]Ps 119:56 119:70 [a]Lit *gross like fat* [A]Deut 32:15; Job 15:27; Ps 17:10; Is 6:10; Jer 5:28; Acts 28:27 [B]Ps 119:16 119:71 [A]Ps 119:67, 75 119:72 [A]Ps 19:10; 119:127; Prov 8:10, 11, 19 119:73 [a]Lit *established* [A]Job 10:8; 31:15; Ps 100:3; 138:8; 139:15, 16 [B]Ps 119:34 119:74 [a]Or *revere* [b]Or *hope in* [A]Ps 34:2; 35:27; 107:42 [B]Ps 119:43 119:75 [A]Ps 119:138 [B]Heb 12:10 119:76 [a]Lit *be for my comfort* [b]Or *promise* 119:77 [A]Ps 119:41 [B]Ps 119:16 119:78 [A]Jer 50:32 [B]Ps 119:86 [C]Ps 119:15

119:47, 48 **Which I love.** The psalmist expresses his great affection for the Word (cf. vv. 97, 113, 127, 140, 159, 163, 165, 167).

119:50 **comfort.** What the psalmist found in God's Word (cf. vv. 52, 76, 82).

119:68 **You are good.** The psalmist frequently appeals to the character of God: 1) His faithfulness (vv. 75, 90); 2) His compassion (v. 77); 3) His righteousness (vv. 137, 142); and 4) His mercy (v. 156).

119:70 **covered with fat.** Refers to the proud of v. 69 whose hearts are thick and thus the Word is unable to penetrate.

119:73 **Your hands.** Figuratively refers to God's involvement in human life (Ps 139:13–16).

119:75 **You have afflicted me.** The psalmist expresses his confidence in God's sovereignty over human affliction referred to in 119:67, 71 (cf. Dt 32:39; Is 45:7; La 3:37, 38).

79 May those who [a]fear You turn to me,
Even those who know Your testimonies.
80 May my heart be [a,A]blameless
in Your statutes,
So that I will not [B]be ashamed.

כ KAPH.

81 My [A]soul languishes for Your salvation;
I [a,B]wait for Your word.
82 My [A]eyes fail *with longing* for Your [a]word,
[b]While I say, "When will You comfort me?"
83 Though I have [A]become like a
wineskin in the smoke,
I do [B]not forget Your statutes.
84 How many are the [A]days of Your servant?
When will You [B]execute judgment
on those who persecute me?
85 The arrogant have [A]dug pits for me,
Men who are not [a]in accord with Your law.
86 All Your commandments are [A]faithful;
They have [B]persecuted me
with a lie; [C]help me!
87 They almost destroyed me [a]on earth,
But as for me, I [A]did not
forsake Your precepts.
88 Revive me according to Your
lovingkindness,
So that I may keep the testimony
of Your mouth.

ל LAMEDH.

89 [A]Forever, O LORD,
Your word [a]is settled in heaven.
90 Your [A]faithfulness *continues*
[a]throughout all generations;
You [B]established the earth, and it [C]stands.
91 They stand this day according
to Your [A]ordinances,
For [B]all things are Your servants.
92 If Your law had not been my [A]delight,
Then I would have perished
[B]in my affliction.
93 I will [A]never forget Your precepts,
For by them You have [a,B]revived me.
94 I am Yours, [A]save me;
For I have [B]sought Your precepts.
95 The wicked [A]wait for me to destroy me;
I shall diligently consider
Your testimonies.
96 I have seen [a]a limit to all perfection;
Your commandment is exceedingly broad.

מ MEM.

97 O how I [A]love Your law!
It is my [B]meditation all the day.
98 Your [A]commandments make me
wiser than my enemies,
For they are ever [a]mine.
99 I have more insight than all my teachers,
For Your testimonies are my [A]meditation.
100 I understand [A]more than the aged,
Because I have [B]observed Your precepts.
101 I have [A]restrained my feet
from every evil way,
That I may keep Your word.
102 I have not [A]turned aside from
Your ordinances,
For You Yourself have taught me.
103 How [A]sweet are Your [a]words to my [b]taste!
Yes, sweeter than honey to my mouth!
104 From Your precepts I [A]get understanding;
Therefore I [B]hate every false way.

נ NUN.

105 Your word is a [A]lamp to my feet
And a light to my path.
106 I have [A]sworn and I will confirm it,
That I will keep Your righteous ordinances.
107 I am exceedingly [A]afflicted;
[a,B]Revive me, O LORD, according
to Your word.
108 O accept the [A]freewill offerings
of my mouth, O LORD,
And [B]teach me Your ordinances.
109 My [a,A]life is continually [b]in my hand,
Yet I do not [B]forget Your law.
110 The wicked have [A]laid a snare for me,
Yet I have not [B]gone astray
from Your precepts.
111 I have [A]inherited Your testimonies forever,
For they are the [B]joy of my heart.
112 I have [A]inclined my heart to
perform Your statutes
Forever, *even* [B]to the end.

ס SAMEKH.

113 I hate those who are [A]double-minded,
But I love Your [B]law.
114 You are my [A]hiding place and my [B]shield;
I [a,C]wait for Your word.
115 [A]Depart from me, evildoers,
That I may [B]observe the
commandments of my God.

119:79 [a]Or *revere* 119:80 [a]Lit *complete;* or *having integrity* [A]Ps 119:1 [B]Ps 119:46 119:81 [a]Or *hope in* [A]Ps 84:2 [B]Ps 119:43 119:82 [a]Or *promise* [b]Lit *Saying* [A]Ps 69:3; 119:123; Is 38:14; Lam 2:11 119:83 [A]Job 30:30 [B]Ps 119:61 119:84 [A]Ps 39:4 [B]Rev 6:10 119:85 [a]Lit *according to Your law* [A]Ps 7:15; 35:7; 57:6; Jer 18:22 119:86 [A]Ps 119:138 [B]Ps 35:19; 119:78, 161 [C]Ps 109:26 119:87 [a]Lit *in the earth* [A]Is 58:2 119:89 [a]Lit *stands firm* [A]Ps 89:2; 119:160; Is 40:8; Matt 24:35; 1 Pet 1:25 119:90 [a]Lit *to* [A]Ps 36:5; 89:1, 2 [B]Ps 148:6 [C]Eccl 1:4 119:91 [A]Jer 31:35; 33:25 [B]Ps 104:2-4 119:92 [A]Ps 119:16 [B]Ps 119:50 119:93 [a]Or *kept me alive* [A]Ps 119:16, 83 [B]Ps 119:25 119:94 [A]Ps 119:146 [B]Ps 119:45 119:95 [A]Ps 40:14; Is 32:7 119:96 [a]Lit *an end of* 119:97 [A]Ps 119:47, 48, 127, 163, 165 [B]Ps 1:2; 119:15 119:98 [a]Or *with me* [A]Deut 4:6; Ps 119:130 119:99 [A]Ps 119:15 119:100 [A]Job 32:7-9 [B]Ps 119:22, 56 119:101 [A]Prov 1:15 119:102 [A]Deut 17:20; Josh 23:6; 1 Kin 15:5 119:103 [a]Or *promises* [b]Lit *palate* [A]Ps 19:10; Prov 8:11; 24:13, 14 119:104 [A]Ps 119:130 [B]Ps 119:128 119:105 [A]Prov 6:23 119:106 [A]Neh 10:29 119:107 [a]Or *Keep me alive* [A]Ps 119:25, 50 [B]Ps 119:25 119:108 [A]Hos 14:2; Heb 13:15 [B]Ps 119:12 119:109 [a]Lit *soul* [b]I.e. in danger [A]Judg 12:3; Job 13:14 [B]Ps 119:16 119:110 [A]Ps 91:3; 140:5; 141:9 [B]Ps 119:10 119:111 [A]Deut 33:4 [B]Ps 119:14, 162 119:112 [A]Ps 119:36 [B]Ps 119:33 119:113 [A]1 Kin 18:21; James 1:8; 4:8 [B]Ps 119:47 119:114 [a]Or *hope in* [A]Ps 31:20; 32:7; 61:4; 91:1 [B]Ps 84:9 [C]Ps 119:74 119:115 [A]Ps 6:8; 139:19; Matt 7:23 [B]Ps 119:22

119:83 a wineskin in the smoke. Just as smoke will dry out, stiffen, and crack a wineskin, thus making it useless, so the psalmist's affliction has debilitated him.

119:89 Forever … settled in heaven. God's Word will not change and is always spiritually relevant.

119:98–100 The wisdom of God always far surpasses the wisdom of man.

119:105 lamp … light. God's Word provides illumination to walk without stumbling.

119:111 joy. Cf. v. 162.

116 [A]Sustain me according to Your
[a]word, that I may live;
And [B]do not let me be
[b]ashamed of my hope.
117 Uphold me that I may be [A]safe,
That I may [B]have regard for
Your statutes continually.
118 You have [a]rejected all those [A]who
wander from Your statutes,
For their deceitfulness is [b]useless.
119 You have [a]removed all the wicked
of the earth *like* [A]dross;
Therefore I [B]love Your testimonies.
120 My flesh [a,A]trembles for fear of You,
And I am [B]afraid of Your judgments.

ע AYIN.

121 I have [A]done justice and righteousness;
Do not leave me to my oppressors.
122 Be [A]surety for Your servant for good;
Do not let the arrogant [B]oppress me.
123 My [A]eyes fail *with longing*
for Your salvation
And for Your righteous [a]word.
124 Deal with Your servant [A]according
to Your lovingkindness
And [B]teach me Your statutes.
125 [A]I am Your servant; [B]give me understanding,
That I may know Your testimonies.
126 It is time for the LORD to [A]act,
For they have broken Your law.
127 Therefore I [A]love Your commandments
Above gold, yes, above fine gold.
128 Therefore I esteem right all *Your*
[A]precepts concerning everything,
I [B]hate every false way.

פ PE.

129 Your testimonies are [A]wonderful;
Therefore my soul [B]observes them.
130 The [A]unfolding of Your words gives light;
It gives [B]understanding to the simple.
131 I [A]opened my mouth wide and [B]panted,
For I [C]longed for Your commandments.
132 [A]Turn to me and be gracious to me,
After Your manner [a]with those
who love Your name.
133 Establish my [A]footsteps in Your [a]word,
And do not let any iniquity
[B]have dominion over me.
134 [A]Redeem me from the
oppression of man,
That I may keep Your precepts.
135 [A]Make Your face shine upon Your servant,
And [B]teach me Your statutes.
136 My eyes [a]shed [A]streams of water,
Because they [B]do not keep Your law.

צ TSADHE.

137 [A]Righteous are You, O LORD,
And upright are Your judgments.
138 You have commanded Your
testimonies in [A]righteousness
And exceeding [B]faithfulness.
139 My [A]zeal has [a]consumed me,
Because my adversaries have
forgotten Your words.
140 Your [a,A]word is very [b]pure,
Therefore Your servant [B]loves it.
141 I am small and [A]despised,
Yet I do not [B]forget Your precepts.
142 Your righteousness is an
everlasting righteousness,
And [A]Your law is truth.
143 Trouble and anguish have
[a]come upon me,
Yet Your commandments
are my [A]delight.
144 Your [A]testimonies are righteous forever;
[B]Give me understanding that I may live.

ק QOPH.

145 I cried [A]with all my heart;
answer me, O LORD!
I will [B]observe Your statutes.
146 I cried to You; [A]save me
And I shall keep Your testimonies.
147 I [a,A]rise before dawn and cry for help;
I [b]wait for Your words.
148 My eyes anticipate the [A]night watches,
That I may [B]meditate on Your [a]word.
149 Hear my voice [A]according to
Your lovingkindness;
[B]Revive me, O LORD, according
to Your ordinances.
150 Those who follow after
wickedness draw near;
They are far from Your law.
151 You are [A]near, O LORD,
And all Your commandments are [B]truth.

119:116 [a]Or *promise* [b]Lit *put to shame because of* [A]Ps 37:17, 24; 54:4 [B]Ps 25:2, 20; 31:1, 17; Rom 5:5; 9:33; Phil 1:20 119:117 [A]Ps 12:5; Prov 29:25 [B]Ps 119:6, 15 119:118 [a]Lit *made light of* [b]Lit *falsehood* [A]Ps 119:10, 21 119:119 [a]Lit *caused to cease* [A]Is 1:22, 25; Ezek 22:18, 19 [B]Ps 119:47 119:120 [a]Lit *bristles up from* [A]Job 4:14; Hab 3:16 [B]Ps 119:161 119:121 [A]2 Sam 8:15; Job 29:14 119:122 [A]Job 17:3; Heb 7:22 [B]Ps 119:134 119:123 [a]Or *promise* [A]Ps 119:82 119:124 [A]Ps 51:1; 106:45; 109:26; 119:88, 149, 159 [B]Ps 119:12 119:125 [A]Ps 116:16 [B]Ps 119:27 119:126 [A]Jer 18:23; Ezek 31:11 119:127 [A]Ps 19:10; 119:47 119:128 [A]Ps 19:8 [B]Ps 119:104 119:129 [A]Ps 119:18 [B]Ps 119:22 119:130 [A]Prov 6:23 [B]Ps 19:7 119:131 [A]Job 29:23; Ps 81:10 [B]Ps 42:1 [C]Ps 119:20 119:132 [a]Lit *to* [A]Ps 25:16; 106:4 119:133 [a]Or *promise* [A]Ps 17:5 [B]Ps 19:13; Rom 6:12 119:134 [A]Ps 119:84; 142:6; Luke 1:74 119:135 [A]Num 6:25; Ps 4:6; 31:16; 67:1; 80:3, 7, 19 [B]Ps 119:12 119:136 [a]Lit *run down* [A]Jer 9:1, 18; 14:17; Lam 3:48 [B]Ps 119:158 119:137 [A]Ezra 9:15; Neh 9:33; Ps 116:5; 129:4; 145:17; Jer 12:1; Lam 1:18; Dan 9:7, 14 119:138 [A]Ps 19:7-9; 119:144, 172 [B]Ps 119:86, 90 119:139 [a]Lit *put an end to* [A]Ps 69:9; John 2:17 119:140 [a]Or *promise* [b]Lit *refined* [A]Ps 12:6; 19:8 [B]Ps 119:47 119:141 [A]Ps 22:6 [B]Ps 119:61 119:142 [A]Ps 19:9; 119:151, 160 119:143 [a]Lit *found me* [A]Ps 119:24 119:144 [A]Ps 19:9 [B]Ps 119:27 119:145 [A]Ps 119:10 [B]Ps 119:22, 55 119:146 [A]Ps 3:7 119:147 [a]Lit *anticipate the dawn* [b]Or *hope in* [A]Ps 5:3; 57:8; 108:2 119:148 [a]Or *promise* [A]Ps 63:6 [B]Ps 119:15 119:149 [A]Ps 119:124 [B]Ps 119:25 119:151 [A]Ps 34:18; 145:18; Is 50:8 [B]Ps 119:142

119:118, 119 have rejected … have removed. God righteously judges the wicked by His Word.

119:128 *See note on v. 21.*

119:130 light … understanding. Refers to illumination in comprehending the meaning of Scripture.

119:131 panted. As after God Himself (cf. Ps 42:1, 2).

119:136 streams of water. The psalmist is brought to sobbing over the sin of others.

119:140 very pure. Like silver refined 7 times (cf. Ps 12:6), the Word is without impurity, i.e., it is inerrant in all that it declares.

152 Of old I have [A]known from
Your testimonies
That You have founded them [B]forever.

ר RESH.

153 [A]Look upon my [B]affliction and rescue me,
For I do not [C]forget Your law.
154 [A]Plead my cause and [B]redeem me;
Revive me according to Your [a]word.
155 Salvation is [A]far from the wicked,
For they [B]do not seek Your statutes.
156 [a,A]Great are Your mercies, O LORD;
Revive me according to Your ordinances.
157 Many are my [A]persecutors
and my adversaries,
Yet I do not [B]turn aside from
Your testimonies.
158 I behold the [A]treacherous
and [B]loathe *them,*
Because they do not keep Your [a]word.
159 Consider how I [A]love Your precepts;
[B]Revive me, O LORD, according
to Your lovingkindness.
160 The [A]sum of Your word is [B]truth,
And every one of Your righteous
ordinances [C]is everlasting.

ש SHIN.

161 [A]Princes persecute me without cause,
But my heart [B]stands in
awe of Your words.
162 I [A]rejoice at Your [a]word,
As one who [B]finds great spoil.
163 I [A]hate and despise falsehood,
But I [B]love Your law.
164 Seven times a day I praise You,
Because of Your [A]righteous ordinances.
165 Those who love Your law
have [A]great peace,
And [a,B]nothing causes them to stumble.
166 I [A]hope for Your salvation, O LORD,
And do Your commandments.
167 My [A]soul keeps Your testimonies,
And I [B]love them exceedingly.
168 I [A]keep Your precepts and
Your testimonies,
For all my [B]ways are before You.

ת TAV.

169 Let my [A]cry [a]come before You, O LORD;
[B]Give me understanding
[C]according to Your word.
170 Let my [A]supplication come before You;
[B]Deliver me according to Your [a]word.
171 Let my [A]lips utter praise,
For You [B]teach me Your statutes.
172 Let my [A]tongue sing of Your [a]word,
For all Your [B]commandments
are righteousness.
173 Let Your [A]hand be [a]ready to help me,
For I have [B]chosen Your precepts.
174 I [A]long for Your salvation, O LORD,
And Your law is my [B]delight.
175 Let my [A]soul live that it may praise You,
And let Your ordinances help me.
176 I have [A]gone astray like a lost
sheep; seek Your servant,
For I do [B]not forget Your commandments.

PSALM 120

PRAYER FOR DELIVERANCE FROM THE TREACHEROUS.

A Song of [†]Ascents.

1 [A]In my trouble I cried to the LORD,
And He answered me.
2 Deliver my soul, O LORD, from [A]lying lips,
From a [B]deceitful tongue.
3 What shall be given to you, and what
more shall be done to you,
You [A]deceitful tongue?

119:152 [A]Ps 119:125 [B]Ps 119:89; Luke 21:33 119:153 [A]Lam 5:1 [B]Ps 119:50 [C]Ps 119:16; Prov 3:1; Hos 4:6 119:154 [a]Or *promise* [A]1 Sam 24:15; Ps 35:1; Mic 7:9 [B]Ps 119:134 119:155 [A]Job 5:4 [B]Ps 119:45, 94 119:156 [a]Or *Many* [A]2 Sam 24:14 119:157 [A]Ps 7:1; 119:86, 161 [B]Ps 119:51 119:158 [a]Or *promise* [A]Is 21:2; 24:16 [B]Ps 139:21 119:159 [A]Ps 119:47 [B]Ps 119:25 119:160 [A]Ps 139:17 [B]Ps 119:142 [C]Ps 119:89, 152 119:161 [A]1 Sam 24:11; 26:18; Ps 119:23 [B]Ps 119:120 119:162 [a]Or *promise* [A]Ps 119:14, 111 [B]1 Sam 30:16; Is 9:3 119:163 [A]Ps 31:6; 119:104, 128; Prov 13:5 [B]Ps 119:47 119:164 [A]Ps 119:7, 160 119:165 [a]Lit *they have no stumbling block* [A]Ps 37:11; Prov 3:2; Is 26:3; 32:17 [B]Prov 3:23; Is 63:13; 1 John 2:10 119:166 [A]Gen 49:18; Ps 119:81, 174 119:167 [A]Ps 119:129 [B]Ps 119:47 119:168 [A]Ps 119:22 [B]Job 24:23; Ps 139:3; Prov 5:21 119:169 [a]Lit *come near before* [A]Job 16:18; Ps 18:6; 102:1 [B]Ps 119:27, 144 [C]Ps 119:65, 154 119:170 [a]Or *promise* [A]Ps 28:2; 130:2; 140:6; 143:1 [B]Ps 22:20; 31:2; 59:1 119:171 [A]Ps 51:15; 63:3 [B]Ps 94:12; 119:12; Is 2:3; Mic 4:2 119:172 [a]Or *promise* [A]Ps 51:14 [B]Ps 119:138 119:173 [a]Lit *to help me* [A]Ps 37:24; 73:23 [B]Josh 24:22; Luke 10:42 119:174 [A]Ps 119:166 [B]Ps 119:16, 24 119:175 [A]Is 55:3 119:176 [A]Is 53:6; Jer 50:6; Matt 18:12; Luke 15:4 [B]Ps 119:16 120:1 [†]Ex 34:24; 1 Kin 12:27 [A]Ps 18:6; 66:14; 102:2; Jon 2:2 120:2 [A]Ps 109:2; Prov 12:22 [B]Ps 52:4; Zeph 3:13 120:3 [A]Ps 52:4; Zeph 3:13

119:155 Salvation ... far. Salvation is clearly revealed in the Scripture and nowhere else with such perspicuity.

119:160 The sum ... truth. There is not a speck of untruth in Scripture.

119:161 in awe. Just as one stands in awe of God Himself.

119:163 I hate ... falsehood. Cf. vv. 29, 30.

119:164 Seven times. Seven is perhaps used in the sense of perfection/completion meaning here that a continual attitude of praise characterizes the psalmist's life.

119:173 Your hand. An anthropomorphic figure of speech.

119:176 I have gone astray. In spite of all that he has affirmed regarding Scripture's power in his life, the psalmist confesses that sin has not yet been eliminated from his life (cf. Ro 7:15–25). Any decrease of sin in his life should be attributed to the suppression of unrighteousness by the working of God's Word (cf. vv. 9–11).

120:1–7 Psalms 120–136 comprise "The Great Hallel"; cf. "The Egyptian Hallel" (Pss 113–118) and "The Final Hallel" (Pss 145–150). Almost all these psalms (15 of 17) are "Songs of Ascent" (Pss 120–134), which the Jewish pilgrims sang on their way up to Jerusalem (about 2,700 ft. in elevation) on 3 prescribed annual occasions. These feasts included: 1) Unleavened Bread; 2) Weeks/Pentecost/Harvest; and 3) Ingathering/Tabernacles/Booths. Cf. Ex 23:14–17; 34:22, 23; Dt 16:16. David authored 4 of these songs (Pss 122, 124, 131, 133), Solomon one (Ps 127), while 10 remain anonymous. When these psalms were assembled in this way is unknown. It appears that these songs begin far away from Jerusalem (cf. Meschech and Kedar in Ps 120:5) and progressively move toward Jerusalem until the pilgrims have actually reached the temple and finished their worship (cf. Ps 134:1, 2). With regard to Ps 120, the author and circumstances are unknown, although it seems as if the worshiper lives at a distance among unbelieving people (cf. Ps 120:5).

I. Petition (120:1, 2)
II. Indictment (120:3, 4)
III. Lament (120:5–7)

120:2 lying lips ... deceitful tongue. Cf. Pss 52:2–4; 109:2; Ro 3:9–18.

4 [A]Sharp arrows of the warrior,
With the *burning* [B]coals
of the broom tree.

5 Woe is me, for I sojourn in [A]Meshech,
For I dwell among the [B]tents of [C]Kedar!
6 Too long has my soul had its dwelling
With those who [A]hate peace.
7 I [A]am *for* peace, but when I speak,
They are [B]for war.

PSALM 121

THE LORD THE KEEPER OF ISRAEL.

A Song of Ascents.

1 I will [A]lift up my eyes to [B]the mountains;
From where shall my help come?
2 My [A]help *comes* from the LORD,
Who [B]made heaven and earth.
3 He will not [A]allow your foot to slip;
He who [B]keeps you will not slumber.
4 Behold, He who keeps Israel
Will neither slumber nor sleep.

5 The LORD is your [A]keeper;
The LORD is your [B]shade on
your right hand.
6 The [A]sun will not smite you by day,
Nor the moon by night.
7 The LORD will [a,A]protect you from all evil;
He will keep your soul.
8 The LORD will [a,A]guard your going
out and your coming in
[B]From this time forth and forever.

PSALM 122

PRAYER FOR THE PEACE OF JERUSALEM.

A Song of Ascents, of David.

1 I was glad when they said to me,
"Let us [A]go to the house of the LORD."
2 Our feet are standing
Within your [A]gates, O Jerusalem,
3 Jerusalem, that is [A]built
As a city that is [B]compact together;
4 To which the tribes [A]go up, even
the tribes of [a]the LORD—
[b]An ordinance for Israel—
To give thanks to the name of the LORD.
5 For there [A]thrones were set for judgment,
The thrones of the house of David.

6 Pray for the [A]peace of Jerusalem:
"May they prosper who [B]love you.
7 "May peace be within your [A]walls,
And prosperity within your [B]palaces."
8 For the sake of my [A]brothers and my friends,
I will now say, "[B]May peace be within you."
9 For the sake of the house of
the LORD our God,
I will [A]seek your good.

PSALM 123

PRAYER FOR THE LORD'S HELP.

A Song of Ascents.

1 To You I [A]lift up my eyes,
O You who [B]are enthroned in the heavens!

120:4 [A]Ps 45:5; Prov 25:18; Is 5:28 [B]Ps 140:10 120:5 [A]Gen 10:2; 1 Chr 1:5; Ezek 27:13; 38:2, 3; 39:1 [B]Song 1:5 [C]Gen 25:13; Is 21:16; 60:7; Jer 2:10; 49:28; Ezek 27:21 120:6 [A]Ps 35:20 120:7 [A]Ps 109:4 [B]Ps 55:21 121:1 [A]Ps 123:1; Is 40:26 [B]Ps 87:1 121:2 [A]Ps 124:8 [B]Ps 115:15 121:3 [A]1 Sam 2:9; Ps 66:9 [B]Ps 41:2; 127:1; Is 27:3 121:5 [A]Ps 91:4 [B]Ps 16:8; 91:1; Is 25:4 121:6 [A]Ps 91:5; Is 49:10; Jon 4:8; Rev 7:16 121:7 [a]Or *keep* [A]Ps 41:2; 91:10-12 121:8 [a]Or *keep* [A]Deut 28:6 [B]Ps 113:2; 115:18 122:1 [A]Ps 42:4; Is 2:3; Mic 4:2; Zech 8:21 122:2 [A]Ps 9:14; 87:2; 116:19; Jer 7:2 122:3 [A]Ps 48:13; 147:2 [B]2 Sam 5:9; Neh 4:6 122:4 [a]Heb *YAH* [b]Or *A testimony* [A]Ex 23:17; Deut 16:16; Ps 84:5 122:5 [A]Deut 17:8; 2 Chr 19:8; Ps 89:29 122:6 [A]Ps 29:11; Jer 29:7 [B]Ps 102:14 122:7 [A]Ps 51:18; Is 62:6 [B]Ps 48:3, 13; Jer 17:27 122:8 [A]Ps 133:1 [B]1 Sam 25:6; John 20:19 122:9 [A]Neh 2:10; Esth 10:3 123:1 [A]Ps 121:1; 141:8 [B]Ps 2:4; 11:4

120:4 Sharp arrows … coals. Lies and false accusations are likened to 1) the pain/injury inflicted in battle by arrows, and 2) the pain of being burned with charcoal made from the wood of a broom tree (a desert bush that grows 10 to 15 ft. high).

120:5–7 The psalmist actually lives among pagans who do not embrace his desire for peace.

120:5 Meshech … Kedar! In Asia Minor (cf. Ge 10:2) and Arabia (Is 21:16) respectively.

121:1–8 *See note on Ps 120:1–7.* The author and circumstances are unknown. This song strikes a strong note of assurance in 4 stages that God is help and protection to keep both Israel and individual believers safe from harm.

I. God—Helper (121:1, 2)
II. God—Keeper (121:3, 4)
III. God—Protector (121:5, 6)
IV. God—Preserver (121:7, 8)

121:1 mountains. Most likely those in the distance as the pilgrim looks to Jerusalem, especially the temple.

121:2 My help. The psalmist does not look to the creation, but rather the Creator for his help.

121:3 slip. Cf. Ps 37:23, 24.

121:3, 4 slumber. Cf. the appearance of sleep, Ps 44:23. The living God is totally unlike the pagan gods/dead idols (cf. 1Ki 18:27).

121:5 your right hand. This represents the place of human need.

121:6 by day … by night. Around the clock protection.

121:7, 8 While this seems to have a temporal sense at first glance, there are indications that it looks beyond to eternal life, e.g., all evil (v. 7) and forevermore (v. 8).

122:1–9 *See note on Ps 120:1–7.* David expressed his great joy over Jerusalem, which he had settled by defeating the Jebusites (cf. 2Sa 5) and bringing the tabernacle and ark for permanent residency (cf. 2Sa 6). David's desire/prayer was temporarily fulfilled in Solomon's reign (cf. 1Ki 4:24, 25). It is ironic that Jerusalem, which means "city of peace," has been fought over through history more than any other city in the world. Prophetically, David's desire will not be experienced in its fullness until the Prince of Peace (Is 9:6) comes to rule permanently (Zec 14:9, 11) as the promised Davidic King (cf. 2Sa 7:12, 13, 16; Eze 37:24–28).

I. Joy Over Worship (122:1–5)
II. Prayer Over Jerusalem (122:6–9)

122:1 the house of the LORD. A term used of the tabernacle (cf. Ex 23:19; 34:26; 2Sa 12:20), not the temple that would be built later by Solomon.

122:2 standing Within your gates. Sometime after the tabernacle and ark of the covenant had arrived in the city of David (2Sa 6). David's joy is that the ark has found its proper location.

122:3 compact together. The Jerusalem of David's day (Zion) was smaller than the enlargement by Solomon.

122:4 An ordinance for Israel. Refers to God's command to go up to Jerusalem 3 times annually (*see note on Ps 120:1–7*).

122:6–9 A most appropriate prayer for a city whose name means peace and is the residency of the God of peace (Is 9:6; Ro 15:33; Heb 13:20). Compare prayers for the peace of Israel (Pss 125:5; 128:6) and other psalms which exalt Jerusalem (Pss 128, 132, 147). History would prove that bad times had to come (Pss 79, 137) before the best of times (Rev 21, 22).

123:1–4 *See note on Ps 120:1–7.* The author and situation are unknown.

I. Exalting God (123:1, 2)
II. Enlisting God's Mercy (123:3, 4)

123:1 my eyes. The progression from Ps

2 Behold, as the eyes of [A]servants *look*
to the hand of their master,
As the eyes of a maid to the
hand of her mistress,
So our [B]eyes *look* to the LORD our God,
Until He is gracious to us.

3 [A]Be gracious to us, O LORD, be gracious to us,
For we are greatly filled [B]with contempt.
4 Our soul is greatly filled
With the [A]scoffing of [B]those who are at ease,
And with the [C]contempt of the proud.

PSALM 124

PRAISE FOR RESCUE FROM ENEMIES.

A Song of Ascents, of David.

1 "[A]Had it not been the LORD
who was on our side,"
[B]Let Israel now say,
2 "Had it not been the LORD
who was on our side
When men rose up against us,
3 Then they would have [A]swallowed us alive,
When their [B]anger was kindled against us;
4 Then the [A]waters would have engulfed us,
The stream would have
[a]swept over our soul;
5 Then the [A]raging waters would
have [a]swept over our soul."

6 Blessed be the LORD,
Who has not given us [a]to be
[A]torn by their teeth.
7 Our soul has [A]escaped [B]as a bird out
of the [C]snare of the trapper;
The snare is broken and we have escaped.
8 Our [A]help is in the name of the LORD,
Who [B]made heaven and earth.

PSALM 125

THE LORD SURROUNDS HIS PEOPLE.

A Song of Ascents.

1 Those who trust in the LORD
Are as Mount Zion, which [A]cannot
be moved but [B]abides forever.
2 As the mountains surround Jerusalem,
So [A]the LORD surrounds His people
[B]From this time forth and forever.
3 For the [A]scepter of wickedness
shall not rest upon the
[a]land of the righteous,
So that the righteous [B]will not put
forth their hands to do wrong.

4 [A]Do good, O LORD, to those who are good
And to those who are [B]upright
in their hearts.
5 But as for those who [A]turn aside
to their [B]crooked ways,
The LORD will lead them away
with the [C]doers of iniquity.
[D]Peace be upon Israel.

PSALM 126

THANKSGIVING FOR RETURN FROM CAPTIVITY.

A Song of Ascents.

1 When the LORD [A]brought back
[a]the captive ones of Zion,
We were [B]like those who dream.

123:2 [A]Prov 27:18; Mal 1:6 [B]Ps 25:15 123:3 [A]Ps 4:1; 51:1 [B]Neh 4:4; Ps 119:22 123:4 [A]Neh 2:19; Ps 79:4 [B]Job 12:5; Is 32:9, 11; Amos 6:1 [C]Neh 4:4; Ps 119:22 124:1 [A]Ps 94:17 [B]Ps 129:1 124:3 [A]Num 16:30; Ps 35:25; 56:1; 57:3; Prov 1:12 [B]Gen 39:19; Ps 138:7 124:4 [a]Or *passed over* [A]Job 22:11; Ps 18:16; 32:6; 69:2; 144:7 124:5 [a]Or *passed over* [A]Job 38:11 124:6 [a]Lit *as a prey to* [A]Ps 27:2; Prov 30:14 124:7 [A]Ps 141:10; 2 Cor 11:33; Heb 11:34 [B]Prov 6:5 [C]Ps 91:3; Hos 9:8 124:8 [A]Ps 121:2 [B]Gen 1:1; Ps 134:3 125:1 [A]Ps 46:5 [B]Ps 61:7; Eccl 1:4 125:2 [A]Zech 2:5 [B]Ps 121:8 125:3 [a]Lit *lot* [A]Ps 89:22; Prov 22:8; Is 14:5 [B]1 Sam 24:10; Ps 55:20; Acts 12:1 125:4 [A]Ps 119:68 [B]Ps 7:10; 11:2; 32:11; 36:10; 94:15 125:5 [A]Job 23:11; Ps 40:4; 101:3 [B]Prov 2:15; Is 59:8 [C]Ps 92:7; 94:4 [D]Ps 128:6; Gal 6:16 126:1 [a]Or *those who returned to* [A]Ps 85:1; Jer 29:14; Hos 6:11 [B]Acts 12:9

121:1. **enthroned in the heavens**. Cf. Pss 11:4; 103:19; 113:5.

123:2 servants … master. The psalmist reasons from the lesser to the greater (human to the divine; earthly to the heavenly). One's eyes should be on the Lord to mercifully meet one's needs.

123:3, 4 contempt … scoffing. From unbelieving pagans, perhaps the Samaritans (cf. Ne 1:3; 2:19).

124:1–8 *See note on Ps 120:1–7.* A Davidic psalm which generically recalls past deliverances, possibly the Exodus (v. 5).

I. God's Protection (124:1–5)
II. God's Provision (124:6–8)

124:1, 2 God has preserved Israel from extinction.

124:2 When men rose up. A general statement which could cover the history of Israel from Abraham to David.

124:4, 5 waters … stream … raging waters. The Red Sea crossing (Ex 14) and/or the Jordan crossing (Jos 3) are pictured.

124:8 Our help. Cf. Ps 121:1, 2.

125:1–5 *See note on Ps 120:1–7.* The author and circumstances are unknown, although the times of Hezekiah (2Ki 18:27–35) or Nehemiah (Ne 6:1–19) have been suggested.

I. The Security of Jerusalem (125:1–3)
II. The Spiritual Purity of Jerusalem (125:4, 5)

125:1 Mount Zion. The SW mount representing Jerusalem and an emblem of permanence, supported by God's covenant promise.

125:1, 2 forever. More than a temporal promise is involved here.

125:2 His people. Those who trust in the Lord (cf. v. 1).

125:3 scepter of wickedness. Assyrian rule if in Hezekiah's time, or Medo-Persian rule if in Nehemiah's day. **the land.** This would be the land promised to Abraham (Ge 15:18–21).

125:4, 5 The outcome of the upright (v. 4) is contrasted with the crooked (v. 5). The true Israel is distinguished from the false (cf. Ro 2:28, 29; 9:6, 7).

125:5 lead them away. Eternal rather than temporal judgment seems to be in view. **Peace.** God will one day institute a lasting covenant of peace (cf. Eze 37:26).

126:1–6 *See note on Ps 120:1–7.* The author and occasion are not named in the psalm. However, v. 1 points to a time of return from captivity. Most likely this refers to the Babylonian Captivity, from which there were 3 separate returns: 1) under Zerubbabel in Ezr 1–6 (ca. 538 B.C.); 2) under Ezra in Ezr 7–10 (ca. 458 B.C.); and 3) under Nehemiah in Ne 1, 2 (ca. 445 B.C.). The occasion could be 1) when the foundation for the second temple had been laid (cf. Ezr 3:8–10), or 2) when the Feast of Booths, or Tabernacles, was reinstated (cf. Ne 8:13–14). This psalm is similar to Ps 85, which rejoices over Israel's return from Exile, but contrasts with Ps 137, which laments the pain of the Babylonian Captivity.

I. The Testimony of Restoration (126:1–3)
II. The Prayer for Riches (126:4)
III. The Wisdom of Righteousness (126:5, 6)

126:1 those who dream. The actual experience of liberation, so unexpected, seemed more like a dream than reality.

2 Then our [A]mouth was
filled with laughter
And our [B]tongue with
joyful shouting;
Then they said among the nations,
"The LORD has [C]done great
things for them."
3 The LORD has done great things for us;
We are [A]glad.

4 Restore our captivity, O LORD,
As the [a,A]streams in the [b]South.
5 Those who sow in [A]tears shall
reap with [B]joyful shouting.
6 He who goes to and fro weeping,
carrying *his* bag of seed,
Shall indeed come again with a shout of
joy, bringing his sheaves *with him.*

PSALM 127

PROSPERITY COMES FROM THE LORD.

A Song of Ascents, of Solomon.

1 Unless the LORD [A]builds the house,
They labor in vain who build it;
Unless the LORD [B]guards the city,
The watchman keeps awake in vain.
2 It is vain for you to rise up early,
To [a]retire late,
To [A]eat the bread of [b]painful labors;
For He gives to His [B]beloved
[C]*even in his* sleep.

3 Behold, [A]children are a
[a]gift of the LORD,
The [B]fruit of the womb is a reward.
4 Like arrows in the hand
of a [A]warrior,
So are the children of one's youth.
5 How [A]blessed is the man whose
quiver is full of them;
[B]They will not be ashamed
When they [C]speak with their
enemies [D]in the gate.

PSALM 128

BLESSEDNESS OF THE FEAR OF THE LORD.

A Song of Ascents.

1 [A]How blessed is everyone
who fears the LORD,
Who [B]walks in His ways.
2 When you shall [A]eat of the
[a,B]fruit of your hands,
You will be happy and [C]it will
be well with you.
3 Your wife shall be like
a [A]fruitful vine
[a]Within your house,
Your children like [B]olive plants
Around your table.
4 Behold, for thus shall the
man be blessed
Who fears the LORD.

5 [A]The LORD bless you [B]from Zion,
And may you see the
prosperity of Jerusalem
all the days of your life.
6 Indeed, may you see your
[A]children's children.
[B]Peace be upon Israel!

126:2 [A]Job 8:21 [B]Ps 51:14; Is 35:6 [C]1 Sam 12:24; Ps 71:19; Luke 1:49 **126:3** [A]Is 25:9; Zeph 3:14 **126:4** [a]Lit *stream-beds* [b]Heb *Negev* [A]Is 35:6; 43:19 **126:5** [A]Ps 80:5; Jer 31:9, 16; Lam 1:2 [B]Is 35:10; 51:11; 61:7; Gal 6:9 **127:1** [A]Ps 78:69 [B]Ps 121:4 **127:2** [a]Lit *delay sitting* [b]Lit *toils* [A]Gen 3:17, 19 [B]Ps 60:5 [C]Job 11:18, 19; Prov 3:24; Eccl 5:12 **127:3** [a]Or *heritage* [A]Gen 33:5; 48:4; Josh 24:3, 4; Ps 113:9 [B]Deut 7:13; 28:4; Is 13:18 **127:4** [A]Ps 112:2; 120:4 **127:5** [A]Ps 128:2, 3 [B]Prov 27:11 [C]Is 29:21; Amos 5:12 [D]Gen 34:20 **128:1** [A]Ps 112:1; 119:1 [B]Ps 119:3 **128:2** [a]Lit *labor* [A]Is 3:10 [B]Ps 109:11; Hag 2:17 [C]Eccl 8:12; Eph 6:3 **128:3** [a]Lit *In the innermost parts of* [A]Ezek 19:10 [B]Ps 52:8; 144:12 **128:5** [A]Ps 134:3 [B]Ps 20:2; 135:21 **128:6** [A]Gen 48:11; 50:23; Job 42:16; Ps 103:17; Prov 17:6 [B]Ps 125:5

126:2, 3 The LORD has done. First recognized by the surrounding nations (v. 2) and then the returning remnant (v. 3).

126:4 Restore. A prayer to restore the nation's fortunes at their best. **streams in the South.** The arid region S of Beersheba (called the Negev) which is utterly dry in the summer, but whose streams quickly fill and flood with the rains of spring. In this manner, the psalmist prays that Israel's fortunes will rapidly change from nothing to everything.

126:5, 6 sow … reap. By sowing tears of repentance over sin, the nation reaped the harvest of a joyful return to the land of Israel.

127:1–5 *See note on Ps 120:1–7.* The author is Solomon (cf. Ecc 12:10), but the occasion is unknown. The major message of God being central to and sovereign in life sounds much like portions of Solomon's Ecclesiastes (cf. Ecc 2:24, 25; 5:18–20; 7:13, 14; 9:1). Psalms 112 and 128 also develop a strong message on the family.

I. God's Sovereignty in Everyday Life (127:1, 2)
II. God's Sovereignty in Family Life (127:3–5)

127:1, 2 God's sovereignty is seen in 3 realms: 1) building a house, 2) protecting a city, and 3) earning a living. In all 3 instances, the sovereign intention of God is far more crucial to the outcome than man's efforts. Otherwise, a man's endeavor is in vain (cf. Ecc 1:2; 12:8).

127:2 the bread of painful labors. Food earned with painful labor.

127:3–5 The same principle of God's sovereignty applies to raising a family.

127:3 gift … reward. Children are a blessing from the Lord. There are overtones of God's promise to Abraham to make his offspring like the dust of the earth and the stars of heaven (Ge 13:16; 15:5).

127:4, 5 As arrows are indispensable for a warrior to succeed in battle, so children are invaluable as defenders of their father and mother in time of war or litigation. The more such defenders, the better.

128:1–6 *See note on Ps 120:1–7.* The author and occasion are unknown. Psalms 112 and 127 also address issues of the home.

I. The Basics of Fearing the Lord (128:1, 4)
II. The Blessings of Fearing the Lord (128:2, 3, 5, 6)
   A. In the Present (128:2, 3)
   B. In the Future (128:5, 6)

128:1 who fears the LORD. *See note on Pr 1:7.* Psalm 112:1–6 also develops this theme. A good working definition is provided by the parallel line, "Who walks in His ways." Fathers (Ps 128:1, 4), mothers (Pr 31:30), and children (Ps 34:11) are to fear the Lord. This psalm may have been the basis for Jesus' illustration of the two builders (cf. Mt 7:24–27).

128:2, 3 Four blessings are recounted: 1) provisions, 2) prosperity, 3) reproducing partner, and 4) flourishing progeny.

128:3 olive plants. Shoots grow off of the main root of an olive tree to reproduce.

128:5, 6 Two realms of blessing are mentioned: 1) personal blessing and 2) national blessing.

128:6 children's children. Cf. Pss 103:17; 112:2; Pr 13:22; 17:6 on grand-children. This is a prayer for prosperity for God's people.

PSALM 129

PRAYER FOR THE OVERTHROW OF ZION'S ENEMIES.

A Song of Ascents.

1 "[a]Many times they have [b,A]persecuted
me from my [B]youth up,"
[C]Let Israel now say,
2 "[a]Many times they have [b]persecuted
me from my youth up;
Yet they have [A]not prevailed against me.
3 "The plowers plowed upon my back;
They lengthened their furrows."
4 The LORD [A]is righteous;
He has cut in two the
[B]cords of the wicked.

5 May all who [A]hate Zion
Be [B]put to shame and turned backward;
6 Let them be like [A]grass upon
the housetops,
Which withers before it [a]grows up;
7 With which the reaper does
not fill his [a]hand,
Or the binder of sheaves his [A]bosom;
8 Nor do those who pass by say,
"The [A]blessing of the LORD be upon you;
We bless you in the name of the LORD."

PSALM 130

HOPE IN THE LORD'S FORGIVING LOVE.

A Song of Ascents.

1 Out of the [A]depths I have
cried to You, O LORD.
2 Lord, [A]hear my voice!
Let [B]Your ears be attentive
To the [C]voice of my supplications.
3 If You, [a]LORD, should mark iniquities,
O Lord, who could [A]stand?
4 But there is [A]forgiveness with You,
That You may be [B]feared.

5 I wait for the LORD, my
[A]soul does wait,
And [a,B]in His word do I hope.
6 My soul *waits* for the Lord
More than the watchmen
[A]for the morning;
Indeed, more than the watchmen
for the morning.
7 O Israel, [A]hope in the LORD;
For with the LORD there is
[B]lovingkindness,
And with Him is [C]abundant
redemption.
8 And He will [A]redeem Israel
From all his iniquities.

PSALM 131

CHILDLIKE TRUST IN THE LORD.

A Song of Ascents, of David.

1 O LORD, my heart is not [A]proud,
nor my eyes [a,B]haughty;
Nor do I [b]involve myself
in [C]great matters,
Or in things [D]too [c]difficult for me.
2 Surely I have [A]composed and
quieted my soul;
Like a weaned [B]child *rests*
[a]against his mother,
My soul is like a weaned
child [a]within me.
3 O Israel, [A]hope in the LORD
[B]From this time forth and forever.

129:1 [a]Lit *Much* [b]Lit *showed hostility toward* [A]Ex 1:11; Judg 3:8; Ps 88:15 [B]Is 47:12; Jer 2:2; 22:21; Ezek 16:22; Hos 2:15; 11:1 [C]Ps 124:1 129:2 [a]Lit *Much* [b]Lit *showed hostility toward* [A]Jer 1:19; 15:20; 20:11; Matt 16:18; 2 Cor 4:8, 9 129:4 [A]Ps 119:137 [B]Ps 140:5 129:5 [A]Mic 4:11 [B]Ps 70:3; 71:13 129:6 [a]Lit *draws out* [A]2 Kin 19:26; Ps 37:2; Is 37:27 129:7 [a]Lit *palm* [A]Ps 79:12 129:8 [A]Ruth 2:4; Ps 118:26 130:1 [A]Ps 42:7; 69:2; Lam 3:55 130:2 [A]Ps 64:1; 119:149 [B]2 Chr 6:40; Neh 1:6, 11 [C]Ps 28:2; 140:6 130:3 [a]Heb *YAH* [A]Ps 76:7; 143:2; Nah 1:6; Mal 3:2; Rev 6:17 130:4 [A]Ex 34:7; Neh 9:17; Ps 86:5; Is 55:7; Dan 9:9 [B]1 Kin 8:39, 40; Jer 33:8, 9 130:5 [a]Lit *for* [A]Ps 27:14; 33:20; 40:1; 62:1, 5; Is 8:17; 26:8 [B]Ps 119:74, 81 130:6 [A]Ps 63:6; 119:147 130:7 [A]Ps 131:3 [B]Ps 86:5; 103:4 [C]Ps 111:9; Rom 3:24; Eph 1:7 130:8 [A]Ps 103:3, 4; Luke 1:68; Titus 2:14 131:1 [a]Or *lofty* [b]Lit *go after,* walk [C]Or *marvelous* [A]2 Sam 22:28; Ps 101:5; Is 2:12; Zeph 3:11 [B]Prov 30:13; Is 5:15 [C]Jer 45:5; Rom 12:16 [D]Job 42:3; Ps 139:6 131:2 [a]Or *upon* [A]Ps 62:1 [B]Matt 18:3; 1 Cor 14:20 131:3 [A]Ps 130:7 [B]Ps 113:2

129:1–8 *See note on Ps 120:1–7.* The author and occasion are not specified. However, v. 4 indicates a release from captivity, most likely the Babylonian captivity.

I. Israel's Freedom Celebrated (129:1–4)
II. Israel's Foe Imprecated (129:5–8)

129:1 persecuted. From living in Egypt (ca. 1875–1445 B.C.), to enduring the Babylonian Captivity (ca. 605–538 B.C.), Israel had enjoyed little rest from her enemies.

129:2 prevailed. As the Lord had promised Abraham (cf. Ge 12:1–3).

129:3 plowed upon my back. A farming analogy used to describe the deep, but nonfatal, wounds inflicted on Israel by her enemies.

129:4 cut . . . the cords. These cords tied the ox to the plow, and refer to God ending the persecution (cf. Pss 121, 124).

129:5–8 A 3-part imprecatory prayer: 1) be put to shame and defeat (v. 5), 2) be few and short lived (vv. 6, 7), and 3) be without God's blessing (v. 8).

129:6 grass . . . the housetops. Grass with shallow roots, which quickly dies with the first heat, depicts the wicked.

130:1–8 *See note on Ps 120:1–7.* The author and occasion are not mentioned. This is the sixth of 7 penitential psalms (cf. Pss 6, 32, 38, 51, 102, 143).

I. Urgent Prayer of the Psalmist (130:1, 2)
II. Magnified Forgiveness of God (130:3, 4)
III. Waiting Patience of the Psalmist (130:5, 6)
IV. Unique Hope of Israel (130:7, 8)

130:1 Out of the depths. A figurative expression of severe distress.

130:3, 4 The psalmist basks in the glow of God's never-ending forgiveness (cf. Ps 143:2).

130:5 in His word do I hope. The psalmist expresses a certain hope since God's Word cannot fail (cf. Mt 5:18; Lk 16:17; Jn 10:35).

130:6 watchmen for the morning. Probably refers to shepherds with a night watch which ends with the sun's rising.

130:7 hope in the LORD. The psalmist's hope in God's Word (v. 5) parallels Israel's hope in the Lord.

130:8 He will redeem Israel. This can be taken in both a historical and a soteriological sense (cf. Mt 1:21; Lk 1:68; Ro 9–11).

131:1–3 *See note on Ps 120:1–7.* David is the author, but the circumstances are not apparent.

I. A Personal Testimony (131:1, 2)
II. A National Exhortation (131:3)

131:1 proud . . . haughty. God gives grace to the humble (cf. Pr 3:34; 16:5; Jas 4:6). David expresses the greatest of God's ways (cf. Ps 139:6; Ro 11:33–36).

131:2 Like a weaned child. David has been trained to trust God to supply his needs as a weaned child trusts his mother.

131:3 David exhorts the nation to forever embrace his own personal hope in the Lord.

PSALM 132

PRAYER FOR THE LORD'S BLESSING UPON THE SANCTUARY.

A Song of Ascents.

1 Remember, O LORD, on
David's behalf,
All [A]his affliction;
2 How he swore to the LORD
And vowed to [A]the Mighty
One of Jacob,
3 "Surely I will not [a]enter [A]my house,
Nor [b]lie on my bed;
4 I will not [A]give sleep to my eyes
Or slumber to my eyelids,
5 Until I find a [A]place for the LORD,
[a]A dwelling place for [B]the
Mighty One of Jacob."

6 Behold, we heard of it
in [A]Ephrathah,
We found it in the [B]field of [a]Jaar.
7 Let us go into His [a,A]dwelling place;
Let us [B]worship at His [C]footstool.
8 [A]Arise, O LORD, to Your
[B]resting place,
You and the ark of Your [C]strength.
9 Let Your priests be [A]clothed
with righteousness,
And let Your [B]godly ones
sing for joy.
10 For the sake of David Your servant,
Do not turn away the face
of Your [A]anointed.
11 The LORD has [A]sworn to David
A truth from which He
will not turn back:
"[B]Of the fruit of your body I will
set upon your throne.
12 "If your sons will keep My covenant
And My testimony which I
will teach them,
Their sons also shall [A]sit upon
your throne forever."

13 For the LORD has [A]chosen Zion;
He has [B]desired it for His habitation.
14 "This is My [A]resting place forever;
Here I will [B]dwell, for I have desired it.
15 "I will abundantly [A]bless her provision;
I will [B]satisfy her needy with bread.
16 "Her [A]priests also I will clothe
with salvation,
And her [A]godly ones will
sing aloud for joy.
17 "There I will cause the [A]horn of
David to spring forth;
I have prepared a [B]lamp
for Mine anointed.
18 "His enemies I will [A]clothe with shame,
But upon himself his
[B]crown shall shine."

132:1 [A]Gen 49:24; 2 Sam 16:12 132:2 [A]Gen 49:24; Is 49:26; 60:16 132:3 [a]Lit *come into the tabernacle of* [b]Lit *go up into the couch of* [A]Job 21:28 132:4 [A]Prov 6:4 132:5 [a]Lit *Dwelling places* [A]1 Kin 8:17; 1 Chr 22:7; Ps 26:8; Acts 7:46 [B]Ps 132:2 132:6 [a]Or *the wood* [A]Gen 35:19; 1 Sam 17:12 [B]1 Sam 7:1 132:7 [a]Lit *dwelling places* [A]Ps 43:3 [B]Ps 5:7; 99:5 [C]1 Chr 28:2 132:8 [A]Num 10:35; 2 Chr 6:41; Ps 68:1 [B]Ps 132:14 [C]Ps 78:61 132:9 [A]Job 29:14 [B]Ps 30:4; 132:16; 149:5 132:10 [A]Ps 2:2; 132:17 132:11 [A]Ps 89:3, 35 [B]2 Sam 7:12-16; 1 Chr 17:11-14; 2 Chr 6:16; Ps 89:4; Acts 2:30 132:12 [A]Luke 1:32; Acts 2:30 132:13 [A]Ps 48:1, 2; 78:68 [B]Ps 68:16 132:14 [A]Ps 132:8 [B]Ps 68:16; Matt 23:21 132:15 [A]Ps 147:14 [B]Ps 107:9 132:16 [A]2 Chr 6:41; Ps 132:9 132:17 [A]Ezek 29:21; Luke 1:69 [B]1 Kin 11:36; 15:4; 2 Kin 8:19; 2 Chr 21:7; Ps 18:28 132:18 [A]Job 8:22; Ps 35:26; 109:29 [B]Ps 21:3

132:1–18 *See note on Ps 120:1–7.* The author and occasion are not specifically mentioned. However, the bringing of the tabernacle to Jerusalem in David's time seems likely (cf. 2Sa 6:12–19 with 132:6–9). Further, Solomon's quote of vv. 8–10 in his dedication of the temple (2Ch 6:41, 42) makes that time probable. Psalm 132 has strong historical implications with regard to the Davidic Covenant (cf. 2Sa 7:10–14, 16; Pss 89; 132:10, 11) and pronounced messianic and millennial overtones (Ps 132:12–18). Essentially, this psalm contains the nation's prayers for David's royal descendants which look ahead, even to Messiah.

I. Israel's First Prayer (132:1)
II. David's Vow to God (132:2–9)
III. Israel's Second Prayer (132:10)
IV. God's Vow to David (132:11–18)

132:1–9 This section focuses on David fulfilling his vow to God to bring the tabernacle to rest in Jerusalem and thus his descendants are to be remembered by the Lord.

132:1 his affliction. This seems to be inclusive from the times of being pursued by Saul (cf. 1Sa 18–26) through God's judgment because David numbered the people (cf. 2Sa 24). Perhaps it focuses on David's greatest affliction, which came from not having the ark in Jerusalem.

132:2–5 Although this specific vow is not recorded elsewhere in Scripture, the historical circumstances can be found in 2Sa 6; 1Ch 13–16.

132:2 the Mighty One of Jacob. A title last used by Jacob in Ge 49:24.

132:6–9 The ark was brought from Kiriath-jearim to Jerusalem (cf. 2Sa 6; 1Ch 13, 15).

132:6 heard of it in Ephrathah. Probably referring to David's younger days in Ephrathah, which was an earlier name for Bethlehem (cf. Ru 1:1, 2; 4:11), when he and his family had heard of the ark but had not seen it. **found it in the field of Jaar.** After the ark of the covenant was returned by the Philistines in the days of Saul (cf. 1Sa 7:1, 2), it rested at the house of Abinadab in Kiriath-jearim until David decided to move to Jerusalem (cf. 2Sa 6; 1Ch 13–16).

132:7 His footstool. God's throne is in heaven (cf. Is 66:1) and His footstool is on earth (cf. Ps 99:5), figuratively speaking. Thus to worship at the ark of the covenant on earth would be, so to speak, at God's footstool.

132:8 Arise, O LORD. Since the Holy Place contained the bread of the presence (Ex 25:30; 1Sa 21:6), the psalmist refers to moving the ark to Jerusalem.

132:9 Describes the proper inward attire for the priests who would oversee the move.

132:10–18 This section focuses on God's fulfilling His vow to David to perpetuate the Davidic throne and thus his descendants are to be remembered by the Lord.

132:10 A prayer that God's promise and favor would not be withheld from David's descendants on the throne of Judah. **Your anointed.** As David had been anointed king (1Sa 16:13), so a greater King had been anointed, namely Christ, but not yet seated on the throne (cf. Is 61:1; Lk 4:18, 19).

132:11, 12 God's covenant with David (2Sa 23:5) is summarized here from 2Sa 7:11–16 and 1Ki 9:1–9.

132:12 This conditional aspect could interrupt the occupation of the throne, but it would not invalidate God's promise to one day seat the Messiah as king forever (cf. Eze 37:24–28).

132:13–18 This section looks forward prophetically to the day that Jesus Christ, the son of David and the son of Abraham (Mt 1:1), will be installed by God on the throne of David in the city of God to rule and bring peace on earth, especially Israel (cf. Pss 2, 89, 110; Is 25, 26; Jer 23:5, 6; 33:14–18; Eze 37; Da 2:44, 45; Zec 14:1–11).

132:13 Zion. Refers to earthly Jerusalem.

PSALM 133

THE EXCELLENCY OF BROTHERLY UNITY.

A Song of Ascents, of David.

1 Behold, how good and how pleasant it is
For [A]brothers to dwell together in unity!
2 It is like the precious [A]oil upon the head,
Coming down upon the beard,
Even Aaron's beard,
Coming down upon the
[B]edge of his robes.
3 It is like the [A]dew of [B]Hermon
Coming down upon the
[C]mountains of Zion;
For there the LORD [D]commanded
the blessing—[E]life forever.

PSALM 134

GREETINGS OF NIGHT WATCHERS.

A Song of Ascents.

1 Behold, [A]bless the LORD, all
[B]servants of the LORD,
Who [a,C]serve [D]by night in the
house of the LORD!
2 [A]Lift up your hands to the [B]sanctuary
And bless the LORD.
3 May the LORD [A]bless you from Zion,
He who [B]made heaven and earth.

PSALM 135

PRAISE THE LORD'S WONDERFUL WORKS. VANITY OF IDOLS.

1 [a,A]Praise [b]the LORD!
Praise the name of the LORD;
Praise *Him,* O [B]servants of the LORD,
2 You who stand in the house of the LORD,
In the [A]courts of the house of our God!
3 [a]Praise [b]the LORD, for [A]the LORD is good;
[B]Sing praises to His name, [C]for it is lovely.
4 For [a]the LORD has [A]chosen
Jacob for Himself,
Israel for His [b,B]own possession.

5 For I know that [A]the LORD is great
And that our Lord is [B]above all gods.
6 [A]Whatever the LORD pleases, He does,
In heaven and in earth, in the
seas and in all deeps.
7 [a]He [A]causes the [b]vapors to ascend
from the ends of the earth;
Who [B]makes lightnings for the rain,
Who [A]brings forth the wind
from His treasuries.

8 [a]He [A]smote the firstborn of Egypt,
[b]Both of man and beast.
9 [a]He sent [A]signs and wonders into
your midst, O Egypt,
Upon [B]Pharaoh and all his servants.

133:1 [A]Gen 13:8; Heb 13:1 133:2 [A]Ex 29:7; 30:25, 30; Lev 8:12 [B]Ex 28:33; 39:24 133:3 [A]Prov 19:12; Hos 14:5; Mic 5:7 [B]Deut 3:9; 4:48 [C]Ps 48:2; 74:2; 78:68 [D]Lev 25:21; Deut 28:8; Ps 42:8 [E]Ps 21:4 134:1 [a]Lit *stand* [A]Ps 103:21 [B]Ps 135:1, 2 [C]Deut 10:8; 1 Chr 23:30; 2 Chr 29:11 [D]1 Chr 9:33 134:2 [A]Ps 28:2; 1 Tim 2:8 [B]Ps 63:2 134:3 [A]Ps 128:5 [B]Ps 124:8 135:1 [a]Or *Hallelujah!* [b]Heb *YAH* [A]Ps 113:1 [B]Ps 134:1 135:2 [A]Ps 92:13; 116:19 135:3 [a]Or *Hallelujah!* [b]Heb *YAH* [A]Ps 100:5; 119:68 [B]Ps 68:4 [C]Ps 147:1 135:4 [a]Heb *YAH* [b]Or *special treasure* [A]Deut 7:6; 10:15; Ps 105:6 [B]Ex 19:5; Mal 3:17; Titus 2:14; 1 Pet 2:9 135:5 [A]Ps 48:1; 95:3; 145:3 [B]Ps 97:9 135:6 [A]Ps 115:3 135:7 [a]Lit *The one who* [b]I.e. clouds [A]Jer 10:13; 51:16 [B]Job 28:25, 26; 38:25, 26; Zech 10:1 135:8 [a]Lit *The one who* [b]Lit *From man to beast* [A]Ex 12:12; Ps 78:51; 105:36 135:9 [a]Lit *The one who* [A]Ex 7:10; Deut 6:22; Ps 78:43 [B]Ps 136:15

133:1–3 *See note on Ps 120:1–7.* The occasion for this Davidic psalm is unknown. Perhaps it was prompted by the nation's coming together in unity at his coronation (cf. 2Sa 5:1–3; 1Ch 11:1–3). Its teaching on fraternal unity would have been instructive to David's sons, who were antagonistic toward one another, e.g., Absalom murdered Amnon (2Sa 13:28–33) and Adonijah tried to preempt Solomon's right to the throne (1Ki 1:5–53).

I. Praise of Unity (133:1)
II. Pictures of Unity (133:2, 3)
  A. Oil on Aaron's head (133:2)
  B. Dew on Mt. Zion (133:3)

133:1 brothers. Those whose lineage can be traced to Abraham, Isaac, and Jacob. **unity.** While national unity might be on the surface, the foundation must always be spiritual unity. This would be the emphasis here, since these songs were sung by Jewish pilgrims traveling to the 3 great feasts.

133:2 oil upon. Most likely refers to the anointing of Aaron as High Priest of the nation (cf. Ex 29:7; 30:30), which would picture a rich spiritual blessing as a first priority.

133:3 the dew of Hermon. Mt. Hermon, a 9,200 ft. peak at the extreme northern portion of Israel, provided the major water supply for the Jordan River by its melting snow. This reference could be to the Jordan water supply or figuratively to the actual prevalent dew of Hermon being hypothetically transported to Zion. Either way, this pictures a refreshing material blessing as a second, lesser priority. **there.** Seems to refer to Zion. **life forever.** Cf. Ps 21:4–6.

134:1–3 *See note on Ps 120:1–7.* This final song in the "songs of ascent" seems to picture the worshipers exhorting the priests to continued faithfulness (134:1, 2) while the priests bestow a final blessing on the faithful as the feast ends and the pilgrims depart Zion for home (134:3).

I. Exhortation to Faithfulness (134:1, 2)
II. Solicitation of Blessing (134:3)

134:1 servants. Levites who ministered to God's people. **by night.** The burnt offerings continued day and night (cf. Lv 6:8–13), as did the Levitical service (cf. 1Ch 9:33). **house of the LORD!** Refers to the tabernacle up to the time of David (Ex 23:19; 2Sa 12:20) and to the temple from Solomon on (1Ki 9:10).

134:2 Lift up your hands. A common OT praise practice (cf. Pss 28:2; 63:4; 119:48; 141:2; La 2:19), which was understood figuratively in the NT (1Ti 2:8).

134:3 the LORD. The Creator blesses His human creation. **bless you from Zion.** Since God's presence resided in the tabernacle/temple on Zion, from a human perspective it would be the source of divine blessing.

135:1–21 Psalms 135 and 136 conclude the "Great Hallel." The composer and occasion of Ps 135 are unknown but likely post-Exilic. Psalm 135:15–20 is strikingly similar to Ps 115:4–11.

I. Call to Praise (135:1, 2)
II. Causes for Praise (135:3–18)
  A. God's Character (135:3)
  B. God's Choice of Jacob (135:4)
  C. God's Sovereignty in Creation (135:5–7)
  D. God's Deliverance of Israel (135:8–12)
  E. God's Unique Nature (135:13–18)
III. Concluding Praise (135:19–21)

135:1, 2 servants . . . stand . . . In the courts. Addressed to the priests and Levites (cf. 134:1).

135:3 the LORD is good. A consistent theme in the psalms (cf. Pss 16:2; 25:8; 34:8; 73:1; 86:5; 100:5; 106:1; 107:1; 118:1; 136:1; 145:9).

135:4 the LORD has chosen. Refers to God's unique selection of the offspring of Abraham, Isaac, and Jacob to enjoy God's covenant blessing (cf. Dt 7:6–8; 14:2; Ps 105:6; Is 41:8, 9; 43:20; 44:1; 49:7). **His own possession.** Cf. Dt 26:18, 19. *See note on Ps 148:14.*

135:5 the LORD is great. A common superlative to distinguish the true God of Israel from the false gods of the other nations (cf. Dt 7:21; Pss 48:1; 77:13; 86:10; 95:3; 104:1; 145:3; 147:5).

135:7 vapors to ascend. Refers to the water cycle of earthly evaporation and condensation in the clouds.

135:8–12 In reference to God's deliverance of Israel from Egypt to the Promised Land.

135:8 smote. The final plague in Egypt (cf. Ex 11).

135:9 signs and wonders. Cf. Dt 26:8; 29:3; 34:11.

10 [a,A]He [B]smote many nations
And slew mighty kings,
11 [A]Sihon, king of the Amorites,
And [B]Og, king of Bashan,
And [C]all the kingdoms of Canaan;
12 And He [A]gave their land as a heritage,
A heritage to Israel His people.
13 Your [A]name, O LORD, is everlasting,
Your [a]remembrance, O LORD,
[b]throughout all generations.
14 For the LORD will [A]judge His people
And [B]will have compassion
on His servants.
15 The [A]idols of the nations are
but silver and gold,
The work of man's hands.
16 They have mouths, but
they do not speak;
They have eyes, but they do not see;
17 They have ears, but they do not hear,
Nor is there any breath at
all in their mouths.
18 Those who make them
will be like them,
Yes, everyone who trusts in them.

19 O house of [A]Israel, bless the LORD;
O house of Aaron, bless the LORD;
20 O house of Levi, bless the LORD;
You [A]who [a]revere the LORD,
bless the LORD.
21 Blessed be the LORD [A]from Zion,
Who [B]dwells in Jerusalem.
[a]Praise [b]the LORD!

PSALM 136

THANKS FOR THE LORD'S GOODNESS TO ISRAEL.

1 [A]Give thanks to the LORD, for [B]He is good,
For [C]His lovingkindness is everlasting.
2 Give thanks to the [A]God of gods,
For His lovingkindness is everlasting.
3 Give thanks to the [A]Lord of lords,
For His lovingkindness is everlasting.
4 To Him who [A]alone does great [a]wonders,
For His lovingkindness is everlasting;
5 To Him who [A]made the
heavens [a,B]with skill,
For His lovingkindness is everlasting;
6 To Him who [A]spread out the
earth above the waters,
For His lovingkindness is everlasting;
7 To Him who [A]made *the* great lights,
For His lovingkindness is everlasting:
8 The [A]sun to rule [a]by day,
For His lovingkindness is everlasting,
9 The [A]moon and stars to rule [a]by night,
For His lovingkindness is everlasting.

10 To Him who [A]smote [a]the Egyptians
in their firstborn,
For His lovingkindness is everlasting,
11 And [A]brought Israel out
from their midst,
For His lovingkindness is everlasting,
12 With a [A]strong hand and an
[B]outstretched arm,
For His lovingkindness is everlasting.
13 To Him who [A]divided the
[a]Red Sea [b]asunder,
For His lovingkindness is everlasting,
14 And [A]made Israel pass through
the midst of it,
For His lovingkindness is everlasting;
15 But [A]He [a]overthrew Pharaoh and
his army in the [b]Red Sea,
For His lovingkindness is everlasting.
16 To Him who [A]led His people
through the wilderness,
For His lovingkindness is everlasting;
17 To Him who [A]smote great kings,
For His lovingkindness is everlasting,
18 And [A]slew [a]mighty kings,
For His lovingkindness is everlasting:
19 [A]Sihon, king of the Amorites,
For His lovingkindness is everlasting,

135:10 [a]Lit *The one who* [A]Num 21:24; Ps 135:10-12; 136:17-21 [B]Ps 44:2 135:11 [A]Num 21:21-26; Deut 29:7 [B]Num 21:33-35 [C]Josh 12:7-24 135:12 [A]Deut 29:8; Ps 78:55; 136:21, 22 135:13 [a]Or *memorial* [b]Lit *to* [A]Ex 3:15; Ps 102:12 135:14 [A]Deut 32:36; Ps 50:4 [B]Ps 90:13; 106:46 135:15 [A]Ps 115:4-8; 135:15-18 135:19 [A]Ps 115:9 135:20 [a]Lit *fear* [A]Ps 118:4 135:21 [a]Or *Hallelujah!* [b]Heb *YAH* [A]Ps 128:5; 134:3 [B]Ps 132:14 136:1 [A]1 Chr 16:34; Ps 106:1; 107:1; 118:1; Jer 33:11 [B]2 Chr 5:13; 7:3; Ezra 3:11; Ps 100:5 [C]1 Chr 16:41; 2 Chr 20:21; Ps 118:1-4 136:2 [A]Deut 10:17 136:3 [A]Deut 10:17 136:4 [a]I.e. wonderful acts [A]Deut 6:22; Job 9:10; Ps 72:18 136:5 [a]Lit *with understanding* [A]Gen 1:1 [B]Ps 104:24; Prov 3:19; Jer 10:12; 51:15 136:6 [A]Gen 1:2, 6, 9; Ps 24:2; Is 42:5; 44:24; Jer 10:12 136:7 [A]Gen 1:14-18; Ps 74:16 136:8 [a]Or *over the* [A]Gen 1:16 136:9 [a]Or *over the* [A]Gen 1:16 136:10 [a]Lit *Egypt* [A]Ex 12:29; Ps 78:51; 135:8 136:11 [A]Ex 12:51; 13:3; Ps 105:43 136:12 [A]Ex 6:1; 13:9; 1 Kin 8:42; Neh 1:10; Ps 44:3; Jer 32:21 [B]Ex 6:6; Deut 4:34; 5:15; 7:19; 9:29; 11:2; 2 Kin 17:36; 2 Chr 6:32; Jer 32:17 136:13 [a]Lit *Sea of Reeds* [b]Lit *in parts* [A]Ex 14:21; Ps 66:6; 78:13 136:14 [A]Ex 14:22; Ps 106:9 136:15 [a]Lit *shook off* [b]Lit *Sea of Reeds* [A]Ex 14:27; Ps 78:53; 106:11 136:16 [A]Ex 13:18; 15:22; Deut 8:15; Ps 78:52 136:17 [A]Ps 135:10-12; 136:17-22 136:18 [a]Lit *majestic* [A]Deut 29:7 136:19 [A]Num 21:21-24

135:11 Sihon. Cf. Nu 21:21, 32, which recounts Israel's defeat of Sihon, king of the Amorites. **Og.** Cf. Nu 21:33–35, which recounts Israel's defeat of Og, king of Bashan. **kingdoms of Canaan.** Joshua 6–12 recounts Joshua's conquest of the Land.

135:12 gave their land … to Israel. As promised to Abraham (cf. Ge 15:18–21).

135:13–18 The living God of Israel (vv. 13–14) stands decidedly superior to the imaginary gods of the nations (vv. 15–18).

135:18 make them … like them. Both are worthless and will know nothing of eternal life.

135:19–20 The categories 1) Israel, 2) Aaron, 3) Levi, and 4) you who fear the Lord, refer to the nation as a whole (Israel), the priesthood (Aaron and Levi), and the true believers (who fear the Lord).

136:1–26 This psalm, extremely similar to Ps 135, closes the Great Hallel. Unique to all the psalms, Ps 136 uses the antiphonal refrain "For His lovingkindness is everlasting" after each stanza, perhaps spoken by the people in responsive worship. The author and occasion remain unknown.

I. Call to Praise (136:1–3)
II. Causes for Praise (136:4–22)
  A. God's Creation (136:4–9)
  B. God's Deliverance (136:10–15)
  C. God's Care and Gift (136:16–22)
III. Concluding Praise (136:23–26)

136:1 He is good. *See note on Ps 135:3.*

136:4–9 Cf. Ge 1.

136:10–15 Cf. Ex 11–14.

136:16–22 Cf. Nu 14–36.

136:19 Sihon. *See note on Ps 135:11.*

20 And [A]Og, king of Bashan,
For His lovingkindness is everlasting,
21 And [A]gave their land as a heritage,
For His lovingkindness is everlasting,
22 Even a heritage to Israel His [A]servant,
For His lovingkindness is everlasting.

23 Who [A]remembered us in our low estate,
For His lovingkindness is everlasting,
24 And has [A]rescued us from
our adversaries,
For His lovingkindness is everlasting;
25 Who [A]gives food to all flesh,
For His lovingkindness is everlasting.
26 Give thanks to the [A]God of heaven,
For His lovingkindness is everlasting.

PSALM 137

AN EXPERIENCE OF THE CAPTIVITY.

1 By the [A]rivers of Babylon,
There we sat down and [B]wept,
When we remembered Zion.
2 Upon the [a,A]willows in the midst of it
We [B]hung our [b]harps.
3 For there our captors
[a,A]demanded of us [b]songs,
And [B]our tormentors mirth, *saying,*
"Sing us one of the songs of Zion."

4 How can we sing [A]the LORD'S song
In a foreign land?
5 If I [A]forget you, O Jerusalem,
May my right hand [a]forget *her skill.*
6 May my [A]tongue cling to the
roof of my mouth
If I do not remember you,
If I do not [a,B]exalt Jerusalem
Above my chief joy.

7 Remember, O LORD, against
the sons of [A]Edom
The day of Jerusalem,
Who said, "Raze it, raze it
[B]To its very foundation."
8 O daughter of Babylon, you
[a,A]devastated one,
How blessed will be the one
who [B]repays you
With [b]the recompense with
which you have repaid us.
9 How blessed will be the one who
seizes and [A]dashes your little ones
Against the rock.

PSALM 138

THANKSGIVING FOR THE LORD'S FAVOR.

A Psalm of David.

1 [A]I will give You thanks with all my heart;
I will sing praises to You
before the [B]gods.
2 I will bow down [A]toward
Your holy temple
And [B]give thanks to Your
name for Your lovingkindness
and Your [a]truth;
For You have [C]magnified Your [b]word
[c]according to all Your name.
3 On the day I [A]called, You answered me;
You made me bold with
[B]strength in my soul.

136:20 [A]Num 21:33-35 136:21 [A]Josh 12:1 136:22 [A]Ps 105:6; Is 41:8; 44:1; 45:4 136:23 [A]Ps 9:12; 103:14; 106:45 136:24 [A]Judg 6:9; Neh 9:28; Ps 107:2 136:25 [A]Ps 104:27; 145:15 136:26 [A]Gen 24:3, 7; 2 Chr 36:23; Ezra 1:2; 5:11; Neh 1:4 137:1 [A]Ezek 1:1, 3 [B]Neh 1:4 137:2 [a]Or *poplars* [b]Lit *lyres* [A]Lev 23:40; Is 44:4 [B]Job 30:31; Is 24:8; Ezek 26:13 137:3 [a]Lit *asked* [b]Lit *words of song* [A]Ps 80:6 [B]Is 49:17 137:4 [A]2 Chr 29:27; Neh 12:46 137:5 [a]I.e. become lame [A]Is 65:11 137:6 [a]Lit *cause to ascend* [A]Job 29:10; Ps 22:15; Ezek 3:26 [B]Neh 2:3 137:7 [A]Ps 83:4-8; Is 34:5, 6; Jer 49:7-22; Lam 4:21; Ezek 25:12-14; 35:2; Amos 1:11; Obad 10-14 [B]Ps 74:7; Hab 3:13 137:8 [a]Or *devastator* [b]Lit *your recompense* [A]Is 13:1-22; 47:1-15; Jer 25:12; 50:1-46; 51:1-64 [B]Jer 50:15; 51:24, 35, 36, 49; Rev 18:6 137:9 [A]2 Kin 8:12; Is 13:16; Hos 13:16; Nah 3:10 138:1 [A]Ps 111:1 [B]Ps 95:3; 96:4; 97:7 138:2 [a]Or *faithfulness* [b]Or *promise* [C]Or *together with* [A]1 Kin 8:29; Ps 5:7; 28:2 [B]Ps 140:13 [C]Is 42:21 138:3 [A]Ps 118:5 [B]Ps 28:7; 46:1

136:20 Og. *See note on Ps 135:11.*

136:23 low estate. Cf. Dt 7:7; 9:4, 5; Eze 16:1–5.

137:1–9 A psalm, explicitly about the Babylonian captivity of Judah. Its author and date are unknown.

I. Lamentations (137:1–4)
II. Conditions (137:5, 6)
III. Imprecations (137:7–9)

137:1 the rivers of Babylon. The Tigris and Euphrates Rivers. **we … wept.** They even wept when the exile was over and the second temple was being built (cf. Ezr 3:12), so deep was their sorrow. **Zion.** The dwelling place of God on earth (Pss 9:11; 76:2) which was destroyed by the Babylonians (2Ch 36:19; Pss 74:6–8; 79:1; Is 64:10, 11; Jer 52:12–16; La 2:4, 6–9; Mic 3:12).

137:2 hung our harps. In captivity, there was no use for an instrument of joy (cf. Is 24:8).

137:3 our captors. The Babylonians taunted the Jews to sing of their once beautiful, but now destroyed, Zion. **the songs of Zion.** Cf. Pss 46, 48, 76, 84, 87, 122.

137:4 How can we sing. A rhetorical question whose answer is, "We can't!" **the LORD's song.** A unique way to refer to divine inspiration of the psalms.

137:5, 6 Their refusal to sing was not caused by either of 2 unthinkable situations: 1) they forgot Jerusalem; 2) they did not have Jerusalem as their chief joy. The worst of punishments should be imposed if any one or a combination of these factors were to become true.

137:7 the sons of Edom. Edomites had been allied with the Babylonians in the fall and destruction of Jerusalem (cf. Is 21:11, 12; Jer 49:7–12; La 4:21; Eze 25:12–14; 35:1–15; Ob 11–14). The psalmist only prayed for that which the Lord had always promised. **The day of Jerusalem.** The day Jerusalem was destroyed. *See notes on Ps 137:1.*

137:8 devastated. Cf. Is 13:1–14:23, 46, 47; Jer 50; 51; Hab 1:11; 2:6–17.

137:8, 9 blessed … the one. For these will be God's human instruments used to carry out His prophesied will for the destruction of Babylon.

138:1–8 The next 8 psalms were written by David (Pss 138–145) and are his last in the Psalter. The occasion is unknown, although it's possible that David wrote them in response to the Davidic Covenant (cf. 2Sa 7:12–14, 16).

I. Individual Praise (138:1–3)
II. International Praise (138:4, 5)
III. Invincible Praise (138:6–8)

138:1 the gods. This can refer to either pagan royalty (cf. Ps 82:1) and/or to the idols they worship.

138:2 holy temple. Refers to the tabernacle since Solomon's temple has not yet been built. **Your word … Your name.** Most likely this means that God's latest revelation ("Your word") exceeded all previous revelation about God. This would be in concert with David's prayer (2Sa 7:18–29) after he received the Davidic promise (2Sa 7:12–14, 16).

4 [A]All the kings of the earth will give
thanks to You, O LORD,
When they have heard the
words of Your mouth.
5 And they will [A]sing of the
ways of the LORD,
For [B]great is the glory of the LORD.
6 For [A]though the LORD is exalted,
Yet He [B]regards the lowly,
But the [C]haughty He knows from afar.

7 Though I [A]walk in the midst of
trouble, You will [a,B]revive me;
You will [C]stretch forth Your hand
against the wrath of my enemies,
And Your right hand will [D]save me.
8 The LORD will [A]accomplish
what concerns me;
Your [B]lovingkindness, O LORD,
is everlasting;
[C]Do not forsake the [D]works of Your hands.

PSALM 139

GOD'S OMNIPRESENCE AND OMNISCIENCE.

For the choir director. A Psalm of David.

1 O LORD, You have [A]searched
me and known *me.*
2 You [A]know [a]when I sit down
and [b]when I rise up;
You [B]understand my thought from afar.
3 You [a,A]scrutinize my [b]path
and my lying down,
And are intimately acquainted
with all my ways.
4 [a]Even before there is a word on my tongue,
Behold, O LORD, You [A]know it all.
5 You have [A]enclosed me
behind and before,
And [B]laid Your hand upon me.
6 *Such* [A]knowledge is [B]too
wonderful for me;
It is *too* high, I cannot attain to it.

7 [A]Where can I go from Your Spirit?
Or where can I flee from Your presence?
8 [A]If I ascend to heaven, You are there;
If I make my bed in [a]Sheol,
behold, [B]You are there.
9 If I take the wings of the dawn,
If I dwell in the remotest part of the sea,
10 Even there Your hand will [A]lead me,
And Your right hand will lay hold of me.
11 If I say, "Surely the [A]darkness
will [a]overwhelm me,
And the light around me will be night,"
12 Even the [A]darkness is not dark [a]to You,
And the night is as bright as the day.
[B]Darkness and light are alike *to You.*

13 For You [A]formed my [a]inward parts;
You [B]wove me in my mother's womb.
14 I will give thanks to You, for [a]I am
fearfully and wonderfully made;
[A]Wonderful are Your works,
And my soul knows it very well.
15 My [a,A]frame was not hidden from You,
When I was made in secret,
And skillfully wrought in the
[B]depths of the earth;
16 Your [A]eyes have seen my
unformed substance;
And in [B]Your book were all written
The [C]days that were ordained *for me,*
When as yet there was not one of them.

17 How precious also are Your
[A]thoughts to me, O God!
How vast is the sum of them!
18 If I should count them, they would
[A]outnumber the sand.
When [B]I awake, I am still with You.

138:4 [A]Ps 72:11; 102:15 138:5 [A]Ps 145:7 [B]Ps 21:5 138:6 [A]Ps 113:4-7 [B]Prov 3:34; Is 57:15; Luke 1:48; James 4:6; 1 Pet 5:5 [C]Ps 40:4; 101:5 138:7 [a]Or *keep me alive* [A]Ps 23:4; 143:11 [B]Ezra 9:8, 9; Ps 71:20; Is 57:15 [C]Ex 7:5; 15:12; Is 5:25; Jer 51:25; Ezek 6:14; 25:13 [D]Ps 20:6; 60:5 138:8 [A]Ps 57:2; Phil 1:6 [B]Ps 136:1 [C]Job 10:8; Ps 27:9; 71:9; 119:8 [D]Job 10:3; 14:15; Ps 100:3 139:1 [A]Ps 17:3; 44:21; Jer 12:3 139:2 [a]Lit *my sitting* [b]Lit *my rising* [A]2 Kin 19:27 [B]Ps 94:11; Is 66:18; Matt 9:4 139:3 [a]Lit *winnow* [b]Or *journeying* [A]Job 14:16; 31:4 139:4 [a]Lit *For there is not* [A]Heb 4:13 139:5 [A]Ps 34:7; 125:2 [B]Job 9:33 139:6 [A]Rom 11:33 [B]Job 42:3 139:7 [A]Jer 23:24 139:8 [a]I.e. the nether world [A]Amos 9:2-4 [B]Job 26:6; Prov 15:11 139:10 [A]Ps 23:2, 3 139:11 [a]Lit *bruise;* some commentators read *cover* [A]Job 22:13 139:12 [a]Lit *from* [A]Job 34:22; Dan 2:22 [B]1 John 1:5 139:13 [a]Lit *kidneys* [A]Ps 119:73; Is 44:24 [B]Job 10:11 139:14 [a]Some ancient versions read *You are fearfully wonderful* [A]Ps 40:5 139:15 [a]Lit *bones were* [A]Job 10:8-10; Eccl 11:5 [B]Ps 63:9 139:16 [A]Job 10:8-10; Eccl 11:5 [B]Ps 56:8 [C]Job 14:5 139:17 [A]Ps 40:5; 92:5 139:18 [A]Ps 40:5 [B]Ps 3:5

138:4 All the kings. In contrast to Ps 2:1–3, cf. Pss 68:32; 72:11, 12; 96:1, 3, 7, 8; 97:1; 98:4; 100:1; 102:15; 148:11.

138:6, 7 David sees himself as "the lowly" and his enemies as "the haughty."

138:8 accomplish. Refers to God's work in David's life, especially the Davidic Covenant (cf. 2Sa 7:12–14, 16).

139:1–24 This intensely personal Davidic psalm expresses the psalmist's awe that God knew him, even to the minutest detail. David might have remembered the Lord's words, "the LORD looks at the heart" (1Sa 16:7). The exact occasion is unknown.

I. God's Omniscience (139:1–6)
II. God's Omnipresence (139:7–12)
III. God's Omnipotence (139:13–18)
IV. David's Obeisance (139:19–24)

139:1–6 God knows everything about David.

139:1 searched me. As it has been in David's life, he prays later that it will continue to be (cf. vv. 23, 24). David understands that nothing inside of him can be hidden from God.

139:5 enclosed me. God used circumstances to limit David's actions.

139:6 too wonderful. Cf. Ps 131:1; Ro 11:33–36.

139:7–12 God was always watching over David, and thus it was impossible to do anything over which God is not a spectator.

139:7 Your Spirit. A reference to the Holy Spirit (cf. Pss 51:11; 143:10). See "The Anointing of the Holy Spirit in the OT" at Ps 51.

139:9 the wings of the dawn. In conjunction with "the remotest part of the sea," David uses this literary figure to express distance.

139:13–18 God's power is magnified in the development of human life before birth.

139:13 formed ... wove. By virtue of the divinely designed period of pregnancy, God providentially watches over the development of the child while yet in the mother's womb.

139:15 secret ... depths of the earth. Used figuratively of the womb.

139:16 Your book. This figure of speech likens God's mind to a book of remembrance. **not one of them.** God sovereignly ordained David's life before he was conceived.

139:17, 18 David expresses his amazement at the infinite mind of God compared to the limited mind of man, especially as it relates to the physiology of human life (cf. vv. 13–16).

19 O that You would [A]slay the wicked, O God;
[B]Depart from me, therefore,
[C]men of bloodshed.
20 For they [A]speak [a]against You wickedly,
And Your enemies [b,B]take
Your name in vain.
21 Do I not [A]hate those who
hate You, O LORD?
And do I not [B]loathe those who
rise up against You?
22 I hate them with the utmost hatred;
They have become my enemies.

23 [A]Search me, O God, and know my heart;
[B]Try me and know my anxious thoughts;
24 And see if there be any
[a,A]hurtful way in me,
And [B]lead me in the [C]everlasting way.

PSALM 140

PRAYER FOR PROTECTION AGAINST THE WICKED.

For the choir director. A Psalm of David.

1 [A]Rescue me, O LORD, from evil men;
Preserve me from [B]violent men
2 Who [A]devise evil things in *their* hearts;
They [B]continually stir up wars.
3 They [A]sharpen their tongues as a serpent;
[B]Poison of a viper is under their lips.
[a]*Selah*

4 [A]Keep me, O LORD, from the
hands of the wicked;
[B]Preserve me from violent men
Who have [a]purposed to [b,C]trip up my feet.
5 The proud have [A]hidden a trap
for me, and cords;
They have spread a [B]net by the [a]wayside;
They have set [C]snares for me. *Selah*

6 I [A]said to the LORD, "You are my God;
[B]Give ear, O LORD, to the [C]voice
of my supplications.
7 "O [a]GOD the Lord, [A]the strength
of my salvation,
You have [B]covered my head
in the day of [b]battle.
8 "Do not grant, O LORD, the
[A]desires of the wicked;
Do not promote [B]his *evil* device, *that* they
not be exalted. *Selah*

9 "As for the head of those who surround me,
May the [A]mischief of their lips cover them.
10 "May [A]burning coals fall upon them;
May they be [B]cast into the fire,
Into [a]deep pits from which
they [C]cannot rise.
11 "May a [a]slanderer not be
established in the earth;
[A]May evil hunt the violent man [b]speedily."

12 I know that the LORD will [A]maintain
the cause of the afflicted
And [B]justice for the poor.
13 Surely the [A]righteous will give
thanks to Your name;
The [B]upright will dwell in Your presence.

PSALM 141

AN EVENING PRAYER FOR SANCTIFICATION AND PROTECTION.

A Psalm of David.

1 O LORD, I call upon You; [A]hasten to me!
[B]Give ear to my voice when I call to You!
2 May my prayer be [a]counted as
[A]incense before You;
The [B]lifting up of my hands as
the [C]evening offering.

139:19 [A]Is 11:4 [B]Ps 6:8; 119:115 [C]Ps 5:6; 26:9 139:20 [a]Or *of* [b]Some mss read *lift themselves up* against You [A]Jude 15 [B]Ex 20:7; Deut 5:11 139:21 [A]2 Chr 19:2; Ps 26:5; 31:6 [B]Ps 119:158 139:23 [A]Job 31:6; Ps 26:2 [B]Ps 7:9; Prov 17:3; Jer 11:20; 1 Thess 2:4 139:24 [a]Lit *way of pain* [A]Ps 146:9; Prov 15:9; 28:10; Jer 25:5; 36:3 [B]Ps 5:8; 143:10 [C]Ps 16:11 140:1 [A]Ps 17:13; 59:2; 71:4 [B]Ps 18:48; 86:14; 140:11 140:2 [A]Ps 7:14; 36:4; 52:2; Prov 6:14; Is 59:4; Hos 7:15 [B]Ps 56:6 140:3 [a]*Selah* may mean: *Pause, Crescendo* or *Musical interlude* [A]Ps 57:4; 64:3 [B]Ps 58:4; Rom 3:13; James 3:8 140:4 [a]Or *devised* [b]Lit *push violently* [A]Ps 71:4 [B]Ps 140:1 [C]Ps 36:11 140:5 [a]Lit *track* [A]Job 18:9; Ps 35:7; 141:9; 142:3 [B]Ps 31:4; 57:6; Lam 1:13 [C]Ps 141:9; Is 8:14; Amos 3:5 140:6 [A]Ps 16:2; 31:14 [B]Ps 143:1 [C]Ps 116:1; 130:2 140:7 [a]Heb *YHWH*, usually rendered *LORD* [b]Lit *weapons* [A]Ps 28:8; 118:14 [B]Ps 144:10 140:8 [A]Ps 112:10 [B]Esth 9:25; Ps 10:2, 3 140:9 [A]Ps 7:16; Prov 18:7 140:10 [a]Lit *watery* [A]Ps 11:6 [B]Ps 21:9; Matt 3:10 [C]Ps 36:12 140:11 [a]Lit *man of tongue* [b]Lit *thrust upon thrust* [A]Ps 34:21 140:12 [A]1 Kin 8:45, 49; Ps 9:4; 18:27; 82:3 [B]Ps 12:5; 35:10 140:13 [A]Ps 97:12 [B]Ps 11:7; 16:11; 17:15 141:1 [A]Ps 22:19; 38:22; 70:5 [B]Ps 5:1; 143:1 141:2 [a]Lit *fixed* [A]Ex 30:8; Luke 1:10; Rev 5:8; 8:3, 4 [B]1 Tim 2:8 [C]Ex 29:39, 41; 1 Kin 18:29, 36; Dan 9:21

139:22 utmost hatred. David has no other response to God's enemies than that of hatred, i.e., he is not neutral toward them nor will he ever ally himself with them.

139:23, 24 In light of vv. 19–22, David invites God to continue searching his heart to root out any unrighteousness, even when it is expressed against God's enemies.

139:24 the everlasting way. David expresses his desire/expectation of eternal life (*see notes on Php 1:6*).

140:1–13 Davidic authorship is stated here, but the circumstances are unknown. It is like the psalms earlier in the Psalter that feature the usual complaint, prayer, and confident hope of relief.

I. Concerning David (140:1–5)
  A. "Deliver Me" (140:1–3)
  B. "Protect Me" (140:4, 5)
II. Concerning David's Enemies (140:6–11)
  A. "Thwart Them" (140:6–8)
  B. "Punish Them" (140:9–11)
III. Concerning the Lord (140:12, 13)

140:1–3 The emphasis here is deliverance from evil plans.

140:3 viper. A type of snake (cf. Ro 3:13), signifying cunning and venom.

140:4, 5 The emphasis here is protection from being captured.

140:6–8 The emphasis here is upon God's thwarting the plans of David's enemy.

140:7 covered my head. God has figuratively been David's helmet in battle.

140:9–11 The emphasis here is upon God's turning their evil plans back on them in judgment.

140:12, 13 David expresses unshakeable confidence in the character of God and the outcome for the righteous (cf. Pss 10:17, 18; 74:21; 82:3, 4).

141:1–10 Another psalm of lament by David whose occasion is unknown. This psalm is comprised of 4 prayers that have been combined into one.

I. Prayer for God's Haste (141:1, 2)
II. Prayer for Personal Righteousness (141:3–5)
III. Prayer for Justice (141:6, 7)
IV. Prayer for Deliverance (141:8–10)

141:2 incense ... evening offering. David desired that his prayers and stretching forth for God's help (Pss 68:31; 77:2) be as disciplined and regular as the offering of incense (Ex 30:7, 8) and burnt offerings (Ex 29:38, 39) in the tabernacle.

3 Set a [A]guard, O LORD, [a]over my mouth;
Keep watch over the [B]door of my lips.
4 [A]Do not incline my heart
to any evil thing,
To practice deeds [a]of wickedness
With men who [B]do iniquity;
And [C]do not let me eat of their delicacies.

5 Let the [A]righteous smite me [a]in
kindness and reprove me;
It is [B]oil upon the head;
Do not let my head refuse it,
[b]For still my prayer [C]is [c]against
their wicked deeds.
6 Their judges are [A]thrown down
by the sides of the rock,
And they hear my words, for
they are pleasant.
7 As when one [A]plows and
breaks open the earth,
Our [B]bones have been scattered
at the [C]mouth of [a]Sheol.

8 For my [A]eyes are toward You,
O [a]GOD, the Lord;
In You I [B]take refuge; [C]do not
[b]leave me defenseless.
9 Keep me from the [a,A]jaws of the trap
which they have set for me,
And from the [B]snares of those
who do iniquity.
10 Let the wicked [A]fall into their own nets,
While I pass by [a,B]safely.

PSALM 142

PRAYER FOR HELP IN TROUBLE.

[†]Maskil of David, when he was
[•]in the cave. A Prayer.

1 I [A]cry aloud with my voice to the LORD;
I [B]make supplication with my
voice to the LORD.
2 I [A]pour out my complaint before Him;
I declare my [B]trouble before Him.
3 When [A]my spirit [a]was
overwhelmed within me,
You knew my path.
In the way where I walk
They have [B]hidden a trap for me.
4 Look to the right and see;
For there is [A]no one who regards me;
[a]There is no [B]escape for me;
[C]No one cares for my soul.

5 I cried out to You, O LORD;
I said, "You are [A]my refuge,
My [B]portion in the [C]land of the living.
6 "[A]Give heed to my cry,
For I am [B]brought very low;
Deliver me from my persecutors,
For they are too [C]strong for me.
7 "[A]Bring my soul out of prison,
So that I may give thanks
to Your name;
The righteous will surround me,
For You will [B]deal bountifully with me."

PSALM 143

PRAYER FOR DELIVERANCE AND GUIDANCE.

A Psalm of David.

1 Hear my prayer, O LORD,
[A]Give ear to my supplications!
Answer me in Your [B]faithfulness,
in Your [C]righteousness!
2 And [A]do not enter into judgment
with Your servant,
For in Your sight [B]no man
living is righteous.
3 For the enemy has persecuted my soul;
He has crushed my life [A]to the ground;
He [B]has made me dwell in dark places,
like those who have long been dead.

141:3 [a]Lit *to* [A]Ps 34:13; 39:1; Prov 13:3; 21:23 [B]Mic 7:5 141:4 [a]Lit *in* [A]Ps 119:36 [B]Is 32:6; Hos 6:8; Mal 3:15 [C]Prov 23:6 141:5 [a]Or *lovingly* [b]Lit *And my prayer* [c]Or *in spite of their calamities* [A]Prov 9:8; 19:25; 25:12; 27:6; Eccl 7:5; Gal 6:1 [B]Ps 23:5; 133:2 [C]Ps 35:14 141:6 [A]2 Chr 25:12 141:7 [a]I.e. the nether world [A]Ps 129:3 [B]Ps 53:5 [C]Num 16:32, 33; Ps 88:3-5 141:8 [a]Heb *YHWH*, usually rendered *LORD* [b]Lit *pour out my soul* [A]Ps 25:15; 123:2 [B]Ps 2:12; 11:1 [C]Ps 27:9 141:9 [a]Lit *hands of the trap* [A]Ps 38:12; 64:5; 91:3; 119:110 [B]Ps 140:5 141:10 [a]Lit *altogether* [A]Ps 7:15; 35:8; 57:6 [B]Ps 124:7 142:1 [†]Possibly *Contemplative*, or *Didactic*, or *Skillful Psalm* [•]1 Sam 22:1; 24:3 [A]Ps 77:1 [B]Ps 30:8 142:2 [A]Ps 102: title [B]Ps 77:2 142:3 [a]Lit *fainted* [A]Ps 77:3; 143:4 [B]Ps 140:5 142:4 [a]Lit *Escape has perished from me* [A]Ps 31:11; 88:8, 18 [B]Job 11:20; Jer 25:35 [C]Jer 30:17 142:5 [A]Ps 91:2, 9 [B]Ps 16:5; 73:26 [C]Ps 27:13 142:6 [A]Ps 17:1 [B]Ps 79:8; 116:6 [C]Ps 18:17 142:7 [A]Ps 143:11; 146:7 [B]Ps 13:6 143:1 [A]Ps 140:6 [B]Ps 89:1, 2 [C]Ps 71:2 143:2 [A]Job 14:3; 22:4 [B]1 Kin 8:46; Job 4:17; 9:2; 25:4; Ps 130:3; Eccl 7:20; Rom 3:10, 20; Gal 2:16 143:3 [A]Ps 44:25 [B]Ps 88:6; Lam 3:6

141:3, 4 David prayed that God would protect him from the kind of evil that characterized his own enemy.

141:5 David acknowledged that God would use other righteous men to answer his prayer in vv. 3, 4 (cf. Pr 9:8; 19:25; 27:6; 27:17).

141:6 **judges . . . thrown down.** That the leaders of the wicked would be punished by being thrown over a cliff (cf. Lk 4:28, 29) is at the heart of David's prayer (cf. v. 5). **my words . . . pleasant.** In the sense that David's words were true.

141:7 **Our bones.** The basis on which the judges were thrown over the cliff—they had first done this to the righteous (cf. v. 10).

141:10 **fall into their own nets.** David prays that the wicked will be destroyed by their own devices.

142:1–7 Under the same circumstances as Ps 57 (according to the superscription), David recounted his desperate days hiding in the cave of Adullam (1Sa 22:1) while Saul sought him to take his life (1Sa 18–24). It appears that David's situation, for the moment at least, seems hopeless without God's intervention. Psalm 91 provides the truths that bring the solution.

I. Cry of David (142:1, 2)
II. Circumstances of David (142:3, 4)
III. Confidence of David (142:5–7)

142:4 **no one.** It appears to David that he has been totally abandoned.

142:5 **You are my refuge.** A frequent claim in the psalms (cf. Pss 7:1; 11:1; 16:1; 18:2; 25:20; 31:1; 46:1; 57:1; 61:3; 62:7; 91:2; 94:22; 141:8; 143:9; 144:2).

142:7 **prison.** The cave in which David was hidden.

143:1–12 No specific background is known for this Davidic psalm which is the final penitential psalm (cf. Pss 6, 32, 38, 51, 102, 130).

I. David's Passion (143:1, 2)
II. David's Predicament (143:3–6)
III. David's Plea (143:7–12)

143:1 **faithfulness . . . righteousness!** David fervently appeals to God's character.

143:2 **no man living is righteous.** David admits his own unrighteousness and realizes that if he is to be delivered for righteousness' sake (cf. 143:11), it will be because of God's righteousness, not his own.

4 Therefore [A]my spirit [a]is
overwhelmed within me;
My heart is [b,B]appalled
within me.

5 I [A]remember the days of old;
I [B]meditate on all Your doings;
I [C]muse on the work
of Your hands.
6 I [A]stretch out my hands to You;
My [B]soul *longs* for You, as
a [a]parched land. [b]*Selah*

7 [A]Answer me quickly, O LORD,
my [B]spirit fails;
[C]Do not hide Your face from me,
Or I will become like [D]those
who go down to the pit.
8 Let me hear Your [A]lovingkindness
[B]in the morning;
For I trust [C]in You;
Teach me the [D]way in which
I should walk;
For to You I [E]lift up my soul.
9 [A]Deliver me, O LORD,
from my enemies;
[a]I take refuge in You.

10 [A]Teach me to do Your will,
For You are my God;
Let [B]Your good Spirit [C]lead
me on level [a]ground.
11 [A]For the sake of Your name,
O LORD, [B]revive me.
[C]In Your righteousness bring
my soul out of trouble.
12 And in Your lovingkindness,
[a,A]cut off my enemies
And [B]destroy all those
who afflict my soul,
For [C]I am Your servant.

PSALM 144

PRAYER FOR RESCUE AND PROSPERITY.

A Psalm of David.

1 Blessed be the LORD, [A]my rock,
Who [B]trains my hands for war,
And my fingers for battle;
2 My lovingkindness and [A]my fortress,
My [B]stronghold and my deliverer,
My [C]shield and He in whom I take refuge,
Who [D]subdues [a]my people under me.
3 O LORD, [A]what is man, that You
take knowledge of him?
Or the son of man, that You think of him?
4 [A]Man is like a mere breath;
His [B]days are like a passing shadow.

5 [A]Bow Your heavens, O LORD,
and [B]come down;
[C]Touch the mountains, that they may smoke.
6 Flash forth [A]lightning and scatter them;
Send out Your [B]arrows and confuse them.
7 Stretch forth Your hand [A]from on high;
Rescue me and [B]deliver me
out of great waters,
Out of the hand of [C]aliens
8 Whose mouths [A]speak deceit,
And whose [B]right hand is a
right hand of falsehood.

9 I will sing a [A]new song to You, O God;
Upon a [B]harp of ten strings I
will sing praises to You,
10 Who [A]gives salvation to kings,
Who [B]rescues David His servant
from the evil sword.
11 Rescue me and deliver me out
of the hand of [A]aliens,
Whose mouth [B]speaks deceit
And whose [C]right hand is a
right hand of falsehood.

143:4 [a]Lit *faints* [b]Or *desolate* [A]Ps 77:3; 142:3 [B]Lam 3:11 143:5 [A]Ps 77:5, 10, 11 [B]Ps 77:12 [C]Ps 105:2 143:6 [a]Lit *weary* [b]*Selah* may mean: *Pause, Crescendo* or *Musical interlude* [A]Job 11:13; Ps 88:9 [B]Ps 42:2; 63:1 143:7 [A]Ps 69:17 [B]Ps 73:26; 84:2; Jer 8:18; Lam 1:22 [C]Ps 27:9; 69:17; 102:2 [D]Ps 28:1; 88:4 143:8 [A]Ps 90:14 [B]Ps 46:5 [C]Ps 25:2 [D]Ps 27:11; 32:8; 86:11 [E]Ps 25:1; 86:4 143:9 [a]Lit *To You have I hidden* [A]Ps 31:15; 59:1 143:10 [a]Lit *land* [A]Ps 25:4, 5; 119:12 [B]Neh 9:20 [C]Ps 23:3 143:11 [A]Ps 25:11 [B]Ps 119:25 [C]Ps 31:1; 71:2 143:12 [a]Or *silence* [A]Ps 54:5 [B]Ps 52:5 [C]Ps 116:16 144:1 [A]Ps 18:2 [B]2 Sam 22:35; Ps 18:34 144:2 [a]Another reading is *peoples* [A]Ps 18:2; 91:2 [B]Ps 59:9 [C]Ps 3:3; 28:7; 84:9 [D]Ps 18:39 144:3 [A]Job 7:17; Ps 8:4; Heb 2:6 144:4 [A]Ps 39:11 [B]Job 8:9; 14:2; Ps 102:11; 109:23 144:5 [A]Ps 18:9 [B]Is 64:1 [C]Ps 104:32 144:6 [A]Ps 18:14 [B]Ps 7:13; 58:7; Hab 3:11; Zech 9:14 144:7 [A]Ps 18:16 [B]Ps 69:1, 14 [C]Ps 18:44; 54:3 144:8 [A]Ps 12:2; 41:6 [B]Gen 14:22; Deut 32:40; Ps 106:26; Is 44:20 144:9 [A]Ps 33:3; 40:3 [B]Ps 33:2 144:10 [A]Ps 18:50 [B]2 Sam 18:7; Ps 140:7 144:11 [A]Ps 18:44; 54:3 [B]Ps 12:2; 41:6 [C]Gen 14:22; Deut 32:40; Ps 106:26; Is 44:20

143:6 a parched land. As a drought-struck land yearns for life-giving water, so persecuted David longs for his life-giving Deliverer.

143:7 Your face. An anthropomorphism picturing God's attention to the psalmist's plight.

143:10 Your ... Spirit. Refers to the Holy Spirit (cf. Pss 51:11; 139:7). *See note on Ps 51:11.*

143:11 sake of Your name. David appeals to God's benefit and honor, not his own (cf. Pss 23:3; 31:3; 79:9).

143:12 Your servant. To attack God's servant is to attack God, thus bringing God to the rescue.

144:1–15 This Davidic psalm, in part (144:1–8), is very similar to Ps 18:1–15. It could be that this psalm was written under the same kind of circumstances as the former, i.e., on the day that the Lord delivered him from the hand of all his enemies and from the hand of Saul (cf. 2Sa 22:1–18).

I. God's Greatness (144:1, 2)
II. Man's Insignificance (144:3, 4)
III. God's Power (144:5–8)
IV. Man's Praise (144:9, 10)
V. God's Blessing (144:11–15)

144:1 my rock. David's foundation is God—solid and unshakeable (cf. Pss 19:14; 31:3; 42:9; 62:2; 71:3; 89:26; 92:15; 95:1). **trains my hands for war.** David lived in the days of Israel's theocracy, not the NT church. God empowered the king to subdue His enemies.

144:2 God provided 6 benefits: 1) lovingkindness, 2) a fortress, 3) a stronghold, 4) a deliverer, 5) a shield, and 6) a refuge.

144:3, 4 Eternal God is contrasted with short-lived man (cf. Ps 8:4).

144:5–8 Highly figurative language is used to portray God as the heavenly warrior who comes to fight on earth on behalf of David against God's enemies.

144:9 a new song. A song of victory that celebrates deliverance/salvation (cf. Pss 33:3; 40:3; 96:1; 98:1; 144:9; 149:1; Rev 5:9; 14:3).

144:11 Cf. vv. 7, 8.

12 Let our sons in their youth be
as [A]grown-up plants,
And our daughters as [B]corner pillars
[a]fashioned as for a palace;
13 Let our [A]garners be full, furnishing
every kind of produce,
And our flocks bring forth thousands
and ten thousands in our [a]fields;
14 Let our [A]cattle [a]bear
Without [b,B]mishap and without [c,C]loss,
Let there be no [D]outcry in our streets!
15 How blessed are the people
who are so situated;
How [A]blessed are the people
whose God is the LORD!

PSALM 145

THE LORD EXTOLLED FOR HIS GOODNESS.

A Psalm of Praise, of David.

1 I will [A]extol You, [B]my God, O King,
And I will [C]bless Your name
forever and ever.
2 Every day I will bless You,
And I will [A]praise Your name
forever and ever.
3 [A]Great is the LORD, and highly to be praised,
And His [B]greatness is unsearchable.
4 One [A]generation shall praise
Your works to another,
And shall declare Your mighty acts.
5 On the [A]glorious [a]splendor
of Your majesty
And [B]on Your wonderful
works, I will meditate.
6 Men shall speak of the [a]power
of Your [A]awesome acts,
And I will [B]tell of Your greatness.
7 They shall [a]eagerly utter the memory
of Your [A]abundant goodness
And will [B]shout joyfully of
Your righteousness.
8 The LORD is [A]gracious and merciful;
Slow to anger and great in
lovingkindness.
9 The LORD is [A]good to all,
And His [B]mercies are over all His works.
10 [A]All Your works shall give
thanks to You, O LORD,
And Your [B]godly ones shall bless You.
11 They shall speak of the [A]glory
of Your kingdom
And talk of Your power;
12 To [A]make known to the sons of
men [a]Your mighty acts
And the [B]glory of the majesty
of [a]Your kingdom.
13 Your kingdom is [a]an
[A]everlasting kingdom,
And Your dominion *endures*
throughout all generations.

14 The LORD [A]sustains all who fall
And [B]raises up all who are bowed down.
15 The eyes of all [a]look to You,
And You [A]give them their
food in due time.
16 You [A]open Your hand
And satisfy the desire of
every living thing.

17 The LORD is [A]righteous in all His ways
And kind in all His deeds.
18 The LORD is [A]near to all
who call upon Him,
To all who call upon Him [B]in truth.
19 He will [A]fulfill the desire of
those who fear Him;
He will also [B]hear their cry
and will save them.
20 The LORD [A]keeps all who love Him,
But all the [B]wicked He will destroy.
21 My [A]mouth will speak the
praise of the LORD,
And [B]all flesh will [C]bless His holy
name forever and ever.

144:12 [a]Lit *cut after the pattern of* [A]Ps 92:12-14; 128:3 [B]Song 4:4; 7:4 144:13 [a]Lit *outside* [A]Prov 3:9, 10 144:14 [a]Lit *be laden* [b]Lit *bursting forth* [c]Lit *going out* [A]Prov 14:4 [B]2 Kin 25:10, 11 [C]Amos 5:3 [D]Is 24:11; Jer 14:2 144:15 [A]Ps 33:12 145:1 [A]Ps 30:1; 66:17 [B]Ps 5:2 [C]Ps 34:1 145:2 [A]Ps 71:6 145:3 [A]Ps 48:1; 86:10; 147:5 [B]Job 5:9; 9:10; 11:7; Is 40:28; Rom 11:33 145:4 [A]Ps 22:30, 31; Is 38:19 145:5 [a]Or *majesty of Your splendor* [A]Ps 145:12 [B]Ps 119:27 145:6 [a]Or *strength* [A]Deut 10:21; Ps 66:3; 106:22 [B]Deut 32:3 145:7 [a]Or *bubble over with* [A]Ps 31:19; Is 63:7 [B]Ps 51:14 145:8 [A]Ex 34:6; Num 14:18; Ps 86:5, 15; 103:8 145:9 [A]Ps 100:5; 136:1; Jer 33:11; Nah 1:7; Matt 19:17; Mark 10:18 [B]Ps 145:15 145:10 [A]Ps 19:1; 103:22 [B]Ps 68:26 145:11 [A]Jer 14:21 145:12 [a]Lit *His* [A]Ps 105:1 [B]Ps 145:5; Is 2:10, 19, 21 145:13 [a]Lit *a kingdom of all ages* [A]Ps 10:16; 29:10; 1 Tim 1:17; 2 Pet 1:11 145:14 [A]Ps 37:24 [B]Ps 146:8 145:15 [a]Lit *wait; or hope for* [A]Ps 104:27; 136:25 145:16 [A]Ps 104:28 145:17 [A]Ps 116:5 145:18 [A]Deut 4:7; Ps 34:18; 119:151 [B]John 4:24 145:19 [A]Ps 21:2; 37:4 [B]Ps 10:17; Prov 15:29; 1 John 5:14 145:20 [A]Ps 31:23; 91:14; 97:10 [B]Ps 9:5; 37:38 145:21 [A]Ps 71:8 [B]Ps 65:2; 150:6 [C]Ps 145:1, 2

144:12 sons … daughters. God's rescue of David's kingdom from foreigners would bring blessing on families.

144:13, 14 garners … flocks … cattle. Blessing would also come to the agricultural efforts.

144:14 Without mishap … loss … outcry. Peace, not strife, would characterize the land.

145:1–21 David penned this most exquisite conclusion to his 73 psalms in the Psalter. Here, the king of Israel extols and celebrates the King of Eternity for who He is, what He has done, and what He has promised. Not only rich in content, this psalm also duplicates a majestic acrostic design using the 22 letters of the Heb. alphabet. Psalm 145 begins the great crescendo of praise that completes the Psalter and might be called "The Final Hallel" (Pss 145–150).

I. Commitment to Praise (145:1, 2)
II. God's Awesome Greatness (145:3–7)
III. God's Great Grace (145:8–13)
IV. God's Unfailing Faithfulness (145:14–16)
V. God's Unblemished Righteousness (145:17–20)
VI. Recommitment/Exhortation to Praise (145:21)

145:1 my God, O King. David, king of Israel, recognized God as his sovereign (cf. Pss 5:2; 84:3).

145:11–13 kingdom. David refers here to the broadest use of kingdom in Scripture—i.e., God the eternal king ruling over all from before creation and eternally thereafter (cf. Ps 10:16; Da 4:3; 7:27).

145:14–16 The emphasis is on God's common grace to all of humanity (cf. Mt 5:45; Lk 6:35; Ac 14:17; 17:25).

145:20 the wicked … destroy. The wicked await an eternity of living forever, away from the presence of God in the lake of fire (cf. 2Th 1:9; Rev 20:11–15).

PSALM 146

THE LORD AN ABUNDANT HELPER.

1 [a]Praise [b]the LORD!
[A]Praise the LORD, O my soul!
2 I will praise the LORD
[A]while I live;
I will [B]sing praises to my God
while I have my being.
3 [A]Do not trust in princes,
In [a]mortal [B]man, in whom
there is [C]no salvation.
4 His [A]spirit departs, he
[B]returns to [a]the earth;
In that very day his
[C]thoughts perish.
5 How [A]blessed is he whose help
is the God of Jacob,
Whose [B]hope is in the
LORD his God,
6 Who [A]made heaven and earth,
The [B]sea and all that is in them;
Who [C]keeps [a]faith forever;
7 Who [A]executes justice
for the oppressed;
Who [B]gives food to the hungry.
The LORD [C]sets the prisoners free.

8 The LORD [A]opens *the eyes*
of the blind;
The LORD [B]raises up those
who are bowed down;
The LORD [C]loves the righteous;
9 The LORD [a,A]protects the [b]strangers;
He [c,B]supports the fatherless
and the widow,
But He [d]thwarts [C]the
way of the wicked.
10 The LORD will [A]reign forever,
Your God, O Zion, to all generations.
[a]Praise [b]the LORD!

PSALM 147

PRAISE FOR JERUSALEM'S RESTORATION AND PROSPERITY.

1 [a]Praise [b]the LORD!
For [A]it is good to sing praises to our God;
For [c]it is pleasant *and* praise is [B]becoming.
2 The LORD [A]builds up Jerusalem;
He [B]gathers the outcasts of Israel.
3 He heals the [A]brokenhearted
And [B]binds up their [a]wounds.
4 He [A]counts the number of the stars;
He [a,B]gives names to all of them.
5 [A]Great is our Lord and abundant in strength;
His [B]understanding is [a]infinite.
6 The LORD [a,A]supports the afflicted;
He brings down the wicked to the ground.

7 [A]Sing to the LORD with thanksgiving;
Sing praises to our God on the lyre,
8 Who [A]covers the heavens with clouds,
Who [B]provides rain for the earth,
Who [C]makes grass to [a]grow
on the mountains.
9 He [A]gives to the beast its food,
And to the [B]young ravens which cry.
10 He does not delight in the
strength of the [A]horse;
He [B]does not take pleasure
in the legs of a man.
11 The LORD [A]favors those who fear Him,
[B]Those who wait for His lovingkindness.

12 Praise the LORD, O Jerusalem!
Praise your God, O Zion!
13 For He has strengthened the
[A]bars of your gates;
He has [B]blessed your sons within you.
14 He [A]makes [a]peace in your borders;
He [B]satisfies you with [C]the
[b]finest of the wheat.

146:1 [a]Or *Hallelujah!* [b]Heb *YAH* [A]Ps 103:1 146:2 [A]Ps 63:4 [B]Ps 104:33 146:3 [a]Lit *a son of a man* [A]Ps 118:9 [B]Ps 118:8; Is 2:22 [C]Ps 60:11; 108:12 146:4 [a]Lit *his earth* [A]Ps 104:29 [B]Eccl 12:7 [C]Ps 33:10; 1 Cor 2:6 146:5 [A]Ps 144:15; Jer 17:7 [B]Ps 71:5 146:6 [a]Or *truth* [A]Ps 115:15; Rev 14:7 [B]Acts 14:15 [C]Ps 117:2 146:7 [A]Ps 103:6 [B]Ps 107:9; 145:15 [C]Ps 68:6; Is 61:1 146:8 [A]Matt 9:30; John 9:7 [B]Ps 145:14 [C]Ps 11:7 146:9 [a]Or *keeps* [b]Or *sojourners* [c]Or *relieves* [d]Lit *makes crooked* [A]Ex 22:21; Lev 19:34 [B]Deut 10:18; Ps 68:5 [C]Ps 147:6 146:10 [a]Or *Hallelujah!* [b]Heb *YAH* [A]Ex 15:18; Ps 10:16 147:1 [a]Or *Hallelujah!* [b]Heb *YAH* [c]Or *He is gracious* [A]Ps 92:1; 135:3 [B]Ps 33:1 147:2 [A]Ps 51:18; 102:16 [B]Deut 30:3; Ps 106:47; Is 11:12; 56:8; Ezek 39:28 147:3 [a]Lit *sorrows* [A]Ps 34:18; 51:17; Is 61:1 [B]Job 5:18; Is 30:26; Ezek 34:16 147:4 [a]Or *calls them all by* their *names* [A]Gen 15:5 [B]Is 40:26 147:5 [a]Lit *innumerable* [A]Ps 48:1; 145:3 [B]Is 40:28 147:6 [a]Or *relieves* [A]Ps 37:24; 146:8, 9 147:7 [A]Ps 33:2; 95:1, 2 147:8 [a]Lit *spring forth* [A]Job 26:8 [B]Job 5:10; 38:26; Ps 104:13 [C]Job 38:27; Ps 104:14 147:9 [A]Ps 104:27, 28; 145:15 [B]Job 38:41; Matt 6:26 147:10 [A]Ps 33:17 [B]1 Sam 16:7 147:11 [A]Ps 149:4 [B]Ps 33:18 147:13 [A]Neh 3:3; 7:3 [B]Ps 37:26 147:14 [a]Lit *your borders peace* [b]Lit *fat* [A]Ps 29:11; Is 54:13; 60:17, 18 [B]Ps 132:15 [C]Deut 32:14; Ps 81:16

146:1–10 From this psalm to the conclusion of the Psalter, each psalm begins and ends with "Praise the LORD!" (Pss 146–150). Neither the composer nor the occasions are known. Psalm 146 appears similar in content to Pss 113, 145.

I. Commitment to Praise (146:1, 2)
II. Misplaced Trust (146:3, 4)
III. Blessed Hope (146:5–10)

146:1 O my soul! Cf. the beginnings and ends of Pss 103, 104.

146:3, 4 Do not trust. This could be 1) a general principle, 2) a reference to the people wanting a human king like the nations (1Sa 8:5), or 3) Judah's later dependence on foreign kings for protection (2Ki 16:7–9).

146:5 the God of Jacob. Also the God of Abraham and Isaac, thus the recipients of God's blessing through the Abrahamic Covenant (cf. Ge 12:1–3; Ps 144:15).

146:6 Man's trust is best placed in the Creator of heaven and earth and the Revealer of all truth.

146:7–9b God righteously and mercifully reaches out to those in need.

146:9c the way of the wicked. Cf. Pss 1:4–6; 145:20.

146:10 will reign forever. In contrast to man who perishes (cf. v. 4), the truths of vv. 5–9 are not faddish or temporal but rather eternal (cf. Rev 22:5).

147:1–20 *See note on Ps 146:1–10.* This seems to be a post-Exilic psalm (cf. vv. 2, 3) which might have been used to celebrate the rebuilt walls of Jerusalem (cf. vv. 2, 13; Ne 12:27, 43). The hard questions that God posed to Job (Job 38–41) and Israel (Is 40), the psalmist here turns into declarations worthy of praise. Verses 1, 7, 12 each introduce a stanza of praise in this 3-part hymn. Verses 2, 3, 19, 20 specifically speak of God's involvement with Israel.

I. Praise the Lord—Part 1 (147:1–6)
II. Praise the Lord—Part 2 (147:7–11)
III. Praise the Lord—Part 3 (147:12–20)

147:2 builds up Jerusalem. Ezra and Nehemiah chronicle this portion of Israel's history.

147:3 heals the brokenhearted. Cf. Ps 137 (brokenhearted) with Ps 126 (healed).

147:6 Each part of the psalm ends with a contrast—here the humble and the wicked (cf. vv. 10, 11, 19, 20).

147:13 He has strengthened. Refers to a means of defense, most likely in reference to the rebuilding of Jerusalem's walls in Nehemiah's time.

15 He sends forth His [A]command
to the earth;
His [B]word runs very swiftly.
16 He gives [A]snow like wool;
He scatters the [B]frost like ashes.
17 He casts forth His [A]ice as fragments;
Who can stand before His [B]cold?
18 He [A]sends forth His word and melts them;
He [B]causes His wind to blow
and the waters to flow.
19 He [A]declares His words to Jacob,
His [B]statutes and His ordinances to Israel.
20 He [A]has not dealt thus with any nation;
And as for His ordinances, they
have [B]not known them.
[a]Praise [b]the LORD!

PSALM 148

THE WHOLE CREATION INVOKED TO PRAISE THE LORD.

1 [a]Praise [b]the LORD!
Praise the LORD [A]from the heavens;
Praise Him [B]in the heights!
2 Praise Him, [A]all His angels;
Praise Him, [B]all His hosts!
3 Praise Him, sun and moon;
Praise Him, all stars of light!
4 Praise Him, [a,A]highest heavens,
And the [B]waters that are
above the heavens!
5 Let them praise the name of the LORD,
For [A]He commanded and
they were created.
6 He has also [A]established them
forever and ever;
He has made a [B]decree which
will not pass away.
7 Praise the LORD from the earth,
[A]Sea monsters and all [B]deeps;
8 [A]Fire and hail, [B]snow and [C]clouds;
[D]Stormy wind, [E]fulfilling His word;
9 [A]Mountains and all hills;
Fruit [B]trees and all cedars;
10 [A]Beasts and all cattle;
[B]Creeping things and winged fowl;
11 [A]Kings of the earth and all peoples;
Princes and all judges of the earth;
12 Both young men and virgins;
Old men and children.

13 Let them praise the name of the LORD,
For His [A]name alone is exalted;
His [B]glory is above earth and heaven.
14 And He has [A]lifted up a horn
for His people,
[B]Praise for all His godly ones;
Even for the sons of Israel, a
people [C]near to Him.
[a]Praise [b]the LORD!

PSALM 149

ISRAEL INVOKED TO PRAISE THE LORD.

1 [a]Praise [b]the LORD!
Sing to the LORD a [A]new song,
And His praise [B]in the congregation
of the godly ones.
2 Let Israel be glad in [A]his Maker;
Let the sons of Zion rejoice
in their [B]King.
3 Let them praise His name
with [A]dancing;
Let them sing praises to Him
with [B]timbrel and lyre.

147:15 [A]Job 37:12; Ps 148:5 [B]Ps 104:4 147:16 [A]Job 37:6; Ps 148:8 [B]Job 38:29 147:17 [A]Job 37:10 [B]Job 37:9 147:18 [A]Ps 33:9; 107:20; 147:15 [B]Ps 107:25 147:19 [A]Deut 33:3, 4 [B]Mal 4:4 147:20 [a]Or *Hallelujah!* [b]Heb *YAH* [A]Deut 4:7, 8, 32-34; Rom 3:1, 2 [B]Ps 79:6; Jer 10:25 148:1 [a]Or *Hallelujah!* [b]Heb *YAH* [A]Ps 69:34 [B]Job 16:19; Ps 102:19; Matt 21:9 148:2 [A]Ps 103:20 [B]Ps 103:21 148:4 [a]Lit *heavens of heavens* [A]Deut 10:14; 1 Kin 8:27; Neh 9:6; Ps 68:33 [B]Gen 1:7 148:5 [A]Gen 1:1; Ps 33:6, 9 148:6 [A]Ps 89:37; Jer 31:35, 36; 33:20, 25 [B]Job 38:33 148:7 [A]Gen 1:21; Ps 74:13 [B]Gen 1:2; Deut 33:13; Hab 3:10 148:8 [A]Ps 18:12 [B]Ps 147:16 [C]Ps 135:7 [D]Ps 107:25 [E]Job 37:12; Ps 103:20 148:9 [A]Is 44:23; 49:13 [B]Is 55:12 148:10 [A]Is 43:20 [B]Hos 2:18 148:11 [A]Ps 102:15 148:13 [A]Is 12:4 [B]Ps 8:1; 113:4 148:14 [a]Or *Hallelujah!* [b]Heb *YAH* [A]1 Sam 2:1; Ps 75:10 [B]Deut 10:21; Ps 109:1; Jer 17:14 [C]Lev 10:3; Eph 2:17 149:1 [a]Or *Hallelujah!* [b]Heb *YAH* [A]Ps 33:3 [B]Ps 35:18; 89:5 149:2 [A]Ps 95:6 [B]Judg 8:23; Ps 47:6; Zech 9:9 149:3 [A]2 Sam 6:14; Ps 150:4 [B]Ex 15:20; Ps 81:2

147:15–18 Describes the cold weather that Jerusalem can experience. God sovereignly oversees the normal and the extraordinary.

147:19, 20 The psalmist acknowledges God's unique election of Israel from among all the nations (cf. Ge 12:1–3; Ex 19:5, 6; Dt 7:6–8; 14:2; 26:18, 19; 2Sa 7:23, 24; Eze 16:1–7).

148:1–14 *See note on Ps 146:1–10.* The author and background for this psalm, which calls for all of God's creation to praise Him, is unknown. There is a connection between the creation praising God and His involvement with Israel.

I. Heaven's Praise (148:1–6)
   A. Who? (148:1–4)
   B. Why? (148:5, 6)
II. Earth's Praise (148:7–14)
   A. Who? (148:7–12)
   B. Why? (148:13, 14)

148:1–4 A representative sample of God's creation in the skies and heavens.

148:2 **all His hosts!** Another term for angels.

148:4 **waters … above the heavens!** Cf. Ge 1:7.

148:5, 6 He emphatically ascribes creation to God alone.

148:6 Jeremiah 31:35–37; 33:20–22 might be in mind in the sense that the certain, fixed order of creation was a witness to God's unbreakable covenants with Abraham and David.

148:8 **fulfilling His word.** Another way of saying that God sovereignly oversees weather.

148:13, 14 Two reasons are given for earth's praise: 1) His name alone is exalted in heaven (148:13) and 2) He has exalted Israel on earth (148:14).

148:14 **a horn.** Refers in general to the strength and prosperity of the nation, which became the cause of praise for Israel. This suggests that Israel will enjoy better times than in the past, e.g., during David's and Solomon's reigns or after returning from the Babylonian Captivity. **a people near to Him.** Cf. also "My chosen people" (Is 43:20) and "His own possession" (Ps 135:4).

149:1–9 *See note on Ps 146:1–10.* The composer and occasion for this psalm are unknown.

I. Israel's Praise of God (149:1–5)
II. Israel's Punishment of the Nations (149:6–9)

149:1 **a new song.** A song of testimony concerning salvation (cf. 149:4). **the congregation.** The gathering of the nation for worship.

149:3 **dancing.** Either individual or group, perhaps like David when he brought the ark to Jerusalem (2Sa 6:15, 16). **timbrel.** A tambourine-like instrument which accompanied dancing and singing (cf. Ex 15:20; 1Sa 18:6). *See note on 2Sa 6:14.*

4 For the LORD [A]takes pleasure
in His people;
He will [B]beautify the afflicted
ones with salvation.

5 Let the [A]godly ones exult in glory;
Let them [B]sing for joy on their beds.
6 *Let* the [A]high praises of God
be in their [a]mouth,
And a [B]two-edged [C]sword
in their hand,
7 To [A]execute vengeance
on the nations
And punishment on the peoples,
8 To bind their kings [A]with chains
And their [B]nobles with fetters of iron,
9 To [A]execute on them the
judgment written;
This is an [B]honor for all His godly ones.
[a]Praise [b]the LORD!

PSALM 150

A PSALM OF PRAISE.

1 [a]Praise [b]the LORD!
Praise God in His [A]sanctuary;
Praise Him in His mighty [c,B]expanse.
2 Praise Him for His [A]mighty deeds;
Praise Him according to His
excellent [B]greatness.

3 Praise Him with [A]trumpet sound;
Praise Him with [B]harp and lyre.
4 Praise Him with [A]timbrel and dancing;
Praise Him with [B]stringed
instruments and [C]pipe.
5 Praise Him with loud [A]cymbals;
Praise Him with resounding cymbals.
6 Let [A]everything that has breath
praise [a]the LORD.
[b]Praise [a]the LORD!

149:4 [A]Job 36:11; Ps 16:11; 35:27; 147:11 [B]Ps 132:16; Is 61:3 149:5 [A]Ps 132:16 [B]Job 35:10; Ps 42:8 149:6 [a]Lit *throat* [A]Ps 66:17 [B]Heb 4:12 [C]Neh 4:17 149:7 [A]Ezek 25:17; Mic 5:15 149:8 [A]Job 36:8 [B]Nah 3:10 149:9 [a]Or *Hallelujah!* [b]Heb *YAH* [A]Deut 7:12; Ezek 28:26 [B]Ps 112:9; 148:14 150:1 [a]Or *Hallelujah!* [b]Heb *YAH* [c]Or *firmament* [A]Ps 73:17; 102:19 [B]Ps 19:1 150:2 [A]Ps 145:12 [B]Deut 3:24; Ps 145:3 150:3 [A]Ps 98:6 [B]Ps 33:2 150:4 [A]Ps 149:3 [B]Ps 45:8; Is 38:20 [C]Gen 4:21; Job 21:12 150:5 [A]2 Sam 6:5; 1 Chr 13:8; 15:16; Ezra 3:10; Neh 12:27 150:6 [a]Heb *YAH* [b]Or *Hallelujah!* [A]Ps 103:22; 145:21

149:6–9 It would appear that this section is eschatological in nature and looks 1) to the Millennium when all nations and peoples will acknowledge Christ as king and 2) to Jerusalem as His royal capital (cf. Eze 28:25, 26; Joel 3:9–17; Mic 5:4–15).

149:9 **the judgment written.** Another way of saying "according to the Scriptures," as God has prophesied the subjection of the nations. **This … honor.** The privilege of carrying out God's will.

150:1–6 *See note on Ps 146:1–10.* This concluding psalm fitly caps the Psalter and the Final Hallel (Pss 145–150) by raising and then answering some strategic questions about praise: 1) where? (150:1); 2) what for? (150:2); 3) with what? (150:3–5); and 4) who? (150:6). The author and occasion are unknown.

I. Place of Praise (150:1)
II. Points of Praise (150:2)
III. Proper Means of Praise (150:3–5)
IV. Practitioners of Praise (150:6)

150:1 **sanctuary … mighty expanse.** "Sanctuary" most likely refers to the temple in Jerusalem, so the sense would be "Praise God on earth and in heaven."

150:2 Praise should be for 1) what God has done and 2) who God is.

150:3 **lyre.** A smaller, portable version of the harp, most likely played with a plectrum (pick).

150:4 **timbrel and dancing.** *See note on Ps 149:3.*

150:6 **everything.** All of God's living creation. This is the fitting conclusion to Book Five of the Psalms (Pss 107–150) and to the entire Psalter.

THE BOOK OF

PROVERBS

TITLE

The title in the Hebrew Bible is "The Proverbs of Solomon" (1:1), as also in the Greek Septuagint (LXX). Proverbs pulls together the most important 513 of the over 3,000 proverbs pondered by Solomon (1Ki 4:32; Ecc 12:9), along with some proverbs of others whom Solomon likely influenced. The word "proverb" means "to be like," thus Proverbs is a book of comparisons between common, concrete images and life's most profound truths. Proverbs are simple, moral statements (or illustrations) that highlight and teach fundamental realities about life. Solomon sought God's wisdom (2Ch 1:8–12) and offered "pithy sayings" designed to make men contemplate 1) the fear of God and 2) living by His wisdom (1:7; 9:10). The sum of this wisdom is personified in the Lord Jesus Christ (1Co 1:30).

AUTHOR AND DATE

The phrase "Proverbs of Solomon" is more a title than an absolute statement of authorship (1:1). While King Solomon, who ruled Israel from 971–931 B.C. and was granted great wisdom by God (see 1Ki 4:29–34), is the author of the didactic section (chaps. 1–9) and the proverbs of 10:1–22:16, he is likely only the compiler of the "sayings of the wise" in 22:17–24:34, which are of an uncertain date before Solomon's reign. The collection in chaps. 25–29 was originally composed by Solomon (25:1) but copied and included later by Judah's king Hezekiah (ca. 715–686 B.C.). Chapter 30 reflects the words of Agur and chap. 31 the words of Lemuel, who perhaps was Solomon. Proverbs was not assembled in its final form until Hezekiah's day or after. Solomon authored his proverbs before his heart was turned away from God (1Ki 11:1–11), since the book reveals a godly perspective and is addressed to the "naive" and "young" who need to learn the fear of God. Solomon also wrote Psalms 72 and 127, Ecclesiastes, and Song of Solomon. See Introduction: Author and Date for Ecclesiastes and Song of Solomon.

BACKGROUND AND SETTING

The book reflects a 3-fold setting as: 1) general wisdom literature; 2) insights from the royal court; and 3) instruction offered in the tender relationship of a father and mother with their children, all designed to produce meditation on God. Since Proverbs is Wisdom literature, by nature it is sometimes difficult to understand (1:6). Wisdom literature is part of the whole of OT truth; the Priest gave the *Law,* the Prophet gave a *Word* from the Lord, and the Sage (or wise man) gave his wise *Counsel* (Jer 18:18; Eze 7:26). In Proverbs, Solomon the Sage gives insight into the "knotty" issues of life (1:6) which are not directly addressed in the Law or the Prophets. Though it is practical, Proverbs is not superficial or external because it contains moral and ethical elements stressing upright living which flow out of a right relationship with God. In 4:1–4, Solomon connected 3 generations as he entrusted to his son Rehoboam what he learned at the feet of David and Bathsheba. Proverbs is both a pattern for the tender impartation of truth from generation to generation, as well as a vast resource for the content of the truth to be imparted. Proverbs contains the principles and applications of Scripture which the godly characters of the Bible illustrate in their lives.

HISTORICAL AND THEOLOGICAL THEMES

Solomon came to the throne with great promise, privilege, and opportunity. God had granted his request for understanding (1Ki 3:9–12; 2Ch 1:10–12), and his wisdom exceeded all others (1Ki 4:29–31). However, the shocking reality is that he failed to live out the truth that he knew and even taught his son Rehoboam (1Ki 11:1, 4, 6, 7–11), who subsequently rejected his father's teaching (1Ki 12:6–11).

Proverbs contains a gold mine of biblical theology, reflecting themes of Scripture brought to the level of practical righteousness (1:3), by addressing man's ethical choices, calling into question how he thinks, lives, and manages his daily life in light of divine truth. More specifically, Proverbs calls man to live as the Creator intended him to live when He made man (Ps 90:1, 2, 12).

The recurring promise of Proverbs is that generally the wise (the righteous who obey God) live longer (9:11), prosper (2:20–22), experience joy (3:13–18) and the goodness of God temporally (12:21), while fools suffer shame (3:35) and death (10:21). On the other hand, it must be remembered that this general principle is balanced by the reality that the wicked sometimes prosper (Ps 73:3, 12), though only temporarily

(Ps 73:17–19). Job illustrates that there are occasions when the godly wise are struck with disaster and suffering.

There are a number of important themes addressed in Proverbs, which are offered in random order and address different topics, so that it is helpful to study the proverbs thematically as illustrated.

I. Man's Relationship to God

A. His Trust—Pr 22:19
B. His Humility—Pr 3:34
C. His Fear of God—Pr 1:7
D. His Righteousness—Pr 10:25
E. His Sin—Pr 28:13
F. His Obedience—Pr 6:23
G. Facing Reward—Pr 12:28
H. Facing Tests—Pr 17:3
I. Facing Blessing—Pr 10:22
J. Facing Death—Pr 15:11

II. Man's Relationship to Himself

A. His Character—Pr 20:11
B. His Wisdom—Pr 1:5
C. His Foolishness—Pr 26:10, 11
D. His Speech—Pr 18:21
E. His Self-Control—Pr 6:9–11
F. His Kindness—Pr 3:3
G. His Wealth—Pr 11:4
H. His Pride—Pr 27:1
I. His Anger—Pr 29:11
J. His Laziness—Pr 13:4

III. Man's Relationship to Others

A. His Love—Pr 8:17
B. His Friends—Pr 17:17
C. His Enemies—Pr 16:7
D. His Truthfulness—Pr 23:23
E. His Gossip—Pr 20:19
F. As a Father—Pr 20:7; 31:2–9
G. As a Mother—Pr 31:10–31
H. As Children—Pr 3:1–3
I. In Educating Children—Pr 4:1–4
J. In Disciplining Children—Pr 22:6

The two major themes which are interwoven and overlapping throughout Proverbs are wisdom and folly. Wisdom, which includes knowledge, understanding, instruction, discretion, and obedience, is built on the fear of the Lord and the Word of God. Folly is everything opposite to wisdom.

INTERPRETIVE CHALLENGES

The first challenge is the generally elusive nature of Wisdom literature itself. Like the parables, the intended truths are often veiled from understanding if given only a cursory glance, and thus must be pondered in the heart (1:6; 2:1–4; 4:4–9).

Another challenge is the extensive use of parallelism, which is the placing of truths side by side so that the second line expands, completes, defines, emphasizes, or reaches the logical conclusion, the ultimate end, or, in some cases, the contrasting point of view. Often the actual parallel is only implied. For example, 12:13 contains an unstated, but clearly implied parallel, in that the righteous one comes through trouble because of his virtuous speech (cf. 28:7). In interpreting the Proverbs, one must: 1) determine the parallelism and often complete what is assumed and not stated by the author; 2) identify the figures of speech and rephrase the thought without those figures; 3) summarize the lesson or principle of the proverb in a few words; 4) describe the behavior that is taught; and 5) find examples inside Scripture.

Challenges are also found in the various contexts of Proverbs, all of which affect interpretation and understanding. First, there is the setting in which they were spoken; this is largely the context of the young men in the royal court of the king. Second, there is the setting of the book as a whole and how its teachings are to be understood in light of the rest of Scripture. For example, there is much to be gained by comparing the wisdom Solomon taught with the wisdom Christ personified. Third, there is the historical context in which the principles and truths draw on illustrations from their own day.

A final area of challenge comes in understanding that proverbs are divine guidelines and wise observations, i.e., teaching underlying principles (24:3, 4) which are not always inflexible laws or absolute promises. These expressions of general truth (cf. 10:27; 22:4) generally do have "exceptions," due to the uncertainty of life and unpredictable behavior of fallen men. God does not guarantee uniform outcome or application for each proverb, but in studying them and applying them, one comes to contemplate the mind of God, His character, His attributes, His works, and His blessings. All of the treasures of wisdom and knowledge expressed in Proverbs are hidden in Christ (Col 2:3).

OUTLINE

I. Prologue (1:1–7)
- A. Title (1:1)
- B. Purpose (1:2–6)
- C. Theme (1:7)

II. Praise and Wisdom to the Young (1:8–9:18)

III. Proverbs for Everyone (10:1–29:27)
- A. From Solomon (10:1–22:16)
- B. From Wise Men (22:17–24:34)
- C. From Solomon Collected by Hezekiah (25:1–29:27)

IV. Personal Notes (30:1–31:31)
- A. From Agur (30:1–33)
- B. From Lemuel (31:1–31)

THE USEFULNESS OF PROVERBS

1 The [A]proverbs of Solomon [B]the son of David, king of Israel:

2 To know [A]wisdom and instruction,
To discern the sayings
of [B]understanding,
3 To [A]receive instruction in wise behavior,
[B]Righteousness, justice and equity;
4 To give [A]prudence to the [a]naive,
To the youth [B]knowledge and discretion,
5 A wise man will hear and
[A]increase in learning,
And a [B]man of understanding
will acquire wise counsel,
6 To understand a proverb and a figure,
The words of the wise
and their [A]riddles.

7 [A]The fear of the LORD is the
beginning of knowledge;
Fools despise wisdom and instruction.

1:1 [A]1 Kin 4:32; Prov 10:1; 25:1; Eccl 12:9 [B]Eccl 1:1 1:2 [A]Prov 15:33 [B]Prov 4:1 1:3 [A]Prov 2:1; 19:20 [B]Prov 2:9 1:4 [a]Lit *simple ones* [A]Prov 8:5, 12 [B]Prov 2:10, 11; 3:21 1:5 [A]Prov 9:9 [B]Prov 14:6; Eccl 9:11 1:6 [A]Num 12:8; Ps 49:4; 78:2; Dan 8:23 1:7 [A]Job 28:28; Ps 111:10; Prov 9:10; 15:33; Eccl 12:13

1:1–7 These verses form the Prologue, where the reader is called to serious study for his own benefit. In a few brief words, he is introduced to: 1) the genre of this literature (v. 1); 2) a clear two-fold purpose (vv. 2–6); and 3) an all-important motto (v. 7).

1:1 proverbs. See Introduction: Title. The proverbs are short, pithy sayings which express timeless truth and wisdom. They arrest one's thoughts, causing the reader to reflect on how one might apply divine principles to life situations (e.g., 2:12). Proverbs contains insights both in poetry and prose; yet, at the same time, it includes commands to be obeyed. God's proverbs are not limited to this book alone (see Ge 10:9; 1Sa 10:12; 24:13; Jer 31:29; Eze 12:22; 18:2). **Solomon.** See Introduction: Author and Date. As Solomon became king of Israel, he sought and received wisdom and knowledge from the Lord (2Ch 1:7–12), which led him to wealth, honor, and fame.

1:2–6 The two-fold purpose of the book is 1) to produce the skill of godly living by wisdom and instruction (v. 2a; expanded in vv. 3, 4), and 2) to develop discernment (v. 2b, expanded in v. 5).

1:2 wisdom. See Introduction: Historical and Theological Themes. To the Hebrew mind, wisdom was not knowledge alone, but the skill of living a godly life as God intended man to live (cf. Dt 4:5–8). **instruction.** This refers to the discipline of the moral nature. **understanding.** This word looks at the mental discipline which matures one for spiritual discernment.

1:3 wise behavior, righteousness, justice and equity. Expanding the purpose and terms of v. 2a, Proverbs engages in a process of schooling a son in the disciplines of: 1) wise behavior (a different Heb. word from that in v. 2) which means discreet counsel or the ability to govern oneself by choice; 2) righteousness, the application of God's standards in dealing with others; 3) justice, the ability to conform to the will and standard of God; a practical righteousness that matches one's positional righteousness; and 4) equity, the living of life in a fair, pleasing way.

1:4 prudence … naive. The purpose is to impart discernment to the naive and the ignorant. The root of "naive" is a word meaning "an open door," an apt description of the undiscerning, who do not know what to keep in or out of their minds. **youth knowledge and discretion.** To make one ponder before sinning, thus to make a responsible choice.

1:5 counsel. The wise believer will have the ability to guide or govern others with truth.

1:6 understand a proverb … figure. Proverbs seeks to sharpen the mind by schooling one in "parabolic speech" and "dark sayings" that need reflection and interpretation. **riddles.** Study of the Scriptures is sufficient to provide the wisdom for the perplexities of life.

1:7 The fear of the LORD. The overarching theme of this book and particularly the first 9 chapters is introduced—reverence for God (see v. 29; 2:5; 3:7; 8:13; 9:10; 14:26, 27; cf. also Job 28:28; Ps 34:11; Ac 9:31). See Introduction: Historical and Theological Themes. This reverential awe and admiring, submissive fear is foundational for all spiritual knowledge and wisdom (cf. 2:4–6; 9:10; 15:33; Job 28:28; Ps 111:10; Ecc 12:13). While the unbeliever may make statements about life and truth, he does not have true or ultimate knowledge until he is in a redemptive relationship of reverential awe with God. Note the progression here: 1) teaching about God; 2) learning about God; 3) fearing God; 4) knowing God; and 5) imitating God's wisdom. The fear of the Lord is a state of mind in which one's own attitudes, will, feelings, deeds, and goals are exchanged for God's (cf. Ps 42:1).

NOTABLE TEACHERS IN SCRIPTURE

Name	Description	Reference(s)
Moses	Renowned as the leader of Israel who first taught God's Law	Dt 4:5
Bezalel and Oholiab	Two master craftsmen who were gifted and called to teach others in the construction of the tabernacle	Ex 35:30–35
Samuel	The last of Israel's judges before the monarchy, who taught the people "the good and right way"	1Sa 12:23
David	Prepared his son Solomon to build and staff the temple	1Ch 28:9–21
Solomon	Known for his outstanding wisdom, which he used to teach numerous subjects	1Ki 4:29–34
Ezra	A scribe and priest who was committed not only to keeping the Law himself but also to teaching it to others	Ezr 7:10
Jesus	Called Rabbi ("teacher," Jn 1:38; cf. Mt 9:11; 26:18; Jn 13:13), whose teaching revealed the good news of salvation	Eph 4:20, 21
Barnabas	One of the teachers among the believers at Antioch (Ac 13:1), who had a lasting impact on Saul after his conversion to the faith	Ac 9:26–30
Gamaliel	A renowned Jewish rabbi who was the teacher of Saul during his youth	Ac 18:26
Paul	Perhaps the early church's most gifted teacher, known to have taught throughout the Roman world	Ac 13:1; 19:9
Priscilla and Aquila	Two believers who taught the way of God to a talented young orator named Apollos	Ac 18:26
Apollos	A powerful teacher from Alexandria in Egypt, whose teaching paved the way for the gospel at Ephesus	Ac 18:24–26
Timothy	Pastor-teacher of the church at Ephesus	1Ti 1:3; 2Ti 4:2
Titus	Pastor-teacher of a church on the island of Crete	Titus 2:1–15

THE ENTICEMENT OF SINNERS

8 [A]Hear, my son, your father's instruction
And [B]do not forsake your
mother's teaching;
9 Indeed, they are a [A]graceful
wreath to your head
And [a,B]ornaments about your neck.
10 My son, if sinners [A]entice you,
[B]Do not consent.
11 If they say, "Come with us,
Let us [A]lie in wait for blood,
Let us [B]ambush the innocent
without cause;
12 Let us [A]swallow them alive like Sheol,
Even whole, as those who
[B]go down to the pit;
13 We will find all *kinds* of precious wealth,
We will fill our houses with spoil;
14 Throw in your lot [a]with us,
We shall all have one purse,"
15 My son, [A]do not walk in the
way with them.
[B]Keep your feet from their path,
16 For [A]their feet run to evil
And they hasten to shed blood.
17 Indeed, it is [a]useless to
spread the *baited* net
In the sight of any [b]bird;
18 But they [A]lie in wait for their own blood;
They ambush their own lives.
19 So are the ways of everyone
who [A]gains by violence;
It takes away the life of its possessors.

WISDOM WARNS

20 [A]Wisdom shouts in the street,
She [a]lifts her voice in the square;
21 At the head of the noisy
streets she cries out;
At the entrance of the gates in the
city she utters her sayings:
22 "How long, O [a,A]naive ones, will you
love [b]being simple-minded?
And [B]scoffers delight
themselves in scoffing
And fools [C]hate knowledge?
23 "Turn to my reproof,
Behold, I will [A]pour out my spirit on you;
I will make my words known to you.
24 "Because [A]I called and you [B]refused,
I [C]stretched out my hand and
no one paid attention;
25 And you [A]neglected all my counsel
And did not [B]want my reproof;
26 I will also [A]laugh at your [B]calamity;
I will mock when your [C]dread comes,
27 When your dread comes like a storm
And your calamity comes
like a [A]whirlwind,
When distress and anguish
come upon you.
28 "Then they will [A]call on me,
but I will not answer;
They will [B]seek me diligently
but they will not find me,
29 Because they [A]hated knowledge
And did not choose the fear of the LORD.

1:8 [A]Prov 4:1 [B]Prov 6:20 1:9 [a]Lit *necklaces* [A]Prov 4:9 [B]Gen 41:42; Dan 5:29 1:10 [A]Prov 16:29 [B]Gen 39:7-10; Deut 13:8; Ps 50:18; Eph 5:11 1:11 [A]Prov 12:6; Jer 5:26 [B]Ps 10:8; Prov 1:18 1:12 [A]Ps 124:3 [B]Ps 28:1 1:14 [a]Lit *in the midst of us* 1:15 [A]Ps 1:1; Prov 4:14 [B]Ps 119:101 1:16 [A]Prov 6:17, 18; Is 59:7 1:17 [a]Lit *in vain* [b]Lit *possessor of wing* 1:18 [A]Prov 11:19 1:19 [A]Prov 15:27 1:20 [a]Lit *gives* [A]Prov 8:1-3; 9:3 1:22 [a]Lit *simple ones* [b]Or *naivete* [A]Prov 1:4, 32; 8:5; 9:4; 22:3 [B]Ps 1:1 [C]Prov 1:29; 5:12 1:23 [A]Is 32:15; Joel 2:28; John 7:39 1:24 [A]Is 65:12; 66:4; Jer 7:13 [B]Zech 7:11 [C]Is 65:2; Rom 10:21 1:25 [A]Ps 107:11; Luke 7:30 [B]Prov 15:10 1:26 [A]Ps 2:4 [B]Prov 6:15 [C]Prov 10:24 1:27 [A]Prov 10:25 1:28 [A]1 Sam 8:18; Job 27:9; 35:12; Ps 18:41; Is 1:15; Jer 11:11; 14:12; Ezek 8:18; Mic 3:4; Zech 7:13; James 4:3 [B]Prov 8:17 1:29 [A]Job 21:14; Prov 1:22

1:8–9:18 This lengthy section features parental praise of wisdom in the form of didactic addresses. These chapters prepare the reader for the actual proverbs that begin in 10:1ff.

1:10–19 Here is a warning against enticement by sinners who will succeed if his son fails to embrace wisdom (v. 8).

1:10 sinners. This term is reserved in Scripture to describe unbelievers for whom sin is continual and who endeavor to persuade even believers to sin with them (*see note on Jas 4:8*). The sins of murder and robbery are used as illustrations of such folly.

1:11 Come with us. The intimidating force of peer pressure is often the way to entice those who lack wisdom.

1:12 swallow. The wicked devise a plot of deception in which the innocent are captured and victimized like one who is taken by death itself—as with Joseph (Ge 37:20ff.), Jeremiah (Jer 38:6–13), and Daniel (Da 6:16, 17). "Sheol" is the place of death. For the wicked it is a place of no return (Job 7:9), darkness (Ps 143:3), and torment (Is 14:11).

1:13 We … spoil. This is the enlisting of the innocent without full disclosure of intent. Abundant spoil is promised by this outright robbery, which is made to appear easy and safe for the thieves and murderers.

1:15 do not walk. This directly confronts the invitation of v. 11. Sin must be rejected at the first temptation (cf. Ps 119:114,115; Jas 1:15) by refusing even the association that can lead to sin (cf. Ps 1:1–6). Avoid the beginnings of sin (see 4:14).

1:17 spread the *baited* net. It would be ineffective to set up a net for catching a bird in full view of the bird. Taken with v. 18, this analogy means that the sinner sets up his trap for the innocent in secret, but in the end the trap is sprung on him (v. 19). This greed entraps him (cf. 1Ti 6:9–11). Stupid sinners rush to their own ruin.

1:20–33 In this section, wisdom is personified and speaks in the first person, emphasizing the serious consequences that come to those who reject it. Similar personifications of wisdom occur in 3:14–18; 8:1–36; 9:1–12.

1:21 cries out … in the city. While enticement is covert and secret (v. 10), wisdom, with nothing to hide, is available to everyone, being found in the most prominent of public places.

1:22 How long. Three questions reveal 3 classes of those needing wisdom, and the downward progression of sin: 1) the naive or simple-minded, who are ignorant; 2) scoffers or mockers, who commit more serious, determined acts; and 3) fools or obstinate unbelievers, who will not listen to the truth. Proverbs aims its wisdom primarily at the first group.

1:23 reproof. God's wisdom brings to bear against the sinner indictments for sin that demand repentance. To the one who does repent, God promises the spirit or essence of true wisdom linked to divine revelation.

1:24–26 Sinners who respond with indifference and mockery at God's indictments increase their guilt (cf. Ro 2:5) and bring upon themselves the wrath of God's mockery and indifference (vv. 26, 27). Some wait to seek God until it is too late. See Dt 1:45; 1Sa 28:6; Ps 18:41.

1:26, 27 calamity … dread … distress and anguish. All these terms describe the severe troubles of divine judgment. When sinners who have rejected wisdom call on God in the day of judgment, God will respond to their distress with derision.

1:28–32 God's rejection of sinners is carefully detailed. This is the aspect of God's wrath expressed in His abandonment of sinners. *See notes on Ro 1:24–28*. No prayers or diligent seeking will help them (cf. 8:17).

1:28–30 I will not answer. God will withdraw His invitation to sinners because they have rejected Him. Note the rejection of wisdom (v. 7), knowledge (v. 22), reproof (vv. 23, 24), and counsel (v. 25).

30 "They [A]would not accept my counsel,
They spurned all my reproof.
31 "So they shall [A]eat of the fruit
of their own way
And be [B]satiated with
their own devices.
32 "For the [A]waywardness of the
[a]naive will kill them,
And the complacency of fools
will destroy them.
33 "But [A]he who listens to me
shall [a]live securely
And will be at ease from
the dread of evil."

THE PURSUIT OF WISDOM BRINGS SECURITY

2 My son, if you will [A]receive my words
And [B]treasure my commandments
within you,
2 [A]Make your ear attentive to wisdom,
Incline your heart to understanding;
3 For if you cry for discernment,
[a]Lift your voice for understanding;
4 If you seek her as [A]silver
And search for her as for
[B]hidden treasures;
5 Then you will discern the
[A]fear of the LORD
And discover the knowledge of God.
6 For [A]the LORD gives wisdom;
From His mouth *come* knowledge
and understanding.
7 He stores up sound wisdom
for the upright;
He is a [A]shield to those who
walk in integrity,
8 Guarding the paths of justice,
And He [A]preserves the way
of His godly ones.
9 Then you will discern
[A]righteousness and justice
And equity *and* every [B]good course.
10 For [A]wisdom will enter your heart
And [B]knowledge will be
pleasant to your soul;
11 Discretion will [A]guard you,
Understanding will watch over you,
12 To [A]deliver you from the way of evil,
From the man who speaks
[B]perverse things;
13 From those who [A]leave the
paths of uprightness
To walk in the [B]ways of darkness;
14 Who [A]delight in doing evil
And rejoice in the perversity of evil;
15 Whose paths are [A]crooked,
And who are devious in their ways;
16 To [A]deliver you from the strange woman,
From the [a,B]adulteress who
flatters with her words;
17 That leaves the [A]companion of her youth
And forgets the [B]covenant of her God;
18 For [A]her house [a]sinks down to death
And her tracks *lead* to the [b]dead;
19 None [A]who go to her return again,
Nor do they reach the [B]paths of life.
20 So you will [A]walk in the way of good men
And keep to the [B]paths of the righteous.
21 For [A]the upright will [a]live in the land
And [B]the blameless will remain in it;
22 But [A]the wicked will be cut off from the land
And [B]the treacherous will be
[C]uprooted from it.

1:30 [A]Ps 81:11; Prov 1:25 1:31 [A]Job 4:8; Prov 5:22, 23; 22:8; Is 3:11; Jer 6:19 [B]Prov 14:14 1:32 [a]Lit *simple ones* [A]Jer 2:19 1:33 [a]Lit *dwell* [A]Ps 25:12, 13; Prov 3:24-26 2:1 [A]Prov 4:10 [B]Prov 3:1 2:2 [A]Prov 22:17 2:3 [a]Lit *Give* 2:4 [A]Prov 3:14 [B]Job 3:21; Matt 13:44 2:5 [A]Prov 1:7 2:6 [A]1 Kin 3:12; Job 32:8; James 1:5 2:7 [A]Ps 84:11; Prov 30:5 2:8 [A]1 Sam 2:9; Ps 66:9 2:9 [A]Prov 8:20 [B]Prov 4:18 2:10 [A]Prov 14:33 [B]Prov 22:18 2:11 [A]Prov 4:6; 6:22 2:12 [A]Prov 28:26 [B]Prov 6:12 2:13 [A]Prov 21:16 [B]Ps 82:5; Prov 4:19; John 3:19, 20 2:14 [A]Prov 10:23; Jer 11:15 2:15 [A]Ps 125:5; Prov 21:8 2:16 [a]Lit *strange woman* [A]Prov 6:24; 7:5 [B]Prov 23:27 2:17 [A]Mal 2:14, 15 [B]Gen 2:24 2:18 [a]Lit *bows down* [b]Lit *departed spirits* [A]Prov 7:27 2:19 [A]Eccl 7:26 [B]Ps 16:11; Prov 5:6 2:20 [A]Heb 6:12 [B]Prov 4:18 2:21 [a]Or *dwell* [A]Ps 37:9, 29; Prov 10:30 [B]Prov 28:10 2:22 [A]Ps 37:38; Prov 10:30 [B]Prov 11:3 [C]Deut 28:63; Ps 52:5

1:31 eat of the fruit of their own way. The ultimate punishment is God's giving a people up to the result of their wickedness. Cf. Ro 1:24–28.

1:32 complacency. Willful carelessness or lack of appropriate care is intended.

2:1 my words. Solomon has taken God's law and made it his own by faith and obedience, as well as teaching. The wisdom of these words is available to those who, first of all, understand the rich value ("treasure") that wisdom possesses. Appropriating wisdom begins when one values it above all else.

2:2 ear … heart. *See note on 4:21–23.* Once wisdom is properly valued, both the ear and mind are captivated by it.

2:3 cry for discernment. This shows the passionate pleading of one who is desperate to know and apply the truth of God. The least bit of indifference will leave one bereft of the fullness of wisdom.

2:4 seek … search. A desiring search, the most intensive of a lifetime. Cf. Job 28:1–28 for a parallel.

2:6 His mouth. The words of His mouth are contained in Scripture. It is there that God speaks (cf. Heb 1:1, 2; 2Pe 1:20, 21). Wisdom comes only by revelation.

2:7, 8 the upright. This identifies those who are true believers, who seek to know, love, and obey God and to live righteously. These covenant keepers alone can know wisdom and experience God's protection.

2:9 righteousness and justice and equity. The ethical triad of 1:3.

2:10 wisdom will enter your heart. *See note on 4:21–23.*

2:11 Discretion … Understanding. Truth is the protector from all evil (see Ps 119:11, 97–104).

2:12 speaks perverse things. Twisted speech is typical of those who reject wisdom (cf. Pr 8:13; 10:31, 32).

2:14 Fools love most what is worst.

2:16 strange woman. She is the harlot repeatedly condemned in Proverbs (cf. 5:1–23; 6:20–29; 7:1–27; 22:14; 23:27), as in the rest of Scripture (Ex 20:14; Lv 20:10). She is "foreign" or "strange" because such women were at first from outside Israel, but came to include any prostitute or adulteress. Her words are the flattering or smooth words of Pr 7:14–20.

2:17 leaves the companion. She leaves the guidance and friendship of her husband (cf. 16:28; 17:9). **forgets the covenant.** In a wide sense this could be the covenant of Sinai (Ex 20:14), but specifically looks to the marriage covenant of Ge 2:24, with its commitment to fidelity.

2:18 sinks down to death. The destructive nature of this blinding sin leads one to walk alongside death (see vv. 8, 9, 12, 15). Death in Proverbs is presented as both a gradual descent (5:23) and a sudden end (29:1).

2:19 None who go … return. The irreversible nature of continuing in this sin points to its devastating consequences. It leads to physical death, as expressed in the Heb. euphemisms of v. 22 ("cut off" and "uprooted"). After that comes the reality of eternal death.

2:21 live in the land … remain. Exactly opposite to those who live in sexual sin and are headed for death, those who belong to the Lord will live. *See note on 8:18–21.*

THE REWARDS OF WISDOM

3 My son, [A]do not forget my [a]teaching,
But let your heart [B]keep my
commandments;
2 For [A]length of days and years of life
And peace they will add to you.
3 Do not let [A]kindness and truth leave you;
[B]Bind them around your neck,
[C]Write them on the tablet of your heart.
4 So you will [A]find favor and [B]good [a]repute
In the sight of God and man.
5 [A]Trust in the LORD with all your heart
And [B]do not lean on your
own understanding.
6 In all your ways [A]acknowledge Him,
And He will [B]make your paths straight.
7 [A]Do not be wise in your own eyes;
[B]Fear the LORD and turn away from evil.
8 It will be [A]healing to your [a]body
And [B]refreshment to your bones.
9 [A]Honor the LORD from your wealth
And from the [B]first of all your produce;
10 So your [A]barns will be filled with plenty
And your [B]vats will overflow
with new wine.
11 [A]My son, do not reject the
[a]discipline of the LORD
Or loathe His reproof,
12 For [A]whom the LORD loves He reproves,
Even [B]as a father *corrects* the
son in whom he delights.

13 [A]How blessed is the man
who finds wisdom
And the man who gains understanding.
14 For her [A]profit is better than
the profit of silver
And her gain better than fine gold.
15 She is [A]more precious than [a]jewels;
And nothing you desire compares with her.
16 [a,A]Long life is in her right hand;
In her left hand are [B]riches and honor.
17 Her [A]ways are pleasant ways
And all her paths are [B]peace.
18 She is a [A]tree of life to those
who take hold of her,
And happy are all who hold her fast.
19 The LORD [A]by wisdom founded the earth,
By understanding He
[B]established the heavens.
20 By His knowledge the [A]deeps
were broken up
And the [B]skies drip with dew.
21 My son, [A]let them not [a]vanish
from your sight;
Keep sound wisdom and discretion,
22 So they will be [A]life to your soul
And [B]adornment to your neck.
23 Then you will [A]walk in your way securely
And your foot will not [B]stumble.
24 When you [A]lie down, you
will not be afraid;
When you lie down, your
sleep will be sweet.
25 [A]Do not be afraid of sudden fear
Nor of the [a,B]onslaught of the
wicked when it comes;
26 For the LORD will be [a]your confidence
And will [A]keep your foot
from being caught.

3:1 [a]Or *law* [A]Ps 119:61; Prov 4:5 [B]Ex 20:6; Deut 30:16 3:2 [A]Ps 91:16; Prov 3:16; 4:10; 9:11; 10:27 3:3 [A]2 Sam 15:20; Prov 14:22 [B]Deut 6:8; 11:18; Prov 1:9; 6:21 [C]Prov 7:3; Jer 17:1; 2 Cor 3:3 3:4 [a]Lit *understanding* [A]1 Sam 2:26; Prov 8:35; Luke 2:52 [B]Ps 111:10 3:5 [A]Ps 37:3, 5; Prov 22:19 [B]Prov 23:4; Jer 9:23 3:6 [A]1 Chr 28:9; Prov 16:3; Phil 4:6; James 1:5 [B]Is 45:13; Jer 10:23 3:7 [A]Rom 12:16 [B]Job 1:1; 28:28; Prov 8:13; 16:6 3:8 [a]Lit *navel* [A]Prov 4:22 [B]Job 21:24 3:9 [A]Is 43:23 [B]Ex 23:19; Deut 26:2; Mal 3:10 3:10 [A]Deut 28:8 [B]Joel 2:24 3:11 [a]Or *instruction* [A]Job 5:17; Heb 12:5, 6 3:12 [A]Rev 3:19 [B]Deut 8:5; Prov 13:24 3:13 [A]Prov 8:32, 34 3:14 [A]Job 28:15-19; Prov 8:10, 19; 16:16 3:15 [a]Lit *corals* [A]Job 28:18; Prov 8:11 3:16 [a]Lit *Length of days* [A]Prov 3:2 [B]Prov 8:18; 22:4 3:17 [A]Matt 11:29 [B]Ps 119:165; Prov 16:7 3:18 [A]Gen 2:9; Prov 11:30; 13:12; 15:4; Rev 2:7 3:19 [A]Ps 104:24; Prov 8:27 [B]Prov 8:27, 28 3:20 [A]Gen 7:11 [B]Deut 33:28; Job 36:28 3:21 [a]Lit *depart* [A]Prov 4:21 3:22 [A]Deut 32:47; Prov 4:22; 8:35; 16:22; 21:21 [B]Prov 1:9 3:23 [A]Prov 4:12; 10:9 [B]Ps 91:12; Is 5:27; 63:13 3:24 [A]Job 11:19; Ps 3:5; Prov 1:33; 6:22 3:25 [a]Lit *storm* [A]Ps 91:5; 1 Pet 3:14 [B]Job 5:21 3:26 [a]Or *at your side* [A]1 Sam 2:9

3:1–35 Here the study of truth leading to wisdom is commended to all. This is enforced by a contrast of the destinies of the wise and wicked.

3:1–20 Solomon instructs that wisdom is: 1) rooted in sound teaching (vv. 1–4); 2) rests in trust in God (vv. 5, 6), and 3) rewards those who obey (vv. 7–10). While wisdom demands chastening, it brings profound benefits (vv. 13–18), and its importance is clear since it undergirded God's creation (vv. 19, 20).

3:1 my teaching. Heb. "Torah," from the verb "to throw, distribute, or teach," hence "teaching." It is used of God's law (29:18), but here it is used of the commands and principles that God gave through Solomon. **heart.** *See note on 4:21–23.*

3:3 neck ... heart. The virtues of mercy (the Heb. word for lovingkindness and loyal love) and truth that come from God are to become part of us—outwardly in our behavior for all to see as an adornment of spiritual beauty, and inwardly as the subject of our meditation (cf. Dt 6:4–9). Such inward and outward mercy and truth is evidence of New Covenant salvation (cf. Jer 31:33, 34).

3:4 God and man. Cf. Christ in Lk 2:52.

3:7 This is alluded to by Paul in Ro 12:16.

3:8 healing ... refreshment. The renewal here is in the marrow, the inner parts (Job 21:24). God is promising physical well-being for those who live wisely according to His will. Such physical well-being is what David forfeited before he confessed that he had sinned against Bathsheba and Uriah (see Pss 32:3, 4; 51:8).

3:9, 10 Honor the LORD ... wealth. A biblical view of wealth demands using possessions for honoring God. This is accomplished by trusting God (v. 5); by giving the best to God ("first"; cf. Ex 22:29; 23:19; Dt 18:4); by being fair (vv. 27, 28); by giving generously (11:25); and by expressing gratitude for all He gives (Dt 6:10–12). The result of such faithfulness to honor Him is prosperity and satisfaction.

3:11, 12 not reject ... discipline. Since even the wisest of God's children are subject to sin, there is necessity of God's fatherly discipline to increase wisdom and blessing. Such correction should not be resisted. *See notes on Heb 12:5–11.*

3:14, 15 Cf. Ps 19:10, 11. Divine wisdom yields the richest treasures, described in vv. 14–18 as "profit," "long life," "riches," "honor," "pleasant ways," "peace," "life," and "happy."

3:18 tree of life. This expression is a metaphor referring to temporal and spiritual renewal and refreshment (cf. 11:30; 13:12; 15:4).

3:19, 20 Solomon is indicating that wisdom is basic to all of life, for by it God created everything. Since God used it to create the universe, how eager must we be to use it to live in this universe.

3:22 life to your soul. The association of wisdom with the inner spiritual life (cf. vv. 2, 16) unfolds throughout the book (cf. 4:10, 22; 7:2; 8:35; 9:11; 10:11, 16, 17; 11:19, 30; 12:28; 13:14; 14:27; 15:4, 24; 16:22; 19:23; 21:21; 22:4). **adornment to your neck.** The wisdom of God will adorn one's life for all to see its beauty (cf. 1:9).

3:25, 26 afraid ... confidence. Living in God's wisdom provides the basis for the believer's peace of mind (v. 24) and removes fear (v. 25).

27 [A]Do not withhold good from
[a]those to whom it is due,
When it is in your power to do *it*.
28 [A]Do not say to your neighbor,
"Go, and come back,
And tomorrow I will give *it*,"
When you have it with you.
29 [A]Do not devise harm against
your neighbor,
While he lives securely beside you.
30 [A]Do not contend with a man without cause,
If he has done you no harm.
31 [A]Do not envy a man of violence
And do not choose any of his ways.
32 For the [A]devious are an
abomination to the LORD;
But [a]He is [B]intimate with the upright.
33 The [A]curse of the LORD is on
the house of the wicked,
But He [B]blesses the dwelling
of the righteous.
34 Though [A]He scoffs at the scoffers,
Yet [B]He gives grace to the afflicted.
35 [A]The wise will inherit honor,
But fools [a]display dishonor.

A FATHER'S INSTRUCTION

4 Hear, *O* sons, the [A]instruction of a father,
And [B]give attention that you
may [a]gain understanding,
2 For I give you [a]sound [A]teaching;
[B]Do not abandon my [b]instruction.
3 When I was a son to my father,
[A]Tender and [B]the only son in
the sight of my mother,
4 Then he [A]taught me and said to me,
"Let your heart [B]hold fast my words;
[C]Keep my commandments and live;
5 [A]Acquire wisdom! [B]Acquire understanding!
Do not forget nor turn away from
the words of my mouth.
6 "Do not forsake her, and she
will guard you;
[A]Love her, and she will watch over you.
7 "[A]The [a]beginning of wisdom
is: [B]Acquire wisdom;
And with all your acquiring,
get understanding.
8 "[A]Prize her, and she will exalt you;
She will honor you if you embrace her.
9 "She will place [A]on your head
a garland of grace;
She will present you with a
crown of beauty."

10 Hear, my son, and [A]accept my sayings
And the [B]years of your life will be many.
11 I have [A]directed you in the
way of wisdom;
I have led you in upright paths.
12 When you walk, your [A]steps
will not be impeded;
And if you run, you [B]will not stumble.
13 [A]Take hold of instruction; do not let go.
Guard her, for she is your [B]life.
14 [A]Do not enter the path of the wicked
And do not proceed in the
way of evil men.
15 Avoid it, do not pass by it;
Turn away from it and pass on.
16 For they [A]cannot sleep unless they do evil;
And [a]they are robbed of sleep unless
they make *someone* stumble.
17 For they [A]eat the bread of wickedness
And drink the wine of violence.
18 But the [A]path of the righteous
is like the [B]light of dawn,
That [C]shines brighter and
brighter until the [D]full day.
19 The [A]way of the wicked is like darkness;
They do not know over what
they [a,B]stumble.

3:27 [a]Lit *its owners* [A]Rom 13:7; Gal 6:10 3:28 [A]Lev 19:13; Deut 24:15 3:29 [A]Prov 6:14; 14:22 3:30 [A]Prov 26:17; Rom 12:18 3:31 [A]Ps 37:1; Prov 24:1 3:32 [a]Lit *His private counsel is* [A]Prov 11:20 [B]Job 29:4; Ps 25:14 3:33 [A]Lev 26:14, 16; Deut 11:28; Zech 5:3, 4; Mal 2:2 [B]Job 8:6; Ps 1:3 3:34 [A]James 4:6 [B]1 Pet 5:5 3:35 [a]Lit *raise high* [A]Dan 12:3 4:1 [a]Lit *know* [A]Ps 34:11; Prov 1:8 [B]Prov 1:2; 2:2 4:2 [a]Lit *good* [b]Or *law* [A]Deut 32:2; Job 11:4 [B]Ps 89:30; 119:87; Prov 3:1 4:3 [A]1 Chr 22:5; 29:1 [B]Zech 12:10 4:4 [A]Eph 6:4 [B]Ps 119:168 [C]Prov 7:2 4:5 [A]Prov 4:7 [B]Prov 16:16 4:6 [A]2 Thess 2:10 4:7 [a]Or *the primary thing is wisdom* [A]Prov 8:23 [B]Prov 23:23 4:8 [A]1 Sam 2:30 4:9 [A]Prov 1:9 4:10 [A]Prov 2:1 [B]Prov 3:2 4:11 [A]1 Sam 12:23 4:12 [A]Job 18:7; Ps 18:36 [B]Ps 91:11; Prov 3:23 4:13 [A]Prov 3:18 [B]Prov 3:22; John 6:63 4:14 [A]Ps 1:1; Prov 1:15 4:16 [a]Lit *their sleep is robbed* [A]Ps 36:4; Mic 2:1 4:17 [A]Prov 13:2 4:18 [A]Is 26:7; Matt 5:14; Phil 2:15 [B]2 Sam 23:4 [C]Dan 12:3 [D]Job 11:17 4:19 [a]Or *may stumble* [A]Job 18:5, 6; Prov 2:13; Is 59:9, 10; Jer 23:12; John 12:35 [B]John 11:10

3:28 neighbor. A neighbor is anyone in need whom God brings across one's path. See Lk 10:29–37.

3:29 devise ... lives. Do not plan evil against one trusting in your protection.

3:30 contend. This can mean "come to hand blows," or, with legal overtones, "accuse a man."

3:31 envy. Many law-keepers wish they were law-breakers (Ps 37:1–7). They would like to be oppressors rather than the oppressed.

3:32 abomination. Specifically, an abomination is an attitude or act that is incompatible with God's nature and intolerable to Him, leading to His anger and judgment. This is an important theme in Proverbs (*see note on 6:16–19*). **intimate.** This means that God discloses Himself and His truth to the upright (cf. Ps 25:14).

3:34 afflicted. Lit. "he who bends himself" (Jas 4:6; 1Pe 5:5).

4:2 sound teaching ... my instruction. There is no wisdom but that which is linked to sound teaching, which should be the focal point of all instruction (cf. 1Ti 1:10; 4:13, 16; 5:17; 2Ti 3:10, 16; 4:2; Titus 1:9; 2:1, 10).

4:3–5 son to my father ... my mother. This is Solomon's reference to David and Bathsheba (2Sa 12:24).

4:8 Prize ... exalt ... honor ... embrace. The more highly one esteems wisdom, the more highly wisdom lifts that person.

4:9 head. *See note on 3:22.*

4:13 Take ... do not let go. Guard. The father commanded his son in v. 5 to "acquire wisdom"; here he commands him to hold on to it.

4:14 Do not enter the path of the wicked. Sin is best dealt with at its beginning by the application of necessary wisdom to suit the initial temptation (cf. Ps 1:1).

4:15 Four verbs identify aspects necessary in urgently dealing with sin at its start (v. 14): 1) avoid the sinful situation; 2) pass as far from it as possible; 3) turn away from the sin; and 4) pass beyond or escape the sin. The plan here fits exactly with the pattern of sin's enticement outlined in Jas 1:13–15.

4:16, 17 they cannot sleep. Cf. 3:24. They have to sin before they can sleep, and they view their sin as food for their hungry, wicked souls.

4:18 path of the ... light of dawn. The path of the believer is one of increasing light, just as a sunrise begins with the faint glow of dawn and proceeds to the splendor of noonday.

20 My son, [A]give attention to my words;
[B]Incline your ear to my sayings.
21 [A]Do not let them depart
from your sight;
[B]Keep them in the midst of your heart.
22 For they are [A]life to those who find them
And [B]health to all [a]their body.
23 Watch over your heart with all diligence,
For [A]from it *flow* the springs of life.
24 Put away from you a [A]deceitful mouth
And [B]put devious [a]speech far from you.
25 Let your eyes look directly ahead
And let your [a]gaze be fixed
straight in front of you.
26 [A]Watch the path of your feet
And all your [B]ways will be established.
27 [A]Do not turn to the right nor to the left;
[B]Turn your foot from evil.

PITFALLS OF IMMORALITY

5 My son, [A]give attention to my wisdom,
[B]Incline your ear to my understanding;
2 That you may [A]observe discretion
And your [B]lips may reserve knowledge.
3 For the lips of an
[a,A]adulteress [B]drip honey
And [C]smoother than oil is her [b]speech;
4 But in the end she is [A]bitter
as wormwood,
[B]Sharp as a two-edged sword.
5 Her feet [A]go down to death,
Her steps take hold of Sheol.
6 [a]She does not ponder the [A]path of life;
Her ways are [B]unstable, she
[C]does not know *it*.
7 [A]Now then, *my* sons, listen to me
And [B]do not depart from the
words of my mouth.
8 [A]Keep your way far from her
And do not go near the [B]door of her house,
9 Or you will give your vigor to others
And your years to the cruel one;
10 And strangers will be filled
with your strength
And your hard-earned goods *will*
go to the house of an alien;
11 And you groan at your [a]final end,
When your flesh and your
body are consumed;
12 And you say, "How I have [A]hated instruction!
And my heart [B]spurned reproof!
13 "I have not listened to the
voice of my [A]teachers,
Nor inclined my ear to my instructors!
14 "I was almost in utter ruin
In the midst of the assembly
and congregation."

15 Drink water from your own cistern
And [a]fresh water from your own well.
16 Should your [A]springs be
dispersed abroad,
Streams of water in the streets?
17 Let them be yours alone
And not for strangers with you.
18 Let your [A]fountain be blessed,
And [B]rejoice in the [C]wife of your youth.
19 *As* a loving [A]hind and a graceful doe,
Let her breasts satisfy you at all times;
Be [a]exhilarated always with her love.

4:20 [A]Prov 5:1 [B]Prov 2:2 4:21 [A]Prov 3:21 [B]Prov 7:1, 2 4:22 [a]Lit *his* [A]Prov 3:22 [B]Prov 3:8; 12:18 4:23 [A]Matt 12:34; 15:18, 19; Mark 7:21; Luke 6:45 4:24 [a]Or *lips* [A]Prov 6:12; 10:32 [B]Prov 19:1 4:25 [a]Or *eyelids* 4:26 [A]Prov 5:21; Heb 12:13 [B]Ps 119:5 4:27 [A]Deut 5:32; 28:14 [B]Prov 1:15; Is 1:16 5:1 [A]Prov 4:20 [B]Prov 22:17 5:2 [A]Prov 3:21 [B]Mal 2:7 5:3 [a]Lit *strange woman* [b]Lit *palate* [A]Prov 2:16; 5:20; 7:5; 22:14 [B]Song 4:11 [C]Ps 55:21 5:4 [A]Eccl 7:26 [B]Ps 57:4; Heb 4:12 5:5 [A]Prov 7:27 5:6 [a]Lit *That she not watch* [A]Prov 4:26; 5:21 [B]2 Pet 2:14 [C]Prov 30:20 5:7 [A]Prov 7:24 [B]Ps 119:102 5:8 [A]Prov 7:25 [B]Prov 9:14 5:11 [a]Or *latter* 5:12 [A]Prov 1:7, 22, 29 [B]Prov 1:25; 12:1 5:13 [A]Prov 1:8 5:15 [a]Lit *flowing* 5:16 [A]Prov 5:18; 9:17; Song 4:12, 15 5:18 [A]Prov 9:17; Song 4:12, 15 [B]Eccl 9:9 [C]Mal 2:14 5:19 [a]Lit *intoxicated* [A]Song 2:9, 17; 4:5; 7:3

4:21–23 **heart.** The "heart" commonly refers to the mind as the center of thinking and reason (3:3; 6:21; 7:3), but also includes the emotions (15:15, 30), the will (11:20; 14:14), and thus, the whole inner being (3:5). The heart is the depository of all wisdom and the source of whatever affects speech (v. 24), sight (v. 25), and conduct (vv. 26, 27).

5:1, 2 **give attention.** The wise father marshals all the essential terms to sum up his call to wisdom (cf. 1:2; 2:2; 3:13; 4:5).

5:3 **lips ... speech.** Seduction begins with deceptive flattery (cf. 2:16). Lips of honey should be part of true love in marriage (SS 4:11).

5:4, 5 **in the end.** Lit. "the future" of tasting her lips is like "wormwood," a symbol of suffering (cf. Dt 29:18), and a "sword," the symbol of death. She travels on the road to death and hell (cf. 2:18).

5:5 **Sheol.** *See note on 1:12.*

5:6 **Her ways are unstable.** Her steps willfully and predictably stagger here and there, as she has no concern for the abyss ahead.

5:7–14 These verses describe the high price of infidelity. The focus here is on the guilty suffering of the one who yields to lust rather than obeying God's law. Contrast the proper response to such temptation in the case of Joseph (Ge 39:1–12).

5:9, 10 **your vigor to others.** The consequences of this sin may include slavery, as a commuted punishment, instead of death that should have come for adultery (Dt 22:22). In that case, "the cruel one" was the judge, and the "others" were the masters to whom all the energy of youth was directed in slavery. All personal wealth was lost to outsiders, and one served in a stranger's house helping him to prosper.

5:11 **flesh and ... body.** This could be a reference to venereal disease (cf. 1Co 6:18), or to the natural end of life. At that point, filled with an irreversible regret (v. 12), the ruined sinner vainly laments his neglect of warning and his sad disgrace.

5:14 **midst of the assembly.** A most painful loss in such a situation is public disgrace in the community. There can be public confession, discipline, and forgiveness, but not restoration to one's former place of honor and service. See 6:33.

5:15–19 Using the imagery of water, the joy of a faithful marriage is contrasted with the disaster of infidelity (vv. 9–14). "Cistern" and "well" refer to the wife from whom the husband is to draw all his satisfying refreshment, sexually and affectionately (v. 19; cf. 9:17, 18; SS 4:9–11).

5:16, 17 **springs ... streams.** The euphemism refers to the male procreation capacity with the idea of the foolish as a fountain ("spring") scattering precious water—a picture of the wastefulness of sexual promiscuity. The result of such indiscriminate sin is called "streams of waters in the streets," a graphic description of the illegitimate street children of harlotry. Rather, says Solomon, "let them be yours alone" and not the children of such immoral strangers.

5:18 **fountain be blessed.** God offers to bless male procreation when it is confined to one's wife. It should be noted that, in spite of the sinful polygamy of David and Solomon, as well as the disastrous polygamy of Rehoboam (cf. 2Ch 11:21), the instruction here identifies God's ideal as one wife from youth on.

5:19 **graceful doe.** The doe has graceful beauty in her face and form and is often used in the poetry of Bible times for the beauty of a woman. **breasts.** This is imagery of affection (cf. SS 1:13; 4:1–7; 7:7, 8).

20 For why should you, my son, be
exhilarated with an [a,A]adulteress
And embrace the bosom of a [B]foreigner?
21 For the [A]ways of a man are before
the eyes of the LORD,
And He [B]watches all his paths.
22 His [A]own iniquities will capture the wicked,
And he will be held with
the cords of his sin.
23 He will [A]die for lack of instruction,
And in the greatness of his
folly he will go astray.

PARENTAL COUNSEL

6 My son, if you have become
[A]surety for your neighbor,
Have [a]given a pledge for a stranger,
2 *If* you have been snared with
the words of your mouth,
Have been caught with the
words of your mouth,
3 Do this then, my son, and deliver yourself;
Since you have come into the
[a]hand of your neighbor,
Go, humble yourself, and
importune your neighbor.
4 Give no [A]sleep to your eyes,
Nor slumber to your eyelids;
5 Deliver yourself like a gazelle
from *the hunter's* hand
And like a [A]bird from the
hand of the fowler.

6 Go to the [A]ant, O [B]sluggard,
Observe her ways and be wise,
7 Which, having [A]no chief,
Officer or ruler,
8 Prepares her food [A]in the summer
And gathers her provision in the harvest.
9 How long will you lie down, O sluggard?
When will you arise from your sleep?
10 "[A]A little sleep, a little slumber,
A little folding of the hands to [a]rest"—
11 [A]Your poverty will come in like a [a]vagabond
And your need like [b]an armed man.

12 A [A]worthless person, a wicked man,
Is the one who walks with
a [B]perverse mouth,
13 Who [A]winks with his eyes, who
[a]signals with his feet,
Who [b]points with his fingers;
14 Who *with* [A]perversity in his heart
continually [B]devises evil,
Who [a,C]spreads strife.
15 Therefore [A]his calamity will come suddenly;
[B]Instantly he will be broken and
there will be [C]no healing.

16 There are six things which
the LORD hates,
Yes, seven which are an
abomination [a]to Him:
17 [A]Haughty eyes, a [B]lying tongue,
And hands that [C]shed innocent blood,
18 A heart that devises [A]wicked plans,
[B]Feet that run rapidly to evil,
19 A [A]false witness *who* utters lies,
And one who [a,B]spreads strife
among brothers.

5:20 [a]Lit *strange woman* [A]Prov 5:3 [B]Prov 2:16; 6:24; 7:5; 23:27 5:21 [A]Job 14:16; 31:4; 34:21; Ps 119:168; Prov 15:3; Jer 16:17; 32:19; Hos 7:2; Heb 4:13 [B]Prov 4:26 5:22 [A]Num 32:23; Ps 7:15; 9:15; 40:12; Prov 1:31, 32 5:23 [A]Job 4:21; 36:12 6:1 [a]Lit *clapped your palms* [A]Prov 11:15; 17:18; 20:16; 22:26; 27:13 6:3 [a]Lit *palm* 6:4 [A]Ps 132:4 6:5 [A]Ps 91:3; 124:7 6:6 [A]Prov 30:24, 25 [B]Prov 6:9; 10:26; 13:4; 20:4; 26:16 6:7 [A]Prov 30:27 6:8 [A]Prov 10:5 6:10 [a]Lit *lie down* [A]Prov 24:33 6:11 [a]Lit *one who walks* [b]Lit *a man with a shield* [A]Prov 24:34 6:12 [A]Prov 16:27 [B]Prov 4:24; 10:32 6:13 [a]Lit *scrapes* [b]Lit *instructs with* [A]Job 15:12; Ps 35:19; Prov 10:10 6:14 [a]Lit *sends out* [A]Prov 17:20 [B]Prov 3:29; Mic 2:1 [C]Prov 6:19; 16:28 6:15 [A]Prov 24:22 [B]Is 30:13, 14; Jer 19:11 [C]2 Chr 36:16 6:16 [a]Lit *of His soul* 6:17 [A]Ps 18:27; 101:5; Prov 21:4; 30:13 [B]Ps 31:18; 120:2; Prov 12:22; 17:7 [C]Deut 19:10; Prov 28:17; Is 1:15; 59:7 6:18 [A]Gen 6:5; Prov 24:2 [B]Prov 1:16; Is 59:7; Rom 3:15 6:19 [a]Lit *sends out* [A]Ps 27:12; Prov 12:17; 19:5, 9; 21:28 [B]Prov 6:14

5:20 Such behavior is presented as having no benefit; thus, to justify such folly is senseless.

5:21, 22 watches … held. The Lord sees all that man does and in mercy withholds immediate judgment, allowing the sinner time to repent or to be caught in his own sin (cf. Nu 32:23; Pss 7:15, 16; 57:6; Pr 1:17; Gal 6:7, 8). Note the example of Haman (Est 5:9–14; 7:1–10).

5:23 He will die. *See note on 2:18.*

6:1 surety … pledge. The foolishness here is making one's self responsible for another's debt and pledging to pay if the other defaults (cf. 11:15; 17:18; 20:16; 22:26). While there is precedent for such a practice, it is far better to give to those in need (see 19:17; Dt 15:1–15) or lend without interest (see 28:8; Lv 25:35–38).

6:2–4 snared … come into the hand. Cf. 22:26, 27. Anyone who becomes responsible for another person's debt is trapped and controlled because he has yielded control of what God has given him as a stewardship. The situation is so serious that it is imperative to take control of one's own God-given resources and get out of such an intolerable arrangement immediately ("deliver yourself," vv. 3, 4) before coming to poverty or slavery. Cf. Ge 43:9; 44:32, 33.

6:6–11 A warning against laziness is appropriate after the discussion on the folly of guaranteeing someone else's debt, since it is often lazy people who want sureties.

6:6 ant … sluggard. Cf. 30:25. The ant is an example of industry, diligence, and planning (vv. 7, 8) and serves as a rebuke to a sluggard (a lazy person who lacks self-control). Wisdom sends a lazy man to learn from an ant (see 10:4, 26; 12:24; 13:4; 15:19; 19:15; 20:4; 26:14–16).

6:11 vagabond … armed man. The lazy man, with his inordinate devotion to sleep rather than work (vv. 9, 10), learns too late, thus coming to inescapable poverty just as a victim is overpowered by a robber (see 24:33, 34). While laziness leads to poverty (cf. 10:4, 5; 13:4; 20:4, 13), laziness is not always the cause of poverty (cf. 14:31; 17:5; 19:1, 17, 22; 21:12; 28:3, 11).

6:12 A worthless person. A scoundrel (1Sa 25:25; Job 34:18), lit. a "man of Belial" (useless; cf. 1Sa 2:12; 30:22), a term which came to be used of the Devil himself (see 2Co 6:15).

6:13 winks … signals … points. Apparently this was common in the East. Fearing detection, and to hide his intention, the deceiver spoke lies to the victim while giving signals with his eyes, hands, and feet to someone else who was in on the deception to carry out the intrigue.

6:14 strife. The sin of discord, dissent, or creating conflict intentionally recurs in Proverbs (15:18; 16:28; 17:14; 18:19; 21:9, 19; 22:10; 23:29; 25:24; 26:21; 27:15; 28:25; 29:22).

6:15 no healing. The results of iniquity can be irreversible. His punishment will fit his crime when God judges.

6:16–19 six … seven. The sequence of these two numbers was used both to represent totality and as a means of arresting attention (cf. 30:15, 18; Job 5:19; Am 1:3). These 7 detestable sins provide a profound glimpse into the sinfulness of man. These verses act as a summary of the previous warnings: 1) haughty eyes (v. 13a, "winks"); 2) lying tongue (v. 12b, "perverse mouth"); 3) hands (v. 13c, "fingers"); 4) heart (v. 14a); 5) feet (v. 13b); 6) false witness (v. 12b); and 7) strife (v. 14c).

20 [A]My son, observe the commandment
of your father
And do not forsake the [a]teaching
of your mother;
21 [A]Bind them continually on your heart;
Tie them around your neck.
22 When you [A]walk about, [a]they will guide you;
When you sleep, [a]they will watch over you;
And when you awake, [a]they will talk to you.
23 For [A]the commandment is a lamp
and the [a]teaching is light;
And reproofs for discipline
are the way of life
24 To [A]keep you from the evil woman,
From the smooth tongue of the [a]adulteress.
25 [A]Do not desire her beauty in your heart,
Nor let her capture you with her [B]eyelids.
26 For [A]on account of a harlot *one is*
reduced to a loaf of bread,
And [a]an adulteress [B]hunts
for the precious life.
27 Can a man [a]take fire in his bosom
And his clothes not be burned?
28 Or can a man walk on hot coals
And his feet not be scorched?
29 So is the one who [A]goes in to
his neighbor's wife;
Whoever touches her [B]will
not [a]go unpunished.
30 [a]Men do not despise a thief if he steals
To [A]satisfy [b]himself when he is hungry;
31 But when he is found, he must
[A]repay sevenfold;
He must give all the [a]substance
of his house.
32 The one who commits adultery with
a woman is [A]lacking [a]sense;
He who would [B]destroy [b]himself does it.
33 Wounds and disgrace he will find,
And his reproach will not be blotted out.
34 For [A]jealousy [a]enrages a man,
And he will not spare in the
[B]day of vengeance.
35 He will not [a]accept any ransom,
Nor will he be [b]satisfied though
you give many [c]gifts.

6:20 [a]Or *law* [A]Eph 6:1 6:21 [A]Prov 3:3 6:22 [a]Lit *she* [A]Prov 3:23 6:23 [a]Or *law* [A]Ps 19:8; 119:105 6:24 [a]Lit *foreign woman* [A]Prov 5:3; 7:5, 21 6:25 [A]Matt 5:28 [B]2 Kin 9:30; Jer 4:30; Ezek 23:40 6:26 [a]Lit *a man's wife* [A]Prov 5:9, 10; 29:3 [B]Prov 7:23; Ezek 13:18 6:27 [a]Lit *snatch up* 6:29 [a]Lit *be innocent* [A]Ezek 18:6; 33:26 [B]Prov 16:5 6:30 [a]Lit *They do not;* or *Do not men...?* [b]Lit *his soul* [A]Job 38:39 6:31 [a]Or *wealth* [A]Ex 22:1-4 6:32 [a]Lit *heart* [b]Lit *his soul* [A]Prov 7:7; 9:4, 16; 10:13, 21; 11:12; 12:11 [B]Prov 7:22, 23 6:34 [a]Lit *is the rage of* [A]Prov 27:4; Song 8:6 [B]Prov 11:4 6:35 [a]Lit *lift up the face of any* [b]Lit *willing* [c]Or *bribes*

6:20, 21 *See notes on 3:1, 3.*

6:22 walk about … sleep … awake. Cf. 3:23, 24. This parallels the 3 circumstances of life in Dt 6:6–9; 11:18–20, for which wisdom provides direction, protection, and meditation. The biblical instruction for parents prevents the entrance of evil by supplying good and true thoughts, even when sleeping.

6:23 the commandment … the teaching … discipline. These all identify the Word of God, which provides the wisdom leading to abundant and eternal life.

6:24 *See notes on 2:16; 5:3.* Parental instruction in wisdom is crucial to strengthen a person against the strong attraction of sexual sin. By loving truth and being elevated to wisdom, men are not seduced by lying flattery.

6:25 desire. Sexual sin is rooted in desire (imagination of the sinful act), as implied in Ex 20:17 and addressed by Christ in Mt 5:28. This initial attraction must be consistently rejected (Jas 1:14, 15).

6:26 loaf of bread. Here a loaf of bread demonstrates how the prostitute reduces the life of a man to insignificance, including the loss of his wealth (see 29:3), freedom, family, purity, dignity, and even his soul (v. 32).

6:27–29 Powerful metaphors are given here to describe the obvious danger and destructive consequences of adultery, showing that punishment is a natural and expected consequence.

6:29 touches her. This refers to a touch intended to inflame sexual passion. Paul uses the same expression with the same meaning in 1Co 7:1.

6:30–35 Adultery is compared to a thief. Unlike the pity extended to a starving thief, who, though it may cost all he has, can make restitution and put the crime behind him permanently (vv. 30, 31), for the adulterer there is no restitution, as he destroys his soul (v. 32; cf. Dt 22:22). If he lives, he is disgraced for life (v. 33) with a reproach which will never go away. The jealous husband will have no mercy on him either (vv. 34, 35; cf. 27:4; SS 8:6).

6:31 sevenfold. Varying measures of restitution occur in Scripture (cf. Ex 22:1ff.; Lv 6:5; Nu 5:7; 2Sa 12:6; Lk 19:8), but none are so severe as for the thief.

SYMBOLS FOR THE BIBLE

Symbol	Reality	Texts
1. Jesus Christ	Personification of the Word	Jn 1:1; Rev 19:13
2. Valuable Metals	Incalculable worth	Ps 12:6 (silver) Pss 19:10; 119:127 (gold)
3. Seed	Source of new life	Mt 13:10–23; Jas 1:18; 1Pe 1:23
4. Water	Cleansing from sin	Eph 5:25–27; Rev 21:6; 22:17
5. Mirror	Self-examination	Jas 1:22–25
6. Food	Nourishment to the soul	1Co 3:2; 1Pe 2:1–3 (milk) Dt 8:3; Mt 4:4 (bread) 1Co 3:3; Heb 5:12–14 (meat) Ps 19:10 (honey)
7. Clothing	A life dressed in truth	Titus 2:10; 1Pe 3:5
8. Lamp	Light for direction	Ps 119:105; Pr 6:23; 2Pe 1:19
9. Sword	Spiritual weapon	Eph 6:17 (outwardly) Heb 4:12 (inwardly)
10. Plumb line	Benchmark of spiritual reality	Am 7:8
11. Hammer	Powerful judgment	Jer 23:29
12. Fire	Painful judgment	Jer 5:14; 20:9; 23:29

THE WILES OF THE HARLOT

7 My son, [A]keep my words
And treasure my commandments
within you.
2 [A]Keep my commandments and live,
And my [a]teaching [B]as the [b]apple of your eye.
3 [A]Bind them on your fingers;
[B]Write them on the tablet of your heart.
4 Say to wisdom, "You are my sister,"
And call understanding *your*
intimate friend;
5 That they may keep you
from an [a]adulteress,
From the foreigner who
[b]flatters with her words.

6 For [A]at the window of my house
I looked out [B]through my lattice,
7 And I saw among the [a,A]naive,
And discerned among the [b]youths
A young man [B]lacking [c]sense,
8 Passing through the street near [A]her corner;
And he [a]takes the way to [B]her house,
9 In the [A]twilight, in the [a]evening,
In the [b]middle of the night
and *in* the darkness.
10 And behold, a woman *comes* to meet him,
[A]Dressed as a harlot and cunning of heart.
11 She is [A]boisterous and rebellious,
Her [B]feet do not remain at home;
12 *She is* now in the streets,
now [A]in the squares,
And [B]lurks by every corner.
13 So she seizes him and kisses him
[a]And with a [A]brazen face she says to him:
14 "[a]I was due to offer [A]peace offerings;
Today I have [B]paid my vows.
15 "Therefore I have come out to meet you,
To seek your presence earnestly,
and I have found you.
16 "I have spread my couch with [A]coverings,
With colored [B]linens of Egypt.
17 "I have sprinkled my bed
With [A]myrrh, aloes and [B]cinnamon.
18 "Come, let us drink our fill of
love until morning;
Let us delight ourselves with caresses.
19 "For [a]my husband is not at home,
He has gone on a long journey;
20 He has taken a [A]bag of money [a]with him,
At the full moon he will come home."
21 With her many persuasions
she entices him;
With her [a,A]flattering lips she seduces him.
22 Suddenly he follows her
As an ox goes to the slaughter,
Or as [a]*one in* fetters to the
discipline of a fool,
23 Until an arrow pierces through his liver;
As a [A]bird hastens to the snare,
So he does not know that it
will cost him his life.

24 Now therefore, *my* sons, [A]listen to me,
And pay attention to the
words of my mouth.
25 Do not let your heart [A]turn
aside to her ways,
Do not stray into her paths.
26 For many are the [a]victims
she has cast down,
And [A]numerous are all her slain.
27 Her [A]house is the way to Sheol,
Descending to the chambers of death.

7:1 [A]Prov 2:1; 6:20 7:2 [a]Or *law* [b]Lit *pupil* [A]Prov 4:4 [B]Deut 32:10; Ps 17:8; Zech 2:8 7:3 [A]Deut 6:8; 11:18; Prov 6:21 [B]Prov 3:3 7:5 [a]Lit *strange woman* [b]Lit *is smooth* 7:6 [A]Judg 5:28 [B]Song 2:9 7:7 [a]Lit *simple ones* [b]Lit *sons* [c]Lit *heart* [A]Prov 1:22 [B]Prov 6:32; 9:4 7:8 [a]Lit *steps* [A]Prov 7:12 [B]Prov 7:27 7:9 [a]Lit *evening of the day* [b]Lit *pupil* (of the eye) [A]Job 24:15 7:10 [A]Gen 38:14, 15; 1 Tim 2:9 7:11 [A]Prov 9:13 [B]1 Tim 5:13; Titus 2:5 7:12 [A]Prov 9:14 [B]Prov 23:28 7:13 [a]Lit *She makes bold her face and says* [A]Prov 21:29 7:14 [a]Lit *Sacrifices of peace offerings are with me* [A]Lev 7:11 [B]Lev 7:16 7:16 [A]Prov 31:22 [B]Is 19:9; Ezek 27:7 7:17 [A]Ps 45:8 [B]Ex 30:23 7:19 [a]Lit *the man* 7:20 [a]Lit *in his hand* [A]Gen 42:35 7:21 [a]Lit *smooth* [A]Prov 5:3; 6:24 7:22 [a]Or *as a stag goes into a trap;* so some ancient versions 7:23 [A]Eccl 9:12 7:24 [A]Prov 5:7 7:25 [A]Prov 5:8 7:26 [a]Lit *mortally wounded* [A]Prov 9:18 7:27 [A]Prov 2:18; 5:5; 9:18; 1 Cor 6:9, 10; Rev 22:15

7:1–4 Cf. 2:1–4; 3:1–3; 4:10.

7:2 apple of your eye. This expression refers to the pupil of the eye which, because it is the source of sight, is carefully protected (see Dt 32:10; Ps 17:8; Zec 2:8). The son is to guard and protect his father's teachings because they give him spiritual and moral sight.

7:3 Bind. This is a call to give the truth of divine wisdom a permanent place in the mind and in conduct. Cf. 3:3; 6:21; Dt 6:8.

7:6 The drama of seduction by the adulteress, introduced in v. 5 and unfolding to v. 23, is described from the viewpoint of one who is watching from his window.

7:7 naive ... lacking sense. *See notes on 1:2–4.*

7:8 takes the way. Against the advice of 4:14, 15, he put himself right in the harlot's place. "Fleeing immorality" (1Co 6:18) starts by not being in the harlot's neighborhood at night. Cf. v. 25.

7:10 cunning of heart. Lit. "hidden." This is an unfair contest between the naive young man, who lacks wisdom and is void of the truth, and the evil woman, who knows her goal, but hides her true intentions. *See notes on 6:26; 23:27, 28.*

7:11, 12 These verses break the narrative to describe the woman's modes of operation leading to her successful seduction of the naive man.

7:14 peace offerings. According to the law of peace offerings (Lv 7:11–18), the meat left over after the sacrifice was to be eaten before the end of the day. She appears very religious in making the invitation that the man join her because she had made her offering and is bringing home the meat that must be eaten.

7:15 It is already night (v. 9), and the meal must be consumed. It cannot be left for morning. Such hypocrisy is concerned about the ceremonial law while aggressively seducing someone to violate God's moral law.

7:16, 17 linens of Egypt. Fine linen was a sign of wealth (31:22; Is 19:9; Eze 27:7). Here the solicitation is direct, as she describes the comfort of her bed with its aromatic spices (cf. SS 1:13; 3:6).

7:18 fill of love. Adultery is not true love, but mere physical gratification.

7:19, 20 She gives the naive man the assurance that there is no fear of discovery of their act, since her husband has taken a large sum of cash, needed because he will be away for a long time (lit. "the full moon"), returning at a set time and not before.

7:21 When the location, time, and setting were allowed, the seduction was easy (cf. v. 26).

7:22 slaughter ... fetters. Ignorant of the real danger and incapable of resistance, he quickly succumbs like a beast to be butchered or a criminal put in chains.

7:23 arrow ... bird. This refers to a mortal wound, as the liver represents the seat of life (La 2:11) and the bird is snared to be eaten (cf. 6:26).

7:24 The appropriate application of this drama is made in the admonition of these verses to avoid her deadly seduction.

7:26 It is not just weak men who fall, but strong men in the wrong place at the wrong time with the wrong thoughts for the wrong reasons.

7:27 Cf. 5:5.

THE COMMENDATION OF WISDOM

8 Does not [A]wisdom call,
And understanding [a]lift up her voice?
2 On top of [A]the heights beside the way,
Where the paths meet, she
takes her stand;
3 Beside the [A]gates, at the
opening to the city,
At the entrance of the doors, she cries out:
4 "To you, O men, I call,
And my voice is to the sons of men.
5 "O [a,A]naive ones, understand prudence;
And, O [B]fools, understand [b]wisdom.
6 "Listen, for I will speak [A]noble things;
And the opening of my lips *will
reveal* [B]right things.
7 "For my [A]mouth will utter truth;
And wickedness is an
abomination to my lips.
8 "All the utterances of my mouth
are in righteousness;
There is nothing [A]crooked or
perverted in them.
9 "They are all [A]straightforward to
him who understands,
And right to those who [B]find knowledge.
10 "Take my [A]instruction and not silver,
And knowledge rather than choicest gold.
11 "For wisdom is [A]better than [a]jewels;
And [B]all desirable things cannot
compare with her.

12 "I, wisdom, [A]dwell with prudence,
And I find [B]knowledge *and* discretion.
13 "The [A]fear of the LORD is to hate evil;
[B]Pride and arrogance and [C]the evil way
And the [D]perverted mouth, I hate.
14 "[A]Counsel is mine and [B]sound wisdom;
I am understanding, [C]power is mine.
15 "By me [A]kings reign,
And rulers decree justice.
16 "By me princes rule, and nobles,
All who judge rightly.
17 "I [A]love those who love me;
And [B]those who diligently
seek me will find me.
18 "[A]Riches and honor are with me,
Enduring [B]wealth and righteousness.
19 "My fruit is [A]better than gold, even pure gold,
And my yield *better* than [B]choicest silver.
20 "I walk in the way of righteousness,
In the midst of the paths of justice,
21 To endow those who love me with wealth,
That I may [A]fill their treasuries.

22 "The LORD possessed me [A]at the
beginning of His way,
Before His works [a]of old.
23 "From everlasting I was [a,A]established,
From the beginning, [B]from the
earliest times of the earth.
24 "When there were no [A]depths
I was [a]brought forth,
When there were no springs
abounding with water.
25 "[A]Before the mountains were settled,
Before the hills I was [a]brought forth;
26 While He had not yet made the
earth and the [a]fields,
Nor the first dust of the world.
27 "When He [A]established the
heavens, I was there,
When [B]He inscribed a circle
on the face of the deep,
28 When He made firm the skies above,
When the springs of the
deep became [a]fixed,
29 When [A]He set for the sea its boundary
So that the water would not
transgress His [a]command,
When He marked out [B]the
foundations of the earth;

8:1 [a]Lit *give* [A]Prov 1:20, 21; 8:1-3; 9:3; 1 Cor 1:24 8:2 [A]Prov 9:3, 14 8:3 [A]Job 29:7 8:5 [a]Lit *simple* [b]Lit *heart* [A]Prov 1:4 [B]Prov 1:22, 32; 3:35 8:6 [A]Prov 22:20 [B]Prov 23:16 8:7 [A]Ps 37:30; John 8:14; Rom 15:8 8:8 [A]Deut 32:5; Prov 2:15; Phil 2:15 8:9 [A]Prov 14:6 [B]Prov 3:13 8:10 [A]Prov 3:14, 15; 8:19 8:11 [a]Lit *corals* [A]Job 28:15, 18; Ps 19:10 [B]Prov 3:15 8:12 [A]Prov 8:5 [B]Prov 1:4 8:13 [A]Prov 3:7; 16:6 [B]1 Sam 2:3; Prov 16:18; Is 13:11 [C]Prov 15:9 [D]Prov 6:12 8:14 [A]Prov 1:25; 19:20; Is 28:29; Jer 32:19 [B]Prov 2:7; 3:21; 18:1 [C]Eccl 7:19; 9:16 8:15 [A]2 Chr 1:10; Prov 29:4; Dan 2:21; Matt 28:18; Rom 13:1 8:17 [A]1 Sam 2:30; Prov 4:6; John 14:21 [B]Prov 2:4, 5; John 7:37; James 1:5 8:18 [A]Prov 3:16 [B]Ps 112:3; Matt 6:33 8:19 [A]Job 28:15; Prov 3:14 [B]Prov 10:20 8:21 [A]Prov 24:4 8:22 [a]Lit *from then* [A]Job 28:26-28; Ps 104:24; Prov 3:19 8:23 [a]Or *consecrated* [A]John 1:1-3 [B]John 17:5 8:24 [a]Or *born* [A]Gen 1:2; Ex 15:5; Job 38:16; Prov 3:20 8:25 [a]Or *born* [A]Job 15:7; Ps 90:2 8:26 [a]Lit *outside places* 8:27 [A]Prov 3:19 [B]Job 26:10 8:28 [a]Lit *strong* 8:29 [a]Lit *mouth* [A]Job 38:10; Ps 104:9 [B]Job 38:6; Ps 104:5

8:1–3 **wisdom.** *See note on 1:21.* The openness and public exposure of wisdom contrasts with the secrecy and intrigues of the wicked adulterers in chap. 7.

8:4, 5 **naive ones.** *See note on 1:4.*

8:6–8 The virtues of wisdom are summarized in all that is noble, right, true, and righteous.

8:9 **straightforward.** Lit. "clear." The one who applies his mind to the wisdom of God will understand and gain moral knowledge and the insight to recognize truth. Cf. 1Co 1:18–25.

8:10, 11 The most valuable reality a young person can attain is the insight to order his life by the standard of truth (*see notes on 3:14, 15; 8:18–21;* also Job 28:12–28; Ps 19:10).

8:13 **The fear of the LORD.** *See note on 1:7.* **arrogance … hate.** Wisdom hates what God hates (cf. 6:16–19; Ps 5:5). The highest virtue is humility (submission to God), and thus wisdom hates pride and self-exaltation above all.

8:15, 16 **kings … rulers … princes … nobles.** In this royal court setting, Solomon addresses his son as a future king. All these leaders should do their work by God's wisdom and justice.

8:17 **love.** Wisdom's love for the one who receives it is proven by the benefits mentioned in vv. 18–21.

8:18–21 **Riches and honor.** Cf. 3:16; 22:4. Solomon, who was given great wisdom, experienced its wealth of benefits firsthand as a young king (cf. 1Ki 3:12–14; 10:14–29).

8:22–31 **The LORD possessed me.** Cf. 3:19, 20. Wisdom personified claims credit for everything that God created, so that wisdom was first, as God was eternally first. Christ used His eternal wisdom in creation (Jn 1:1–3; 1Co 1:24, 30).

8:24–26 Note how these verses parallel the creation account. The earth (v. 23) with day one in Ge 1:1–5; water (v. 24) with day two in Ge 1:6–8; and land (vv. 25, 26) with day three in Ge 1:9–13.

8:27 **circle on the face of the deep.** The Heb. word for circle indicates that the earth is a globe; therefore, the horizon is circular (cf. Is 40:22). This "deep" that surrounds the earth was the original world ocean that covered the surface of the earth before it was fully formed and given life (cf. Ge 1:2).

8:29 **sea its boundary.** In creation, God limited the waters on the earth (cf. Ge 1:9; 7:11; 8:2), commanding into existence shorelines beyond which the oceans cannot go. **foundations.** This figuratively denotes the solid structure of the earth (cf. Job 38:4; Ps 24:2).

30 Then [A]I was beside Him, *as*
a master workman;
And I was daily *His* delight,
[a]Rejoicing always before Him,
31 [a]Rejoicing in the world, His earth,
And *having* [A]my delight in
the sons of men.

32 "Now therefore, *O* sons, [A]listen to me,
For [B]blessed are they who
keep my ways.
33 "[A]Heed instruction and be wise,
And do not neglect *it*.
34 "[A]Blessed is the man who listens to me,
Watching daily at my gates,
Waiting at my doorposts.
35 "For [A]he who finds me finds life
And [B]obtains favor from the LORD.
36 "But he who [a]sins against me
[A]injures himself;
All those who [B]hate me [C]love death."

WISDOM'S INVITATION

9 Wisdom has [A]built her house,
She has hewn out her seven pillars;
2 She has [a,A]prepared her food,
she has [B]mixed her wine;
She has also [C]set her table;
3 She has [A]sent out her
maidens, she [B]calls
From the [C]tops of the
heights of the city:
4 "[A]Whoever is [a]naive, let him turn in here!"
To him who [B]lacks
[b]understanding she says,
5 "Come, [A]eat of my food
And drink of the wine I have mixed.
6 "[a]Forsake *your* folly and [A]live,
And [B]proceed in the way of
understanding."

7 He who [A]corrects a scoffer gets
dishonor for himself,
And he who reproves a wicked
man *gets* [a]insults for himself.
8 [A]Do not reprove a scoffer, or he will hate you,
[B]Reprove a wise man and he will love you.
9 Give *instruction* to a wise man
and he will be still wiser,
Teach a righteous man and he
will [A]increase *his* learning.
10 The [A]fear of the LORD is the
beginning of wisdom,
And the knowledge of the Holy
One is understanding.
11 For [A]by me your days will be multiplied,
And years of life will be added to you.
12 If you are wise, you are wise [A]for yourself,
And if you [B]scoff, you alone will bear it.

13 The [a]woman of folly is [A]boisterous,
She is [b]naive and [B]knows nothing.
14 She sits at the doorway of her house,
On a seat by [A]the high places of the city,
15 Calling to those who pass by,
Who are making their paths straight:
16 "[A]Whoever is [a]naive, let him turn in here,"
And to him who lacks
[b]understanding she says,
17 "Stolen water is sweet;
And [A]bread *eaten* in secret is pleasant."
18 But he does not know that
the [a]dead are there,
That her guests are in the [A]depths of Sheol.

CONTRAST OF THE RIGHTEOUS AND THE WICKED

10 The [A]proverbs of Solomon.

[B]A wise son makes a father glad,
But [C]a foolish son is a grief to his mother.

8:30 [a]Or *Playing* [A]John 1:2, 3 8:31 [a]Or *Playing* [A]Ps 16:3; John 13:1 8:32 [A]Prov 5:7; 7:24 [B]Ps 119:1, 2; 128:1; Prov 29:18; Luke 11:28 8:33 [A]Prov 4:1 8:34 [A]Prov 3:13, 18 8:35 [A]Prov 4:22; John 17:3 [B]Prov 3:4; 12:2 8:36 [a]Or *misses me* [A]Prov 1:31, 32; 15:32 [B]Prov 5:12; 12:1 [C]Prov 21:6 9:1 [A]1 Cor 3:9, 10; Eph 2:20-22; 1 Pet 2:5 9:2 [a]Lit *slaughtered her slaughter* [A]Matt 22:4 [B]Song 8:2 [C]Luke 14:16, 17 9:3 [A]Ps 68:11; Matt 22:3 [B]Prov 8:1, 2 [C]Prov 9:14 9:4 [a]Lit *simple* [b]Lit *heart* [A]Prov 8:5; 9:16 [B]Prov 6:32 9:5 [A]Song 5:1; Is 55:1; John 6:27 9:6 [a]Or *Forsake the simple ones* [A]Prov 8:35; 9:11 [B]Ezek 11:20; 37:24 9:7 [a]Lit *a blemish* [A]Prov 23:9 9:8 [A]Prov 15:12; Matt 7:6 [B]Ps 141:5; Prov 10:8 9:9 [A]Prov 1:5 9:10 [A]Job 28:28; Ps 111:10; Prov 1:7 9:11 [A]Prov 3:16; 10:27 9:12 [A]Job 22:2; Prov 14:14 [B]Prov 19:29 9:13 [a]Or *foolish woman* [b]Lit *simple* [A]Prov 7:11 [B]Prov 5:6 9:14 [A]Prov 9:3 9:16 [a]Lit *simple* [b]Lit *heart* [A]Prov 9:4 9:17 [A]Prov 20:17 9:18 [a]Lit *departed spirits* [A]Prov 7:27 10:1 [A]Prov 1:1 [B]Prov 15:20; 29:3 [C]Prov 17:25; 29:15

8:30 master workman. As translated in SS 7:1 and Jer 52:15, this term describes wisdom as competent and experienced in the craft of creation.

8:31 my delight. When God rejoiced over His creation (Ge 1:31; Job 38:7), wisdom was also rejoicing, especially in the creation of mankind, who alone in the physical creation has the capacity to appreciate wisdom and truth.

8:36 hate me love death. Since wisdom is the source of life (see 3:18), anyone hating wisdom, so as to spurn it, is acting as if he loves death.

9:1 seven pillars. The significance of 7 is to convey the sufficiency of this house as full in size and fit for a banquet.

9:2 mixed her wine. Cf. 23:29, 30. Wine was diluted with water as much as 1 to 8, to reduce its power to intoxicate. It was also mixed with spices for flavor (SS 8:2). Unmixed wine is called strong drink (cf. 20:1; 31:6; Lv 10:9; Is 28:7; Lk 1:15).

9:3–5 The call of wisdom is not secret, but public. *See note on 1:21.*

9:5 Come, eat … drink. Cf. God's banquet call (Is 55:1–3; Lk 14:16–24; Rev 22:17).

9:7–9 Wise people receive reproof and rebuke with appreciation; fools do not.

9:10 The fear of the LORD. *See note on 1:7.*

9:11 See Introduction: Historical and Theological Themes.

9:12 Every individual is responsible for his own conduct, so that the choices we make affect our own lives.

9:13–18 The feast of folly is described as offered by the foolish hostess. Note the contrast with lady wisdom in vv. 1–6 and similarities to the immoral woman in 7:6–23.

9:13 boisterous. Cf. 7:11, 12.

9:17 Forbidden delights sometimes seem sweeter and more pleasant because of their risk and danger.

9:18 Sheol. *See note on 1:12.* Like the adulterer, the flattering words of folly lead to death (see 2:18, 19; 5:5; 7:21–23, 26, 27).

10:1–22:16 This large section contains 375 of Solomon's individual proverbs. They are in no apparent order, with only occasional grouping by subject, and are often without a context to qualify their application. They are based on Solomon's inspired knowledge of the Law and the Prophets. The parallel, two-line proverbs of chaps. 10–15 are mostly contrasts or opposites (antithetical), while those of chaps. 16–22 are mostly similarities or comparisons (synthetical).

10:1 grief to his mother. *See note on 23:15, 16.* This parental grief is most deeply felt by the mother, who plays a more intimate role in raising a child.

2 [a,A]Ill-gotten gains do not profit,
But righteousness delivers from death.
3 The LORD [A]will not allow the
[a]righteous to hunger,
But He [B]will [b]reject the
craving of the wicked.
4 Poor is he who works with
a negligent hand,
But the [A]hand of the diligent makes rich.
5 He who gathers in summer is
a son who acts wisely,
But he who sleeps in harvest is a
son who acts shamefully.
6 [A]Blessings are on the head
of the righteous,
But [B]the mouth of the wicked
conceals violence.
7 The [A]memory of the
righteous is blessed,
But [B]the name of the wicked will rot.
8 The [A]wise of heart will
receive commands,
But [a]a babbling fool will be [b]ruined.
9 He [A]who walks in integrity
walks securely,
But [B]he who perverts his ways
will be found out.
10 He [A]who winks the eye causes trouble,
And [a,B]a babbling fool will be [b]ruined.
11 The [A]mouth of the righteous
is a fountain of life,
But [B]the mouth of the wicked
conceals violence.
12 Hatred stirs up strife,
But [A]love covers all transgressions.
13 On [A]the lips of the discerning,
wisdom is found,
But [B]a rod is for the back of him
who lacks [a]understanding.
14 Wise men [A]store up knowledge,
But with [B]the mouth of the
foolish, ruin is at hand.
15 The [A]rich man's wealth is his [a]fortress,
The [B]ruin of the poor is their poverty.
16 The [a,A]wages of the righteous is life,
The income of the wicked, punishment.
17 He [A]is *on* the path of life who
heeds instruction,
But he who ignores reproof goes astray.
18 He [A]who conceals hatred *has* lying lips,
And he who spreads slander is a fool.
19 When there are [A]many words,
transgression is unavoidable,
But [B]he who restrains his lips is wise.
20 The tongue of the righteous
is *as* [A]choice silver,
The heart of the wicked is *worth* little.
21 The [A]lips of the righteous feed many,
But fools [B]die for lack
of [a]understanding.
22 It is the [A]blessing of the LORD
that makes rich,
And He adds no sorrow to it.
23 Doing wickedness is like [A]sport to a fool,
And *so is* wisdom to a man
of understanding.

10:2 [a]Lit *Treasures of wickedness* [A]Ps 49:7; Prov 11:4; 21:6; Ezek 7:19; Luke 12:19, 20 10:3 [a]Lit *soul of the righteous* [b]Lit *thrust away* [A]Ps 34:9, 10; 37:25; Prov 28:25; Matt 6:33 [B]Ps 112:10; Prov 28:9 10:4 [A]Prov 13:4; 21:5 10:6 [A]Prov 28:20 [B]Prov 10:11; Obad 10 10:7 [A]Ps 112:6 [B]Ps 9:5, 6; 109:13; Eccl 8:10 10:8 [a]Lit *the foolish of lips* [b]Lit *thrust down* [A]Prov 9:8; Matt 7:24 10:9 [A]Ps 23:4; Prov 3:23; 28:18; Is 33:15, 16 [B]Prov 26:26; Matt 10:26; 1 Tim 5:25 10:10 [a]Lit *the foolish of lips* [b]Lit *thrust down* [A]Ps 35:19; Prov 6:13 [B]Prov 10:8 10:11 [A]Ps 37:30; Prov 13:14; 18:4 [B]Prov 10:6 10:12 [A]Prov 17:9; 1 Cor 13:4-7; James 5:20; 1 Pet 4:8 10:13 [a]Lit *heart* [A]Prov 10:31 [B]Prov 19:29; 26:3 10:14 [A]Prov 9:9 [B]Prov 10:8, 10; 13:3; 18:7 10:15 [a]Lit *strong city* [A]Job 31:24; Ps 52:7; Prov 18:11 [B]Prov 19:7 10:16 [a]Or *work* [A]Prov 11:18, 19 10:17 [A]Prov 6:23 10:18 [A]Prov 26:24 10:19 [A]Job 11:2; Prov 18:21; Eccl 5:3 [B]Prov 17:27; James 1:19; 3:2 10:20 [A]Prov 8:19 10:21 [a]Lit *heart* [A]Prov 10:11 [B]Prov 5:23; Hos 4:6 10:22 [A]Gen 24:35; 26:12; Deut 8:18; Prov 8:21 10:23 [A]Prov 2:14; 15:21

10:2 death. The greatest of all treasures, life, is gained by righteousness.

10:3 craving of the wicked. For a while, the wicked may seem to realize their desires; in the end, God removes their accomplishments because they are evil (cf. Ps 37:16–20).

10:4 diligent. This is in contrast to the sluggard (*see notes on 6:6–11*). Poverty by itself is not evil, unless it is the product of laziness.

10:5 gathers ... sleeps. Cf. 6:6–11; 13:4; 15:19; 24:30–34; 28:19, 20. The timing necessary in agriculture can be applied to the general laying hold of life's opportunities.

10:6 violence. See 10:13; 12:13; 14:3; 18:6, 7. The violence, which has gone forth from the wicked, later falls back upon his foul mouth (cf. Hab 2:17; Mal 2:16).

10:7 memory ... name. This refers to the way a righteous person is remembered by man and God after his death.

10:8 receive commands. To finish the parallelism, the wise listens and is teachable and, therefore, will be lifted up. The fool, always talking, falls because he rejects God's commands.

10:9 Those who have integrity (who live what they believe) exist without fear of some evil being discovered, while those who are perverse and have secret wickedness will not be able to hide it. Cf. 11:3; 19:1; 20:7.

10:10 winks the eye. See 6:13, 14.

10:11 fountain of life. The Lord is the source of this fountain (Ps 36:9), which then springs up in the wise man as wise speech (10:11), wise laws (13:14), the fear of the Lord (14:27), and understanding (16:22). *See notes on 3:18; Eze 47:1–12; Jn 4:10; 7:38, 39.* **violence.** *See note on 10:6.*

10:12 love. True love seeks the highest good for another (cf. 1Co 13:4–7). First Peter 4:8 quotes this verse.

10:13 rod. This first reference to corporal punishment applied to the backside (cf. 19:29; 26:3) recommends it as the most effective way of dealing with children and fools. See also 13:24; 18:6; 19:29; 22:15; 23:13, 14; 26:3; 29:15.

10:14 mouth of the foolish. The loose tongue of the fool is a recurring subject in Proverbs (cf. vv. 6, 8, 13, 18, 19, 31, 32; 12:23; 13:3; 15:1, 2, 23, 26, 28, 31–33; 17:28; 18:2, 6–8). James parallels this emphasis concerning the tongue (Jas 1:26; 3:1–12).

10:15 rich man's ... poor. While the rich man thinks he has his walled city for protection (cf. 18:11; 28:11), the poor man knows he has nothing. Both should trust in the Lord as their only protection (cf. 3:5, 6; 11:4, 28; 18:10, 11; Ps 20:7; Ecc 9:11–18; Jas 5:1–6).

10:16 wages. The industry alone of the righteous makes him truly successful, while the earnings of the wicked provide more opportunities for sinning.

10:18 hatred ... slander. Both the harboring and venting of hatred are wrong and will be punished. Slander (gossip or lies) is forbidden (cf. 25:10; also 16:28; 18:8; 20:19; 26:20, 22).

10:19 Wisdom is to restrain the tongue, since much speech risks sin. Cf. Ps 39:1; Jas 1:26; 3:2–8.

10:20 tongue ... heart. These words are used as parallel terms because they are inseparably linked. Cf. Mt 15:18, 19. **choice silver.** Good words are scarce, precious, and valuable (cf. 15:23; Is 50:4).

10:21 feed ... die. Sound teaching benefits many; the fool starves himself to death spiritually by his lack of wise teaching (cf. Hos 4:6).

10:22 rich. While having more than what one needs is not the object of wisdom, it is generally the result (cf. Dt 6:11–15; 1Ki 3:10–14). See Introduction: Historical and Theological Themes. **no sorrow.** None of the sorrow that is associated with ill-gotten wealth (cf. 13:11; 15:6; 16:19; 21:6; 28:6) is associated with wealth provided by the Lord.

24 What [A]the wicked fears will come upon him,
But the [B]desire of the righteous
will be granted.
25 When the [A]whirlwind passes,
the wicked is no more,
But the [B]righteous *has* an
everlasting foundation.
26 Like vinegar to the teeth and
smoke to the eyes,
So is the [A]lazy one to those who send him.
27 The [A]fear of the LORD prolongs [a]life,
But the [B]years of the wicked
will be shortened.
28 The [A]hope of the righteous is gladness,
But the [B]expectation of the wicked perishes.
29 The [A]way of the LORD is a
stronghold to the upright,
But [B]ruin to the workers of iniquity.
30 The [A]righteous will never be shaken,
But [B]the wicked will not dwell in the land.
31 The [A]mouth of the righteous
flows with wisdom,
But the [B]perverted tongue will be cut out.
32 The lips of the righteous bring
forth [A]what is acceptable,
But the [B]mouth of the wicked
what is perverted.

CONTRAST THE UPRIGHT AND THE WICKED

11 A [A]false balance is an
abomination to the LORD,
But a [B]just weight is His delight.
2 When [A]pride comes, then comes dishonor,
But with the humble is wisdom.
3 The [A]integrity of the upright
will guide them,
But the [B]crookedness of the
treacherous will destroy them.
4 [A]Riches do not profit in the day of wrath,
But [B]righteousness delivers from death.
5 The [A]righteousness of the blameless
will smooth his way,
But [B]the wicked will fall by
his own wickedness.
6 The righteousness of the upright
will deliver them,
But the treacherous will [A]be
caught by *their own* greed.
7 When a wicked man dies, *his*
[A]expectation will perish,
And the [B]hope of strong men perishes.
8 The righteous is delivered from trouble,
But the wicked [a]takes his place.
9 With *his* [A]mouth the godless man
destroys his neighbor,
But through knowledge the
[B]righteous will be delivered.
10 When it [A]goes well with the
righteous, the city rejoices,
And when the wicked perish,
there is joyful shouting.
11 By the blessing of the upright
a city is exalted,
But by the mouth of the
wicked it is torn down.
12 He who despises his neighbor lacks [a]sense,
But a man of understanding keeps silent.
13 He [A]who goes about as a
talebearer reveals secrets,
But he who is [a]trustworthy
[B]conceals a matter.
14 Where there is no [A]guidance the people fall,
But in abundance of counselors
there is [a]victory.
15 He who is [A]guarantor for a stranger
will surely suffer for it,
But he who hates [a]being a
guarantor is secure.
16 A [A]gracious woman attains honor,
And ruthless men attain riches.
17 The [A]merciful man does [a]himself good,
But the cruel man [b]does himself harm.
18 The wicked earns deceptive wages,
But he who [A]sows righteousness
gets a true reward.

10:24 [A]Job 15:21; Prov 1:27; Is 66:4 [B]Ps 145:19; Prov 15:8; Matt 5:6; 1 John 5:14, 15 10:25 [A]Job 21:18; Ps 58:9; Prov 12:7 [B]Ps 15:5; Prov 12:3; Matt 7:24, 25 10:26 [A]Prov 26:6 10:27 [a]Lit *days* [A]Prov 3:2; 9:11; 14:27 [B]Job 15:32, 33; 22:16; Ps 55:23 10:28 [A]Prov 11:23 [B]Job 8:13; 11:20; Prov 11:7 10:29 [A]Prov 13:6 [B]Prov 21:15 10:30 [A]Ps 37:29; 125:1; Prov 2:21 [B]Prov 2:22 10:31 [A]Ps 37:30; Prov 10:13 [B]Prov 17:20 10:32 [A]Eccl 12:10 [B]Prov 2:12; 6:12 11:1 [A]Lev 19:35, 36; Deut 25:13-16; Prov 20:10, 23; Mic 6:11 [B]Prov 16:11 11:2 [A]Prov 16:18; 18:12; 29:23 11:3 [A]Prov 13:6 [B]Prov 19:3; 22:12 11:4 [A]Prov 10:2; Ezek 7:19; Zeph 1:18 [B]Gen 7:1 11:5 [A]Prov 3:6 [B]Prov 5:22 11:6 [A]Ps 7:15, 16; 9:15; Eccl 10:8 11:7 [A]Prov 10:28 [B]Job 8:13, 14 11:8 [a]Lit *enters* 11:9 [A]Prov 16:29 [B]Prov 11:6 11:10 [A]Prov 28:12 11:12 [a]Lit *heart* 11:13 [a]Lit *faithful of spirit* [A]Lev 19:16; Prov 20:19; 1 Tim 5:13 [B]Prov 19:11 11:14 [a]Lit *deliverance* [A]Prov 15:22; 20:18; 24:6 11:15 [a]Lit *those who strike hands* [A]Prov 6:1; 27:13 11:16 [A]Prov 31:28, 30 11:17 [a]Lit *good to his own soul* [b]Lit *troubles his flesh* [A]Matt 5:7; 25:34-36 11:18 [A]Hos 10:12; Gal 6:8, 9; James 3:18

10:24 What the wicked fears. The righteous receive what they desire, while the wicked receive what they fear (cf. Heb 10:26–29).

10:25 whirlwind. See 1:27; 6:15; 29:1.

10:27 fear of the LORD. *See note on 1:7.*

10:29 The way of the LORD. This is the spiritual path in which God directs man to walk (*see note on Ac 18:25*).

10:30 Cf. Ps 37:9–11.

11:1 A false balance. Cf. 16:11; 20:10, 23. As indicated in Lv 19:35, 36; Dt 25:13–16; Eze 45:10; Am 8:5; Mic 6:10, God detests dishonesty.

11:2 pride. From a root meaning "to boil," or "to run over," indicating an overwhelmingly arrogant attitude or behavior. It is used of ordinary men (Dt 17:12, 13); kings (Ne 9:10); Israel (Ne 9:16, 29); false prophets (Dt 18:20); and murderers (Ex 21:14). **the humble.** A rare word, which appears in Mic 6:8: "walk humbly with your God." This humble and teachable spirit is first of all directed toward God (cf. 15:33; 16:18, 19; 18:12; 22:4).

11:4 day of wrath. Money buys no escape from death in the day of final accounting to God, the divine Judge (cf. Is 10:3; Eze 7:19; Zep 1:18; Lk 12:16–21).

11:11 Social influence for good or bad is in view.

11:12 despises. Lit. one who gossips, slanders, or destroys with words, in contrast to the silence of the wise. *See notes on 10:14, 18.*

11:13 talebearer. This depicts someone who is a peddler in scandal, who speaks words deliberately intended to harm rather than merely unguarded speech (cf. Lv 19:16).

11:14 abundance of counselors. As in 15:22; 20:18; 24:6, a good decision is made with multiple wise advisers. The more crucial the decision, the more appropriate is corporate wisdom. Note the example of David (2Sa 15:30–17:23).

11:15 *See note on 6:1.*

11:16 gracious woman … ruthless men. While evil men may grasp at wealth, they will never attain the honor due a gracious woman (cf. 31:30).

11:18 deceptive wages. The efforts of the wicked deceiver do not yield the riches his deception seeks, but the righteous receive a reward from God.

19 He who is steadfast in [A]righteousness
will attain to life,
And [B]he who pursues evil *will*
bring about his own death.
20 The perverse in heart are an
abomination to the LORD,
But the [A]blameless in *their*
[a]walk are His [B]delight.
21 [a]Assuredly, the evil man will
not go unpunished,
But the [b]descendants of the
righteous will be delivered.
22 *As* a [A]ring of gold in a swine's snout
So is a beautiful woman who
lacks [a]discretion.
23 The desire of the righteous is only good,
But the [A]expectation of the
wicked is wrath.
24 There is one who scatters, and
yet increases all the more,
And there is one who withholds
what is justly due, *and yet*
it results only in want.
25 The [a,A]generous man will be [b]prosperous,
And he who [B]waters will
himself be watered.
26 He who withholds grain, the
[A]people will curse him,
But [B]blessing will be on the
head of him who [C]sells *it*.
27 He who diligently seeks good seeks favor,
But [A]he who seeks evil, evil
will come to him.
28 He who [A]trusts in his riches will fall,
But [B]the righteous will flourish
like the *green* leaf.
29 He who [A]troubles his own house
will [B]inherit wind,
And [C]the foolish will be servant
to the wisehearted.
30 The fruit of the righteous is [A]a tree of life,
And [B]he who is wise [a]wins souls.
31 If [A]the righteous will be
rewarded in the earth,
How much more the wicked
and the sinner!

CONTRAST THE UPRIGHT AND THE WICKED

12 Whoever loves [a]discipline
loves knowledge,
But he who hates reproof is stupid.
2 A [A]good man will obtain
favor from the LORD,
But He will condemn a man
[a]who devises evil.
3 A man will [A]not be established
by wickedness,
But the root of the [B]righteous
will not be moved.
4 An [a,A]excellent wife is the
crown of her husband,
But she who shames *him* is like
[B]rottenness in his bones.
5 The thoughts of the righteous are just,
But the counsels of the wicked are deceitful.
6 The [A]words of the wicked lie
in wait for blood,
But the [B]mouth of the upright
will deliver them.
7 The [A]wicked are overthrown
and are no more,
But the [B]house of the righteous will stand.
8 A man will be praised according
to his insight,
But one of perverse [a]mind will be despised.
9 Better is he who is lightly
esteemed and has a servant
Than he who honors himself
and lacks bread.

11:19 [A]Prov 10:16; 12:28; 19:23 [B]Prov 21:16; Rom 6:23; James 1:15 11:20 [a]Lit *way* [A]Ps 119:1; Prov 13:6 [B]1 Chr 29:17 11:21 [a]Lit *Hand to hand* [b]Lit *seed* 11:22 [a]Lit *taste* [A]Gen 24:47 11:23 [A]Prov 10:28; Rom 2:8, 9 11:25 [a]Lit *soul of blessing* [b]Lit *made fat* [A]Prov 3:9, 10; 2 Cor 9:6, 7 [B]Matt 5:7 11:26 [A]Prov 24:24 [B]Job 29:13 [C]Gen 42:6 11:27 [A]Esth 7:10; Ps 7:15, 16; 57:6 11:28 [A]Ps 49:6; Mark 10:25; 1 Tim 6:17 [B]Ps 1:3; 92:12; Jer 17:8 11:29 [A]Prov 15:27 [B]Eccl 5:16 [C]Prov 14:19 11:30 [a]Lit *takes* [A]Prov 3:18 [B]Prov 14:25; Dan 12:3; 1 Cor 9:19-22; James 5:20 11:31 [A]2 Sam 22:21, 25; Prov 13:21; 1 Pet 4:18 12:1 [a]Or *instruction* 12:2 [a]Lit of *evil devices* [A]Prov 3:4; 8:35 12:3 [A]Prov 11:5 [B]Prov 10:25 12:4 [a]Or *virtuous* [A]Prov 31:11; 1 Cor 11:7 [B]Prov 14:30; Hab 3:16 12:6 [A]Prov 1:11, 16 [B]Prov 14:3 12:7 [A]Job 34:25; Prov 10:25 [B]Matt 7:24-27 12:8 [a]Lit *heart*

11:20 **abomination.** Defined throughout Scripture as attitudes, this involves words and behaviors which God hates (see 6:16).

11:21 Individually or in collaboration, the power of the wicked cannot free them from just punishment, while the unaided children of the righteous find deliverance by reason of their relationship with God.

11:22 **ring of gold.** A nose ring was an ornament intended to beautify a woman in OT times (cf. Ge 24:47; Is 3:21; Eze 16:12). It was as out of place in a pig's nose as the lack of discretion was in a lovely lady.

11:23 **desire ... expectation.** These terms refer to outcomes from God's perspective.

11:24–26 **scatters, and *yet* increases.** The principle here is that generosity, by God's blessing, secures increase, while stinginess leads to poverty instead of expected gain. The one who gives receives far more in return (Ps 112:9; Ecc 11:1; Jn 12:24, 25; Ac 20:35; 2Co 9:6–9).

11:28 **trusts in his riches.** Cf. 23:4, 5; *see notes on 1Ti 6:17, 19.*

11:29 **inherit wind.** The one who mismanages his house will see all he has blown away, and he will have nothing left in the end. He will serve the one who manages well (15:27).

11:30 **tree of life.** *See note on 3:18.* **wins souls.** Lit. "to take lives," in the sense of doing them good or influencing them with wisdom's ways (cf. Lk 5:10). The word is also used for capturing people for evil purposes as in 6:25; Ps 31:13; Eze 13:18.

11:31 **rewarded.** God's final blessing and reward to the "righteous," and His judgment and punishment of the "wicked" and "sinners" come after life on this earth has ended. But there are foretastes of both during life on the earth, as the righteous experience God's personal care and goodness, while the wicked are void of it.

12:1 **stupid.** From the Heb. "to graze"; he is as stupid as the brute cattle (cf. Pss 49:20; 73:22).

12:3 **root.** The familiar image is of the righteous being firm like a flourishing tree (Ps 1; Jer 17:7, 8).

12:4 **excellent wife.** *See notes on 31:10; Ru 3:11.* For the opposite see 19:13; 21:9, 19; 25:24; 27:15. **rottenness in his bones.** This speaks of suffering that is like a painful and incurable condition.

12:6 **lie in wait.** *See notes on 1:11, 12.*

12:7 **house.** The rewards of wise living are not only to individuals, but extend to one's household or family.

12:9 **Better ... Than.** This is one of several proverbs which makes a distinct comparison using "Better ... Than" (cf. 15:16, 17; 16:8, 19, 32; 17:1; 19:1; 21:9, 19; 25:7, 24; 27:5, 10; 28:6). **lightly esteemed ... honors himself.** The obscure person of lowly rank, who can at least afford to hire a servant because of his honest gain, is better than the one who falsely boasts about his prominence but is really poor.

10 A [A]righteous man has regard
for the life of his animal,
But *even* the compassion of
the wicked is cruel.
11 He [A]who tills his land will
have plenty of bread,
But he who pursues worthless
things lacks [a]sense.
12 The [A]wicked man desires the
[a]booty of evil men,
But the root of the righteous [B]yields *fruit*.
13 [a]An evil man is ensnared by the
transgression of his lips,
But the [A]righteous will escape from trouble.
14 A man will be [A]satisfied with good
by the fruit of his [a]words,
And the [B]deeds of a man's hands
will return to him.
15 The [A]way of a fool is right in his own eyes,
But a wise man is he who
listens to counsel.
16 A [A]fool's anger is known at once,
But a prudent man conceals dishonor.
17 He who [a]speaks truth tells what is right,
But a false witness, deceit.
18 There is one who [A]speaks rashly
like the thrusts of a sword,
But the [B]tongue of the wise brings healing.
19 Truthful lips will be established forever,
But a [A]lying tongue is only for a moment.
20 Deceit is in the heart of those
who devise evil,
But counselors of peace have joy.
21 [A]No harm befalls the righteous,
But the wicked are filled with trouble.
22 [A]Lying lips are an abomination
to the LORD,
But those who deal faithfully
are His delight.
23 A [A]prudent man conceals knowledge,
But the heart of fools proclaims folly.
24 The hand of the diligent will rule,
But the [a]slack *hand* will be
[A]put to forced labor.
25 [A]Anxiety in a man's heart weighs it down,
But a [B]good word makes it glad.
26 The righteous is a guide to his neighbor,
But the way of the wicked
leads them astray.
27 A [a]lazy man does not [b]roast his prey,
But the [A]precious possession
of a man *is* diligence.
28 [A]In the way of righteousness is life,
And in *its* pathway there is no death.

CONTRAST THE UPRIGHT AND THE WICKED

13 A [A]wise son *accepts his* father's discipline,
But a [B]scoffer does not listen to rebuke.
2 From the fruit of a man's mouth
he [a,A]enjoys good,
But the [b]desire of the
treacherous is [B]violence.
3 The one who [A]guards his mouth
preserves his life;
The one who [B]opens wide his
lips [a]comes to ruin.
4 The soul of the sluggard craves
and *gets* nothing,
But the soul of the diligent is made fat.
5 A righteous man [A]hates falsehood,
But a wicked man [a,B]acts
disgustingly and shamefully.
6 Righteousness [A]guards the [a]one
whose way is blameless,
But wickedness subverts the [b]sinner.
7 There is one who [A]pretends to
be rich, but has nothing;
Another [a]pretends to be [B]poor,
but has great wealth.
8 The ransom of a man's life is his wealth,
But the poor hears no rebuke.

12:10 [A]Deut 25:4 12:11 [a]Lit *heart* [A]Prov 28:19 12:12 [a]Lit *net* [A]Prov 21:10 [B]Prov 11:30 12:13 [a]Lit *In the transgression of the lips is an evil snare* [A]Prov 11:8; 21:23; 2 Pet 2:9 12:14 [a]Lit *mouth* [A]Prov 13:2; 15:23; 18:20 [B]Job 34:11; Prov 1:31; 24:12; Is 3:10, 11; Hos 4:9 12:15 [A]Prov 14:12; 16:2; 21:2 12:16 [A]Prov 14:33; 27:3; 29:11 12:17 [a]Lit *breathes* 12:18 [A]Ps 57:4 [B]Prov 4:22; 15:4 12:19 [A]Ps 52:4, 5; Prov 19:9 12:21 [A]Ps 91:10; 121:7; Prov 1:33; 1 Pet 3:13 12:22 [A]Rev 22:15 12:23 [A]Prov 10:14; 11:13; 13:16; 15:2; 29:11 12:24 [a]Lit *slackness* [A]Gen 49:15; Judg 1:28; 1 Kin 9:21 12:25 [A]Prov 15:13 [B]Is 50:4 12:27 [a]Lit *slackness* [b]Or *catch* [A]Prov 10:4; 13:4 12:28 [A]Deut 30:15f; 32:46f; Jer 21:8 13:1 [A]Prov 10:1; 15:20 [B]Prov 9:7, 8; 15:12 13:2 [a]Lit *eats* [b]Lit *soul* [A]Prov 12:14 [B]Prov 1:31; Hos 10:13 13:3 [a]Lit *ruin is his* [A]Prov 18:21; 21:23; James 3:2 [B]Prov 18:7; 20:19 13:5 [a]Lit *causes a bad odor and causes shame* [A]Col 3:9 [B]Prov 3:35 13:6 [a]Lit *blamelessness of way* [b]Lit *sin* [A]Prov 11:3 13:7 [a]Lit *impoverishes himself* [A]Prov 11:24; Luke 12:20, 21 [B]Luke 12:33; 2 Cor 6:10; James 2:5

12:10 has regard ... cruel. Lit. he has concern for the condition of his beast, while the wicked has no concern for people.

12:11 worthless *things*. Energy expended in worthless pursuits and fantasies is as useless as outright laziness. *See notes on 6:6–11; 20:4; 24:30–34.*

12:12 desires the booty. This refers to the desire for spoils gained by the schemes of the wicked, contrasted with a simple life of obedience that produces blessing.

12:14 fruit of his words. This deals with the power of words; the reward of wise words is like the reward for physical labor (cf. 10:11; 15:4; 18:4).

12:16 conceals dishonor. A model of self-control, the prudent man ignores an insult (cf. 9:7; 10:12).

12:17 speaks truth. In the court, the truthful witness promotes justice.

12:18 speaks ... thrusts. The contrast here is between cutting words that are spoken "rashly" (Ps 106:33) and thoughtful words that bring health. Cf. Eph 4:29, 30.

12:20 Deceit. The contrasting parallel is implied, not stated. Those who plan evil by deceit have no joy because of the risks and dangers in their plan, but the righteous who lead by peace fear nothing, and thus have joy.

12:23 conceals. Unlike the fool who makes all hear his folly, the wise person is a model of restraint and humility, speaking what he knows at an appropriate time (cf. 29:11). *See notes on 1:4; 10:14.*

12:24 forced labor. Unlike the hardworking people who have charge over their work, the lazy are eventually forced to go to work for the diligent to survive.

12:26 astray. Cf. 1Co 15:33. This verse could be understood as saying that the righteous "guides" his friends carefully, unlike the wicked who leads his companions astray.

12:27 does not roast. The sluggard lacks commitment to make something of his opportunities (cf. vv. 11, 25).

13:2, 3 The parallels here are implied. A man of good words prospers, but a man of evil words (thus unfruitful to God) provokes violence against himself.

13:4 *See notes on 6:6, 11.*

13:7 pretends to be rich ... pretends to be poor. The same pretense is presented in two contrasting weaknesses; one pretends to be rich while the other pretends to be poor. In contrast, men should be honest and unpretentious (cf. 11:24; 2 Cor 6:10).

13:8 ransom ... wealth ... poor ... rebuke. Riches deliver some people from punishment,

9 The [A]light of the righteous [a]rejoices,
But the [B]lamp of the wicked goes out.
10 Through insolence [a]comes
nothing but strife,
But wisdom is with those
who receive counsel.
11 Wealth *obtained* by [a]fraud dwindles,
But the one who gathers [b]by
labor increases *it.*
12 Hope deferred makes the heart sick,
But desire [a]fulfilled is a tree of life.
13 The one who [A]despises the word
will be [a]in debt to it,
But the one who fears the
commandment will be [B]rewarded.
14 The [a]teaching of the wise is
a [A]fountain of life,
To turn aside from the [B]snares of death.
15 [A]Good understanding produces favor,
But the way of the treacherous is hard.
16 Every [A]prudent man acts with knowledge,
But a fool [a]displays folly.
17 A wicked messenger falls into adversity,
But [A]a faithful envoy *brings* healing.
18 Poverty and shame *will come* to
him who [A]neglects [a]discipline,
But he who regards reproof
will be honored.
19 Desire realized is sweet to the soul,
But it is an abomination to fools
to turn away from evil.
20 [A]He who walks with wise
men will be wise,
But the companion of fools
will suffer harm.
21 [A]Adversity pursues sinners,
But the [B]righteous will be
rewarded with prosperity.
22 A good man [A]leaves an inheritance
to his [a]children's children,
And the [B]wealth of the sinner is
stored up for the righteous.
23 [A]Abundant food *is in* the fallow
ground of the poor,
But [a]it is swept away by injustice.
24 He who [A]withholds his
[a]rod hates his son,
But he who loves him [b,B]disciplines
him diligently.
25 The [A]righteous [a]has enough
to satisfy his appetite,
But the stomach of the [B]wicked is in need.

CONTRAST THE UPRIGHT AND THE WICKED

14 The [A]wise woman builds her house,
But the foolish tears it down
with her own hands.
2 He who [A]walks in his uprightness
fears the LORD,
But he who is [B]devious in his
ways despises Him.
3 In the mouth of the foolish
is a rod [a]for *his* back,
But [A]the lips of the wise will protect them.
4 Where no oxen are, the manger is clean,
But much revenue *comes* by
the strength of the ox.
5 A [A]trustworthy witness will not lie,
But a [B]false witness [a,C]utters lies.
6 A scoffer seeks wisdom and *finds* none,
But knowledge is easy to one
who has understanding.
7 Leave the [A]presence of a fool,
Or you will not [a]discern
[b]words of knowledge.

13:9 [a]I.e. shines brightly [A]Job 29:3; Prov 4:18 [B]Job 18:5; Prov 24:20 13:10 [a]Lit *gives* 13:11 [a]Lit *vanity* [b]Or *gradually;* lit *on the hand* 13:12 [a]Lit *coming* 13:13 [a]Lit *pledged to it* [A]Num 15:31; 2 Chr 36:16 [B]Prov 13:21 13:14 [a]Or *law* [A]Prov 10:11; 14:27 [B]Ps 18:5 13:15 [A]Ps 111:10; Prov 3:4 13:16 [a]Lit *spreads out* [A]Prov 12:23 13:17 [A]Prov 25:13 13:18 [a]Or *instruction* [A]Prov 15:5, 32 13:20 [A]Prov 2:20; 15:31 13:21 [A]Ps 32:10; 54:5; Is 47:11 [B]Prov 11:31; 13:13; Is 3:10 13:22 [a]Lit *sons' sons* [A]Ezra 9:12; Ps 37:25 [B]Job 27:16, 17; Prov 28:8; Eccl 2:26 13:23 [a]Lit *there is what is swept* [A]Prov 12:11 13:24 [a]I.e. correction or discipline [b]Lit *seeks him diligently with discipline* [A]Prov 19:18; 22:15; 23:13, 14; 29:15, 17 [B]Deut 8:5; Prov 3:12; Heb 12:7 13:25 [a]Lit *eats to the satisfaction of his soul* [A]Ps 34:10; 103:5; 132:15; Prov 10:3 [B]Prov 13:18; Luke 15:14 14:1 [A]Ruth 4:11; Prov 31:10-27 14:2 [A]Prov 19:1; 28:6 [B]Prov 2:15 14:3 [a]Lit *of pride* [A]Prov 12:6 14:5 [a]Lit *breathes out* [A]Rev 1:5; 3:14 [B]Ex 23:1; Deut 19:16; Prov 6:19; 12:17 [C]Prov 19:5 14:7 [a]Lit *know* [b]Lit *lips* [A]Prov 23:9

while others suffer, because they will not heed the rebuke of laziness, which keeps them poor.

13:9 **light … lamp.** This image of life, prosperity, and joy is contrasted with adversity and death (cf. Job 3:20).

13:10 The proud spurn advice from others; the wise accept it.

13:11 Cf. 20:21.

13:12 **tree of life.** *See note on 3:18.*

13:13 **word … commandment.** These terms refer to divine revelation.

13:14 **fountain of life.** *See note on 10:11.*

13:16 **displays.** The language vividly shows that a fool displays folly, like a peddler openly spreads out his wares for others to gaze upon. Cf. 12:23; 15:2.

13:19 The fool's relentless pursuit of evil and hatred of good does not ever let him taste the sweet blessings of obedience.

13:20 **walks … companion.** This speaks of the power of association to shape character. Cf. 1:10, 18; 2:12; 4:14; 16:29; 22:24, 25; 23:20; 28:7, 19; Ps 1.

13:21 This is a basic theme/general principle throughout Proverbs and is illustrated throughout the OT, which establishes that righteousness brings divine blessing and evil brings divine cursing.

13:22 **leaves an inheritance.** While good men's estates remain with their families, the wealth of the wicked does not. In the providence of God, it will ultimately belong to the righteous. Cf. 28:8; Job 27:16, 17.

13:23 **injustice.** The contrast here is between the poor, but industrious, man who will be rewarded with provision from his efforts, and the rich man whose efforts are brought to ruin by his deeds of injustice (cf. Jas 5:1–6).

13:24 **rod … disciplines … diligently.** Early childhood teaching (*see note on 22:6*) requires both parental discipline, including corporal punishment (cf. 10:13; 19:18; 22:15; 29:15, 17), and balanced kindness and love. There is great hope that the use of the "divine ordinance" of the rod will produce godly virtue (cf. 23:13, 14) and parental joy (cf. 10:1; 15:20; 17:21; 23:15, 16, 24, 25; 28:7; 29:1, 15, 17). Such discipline must have the right motivation (Heb 12:5–11) and appropriate severity (Eph 6:4). One who has genuine affection for his child, but withholds corporal punishment, will produce the same kind of child as a parent who hates his offspring.

13:25 This states more directly the teaching of vv. 13, 18, 21.

14:1 **builds her house.** Cf. the wise woman building her house (31:10–31) with lady wisdom building her house (9:1–6).

14:3 **rod.** A rare Heb. word that refers to a small shoot (see Is 11:1). Here it is metaphoric for the proud, inflicting tongue in a fool's mouth, which destroys the fool and others (cf. 11:2; 16:18; 29:23).

14:7 **Leave.** Avoid association with all who cannot teach you wisdom. Cf. 1 Tim 4:6, 7; 6:3–5.

8 The wisdom of the sensible is
to understand his way,
But [A]the foolishness of fools is deceit.
9 Fools mock at [a]sin,
But [A]among the upright
there is [b]good will.
10 The heart knows its own [A]bitterness,
And a stranger does not share its joy.
11 The [A]house of the wicked
will be destroyed,
But the tent of the upright will flourish.
12 There [A]is a way *which seems*
right to a man,
But its [B]end is the way of death.
13 Even in laughter the heart may be in pain,
And the [A]end of joy may be grief.
14 The backslider in heart will have
his [A]fill of his own ways,
But a good man will [B]*be*
satisfied [a]with his.
15 The [a]naive believes everything,
But the sensible man considers his steps.
16 A wise man [a]is cautious and
[A]turns away from evil,
But a fool is arrogant and careless.
17 A quick-tempered man acts foolishly,
And a man of evil devices is hated.
18 The [a]naive inherit foolishness,
But the sensible are crowned
with knowledge.
19 The [A]evil will bow down before the good,
And the wicked at the gates
of the righteous.
20 The [A]poor is hated even by his neighbor,
But those who love the rich are many.
21 He who [A]despises his neighbor sins,
But [B]happy is he who is
gracious to the [a]poor.
22 Will they not go astray who [A]devise evil?
But kindness and truth *will be*
to those who devise good.
23 In all labor there is profit,
But [a]mere talk *leads* only to poverty.
24 The [A]crown of the wise is their riches,
But the folly of fools is foolishness.
25 A truthful witness saves lives,
But he who [a,A]utters lies is [b]treacherous.
26 In the [a,A]fear of the LORD there
is strong confidence,
And [b]his children will have refuge.
27 The [a]fear of the LORD is a fountain of life,
That one may avoid the snares of death.
28 In a multitude of people is a king's glory,
But in the dearth of people
is a prince's ruin.
29 He who is [A]slow to anger has
great understanding,
But he who is [a]quick-tempered exalts folly.
30 A [A]tranquil heart is life to the body,
But passion is [B]rottenness to the bones.
31 He [A]who oppresses the poor
taunts [B]his Maker,
But he who is gracious to the
needy honors Him.
32 The wicked is [A]thrust down
by his [a]wrongdoing,
But the [B]righteous has a
refuge when he dies.
33 Wisdom rests in the heart of one
who has understanding,
But in the [a]hearts of fools
it is made known.
34 Righteousness exalts a nation,
But sin is a disgrace to *any* people.
35 The king's favor is toward a
[A]servant who acts wisely,
But his anger is toward him
who acts shamefully.

14:8 [A]1 Cor 3:19 14:9 [a]Lit *guilt* [b]Or the *favor* of God [A]Prov 3:34; 11:20 14:10 [A]1 Sam 1:10; Job 21:25 14:11 [A]Job 8:15 14:12 [A]Prov 12:15; 16:25 [B]Rom 6:21 14:13 [A]Eccl 2:1, 2 14:14 [a]Lit *from himself* [A]Prov 1:31; 12:21 [B]Prov 12:14; 18:20 14:15 [a]Lit *simple* 14:16 [a]Lit *fears* [A]Job 28:28; Ps 34:14; Prov 3:7; 22:3 14:18 [a]Lit *simple* 14:19 [A]1 Sam 2:36; Prov 11:29 14:20 [A]Prov 19:7 14:21 [a]Or *afflicted* [A]Prov 11:12 [B]Ps 41:1; Prov 19:17; 28:8 14:22 [A]Ps 36:4; Prov 3:29; 12:2; Mic 2:1 14:23 [a]Lit *word of lips* 14:24 [A]Prov 10:22; 13:8; 21:20 14:25 [a]Lit *breathes out* [b]Lit *treachery* [A]Prov 14:5 14:26 [a]Or *reverence* [b]Or *His* [A]Prov 18:10; 19:23; Is 33:6 14:27 [a]Or *reverence* 14:29 [a]Lit *short of spirit* [A]Prov 16:32; 19:11; Eccl 7:9; James 1:19 14:30 [A]Prov 15:13 [B]Prov 12:4; Hab 3:16 14:31 [A]Prov 17:5; Matt 25:40; 1 John 3:17 [B]Job 31:15; Prov 22:2 14:32 [a]Or *calamity* [A]Prov 6:15; 24:16 [B]Gen 49:18; Ps 16:11; 17:15; 37:37; 73:24; 2 Cor 1:9; 5:8; 2 Tim 4:18 14:33 [a]Lit *inward part* 14:35 [A]Matt 24:45, 47; 25:21, 23

14:9 Fools mock at sin. While fools ridicule their impending judgment (cf. 1:26), the wise are promised favor with God (cf. Is 1:11–20) and man (cf. 10:32; 11:27). Cf. 1Sa 2:26; Lk 2:40, 52.

14:10 At its depth, suffering and rejoicing are personal and private. No one is able to communicate them fully (1Sa 1:10; 1Ki 8:38; Mt 2:18; 26:39–42, 75).

14:12 way of death. *See notes on Mt 7:13, 14.*

14:14 backslider in heart. This term, so often used by the prophets (Is 57:17; Jer 3:6, 8, 11, 12, 14, 22; 8:5; 31:22; 49:4; Hos 11:7; 14:4), is here used in such a way as to clarify who is a backslider. He belongs in the category of the fool, the wicked, and the disobedient, and he is contrasted with the godly wise. It is a word that the prophets used of apostate unbelievers.

14:17 quick-tempered ... evil devices. The contrast is between the hasty anger that is labeled as folly and the deliberate malice which produces hatred (Ps 37:7).

14:19 evil will bow. The ancient custom was for the inferior to prostrate himself before the superior or wait humbly before the great one's gate seeking favor. Good will humble evil.

14:20 This sad-but-true picture of human nature is not given approvingly, but only as a fact.

14:24 folly of fools is foolishness. This is emphatic language, playing on the word "fool" and showing that the only reward for fools is more folly.

14:25 The truth produces justice, on which the lives of people may depend.

14:26 fear of the LORD. *See note on 1:7.*

14:27 fountain of life. *See note on 10:11.*

14:28 multitude of people. This is a truism stating that a king's honor comes from the support of his people as they increase and prosper (cf. 30:29–31).

14:29 Cf. v. 17.

14:30 tranquil heart ... body. A healthy mind filled with wisdom is associated with a healthy body (cf. 3:5–8; 17:22). **rottenness to the bones.** *See note on 12:4.*

14:31 oppresses the poor ... Maker. It offends the Creator when one neglects the poor, who are part of His creation (cf. 14:21; 17:5; 19:17; 21:13; 22:2, 7; 28:8; 29:13).

14:32 righteous ... dies. Cf. 23:18. Hope in death for the righteous is a central OT theme (cf. Job 19:25, 26; Pss 31:5; 49:14, 15; 73:24; Ecc 11:9; Is 26:19; Da 12:1, 2).

14:33 is made known. Wisdom is quietly preserved in the heart of the wise for the time of proper use, while fools are eager to blurt out their folly (cf. 12:23; 13:16; 15:2, 14).

14:34 exalts. While just principles and actions preserve and even exalt a society, their absence shames a society (cf. 11:11).

14:35 acts shamefully. Cf. 10:5; 12:4.

CONTRAST THE UPRIGHT AND THE WICKED

15 A [A]gentle answer turns away wrath,
But a [a,B]harsh word stirs up anger.
2 The [A]tongue of the wise makes
knowledge [a]acceptable,
But the [B]mouth of fools spouts folly.
3 The [A]eyes of the LORD are in every place,
Watching the evil and the good.
4 A [a]soothing tongue is a tree of life,
But perversion in it [b]crushes the spirit.
5 A fool [a]rejects his father's discipline,
But he who regards reproof is sensible.
6 Great wealth is *in* the house
of the [A]righteous,
But trouble is in the income of the wicked.
7 The lips of the wise spread knowledge,
But the hearts of fools are not so.
8 The [A]sacrifice of the wicked is an
abomination to the LORD,
But [B]the prayer of the upright
is His delight.
9 The way of the wicked is an
abomination to the LORD,
But He loves one who [A]pursues
righteousness.
10 Grievous punishment is for him
who forsakes the way;
He who hates reproof will die.
11 [a,A]Sheol and [b]Abaddon *lie open*
before the LORD,
How much more the [B]hearts of [c]men!
12 A [A]scoffer does not love one
who reproves him,
He will not go to the wise.
13 A [A]joyful heart makes a [a]cheerful face,
But [b]when the heart is [B]sad,
the [C]spirit is broken.
14 The [A]mind of the intelligent
seeks knowledge,
But the mouth of fools feeds on folly.
15 All the days of the afflicted are bad,
But a [a]cheerful heart *has* a continual feast.
16 [A]Better is a little with the [a]fear of the LORD
Than great treasure and turmoil with it.
17 [A]Better is a [a]dish of [b]vegetables where love is
Than a [B]fattened ox *served* with hatred.
18 A [A]hot-tempered man stirs up strife,
But the [B]slow to anger [C]calms a dispute.
19 The way of the lazy is as a hedge of thorns,
But the path of the upright is a highway.
20 A [A]wise son makes a father glad,
But a foolish man [B]despises his mother.
21 Folly is joy to him who lacks [a]sense,
But a man of understanding
[A]walks straight.
22 Without consultation, plans are frustrated,
But with many counselors they [a]succeed.
23 A [A]man has joy in an [a]apt answer,
And how delightful is a timely [B]word!
24 The [A]path of life *leads*
upward for the wise
That he may keep away
from [a]Sheol below.
25 The LORD will [A]tear down the
house of the proud,
But He will [B]establish the
boundary of the [C]widow.
26 Evil plans are an abomination
to the LORD,
But pleasant words are pure.
27 He who [A]profits illicitly
troubles his own house,
But he who [B]hates bribes will live.
28 The heart of the righteous
[A]ponders how to answer,
But the [B]mouth of the wicked
pours out evil things.
29 The LORD is [A]far from the wicked,
But He [B]hears the prayer of the righteous.
30 [a]Bright eyes gladden the heart;
Good news puts fat on the bones.

15:1 [a]Lit *painful* [A]Judg 8:1-3; Prov 15:18; 25:15 [B]1 Sam 25:10-13 15:2 [a]Lit *good* [A]Prov 15:7 [B]Prov 12:23; 13:16; 15:28 15:3 [A]2 Chr 16:9; Job 31:4; Jer 16:17; Zech 4:10; Heb 4:13 15:4 [a]Lit *healing* [b]Lit *is the crushing of the spirit* 15:5 [a]Or *despises* 15:6 [A]Prov 8:21 15:8 [A]Prov 21:27; Eccl 5:1; Is 1:11; Jer 6:20; Mic 6:7 [B]Prov 15:29 15:9 [A]1 Tim 6:11 15:11 [a]I.e. the nether world [b]I.e. place of destruction [c]Lit *sons of Adam* [A]Job 26:6; Ps 139:8 [B]1 Sam 16:7; 2 Chr 6:30; Ps 44:21; Acts 1:24 15:12 [A]Prov 13:1; Amos 5:10 15:13 [a]Lit *good* [b]Lit *in sadness of heart* [A]Prov 17:22 [B]Prov 12:25 [C]Prov 17:22; 18:14 15:14 [A]Prov 18:15 15:15 [a]Lit *good* 15:16 [a]Or *reverence* [A]Ps 37:16; Prov 16:8; Eccl 4:6; 1 Tim 6:6 15:17 [a]Or *portion* [b]Or *herbs* [A]Prov 17:1 [B]Matt 22:4; Luke 15:23 15:18 [A]Prov 16:28; 26:21; 29:22 [B]Prov 14:29 [C]Gen 13:8; Prov 16:14; Eccl 10:4 15:20 [A]Prov 10:1; 29:3 [B]Prov 30:17 15:21 [a]Lit *heart* [A]Prov 14:8; Eph 5:15 15:22 [a]Or *are established* 15:23 [a]Lit *answer of his mouth* [A]Prov 12:14 [B]Prov 25:11; Is 50:4 15:24 [a]I.e. the nether world [A]Prov 4:18 15:25 [A]Prov 12:7; 14:11 [B]Deut 19:14; Prov 23:10 [C]Ps 68:5; 146:9 15:27 [A]Prov 1:19; 28:25; 1 Tim 6:10 [B]Ex 23:8; Deut 16:19; 1 Sam 12:3; Is 33:15 15:28 [A]1 Pet 3:15 [B]Prov 10:32; 15:2 15:29 [A]Ps 18:41; Prov 1:28 [B]Ps 145:18, 19 15:30 [a]Lit *The light of the eyes gladdens*

15:2 *See note on 14:33.*

15:3 eyes of the LORD. Cf. 5:21. This refers to God's omniscience. Cf. 1 Sam 16:7; 2Ch 16:9; Job 24:23; Pss 33:13–15; 139:1–16; Jer 17:10.

15:4 tree of life. *See note on 3:18.* **crushes the spirit.** To break or wound, thus to destroy one's morale (cf. Is 65:14).

15:8 External acts of worship, though according to biblical prescription, are repulsive to God when the heart of the worshiper is wicked (cf. Is 1:12–15; Am 5:21; Mal 1:11–14; Heb 11:4, 6).

15:10 the way. The way of truth and righteousness (see 2:13; 10:17).

15:11 Sheol and Abaddon. Cf. 27:20. Hell or Sheol is the place of the dead (*see note on 1:12*). "Abaddon" or destruction refers to the experience of eternal punishment. Cf. Job 26:6.

15:13 Cf. v. 4.

15:15 continual feast. The joyous, inward condition of the wise man's heart (14:21) is described as a perpetual feast. Real happiness is always determined by the state of the heart (cf. Hab 3:17, 18; 1Ti 4:6–8).

15:16, 17 *See note on 12:9* for other "Better … Than" references.

15:16 fear of the LORD. *See note on 1:7.*

15:17 dish of vegetables. The typical dinner of the poor.

15:18 "Hotheads" are contrasted with "peacemakers" (cf. 14:17, 29; 15:1; 28:25; 29:11, 22).

15:19 thorns. He is too lazy to remove them. *See notes on 6:6, 11.*

15:22 *See note on 11:14.*

15:24 Sheol below. *See note on 1:12.*

15:25 When evil men try to take the property of widows, God will intervene (cf. 22:28; 23:10, 11). The most desolate (widows) who have God's help possess a more permanent dwelling place than the prosperous and self-reliant sinners.

15:27 bribes. Cf. 18:5; 24:23; 29:4; Ex 23:8; Dt 16:19; Ecc. 7:7; Is 1:23.

15:28 mouth of the wicked pours out. Wicked people don't guard their words. *See note on 12:23*; cf. Eph 4:29.

15:30 Bright eyes. This is a comparison, so that the "Good news" defines this term. Whatever is good, sound truth and wisdom stirs the heart by relieving anxiety and producing a cheerful face (cf. 14:30; 15:13; 17:22).

31 He whose ear listens to the
life-giving reproof
Will dwell among the wise.
32 He who [A]neglects discipline
[B]despises himself,
But he who [C]listens to reproof
acquires [a]understanding.
33 The [a]fear of the LORD is the
instruction for wisdom,
And before honor *comes* humility.

CONTRAST THE UPRIGHT AND THE WICKED

16 The [A]plans of the heart belong to man,
But the answer of the tongue
is from the LORD.
2 All the ways of a man are
clean in his own sight,
But the [A]LORD weighs the [a]motives.
3 [a,A]Commit your works to the LORD
And your plans will be established.
4 The LORD [A]has made everything
for [a]its own purpose,
Even the [B]wicked for the day of evil.
5 Everyone who is proud in heart is
an abomination to the LORD;
Assuredly, he will not be unpunished.
6 By [A]lovingkindness and truth
iniquity is atoned for,
And by the [a,B]fear of the LORD
one keeps away from evil.
7 When a man's ways are
pleasing to the LORD,
He [A]makes even his enemies to
be at peace with him.
8 Better is a little with righteousness
Than great income with injustice.
9 The mind of [A]man plans his way,
But [B]the LORD directs his steps.
10 A divine [A]decision is in the lips of the king;
His mouth should not [a]err in judgment.
11 A [A]just balance and scales
belong to the LORD;
All the [a]weights of the bag are His [b]concern.
12 It is an abomination for kings
to commit wicked acts,
For a [A]throne is established
on righteousness.
13 Righteous lips are the delight of kings,
And he who speaks right is loved.
14 The fury of a king is *like*
messengers of death,
But a wise man will appease it.
15 In the light of a king's face is life,
And his favor is like a cloud
with the [a,A]spring rain.
16 How much [A]better it is to get
wisdom than gold!
And to get understanding is to
be chosen above silver.
17 The [A]highway of the upright
is to depart from evil;
He who watches his way preserves his [a]life.
18 [A]Pride *goes* before destruction,
And a haughty spirit before stumbling.
19 It is better to be [A]humble in
spirit with the lowly
Than to [B]divide the spoil with the proud.
20 He who gives attention to the
word will [A]find good,
And [B]blessed is he who trusts in the LORD.
21 The [A]wise in heart will be
called understanding,
And sweetness of [a]speech
[B]increases [b]persuasiveness.
22 Understanding is a fountain of
life to one who has it,
But the discipline of fools is folly.
23 The [A]heart of the wise instructs his mouth
And adds [a]persuasiveness to his lips.

15:32 [a]Lit *heart* [A]Prov 1:7; 8:33 [B]Prov 8:36 [C]Prov 15:5 15:33 [a]Or *reverence* 16:1 [A]Prov 16:9; 19:21 16:2 [a]Lit *spirits* [A]1 Sam 16:7; Dan 5:27 16:3 [a]Lit *Roll* [A]Ps 37:5; 55:22; Prov 3:6; 1 Pet 5:7 16:4 [a]Or *His* [A]Gen 1:31; Eccl 3:11 [B]Rom 9:22 16:6 [a]Or *reverence* [A]Dan 4:27; Luke 11:41 [B]Prov 8:13; 14:16 16:7 [A]Gen 33:4; 2 Chr 17:10 16:9 [A]Prov 16:1; 19:21 [B]Ps 37:23; Prov 20:24; Jer 10:23 16:10 [a]Lit *be unfaithful* [A]1 Kin 3:28 16:11 [a]Lit *stones* [b]Lit *work* [A]Prov 11:1 16:12 [A]Prov 25:5 16:15 [a]Lit *latter* [A]Job 29:23 16:16 [A]Prov 8:10, 19 16:17 [a]Lit *soul* [A]Is 35:8 16:18 [A]Prov 11:2; 18:12; Jer 49:16; Obad 3, 4 16:19 [A]Prov 3:34; 29:23; Is 57:15 [B]Ex 15:9; Judg 5:30; Prov 1:13, 14 16:20 [A]Prov 19:8 [B]Ps 2:12; 34:8; Jer 17:7 16:21 [a]Lit *lips* [b]Or *learning* [A]Hos 14:9 [B]Prov 16:23 16:23 [a]Or *learning* [A]Ps 37:30; Prov 15:28; Matt 12:34

15:31 ear listens ... wise. The acquiring of wisdom demands a teachable spirit.

15:33 fear of the LORD. *See note on 1:7.*

16:1 plans ... answer. Human responsibility is always subject to God's absolute sovereignty (cf. 3:6; 16:2, 9, 33; 19:21; 20:24; 21:1, 30, 31).

16:2 motives. While man can be self-deceived, God determines his true motives (cf. 21:2; 24:12; 1Sa 16:7; 1Co 4:4).

16:3 Commit. Lit. "roll upon" in the sense of both total trust (3:5–6) and submission to the will of God (Pss 22:8; 37:5; 119:133); He will fulfill your righteous plans.

16:4 The wicked will bring glory to God in the day of their judgment and eternal punishment. *See notes on Ro 9:17–23.*

16:6 By God's "lovingkindness and truth," He affects the atonement or covering of sin, which for the believing sinner inclines him to keep away from evil. *See notes on Lv 16:1–34; 17:11* for explanation of atonement. **fear of the LORD.** *See note on 1:7.*

16:7 This general rule does not preclude persecution from some. *See note on 2Ti 3:12.*

16:9 *See notes on vv. 1, 2.* Sovereign God overrules the plans of men to fulfill His purposes. See Ge 50:20; 1Ki 12:15; Ps 119:133; Jer 10:23; Da 5:23–30; 1Co 3:19, 20.

16:10 divine decision. This does not imply any occultic practice forbidden in Lv 19:26, but is literally a decision from divine wisdom, in the words of the king who represented God. The king was under mandate (Dt 17:18–20) to seek out and speak God's wisdom (cf. David in 2Sa 14:17–20; Solomon in 1Ki 3:9–12; and Christ as King in Is 11:2).

16:11 *See note on 11:1.*

16:12 *See note on 14:34.*

16:14 This points to the king's power of "life or death," which can be abused (cf. 1Sa 22:16–18; Est 7–10; Da 2:5) or used for good (cf. 2Sa 1:1–16; 4:5–12).

16:15 cloud with the spring rain. The late spring rain, which matured the crop, fell before the harvest (cf. 2Sa 23:3, 4; Ps 72:6) and is here compared to the king's power to grace his subjects with encouragement.

16:16 better. Cf. 3:13–16; 8:10, 11, 18, 19.

16:17 A plain road represents the habitual course of the righteous in departing from evil. As long as he stays on it, he is safe.

16:19 The proud are those who have plundered the poor.

16:21 sweetness of speech. "Honeyed words," which reflect intelligence, judiciousness, and discernment in speech. This refers to eloquent discourse from the wise (cf. v. 24).

16:22 fountain of life. *See note on 10:11.* The advice of the understanding person brings blessing, while the correction offered by a fool is useless.

16:23 heart. *See note on 4:21–23.*

24 [A]Pleasant words are a honeycomb,
Sweet to the soul and [B]healing
to the bones.
25 [A]There is a way *which seems*
right to a man,
But its end is the way of death.
26 A worker's appetite works for him,
For his [a]hunger urges him *on*.
27 A [A]worthless man digs up evil,
While [a]his words are like [B]scorching fire.
28 A perverse man spreads strife,
And a slanderer separates
intimate friends.
29 A man of violence [A]entices
his neighbor
And leads him in a way that
is not good.
30 He who winks his eyes *does so*
to devise perverse things;
He who compresses his lips
brings evil to pass.
31 A [A]gray head is a crown of glory;
It [B]is found in the way of righteousness.
32 He who is slow to anger is
better than the mighty,
And he who rules his spirit, than
he who captures a city.
33 The [A]lot is cast into the lap,
But its every [B]decision is from the LORD.

CONTRAST THE UPRIGHT AND THE WICKED

17 [A]Better is a dry morsel and
quietness with it
Than a house full of [a]feasting with strife.
2 A servant who acts wisely will rule
over a son who acts shamefully,
And will share in the inheritance
among brothers.
3 The [A]refining pot is for silver
and the furnace for gold,
But [B]the LORD tests hearts.
4 An [A]evildoer listens to wicked lips;
A [a]liar pays attention to a
destructive tongue.
5 He who mocks the [A]poor taunts his Maker;
He who [B]rejoices at calamity
will not go unpunished.
6 [A]Grandchildren are the crown of old men,
And the [B]glory of sons is their fathers.
7 [a,A]Excellent speech is not fitting for a fool,
Much less are [B]lying lips to a prince.
8 A [A]bribe is a [a]charm in the
sight of its owner;
Wherever he turns, he prospers.
9 He who [A]conceals a
transgression seeks love,
But he who repeats a matter
[B]separates intimate friends.
10 A rebuke goes deeper into one
who has understanding
Than a hundred blows into a fool.
11 A rebellious man seeks only evil,
So a cruel messenger will be
sent against him.
12 Let a [A]man meet a [B]bear
robbed of her cubs,
Rather than a fool in his folly.
13 He who [A]returns evil for good,
[B]Evil will not depart from his house.
14 The beginning of strife is *like*
letting out water,
So [A]abandon the quarrel
before it breaks out.
15 He who [A]justifies the wicked and he
who condemns the righteous,
Both of them alike are an
abomination to the LORD.

16:24 [A]Ps 19:10; Prov 15:26; 24:13, 14 [B]Prov 4:22; 17:22 16:25 [A]Prov 12:15; 14:12 16:26 [a]Lit *mouth* 16:27 [a]Lit *on his lips* [A]Prov 6:12, 14, 18 [B]James 3:6 16:29 [A]Prov 1:10; 12:26 16:31 [A]Prov 20:29 [B]Prov 3:1, 2 16:33 [A]Prov 18:18 [B]Prov 29:26 17:1 [a]Lit *sacrifices of strife* [A]Prov 15:17 17:3 [A]Prov 27:21 [B]1 Chr 29:17; Ps 26:2; Prov 15:11; Jer 17:10; Mal 3:3 17:4 [a]Lit *falsehood* [A]Prov 14:15 17:5 [A]Prov 14:31 [B]Job 31:29; Prov 24:17; Obad 12 17:6 [A]Gen 48:11; Prov 13:22 [B]Ex 20:12; Mal 1:6 17:7 [a]Lit *A lip of abundance* [A]Prov 24:7 [B]Ps 31:18; Prov 12:22 17:8 [a]Lit *stone of favor* [A]Prov 21:14; Is 1:23; Amos 5:12 17:9 [A]Prov 10:12; James 5:20; 1 Pet 4:8 [B]Prov 16:28 17:12 [A]Prov 29:9 [B]2 Sam 17:8; Hos 13:8 17:13 [A]Ps 35:12; 109:5; Jer 18:20 [B]2 Sam 12:10; 1 Kin 21:22; Prov 13:21 17:14 [A]Prov 20:3; 25:8; 1 Thess 4:11 17:15 [A]Ex 23:7; Prov 18:5; 24:24; Is 5:23

16:24 Pleasant words. *See note on v. 21*; cf. 24:13, 14; Ps 19:10.

16:25 way of death. Cf. 14:12.

16:26 works for him. Labor is hard and often grievous, but necessary, even for the lazy (cf. Ecc 6:7; Eph 4:28; 6:7; 2Th 3:10–12).

16:27 worthless man. *See note on 6:12.* He literally digs a pit for his neighbor as a hunter would for prey (cf. Pss 7:15; 62:6), and his speech is incendiary (cf. Jas 3:6).

16:28 spreads. The same root word is used for the release of flaming foxes in the grain fields of the Philistines (Jdg 15:4, 5; cf. 17:9). **slanderer.** A whisperer or gossip. *See note on 6:14*; cf. 8:8; 26:20, 22 for the same Heb. term.

16:30 compresses. The idea of winking or squinting the eyes and compressing one's lips was to express the posture connoting deep thought and determined purpose.

16:31 This calls for respecting elders. Cf. 20:29.

16:32 slow to anger. *See notes on 14:17; 25:28.* Cf. Ecc 9:17, 18; Jas 1:19, 20.

16:33 lot. *See note on 16:1.* Casting lots was a method often used to reveal God's purposes in a matter (cf. Jos 14:1, 2; 1Sa 14:38–43; 1Ch 25:8–31; Jon 1:7; Ac 1:26). The High Priest may have carried lots in his sacred vest, along with the Urim and Thummim (*see note on Ex 28:30*).

17:1 Cf. 15:17.

17:2 servant who acts wisely … inheritance. A faithful servant will rise above an unworthy son and receive an inheritance (cf. 11:29; 1Ki 11:26, 28–38; Mt 8:11, 12).

17:3 refining pot. This was a heated crucible used to test and refine precious metal. Cf. Ps 66:10; Is 1:25; 48:10; Jer 6:29; Eze 22:17–22; Dan 12:10; Mal 3:3.

17:5 Cf. 14:21, 31.

17:6 Grandchildren. Godly influence generates mutual love and respect in a family, which extends from generation to generation (cf. Ps 90 with Ex 20:12).

17:8 bribe. This refers to a bribe that brings prosperity to its recipient (v. 23; 15:27).

17:9 Cf. 16:28; 18:8.

17:10 For the theme of a teachable spirit, cf. 9:7, 8; 15:31–33.

17:11 Just retribution comes against people who rebel, and thus the king's messenger will have no mercy (cf. 16:14; 2Sa 20:1–22; 1Ki 2:25, 29, 34, 46).

17:12 Fools are less rational in anger than wild bears.

17:13 evil for good. Solomon knew this proverb well, since his father mistreated Uriah (cf. 2Sa 12:10–31). Contrast this with the man who repays evil with good (cf. 20:22; Mt 5:43–48; 1Pe 3:9).

17:14 letting out water. The smallest break in the dam sets loose an uncontrollable flood force.

17:15 The unjust judge is controlled by his pride, prejudice, bribes, and passions. *See note on 24:23b–25*; cf. Ex 23:7; Is 5:23.

16 Why is there a price in the hand
of a fool to [A]buy wisdom,
When [a]he has no sense?
17 A [A]friend loves at all times,
And a brother is born for adversity.
18 A man lacking in [a]sense [b,A]pledges
And becomes guarantor in the
presence of his neighbor.
19 He who [A]loves transgression loves strife;
He who [B]raises his door
seeks destruction.
20 He who has a crooked [a]mind
[A]finds no good,
And he who is [B]perverted in his
language falls into evil.
21 He who [A]sires a fool *does*
so to his sorrow,
And the father of a fool has no joy.
22 A [A]joyful heart [a]is good medicine,
But a broken spirit [B]dries up the bones.
23 A wicked man receives a
[A]bribe from the bosom
To [B]pervert the ways of justice.
24 Wisdom is in the presence of the
one who has understanding,
But the [A]eyes of a fool are on
the ends of the earth.
25 A [A]foolish son is a grief to his father
And [B]bitterness to her who bore him.
26 It is also not good to [A]fine the righteous,
Nor to strike the noble for
their uprightness.
27 He who [A]restrains his words
[a]has knowledge,
And he who has a [B]cool spirit is
a man of understanding.
28 Even a fool, when he [A]keeps
silent, is considered wise;
When he closes his lips, he is
considered prudent.

CONTRAST THE UPRIGHT AND THE WICKED

18 He who separates himself
seeks *his own* desire,
He [a,A]quarrels against all sound wisdom.
2 A fool does not delight in understanding,
But only [A]in revealing his own [a]mind.
3 When a wicked man comes,
contempt also comes,
And with dishonor *comes* scorn.
4 The words of a man's mouth
are [A]deep waters;
[a]The fountain of wisdom is a bubbling brook.
5 To [A]show partiality to the
wicked is not good,
Nor to [B]thrust aside the
righteous in judgment.
6 A fool's lips [a]bring strife,
And his mouth calls for [A]blows.
7 A [A]fool's mouth is his ruin,
And his lips are the snare of his soul.
8 The words of a whisperer are
like dainty morsels,
And they go down into the
[a]innermost parts of the body.
9 He also who is [A]slack in his work
[B]Is brother to him who destroys.
10 The [A]name of the LORD is a [B]strong tower;
The righteous runs into it and [C]is [a]safe.
11 A [A]rich man's wealth is his strong city,
And like a high wall in his
own imagination.
12 [A]Before destruction the heart
of man is haughty,
But [B]humility *goes* before honor.
13 He who [A]gives an answer before he hears,
It is folly and shame to him.
14 The [A]spirit of a man can
endure his sickness,
But *as for* a [B]broken spirit who can bear it?

17:16 [a]Lit *there is no heart* [A]Prov 23:23 17:17 [A]Ruth 1:16; Prov 18:24 17:18 [a]Lit *heart* [b]Lit *shakes hands* [A]Prov 6:1; 11:15; 22:26 17:19 [A]Prov 29:22 [B]Prov 16:18; 29:23 17:20 [a]Lit *heart* [A]Prov 24:20 [B]James 3:8 17:21 [A]Prov 10:1; 17:25; 19:13 17:22 [a]Lit *causes good healing* [A]Prov 15:13 [B]Ps 22:15 17:23 [A]Prov 17:8 [B]Ex 23:8; Mic 3:11; 7:3 17:24 [A]Eccl 2:14 17:25 [A]Prov 19:13 [B]Prov 10:1 17:26 [A]Prov 17:15; 18:5 17:27 [a]Lit *knows* [A]Prov 10:19; James 1:19 [B]Prov 14:29 17:28 [A]Job 13:5 18:1 [a]Lit *breaks out* [A]Prov 3:21; 8:14 18:2 [a]Lit *heart* [A]Prov 12:23; 13:16; Eccl 10:3 18:4 [a]Or *A bubbling brook, a fountain of wisdom* [A]Prov 20:5 18:5 [A]Lev 19:15; Deut 1:17; 16:19; Ps 82:2; Prov 17:15; 24:23; 28:21 [B]Ex 23:2, 6; Prov 17:26; 31:5; Mic 3:9 18:6 [a]Lit *come with* [A]Prov 19:29 18:7 [A]Ps 64:8; 140:9; Prov 10:14; 12:13; 13:3; Eccl 10:12 18:8 [a]Lit *chambers of the belly* 18:9 [A]Prov 10:4 [B]Prov 28:24 18:10 [a]Lit *set on high* [A]Ex 3:15 [B]2 Sam 22:2, 3, 33; Ps 18:2; 61:3; 91:2; 144:2 [C]Prov 29:25 18:11 [A]Prov 10:15 18:12 [A]Prov 11:2; 16:18; 29:23 [B]Prov 15:33 18:13 [A]Prov 20:25; John 7:51 18:14 [A]Prov 17:22 [B]Prov 15:13

17:16 Even wealth cannot buy wisdom for those who do not love it. Cf. 4:7.

17:17 The difference between a friend and brother is noted here. A true friend is a constant source of love, while a brother in one's family may not be close, but is drawn near to help in trouble. Friends are closer than brothers because they are available all the time, not just in the crisis. Cf. 18:24.

17:18 *See notes on 6:1, 2–4.*

17:19 raises his door. The image here is of the proud person who flaunts his wealth with a huge house having a large front door and who thus invites death (cf. Jer 22:13–19).

17:20 perverted. Cf. 10:31.

17:21 Cf. 10:1; 15:20; 17:25; 19:26.

17:22 Cf. 14:30; 15:13, 30; 16:14; Job 29:24.

17:23 *See note on v. 8.*

17:24 ends of the earth. This refers to the fool's roving fixations in the absence of wisdom.

17:25 Cf. v. 21.

17:26 fine ... strike. Here is a clear statement on political and religious injustice, focusing on the equally bad mistreatment of the innocent and the noble.

17:27 restrains. Cf. 10:19; 14:29; 15:18; 16:27, 32; 29:20.

17:28 fool ... is considered wise. This is not saying that fools show wisdom in their silence, but that silence conceals their folly.

18:1 separates himself. This man seeks selfish gratification and accepts advice from no one.

18:2 Cf. Ecc 10:12–14.

18:3 Sin and punishment are inseparably connected, as evil produces both the feeling of contempt in others and its manifestation, scorn.

18:4 words ... deep waters. Wise speech is like a deep, inexhaustible stream of blessing.

18:5 Cf. 17:26; 28:21.

18:6, 7 The fool self-destructs. Cf. 12:13; 17:14, 19, 28; 19:29; 20:3.

18:8 dainty morsels. This comes from a Heb. word, meaning "to swallow greedily." The proverb is repeated in 26:22.

18:9 slack ... destroys. To leave a work half done or poorly done is to destroy it. *See notes on 6:1, 11.*

18:10 The name of the LORD. This expression, found only here in Proverbs, stands for the manifest perfections of God such as faithfulness, power, mercy, and wisdom, on which the righteous rely for security (cf. Ex 3:15; 15:1–3; Ps 27:4, 5)

18:11 This proverb repeats 10:15 and contrasts with v. 10.

18:12 Cf. 16:18.

18:14 broken spirit. Cf. 12:25; 15:13. When the spirit is broken, people lose hope.

15 The [a,A]mind of the prudent
acquires knowledge,
And the [B]ear of the wise seeks knowledge.
16 A man's [A]gift makes room for him
And brings him before great men.
17 The first [a]to plead his case *seems* right,
Until [b]another comes and examines him.
18 The *cast* [A]lot puts an end to strife
And [a]decides between the mighty ones.
19 A brother offended *is harder to
be won* than a strong city,
And contentions are like the
bars of a citadel.
20 With the [a,A]fruit of a man's mouth
his stomach will be satisfied;
[B]He will be satisfied *with* the
product of his lips.
21 [A]Death and life are in the
[a]power of the tongue,
And those who love it will eat its [B]fruit.
22 He who finds a [A]wife finds a good thing
And [B]obtains favor from the LORD.
23 The [A]poor man utters supplications,
But the [B]rich man [C]answers roughly.
24 A man of *too many* friends *comes* to [a]ruin,
But there is [A]a [b]friend who sticks
closer than a brother.

ON LIFE AND CONDUCT

19 [A]Better is a poor man who
[B]walks in his integrity
Than he who is perverse in
[a]speech and is a fool.
2 Also it is not good for a person
to be without knowledge,
And he who hurries [a,A]his footsteps [b]errs.
3 The [A]foolishness of man ruins his way,
And his heart [B]rages against the LORD.
4 [A]Wealth adds many friends,
But a poor man is separated
from his friend.
5 A [A]false witness will not go unpunished,
And he who [a,B]tells lies will not escape.
6 [A]Many will seek the favor of
a [a]generous man,
And every man is a friend to
him who [B]gives gifts.
7 All the brothers of a poor man hate him;
How much more do his
[A]friends abandon him!
He [B]pursues *them with* words,
but they are [a]gone.
8 He who gets [a]wisdom loves his own soul;
He who keeps understanding
will [A]find good.
9 A [A]false witness will not go unpunished,
And he who [a]tells lies will perish.
10 Luxury is [A]not fitting for a fool;
Much less for a [B]slave to
rule over princes.
11 A man's [A]discretion makes
him slow to anger,
And it is his glory [B]to overlook
a transgression.
12 The [A]king's wrath is like the
roaring of a lion,
But his favor is like [B]dew on the grass.
13 A [A]foolish son is destruction
to his father,
And the [B]contentions of a wife
are a constant dripping.
14 House and wealth are an
[A]inheritance from fathers,
But a prudent wife is from the LORD.
15 [A]Laziness casts into a deep sleep,
And an idle [a]man will suffer hunger.

18:15 [a]Lit *heart* [A]Prov 15:14; Eph 1:17 [B]Prov 15:31 18:16 [A]Gen 32:20; 1 Sam 25:27 18:17 [a]Lit *in his plea* [b]Lit *his neighbor* 18:18 [a]Lit *makes a division* [A]Prov 16:33 18:20 [a]I.e. speech [A]Prov 12:14 [B]Prov 14:14 18:21 [a]Lit *hand* [A]Prov 12:13; 13:3; Matt 12:37 [B]Prov 13:2; Is 3:10; Hos 10:13 18:22 [A]Gen 2:18; Prov 12:4; 19:14; 31:10-31 [B]Prov 8:35 18:23 [A]Prov 19:7 [B]James 2:3, 6 [C]1 Kin 12:13; 2 Chr 10:13 18:24 [a]Lit *be broken in pieces* [b]Or *lover* [A]Prov 17:17; John 15:14, 15 19:1 [a]Lit *his lips* [A]Prov 28:6 [B]Ps 26:11; Prov 14:2; 20:7 19:2 [a]Lit *with his feet* [b]Lit *sins* [A]Prov 21:5; 28:20; 29:20 19:3 [A]Prov 11:3 [B]Is 8:21 19:4 [A]Prov 14:20 19:5 [a]Lit *breathes* [A]Ex 23:1; Deut 19:16-19; Prov 19:9; 21:28 [B]Prov 6:19 19:6 [a]Or *noble* [A]Prov 29:26 [B]Prov 18:16; 21:14 19:7 [a]Lit *not* [A]Ps 38:11 [B]Prov 18:23 19:8 [a]Lit *heart* [A]Prov 16:20 19:9 [a]Lit *breathes* [A]Prov 19:5; Dan 6:24 19:10 [A]Prov 17:7; 26:1; Eccl 10:6, 7 [B]Prov 30:22 19:11 [A]Prov 14:29; 16:32 [B]Matt 5:44; Eph 4:32; Col 3:13 19:12 [A]Prov 16:14 [B]Gen 27:28; Deut 33:28; Ps 133:3; Hos 14:5; Mic 5:7 19:13 [A]Prov 17:25 [B]Prov 21:9, 19; 27:15 19:14 [A]2 Cor 12:14 19:15 [a]Lit *soul* [A]Prov 6:9, 10; 24:33

18:16 man's gift. This is not the word for a bribe (cf. 17:23), but rather the word for a present given to someone (cf. Jacob's gift, Ge 32:20, 21; Joseph's gift, Ge 43:11; David's gift, 1Sa 17:17, 18; and Abigail's gift, 1Sa 25:27).

18:17 See v. 13. Cross-examination avoids hasty judgment.

18:18 lot. *See note on 16:33.*

18:19 There are no feuds as difficult to resolve as those with relatives; no barriers are so hard to bring down. Hence, great care should be taken to avoid such conflicts. bars of a citadel. Cf. Jdg 16:3; 1Ki 4:13; Ne 3:3; Is 45:2.

18:20 the product of his lips. *See notes on 12:14; 13:2, 3.* The consequences of one's words should produce satisfaction and fulfillment.

18:21 Death and life. The greatest good and the greatest harm are in the power of the tongue (cf. Jas 3:6–10).

18:22 Cf. 12:4; 19:14; 31:10–31.

18:23 The rich do not need favors from others, so they do not care how they treat people.

18:24 *comes to ruin.* The person who makes friends too easily and indiscriminately does so to his own destruction. On the other hand, a friend chosen wisely is more loyal than a brother. friend. This is a strong word meaning "one who loves" and was used of Abraham, God's friend (2Ch 20:7; Is 41:8; cf. 1Sa 18:1; 2Sa 1:26).

19:1 Integrity is better than wealth. Cf. 15:16, 17; 16:8.

19:2 hurries his footsteps. Rashness, the result of ignorance, brings trouble. errs. Lit. "to miss the mark."

19:3 his heart rages. The fool blames God for his troubles and failures (cf. Ge 4:5; Is 8:21; La 3:39–41).

19:4 Wealth adds. Cf. v. 7; 14:20. Lit. wealth adds new friends while poverty alienates existing friends who grow weary of the demands of the poor.

19:5, 9 For the sin of perjury, cf. 6:19; 12:17; 14:5, 25; 19:9; Dt 19:18–21.

19:6 Generosity or bribery could be the issue.

19:7 *See note on v. 4.*

19:10 Neither are suited for possessions or responsibilities beyond their capabilities of managing wisely (cf. 30:21–23).

19:11 slow to anger. *See note on 14:17.*

19:12 This is a call to submit to governmental authority. Cf. Ro 13:1–4; 1Pe 2:13–17.

19:13 constant dripping. An obstinate, argumentative woman is literally like a leak so unrelenting that one has to run from it or go mad. Here are two ways to devastate a man: an ungodly son and an irritating wife.

19:14 One receives inheritance as a family blessing (a result of human birth), but a wise wife (cf. 31:10–31) is a result of divine blessing. Cf. 12:4; 18:22; 31:10–31.

19:15 *See notes on 6:6, 11.*

16 He who [A]keeps the commandment
keeps his soul,
But he who [a]is careless of
[b]conduct will die.
17 One who [A]is gracious to a poor
man lends to the LORD,
And He will repay him for
his [a,B]good deed.
18 [A]Discipline your son while there is hope,
And do not desire [a]his death.
19 *A man of* great anger will
bear the penalty,
For if you rescue *him,* you will
only have to do it again.
20 [A]Listen to counsel and accept discipline,
That you may be wise [a]the
rest of your days.
21 Many [A]plans are in a man's heart,
But the [B]counsel of the LORD will stand.
22 What is desirable in a man
is his [a]kindness,
And *it is* better to be a poor
man than a liar.
23 The [a,A]fear of the LORD *leads* to life,
So that one may sleep [B]satisfied,
[b,C]untouched by evil.
24 The [A]sluggard buries his
hand [B]in the dish,
But will not even bring it
back to his mouth.
25 [A]Strike a scoffer and the [a]naive
may become shrewd,
But [B]reprove one who has
understanding and he
will [b]gain knowledge.
26 He [A]who assaults *his* father *and*
drives *his* mother away
Is a shameful and disgraceful son.
27 Cease listening, my son, to discipline,
And you will stray from the
words of knowledge.
28 A rascally witness makes a
mockery of justice,
And the mouth of the wicked
[a,A]spreads iniquity.
29 [a]Judgments are prepared for [A]scoffers,
And [B]blows for the back of fools.

ON LIFE AND CONDUCT

20 [A]Wine is a mocker, [B]strong
drink a brawler,
And whoever [a]is intoxicated
by it is not wise.
2 The terror of a king is like the
growling of a lion;
He who provokes him to anger
[a,A]forfeits his own life.
3 [a,A]Keeping away from strife is
an honor for a man,
But any fool will [b]quarrel.
4 The [A]sluggard does not plow
after the autumn,
So he [a]begs during the harvest
and has nothing.
5 A plan in the heart of a man
is *like* deep water,
But a man of understanding draws it out.
6 Many a man [A]proclaims his own loyalty,
But who can find a [B]trustworthy man?
7 A righteous man who [A]walks
in his integrity—
[B]How blessed are his sons after him.
8 [A]A king who sits on the throne of justice
[a]Disperses all evil with his eyes.
9 [A]Who can say, "I have cleansed my heart,
I am pure from my sin"?

19:16 [a]Lit *despises* [b]Lit *ways* [A]Prov 13:13; 16:17; Luke 10:28; 11:28 19:17 [a]Or *benefits* [A]Deut 15:7, 8; Prov 14:31; 28:27; Eccl 11:1, 2; Matt 10:42; 25:40; 2 Cor 9:6-8; Heb 6:10 [B]Prov 12:14; Luke 6:38 19:18 [a]Lit *causing him to die* [A]Prov 13:24; 23:13; 29:15, 17 19:20 [a]Lit *in your latter end* [A]Prov 4:1; 8:33; 12:15 19:21 [A]Prov 16:1, 9 [B]Ps 33:10, 11; Is 14:26, 27 19:22 [a]Or *loyalty* 19:23 [a]Or *reverence* [b]Lit *not visited* [A]Prov 14:27; 1 Tim 4:8 [B]Ps 25:13 [C]Ps 91:10; Prov 12:21 19:24 [A]Prov 26:15 [B]Matt 26:23; Mark 14:20 19:25 [a]Lit *simple* [b]Lit *discern* [A]Prov 21:11 [B]Prov 9:8 19:26 [A]Prov 28:24 19:28 [a]Or *swallows* [A]Job 15:16; 20:12, 13; 34:7 19:29 [a]Gr *Rods* [A]Ps 1:1; Prov 9:12 [B]Prov 10:13; 18:6; 26:3 20:1 [a]Lit *errs* [A]Gen 9:21; Prov 23:29, 30; Is 28:7; Hos 4:11 [B]Prov 31:4; Is 5:22; 56:12 20:2 [a]Lit *sins against* [A]Num 16:38; 1 Kin 2:23; Prov 8:36; Hab 2:10 20:3 [a]Lit *Ceasing* [b]Lit *burst out* [A]Gen 13:7f; Prov 17:14 20:4 [a]Lit *asks* [A]Prov 13:4; 21:25 20:6 [A]Prov 25:14; Matt 6:2; Luke 18:11 [B]Ps 12:1; Luke 18:8 20:7 [A]Prov 19:1 [B]Ps 37:26; 112:2 20:8 [a]Or *Sifts* [A]Prov 20:26; 25:5 20:9 [A]1 Kin 8:46; 2 Chr 6:36; Job 14:4; Eccl 7:20; Rom 3:9; 1 John 1:8

19:16 commandment. Wisdom is equated with God's commandments. In a sense, Proverbs contains the applications and implications of all that is in God's moral law.

19:17 *See note on 14:31.*

19:18 Discipline. *See notes on 3:11, 12; 13:24; 22:6.*

19:19 Repeated acts of kindness are wasted on ill-natured people.

19:21 *See note on 16:1.*

19:22 Rich liars are not kind since their lies bring harm; a kind poor man is more desirable.

19:23 fear of the LORD. *See note on 1:7.*

19:24 The lazy man's lack of action to move his hand from the flat, metal food saucer up to his mouth is because he is too lazy, as explained in 26:15.

19:25 scoffer ... naive ... understanding. Three classes of people are noted: 1) scoffers are rebuked for learning nothing; 2) naive people are warned by observing the rebuke of the scoffer; and 3) the understanding deepen their wisdom from any reproof.

19:26 assaults. Cf. 10:1; 15:20; 17:21, 25; 28:24. The son appears to come into possession of his father's property during his parents' lifetime, but rather than caring for them, he drives them out (cf. Ex 20:12; 21:15, 17).

19:28 rascally witness. *See note on 12:17.*

19:29 *See note on 10:13.*

20:1 Wine ... strong drink. This begins a new theme of temperance (see 23:20, 21, 29–35; 31:4, 5). Wine was grape juice mixed with water to dilute it, but strong drink was unmixed (*see note on Eph 5:18*). While the use of these beverages is not specifically condemned (Dt 14:26), being intoxicated always is (Is 28:7). Rulers were not to drink, so their judgment would not be clouded nor their behavior less than exemplary (see 31:4, 5). *See note on 1 Tim 3:3.* **mocker ... brawler.** "Mocker" is the same word as "scoffer" in 19:25, 29; a brawler is violent, loud, and uncontrolled. Both words describe the personality of the drunkard.

20:2 *See notes on 16:14; 19:12.* Men who resist governmental authority injure themselves. *See notes on Ro 13:1–5.*

20:3 Cf. 15:18; 17:14; 19:11.

20:4 sluggard *See notes on 6:6, 11.*

20:5 deep water. The wise man has keen discernment reaching to the deepest intentions of the heart to grasp wise counsel (cf. 18:4; Heb 4:12).

20:6 There are a lot more people who are eager to brag about themselves than there are those who are truly faithful to testify of God's goodness.

20:7 integrity. *See note on 10:9.*

20:8 Disperses. The king as judge lit. "winnows" or "sifts" (as in v. 26) data as he discerns evil and good (cf. Is 11:3, 4).

20:9 No one can make himself sinless. Cf. Job 14:4; Ro 3:10, 23; 1 Jn 1:8. Those whose sin has been forgiven are pure before God (Ps 51:1, 2, 9, 10).

10 [a,A]Differing weights and differing measures,
Both of them are abominable to the LORD.
11 It is by his deeds that a lad
[a,A]distinguishes himself
If his conduct is pure and right.
12 The hearing [A]ear and the seeing eye,
The LORD has made both of them.
13 [A]Do not love sleep, or you
will become poor;
Open your eyes, *and* you will
be satisfied with [a]food.
14 "Bad, bad," says the buyer,
But when he goes his way, then he boasts.
15 There is gold, and an
abundance of [a]jewels;
But the lips of knowledge are
a more precious thing.
16 Take his garment when he becomes
surety for a stranger;
And for foreigners, hold him in pledge.
17 [A]Bread obtained by falsehood
is sweet to a man,
But afterward his mouth will
be filled with gravel.
18 Prepare [A]plans by consultation,
And [B]make war by wise guidance.
19 He who [A]goes about as a
slanderer reveals secrets,
Therefore do not associate
with [a,B]a gossip.
20 He who [A]curses his father or his mother,
His [B]lamp will go out in
[a]time of darkness.
21 An inheritance gained hurriedly
at the beginning
Will not be blessed in the end.
22 [A]Do not say, "I will repay evil";
[B]Wait for the LORD, and He will save you.
23 [a,A]Differing weights are an
abomination to the LORD,
And a [b,B]false scale is not good.
24 [A]Man's steps are *ordained* by the LORD,
How then can man understand his way?
25 It is a trap for a man to say
rashly, "It is holy!"
And [A]after the vows to make inquiry.
26 A [A]wise king winnows the wicked,
And [a]drives the [B]*threshing*
wheel over them.
27 The [a,A]spirit of man is the
lamp of the LORD,
Searching all the [b]innermost
parts of his being.
28 [a]Loyalty and [A]truth preserve the king,
And he upholds his throne
by [a]righteousness.
29 The glory of young men is their strength,
And the [a,A]honor of old men
is their gray hair.
30 [A]Stripes that wound scour away evil,
And strokes *reach* the [a]innermost parts.

ON LIFE AND CONDUCT

21 The king's heart is *like* channels of
water in the hand of the LORD;
He [A]turns it wherever He wishes.
2 [A]Every man's way is right in his own eyes,
But the LORD [B]weighs the hearts.
3 To do [A]righteousness and justice
Is desired by the LORD more than sacrifice.
4 Haughty eyes and a proud heart,
The [A]lamp of the wicked, is sin.
5 The plans of the [A]diligent *lead*
surely to advantage,
But everyone [B]who is hasty
comes surely to poverty.

20:10 [a]Lit *A stone and a stone, an ephah and an ephah* [A]Prov 11:1; 20:23 20:11 [a]Or *makes himself known* [A]Matt 7:16 20:12 [A]Ex 4:11; Ps 94:9 20:13 [a]Lit *bread* [A]Prov 6:9, 10; 19:15; 24:33 20:15 [a]Or *corals* 20:17 [A]Prov 9:17 20:18 [A]Prov 11:14; 15:22 [B]Prov 24:6; Luke 14:31 20:19 [a]Lit *one who opens his lips* [A]Prov 11:13 [B]Prov 13:3 20:20 [a]Lit *pupil* (of eye) [A]Ex 21:17; Lev 20:9; Prov 30:11; Matt 15:4 [B]Job 18:5; Prov 13:9; 24:20 20:22 [A]Prov 24:29; Matt 5:39; Rom 12:17, 19; 1 Thess 5:15; 1 Pet 3:9 [B]Ps 27:14 20:23 [a]Lit *A stone and a stone* [b]Lit *balance of deceit* [A]Prov 20:10 [B]Prov 11:1 20:24 [A]Prov 16:9 20:25 [A]Eccl 5:4, 5 20:26 [a]Lit *turns* [A]Prov 20:8 [B]Is 28:27 20:27 [a]Lit *breath* [b]Lit *chambers of the body* [A]1 Cor 2:11 20:28 [a]Lit *Covenant loyalty* [A]Prov 29:14 20:29 [a]Or *splendor* [A]Prov 16:31 20:30 [a]Lit *chambers of the body* [A]Ps 89:32; Prov 22:15; Is 53:5; 1 Pet 2:24 21:1 [A]Ezra 6:22 21:2 [A]Prov 16:2 [B]Prov 16:2; 24:12; Luke 16:15 21:3 [A]1 Sam 15:22; Prov 15:8; Is 1:11, 16, 17; Hos 6:6; Mic 6:7, 8 21:4 [A]Prov 24:20; Luke 11:34 21:5 [A]Prov 10:4; 13:4 [B]Prov 28:22

20:10 *See note on 11:1*; cf. 20:23.

20:12 Because God has given man the ability to hear and see, it should be obvious that He hears and sees everything (see Ps 94:9).

20:13 *See notes on 6:6, 11.*

20:14 The buyer purposely undervalues the thing he is negotiating to purchase in order to bring down the price. Afterward, he brags about his cleverness.

20:15 Wealth is a blessing when honestly gained, but wisdom is more desirable. *See notes on 3:14, 15; 8:10, 11, 18–21; 16:16.*

20:16 *See note on 6:1.* Garments were common security for a loan, but they always had to be returned by sundown (Ex 22:26, 27; Dt 24:10–13). Anyone who foolishly has taken on the responsibility for the debt of a stranger will likely never be paid back, so he will never pay his creditor unless his own garment is taken as security.

20:18 wise guidance. Cf. 11:14; 15:22; Lk 14:28–32.

20:19 slanderer. Those who love to spread secrets will flatter to learn them.

20:20 lamp will go out. Cf. 13:9. This grievous sin (cf. 30:11, 17; Ex 21:17; Lv 20:9) will result in death.

20:21 gained hurriedly. This implies an unjust method in gaining the inheritance, so that it will be lost by the same unjust ways or by punishment (cf. 13:11; 21:5, 6; 28:20, 22).

20:22 I will repay evil. God, not man, avenges evil (cf. Dt 32:35; Ro 12:17, 19; Heb 10:30) and delivers from the wicked.

20:23 Cf. v. 10; *see note on 11:1.*

20:24 *See notes on 16:1, 9, 33.* Since a man cannot comprehend the unfolding purposes of God's providence in his life, he has to walk in faith.

20:25 to say rashly. To declare something sacred, i.e., promising it to God in consecration as an offering, was irreversible and, therefore, serious. See Ecc 5:4–6; cf. Nu 30:2; Dt 23:21–23; Pss 50:14; 78:11.

20:26 *See note on v. 8.*

20:27 the lamp of the LORD. The "spirit" represents the conscience of man which searches every secret place. Cf. Ro 2:15; *see note on 2Co 1:12.*

20:28 Loyalty and truth. *See note on 3:3.*

20:30 Wise use of corporal punishment deters evil behavior. *See note on 10:13.*

21:1 He turns it. *See notes on 16:1, 9, 33*; cf. 19:21; 20:24. Note the examples of the divine hand of God in the cases of Artaxerxes (Ezr 7:21–23), Tiglath-pileser (Is 10:5–7), Cyrus (Is 45:1–4), and Nebuchadnezzar (Da 4:34) and Belshazzar (Da 5:23–25).

21:2 *See note on 16:2.*

21:3 *See note on 15:8* (cf. 1Sa 15:22; Is 1:10–20; Hos 6:6; Mic 6:6–8).

21:4 lamp of the wicked. Cf. 6:17; 30:13; Pss 18:27; 131:1. "Lamp" is used as a symbol for the eyes, which conveys their pride.

21:5–7 These verses address the evils of ill-gotten gain. They show 3 major defects in the way this gain is acquired: 1) hastily (v. 5; cf. 19:2; 28:20); 2) deceitfully (v. 6; cf. 13:11); and 3) violently (v. 7; cf. 12:6).

6 The [A]acquisition of treasures
by a lying tongue
Is a fleeting vapor, the [a]pursuit of [B]death.
7 The violence of the wicked
will drag them away,
Because they [A]refuse to act with justice.
8 The way of a guilty man is [A]crooked,
But as for the pure, his conduct is upright.
9 It is better to live in a corner of a roof
Than [a]in a house shared with
a contentious woman.
10 The soul of the wicked desires evil;
His [A]neighbor finds no favor in his eyes.
11 When the [A]scoffer is punished,
the [a]naive becomes wise;
But when the wise is instructed,
he receives knowledge.
12 The righteous one considers
the house of the wicked,
Turning the [A]wicked to ruin.
13 He who [A]shuts his ear to
the cry of the poor
Will also cry himself and not be [B]answered.
14 A [A]gift in secret subdues anger,
And a bribe in the bosom, strong wrath.
15 The exercise of justice is joy
for the righteous,
But is [A]terror to the workers of iniquity.
16 A man who wanders from the
way of understanding
Will [A]rest in the assembly of the [a]dead.
17 He who [A]loves pleasure *will
become* a poor man;
He who loves wine and oil
will not become rich.
18 The wicked is a [A]ransom for the righteous,
And the [B]treacherous is in the
place of the upright.
19 [A]It is better to live in a desert land
Than with a contentious
and vexing woman.
20 There is precious [A]treasure and oil
in the dwelling of the wise,
But a foolish man [B]swallows it up.
21 He who [A]pursues righteousness
and loyalty
Finds life, righteousness and honor.
22 A [A]wise man scales the
city of the mighty
And brings down the [a]stronghold
in which they trust.
23 He who [A]guards his mouth
and his tongue,
Guards his soul from troubles.
24 "Proud," "Haughty," "[A]Scoffer,"
are his names,
Who acts with [B]insolent pride.
25 The [A]desire of the sluggard
puts him to death,
For his hands refuse to work;
26 All day long he [a]is craving,
While the righteous [A]gives and
does not hold back.
27 The [A]sacrifice of the wicked
is an abomination,
How much more when he
brings it with evil intent!
28 A [A]false witness will perish,
But the man who listens *to the
truth* will speak forever.
29 A wicked man [a,A]displays
a bold face,
But as for the [B]upright, he
makes his way sure.
30 There is [A]no wisdom and
no understanding
And no counsel against the LORD.
31 The [A]horse is prepared for
the day of battle,
But [B]victory belongs to the LORD.

ON LIFE AND CONDUCT

22 A [A]*good* name is to be more
desired than great wealth,
Favor is better than silver and gold.
2 The rich and the poor [a]have
a common bond,
The LORD is the [A]maker of them all.

21:6 [a]Lit *seekers* [A]Prov 13:11; 20:21 [B]Prov 8:36 21:7 [A]Amos 5:7; Mic 3:9 21:8 [A]Prov 2:15 21:9 [a]Lit *with a woman of contentions and a house of association* 21:10 [A]Ps 52:3; Prov 2:14; 14:21 21:11 [a]Lit *simple* [A]Prov 19:25 21:12 [A]Prov 14:11 21:13 [A]Matt 18:30-34; 1 John 3:17 [B]James 2:13 21:14 [A]Prov 18:16; 19:6 21:15 [A]Prov 10:29 21:16 [a]Lit *departed spirits* [A]Ps 49:14 21:17 [A]Prov 23:21 21:18 [A]Is 43:3 [B]Prov 11:8 21:19 [A]Prov 21:9 21:20 [A]Ps 112:3; Prov 8:21; 22:4 [B]Job 20:15, 18 21:21 [A]Prov 15:9; Matt 5:6; 1 Cor 15:58 21:22 [a]Lit *strength of trust* [A]2 Sam 5:6-9; Prov 24:5; Eccl 7:19; 9:15, 16 21:23 [A]Prov 12:13; 13:3; 18:21; James 3:2 21:24 [A]Ps 1:1; Prov 1:22; 3:34; 24:9; Is 29:20 [B]Is 16:6; Jer 48:29 21:25 [A]Prov 13:4 21:26 [a]Lit *desires desire* [A]Ps 37:26; 112:5, 9; Matt 5:42; Eph 4:28 21:27 [A]Prov 15:8; Is 66:3; Jer 6:20; Amos 5:22 21:28 [A]Prov 19:5, 9 21:29 [a]Lit *makes firm with his face* [A]Eccl 8:1 [B]Ps 119:5; Prov 11:5 21:30 [A]Jer 9:23; Acts 5:38, 39; 1 Cor 3:19, 20 21:31 [A]Ps 20:7; 33:17; Is 31:1 [B]Ps 3:8; Jer 3:23; 1 Cor 15:57 22:1 [A]Prov 10:7; Eccl 7:1 22:2 [a]Lit *meet together* [A]Job 31:15; Prov 14:31

21:7 Cf. 1:18, 19.

21:9 corner of a roof. Since roofs were open like patios (cf. Dt 22:8; 1Sa 9:25; 2Ki 4:10), a small arbor or enclosure in the corner of a flat roof was a very inconvenient place to live. **contentious woman.** Cf. v. 19; 19:13; 25:24; 27:15, 16; *see note on 19:13.*

21:10 wicked desires evil. So strongly does he seek to do evil (cf. Ecc 8:11) that he will not even spare his neighbor if he gets in his way.

21:11 *See note on 19:25.*

21:12 *See note on 20:22;* cf. 10:25; 14:11.

21:13 poor. *See note on 14:31.*

21:14 Cf. 17:8; 18:16; 19:6.

21:16 This is proven in the account of the simple man who was seduced (2:18; 7:22, 23; 9:18).

21:17 wine and oil. These are associated with unbridled luxury in feasting (Dt 14:26; Ne 8:12; Ps 104:15; Am 6:6; Jn 12:5). Costly indulgences impoverish.

21:18 By suffering the very thing they had devised for the righteous, or brought on them, the wicked became their ransom, in the sense of being a substitute in judgment.

21:19 *See note on 19:13.*

21:21 Those who pursue "righteousness" and "loyalty" receive more than they seek (see Mt 5:6, 7; 6:33).

21:22 Cf. 24:5. Wisdom is better than strength (cf. Ecc 7:19; 9:15).

21:26 The sin of covetousness marks the lazy man as the virtue of benevolence marks the righteous.

21:27 *See note on 15:8;* cf. v. 3; Is 1:13–15.

21:28 false witness. *See note on 12:17.*

21:29 The wicked become obstinate, maintaining what suits them without regard for others or the truth, while good people proceed with integrity.

21:31 prepared ... victory. This is not a condemnation of adequate preparation but rather of reliance on it for victory, instead of on the Lord (cf. Ezr 8:22; Ps 20:7; Is 31:1–3; Hos 1:7).

3 The [A]prudent sees the evil
and hides himself,
But the [a]naive go on, and
are punished for it.
4 The reward of humility *and*
the [a]fear of the LORD
Are riches, honor and life.
5 [A]Thorns *and* snares are in the
way of the perverse;
He who guards himself will
be far from them.
6 [A]Train up a child [a]in the way he should go,
Even when he is old he will
not depart from it.
7 The [A]rich rules over the poor,
And the borrower *becomes*
the lender's slave.
8 He who [A]sows iniquity will reap vanity,
And the [B]rod of his fury will perish.
9 He who [a]is [A]generous will be blessed,
For he [B]gives some of his food to the poor.
10 [A]Drive out the scoffer, and
contention will go out,
Even strife and dishonor will cease.
11 He who loves [A]purity of heart
And [a]whose speech is [B]gracious,
the king is his friend.
12 The eyes of the LORD
preserve knowledge,
But He overthrows the words
of the treacherous man.
13 The [A]sluggard says, "There
is a lion outside;
I will be killed in the streets!"
14 The mouth of [a,A]an adulteress
is a deep pit;
He who is [B]cursed of the
LORD will fall [b]into it.
15 Foolishness is bound up in
the heart of a child;
The [A]rod of discipline will
remove it far from him.
16 He [A]who oppresses the poor to
make [a]more for himself
Or who gives to the rich, [B]*will*
only *come to* poverty.

17 [A]Incline your ear and hear the
words of the wise,
And apply your mind to my knowledge;
18 For it will be [A]pleasant if you
keep them within you,
[a]That they may be ready on your lips.
19 So that your [A]trust may be in the LORD,
I have [a]taught you today, even you.
20 Have I not written to you [a,A]excellent things
Of counsels and knowledge,
21 To make you [A]know the [a]certainty
of the words of truth
That you may [b,B]correctly answer
him who sent you?

22 [A]Do not rob the poor because he is poor,
Or [B]crush the afflicted at the gate;
23 For the LORD will [A]plead their case
And [a]take the life of those who rob them.

24 Do not associate with a man *given* to anger;
Or go with a [A]hot-tempered man,
25 Or you will [A]learn his ways
And [a]find a snare for yourself.

26 Do not be among those who
[A]give [a]pledges,
Among those who become
guarantors for debts.

22:3 [a]Lit *simple* [A]Prov 14:16; 27:12; Is 26:20 22:4 [a]Or *reverence* 22:5 [A]Prov 15:19 22:6 [a]Lit *according to his way* [A]Eph 6:4 22:7 [A]Prov 18:23; James 2:6 22:8 [A]Job 4:8 [B]Ps 125:3 22:9 [a]Lit *has a good eye* [A]Prov 19:17; 2 Cor 9:6 [B]Luke 14:13 22:10 [A]Gen 21:9, 10; Prov 18:6; 26:20 22:11 [a]Lit *has grace on his lips* [A]Ps 24:4; Matt 5:8 [B]Prov 14:35; 16:13 22:13 [A]Prov 26:13 22:14 [a]Lit *strange woman* [b]Lit *there* [A]Prov 2:16; 5:3; 7:5; 23:27 [B]Eccl 7:26 22:15 [A]Prov 13:24; 23:14 22:16 [a]Lit *much* [A]Eccl 5:8; James 2:13 [B]Prov 28:22 22:17 [A]Prov 5:1 22:18 [a]Lit *They together* [A]Prov 2:10 22:19 [a]Lit *made you know* [A]Prov 3:5 22:20 [a]Or *previous* [A]Prov 8:6 22:21 [a]Lit *truth* [b]Lit *return to words of truth* [A]Luke 1:3, 4 [B]Prov 25:13; 1 Pet 3:15 22:22 [A]Ex 23:6; Job 31:16; Prov 22:16 [B]Zech 7:10; Mal 3:5 22:23 [a]Lit *rob the soul* [A]1 Sam 25:39; Ps 12:5; 35:10; 140:12; Prov 23:11; Jer 51:36 22:24 [A]Prov 29:22 22:25 [a]Lit *take* [A]1 Cor 15:33 22:26 [a]Lit *strike hands* [A]Prov 17:18

22:3 Wise people see the approach of sin and remove themselves from it, while naive people walk right into it and suffer the consequences.

22:4 fear of the LORD. *See note on 1:7.*

22:6 way he should go. There is only one right way, God's way, the way of life. That way is specified in great detail in Proverbs. Since it is axiomatic that early training secures lifelong habits, parents must insist upon this way, teaching God's Word and enforcing it with loving discipline consistently throughout the child's upbringing. *See note on 13:24.* Cf. Dt 4:9; 6:6–8; 11:18–21; Jos 24:15; Eph 6:4.

22:7 rich rules. While this is naturally true, the Law and Prophets condemned those who were oppressive (cf. 22:22, 23; Dt 24:14–18; Is 5:8; Jer 34:13, 17; Mic 2:2).

22:8, 9 generous. The principle of sowing and reaping is emphasized. Cf. Job 4:8; Hos 8:7; 10:13; 2Co 9:6; Gal 6:7–9.

22:11 Even the most powerful are drawn to the wise (cf. Ecc 10:12).

22:12 The eyes of the LORD. *See note on 15:3.* God's sovereign omniscience protects the principles and possessors of divine knowledge.

22:13 a lion outside. Cf. 26:13. The lazy give lame excuses for not leaving the house to work. *See notes on 6:6, 11.*

22:14 The flattering seductions of such a woman lure men into a pit as God makes their sin its own punishment. *See note on 2:16*; cf. 5:3; 7:5.

22:15 *See note on 13:24.*

22:16 These two vices reflect the same selfish attitude: withholding from the poor to keep what one has, and giving to the rich to induce them to give one more. Both are unacceptable to God and incur punishment.

22:17–24:34 Solomon did not author, but did compile, this collection containing 77 proverbs which were most likely spoken by godly men prior to Solomon's reign. The section begins with an introduction (22:17–21), followed by a collection of proverbs in random order, one, two, or three verses each (as opposed to the one verse, two line proverbs in the previous section). This is followed by two collections of additional proverbs (22:22–24:22 and 24:23–34), which continue and enlarge upon the wisdom themes of this book.

22:17–21 This introductory section offers an exhortation, reminiscent of 2:1–5; 5:1, 2, to be alert to hear and speak the wisdom of God.

22:20 excellent things. This term is lit. "chief proverbs" (cf. 8:6).

22:21 certainty. Solomon is especially concerned about accuracy so that his reader can teach others.

22:22–24:22 The first collection of words for wise men is recorded.

22:22, 23 *See note on 14:31.*

22:22 gate. Beggars typically sat at the gate because of the large number of people passing by. The gate was also the place for civic and legal issues to be settled (cf. 31:23). The "afflicted" were there begging or seeking justice or mercy and were to be fairly treated.

22:24, 25 Cf. 12:26.

22:26, 27 *See note on 6:1.*

27 If you have nothing with which to pay,
Why should he [A]take your
bed from under you?

28 [A]Do not move the ancient boundary
Which your fathers have set.

29 Do you see a man skilled in his work?
He will [A]stand before kings;
He will not stand before obscure men.

ON LIFE AND CONDUCT

23 When you sit down to dine with a ruler,
Consider carefully [a]what is before you,
2 And put a knife to your throat
If you are a [A]man of *great* appetite.
3 Do not [A]desire his delicacies,
For it is deceptive food.

4 [A]Do not weary yourself to gain wealth,
[B]Cease from your [a]consideration *of it.*
5 [a]When you set your eyes on it, it is gone.
For [A]*wealth* certainly makes itself wings
Like an eagle that flies
toward the heavens.

6 [A]Do not eat the bread of [a]a [B]selfish man,
Or desire his delicacies;
7 For as he [a]thinks within himself, so he is.
He says to you, "Eat and drink!"
But [A]his heart is not with you.
8 You will [A]vomit up [a]the morsel
you have eaten,
And waste your [b]compliments.

9 [A]Do not speak in the [a]hearing of a fool,
For he will [B]despise the
wisdom of your words.

10 Do not move the ancient boundary
Or [A]go into the fields of the fatherless,
11 For their [A]Redeemer is strong;
[B]He will plead their case against you.
12 Apply your heart to discipline
And your ears to words of knowledge.

13 [A]Do not hold back discipline
from the child,
Although you [a]strike him with
the rod, he will not die.
14 You shall [a]strike him with the rod
And [A]rescue his soul from Sheol.

15 My son, if your heart is [A]wise,
My own heart also will be glad;
16 And my [a]inmost being will rejoice
When your lips speak [A]what is right.

17 [A]Do not let your heart envy sinners,
But *live* in the [a,B]fear of the LORD [b]always.
18 Surely there is a [a,A]future,
And your [B]hope will not be cut off.
19 Listen, my son, and [A]be wise,
And [B]direct your heart in the way.
20 Do not be with [A]heavy drinkers of wine,
Or with [B]gluttonous eaters of meat;
21 For the [A]heavy drinker and the
glutton will come to poverty,
And [B]drowsiness will clothe
one with rags.

22 [A]Listen to your father who begot you,
And [B]do not despise your
mother when she is old.
23 [A]Buy truth, and do not sell *it,*
Get wisdom and instruction
and understanding.

22:27 [A]Ex 22:26; Prov 20:16 22:28 [A]Deut 19:14; 27:17; Job 24:2; Prov 23:10 22:29 [A]Gen 41:46; 1 Kin 10:8 23:1 [a]Or *who* 23:2 [A]Prov 23:20 23:3 [A]Ps 141:4; Prov 23:6; Dan 1:5, 8, 13, 15, 16 23:4 [a]Or *understanding* [A]Prov 15:27; 28:20; Matt 6:19; 1 Tim 6:9; Heb 13:5 [B]Prov 3:5, 7 23:5 [a]Lit *Will your eyes fly upon it and it is not?* [A]Prov 27:24; 1 Tim 6:17 23:6 [a]Lit *an evil eye* [A]Ps 141:4 [B]Deut 15:9; Prov 28:22 23:7 [a]Lit *reckons in his soul* [A]Prov 26:24, 25 23:8 [a]Lit *your* [b]Lit *pleasant words* [A]Prov 25:16 23:9 [a]Lit *ears* [A]Matt 7:6 [B]Prov 1:7 23:10 [A]Jer 22:3; Zech 7:10 23:11 [A]Job 19:25; Jer 50:34 [B]Prov 22:23 23:13 [a]Lit *smite* [A]Prov 13:24; 19:18 23:14 [a]Lit *smite* [A]1 Cor 5:5 23:15 [A]Prov 23:24f; 27:11; 29:3 23:16 [a]Lit *kidneys* [A]Prov 8:6 23:17 [a]Or *reverence* [b]Lit *all the day* [A]Ps 37:1; Prov 24:1, 19 [B]Prov 28:14 23:18 [a]Lit *latter end* [A]Ps 19:11; 58:11; Prov 24:14 [B]Ps 9:18 23:19 [A]Prov 6:6 [B]Prov 4:23; 9:6 23:20 [A]Prov 20:1; 23:29, 30; Is 5:22; Matt 24:49; Luke 21:34; Rom 13:13; Eph 5:18 [B]Deut 21:20; Prov 28:7 23:21 [A]Prov 21:17 [B]Prov 6:10, 11 23:22 [A]Prov 1:8; Eph 6:1 [B]Prov 15:20; 30:17 23:23 [A]Prov 4:7; 18:15; Matt 13:44

22:28 boundary. This refers to stealing land by moving the boundaries. *See note on 15:25;* cf. Lv 25:23; Dt 19:14.

23:1–3 Here is a warning to exercise restraint when confronted with the luxuries of a wealthy ruler who seeks to lure you into his schemes and intrigues. Daniel is the classic illustration of one who lived by this proverb, refusing the allurements of the pagan monarch, which he knew could corrupt him (see Da 1:8ff.).

23:4, 5 Cf. 11:28; 28:22; 1Ti 6:9, 10, 17. Rather than wearing one's self out pursuing wealth, pursue the wisdom of God and what glorifies Him, and He will bless with prosperity as He chooses. See 2:1–11; 3:5–10.

23:6–8 selfish man. This is the greedy one who, to be rich, hoards his riches, withholding from the poor and needy to keep and increase his own wealth. He invites someone to enjoy his courtesies, feigning generosity, while really being sickeningly hypocritical, as his real goal is to take advantage in some way so as to increase his wealth at his guest's expense. Cf. 26:24–26.

23:9 This is true because fools hate wisdom (cf. 1:22; 9:8; 12:1).

23:10, 11 ancient boundary. *See note on 15:25;* cf. 22:22, 23.

23:11 Redeemer. In a normal situation the near kinsman would rescue the one who had fallen upon hard times (cf. Lv 25:25; Ru 2:20; 3:12, 13; 4:1–12) or avenge in the case of a murder (Nu 35:19). "Redeemer" is applied to God as the Savior of His people (e.g., Ge 48:16; Ex 6:6; Job 19:25; Ps 19:14; Is 41:14; 43:14; 44:24) since the helpless had no voice.

23:13, 14 discipline. *See notes on 13:24; 22:6.* The child will survive the punishment and thus avoid an untimely or premature death due to sinful conduct (cf. Dt 21:18–21).

23:14 Sheol. *See note on 1:12.*

23:15, 16 son ... wise. The result of discipline (vv. 13, 14) is the child's wise choices, bringing the parents joy (cf. vv. 24, 25; 10:1; 15:20; 17:21; 28:7; 29:3).

23:16 inmost being. Lit. "the kidney," which, along with the heart (cf. 3:5; 4:21–23), are figurative expressions for the inner man or the seat of one's thoughts and feelings.

23:17 fear of the LORD. *See note on 1:7.*

23:18 there is a future. Cf. v. 24. Anyone who might envy sinners needs to know that their prosperity is brief. They will die ("be cut off"); then there will be a time when all iniquities will be dealt with and divine justice will prevail (cf. Ps 37:28–38). The righteous will live forever (*see note on 14:32*).

23:19 the way. The way of wisdom is the only right way (4:10, 11).

23:20 heavy drinkers of wine. Cf. vv. 29–35; Dt 21:20.

23:22 Cf. 1:8; 2:1; 3:1; 4:1; 5:1; Eph 6:1.

23:23 Buy truth. Obtain the truth at all costs. Cf. 4:5–7; Mt 13:44–46. Then never relinquish it at any price (see Da 1:8ff.).

24 The father of the righteous
will greatly rejoice,
And [A]he who sires a wise son
will be glad in him.
25 Let your [A]father and your mother be glad,
And let her rejoice who
gave birth to you.

26 [A]Give me your heart, my son,
And let your eyes [a,B]delight in my ways.
27 For a harlot is a [A]deep pit
And an [a,B]adulterous woman
is a narrow well.
28 Surely she [A]lurks as a robber,
And increases the [a]faithless among men.

29 Who has [A]woe? Who has sorrow?
Who has contentions? Who
has complaining?
Who has wounds without cause?
Who has redness of eyes?
30 Those who [A]linger long over wine,
Those who go to [a]taste [B]mixed wine.
31 Do not look on the wine when it is red,
When it [a]sparkles in the cup,
When it [A]goes down smoothly;
32 At the last it [A]bites like a serpent
And stings like a [B]viper.
33 Your eyes will see strange things
And your [a]mind will [A]utter
perverse things.
34 And you will be like one who lies
down in the [a]middle of the sea,
Or like one who lies down on
the top of a [b]mast.
35 "They [A]struck me, *but* I did
not become [a]ill;
They beat me, *but* I did not know *it*.
When shall I awake?
I will [B]seek [b]another drink."

PRECEPTS AND WARNINGS

24 Do not be [A]envious of evil men,
Nor desire to [B]be with them;
2 For their [a]minds devise [A]violence,
And their lips [B]talk of trouble.

3 [A]By wisdom a house is built,
And by understanding it is established;
4 And by knowledge the rooms are [A]filled
With all precious and pleasant riches.

5 A [A]wise man is [a]strong,
And a man of knowledge
[b]increases power.
6 For [A]by wise guidance you will [a]wage war,
And [B]in abundance of counselors
there is victory.

7 Wisdom is [A]*too* exalted for a fool,
He does not open his mouth [B]in the gate.

8 One who [A]plans to do evil,
Men will call a [a]schemer.
9 The [A]devising of folly is sin,
And the scoffer is an abomination to men.

10 If you [A]are slack in the day of distress,
Your strength is limited.

11 [A]Deliver those who are being
taken away to death,
And those who are staggering to
slaughter, Oh hold *them* back.
12 If you say, "See, we did not know this,"
Does He not [A]consider *it* [B]who
weighs the hearts?
And [C]does He not know *it*
who [D]keeps your soul?
And will He not [a,E]render to man
according to his work?

23:24 [A]Prov 10:1; 15:20; 29:3 23:25 [A]Prov 27:11 23:26 [a]Another reading is *observe* [A]Prov 3:1; 4:4 [B]Ps 1:2; 119:24 23:27 [a]Lit *strange* [A]Prov 22:14 [B]Prov 5:20 23:28 [a]Lit *treacherous* [A]Prov 6:26; 7:12; Eccl 7:26 23:29 [A]Is 5:11, 22 23:30 [a]Or *search out* [A]1 Sam 25:36; Prov 20:1; Is 5:11; 28:7; Eph 5:18 [B]Ps 75:8 23:31 [a]Lit *gives its eye* [A]Song 7:9 23:32 [A]Job 20:16; Prov 20:1; Eph 5:18 [B]Ps 91:13; Is 11:8 23:33 [a]Lit *heart* [A]Prov 2:12 23:34 [a]Lit *heart* [b]Or *lookout* 23:35 [a]I.e. from the effect of wounds [b]Lit *it yet again* [A]Prov 27:22; Jer 5:3 [B]Prov 26:11; Is 56:12 24:1 [A]Ps 37:1; Prov 3:31; 23:17; 24:19 [B]Ps 1:1; Prov 1:15 24:2 [a]Lit *hearts* [A]Is 30:12; Jer 22:17 [B]Job 15:35; Ps 10:7; 38:12 24:3 [A]Prov 9:1; 14:1 24:4 [A]Prov 8:21 24:5 [a]Lit *in strength* [b]Lit *strengthens power* [A]Prov 21:22 24:6 [a]Lit *make battle for yourself* [A]Prov 20:18 [B]Prov 11:14 24:7 [A]Ps 10:5; Prov 14:6; 17:16 [B]Job 5:4; Ps 127:5 24:8 [a]Or *deviser of evil* [A]Prov 6:14; 14:22; Rom 1:30 24:9 [A]Matt 15:19; Acts 8:22 24:10 [A]Deut 20:8; Job 4:5; Jer 51:46; Heb 12:3 24:11 [A]Ps 82:4; Is 58:6, 7 24:12 [a]Lit *bring back* [A]Eccl 5:8 [B]1 Sam 16:7; Prov 21:2 [C]Ps 94:9-11 [D]Ps 121:3-8 [E]Job 34:11; Prov 12:14

23:24, 25 *See notes on vv. 15, 16; 13:24.*

23:27, 28 harlot . . . adulterous woman. Cf. 22:14. The terms refer to any immoral woman. *See notes on 2:16; 5:3–5; 7:6–27; 9:13–18.* Falling into her clutches should be as frightening as the prospect of falling into a deep pit or well, from which there is no escape.

23:29–35 This passage offers a powerful warning against drunkenness, presented as a riddle (v. 29) with its answer (v. 30). Following the riddle, come exhortations (vv. 31, 32) and descriptions of the drunkard's delirious thoughts (vv. 33, 35).

23:30 mixed wine. *See note on 20:1.* Lingering long at the wine is indicative of constant drinking, so as to induce drunkenness (cf. 1Ti 3:3; Titus 1:7). Searching for more to drink indicates the same pursuit.

23:31 wine when it is red. This describes wine when it is especially desirable and when it is most intoxicating, perhaps as "strong drink" or mixed with spices only and not water, as opposed to the "new wine" (3:10), which was fresh and unfermented or less fermented (cf. Hos 4:11).

23:32 bites . . . stings. This recounts the hangover, but also the more than likely destructive consequences (cf. Is 59:5; Jer 8:17).

23:33 The delirium and distortion of reality are part of the drunkard's miserable experience (*see note on 1Co 6:12*).

23:34 Here is the warning about the dizziness, sickness, and confusion of the drunkard, like being seasick at the top of the mast, the most agitated point on a ship in strong seas.

23:35 The drunkard's lack of sense is so severe that his first waking thought is to repeat his debauchery and dangerous sin.

24:1, 2 Cf. 23:3, 17.

24:3, 4 house is built. House can refer to a physical structure (cf. 14:1), a family (see Jos 24:15), or even a dynasty (see 2Sa 7:11, 12; 1Ki 11:38; 1Ch 17:10).

24:5, 6 Wisdom and wise counsel are associated with strength. *See notes on 11:14; 13:20*; cf. Ecc 9:16–18.

24:7 the gate. *See note on 22:22.* Since the leading minds were there debating the issues of life, it was no place for fools.

24:11 The danger here may be from unjust treatment or violence. Deliverance can either be by giving a true testimony on their behalf, by providing what they need to survive, or by rescuing them from a fatal course.

24:12 who weighs the hearts. *See note on 16:2.* God is the One who knows the truth about the motives of the heart and the excuses for failing to do what is right (cf. Jas 4:17). **render to man according to his work.** Cf. v. 29; Job 34:11; Jer 25:14; 50:29.

13 My son, eat [A]honey, for it is good,
Yes, the [B]honey from the comb
is sweet to your taste;
14 Know *that* [A]wisdom is thus for your soul;
If you find *it,* then there will be a [a,B]future,
And your hope will not be cut off.

15 [A]Do not lie in wait, O wicked man, against
the dwelling of the righteous;
Do not destroy his resting place;
16 For a [A]righteous man falls seven
times, and rises again,
But the [B]wicked stumble in
time of calamity.

17 [A]Do not rejoice when your enemy falls,
And do not let your heart be
glad when he stumbles;
18 Or the LORD will see *it*
and [a]be displeased,
And turn His anger away from him.

19 [A]Do not fret because of evildoers
Or be [B]envious of the wicked;
20 For [A]there will be no [a,B]future
for the evil man;
The [C]lamp of the wicked will be put out.

21 My son, [a,A]fear the LORD and the king;
Do not associate with those
who are given to change,
22 For their [A]calamity will rise suddenly,
And who knows the ruin *that*
comes from both of them?

23 These also are [A]sayings of the wise.
To [a,B]show partiality in
judgment is not good.
24 He [A]who says to the wicked,
"You are righteous,"
[B]Peoples will curse him, nations
will abhor him;
25 But [A]to those who rebuke the
wicked will be delight,
And a good blessing will
come upon them.
26 He kisses the lips
Who gives [a]a right answer.

27 Prepare your work outside
And [A]make it ready for
yourself in the field;
Afterwards, then, build your house.

28 Do not be a [A]witness against your
neighbor without cause,
And [B]do not deceive with your lips.
29 [A]Do not say, "Thus I shall do to
him as he has done to me;
I will [a]render to the man
according to his work."

30 I passed by the field of the sluggard
And by the vineyard of the
man [A]lacking [a]sense,
31 And behold, it was completely
[A]overgrown with thistles;
Its surface was covered with [a,B]nettles,
And its stone [C]wall was broken down.
32 When I saw, I [a]reflected upon it;
I looked, *and* received instruction.
33 "[A]A little sleep, a little slumber,
A little folding of the hands to rest,"
34 Then your poverty will come *as* [a]a robber
And your want like [b]an armed man.

SIMILITUDES, INSTRUCTIONS

25 These also are [A]proverbs of Solomon which the men of Hezekiah, king of Judah, transcribed.

24:13 [A]Ps 19:10; 119:103; Prov 25:16; Song 5:1 [B]Prov 16:24; 27:7; Song 4:11 24:14 [a]Lit *latter end* [A]Prov 2:10 [B]Prov 23:18 24:15 [A]Ps 10:9, 10 24:16 [A]Job 5:19; Ps 37:24; Mic 7:8 [B]Prov 6:15; 14:32; 24:22; Jer 18:17 24:17 [A]Job 31:29; Ps 35:15, 19; Prov 17:5; Obad 12 24:18 [a]Lit *it is evil in His eyes* 24:19 [A]Ps 37:1 [B]Prov 23:17; 24:1 24:20 [a]Lit *latter end* [A]Job 15:31 [B]Prov 23:18 [C]Job 18:5, 6; 21:17; Prov 13:9; 20:20 24:21 [a]Or *reverence* [A]Rom 13:1-7; 1 Pet 2:17 24:22 [A]Prov 24:16 24:23 [a]Lit *regard the face* [A]Prov 1:6; 22:17 [B]Prov 18:5; 28:21 24:24 [A]Prov 17:15; Is 5:23 [B]Prov 11:26 24:25 [A]Prov 28:23 24:26 [a]Or *an honest* 24:27 [A]Prov 27:23-27 24:28 [A]Prov 25:18 [B]Lev 6:2, 3; 19:11; Eph 4:25 24:29 [a]Lit *bring back* [A]Prov 20:22; Matt 5:39; Rom 12:17 24:30 [a]Lit *heart* [A]Prov 6:32 24:31 [a]I.e. a kind of weed [A]Gen 3:18 [B]Job 30:7 [C]Is 5:5 24:32 [a]Lit *set my heart* 24:33 [A]Prov 6:10 24:34 [a]Or *a vagabond;* lit *one who walks* [b]Lit *a man with a shield* 25:1 [A]Prov 1:1

24:13, 14 This is not a command to eat honey, but an analogy to seek the sweetness of wisdom's rewards. Cf. Ps 19:10.

24:14 hope … cut off. *See note on 23:18.*

24:15, 16 seven times. This stands for "often" or "many" (see 26:16; Job 5:19). The plots of the wicked against the righteous, though partially and temporarily successful, shall not be ultimately successful; while the wicked will fall under God's eternal judgment and find no help or deliverance.

24:17, 18 when your enemy falls. *See note on 25:21, 22.* Gloating over a fallen enemy can be more serious than the sin the enemy committed.

24:19 Do not fret. Do not become angrily excited or envious at the apparent prosperity of the wicked. Cf. 3:31; 23:17, 18; 24:1.

24:20 lamp of the wicked. *See note on 13:9.*

24:21 fear the LORD. *See note on 1:7.* **the king.** Loyalty to the king is proper because he is the agent of the Lord's wisdom (cf. Dt 17:14–20; Ro 13:1–7). That loyalty includes having no part with rebels who seek to subvert or overthrow him ("change"). Peter draws on this verse in his call to good citizenship in 1Pe 1:17; 2:17.

24:22 the ruin *that comes* from both. A reference to the retributive power of the king and the Lord (cf. Job 31:23).

24:23a These words introduce a brief section forming an appendix of further wise sayings (vv. 23b–34) that finish the first group of proverbs compiled by Solomon to add to his own. *See note on 22:17–24:34.*

24:23b–25 partiality in judgment. Injustice is evil and destabilizes society. *See note on 17:15.*

24:26 kisses the lips. A just and righteous response is as desirable as this most intimate expression of friendship.

24:27 First, secure by diligent work and planning a good living in your fields, then build. In other words, provide a financial base so that all the necessities and contingencies are secured, then move from the tents (which were acceptable) to a house (which was desirable).

24:28, 29 Avenging the evil done by one's neighbor by offering false witness (cf. 14:5; 19:5) against him is forbidden. *See notes on 6:16–19; 20:22.*

24:30–34 *See notes on 6:6, 11.* Thorns also appear in his life in 15:19 (*see note there*).

25:1–29:27 Hezekiah's collection of Solomon's proverbs.

25:1 men of Hezekiah … transcribed. This collection of 137 proverbs was spoken by Solomon and most likely copied into a collection during the reign of Judah's king, Hezekiah (ca. 715–686 B.C.) over 200 years later. See Introduction: Author and Date. This is consistent

2 It is the glory of God to [A]conceal a matter,
But the glory of [B]kings is to
search out a matter.
3 *As* the heavens for height and
the earth for depth,
So the heart of kings is unsearchable.
4 Take away the [A]dross from the silver,
And there comes out a vessel
for the [B]smith;
5 Take away the [A]wicked before the king,
And his [B]throne will be established
in righteousness.
6 Do not claim honor in the
presence of the king,
And do not stand in the place of great men;
7 For [A]it is better that it be said
to you, "Come up here,"
Than for you to be placed lower in
the presence of the prince,
Whom your eyes have seen.

8 Do not go out [A]hastily to [a]argue *your case;*
[b]Otherwise, what will you do in [c]the end,
When your neighbor humiliates you?
9 [a,A]Argue your case with your neighbor,
And [B]do not reveal the secret of another,
10 Or he who hears *it* will reproach you,
And the evil report about you
will not [a]pass away.

11 *Like* apples of gold in settings of silver
Is a [A]word spoken in [a]right circumstances.
12 *Like* [a]an [A]earring of gold and an
[B]ornament of [C]fine gold
Is a wise reprover to a [D]listening ear.
13 Like the cold of snow in the
[a]time of harvest
Is a [A]faithful messenger to
those who send him,
For he refreshes the soul of his masters.
14 *Like* [A]clouds and [B]wind without rain
Is a man who boasts [a]of
his gifts falsely.
15 By [a,A]forbearance a ruler
may be persuaded,
And a soft tongue breaks the bone.
16 Have you [A]found honey? Eat
only [a]what you need,
That you not have it in
excess and vomit it.
17 Let your foot rarely be in your
neighbor's house,
Or he will become [a]weary of
you and hate you.
18 *Like* a club and a [A]sword
and a sharp [B]arrow
Is a man who bears [C]false witness
against his neighbor.
19 *Like* a bad tooth and [a]an unsteady foot
Is confidence in a [A]faithless
man in time of trouble.
20 *Like* one who takes off a garment on a
cold day, *or like* vinegar on [a]soda,
Is he who sings songs to
[b]a troubled heart.
21 [A]If [a]your enemy is hungry,
give him food to eat;
And if he is thirsty, give him
water to drink;
22 For you will [a]heap burning
coals on his head,
And [A]the LORD will reward you.
23 The north wind brings forth rain,
And a [a,A]backbiting tongue, an
angry countenance.
24 It is [A]better to live in a corner of the roof
Than [a]in a house shared with
a contentious woman.
25 *Like* cold water to a weary soul,
So is [A]good news from a distant land.

25:2 [A]Deut 29:29; Rom 11:33 [B]Ezra 6:1 25:4 [A]Prov 26:23; Ezek 22:18 [B]Mal 3:2, 3 25:5 [A]Prov 20:8 [B]Prov 16:12 25:7 [A]Luke 14:7-11 25:8 [a]Lit *contend* [b]Lit *Lest* [c]Lit *its* [A]Prov 17:14; Matt 5:25 25:9 [a]Lit *Contend* [A]Matt 18:15 [B]Prov 11:13 25:10 [a]Lit *return* 25:11 [a]Lit *its* [A]Prov 15:23 25:12 [a]Or *a nose ring* [A]Ex 32:2; 35:22; Ezek 16:12 [B]2 Sam 1:24 [C]Job 28:17 [D]Prov 15:31; 20:12 25:13 [a]Lit *day* [A]Prov 13:17 25:14 [a]Lit *in a gift of falsehood* [A]Jude 12 [B]Jer 5:13; Mic 2:11 25:15 [a]Lit *length of anger* [A]Gen 32:4; 1 Sam 25:24; Eccl 10:4 25:16 [a]Lit *your sufficiency* [A]Judg 14:8; 1 Sam 14:25 25:17 [a]Lit *surfeited with* 25:18 [A]Ps 57:4; Prov 12:18 [B]Jer 9:8 [C]Ex 20:16; Prov 24:28 25:19 [a]Lit *a slipping foot* [A]Job 6:15; Is 36:6 25:20 [a]I.e. natron [b]Lit *an evil* 25:21 [a]Lit *one who hates you* [A]Ex 23:4, 5; 2 Kin 6:22; 2 Chr 28:15; Matt 5:44; Rom 12:20 25:22 [a]Lit *snatch up* [A]2 Sam 16:12; Matt 6:4, 6 25:23 [a]Lit *tongue of secrecy* [A]Ps 101:5 25:24 [a]Lit *with a woman of contentions and a house of association* [A]Prov 21:9 25:25 [A]Prov 15:30

with Hezekiah's efforts to bring revival to Judah (2Ch 29:30; 32:26), as he elevated the forgotten wisdom of David and Solomon (cf. 2Ch 29:31; 30:26).

25:2, 3 God ... kings. The roles of God and the king are compared. God, whose knowledge is above all human knowledge (cf. Ps 92:5; Ecc 3:11; Is 46:10; Ac 15:18; Heb 4:13), and whose ways are unsearchable (cf. Job 5:9; Ps 145:3; Is 40:28), keeps things to Himself because He needs no counsel (see Ro 11:34). On the contrary, kings should rightly seek to know what they must know in order to rule righteously.

25:4, 5 A nation is established as wisdom replaces and purifies wickedness (cf. 14:34; 16:12).

25:6, 7 In the royal court as in all of life, self-seeking and pride bring a person down. Do not intrude into such a place, for the elevating of the humble is honorable, but the humbling of the proud is disgraceful (cf. Lk 14:8–10; Jas 4:7–10).

25:8–10 go out hastily to argue. When conflict arises, the man with a contentious spirit is quick to go to court, but he is better off to talk it over with his neighbor than to expose himself to public shame in court, where everything will be told.

25:11, 12 The imagery of beauty describes well chosen words, including words of rebuke. Cf. 15:23; 24:26.

25:13 cold of snow. A faithful messenger (cf. v. 25; 26:6) was as refreshing as snow would be in the heat of the summer harvest.

25:15 forbearance. Patience is a mighty weapon. See 15:1; 16:32.

25:16 This may be a parable that goes with v. 17, instructing the wise not to overdo anything that may lead to disgust and rejection, including overstaying or being overbearing with a friend who may begin to resent him.

25:18 He is as destructive to reputation as those weapons are to the body.

25:20 vinegar on soda. Pouring vinegar on an alkali (e.g., baking soda) produces a reaction like boiling or turning tranquility into agitation. So is the effect of singing joyful songs without sympathy to the sorrowful. Cf. Ps 137:3, 4.

25:21, 22 As metals are melted by placing fiery coals on them, so is the heart of an enemy softened by such kindness. Contrast the coals of judgment in Ps 140:10. Paul quotes this proverb in Ro 12:20. Cf. Mt 5:43–48.

25:23 The theme is cause and effect; as surely as a rain cloud brings the rain, slander, or "a backbiting tongue," produces anger.

25:24 *See notes on 19:13; 21:9.*

25:25 *See note on v. 13.*

26 *Like* a [A]trampled spring and a [a]polluted well
Is a righteous man who gives
way before the wicked.
27 It is not good to eat much honey,
Nor is it glory to [A]search out
[a]one's own glory.
28 *Like* a [A]city that is broken into
and without walls
Is a man [B]who has no control over his spirit.

SIMILITUDES, INSTRUCTIONS

26 Like snow in summer and
like [A]rain in harvest,
So honor is not [B]fitting for a fool.
2 Like a [A]sparrow in *its* [a]flitting,
like a swallow in *its* flying,
So a [B]curse without cause does not [b]alight.
3 A [A]whip is for the horse, a
bridle for the donkey,
And a [B]rod for the back of fools.
4 [A]Do not answer a fool
according to his folly,
Or you will also be like him.
5 [A]Answer a fool as his folly *deserves,*
That he not be [B]wise in his own eyes.
6 He cuts off *his own* feet *and*
drinks violence
Who sends a message by
the hand of a fool.
7 *Like* the legs *which* [a]are
useless to the lame,
So is a proverb in the mouth of fools.
8 Like [a]one who binds a stone in a sling,
So is he who gives honor to a fool.
9 *Like* a thorn *which* [a]falls into
the hand of a drunkard,
So is a proverb in the mouth of fools.
10 [a]*Like* an archer who wounds everyone,
So is he who hires a fool or who
hires those who pass by.
11 Like [A]a dog that returns to its vomit
Is a fool who [B]repeats [a]his folly.
12 Do you see a man [A]wise in his own eyes?
[B]There is more hope for a
fool than for him.
13 The [A]sluggard says, "There
is a lion in the road!
A lion is [a]in the open square!"
14 *As* the door turns on its hinges,
So *does* the [A]sluggard on his bed.
15 The [A]sluggard buries his
hand in the dish;
He is weary of bringing it
to his mouth again.
16 The sluggard is [A]wiser in his own eyes
Than seven men who can [a]give
a discreet answer.
17 *Like* one who takes a dog by the ears
Is he who passes by *and* [a]meddles
with [A]strife not belonging to him.
18 Like a madman who throws
[A]Firebrands, arrows and death,
19 So is the man who [A]deceives his neighbor,
And says, "[B]Was I not joking?"
20 For lack of wood the fire goes out,
And where there is no [A]whisperer,
[B]contention quiets down.
21 *Like* charcoal to hot embers
and wood to fire,
So is a [A]contentious man to kindle strife.
22 The [A]words of a whisperer are
like dainty morsels,
And they go down into the
[a]innermost parts of the body.

25:26 [a]Lit *ruined* [A]Ezek 32:2; 34:18, 19 25:27 [a]Lit *their* [A]Prov 27:2; Luke 14:11 25:28 [A]Prov 16:32 [B]2 Chr 32:5; Neh 1:3 26:1 [A]1 Sam 12:17 [B]Prov 17:7 26:2 [a]Lit *wandering* [b]Lit *come* [A]Prov 27:8; Is 16:2 [B]Num 23:8; Deut 23:5; 2 Sam 16:12 26:3 [A]Ps 32:9 [B]Prov 10:13; 19:29 26:4 [A]Prov 23:9; 29:9; Is 36:21; Matt 7:6 26:5 [A]Matt 16:1-4; 21:24-27 [B]Prov 3:7; 28:11; Rom 12:16 26:7 [a]Lit *hang down from* 26:8 [a]Lit *the binding of* 26:9 [a]Lit *goes up* 26:10 [a]Or *A master* workman *produces all things, But he who hires a fool is* like *one who hires those who pass by* 26:11 [a]Lit *with his* [A]2 Pet 2:22 [B]Ex 8:15 26:12 [A]Prov 3:7; 26:5 [B]Prov 29:20 26:13 [a]Lit *within* [A]Prov 22:13 26:14 [A]Prov 6:9 26:15 [A]Prov 19:24 26:16 [a]Lit *return discreetly* [A]Prov 27:11 26:17 [a]Lit *infuriates himself* [A]Prov 3:30 26:18 [A]Is 50:11 26:19 [A]Prov 24:28 [B]Eph 5:4 26:20 [A]Prov 16:28 [B]Prov 22:10 26:21 [A]Prov 15:18; 29:22 26:22 [a]Lit *chambers of the belly* [A]Prov 18:8

25:26 trampled spring. The righteous one who sins muddies the water for the wicked who see him and for whom he should serve as an example of righteousness (cf. Ps 17:5).

25:27 Eating honey is analogous to enjoying the sweetness of your own self-glory. *See notes on vv. 6, 7, 16.*

25:28 city that is broken. Such are exposed and vulnerable to the incursion of evil thoughts and successful temptations. For the opposite, *see note on 16:32.*

26:1–12 The fool is described in every verse. Most verses compare aspects of natural order that are violated with the behavior of a fool. The deteriorating nature of foolishness is seen as the description progresses from drink (v. 6) to vomit (v. 11).

26:1 These damaging incongruities of nature illustrate those in the moral realm. Cf. 17:7; 19:10.

26:2 curse without cause. A bird's aimless motion without landing is compared to a fool who utters an undeserved curse—it does not land either.

26:4, 5 answer a fool. Taken together, these verses teach the appropriate way to answer a fool (e.g., an unbeliever who rejects truth). He should not be answered with agreement to his own ideas and presuppositions, or he will think he is right (v. 4), but rather he should be rebuked on the basis of his folly and shown the truth so he sees how foolish he is (v. 5).

26:6 Self-inflicted wounds come to the person who chooses to depend upon a fool (cf. 25:13).

26:7 Awkward and useless.

26:8 binds a stone. As it is nonsense to fasten a stone to a slingshot so that it will not release, so it is nonsense to honor a fool.

26:10 The Heb. language is obscure here, so as to produce many interpretations of what this is saying. Since it is impossible to know exactly what it said in the original, it is impossible to know exactly what it means. The translation might be: "Much brings forth from itself all; but the reward and the wages of the fool pass away." This could mean, reasonably, that although he who possesses much and has great ability may be able to accomplish all he wants, that is not the case when he makes use of the work of fools, who not only do not accomplish anything, but destroy everything.

26:11 Peter quotes this disgusting proverb in 2Pe 2:22.

26:12 wise in his own eyes. There are degrees of foolishness, with intellectual conceit being the most stupid and hard to remedy. This is applied to the lazy man in v. 16 and the rich in 28:11.

26:13–16 The sluggard *See notes on 6:6, 11; 22:13.*

26:16 The ignorant are ignorant of their ignorance. **seven.** *See note on 24:15, 16.*

26:17–28 Here is a picturesque discourse on the evil speaking of fools and lazy people and its harmful effects.

26:17 dog by the ears. The dog was not domesticated in Israel and thus to grab any dog was dangerous. The aggressor deserved to be bitten for his unprovoked act.

26:18, 19 The serious damage done by deceit cannot be dismissed as a joke (cf. Is 50:11).

26:20–22 whisperer. *See notes on 6:14; 16:28.* Slander fuels this fire.

26:22 morsels. *See note on 18:8.*

23 *Like* an earthen [A]vessel overlaid
with silver [B]dross
Are burning lips and a wicked heart.
24 He who [A]hates disguises *it* with his lips,
But he lays up [B]deceit in his [a]heart.
25 When [a]he [A]speaks graciously,
do not believe him,
For there are seven abominations
in his heart.
26 *Though his* hatred [A]covers itself with guile,
His wickedness will be [B]revealed
before the assembly.
27 He who [A]digs a pit will fall into it,
And he who rolls a stone, it
will come back on him.
28 A lying tongue hates [a]those it crushes,
And a [A]flattering mouth works ruin.

WARNINGS AND INSTRUCTIONS

27 [A]Do not boast about tomorrow,
For you [B]do not know what a
day may bring forth.
2 Let [A]another praise you, and
not your own mouth;
A stranger, and not your own lips.
3 A stone is heavy and the sand weighty,
But the provocation of a fool is
heavier than both of them.
4 Wrath is fierce and anger is a flood,
But [A]who can stand before jealousy?
5 Better is [A]open rebuke
Than love that is concealed.
6 Faithful are the [A]wounds of a friend,
But [a]deceitful are the [B]kisses of an enemy.
7 A sated [a]man [b]loathes honey,
But to a famished [a]man any
bitter thing is sweet.
8 Like a [A]bird that wanders from her nest,
So is a man who [B]wanders from his [a]home.
9 [A]Oil and perfume make the heart glad,
So a [a]man's counsel is sweet to his friend.
10 Do not forsake your own [A]friend
or [B]your father's friend,
And do not go to your brother's house
in the day of your calamity;
Better is a neighbor who is near
than a brother far away.
11 [A]Be wise, my son, and make my heart glad,
That I may [B]reply to him
who reproaches me.
12 A prudent man sees evil *and* hides himself,
The [a]naive proceed *and* pay the penalty.
13 [A]Take his garment when he becomes
surety for a stranger;
And for an [a]adulterous woman
hold him in pledge.
14 [A]He who blesses his friend with a
loud voice early in the morning,
It will be reckoned a curse to him.
15 A [A]constant dripping on a
day of steady rain
And a contentious woman are alike;
16 He who would [a]restrain her
[a]restrains the wind,
And [b]grasps oil with his right hand.
17 Iron sharpens iron,
So one man sharpens another.
18 He who tends the [A]fig tree will eat its fruit,
And he who [B]cares for his
master will be honored.
19 As in water face *reflects* face,
So the heart of man *reflects* man.
20 [a,A]Sheol and [b]Abaddon are [B]never satisfied,
Nor are the [C]eyes of man ever satisfied.
21 The [A]crucible is for silver and
the furnace for gold,
And each [B]*is tested* by the
praise accorded him.
22 Though you [A]pound a fool in a mortar
with a pestle along with crushed grain,
Yet his foolishness will not
depart from him.

26:23 [A]Matt 23:27; Luke 11:39 [B]Prov 25:4 26:24 [a]Lit *inward part* [A]Ps 41:6; Prov 10:18 [B]Prov 12:20 26:25 [a]Lit *his voice is gracious* [A]Ps 28:3; Prov 26:23; Jer 9:8 26:26 [A]Matt 23:28 [B]Luke 8:17 26:27 [A]Esth 7:10; Prov 28:10 26:28 [a]Lit *its crushed ones* [A]Prov 29:5 27:1 [A]James 4:13-16 [B]Luke 12:19, 20; James 4:14 27:2 [A]Prov 25:27; 2 Cor 10:12, 18; 12:11 27:4 [A]Prov 6:34; 1 John 3:12 27:5 [A]Prov 28:23; Gal 2:14 27:6 [a]Or *excessive* [A]Ps 141:5; Prov 20:30 [B]Matt 26:49 27:7 [a]Lit *soul* [b]Lit *tramples on* 27:8 [a]Lit *place* [A]Prov 26:2; Is 16:2 [B]Gen 21:14 27:9 [a]Lit *soul's* [A]Ps 23:5; 141:5 27:10 [A]Prov 18:24 [B]1 Kin 12:6-8; 2 Chr 10:6-8 27:11 [A]Prov 10:1; 23:15; 29:3 [B]Ps 119:42 27:12 [a]Lit *simple* 27:13 [a]Lit *strange* [A]Prov 20:16 27:14 [A]Ps 12:2 27:15 [A]Prov 19:13 27:16 [a]Lit *hide(s)* [b]Lit *encounters* 27:18 [A]2 Kin 18:31; Song 8:12; Is 36:16; 1 Cor 3:8; 9:7; 2 Tim 2:6 [B]Luke 12:42-44; 19:17 27:20 [a]I.e. The nether world [b]I.e. the place of destruction [A]Job 26:6; Prov 15:11 [B]Prov 30:15, 16; Hab 2:5 [C]Eccl 1:8; 4:8 27:21 [A]Prov 17:3 [B]Luke 6:26 27:22 [A]Prov 23:35; 26:11; Jer 5:3

26:23 **earthen vessel overlaid.** A cheap veneer of silver over a common clay pot hiding its commonness and fragility is like the deception spoken by evil people. This thought is expanded in vv. 24–28.

26:27 The ruin intended for others will come back on the person who spoke it.

27:1 **boast about tomorrow.** Fools think they know the future or can affect its outcome, but the future rests with sovereign God. *See notes on 16:1, 9*; cf. Ps 37; Jas 4:13–16.

27:4 **jealousy.** Cf. 6:34; SS 8:6. The most uncontrollable sin.

27:5, 6 **open rebuke.** To genuinely love is to manifest the truth, even if it means to rebuke (cf. 28:23; Ps 141:5; Gal 4:16).

27:6 **the kisses of an enemy.** Cf. 5:3–5; 26:23, 24.

27:7 The luxury and indolence of wealth make the best things tasteless, while the hard-working person who hungers finds every bitter thing sweet. This proverb extends beyond food to things in general, which means so much more to those with little.

27:8 **man who wanders.** Such are not only out of place, but off duty and in danger. Stay close to home.

27:10 Adhere to tried and true friends. The ties of blood may be less reliable than those of genuine friendship. *See notes on 17:17; 18:24.*

27:11 A wise son accredits his father and also aides him in difficulty with appropriate answers (cf. 10:1; 15:20). This proverb is true in reverse as well (cf. 17:25; 19:13; 22:21; 23:15).

27:12 Cf. 22:3.

27:13 *See note on 20:16.*

27:14 **blesses his friend.** Excessive flattery all day raises suspicion of selfishness.

27:15, 16 *See notes on 19:13; 21:9.* This kind of woman is impossible to restrain or tame.

27:17 **Iron sharpens iron.** The benefits of intellectual and theological discussion encourage joy through a keener mind and the improvement of good character which the face will reveal.

27:20 **Sheol and Abaddon.** Man's desires are never filled up. They are as insatiable as the place of eternal punishment which never overfills (cf. 30:15, 16).

27:21 **crucible . . . praise accorded him.** Popularity and praise "test" personal character. *See note on 17:3.*

27:22 **mortar . . . pestle.** A bowl and rod of stone which were used to crush solid grain into powder.

23 [A]Know well the [a]condition of your flocks,
And pay attention to your herds;
24 For riches are not forever,
Nor does a [A]crown *endure*
to all generations.
25 *When* the grass disappears, the
new growth is seen,
And the herbs of the mountains
are [A]gathered in,
26 The lambs *will be* for your clothing,
And the goats *will bring* the price of a field,
27 And *there will be* goats' milk
enough for your food,
For the food of your household,
And sustenance for your maidens.

WARNINGS AND INSTRUCTIONS

28 The wicked [A]flee when no one is pursuing,
But the righteous are [a]bold as a lion.
2 By the transgression of a land
[A]many are its princes,
But [B]by a man of understanding
and knowledge, so it endures.
3 A [A]poor man who oppresses the lowly
Is *like* a driving rain [a]which leaves no food.
4 Those who forsake the law
[A]praise the wicked,
But those who keep the law
[B]strive with them.
5 Evil men [A]do not understand justice,
But those who seek the LORD
[B]understand all things.
6 [A]Better is the poor who walks
in his integrity
Than he who is [a]crooked
though he be rich.
7 He who keeps the law is a discerning son,
But he who is a companion of
[A]gluttons humiliates his father.
8 He who increases his wealth
by [A]interest and usury
Gathers it [B]for him who is
gracious to the poor.
9 He who turns away his ear from
listening to the law,
Even his [A]prayer is an abomination.
10 He who leads the upright
astray in an evil way
Will [A]himself fall into his own pit,
But the [B]blameless will inherit good.
11 The rich man is [A]wise in his own eyes,
But the poor who has understanding
[a]sees through him.
12 When the [A]righteous triumph,
there is great glory,
But [B]when the wicked rise,
men [a]hide themselves.
13 He who [A]conceals his transgressions
will not prosper,
But he who [B]confesses and forsakes
them will find compassion.
14 How blessed is the man
who [A]fears always,
But he who [B]hardens his heart
will fall into calamity.
15 *Like* a [A]roaring lion and a rushing bear
Is a [B]wicked ruler over a poor people.
16 A [A]leader who is a great oppressor
lacks understanding,
But he who hates unjust gain
will prolong *his* days.
17 A man who is [A]laden with the
guilt of human blood
Will [a]be a fugitive until death;
let no one support him.
18 He who walks blamelessly
will be delivered,
But he who is [a,A]crooked will fall all at once.

27:23 [a]Lit *face* [A]Jer 31:10; Ezek 34:12; John 10:3 27:24 [A]Job 19:9; Ps 89:39; Jer 13:18; Lam 5:16; Ezek 21:26 27:25 [A]Is 17:5; Jer 40:10, 12 28:1 [a]Lit *confident* [A]Lev 26:17, 36; Ps 53:5 28:2 [A]1 Kin 16:8-28; 2 Kin 15:8-15 [B]Prov 11:11 28:3 [a]Lit *and there is no bread* [A]Matt 18:28 28:4 [A]Ps 49:18; Rom 1:32 [B]1 Kin 18:18; Neh 13:11, 15; Matt 3:7; 14:4; Eph 5:11 28:5 [A]Ps 92:6; Is 6:9; 44:18 [B]Ps 119:100; Prov 2:9; John 7:17; 1 Cor 2:15; 1 John 2:20, 27 28:6 [a]Lit *perverse of two ways* [A]Prov 19:1 28:7 [A]Prov 23:20 28:8 [A]Ex 22:25; Lev 25:36 [B]Job 27:17; Prov 13:22; 14:31 28:9 [A]Ps 66:18; 109:7; Prov 15:8; 21:27 28:10 [A]Ps 7:15; Prov 26:27 [B]Matt 6:33; Heb 6:12; 1 Pet 3:9 28:11 [a]Lit *examines him* [A]Prov 3:7; 26:5, 12 28:12 [a]Lit *will be searched for* [A]Prov 11:10; 29:2 [B]Prov 28:28; Eccl 10:5, 6 28:13 [A]Job 31:33; Ps 32:3 [B]Ps 32:5; 1 John 1:9 28:14 [A]Prov 23:17 [B]Ps 95:8; Rom 2:5 28:15 [A]Prov 19:12; 1 Pet 5:8 [B]Ex 1:14; Prov 29:2; Matt 2:16 28:16 [A]Eccl 10:16; Is 3:12 28:17 [a]Lit *flee to the pit* [A]Gen 9:6; Ex 21:14 28:18 [a]Lit *perverse of two ways* [A]Prov 10:27

27:23–27 This portion contrasts the common shepherd's labor and God's provision with the fleeting nature of uncertain riches and power (v. 24). Since all lands reverted to the original owners every 50 years, flocks were the staple wealth. Only by care and diligence could they be perpetuated and profitable. God's providence aids this effort (cf. Ps 65:9–13) to properly use the blessings of the land (vv. 25–27).

28:1 A guilty conscience imagines accusers everywhere (cf. Nu 32:23; Ps 53:5), while a clear conscience has boldness to face everyone.

28:2 **many are its princes.** Unrighteousness in a nation produces political instability, with many vying for power, thus the tenure of each leader is shortened. Wisdom promotes social order and long rule.

28:3 **oppresses the lowly.** When the poor come to power and oppress their own, it is as bad as a destructive storm washing the fields clean instead of watering the crop.

28:7 The son who obeyed God's law would not be a glutton and shame his father. Cf. 23:19–25.

28:8 **interest and usury.** The law forbade the charging of interest to fellow Jews (see Dt 23:19, 20), but this was often violated (cf. Ne 5:7, 11; Eze 22:12). **Gathers it for him.** In the providence and justice of God, such wealth will be forfeited to someone who treats the poor fairly. *See notes on 13:22; 14:31.*

28:9 *See note on 15:8.*

28:10 The attempted corruption of the righteous is a wicked sin (Mt 5:19; 18:6; 23:15). **fall into his own pit.** *See note on 26:27.*

28:11 **rich man is wise in his own eyes.** This contrasts the discerning poor with the rich man, who is deceived by his self-confidence. Riches are not always possessed by the unrighteous and wisdom by the poor, but, more often than not, this is the case due to the blinding nature of wealth (cf. 11:28; 18:23; Mt 19:23, 24).

28:12 When wicked people come into power, the righteous "groan" (29:2) and "hide" (28:28).

28:13 **conceals ... confesses.** Sin must not be hidden but confessed. *See notes on Ps 32:1–11; 1Jn 1:6–9.*

28:14 **hardens his heart.** Cf. Ex 7:13; 17:7; Ps 95:8; Ro 2:5.

28:16 **great oppressor.** The tyrannical leader who is covetous (implied) is foolish and short-lived.

28:17 Whoever is inwardly tormented by the murder of someone takes to ceaseless flight to escape the avenger of blood and the punishment of his crime. He flees and finds no rest until the grave receives him. The exhortation is to avoid helping a murderer with any support, refuge, or security against the vengeance which pursues him from the arm of justice.

19 [A]He who tills his land will
[B]have plenty of food,
But he who follows empty *pursuits*
will have poverty in plenty.
20 A [A]faithful man will abound
with blessings,
But he who [B]makes haste to be
rich will not go unpunished.
21 To [a,A]show partiality is not good,
[B]Because for a piece of bread a
man will transgress.
22 A man with an [A]evil eye
[B]hastens after wealth
And does not know that want
will come upon him.
23 He who [A]rebukes a man will
afterward find *more* favor
Than he who [B]flatters with the tongue.
24 He who [A]robs his father or his mother
And says, "It is not a transgression,"
Is the [B]companion of a
man who destroys.
25 An [a]arrogant man [A]stirs up strife,
But he who [B]trusts in the
LORD [C]will [b]prosper.
26 He who [A]trusts in his own heart is a fool,
But he who walks wisely will be delivered.
27 He who [A]gives to the poor will never want,
But he who [a]shuts his eyes
will have many curses.
28 When the wicked rise, men
hide themselves;
But when they perish, the
righteous increase.

WARNINGS AND INSTRUCTIONS

29 A man who hardens *his* neck
after [A]much reproof
Will [B]suddenly be broken [a]beyond remedy.
2 When the [A]righteous [a]increase,
the people rejoice,
But when a wicked man
rules, people groan.
3 A man who [A]loves wisdom
makes his father glad,
But he who [B]keeps company with
harlots wastes *his* wealth.
4 The [A]king gives stability to
the land by justice,
But a man who takes bribes overthrows it.
5 A man who [A]flatters his neighbor
Is spreading a net for his steps.
6 By transgression an evil
man is [A]ensnared,
But the righteous [B]sings and rejoices.
7 The [A]righteous [a]is concerned
for the rights of the poor,
The wicked does not understand
such [b]concern.
8 Scorners [A]set a city aflame,
But [B]wise men turn away anger.
9 When a wise man has a controversy
with a foolish man,
[a]The foolish man either rages or
laughs, and there is no rest.
10 Men of [A]bloodshed hate the blameless,
But the upright [a]are concerned for his life.
11 A [A]fool [a]always loses his temper,
But a [B]wise man holds it back.
12 If a [A]ruler pays attention to falsehood,
All his ministers *become* wicked.
13 The [A]poor man and the oppressor
[a]have this in common:
The LORD gives [B]light to
the eyes of both.
14 If a [A]king judges the poor with truth,
His [B]throne will be established forever.
15 The [A]rod and reproof give wisdom,
But a child [a]who gets his own way
[B]brings shame to his mother.
16 When the wicked [a]increase,
transgression increases;
But the [A]righteous will see their fall.
17 [A]Correct your son, and he will
give you comfort;
He will also [a,B]delight your soul.

28:19 [A]Prov 12:11 [B]Prov 20:13 28:20 [A]Prov 10:6; Matt 24:45; 25:21 [B]Prov 20:21; 28:22; 1 Tim 6:9 28:21 [a]Lit *regard the face* [A]Prov 24:23 [B]Ezek 13:19 28:22 [A]Prov 23:6 [B]Prov 21:5 28:23 [A]Prov 27:5, 6 [B]Prov 29:5 28:24 [A]Prov 19:26 [B]Prov 18:9 28:25 [a]Lit *broad soul* [b]Lit *be made fat* [A]Prov 15:18 [B]Prov 29:25; 1 Tim 6:6 [C]Prov 11:25 28:26 [A]Prov 3:5 28:27 [a]Lit *hides* [A]Prov 11:24; 19:17 29:1 [a]Lit *and there is no remedy* [A]1 Sam 2:25; 2 Chr 36:16; Prov 1:24-31 [B]Prov 6:15 29:2 [a]Or *become great* [A]Esth 8:15; Prov 11:10; 28:12 29:3 [A]Prov 10:1; 15:20; 27:11; 28:7 [B]Prov 5:10; 6:26; Luke 15:30 29:4 [A]2 Chr 9:8; Prov 8:15; 29:14 29:5 [A]Ps 5:9 29:6 [A]Prov 22:5; Eccl 9:12 [B]Ex 15:1 29:7 [a]Lit *knows the cause* [b]Lit *knowledge* [A]Job 29:16; Ps 41:1; Prov 31:8, 9 29:8 [A]Prov 11:11 [B]Prov 16:14 29:9 [a]Lit *He* 29:10 [a]Lit *seek his soul* [A]Gen 4:5-8; 1 John 3:12 29:11 [a]Lit *sends forth all his spirit* [A]Prov 12:16; 14:33 [B]Prov 19:11 29:12 [A]1 Kin 12:14 29:13 [a]Lit *meet together* [A]Prov 22:2 [B]Ezra 9:8; Ps 13:3 29:14 [A]Ps 72:4; Is 11:4 [B]Prov 16:12; 25:5 29:15 [a]Lit *left to himself* [A]Prov 13:24; 22:15 [B]Prov 10:1; 17:25 29:16 [a]Or *become great* [A]Ps 37:34, 36; 58:10; 91:8; 92:11; Prov 21:12 29:17 [a]Lit *give delight to* [A]Prov 13:24; 29:15 [B]Prov 10:1

28:20 abound with blessings. Blessings are the product of honest labor. *See notes on 10:22; 11:24–26;* cf. Ge 49:25; Mal 3:10. makes haste to be rich. *See note on 20:21;* cf. 1Ti 6:9.

28:21 piece of bread. A small bribe. Cf. 15:27; 18:5; 24:23.

28:22 man with an evil eye. A miser is motivated by greed. *See notes on 21:5–7.*

28:23 Flattery has no value but reproof does, so it leads to gratitude. Cf. 16:13; 27:5, 6.

28:24 robs his father ... mother. *See note on 19:26.* To plunder one's own family is an unthinkable crime, but it is worse yet when denied.

28:25 arrogant man ... strife. This is arrogance that satisfies itself at the expense of conflict with others and never knows the prosperity of humble trust in God.

28:27 shuts his eyes. This refers to one who does not respond to the needs of the poor. *See note on 14:31;* cf. 1Jn 3:16–18.

28:28 *See note on v. 12.*

29:1 hardens *his* neck. This refers to a state of increasing obstinance, along with an unteachable spirit. *See note on 28:14.*

29:2 righteous ... wicked. *See note on 28:12.* This could describe the political turmoil of the northern kingdom of Israel in the time of Hezekiah, who collected these proverbs (*see note on 25:1*).

29:4 bribes. *See note on 15:27.*

29:5 Flattery is a trap. Cf. 26:28; 28:23.

29:8 These angry, arrogant men fan the flames of strife that trap a city as if engulfed in flames (cf. 26:21).

29:9 controversy. A fool may respond to wisdom with anger or laughter, but in either case, no agreement can be reached. Cf. 26:4, 5.

29:12 ruler pays attention to falsehood. A corrupt leader will draw around him corrupt people. Allow lies and you will be surrounded by liars.

29:13 gives light to the eyes. This phrase means to sustain life. God gives life to both the poor and the rich oppressor, and He holds each responsible for His truth. Cf. 22:2.

29:15 *See notes on 13:24; 22:6.*

29:17 Correct your son. *See notes on 13:24; 22:6.*

18 Where there is [A]no [a]vision, the
people [B]are unrestrained,
But [C]happy is he who keeps the law.
19 A slave will not be instructed
by words *alone;*
For though he understands,
there will be no response.
20 Do you see a man who is
[A]hasty in his words?
There is [B]more hope for a fool than for him.
21 He who pampers his slave from childhood
Will in the end find him to be a son.
22 An [A]angry man stirs up strife,
And a hot-tempered man
abounds in transgression.
23 A man's [A]pride will bring him low,
But a [B]humble spirit will obtain honor.
24 He who is a partner with a
thief hates his own life;
He [A]hears the oath but tells nothing.
25 The [A]fear of man [a]brings a snare,
But he who [B]trusts in the
LORD will be exalted.
26 [A]Many seek the ruler's [a]favor,
But [B]justice for man *comes* from the LORD.
27 An [A]unjust man is abominable
to the righteous,
And he who is [B]upright in the way
is abominable to the wicked.

THE WORDS OF AGUR

30 The words of Agur the son of Jakeh, the [a]oracle.
The man declares to Ithiel, to Ithiel and Ucal:

2 Surely I am more [A]stupid than any man,
And I do not have the
understanding of a man.
3 Neither have I learned wisdom,
Nor do I have the [A]knowledge
of the Holy One.
4 Who has [A]ascended into heaven
and descended?
Who has gathered the [B]wind in His fists?
Who has [C]wrapped the waters
in [a]His garment?
Who has [D]established all the
ends of the earth?
What is His [E]name or His son's name?
Surely you know!

5 Every [A]word of God is tested;
He is a [B]shield to those who
take refuge in Him.
6 [A]Do not add to His words
Or He will reprove you, and you
will be proved a liar.

7 Two things I asked of You,
Do not refuse me before I die:
8 Keep deception and
[a]lies far from me,
Give me neither poverty nor riches;
Feed me with the [A]food
that is my portion,
9 That I not be [A]full and deny [B]*You*
and say, "Who is the LORD?"
Or that I not be [C]in want and steal,
And [D]profane the name of my God.

29:18 [a]Or *revelation* [A]1 Sam 3:1; Ps 74:9; Amos 8:11, 12 [B]Ex 32:25 [C]Ps 1:1, 2; 106:3; 119:2; Prov 8:32; John 13:17 29:20 [A]James 1:19 [B]Prov 26:12 29:22 [A]Prov 15:18; 26:21 29:23 [A]Prov 11:2; 16:18; Dan 4:30, 31; Matt 23:12; James 4:6 [B]Prov 15:33; 18:12; 22:4; Is 66:2; Luke 14:11; 18:14; James 4:10 29:24 [A]Lev 5:1 29:25 [a]Lit *gives* [A]Gen 12:12; 20:2; Luke 12:4; John 12:42, 43 [B]Ps 91:1-16; Prov 18:10; 28:25 29:26 [a]Lit *face* [A]Prov 19:6 [B]Is 49:4; 1 Cor 4:4 29:27 [A]Ps 6:8; 139:21, 22; Prov 12:8 [B]Ps 69:4; Prov 29:10; Matt 10:22; 24:9; John 15:18; 17:14; 1 John 3:13 30:1 [a]Or *burden* 30:2 [A]Ps 49:10; 73:22; Prov 12:1 30:3 [A]Prov 9:10 30:4 [a]Lit *the* [A]Ps 68:18; John 3:13; Eph 4:8 [B]Ex 15:10; Ps 135:7 [C]Job 26:8; 38:8, 9 [D]Ps 24:2; Is 45:18 [E]Rev 19:12 30:5 [A]Ps 12:6; 18:30 [B]Ps 3:3; 84:11; Prov 2:7 30:6 [A]Deut 4:2; 12:32; Rev 22:18 30:8 [a]Lit *words of falsehood* [A]Job 23:12; Matt 6:11 30:9 [A]Deut 8:12; 31:20; Neh 9:25; Hos 13:6 [B]Josh 24:27; Job 31:28 [C]Prov 6:30 [D]Ex 20:7

29:18 **no vision.** This proverb looks both to the lack of the Word (i.e., 1Sa 3:1) and the lack of hearing the Word (Am 8:11, 12), which lead to lawless rebellion (cf. Ex 32:25; Lv 13:45; Nu 5:18). The proverb then contrasts the joy and glory of a lawful society (28:14; Mal 4:4).

29:19 **will not be instructed.** This verse views the mind-set of an unprincipled and foolish slave who is unresponsive and irresponsible.

29:20 **hasty in his words.** *See note on 10:19.*

29:21 The idea is of overindulging a servant, so that the servant will ultimately want to be cared for like a son, rather than one who serves the master.

29:22 Cf. 15:18.

29:23 Cf. 16:18, 19.

29:24 **partner with a thief.** By refusing to testify with full disclosure to avoid incrimination, one commits perjury which leads to punishment. *See note on Mt 26:63.*

29:26 **the ruler's favor.** The moral is to seek the Lord's favor, since He alone can and will exact justice.

30:1–33 **The words of Agur.** This is a collection of proverbs written by an unknown sage who was likely a student of wisdom at the time of Solomon (cf. 1Ki 4:30, 31). Agur reflects humility (vv. 1–4), a deep hatred for arrogance (vv. 7–9), and a keen theological mind (vv. 5, 6).

30:1 **oracle.** This word is often used of a prophet (cf. Zec 9:1; Mal 1:1) and can be translated "burden" for its weighty character as a divine word or prophecy (cf. Mal 1:1). **Ithiel and Ucal.** Agur addressed his wisdom perhaps to his favorite pupils, as Luke to Theophilus (Lk 1:1–4; Ac 1:1, 2).

30:2, 3 **more stupid … Neither have I learned.** This is a statement of humility and a recognition of the reality that, apart from divine revelation, there would be no true wisdom at all (*see notes on 1:7; 9:10*). This is illustrated in the pursuits of Job (Job 3:3–26) and Solomon (Ecc 3:1–15). Agur was wise because he first admitted what he could not know (1Co 2:6–16).

30:3 **knowledge of the Holy One.** Agur knew that he could not gain wisdom through human searching alone. Understanding is here associated with the holiness of God. Cf. 9:10; 1Co 8:2.

30:4 **Who …. What … ?** These questions can be answered only by revelation from God. A man can know the "what" about creative wisdom through observation of the physical world and its inner workings, but cannot know the "who." The "who" can be known only when God reveals Himself, which He has in Scripture. This is the testimony and conclusion of Job (Job 42:1–6), Solomon (Ecc 12:1–14), Isaiah (Is 40:12–17; 46:8–11; 66:18, 19), and Paul (Ro 8:18–39). **His son's name.** Jesus Christ. Cf. Jn 1:1–18.

30:5, 6 These verses move from the uncertainty of human speculation to the certainty of divine revelation. Agur quotes from David (2Sa 22:31; Ps 18:30).

30:5 **tested.** Lit. "tried," and found to be without dross or error. Cf. Ps 12:6.

30:6 **Do not add.** A powerful statement on the inspired nature of God's canonical Word to Israel. To add to God's Word is to deny God as the standard of truth (cf. Ge 2:16, 17 with 3:2, 3). *See notes on Dt 4:2; Rev 22:18, 19.*

30:7–9 The prayer of a true wisdom-seeker. He seeks from the Lord honesty in heart and sufficiency in Him (away from the dangers posed by the extremes of poverty or wealth). If he has too much, he could cease depending on God (*see 10:15; 18:11; Dt 8:11–20*), and if he has too little, he could be tempted to be as the sluggard (6:6–11).

30:9 **Who is the LORD?** This is a question reflecting extreme arrogance, e.g., "Who is the Almighty, that we should serve Him?" (Job 21:14–16). Cf. Dt 8:10–18; Lk 12:16–21.

10 Do not slander a slave to his master,
Or he will [A]curse you and you
will be found guilty.

11 There is a [a]kind of *man* who
[A]curses his father
And does not bless his mother.
12 There is a [a]kind who is [A]pure
in his own eyes,
Yet is not washed from his filthiness.
13 There is a [a]kind—oh how
[A]lofty are his eyes!
And his eyelids are raised *in arrogance*.
14 There is a [a]kind of *man* whose
[A]teeth are *like* swords
And his [B]jaw teeth *like* knives,
To [C]devour the afflicted from the earth
And the needy from among men.

15 The leech has two daughters,
"Give," "Give."
There are three things that
will not be satisfied,
Four that will not say, "Enough":
16 [a,A]Sheol, and the [B]barren womb,
Earth that is never satisfied with water,
And fire that never says, "Enough."
17 The eye that [A]mocks a father
And [a,B]scorns a mother,
The [C]ravens of the valley will pick it out,
And the young [C]eagles will eat it.

18 There are three things which
are too wonderful for me,
Four which I do not understand:
19 The way of an [A]eagle in the sky,
The way of a serpent on a rock,
The way of a ship in the
middle of the sea,
And the way of a man with a maid.
20 This is the way of an
[A]adulterous woman:
She eats and wipes her mouth,
And says, "I have done no wrong."

21 Under three things the earth quakes,
And under four, it cannot bear up:
22 Under a [A]slave when he becomes king,
And a fool when he is satisfied with food,
23 Under an unloved woman when
she gets a husband,
And a maidservant when she
supplants her mistress.

24 Four things are small on the earth,
But they are exceedingly wise:
25 The [A]ants are not a strong people,
But they prepare their food
in the summer;
26 The [a,A]shephanim are not mighty people,
Yet they make their houses in the rocks;
27 The locusts have no king,
Yet all of them go out in [A]ranks;
28 The lizard you may grasp with the hands,
Yet it is in kings' palaces.

29 There are three things which
are stately in *their* march,
Even four which are stately
when they walk:
30 The lion *which* is [A]mighty among beasts
And does not [a,B]retreat before any,
31 The [a]strutting rooster, the male goat also,
And a king *when his* army is with him.

30:10 [A]Eccl 7:21 30:11 [a]Or *generation* [A]Ex 21:17; Prov 20:20 30:12 [a]Or *generation* [A]Prov 16:2; Is 65:5; Luke 18:11; Titus 1:15, 16 30:13 [a]Or *generation* [A]Prov 6:17; Is 2:11; 5:15 30:14 [a]Or *generation* [A]Ps 57:4 [B]Job 29:17 [C]Ps 14:4; Amos 8:4 30:16 [a]I.e. The nether world [A]Prov 27:20 [B]Gen 30:1 30:17 [a]Lit *despises to obey* [A]Gen 9:22 [B]Prov 15:20 [C]Deut 28:26 30:19 [A]Deut 28:49; Jer 48:40; 49:22 30:20 [A]Prov 5:6 30:22 [A]Prov 19:10; Eccl 10:7 30:25 [A]Prov 6:6 30:26 [a]Small, shy, furry animals *(Hyrax syriacus)* found in the peninsula of the Sinai, northern Israel, and the region round the Dead Sea; KJV *coney,* orig NASB *badgers* [A]Lev 11:5; Ps 104:18 30:27 [A]Joel 2:7 30:30 [a]Lit *turn back* [A]Judg 14:18; 2 Sam 1:23 [B]Mic 5:8 30:31 [a]Lit *girt in the loins*

30:11–14 There is a kind. These proverbs condemn various forms of unwise behavior and are connected with this common phrase which points to the fact that certain sins can uniquely permeate a whole society or time period.

30:11 *See note on 20:20.* Cf. Ex 21:17; Pss 14:5; 24:6.

30:12 *See notes on 16:2; 20:9;* cf. Mt 23:23–26.

30:13 *See note on 21:4.*

30:14 *See note on 14:31.*

30:15, 16 leech … "Give," "Give." These two blood-sucking mouths of the horse leech, which lived off the blood of its victim, are used to picture the insatiably greedy.

30:16 Sheol … fire. Four illustrations of the greedy are given, all of which are parasitic in nature and characterize the heart of human greed. Cf. Ge 16:2; 20:18; 30:1.

30:17 eye that mocks. This proverb vividly speaks to the tragic results of disregarding parental respect and authority and the destruction it brings. *See notes on 10:1; 17:21; 29:15, 17;* cf. Ex 20:12. **ravens … young eagles.** These birds scavenge the unburied corpse of a child who dies prematurely because of rebellion. Cf. 1Sa 17:44; 1Ki 14:11; Jer 16:4; Eze 29:5; 39:7.

30:18–20 Hypocrisy is illustrated by 4 natural analogies of concealment: 1) an eagle leaves no trail in the air; 2) a slithering snake leaves no trail on the rock; 3) a ship leaves no trail in the sea; 4) a man leaves no marks after he has slept with a virgin. These actions are all concealed and thus serve to illustrate the hypocrisy of the adulterous woman who hides the evidences of her shame while professing innocence.

30:21–23 earth quakes. *See notes on 19:10; 28:3.* Society is greatly agitated when normal roles are overturned, e.g., servants reigning, fools made rich, hated women married, and maidservants becoming wives (cf. Ge 16:1–6).

30:24–28 Four things are small. These verses picture 4 creatures which survive due to natural instinct. The wisdom seen in each of these reveals the beauty of the wise Creator and His creation (cf. Ps 8:3–9) and becomes a model for the principle that labor, diligence, organization, planning, and resourcefulness are better than strength, thus implying the superiority of wisdom over might.

30:25 ants. These survive through planning and labor. *See note on 6:6.*

30:26 shephanim. This word probably refers to rock badgers (see marginal note) who, though weak, survive by being diligent enough to climb and find sanctuary in high places. Cf. Lv 11:5; Ps 104:18.

30:27 locusts. These survive through careful organization.

30:28 lizard. These creatures are resourceful and can make their home in inaccessible places—even in a palace.

30:29–31 three things … stately in *their* march … four. The 3 creatures and the king all picture wise, stately, and orderly deportment. Each offers a glimpse of the Creator's power and wisdom (cf. Job 38:1–42:6) and illustrates the dignity and confidence of those who walk wisely.

30:31 strutting rooster. The meaning in Heb. is uncertain. Other possibilities are 1) a greyhound or 2) a warhorse ready for battle. Cf. Job 39:19–25. **male goat.** This is the he-goat that was the leader of the flock. Cf. Da 8:5.

32 If you have been foolish in
exalting yourself
Or if you have plotted *evil,* [A]*put*
your hand on your mouth.
33 For the [a]churning of milk produces butter,
And pressing the nose brings forth blood;
So the [a]churning of [A]anger
produces strife.

THE WORDS OF LEMUEL

31 The words of King Lemuel, the [a]oracle which
his mother taught him:

2 What, O my son?
And what, O [A]son of my womb?
And what, O son of my [B]vows?
3 [A]Do not give your strength to women,
Or your ways to that which
[B]destroys kings.
4 It is not for [A]kings, O Lemuel,
It is not for kings to [B]drink wine,
Or for rulers to desire strong drink,
5 For they will drink and forget
what is decreed,
And [A]pervert the [a]rights of
all the [b]afflicted.
6 Give strong drink to him
who is [A]perishing,
And wine to him [a,B]whose life is bitter.
7 Let him drink and forget his poverty
And remember his trouble no more.
8 [A]Open your mouth for the mute,
For the [a]rights of all the [b]unfortunate.
9 Open your mouth, [A]judge righteously,
And [a]defend the [B]rights of the
afflicted and needy.

DESCRIPTION OF A WORTHY WOMAN

10 An [A]excellent wife, who can find?
For her worth is far [B]above jewels.
11 The heart of her husband trusts in her,
And he will have no lack of gain.
12 She does him good and not evil
All the days of her life.
13 She looks for wool and flax
And works with her [a]hands [b]in delight.
14 She is like [A]merchant ships;
She brings her food from afar.
15 She [A]rises also while it is still night
And [B]gives food to her household
And [a]portions to her maidens.
16 She considers a field and buys it;
From [a]her earnings she
plants a vineyard.
17 She [A]girds [a]herself with strength
And makes her arms strong.
18 She senses that her gain is good;
Her lamp does not go out at night.

30:32 [A]Job 21:5; 40:4; Mic 7:16 30:33 [a]Lit *pressing* [A]Prov 10:12; 29:22 31:1 [a]Or *burden* 31:2 [A]Is 49:15 [B]1 Sam 1:11 31:3 [A]Prov 5:9 [B]Deut 17:17; 1 Kin 11:1; Neh 13:26 31:4 [A]Eccl 10:17 [B]Prov 20:1; Is 5:22; Hos 4:11 31:5 [a]Lit *judgment* [b]Lit *sons of affliction* [A]Ex 23:6; Deut 16:19; Prov 17:15 31:6 [a]Lit *bitter of soul* [A]Job 29:13 [B]Job 3:20; Is 38:15 31:8 [a]Lit *judgment* [b]Lit *sons of passing away* [A]Job 29:12-17; Ps 82 31:9 [a]Lit *judge the afflicted* [A]Lev 19:15; Deut 1:16 [B]Is 1:17; Jer 22:16 31:10 [A]Ruth 3:11; Prov 12:4; 19:14 [B]Job 28:18; Prov 8:11 31:13 [a]Lit *palms* [b]Or *willingly* 31:14 [A]Ezek 27:25 31:15 [a]Or *prescribed tasks* [A]Prov 20:13; Rom 12:11 [B]Luke 12:42 31:16 [a]Lit *the fruit of her palms* 31:17 [a]Lit *her loins* [A]1 Kin 18:46; 2 Kin 4:29; Job 38:3

30:32 *put your* **hand on your mouth.** Lit. "stop your scheming and talking"—a gesture of awestruck, self-imposed silence. Cf. Job 21:5; 29:9; 40:4.

30:33 **produces ... brings forth ... produces.** The verb is the same in all 3 instances. These are natural causes and effects to show that anger pressed beyond certain limits produces conflict.

31:1–31 This concluding chapter contains two poems: 1) The Wise King (31:2–9) and 2) The Excellent Wife (31:10–31). Both are the teachings of a godly mother (v. 1) to King Lemuel, whom ancient Jewish tradition identified as King Solomon, but who is otherwise unknown.

31:1 **oracle.** *See note on 30:1.* **mother taught him.** See 1:8.

31:2–9 The godly king is addressed (v. 2) and told that his reign should be characterized by: 1) holiness (v. 3); 2) sobriety (vv. 4–7); and 3) compassion (vv. 8, 9). This section is filled with succinct and solemn warnings against vices to which kings are particularly susceptible—immorality, overindulgence, unrighteous rule, and indifference to those in need.

31:2 **my son.** The phrase is repeated 3 times to indicate the serious passion of a mother's heart. **son of my vows.** Like Hannah, she had dedicated her child to the Lord (cf. 1Sa 1:11, 27, 28).

31:3 **Do not give your strength to women.** Multiplying foreign wives destroys a king as it did Solomon (cf. Dt 17:17; 1Ki 11:1–4). *See notes on 5:9–11.*

31:4, 5 *See notes on 20:1; 23:29–35.* Intoxicating drinks can weaken reason and judgment, loosen convictions, or pervert the heart. They do not suit rulers who need clear, steady minds and keen judgment.

31:6, 7 **Give strong drink.** Such extreme situations, possibly relating to a criminal on death row or someone agonizing in pain with a terminal illness or tragic circumstance, are in utter contrast to that of the king (cf. Ps 104:15).

31:8, 9 **Open your mouth.** Plead for those who cannot plead their own case, namely those who are otherwise ruined by their condition of weakness. The king's duty was to righteously uphold the case of the helpless in both physical (v. 6) and material (v. 9) crises. The monarch thus mediates the compassion of God. *See note on 14:31.*

31:10–31 This poem offers a beautiful description of the excellent wife as defined by a wife and mother (v. 1). Spiritual and practical wisdom plus moral virtues mark the character of this woman in contrast to the immoral women of v. 3. While the scene here is of a wealthy home and the customs of the ancient Near East, the principles apply to every family. They are set forth as the prayer of every mother for the future wife of her son, and literarily arranged with each of the 22 verses beginning with the 22 letters of the Hebrew alphabet in consecutive order.

31:10–12 This section describes her marriage.

31:10 **excellent.** *See note on 12:4;* cf. Ru 3:11. **who can find?** She does exist, but is very hard to find. Cf. 18:22.

31:11 **trusts in her.** He does not maintain jealous guard over her or keep his valuables locked up so that she cannot access them as was a common ancient practice in a house of distrust. She demonstrates impeccable loyalty to her husband, and her thrift and industry will add to his wealth.

31:13–24 This section describes her behavior.

31:13 **looks for wool and flax.** Excellent women gathered the material for making clothes (v. 19).

31:14 **like merchant ships.** Excellent women would go far to secure the best food for their families.

31:15 **rises ... while it is still night.** In order to have the food prepared for the family each day, she had to rise before dawn to begin the work, which she would do gladly.

31:16 **considers a field.** She was resourceful and entrepreneurial in her investing and reinvesting.

31:17 Such women were not soft, but by virtue of rigorous work, strong.

31:18 **gain is good.** That which she produced for the family of clothing, food, and wealth was good and profitable. **lamp ... night.** Lamp is to be understood literally (cf. v. 15). She planted the vineyard during the day (v. 16) and wove late at night (v. 19). She rose early before dawn to prepare the food (v. 15), thus keeping a before-sunrise to after-dark schedule to care for her household, which was the foremost priority of her life (cf. Titus 2:5).

19 She stretches out her hands to the distaff,
And her [a]hands grasp the spindle.
20 She [a,A]extends her hand to the poor,
And she stretches out her
hands to the needy.
21 She is not afraid of the snow
for her household,
For all her household are
[A]clothed with scarlet.
22 She makes [A]coverings for herself;
Her clothing is [B]fine linen and [C]purple.
23 Her husband is known [A]in the gates,
When he sits among the elders of the land.
24 She makes [A]linen garments
and sells *them,*
And [a]supplies belts to the [b]tradesmen.
25 Strength and [A]dignity are her clothing,
And she smiles at the [a]future.
26 She [A]opens her mouth in wisdom,
And the [a]teaching of kindness
is on her tongue.
27 She looks well to the ways
of her household,
And does not eat the
[A]bread of idleness.
28 Her children rise up and bless her;
Her husband *also,* and he
praises her, *saying:*
29 "Many daughters have done nobly,
But you excel them all."
30 Charm is deceitful and beauty is vain,
But a woman who [a,A]fears the
LORD, she shall be praised.
31 Give her the [a]product of her hands,
And let her works praise
her in the gates.

31:19 [a]Lit *palms* 31:20 [a]Lit *spreads out her palm* [A]Deut 15:11; Job 31:16-20; Prov 22:9; Rom 12:13; Eph 4:28 31:21 [A]2 Sam 1:24 31:22 [A]Prov 7:16 [B]Gen 41:42; Rev 19:8, 14 [C]Judg 8:26; Luke 16:19 31:23 [A]Deut 16:18; Ruth 4:1, 11 31:24 [a]Lit *gives* [b]Lit *Canaanite* [A]Judg 14:12 31:25 [a]Lit *latter days* [A]1 Tim 2:9, 10 31:26 [a]Or *law* [A]Prov 10:31 31:27 [A]Prov 19:15 31:30 [a]Or *reverences* [A]Ps 112:1; Prov 22:4 31:31 [a]Lit *fruit*

31:19 distaff … spindle. These tools are used to turn wool into thread for making clothing. Cf. Ex 35:25.

31:20–24 Her activities, driven by the priority of caring for her family, resulted in multiplied fruitfulness for: 1) the poor and needy (v. 20); 2) her own household (v. 21); 3) herself (v. 22); 4) her husband (v. 23); and 5) the tradesmen (v. 24).

31:21 snow. Snow indicates the cold that occurs in the high altitudes of Israel. Her labors anticipated her family's need for warm clothing in such cold places and seasons.

31:22 fine linen and purple. The efforts she makes to honor others are rewarded to her. These silk and purple garments are expensive evidences of the blessings returned to her by God's grace.

31:23 known in the gates. This woman made a significant contribution to her husband's position in the community and to his success (vv. 10–12). His domestic comfort promoted his advancement in public honor. A man's good reputation begins with his home and thus the virtue of his wife (cf 18:22).

31:24 makes … sells *them.* With all her other responsibilities faithfully discharged, she took time to make items of clothing for the purposes of trade.

31:25–27 This section emphasizes her character.

31:25 Strength and dignity. These words describe the character of the woman who fears the Lord. Her inward clothing displays divine wisdom, giving her confidence to face the future with its unexpected challenges.

31:26 opens her mouth … teaching of kindness. Her teaching of wisdom and the law is tempered with mercy.

31:27 She was a skilled manager of the home. *See note on Titus 2:4, 5.* **bread of idleness.** Lit. "eyes looking everywhere" as in the lazy man (cf. 6:6, 9) of whom the same root word is used.

31:28, 29 This section describes her family life.

31:28 rise up and bless her. She was greatly respected because she has earned the praise of her family. *See note on 29:17.* There can be no higher joy for a mother than for her children to grow up to praise her as the source of the wisdom that made them godly. *See note on 1Ti 2:15.*

31:29, 30 you excel them all. This was her husband's superlative praise (v. 28) which was well-deserved, in which he used the same word for "excellent" found in v. 10.

31:30, 31 This portion summarizes her spiritual life.

31:30 Charm … beauty. True holiness and virtue command permanent respect and affection, far more than charm and beauty of face and form. Cf. 1Ti 2:9, 10; 1Pe 3:1–6. **a woman who fears the LORD.** Proverbs ends where it began with a reference to the fear of the Lord. *See note on 1:7.*

31:31 product … works. See vv. 10–29. While she receives material reward (v. 22), the praise and success she labored to bring to her family and community will be her praise. The result of all her efforts is her best eulogy.

THE BOOK OF ECCLESIASTES

TITLE

The English title, Ecclesiastes, comes from the Greek and Latin translations of Solomon's book. The LXX used the Greek term *ekklēsiastēs* for its title. It means "preacher," derived from the word *ekklēsia,* translated "assembly" or "congregation" in the NT. Both the Greek and Latin versions derive their titles from the Hebrew title, *Qoheleth,* which means "one who calls or gathers" the people. It refers to the one who addresses the assembly; hence, the preacher (cf. 1:1, 2, 12; 7:27; 12:8–10). Along with Ruth, Song of Solomon, Esther, and Lamentations, Ecclesiastes stands with the OT books of the Megilloth, or "five scrolls." Later rabbis read these books in the synagogue on 5 special occasions during the year—Ecclesiastes being read on Pentecost.

AUTHOR AND DATE

The autobiographical profile of the book's writer unmistakably points to Solomon. Evidence abounds such as: 1) the titles fit Solomon, "son of David, king in Jerusalem" (1:1) and "king over Israel in Jerusalem" (1:12); 2) the author's moral odyssey chronicles Solomon's life (1Ki 2–11); and 3) the role of one who "taught the people knowledge" and wrote "many proverbs" (12:9) corresponds to his life. All point to Solomon, the son of David, as the author.

Once Solomon is accepted as the author, the date and occasion become clear. Solomon was writing, probably in his latter years (no later than ca. 931 B.C.), primarily to warn the young people of his kingdom, without omitting others. He warned them to avoid walking through life on the path of human wisdom; he exhorted them to live by the revealed wisdom of God (12:9–14).

BACKGROUND AND SETTING

Solomon's reputation for possessing extraordinary wisdom fits the Ecclesiastes profile. David recognized his son's wisdom (1Ki 2:6, 9) before God gave Solomon an additional measure. After he received a "wise and discerning heart" from the Lord (1Ki 3:7–12), Solomon gained renown for being exceedingly wise by rendering insightful decisions (1Ki 3:16–28), a reputation that attracted "all the kings of the earth" to his courts (1Ki 4:34). In addition, he composed songs and proverbs (1Ki 4:32; cf. 12:9), activity befitting only the ablest of sages. Solomon's wisdom, like Job's wealth, surpassed the wisdom "of all the sons of the east" (1Ki 4:30; Job 1:3).

The book is applicable to all who would listen and benefit, not so much from Solomon's experiences, but from the principles he drew as a result. Its aim is to answer some of life's most challenging questions, particularly where they seem contrary to Solomon's expectations. This has led some unwisely to take the view that Ecclesiastes is a book of skepticism. But in spite of amazingly unwise behavior and thinking, Solomon never let go of his faith in God (12:13, 14).

HISTORICAL AND THEOLOGICAL THEMES

As is true with most biblical Wisdom literature, little historical narrative occurs in Ecclesiastes, apart from Solomon's own personal pilgrimage. The kingly sage studied life with high expectations but repeatedly bemoaned its shortcomings, which he acknowledged were due to the curse (Ge 3:14–19). Ecclesiastes represents the painful autobiography of Solomon who, for much of his life, squandered God's blessings on his own personal pleasure rather than God's glory. He wrote to warn subsequent generations not to make the same tragic error, in much the same manner as Paul wrote to the Corinthians (cf. 1Co 1:18–31; 2:13–16).

The Heb. word translated "vanity," "vanities," and "vain life" expresses the futile attempt to be satisfied apart from God. This word is used 38 times expressing the many things hard to understand about life. All earthly goals and ambitions when pursued as ends in themselves produce only emptiness. Paul was probably echoing Solomon's dissatisfaction when he wrote, " … the creation was subjected to futility" (Solomon's "vanity"; Ro 8:19–21). Solomon's experience with the effects of the curse (see Ge 3:17–19) led him to view life as "chasing after the wind."

Solomon asked, "What advantage does a man have in all his work … ?" (1:3), a question he repeated in 2:22 and 3:9. The wise king gave over a considerable portion of the book to addressing this dilemma. The impossibility of discovering both the inner workings of God's creation and the personal providence of God in Solomon's life was also deeply troubling to the king, as it was to Job. But the reality of judgment for all, despite many unknowns, emerged as the great certainty. In light of this judgment by God, the only fulfilled life is one lived in proper recognition of God and service to Him. Any other kind of life is frustrating and pointless.

A proper balance of the prominent "enjoy life" theme with that of "divine judgment" tethers the reader to Solomon's God with the sure cord of faith. For a time, Solomon suffered from the imbalance of trying to enjoy life without regard for the fear of Yahweh's judgment holding him on the path of obedience. In the end, he came to grasp the importance of obedience. The tragic results of Solomon's personal experience, coupled with the insight of extraordinary wisdom, make Ecclesiastes a book from which all believers can be warned and grow in their faith (cf. 2:1–26). This book shows that if one perceives each day of existence, labor, and basic provision as a gift from God, and accepts whatever God gives, then that person lives an abundant life (cf. Jn 10:10). However, one who looks to be satisfied apart from God will live with futility regardless of their accumulations.

INTERPRETIVE CHALLENGES

The author's declaration that "all is vanity" envelops the primary message of the book (cf. 1:2; 12:8). The word translated "vanity" is used in at least 3 ways throughout the book. In each case, it looks at the nature of man's activity "under the sun" as: 1) "fleeting," which has in view the vapor-like (cf. Jas 4:14) or transitory nature of life; 2) "futile" or "meaningless," which focuses on the cursed condition of the universe and the debilitating effects it has on man's earthly experience; or 3) "incomprehensible" or "enigmatic," which gives consideration to life's unanswerable questions. Solomon draws upon all 3 meanings in Ecclesiastes.

While the context in each case will determine which meaning Solomon is focusing upon, the most recurring meaning of *vanity* is "incomprehensible" or "unknowable," referring to the mysteries of God's purposes. Solomon's conclusion to "fear God and keep His commandments" (12:13, 14) is more than the book's summary; it is the only hope of the good life and the only reasonable response of faith and obedience to sovereign God. He precisely works out all activities under the sun, each in its time according to His perfect plan, but also discloses only as much as His perfect wisdom dictates and holds all men accountable. Those who refuse to take God and His Word seriously are doomed to lives of the severest vanity.

OUTLINE

The book chronicles Solomon's investigations and conclusions regarding man's lifework, which combine all of his activity and its potential outcomes including limited satisfaction. The role of wisdom in experiencing success surfaces repeatedly, particularly when Solomon must acknowledge that God has not revealed all of the details. This leads Solomon to the conclusion that the primary issues of life after the Edenic fall involve divine blessings to be enjoyed and the divine judgment for which all must prepare.

OUTLINE

I. Introduction
- A. Title (1:1)
- B. Poem—A Life of Activity That Appears Wearisome (1:2–11)

II. Solomon's Investigation (1:12–6:9)
- A. Introduction—The King and His Investigation (1:12–18)
- B. Investigation of Pleasure-Seeking (2:1–11)
- C. Investigation of Wisdom and Folly (2:12–17)
- D. Investigation of Labor and Rewards (2:18–6:9)
  1. One has to leave them to another (2:18–26)
  2. One cannot find the right time to act (3:1–4:6)
  3. One often must work alone (4:7–16)
  4. One can easily lose all he acquires (5:1–6:9)

III. Solomon's Conclusions (6:10–12:8)
- A. Introduction—The Problem of Not Knowing (6:10–12)
- B. Man Cannot Always Find Out Which Route Is the Most Successful for Him to Take Because His Wisdom Is Limited (7:1–8:17)
  1. On prosperity and adversity (7:1–14)
  2. On justice and wickedness (7:15–24)
  3. On women and folly (7:25–29)
  4. On the wise man and the king (8:1–17)
- C. Man Does Not Know What Will Come After Him (9:1–11:6)
  1. He knows he will die (9:1–4)
  2. He has no knowledge in the grave (9:5–10)
  3. He does not know his time of death (9:11, 12)
  4. He does not know what will happen (9:13–10:15)
  5. He does not know what evil will come (10:16–11:2)
  6. He does not know what good will come (11:3–6)
- D. Man Should Enjoy Life, But Not Sin, Because Judgment Will Come to All (11:7–12:8)

IV. Solomon's Final Advice (12:9–14)

THE FUTILITY OF ALL ENDEAVOR

1 The words of the [A]Preacher, the son of David,
king in Jerusalem.

2 "[a,A]Vanity of vanities," says the Preacher,
"[a]Vanity of vanities! All is [b]vanity."

3 [A]What advantage does man
have in all his work
Which he does under the sun?
4 A generation goes and a generation comes,
But the [A]earth [a]remains forever.
5 Also, [A]the sun rises and the sun sets;
And [a]hastening to its place
it rises there *again*.
6 [a,A]Blowing toward the south,
Then turning toward the north,
The wind continues [b]swirling along;
And on its circular courses the wind returns.
7 All the rivers [a]flow into the sea,
Yet the sea is not full.
To the place where the rivers [a]flow,
There they [a]flow again.
8 All things are wearisome;
Man is not able to tell *it*.
[A]The eye is not satisfied with seeing,
Nor is the ear filled with hearing.
9 [A]That which has been is that which will be,
And that which has been done is
that which will be done.
So there is nothing new under the sun.
10 Is there anything of which one might say,
"See this, it is new"?
Already it has existed for ages
Which were before us.
11 There is [A]no remembrance
of [a]earlier things;
And also of the [b]later things
which will occur,
There will be for them no remembrance
Among those who will come [b]later *still*.

THE FUTILITY OF WISDOM

12 I, the [A]Preacher, have been king over Israel in
Jerusalem. 13 And I [A]set my [a]mind to seek and [B]ex-
plore by wisdom concerning all that has been done
under heaven. *It is* [b]a grievous [C]task *which* God has
given to the sons of men to be afflicted with. 14 I have
seen all the works which have been done under the
sun, and behold, all is [a,A]vanity and striving after
wind. 15 What is [A]crooked cannot be straightened
and what is lacking cannot be counted.

1:1 [A]Eccl 1:12; 7:27; 12:8-10 1:2 [a]Or *Futility of futilities* [b]Or *futile* [A]Ps 39:5, 6; 62:9; 144:4; Eccl 12:8; Rom 8:20 1:3 [A]Eccl 2:11; 3:9; 5:16 1:4 [a]Lit *stands* [A]Ps 104:5; 119:90 1:5 [a]Lit *panting* [A]Ps 19:6 1:6 [a]Lit *Going* [b]Lit *turning* [A]Eccl 11:5; John 3:8 1:7 [a]Lit *go* 1:8 [A]Prov 27:20; Eccl 4:8 1:9 [A]Eccl 1:10; 2:12; 3:15; 6:10 1:11 [a]Lit *first* or *former* [b]Lit *latter* or *after* [A]Eccl 2:16; 9:5 1:12 [A]Eccl 1:1; 7:27; 12:8-10 1:13 [a]Lit *heart* [b]Lit *an evil* [A]Eccl 1:17 [B]Eccl 3:10, 11; 7:25; 8:17 [C]Eccl 2:23, 26; 3:10; 4:8 1:14 [a]Or *futility* [A]Eccl 2:11, 17; 4:4; 6:9 1:15 [A]Eccl 7:13

1:1 **The words.** The matters of the book are the crucial issues for Solomon's faith. They resemble the subject matter of Pss 39; 49. **the Preacher.** The title of one who gathers the assembly together for instruction. See Introduction: Title.

1:2 **Vanity of vanities.** Solomon's way of saying "the greatest vanity." Cf. the discussion of "vanity" in Introduction: Interpretive Challenges.

1:3 **advantage.** Advantage to or gain from one's labor. A very important and repeated word for Solomon (cf. 3:19; 5:9, 11, 16; 6:7, 11; 7:11, 12; 10:10). Solomon looks at the fleeting moments of life and the seemingly small gain for man's activity under the sun. The only lasting efforts are those designed to accomplish God's purposes for eternity. **work.** Work is not just one's livelihood, but all of man's activity in life. **under the sun.** The phrase appears about 30 times to describe daily life.

1:4–7 These pictures from God's creation illustrate and underscore the futile repetition of human activity.

1:4 **generation … earth.** The essence of this comparison is permanence/impermanence without profit or "advantage." The observer perceives life as an endless cycle of activity which, by itself, does not bring security or meaning to man's experience.

1:8–11 This is a summary of sorts. Solomon looks at the effect of repetitious, enduring activity in God's creation over many generations as compared to the brief, comparatively profitless activity of one man which fails to produce an enduring satisfaction, and he concludes that it is wearisome. Another harsh reality comes with the realization that nothing is new and nothing will be remembered.

1:11 **no remembrance.** A written record or some other object which serves as a reminder of these events, people, and things will be short-lived.

1:12–6:9 This section records Solomon's ill-advised quest for greater wisdom.

1:12 **king over Israel.** See Introduction: Author and Date.

1:13 **wisdom.** Solomon's use of the term, in typical Hebrew fashion, is more practical than philosophical and implies more than knowledge. It carries notions of ability for proper behavior, success, common sense, and wit. **grievous task.** Man's search to understand is at times difficult, yet God-given (cf. 2:26; 3:10; 5:16–19; 6:2; 8:11, 15; 9:9; 12:11). **God.** The covenant name, Lord, is never used in Ecclesiastes. However, "God" is found almost 40 times. The emphasis is more on God's sovereignty in creation and providence than His covenant relationship through redemption.

1:14 **striving after wind.** One aspect of life's vanity is its fleeting character. Like the wind, much of what is desirable in life cannot be held in one's hand (cf. 1:14, 17; 2:11, 17, 26; 4:4, 6, 16; 5:16; 6:9).

1:15 **crooked … lacking.** With no necessarily moral implications being made, these words measure wisdom as the ability to resolve issues

THE "VANITIES" OF ECCLESIASTES (1:2; 12:8)	
1. Human wisdom	2:14–16
2. Human effort	2:18–23
3. Human achievement	2:26
4. Human life	3:18–22
5. Human rivalry	4:4
6. Human selfish sacrifice	4:7, 8
7. Human power	4:16
8. Human greed	5:10
9. Human accumulation	6:1–12
10. Human religion	8:10–14

16 I [a]said to myself, "Behold, I have magnified and
increased [A]wisdom more than all who were over Jerusalem before me; and my [b]mind has observed [c]a
wealth of wisdom and knowledge." 17 And I [A]set my
[a]mind to know wisdom and to [B]know madness and
folly; I realized that this also is [C]striving after wind.
18 Because [A]in much wisdom there is much grief, and
increasing knowledge *results in* increasing pain.

THE FUTILITY OF PLEASURE AND POSSESSIONS

2 I said [a]to myself, "Come now, I will test you with
[A]pleasure. So [b]enjoy yourself." And behold, it too
was futility. 2 [A]I said of laughter, "It is madness," and
of pleasure, "What does it accomplish?" 3 I explored
with my [a]mind *how* to [A]stimulate my body with wine
while my [a]mind was guiding *me* wisely, and how to
take hold of [B]folly, until I could see [C]what good there
is for the sons of men [b]to do under heaven the few
[c]years of their lives. 4 I enlarged my works: I [A]built
houses for myself, I planted [B]vineyards for myself; 5 I
made [A]gardens and [B]parks for myself and I planted
in them all kinds of fruit trees; 6 I made [A]ponds of
water for myself from which to irrigate a forest of
growing trees. 7 I bought male and female slaves
and I had [a,A]homeborn slaves. Also I possessed flocks
and [B]herds larger than all who preceded me in Jerusalem. 8 Also, I collected for myself silver and
[A]gold and the treasure of kings and provinces. I
provided for myself [B]male and female singers and
the pleasures of men—many concubines.
9 Then I became [A]great and increased more than
all who preceded me in Jerusalem. My wisdom also
stood by me. 10 [A]All that my eyes desired I did not
refuse them. I did not withhold my heart from any
pleasure, for my heart was pleased because of all
my labor and this was my [B]reward for all my labor. 11 Thus I considered all my activities which my
hands had done and the labor which I had [a]exerted,
and behold all was [b,A]vanity and striving after wind
and there was [B]no profit under the sun.

WISDOM EXCELS FOLLY

12 So I turned to [A]consider wisdom, madness
and folly; for what *will* the man *do* who will come
after the king *except* [B]what has already been done?
13 And I saw that [A]wisdom excels folly as light excels darkness. 14 The wise man's eyes are in his
head, but the [A]fool walks in darkness. And yet I
know that [B]one fate befalls them both. 15 Then I
said [a]to myself, "[A]As is the fate of the fool, it will
also befall me. [B]Why then have I been extremely
wise?" So [b]I said to myself, "This too is vanity."
16 For there is [A]no [a]lasting remembrance of the
wise man *as* with the fool, inasmuch as *in* the
coming days all will be forgotten. And [B]how the
wise man and the fool alike die! 17 So I [A]hated life,
for the work which had been done under the sun
was [a]grievous to me; because everything is futility
and striving after wind.

THE FUTILITY OF LABOR

18 Thus I hated [A]all the fruit of my labor for which
I had labored under the sun, for I must [B]leave it to
the man who will come after me. 19 And who knows
whether he will be a wise man or [A]a fool? Yet he will
have [a]control over all the fruit of my labor for which
I have labored by acting wisely under the sun. This
too is [B]vanity. 20 Therefore I [a]completely despaired
of all the fruit of my labor for which I had labored
under the sun. 21 When there is a man who has labored with wisdom, knowledge and [A]skill, then he
[B]gives his [a]legacy to one who has not labored with
them. This too is vanity and a great evil. 22 For what
does a man get in [A]all his labor and in [a]his striving
with which he labors under the sun? 23 Because all

1:16 [a]Lit *spoke with my heart, saying* [b]Lit *heart* [c]Lit *an abundance* [A]1 Kin 3:12; 4:30; 10:23; Eccl 2:9 1:17 [a]Lit *heart* [A]Eccl 1:13; 7:25 [B]Eccl 2:12; 7:25 [C]Eccl 1:14; 2:11, 17; 4:4, 6, 16; 6:9 1:18 [A]Eccl 2:23; 12:12 2:1 [a]Lit *in my heart* [b]Lit *consider with goodness* [A]Eccl 7:4; 8:15 2:2 [A]Prov 14:13; Eccl 7:3, 6 2:3 [a]Lit *heart* [b]Lit *which they do* [c]Lit *days* [A]Judg 9:13; Ps 104:15; Eccl 10:19 [B]Eccl 7:25 [C]Eccl 2:24; 3:12, 13; 5:18; 6:12; 8:15; 12:13 2:4 [A]1 Kin 7:1-12 [B]Song 8:11 2:5 [A]Song 4:16; 5:1 [B]Neh 2:8 2:6 [A]Neh 2:14; 3:15, 16 2:7 [a]Lit *sons of the house* [A]Gen 14:14; 15:3 [B]1 Kin 4:23 2:8 [A]1 Kin 9:28; 10:10, 14, 21 [B]2 Sam 19:35 2:9 [A]1 Chr 29:25; Eccl 1:16 2:10 [A]Eccl 6:2 [B]Eccl 3:22; 5:18; 9:9 2:11 [a]Lit *labored to do* [b]Or *futility,* and so throughout the ch [A]Eccl 1:14; 2:22, 23 [B]Eccl 1:3; 3:9; 5:16 2:12 [A]Eccl 1:17 [B]Eccl 1:9, 10; 3:15 2:13 [A]Eccl 7:11, 12, 19; 9:18; 10:10 2:14 [A]1 John 2:11 [B]Ps 49:10; Eccl 3:19; 6:6; 7:2; 9:2, 3 2:15 [a]Lit *in my heart* [b]Lit *I spoke in my heart* [A]Eccl 2:16 [B]Eccl 6:8, 11 2:16 [a]Lit *forever* [A]Eccl 1:11; 9:5 [B]Eccl 2:14 2:17 [a]Lit *evil* [A]Eccl 4:2, 3 2:18 [A]Eccl 1:3; 2:11 [B]Ps 39:6; 49:10 2:19 [a]Lit *dominion* [A]1 Kin 12:13 [B]1 Tim 6:10 2:20 [a]Lit *turned aside my heart to despair* 2:21 [a]Lit *share* [A]Eccl 4:4 [B]Eccl 2:18 2:22 [a]Lit *the striving of his heart* [A]Eccl 1:3; 2:11

in life. In spite of man's grandest efforts, some crooked matters will remain unstraightened.

1:16 wisdom. Cf. Introduction: Background and Setting.

1:17 I set my mind to know. When Solomon depended on empirical research rather than divine revelation to understand life, he found it to be an empty experience.

1:18 wisdom ... much grief. The expected outcome of wisdom is success. Success, in turn, should bring happiness. But Solomon concluded that there were no guarantees. This grieves the one who places his hope in human achievement alone.

2:1–11 Pleasure, although not necessarily evil, has its shortcomings, much like human wisdom. Solomon reflected upon his tragic experiences in attempting to draw satisfaction purely out of pleasure.

2:1, 2 test. The investigation or test was crucial for Solomon. But the test was not scientific; rather it was a practical experiment to see what worked. He was interested in what a given act accomplished.

2:3 stimulate. In further tests on the human level, Solomon overemphasized human gratification at the expense of God's glory.

2:4–8 Cf. 1Ki 4–10 for an amplified account of Solomon's riches.

2:8 many concubines. This fits Solomon's 700 wives and 300 concubines (1Ki 11:3). Most likely this should be translated "harem," which would refer to Solomon's many women (cf. 1Ki 11:3).

2:10 reward. Solomon's portion in life. This was what he received for all his activity and effort.

2:11 no profit. "Vanity" is defined in this context. The futility of the labor process is that Solomon had nothing of enduring and satisfying substance to show for it. Wisdom is no guarantee that one will achieve satisfaction, even in accomplishments comparable to Solomon's. To expend God-given resources for human accomplishment alone is empty.

2:12–17 Human wisdom suffers another crucial shortcoming—it leaves both the wise and the fool empty-handed at the threshold of death.

2:14 fool walks in darkness. The fool is not one who is mentally deficient, but is morally bankrupt. It is not that he cannot learn wisdom, but that he won't. He refuses to know, fear, and obey God.

2:17 for the work which had been done. Since it had no more lasting value than the folly of a fool, Solomon viewed even the great reward of his labor as a source of pain.

2:18–22 Cf. 4:7, 8

2:18 hated all ... my labor. Solomon left the kingdom divided to Jeroboam and his son Rehoboam, both of whom squandered their opportunities (1Ki 12–14).

2:21 legacy. The portion of one's life that he must leave behind at death.

his days his task is painful and [A]grievous; even at
night his [a]mind [B]does not rest. This too is vanity.
24 There is [A]nothing better for a man *than* to eat
and drink and [a]tell himself that his labor is good.
This also I have seen that it is [B]from the hand of
God. 25 For who can eat and who can have enjoyment without [a]Him? 26 For to a person who is good
in His sight [A]He has given wisdom and knowledge
and joy, while to the sinner He has given the task
of gathering and collecting so that he may [B]give to
one who is good in God's sight. This too is [C]vanity
and striving after wind.

A TIME FOR EVERYTHING

3 There is an appointed time for everything. And
there is a [A]time for every [a]event under heaven—

2 A time to give birth and a [A]time to die;
A time to plant and a time to
uproot what is planted.
3 A [A]time to kill and a time to heal;
A time to tear down and a
time to build up.
4 A time to [A]weep and a time to [B]laugh;
A time to mourn and a time to [C]dance.
5 A time to throw stones and a
time to gather stones;
A time to embrace and a time
to shun embracing.
6 A time to search and a time
to give up as lost;
A time to keep and a time
to throw away.
7 A time to tear apart and a
time to sew together;
A time to [A]be silent and a time to speak.
8 A time to love and a time to [A]hate;
A time for war and a time for peace.

9 [A]What profit is there to the worker from that in
which he toils? 10 I have seen the [A]task which God
has given the sons of men with which to occupy
themselves.

GOD SET ETERNITY IN THE HEART OF MAN

11 He has [A]made everything [a]appropriate in its
time. He has also set eternity in their heart, [b]yet so
that man [B]will not find out the work which God has
done from the beginning even to the end.
12 I know that there is [A]nothing better for them
than to rejoice and to do good in one's lifetime;
13 moreover, that every man who eats and drinks
sees good in all his labor—it is the [A]gift of God. 14 I
know that everything God does will remain forever;
there is nothing to add to it and there is nothing to
take from it, for God has *so* worked that men should
[a,A]fear Him. 15 That [A]which is has been already and
that which will be has already been, for God seeks
what has passed by.
16 Furthermore, I have seen under the sun *that*
in the place of justice there is [A]wickedness and in
the place of righteousness there is wickedness. 17 I
said [a]to myself, "[A]God will judge both the righteous
man and the wicked man," for a [B]time for every
[b]matter and for every deed is there. 18 I said [a]to myself concerning the sons of men, "God has surely
tested them in order for them to see that they are
but [A]beasts." 19 [A]For the fate of the sons of men and
the fate of beasts [a]is the same. As one dies so dies
the other; indeed, they all have the same breath
and there is no advantage for man over beast, for
all is [b]vanity. 20 All go to the same place. All came
from the [A]dust and all return to the dust. 21 Who
knows that the [A]breath of man ascends upward
and the breath of the beast descends downward
to the earth? 22 I have seen that [A]nothing is better

2:23 [a]Lit *heart* [A]Job 5:7; 14:1; Eccl 1:18; 5:17 [B]Ps 127:2 2:24 [a]Lit *cause his soul to see good in his labor* [A]Eccl 2:3; 3:12, 13, 22; 5:18; 6:12; 8:15; 9:7; Is 56:12; Luke 12:19; 1 Cor 15:32; 1 Tim 6:17 [B]Eccl 3:13 2:25 [a]So Gr; Heb *me* 2:26 [A]Job 32:8; Prov 2:6 [B]Job 27:16, 17; Prov 13:22 [C]Eccl 1:14 3:1 [a]Lit *delight* [A]Eccl 3:17; 8:6 3:2 [A]Job 14:5; Heb 9:27 3:3 [A]Gen 9:6; 1 Sam 2:6; Hos 6:1, 2 3:4 [A]Rom 12:15 [B]Ps 126:2 [C]Ex 15:20 3:7 [A]Amos 5:13 3:8 [A]Ps 101:3; Prov 13:5 3:9 [A]Eccl 1:3; 2:11; 5:16 3:10 [A]Eccl 1:13; 2:26 3:11 [a]Lit *beautiful* [b]Or *without which man* [A]Gen 1:31 [B]Job 5:9; Eccl 7:23; 8:17; Rom 11:33 3:12 [A]Eccl 2:24 3:13 [A]Eccl 2:24; 5:19 3:14 [a]Or *be in awe before Him* [A]Eccl 5:7; 7:18; 8:12, 13; 12:13 3:15 [A]Eccl 1:9; 6:10 3:16 [A]Eccl 4:1; 5:8; 8:9 3:17 [a]Lit *in my heart* [b]Or *delight* [A]Gen 18:25; Ps 96:13; 98:9; Eccl 11:9; Matt 16:27; Rom 2:6-10; 2 Thess 1:6-9 [B]Eccl 3:1; 8:6 3:18 [a]Lit *in my heart* [A]Ps 49:12, 20; 73:22 3:19 [a]Lit *and they have one fate* [b]Or *futility* [A]Ps 49:12; Eccl 9:12 3:20 [A]Gen 3:19; Ps 103:14; Eccl 12:7 3:21 [A]Eccl 12:7 3:22 [A]Eccl 2:24

2:24 nothing better. Even with the limitations of this present life (cf. 3:12, 13, 22; 5:18, 19; 8:15; 9:7), humanity should rejoice in its temporal goodness. **from the hand of God.** Solomon's strong view of God's sovereignty brings comfort after an honest critique of what life in a cursed world entails.

2:25 without Him. Lit. "outside of Him" (i.e., God).

2:26 give to one who is good. The qualifier "in God's sight" makes God's prerogative the standard.

3:1–8 an appointed time. Not only does God fix the standard and withhold or dispense satisfaction (2:26), but He also appoints "times." Earthly pursuits are good in their proper place and time, but unprofitable when pursued as the chief goal (cf. vv. 9, 10).

3:9, 10 Earthly pursuits (vv. 1–8) are unprofitable when considered as life's chief good, which was never intended by God.

3:11 everything. Every activity or event for which a culmination point may be fixed. **appropriate.** The phrase echoes "God saw … it was good" (Ge 1:31). Even in a cursed universe, activity should not be meaningless. Its futility lies in the fickle satisfaction of man and his failure to trust the wisdom of sovereign God. **set eternity in their heart.** God made men for His eternal purpose, and nothing in post-Fall time can bring them complete satisfaction.

3:12 to rejoice and to do good. These words capture the goal of Solomon's message which he echoes and elaborates on in 11:9, 10 and again in 12:13, 14.

3:13 sees good in all his labor. In accepting everything as a gift of his Creator, even in a cursed world, man is enabled to see "good" in all his work (cf. 2:24, 25; 5:19).

3:14 fear Him. Acknowledging God's enduring and perfect work becomes grounds for reverence, worship, and meaning. Apart from God, man's works are pitifully inadequate. The theme, "fear God," also appears in 5:7; 8:12, 13; 12:13.

3:17 God will judge … for a time … is there. The culminating issue of Solomon's "appointed time" discussion is that there is a time for judgment (cf. Jn 5:28, 29). God's judgment is a central theme in Solomon's message for this book (cf. 11:9; 12:14). Even where the word "judgment" is absent, the greater issue of divine retribution is often pervasive.

3:18, 19 fate. The ultimate fate of man and beast is to die. Solomon isn't looking at eternal destinies, but rather at what all earthly flesh shares in common.

3:20 from the dust … to the dust. Genesis 3:19 is alluded to in the broadest sense, i.e., all of living creation will die and go to the grave. Neither heaven nor hell is considered here.

3:21 the breath. Man's breath or physical life appears on the surface to be little different than that of an animal. In reality, man's soul differs in that God has made him eternal (cf. v. 11).

3:22 after him. Once again, death becomes the overshadowing reality.

than that man should be happy in his activities, for
that is his lot. For who will bring him to see [B]what
will occur after him?

THE EVILS OF OPPRESSION

4 Then I looked again at all the acts of [A]oppres-
sion which were being done under the sun. And
behold *I saw* the tears of the oppressed and *that*
they had [B]no one to comfort *them;* and on the side
of their oppressors was power, but they had no one
to comfort *them.* 2 So [A]I congratulated the dead who
are already dead more than the living who are still
living. 3 But [A]better *off* than both of them is the one
who has never existed, who has never seen the evil
activity that is done under the sun.
4 I have seen that every labor and every [A]skill
which is done is *the result of* rivalry between a man
and his neighbor. This too is [a,B]vanity and striving
after wind. 5 The fool [A]folds his hands and [B]con-
sumes his own flesh. 6 One hand full of rest is [A]better
than two fists full of labor and striving after wind.
7 Then I looked again at vanity under the sun.
8 There was a certain man without a [a]dependent,
having neither a son nor a brother, yet there was
no end to all his labor. Indeed, [A]his eyes were not
satisfied with riches *and he never asked,* "And [B]for
whom am I laboring and depriving myself of pleasure?" This too is vanity and it is a [C]grievous task.
9 Two are better than one because they have a
good return for their labor. 10 For if [a]either of them
falls, the one will lift up his companion. But woe
to the one who falls when there is not [b]another to
lift him up. 11 Furthermore, if two lie down together
they [a]keep warm, but [A]how can one be warm *alone?*
12 And if [a]one can overpower him who is alone, two
can resist him. A cord of three *strands* is not quickly
torn apart.
13 A [A]poor yet wise lad is better than an old and
foolish king who no longer knows *how* to receive
[a]instruction. 14 For he has come [A]out of prison to
become king, even though he was born poor in
his kingdom. 15 I have seen all the living under the
sun throng to the side of the second lad who [a]re-
places him. 16 There is no end to all the people, to
all who were before them, and even the ones who
will come later will not be happy with him, for this
too is [A]vanity and striving after wind.

YOUR ATTITUDE TOWARD GOD

5 [a,A]Guard your steps as you go to the house of
God and draw near to listen rather than to offer
the [B]sacrifice of fools; for they do not know they are

3:22 [B]Eccl 2:18; 6:12; 8:7; 10:14 4:1 [A]Job 35:9; Ps 12:5; Eccl 3:16; 5:8; Is 5:7 [B]Jer 16:7; Lam 1:9 4:2 [A]Job 3:11-26; Eccl 2:17; 7:1 4:3 [A]Job 3:11-22; Eccl 6:3; Luke 23:29 4:4 [a]Or *futility,* and so throughout the ch [A]Eccl 2:21 [B]Eccl 1:14 4:5 [A]Prov 6:10; 24:33 [B]Is 9:20 4:6 [A]Prov 15:16, 17; 16:8 4:8 [a]Lit *second* [A]Prov 27:20; Eccl 1:8; 5:10 [B]Eccl 2:21 [C]Eccl 1:13 4:10 [a]Lit *they fall* [b]Lit *a second* 4:11 [a]Lit *have warmth* [A]1 Kin 1:1-4 4:12 [a]Lit *he* 4:13 [a]Or *warning* [A]Eccl 7:19; 9:15 4:14 [A]Gen 41:14, 41-43 4:15 [a]Lit *stands in his stead* 4:16 [A]Eccl 1:14 5:1 [a]Ch 4:17 in Heb [A]Ex 3:5; 30:18-20; Is 1:12 [B]1 Sam 15:22; Prov 15:8; 21:27

4:1–3 The oppressiveness of some lives renders death more appealing.

4:3 **evil activity.** Earthly life can be so disheartening as to make nonexistence preferable.

4:4 ***the result of* rivalry.** The lack of satisfaction with life leads some to conclude that everyone else has it better.

4:5 **folds his hands ... consumes his own flesh.** Even the man who settles into idleness, living on what he takes from others, is self-tormented and never satisfied (cf. Is 9:20; 44:20).

4:7–12 The futility of labor alone without satisfaction and without any heir to experience its value is addressed (cf. 2:18–22, a complementary message). Life is better with companionship.

4:13–16 The cherished popularity of kings is precarious and short-lived.

4:15 **second lad.** This refers to the legitimate successor to the "old and foolish king," as opposed to the "poor yet wise lad" (cf. v. 13) who rises on his ability to reign.

5:1–7 A prelude to the book's concluding admonition to approach God with reverence.

5:1 **the house of God.** The temple Solomon built in Jerusalem (cf. 1Ki 8:15–21).

SOLOMON REFLECTS ON GENESIS

Toward the end of his life, the penitent King Solomon pondered life in the wake of the fall and the outworking of man's sin.

Solomon drew the following conclusions, possibly from his own study of Genesis:

1. God created the heavens and earth with laws of design and regularity (Ecc 1:2–7; 3:1–8; cf. Ge 1:1–31; 8:22).
2. Man is created from dust and returns to dust (Ecc 3:20; 12:7; cf. Ge 2:7; 3:19).
3. God placed in man His life-giving breath (Ecc 12:7; cf. Ge 2:7).
4. As God ordained it, marriage is one of life's most enjoyable blessings (Ecc 9:9; cf. Ge 2:18–25).
5. Divine judgment results from the fall (Ecc 3:14–22; 11:9; 12:14; cf. Ge 2:17; 3:1–19).
6. The effect of the curse on creation is "vanity," i.e., futility (Ecc 1:5–8; cf. Ge 3:17–19).
7. Labor after the fall is difficult and yields little profit (Ecc 1:3, 13; 2:3; 3:9–11; cf. Ge 3:17–19).
8. Death overcomes all creatures after the fall (Ecc 8:8; 9:4, 5; cf. Ge 2:17; 3:19).
9. After the fall, man's heart is desperately wicked (Ecc 7:20, 29; 8:11; 9:3; cf. Ge 3:22; 6:5; 8:21).
10. God withholds certain knowledge and wisdom from man for His wise, but unspoken, reasons (Ecc 6:12; 8:17; cf. Ge 3:22).

doing evil. 2[a]Do not be [A]hasty [b]in word or [c]impulsive
in thought to bring up a matter in the presence of
God. For God is in heaven and you are on the earth;
therefore let your [B]words be few. 3 For the dream
comes through much [a]effort and the voice of a [A]fool
through many words.
4 When you [A]make a vow to God, do not be late
in paying it; for *He takes* no delight in fools. [B]Pay
what you vow! 5 It is [A]better that you should not vow
than that you should vow and not pay. 6 Do not let
your [a]speech cause [b]you to sin and do not say in
the presence of the messenger *of God* that it was
a [A]mistake. Why should God be angry on account
of your voice and destroy the work of your hands?
7 For in many dreams and in many words there is
[a]emptiness. Rather, [b,A]fear God.
8 If you see [A]oppression of the poor and [B]denial
of justice and righteousness in the province, do not
be [C]shocked at the [a]sight; for one [b]official watches
over another [b]official, and there are higher [c]officials
over them. 9 After all, a king who cultivates the field
is an advantage to the land.

THE FOLLY OF RICHES

10[A]He who loves money will not be satisfied with
money, nor he who loves abundance *with its* income. This too is [a]vanity. 11[A]When good things increase, those who consume them increase. So what
is the advantage to their owners except to [a]look
on? 12 The sleep of the working man is [A]pleasant,
whether he eats little or much; but the [a]full stomach of the rich man does not allow him to sleep.
13 There is a grievous evil *which* I have seen under
the sun: [A]riches being [a]hoarded by their owner to his
hurt. 14 When those riches were lost through [a]a bad
investment and he had fathered a son, then there
was nothing [b]to support him. 15[A]As he had come
naked from his mother's womb, so will he return as
he came. He will [B]take nothing from the fruit of his
labor that he can carry in his hand. 16 This also is a
grievous evil—exactly as a man [a]is born, thus will
he [b]die. So [A]what is the advantage to him who [B]toils
for the wind? 17 Throughout his life [A]*he* also eats in
darkness with [B]great vexation, sickness and anger.
18 Here is what I have seen to be [A]good and [a]fit-
ting: to eat, to drink and [b]enjoy oneself in all one's
labor in which he toils under the sun *during* the few
[c]years of his life which God has given him; for this
is his [d,B]reward. 19 Furthermore, as for every man to
whom [A]God has given riches and wealth, He has also
[B]empowered him to eat from them and to receive
his [a]reward and rejoice in his labor; this is the [C]gift
of God. 20 For he will not often [a]consider the [b]years
of his life, because [A]God keeps [c]him occupied with
the gladness of his heart.

THE FUTILITY OF LIFE

6 There is an [A]evil which I have seen under the
sun and it is prevalent [a]among men— 2 a man
to whom God has [A]given riches and wealth and
honor so that his soul [B]lacks nothing of all that he
desires; yet God has not empowered him to eat
from them, for a foreigner [a]enjoys them. This is
[b]vanity and a severe affliction. 3 If a man fathers a
hundred *children* and lives many years, however
many [a]they be, but his soul is not satisfied with good
things and he does not even have a *proper* [A]burial,
then I say, "Better [B]the miscarriage than he, 4 for it
comes in futility and goes into obscurity; and its
name is covered in obscurity. 5 It never sees the sun
and it never knows *anything;* [a]it is better off than
he. 6 Even if the *other* man lives a thousand years
twice and does not [a]enjoy good things—[A]do not all
go to one place?"
7[A]All a man's labor is for his mouth and yet the
[a]appetite is not [b]satisfied. 8 For [A]what advantage
does the wise man have over the fool? What *advantage* does the poor man have, knowing *how* to

5:2 [a]Ch 5:1 in Heb [b]Lit *with your mouth* [c]Lit *hurry your heart* [A]Prov 20:25 [B]Prov 10:19; Matt 6:7 5:3 [a]Lit *task* [A]Job 11:2; Prov 15:2; Eccl 10:14 5:4 [A]Num 30:2; Ps 50:14; 76:11 [B]Ps 66:13, 14 5:5 [A]Prov 20:25; Acts 5:4 5:6 [a]Lit *mouth* [b]Lit *your body* [A]Lev 4:2, 22; Num 15:25 5:7 [a]Lit *vanity* [b]Or *revere* [A]Eccl 3:14; 7:18; 8:12, 13; 12:13 5:8 [a]Lit *delight* [b]Lit *high one* [c]Lit *ones* [A]Eccl 4:1 [B]Ezek 18:18 [C]1 Pet 4:12 5:10 [a]Or *futility* [A]Eccl 1:8; 2:10, 11; 4:8 5:11 [a]Lit *see with their eyes* [A]Eccl 2:9 5:12 [a]Lit *satiety* [A]Prov 3:24 5:13 [a]Lit *guarded* [A]Eccl 6:2 5:14 [a]Lit *an evil task* [b]Lit *in his hand* 5:15 [A]Job 1:21 [B]Ps 49:17; 1 Tim 6:7 5:16 [a]Lit *comes* [b]Lit *go* [A]Eccl 1:3; 2:11; 3:9 [B]Prov 11:29 5:17 [A]Ps 127:2 [B]Eccl 2:23 5:18 [a]Lit *beautiful* [b]Lit *see good* [c]Or *days* [d]Or *share* [A]Eccl 2:24 [B]Eccl 2:10 5:19 [a]Or *share* [A]2 Chr 1:12; Eccl 6:2 [B]Eccl 6:2 [C]Eccl 3:13 5:20 [a]Lit *remember* [b]Or *days* [c]So with Gr [A]Ex 23:25 6:1 [a]Lit *upon* [A]Eccl 5:13 6:2 [a]Lit *eats from them* [b]Or *futility* [A]1 Kin 3:13 [B]Ps 17:14; 73:7; Eccl 2:10 6:3 [a]Lit *the days of his years* [A]Is 14:20; Jer 8:2; 22:19 [B]Job 3:16; Eccl 4:3 6:5 [a]Lit *more rest has this one than that* 6:6 [a]Lit *see* [A]Eccl 2:14 6:7 [a]Lit *soul* [b]Lit *filled* [A]Prov 16:26 6:8 [A]Eccl 2:15

5:2 heaven … earth. Because God is in heaven and man is on earth, rash promises and arguments before Him are foolish.

5:4, 5 vow and not pay. Promises made to God have serious implications. The OT background for this admonition is found in Dt 23:21–23; Jdg 11:35. Ananias and Sapphira learned the hard way (cf. Ac 5:1–11).

5:6 speech cause you to sin. Don't vow something that your fleshly desire will cause you to break. messenger. The priest in the house of God (cf. Mal 2:7). Both priests and prophets are called messengers, commissaries who deliver and report back messages for the Heavenly King (cf. Is 6:1–13). Don't tell them your broken vow was a small thing.

5:7 fear God. Cf. 3:14; 8:12, 13; 12:13.

5:8, 9 Officials have an unfair advantage to attain wealth.

5:10 The love of money is never satisfied (cf. 1Ti 6:9, 10).

5:11 those who consume them increase. This refers to the rich man's dependents.

5:12–17 Earthly treasures are precarious and bring disadvantages; they produce anxiety (v. 12) and pain (v. 13). They disappear through bad business (v. 14) and are left at death (v. 15). They can even produce fear (v. 17).

5:18–20 In contrast to the anxiety of those just described (vv. 12–17), for those who consider God as the source of wealth, there are pleasures, riches, and the ability to enjoy them (see 2:24).

5:18 fitting. The same word translated in 3:11 "appropriate." Once again, Solomon uses an admonition to enjoy the richness of life that God gives.

5:19 the gift of God. To understand this is to enjoy the satisfaction of His good gifts.

5:20 God keeps him occupied. When a person recognizes the goodness of God, he rejoices and does not dwell unduly on the troubles detailed in the previous context.

6:2 God has not empowered him to eat. The Lord gives and takes away for His own purposes. So, the blessings of God cannot be assumed or taken for granted. But they should be enjoyed with thankfulness while they are available.

6:3–6 Not having a burial, as in the case of King Jehoiakim (Jer 22:18, 19), indicated complete disrespect and disregard for one's life. To die without mourners or honors was considered worse than being born dead, even if one had many children and a full life.

6:3 This is hyperbole.

6:7–12 Lack of soul satisfaction comes from working only for what is consumed (v. 7), seeing little difference in the end between the wise and foolish (v. 8), not knowing the future (v. 9), realizing that God alone controls everything (v. 10), and true

walk before the living? 9 What the eyes [A]see is better
than what the soul [a]desires. This too is [B]futility and
a striving after wind.
10 Whatever [A]exists has already been named, and
it is known what man is; for he [B]cannot dispute
with him who is stronger than he is. 11 For there are
many words which increase futility. What *then* is
the advantage to a man? 12 For who knows what is
good for a man during *his* lifetime, *during* the few
[a]years of his futile life? He will [b]spend them like a
shadow. For who can tell a man [A]what will be after
him under the sun?

WISDOM AND FOLLY CONTRASTED

7 A [A]good name is better than
a good ointment,
And the [B]day of *one's* death is better
than the day of one's birth.
2 It is better to go to a house of mourning
Than to go to a house of feasting,
Because [a]that is the [A]end of every man,
And the living [b,B]takes *it* to [c]heart.
3 [A]Sorrow is better than laughter,
For [B]when a face is sad a
heart may be happy.
4 The [a]mind of the wise is in the
house of mourning,
While the [a]mind of fools is in
the house of pleasure.
5 It is better to [A]listen to the
rebuke of a wise man
Than for one to listen to
the song of fools.
6 For as the [a]crackling of [A]thorn
bushes under a pot,
So is the [B]laughter of the fool;
And this too is futility.
7 For [A]oppression makes a wise man mad,
And a [B]bribe [a]corrupts the heart.
8 The [A]end of a matter is better
than its beginning;
[B]Patience of spirit is better than
haughtiness of spirit.
9 Do not be [a,A]eager in your
heart to be angry,
For anger resides in the bosom of fools.
10 Do not say, "Why is it that the former
days were better than these?"
For it is not from wisdom that
you ask about this.
11 Wisdom along with an
inheritance is good
And an [A]advantage to those
who see the sun.
12 For [A]wisdom is [a]protection *just*
as money is [a]protection,
But the advantage of knowledge
is that [B]wisdom preserves the
lives of its possessors.
13 Consider the [A]work of God,
For who is [B]able to straighten
what He has bent?
14 [A]In the day of prosperity be happy,
But [B]in the day of adversity consider—
God has made the one as well as the other
So that man will [C]not discover
anything *that will be* after him.

15 I have seen everything during my [a,A]lifetime of
futility; there is [B]a righteous man who perishes in
his righteousness and there is [C]a wicked man who
prolongs *his life* in his wickedness. 16 Do not be excessively [A]righteous and do not [B]be overly wise. Why
should you ruin yourself? 17 Do not be excessively
wicked and do not be a fool. Why should you [A]die
before your time? 18 It is good that you grasp one
thing and also not [a]let go of the other; for the one
who [A]fears God comes forth with [b]both of them.
19 [A]Wisdom strengthens a wise man more than
ten rulers who are in a city. 20 Indeed, [A]there is not a
righteous man on earth who *continually* does good
and who never sins. 21 Also, do not [a]take seriously
all words which are spoken, so that you will not
hear your servant [A]cursing you. 22 For [a]you also
have realized that you likewise have many times
cursed others.

6:9 [a]Lit *goes after* [A]Eccl 11:9 [B]Eccl 1:14 6:10 [A]Eccl 1:9; 3:15 [B]Job 9:32; 40:2; Prov 21:30; Is 45:9 6:12 [a]Lit *days* [b]Lit *do* [A]Eccl 3:22 7:1 [A]Prov 22:1 [B]Eccl 4:2; 7:8 7:2 [a]I.e. death [b]Lit *gives* [c]Lit *his heart* [A]Eccl 2:14, 16; 3:19, 20; 6:6; 9:2, 3 [B]Ps 90:12 7:3 [A]Eccl 2:2 [B]2 Cor 7:10 7:4 [a]Lit *heart* 7:5 [A]Ps 141:5; Prov 6:23; 13:18; 15:31, 32; 25:12; Eccl 9:17 7:6 [a]Lit *voice* [A]Ps 58:9; 118:12 [B]Eccl 2:2 7:7 [a]Lit *destroys* [A]Eccl 4:1; 5:8 [B]Ex 23:8; Deut 16:19; Prov 17:8, 23 7:8 [A]Eccl 7:1 [B]Prov 14:29; 16:32; Gal 5:22; Eph 4:2 7:9 [a]Lit *hasty in your spirit* [A]Prov 14:17; James 1:19 7:11 [A]Prov 8:10, 11; Eccl 2:13 7:12 [a]Lit *in a shadow* [A]Eccl 7:19; 9:18 [B]Prov 3:18; 8:35 7:13 [A]Eccl 3:11; 8:17 [B]Eccl 1:15 7:14 [A]Deut 26:11; Eccl 3:22; 9:7; 11:9 [B]Deut 8:5; Job 2:10 [C]Eccl 3:22 7:15 [a]Lit *days* [A]Eccl 6:12; 9:9 [B]Eccl 8:14 [C]Eccl 8:12, 13 7:16 [A]Prov 25:16; Phil 3:6 [B]Rom 12:3 7:17 [A]Job 22:16; Ps 55:23; Prov 10:27 7:18 [a]Lit *rest your hand* [b]Lit *all* [A]Eccl 3:14; 5:7; 8:12, 13; 12:13 7:19 [A]Eccl 7:12; 9:13-18 7:20 [A]1 Kin 8:46; 2 Chr 6:36; Ps 143:2; Prov 20:9; Rom 3:23 7:21 [a]Lit *give your heart to* [A]Prov 30:10 7:22 [a]Lit *your heart knows also*

understanding of the present and future is limited (vv. 11, 12).

7:1 good name. Where a man has so lived to earn a good reputation, the day of his death can be a time of honor.

7:2–6 The point of this section is to emphasize that more is learned from adversity than from pleasure. True wisdom is developed in the crucible of life's trials, though the preacher wishes that were not the case when he writes "this too is futility" (v. 6).

7:10 former days. In the midst of trouble and discontent, it is easy to lose touch with reality.

7:12 wisdom is protection. Wisdom is better than money because it provides the fulfilled life.

7:13 straighten what He has bent? Man should consider God's activity because God is sovereign, decreeing and controlling everything under the sun (cf. 1:15).

7:14 prosperity … adversity. God ordains both kinds of days and withholds knowledge of the future.

7:15–18 The focus on the nature of righteousness is made clear in the statement "For the one who fears God comes forth with both of them" (v. 18).

7:15 perishes … prolongs. The fact that some righteous men die young and some wicked men live long is enigmatic (cf. 8:11, 12).

7:16 excessively righteous … overly wise. Solomon has already exhorted his readers to be righteous and wise (cf. v. 19). The warning here is against being self-righteous or pharisaical.

7:19 Wisdom strengthens. The measure of wisdom is its ability to bring good outcomes in life.

7:20 does good … never sins. Solomon gave great emphasis to the general effects of sin (cf. Ge 3:1–24) and also pointed out the universality of personal transgressions. Paul may have recalled this passage when he wrote Ro 3:10.

7:21, 22 words which are spoken. Since you have many offensive words to be forgiven, don't keep strict accounts of other's offensive words against you.

23 I tested all this with wisdom, *and* I said, "I will be wise," [A]but it was far from me. 24 What has been is remote and [A]exceedingly [a]mysterious. [B]Who can discover it? 25 I [a,A]directed my [b]mind to know, to investigate and to seek wisdom and an explanation, and to know the evil of folly and the foolishness of madness. 26 And I discovered more [A]bitter than death the woman whose heart is [B]snares and nets, whose hands are chains. [C]One who is pleasing to God will escape from her, but [D]the sinner will be captured by her.

27 "Behold, I have discovered this," says the Preacher, "*adding* one thing to another to find an explanation, 28 which [a]I am still seeking but have not found. I have found one man among a thousand, but I have not found a [A]woman among all these. 29 Behold, I have found only this, that [A]God made men upright, but they have sought out many devices."

OBEY RULERS

8 Who is like the wise man and who knows the interpretation of a matter? A man's wisdom [A]illumines [a]him and causes his [B]stern face to [b]beam.

2 I say, "Keep the [a]command of the king because of the [A]oath [b]before God. 3 Do not be in a hurry [a,A]to leave him. Do not join in an evil matter, for he will do whatever he pleases." 4 Since the word of the king is authoritative, [A]who will say to him, "What are you doing?"

5 He who [A]keeps a *royal* command [B]experiences no [a]trouble, for a wise heart knows the proper time and procedure. 6 For [A]there is a proper time and procedure for every delight, though a man's trouble is heavy upon him. 7 If no one [A]knows what will happen, who can tell him when it will happen? 8 [A]No man has authority to restrain the wind with the wind, or authority over the day of death; and there is no discharge in the time of war, and [B]evil will not deliver [a]those who practice it. 9 All this I have seen and applied my [a]mind to every deed that has been done under the sun wherein a man has exercised [A]authority over *another* man to his hurt.

10 So then, I have seen the wicked buried, those who used to go in and out from the holy place, and they are [A]*soon* forgotten in the city where they did thus. This too is futility. 11 Because the [A]sentence against an evil deed is not executed quickly, therefore [B]the hearts of the sons of men among them are given fully to do evil. 12 Although a sinner does evil a hundred *times* and may [A]lengthen his *life*, still I know that it will be [B]well for those who fear God, who fear [a]Him openly. 13 But it will [A]not be well for the evil man and he will not lengthen his days like a [B]shadow, because he does not fear God.

14 There is futility which is done on the earth, that is, there are [A]righteous men to whom it [a]happens according to the deeds of the wicked. On the other hand, there are [B]evil men to whom it [a]happens according to the deeds of the righteous. I say that this too is futility. 15 So I commended pleasure, for there is nothing good for [A]a man under the sun except to eat and to drink and to be merry, and this will stand by him in his [a]toils *throughout* the days of his life which God has given him under the sun.

16 When I [A]gave my heart to know wisdom and to see the task which has been done on the earth (even though one should [a,B]never sleep day or night), 17 and I saw every work of God, *I concluded* that [A]man cannot discover the work which has been done under the sun. Even though man should seek laboriously, he will not discover; and [B]though the wise man should say, "I know," he cannot discover.

MEN ARE IN THE HAND OF GOD

9 For I have taken all this to my heart and explain [a]it that righteous men, wise men, and their deeds are [A]in the hand of God. [B]Man does not know whether *it will be* [C]love or hatred; anything [b]awaits him.

7:23 [A]Eccl 3:11; 8:17 7:24 [a]Lit *deep* [A]Rom 11:33 [B]Job 11:7; 37:23; Eccl 8:17 7:25 [a]Lit *turned about* [b]Lit *heart* [A]Eccl 1:15, 17; 10:13 7:26 [A]Prov 5:4 [B]Prov 7:23 [C]Prov 6:23, 24 [D]Prov 22:14 7:28 [a]Lit *my soul still seeks* [A]1 Kin 11:3 7:29 [A]Gen 1:27 8:1 [a]Lit *his face* [b]Or *change* [A]Ex 34:29, 30 [B]Deut 28:50 8:2 [a]Lit *mouth* [b]Lit *of* [A]Ex 22:11; 2 Sam 21:7; Ezek 17:18 8:3 [a]Lit *to go out from his presence* [A]Eccl 10:4 8:4 [A]Job 9:12; Dan 4:35 8:5 [a]Lit *evil thing* [A]Eccl 12:13 [B]Prov 12:21 8:6 [A]Eccl 3:1, 17 8:7 [A]Eccl 3:22; 6:12; 7:14; 9:12 8:8 [a]Lit *its possessors* [A]Ps 49:7 [B]Eccl 8:13 8:9 [a]Lit *heart* [A]Eccl 4:1; 5:8; 7:7 8:10 [A]Eccl 1:11; 2:16; 9:5, 15 8:11 [A]Ex 34:6; Ps 86:15; Rom 2:4; 2 Pet 3:9 [B]Eccl 9:3 8:12 [a]Lit *before Him* [A]Eccl 7:15 [B]Deut 4:40; 12:25; Ps 37:11; Prov 1:33; Is 3:10 8:13 [A]Eccl 8:8; Is 3:11 [B]Job 14:2; Eccl 6:12 8:14 [a]Lit *strikes* [A]Ps 73:14; Eccl 7:15 [B]Job 21:7; Ps 73:3, 12; Jer 12:1; Mal 3:15 8:15 [a]Lit *labor* [A]Eccl 2:24; 3:12, 13; 5:18; 9:7 8:16 [a]Lit *see no sleep in his eyes* [A]Eccl 1:13, 14 [B]Eccl 2:23 8:17 [A]Eccl 3:11 [B]Ps 73:16; Eccl 7:23; Rom 11:33 9:1 [a]Lit *all this* [b]Lit *is before them* [A]Deut 33:3; Job 12:10; Ps 119:109 [B]Eccl 10:14 [C]Eccl 9:6

7:23, 24 "I will be wise" … Who can discover it? The already wise king resolves to be even wiser. But upon further investigation, the limitations of wisdom become apparent. Some things are unknowable. This realization quickly dampens his enthusiasm.

7:26 the woman. This is the seductress about whom Solomon warns young men in Proverbs (Pr 2:16–19; 5:1–14; 6:24–29; 7:1–27). Elsewhere, Solomon exalts the virtues of man's lifetime companion (Ecc 9:9; cf. Pr 5:15–23; 31:10–31).

7:27–29 Empirical acquisition of knowledge, that is man seeking righteousness through his many schemes, fails. Only God can make man upright.

7:29 many devices. The same word is translated "intent" and reflects the evil imaginations of all human beings since Adam and Eve.

8:2, 3 the oath before God. This refers to Israel's promises to serve King Solomon (1Ch 29:24).

8:5, 6 proper time and procedure. A wise man knows when to apply the proper course of action for the best outcome, whether in an earthly sense before the king (8:2) or an eternal sense before God (cf. 12:13, 14).

8:7 what … when. God has appointed a time for everything, but man knows neither the time nor the outcome. These uncertainties can increase his misery.

8:8 wind. Death is as precarious and uncontrollable as the wind.

8:10 the holy place. This refers to the temple at Jerusalem (cf. 5:1). **futility.** Lessons that should be gained from the death of the hypocritically wicked are quickly forgotten.

8:11 the sentence. The gracious delay of God's retribution leads to further disobedience. This delay, in actuality, in no way diminishes the certainty of final judgment.

8:12, 13 those who fear God … the evil man. There is no real advantage for the wicked, although at times it might seem so (cf. 5:7; 12:13, 14). Temporal patience does not eliminate eternal judgment.

8:14 futility. Temporally speaking, God generally rewards obedience and punishes disobedience. Solomon regards the exceptions to this principle as enigmatic and discouraging (see Ps 73).

8:15 pleasure. In no way does Solomon commend unbridled, rampant indulgence in sin, which is implied in Christ's account of the man whose barns were full. That man may have justified his sin by quoting this passage (cf. Lk 12:19). His focus here is on the resolve to enjoy life in the face of the injustice which surrounded him (see 2:24).

8:16, 17 every work of God. God's work is wonderful, but at times incomprehensible.

9:1 in the hand of God. There will be no inequities in the final judgment of the righteous

2 [A]It is the same for all. There is [B]one fate for the
righteous and for the wicked; for the good, for the
clean and for the unclean; for the man who offers
a sacrifice and for the one who does not sacrifice.
As the good man is, so is the sinner; as the swearer
is, so is the one who [a]is afraid to swear. 3 This is an
evil in all that is done under the sun, that there is
[A]one fate for all men. Furthermore, [B]the hearts of
the sons of men are full of evil and [C]insanity is in
their hearts throughout their lives. Afterwards they
go to the dead. 4 For whoever is joined with all the
living, there is hope; surely a live dog is better than
a dead lion. 5 For the living know they will die; but
the dead [A]do not know anything, nor have they any
longer a reward, for their [B]memory is forgotten.
6 Indeed their love, their hate and their zeal have
already perished, and they will no longer have a
[A]share in all that is done under the sun.
7 Go *then,* [A]eat your bread in happiness and drink
your wine with a cheerful heart; for God has already
approved your works. 8 Let your [A]clothes be white
all the time, and let not [B]oil be lacking on your head.
9 Enjoy life with the woman whom you love all the
days of your [a,A]fleeting life which He has given to you
under the sun[b]; for this is your [B]reward in life and in
your toil in which you have labored under the sun.

WHATEVER YOUR HAND FINDS TO DO

10 Whatever your hand finds to do, [A]do *it* with *all*
your might; for there is no [B]activity or planning or
knowledge or wisdom in [C]Sheol where you are going.
11 I again saw under the sun that the [A]race is not
to the swift and the [B]battle is not to the warriors,
and neither is bread to the wise nor [C]wealth to the
discerning nor favor to men of ability; for time and
[D]chance overtake them all. 12 Moreover, man does
not [A]know his time: like fish caught in a treacherous net and [B]birds trapped in a snare, so the sons
of men are [C]ensnared at an evil time when it [D]sud-
denly falls on them.
13 Also this I came to see as wisdom under the
sun, and [a]it impressed me. 14 There [A]was a small
city with few men in it and a great king came to it,
surrounded it and constructed large siegeworks
against it. 15 But there was found in it a [A]poor wise
man and he [a]delivered the city [B]by his wisdom. Yet
[C]no one remembered that poor man. 16 So I said,
"[A]Wisdom is better than strength." But the wisdom
of the poor man is despised and his words are not
heeded. 17 The [A]words of the wise heard in quietness
are *better* than the shouting of a ruler among fools.
18 [A]Wisdom is better than weapons of war, but [B]one
sinner destroys much good.

A LITTLE FOOLISHNESS

10 Dead flies make a [A]perfumer's oil stink, so a
little foolishness is weightier than wisdom
and honor. 2 A wise man's heart *directs him* toward
the right, but the foolish [A]man's heart *directs him*
toward the left. 3 Even when the fool walks along the
road, his [a]sense is lacking and he [b,A]demonstrates
to everyone *that* he is a fool. 4 If the ruler's [a]temper
rises against you, [A]do not abandon your position,
because [B]composure allays great offenses.
5 There is an evil I have seen under the sun, like
an error which goes forth from the ruler— 6 [A]folly
is set in many exalted places while rich men sit
in humble places. 7 I have seen [A]slaves *riding* [B]on
horses and princes walking like slaves on the land.
8 [A]He who digs a pit may fall into it, and a [B]ser-
pent may bite him who breaks through a wall. 9 He
who quarries stones may be hurt by them, and he
who splits logs may be endangered by them. 10 If
the [a]axe is dull and he does not sharpen *its* edge,
then he must [b]exert more strength. Wisdom has the
advantage of giving success. 11 If the serpent bites
[a,A]before being charmed, there is no profit for the
charmer. 12 [A]Words from the mouth of a wise man
are gracious, while the lips of a [B]fool consume him;
13 the beginning of [a]his talking is folly and the end
of [b]it is wicked [A]madness. 14 Yet the [A]fool multiplies
words. No man knows what will happen, and who
can tell him [B]what will come after him? 15 The toil of
[a]a fool *so* wearies him that he does not *even* know

9:2 [a]Lit *fears an oath* [A]Job 9:22; Eccl 9:11 [B]Eccl 2:14; 3:19; 6:6; 7:2 9:3 [A]Eccl 9:2; Jer 17:10 [B]Eccl 8:11 [C]Eccl 1:17 9:5 [A]Job 14:21 [B]Ps 88:12; Eccl 1:11; 2:16; 8:10; Is 26:14 9:6 [A]Eccl 2:10; 3:22 9:7 [A]Eccl 2:24; 8:15 9:8 [A]Rev 3:4 [B]Ps 23:5 9:9 [a]Lit *life of vanity* [b]Heb adds *all the days of your vanity* [A]Eccl 6:12; 7:15 [B]Eccl 2:10 9:10 [A]Eccl 11:6; Rom 12:11; Col 3:23 [B]Eccl 9:5 [C]Gen 37:35; Job 21:13; Is 38:10 9:11 [A]Amos 2:14, 15 [B]2 Chr 20:15; Ps 76:5; Zech 4:6 [C]Deut 8:17, 18 [D]1 Sam 6:9 9:12 [A]Eccl 8:7 [B]Prov 7:23 [C]Prov 29:6; Is 24:18; Hos 9:8 [D]Luke 21:34, 35 9:13 [a]Lit *great it was to me* 9:14 [A]2 Sam 20:16-22 9:15 [a]Or *might have delivered* [A]Eccl 4:13 [B]2 Sam 20:22 [C]Eccl 2:16; 8:10 9:16 [A]Prov 21:22; Eccl 7:12, 19 9:17 [A]Eccl 7:5; 10:12 9:18 [A]Eccl 9:16 [B]Josh 7:1-26; 2 Kin 21:2-17 10:1 [A]Ex 30:25 10:2 [A]Matt 6:33; Col 3:1 10:3 [a]Lit *heart* [b]Lit *says* [A]Prov 13:16; 18:2 10:4 [a]Lit *spirit* [A]Eccl 8:3 [B]1 Sam 25:24-33; Prov 25:15 10:6 [A]Esth 3:1, 5f; Prov 28:12; 29:2 10:7 [A]Prov 19:10 [B]Esth 6:8-10 10:8 [A]Ps 7:15; Prov 26:27 [B]Amos 5:19 10:10 [a]Lit *iron* [b]Lit *strengthen* 10:11 [a]Lit *without enchantment* [A]Ps 58:4, 5; Jer 8:17 10:12 [A]Prov 10:32; 22:11; Luke 4:22 [B]Prov 10:14; 18:7; Eccl 4:5 10:13 [a]Lit *the words of his mouth* [b]Lit *his mouth* [A]Eccl 7:25 10:14 [A]Prov 15:2; Eccl 5:3 [B]Eccl 3:22; 6:12; 7:14; 8:7 10:15 [a]Lit *fools*

or the wicked, because God remembers both in perfect detail.

9:2, 3 **one fate for all men.** Death because of universal depravity.

9:7 **eat … drink.** *See notes on 2:24.*

9:9 **the woman.** Cf. Pr 5:15–19 and Solomon's Song.

9:11 **time and chance.** Wisdom cannot guarantee good outcomes because of what appear to be so many unpredictable contingencies.

9:12 **his time.** The time of his misfortune, especially death (cf. 11:8, "days of darkness"; 12:1, "evil days").

9:13–15 Wisdom may not receive its due in this life.

9:16 This is true because he lacks status and position.

10:1–20 Solomon draws together assorted examples of the wisdom he has both scrutinized and touted.

10:2 **right … left.** This proverb is based on the fact that, commonly, the right hand is more deft than the left.

10:3 **fool.** *See note on 2:14.* **walks.** A person lacking wisdom will manifest that in daily conduct.

10:5 It is a great and far-reaching evil when leaders make bad judgments.

10:6, 7 **rich men … princes.** Life presents some strange ironies and is not, in this world, always fair.

10:8–10 **digs … does not sharpen.** Dangers and uncertainties abound in life.

10:10 **Wisdom … giving success.** A little wisdom will ease the efforts of life. Even though life's experiences often don't turn out the way one would have hoped, wise living usually produces a good outcome. This is a very important conclusion for Solomon's testing of wisdom.

10:12–14 **Words.** Man demonstrates wisdom in words as well as works. Foolish words yield unfavorable outcomes.

10:15 **to go to a city.** A proverb for ignorance with regard to the most ordinary matters, which extends even to spiritual realities. If a fool can't find a town, how could he possibly locate God?

how to go to a city. 16 Woe to you, O land, whose [A]king
is a lad and whose princes [a]feast in the morning.
17 Blessed are you, O land, whose king is of nobility
and whose princes eat at the appropriate time—
for strength and not for [A]drunkenness. 18 Through
[A]indolence the rafters sag, and through slackness
the house leaks. 19 *Men* prepare a meal for enjoyment, and [A]wine makes life merry, and [B]money
[a]is the answer to everything. 20 Furthermore, [A]in
your bedchamber do not [B]curse a king, and in your
sleeping rooms do not curse a rich man, for a bird
of the heavens will carry the sound and the winged
creature will make the matter known.

CAST YOUR BREAD ON THE WATERS

11 [A]Cast your bread on the surface of the waters,
for you [A]will find it [a]after many days. 2 [A]Divide
your portion to seven, or even to eight, for you do
not know what [B]misfortune may occur on the earth.
3 If the clouds are full, they pour out rain upon the
earth; and whether a tree falls toward the south or
toward the north, wherever the tree falls, there it
[a]lies. 4 He who watches the wind will not sow and
he who looks at the clouds will not reap. 5 Just as
you do not [A]know [a]the path of the wind and [B]how
bones *are formed* in the womb of the [b]pregnant
woman, so you do not [C]know the activity of God
who makes all things.

6 Sow your seed [A]in the morning and do not [a]be
idle in the evening, for you do not know whether
[b]morning or evening sowing will succeed, or
whether both of them alike will be good.

7 The light is pleasant, and *it is* good for the eyes
to [A]see the sun. 8 Indeed, if a man should live many
years, let him [A]rejoice in them all, and let him remember the [B]days of darkness, for they will be
many. Everything that is to come *will be* futility.

9 Rejoice, young man, during your childhood,
and let your heart be pleasant during the days of
young manhood. And follow the [a]impulses of your
heart and the [b,A]desires of your eyes. Yet know that
[B]God will bring you to judgment for all these things.
10 So, remove grief and anger from your heart and
put away [a,A]pain from your body, because childhood
and the prime of life are fleeting.

REMEMBER GOD IN YOUR YOUTH

12 [A]Remember also your Creator in the days of
your youth, before the [B]evil days come and
the years draw near when you will say, "I have
no delight in them"; 2 before the [A]sun and the
light, the moon and the stars are darkened, and
clouds return after the rain; 3 in the day that the
watchmen of the house tremble, and mighty men
[A]stoop, the grinding ones stand idle because they
are few, and [B]those who look through [a]windows
grow dim; 4 and the doors on the street are shut
as the [A]sound of the grinding mill is low, and one
will arise at the sound of the bird, and all the
[B]daughters of song will [a]sing softly. 5 Furthermore,
[a]men are afraid of a high place and of terrors on
the road; the almond tree blossoms, the grasshopper drags himself along, and the caperberry
is ineffective. For man goes to his eternal [A]home
while [B]mourners go about in the street. 6 *Remember Him* before the silver cord is [a]broken and the
[A]golden bowl is crushed, the pitcher by the well is
shattered and the wheel at the cistern is crushed;

10:16 [a]Lit *eat* [A]Is 3:4, 12 10:17 [A]Prov 31:4; Is 5:11 10:18 [A]Prov 24:30-34 10:19 [a]Lit *answers all* [A]Judg 9:13; Ps 104:15; Eccl 2:3 [B]Eccl 7:12 10:20 [A]2 Kin 6:12; Luke 12:3 [B]Ex 22:28; Acts 23:5 11:1 [a]Lit *in, within* [A]Deut 15:10; Prov 19:17; Matt 10:42; Gal 6:9; Heb 6:10 11:2 [A]Ps 112:9; Matt 5:42; Luke 6:30; 1 Tim 6:18, 19 [B]Eccl 11:8; 12:1 11:3 [a]Lit *is* 11:5 [a]Or with many mss *how the spirit* enters *the bones in the womb* [b]Lit *full* [A]John 3:8 [B]Ps 139:13-16 [C]Eccl 1:13; 3:10, 11; 8:17 11:6 [a]Lit *let down your hand* [b]Lit *this or that* [A]Eccl 9:10 11:7 [A]Eccl 6:5; 7:11 11:8 [A]Eccl 9:7 [B]Eccl 12:1 11:9 [a]Lit *ways* [b]Lit *sights* [A]Num 15:39; Job 31:7; Eccl 2:10 [B]Eccl 3:17; 12:14; Rom 14:10 11:10 [a]Lit *evil* [A]2 Cor 7:1; 2 Tim 2:22 12:1 [A]Deut 8:18; Neh 4:14; Ps 63:6; 119:55 [B]Eccl 11:8 12:2 [A]Is 5:30; 13:10; Ezek 32:7, 8; Joel 3:15; Matt 24:29 12:3 [a]Or *holes* [A]Ps 35:14; 38:6 [B]Gen 27:1; 48:10; 1 Sam 3:2 12:4 [a]Lit *be brought low* [A]Jer 25:10; Rev 18:22 [B]2 Sam 19:35 12:5 [a]Lit *they* [A]Job 17:13; 30:23 [B]Gen 50:10; Jer 9:17 12:6 [a]So with Gr; Heb *removed* [A]Zech 4:2, 3

10:18 rafters sag … house leaks. This is likely an analogy for the kingdom of a lazy monarch.

10:19 money is the answer to everything. The partying king of v. 18 thinks he can fix all the disasters of his inept reign by raising taxes.

11:1 Cast your bread. Take a calculated and wise step forward in life, like a farmer who throws his seed on the wet or marshy ground and waits for it to grow (cf. Is 32:20).

11:2 Divide. Be generous while there is plenty, and make friends while time remains, because one never knows when he might need them to return the favor.

11:3–6 The world is full of things over which one has no control, including the purposes of God. There is no virtue in wishful wondering, but there is hope for those who get busy and do their work.

11:7–12:8 Solomon crystallizes the book's message. Death is imminent and with it comes retribution. Enjoyment and judgment, though strange partners, come together in this section because both clamor for man's deepest commitment. Surprisingly, one does not win out over the other. In a world created for enjoyment but damaged by sin, judgment and enjoyment/pleasure are held in tension. With too much pleasure, judgment stands as a threatening force; with too much judgment, enjoyment suffers. In the final analysis, both are prominent themes of life that are resolved in our relationship to God, the primary issue of life and this book.

11:7 light. Good times in contrast to "darkness" (v. 8), meaning bad times. Cf. 12:1.

11:9 Rejoice … judgment. The two terms seem to cancel out the other. How can this be explained? Enjoy life but do not commit iniquity. The balance that is called for ensures that enjoyment is not reckless, sinful abandonment. Pleasure is experienced in faith and obedience, for as Solomon has said repeatedly, one can only receive true satisfaction as a gift from God.

11:10 fleeting. Enjoy childhood and youth while you can because they are soon gone.

12:1 Remember … your Creator … evil days. Remember you are God's property, so serve Him from the start of your years, not the end of your years, when service is very limited.

12:2–6 Solomon uses the imagery of aging, incorporating elements of a dilapidated house, nature, and a funeral procession to heighten the emphasis of 11:7–12:1.

12:2 sun … moon … clouds. Youth is typically the time of dawning light, old age the time of twilight's gloom.

12:3 watchmen of the house tremble. The hands and arms which protect the body, as guards do a palace, shake in old age. **mighty men stoop.** The legs, like supporting pillars, weaken. **grinding ones.** Teeth. **those who look through windows.** Eyes.

12:4 doors. Lips that do not have much to say. **sound of the grinding.** This refers to little eating, when the sound of masticating is low. **arise.** Light sleep. **daughters of song.** The ear and voice that once loved music.

12:5 afraid of a high place. For fear of falling. **almond tree blossoms.** A white blossoming tree among dark trees speaks of hair. **mourners.** The funeral is near.

12:6, 7 Here are the images of death.

12:6 silver cord is broken. Perhaps this pictures a lamp hanging from a silver chain, which breaks with age, smashing the lamp. Some suggest this refers to the spinal cord. **golden bowl.** Possibly this refers to the brain. **pitcher … well … wheel.** Wells required a wheel with a rope attached in order to lower the pitcher for water. Perhaps this pictures

7 then the [A]dust will return to the earth as it was,
and the [a,B]spirit will return to [C]God who gave it.
8 "[A]Vanity of vanities," says the Preacher, "all is
vanity!"

PURPOSE OF THE PREACHER

9 In addition to being a wise man, the Preacher
also taught the people knowledge; and he pondered,
searched out and arranged [A]many proverbs. 10 The
Preacher sought to find [A]delightful words and to
write [B]words of truth correctly.

11 The [A]words of wise men are like [B]goads, and
masters of *these* collections are like [a]well-driven
[C]nails; they are given by one Shepherd. 12 But beyond this, my son, be warned: the [a]writing of [A]many
books is endless, and excessive [B]devotion *to books*
is wearying to the body.
13 The conclusion, when all has been heard, *is:*
[A]fear God and [B]keep His commandments, because
this *applies to* [C]every person. 14 For [A]God will bring
every act to judgment, everything which is hidden,
whether it is good or evil.

12:7 [a]Or *breath* [A]Gen 3:19; Job 34:15; Ps 104:29; Eccl 3:20 [B]Job 34:14; Eccl 3:21; Luke 23:46; Acts 7:59 [C]Num 16:22; 27:16; Is 57:16; Zech 12:1 12:8 [A]Eccl 1:2 12:9 [A]1 Kin 4:32 12:10 [A]Prov 10:32 [B]Prov 22:20, 21 12:11 [a]Lit *planted* [A]Prov 1:6; 22:17; Eccl 7:5; 10:12 [B]Acts 2:37 [C]Ezra 9:8; Is 22:23 12:12 [a]Lit *making* [A]1 Kin 4:32 [B]Eccl 1:18 12:13 [A]Eccl 3:14; 5:7; 7:18; 8:12 [B]Deut 4:2; Eccl 8:5 [C]Deut 10:12; Mic 6:8 12:14 [A]Eccl 3:17; 11:9; Matt 10:26; Rom 2:16; 1 Cor 4:5

the fountain of blood, the heart. **broken … crushed … shattered … crushed.** All of these actions portray death as tragic and irreversible.

12:7 dust … spirit. Solomon recalls Ge 2:7 and 3:19 as he contemplates the end of the aging process. **spirit … return to … who gave it.** The sage ends his message with the culmination of a human life. "The LORD gave and the LORD has taken away" (Job 1:21; 1Ti 6:7).

12:7, 8 This gloomy picture of old age does not negate the truth that old age can be blessed for the godly (Pr 16:31), but it does remind the young that they will not have the ability to enjoy that blessing of a godly old age and a life of strong service to God if they do not remember their Creator while young (v. 1).

12:9–14 Solomon's final words of advice.

12:11 goads … well-driven nails. Two shepherd's tools are in view: one used to motivate reluctant animals, the other to secure those who might otherwise wander into dangerous territory. Both goads and nails picture aspects of applied wisdom. **one Shepherd.** True wisdom has its source in God alone.

12:12 books. Books written on any other subject than God's revealed wisdom will only proliferate the uselessness of man's thinking.

12:13, 14 fear God. Solomon's final word on the issues raised in this book, as well as life itself, focuses on one's relationship to God. All of the concern for a life under the sun, with its pleasures and uncertainties, was behind Solomon. Such things seemed comparatively irrelevant to him as he faced the end of his life. But death, in spite of the focused attention he had given to it in Ecclesiastes, was not the greatest equalizer. Judgment/retribution is the real equalizer as Solomon saw it, for God will bring every person's every act to judgment. Unbelievers will stand at the Great White Throne judgment (cf. Rev 20:11–15) and believers before Christ at the Bema judgment (cf. 1Co 3:10–15; 2Co 5:9, 10). When all is said and done, the certainty and finality of retribution give life the meaning for which David's oft-times foolish son had been searching. Whatever may be one's portion in life, accountability to God, whose ways are often mysterious, is both eternal and irrevocable.

THE

SONG OF SOLOMON

TITLE

The Greek Septuagint (LXX) and Latin Vulgate (Vg.) versions follow the Hebrew (Masoretic Text) with literal translations of the first two words in 1:1—"Song of Songs." Several English versions read "The Song of Solomon," thus giving the fuller sense of 1:1. The superlative, "Song of Songs" (cf. "Holy of Holies" in Ex 26:33, 34 and "King of kings" in Rev 19:16), indicates that this song is the best among Solomon's 1,005 musical works (1Ki 4:32). The word translated "song" frequently refers to music that honors the Lord (cf. 1Ch 6:31, 32; Pss 33:3; 40:3; 144:9).

AUTHOR AND DATE

Solomon, who reigned over the united kingdom 40 years (971–931 B.C.), appears 7 times by name in this book (1:1, 5; 3:7, 9, 11; 8:11, 12). In view of his writing skills, musical giftedness (1Ki 4:32), and the authorial, not dedicatory, sense of 1:1, this piece of Scripture could have been penned at any time during Solomon's reign. Since cities to the N and to the S are spoken of in Solomon's descriptions and travels, both the period depicted and the time of actual writing point to the united kingdom before it divided after Solomon's reign ended. Knowing that this portion of Scripture comprises one song by one author, it is best taken as a unified piece of poetic, Wisdom literature rather than a series of love poems without a common theme or author.

BACKGROUND AND SETTING

Two people dominate this true-life, dramatic love song. Solomon, whose kingship is mentioned 5 times (1:4, 12; 3:9, 11; 7:5), appears as "the beloved." The Shulammite maiden (6:13) remains obscure; most likely she was a resident of Shunem, 3 mi. N of Jezreel in lower Galilee. Some suggest she is Pharaoh's daughter (1Ki 3:1), although the Song provides no evidence for this conclusion. Others favor Abishag, the Shunammite who cared for King David (1Ki 1:1–4, 15). An unknown maiden from Shunem, whose family had possibly been employed by Solomon (8:11), seems most reasonable. She would have been Solomon's first wife (Ecc 9:9), before he sinned by adding 699 other wives and 300 concubines (1Ki 11:3).

Minor roles feature several different groups in this book. First, note the not-infrequent commentary by "the daughters of Jerusalem" (1:4b, 8, 11; 3:6–11; 5:9; 6:1, 10, 13a; 7:1–5; 8:5a), who might be part of Solomon's household staff (cf. 3:10). Second, the affirmation of 5:1b would most likely be God's blessing on the couple's union. Third, the Shulammite's brothers speak (8:8, 9).

The setting combines both rural and urban scenes. Portions take place in the hill country N of Jerusalem, where the Shulammite lived (6:13) and where Solomon enjoyed prominence as a vinegrower and shepherd (Ecc 2:4–7). The city section includes the wedding and time afterward at Solomon's abode in Jerusalem (3:6–7:13).

The first spring appears in 2:11–13 and the second in 7:12. Assuming a chronology without gaps, the Song of Solomon took place over a period of time at least one year in length, but probably no longer than two years.

HISTORICAL AND THEOLOGICAL THEMES

All 117 verses in Solomon's Song have been recognized by the Jews as a part of their sacred writings. Along with Ruth, Esther, Ecclesiastes, and Lamentations, it is included among the OT books of the Megilloth, or "five scrolls." The Jews read this song at Passover, calling it "the Holy of Holies." Surprisingly, God is not mentioned explicitly except possibly in 8:6. No formal theological themes emerge. The NT never quotes Solomon's Song directly (nor Esther, Obadiah, and Nahum).

In contrast to the two distorted extremes of ascetic abstinence and lustful perversion outside of marriage, Solomon's ancient love song exalts the purity of marital affection and romance. It parallels and enhances other portions of Scripture which portray God's plan for marriage, including the beauty and sanctity of sexual intimacy between husband and wife. The Song rightfully stands alongside other classic Scripture passages which expand on this theme, e.g., Ge 2:24; Ps 45; Pr 5:15–23; 1Co 7:1–5; 13:1–8; Eph 5:18–33; Col 3:18, 19; and 1Pe 3:1–7. Hebrews 13:4 captures the heart of this song, "Marriage *is to be held* in honor among all, and the *marriage* bed *is to be* undefiled; for fornicators and adulterers God will judge."

INTERPRETIVE CHALLENGES

The Song has suffered strained interpretations over the centuries by those who use the "allegorical" method of interpretation, claiming that this song has no actual historical basis, but rather that it depicts God's love for Israel and/or Christ's love for the church. The misleading idea from hymnology that Christ is the rose of Sharon and the lily of the valleys results from this method (2:1). The "typological" variation admits the historical reality, but concludes that it ultimately pictures Christ's bridegroom love for His bride the church.

A more satisfying way to approach Solomon's Song is to take it at face value and interpret it in the normal historical sense, understanding the frequent use of poetic imagery to depict reality. To do so understands that Solomon recounts 1) his own days of courtship, 2) the early days of his first marriage, followed by 3) the maturing of this royal couple through the good and bad days of life. The Song of Solomon expands on the ancient marriage instructions of Ge 2:24, thus providing spiritual music for a lifetime of marital harmony. It is given by God to demonstrate His intention for the romance and loveliness of marriage, the most precious of human relations and "the grace of life" (1Pe 3:7).

The metaphoric and euphemistic nature of this book is designed by God to veil the private intimacy of marriage. Its beautiful expressions of romantic love are purposefully shrouded in poetic language—intended only to give general insight into the joys of passion, desire, and romance. In this way, the Song expresses the wonders of marital love while distancing itself from anything crass or explicitly sensual. Interpreters of this book must be careful to maintain the dignified character of the book and must not read anything into it that is not actually there.

OUTLINE

I. The Courtship: "Leaving" (1:2–3:5)
- A. The Lovers' Remembrances (1:2–2:7)
- B. The Lovers' Expression of Reciprocal Love (2:8–3:5)

II. The Wedding: "Cleaving" (3:6–5:1)
- A. The Kingly Bridegroom (3:6–11)
- B. The Wedding and First Night Together (4:1–5:1a)
- C. God's Approval (5:1b)

III. The Marriage: "Weaving" (5:2–8:14)
- A. The First Major Disagreement (5:2–6:3)
- B. The Restoration (6:4–8:4)
- C. Growing in Grace (8:5–14)

THE YOUNG SHULAMMITE BRIDE AND JERUSALEM'S DAUGHTERS

1 The [a]Song of [A]Songs, which is Solomon's.

2 "[a]May he kiss me with the kisses of his mouth!
For your [A]love is better than wine.
3 "Your [A]oils have a pleasing fragrance,
Your [B]name is *like* [a]purified oil;
Therefore the [b,C]maidens love you.
4 "Draw me after you *and* let us run *together!*
The [A]king has brought me
into his chambers."

"[a]We will rejoice in you and be glad;
We will [b]extol your [B]love more than wine.
Rightly do they love you."

5 "[a]I am black but [A]lovely,
O [B]daughters of Jerusalem,
Like the [C]tents of [D]Kedar,
Like the curtains of Solomon.
6 "Do not stare at me because I am [a]swarthy,
For the sun has burned me.
My [A]mother's sons were angry with me;
They made me [B]caretaker of the vineyards,
But I have not taken care of
my own vineyard.
7 "Tell me, O you [A]whom my soul loves,
Where do you [B]pasture *your flock,*
Where do you make *it* [C]lie down at noon?
For why should I be like one
who [a]veils herself
Beside the flocks of your [D]companions?"

SOLOMON, THE LOVER, SPEAKS

8 "[a]If you yourself do not know,
[A]Most beautiful among women,
Go forth on the trail of the flock
And pasture your young goats
By the tents of the shepherds.

9 "[a]To me, [A]my darling, you are like
My [B]mare among the
chariots of Pharaoh.
10 "Your [A]cheeks are lovely with ornaments,
Your neck with strings of [B]beads."

11 "[a]We will make for you ornaments of gold
With beads of silver."

12 "[a]While the king was at his [b]table,
My [c,A]perfume gave forth its fragrance.
13 "My beloved is to me a pouch of [A]myrrh
Which lies all night between my breasts.
14 "My beloved is to me a cluster
of [A]henna blossoms
In the vineyards of [B]Engedi."

15 "[a,b,A]How beautiful you are, my darling,
[b]How beautiful you are!
Your [B]eyes are *like* doves."

16 "[a,b]How handsome you are, [A]my beloved,
And so pleasant!
Indeed, our couch is luxuriant!
17 "The beams of our houses are [A]cedars,
Our rafters, [a,B]cypresses.

THE BRIDE'S ADMIRATION

2 "[a]I am the [b,A]rose of [B]Sharon,
The [C]lily of the valleys."

2 "[a]Like a lily among the thorns,
So is [A]my darling among the [b]maidens."

3 "[a]Like an [b,A]apple tree among
the trees of the forest,
So is my beloved among the [c]young men.
In his shade I took great
delight and sat down,
And his [B]fruit was sweet to my [d]taste.

1:1 [a]Or *Best of the Songs* [A]1 Kin 4:32 1:2 [a]BRIDE [A]Song 1:4; 4:10 1:3 [a]Lit *oil which is emptied* (from one vessel to another) [b]Or *virgins* [A]Song 4:10; John 12:3 [B]Eccl 7:1 [C]Ps 45:14 1:4 [a]CHORUS [b]Lit *mention with praise* [A]Ps 45:14, 15 [B]Song 1:4; 4:10 1:5 [a]BRIDE [A]Song 2:14; 4:3; 6:4 [B]Song 2:7; 3:5, 10; 5:8, 16; 8:4 [C]Ps 120:5 [D]Is 60:7 1:6 [a]Or *black* [A]Ps 69:8 [B]Song 8:11 1:7 [a]Some versions read *wanders* [A]Song 3:1-4 [B]Song 2:16; 6:3 [C]Is 13:20; Jer 33:12 [D]Song 8:13 1:8 [a]BRIDEGROOM [A]Song 5:9; 6:1 1:9 [a]Lit *I have compared you to* [A]Song 1:15; 2:2, 10, 13 [B]2 Chr 1:16, 17 1:10 [A]Song 5:13 [B]Gen 24:53; Is 61:10 1:11 [a]CHORUS 1:12 [a]BRIDE [b]Or *couch* [c]Lit *nard* [A]Song 4:14; Mark 14:3; John 12:3 1:13 [A]Ps 45:8; John 19:39 1:14 [A]Song 4:13 [B]1 Sam 23:29 1:15 [a]BRIDEGROOM [b]Lit *Behold* [A]Song 1:16; 2:10, 13; 4:1, 7; 6:4, 10 [B]Song 4:1; 5:12 1:16 [a]BRIDE [b]Lit *Behold* [A]Song 2:3, 9, 17; 5:2, 5, 6, 8 1:17 [a]Or *junipers* [A]1 Kin 6:9, 10; Jer 22:14 [B]2 Chr 3:5 2:1 [a]BRIDE [b]Lit *crocus* [A]Is 35:1 [B]Is 33:9; 35:2 [C]Song 5:13; 7:2; Hos 14:5 2:2 [a]BRIDEGROOM [b]Lit *daughters* [A]Song 1:9 2:3 [a]BRIDE [b]Or *apricot* [c]Lit *sons* [d]Lit *palate* [A]Song 8:5 [B]Song 4:13, 16; 8:11, 12

1:1 See Introduction: Title; Author and Date.

1:2–3:5 In this first of 3 major sections to the Song, 32 out of 39 verses are spoken by the Shulammite, with brief interludes by her beloved and the daughters of Jerusalem. This portion most likely represents her remembrances of past events combined with the desires of her heart to marry the king, as she anticipates his arrival to take her to Jerusalem for the wedding in 3:6ff.

1:2, 3 Four features of Solomon attracted *the beloved: 1) his lips, 2) his love, 3) his lo*tion, and 4) his pure lifestyle. Later Solomon noticed these same features in her (4:9–11).

1:3 **the maidens.** The daughters of Jerusalem (v. 5).

1:4 **let us run.** This is better understood as spoken by the Shulammite, rather than the daughters of Jerusalem, in the sense of "let us hurry." **The king has brought me.** This is better understood as the desire of her heart—"Let the king bring me into his chambers"—rather than a statement of fact. **We will extol your love.** The daughters of Jerusalem affirmed the Shulammite's praise in v. 2.

1:5, 6 **I am black.** The Shulammite was concerned that the sun (from working outdoors) had marred her complexion (cf. vineyard, 7:12; 8:11).

1:6 **my own vineyard.** Speaks of herself (cf. 8:12).

1:7 **veils herself.** Valuing purity, she disclaimed the veil of the prostitute, unlike Tamar (Ge 38:14–16). Rather, she would go as a shepherdess to a shepherd.

1:8 This could have been spoken by the daughters of Jerusalem. **Most beautiful among women.** The Shulammite received accolades as the best (cf. 5:9; 6:1). This is reminiscent of the Pr 31 woman (v. 29).

1:9 **my darling.** The first of 9 uses (1:15; 2:2, 10, 13; 4:1, 7; 5:2; 6:4) **my mare.** Coming from an accomplished horseman (1Ki 10:26–29), this speech figure makes perfect sense as a striking compliment of her dazzling beauty.

1:13 **My beloved.** The first of 24 appearances.

1:15 **How beautiful you are!** Verbal affirmation fueled this romance. He used "beautiful" at least 10 times (1:15; 2:10, 13; 4:1, 7; 6:4, 10; 7:6). **eyes . . . *like* doves.** She returned the compliment in 5:12, which is best understood as beautiful eyes representing a beautiful personality.

1:16, 17 Actually an outdoor setting in the forest.

2:3–6 This scene pictures the loving desire of the Shulammite rather than her actual experience.

4 "He has [A]brought me to *his* [a]banquet hall,
And his [B]banner over me is love.
5 "Sustain me with [A]raisin cakes,
Refresh me with [a,B]apples,
Because [C]I am lovesick.
6 "Let [A]his left hand be under my head
And [A]his right hand [B]embrace me."

7 "[a]I [A]adjure you, O [B]daughters
of Jerusalem,
By the [C]gazelles or by the
[D]hinds of the field,
[A]That you do not arouse or
awaken *my* love
Until [b]she pleases."

2:4 [a]Lit *house of wine* [A]Song 1:4 [B]Ps 20:5 2:5 [a]Or *apricots* [A]2 Sam 6:19; 1 Chr 16:3; Hos 3:1 [B]Song 7:8 [C]Song 5:8 2:6 [A]Song 8:3 [B]Prov 4:8
2:7 [a]BRIDEGROOM [b]Or *it* [A]Song 3:5; 5:8, 9; 8:4 [B]Song 1:5 [C]Prov 6:5; Song 2:9, 17; 3:5; 8:14 [D]Gen 49:21; Ps 18:33; Hab 3:19

2:4 banquet hall. The scene continues in the outdoors. This "house of wine" symbolizes the vineyard, just as the beams and rafters of 1:17 refer to the forest. **his banner.** As a military flag indicates location or possession, so Solomon's love flew over his beloved one (cf. Nu 1:52; Ps 20:5).

2:7 I adjure you. This refrain, which is repeated before the wedding (3:5) and also afterward (8:4), explicitly expresses her commitment to a chaste life before and during marriage. She invites accountability to the daughters of Jerusalem.

LOCAL COLOR IN THE SONG OF SOLOMON

1:5	"tents of Kedar"	nomadic tribal tents made of dark goat hair
1:5	"curtains of Solomon"	most likely the beautiful curtains of Solomon's palace
1:9	"my mare"	a young, female horse
1:12; 4:13, 14	"perfume" (nard)	an aromatic oil taken from an Indian herb
1:13; 3:6; 4:6, 14; 5:1, 5, 13	"myrrh"	an aromatic gum from the bark of a balsam tree made into perfume in either liquid or solid form
1:14; 4:13	"henna blossoms"	a common shrub whose white, spring blossoms give off a fragrant scent
1:14	"Engedi"	a lush oasis just west of the Dead Sea
1:15; 4:1; 5:12	"dove's eyes"	beautiful, deep, smoke gray eyes of the dove
2:1	"rose of Sharon"	probably a bulb flower like crocus, narcissus, iris, or daffodil growing in the low country (plain of Sharon), south of Mt. Carmel
2:1, 16	"lily of the valleys"	possibly a six-petaled flower that grew in the fertile, watered areas
2:3, 5; 7:8; 8:5	"apple"	an aromatic, sweet fruit—possibly an apricot
2:5	"raisin cakes"	a food associated with religious festivals, having possible erotic significance (cf. 2Sa 6:19; Hos 3:1)
2:7, 9, 17; 3:5; 8:14	"gazelles"	graceful members of the antelope family
2:7; 3:5	"hind"	female deer
2:9, 17; 8:14	"stag"	a male deer
2:14; 5:2; 6:9	"dove"	a common symbol of love
2:17	"mountains of Bether"	a ravine or rugged hills in an unidentifiable location in Israel
3:6; 4:6, 14	"frankincense"	amber resin extracted from trees and used for incense/spice
3:6	"scented powders"	various spices
3:7, 9	"couch," "sedan chair"	a chair that transported the king and his bride
3:9; 4:8, 11, 15; 5:15	"Lebanon"	a beautiful country, north of Israel on the coast, with rich natural resources
4:1; 6:5	"Mount Gilead"	the high plateau east of Galilee and Samaria
4:4	"tower of David"	probably the armory tower of Ne 3:19, 25
4:8	"summit of Amana"	the hill in which the Amana River has its source in Syria
4:8	"summit of Senir and Hermon"	the Amorite and Hebrew names for the tallest summit in northern Israel (over 9,200 ft., cf. Dt 3:9)
4:10, 14, 16; 5:1, 13; 6:2; 8:14	"spices"	the sweet smelling oil from the balsam
4:14	"saffron"	the dried, powdered pistils and stamens of a small crocus
4:14	"calamus"	a wild grass with a gingery scent
4:14	"cinnamon"	a spice taken from the bark of a tree
4:14	"aloes"	a spicy drug with a strong scent
5:14	"beryl"	possibly a yellowish or greenish stone such as topaz
5:14	"sapphires"	the azure-blue lapis lazuli which was abundant in the East
6:4	"Tirzah"	a site known for its natural beauty and gardens located seven miles northeast of Shechem in Samaria
6:13	"the dance of the two companies"	possibly a dance of unknown origin associated with the place of Mahanaim (cf. Ge 32:2)
7:4	"the pools in Heshbon"	water reservoirs in the Moabite city of Heshbon near modern Amman
7:4	"the gate of Bath-rabbim"	possibly a gate name in Heshbon
7:4	"the tower of Lebanon"	most likely refers to the white color of the mountain rather than its elevation of 10,000 feet
7:4	"Damascus"	the capital city of Syria to the east of the Lebanon mountains
7:5	"Carmel"	a prominent wooded mountain in northern Israel
7:13	"mandrakes"	a pungently fragrant herb considered to be an aphrodisiac (cf. Ge 30:14)
8:11	"Baal-hamon"	an unknown location in the hill country north of Jerusalem

8 “[a]Listen! My beloved!
Behold, he is coming,
Climbing [A]on the mountains,
Leaping on the hills!
9 “My beloved is like a [A]gazelle
or a [B]young [a]stag.
Behold, he is standing behind our wall,
He is looking through the windows,
He is peering [C]through the lattice.

10 “My beloved responded and said to me,
‘[A]Arise, my darling, my beautiful one,
And come along.
11 ‘For behold, the winter is past,
The rain is over *and* gone.
12 ‘The flowers have *already*
appeared in the land;
The time has arrived for
[a]pruning *the vines,*
And the voice of the [A]turtledove
has been heard in our land.
13 ‘The [A]fig tree has ripened its figs,
And the [B]vines in blossom have
given forth *their* fragrance.
Arise, my darling, my beautiful one,
And come along!’ ”

14 “[a]O [A]my dove, [B]in the clefts of the [b]rock,
In the secret place of the steep [c]pathway,
Let me see your [d]form,
[C]Let me hear your voice;
For your voice is sweet,
And your [d]form is [D]lovely.”

15 “[a,A]Catch the foxes for us,
The [b]little foxes that are
ruining the vineyards,
While our [B]vineyards are in blossom.”

16 “[a,A]My beloved is mine, and I am his;
He [B]pastures *his flock* among the lilies.
17 “[A]Until [a]the cool of the day when
the shadows flee away,
Turn, my beloved, and be like a [B]gazelle
Or a young stag [C]on the
mountains of [b]Bether.”

THE BRIDE’S TROUBLED DREAM

3 “[a]On my bed night after night I sought him
[A]Whom my soul loves;
I [B]sought him but did not find him.
2 ‘[a]I must arise now and [a]go about the city;
In the [A]streets and in the squares
[b]I must seek him whom my soul loves.’
I sought him but did not find him.
3 “[A]The watchmen who make the
rounds in the city found me,
And I said, ‘Have you seen him
whom my soul loves?’
4 “[A]Scarcely had I [a]left them
When I found him whom my soul loves;
I [B]held on to him and would
not let him go
Until I had [C]brought him to
my mother’s house,
And into the room of her
who conceived me.”

5 “[a]I [A]adjure you, O daughters of Jerusalem,
By the [B]gazelles or by the
hinds of the field,
That you will not arouse or
awaken *my* love
Until [b]she pleases.”

SOLOMON’S WEDDING DAY

6 “[a,b,A]What is this coming up from
the wilderness
Like [B]columns of smoke,
Perfumed with [C]myrrh and [D]frankincense,
With all scented powders
of the merchant?
7 “Behold, it is the *traveling*
couch of Solomon;
Sixty mighty men around it,
Of the mighty men of Israel.

2:8 [a]BRIDE [A]Song 2:17; Is 52:7 2:9 [a]Lit *of the stags* [A]Prov 6:5; Song 2:17; 3:5; 8:14 [B]Song 2:17; 8:14 [C]Judg 5:28 2:10 [A]Song 2:13 2:12 [a]Or *singing* [A]Gen 15:9; Ps 74:19; Jer 8:7 2:13 [A]Matt 24:32 [B]Song 7:12 2:14 [a]BRIDEGROOM [b]Or *crag* [c]Or *cliff* [d]Lit *appearance* [A]Song 5:2; 6:9 [B]Jer 48:28 [C]Song 8:13 [D]Song 1:5 2:15 [a]CHORUS [b]Or *young* [A]Ezek 13:4; Luke 13:32 [B]Song 2:13 2:16 [a]BRIDE [A]Song 6:3; 7:10 [B]Song 4:5; 6:2, 3 2:17 [a]Lit *the day blows* [b]Or *cleavage or a kind of spice* [A]Song 4:6 [B]Song 2:9 [C]Song 2:8 3:1 [a]BRIDE [A]Song 1:7 [B]Song 5:6 3:2 [a]Or *Let me arise* [b]Or *Let me seek* [A]Jer 5:1 3:3 [A]Song 5:7; Is 21:6-8, 11, 12 3:4 [a]Lit *passed* [A]Prov 8:17 [B]Prov 4:13; Rom 8:35, 39 [C]Song 8:2 3:5 [a]BRIDEGROOM [b]Or *it* [A]Song 2:7; 5:8; 8:4 [B]Song 2:7 3:6 [a]CHORUS [b]Lit *Who* [A]Song 8:5 [B]Ex 13:21; Joel 2:30 [C]Song 1:13; 4:6, 14; Matt 2:11 [D]Ex 30:34; Rev 18:13

2:11–13 Winter past, rains over, flowers appearing, and vines blooming use springtime as a picture of their robust, growing love for one another.

2:14 This is best taken as a continuation of what Solomon said as quoted by the Shulammite (vv. 10–15).

2:15 Catch the foxes. Perhaps, as she literally did in the vineyards, Solomon wanted her to do by analogy in their relationship, i.e., to remove those things in their relationship that would spoil their blossoming love. It could also be thought of as “Let us ….”

2:16 My beloved is mine, and I am his. This clearly expresses the sanctity of a monogamous relationship that is built on mutual love (cf. 6:3; 7:10).

3:1–4 As the wedding time approaches, the Shulammite’s expectations grew more intense. It’s best to understand this as her dream, rather than a historical remembrance.

3:1 whom my soul loves. She repeated this phrase once in each of the first 4 verses, expressing her exclusive love for Solomon.

3:3 watchmen. This imagined encounter resembles a later real experience (cf. 5:6–8).

3:4 The Shulammite finds Solomon in her dreams and brings him to where she actually resides—her mother’s house.

3:5 As in 2:7, the beloved knows that the intensity of her love for Solomon cannot yet be experienced until the wedding, so she invites the daughters of Jerusalem to keep her accountable regarding sexual purity. Up to this point, the escalating desire of the Shulammite for Solomon has been expressed in veiled and delicate ways as compared to the explicit and open expressions which follow, as would be totally appropriate for a married couple (cf. 4:1ff.).

3:6–5:1 This second major section portrays the king actually coming for his bride and their return to Jerusalem (3:6–11), the wedding (4:1–7), and the couple’s consummation of their union (4:8–5:1). Unlike the previous section, Solomon does a majority of the speaking (15 of 23 verses).

3:6–11 This narrative would be better understood as spoken by the daughters of Jerusalem who are also called the “daughters of Zion” (v. 11).

8 "All of them are wielders of the sword,
[A]Expert in war;
Each man has his [B]sword at his side,
Guarding against the [a,C]terrors
of the night.
9 "King Solomon has made for
himself a sedan chair
From the timber of Lebanon.
10 "He made its posts of silver,
Its [a]back of gold
And its seat of purple fabric,
With its interior lovingly fitted out
By the [A]daughters of Jerusalem.
11 "Go forth, O [A]daughters of Zion,
And gaze on King Solomon
with the [a]crown
With which his mother has crowned him
On the [B]day of his wedding,
And on the day of his gladness of heart."

SOLOMON'S LOVE EXPRESSED

4 "[a,b]How beautiful [A]you are, my darling,
[b]How beautiful you are!
Your [B]eyes are *like* doves
[C]behind your veil;
Your [D]hair is like a flock of goats
That have descended from Mount [E]Gilead.
2 "Your [A]teeth are like a flock
of *newly* shorn ewes
Which have come up from *their* washing,
All of which bear twins,
And not one among them
has [a]lost her young.
3 "Your lips are like a [A]scarlet thread,
And your [B]mouth is lovely.
Your [C]temples are like a slice
of a pomegranate
Behind your veil.
4 "Your [A]neck is like the tower of David,
Built [a]with rows of stones
On which are [B]hung a thousand shields,
All the round [C]shields of the mighty men.
5 "Your [A]two breasts are like two fawns,
Twins of a gazelle
Which [B]feed among the lilies.
6 "[A]Until [a]the cool of the day
When the shadows flee away,
I will go my way to the
mountain of [B]myrrh
And to the hill of [B]frankincense.

PLACES NAMED IN THE SONG OF SOLOMON

© 1996 Thomas Nelson, Inc.

From the peaks of Lebanon to the streets of Jerusalem (4:8; 6:4), the love story in the Song of Solomon takes place in a variety of settings. The lovers speak of, and to, each other with several word pictures, including "the rose of Sharon" (2:1), "the lily of the valleys" (2:1), and "the vineyards of Engedi" (1:14).

7 "[A]You are altogether beautiful, my darling,
And there is no blemish in you.
8 "*Come* with me from [A]Lebanon, *my* [B]bride,
May you come with me from Lebanon.
[a]Journey down from the summit of [C]Amana,
From the summit of [D]Senir and Hermon,
From the dens of lions,
From the mountains of leopards.
9 "You have made my heart beat
faster, [A]my sister, *my* bride;
You have made my heart beat faster
with a single *glance* of your eyes,
With a single strand of your [B]necklace.

3:8 [a]Lit *terror in the nights* [A]Jer 50:9 [B]Ps 45:3 [C]Ps 91:5 3:10 [a]Or *support* [A]Song 1:5 3:11 [a]Or *wreath* [A]Is 3:16, 17; 4:4 [B]Is 62:5 4:1 [a]BRIDEGROOM [b]Lit *Behold* [A]Song 1:15 [B]Song 1:15; 5:12 [C]Song 6:7 [D]Song 6:5 [E]Mic 7:14 4:2 [a]Or *miscarried* [A]Song 6:6 4:3 [A]Josh 2:18 [B]Song 5:16 [C]Song 6:7 4:4 [a]Or *for an arsenal* [A]Song 7:4 [B]Ezek 27:10, 11 [C]2 Sam 1:21 4:5 [A]Song 7:3 [B]Song 2:16; 6:2, 3 4:6 [a]Lit *the day blows* [A]Song 2:17 [B]Song 4:14 4:7 [A]Song 1:15; Eph 5:27 4:8 [a]Or *Look* [A]1 Kin 4:33; Ps 72:16 [B]Song 5:1; Is 62:5 [C]2 Kin 5:12 [D]Deut 3:9; 1 Chr 5:23; Ezek 27:5 4:9 [A]Song 4:10, 12; 5:1, 2 [B]Gen 41:42; Prov 1:9; Ezek 16:11; Dan 5:7

4:1–5:1 Until 3:11, there has been no hint of a wedding or marriage; thus the scenario of events support the idea that 1:2–3:5 refers to premarital days, while 4:1ff. rehearses the wedding and their love life that followed. Several reasons support this explanation: 1) "wedding" is not mentioned before 3:11; 2) "bride" does not appear until 4:8, and then it is mentioned 6 times from 4:8 to 5:1; and 3) prior to 4:1 the beloved has a holy preoccupation with sexual restraint (cf. 2:7; 3:5), but not afterwards in the holy bonds of matrimony.

4:1–15 Possibly Solomon speaks vv. 1–7 in public and the far more intimate words of vv. 8–15 in private as they prepare to consummate their marriage in v. 16 and 5:1.

4:1–7 For other specific descriptions of the Shulammite's beauty, see 6:4–9 and 7:1–7. He begins v. 1 and closes v. 7 with the same refrain, "you are … beautiful, my darling."

4:1, 3 veil. Not the veil of a prostitute (1:7), but rather the bride.

4:8 from Lebanon. This figuratively describes the distance that the couple had kept sexually, which is further described in v. 12 as a locked garden and a sealed spring.

4:9 my sister. A common ancient Near Eastern term of endearment by a husband for his wife, which expresses closeness and permanence of relationship (cf. 4:10, 12; 5:1, 2).

10 "[A]How beautiful is your love,
my sister, *my* bride!
How much [B]better is your love than wine,
And the [C]fragrance of your oils
Than all *kinds* of [a]spices!
11 "Your lips, *my* bride, [A]drip [B]honey;
Honey and milk are under your tongue,
And the fragrance of your garments
is like the [C]fragrance of Lebanon.
12 "A garden locked is my sister, *my* bride,
A [a]rock garden locked, a [A]spring [B]sealed up.
13 "Your shoots are an [a,A]orchard
of [B]pomegranates
With [C]choice fruits, [D]henna
with nard plants,
14 [A]Nard and saffron, calamus and [B]cinnamon,
With all the trees of [C]frankincense,
[D]Myrrh and aloes, along with
all the finest [a]spices.
15 "*You are* a garden spring,
A well of [a,A]fresh water,
And streams *flowing* from Lebanon."

16 "[a]Awake, O north *wind*,
And come, *wind of* the south;
Make my [A]garden breathe out *fragrance*,
Let its [b]spices [c]be wafted abroad.
May [B]my beloved come into his garden
And eat its [C]choice fruits!"

THE TORMENT OF SEPARATION

5 "[a]I have [A]come into my garden,
[B]my sister, *my* bride;
I have gathered my [C]myrrh
along with my balsam.
I have eaten my honeycomb
[b]and my [D]honey;
I have [E]drunk my wine [b]and my milk.
Eat, [F]friends;
Drink and [c]imbibe deeply, O lovers."

2 "[a]I was asleep but my heart was awake.
A voice! My beloved was knocking:
'Open to me, [A]my sister, my darling,
[B]My dove, my perfect one!
For my head is [b]drenched with dew,
My [C]locks with the [c]damp of the night.'
3 "I have [A]taken off my dress,
How can I put it on *again?*
I have [B]washed my feet,
How can I dirty them *again?*
4 "My beloved extended his hand
through the opening,
And my [a,A]feelings were aroused for him.
5 "I arose to open to my beloved;
And my hands [A]dripped with myrrh,
And my fingers with [a]liquid myrrh,
On the handles of the bolt.
6 "I opened to my beloved,
But my beloved had [A]turned
away *and* had gone!
My [a]heart went out *to him* as he [B]spoke.
I [C]searched for him but I
did not find him;
I [D]called him but he did not answer me.
7 "The [A]watchmen who make the
rounds in the city found me,
They struck me *and* wounded me;
The guardsmen of the walls took
away my shawl from me.
8 "I [A]adjure you, O daughters of Jerusalem,
If you find my beloved,
As to what you will tell him:
For [B]I am lovesick."

9 "[a,b]What kind of beloved is your beloved,
O [A]most beautiful among women?
[b]What kind of beloved is your beloved,
That thus you adjure us?"

ADMIRATION BY THE BRIDE

10 "[a]My beloved is dazzling and [A]ruddy,
[b,B]Outstanding among ten thousand.
11 "His head is *like* gold, pure gold;
His [A]locks are *like* clusters of dates
And black as a raven.

4:10 [a]Or *balsam odors* [A]Song 7:6 [B]Song 1:2, 4 [C]Song 1:3 4:11 [A]Prov 5:3 [B]Ps 19:10; Prov 24:13 [C]Gen 27:27; Hos 14:6 4:12 [a]Lit *stone heap* [A]Prov 5:15-18 [B]Gen 29:3 4:13 [a]Or *park or paradise* [A]Eccl 2:5 [B]Song 6:11; 7:12 [C]Song 2:3; 4:16; 7:13 [D]Song 1:14 4:14 [a]Or *balsam odors* [A]Song 1:12 [B]Ex 30:23 [C]Song 4:6 [D]Ps 45:8; Song 3:6; John 19:39 4:15 [a]Lit *living* [A]Zech 14:8; John 4:10 4:16 [a]BRIDE [b]Or *balsam odors* [c]Lit *flow forth* [A]Song 5:1; 6:2 [B]Song 1:13; 2:3, 8; 6:2 [C]Song 4:13 5:1 [a]BRIDEGROOM [b]Lit *with* [c]Or *become drunk* [A]Song 6:2 [B]Song 4:9 [C]Song 1:13; 4:14 [D]Song 4:11 [E]Prov 9:5; Is 55:1 [F]Judg 14:11, 20; John 3:29 5:2 [a]BRIDE [b]Lit *filled* [c]Lit *drops* [A]Song 4:9 [B]Song 2:14; 6:9 [C]Song 5:11 5:3 [A]Luke 11:7 [B]Gen 19:2 5:4 [a]Lit *bowels* [A]Jer 31:20 5:5 [a]Lit *passing* [A]Song 5:13 5:6 [a]Lit *soul* [A]Song 6:1 [B]Song 5:2 [C]Song 3:1 [D]Prov 1:28 5:7 [A]Song 3:3 5:8 [A]Song 2:7; 3:5 [B]Song 2:5 5:9 [a]CHORUS [b]Or *What is your beloved more than another beloved* [A]Song 1:8; 6:1 5:10 [a]BRIDE [b]Lit *Lifted up banner* [A]1 Sam 16:12 [B]Ps 45:2 5:11 [A]Song 5:2

4:15 a well of fresh water. Solomon testified that whereas she was closed to his physical love before marriage (vv. 8, 12), now she is appropriately open to it (cf. Pr 5:15–20).

4:16 The Shulammite then portrays herself as an open garden, whereas before she was closed (4:12). She describes herself as "his garden" signifying voluntary sexual surrender (cf. 1Co 7:3–5).

5:1 I have. While the guests feasted, the couple consummated their marriage (cf. Ge 29:23; Dt 22:13–21) and Solomon announced the blessing (cf. Ge 2:25). **Eat, friends.** Given the intimate and private nature of sexual union, it seems difficult to understand anyone but God speaking these words (cf. Pr 5:21). This is the divine affirmation of sexual love between husband and wife as holy and beautiful.

5:2–8:14 This third major section features the couple's first argument (5:2–6:3) and their reconciliation (6:4–8:14).

5:2–6:3 Inevitable discord comes to even the most idyllic marriage. The "little foxes" of 2:15 have visited the home in this segment.

5:2 I was asleep but my heart was awake. Some have suggested the beloved dreams here, as in 3:1–4. However, she acknowledges "my heart was awake," indicating that she was not sound asleep. To make this a dream would make the rest of the book a dream, which is highly unlikely. **Open to me.** It appears that Solomon returned home earlier than expected and wanted to give his bride a romantic surprise.

5:3 How can I . . . ? Her groggy response to Solomon.

5:4–6 By the time she awakens fully and opens the door, Solomon has departed.

5:7 Unlike what happened in her dream (3:3), the watchmen treat her badly. Between the darkness and the unfamiliar features of the new bride, this could easily have happened.

5:9 The wise daughters of Jerusalem twice ask a question that prompts this bride to recall the superlative features of her new husband in vv. 10–16.

5:10–16 She responds that he is "outstanding among ten thousand" which is another way to say, "He is the best of the best."

12 "His [A]eyes are like doves
Beside streams of water,
Bathed in milk,
And [a]reposed in *their* [B]setting.
13 "His cheeks are like a [A]bed of balsam,
Banks of sweet-scented herbs;
His lips are [B]lilies
[C]Dripping with liquid myrrh.
14 "His hands are rods of gold
Set with [A]beryl;
His abdomen is carved ivory
Inlaid with [a,B]sapphires.
15 "His legs are pillars of alabaster
Set on pedestals of pure gold;
His appearance is like [A]Lebanon
Choice as the [B]cedars.
16 "His [a,A]mouth is *full of* sweetness.
And he is wholly [B]desirable.
This is my beloved and
this is my friend,
O daughters of Jerusalem."

MUTUAL DELIGHT IN EACH OTHER

6 "[a,A]Where has your beloved gone,
O [B]most beautiful among women?
Where has your beloved turned,
That we may seek him with you?"

2 "[a]My beloved has gone down to his [A]garden,
To the [B]beds of balsam,
To [C]pasture *his flock* in the gardens
And gather [D]lilies.
3 "[A]I am my beloved's and my
beloved is mine,
He who [B]pastures *his flock*
among the lilies."

4 "[a,A]You are as beautiful as
[B]Tirzah, my darling,
As [C]lovely as [D]Jerusalem,
As [E]awesome as [b]an army with banners.
5 "Turn your eyes away from me,
For they have confused me;
[A]Your hair is like a flock of goats
That have descended from Gilead.
6 "[A]Your teeth are like a flock of ewes
Which have come up from *their* washing,
All of which bear twins,
And not one among them
has [a]lost her young.
7 "[A]Your temples are like a slice
of a pomegranate
Behind your veil.
8 "There are sixty [A]queens and
eighty concubines,
And [a,B]maidens without number;
9 *But* [A]my dove, my perfect
one, is [a]unique:
She is her mother's [a]only *daughter;*
She is the pure *child* of the
one who bore her.
The [b,B]maidens saw her and
called her blessed,
The [C]queens and the concubines *also,*
and they praised her, *saying,*

10 'Who is this that [a]grows like the dawn,
As beautiful as the full [A]moon,
As pure [B]as the sun,
As [C]awesome as [b]an army with banners?'
11 "I went down to the orchard of nut trees
To see the blossoms of the valley,
To see whether [A]the vine had budded
Or the [B]pomegranates had bloomed.
12 "Before I was aware, my soul set me
Over the chariots of [a]my noble people."

13 "[a,b]Come back, come back,
O Shulammite;
Come back, come back, that
we may gaze at you!"

"[c]Why should you gaze at
the Shulammite,
As at the [A]dance of [d,B]the
two companies?

5:12 [a]Lit *sitting upon* [A]Song 1:15; 4:1 [B]Ex 25:7 5:13 [A]Song 6:2 [B]Song 2:1 [C]Song 5:5 5:14 [a]Lit *lapis lazuli* [A]Ex 28:20; 39:13; Ezek 1:16; Dan 10:6 [B]Ex 24:10; 28:18; Job 28:16; Is 54:11 5:15 [A]Song 7:4 [B]1 Kin 4:33; Ps 80:10; Ezek 17:23; 31:8 5:16 [a]Lit *palate* [A]Song 7:9 [B]2 Sam 1:23 6:1 [a]CHORUS [A]Song 5:6 [B]Song 1:8 6:2 [a]BRIDE [A]Song 4:16; 5:1 [B]Song 5:13 [C]Song 1:7 [D]Song 2:1; 5:13 6:3 [A]Song 2:16; 7:10 [B]Song 2:16; 4:5 6:4 [a]BRIDEGROOM [b]Lit *bannered ones* [A]Song 1:15 [B]1 Kin 14:17 [C]Song 1:5 [D]Ps 48:2; 50:2 [E]Song 6:10 6:5 [A]Song 4:1 6:6 [a]Or *miscarried* [A]Song 4:2 6:7 [A]Song 4:3 6:8 [a]Or *virgins* [A]1 Kin 11:3 [B]Song 1:3 6:9 [a]Lit *one* [b]Lit *daughters* [A]Song 2:14; 5:2 [B]Gen 30:13 [C]1 Kin 11:3 6:10 [a]Lit *looks down* [b]Lit *bannered ones* [A]Job 31:26 [B]Matt 17:2; Rev 1:16 [C]Song 6:4 6:11 [A]Song 7:12 [B]Song 4:13 6:12 [a]Another reading is *Ammi-nadib* 6:13 [a]CHORUS [b]Ch 7:1 in Heb [C]BRIDEGROOM [d]Or *Mahanaim* [A]Judg 21:21 [B]Gen 32:2; 2 Sam 17:24

6:1 Having established why they should look (5:9), the daughters ask where they should look.

6:2, 3 She believed Solomon had gone back to the garden and reaffirmed her exclusive love (cf. 2:16; 7:10).

6:4–8:4 The couple works through their difficulties and rekindles their love.

6:4–9 Apparently a reunion has occurred, and Solomon once again assured her of his love.

6:4 **lovely as Jerusalem.** The nation's capital city was known as "the perfection of beauty, a joy to all the earth" (cf. Ps 48:1, 2; La 2:15).

6:8, 9 Solomon reaches new heights in telling his bride she remains the best of the best (cf. 2:2; 4:7; 5:2).

6:8 **queens ... concubines ... maidens.** Are these Solomon's other women? There is no language of ownership or relationship. The numerical progression from 60 to 80 to "without number" points to the use of various categories for effect only. Solomon tells his beloved that she stands above all women.

6:10 This is better understood as being said by the daughters of Jerusalem as the third question in a series of 3 (cf. 5:9; 6:1). This time they exalt the Shulammite as one who ranks with the great beauties of God's creation.

6:11–13 This represents the most difficult portion to interpret in the entire song.

6:11, 12 This is best understood as being spoken by the beloved. Solomon acknowledges that when he left home hastily (cf. 5:2–6), he returned to agricultural (v. 11) and military (v. 12) matters.

6:13 **Come back, come back.** This is best understood as being spoken by the daughters of Jerusalem. In effect, they beckon the bride back to the royal palace. **Shulammite.** A resident of Shunem, a part of the Land allotted to Issachar (cf. Jos 19:18). **Why should you gaze.** This is best understood as being spoken by the beloved. This probably refers to some form of marital dance associated with the city of Mahanaim which would be inappropriate for anyone other than Solomon to witness.

ADMIRATION BY THE BRIDEGROOM

7 "[a]How beautiful are your [b]feet in sandals,
O [c,A]prince's daughter!
The curves of your hips are like [d]jewels,
The work of the hands of an artist.
2 "Your navel is *like* a round goblet
Which never lacks mixed wine;
Your belly is like a heap of wheat
Fenced about with lilies.
3 "Your [A]two breasts are like two fawns,
Twins of a gazelle.
4 "Your [A]neck is like a tower of ivory,
Your eyes *like* the pools in [B]Heshbon
By the gate of Bath-rabbim;
Your nose is like the tower of Lebanon,
Which faces toward Damascus.
5 "Your head [a]crowns you like [A]Carmel,
And the flowing locks of your
head are like purple threads;
The king is captivated by *your* tresses.
6 "How [A]beautiful and how
delightful you are,
[a]*My* love, with *all* your charms!
7 "[a]Your stature is like a palm tree,
And your breasts are *like its* clusters.
8 "I said, 'I will climb the palm tree,
I will take hold of its fruit stalks.'
Oh, may your breasts be like
clusters of the vine,
And the fragrance of your
[a]breath like [b,A]apples,
9 And your [a,A]mouth like the best wine!"

"[b]It [B]goes *down* smoothly for my beloved,
Flowing gently *through* the lips
of those who fall asleep.

THE UNION OF LOVE

10 "[A]I am my beloved's,
And his [B]desire is for me.
11 "Come, my beloved, let us go
out into the [a]country,
Let us spend the night in the villages.
12 "Let us rise early *and go* to the vineyards;
Let us [A]see whether the vine has budded
And its blossoms have opened,
And whether the pomegranates
have bloomed.
There I will give you my love.
13 "The [A]mandrakes have given
forth fragrance;
And over our doors are all [B]choice *fruits,*
Both new and old,
Which I have saved up for
you, my beloved.

THE LOVERS SPEAK

8 "Oh that you were like a brother to me
Who nursed at my mother's breasts.
If I found you outdoors, I would kiss you;
No one would despise me, either.
2 "I would lead you *and* [A]bring you
Into the house of my mother,
who used to instruct me;
I would give you spiced wine to drink
from the juice of my pomegranates.
3 "Let [A]his left hand be under my head
And his right hand embrace me."

4 "[a,A]I want you to swear, O daughters
of Jerusalem,
[b]Do not arouse or awaken *my* love
Until [c]she pleases."

5 "[a,A]Who is this coming up from
the wilderness
Leaning on her beloved?"

"[b]Beneath the [c,B]apple tree I awakened you;
There your mother was in labor with you,
There she was in labor *and* gave you birth.
6 "Put me like a [a]seal over your heart,
Like a [A]seal on your arm.
For love is as strong as death,
[b,B]Jealousy is as severe as Sheol;
Its flashes are flashes of fire,
[c]The *very* flame of the LORD.
7 "Many waters cannot quench love,
Nor will rivers overflow it;
[A]If a man were to give all the
riches of his house for love,
It would be utterly despised."

7:1 [a]Ch 7:2 in Heb [b]Lit *footsteps* [c]Or *nobleman's* [d]Or *ornaments* [A]Ps 45:13 7:3 [A]Song 4:5 7:4 [A]Song 4:4 [B]Num 21:26 7:5 [a]Lit *is upon* [A]Is 35:2 7:6 [a]Or *With love among your delights* [A]Song 1:15, 16; 4:10 7:7 [a]Lit *This stature of yours* 7:8 [a]Lit *nose* [b]Or *apricots* [A]Song 2:5 7:9 [a]Lit *palate* [b]BRIDE [A]Song 5:16 [B]Prov 23:31 7:10 [A]Song 2:16; 6:3 [B]Ps 45:11; Gal 2:20 7:11 [a]Lit *field* 7:12 [A]Song 6:11 7:13 [A]Gen 30:14 [B]Song 2:3; 4:13, 16; Matt 13:52 8:2 [A]Song 3:4 8:3 [A]Song 2:6 8:4 [a]BRIDEGROOM [b]Or *Why should you arouse* [c]Or *it* [A]Song 2:7; 3:5 8:5 [a]CHORUS [b]BRIDE [c]Or *apricot* [A]Song 3:6 [B]Song 2:3 8:6 [a]Or *signet* [b]Or Its *ardor is as inflexible* [c]Another reading is *A vehement flame* [A]Is 49:16; Jer 22:24; Hag 2:23 [B]Prov 6:34 8:7 [A]Prov 6:35

7:1–5 It is better to understand this as the friends answering Solomon. Verses 1 and 5 fit far better this way.

7:1 O prince's daughter! She appeared by beauty and dress to be of royal lineage, although she really came from a humble background.

7:6–9a Solomon and his bride start all over again. He picked up where he left off at 5:2.

7:9b–8:4 Unlike the response in 5:3, this time Solomon's beloved one responded with reciprocal love.

7:10 I am my beloved's. She expressed her loyal love for the third time (cf. 2:16; 6:3).

8:1 like a brother to me. This way she could have publicly bestowed her affection without embarrassment.

8:3, 4 It will be just as it was when they courted (cf. 2:6, 7). This time the restraint involves waiting for lovemaking until they are in private circumstances rather than public.

8:5–14 This final scene portrays the original "marriage encounter" where they reaffirm their love for each other.

8:5b I awakened you. This is better understood as being spoken by Solomon. The Shulammite's dream of 3:4 has actually been realized now in their marriage. **mother.** This is the sixth reference to the Shulammite's mother (cf. 1:6; 3:4; 6:9; 8:1; 8:2). In contrast, Solomon's mother Bathsheba is mentioned only once (cf. 3:11).

8:6 seal. The Shulammite is the seal, and Solomon would do the sealing. This represents their publicly declared mutual love for each other.

8:6, 7 For love. This represents the 1Co 13:1–8 of the OT. Four qualities of love appear: 1) love is unyielding in marriage, as death is to life; 2) love is intense like the brightest flame, perhaps as bright as the glory of the Lord; 3) love is invincible or unquenchable, even when flooded by difficulty; and 4) love is so priceless that it cannot be bought, only given away.

8 “[a]We have a little sister,
And she [A]has no breasts;
What shall we do for our sister
On the day when she is spoken for?
9 “If she is a wall,
We will build on her a
battlement of silver;
But if she is a door,
We will barricade her with
[A]planks of cedar.”

10 “[a]I was a wall, and [A]my breasts
were like towers;
Then I became in his eyes as
one who finds peace.
11 “Solomon had a [A]vineyard at Baal-hamon;
He [B]entrusted the vineyard to [C]caretakers.
Each one was to bring a [D]thousand
shekels of silver for its [E]fruit.
12 “My very own vineyard
is [a]at my disposal;
The thousand *shekels* are
for you, Solomon,
And two hundred are for those
who take care of its fruit.”

13 “[a]O you who sit in the gardens,
My [A]companions are listening
for your voice—
[B]Let me hear it!”

14 “[a,b]Hurry, my beloved,
And be [A]like a gazelle or a young [c]stag
On the [B]mountains of spices.”

8:8 [a]CHORUS [A]Ezek 16:7 8:9 [A]1 Kin 6:15 8:10 [a]BRIDE [A]Ezek 16:7 8:11 [A]Eccl 2:4 [B]Matt 21:33 [C]Song 1:6 [D]Is 7:23 [E]Song 2:3; 8:12 8:12 [a]Lit *before me* 8:13 [a]BRIDEGROOM [A]Song 1:7 [B]Song 2:14 8:14 [a]BRIDE [b]Lit *Flee* [c]Lit *of the stags* [A]Song 2:7, 9, 17 [B]Song 4:6

8:8, 9 The bride’s brothers reminded everyone that they did their brotherly duty of keeping their sister pure before marriage (cf. the brothers of Rebekah in Ge 24:50–60; Dinah in Ge 34:13–27; and Tamar in 2Sa 13:1–22). The same standard of purity is taught in the NT (cf. 1Th 4:1–8).

8:9 wall . . . door. Wall represents sexual purity; door portrays an openness to immorality.

8:10 wall. She reaffirmed that she lived a premarital life of a wall, successfully rebuffing all attempts on her honor. Thus her husband took great delight and contentment in her moral purity.

8:11, 12 While Solomon might have leased out his real vineyard for profit, she gave the vineyard of her love to Solomon.

8:13 *My companions*. These could be 1) Solomon’s shepherd companions (cf. 1:7), 2) the daughters of Jerusalem (cf. 6:13), or 3) those who escorted the bride to Jerusalem (cf. 3:7).

THE
BOOK OF

ISAIAH

TITLE

The book derives its title from the author, whose name means "The Lord is salvation," and is similar to the names Joshua, Elisha, and Jesus. Isaiah is quoted directly in the NT over 65 times, far more than any other OT prophet, and mentioned by name over 20 times.

AUTHOR AND DATE

Isaiah, the son of Amoz, ministered in and around Jerusalem as a prophet to Judah during the reigns of 4 kings of Judah: Uzziah (called "Azariah" in 2 Kings), Jotham, Ahaz, and Hezekiah (1:1), from ca. 739–686 B.C. He evidently came from a family of some rank, because he had easy access to the king (7:3). He was married and had two sons who bore symbolic names: "Shear-jashub" ("a remnant shall return," 7:3) and "Maher-shalal-hash-baz" ("hasting to the spoil, hurrying to the prey," 8:3). When called by God to prophesy, in the year of King Uzziah's death (ca. 739 B.C.), he responded with a cheerful readiness, though he knew from the beginning that his ministry would be one of fruitless warning and exhortation (6:9–13). Having been reared in Jerusalem, he was an appropriate choice as a political and religious counselor to the nation.

Isaiah was a contemporary of Hosea and Micah. His writing style has no rival in its versatility of expression, brilliance of imagery, and richness of vocabulary. The early church father Jerome likened him to Demosthenes, the legendary Greek orator. His writing features a range of 2,186 different words, compared to 1,535 in Ezekiel, 1,653 in Jeremiah, and 2,170 in the Psalms. Second Chronicles 32:32 records that he wrote a biography of King Hezekiah also. The prophet lived until at least 681 B.C. when he penned the account of Sennacherib's death (cf. 37:38). Tradition has it that he met his death under King Manasseh (ca. 695–642 B.C.) by being cut in two with a wooden saw (cf. Heb 11:37).

BACKGROUND AND SETTING

During Uzziah's prosperous 52 year reign (ca. 790–739 B.C.), Judah developed into a strong commercial and military state with a port for commerce on the Red Sea and the construction of walls, towers, and fortifications (2Ch 26:3–5, 8–10, 13–15). Yet the period witnessed a decline in Judah's spiritual status. Uzziah's downfall resulted from his attempt to assume the privileges of a priest and burn incense on the altar (2Ki 15:3, 4; 2Ch 26:16–19). He was judged with leprosy, from which he never recovered (2Ki 15:5; 2 Chr 26:20, 21).

His son Jotham (ca. 750–731 B.C.) had to take over the duties of king before his father's death. Assyria began to emerge as a new international power under Tiglath-Pileser (ca. 745–727 B.C.) while Jotham was king (2Ki 15:19). Judah also began to incur opposition from Israel and Syria to her north during his reign (2Ki 15:37). Jotham was a builder and a fighter like his father, but spiritual corruption still existed in the Land (2Ki 15:34, 35; 2Ch 27:1, 2).

Ahaz was 25 when he began to reign in Judah and he reigned until age 41 (2Ch 28:1, 8; ca. 735–715 B.C.). Israel and Syria formed an alliance to combat the rising Assyrian threat from the E, but Ahaz refused to bring Judah into the alliance (2Ki 16:5; Is 7:6). For this, the northern neighbors threatened to dethrone him, and war resulted (734 B.C.). In panic, Ahaz sent to the Assyrian king for help (2Ki 16:7) and the Assyrian king gladly responded, sacking Gaza, carrying all of Galilee and Gilead into captivity, and finally capturing Damascus (732 B.C.). Ahaz's alliance with Assyria led to his introduction of a heathen altar, which he set up in Solomon's temple (2Ki 16:10–16; 2Ch 28:3). During his reign (722 B.C.), Assyria captured Samaria, capital of the northern kingdom, and carried many of Israel's most capable people into captivity (2Ki 17:6, 24).

Hezekiah began his reign over Judah in 715 B.C. and continued for 29 years to ca. 686 B.C. (2Ki 18:1, 2). Reformation was a priority when he became king (2Ki 18:4, 22; 2Ch 30:1). The threat of an Assyrian invasion forced Judah to promise heavy tribute to that eastern power. In 701 B.C. Hezekiah became very ill with a life-threatening disease, but he prayed and God graciously extended his life for 15 years (2Ki 20; Is 38) until 686 B.C. The ruler of Babylon used the opportunity of his illness and recovery to send congratulations to him, probably seeking to form an alliance with Judah against Assyria at the same time (2Ki 20:12 ff.; Is 39). When Assyria became weak through internal strife, Hezekiah refused to pay any further tribute to that power (2Ki 18:7). So in 701 B.C. Sennacherib, the Assyrian king, invaded the coastal areas of Israel, marching toward Egypt on Israel's southern flank. In the process he overran many Judean towns, looting and carrying many people back to Assyria. While besieging Lachish, he sent a contingent of forces to besiege Jerusalem (2Ki 18:17–19:8; Is 36:2–37:8). The side-expedition failed, however, so in a second attempt he sent messengers to Jerusalem demanding an immediate surrender of the city (2Ki 19:9ff.; Is 37:9ff.). With Isaiah's encouragement, Hezekiah refused to surrender, and when Sennacherib's army fell prey to a sudden disaster, he returned to Nineveh and never threatened Judah again.

HISTORICAL AND THEOLOGICAL THEMES

Isaiah prophesied during the period of the divided kingdom, directing the major thrust of his message to the southern kingdom of Judah. He condemned the empty ritualism of his day (e.g., 1:10–15) and the idolatry into which so many of the people had fallen (e.g., 40:18–20). He foresaw the coming Babylonian captivity of Judah because of this departure from the Lord (39:6, 7).

Fulfillment of some of his prophecies in his own lifetime provided his credentials for the prophetic office. Sennacherib's effort to take Jerusalem failed, just as Isaiah had said it would (37:6, 7, 36–38). The Lord healed Hezekiah's critical illness, as Isaiah had predicted (38:5; 2Ki 20:7). Long before Cyrus, king of Persia, appeared on the scene, Isaiah named him as Judah's deliverer from the Babylonian captivity (44:28; 45:1). Fulfillment of his prophecies of Christ's first coming have given Isaiah further vindication (e.g., 7:14). The pattern of literal fulfillment of his already-fulfilled prophecies gives assurance that prophecies of Christ's second coming will also see literal fulfillment.

Isaiah provides data on the future day of the Lord and the time following. He details numerous aspects of Israel's future kingdom on earth not found elsewhere in the OT or NT, including changes in nature, the animal world, Jerusalem's status among the nations, the Suffering Servant's leadership, and others.

Through a literary device called "prophetic foreshortening," Isaiah predicted future events without delineating exact sequences of the events or time intervals separating them. For example, nothing in Isaiah reveals the extended period separating the two comings of the Messiah. Also, he does not provide as clear a distinction between the future temporal kingdom and the eternal kingdom as John does in Rev 20:1–10; 21:1–22:5. In God's program of progressive revelation, details of these relationships awaited a prophetic spokesman of a later time.

Also known as the "evangelical Prophet," Isaiah spoke much about the grace of God toward Israel, particularly in his last 27 chapters. The centerpiece is Isaiah's unrivaled chap. 53, portraying Christ as the slain Lamb of God.

INTERPRETIVE CHALLENGES

Interpretive challenges in a long and significant book such as Isaiah are numerous. The most critical of them focuses on whether Isaiah's prophecies will receive literal fulfillment or not, and on whether the Lord, in His program, has abandoned national Israel and permanently replaced the nation with the church, so that there is no future for national Israel.

On the latter issue, numerous portions of Isaiah support the position that God has not replaced ethnic Israel with an alleged "new Israel." Isaiah has too much to say about God's faithfulness to Israel, that He would not reject the people whom He has created and chosen (43:1). The nation is on the palms of His hands, and Jerusalem's walls are ever before His eyes (49:16). He is bound by His own Word to fulfill the promises He has made to bring them back to Himself and bless them in that future day (55:10–12).

On the former issue, literal fulfillment of many of Isaiah's prophecies has already occurred, as illustrated in Introduction: Historical and Theological Themes. To contend that those yet unfulfilled will see nonliteral fulfillment is biblically groundless. This fact disqualifies the case for proposing that the church receives some of the promises made originally to Israel. The kingdom promised to David belongs to Israel, not the church. The future exaltation of Jerusalem will be on earth, not in heaven. Christ will reign personally on this earth as we know it, as well as in the new heavens and new earth (Rev 22:1, 3).

OUTLINE

I. Judgment (1:1–35:10)

- A. Prophecies Concerning Judah and Jerusalem (1:1–12:6)
    1. Judah's social sins (1:1–6:13)
    2. Judah's political entanglements (7:1–12:6)
- B. Oracles of Judgment and Salvation (13:1–23:18)
    1. Babylon and Assyria (13:1–14:27)
    2. Philistia (14:28–32)
    3. Moab (15:1–16:14)
    4. Syria and Israel (17:1–14)
    5. Ethiopia (18:1–7)
    6. Egypt (19:1–20:6)
    7. Babylon continued (21:1–10)
    8. Edom (21:11, 12)
    9. Arabia (21:13–17)
    10. Jerusalem (22:1–25)
    11. Tyre (23:1–18)

C. Redemption of Israel through World Judgment (24:1–27:13)
1. God's devastation of the earth (24:1–23)
2. First song of thanksgiving for redemption (25:1–12)
3. Second song of thanksgiving for redemption (26:1–19)
4. Israel's chastisements and final prosperity (26:20–27:13)

D. Warnings Against Alliance with Egypt (28:1–35:10)
1. Woe to drunken politicians (28:1–29)
2. Woe to religious formalists (29:1–14)
3. Woe to those who hide plans from God (29:15–24)
4. Woe to the pro-Egyptian party (30:1–33)
5. Woe to those who trust in horses and chariots (31:1–32:20)
6. Woe to the Assyrian destroyer (33:1–24)
7. A cry for justice against the nations, particularly Edom (34:1–35:10)

II. Historical Interlude (36:1–39:8)

A. Sennacherib's Attempt to Capture Jerusalem (36:1–37:38)

B. Hezekiah's Sickness and Recovery (38:1–22)

C. Babylonian Emissaries to Jerusalem (39:1–8)

III. Salvation (40:1–66:24)

A. Deliverance from Captivity (40:1–48:22)
1. Comfort to the Babylonian exiles (40:1–31)
2. The end of Israel's misery (41:1–48:22)

B. Sufferings of the Servant of the Lord (49:1–57:21)
1. The Servant's mission (49:1–52:12)
2. Redemption by the Suffering Servant (52:13–53:12)
3. Results of the Suffering Servant's redemption (54:1–57:21)

C. Future Glory of God's People (58:1–66:24)
1. Two kinds of religion (58:1–14)
2. Plea to Israel to forsake their sins (59:1–19)
3. Future blessedness of Zion (59:20–61:11)
4. Nearing of Zion's deliverance (62:1–63:6)
5. Prayer for national deliverance (63:7–64:12)
6. The Lord's answer to Israel's supplication (65:1–66:24)

REBELLION OF GOD'S PEOPLE

1 The vision of Isaiah the son of Amoz concerning [A]Judah and Jerusalem, which he saw during the [a]reigns of [B]Uzziah, [C]Jotham, [D]Ahaz *and* [E]Hezekiah, kings of Judah.

2 [A]Listen, O heavens, and hear, O [B]earth;
For the LORD speaks,
"[C]Sons I have reared and brought up,
But they have [D]revolted against Me.
3 "An ox knows its owner,
And a donkey its master's manger,
But Israel [A]does not know,
My people [B]do not understand."

4 Alas, sinful nation,
People weighed down with iniquity,
[a,A]Offspring of evildoers,
Sons who [B]act corruptly!
They have [C]abandoned the LORD,
They have [D]despised the
Holy One of Israel,
They have turned away [b]from Him.

5 Where will you be stricken again,
As you [A]continue in *your* rebellion?
The whole head is [B]sick
And the whole heart is faint.
6 [A]From the sole of the foot even to the head
There is [B]nothing sound in it,
Only bruises, welts and raw wounds,
[C]Not pressed out or bandaged,
Nor softened with oil.

7 Your [A]land is desolate,
Your cities are burned with fire,
Your fields—strangers are devouring
them in your presence;
It is desolation, as overthrown
by strangers.
8 The daughter of Zion is left like
a shelter in a vineyard,
Like a watchman's hut in a cucumber
field, like a besieged city.
9 [A]Unless the LORD of hosts
Had left us a few [B]survivors,
We would be like [C]Sodom,
We would be like Gomorrah.

GOD HAS HAD ENOUGH

10 Hear [A]the word of the LORD,
You rulers of [B]Sodom;
Give ear to the instruction of our God,
You people of Gomorrah.
11 "[A]What are your multiplied
sacrifices to Me?"
Says the LORD.
"I [a]have had enough of burnt
offerings of rams
And the fat of fed cattle;
And I take no pleasure in the blood
of bulls, lambs or goats.
12 "When you come [A]to appear before Me,
Who requires [a]of you this
trampling of My courts?
13 "Bring your worthless
offerings no longer,
[A]Incense is an abomination to Me.
[B]New moon and sabbath, the
[C]calling of assemblies—
I cannot [D]endure iniquity and
the solemn assembly.

1:1 [a]Lit *days* [A]Is 2:1; 40:9 [B]2 Kin 15:1-7, 13; 2 Chr 26:1-23 [C]2 Kin 15:32-38; 2 Chr 27:1-9 [D]2 Kin 16:1-20; 2 Chr 28:1-27; Is 7:1 [E]2 Kin 18:1-20:21; 2 Chr 29:1-32:33 1:2 [A]Deut 32:1 [B]Mic 1:2 [C]Jer 3:22 [D]Is 30:1, 9; 65:2 1:3 [A]Jer 9:3, 6 [B]Is 44:18 1:4 [a]Lit *Seed* [b]Lit *backward* [A]Is 14:20 [B]Neh 1:7 [C]Is 1:28 [D]Is 5:24 1:5 [A]Is 31:6 [B]Is 33:24; Ezek 34:4, 16 1:6 [A]Job 2:7 [B]Ps 38:3 [C]Jer 8:22 1:7 [A]Lev 26:33; Jer 44:6 1:9 [A]Rom 9:29 [B]Is 10:20-22; 11:11, 16; 37:4, 31, 32; 46:3 [C]Gen 19:24 1:10 [A]Is 8:20; 28:14 [B]Is 3:9; Ezek 16:49; Rom 9:29; Rev 11:8 1:11 [a]Or *am sated with* [A]Ps 50:8; Jer 6:20; Amos 5:21, 22; Mal 1:10 1:12 [a]Lit *of your hand* [A]Ex 23:17 1:13 [A]Is 66:3 [B]1 Chr 23:31 [C]Ex 12:16 [D]Jer 7:9, 10

1:1 See Introduction: Title; Author and Date.

1:2–9 This is a courtroom scene in which the Lord is the plaintiff and the nation of Israel is the defendant. Instead of responding to God's ultimate care and provision for them, these people have failed to give Him the loving obedience that is His due.

1:2 heavens … earth. God intended Israel to be a channel of blessing to the nations (19:24, 25; 42:6; Ge 12:2, 3), but instead He must call the nations to look on Israel's shame. **Sons.** The physical descendants of Abraham are God's chosen people, in spite of their disobedience (cf. Ge 18:18, 19).

1:3 ox … donkey. Animals appear to have more powers of reason than God's people who break fellowship with Him.

1:4 the Holy One of Israel. This is Isaiah's special title for God, found 25 times in this book (1:4; 5:19, 24; 10:20; 12:6; 17:7; 29:19; 30:11, 12, 15; 31:1; 37:23; 41:14, 16, 20; 43:3, 14; 45:11; 47:4; 48:17; 49:7; 54:5; 55:5; 60:9, 14), but only 6 times in the rest of the OT (2Ki 19:22; Pss 71:22; 78:41; 89:18; Jer 50:29; 51:5). Isaiah also uses "Holy One" as a title 4 times (10:17; 40:25; 43:15; 49:7) and "Holy One of Jacob" once (29:23). In many contexts the name contrasts the holiness of God with the sinfulness of Israel.

1:5 Where … stricken again … ? Already in ruins because of rebellion against God (vv. 7, 8), the nation behaved irrationally by continuing their rebellion.

1:8 daughter of Zion. The phrase occurs 28 times in the OT, 6 of which are in Isaiah (1:8; 10:32; 16:1; 37:22; 52:2; 62:11). It is a personification of Jerusalem, standing in this case for all of Judah.

1:9 LORD of hosts. Isaiah used this title or the similar "Lord GOD of hosts" 60 times. It pictured God as a mighty warrior, a leader of armies, capable of conquering all of Israel's enemies and providing for her survival. **survivors.** Sometimes rendered "remnant," this term designated the faithful among the Israelites. Paul cited this verse to prove the ongoing existence of faithful Israelites even in his day (Ro 9:29). Such a remnant will constitute the nucleus of returning Israelites in the nation's regathering when the Messiah returns to earth. See 10:20, 22; Hos 1:10, 11. **Sodom … Gomorrah.** In destroying them, God rained brimstone and fire on these two Canaanite cities because of their aggravated sinfulness (Ge 18:20; 19:24, 25, 28). The two thereby became a proverbial expression for the ultimate in God's temporal judgment against any people (e.g., 13:19; Dt 29:23; Jer 23:14; 49:18; 50:40; Am 4:11; Zep 2:9; Mt 10:15; 2Pe 2:6; Jude 7). Had God's grace not intervened, He would have judged Israel in the same way.

1:10–17 The prophet applied the names of the sinful cities, Sodom and Gomorrah, to Judah and Jerusalem in decrying their empty formalism in worship. God found their activities utterly repulsive when they engaged in the rituals prescribed by Moses, because when doing so they persisted in iniquity.

1:11 I have had enough … take no pleasure. Cf. 1Sa 15:22, 23. God found all sacrifices meaningless and even abhorrent if the offerer failed in obedience to His laws. Rebellion is equated to the sin of witchcraft and stubbornness to iniquity and idolatry.

1:13, 14 New moon and sabbath, the calling of assemblies … appointed feasts. These were all occasions prescribed by the law of Moses (cf. Ex 12:16; Lv 23; Nu 10:10; 28:11–29:40; Dt 16:1–17).

14 "I hate your new moon *festivals*
and your [A]appointed feasts,
They have become a burden to Me;
I am [B]weary of bearing *them*.
15 "So when you [A]spread out
your hands *in prayer*,
[B]I will hide My eyes from you;
Yes, even though you [C]multiply prayers,
I will not listen.
[D]Your hands are [a]covered with blood.

16 "[A]Wash yourselves, [B]make
yourselves clean;
[C]Remove the evil of your
deeds from My sight.
[D]Cease to do evil,
17 Learn to do good;
[A]Seek justice,
Reprove the ruthless,
[a,B]Defend the orphan,
Plead for the widow.

"LET US REASON"

18 "Come now, and [A]let us reason together,"
Says the LORD,
"[B]Though your sins are as scarlet,
They will be as white as snow;
Though they are red like crimson,
They will be like wool.
19 "[A]If you consent and obey,
You will [B]eat the best of the land;
20 But if you refuse and rebel,
You will be [A]devoured by the sword."
Truly, [B]the mouth of the LORD has spoken.

ZION CORRUPTED, TO BE REDEEMED

21 How the faithful city has
become a [A]harlot,
She *who* was full of justice!
Righteousness once lodged in her,
But now murderers.
22 Your silver has become dross,
Your drink diluted with water.
23 Your [A]rulers are rebels
And companions of thieves;
Everyone [B]loves a bribe
And chases after rewards.
They [C]do not [a]defend the [b]orphan,
Nor does the widow's plea
come before them.

24 Therefore the Lord [a]GOD of hosts,
The [A]Mighty One of Israel, declares,
"Ah, I will be relieved of My adversaries
And [B]avenge Myself on My foes.
25 "I will also turn My hand against you,
And will [A]smelt away your
dross as with lye
And will remove all your alloy.
26 "Then I will restore your
[A]judges as at the first,
And your counselors as at the beginning;
After that you will be called the
[B]city of righteousness,
A faithful city."

27 Zion will be [A]redeemed with justice
And her [a]repentant ones
with righteousness.

1:14 [A]Is 29:1, 2 [B]Is 7:13; 43:24 1:15 [a]Lit *full of* [A]1 Kin 8:22; Lam 1:17 [B]Is 8:17; 59:2 [C]Mic 3:4 [D]Is 59:3 1:16 [A]Ps 26:6 [B]Is 52:11 [C]Is 55:7 [D]Jer 25:5 1:17 [a]Or *Vindicate the fatherless* [A]Jer 22:3; Zeph 2:3 [B]Ps 82:3 1:18 [A]Is 41:1, 21; 43:26; Mic 6:2 [B]Ps 51:7; Is 43:25; 44:22; Rev 7:14 1:19 [A]Deut 28:1; 30:15, 16 [B]Is 55:2 1:20 [A]Is 3:25; 65:12 [B]Is 40:5; 58:14; Mic 4:4; Titus 1:2 1:21 [A]Is 57:3-9; Jer 2:20 1:23 [a]Or *vindicate* [b]Or *fatherless* [A]Hos 5:10; Mic 7:3 [B]Ex 23:8; Mic 7:3 [C]Is 10:2; Jer 5:28; Ezek 22:7; Zech 7:10 1:24 [a]Heb *YHWH*, usually rendered *LORD* [A]Ps 132:2; Is 49:26; 60:16 [B]Deut 28:63; Is 35:4; 59:18; 61:2; 63:4 1:25 [A]Ezek 22:19-22; Mal 3:3 1:26 [A]Is 60:17 [B]Is 33:5; 60:14; 62:1, 2; Zech 8:3 1:27 [a]Or *returnees* [A]Is 35:9f; 62:12; 63:4

1:14 I hate. It is impossible to doubt the Lord's total aversion toward hypocritical religion. Other practices God hates include robbery for burnt offering (61:8), serving other gods (Jer 44:4), harboring evil against a neighbor and love for a false oath (Zec 8:16), divorce (Mal 2:16), and the one who loves violence (Ps 11:5).

1:16, 17 Remove the evil ... Seek justice. The outward evidence of the emptiness of Jerusalem's ritualism was the presence of evil works and the absence of good works.

1:17 the orphan ... the widow. Illustrative of good works are deeds done on behalf of those in need (v. 23; Dt 10:17, 18; 14:29; 24:17, 19, 20, 21; 26:12, 13; 27:19; Jas 1:27).

1:18–20 In developing His call for cleanliness in v. 16, the Lord pardoned the guilty who desire forgiveness and obedience. This section previews the last 27 chapters of Isaiah, which focus more on grace and forgiveness than on judgment.

1:18 scarlet ... crimson. The two colors speak of the guilt of those whose hands were "covered with blood" (v. 15). Being covered with blood speaks of extreme iniquity and perversity (cf. 59:3; Eze 9:9, 10; 23:37, 45). **white as snow ... like wool.** Snow and wool are substances that are naturally white, and therefore portray what is clean, the blood-guilt (v. 15) having been removed (cf. Ps 51:7). Isaiah was a prophet of grace, but forgiveness is not unconditional. It comes through repentance as v. 19 indicates.

1:19, 20 consent and obey ... refuse and rebel. The prophet offered his readers the same choice God gave Moses in Dt 28, a choice between a blessing and a curse. They may choose repentance and obedience and reap the benefits of the land or refuse to do so and become victims of foreign oppressors. **eat ... be devoured.** To accentuate the opposite outcomes, the Lord used the same Heb. word to depict both destinies. On one hand, they may eat the fruit of the land; on the other, they may be eaten by conquering powers.

1:21–31 Verses 21–23 recount Jerusalem's current disobedience, with an account of God's actions to purge her in vv. 24–31.

1:21 harlot. Often in the OT, spiritual harlotry pictured the idolatry of God's people (e.g., Jer 2:20; 3:1; Hos 2:2; 3:1; Eze 16:22–37). In this instance, however, Jerusalem's unfaithfulness incorporated a wider range of wrongs, including murders and general corruption (vv. 21, 23). **justice ... Righteousness.** As Isaiah prophesied, ethical depravity had replaced the city's former virtues.

1:24 the Lord GOD of hosts, the Mighty One of Israel. These titles of God emphasized His role as the rightful judge of His sinful people. "The Mighty One of Israel" occurs only here in the Bible, though "the Mighty One of Jacob" appears 5 times (49:26; 60:16; Ge 49:24; Ps 132:2, 5).

1:25, 26 I will ... smelt away .... will restore. God's judgment of His people has future restoration as its goal. They were subsequently restored from the Babylonian captivity (Jer 29:10), but this promise has in view a greater and more lasting restoration. It anticipates a complete and permanent restoration, which will make Jerusalem supreme among the nations (Jer 3:17; Eze 5:5; Mic 4:2; Zec 8:22; 14:16). The only such purging and restoration in Scripture is that spoken of in conjunction with the yet-future "time of Jacob's distress" (Jer 30:6, 7; i.e., Daniel's 70th week, cf. Da 9:24–27) and the second advent of the Messiah (Zec 14:4).

1:27 Zion. Originally a designation for the hill Ophel, this name became a synonym for the entire city of Jerusalem. Isaiah always uses it that way. **be redeemed ... repentant ones.** That remnant of the city who repented of their sins would find redemption in conjunction with God's future restoration of Israel's prosperity (cf. 59:20).

28 But [a]transgressors and sinners
will be [A]crushed together,
And those who forsake the LORD
will come to an end.
29 Surely [a]you will be ashamed of the
[b,A]oaks which you have desired,
And you will be embarrassed at the
[B]gardens which you have chosen.
30 For you will be like an [a]oak
whose [A]leaf fades away
Or as a garden that has no water.
31 The strong man will become tinder,
His work also a spark.
Thus they shall both [A]burn together
And there will be [B]none to quench *them*.

GOD'S UNIVERSAL REIGN

2 The word which [A]Isaiah the son of Amoz saw
concerning Judah and Jerusalem.

2 Now it will come about that
[A]In the last days
The [B]mountain of the house of the LORD
Will be established [a]as the
chief of the mountains,
And will be raised above the hills;
And [C]all the nations will stream to it.
3 And many peoples will come and say,
"Come, let us go up to the
mountain of the LORD,
To the house of the God of Jacob;
That He may teach us
[a]concerning His ways
And that we may walk in His paths."
For the [b]law will go forth [A]from Zion
And the word of the LORD
from Jerusalem.
4 And He will judge between the nations,
And will [a]render decisions
for many peoples;
And [A]they will hammer their
swords into plowshares and their
spears into pruning hooks.
[B]Nation will not lift up sword
against nation,
And never again will they learn war.

5 Come, [A]house of Jacob, and let us
walk in the [B]light of the LORD.
6 For You have [A]abandoned Your
people, the house of Jacob,
Because they are filled *with*
influences from the east,
And *they are* soothsayers
[B]like the Philistines,
And they [C]strike *bargains* with
the children of foreigners.
7 Their land has also been filled
with silver and gold
And there is no end to their treasures;
Their land has also been
filled with [A]horses
And there is no end to their chariots.
8 Their land has also been
[A]filled with idols;
They worship the [B]work of their hands,
That which their fingers have made.
9 So [A]the *common* man has been humbled
And the man *of importance*
has been abased,
But [B]do not forgive them.
10 [A]Enter the rock and hide in the dust
[B]From the terror of the LORD and from
the splendor of His majesty.

1:28 [a]Lit *crushing of transgressors and sinners shall be together* [A]Ps 9:5; Is 66:24; 2 Thess 1:8, 9 1:29 [a]So with some mss; M.T. *they* [b]Or *terebinths* [A]Is 57:5 [B]Is 65:3; 66:17 1:30 [a]Or *terebinth* [A]Is 64:6 1:31 [A]Is 5:24; 9:19; 26:11; 33:11-14 [B]Is 66:24; Matt 3:12; Mark 9:43 2:1 [A]Is 1:1 2:2 [a]Lit *on* [A]Mic 4:1-3 [B]Is 27:13; 66:20 [C]Is 56:7 2:3 [a]Or *some of* [b]Or *instruction* [A]Is 51:4, 5; Luke 24:47 2:4 [a]Or *reprove many* [A]Is 32:17, 18; Joel 3:10 [B]Is 9:5, 7; 11:6-9; Hos 2:18; Zech 9:10 2:5 [A]Is 58:1 [B]Is 60:1, 2, 19, 20; 1 John 1:5 2:6 [A]Deut 31:17 [B]2 Kin 1:2 [C]2 Kin 16:7, 8; Prov 6:1 2:7 [A]Deut 17:16; Is 30:16; 31:1; Mic 5:10 2:8 [A]Is 10:11 [B]Ps 115:4-8; Is 17:8; 37:19; 40:19; 44:17 2:9 [A]Ps 49:2; 62:9; Is 5:15 [B]Neh 4:5 2:10 [A]Is 2:19, 21; Rev 6:15, 16 [B]2 Thess 1:9

1:28 transgressors ... sinners ... those who forsake. Concurrent with the future blessing of the faithful remnant, the Lord will relegate the unrepentant to destruction. This is the only way Zion can become pure.

1:29 oaks ... gardens. These were settings where Israel practiced idolatrous worship. It is ironic that the Lord had chosen Israel while some citizens of Jerusalem have chosen the "gardens." When God calls them to account for their rebellious choice, they will be ashamed and embarrassed.

1:31 burn together ... none to quench. Both the rebel and his works will perish. This is final judgment, not merely another captivity.

2:1–5:30 Chapters 2–5 comprise a single connected discourse.

2:1–5 The first of 3 pictures of Zion (Jerusalem) in this discourse that depicts her future exaltation.

2:2–4 The book of Micah contains this portion of Isaiah's prophecy almost word for word (Mic 4:1–3), indicating that the younger contemporary of Isaiah may have obtained the words from him. Both passages present a prophetic picture of Zion in the future messianic kingdom when all people will recognize Jerusalem as the capital of the world.

2:2 In the last days. The "last days" is a time designation looking forward to the messianic era (Eze 38:16; Hos 3:5; Mic 4:1). The NT applied the expression to the period beginning with the first advent of Jesus Christ (Ac 2:17; 2Ti 3:1; Heb 1:2; Jas 5:3; 2Pe 3:3). Old Testament prophets, being without a clear word regarding the time between the Messiah's two advents, linked the expression to the Messiah's return to establish His earthly kingdom, i.e., the millennial kingdom spoken about in Rev 20:1–10. **The mountain of the house of the LORD.** The reference is to Mt. Zion, the location of the temple in Jerusalem. The expression occurs two other times in the OT (2Ch 33:15; Mic 4:1).

2:3 mountain of the LORD. Isaiah frequently calls Mt. Zion the "holy mountain" (11:9; 27:13; 56:7; 57:13; 65:11, 25; 66:20).

2:4 swords into plowshares ... spears into pruning hooks. With the Messiah on His throne in Jerusalem, the world will enjoy uninterrupted peaceful conditions. Warfare will continue to characterize human history until the Prince of Peace (9:6) returns to earth to put an end to it.

2:6–4:1 After a glimpse of Judah's glorious future (2:1–5), the prophet returned to the present for a scathing rebuke of her idolatry and the judgment of God it evokes.

2:6–9 Isaiah stated the Lord's formal charge against the people of Jerusalem.

2:6 *influences* from the east. Through caravans from the E, an influx of religious superstitions had filled Jerusalem and its environs.

2:8 filled with idols. Jotham and Ahaz, two of the kings under whom Isaiah prophesied, failed to remove the idolatrous high places from the land (2Ki 15:35; 16:4).

2:10–22 This section pictures conditions during the future day of the Lord. Though some elements of the description could fit what Judah experienced in the Babylonian captivity, the intensity of judgment predicted here could not have found fulfillment at that time. The tribulation period before Christ's return will be the time for these judgmental horrors.

11 The [a,A]proud look of man will be abased
And the [B]loftiness of man will be humbled,
And the LORD alone will be
exalted in that day.

A DAY OF RECKONING COMING

12 For the LORD of hosts will have
a day *of reckoning*
Against [A]everyone who is proud and lofty
And against everyone who is lifted up,
That he may be abased.
13 And *it will be* against all the cedars of
Lebanon that are lofty and lifted up,
Against all the [A]oaks of Bashan,
14 Against all the [A]lofty mountains,
Against all the hills that are lifted up,
15 Against every [A]high tower,
Against every fortified wall,
16 Against all the [A]ships of Tarshish
And against all the beautiful craft.
17 The pride of man will be humbled
And the loftiness of men will be abased;
And the LORD alone will be
exalted in that day,
18 But the [A]idols will completely vanish.
19 *Men* will [A]go into caves of the rocks
And into holes of the [a]ground
Before the terror of the LORD
And the splendor of His majesty,
When He arises [B]to make the earth tremble.
20 In that day men will [A]cast away
to the moles and the [B]bats
Their idols of silver and their idols of gold,
Which they made for
themselves to worship,
21 In order to [A]go into the caverns of the
rocks and the clefts of the cliffs
Before the terror of the LORD and
the splendor of His majesty,
When He arises to make
the earth tremble.
22 [a,A]Stop regarding man, whose breath
of life is in his nostrils;
For [b,B]why should he be esteemed?

GOD WILL REMOVE THE LEADERS

3 For behold, the Lord [a]GOD of
hosts [A]is going to remove
from Jerusalem and Judah
Both [b]supply and support, the
whole [b]supply of bread
And the whole [b]supply of water;
2 [A]The mighty man and the warrior,
The judge and the prophet,
The diviner and the elder,
3 The captain of fifty and the honorable man,
The counselor and the expert artisan,
And the skillful enchanter.
4 And I will make mere [A]lads their princes,
And [a]capricious children
will rule over them,
5 And the people will be [A]oppressed,
Each one by another, and each
one by his [B]neighbor;
The youth will storm against the elder
And the inferior against the honorable.
6 When a man [A]lays hold of his brother
in his father's house, *saying,*
"You have a cloak, you shall be our ruler,
And these ruins will be
under your [a]charge,"
7 He will [a]protest on that day, saying,
"I will not be *your* [b,A]healer,
For in my house there is neither
bread nor cloak;
You should not appoint me
ruler of the people."
8 For [A]Jerusalem has stumbled
and Judah has fallen,
Because their [a,B]speech and their
actions are against the LORD,
To [C]rebel against [b]His glorious presence.

2:11 [a]Lit *eyes of the loftiness of men* [A]Is 5:15; 37:23 [B]Ps 18:27; Is 13:11; 23:9; 2 Cor 10:5 2:12 [A]Job 40:11, 12; Is 24:4, 21; Mal 4:1 2:13 [A]Zech 11:2 2:14 [A]Is 40:4 2:15 [A]Is 25:12 2:16 [A]1 Kin 10:22; Is 23:1, 14; 60:9 2:18 [A]Is 21:9; Mic 1:7 2:19 [a]Lit *dust* [A]Is 2:10 [B]Ps 18:7; Is 2:21; 13:13; 24:1, 19, 20; Hag 2:6, 7; Heb 12:26 2:20 [A]Is 30:22; 31:7 [B]Lev 11:19 2:21 [A]Is 2:19 2:22 [a]Lit *Cease from man* [b]Lit *in what* [A]Ps 146:3; Jer 17:5 [B]Ps 8:4; 144:3, 4; Is 40:15, 17; James 4:14 3:1 [a]Heb *YHWH*, usually rendered *LORD* [b]Lit *staff* [A]Lev 26:26; Is 5:13; 9:20; Ezek 4:16 3:2 [A]2 Kin 24:14; Is 9:14, 15; Ezek 17:12, 13 3:4 [a]Lit *arbitrary power will rule* [A]Eccl 10:16 3:5 [A]Mic 7:3-6 [B]Is 9:19; Jer 9:3-8 3:6 [a]Lit *hand* [A]Is 4:1 3:7 [a]Lit *lift up his voice* [b]Lit *binder of wounds* [A]Ezek 34:4; Hos 5:13 3:8 [a]Lit *tongue* [b]Lit *the eyes of His glory* [A]Is 1:7; 6:11 [B]Ps 73:9-11; Is 9:17; 59:3 [C]Is 65:3

2:12 LORD of hosts will have a day *of reckoning*. The phrase "day of reckoning" or "day of the LORD" appears 19 times in the OT (Ob 15; Joel 1:15; 2:1, 11, 31; 3:14; Am 5:18, 20; Is 2:12; 13:6, 9; Zep 1:7, 14; Eze 13:5; 30:3; Zec 14:1; Mal 4:5) and 4 times in the NT (Ac 2:20; 1Th 5:2; 2Th 2:2; 2Pe 3:10) to express the time of God's extreme wrath. The day of reckoning can refer to a near future judgment (Eze 13:5; 30:3) or a far future judgment (Zec 14:1; 2Th 2:2). Two "day of the LORD" expressions remain to be fulfilled: 1) at the end of Daniel's 70th week (see Joel 3:14; Mal 4:5; 1Th 5:2) and 2) at the end of the Millennium (see 2Pe 3:10). The day of reckoning can occur through providential means (Eze 30:3) or directly at the hand of God (2Pe 3:10). At times, the near fulfillment (Joel 1:15) prefigures the far fulfillment (Joel 3:14); on other occasions, both kinds of fulfillment are included in one passage (13:6, 9; Zeph 1:7, 14). Here Isaiah looks to the far fulfillment at the end of the time of Jacob's trouble (Jer 30:7).

2:13 cedars of Lebanon … oaks of Bashan. The cedars and oaks were objects of great admiration to people of OT times (Pss 92:12; 104:16; Eze 27:6; 31:3). Yet even these impressive created objects would face destruction because of human rebellion.

2:19 caves of the rocks … holes of the ground. Revelation 6:12, 15, 16 uses this passage and 2:21 to describe man's flight from the terrors of tribulation during the period before Christ's personal return to earth. This shows that the final fulfillment of this prophecy will be during Daniel's 70th week.

2:22 Stop regarding man. This calls readers to stop depending on other humans and to trust only in God, who alone is worthy.

3:1–4:1 The Lord's indictment against and judgment of Jerusalem and Judah continued.

3:1 the Lord GOD of hosts. Emphasizing His ultimate authority, God refers to Himself by the title Adonai ("the Lord"), the sovereign Lord of all, and by the mighty and warlike "GOD of hosts."

3:1–3 remove … diviner. God's judgment was to include a removal of the people's leadership.

3:4, 5 children … honorable. Inexperience in government was to lead to degeneration and irresponsibility at every level of national life.

3:6, 7 these ruins … ruler of the people. Conditions of anarchy were to be so bad that no one would accept a position of authority over the people.

3:8 Jerusalem … Judah. The fall of Jerusalem in 586 B.C. was only a partial fulfillment of this prophecy. The final fulfillment awaits

9 [a]The expression of their faces
bears witness against them,
And they display their sin like [A]Sodom;
They do not *even* conceal *it.*
Woe to [b]them!
For they have [B]brought evil on themselves.
10 Say to the [A]righteous that *it*
will go well *with them,*
For they will eat the fruit of their actions.
11 Woe to the wicked! *It will go* badly *with him,*
For [a,A]what he deserves will be done to him.
12 O My people! Their oppressors
[a]are [A]children,
And women rule over them.
O My people! [B]Those who guide
you lead *you* astray
And confuse the direction of your paths.

GOD WILL JUDGE

13 [A]The LORD arises to contend,
And stands to judge the people.
14 The LORD [A]enters into judgment with
the elders and princes of His people,
"It is you who have [B]devoured
the vineyard;
The [C]plunder of the poor
is in your houses.
15 "What do you mean by
[A]crushing My people
And grinding the face of the poor?"
Declares the Lord [a]GOD of hosts.

JUDAH'S WOMEN DENOUNCED

16 Moreover, the LORD said, "Because
the [A]daughters of Zion are proud
And walk with [a]heads held high
and seductive eyes,
And go along with mincing steps
And tinkle the bangles on their feet,
17 Therefore the Lord will afflict the scalp
of the daughters of Zion with scabs,
And the LORD will make their
foreheads bare."

18 In that day the Lord will take away the beauty
of *their* anklets, headbands, [A]crescent ornaments,
19 dangling earrings, bracelets, veils, 20 [A]head-
dresses, ankle chains, sashes, perfume boxes, amulets, 21 [a]finger rings, [A]nose rings, 22 festal robes,
outer tunics, cloaks, money purses, 23 hand mirrors,
undergarments, turbans and veils.

24 Now it will come about that
instead of [a]sweet [A]perfume
there will be putrefaction;
Instead of a belt, a rope;
Instead of [B]well-set hair, a
[C]plucked-out scalp;
Instead of fine clothes, a
[D]donning of sackcloth;
And branding instead of beauty.
25 Your men will [A]fall by the sword
And your [a]mighty ones in battle.
26 And her [a,A]gates will lament and mourn,
And deserted she will [B]sit on the ground.

A REMNANT PREPARED

4 For seven women will take hold of [A]one man
in that day, saying, "We will eat our own bread
and wear our own clothes, only let us be called by
your name; [B]take away our reproach!"
2 In that day the [A]Branch of the LORD will be beautiful and glorious, and the [B]fruit of the earth *will*
be the pride and the adornment of the [C]survivors
of Israel. 3 It will come about that he who is [A]left in
Zion and remains in Jerusalem will be called [B]holy—
everyone who is [C]recorded for life in Jerusalem.
4 When the Lord has washed away the filth of the
[A]daughters of Zion and [a]purged the [B]bloodshed of
Jerusalem from her midst, by the [C]spirit of judgment and the [D]spirit of burning, 5 then the LORD
will create over the whole area of Mount Zion and
over her assemblies [A]a cloud by day, even smoke,
and the brightness of a flaming fire by night; for
over all the [B]glory will be a canopy. 6 There will be
a [A]shelter to *give* shade from the heat by day, and
refuge and [a]protection from the storm and the rain.

3:9 [a]Or *Their partiality bears* [b]Lit *their soul* [A]Gen 13:13; Is 1:10-15 [B]Prov 8:36; 15:32; Rom 6:23 3:10 [A]Deut 28:1-14; Eccl 8:12; Is 54:17 3:11 [a]Lit *the dealing of his hands* [A]Deut 28:15-68; Is 65:6, 7 3:12 [a]Or *deal severely* [A]Is 3:4 [B]Is 9:16; 28:14, 15 3:13 [A]Is 66:16; Hos 4:1; Mic 6:2 3:14 [A]Job 22:4; Ps 143:2; Ezek 20:35, 36 [B]Ps 14:4; Mic 3:3 [C]Job 24:9, 14; Ps 10:9; Prov 30:14; Is 10:1, 2; Ezek 18:12; James 2:6 3:15 [a]Heb *YHWH*, usually rendered *LORD* [A]Ps 94:5 3:16 [a]Lit *outstretched necks* [A]Song 3:11; Is 3:16-4:1, 4; 32:9-15 3:18 [A]Judg 8:21, 26 3:20 [A]Ex 39:28 3:21 [a]Or *signet rings* [A]Gen 24:47; Ezek 16:12 3:24 [a]Or *balsam oil* [A]Esth 2:12 [B]1 Pet 3:3 [C]Is 22:12; Ezek 27:31; Amos 8:10 [D]Is 15:3; Lam 2:10 3:25 [a]Lit *strength* [A]Is 1:20; 65:12 3:26 [a]Lit *entrances* [A]Jer 14:2; Lam 1:4 [B]Lam 2:10 4:1 [A]Is 13:12 [B]Gen 30:23; Is 54:4 4:2 [A]Is 11:1; 53:2; Jer 23:5; 33:15; Zech 3:8; 6:12 [B]Ps 72:16 [C]Is 10:20; 37:31, 32; Joel 2:32; Obad 17 4:3 [A]Is 28:5; 46:3; Rom 11:4, 5 [B]Is 52:1; 62:12 [C]Ex 32:32; Ps 69:28; Luke 10:20 4:4 [a]Lit *rinsed away* [A]Is 3:16 [B]Is 1:15 [C]Is 28:6 [D]Is 1:31; 9:19; Matt 3:11 4:5 [A]Ex 13:21, 22; 24:16; Num 9:15-23 [B]Is 60:1, 2 4:6 [a]Lit *a hiding place* [A]Ps 27:5; Is 25:4; 32:1, 2

the times just prior to Christ's second coming. **against the LORD.** The root of Zion's problem surfaces: overt rebellion against the Lord. The people sinned shamelessly; they made no effort to conceal it (3:9).

3:12 children ... women. Children and women were considered ill-suited for governmental leadership, so they figuratively depicted the incompetent rulers.

3:14 vineyard. The spoiling of the vineyard by the leaders amounts to their inequities in ruling the nation. Isaiah gave a more detailed comparison of God's people to a vineyard in 5:1–7.

3:16 daughters of Zion. When women cultivate beauty for beauty's sake, they thereby reflect the moral decay of the nations and detract from the glory of God. Rather than emphasizing outward apparel and activities (vv. 16–24), ladies should cultivate the beauty of the inner person (1Ti 2:9, 10; 1Pe 3:3, 4). **mincing steps.** Ornamental chains about the ankles necessitated shorter steps and produced tinkling sounds to attract attention.

4:1 seven women ... one man. In the day of reckoning, or the day of the Lord (*see note on 2:12*), He will judge wicked women indirectly by allowing a slaughtering of males, thereby producing a shortage of husbands.

4:2–6 The third picture of Zion resembles the first (2:1–5): an eventual purification and prosperity in the Land.

4:2 Branch. This messianic title occurs also in Jer 23:5; 33:15; Zec 3:8; 6:12. The thought behind the title relates to 2Sa 23:5, that of growth. The life of the Branch will bear spiritual fruit (cf. Jn 15:4, 5).

4:3 he who is left ... holy. "Holy" or "set apart" is another way of describing the remnant who will inherit God's prosperity in that day (cf. 1:9, 27; 3:10).

4:4 spirit of burning. For other instances of purging by burning, see 1:25; 6:6, 7.

4:5, 6 canopy ... shelter. The future inhabitants of Jerusalem will enjoy the Lord's protective covering over the glory on Mt. Zion. This recalls Ezekiel's prophecy of the return of the Shekinah to the temple (Eze 43:2–5).

PARABLE OF THE VINEYARD

5 Let me sing now for my well-beloved
A song of my beloved
concerning His vineyard.
My well-beloved had a [A]vineyard
on [a]a fertile hill.
2 He dug it all around, removed its stones,
And planted it with [a]the [A]choicest vine.
And He built a tower in the middle of it
And also hewed out a [b]wine vat in it;
Then He [B]expected *it* to
produce *good* grapes,
But it produced *only* [c]worthless ones.

3 "And now, O inhabitants of
Jerusalem and men of Judah,
[A]Judge between Me and My vineyard.
4 "[A]What more was there to do for My
vineyard [a]that I have not done in it?
Why, when I expected *it* to produce
good grapes did it produce
[b]worthless ones?
5 "So now let Me tell you what I am
going to do to My vineyard:
I will [A]remove its hedge and
it will be consumed;
I will [B]break down its wall and it
will become [C]trampled ground.
6 "I will [A]lay it waste;
It will not be pruned or hoed,
But briars and thorns will come up.
I will also charge the clouds
to [B]rain no rain on it."

7 For the [A]vineyard of the LORD of
hosts is the house of Israel
And the men of Judah His
delightful plant.
Thus He looked for justice, but
behold, [B]bloodshed;
For righteousness, but behold,
a cry of distress.

WOES FOR THE WICKED

8 Woe to those who [A]add house to
house *and* join field to field,
Until there is no more room,
So that you have to live alone
in the midst of the land!
9 In my ears the LORD of hosts *has*
sworn, "Surely, [A]many houses
shall become [B]desolate,
Even great and fine ones,
without occupants.
10 "For [A]ten acres of vineyard will
yield *only* one [a]bath *of wine,*
And a [B]homer of seed will yield
but an [b]ephah of grain."
11 Woe to those who rise early in
the morning that they may
pursue [A]strong drink,
Who stay up late in the evening
that wine may inflame them!
12 Their banquets are *accompanied*
by lyre and [A]harp, by tambourine
and flute, and by wine;
But they [B]do not pay attention
to the deeds of the LORD,
Nor do they consider the
work of His hands.

13 Therefore My people go into exile
for their [A]lack of knowledge;
And [a]their [B]honorable men are famished,
And their multitude is
parched with thirst.
14 Therefore [A]Sheol has enlarged
its [a]throat and opened its
mouth without measure;
And [b]Jerusalem's splendor, her multitude,
her din *of revelry* and the jubilant
within her, descend *into it.*
15 So the *common* man will be humbled
and the man of *importance* abased,
[A]The eyes of the proud also will be abased.

5:1 [a]Lit *a horn, the son of fatness* [A]Ps 80:8; Jer 12:10; Matt 21:33; Mark 12:1; Luke 20:9 5:2 [a]Lit *a bright red grape* [b]Or *wine press* [c]Or *wild grapes* [A]Jer 2:21 [B]Matt 21:19; Mark 11:13; Luke 13:6 5:3 [A]Matt 21:40 5:4 [a]Lit *and I have not done* [b]Or *wild grapes* [A]2 Chr 36:16; Jer 2:5; 7:25, 26; Mic 6:3; Matt 23:37 5:5 [A]Ps 89:40 [B]Ps 80:12 [C]Is 10:6; 28:18; Lam 1:15; Luke 21:24; Rev 11:2 5:6 [A]2 Chr 36:19-21; Is 7:19-25; 24:1, 3; Jer 25:11 [B]1 Kin 8:35; 17:1; Jer 14:1-22 5:7 [A]Ps 80:8-11 [B]Is 3:14, 15; 30:12; 59:13 5:8 [A]Jer 22:13-17; Mic 2:2; Hab 2:9-12 5:9 [A]Is 6:11, 12 [B]Matt 23:38 5:10 [a]I.e. Approx 10 1/2 gal. [b]I.e. Approx one bu [A]Lev 26:26; Is 7:23; Hag 1:6; 2:16 [B]Ezek 45:11 5:11 [A]Prov 23:29, 30; Eccl 10:16, 17; Is 5:22; 22:13; 28:1, 3, 7, 8 5:12 [A]Amos 6:5, 6 [B]Job 34:27; Ps 28:5 5:13 [a]Lit *their glory are men of famine* [A]Is 1:3; 27:11; Hos 4:6 [B]Is 3:3 5:14 [a]Or *appetite* [b]Lit *her* [A]Prov 30:16; Hab 2:5 5:15 [A]Is 2:11; 10:33

5:1–30 The conclusion of the extended discourse begun at 2:1 comes by way of a comparison of God's people to a vineyard which He cultivated, but which did not bear fruit.

5:1 well-beloved. The Lord is the friend who is well-beloved by Isaiah. The vineyard belongs to Him (5:7).

5:2 *good* grapes ... worthless ones. The owner made every conceivable provision for the vine's productivity and protection, illustrating the Lord's purely gracious choice of Israel. Justifiably, He expected a good yield from His investment, but the vine's produce was "sour berries," inedible and fit only for dumping.

5:5 consumed ... trampled ground. As punishment for her unfruitfulness, Israel became desolate and accessible to any nation wishing to invade her, such as happened in the Babylonian invasion of 586 B.C., and will happen repeatedly until her national repentance at the second coming of the Messiah.

5:7 justice ... bloodshed ... righteousness ... cry. The Eng. words "equity ... iniquity ... right ... riot" illustrate the effective play on words in the underlying Heb. behind v. 7.

5:8–23 The prophet pronounced 6 woes (judgments) against the unresponsive people of Israel.

5:8–10 The first woe was against real estate owners because of their greedy materialism.

5:8 house to house ... field to field. God gave the land to the Israelites with the intention that the original allocation remain with each family (Lv 25:23–25). By Isaiah's time, land speculators had begun putting together huge estates (Mic 2:2, 9), and the powerful rich used legal processes to deprive the poor of what was rightfully theirs (Am 2:6, 7).

5:10 one bath ... an ephah. God judged the greedy rich by reducing the productivity of their land to a small fraction of what it would have been normally. One bath was roughly equivalent to six gallons (contra. marginal note). About one-half bushel would be produced from about six bushels of planted seed. Such amounts indicate famine conditions.

5:11, 12 The second woe addressed the drunkards for their neglect of the Lord's work of judgment and redemption, and their devotion to pleasure.

5:14 Sheol. This term in this context pictures death as a great monster with wide-open jaws, ready to receive its victims. Such was to be the fate of those who perish in the captivity God will send to punish the people's sinfulness.

16 But the [A]LORD of hosts will be
[B]exalted in judgment,
And the holy God will show Himself
[C]holy in righteousness.
17 [A]Then the lambs will graze
as in their pasture,
And strangers will eat in the waste
places of the [a]wealthy.

18 Woe to those who drag [A]iniquity
with the cords of [a]falsehood,
And sin as if with cart ropes;
19 [A]Who say, "Let Him make speed, let Him
hasten His work, that we may see *it;*
And let the purpose of the Holy
One of Israel draw near
And come to pass, that we may know *it!*"
20 Woe to those who [A]call evil
good, and good evil;
Who [a,B]substitute darkness for
light and light for darkness;
Who [a]substitute bitter for sweet
and sweet for bitter!
21 Woe to those who are [A]wise
in their own eyes
And clever in their own sight!
22 [A]Woe to those who are heroes
in drinking wine
And valiant men in mixing strong drink,
23 [A]Who justify the wicked for a bribe,
And [B]take away the [a]rights of the
ones who are in the right!

24 Therefore, [A]as a tongue of fire
consumes stubble
And dry grass collapses into the flame,
So their [B]root will become [C]like rot and
their blossom [a]blow away as dust;
For they have [D]rejected the law
of the LORD of hosts
And despised the word of the
Holy One of Israel.
25 On this account the [A]anger of the LORD
has burned against His people,
And He has stretched out His hand
against them and struck them down.
And the [B]mountains quaked, and
their [C]corpses [a]lay like refuse
in the middle of the streets.
[D]For all this His anger [b]is not spent,
But His [E]hand is still stretched out.

26 He will also lift up a [A]standard
to the [a]distant nation,
And will [B]whistle for it [C]from
the ends of the earth;
And behold, it will [D]come
with speed swiftly.
27 [A]No one in it is weary or stumbles,
None slumbers or sleeps;
Nor is the [B]belt at its waist undone,
Nor its sandal strap broken.
28 [a,A]Its arrows are sharp and all
its bows are bent;
The hoofs of its horses [b]seem like flint and
its *chariot* [B]wheels like a whirlwind.
29 Its [A]roaring is like a lioness, and
it roars like young lions;
It growls as it [B]seizes the prey
And carries *it* off with [C]no
one to deliver *it.*
30 And it will [A]growl over it in that
day like the roaring of the sea.
If one [B]looks to the land, behold,
there is darkness *and* distress;
Even the light is darkened by its clouds.

ISAIAH'S VISION

6 In the year of [A]King Uzziah's death [B]I saw the
Lord sitting on a throne, lofty and exalted, with

5:16 [A]Is 28:17; 30:18; 61:8 [B]Is 2:11, 17; 33:5, 10 [C]Is 8:13; 29:23; 1 Pet 3:15 5:17 [a]Lit *the fat* [A]Is 7:25; Mic 2:12; Zeph 2:6 5:18 [a]Or *worthlessness* [A]Is 59:4-8; Jer 23:10-14 5:19 [A]Ezek 12:22; 2 Pet 3:4 5:20 [a]Lit *set* [A]Prov 17:15; Amos 5:7 [B]Job 17:12; Matt 6:22, 23; Luke 11:34, 35 5:21 [A]Prov 3:7; Rom 12:16; 1 Cor 3:18-20 5:22 [A]Prov 23:20; Is 5:11; 56:12; Hab 2:15 5:23 [a]Lit *righteousness* [A]Ex 23:8; Is 1:23; 10:1, 2; Mic 3:11; 7:3 [B]Ps 94:21; James 5:6 5:24 [a]Lit *ascend* [A]Is 9:18, 19; Joel 2:5 [B]Job 18:16 [C]Hos 5:12 [D]Is 8:6; 30:9, 12; Acts 13:41 5:25 [a]Lit *were* [b]Lit *has not turned away* [A]2 Kin 22:13, 17; Is 66:15 [B]Ps 18:7; Is 64:3; Jer 4:24; Nah 1:5 [C]2 Kin 9:37; Is 14:19; Jer 16:4 [D]Is 9:12, 17, 19, 21; 10:4; Jer 4:8; Dan 9:16 [E]Ex 7:19; Is 23:11 5:26 [a]Lit *nations;* probably Assyria [A]Is 13:2, 3 [B]Is 7:18; Zech 10:8 [C]Deut 28:49 [D]Is 13:4, 5 5:27 [A]Joel 2:7, 8 [B]Job 12:18 5:28 [a]Lit *Which, its arrows* [b]Lit *are regarded as* [A]Ps 7:12, 13; 45:5; Is 13:18 [B]Is 21:1; Jer 4:13 5:29 [A]Jer 51:38; Zeph 3:3; Zech 11:3 [B]Is 10:6; 49:24, 25; Mic 5:8 [C]Is 42:22 5:30 [A]Is 17:12; Jer 6:23; Luke 21:25 [B]Is 8:22; Jer 4:23-28; Joel 2:10; Luke 21:25, 26 6:1 [A]2 Kin 15:7; 2 Chr 26:23; Is 1:1 [B]John 12:41; Rev 4:2, 3; 20:11

5:18, 19 The third woe was against those who defied the Lord and ridiculed His prophet.

5:19 **Let Him make speed.** The taunting unbelievers said, "Where is the judgment of which you have spoken, Isaiah? Bring it on. We will believe it when we see it." This challenge for God to hasten His judgment represented their disbelief that the Holy One of Israel would judge the people. See Isaiah's response in the naming of his son: "Swift is the booty, speedy is the prey" (8:1; cf. 5:26).

5:20 **evil good, and good evil.** The fourth woe condemned the reversal of morality which dominated the nation. They utterly confused all moral distinctions.

5:21 **wise in their own eyes.** The object of the fifth woe was the people's arrogance. "Pride *goes* before destruction ..." (Pr 16:18).

5:22, 23 **justify the wicked.** The sixth woe pointed to the unjust sentences passed by drunken and bribed judges.

5:24–30 The conclusion of the discourse announced God's action in sending a mighty army against Judah to conquer and leave the land in darkness and distress.

5:26 **distant nation.** Principal among the nations God would bring against Israel were: 1) Assyria, which conquered the northern kingdom in 722 B.C., and 2) Babylon, which completed its invasion of Jerusalem in 586 B.C. and destroyed the temple.

5:30 **darkness.** God's wrath against the people was to eliminate light (8:22; 42:7), but His promised deliverance of the remnant will ultimately turn that darkness into light at the coming of the Messiah (9:2; 42:16; 58:10; 60:2).

6:1–5 In preparation for calling Isaiah to be the prophet who would proclaim the coming judgment, God gave him a vision of His majestic holiness so overwhelming that it devastated him and made him realize his own sinfulness.

6:1 **King Uzziah's death.** After 52 years of reigning, leprosy caused the death of Uzziah in 739 B.C. (cf. 2Ch 26:16–23). Isaiah began his prophetic ministry that year. He received the prophecies of the first 5 chapters after his call, but at 6:1 he returns to authenticate what he has already written by describing how he was called. **I saw.** The prophet became unconscious of the outside world and with his inner eye saw what God revealed to him. This experience recalls the experience of John's prophetic vision in Rev 4:1–11. **lofty and exalted.** The throne was greatly elevated, emphasizing the Most High God. **train.** This refers to the hem or fringe of the Lord's glorious robe that filled the temple. **temple.** Though Isaiah may have been at the earthly temple, this describes a vision which transcends the

the train of His robe filling the temple. [2]Seraphim
stood above Him, [A]each having six wings: with two
he covered his face, and with two he covered his
feet, and with two he flew. [3]And one called out to
another and said,

"[A]Holy, Holy, Holy, is the LORD of hosts,
The [a,B]whole earth is full of His glory."

[4]And the [a]foundations of the thresholds trembled at
the voice of him who called out, while the [b,A]temple
was filling with smoke. [5]Then I said,

"[A]Woe is me, for I am ruined!
Because I am a man of [B]unclean lips,
And I live among a [C]people
of unclean lips;
For my eyes have seen the [D]King,
the LORD of hosts."

[6]Then one of the seraphim flew to me with a
burning coal in his hand, which he had taken from
the [A]altar with tongs. [7]He [A]touched my mouth *with*
it and said, "Behold, this has touched your lips;
and [B]your iniquity is taken away and your sin is
[a]forgiven."

ISAIAH'S COMMISSION

[8]Then I heard the [A]voice of the Lord, saying,
"Whom shall I send, and who will go for Us?" Then
[B]I said, "Here am I. Send me!" [9]He said, "Go, and
tell this people:

'Keep on [A]listening, but do not perceive;
Keep on looking, but do not understand.'

10 "[A]Render the hearts of this
people [a,B]insensitive,
Their ears [b]dull,
And their eyes [c]dim,
[C]Otherwise they might see
with their eyes,
Hear with their ears,
Understand with their hearts,
And return and be healed."

[11]Then I said, "Lord, [A]how long?" And He answered,

"Until [B]cities are devastated *and*
without inhabitant,
Houses are without people
And the land is utterly desolate,
12 The LORD has [A]removed men far away,
And the [a,B]forsaken places are many
in the midst of the land.
13 "Yet there will be a tenth portion in it,
And it will again be *subject* to burning,
Like a terebinth or an [A]oak
Whose stump remains when it is felled.
The [B]holy seed is its stump."

WAR AGAINST JERUSALEM

7 Now it came about in the days of [A]Ahaz, the son
of Jotham, the son of Uzziah, king of Judah, that
[B]Rezin the king of Aram and [C]Pekah the son of Remaliah, king of Israel, went up to Jerusalem to *wage*
war against it, but [D]could not [a]conquer it. [2]When it
was reported to the [A]house of David, saying, "The
Arameans [a,B]have camped in [C]Ephraim," his heart
and the hearts of his people shook as the trees of
the forest shake [b]with the wind.

6:2 [A]Rev 4:8 6:3 [a]Lit *fullness of the whole earth is His glory* [A]Rev 4:8 [B]Num 14:21; Ps 72:19 6:4 [a]Lit *door sockets* [b]Lit *house* [A]Rev 15:8 6:5 [A]Ex 33:20; Luke 5:8 [B]Ex 6:12, 30 [C]Is 59:3; Jer 9:3-8 [D]Jer 51:57 6:6 [A]Rev 8:3 6:7 [a]Lit *atoned for* [A]Jer 1:9; Dan 10:16 [B]Is 40:2; 53:5, 6, 11; 1 John 1:7 6:8 [A]Ezek 10:5; Acts 9:4 [B]Acts 26:19 6:9 [A]Is 43:8; Matt 13:14; Mark 4:12; Luke 8:10; John 12:40; Acts 28:26; Rom 11:8 6:10 [a]Lit *fat* [b]Lit *heavy* [c]Lit *besmeared* [A]Matt 13:15 [B]Deut 31:20; 32:15 [C]Jer 5:21 6:11 [A]Ps 79:5 [B]Lev 26:31; Is 1:7; 3:8, 26 6:12 [a]Or *forsakenness will be great* [A]Deut 28:64 [B]Jer 4:29 6:13 [A]Job 14:7 [B]Deut 7:6; Ezra 9:2 7:1 [a]Lit *fight against* [A]2 Kin 16:1; Is 1:1 [B]2 Kin 15:37 [C]2 Kin 15:25; 2 Chr 28:6 [D]Is 7:6, 7 7:2 [a]Lit *has settled down on* [b]Lit *from before* [A]Is 7:13; 22:22 [B]Is 8:12 [C]Is 9:9

earthly. The throne of God is in the heavenly temple (Rev 4:1–6; 5:1–7; 11:19; 15:5–8).

6:2 Seraphim. The seraphim are an order of angelic creatures who bear a similarity to the 4 living creatures of Rev 4:6, which in turn resemble the cherubim of Eze 10:1ff. **six wings.** Two wings covered the faces of the seraphim because they dared not gaze directly at God's glory. Two covered their feet, acknowledging their lowliness even though engaged in divine service. With two they flew in serving the One on the throne. Thus, 4 wings related to worship, emphasizing the priority of praise.

6:3 called out to another. The seraphs were speaking to each other in antiphonal praise. **Holy, Holy, Holy.** The primary thrust of the 3-fold repetition of God's holiness (called the *trihagion*) is to emphasize God's separateness from and independence of His fallen creation, though it implies secondarily that God is 3 Persons. See Rev 4:8, where the 4 living creatures utter the *trihagion*. **full of His glory.** The earth is the worldwide display of His immeasurable glory, perfections, and attributes as seen in creation (see Ro 1:20). Fallen man has nevertheless refused to glorify Him as God (Ro 1:23).

6:4 trembled … smoke. The trembling and smoke symbolize God's holiness as it relates to His wrath and judgment (cf. Ex 19:16–20; Rev 15:8).

6:5 unclean lips. If the lips are unclean, so is the heart. This vision of God's holiness vividly reminded the prophet of his own unworthiness which deserved judgment. Job (Job 42:6) and Peter (Lk 5:8) came to the same realization about themselves when confronted with the presence of the Lord (cf. Eze 1:28–2:7; Rev 1:17).

6:6–13 Isaiah's vision has made him painfully aware of his sin and has broken him (cf. 66:2, 5); in this way God has prepared him for his cleansing and his commission.

6:6 coal … altar. The hot coal taken from the altar of incense in heaven (cf. Rev 8:3–5) is emblematic of God's purifying work. Repentance is painful.

6:7 taken away … forgiven. Spiritual cleansing for special service to the Lord, not salvation, is in view.

6:8 Us. This plural pronoun does not prove the doctrine of the Trinity, but does strongly imply it (see Ge 1:26). **Here am I. Send me!** This response evidenced the humble readiness of complete trust. Though profoundly aware of his sin, he was available.

6:9, 10 do not perceive … do not understand. Isaiah's message was to be God's instrument for hiding the truth from an unreceptive people. Centuries later, Jesus' parables were to do the same (Mt 13:14, 15; Mk 4:12; Lk 8:10; cf. 29:9, 10; 42:18; 43:8; Dt 29:4; Jn 12:40; Ac 28:26, 27; Ro 11:8).

6:11, 12 how long? Because of such rejection from his people, the prophet asked how long he should preach this message of divine judgment. God replied that it must continue until the cities are desolate (v. 11) and the people have gone into exile (v. 12).

6:13 a tenth. Though most will reject God, the tenth, also called "stump" and "holy seed," represents the faithful remnant in Israel who will be the nucleus who hear and believe.

7:1, 2 An unsuccessful invasion of Judah by Aram, or Syria, and Israel (i.e., the northern 10 tribes) led to a continued presence of King Tiglath-Pileser's Assyrian forces in Israel. Shortly after Ahaz assumed the throne (ca. 735 B.C.), this threat to Judah's security brought great fear to the king and the people of Judah. See 2Ch 28:5–8, 17–19.

7:2 house of David. This expression refers to the Davidic dynasty, personified in the current king, Ahaz.

3 Then the LORD said to Isaiah, "Go out now to
meet Ahaz, you and your son [a]Shear-jashub, at
the end of the [A]conduit of the upper pool, on the
highway to the [b]fuller's field, 4 and say to him,
'Take care and be [A]calm, have no [B]fear and [C]do
not be fainthearted because of these two stubs of
smoldering [D]firebrands, on account of the fierce
anger of Rezin and Aram and the [E]son of Remaliah. 5 Because [A]Aram, *with* Ephraim and the son
of Remaliah, has planned evil against you, saying,
6 "Let us go up against Judah and [a]terrorize it, and
make for ourselves a breach in [b]its walls and set up
the son of Tabeel as king in the midst of it," 7 thus
says the Lord [a]GOD: "[A]It shall not stand nor shall it
come to pass. 8 For the head of Aram is [A]Damascus
and the head of Damascus is Rezin (now within
another 65 years Ephraim will be shattered, *so
that it is* no longer a people), 9 and the head of
Ephraim is Samaria and the head of Samaria is
the son of Remaliah. [A]If you will not believe, you
surely shall not [a]last." ' "

THE CHILD IMMANUEL

10 Then the LORD spoke again to Ahaz, saying,
11 "Ask a [A]sign for yourself from the LORD your God;
[a]make *it* deep as Sheol or high as [b]heaven." 12 But
Ahaz said, "I will not ask, nor will I test the LORD!"
13 Then he said, "Listen now, O [A]house of David! Is
it too slight a thing for you to try the patience of
men, that you will [B]try the patience of [C]my God as
well? 14 Therefore the Lord Himself will give you a
sign: Behold, [A]a [a]virgin will be with child and bear
a son, and she will call His name [b,B]Immanuel. 15 He
will eat [A]curds and honey [a]at the time He knows
enough to refuse evil and choose good. 16 [A]For before the boy will know *enough* to refuse evil and
choose good, [B]the land whose two kings you dread
will be forsaken.

TRIALS TO COME FOR JUDAH

17 The LORD will bring on you, on your people,
and on your father's house such days as have never
come since the day that [A]Ephraim separated from
Judah, the [B]king of Assyria."
18 In that day the LORD will [A]whistle for the fly
that is in the [a,B]remotest part of the rivers of Egypt
and for the bee that is in the land of Assyria. 19 They
will all come and settle on the steep [a]ravines, on the
[A]ledges of the cliffs, [B]on all the thorn bushes and
on all the [b]watering places.
20 In that day the Lord will [A]shave with a [B]razor,
[C]hired from regions beyond [D]the [a]Euphrates (*that
is,* with the king of Assyria), the head and the hair
of the legs; and it will also remove the beard.
21 Now in that day a man may keep alive a [A]heifer
and a pair of sheep; 22 and because of the abundance
of the milk produced he will eat curds, for everyone
that is left within the land will eat [A]curds and honey.
23 And it will come about in that day, [A]that every
place where there used to be a thousand vines,
valued at a thousand *shekels* of silver, will become [B]briars and thorns. 24 *People* will come there
with bows and arrows because all the land will
be briars and thorns. 25 As for all the hills which
used to be cultivated with the hoe, you will not go
there for fear of briars and thorns; but they will
become a place for [a,A]pasturing oxen and for sheep
to trample.

7:3 [a]I.e. a remnant shall return [b]I.e. laundryman's [A]2 Kin 18:17; Is 36:2 7:4 [A]Ex 14:13; Is 30:15; Lam 3:26 [B]Is 10:24; Matt 24:6 [C]Deut 20:3; 1 Sam 17:32; Is 35:4 [D]Amos 4:11; Zech 3:2 [E]Is 7:1, 9 7:5 [A]Is 7:2 7:6 [a]Lit *cause it a sickening dread* [b]Lit *it* 7:7 [a]Heb *YHWH*, usually rendered *LORD* [A]Is 8:10; 28:18; Acts 4:25, 26 7:8 [A]Gen 14:15; Is 17:1-3 7:9 [a]Or *be established* [A]2 Chr 20:20; Is 5:24; 8:6-8; 30:12-14 7:11 [a]So with the versions; M.T. *make the request deep or high* [b]Lit *heights* [A]2 Kin 19:29; Is 37:30; 38:7, 8; 55:13 7:13 [A]Is 7:2 [B]Is 1:14; 43:24 [C]Is 25:1 7:14 [a]Or *maiden* [b]I.e. God is with us [A]Matt 1:23 [B]Is 8:8, 10 7:15 [a]Lit *with respect to his knowing* [A]Is 7:22 7:16 [A]Is 8:4 [B]Is 8:14; 17:3; Jer 7:15; Hos 5:3, 9, 14; Amos 1:3-5 7:17 [A]1 Kin 12:16 [B]2 Chr 28:20; Is 8:7, 8; 10:5, 6 7:18 [a]Or *mouth of the rivers;* i.e. the Nile Delta [A]Is 5:26 [B]Is 13:5 7:19 [a]Or *wadis* [b]Or *pastures* [A]Is 2:19; Jer 16:16 [B]Is 7:24, 25 7:20 [a]Lit *River* [A]2 Kin 18:13-16; Is 24:1 [B]Ezek 5:1-4 [C]Is 10:5, 15 [D]Is 8:7; 11:15; Jer 2:18 7:21 [A]Is 14:30; 27:10; Jer 39:10 7:22 [A]Is 8:15 7:23 [A]Is 5:10; 32:13, 14 [B]Is 5:6 7:25 [a]Lit *sending* [A]Is 5:17

7:3 Shear-jashub. The name means "a remnant shall return." The presence of Isaiah's son is an object lesson of God's faithfulness to believers among the people.

7:4 have no fear. Isaiah's message to Ahaz is one of reassurance. The two invading kings will not prevail.

7:8 Ephraim will be shattered. This tribe represented all the northern 10 tribes. The prophet predicted the coming demise because of idolatry (cf. Hos 4:17). In 65 years they would cease to be a people, first through the captivity of most of them in 722 B.C. (2Ki 17:6) and then with the importation of foreign settlers into the land in ca. 670 B.C. (2Ki 17:24; 2Ch 33:11; Ezr 4:2).

7:9 not believe ... not last. The choice belonged to Ahaz. He could trust the Lord's word or fall into the enemy's hands or, even worse, experience a final heart-hardening (6:9, 10).

7:11 a sign. To encourage his faith, the Lord offered Ahaz a sign, but Ahaz feigned humility in refusing the sign (v. 12).

7:13 house of David. Upon hearing Ahaz's refusal, the prophet broadened his audience beyond Ahaz (see v. 2) to include the whole faithless house of David. The nation was guilty of wearying God (1:14).

7:14 a sign. Since Ahaz refused to choose a sign (vv. 11, 12), the Lord chose His own sign, whose implementation would occur far beyond Ahaz's lifetime. **a virgin.** This prophecy reached forward to the virgin birth of the Messiah, as the NT notes (Mt 1:23). The Heb. word refers to an unmarried woman and means "virgin" (Ge 24:43; Prov 30:19; SS 1:3; 6:8), so the birth of Isaiah's own son (8:3) could not have fully satisfied the prophecy. Cf. Ge 3:15. **Immanuel.** The title, applied to Jesus in Mt 1:23, means "God with us."

7:15 curds and honey. Curds result from coagulated milk, something like cottage cheese. This diet indicated the scarcity of provisions which characterized the period after foreign invaders had decimated the land.

7:16 refuse evil. Before the promised son of Isaiah was old enough to make moral choices, the kings of Aram, or Syria, and Ephraim were to meet their doom at the hands of the Assyrians.

7:17 bring on you ... the king of Assyria. Not only did the Lord use the Assyrians to judge the northern kingdom, He also used them to invade Ahaz's domain of Judah. This coming of the Assyrian king was the beginning of the end for the nation and eventually led to her captivity in Babylon.

7:18–25 The desolation prophesied in this section began in the days of Ahaz and reached its climax when the Babylonians conquered Judah. Its results continue to the time when the Messiah will return to deliver Israel and establish His kingdom on earth.

7:18 fly ... bee. Egypt was full of flies, and Assyria was a country noted for beekeeping. These insects represented the armies from the powerful countries which the Lord would summon to overrun Judah and take the people into exile.

7:19 steep ravines ... ledges of the cliffs. Not even inaccessible areas of the land were free from the invading armies.

7:20 razor, hired. The Assyrians were the Lord's hired blade to shave and disgrace the entire body of Judah (cf. 1:6).

7:21, 22 a heifer and a pair of sheep. The foreign invasion would cause a change from an agricultural economy to a pastoral one. Not enough men would remain in the land to farm. It was to be a time of great poverty.

7:23–25 briars and thorns. The presence of these uncultivated growths was a sign of desolation, as in 5:6.

DAMASCUS AND SAMARIA FALL

8 Then the LORD said to me, "Take for yourself a
large tablet and [A]write on it [a]in ordinary letters:
[b,B]Swift is the booty, speedy is the prey. 2 And [a]I will
take to Myself faithful witnesses for testimony, [A]Uriah
the priest and Zechariah the son of Jeberechiah." 3 So
I approached the prophetess, and she conceived and
gave birth to a son. Then the LORD said to me, "Name
him [a,A]Maher-shalal-hash-baz; 4 for [A]before the boy
knows how to cry out 'My father' or 'My mother,' the
wealth of [B]Damascus and the spoil of Samaria will
be carried away before the king of Assyria."

8:1 [a]Lit *with the stylus of man* [b]Heb *Maher-shalal-hash-baz* [A]Is 30:8; Hab 2:2 [B]Is 8:3 8:2 [a]Another reading is *take for me* [A]2 Kin 16:10, 11, 15, 16 8:3 [a]I.e. swift is the booty, speedy is the prey [A]Is 8:1 8:4 [A]Is 7:16 [B]Is 7:8, 9

8:1 large tablet. Isaiah was to prepare a large placard for public display. That placard reiterated, from another perspective, the prophecies just concluded in 7:18–25.

8:2 faithful witnesses. After the prophecy's fulfillment, the respected leaders Uriah and Zechariah verified to the people that Isaiah had spoken it on a given date before the Assyrian invasion. This verification accredited the Lord's word and upheld His honor (Dt 18:21, 22; Jer 28:9).

8:3 prophetess. Isaiah's wife was called a prophetess because the son to whom she gave birth was prophetic of the Assyrian conquest. **Maher-shalal-hash-baz.** *Maher-shalal* ("swift is the booty") told the Assyrian invaders with no doubt as to who was to win the battle. *Hash-baz* ("speedy is the prey") told them to reap the benefits of the conquered land quickly (5:26).

8:4 before the boy. The time before the plunder of Aram, or Syria, and the northern kingdom of Israel began was very short. The Assyrians initiated their invasion before Isaiah's child learned to talk. That prophetic limit resembled the one set in 7:16, but there the prophecy was more far-reaching. Fulfillment of the closer prophecy verified the one relating to the distant future.

PROPHECIES OF ISAIAH FULFILLED AT CHRIST'S FIRST ADVENT

Reference	Fulfilled Literally	Fulfilled Typically
7:14	The virgin birth of Christ (Mt 1:23)	
8:14, 15		A stone of stumbling and a rock of offense (Ro 9:33; 1Pe 2:8)
8:17		Christ's hope and trust in God (Heb 2:13a)
8:18		The Son of God and the sons of God (Heb 2:13b)
9:1, 2		The arrival of Jesus in the area of Zebulun and Naphtali (Mt 4:12–16)
9:6a	The birth of Immanuel (Mt 1:23; Lk 1:31–33; 2:7, 11)	
11:1	Revival of the Davidic dynasty (Mt 1:6, 16; Ac 13:23; Rev 5:5; 22:16)	
12:3		Water from the wells of salvation (Jn 4:10, 14)
25:8		The swallowing up of death (1Co 15:54)
28:11		The gift of tongues as an authenticating sign of God's messengers (1Co 14:21, 22)
28:16	Incarnation of Jesus Christ (Mt 21:42)	
29:18; 35:5	Jesus' healing of the physically deaf and blind (Mt 11:5)	
40:3–5	Preaching of John the Baptist (Mt 3:3; Mk 1:3; Lk 3:4–6; Jn 1:23)	
42:1a, 2, 3	Christ at His baptism (Mt 3:16, 17) and transfiguration (Mt 17:5) and His general demeanor throughout His first advent	
42:6		Christ extended the benefits of the New Covenant to the church (Heb 8:6, 10–12)
42:7		Jesus healed physical blindness and provided liberty for the spiritual captives (Mt 11:5; Lk 4:18)
42:7		Jesus removed spiritual darkness at His first coming (Mt 4:16)
50:6	Jesus beaten and spat upon (Mt 26:67; 27:26, 30; Mk 14:65; 15:19; Lk 22:63; Jn 18:22)	
50:7	Jesus resolutely setting His face to go to Jerusalem (Lk 9:51)	
53:1	Israel failed to recognize her Messiah (Jn 12:38)	
53:4		Jesus healed sick people as a symbol of His bearing of sin (Mt 8:16, 17)
53:7, 8	Philip identifies Jesus as the one about whom the prophet wrote (Ac 8:32, 33)	
53:7	Jesus remained silent at all phases of His trial (Mt 26:63; 27:12–14; Mk 14:61; 15:5; Lk 23:9; Jn 19:9; 1Pe 2:23)	
53:7	Jesus was the Lamb of God who takes away the sin of the world (Jn 1:29; 1Pe 1:18, 19; Rev 5:6)	
53:9	Jesus was completely innocent of all charges against Him (1Pe 2:22)	
53:12	Jesus saw the need to be crucified between two criminals (Lk 22:37)	
54:13		Jesus saw those who came to Him at His first advent as taught by God (Jn 6:45)
55:3	Christ's resurrection was prerequisite to His some day occupying David's throne on earth (Ac 13:34)	
61:1, 2a		Jesus saw His first-advent ministry as a spiritual counterpart of His second-advent deliverance of Israel (Lk 4:18, 19)
62:11	Jesus fulfilled the call to the daughter of Zion in His triumphal entry (Mt 21:5)	

5 Again the LORD spoke to me further, saying,

6 “Inasmuch as these people have [A]rejected
the gently flowing waters of Shiloah
And rejoice in [B]Rezin and
the son of Remaliah;
7 Now therefore, behold, the Lord is about
to bring on them the [A]strong and
abundant waters of the [a,B]Euphrates,
Even the [C]king of Assyria and all his glory;
And it will [D]rise up over all its channels
and go over all its banks.
8 “Then [A]it will sweep on into Judah, it
will overflow and pass through,
It will [B]reach even to the neck;
And the spread of its wings will [a]fill the
breadth of [b]your land, O [C]Immanuel.

A BELIEVING REMNANT

9 “[A]Be broken, O peoples, and be [a,B]shattered;
And give ear, all remote places of the earth.
Gird yourselves, yet be [a]shattered;
Gird yourselves, yet be [a]shattered.
10 “[A]Devise a plan, but it will be thwarted;
State a [a]proposal, but [B]it will not stand,
For [b,C]God is with us.”

11 For thus the LORD spoke to me [a]with [A]mighty
power and instructed me [B]not to walk in the way
of this people, saying,

12 “You are not to say, ‘*It is* a [A]conspiracy!’
In regard to all that this people
call a conspiracy,
And [B]you are not to fear [a]what
they fear or be in dread of *it*.
13 “It is the [A]LORD of hosts [B]whom
you should regard as holy.
And He shall be your fear,
And He shall be your dread.
14 “Then He shall become a [A]sanctuary;
But to both the houses of
Israel, a [B]stone to strike
and a rock to stumble over,
And a snare and a [C]trap for the
inhabitants of Jerusalem.
15 “Many [A]will stumble over them,
Then they will fall and be broken;
They will even be snared
and caught.”

16 [A]Bind up the testimony, [B]seal the [a]law among
[C]my disciples. 17 And I will [A]wait for the LORD [B]who
is hiding His face from the house of Jacob; I will
even look eagerly for Him. 18 [A]Behold, I and the children whom the LORD has given me are for [B]signs
and wonders in Israel from the LORD of hosts, who
[C]dwells on Mount Zion.
19 When they say to you, “[A]Consult the mediums
and the spiritists who whisper and mutter,” should
not a people [B]consult their God? *Should they* [C]*con-*
sult the dead on behalf of the living? 20 To the [a,A]law
and to the testimony! If they do not speak according to this word, it is because [B]they have no dawn.
21 They will pass through [a]the land [A]hard-pressed
and famished, and it will turn out that when they
are hungry, they will be enraged and curse [b]their
king and their God as they face upward. 22 Then

8:6 [A]Is 1:20; 5:24; 7:9; 30:12 [B]Is 7:1 8:7 [a]Lit *River* [A]Is 17:12, 13 [B]Is 7:20; 11:15 [C]Is 7:17; 10:5 [D]Amos 8:8; 9:5 8:8 [a]Lit *be the fullness of* [b]Or *Your* [A]Is 10:6 [B]Is 30:28 [C]Is 7:14 8:9 [a]Or *dismayed* [A]Is 17:12-14 [B]Dan 2:34, 35 8:10 [a]Lit *word* [b]Heb *Immanu-el* [A]Job 5:12; Is 28:18 [B]Is 7:7 [C]Is 8:8; Rom 8:31 8:11 [a]Lit *with strength of the hand* [A]Ezek 3:14 [B]Ezek 2:8 8:12 [a]Lit *their fear* [A]Is 7:2; 30:1 [B]1 Pet 3:14, 15 8:13 [A]Is 5:16; 29:23 [B]Num 20:12 8:14 [A]Is 4:6; 25:4; Ezek 11:16 [B]Luke 2:34; Rom 9:33; 1 Pet 2:8 [C]Is 24:17, 18 8:15 [A]Is 28:13; 59:10; Luke 20:18; Rom 9:32 8:16 [a]Or *teaching* [A]Is 8:1, 2; 29:11, 12 [B]Dan 12:4 [C]Is 50:4 8:17 [A]Is 25:9; 30:18; Hab 2:3 [B]Deut 31:17; Is 1:15; 45:15; 54:8 8:18 [A]Heb 2:13 [B]Luke 2:34 [C]Ps 9:11; Zech 8:3 8:19 [A]Lev 20:6; 2 Kin 21:6; 23:24; Is 19:3; 29:4; 47:12, 13 [B]Is 30:2; 45:11 [C]1 Sam 28:8-11 8:20 [a]Or *teaching* [A]Is 1:10; 8:16; Luke 16:29 [B]Is 8:22; Mic 3:6 8:21 [a]Lit *it* [b]Or *by their king* [A]Is 9:20, 21

8:6 these people. Lit. “this people” (the Heb. is sing.). These were the people of Judah (cf. 6:9), but perhaps secondarily the whole nation of Israel. Ahaz had called on Assyria for help rather than relying on the Lord. **waters of Shiloah.** This was the stream from the Gihon Spring outside Jerusalem’s city wall flowing to the Pool of Siloam inside the city which supplied the city’s water (see 7:3). It symbolized the city’s dependence on the Lord and His defense of the city, if they were to survive. First, the northern 10 tribes refused that dependence; later, King Ahaz of Judah in the S did the same.

8:7 waters of the Euphrates. In place of the waters of Shiloah, the waters of the River Euphrates were to overflow its banks and flood all the way to and including Judah. In other words, the King of Assyria was to sweep through the Land with his devastating destruction. Though outwardly Ahaz’s submission to the Assyrians brought peace to Judah (2Ki 16:7–18), Isaiah saw the reality that David’s throne was merely a hollow sham.

8:8 O Immanuel. Because of the Assyrian onslaught, the land of Immanuel (7:14) was to be stripped of all its earthly glory. What a pity that He who owns and will someday possess the land must see it in such a devastated condition!

8:9 Be broken. Lest Assyria and other foreign powers think they conquered in their own strength, the prophet reminded them that they were only instruments for the Lord’s use and would eventually come to nothing.

8:10 God is with us. The Heb. is *Immanuel.* The name of the virgin’s child (7:14) guaranteed the eventual triumph of the faithful remnant of Israel.

8:11 with mighty power. God inspired Isaiah with compelling power to speak a message that by its nature distanced him from the people he ministered to.

8:12 conspiracy. Many in Israel considered Isaiah, Jeremiah, and other prophets to be servants of the enemy when they advocated a policy of nonreliance on foreign powers and complete dependence on the Lord alone (see Jer 37:13–15).

8:14 sanctuary … rock to stumble over. Isaiah found encouragement in the Lord as his holy place of protection from his accusers. The NT applies this verse to corporate Israel in her ongoing rejection of Jesus as Messiah (Lk 2:34; Ro 9:32, 33; 1Pe 2:8). **both the houses of Israel.** They will be collapsed until the return of the Messiah to the earth restores them.

8:15 Many will stumble. Another prediction anticipated the stumbling of Israel, which included her rejection of her Messiah at His first advent (Lk 20:18; Ro 9:32; cf. 28:16).

8:16 my disciples. These were God’s faithful remnant, and hence disciples of Isaiah in a secondary sense. They had the responsibility of maintaining written records of his prophecies so that they could become public after the prophesied Assyrian invasion (see 8:2).

8:17 I will wait … look eagerly. The speaker is Isaiah, whose disposition was to await the Lord’s deliverance, the national salvation promised to the faithful remnant (40:31; 49:23). *See note on Heb 2:13.*

8:18 I and the children. In their historical setting, the words refer to Isaiah and his two sons, whose names had prophetic significance (i.e., as “signs and wonders”). *See note on Heb 2:13.*

8:19 *consult* the dead. People of Isaiah’s day were using spiritualists to communicate with the dead as King Saul did through the medium at En-dor (1Sa 28:8–19). The law strictly forbade such consultations (Lv 19:26; Dt 18:10, 11).

8:20 law … testimony. See 8:16. Light came through the prophecies of God’s spokesman, Isaiah.

8:21, 22 This is a dismal picture of those who were frustrated, desperate, and angry

they will [A]look to the earth, and behold, distress and darkness, the gloom of anguish; and *they will be* [B]driven away into darkness.

BIRTH AND REIGN OF THE PRINCE OF PEACE

9 [a]But there will be no *more* [A]gloom for her who was in anguish; in earlier times He [B]treated the [C]land of Zebulun and the land of Naphtali with contempt, but later on He shall make *it* glorious, by the way of the sea, on the other side of Jordan, Galilee of the [b]Gentiles.

2 [a,A]The people who walk in darkness
Will see a great light;
Those who live in a dark land,
The light will shine on them.
3 [A]You shall multiply the nation,
You [B]shall [a]increase [b]their gladness;
They will be glad in Your presence
As with the gladness [c]of harvest,
As [d,C]men rejoice when they divide the spoil.
4 For [A]You shall break the yoke of their
burden and the staff on their shoulders,
The rod of their [B]oppressor, as
[a]at the battle of [C]Midian.
5 For every boot of the booted
warrior in the *battle* tumult,
And cloak rolled in blood, will be
for burning, fuel for the fire.
6 For a [A]child will be born to us, a
[B]son will be given to us;
And the [C]government will [a]rest
[D]on His shoulders;
And His name will be called [E]Wonderful
Counselor, [F]Mighty God,
Eternal [G]Father, Prince of [H]Peace.
7 There will be [A]no end to the increase
of *His* government or of peace,
On the [B]throne of David and
over his kingdom,
To establish it and to uphold it with
[C]justice and righteousness
From then on and forevermore.
[D]The zeal of the LORD of hosts
will accomplish this.

GOD'S ANGER WITH ISRAEL'S ARROGANCE

8 The Lord sends a [a]message against Jacob,
And it falls on Israel.
9 And all the people know *it,*
That is, [A]Ephraim and the
inhabitants of Samaria,
Asserting in pride and in
[B]arrogance of heart:
10 "The bricks have fallen down,
But we will [A]rebuild with smooth stones;
The sycamores have been cut down,
But we will replace *them* with cedars."
11 Therefore the LORD raises against
them adversaries from [A]Rezin
And spurs their enemies on,
12 The Arameans on the east and
the [A]Philistines on the west;
And they [B]devour Israel
with [a]gaping jaws.
[C]In *spite of* all this, His anger
does not turn away
And His hand is still stretched out.

13 Yet the people [A]do not turn back
to Him who struck them,
Nor do they [B]seek the LORD of hosts.

8:22 [A]Is 5:30; 59:9; Jer 13:16; Amos 5:18, 20; Zeph 1:14, 15 [B]Is 8:20 9:1 [a]Ch 8:23 in Heb [b]Or *nations* [A]Is 8:22 [B]2 Kin 15:29; 2 Chr 16:4 [C]Matt 4:15, 16 9:2 [a]Ch 9:1 in Heb [A]Matt 4:16; Luke 1:79; Eph 5:8 9:3 [a]Another reading is *not increase* [b]Lit *the* [c]Lit *in* [d]Lit *they* [A]Is 26:15 [B]Is 35:10; 65:14, 18, 19; 66:10 [C]1 Sam 30:16 9:4 [a]Lit *in the day of Midian* [A]Is 10:27; 14:25 [B]Is 14:4; 49:26; 51:13; 54:14 [C]Judg 7:25; Is 10:26 9:6 [a]Lit *be* [A]Is 7:14; 11:1, 2; 53:2; Luke 2:11 [B]John 3:16 [C]Matt 28:18; 1 Cor 15:25 [D]Is 22:22 [E]Is 28:29 [F]Deut 10:17; Neh 9:32; Is 10:21 [G]Is 63:16; 64:8 [H]Is 26:3, 12; 54:10; 66:12 9:7 [A]Dan 2:44; Luke 1:32, 33 [B]Is 16:5 [C]Is 11:4, 5; 32:1; 42:3, 4; 63:1 [D]Is 37:32; 59:17 9:8 [a]Lit *word* 9:9 [A]Is 7:8, 9; 28:1, 3 [B]Is 46:12 9:10 [A]Mal 1:4 9:11 [A]Is 7:1, 8 9:12 [a]Lit *the whole mouth* [A]2 Chr 28:18 [B]Ps 79:7; Jer 10:25 [C]Is 5:25 9:13 [A]Jer 5:3; Hos 7:10 [B]Is 31:1; Hos 3:5

even to the point of cursing God, all because they refused to accept the truthfulness of what Isaiah had predicted regarding the nation's future hardships.

9:1 Zebulun ... Naphtali ... Galilee. Zebulun and Naphtali on the northern border in NE Galilee W of the Jordan River were the first to suffer from the invasion by the Assyrian king (2Ki 15:29), marking the beginning of dark days for Israel. **shall make *it* glorious.** "In earlier times" the days were to be full of gloom, but "later on" God would transform that gloom into honor. The NT applies this prophecy of Galilee's honor to the time of Jesus Christ's first advent (Mt 4:12–16). Matthew 4:15, 16 quotes Is 9:1, 2 directly. Ultimately, its fulfillment will come at His second advent when the area is freed from the yoke of foreign invaders.

9:2 a great light ... light. The coming of the Messiah is synonymous with the coming of light to remove the darkness of captivity (42:16; 49:6; 58:8; 60:1, 19, 20).

9:3 multiply the nation. Once again the Lord confirmed His covenant with Abraham to multiply his physical descendants as the sands of the seashore (Ge 22:17).

9:4 break the yoke. Eventually the Lord will free national Israel from bondage to Assyria, Babylon, and every other foreign power that has oppressed her.

9:5 burning, fuel for the fire. The world will no longer need the accessories of warfare because a time of universal peace will follow the return of Christ.

9:6 child ... son. These terms elaborate further on Immanuel, the child to be born to the virgin (7:14). The virgin's child will also be the royal Son of David, with rights to the Davidic throne (9:7; cf. Mt 1:21; Lk 1:31–33; 2:7, 11). **government.** In fulfillment of this verse and Ps 2:9, the Son will rule the nations of the world (Rev 2:27; 19:15). **Wonderful Counselor.** In contrast to Ahaz, this King will implement supernatural wisdom in discharging His office (cf. 2Sa 16:23; 1Ki 3:28). **Mighty God.** As a powerful warrior, the Messiah will accomplish the military exploits mentioned in 9:3–5 (cf. 10:21; Dt 10:17; Ne 9:32). **Eternal Father.** The Messiah will be a Father to His people eternally. As Davidic King, He will compassionately care for and discipline them (40:11; 63:16; 64:8; Pss 68:5, 6; 103:13; Pr 3:12). **Prince of Peace.** The government of Immanuel will procure and perpetuate peace among the nations of the world (2:4; 11:6–9; Mic 4:3).

9:7 throne of David. The virgin's Son will be the rightful heir to David's throne and will inherit the promises of the Davidic Covenant (2Sa 7:12–16; cf. Ps 89:1–37; Mt 1:1).

9:8–10:4 This poem tells of great warning calamities sent by the Lord that have gone unheeded by Israel. The same refrain recurs 4 times (9:12, 17, 21; 10:4), dividing it into 4 strophes.

9:9 pride and in arrogance. Israel's downfall was her feeling of self-sufficiency whereby she thought she could handle any eventuality (v. 10).

9:11 adversaries from Rezin. The Aramean, or Syrian, king's enemies were the Assyrians.

9:12 His hand is still stretched out. The outstretched hand will punish (cf. 5:25) beyond what the people had already experienced.

14 So the LORD cuts off [A]head
and tail from Israel,
Both palm branch and bulrush
[B]in a single day.
15 The head is [A]the elder and
honorable man,
And the prophet who teaches
[B]falsehood is the tail.
16 [A]For those who guide this people
are leading *them* astray;
And those who are guided by them
are [a]brought to confusion.
17 Therefore the Lord does [A]not take
pleasure in their young men,
[B]Nor does He have pity on their
[a]orphans or their widows;
For every one of them is [C]godless
and an [D]evildoer,
And every [E]mouth is speaking foolishness.
[F]In *spite of* all this, His anger
does not turn away
And His hand is still stretched out.

18 [A]For wickedness burns like a fire;
It consumes briars and thorns;
It even sets the thickets of
the forest aflame
And they roll upward in a
column of smoke.
19 By the [A]fury of the LORD of hosts
the [B]land is burned up,
And the [C]people are like fuel for the fire;
No [D]man spares his brother.
20 [a]They slice off *what is* on the right
hand but *still* are [A]hungry,
And [b]they eat *what is* on the left
hand but they are not satisfied;
Each of them eats the [B]flesh
of his own arm.
21 Manasseh *devours* Ephraim,
and Ephraim Manasseh,
[A]*And* together they are against Judah.
[B]In *spite of* all this, His anger
does not turn away
And His hand is still stretched out.

ASSYRIA IS GOD'S INSTRUMENT

10 Woe to those who [A]enact evil statutes
And to those who constantly
record [a]unjust decisions,
2 So as [A]to [a]deprive the needy of justice
And rob the poor of My
people of *their* rights,
So [B]that widows may be their spoil
And that they may plunder
the [b]orphans.
3 Now [A]what will you do in the
[B]day of punishment,
And in the devastation which
will come [C]from afar?
[D]To whom will you flee for help?
And where will you leave your [a]wealth?
4 Nothing *remains* but to crouch
[a]among the [A]captives
Or fall [a]among the [B]slain.
[C]In *spite of* all this, His anger
does not turn away
And His hand is still stretched out.

5 Woe to [A]Assyria, the [B]rod of My anger
And the staff in whose hands
is [C]My indignation,
6 I send it against a [A]godless nation
And commission it against
the [B]people of My fury
To capture booty and [C]to seize plunder,
And to [a]trample them down
like [D]mud in the streets.
7 Yet it [A]does not so intend,
Nor does [a]it plan so in its heart,
But rather it is [b]its purpose to destroy
And to cut off [c]many nations.
8 For it says, "Are not my
princes [a]all kings?
9 "Is not [A]Calno like [B]Carchemish,
Or [C]Hamath like Arpad,
Or [D]Samaria like [E]Damascus?
10 "As my hand has reached to the
[A]kingdoms of the idols,
Whose graven images *were* greater than
those of Jerusalem and Samaria,

9:14 [A]Is 19:15 [B]Rev 18:8 9:15 [A]Is 3:2, 3 [B]Is 28:15; 59:3, 4; Jer 23:14, 32; Matt 24:24 9:16 [a]Or *swallowed up* [A]Is 3:12; Matt 15:14; 23:16, 24 9:17 [a]Or *fatherless* [A]Jer 18:21; Amos 4:10; 8:13 [B]Is 27:11 [C]Is 10:6; 32:6 [D]Is 1:4; 14:20; 31:2 [E]Matt 12:34 [F]Is 5:25 9:18 [A]Ps 83:14; Is 1:7; Nah 1:10; Mal 4:1 9:19 [A]Is 10:6; 13:9, 13; 42:25 [B]Joel 2:3 [C]Is 1:31; 24:6 [D]Mic 7:2, 6 9:20 [a]Lit *he slices* [b]Lit *he eats* [A]Is 8:21, 22 [B]Is 49:26 9:21 [A]2 Chr 28:6, 8; Is 11:13 [B]Is 5:25 10:1 [a]Lit *mischief* or *misfortune* [A]Ps 94:20; Is 29:21; 59:4, 13 10:2 [a]Lit *turn aside from* [b]Or *fatherless* [A]Is 5:23 [B]Is 1:23; 3:14, 15 10:3 [a]Lit *glory* [A]Job 31:14 [B]Is 13:6; 26:14, 21; 29:6; Jer 9:9; Hos 9:7; Luke 19:44 [C]Is 5:26 [D]Is 20:6; 30:5, 7; 31:3 10:4 [a]Lit *under* [A]Is 24:22 [B]Is 22:2; 34:3; 66:16 [C]Is 5:25 10:5 [A]Is 7:17; 8:7; 14:24-27; Zeph 2:13-15 [B]Jer 51:20 [C]Is 13:5; 30:30; 34:2; 66:14 10:6 [a]Lit *make them a trampled place* [A]Is 9:17 [B]Is 9:19 [C]Is 5:29 [D]Is 5:25 10:7 [a]Lit *its heart so plan* [b]Lit *in its heart* [c]Lit *not a few* [A]Gen 50:20; Mic 4:11, 12; Acts 2:23, 24 10:8 [a]Lit *altogether* 10:9 [A]Gen 10:10; Amos 6:2 [B]2 Chr 35:20 [C]Num 34:8 [D]2 Kin 17:6 [E]2 Kin 16:9 10:10 [A]2 Kin 19:17, 18

9:16 those who guide . . . those who are guided. The aggravated wickedness of Israel extended to all classes, even the fatherless and widows (v. 17) who often were the objects of special mercy (1:17).

9:19 No man spares his brother. God's wrath allowed wickedness to cause the society to self-destruct. A senseless mutual exploitation resulted in anarchy and confusion (v. 20).

9:21 Manasseh . . . Ephraim . . . Judah. Descendants of Joseph's two sons (Manasseh and Ephraim) had engaged in civil war with each other before (see Jdg 12:4) and unite only in their opposition to Judah.

10:1, 2 evil statutes . . . deprive the needy. The prophet returned to assign reasons for God's wrath again: 1) inequities in administering the laws, and 2) harsh treatment of those in need.

10:2 widows . . . orphans. See 1:17.

10:3 day of punishment. The Assyrians were the first to invade, then Babylon and other foreign powers followed.

10:5 rod of My anger. God used Assyria as His instrument of judgment against Israel and Judah. He did the same with Babylon against Judah later on (Hab 1:6).

10:6 a godless nation. "My people" (v. 2), the people of Israel and Judah.

10:7 it does not so intend. Assyria did not realize that she was the Lord's instrument, but thought her conquests were the result of her own power.

10:9 Calno . . . Damascus. These cities and territories all capitulated to the Assyrian invaders.

10:10, 11 Shall I not do to Jerusalem. Proud Assyria warned Jerusalem that she would overcome that city just as she had been the instrument used by God against other nations.

11 Shall I not [a]do to Jerusalem
and her images
Just as I have done to Samaria
and [A]her idols?"

12 So it will be that when the Lord has completed
all His [A]work on Mount Zion and on Jerusalem, *He
will say,* "I will [a]punish the fruit of the arrogant
heart of the king of Assyria and [B]the pomp of [b]his
haughtiness." 13 For [A]he has said,

"By the power of my hand and
by my wisdom I did *this,*
For I have understanding;
And I [B]removed the boundaries
of the peoples
And plundered their treasures,
And like a mighty man I brought
down [a]*their* inhabitants,
14 And my hand reached to the riches
of the peoples like a [A]nest,
And as one gathers abandoned
eggs, I gathered all the earth;
And there was not one that
flapped its wing or opened
its beak or chirped."

15 Is the [A]axe to [B]boast itself over
the one who chops with it?
Is the saw to exalt itself over
the one who wields it?
That would be like [C]a [a]club
wielding those who lift it,
Or like [C]a rod lifting *him*
who is not wood.
16 Therefore the Lord, the [a]GOD of
hosts, will send a [A]wasting disease
among his [B]stout warriors;
And under his [C]glory a fire will be
kindled like a burning flame.
17 And the [A]light of Israel will become
a fire and his [B]Holy One a flame,
And it will [C]burn and
devour his thorns and his
briars in a single day.
18 And He will [A]destroy the glory
of his forest and of his fruitful
garden, both soul and body,
And it will be as when a sick
man wastes away.
19 And the [A]rest of the trees of his forest
will be so small in number
That a child could write them down.

A REMNANT WILL RETURN

20 Now in that day the [A]remnant of Israel, and
those of the house of Jacob [B]who have escaped, will
never again rely on the one who struck them, but
will truly [C]rely on the LORD, the Holy One of Israel.

21 A [A]remnant will return, the remnant
of Jacob, to the [B]mighty God.

10:11 [a]Lit *do thus* [A]Is 2:8 10:12 [a]Lit *visit* [b]Lit *haughtiness of his eyes* [A]2 Kin 19:31; Is 28:21, 22; 29:14; 65:7 [B]Is 37:23 10:13 [a]Or *those who sit* on thrones [A]2 Kin 19:22-24; Is 37:24-27; Ezek 28:4; Dan 4:30 [B]Hab 2:6-11 10:14 [A]Jer 49:16; Obad 4 10:15 [a]Lit *staff* [A]Jer 51:20 [B]Is 29:16; 45:9; Rom 9:20, 21 [C]Is 10:5 10:16 [a]Heb *YHWH*, usually rendered *LORD* [A]Ps 106:15 [B]Is 17:4 [C]Is 8:7; 10:18 10:17 [A]Is 30:33; 31:9 [B]Is 37:23 [C]Num 11:1-3; Is 27:4; 33:12; Jer 4:4; 7:20 10:18 [A]Is 10:33, 34 10:19 [A]Is 21:17 10:20 [A]Is 1:9; 11:11, 16; 46:3 [B]Is 4:2; 37:31, 32 [C]2 Chr 14:11; Is 17:7, 8; 50:10 10:21 [A]Is 7:3 [B]Is 9:6

10:12 punish … the king of Assyria. The Lord expressed His intention of punishing proud Assyria after He had finished using that nation to punish Jerusalem.

10:13, 14 The prophet proved the Assyrian king's pride by reiterating his boast (cf. vv. 8–11).

10:15 axe … saw … club … rod. Nothing more than an instrument of the Lord (vv. 5, 24), Assyria had no power or wisdom of her own.

10:16–19 burning … fire … flame … burn … devour. When He had finished using Assyria as His instrument, the Lord terminated the kingdom's existence (see v. 12).

10:20 the remnant of Israel. Cf. 1:9. A small nucleus of God's people, preserved by His sovereign grace, form this righteous remnant in the midst of national apostasy. There were always the obedient few who preserved, obeyed, and passed on God's law. There will always be a remnant because God will never forsake the Abrahamic Covenant (cf. Mic 2:12, 13; Ro 9:27; 11:5).

GOD'S JUDGMENT ON THE NATIONS

	Obadiah	Amos	Isaiah	Jeremiah	Habakkuk	Ezekiel
Ammon		*1:13–15* Judgment		*49:1–6* Judgment; Restoration		*25:1–7* Judgment
Babylon			*13:1–14:23* Judgment	*50, 51* Judgment	*2:6–17* Judgment	
Damascus		*1:3–5* Judgment	*17:1–3* Judgment; Remnant	*49:23–27* Judgment		
Edom	Judgment	*1:11, 12* Judgment	*21:11, 12* Judgment	*49:7–22* Judgment		*25:12–14* Judgment
Egypt			*19* Judgment; Restoration	*46:1–26* Judgment		*29–32* Judgment
Moab		*2:1–3* Judgment	*15, 16* Judgment; Remnant	*48* Judgment; Restoration		*25:8–11* Judgment
Philistia		*1:6–8* Judgment	*14:29–32* Judgment	*47* Judgment; Remnant		*25:15–17* Judgment
Tyre		*1:9, 10* Judgment	*23* Judgment; Restoration			*26–28* Judgment

22 For [A]though your people, O Israel,
may be like the sand of the sea,
Only a remnant within them will return;
A [B]destruction is determined,
overflowing with righteousness.

23 For a complete destruction, one that is decreed,
[A]the Lord [a]GOD of hosts will execute in the midst
of the whole land.
24 Therefore thus says the Lord [a]GOD of hosts,
"O My people who dwell in [A]Zion, [B]do not fear the
Assyrian [b]who [C]strikes you with the rod and lifts
up his staff against you, the way Egypt *did.* 25 For
in a very [A]little while [B]My indignation *against you*
will be spent and My anger *will be directed* to their
destruction." 26 The LORD of hosts will [A]arouse a
scourge against him like the slaughter of [B]Midian
at the rock of Oreb; and His [C]staff will be over the
sea and He will lift it up [D]the way *He did* in Egypt.
27 So it will be in that day, that [a]his [A]burden will be
removed from your shoulders and his yoke from
your neck, and the yoke will be broken because
[B]of fatness.

28 He has come against Aiath,
He has passed through [A]Migron;
At [B]Michmash he deposited his [C]baggage.
29 They have gone through
[A]the pass, *saying,*
"[B]Geba will be our lodging place."
[C]Ramah is terrified, and [D]Gibeah
of Saul has fled away.
30 Cry aloud with your voice,
O daughter of [A]Gallim!
Pay attention, Laishah *and*
[a]wretched [B]Anathoth!
31 Madmenah has fled.
The inhabitants of Gebim
have sought refuge.
32 Yet today he will halt at [A]Nob;
He [B]shakes his fist at the mountain
of the [a,C]daughter of Zion,
the hill of Jerusalem.

33 Behold, the Lord, the [a]GOD of hosts, will
lop off the boughs with a terrible crash;
Those also who are [A]tall in
stature will be cut down
And those who are lofty will be abased.
34 He will cut down the thickets of
the forest with an iron *axe,*
And [A]Lebanon will fall [a]by
the Mighty One.

RIGHTEOUS REIGN OF THE BRANCH

11 Then a [A]shoot will spring from
the [B]stem of Jesse,
And a [C]branch from [D]his
roots will bear fruit.
2 The [A]Spirit of the LORD will rest on Him,
The spirit of [B]wisdom and understanding,
The spirit of counsel and [C]strength,
The spirit of knowledge and
the fear of the LORD.
3 And He will delight in the
fear of the LORD,
And He will not judge by
what His eyes [A]see,
Nor make a decision by
what His ears hear;
4 But with [A]righteousness He
will judge the [B]poor,
And decide with fairness for the
[C]afflicted of the earth;
And He will strike the earth with
the [D]rod of His mouth,
And with the [E]breath of His lips
He will slay the wicked.

10:22 [A]Rom 9:27, 28 [B]Is 28:22; Dan 9:27; Rom 9:28 10:23 [a]Heb *YHWH*, usually rendered *LORD* [A]Is 28:22; Dan 9:27; Rom 9:28 10:24 [a]Heb *YHWH*, usually rendered *LORD* [b]Lit *he* [A]Ps 87:5, 6 [B]Is 7:4; 12:2; 37:6 [C]Ex 5:14-16 10:25 [A]Is 17:14; Hag 2:6 [B]Is 10:5; 26:20; Dan 11:36 10:26 [A]Is 37:36-38 [B]Judg 7:25; Is 9:4 [C]Ex 14:16 [D]Ex 14:27 10:27 [a]I.e. the Assyrian [A]Is 9:4; 14:25 [B]Is 30:23; 55:2 10:28 [A]1 Sam 14:2 [B]1 Sam 13:2, 5 [C]Judg 18:21; 1 Sam 17:22 10:29 [A]1 Sam 13:23 [B]Josh 21:17; 1 Sam 13:16 [C]Josh 18:25; 1 Sam 7:17 [D]1 Sam 10:26 10:30 [a]An ancient version reads *Answer her, O Anathoth* [A]1 Sam 25:44 [B]Josh 21:18; Jer 1:1 10:32 [a]Another reading is *house of* [A]1 Sam 21:1; 22:9 [B]Is 19:16; Zech 2:9 [C]Is 1:8; Jer 6:23 10:33 [a]Heb *YHWH*, usually rendered *LORD* [A]Is 37:24, 36-38; Ezek 31:3; Amos 2:9 10:34 [a]Or *as a mighty one* [A]Is 2:13; 33:9; 37:24 11:1 [A]Is 4:2; 53:2 [B]Is 9:7; 11:10; Acts 13:23 [C]Is 6:13; Jer 23:5; Zech 3:8 [D]Rev 5:5; 22:16 11:2 [A]Is 42:1; 48:16; 61:1; Matt 3:16; John 1:32 [B]John 16:13; 1 Cor 1:30; Eph 1:17, 18 [C]2 Tim 1:7 11:3 [A]John 2:25; 7:24 11:4 [A]Is 9:7; 16:5; 32:1 [B]Ps 72:2, 13, 14; Is 3:14 [C]Is 29:19; 32:7; 61:1 [D]Ps 2:9; Is 49:2; Mal 4:6 [E]Job 4:9; Is 30:28, 33; 2 Thess 2:8

10:22 sand of the sea. Cf. Ge 22:17.

10:23 will execute. They must face the wrath of God. See Paul's use of this verse in Ro 9:28.

10:25 My indignation. The indignation covers the entire period of Israel's exile (26:20; Da 11:36). Here is the promise that it will end with the return of the Messiah (11:1–16).

10:26 Midian … Egypt. Isaiah selected two examples from the past to illustrate the Lord's future deliverance of Israel: Gideon's victory over the Midianites (Jdg 7:25) and the slaughter of the Egyptians who pursued the Israelites through the Red Sea (Ex 14:16, 26, 27).

10:27 burden … yoke. The removal of this yoke speaks of the future freeing of Israel from compulsion to render service to foreign oppressors.

10:28–32 Isaiah visualized the Assyrian army approaching Jerusalem from the N. The place names grew closer to Jerusalem as his vision progressed.

10:33 lop off … cut down … abased. Though the Assyrian army reached the walls of Jerusalem, the sovereign Lord, the Lord of hosts, intervened and sent them away in defeat. Later Isaiah recorded the literal fulfillment of this prophecy (37:24, 36–38; cf. 2Ki 19:35–37; 2Ch 32:21).

10:34 Lebanon. The OT equates Assyria to Lebanon (Eze 31:3; cf. 2:13; 37:24).

11:1 stem … roots. With the Babylonian captivity of 586 B.C., the Davidic dynasty appeared as decimated as the Assyrian army. A major difference between the two was the life remaining in the stump and roots of the Davidic line. That life was to manifest itself in new growth in the form of the Rod and Branch. **Jesse.** Jesse was David's father through whose line the messianic king was to come (Ru 4:22; 1Sa 16:1, 12, 13). **branch.** This is a title for the Messiah (see 4:2).

11:2 The Spirit of the LORD. As the Spirit of the Lord came upon David when he was anointed king (1Sa 16:13; Ps 51:11), so He will rest upon David's descendant, Christ, who will rule the world. **Spirit … the LORD … Him.** This verse refers to the 3 persons of the Holy Trinity (see 6:3). **wisdom and understanding … counsel and strength … knowledge … fear of the LORD.** These are Spirit-imparted qualifications that will enable the Messiah to rule justly and effectively. Compare the 7-fold Spirit in Rev 1:4.

11:3 what His eyes see … what His ears hear. These are ordinary avenues for a king to obtain information needed to govern, but the future King will have supernatural perception beyond these usual sources.

11:4 poor … afflicted. The Messiah will reverse Israel's earlier dealings with the underprivileged (3:14, 15; 10:2). **rod of His mouth.** The Branch's rule over the nations will be forceful. The NT uses equivalent terminology

5 Also [A]righteousness will be the
belt about His loins,
And [B]faithfulness the belt about His waist.

6 And the [A]wolf will dwell with the lamb,
And the leopard will lie down
with the young goat,
And the calf and the young lion
[a]and the fatling together;
And a little boy will lead them.
7 Also the cow and the bear will graze,
Their young will lie down together,
And the [A]lion will eat straw like the ox.
8 The nursing child will play by
the hole of the cobra,
And the weaned child will put his
hand on the viper's den.
9 They will [A]not hurt or destroy
in all My holy mountain,
For the [B]earth will be full of the
knowledge of the LORD
As the waters cover the sea.

10 Then in that day
The [A]nations will resort to
the [B]root of Jesse,
Who will stand as a [a,C]signal for the peoples;
And His [D]resting place will be [b]glorious.

THE RESTORED REMNANT

11 Then it will happen on that
day that the Lord
Will again recover the second
time with His hand
The [A]remnant of His people,
who will remain,
From [B]Assyria, [C]Egypt, Pathros,
Cush, [D]Elam, Shinar, Hamath,
And from the [a,E]islands of the sea.

12 And He will lift up a [A]standard
for the nations
And [B]assemble the banished
ones of Israel,
And will gather the dispersed of Judah
From the four corners of the earth.
13 Then the [A]jealousy of Ephraim will depart,
And those who harass Judah
will be cut off;
Ephraim will not be jealous of Judah,
And Judah will not harass Ephraim.
14 They will [A]swoop down on the slopes
of the Philistines on the [B]west;
Together they will [C]plunder
the sons of the east;
[a]They will possess [D]Edom and [E]Moab,
And the sons of Ammon will
be [b]subject to them.
15 And the LORD will [a,A]utterly destroy
The tongue of the [b]Sea of Egypt;
And He will [B]wave His hand
over the [c,C]River
With His scorching wind;
And He will strike it into seven streams
And make *men* walk over [d]dry-shod.
16 And there will be a [A]highway
from Assyria
For the [B]remnant of His people
who will be left,
Just as there was for Israel
In [C]the day that they came up
out of the land of Egypt.

THANKSGIVING EXPRESSED

12 Then you will say on that day,
"[A]I will give thanks to You, O LORD;
For [B]although You were angry with me,
Your anger is turned away,
And You comfort me.

11:5 [A]Eph 6:14 [B]Is 25:1 11:6 [a]Some versions read *will feed together* [A]Is 65:25 11:7 [A]Is 65:25 11:9 [A]Job 5:23; Is 65:25; Ezek 34:25; Hos 2:18 [B]Ps 98:2, 3; Is 45:6; 52:10; 66:18-23; Hab 2:14 11:10 [a]Or *standard* [b]Lit *glory* [A]Luke 2:32; Acts 11:18 [B]Is 11:1; Rom 15:12 [C]Is 11:12; 49:22; 62:10; John 3:14, 15; 12:32 [D]Is 14:3; 28:12; 32:17, 18 11:11 [a]Or *coastlands* [A]Is 10:20-22; 37:4, 31, 32; 46:3 [B]Is 19:23-25; Hos 11:11; Zech 10:10 [C]Is 19:21, 22; Mic 7:12 [D]Gen 10:22; 14:1 [E]Is 24:15; 42:4, 10, 12; 49:1; 51:5; 60:9; 66:19 11:12 [A]Is 11:10 [B]Is 56:8; Zeph 3:10; Zech 10:6 11:13 [A]Is 9:21; Jer 3:18; Ezek 37:16, 17, 22; Hos 1:11 11:14 [a]Lit *Edom and Moab will be the outstretching of their hand* [b]Lit *their obedience* [A]Jer 48:40; 49:22; Hab 1:8 [B]Is 9:12 [C]Jer 49:28 [D]Is 63:1; Dan 11:41; Joel 3:19; Amos 9:12 [E]Is 16:14; 25:10 11:15 [a]Another reading is *dry up the tongue* [b]Perhaps the Red Sea [c]I.e. Euphrates [d]Lit *in sandals* [A]Is 43:16; 44:27; 50:2; 51:10, 11 [B]Is 19:16 [C]Is 7:20; 8:7; Rev 16:12 11:16 [A]Is 19:23; 35:8; 40:3; 62:10 [B]Is 11:11 [C]Ex 14:26-29 12:1 [A]Ps 9:1; Is 25:1 [B]Ps 30:5; Is 40:1, 2; 54:7-10

to describe the Warrior-King at His triumphant return to earth (Rev 19:15; cf. 49:2; Ps 2:9). **breath of His lips.** This is another figure for the Messiah's means of inflicting physical harm. Paul draws upon this to tell of the destruction of the man of lawlessness at Christ's second advent (2Th 2:8).

11:5 belt … belt. The belt, which gathered the loose garments together, is figurative for the Messiah's readiness for conflict. Righteousness and faithfulness are His preparation. Cf. Eph 6:14.

11:6–9 Conditions of peace will prevail to the extent that all enmity among men, among animals—rapacious or otherwise—and between men and animals will disappear. Such will characterize the future millennial kingdom in which the Prince of Peace (9:6) will reign.

11:9 full of the knowledge of the LORD. Everyone will know the Lord when He returns to fulfill His New Covenant with Israel (Jer 31:34).

11:10 in that day. The time of universal peace will come in the future reign of the Lord. **a signal for the peoples.** The Root of Jesse will also attract non-Jews who inhabit the future kingdom (49:6; 52:10; 60:3; 66:18). Paul saw God's ministry to Gentiles during the church age as an additional implication of this verse (Ro 15:12).

11:11 second time. The first return of Israel to her land was from Egyptian captivity (Ex 14:26–29). The second will be from her worldwide dispersion (51:9–11; *see note on 10:20*).

11:12 four corners of the earth. This figurative expression depicts the whole world (Rev 20:8). The faithful remnant of Israel will return from a worldwide dispersion to their land.

11:13 Ephraim … Judah. These were the two major divisions of Israel after the schism under Jeroboam (1Ki 12:16–20). Ephraim was the name representing the northern 10 tribes, and Judah the southern two. When the Messiah returns, they will reunite in a lasting peace.

11:14 west … east. In that day Israel will be free from all foreign oppression and will be the dominant political force.

11:15 the River. Just as He dried up the Red Sea in the deliverance from Egypt, the Lord will in the future dry up the Euphrates in connection with the final deliverance of His people. *See note on Rev 16:12.*

11:16 highway. Isaiah has much to say about a way for the remnant returning to Jerusalem (35:8, 9; 42:16; 43:19; 48:21; 49:11; 57:14; 62:10).

12:1–6 Two brief songs of praise (vv. 1–3, 4–6) which redeemed Israel will sing at the outset of the millennial kingdom. They are the earthly counterpart to the heavenly doxology in Rev 19:6, 7.

12:1 Your anger is turned away. For the future remnant who will recognize the substitutionary death of Christ for their sins, Christ

2 “Behold, [A]God is my salvation,
I will [B]trust and not be afraid;
For [C]the LORD GOD is my strength and song,
And He has become my salvation.”
3 Therefore you will joyously [A]draw water
From the [B]springs of salvation.
4 And in that day you will [A]say,
“[B]Give thanks to the LORD, call on His name.
[C]Make known His deeds among the peoples;
[a]Make *them* remember that
His name is exalted.”
5 [A]Praise the LORD in song, for He
has done [a]excellent things;
Let this be known throughout the earth.
6 [A]Cry aloud and shout for joy,
O inhabitant of Zion,
For [B]great in your midst is the
Holy One of Israel.

PROPHECIES ABOUT BABYLON

13 The [a,A]oracle concerning [B]Babylon which [C]Isa-
iah the son of Amoz saw.

2 [A]Lift up a standard on the [a,B]bare hill,
Raise your voice to them,
[C]Wave the hand that they may [D]enter
the doors of the nobles.
3 I have commanded My consecrated ones,
I have even called My [A]mighty warriors,
My proudly exulting ones,
To *execute* My anger.
4 A [A]sound of tumult on the mountains,
Like that of many people!
A sound of the uproar of kingdoms,
Of nations gathered together!
The LORD of hosts is mustering
the army for battle.
5 They are coming from a far country,
From the [a,A]farthest horizons,
The LORD and His instruments
of [B]indignation,
To [C]destroy the whole land.

JUDGMENT ON THE DAY OF THE LORD

6 Wail, for the [A]day of the LORD is near!
It will come as [B]destruction
from [a]the Almighty.
7 Therefore [A]all hands will fall limp,
And every man’s [B]heart will melt.
8 They will be [A]terrified,
Pains and anguish will take hold of *them;*
They will [B]writhe like a woman in labor,
They will look at one another
in astonishment,
Their faces aflame.
9 Behold, [A]the day of the LORD is coming,
Cruel, with fury and burning anger,
To make the land a desolation;
And He will exterminate its sinners from it.
10 For the [A]stars of heaven and
their constellations
Will not flash forth their light;
The [B]sun will be dark when it rises
And the moon will not shed its light.

12:2 [A]Is 32:2; 45:17; 62:11 [B]Is 26:3 [C]Ex 15:2; Ps 118:14 12:3 [A]John 4:10; 7:37, 38 [B]Is 41:18; Jer 2:13 12:4 [a]Or *Proclaim* to them *that* [A]Is 24:15; 42:12; 48:20 [B]Ps 105:1 [C]Ps 145:4 12:5 [a]Or *gloriously* [A]Ex 15:1; Ps 98:1; Is 24:14; 42:10, 11; 44:23 12:6 [A]Is 52:9; 54:1; Zeph 3:14 [B]Is 1:24; 49:26; 60:16; Zeph 3:15-17; Zech 2:5, 10, 11 13:1 [a]Or *burden of* [A]Is 14:28; 15:1 [B]Is 13:19; 14:4; 47:1-15; Jer 24:1; 50:1-51:64; Matt 1:11; Rev 14:8 [C]Is 1:1 13:2 [a]Or *wind-swept mountain* [A]Is 5:26; Jer 50:2 [B]Jer 51:25 [C]Is 10:32; 19:16 [D]Is 45:1-3; Jer 51:58 13:3 [A]Joel 3:11 13:4 [A]Is 5:30; 17:12; Joel 3:14 13:5 [a]Lit *end of heaven* [A]Is 5:26; 7:18 [B]Is 10:5 [C]Is 24:1 13:6 [a]Heb *Shaddai* [A]Is 2:12; 10:3; 13:9; 34:2, 8; 61:2; Ezek 30:3; Amos 5:18; Zeph 1:7 [B]Is 10:25; 14:23; Joel 1:15 13:7 [A]Ezek 7:17 [B]Is 19:1; Ezek 21:7; Nah 2:10 13:8 [A]2 Kin 19:26; Is 21:3; Jer 46:5 [B]Is 26:17; Jer 4:31; John 16:21 13:9 [A]Is 13:6 13:10 [A]Is 5:30; Ezek 32:7; Joel 2:10; Matt 24:29; Mark 13:24; Luke 21:25; Rev 6:13; 8:12 [B]Is 24:23; 50:3; Ezek 32:7; Acts 2:20; Rev 6:12

bore God’s anger in their place. Otherwise, that anger against them would remain.

12:2 God is my salvation. God will deliver the faithful of Israel from both their political opponents and the spiritual consequences of their sins. **LORD GOD.** The doubling of the personal name of God serves to emphasize His role as the covenant-keeping One. **my strength and song … my salvation.** Moses and the Israelites sang a similar song to celebrate their deliverance from the Egyptians (Ex 15:2; cf. Ps 118:14).

12:3 water … springs. Isaiah’s readers doubtless thought of how God satisfied the physical thirst of their ancestors in the Wilderness of Sin (Ex 17:1–7). The same provision will apply for their descendants when the Messiah comes to deliver the nation (41:17, 18; cf. 30:25; 35:6, 7; 43:19; Ps 107:35). The NT amplifies this provision to include the supply of spiritual water for the thirsty soul (Jn 4:10, 14; 7:37; Rev 7:16, 17; 21:6; 22:17).

12:4, 5 among the peoples … throughout the earth. Following the future day of the Lord, Israel will testify to the rest of the world about His greatness and majesty. This was His purpose for His earthly people from the beginning.

12:6 O inhabitant of Zion. The Heb. of this verse personifies Zion as a woman by commanding her to “cry aloud and shout” in celebration of the Lord’s greatness.

13:1–23:18 These 11 chapters group together prophecies against foreign nations, much the same as those in Jer 46–51 and Eze 25–32.

13:1–14:27 The section 13:1–14:24 deals specifically with Babylon and vv. 25–27 with Assyria, though Babylon was not yet a world power at the time of this prophecy. Isaiah foresaw a time when Babylon would overthrow the current dominant nation Assyria and be an international force.

13:1 oracle. In the sense of his having heavy responsibility to deliver the message. It is used 15 other times in the OT in superscriptions like this (14:28; 15:1; 17:1; 19:1; 21:1, 11, 13; 22:1; 23:1; La 2:14; Na 1:1; Hab 1:1; Zec 9:1; 12:1; Mal 1:1). **Babylon … Isaiah … saw.** This chapter foretold the city’s destruction. Even during the Assyrian Empire the city of Babylon was formidable and stood at the head in the list of Israel’s enemies to be conquered.

13:2 Lift up a standard. As in 5:26, the Lord summoned foreign armies to conquer Babylon in all her greatness.

13:3 I have commanded … called. The Lord told of His gathering of armies to overcome Babylon. **My anger.** God’s anger had turned away from Israel (12:1) and toward this oppressive foreign power.

13:4 The LORD of hosts is mustering the army. Lit. “the Lord of armies musters the army.” *See note at 1:9.* This anticipated the end-time coming of the Lord to crush the final Babylon and to dash His enemies in pieces and establish a kingdom over all nations (Rev 19:11–16).

13:5 From the farthest horizons. The fall of Babylon to the Medes was merely a short-term glimpse of the ultimate fall of Babylon at the hands of the universal forces of God (Rev 18:2).

13:6 the day of the LORD is near! The prophecy looked beyond the more immediate conquest of the city by the Medes to a greater day of the Lord and anticipated the final destruction of Babylon by the personal intervention of the Messiah. *See note on 2:12.*

13:7 heart will melt. Courage was to vanish (19:1; Eze 21:7; Na 2:10).

13:8 like a woman in labor. The comparison of labor pains is often a figure to describe human sufferings in the period just before the final deliverance of Israel (21:3; 26:17, 18; 66:7ff.; Jer 4:31; 13:21; 22:23; Hos 13:13; Mic 4:10; 5:2, 3; Mt 24:8; 1Th 5:3). Usually, it was the suffering of Israel, but here it pictured the misery of Babylon.

13:9 exterminate its sinners. This occurs when Messiah returns in judgment of all living on earth. In this case the prophet moves forward to the Babylon which is the final evil world city to be destroyed with all its inhabitants (see Rev 17, 18).

13:10 stars … sun … moon. Scripture frequently associates cosmic upheavals with

11 Thus I will [A]punish the world for its evil
And the [B]wicked for their iniquity;
I will also put an end to the
[C]arrogance of the proud
And abase the [D]haughtiness
of the [a,E]ruthless.
12 I will make mortal man
[a,A]scarcer than pure gold
And mankind than the [B]gold of Ophir.
13 Therefore I will make the
[A]heavens tremble,
And [B]the earth will be shaken
from its place
At the fury of the LORD of hosts
In [C]the day of His burning anger.
14 And it will be that like a hunted gazelle,
Or like [A]sheep with none
to gather *them,*
They will each turn to his own people,
And each one flee to his own land.
15 Anyone who is found will
be [A]thrust through,
And anyone who is captured
will fall by the sword.
16 Their [A]little ones also will
be dashed to pieces
Before their eyes;
Their houses will be plundered
And their wives ravished.

BABYLON WILL FALL TO THE MEDES

17 Behold, I am going to [A]stir up
the Medes against them,
Who will not value silver or
[B]take pleasure in gold.
18 And *their* bows will [a]mow
down the [A]young men,
They will not even have compassion
on the fruit of the womb,
Nor will their [B]eye pity [b]children.
19 And [A]Babylon, the [B]beauty of kingdoms,
the glory of the Chaldeans' pride,
Will be as when God [C]overthrew
Sodom and Gomorrah.
20 It will [A]never be inhabited or lived in
from generation to generation;
Nor will the [B]Arab pitch *his* tent there,
Nor will shepherds make *their*
flocks lie down there.
21 But [A]desert creatures will lie down there,
And their houses will be full of [a]owls;
Ostriches also will live there, and
[b]shaggy goats will frolic there.
22 [a]Hyenas will howl in their
fortified towers
And jackals in their luxurious [A]palaces.
Her *fateful* time also [b]will soon come
And her days will not be prolonged.

ISRAEL'S TAUNT

14 When the LORD will [A]have compassion on Jacob and again [B]choose Israel, and settle them
in their own land, then [C]strangers will join them
and attach themselves to the house of Jacob. 2 The
peoples will take them along and bring them to
their place, and the [A]house of Israel will possess
them as an inheritance in the land of the LORD [B]as
male servants and female servants; and [a]they will
take their captors captive and will rule over their
oppressors.

13:11 [a]Or *tyrants, despots* [A]Is 26:21 [B]Is 3:11; 11:4; 14:5 [C]Is 2:11; 23:9; Dan 5:22, 23 [D]Jer 48:29 [E]Is 25:3; 29:5, 20 13:12 [a]Lit *more precious* [A]Is 4:1; 6:11, 12 [B]1 Kin 9:28; Job 28:16; Ps 45:9 13:13 [A]Is 34:4; 51:6 [B]Ps 18:7; Is 2:19; 24:1, 19, 20; Hag 2:6 [C]Lam 1:12 13:14 [A]1 Kin 22:17; Matt 9:36; Mark 6:34; 1 Pet 2:25 13:15 [A]Is 14:19; Jer 50:25; 51:3, 4 13:16 [A]Ps 137:8, 9; Is 13:18; 14:21; Hos 10:14; Nah 3:10 13:17 [A]Jer 51:11; Dan 5:28 [B]Prov 6:34, 35 13:18 [a]Lit *dash in pieces* [b]Lit *sons* [A]2 Kin 8:12; 2 Chr 36:17 [B]Ezek 9:5, 10 13:19 [A]Is 21:9; 48:14 [B]Dan 4:30; Rev 18:11-16, 19, 21 [C]Gen 19:24; Deut 29:23; Jer 49:18; Amos 4:11 13:20 [A]Is 14:23; 34:10-15; Jer 51:37-43 [B]2 Chr 17:11 13:21 [a]Or *howling creatures* [b]Or *goat demons* [A]Is 34:11-15; Zeph 2:14; Rev 18:2 13:22 [a]Or *howling creatures* [b]Lit *is near to come* [A]Is 25:2; 32:14; 34:13 14:1 [A]Ps 102:13; Is 49:13, 15; 54:7, 8 [B]Is 41:8, 9; 44:1; 49:7; Zech 1:17; 2:12 [C]Is 56:3, 6; Eph 2:12-19 14:2 [a]Lit *the captors will become their captives* [A]Is 45:14; 49:23; 54:3 [B]Is 60:10; 61:5; Dan 7:18, 27

the period of tribulation just before Christ's return (24:23; Eze 32:7, 8; Joel 2:10, 30, 31; Am 8:9; Mt 24:29; Mk 13:24, 25; Lk 21:25; Rev 6:12–14).

13:11 arrogance. The same sin of pride that led to Israel's judgment (5:21; 9:9) will cause Babylon's downfall (47:5, 7, 8; Rev 18:7).

13:12 scarcer. Because of this visitation human mortality will be extremely high, but not complete. God will spare a faithful remnant.

13:13 make the heavens tremble … earth will be shaken. These upheavals are associated with the ones in v. 10 (Joel 2:10; Hag 2:6; Rev 6:12–14; cf. 2:19, 21; 24:1, 19, 20; 34:4; 51:6).

13:14 gazelle … sheep. Humans are frightening to the shy gazelle, but indispensable to the helpless sheep. The Babylonians will find the Lord as their enemy and lose Him as their shepherd. All they can do is flee the land.

13:15, 16 thrust through … captured … dashed to pieces … plundered … ravished. The prophet for the moment returned to the immediate future, when the Medes committed all those cruel atrocities in captured Babylon. For more brutal acts, see v. 18.

13:17 Medes. This people from an area SW of the Caspian Sea, N of Persia, E of Assyria, and NE of Babylon later allied themselves with the Babylonians to conquer Assyria ca. 610 B.C. and later with the Persians to cause the fall of Babylon (539 B.C.).

13:19–22 From the near future, Isaiah returned to the distant future. The ultimate fulfillment of these prophecies of Babylon's desolation will come in conjunction with Babylon's rebuilding and utter destruction when Christ returns (Rev 14:8; 18:2). Obviously, Isaiah was unable to see the many centuries that separated Babylon's fall to the Medes from the destruction of the final Babylon by God (see Rev 17, 18).

13:19 Sodom and Gomorrah. God will overthrow rebuilt Babylon in the same supernatural way He did these two ancient cities (Ge 19:24; Rev 18:8).

13:20 never be inhabited. Though nothing like its glorious past, the site of Babylon has never been void of inhabitants. A city or town of one type or another has always existed there, so this prophecy must point toward a yet future desolation.

13:21, 22 desert creatures … jackals. This is the utter devastation referred to in 21:9 and further described in Rev 18:2 (cf. 34:11–17; Jer 51:37).

13:22 will soon come. As already noted in v. 6, once Babylon becomes great, her days are numbered.

14:1–3 While having some reference to the release from Babylonian captivity, the primary view in this chapter is identified in these opening verses. The prophet looked at the final Babylon at the end of the tribulation. The language is that which characterizes conditions during the millennial kingdom after the judgment of the final Babylon. The destruction of future Babylon is integrally connected with the deliverance of Israel from bondage. Babylon must perish so that the Lord may exalt His people. God's compassion for physical Israel receives fuller development in chaps. 40–46.

14:1 strangers. These are Jewish proselytes who join themselves to the nation in the final earthly kingdom of Christ.

14:2 take their captors captive. Here is the great role reversal. Instead of their miserable state of captivity, endured in the tribulation under Antichrist, the Israelites will be the rulers of those nations that once dominated them.

3 And it will be in the day when the LORD gives
you [A]rest from your pain and turmoil and harsh
service in which you have been enslaved, 4 that
you will [A]take up this [a]taunt against the king of
Babylon, and say,

"How [B]the oppressor has ceased,
And how [b]fury has ceased!
5 "The LORD has broken the staff of the wicked,
The scepter of rulers
6 [A]Which used to strike the peoples in
fury with unceasing strokes,
Which [a]subdued the nations in anger
with unrestrained persecution.
7 "The whole earth is at rest *and* is quiet;
They [A]break forth into shouts of joy.
8 "Even the [A]cypress trees rejoice over you,
and the cedars of Lebanon, *saying,*
'Since you were laid low, no *tree*
cutter comes up against us.'
9 "[A]Sheol from beneath is excited over
you to meet you when you come;
It arouses for you the [a]spirits of the
dead, all the [b]leaders of the earth;
It raises all the kings of the
nations from their thrones.
10 "[A]They will all respond and say to you,
'Even you have been made weak as we,
You have become like us.
11 'Your [A]pomp *and* the music of your harps
Have been brought down to Sheol;
Maggots are spread out *as*
your bed beneath you
And worms are your covering.'
12 "How you have [A]fallen from heaven,
O [a,B]star of the morning, son of the dawn!
You have been cut down to the earth,
You who have weakened the nations!
13 "But you said in your heart,
'I will [A]ascend to heaven;
I will [B]raise my throne above
the stars of God,
And I will sit on the mount of assembly
In the recesses of the north.
14 'I will ascend above the
heights of the clouds;
[A]I will make myself like the Most High.'
15 "Nevertheless you [A]will be
thrust down to Sheol,
To the recesses of the pit.
16 "Those who see you will gaze at you,
They will [a]ponder over you, *saying,*
'Is this the man who made the earth tremble,
Who shook kingdoms,
17 Who made the world like a [A]wilderness
And overthrew its cities,
Who [B]did not [a]allow his
prisoners to *go* home?'
18 "All the kings of the nations lie in glory,
Each in his own [a]tomb.
19 "But you have been [A]cast out of your tomb
Like [a]a rejected branch,
[b]Clothed with the slain who are
pierced with a sword,
Who go down to the stones of the [B]pit
Like a [C]trampled corpse.
20 "You will not be united with them in burial,
Because you have ruined your country,
You have slain your people.
May the [A]offspring of evildoers
not be mentioned forever.
21 "Prepare for his sons a place of slaughter
Because of the [A]iniquity of their fathers.
They must not arise and take
possession of the earth
And fill the face of the world with cities."

14:3 [A]Ezra 9:8, 9; Is 11:10; 40:2; Jer 30:10; 46:27 14:4 [a]Or *proverb* [b]Amended from the meaningless *medhebah* to *marhebah* [A]Hab 2:6 [B]Is 9:4; 16:4; 49:26; 51:13; 54:14 14:6 [a]Or *ruled* [A]Is 10:14; 47:6 14:7 [A]Ps 47:1-3; 98:1-9; 126:1-3 14:8 [A]Is 55:12; Ezek 31:16 14:9 [a]Or *shades* (Heb *Repha'im*) [b]Lit *male goats* [A]Is 5:14 14:10 [A]Ezek 32:21 14:11 [A]Is 5:14 14:12 [a]Heb *Helel;* i.e. shining one [A]Is 34:4; Luke 10:18; Rev 8:10; 9:1 [B]2 Pet 1:19; Rev 2:28; 22:16 14:13 [A]Ezek 28:2 [B]Dan 5:22, 23; 8:10; 2 Thess 2:4 14:14 [A]Is 47:8; 2 Thess 2:4 14:15 [A]Ezek 28:8; Matt 11:23; Luke 10:15 14:16 [a]Lit *show themselves attentive to* 14:17 [a]Lit *open* [A]Joel 2:3 [B]Is 45:13 14:18 [a]Lit *house* 14:19 [a]Lit *an abhorred branch* [b]Or *As the clothing of those who are slain* [A]Is 22:16-18 [B]Jer 41:7, 9 [C]Is 5:25 14:20 [A]Job 18:16, 19; Ps 21:10; 37:28; Is 1:4; 31:2 14:21 [A]Ex 20:5; Lev 26:39; Is 13:16; Matt 23:35

14:3 **rest.** The future earthly kingdom of Messiah is in view. Cf. Ac 3:19–21.

14:4 **you will take up this taunt.** The prophet instructed the delivered nation to sing the song of vv. 4–21, celebrating the downfall of the king of Babylon. **the king of Babylon.** This could refer to the final Antichrist, who will rule Babylon, which will rule the earth (cf. Rev 17:17, 18) **oppressor has ceased.** The nation that made life bitter for God's people disappeared.

14:6 **strike the peoples ... subdued the nations.** These picture the tyranny of the Babylonian king.

14:7 **The whole earth is at rest *and* is quiet.** With the tyrant off the throne, the whole world will have peace. This has to refer to the millennium.

14:9–11 **Sheol.** Those kings of the nations already in the place of the dead stage a welcome party for the arriving king of Babylon.

14:10 **You have become like us.** The kings mock the king of Babylon, reminding him that human distinctions are meaningless among the dead.

14:11 **Maggots.** Human pride becomes a rotting corpse covered with worms.

14:12–14 **fallen from heaven ... make myself like the Most High.** Jesus' use of v. 12 to describe Satan's fall (Lk 10:18; cf. Rev 12:8–10) has led many to see more than a reference to the king of Babylon. Just as the Lord addressed Satan in His words to the serpent (Ge 3:14, 15), this inspired dirge speaks to the king of Babylon and to the devil who energized him. See Eze 28:12–17 for similar language to the king of Tyre and Satan behind him.

14:12 **heaven.** The scene suddenly shifts from the underworld to heaven to emphasize the unbridled pride of the king and Satan energizing him. **star of the morning.** Tradition of the time saw the stars as representing gods battling among themselves for places of preeminence.

14:13, 14 **I will.** Five "I wills" emphasize the arrogance of the king of Babylon, and of Satan, from whom he takes his cue.

14:13 **mount of assembly.** This was a mountain in northern Syria, according to local tradition, where the Canaanite gods assembled. The human king aspired to kingship over those gods.

14:15 **Sheol ... the pit.** Death awaits those who try to be like God (cf. vv. 9, 11; Ge 3:5, 22).

14:16–21 The final section of the dirge elaborates on the disgrace of the king, on display before all as an unburied corpse.

14:16 **Is this the man ... ?** The complete role reversal from the most powerful to utter humiliation will provoke universal amazement.

14:18 **All the kings ... lie in glory.** The king of Babylon is the sole exception. The rest of the kings received honorable burials.

14:19 **trampled corpse.** Among the ancients, this was the deepest degradation. *See note on Ecc 6:3–6.*

14:20 **not be mentioned forever.** Because the king of Babylon was an evildoer, he had no monument or posterity to keep his memory alive.

22 "I will rise up against them," declares the LORD of
hosts, "and will cut off from Babylon [A]name and survivors, [B]offspring and posterity," declares the LORD.
23 "I will also make it a possession for the [A]hedgehog
and swamps of water, and I will sweep it with the
broom of [B]destruction," declares the LORD of hosts.

JUDGMENT ON ASSYRIA

24 The LORD of hosts has sworn saying, "Surely,
[A]just as I have intended so it has happened, and
just as I have planned so it will stand, 25 to [A]break
Assyria in My land, and I will trample him on My
mountains. Then his [B]yoke will be removed from
them and his burden removed from their shoulder. 26 This is the [A]plan [a]devised against the whole
earth; and this is the [B]hand that is stretched out
against all the nations. 27 For [A]the LORD of hosts has
planned, and who can frustrate *it?* And as for His
stretched-out hand, who can turn it back?"
28 In the [A]year that King Ahaz died this [a,B]oracle
came:

JUDGMENT ON PHILISTIA

29 "Do not rejoice, O [A]Philistia, all of you,
Because the rod that [B]struck
you is broken;
For from the serpent's root a
[C]viper will come out,
And its fruit will be a [D]flying serpent.
30 "[a]Those who are most [A]helpless will eat,
And the needy will lie down in security;
I will [b]destroy your root with [B]famine,
And it will kill off your survivors.
31 "Wail, O [A]gate; cry, O city;
[a]Melt away, O [B]Philistia, all of you;
For smoke comes from the [C]north,
And [D]there is no straggler in his ranks.
32 "How then will one answer the
[A]messengers of the nation?
That [B]the LORD has founded Zion,
And [C]the afflicted of His people
will seek refuge in it."

JUDGMENT ON MOAB

15 The [a]oracle concerning [A]Moab.

Surely in a night [B]Ar of Moab is
devastated *and* ruined;
Surely in a night Kir of Moab is
devastated *and* ruined.
2 They have gone up to the [a]temple and *to*
[A]Dibon, *even* to the high places to weep.
Moab wails over Nebo and Medeba;
Everyone's head is [B]bald *and*
every beard is cut off.
3 In their streets they have girded
themselves with [A]sackcloth;
[B]On their housetops and in their squares
Everyone is wailing, [a,C]dissolved in tears.
4 [A]Heshbon and Elealeh also cry out,
Their voice is heard all the way to Jahaz;
Therefore the [a]armed men
of Moab cry aloud;
His soul trembles within him.
5 My heart cries out for Moab;
His fugitives are as far as [A]Zoar
and Eglath-shelishiyah,
For they go up the [B]ascent
of Luhith weeping;
Surely on the road to Horonaim they
raise a cry of distress [C]over *their* ruin.
6 For the [A]waters of Nimrim are [a]desolate.
Surely the grass is withered, the
tender grass [b]died out,
There is [B]no green thing.
7 Therefore the [A]abundance *which* they
have acquired and stored up
They carry off over the brook of [a]Arabim.

14:22 [A]Prov 10:7 [B]Job 18:19; Is 47:9 14:23 [A]Is 34:11; Zeph 2:14 [B]1 Kin 14:10; Is 13:6 14:24 [A]Job 23:13; Is 46:11; 55:8, 9; Acts 4:28 14:25 [A]Is 10:12; 30:31; 31:8 [B]Is 9:4; 10:27; Nah 1:13 14:26 [a]Lit *planned* [A]Is 23:9; Zeph 3:6, 8 [B]Ex 15:12 14:27 [A]2 Chr 20:6; Is 43:13; Dan 4:31, 35 14:28 [a]Or *burden* [A]2 Kin 16:20; 2 Chr 28:27 [B]Is 13:1 14:29 [A]Is 2:6; 11:14; Jer 47:1-7; Ezek 25:15-17; Joel 3:4-8; Amos 1:6-8; Zeph 2:4-7; Zech 9:5-7 [B]2 Chr 26:6 [C]Is 11:8 [D]Is 30:6 14:30 [a]Lit *The firstborn of the helpless* [b]Lit *put to death* [A]Is 3:14, 15; 7:21, 22; 11:4 [B]Is 8:21; 9:20; 51:19 14:31 [a]Or *Become demoralized* [A]Is 3:26; 24:12; 45:2 [B]Is 14:29 [C]Jer 1:14 [D]Is 34:16 14:32 [A]Is 37:9 [B]Ps 87:1, 5; 102:16; Is 28:16; 44:28; 54:11 [C]Is 4:6; 25:4; 57:13; Zeph 3:12; Heb 11:10; James 2:5 15:1 [a]Or *burden of* [A]Is 11:14; 25:10; Jer 48:1; Ezek 25:8-11; Amos 2:1-3; Zeph 2:8-11 [B]Num 21:28 15:2 [a]Lit *house* [A]Jer 48:18, 22 [B]Lev 21:5; Jer 48:37 15:3 [a]Lit *going down in weeping* [A]Jon 3:6-8 [B]Jer 48:38 [C]Is 22:4 15:4 [a]Another reading is *the loins of* [A]Num 21:28; 32:3; Jer 48:34 15:5 [A]Jer 48:34 [B]Jer 48:5 [C]Is 59:7; Jer 4:20 15:6 [a]Lit *desolations* [b]Lit *come to an end* [A]Is 19:5-7; Jer 48:34 [B]Joel 1:10-12; 2:3 15:7 [a]Or *the poplars* [A]Is 30:6; Jer 48:36

14:22 cut off. Israel will have a remnant, but not Babylon, according to the Lord's promise in vv. 22, 23. Cf. Rev 18:2, 21.

14:26 the plan devised. The scope of this judgment against the whole earth represents His final wrath against the ungodly in Israel (5:25; 9:17) and the nations (23:11).

14:28 Ahaz died. The year of Ahaz's death is uncertain. It came when Hezekiah began his reign, either 727 B.C. (2Ki 18:1, 9, 10) or 716/15 B.C. (2Ki 18:13).

14:29 Philistia. Israel need not think an alliance with the Philistines would save them from the Assyrians, since Assyria would conquer this neighbor of Israel too. **rod … broken.** The prophet pictured the Assyrian weakness, their conquest of Philistia notwithstanding.

14:30–32 needy. The poor of Judah who depend on the Lord are to find Him to be a refuge, but the Philistine oppressors are to meet their doom.

14:32 messengers. These were the Philistine envoys who sought an alliance with Israel. Isaiah's answer saw the Lord as Zion's only security.

15:1–16:14 The demise of Moab taught Israel not to depend on that nation any more than others, but to depend on the Lord.

15:1 Moab. Moab was a country about 30 mi. sq., E of the Dead Sea, S of the Arnon River, and N of the Zered River. **Ar … Kir.** These were the two major cities of Moab.

15:2 Dibon. Moab chose the temple of the Moabite god Chemosh—3 mi. N of the Arnon—as the place of weeping because that god had failed to deliver the nation. **Nebo … Medeba.** Nebo is the mountain at the N end of the Dead Sea where the Lord took Moses to view the Promised Land (Dt 34:1). Medeba is 5 mi. SE of Nebo. **bald … every beard.** Shaving heads and beards expressed disgrace and humiliation (22:12; Lv 21:5; Jer 41:5; 48:37).

15:3 sackcloth. Wearing of sackcloth occurs 46 times in the Bible as a sign of mourning.

15:4 Heshbon … Elealeh … Jahaz. The city Heshbon was just under 20 mi. E of the northern end of the Dead Sea in a territory claimed by both Israel and Moab (Dt 2:32, 33). Elealeh was about a mi. away from Heshbon. The location of Jahaz was over 10 mi. S of Heshbon.

15:5 My heart cries out. The prophecy expresses much greater sympathy for Moab's plight than for the other nations to be judged, even allowing for a surviving remnant (16:11, 14). **Eglath-shelishiyah.** A city of unknown location. **Luhith … Horonaim.** These are two more cities whose locations are unknown.

15:6 Nimrim. This is possibly the Wadi Numeira, the drying up of whose waters, along with the dead grass, pictures widespread devastation in Moab.

15:7 brook of Arabim. Probably the Zered River; the refugees from Moab had to cross this to pass over into Edom to escape their invaders.

8 For the cry of distress has gone
around the territory of Moab,
Its wail *goes* as far as Eglaim and
its wailing even to Beer-elim.
9 For the waters of Dimon are full of [a]blood;
Surely I will bring added
woes upon Dimon,
A [A]lion upon the fugitives of Moab and
upon the remnant of the land.

PROPHECY OF MOAB'S DEVASTATION

16 [A]Send the *tribute* lamb to the
ruler of the land,
From [a,B]Sela by way of the wilderness to
the [C]mountain of the daughter of Zion.
2 Then, like [a,A]fleeing birds *or*
scattered [b]nestlings,
The daughters of [B]Moab will be
at the fords of the [C]Arnon.
3 "[a]Give *us* advice, make a decision;
[b]Cast your [A]shadow like night [c]at high noon;
[B]Hide the outcasts, do not
betray the fugitive.
4 "Let the [a]outcasts of Moab stay with you;
Be a hiding place to them
from the destroyer."
For the extortioner has come to an
end, destruction has ceased,
[A]Oppressors have completely
disappeared from the land.
5 A [A]throne will even be established
in lovingkindness,
And a judge will sit on it in
faithfulness in the tent of [B]David;
Moreover, he will seek justice
And be prompt in righteousness.

6 [A]We have heard of the pride of
Moab, an excessive pride;
Even of his arrogance, pride, and fury;
[B]His idle boasts are [a]false.
7 Therefore Moab will wail;
everyone of Moab will wail.
You will moan for the [A]raisin
cakes of [B]Kir-hareseth
As those who are utterly stricken.
8 For the fields of [A]Heshbon have [a]withered,
the vines of [B]Sibmah *as well;*
The lords of the nations have trampled
down its choice clusters
Which reached as far as Jazer *and*
wandered to the deserts;
[C]Its tendrils spread themselves out
and passed over the sea.
9 Therefore I will [A]weep bitterly for
Jazer, for the vine of Sibmah;
I will drench you with my tears,
O [B]Heshbon and Elealeh;
For the shouting over your [C]summer
fruits and your harvest has fallen away.
10 [A]Gladness and joy are taken away
from the fruitful field;
In the [B]vineyards also there will be no
cries of joy or jubilant shouting,
No [C]treader treads out wine in the presses,
For I have made the shouting to cease.
11 Therefore my [a,A]heart intones
like a harp for Moab
And my [b]inward feelings for Kir-hareseth.
12 So it will come about when
Moab [A]presents himself,
When he [B]wearies himself
upon *his* [C]high place
And comes to his sanctuary to pray,
That he will not prevail.

13 This is the word which the LORD spoke earlier
concerning Moab. 14 But now the LORD speaks, saying, "Within three years, as [a,A]a hired man would
count them, the glory of [B]Moab will be degraded
along with all *his* great population, and *his* remnant
will be very small *and* [b]impotent."

15:9 [a]Heb *dam* (a wordplay) [A]2 Kin 17:25; Jer 50:17 16:1 [a]I.e. Petra in Edom [A]2 Kin 3:4; Ezra 7:17 [B]2 Kin 14:7; Is 42:11 [C]Is 10:32 16:2 [a]Or *fluttering* [b]Lit *nest* [A]Prov 27:8 [B]Jer 48:20, 46 [C]Num 21:13, 14 16:3 [a]Lit *Bring* [b]Lit *Set* [c]Lit *in the midst of the noon* [A]Is 25:4; 32:2 [B]1 Kin 18:4 16:4 [a]So the versions; M.T. *My outcasts, as for Moab* [A]Is 9:4; 14:4; 49:26; 51:13; 54:14 16:5 [A]Is 9:6, 7; 32:1; 55:4; Dan 7:14; Mic 4:7; Luke 1:33 [B]Is 9:7 16:6 [a]Lit *not so* [A]Jer 48:29; Amos 2:1; Obad 3, 4; Zeph 2:8, 10 [B]Jer 48:30 16:7 [A]1 Chr 16:3 [B]2 Kin 3:25; Jer 48:31 16:8 [a]Or *languished* [A]Is 15:4 [B]Num 32:38 [C]Jer 48:32 16:9 [A]Jer 48:32 [B]Is 15:4 [C]Jer 40:10, 12; 48:32 16:10 [A]Is 24:8; Jer 48:33 [B]Judg 9:27; Is 24:7; Amos 5:11, 17 [C]Job 24:11; Amos 9:13 16:11 [a]Lit *entrails murmur* [b]Lit *inward part* [A]Is 15:5; 63:15; Jer 48:36; Hos 11:8; Phil 2:1 16:12 [A]Num 22:39-41; Jer 48:35 [B]1 Kin 18:29 [C]Is 15:2 16:14 [a]Lit *the years of a hireling* [b]Lit *not mighty* [A]Job 7:1; 14:6; Is 21:16 [B]Is 25:10; Jer 48:42

15:8 Eglaim ... Beer-elim. The shouts of the fugitives reached all the way from the northern part of Edom (Eglaim) to its southern extremity (Beer-elim).

15:9 Dimon. Perhaps another spelling of "Dibon" (cf. v. 2), this religious center of heathendom is appropriate as a closing representation of the whole land of Moab. **lion.** Flight from invading armies would not bring security, but new dangers from the beasts of the wilderness.

16:1 Send the *tribute* lamb. This was an action showing submission to an overlord, as Mesha did to Omri, king of Israel (2Ki 3:4). **Sela.** This was a place in Edom not far from Petra (2Ki 14:7), from which fugitives of Moab were to send to Judah for help. **mountain of the daughter of Zion.** This speaks figuratively of Jerusalem and her inhabitants.

16:2 fords of the Arnon. The fugitives fled to the S to escape the Assyrians entering Moab from the N.

16:3 night at high noon. Moab asked Judah for shade from the wilting noonday sun, i.e., from their invaders.

16:4 a hiding place. Moab continued its plea to Judah for refuge. **destruction has ceased.** The prophet anticipated the day when the oppression by the Assyrians would be no more.

16:5 throne ... tent of David. The Davidic king will some day sit on His throne in Zion (Am 9:11, 12), ending all injustices such as those committed by the Assyrians.

16:6 pride of Moab ... excessive pride. Though a small nation, Moab's pride was well known (25:10, 11; Jer 48:29, 42).

16:7 Kir-hareseth. This is probably the same city called Kir in 15:1.

16:8 Sibmah. Sibmah was a suburb of Heshbon (cf. Jer 48:32). **Jazer ... sea.** Moab's vines, rather than being on stakes, ran along the ground to Moab's extreme northern border, stretching from the desert on the E to the Dead Sea on the W. This perhaps signified the export of raisins and wine to Judah.

16:9 I will weep bitterly. Isaiah displayed genuine emotion over the destruction of so rich an agricultural resource. This reflected the Lord's response too.

16:10 Gladness ... joy. The normal celebration at harvesttime is not to take place.

16:11 my heart ... my inward feelings. The prophet and the Lord reflected deeply felt sorrow over this necessary judgment of Moab.

16:12 wearies himself upon *his* high place. Moab's religion had utterly failed. Rather than deliverance, the nation found weariness in their repeated rituals to their national god.

16:14 Within three years. Moab had 3 more years of "glory," perhaps till ca. 715 B.C., when

PROPHECY ABOUT DAMASCUS

17 The [a,A]oracle concerning [B]Damascus.

"Behold, Damascus is about to be
[C]removed from being a city
And will become a [D]fallen ruin.
2 "The cities [a]of [A]Aroer are forsaken;
They will be for [B]flocks [b]to lie down in,
And there will be [C]no one to frighten *them*.
3 "The [a,A]fortified city will
disappear from Ephraim,
And [b]sovereignty from Damascus
And the remnant of Aram;
They will be like the [B]glory
of the sons of Israel,"
Declares the LORD of hosts.

4 Now in that day the [A]glory
of Jacob will [a]fade,
And [B]the fatness of his flesh
will become lean.
5 It will be [A]even like the [a]reaper
gathering the standing grain,
As his arm harvests the ears,
Or it will be like one gleaning ears of grain
In the [B]valley of Rephaim.
6 Yet [A]gleanings will be left in it like
the [a]shaking of an olive tree,
Two *or* three olives on the topmost bough,
Four *or* five on the branches
of a fruitful tree,
Declares the LORD, the God of Israel.
7 In that day man will [A]have
regard for his Maker
And his eyes will look to the
Holy One of Israel.
8 He will not have regard for the
[A]altars, the work of his hands,
Nor will he look to that which
his [B]fingers have made,
Even the [a,C]Asherim and [b]incense stands.
9 In that day [a]their strong cities will be
like [b]forsaken places in the forest,
Or like [c]branches which they abandoned
before the sons of Israel;
And [d]the land will be a desolation.
10 For [A]you have forgotten the
[B]God of your salvation
And have not remembered the
[C]rock of your refuge.
Therefore you plant delightful plants
And set them with vine slips
of a strange *god*.
11 In the day that you plant *it* you
carefully fence *it* in,
And in the [A]morning you bring
your seed to blossom;
But the harvest will [B]*be* a heap
In a day of sickliness
and incurable pain.

12 Alas, the uproar of many peoples
[A]Who roar like the roaring of the seas,
And the rumbling of nations
Who rush on like the [B]rumbling
of mighty waters!
13 The [A]nations rumble on like the
rumbling of many waters,
But He will [B]rebuke them and
they will flee far away,
And be chased [C]like chaff in the
mountains before the wind,
Or like whirling dust before a gale.
14 At evening time, behold, *there is* terror!
Before morning [A]they are no more.
[a]Such *will be* the portion of
those who plunder us
And the lot of those who pillage us.

MESSAGE TO ETHIOPIA

18 Alas, oh land of whirring wings
Which lies beyond the rivers of [a,A]Cush,

17:1 [a]Or *burden of* [A]Is 13:1 [B]Gen 14:15; 15:2; 2 Kin 16:9; Jer 49:23; Amos 1:3-5; Zech 9:1; Acts 9:2 [C]Is 7:16; 8:4; 10:9 [D]Is 25:2; Jer 49:2; Mic 1:6 17:2 [a]Gr reads *forever and ever* [b]Lit *and they will lie down* [A]Num 32:34 [B]Is 7:21, 22; Ezek 25:5; Zeph 2:6 [C]Mic 4:4 17:3 [a]Or *fortification* [b]Or *royal power, kingdom* [A]Is 7:8, 16; 8:4 [B]Is 17:4; Hos 9:11 17:4 [a]Lit *become thin* [A]Is 10:3 [B]Is 10:16 17:5 [a]Lit *gathering of the harvest, the standing grain* [A]Is 17:11; Jer 51:33; Joel 3:13; Matt 13:30 [B]2 Sam 5:18, 22 17:6 [a]Lit *striking* [A]Deut 4:27; Is 24:13; 27:12; Obad 5 17:7 [A]Is 10:20; Hos 3:5; 6:1; Mic 7:7 17:8 [a]I.e. wooden symbols of a female deity [b]Or *sun pillars* [A]2 Chr 34:7; Is 27:9 [B]Is 2:8, 20; 30:22; 31:7 [C]Ex 34:13; Deut 7:5; Mic 5:14 17:9 [a]I.e. man's [b]Gr reads *the deserted places of the Amorites and the Hivites which they abandoned* [c]Or *the treetop* [d]Lit *it* 17:10 [A]Is 51:13 [B]Ps 68:19; Is 12:2; 33:2; 61:10; 62:11 [C]Deut 32:4, 18, 31; Is 26:4; 30:29; 44:8 17:11 [A]Ps 90:6 [B]Job 4:8; Hos 8:7; 10:13 17:12 [A]Is 5:30; Jer 6:23; Ezek 43:2; Luke 21:25 [B]Ps 18:4 17:13 [A]Is 33:3 [B]Ps 9:5; Is 41:11 [C]Job 21:18; Ps 1:4; 83:13; Is 29:5; 41:15, 16 17:14 [a]Lit *This* [A]2 Kin 19:35; Is 41:12 18:1 [a]Or *Ethiopia* [A]2 Kin 19:9; Is 20:3-5; Ezek 30:4, 5, 9; Zeph 2:12; 3:10

the Assyrian king, Sargon, overran the country. ***his* remnant.** Assyria was not to completely obliterate Moab. Babylon received no such promise.

17:1 Damascus. This city served as the capital of Aram, or Syria. Its location NE of Mt. Hermon on the main land route between Mesopotamia and Egypt made it very influential. Its destruction by the Assyrians in 732 B.C. is the subject of this chapter.

17:2 Aroer. Aram's, or Syria's, domain extended as far S as Aroer E of the Dead Sea, on the Arnon River (2Ki 10:32, 33).

17:3 Ephraim. The northern 10 tribes, also known as "Israel," joined with Syria as objects of this oracle. They formed an alliance with Syria to combat the Assyrians, but many of their cities fell victim to the campaign in which Syria fell (see v. 1). **remnant of Aram.** Aram, or Syria, was to have a remnant, but not a kingdom, left after the Assyrian onslaught.

17:4 glory of Jacob. The waning of this glory pictured the judgment of God against the northern 10 tribes, descendants of Jacob.

17:5 valley of Rephaim. As harvesters stripped bare that fertile valley W of Jerusalem, so God's judgment would leave nothing fruitful in the northern kingdom.

17:6 Two *or* three ... Four *or* five. God's judgment against Ephraim was to leave only sparse pieces of her original abundance of olives.

17:7 have regard for his Maker. In the future, severe judgments are to awaken a remnant of Ephraim to their failure to depend on the Lord. Then they will repent.

17:8 work of his hands. Repentance is to lead to the forsaking of idolatry, which for so long beset the nation (see 2:6–22; 44:9–18).

17:10 forgotten the God of your salvation. Failure to remember God had left Israel unprotected.

17:11 that you plant. The prophet reminded his readers of the futility of trying to meet their needs without the Lord's help.

17:12 many peoples. The prophet turned his attention to the coming armies of Judah's enemies and pronounced a "woe" upon them.

17:13 He will rebuke them. God's rebuke put those enemies to flight.

17:14 they are no more. When morning came, the invading force had disappeared. God protects His people.

18:1 whirring wings. These may speak of Ethiopia's strong armada of ships. **Cush.** The Heb. word for Ethiopia. The country was S

2 Which sends envoys by the sea,
Even in [A]papyrus vessels on the
surface of the waters.
Go, swift messengers, to a
nation [a,B]tall and smooth,
To a people [C]feared [b]far and wide,
A powerful and oppressive nation
Whose land the rivers divide.
3 [A]All you inhabitants of the world
and dwellers on earth,
As soon as a standard is raised on
the mountains, [B]you will see *it,*
And as soon as the trumpet is
blown, you will hear *it.*

4 For thus the LORD has told me,

"I will look [a]from My [A]dwelling place quietly
Like dazzling heat in the [b,B]sunshine,
Like a cloud of [C]dew in the heat of harvest."
5 For [A]before the harvest, as soon
as the bud [a]blossoms
And the flower becomes a ripening grape,
Then He will cut off the sprigs
with pruning knives
And remove *and* cut away the
spreading branches.
6 They will be left together for
mountain birds [A]of prey,
And for the beasts of the earth;
And the birds of prey will spend
the summer *feeding* on them,
And all the beasts of the earth will
spend harvest time on them.
7 At that time a gift of homage will be
brought to the LORD of hosts
[a]From a [A]people [b]tall and smooth,
Even from a people feared [c]far and wide,
A powerful and oppressive nation,
Whose land the rivers divide—
To the [B]place of the name of the LORD
of hosts, *even* Mount Zion.

MESSAGE TO EGYPT

19 The [a,A]oracle concerning [B]Egypt.

Behold, the LORD is [C]riding on a swift
cloud and is about to come to Egypt;
The [D]idols of Egypt will tremble
at His presence,
And the [E]heart of the Egyptians
will melt within them.
2 "So I will incite Egyptians
against Egyptians;
And they will [A]each fight against his
brother and each against his neighbor,
City against city *and* kingdom
against kingdom.
3 "Then the spirit of the Egyptians will
be demoralized within them;
And I will confound their strategy,
So that [A]they will resort to idols
and ghosts of the dead
And to [a]mediums and spiritists.
4 "Moreover, I will deliver the Egyptians
into the hand of a [A]cruel master,
And a [a]mighty king will rule over them,"
declares the Lord [b]GOD of hosts.

5 [A]The waters from the sea will dry up,
And the river will be parched and dry.
6 The [a,A]canals will emit a stench,
The [b,B]streams of Egypt will
thin out and dry up;
[C]The reeds and rushes will rot away.
7 The bulrushes by the [A]Nile, by
the [a]edge of the Nile
And all the sown fields by the Nile
Will become dry, be driven
away, and be no more.
8 And the [A]fishermen will lament,
And all those who cast a [a]line
into the Nile will mourn,
And those who spread nets on
the waters will [b]pine away.

18:2 [a]Lit *drawn out* [b]Lit *from it and beyond* [A]Ex 2:3 [B]Is 18:7 [C]Gen 10:8, 9; 2 Chr 12:2-4; 14:9; 16:8 18:3 [A]Ps 49:1; Mic 1:2 [B]Is 26:11 18:4 [a]Lit *in* [b]Lit *light* [A]Is 26:21; Hos 5:15 [B]2 Sam 23:4 [C]Prov 19:12; Is 26:19; Hos 14:5 18:5 [a]Lit *is finished* [A]Is 17:10, 11; Ezek 17:6-10 18:6 [A]Is 46:11; 56:9; Jer 7:33; Ezek 32:4-6; 39:17-20 18:7 [a]So with some ancient versions and DSS; M.T. implies *Consisting of a people* [b]Lit *drawn out* [c]Lit *from it and beyond* [A]Ps 68:31; Is 45:14; Zeph 3:10; Acts 8:27-38 [B]Zech 14:16, 17 19:1 [a]Or *burden of* [A]Is 13:1 [B]Joel 3:19 [C]Ps 18:9, 10; 104:3; Matt 26:64; Rev 1:7 [D]Ex 12:12; Jer 43:12; 44:8 [E]Josh 2:11; Is 13:7 19:2 [A]Judg 7:22; 1 Sam 14:20; 2 Chr 20:23; Matt 10:21, 36 19:3 [a]Or *ghosts and spirits* [A]1 Chr 10:13; Is 8:19; Dan 2:2 19:4 [a]Or *fierce* [b]Heb *YHWH*, usually rendered *LORD* [A]Is 20:4; Jer 46:26; Ezek 29:19 19:5 [A]Is 50:2; Jer 51:36; Ezek 30:12 19:6 [a]Lit *rivers* [b]Or *Nile branches;* i.e. the delta [A]Ex 7:18 [B]Is 37:25 [C]Ex 2:3; Job 8:11; Is 15:6 19:7 [a]Or *mouth* [A]Is 23:3, 10 19:8 [a]Lit *hook* [b]Or *languish* [A]Ezek 47:10; Hab 1:15

of Egypt, including territory belonging to modern Ethiopia.

18:2 sea . . . waters . . . rivers. These all apparently refer to the Nile River and its tributaries.

18:3 All you inhabitants . . . and dwellers. The prophet calls upon the whole human race to be alert for the signals that God is at work in the world.

18:4 I will look from My dwelling place quietly. The Lord will wait patiently until the appropriate time to intervene in human affairs, until sunshine and dew have built to an opportune climactic moment.

18:5 cut off . . . remove *and* cut away. As an all-wise farmer, God's pruning activity (i.e., His direct intervention) will be neither too early nor too late.

18:6 birds of prey. Dropping his metaphorical language, Isaiah describes in grotesque language the fallen carcasses of the victims of God's judgment.

18:7 place of the name of the LORD of hosts. Jerusalem was and remains the location on earth where the Lord has chosen to dwell (Dt 12:5). Isaiah's prediction here extends to the future bringing of tribute to Jerusalem in the Messiah's kingdom.

19:1–4 Disunity and internal strife because of idolatry are to spell the end of Egypt's greatness.

19:1 riding on a swift cloud. Clouds are vehicles for the Lord's coming to execute judgment elsewhere (Pss 18:10, 11; 104:3; Da 7:13).

19:2 Egyptians against Egyptians. Noted for its internal strife through the centuries, the nation will experience even worse under God's judgment.

19:3 mediums and spiritists. Internal strife will lead to disorientation and depression. With nowhere else to turn, the Egyptians will consult spiritists. Israelites of Isaiah's day did the same (8:19).

19:4 mighty king. Egypt was subject to foreign rule beginning with the Assyrian conquest of the middle-seventh century B.C.

19:5–10 A disruption of the Nile River will wreak havoc in Egypt.

19:5, 6 parched and dry . . . dry up. God will act to take away the country's only water resource, the Nile and its tributaries.

19:7 sown fields by the Nile. The alluvial deposits left by the flooding of the Nile yielded rich agricultural crops, permitting Egypt to export grain to the rest of the world.

19:8 cast a line . . . spread nets. The loss of the Nile's important fishing business would mean a great loss to Egypt's population.

9 Moreover, the manufacturers of
linen made from combed flax
And the weavers of white [A]cloth
will be [a]utterly dejected.
10 And [a]the [A]pillars *of Egypt* will be crushed;
All the hired laborers will
be grieved in soul.

11 The princes of [a,A]Zoan are mere fools;
The advice of Pharaoh's wisest
advisers has become [b]stupid.
How can you *men* say to Pharaoh,
"I am a son of the [B]wise, a son
of ancient kings"?
12 Well then, where are your wise men?
Please let them tell you,
And let them [a]understand
what the LORD of hosts
Has [A]purposed against Egypt.
13 The princes of [a]Zoan have acted foolishly,
The princes of [A]Memphis are deluded;
Those who are the [B]cornerstone
of her tribes
Have [b]led Egypt astray.
14 The LORD has mixed within her
a spirit of [A]distortion;
[B]They have led Egypt astray
in all [a]that it does,
As a [C]drunken man [b]staggers in his vomit.
15 There will be no work for Egypt
[A]Which *its* head or tail, *its* palm
branch or bulrush, may do.

16 In that day the Egyptians will become like
women, and they will tremble and be in [A]dread
because of the [B]waving of the hand of the LORD of
hosts, which He is going to wave over them. 17 The
land of Judah will become a [a]terror to Egypt; everyone [b]to whom it is mentioned will be in dread
of it, because of the [A]purpose of the LORD of hosts
which He is purposing against them.
18 In that day five cities in the land of Egypt will
be speaking the language of Canaan and [A]swearing
allegiance to the LORD of hosts; one will be called
the City of [a]Destruction.
19 In that day there will be an [A]altar to the LORD
in the midst of the land of Egypt, and a [B]pillar to
the LORD near its border. 20 It will become a sign
and a witness to the LORD of hosts in the land of
Egypt; for they will cry to the LORD because of oppressors, and He will send them a [A]Savior and a
[a,B]Champion, and He will deliver them. 21 Thus the
LORD will make Himself known to Egypt, and the
Egyptians will know the LORD in that day. They will
even worship with [A]sacrifice and offering, and will
make a vow to the LORD and perform it. 22 The LORD
will strike Egypt, striking but [A]healing; so they will
[B]return to the LORD, and He will respond to them
and will heal them.
23 In that day there will be a [A]highway from Egypt
to Assyria, and the Assyrians will come into Egypt
and the Egyptians into Assyria, and the Egyptians
will [B]worship with the Assyrians.
24 In that day Israel will be the third *party* with
Egypt and Assyria, a blessing in the midst of the

19:9 [a]Lit *ashamed* [A]Prov 7:16; Ezek 27:7 19:10 [a]Lit *her pillars* or, *her weavers* [A]Ps 11:3 19:11 [a]Or *Tanis* [b]Or *brutish* [A]Num 13:22; Ps 78:12, 43; Is 30:4 [B]Gen 41:38, 39; 1 Kin 4:30; Acts 7:22 19:12 [a]Or *know* [A]Is 14:24; Rom 9:17 19:13 [a]Or *Tanis* [b]Or *have caused Egypt to stagger* [A]Jer 2:16; 46:14, 19; Ezek 30:13 [B]Zech 10:4 19:14 [a]Lit *its work* [b]Or *goes astray* [A]Prov 12:8; Matt 17:17 [B]Is 3:12; 9:16 [C]Is 28:7 19:15 [A]Is 9:14, 15 19:16 [A]2 Cor 5:11; Heb 10:31 [B]Is 11:15 19:17 [a]Or *cause of shame* [b]Lit *who mentions it will be in dread to it* [A]Is 14:24; Dan 4:35 19:18 [a]Some ancient mss and versions read *the Sun* [A]Is 45:23; 65:16 19:19 [A]Is 56:7; 60:7 [B]Gen 28:18; Ex 24:4; Josh 22:10, 26, 27 19:20 [a]Lit *Mighty One* [A]Is 43:3, 11; 45:15, 21; 49:26; 60:16; 63:8 [B]Is 49:25 19:21 [A]Is 56:7; 60:7; Zech 14:16-18 19:22 [A]Deut 32:39; Is 30:26; 57:18; Heb 12:11 [B]Is 27:13; 45:14; Hos 14:1 19:23 [A]Is 11:16; 35:8; 49:11; 62:10 [B]Is 27:13

19:9 combed flax … white cloth. Egypt was famous for its production of linen from flax. Both the growth of the plant and the manufacture of the cloth depended on water.

19:10 pillars. God was to remove the foundations, or "pillars," on which the working class depended. The word refers either generally to the economic structure of the society or specifically to the upper class which organized the businesses of the land.

19:11–15 God's judgment was to confound Egypt's famed wisdom (cf. 1Ki 4:30).

19:11 Zoan. This major city of northern Egypt E of the Nile Delta region was the first large city a Semite would encounter in traveling toward the Nile. "Tanis" was also a name of this city that was a capital of northern Egypt at one point when the country split into two parts.

19:11, 12 advisers … stupid. Whatever wisdom Egypt's experts may have possessed formerly, they were helpless to deal with the crisis because they were ignorant of the Lord's judgment against the land.

19:13 Memphis. The capital of northern Egypt at one time. This city had leaders who were in a state of confusion regarding a true perspective on Egypt's crisis. **cornerstone of her tribes.** If the cornerstones of a society suffer from delusion, they can do nothing else than delude the people they lead.

19:14, 15 The LORD has mixed. The Lord had caused dizziness that resulted in a complete loss of productivity, when the invaders came.

19:16–24 Turning from Egypt's destitution just described in vv. 1–15, the prophet proceeds to describe Egypt's eventual turning to the true God, "in that day" (v. 16), referring to the time of the millennial rule of Christ. These features have not been true of Egypt yet.

19:16 women … tremble and be in dread. God's judgment will immobilize mighty Egypt to the point that the nation realizes it is defenseless and helpless.

19:17 Judah …. terror to Egypt. Instead of Judah fearing Egypt, the reverse will be true. God's great power on behalf of Israel will cause this to happen (cf. Ex 10:7; 12:33). Such will occur at Christ's second advent.

19:18 five cities. Humanly speaking, the chances of even one Egyptian city turning to the Lord were remote, but divinely speaking, there will be 5 times that many. **language of Canaan.** Egypt is to speak the language of Judah. Not only are they to fear Judah (v. 17), they are also to convert to Judah's form of worship. **swearing *allegiance* to the LORD of hosts.** Egypt will "in that day" turn to God in a dramatic way. This prophecy anticipates the personal reign of the Davidic King on earth. **City of Destruction.** More probably this was the "City of the Sun," i.e., Heliopolis, which was the home of the Egyptian sun-god (see "Beth-shemesh," Jer 43:12, 13).

19:19 altar … pillar. These speak figuratively of Egypt's conversion to the Lord "in that day" of the Messiah's reign on earth (cf. Ge 28:22).

19:20 Savior. God is to act on behalf of Egypt as He did earlier in delivering Israel (Jdg 2:18; 3:9, 15; 6:7–9; 10:11, 12).

19:21 know the LORD in that day. The future kingdom will be a time when everyone will know the Lord, because the New Covenant will dominate (Jer 31:31–34: Heb 8:11; cf. 11:9; Hab 2:14).

19:22 striking … healing. Just as a parent disciplines a child for purposes of betterment, so the Lord had dealt and would deal with Egypt (cf. Hos 6:1).

19:23 a highway from Egypt to Assyria. The two great warring nations of Isaiah's time are to reach a lasting peace with each other during "that day" of Christ's reign (27:13; cf. 2:2–4).

19:24 a blessing in the midst of the earth. Israel "in that day" will become what God intended her to be—a blessing to the rest of the world (Ge 12:3; 42:6; contra 1:2).

earth, 25 whom the LORD of hosts has blessed, saying, "Blessed is [A]Egypt My people, and Assyria [B]the
work of My hands, and Israel My inheritance."

PROPHECY ABOUT EGYPT AND ETHIOPIA

20 In the year that the [a,A]commander came to
[B]Ashdod, when Sargon the king of Assyria
sent him and he fought against Ashdod and captured it, 2 at that time the LORD spoke through [A]Isa-
iah the son of Amoz, saying, "Go and loosen the
[B]sackcloth from your hips and take your [C]shoes off
your feet." And he did so, going [D]naked and barefoot.
3 And the LORD said, "Even as My servant Isaiah has
gone naked and barefoot three years as a [a,A]sign and
token against Egypt and [b,B]Cush, 4 so the [A]king of Assyria will lead away the captives of Egypt and the
exiles of Cush, [B]young and old, naked and barefoot
with buttocks uncovered, to the [a]shame of Egypt.
5 Then they will be [A]dismayed and ashamed because
of Cush their hope and Egypt their [B]boast. 6 So the
inhabitants of this coastland will say in that day,
'Behold, such is our hope, where we fled [A]for help
to be delivered from the king of Assyria; and we,
[B]how shall we escape?' "

GOD COMMANDS THAT BABYLON BE TAKEN

21 The [a,A]oracle concerning the [b,B]wilderness of
the sea.

As [C]windstorms in the
[C]Negev sweep on,
It comes from the wilderness,
from a terrifying land.

2 A [A]harsh vision has been shown to me;
The [B]treacherous one *still*
deals treacherously, and the
destroyer *still* destroys.
Go up, [C]Elam, lay siege, Media;
I have made an end of all [a]the
groaning she has caused.
3 For this reason my [A]loins
are full of anguish;
Pains have seized me like the
pains of a [B]woman in labor.
I am so bewildered I cannot hear,
so terrified I cannot see.
4 My [a]mind reels, [b]horror overwhelms me;
The twilight I longed for has been
[A]turned for me into trembling.
5 They [A]set the table, they [a]spread out
the cloth, they eat, they drink;
"Rise up, captains, oil the shields,"

6 For thus the Lord says to me,

"Go, station the lookout, let him
[A]report what he sees.
7 "When he sees [A]riders, horsemen in pairs,
A train of donkeys, a train of camels,
Let him pay close attention,
very close attention."

8 Then [a]the lookout called,

"[A]O Lord, I stand continually by
day on the watchtower,
And I am stationed every night
at my guard post.

19:25 [A]Is 45:14 [B]Ps 100:3; Is 29:23; 45:11; 60:21; 64:8; Eph 2:10 20:1 [a]Heb *Tartan* [A]2 Kin 18:17 [B]1 Sam 5:1 20:2 [A]Is 1:1; 13:1 [B]Zech 13:4; Matt 3:4 [C]Ezek 24:17, 23 [D]1 Sam 19:24; Mic 1:8 20:3 [a]Or *wonder* [b]Or *Ethiopia*, so in vv 4, 5 [A]Is 8:18 [B]Is 37:9; 43:3 20:4 [a]Lit *nakedness* [A]Is 19:4 [B]Is 47:2, 3 20:5 [A]2 Kin 18:21; Is 30:3-5; 31:1; Ezek 29:6, 7 [B]Jer 9:23, 24; 17:5; 1 Cor 3:21 20:6 [A]Is 10:3; 30:7; 31:3; Jer 30:1, 7, 15-17; 31:1-3 [B]Matt 23:33; 1 Thess 5:3; Heb 2:3 21:1 [a]Or *burden of* [b]Or *sandy wastes, sea country* [C]I.e. South country [A]Is 13:1 [B]Is 13:20-22; 14:23; Jer 51:42 [C]Zech 9:14 21:2 [a]Lit *her groaning* [A]Ps 60:3 [B]Is 24:16; 33:1 [C]Is 22:6; Jer 49:34 21:3 [A]Is 13:8; 16:11 [B]Ps 48:6; Is 13:8; 26:17; 1 Thess 5:3 21:4 [a]Lit *heart has wandered* [b]Lit *shuddering* [A]Deut 28:67 21:5 [a]Or *spread out the rugs* or possibly *they arranged the seating* [A]Jer 51:39, 57; Dan 5:1-4 21:6 [A]2 Kin 9:17-20 21:7 [A]Is 21:9 21:8 [a]So DSS; M.T. *he called* like *a lion* [A]Hab 2:1

19:25 My people ... the work of My hands. Elsewhere Scripture uses these epithets to speak only of Israel (10:24; 29:23; 43:6, 7; 45:11; 60:21; 64:8; Pss 100:3; 110:3; 138:8; Jer 11:4; Hos 1:10; 2:23). In the future kingdom, Israel is to be God's instrument for drawing other nations into His fold.

20:1 Ashdod ... Sargon. Ashdod was one of the 5 largest Philistine cities, all located SW of Jerusalem. Sargon, mentioned only here in the Bible, was Sargon II, king of Assyria from ca. 722–705 B.C. **captured it.** The Assyrians captured Ashdod in 711 B.C., and so frightened the Egyptians that they backed away, thus teaching Judah the folly of reliance on a foreign power such as Egypt for protection.

20:2 at that time. Isaiah began his object lesson 3 years (v. 3) before his speech in vv. 3–6, which came just prior to the Assyrian attack in 711 B.C. **sackcloth.** This apparel may denote Isaiah's mourning (Ge 37:34; 2Ki 6:30), or it may signify his prophetic office (2Ki 1:8; Mt 3:4). **naked and barefoot.** The Lord commanded stripping off all of his outer garments as an act denoting disgrace and humiliation.

20:3 My servant. This designation places Isaiah among a select group: Others include: Abraham (Ge 26:24); Moses (Nu 12:7, 8; Jos 1:2, 7; 2Ki 21:8; Mal 4:4); Caleb (Nu 14:24); David (2Sa 3:18; 7:5, 8; 1Ki 11:32, 34, 36, 38; 14:8; 2Ki 19:34; 20:6; 1Ch 17:4, 7; Ps 89:3; Is 37:35; Jer 33:21, 22, 26; Eze 34:23, 24; 37:24, 25); Job (Job 1:8; 2:3; 42:7, 8); Eliakim (22:20); the Servant of the Lord (42:1; 49:5, 6, 7; 52:13; 53:11; Zec 3:8; Mt 12:18); Israel (41:8, 9; 42:19; 43:10; 44:1, 2, 21, 26; 44:21; 45:4; 48:20; 50:10; Jer 30:10; 46:27, 28; Eze 28:25; 37:25); Nebuchadnezzar (Jer 25:9; 27:6; 43:10); Zerubbabel (Hag 2:23); and Christ's follower (Jn 12:26). **sign ... token.** Isaiah's nakedness and bare feet symbolized the coming desolation and shame of Egypt and Ethiopia at the hands of the Assyrians (cf. 19:4).

20:4 captives ... exiles. Esarhaddon, king of Assyria, fulfilled this prophecy in 671 B.C. (cf. 37:38; 2Ki 19:37; Ezr 4:2). Far from being a suitable object of Judah's trust, mighty Egypt will go off in shame.

20:6 how shall we escape? "We" refers to the people of Judah. Trust in Egypt has proven itself misplaced. Is there any adequate source of help?

21:1 wilderness of the sea. The prophet referred to an area of southern Babylon near the Persian Gulf known for its fertility. **As windstorms in the Negev.** The simile drew from the suddenness with which storm winds come from the Negev and sweep through the land of Israel. So sudden is to be Babylon's overthrow.

21:2 Elam ... Media. The Elamites and Medes were part of the Persian army that defeated Babylon in 539 B.C.

21:3, 4 anguish ... Pains ... bewildered ... terrified. The severity of the violence about which Isaiah must prophesy caused him extreme agitation.

21:5 eat ... drink ... oil the shields. This part of the oracle recalled Belshazzar's feast in Da 5, when amid the celebration came a call to fight the attacking enemy invading the city.

21:6 station the lookout. Isaiah stationed a watchman on the city walls.

21:7 horsemen ... donkeys ... camels. Isaiah heard the watchman warn of an approaching military force.

21:8 lookout called, "O Lord." The Dead Sea Scrolls correctly read, "the watchman cried, my Lord." The watchman whom Isaiah had stationed (v. 6) continued his report.

9 "Now behold, here comes a troop of
riders, horsemen in pairs."
And one said, "[A]Fallen, fallen is Babylon;
And all the [B]images of her gods
[a]are shattered on the ground."
10 O my [A]threshed *people,* and my
[a]afflicted of the threshing floor!
What I have heard from the LORD of hosts,
The God of Israel, I make known to you.

ORACLES ABOUT EDOM AND ARABIA

11 The [a]oracle concerning [b,A]Edom.

One keeps calling to me from [B]Seir,
"Watchman, [c]how far gone is the night?
Watchman, [c]how far gone is the night?"
12 The watchman says,
"Morning comes but also night.
If you would inquire, inquire;
Come back again."

13 The [a]oracle about [A]Arabia.

In the thickets of Arabia you
[b]must spend the night,
O caravans of [B]Dedanites.
14 Bring water [a]for the thirsty,
O inhabitants of the land of [A]Tema,
Meet the fugitive with bread.
15 For they have [A]fled from the swords,
From the drawn sword, and
from the bent bow
And from the press of battle.

16 For thus the Lord said to me, "In a [A]year, as [a]a
hired man would count it, all the splendor of [B]Kedar
will terminate; 17 and the [A]remainder of the number
of bowmen, the mighty men of the sons of Kedar,
will be few; for the LORD God of Israel [B]has spoken."

THE VALLEY OF VISION

22 The [a]oracle concerning the [A]valley of vision.

What is the matter with you now, that you
have all gone up to the [B]housetops?
2 You who were full of noise,
You boisterous town, you [A]exultant city;
Your slain were [B]not slain with the sword,
Nor [a]did they die in battle.
3 [A]All your rulers have fled together,
And have been captured [a]without the bow;
All of you who were found were
taken captive together,
[b]Though they had fled far away.
4 Therefore I say, "Turn your
eyes away from me,
Let me [A]weep bitterly,
Do not [a]try to comfort me
concerning the destruction of
the daughter of my people."
5 [A]For the Lord [a]GOD of hosts has a [B]day of
panic, [C]subjugation and confusion
[D]In the valley of vision,
A breaking down of walls
And a crying [b]to the mountain.
6 [A]Elam took up the quiver
With the chariots, [a]infantry *and* horsemen;
And [B]Kir uncovered the shield.
7 Then your choicest valleys
were full of chariots,
And the horsemen took up fixed
positions at the gate.

21:9 [a]Lit *he has shattered to the earth* [A]Is 13:19; 47:5, 9; 48:14; Jer 51:8; Rev 14:8; 18:2 [B]Is 46:1; Jer 50:2; 51:44 21:10 [a]Lit *son* [A]Jer 51:33; Mic 4:13 21:11 [a]Or *burden* [b]So the Gr; Heb *Dumah, silence* [c]Lit *what* is the time *of the night?* [A]Gen 25:14 [B]Gen 32:3 21:13 [a]Or *burden* [b]Or *will spend* [A]Jer 25:23, 24; 49:28 [B]Gen 10:7; Ezek 27:15 21:14 [a]Lit *to meet* [A]Gen 25:15; Job 6:19 21:15 [A]Is 13:14, 15; 17:13 21:16 [a]Lit *the years of a hireling* [A]Is 16:14 [B]Ps 120:5; Song 1:5; Is 42:11; 60:7; Ezek 27:21 21:17 [A]Is 10:19 [B]Num 23:19; Zech 1:6 22:1 [a]Or *burden of* [A]Ps 125:2; Jer 21:13; Joel 3:12, 14 [B]Is 15:3 22:2 [a]Lit *dead in battle* [A]Is 23:7; 32:13 [B]Jer 14:18; Lam 2:20 22:3 [a]Lit *from a bow* [b]So with ancient versions; Heb *They fled far away* [A]Is 21:15 22:4 [a]Lit *insist* [A]Is 15:3; Jer 9:1; Luke 19:41 22:5 [a]Heb *YHWH,* usually rendered *LORD* [b]Or *against* [A]Lam 1:5; 2:2 [B]Is 37:3 [C]Is 10:6; 63:3 [D]Is 22:1 22:6 [a]Lit *man* [A]Is 21:2; Jer 49:35 [B]2 Kin 16:9; Amos 1:5; 9:7

21:9 Fallen, fallen is Babylon. The watchman proclaimed the tragic end of mighty Babylon, which initially fell to the Assyrians in 689 B.C. and again to the Persians in 539 B.C. Yet Isaiah's prediction looked forward to the ultimate fall of the great enemy of God, as verified by John's citation of this verse in Rev 14:8; 18:2 (cf. Jer 50:2; 51:8, 49).

21:10 my threshed *people* ... afflicted of the threshing floor! The violent threshing of grain portrayed Babylon's oppression of Israel, and the resultant grain was Israel's deliverance by God. The concise saying offered God's people hope.

21:11 Seir. Another name for Edom—located S of the Dead Sea and the home of Esau's descendants—this is the source of an inquiry directed to Isaiah. **how far gone is the night?** How long was the Assyrian oppression to last?

21:12 Morning ... night. The prophet promises a short-lived deliverance from Assyrian oppression, but quickly added the threat of Babylonian domination to follow soon.

21:13 Dedanites. Dedan was on the route to the Red Sea about 290 mi. SE of Dumah, in the northwestern part of the Arabian desert.

21:14 water ... bread. The prophet indicated that those fleeing the Assyrian army will need supplies. **Tema.** Tema was on the Red Sea route about 200 mi. SE of Dumah, in the northwestern part of the Arabian desert.

21:15 they have fled. The interior area of Arabia was a place of refuge for fugitives fleeing from the sophisticated armament of the Assyrians.

21:16 Kedar. Kedar covers the area in the northwestern part of the Arabian desert. **splendor of Kedar will terminate.** This prophecy anticipated the conquest of the region by Nebuchadnezzar, king of Babylon (Jer 49:28).

22:1 valley of vision. This referred to Israel, since God often revealed Himself to Jerusalem in visions. However, the unrepentant inhabitants displayed a marked lack of vision in their oblivion to the destruction that awaited them. **What is the matter with you ... ?** The prophet reproached the people for celebrating with wild parties when they should have been in deep repentance because of their sins. Apparently he anticipated a condition that arose in conjunction with Jerusalem's fall to the Babylonians in 586 B.C. But similar incursions by the Assyrians in either 711 or 701 B.C., from which the Lord delivered the city, had prompted the revelry among the people.

22:2 sword ... battle. Death came through starvation or disease as the Babylonians besieged the city.

22:3 rulers have fled. Rather than defend the city the way they ought, the leaders fled to save their own necks and in doing so, were captured (2Ki 25:4–7).

22:4 weep bitterly. Isaiah's pain was deep. He could not participate in the revelry because he saw the reality of the spiritual issues.

22:5 Lord GOD of hosts has a day. On a former occasion when the city was about to fall, terror had reigned among the citizens. It was to occur again, leaving no room for merriment.

22:6 Elam ... Kir. These lands had representatives in the Assyrian army that besieged Jerusalem.

22:7 choicest valleys. Valleys lying both in and around Jerusalem are to be full of enemy troops.

8 And He removed the
[a]defense of Judah.
In that day you [b]depended on the
weapons of the [A]house of the forest,
9 And you saw that the breaches
In the *wall* of the city of
David were many;
And you [A]collected the waters
of the lower pool.
10 Then you counted the
houses of Jerusalem
And tore down houses to
fortify the wall.
11 And you made a reservoir
[A]between the two walls
For the waters of the [B]old pool.
But you did not [a]depend on
Him who made it,
Nor did you [b]take into consideration
Him who planned it long ago.

12 Therefore in that day the Lord
[a]GOD of hosts called *you* to
[A]weeping, to wailing,
To [B]shaving the head and to
wearing sackcloth.
13 Instead, there is [A]gaiety and gladness,
Killing of cattle and
slaughtering of sheep,
Eating of meat and drinking of wine:
"[B]Let us eat and drink, for
tomorrow we may die."
14 But the LORD of hosts revealed
Himself [a]to me,
"Surely this [A]iniquity [B]shall
not be [b]forgiven you
[C]Until you die," says the
Lord [c]GOD of hosts.

15 Thus says the Lord [a]GOD of hosts,

"Come, go to this steward,
To [A]Shebna, who is in charge
of the *royal* household,
16 'What right do you have here,
And whom do you have here,
That you have [A]hewn a tomb
for yourself here,
You who hew a tomb on the height,
You who carve a resting place
for [a]yourself in the rock?
17 'Behold, the LORD is about to hurl
you headlong, O man.
And He is about to grasp you firmly
18 *And* roll you tightly like a ball,
To be [A]*cast* into a vast country;
There you will die
And there your splendid chariots will be,
You shame of your master's house.'
19 "I will [A]depose you from your office,
And [a]I will pull you down from your station.
20 "Then it will come about in that day,
That I will summon My servant
[A]Eliakim the son of Hilkiah,
21 And I will clothe him with your tunic
And tie your sash securely about him.
I will entrust him with your [a]authority,
And he will become a [A]father to
the inhabitants of Jerusalem
and to the house of Judah.
22 "Then I will set [A]the key of the [B]house
of David on his shoulder,
When he opens no one will shut,
When he shuts no one will [C]open.
23 "I will drive him *like* a [A]peg in a firm place,
And he will become a [B]throne of
glory to his father's house.

22:8 [a]Lit *screen, covering* [b]Or *looked to, considered* [A]1 Kin 7:2; 10:17 22:9 [A]2 Kin 20:20; Neh 3:16 22:11 [a]Or *look to, consider* [b]Lit *see...Him* [A]2 Kin 25:4; Jer 39:4 [B]2 Kin 20:20; 2 Chr 32:3, 4 22:12 [a]Heb *YHWH*, usually rendered *LORD* [A]Is 32:11; Joel 1:13; 2:17 [B]Mic 1:16 22:13 [A]Is 5:11, 22; 28:7, 8; Luke 17:26-29 [B]Is 56:12; 1 Cor 15:32 22:14 [a]Lit *in my ears* [b]Lit *atoned for* [c]Heb *YHWH*, usually rendered *LORD* [A]Is 13:11; 26:21; 30:13; 65:7 [B]1 Sam 3:14; Ezek 24:13 [C]Is 65:20 22:15 [a]Heb *YHWH*, usually rendered *LORD* [A]2 Kin 18:18, 26, 37; Is 36:3, 11, 22; 37:2 22:16 [a]Lit *himself* [A]2 Sam 18:18; 2 Chr 16:14; Matt 27:60 22:18 [A]Job 18:18; Is 17:13 22:19 [a]So with many ancient versions; Heb *He* [A]Job 40:11, 12; Ezek 17:24 22:20 [A]2 Kin 18:18; Is 36:3, 22; 37:2 22:21 [a]Lit *rule* [A]Gen 45:8; Job 29:16 22:22 [A]Rev 3:7 [B]Is 7:2, 13 [C]Job 12:14 22:23 [A]Ezra 9:8; Zech 10:4 [B]1 Sam 2:8; Job 36:7

22:8 house of the forest. Constructed by Solomon out of cedars (1Ki 7:2–6), the structure housed weaponry (1Ki 10:17) and other valuables (2Ch 9:20; Is 39:2).

22:9 city of David. Jerusalem bore this name (2Sa 5:6, 7, 9). *See note on 29:1.* **lower pool.** The pool of Siloam furnished the city's water supply. Hezekiah's lengthy underground conduit fed the pool from the Gihon Spring.

22:10 fortify the wall. Hezekiah rebuilt the damaged wall (2Ch 32:5), but did so while trusting God. His faith contrasts with that of the people Isaiah currently addresses (v. 11b).

22:11 old pool. This refers to the Gihon Spring, which the prophet sometimes referred to as the "upper pool" (7:3; 36:2; cf. 2Ki 18:17). **did not depend on Him who made it.** Preparations for the city's defense were purely external. The people gave no thought to the Creator of the city, the pool, or the present crisis (cf. 31:1), against whom their physical defenses were useless.

22:12, 13 sackcloth . . . gaiety and gladness. In the face of a crisis that required genuine repentance, the people responded with hilarity and self-indulgence. Contrast this spirit with the legitimate joy and gladness of God's people in 35:10; 51:11.

22:13 Let us eat and drink, for tomorrow we may die. Paul cites the same philosophy (1Co 15:32): If there is no resurrection, enjoyment in this life is all that matters. It utterly disregards God's eternal values.

22:14 shall not be forgiven. The Lord's prediction about the outcome of Isaiah's ministry (6:9, 10) found fulfillment.

22:15 Shebna, who is in charge of the *royal* household. Possibly of Egyptian extraction, this man was second in authority only to the king. Other OT references to Shebna refer to him as a "scribe" (36:22; 37:2; 2Ki 18:37; 19:2), his position after his demotion from steward as prophesied by Isaiah (see v. 19).

22:16 hewn a tomb. Shebna arranged construction of a tomb fit for a king as a memorial for himself, when he should have been attending to the spiritual affairs of Judah. The prophet condemns his arrogance.

22:17 O man. Literally, mighty or valiant man. Isaiah referred to Shebna's glorious estimate of himself.

22:18 vast country . . . die . . . shame. Far from receiving a luxurious burial in Jerusalem, Shebna died a shameful death in a foreign country.

22:19 depose you from your office. Arrogance caused Shebna's demotion from steward to scribe some time later in Hezekiah's reign but before 701 B.C. (36:1, 2).

22:20 My servant Eliakim. Eliakim, who replaced Shebna as steward or prime minister, was highly honored in being called "My servant" (*see note on 20:3*).

22:21 father . . . Judah. The steward had supreme authority under the king's oversight.

22:22 key of the house of David. This authority to admit or refuse admittance into the king's presence evidenced the king's great confidence in Eliakim. Jesus applied this terminology to Himself as one who could determine who would enter His future Davidic kingdom (Rev 3:7).

22:23 throne of glory. The "throne"

24 So they will hang on him all the glory of his father's house, offspring and [a]issue, all the least of
vessels, from bowls to all the jars. 25 In that day,"
declares the LORD of hosts, "the [A]peg driven in a
firm place will give way; it will even [B]break off and
fall, and the load hanging on it will be cut off, for
the [C]LORD has spoken."

THE FALL OF TYRE

23 The [a]oracle concerning [A]Tyre.

Wail, O [B]ships of [C]Tarshish,
For *Tyre* is destroyed, without
house *or* [b,D]harbor;
It is reported to them from
the land of [c,E]Cyprus.
2 [A]Be silent, you inhabitants
of the coastland,
You merchants of Sidon;
[a]Your messengers crossed the sea
3 And *were* on many waters.
[A]The grain of the [a,B]Nile, the harvest
of the River was her revenue;
And she was the [C]market of nations.
4 Be ashamed, O [A]Sidon;
For the sea speaks, the stronghold
of the sea, saying,
"I have neither travailed
nor given birth,
I have neither brought up young
men *nor* reared virgins."
5 When the report *reaches* Egypt,
They will be in [A]anguish at
the report of Tyre.
6 Pass over to [A]Tarshish;
Wail, O inhabitants of the coastland.
7 Is this your [A]jubilant *city,*
Whose origin is from antiquity,
Whose feet used to carry her to
[a]colonize distant places?

8 Who has planned this against Tyre,
[A]the bestower of crowns,
Whose merchants were
princes, whose traders were
the honored of the earth?
9 [A]The LORD of hosts has
planned it, to [B]defile the
pride of all beauty,
To despise all the [C]honored of the earth.
10 [a]Overflow your land like the Nile,
O daughter of Tarshish,
There is no more [b]restraint.
11 He has [A]stretched His hand
out [B]over the sea,
He has [C]made the kingdoms tremble;
The LORD has given a command
concerning Canaan to
[D]demolish its strongholds.

12 He has said, "[A]You shall exult no more,
O crushed virgin daughter of Sidon.
Arise, pass over to [a,B]Cyprus; even
there you will find no rest."

13 Behold, the land of the Chaldeans—this is the people *which* was not; [A]Assyria appointed it for [B]desert creatures—they erected their siege towers, they stripped its palaces, [C]they made it a ruin.

14 Wail, O [A]ships of Tarshish,
For your stronghold is destroyed.

22:24 [a]Or perhaps, *leaf* 22:25 [A]Is 22:23 [B]Esth 9:24, 25 [C]Is 46:11; Mic 4:4 23:1 [a]Or *burden of* [b]Lit *entering* [c]Heb *Kittim* [A]Josh 19:29; 1 Kin 5:1; Jer 25:22; 47:4; Ezek 26:1-27:36; Joel 3:4-8; Amos 1:9; Zech 9:2-4 [B]Is 2:16 [C]Gen 10:4; 1 Kin 10:22 [D]Is 24:10 [E]Gen 10:4; Is 23:12; Ezek 27:6 23:2 [a]So DSS; M.T. *Who passed over the sea, they replenished you* [A]Is 47:5 23:3 [a]Heb *Shihor* [A]Is 19:7-9 [B]Josh 13:3; 1 Chr 13:5; Jer 2:18 [C]Ezek 27:3-23 23:4 [A]Gen 10:15, 19; Josh 11:8; Judg 10:6; Jer 25:22; 27:3; 47:4; Ezek 28:21, 22 23:5 [A]Ex 15:14-16; Josh 2:9-11 23:6 [A]Is 23:1 23:7 [a]Lit *sojourn afar off* [A]Is 22:2; 32:13 23:8 [A]Ezek 28:2 23:9 [A]Is 2:11; 13:11 [B]Job 40:11, 12; Dan 4:37 [C]Is 5:13; 9:15 23:10 [a]Lit *Pass over* [b]Perhaps *girdle* or *shipyard* 23:11 [A]Ex 14:21; Is 14:26 [B]Is 19:5; 50:2 [C]Is 13:13 [D]Is 25:2; Zech 9:3, 4 23:12 [a]Heb *Kittim* [A]Ezek 26:13, 14; Rev 18:22 [B]Is 23:1 23:13 [A]Is 10:5 [B]Is 13:21; 18:6 [C]Is 10:7 23:14 [A]Is 2:16; Ezek 27:25, 26

symbolized the honor Eliakim was to bring to his family.

22:24 hang on him. Returning to the figure of a peg (v. 23), Isaiah noted how Eliakim's posterity will use him to gain glory for themselves.

22:25 peg … give way. After a time of faithful service, Eliakim faltered and fell, and all "hanging" on him fell as well.

23:1 Tyre. A Phoenician seaport on the Mediterranean Sea, located about 35 mi. N of Mt. Carmel and 28 mi. W of Mt. Hermon, Tyre supplied lumber for King Solomon's temple (1Ki 5:1, 7–12) and sailors for his navy (1Ki 9:26, 27). **ships of Tarshish.** Tarshish was most likely in Spain, so "ships of Tarshish" were large trading vessels capable of making distant voyages on the open sea all the way to the port of Tyre. The OT refers to them frequently (2:16; 60:9; 1Ki 10:22; 22:48; Ps 48:7; Eze 27:25; Jon 1:3). **destroyed.** Tyre was under siege 5 times between this prophecy and 332 B.C. Only the last of these attacks (in 332 B.C., by Alexander the Great) completely leveled and subdued the city. Ezekiel prophesied this destruction in Eze 26:3–27:36. **without house *or* harbor.** Weary from their long, difficult journey, sailors would find no customary haven of rest upon arrival at their destination, Tyre. **Cyprus.** Upon reaching this island in the eastern Mediterranean, the seamen would learn of Tyre's overthrow.

23:2 Sidon. Sidon was the other important Phoenician seaport, along with Tyre. Here it represented the rest of Phoenicia as reflecting the country's response to Tyre's overthrow.

23:3 grain of the Nile. Phoenicians carried much grain grown in Egypt aboard their ships. They also bought and sold much of the commodity.

23:4 neither travailed nor given birth. Isaiah spoke of barrenness, labor, and childbirth frequently (7:14; 8:3; 9:6; 26:16–18; 37:3; 44:3–5; 45:10, 11; 47:8; 49:21; 54:1–3; 66:9). Here the figure described Tyre, "the stronghold of the sea," bemoaning her desolate condition.

23:6, 7 Tarshish … distant places. Tyre's refugees had traveled throughout the Mediterranean world (see v. 1). They too lamented the city's fall.

23:7 from antiquity. Tyre was a very old city, dating from about two millennia before Christ.

23:8 bestower of crowns … princes … honored. Tyre had very high international prestige.

23:9 pride of all beauty. This furnished the reason the Lord of Hosts brought the overthrow of Tyre—their arrogance stemming from the city's prestige. They were foolish to rely on human glory.

23:10 no more restraint. The oracle invited the colonies of Tyre to exercise their freedom in taking advantage of the city's fall.

23:11 The LORD has given a command concerning Canaan. The Lord had caused the downfall of the territory of Canaan, which included Tyre and Sidon.

23:12 virgin daughter of Sidon. A city once noted for its freshness and revelry (cf. v. 7) will become like a used-up old woman, piecing together what is left. God used the Assyrians to crush her (contrast the virgin daughter of Zion in 37:22).

23:13 Chaldeans … Assyria. The example of the Chaldeans, another name for the Babylonians, reminded Tyre of their hopelessness against Assyria. Assyria ravaged Babylon in 689 B.C.

15 Now in that day Tyre will be forgotten for [A]sev-
enty years like the days of one king. At the end of
seventy years it will happen to Tyre as *in* the song
of the harlot:

16 Take *your* harp, walk about the city,
O forgotten harlot;
Pluck the strings skillfully,
sing many songs,
That you may be remembered.

17 It will come about at [A]the end of seventy years that
the LORD will visit Tyre. Then she will go back to her
harlot's wages and will [B]play the harlot with all the
kingdoms [a]on the face of the earth. 18 Her [A]gain and
her harlot's wages will be [B]set apart to the LORD; it
will not be stored up or hoarded, but her gain will
become sufficient food and choice attire for those
who dwell in the presence of the LORD.

JUDGMENT ON THE EARTH

24 Behold, the LORD [A]lays the earth waste, devastates it, distorts its surface and scatters its
inhabitants. 2 And the people will be like the priest,
the servant like his master, the maid like her mistress, the buyer like the seller, the lender like the borrower, the [A]creditor like the debtor. 3 The earth will
be completely laid waste and completely despoiled,
for the LORD has spoken this word. 4 The [A]earth
mourns *and* withers, the world fades *and* withers,
the [B]exalted of the people of the earth fade away.
5 The earth is also [A]polluted [a]by its inhabitants, for
they transgressed laws, violated statutes, [B]broke the
everlasting covenant. 6 Therefore, a [A]curse devours
the earth, and those who live in it are held guilty.
Therefore, the [B]inhabitants of the earth are burned,
and few men are left.

7 The [A]new wine mourns,
The vine decays,
All the merry-hearted sigh.
8 The [A]gaiety of tambourines ceases,
The noise of revelers stops,
The gaiety of the harp ceases.
9 They do not drink wine with song;
[A]Strong drink is [B]bitter to those who drink it.
10 The [A]city of chaos is broken down;
[B]Every house is shut up so
that none may enter.
11 There is an [A]outcry in the streets
concerning the wine;
[B]All joy [a]turns to gloom.
The gaiety of the earth is banished.
12 Desolation is left in the city
And the [A]gate is battered to ruins.
13 For [A]thus it will be in the midst of
the earth among the peoples,
As the [a]shaking of an olive tree,
As the gleanings when the
grape harvest is over.
14 [A]They raise their voices, they shout for joy;
They cry out from the [a]west concerning
the majesty of the LORD.
15 Therefore [A]glorify the LORD in the [a]east,
The [B]name of the LORD, the God of Israel,
In the [b,C]coastlands of the sea.
16 From the [A]ends of the earth we hear
songs, "[B]Glory to the Righteous One,"
But I say, "[a,C]Woe to me! [a]Woe
to me! Alas for me!
The [D]treacherous deal treacherously,
And the treacherous deal
very treacherously."
17 [A]Terror and pit and snare
[a]Confront you, O inhabitant of the earth.

23:15 [A]Jer 25:11, 22 23:17 [a]Lit *of the earth on the face of the land* [A]Is 23:15 [B]Ezek 16:25-29; Nah 3:4 23:18 [A]Ps 72:10, 11; Is 60:5-9; Mic 4:13 [B]Ex 28:36; Zech 14:20 24:1 [A]Is 2:19; 13:13; 24:19, 20; 30:32; 33:9 24:2 [A]Lev 25:36, 37; Deut 23:19, 20 24:4 [A]Is 33:9 [B]Is 2:12; 24:21 24:5 [a]Lit *under* [A]Gen 3:17; Num 35:33; Is 9:17; 10:6 [B]Is 33:8 24:6 [A]Josh 23:15; Is 34:5; 43:28; Zech 5:3, 4 [B]Is 1:31; 5:24; 9:19 24:7 [A]Is 16:10; Joel 1:10, 12 24:8 [A]Is 5:12, 14; Ezek 26:13; Hos 2:11; Rev 18:22 24:9 [A]Is 5:11, 22 [B]Is 5:20 24:10 [A]Is 34:11 [B]Is 23:1 24:11 [a]Lit is *darkened* [A]Jer 14:2; 46:12 [B]Is 16:10; 32:13 24:12 [A]Is 14:31; 45:2 24:13 [a]Lit *striking* [A]Is 17:6; 27:12 24:14 [a]Lit *sea* [A]Is 12:6; 48:20; 52:8; 54:1 24:15 [a]Lit *region of light* [b]Or *islands* [A]Is 25:3 [B]Mal 1:11 [C]Is 11:11; 42:4, 10, 12; 49:1; 51:5; 60:9; 66:19 24:16 [a]Lit *Wasting to me!* [A]Is 11:12; 42:10 [B]Is 28:5; 60:21 [C]Lev 26:39 [D]Is 21:2; 33:1; Jer 3:20; 5:11 24:17 [a]Lit *Are upon you* [A]Jer 48:43; Amos 5:19

23:15 seventy years. The devastation of Tyre was not permanent. A little village remains on the site of the ancient city to the present day. The time frame of the 70 years is obscure.

23:15, 16 song of the harlot . . . forgotten . . . remembered. Harlots sang to draw attention to themselves, attention not so hard to obtain in ancient days. Like those harlots, the people of Tyre were invited to sing songs drawing attention to their earlier prosperity.

23:17 the LORD will visit. With God's help, the city was to return.

23:18 set apart to the LORD. Even Tyre's sinful gain was to support Judah as her colonies once supported her.

24:1–27:13 These 4 chapters give praise to God for His future victory over all enemies and the final deliverance of Israel in the day of the Lord. The judgments in this chapter (24) look forward to the tribulation as described in Rev 6ff.

24:1 waste . . . distorts . . . scatters. The prophet generalized and broadened the destruction about which he had written more specifically in chaps. 13–23. The Lord is to deal with the whole earth more severely than He did at the tower of Babel or through the Noahic Flood.

24:2 people . . . priest . . . creditor . . . debtor. Neither rank, wealth, nor power were able to deliver from God's judgment.

24:3 the LORD has spoken. Isaiah used this expression or a comparable one 9 other times to emphasize the certainty of his predictions (1:20; 21:17; 22:25; 25:8; 37:22; 38:7; 38:15; 40:5; 58:14).

24:4 exalted of the people. The prophet again called attention to pride as the reason for God's judgment (cf. 23:9).

24:5 everlasting covenant. Likely, this referred to the Abrahamic Covenant, frequently referred to as "everlasting" (cf. Ge 17:7, 13, 19; 1Ch 16:15, 17; Pss 105:8, 10; 111:5, 9), which contained devotion to God's moral law and salvation by faith in Him.

24:6 few men are left. This Gentile remnant differed from that of Israel. Presumably they will join in support of Israel when the Messiah returns.

24:7–9 merry-hearted sigh. The future day of judgment will terminate all merriment derived from natural sources. Cf. Rev 18:22.

24:10 Every house. Houses normally provided security from outside harm, but they became inaccessible.

24:13 shaking of an olive tree. The same figure spoke of leanness in the judgment against Ephraim in 17:6.

24:14 raise their voices . . . shout. The songs of the godly remnant (cf. v. 6), celebrating God's righteous judgment, replace the drunken music (cf. v. 9).

24:15 glorify the LORD. This call summoned all people worldwide to attribute to the Lord what was due Him.

24:16 Glory to the Righteous One. This refers to God. **But I.** Isaiah could not yet join in the celebration of God's glory because he pondered the grief and corruption in the world before that final celebration of God's victory.

24:17, 18 pit . . . snare. The figure of an animal caught in a trap set by humans frequently

18 Then it will be that he who flees the
[a]report of disaster will fall into the pit,
And he who [b]climbs out of the pit
will be caught in the snare;
For the [A]windows [c]above are opened, and
the [B]foundations of the earth shake.
19 [A]The earth is broken asunder,
The earth is [B]split through,
The earth is shaken violently.
20 The earth [A]reels to and fro like a drunkard
And it totters like a [a]shack,
For its [B]transgression is heavy upon it,
And it will fall, [C]never to rise again.
21 So it will happen in that day,
That the LORD will [A]punish the
host of [a]heaven on high,
And the [B]kings of the earth on earth.
22 They will be gathered together
Like [A]prisoners in the [a]dungeon,
And will be confined in prison;
And after many days they
will [B]*be* punished.
23 Then the [A]moon will be abashed
and the sun ashamed,
For the [B]LORD of hosts will reign on
[C]Mount Zion and in Jerusalem,
And *His* glory will be before His elders.

SONG OF PRAISE FOR GOD'S FAVOR

25 O LORD, You are [A]my God;
I will exalt You, I will give
thanks to Your name;
For You have [B]worked wonders,
[C]Plans *formed* long ago, with
perfect faithfulness.
2 For You have made a city into a [A]heap,
A [B]fortified city into a ruin;
A [C]palace of strangers is a city no more,
It will never be rebuilt.
3 Therefore a strong people
will [A]glorify You;
[B]Cities of ruthless nations will revere You.
4 For You have been a [A]defense
for the helpless,
A defense for the needy in his distress,
A [B]refuge from the storm, a
shade from the heat;
For the breath of the [C]ruthless
Is like a *rain* storm *against* a wall.
5 Like heat in drought, You subdue
the [A]uproar of aliens;
Like heat by the shadow of a cloud, the
song of the ruthless is [a]silenced.

6 [A]The LORD of hosts will prepare
a [a]lavish banquet for [B]all
peoples on this mountain;
A banquet of [b]aged wine, [c]choice
pieces with marrow,
And [d]refined, aged wine.
7 And on this mountain He will swallow up
the [a,A]covering which is over all peoples,
Even the veil which is [b]stretched
over all nations.
8 He will [A]swallow up death for all time,
And the Lord [a]GOD will [B]wipe
tears away from all faces,
And He will remove the [C]reproach of
His people from all the earth;
For the LORD has spoken.

24:18 [a]Lit *sound of terror* [b]Lit *goes up from the midst of* [C]Lit *from the height;* i.e. heaven [A]Gen 7:11 [B]Ps 18:7; 46:2; Is 2:19, 21; 13:13 24:19 [A]Is 24:1 [B]Num 16:31, 32; Deut 11:6 24:20 [a]Or *hut* [A]Is 19:14; 24:1; 28:7 [B]Is 1:28; 43:27; 66:24 [C]Dan 11:19; Amos 8:14 24:21 [a]Lit *the height in the height* [A]Is 10:12; 13:11 [B]Ps 76:12 24:22 [a]Lit *pit* [A]Is 10:4; 42:22 [B]Ezek 38:8; Zech 9:11, 12 24:23 [A]Is 13:10 [B]Is 60:19, 20; Zech 14:6, 7; Rev 21:23; 22:5 [C]Mic 4:7; Heb 12:22 25:1 [A]Ex 15:2; Ps 118:28; Is 7:13; 49:4, 5; 61:10 [B]Ps 40:5; 98:1 [C]Eph 1:11 25:2 [A]Is 17:1; 26:5; 27:10; 32:19 [B]Is 17:3; 25:12 [C]Is 13:22; 32:14; 34:13 25:3 [A]Is 24:15 [B]Is 13:11 25:4 [A]Is 14:32; 17:10; 27:5; 33:16 [B]Is 4:6; 32:2 [C]Is 29:5, 20; 49:25 25:5 [a]Lit *humbled* [A]Jer 51:54-56 25:6 [a]Lit *feast of fat things;* i.e. abundance [b]Lit *wine on the lees* [c]Lit *fat pieces* [d]Lit *wine refined on the lees* [A]Is 1:19 [B]Is 2:2-4; 56:7 25:7 [a]Lit *face of the covering* [b]Lit *woven* [A]2 Cor 3:15, 16; Eph 4:18 25:8 [a]Heb *YHWH,* usually rendered *LORD* [A]Hos 13:14; 1 Cor 15:54 [B]Is 30:19; 35:10; 51:11; 65:19; Rev 7:17; 21:4 [C]Ps 69:9; 89:50, 51; Is 51:7; 54:4; Matt 5:11; 1 Pet 4:14

symbolized the principle that life is a series of inescapable traps (2Sa 22:6; Job 18:8–10; 22:10; Pss 18:5; 64:5; 106:36; 124:7; Jer 48:43, 44; La 3:47; Am 5:19).

24:18 windows above. In Noah's day, God judged with a flood (Ge 7:11). He will judge again from heaven, but not with a flood. Cf. Rev 6:13, 14; 8:3–13; 16:1–21. **foundations of the earth.** Unparalleled earthquakes will mark the future visitation during and after the fulfillment of Daniel's 70-week prophecy (*see note on 13:13*; cf. Mt 24:7; Rev 6:12, 14; 8:5; 11:19; 16:18).

24:20 drunkard ... shack. Two more comparisons picture the ultimate collapse of the presumably strong and dependable planet earth: a staggering drunkard and a flimsy lean-to shack.

24:21 the host of heaven on high ... kings. In the climactic phase of the day of the Lord, He will strike against rebelling forces, both angelic (Eph 6:12) and human. *See note on 2:12.*

24:22 confined in prison. The NT teaches more about the imprisonment of fallen angels before their final assignment to the lake of fire (2Pe 2:4; Jude 6; Rev 9:2, 3, 11; 11:7; 17:8; 20:1–10). It does the same regarding unbelieving humans (Lk 16:19–31; Rev 20:11–15).

24:23 moon ... abashed ... sun ashamed. In the eternal state after Christ's millennial reign, the glory of God and of the Lamb will replace the sun and moon as sources of light (Rev 21:23). **reign ... in Jerusalem.** In Rev 11:15–17; 19:6, 16 (cf. Lk 1:31–33), John confirmed this clear prophecy of Messiah's future earthly reign in Jerusalem.

25:1 wonders, plans *formed* long ago. Isaiah responded to God's final judgment of the world (chap. 24) with praise to Him for planning His actions long before their implementation.

25:2 a city into a heap ... never be rebuilt. The prophet did not stipulate which city, but a prophecy of Babylon's final destruction is in keeping with the context (21:9; cf. Jer 51:37; Rev 18).

25:3 strong people ... ruthless nations. When Christ reigns on earth, nations from the whole world will glorify and fear Him (see 24:14–16).

25:4 helpless ... needy. Another indicator of God's worthiness to be glorified is His upholding of the oppressed (cf. 11:4; 14:32).

25:4, 5 storm ... heat. Two weather extremes of Judah's climate illustrate how God will harbor the poor and needy: the sudden thunderstorm and the relentless heat.

25:6 this mountain. In the kingdom the Lord will host His great banquet on Mt. Zion for the faithful remnant (*see notes on 1:27; 2:2*).

25:7 covering ... veil. God will remove the death shrouds from those in attendance at His banquet.

25:8 swallow up death. God will swallow up death, which itself functions as a swallower of human beings (5:14; Pr 1:12). Paul notes the fulfillment of this promise in the resurrection of believers (1Co 15:54). **wipe tears away.** The Lord God will remove the sorrow associated with death (cf. 65:19). Revelation alludes to the tender action of this verse twice—once in 7:17 to describe the bliss of the redeemed in heaven, and once in 21:4 to describe ideal conditions in the New Jerusalem. **remove the reproach.** Israel will be the head of the nations and no longer the tail (Dt 28:13).

9 And it will be said in that day,
"Behold, [A]this is our God for whom we
have [B]waited that [C]He might save us.
This is the LORD for whom we have waited;
[D]Let us rejoice and be glad in His salvation."
10 For the hand of the LORD will
rest on this mountain,
And [A]Moab will be trodden
down in his place
As straw is trodden down in the
water of a manure pile.
11 And he will [A]spread out his
hands in the middle of it
As a swimmer spreads out
his hands to swim,
But *the Lord* will [B]lay low his pride
together with the trickery of his hands.
12 The [A]unassailable fortifications of
your walls He will bring down,
Lay low *and* cast to the ground,
even to the dust.

SONG OF TRUST IN GOD'S PROTECTION

26 [A]In that day this song will be sung in the
land of Judah:

"We have a [B]strong city;
He sets up walls and ramparts
for [a,C]security.
2 "Open the [A]gates, that the [B]righteous
nation may enter,
The one that [a]remains faithful.
3 "The steadfast of mind You will
keep in perfect [A]peace,
Because he trusts in You.
4 "[A]Trust in the LORD forever,
For in [a]GOD the LORD, *we have*
an everlasting [B]Rock.
5 "For He has brought low those who dwell
on high, the [A]unassailable city;
[B]He lays it low, He lays it low to the
ground, He casts it to the dust.
6 "[A]The foot will trample it,
The feet of the [B]afflicted, the
steps of the helpless."

7 The [A]way of the righteous is smooth;
O Upright One, [B]make the path
of the righteous level.
8 Indeed, *while following* the way of
[A]Your judgments, O LORD,
We have waited for You eagerly;
[B]Your name, even Your [C]memory,
is the desire of *our* souls.
9 [A]At night [a]my soul longs for You,
Indeed, [b]my spirit within me
[B]seeks You diligently;
For when the earth [c]experiences
Your judgments
The inhabitants of the world
[C]learn righteousness.
10 *Though* the wicked is shown favor,
He does not [A]learn righteousness;
He [B]deals unjustly in the
land of uprightness,
And does not perceive the
majesty of the LORD.

11 O LORD, Your hand is lifted up
yet they [A]do not see it.
[a]They see [B]*Your* zeal for the people
and are put to shame;
Indeed, [b,C]fire will devour
Your enemies.
12 LORD, You will establish [A]peace for us,
Since You have also performed
for us all our works.

25:9 [A]Is 35:2; 40:9; 52:10 [B]Is 8:17; 30:18; 33:2 [C]Is 33:22; 35:4; 49:25, 26; 60:16 [D]Ps 20:5; Is 35:1, 2, 10; 65:18; 66:10 25:10 [A]Is 16:14; Jer 48:1-47; Ezek 25:8-11; Amos 2:1-3; Zeph 2:9 25:11 [A]Is 5:25; 14:26 [B]Job 40:11; Is 2:10-12, 15-17; 16:6, 14 25:12 [A]Is 15:1; 25:2; 26:5 26:1 [a]Or *salvation* [A]Is 4:2; 12:1 [B]Is 14:31; 31:5, 9; 33:5, 6, 20-24 [C]Is 60:18 26:2 [a]Lit *keeps faithfulness* [A]Is 60:11, 18; 62:10 [B]Is 45:25; 54:14, 17; 58:8; 60:21; 61:3; 62:1, 2 26:3 [A]Is 26:12; 27:5; 57:19; 66:12 26:4 [a]Heb *YAH*, usually rendered *LORD* [A]Is 12:2; 50:10; 51:5 [B]Is 17:10; 30:29; 44:8 26:5 [A]Is 25:12 [B]Job 40:11-13 26:6 [A]Is 28:3 [B]Is 3:14, 15; 11:4; 29:19 26:7 [A]Is 57:2 [B]Ps 25:4, 5; 27:11; Is 42:16; 52:12 26:8 [A]Is 51:4; 56:1 [B]Is 12:4; 24:15; 25:1; 26:13 [C]Ex 3:15 26:9 [a]Lit with *my soul I long* [b]Lit with *my spirit…I seek* [c]Lit *has* [A]Ps 63:5, 6; 77:2; 119:62; Is 50:10; Luke 6:12 [B]Ps 63:1; 78:34; Matt 6:33 [C]Is 55:6; Hos 5:15 26:10 [A]Is 22:12, 13; 32:6, 7 [B]Hos 11:7; John 5:37, 38 26:11 [a]Or *Let them see…and be* [b]Or *let the fire for Your adversaries devour them* [A]Is 44:9, 18 [B]Is 9:7; 37:32; 59:17 [C]Is 5:24; 9:18, 19; 10:17; 66:15, 24; Heb 10:27 26:12 [A]Is 26:3

25:9 **LORD for whom we have waited.** To wait for God entails an ultimate trust in Him, not becoming impatient when His timetable for final salvation differs from ours (cf. 26:8; 33:2; 40:31).

25:10 **Moab.** Moab represented the rest of the nations as does Edom elsewhere (34:5–15; 63:1–6; Ob 1–9).

25:12 **fortifications … walls.** Moabite cities had highly fortified and elevated walls. Even these will not withstand God's judgment.

26:1–4 The redeemed remnant will sing praise to God over their impregnable city, Jerusalem.

26:1 **strong city.** In contrast to the typical city of confusion (24:10; 25:2; 26:5) that was doomed, God has a future city of prominence, the millennial Jerusalem (Zec 14:11).

26:2 **Open the gates.** Isaiah envisions the future Jerusalem, where only righteous Israel may enter. The redeemed remnant from other nations will come periodically to worship (Zec 14:16–19).

26:3 **perfect peace … trusts in You.** A fixed disposition of trust in the Lord brings a peace that the wicked can never know (48:22; 57:21). Such reliance precludes double-mindedness (Jas 1:6–8) and serving two masters (Mt 6:24).

26:4 **everlasting Rock.** Lit. the expression is "Rock of Ages," a rocky cliff where the trusting one may find shelter from attackers (cf. 12:2).

26:5, 6 **those who dwell on high … afflicted.** The arrogant inhabit the lofty city during its overthrow; the humble inhabit the strong city (v. 1) in its exaltation (cf. Jas 1:9, 10; 1Pe 5:5).

26:7 **path of the righteous level.** In a land of hilly, twisting roads, Isaiah spoke of a straight and level path for the feet of the poor and needy (cf. 40:3, 4; 42:16; 45:13).

26:8 **waited for You.** The future remnant divulges the key to its redemption—their complete dependence on the Lord, not humanly devised schemes.

26:9 **At night.** The pious long for God at all times. **judgments … learn righteousness.** God's punishing hand benefits sinners in leading them to repentance.

26:10 **not learn righteousness.** God evidences His love and mercy toward other wicked ones, but they turn their back on it.

26:11 **they do not see … They see.** The wicked, who are blind to God's authority and imminent judgment upon them, will be conscious of His compassion for His people Israel, to their own shame.

26:12 **will establish peace.** Though Israel's immediate future looks bleak, Isaiah expresses strong confidence that the nation will ultimately prosper.

13 O LORD our God, [A]other masters
besides You have ruled us;
But through You alone we
[a,B]confess Your name.
14 [A]The dead will not live, the [a]departed
spirits will not rise;
Therefore You have [B]punished
and destroyed them,
And You have wiped out all
remembrance of them.
15 [A]You have increased the nation, O LORD,
You have increased the nation,
You are glorified;
You have [B]extended all the
borders of the land.
16 O LORD, they sought You [A]in distress;
They [a]could only whisper a prayer,
Your chastening was upon them.
17 [A]As the pregnant woman approaches
the time to give birth,
She writhes *and* cries out
in her labor pains,
Thus were we before You, O LORD.
18 We were pregnant, we writhed *in labor,*
We [A]gave birth, as it seems, *only* to wind.
We could not accomplish
deliverance for the earth,
Nor were [B]inhabitants
of the world [a]born.
19 Your [A]dead will live;
[a]Their corpses will rise.
You who lie in the dust, [B]awake
and shout for joy,
For your dew *is as* the dew of the [b]dawn,
And the earth will [c]give birth
to the [d]departed spirits.

20 Come, my people, [A]enter into your rooms
And close your doors behind you;
Hide for a little [a,B]while
Until [C]indignation [b]runs *its* course.
21 For behold, the LORD is about to
[A]come out from His place
To [B]punish the inhabitants of the
earth for their iniquity;
And the earth will [C]reveal
her bloodshed
And will no longer cover her slain.

THE DELIVERANCE OF ISRAEL

27 In that day [A]the LORD will punish
[a,B]Leviathan the fleeing serpent,
With His fierce and great
and mighty sword,
Even [a]Leviathan the twisted serpent;
And [C]He will kill the dragon
who *lives* in the sea.

2 In that day,
"A [a,A]vineyard of wine, sing of it!
3 "I, the LORD, am its keeper;
[A]I water it every moment.
So that no one will [a]damage it,
I [B]guard it night and day.
4 "I have no wrath.
Should [a]someone give Me [A]briars
and thorns in battle,
Then I would step on them, [B]I would
burn them [b]completely.
5 "Or let him [a,A]rely on My protection,
Let him make peace with Me,
Let him [B]make peace with Me."
6 [a]In the days to come Jacob
[A]will take root,
Israel will [B]blossom and sprout,
And they will fill the [b]whole
world with [C]fruit.

7 Like the striking of Him who has
struck them, has [A]He struck them?
Or like the slaughter of His slain,
[a]have they been slain?

26:13 [a]Or *cause to be remembered* [A]Is 2:8; 10:11 [B]Is 63:7 26:14 [a]Or *shades* [A]Deut 4:28; Ps 135:17; Is 8:19; Hab 2:19 [B]Is 10:3 26:15 [A]Is 9:3 [B]Is 33:17; 54:2, 3 26:16 [a]Lit *sound forth a whisper* [A]Is 37:3; Hos 5:15 26:17 [A]Is 13:8; 21:3; John 16:21 26:18 [a]Lit *fallen* [A]Is 33:11; 59:4 [B]Ps 17:14 26:19 [a]So with some ancient versions; Heb *My* [b]Lit *lights* [c]Lit *cause to fall* [d]Or *shades* [A]Is 25:8; Ezek 37:1-14; Dan 12:2; Hos 13:14 [B]Eph 5:14 26:20 [a]Lit *moment* [b]Lit *passes over* [A]Ex 12:22, 23; Ps 91:1, 4 [B]Ps 30:5; Is 54:7, 8; 2 Cor 4:17 [C]Is 10:5, 25; 13:5; 34:2; 66:14 26:21 [A]Mic 1:3; Jude 14 [B]Is 13:11; 30:12-14; 65:6, 7 [C]Job 16:18; Luke 11:50 27:1 [a]Or *sea monster* [A]Is 66:16 [B]Job 3:8; 41:1; Ps 74:14; 104:26 [C]Is 51:9 27:2 [a]Some mss read *a vineyard of delight* [A]Ps 80:8; Is 5:7; Jer 2:21 27:3 [a]Lit *punish* [A]Is 58:11 [B]1 Sam 2:9; Is 31:5; John 10:28 27:4 [a]Lit *who* [b]Lit *altogether* [A]2 Sam 23:6; Is 10:17 [B]Is 33:12; Matt 3:12; Heb 6:8 27:5 [a]Lit *take hold of* [A]Is 12:2; 25:4 [B]Job 22:21; Is 26:3, 12; Rom 5:1; 2 Cor 5:20 27:6 [a]Lit *Those coming* [b]Lit *face of* [A]Is 37:31 [B]Is 35:1, 2; Hos 14:5, 6 [C]Is 4:2 27:7 [a]Lit *he was slain* [A]Is 10:12, 17; 30:31-33; 31:8, 9; 37:36-38

26:13 masters besides You. Israel's history was replete with periods of foreign domination by the likes of Egypt and Assyria.

26:14 departed spirits will not rise. These foreign overlords are to be a thing of the past; they are not to appear again on the earthly scene.

26:15 have increased the nation. With prophetic certainty from the perspective of Israel's future restoration, Isaiah saw the expansion of Israel's borders as an accomplished fact.

26:16 distress ... chastening. The hard experiences of Israel's history drove her to call on God.

26:17, 18 pregnant woman. Israel's tumultuous history is compared to a pregnant woman in labor.

26:18 not accomplish deliverance. All the nation's effort was to no avail because they did not depend on the Lord.

26:19 dead will live. This speaks of the raising of corporate Israel to participate in the great future banquet (cf. Eze 37). Daniel 12:2 speaks of the resurrection of individual OT saints.

26:20 for a little while. Israel's final restoration was not immediately at hand. Hence she had to continue praying in solitude for that restoration until the time of God's indignation would pass.

26:21 reveal her bloodshed. The innocent killed by their oppressors are to come to life (cf. v. 19) and testify against their murderers.

27:1 Leviathan. *See note on Job 41:1.*

27:2–6 This vineyard of the Lord contrasts sharply with the one in 5:1–7. Far from a disappointment to the vinekeeper, this one bore abundant fruit (v. 6).

27:2 vineyard. Verse 6 identifies this vineyard as Israel.

27:3 I guard it night and day. God's future provisions for restored Israel will be complete.

27:4 I have no wrath. The time for Israel's punishment by God will pass. **briars *and* thorns ... burn them.** I.e., the enemies of His people.

27:5 make peace with Me. The enemies of Israel may make peace with God.

27:6 fill the whole world. In the future kingdom of the Messiah, restored Israel will rule with Him and fill the earth with the fruit of righteousness and peace.

27:7 striking ... struck. God has tempered His dealings with Israel, but not so with those He used to punish Israel. His compassion for the other nations has come to an end.

8 You contended with them [a]by banishing
them, by [A]driving them away.
With His fierce wind He has expelled
them on the day of the [B]east wind.
9 Therefore through this Jacob's
iniquity will be [A]forgiven;
And this will be [a]the full price of
the [b,B]pardoning of his sin:
When he makes all the [C]altar stones
like pulverized chalk stones;
When [c]Asherim and incense
altars will not stand.
10 For the fortified city is [A]isolated,
A [a]homestead forlorn and
forsaken like the desert;
[B]There the calf will graze,
And there it will lie down and
[b]feed on its branches.
11 When its [A]limbs are dry, they are broken off;
Women come *and* make a fire with them,
For they are not a people of [B]discernment,
Therefore [C]their Maker [D]will not
have compassion on them.
And their Creator will not be
gracious to them.

12 In that day the LORD [A]will start *His* threshing
from the flowing stream of the [B]Euphrates to the
brook of Egypt, and you will be [C]gathered up one by
one, O sons of Israel. 13 It will come about also in that
day that a great [A]trumpet will be blown, and those
who were perishing in the land of [B]Assyria and who
were scattered in the land of Egypt will come and
[C]worship the LORD in the holy mountain at Jerusalem.

EPHRAIM'S CAPTIVITY PREDICTED

28 Woe to the proud crown of the
[A]drunkards of [B]Ephraim,
And to the fading flower of
its glorious beauty,
Which is at the head of the [a]fertile valley
Of those who are [b]overcome with wine!
2 Behold, the Lord has a strong
and [A]mighty *agent;*
As a storm of [B]hail, a tempest
of destruction,
Like a storm of [C]mighty overflowing waters,
He has cast *it* down to the
earth with *His* hand.
3 The proud crown of the drunkards of
Ephraim is [A]trodden under foot.
4 And the fading flower of its glorious beauty,
Which is at the head of the [a]fertile valley,
Will be like the [A]first-ripe fig
prior to summer,
Which [b]one sees,
And [c]as soon as it is in his [d]hand,
He swallows it.
5 In that day the [A]LORD of hosts will
become a beautiful [B]crown
And a glorious diadem to the
remnant of His people;
6 A [A]spirit of justice for him
who sits in judgment,
A [B]strength to those who repel
the [a]onslaught at the gate.
7 And these also [A]reel with wine and
stagger from strong drink:
[B]The priest and [C]the prophet
reel with strong drink,
They are confused by wine, they
stagger from [D]strong drink;
They reel while [a]having [E]visions,
They totter *when rendering* judgment.
8 For all the tables are full of filthy [A]vomit,
without a *single clean* place.

9 "To [A]whom would He teach knowledge,
And to whom would He
interpret the message?
Those *just* [B]weaned from milk?
Those *just* taken from the breast?

27:8 [a]Some ancient versions read *by exact measure* [A]Is 50:1; 54:7 [B]Jer 4:11; Ezek 19:12; Hos 13:15 27:9 [a]Lit *all the fruit* [b]Lit *removing* [c]I.e. wooden symbols of a female deity [A]Is 1:25; 48:10; Dan 11:35 [B]Rom 11:27 [C]Ex 34:13; Deut 12:3; 2 Kin 10:26; Is 17:8 27:10 [a]Lit *pasture* [b]Lit *consume* [A]Is 32:13, 14 [B]Is 17:2 27:11 [A]Is 18:5 [B]Deut 32:28; Is 1:3; 5:13; Jer 8:7 [C]Deut 32:18; Is 43:1, 7; 44:2, 21, 24 [D]Is 9:17 27:12 [A]Is 11:11; 17:6; 24:13; 56:8 [B]Gen 15:18 [C]Deut 30:3, 4; Neh 1:9 27:13 [A]Lev 25:9; 1 Chr 15:24; Matt 24:31; Rev 11:15 [B]Is 19:24, 25 [C]Is 19:21, 23; 49:7; 66:23; Zech 14:16; Heb 12:22 28:1 [a]Lit *valley of fatness* [b]Lit *smitten* [A]Is 28:7; Hos 7:5 [B]Is 9:9 28:2 [A]Is 8:7; 40:10 [B]Is 28:17; 30:30; 32:19; Ezek 13:11 [C]Is 8:6, 7; 30:28; Nah 1:8 28:3 [A]Is 26:6; 28:18 28:4 [a]Lit *valley of fatness* [b]Lit *the one seeing sees* [c]Lit *while it is yet* [d]Lit *palm* [A]Hos 9:10; Mic 7:1; Nah 3:12 28:5 [A]Is 41:16; 45:25; 60:1, 19 [B]Is 62:3 28:6 [a]Lit *battle* [A]1 Kin 3:28; Is 11:2; 32:15, 16; John 5:30 [B]2 Chr 32:6-8; Is 25:4 28:7 [a]Lit *seeing* [A]Is 5:11, 22; 22:13; 56:12; Hos 4:11 [B]Is 24:2 [C]Is 9:15 [D]Hab 2:15, 16 [E]Is 29:11 28:8 [A]Jer 48:26 28:9 [A]Is 2:3; 28:26; 30:20; 48:17; 50:4; 54:13 [B]Ps 131:2

27:8 driving them away. The Lord sent Judah into captivity to awaken the nation to trust in Him.

27:9 iniquity will be forgiven. Jacob atoned for his iniquity by undergoing punishment from God.

27:10 fortified city. The city symbolized Judah's oppressors (cf. 24:10; 25:2; 26:5).

27:11 will not have compassion on them. In contrast with His dealings with Israel, the Creator will deal a fatal blow to her enemies.

27:12 gathered up one by one. After the judgment of her enemies at the end of Daniel's 70th week, the faithful remnant of Israelites will return to their land (Mt 24:31).

27:13 worship the LORD ... at Jerusalem. The prophet reiterates one of his great themes: future worship of regathered Israel on Mt. Zion (24:23; 25:6, 7, 10).

28:1 Woe. The prominent thought in this word is impending disaster. **crown.** The walls of Samaria were the "crown" of a beautiful hill overlooking a lush valley leading toward the Mediterranean coast. **Ephraim.** The northern kingdom of Israel had fallen to the Assyrians, leaving a lesson for Jerusalem under similar circumstances to learn about foreign alliances. **overcome with wine.** Licentious living prevailed in Ephraim before her fall (vv. 3, 7; Am 4:1; 6:1, 6).

28:2 a storm of mighty ... waters. Isaiah drew on forceful figures of speech to wake his readers from their lethargy in the face of the awfulness of an impending Assyrian invasion.

28:4 first-ripe fig prior to summer. Figs ripened before the end-of-summer harvest were devoured immediately. So the Assyrian conquest of Ephraim would be rapid.

28:5 a beautiful crown. The true crown will replace the fraudulent "proud crown" (v. 1). **remnant of His people.** Isaiah again sounded the note of a faithful remnant in the day of the Lord (cf. 10:20–22; 11:11, 16; 37:31, 32; 46:3).

28:6 spirit of justice. In that day of Messiah's reign, the empowering Spirit will prevail in bringing justice to the world (cf. 11:2).

28:7 priest ... prophet ... totter. Drunkenness had infected even the religious leadership of the nation, resulting in false spiritual guidance of the people.

28:8 without a *single clean* place. When leaders wallowed in filth, what hope did the nation have?

28:9 weaned from milk. The drunken leaders resented it when Isaiah and other true prophets treated them as toddlers, by reminding them of elementary truths of right and wrong.

10 "For *He says,*
'[a,A]Order on order, order on order,
Line on line, line on line,
A little here, a little there.' "
11 Indeed, He will speak
to this people
Through [A]stammering lips
and a foreign tongue,
12 He who said to them, "Here is
[A]rest, give rest to the weary,"
And, "Here is repose," but
they would not listen.
13 So the word of the LORD
to them will be,
"[a]Order on order, order on order,
Line on line, line on line,
A little here, a little there,"
That they may go and [A]stumble
backward, be broken, snared
and taken captive.

JUDAH IS WARNED

14 Therefore, [A]hear the word of
the LORD, O [B]scoffers,
Who rule this people who
are in Jerusalem,
15 Because you have said, "We have
made a [A]covenant with death,
And with [a]Sheol we have
made a [b]pact.
[B]The overwhelming [c]scourge
will not reach us when
it passes by,
For we have made [C]falsehood our
refuge and we have [D]concealed
ourselves with deception."
16 Therefore thus says the Lord [a]GOD,
"[A]Behold, I am laying in Zion a
stone, a tested [B]stone,
A costly cornerstone *for* the
foundation, [b]firmly placed.
He who believes *in it* will not be [c]disturbed.
17 "I will make [A]justice the measuring line
And righteousness the level;
Then [B]hail will sweep away
the refuge of lies
And the waters will overflow
the secret place.
18 "Your [A]covenant with death
will be [a,B]canceled,
And your pact with Sheol will not stand;
When the [A]overwhelming
scourge passes through,
Then you become its [C]trampling *place.*
19 "As [A]often as it passes through,
it will [a]seize you;
For [B]morning after morning it
will pass through, *anytime*
during the day or night,
And it will be [b]sheer [C]terror to
understand [c]what it means."
20 The bed is too short on which to stretch out,
And the [A]blanket is too [a]small
to wrap oneself in.
21 For the LORD will rise up as
at Mount [A]Perazim,
He will be stirred up as in the
valley of [B]Gibeon,
To do His [C]task, His [a,D]unusual task,
And to work His work, His
[b]extraordinary work.

28:10 [a]Heb *Sav lasav, sav lasav, Kav lakav, kav lakav, Ze'er sham, ze'er sham* These Hebrew monosyllables, imitating the babbling of a child, mock the prophet's preaching [A]2 Chr 36:15; Neh 9:30 28:11 [A]Is 33:19; 1 Cor 14:21 28:12 [A]Is 11:10; 30:15; 32:17, 18; Jer 6:16; Matt 11:28, 29 28:13 [a]V 10, note 1 The LORD responds to their scoffing by imitating their mockery, to represent the unintelligible language of a conqueror [A]Is 8:15; Matt 21:44 28:14 [A]Is 1:10; 28:22 [B]Is 29:20 28:15 [a]I.e. the nether world [b]So some ancient versions; Heb *seer* [c]Or *flood* [A]Is 28:18 [B]Is 8:8; 28:2; 30:28; Dan 11:22 [C]Is 9:15; 30:9; 44:20; 59:3, 4; Ezek 13:22 [D]Is 29:15 28:16 [a]Heb *YHWH,* usually rendered *LORD* [b]Lit *well-laid* [c]Lit *in a hurry* [A]Rom 9:33; 10:11; 1 Pet 2:6 [B]Ps 118:22; Is 8:14, 15; Matt 21:42; Mark 12:10; Luke 20:17; Acts 4:11; Eph 2:20 28:17 [A]2 Kin 21:13; Is 5:16; 30:18; 61:8; Amos 7:7-9 [B]Is 28:2 28:18 [a]Lit *covered over* [A]Is 28:15 [B]Is 7:7; 8:10 [C]Is 28:3; Dan 8:13 28:19 [a]Lit *take* [b]Lit *only* [c]Lit *the report,* or, *the message* [A]2 Kin 24:2 [B]Is 50:4 [C]Job 6:4; 18:11; 24:17; Ps 55:4; 88:15; Lam 2:22 28:20 [a]Lit *narrow* [A]Is 59:6 28:21 [a]Lit *task is strange* [b]Lit *work is alien* [A]2 Sam 5:20; 1 Chr 14:11 [B]Josh 10:10, 12; 2 Sam 5:25; 1 Chr 14:16 [C]Is 10:12; 29:14; 65:7 [D]Lam 2:15; 3:33; Luke 19:41-44

28:10 order on order .... little there. This is the drunkard's sarcastically mocking response to corrective advice from the prophet. Transliterated, the Hebrew monosyllables are *Sav lasav, sav lasav, Kav lakav, kav lakav, Ze'er sham, ze'er sham.* These imitations of a young child's babbling ridicule Isaiah's preaching.

28:11 foreign tongue. Since the drunkards would not listen to God's prophet, he responded to them by predicting their subservience to Assyrian taskmasters, who would give them instructions in a foreign language. The NT divulges an additional meaning of this verse that anticipates God's use of the miraculous gift of tongues as a credential of His NT messengers (*see notes on 1Co 14:21, 22*; cf. Dt 28:49; Jer 5:15; 1Co 14:21).

28:12 Here is rest ... repose ... not listen. In simple language they could understand, God offered them relief from their oppressors, but they would not listen.

28:13 order on order .... little there. In light of their rejection, the Lord imitated the mockery of the drunkards in jabber they could not understand (see v. 10).

28:14 Therefore. In light of the tragedies that had befallen Ephraim (vv. 1–13), the scornful leaders in Jerusalem needed to steer a course different from relying on foreign powers for deliverance.

28:15 covenant with death. Scornful leaders in Jerusalem had made an agreement with Egypt to help defend themselves against the Assyrians. **overwhelming scourge.** Combining images of an overflowing river and a whip, the people bragged about their invincibility to foreign invasion. **falsehood ... deception.** Jerusalem's leaders yielded to expediency for the sake of security. Without directly admitting it, they had taken refuge in deceit and falsehood.

28:16 cornerstone *for* the foundation. The Lord God contrasted the only sure refuge with the false refuge of relying on foreigners (v. 15). This directly prophesied the coming of the Messiah (Mt 21:42; Mk 12:10; Lk 20:17; Ac 4:11; Ro 9:33; Eph 2:20; 1Pe 2:6–8; cf. 8:14, 15; Ps 118:22). **disturbed.** The Heb. word is "hurry." The Greek OT interprets this Hebrew verb for "hurry" in the sense of "put to shame," furnishing the basis of the NT citations of this verse (Ro 9:33; 10:11; 1Pe 2:6).

28:17 justice the measuring line. When the Messiah rules His kingdom, the system of justice will contrast strongly with the refuge of lies in which Jerusalem's leaders engaged (see v. 15).

28:18 covenant with death ... will not stand. Trusting in foreign deliverers will utterly fail (see. v. 15).

28:19 morning after morning. The Assyrians repeatedly plundered the area around Jerusalem, provoking great terror among the city's inhabitants.

28:20 bed is too short ... blanket is too small. A proverbial expression about short beds and narrow sheets, telling Jerusalem that foreign alliances are inadequate preparations for the defense of the city.

28:21 Mount Perazim ... valley of Gibeon. Just as the Lord defeated the Philistines at Mt. Perazim (2Sa 5:19, 20; 1Ch 14:10, 11) and

22 And now do not carry
on as [A]scoffers,
Or your fetters will be made stronger;
For I have heard from the
Lord [a]GOD of hosts
Of decisive [B]destruction
on all the earth.

23 Give ear and hear my voice,
Listen and hear my words.
24 Does the [a]farmer plow
[b]continually to plant seed?
Does he *continually* [c]turn and
harrow the ground?
25 Does he not level its surface
And sow dill and scatter [A]cummin
And [a]plant [B]wheat in rows,
Barley in its place and rye
within its [b]area?
26 For his God instructs and
teaches him properly.
27 For dill is not threshed with
a [A]threshing sledge,
Nor is the cartwheel [a]driven
over cummin;
But dill is beaten out with a rod,
and cummin with a club.
28 *Grain for* bread is crushed,
Indeed, he does not continue
to thresh it forever.
Because the wheel of *his*
cart and his horses
eventually [a]damage *it,*
He does not thresh it longer.
29 This also comes from the
LORD of hosts,
Who has made *His* counsel [A]wonderful
and *His* wisdom [B]great.

JERUSALEM IS WARNED

29 Woe, O [a]Ariel, [a]Ariel the city
where David *once* [A]camped!
Add year to year, [b,B]observe
your feasts on schedule.
2 I will bring distress to Ariel,
And she will be *a city of*
lamenting and [A]mourning;
And she will be like an Ariel to me.
3 I will [A]camp against you [a]encircling *you,*
And I will set siegeworks against you,
And I will raise up battle
towers against you.
4 Then you will [A]be brought low;
From the earth you will speak,
And from the dust *where*
you are prostrate
Your words *will come.*
Your voice will also be like that of
a [a]spirit from the ground,
And your speech will whisper
from the dust.

5 But the multitude of your [a]enemies
will become like fine [A]dust,
And the multitude of the [B]ruthless ones
like the chaff which [b]blows away;
And it will happen [C]instantly, suddenly.
6 From the LORD of hosts you will
be [A]punished with [B]thunder and
earthquake and loud noise,
With whirlwind and tempest and
the flame of a consuming fire.
7 And the [A]multitude of all the nations
who wage war against [a]Ariel,
Even all who wage war against her and
her stronghold, and who distress her,
Will be like a dream, a [B]vision of the night.

28:22 [a]Heb *YHWH*, usually rendered *LORD* [A]Is 28:14 [B]Is 10:22, 23 28:24 [a]Lit *plowman* [b]Lit *all day* [c]Lit *open* 28:25 [a]Lit *put* [b]Lit *region* [A]Matt 23:23 [B]Ex 9:32 28:27 [a]Lit *rolled* [A]Amos 1:3 28:28 [a]Lit *discomfit* 28:29 [A]Is 9:6 [B]Is 31:2; Rom 11:33 29:1 [a]I.e. Lion of God, or Jerusalem [b]Lit *let your feasts run their round* [A]2 Sam 5:9 [B]Is 1:14; 5:12; 22:12, 13; 29:9, 13 29:2 [A]Is 3:26; Lam 2:5 29:3 [a]Lit *like a circle* [A]Luke 19:43, 44 29:4 [a]Or *ghost* [A]Is 8:19 29:5 [a]Lit *strangers* [b]Lit *passes away* [A]Is 17:13; 41:15, 16 [B]Is 13:11; 25:3; 29:20 [C]Is 17:14; 30:13; 47:11; 1 Thess 5:3 29:6 [A]Is 10:3; 26:14, 21 [B]1 Sam 2:10; Matt 24:7; Mark 13:8; Luke 21:11; Rev 11:13, 19; 16:18 29:7 [a]V 1, note 1 [A]Mic 4:11, 12; Zech 12:9 [B]Job 20:8; Ps 73:20; Is 17:14

the Canaanites in the Valley of Gibeon (Jos 10:6–11), He will do so against any who mock Him, even Jerusalemites.

28:22 decisive destruction. God had decreed something unusual (v. 21), the destruction of His own wicked people. Yet, they could escape if they repented.

28:23 Give ear. The parable of a farmer underlined the lessons of judgment threats in vv. 18–22. As the farmer does his different tasks, each in the right season and proportion, so God adopts His measures to His purposes: now mercy, then judgment; punishing sooner, then later. His purpose was not to destroy His people, any more than the farmer's object in his threshing or plowing is to destroy his crop.

28:24 plow continually … *continually* turn. No ordinary farmer plows and turns the soil endlessly. He sows also in accord with what is proper.

28:25 sow … scatter … plant. After preparing the soil, the farmer carefully plants the seed.

28:26 God instructs … him. Farming intelligently is a God-given instinct.

28:27, 28 God-given understanding prevails in the threshing of various types of grain.

28:29 counsel wonderful. If God's way in the physical realm of farming is best, why did Jerusalem persist in refusing to accept His spiritual guidance?

29:1 Ariel. The word means "lion of God," referring to the city's strength, and perhaps "hearth of God," referring to the place where the altar of God always burns. Verses 7, 8 show this to be a name for Jerusalem, and the chapter looks to the invasion of Jerusalem because of unbelief. ***where* David *once* camped.** David named Jerusalem "the city of David" (22:9; 2Sa 5:7, 9; cf. 2Sa 6:10, 12, 16; 1Ki 2:10; 3:1; 8:1; 9:24; 14:31; 15:8; 2Ki 8:24; 9:28; 12:21; 14:20; 15:7, 38; 16:20; 1Ch 11:5, 7; 13:13; 15:1, 29; 2Ch 5:2; 8:11; 12:16; 14:1; 16:14; 21:1, 20; 24:16, 25; 27:9; 32:5, 30; 33:14; Ne 3:15; 12:37; Lk 2:4, 11). **feasts.** Jerusalem's cycle of religious ceremonies was meaningless to God.

29:3 set siegeworks. God encamped against Jerusalem through His instruments, first the Assyrians (701 B.C.) and then the Babylonians (586 B.C.).

29:4 From the earth … from the dust. Jerusalem will be like a captive, humbled to the dust. Her voice will come from the earth like that of a medium spirit, like the voice of the dead was supposed to be. This would be fitting for her sins of necromancy.

29:5–8 In God's time, after Jerusalem's punishment, those who fought against the city will themselves come under God's judgment.

29:5 instantly, suddenly. God's demolition of Israel's enemies will be very abrupt, as was the repulsion of the Assyrians from Jerusalem in 701 B.C.

29:6 thunder and earthquake and loud noise. This terminology points to the storm theophany marking the termination of the seals, trumpets, and bowls in Revelation (Rev 8:5; 11:19; 16:18).

29:7 dream. All the threat to the city from enemy nations will fade like a bad dream when one awakens.

8 It will be as when a hungry man dreams—
And behold, he is eating;
But when he awakens, his
[a]hunger is not satisfied,
Or as when a thirsty man dreams—
And behold, he is drinking,
But when he awakens, behold, he is faint
And his [a]thirst is not quenched.
[A]Thus the multitude of all
the nations will be
Who wage war against Mount Zion.

9 [A]Be delayed and wait,
Blind yourselves and be blind;
They [B]become drunk, but not with wine,
They stagger, but not with strong drink.
10 For the LORD has poured over
you a spirit of deep [A]sleep,
He has [B]shut your eyes, the prophets;
And He has covered your heads, the seers.

11 The entire vision will be to you like the words of
a sealed [a,A]book, which when they give it to the one
who [b]is literate, saying, "Please read this," he will
say, "I cannot, for it is sealed." 12 Then the [a]book will
be given to the one who [b]is illiterate, saying, "Please
read this." And he will say, "I [c]cannot read."
13 Then the Lord said,

"Because [A]this people draw
near with their [a]words
And honor Me with their [b]lip service,
But they remove their hearts far from Me,
And their [c]reverence for Me [d]consists
of [e]tradition learned *by rote,*
14 Therefore behold, I will once again
deal [A]marvelously with this
people, wondrously marvelous;
And [B]the wisdom of their
wise men will perish,
And the discernment of their
discerning men will be concealed."

15 Woe to those who deeply [A]hide
their [a]plans from the LORD,
And whose [B]deeds are *done*
in a dark place,
And they say, "[C]Who sees us?"
or "Who knows us?"
16 You turn *things* around!
Shall the potter be considered
[a]as equal with the clay,
That [A]what is made would say to its
maker, "He did not make me";
Or what is formed say to
him who formed it, "He has
no understanding"?

BLESSING AFTER DISCIPLINE

17 Is it not yet just a little while
[a]Before Lebanon will be turned
into a [A]fertile field,
And the fertile field will be
considered as a forest?
18 On that day the [A]deaf will
hear [B]words of a book,
And out of *their* gloom and darkness
the [C]eyes of the blind will see.
19 The [A]afflicted also will increase
their gladness in the LORD,
And the [B]needy of mankind will
rejoice in the Holy One of Israel.
20 For the [A]ruthless will come to an end
and the [B]scorner will be finished,
Indeed [C]all who [a]are intent on
doing evil will be cut off;

29:8 [a]Lit *soul* [A]Is 54:17 29:9 [A]Is 29:1 [B]Is 51:17, 21, 22; 63:6 29:10 [A]Ps 69:23; Is 6:9, 10; Mic 3:6; Rom 11:8 [B]Is 44:18; 2 Thess 2:9-12 29:11 [a]Or *scroll* [b]Lit *knows books* [A]Is 8:16; Dan 12:4, 9; Matt 13:11 29:12 [a]Or *scroll* [b]Lit *does not know books* [c]Lit *do not know books* 29:13 [a]Lit *mouth* [b]Lit *lips* [c]Lit *fear of Me* [d]Lit *is* [e]Lit *commandment of rulers* [A]Ezek 33:31; Matt 15:8, 9; Mark 7:6, 7 29:14 [A]Is 6:9, 10; 28:21; 65:7; Hab 1:5 [B]Is 44:25; Jer 8:9; 49:7; 1 Cor 1:19 29:15 [a]Lit *counsel* [A]Ps 10:11, 13; Is 28:15; 30:1 [B]Job 22:13; Is 57:12; Ezek 8:12 [C]Ps 94:7; Is 47:10; Mal 2:17 29:16 [a]Lit *like* [A]Is 45:9; 64:8; Jer 18:1-6; Rom 9:19-21 29:17 [a]Lit *And* [A]Ps 84:6; 107:33, 35; Is 32:15 29:18 [A]Is 35:5; 42:18, 19; 43:8; Matt 11:5; Mark 7:37 [B]Is 29:11 [C]Ps 119:18; Prov 20:12; Is 32:3 29:19 [A]Ps 25:9; 37:11; Is 11:4; 61:1; Matt 5:5; 11:29 [B]Is 3:14, 15; 11:4; 14:30, 32; 25:4; 26:6; Matt 11:5; James 1:9; 2:5 29:20 [a]Lit *watch evil* [A]Is 29:5 [B]Is 28:14 [C]Is 59:4; Mic 2:1

29:8 not satisfied … faint. Jerusalem's attackers will frustrate themselves, as a dreamer who has the illusion that he eats and drinks, but awakens to find himself still hungry and thirsty.

29:9–14 The prophet returned to the theme of the blindness of mechanical religion.

29:9 Blind … drunk. The blindness and drunkenness came from the people's inability to comprehend Isaiah's message about trusting God instead of Egypt.

29:10 spirit of deep sleep. Because Israel refused to hear her true prophets initially, their ability to hear has been impaired. God gave them up judicially to their own hardness of heart. Paul applied this verse specifically to the general condition of Israel's blindness during the age of the church (Ro 11:8). **prophets … seers.** False prophets and seers have blinded their listeners with their false prophecies.

29:11 one who is literate. Those with ability to read could not do so because they had surrendered their spiritual sensitivity (cf. 6:9, 10; Mt 13:10–17).

29:12 one who is illiterate. The uneducated had two reasons for not knowing the book's contents: 1) the book was sealed, and 2) he could not read it even if it were not. It is deplorable when no one is capable of receiving God's rich revelation.

29:13 hearts far from Me. Empty ritualism does not bring closeness to God. Jesus used this verse to describe the Judaism of His day (Mt 15:7–9; Mk 7:6, 7).

29:14 wisdom … perish … discernment … concealed. The principle of resorting to human wisdom rather than divine wisdom was the spiritual plague of Jerusalem. The same principle was the downfall of the Greek world in Paul's day (1Co 1:19).

29:15 hide … from the LORD. The prophet probably referred to a secret plan of the leaders to join with Egypt to combat the Assyrians. The Lord had counseled otherwise, so they hid their strategy from Him.

29:16 He did not make me. For man to make plans on his own without God is a rejection of God as Creator. Paul reasons that it is also a questioning of the sovereignty of God (Ro 9:19–21). Does the clay think itself equal to the potter?

29:17 fertile field …. forest. In the future, a reversal of roles between the mighty and the weak will transpire, when God intervenes to bless Jerusalem. The moral change in the Jewish nation will be as great as if the usually forested Lebanon were turned into a field and vice versa.

29:18 deaf will hear … blind will see. The spiritual blindness of Israel will no longer exist. Jesus gives the words an additional meaning, applying it to His ministry of physical healing for the deaf and blind (Mt 11:5; cf. 35:5).

29:19, 20 increase their gladness … cut off. The future messianic age will bring a reversal of status. Rejoicing will replace the hardships of the oppressed; the oppressors' dominance will end.

21 Who [a]cause a person to be
indicted by a word,
And [A]ensnare him who
adjudicates at the gate,
And [b,B]defraud the one in the right
with [c]meaningless arguments.

22 Therefore thus says the LORD, who redeemed
[A]Abraham, concerning the house of Jacob:

"Jacob [B]shall not now be ashamed,
nor shall his face now turn pale;
23 But when [a]he sees his [A]children, the
[B]work of My hands, in his midst,
They will sanctify My name;
Indeed, they will [C]sanctify
the Holy One of Jacob
And will stand in awe of the God of Israel.
24 "Those who [A]err in [a]mind will
[B]know [b]the truth,
And those who [c]criticize will
[d,C]accept instruction.

JUDAH WARNED AGAINST EGYPTIAN ALLIANCE

30 "Woe to the [A]rebellious children,"
declares the LORD,
"Who [B]execute a plan, but not Mine,
And [a,C]make an alliance, but not of My Spirit,
In order to add sin to sin;
2 Who [A]proceed down to Egypt
Without [B]consulting [a]Me,
[C]To take refuge in the safety of Pharaoh
And to seek shelter in the shadow of Egypt!
3 "Therefore the safety of Pharaoh
will be [A]your shame
And the shelter in the shadow of
Egypt, your humiliation.
4 "For [A]their princes are at Zoan
And their ambassadors arrive at Hanes.
5 "Everyone will be [A]ashamed because of
a people who cannot profit them,
Who are [B]not for help or profit, but
for shame and also for reproach."

6 The [a]oracle concerning the [A]beasts of the [B]Negev.

Through a land of [C]distress and anguish,
From [b]where *come* lioness and lion,
viper and [D]flying serpent,
They [E]carry their riches on the
[c]backs of young donkeys
And their treasures on [F]camels' humps,
To a people who cannot profit *them;*
7 Even Egypt, whose [A]help is
vain and empty.
Therefore, I have called [a]her
"[b,B]Rahab who has been exterminated."
8 Now go, [A]write it on a tablet before them
And inscribe it on a scroll,
That it may [a]serve in the time to come
[b]As a witness forever.
9 For this is a [A]rebellious
people, [B]false sons,
Sons who [a]refuse to [C]listen
To the [b]instruction of the LORD;
10 Who say to the [A]seers, "You
must not see *visions*";
And to the prophets, "You must not
[B]prophesy to us what is right,
[C]Speak to us [a]pleasant words,
Prophesy illusions.
11 "Get out of the way, [A]turn
aside from the path,
[a,B]Let us hear no more about
the Holy One of Israel."

29:21 [a]Lit *bring a person under condemnation* [b]Lit *turn aside* [c]Lit *confusion* [A]Amos 5:10 [B]Is 32:7; Amos 5:12 29:22 [A]Is 41:8; 51:2; 63:16 [B]Is 45:17; 49:23; 50:7; 54:4 29:23 [a]Or *his children see* [A]Is 49:20-26 [B]Is 26:12; 45:11; Eph 2:10 [C]Is 5:16; 8:13 29:24 [a]Lit *spirit* [b]Lit *understanding* [c]Lit *murmur* [d]Lit *learn* [A]Is 30:21; Heb 5:2 [B]Is 41:20; 60:16 [C]Is 54:13 30:1 [a]Lit *pour out a drink offering* [A]Is 1:2, 23; 30:9; 65:2 [B]Is 29:15 [C]Is 8:11, 12 30:2 [a]Lit *My mouth* [A]Is 31:1; Jer 43:7 [B]Is 8:19 [C]Is 36:9 30:3 [A]Is 20:5, 6; 36:6; Jer 42:18, 22 30:4 [A]Is 19:11 30:5 [A]Jer 2:36 [B]Is 10:3; 30:7; 31:3 30:6 [a]Or *burden of* [b]Lit *them* [c]Lit *shoulders* [A]Is 46:1, 2 [B]Gen 12:9 [C]Ex 5:10, 21; Deut 4:20; 8:15; Is 5:30; 8:22; Jer 11:4 [D]Deut 8:15; Is 14:29 [E]Is 15:7; 46:1, 2 [F]1 Kin 10:2 30:7 [a]Lit *this* one [b]M.T. reads *They are Rahab* (or *arrogance*), *to remain* [A]Is 30:5 [B]Job 9:13; Ps 87:4; 89:10; Is 51:9 30:8 [a]Lit *be* [b]So the versions; Heb *Forever and ever* [A]Is 8:1 30:9 [a]Lit *are not willing* [b]Or *law* [A]Is 30:1 [B]Is 28:15; 59:3, 4 [C]Is 1:10; 5:24; 24:5 30:10 [a]Lit *smooth things* [A]Is 29:10 [B]Is 5:20; Jer 11:21; Amos 2:12; 7:13 [C]1 Kin 22:8, 13; Jer 6:14; 23:17, 26; Ezek 13:7; Rom 16:18; 2 Tim 4:3, 4 30:11 [a]Lit *Cause to cease from our presence* the [A]Acts 13:8 [B]Job 21:14

29:21 indicted … defraud. Those with political and judicial authority are no longer to misuse their power to oppress.

29:22 redeemed Abraham. God delivered Abraham from his pagan background when He brought him from beyond the Euphrates River into the land of Canaan (Jos 24:2, 3). Paul elaborates on this theme in Ro 4:1–22. **not now be ashamed.** Israel in her history had frequently suffered disgrace, but the personal presence of the Messiah is to change that (45:17; 49:23; 50:7; 54:4). After the salvation of Israel in the end time, the children of Jacob will no longer cause their forefathers to blush over their wickedness.

29:23 sanctify … stand in awe. Jacob's descendants will marvel at the strong deliverance of the Lord and set Him apart as the only one worthy of utmost respect. God will cleanse Israel (cf. 54:13, 14).

29:24 err … criticize. With their newfound respect for God, the formerly wayward ones were to gain the capacity for spiritual perception.

30:1 not Mine … not of My Spirit. Hezekiah's advisers urged him to turn to the Egyptians, not to God, for help against the invading Assyrians. Isaiah denounced this reliance on Egypt rather than God, who had forbidden such alliances.

30:2 Without consulting Me. They had failed to consult God's prophet. **Egypt … Pharaoh … Egypt.** The Lord had warned Israel against returning to Egypt (Dt 17:16). Now He warns them against an alliance with Egypt (31:1). Note the similar advice from the Assyrian Rabshakeh, while laying siege to Jerusalem (36:9).

30:3 shame … humiliation. The Assyrians had already defeated the Egyptian army only 100 mi. from the Egyptian border.

30:4 Zoan … Hanes. Judah's emissaries had penetrated from Zoan in the NE of Egypt to Hanes fifty mi. S of Memphis.

30:6 land of distress and anguish … camels' humps. Isaiah pictured a rich caravan, trudging slowly through rugged territory fraught with dangers, on its way to Egypt to purchase assistance.

30:7 help is vain … Rahab. Egypt was unwilling to help so the prophet calls the powerful Egypt "Rahab," meaning "strength," or "sitting idle" (Hebrew). "Rahab" is used of Egypt in Pss 87:4; 89:10.

30:8 in the time to come. The Lord's instruction to Isaiah was to make a permanent written record so that future generations could learn Israel's folly of trusting in Egypt instead of in the Lord.

30:9 rebellious people, false sons. The people's unwillingness to obey the Lord necessitated the keeping of a permanent record of their misdeeds.

30:10, 11 Prophesy illusions … turn aside from the path. Isaiah's listeners tired of hearing counsel that was contrary to the path they desired to follow and wanted him to change his message to accommodate them.

12 Therefore thus says the Holy One of Israel,

"[A]Since you have rejected this word
And have put your trust
in [B]oppression and guile,
and have relied on them,
13 Therefore this [A]iniquity
will be to you
Like a [B]breach about to fall,
A bulge in a high wall,
Whose collapse comes
[C]suddenly in an instant,
14 Whose collapse is like the
smashing of a [A]potter's jar,
[a]So ruthlessly shattered
That a sherd will not be found
among its pieces
To [b]take fire from a hearth
Or to scoop water from a cistern."

15 For thus the Lord [a]GOD, the Holy One of Israel,
has said,

"In [b]repentance and [A]rest
you will be saved,
In [B]quietness and trust
is your strength."
But you were not willing,
16 And you said, "No, for we
will flee on [A]horses,"
Therefore you shall flee!
"And we will ride on swift *horses,*"
Therefore those who pursue
you shall be swift.
17 [A]One thousand *will flee* at the
threat of one *man;*
You will flee at the threat of five,
Until you are left as a [a]flag
on a mountain top
And as a signal on a hill.

GOD IS GRACIOUS AND JUST

18 Therefore the LORD [a,A]longs
to be gracious to you,
And therefore He [b]waits on [B]high
to have compassion on you.
For the LORD is a [C]God of justice;
How blessed are all those
who [c,D]long for Him.

19 [a]O people in Zion, [A]inhabitant in Jerusalem, you
will [B]weep no longer. He will surely be gracious to
you at the sound of your cry; when He hears it, He
will [C]answer you. 20 Although the Lord has given you
[A]bread of privation and water of oppression, *He,* your
Teacher will no longer [B]hide Himself, but your eyes
will behold your Teacher. 21 Your ears will hear a word
behind you, "[a]This is the [A]way, walk in it," whenever
you [B]turn to the right or to the left. 22 And you will
defile your graven [A]images overlaid with silver, and
your molten [A]images plated with gold. You will scatter
them as an impure thing, *and* say to [a]them, "[B]Be gone!"
23 Then He will [A]give *you* rain for [a]the seed which
you will sow in the ground, and bread *from* the yield
of the ground, and it will be [b]rich and [c]plenteous; on
that day [B]your livestock will graze in a roomy pasture. 24 Also the oxen and the donkeys which work the
ground will eat salted fodder, which [a]has been [A]win-
nowed with shovel and fork. 25 On every lofty mountain and on [A]every high hill there will be [a]streams
running with water on the day of the great [B]slaughter,
when the towers fall. 26 [A]The light of the moon will be
as the light of the sun, and the light of the sun will be
seven times *brighter,* like the light of seven days, on
the day [B]the LORD binds up the [C]fracture of His people
and [D]heals the bruise [a]He has inflicted.

27 Behold, [A]the name of the LORD
comes from a [a]remote place;
[B]Burning is His anger and
[b]dense is *His* [c]smoke;

30:12 [A]Is 5:24; 7:9; 8:6 [B]Is 3:14, 15; 5:7; 59:13 30:13 [A]Is 26:21 [B]1 Kin 20:30; Ps 62:4; Is 58:12 [C]Is 29:5; 47:11 30:14 [a]Lit *Crushed, it will not be spared* [b]Lit *snatch up* [A]Ps 2:9; Jer 19:10, 11 30:15 [a]Heb *YHWH,* usually rendered *LORD* [b]Lit *returning* [A]Ps 116:7; Is 28:12 [B]Is 7:4; 32:17 30:16 [A]Is 2:7; 31:1, 3 30:17 [a]Lit *pole* [A]Lev 26:36; Deut 28:25; 32:30; Josh 23:10; Prov 28:1 30:18 [a]Lit *waits* [b]Lit *is on high* [c]Lit *wait* [A]Is 42:14, 16; 48:9; Jon 3:4, 10; 2 Pet 3:9, 15 [B]Is 2:11, 17; 33:5 [C]Is 5:16; 28:17; 61:8 [D]Is 8:17; 25:9; 26:8; 33:2 30:19 [a]M.T. reads *A people will inhabit Zion, Jerusalem* [A]Is 65:9; Ezek 37:25, 28 [B]Is 25:8; 60:20; 61:1-3 [C]Ps 50:15; Is 58:9; 65:24; Matt 7:7-11 30:20 [A]1 Kin 22:27; Ps 80:5 [B]Ps 74:9; Amos 8:11 30:21 [a]Lit *saying, "This* [A]Ps 25:8, 9; Prov 3:6; Is 35:8, 9; 42:16 [B]Is 29:24 30:22 [a]Lit *it "Go out"* [A]Ex 32:2, 4; Judg 17:3, 4; Is 46:6 [B]Matt 4:10 30:23 [a]Lit *your* [b]Lit *fatness* [c]Lit *fat* [A]Ps 65:9-13; 104:13, 14 [B]Ps 144:13; Is 32:20; Hos 4:16 30:24 [a]Lit *one winnows* [A]Matt 3:12; Luke 3:17 30:25 [a]Lit *canals, streams of water* [A]Is 35:6, 7; 41:18; 43:19, 20 [B]Is 34:2 30:26 [a]Lit *of His blow* [A]Is 24:23; 60:19, 20; Rev 21:23; 22:5 [B]Is 61:1 [C]Is 1:6; 30:13, 14 [D]Deut 32:39; Job 5:18; Is 33:24; Jer 33:6; Hos 6:1, 2 30:27 [a]Lit *distance* [b]Lit *heaviness* [c]Lit *uplifting* [A]Is 59:19 [B]Is 10:17

30:12–14 Since the people opted not to hear the word of the Lord's prophet, they will hear from the Lord's judgment.

30:12 this word. The reference is to the instruction of the Lord through Isaiah.

30:13, 14 high wall … potter's jar. Two comparisons portrayed the coming sudden disaster to befall the rebels, a high wall that collapses suddenly and a clay jar that shatters into many pieces when dropped.

30:15 rest … trust. The Israelite rebels refused the true avenue of salvation and strength, i.e., resting and confidence in the Lord.

30:16 horses … swift *horses.* The people put their trust in Egypt's horses instead of the Lord. No horse could deliver them from their God-appointed oppressors (cf. Dt 17:16; Pss 33:17; 147:10).

30:17 One thousand … one. Similar figures elsewhere describe Israel's victories (Lv 26:36; Jos 23:10) and defeats (Dt 32:30).

30:18 the LORD … waits. Since Judah would not wait on the Lord to deliver (25:9; 26:8; 33:2; cf. 30:15), He must wait to be gracious to the nation.

30:19 inhabitant in Jerusalem. The prophet emphatically pointed to a result of God's grace toward Israel—the survival of the city of Jerusalem as the center of her domain (65:9; Eze 37:25, 28).

30:20 eyes will behold. After their period of judgment because of disobedience, God is to open Israel's eyes to the soundness of the message of His prophets (29:24).

30:21 a word behind you. The teachers will be near and the pupils sensitive to the Lord's prophets, in strong contrast to the callousness formerly manifest (29:10, 11).

30:22 scatter them. The Babylonian captivity rid Israel of her idolatry in fulfillment of this prophecy.

30:23–25 In the messianic kingdom of that future day, agriculture, cattle raising, food production, and water resources will prosper. The prophet predicted the redemption of nature (cf. Ro 8:19–21).

30:25 towers fall. Powerful nations that oppress Israel will come to an end (contra. 29:17).

30:26 light of the moon … light of the sun. The benefits from the natural bodies of light will be much greater. Increase in the intensity of their light will work to people's advantage (60:19, 20), not to their detriment as in Rev 16:8, 9.

30:27–33 Isaiah followed the promise of Judah's redemption (vv. 19–26) with a promise of Assyria's destruction.

30:27 the name of the LORD. His name focuses particularly on His revealed character as Sovereign and Savior (Dt 12:5).

30:27, 28 comes from a remote place …

His lips are filled with [C]indignation
And His tongue is like a [D]consuming fire;
28 His [A]breath is like an overflowing torrent,
Which [B]reaches to the neck,
To [C]shake the nations back
and forth in a [a]sieve,
And to *put* in the jaws of the peoples
[D]the bridle which [b]leads to ruin.
29 You will have [a]songs as in the night
when you keep the festival,
And gladness of heart as when one
marches to *the sound of* the flute,
To go to the mountain of the
LORD, to the Rock of Israel.
30 And the LORD will cause [a]His voice
of authority to be heard,
And the [b]descending of His arm
to be seen in fierce anger,
And *in* the flame of a consuming fire
In cloudburst, downpour
and hailstones.
31 For [A]at the voice of the LORD
[B]Assyria will be terrified,
When He strikes with the [C]rod.
32 And every [a]blow of the [b,A]rod
of punishment,
Which the LORD will lay on him,
Will be with *the music of*
[B]tambourines and lyres;
And in battles, [C]brandishing
weapons, He will fight them.
33 For [a,A]Topheth has long been ready,
Indeed, it has been prepared for the king.
He has made it deep and large,
[b]A pyre of fire with plenty of wood;
The [B]breath of the LORD, like a torrent
of [C]brimstone, sets it afire.

HELP NOT IN EGYPT BUT IN GOD

31 Woe to those who go down
to [A]Egypt for help
And [B]rely on horses,
And trust in chariots because
they are many
And in horsemen because
they are very strong,
But they do not [C]look to the [D]Holy
One of Israel, nor seek the LORD!
2 Yet He also is [A]wise and
will [B]bring disaster
And does [C]not retract His words,
But will arise against the
house of [D]evildoers
And against the help of the
[E]workers of iniquity.
3 Now the Egyptians are [A]men and not God,
And their [B]horses are flesh
and not spirit;
So the LORD will [C]stretch out His hand,
And [D]he who helps will stumble
And he who is helped will fall,
And all of them will come
to an end together.

4 For thus says the LORD to me,
"As the [A]lion or the young lion
growls over his prey,
Against which a band of
shepherds is called out,
And he will not be terrified at their
voice nor disturbed at their noise,
So will the LORD of hosts come
down to wage [B]war on Mount
Zion and on its hill."
5 Like [a]flying [A]birds so the LORD of
hosts will protect Jerusalem.
He will [B]protect and deliver *it;*
He will pass over and rescue *it.*

6 [A]Return to Him from whom [a]you have [B]deeply
defected, O sons of Israel. 7 For in that day every
man will [A]cast away his silver idols and his gold
idols, which your [B]sinful hands have made for you
as [B]a sin.

30:27 [C]Is 10:5; 13:5; 66:14 [D]Is 66:15 30:28 [a]Lit *sifting of the worthless* [b]Lit *misleads* [A]Is 11:4; 30:33; 2 Thess 2:8 [B]Is 8:8 [C]Amos 9:9 [D]2 Kin 19:28; Is 37:29 30:29 [a]Lit *the song* 30:30 [a]Lit *the majesty of His voice* [b]Lit *descent* 30:31 [A]Is 11:4 [B]Is 10:12; 14:25; 31:8 [C]Is 10:26; 11:4 30:32 [a]Lit *passing* [b]Lit *staff of foundation* [A]Is 10:24 [B]1 Sam 18:6; Jer 31:4 [C]Ezek 32:10 30:33 [a]I.e. the place of human sacrifice to Molech [b]Lit *Its pile* [A]2 Kin 23:10; Jer 7:31; 19:6 [B]Is 11:4; 30:28 [C]Gen 19:24; Is 34:9 31:1 [A]Is 30:2, 7; 36:6 [B]Deut 17:16; Ps 20:7; 33:17; Is 2:7; 30:16 [C]Is 9:13; Dan 9:13; Amos 5:4-8 [D]Is 10:17; 43:15; Hos 11:9; Hab 1:12; 3:3 31:2 [A]Is 28:29; Rom 16:27 [B]Is 45:7 [C]Num 23:19; Jer 44:29 [D]Is 1:4; 9:17; 14:20 [E]Is 22:14; 32:6 31:3 [A]Ezek 28:9; 2 Thess 2:4 [B]Is 36:9 [C]Is 9:17; Jer 15:6; Ezek 20:33, 34 [D]Is 30:5, 7; Matt 15:14 31:4 [A]Num 24:9; Hos 11:10; Amos 3:8 [B]Is 42:13; Zech 12:8 31:5 [a]Or *hovering* [A]Deut 32:11; Ps 91:4 [B]Is 37:35; 38:6 31:6 [a]Lit *they* [A]Is 44:22; 55:7; Jer 3:10, 14, 22; Ezek 18:31, 32 [B]Is 1:2, 5 31:7 [A]Is 2:20; 30:22 [B]1 Kin 12:30

overflowing torrent. The Lord will come suddenly upon His enemies as a great storm with its accompanying flood, to overwhelm them.

30:29 songs … festival. While God's judgment devastated the Assyrians, the people of Jerusalem conducted a time of joyful celebration at one of their feasts, perhaps a Passover.

30:30, 31 Assyria … terrified. Assyria in particular, but in the long range, any enemy of God's people will fall victim to divine storm and flood (vv. 27, 28).

30:32 rod of punishment … tambourines and lyres. With each blow of punishment against the Assyrians will come joyful celebration in Jerusalem.

30:33 Topheth. Lit. a place of abomination. Idolatrous Israel had burned to death human victims in this valley just S of Jerusalem, an area sometimes called the Valley of Hinnom (2Ki 23:10; *see note on Jer 19:6*). Later it became known as Gehenna, the place of refuse for the city, with constantly burning fires, symbolizing hell. The defeat was to be so complete that the fire burns continually.

31:1 horses … chariots. Egypt's horses and chariots were numerous (1Ki 10:28, 29). Its flat topography was well suited for chariotry. They would be useful to Israel against the Assyrian cavalry. **nor seek the LORD.** What made Israel's turning to Egypt most despicable was her accompanying turning away from the Lord.

31:2 He also is wise. Sarcastically, Isaiah countered the unwise royal counselors who had advised dependence on Egypt. **does not retract His words.** The implied exception is, of course, when the sinful nation repented, as in the case of Nineveh (Jon 3:5–10).

31:3 flesh … spirit. For example, Hezekiah wisely chose to rely on the Lord, not on the arm of flesh (2Ch 32:8).

31:4 not be terrified … nor disturbed. In His defense of Jerusalem, the Lord is to be like a strong and determined lion, unafraid of shepherds summoned against him.

31:5 flying birds. The Lord is like a hovering mother bird with a strong attachment to her little ones and a willingness to do whatever is necessary for their safety.

31:6 Return to Him. The prophet called rebellious Israel to repent in light of God's gracious dealings with them (vv. 4, 5; cf. 30:18, 19).

31:7 cast away his … idols. The obvious helplessness of the idols to deliver rendered them completely useless.

8 And the [A]Assyrian will fall by
a sword not of man,
And a [B]sword not of man will devour him.
So he will [a,C]not escape the sword,
And his young men will become
[D]forced laborers.
9 "His [A]rock will pass away because of panic,
And his princes will be terrified
at the [B]standard,"
Declares the LORD, whose [C]fire is in Zion
and whose furnace is in Jerusalem.

THE GLORIOUS FUTURE

32 Behold, a [A]king will reign righteously
And princes will rule justly.
2 Each will be like a [A]refuge from the wind
And a shelter from the storm,
Like [a,B]streams of water in a dry country,
Like the [A]shade of a [b]huge rock
in [c]a parched land.
3 Then [A]the eyes of those who
see will not be [a]blinded,
And the ears of those who hear will listen.
4 The [a]mind of the [A]hasty will
discern the [b]truth,
And the tongue of the stammerers
will hasten to speak clearly.
5 No longer will the [A]fool be called noble,
Or the rogue be spoken of *as* generous.
6 For a fool speaks nonsense,
And his heart [a,A]inclines toward wickedness:
To practice [B]ungodliness and to
speak error against the LORD,
To [b,C]keep the hungry person unsatisfied
And [c]to withhold drink from the thirsty.
7 As for a rogue, his weapons are evil;
He [A]devises wicked schemes
To [B]destroy *the* afflicted with [a]slander,
[C]Even though *the* needy one
speaks [b]what is right.
8 But [A]the noble man devises noble plans;
And by noble plans he stands.

9 Rise up, you [A]women who are at ease,
And hear my voice;
[B]Give ear to my word,
You complacent daughters.
10 Within a year and *a few* days
You will be troubled,
O complacent *daughters;*
[A]For the vintage is ended,
And the *fruit* gathering will not come.
11 Tremble, you *women* who are at ease;
[A]Be troubled, you complacent *daughters;*
[B]Strip, undress and put *sackcloth*
on *your* waist,
12 [A]Beat your breasts for the pleasant
fields, for the fruitful vine,
13 [A]For the land of my people *in which*
thorns *and* briars shall come up;
Yea, for all the joyful houses
and for the [B]jubilant city.
14 Because [A]the palace has been abandoned,
the [a]populated [B]city forsaken.
[b]Hill and watch-tower have
become [C]caves forever,
A delight for [D]wild donkeys,
a pasture for flocks;
15 Until the [A]Spirit is poured out
upon us from on high,
And the wilderness becomes
a [B]fertile field,
And the fertile field is
considered as a forest.

31:8 [a]Lit *flee* [A]Is 10:12; 14:25; 30:31-33; 37:7, 36-38 [B]Is 66:16 [C]Is 21:15 [D]Gen 49:15; Is 14:2 31:9 [A]Deut 32:31, 37 [B]Is 5:26; 13:2; 18:3 [C]Is 10:16, 17; 30:33; Zech 2:5 32:1 [A]Ps 72:1-4; Is 9:6, 7; 11:4, 5; Jer 23:5; 33:15; Ezek 37:24; Zech 9:9 32:2 [a]Lit *canals* [b]Lit *heavy* [c]Lit *an exhausted* [A]Is 4:6; 25:4 [B]Is 35:6; 41:18; 43:19, 20 32:3 [a]Or *turned away* [A]Is 29:18 32:4 [a]Lit *heart* [b]Lit *knowledge* [A]Is 29:24 32:5 [A]1 Sam 25:25 32:6 [a]Or *does* [b]Lit *make empty the hungry soul* [c]Lit *he causes to lack* [A]Prov 19:3; 24:7-9; Is 59:7, 13 [B]Is 9:17; 10:6 [C]Is 3:15; 10:2 32:7 [a]Lit *words of falsehood* [b]Lit *justly* [A]Jer 5:26-28; Mic 7:3 [B]Is 11:4; 61:1 [C]Is 5:23 32:8 [A]Prov 11:25 32:9 [A]Is 47:8; Amos 6:1; Zeph 2:15 [B]Is 28:23 32:10 [A]Is 5:5, 6; 7:23; 24:7 32:11 [A]Is 22:12 [B]Is 47:2 32:12 [A]Nah 2:7 32:13 [A]Is 5:6, 10, 17; 27:10 [B]Is 22:2; 23:9 32:14 [a]Lit *multitude of the* [b]Or *Ophel* [A]Is 13:22; 25:2; 34:13 [B]Is 6:11; 22:2; 24:10, 12 [C]Is 13:21; 34:13 [D]Ps 104:11; Jer 14:6 32:15 [A]Is 11:2; 44:3; 59:21; Ezek 39:29; Joel 2:28 [B]Ps 107:35; Is 29:17; 35:1, 2

31:8 Assyrian will fall. The defeat of Assyria by other-than-human means matched this prophecy well (see 37:36, 37), but other such foreign oppressors meet the same fate in the distant future of Israel, during the time of Jacob's trouble (cf. Jer 30:7).

31:9 fire is in Zion … furnace is in Jerusalem. Both in Isaiah's near future and in the distant future, Jerusalem will be God's headquarters for bringing judgment on foreign nations. God Himself is the fire, waiting for all the enemies who attack Jerusalem.

32:1 a king … princes. In contrast to bad leaders already discussed (e.g., 28:14, 15; 29:15), the prophet turned to the messianic king and His governmental assistants during the future day of righteousness. These will be the apostles (Lk 22:30) and the saints (1Co 6:2; 2Ti 2:12; Rev 2:26, 27; 3:21).

32:2 shade … land. During the millennial reign of Christ, leaders will provide protection like "the shade of a huge rock in a parched land," instead of posing threats to the people's well-being.

32:3 eyes … not … blinded … ears … listen. A future generation of Israelites will experience a reversal of receptivity compared to Isaiah's generation (6:9, 10; cf. 29:18, 24; 30:20).

32:4 stammerers. The stammerers were former drunkards who uttered nonsense in their drunken stupor (28:7, 8; 29:9).

32:5 fool … noble … rogue … generous. In the future earthly kingdom envisioned by Isaiah, false appraisals of leadership qualities will be impossible, because everyone will see and speak clearly.

32:6–8 fool … noble man. An unwillingness to care for the needy reflects the character of a fool, but the noble person in dependence on God provides for the poor. These qualities will be evident to all in the age to come.

32:9–14 The prophet warns the women of Judah against complacency (cf. 3:16–4:1). God's eventual blessing on their nation gave no excuse for business as usual, i.e., dependence on Egypt instead of God.

32:9 at ease … complacent. The words translated "at ease" and "complacent" are translated as "quiet" and "secure," respectively, in v. 18. The difference between the bad senses here and the good senses in v. 18 is the object of trust, Egypt or God. Ease and security in God are proper.

32:10 year and *a few* days. Perhaps specifying a time when the Assyrian army came and pillaged the land, the prophet warned of how God's coming judgment was to spoil agricultural production.

32:11, 12 Tremble … Beat your breasts. Present satisfaction with the status quo shortly gave way to an entirely different set of emotions.

32:13 thorns … briars. Without harmony with God, the land of God's people became just as desolate as any other forsaken territory (1:7; 5:6; 7:23).

32:14 populated city. Jerusalem too was to become desolate through the Lord's purging judgments of the nation (Lk 21:24).

32:15–20 The promised kingdom was to eventually come to Israel with its accompanying fruitfulness, peace, and security.

32:15 the Spirit is poured out upon us. The

16 Then [A]justice will dwell in the wilderness
And righteousness will abide
in the fertile field.
17 And the [A]work of righteousness
will be peace,
And the service of righteousness,
[B]quietness and [a]confidence forever.
18 Then my people will live in a
[A]peaceful habitation,
And in secure dwellings and in
undisturbed [B]resting places;
19 And it will [A]hail when the
[B]forest comes down,
And [C]the city will be utterly laid low.
20 How [A]blessed will you be, you
who sow beside all waters,
Who [a]let out freely the ox and the donkey.

THE JUDGMENT OF GOD

33 Woe [A]to you, O destroyer,
While you were not destroyed;
And he [B]who is treacherous, while *others*
did not deal treacherously with him.
As soon as you finish destroying,
[C]you will be destroyed;
As soon as you cease to deal
treacherously, *others* will [D]deal
treacherously with you.
2 O LORD, [A]be gracious to us; we
have [B]waited for You.
Be [a]their [b,C]strength every morning,
Our salvation also in the [D]time of distress.
3 At the sound of the tumult [A]peoples flee;
At the [B]lifting up of Yourself
nations disperse.
4 Your spoil is gathered *as* the
caterpillar gathers;
As locusts rushing about
men rush about on it.
5 The LORD is [A]exalted, for He dwells on high;
He has [B]filled Zion with justice
and righteousness.
6 And He will be the [a,A]stability of your times,
A [B]wealth of salvation, wisdom
and [C]knowledge;
The [D]fear of the LORD is his treasure.
7 Behold, their brave men cry in [a]the streets,
The [b,A]ambassadors of peace weep bitterly.
8 The highways are desolate, [a]the
[A]traveler has ceased,
He has [B]broken the covenant, he
has despised the cities,
He has no regard for man.
9 [A]The land mourns *and* pines away,
[B]Lebanon is shamed *and* withers;
[C]Sharon is like a desert plain,
And Bashan and Carmel
[a]lose *their foliage.*
10 "Now [A]I will arise," says the LORD,
"Now I will be exalted, now
I will be lifted up.
11 "You have [A]conceived [a]chaff, you
will give birth to stubble;
[b]My [B]breath will consume you like a fire.
12 "The peoples will be burned to lime,
[A]Like cut thorns which are
burned in the fire.

13 "You who are far away, [A]hear
what I have done;
And you who are near,
[a]acknowledge My might."
14 [A]Sinners in Zion are terrified;
[B]Trembling has seized the godless.
"Who among us can live with
[C]the consuming fire?
Who among us can live with
[a]continual [D]burning?"

32:16 [A]Is 33:5; Zech 8:3 32:17 [a]Or *security* [A]Ps 72:2, 3; 85:8; 119:165; Is 2:4; Rom 14:17; James 3:18 [B]Is 30:15 32:18 [A]Is 26:3, 12 [B]Is 11:10; 14:3; 30:15; Hos 2:18-23; Zech 2:5; 3:10 32:19 [A]Is 28:2, 17; 30:30 [B]Is 10:18, 19, 34 [C]Is 24:10, 12; 26:5; 27:10; 29:4 32:20 [a]Lit *send out the foot of the ox* [A]Eccl 11:1; Is 30:23, 24 33:1 [A]Is 10:6; 21:2 [B]Is 24:16; 48:8 [C]Is 10:12; 14:25; 31:8; Hab 2:8 [D]Jer 25:12-14; Matt 7:2 33:2 [a]Some versions read *our* [b]Lit *arm* [A]Is 30:18, 19 [B]Is 25:9 [C]Is 40:10; 51:5; 59:16 [D]Is 37:3 33:3 [A]Is 17:13; 21:15 [B]Is 10:33; 17:13; 59:16-18; Jer 25:30, 31 33:5 [A]Ps 97:9 [B]Is 1:26; 28:6; 32:16 33:6 [a]Or *faithfulness* [A]Is 33:20 [B]Is 45:17; 51:6 [C]Is 11:9 [D]2 Kin 18:7; Ps 112:1-3; Is 11:3; Matt 6:33 33:7 [a]Lit *the outside* [b]Lit *messengers* [A]2 Kin 18:18, 37 33:8 [a]Lit *he who passes along the way* [A]Is 35:8 [B]Is 24:5 33:9 [a]Lit *shake off* [A]Is 3:26; 24:4; 29:2 [B]Is 2:13; 10:34 [C]Is 35:2; 65:10 33:10 [A]Ps 12:5; Is 2:19, 21 33:11 [a]Lit *dry grass* [b]So one ancient version; M.T. reads *Your breath will* [A]Ps 7:14; Is 26:18; 59:4; James 1:15 [B]Is 1:31 33:12 [A]2 Sam 23:6, 7; Is 10:17; 27:4 33:13 [a]Lit *know* [A]Ps 48:10; Is 49:1 33:14 [a]Lit *everlasting* [A]Is 1:28 [B]Is 32:11 [C]Is 30:27, 30; Heb 12:29 [D]Is 9:18, 19; 10:16; 47:14

infusion of God's Spirit was to transform the land into productive fruitfulness (Joel 2:28–3:1).

32:16 justice ... righteousness. Noble spiritual values were to thrive in the future messianic reign.

32:18 my people ... peaceful ... secure ... undisturbed. The people of Israel will enjoy lasting security with the Messiah personally present to ensure peace.

32:19 city ... laid low. Jerusalem must learn humility before the prophesied ideal conditions can become reality.

32:20 blessed. As with the beatitudes of Christ (Mt 5:3–12), Isaiah pronounced the blessedness of those who participate in the future glory of Christ's kingdom.

33:1 O destroyer. Though the immediate reference is to Assyria (2Ki 18:13–16; 19:32–37), the prophecy looks beyond Assyria to any power that sets itself against Israel.

33:2 we have waited for You. Israel refused to do this earlier (30:15; 31:6), but had repented (25:9; 26:8; 33:2).

33:3, 4 Just as Sennacherib took flight suddenly (cf. 37:37; 2Ch 32:21), so the nations will scatter before the Lord, leaving their spoils behind.

33:6 fear of the LORD. The same Spirit-imparted qualification possessed by the Messiah (11:2) will belong to His people when He returns.

33:7–9 From the vision of future glory, Isaiah returns to the disastrous present. Jerusalem's situation was hopeless when in 701 B.C. the Assyrian army had the city surrounded and was ready to move in.

33:7 brave men ... ambassadors. Both men of war and diplomats had failed in their attempts to thwart the invaders.

33:8 highways are desolate. The enemy surrounding the city had cut off all travel and trade with the outside world.

33:9 Lebanon ... Sharon ... Bashan ... Carmel. The enemy had spoiled places renowned for their lush fertility.

33:10 Now I will arise. When the oppressor's power had reached its zenith, the time had arrived for the Lord to assert Himself in judging the plunderer, in Isaiah's case the Assyrian troops.

33:11 chaff ... stubble. References to Assyria reaffirm that the plunderer is to be plundered (v. 1).

33:12 lime ... thorns. Burned limestone became dust; thorn bushes burned rapidly.

33:13 far away ... near. When God puts down the final enemies of Israel, He will receive worldwide acknowledgment of His might.

33:14 terrified. When sinners (false professors among the elect) comprehend the might of God, fear takes hold of their lives (Ac 5:11; Heb 12:29).

15 He who [A]walks righteously and
speaks with sincerity,
He who rejects [a]unjust gain
And shakes his hands so that
they hold no bribe;
He who stops his ears from
hearing about bloodshed
And [B]shuts his eyes from
looking upon evil;
16 He will dwell on the heights,
[A]His refuge will be the [a]impregnable rock;
[B]His bread will be given *him*,
His water will be sure.

17 Your eyes will see [A]the
King in His beauty;
They will behold [B]a far-distant land.
18 Your heart will meditate on [A]terror:
"Where is [B]he who counts?
Where is he who weighs?
Where is he who counts the towers?"
19 You will no longer see a fierce people,
A people of [a,A]unintelligible speech
[b]which no one comprehends,
Of a stammering tongue [c]which
no one understands.
20 [A]Look upon Zion, the city of
our appointed feasts;
Your eyes will see Jerusalem, an
[B]undisturbed habitation,
[C]A tent which will not be folded;
Its stakes will never be pulled up,
Nor any of its cords be torn apart.
21 But there the majestic *One*, the
LORD, will be for us
A place of [A]rivers *and* wide canals
On which no boat with oars will go,
And on which no mighty ship will pass—
22 For the LORD is our [A]judge,
The LORD is [B]our lawgiver,
The LORD is [C]our king;
[D]He will save us—
23 Your tackle hangs slack;
It cannot hold the base of its mast firmly,
Nor spread out the sail.
Then the [A]prey of an abundant
spoil will be divided;
[B]The lame will take the plunder.
24 And no resident will say, "I am [A]sick";
The people who dwell [a]there will
be [B]forgiven *their* iniquity.

GOD'S WRATH AGAINST NATIONS

34 Draw near, [A]O nations, to hear;
and listen, O peoples!
[B]Let the earth and [a]all it contains hear, and
the world and all that springs from it.
2 For the LORD'S [A]indignation is
against all the nations,
And *His* wrath against all their armies;
He has [a,B]utterly destroyed them,
He has given them over to [C]slaughter.
3 So their slain will be [A]thrown out,
And their corpses [a]will give
off their [B]stench,
And the mountains will [b]be
drenched with their [C]blood.
4 And [A]all the host of heaven
will [a]wear away,
And the [B]sky will be rolled up like a scroll;
All their hosts will also wither away
As a leaf withers from the vine,
Or as *one* withers from the fig tree.
5 For [A]My sword is satiated in heaven,
Behold it shall descend for
judgment upon [B]Edom
And upon the people whom I have
[C]devoted to destruction.
6 The sword of the LORD is
filled with blood,

33:15 [a]Lit *gain of extortioners* [A]Ps 15:2; 24:4; Is 58:6-11 [B]Ps 119:37 33:16 [a]Lit *stronghold of rock* [A]Is 25:4 [B]Is 49:10 33:17 [A]Is 6:5; 24:23; 33:21, 22 [B]Is 26:15 33:18 [A]Is 17:14 [B]1 Cor 1:20 33:19 [a]Lit *deepness of lip* [b]Lit *from hearing* [c]Lit *there is no understanding* [A]Deut 28:49, 50; Is 28:11; Jer 5:15 33:20 [A]Ps 48:12 [B]Ps 46:5; 125:1, 2; Is 32:18 [C]Is 54:2 33:21 [A]Is 41:18; 43:19, 20; 48:18; 66:12 33:22 [A]Is 2:4; 11:4; 16:5; 51:5 [B]Is 1:10; 51:4, 7; James 4:12 [C]Ps 89:18; Is 33:17; Zech 9:9 [D]Is 25:9; 35:4; 49:25, 26; 60:16 33:23 [A]2 Kin 7:16 [B]2 Kin 7:8; Is 35:6 33:24 [a]Lit *in it* [A]Is 30:26; 58:8; Jer 30:17 [B]Is 40:2; 44:22; Jer 50:20; Mic 7:18, 19; 1 John 1:7-9 34:1 [a]Lit *its fullness* [A]Ps 49:1; Is 41:1; 43:9 [B]Deut 32:1; Is 1:2 34:2 [a]Lit *put under the ban* [A]Is 26:20 [B]Is 13:5; 24:1 [C]Is 30:25; 63:6; 65:12 34:3 [a]Lit *their stench will go up* [b]Lit *dissolve* [A]Is 14:19 [B]Joel 2:20; Amos 4:10 [C]Ezek 14:19; 35:6; 38:22 34:4 [a]Lit *rot* [A]Is 13:13; 51:6; Ezek 32:7, 8; Joel 2:31; Matt 24:29; 2 Pet 3:10 [B]Rev 6:12-14 34:5 [A]Deut 32:41, 42; Jer 46:10; Ezek 21:3-5 [B]Is 63:1; Jer 49:7, 8, 20; Ezek 25:12-14; 35:1-15; Amos 1:11, 12; Obad 1-14; Mal 1:4 [C]Is 24:6; 43:28

33:15 walks righteously and speaks with sincerity. The only survivors in the presence of mighty God will be the righteous (Pss 15:1–5; 24:3, 4).

33:16 refuge … bread … water. Those who are right with God will enjoy perfect security and ample provisions (32:15, 17, 18).

33:17 King in His beauty. The prophecy moves beyond Hezekiah in his sackcloth, oppressed by his enemy, to Messiah in His beauty. Seeing Him in glory is another reward of the righteous. The near-future deliverance from Sennacherib anticipates a more distant wonder when the Messiah will sit on His throne.

33:18, 19 In that future day God's people will remember past hardships under foreign domination.

33:20 tent … not be folded. God's presence is to permanently inhabit restored Jerusalem in the millennial kingdom.

33:21 rivers *and* wide canals. God is to restore wide rivers and streams as a means of defending the city.

33:22 He will save us. In explicit language, God, not the surrounding nations, is to deliver Israel.

33:23 tackle hangs slack. In her own strength, Jerusalem is as helpless to defend herself as a ship deprived of its ropes and pulleys is unable to. **lame will take the plunder.** The weak city defeats the invaders with the Lord's enablement.

33:24 forgiven *their* iniquity. When Christ returns to rule, Jerusalem will be free of physical and spiritual problems.

34:1 Draw near. Isaiah invited the nations to approach to hear God's sentence of judgment against them.

34:3 their stench. Prolonged exposure of dead corpses was and is repulsive and disgraceful (see 14:19).

34:4 heaven … scroll. Not even the heavens are to escape the effects of God's wrath. Revelation 6:14 affirms the future fulfillment of this prophecy during Daniel's 70th week (see 2:19; 13:10).

34:5 Edom. The prophet selects Edom as a representative of the rest of the nations (cf. 63:1; Ge 25:23; Nu 20:14–21; Eze 35:1–15; Ob 1–14; Mal 1:2, 3; cf. 25:10). **people … devoted to destruction.** The expression's negative connotation stems from their involuntary devotion to God.

34:6, 7 lambs … goats … rams … Wild oxen … bulls. Since the nations had not repented and obeyed God's way of sacrifice for sins, they became the sacrificial penalty for their own sins.

34:6 Bozrah. A chief city of Edom located

It is [a]sated with fat, with the
blood of lambs and goats,
With the fat of the kidneys of rams.
For the LORD has a sacrifice in [A]Bozrah
And a great slaughter in
the land of [B]Edom.
7 [A]Wild oxen will also [a]fall with them
And [B]young bulls with strong ones;
Thus their land will be [C]soaked with blood,
And their dust [b]become greasy with fat.
8 For the LORD has a day of [A]vengeance,
A year of recompense for
the [a]cause of Zion.
9 [a]Its streams will be turned into pitch,
And its loose earth into [A]brimstone,
And its land will become burning pitch.
10 It will [A]not be quenched night or day;
Its [B]smoke will go up forever.
From [C]generation to generation
it will be desolate;
[D]None will pass through it
forever and ever.
11 But [a,A]pelican and hedgehog will possess it,
And [b]owl and raven will dwell in it;
And He will stretch over it the
[B]line of [c]desolation
And the [d]plumb line of emptiness.
12 Its nobles—there is [A]no one there
Whom they may proclaim king—
And all its princes will be [B]nothing.
13 Thorns will come up in its
[A]fortified towers,
Nettles and thistles in its fortified cities;
It will also be a haunt of [B]jackals
And an abode of ostriches.
14 The desert [A]creatures will
meet with the [a]wolves,
The [b,A]hairy goat also will cry to its kind;
Yes, the [c]night monster will settle there
And will find herself a resting place.
15 The tree snake will make its
nest and lay *eggs* there,
And it will hatch and gather
them under its [a]protection.
Yes, [A]the [b]hawks will be gathered there,
Every one with its kind.

16 Seek from the [A]book of the LORD, and read:

Not one of these will be missing;
None will lack its mate.
For [a,B]His mouth has commanded,
And His Spirit has gathered them.
17 He has cast the [A]lot for them,
And His hand has divided
it to them by [B]line.
They shall possess it forever;
From [C]generation to generation
they will dwell in it.

ZION'S HAPPY FUTURE

35 The [A]wilderness and the
desert will be glad,
And the [a,B]Arabah will rejoice and blossom;
Like the crocus
2 It will [A]blossom profusely
And [B]rejoice with rejoicing
and shout of joy.
The [C]glory of Lebanon will be given to it,
The majesty of [D]Carmel and Sharon.
They will see the [E]glory of the LORD,
The majesty of our God.
3 [A]Encourage the [a]exhausted, and
strengthen the [b]feeble.
4 Say to those with [A]anxious heart,
"Take courage, fear not.
Behold, your God will come
with [B]vengeance;
The [C]recompense of God will come,
But He will [D]save you."

34:6 [a]Lit *made fat* [A]Is 63:1; Jer 49:13 [B]Is 63:1 34:7 [a]Lit *go down* [b]Lit *made fat* [A]Num 23:22; Ps 22:21 [B]Ps 68:30; Jer 50:27 [C]Is 63:6 34:8 [a]Or *controversy* [A]Is 13:6; 35:4; 47:3; 61:2; 63:4 34:9 [a]I.e. Edom's [A]Deut 29:23; Ps 11:6; Is 30:33 34:10 [A]Is 1:31; 66:24 [B]Rev 14:11; 19:3 [C]Is 13:20-22; 24:1; 34:10-15; Mal 1:3, 4 [D]Ezek 29:11 34:11 [a]Or *owl* or *jackdaw* [b]Or *great horned owl* [c]Or *formlessness* [d]Lit *stones of void* [A]Zeph 2:14 [B]2 Kin 21:13; Is 24:10; Lam 2:8 34:12 [A]Jer 27:20; 39:6 [B]Is 41:11, 12 34:13 [A]Is 13:22; 25:2; 32:13 [B]Ps 44:19; Jer 9:11; 10:22 34:14 [a]Or *howling creatures* [b]Or *demon* [c]Heb *Lilith* [A]Is 13:21 34:15 [a]Lit *shade* [b]Or *kites* [A]Deut 14:13 34:16 [a]So DSS; M.T. *My* [A]Is 30:8 [B]Is 1:20; 40:5; 58:14 34:17 [A]Is 17:13, 14; Jer 13:25 [B]Is 34:11 [C]Is 34:10 35:1 [a]Or *desert* [A]Is 6:11; 7:21-25; 27:10; 41:18; 55:12, 13 [B]Is 41:19; 51:3 35:2 [A]Is 27:6; 32:15 [B]Is 25:9; 35:10; 55:12, 13; 66:10, 14 [C]Is 60:13 [D]Song 7:5 [E]Is 25:9 35:3 [a]Lit *slack hands* [b]Lit *tottering knees* [A]Job 4:3, 4; Heb 12:12 35:4 [A]Is 32:4 [B]Is 1:24; 47:3; 61:2; 63:4 [C]Is 34:8; 59:18 [D]Ps 145:19; Is 33:22; 35:4

about 20 mi. SE of the southern end of the Dead Sea.

34:8 the LORD has a day of vengeance. *See note on 2:10–22.* God's day of vengeance on Edom (63:4) will be the same as on the rest of the nations (59:17, 18; 61:2).

34:9, 10 God's judgment is to reduce the nations to a state of perpetual volcanic waste.

34:9 brimstone … burning pitch. Genesis 19:24, 28 describes Sodom in similar terms (cf. 30:33; Dt 29:23; Ps 11:6; Jer 49:18; Eze 38:22).

34:10 smoke will go up forever. Revelation forecasts this destiny for final Babylon, the great end-time world empire (Rev 14:10, 11; 18:18; 19:3).

34:11–15 Various forms of animal and bird life symbolize the depopulated condition into which the nations fall after God's judgment upon them (13:21, 22; 14:23).

34:11, 13 pelican … owl … raven … ostriches. The presence of unclean birds was a sign of desolation and wilderness. Similar symbolism portrays the final state of Babylon in the future (Rev 18:2; cf. 13:21; Jer 50:39; Zep 2:13, 14).

34:16 His mouth has commanded. The prophecies against the nation in vv. 1–15 were just as certain as God's sovereign command through His prophet.

34:17 divided it … by line. God had partitioned off Edom just as He once did Canaan (Nu 26:55, 56; Jos 18:4–6) and allotted it to the wild animals listed in vv. 11–15.

35:1–4 In contrast to luxuriant Edom that is to become a desert (34:1–17), during Messiah's reign on earth the whole world is to become a flourishing garden and this will offer encouragement to the weak.

35:1 desert … Like the crocus. Dramatic changes in the land are to come during the messianic age (see 30:23–25; 32:15–20).

35:2 Lebanon … Carmel and Sharon. Areas near the sea noted for their agricultural fertility. They will see. Israel is to recognize the earth's newfound fruitfulness as coming from the Lord and attribute to Him the appropriate credit.

35:3 exhausted … feeble. The future change in Israel's international role is to serve to encourage the discouraged among the people. The writer of Hebrews gave an additional application of this verse to strengthen endurance among Christians suffering persecution for their faith (Heb 12:12).

35:4 vengeance … save you. The vengeance of God (34:8) is to furnish the means to redeem His long-oppressed people of Israel.

5 Then the [A]eyes of the blind will be opened
And the ears of the deaf
will be unstopped.
6 Then the [A]lame will leap like a deer,
And the [B]tongue of the mute
will shout for joy.
For waters will break forth
in the [C]wilderness
And streams in the [a]Arabah.
7 The [a]scorched land will become a pool
And the thirsty ground [A]springs of water;
In the [B]haunt of jackals, its resting place,
Grass *becomes* reeds and rushes.
8 [A]A highway will be there, [B]a roadway,
And it will be called the
Highway of [C]Holiness.
The unclean will not travel on it,
But it *will* be for him who
walks *that* way,
And [D]fools will not wander *on it.*
9 No [A]lion will be there,
Nor will any vicious beast go up on it;
[a]These will not be found there.
But [B]the redeemed will walk *there,*
10 And [A]the ransomed of the
LORD will return
And come with joyful shouting to Zion,
With everlasting joy upon their heads.
They will [a]find gladness and joy,
And [B]sorrow and sighing will flee away.

SENNACHERIB INVADES JUDAH

36 [A]Now in the fourteenth year of King Hezekiah, [B]Sennacherib king of Assyria came up against all the fortified cities of Judah and seized them. 2 And the [A]king of Assyria sent Rabshakeh from Lachish to Jerusalem to King Hezekiah with a large army. And he stood by the [B]conduit of the upper pool on the highway of the [a]fuller's field. 3 Then [A]Eliakim the son of Hilkiah, who was over the household, and [B]Shebna the scribe, and Joah the son of Asaph, the recorder, came out to him.

4 Then [A]Rabshakeh said to them, "Say now to Hezekiah, 'Thus says the great king, the king of Assyria, "What is this confidence that you [a]have? 5 I say, 'Your counsel and strength for the war are only [a]empty words.' Now on whom do you rely, that [A]you have rebelled against me? 6 Behold, you rely on the [A]staff of this crushed reed, *even* on Egypt, on which if a man leans, it will go into his [a]hand and pierce it. [B]So is Pharaoh king of Egypt to all who rely on him. 7 But if you say to me, 'We trust in the LORD our God,' is it not He [A]whose high places and whose altars Hezekiah has taken away and has said to Judah and to Jerusalem, 'You shall worship before this altar'? 8 Now therefore, [a]come make a bargain with my master the king of Assyria, and I will give you two thousand horses, if you are able on your part to set riders on them. 9 How then can you [a]repulse one [b]official of the least of my master's servants and [c,A]rely on Egypt for chariots and for

35:5 [A]Is 29:18; 32:3, 4; 42:7, 16; 50:4; Matt 11:5; John 9:6, 7 35:6 [a]Or *desert* [A]Matt 15:30; John 5:8, 9; Acts 3:8 [B]Matt 9:32; Luke 11:14 [C]Is 35:1; 41:18; 43:19; 49:10; 51:3; John 7:38 35:7 [a]Or *mirage* [A]Is 49:10 [B]Is 13:22; 34:13 35:8 [A]Is 11:16; 19:23; 40:3; 49:11; 62:10 [B]Is 30:21; 51:10 [C]Is 4:3; 52:1; Matt 7:13, 14; 1 Pet 1:15, 16 [D]Is 33:8 35:9 [a]Lit *It* [A]Is 5:29; 30:6 [B]Is 51:10; 62:12; 63:4 35:10 [a]Lit *overtake* [A]Is 1:27; 51:11 [B]Is 25:8; 30:19; 65:19; Rev 7:17; 21:4 36:1 [A]2 Kin 18:13 [B]2 Chr 32:1 36:2 [a]I.e. launderer's [A]2 Kin 18:17-20:11; 2 Chr 32:9-24; Is 36:2-38:8 [B]Is 7:3 36:3 [A]Is 22:20 [B]Is 22:15 36:4 [a]Lit *trust* [A]2 Kin 18:19 36:5 [a]Lit *words of lips* [A]2 Kin 18:7 36:6 [a]Lit *palm* [A]Ezek 29:6, 7 [B]Ps 146:3; Is 30:3, 5, 7 36:7 [A]Deut 12:2-5; 2 Kin 18:4, 5 36:8 [a]Lit *please exchange pledges* 36:9 [a]Lit *turn away the face of* [b]Or *governor* [C]Lit *rely on for yourself* [A]Is 20:5; 30:2-5, 7; 31:3

35:5 eyes … opened … ears … unstopped. This is to reverse the spiritual condition of the immediate objects of Isaiah's ministry (see 29:18; 32:3).

35:6 lame … shout. God's restoration in the millennial age is to include physical restoration to the afflicted. Jesus' first coming gave a foretaste of that future day (Mt 11:5; 12:22; Mk 7:37; Lk 7:21; Ac 3:8).

35:6, 7 streams in the Arabah … springs of water. Water was and is a precious commodity in Israel (41:18). In the Millennium, there will be no scarcity.

35:7 haunt of jackals. The rocky crags normally inhabited by jackals (34:13) are to become splashy meadows.

35:8 Highway of Holiness. This refers to the way leading the redeemed back to Jerusalem, the throne of Messiah, literally and spiritually. Christ Himself is to be the leader on that way, called in 40:3, the "way for the LORD."

35:9 lion … vicious beast. No ferocious beasts are to threaten the safety of those traveling the Highway of Holiness. **the redeemed.** Mentioned only rarely in chaps. 1–39 (1:27; 29:22) whose theme is judgment; terms for redemption occur frequently in chaps. 40–66.

35:10 the ransomed … flee away. See 51:11 where the words occur again. Gladness is to replace sadness across the board in the day of Israel's restoration.

36:1–39:8 The 4 chapters duplicate almost verbatim 2Ki 18:13–20:19 (cf. 2Ch 32:1–23). *See 2 Kings notes* for amplification. Isaiah added this material to make the references to Assyria more understandable. It is most probable that Isaiah is the author of this section, since 2Ch 32:32 says Isaiah also wrote the acts of Hezekiah. Isaiah's record was incorporated into 2 Kings by the author of that record. These chapters form the transition closing the first division of Isaiah's prophecy. Chapters 36, 37 are the historical consummation of chaps. 1–35—Jerusalem's deliverance from Assyria—and chaps. 38, 39 are the historical basis for chaps. 40–66—a preview of the Babylonian captivity.

36:1 fourteenth year of King Hezekiah. Since Sennacherib's attack came in 701 B.C., this places the beginning of Hezekiah's reign in 715 B.C. But since 2Ki 18:1 says he began to reign in the third year of Hoshea, ca. 729 B.C., Hezekiah served as co-regent with Ahaz (ca. 729–716 B.C.) before assuming the throne exclusively. It was customary for the later kings of Israel to assume their sons into partnership in the government during their lives. **Sennacherib.** The king of Assyria (ca. 705 to 681 B.C.). **fortified cities.** The discovery of the ancient *Annals of Sennacherib* reveals the cities he conquered in his campaign southward from Sidon on the Mediterranean coast.

36:2 Rabshakeh. The spokesman for Sennacherib's 3 highest officials, who represented the king against Jerusalem on this occasion, according to 2Ki 18:17. **large army.** This was a token force of the main army (37:36), with which Sennacherib hoped to bluff Judah into submitting. **Lachish.** A city about 25 mi. SW of Jerusalem. Sennacherib's conquest of this city was in its closing phase when he sent the messengers. **conduit of the upper pool.** Isaiah met Ahaz at the same spot to try unsuccessfully to dissuade him from trusting in foreign powers (7:3).

36:3 Eliakim … Shebna. *See notes on 22:19–22.* **Joah … the recorder.** The position was that of an intermediary between the king and the people.

36:4–10 Rabshakeh's logic was twofold: (1) Egypt was to be unable to deliver Jerusalem (vv. 4–6, 8, 9), and (2) the Lord had called on the Assyrians to destroy Judah (vv. 7, 10).

36:4 the great king, the king of Assyria. The self-appropriated title of Assyrian kings. In contrast, Rabshakeh rudely omitted any title for Hezekiah (vv. 4, 14, 15, 16).

36:5 empty words. Words amounted to nothing when it came to warfare. In other words, Judah was defenseless.

36:6 crushed reed … Egypt. The Assyrian's advice strongly resembled that of Isaiah (19:14–16; 30:7; 31:3).

36:7 He whose high places and whose altars. Rabshakeh mistakenly thought Hezekiah's reforms in removing idols (2Ki 18:4; 2Ch 31:1) had removed opportunities to worship the Lord. **this altar.** That all worship should center in Solomon's temple was utterly foreign to the polytheistic Assyrians.

36:8, 9 Rabshakeh taunted and minimized Judah's best defensive efforts, even with Egypt's help.

horsemen? 10 Have I now come up [a]without the
LORD'S approval against this land to destroy it?
[A]The LORD said to me, 'Go up against this land and
destroy it.' " ' "
11 Then Eliakim and Shebna and Joah said to Rabshakeh, "Speak now to your servants in [A]Aramaic,
for we [a]understand *it;* and do not speak with us in
[b,B]Judean in the hearing of the people who are on
the wall." 12 But Rabshakeh said, "Has my master
sent me only to your master and to you to speak
these words, *and* not to the men who sit on the wall,
doomed to eat their own dung and drink their own
urine with you?"
13 Then Rabshakeh stood and [A]cried with a loud
voice in Judean and said, "Hear the words of the
great king, the king of Assyria. 14 Thus says the king,
'Do not let Hezekiah [A]deceive you, for he will not
be able to deliver you; 15 nor let Hezekiah make you
[A]trust in the LORD, saying, "The LORD will surely deliver us, this city will not be given into the hand of
the king of Assyria." 16 Do not listen to Hezekiah,' for
thus says the king of Assyria, '[a]Make your peace with
me and come out to me, and eat each of his [A]vine
and each of his fig tree and drink each of the [B]waters
of his own cistern, 17 until I come and take you away
to a land like your own land, a land of grain and
new wine, a land of bread and vineyards. 18 *Beware*
that Hezekiah does not mislead you, saying, "[A]The
LORD will deliver us." Has any one of the gods of
the nations delivered his land from the hand of the
king of Assyria? 19 Where are the gods of [A]Hamath
and Arpad? Where are the gods of [A]Sepharvaim?
And when have they [B]delivered Samaria from my
hand? 20 Who among all the [A]gods of these lands
have delivered their land from my hand, that the
[B]LORD would deliver Jerusalem from my hand?' "
21 But they were silent and [A]answered him not a
word; for the king's commandment was, "Do not
answer him." 22 Then [A]Eliakim the son of Hilkiah,
who was over the household, and [B]Shebna the scribe
and Joah the son of Asaph, the recorder, came to
Hezekiah with their clothes torn and told him the
words of Rabshakeh.

HEZEKIAH SEEKS ISAIAH'S HELP

37 And [A]when King Hezekiah heard *it,* he tore
his clothes, covered himself with sackcloth
and entered the house of the LORD. 2 Then he sent
[A]Eliakim who was over the household with [B]Shebna
the scribe and the elders of the priests, covered with
sackcloth, to [C]Isaiah the prophet, the son of Amoz.
3 They said to him, "Thus says Hezekiah, 'This day
is a [A]day of distress, rebuke and rejection; for [B]chil-
dren have come to birth, and there is no strength to
[a]deliver. 4 Perhaps the LORD your God will hear the
words of Rabshakeh, whom his master the king of
Assyria has sent to [A]reproach the living God, and
will rebuke the words which the LORD your God has
heard. Therefore, offer a prayer for [B]the remnant
that is left.' "
5 So the servants of King Hezekiah came to Isaiah.
6 Isaiah said to them, "Thus you shall say to your
master, 'Thus says the LORD, "[A]Do not be afraid because of the words that you have heard, with which
the servants of the king of Assyria have blasphemed
Me. 7 Behold, I will put a spirit in him so that he will
[A]hear a rumor and [B]return to his own land. And I
will make him fall by the sword in his own land." ' "
8 Then Rabshakeh returned and found the king of
Assyria fighting against [A]Libnah, for he had heard
that [a]the king had left [B]Lachish. 9 When he [A]heard
them say concerning Tirhakah king of [a,B]Cush, "He

36:10 [a]Lit *without the LORD* [A]1 Kin 13:18; 22:6, 12 36:11 [a]Lit *hear* [b]I.e. Hebrew [A]Ezra 4:7; Dan 2:4 [B]Is 36:13 36:13 [A]2 Chr 32:18 36:14 [A]Is 37:10 36:15 [A]Is 36:18, 20; 37:10, 11 36:16 [a]Lit *Make with me a blessing* [A]1 Kin 4:25; Mic 4:4; Zech 3:10 [B]Prov 5:15 36:18 [A]Is 36:15 36:19 [A]Is 10:9-11; 37:11-13; Jer 49:23 [B]2 Kin 17:6 36:20 [A]1 Kin 20:23, 28 [B]Is 36:15 36:21 [A]Prov 9:7, 8; 26:4 36:22 [A]Is 22:20; 36:3 [B]Is 22:15 37:1 [A]2 Kin 19:1-37; Is 37:1-38 37:2 [A]Is 22:20 [B]Is 22:15 [C]Is 1:1; 20:2 37:3 [a]Lit *give birth* [A]Is 22:5; 26:16; 33:2 [B]Is 26:17, 18; 66:9; Hos 13:13 37:4 [A]Is 36:13-15, 18, 20 [B]Is 1:9; 10:20-22; 37:31, 32; 46:3 37:6 [A]Is 7:4; 35:4 37:7 [A]Is 37:9 [B]Is 37:37, 38 37:8 [a]Lit *he* [A]Num 33:20; Josh 10:29 [B]Josh 10:31, 32 37:9 [a]Or *Ethiopia* [A]Is 37:7 [B]Is 18:1; 20:5

36:10 The LORD said. Rabshakeh's boastful claim of the authority from Judah's God for his mission may have been a ploy on his part to get a surrender, but it aligned with Isaiah's prophecy that the Assyrians would be His instrument to punish His people (8:7, 8; 10:5, 6). The Assyrians may have heard this from partisans or may not have known this, but Judah did.

36:11 Aramaic ... Judean. Hezekiah's representatives, aware of the alarm created by the suggestion that the Lord was on the Assyrian side, asked Rabshakeh to change from Hebrew, or Judean, to Aramaic, the language of diplomacy, so the people on the wall could not understand his words and be terrified.

36:12 men ... on the wall. The foreign emissary continued his efforts to damage the city's morale by speaking of the horrors of famine that a long siege would entail.

36:13–17 Rabshakeh spoke longer and louder, suggesting that Hezekiah could not save the city, but the great king, the king of Assyria, would fill the people with abundance (vv. 16, 17).

36:16 Make your peace. Lit. "Make a blessing with me." The official invited the people to make a covenant with Assyria by surrendering.

36:17 take you away. Rabshakeh did not hide Assyria's well-known practice of deporting conquered peoples to distant places.

36:18–20 In Rabshakeh's eyes, the Lord was one of the many gods worshiped by nations conquered by the Assyrians (cf. 10:8–11).

36:21 were silent. Hezekiah had apparently anticipated the ultimatum of the Assyrians and had told his representatives and the men on the wall not to respond.

36:22 clothes torn. The king's representatives reported to him in a state of grief and shock at the blasphemy they thought they had heard.

37:1 tore ... sackcloth. A reaction that symbolized Hezekiah's grief, repentance and contrition. The nation was to repent and the king was to lead the way. **house of the LORD.** God designated the temple as His "house of prayer" (56:7; Mt 21:13; Mk 11:17; Lk 19:46), so it was the proper place to go to confess sins and seek forgiveness (cf. Ps 73:16, 17).

37:2 elders of the priests. Senior religious leaders in Israel.

37:3 come to birth ... no strength. Hezekiah compared his dilemma with a mother in labor unable to deliver her child. Jerusalem had to be delivered, but he was helpless to make it happen.

37:4 reproach the living God. Hezekiah received a report of Rabshakeh's belittling of the Lord by equating Him with other gods and points out the distinction between God who is living and gods who are lifeless and helpless (40:18–20; 46:5–7). **remnant that is left.** Only Jerusalem remained unconquered. Hezekiah asked Isaiah's prayer for the city.

37:6 Do not be afraid. The same assurance Isaiah had given Ahaz (7:4).

37:7 spirit. The Lord promised to incline Sennacherib's attitude in such a way that he would leave Jerusalem unharmed and return home.

37:8 Libnah. After conquering Lachish, Sennacherib moved on to this smaller town to the N of Lachish.

37:9 Tirhakah king of Cush. Tirhakah did not become king of Cush, or Ethiopia (and Egypt), until 11 years after the 701 B.C. siege, so Isaiah's use of "king" anticipates his future title. At that moment, however, he represented a threat to Sennacherib from the S that caused him to renew his call for Jerusalem's surrender to the N.

has come out to fight against you," and when he
heard *it* he sent messengers to Hezekiah, saying,
10 "Thus you shall say to Hezekiah king of [a]Judah,
'[A]Do not let your God in whom you trust deceive
you, saying, "Jerusalem will not be given into the
hand of the king of Assyria." 11 [A]Behold, you have
heard what the kings of Assyria have done to all the
lands, destroying them completely. So will you be
[a]spared? 12 Did the gods of [a]those nations which my
fathers have destroyed deliver them, *even* [A]Gozan
and [B]Haran and Rezeph and the sons of Eden who
were in Telassar? 13 Where is the king of Hamath, the
king of Arpad, the king of the city of Sepharvaim,
and of Hena and Ivvah?'"

HEZEKIAH'S PRAYER IN THE TEMPLE

14 Then Hezekiah took the [a]letter from the hand
of the messengers and read it, and he went up to
the house of the LORD and [b]spread it out before
the LORD. 15 Hezekiah prayed to the LORD saying,
16 "O LORD of hosts, the God of Israel, [A]who is enthroned *above* the cherubim, You are the [B]God, You
alone, of all the kingdoms of the earth. [C]You have
made heaven and earth. 17 [A]Incline Your ear, O LORD,
and hear; open Your eyes, O LORD, and see; and [B]lis-
ten to all the words of Sennacherib, who sent *them*
to [C]reproach the living God. 18 Truly, O LORD, the
[A]kings of Assyria have devastated all the countries
and their lands, 19 and have cast their gods into the
fire, for they were not gods but the [A]work of men's
hands, wood and stone. So they have [B]destroyed
them. 20 Now, O LORD our God, [A]deliver us from his
hand that [B]all the kingdoms of the earth may know
that You alone, LORD, [a]are God."

GOD ANSWERS THROUGH ISAIAH

21 Then [A]Isaiah the son of Amoz sent *word* to Hezekiah, saying, "Thus says the LORD, the God of Israel,
'Because you have prayed to Me about Sennacherib
king of Assyria, 22 this is the word that the LORD has
spoken against him:

"She has despised you and mocked you,
The [A]virgin [B]daughter of Zion;
She has [C]shaken *her* head behind you,
The daughter of Jerusalem!

23 "Whom have you [A]reproached
and blasphemed?
And against whom have you
raised *your* voice
And [a]haughtily [B]lifted up your eyes?
Against the [C]Holy One of Israel!

24 "Through your servants you have
reproached the Lord,
And you have said, 'With my
many chariots I came up to the
heights of the mountains,
To the remotest parts of [A]Lebanon;
And I cut down its tall [B]cedars
and its choice cypresses.
And I will go to its [a]highest
peak, its thickest [C]forest.

25 'I dug *wells* and drank waters,
And [A]with the sole of my
feet I dried up
All the rivers of [a]Egypt.'

26 "[A]Have you not heard?
Long ago I did it,
From ancient times I [B]planned it.
Now [C]I have brought it to pass,
That [D]you should turn fortified
cities into [E]ruinous heaps.

27 "Therefore their inhabitants
were short of strength,
They were dismayed
and put to shame;
They were *as* the [A]vegetation of the
field and *as* the green herb,
As [B]grass on the housetops [a]is
scorched before it is grown up.

28 "But I [A]know your sitting down
And your going out and your coming in
And your raging against Me.

37:10 [a]Lit *Judah, saying* [A]Is 36:15 37:11 [a]Lit *delivered* [A]Is 10:9-11; 36:18-20 37:12 [a]Lit *the* [A]2 Kin 17:6; 18:11 [B]Gen 11:31; 12:1-4; Acts 7:2 37:14 [a]Lit *letters* [b]Lit *Hezekiah spread* 37:16 [A]Ex 25:22; 1 Sam 4:4; Ps 80:1; 99:1 [B]Deut 10:17; Ps 86:10; 136:2, 3 [C]Is 42:5; 45:12; Jer 10:12 37:17 [A]2 Chr 6:40; Ps 17:6; Dan 9:18 [B]Ps 74:22 [C]Is 37:4 37:18 [A]2 Kin 15:29; 16:9; 17:6, 24; 1 Chr 5:26 37:19 [A]Is 2:8; 17:8; 41:24, 29 [B]Is 26:14 37:20 [a]So DSS and 2 Kin 19:19; M.T. omits *God* [A]Is 25:9; 33:22; 35:4 [B]1 Kin 18:36, 37; Ps 46:10; Is 37:16; Ezek 36:23 37:21 [A]Is 37:2 37:22 [A]Jer 14:17; Lam 2:13 [B]Ps 9:14; Zeph 3:14; Zech 2:10 [C]Job 16:4 37:23 [a]Lit *on high* [A]Is 37:4 [B]Is 2:11; 5:15, 21 [C]Ezek 39:7; Hab 1:12 37:24 [a]Lit *farthest height* [A]Is 10:33, 34 [B]Is 14:8 [C]Is 10:18 37:25 [a]Or *the besieged place* [A]Deut 11:10; 1 Kin 20:10 37:26 [A]Is 40:21, 28 [B]Acts 2:23; 4:27, 28; 1 Pet 2:8 [C]Is 46:11 [D]Is 10:6 [E]Is 17:1; 25:2 37:27 [a]So DSS and 2 Kin 19:26; M.T. as *a plowed field* [A]Is 40:7 [B]Ps 129:6 37:28 [A]Ps 139:1

37:10–13 The king of Assyria sent messengers to summarize the arguments given in Rabshakeh's ultimatum of 36:4–19.

37:10 deceive. The accusation of deception was first against Hezekiah (36:14), then against the Lord.

37:11–13 The threat repeats the thrust of 36:18–20.

37:12 The conquered cities mentioned here lay between the Tigris and Euphrates Rivers in Mesopotamia.

37:13 These were cities of Syria that had fallen to the Assyrians recently.

37:14 house of the LORD. Godly Hezekiah returned to the house of the Lord (cf. v. 1) as he should have, in contrast to Ahaz, who in a similar crisis refused even to ask a sign from the Lord (7:11, 12).

37:16 who is enthroned … made heaven and earth. The basis for Hezekiah's plea was God's role as the Sovereign and Creator of the universe, not Judah's worthiness to be delivered.

37:17 hear … see … listen. In contrast to the gods of other nations (Ps 115:4–7), the God of Israel heard and saw all.

37:18, 19 Hezekiah exploded the Assyrian theory that the Lord was no different from gods of the other nations that could not deliver their worshipers.

37:20 You alone. Hezekiah displayed the highest motivation of all in requesting the salvation of Jerusalem: that the world may know that the Lord alone is God (cf. Da 9:16–19).

37:21 Isaiah the son of Amoz. Immediately upon the conclusion of Hezekiah's prayer, Isaiah had a response from the Lord.

37:22 mocked you. Jerusalem, portrayed as a virgin helpless before a would-be rapist, had the "last laugh" against Sennacherib.

37:23 you reproached and blasphemed. The Lord had heard Sennacherib's reproach against Him (37:17).

37:24, 25 Even the servants of Sennacherib had bragged about Assyria's being unstoppable.

37:26 I have brought it to pass. God corrected Sennacherib's vanity; he conquered nothing on his own, but was a mere instrument in the Lord's hand.

37:27 They were dismayed. Assyria had utterly overwhelmed populations included in their conquests.

37:28 your raging against Me. Sennacherib's ignorance of being a mere tool in the Lord's hand was bad, but his belittling of God, the source of his life, was far worse.

29 “Because of your raging against Me
And because your [a,A]arrogance
has come up to My ears,
Therefore I will put My [B]hook in your nose
And My [C]bridle in your lips,
And I will turn you back [D]by the
way which you came.

30 “Then this shall be the sign for you: [a]you will
eat this year what [A]grows of itself, in the second
year what springs from the same, and in the third
year sow, reap, plant vineyards and eat their fruit.
31 The [A]surviving [B]remnant of the house of Judah will
again [C]take root downward and bear fruit upward.
32 For out of Jerusalem will go forth a [A]remnant and
out of Mount Zion [a]survivors. The [B]zeal of the LORD
of hosts will perform this.” ’
33 “Therefore, thus says the LORD concerning the
king of Assyria, ‘He will not come to this city or
shoot an arrow there; and he will not come before
it with a shield, or throw up a [A]siege ramp against
it. 34 [A]By the way that he came, by the same he will
return, and he will not come to this city,’ declares
the LORD. 35 ‘For I will [A]defend this city to save it
[B]for My own sake and for My servant David’s sake.’ ”

ASSYRIANS DESTROYED

36 Then the [A]angel of the LORD went out and
struck 185,000 in the camp of the Assyrians; and
when [a]men arose early in the morning, behold, all of
these were [b]dead. 37 So Sennacherib king of Assyria
departed and [a]returned *home* and lived at [A]Nineveh.
38 It came about as he was worshiping in the house
of Nisroch his god, that Adrammelech and Sharezer
his sons killed him with the sword; and they escaped
into the land of [A]Ararat. And [B]Esarhaddon his son
became king in his place.

HEZEKIAH HEALED

38 [A]In those days Hezekiah became [a]mortally
ill. And [B]Isaiah the prophet the son of Amoz
came to him and said to him, “Thus says the LORD,
‘[C]Set your house in order, for you shall die and not
live.’ ” 2 Then Hezekiah turned his face to the wall
and prayed to the LORD, 3 and said, “[A]Remember
now, O LORD, I beseech You, how I have [B]walked
before You in truth and with a [C]whole heart, and
[D]have done what is good in Your sight.” And Hezekiah [E]wept [a]bitterly.
4 Then the word of the LORD came to Isaiah, saying, 5 “Go and say to Hezekiah, ‘Thus says the LORD,
the God of your father David, “I have heard your
prayer, I have seen your tears; behold, I will add
[A]fifteen years to your [a]life. 6 I will [A]deliver you and
this city from the hand of the king of Assyria; and
I will defend this city.” ’
7 “This shall be the [A]sign to you from the LORD, that
the LORD will do this thing that He has spoken: 8 Behold, I will [A]cause the shadow on the stairway, which
has gone down with the sun on the stairway of Ahaz,
to go back ten steps.” So the [B]sun’s *shadow* went back
ten steps on the stairway on which it had gone down.
9 A writing of Hezekiah king of Judah after his
illness and [a]recovery:

37:29 [a]Lit *complacency* [A]Is 10:12 [B]Ezek 29:4; 38:4 [C]Is 30:28 [D]Is 37:34 37:30 [a]Lit *eating* [A]Lev 25:5, 11 37:31 [A]Is 4:2; 10:20 [B]Is 37:4 [C]Is 27:6 37:32 [a]Lit *those who escape* [A]Is 37:4 [B]2 Kin 19:31; Is 9:7; 59:17; Joel 2:18; Zech 1:14 37:33 [A]Jer 6:6; 32:24 37:34 [A]Is 37:29 37:35 [A]2 Kin 20:6; Is 31:5; 38:6 [B]Is 43:25; 48:9, 11 37:36 [a]Lit *they* [b]Lit *dead bodies* [A]2 Kin 19:35; Is 10:12, 33, 34 37:37 [a]Lit *went and returned* [A]Gen 10:11; Jon 1:2; 3:3; 4:11; Zeph 2:13 37:38 [A]Gen 8:4; Jer 51:27 [B]Ezra 4:2 38:1 [a]Lit *sick to the point of death* [A]2 Kin 20:1-6, 9-11; 2 Chr 32:24; Is 38:1-8 [B]Is 1:1; 37:2 [C]2 Sam 17:23 38:3 [a]Lit *great weeping* [A]Neh 13:14 [B]2 Kin 18:5, 6; Ps 26:3 [C]1 Chr 28:9; 29:19 [D]Deut 6:18 [E]Ps 6:6-8 38:5 [a]Lit *days* [A]2 Kin 18:2, 13 38:6 [A]Is 31:5; 37:35 38:7 [A]Judg 6:17, 21, 36-40; Is 7:11, 14; 37:30 38:8 [A]2 Kin 20:9-11 [B]Josh 10:12-14 38:9 [a]Lit *he lived after his illness*

37:29 hook in your nose … bridle in your lips. In judging Sennacherib, the Lord treated him as an obstinate animal with a ring in his nose and/or a bridle in his mouth. Some ancient sources indicate that captives were led before a king by a cord attached to a hook or ring through the upper lip and nose. Thus, he was to be brought back to his own country.

37:30 sign. The two years in which they were sustained by the growth of the crops were the two in which Sennacherib ravaged them (cf. 32:10). He left immediately after the deliverance (37:37), so in the third year, the people left could plant again.

37:31, 32 remnant … remnant. From the remnant of survivors in Jerusalem came descendants who covered the Land once again (1:9, 27; 3:10; 4:3; 6:13; 8:16, 17; 10:20, 22; 11:12, 16; 26:1–4, 8; 27:12; 28:5; 37:4).

37:32 zeal of the LORD of hosts. The same confirmation of God’s promise in 9:7 assured the future establishment of the messianic kingdom. Deliverance from Sennacherib in Hezekiah’s day was a down payment on the literal, final restoration of Israel.

37:33 will not come … throw up a siege ramp. God promised that the Assyrians would not even pose a physical threat to Jerusalem. They came near, but never engaged in a true siege of the city.

37:34 he will return. In contrast with his arrival in Judah as an overbearing, invincible monarch, he returned to Assyria as a defeated, dejected “has-been.” In his own *Annals* he claimed only to have “shut up” Jerusalem, not to have conquered it.

37:35 for My own sake. Since Sennacherib had directly challenged the Lord’s faithfulness to His word (v. 10), the faithfulness of God was at stake in this contest with the Assyrians (cf. Eze 36:22, 23). **for My servant David’s sake.** God pledged to perpetuate David’s line on his throne (2Sa 7:16; cf. 9:6, 7; 11:1; 55:3).

37:36 the angel of the LORD. This was Isaiah’s only use of a title that is frequent in the OT, one referring to the Lord Himself. For identification, *see note on Ex 3:2.* **struck.** Secular records also mention this massive slaughter of Assyrian troops, without noting its supernatural nature, of course (cf. Ex 12:12, 29).

37:37 Nineveh. The capital of Assyria.

37:38 his god. The place of Sennacherib’s death (ca. 681 B.C.) recalled the impotence of his god, Nisroch, compared with the omnipotence of Hezekiah’s God. **killed him.** Sennacherib’s pitiful death came 20 years after his confrontation with the Lord regarding the fate of Jerusalem. **Ararat.** Mountain region N of Israel, W of Assyria (cf. Ge 8:4; 2Ki 19:37; Jer 51:27). **Esarhaddon.** Successor to Sennacherib (ca. 681–669 B.C.).

38:1 In those days … ill. Hezekiah’s sickness occurred before the Assyrian siege of Jerusalem described in chaps. 36, 37. Isaiah placed the description of that illness here, along with chap. 39, to introduce chaps. 40–66. *See note on 2Ki 20:1.* **Set your house in order.** An instruction telling Hezekiah to make his final will known to his family (cf. 2Sa 17:23; 1Ki 2:1–9). **you shall die and not live.** The prediction sounded final, but Hezekiah knew God was willing to hear his appeal (cf. Ex 32:7–14).

38:2, 3 prayed … wept bitterly. *See note on 2Ki 20:2, 3.*

38:3 whole heart. Hezekiah based his implied request for an extension of his life on an undivided desire to please the Lord.

38:5 fifteen years. The Lord’s immediate (2Ki 20:4) response granted the king’s request. Having to reverse a prophecy so quickly did not alarm Isaiah as it did Jonah later on (Jon 4:2, 3). Isaiah resembled Nathan in this respect (2Sa 7:3–6).

38:6 I will deliver … this city. The deliverance described in the previous chapter.

38:7, 8 sign … back ten steps. Here is the first biblical mention of any means of marking time. According to 2Ki 20:8–10, Hezekiah requested this sign to confirm the Lord’s promise of healing.

38:9 writing of Hezekiah. In response to his healing, Hezekiah wrote the record of his helplessness when facing death (vv. 10–14)

10 I said, "[A]In the middle of my [a]life
I am to enter the [B]gates of Sheol;
I am to be [C]deprived of the
rest of my years."
11 I said, "I will not see the LORD,
The LORD [A]in the land of the living;
I will look on man no more among
the inhabitants of the world.
12 "Like a shepherd's [A]tent my dwelling is
pulled up and removed from me;
As a [B]weaver I [C]rolled up my life.
He [D]cuts me off from the loom;
From [E]day until night You
make an end of me.
13 "I composed *my soul* until morning.
[A]Like a lion—so He [B]breaks all my bones,
From [C]day until night You
make an end of me.
14 "[A]Like a swallow, *like* a crane, so I twitter;
I [B]moan like a dove;
My [C]eyes look wistfully to the heights;
O Lord, I am oppressed, be my [D]security.

15 "[A]What shall I say?
[a]For He has spoken to me, and
He Himself has done it;
I will [B]wander about all my years
because of the [C]bitterness of my soul.
16 "O Lord, [A]by *these* things *men* live,
And in all these is the life of my spirit;
[a,B]O restore me to health and [C]let me live!
17 "Lo, for *my own* welfare I had
great bitterness;
It is You who has [a,A]kept my soul
from the pit of [b]nothingness,
For You have [B]cast all my sins
behind Your back.
18 "For [A]Sheol cannot thank You,
Death cannot praise You;
Those who go down [B]to the pit cannot
hope for Your faithfulness.
19 "It is the [A]living who give thanks
to You, as I do today;
A [B]father tells his sons about
Your faithfulness.
20 "The LORD will surely save me;
So we will [A]play my songs on
stringed instruments
[B]All *the* days of our life [C]at the
house of the LORD."

21 Now [A]Isaiah had said, "Let them take a cake of
figs and apply it to the boil, that he may recover."
22 Then Hezekiah had said, "What is the [A]sign that
I shall go up to the house of the LORD?"

HEZEKIAH SHOWS HIS TREASURES

39 [A]At that time Merodach-baladan son of Bal-
adan, king of Babylon, sent letters and a
present to Hezekiah, for he heard that he had been
sick and had recovered. 2 Hezekiah [a]was [A]pleased,
and showed them *all* his treasure house, the [B]silver
and the gold and the spices and the precious oil
and his whole armory and all that was found in his
treasuries. There was nothing in his house nor in
all his dominion that Hezekiah did not show them.
3 Then Isaiah the [A]prophet came to King Hezekiah
and said to him, "What did these men say, and from
where have they come to you?" And Hezekiah said,
"They have come to me from a far [B]country, from
Babylon." 4 He said, "What have they seen in your
house?" So Hezekiah [a]answered, "They have seen
all that is in my house; there is nothing among my
treasuries that I have not shown them."

38:10 [a]Lit *days* [A]Ps 102:24 [B]Ps 107:18 [C]Job 17:11, 15; 2 Cor 1:9 38:11 [A]Ps 27:13; 116:9 38:12 [A]2 Cor 5:1, 4; 2 Pet 1:13, 14 [B]Job 7:6 [C]Heb 1:12 [D]Job 6:9 [E]Job 4:20; Ps 73:14 38:13 [A]Job 10:16 [B]Ps 51:8; Dan 6:24 [C]Ps 32:4 38:14 [A]Job 30:29; Ps 102:6 [B]Is 59:11; Ezek 7:16; Nah 2:7 [C]Ps 119:123 [D]Job 17:3; Ps 119:122 38:15 [a]Targum and DSS read *And what shall I say for He* [A]Ps 39:9 [B]1 Kin 21:27 [C]Job 7:11; 10:1; Is 38:17 38:16 [a]Lit *You will* [A]Ps 119:71, 75 [B]Ps 39:13 [C]Ps 119:25 38:17 [a]So some versions; Heb *loved* [b]Or *destruction* [A]Ps 30:3; 86:13; Jon 2:6 [B]Is 43:25; Jer 31:34; Mic 7:19 38:18 [A]Ps 6:5; 30:9; 88:11; Eccl 9:10 [B]Num 16:33; Ps 28:1 38:19 [A]Ps 118:17; 119:175 [B]Deut 6:7; 11:19; Ps 78:5-7 38:20 [A]Ps 33:1-3; 68:24-26 [B]Ps 104:33; 116:2; 146:2 [C]Ps 116:17-19 38:21 [A]2 Kin 20:7, 8 38:22 [A]Is 38:7 39:1 [A]2 Kin 20:12-19; 2 Chr 32:31; Is 39:1-8 39:2 [a]Lit *rejoiced over them* [A]2 Chr 32:25, 31; Job 31:25 [B]2 Kin 18:15, 16 39:3 [A]2 Sam 12:1; 2 Chr 16:7 [B]Deut 28:49; Jer 5:15 39:4 [a]Lit *said*

and told of God's response to his condition (vv. 15–20). This poetry is missing from the parallel account in 2 Kings.

38:10 In the middle of my life. The king was probably in his thirties or forties when he fell sick.

38:11 I will not see. Hezekiah feared that death would terminate his fellowship with the Lord. **LORD, the LORD.** The Heb. repeats the name: "Yah, Yah." The KJV rendered it, "Lord, even the Lord." See 12:2; 26:4 for other such repetitions.

38:12 shepherd's tent .... weaver. Two comparisons with transient articles illustrate how death removes in a moment what may have seemed so permanent.

38:14 I moan ... be my security. In his helplessness, Hezekiah pleaded with God to deliver him from impending death.

38:15 He Himself has done it. The king had complete confidence in God.

38:16 restore me ... let me live! The king's survival was God's accomplishment.

38:17 my sins behind Your back. Hezekiah felt his sickness was somehow related to his sinfulness. To be rid of the latter was to be rid of the former also.

38:18 cannot hope. Hezekiah's understanding of the resurrection of believers was incomplete. The same was true of others throughout much of the OT. But he was right in recognizing that death ended his opportunity for earthly praise and worship in the presence of men.

38:19 father ... sons. Word about God's faithfulness passed from generation to generation (Dt 4:9; 6:7; Ps 78:3, 4). Even if Hezekiah at this point had no heir, he had another reason for frustration over dying in the prime of life.

38:20 play my songs ... at the house of the LORD. Hezekiah was so overwhelmed with gratitude to God that he felt compelled to express it appropriately throughout the 15 years he had left on earth.

38:21, 22 These two verses furnish background details of the account in vv. 1–8.

38:21 cake of figs. The medicine for healing the king's sickness (2Ki 20:7).

38:22 sign. Hezekiah's request explained why the Lord gave him a sign that he would be healed (v. 7; cf. 2Ki 20:8). **the house of the LORD.** Hezekiah went to the temple (v. 20) as Isaiah had instructed him to do (2Ki 20:5, 8).

39:1 At that time. Just after Hezekiah's sickness and recovery. **Merodach-baladan.** *See note on 2Ki 20:12.*

39:2 Hezekiah was pleased. The text does not say whether it was because of flattery or of a desire for help against the increasing Assyrian threat. Cf. 2Ki 20:13. **treasure house ... treasuries.** Doubtless to try to impress his visitors (2Ch 32:25), Hezekiah showed all he could contribute in an alliance against the Assyrians.

39:3 Isaiah the prophet came. God's spokesman showed up without being invited to confront the king, as often happened (e.g., 7:3; 2Sa 12:1; 1Ki 13:1; 18:16, 17).

5 Then Isaiah said to Hezekiah, "Hear the [A]word
of the LORD of hosts, 6 'Behold, the days are coming
when [A]all that is in your house and all that your
fathers have laid up in store to this day will be carried to Babylon; nothing will be left,' says the LORD.
7 'And *some* of your sons who will issue from you,
whom you will beget, [A]will be taken away, and [B]they
will become officials in the palace of the king of
Babylon.' " 8 [A]Then Hezekiah said to Isaiah, "The
word of the LORD which you have spoken is good."
For he [a]thought, "For there will be peace and truth
[B]in my days."

THE GREATNESS OF GOD

40 "[A]Comfort, O comfort My
people," says your God.
2 "[A]Speak [a]kindly to Jerusalem;
And call out to her, that her
[b,B]warfare has ended,
That her [c,C]iniquity has been removed,
That she has received of
the LORD'S hand
[D]Double for all her sins."

3 [A]A voice [a]is calling,
"[B]Clear the way for the LORD
in the wilderness;
Make smooth in the desert a
highway for our God.
4 "Let every valley be lifted up,
And every mountain and
hill be made low;
And let the rough ground
become a plain,
And the rugged terrain a broad valley;
5 [a]Then the [A]glory of the LORD
will be revealed,
And [B]all flesh will see *it* together;
For the [C]mouth of the LORD has spoken."
6 A voice says, "Call out."
Then [a]he answered, "What
shall I call out?"
[A]All flesh is grass, and all its [b]loveliness
is like the flower of the field.
7 The [A]grass withers, the flower fades,
[a]When the [B]breath of the
LORD blows upon it;
Surely the people are grass.
8 The grass withers, the flower fades,
But [A]the word of our God stands forever.

9 Get yourself up on a [A]high mountain,
O Zion, bearer of [B]good news,
Lift up your voice mightily,
O Jerusalem, bearer of good news;
Lift *it* up, do not fear.
Say to the [C]cities of Judah,
"[D]Here is your God!"

39:5 [A]1 Sam 13:13, 14; 15:16 39:6 [A]2 Kin 24:13; 25:13-15; Jer 20:5 39:7 [A]2 Kin 24:10-16; 2 Chr 36:10 [B]Dan 1:1-7 39:8 [a]Lit *said* [A]2 Chr 32:26 [B]2 Chr 34:28
40:1 [A]Is 12:1; 49:13; 51:3, 12; 52:9; 61:2; 66:13; Jer 31:10-14; Zeph 3:14-17; 2 Cor 1:4 40:2 [a]Lit *to the heart of* [b]Or *hard service* [c]Or *penalty of iniquity accepted as paid off* [A]Is 35:4; Zech 1:13 [B]Is 41:11-13; 49:25; 54:15, 17 [C]Is 33:24; 53:5, 6, 11 [D]Jer 16:18; Zech 9:12; Rev 18:6 40:3 [a]Or *of one calling out* [A]Matt 3:3; Mark 1:3; Luke 3:4-6; John 1:23 [B]Mal 3:1; 4:5, 6 40:5 [a]Or *In order that the* [A]Is 6:3; Hab 2:14 [B]Is 52:10; Joel 2:28 [C]Is 1:20; 34:16; 58:14
40:6 [a]Another reading is *I said* [b]Or *constancy* [A]Job 14:2; Ps 102:11; 103:15; 1 Pet 1:24, 25 40:7 [a]Or *Because* [A]Ps 90:5, 6; James 1:10, 11 [B]Job 4:9; 41:21; Is 11:4; 40:24 40:8 [A]Is 55:11; 59:21; Matt 5:18 40:9 [A]Is 52:7 [B]Is 61:1 [C]Is 44:26 [D]Is 25:9; 35:2

39:5, 6 word of the LORD ... carried to Babylon. Isaiah predicted the Babylonian captivity that would come over a century later (586 B.C.), another prophecy historically fulfilled in all of its expected detail.

39:6 nothing will be left. Hezekiah's sin of parading his wealth before the visitors backfired, though this sin was only symptomatic of the ultimate reason for the captivity. The major cause was the corrupt leadership of Manasseh, Hezekiah's son (2Ki 21:11–15).

39:7 sons who will issue from you. To a king without an heir, this was good news (that he would have one some day) and bad news (that his sons must go into captivity). See 2Ki 24:12–16; 2Ch 33:11; Da 1:3, 4, 6 for the prophecy's fulfillment.

39:8 word of the LORD ... is good. A surprising response to the negative prophecy of vv. 5–7! It perhaps acknowledged Isaiah as God's faithful messenger. **peace and truth in my days.** Hezekiah perhaps reacted selfishly, or perhaps he looked for a bright spot to lighten the gloomy fate of his descendants.

40:1–66:24 The prophecies of chaps. 1–39 addressed Judah in her situation during Isaiah's ministry (739 B.C. until ca. 686 B.C.). The prophecies of chaps. 40–66 address Judah as though the prophesied Babylonian captivity (39:5–7) were already a present reality, though that captivity did not begin until 605–586 B.C. The words "There is no peace for the wicked" (48:22; 57:21) signal the divisions of this section into three parts: chaps. 40–48, chaps. 49–57, and chaps. 58–66.

40:1–48:22 This section looks at the hope and comfort of a blessed future subsequent to God's judgment in the forthcoming Babylonian captivity.

40:1, 2 Comfort ... comfort. The prophecy addressed God's prophets, instructing them to emphasize the theme of comfort to a captive people in a foreign land many mi. from their home city of Jerusalem. God has good plans for great blessing to Israel in the future because they are His covenant people, who are never to be permanently cast away (cf. Ro 11:2).

40:2 iniquity has been removed ... Double for all her sins. Cruel slaughter and captivity at the hands of the Babylonians were sufficient payment for past sins; so someday after worldwide dispersion, Israel will return to her land in peace and in the glory of Messiah's kingdom.

40:3–5 A prophetic exhortation told Israel to prepare for the revelation of the Lord's glory at the arrival of Messiah. Scripture sees John the Baptist in this role (Mt 3:3; Mk 1:3; Lk 3:4–6; Jn 1:23). It likewise sees the future forerunner who is to be like Elijah preparing for Christ's second coming (Mal 3:1; 4:5, 6).

40:3, 4 Clear the way. The remnant of Israel could remove obstacles from the coming Messiah's path through repentance from their sins. John the Baptist reminded his listeners of this necessity (Mt 3:2), as did Jesus (Mt 4:17; Mk 1:15). These verses reflect the custom of some eastern monarchs to send heralds before them to clear away obstacles, make causeways, straighten crooked roads and valleys, and level hills (cf. 45:1, 2). John had the task of getting people ready for Messiah's arrival.

40:5 glory of the LORD ... revealed. Jerusalem's misery is to end and the Lord's glory to replace it, so comfort will come to the city (v. 2), and every person will see God's glorious salvation (cf. 52:10) in Messiah's future kingdom (Hab 2:14; Rev 21:23; cf. 11:9). **mouth of the LORD has spoken.** Used for confirmations also in 1:20; 58:14; 62:2.

40:6–8 All flesh ... flower fades. Isaiah elaborated on how transitory humanity is: here today, gone tomorrow. People pass away like plants under the hot breath of the withering E wind. James used this illustration to teach the folly of trusting in material wealth (Jas 1:10, 11). Peter used it to illustrate the passing nature of everything related to humanity (1Pe 1:24, 25).

40:8 the word of our God stands forever. The permanence of God's word guarantees against any deviation from the divine plan (55:11). He has promised Jerusalem's deliverance (v. 2) through His coming (vv. 3–5), so it must happen that way (cf. Mt 5:18; Lk 16:17).

40:9 Zion ... good news ... Jerusalem ... good news. Like a messenger on a mountain, to be seen and heard by all, the prophet called on the city to proclaim loudly to the rest of Judah's cities the good news of God's presence there (cf. 2:3). **Here is your God!** The restoration of Israel to the land is to include the resumption of God's presence in Jerusalem after many centuries (Eze 43:1–7; Rev 21:22, 23; cf. Eze 11:22, 23).

10 Behold, the Lord [a]GOD will
come [A]with might,
With His [B]arm ruling for Him.
Behold, His [C]reward is with Him
And His recompense before Him.
11 Like a shepherd He will [A]tend His flock,
In His arm He will gather the lambs
And carry *them* in His bosom;
He will gently lead the nursing *ewes.*

12 Who has [A]measured the [a]waters
in the hollow of His hand,
And marked off the heavens by the [b]span,
And [c]calculated the dust of the
earth by the measure,
And weighed the mountains in a balance
And the hills in a pair of scales?
13 [A]Who has [a]directed the
Spirit of the LORD,
Or as His [B]counselor has informed Him?
14 [A]With whom did He consult and *who*
[B]gave Him understanding?
And *who* taught Him in the path of
justice and taught Him knowledge
And informed Him of the way
of understanding?
15 Behold, the [A]nations are like
a drop from a bucket,
And are regarded as a speck
of [B]dust on the scales;
Behold, He lifts up the
[a]islands like fine dust.
16 Even Lebanon is not enough to burn,
Nor its [A]beasts enough for
a burnt offering.
17 [A]All the nations are as nothing before Him,
They are regarded by Him as less
than nothing and [a]meaningless.

18 [A]To whom then will you liken God?
Or what likeness will you
compare with Him?
19 *As for* the [a,A]idol, a craftsman casts it,
A goldsmith [B]plates it with gold,
And a silversmith *fashions* chains of silver.
20 He who is too impoverished
for *such* an offering
Selects a [A]tree that does not rot;
He seeks out for himself a skillful craftsman
To [a]prepare [b]an idol that [B]will not totter.

21 [A]Do you not know? Have you not heard?
Has it not been declared to you
from the beginning?
Have you not understood [B]from
the foundations of the earth?
22 It is He who [a]sits above the
[b,A]circle of the earth,
And its inhabitants are like [B]grasshoppers,
Who [C]stretches out the
heavens like a [D]curtain
And spreads them out like
a [E]tent to dwell in.
23 He *it is* who reduces [A]rulers to nothing,
Who [B]makes the judges of the
earth [a]meaningless.
24 [a]Scarcely have they been planted,
[a]Scarcely have they been sown,
[a]Scarcely has their stock taken
root in the earth,
But He merely blows on them,
and they wither,
And the [A]storm carries them
away like stubble.
25 "[A]To whom then will you liken Me
That I would be *his* equal?"
says the Holy One.

40:10 [a]Heb *YHWH*, usually rendered *LORD* [A]Is 9:6, 7 [B]Is 59:16, 18 [C]Is 62:11; Rev 22:12 40:11 [A]Jer 31:10; Ezek 34:12-14, 23, 31; Mic 5:4; John 10:11, 14-16 40:12 [a]DSS reads *waters of the sea* [b]Or *half cubit;* i.e. 9 in. [c]Lit *contained* or *comprehended* [A]Job 38:8-11; Ps 102:25, 26; Is 48:13; Heb 1:10-12 40:13 [a]Or *measured, marked off* [A]Rom 11:34; 1 Cor 2:16 [B]Is 41:28 40:14 [A]Job 38:4 [B]Job 21:22; Col 2:3 40:15 [a]Or *coastlands* [A]Jer 10:10 [B]Is 17:13; 29:5 40:16 [A]Ps 50:9-11; Mic 6:6, 7; Heb 10:5-9 40:17 [a]Or *void* [A]Is 29:7 40:18 [A]Ex 8:10; 15:11; 1 Sam 2:2; Is 40:25; 46:5; Mic 7:18; Acts 17:29 40:19 [a]Or *graven image* [A]Ps 115:4-8; Is 41:7; 44:10; Hab 2:18, 19 [B]Is 2:20; 30:22 40:20 [a]Or *set up* [b]Or *a graven image* [A]Is 44:14 [B]1 Sam 5:3, 4; Is 41:7; 46:7 40:21 [A]Ps 19:1; 50:6; Is 37:26; Acts 14:17; Rom 1:19 [B]Is 48:13; 51:13 40:22 [a]Or *is enthroned* [b]Or *vault* [A]Job 22:14; Prov 8:27 [B]Num 13:33 [C]Job 9:8; Is 37:16; 42:5; 44:24 [D]Ps 104:2 [E]Job 36:29; Ps 18:11; 19:4 40:23 [a]Or *void* [A]Job 12:21; Ps 107:40; Is 34:12 [B]Is 5:21; Jer 25:18-27 40:24 [a]Or *Not even* [A]Is 17:13; 41:16 40:25 [A]Is 40:18

40:10 the Lord GOD will come with might. At His second coming, Christ returns with power to defeat His enemies and gather the dispersed of Israel to their land (Mt 24:31; Rev 19:11–21).

40:11 His arm. A picture of God's omnipotence. The same arm that powerfully scatters the Jews all over the earth in judgment is to overcome Israel's oppressors (v. 10) and to tenderly feed and lead His flock (Ps 23:1, 2; Jer 31:10; Eze 34:11–16; Mic 2:12).

40:12–14 By a series of questions, to which the implied answer is "no one," the prophet emphasized the omnipotence and omniscience of God, the God whose coming is to bring comfort to Israel according to vv. 1–11.

40:12 Who has measured … in a balance … ? God alone has power to create the physical universe and the earth in perfect balance, weighing mountains and seas perfectly, so that the earth moves perfectly in space. This matter of the amazing balance of our planet is called the science of isostasy.

40:13, 14 directed the Spirit of the LORD. Isaiah pointed to the incomparable wisdom of God. Paul alluded to this verse in connection with God's wisdom in dealing with Jews and Gentiles (Ro 11:34) and with God's impartation of wisdom to the spiritual believer (1Co 2:16).

40:15–17 Since the surrounding nations who had oppressed Israel were utterly insignificant in comparison to the Lord's greatness and power, they could not prevent His purposes from being accomplished. His deliverance of Israel was certain.

40:16 burn … burnt offering. God is so great and worthy of so much worship that even the large wood and animal resources of Lebanon were insufficient for appropriate offerings to Him.

40:18–20 The prophet sarcastically indicated the futility of trying to portray the immensity of God—His power, wisdom, and resources—in the form of a man-made idol, no matter how ornate, durable, and immovable.

40:21–31 Isaiah extolled God as Creator, in whom the Jews were to put their full trust.

40:21 declared to you … understood. Throughout human history people had heard by special revelation from God that the Lord, not idols, created all things. They had also understood it from natural revelation as reason looks at creation (cf. Ro 1:20).

40:22 sits above the circle of the earth. The word "circle" is applicable to the spherical form of the earth, above which He sits. This implies that God upholds and maintains His creation on a continuing basis (Col 1:17; Heb 1:3). As He looks down, men seem like insects to the One who has stretched and spread out the universal heavens.

40:23 rulers … judges. God disposes of human leaders according to His will (34:12; Job 12:17–21; Ps 107:40; Da 2:21). Verse 24 expands on how suddenly God removes them.

40:25 liken … be *his* equal. Israel was foolish to compare such a sovereign, almighty Lord with the gods of their Babylonian captors (see v. 18).

26 [A]Lift up your eyes on high
And see [B]who has created these *stars,*
The [C]One who leads forth
their host by number,
He calls them all by name;
Because of the [D]greatness of His might
and the [a]strength of *His* power,
[E]Not one *of them* is missing.

27 [A]Why do you say, O Jacob,
and assert, O Israel,
"My way is [B]hidden from the LORD,
And the [C]justice due me [a]escapes
the notice of [D]my God"?
28 [A]Do you not know? Have you not heard?
The [B]Everlasting God, the LORD, the
Creator of the ends of the earth
Does not become weary or tired.
His understanding is [C]inscrutable.
29 He gives strength to the [A]weary,
And to *him who* lacks might
He [B]increases power.
30 Though [A]youths grow weary and tired,
And vigorous [B]young men
stumble badly,
31 Yet those who [a]wait for the LORD
Will [A]gain new strength;
They will [b,B]mount up *with*
[c]wings like eagles,
They will run and not get tired,
They will walk and not become weary.

ISRAEL ENCOURAGED

41 "[A]Coastlands, listen to Me [B]in silence,
And let the peoples [C]gain new strength;
[D]Let them come forward,
then let them speak;
[E]Let us come together for judgment.
2 "[A]Who has aroused one from the east
Whom He [B]calls in righteousness
to His [a]feet?
He [C]delivers up nations before him
And subdues kings.
He makes them like [D]dust with his sword,
As the wind-driven [E]chaff with his bow.
3 "He pursues them, passing on in safety,
By a way he had not been
[a]traversing with his feet.
4 "[A]Who has performed and accomplished *it,*
Calling forth the generations
from the beginning?
'[B]I, the LORD, am the first, and
with the last. [C]I am He.' "

5 The [A]coastlands have seen and are afraid;
The [B]ends of the earth tremble;
They have drawn near and have come.
6 Each one helps his neighbor
And says to his brother, "Be strong!"
7 So the [A]craftsman encourages
the [B]smelter,
And he who smooths *metal*
with the hammer *encourages*
him who beats the anvil,
Saying of the soldering, "It is good";
And he fastens it with nails,
[C]*So that* it will not totter.
8 "But you, Israel, [A]My servant,
Jacob whom I have chosen,
Descendant of [B]Abraham My [C]friend,

40:26 [a]So DSS and ancient versions; M.T. *strong* [A]Is 51:6 [B]Is 42:5; 48:12, 13 [C]Ps 147:4 [D]Ps 89:11-13 [E]Is 34:16; 48:13 40:27 [a]Lit *passes by my God* [A]Is 49:4, 14 [B]Is 54:8 [C]Job 27:2; 34:5; Luke 18:7, 8 [D]Is 25:1 40:28 [A]Is 40:21 [B]Gen 21:33; Ps 90:2 [C]Ps 147:5; Rom 11:33 40:29 [A]Is 50:4; Jer 31:25 [B]Is 41:10 40:30 [A]Jer 6:11; 9:21 [B]Is 9:17 40:31 [a]Or *hope in* [b]Or *sprout wings* [c]Or *pinions* [A]Job 17:9; Ps 103:5; 2 Cor 4:8-10, 16 [B]Ex 19:4; Deut 32:11; Luke 18:1; 2 Cor 4:1, 16; Gal 6:9; Heb 12:3 41:1 [A]Is 11:11 [B]Hab 2:20; Zech 2:13 [C]Is 40:31 [D]Is 34:1; 48:16 [E]Is 1:18; 43:26; 50:8 41:2 [a]Lit *foot* [A]Is 41:25; 45:1-3; 46:11 [B]Is 42:6 [C]2 Chr 36:23; Ezra 1:2 [D]2 Sam 22:43 [E]Is 40:24 41:3 [a]Lit *going* 41:4 [A]Is 41:26; 44:7; 46:10 [B]Is 43:10; 44:6; Rev 1:8, 17; 22:13 [C]Is 43:13; 46:4; 48:12 41:5 [A]Is 41:1; Ezek 26:15, 16 [B]Josh 5:1; Ps 67:7 41:7 [A]Is 44:12, 13 [B]Is 40:19 [C]Is 40:20; 46:7 41:8 [A]Is 42:19; 43:10; 44:1, 2, 21 [B]Is 29:22; 51:2; 63:16 [C]2 Chr 20:7; James 2:23

40:26 created these *stars.* Rather than worshiping the stars (47:13; Dt 4:19; Jer 7:18; 8:2; 44:17), Israel should have seen in them the evidence of God's creatorship (Ps 19:1). As innumerable as the stars are, He knows every one and named each. Not one of the stars runs astray, but all are held by the forces with which He has endowed the universe to keep them in their orbit and place.

40:27–31 The prophet applied the comforting truths in vv. 1–26 about God to Israel's situation in Babylon during the coming captivity.

40:27 Why do you say . . . ? In light of who God is, how could His people in exile have thought He had forgotten them or was ignorant of their condition?

40:28 Does not become weary or tired. God was not too weak to act on their behalf, nor was fatigue an obstacle for the Creator in caring for His people (cf. vv. 29, 30). Though even the young and strong become tired and fall, the Ancient of Days never does. **inscrutable.** To the human mind, God's wisdom is not fully comprehensible in how He chooses to fulfill His promises to deliver Israel. Paul saw a further illustration of this truth in God's plan for the final restoration of Israel (Ro 11:33; see Is 40:13).

40:31 wait for the LORD. See 8:17; 49:23. There is a general principle here that patient, praying believers are blessed by God with strength in their trials (cf. 2Co 12:8–10). The Lord also expected His people to be patient and await His coming in glory at the end to fulfill the promises of national deliverance, when believing Israel would become stronger than they had ever been.

41:1 Coastlands. The coasts of lands around the Mediterranean Sea and the islands represent the nations. **gain new strength.** The Lord challenged the nations that refused to wait on Him to be silent in awe and then move to renew their strength (cf. 40:31), meaning to collect their best arguments to plead their cause before Him.

41:2 one from the east. The Lord anointed Cyrus the Great, king of Persia, to accomplish His righteous will by conquering Babylon in 539 B.C. and allowing some of the Jewish exiles to return to Jerusalem (cf. 41:25; 44:28; 45:1). He founded the Persian Empire and ruled from ca. 550 to 530 B.C.

41:3 pursues . . . traversing with his feet. Cyrus accomplished his conquests with great ease in territories he had never before visited.

41:4 first . . . last. He existed before history and will exist after it (cf. 44:6; 48:12; Rev 1:17; 2:8; 22:13). **I am He.** It is legitimate to translate the two Heb. words thus represented by "I am" (see also 42:8; 43:10, 13; 46:4), a messianic title appropriated by Jesus frequently as explicit testimony to His deity (e.g., Mk 13:6; 14:62; Lk 21:8; Jn 8:28, 58; 13:19). The title comes originally from the Lord's self-revelation to Moses in Ex 3:14.

41:5–7 Instead of turning to the Lord when they saw His anointed one, Cyrus, approaching, the nations turned to one another for help and made more idols. See 40:18–20 regarding Isaiah's description of idols and their makers.

41:8 Israel, My servant. The faithful of the nation receive the honored corporate designation as the servant of the Lord (*see note on 20:3*). As His servant, they stood in bold contrast to the rest of the nations (vv. 5–7). Cf. Israel as the servant in 42:18–25. **Abraham My friend.** "Friend" is an even higher designation than "servant" (Jn 15:14, 15; cf. 2Ch 20:7; Jas 2:23) and speaks of a greater faithfulness.

9 You whom I have [a,A]taken from
the ends of the earth,
And called from its [B]remotest parts
And said to you, 'You are [C]My servant,
I have [D]chosen you and not rejected you.
10 'Do not [A]fear, for I am with you;
Do not anxiously look about
you, for I am your God.
I will strengthen you, surely
[B]I will help you,
Surely I will uphold you with My
righteous [C]right hand.'
11 "Behold, [A]all those who are angered at
you will be shamed and dishonored;
[B]Those who contend with you will
be as nothing and will perish.
12 "[A]You will seek those who quarrel with
you, but will not find them,
Those who war with you will be as
nothing and non-existent.
13 "For I am the LORD your God, [A]who
upholds your right hand,
Who says to you, '[B]Do not
fear, I will help you.'
14 "Do not fear, you [A]worm Jacob,
you men of Israel;
I will help you," declares the
LORD, "[a]and [B]your Redeemer
is the Holy One of Israel.
15 "Behold, I have made you a new, sharp
threshing sledge with double edges;
[A]You will thresh the [B]mountains
and pulverize *them,*
And will make the hills like chaff.
16 "You will [A]winnow them, and the
wind will carry them away,
And the storm will scatter them;
But you will [B]rejoice in the LORD,
You will glory in the
Holy One of Israel.
17 "The [a]afflicted and needy are seeking
[A]water, but there is none,
And their tongue is parched with thirst;
I, the LORD, [B]will answer them Myself,
As the God of Israel I [C]will
not forsake them.
18 "I will open [A]rivers on the bare heights
And springs in the midst of the valleys;
I will make [B]the wilderness a pool of water
And the dry land fountains of water.
19 "I will put the cedar in the wilderness,
The acacia and the [A]myrtle
and the [a]olive tree;
I will place the [A]juniper in the desert
Together with the box tree
and the cypress,
20 That [A]they may see and recognize,
And consider and gain insight as well,
That the [B]hand of the LORD has done this,
And the Holy One of Israel has created it.

21 "[a]Present your case," the LORD says.
"Bring forward your strong *arguments,*"
The [A]King of Jacob *says.*
22 [A]Let them bring forth and declare to
us what is going to take place;
As for the [B]former *events,*
declare what they *were,*
That we may consider them
and know their outcome.
Or announce to us what is coming;
23 [A]Declare the things that are
going to come afterward,
That we may know that you are gods;
Indeed, [B]do good or evil, that
we may anxiously look about
us and fear together.
24 Behold, [A]you are of [a]no account,
And [B]your work amounts to nothing;
He who chooses you is an [C]abomination.

41:9 [a]Or *taken hold of* [A]Is 11:11 [B]Is 43:5-7 [C]Is 42:1; 44:1 [D]Deut 7:6; 14:2; Ps 135:4 41:10 [A]Deut 20:1; 31:6; Josh 1:9; Ps 27:1; Is 41:13, 14; 43:2, 5; Rom 8:31 [B]Is 41:14; 44:2; 49:8 [C]Ps 89:13, 14 41:11 [A]Is 45:24 [B]Is 17:13; 29:5, 7, 8 41:12 [A]Job 20:7-9; Ps 37:35, 36; Is 17:14 41:13 [A]Is 42:6; 45:1 [B]Is 41:10 41:14 [a]Or *even your Redeemer, the Holy One* [A]Job 25:6; Ps 22:6 [B]Is 35:10; 43:14; 44:6, 22-24 41:15 [A]Mic 4:13; Hab 3:12 [B]Is 42:15; 64:1; Jer 9:10; Ezek 33:28 41:16 [A]Jer 51:2 [B]Is 25:9; 35:10; 51:3; 61:10 41:17 [a]Or *poor* [A]Is 43:20; 44:3; 49:10; 55:1 [B]Is 30:19; 65:24 [C]Is 42:16; 62:12 41:18 [A]Is 30:25; 43:19 [B]Ps 107:35; Is 35:6, 7 41:19 [a]Or *oleaster* [A]Is 35:1; 55:13; 60:13 41:20 [A]Is 40:5; 43:10 [B]Job 12:9; Is 66:14 41:21 [a]Lit *Bring near* [A]Is 44:6 41:22 [A]Is 44:7; 45:21; 46:10 [B]Is 43:9 41:23 [A]Is 42:9; 44:7, 8; 45:3; John 13:19 [B]Jer 10:5 41:24 [a]Lit *nothing* [A]Ps 115:8; Is 44:9; 1 Cor 8:4 [B]Is 37:19; 41:29 [C]Prov 3:32; 28:9

41:9 taken from the ends of the earth. In the last days, God will regather Israel from her worldwide dispersion as He did from Egypt and Babylon because Israel is God's chosen nation (cf. 45:4; Am 3:2).

41:10 Do not fear. Israel need not fear God's destructive judgment, as the rest of the nations do (vv. 5, 13, 14; 43:1, 5), because He is their God and faithful to His promise to restore the nation.

41:11–13 Through the Lord's help, the enemies of Israel were to be weakened and vanish (60:12; Zec 12:3) while God strengthened *Israel.*

41:14 worm. This refers to the contempt of Israel by the ungodly nations, and the same term is used similarly of the Messiah on the cross (Ps 22:6). **Redeemer is the Holy One of Israel.** The Heb. for "Redeemer" refers to a near relative who has the opportunity and responsibility to buy back what a relative has lost (*see note on Ru 2:20*). The term occurs 5 more times in connection with the title "Holy One of Israel." *See notes on 43:14; 48:17–19; 49:7; 54:5 (cf. 47:4).* As the Lord purchased His people from the bondage of Egypt by the blood of the Passover Lamb, He is to do the same from their worldwide exile by the blood of the True Lamb, Jesus Christ, when they turn to Him in faith (cf. Zec 12:10–13:1).

41:15, 16 mountains ... hills. Figurative representations of foreign nations, whom Israel is to grind into nothingness in the time of her kingdom, when the Lord Jesus sets Himself up as King in Jerusalem.

41:17, 18 afflicted and needy. Israel in her deprived state as a captive of foreign nations is spoken of as thirsty for blessing and joy. In the Messiah's future kingdom, the land of Israel will be well-watered (cf. 12:2, 3; 35:6, 7; 43:19, 20; 44:3, 4; 48:20, 21), a real physical blessing, but symbolizing here the spiritual quenching that will be Israel's in the Millennium.

41:19 myrtle ... olive tree ... juniper ... box ... cypress. Luxuriant vegetation will enrich the land when God redeems His creation (35:1, 2, 7; Ro 8:19–21).

41:22, 23 what is going to take place ... come afterward. God challenged the idols to prove their competence by predicting future events, as the Lord has done regarding "the former *events,*" i.e., the raising of Cyrus (v. 2), the repulsion of the Assyrians from Jerusalem (chaps. 36, 37), and the healing of Hezekiah (chap. 38).

41:23 do good or evil. God invited the idols to proclaim and execute either deliverance or judgment, as He had done.

41:24 no account ... nothing. The idols were not what humans claimed they were, because they could not predict the future, nor could they judge or deliver. They were useless (44:9; Ps 115:2–8; 1Co 8:4; 10:19; Gal 4:8).

25 "I have aroused [A]one from the north, and he has come;
From the rising of the sun he will call on My name;
And he will come upon rulers as *upon* [B]mortar,
Even as the potter treads clay."
26 Who has [A]declared *this* from the beginning, that we might know?
Or from former times, that we may say, "*He is* right!"?
Surely there was [B]no one who declared,
Surely there was no one who proclaimed,
Surely there was no one who heard your words.
27 "[A]Formerly *I said* to Zion,
'Behold, here they are.'
And to Jerusalem, 'I will give a [B]messenger of good news.'
28 "But [A]when I look, there is no one,
And there is no [B]counselor [a]among them
Who, if I ask, can [C]give an answer.
29 "Behold, all of them are [a]false;
Their [A]works are [B]worthless,
Their molten images are [C]wind and emptiness.

GOD'S PROMISE CONCERNING HIS SERVANT

42 "[A]Behold, My [B]Servant, whom I [a]uphold;
My [C]chosen one *in whom* My [D]soul delights.
I have put My [E]Spirit upon Him;
He will bring forth [F]justice to the [b]nations.
2 "He will not cry out or raise *His voice*,
Nor make His voice heard in the street.
3 "A bruised reed He will not break
And a dimly burning wick He will not extinguish;
He will faithfully bring forth [A]justice.
4 "He will not be [A]disheartened or crushed
Until He has established justice in the earth;
And the [B]coastlands will wait expectantly for His [a]law."

5 Thus says God the LORD,

Who [A]created the heavens and [B]stretched them out,
Who spread out the [C]earth and its [a]offspring,
Who [D]gives breath to the people on it
And spirit to those who walk in it,
6 "I am the LORD, I have [A]called You in righteousness,
I will also [B]hold You by the hand and [C]watch over You,
And I will appoint You as a [D]covenant to the people,
As a [E]light to the nations,
7 To [A]open blind eyes,
To [B]bring out prisoners from the dungeon
And those who dwell in darkness from the prison.
8 "[A]I am the LORD, that is [B]My name;
I will not give My [C]glory to another,
Nor My praise to [a]graven images.

41:25 [A]Is 41:2; Jer 50:3 [B]2 Sam 22:43; Is 10:6; Mic 7:10; Zech 10:5 41:26 [A]Is 41:22; 44:7; 45:21 [B]Hab 2:18, 19 41:27 [A]Is 48:3-8 [B]Is 40:9; 44:28; 52:7; Nah 1:15 41:28 [a]Lit *out of those* [A]Is 50:2; 59:16; 63:5 [B]Is 40:13, 14 [C]Is 46:7 41:29 [a]Another reading is *nothing* [A]Is 2:8; 17:8; 41:24 [B]Is 44:9 [C]Jer 5:13 42:1 [a]Or *hold fast* [b]Or *Gentiles* [A]Matt 12:18-21 [B]Is 41:8; 43:10; 49:3-6; 52:13; 53:11; Matt 12:18-21; Phil 2:7 [C]Luke 9:35; 1 Pet 2:4, 6 [D]Matt 3:17; 17:5; Mark 1:11; Luke 3:22 [E]Is 11:2; 59:21; 61:1; Matt 3:16; Luke 4:18, 19, 21 [F]Is 2:4 42:3 [A]Ps 72:2, 4; 96:13 42:4 [a]Or *instruction* [A]Is 40:28 [B]Is 11:11; 24:15; 42:10, 12; 49:1; 51:5; 60:9; 66:19 42:5 [a]Or *vegetation* [A]Ps 102:25, 26; Is 45:18 [B]Ps 104:2; Is 40:22 [C]Ps 24:1, 2; 136:6 [D]Job 12:10; 33:4; Is 57:16; Dan 5:23; Acts 17:25 42:6 [A]Is 41:2; Jer 23:5, 6 [B]Is 41:13; 45:1 [C]Is 26:3; 27:3 [D]Is 49:8 [E]Is 49:6; 51:4; 60:1, 3; Luke 2:32; Acts 13:47; 26:23 42:7 [A]Is 29:18; 35:5 [B]Is 49:9; 61:1 42:8 [a]Or *idols* [A]Is 43:3, 11, 15 [B]Ex 3:15; Ps 83:18 [C]Ex 20:3-5; Is 48:11

41:25 from the north … From the rising of the sun. Cyrus, king of Persia, a land E of Babylon, approached Babylon from the N where he had conquered Media before coming to Babylon. **call on My name.** Apparently fulfilled by Cyrus' proclamation in Ezr 1:1–4.

41:26 no one. No soothsayer had predicted future happenings as the Lord had.

41:27–29 Idols were helpless in giving "good news" of future events (v. 27) and counsel to people (v. 28), and thus were useless.

42:1–9 This is the first of 4 Servant-songs referring to Messiah (cf. 49:1–13; 50:4–11; 52:13–53:12). They speak of the Servant's gentle manner and worldwide mission. Verses 1–3 are applied to Jesus Christ at His first coming in Mt 12:18–20.

42:1 My Servant. Others deserve the title "my servant" (*see note on 20:3*), but this personal Servant of the Lord is the Messiah, who was chosen (Lk 9:35; 1Pe 1:20; Rev 13:8) because the Lord delights in Him (Mt 3:17; 17:5) and puts His Spirit upon Him (11:2; 59:21; Mt 3:16; Lk 4:18). **justice to the nations.** At His second coming, Christ will rule over a kingdom in which justice prevails throughout the world. The millennial kingdom is not for Israel alone, though the Messiah will reign on the throne of David in Jerusalem, and Israel will be the glorious people. In fact, all the nations of the world will experience the righteousness and justice of the Messiah King.

42:2 not cry out … in the street. The quiet and submissive demeanor of Christ at His first advent fulfilled this prophecy (Mt 11:28–30; 1Pe 2:23).

42:3 bruised reed … burning wick. The Servant will bring comfort and encouragement to the weak and oppressed. Cf. 40:11; 50:4; 61:1 and *see notes on Mt 12:18–20.*

42:4 justice in the earth. Isaiah looked beyond the first coming of Christ to His second coming. Jesus fulfilled vv. 1a, 2, 3 at His first coming and will fulfill vv. 1b, 4 at His second coming, when He rules the earth in perfect justice with "a rod of iron" (Ps 2:8, 9; Rev 2:27).

42:5 Thus says God the LORD, Who created … walk in it. Here God spoke directly to the Messiah, identified as "You" (v. 6). God's role as Creator of the universe (cf. 40:21, 22) is the basis of certainty for the fulfilling of His will by His Servant the Messiah.

42:6 I am the LORD. Beginning with 41:13, the Lord's self-identification is frequent (41:13; 42:6, 8; 43:3, 11, 15; 45:5, 6, 7, 18; 48:17; 49:23; 51:15). His personal name is the one He explained to Moses as specially symbolic of the unique relationship He bore to Israel (Ex 3:15; 6:3). Here that covenant name guarantees His ministry through the Messiah-Servant. **covenant to the people.** The Servant is a covenant in that He personifies and provides the blessings of salvation to God's people Israel. He is the Mediator of a better covenant than the one with Moses, i.e., the New Covenant (Jer 31:31–34; Heb 8:6, 10–12). *See note on 49:8.* **light to the nations.** Simeon saw the beginning of this fulfillment at Christ's first coming (Lk 2:32). He came as the Messiah of Israel, yet the Savior of the world, who revealed Himself to a non-Jewish immoral woman by the well in Samaria (cf. Jn 4:25, 26) and commanded His followers to preach the gospel of salvation to everyone in the world (Mt 28:19, 20). Certainly the church, made up mostly of Gentiles grafted into the trunk of blessing (cf. Ro 9:24–30; 11:11–24), fulfills this promise, as does the future kingdom on earth when the Servant will use Israel to shine and enlighten all the nations of the earth (49:6; cf. 19:24).

42:7 open blind eyes … bring out prisoners. Jesus fulfilled these words (9:1, 2; Mt 4:13–16) when He applied them to miracles of physical healing and freedom from spiritual bondage during His incarnation (Mt 11:5; Lk 4:18). Under the Servant's millennial reign on earth, spiritual perception will replace Israel's

9 "Behold, the [A]former things
have come to pass,
Now I declare [B]new things;
Before they spring forth I
proclaim *them* to you."

10 Sing to the LORD a [A]new song,
Sing His praise from the [B]end of the earth!
[C]You who go down to the sea,
and [D]all that is in it.
You [E]islands, and those who dwell on them.
11 Let the [A]wilderness and its
cities lift up *their voices,*
The settlements where [B]Kedar inhabits.
Let the inhabitants of [C]Sela sing aloud,
Let them shout for joy from the
tops of the [D]mountains.
12 Let them [A]give glory to the LORD
And declare His praise in the [B]coastlands.
13 [A]The LORD will go forth like a warrior,
He will arouse *His* [B]zeal like a man of war.
He will utter a shout, yes, He
will raise a war cry.
He will [C]prevail against His enemies.

THE BLINDNESS OF THE PEOPLE

14 "[A]I have kept silent for a long time,
I have kept still and restrained Myself.
Now like a woman in labor I will groan,
I will both gasp and pant.
15 "I will [A]lay waste the mountains and hills
And wither all their vegetation;
I will [B]make the rivers into coastlands
And dry up the ponds.
16 "I will [A]lead the blind by a way
they do not know,
In paths they do not know
I will guide them.
I will [B]make darkness into
light before them
And [C]rugged places into plains.
These are the things I will do,
And I will [D]not leave them undone."
17 They will be turned back *and*
be [A]utterly put to shame,
Who trust in [a]idols,
Who say to molten images,
"You are our gods."

18 [A]Hear, you deaf!
And look, you blind, that you may see.
19 Who is blind but My [A]servant,
Or so deaf as My [B]messenger whom I send?
Who is so blind as he that is
[a,C]at peace *with Me,*
Or so blind as the servant of the LORD?
20 [A]You have seen many things, but
you do not observe *them;*
Your ears are open, but none hears.
21 The LORD was pleased for His
righteousness' sake
To make the law [A]great and glorious.
22 But this is a people plundered
and despoiled;
All of them are [A]trapped in [a]caves,
Or are [B]hidden away in prisons;
They have become a prey with
none to deliver *them,*
And a spoil, with none to say,
"Give *them* back!"

23 Who among you will give ear to this?
Who will give heed and listen hereafter?
24 Who gave Jacob up for spoil,
and Israel to plunderers?
Was it not the LORD, against
whom we have sinned,
And in whose ways they [A]were
not willing to walk,
And whose law they did not [B]obey?

42:9 [A]Is 48:3 [B]Is 43:19; 48:6 42:10 [A]Ps 33:3; 40:3; 98:1 [B]Is 49:6; 62:11 [C]Ps 65:5; 107:23 [D]Ex 20:11; 1 Chr 16:32; Ps 96:11 [E]Is 42:4 42:11 [A]Is 32:16; 35:1, 6 [B]Is 21:16; 60:7 [C]Is 16:1 [D]Is 52:7; Nah 1:15 42:12 [A]Is 24:15 [B]Is 42:4 42:13 [A]Ex 15:3 [B]Is 9:7; 26:11; 37:32; 59:17 [C]Is 66:14-16 42:14 [A]Ps 50:21; Is 57:11 42:15 [A]Is 2:12-16; Ezek 38:19, 20 [B]Is 44:27; 50:2; Nah 1:4-6 42:16 [A]Is 29:18; 30:21; 32:3; Jer 31:8, 9; Luke 1:78, 79 [B]Is 29:18; Eph 5:8 [C]Is 40:4; Luke 3:5 [D]Josh 1:5; Ps 94:14; Is 41:17; Heb 13:5 42:17 [a]Or *graven images* [A]Ps 97:7; Is 1:29; 44:9, 11; 45:16 42:18 [A]Is 29:18; 35:5 42:19 [a]Or *the devoted one* [A]Is 41:8 [B]Is 44:26 [C]Is 26:3; 27:5 42:20 [A]Rom 2:21 42:21 [A]Is 42:4; 51:4 42:22 [a]Or *holes* [A]Is 24:18 [B]Is 24:22 42:24 [A]Is 30:15 [B]Is 48:18; 57:17

spiritual blindness and her captives will receive their freedom (29:18; 32:3; 35:5; 61:1).

42:9 former things … new things. The "former things" are already fulfilled or about to be fulfilled prophecies of Isaiah (cf. 41:22). The "new things" pertain to the future accomplishments of the Lord through His Messiah-Servant when He comes.

42:10 Sing …. new song … His praise. This "new song" never before sung, called for by new manifestations of God's grace, will match the newness of conditions created by the Servant's work of redemption in the kingdom, for which earth's inhabitants will also sing "His praise." Cf. 2:2; 26:1; Rev 4:11; 5:9.

42:11 Kedar … Sela. See 16:1 and 21:16.

42:13 warrior … man of war. As a mighty warrior, the Lord will work through His Servant to overcome all enemies (40:10; cf. 9:7; 37:32; 59:17).

42:14 kept silent … kept still and restrained Myself. From the beginning of creation God remained silent, until the time was ripe to intervene in human affairs. He has not been indifferent to wickedness in the world, but will send His Servant in "the fullness of the time" (Gal 4:4).

42:15 lay waste … wither … dry up. God's judgment through His Servant will wreak devastation on the earth (cf. Rev 6–19). The reverse of that will be His blessing through the same Messiah subsequently in the millennial kingdom (see 35:1–4; 41:18).

42:16 I will lead … guide … make … do. God's sovereignty will be evident to all as He guides the blind over previously uncharted courses (cf. Ex 13:21, 22). The spiritually blind (9:1, 2) will see the way (see 42:7). Cf. Eph 5:8.

42:17 idols … molten images. God will utterly repudiate idolaters (cf. Ex 32:4).

42:18–24 The Lord charged Israel, His servant, with unfaithfulness. In an important comparison, positive qualities of the Servant (42:1–7) are personified into an individual, the Messiah, but terms of reproach toward God's servant (42:18, 19, 22–24) are personified in the nation, Israel.

42:18–20 deaf … blind. Though they are called "My servant" (v. 19; 41:8; 44:21) and "My messenger" and were perfectly fitted with the truth, Isaiah's commission to prophesy highlighted the spiritual deafness and blindness of Israel (6:9, 10; cf. 22:14; 29:11; 32:3). They were deaf to the voice of God and blind to spiritual reality and duty.

42:21 His righteousness' sake. In spite of Israel's deafness, blindness, and defective righteousness (v. 24), God will staunchly uphold His principles of righteousness. Cf. 59:14–17.

42:22 plundered and despoiled … trapped … hidden. Exiled and dispersed, Israel was like a caravan in the desert, attacked unmercifully by bandits and imprisoned in caves or dungeons, so that no human deliverer could restore them (cf. 63:5).

42:24 Was it not the LORD …? The nation went into Babylonian exile and worldwide

25 So He poured out on him the
heat of His anger
And the [A]fierceness of battle;
And it set him aflame all around,
Yet he did not recognize *it;*
And it burned him, but he
[a,B]paid no attention.

ISRAEL REDEEMED

43 But now, thus says the LORD,
your [A]Creator, O Jacob,
And He who [B]formed you, O Israel,
"Do not [C]fear, for I have [D]redeemed you;
I have [E]called you by name;
you are [F]Mine!
2 "When you [A]pass through the
waters, [B]I will be with you;
And through the rivers, they
will not overflow you.
When you [C]walk through the fire,
you will not be scorched,
Nor will the flame burn you.
3 "For [A]I am the LORD your God,
The Holy One of Israel, your [B]Savior;
I have given Egypt as your ransom,
[a,C]Cush and Seba in your place.
4 "Since you are [A]precious in My sight,
Since you are [B]honored and I [C]love you,
I will give *other* men in your place and
other peoples in exchange for your life.
5 "Do not fear, for [A]I am with you;
I will bring [B]your offspring from the east,
And [C]gather you from the west.
6 "I will say to the [A]north, 'Give *them* up!'
And to the south, 'Do not
hold *them* back.'
Bring My [B]sons from afar
And My daughters from the
[C]ends of the earth,
7 Everyone who is [A]called by My name,
And whom I have [B]created
for My [C]glory,
[D]Whom I have formed, even
whom I have made."

ISRAEL IS GOD'S WITNESS

8 Bring out the people who are [A]blind,
even though they have eyes,
And the deaf, even though
they have ears.
9 All the nations have [A]gathered together
So that the peoples may be assembled.
Who among them can [B]declare this
And proclaim to us the former things?
Let them present [C]their witnesses
[D]that they may be justified,
Or let them hear and say, "It is true."
10 "You are [A]My witnesses,"
declares the LORD,
"And [B]My servant whom I have chosen,
So that you may know and believe Me
And understand that [C]I am He.
[D]Before Me there was no God formed,
And there will be none after Me.
11 "I, even I, am the LORD,
And there is no [A]savior [B]besides Me.

42:25 [a]Lit *did not lay it to heart* [A]Is 5:25; 9:19 [B]Is 29:13; 47:7; 57:1; Hos 7:9 43:1 [A]Is 43:15 [B]Is 43:7, 21; 44:2, 21, 24 [C]Is 43:5 [D]Is 44:22, 23; 48:20 [E]Gen 32:28; Is 43:7; 45:3, 4 [F]Is 43:21 43:2 [A]Ps 66:12; Is 8:7, 8 [B]Deut 31:6, 8 [C]Is 29:6; 30:27-29; Dan 3:25, 27 43:3 [a]Or *Ethiopia* [A]Ex 20:2 [B]Is 19:20; 43:11; 45:15, 21; 49:26; 60:16; 63:8 [C]Is 20:3-5 43:4 [A]Ex 19:5, 6 [B]Is 49:5 [C]Is 63:9 43:5 [A]Is 8:10; 43:2 [B]Is 41:8; 49:12; 61:9 [C]Is 49:12 43:6 [A]Ps 107:3 [B]2 Cor 6:18 [C]Is 45:22 43:7 [A]Is 56:5; 62:2; James 2:7 [B]Ps 100:3; Is 29:23; Eph 2:10 [C]Is 44:23; 46:13 [D]Is 43:1 43:8 [A]Is 6:9; 42:19; Ezek 12:2 43:9 [A]Is 34:1; 41:1 [B]Is 41:22, 23, 26 [C]Is 44:9 [D]Is 43:26 43:10 [A]Is 44:8 [B]Is 41:8 [C]Is 41:4 [D]Is 45:5, 6 43:11 [A]Is 43:3; 45:21; Hos 13:4 [B]Is 44:6, 8

dispersion as punishment by God for their rebellion against Him (30:15; 57:17; 65:2).

42:25 **the heat of His anger.** The fall of Jerusalem to Babylon in 586 B.C. did not result from the strength of Babylon. Rather, Israel had to taste the wrath of God because they paid no attention to the Lord (1:3; 5:13; 29:13; 47:7; 51:1; Hos 7:9). **set him aflame.** Nebuchadnezzar, king of Babylon, burned Jerusalem when he conquered the city (2Ki 25:8, 9).

43:1 **formed.** The only explanation for the ongoing existence of the nation of Israel is God's sovereign grace, which brought her into existence from nothing (cf. Dt 7:6–11) and sustains her. Since she was God's creation, she could find comfort in knowing that no one or nothing can destroy her, not even her own wickedness (cf. 43:18–25; Ro 11:1, 2, 25–27). **Jacob … Israel.** This double designation (cf. Ge 32:28) for God's chosen nation is used by Isaiah 21 times, 16 of them in chaps. 40–49 (9:8; 10:20; 14:1; 27:6; 29:23; 40:27; 41:8, 14; 42:24; 43:1, 22, 28; 44:1, 21, 23; 45:4; 46:3; 48:1, 12; 49:5, 6). This speaks of the Lord's special attachment to Abraham's physical seed. **Do not fear.** The Lord repeated His word, relieving Israel's fear (35:4; 41:10, 13, 14; cf. 7:4). **redeemed.** God's redemption of His people from exile is not to be complete until His Servant returns to reign over the faithful remnant in the land of Israel who have believed on Jesus Christ (cf. Zec 12:10–13:1; Ro 11:25–27; Rev 11:13). The limited return from Babylon only typified the final return. *See note on 43:14.*

43:2 **waters … rivers … fire … flame.** Many perils symbolized by these words have confronted the Israelites through the centuries and will continue to do so until the nation's final redemption, but the Lord promises the nation's survival through them all. The passage of Moses' and Joshua's generations through the Red Sea (Ex 14:21, 22) and the Jordan River (Jos 3:14–17) and the preservation of Shadrach, Meshach, and Abed-nego in the fiery furnace illustrate His care for Israel.

43:3 **your Savior.** God is by nature a Savior (v. 11; 45:21), both temporally and eternally (*see note on 1Ti 4:10*; cf. Tit 1:3; 2:10; 3:4). God delivered Israel from Egypt and will deliver her from Babylon and all future exiles, as well as bring her to spiritual salvation (Zec 12:10–13:1; Ro 11:25–27). **Cush.** See 18:1. **Seba.** A country either in southern Arabia or across the Red Sea in NE Africa, near Cush, or Ethiopia. Egypt, Cush, and Seba became a vicarious compensation so that God could spare Israel. "Sabeans" is another name for the inhabitants of Seba (cf. 45:14).

43:5, 6 **east … west … north … south … ends of the earth.** The Lord will regather to the land of Israel the faithful remnant of His people from their worldwide dispersion in conjunction with the institution of the Messiah's kingdom on earth (cf. 11:12).

43:7 **called by My name … created for My glory.** The faithful remnant of Israel will bear the Lord's name and exist for one primary purpose: to glorify Him (44:23).

43:8 **blind … have eyes … deaf … have ears.** Restored Israel (vv. 5–7) will have their spiritual eyesight and hearing restored (29:18; contra. 42:18, 19).

43:9 **their witnesses.** Who among the idolatrous soothsayers could predict Cyrus would deliver Israel from Babylon, or make prophecies of any kind that already were fulfilled? The gods of the nations showed no ability to reveal accurately "the former *events*" (41:21–23) as the Lord had. So the nations had no witnesses to accredit that their gods could speak prophetic truth.

43:10 **You are My witnesses … My servant.** Israel's God repeatedly predicted the future accurately, enabling Israel to witness to His truthful accuracy (v. 13), and thus the reality that He was the only eternal, living God. This witnessing they will do again in the millennial kingdom (cf. Joel 2:28–32).

12 "It is I who have declared and
saved and proclaimed,
And there was no [A]strange *god* among you;
So you are My witnesses,"
declares the LORD,
"And I am God.
13 "Even [a,A]from eternity [B]I am He,
And there is [C]none who can
deliver out of My hand;
[D]I act and who can reverse it?"

BABYLON TO BE DESTROYED

14 Thus says the LORD your [A]Redeemer, the Holy
One of Israel,

"For your sake I have sent to Babylon,
And will bring them all down as fugitives,
[a]Even the [B]Chaldeans, into the
[C]ships [b]in which they rejoice.
15 "I am the LORD, your Holy One,
[A]The Creator of Israel, your [B]King."

16 Thus says the LORD,

Who [A]makes a way through the sea
And a path through the mighty waters,
17 Who brings forth the [A]chariot
and the horse,
The army and the mighty man
(They will lie down together
and not rise again;
They have been [B]quenched *and*
extinguished like a wick):
18 "[A]Do not call to mind the former things,
Or ponder things of the past.
19 "Behold, I will do something [A]new,
Now it will spring forth;
Will you not be aware of it?
I will even [B]make a roadway
in the wilderness,
Rivers in the desert.
20 "The beasts of the field will glorify Me,
The [A]jackals and the ostriches,
Because I have [B]given waters
in the wilderness
And rivers in the desert,
To give drink to My chosen people.
21 "The people whom [A]I formed for Myself
[B]Will declare My praise.

THE SHORTCOMINGS OF ISRAEL

22 "Yet you have not called on Me, O Jacob;
But you have become [A]weary
of Me, O Israel.
23 "You have [A]not brought to Me the
sheep of your burnt offerings,
Nor have you [B]honored Me
with your sacrifices.
I have not [C]burdened you with [a]offerings,
Nor wearied you with [D]incense.
24 "You have bought Me not [a,A]sweet
cane with money,
Nor have you [b]filled Me with
the fat of your sacrifices;
Rather you have burdened
Me with your sins,
You have [B]wearied Me with
your iniquities.
25 "I, even I, am the one who [A]wipes out your
transgressions [B]for My own sake,
And I will [C]not remember your sins.
26 "[a]Put Me in remembrance, [A]let us
argue our case together;
State your *cause*, [B]that you
may be proved right.

43:12 [A]Deut 32:16; Ps 81:9 43:13 [a]So with Gr; Heb *from the day* [A]Ps 90:2; Is 48:16 [B]Is 41:4 [C]Ps 50:22 [D]Job 9:12; Is 14:27 43:14 [a]Another reading is *As for the Chaldeans, their rejoicing* is turned *into lamentations* [b]Lit *of their rejoicing* [A]Is 41:14 [B]Is 23:13 [C]Jer 51:13 43:15 [A]Is 43:1 [B]Is 41:20; 44:6 43:16 [A]Ex 14:21, 22; Ps 77:19; Is 11:15; 44:27; 50:2; 51:10; 63:11, 12 43:17 [A]Ex 15:19 [B]Ps 118:12; Is 1:31 43:18 [A]Is 65:17; Jer 23:7 43:19 [A]Is 42:9; 48:6; 2 Cor 5:17 [B]Ex 17:6; Num 20:11; Deut 8:15; Ps 78:16; Is 35:1, 6; 41:18, 19; 49:10; 51:3 43:20 [A]Is 13:22; 35:7 [B]Is 41:17, 18; 48:21 43:21 [A]Is 43:1 [B]Ps 102:18; Is 42:12; Luke 1:74, 75; 1 Pet 2:9 43:22 [A]Mic 6:3; Mal 1:13; 3:14 43:23 [a]Or *a meal offering* [A]Amos 5:25 [B]Zech 7:5, 6; Mal 1:6-8 [C]Jer 7:21-26 [D]Ex 30:34; Lev 2:1; 24:7 43:24 [a]Or *calamus* [b]Or *saturated* [A]Ex 30:23; Jer 6:20 [B]Ps 95:10; Is 1:14; 7:13; Ezek 6:9; Mal 2:17 43:25 [A]Is 44:22; 55:7; Jer 50:20 [B]Is 37:35; 48:9, 11; Ezek 36:22 [C]Is 38:17; Jer 31:34 43:26 [a]Or *Report to Me* [A]Is 1:18; 41:1; 50:8 [B]Is 43:9

43:12 declared and saved and proclaimed. As in the deliverance from Egypt (Ex 3, 4), God declared in advance how He would redeem Israel from their captivity. Then came the actual events of the saving process, followed by the Lord's proclamation of that deliverance by way of reminder. The people, on the basis of such omniscience and omnipotence, gave testimony to the true and only living God.

43:13 from eternity. Before the first day of creation when time began and throughout all periods of history, God exists and manifests His will and purpose. **none . . . My hand.** The Heb. behind this clause is identical with the comparable clause in Dt 32:39. God's actions are irreversible and can never end in frustration.

43:14 Redeemer, the Holy One of Israel. The former title characterizes the Lord's role in the salvation of His people in chaps. 40–66 (41:14; 43:14; 44:6, 24; 47:4; 48:17; 49:7, 26; 54:5, 8; 59:20; 60:16; 63:16). The latter title represents His holiness throughout the book (*see note on 1:4*). The Lord's Servant retains His holiness in implementing His redemption of Israel. **Chaldeans . . . the ships.** When God sent a conqueror against Babylon (i.e., Cyrus, 45:1), the proud Babylonian fleet provided a means of flight for the country's fugitives. Babylon was accessible by ship through the Persian Gulf and the Tigris and Euphrates Rivers.

43:15 your King. The Lord was King over Israel from her inception, but the people asked for a human king instead (1Sa 8:4–7). The restoration will put Him back on the throne in the Person of His Servant the Messiah (Lk 1:31–33; cf. 6:1; 41:21).

43:16, 17 sea . . . mighty waters . . . chariot and the horse. To bring assurance of the greater future deliverance He will bring through His Servant, the Lord reminded Isaiah's readers of His deliverance of their ancestors from Egypt (Ex 14:16, 21, 26–28; Jos 3:13).

43:18, 19 former things . . . things of the past . . . something new. Deliverances of the nation in the past will pale into insignificance in comparison with the future deliverance the Lord will give His people (42:9; 48:6; Jer 16:14, 15).

43:19, 20 Rivers . . . waters . . . rivers. In the Messiah's future kingdom, the barren places of Israel will be well-watered (41:18) and will supply refreshment for God's chosen people (43:1).

43:21 declare My praise. In the messianic age, Israel will finally give the Lord the credit that is due Him (contra. Jer 13:11).

43:22–24 Even though the Lord has chosen Israel, Israel throughout her history has not chosen Him. Rather, they have wearied Him with their iniquities and empty ritualism (1:11–15).

43:25 I, even I . . . will not remember your sins. This verse is probably the high point of grace in the OT. In spite of Israel's utter unworthiness, the Lord in His grace has devised a way that He can forgive their sins and grant righteousness (*see note on 61:10*), without compromising His holiness. This He would accomplish through the work of His Servant (53:6). In spite of her failures, Israel will always be God's chosen people.

43:26 State your *cause*. God gives the nation opportunity to come into the court and plead her case. The strongest plea is not to

27 “Your [A]first [a]forefather sinned,
And your [b,B]spokesmen have
[c]transgressed against Me.
28 “So I will [a]pollute the [b]princes
of the sanctuary,
And I will consign Jacob to the [A]ban
and Israel to [B]revilement.

THE BLESSINGS OF ISRAEL

44 “But now listen, O Jacob, My [A]servant,
And Israel, whom I have chosen:
2 Thus says the LORD who made you
And [A]formed you from the
womb, who [B]will help you,
‘[C]Do not fear, O Jacob My servant;
And you [D]Jeshurun whom I have chosen.
3 ‘For [A]I will pour out water
on [a]the thirsty *land*
And streams on the dry ground;
I will [B]pour out My Spirit on your [C]offspring
And My blessing on your descendants;
4 And they will spring up [a]among the grass
Like [A]poplars by streams of water.’
5 “This one will say, ‘I am the LORD’S’;
And that one [a]will call on
the name of Jacob;
And another will [A]write [b]*on* his
hand, ‘Belonging to the LORD,’
And will name Israel’s name with honor.

6 “Thus says the LORD, the [A]King of Israel and his
[B]Redeemer, the LORD of hosts:

‘I am the [C]first and I am the last,
And there is no God [D]besides Me.
7 ‘Who is like Me? [A]Let him
proclaim and declare it;
Yes, let him recount it to Me in order,
[a]From the time that I established
the ancient [b]nation.
And let them declare to them the
things that are coming
And the events that are going to take place.
8 ‘Do not tremble and do not be afraid;
[A]Have I not long since announced
it to you and declared *it?*
And [B]you are My witnesses.
Is there any God [C]besides Me,
Or is there any *other* [D]Rock?
I know of none.’ ”

THE FOLLY OF IDOLATRY

9 Those who fashion [a]a graven image are all of
them futile, and their precious things are of no
profit; even their own witnesses fail to see or know,
so that they will be [A]put to shame. 10 Who has fashioned a god or cast [a]an idol to [A]no profit? 11 Behold,
all his companions will be [A]put to shame, for the
craftsmen themselves are mere men. Let them all
assemble themselves, let them stand up, let them
tremble, let them together be put to shame.
12 The [A]man shapes iron into a cutting tool and
does his work over the coals, [a]fashioning it with
hammers and working it with his strong arm. He
also gets hungry and [b]his strength fails; he drinks no
water and becomes weary. 13 [A]*Another* shapes wood,
he extends a measuring line; he outlines it with red
chalk. He works it with planes and outlines it with a
compass, and makes it like the form of a man, like
the beauty of [B]man, so that it may sit in a [C]house.

43:27 [a]Lit *father* [b]Or *interpreters* [c]Or *rebelled* [A]Is 51:2; Ezek 16:3 [B]Is 9:15; 28:7; 29:10; Jer 5:31 43:28 [a]Or *pierce through* [b]Or *holy princes* [A]Is 24:6; 34:5; Jer 24:9; Dan 9:11; Zech 8:13 [B]Ps 79:4; Ezek 5:15 44:1 [A]Is 41:8; Jer 30:10; 46:27, 28 44:2 [A]Is 44:21, 24 [B]Is 41:10 [C]Is 43:5 [D]Deut 32:15; 33:5, 26 44:3 [a]Or *him who is thirsty* [A]Is 41:17; Ezek 34:26; Joel 3:18 [B]Is 32:15; Joel 2:28 [C]Is 61:9; 65:23 44:4 [a]Another reading is *like grass among the waters* [A]Lev 23:40; Job 40:22 44:5 [a]Another reading is *will be called by the name of Jacob* [b]Or *with* [A]Ex 13:9; Neh 9:38 44:6 [A]Is 41:21; 43:15 [B]Is 41:14; 43:1, 14 [C]Is 41:4; 43:10; 48:12; Rev 1:8, 17; 22:13 [D]Is 43:11; 44:8; 45:5, 6, 21 44:7 [a]Lit *From My establishing of* [b]Or *people* [A]Is 41:22, 26 44:8 [A]Is 42:9; 48:5 [B]Is 43:10 [C]Deut 4:35, 39; 1 Sam 2:2; Is 45:5; Joel 2:27 [D]Is 17:10; 26:4; 30:29 44:9 [a]Or *an idol* [A]Ps 97:7; Is 42:17; 44:11; 45:16 44:10 [a]Or *a graven image* [A]Is 41:29; Jer 10:5; Hab 2:18; Acts 19:26 44:11 [A]Ps 97:7; Is 42:17; 44:9; 45:16 44:12 [a]Lit *and fashions* [b]Lit *there is no strength* [A]Is 40:19, 20; 41:6, 7; 46:6, 7; Jer 10:3-5; Hab 2:18 44:13 [A]Is 41:7 [B]Ps 115:5-7 [C]Judg 17:4, 5; Ezek 8:10, 11

claim personal worthiness, but to confess their sin and repent, thus pleading for mercy and forgiveness based on God’s gracious promise in v. 25 and based on what Jesus Christ would do on the cross (cf. 55:6, 7; Ro 3:21–26).

43:27 first forefather … spokesmen. Sins of even the respected patriarchal ancestors of the Jewish race, like Abraham, kept them from claiming personal merit (e.g., Ge 12:11–13; 20:2). Even such honored intermediaries between God and Israel as the priests needed cleansing from sin (6:5–7).

43:28 Jacob to the ban … Israel to revilement. Even though God will forgive the nation in the messianic age, she still must suffer in the intervening interval.

44:1–5 Under the shadow of more punishment to come (43:26–28), the prophet spoke of abundant blessing that was to be the nation’s portion during the Millennium.

44:1, 2 My servant … whom I have chosen … made you … formed you. God has chosen His servant Israel to be His own eternally (43:1, 21, 25), and they need not fear abandonment.

44:2 Jeshurun. An honored name for Israel whose root meaning is “right” or “straight,” in contrast to the root of “Jacob” which means “over-reacher” or “deceiver” (cf. Dt 32:15).

44:3 water … streams. The extensive blessing of physical conditions will favor the nation in the coming kingdom age (43:19, 20); they were also symbolic of spiritual refreshment from the Holy Spirit and God Himself (32:15; Joel 2:28, 29).

44:5 the LORD’s … name of Jacob … Israel’s name. In the future golden age of Israel, belonging to the Lord and belonging to God’s chosen people will be synonymous, and it will be a badge of honor gladly worn without fear.

44:6 King … Redeemer … LORD of hosts … first … last. The Lord identified Himself as Israel’s King (43:15), Redeemer (43:14), and Eternal One (41:4; cf. 48:12). Jesus, in a direct affirmation of His deity, called Himself the First and the Last (cf. Rev 1:17; 2:8; 22:13). **no God besides Me.** God’s exclusive claim to deity prepared the way for another challenge to false gods in vv. 7–20 (cf. 43:10).

44:7 let them declare. If idols can foretell “the things that are coming,” let them predict accurately, as the Lord has. Since the Jews have had predictions of the future ever since God chose them as His people, they are qualified to be His witnesses (v. 8).

44:9–11 shame … shame … shame. The workmen who manufactured idols were mere men and could make nothing as good as or greater than man. They and others who put their trust in idols had ample reason to fear and be ashamed of such folly (v. 11; contra. v. 8).

44:12–19 Human workers expended all their energy to produce a beautiful idol, but the best they could make was the likeness of a man (Dt 4:15–18; Ro 1:23), and that could not renew their strength. Yet they who wait on the Lord will renew their strength (40:28–31). The same humanly nurtured trees used as fuel for fires to furnish warmth and to cook also provides wood for people to make idols, which they worship and to which they entrust their prayers and themselves. Nothing could be more foolish than worshiping as deity a piece of wood, while burning the same wood in a fire to keep warm. Idol-makers cannot comprehend the idiocy of creating gods from materials used for the most trivial domestic purposes. Cf. 6:9, 10; Dt 27:15.

14 Surely he cuts cedars for himself, and takes a [a]cy-
press or an oak and [b]raises *it* for himself among the
trees of the forest. He plants a fir, and the rain makes
it grow. 15 Then it becomes *something* for a man to
burn, so he takes one of them and warms himself;
he also makes a fire to bake bread. He also [A]makes a
god and worships it; he makes it a graven image and
[B]falls down before it. 16 Half of it he burns in the fire;
over *this* half he eats meat as he roasts a roast and
is satisfied. He also warms himself and says, "Aha! I
am warm, I have seen the fire." 17 But the rest of it he
[A]makes into a god, his graven image. He falls down
before it and worships; he also [B]prays to it and says,
"Deliver me, for you are my god."

18 They do not [A]know, nor do they understand,
for He has [B]smeared over their eyes so that they
cannot see and their hearts so that they cannot
comprehend. 19 No one [a]recalls, nor is there [A]knowl-
edge or understanding to say, "I have burned half
of it in the fire and also have baked bread over its
coals. I roast meat and eat *it*. Then [b]I make the rest
of it into an [B]abomination, [c]I fall down before a
block of wood!" 20 He [a,A]feeds on ashes; a [B]deceived
heart has turned him aside. And he cannot deliver [b]himself, nor say, "[C]Is there not a lie in my
right hand?"

GOD FORGIVES AND REDEEMS

21 "[A]Remember these things, O Jacob,
And Israel, for you are [B]My servant;
I have formed you, you are My servant,
O Israel, you will [C]not
be forgotten by Me.
22 "I have [A]wiped out your transgressions
like a thick cloud
And your sins like a [a]heavy mist.
[B]Return to Me, for I have [C]redeemed you."
23 [A]Shout for joy, O heavens, for
the LORD has done *it!*
Shout joyfully, you lower
parts of the earth;
[B]Break forth into a shout of
joy, you mountains,
O forest, and every tree in it;
For [C]the LORD has redeemed Jacob
And in Israel He [D]shows
forth His glory.

24 Thus says the LORD, your [A]Redeemer, and the
one who [B]formed you from the womb,

"I, the LORD, am the maker
of all things,
[C]Stretching out the heavens by Myself
And spreading out the earth [a]all alone,
25 [A]Causing the [a]omens of boasters to fail,
[b]Making fools out of diviners,
[B]Causing wise men to draw back
And [c]turning their knowledge
into foolishness,
26 [A]Confirming the word of His servant
And [a]performing the purpose
of His messengers.
It is I who says of Jerusalem,
'She shall be inhabited!'
And of the [B]cities of Judah,
'[C]They shall be built.'
And I will raise up her ruins *again*.
27 "*It is I* who says to the depth of
the sea, 'Be dried up!'
And I will make your rivers [A]dry.
28 "*It is I* who says of [A]Cyrus,
'*He is* My shepherd!
And he will perform all My desire.'
And [a]he declares of Jerusalem,
'[B]She will be built,'
And of the temple, '[b]Your
foundation will be laid.' "

44:14 [a]Or *holm-oak* [b]Lit *makes strong* 44:15 [A]Is 44:17 [B]2 Chr 25:14 44:17 [A]Is 44:15 [B]1 Kin 18:26, 28; Is 45:20 44:18 [A]Is 1:3; Jer 10:8, 14 [B]Ps 81:12; Is 6:9, 10; 29:10 44:19 [a]Lit *returns to his heart* [b]Or *shall I make?* [c]Or *shall I fall...?* [A]Is 5:13; 44:18, 19; 45:20 [B]Deut 27:15; 1 Kin 11:5, 7; 2 Kin 23:13, 14 44:20 [a]Or *is a companion of ashes* [b]Lit *his soul* [A]Ps 102:9 [B]Job 15:31; Hos 4:12; Rom 1:21, 22; 2 Thess 2:11; 2 Tim 3:13 [C]Is 57:11; 59:3, 4, 13; Rom 1:25 44:21 [A]Is 46:8; Zech 10:9 [B]Is 44:1, 2 [C]Is 49:15 44:22 [a]Or *cloud* [A]Ps 51:1, 9; Is 43:25; Acts 3:19 [B]Is 31:6; 55:7 [C]Is 43:1; 48:20; 1 Cor 6:20; 1 Pet 1:18, 19 44:23 [A]Ps 69:34; 96:11, 12; Is 42:10; 49:13 [B]Ps 98:7, 8; 148:7, 9; Is 55:12 [C]Is 43:1 [D]Is 49:3; 61:3 44:24 [a]Or *who was with Me?* [A]Is 41:14; 43:14 [B]Is 44:2 [C]Is 40:22; 42:5; 45:12, 18; 51:13 44:25 [a]Lit *signs* [b]Lit *He makes* [c]Lit *He turns* [A]Is 47:13 [B]2 Sam 15:31; Job 5:12-14; Ps 33:10; Is 29:14; Jer 51:57; 1 Cor 1:20, 27 44:26 [a]Lit *He performs* [A]Zech 1:6; Matt 5:18 [B]Is 40:9 [C]Jer 32:15, 44 44:27 [A]Is 42:15; 50:2; Jer 50:38; 51:36 44:28 [a]Lit *to say* [b]Lit *You will be founded* [A]Is 45:1 [B]2 Chr 36:22, 23; Ezra 1:1; Is 14:32; 45:13; 54:11

44:20 deceived heart ... lie. Like eating ashes, which provide no nourishment, idolatry is a deception, from which the sinner gets nothing but judgment (cf. Pr 15:14; Hos 12:1).

44:22 wiped out ... your sins. Further reassurances of God's sovereign grace at work on behalf of Israel were given (43:25). God had blotted out their sins written in His book against them (cf. Rev 20:12). As a person can't see what is ahead because it is blocked by a "thick cloud," so God obliterated the sins of those He redeemed. **Return to Me.** God has already provided for redemption, even before the cross, but based on it alone. For those who turn from sin and return to Him, there is redemption (because the purchase price for the sinner was paid by the sacrifice of Christ). The Lord calls on His people to repent so they may receive the promised redemption (cf. Ne 1:9; Jer 4:1; 24:7; Joel 2:12; Zec 1:3; Mal 3:7; Mt 3:2; 4:17; Ro 3:25, 26; Heb 9:15).

44:23 heavens ... every tree ... redeemed Jacob. The national redemption of Israel at Christ's second coming entails also the redemption of all nature (Ro 8:19–22), so the prophet calls on the whole creation to rejoice.

44:25 boasters ... diviners. False prophets must suffer the consequences of their deceptive counsel (47:12–14; Dt 13:1–5; Jos 13:22; Jer 27:9; 29:8; 50:36; Mic 3:7).

44:26 His servant ... His messengers. In contrast with His breaking the word of false prophets (v. 25), the Lord confirmed the word of His true prophets such as of Isaiah (Zec 1:6). Most specially, God confirmed the Word of the Messiah, who is the consummate embodiment of all the prophets and messengers of God (Mal 3:1; Mt 21:34, 36, 37). **raise up her ruins.** The fall of Jerusalem came in 586 B.C. when the Babylonians invaded the Land. God promised to restore the Land to prosperity, the foretaste of restoration coming after 70 years with the help of the Persians (41:2), but the greater restoration to come in Messiah's kingdom.

44:27 Be dried up! The Lord demonstrated His power by drying up the Red Sea and the Jordan River when delivering His people from Egypt (43:2).

44:28 Cyrus ... My shepherd. The prophecy—given a century and a half before Cyrus lived and became king of Persia—predicted God's use of the Persian king to gather the faithful remnant of Israel back to the land. In this role, Cyrus prefigured the Lord's Servant, who will shepherd the sheep of Israel in their final regathering (Mic 5:4). The title "shepherd" applied to kings as leaders of God's people (2Sa 5:2; Jer 3:15). In Ac 13:22, Paul compares David to the standard of Cyrus' obedience. **Jerusalem ... the temple.** In 538 B.C. Cyrus decreed the rebuilding of the temple (Ezr 1:1, 2; 6:3), thus fulfilling Isaiah's prophecy. The returning Jews completed the work in 516 B.C. (Ezr 6:15).

GOD USES CYRUS

45 Thus says the LORD to
[A]Cyrus His anointed,
Whom I have taken by
the right [B]hand,
To [C]subdue nations before him
And [a]to [D]loose the loins of kings;
To open doors before him so that
gates will not be shut:
2 "I will go before you and [A]make
the [a]rough places smooth;
I will [B]shatter the doors of bronze
and cut through their iron [C]bars.
3 "I will give you the [a,A]treasures
of darkness
And hidden wealth of secret places,
So that you may know that it is I,
The LORD, the God of Israel, who
[B]calls you by your name.
4 "For the sake of [A]Jacob My servant,
And Israel My chosen *one,*
I have also [B]called you
by your name;
I have given you a title of honor
Though you have [C]not known Me.
5 "I am the LORD, and [A]there
is no other;
[B]Besides Me there is no God.
I will [a,C]gird you, though you
have not known Me;
6 That [a,A]men may know from the
rising to the setting of the sun
That there is [B]no one besides Me.
I am the LORD, and there
is no other,
7 The One [A]forming light and
[B]creating darkness,
Causing [a]well-being and
[C]creating calamity;
I am the LORD who does all these.

GOD'S SUPREME POWER

8 "[A]Drip down, O heavens, from above,
And let the clouds pour
down righteousness;
Let the [B]earth open up and
salvation bear fruit,
[C]And righteousness spring up with it.
I, the LORD, have created it.

9 "Woe to *the one* who [A]quarrels
with his [a]Maker—
An earthenware vessel [b]among
the vessels of earth!
Will the [B]clay say to the [a]potter,
'What are you doing?'
Or the thing you are making
say, 'He has no hands'?
10 "Woe to him who says to a father,
'What are you begetting?'
Or to a woman, 'To what are
you [a]giving birth?' "

11 Thus says the [A]LORD, the Holy One of Israel,
and his [a,B]Maker:

"[b,C]Ask Me about the things to come
[c]concerning My [D]sons,
And you shall commit to Me
[E]the work of My hands.
12 "It is I who [A]made the earth, and
created man upon it.
I [B]stretched out the heavens
with My hands
And I [a]ordained [C]all their host.
13 "I have aroused him in [A]righteousness
And I will [B]make all his ways smooth;
He will [C]build My city and will
let My exiles go [D]free,
Without any payment or reward,"
says the LORD of hosts.

45:1 [a]Lit *I will loose* [A]Is 44:28 [B]Ps 73:23; Is 41:13; 42:6 [C]Is 41:2, 25; Jer 50:3, 35; 51:11, 20, 24 [D]Job 12:21; Is 45:5 45:2 [a]Another reading is *mountains* [A]Is 40:4 [B]Ps 107:16 [C]Jer 51:30 45:3 [a]Or *hoarded treasures* [A]Jer 41:8; 50:37 [B]Ex 33:12, 17; Is 43:1; 49:1 45:4 [A]Is 41:8, 9; 44:1 [B]Is 43:1 [C]Acts 17:23 45:5 [a]Or *arm* [A]Is 45:6, 14, 18, 21; 46:9 [B]Is 44:6, 8 [C]Ps 18:39 45:6 [a]Lit *they* [A]Ps 102:15; Mal 1:11 [B]Is 45:5 45:7 [a]Or *peace* [A]Is 42:16 [B]Ps 104:20; 105:28 [C]Is 31:2; 47:11; Amos 3:6 45:8 [A]Ps 72:6; Hos 10:12; 14:5; Joel 3:18 [B]Ps 85:11 [C]Is 60:21; 61:11 45:9 [a]Lit *Fashioner* [b]Lit *with* [A]Job 15:25; 40:8, 9; Ps 2:2, 3; Prov 21:30; Jer 50:24 [B]Is 29:16; 64:8; Jer 18:6; Rom 9:20, 21 45:10 [a]Lit *in labor pains with* 45:11 [a]Lit *Fashioner* [b]Or *Will you ask* [c]Or *upon* [A]Is 43:15; 48:17; Ezek 39:7 [B]Is 44:2; 54:5 [C]Is 8:19 [D]Jer 31:9 [E]Is 19:25; 29:23; 60:21; 64:8 45:12 [a]Or *commanded* [A]Is 42:5; 45:18; Jer 27:5 [B]Ps 104:2; Is 42:5; 44:24 [C]Gen 2:1; Neh 9:6 45:13 [A]Is 41:2 [B]Is 45:2 [C]2 Chr 36:22, 23; Is 44:28 [D]Is 52:3

45:1, 2 doors … gates … doors of bronze. Probably this was a reference to the many gates in the city wall of Babylon which Cyrus entered with relative ease. The inner gates leading from the river to the city were left open, as were the palace doors. Herodotus, the Greek historian, reported that the openness of the city was so great that the Persians were taking prisoners as they moved to the palace in the center.

45:1 His anointed. This word is the one translated from the Heb. by the transliteration—"Messiah." It is the word used for the messianic Redeemer King in Ps 2:2 and Da 9:25, 26, but here refers to Cyrus, as the king set apart by God's providence for divine purposes. Though not a worshiper of the Lord, the Persian monarch played an unusual role as Israel's shepherd (44:28) and God's anointed judge on nations.

45:3 that you may know. God intended Cyrus to be aware that the God of the Jews was giving him victorious conquests. According to Josephus, the Jewish historian, who indicated that Daniel influenced Cyrus with the prophecy of Isaiah, the king did know that the God of Israel was with him.

45:4 Jacob … have not known Me. For His servant Israel's sake, the Lord raised up Cyrus, calling him by name, even though Cyrus did not have a personal relationship to Him. At some point, Cyrus certainly became aware of the true God and His sovereign control over human affairs, perhaps through the influence of Daniel (cf. Ezr 1:1–4).

45:6 from the rising to the setting of the sun. This expression, meaning the whole earth, points to the fact that through the eventual, final regathering of Israel (of which Cyrus' exploits were a foretaste), the whole earth will know the Lord alone is God (cf. 43:10; 44:6).

45:8 righteousness … salvation … righteousness. Eventually the Lord will cause righteous goodness to prevail throughout the world, just as He has promised Israel that it would (v. 13; Hos 10:12).

45:9, 10 Woe … Woe. Figures of the potter and the clay and of parent and child show how absurd it is to contend with God over His plans for the future. This anticipated the objections by the Jews against 1) their captivity and restoration by a pagan king, and 2) ultimately God's sovereign plan to redeem Gentiles as well as Jews worldwide (cf. Ro 9:20–24).

45:11 Ask Me about the things to come. The Lord commands Israel to seek information about what He will do for the nation in the future, for He will reveal it.

45:12, 13 I who made … He will build My city. As the omnipotent Creator, God can save the nation through Cyrus as He has promised.

14 Thus says the LORD,

"The [a]products of [A]Egypt and the
merchandise of [b,B]Cush
And the Sabeans, men of stature,
Will [C]come over to you
and will be yours;
They will walk behind you, they
will come over in [D]chains
And will [E]bow down to you;
They will make supplication to you:
'[c]Surely, [F]God is [d]with you, and
[G]there is none else,
No other God.' "
15 Truly, You are a God who [A]hides Himself,
O God of Israel, [B]Savior!
16 They will be [A]put to shame and
even humiliated, all of them;
The [B]manufacturers of idols will go
away together in humiliation.
17 Israel has been saved by the LORD
With an [A]everlasting salvation;
You [B]will not be put to shame
or humiliated
To all eternity.

18 For thus says the LORD, who [A]created the heavens (He is the God who [B]formed the earth and made
it, He established it *and* did not create it [a]a [C]waste
place, *but* formed it to be [D]inhabited),

"I am the LORD, and [E]there is none else.
19 "[A]I have not spoken in secret,
In [a]some dark land;
I did not say to the [b,B]offspring of Jacob,
'[C]Seek Me in [c]a waste place';
I, the LORD, [D]speak righteousness,
[E]Declaring things that are upright.
20 "[A]Gather yourselves and come;
Draw near together, you
fugitives of the nations;
[B]They have no knowledge,
Who [C]carry about [a]their wooden idol
And [D]pray to a god who cannot save.
21 "[A]Declare and set forth *your case;*
Indeed, let them consult together.
[B]Who has announced this from of old?
Who has long since declared it?
Is it not I, the LORD?
And there is [C]no other God besides Me,
A righteous God and a [D]Savior;
There is none except Me.
22 "[A]Turn to Me and [B]be saved, all
the ends of the earth;
For I am God, and there is no other.
23 "[A]I have sworn by Myself,
The [B]word has gone forth from
My mouth in righteousness
And will not turn back,
That to Me [C]every knee will bow, every
tongue will [D]swear *allegiance.*
24 "They will say of Me, 'Only [A]in the LORD
are righteousness and strength.'
Men will come to Him,
And [B]all who were angry at Him
will be put to shame.
25 "In the LORD all the offspring of Israel
Will be [A]justified and will [B]glory."

BABYLON'S IDOLS AND THE TRUE GOD

46 [A]Bel has bowed down, Nebo stoops over;
Their images are *consigned* to
the beasts and the cattle.
The things [a]that you carry are burdensome,
A load for the weary *beast.*

45:14 [a]Lit *labor* [b]Or *Ethiopia* [c]Or *God is with you alone* [d]Or *in* [A]Ps 68:31; Is 19:21 [B]Is 18:1; 43:3 [C]Is 14:1, 2; 49:23; 54:3 [D]Ps 149:8 [E]Is 49:23; 60:14 [F]Jer 16:19; Zech 8:20-23; 1 Cor 14:25 [G]Is 45:5 45:15 [A]Ps 44:24; Is 1:15; 8:17; 57:17 [B]Is 43:3 45:16 [A]Is 42:17; 44:9 [B]Is 44:11 45:17 [A]Is 26:4; 51:6; Rom 11:26 [B]Is 49:23; 50:7; 54:4 45:18 [a]Or *in vain* [A]Is 42:5 [B]Is 45:12 [C]Gen 1:2 [D]Gen 1:26; Ps 115:16 [E]Is 45:5 45:19 [a]Lit *a place of a land of darkness* [b]Lit *seed* [c]Or *vain* [A]Is 48:16 [B]Is 45:25; 65:9 [C]2 Chr 15:2; Ps 78:34; Jer 29:13, 14 [D]Ps 19:8; Is 45:23; 63:1 [E]Is 43:12; 44:8 45:20 [a]Lit *the wood of their graven image* [A]Is 43:9 [B]Is 44:18, 19; 48:5-7 [C]Is 46:1, 7; Jer 10:5 [D]Is 44:17; 46:6, 7 45:21 [A]Is 41:23; 43:9 [B]Is 41:26; 44:7; 48:14 [C]Is 45:5 [D]Is 43:3, 11 45:22 [A]Num 21:8, 9; 2 Chr 20:12; Mic 7:7; Zech 12:10 [B]Is 30:15; 49:6, 12; 52:10 45:23 [A]Gen 22:16; Is 62:8; Heb 6:13 [B]Is 55:11 [C]Rom 14:11; Phil 2:10 [D]Deut 6:13; Ps 63:11; Is 19:18; 65:16 45:24 [A]Jer 33:16 [B]Is 41:11 45:25 [A]1 Kin 8:32; Is 53:11 [B]Is 41:16; 60:19 46:1 [a]Lit *carried by you* [A]Is 2:18; 21:9; Jer 50:2-4; 51:44

45:14 Egypt … Cush … Sabeans. Three countries to the S (cf. 43:3) illustrate the worldwide submission to Israel that will prevail during the messianic kingdom age. **Surely, God is with you.** All nations will acknowledge the presence of the one true God among His people Israel (49:23; 60:14). Paul the apostle found a fuller sense in these words when he advised the Corinthians on exercising prophecy rather than tongues in their meetings. This brought an acknowledgment from visitors of God's presence among them (1Co 14:25).

45:15 hides Himself. The contemporary situation hid God's purposes of mercy toward Israel, i.e., that they would repent and He would eventually regather them and make Jerusalem the center of world attention (cf. 8:17; 54:8; 57:17; Ps 44:24).

45:16, 17 Israel has been saved. Makers of idols are to find disillusionment because of the failure of their gods to deliver, but Israel is to find eternal salvation in the Lord (44:9–11; Ro 11:25–27).

45:19 not spoken in secret. Unlike mysterious utterances of the false gods (8:19; 29:4), God's revelations through His true prophets are open and accessible.

45:21 Who has announced this from of old? The Lord's case to prove He is the only true God is unanswerable; only He foretold the captivity of Judah and the deliverance from that captivity, as well as other future events that happened just as He had predicted. **there is no other … There is none.** The Lord restated the truth expressed by Moses in Dt 4:35 (cf. 43:10; 44:6; 45:6). The scribe who asked Jesus about the greatest commandment cited this same principle in agreeing with Jesus' answer to his question (Mk 12:32).

45:22 be saved, all the ends of the earth. When the Messiah sits on His throne in Jerusalem, all people will enjoy His temporal salvation in the physical blessings of the millennial earth and will have opportunity for spiritual salvation (49:6).

45:23 every knee will bow. In the kingdom age, all nations will worship the one true God of Israel. A further meaning, justified by the NT, applies this verse to believers' accountability to God when He evaluates their works (Ro 14:11). In assigning the words another meaning, Paul relates the words to the coming universal acknowledgment that "Jesus Christ is Lord, to the glory of God the Father" (Php 2:10, 11).

45:25 all the offspring of Israel. Physical descent from Abraham alone cannot bring justification. Only the faithful remnant of Israel will be saved (v. 17; Ro 11:25–27). "Justified" means to be declared righteous, to be treated as if one is not sinful, but holy through the application of Christ's righteousness to the one who believes (cf. 61:10; 2Co 5:21).

46:1 Bel … Nebo. The two most prominent gods in Babylon. "Bel" is another spelling for "Baal," the Phoenician chief god of Babylon. That "Nebo" was extensively worshiped is shown by the proper names compounded from his: Nebuchadnezzar, Nabopolassar, and Nebuzaradan.

2 They stooped over, they have
bowed down together;
They could not rescue the burden,
But [a]have themselves [A]gone into captivity.

3 "[A]Listen to Me, O house of Jacob,
And all [B]the remnant of the house of Israel,
You who have been [C]borne
by Me from [a]birth
And have been carried from the womb;
4 Even to *your* old age [A]I [a]will be the same,
And even to *your* [b,B]graying
years I will bear *you!*
I have [c]done *it,* and I will carry *you;*
And I will bear *you* and I will deliver *you.*

5 "[A]To whom would you liken Me
And make Me equal and compare Me,
That we would be alike?
6 "Those who [A]lavish gold from the purse
And weigh silver on the scale
Hire a goldsmith, and he
makes it *into* a god;
They [B]bow down, indeed they worship it.
7 "They [A]lift it upon the shoulder
and carry it;
They set it in its place and it stands *there.*
[B]It does not move from its place.
Though one may cry to it,
it [C]cannot answer;
It [D]cannot deliver him from his distress.

8 "[A]Remember this, and be [a]assured;
[B]Recall it to [b]mind, you [C]transgressors.
9 "Remember the [A]former things long past,
For I am God, and there is [B]no other;
I am God, and there is [C]no one like Me,
10 Declaring the end from the beginning,
And from ancient times things
which have not been done,
Saying, '[A]My purpose will
be established,
And I will accomplish all
My good pleasure';
11 Calling a [A]bird of prey from the [B]east,
The man of [a]My purpose
from a far country.
Truly I have [C]spoken; truly I
will bring it to pass.
I have planned *it, surely* I will do it.

12 "[A]Listen to Me, you [B]stubborn-minded,
Who are [C]far from righteousness.
13 "I [A]bring near My righteousness,
it is not far off;
And My salvation will not delay.
And I will grant [B]salvation in Zion,
And My [C]glory for Israel.

LAMENT FOR BABYLON

47 "[A]Come down and sit in the dust,
O [B]virgin [C]daughter of Babylon;
Sit on the ground without a throne,
O daughter of the Chaldeans!
For you shall no longer be called
[D]tender and delicate.
2 "Take the [A]millstones and [B]grind meal.
Remove your [C]veil, [D]strip off the skirt,
Uncover the leg, cross the rivers.
3 "Your [A]nakedness will be uncovered,
Your shame also will be exposed;
I will [B]take vengeance and
will not [a]spare a man."
4 Our [A]Redeemer, the LORD of
hosts is His name,
The Holy One of Israel.
5 "[A]Sit silently, and go into [B]darkness,
O daughter of the Chaldeans,
For you will no longer be called
The [C]queen of [D]kingdoms.

46:2 [a]Or *their soul has* [A]Judg 18:17, 18, 24; 2 Sam 5:21; Jer 43:12, 13; 48:7; Hos 10:5, 6 46:3 [a]Lit *the belly* [A]Is 46:12 [B]Is 10:21, 22 [C]Ps 71:6; Is 49:1 46:4 [a]Lit *I am He* [b]Lit *gray hairs* [c]Or *made* you [A]Is 41:4; 43:13; 48:12 [B]Ps 71:18 46:5 [A]Is 40:18, 25 46:6 [A]Is 40:19; 41:7; 44:12-17; Jer 10:4 [B]Is 44:15, 17 46:7 [A]Is 45:20; 46:1; Jer 10:5 [B]Is 40:20; 41:7 [C]Is 41:28 [D]Is 45:20 46:8 [a]Lit *firm* [b]Lit *heart* [A]Is 44:21 [B]Is 44:19 [C]Is 50:1 46:9 [A]Deut 32:7; Is 42:9; 65:17 [B]Is 45:5, 21 [C]Is 41:26, 27 46:10 [A]Ps 33:11; Prov 19:21; Is 14:24; 25:1; 40:8; Acts 5:39 46:11 [a]Lit *His* [A]Is 18:6 [B]Is 41:2 [C]Num 23:19; Is 14:24; 37:26 46:12 [A]Is 46:3 [B]Ps 76:5; Is 48:4; Zech 7:11, 12; Mal 3:13 [C]Ps 119:150; Is 48:1; Jer 2:5 46:13 [A]Is 51:5; 61:11; Rom 3:21 [B]Is 61:3; 62:11; Joel 3:17; 1 Pet 2:6 [C]Is 43:7; 44:23 47:1 [A]Is 3:26; Jer 48:18 [B]Is 23:12; 37:22; Jer 46:11 [C]Ps 137:8; Jer 50:42; 51:33; Zech 2:7 [D]Deut 28:56 47:2 [A]Ex 11:5; Jer 25:10 [B]Job 31:10; Eccl 12:4; Matt 24:41 [C]Gen 24:65; Is 3:23; 1 Cor 11:5 [D]Is 32:11 47:3 [a]Lit *meet* [A]Ezek 16:37; Nah 3:5 [B]Is 34:8; 63:4 47:4 [A]Is 41:14 47:5 [A]Is 23:2; Jer 8:14; Lam 2:10 [B]Is 13:10 [C]Is 47:7 [D]Is 13:19; Dan 2:37

46:2 gone into captivity. When Cyrus came, even the gods were taken into exile. These idols couldn't save themselves from being laid down on the backs of beasts and hauled away, let alone save the people who worshiped them.

46:3, 4 all the remnant of the house of Israel. The God of Israel is not helpless like idols. In His strength He has sustained and will sustain helpless Israel through every circumstance. In v. 4, the Lord uses the first person pronoun 6 times to emphasize His personal involvement in delivering Israel.

46:5–8 The human origin and utter impotence of idols renders them unfit for comparison with the God of Israel (40:18–20). In v. 8, the prophet calls on the readers to recall the impotence of the idols they worship in transgression of God's law.

46:9 Remember the former things long past. The readers are to recall: 1) all the past history of fulfilled prophecies, as well as 2) miraculous deliverances such as that from Egypt, and 3) providential blessings Israel has experienced. All of these are ample evidence that He alone is God.

46:11 man . . . from a far country. Cyrus was this man whom God summoned to conquer Babylon and return a remnant of Israel to end the 70-year captivity a century and a half after Isaiah wrote this prophecy (44:28; 45:1).

46:13 righteousness . . . salvation in Zion. At God's appointed time, the salvation of Israel will become reality and result in the Messiah's righteous kingdom (61:3; 62:11; Joel 3:17; Zec 12:10–13:1; Ro 11:25–27).

47:1–3 O virgin daughter of Babylon. The prophet depicted Babylon as a virgin in the sense of never before having been captured. Babylon sat like a royal virgin in the dust, experiencing complete humiliation. The "throne" was gone, taken by Persian power, and the empire never recovered from being robbed of its power, its people, and its name. The former royal virgin is depicted as a slave woman forced to exchange royal garments for working clothes, who must lift her garment to wade through the water as she serves like a slave traversing the river in her duties. Such duties in the E belonged to women of low rank, fitting imagery for Babylon's fall into degradation.

47:5 queen of kingdoms. The title continues the analogy of v. 1 and speaks of the exalted position from which Babylon was to fall. She was mistress of the world, but would later become a slave woman (cf. v. 7), degraded by pride and false security (v. 8).

6 "I was angry with My people,
I profaned My heritage
And gave them into your hand.
You did not show mercy to them,
On the [A]aged you made your
yoke very heavy.
7 "Yet you said, 'I will be a [A]queen forever.'
These things you did not [B]consider
Nor remember the [C]outcome of [a]them.

8 "Now, then, hear this, you [A]sensual one,
Who [B]dwells securely,
Who says in [a]your heart,
'[C]I am, and there is no one besides me.
I will [D]not sit as a widow,
Nor know loss of children.'
9 "But these [A]two things will come on
you [B]suddenly in one day:
Loss of children and widowhood.
They will come on you in full measure
In spite of your many [C]sorceries,
In spite of the great power
of your spells.
10 "You felt [A]secure in your
wickedness and said,
'[B]No one sees me,'
Your [C]wisdom and your knowledge,
[a]they have deluded you;
For you have said in your heart,
'[D]I am, and there is no one besides me.'
11 "But [A]evil will come on you
Which you will not know
how to charm away;
And disaster will fall on you
For which you cannot atone;
And [B]destruction about which
you do not know
Will come on you [C]suddenly.
12 "Stand *fast* now in your [A]spells
And in your many sorceries
With which you have labored
from your youth;
Perhaps you will be able to profit,
Perhaps you may cause trembling.
13 "You are [A]wearied with your
many counsels;
Let now the [B]astrologers,
Those who prophesy by the stars,
Those who predict by the new moons,
Stand up and [C]save you from
what will come upon you.
14 "Behold, they have become [A]like stubble,
[B]Fire burns them;
They cannot deliver themselves
from the power of the flame;
There will be [C]no coal to warm by
Nor a fire to sit before!
15 "So have those become to you with
whom you have labored,
Who have [A]trafficked with
you from your youth;
Each has wandered in his own [a]way;
There is [B]none to save you.

ISRAEL'S OBSTINACY

48 "[A]Hear this, O house of Jacob,
who are named Israel
And who came forth from
the [a,B]loins of Judah,
Who [C]swear by the name of the LORD
And invoke the God of Israel,
But not in truth nor in [D]righteousness.
2 "For they call themselves
after the [A]holy city
And [B]lean on the God of Israel;
The LORD of hosts is His name.

47:6 [A]Deut 28:50 47:7 [a]Lit *it* [A]Is 47:5 [B]Is 42:25; 57:11 [C]Deut 32:29; Jer 5:31; Ezek 7:2, 3 47:8 [a]Lit *her* [A]Is 22:13; 32:9; Jer 50:11 [B]Is 32:9, 11; Zeph 2:15 [C]Is 45:5, 6, 18; 47:10; Zeph 2:15 [D]Rev 18:7 47:9 [A]Is 13:16, 18; 14:22 [B]Ps 73:19; 1 Thess 5:3; Rev 18:8, 10 [C]Is 47:13; Nah 3:4; Rev 18:23 47:10 [a]Lit *it has* [A]Ps 52:7; 62:10; Is 59:4 [B]Is 29:15; Ezek 8:12; 9:9 [C]Is 5:21; 44:20 [D]Is 47:8 47:11 [A]Is 57:1 [B]Is 13:6; Jer 51:8, 43; Luke 17:27; 1 Thess 5:3 [C]Is 47:9 47:12 [A]Is 47:9 47:13 [A]Jer 51:58, 64 [B]Is 8:19; 44:25; 47:9; Dan 2:2, 10 [C]Is 47:15 47:14 [A]Is 5:24; Nah 1:10; Mal 4:1 [B]Is 10:17; Jer 51:30, 32, 58 [C]Is 44:16 47:15 [a]Lit *side, region* [A]Rev 18:11 [B]Is 5:29; 43:13; 46:7 48:1 [a]Lit *waters* [A]Is 46:12 [B]Num 24:7; Deut 33:28; Ps 68:26 [C]Deut 6:13; Is 45:23; 65:16 [D]Is 58:2; Jer 4:2 48:2 [A]Is 52:1; 64:10 [B]Is 10:20; Jer 7:4; 21:2; Mic 3:11; Rom 2:17

47:6 did not show mercy. Though God was punishing Israel in captivity, Babylon's cruel oppression of the captive Israelites was cause for the kingdom's overthrow. Cf. Jer 50:17, 18; 51:33–40; Zec 1:15.

47:7–9 In Rev 18:7, 8, 10, 16, 19, John alludes to these verses in describing the downfall of Babylon just before Christ's return. Compare "a queen forever" with 18:7, "not sit as a widow" with 18:7, and "in one day" with 18:8.

47:8 no one besides me. This pinnacle of Babylon's pride was mockery of the true God in its frivolous presumption of deity (v. 10; cf. 44:6).

47:9 suddenly in one day. Babylon did not decay slowly, but went from being the wealthy lady, the unconquered virgin, the proud, invincible mother of many to a degraded, slave woman in the dust who lost her throne, her children, and her life. It happened in one night, suddenly and unexpectedly, when Cyrus and the Persian army entered the city (cf. Da 5:28, 30). **Loss of children and widowhood.** Babylon did lose its inhabitants, many of whom were killed and taken captive under Cyrus. This prophecy was fulfilled again when Babylon revolted against Darius; and in order to hold out in the siege, each man chose one woman of his family and strangled the rest to save provisions. Darius impaled 3,000 of the revolters.

47:10 Sinners foolishly think they are safe, and there is none to judge them. Cf. Pss 10:11; 94:7.

47:11 evil ... disaster ... destruction. The Persians under Cyrus suddenly initiated (cf. v. 9) the visitation that ultimately obliterated Babylon. Its culmination is to come in conjunction with the destruction of a revived Babylon, the world headquarters of evil at the second coming of Christ (51:8; Rev 18:2–24).

47:12 spells ... sorceries. The magical practices of Babylon, designed to aid against enemies (also v. 9), will characterize the Babylon of the future also (Rev 18:23).

47:13 Let now the astrologers ... save you. Babylon relied heavily on those who looked for combinations of stars, who watched conjunctions of heavenly bodies, who made much of months of birth, and who relied on the movements of stars to predict the future (Da 2:2, 10). The prophet sarcastically points out the futility of such trust. This ancient deception is still popular today in the widespread use of horoscopes.

47:14 They cannot deliver themselves. The astrologers were helpless to save themselves, much less the Babylonians who depended on them, or anyone else. The divine fire that came was not to be a fire to warm them, but to consume them.

47:15 none to save you. When judgment comes, the astrologers with whom the people trafficked and spent their money will run to their homes, unable to save themselves or anyone else.

48:1, 2 swear by the name of the LORD ... not in truth. The people were nominally Israelites, but their hearts were far from God. This hypocrisy was common all through Israel's history, even to the time of the Lord Jesus. Cf. Mt 23:3, 13–39.

3 “I [A]declared the former things long ago
And they went forth from My mouth,
and I proclaimed them.
[B]Suddenly I acted, and they
[C]came to pass.
4 “Because I know that you are [a,A]obstinate,
And your [B]neck is an iron sinew
And your [C]forehead bronze,
5 Therefore I declared *them*
to you long ago,
Before [a]they took place I
proclaimed *them* to you,
So that you would not say, ‘My
[A]idol has done them,
And my graven image and my molten
image have commanded them.’
6 “You have heard; look at all this.
And you, will you not declare it?
I proclaim to you [A]new things
from this time,
Even hidden things which
you have not known.
7 “They are created now and not long ago;
And before today you have
not heard them,
So that you will not say,
‘Behold, I knew them.’
8 “You have not [A]heard, you have not known.
Even from long ago your ear
has not been open,
Because I knew that you would
deal very treacherously;
And you have been called a
[a,B]rebel from [b]birth.
9 “[A]For the sake of My name I
[B]delay My wrath,
And *for* My praise I restrain *it* for you,
In order not to cut you off.
10 “Behold, I have refined you,
but [A]not as silver;
I have tested you in the
[B]furnace of affliction.
11 “[A]For My own sake, for My
own sake, I will act;
For how can *My name* be profaned?
And My [B]glory I will not give to another.

DELIVERANCE PROMISED

12 “Listen to Me, O Jacob, even
Israel [a]whom I called;
[A]I am He, [B]I am the first,
I am also the last.
13 “Surely My hand [A]founded the earth,
And My right hand spread
out the heavens;
When I [B]call to them, they stand together.
14 “[A]Assemble, all of you, and listen!
[B]Who among them has
declared these things?
The LORD loves him; he will [C]carry out
His good pleasure on [D]Babylon,
And His arm *will be against*
the Chaldeans.
15 “I, even I, have spoken; indeed
I have [A]called him,
I have brought him, and He will
make his ways successful.
16 “[A]Come near to Me, listen to this:
From the first I have [B]not
spoken in secret,
[C]From the time it took place, I was there.
And now [D]the Lord [a]GOD has
sent Me, and His Spirit.”

17 Thus says the LORD, your [A]Redeemer, the Holy
One of Israel,

“I am the LORD your God, who
teaches you to profit,
Who [B]leads you in the way you should go.

48:3 [A]Is 41:22; 42:9; 43:9; 44:7, 8; 45:21; 46:10 [B]Is 29:5; 30:13 [C]Josh 21:45; Is 42:9 48:4 [a]Or *harsh* [A]Ex 32:9; Deut 31:27; Ezek 2:4; 3:7 [B]2 Chr 36:13; Prov 29:1; Acts 7:51 [C]Ezek 3:7-9 48:5 [a]Lit *it* [A]Jer 44:15-18 48:6 [A]Is 42:9; 43:19 48:8 [a]Or *transgressor* [b]Lit *the belly* [A]Is 42:25; 47:11; Hos 7:9 [B]Deut 9:7, 24; Ps 58:3; Is 46:8 48:9 [A]Is 48:11 [B]Neh 9:30, 31; Ps 78:38; 103:8-10; Is 30:18; 65:8 48:10 [A]Jer 9:7; Ezek 22:18-22 [B]Deut 4:20; 1 Kin 8:51; Jer 11:4 48:11 [A]1 Sam 12:22; Ps 25:11; 106:8; Is 37:35; 43:25; Jer 14:7; Ezek 20:9, 14, 22, 44; Dan 9:17-19 [B]Deut 32:26, 27; Is 42:8 48:12 [a]Lit *My called one* [A]Is 41:4; 43:10-13; 46:4 [B]Is 44:6; Rev 1:17; 22:13 48:13 [A]Ex 20:11; Ps 102:25; Is 42:5; 45:12, 18; Heb 1:10-12 [B]Is 40:26 48:14 [A]Is 43:9; 45:20 [B]Is 45:21 [C]Is 46:10, 11 [D]Is 13:4, 5, 17-19; Jer 50:21-29; 51:24 48:15 [A]Is 41:2; 45:1, 2 48:16 [a]Heb *YHWH*, usually rendered *LORD* [A]Is 34:1; 41:1; 57:3 [B]Is 45:19 [C]Is 43:13 [D]Zech 2:9, 11 48:17 [A]Is 41:14; 43:14; 49:7, 26; 54:5, 8 [B]Ps 32:8; Is 30:21; 49:9, 10

48:3–5 The Lord predicted events that have happened as He predicted them (41:2–4; 46:10), so the people would not ascribe these events to other gods.

48:3 **former things.** *See note on 46:9.*

48:6 **new things.** From this point onward, the prophecies of Messiah’s first and second coming and the restoration of Israel have a new distinctiveness. Babylon becomes the Babylon of Revelation (v. 20), and God uses Isaiah to communicate truths about the messianic kingdom on earth and the new heavens and new earth that follow it (e.g., 11:1–5; 65:17). Verse 7 indicates that God had never before revealed these features about the future.

48:9 **For the sake of My name.** The nation Israel had no merit to prompt God’s favor toward them (v. 8). They deserved wrath and death, but His mercy toward them originates in His desire to be glorified and His desire to display the integrity of His own name.

48:10, 11 **refined … tested.** Since Isaiah’s time, Israel’s testings have included the Babylonian captivity and present worldwide dispersion from her land; unlike silver purged in the furnace, the purging of Israel is not complete, and they are not refined. But God keeps up the afflictions until they are, so His name is not defamed through the destruction of Israel. The nation will be purged (cf. Zec 13:1). God’s plan is such that He alone, not man or man-made idols, will receive credit for Israel’s salvation (42:8; cf. Ro 11:25–27, 33–36). The adversaries of God are never to be given legitimate reasons for scoffing at God and His work.

48:14, 15 **him … he … His arm … him … him … his ways.** Beginning with v. 6, the prophet began to write of the new things. Babylon is the final one of Rev 18, and the instrument of God’s judgment is Messiah. The pronouns refer to Jesus Christ, whom the Lord will anoint to defeat the final Babylon at His second coming and bring Israel to her land and kingdom. That it is not Cyrus is also clear from the statement, “The LORD loves him,” which is too strong to apply to the pagan king—but not to God’s Beloved, the Lord Jesus.

48:16 **sent Me.** Here it was not the prophet who spoke, but the Messiah, the Servant of the Lord whom the Lord God and the Holy Spirit will send for the final regathering of Israel and establishment of His kingdom as described in 61:1–7.

48:17–19 Chastisements of Israel by the Redeemer and Holy One of Israel are for discipline (42:18–43:13; cf. Heb 12:10). Some day they will end, when Israel heeds the Lord’s commandments and God’s punishments will turn to prosperity. A future generation will do so and enjoy the refreshment of a continuous stream of God’s peace and righteousness that rolls over them like the relentless sea (65:18).

18 "If only you had [A]paid attention
to My commandments!
Then your [a,B]well-being would
have been like a river,
And your [C]righteousness like
the waves of the sea.
19 "Your [a,A]descendants would
have been like the sand,
And [b]your offspring like its grains;
[B]Their name would never be cut off or
destroyed from My presence."

20 [A]Go forth from Babylon! Flee
from the Chaldeans!
Declare with the sound of [B]joyful
shouting, proclaim this,
[C]Send it out to the end of the earth;
Say, "[D]The LORD has redeemed
His servant Jacob."
21 They did not [A]thirst when He led
them through the deserts.
He [B]made the water flow out
of the rock for them;
He split the rock and [C]the
water gushed forth.
22 "[A]There is no peace for the
wicked," says the LORD.

SALVATION REACHES TO THE END OF THE EARTH

49 Listen to Me, O [A]islands,
And pay attention, you peoples from afar.
[B]The LORD called Me from the womb;
From the [a]body of My mother
He named Me.
2 He has made My [A]mouth
like a sharp sword,
In the [B]shadow of His hand
He has concealed Me;
And He has also made Me a [a]select [C]arrow,
He has hidden Me in His quiver.
3 He said to Me, "[A]You are
My Servant, Israel,
[B]In Whom I will [a]show My glory."
4 But I said, "I have [A]toiled in vain,
I have spent My strength for
nothing and vanity;
Yet surely the justice *due* to
Me is with the LORD,
And My [B]reward with My God."
5 And now says [A]the LORD, who formed
Me from the womb to be His Servant,
To bring Jacob back to Him, so that
[B]Israel might be gathered to Him
(For I am [C]honored in the
sight of the LORD,
And My God is My [D]strength),
6 He says, "It is too [a]small a thing that
You should be My Servant
To raise up the tribes of Jacob and to
restore the [A]preserved ones of Israel;
I will also make You a [B]light
[b]of the nations
So that My salvation may [c]reach
to the [C]end of the earth."

48:18 [a]Or *peace* [A]Deut 5:29; 32:29; Ps 81:13-16 [B]Ps 119:165; Is 32:16-18; 66:12 [C]Is 45:8; 61:10, 11; 62:1; Hos 10:12; Amos 5:24 **48:19** [a]Lit *seed* [b]Lit *the offspring of your inward parts* [A]Gen 22:17; Is 10:22; 44:3, 4; 54:3; Jer 33:22 [B]Is 56:5; 66:22 **48:20** [A]Jer 50:8; 51:6, 45; Zech 2:6, 7; Rev 18:4 [B]Is 42:10; 49:13; 52:9 [C]Is 62:11; Jer 31:10; 50:2 [D]Is 43:1; 52:9; 63:9 **48:21** [A]Is 30:25; 35:6, 7; 41:17, 18; 43:19, 20; 49:10 [B]Ex 17:6; Ps 78:15, 16 [C]Ps 78:20; 105:41 **48:22** [A]Is 57:21 **49:1** [a]Lit *inward parts* [A]Is 42:4 [B]Is 44:2, 24; 46:3; Jer 1:5 **49:2** [a]Or *sharpened* [A]Is 11:4; Heb 4:12; Rev 1:16; 2:12, 16 [B]Is 51:16 [C]Hab 3:11 **49:3** [a]Or *glorify Myself* [A]Zech 3:8 [B]Is 44:23 **49:4** [A]Is 65:23 [B]Is 35:4; 59:18 **49:5** [A]Is 44:2 [B]Is 11:12; 27:12 [C]Is 43:4 [D]Is 12:2 **49:6** [a]Lit *light* [b]Or *to* [c]Lit *be* [A]Ps 37:28; 97:10 [B]Is 42:6; 51:4; Luke 2:32; Acts 13:47; 26:23 [C]Is 48:20

48:19 like the sand … like its grains. Because of Israel's disobedience, God's promise to Abraham to multiply his descendants (Ge 22:17) has not yet been finally fulfilled. Even though the nation was temporarily set aside during the Babylonian captivity and during the dispersion before 1948 A.D., and will suffer deadly assaults in the coming time of Jacob's trouble (cf. Jer 30:7), God will be true to His promise.

48:20 Go forth from Babylon! The worldwide proclamation of deliverance, along with the statement that "the LORD has redeemed … Jacob" shows that it is not the return of a meager 50,000 Jews from historic Babylon while most stayed in that pagan land, but the final redemption of the nation as Zechariah spoke of it in Zec 12:10–13:1 and Paul in Ro 11:1, 2, 25–27. A redeemed Israel is to make a complete separation from the final Babylon and its wicked system, and proclaim to the world the Lord's grace toward the nation. John repeats this command in Rev 18:4.

48:21 They did not thirst. Isaiah pointed to the way that God miraculously provided for Moses' generation, after He delivered them from Egypt (Ex 17:6; cf. Is 41:17, 18), as an illustration of how He will provide for redeemed Israel when they escape the final world empire of Babylon.

48:22 no peace for the wicked. Cf. 57:21. Not every Israelite will enjoy the Lord's salvation, but only the faithful remnant who have turned from their wicked ways. The wicked will be purged out before the kingdom of peace is established (cf. Zec 13:7–9).

49:1–57:21 This section defines the Messiah/Servant's prophetic and priestly functions, His equipment for His task, His sufferings and humiliation, and His final exaltation. The word "servant" occurs about 20 times in this portion, which magnifies Jesus Christ as the Lamb of God who was slain to redeem God's elect.

49:1–13 The second of 4 Servant-songs (cf. 42:1–9; 50:4–11; 52:13–53:12). This one tells of the Servant's mission and spiritual success.

49:1 from the womb … the body of My mother. The whole world, including Gentiles ("islands," "peoples from afar") are called to recognize two significant points: (1) the Messiah/Servant will be a human being, born as others are of a woman, yet virgin born (cf. 7:14; Lk 1:30–33), and (2) He will be an individual as distinct from a personified group such as the nation of Israel, which has also been called the Lord's servant (41:8, 9; 42:19; 43:10; 44:1, 2, 21, 26; 45:4; 48:20; 50:10).

49:2 My mouth like a sharp sword. The Lord has given power to His Servant to speak effectively and thereby to conquer His enemies (11:4; cf. Ps 2:9; Rev 1:16; 2:12, 16; 19:15). His Word is always effective (55:11; Eph 6:17; Heb 4:12) **concealed Me.** Messiah, before His appearing, was hidden with God, ready to be drawn out at the precise moment (cf. Gal 4:4, 5).

49:3 You are My servant, Israel. That the Lord's use of the name Israel refers here to Messiah (42:1; 49:5, 6, 7; 52:13; 53:11) is explainable through the intimate relationship that exists between the nation and her King.

49:4 in vain … for nothing and vanity. At His first coming, the Servant met with rejection by His nation. It may have appeared to some that His mission was a failure because of the suffering and rejection He endured (cf. Jn 1:9–11). The last two Servant-songs also emphasize the Servant's suffering (50:4–11; 52:13–53:12). But, though rejected by men, the Servant expresses His strong assurance that He is doing God's work and will be rewarded with complete success.

49:5 back to Him … gathered to Him. The Servant's mission will include the priority of bringing Israel to the Lord. Cf. Mt 10:5, 6; 15:24; Ro 1:16; 11:25–27. He will complete this at His second advent (cf. Zec 12:10–13:1).

49:6 raise up the tribes of Jacob … My salvation may reach to the end of the earth. The Servant's goal is the salvation and restoration of Israel for the fulfillment of the covenant promise. But not limited to Israel,

7 Thus says the LORD, the [A]Redeemer
of Israel *and* its Holy One,
To the [B]despised One,
To the One abhorred by the nation,
To the Servant of rulers,
"[C]Kings will see and arise,
Princes will also [D]bow down,
Because of the LORD who is
faithful, the Holy One of Israel
who has chosen You."

8 Thus says the LORD,
"In a [A]favorable time I have answered You,
And in a day of salvation I
have helped You;
And I will [B]keep You and [C]give You
for a covenant of the people,
To [a,D]restore the land, to make *them*
inherit the desolate heritages;
9 Saying to those who are
[A]bound, 'Go forth,'
To those who are in darkness,
'Show yourselves.'
Along the roads they will feed,
And their pasture *will be* on
all [B]bare heights.
10 "They will [A]not hunger or thirst,
Nor will the scorching [B]heat or
sun strike them down;
For [C]He who has compassion
on them will [D]lead them
And will guide them to [E]springs of water.
11 "I will make all [A]My mountains a road,
And My [B]highways will be raised up.
12 "Behold, these will come [A]from afar;
And lo, these *will come* from the
[B]north and from the west,
And these from the land of Sinim."

13 [A]Shout for joy, O heavens!
And rejoice, O earth!
Break forth into joyful
shouting, O mountains!
For the [B]LORD has comforted His people
And will [C]have compassion
on His afflicted.

PROMISE TO ZION

14 But Zion said, "The LORD has forsaken me,
And the Lord has forgotten me."
15 "Can a woman forget her nursing child
And have no compassion on
the son of her womb?
Even these may forget, but [A]I
will not forget you.
16 "Behold, I have [A]inscribed you on
the palms *of My hands;*
Your [B]walls are continually before Me.
17 "Your [a]builders hurry;
Your [A]destroyers and devastators
Will depart from you.
18 "[A]Lift up your eyes and look around;
[B]All of them gather together,
[C]they come to you.
[D]As I live," declares the LORD,
"You will surely [E]put on all of them as
[a]jewels and bind them on as a bride.
19 "For [A]your waste and desolate places
and your destroyed land—
Surely now you will be [B]too
cramped for the inhabitants,
And those who [C]swallowed
you will be far away.
20 "The [A]children of [a]whom you were
bereaved will yet say in your ears,
'The place is too cramped for me;
Make room for me that I may live *here.*'

49:7 [A]Is 48:17 [B]Ps 22:6-8; 69:7-9; Is 53:3 [C]Is 52:15 [D]Is 19:21, 23; 27:13; 66:23 **49:8** [a]Lit *establish* [A]Ps 69:13; 2 Cor 6:2 [B]Is 26:3; 27:3; 42:6 [C]Is 42:6 [D]Is 44:26 **49:9** [A]Is 42:7; 61:1; Luke 4:18 [B]Is 41:18 **49:10** [A]Is 33:16; 48:21; Rev 7:16 [B]Ps 121:6 [C]Is 14:1 [D]Ps 23:2; Is 40:11 [E]Is 35:7; 41:17 **49:11** [A]Is 40:4 [B]Is 11:16; 19:23; 35:8; 62:10 **49:12** [A]Is 49:1; 60:4 [B]Is 43:5, 6 **49:13** [A]Is 44:23 [B]Is 40:1; 51:3, 12 [C]Is 54:7, 8, 10 **49:15** [A]Is 44:21 **49:16** [A]Song 8:6; Hag 2:23 [B]Ps 48:12, 13; Is 62:6, 7 **49:17** [a]So ancient versions and DSS; M.T. reads *sons* [A]Is 10:6; 37:18 **49:18** [a]Lit *an ornament* [A]Is 60:4; John 4:35 [B]Is 43:5; 54:7; 60:4 [C]Is 49:12 [D]Is 45:23; 54:9 [E]Is 52:1; 61:10 **49:19** [A]Is 1:7; 3:8; 5:6; 51:3 [B]Is 54:1, 2; Zech 10:10 [C]Ps 56:1, 2 **49:20** [a]Lit *your bereavement* [A]Is 54:1-3

He is to function as a light bringing salvation to the Gentiles. Israel's mission had always been to bring the nations to God (19:24; 42:6). This she will finally do very effectively in the tribulation after the conversion of the 144,000 witnesses (Rev 7:1–10; 14:1–5) and when she is restored to her land at the Servant's return to earth. Cf. 9:2; 11:10; 42:6; 45:22; Lk 2:32. Paul applied this verse to his ministry to the Gentiles on his first missionary journey (Ac 13:47).

49:7 despised ... abhorred. This speaks to the humiliating treatment of the Servant at His first advent, a theme emphasized by Isaiah (50:6–9; 52:14, 15; 53:3). The "nation" is used collectively for all who reject Him, particularly Gentiles, who are the rulers, kings, and princes referred to as someday giving exalted treatment to the Servant at His second advent. Former oppressors will bow down to Him as in 52:15, because of the salvation of Israel.

49:8 favorable time ... day of salvation. Messiah is represented as asking for the grace of God to be given to sinners. God gives His favorable answer in a time of grace (cf. 61:1) when salvation's day comes to the world (cf. Gal 4:4, 5; Heb 4:7). At His appointed time in the future, the Lord will, by His Servant, accomplish the final deliverance of Israel. Paul applied these words to his ministry of proclaiming the gospel of God's grace to all people (2Co 6:2). **a covenant of the people.** *See note on 42:6.* When the Lord saves and regathers Israel, they will return to the land, to which Joshua brought their ancestors after their exit from Egypt, now restored and glorious (44:26; Jos 13:1–8).

49:9, 10 bound ... darkness ... feed ... pasture. At the Messiah's second advent, Israel's condition will change from captivity and oppression to contentment and prosperity such as that enjoyed by a well-fed, protected, and watered flock of sheep. These ideal conditions will be enjoyed by the faithful remnant returning for their kingdom in Israel. John reveals that this condition is a foretaste of heaven (Rev 7:16, 17).

49:12 come from afar. Israel's regathering will be from a worldwide exile (43:5, 6), even far away places like Sinim, probably an ancient name for what is China.

49:13 Cf. Rev 12:12.

49:14 Here is the summary of the history of lament by the nation during its long period of suffering. Verses 15–23 follow with words of assurance responding to the despondency.

49:16 The Lord is referring here to the Jews' custom, perhaps drawn from Ex 13:9, of puncturing their hands with a symbol of their city and temple, as a sign of devotion (cf. SS 8:6).

49:17, 18 Your builders ... put on ... jewels. Zion's inhabitants will return as the city's destroyers depart and will adorn the city. Israel will be the means of the conversion of the nations in the end (cf. Rom 11:11, 12, 15).

49:19–21 After the faithful remnant is regathered in salvation, and Gentiles come to faith in the kingdom through Jewish witnesses, millennial Jerusalem will not be large enough to contain all her inhabitants.

21 "Then you will [A]say in your heart,
'Who has begotten these for me,
Since I have been bereaved of my children
And am [B]barren, an [C]exile
and a wanderer?
And who has reared these?
Behold, I was [D]left alone;
[a,E]From where did these come?' "

22 Thus says the Lord [a]GOD,

"Behold, I will lift up My
hand to the nations
And set up My [A]standard to the peoples;
And they will [B]bring your
sons in *their* bosom,
And your daughters will be
carried on *their* shoulders.
23 "[A]Kings will be your guardians,
And their princesses your nurses.
They will [B]bow down to you with
their faces to the earth
And [C]lick the dust of your feet;
And *you* will [D]know that I am the LORD;
Those who hopefully [E]wait for Me
will [F]not be put to shame.

24 "[A]Can the prey be taken from
the mighty man,
Or the captives of [a]a tyrant be rescued?"

25 Surely, thus says the LORD,

"Even the [A]captives of the mighty
man will be taken away,
And the prey of the tyrant will be rescued;
For I will contend with the one
who contends with you,
And I will [B]save your sons.
26 "I will feed your [A]oppressors
with their [B]own flesh,
And they will become drunk with their
own blood as with sweet wine;
And [C]all flesh will know that I,
the LORD, am your [D]Savior
And your [E]Redeemer, the
Mighty One of Jacob."

GOD HELPS HIS SERVANT

50 Thus says the LORD,

"Where is the [A]certificate of divorce
By which I have [B]sent your mother away?
Or to whom of My creditors did I [C]sell you?
Behold, you were sold for your [D]iniquities,
And for your [E]transgressions your
mother [F]was sent away.
2 "Why was there [A]no man when I came?
When I called, *why* was there
none to answer?
Is My [B]hand so short that it cannot ransom?
Or have I no power to deliver?
Behold, I [C]dry up the sea with My rebuke,
I [D]make the rivers a wilderness;
Their fish stink for lack of water
And die of thirst.
3 "I [A]clothe the heavens with blackness
And make sackcloth their covering."

4 The Lord [a]GOD has given Me
the tongue of [A]disciples,
That I may know how to [B]sustain
the weary one with a word.
He awakens *Me* [C]morning by morning,
He awakens My ear to listen as a disciple.
5 The Lord GOD has [A]opened My ear;
And I was [B]not disobedient
Nor did I turn back.

49:21 [a]Lit *These, where are they?* [A]Is 29:23; 54:6, 7 [B]Is 27:10; Lam 1:1 [C]Is 5:13 [D]Is 1:8 [E]Is 60:8 49:22 [a]Heb *YHWH*, usually rendered *LORD* [A]Is 11:10, 12; 18:3; 62:10 [B]Is 14:2; 43:6; 60:4 49:23 [A]Is 14:1, 2; 60:3, 10, 11 [B]Is 45:14; 60:14 [C]Ps 72:9; Mic 7:17 [D]Is 41:20; 43:10; 60:16 [E]Ps 37:9; Is 25:9; 26:8 [F]Ps 25:3; Is 45:17; Joel 2:27 49:24 [a]So ancient versions and DSS; M.T. reads *the righteous,* cf v 25 [A]Matt 12:29; Luke 11:21 49:25 [A]Is 10:6; 14:1, 2; Jer 50:33, 34 [B]Is 25:9; 33:22; 35:4 49:26 [A]Is 9:4; 14:4; 16:4; 51:13; 54:14 [B]Is 9:20 [C]Is 45:6; Ezek 39:7 [D]Is 43:3 [E]Is 49:7 50:1 [A]Deut 24:1, 3; Jer 3:8 [B]Is 54:6, 7 [C]Deut 32:30; 2 Kin 4:1; Neh 5:5 [D]Is 52:3; 59:2 [E]Is 1:28; 43:27 [F]Jer 3:8 50:2 [A]Is 41:28; 59:16; 66:4 [B]Gen 18:14; Num 11:23; Is 59:1 [C]Ex 14:21; Is 19:5; 43:16; 44:27 [D]Josh 3:16; Is 42:15 50:3 [A]Is 13:10; Rev 6:12 50:4 [a]Heb *YHWH*, usually rendered *LORD*, and so throughout the ch [A]Is 8:16; 54:13 [B]Is 57:19; Jer 31:25 [C]Ps 5:3; 88:13; 119:147; 143:8 50:5 [A]Ps 40:6; Is 35:5 [B]Matt 26:39; John 8:29; 14:31; 15:10; Acts 26:19; Phil 2:8; Heb 5:8; 10:7

49:22 nations … will bring your sons … your daughters. The promise will find literal fulfillment as the nations of the world assist the faithful remnant of Israel to their land (14:2; 43:6; 60:4; 66:20). At the outset of the kingdom, when this regathering takes place, all the Gentiles will be believers in Jesus Christ who, by faith, escaped the wrath of the Lamb on the day of the Lord and entered the kingdom (*see notes on Mt 25:31–46*). Nations and leaders who throughout history oppressed Israel, will humble themselves before the redeemed people of God's covenant, and Israel will know that waiting on the Lord will not disappoint (8:17; 40:31).

49:24 prey be taken … captives … be rescued. As in v. 14, Isaiah speaks of Zion again expressing her despondency over her captivity and wondering about deliverance. The Lord replies again with encouraging words in vv. 25, 26.

49:25, 26 feed … with their own flesh … drunk with their own blood. Strong language against Israel's enemies reassures her of eventual deliverance from her exile. The angel of the waters draws on this terminology in celebrating the third bowl judgment in Rev 16:6. The destruction of Israel's enemies, led by Satan in the tribulation (cf. Rev 12:15, 16), also fulfills this pledge.

49:26 all flesh will know. God's deliverance of Israel will be so dramatic that the world will recognize that the Lord, the Savior, Redeemer, and Mighty One of Israel is the true God (11:9; 45:6; Eze 39:7; Hab 2:14).

50:1 certificate of divorce … My creditors. Though the sufferings of Judah were the necessary result of sin, no certificate of divorce or sale to creditors occurred because Zion's separation from the Lord was only temporary. In fact, God gave the non-Davidic northern kingdom a certificate of divorce (*see note on Jer 3:8*). However, the unconditional promises of the Davidic Covenant (2Sa 7) precluded such a divorce for Judah, although there would be a time of separation (cf. 54:6, 7).

50:2 Why … ? God asked why no one was willing to believe and obey Him, even after all had seen His redemptive power in Egypt, when He dried up the Red Sea (Ex 14:21), opened the river Jordan by turning it into dry land (Jos 4:23), and killed the fish in Egypt (Ex 7:18–21). The Lord's power to redeem was indisputable (59:1). He proved it by His deliverance from Egypt (43:16, 17; 44:27; 46:9; 48:3, 21).

50:4–11 This is the third of 4 Servant-songs (cf. 42:1–9; 49:1–13; 52:13–53:12), and it is Messiah's soliloquy about being perfected through obedience (vv. 4, 5) and sufferings (v. 6). The apostle John writes much about Jesus' obedience to God in fulfilling His will (cf. Jn 5:19, 36; 6:38; 7:16, 29; 12:49, 50). Cf. Php 2:8; Heb 5:8; 10:7.

6 I [A]gave My back to those who strike *Me,*
And My cheeks to those who
pluck out the beard;
I did not cover My face from
humiliation and spitting.
7 For the Lord GOD [A]helps Me,
Therefore, I am [B]not disgraced;
Therefore, I have set My face like [C]flint,
And I know that I will not be ashamed.
8 He who [A]vindicates Me is near;
Who will contend with Me?
Let us [B]stand up to each other;
Who has a case against Me?
Let him draw near to Me.
9 Behold, [A]the Lord GOD helps Me;
[B]Who is he who condemns Me?
Behold, [C]they will all wear
out like a garment;
The moth will eat them.
10 Who is among you that fears the LORD,
That obeys the voice of His [A]servant,
That [B]walks in darkness and has no light?
Let him [C]trust in the name of the
LORD and rely on his God.
11 Behold, all you who [A]kindle a fire,
Who [a]encircle yourselves with firebrands,
Walk in the light of your fire
And among the brands you have set ablaze.
This you will have from My hand:
You will [B]lie down in torment.

ISRAEL EXHORTED

51 "[A]Listen to me, you who [B]pursue
righteousness,
Who seek the LORD:
Look to the [C]rock from which
you were hewn
And to the [a]quarry from
which you were dug.
2 "Look to [A]Abraham your father
And to Sarah who gave
birth to you in pain;
When *he* [B]*was but* one I called him,
Then I blessed him and multiplied him."
3 Indeed, [A]the LORD will comfort Zion;
He will comfort all her [B]waste places.
And her [C]wilderness He will
make like [D]Eden,
And her desert like the
[E]garden of the LORD;
[F]Joy and gladness will be found in her,
Thanksgiving and sound of a melody.

4 "[A]Pay attention to Me, O My people,
And give ear to Me, O My [a]nation;
For a [B]law will go forth from Me,
And I will [b]set My [C]justice for
a [D]light of the peoples.
5 "My [A]righteousness is near, My
salvation has gone forth,
And My [B]arms will judge the peoples;
The [C]coastlands will wait for Me,
And for My [D]arm they will
wait expectantly.
6 "[A]Lift up your eyes to the sky,
Then look to the earth beneath;
For the [B]sky will vanish like smoke,
And the [B]earth will wear
out like a garment
And its inhabitants will die
[a]in like manner;
But My [C]salvation will be forever,
And My righteousness will not [b]wane.
7 "[A]Listen to Me, you who know
righteousness,
A people in whose [B]heart is My law;
Do not fear the [C]reproach of man,
Nor be dismayed at their revilings.

50:6 [A]Matt 26:67; 27:30; Mark 14:65; 15:19; Luke 22:63 50:7 [A]Is 42:1; 49:8 [B]Is 45:17; 54:4 [C]Ezek 3:8, 9 50:8 [A]Is 45:25; Rom 8:33, 34 [B]Is 1:18; 41:1; 43:26 50:9 [A]Is 41:10 [B]Is 54:17 [C]Job 13:28; Is 51:8 50:10 [A]Is 49:2, 3; 50:4 [B]Is 9:2; 26:9; Eph 5:8 [C]Is 12:2; 26:4 50:11 [a]Lit *gird* [A]Prov 26:18; Is 9:18; James 3:6 [B]Is 8:22; 65:13-15; Amos 4:9, 10 51:1 [a]Lit *excavation of a pit* [A]Is 46:3; 48:12; 51:7 [B]Ps 94:15; Prov 15:9 [C]Gen 17:15-17 51:2 [A]Is 29:22; 41:8; 63:16 [B]Gen 12:1; 15:5; Deut 1:10; Ezek 33:24 51:3 [A]Is 40:1; 49:13 [B]Is 52:9 [C]Is 35:1; 41:19 [D]Gen 2:8; Joel 2:3 [E]Gen 13:10 [F]Is 25:9; 41:16; 65:18; 66:10 51:4 [a]Or *people* [b]Lit *cause to rest* [A]Ps 50:7; 78:1 [B]Deut 18:18; Is 2:3; Mic 4:2 [C]Is 1:27; 42:4 [D]Is 42:6; 49:6 51:5 [A]Is 46:13; 54:17 [B]Is 40:10 [C]Is 42:4; 60:9 [D]Is 59:16; 63:5 51:6 [a]Or *like gnats* [b]Lit *be broken* [A]Is 40:26 [B]Ps 102:25, 26; Is 13:13; 34:4; Matt 24:35; Heb 1:10-12; 2 Pet 3:10 [C]Is 45:17; 51:8 51:7 [A]Is 51:1 [B]Ps 37:31 [C]Is 25:8; 54:4; Matt 5:11; Acts 5:41

50:6 My back ... My cheeks ... My face. The Servant remained obedient though provoked to rebel by excessively vile treatment. Jesus fulfilled this prophecy by remaining submissive to the Father's will (Mt 26:67; 27:26, 30; Mk 14:65; 15:19; Lk 22:63; Jn 18:22).

50:7 set My face like flint. So sure was He of the Lord God's help that He resolutely determined to remain unswayed by whatever hardship might await Him (cf. Eze 3:8, 9). Jesus demonstrated this determination in setting His face to go to Jerusalem to be crucified (Lk 9:51).

50:8, 9 No matter how He was mistreated, mocked, and repudiated, the Servant had full confidence of the Lord God's support, so He welcomed an adversary to come.

50:10, 11 Here was a call to the unconverted to believe and be saved, along with a warning that those who tried to escape moral, spiritual darkness by lighting their own fire (man-made religion, works righteousness) were to end up in eternal torment.

51:1, 2 The prophet assured the nation of deliverance by pointing to God's past covenant with Abraham (Ge 12:1–3), who was the rock in the quarry from which they were hewn as a people. Originally, Abraham was only one person, but God multiplied his descendants as He had promised (Ge 13:16; 15:5; 17:5; 22:17).

51:3 waste places ... Eden ... desert ... garden of the LORD. The same God whose power fulfilled His promises to Abraham is to transform Israel's desolation into a primeval paradise, both nationally and spiritually, causing joy and songs of thanksgiving to ring from it.

51:4 law ... justice ... light of the peoples. The Servant's rule over Israel's earthly kingdom is to cause righteousness to prevail for the benefit of all nations.

51:5 near ... gone forth. The Servant's power to restore His people and bring justice, righteousness, and salvation to the world was at work, but God's perspective differs from man's reckoning of time. Though near by God's reckoning in timeless eternity, the fruition of His deliverance was still many centuries from Isaiah's day. The nations who survive judgment will trust in Him and enter His kingdom.

51:6 sky will vanish ... earth will wear out. This begins to take place in the time of tribulation (cf. Rev 6:12–14; 8:12, 13; 16:8–10, 21), setting the stage, along with the earthly judgments on land, sea, and fresh water (cf. Rev 6:14; 8:6–11; 16:3–5), for a renewed earth during the Millennium. The actual "uncreation" or destruction of the present universe, of which Peter wrote (2Pe 3:10–13), occurs at the end of Christ's millennial reign on the earth, when a new heaven and a new earth will replace the present creation (2Pe 3:10; Rev 21:1).

51:7, 8 Israel's enemies will perish, but the Servant's salvation will be permanent.

8 "For the [A]moth will eat them like a garment,
And the [B]grub will eat them like wool.
But My [C]righteousness will be forever,
And My salvation to all generations."

9 [A]Awake, awake, put on strength,
O arm of the LORD;
Awake as in the [B]days of old, the
generations of long ago.
[C]Was it not You who cut Rahab in pieces,
Who pierced the [D]dragon?
10 Was it not You who [A]dried up the sea,
The waters of the great deep;
Who made the depths of the sea a pathway
For the [B]redeemed to cross over?
11 So the [A]ransomed of the LORD will return
And come with joyful shouting to Zion,
And [B]everlasting joy *will be* on their heads.
They will obtain gladness and joy,
And [C]sorrow and sighing will flee away.

12 "I, even I, am He who [A]comforts you.
Who are you that you are
afraid of [B]man who dies
And of the son of man who
is made [C]like grass,
13 That you have [A]forgotten the
LORD your Maker,
Who [B]stretched out the heavens
And laid the foundations of the earth,
That you [C]fear continually all day long
because of the fury of the oppressor,
As he makes ready to destroy?
But where is the fury of the [D]oppressor?

51:8 [A]Is 50:9 [B]Is 14:11; 66:24 [C]Is 51:6 51:9 [A]Is 51:17; 52:1 [B]Ex 6:6; Deut 4:34 [C]Job 26:12; Ps 89:10; Is 30:7 [D]Ps 74:13; Is 27:1 51:10 [A]Is 11:15, 16; 50:2; 63:11, 12 [B]Ex 15:13; Ps 106:10; Is 63:9 51:11 [A]Is 35:10; Jer 31:11, 12 [B]Is 60:19; 61:7 [C]Is 25:8; 60:20; 65:19; Rev 7:17; 21:1, 4; 22:3 51:12 [A]Is 51:3 [B]Ps 118:6; Is 2:22 [C]Is 40:6, 7; 1 Pet 1:24 51:13 [A]Deut 6:12; 8:11; Is 17:10 [B]Job 9:8; Ps 104:2; Is 40:22; 45:12, 18; 48:13 [C]Is 7:4; 10:24 [D]Is 49:26; 54:14

51:9, 10 This prayer for deliverance in the future was based on times past when the Lord overcame Rahab, which was a term widely used to refer to things that wreak havoc, often, as in this case, Egypt (see Ps 87:4).

51:11–16 Again, Isaiah summarized a constant theme: that instead of hearing dying men (v. 12), Israel should trust the Creator of all things. He had delivered Israel in the past and is to do so permanently in the future before the nations can be destroyed (v. 14), so they have no need to fear oppressors. The blessing of restored Israel will be evidenced in the joy of v. 11.

ISAIAH'S DESCRIPTION OF ISRAEL'S FUTURE KINGDOM

Description	Isaiah passages
1. The Lord will restore the faithful remnant of Israel to the land to inhabit the kingdom at its beginning.	1:9, 25–27; 3:10; 4:3; 6:13; 8:10; 9:1; 10:20, 22, 25, 27; 11:11, 12, 16; 14:1, 2; 14:22, 26; 26:1–4; 27:12; 28:5; 35:9; 37:4, 31, 32; 40:2, 3; 41:9; 43:5, 6; 46:3, 4; 49:5, 8; 49:12, 22; 51:11; 54:7–10; 55:12; 57:13, 18; 60:4, 9; 61:1–4, 7; 65:8–10; 66:8, 9, 19
2. As the Lord defeats Israel's enemies, He will provide protection for His people.	4:5, 6; 9:1, 4; 12:1–6; 13:4; 14:2; 21:9; 26:4, 5; 27:1–4; 30:30, 31; 32:2; 33:16, 22; 35:4; 49:8, 9; 49:17, 18; 52:6; 54:9, 10; 55:10, 11; 58:12; 60:10, 12, 18; 62:9; 66:16
3. In her kingdom, Israel will enjoy great prosperity of many kinds.	26:15, 19; 27:2, 13; 29:18–20; 22:22, 23; 30:20; 32:3; 32:15–20; 33:6, 24; 35:3, 5, 6, 8–10; 40:11; 42:6, 7, 16; 43:5, 6, 8, 10, 21; 44:5, 14; 46:13; 48:6; 49:10; 52:9; 54:2, 3; 55:1, 12; 58:9, 14; 60:5, 16, 21; 61:4, 6–10; 62:5; 65:13–15, 18, 24; 66:21, 22
4. The city of Jerusalem will rise to world preeminence in the kingdom.	2:2–4; 18:7; 25:6; 40:5, 9; 49:19–21; 60:1–5, 13–15, 17; 62:3, 4
5. Israel will be the center of world attention in the kingdom.	23:18; 54:1–3; 55:5; 56:6–8; 60:5–9; 66:18–21
6. Israel's mission in the kingdom will be to glorify the Lord.	60:21; 61:3
7. Gentiles in the kingdom will receive blessing through the channel of faithful Israel.	11:10; 19:18, 24, 25; 42:6; 45:22, 23; 49:6; 51:5; 56:3, 6–8; 60:3, 7, 8; 61:5; 66:19
8. Worldwide peace will prevail in the kingdom under the rule of the Prince of Peace.	2:4; 9:5, 6; 11:10; 19:23; 26:12; 32:18; 54:14; 57:19; 66:12
9. Moral and spiritual conditions in the kingdom will reach their highest plane since the fall of Adam.	27:6; 28:6, 17; 32:16; 42:7; 44:3; 45:8; 51:4; 61:11; 65:21, 22
10. Governmental leadership in the kingdom will be superlative with the Messiah heading it up.	9:6, 7; 11:2, 3; 16:5; 24:23; 25:3; 32:1; 32:5; 33:22; 42:1, 4; 43:15; 52:13; 53:12; 55:3–5
11. Humans will enjoy long life in the kingdom.	65:20, 22
12. Knowledge of the Lord will be universal in the kingdom.	11:9; 19:21; 33:13; 40:5; 41:20; 45:6, 14; 49:26; 52:10, 13, 15; 54:13; 66:23
13. The world of nature will enjoy a great renewal in the kingdom.	12:3; 30:23–26; 32:15; 35:1–4, 6, 7; 41:18, 19; 43:19, 20; 44:3, 23; 55:1, 2, 13; 58:10, 11
14. "Wild" animals will be tame in the kingdom.	11:6–9; 35:9; 65:25
15. Sorrow and mourning will not exist in the kingdom.	25:8; 60:20
16. An eternal kingdom, as a part of God's new creation, will follow the millennial kingdom.	24:23; 51:6; 51:16; 54:11, 12; 60:11, 19; 65:17
17. The King will judge overt sin in the kingdom.	66:24

14 The [a,A]exile will soon be set free, and will not die
in the dungeon, [B]nor will his bread be lacking. 15 For
I am the LORD your God, who [A]stirs up the sea and
its waves roar (the LORD of hosts is His name). 16 I
have [A]put My words in your mouth and have [B]cov-
ered you with the shadow of My hand, to [a,C]establish
the heavens, to found the earth, and to say to Zion,
'You are My people.' "

17 [A]Rouse yourself! Rouse yourself!
Arise, O Jerusalem,
You who have [B]drunk from the LORD'S
hand the cup of His anger;
The [a]chalice of reeling you have
[b]drained to the dregs.
18 There is [A]none to guide her among
all the sons she has borne,
Nor is there one to take her by the hand
among all the sons she has reared.
19 These two things have befallen you;
Who will mourn for you?
The [A]devastation and destruction,
famine and sword;
How shall I comfort you?
20 Your sons have fainted,
They [A]lie *helpless* at the
head of every street,
Like an [B]antelope in a net,
Full of the wrath of the LORD,
The [C]rebuke of your God.

21 Therefore, please hear this, you [A]afflicted,
Who are [B]drunk, but not with wine:
22 Thus says your Lord, the
LORD, even your God
Who [A]contends for His people,
"Behold, I have taken out of your
hand the [B]cup of reeling,
The [a]chalice of My anger;
You will never drink it again.
23 "I will [A]put it into the hand of
your tormentors,
Who have said to [a]you, '[B]Lie down
that we may walk over *you*.'
You have even made your
back like the ground
And like the street for those
who walk over *it*."

CHEER FOR PROSTRATE ZION

52 [A]Awake, awake,
Clothe yourself in your strength, O Zion;
Clothe yourself in your [B]beautiful garments,
O Jerusalem, the [C]holy city;
For the uncircumcised and the [D]unclean
Will no longer come into you.
2 Shake yourself [A]from the dust, [B]rise up,
O captive Jerusalem;
[C]Loose yourself from the chains
around your neck,
O captive daughter of Zion.

3 For thus says the LORD, "You were [A]sold for nothing and you will be [B]redeemed [C]without money." 4 For
thus says the Lord [a]GOD, "My people [A]went down at
the first into Egypt to reside there; then the Assyrian
oppressed them without cause. 5 Now therefore, what
do I have here," declares the LORD, "seeing that My
people have been taken away without cause?" *Again*
the LORD declares, "Those who rule over them howl,
and My [A]name is continually blasphemed all day long.
6 Therefore My people shall [A]know My name; therefore
in that day I am the one who is speaking, 'Here I am.' "

7 How lovely on the mountains
Are the feet of him who brings [A]good news,
Who announces [a]peace
And brings good news of [b]happiness,
Who announces salvation,
And says to Zion, "Your [B]God [c]reigns!"

51:14 [a]Lit *one in chains* [A]Is 48:20; 52:2 [B]Is 33:6; 49:10 51:15 [A]Ps 107:25; Jer 31:35 51:16 [a]Lit *plant* [A]Deut 18:18; Is 59:21 [B]Ex 33:22; Is 49:2 [C]Is 66:22 51:17 [a]Lit *bowl of the cup of reeling* [b]Lit *drunk* [A]Is 51:9; 52:1 [B]Job 21:20; Is 29:9; 63:6; Jer 25:15; Rev 14:10; 16:19 51:18 [A]Ps 88:18; 142:4; Is 49:21 51:19 [A]Is 8:21; 9:20; 14:30 51:20 [A]Is 5:25; Jer 14:16 [B]Deut 14:5 [C]Is 66:15 51:21 [A]Is 54:11 [B]Is 29:9; 51:17; 63:6 51:22 [a]Lit *bowl of the cup of* [A]Is 3:12, 13; 49:25; Jer 50:34 [B]Is 51:17 51:23 [a]Lit *your soul* [A]Is 49:26; Jer 25:15-17, 26, 28; Zech 12:2 [B]Josh 10:24 52:1 [A]Is 51:9, 17 [B]Ex 28:2, 40; 1 Chr 16:29; Ps 110:3; Is 49:18; 61:3, 10; Zech 3:4 [C]Neh 11:1; Is 48:2; 64:10; Zech 14:20, 21; Matt 4:5; Rev 21:2-27 [D]Is 35:8 52:2 [A]Is 29:4 [B]Is 60:1 [C]Is 9:4; 10:27; 14:25; Zech 2:7 52:3 [A]Ps 44:12; Jer 15:13 [B]Is 1:27; 62:12; 63:4 [C]Is 45:13 52:4 [a]Heb *YHWH*, usually rendered *LORD* [A]Gen 46:6 52:5 [A]Ezek 36:20, 23; Rom 2:24 52:6 [A]Is 49:23 52:7 [a]Or *well-being* [b]Lit *good* [c]Or *is King* [A]Is 40:9; 61:1; Nah 1:15; Rom 10:15; Eph 6:15 [B]Ps 93:1; Is 24:23

51:16 My words in your mouth. Israel had been the unfaithful depository of divine revelation (cf. Ro 9:1–5), but the time is coming when God will put words into the mouths of His future faithful remnant (59:21) when He sets up the kingdom of Messiah in Zion on a renewed earth. Cf. 51:6; 65:17; 66:22.

51:17, 18 Jerusalem … drunk … cup of His anger. Jerusalem experienced the Lord's anger through her extended subservience to foreign powers with no human to deliver her (v. 18), but the punishment will end (v. 22; 40:1, 2; cf. 29:9). On the other hand, Babylon will drink from the cup of His anger forever (Rev 14:8–11; 16:19).

51:19 two things. The city of Jerusalem (v. 17) had suffered the twofold loss of property ("devastation and destruction") and human life ("famine and sword").

51:20 Your sons have fainted. The city's inhabitants lay helpless in the streets, having expended all their strength in fighting unsuccessfully against the Lord's fury (40:30).

51:21, 22 drunk, but not with wine. Jerusalem was drunk through drinking the cup of God's wrath (63:6). But, in contrast to Babylon, which drank the fury of God's wrath to the last drop (v. 17; Rev 18:6), Israel will have the cup removed before all the wrath is consumed. It will be handed to Israel's oppressors for them to drink the full fury (49:26; Jer 25:15, 26, 28; Zec 12:2).

52:1, 2 your strength … beautiful garments. A call is given for Zion to awake from drunkenness and clothe herself in garments of honor and dignity provided by the Lord. Foreign invaders will no longer control the city at the time of her final restoration.

52:3 sold for nothing … redeemed without money. The Jews became the servants of their foreign conquerors, who paid nothing for Israel, so the Lord will redeem Israel gratuitously from sin (45:13; 55:1).

52:5 Those who rule over them. A reference to the Babylonians and their cruelty to captive Israelites. **My name is … blasphemed.** Foreign rulers despised the God of Israel as long as His people were in bondage. God delivered His people, not for their goodness, but for the sake of His holy name—to prove He was truthful, faithful, and powerful (Eze 20:9, 14). Paul cited the blasphemy to Israel's God that resulted from the hypocrisy of first-century Jews not applying to themselves the standards of God that they knew and taught others (Ro 2:24).

52:6 in that day I am the one. After the day of the Lord, when Israel experiences deliverance from her worldwide dispersion, she will recognize the fulfillment of prophecies through Isaiah and others and enjoy full assurance that the Lord had spoken and fulfilled His promises of deliverance. They will connect these events with the great "I AM" (43:11; Ex 3:13–15).

52:7 How lovely … good news. Messengers will traverse the mountains around

8 Listen! Your watchmen lift up *their* [A]voices,
They shout joyfully together;
For they will see [a]with their own eyes
When the LORD restores Zion.
9 [A]Break forth, shout joyfully together,
You [B]waste places of Jerusalem;
For the LORD has comforted His people,
He has [C]redeemed Jerusalem.
10 The LORD has bared His holy [A]arm
In the sight of all the nations,
[a]That [B]all the ends of the earth may see
The salvation of our God.

11 [A]Depart, depart, go out from there,
[B]Touch nothing unclean;
Go out of the midst of her, [C]purify yourselves,
You who carry the vessels of the LORD.
12 But you will not go out in [A]haste,
Nor will you go [a]as fugitives;
For the [B]LORD will go before you,
And [C]the God of Israel *will*
be your rear guard.

THE EXALTED SERVANT

13 Behold, My [A]servant will prosper,
He will be high and lifted up
and [a]greatly [B]exalted.
14 Just as many were astonished
at you, *My people,*
So His [A]appearance was marred
more than any man
And His form more than the sons of men.
15 Thus He will [A]sprinkle many nations,
Kings will [B]shut their mouths
on account of Him;
For [C]what had not been told
them they will see,
And what they had not heard
they will understand.

THE SUFFERING SERVANT

53 [A]Who has believed our message?
And to whom has the arm of
the LORD been revealed?
2 For He grew up before Him
like a [A]tender [a]shoot,
And like a root out of parched ground;
He has [B]no *stately* form or majesty
That we should look upon Him,
Nor appearance that we should
[b]be attracted to Him.
3 He was [A]despised and forsaken of men,
A man of [a]sorrows and
[B]acquainted with [b]grief;
And like one from whom
men hide their face
He was [C]despised, and we
did not [D]esteem Him.

52:8 [a]Lit *eye to eye* [A]Is 62:6 52:9 [A]Ps 98:4; Is 44:23 [B]Is 44:26; 51:3; 61:4 [C]Is 43:1; 48:20 52:10 [a]Lit *And...earth will see* [A]Ps 98:1-3; Is 51:9; 66:18, 19 [B]Is 45:22; 48:20 52:11 [A]Is 48:20; Jer 50:8; Zech 2:6, 7; 2 Cor 6:17 [B]Num 19:11, 16 [C]Lev 22:2; Is 1:16 52:12 [a]Lit *in flight* [A]Ex 12:11, 33; Deut 16:3 [B]Is 26:7; 42:16; 49:10, 11 [C]Ex 14:19, 20; Is 58:8 52:13 [a]Or *very high* [A]Is 42:1; 49:1-7; 53:11 [B]Is 57:15; Phil 2:9 52:14 [A]Is 53:2, 3 52:15 [A]Num 19:18-21; Ezek 36:25 [B]Job 21:5 [C]Rom 15:21; Eph 3:5 53:1 [A]John 12:38; Rom 10:16 53:2 [a]Lit *suckling* [b]Lit *desire* [A]Is 11:1 [B]Is 52:14 53:3 [a]Or *pains* [b]Or *sickness* [A]Ps 22:6; Is 49:7; Luke 18:31-33 [B]Is 53:10 [C]Mark 10:33, 34 [D]John 1:10, 11

Jerusalem to spread the good news of the return of redeemed Israel to the land (40:9; 61:1; Na 1:15). Paul broadened this millennial reference to the preaching of the gospel in the kingdom to include spreading the gospel of God's grace from the time of Jesus Christ on (Ro 10:15; cf. Eph 6:15). **happiness … salvation … "Your God reigns!"** The good news pertains to the ideal conditions of Israel's golden age, during which Christ will reign personally over His kingdom (24:23; Ps 93:1).

52:8 with their own eyes. See Nu 14:14. This Heb. expression portrayed two people so close to each other that they can look into one another's eyes. The point is that the messengers of the truth ("watchmen") will see the Lord return to Zion (a better translation) as vividly as they see each other looking eye to eye.

52:9, 10 comforted … redeemed. The ruined city will respond to the call to sing for joy because the Lord has provided comfort (40:1, 2; 49:13; 51:12) and redemption (41:14; 43:1, 12, 14; 44:6, 23, 24; 47:4).

52:11 Depart, depart. The prophet commands the Israelites to leave the lands of their exiles to return to Jerusalem (48:20; Jer 50:8; Zec 2:6, 7; Rev 18:4). Under Cyrus there was only a limited return (50,000), but the final fulfillment in view here is in the future. **Touch nothing unclean … purify yourselves.** Returning exiles were not to defile themselves by taking property home from their exile (cf. Jos 6:18; 7:1). The NT gave these prophetic words an application in principle by using them as an exhortation forbidding Christians to involve themselves with spiritual ties to forces of heathendom (2Co 6:17).

52:12 not go out in haste. Delivered captives will not have to hurry in their return to Jerusalem, as their ancestors did when delivered from Egypt (Ex 12:11, 33, 39; Dt 16:3). They can move deliberately and safely, with the Messiah in front and God in back. Cf. 58:8.

52:13–53:12 This is the last and most memorable of the 4 Messiah/Servant-songs (cf. 42:1–9; 49:1–13; 50:4–11). This section contains unarguable, incontrovertible proof that God is the author of Scripture and Jesus is the fulfillment of messianic prophecy. The details are so minute that no human could have predicted them by accident, and no imposter fulfilled them by cunning. Clearly this refers to Messiah Jesus, as the NT attests (cf. Matt 8:17; Mk 15:28; Lk 22:37; Jn 12:38; Ac 8:28–35; Ro 10:16; 1Pe 2:21–25). It is often alluded to without being quoted (cf. Mk 9:12; Ro 4:25; 1Co 15:3; 2Co 5:21; 1Pe 1:19; 1Jn 3:5).

52:13–15 Here is a summary and preview of the humiliation and exaltation of the Servant, described in more detail in 53:1–12. The details cover the work of Christ in His substitutionary death, His burial, His resurrection, His saving of sinners, His intercession, and His kingdom.

52:13 high … lifted up … exalted. Ultimately, when the Servant rules over His kingdom, He will receive international recognition for the effectiveness of His reign (cf. Phil 2:9).

52:14 His appearance was marred. The Servant must undergo inhuman cruelty to the point that He no longer looks like a human being. His appearance is so awful that people look at Him in astonishment (53:2, 3; Ps 22:6; Mt 26:67; 27:30; Jn 19:3).

52:15 sprinkle many nations. The verb can have the sense of causing them to spring up in astonishment. They are electrified—startled, so much so that they are left speechless. The context best supports this understanding of "startle." **shut their mouths.** At His exaltation, human leaders in the highest places will be speechless and in awe before the once-despised Servant (cf. Ps 2). When He takes His throne, they will see the unfolding of power and glory such as they have never heard. Paul applied the principle in this verse to his apostolic mission of preaching the gospel of Christ where Christ was yet unknown (Ro 15:21).

53:1 Who has believed our message? The question implied that, in spite of these and other prophecies, only a few would recognize the Servant when He appeared. This anticipation found literal fulfillment at Christ's first advent. Israel did not welcome Him at His first advent (Jn 1:9–11; 12:38). Paul applied the same prophecy to the world at large (Ro 10:16). **the arm of the LORD.** At His first coming, the nation did not recognize the mighty, incarnate power of God in the person of Jesus, their Deliverer.

53:2 before Him. Though unrecognized by the world (v. 1), Messiah Jesus was observed carefully by God, who ordered every minute circumstance of His life. **parched ground … Nor appearance that we should be attracted to Him.** The Servant will arise in lowly conditions and wear none of the usual emblems of royalty, making His true identity visible only to the discerning eye of faith.

53:3 despised … forsaken … despised. The prophet foresees the hatred and rejection by

4 Surely our [a]griefs He Himself [A]bore,
And our [b]sorrows He carried;
Yet we ourselves esteemed Him stricken,
[c]Smitten of [B]God, and afflicted.
5 But He was [a]pierced through
for [A]our transgressions,
He was crushed for [B]our iniquities;
The [C]chastening for our
[b]well-being *fell* upon Him,
And by [D]His scourging we are healed.
6 All of us like sheep have gone astray,
Each of us has turned to his own way;
But the LORD has caused the
iniquity of us all
To [a]fall on Him.

7 He was oppressed and He was afflicted,
Yet He did not [A]open His mouth;
[B]Like a lamb that is led to slaughter,
And like a sheep that is silent
before its shearers,
So He did not open His mouth.
8 By oppression and judgment
He was taken away;
And as for His generation,
who considered
That He was cut off out of the
land of the [a]living
[A]For the transgression of my people,
to whom the stroke *was due?*
9 His grave was assigned with wicked men,
Yet He was with a [A]rich man in His death,
[B]Because He had [C]done no violence,
Nor was there any deceit in His mouth.

10 But the LORD was pleased
To [A]crush Him, [a,B]putting *Him* to grief;
If [b]He would render Himself
as a guilt [C]offering,
He will see [D]*His* [c]offspring,
He will prolong *His* days,
And the [d]good [E]pleasure of the LORD
will prosper in His hand.
11 As a result of the [a]anguish of His soul,
He will [A]see [b]*it and* be satisfied;
By His [B]knowledge the Righteous One,
My Servant, will justify the many,
As He will [C]bear their iniquities.
12 Therefore, I will allot Him a
[A]portion with the great,
And He will divide the booty
with the strong;
Because He poured out [a,B]Himself to death,
And was [C]numbered with the transgressors;
Yet He Himself [D]bore the sin of many,
And interceded for the transgressors.

53:4 [a]Or *sickness* [b]Or *pains* [c]Or *Struck down by* [A]Matt 8:17 [B]John 19:7 53:5 [a]Or *wounded* [b]Or *peace* [A]Is 53:8; Heb 9:28 [B]Is 53:10; Rom 4:25; 1 Cor 15:3 [C]Deut 11:2; Heb 5:8 [D]1 Pet 2:24, 25 53:6 [a]Lit *encounter Him* 53:7 [A]Matt 26:63; 27:12-14; Mark 14:61; 15:5; Luke 23:9; John 19:9 [B]Acts 8:32, 33; Rev 5:6 53:8 [a]Or *life* [A]Is 53:5, 12 53:9 [A]Matt 27:57-60 [B]Is 42:1-3 [C]1 Pet 2:22 53:10 [a]Lit *He made Him sick* [b]Lit *His soul* [c]Lit *seed* [d]Or *will of* [A]Is 53:5 [B]Is 53:3, 4 [C]Is 53:6, 12; John 1:29 [D]Ps 22:30; Is 54:3; 61:9; 66:22 [E]Is 46:10 53:11 [a]Or *toilsome labor* [b]Another reading is *light* [A]John 10:14-18 [B]Is 45:25; Rom 5:18, 19 [C]Is 53:5, 6 53:12 [a]Lit *His soul* [A]Is 52:13; Phil 2:9-11 [B]Matt 26:38, 39, 42 [C]Mark 15:28; Luke 22:37 [D]Is 53:6, 11; 2 Cor 5:21

mankind toward the Messiah/Servant, who suffered not only external abuse, but also internal grief over the lack of response from those He came to save (e.g., Mt 23:37; Lk 13:34). **hide their face … we did not esteem.** By using the first person, the prophet spoke for his unbelieving nation's aversion to a crucified Messiah and their lack of respect for the incarnate Son of God.

53:4 bore … carried. Cf. vv. 11, 12. Even though the verbs are past tense, they predict happenings future to Isaiah's time, i.e., "prophetic perfects" in Heb. here and elsewhere in this Servant-song. Isaiah was saying that the Messiah would bear the consequences of the sins of men, namely the griefs and sorrows of life, though incredibly the Jews who watched Him die thought He was being punished by God for His own sins. Matthew found an analogical fulfillment of these words in Jesus' healing ministry (*see notes on Mt 8:16, 17*), because sickness results from sin for which the Servant paid with His life (vv. 7, 8; cf. 1Pe 2:24). In eternity, all sickness will be removed, so ultimately it is included in the benefits of the atonement.

53:5 pierced through for our transgressions … crushed for our iniquities. This verse is filled with the language of substitution. The Servant suffered not for His own sin, since He was sinless (cf. Heb 4:15; 7:26), but as the substitute for sinners. The emphasis here is on Christ being the substitute recipient of God's wrath on sinners (cf. 2Co 5:21; Gal 1:3, 4; Heb 10:9, 10). **chastening for our well-being.** He suffered the chastisement of God in order to procure our peace with God. **by His scourging we are healed.** The stripe (the Heb. noun is singular) that caused His death has brought salvation to those for whose sins He died. Peter confirms this in 1Pe 2:24.

53:6 All of us … Each of us … us all. Every person has sinned (Ro 3:9, 23), but the Servant has sufficiently shouldered the consequences of sin and the righteous wrath deserved by sinners (cf. 1Ti 2:5, 6; 4:10; 1Jn 2:2). The manner in which God laid our iniquity on Him was that God treated Him as if He had committed every sin ever committed by every person who would ever believe, though He was perfectly innocent of any sin. God did so to Him, so that wrath being spent and justice satisfied, God could then give to the account of sinners who believe the righteousness of Christ, treating them as if they had done only the righteous acts of Christ. In both cases, this is substitution. *See notes on 2Co 5:21.*

53:7, 8 This is the portion of Scripture read by the Ethiopian eunuch and subsequently explained to him by Philip as referring to Jesus (Ac 8:32, 33).

53:7 did not open His mouth. The Servant will utter no protest and will be utterly submissive to those who oppress Him. Jesus fulfilled this (Mt 26:63; 27:12–14; Mk 14:61; 15:5; Lk 23:9; Jn 19:9; 1Pe 2:23). **lamb … led to slaughter.** The Servant was to assume the role of a sacrificial lamb (Ex 12:3, 6). Jesus fulfilled this figurative role literally (Jn 1:29; 1Pe 1:18, 19; Rev 5:6).

53:8 cut off … For the transgression of my people. The Servant lost His life to be the substitute object of wrath in the place of the Jews, who by that substitution will receive salvation and the righteousness of God imputed to them. Similar terminology applies to the Messiah in Da 9:26.

53:9 with wicked men … with a rich man. Because of His disgraceful death, the Jews intended the Servant to have a disgraceful burial along with the thieves (cf. Jn 19:31), but instead He was buried with "a rich man" in an honorable burial through the donated tomb of Joseph of Arimathea (Mt 27:57–60; Mk 15:42–46; Lk 23:50–53; Jn 19:38–40). **no violence … deceit.** The Servant's innocence meant that His execution was totally undeserved. Peter notes the fulfillment of this in 1Pe 2:22.

53:10 the LORD was pleased. Though the Servant did not deserve to die, it was the Lord's will for Him to do so (Mt 26:39; Lk 22:42; Jn 12:27; Ac 2:23). **a guilt offering.** Fulfilled by the Servant as the Lamb of God (v. 7; Jn 1:29). Christ is the Christian's Passover (1Co 5:7). This conclusively eliminates the error that Christ's atonement provides present-day healing for those who pray in faith. His death was an atonement for sin, not sickness. *See note on 53:4.* **see *His* offspring … prolong *His* days.** To see His offspring, the Servant must rise from the dead. He will do this and live to reign forever (2Sa 7:13, 16; Pss 21:4; 89:4; 132:12).

53:11 He will … be satisfied. The one sacrifice of the Servant will provide complete satisfaction in settling the sin issue (1Jn 2:2; cf. 1:11). **By His knowledge.** Knowledge of Him (Php 3:10), i.e., faith in Him (Jn 17:3). **justify the many.** Through the divine "knowledge" of how to justify sinners, the plan was accomplished that by His one sacrifice He declared many righteous before God (Ro 5:19; 2Co 5:21).

53:12 portion with the great … booty with the strong. The Servant's reward for His work

THE FERTILITY OF ZION

54 "[A]Shout for joy, O barren one, you
who have borne no *child;*
Break forth into joyful shouting and cry
aloud, you who have not travailed;
For the sons of the [B]desolate one
will be [C]more numerous
Than the sons of the married
woman," says the LORD.
2 "[A]Enlarge the place of your tent;
[a]Stretch out the curtains of your
dwellings, spare not;
Lengthen your [B]cords
And strengthen your [B]pegs.
3 "For you will [A]spread abroad to
the right and to the left.
And your [a]descendants will
[B]possess nations
And will [C]resettle the desolate cities.

4 "Fear not, for you will [A]not be put to shame;
And do not feel humiliated, for
you will not be disgraced;
But you will forget the [B]shame
of your youth,
And the [C]reproach of your widowhood
you will remember no more.
5 "For your [A]husband is your Maker,
Whose name is the LORD of hosts;
And your [B]Redeemer is the
Holy One of Israel,
Who is called the [C]God of all the earth.
6 "For the LORD has called you,
Like a wife [A]forsaken and grieved in spirit,
Even like a wife of *one's* youth
when she is rejected,"
Says your God.
7 "[a]For a [A]brief moment I forsook you,
But with great compassion
I will [B]gather you.
8 "In an [a,A]outburst of anger
I hid My face from you for a moment,
But with everlasting [B]lovingkindness
I will [C]have compassion on you,"
Says the LORD your [D]Redeemer.

9 "For [a]this is like the days of Noah to Me,
When I swore that the waters of Noah
Would [A]not [b]flood the earth again;
So I have sworn that I will
[B]not be angry with you
Nor will I rebuke you.
10 "For the [A]mountains may be removed
and the hills may shake,
But My lovingkindness will not
be removed from you,
And My [B]covenant of peace
will not be shaken,"
Says [C]the LORD who has
compassion on you.

11 "O [A]afflicted one, storm-tossed,
and [B]not comforted,
Behold, I will set your
stones in antimony,
And your foundations I will
[C]lay in [a,D]sapphires.
12 "Moreover, I will make your
battlements of [a]rubies,
And your gates of [b]crystal,
And your entire [c]wall of precious stones.
13 "[A]All your sons will be [a]taught of the LORD;
And the well-being of your
sons will be [B]great.
14 "In [A]righteousness you will
be established;
You will be far from [B]oppression,
for you will [C]not fear;
And from [D]terror, for it will
not come near you.

54:1 [A]Gal 4:27 [B]Is 62:4 [C]1 Sam 2:5; Is 49:20 54:2 [a]Lit *Let them stretch out* [A]Is 33:20; 49:19, 20 [B]Ex 35:18; 39:40 54:3 [a]Lit *seed* [A]Gen 28:14; Is 43:5, 6; 60:3 [B]Is 14:1, 2 [C]Is 49:19 54:4 [A]Is 45:17 [B]Jer 31:19 [C]Is 4:1; 25:8; 51:7 54:5 [A]Jer 3:14; Hos 2:19 [B]Is 43:14; 48:17 [C]Is 6:3; 11:9; 65:16 54:6 [A]Is 49:14-21; 50:1, 2; 62:4 54:7 [a]Lit *In* [A]Is 26:20 [B]Is 11:12; 43:5; 49:18 54:8 [a]Lit *overflowing* [A]Is 60:10 [B]Is 54:10; 63:7 [C]Is 49:10, 13 [D]Is 54:5 54:9 [a]Some mss read *the waters of Noah this is to Me* [b]Lit *cross over* [A]Gen 9:11 [B]Is 12:1; Ezek 39:29 54:10 [A]Ps 102:26; Is 51:6 [B]2 Sam 23:5; Ps 89:34; Is 55:3; 59:21; 61:8 [C]Is 54:8 54:11 [a]Or *lapis lazuli* [A]Is 51:21 [B]Is 51:18, 19 [C]Is 14:32; 28:16; 44:28 [D]Job 28:16; Rev 21:19 54:12 [a]I.e. bright red [b]Or *carbuncles* [c]Lit *border, boundary* 54:13 [a]Or *disciples* [A]John 6:45 [B]Is 48:18; 66:12 54:14 [A]Is 1:26, 27; 9:7; 62:1 [B]Is 9:4; 14:4 [C]Is 54:4 [D]Is 33:18

will be to enjoy the "booty" of His spiritual victories during His millennial reign. **numbered with the transgressors.** The Servant assumes a role among sinful human beings, fulfilled by Jesus when He was crucified between two criminals (Lk 22:37). **interceded for the transgressors.** This speaks of the office of intercessory High Priest, which began on the cross (Lk 23:34) and continues in heaven (cf. Heb 7:25; 9:24).

54:1 barren … have borne no *child* … have not travailed … desolate. In her exile and dispersion, Israel has been destitute, disgraced as a woman who had borne no children (49:21). The prophet calls for singing, however, because of the Lord's promise of future fruitfulness for the nation (49:19, 20). The NT supplies an additional application of the principle in this verse, citing it as evidence that the Jerusalem above, mother of the children of promise through Sarah, will enjoy great fruitfulness (Gal 4:27).

54:2 Enlarge … Stretch out … Lengthen. The prophet commanded barren Israel to prepare for the day when her numerous inhabitants will require larger space to dwell in (26:15; 49:19, 20).

54:3 spread abroad … possess nations. The Messiah's future kingdom is to be worldwide, far greater in extent than the former kingdoms of David and Solomon.

54:4 shame of your youth … reproach of your widowhood. Israel's sins brought on the Egyptian captivity, the Babylonian exile, and her current dispersion, but the glories of the future kingdom will be so great that they will overshadow past failures.

54:5 husband … Redeemer. The basis for forgetting past failures is Israel's relationship to the Lord as her husband (62:4, 5) and Redeemer (41:14).

54:6–8 forsaken … grieved … rejected. Israel in exile and dispersion has been like a wife whose husband has rejected her. But this is only for a brief time compared to the everlasting kindness she will enjoy when the Messiah returns to gather the woeful wife (26:20).

54:9 waters of Noah. Just as God swore He would never again judge the whole earth with a flood (Ge 8:21; 9:11), so He has taken an oath never to be angry with His people again. He will fulfill this promise after their final restoration.

54:10 mountains … hills … My lovingkindness … My covenant. In the Millennium (48:6, 7; 51:6, 16) topography will change (see Eze 38:20; Mic 1:4; Zec 14:4, 10), but not God's pledge of well-being for Israel as a result of the New Covenant (55:3; 59:21; 61:8).

54:11, 12 antimony … sapphires … rubies … crystal … precious stones. The elaborate ornamentation will outfit Jerusalem to be the center of the future, eternal messianic reign following the Millennium (Rev 21:18–21). As magnificent as this is, it is

15 "If anyone fiercely assails *you*
it will not be from Me.
[A]Whoever assails you will
fall because of you.
16 "Behold, I Myself have created the
smith who blows the fire of coals
And brings out a weapon for its work;
And I have created the destroyer to ruin.
17 "[A]No weapon that is formed
against you will prosper;
And [B]every tongue that [a]accuses you
in judgment you will condemn.
This is the heritage of the
servants of the LORD,
And their [C]vindication is from
Me," declares the LORD.

THE FREE OFFER OF MERCY

55 "Ho! Every one who [A]thirsts,
come to the waters;
And you who have [B]no [a]money
come, buy and eat.
Come, buy [C]wine and milk
[D]Without money and without cost.
2 "Why do you [a]spend money for
what is [A]not bread,
And your wages for what
does not satisfy?
Listen carefully to Me, and
[B]eat what is good,
And [C]delight yourself in abundance.
3 "[A]Incline your ear and come to Me.
Listen, that [a]you may [B]live;
And I will make [C]an everlasting
covenant with you,
According to the [D]faithful
mercies [b]shown to David.
4 "Behold, I have made [A]him a
witness to the peoples,
A [B]leader and commander for the peoples.
5 "Behold, you will call a [A]nation
you do not know,
And a nation which knows you
not will [B]run to you,
Because of the LORD your God,
even the Holy One of Israel;
For He has [C]glorified you."

6 [A]Seek the LORD while He may be found;
[B]Call upon Him while He is near.
7 [A]Let the wicked forsake his way
And the unrighteous man his [B]thoughts;
And let him [C]return to the LORD,
And He will have [D]compassion on him,
And to our God,
For He will [E]abundantly pardon.
8 "For My thoughts are not [A]your thoughts,
Nor are [B]your ways My ways,"
declares the LORD.
9 "For [A]*as* the heavens are
higher than the earth,
So are My ways higher than your ways
And My thoughts than your thoughts.
10 "For as the [A]rain and the snow
come down from heaven,
And do not return there without
watering the earth
And making it bear and sprout,
And furnishing [B]seed to the sower
and bread to the eater;

54:15 [A]Is 41:11-16 54:17 [a]Lit *rises against* [A]Is 17:12-14; 29:8 [B]Is 50:8, 9 [C]Is 45:24; 46:13 55:1 [a]Lit *silver* [A]Ps 42:1, 2; 63:1; 143:6; Is 41:17; 44:3; John 4:14; 7:37; Rev 21:6 [B]Lam 5:4 [C]Song 5:1; Joel 3:18 [D]Hos 14:4; Matt 10:8 55:2 [a]Lit *weigh out silver* [A]Eccl 6:2; Hos 8:7 [B]Ps 22:26; Is 1:19; 62:8, 9 [C]Is 25:6; Jer 31:14 55:3 [a]Lit *your soul* [b]Lit *of David* [A]Is 51:4 [B]Lev 18:5; Rom 10:5 [C]Is 61:8 [D]Acts 13:34 55:4 [A]Ps 18:43; Jer 30:9; Hos 3:5 [B]Ezek 34:24; 37:24, 25; Dan 9:25; Mic 5:2 55:5 [A]Is 45:14, 22-24; 49:6, 12, 23 [B]Zech 8:22 [C]Is 60:9 55:6 [A]Ps 32:6; Is 45:19, 22; 49:8; Amos 5:6 [B]Is 58:9; 65:24 55:7 [A]Is 1:16, 19; 58:6 [B]Is 32:7; 59:7 [C]Is 31:6; 44:22 [D]Is 14:1; 54:8, 10 [E]Is 1:18; 40:2; 43:25; 44:22 55:8 [A]Is 65:2; 66:18 [B]Is 53:6 55:9 [A]Ps 103:11 55:10 [A]Is 30:23 [B]2 Cor 9:10

not as important as the spiritual richness of the kingdom, when truth and peace (v. 13) prevail along with righteousness (v. 14). The Lord Himself will teach everyone during the messianic kingdom, so everyone will know His righteousness (11:9; Jer 31:34). Jesus gave this verse an additional focus, applying it to those with spiritual insight to come to Him during His first advent (Jn 6:45).

54:15–17 Whoever assails you will fall. In the millennial kingdom this will occur, as prophesied by John in Rev 20:7–9. The Lord will burn up all Israel's enemies. The heritage of the Lord's servants in the Messiah's kingdom will include His protection from would-be conquerors. It should be noted that after the Servant-song of Isaiah 53, Israel is always referred to as God's "servants" (plural) rather than His servant (54:17; 56:6; 63:17; 65:8, 9, 13, 14, 15; 66:14).

55:1 Every one. The Servant's redemptive work and glorious kingdom are for the benefit of all who are willing to come (53:6). The prophet invites his readers to participate in the benefits obtained by the suffering of the Servant in chap. 53 and described in chap. 54. **no money ... Without money ... without cost.** Benefits in the Servant's kingdom will be free because of His redemptive work (53:6, 8, 11; Eph 2:8, 9). **wine and milk.** Symbols for abundance, satisfaction, and prosperity (SS 5:1; Joel 3:18).

55:2 not bread. This is the "bread of deceit" (Pr 20:17) and not the "bread of life" (Jn 6:32–35).

55:3 everlasting covenant. The New Covenant that God will give to Israel (54:8; 61:8; Jer 31:31–34; 32:40; 50:5; Eze 16:60; 37:26; Heb 13:20). **faithful mercies shown to David.** The Davidic Covenant promised David that his seed would be ruler over Israel in an everlasting kingdom (2Sa 7:8, 16; Ps 89:27–29). Paul connected the resurrection of Christ with this promise (Ac 13:34), since it was an essential event in fulfilling this promise. If He had not fully satisfied God by His atoning death, He would not have risen; if He had not risen from the dead, He could not eventually sit on David's earthly throne. But He did rise and will fulfill the kingly role (v. 4). Cf. Jer 30:9; Eze 34:23, 24; 37:24, 25; Da 9:25; Hos 3:5; Mic 5:2. The whole world will come to Him as the Great King (v. 5).

55:6, 7 Here is one of the clearest OT invitations to salvation now and kingdom blessing later. It gives an excellent example of how people were saved during the OT period. Salvation grace and mercy were available to the soul that was willing to 1) seek the Lord (Dt 4:29; 2Ch 15:4) and 2) call on Him while He is still available (65:1; Ps 32:6; Pr 8:17; Mt 25:1–13; Jn 7:34; 8:21; 2Co 6:2; Heb 2:3; 3:13, 15). Such true seeking in faith is accompanied by repentance, which is described as forsaking ways and thoughts and turning from sinful living to the Lord. A sinner must come, believing in God, recognizing his sin and desiring forgiveness and deliverance from that sin. At the same time he must recognize his own inability to be righteous or to satisfy God and cast himself on God's mercy. It is then that he receives a complete pardon. His sin has been covered by the substitution of the Messiah in his place (chap. 53). This OT pattern of salvation is illustrated in Lk 18:9–14.

55:7 forsake. An integral part of seeking the Lord (v. 6) is a turning from sin (1:16).

55:8, 9 My thoughts ... My ways. Some may doubt such willingness as is described in v. 7, but God's grace is far beyond human comprehension, especially as manifested toward Israel.

55:10, 11 rain ... snow ... My word. Moisture from heaven invariably accomplishes its intended purpose in helping meet human

11 So will My [A]word be which goes
forth from My mouth;
It will [B]not return to Me empty,
Without [C]accomplishing what I desire,
And without succeeding *in the*
matter for which I sent it.
12 "For you will go out with [A]joy
And be led forth with [B]peace;
The [C]mountains and the hills will break
forth into shouts of joy before you,
And all the [D]trees of the field
will clap *their* hands.
13 "Instead of the [A]thorn bush the
[B]cypress will come up,
And instead of the [C]nettle the
myrtle will come up,
And [a]it will be a [b,D]memorial to the LORD,
For an everlasting [E]sign which
[F]will not be cut off."

REWARDS FOR OBEDIENCE TO GOD

56 Thus says the LORD,
"[A]Preserve justice and do righteousness,
For My [B]salvation is about to come
And My righteousness to be revealed.
2 "How [A]blessed is the man who does this,
And the son of man who
[B]takes hold of it;
Who [C]keeps from profaning the sabbath,
And keeps his hand from doing any evil."
3 Let not the [A]foreigner who has
joined himself to the LORD say,
"The LORD will surely separate
me from His people."
Nor let the [B]eunuch say, "Behold,
I am a dry tree."
4 For thus says the LORD,
"To the eunuchs who [A]keep My sabbaths,
And choose what pleases Me,
And [B]hold fast My covenant,
5 To them I will give in My [A]house and
within My [B]walls a memorial,
And a name better than that
of sons and daughters;
I will give [a]them an everlasting
[C]name which [D]will not be cut off.
6 "Also the [A]foreigners who join
themselves to the LORD,
To minister to Him, and to love
the name of the LORD,
To be His servants, every one who
[B]keeps from profaning the sabbath
And holds fast My covenant;
7 Even [A]those I will bring to
My [B]holy mountain
And [C]make them joyful in
My house of prayer.
Their burnt offerings and their sacrifices
will be acceptable on [D]My altar;
For [E]My house will be called a house
of prayer for all the peoples."
8 The Lord [a]GOD, who [A]gathers the
dispersed of Israel, declares,
"Yet [B]*others* I will gather to [b]them,
to those *already* gathered."

9 All you [A]beasts of the field,
All you beasts in the forest,
Come to eat.
10 His [A]watchmen are [B]blind,
All of them know nothing.
All of them are mute dogs unable to bark,
[a]Dreamers lying down, who love to slumber;
11 And the dogs are [a,A]greedy,
they [b]are not satisfied.
And they are shepherds who
have [B]no understanding;
They have all [C]turned to their own way,
Each one to his unjust gain, to the last one.

55:11 [A]Is 45:23; Matt 24:35 [B]Is 44:26; 59:21 [C]Is 46:10; 53:10 55:12 [A]Ps 105:43; Is 51:11; 52:9 [B]Is 54:10, 13; Jer 29:11 [C]Is 44:23; 49:13 [D]1 Chr 16:33 55:13 [a]I.e. the transformation of the desert [b]Lit *name* [A]Is 7:19 [B]Is 60:13 [C]Is 5:6; 7:24; 32:13 [D]Is 63:12, 14; Jer 33:9 [E]Is 19:20 [F]Is 56:5 56:1 [A]Is 1:17; 33:5; 61:8 [B]Ps 85:9; Is 46:13; 51:5 56:2 [A]Ps 112:1; 119:1, 2 [B]Is 56:4, 6 [C]Ex 20:8-11; 31:13-17; Is 56:6; 58:13; Jer 17:21, 22; Ezek 20:12, 20 56:3 [A]Is 14:1; 56:6 [B]Deut 23:1; Jer 38:7; Acts 8:27 56:4 [A]Is 56:2, 6 [B]Is 56:6 56:5 [a]So DSS; M.T. reads *him* [A]Is 2:2, 3; 56:7; 66:20 [B]Is 26:1; 60:18 [C]Is 62:2 [D]Is 48:19; 55:13 56:6 [A]Is 56:3; 60:10; 61:5 [B]Is 56:2, 4 56:7 [A]Is 2:2, 3; 60:11; Mic 4:1, 2 [B]Is 11:9; 65:25 [C]Is 61:10 [D]Is 60:7 [E]Matt 21:13; Mark 11:17; Luke 19:46 56:8 [a]Heb *YHWH*, usually rendered *LORD* [b]Lit *him* [A]Is 11:12 [B]Is 60:3-11; 66:18-21; John 10:16 56:9 [A]Is 18:6; 46:11 56:10 [a]So DSS; M.T. *Ravers* [A]Ezek 3:17 [B]Is 29:9-14; Jer 14:13, 14 56:11 [a]Lit *strong of soul/appetite* [b]Lit *do not know satisfaction* [A]Is 28:7; Ezek 13:19; Mic 3:5, 11 [B]Is 1:3 [C]Is 57:17; Jer 22:17

physical needs. The Word of God will likewise produce its intended results in fulfilling God's spiritual purposes, especially the establishment of the Davidic kingdom on earth (vv. 1–5).

55:12 go out with joy … led forth with peace. Exiled Israel will return from her dispersion rejoicing in her deliverance and unbothered by her enemies.

55:13 Instead of the thorn … myrtle. In the Davidic kingdom positive changes in nature, including the reverse of the curse (Ge 3:17), will be an ongoing testimony to the Lord's redemption of His people (44:23; Ro 8:19–23).

56:1 about to come … revealed. Incentives to comply with 55:6, 7 include the nearness of God's kingdom of salvation and righteousness (51:5).

56:2 keeps from profaning the sabbath. Sabbath observance, established after the deliverance from Egypt (Ex 20:8–11), became a sign of fulfilling the covenant God made with Moses (Ex 31:13–17).

56:3 foreigner … eunuch. Such individuals, excluded from Israel by the law (Ex 12:43; Dt 23:1, 3, 7, 8), will find in the coming of the messianic kingdom the removal of such exclusions.

56:4, 5 hold fast My covenant … an everlasting name. Eunuchs with hearts inclined to comply with the Mosaic Covenant may anticipate an endless posterity. It is never works that save (cf. Ro 3:20; Eph 2:8, 9); rather, obeying God's law, doing what pleases Him or desiring to keep the promises of obedience are the evidences that one has been saved, and will thus enjoy all salvation blessings.

56:6, 7 holds fast My covenant … acceptable on My altar. The foreigner who loves God, whose heart is inclined to serve Him and obey the Mosaic law, will find his sacrifices welcome, in the coming kingdom as well.

56:7 My house … for all the peoples. In the kingdom of the Messiah, the Jerusalem temple will be the focal point for worship of the Lord by people of all ethnic backgrounds. Jesus cited a violation of this anticipation by His contemporaries in His second cleansing of the temple: Jewish leaders had made the temple a commercial venture (Mt 21:13; Mk 11:17; Lk 19:46).

56:8 *others* … those *already* gathered. Besides gathering Israel's exiles into His kingdom, the Lord will bring in non-Jews also (49:6).

56:9–12 A commentary on Israel's false prophets and irresponsible leaders who led them astray.

56:9–11 beasts … watchmen … shepherds. These titles identify the wicked; other prophets refer to Israel's enemies as beasts (Jer 12:9; Eze 34:5, 8). Prophets, who should have been watchmen and warned Israel to

12 "Come," *they say,* "let [a]us get [A]wine, and
let us drink heavily of strong drink;
And [B]tomorrow will be like
today, only more so."

EVIL LEADERS REBUKED

57 The righteous man perishes, and
no man [A]takes it to heart;
And devout men are taken away,
while no one understands.
For the righteous man is
taken away from [B]evil,
2 He enters into peace;
They rest in their [a]beds,
Each one who [A]walked in his upright way.
3 "But come here, you sons of a [A]sorceress,
[B]Offspring of an adulterer
and [a]a [C]prostitute.
4 "Against whom do you jest?
Against whom do you open
wide your mouth
And stick out your tongue?
Are you not children of [A]rebellion,
Offspring of deceit,
5 *Who* inflame yourselves among the [a,A]oaks,
[B]Under every luxuriant tree,
Who [C]slaughter the children
in the [b]ravines,
Under the clefts of the crags?
6 "Among the [a,A]smooth *stones* of the [b]ravine
Is your portion, [c]they are your lot;
Even to them you have [B]poured
out a drink offering,
You have made a grain offering.
Shall I [d,C]relent concerning these things?
7 "Upon a [A]high and lofty mountain
You have [B]made your bed.
You also went up there to offer sacrifice.
8 "Behind the door and the doorpost
You have set up your sign;
Indeed, far removed from Me, you
have [A]uncovered yourself,
And have gone up and made
your bed wide.
And you have made an agreement
for yourself with them,
You have loved their [a]bed,
You have looked on *their* [b]manhood.
9 "You have journeyed to the king with oil
And increased your perfumes;
You have [A]sent your envoys
a great distance
And made *them* go down to [a]Sheol.
10 "You were tired out by the
length of your road,
Yet you did not say, '[A]It is hopeless.'
You found [a]renewed strength,
Therefore you did not [b]faint.

11 "Of [A]whom were you worried and fearful
When you lied, and did
[B]not remember Me
[a]Nor [C]give *Me* a thought?
Was I not silent even for a long time
So you do not fear Me?
12 "I will [A]declare your righteousness
and your [B]deeds,
But they will not profit you.
13 "When you cry out, [A]let your
collection *of idols* deliver you.
But the wind will carry all of them up,
And a breath will take *them away.*
But he who [B]takes refuge in Me
will [C]inherit the land
And will [D]possess My holy mountain."

14 And it will be said,
"[A]Build up, build up, prepare the way,
Remove *every* obstacle out of
the way of My people."

56:12 [a]So DSS and many versions; M.T. *me* [A]Is 5:11, 12, 22 [B]Ps 10:6; Luke 12:19, 20 57:1 [A]Is 42:25; 47:7 [B]2 Kin 22:20; Is 47:11; Jer 18:11 57:2 [a]I.e. graves [A]Is 26:7 57:3 [a]So ancient versions; Heb *she prostitutes herself* [A]Mal 3:5 [B]Is 1:4; Matt 16:4 [C]Is 1:21; 57:7-9 57:4 [A]Is 48:8 57:5 [a]Or *terebinths* [b]Or *wadis* [A]Is 1:29 [B]2 Kin 16:4; Jer 2:20; 3:13 [C]2 Kin 23:10; Ps 106:37, 38; Jer 7:31 57:6 [a]I.e. symbols of fertility gods [b]Or *wadi* [c]Lit *they, they* [d]Or *repent* [A]Jer 3:9; Hab 2:19 [B]Jer 7:18 [C]Jer 5:9, 29; 9:9 57:7 [A]Jer 3:6; Ezek 16:16 [B]Ezek 23:41 57:8 [a]Or *lying down* [b]Lit *hand* [A]Ezek 23:18 57:9 [a]I.e. the nether world [A]Ezek 23:16, 40 57:10 [a]Lit *the life of your hand* [b]Or *become sick* [A]Jer 2:25; 18:12 57:11 [a]Lit *You did not set it upon your heart* [A]Prov 29:25; Is 51:12, 13 [B]Jer 2:32; 3:21 [C]Ps 50:21; Is 42:14 57:12 [A]Is 58:1, 2 [B]Is 29:15; 59:6; 65:7; 66:18; Mic 3:2-4 57:13 [A]Jer 22:20; 30:14 [B]Ps 37:3, 9; Is 25:4 [C]Is 49:8; 60:21 [D]Is 65:9 57:14 [A]Is 62:10; Jer 18:15

repent, ignored their responsibility (cf. Eze 3:17). Priests also failed to lead Israel in paths of righteousness (Eze 34:1–6; Zec 11:15–17).

56:12 wine ... strong drink. This is indicative of the self-indulgent irresponsibility of the leaders. Drunkenness completely obliterated any concern that leaders had for their people. *See notes on Pr 31:4–7.*

57:1, 2 In contrast to the evil leaders, who were engaged in debauchery and self-indulgence, were the righteous who were removed from impending divine judgments. The righteous do suffer by oppression and distress at what is going on around them, but they die in faith and enjoy their eternal reward.

57:3 sorceress ... adulterer ... prostitute. Sorcery and adultery were figurative designations for idolatry. God summoned the wicked to give an account.

57:4 stick out your tongue. The ungodly blatantly ridiculed God's messengers (e.g., 28:9, 10).

57:5, 6 These verses feature elements of idolatry such as child sacrifice, which were a part of worshiping the Ammonite god Molech (Jer 32:35; Eze 20:26, 31). In response to Israel's offerings to idols, what was the Lord's appropriate response—to be satisfied or to take vengeance? Jeremiah had the answer (Jer 5:9, 29; 9:9).

57:7, 8 The location of idol altars where Israel committed spiritual adultery in offering sacrifices (Jer 3:6; Eze 16:16) to Baal and Astarte.

57:9 journeyed to the king. An example of this was Ahaz, who called on the king of Assyria for help and spared no expense in copying the idolatry of Assyria (2Ki 16:7–18).

57:10 found renewed strength. Rather than recognizing the hopelessness of idolatry, and in spite of the weariness of idol worship, the Israelites found renewed strength to pursue their idolatrous course.

57:11 you lied. These wicked people feared false gods more than the true God to whom they played the hypocrite, trading on God's patience.

57:12, 13 I will declare your righteousness. God will break His silence by elaborating on Israel's sham righteousness, a sarcastic way of saying they have no real righteousness. The folly of such devotion to nonexistent gods will show up when judgment comes and they all are blown away, while the worshipers of the true God enjoy the blessings of the kingdom. See Ps 37:11; Mt 5:5.

57:14–20 In contrast with the threats of judgment for idolatry (vv. 3–13), vv. 14–20 give promises of blessing.

57:14 Remove *every* obstacle. The command is to remove all barriers to prepare the way for God's people to return to Him (62:10).

15 For thus says the [A]high and exalted One
Who [a,B]lives forever, whose name is Holy,
"I [C]dwell *on* a high and holy place,
And *also* with the [D]contrite
and lowly of spirit
In order to [E]revive the spirit of the lowly
And to revive the heart of the contrite.
16 "For I will [A]not contend forever,
[B]Nor will I always be angry;
For the spirit would grow faint before Me,
And the [C]breath *of those*
whom I have made.
17 "Because of the iniquity of his [A]unjust
gain I was angry and struck him;
I hid *My face* and was angry,
And he went on [B]turning away,
in the way of his heart.
18 "I have seen his ways, but I will [A]heal him;
I will [B]lead him and [C]restore comfort
to him and to his mourners,
19 Creating the [a,A]praise of the lips.
[B]Peace, peace to him who is [C]far
and to him who is near,"
Says the LORD, "and I will heal him."
20 But the [A]wicked are like the tossing sea,
For it cannot be quiet,
And its waters toss up refuse and mud.
21 "[A]There is no peace," says [B]my
God, "for the wicked."

OBSERVANCES OF FASTS

58 "[A]Cry loudly, do not hold back;
Raise your voice like a trumpet,
And declare to My people
their [B]transgression
And to the house of Jacob their sins.
2 "Yet they [A]seek Me day by day and
delight to know My ways,
As a nation that has done [B]righteousness
And [C]has not forsaken the
ordinance of their God.
They ask Me *for* just decisions,
They delight [D]in the nearness of God.
3 'Why have we [A]fasted and You do not see?
Why have we humbled ourselves
and You do not [a]notice?'
Behold, on the [B]day of your fast
you find *your* desire,
And drive hard all your workers.
4 "Behold, you fast for contention and
[A]strife and to strike with a wicked fist.
You do not fast like *you do* today to
[B]make your voice heard on high.
5 "Is it a fast like this which I choose, a
day for a man to humble himself?
Is it for bowing [a]one's head like a reed
And for spreading out [A]sackcloth
and ashes as a bed?
Will you call this a fast, even an
[B]acceptable day to the LORD?
6 "Is this not the fast which I choose,
To [A]loosen the bonds of wickedness,
To undo the bands of the yoke,
And to [B]let the oppressed go free
And [C]break every yoke?
7 "Is it not to [A]divide your bread
[a]with the hungry
And [B]bring the homeless
poor into the house;
When you see the [C]naked, to cover him;
And not to [D]hide yourself
from your own flesh?
8 "Then your [A]light will break
out like the dawn,
And your [B]recovery will
speedily spring forth;
And your [C]righteousness
will go before you;
The glory of the [D]LORD will
be your rear guard.
9 "Then you will [A]call, and the
LORD will answer;
You will cry, and He will say, 'Here I am.'
If you [B]remove the yoke from your midst,
The [a,C]pointing of the finger and
[D]speaking wickedness,

57:15 [a]Or *dwells in eternity* [A]Is 52:13 [B]Deut 33:27; Is 40:28 [C]Is 33:5; 66:1 [D]Ps 34:18; 51:17; Is 66:2 [E]Ps 147:3; Is 61:1-3 57:16 [A]Gen 6:3 [B]Ps 85:5; 103:9; Mic 7:18 [C]Is 42:5 57:17 [A]Is 2:7; 56:11; Jer 6:13 [B]Is 1:4; Jer 3:14, 22 57:18 [A]Is 19:22; 30:26; 53:5 [B]Is 52:12 [C]Is 61:1-3 57:19 [a]Lit *fruit of the lips* [A]Is 6:7; 51:16; 59:21; Heb 13:15 [B]Is 26:12; 32:17 [C]Acts 2:39; Eph 2:17 57:20 [A]Job 18:5-14; Is 3:9, 11 57:21 [A]Is 48:22; 59:8 [B]Is 49:4 58:1 [A]Is 40:6 [B]Is 43:27; 50:1; 59:12 58:2 [A]Is 1:11; Titus 1:16 [B]Is 48:1; Jer 7:9, 10 [C]Is 1:4, 28; 59:13 [D]Ps 119:151; Is 29:13; 57:3; James 4:8 58:3 [a]Lit *know* [A]Mal 3:14; Luke 18:12 [B]Is 22:12, 13; Zech 7:5, 6 58:4 [A]Is 3:14, 15; 59:6 [B]Is 1:15; 59:2; Joel 2:12-14 58:5 [a]Lit *his* [A]1 Kin 21:27 [B]Is 49:8; 61:2 58:6 [A]Neh 5:10-12; Jer 34:8 [B]Is 1:17 [C]Is 58:9 58:7 [a]Lit *for* [A]Job 31:19, 20; Is 58:10; Ezek 18:7, 16 [B]Is 16:3, 4; Heb 13:2 [C]Matt 25:35, 36; Luke 3:11 [D]Deut 22:1-4; Luke 10:31, 32 58:8 [A]Is 58:10 [B]Is 30:26; 33:24; Jer 30:17; 33:6 [C]Ps 85:13; Is 62:1 [D]Ex 14:19; Is 52:12 58:9 [a]Lit *sending out* [A]Ps 50:15; Is 55:6; 65:24 [B]Is 58:6 [C]Prov 6:13 [D]Ps 12:2; Is 59:13

57:15, 18 revive the spirit ... revive the heart. The Lord sends true revival, which comes to the humble and contrite (61:1–3; contra. v. 10). After all the years of Israel's sin and backsliding, and of Israel's punishment, God's grace will prevail (43:25), and spiritual healing and restoration will come.

57:17 turning away. *See note on Pr 14:14.*

57:19 praise of the lips. According to Heb 13:15, this phrase refers to praising and thanking God. Cf. Hos 14:2. In this context, it is the voice crying "peace, peace" in a call to people far and near to come to the Lord and receive spiritual healing.

57:20, 21 like the tossing sea. In contrast to those in v. 19, the wicked enjoy anything but peace (Jude 13). Cf. 48:22.

58:1–66:24 This section describes the future glory for God's people Israel.

58:1–5 A description of religious formalism that manifests itself in improper fasting.

58:1 Cry loudly. The prophet was to tell the people of Israel in plain language those areas of their behavior with which the Lord was displeased.

58:2 delight in the nearness of God. Israel was merely "going through the motions." Their appearance of righteousness was mere pretense (1:11).

58:3–7 Why ... ? The people complained when God did not recognize their religious actions, but God responded that their fastings had been only half-hearted. Hypocritical fasting resulted in contention, quarreling, and pretense, excluding the possibility of genuine prayer to God. Fasting consisted of more than just an outward ritual and a mock repentance. It involved penitence over sin and consequent humility, disconnecting from sin and oppression of others, feeding the hungry, and acting humanely toward those in need.

58:8 your righteousness ... rear guard. When Israel learned the proper way to fast, she would enjoy the blessings of salvation and the Messiah's kingdom (52:12).

58:9 Here I am. See 65:1. In contrast with the complaint of v. 3, a time will come when the Lord will be completely responsive to the prayers of His people (65:24). This will be done when they are converted and giving evidence of the transformation in the kind of works

10 And if you [a,A]give yourself to the hungry
And satisfy the [b]desire of the afflicted,
Then your [B]light will rise in darkness
And your gloom *will become* like midday.
11 "And the [A]LORD will continually guide you,
And [B]satisfy your [a]desire in scorched places,
And [C]give strength to your bones;
And you will be like a [D]watered garden,
And like a [E]spring of water
whose waters do not [b]fail.
12 "Those from among you will
[A]rebuild the ancient ruins;
You will [B]raise up the age-old foundations;
And you will be called the
repairer of the [C]breach,
The restorer of the [a]streets
in which to dwell.

KEEPING THE SABBATH

13 "If because of the sabbath,
you [A]turn your foot
From doing your *own* pleasure
on My holy day,
And call the sabbath a [B]delight, the
holy *day* of the LORD honorable,
And honor it, desisting from
your [C]*own* ways,
From seeking your *own* pleasure
And [D]speaking *your own* word,
14 Then you will take [A]delight in the LORD,
And I will make you ride [B]on
the heights of the earth;
And I will feed you *with* the
heritage of Jacob your father,
For the [C]mouth of the LORD has spoken."

SEPARATION FROM GOD

59 Behold, [A]the LORD'S hand is not so short
That it cannot save;
[B]Nor is His ear so dull
That it cannot hear.
2 But your [A]iniquities have made a
separation between you and your God,
And your sins have hidden *His* [a]face
from you so that He does [B]not hear.
3 For your [A]hands are defiled with blood
And your fingers with iniquity;
Your lips have spoken [B]falsehood,
Your tongue mutters wickedness.
4 [A]No one sues righteously and
[B]no one pleads [a]honestly.
They [C]trust in confusion and speak lies;
They [D]conceive mischief and
bring forth iniquity.
5 They hatch adders' eggs and
[A]weave the spider's web;
He who eats of their eggs dies,
And *from* that which is crushed
a snake breaks forth.
6 Their webs will not become clothing,
Nor will they [A]cover themselves
with their works;
Their [B]works are works of iniquity,
And an [C]act of violence is in their [a]hands.
7 [A]Their feet run to evil,
And they hasten to shed
innocent blood;
[B]Their thoughts are thoughts of iniquity,
Devastation and destruction
are in their highways.
8 They do not know the [A]way of peace,
And there is [B]no justice in their tracks;
They have made their paths crooked,
[C]Whoever treads on [a]them
does not know peace.

A CONFESSION OF WICKEDNESS

9 Therefore [A]justice is far from us,
And righteousness does not overtake us;
We [B]hope for light, but behold, darkness,
For brightness, but we walk in gloom.
10 We [A]grope along the wall like blind men,
We grope like those who have no eyes;
We [B]stumble at midday as in the twilight,
Among those who are vigorous
we are [C]like dead men.

58:10 [a]Lit *furnish* [b]Or *soul* [A]Deut 15:7; Is 58:7 [B]Job 11:17; Ps 37:6; Is 42:16; 58:8 58:11 [a]Or *soul* [b]Or *deceive* [A]Is 49:10; 57:18 [B]Ps 107:9; Is 41:17 [C]Is 66:14 [D]Song 4:15; Is 27:3; Jer 31:12 [E]John 4:14; 7:38 58:12 [a]Lit *paths* [A]Is 49:8; 61:4; Ezek 36:10 [B]Is 44:28 [C]Is 30:13; Amos 9:11 58:13 [A]Ex 31:16, 17; 35:2, 3; Is 56:2, 4, 6; Jer 17:21-27 [B]Ps 27:4; 42:4; 84:2, 10 [C]Is 55:8 [D]Is 59:13 58:14 [A]Job 22:26; Is 61:10 [B]Deut 32:13; 33:29; Is 33:16; Hab 3:19 [C]Is 1:20; 40:5 59:1 [A]Num 11:23; Is 50:2; Jer 32:17 [B]Is 58:9; 65:24; Ezek 8:18 59:2 [a]So versions; M.T. *faces* [A]Is 1:15; 50:1 [B]Is 58:4 59:3 [A]Is 1:15, 21; Jer 2:30, 34; Ezek 7:23; Hos 4:2 [B]Is 28:15; 30:9; 59:13 59:4 [a]Lit *in truth* [A]Is 5:7; 59:14 [B]Is 59:14, 15 [C]Is 30:12; Jer 7:4, 8 [D]Job 15:35; Ps 7:14; Is 33:11 59:5 [A]Job 8:14 59:6 [a]Lit *palms* [A]Is 28:20 [B]Is 57:12; Jer 6:7 [C]Is 58:4; Ezek 7:11 59:7 [A]Prov 1:16; 6:17; Rom 3:15-17 [B]Is 65:2; 66:18; Mark 7:21, 22 59:8 [a]Lit *it* [A]Luke 1:79 [B]Is 59:9, 11; Hos 4:1 [C]Is 57:20, 21 59:9 [A]Is 59:14 [B]Is 5:30; 8:21, 22 59:10 [A]Deut 28:29; Job 5:14 [B]Is 8:14, 15; 28:13 [C]Lam 3:6

that reflect a truly repentant heart (vv. 9, 10). At the time of Christ's return, Israel will demonstrate true repentance and the fullness of blessing will be poured out (vv. 10b, 11).

58:12 rebuild the ancient ruins. In view here is the final restoration of the millennial Jerusalem, of which Nehemiah's rebuilding of the walls (Ne 2:17) was only a foretaste (61:4; Am 9:11).

58:13 turn your foot … the sabbath. The Sabbath was holy ground on which no one should walk. Keeping the Sabbath was symbolic of obedience to all the law of Moses (56:2). For the setting aside of Sabbath law in the NT, *see notes on Ro 14:5, 6 and Col 2:16, 17.*

58:14 take delight in the LORD. Repentant people walking in fellowship with the Lord experience satisfaction of soul (Ps 37:4). Their satisfaction will not come from material goods (contra. 55:2).

59:1 LORD's hand … His ear. The Lord's strength is more than adequate to bring deliverance to captive Israel (50:2). His ear is attuned to the call of His repentant people (58:9; 65:24).

59:2 iniquities … sins. Abraham's physical lineage had not yet experienced the Lord's deliverance because of the barrier created by their wrongdoing. This is a universal truth applying to all men—sin separates people from God (cf. Ro 3:23).

59:5 adders' eggs … spider's web. It is sad when persons do evil, but even sadder when they delight in poisoning or ensnaring others with their evil habits (Ro 1:32). Israel had reached this latter state.

59:6 webs … works. Just as spiders' webs are too flimsy to serve as clothing, so were Israel's evil works. Spiritually, they did not suffice.

59:7, 8 Their feet … do not know … peace. From Isaiah's pen, the words focused on the national depravity of Israel that stood in the way of God's deliverance. Paul showed that what was true of sinful Israel is indicative of the depravity of all mankind (Ro 3:15–17).

59:10, 11 grope … stumble. Here is a picture of men seeking unsuccessfully to escape their depraved condition through their own strength. They wind up growling and lamenting their inability to gain salvation (Dt 28:29).

11 All of us growl like bears,
And [A]moan sadly like doves;
We hope for [B]justice, but there is none,
For salvation, *but* it is far from us.
12 For our [A]transgressions are
multiplied before You,
And our [B]sins [a]testify against us;
For our transgressions are with us,
And [b]we know our iniquities:
13 Transgressing and [A]denying the LORD,
And turning away from our God,
Speaking [B]oppression and revolt,
Conceiving *in* and [C]uttering from
the heart lying words.
14 [A]Justice is turned back,
And [B]righteousness stands far away;
For truth has stumbled in the street,
And uprightness cannot enter.
15 Yes, truth is lacking;
And he who turns aside from
evil [A]makes himself a prey.

Now the LORD saw,
And it was [a]displeasing in His sight
[B]that there was no justice.
16 And He saw that there was [A]no man,
And was astonished that there
was no one to intercede;
Then His [B]own arm brought
salvation to Him,
And His righteousness upheld Him.
17 He put on [A]righteousness
like a breastplate,
And a [B]helmet of salvation on His head;
And He put on [C]garments of
vengeance for clothing
And wrapped Himself with
[D]zeal as a mantle.
18 [A]According to *their* [a]deeds, [b]so He will repay,
Wrath to His adversaries,
recompense to His enemies;
To the coastlands He will
[c]make recompense.
19 So they will fear the name of
the LORD from the [A]west
And His glory from the [B]rising of the sun,
For He will [C]come like a [a]rushing stream
Which the wind of the LORD drives.
20 "A [A]Redeemer will come to Zion,
And to those who [B]turn from
transgression in Jacob,"
declares the LORD.

21 "As for Me, this is My [A]covenant with them," says
the LORD: "My [B]Spirit which is upon you, and My
[C]words which I have put in your mouth shall not depart from your mouth, nor from the mouth of your
[a]offspring, nor from the mouth of your [a]offspring's
offspring," says the LORD, "from now and forever."

A GLORIFIED ZION

60 "[A]Arise, shine; for your [B]light has come,
And the [C]glory of the LORD
has risen upon you.
2 "For behold, [A]darkness will cover the earth
And deep darkness the peoples;
But the LORD will rise upon you
And His [B]glory will appear upon you.
3 "[A]Nations will come to your light,
And kings to the brightness of your rising.

4 "[A]Lift up your eyes round about and see;
They all gather together, they [B]come to you.
Your sons will come from afar,
And your [C]daughters will be
[a]carried in the arms.

59:11 [A]Is 38:14; Ezek 7:16 [B]Is 59:9, 14 59:12 [a]Lit *answer* [b]Lit *our iniquities we know them* [A]Ezra 9:6; Is 58:1 [B]Is 3:9; Jer 14:7; Hos 5:5 59:13 [A]Josh 24:27; Prov 30:9; Matt 10:33; Titus 1:16 [B]Is 5:7; 30:12; Jer 9:3, 4 [C]Is 59:3, 4; Mark 7:21, 22 59:14 [A]Is 1:21; 5:7 [B]Is 46:12; Hab 1:4 59:15 [a]Or *evil* [A]Is 5:23; 10:2; 29:21; 32:7 [B]Is 1:21-23 59:16 [A]Is 41:28; 63:5; Ezek 22:30 [B]Ps 98:1; Is 52:10; 63:5 59:17 [A]Eph 6:14 [B]Eph 6:17; 1 Thess 5:8 [C]Is 63:2, 3 [D]Is 9:7; 37:32; Zech 1:14 59:18 [a]Lit *recompense* [b]Lit *accordingly* [c]Lit *repay* [A]Job 34:11; Is 65:6, 7; 66:6; Jer 17:10 59:19 [a]Lit *narrow* [A]Is 49:12 [B]Ps 113:3 [C]Is 30:28; 66:12 59:20 [A]Rom 11:26 [B]Ezek 18:30, 31; Acts 2:38, 39 59:21 [a]Lit *seed* [A]Jer 31:31-34; Rom 11:27 [B]Is 11:2; 32:15; 44:3 [C]Is 55:11 60:1 [A]Is 52:2 [B]Is 60:19, 20 [C]Is 24:23; 35:2; 58:8 60:2 [A]Is 58:10; Jer 13:16; Col 1:13 [B]Is 4:5 60:3 [A]Is 2:3; 45:14, 22-25; 49:23 60:4 [a]Lit *nursed upon the side* [A]Is 11:12; 49:18 [B]Is 49:20-22 [C]Is 43:6; 49:22

59:12–14 transgressions … sins. The prophet supplies the answer to the nation's frustrations: their sins and transgressions remain as an obstacle to God's deliverance. Though their external rituals may be proper, the hindrance of impure motives remains between God and His people (Mt 12:34; Mk 7:21, 22). The presence of iniquity eliminates righteousness.

59:15 makes himself a prey. In an environment where evil prevailed, anyone who departed from it became a victim of his environment because he did not fit in.

59:15, 16 the LORD saw … no one to intercede. The Lord was aware of Israel's tragic condition and of the absence of anyone to intervene on His behalf. The Lord took it on Himself to change Israel's condition through the intervention of His Suffering Servant (53:12).

59:17 righteousness like a breastplate … helmet of salvation. Figuratively speaking, the Lord armed Himself for the deliverance of His people and for taking vengeance on enemies who would seek His destruction. Paul drew on this terminology in describing a believer's spiritual preparation for warding off the attacks of Satan (Eph 6:14, 17; 1Th 5:8).

59:17, 18 garments of vengeance … recompense to His enemies. In the process of delivering the faithful remnant of Israel, the Lord executes decisive judgment against all rebellious nations ("coastlands") as well as the wicked Israelites (63:1–6).

59:19 they will fear. All surviving peoples throughout the world are to have added reason to worship the Lord, seeing how He defeated all enemies by the power of His Spirit in bringing salvation to His people Israel. All over the earth, submission to Him is to be the only path to survival in the coming kingdom.

59:20, 21 A Redeemer will come. The Messiah, the Suffering Servant, will redeem Zion and all faithful Israelites. This unalterable promise to the nation was the basis for Paul's reassurance of the future salvation of Israel (Ro 11:26, 27).

59:21 My covenant … forever. Because God's New Covenant with Israel is "everlasting" (55:3; cf. Jer 31:31–34), God's Spirit and His words are to remain objects of their attention continually.

60:1, 2 glory of the LORD … darkness … deep darkness … His glory. Addressing Zion (59:20; 60:14), Isaiah told the city and thus the nation Israel that her light has come, putting her in contrast with the rest of the darkened world. This expressed the glory of Jerusalem during the millennial kingdom.

60:3 Nations will come. Jerusalem's light will attract other nations seeking relief from their darkness (2:3). Only believing Jews and Gentiles will enter the earthly kingdom after the day of the Lord, but as the 1,000 years goes along children will be born, and nations will become populated by those who reject Jesus Christ. The glory of the King in Jerusalem and His mighty power will draw those Gentiles to His light.

60:4 gather … sons … daughters. Another promise of the regathering of Israel's faithful remnant (49:18, 22).

5 "Then you will see and be [A]radiant,
And your heart will [a]thrill and rejoice;
Because the [B]abundance of the
sea will be turned to you,
The [C]wealth of the nations
will come to you.
6 "A multitude of camels will cover you,
The young camels of Midian and [A]Ephah;
All those from [B]Sheba will come;
They will bring [C]gold and frankincense,
And will [D]bear good news of
the praises of the LORD.
7 "All the flocks of [A]Kedar will be
gathered together to you,
The rams of Nebaioth will
minister to you;
They will go up with acceptance
on My [B]altar,
And I shall [a,C]glorify My [b]glorious house.
8 "[A]Who are these who fly like a cloud
And like the doves to their [a]lattices?
9 "Surely the [A]coastlands will wait for Me;
And the [B]ships of Tarshish *will come* first,
To [C]bring your sons from afar,
Their silver and their gold with them,
For the name of the LORD your God,
And for the Holy One of Israel
because He has [a,D]glorified you.

10 "[A]Foreigners will build up your walls,
And their [B]kings will minister to you;
For in My [C]wrath I struck you,
And in My favor I have had
compassion on you.
11 "Your [A]gates will be open continually;
They will not be closed day or night,
So that *men* may [B]bring to you
the wealth of the nations,
With [C]their kings led in procession.
12 "For the [A]nation and the
kingdom which will not
serve you will perish,
And the nations will be
utterly ruined.
13 "The [A]glory of Lebanon will
come to you,
The [B]juniper, the box tree and
the cypress together,
To beautify the place of My sanctuary;
And I shall make the [C]place
of My feet glorious.
14 "The [A]sons of those who afflicted
you will come bowing to you,
And all those who despised
you will bow themselves
at the soles of your feet;
And they will call you the
[B]city of the LORD,
The [C]Zion of the Holy One of Israel.

15 "Whereas you have been
[A]forsaken and [B]hated
With no one passing through,
I will make you an everlasting [C]pride,
A joy from generation to generation.
16 "You will also [A]suck the milk of nations
And suck the breast of kings;
Then you will know that I, the
LORD, am your [B]Savior
And your [C]Redeemer, the
Mighty One of Jacob.
17 "Instead of bronze I will bring gold,
And instead of iron I will bring silver,
And instead of wood, bronze,
And instead of stones, iron.
And I will make peace your
administrators
And righteousness your overseers.

60:5 [a]Lit *tremble and be enlarged* [A]Ps 34:5 [B]Is 23:18; 24:14 [C]Is 61:6 60:6 [A]Gen 25:4 [B]Gen 25:3; Ps 72:10 [C]Is 60:9; Matt 2:11 [D]Is 42:10 60:7 [a]Or *beautify* [b]Or *beautiful* [A]Gen 25:13 [B]Is 19:19; 56:7 [C]Is 60:13; Hag 2:7, 9 60:8 [a]Or *dovecotes, windows* [A]Is 49:21 60:9 [a]Lit *beautified* [A]Is 11:11; 24:15; 42:4, 10, 12; 49:1; 51:5; 66:19 [B]Ps 48:7; Is 2:16 [C]Is 14:2; 43:6; 49:22 [D]Is 55:5 60:10 [A]Is 14:1, 2; 61:5; Zech 6:15 [B]Is 49:23; Rev 21:24 [C]Is 54:8 60:11 [A]Is 26:2; 60:18; 62:10; Rev 21:25, 26 [B]Is 60:5 [C]Ps 149:8; Is 24:21 60:12 [A]Is 14:2; Zech 14:17 60:13 [A]Is 35:2 [B]Is 41:19 [C]1 Chr 28:2; Ps 99:5; 132:7 60:14 [A]Is 14:1, 2; 45:14, 23; 49:23; Rev 3:9 [B]Is 1:26 [C]Heb 12:22 60:15 [A]Is 1:7-9; 6:11-13; Jer 30:17 [B]Is 66:5 [C]Is 4:2; 65:18 60:16 [A]Is 66:11 [B]Is 19:20; 43:3, 11; 45:15, 21; 63:8 [C]Is 59:20; 63:16

60:5 rejoice … wealth. Two more benefits of Israel's future kingdom will be rejoicing and an abundance of material possessions as symbolized in vv. 6, 7 (23:18; 24:14; 61:6).

60:6 Midian … Ephah … Sheba. The descendants of Midian, Abraham's son through Keturah (Ge 25:1, 2), inhabited the desert areas E of the Jordan River. Ephah was one of the sons of Midian (Ge 25:4) whose descendants settled on the E coast of the Elanitic Gulf. Sheba was a district in Arabia noted for its wealth (1Ki 10:1, 2).

60:7 Kedar … Nebaioth. The descendants of Kedar, a son of Ishmael (Ge 25:13), lived in the desert between Syria and Mesopotamia. The Nabateans, inhabitants of the Arabian city Petra, were probably the descendants of Nebaioth, the oldest son of Ishmael (Ge 25:13). **acceptance on My altar.** Animal sacrifices brought by other nations during the millennial kingdom will glorify the house of God's glory even more (v. 13). *See notes on Eze 40–48* for the description of the operation of sacrifices in the millennial temple.

60:8 fly like a cloud … doves. Figurative language to describe the rapid influx of Gentiles into Jerusalem.

60:9 coastlands … ships of Tarshish … your sons … silver … gold. Because of the Lord's favor toward Zion, the city will attract worldwide attention (23:1; 41:1). Trading vessels will return Israel's faithful remnant as they bring rich treasures to Jerusalem.

60:10 build up your walls. The rebuilding of Jerusalem's walls, helped by Persian kings, was merely a foretaste of the final rebuilding of the city assisted by Gentiles when Christ returns to earth. **in My wrath … in My favor.** God's past dealings with Israel have been largely in wrath, but His future merciful work will demonstrate His favor.

60:11 gates … open continually. Unrestricted access to Jerusalem will prevail in the future kingdom (26:2; 62:10; Rev 21:25, 26).

60:12 nation … perish. Survival in the future kingdom will be impossible for those nations who do not come to terms with Israel (11:13, 14; 14:2; 49:23). The Lord will rule the nations with a rod of iron (cf. Ps 2:7–12).

60:13 glory of Lebanon. Timber was Lebanon's claim to fame. As in Solomon's temple (1Ki 5:10, 18), but even more so, the timber taken from Lebanon's forests will enrich the Lord's temple in Jerusalem.

60:14 the city of the LORD. Nations which formerly were oppressors of Israel will acknowledge Zion's supremacy as the city that belongs to the Lord.

60:15 forsaken and hated … everlasting pride. Jerusalem will switch roles from having been despised to being exalted forever.

60:16 milk … breast. As a mother feeds her infant, so Gentiles and kings will provide wealth and power to Zion. The city will recognize the Lord as her Savior and Redeemer, "the Mighty One of Jacob," as will "all flesh" (49:26).

60:17 gold … silver … peace … righteousness. Jerusalem in the future kingdom will be a place of beauty and peace where right will prevail.

18 "[A]Violence will not be heard
again in your land,
Nor [B]devastation or destruction
within your borders;
But you will call your [C]walls salvation,
and your [D]gates praise.
19 "No longer will you have the
[A]sun for light by day,
Nor for brightness will the
moon give you light;
But you will have the [B]LORD
for an everlasting light,
And your [C]God for your [a]glory.
20 "Your [A]sun will no longer set,
Nor will your moon wane;
For you will have the LORD for
an everlasting light,
And the days of your
[B]mourning will be over.
21 "Then all your [A]people *will be* righteous;
They will [B]possess the land forever,
The branch of [a]My planting,
The [C]work of My hands,
That I may be [D]glorified.
22 "The [A]smallest one will become a [a]clan,
And the least one a mighty nation.
I, the LORD, will hasten it in its time."

EXALTATION OF THE AFFLICTED

61 The [A]Spirit of the Lord [a]GOD is upon me,
Because the LORD has anointed me
To [B]bring good news
to the [b,C]afflicted;
He has sent me to [D]bind up
the brokenhearted,
To [E]proclaim liberty to captives
And [c]freedom to prisoners;
2 To [A]proclaim the favorable
year of the LORD
And the [B]day of vengeance of our God;
To [C]comfort all who mourn,
3 To [A]grant those who mourn *in* Zion,
Giving them a garland instead of ashes,
The [B]oil of gladness instead
of mourning,
The mantle of praise instead
of a spirit of fainting.
So they will be called [a,C]oaks
of righteousness,
The planting of the LORD, that
He may be glorified.

4 Then they will [A]rebuild the ancient ruins,
They will raise up the former
devastations;
And they will repair the ruined cities,
The desolations of many generations.
5 [A]Strangers will stand and
pasture your flocks,
And [a]foreigners will be your farmers
and your vinedressers.
6 But you will be called the
[A]priests of the LORD;
You will be spoken of *as*
[B]ministers of our God.
You will eat the [C]wealth of nations,
And in their [a]riches you will boast.
7 Instead of your [A]shame *you will*
have a [B]double *portion,*
And *instead of* humiliation they will
shout for joy over their portion.
Therefore they will possess a
double *portion* in their land,
[C]Everlasting joy will be theirs.

60:18 [A]Is 54:14 [B]Is 51:19 [C]Is 26:1 [D]Is 60:11 60:19 [a]Or *beauty* [A]Rev 21:23; 22:5 [B]Is 2:5; 9:2 [C]Is 41:16; 45:25; Zech 2:5 60:20 [A]Is 30:26 [B]Is 35:10; 65:19; Rev 21:4 60:21 [a]Lit *His* [A]Is 45:24, 25; 52:1 [B]Ps 37:11, 22; Is 57:13; 61:7 [C]Is 19:25; 29:23; 45:11; 64:8 [D]Is 61:3 60:22 [a]Or *thousand* [A]Is 10:22; 51:2 61:1 [a]Heb *YHWH,* usually rendered *LORD* [b]Or *humble* [c]Lit *opening to those who are bound* [A]Is 11:2; 48:16; Luke 4:18 [B]Matt 11:5; Luke 7:22 [C]Is 11:4; 29:19; 32:7 [D]Is 57:15 [E]Is 42:7; 49:9 61:2 [A]Is 49:8; 60:10 [B]Is 2:12; 13:6; 34:2, 8 [C]Is 57:18; Jer 31:13; Matt 5:4 61:3 [a]Or *terebinths* [A]Is 60:20 [B]Ps 23:5; 45:7; 104:15 [C]Is 60:21; Jer 17:7, 8 61:4 [A]Is 49:8; 58:12; Ezek 36:33; Amos 9:14 61:5 [a]Lit *sons of the foreigner* [A]Is 14:2; 60:10 61:6 [a]Or *glory* [A]Is 66:21 [B]Is 56:6 [C]Is 60:5, 11 61:7 [A]Is 54:4 [B]Is 40:2; Zech 9:12 [C]Ps 16:11

60:18 salvation … praise. The walls and gates of the city that will take on those names refer to the divine protection the Lord provides from any form of violence or destruction.

60:19 No longer … have the sun … everlasting light. Isaiah, looking beyond the millennial kingdom, sees a view of the new Jerusalem following the Millennium (Rev 21:23; 22:5). His prophetic perspective did not allow him to distinguish the eternal phase of the future kingdom from the temporal one, just as the OT prophets could not distinguish between the first and second advent of Christ (cf. 1Pe 1:10, 11).

60:20 mourning will be over. In the eternal kingdom of the new creation, subjects will shed no more tears (Rev 21:4).

60:21 possess the land forever. Israel will inherit the land promised to Abraham (Ge 12:1, 7; 13:15; 15:18). During the millennial kingdom, that will be the land of Israel as we know it today. In the eternal kingdom, it will be the New Jerusalem, capital of the new creation. **I may be glorified.** The ultimate mission of Israel is to glorify the Lord (49:3; 61:3).

60:22 smallest one … mighty nation. Israel's great increase in numbers and power resulting from the Lord's working will bring them into never-before-experienced world prominence.

61:1, 2a The Spirit … favorable year of the LORD. The Servant of the Lord (42:1) will be the ultimate Preacher and the Redeemer of Israel who rescues them. Jesus speaks of the initial fulfillment of this promise, referring it to His ministry of providing salvation's comfort to the spiritually oppressed (Lk 4:18, 19). He says specifically, "Today this Scripture has been fulfilled in your hearing" (Lk 4:21). The Jews were saved during Christ's ministry, and those being saved during this church age, still do not fulfill the promise of the salvation of the nation to come in the end time (cf. Zec 12:10–13:1; Ro 11:25–27).

61:1 Spirit … Lord GOD … me. The 3 persons of the Holy Trinity function together in this verse (6:8; cf. Mt 3:16, 17). **liberty to captives.** The "captives" are Israelites remaining in the dispersion following the Babylonian captivity (42:7).

61:2 favorable year. The same as "a day of salvation" (49:8) and "My year of redemption" (63:4). This is where Jesus stopped reading in the synagogue (Lk 4:19), indicating that the subsequent writing in the rest of the chapter (vv. 2b–11) awaited the second coming of Christ. **day of vengeance.** As part of His deliverance of Israel, the Lord will pour out wrath on all who oppose Him (59:17–18). Cf. Rev 6–19.

61:3 grant … glorified. The purpose of the Lord's consolation of the mourners after centuries of suffering (60:20) will be to glorify Himself (60:21).

61:4 rebuild. The rebuilding of Israel's cities is part of God's future plan for the nation (49:8; 58:12; 60:10).

61:6 priests of the LORD. In fulfillment of Ex 19:6, Israel will be a kingdom of priests when Christ establishes His kingdom. In the meantime, Peter applied the same terminology to the church (1Pe 2:9).

61:7 double *portion*. Israel will receive double portions of blessing to replace the double punishment of her exile (40:2).

8 For I, the LORD, [A]love justice,
I hate robbery [a]in the burnt offering;
And I will faithfully give them
their recompense
And make an [B]everlasting
covenant with them.
9 Then their offspring will be
known among the nations,
And their descendants in the
midst of the peoples.
All who see them will recognize them
Because they are the [A]offspring
whom the LORD has blessed.

10 I will [A]rejoice greatly in the LORD,
My soul will exult in [B]my God;
For He has [C]clothed me with
garments of salvation,
He has wrapped me with a
robe of righteousness,
As a bridegroom decks himself
with a garland,
And [D]as a bride adorns herself
with her jewels.
11 For as the [A]earth brings
forth its sprouts,
And as a garden causes the things
sown in it to spring up,
So the Lord [a]GOD will [B]cause
[C]righteousness and praise
To spring up before all the nations.

ZION'S GLORY AND NEW NAME

62 For Zion's sake I will not keep silent,
And for Jerusalem's sake I
will not keep quiet,
Until her [A]righteousness goes
forth like brightness,
And her [B]salvation like a
torch that is burning.
2 The [A]nations will see your righteousness,
And all kings your glory;
And you will be called by a new [B]name
Which the mouth of the
LORD will designate.
3 You will also be a [A]crown of beauty
in the hand of the LORD,
And a royal [a]diadem in the
hand of your God.
4 It will no longer be said to you, "[a,A]Forsaken,"
Nor to your land will it any
longer be said, "[b]Desolate";
But you will be called, "[c]My delight is in her,"
And your land, "[d,B]Married";
For the [C]LORD delights in you,
And *to Him* your land will be married.
5 For *as* a young man marries a virgin,
So your sons will marry you;
And *as* the [a]bridegroom
rejoices over the bride,
So your [A]God will rejoice over you.

6 On your walls, O Jerusalem, I have
appointed [A]watchmen;
All day and all night they will
never keep silent.
You who [B]remind the LORD, take
no rest for yourselves;
7 And [A]give Him no rest until He establishes
And makes [B]Jerusalem a praise in the earth.
8 [A]The LORD has sworn by His right
hand and by His strong arm,
"I will [B]never again give your grain
as food for your enemies;
Nor will [a]foreigners drink your new
wine for which you have labored."
9 But those who [A]garner it will eat
it and praise the LORD;
And those who gather it will drink it
in the courts of My sanctuary.

10 Go through, [A]go through the gates,
Clear the way [a]for the people;
[B]Build up, build up the [C]highway,
Remove the stones, lift up a
[D]standard over the peoples.
11 Behold, the LORD has proclaimed
to the [A]end of the earth,
[B]Say to the daughter of Zion, "Lo,
your [C]salvation comes;

61:8 [a]Or *with iniquity* [A]Is 5:16; 28:17; 30:18 [B]Gen 17:7; Ps 105:10; Is 55:3; Jer 32:40 61:9 [A]Is 44:3 61:10 [A]Is 12:1, 2; 25:9; 41:16; 51:3 [B]Is 49:4 [C]Is 49:18; 52:1 [D]Rev 21:2 61:11 [a]Heb *YHWH*, usually rendered *LORD* [A]Is 4:2; 55:10 [B]Is 45:23, 24; 60:18, 21 [C]Ps 72:3; 85:11 62:1 [A]Is 1:26; 58:8; 61:11 [B]Is 46:13; 52:10 62:2 [A]Is 60:3 [B]Is 56:5; 62:4, 12; 65:15 62:3 [a]Lit *turban* [A]Is 28:5; Zech 9:16; 1 Thess 2:19 62:4 [a]I.e. Azubah [b]I.e. Shemamah [c]I.e. Hephzibah [d]I.e. Beulah [A]Is 54:6, 7; 60:15, 18 [B]Hos 2:19, 20 [C]Jer 32:41; Zeph 3:17 62:5 [a]Lit *exultation of the bridegroom* [A]Is 65:19 62:6 [A]Is 52:8; Jer 6:17; Ezek 3:17; 33:7 [B]Ps 74:2; Jer 14:21; Lam 5:1, 20 62:7 [A]Luke 18:1-8 [B]Is 60:18; Jer 33:9; Zeph 3:19, 20 62:8 [a]Lit *sons of foreigners* [A]Is 45:23; 54:9 [B]Lev 26:16; Deut 28:31, 33; Judg 6:3-6; Is 1:7; Jer 5:17 62:9 [A]Is 65:13, 21-23 62:10 [a]Lit *of* [A]Is 26:1; 60:11, 18 [B]Is 57:14 [C]Is 11:16; 19:23; 35:8; 49:11 [D]Is 11:10, 12; 49:22 62:11 [A]Is 42:10; 49:6 [B]Matt 21:5; Zech 9:9 [C]Is 51:5

61:8 everlasting covenant. This refers to the New Covenant. *See note on 55:3.*

61:10 clothed me … wrapped me. Here is the OT picture of imputed righteousness, the essential heart of the New Covenant. When a penitent sinner recognizes he can't achieve his own righteousness by works (*see notes on Ro 3:19–22; 2Co 5:21; Php 3:8, 9*), and repents and calls on the mercy of God, the Lord covers him with His own divine righteousness by grace through his faith.

62:1 not keep silent … not keep quiet. The Lord expresses His determination to make Jerusalem a lighthouse for the world (58:8; 60:1–3).

62:2 new name. Jerusalem's new name will reflect Israel's new favored status (vv. 4, 12; 65:15).

62:4 My delight is in her … Married. These terms reflect a full restored relationship with the Lord.

62:5 sons will marry you. "Marry" in the sense of occupying and possessing the city.

62:6, 7 never keep silent … give Him no rest. The prophets of Israel issued constant warnings about lurking enemies and prayed for Jerusalem to be "a praise" (60:18; 61:11). There will be more prophets in the kingdom who continually proclaim the honor of the Lord.

62:8, 9 The LORD has sworn. The end of foreign domination over Jerusalem is as certain as the oath of God.

62:9 courts of My sanctuary. This refers to the millennial temple (cf. Eze 40–46).

62:10 Clear the way. This and the accompanying commands prepare the people for the exaltation of Zion and the manifestation of her salvation (11:12; 40:3; 57:14).

62:11 Say to the daughter … Behold. Matthew may also have alluded to these words when he was quoting from Zec 9:9 as it related to Jesus' triumphal entry into Jerusalem (see Mt 21:5). **His reward … His recompense.** See 40:9, 10.

[D]Behold His reward is with Him, and
His recompense before Him."
12 And they will call them,
"[A]The holy people,
The [B]redeemed of the LORD";
And you will be called, "Sought
out, a city [C]not forsaken."

GOD'S VENGEANCE ON THE NATIONS

63 Who is this who comes from [A]Edom,
With [B]garments of [a]glowing
colors from [C]Bozrah,
This One who is majestic in His apparel,
[b]Marching in the greatness
of His strength?
"It is I who speak in righteousness,
[D]mighty to save."
2 Why is Your apparel red,
And Your garments like the one
who [A]treads in the wine press?
3 "[A]I have trodden the wine trough alone,
And from the peoples there
was no man with Me.
I also [B]trod them in My anger
And [C]trampled them in My wrath;
And [D]their [a]lifeblood is sprinkled
on My garments,
And I [b]stained all My raiment.
4 "For the [A]day of vengeance
was in My heart,
And My year of redemption has come.
5 "I looked, and there was [A]no one to help,
And I was astonished and there
was no one to uphold;
So My [B]own arm brought salvation to Me,
And My wrath upheld Me.
6 "I [A]trod down the peoples in My anger
And made them [B]drunk in My wrath,
And I [a]poured out their
lifeblood on the earth."

GOD'S ANCIENT MERCIES RECALLED

7 I shall make mention of the
[A]lovingkindnesses of the LORD,
the praises of the LORD,
According to all that the
LORD has granted us,
And the great [B]goodness toward
the house of Israel,
Which He has granted them
according to His [C]compassion
And according to the abundance
of His lovingkindnesses.
8 For He said, "Surely,
they are [A]My people,
Sons who will not deal falsely."
So He became their [B]Savior.
9 In all their affliction [a][A]He was afflicted,
And the [B]angel of His
presence saved them;
In His [C]love and in His mercy
He [D]redeemed them,
And He [E]lifted them and carried
them all the days of old.
10 But they [A]rebelled
And grieved His [B]Holy Spirit;
Therefore He turned Himself
to become their enemy,
He fought against them.
11 Then [A]His people remembered
the days of old, of Moses.
Where is [B]He who brought them
up out of the sea with the
[a]shepherds of His flock?
Where is He who [C]put His Holy
Spirit in the midst of [b]them,

62:11 [D]Is 40:10; Rev 22:12 62:12 [A]Deut 7:6; Is 4:3; 1 Pet 2:9 [B]Is 35:9; 51:10 [C]Is 41:17; 42:16; 62:4 63:1 [a]Or *crimson* [b]Lit *Inclining* [A]Ps 137:7; Is 34:5, 6; Ezek 25:12-14; 35:1-15; Obad 1-14; Mal 1:2-5 [B]Is 63:2 [C]Is 34:6; Jer 49:13; Amos 1:12 [D]Zeph 3:17 63:2 [A]Rev 19:13, 15 63:3 [a]Lit *juice* [b]Lit *defiled* [A]Rev 14:20; 19:15 [B]Is 22:5; 28:3 [C]Mic 7:10 [D]Rev 19:13 63:4 [A]Is 34:8; 35:4; 61:2; Jer 51:6 63:5 [A]Is 59:16 [B]Ps 44:3; Is 40:10; 52:10 63:6 [a]Lit *brought down their juice to the earth* [A]Is 22:5; 34:2; 65:12 [B]Is 29:9; 51:17, 21 63:7 [A]Ps 25:6; 92:2; Is 54:8, 10 [B]1 Kin 8:66; Neh 9:25, 35 [C]Ps 51:1; 86:5, 15; Is 54:7, 8; Eph 2:4 63:8 [A]Ex 6:7; Is 3:15; 51:4 [B]Is 60:16 63:9 [a]Another reading is *He was not an adversary* [A]Judg 10:16 [B]Ex 23:20-23; 33:14, 15 [C]Deut 7:7, 8 [D]Is 43:1; 52:9 [E]Deut 1:31; 32:10-12; Is 46:3 63:10 [A]Ps 78:40; 106:33; Acts 7:51; Eph 4:30 [B]Ps 51:11; Is 63:11 63:11 [a]Some mss read *shepherd* [b]Lit *him* [A]Ps 106:44, 45 [B]Is 51:10 [C]Num 11:17, 25, 29; Hag 2:5

62:12 a city not forsaken. See v. 4 and cf. Zion's complaint in 49:14.

63:1 Edom … Bozrah. Edom represents a God-hating world (34:5). Bozrah was a capital city in Edom at one time (34:6). Messiah, coming as the avenger approaching Jerusalem to reign after having avenged His people on His and their enemies, is presented in imagery taken from the destruction of Edom, the representative in this picture of the last and most bitter foes of God and His people. He alone is "mighty to save."

63:3 anger … wrath … lifeblood. The Savior explains the red coloring of His clothing (v. 2) as resulting from His judgmental activity against Israel's enemies (61:2). The splattered grape juice staining His clothing is, in reality, "blood" from those destroyed in judgment. John alludes to vv. 1–3 in describing the second coming of Christ, the Warrior-King. *See notes on Rev 19:13, 15.*

63:4 day of vengeance … My year of redemption. The Messiah's future reckoning with the wicked will coincide with His redemption of Israel (61:2).

63:5 no one to help … My own arm. The future salvation of Israel will be a singlehanded accomplishment of the Lord (v. 3; 59:15, 16).

63:6 made them drunk. See 51:17, 21–23. Revelation compares God's wrath to wine several times (e.g., Rev 14:10, 19; 16:19; 19:15).

63:7–64:12 As one of Israel's watchmen, Isaiah, on behalf of the faithful remnant, prays this penitential confession and prayer for Israel's restoration (cf. 62:6, 7).

63:7–14 The prayer reviews God's compassionate acts toward His people in spite of their unfaithfulness to Him.

63:7, 8 lovingkindnesses … lovingkindnesses. All the plurals in this verse imply that language is inadequate to recite all the goodness and undeserved mercies God has showered on the nation time after time because of His everlasting covenant with them. By His elective choice, they became His people and He their Savior (43:1, 3); this guarantees that they will not always be false, but someday true and faithful to God because of His sovereign election of them. Cf. Eph 1:3, 4.

63:9 angel of His presence. The angel, who delivered the Israelites from Egypt, was none other than the Lord Himself (Ex 14:19; 23:20–23; 33:12, 14, 15; Nu 20:16). He is sometimes identified as the Angel of the Lord. He was close enough to His people that He felt their afflictions as if they were His own. *See note on Ex 3:2.*

63:10 rebelled … grieved His Holy Spirit. In spite of the Lord's loving choice and sympathy, Israel continually turned their backs on Him and spurned His lovingkindnesses toward them (Nu 20:10; Pss 78:40; 106:33; Ac 7:51; cf. Eph 4:30). Here is an illustration of the reality that the Holy Spirit is a Person, since only a person can be grieved.

63:11–13 His people remembered … did not stumble. The Lord, in spite of their perversity, did not forget His covenant nor fully forsake them (Lv 26:40–45; Ps 106:45, 46). In

12 Who caused His [A]glorious arm to
go at the right hand of Moses,
Who [B]divided the waters before them to
make for Himself an everlasting name,
13 Who led them through the depths?
Like the horse in the wilderness,
they did not [A]stumble;
14 As the cattle which go down into the valley,
The Spirit of the [A]LORD gave [a]them rest.
So You [B]led Your people,
To make for Yourself a glorious name.

"YOU ARE OUR FATHER"

15 [A]Look down from heaven and see from
Your holy and glorious [B]habitation;
Where are Your [C]zeal and
Your mighty deeds?
The [D]stirrings of Your heart and Your
compassion are restrained toward me.
16 For You are our [A]Father, though
[B]Abraham does not know us
And Israel does not recognize us.
You, O LORD, are our Father,
Our [C]Redeemer from of old is Your name.
17 Why, O LORD, do You [A]cause us
to stray from Your ways
And [B]harden our heart from fearing You?
[C]Return for the sake of Your servants,
the tribes of Your heritage.
18 Your holy people possessed Your
sanctuary for a little while,
Our adversaries have [A]trodden *it* down.
19 We have become *like* those over
whom You have never ruled,
Like those who were not
called by Your name.

PRAYER FOR MERCY AND HELP

64 [a]Oh, that You would rend the
heavens *and* [A]come down,
That the mountains might
[B]quake at Your presence—
2 [a]As fire kindles the brushwood, *as*
fire causes water to boil—
To make Your name known
to Your adversaries,
That the [A]nations may tremble
at Your presence!
3 When You did [A]awesome things
which we did not expect,
You came down, the mountains
quaked at Your presence.
4 For from days of old [A]they have not
heard or perceived by ear,
Nor has the eye seen a
God besides You,
Who acts in behalf of the one
who [B]waits for Him.
5 You [A]meet him who rejoices in
[B]doing righteousness,
Who [C]remembers You in
Your ways.
Behold, [D]You were angry,
for we sinned,
We continued in them a long time;
And shall we be saved?
6 For all of us have become like
one who is [A]unclean,
And all our [B]righteous deeds
are like a filthy garment;
And all of us [C]wither like a leaf,
And our [D]iniquities, like the
wind, take us away.

63:12 [A]Ex 6:6; 15:16 [B]Ex 14:21, 22; Is 11:15; 51:10 63:13 [A]Jer 31:9 63:14 [a]Lit *him* [A]Josh 21:44; 23:1 [B]Deut 32:12 63:15 [A]Deut 26:15; Ps 80:14 [B]Ps 68:5; 123:1 [C]Is 9:7; 26:11; 37:32; 42:13; 59:17 [D]Jer 31:20; Hos 11:8 63:16 [A]Is 1:2; 64:8 [B]Is 29:22; 41:8; 51:2 [C]Is 41:14; 44:6; 60:16 63:17 [A]Is 30:28; Ezek 14:7-9 [B]Is 29:13, 14 [C]Num 10:36 63:18 [A]Ps 74:3-7; Is 64:11 64:1 [a]Ch 63:19b in Heb [A]Ex 19:18; Ps 18:9; 144:5; Mic 1:3, 4; Hab 3:13 [B]Judg 5:5; Ps 68:8; Nah 1:5 64:2 [a]Ch 64:1 in Heb [A]Ps 99:1; Jer 5:22; 33:9 64:3 [A]Ps 65:5; 66:3, 5; 106:22 64:4 [A]1 Cor 2:9 [B]Is 25:9; 30:18; 40:31 64:5 [A]Ex 20:24 [B]Is 56:1 [C]Is 26:13; 63:7 [D]Is 12:1 64:6 [A]Is 6:5 [B]Is 46:12; 48:1 [C]Ps 90:5, 6; Is 1:30 [D]Is 50:1

contrasting their present state of destitution with that of blessing experienced by Moses' generation, the people of Israel lamented the loss of God's mighty works on their behalf and pleaded with the Lord that He would not forsake them. **brought them up out of the sea ... put His Holy Spirit in the midst of them ... divided the waters.** Letting the people pass through the sea on dry ground was a typical mighty work of God (Ex 14:29, 30), and the Holy Spirit ministered among them (Nu 11:17, 25, 29). Another reference is made to the miracle of the Red Sea (Ex 14:21, 22).

63:14 make for Yourself a glorious name. The Lord's purpose for Israel was and is to make them great so as to magnify His name in the world. Cf. v. 12.

63:15–19 After having extolled God's goodness (vv. 7–9) and rehearsed God's past faithfulness to Israel for the sake of His glory (vv. 11–13), the prophet offered a prayer of repentance by the nation in its desolate condition.

63:15 Your compassion ... toward me. On behalf of the people, Isaiah asked if God had changed how He felt about Israel and prayed for new mercies such as He had exhibited toward the nation in the past.

63:16 Abraham ... Israel. The nation's physical ancestors, Abraham and Jacob (Israel), played a crucial role in Jewish thinking. It had been the besetting temptation and sin of the Jews to rest on the mere privilege of descent from Abraham and Jacob (cf. Mt 3:9; Jn 4:12; 8:39), but at last they renounce that to trust God alone as Father.

63:17 cause us to stray ... harden our heart. The sense is that God allowed them to stray and be burdened in their hearts. They were not denying their own guilt, but confessing that because of it, God gave them up to the consequences of their iniquitous choices. Cf. 6:9, 10; Ps 81:11, 12; Hos 4:17; Ro 1:24–28.

63:18 sanctuary ... trodden ... down. The Babylonians, among others, had possessed the land given to Israel and desecrated God's sanctuary (Ps 74:3–7).

63:19 never ... not called. Israel's complaint was that her desolate condition was comparable to that of nations who had no unique relationship with the Lord.

64:1–5 A plea for the Lord to demonstrate His power as He did in earlier days.

64:1, 2 rend the heavens ... quake at Your presence. Israel's response to her own complaint (63:19) was a plea that God would burst forth to execute vengeance suddenly on His people's foes (cf. Pss 18:7–9; 144:5; Hab 3:5, 6), manifesting Himself in judgment again as He did at Mt. Sinai (Ex 19:18; Jdg 5:5; Ps 68:8; Heb 12:18–20). As God's name is to receive glory through His redemption of Israel (63:14), it also is to have widespread recognition because of His judgment against Israel's enemies (Ps 99:1).

64:3 awesome things. Another reference to God's acts at Sinai (Dt 10:21).

64:4 ear ... eye. God's judgmental manifestations are unique. No one has witnessed the likes of His awesome works on behalf of His own. Paul adapts words from this verse to speak of direct revelation of God imparted to His apostles and prophets and pertaining to mysteries hidden from mankind before the birth of the church (1Co 2:9).

64:5 shall we be saved? Direct exposure to the awesome character of God's judgment brings a realization of sinners' need of salvation (cf. Ac 16:26–30).

64:6 unclean ... filthy garment. As in 53:6, the prophet included himself among those confessing their utter unworthiness to be in God's presence. Isaiah employed the imagery of menstrual cloths used during a woman's

7 There is [A]no one who calls on Your name,
Who arouses himself to take hold of You;
For You have [B]hidden Your face from us
And have [a]delivered us into the
power of our iniquities.
8 But now, O LORD, [A]You are our Father,
We are the [B]clay, and You our potter;
And all of us are the [C]work
of Your hand.
9 Do not be [A]angry beyond
measure, O LORD,
[B]Nor remember iniquity forever;
Behold, look now, all of us
are [C]Your people.
10 Your [A]holy cities have become
a [B]wilderness,
Zion has become a wilderness,
Jerusalem a desolation.
11 Our holy and beautiful [A]house,
Where our fathers praised You,
Has been burned *by* fire;
And [B]all our precious things
have become a ruin.
12 Will You [A]restrain Yourself at
these things, O LORD?
Will You keep silent and afflict
us beyond measure?

A REBELLIOUS PEOPLE

65 "I permitted Myself to be sought by
[A]those who did not ask *for Me;*
I permitted Myself to be found by
those who did not seek Me.
I said, 'Here am I, here am I,'
To a nation which [B]did not
call on My name.
2 "[A]I have spread out My hands all day
long to a [B]rebellious people,
Who walk *in* the way which is not good,
[a]following their own [C]thoughts,
3 A people who continually
[A]provoke Me to My face,
Offering sacrifices in [B]gardens and
[C]burning incense on bricks;
4 Who sit among graves and spend
the night in secret places;
Who [A]eat swine's flesh,
And the broth of unclean
meat is *in* their pots.
5 "Who say, '[A]Keep to yourself,
do not come near me,
For I am holier than you!'
These are smoke in My [a]nostrils,
A fire that burns all the day.
6 "Behold, it is written before Me,
I will [A]not keep silent, but [B]I will repay;
I will even repay into their bosom,
7 Both [a]their own [A]iniquities and
the iniquities of their fathers
together," says the LORD.
"Because they have [B]burned
incense on the mountains
And [C]scorned Me on the hills,
Therefore I will [D]measure their
former work into their bosom."

8 Thus says the LORD,

"As the new wine is found in the cluster,
And one says, 'Do not destroy it,
for there is [a]benefit in it,'
So I will act on behalf of My servants
In order [A]not to destroy [b]all of them.
9 "I will bring forth [A]offspring from Jacob,
And an [B]heir of My mountains from Judah;
Even [C]My chosen ones shall inherit it,
And [D]My servants will dwell there.

64:7 [a]Reading with the DSS and versions; M.T. *melted* [A]Is 59:4; Ezek 22:30 [B]Deut 31:18; Is 1:15; 54:8 64:8 [A]Is 63:16 [B]Is 29:16; 45:9 [C]Ps 100:3; Is 60:21 64:9 [A]Is 57:17; 60:10 [B]Is 43:25; Mic 7:18 [C]Ps 79:13; Is 63:8 64:10 [A]Is 48:2; 52:1 [B]Is 1:7; 6:11 64:11 [A]2 Kin 25:9; Ps 74:5-7; Is 63:18 [B]Lam 1:7, 10, 11 64:12 [A]Ps 74:10, 11, 18, 19; Is 42:14; 63:15 65:1 [A]Rom 9:24-26; 10:20 [B]Is 63:19; Hos 1:10 65:2 [a]Lit *after* [A]Rom 10:21 [B]Is 1:2, 23; 30:1, 9 [C]Ps 81:11, 12; Is 59:7; 66:18 65:3 [A]Job 1:11; 2:5; Is 3:8 [B]Is 1:29; 66:17 [C]Is 66:3 65:4 [A]Lev 11:7; Is 66:3, 17 65:5 [a]Lit *nose* [A]Matt 9:11; Luke 7:39; 18:9-12 65:6 [A]Ps 50:3, 21; Is 42:14; 64:12 [B]Jer 16:18 65:7 [a]Lit *your* [A]Is 13:11; 22:14; 26:21; 30:13, 14 [B]Is 57:7; Hos 2:13 [C]Ezek 20:27, 28 [D]Jer 5:29; 13:25 65:8 [a]Lit *blessing* [b]Lit *the whole* [A]Is 1:9; 10:21, 22; 48:9 65:9 [A]Is 45:19, 25; Jer 31:36, 37 [B]Is 49:8; 60:21; Amos 9:11-15 [C]Is 57:13 [D]Is 32:18

period to picture uncleanness (cf. Lv 15:19–24). This is true of the best behavior of unbelievers (cf. Php 3:5–8).

64:7–9 no one who calls. The prophet finds no exception among a people whose iniquities had separated them from God. *See notes on Ro 3:10–18.* Such seeking and calling on the Lord as Isaiah describes in 55:6, 7 cannot occur apart from the powerful conviction and awakening of the sinful heart by the Holy Spirit. Thus the prayer recognizes God as a potter in control of clay and pleads for Him to do a saving work (v. 8). Cf. 45:9, 10; 60:21; 63:16. Such a work is what God promised to end His fury (54:7, 8) and His memory of sin (v. 9; 43:25).

64:11 burned *by* fire … become a ruin. Through prophetic revelation Isaiah uttered these words many years before the fall of Jerusalem and the destruction of the temple in 586 B.C. Yet, he lamented over the fallen state as though it had already occurred. God's people were in desperate straits and their prayers urgent and persistent: "How can You stand by when Your people and Your land are so barren?"

65:1–7 In response to the prayer of 63:7–64:12, the Lord repeated the warnings of His judgment.

65:1 not ask … not seek … not call. Though Israel sought the Lord, they did so only superficially. They did not genuinely seek Him. The NT assigns an additional sense to the words in Ro 10:20, applying them to Gentiles who find Him through the work of His sovereign grace.

65:2 I have spread out … rebellious people. God had continually taken the initiative in inviting His people Israel to walk in His ways, but time after time they rebuffed Him. Using this verse, Paul concurred in citing the rebelliousness of his fellow Jews (Ro 10:21).

65:3, 4 Here Isaiah gave more references to Israel's sin, such as defiance in practicing idolatry, communing with the spirits of the dead (a forbidden practice according to Dt 18:10, 11), eating in ways forbidden by the Mosaic law (Lv 11:7, 8), consuming food connected with idol sacrifices, and the arrogance of self-righteousness (cf. Mt 9:11; Lk 5:30; 18:11).

65:5 smoke in My nostrils. This alluded to the smoke of their self-righteous sacrifices, an endless irritation to God who responds in judgment.

65:6 I will not keep silent. The Lord's response to the prayer asking Him not to restrain Himself in granting deliverance (64:12) was that He will act in judgment, not deliverance, to punish sin (v. 7).

65:8–10 In the midst of the final fury of judgment when the time of Jacob's trouble comes (cf. Jer 30:7) and God purges out the rebels in Israel (cf. Eze 20:38), there will also be the restoration of the faithful remnant to the land. Though judgment comes to the nation as a whole, God will spare and save

10 "[A]Sharon will be a pasture land for flocks,
And the [B]valley of Achor a
resting place for herds,
For My people who [C]seek Me.
11 "But you who [A]forsake the LORD,
Who forget My [B]holy mountain,
Who set a table for [a]Fortune,
And who fill *cups* with mixed
wine for [b]Destiny,
12 I will destine you for the [A]sword,
And all of you will bow down
to the [B]slaughter.
Because I called, but you
[C]did not answer;
I spoke, but you did not hear.
And you did evil in My sight
And chose that in which I did not delight."

13 Therefore, thus says the Lord [a]GOD,
"Behold, My servants will [A]eat,
but you will be [B]hungry.
Behold, My servants will [C]drink,
but you will be [D]thirsty.
Behold, My servants will [E]rejoice,
but you will be [F]put to shame.
14 "Behold, My servants will [A]shout
joyfully with a glad heart,
But you will [B]cry out with a [a]heavy heart,
And you will wail with a broken spirit.
15 "You will leave your name for a
[A]curse to My chosen ones,
And the Lord [a]GOD will slay you.
But [b]My servants will be called
by [B]another name.
16 "Because he who [a]is blessed in the earth
Will [a]be blessed by the [A]God of truth;
And he who swears in the earth
Will [B]swear by the God of truth;
Because the former troubles
are forgotten,
And because they are hidden
from My sight!

NEW HEAVENS AND A NEW EARTH

17 "For behold, I create [A]new
heavens and a new earth;
And the [B]former things will not be
remembered or come to [a]mind.
18 "But be [A]glad and rejoice forever
in what I create;
For behold, I create Jerusalem
for rejoicing
And her people *for* gladness.
19 "I will also [A]rejoice in Jerusalem
and be glad in My people;
And there will no longer be heard in her
The voice of [B]weeping and
the sound of crying.
20 "No longer will there be [a]in it an
infant *who lives but a few* days,
Or an old man who does [A]not
[b]live out his days;
For the youth will die at the
age of one hundred
And the [c,B]one who does not reach
the age of one hundred
Will be *thought* accursed.
21 "They will [A]build houses and inhabit *them;*
They will also [B]plant vineyards
and eat their fruit.
22 "They will not build and [A]another inhabit,
They will not plant and another eat;
For [B]as the [a]lifetime of a tree, *so*
will be the days of My people,
And My chosen ones will [C]wear
out the work of their hands.

65:10 [A]Is 33:9; 35:2 [B]Josh 7:24, 26; Hos 2:15 [C]Is 51:1; 55:6 65:11 [a]Heb *Gad* [b]Heb *Meni* [A]Deut 29:24, 25; Is 1:4, 28 [B]Is 2:2, 3; 66:20 65:12 [A]Is 27:1; 34:5, 6; 66:16 [B]Is 63:6 [C]2 Chr 36:15, 16; Prov 1:24; Is 41:28; 50:2; 66:4; Jer 7:13 65:13 [a]Heb *YHWH*, usually rendered *LORD* [A]Is 1:19 [B]Is 8:21 [C]Is 41:17, 18; 49:10 [D]Is 5:13 [E]Is 61:7; 66:14 [F]Is 42:17; 44:9, 11; 66:5 65:14 [a]Lit *pain of* [A]Ps 66:4; Is 51:11; James 5:13 [B]Is 13:6; Matt 8:12 65:15 [a]Heb *YHWH*, usually rendered *LORD* [b]So with Gr; Heb *He will call His servants* [A]Jer 24:9; 25:18; Zech 8:13 [B]Is 62:2 65:16 [a]Or *bless(es) himself* [A]Ex 34:6; Ps 31:5 [B]Is 19:18; 45:23 65:17 [a]Lit *heart* [A]Is 66:22; 2 Pet 3:13; Rev 21:1 [B]Is 43:18; Jer 3:16 65:18 [A]Ps 98; Is 12:1, 2; 25:9; 35:10; 41:16; 51:3; 61:10 65:19 [A]Is 62:4, 5; Jer 32:41 [B]Is 25:8; 30:19; 35:10; 51:11; Rev 7:17; 21:4 65:20 [a]Lit *from there* [b]Lit *fill out* [C]Lit *one who misses the mark* [A]Deut 4:40; Job 5:26; Ps 34:12 [B]Eccl 8:12, 13; Is 3:11; 22:14 65:21 [A]Is 32:18; Amos 9:14 [B]Is 30:23; 37:30; Jer 31:5 65:22 [a]Lit *days* [A]Is 62:8, 9 [B]Ps 92:12-14 [C]Ps 21:4; 91:16

(cf. Zec 12:10–13:1; Ro 11:25–27) the faithful remnant, "My servants" (1:9), in the future kingdom. This will include a physical return of God's elect, believing Jews, to the land of Israel (57:13).

65:10 Sharon ... valley of Achor. Sharon was the western fertile territory on the Mediterranean coast, S of Mt. Carmel (35:2). The eastern Valley of Achor was near Jericho and the Jordan River (Jos 7:24, 26). Together they represented the whole land.

65:11, 12 Another pronouncement of judgment was given on the rebellious Israelites, who resorted to the worship of pagan gods, like Fortune (Heb. Gad) and Destiny (Heb. Meni), and had no one to blame but themselves for the sword of damnation that fell on them.

65:13, 14 Continuing to address the rebel idolaters, the Lord Himself gave contrasts between the faithful and unfaithful of Israel.

65:15 your name for a curse ... another name. Israel's new name was to reflect her favored status among the nations (62:2–4). Delinquent Israelites, on the other hand, were to endure the reproach of men, so that the very name "Jew" would be disclaimed.

65:16 God of truth. Lit. this is "God of Amen," referring to the very God, the True God, who will honor His promises to Israel, thus vindicating Himself in the eyes of all people. Someday the rebels will be purged out, and the redeemed remnant will be left. In that time, all blessing and swearing will be by the one and only True God, because all idols will be vanquished and forgotten in the glory of the kingdom of Messiah.

65:17–25 The blessings of faithful Israel in the coming kingdom are described.

65:17 new heavens and a new earth. Israel's future kingdom will include a temporal kingdom of a thousand years (*see notes on Rev 20:1–10*) and an eternal kingdom in God's new creation (51:6, 16; 54:10; 66:22; cf. Rev 21:1–8). The prophet uses the eternal kingdom here as a reference point for both. Isaiah's prophecy does not make clear the relationship between the kingdom's two aspects as does later prophecy (Rev 20:1–21:8). This is similar to the compression of Christ's first and second advents, so that in places they are indistinguishable (cf. 61:1, 2).

65:20 No longer will ... an infant ... Or an old man. Long life will prevail in the millennial kingdom. In the temporal phase of the kingdom, death will happen, but not nearly so early as in the time of Isaiah. **accursed.** In the millennial phase of Israel's kingdom, a sinful person may die at age 100, but will be considered a mere youth at the time of his premature death. Having died an untimely death at such a youthful time, it will be assumed that God has taken his life for sin. The curse will be reversed in the Millennium, but it will not be removed until the eternal state (cf. Rev 22:3).

65:21, 22 build ... inhabit ... plant ... eat. Social justice will prevail in Israel's kingdom. No enemies will deprive people of what is rightfully theirs (contra. Dt 28:30).

23 "They will [A]not labor in vain,
Or bear *children* for calamity;
For they are the [a,B]offspring of
those blessed by the LORD,
And their descendants with them.

24 It will also come to pass that before they call, I
will [A]answer; and while they are still speaking, I will
hear. 25 The [A]wolf and the lamb will graze together,
and the [B]lion will eat straw like the ox; and [C]dust
will be the serpent's food. They will [D]do no evil or
harm in all My [E]holy mountain," says the LORD.

HEAVEN IS GOD'S THRONE

66

Thus says the LORD,
"[A]Heaven is My throne and the
earth is My footstool.
Where then is a [B]house you
could build for Me?
And where is a place that [a]I may rest?
2 "For [A]My hand made all these things,
Thus all these things came into
being," declares the LORD.
"But to this one I will look,
To him who is humble and
[B]contrite of spirit, and who
[C]trembles at My word.

HYPOCRISY REBUKED

3 "*But* he who kills an ox is *like*
one who slays a man;
He who sacrifices a lamb is *like* the
one who breaks a dog's neck;
He who offers a grain offering *is like*
one who offers [A]swine's blood;
He who [a,B]burns incense is *like* the
one who blesses an idol.
As they have chosen their [C]*own* ways,
And their soul delights in
their [D]abominations,
4 So I will [A]choose their [a]punishments
And will [B]bring on them what they dread.
Because I called, but [C]no one answered;
I spoke, but they did not listen.
And they did [D]evil in My sight
And chose that in which I did not delight."
5 Hear the word of the LORD, you
who [A]tremble at His word:
"Your brothers who [B]hate you, who
[C]exclude you for My name's sake,
Have said, 'Let the LORD be glorified,
that we may see your joy.'
But [D]they will be put to shame.
6 "A voice of uproar from the city,
a voice from the temple,
The voice of the LORD who is [A]rendering
recompense to His enemies.

7 "Before she travailed, [A]she brought forth;
Before her pain came, [B]she
gave birth to a boy.
8 "[A]Who has heard such a thing?
Who has seen such things?
Can a land be [a]born in one day?
Can a nation be brought forth all at once?
As soon as Zion travailed, she also
brought forth her sons.
9 "Shall I bring to the point of birth and
[A]not give delivery?" says the LORD.
"Or shall I who gives delivery shut
the womb?" says your God.

JOY IN JERUSALEM'S FUTURE

10 "Be [A]joyful with Jerusalem and rejoice
for her, all you who [B]love her;
Be exceedingly [C]glad with her, all
you who mourn over her,

65:23 [a]Lit *seed* [A]Deut 28:3-12; Is 55:2 [B]Is 61:9; Jer 32:38, 39; Acts 2:39 65:24 [A]Ps 91:15; Is 55:6; 58:9; Dan 9:20-23; 10:12 65:25 [A]Is 11:6 [B]Is 11:7 [C]Gen 3:14; Mic 7:17 [D]Is 11:9; Mic 4:3 [E]Is 65:11 66:1 [a]Lit *is My resting place?* [A]1 Kin 8:27; Ps 11:4; Matt 5:34, 35; 23:22 [B]2 Sam 7:5-7; Jer 7:4; John 4:20, 21; Acts 7:48-50 66:2 [A]Is 40:26 [B]Ps 34:18; Is 57:15; Matt 5:3, 4; Luke 18:13, 14 [C]Ps 119:120; Is 66:5 66:3 [a]Lit *offers a memorial of incense* [A]Is 65:4 [B]Lev 2:2; Is 1:13 [C]Is 57:17; 65:2 [D]Is 44:19 66:4 [a]Lit *ill treatments* [A]Prov 1:31, 32; Is 65:7 [B]Prov 10:24 [C]Prov 1:24; Is 65:12; Jer 7:13 [D]2 Kin 21:2, 6; Is 59:7; 65:12; Jer 7:30 66:5 [A]Is 66:2 [B]Ps 38:20; Is 60:15 [C]Matt 5:10-12; 10:22; John 9:34; 15:18-20 [D]Luke 13:17 66:6 [A]Is 59:18; 65:6; Joel 3:7 66:7 [A]Is 37:3; 54:1 [B]Rev 12:5 66:8 [a]Lit *travailed with* [A]Is 64:4 66:9 [A]Is 37:3 66:10 [A]Deut 32:43; Is 65:18; Rom 15:10 [B]Ps 26:8; 122:6 [C]Ps 137:6

65:23 for calamity. Lit. this means "for sudden death." Subjects in the kingdom will enjoy freedom from ordinary misfortunes related to the premature death of infants. There will be the lowest infant mortality rate ever. Along with longer life (v. 20), this means the earth will be greatly populated at an exponential rate of reproduction. Cf. Rev 20:7–9 for the massive collection of people at the end of the kingdom who come against Christ.

65:24 before they call ... while they are still speaking. Relationship with the Lord will be so close that He will anticipate and provide for every need (58:9).

65:25 wolf ... lamb ... lion ... ox ... serpent's. Dangers from the animal world will be nonexistent during the reign of the Servant of the Lord (11:6–9).

66:1, 2 Isaiah began the final summary of his prophecy with a reminder that God is not looking for a temple of stone, since as Creator of all things, the whole universe is His dwelling place. Stephen cited this passage before the Sanhedrin to point out their error in limiting God to a temple made with hands (Ac 7:49, 50). On the contrary, God is looking for a heart to dwell in, a heart that is tender and broken, not one concerned with the externalities of religion (cf. Mt 5:3–9). God is looking to dwell in the heart of a person who takes His Word seriously (cf. 66:5; Jn 14:23).

66:3 *like* one who slays a man. God loathes even the sacrifices of the wicked (cf. Pr 15:8; 28:9). They often killed children to offer in sacrifice (cf. Eze 23:39). Some of the Jews were offering bulls as sacrifices with the same empty heartedness as the pagans offering "a man" on the altar. **breaks a dog's neck.** This refers to offering dogs in sacrifice, which, as unclean (Jer 15:3; cf. 56:10, 11), are associated with swine (Mt 7:6; 2Pe 2:22). To sacrifice a lamb with an attitude no different than if it were a dog betrayed the emptyheartedness of the offerer. All of these images are meant to illustrate the shallow hypocrisy of one who makes an offering to God, but with no more heartbrokenness than a pagan who kills a child, offers a dog, sacrifices pig's blood, blesses an idol, and loves such abominations. God will judge such (v. 4).

66:5 Your brothers who hate you. The apostate Israelites intensified their rivalry with the faithful remnant (65:11–15) and blasphemously said, "Let the LORD be glorified," words uttered in the sarcastic spirit of 5:19 by these apostates. In the end, "they will be put to shame" because God's judgment will fall.

66:7–9 Here is another comparison with the human birth process (see 13:8), this time to teach two lessons: 1) no birth can come until labor pains have occurred (vv. 7, 8); and 2) when labor occurs, birth will surely follow (v. 9). Cf. Jer 30:6, 7; Mt 24:8; 1Th 5:3. The point is that Israel's suffering will end with a delivery! The Lord will not impose travail on the remnant without bringing them to the kingdom (v. 10).

11 That you may nurse and [A]be satisfied
with her comforting breasts,
That you may suck and be delighted
with her [B]bountiful bosom."
12 For thus says the LORD, "Behold, I
extend [A]peace to her like a river,
And the [B]glory of the nations like
an overflowing stream;
And you will [a]be nursed, you
will be [C]carried on the [b]hip
and fondled on the knees.
13 "As one whom his mother comforts,
so I will [A]comfort you;
And you will be comforted in Jerusalem."
14 Then you will [A]see *this,* and
your [B]heart will be glad,
And your [C]bones will flourish
like the new grass;
And the [D]hand of the LORD will be
made known to His servants,
But He will be [E]indignant
toward His enemies.
15 For behold, the LORD will come in [A]fire
And His [B]chariots like the whirlwind,
To render His anger with fury,
And His rebuke with flames of fire.
16 For the LORD will execute judgment by [A]fire
And by His [B]sword on all flesh,
And those slain by the LORD will be many.
17 "Those who sanctify and purify
themselves *to go* to the [A]gardens,
[a]Following one in the center,
Who eat [B]swine's flesh, detestable
things and mice,
Will [C]come to an end altogether,"
declares the LORD.

18 "For I [a]know their works and their [A]thoughts;
[b]the time is coming to [B]gather all nations and
tongues. And they shall come and see My glory.
19 I will set a [A]sign among them and will send survivors from them to the nations: [B]Tarshish, [a]Put, [C]Lud,
[b]Meshech, [D]Tubal and [c]Javan, to the distant [E]coast-
lands that have neither heard My fame nor seen My
glory. And they will [F]declare My glory among the
nations. 20 Then they shall [A]bring all your brethren
from all the nations as a grain offering to the LORD,
on horses, in chariots, in litters, on mules and on
camels, to My [B]holy mountain Jerusalem," says the
LORD, "just as the sons of Israel bring their grain
offering in a [C]clean vessel to the house of the LORD.
21 I will also take some of them for [A]priests *and* for
Levites," says the LORD.

22 "For just as the [A]new heavens
and the new earth
Which I make will endure before
Me," declares the LORD,
"So your [B]offspring and your
[C]name will endure.
23 "And it shall be from [A]new
moon to new moon
And from sabbath to sabbath,
All [a]mankind will come to
[B]bow down before Me,"
says the LORD.
24 "Then they will go forth and look
On the [A]corpses of the men
Who have [a,B]transgressed against Me.
For their [C]worm will not die
[D]And their fire will not be quenched;
And they will be an [E]abhorrence
to all [b]mankind."

66:11 [A]Is 49:23; 60:16; Joel 3:18 [B]Is 60:1, 2; 62:2 66:12 [a]Lit *nurse* [b]Lit *side* [A]Ps 72:3, 7; Is 48:18 [B]Is 60:5; 61:6 [C]Is 60:4 66:13 [A]Is 12:1; 40:1, 2; 49:13; 51:3; 2 Cor 1:3, 4 66:14 [A]Is 33:20 [B]Zech 10:7 [C]Prov 3:8; Is 58:11 [D]Ezra 7:9; 8:31 [E]Is 10:5; 13:5; 34:2 66:15 [A]Is 10:17; 30:27, 33; 31:9 [B]Ps 68:17; Is 5:28; Hab 3:8 66:16 [A]Is 30:30; Ezek 38:22 [B]Is 65:12; Ezek 38:21 66:17 [a]Lit *After* [A]Is 1:29; 65:3 [B]Lev 11:7; Is 65:4 [C]Is 1:28, 31 66:18 [a]So with Gr; Heb omits *know* [b]Lit *it is coming* [A]Is 59:7; 65:2 [B]Is 45:22-25; Jer 3:17 66:19 [a]So with Gr; Heb *Pul* [b]So with Gr; Heb *those who draw the bow* [c]I.e. Greece [A]Is 11:10, 12; 49:22; 62:10 [B]Is 2:16; 60:9 [C]Ezek 27:10 [D]Gen 10:2 [E]Is 11:11; 24:15; 60:9 [F]1 Chr 16:24; Is 42:12 66:20 [A]Is 43:6; 49:22; 60:4 [B]Is 2:2, 3; 11:9; 56:7; 65:11, 25 [C]Is 52:11 66:21 [A]Ex 19:6; Is 61:6; 1 Pet 2:5, 9 66:22 [A]Is 65:17; Heb 12:26, 27; 2 Pet 3:13; Rev 21:1 [B]Is 61:8, 9; 65:22, 23; John 10:27-29; 1 Pet 1:4, 5 [C]Is 56:5 66:23 [a]Lit *flesh* [A]Is 1:13, 14; Ezek 46:1, 6 [B]Is 19:21, 23; 27:13; 49:7 66:24 [a]Or *rebelled* [b]Lit *flesh* [A]Is 5:25; 34:3 [B]Is 1:28; 24:20 [C]Is 14:11; Mark 9:48 [D]Is 1:31; Matt 3:12 [E]Dan 12:2

66:11 nurse and be satisfied. The prophet compares Jerusalem to a nursing mother.

66:12 peace … like a river. The picture is of abundant peace that compares to a wadi filled with a rushing torrent of water.

66:14 to His servants … toward His enemies. Prosperity will belong to the faithful remnant, but wrath to those who oppose the Lord.

66:15 whirlwind … flames of fire. That the wrath of God will come to the rebels is expressed in language describing the end-time judgment (cf. 29:6).

66:16 slain … will be many. The many who fight against the Lord when He comes to establish His kingdom will die (34:6, 7; Rev 19:21).

66:17 sanctify and purify themselves. Sanctification and purification for right purposes are right, but when done for purposes of idol worship, will draw judgment from the one true God.

66:18 their works and their thoughts. The Lord was aware of the motivations behind the actions of apostate Israelites (v. 17). **gather all nations and tongues.** See 2:2–4. Jerusalem will be the center of world attention because of the presence of the Messiah there.

66:19 survivors. The faithful remnant of Israel are in view, who had escaped both the persecutions of their enemies and the judgment of God against those enemies (v. 16). **Tarshish, Put, Lud … Tubal and Javan.** Tarshish was possibly in Spain, Put and Lud in North Africa, Tubal in NE Asia Minor, and Javan in Greece. These were representative Gentile populations that will hear of God's glory through the faithful remnant.

66:20 bring all your brethren. As their offering to the Lord, the Gentiles who hear of God's glory will expedite the return of Israel's faithful remnant (43:6; 49:22).

66:21 for priests *and* for Levites. Some of the returning remnant will function in these specialized roles in the services of the millennial temple and memorial sacrifices (cf. Eze 44–46).

66:22 your offspring … endure. National Israel will have a never-ending existence through the Millennium, and on into the new heavens and the new earth throughout eternity.

66:23 All mankind … bow down before Me. All humanity will participate in worshiping the Lord at stipulated times during the temporal phase of the messianic kingdom.

66:24 worm will not die … fire will not be quenched. The corpses of those enduring everlasting torment will serve as a vivid reminder to all of the grievous nature and terrible consequences of rebellion against God. In referring to this verse, Jesus referred to the Valley of Hinnom—i.e., Gehenna—where a continually burning trash-heap pictured the never-ending pain of the lost (Mk 9:47, 48). *See note on Jer 19:6.*

THE BOOK OF JEREMIAH

TITLE

This book gains its title from the human author, who begins with "the words of Jeremiah . . . ." (1:1). Jeremiah recounts more of his own life than any other prophet, telling of his ministry, the reactions of his audiences, testings, and his personal feelings. His name means "Jehovah throws," in the sense of laying down a foundation, or "Jehovah establishes, appoints, or sends."

Seven other Jeremiahs appear in Scripture (2Ki 23:31; 1Ch 5:24; 12:4; 12:10; 12:13; Ne 10:2; 12:1), and Jeremiah the prophet is named at least 9 times outside of his book (cf. 2Ch 35:25; 36:12; 36:21, 22; Ezr 1:1; Da 9:2; Mt 2:17; 16:14; 27:9). The Old and New Testaments quote Jeremiah at least 7 times: 1) Da 9:2 (25:11, 12; 29:10); 2) Mt 2:18 (31:15); 3) Mt 27:9 (18:2; 19:2, 11; 32:6–9); 4) 1Co 1:31 (9:24); 5) 2Co 10:17 (9:24); 6) Heb 8:8–12 (31:31–34); and 7) Heb 10:16, 17 (31:33, 34).

AUTHOR AND DATE

Jeremiah, who served as both a priest and a prophet, was the son of a priest named Hilkiah (not the High Priest of 2Ki 22:8 who discovered the Book of the Law). He was from the small village of Anathoth (1:1), today called Anata, about 3 mi. NE of Jerusalem in Benjamin's tribal inheritance. As an object lesson to Judah, Jeremiah remained unmarried (16:1–4). He was assisted in ministry by a scribe, named Baruch, to whom Jeremiah dictated and who copied and had custody over the writings compiled from the prophet's messages (36:4, 32; 45:1). Jeremiah has been known as "the weeping prophet" (cf. 9:1; 13:17; 14:17), living a life of conflict because of his predictions of judgment by the invading Babylonians. He was threatened, tried for his life, put in stocks, forced to flee from Jehoiakim, publicly humiliated by a false prophet, and thrown into a pit.

Jeremiah carried out a ministry directed mostly to his own people in Judah, but which expanded to other nations at times. He appealed to his countrymen to repent and avoid God's judgment via an invader (chaps. 7, 26). Once invasion was certain after Judah refused to repent, he pled with them not to resist the Babylonian conqueror in order to prevent total destruction (chap. 27). He also called on delegates of other nations to heed his counsel and submit to Babylon (chap. 27), and he predicted judgments from God on various nations (25:12–38; chaps. 46–51).

The dates of his ministry, which spanned 5 decades, are from the Judean king Josiah's 13th year, noted in 1:2 (627 B.C.), to beyond the fall of Jerusalem to Babylon in 586 B.C. (Jer 39, 40, 52). After 586 B.C., Jeremiah was forced to go with a fleeing remnant of Judah to Egypt (Jer 43, 44). He was possibly still ministering in 570 B.C. (*see note on 44:29, 30*). A rabbinic note claims that when Babylon invaded Egypt in 568/67 B.C. Jeremiah was taken captive to Babylon. He could have lived even to pen the book's closing scene ca. 561 B.C. in Babylon, when Judah's king Jehoiachin, captive in Babylon since 597 B.C., was allowed liberties in his last days (52:31–34). Jeremiah, if still alive at that time, was between 85 and 90 years old.

BACKGROUND AND SETTING

Background details of Jeremiah's times are portrayed in 2Ki 22–25 and 2Ch 34–36. Jeremiah's messages paint pictures of: 1) his people's sin; 2) the invader God would send; 3) the rigors of siege; and 4) calamities of destruction. Jeremiah's message of impending judgment for idolatry and other sins was preached over a period of 40 years (ca. 627–586 B.C. and beyond). His prophecy took place during the reigns of Judah's final 5 kings (Josiah 640–609 B.C., Jehoahaz 609 B.C., Jehoiakim 609–598 B.C., Jehoiachin 598–597 B.C., and Zedekiah 597–586 B.C.).

The spiritual condition of Judah was one of flagrant idol worship (cf. chap. 2). King Ahaz, preceding his son Hezekiah long before Jeremiah in Isaiah's day, had set up a system of sacrificing children to the god Molech in the Valley of Hinnom just outside Jerusalem (735–715 B.C.). Hezekiah led in reforms and clean-up (Is 36:7), but his son Manasseh continued to foster child sacrifice along with gross idolatry, which continued into Jeremiah's time (7:31; 19:5; 32:35). Many also worshiped the "queen of heaven" (7:18; 44:19). Josiah's reforms, reaching their apex in 622 B.C., forced a repressing of the worst practices outwardly, but the deadly cancer of sin was deep and flourished quickly again after a shallow revival.

Religious insincerity, dishonesty, adultery, injustice, tyranny against the helpless, and slander prevailed as the norm not the exception.

Politically momentous events occurred in Jeremiah's day. Assyria saw its power wane gradually; then Ashurbanipal died in 626 B.C. Assyria grew so feeble that in 612 B.C. her seemingly invincible capital, Nineveh, was destroyed (cf. the book of Nahum). The Neo-Babylonian empire under Nabopolassar (625–605 B.C.) became dominant militarily with victories against Assyria (612 B.C.), Egypt (609–605 B.C.), and Israel in 3 phases (605 B.C., as in Da 1; 597 B.C., as in 2Ki 24:10–16; and 586 B.C., as in Jer 39, 40, 52).

While Joel and Micah had earlier prophesied of Judah's judgment, during Josiah's reign, God's leading prophets were Jeremiah, Habakkuk, and Zephaniah. Later, Jeremiah's contemporaries, Ezekiel and Daniel, played prominent prophetic roles.

HISTORICAL AND THEOLOGICAL THEMES

The main theme of Jeremiah is judgment upon Judah (chaps. 1–29) with restoration in the future messianic kingdom (23:3–8; 30–33). Whereas Isaiah devoted many chapters to a future glory for Israel (Is 40–66), Jeremiah gave far less space to this subject. Since God's judgment was imminent, he concentrated on current problems as he sought to turn the nation back from the point of no return.

A secondary theme is God's willingness to spare and bless the nation only if the people repent. Though this is a frequent emphasis, it is most graphically portrayed at the potter's shop (18:1–11). A further focus is God's plan for Jeremiah's life, both in his proclamation of God's message and in his commitment to fulfill all of His will (1:5–19; 15:19–21). Other themes include: 1) God's longing for Israel to be tender toward Him, as in the days of first love (2:1–3); 2) Jeremiah's servant tears, as "the weeping prophet" (9:1; 14:17); 3) the close, intimate relationship God had with Israel and that He yearned to keep (13:11); 4) suffering, as in Jeremiah's trials (11:18–23; 20:1–18) and God's sufficiency in all trouble (20:11–13); 5) the vital role that God's Word can play in life (15:16); 6) the place of faith in expecting restoration from the God for whom nothing is too difficult (chap. 32, especially vv. 17, 27); and 7) prayer for the coordination of God's will with God's action in restoring Israel to its land (33:3, 6–18).

INTERPRETIVE CHALLENGES

A number of questions arise, such as: 1) How can one explain God's forbidding prayer for the Jews (7:16) and saying that even Moses' and Samuel's advocacy could not avert judgment (15:1)? 2) Did Jeremiah make an actual trek of several hundred miles to the Euphrates River, or did he bury his loin cloth nearby (13:4–7)? 3) How could he utter such severe things about the man who announced his birth (20:14–18)? 4) Does the curse on Jeconiah's kingly line relate to Christ (22:30)? 5) How is one to interpret the promises of Israel's return to its ancient land (chaps. 30–33)? and 6) How will God fulfill the New Covenant in relation to Israel and the church (31:31–34)? The answers to these will be included in the study notes at the appropriate passages.

A frequent challenge is to understand the prophet's messages in their right time setting, since the book of Jeremiah is not always chronological, but loosely arranged, moving back and forth in time for thematic effect. Ezekiel, by contrast, usually places his material in chronological order.

OUTLINE

I. Preparation of Jeremiah (1:1–19)

- A. The Context of Jeremiah (1:1–3)
- B. The Choice of Jeremiah (1:4–10)
- C. The Charge to Jeremiah (1:11–19)

II. Proclamations to Judah (2:1–45:5)

- A. Condemnation of Judah (2:1–29:32)
    1. First message (2:1–3:5)
    2. Second message (3:6–6:30)
    3. Third message (7:1–10:25)
    4. Fourth message (11:1–13:27)
    5. Fifth message (14:1–17:18)
    6. Sixth message (17:19–27)
    7. Seventh message (18:1–20:18)
    8. Eighth message (21:1–14)
    9. Ninth message (22:1–23:40)
    10. Tenth message (24:1–10)
    11. Eleventh message (25:1–38)
    12. Twelfth message (26:1–24)
    13. Thirteenth message (27:1–28:17)
    14. Fourteenth message (29:1–32)
- B. Consolation to Judah—New Covenant (30:1–33:26)
    1. The forecast of restoration (30:1–31:40)
    2. The faith in restoration (32:1–44)
    3. The forecast of restoration—Part 2 (33:1–26)

- C. Calamity on Judah (34:1–45:5)
  - 1. Before Judah's fall (34:1–38:28)
  - 2. During Judah's fall (39:1–18)
  - 3. After Judah's fall (40:1–45:5)

III. Proclamations of Judgment on the Nations (46:1–51:64)

- A. Introduction (46:1; cf. 25:15–26)
- B. Against Egypt (46:2–28)
- C. Against Philistia (47:1–7)
- D. Against Moab (48:1–47)
- E. Against Ammon (49:1–6)
- F. Against Edom (49:7–22)
- G. Against Damascus (49:23–27)
- H. Against Kedar and Hazor [Arabia] (49:28–33)
- I. Against Elam (49:34–39)
- J. Against Babylon (50:1–51:64)

IV. The Fall of Jerusalem (52:1–34)

- A. The Destruction of Jerusalem (52:1–23)
- B. The Deportation of Jews (52:24–30)
- C. The Deliverance of Jehoiachin (52:31–34)

JEREMIAH'S CALL AND COMMISSION

1 The words of [A]Jeremiah the son of Hilkiah, of
the priests who were in [B]Anathoth in the land of
Benjamin, 2 to whom the word of the LORD came in
the days of [A]Josiah the son of [B]Amon, king of Judah,
in the [C]thirteenth year of his reign. 3 It came also
in the days of [A]Jehoiakim the son of Josiah, king of
Judah, until the end of the eleventh year of [B]Zede-
kiah the son of Josiah, king of Judah, until the exile
of Jerusalem in the fifth month.
4 Now the word of the LORD came to me saying,

5 "Before I [A]formed you in the
womb I knew you,
And [B]before you were born
I consecrated you;
I have [C]appointed you a
prophet to the nations."
6 Then [A]I said, "Alas, Lord [a]GOD!
Behold, I do not know how to speak,
Because [B]I am a youth."
7 But the LORD said to me,
"Do not say, 'I am a youth,'
[A]Because everywhere I send
you, you shall go,
And [B]all that I command
you, you shall speak.
8 "[A]Do not be afraid of them,
For [B]I am with you to deliver
you," declares the LORD.

9 Then the LORD stretched out His hand and
[A]touched my mouth, and the LORD said to me,

"Behold, I have [B]put My words
in your mouth.
10 "See, [A]I have appointed you this day over
the nations and over the kingdoms,
[B]To pluck up and to break down,
To destroy and to overthrow,
[C]To build and to plant."

THE ALMOND ROD AND BOILING POT

11 The word of the LORD came to me saying, "What
do you see, [A]Jeremiah?" And I said, "I see a rod of
an [a]almond tree." 12 Then the LORD said to me, "You

1:1 [A]2 Chr 35:25; 36:12, 21, 22; Ezra 1:1; Dan 9:2; Matt 2:17; 16:14; 27:9 [B]Josh 21:18; 1 Kin 2:26; 1 Chr 6:60; Is 10:30; Jer 11:21; 32:7 1:2 [A]1 Kin 13:2; 2 Kin 21:24; 22:3; 2 Chr 34:1; Jer 3:6; 36:2 [B]2 Kin 21:18, 24 [C]Jer 25:3 1:3 [A]2 Kin 23:34; 1 Chr 3:15; 2 Chr 36:5-8; Jer 25:1 [B]2 Kin 24:17; 1 Chr 3:15; 2 Chr 36:11-13; Jer 39:2 1:5 [A]Ps 139:15, 16 [B]Is 49:1, 5; Luke 1:15 [C]Jer 1:10; 25:15-26 1:6 [a]Heb *YHWH*, usually rendered *LORD* [A]Ex 4:10 [B]1 Kin 3:7 1:7 [A]Ezek 2:3, 4 [B]Num 22:20; Jer 1:17 1:8 [A]Ex 3:12; Deut 31:6; Josh 1:5; Jer 15:20 [B]Ezek 2:6 1:9 [A]Is 6:7; Mark 7:33-35 [B]Ex 4:11-16; Deut 18:18; Is 51:16 1:10 [A]Rev 11:3-6 [B]Jer 18:7-10; Ezek 32:18; 2 Cor 10:4 [C]Is 44:26-28; Jer 24:6; 31:28, 40 1:11 [a]Heb *shaqed* [A]Jer 24:3; Amos 7:8

1:1 Anathoth. A town in the territory of Benjamin, 3 mi. N of Jerusalem, assigned to the Levites (cf. Jos 21:18) where Abiathar had once lived (1Ki 2:26).

1:2 in the days of. Jeremiah's ministry spanned at least 5 decades—from Judah's king Josiah (13th year, 627 B.C.) to the final king, Zedekiah, in his last year (586 B.C.).

1:3 fifth month. Babylonian conquerors began deporting Judeans into captivity in the Heb. month Ab (July–Aug.) in 586 B.C. (52:12; 2Ki 25:8–11), shortly after breaking into Jerusalem on the fourth month and ninth day (39:2; 52:6).

1:5 Before I formed you. This is not reincarnation; it is God's all-knowing cognizance of Jeremiah and sovereign plan for him before he was conceived (cf. Paul's similar realization, Gal 1:15).

1:6 Jeremiah's response points out his inability and his inexperience. If as a young man he was 20–25 years old in 626 B.C., he was 60–65 in 586 B.C. when Jerusalem fell (chap. 39), and 85–90 if he lived to the time of 52:31–34 (ca. 561 B.C.).

1:7–10 The power backing Jeremiah's service was God's presence and provision (cf. 2Co 3:5).

1:9 My words in your mouth. God used him as His mouthpiece, speaking His message (15:19); thus, Jeremiah's fitting response was to receive God's Word (15:16).

1:10 appointed you ... over. Because God spoke through Jeremiah, the message has divine authority.

1:11–16 Illustrations of God's charge were twofold. First, there was the sign of the almond

ILLUSTRATIONS OF GOD'S JUDGMENT IN JEREMIAH

Illustration	Reference(s)
An Almond Branch	1:11, 12
A Boiling Caldron	1:13–16
Lions	2:15; 4:7; 5:6; 50:17
A Scorching Storm Wind	4:11, 12; 18:17; 23:19; 25:32
Wolf	5:6
Leopard	5:6
Stripping Away Judah's Branches	5:10
Fire	5:14
Making This House (Worship Center) like Shiloh	7:14
Serpents, Adders	8:17
Destroying Olive Branches	11:16–17
Uprooting	12:17
Linen Waistband Made Worthless	13:1–11
Jugs Filled with Wine and Dashed Against One Another	13:12–14
A Potter's Jar Shattered	19:10, 11; cf. 22:28
A Hammer [God's Word] Crushing a Rock	23:29
A Cup of Wrath	25:15
Zion Plowed as a Field	26:18
Wearing Yokes of Wood and Iron	27:2; 28:13
A Hammer [Babylon]	50:23
A Mountain of Destruction [Babylon]	51:25

have seen well, for [A]I am [a]watching over My word
to perform it."
13 The word of the LORD came to me a second
time saying, "[A]What do you see?" And I said, "I see
a boiling [B]pot, facing away from the north." 14 Then
the LORD said to me, "[A]Out of the north the evil [a]will
break forth on all the inhabitants of the land. 15 For,
behold, I am calling [A]all the families of the kingdoms of the north," declares the LORD; "and they
will come and they will [B]set each one his throne at
the entrance of the gates of Jerusalem, and against
all its walls round about and against all the [C]cities
of Judah. 16 I will [a]pronounce My judgments on
them concerning all their wickedness, whereby
they have [A]forsaken Me and have [b,B]offered sacrifices to other gods, and worshiped the [C]works of
their own hands. 17 Now, [A]gird up your loins and
arise, and speak to them all which I command you.
[B]Do not be dismayed before them, or I will dismay
you before them. 18 Now behold, I have made you
today as a fortified city and as a pillar of iron and
as walls of bronze against the whole land, to the
kings of Judah, to its princes, to its priests and to
the people of the land. 19 They will fight against you,
but they will not overcome you, for [A]I am with you
to deliver you," declares the LORD.

JUDAH'S APOSTASY

2 Now the word of the LORD came to me saying,
2 "Go and [A]proclaim in the ears of Jerusalem,
saying, 'Thus says the LORD,

"I remember concerning you the
[a,B]devotion of your youth,
The love of your betrothals,
[C]Your following after Me
in the wilderness,
Through a land not sown.
3 "Israel was [A]holy to the LORD,
The [B]first of His harvest.
[C]All who ate of it became guilty;
Evil came upon them,"
declares the LORD.' "

4 Hear the word of the LORD, O house of Jacob,
and all the families of the house of Israel. 5 Thus
says the LORD,

"[A]What injustice did your fathers find in Me,
That they went far from Me
And walked after [B]emptiness
and became empty?
6 "They did not say, 'Where is the LORD
Who [A]brought us up out of
the land of Egypt,
Who [B]led us through the wilderness,
Through a land of deserts and of pits,
Through a land of drought
and of [a]deep darkness,
Through a land that no one crossed
And where no man dwelt?'
7 "I brought you into the [A]fruitful land
To eat its fruit and its good things.
But you came and [B]defiled My land,
And My inheritance you made
an abomination.
8 "The [A]priests did not say,
'Where is the LORD?'
And those who handle the
law [B]did not know Me;
The [a]rulers also transgressed against Me,
And the [C]prophets prophesied by Baal
And walked after [D]things that did not profit.

9 "Therefore I will yet [A]contend with
you," declares the LORD,
"And with your sons' sons I will contend.
10 "For [A]cross to the coastlands
of [a]Kittim and see,
And send to [B]Kedar and observe closely
And see if there has been
such *a thing* as this!
11 "Has a nation changed gods
When [A]they were not gods?
But My people have [B]changed their glory
For that which does not profit.
12 "Be appalled, [A]O heavens, at this,
And shudder, be very desolate,"
declares the LORD.
13 "For My people have committed two evils:
They have forsaken Me,
The [A]fountain of living waters,
To hew for themselves [B]cisterns,
Broken cisterns
That can hold no water.

1:12 [a]Heb *shoqed* [A]Jer 31:28 1:13 [A]Zech 4:2 [B]Ezek 11:3, 7 1:14 [a]Lit *will be opened* [A]Is 41:25; Jer 4:6; 10:22 1:15 [A]Jer 25:9 [B]Is 22:7; Jer 39:3 [C]Jer 4:16; 9:11 1:16 [a]Lit *speak* [b]Or *burned incense* [A]Deut 28:20 [B]Jer 7:9; 19:4; 44:17 [C]Is 2:8; 37:19; Jer 10:3-5 1:17 [A]1 Kin 18:46; Job 38:3 [B]Ezek 2:6; 3:16-18 1:19 [A]Num 14:9; Jer 1:8; 20:11 2:2 [a]Or *lovingkindness* [A]Is 58:1; Jer 7:2; 11:6 [B]Ezek 16:8; Hos 2:15 [C]Deut 2:7; Jer 2:6 2:3 [A]Ex 19:5, 6; Deut 7:6; 14:2 [B]James 1:18; Rev 14:4 [C]Is 41:11; Jer 30:16; 50:7 2:5 [A]Is 5:4; Mic 6:3 [B]2 Kin 17:15; Jer 8:19; Rom 1:21 2:6 [a]Or *the shadow of death* [A]Ex 20:2; Is 63:11 [B]Deut 8:15; 32:10 2:7 [A]Deut 8:7-9; 11:10-12 [B]Ps 106:38; Jer 3:2; 16:18 2:8 [a]Lit *shepherds* [A]Jer 10:21 [B]Jer 4:22; Mal 2:7, 8 [C]Jer 23:13 [D]Jer 16:19; Hab 2:18 2:9 [A]Jer 2:35; Ezek 20:35, 36 2:10 [a]I.e. Cyprus and other islands [A]Is 23:12 [B]Ps 120:5; Is 21:16; Jer 49:28 2:11 [A]Is 37:19; Jer 5:7; 16:20 [B]Ps 106:20; Rom 1:23 2:12 [A]Is 1:2; Jer 4:23 2:13 [A]Ps 36:9; Jer 17:13; John 4:14 [B]Jer 14:3

rod. The almond tree was literally "the wakeful tree," because it awakened from the sleep of winter earlier than the other trees, blooming in Jan. It was a symbol of God's early judgment, as Jeremiah announced (605–586 B.C.). Second, the boiling pot pictured the Babylonian invaders bringing judgment on Judah (cf. 20:4).

1:17–19 Jeremiah's part was proclamation, as God's mouthpiece (v. 17); God's part was preservation in defending the prophet (vv. 18, 19). God did protect him often, e.g., 11:18–23; 20:1ff., and 38:7–13.

2:1–3 Jerusalem … Israel. Jeremiah pointed to the sensitivity of the Lord and His care for them in the early history (v. 21). After centuries, many were: 1) far from God, whom they had forsaken (vv. 5, 31); 2) deep in idolatry (vv. 11, 27, 28); and 3) without true salvation (as v. 8; 5:10a).

2:3 first of His harvest. Israel was first to worship the true God (Ex 19:5, 6) through His covenant with Abraham (Ge 12:1–3), which also assured His intent to bless peoples from all nations (16:19–21; Da 7:27).

2:8 priests … prophets. Leaders, who did not really know the Lord, set the idolatrous pattern for others (cf. Hos 4:6).

2:13 two evils. First, Israel had abandoned the Lord, the source of spiritual salvation and sustenance (cf. 17:8; Ps 36:9; Jn 4:14). Second, Israel turned to idolatrous objects of trust; Jeremiah compared these with underground water storage devices for rainwater, which were broken and let water seep out, thus proving useless.

14 "Is Israel [A]a slave? Or is he a
homeborn servant?
Why has he become a prey?
15 "The young [A]lions have roared at him,
They have [a]roared loudly.
And they have [B]made his land a waste;
His cities have been destroyed,
without inhabitant.
16 "Also the [a]men of [A]Memphis and Tahpanhes
Have [b]shaved the [B]crown of your head.
17 "Have you not [A]done this to yourself
By your forsaking the LORD your God
When He [A]led you in the way?
18 "But now what are you doing
[A]on the road to Egypt,
To drink the waters of the [a,B]Nile?
Or what are you doing on
the road to Assyria,
To drink the waters of the [b]Euphrates?
19 "[A]Your own wickedness will correct you,
And your [B]apostasies will reprove you;
Know therefore and see that
it is evil and [C]bitter
For you to forsake the LORD your God,
And [D]the dread of Me is not in you,"
declares the Lord [a]GOD of hosts.

20 "For long ago [a,A]I broke your yoke
And tore off your bonds;
But you said, 'I will not serve!'
For on every [B]high hill
And under every green tree
You have lain down as a harlot.
21 "Yet I [A]planted you a choice vine,
A completely faithful seed.
How then have you turned
yourself before Me
Into the [B]degenerate shoots
of a foreign vine?
22 "Although you [A]wash yourself with lye
And [a]use much soap,
The [B]stain of your iniquity is before
Me," declares the Lord [b]GOD.
23 "[A]How can you say, 'I am not defiled,
I have not gone after the [B]Baals'?
Look at your way in the [C]valley!
Know what you have done!
You are a swift young camel
[D]entangling her ways,
24 A [A]wild donkey accustomed
to the wilderness,
That sniffs the wind in her passion.
In *the time of* her [a]heat who
can turn her away?
All who seek her will not become weary;
In her month they will find her.
25 "Keep your feet from being unshod
And your throat from thirst;
But you said, '[A]It is [a]hopeless!
No! For I have [B]loved strangers,
And after them I will walk.'

26 "As the [A]thief is shamed when
he is discovered,
So the house of Israel is shamed;
They, their kings, their princes
And their priests and their prophets,
27 Who say to a tree, 'You are my father,'
And to a stone, 'You gave me birth.'
For they have turned *their* [A]back to Me,
And not *their* face;
But in the [B]time of their
[a]trouble they will say,
'Arise and save us.'
28 "But where are your [A]gods
Which you made for yourself?
Let them arise, if they can [B]save you
In the time of your [a]trouble;
For [C]*according to* the number of your cities
Are your gods, O Judah.

29 "Why do you contend with Me?
You have [A]all transgressed against
Me," declares the LORD.
30 "[A]In vain I have struck your sons;
They accepted no chastening.
Your [B]sword has devoured your prophets
Like a destroying lion.
31 "O generation, heed the word of the LORD.
Have I been a wilderness to Israel,
Or a [A]land of thick darkness?
Why do My people say, '[B]We
are free to roam;
We will no longer come to You'?
32 "Can a virgin forget her ornaments,
Or a bride her attire?
Yet My people have [A]forgotten Me
Days without number.

2:14 [A]Jer 5:19; 17:4 2:15 [a]Lit *given their voice* [A]Jer 50:17 [B]Jer 4:7 2:16 [a]Or *sons* [b]Lit *grazed* [A]Is 19:13; Jer 44:1; Hos 9:6 [B]Deut 33:20; Jer 48:45 2:17 [A]Deut 32:10; Jer 4:18 2:18 [a]Heb *Shihor* [b]Lit *River* [A]Is 30:2 [B]Josh 13:3 2:19 [a]Heb *YHWH*, usually rendered *LORD* [A]Is 3:9; Jer 4:18; Hos 5:5 [B]Jer 3:6, 8, 11, 14; Hos 11:7 [C]Job 20:12-16; Amos 8:10 [D]Ps 36:1; Jer 5:24 2:20 [a]Or *you* [A]Lev 26:13 [B]Deut 12:2; Is 57:5, 7; Jer 3:2, 6; 17:2 2:21 [A]Ex 15:17; Ps 44:2; 80:8; Is 5:2 [B]Is 5:4 2:22 [a]Lit *cause to be great to you* [b]Heb *YHWH*, usually rendered *LORD* [A]Jer 4:14 [B]Job 14:17; Hos 13:12 2:23 [A]Prov 30:12 [B]Jer 9:14 [C]Jer 7:31 [D]Jer 2:33, 36; 31:22 2:24 [a]Lit *occasion* [A]Jer 14:6 2:25 [a]Or *desperate* [A]Jer 18:12 [B]Deut 32:16; Jer 14:10 2:26 [A]Jer 48:27 2:27 [a]Or *evil* [A]Jer 18:17; 32:33 [B]Judg 10:10; Is 26:16 2:28 [a]Or *evil* [A]Deut 32:37; Judg 10:14; Is 45:20; Jer 1:16 [B]Jer 11:12 [C]2 Kin 17:30, 31; Jer 11:13 2:29 [A]Jer 5:1; 6:13; Dan 9:11 2:30 [A]Is 1:5; Jer 5:3; 7:28 [B]Neh 9:26; Jer 26:20-24; Acts 7:52; 1 Thess 2:15 2:31 [A]Is 45:19 [B]Deut 32:15; Jer 2:20, 25 2:32 [A]Ps 106:21; Is 17:10; Jer 3:21; 13:25; Hos 8:14

2:14 How is it that a people under God's special care are left at the mercy of an enemy, like a worthless slave?

2:15 young lions. The figure represents invading soldiers that burned cities (cf. 4:7), perhaps a reference to the disaster from the Babylonians during Jehoiakim's fourth year, and again 3 years later when he relied on Egypt (cf. 20:4; 46:2; 2Ki 24:1, 2).

2:16 Memphis … Tahpanhes. These two cities in Egypt stood for the country itself.

2:18 Dependence on alliances with Egypt and Assyria was part of national undoing, a source of shame (vv. 36, 37).

2:19 apostasies. Cf. 3:6, 8, 11, 12, 14, 22; 8:5; 31:22; 49:4; Is 57:17; Hos 11:7; 14:4. For clarification of the meaning, *see note on Pr 14:14*.

2:23 the Baals. An inclusive term referring collectively to false deities. **camel.** The nation, in chasing other idols, is depicted as a female camel pursuing its instinct, and as a wild donkey in heat sniffing the wind to find a mate, craving to attract others of its kind. Other pictures of Israel are that of a thief, who is ashamed when exposed (v. 26), and that of a virgin or a bride who forgets what beautifies her (v. 32).

33 "How well you prepare your way
To seek love!
Therefore even [a]the wicked women
You have taught your ways.
34 "Also on your skirts is found
The [A]lifeblood of the innocent poor;
You did not find them [B]breaking in.
But in spite of all these things,
35 Yet you said, 'I am innocent;
Surely His anger is turned
away from me.'
Behold, I will [A]enter into
judgment with you
Because you [B]say, 'I have not sinned.'
36 "Why do you [A]go around so much
Changing your way?
Also, [B]you will be put to shame by Egypt
As you were put to shame by [C]Assyria.
37 "From this *place* also you will go out
With [A]your hands on your head;
For the LORD has rejected [B]those
in whom you trust,
And you will not prosper with them."

THE POLLUTED LAND

3 *God* [a]says, "[A]If a husband divorces his wife
And she goes from him
And belongs to another man,
Will he still return to her?
Will not that land be
completely [b]polluted?
But you [B]are a harlot *with* many [c]lovers;
Yet you [C]turn to Me," declares the LORD.
2 "Lift up your eyes to the [A]bare
heights and see;
Where have you not been violated?
By the roads you have [B]sat for them
Like an Arab in the desert,
And you have [C]polluted a land
With your harlotry and with
your wickedness.
3 "Therefore the [A]showers have
been withheld,
And there has been no spring rain.
Yet you had a [B]harlot's forehead;
You refused to be ashamed.
4 "Have you not just now called to Me,
'[A]My Father, You are the
[a,B]friend of my [C]youth?
5 '[A]Will He be angry forever?
Will He [a]be indignant to the end?'
Behold, you have spoken
And have done evil things,
And you have [b]had your way."

FAITHLESS ISRAEL

6 Then the LORD said to me in the days of Josiah the king, "Have you seen what faithless Israel
did? She [A]went up on every high hill and under
every green tree, and she was a harlot there. 7 [A]I
[a]thought, 'After she has done all these things she
will return to Me'; but she did not return, and her
[B]treacherous sister Judah saw it. 8 And I saw that
for all the adulteries of faithless Israel, I had sent
her away and [A]given her a writ of divorce, yet her
[B]treacherous sister Judah did not fear; but she went
and was a harlot also. 9 Because of the lightness of
her harlotry, she [A]polluted the land and committed
adultery with [B]stones and trees. 10 Yet in spite of
all this her treacherous sister Judah did not return
to Me with all her heart, but rather in [A]deception,"
declares the LORD.

GOD INVITES REPENTANCE

11 And the LORD said to me, "[A]Faithless Israel has
proved herself more righteous than treacherous
Judah. 12 Go and proclaim these words toward the
north and say,

'[A]Return, faithless Israel,'
declares the LORD;
'[B]I will not [a]look upon you in anger.
For I am [C]gracious,' declares the LORD;
'I will not be angry forever.
13 'Only [a,A]acknowledge your iniquity,
That you have transgressed
against the LORD your God
And have [B]scattered your
[b]favors to the strangers
[C]under every green tree,
And you have not obeyed My
voice,' declares the LORD.
14 'Return, O faithless sons,'
declares the LORD;
'For I am a [A]master to you,
And I will take you one from a
city and two from a family,
And [B]I will bring you to Zion.'

2:33 [a]Or *in wickedness* 2:34 [A]2 Kin 21:16; 24:4; Ps 106:38; Jer 7:6; 19:4 [B]Ex 22:2 2:35 [A]Jer 25:31 [B]Prov 28:13; 1 John 1:8, 10 2:36 [A]Jer 2:23; 31:22; Hos 12:1 [B]Is 30:3 [C]2 Chr 28:16, 20, 21 2:37 [A]2 Sam 13:19; Jer 14:3, 4 [B]Jer 37:7-10 3:1 [a]Lit *saying* [b]Or *alienated* [c]Lit *companions* [A]Deut 24:1-4 [B]Jer 2:20; Ezek 16:26, 28, 29 [C]Jer 4:1; Zech 1:3 3:2 [A]Deut 12:2; Jer 2:20; 3:21; 7:29 [B]Gen 38:14; Ezek 16:25 [C]Jer 2:7 3:3 [A]Lev 26:19; Jer 14:3-6 [B]Jer 6:15; 8:12 3:4 [a]Lit *leader* [A]Jer 3:19; 31:9 [B]Ps 71:17; Prov 2:17 [C]Jer 2:2; Hos 2:15 3:5 [a]Lit *keep it* [b]Lit *been able* [A]Ps 103:9; Is 57:16; Jer 3:12 3:6 [A]Jer 17:2; Ezek 23:4-10 3:7 [a]Lit *said* [A]2 Kin 17:13 [B]Jer 3:11; Ezek 16:47 3:8 [A]Deut 24:1, 3; Is 50:1 [B]Ezek 16:46, 47; 23:11 3:9 [A]Jer 2:7; 3:2 [B]Is 57:6; Jer 2:27; 10:8 3:10 [A]Jer 12:2; Hos 7:14 3:11 [A]Ezek 16:51, 52; 23:11 3:12 [a]Lit *cause My countenance to fall* [A]Jer 3:14, 22; Ezek 33:11 [B]Jer 3:5 [C]Ps 86:15; Jer 12:15; 31:20; 33:26 3:13 [a]Lit *know* [b]Lit *ways* [A]Deut 30:1-3; Jer 3:25; 14:20; 1 John 1:9 [B]Jer 2:20, 25; 3:2, 6 [C]Deut 12:2 3:14 [A]Jer 31:32; Hos 2:19 [B]Jer 31:6, 12

3:1 If a husband divorces. Such a man was not to take that woman as his wife again, for this would defile her (Dt 24:4) and be a scandal. Jeremiah used this analogy to picture Israel as a harlot in the spiritual realm, with many lovers, i.e., nations (2:18, 25) and idols (2:23–25; 3:2, 6–9). Yet, the Lord would graciously receive Israel or Judah back as His wife if she would repent (3:12–14).

3:6 faithless. Also 3:8, 11, 12, 14. *See note on Pr 14:14.*

3:8 I had sent her away and given her a writ of divorce. Though God hates divorce (Mal 2:16), it is tolerated for unrepentant adultery (*see notes on Mt 5:32; 19:8, 9*), as indicated by this analogy of God's divorcing Israel for that continual sin in the spiritual realm. God had divorced Israel but not yet Judah (cf. Is 50:1). Cf. Ezr 10:3, where divorce is the right action of God's people to separate from idolatrous wives.

3:14 I am a master to you. God pictured His covenant relationship with Israel as a marriage, and pleaded with mercy for Judah to repent and return. He will take her back. Cf. Hosea's restoration of Gomer as a picture of God taking back His wicked, adulterous people.

15 "Then I will give you [A]shepherds after My own
heart, who will [B]feed you on knowledge and understanding. 16 It shall be in those days when you
are multiplied and increased in the land," declares
the LORD, "they will [A]no longer say, 'The ark of the
covenant of the LORD.' And it will not come to mind,
nor will they remember it, nor will they miss *it,* nor
will it be made again. 17 At that time they will call
Jerusalem 'The [A]Throne of the LORD,' and [B]all the
nations will be gathered to it, to Jerusalem, for the
[C]name of the LORD; nor will they [D]walk anymore after the stubbornness of their evil heart. 18 [A]In those
days the house of Judah will walk with the house of
Israel, and they will come together [B]from the land
of the north to the [C]land that I gave your fathers as
an inheritance.

19 "Then I said,

'How I would set you among [a]My sons
And give you a pleasant land,
The most [A]beautiful inheritance
of the nations!'
And I said, 'You shall call
Me, [B]My Father,
And not turn away from following Me.'

20 "Surely, as a woman treacherously
departs from her [a]lover,
So you have [A]dealt treacherously with Me,
O house of Israel," declares the LORD.

21 A voice is heard on the [A]bare heights,
The weeping *and* the supplications
of the sons of Israel;
Because they have perverted their way,
They have [B]forgotten the LORD their God.
22 "Return, O faithless sons,
[A]I will heal your faithlessness."
"Behold, we come to You;
For You are the LORD our God.
23 "Surely, [A]the hills are a deception,
A tumult *on* the mountains.
Surely in the [B]LORD our God
Is the salvation of Israel.

24 "But [A]the shameful thing has consumed the labor
of our fathers since our youth, their flocks and their
herds, their sons and their daughters. 25 Let us lie
down in our [A]shame, and let our humiliation cover
us; for we have sinned against the LORD our God, we
and our fathers, [B]from our youth even to this day. And
we have not obeyed the voice of the LORD our God."

JUDAH THREATENED WITH INVASION

4 "If you will [A]return, O Israel,"
declares the LORD,
"*Then* you should return to Me.
And [B]if you will put away your detested
things from My presence,
And will not waver,
2 And you will [A]swear, 'As the LORD lives,'
[B]In truth, in justice and in righteousness;
Then the [C]nations will bless
themselves in Him,
And [D]in Him they will glory."

3 For thus says the LORD to the men of Judah and
to Jerusalem,

"[a,A]Break up your fallow ground,
And [B]do not sow among thorns.
4 "[A]Circumcise yourselves to the LORD
And remove the foreskins of your heart,
Men of Judah and inhabitants of Jerusalem,
Or else My [B]wrath will go forth like fire
And burn with [C]none to quench it,
Because of the evil of your deeds."

5 Declare in Judah and proclaim
in Jerusalem, and say,
"[A]Blow the trumpet in the land;
Cry aloud and say,
'[B]Assemble yourselves, and let us go
Into the fortified cities.'
6 "Lift up a [A]standard toward Zion!
Seek refuge, do not stand *still,*
For I am bringing [B]evil from the north,
And great destruction.

3:15 [A]Jer 23:4; 31:10; Ezek 34:23; Eph 4:11 [B]Acts 20:28 3:16 [A]Is 65:17 3:17 [A]Jer 17:12; Ezek 43:7 [B]Jer 3:19; 4:2; 12:15, 16; 16:19 [C]Is 60:9 [D]Jer 11:8 3:18 [A]Is 11:13; Jer 50:4, 5; Hos 1:11 [B]Jer 16:15; 31:8 [C]Amos 9:15 3:19 [a]Lit *the* [A]Ps 16:6 [B]Is 63:16; Jer 3:4 3:20 [a]Or *companion* [A]Is 48:8 3:21 [A]Is 15:2; Jer 3:2; 7:29 [B]Is 17:10; Jer 2:32; 13:25 3:22 [A]Jer 30:17; 33:6; Hos 6:1; 14:4 3:23 [A]Jer 17:2 [B]Ps 3:8; Jer 17:14; 31:7 3:24 [A]Hos 9:10 3:25 [A]Ezra 9:6, 7 [B]Jer 22:21 4:1 [A]Jer 3:22; 15:19; Joel 2:12 [B]Jer 7:3, 7; 35:15 4:2 [A]Deut 10:20; Is 45:23; 65:16; Jer 12:16 [B]Is 48:1 [C]Gen 22:18; Jer 3:17; 12:15, 16; Gal 3:8 [D]Is 45:25; Jer 9:24; 1 Cor 1:31 4:3 [a]Lit *Plow for yourselves plowed ground* [A]Hos 10:12 [B]Matt 13:7 4:4 [A]Deut 10:16; 30:6; Jer 9:25, 26; Rom 2:28, 29; Col 2:11 [B]Is 30:27, 33; Jer 21:12; Zeph 2:2 [C]Amos 5:6; Mark 9:43, 48 4:5 [A]Jer 6:1; Hos 8:1 [B]Josh 10:20; Jer 8:14 4:6 [A]Is 62:10; Jer 4:21; 50:2 [B]Jer 1:14, 15; 6:1, 22

3:15–18 It shall be in those days. When Israel repents (vv. 13, 14, 22), which has not happened, but will in the millennial era of God's restoration that the prophets often describe (Jer 23:5, 6; 30–33; Eze 36), God will bring these blessings: 1) shepherds to teach them the truth; 2) His own immediate presence on the throne in Jerusalem, not just the ark of His covenant; 3) allegiance even of Gentile nations; 4) righteousness; 5) genuineness in worship; 6) unity of Israel (north) and Judah (south) into one kingdom; and 7) reestablishment in their own Promised Land.

3:19 set you among My sons. Here is a reference to adoption into God's family, when the people turn back from idols to acknowledge Him as "Father."

3:20 a woman treacherously departs. Hosea had earlier used this same imagery (ca. 755–710 B.C.). Thus God had given the divorce because the spiritual adultery was unrepentant. But when repentance comes, He will take Israel back (cf. 3:1). **O … Israel.** Since the irretrievable dispersion of Israel in the N (722 B.C.) Judah alone was left to be called by the name Israel, as Jeremiah sometimes chose to do (e.g., 3:20–23).

4:3 Break up. Jeremiah appealed for a spiritual turnabout from sinful, wasteful lives. He pictured this as the plowing of ground, formerly hard and unproductive due to weeds, in order to make it useful for sowing (cf. Mt 13:18–23).

4:4 Circumcise. This surgery (Ge 17:10–14) was to cut away flesh that could hold disease in its folds and could pass the disease on to wives. It was important for the preservation of God's people physically. But it was also a symbol of the need for the heart to be cleansed from sin's deadly disease. The really essential surgery needed to happen on the inside, where God calls for taking away fleshly things that keep the heart from being spiritually devoted to Him and from true faith in Him and His will. Jeremiah later expanded on this theme (31:31–34; cf. Dt 10:16; 30:6; Ro 2:29). God selected the reproductive organ as the location of the symbol for man's need of cleansing for sin, because it is the instrument most indicative of his depravity, since by it he reproduces generations of sinners.

4:6, 7 evil from the north. This evil is Babylon's army, which would invade from that direction. The "lion" on the prowl fit Babylon because of its conquering power, and Babylon was symbolized by the winged lions guarding

7 "A [A]lion has gone up from his thicket,
And a [B]destroyer of nations has set out;
He has gone out from his place
To [C]make your land a waste.
Your cities will be ruins
Without inhabitant.
8 "For this, [A]put on sackcloth,
Lament and wail;
For the [B]fierce anger of the LORD
Has not turned back from us."

9 "It shall come about in that day," declares the LORD,
"that the [A]heart of the king and the heart of the
princes will fail; and the priests will be appalled
and the [B]prophets will be astounded."
10 Then I said, "Ah, Lord [a]GOD! Surely You have
utterly [A]deceived this people and Jerusalem, saying,
'[B]You will have peace'; whereas a sword touches
the [b]throat."
11 In that time it will be said to this people and
to Jerusalem, "A [A]scorching wind from the bare
heights in the wilderness in the direction of the
daughter of My people—not to winnow and not to
cleanse, 12 a wind too strong for [a]this—will come [b]at
My command; now I will also pronounce judgments
against them.

13 "Behold, he [A]goes up like clouds,
And his [B]chariots like the whirlwind;
His horses are [C]swifter than eagles.
Woe to us, for [D]we are ruined!"

14 Wash your heart from evil, O Jerusalem,
That you may be saved.
How long will your [A]wicked thoughts
Lodge within you?
15 For a voice declares from [A]Dan,
And proclaims wickedness
from Mount Ephraim.
16 "Report *it* to the nations, now!
Proclaim over Jerusalem,
'Besiegers come from a [A]far country,
And [B]lift their voices against
the cities of Judah.
17 'Like watchmen of a field they are
[A]against her round about,
Because she has [B]rebelled against
Me,' declares the LORD.

18 "Your [A]ways and your deeds
Have [a]brought these things to you.
This is your evil. How [B]bitter!
How it has touched your heart!"

LAMENT OVER JUDAH'S DEVASTATION

19 [A]My [a]soul, my [a]soul! I am in
anguish! [b]Oh, my heart!
My [B]heart is pounding in me;
I cannot be silent,
Because [c]you have heard, O my soul,
The [C]sound of the trumpet,
The alarm of war.
20 [A]Disaster on disaster is proclaimed,
For the [B]whole land is devastated;
Suddenly my [C]tents are devastated,
My curtains in an instant.
21 How long must I see the standard
And hear the sound of the trumpet?
22 "[A]For My people are foolish,
They know Me not;
They are stupid children
And have no understanding.
They are shrewd to [B]do evil,
But to do good they do not know."

23 I looked on the earth, and behold,
it was [a,A]formless and void;
And to the heavens, and they had no light.
24 I looked on the mountains, and
behold, they were [A]quaking,
And all the hills [a]moved to and fro.
25 I looked, and behold, there was no man,
And all the [A]birds of the heavens had fled.
26 I looked, and behold, [a]the [A]fruitful
land was a wilderness,
And all its cities were pulled down
Before the LORD, before His fierce anger.

27 For thus says the LORD,
"The [A]whole land shall be a desolation,
Yet I will [B]not execute a
complete destruction.
28 "For this the [A]earth shall mourn
And the [B]heavens above be dark,
Because I have [C]spoken, I have purposed,
And I will not [a]change My mind,
nor will I turn from it."

4:7 [A]Jer 5:6; 25:38; 50:17 [B]Jer 25:9; Ezek 26:7-10 [C]Is 1:7; 6:11; Jer 2:15 4:8 [A]Is 22:12; Jer 6:26 [B]Is 5:25; 10:4; Jer 30:24 4:9 [A]Is 22:3-5; Jer 48:41 [B]Is 29:9, 10; Ezek 13:9-16 4:10 [a]Heb *YHWH*, usually rendered *LORD* [b]Or *life* [A]Ezek 14:9; 2 Thess 2:11 [B]Jer 5:12; 14:13 4:11 [A]Jer 13:24; 51:1; Ezek 17:10; Hos 13:15 4:12 [a]Lit *these* [b]Lit *for Me* 4:13 [A]Is 19:1; Nah 1:3 [B]Is 5:28; 66:15 [C]Lam 4:19; Hab 1:8 [D]Is 3:8 4:14 [A]Prov 1:22; Jer 6:19; 13:27; James 4:8 4:15 [A]Jer 8:16 4:16 [A]Is 39:3; Jer 5:15 [B]Ezek 21:22 4:17 [A]2 Kin 25:1, 4 [B]Is 1:20, 23; Jer 5:23 4:18 [a]Lit *done* [A]Ps 107:17; Is 50:1; Jer 2:17, 19 [B]Jer 2:19 4:19 [a]Lit *inward parts* [b]Lit *The walls of my heart* [c]Or *I, my soul, heard* [A]Is 15:5; 16:11; 21:3; 22:4; Jer 9:1, 10; 20:9 [B]Hab 3:16 [C]Num 10:9 4:20 [A]Ps 42:7; Ezek 7:26 [B]Jer 4:27 [C]Jer 10:20 4:22 [A]Jer 5:4, 21; 10:8; Rom 1:22 [B]Jer 9:3; 13:23; Rom 16:19; 1 Cor 14:20 4:23 [a]Or *a waste and emptiness* [A]Gen 1:2; Is 24:19 4:24 [a]Lit *moved lightly* [A]Is 5:25; Jer 10:10; Ezek 38:20 4:25 [A]Jer 9:10; 12:4; Zeph 1:3 4:26 [a]Or *Carmel* [A]Jer 9:10 4:27 [A]Jer 12:11, 12; 25:11 [B]Jer 5:10, 18; 30:11; 46:28 4:28 [a]Lit *be sorry* [A]Jer 12:4, 11; 14:2; Hos 4:3 [B]Is 5:30; 50:3; Joel 2:30, 31 [C]Num 23:19; Jer 23:20; 30:24

its royal court. Babylon is later identified in 20:4. Many details in chap. 4 graphically depict warriors in conquest (vv. 7, 13, 29).

4:10 deceived. Like Habakkuk (1:12–17), Jeremiah was horrified at these words of judgment, contrasting the prevailing hope of peace. God is sometimes described as if doing a thing He merely permits, such as allowing false prophets who delude themselves to also deceive a sinful people into thinking peace would follow (cf. 6:14; 8:11; 1Ki 22:21–24). God sees how people insist on their delusions, and lets it happen.

4:14 Wash. Jeremiah continued to appeal for a dealing with sin so that national destruction might be averted (v. 20), while there was still time to repent (cf. chaps. 7, 26).

4:22 shrewd to do evil. Israelites were wise or clever in doing evil but were dull in knowing to do the good, i.e., God's will. Paul, applying the principle but turning it to the positive, wanted the believers at Rome to be wise to do good but unlearned in the skill of doing evil (Ro 16:19).

4:23 formless. Jeremiah may be borrowing the language, but the description in its context is not of creation in Ge 1:2, but of judgment on the land of Israel and its cities (v. 20). The invader left it desolate of the previous form and void of inhabitants due to slaying and flight (v. 25). The heavens gave no light, possibly due to smoke from fires that were destroying cities (vv. 7, 20).

29 At the sound of the horseman and
bowman [A]every city flees;
They [B]go into the thickets and
climb among the rocks;
[C]Every city is forsaken,
And no man dwells in them.
30 And you, O desolate one,
[A]what will you do?
Although you dress in scarlet,
Although you decorate *yourself*
with ornaments of gold,
Although you [B]enlarge your
eyes with paint,
In vain you make yourself beautiful.
Your [a,C]lovers despise you;
They seek your life.
31 For I heard a [a]cry as of a woman in labor,
The anguish as of one giving
birth to her first child,
The [a]cry of the daughter of Zion
[A]gasping for breath,
[B]Stretching out her [b]hands, *saying,*
"Ah, woe is me, for [c]I faint
before murderers."

JERUSALEM'S GODLESSNESS

5 "[A]Roam to and fro through the
streets of Jerusalem,
And look now and take note.
And seek in her open squares,
If you can [B]find a man,
[C]If there is one who does justice,
who seeks [a]truth,
Then I will pardon her.
2 "And [A]although they say, 'As
the LORD lives,'
Surely they swear falsely."
3 O LORD, do not [A]Your eyes *look* for [a]truth?
You have [B]smitten them,
But they did not [b]weaken;
You have consumed them,
But they [C]refused to take correction.
They have [D]made their faces
harder than rock;
They have refused to repent.

4 Then I said, "They are only the poor,
They are foolish;
For they [A]do not know the way of the LORD
Or the ordinance of their God.
5 "I will go to the great
And will speak to them,
For [A]they know the way of the LORD
And the ordinance of their God."
But they too, with one accord,
have [B]broken the yoke
And burst the bonds.
6 Therefore [A]a lion from the
forest will slay them,
A [B]wolf of the deserts will
destroy them,
A [C]leopard is watching their cities.
Everyone who goes out of them
will be torn in pieces,
Because their [D]transgressions
are many,
Their apostasies are numerous.

7 "Why should I pardon you?
Your sons have forsaken Me
And [A]sworn by those who
are [B]not gods.
When I had fed them to the full,
They [C]committed adultery
And trooped to the harlot's house.
8 "They were well-fed lusty horses,
Each one neighing after his
[A]neighbor's wife.
9 "Shall I not punish [a]these *people,*"
declares the LORD,
"And on a nation such as this
[A]Shall I not avenge Myself?

10 "Go up through her vine
rows and destroy,
But do not execute a complete
destruction;
Strip away her branches,
For they are not the LORD'S.
11 "For the [A]house of Israel and
the house of Judah
Have dealt very treacherously
with Me," declares the LORD.
12 They have [A]lied about the LORD
And said, "[a,B]Not He;
Misfortune will [C]not come on us,
And we [D]will not see sword or famine.
13 "The [A]prophets are *as* wind,
And the word is not in them.
Thus it will be done to them!"

4:29 [A]2 Kin 25:4 [B]Is 2:19-21; Jer 16:16 [C]Jer 4:7 4:30 [a]Lit *paramours* [A]Is 10:3; 20:6; Jer 13:21 [B]2 Kin 9:30; Ezek 23:40 [C]Jer 22:20, 22; Lam 1:2, 19; Ezek 23:9, 10, 22 4:31 [a]Lit *sound* [b]Lit *palms* [c]Lit *my soul faints* [A]Is 42:14 [B]Is 1:15; Lam 1:17 5:1 [a]Lit *faithfulness* [A]2 Chr 16:9; Dan 12:4 [B]Ezek 22:30 [C]Gen 18:26, 32 5:2 [A]Is 48:1; Titus 1:16 5:3 [a]Lit *faithfulness* [b]Or *become sick* [A]2 Chr 16:9 [B]Is 1:5; 9:13; Jer 2:30 [C]Jer 7:28; 8:5; Zeph 3:2 [D]Jer 7:26; 19:15; Ezek 3:8 5:4 [A]Is 27:11; Jer 8:7; Hos 4:6 5:5 [A]Mic 3:1 [B]Ex 32:25; Ps 2:3; Jer 2:20 5:6 [A]Jer 4:7 [B]Ezek 22:27; Hab 1:8; Zeph 3:3 [C]Hos 13:7 [D]Jer 30:14, 15 5:7 [A]Josh 23:7; Jer 12:16; Zeph 1:5 [B]Deut 32:21; Jer 2:11; Gal 4:8 [C]Jer 7:9 5:8 [A]Jer 13:27; 29:23; Ezek 22:11 5:9 [a]Or *for these things* [A]Jer 9:9 5:11 [A]Jer 3:6, 7, 20 5:12 [a]Lit *He is not* [A]2 Chr 36:16 [B]Prov 30:9; Jer 14:22; 43:1-4 [C]Jer 23:17 [D]Jer 14:13 5:13 [A]Job 8:2; Jer 14:13, 15; 22:22

5:1 find a man. The city was too sinful to have even one man who, by truth and justice, could qualify to be an advocate to secure pardon for Judah. Refusal to repent was the norm (v. 3) for the common people (v. 4) and for the leaders (v. 5).

5:6 lion. Three animals which tear and eat their victims represented the invader: the lion (*see note on 4:6, 7*), the wolf, and the leopard, picturing vicious judgment on both poor (v. 4) and great (v. 5).

5:7 adultery. Often the idea of adultery is figurative for idolatry or political alliances (*see note on 3:1*), but the language here refers to physical adultery by men seeking out a prostitute or going to neighbors' wives (v. 8), thus violating the seventh commandment (Ex 20:14).

5:10 not the LORD's. The people, depicted as vine branches to be destroyed (cf. 11:16, 17), did not genuinely know the Lord in a saving relationship, but had forsaken Him and given allegiance to other gods. The description of having eyes but not seeing, and ears but not hearing (v. 21) is used by Isaiah (6:9) and Jesus Christ (Mt 13:13) for such false professors as these branches. Jesus also referred to false branches in Jn 15:2, 6 which were burned.

JUDGMENT PROCLAIMED

14 Therefore, thus says the LORD,
the God of hosts,
"Because you have spoken this word,
Behold, I am [A]making My words
in your mouth fire
And this people wood, and it
will consume them.
15 "Behold, I am [A]bringing a nation
against you from afar, O house
of Israel," declares the LORD.
"It is an enduring nation,
It is an ancient nation,
A nation whose [B]language
you do not know,
Nor can you understand what they say.
16 "Their [A]quiver is like an [B]open grave,
All of them are mighty men.
17 "They will [A]devour your harvest
and your food;
They will devour your sons
and your daughters;
They will devour your flocks
and your herds;
They will devour your [B]vines
and your fig trees;
They will demolish with the sword your
[C]fortified cities in which you trust.

18 "Yet even in those days," declares the LORD, "I
will not make you a complete destruction. 19 It shall
come about [A]when [a]they say, 'Why has the LORD our
God done all these things to us?' then you shall say
to them, 'As you have forsaken Me and served foreign gods in your land, so you will [B]serve strangers
in a land that is not yours.'

20 "Declare this in the house of Jacob
And proclaim it in Judah, saying,
21 'Now hear this, O foolish and
[a]senseless people,
Who have [A]eyes but do not see;
Who have ears but do not hear.
22 'Do you not [A]fear Me?' declares the LORD.
'Do you not tremble in My presence?
For I have [B]placed the sand as
a boundary for the sea,
An eternal decree, so it cannot cross over it.
Though the waves toss, yet
they cannot prevail;
Though they roar, yet they
cannot cross over it.
23 'But this people has a [A]stubborn
and rebellious heart;
They have turned aside and departed.
24 'They do not say in their heart,
"Let us now fear the LORD our God,
Who [A]gives rain in its season,
Both [B]the autumn rain and the spring rain,
Who keeps for us
The [C]appointed weeks of the harvest."
25 'Your [A]iniquities have turned these away,
And your sins have withheld
good from you.
26 'For wicked men are found
among My people,
They [A]watch like fowlers [a]lying in wait;
They set a trap,
They catch men.
27 'Like a cage full of birds,
So their houses are full of [A]deceit;
Therefore they have become great and rich.
28 'They are [A]fat, they are sleek,
They also [a]excel in deeds of wickedness;
They do not plead the cause,
The cause of the [b,B]orphan,
that they may prosper;
And they do not [c]defend the
rights of the poor.
29 '[A]Shall I not punish [a]these *people?*'
declares the LORD,
'On a nation such as this
Shall I not avenge Myself?'

30 "An appalling and [A]horrible thing
Has happened in the land:
31 The [A]prophets prophesy falsely,
And the priests rule [a]on
their *own* authority;
And My people [B]love it so!
But what will you do at the end of it?

DESTRUCTION OF JERUSALEM IMPENDING

6 "Flee for safety, O sons of [A]Benjamin,
From the midst of Jerusalem!
Now blow a trumpet in Tekoa
And raise a signal over [a,B]Beth-haccerem;
For evil looks down from the [C]north,
And a great destruction.

5:14 [A]Is 24:6; Jer 1:9; 23:29; Hos 6:5; Zech 1:6 5:15 [A]Deut 28:49; Is 5:26; Jer 4:16 [B]Is 28:11 5:16 [A]Is 5:28; 13:18 [B]Ps 5:9 5:17 [A]Lev 26:16; Deut 28:31, 33; Jer 8:16; 50:7, 17 [B]Jer 8:13 [C]Hos 8:14 5:19 [a]Or *you* [A]Deut 29:24-26; 1 Kin 9:8, 9; Jer 13:22; 16:10-13 [B]Deut 28:48; Jer 16:13 5:21 [a]Lit *without heart* [A]Is 6:9; 43:8; Ezek 12:2; Matt 13:14; Mark 8:18; John 12:40; Acts 28:26; Rom 11:8 5:22 [A]Deut 28:58; Ps 119:120; Jer 2:19; 10:7; Rev 15:4 [B]Job 38:8-11; Ps 104:9; Prov 8:29 5:23 [A]Deut 21:18; Ps 78:8; Jer 4:17; 6:28 5:24 [A]Ps 147:8; Jer 3:3; Matt 5:45; Acts 14:17 [B]Joel 2:23 [C]Gen 8:22 5:25 [A]Jer 2:17; 4:18 5:26 [a]Perhaps, *crouching down* [A]Ps 10:9; Prov 1:11; Jer 18:22; Hab 1:15 5:27 [A]Jer 9:6 5:28 [a]Lit *pass over,* or, *overlook deeds* [b]Or *fatherless* [c]Lit *judge* [A]Deut 32:15 [B]Is 1:23; Jer 7:6; 22:3; Zech 7:10 5:29 [a]Or *for these things* [A]Jer 5:9; Mal 3:5 5:30 [A]Jer 23:14; Hos 6:10 5:31 [a]Lit *over their own hands* [A]Ezek 13:6 [B]Mic 2:11 6:1 [a]I.e. house of the vineyard [A]Josh 18:28 [B]Neh 3:14 [C]Jer 1:14; 4:6; 6:22

5:14 My words ... fire. The judgment of Judah prophesied in God's Word by Jeremiah will bring destruction, but not elimination (v. 18), to the nation, cf. 23:29.

5:22 sand ... for the sea. God's providential acts in the natural world such as 1) creating the seashore to prevent flooding, 2) giving rain at the appropriate times (v. 24), and 3) providing time for harvest (v. 24) are witness enough to the Lord's reality and grace. As the nation turns away from God, He will take these unappreciated gifts away (v. 25).

5:31 prophesy falsely. These included prophets with bogus messages, priests who asserted their own authority, and also followers who indulged such falseness. All are guilty before God.

6:1 Tekoa ... Beth-haccerem. Tekoa, the home of Amos, is 6 mi. S of Bethlehem. The location of Beth-haccerem ("vineyard house") is unknown, but probably near Tekoa. As the enemy came from the N, the people would flee S. **north.** *See note on 4:6, 7.*

2 "The comely and [A]dainty one, [B]the
daughter of Zion, I will cut off.
3 "[A]Shepherds and their flocks will come to her,
They will [B]pitch *their* tents [a]around her,
They will pasture each in his [b]place.
4 "[a,A]Prepare war against her;
Arise, and let us [b]attack at [B]noon.
Woe to us, for the day declines,
For the shadows of the evening lengthen!
5 "Arise, and let us [a]attack by night
And [A]destroy her [b]palaces!"
6 For thus says the LORD of hosts,
"[A]Cut down her trees
And cast up a [B]siege against Jerusalem.
This is the city to be punished,
In whose midst there is only [C]oppression.
7 "[A]As a well [a]keeps its waters fresh,
So she [a]keeps fresh her wickedness.
[B]Violence and destruction are heard in her;
[C]Sickness and wounds are ever before Me.
8 "[A]Be warned, O Jerusalem,
Or [a,B]I shall be alienated from you,
And make you a desolation,
A land not inhabited."

9 Thus says the LORD of hosts,
"They will [A]thoroughly glean as the
vine the [B]remnant of Israel;
Pass your hand again like a grape gatherer
Over the branches."
10 To whom shall I speak and give warning
That they may hear?
Behold, their [A]ears are [a]closed
And they cannot listen.
Behold, [B]the word of the LORD has
become a reproach to them;
They have no delight in it.
11 But I am [A]full of the wrath of the LORD;
I am [B]weary with holding *it* in.
"[C]Pour *it* out on the children in the street
And on the [a]gathering of
young men together;
For both husband and wife shall be taken,
The aged [b]and the very old.
12 "Their [A]houses shall be turned over to others,
Their fields and their wives together;
For I will [B]stretch out My hand
Against the inhabitants of the
land," declares the LORD.
13 "For [A]from the least of them even
to the greatest of them,
Everyone is [B]greedy for gain,
And from the prophet even to the priest
Everyone [a]deals falsely.
14 "They have [A]healed the brokenness
of My people superficially,
Saying, 'Peace, peace,'
But there is no peace.
15 "Were they [A]ashamed because of the
abomination they have done?
They were not even ashamed at all;
They did not even know how to blush.
Therefore they shall fall
among those who fall;
At the time that I punish them,
They shall be cast down," says the LORD.

16 Thus says the LORD,
"Stand by the ways and see and
ask for the [A]ancient paths,
Where the good way is, and walk in it;
And [B]you will find rest for your souls.
But they said, 'We will not walk *in it.*'
17 "And I set [A]watchmen over you, *saying,*
'Listen to the sound of the trumpet!'
But they said, 'We will not listen.'
18 "Therefore hear, O nations,
And know, O congregation,
what is among them.
19 "[A]Hear, O earth: behold, I am bringing
disaster on this people,
The [B]fruit of their [a]plans,
Because they have not
listened to My words,
And as for My law, they have
[C]rejected it also.
20 "[A]For what purpose does [B]frankincense
come to Me from Sheba
And the [a,C]sweet cane from a distant land?
[D]Your burnt offerings are not acceptable
And your sacrifices are not
pleasing to Me."
21 Therefore, thus says the LORD,
"Behold, [A]I am [a]laying stumbling
blocks before this people.
And they will stumble against them,
[B]Fathers and sons together;
Neighbor and [b]friend will perish."

6:2 [A]Deut 28:56 [B]Is 1:8; Jer 4:31 6:3 [a]Lit *against her round about* [b]Lit *hand* [A]Jer 12:10 [B]2 Kin 25:1; Jer 4:17; Luke 19:43 6:4 [a]Lit *Sanctify* [b]Lit *go up* [A]Jer 6:23; Joel 3:9 [B]Jer 15:8; Zeph 2:4 6:5 [a]Lit *go up* [b]Or *fortified towers* [A]Is 32:14; Jer 52:13 6:6 [A]Deut 20:19, 20 [B]Jer 32:24; 33:4 [C]Jer 22:17 6:7 [a]Lit *keeps cold* [A]James 3:11f [B]Jer 20:8; Ezek 7:11, 23 [C]Jer 30:12, 13 6:8 [a]Lit *my soul* [A]Jer 7:28; 17:23 [B]Ezek 23:18; Hos 9:12 6:9 [A]Jer 16:16; 49:9; Obad 5, 6 [B]Jer 8:3; 11:23 6:10 [a]Lit *uncircumcised* [A]Jer 5:21; 7:26; Acts 7:51 [B]Jer 20:8 6:11 [a]Lit *council* [b]Lit *with fullness of days* [A]Job 32:18, 19; Mic 3:8 [B]Jer 15:6; 20:9 [C]Jer 7:20; 9:21 6:12 [A]Deut 28:30; Jer 8:10; 38:22, 23 [B]Jer 15:6 6:13 [a]Or *makes lies* [A]Jer 8:10 [B]Is 56:11; 57:17; Jer 8:10; 22:17 6:14 [A]Jer 8:11; Ezek 13:10 6:15 [A]Jer 3:3; 8:12 6:16 [A]Is 8:20; Jer 12:16; 18:15; 31:21; Mal 4:4; Luke 16:29 [B]Matt 11:29 6:17 [A]Is 21:11; 58:1; Jer 25:4; Ezek 3:17; Hab 2:1 6:19 [a]Or *devices* [A]Is 1:2; Jer 19:3, 15; 22:29 [B]Prov 1:31 [C]Jer 8:9 6:20 [a]Lit *good* [A]Ps 50:7-9; Is 1:11; 66:3; Mic 6:6 [B]Is 60:6 [C]Ex 30:23 [D]Ps 40:6; Amos 5:22 6:21 [a]Lit *giving* [b]Lit *his friend* [A]Is 8:14; Jer 13:16 [B]Is 9:14-17; Jer 9:21, 22

6:3 Shepherds. These were hostile leaders of the invading Babylonians, whose soldiers were compared with flocks.

6:6 Cut down her trees. A besieging tactic is described in which trees were used to build up ramps against the city walls.

6:9 thoroughly glean. Unlike the benevolent practice of leaving food in the field for the poor to glean (Lv 19:9, 10; Ru 2:5–18), the Babylonians will leave no one when they "harvest" Judah.

6:14 Peace, peace. Wicked leaders among the prophets and priests (v. 13) proclaimed peace falsely and gave weak and brief comfort. They provided no true healing from the spiritual wound, not having discernment to deal with the sin and its effects (v. 15). The need was to return to obedience (v. 16). Cf. 8:11.

6:16 Here is the image of travelers who are lost, stopping to inquire about the right way they once knew before they wandered so far off it.

6:17 watchmen. Prophets.

6:20 not acceptable. Using imported fragrances in their offerings did not make them sweetly acceptable to God when the worshipers rejected His Word (v. 19).

6:21 stumbling blocks. Cf. Is 8:14; Mt 21:44; 1Pe 2:8.

THE ENEMY FROM THE NORTH

22 Thus says the LORD,
"Behold, [A]a people is coming
from the north land,
And a great nation will be
aroused from the [B]remote
parts of the earth.
23 "They seize [A]bow and spear;
They are [B]cruel and have no mercy;
Their voice [C]roars like the sea,
And they ride on horses,
Arrayed as a man for the battle
Against you, O daughter of Zion!"
24 We have [A]heard the report of it;
Our hands are limp.
[B]Anguish has seized us,
Pain as of a woman in childbirth.
25 [A]Do not go out into the field
And [B]do not walk on the road,
For the enemy has a sword,
[C]Terror is on every side.
26 O daughter of my people,
[A]put on sackcloth
And [B]roll in ashes;
[a,C]Mourn as for an only son,
A lamentation most bitter.
For suddenly the destroyer
Will come upon us.

27 "I have [A]made you an assayer *and*
a tester among My people,
That you may know and
assay their way."
28 All of them are stubbornly rebellious,
[A]Going about as a talebearer.
They are [B]bronze and iron;
They, all of them, are corrupt.
29 The bellows blow fiercely,
The lead is consumed by the fire;
In vain the refining goes on,
But the [A]wicked are not [a]separated.
30 [A]They call them rejected silver,
Because the [B]LORD has rejected them.

MESSAGE AT THE TEMPLE GATE

7 The word that came to Jeremiah from the LORD,
saying, 2 "[A]Stand in the gate of the LORD'S house
and proclaim there this word and say, 'Hear the
word of the LORD, all you of Judah, who enter by
these gates to worship the LORD!' " 3 Thus says the
LORD of hosts, the God of Israel, "[A]Amend your ways
and your deeds, and I will let you dwell in this place.
4 [A]Do not trust in deceptive words, saying, '[a]This is
the temple of the LORD, the temple of the LORD, the
temple of the LORD.' 5 For [A]if you truly amend your
ways and your deeds, if you truly [B]practice justice
between a man and his neighbor, 6 *if* you do not
oppress the alien, the [a,A]orphan, or the widow, and
do not shed [B]innocent blood in this place, nor [C]walk
after other gods to your own ruin, 7 then I will let
you [A]dwell in this place, in the [B]land that I gave to
your fathers forever and ever.
8 "Behold, you are trusting in [A]deceptive words
to no avail. 9 Will you steal, murder, and commit
adultery and swear falsely, and [a,A]offer sacrifices to
Baal and walk after [B]other gods that you have not
known, 10 then [A]come and stand before Me in [B]this
house, which is called by My name, and say, 'We are
delivered!'—that you may do all these abominations?
11 Has [A]this house, which is called by My name, become a [B]den of robbers in your sight? Behold, [C]I,
even I, have seen *it*," declares the LORD.
12 "But go now to My place which was in [A]Shiloh,
where I [B]made My name dwell at the first, and [C]see
what I did to it because of the wickedness of My
people Israel. 13 And now, because you have done
all these things," declares the LORD, "and I spoke
to you, [A]rising up early and [B]speaking, but you did
not hear, and I [C]called you but you did not answer,
14 therefore, I will do to the [A]house which is called
by My name, [B]in which you trust, and to the place
which I gave you and your fathers, as I [C]did to Shiloh. 15 I will [A]cast you out of My sight, as I have cast
out all your brothers, all the [a]offspring of [B]Ephraim.
16 "As for you, [A]do not pray for this people, and
do not lift up cry or prayer for them, and do not
intercede with Me; for I do not hear you. 17 Do you

6:22 [A]Jer 1:15; 10:22; 50:41-43 [B]Neh 1:9 6:23 [A]Is 13:18; Jer 4:29 [B]Jer 50:42 [C]Is 5:30 6:24 [A]Is 28:19; Jer 4:19-21 [B]Is 21:3; Jer 4:31; 13:21; 30:6; 49:24; 50:43 6:25 [A]Jer 14:18 [B]Judg 5:6 [C]Jer 20:10; 46:5; 49:29 6:26 [a]Lit *Make for yourself mourning* [A]Jer 4:8 [B]Jer 25:34; Mic 1:10 [C]Amos 8:10; Zech 12:10 6:27 [A]Jer 1:18; 15:20 6:28 [A]Jer 9:4 [B]Ezek 22:18 6:29 [a]Or *drawn off* [A]Jer 15:19 6:30 [A]Ps 119:119; Is 1:22 [B]Jer 7:29; Hos 9:17; Zech 11:8 7:2 [A]Jer 17:19; 26:2 7:3 [A]Jer 4:1; 7:5; 18:11; 26:13 7:4 [a]Lit *They are* [A]Jer 7:8; Mic 3:11 7:5 [A]Is 1:19; Jer 4:1, 2 [B]1 Kin 6:12; Jer 21:12; 22:3 7:6 [a]Or *fatherless* [A]Ex 22:21-24; Jer 5:28 [B]Jer 2:34; 19:4 [C]Deut 6:14, 15; 8:19; 11:28; Jer 13:10 7:7 [A]Deut 4:40 [B]Jer 3:18 7:8 [A]Jer 7:4; 28:15 7:9 [a]Or *burn incense* [A]Jer 11:13, 17 [B]Ex 20:3; Jer 7:6; 19:4 7:10 [A]Ezek 23:39 [B]Jer 7:11, 14, 30; 32:34 7:11 [A]Is 56:7 [B]Matt 21:13; Mark 11:17; Luke 19:46 [C]Jer 29:23 7:12 [A]Judg 18:31; Jer 26:6 [B]Josh 18:1, 10 [C]1 Sam 4:10, 11, 22; Ps 78:60-64 7:13 [A]Jer 7:25 [B]Jer 35:17 [C]Prov 1:24; Is 65:12; 66:4 7:14 [A]Deut 12:5; 1 Kin 9:7 [B]Jer 7:4 [C]Jer 7:12 7:15 [a]Lit *seed* [A]Jer 15:1; 52:3 [B]Ps 78:67; Hos 7:13; 9:13; 12:1 7:16 [A]Ex 32:10; Deut 9:14; Jer 11:14

6:22, 23 A description of the Babylonians.

6:27–30 I have made you. God placed Jeremiah as a kind of assayer to test the people's obedience. He also was a "tester" who works with metals. Their sin prevented them from being pure silver, but rather they were bronze, iron, lead, even impure silver, so that they failed the test.

7:1 The word that came. This was Jeremiah's first temple sermon (v. 2); another is found in chap. 26. God was aroused against the sins He names (vv. 6, 19), especially at His temple becoming a den of robbers (v. 11). The point of this message, however, was that if Israel would repent, even at this late hour, God would still keep the conqueror from coming (vv. 3, 7). They must reject lies such as the false hope that peace is certain, based on the reasoning that the Lord would never bring calamity on His own temple (v. 4). They must turn from their sins (vv. 3, 5, 9), and end their hypocrisy (v. 10).

7:7 the land that I gave … forever. God refers to the unconditional element of the land promise in the Abrahamic Covenant (Ge 12, 15, 17, 22).

7:12 go … to … Shiloh. God calls them to return to Shiloh where the tabernacle dwelt along with the ark of the covenant. He permitted the Philistines to devastate that place (1Sa 4), and He is ready to do similarly with Jerusalem, the place of His temple (vv. 13, 14).

7:13 rising up early. This refers to the daily ministry of the prophets (cf. v. 25).

7:15 as I have cast out … Ephraim. Ephraim represents the northern kingdom of Israel, since it was the leading tribe (cf. 2Ki 17:23). As God exiled them to Assyria (ca. 722 B.C.), though they were more in number and power, so He will do to the southern kingdom.

7:16 do not pray. God told His spokesman not to pray for the people (cf. 11:14). He did not find Judah inclined to repent. Instead, He found the glib use of self-deluding slogans, such as in 7:4, and flagrant idol worship in v. 18 from a people insistent on not hearing (v. 27; 19:15). Cf. 1Jn 5:16.

not see what they are doing in the cities of Judah and in the streets of Jerusalem? 18 The [a]children gather wood, and the fathers kindle the fire, and the women knead dough to make cakes for the queen of heaven; and *they* [A]pour out drink offerings to other gods in order to [B]spite Me. 19 [A]Do they spite Me?" declares the LORD. "Is it not themselves *they spite,* to [a]their own [B]shame?" 20 Therefore thus says the Lord [a]GOD, "Behold, My [A]anger and My wrath will be poured out on this place, on man and on beast and on the [B]trees of the field and on the fruit of the ground; and it will burn and not be quenched."

21 Thus says the LORD of hosts, the God of Israel, "Add your [A]burnt offerings to your sacrifices and [B]eat flesh. 22 For I did not [A]speak to your fathers, or command them in the day that I brought them out of the land of Egypt, concerning burnt offerings and sacrifices. 23 But this is [a]what I commanded them, saying, '[A]Obey My voice, and [B]I will be your God, and you will be My people; and you will walk in all the way which I command you, that it may [C]be well with you.' 24 Yet they [A]did not obey or incline their ear, but walked in *their own* counsels *and* in the stubbornness of their evil heart, and [a,B]went backward and not forward. 25 Since the day that your fathers came out of the land of Egypt until this day, I have [A]sent you all My servants the prophets, daily rising early and sending *them.* 26 Yet they did not listen to Me or incline their ear, but [A]stiffened their neck; they [B]did more evil than their fathers.

27 "You shall [A]speak all these words to them, but they will not listen to you; and you shall call to them, but they will [B]not answer you. 28 You shall say to them, 'This is the nation that [A]did not obey the voice of the LORD their God or accept correction; [a,B]truth has perished and has been cut off from their mouth.

29 '[A]Cut off [a]your hair and cast *it* away,
And [B]take up a lamentation
on the bare heights;
For the LORD has [C]rejected and forsaken
The generation of His wrath.'

30 For the sons of Judah have done that which is evil in My sight," declares the LORD, "they have [A]set their detestable things in the house which is called by My name, to defile it. 31 They have [A]built the high places of Topheth, which is in the valley of the son of Hinnom, to [B]burn their sons and their daughters in the fire, which I [C]did not command, and it did not come into My [a]mind.

32 "[A]Therefore, behold, days are coming," declares the LORD, "when it will no longer be called Topheth, or the valley of the son of Hinnom, but the valley of the Slaughter; for they will [B]bury in Topheth [a]because there is no *other* place. 33 The [A]dead bodies of this people will be food for the birds of the sky and for the beasts of the earth; and no one will frighten *them away.* 34 Then I will make to [A]cease from the cities of Judah and from the streets of Jerusalem the voice of joy and the voice of gladness, the voice of the bridegroom and the voice of the bride; for the [B]land will become a ruin.

THE SIN AND TREACHERY OF JUDAH

8 "At that time," declares the LORD, "they will [A]bring out the bones of the kings of Judah and the bones of its princes, and the bones of the priests and the bones of the prophets, and the bones of the inhabitants of Jerusalem from their graves. 2 They will spread them out to the sun, the moon and to all the [A]host of heaven, which they have loved and which they have served, and which they have gone after and which they have sought, and which they have worshiped. They will not be gathered [B]or buried; [C]they will be as dung on the face of the ground. 3 And [A]death will be chosen rather than life by all the remnant that remains of this evil family, that remains in all the [B]places to which I have driven them," declares the LORD of hosts. 4 "You shall say to them, 'Thus says the LORD,

"Do *men* [A]fall and not get up again?
Does one turn away and not [a]repent?

7:18 [a]Lit *sons* [A]Jer 19:13 [B]Deut 32:16, 21; 1 Kin 14:9; 16:2; Jer 11:17; Ezek 8:17 7:19 [a]Lit *their faces'* [A]Job 35:6; 1 Cor 10:22 [B]Jer 9:19; 15:9; 22:22 7:20 [a]Heb *YHWH*, usually rendered *LORD* [A]Is 42:25; Jer 6:11, 12; 42:18; Lam 2:3-5; 4:11 [B]Jer 8:13; 11:16 7:21 [A]Is 1:11; Jer 6:20; 14:12; Amos 5:22 [B]Ezek 33:25; Hos 8:13 7:22 [A]1 Sam 15:22; Ps 51:16; Hos 6:6 7:23 [a]Lit *the word which* [A]Ex 15:26; 16:32; Deut 6:3 [B]Ex 19:5, 6; Lev 26:12; Jer 11:4; 13:11 [C]Is 3:10; Jer 38:20; 42:6 7:24 [a]Lit *they were* [A]Deut 29:19; Ps 81:11; Jer 11:8; Ezek 20:8, 13, 16, 21 [B]Jer 15:6 7:25 [A]2 Chr 36:15; Jer 25:4; 29:19; Luke 11:49 7:26 [A]Neh 9:16; Jer 17:23; 19:15 [B]Jer 16:12; Matt 23:32 7:27 [A]Jer 1:7; 26:2; Ezek 2:7 [B]Is 50:2; 65:12; Zech 7:13 7:28 [a]Lit *faithfulness* [A]Jer 6:17; 11:10 [B]Is 59:14, 15; Jer 9:5 7:29 [a]Lit *your crown* [A]Job 1:20; Is 15:2; 22:12; Jer 16:6; Mic 1:16 [B]Jer 3:21; 9:17, 18 [C]Jer 6:30; 14:19 7:30 [A]2 Kin 21:3f; 2 Chr 33:3-5, 7; Jer 32:34, 35; Ezek 7:20; Dan 9:27; 11:31 7:31 [a]Lit *heart* [A]2 Kin 23:10; Jer 19:5; 32:35 [B]Lev 18:21; 2 Kin 17:17; Ps 106:38 [C]Deut 17:3 7:32 [a]Or *until there is no place left* [A]Jer 19:6, 11 [B]2 Kin 23:10 7:33 [A]Deut 28:26; Ps 79:2; Jer 12:9; 19:7 7:34 [A]Is 24:7, 8; Jer 16:9; 25:10; Ezek 26:13; Hos 2:11; Rev 18:23 [B]Lev 26:33; Is 1:7; Jer 4:27 8:1 [A]Ezek 6:5 8:2 [A]2 Kin 23:5; Jer 19:13; Zeph 1:5; Acts 7:42 [B]Jer 22:19; 36:30 [C]2 Kin 9:37; Ps 83:10; Jer 9:22 8:3 [A]Job 3:21, 22; 7:15, 16; Jon 4:3; Rev 9:6 [B]Deut 30:1, 4; Jer 23:3, 8; 29:14 8:4 [a]Lit *turn back* [A]Prov 24:16; Amos 5:2; Mic 7:8

7:18 the queen of heaven. Cf. 44:17–19, 25. The Jews were worshiping Ishtar, an Assyrian and Babylonian goddess also called Ashtoreth and Astarte, the wife of Baal or Molech. Because these deities symbolized generative power, their worship involved prostitution.

7:22 I did not … command. Bible writers sometimes use apparent negation to make a comparative emphasis. What God commanded His people at the Exodus was not so much the offerings, as it was the heart obedience which prompted the offerings. See this comparative sense used elsewhere (Dt 5:3; Hos 6:6; 1Jn 3:18).

7:22, 23 offerings … sacrifices … Obey. Here is a crucial emphasis on internal obedience. Cf. Jos 1:8; 1Sa 15:22; Pr 15:8; 21:3; Is 1:11–17; Hos 6:6; Mt 9:13.

7:25 Cf. v. 13.

7:29 Cut off your hair. This is a sign depicting God's cutting the nation off and casting them into exile. Ezekiel used a similar illustration by cutting his hair (Eze 5:1–4). God never casts away the genuinely saved from spiritual salvation (Jn 6:37; 10:28, 29).

7:31 burn their sons. Though God forbade this atrocity (Lv 18:21; 20:2–5; Dt 12:31), Israelites still offered babies as sacrifices at the high places of idol worship (Topheth) in the valley of Hinnom (S end of Jerusalem). They offered them to the fire god Molech, under the delusion that this god would reward them. *See note on 19:6.*

7:32 valley of the Slaughter. God renamed the place because great carnage would be forthcoming in the Babylonian invasion.

8:1 bring out the bones. Conquerors would ransack all the tombs to gain treasures and then humiliate the Jews by scattering the bones of the rich and honored in open spaces as a tribute to the superiority of their gods (v. 2).

8:4 Jeremiah spoke of the natural instinct of one who falls, to get up, and one who leaves, to return, but Judah did not possess this instinct.

5 "Why then has this people, Jerusalem,
[A]Turned away in continual apostasy?
They [B]hold fast to deceit,
They [C]refuse to return.
6 "I [A]have listened and heard,
They have spoken what is not right;
[B]No man repented of his wickedness,
Saying, 'What have I done?'
Everyone turned to his course,
Like a [C]horse charging into the battle.
7 "Even the stork in the sky
[A]Knows her seasons;
And the [B]turtledove and the
swift and the thrush
Observe the time of their [a]migration;
But [C]My people do not know
The ordinance of the LORD.

8 "[A]How can you say, 'We are wise,
And the law of the LORD is with us'?
But behold, the lying pen of the scribes
Has made *it* into a lie.
9 "The wise men are [A]put to shame,
They are dismayed and caught;
Behold, they have [B]rejected
the word of the LORD,
And what kind of wisdom
do they have?
10 "Therefore I will [A]give their
wives to others,
Their fields to [a]new owners;
Because from the least even
to the greatest
Everyone is [B]greedy for gain;
From the prophet even to the priest
Everyone practices deceit.
11 "They [A]heal the brokenness of the
daughter of My people superficially,
Saying, 'Peace, peace,'
But there is no peace.
12 "Were they [A]ashamed because of the
abomination they had done?
They certainly were not ashamed,
And they did not know how to blush;
Therefore they shall [B]fall
among those who fall;
At the [C]time of their punishment
they shall be brought down,"
Says the LORD.
13 "I will [A]surely snatch them away,"
declares the LORD;
"There will be [B]no grapes on the vine
And [C]no figs on the fig tree,
And the leaf will wither;
And what I have given them
will pass away." ' "
14 Why are we sitting still?
[A]Assemble yourselves, and let us
[B]go into the fortified cities
And let us perish there,
Because the LORD our God
has doomed us
And given us [C]poisoned water to drink,
For [D]we have sinned against the LORD.
15 *We* [A]waited for peace, but no good *came;*
For a time of healing, but behold, terror!
16 From [A]Dan is heard the
snorting of his horses;
At the sound of the neighing
of his [B]stallions
The whole land quakes;
For they come and [C]devour the
land and its fullness,
The city and its inhabitants.
17 "For behold, I am [A]sending
serpents against you,
Adders, for which there is [B]no charm,
And they will bite you,"
declares the LORD.

18 [a]My [A]sorrow is beyond healing,
My [B]heart is faint *within me!*
19 Behold, listen! The cry of the daughter
of my people from a [A]distant land:
"Is the LORD not in Zion? Is her
King not within her?"
"Why have they [B]provoked Me with their
graven images, with foreign [a,C]idols?"
20 "Harvest is past, summer is ended,
And we are not saved."
21 For the [A]brokenness of the daughter
of my people I am broken;
I [B]mourn, dismay has taken hold of me.
22 Is there no [A]balm in Gilead?
Is there no physician there?
[B]Why then has not the [a]health
of the daughter of my
people [b]been restored?

8:5 [A]Jer 5:6; 7:24 [B]Jer 5:27; 9:6 [C]Jer 5:3 8:6 [A]Ps 14:2; Mal 3:16 [B]Ezek 22:30; Mic 7:2; Rev 9:20 [C]Job 39:21-25 8:7 [a]Lit *coming* [A]Prov 6:6-8; Is 1:3 [B]Song 2:12 [C]Jer 5:4 8:8 [A]Job 5:12, 13; Jer 4:22; Rom 1:22 8:9 [A]Is 19:11; Jer 6:15; 1 Cor 1:27 [B]Jer 6:19 8:10 [a]Lit *possessing ones* [A]Deut 28:30; Jer 6:12, 13; 38:22f [B]Is 56:11; 57:17; Jer 6:13 8:11 [A]Jer 6:14; 14:13, 14; Lam 2:14; Ezek 13:10 8:12 [A]Ps 52:1, 7; Is 3:9; Jer 3:3; 6:15; Zeph 3:5 [B]Is 9:14; Jer 6:21; Hos 4:5 [C]Deut 32:35; Jer 10:15 8:13 [A]Jer 14:12; Ezek 22:20, 21 [B]Jer 5:17; 7:20; Joel 1:7 [C]Matt 21:19; Luke 13:6 8:14 [A]Jer 4:5 [B]2 Sam 20:6; Jer 35:11 [C]Deut 29:18; Ps 69:21; Jer 9:15; 23:15; Lam 3:19; Matt 27:34 [D]Jer 3:25; 14:20 8:15 [A]Jer 8:11; 14:19 8:16 [A]Judg 18:29; Jer 4:15 [B]Judg 5:22 [C]Jer 3:24; 10:25 8:17 [A]Num 21:6; Deut 32:24 [B]Ps 58:4, 5 8:18 [a]So Gr and versions [A]Is 22:4; Lam 1:16, 17 [B]Jer 23:9; Lam 5:17 8:19 [a]Lit *vanities* [A]Is 13:5; 39:3; Jer 4:16; 9:16 [B]Deut 32:21; Jer 7:19 [C]Ps 31:6 8:21 [A]Jer 4:19; 9:1; 14:17 [B]Jer 14:2; Joel 2:6; Nah 2:10 8:22 [a]Or *healing* [b]Lit *gone up* [A]Gen 37:25; Jer 46:11 [B]Jer 14:19; 30:13

8:5 apostasy. *See note on 2:19.*

8:7 The instinct of the migratory birds leads them with unfailing regularity to return every spring from their winter homes. But God's people will not return, though the winter of divine wrath is arriving.

8:11 Cf. 4:10; 6:14.

8:16 Dan. The territory of this tribe was on the northern border of the land, where the invasion would begin and sweep S.

8:17 sending serpents. This is a figurative picture of the Babylonian victors.

8:19 distant land. This is the cry of the exiled Jews who will come after they are taken captive into Babylon. They will wonder why God would let this happen to His land and people.

8:20–22 we are not saved. The coming devastation is compared with the hopeless anguish when harvesttime has passed but people are still in desperate need. Jeremiah identified with his people's suffering (v. 21) as a man of tears (cf. 9:1), but saw a doom so pronounced that there was no remedy to soothe. There was no healing balm, the kind in abundance in Gilead (E of the Sea of Galilee), and no physician to cure (cf. Ge 37:25; 43:11).

A LAMENT OVER ZION

9 [a,A]Oh that my head were waters
And my eyes a fountain of tears,
That I might weep day and night
For the slain of the [B]daughter of my people!
2 [a,A]Oh that I had in the desert
A wayfarers' lodging place;
That I might leave my people
And go from them!
For all of them are [B]adulterers,
An assembly of [C]treacherous men.
3 "They [A]bend their tongue *like* their bow;
Lies and not truth prevail in the land;
For they [B]proceed from evil to evil,
And they [C]do not know Me,"
declares the LORD.
4 "Let everyone [A]be on guard
against his neighbor,
And [B]do not trust any brother;
Because every [C]brother deals [a]craftily,
And every neighbor [D]goes
about as a slanderer.
5 "Everyone [A]deceives his neighbor
And does not speak the truth,
They have taught their tongue to speak lies;
They [B]weary themselves
committing iniquity.
6 "Your [A]dwelling is in the midst of deceit;
Through deceit they [B]refuse to
know Me," declares the LORD.

7 Therefore thus says the LORD of hosts,

"Behold, I will refine them and [A]assay them;
For [B]what *else* can I do, because of
the daughter of My people?
8 "Their [A]tongue is a deadly arrow;
It speaks deceit;
With his mouth one [B]speaks
peace to his neighbor,
But inwardly he [C]sets an ambush for him.
9 "[A]Shall I not punish them for these
things?" declares the LORD.
"On a nation such as this
Shall I not avenge Myself?

10 "For the [A]mountains I will take up
a weeping and wailing,
And for the pastures of the
[B]wilderness a dirge,
Because they are [C]laid waste so
that no one passes through,
And the lowing of the cattle is not heard;
Both the [D]birds of the sky and the
beasts have fled; they are gone.
11 "I will make Jerusalem a [A]heap of ruins,
A haunt of [B]jackals;
And I will make the cities of Judah a
[C]desolation, without inhabitant."

12 Who is the [A]wise man that may understand
this? And *who is* he to whom [B]the mouth of the
LORD has spoken, that he may declare it? [C]Why is
the land ruined, laid waste like a desert, so that no
one passes through? 13 The LORD said, "Because they
have [A]forsaken My law which I set before them, and
have not obeyed My voice nor walked according to
it, 14 but have [A]walked after the stubbornness of their
heart and after the [B]Baals, as their [C]fathers taught
them," 15 therefore thus says the LORD of hosts, the
God of Israel, "behold, [A]I will feed them, this people,
with wormwood and give them [B]poisoned water
to drink. 16 I will [A]scatter them among the nations,
whom neither they nor their fathers have known;
and I will send the [B]sword after them until I have
annihilated them."
17 Thus says the LORD of hosts,

"Consider and call for the [A]mourning
women, that they may come;
And send for the [a,B]wailing women,
that they may come!
18 "Let them make haste and take
up a wailing for us,
That our [A]eyes may shed tears
And our eyelids flow with water.
19 "For a voice of [A]wailing is
heard from Zion,
'[B]How are we ruined!
We are put to great shame,
For we have [C]left the land,
Because they have cast down
our dwellings.' "
20 Now hear the word of the
LORD, O you [A]women,
And let your ear receive the
word of His mouth;
Teach your daughters wailing,
And everyone her neighbor a dirge.
21 For [A]death has come up
through our windows;
It has entered our palaces
To cut off the [B]children from the streets,
The young men from the town squares.

9:1 [a]Ch 8:23 in Heb [A]Is 22:4; Jer 8:18; 13:17; Lam 2:18 [B]Jer 6:26; 8:21, 22 9:2 [a]Ch 9:1 in Heb [A]Ps 55:6, 7; 120:5, 6 [B]Jer 5:7, 8; 23:10; Hos 4:2 [C]Jer 5:11; 12:1, 6 9:3 [A]Ps 64:3; Is 59:4; Jer 9:8 [B]Jer 4:22 [C]Judg 2:10; 1 Sam 2:12; Jer 4:22; 5:4, 5; Hos 4:1; 1 Cor 15:34 9:4 [a]I.e. like Jacob (a play on words) [A]Ps 12:2; Prov 26:24, 25; Jer 9:8; Mic 7:5, 6 [B]Jer 12:6 [C]Gen 27:35 [D]Ps 15:3; Prov 10:18; Jer 6:28 9:5 [A]Mic 6:12 [B]Jer 12:13; 51:58, 64 9:6 [A]Ps 120:5, 6; Jer 5:27; 8:5 [B]Job 21:14, 15; Prov 1:24; Jer 11:10; 13:10; John 3:19, 20 9:7 [A]Is 1:25; Jer 6:27; Mal 3:3 [B]Hos 11:8 9:8 [A]Jer 9:3 [B]Ps 28:3 [C]Jer 5:26 9:9 [A]Is 1:24; Jer 5:9, 29 9:10 [A]Jer 4:24; 7:29 [B]Jer 4:26; Hos 4:3 [C]Jer 12:4, 10; Ezek 14:15; 29:11; 33:28 [D]Jer 4:25; 12:4; Hos 4:3 9:11 [A]Is 25:2; Jer 51:37 [B]Is 13:22; 34:13 [C]Jer 4:27; 26:9 9:12 [A]Ps 107:43; Is 42:23; Hos 14:9 [B]Jer 9:20; 23:16 [C]Ps 107:34; Jer 23:10 9:13 [A]2 Chr 7:19; Ps 89:30; Jer 5:19; 22:9 9:14 [A]Jer 7:24; 11:8; Rom 1:21-24 [B]Jer 2:8, 23; 23:27 [C]Gal 1:14; 1 Pet 1:18 9:15 [A]Ps 80:5 [B]Deut 29:18; Jer 8:14; 23:15; Lam 3:15 9:16 [A]Lev 26:33; Deut 28:64; Jer 13:24 [B]Jer 44:27; Ezek 5:2, 12 9:17 [a]Lit *skilled* [A]2 Chr 35:25; Eccl 12:5 [B]Amos 5:16 9:18 [A]Is 22:4; Jer 9:1; 14:17 9:19 [A]Jer 7:29; Ezek 7:16-18 [B]Deut 28:29; Jer 4:13 [C]Jer 7:15; 15:1 9:20 [A]Is 32:9 9:21 [A]2 Chr 36:17; Jer 15:7; 18:21; Ezek 9:5, 6; Amos 6:9, 10 [B]Jer 6:11

9:1 waters … tears. Jeremiah cared so deeply that he longed for the relief of flooding tears or a place of retreat to be free of the burden of Judah's sins for a while.

9:2 A wayfarers' lodging place. Simple square buildings with an open court were built in remote areas to accommodate caravans. Though it would be lonely and filthy in the wilderness, Jeremiah preferred it to Jerusalem so as to be removed from the moral pollution of the people, which he described in vv. 3–8.

9:3 do not know Me. *See note on 5:10.*

9:15 wormwood … poisoned water. The Lord pictured the awful suffering of the judgment as wormwood, which had very bitter

22 Speak, "Thus says the LORD,
'The corpses of men will fall [A]like
dung on the open field,
And like the sheaf after the reaper,
But no one will gather *them.*' "

23 Thus says the LORD, "[A]Let not a wise man boast
of his wisdom, and let not the [B]mighty man boast
of his might, let not a [C]rich man boast of his riches;
24 but let him who boasts [A]boast of this, that he
understands and knows Me, that I am the LORD
who [B]exercises lovingkindness, justice and righteousness on earth; for I [C]delight in these things,"
declares the LORD.
25 "Behold, the days are coming," declares the
LORD, "that I will punish all who are circumcised
and yet [A]uncircumcised— 26 Egypt and Judah, and
Edom and the sons of Ammon, and Moab and [A]all
those inhabiting the desert who clip the hair on their
temples; for all the nations are uncircumcised, and
all the house of Israel are [B]uncircumcised of heart."

A SATIRE ON IDOLATRY

10 Hear the word which the LORD speaks to you,
O house of Israel. 2 Thus says the LORD,

"[A]Do not learn the way of the nations,
And do not be terrified by the
signs of the heavens
Although the nations are
terrified by them;
3 For the customs of the peoples
are [a,A]delusion;
Because [B]it is wood cut from the forest,
The work of the hands of a
craftsman with a cutting tool.
4 "They [A]decorate *it* with silver and with gold;
They [B]fasten it with nails
and with hammers
So that it will not totter.
5 "Like a scarecrow in a cucumber
field are they,
And they [A]cannot speak;
They must be [B]carried,
Because they cannot walk!
Do not fear them,
For they [C]can do no harm,
Nor can they do any good."
6 [A]There is none like You, O LORD;
You are [B]great, and great is
Your name in might.
7 [A]Who would not fear You,
O [B]King of the nations?
Indeed it is Your due!
For among all the [C]wise men of the nations
And in all their kingdoms,
There is none like You.
8 But they are altogether [A]stupid and foolish
In their discipline of [a]delusion—[b]their
idol is wood!
9 Beaten [A]silver is brought from [B]Tarshish,
And [C]gold from Uphaz,
The work of a craftsman and of
the hands of a goldsmith;
Violet and purple are their clothing;
They are all the [D]work of skilled men.
10 But the LORD is the [A]true God;
He is the [B]living God and the
[C]everlasting King.
At His wrath the [D]earth quakes,
And the nations cannot [E]endure
His indignation.

11 [a]Thus you shall say to them, "The [A]gods that
did not make the heavens and the earth will [B]per-
ish from the earth and from under the [b]heavens."

12 *It is* [A]He who made the
earth by His power,
Who [B]established the world
by His wisdom;
And by His understanding He has
[C]stretched out the heavens.
13 When He utters His [A]voice, *there is* a
tumult of waters in the heavens,
And He causes the [B]clouds to ascend
from the end of the earth;
He makes lightning for the rain,
And brings out the [C]wind
from His storehouses.
14 Every man is [A]stupid, devoid
of knowledge;
Every goldsmith is put to
shame by his [a]idols;
For his molten images are deceitful,
And there is no breath in them.

9:22 [A]Ps 83:10; Is 5:25; Jer 8:2; 16:4; 25:33 9:23 [A]Eccl 9:11; Is 47:10; Ezek 28:3-7 [B]1 Kin 20:10, 11; Is 10:8-12 [C]Job 31:24, 25; Ps 49:6-9 9:24 [A]Ps 20:7; 44:8; Is 41:16; Jer 4:2; 1 Cor 1:31; 2 Cor 10:17; Gal 6:14 [B]Ex 34:6, 7; Ps 36:5, 7; 51:1 [C]Is 61:8; Mic 7:18 9:25 [A]Jer 4:4; Rom 2:28, 29 9:26 [A]Jer 25:23 [B]Lev 26:41; Jer 4:4; 6:10; Ezek 44:7; Rom 2:28 10:2 [A]Lev 18:3; 20:23; Deut 12:30 10:3 [a]Lit *vanity* [A]Jer 14:22 [B]Is 44:9-20 10:4 [A]Is 40:19 [B]Is 40:20; 41:7 10:5 [A]Ps 115:5; Is 46:7; Jer 10:14; 1 Cor 12:2 [B]Ps 115:7; Is 46:1, 7 [C]Is 41:23, 24 10:6 [A]Ex 15:11; Deut 33:26; Ps 86:8, 10; Jer 10:16 [B]Ps 48:1; 96:4; Is 12:6; Jer 32:18 10:7 [A]Rev 15:4 [B]Ps 22:28 [C]Dan 2:27, 28; 1 Cor 1:19, 20 10:8 [a]Lit *vanities,* or *idols* [b]Lit *it is* [A]Jer 4:22; 5:4; 10:14 10:9 [A]Is 40:19 [B]Ps 72:10; Is 23:6 [C]Dan 10:5 [D]Ps 115:4 10:10 [A]Is 65:16 [B]Jer 4:2 [C]Ps 10:16; 29:10 [D]Jer 4:24; 50:46 [E]Ps 76:7 10:11 [a]This verse is in Aram [b]Or *these heavens* [A]Ps 96:5 [B]Is 2:18; Zeph 2:11 10:12 [A]Gen 1:1, 6; Job 38:4-7; Ps 136:5; 148:4, 5; Jer 51:15, 19 [B]Ps 78:69; Is 45:18 [C]Job 9:8; Is 40:22 10:13 [A]Ps 29:3-9 [B]Job 36:27-29 [C]Ps 135:7 10:14 [a]Or *graven image* [A]Jer 10:8; 51:17, 18

leaves. Their food would be bitterness, and their water as foul as gall, a poisonous herb.

9:22 How galling to the Jews to hear that *their corpses will be trampled* contemptuously.

9:24 understands and knows Me. Nothing but a true knowledge of God can save the nation. Paul refers to this passage twice (cf. 1Co 1:31; 2Co 10:17).

9:26 Egypt … desert. A preview of God's judgment of the nations detailed in chaps. 46–51. **uncircumcised of heart.** *See note on 4:4.*

10:2 signs of the heavens. Gentiles worshiped celestial bodies, including the sun, moon, and stars.

10:4 decorate. Idols were often carved from wood (v. 3) and ornamented with gold or silver (cf. v. 9). Some were molded from clay (Jdg 18:17; Is 42:17). The context points out the impossibility (vv. 3–5) of such nonexistent gods punishing or rewarding humans.

10:7 King. God, who sovereignly created and controls all things (cf. vv. 12, 16; Dt 4:35), is alone the eternal, living God (cf. Pss 47, 145) worthy of trust. By contrast, earthly idols have to be fashioned by men (v. 9), and will perish (v. 15).

10:9 Tarshish. Possibly a commercial port in southern Spain or on the island of Sardinia. Cf. Jon 1:3. **Uphaz.** Location is uncertain.

10:11–16 The true and living Creator God is again contrasted with dead idols.

15 They are [A]worthless, a work of mockery;
In the [B]time of their punishment
they will perish.
16 The [A]portion of Jacob is not like these;
For the [a,B]Maker of all is He,
And [C]Israel is the tribe of His inheritance;
The [D]LORD of hosts is His name.

17 [A]Pick up your bundle from the ground,
You who dwell under siege!
18 For thus says the LORD,
"Behold, I am [A]slinging out the
inhabitants of the land
At this time,
And will cause them distress,
That they may [a]be found."

19 [A]Woe is me, because of my [a]injury!
My [B]wound is incurable.
But I said, "Truly this is a sickness,
And I [C]must bear it."
20 My [A]tent is destroyed,
And all my ropes are broken;
My [B]sons have gone from me
and are no more.
There is [C]no one to stretch
out my tent again
Or to set up my curtains.
21 For the shepherds have become stupid
And [A]have not sought the LORD;
Therefore they have not prospered,
And [B]all their flock is scattered.
22 The sound of a [A]report! Behold, it comes—
A great commotion [B]out of
the land of the north—
To [C]make the cities of Judah
A desolation, a haunt of jackals.

23 I know, O LORD, that [A]a man's
way is not in himself,
[B]Nor is it in a man who walks
to direct his steps.
24 [A]Correct me, O LORD, but with justice;
Not with Your anger, or You will
[a]bring me to nothing.
25 [A]Pour out Your wrath on the nations
that [B]do not know You
And on the families that [C]do
not call Your name;
For they have devoured Jacob;
They have [D]devoured him
and consumed him
And have laid waste his [a]habitation.

THE BROKEN COVENANT

11 The word which came to Jeremiah from the
LORD, saying, 2 "[A]Hear the words of this [B]cov-
enant, and speak to the men of Judah and to the
inhabitants of Jerusalem; 3 and say to them, 'Thus
says the LORD, the God of Israel, "[A]Cursed is the
man who does not heed the words of this covenant
4 which I commanded your forefathers in the [A]day
that I brought them out of the land of Egypt, from
the [B]iron furnace, saying, '[C]Listen to My voice, and
[a]do according to all which I command you; so you
shall be [D]My people, and I will be your God,' 5 in
order to confirm the [A]oath which I swore to your
forefathers, to give them a land flowing with milk
and honey, as *it is* this day." ' " Then I said, "[B]Amen,
O LORD."
6 And the LORD said to me, "[A]Proclaim all these
words in the cities of Judah and in the streets of Jerusalem, saying, '[B]Hear the words of this covenant
and [C]do them. 7 For I solemnly [A]warned your fathers
in the [B]day that I brought them up from the land
of Egypt, even to this day, [a,C]warning persistently,
saying, "[D]Listen to My voice." 8 Yet they [A]did not obey
or incline their ear, but walked, each one, in the
stubbornness of his evil heart; therefore I brought
on them all the [B]words of this covenant, which I
commanded *them* to do, but they did not.' "
9 Then the LORD said to me, "A [A]conspiracy has
been found among the men of Judah and among
the inhabitants of Jerusalem. 10 They have [A]turned
back to the iniquities of their [a]ancestors who [B]re-
fused to hear My words, and they [C]have gone after other gods to serve them; the house of Israel
and the house of Judah have [D]broken My covenant
which I made with their fathers." 11 Therefore thus
says the LORD, "Behold I am [A]bringing disaster
on them which they will [B]not be able to escape;
though they will [C]cry to Me, yet I will not listen to
them. 12 Then the cities of Judah and the inhabitants of Jerusalem will [A]go and cry to the gods to

10:15 [A]Is 41:24; Jer 8:19; 14:22 [B]Jer 8:12; 51:18 10:16 [a]Lit *Fashioner* [A]Ps 16:5; 73:26; 119:57; Jer 51:19; Lam 3:24 [B]Is 45:7; Jer 10:12 [C]Deut 32:9; Ps 74:2 [D]Jer 31:35; 32:18 10:17 [A]Ezek 12:3-12 10:18 [a]Lit *find* [A]1 Sam 25:29 10:19 [a]Lit *breaking* [A]Jer 4:31 [B]Jer 14:17 [C]Mic 7:9 10:20 [A]Jer 4:20; Lam 2:4 [B]Jer 31:15; Lam 1:5 [C]Is 51:18 10:21 [A]Jer 2:8 [B]Jer 23:2 10:22 [A]Jer 4:15 [B]Jer 1:14; 25:9 [C]Jer 9:11; 49:33 10:23 [A]Prov 16:1; 20:24 [B]Is 26:7 10:24 [a]Lit *diminish me* [A]Ps 6:1; 38:1 10:25 [a]Or *pasture* [A]Ps 79:6, 7; Zeph 3:8 [B]Job 18:21; 1 Thess 4:5; 2 Thess 1:8 [C]Zeph 1:6 [D]Jer 8:16; 50:7, 17 11:2 [A]Jer 11:6 [B]Ex 19:5 11:3 [A]Deut 27:26; Jer 17:5; Gal 3:10 11:4 [a]Lit *do them* [A]Ex 24:3-8; Jer 31:32 [B]Deut 4:20; 1 Kin 8:51 [C]Lev 26:3; Deut 11:27; Jer 7:23; 26:13 [D]Jer 24:7; Zech 8:8 11:5 [A]Ex 13:5; Deut 7:12; Ps 105:9; Jer 32:22 [B]Jer 28:6 11:6 [A]Jer 3:12; 7:2 [B]Jer 11:2 [C]John 13:17; Rom 2:13; James 1:22 11:7 [a]Lit *rising early and warning* [A]1 Sam 8:9 [B]Jer 11:4 [C]Ex 15:26; 2 Chr 36:15; Jer 7:25 [D]Jer 11:7 11:8 [A]Jer 7:24; 9:14; 35:15; Ezek 20:8 [B]Lev 26:14-43 11:9 [A]Ezek 22:25; Hos 6:9 11:10 [a]Lit *former fathers* [A]1 Sam 15:11; Jer 3:10, 11; Ezek 20:18 [B]Deut 9:7; Ps 78:8-10; Jer 13:10 [C]Judg 2:11-13 [D]Jer 3:6-11; Ezek 16:59 11:11 [A]2 Kin 22:16; Jer 6:19; 11:17 [B]Is 24:17; Jer 25:35 [C]Ps 18:41; Prov 1:28; Is 1:15; Jer 11:14; 14:12; Ezek 8:18; Mic 3:4; Zech 7:13 11:12 [A]Deut 32:37; Jer 44:17

10:16 portion of Jacob. God is the all sufficient source for His people (Nu 18:20), and He will not fail them as idols do (11:12). **Israel is the tribe of His inheritance.** To this nation, God gave His inheritance in covenant love.

10:20 My tent is destroyed. Jeremiah, using a nomadic metaphor, shifted into words that Israelites will speak when the invaders attack. They will feel despair and cry out over their homes being plundered and their children being killed or scattered to exile.

10:23 a man's way is not in himself. Man is incapable of guiding his own life adequately. This prayer shifts to his need of God (Pr 3:5, 6; 16:9), who had a plan for Jeremiah before he was even born (1:5).

10:24, 25 Jeremiah saw himself ("Correct me") in solidarity with his people (cf. Da 9:1ff.) and understood the nation must be punished, but desired some mercy and moderation; he prayed that God's full fury would be poured on the nations that induced the Jews into idolatry.

11:2 this covenant. The reference is to God's covenant, summarized in vv. 3–5, which promised curses for disobeying and blessings for obeying (cf. Dt 27:26–28:68).

11:4 the iron furnace. A metaphor for the hardship of Egyptian bondage hundreds of years earlier (cf. Ex 1:8–14).

11:9 A conspiracy. This refers to a deliberate resisting of God's appeals for repentance and an insistence upon trusting their own "peace" message and idols.

whom they burn incense, but they surely will not
save them in the time of their disaster. 13 For your
gods are [a,A]as many as your cities, O Judah; and
[a]as many as the streets of Jerusalem are the altars
you have set up to the [B]shameful thing, altars to
[C]burn incense to Baal.
14 "Therefore [A]do not pray for this people, nor
lift up a cry or prayer for them; for I will [B]not listen when they call to Me because of their disaster.

15 "What right has My [A]beloved
in My house
When [B]she has done
many vile deeds?
Can the sacrificial flesh take away
from you your disaster,
[a]So *that* you can rejoice?"
16 The LORD called your name,
"A [A]green olive tree, beautiful
in fruit and form";
With the [B]noise of a great tumult
He has [C]kindled fire on it,
And its branches are worthless.

17 The LORD of hosts, who [A]planted you, has [B]pro-
nounced evil against you because of the evil of the
house of Israel and of the house of Judah, which
they have [a]done to provoke Me by [b,C]offering up
sacrifices to Baal.

PLOTS AGAINST JEREMIAH

18 Moreover, the LORD [A]made it
known to me and I knew it;
Then You showed me their deeds.
19 But I was like a gentle [A]lamb
led to the slaughter;
And I did not know that they had
[B]devised plots against me, *saying,*
"Let us destroy the tree with its [a]fruit,
And [C]let us cut him off from
the [D]land of the living,
That his [E]name be
remembered no more."
20 But, O LORD of hosts, who
[A]judges righteously,
Who [B]tries the [a]feelings and the heart,
Let me see Your vengeance on them,
For to You have I [b]committed my cause.

21 Therefore thus says the LORD concerning the
men of [A]Anathoth, who [B]seek your life, saying, "[C]Do
not prophesy in the name of the LORD, so that you
will not [D]die at our hand"; 22 therefore, thus says
the LORD of hosts, "Behold, I am about to [A]punish
them! The [B]young men will die by the sword, their
sons and daughters will die by famine; 23 and a
remnant [A]will not be left to them, for I will [B]bring
disaster on the men of Anathoth—[C]the year of their
punishment."

11:13 [a]Lit *the number of* [A]2 Kin 23:13; Jer 2:28 [B]Jer 3:24 [C]Jer 7:9 11:14 [A]Ex 32:10; Jer 7:16; 14:11; 1 John 5:16 [B]Ps 66:18; Jer 11:11; Hos 5:6 11:15 [a]Lit *Then* [A]Jer 13:27 [B]Ezek 16:25 11:16 [A]Ps 52:8; Rom 11:17 [B]Ps 83:2 [C]Ps 80:16; Is 27:11; Jer 21:14 11:17 [a]Or *done for themselves* [b]Or *burning incense* [A]Is 5:2; Jer 2:21; 12:2 [B]Jer 1:14; 16:10; 19:15 [C]Jer 7:9; 11:13; 32:29 11:18 [A]1 Sam 23:11, 12; 2 Kin 6:9, 10; Ezek 8:6 11:19 [a]Lit *bread* [A]Is 53:7 [B]Jer 18:18; 20:10 [C]Ps 83:4; Is 53:8 [D]Job 28:13; Ps 52:5 [E]Ps 109:13 11:20 [a]Lit *kidneys* [b]Lit *revealed* [A]Gen 18:25; Ps 7:8; Jer 20:12 [B]1 Sam 16:7; Ps 7:9; Jer 17:10 11:21 [A]Jer 1:1 [B]Jer 12:5, 6; 20:10 [C]Amos 2:12 [D]Jer 26:8; 38:4 11:22 [A]Jer 21:14 [B]2 Chr 36:17; Jer 18:21 11:23 [A]Jer 6:9 [B]Jer 23:12; Hos 9:7; Mic 7:4 [C]Luke 19:44

11:13 Judah was so filled with idolatry that there were false deities for every city and a polluted altar on every street.

11:14 do not pray. Cf. 7:16 and *see note there.* Their own prayers, as long as they rejected God, could not gain the answer they desired (v. 11; Ps 66:18), and the same was true of another's prayers for them.

11:15 My beloved. A phrase showing God's sensitive regard for His relationship to Israel as a nation (cf. 2:2; 12:7). It does not carry the assumption, however, that every individual is spiritually saved (cf. 5:10a). **vile deeds.** Shameful idolatry that defiled all that befits true temple worship, such as the examples in Eze 8:6–13. These were gross violations of the first 3 commandments (cf. Ex 20:2–7). **sacrificial flesh.** In some way, they corrupted the animal sacrifices by committing sin which they enjoyed (cf. 7:10).

11:16, 17 green olive tree. Israel was pictured as a grapevine (2:21), then an olive tree meant to bear good fruit. However, they produced fruit that calls only for the fire of judgment (as 5:10).

11:18–23 You showed me. Jeremiah's fellow townsmen from Anathoth, one of the 48 cities throughout the land dedicated to the Levites, plotted his death. Their words, "Let us destroy the tree," indicate their desire to silence Jeremiah by murder.

11:20 Let me see Your vengeance. Jeremiah pleaded for God's defense on his behalf, actually guaranteed in 1:8, 18, 19.

MAJOR TRIALS OF JEREMIAH
1. Trial By Death Threats (11:18–23)
2. Trial By Isolation (15:15–21)
3. Trial By Stocks (19:14–20:18)
4. Trial By Arrest (26:7–24)
5. Trial By Challenge (28:10–16)
6. Trial By Destruction (36:1–32)
7. Trial By Violence and Imprisonment (37:15)
8. Trial By Starvation (38:1–6)
9. Trial By Chains (40:1)
10. Trial By Rejection (42:1–43:4)

JEREMIAH'S PRAYER

12 [A]Righteous are You, O LORD, that I
would plead *my* case with You;
Indeed I would [B]discuss matters
of justice with You:
Why has the [C]way of the
wicked prospered?
Why are all those who [D]deal
in treachery at ease?
2 You have [A]planted them, they
have also taken root;
They grow, they have even produced fruit.
You are [B]near [a]to their lips
But far from their [b]mind.
3 But You [A]know me, O LORD;
You see me;
And You [B]examine my heart's
attitude toward You.
Drag them off like sheep for the slaughter
And [a]set them apart for a
[C]day of carnage!
4 How long is the [A]land to mourn
And the [B]vegetation of the
countryside to wither?
For the [C]wickedness of those
who dwell in it,
[D]Animals and birds have
been snatched away,
Because *men* have said, "He will
not see our latter [E]ending."

5 "If you have run with footmen and
they have tired you out,
Then how can you compete with horses?
If you fall down in a land of peace,
How will you do in the
[a,A]thicket of the Jordan?
6 "For even your [A]brothers and the
household of your father,
Even they have dealt
treacherously with you,
Even they have cried aloud after you.
Do not believe them, although they
may say [B]nice things to you."

GOD'S ANSWER

7 "I have [A]forsaken My house,
I have abandoned My inheritance;
I have given the [B]beloved of My soul
Into the hand of her enemies.
8 "My inheritance has become to Me
Like a lion in the forest;
She has [a,A]roared against Me;
Therefore I have come to [B]hate her.
9 "Is My inheritance like a speckled
bird of prey to Me?
Are the [A]birds of prey against
her on every side?
Go, gather all the [B]beasts of the field,
Bring them to devour!
10 "Many [A]shepherds have ruined My [B]vineyard,
They have [C]trampled down My field;
They have made My [D]pleasant field
A desolate wilderness.
11 "[a]It has been made a desolation,
Desolate, it [A]mourns [b]before Me;
The [B]whole land has been made desolate,
Because no man [C]lays it to heart.
12 "On all the [a,A]bare heights in the wilderness
Destroyers have come,
For a [B]sword of the LORD is devouring
From one end of the land
even to the [b]other;
There is [C]no peace for [c]anyone.
13 "They have [A]sown wheat and
have reaped thorns,
They have [B]strained themselves
[a]to no profit.
But be ashamed of your [b,C]harvest
Because of the [D]fierce anger of the LORD."

14 Thus says the LORD concerning all My [A]wicked
neighbors who [B]strike at the inheritance with which
I have endowed My people Israel, "Behold I am about
to uproot them from their land and will [C]uproot the
house of Judah from among them. 15 And it will come
about that after I have uprooted them, I will [A]again
have compassion on them; and I will [B]bring them
back, each one to his inheritance and each one to

12:1 [A]Ezra 9:15; Ps 51:4; 129:4; Jer 11:20 [B]Job 13:3 [C]Job 12:6; Jer 5:27, 28; Hab 1:4; Mal 3:15 [D]Jer 3:7, 20; 5:11 12:2 [a]Lit *in their mouth* [b]Lit *kidneys* [A]Jer 11:17; 45:4; Ezek 17:5-10 [B]Is 29:13; Jer 3:10; Ezek 33:31; Titus 1:16 12:3 [a]Lit *sanctify them* [A]Ps 139:1-4 [B]Ps 7:9; 11:5; Jer 11:20 [C]Jer 17:18; 50:27; James 5:5 12:4 [A]Jer 4:28; 9:10; 23:10 [B]Joel 1:10-17 [C]Ps 107:34 [D]Jer 4:25; 7:20; 9:10; Hos 4:3; Hab 3:17 [E]Jer 5:31; Ezek 7:2 12:5 [a]Lit *pride* [A]Jer 49:19; 50:44 12:6 [A]Gen 37:4-11; Job 6:15; Ps 69:8; Jer 9:4, 5 [B]Ps 12:2; Prov 26:25 12:7 [A]Is 2:6; Jer 7:29; 23:39 [B]Jer 11:15; Hos 11:1-8 12:8 [a]Lit *raised her voice* [A]Is 59:13 [B]Hos 9:15; Amos 6:8 12:9 [A]2 Kin 24:2; Ezek 23:22-25 [B]Is 56:9; Jer 7:33; 15:3; 34:20 12:10 [A]Jer 6:3; 23:1 [B]Ps 80:8-16; Is 5:1-7 [C]Is 63:18 [D]Jer 3:19 12:11 [a]Lit *One has made it* [b]Or *upon* [A]Jer 12:4; 14:2; 23:10 [B]Jer 4:20, 27; 25:11 [C]Is 42:25 12:12 [a]Or *caravan trails* [b]Lit *other end of the land* [c]Lit *all flesh* [A]Jer 3:2, 21 [B]Is 34:6; Jer 47:6; Amos 9:4 [C]Jer 16:5; 30:5 12:13 [a]Lit *they do not profit* [b]Lit *products* [A]Lev 26:16; Deut 28:38; Mic 6:15; Hag 1:6 [B]Is 55:2; Jer 9:5 [C]Jer 17:10 [D]Jer 4:26; 25:37, 38 12:14 [A]Jer 49:1, 7; Zeph 2:8-10 [B]Jer 2:3; 50:11, 12; Zech 2:8 [C]Deut 30:3; Ps 106:47; Is 11:11-16 12:15 [A]Jer 48:47; 49:6, 39 [B]Amos 9:14

12:1 **Why . . . ?** The issue of why the wicked escape for a time unscathed has often been raised by God's people (cf. Ps 73; Hab 1:2–4).

12:3 **Drag them off . . . for the slaughter.** The prophet here turned from the sadness of pleading for his people to calling on God to punish them. Such imprecatory prayers are similar to prayers throughout the Psalms.

12:4 **He will not see our latter ending.** Here is the foolish idea that Jeremiah was wrong and didn't know how things would happen.

12:5 **If you have run.** The Lord replied to Jeremiah telling him that if he grew faint with lesser trials and felt like quitting, what would he do when the battle got even harder? **thicket of the Jordan.** The river in flood stage overflowed its banks into a plain that grew up as a thicket. The point is that Jeremiah needed to be ready to deal with tougher testings, pictured by the invader's overwhelming the land like a flood, or posing high danger as in the Jordan thicket where concealed wild animals could terrify a person.

12:6 **even your brothers.** Jeremiah met antagonism not only from fellow townsmen (cf. 11:18–23 and *see note there*), but from his own family! He was separated from them (v. 7).

12:8 **Like a lion.** Jeremiah's own people collectively are like a lion acting ferociously against him.

12:9 **a speckled bird of prey.** God's people, speckled with sin and compromise, are opposed by other birds of prey, i.e., enemy nations.

12:12 **sword of the LORD.** God's strength can be for defending (cf. 47:6; Jdg 7:20) or, in this case, condemning. The Babylonians were God's sword doing His will.

12:14 **wicked neighbors.** Other nations which hurt Israel will, in their turn, also receive judgment from the Lord (cf. 9:26; 25:14–32; chaps. 46–51).

12:15 **bring them back.** God will restore His people to the land of Israel in a future millennial day, as indicated in chaps. 30–33.

his land. 16 Then if they will really [A]learn the ways
of My people, to [B]swear by My name, 'As the LORD
lives,' even as they taught My people to [C]swear by
Baal, they will be [D]built up in the midst of My people.
17 But if they will not listen, then I will [A]uproot that
nation, uproot and destroy it," declares the LORD.

THE RUINED WAISTBAND

13 Thus the LORD said to me, "Go and [A]buy yourself a linen waistband and put it around your
waist, but do not put it in water." 2 So I bought the
waistband in accordance with the [A]word of the LORD
and put it around my waist. 3 Then the word of the
LORD came to me a second time, saying, 4 "Take the
waistband that you have bought, which is around
your waist, and arise, go to [a]the [A]Euphrates and hide
it there in a crevice of the rock." 5 So I went and hid
it by the Euphrates, [A]as the LORD had commanded
me. 6 After many days the LORD said to me, "Arise,
go to the Euphrates and take from there the waistband which I commanded you to hide there." 7 Then I
went to the Euphrates and dug, and I took the waistband from the place where I had hidden it; and lo,
the waistband was ruined, it was totally worthless.
8 Then the word of the LORD came to me, saying, 9 "Thus says the LORD, 'Just so will I destroy
the [A]pride of Judah and the great pride of Jerusalem. 10 This wicked people, who [A]refuse to listen to
My words, who [B]walk in the stubbornness of their
hearts and have gone after other gods to serve them
and to bow down to them, let them be just like this
waistband which is totally worthless. 11 For as the
waistband clings to the waist of a man, so I made the
whole household of Israel and the whole household
of Judah [A]cling to Me,' declares the LORD, 'that they
might be for Me a people, for [a,B]renown, for [C]praise
and for glory; but they [D]did not listen.'

CAPTIVITY THREATENED

12 "Therefore you are to speak this word to them,
'Thus says the LORD, the God of Israel, "Every jug
is to be filled with wine."' And when they say to
you, 'Do we not very well know that every jug is
to be filled with wine?' 13 then say to them, 'Thus
says the LORD, "Behold I am about to fill all the inhabitants of this land—the kings that sit for David
on his throne, the priests, the prophets and all the
inhabitants of Jerusalem—with [A]drunkenness! 14 I
will [A]dash them against each other, both the [B]fathers
and the sons together," declares the LORD. "I will
[C]not show pity nor be sorry nor have compassion
so as not to destroy them."'"

15 Listen and give heed, do not be [A]haughty,
For the LORD has spoken.
16 [A]Give glory to the LORD your God,
Before He brings [B]darkness
And before your [C]feet stumble
On the dusky mountains,
And while you are hoping for light
He makes it into [D]deep darkness,
And turns *it* into gloom.
17 But [A]if you will not listen to it,
My soul will [B]sob in secret for *such* pride;
And my eyes will bitterly weep
And flow down with tears,
Because the [C]flock of the LORD
has been taken captive.

12:16 [A]Is 42:6; 49:6 [B]Jer 4:2; Zeph 1:5 [C]Josh 23:7; Jer 5:7 [D]Jer 3:17; 4:2; 16:19 12:17 [A]Ps 2:8-12; Is 60:12 13:1 [A]Jer 13:11 13:2 [A]Is 20:2; Ezek 2:8 13:4 [a]Or *Parah,* cf Josh 18:23; so through v 7 [A]Jer 51:63 13:5 [A]Ex 39:42, 43; 40:16 13:9 [A]Lev 26:19; Is 2:10-17; 23:9; Jer 13:15-17; Zeph 3:11 13:10 [A]Num 14:11; 2 Chr 36:15, 16; Jer 11:10 [B]Jer 9:14; 11:8; 16:12 13:11 [a]Lit *a name* [A]Ex 19:5, 6; Deut 32:10, 11 [B]Jer 32:20 [C]Is 43:21; Jer 33:9 [D]Ps 81:11; Jer 7:13, 24, 26 13:13 [A]Ps 60:3; 75:8; Is 51:17; 63:6; Jer 25:27; 51:7, 57 13:14 [A]Is 9:20, 21; Jer 19:9-11 [B]Jer 6:21; Ezek 5:10 [C]Deut 29:20; Is 27:11; Jer 16:5; 21:7 13:15 [A]Prov 16:5; Is 28:14-22 13:16 [A]Josh 7:19; Ps 96:8 [B]Is 5:30; 8:22; 59:9; Amos 5:18; 8:9 [C]Prov 4:19; Jer 23:12 [D]Ps 44:19; 107:10, 14; Jer 2:6 13:17 [A]Mal 2:2 [B]Ps 119:136; Jer 9:1; 14:17; Luke 19:41, 42 [C]Ps 80:1; Jer 23:1, 2

13:1 a linen waistband. One of several signs Jeremiah enacted to illustrate God's message (cf. Introduction) involved putting on a linen waistband (generally the inner garment against the skin). This depicted Israel's close intimacy with God in the covenant, so that they could glorify Him (v. 11). **do not put it in water.** Signified the moral filth of the nation. Buried and allowed time to rot (v. 7), the waistband pictured Israel as useless to God because of sin (v. 10). Hiding it by the Euphrates (v. 6) pointed to the land of Babylon, where God would exile Israel to deal with her pride (cf. v. 9).

13:4 Euphrates. This refers literally to a site on the Euphrates River because: 1) the Euphrates is the area of exile (20:4); 2) "many days" fits the round trip of well over 1,000 mi. (v. 6); and 3) the ruining of the nation's pride (v. 9) relates to judgment by Babylon (vv. 10, 11).

13:12–14 Every jug. God pictured inhabitants of Israel in Babylon's invasion as jugs or skins of wine. As wine causes drunkenness, they will be dazed, stumbling in darkness (cf. v. 16), out of control, and victims of destruction (v. 14).

13:16 Give glory to the LORD. Show by repentance and obedience to God that you respect His majesty.

OBJECT LESSONS IN JEREMIAH
The Linen Waistband (13:1–11)
The Vessel Marred and Remade (18:1–11)
The Jar Dashed upon the Rocks (19:10–11)
Two Baskets of Figs (24:1–10)
The Wooden and Iron Yokes (chaps. 27; 28)
The Purchase of Land (32:6–44)
The Stones in Egypt (43:8–10)

18 Say to the [A]king and the queen mother,
"[B]Take a lowly seat,
For your beautiful [C]crown
Has come down from your head."
19 The [A]cities of the Negev have
been locked up,
And there is no one to open *them;*
All [B]Judah has been carried into exile,
Wholly carried into exile.

20 "Lift up your eyes and see
Those coming [A]from the north.
Where is the [B]flock that was given you,
Your beautiful sheep?
21 "What will you say when He
appoints over you—
And you yourself had taught them—
Former [a,A]companions to
be head over you?
Will not [B]pangs take hold of you
Like a woman in childbirth?
22 "If you [A]say in your heart,
'[B]Why have these things happened to me?'
Because of the [C]magnitude
of your iniquity
[D]Your skirts have been removed
And your heels have [a]been exposed.
23 "[A]Can the Ethiopian change his skin
Or the leopard his spots?
Then you also can [B]do good
Who are accustomed to doing evil.
24 "Therefore I will [A]scatter them
like drifting straw
To the desert [B]wind.
25 "This is your [A]lot, the portion
measured to you
From Me," declares the LORD,
"Because you have [B]forgotten Me
And trusted in falsehood.
26 "So I Myself have also [A]stripped
your skirts off over your face,
That your shame may be seen.
27 "As for your [A]adulteries and
your *lustful* neighings,
The [B]lewdness of your prostitution
On the [C]hills in the field,
I have seen your abominations.
Woe to you, O Jerusalem!
[D]How long will you remain unclean?"

DROUGHT AND A PRAYER FOR MERCY

14 That which came as the word of the LORD to
Jeremiah in regard to the [A]drought:

2 "Judah mourns
And [A]her gates languish;
They sit on the ground [B]in mourning,
And the [C]cry of Jerusalem has ascended.
3 "Their nobles have [A]sent their
[a]servants for water;
They have come to the [B]cisterns
and found no water.
They have returned with
their vessels empty;
They have been [C]put to shame
and humiliated,
And they [D]cover their heads.
4 "Because the [A]ground is [a]cracked,
For there has been [B]no rain on the land;
The [C]farmers have been put to shame,
They have covered their heads.
5 "For even the doe in the field has given
birth only to abandon *her young,*
Because there is [A]no grass.
6 "The [A]wild donkeys stand on
the bare heights;
They pant for air like jackals,
Their eyes fail
For there is [B]no vegetation.
7 "Although our [A]iniquities
testify against us,
O LORD, act [B]for Your name's sake!
Truly our [C]apostasies have been many,
We have [D]sinned against You.
8 "O [A]Hope of Israel,
Its [B]Savior in [C]time of distress,
Why are You like a stranger in the land
Or like a traveler who has pitched
his *tent* for the night?
9 "Why are You like a man dismayed,
Like a mighty man who [A]cannot save?
Yet [B]You are in our midst, O LORD,
And we are [C]called by Your name;
Do not forsake us!"

13:18 [A]2 Kin 24:12, 15; Jer 22:26 [B]2 Chr 33:12, 19 [C]Ex 39:28; Is 3:20; Ezek 24:17, 23; 44:18 13:19 [A]Jer 32:44 [B]Jer 20:4; 52:27-30 13:20 [A]Jer 1:15; 6:22; Hab 1:6 [B]Jer 13:17; 23:2 13:21 [a]Or *chieftains* [A]Jer 2:25; 38:22 [B]Is 13:8; Jer 4:31 13:22 [a]Or *suffered violence* [A]Deut 7:17 [B]Jer 5:19; 16:10 [C]Jer 2:17-19; 9:2-9 [D]Is 47:2; Ezek 16:37; Nah 3:5 13:23 [A]Prov 27:22; Is 1:5 [B]Jer 4:22; 9:5 13:24 [A]Lev 26:33; Jer 9:16; Ezek 5:2, 12 [B]Jer 4:11; 18:17 13:25 [A]Job 20:29; Ps 11:6; Matt 24:51 [B]Ps 9:17; Jer 2:32; 3:21 13:26 [A]Lam 1:8; Ezek 23:29; Hos 2:10 13:27 [A]Jer 5:7, 8 [B]Jer 11:15 [C]Is 65:7; Jer 2:20; Ezek 6:13 [D]Prov 1:22; Hos 8:5 14:1 [A]Jer 17:8 14:2 [A]Is 3:26 [B]Jer 8:21 [C]1 Sam 5:12; Jer 11:11; 46:12; Zech 7:13 14:3 [a]Lit *little ones* [A]1 Kin 18:5 [B]2 Kin 18:31; Jer 2:13 [C]Job 6:20; Ps 40:14 [D]2 Sam 15:30 14:4 [a]Lit *shattered* [A]Joel 1:19, 20 [B]Jer 3:3 [C]Joel 1:11 14:5 [A]Is 15:6 14:6 [A]Job 39:5, 6; Jer 2:24 [B]Joel 1:18 14:7 [A]Is 59:12; Hos 5:5 [B]Ps 25:11; Jer 14:21 [C]Jer 5:6; 8:5 [D]Jer 3:25; 8:14; 14:20 14:8 [A]Jer 17:13 [B]Is 43:3; 63:8 [C]Ps 9:9; 50:15 14:9 [A]Num 11:23; Is 50:2; 59:1 [B]Ex 29:45; Ps 46:5; Jer 8:19 [C]Is 63:19; Jer 15:16

13:18 king … queen mother. Jehoiachin and Nehushta, ca. 597 B.C. (cf. 22:24–26; 29:2; 2Ki 24:8–17). Because the king was only 18 years old, she held the real power.

13:19 Wholly carried into exile. "All" and "wholly" do not require absolutely every individual, for Jeremiah elsewhere explains that some were to be slain and a remnant left in the land or fleeing to Egypt (chaps. 39–44).

13:23 Ethiopian … leopard. The vivid analogy assumes that sinners cannot change their sinful natures. Only God can change the heart (31:18, 31–34).

13:26 stripped your skirts off. This was done to shame captive women and prostitutes (cf. Na 3:5).

13:27 *lustful* neighings. Refers to desire at an animal level, without conscience.

14:1 drought. Jeremiah seems to actually give the prophecy of this chapter during a drought in Judah (vv. 2–6).

14:2 gates languish. The "gates" were the place of public concourse, which during drought and consequent famine were empty or occupied by mourners.

14:7 O LORD. Jeremiah from 14:7–15:21, pursues a series of prayers in which he dialogues with the Lord, who hears and responds (as 1:7; 12:5–17, etc.). Five rounds or exchanges occur (14:7–12; 14:13–18; 14:19–15:9; 15:10–14; 15:15–21).

14:7–9 our apostasies. The prophet confesses Judah's guilt but reminds God that His reputation is tied up with what happens to His people (vv. 7, 9). He asks that the Lord be not indifferent as a stranger or overnight visitor (v. 8).

10 Thus says the LORD to this people, "Even so
they have [A]loved to wander; they have not [B]kept
their feet in check. Therefore the LORD does [C]not
accept them; now He will [D]remember their iniquity
and call their sins to account." 11 So the LORD said
to me, "[A]Do not pray for the welfare of this people.
12 When they fast, I am [A]not going to listen to their
cry; and when they offer [B]burnt offering and grain
offering, I am not going to accept them. Rather I
am going to [C]make an end of them by the [D]sword,
famine and pestilence."

FALSE PROPHETS

13 But, "Ah, Lord [a]GOD!" I said, "Look, the prophets
are telling them, 'You [A]will not see the sword nor
will you have famine, but I will give you [b]lasting
[B]peace in this place.' " 14 Then the LORD said to me,
"The [A]prophets are prophesying falsehood in My
name. [B]I have neither sent them nor commanded
them nor spoken to them; they are prophesying
to you a [C]false vision, divination, futility and the
deception of their own [a]minds. 15 Therefore thus
says the LORD concerning the prophets who are
prophesying in My name, although it was not I
who sent them—yet they keep saying, 'There will
be no sword or famine in this land'—[A]by sword and
famine those prophets shall [a]meet their end! 16 The
people also to whom they are prophesying will be
[A]thrown out into the streets of Jerusalem because
of the famine and the sword; and there will be no
one to [B]bury them—*neither* them, *nor* their wives,
nor their sons, nor their daughters—for I will [C]pour
out their *own* wickedness on them.

17 "You will say this word to them,
'[A]Let my eyes flow down with
tears night and day,
And let them not cease;
For the virgin [B]daughter of my people
has been crushed with a mighty blow,
With a sorely [C]infected wound.
18 'If I [A]go out to the country,
Behold, those [a]slain with the sword!
Or if I enter the city,
Behold, diseases of famine!
For [B]both prophet and priest
Have [b]gone roving about in the
land that they do not know.' "
19 Have You completely [A]rejected Judah?
Or have [a]You loathed Zion?
Why have You stricken us so that
we [B]are beyond healing?
We [C]waited for peace, but
nothing good *came;*
And for a time of healing,
but behold, terror!
20 We [A]know our wickedness, O LORD,
The iniquity of our fathers, for [B]we
have sinned against You.
21 Do not despise *us,* [A]for Your
own name's sake;
Do not disgrace the [B]throne of Your glory;
Remember *and* do not annul
Your covenant with us.
22 Are there any among the [a,A]idols of
the nations who [B]give rain?
Or can the heavens grant showers?
Is it not You, O LORD our God?
Therefore we [b,C]hope in You,
For You are the one who has
done all these things.

JUDGMENT MUST COME

15 Then the LORD said to me, "Even [A]though [B]Mo-
ses and [C]Samuel were to [D]stand before Me, My
[a]heart would not be [b]with this people; [E]send them
away from My presence and let them go! 2 And it
shall be that when they say to you, 'Where should we
go?' then you are to tell them, 'Thus says the LORD:

"Those *destined* [A]for death, to death;
And those *destined* for the
sword, to the sword;
And those *destined* for
famine, to famine;
And those *destined* for
captivity, to captivity." '

3 I will [A]appoint over them four kinds *of doom,*"
declares the LORD: "the sword to slay, the [B]dogs to
drag off, and the [C]birds of the sky and the beasts of

14:10 [A]Jer 2:25; 3:13 [B]Ps 119:101 [C]Jer 6:20; Amos 5:22 [D]Jer 44:21-23; Hos 8:13; 9:9 14:11 [A]Ex 32:10; Jer 7:16; 11:14 14:12 [A]Prov 1:28; Is 1:15; Jer 11:11; Ezek 8:18; Mic 3:4; Zech 7:13 [B]Jer 6:20; 7:21 [C]Jer 8:13 [D]Jer 21:9 14:13 [a]Heb *YHWH,* usually rendered *LORD* [b]Lit *peace of truth* [A]Jer 5:12; 23:17 [B]Jer 6:14; 8:11 14:14 [a]Lit *hearts* [A]Jer 5:31; 23:25 [B]Jer 23:21 [C]Jer 23:16, 26; 27:9, 10; Ezek 12:24 14:15 [a]Lit *be finished* [A]Jer 23:15; Ezek 14:10 14:16 [A]Ps 79:2, 3; Jer 7:33; 15:2, 3 [B]Jer 8:1, 2 [C]Prov 1:31; Jer 13:22-25 14:17 [A]Jer 9:1; 13:17; Lam 1:16 [B]Is 37:22; Jer 8:21; Lam 1:15; 2:13 [C]Jer 10:19; 30:14 14:18 [a]Lit *pierced* [b]Or *gone around trading* [A]Jer 6:25; Lam 1:20; Ezek 7:15 [B]Jer 6:13; 8:10 14:19 [a]Lit *Your soul* [A]Jer 6:30; 7:29; 12:7; Lam 5:22 [B]Jer 30:13 [C]Job 30:26; Jer 8:15; 1 Thess 5:3 14:20 [A]Neh 9:2; Ps 32:5; Jer 3:25 [B]Jer 8:14; 14:7; Dan 9:8 14:21 [A]Ps 25:11; Jer 14:7 [B]Jer 3:17; 17:12 14:22 [a]Lit *vanities* [b]Or *wait for* [A]Is 41:29; Jer 10:3 [B]1 Kin 17:1; Jer 5:24 [C]Lam 3:26 15:1 [a]Lit *soul* [b]Lit *toward* [A]Ps 99:6; Ezek 14:14, 20 [B]Ex 32:11-14; Num 14:13-20; Ps 99:6; 106:23 [C]1 Sam 7:9; 12:23 [D]Jer 15:19; 18:20; 35:19 [E]2 Kin 17:20; Jer 7:15; 10:18; 52:3 15:2 [A]Jer 14:12; 24:10; 43:11; Ezek 5:2, 12; Zech 11:9; Rev 13:10 15:3 [A]Lev 26:16, 22, 25; Ezek 14:21 [B]1 Kin 21:23, 24 [C]Deut 28:26; Is 18:6; Jer 7:33

14:10–12 God responded in this first exchange that 1) He must judge Judah for chronic sinfulness, and 2) Jeremiah is not to pray for the sparing of Judah nor will He respond to their prayers since unrepentance must be punished (cf. 11:14, and *see note there*).

14:13 the prophets are telling them. Jeremiah seemed to put forth the excuse that the people cannot help it since the false prophets deluded them with lying assurances of peace.

14:14–18 The excuse was not valid. These were deceits spawned from the prophets' lying hearts. The prophets would suffer for their own sins (vv. 14, 15), but so would the people for their "wickedness" (vv. 16–18; 5:31).

14:17 virgin daughter. Judah is so called, having never before been under foreign bondage.

14:18 the land that they do not know. Babylon.

14:19, 20 Have You completely rejected Judah? Lest the Lord be casting Judah off forever, the prophet in deep contrition confesses the nation's sin (cf. Da 9:4ff.).

14:21 the throne of Your glory. Jerusalem, place of the temple.

15:1–9 It was ineffective at this point to intercede for the nation. Even prayers by Moses (cf. Nu 14:11–25) and Samuel (cf. 1Sa 12:19–25), eminent in intercession, would not defer judgment, where unrepentance persists (cf. 18:8; 26:3). Chief among things provoking judgment was the intense sin of King Manasseh (695–642 B.C.). Noted in v. 4., this provocation is recounted in 2Ki 21:1–18, cf. 2Ki 23:26, which says the Lord did not relent from His anger because of this (see also 2Ki 24:3, 4).

the earth to devour and destroy. 4 I will [A]make them
an object of horror among all the kingdoms of the
earth because of [B]Manasseh, the son of Hezekiah,
the king of Judah, for what he did in Jerusalem.

5 "Indeed, who will have [A]pity
on you, O Jerusalem,
Or who will [B]mourn for you,
Or who will turn aside to ask
about your welfare?
6 "You who have [A]forsaken Me,"
declares the LORD,
"You keep [B]going backward.
So I will [C]stretch out My hand
against you and destroy you;
I am [D]tired of relenting!
7 "I will [A]winnow them with a winnowing fork
At the gates of the land;
I will [B]bereave *them* of children,
I will destroy My people;
[C]They did not [a]repent of their ways.
8 "Their [A]widows will be more
numerous before Me
Than the sand of the seas;
I will bring against them, against
the mother of a young man,
A [B]destroyer at noonday;
I will suddenly bring down on her
Anguish and dismay.
9 "She who [A]bore seven *sons* pines away;
[a]Her breathing is labored.
Her [B]sun has set while it was yet day;
She has been [C]shamed and humiliated.
So I will [D]give over their
survivors to the sword
Before their enemies," declares the LORD.

10 [A]Woe to me, my mother, that
you have borne me
As a [B]man of strife and a man of
contention to all the land!
I have not [C]lent, nor have men
lent money to me,
Yet everyone curses me.
11 The LORD said, "Surely I will [A]set
you free for *purposes of* good;
Surely I will cause the [B]enemy to
make supplication to you
In a time of disaster and a time of distress.

12 "Can anyone smash iron,
[A]Iron from the north, or bronze?
13 "Your [A]wealth and your treasures
I will give for booty [B]without cost,
Even for all your sins
And within all your borders.
14 "Then I will cause your enemies to bring [a]*it*
Into a [A]land you do not know;
For a [B]fire has been kindled in My anger,
It will burn upon you."

JEREMIAH'S PRAYER AND GOD'S ANSWER

15 [A]You who know, O LORD,
Remember me, take notice of me,
And [B]take vengeance for me
on my persecutors.
Do not, in view of Your
patience, take me away;
Know that [C]for Your sake I endure reproach.
16 Your words were found and I [A]ate them,
And Your [B]words became for me a
joy and the delight of my heart;
For I have been [C]called by Your name,
O LORD God of hosts.
17 I [A]did not sit in the circle of merrymakers,
Nor did I exult.
Because of Your hand *upon me* I sat [B]alone,
For You [C]filled me with indignation.
18 Why has my pain been perpetual
And my [A]wound incurable,
refusing to be healed?
Will You indeed be to me [B]like
a deceptive *stream*
With water that is unreliable?

19 Therefore, thus says the LORD,
"[A]If you return, then I will restore you—
[B]Before Me you will stand;
And [C]if you extract the precious
from the worthless,
You will become [a]My spokesman.

15:4 [A]Lev 26:33; Jer 24:9; 29:18; Ezek 23:46 [B]2 Kin 21:1-18; 23:26, 27; 24:3, 4; 2 Chr 33:1-9 15:5 [A]Ps 69:20; Is 51:19; Jer 13:14; 21:7 [B]Nah 3:7 15:6 [A]Jer 6:19; 8:9 [B]Is 1:4; Jer 7:24 [C]Jer 6:12; Zeph 1:4 [D]Jer 6:11; 7:16 15:7 [a]Lit *turn back from* [A]Ps 1:4; Jer 51:2 [B]Jer 18:21; Hos 9:12-16 [C]Is 9:13 15:8 [A]Is 3:25, 26; 4:1 [B]Jer 22:7 15:9 [a]Or *She has breathed out her soul* [A]1 Sam 2:5; Is 47:9 [B]Jer 6:4; Amos 8:9 [C]Jer 50:12 [D]Jer 21:7 15:10 [A]Job 3:1, 3; Jer 20:14 [B]Jer 1:18, 19; 15:20; 20:7, 8 [C]Ex 22:25; Lev 25:36, 37; Deut 23:19 15:11 [A]Ps 138:3; Is 41:10 [B]Jer 21:2; 37:3; 38:14; 42:2 15:12 [A]Jer 28:14 15:13 [A]Jer 17:3; 20:5 [B]Ps 44:12; Is 52:3 15:14 [a]I.e. your possessions [A]Deut 28:36, 64; Jer 16:13 [B]Deut 32:22; Ps 21:9; Jer 17:4 15:15 [A]Jer 12:3 [B]Jer 11:20 [C]Ps 44:22; 69:7-9; Jer 20:8 15:16 [A]Ezek 3:3 [B]Job 23:12; Ps 119:103 [C]Jer 14:9 15:17 [A]Ps 1:1; Jer 16:8; 2 Cor 6:17 [B]Ps 102:7; Jer 13:17; Lam 3:28; Ezek 3:24, 25 [C]Jer 6:11 15:18 [A]Job 34:6; Jer 30:12, 15; Mic 1:9 [B]Job 6:15, 20; Jer 14:3 15:19 [a]Lit *as My mouth* [A]Jer 4:1; Zech 3:7 [B]1 Kin 17:1; Jer 15:1; 35:19 [C]Jer 6:29; Ezek 22:26; 44:23

15:6 **I am tired of relenting!** God often withholds the judgment He threatens (cf. 26:19; Ex 32:14; 1Ch 21:15), sparing men so that His patience might lead them to repentance (cf. Ro 2:4, 5; 3:25).

15:9 **sun … set while … yet day.** Young mothers die in youth and their children are killed.

15:10 **Woe to me.** Overcome by grief (cf. 9:1), Jeremiah wished that he had not been born (as 20:14–18). He had not been a bad or disagreeable creditor or debtor, either of whom kindle hatred. Yet his people cursed him, and he felt the sting.

15:11–14 In the midst of judgment, the Lord promised protection for the obedient remnant in Judah (cf. Mal 3:16, 17). The Babylonians permitted some to stay in the land when they departed (40:5–7). Jeremiah personally received kind treatment from the invader (40:1–6), and his enemies in Judah would later appeal to him (21:1–6; 37:3; 42:1–6). Ultimately, a band of renegade Judeans took Jeremiah to Egypt against God's will (cf. 43:1–7).

15:15–18 **You who know, O LORD.** Jeremiah, in a mood of self-pity, reminded the Lord of his faithfulness in bearing reproach, his love for His Word, and his separation from evil men to stand alone.

15:18 **a deceptive *stream*.** He asked that the Lord not fail him like a wadi that has dried up (v. 18). The answer to this concern is in 2:13 (the Lord is his fountain), 15:19–21, and 17:5–8.

15:19 The Lord reprimanded Jeremiah for self-pity and impatience. He had to have the proper posture before God and repent. If he did so, he would discern true values ("extract the precious," a figure drawn from removing pure metal from dross), and have the further

They for their part may turn to you,
But as for you, you must not turn to them.
20 "Then I will [A]make you to this people
A fortified wall of bronze;
And though they fight against you,
They will not prevail over you;
For [B]I am with you to save you
And deliver you," declares the LORD.
21 "So I will [A]deliver you from the
hand of the wicked,
And I will [B]redeem you from the
[a]grasp of the violent."

DISTRESSES FORETOLD

16 The word of the LORD also came to me saying, 2 "You shall not take a wife for yourself
nor have sons or daughters in this place." 3 For thus
says the LORD concerning the sons and daughters
born in this place, and concerning their [A]mothers
who bear them, and their [B]fathers who beget them
in this land: 4 "They will [A]die of deadly diseases,
they [B]will not be lamented or buried; they will be
as [C]dung on the surface of the ground and come to
an end by sword and famine, and their carcasses
will become food for the [D]birds of the sky and for
the beasts of the earth."

5 For thus says the LORD, "Do not enter a house
of [a,A]mourning, or go to lament or to console them;
for I have [B]withdrawn My peace from this people,"
declares the LORD, "*My* [C]lovingkindness and compassion. 6 Both [A]great men and small will die in
this land; they will not be buried, they will not be
lamented, nor will anyone [B]gash himself or [C]shave
his head for them. 7 Men will not [A]break *bread* in
mourning for them, to comfort anyone for the dead,
nor give them a cup of consolation to drink for anyone's father or mother. 8 Moreover you shall [A]not go
into a house of feasting to sit with them to eat and
drink." 9 For thus says the LORD of hosts, the God of
Israel: "Behold, I am going to [a,A]eliminate from this
place, before your eyes and in your time, the voice
of rejoicing and the voice of gladness, the voice of
the groom and the voice of the bride.

10 "Now when you tell this people all these words,
they will say to you, '[A]For what reason has the LORD
declared all this great calamity against us? And
what is our iniquity, or what is our sin which we
have committed against the LORD our God?' 11 Then
you are to say to them, '*It is* [A]because your forefathers have forsaken Me,' declares the LORD, 'and
have followed [B]other gods and served them and
bowed down to them; but Me they have forsaken
and have not kept My law. 12 You too have done evil,
even [A]more than your forefathers; for behold, you
are each one walking according to the [B]stubborn-
ness of his own [C]evil heart, without listening to Me.
13 So I will [A]hurl you out of this land into the [B]land
which you have not known, neither you nor your
fathers; and there you will [C]serve other gods day
and night, for I will grant you no favor.'

GOD WILL RESTORE THEM

14 "[A]Therefore behold, days are coming," declares
the LORD, "when it will no longer be said, 'As the
LORD lives, who [B]brought up the sons of Israel out
of the land of Egypt,' 15 but, 'As the LORD lives, who
brought up the sons of Israel from the [A]land of
the north and from all the countries where He had
banished them.' For I will restore them to their own
land which I gave to their fathers.

16 "Behold, I am going to send for many [A]fish-
ermen," declares the LORD, "and they will fish for
them; and afterwards I will send for many hunters,
and they will [B]hunt them [C]from every mountain and
every hill and from the clefts of the rocks. 17 [A]For
My eyes are on all their ways; they are not hidden
from My face, [B]nor is their iniquity concealed from
My eyes. 18 I will first [A]doubly repay their iniquity
and their sin, because they have [B]polluted My land;
they have filled My inheritance with the carcasses of
their [C]detestable idols and with their abominations."

19 O LORD, my [A]strength and my stronghold,
And my [B]refuge in the day of distress,
To You the [C]nations will come
From the ends of the earth and say,

15:20 [A]Jer 1:18, 19; Ezek 3:9 [B]Ps 46:7; Is 41:10; Jer 1:8, 19; 15:15; 20:11 15:21 [a]Lit *palm* [A]Ps 37:40; Is 49:25; Jer 20:13; 39:11, 12 [B]Gen 48:16; Is 49:26; 60:16; Jer 31:11; 50:34 16:3 [A]Jer 15:8 [B]Jer 6:21 16:4 [A]Jer 15:2 [B]Jer 25:33 [C]Ps 83:10; Jer 9:22; 25:33 [D]Ps 79:2; Is 18:6; Jer 15:3; 34:20 16:5 [a]Or *banqueting* [A]Ezek 24:16-23 [B]Jer 12:12; 15:1-4 [C]Ps 25:6; Is 27:11; Jer 13:14 16:6 [A]2 Chr 36:17; Ezek 9:6 [B]Deut 14:1; Jer 41:5; 47:5 [C]Is 22:12 16:7 [A]Deut 26:14; Ezek 24:17; Hos 9:4 16:8 [A]Eccl 7:2-4; Is 22:12-14; Jer 15:17; Amos 6:4-6 16:9 [a]Lit *cause to cease* [A]Jer 7:34; 25:10; Ezek 26:13; Hos 2:11; Rev 18:23 16:10 [A]Deut 29:24; 1 Kin 9:8; Jer 5:19; 13:22; 22:8 16:11 [A]Deut 29:25; 1 Kin 9:9; 2 Chr 7:22; Neh 9:26-29; Jer 22:9 [B]Deut 29:26; 1 Kin 9:9; Ps 106:35-41; Jer 5:7-9; 8:2; Ezek 11:21; 1 Pet 4:3 16:12 [A]Jer 7:26 [B]1 Sam 15:23; Jer 7:24; 9:14; 13:10 [C]Eccl 9:3; Mark 7:21 16:13 [A]Deut 4:26, 27; 2 Chr 7:20; Jer 15:1 [B]Jer 15:14; 17:4 [C]Deut 4:28; 28:36; Jer 5:19 16:14 [A]Is 43:18; Jer 23:7 [B]Ex 20:2; Deut 15:15 16:15 [A]Ps 106:47; Is 11:11-16; 14:1; Jer 3:18; 23:8; 24:6 16:16 [A]Amos 4:2; Hab 1:14, 15 [B]1 Sam 26:20; Mic 7:2 [C]Is 2:21; Amos 9:3 16:17 [A]2 Chr 16:9; Job 34:21; Ps 90:8; Prov 5:21; 15:3; Jer 23:24; 32:19; Zech 4:10; Luke 12:2; 1 Cor 4:5; Heb 4:13 [B]Jer 2:22 16:18 [A]Jer 17:18; Rev 18:6 [B]Num 35:33, 34; Jer 2:7; 3:9 [C]Jer 7:30; Ezek 11:18, 21 16:19 [A]Ps 18:1, 2; Is 25:4 [B]Nah 1:7 [C]Ps 22:27; Is 2:2; Jer 3:17; 4:2

privilege of being God's mouthpiece. Let sinners change to his values, but let him never compromise to theirs. As a man who is to assay and test others (6:27–30), he must first assay himself (cf. Moses, in Ex 4:22–26).

15:20, 21 When Jeremiah repents, God will protect him (vv. 20, 21, as 1:18, 19).

16:2 **You shall not take a wife.** Since destruction and exile are soon to fall on Judah, the prophet must not have a wife and family. God's kindness will keep him from anxiety over them in the awful situation of suffering and death (v. 4). Cf. 15:9 and 1Co 7:26.

16:5 **house of mourning.** This was a home where friends prepared a meal for a bereaved family. Don't mourn with them or rejoice, he is told (cf. v. 8).

16:6 **gash … shave his head.** These acts indicated extreme grief.

16:10–13 **For what reason … ?** Jeremiah was to explain the reason for the judgment, i.e., their forsaking God and worshiping false gods (v. 11; 2:13). They would get their fill of idols in Babylon (v. 13).

16:14, 15 **no longer be said.** In view of the Lord's promise of restoration from Babylon, the proof of God's redemptive power and faithfulness in the deliverance from Egypt would give way to a greater demonstration in the deliverance of His people from Babylon. That bondage was to be so severe that deliverance from Babylon was a greater relief than from Egypt.

16:15 **all the countries.** This reference is extensive enough to be fully realized only in the final gathering into Messiah's earthly kingdom.

16:16 **many fishermen … hunters.** These are references to Babylonian soldiers, who were doing God's judgment work (v. 17).

16:18 **doubly repay.** The word for "doubly" signified "full or complete," a fitting punishment for such severe sins.

16:19–21 The result of God's judgment on the Jews will be the end of idolatry; even some

"Our fathers have inherited
nothing but [D]falsehood,
Futility and [a,E]things of no profit."
20 Can man make gods for himself?
Yet they are [A]not gods!

21 "Therefore behold, I am going
to make them know—
This time I will [A]make them know
My [a]power and My might;
And they shall [B]know that My
name is the LORD."

THE DECEITFUL HEART

17 The [A]sin of Judah is written down
with an [B]iron stylus;
With a diamond point it is [C]engraved
upon the tablet of their heart
And on the horns of [a]their altars,
2 As they remember their [A]children,
So they *remember* their altars
and their [a,B]Asherim
By [C]green trees on the high hills.
3 O [A]mountain of Mine in the countryside,
I will [B]give over your wealth and
all your treasures for booty,
Your high places for sin
throughout your borders.
4 And you will, even of yourself,
[A]let go of your inheritance
That I gave you;
And I will make you serve your [B]enemies
In the [C]land which you do not know;
For you have [D]kindled a
fire in My anger
Which will burn forever.

5 Thus says the LORD,
"[A]Cursed is the man who trusts in mankind
And makes [B]flesh his [a]strength,
And whose heart turns away
from the LORD.
6 "For he will be like a [A]bush in the desert
And will not see when prosperity comes,
But will live in stony wastes
in the wilderness,
A [B]land of salt [a]without inhabitant.
7 "[A]Blessed is the man who trusts in the LORD
And whose [B]trust is the LORD.
8 "For he will be like a [A]tree
planted by the water,
That extends its roots by a stream
And will not fear when the heat comes;
But its leaves will be green,
And it will not be anxious in
a year of [B]drought
Nor cease to yield fruit.

9 "The [A]heart is more [B]deceitful than all else
And is desperately [C]sick;
Who can understand it?
10 "I, the LORD, [A]search the heart,
I test the [a]mind,
Even [B]to give to each man
according to his ways,
According to the [b]results of his deeds.
11 "As a partridge that hatches eggs
which it has not laid,
So is he who [A]makes a fortune, but unjustly;
In the midst of his days it will forsake him,
And in [a]the end he will be a [B]fool."

12 [A]A glorious throne on high
from the beginning
Is the place of our sanctuary.
13 O LORD, the [A]hope of Israel,
All who [B]forsake You will be put to shame.
Those who turn [a]away on earth
will be [C]written down,
Because they have forsaken the fountain
of living water, even the LORD.
14 [A]Heal me, O LORD, and I will be healed;
[B]Save me and I will be saved,
For You are my [C]praise.

16:19 [a]Lit *there is nothing profitable in them* [D]Is 44:20; Hab 2:18 [E]Is 44:10 16:20 [A]Ps 115:4-8; Is 37:19; Jer 2:11; 5:7; Hos 8:4-6; Gal 4:8 16:21 [a]Lit *hand* [A]Ps 9:16 [B]Ps 83:18; Is 43:3; Jer 33:2; Amos 5:8 17:1 [a]So ancient versions; M.T. *your* [A]Jer 2:22; 4:14 [B]Job 19:24 [C]Prov 3:3; 7:3; Is 49:16; 2 Cor 3:3 17:2 [a]I.e. wooden symbols of a female deity [A]Jer 7:18 [B]Ex 34:13; 2 Chr 24:18; 33:3; Is 17:8 [C]Jer 3:6 17:3 [A]Jer 26:18; Mic 3:12 [B]2 Kin 24:13; Is 39:4-6; Jer 15:13; 20:5 17:4 [A]Jer 12:7; Lam 5:2 [B]Deut 28:48; Is 14:3; Jer 15:14; 27:12, 13 [C]Jer 16:13 [D]Is 5:25; Jer 7:20; 15:14 17:5 [a]Lit *arm* [A]Ps 146:3; Is 2:22; 30:1; Ezek 29:7 [B]2 Chr 32:8; Is 31:3 17:6 [a]Lit *and is not inhabited* [A]Jer 48:6 [B]Deut 29:23; Job 39:6 17:7 [A]Ps 2:12; 34:8; 84:12; Prov 16:20 [B]Ps 40:4 17:8 [A]Ps 1:3; 92:12-14; Ezek 31:3-9 [B]Jer 14:1-6 17:9 [A]Eccl 9:3; Mark 7:21, 22 [B]Rom 7:11; Eph 4:22 [C]Is 1:5, 6; 6:10; Matt 13:15; Mark 2:17; Rom 1:21 17:10 [a]Lit *kidneys* [b]Lit *fruit* [A]1 Sam 16:7; 1 Chr 28:9; Ps 139:23; Prov 17:3; Jer 11:20; 20:12; Rom 8:27; Rev 2:23 [B]Ps 62:12; Jer 32:19; Rom 2:6 17:11 [a]Lit *his* [A]Jer 6:13; 8:10; 22:13, 17 [B]Luke 12:20 17:12 [A]Jer 3:17; 14:21 17:13 [a]Lit *away from Me* [A]Jer 14:8; 50:7 [B]Is 1:28 [C]Luke 10:20 17:14 [A]Jer 30:17; 33:6 [B]Ps 54:1; 60:5 [C]Deut 10:21; Ps 109:1

Gentiles, witnessing the severity, will renounce idols. After the return from Babylon, this was partly fulfilled as the Jews entirely and permanently renounced idols, and many Gentiles turned from their idols to Jehovah. However, the complete fulfillment will come in the final restoration of Israel (cf. Is 2:1–4; 49:6; 60:3).

17:1 The sin of Judah. Reasons for the judgment (chap. 16) continue here: 1) idolatry (vv. 1–4), 2) relying on the flesh (v. 5), and 3) dishonesty in amassing wealth (v. 11). iron stylus. The names of idols were engraved on the horns of their altars with such a tool. The idea is that Judah's sin was permanent, etched in them as if into stone. How much different to have God's word written on the heart (31:33).

17:3 mountain of Mine in the countryside. Jerusalem in Judah.

17:4 land … you do not know. Babylon.

17:5–8 Cursed is the man. Jeremiah contrasted the person who experiences barrenness (vv. 5, 6) with the one who receives blessing (vv. 7, 8). The difference in attitude is in "trust" placed in man or "trust" vested in the Lord (vv. 5, 7). And the contrast in vitality is between being like a parched dwarf juniper in the desert (v. 6) or a tree drawing sustenance from a stream to bear fruit (v. 8; cf. Ps 1:1–3).

17:10 I … search the heart. For the sin of man (vv. 1–4), for the barren man (vv. 5, 6), or the blessed man (vv. 7, 8), God is the final Judge and renders His judgment for their works (cf. Rev 20:11–15). By Him, actions are weighed (1Sa 2:3).

17:11 a partridge. This referred to a sand grouse which invaded and brooded over a nest not its own, but was forced to leave before the eggs hatched. It depicted a person who unjustly took possession of things he had no right to take and couldn't enjoy the benefits, despite all the effort.

17:14–18 Jeremiah voiced the prayerful cry that God would deliver him from his enemies (v. 14). Surrounded by ungodly people (vv. 1–6, 11, 13), he showed qualities of godliness: 1) God was his praise (v. 14); 2) he had a shepherd's heart to follow God (v. 16); 3) he was a man of prayer open to God's examination (v. 16); 4) God was his hope (v. 17); and 5) he trusted God's delivering faithfulness even in judgment (v. 18).

15 Look, they keep [A]saying to me,
"Where is the word of the LORD?
Let it come now!"
16 But as for me, I have not hurried away
from *being* a shepherd after You,
Nor have I longed for the woeful day;
[A]You Yourself know that the
utterance of my lips
Was in Your presence.
17 Do not be a [A]terror to me;
You are my [B]refuge in the day of disaster.
18 Let those who persecute me be
[A]put to shame, but as for me,
[B]let me not be put to shame;
Let them be dismayed, but let
me not be dismayed.
[C]Bring on them a day of disaster,
And crush them with twofold destruction!

THE SABBATH MUST BE KEPT

19 Thus the LORD said to me, "Go and stand in
the [a]public gate, through which the kings of Judah
come in and go out, as well as in all the gates of
Jerusalem; 20 and say to them, '[A]Listen to the word
of the LORD, [B]kings of Judah, and all Judah and
all inhabitants of Jerusalem who come in through
these gates: 21 Thus says the LORD, "[A]Take heed for
yourselves, and [B]do not carry any load on the sabbath day or bring anything in through the gates of
Jerusalem. 22 You shall not bring a load out of your
houses on the sabbath day [A]nor do any work, but
keep the sabbath day holy, as I [B]commanded your
[a]forefathers. 23 Yet they [A]did not listen or incline
their ears, but [B]stiffened their necks in order not
to listen or take correction.
24 "But it will come about, if you [A]listen atten-
tively to Me," declares the LORD, "to [B]bring no load
in through the gates of this city on the sabbath day,
[C]but to keep the sabbath day holy by doing no work
on it, 25 [A]then there will come in through the gates
of this city kings and princes [B]sitting on the throne
of David, riding in chariots and on horses, they and
their princes, the men of Judah and the inhabitants
of Jerusalem, and this [C]city will be inhabited forever.
26 They will come in from the [A]cities of Judah and
from the environs of Jerusalem, from the land of
Benjamin, from the [B]lowland, from the hill country and from the [C]Negev, bringing burnt offerings,
sacrifices, grain offerings and incense, and bringing
sacrifices of thanksgiving to the house of the LORD.
27 But [A]if you do not listen to Me to keep the sabbath day holy by not carrying a load and coming in
through the gates of Jerusalem on the sabbath day,
then [B]I will kindle a fire in its gates and it will [C]devour
the palaces of Jerusalem and [D]not be quenched." ' "

THE POTTER AND THE CLAY

18 The word which came to Jeremiah from the
LORD saying, 2 "Arise and [A]go down to the
potter's house, and there I will announce My words
to you." 3 Then I went down to the potter's house,
and there he was, making something on the [a]wheel.
4 But the vessel that he was making of clay was
spoiled in the hand of the potter; so he remade it
into another vessel, as it pleased the potter to make.
5 Then the word of the LORD came to me saying,
6 "Can I not, O house of Israel, deal with you as this
potter *does?*" declares the LORD. "Behold, like the
[A]clay in the potter's hand, so are you in My hand,
O house of Israel. 7 At one moment I might speak
concerning a nation or concerning a kingdom to
[A]uproot, to pull down, or to destroy *it;* 8 [A]if that nation against which I have spoken turns from its evil,
I will [a,B]relent concerning the calamity I planned to
bring on it. 9 Or at another moment I might speak
concerning a nation or concerning a kingdom to
[A]build up or to plant *it;* 10 if it does [A]evil in My sight
by not obeying My voice, then I will [a,B]think better
of the good with which I had promised to [b]bless
it. 11 So now then, speak to the men of Judah and
against the inhabitants of Jerusalem saying, 'Thus
says the LORD, "Behold, I am [A]fashioning calamity
against you and devising a plan against you. Oh
[B]turn back, each of you from his evil way, and [a]re-
form your ways and your deeds." ' 12 But [A]they will
say, 'It's hopeless! For we are going to follow our
own plans, and each of us will act according to the
[B]stubbornness of his evil heart.'

17:15 [A]Is 5:19; 2 Pet 3:4 17:16 [A]Jer 12:3 17:17 [A]Ps 88:15 [B]Jer 16:19; Nah 1:7 17:18 [A]Ps 35:4, 26; Jer 17:13; 20:11 [B]Jer 1:17 [C]Ps 35:8 17:19 [a]Lit *gate of the sons of the people* 17:20 [A]Ezek 2:7 [B]Ps 49:1, 2; Jer 19:3, 4 17:21 [A]Deut 4:9, 15, 23; Mark 4:24 [B]Num 15:32-36; Neh 13:15-21; John 5:9-12 17:22 [a]Lit *fathers* [A]Ex 16:23-29; 20:8-10; Deut 5:12-14; Is 56:2-6; 58:13 [B]Ex 31:13-17; Ezek 20:12; Zech 1:4 17:23 [A]Jer 7:24, 28; 11:10 [B]Prov 29:1; Jer 7:26; 19:15 17:24 [A]Ex 15:26; Deut 11:13; Is 21:7; 55:2 [B]Jer 17:21, 22 [C]Ex 20:8-11; Ezek 20:20 17:25 [A]Jer 22:4 [B]2 Sam 7:16; Is 9:7; Jer 33:15, 17, 21; Luke 1:32 [C]Ps 132:13, 14; Heb 12:22 17:26 [A]Jer 32:44; 33:13 [B]Zech 7:7 [C]Ps 107:22; Jer 33:11 17:27 [A]Is 1:20; Jer 22:5; 26:4; Zech 7:11-14 [B]Lam 4:11 [C]2 Kin 25:9; Jer 39:8; Amos 2:5 [D]Jer 7:20; Ezek 20:47 18:2 [A]Jer 19:1, 2 18:3 [a]Lit *pair of stone discs* 18:6 [A]Is 45:9; 64:8; Matt 20:15; Rom 9:21 18:7 [A]Jer 1:10 18:8 [a]Lit *repent of* [A]Jer 7:3-7; 12:16; Ezek 18:21 [B]Ps 106:45; Jer 26:3, 13, 19; Hos 11:8; Joel 2:13, 14; Jon 3:10 18:9 [A]Jer 1:10; 31:28; Amos 9:11-15 18:10 [a]Lit *repent* [b]Lit *do it good* [A]Ps 125:5; Jer 7:24-28; Ezek 33:18 [B]1 Sam 2:30; 13:13 18:11 [a]Lit *make good* [A]Is 5:5; Jer 4:6; 11:11 [B]2 Kin 17:13; Is 1:16-19; Jer 4:1; Acts 26:20 18:12 [A]Is 57:10; Jer 2:25 [B]Deut 29:19; Jer 7:24; 16:12

17:21–24 sabbath day. Not only had the Jews failed to observe Sabbath days, but also the required Sabbath year of rest for the land (Lv 25:1–7) was regularly violated. God had warned that such disobedience would bring judgment (Lv 26:34, 35, 43; 2Ch 36:20, 21). The 70-year captivity was correlated to the 490 years from Saul to the captivity, which included 70 Sabbath years. When the Jews were restored from captivity, special stress was placed on Sabbath faithfulness (cf. Ne 13:19).

17:25–27 For obedience, God would assure the dynasty of David perpetual rule in Jerusalem, safety for the city, and worship at the temple (vv. 25, 26). Continued disobedience would meet with destruction of the city (v. 27).

18:1–20:18 A close link exists between chap. 17 and chaps. 18–20. Destruction is in view (chap. 17), but repentance can yet prevent that (18:7, 8). However, repentance was not present (18:12), so Jeremiah's shattered jar illustrated God's dashing Israel in judgment (chap. 19). Then the rejection spirit (cf. 19:15) led to persecution against God's mouthpiece (chap. 20).

18:2–6 potter's house. God sent Jeremiah to a potter, who gave him an illustration by shaping a vessel. The prophet secured a vessel and used it for his own illustration (19:1ff.). Jeremiah watched the potter at his wheel. The soft clay became misshapen, but the potter shaped it back into a good vessel. God will so do with Judah if she repents.

18:8–10 Though He had announced impending judgment, the "spoiled" nation can be restored as a good vessel by God, who will hold off the judgment (vv. 8, 11). By contrast, if the nation followed sin, He would not bring the blessing desired (vv. 9, 10).

18:12 It's hopeless! Jeremiah brought them to the point where they actually stated their condition honestly. The prophet's threats were useless because they were so far gone—abandoned to their sins and the penalty. All hypocrisy was abandoned in favor of honesty, without repentance. Repentance was

13 "Therefore thus says the LORD,
'[A]Ask now among the nations,
Who ever heard the like of [a]this?
The [B]virgin of Israel
Has done a most [C]appalling thing.
14 'Does the snow of Lebanon forsake
the rock of the open country?
Or is the cold flowing water *from* a
foreign *land* ever snatched away?
15 'For [A]My people have forgotten Me,
[B]They burn incense [a]to worthless gods
And they [b]have stumbled [c]from their ways,
[c]From the [C]ancient paths,
To walk in bypaths,
Not on a [D]highway,
16 To make their land a [A]desolation,
An object of perpetual [B]hissing;
Everyone who passes by it
will be astonished
And [C]shake his head.
17 'Like an [A]east wind I will [B]scatter them
Before the enemy;
I will [a]show them [C]My back and not *My* face
[D]In the day of their calamity.' "

18 Then they said, "Come and let us [A]devise plans against Jeremiah. Surely the [B]law is not going to be lost to the priest, nor [C]counsel to the sage, nor the *divine* [D]word to the prophet! Come on and let us [E]strike at him with *our* tongue, and let us [F]give no heed to any of his words."

19 Do give heed to me, O LORD,
And listen to [a]what my
opponents are saying!
20 [A]Should good be repaid with evil?
For they have [B]dug a pit for [a]me.
Remember how I [C]stood before You
To speak good on their behalf,
So as to turn away Your wrath from them.
21 Therefore, [A]give their children
over to famine
And deliver them up to the
[a]power of the sword;
And let their wives become
[B]childless and [C]widowed.
Let their men also be smitten to death,
Their [D]young men struck down
by the sword in battle.
22 May an [A]outcry be heard from their houses,
When You suddenly bring
raiders upon them;
[B]For they have dug a pit to capture me
And [C]hidden snares for my feet.
23 Yet You, O LORD, know
All their [a]deadly designs against me;
[A]Do not [b]forgive their iniquity
Or blot out their sin from Your sight.
But may they be [c,B]overthrown before You;
Deal with them in the [C]time of Your anger!

THE BROKEN JAR

19 Thus says the LORD, "Go and buy a [A]potter's
earthenware [B]jar, and *take* some of the [C]elders
of the people and some of the [a,D]senior priests. 2 Then
go out to the [A]valley of Ben-hinnom, which is by the
entrance of the potsherd gate, and [B]proclaim there
the words that I tell you, 3 and say, 'Hear the word
of the LORD, O [A]kings of Judah and inhabitants of
Jerusalem: thus says the LORD of hosts, the God of
Israel, "Behold I am about to bring a [B]calamity upon
this place, at which the [C]ears of everyone that hears
of it will tingle. 4 Because they have [A]forsaken Me
and have [B]made this an alien place and have burned
[a]sacrifices in it to [C]other gods, that neither they nor
their forefathers nor the kings of Judah had *ever*
known, and *because* they have filled this place with
the [D]blood of the innocent 5 and have built the [A]high
places of Baal to burn their [B]sons in the fire as burnt
offerings to Baal, a thing which I never commanded
or spoke of, nor did it *ever* enter My [a]mind; 6 therefore, behold, [A]days are coming," declares the LORD,
"when this place will no longer be called [B]Topheth
or [C]the valley of Ben-hinnom, but rather the valley

18:13 [a]Lit *these* [A]Is 66:8; Jer 2:10, 11 [B]Jer 14:17; 31:4 [C]Jer 5:30; 23:14; Hos 6:10 18:15 [a]Lit *to worthlessness* [b]So ancient versions; Heb *caused them to* [c]Or *in* [A]Jer 2:32; 3:21 [B]Is 65:7; Jer 7:9; 10:15; 44:17 [C]Jer 6:16 [D]Is 57:14; 62:10 18:16 [A]Jer 25:9; 49:13; 50:13; Ezek 33:28, 29 [B]1 Kin 9:8; Lam 2:15; Mic 6:16 [C]Ps 22:7; Is 37:22; Jer 48:27 18:17 [a]So ancient versions; M.T. reads *look them in the back and not in the face* [A]Ps 48:7 [B]Job 27:21; Jer 13:24 [C]Jer 2:27; 32:33 [D]Jer 46:21 18:18 [A]Jer 11:19; 18:11 [B]Jer 2:8; Mal 2:7 [C]Job 5:13; Jer 8:8 [D]Jer 5:13 [E]Ps 52:2; Jer 20:10 [F]Jer 43:2 18:19 [a]Lit *the voice of my opponents* 18:20 [a]Lit *my soul* [A]Ps 109:4 [B]Ps 35:7; 57:6; Jer 5:26; 18:22 [C]Ps 106:23 18:21 [a]Lit *hands of* [A]Ps 109:9-20; Jer 11:22; 14:16 [B]1 Sam 15:33; Is 13:18 [C]Jer 15:8; Ezek 22:25 [D]Jer 9:21; 11:22 18:22 [A]Jer 6:26; 25:34, 36 [B]Jer 18:20 [C]Ps 140:5 18:23 [a]Lit *unto death* [b]Lit *cover over, atone for* [c]Lit *ones made to stumble* [A]Neh 4:5; Ps 109:14; Is 2:9 [B]Jer 6:15, 21 [C]Jer 7:20; 17:4 19:1 [a]Or *elders of* [A]Jer 18:2 [B]Jer 19:10 [C]Num 11:16 [D]2 Kin 19:2; Ezek 8:11 19:2 [A]Josh 15:8; 2 Kin 23:10; Jer 7:31, 32; 32:35 [B]Prov 1:20 19:3 [A]Jer 17:20 [B]Jer 6:19; 19:15 [C]1 Sam 3:11 19:4 [a]Or *incense* [A]Deut 28:20; Is 65:11; Jer 2:13, 17, 19; 17:13 [B]Ezek 7:22; Dan 11:31 [C]Jer 7:9; 11:13 [D]2 Kin 21:6, 16; Jer 2:34; 7:6 19:5 [a]Lit *heart* [A]Num 22:41; Jer 32:35 [B]Lev 18:21; 2 Kin 17:17; Ps 106:37, 38 19:6 [A]Jer 7:32 [B]Is 30:33 [C]Josh 15:8

not in Israel (as v. 18; 19:15). This explains a seeming paradox: that Israel can repent and avert judgment, yet Jeremiah is not to pray for Israel (7:16; 11:14). It would do no good to pray for their change since they steeled themselves against any change.

18:13 virgin of Israel. It enhanced their guilt that Israel was the virgin whom God had chosen (cf. 2Ki 19:21).

18:14 snow of Lebanon ... cold flowing water. No reasonable man would forsake such for "the rock of the open country," perhaps a poetic term for Mt. Lebanon, from which the high mountain streams flowed. Yet Israel forsook God, the fountain of living waters, for broken foreign cisterns (cf. 2:13).

18:18 plans against Jeremiah. Plans to indict the prophet with their "tongues" and then to slay him (v. 23) were based on the premise that his message of doom was not true. The business of the priests, the wise, and the prophets continued as usual since God made them lasting institutions (cf. Lv 6:18; 10:11).

18:19–23 give heed to me. This is one of many examples of prayer aligning with God's will as Jeremiah prays for God's work of judgment to be done (vv. 11, 15–17).

18:22 dug a pit. Cf. 38:6.

19:1 elders of the people ... the senior priests. These were chosen to be credible witnesses of the symbolic action with the "earthenware jar," so no one could plead ignorance of the prophesy. The 72 elders who made up the Sanhedrin were partly from the "priests" and the other tribes ("people").

19:2 valley ... Ben-hinnom. *See note on 19:6.* **potsherd gate.** The gate of "broken pottery" was on the S wall of Jerusalem where the potters formed pottery for use in the temple nearby.

19:6 Topheth. Hebrew uses the word *toph* for "drum." This was another name for the Valley of Hinnom, an E-W valley at the S end of Jerusalem where, when children were burned in sacrifice to idols (cf. vv. 4, 5), drums were beaten to drown their cries. Rubbish from Jerusalem was dumped there and continually

of Slaughter. 7I will [A]make void the counsel of Judah
and Jerusalem in this place, and [B]I will cause them
to fall by the sword before their enemies and by the
hand of those who seek their life; and I will give over
their [C]carcasses as food for the birds of the sky and
the beasts of the earth. 8I will also make this city a
[A]desolation and an *object of* hissing; [B]everyone who
passes by it will be astonished and hiss because of
all its [a]disasters. 9I will make them [A]eat the flesh of
their sons and the flesh of their daughters, and they
will eat one another's flesh in the siege and in the
distress with which their enemies and those who
seek their life will distress them." '

10"Then you are to break the [A]jar in the sight of
the men who accompany you 11and say to them,
'Thus says the LORD of hosts, "Just so will I [A]break
this people and this city, even as one breaks a potter's vessel, which cannot again be repaired; and
they will [B]bury in Topheth [a]because there is no *other*
place for burial. 12This is how I will treat this place
and its inhabitants," declares the LORD, "so as to
make this city like Topheth. 13The [A]houses of Jerusalem and the houses of the kings of Judah will be
[B]defiled like the place Topheth, because of all the
[C]houses on whose rooftops they burned [a]sacrifices
to [D]all the heavenly host and [E]poured out drink offerings to other gods." ' "

14Then Jeremiah came from Topheth, where the
LORD had sent him to prophesy; and he stood in
the [A]court of the LORD'S house and said to all the
people: 15"Thus says the LORD of hosts, the God of
Israel, 'Behold, I am about to bring on this city and
all its towns the entire calamity that I have declared
against it, because they have [A]stiffened their necks
so [B]as not to heed My words.' "

PASHHUR PERSECUTES JEREMIAH

20 When Pashhur the priest, the son of [A]Immer,
who was [B]chief officer in the house of the
LORD, heard Jeremiah prophesying these things,
2Pashhur had Jeremiah the prophet [A]beaten and
put him in the [B]stocks that were at the upper [C]Ben-
jamin Gate, which was by the house of the LORD.
3On the next day, when Pashhur released Jeremiah
from the stocks, Jeremiah said to him, "Pashhur is
not the name the LORD has [A]called you, but rather
[a,B]Magor-missabib. 4For thus says the LORD, 'Behold,
I am going to make you a [A]terror to yourself and to
all your friends; and while [B]your eyes look on, they
will fall by the sword of their enemies. So I will [C]give
over all Judah to the hand of the king of Babylon, and
he will carry them away as [D]exiles to Babylon and
will slay them with the sword. 5I will also give over
all the [A]wealth of this city, all its produce and all its
costly things; even all the treasures of the kings of
Judah I will give over to the [B]hand of their enemies,
and they will plunder them, take them away and
bring them to Babylon. 6And you, [A]Pashhur, and all
who live in your house will go into captivity; and
you will enter Babylon, and there you will die and
there you will be buried, you and all your [B]friends
to whom you have [C]falsely prophesied.' "

JEREMIAH'S COMPLAINT

7 O LORD, You have deceived me
  and I was deceived;
You have [A]overcome me and prevailed.
I have become a [B]laughingstock
  all day long;
Everyone [C]mocks me.
8 For each time I speak, I cry aloud;
I [A]proclaim violence and destruction,
Because for me the [B]word of
  the LORD has [a]resulted
In reproach and derision all day long.
9 But if I say, "I will not [A]remember Him
Or speak anymore in His name,"
Then in [B]my heart it becomes
  like a burning fire
Shut up in my bones;
And I am weary of holding *it* in,
And [C]I cannot endure *it*.

19:7 [A]Ps 33:10, 11; Is 28:17, 18; Jer 8:8, 9 [B]Lev 26:17; Deut 28:25; Jer 15:2, 9 [C]Ps 79:2; Jer 16:4 19:8 [a]Lit *blows* [A]Jer 18:16; 49:13; 50:13 [B]1 Kin 9:8; 2 Chr 7:21 19:9 [A]Lev 26:29; Deut 28:53, 55; Is 9:20; Lam 4:10; Ezek 5:10 19:10 [A]Jer 19:1 19:11 [a]Or *until there is no place* left *to bury* [A]Ps 2:9; Is 30:14; Lam 4:2; Rev 2:27 [B]Jer 7:32 19:13 [a]Or *incense* [A]Jer 52:13 [B]2 Kin 23:10; Ps 74:7; 79:1; Ezek 7:21, 22 [C]Jer 32:29; Zeph 1:5 [D]Deut 4:19; 2 Kin 17:16; Jer 8:2 [E]Jer 7:18; 44:18; Ezek 20:28 19:14 [A]2 Chr 20:5; Jer 26:2 19:15 [A]Neh 9:17, 29; Jer 7:26; 17:23 [B]Ps 58:4 20:1 [A]1 Chr 24:14; Ezra 2:37, 38 [B]2 Kin 25:18 20:2 [A]1 Kin 22:27; 2 Chr 16:10; 24:21; Jer 1:19; Amos 7:10-13 [B]Job 13:27; 33:11 [C]Jer 37:13; 38:7; Zech 14:10 20:3 [a]I.e. terror on every side [A]Is 8:3; Hos 1:4, 9 [B]Jer 6:25; 20:10 20:4 [A]Job 18:11-21; Jer 6:25; 46:5; Ezek 26:21 [B]Jer 29:21; 39:6, 7 [C]Jer 21:4-10; 25:9 [D]Jer 13:10; 52:27 20:5 [A]Jer 15:13; 17:3 [B]2 Kin 20:17, 18; 2 Chr 36:10; Jer 27:21, 22 20:6 [A]Jer 20:1 [B]Jer 20:4; 29:21 [C]Jer 14:14, 15; Lam 2:14 20:7 [A]Ezek 3:14 [B]Job 12:4; Lam 3:14 [C]Ps 22:7; Jer 38:19 20:8 [a]Lit *become* [A]Jer 6:7 [B]2 Chr 36:16; Jer 6:10 20:9 [A]1 Kin 19:3, 4; Jon 1:2, 3 [B]Job 32:18-20; Ps 39:3; Jer 4:19; 23:9; Ezek 3:14; Acts 4:20 [C]Job 32:18-20

burned. The place became a symbol for the burning fires of hell, called Gehenna (Mt 5:22). Cf. 7:30–32; Is 30:33. It was to become a place of massacre.

19:9 eat the flesh. Desperate for food during a long siege, some would resort to cannibalism, eating family members and friends (La 4:10).

19:10 Cf. v. 1.

19:13 defiled. Their houses were desecrated by idolatrous worship. **sacrifices to … heavenly host.** Refers to worship of the sun, planets, and stars from flat housetops (cf. 32:29; 2Ki 23:11, 12; Zep 1:5).

20:1 Pashhur. The meaning is either "ease," or "deliverance is round about," both in contrast to the new name God assigns him in v. 3. He was one of several men so named (cf. 21:1; 38:1). **Immer.** He was one of the original "governors of the sanctuary" (cf. 1Ch 24:14). **chief officer.** He was not the High Priest, but the chief official in charge of temple police, who were to maintain order.

20:2 had Jeremiah … beaten. He or others acting on his authority delivered 40 lashes (see Dt 25:3) to the prophet. **put him in the stocks.** Hands, feet, and neck were fastened in holes, bending the body to a distorted posture, causing excruciating pain. **upper Benjamin Gate.** The northern gate of the upper temple court.

20:3 Magor-missabib. "Terror on every side" is the fitting name which the Lord reckons for the leader. The details of that terror are in vv. 4, 6 (cf. 6:25).

20:4 Babylon. This was Jeremiah's direct identification of the conqueror who would come out of the "north" (1:13), from "a far country" (4:16).

20:8 derision all day long. In vv. 7–18, Jeremiah prayerfully lamented the ridicule he was experiencing because of God's role for his life. His feelings wavered between quitting (v. 9a), being encouraged (vv. 9c, 11), petitioning for help (v. 12), praise (v. 13), and waves of depression (vv. 14–18; cf. 11:18–23; 15:10, 15–18).

20:9 I will not … speak anymore. A surge of dejection swept over Jeremiah, making him long to say no more. But he was compelled inside (cf. Job 32:18, 19; Ps 39:3; Ac 18:5; 1Co 9:16, 17) because he did not want his enemies to see him fail (v. 10), he felt the powerful presence of the Lord (v. 11), and he remembered God's previous deliverances (v. 13).

10 For [A]I have heard the whispering of many,
"[B]Terror on every side!
[C]Denounce *him;* yes, let us denounce him!"
[a]All my [D]trusted friends,
Watching for my fall, say:
"Perhaps he will be [b]deceived, so that
we may [E]prevail against him
And take our revenge on him."
11 But the [A]LORD is with me like
a dread champion;
Therefore my [B]persecutors will
stumble and not prevail.
They will be utterly ashamed,
because they have [a]failed,
With an [C]everlasting disgrace
that will not be forgotten.
12 Yet, O LORD of hosts, You who
[A]test the righteous,
Who see the [a]mind and the heart;
Let me [B]see Your vengeance on them;
For [C]to You I have set forth my cause.
13 [A]Sing to the LORD, praise the LORD!
For He has [B]delivered the
soul of the needy one
From the hand of evildoers.

14 Cursed be the [A]day when I was born;
Let the day not be blessed when
my mother bore me!
15 Cursed be the man who
brought the news
To my father, saying,
"A [a,A]baby boy has been born to you!"
And made him very happy.
16 But let that man be like the cities
Which the LORD [A]overthrew
without [a]relenting,
And let him hear an [B]outcry
in the morning
And a [b]shout of alarm at noon;
17 Because he did not [A]kill me [a]before birth,
So that my mother would
have been my grave,
And her womb ever pregnant.
18 Why did I ever come forth from the womb
To [A]look on trouble and sorrow,
So that my [B]days have been
spent in [C]shame?

JEREMIAH'S MESSAGE FOR ZEDEKIAH

21 The word which came to Jeremiah from the
LORD when [A]King Zedekiah sent to him [B]Pash-
hur the son of Malchijah, and [C]Zephaniah the priest,
the son of Maaseiah, saying, 2 "Please [A]inquire of the
LORD on our behalf, for [B]Nebuchadnezzar king of
[C]Babylon is warring against us; perhaps the LORD
will deal with us [D]according to all His [a]wonderful
acts, so that *the enemy* will withdraw from us."
3 Then Jeremiah said to them, "You shall say to
Zedekiah as follows: 4 'Thus says the LORD God of
Israel, "Behold, I am about to [A]turn back the weapons of war which are in your hands, with which you
are warring against the king of Babylon and the
Chaldeans who are besieging you outside the wall;
and I will [B]gather them into the center of this city. 5 I
[A]Myself will war against you with an [B]outstretched
hand and a mighty arm, even in [C]anger and wrath
and great indignation. 6 I will also strike down the
inhabitants of this city, both man and beast; they will
die of a great [A]pestilence. 7 Then afterwards," declares
the LORD, "[A]I will give over Zedekiah king of Judah
and his servants and the people, even those who
survive in this city from the pestilence, the sword
and the famine, into the hand of Nebuchadnezzar
king of Babylon, and into the hand of their foes and
into the hand of those who seek their lives; and he
will strike them down with the edge of the sword. He
[B]will not spare them nor have pity nor compassion." '
8 "You shall also say to this people, 'Thus says the
LORD, "Behold, I [A]set before you the way of life and
the way of death. 9 He who [A]dwells in this city will
die by the [B]sword and by famine and by pestilence;
but he who goes out and falls away to the Chaldeans
who are besieging you will live, and he will have his
own life as booty. 10 For I have [A]set My face against
this city for [a]harm and not for good," declares the
LORD. "It will be [B]given into the hand of the king of
Babylon and he will [C]burn it with fire." '

20:10 [a]Lit *Every man of my peace* [b]Or *persuaded* [A]Ps 31:13 [B]Jer 6:25 [C]Neh 6:6-13; Is 29:21; Jer 18:18 [D]Ps 41:9 [E]1 Kin 19:2 20:11 [a]Lit *not succeeded;* or *not acted wisely* [A]Jer 1:8; 15:20; Rom 8:31 [B]Deut 32:35, 36; Jer 15:15, 20; 17:18 [C]Jer 23:40 20:12 [a]Lit *kidneys* [A]Ps 7:9; 11:5; 17:3; 139:23; Jer 11:20; 17:10 [B]Ps 54:7; 59:10; Jer 11:20 [C]Ps 62:8 20:13 [A]Jer 31:7 [B]Ps 34:6; 69:33; Jer 15:21 20:14 [A]Job 3:3-6; Jer 15:10 20:15 [a]Lit *male child* [A]Gen 21:6, 7 20:16 [a]Lit *being sorry* [b]Or *trumpet blast* [A]Gen 19:25 [B]Jer 18:22; 48:3, 4 20:17 [a]Lit *from the womb* [A]Job 3:10, 11, 16; 10:18, 19 20:18 [A]Job 3:20; 5:7; 14:1; Jer 15:10; Lam 3:1 [B]Ps 90:9; 102:3 [C]Ps 69:19; Jer 3:25; 1 Cor 4:9-13 21:1 [A]2 Kin 24:17, 18; Jer 32:1-3; 37:1; 52:1-3 [B]1 Chr 9:12; Jer 38:1 [C]2 Kin 25:18; Jer 29:25, 29; 37:3; 52:24 21:2 [a]Or *miracles* [A]Ex 9:28; Jer 37:3, 17; Ezek 14:7; 20:1-3 [B]2 Kin 25:1 [C]Gen 10:10; 2 Kin 17:24 [D]Ps 44:1-3; Jer 32:17 21:4 [A]Jer 32:5; 33:5; 37:8-10; 38:2, 3, 17, 18 [B]Is 5:5; 13:4; Jer 39:3; Lam 2:5, 7; Zech 14:2 21:5 [A]Is 63:10 [B]Ex 6:6; Deut 4:34; Jer 6:12 [C]Is 5:25; Jer 32:37 21:6 [A]Jer 14:12; 32:24 21:7 [A]2 Kin 25:5-7, 18-21; Jer 37:17; 39:5-9; 52:9 [B]2 Chr 36:17; Jer 13:14; Ezek 7:9; Hab 1:6-10 21:8 [A]Deut 30:15, 19; Is 1:19, 20 21:9 [A]Jer 38:2, 17-23; 39:18; 45:5 [B]Jer 14:12; 24:10 21:10 [a]Lit *evil* [A]Lev 17:10; Jer 44:11, 27; Amos 9:4 [B]Jer 32:28, 29; 38:3 [C]2 Chr 36:19; Jer 34:2; 37:10; 38:18; 39:8; 52:13

20:14 Cursed be the day. Another tide of depression engulfed the prophet, perhaps when he was in the painful stocks (v. 2). His words are like Job's (Job 3:3, 10, 11).

20:15 Cursed be the man. The servant of God fell into sinful despair, and he questioned the wisdom and purpose of God, for which he should have been thankful.

20:16 the cities ... the LORD overthrew. Sodom and Gomorrah (Ge 19:25).

21:1 King Zedekiah. Cf. 2Ki 24:17–25:7 for details of his reign ca. 597–586 B.C. **Pashhur.** This priest was different from the man by this name in 20:1–6. Cf. 38:1.

21:2 warring against us. This was during the last siege by Babylon (v. 4), ca. 587/86 B.C., resulting in the third deportation of Jews. Zedekiah hoped for God's intervention, such as Hezekiah received against Sennacherib (2Ki 19:35, 36).

21:4 turn back the weapons. The Jews were already fighting the invaders by going outside the walls of the city to battle them on the hillsides and in the valleys as they approached. However, they would soon be driven back into the city where the enemy would collect all their weapons and execute many with those very weapons.

21:5 I Myself will war. God used an invader as His judging instrument (v. 7). The Jews have not only the Babylonians as their enemy, but God.

21:7 strike them ... sword. This was the fate of Zedekiah's son and many nobles. Zedekiah died of grief (cf. 34:4; 2Ki 25:6–8).

21:8, 9 life and ... death. Since a persistent lack of repentance had led to the conquest, Jeremiah urged the Jews to submit and surrender to the besieger so as to be treated as captives of war and live rather than be killed.

11 “Then *say* to the household of the [A]king of Judah, ‘Hear the word of the LORD, 12 O [A]house of David, thus says the LORD:

“[B]Administer justice [a]every [C]morning;
And deliver the *person* who has been
robbed from the [b]power of *his* oppressor,
[D]That My wrath may not go forth like fire
And [E]burn with none to extinguish *it,*
Because of the evil of their deeds.

13 “Behold, [A]I am against you, O [B]valley dweller,
O [a]rocky plain,” declares the LORD,
“You men who say, ‘[C]Who will
come down against us?
Or who will enter into our habitations?’
14 “But I will punish you [A]according to the
[a]results of your deeds,” declares the LORD,
“And I will [B]kindle a fire in its forest
That it may devour all its environs.” ’ ”

WARNING OF JERUSALEM’S FALL

22 Thus says the LORD, “Go down to the house
of the king of Judah, and there speak this
word 2 and say, ‘Hear the word of the LORD, O king
of Judah, who [A]sits on David’s throne, you and your
servants and your people who enter these gates.
3 Thus says the LORD, “[A]Do justice and righteousness,
and deliver the one who has been robbed from the
power of *his* [B]oppressor. Also [C]do not mistreat *or* do
violence to the stranger, the orphan, or the widow;
and do not [D]shed innocent blood in this place. 4 For
if you men will indeed perform this thing, then
[A]kings will enter the gates of this house, sitting [a]in
David’s place on his throne, riding in chariots and on
horses, *even the king* himself and his servants and
his people. 5 [A]But if you will not obey these words,
I [B]swear by Myself,” declares the LORD, “that this
house will become a desolation.” ’ ” 6 For thus says
the LORD concerning the house of the king of Judah:

“You are *like* [A]Gilead to Me,
Like the summit of Lebanon;
Yet most assuredly I will make
you like a [B]wilderness,
Like cities which are not inhabited.
7 “For I will set apart [A]destroyers
against you,
Each with his weapons;
And they will [B]cut down
your choicest cedars
And [C]throw *them* on the fire.

8 “Many nations will pass by this city; and they
will [A]say to one another, ‘Why has the LORD done
thus to this great city?’ 9 Then they will [a]answer,
‘Because they [A]forsook the covenant of the LORD
their God and bowed down to other gods and served
them.’ ”

10 [A]Do not weep for the dead
or mourn for him,
But weep continually for the
one who goes away;
For [B]he will never return
Or see his native land.

11 For thus says the LORD in regard to [a,A]Shallum
the son of Josiah, king of Judah, who became king
in the place of Josiah his father, who went forth
from this place, “He will never return there; 12 but
in the place where they led him captive, there he
will [A]die and not see this land again.

MESSAGES ABOUT THE KINGS

13 “Woe to him who builds his house
[A]without righteousness
And his [a]upper rooms without justice,
Who uses his neighbor’s
services without pay
And [B]does not give him his wages,
14 Who says, ‘I will [A]build myself
a roomy house
With spacious [a]upper rooms,
And cut out its windows,
[b]Paneling *it* with [B]cedar and
painting *it* [c]bright red.’
15 “Do you become a king because
you are competing in cedar?
Did not your father eat and drink
And [A]do justice and righteousness?
Then it was [B]well with him.

21:11 [A]Jer 17:20 21:12 [a]Or *in the* [b]Lit *hand* [A]Is 7:2, 13 [B]Ps 72:1; Is 1:17; Jer 7:5; 22:3; Zech 7:9, 10 [C]Ps 101:8; Zeph 3:5 [D]Jer 4:4; 17:4; Ezek 20:47, 48; Nah 1:6 [E]Is 1:31; Jer 7:20 21:13 [a]Lit *rock of the level place* [A]Jer 23:30-32; Ezek 13:8 [B]Ps 125:2; Is 22:1 [C]2 Sam 5:6, 7; Jer 49:4; Lam 4:12; Obad 3, 4 21:14 [a]Lit *fruit* [A]Is 3:10, 11; Jer 17:10; 32:19 [B]2 Chr 36:19; Is 10:16, 18; Jer 11:16; 17:27; 52:13; Ezek 20:47, 48 22:2 [A]Is 9:7; Jer 17:25; 22:4, 30; Luke 1:32 22:3 [A]Is 58:6, 7; Jer 7:5, 23; 21:12; Mic 6:8; Zech 7:9; 8:16; Matt 23:23 [B]Ps 72:4 [C]Ex 22:21-24 [D]Jer 7:6; 19:4; 22:17 22:4 [a]Lit *for David* [A]Jer 17:25 22:5 [A]Jer 17:27; 26:4 [B]Gen 22:16; Amos 6:8; Heb 6:13 22:6 [A]Gen 37:25; Num 32:1; Song 4:1 [B]Ps 107:34; Is 6:11; Jer 7:34; Mic 3:12 22:7 [A]Is 10:3-6; Jer 4:6, 7 [B]Is 10:33, 34; 37:24 [C]Jer 21:14 22:8 [A]Deut 29:24-26; 1 Kin 9:8, 9; 2 Chr 7:20-22; Jer 16:10 22:9 [a]Lit *say* [A]2 Kin 22:17; 2 Chr 34:25; Jer 11:3 22:10 [A]Eccl 4:2; Is 57:1; Jer 16:7; 22:18 [B]Jer 25:27; 44:14 22:11 [a]I.e. Jehoahaz [A]2 Kin 23:30-34; 1 Chr 3:15; 2 Chr 36:1-4 22:12 [A]2 Kin 23:34; Jer 22:18 22:13 [a]Or *roof chambers* [A]Jer 17:11; Mic 3:10; Hab 2:9 [B]Lev 19:13; James 5:4 22:14 [a]Or *roof chambers* [b]Or *Paneled* [c]Or *vermilion* [A]Is 5:8 [B]2 Sam 7:2; Hag 1:4 22:15 [A]2 Kin 23:25; Jer 7:5; 21:12 [B]Ps 128:2; Is 3:10; Jer 42:6

21:12 O house of David. The royal family and all connected were called to enact justice and righteousness promptly (“morning”). There was still time for them to escape the destruction if there was repentance.

21:13 O valley dweller, O rocky plain. Jerusalem personified, situated among rocks, hills, and valleys.

21:14 I will punish. During the siege Jerusalem will be burned (v. 10), as will the land in general.

22:2, 4 David’s throne. Refers to the Davidic Covenant of 2Sa 7:3–17, in which God promised David that his heirs will rule over Israel.

22:6 Gilead … Lebanon. The beautiful high mountains of the land.

22:7 cut down … choicest cedars. This could primarily refer to the palaces and great houses built from such timber (cf. SS 1:17).

22:10 the dead. Probably a reference to Josiah, who died before the destruction (2Ki 22:20; Is 57:1). Dying saints are to be envied, living sinners pitied. When Josiah died, and on each anniversary of his death, there was open public weeping in which Jeremiah participated (2Ch 35:24, 25).

22:11, 12 Shallum. This is another name for King Jehoahaz (3-month reign, 609 B.C., 2Ki 23:31), the fourth son of Josiah (cf. 1Ch 3:15). It was given to him in irony, because the people called him Shalom (“peace”), but Shallum means “retribution.”

22:13–17 Woe to him. This message indicted Jehoahaz (vv. 13, 14, 17), who was unlike his father, the good king, Josiah (vv. 15, 16).

16 "He pled the cause of the
[A]afflicted and needy;
Then it was well.
[B]Is not that what it means to know Me?"
Declares the LORD.
17 "But your eyes and your heart
Are *intent* only upon your
own [A]dishonest gain,
And on [B]shedding innocent blood
And on practicing oppression
and extortion."

18 Therefore thus says the LORD in regard to [A]Je-
hoiakim the son of Josiah, king of Judah,

"They will not [B]lament for him:
'[C]Alas, my brother!' or, 'Alas, sister!'
They will not lament for him:
'Alas for the master!' or, 'Alas
for his splendor!'
19 "He will be [A]buried with a donkey's burial,
Dragged off and thrown out beyond
the gates of Jerusalem.
20 "Go up to Lebanon and cry out,
And lift up your voice in Bashan;
Cry out also from [A]Abarim,
For all your [B]lovers have been crushed.
21 "I spoke to you in your prosperity;
But [A]you said, 'I will not listen!'
[B]This has been your practice
[C]from your youth,
That you have not obeyed My voice.
22 "The wind will sweep away
all your [A]shepherds,
And your [B]lovers will go into captivity;
Then you will surely be
[C]ashamed and humiliated
Because of all your wickedness.
23 "You who dwell in Lebanon,
Nested in the cedars,
How you will groan when
pangs come upon you,
[A]Pain like a woman in childbirth!

24 "As I live," declares the LORD, "even though
[a,A]Coniah the son of Jehoiakim king of Judah were
a [B]signet *ring* on My right hand, yet I would pull
[a]you [b]off; 25 and I will [A]give you over into the hand
of those who are seeking your life, yes, into the
hand of those whom you dread, even into the hand
of Nebuchadnezzar king of Babylon and into the
hand of the Chaldeans. 26 I will [A]hurl you and your
[B]mother who bore you into another country where
you were not born, and there you will die. 27 But as
for the land to which they desire to return, they will
not return to it.

28 "Is this man Coniah a despised,
shattered jar?
Or is he an [A]undesirable vessel?
Why have he and his descendants
been [B]hurled out
And cast into a [C]land that
they had not known?
29 "[A]O land, land, land,
Hear the word of the LORD!

30 Thus says the LORD,

'Write this man down [A]childless,
A man who will [B]not prosper in his days;
For no man of his [C]descendants
will prosper
Sitting on the throne of David
Or ruling again in Judah.' "

THE COMING MESSIAH: THE RIGHTEOUS BRANCH

23 "[A]Woe to the shepherds who are [B]destroying
and scattering the [C]sheep of My pasture!"
declares the LORD. 2 Therefore thus says the LORD
God of Israel concerning the shepherds who are
[a]tending My people: "You have scattered My flock
and driven them away, and have not attended to
them; behold, I am about to [A]attend to you for the
[B]evil of your deeds," declares the LORD. 3 "Then I Myself will [A]gather the remnant of My flock out of all

22:16 [A]Ps 72:1-4, 12, 13 [B]1 Chr 28:9; Jer 9:24 22:17 [A]Jer 6:13; 8:10; Luke 12:15-20 [B]2 Kin 24:4; Jer 22:3 22:18 [A]2 Kin 23:36-24:6; 2 Chr 36:5 [B]Jer 22:10; 34:5 [C]1 Kin 13:30 22:19 [A]1 Kin 21:23, 24; Jer 36:30 22:20 [A]Num 27:12; Deut 32:49 [B]Jer 2:25; 3:1 22:21 [A]Jer 13:10; 19:15 [B]Jer 3:25 [C]Jer 3:24; 32:30 22:22 [A]Jer 23:1 [B]Jer 30:14 [C]Is 65:13; Jer 20:11 22:23 [A]Jer 4:31; 6:24 22:24 [a]I.e. Jehoiachin [b]Lit *off from there* [A]2 Kin 24:6; 1 Chr 3:16; 2 Chr 36:9; Jer 37:1 [B]Song 8:6; Is 49:16; Hag 2:23 22:25 [A]2 Kin 24:15, 16; Jer 21:7; 34:20, 21 22:26 [A]2 Kin 24:15; Jer 10:18; 16:13 [B]2 Kin 24:8 22:28 [A]Ps 31:12; Jer 48:38; Hos 8:8 [B]Jer 15:1 [C]Jer 17:4 22:29 [A]Deut 4:26; Jer 6:19; Mic 1:2 22:30 [A]1 Chr 3:17; Matt 1:12 [B]Jer 2:37; 10:21 [C]Ps 94:20; Jer 36:30 23:1 [A]Ezek 13:3; 34:2; Zech 11:17 [B]Is 56:9-12; Jer 10:21; 50:6 [C]Ezek 34:31 23:2 [a]Lit *shepherding* [A]Ex 32:34 [B]Jer 21:12; 44:22 23:3 [A]Is 11:11, 12, 16; Jer 31:7, 8; 32:37

22:18, 19 Jehoiakim. Ruling from 609 to 598 B.C., he was also wicked in taxing the people (2Ki 23:35) and making them build his splendid palace without pay, violating God's law in Lv 19:13 and Dt 24:14, 15 (cf. Mic 3:10; Hab 2:9; Jas 5:4). He was slain in Babylon's second siege and his corpse dishonored, being left like a dead donkey on the ground for scavengers to feed on.

22:20 Go up to Lebanon. Sinners dwelling in the NW in Lebanon's cedar land and others to the NE beyond the Sea of Galilee in Bashan will suffer in the invasion. The entirety of the land will come under judgment as Abarim in the SE.

22:24–26 Coniah. A short form of Jeconiah, perhaps used in contempt, who was also called Jehoiachin. He ruled only 3 months and 10 days (2Ch 36:9) in 598–597 B.C., and was taken into captivity, where he lived out his life.

22:24 signet. A ring with a personal insignia on it (cf. Hag 2:23).

22:28 Questions the people who idolized Jeconiah were asking.

22:30 Write ... childless. Jeconiah did have offspring (1Ch 3:17, 18), but he was reckoned childless in the sense that he had no sons who would reign ("Sitting on the throne ... "). The curse continued in his descendants down to Joseph, the husband of Mary. How could Jesus then be the Messiah when His father was under this curse? It was because Joseph was not involved in the blood line of Jesus since He was virgin born (Mt 1:12). Jesus' blood right to the throne of David came through Mary from Nathan, Solomon's brother, not Solomon (Jeconiah's line), thus bypassing this curse (Lk 3:31, 32). Cf. 36:30.

23:1, 2 Woe to the shepherds. These were false leaders who failed in their duty to assure the people's welfare (as v. 2), starting with the kings in chap. 22 and other civil heads, as well as prophets and priests (cf. v. 11). They stood in utter contrast to the shepherds God would later give the nation (v. 4; 3:15). Other significant chapters which condemn evil shepherds and false prophets include chaps. 14, 27, 28; Is 28; Eze 13, 34; Mic 3; Zec 11.

23:3, 4 I ... will gather. God pledged to restore exiled Israelites to their ancient soil. Cf. similar promises in chaps. 30–33, and 16:14, 15. The land in view was lit. Israel, being contrasted with all the other countries (v. 3), thus

the countries where I have driven them and bring
them back to their pasture, and they will be fruitful
and multiply. 4 I will also raise up [A]shepherds over
them and they will [a]tend them; and they will [B]not
be afraid any longer, nor be terrified, [C]nor will any
be missing," declares the LORD.

5 "Behold, *the* [A]days are coming,"
declares the LORD,
"When I will raise up for David
a righteous [a,B]Branch;
And He will [C]reign as king and [b]act wisely
And [D]do justice and righteousness
in the land.
6 "In His days Judah will be saved,
And [A]Israel will dwell securely;
And this is His [B]name by which
He will be called,
'The [C]LORD our righteousness.'

7 "[A]Therefore behold, *the* days are coming," declares the LORD, "when they will no longer say, 'As
the LORD lives, who brought up the sons of Israel
from the land of Egypt,' 8 [A]but, 'As the LORD lives,
who [B]brought up and led back the descendants of
the household of Israel from *the* north land and
from all the countries where I had driven them.'
Then they will live on their own soil."

FALSE PROPHETS DENOUNCED

9 As for the prophets:
My [A]heart is broken within me,
All my bones tremble;
I have become like a drunken man,
Even like a man overcome with wine,
Because of the LORD
And because of His holy words.
10 For the land is full of [A]adulterers;
For the land [B]mourns
because of the curse.
The [C]pastures of the wilderness
have dried up.
Their course also is evil
And their might is not right.
11 "For [A]both prophet and priest are polluted;
Even in My house I have found their
wickedness," declares the LORD.
12 "Therefore their way will be like
[A]slippery paths to them,
They will be driven away into the
[B]gloom and fall down in it;
For I will bring [C]calamity upon them,
The year of their punishment,"
declares the LORD.
13 "Moreover, among the prophets of
Samaria I saw an [A]offensive thing:
They [B]prophesied by Baal and [C]led
My people Israel astray.
14 "Also among the prophets of Jerusalem
I have seen a [A]horrible thing:
The committing of [B]adultery and
walking in falsehood;
And they strengthen the
hands of [C]evildoers,
So that no one has turned back
from his wickedness.
All of them have become to Me like [D]Sodom,
And her inhabitants like Gomorrah.

15 Therefore thus says the LORD of hosts concerning
the prophets,

'Behold, I am going to [A]feed
them wormwood
And make them drink poisonous water,
For from the prophets of Jerusalem
Pollution has gone forth into all the land.' "
16 Thus says the LORD of hosts,
"[A]Do not listen to the words of the prophets
who are prophesying to you.
They are [B]leading you into futility;
They speak a [C]vision of their
own [a]imagination,
Not [D]from the mouth of the LORD.
17 "They keep saying to those
who [A]despise Me,
'The LORD has said, "[B]You
will have peace" ';
And as for everyone who walks in the
[C]stubbornness of his own heart,
They say, '[D]Calamity will not
come upon you.'

23:4 [a]Or *shepherd* [A]Jer 3:15; 31:10; Ezek 34:23 [B]Jer 30:10; 46:27, 28 [C]John 6:39; 10:28; 1 Pet 1:5 23:5 [a]Lit *Sprout* [b]Or *succeed* [A]Jer 33:14 [B]Is 4:2; 11:1-5; 53:2; Jer 30:9; 33:15, 16; Zech 3:8; 6:12, 13 [C]Is 9:7; 52:13; Luke 1:32, 33 [D]Ps 72:2; Is 9:7; 32:1; Dan 9:24 23:6 [A]Deut 33:28; Jer 30:10; Zech 14:11 [B]Is 7:14; 9:6; Matt 1:21-23 [C]Is 45:24; Jer 33:16; Dan 9:24; Rom 3:22; 1 Cor 1:30 23:7 [A]Is 43:18, 19; Jer 16:14, 15 23:8 [A]Jer 16:15 [B]Is 43:5, 6; Ezek 34:13; Amos 9:14, 15 23:9 [A]Jer 8:18; Hab 3:16 23:10 [A]Jer 9:2; Hos 4:2, 3; Mal 3:5 [B]Jer 12:4 [C]Ps 107:34; Jer 9:10 23:11 [A]Jer 6:13; Zeph 3:4 23:12 [A]Ps 35:6; Prov 4:19; Jer 13:16 [B]Is 8:22; John 12:35 [C]Jer 11:23 23:13 [A]Hos 9:7, 8 [B]1 Kin 18:18-21; Jer 2:8; 23:32 [C]Is 9:16 23:14 [A]Jer 5:30 [B]Jer 29:23 [C]Jer 23:22; Ezek 13:22, 23 [D]Gen 18:20; Deut 32:32; Is 1:9, 10; Jer 20:16; 49:18; Matt 11:24 23:15 [A]Deut 29:18; Jer 8:14; 9:15 23:16 [a]Lit *heart* [A]Jer 27:9, 10, 14-17; 1 John 4:1 [B]Matt 7:15; 2 Cor 11:13-15; Gal 1:8, 9 [C]Jer 14:14; Ezek 13:3, 6 [D]Jer 9:12, 20 23:17 [A]Mic 2:11 [B]Jer 8:11; Ezek 13:10 [C]Jer 13:10; 18:12 [D]Jer 5:12; Amos 9:10; Mic 3:11

assuring that the regathering would be as literal as the scattering. The restoration of Judah from Babylon is referred to in language which in its fullness can only refer to the final restoration of God's people ("out of all the countries," and v. 8), under Messiah. "Nor will any be missing" indicates that no one will be missing or detached. These are prophecies not yet fulfilled. Cf. 32:37, 38; Is 60:21; Ezek 34:11–16.

23:4 shepherds … will tend them. Cf. Ezek 34:23–31. Zerubbabel, Ezra, Nehemiah, and others were small fulfillments compared to the consummate shepherding of the Messiah Jesus.

23:5 Branch. The Messiah is pictured as a branch (lit. "shoot") out of David's family tree (cf. 33:15, 16; Is 4:2; 11:1–5; Zec 3:8; 6:12, 13), who will rule over God's people in the future. Cf. 33:14–17 where the same promise is repeated.

23:6 The LORD our righteousness. This emphasis is stated 3 times in vv. 5, 6. Messiah's shepherding is contrasted with that of the false shepherds (vv. 1, 2, 11, 14). Judah and Israel will be reunited (cf. Eze 37:15–23).

23:7, 8 *See note on 16:14, 15.*

23:13, 14 Jerusalem and Judah were worse than Samaria and Israel.

23:14 among the prophets …. horrible thing. The false shepherds told lies, committed adultery, and declared vain dreams (vv. 25, 27). They became like chaff rather than grain (v. 28), while promising peace (v. 17) to those whose sins provoke God to bring calamity, not comfort. The scene was like Sodom and Gomorrah, whose sin so grieved God that He destroyed them by fire (cf. Ge 19:13, 24, 25).

18 "But [A]who has stood in the
council of the LORD,
That he should see and hear His word?
Who has given [B]heed to [a]His
word and listened?
19 "Behold, the [A]storm of the LORD
has gone forth in wrath,
Even a whirling tempest;
It will swirl down on the
head of the wicked.
20 "The [A]anger of the LORD will not turn back
Until He has [B]performed and carried
out the purposes of His heart;
[C]In the last days you will
clearly understand it.
21 "[A]I did not send *these* prophets,
But they ran.
I did not speak to them,
But they prophesied.
22 "But if they had [A]stood in My council,
Then they would have [B]announced
My words to My people,
And would have turned them
back from their evil way
And from the evil of their deeds.

23 "Am I a God who is [A]near,"
declares the LORD,
"And not a God far off?
24 "Can a man [A]hide himself in hiding places
So I do not see him?" declares the LORD.
"[B]Do I not fill the heavens and the
earth?" declares the LORD.

25 "I have [A]heard what the prophets have said
who [B]prophesy falsely in My name, saying, 'I had a
[C]dream, I had a dream!' 26 How long? Is there *any-*
thing in the hearts of the prophets who prophesy
falsehood, even *these* prophets of the [A]deception of
their own heart, 27 who intend to [A]make My people
forget My name by their dreams which they relate
to one another, just as their fathers [B]forgot My name
because of Baal? 28 The prophet who has a dream
may relate *his* dream, but let him who has [A]My word
speak My word in truth. [B]What does straw have *in*
common with grain?" declares the LORD. 29 "Is not
My word like [A]fire?" declares the LORD, "and like a
[B]hammer which shatters a rock? 30 Therefore behold,
[A]I am against the prophets," declares the LORD,
"who steal My words from each other. 31 Behold, I
am against the prophets," declares the LORD, "who
use their tongues and declare, '*The Lord* declares.'
32 Behold, I am against those who have prophesied [A]false dreams," declares the LORD, "and related
them and led My people astray by their falsehoods
and [B]reckless boasting; yet [C]I did not send them or
command them, nor do they [D]furnish this people
the slightest benefit," declares the LORD.
33 "Now when this people or the prophet or a
priest asks you saying, 'What is the [a,A]oracle of the
LORD?' then you shall say to them, 'What [a]oracle?'
The LORD declares, 'I will [B]abandon you.' 34 Then as
for the prophet or the priest or the people who say,
'The [A]oracle of the LORD,' I will bring punishment
upon that man and his household. 35 Thus will each
of you say to his neighbor and to his brother, '[A]What
has the LORD answered?' or, 'What has the LORD
spoken?' 36 For you will no longer remember the
oracle of the LORD, because every man's own word
will become the oracle, and you have [A]perverted
the words of the [B]living God, the LORD of hosts, our
God. 37 Thus you will say to *that* prophet, 'What has
the LORD answered you?' and, 'What has the LORD
spoken?' 38 For if you say, 'The oracle of the LORD!'
surely thus says the LORD, 'Because you said this
word, "The oracle of the LORD!" I have also sent to
you, saying, "You shall not say, 'The oracle of the
LORD!' " ' 39 Therefore behold, [A]I will surely forget
you and cast you away from My presence, along
with the city which I gave you and your fathers.
40 I will put an everlasting [A]reproach on you and an
everlasting humiliation which will not be forgotten."

BASKETS OF FIGS AND THE RETURNEES

24 After [A]Nebuchadnezzar king of Babylon had
carried away captive Jeconiah the son of Jehoiakim, king of Judah, and the officials of Judah
with the craftsmen and smiths from Jerusalem and
had brought them to Babylon, the LORD showed me:
behold, two [B]baskets of figs set before the temple
of the LORD! 2 One basket had very good figs, like

23:18 [a]Another reading is *My* [A]Job 15:8, 9; Jer 23:22; 1 Cor 2:16 [B]Job 33:31 23:19 [A]Jer 25:32; 30:23; Amos 1:14 23:20 [A]2 Kin 23:26, 27; Jer 30:24 [B]Is 55:11; Zech 1:6 [C]Gen 49:1 23:21 [A]Jer 14:14; 23:32; 27:15 23:22 [A]Jer 9:12; 23:18 [B]Jer 35:15; Zech 1:4 23:23 [A]Ps 139:1-10 23:24 [A]Job 22:13, 14; 34:21, 22; Ps 139:7-12; Is 29:15; Jer 49:10; Heb 4:13 [B]1 Kin 8:27; 2 Chr 2:6; Is 66:1 23:25 [A]Jer 8:6; 1 Cor 4:5 [B]Jer 14:14 [C]Num 12:6; Jer 23:28, 32; 29:8; Joel 2:28 23:26 [A]1 Tim 4:1, 2 23:27 [A]Deut 13:1-3; Jer 29:8 [B]Judg 3:7; 8:33, 34 23:28 [A]Jer 9:12, 20 [B]1 Cor 3:12, 13 23:29 [A]Jer 5:14; 20:9 [B]2 Cor 10:4, 5 23:30 [A]Deut 18:20; Ps 34:16; Jer 14:14, 15; Ezek 13:8 23:32 [A]Deut 13:1, 2; Jer 23:25 [B]Zeph 3:4 [C]Jer 23:21; Lam 3:37 [D]Jer 7:8; Lam 2:14 23:33 [a]Or *burden,* and so throughout the ch [A]Is 13:1; Nah 1:1; Hab 1:1; Zech 9:1; Mal 1:1 [B]Jer 12:7; 23:39 23:34 [A]Lam 2:14; Zech 13:3 23:35 [A]Jer 33:3; 42:4 23:36 [A]Gal 1:7, 8; 2 Pet 3:16 [B]2 Kin 19:4; Jer 10:10 23:39 [A]Jer 7:14, 15; 23:33; Ezek 8:18 23:40 [A]Jer 20:11; 42:18; Ezek 5:14, 15 24:1 [A]2 Kin 24:10-16; 2 Chr 36:10; Jer 27:20; 29:1, 2 [B]Amos 8:1

23:18 Here was the reason not to listen to the false prophets (cf. v. 16)—they didn't speak God's Word.

23:20 last days. They wouldn't listen, but the day would come (v. 12) when the judgment would fall and then they would "understand."

23:21, 22 According to the Mosaic law, these false prophets should have been stoned (cf. Dt 13:1–5; 18:20–22).

23:23, 24 God who is near . . . God far off. Let not false prophets think they can hide their devices from God, who declares Himself omnipresent and omniscient, in both an immanent and transcendent sense.

23:25 I had a dream. Here was a claim to divine revelation through dreams (cf. Nu 12:6). But such claims were a deception (vv. 26, 27), utterly unequal in power to God's Word (vv. 28, 29).

23:29 like fire . . . hammer. God's Word has irresistible qualities to prevail over the deception in the shepherds' false messages.

23:33 the oracle of the LORD . . . What oracle? The people asked, in mockery, for Jeremiah to give them his latest prophecy ("oracle"). This ridicule of Jeremiah's faithful preaching demanded a response, and God told the prophet to repeat the question and reply simply "I will abandon you," meaning judgment from God was coming.

23:34–40 The oracle of the LORD. When a person falsely claimed to have a word from God, he would be punished for perverting God's truth. Claiming to have prophecies from God, when not true, is dangerous.

24:1 after Nebuchadnezzar . . . carried away. Babylon's second deportation of Judeans in 597 B.C. (cf. 2Ki 24:10–17).

[A]first-ripe figs, and the other basket had [B]very bad
figs which could not be eaten due to rottenness.
3 Then the LORD said to me, "[A]What do you see, Jeremiah?" And I said, "Figs, the good figs, very good;
and the bad *figs*, very bad, which cannot be eaten
due to rottenness."
4 Then the word of the LORD came to me, saying,
5 "Thus says the LORD God of Israel, 'Like these good
figs, so I will regard [A]as good the captives of Judah,
whom I have sent out of this place *into* the land of
the Chaldeans. 6 For I will set My eyes on them for
good, and I will [A]bring them again to this land; and
I will [B]build them up and not overthrow them, and
I will [C]plant them and not pluck them up. 7 I will
give them a [A]heart to know Me, for I am the LORD;
and they will be [B]My people, and I will be their God,
for they will [C]return to Me with their whole heart.
8 'But like the [A]bad figs which cannot be eaten due
to rottenness—indeed, thus says the LORD—so I will
[a]abandon [B]Zedekiah king of Judah and his officials,
and the [C]remnant of Jerusalem who remain in this
land and the ones who dwell in the land of [D]Egypt.
9 I will [A]make them a terror *and an* evil for all the
kingdoms of the earth, as a [B]reproach and a proverb,
a taunt and a [C]curse in all places where I will scatter
them. 10 I will send the [A]sword, the famine and the
pestilence upon them until they are destroyed from
the land which I gave to them and their forefathers.' "

PROPHECY OF THE CAPTIVITY

25 The word that came to Jeremiah concerning
all the people of Judah, in the [A]fourth year of
[B]Jehoiakim the son of Josiah, king of Judah (that was
the [C]first year of Nebuchadnezzar king of Babylon),
2 which Jeremiah the prophet spoke to all the [A]peo-
ple of Judah and to all the inhabitants of Jerusalem,
saying, 3 "From the [A]thirteenth year of [B]Josiah the
son of Amon, king of Judah, even to this day, [a]these
[C]twenty-three years the word of the LORD has come
to me, and I have spoken to you [b,D]again and again,
but you have not listened. 4 And the LORD has sent
to you all His [A]servants the prophets [a]again and
again, but you have not listened nor inclined your
ear to hear, 5 saying, '[A]Turn now everyone from his
evil way and from the evil of your deeds, and dwell
on the land which the LORD has given to you and
your forefathers [B]forever and ever; 6 and [A]do not
go after other gods to [a]serve them and to [b]worship
them, and do not provoke Me to anger with the work
of your hands, and I will do you no harm.' 7 Yet you
have not listened to Me," declares the LORD, "in order that you might [A]provoke Me to anger with the
work of your hands to your own harm.
8 "Therefore thus says the LORD of hosts, 'Because
you have not obeyed My words, 9 behold, I will [A]send
and take all the families of the north,' declares the
LORD, 'and *I will send* to Nebuchadnezzar king of
Babylon, [B]My servant, and will bring them against
this land and against its inhabitants and against all
these nations round about; and I will [a]utterly destroy them and [C]make them a horror and a hissing,
and an everlasting desolation. 10 Moreover, I will
[a,A]take from them the voice of joy and the voice of
gladness, the voice of the bridegroom and the voice
of the bride, the [B]sound of the millstones and the
light of the lamp. 11 [A]This whole land will be a desolation and a horror, and these nations will serve
the king of Babylon [B]seventy years.

BABYLON WILL BE JUDGED

12 'Then it will be [A]when seventy years are completed I will [B]punish the king of Babylon and that
nation,' declares the LORD, 'for their iniquity, and
the land of the Chaldeans; and [C]I will make it an
everlasting desolation. 13 I will bring upon that land
all My words which I have pronounced against it,
all that is written in [A]this book which Jeremiah has
prophesied against [B]all the nations. 14 ([a]For [A]many
nations and great kings will make slaves of them,
even them; and I will [B]recompense them according

24:2 [A]Mic 7:1; Nah 3:12 [B]Is 5:4, 7; Jer 29:17 24:3 [A]Jer 1:11, 13; Amos 8:2; Zech 4:2 24:5 [A]Nah 1:7; Zech 13:9 24:6 [A]Jer 12:15; 29:10; 32:37; Ezek 11:17 [B]Jer 31:4; 32:41; 33:7; 42:10 [C]Jer 32:41 24:7 [A]Deut 30:6; Jer 31:33; 32:40; Ezek 11:19; 36:26 [B]Is 51:16; Jer 7:23; 30:22; 31:33; 32:38; Ezek 14:11; Zech 8:8; Heb 8:10 [C]1 Sam 7:3; Ps 119:2; Jer 29:13 24:8 [a]Lit *give up* [A]Jer 29:17 [B]Jer 39:5; Ezek 12:12, 13 [C]Jer 39:9 [D]Jer 44:1, 26-30 24:9 [A]Jer 15:4; 29:18; 34:17 [B]1 Kin 9:7; Ps 44:13, 14 [C]Is 65:15 24:10 [A]Is 51:19; Jer 21:9; 27:8; Ezek 5:12-17 25:1 [A]Jer 36:1; 46:2 [B]2 Kin 24:1, 2; 2 Chr 36:4-6; Dan 1:1, 2 [C]Jer 32:1 25:2 [A]Jer 18:11 25:3 [a]Lit *this* [b]Lit *rising early and speaking* [A]Jer 1:2 [B]2 Chr 34:1-3, 8 [C]Jer 36:2 [D]Jer 7:25; 11:7; 26:5 25:4 [a]Lit *rising early and sending* [A]2 Chr 36:15; Jer 26:5 25:5 [A]2 Kin 17:13; Is 55:6, 7; Jer 4:1; 35:15; Ezek 18:30; Jon 3:8-10 [B]Gen 17:8; Jer 7:7; 17:25 25:6 [a]Or *worship* [b]Or *bow down to* [A]Deut 6:14; 8:19; 2 Kin 17:35; Jer 35:15 25:7 [A]2 Kin 17:17; 21:15; Jer 7:19; 32:30-33 25:9 [a]Or *put them under the ban* [A]Jer 1:15; 6:22, 23 [B]Is 13:3; Jer 27:6; 43:10 [C]1 Kin 9:7, 8; Jer 18:16; 25:18 25:10 [a]Lit *cause to perish* [A]Is 24:8-11; Jer 7:34; 16:9; Ezek 26:13; Rev 18:23 [B]Eccl 12:4; Is 47:2 25:11 [A]Jer 4:27; 12:11, 12 [B]2 Chr 36:21; Jer 29:10; Dan 9:2; Zech 7:5 25:12 [A]Ezra 1:1; Jer 29:10; Dan 9:2 [B]Is 13:14; Jer ch 50, 51 [C]Is 13:19 25:13 [A]Jer 36:4, 29, 32 [B]Jer 1:5, 10; 36:2 25:14 [a]Or *For they have served many nations and great kings* [A]Jer 27:7; 50:9, 41; 51:27, 28 [B]Jer 51:6, 24, 56

24:5 Like these good figs. The object lesson of v. 2 is explained. Deported Judeans, captive in Babylon, will have good treatment, not death as shown in 29:5–7, 10. They will be granted privileges as colonists rather than being enslaved as captives.

24:6, 7 While it is true that a remnant returned to Judah in 538 B.C., this promise had greater overtones in regard to the ultimate fulfillment of the Abrahamic (Ge 12), Davidic (2Sa 7), and New (Jer 31) Covenants in the day of Messiah's coming and kingdom (cf. 32:41; 33:7). Their conversion (v. 7) from idolatry to the one true God is expressed in language which, in its fullness, applies to the complete conversion in the final Kingdom after the present dispersion (cf. Ro 11:1–5, 25–27).

24:8–10 like the bad figs. Those remaining at Jerusalem during the 11 years (597–586 B.C.) of Zedekiah's vassal reign would soon face hardship from further scattering to other countries, violent death, famine, and disease; cf. Jer 29:17. See 25:9 and *note there*. These verses quote the curses of Dt 28:25, 37 (cf. 29:18, 22; Ps 44:13, 14) and are also fulfilled in the history of the long dispersion until Messiah returns.

25:1 fourth year. The date is 605/04 B.C., as Jehoiakim reigned in 609–598 B.C. **first year.** Nebuchadnezzar reigned 605–562 B.C.

25:3 thirteenth year. The time is ca. 627/626 B.C. Josiah ruled in 640–609 B.C. **twenty-three years.** Jeremiah began his ministry in the 13th year of Josiah (cf. 1:2) and had been faithful to preach repentance and judgment for 23 years (ca. 605/604 B.C.).

25:9 My servant. God used a pagan king, Nebuchadnezzar, to accomplish His will (cf. Cyrus in Is 45:1).

25:10 Cf. 7:34; Rev 18:23.

25:11 seventy years. Here is the first specific statement on the length of the exile (cf. 29:10). This period probably began in the fourth year of Jehoiakim, when Jerusalem was first captured and the temple treasures were taken. It ends with the decree of Cyrus to let the Jews return, spanning from ca. 605/04 B.C. to 536/35 B.C. The exact number of Sabbath years is 490 years, the period from Saul to the Babylonian captivity. This was retribution for their violation of the Sabbath law (cf. Lv 26:34, 35; 2Ch 36:21).

25:13 all the nations. Jeremiah prophesied judgments on surrounding nations (cf. chaps. 46–49), while Babylon is the focus of judgment in chaps. 50–51.

25:14 make slaves of them. The Babylonians, who made other nations their slaves, would become the servants of nations.

to their deeds and according to the work of their
hands.)' "
15 For thus the LORD, the God of Israel, says to me,
"Take this [A]cup of the wine of wrath from My hand
and cause all the nations to whom I send you to
drink it. 16 They will [A]drink and stagger and go mad
because of the sword that I will send among them."
17 Then I took the cup from the LORD'S hand and
[A]made all the nations to whom the LORD sent me
drink it: 18 [A]Jerusalem and the cities of Judah and its
kings *and* its princes, to make them a ruin, a horror, a
hissing and a curse, as it is this day; 19 [A]Pharaoh king
of Egypt, his servants, his princes and all his people;
20 and all the [a,A]foreign people, all the kings of the [B]land
of Uz, all the kings of the land of the [C]Philistines (even
Ashkelon, Gaza, Ekron and the remnant of [D]Ashdod);
21 [A]Edom, [B]Moab and the sons of [C]Ammon; 22 and all
the kings of [A]Tyre, all the kings of Sidon and the kings
of [B]the coastlands which are beyond the sea; 23 and
[A]Dedan, Tema, [B]Buz and all who [C]cut the corners *of
their hair;* 24 and all the kings of [A]Arabia and all the
kings of the [a,B]foreign people who dwell in the desert;
25 and all the kings of Zimri, all the kings of [A]Elam and
all the kings of [B]Media; 26 and all the kings of the north,
near and far, one with another; and [A]all the kingdoms
of the earth which are upon the face of the ground,
and the king of [a,B]Sheshach shall drink after them.
27 "You shall say to them, 'Thus says the LORD of
hosts, the God of Israel, "[A]Drink, be drunk, vomit, fall
and rise no more because of the [B]sword which I will
send among you." ' 28 And it will be, if they [A]refuse
to take the cup from your hand to drink, then you
will say to them, 'Thus says the LORD of hosts: "[B]You
shall surely drink! 29 For behold, I am [A]beginning
to work calamity in *this* city which is [B]called by My
name, and shall you be completely free from punishment? You will not be free from punishment; for [C]I
am summoning a sword against all the inhabitants
of the earth," declares the LORD of hosts.'
30 "Therefore you shall prophesy against them all
these words, and you shall say to them,

'The [A]LORD will [B]roar from on high
And utter His voice from
His holy habitation;
He will roar mightily against His [a]fold.
He will shout like those who
tread *the grapes,*
Against all the inhabitants of the earth.

31 'A clamor has come to the
end of the earth,
Because the LORD has [A]a
controversy with the nations.
He is entering into [B]judgment
with all flesh;
As for the wicked, He has given them
to the sword,' declares the LORD."

32 Thus says the LORD of hosts,
"Behold, evil is going forth
From [A]nation to nation,
And a great [B]storm is being stirred up
From the remotest parts of the earth.

33 "Those [A]slain by the LORD on that day will be
from one end of the earth to the [a]other. They will
[B]not be lamented, gathered or buried; they will be
like [C]dung on the face of the ground.

34 "Wail, you shepherds, and cry;
And [A]wallow *in ashes,* you
masters of the flock;
For the days of your [B]slaughter and
your dispersions [a]have come,
And you will fall like a choice vessel.
35 "[A]Flight will perish from the shepherds,
And escape from the masters of the flock.
36 "*Hear* the sound of the cry
of the shepherds,
And the wailing of the
masters of the flock!
For the LORD is destroying their pasture,
37 And the peaceful [a,A]folds are made silent
Because of the [B]fierce anger of the LORD.
38 "He has left His hiding place [A]like the lion;
For their land has become a horror
Because of the fierceness of
the [a]oppressing *sword*
And because of His fierce anger."

CITIES OF JUDAH WARNED

26 In the beginning of the reign of [A]Jehoiakim
the son of Josiah, king of Judah, this word
came from the LORD, saying, 2 "Thus says the LORD,
'[A]Stand in the court of the LORD'S house, and speak
to all the cities of Judah who have [B]come to worship
in the LORD'S house [C]all the words that I have commanded you to speak to them. [D]Do not omit a word!

25:15 [A]Job 21:20; Ps 75:8; Is 51:17, 22; Jer 51:7 25:16 [A]Nah 3:11 25:17 [A]Jer 1:10; 25:28 25:18 [A]Ps 60:3; Is 51:17 25:19 [A]Jer 46:2-28; Nah 3:8-10 25:20 [a]Or *mixed multitude* [A]Jer 25:24; 50:37; Ezek 30:5 [B]Job 1:1; Lam 4:21 [C]Jer 47:1-7 [D]Is 20:1 25:21 [A]Ps 137:7; Jer 49:7-22 [B]Jer 48:1-47; Amos 2:1-3 [C]Jer 49:1-6; Amos 1:13-15 25:22 [A]Jer 47:4; Zech 9:2-4 [B]Jer 31:10 25:23 [A]Is 21:13; Jer 49:7, 8 [B]Gen 22:21 [C]Jer 9:26; 49:32 25:24 [a]Or *mixed multitude* [A]2 Chr 9:14 [B]Jer 25:20; 50:37; Ezek 30:5 25:25 [A]Gen 10:22; Is 11:11; Jer 49:34 [B]Is 13:17; Jer 51:11, 28 25:26 [a]Cryptic name for Babylon [A]Jer 25:9; 50:9 [B]Jer 51:41 25:27 [A]Jer 25:16; Hab 2:16 [B]Ezek 21:4, 5 25:28 [A]Job 34:33 [B]Jer 49:12 25:29 [A]Prov 11:31; Is 10:12; Jer 13:13; Ezek 9:6; 1 Pet 4:17 [B]1 Kin 8:43 [C]Ezek 38:21 25:30 [a]Or *pasture* [A]Is 42:13; Jer 25:38 [B]Joel 2:11; 3:16; Amos 1:2 25:31 [A]Hos 4:1; Mic 6:2 [B]Is 66:16; Ezek 20:35, 36; Joel 3:2 25:32 [A]2 Chr 15:6; Is 34:2 [B]Is 30:30; Jer 23:19 25:33 [a]Lit *other end of the earth* [A]Is 34:2, 3; 66:16 [B]Ps 79:3; Jer 16:4; Ezek 39:4, 17 [C]Is 5:25 25:34 [a]Lit *are full* [A]Jer 6:26; Ezek 27:30 [B]Is 34:6, 7; Jer 50:27 25:35 [A]Job 11:20; Jer 11:11; Amos 2:14 25:37 [a]Or *pastures* [A]Is 27:10, 11; Jer 5:17; 13:20 [B]Ps 97:1-3; Is 66:15; Heb 12:29 25:38 [a]Or *oppressor* [A]Jer 4:7; 5:6; Hos 5:14; 13:7, 8 26:1 [A]2 Kin 23:36; 2 Chr 36:4, 5 26:2 [A]2 Chr 24:20, 21; Jer 7:2; 19:14 [B]Deut 12:5 [C]Jer 1:17; 42:4; Matt 28:20; Acts 20:20, 27 [D]Deut 4:2

25:15 cup of the wine. A symbol for stupefying judgments (v. 16).

25:17 made all the nations ... drink. Obviously Jeremiah could not visit all the places listed from vv. 18–26, but in this vision he acted as if representatives from all those nations were present so he could make them drink in the message of wrath (v. 27), and understand there was no escape (vv. 28, 29).

25:29 city ... called by My name. Jerusalem (cf. Da 9:18).

25:30–33 While embracing the judgments soon to come to Judah and other nations, this has end-time language ("one end of the earth to the other") and must be ultimately fulfilled in the time of tribulation described in Rev 6–19.

26:1 In the beginning. The time was 609 B.C. The message is about 4 years earlier than that in 25:1 and about 11 years before 24:1.

26:2 Stand in the court. This was the largest public gathering place at the temple.

3 [A]Perhaps they will listen and everyone will turn
from his evil way, that [B]I may repent of the calamity which I am planning to do to them because of
the evil of their deeds.' 4 And you will say to them,
'Thus says the LORD, "[A]If you will not listen to Me,
to [B]walk in My law which I have set before you, 5 to
listen to the words of [A]My servants the prophets,
whom I have been sending to you [a]again and again,
but you have not listened; 6 then I will make this
house like [A]Shiloh, and this city I will make a [B]curse
to all the nations of the earth." ' "

A PLOT TO MURDER JEREMIAH

7 The [A]priests and the prophets and all the people
heard Jeremiah speaking these words in the house
of the LORD. 8 When Jeremiah finished speaking
all that the LORD had commanded *him* to speak
to all the people, the priests and the prophets and
all the people seized him, saying, "[A]You must die!
9 Why have you prophesied in the name of the LORD
saying, 'This house will be like Shiloh and this city
will be [A]desolate, without inhabitant'?" And [B]all
the people gathered about Jeremiah in the house
of the LORD.
10 When the [A]officials of Judah heard these things,
they came up from the king's house to the house
of the LORD and sat in the [B]entrance of the New
Gate of the LORD'S *house*. 11 Then the priests and
the prophets [A]spoke to the officials and to all the
people, saying, "A [B]death sentence for this man! For
he has prophesied [C]against this city as you have
heard in your hearing."
12 Then Jeremiah spoke to all the officials and
to all the people, saying, "[A]The LORD sent me to
prophesy against this house and against this city
all the words that you have heard. 13 Now therefore [A]amend your ways and your deeds and obey
the voice of the LORD your God; and the LORD will
[a]change His mind about the misfortune which He
has pronounced against you. 14 But as for me, behold, [A]I am in your hands; do with me as is good
and right in your sight. 15 Only know for certain that
if you put me to death, you will bring [A]innocent
blood on yourselves, and on this city and on its
inhabitants; for truly the LORD has sent me to you
to speak all these words in your hearing."

JEREMIAH IS SPARED

16 Then the officials and all the people [A]said to the
priests and to the prophets, "No [B]death sentence for
this man! For he has spoken to us in the name of the
LORD our God." 17 Then [A]some of the elders of the
land rose up and spoke to all the assembly of the
people, saying, 18 "[a,A]Micah of Moresheth prophesied
in the days of Hezekiah king of Judah; and he spoke
to all the people of Judah, saying, 'Thus the LORD
of hosts has said,

"[B]Zion will be plowed *as* a field,
And Jerusalem will become ruins,
And the [C]mountain of
the house as the [b]high
places of a forest." '

19 Did Hezekiah king of Judah and all Judah put him
to death? Did he not [A]fear the LORD and entreat the
favor of the LORD, and [B]the LORD [a]changed His mind
about the misfortune which He had pronounced
against them? But we are [C]committing a great evil
against ourselves."
20 Indeed, there was also a man who prophesied in the name of the LORD, Uriah the son of
Shemaiah from [A]Kiriath-jearim; and he prophesied against this city and against this land words
similar to all those of Jeremiah. 21 When King Jehoiakim and all his mighty men and all the officials heard his words, then the [A]king sought to
put him to death; but Uriah heard *it*, and he was
afraid and [B]fled and went to Egypt. 22 Then King
Jehoiakim sent men to Egypt: [A]Elnathan the son
of Achbor and *certain* men with him *went* into
Egypt. 23 And they brought Uriah from Egypt and
led him to King Jehoiakim, who [A]slew him with
a sword and cast his dead body into the [a]burial
place of the [b]common people.
24 But the hand of [A]Ahikam the son of Shaphan
was with Jeremiah, so that he was [B]not given into
the hands of the people to put him to death.

26:3 [A]Is 1:16-19; Jer 36:3-7 [B]Jer 18:8; Jon 3:8 26:4 [A]Lev 26:14; 1 Kin 9:6; Is 1:20; Jer 17:27; 22:5 [B]Jer 32:23; 44:10, 23 26:5 [a]Lit *rising early and sending* [A]2 Kin 9:7; Ezra 9:11; Jer 7:13; 25:3, 4 26:6 [A]Josh 18:1; 1 Sam 4:12; Ps 78:60, 61; Jer 7:12, 14 [B]2 Kin 22:19; Is 65:15; Jer 24:9; 25:18 26:7 [A]Jer 5:31; Mic 3:11 26:8 [A]Jer 11:19; 18:23; Lam 4:13, 14; Matt 21:35, 36; 23:34, 35; 27:20 26:9 [A]Jer 9:11; 33:10 [B]Acts 3:11; 5:12 26:10 [A]Jer 26:21 [B]Jer 36:10 26:11 [A]Jer 18:23 [B]Deut 18:20; Matt 26:66 [C]Jer 38:4; Acts 6:11-14 26:12 [A]Jer 1:17, 18; 26:15; Amos 7:15; Acts 4:19; 5:29 26:13 [a]Lit *be sorry for* [A]Jer 7:3, 5; 18:8, 11; 26:3; 35:15; Joel 2:14; Jon 3:9; 4:2 26:14 [A]Jer 38:5 26:15 [A]Num 35:33; Prov 6:16, 17; Jer 7:6 26:16 [A]Jer 26:11; 36:19, 25; 38:7, 13 [B]Acts 5:34-39; 23:9, 29; 25:25; 26:31 26:17 [A]Acts 5:34 26:18 [a]Lit *Micaiah the Morasthite* [b]Or *a wooded height* [A]Mic 1:1 [B]Neh 4:2; Ps 79:1; Jer 9:11; Mic 3:12 [C]Is 2:2, 3; Jer 17:3; Mic 4:1; Zech 8:3 26:19 [a]Lit *was sorry for* [A]2 Chr 29:6-11; 32:26; Is 37:1, 4, 15-20 [B]Ex 32:14; 2 Sam 24:16 [C]Jer 44:7; Hab 2:10 26:20 [A]Josh 9:17; 1 Sam 6:21; 7:2 26:21 [A]2 Chr 16:10; 24:21; Jer 36:26; Matt 14:5 [B]1 Kin 19:2-4; Matt 10:23 26:22 [A]Jer 36:12 26:23 [a]Lit *graves* [b]Lit *sons of the people* [A]Jer 2:30 26:24 [A]2 Kin 22:12-14; Jer 39:14; 40:5-7 [B]1 Kin 18:4; Jer 1:18, 19

26:6 like Shiloh. The former dwelling place of God before Jerusalem. Cf. 7:12 and *see note there*.

26:11 Jeremiah was accused of treason. Cf. Paul's arrest in Ac 21:27, 28.

26:12 Jeremiah spoke. Leaders and people threatened to kill him (v. 8). The prophet defended himself while in extreme danger. He did not compromise, but displayed tremendous spiritual courage. He was ready to die (v. 14), yet warned the crowd that God would hold the guilty accountable (v. 15).

26:15 put me to death. Cf. Mt 23:31–37.

26:17–19 elders … spoke. These spokesmen cited the prophet Micah (cf. Mic 3:12), who before and during Hezekiah's reign (ca. 715–686 B.C.) prophesied the destruction of Jerusalem and its temple. They reasoned that because they didn't kill Micah, God rescinded the judgment. They must not kill Jeremiah so God might change His mind. Micah's prophecy and Jeremiah's would come true in time.

26:20–22 also a man who prophesied. Uriah, like Micah and Jeremiah, had warned of doom on Jerusalem, speaking in Jehoiakim's day only a bit earlier than Jeremiah's present warning (609 B.C.). He was executed. The decision could have gone either way since there was precedent for killing and for sparing.

26:22 Elnathan. A high-ranking official who on another occasion sided with Jeremiah (cf. 36:12, 25).

26:23 the burial place. In the Kidron Valley, to the E of the temple (cf. 2Ki 23:6).

26:24 Ahikam. He used his strategic influence to spring Jeremiah free of the death threat. This civil leader under King Josiah (cf. 2Ki 22:12, 14) and father of Gedaliah, was appointed governor over Judah by the Babylonians after Jerusalem's final fall in 586 B.C. (39:14; 40:13–41:3).

THE NATIONS TO SUBMIT TO NEBUCHADNEZZAR

27 In the beginning of the reign of [a,A]Zedekiah the
son of Josiah, king of Judah, this word came
to Jeremiah from the LORD, saying— 2 thus says the
LORD to me—"Make for yourself [A]bonds and [B]yokes
and put them on your neck, 3 and send [a]word to the
king of [A]Edom, to the king of [A]Moab, to the king of the
sons of [A]Ammon, to the king of [A]Tyre and to the king
of [A]Sidon [b]by the messengers who come to Jerusalem
to Zedekiah king of Judah. 4 Command them *to go* to
their masters, saying, 'Thus says the LORD of hosts,
the God of Israel, thus you shall say to your masters,
5 "[A]I have made the earth, the men and the beasts
which are on the face of the earth [B]by My great power
and by My outstretched arm, and I will [C]give it to the
one who is [a]pleasing in My sight. 6 Now I [A]have given
all these lands into the hand of Nebuchadnezzar king
of Babylon, [B]My servant, and I have given him also
the [C]wild animals of the field to serve him. 7 [A]All the
nations shall serve him and his son and his grandson
[B]until the time of his own land comes; then [C]many
nations and great kings will [a]make him their servant.
8 "It will be, *that* the nation or the kingdom which
[A]will not serve him, Nebuchadnezzar king of Babylon, and which will not put its neck under the yoke
of the king of Babylon, I will punish that nation
with the [B]sword, with famine and with pestilence,"
declares the LORD, "until I have destroyed [a]it by his
hand. 9 But as for you, [A]do not listen to your prophets, your diviners, your [a]dreamers, your soothsayers
or your sorcerers who speak to you, saying, 'You will
not serve the king of Babylon.' 10 For they prophesy
a [A]lie to you in order to [B]remove you far from your
land; and I will drive you out and you will perish.
11 But the nation which will [A]bring its neck under
the yoke of the king of Babylon and serve him, I
will [B]let remain on its land," declares the LORD, "and
they will till it and dwell in it." ' "
12 I spoke words like all these to [A]Zedekiah king of
Judah, saying, "Bring your necks under the yoke of
the king of Babylon and serve him and his people,
and live! 13 Why will you [A]die, you and your people,
by the sword, famine and pestilence, as the LORD
has spoken to that nation which will not serve the
king of Babylon? 14 So [A]do not listen to the words
of the prophets who speak to you, saying, 'You will
not serve the king of Babylon,' for they prophesy
a [B]lie to you; 15 for [A]I have not sent them," declares
the LORD, "but they [B]prophesy falsely in My name,
in order that I may [C]drive you out and that you may
perish, [D]you and the prophets who prophesy to you."
16 *Then* I spoke to the priests and to all this people,
saying, "Thus says the LORD: Do not listen to the
words of your prophets who prophesy to you, saying,
'Behold, the [A]vessels of the LORD'S house will now
shortly be brought again from Babylon'; for they are
prophesying a [B]lie to you. 17 Do not listen to them;
serve the king of Babylon, and live! Why should this
city [A]become a ruin? 18 But [A]if they are prophets, and
if the word of the LORD is with them, let them now
[B]entreat the LORD of hosts that the vessels which are
left in the house of the LORD, in the house of the king
of Judah and in Jerusalem may not go to Babylon.
19 For thus says the LORD of hosts concerning the
[A]pillars, concerning the sea, concerning the stands
and concerning the rest of the vessels that are left in
this city, 20 which Nebuchadnezzar king of Babylon
did not take when he [A]carried into exile Jeconiah the
son of Jehoiakim, king of Judah, from Jerusalem to
Babylon, and all the nobles of Judah and Jerusalem.
21 Yes, thus says the LORD of hosts, the God of Israel,
concerning the vessels that are left in the house of
the LORD and in the house of the king of Judah and
in Jerusalem, 22 'They will be [A]carried to Babylon
and they will be there until the [B]day I visit them,'
declares the LORD. 'Then I will [C]bring them [a]back
and restore them to this place.' "

HANANIAH'S FALSE PROPHECY

28 Now in the same year, [A]in the beginning of the
reign of [B]Zedekiah king of Judah, in the fourth
year, in the fifth month, [C]Hananiah the son of Azzur,
the prophet, who was from [D]Gibeon, spoke to me in
the house of the LORD in the presence of the priests
and all the people, saying, 2 "[A]Thus says the LORD of

27:1 [a]Many mss read *Jehoiakim* [A]2 Kin 24:18-20; 2 Chr 36:11-13 27:2 [A]Jer 30:8 [B]Jer 28:10, 13 27:3 [a]Lit *them* [b]Lit *by the hand of* [A]Jer 25:21, 22 27:5 [a]Or *upright* [A]Ps 96:5; 146:5, 6; Is 42:5; 45:12; Jer 10:12; 51:15 [B]Deut 9:29; Jer 32:17; Dan 4:17 [C]Ps 115:15, 16; Acts 17:26 27:6 [A]Jer 21:7; 22:25; Ezek 29:18-20 [B]Is 44:28; Jer 25:9; 43:10 [C]Jer 28:14; Dan 2:38 27:7 [a]Or *enslave him* [A]2 Chr 36:20; Jer 44:30; 46:13 [B]Dan 5:26; Zech 2:8, 9 [C]Is 14:4-6; Jer 25:12 27:8 [a]Lit *them* [A]Jer 38:17-19; 42:15, 16; Ezek 17:19-21 [B]Jer 24:10; 27:13; 29:17, 18; Ezek 14:21 27:9 [a]Lit *dreams* [A]Ex 22:18; Deut 18:10; Prov 19:27; Is 8:19; Mal 3:5; Eph 5:6 27:10 [A]Jer 23:25 [B]Jer 8:19; 32:31 27:11 [A]Jer 27:2, 8, 12 [B]Jer 21:9; 38:2; 40:9-12; 42:10, 11 27:12 [A]Jer 27:3; 28:1; 38:17 27:13 [A]Prov 8:36; Jer 27:8; 38:23; Ezek 18:31 27:14 [A]Jer 27:9; 2 Cor 11:13-15 [B]Jer 14:14; 23:21; 27:10; 29:8, 9; Ezek 13:22 27:15 [A]Jer 23:21; 29:9 [B]Jer 23:25 [C]2 Chr 25:16; Jer 27:10 [D]Jer 6:13-15; 14:15, 16 27:16 [A]2 Kin 24:13; 2 Chr 36:7, 10; Jer 28:3; Dan 1:2 [B]Jer 27:10 27:17 [A]Jer 7:34 27:18 [A]1 Kin 18:24 [B]1 Sam 7:8; 12:19, 23; Jer 18:20 27:19 [A]1 Kin 7:15; 2 Kin 25:13, 17; Jer 52:17-23 27:20 [A]2 Kin 24:12, 14-16; 2 Chr 36:10, 18; Jer 22:28; 24:1 27:22 [a]Lit *up* [A]Jer 34:2, 3 [B]Jer 25:11, 12; 27:7; 29:10; 32:5 [C]Ezra 1:7-11; 5:13-15; 7:19 28:1 [A]Jer 27:1; 49:34 [B]2 Kin 24:18-20; 2 Chr 36:11-13; Jer 27:3, 12 [C]Jer 28:17 [D]Josh 9:3; 10:12; 1 Kin 3:4 28:2 [A]Jer 27:12; 28:11

27:1 reign of Zedekiah. This may refer to Jehoiakim around 609/608 B.C. (as chap. 26; see marginal note). Or, possibly, the correct reading is "Zedekiah" as in vv. 3, 12, and 28:1, which would put the date at the outset of his 597–586 B.C. reign.

27:2 Make ... bonds and yokes. This object lesson symbolized bondage to Babylon. The yoke was bound on Jeremiah's neck to picture Judah's captivity (v. 12), then sent to 6 kings of nearby nations who would also be under Babylon's power (v. 3). Cf. Jer 28:10–12.

27:7 Cf. 25:13, 14.

27:8 yoke of ... Babylon. The point of the object lesson is simple. Any nation that will serve Babylon willingly may stay in their own land, but nations that will not submit voluntarily to Babylon will suffer destruction. Consequently, Judah should submit and not be removed from the land (vv. 9–18).

27:18 entreat the LORD. God would not answer such a prayer, as proven by vv. 19–22. This revealed His indifference to the prayers of these false prophets.

27:20 Ca. 597 B.C.

27:21, 22 vessels. Jeremiah revealed that Judah's temple vessels taken to Babylon (cf. 2Ki 24:13; Da 1:1, 2) would be restored to the temple. Fulfillment around 536 B.C. was spoken of in Ezr 5:13–15. About 516/515 B.C. these articles were placed in the rebuilt temple (Ezr 6:15).

28:1 reign of Zedekiah. Cf. 27:1 and *see note there*. The fourth year would be about 593 B.C. **Hananiah.** This man was one of several by this name in Scripture, in this case a foe of God's true prophet, distinct from the loyal Hananiah of Da 1:6.

28:2, 3 I have broken the yoke. The false prophet, of the kind Jeremiah warned of in 27:14–16, boldly predicted victory over Babylon and the return of the temple vessels within two years. In actuality, Babylon achieved its third and final step in conquering Judah 11 years later (586 B.C.) as in chaps. 39, 40, 52. As to the vessels, *see note on 27:21, 22.*

hosts, the God of Israel, 'I have broken the yoke of
the king of Babylon. 3 Within two years I am going to
bring back to this place [A]all the vessels of the LORD'S
house, which Nebuchadnezzar king of Babylon took
away from this place and carried to Babylon. 4 I am
[A]also going to bring back to this place [B]Jeconiah the
son of Jehoiakim, king of Judah, and all the [C]exiles
of Judah who went to Babylon,' declares the LORD,
'for I will break the [D]yoke of the king of Babylon.' "
5 Then the prophet Jeremiah spoke to the prophet
Hananiah in the presence of the priests and in the
presence of all the people who were standing in
the [A]house of the LORD, 6 and the prophet Jeremiah
said, "[A]Amen! May the LORD do so; may the LORD
[a]confirm your words which you have prophesied
to bring back the vessels of the LORD'S house and
all the exiles, from Babylon to this place. 7 Yet [A]hear
now this word which I am about to speak in your
hearing and in the hearing of all the people! 8 The
prophets who were before me and before you from
ancient times [A]prophesied against many lands and
against great kingdoms, of war and of calamity
and of pestilence. 9 The prophet who prophesies
of peace, [A]when the word of the prophet comes to
pass, then that prophet will be known *as* one whom
the LORD has truly sent."
10 Then Hananiah the prophet took the [A]yoke
from the neck of Jeremiah the prophet and broke it.
11 Hananiah spoke in the presence of all the people,
saying, "[A]Thus says the LORD, 'Even so will I break
within two full years the yoke of Nebuchadnezzar
king of Babylon from the neck of all the nations.' "
Then the prophet Jeremiah went his way.
12 The [A]word of the LORD came to Jeremiah after
Hananiah the prophet had broken the yoke from off
the neck of the prophet Jeremiah, saying, 13 "Go and
speak to Hananiah, saying, 'Thus says the LORD,
"You have broken the yokes of wood, but you have
made instead of them [A]yokes of iron." 14 For thus says
the LORD of hosts, the God of Israel, "I have put a
[A]yoke of iron on the neck of all these nations, that
they may serve Nebuchadnezzar king of Babylon;
and they will [B]serve him. And [C]I have also given
him the beasts of the field." ' " 15 Then Jeremiah the
prophet said to Hananiah the prophet, "Listen now,
Hananiah, the LORD has not sent you, and [A]you have
made this people trust in a lie. 16 Therefore thus
says the LORD, '[A]Behold, I am about to [a]remove you
from the face of the earth. This year you are going
to [B]die, because you have [b,C]counseled rebellion
against the LORD.' "
17 So Hananiah the prophet died in the same year
in the seventh month.

MESSAGE TO THE EXILES

29 Now these are the words of the [A]letter which
Jeremiah the prophet sent from Jerusalem
to the rest of the elders of the exile, the priests, the
prophets and all the people whom Nebuchadnezzar
had taken into exile from Jerusalem to Babylon.
2 (This was after King [A]Jeconiah and the [B]queen
mother, the court officials, the princes of Judah
and Jerusalem, the craftsmen and the smiths had
departed from Jerusalem.) 3 *The letter was sent* by
the hand of Elasah the son of Shaphan, and Gemariah the son of [A]Hilkiah, whom Zedekiah king of
Judah sent to Babylon to Nebuchadnezzar king of
Babylon, saying, 4 "Thus says the LORD of hosts, the
God of Israel, to all the exiles whom I have [A]sent into
exile from Jerusalem to Babylon, 5 '[A]Build houses
and live *in them;* and plant gardens and eat their
[a]produce. 6 Take [A]wives and [a]become the fathers of
sons and daughters, and take wives for your sons
and give your daughters to husbands, that they
may bear sons and daughters; and multiply there
and do not decrease. 7 [A]Seek the [a]welfare of the city
where I have sent you into exile, and [B]pray to the
LORD on its behalf; for in its [a]welfare you will have
[a]welfare.' 8 For thus says the LORD of hosts, the God
of Israel, 'Do not let your [A]prophets who are in your
midst and your diviners [B]deceive you, and do not
listen to [a,C]the dreams which [b]they dream. 9 For they
[A]prophesy falsely to you in My name; [B]I have not
sent them,' declares the LORD.
10 "For thus says the LORD, 'When [A]seventy years
have been completed for Babylon, I will visit you
and fulfill My [B]good word to you, to bring you back
to this place. 11 For I know the [A]plans that I [a]have
for you,' declares the LORD, 'plans for [B]welfare and
not for calamity to give you a future and a [C]hope.

28:3 [A]2 Kin 24:13; 2 Chr 36:10; Jer 27:16; Dan 1:2 28:4 [A]Jer 22:26, 27 [B]2 Kin 25:27; Jer 22:24; 24:1 [C]Jer 22:10 [D]Jer 27:8 28:5 [A]Jer 28:1 28:6 [a]Or *fulfill* [A]1 Kin 1:36; Ps 41:13; Jer 11:5 28:7 [A]1 Kin 22:28 28:8 [A]Lev 26:14-39; 1 Kin 14:15; 17:1; 22:17; Is 5:5-7; Joel 1:20; Amos 1:2; Nah 1:2 28:9 [A]Deut 18:22 28:10 [A]Jer 27:2 28:11 [A]Jer 14:14; 27:10; 28:15 28:12 [A]Jer 1:2 28:13 [A]Ps 107:16; Is 45:2 28:14 [A]Deut 28:48; Jer 27:8 [B]Jer 25:11 [C]Jer 27:6 28:15 [A]Jer 20:6; 29:31; Lam 2:14; Ezek 13:2, 3, 22; 22:28; Zech 13:3 28:16 [a]Lit *send you away* [b]Lit *spoken* [A]Gen 7:4; Ex 32:12; Deut 6:15; 1 Kin 13:34 [B]Jer 20:6 [C]Deut 13:5; Jer 29:32 29:1 [A]2 Chr 30:1, 6; Esth 9:20; Jer 29:25, 29 29:2 [A]2 Kin 24:12-16; 2 Chr 36:9, 10; Jer 22:24-28; 24:1; 27:20 [B]2 Kin 24:12, 15; Jer 13:18; 22:26 29:3 [A]1 Chr 6:13 29:4 [A]Jer 24:5 29:5 [a]Lit *fruit* [A]Jer 29:28 29:6 [a]Lit *beget* [A]Jer 16:2-4 29:7 [a]Or *peace* [A]Dan 4:27; 6:4, 5 [B]Ezra 6:10; 7:23; Dan 4:19; 1 Tim 2:1, 2 29:8 [a]Lit *your* [b]Lit *you* [A]Jer 27:9; 29:1 [B]Jer 14:14; 23:21; 27:14, 15; 28:15; Eph 5:6 [C]Jer 23:25, 27 29:9 [A]Jer 27:15; 29:21 [B]Jer 29:31 29:10 [A]2 Chr 36:21-23; Jer 25:12; 27:22; Dan 9:2; Zech 7:5 [B]Jer 24:6, 7; Zeph 2:7 29:11 [a]Lit *am planning* [A]Ps 40:5; Jer 23:5, 6; 30:9, 10 [B]Is 40:9-11; Jer 30:18-22 [C]Jer 31:17; Hos 2:15

28:4 bring back … Jeconiah. This rash, false claim fell into ignominy. Jeconiah, soon taken to Babylon in 597 B.C., would live out his years there and not return to Jerusalem (52:31–34). Other captives either died in captivity, or didn't return until 61 years later. Cf. 22:24–26.

28:10 took the yoke … broke it. The phony prophet, in foolishness, removed the object lesson from the true spokesman and broke it as a sign of his own prediction coming true (cf. vv. 2–4, 11).

28:13 Go and speak to Hananiah. Jeremiah apparently left the meeting, and later God sent him back to confront the liar, likely wearing yokes of iron (which Hananiah could not break!) to replace the wooden ones (v. 14) and to illustrate his message.

28:15–17 the LORD has not sent you. Jeremiah told Hananiah that 1) God had not approved his message; 2) he was guilty of encouraging the people to trust in a lie, even rebellion; and 3) God would require his life that very year, 597 B.C. The true prophet's word was authenticated by Hananiah's death in two months (cf. v. 17).

29:1 the letter. Jeremiah, shortly after the 597 B.C. deportation of many countrymen (cf. v. 2), wrote to comfort them in exile.

29:4–10 Jeremiah's counsel to Israelites in Babylon was to take all the steps in living as colonists planning to be there for a long time (70 years, 29:10, as 25:11). Further, they were to seek Babylon's peace and intercede in prayer for it, their own welfare being bound with it (v. 7; cf. Ezr 6:10; 7:23).

29:11 plans for welfare. This assured God's intentions to bring about blessing in Israel's future (cf. chaps. 30–33).

12 Then you will [A]call upon Me and come and pray
to Me, and I will [B]listen to you. 13 You will [A]seek Me
and find *Me* when you [B]search for Me with all your
heart. 14 I will be [A]found by you,' declares the LORD,
'and I will [B]restore your [a]fortunes and will [C]gather
you from all the nations and from all the places
where I have driven you,' declares the LORD, 'and I
will [D]bring you back to the place from where I sent
you into exile.'

15 "Because you have said, 'The LORD has raised
up [A]prophets for us in Babylon'— 16 for thus says the
LORD concerning the king who sits on the throne
of David, and concerning all the people who dwell
in this city, your brothers who did [A]not go with you
into exile— 17 thus says the LORD of hosts, 'Behold,
I am sending upon them the [A]sword, famine and
pestilence, and I will make them like [B]split-open
figs that cannot be eaten due to rottenness. 18 I will
pursue them with the sword, with famine and with
pestilence; and I will [A]make them a terror to all the
kingdoms of the earth, to be a [B]curse and a horror
and a [C]hissing, and a reproach among all the nations
where I have driven them, 19 because they have [A]not
listened to My words,' declares the LORD, 'which I
sent to them again and again by [B]My servants the
prophets; but you did not listen,' declares the LORD.
20 You, therefore, hear the word of the LORD, all you
exiles, whom I have [A]sent away from Jerusalem to
Babylon.

21 "Thus says the LORD of hosts, the God of Israel, concerning Ahab the son of Kolaiah and concerning Zedekiah the son of Maaseiah, who are
[A]prophesying to you falsely in My name, 'Behold, I
will deliver them into the hand of Nebuchadnezzar
king of Babylon, and he will slay them before your
eyes. 22 Because of them a [A]curse will be [a]used by
all the exiles from Judah who are in Babylon, saying, "May the LORD make you like Zedekiah and like
Ahab, whom the king of Babylon [B]roasted in the fire,
23 because they have [A]acted foolishly in Israel, and
[B]have committed adultery with their neighbors'
wives and have [C]spoken words in My name falsely,
which I did not command them; and I am He who
[D]knows and am a witness," declares the LORD.' "

24 To [A]Shemaiah the Nehelamite you shall speak,
saying, 25 "Thus says the LORD of hosts, the God of
Israel, 'Because you have sent [A]letters in your own
name to all the people who are in Jerusalem, and
to [B]Zephaniah the son of Maaseiah, the priest, and
to all the priests, saying, 26 "The LORD has made
you priest instead of Jehoiada the priest, to be the
[a,A]overseer in the house of the LORD over every
[B]madman who [C]prophesies, to [D]put him in the stocks
and in the iron collar, 27 now then, why have you
not rebuked Jeremiah of [A]Anathoth who prophesies
to you? 28 For he has [A]sent to us in Babylon, saying,
'*The exile* will be [B]long; [C]build houses and live *in
them* and plant gardens and eat their [a]produce.' " ' "

29 [A]Zephaniah the priest read this letter [a]to Jeremiah the prophet. 30 Then came the word of the
LORD to Jeremiah, saying, 31 "Send to [A]all the exiles,
saying, 'Thus says the LORD concerning [B]Shemaiah
the Nehelamite, "Because Shemaiah has [C]prophe-
sied to you, although I did not send him, and he has
[D]made you trust in a lie," 32 therefore thus says the
LORD, "Behold, I am about to [A]punish Shemaiah the
Nehelamite and his [a]descendants; he will [B]not have
anyone living among this people, [C]and he will not
see the good that I am about to do to My people,"
declares the LORD, "because he has [b,D]preached rebellion against the LORD." ' "

DELIVERANCE FROM CAPTIVITY PROMISED

30 The word which came to Jeremiah from the
LORD, saying, 2 "Thus says the LORD, the God
of Israel, '[A]Write all the words which I have spoken
to you in a book. 3 For behold, [A]days are coming,' declares the LORD, 'when I will [B]restore the [a]fortunes
of My people [C]Israel and Judah.' The LORD says, 'I
will also [D]bring them back to the land that I gave to
their forefathers and they shall possess it.' "

4 Now these are the words which the LORD spoke
concerning Israel and concerning Judah:

5 "For thus says the LORD,

'[a]I have heard a sound of [A]terror,
Of dread, and there is no peace.

29:12 [A]Ps 50:15; Jer 33:3; Dan 9:3 [B]Ps 145:19 29:13 [A]Deut 4:29; Ps 32:6; Matt 7:7 [B]1 Chr 22:19; 2 Chr 22:9; Jer 24:7 29:14 [a]Or *captivity* [A]Deut 30:1-10; Ps 32:6; Is 55:6 [B]Jer 30:3; 32:37-41 [C]Is 43:5, 6; Jer 23:8; 32:37 [D]Jer 3:14; 12:15; 16:15 29:15 [A]Jer 29:21, 24 29:16 [A]Jer 38:2, 3, 17-23 29:17 [A]Jer 27:8; 29:18; 32:24 [B]Jer 24:3, 8-10 29:18 [A]Deut 28:25; 2 Chr 29:8; Jer 15:4; 24:9; 34:17; Ezek 12:15 [B]Is 65:15; Jer 42:18 [C]Jer 25:9; Lam 2:15, 16 29:19 [A]Jer 6:19 [B]Jer 25:4; 26:5; 35:15 29:20 [A]Jer 24:5; Ezek 11:9; Mic 4:10 29:21 [A]Jer 14:14, 15; 29:8, 9; Lam 2:14; 2 Pet 2:1 29:22 [a]Lit *taken* [A]Is 65:15 [B]Dan 3:6, 21 29:23 [A]Gen 34:7; 2 Sam 13:12 [B]Jer 5:8; 23:14 [C]Jer 29:8, 9, 21 [D]Prov 5:21; Jer 7:11; 16:17; Mal 3:5; Heb 4:13 29:24 [A]Jer 29:31, 32 29:25 [A]Jer 29:1 [B]2 Kin 25:18; Jer 21:1; 29:29; 37:3; 52:24 29:26 [a]Lit *overseers* [A]Jer 20:1 [B]2 Kin 9:11; Hos 9:7; Mark 3:21; John 10:20; Acts 26:24, 25; 2 Cor 5:13 [C]Deut 13:1-5; Zech 13:1-5 [D]Jer 20:1, 2; Acts 16:24 29:27 [A]Jer 1:1 29:28 [a]Lit *fruit* [A]Jer 29:1 [B]Jer 29:10 [C]Jer 29:5 29:29 [a]Lit *in the ears of* [A]Jer 29:25 29:31 [A]Jer 29:20 [B]Jer 29:24 [C]Jer 14:14, 15; 29:9, 23; Ezek 13:8-16, 22, 23 [D]Jer 28:15 29:32 [a]Lit *seed* [b]Lit *spoken* [A]Jer 36:31 [B]1 Sam 2:30-34; Jer 22:30 [C]2 Kin 7:2, 19, 20; Jer 17:6; 29:10 [D]Deut 13:5; Jer 28:16 30:2 [A]Is 30:8; Jer 25:13; 36:4, 28, 32; Hab 2:2 30:3 [a]Or *captivity* [A]Jer 29:10 [B]Ps 53:6; Jer 29:14; 30:18; 32:44; Ezek 39:25; Amos 9:14; Zeph 3:20 [C]Jer 3:18 [D]Jer 16:15; 23:7, 8; Ezek 20:42; 36:24 30:5 [a]Lit *We* [A]Is 5:30; Jer 6:25; 8:16; Amos 5:16-18

29:12–14 you will call. What God planned, He also gave the people opportunity to participate in by sincere (v. 13) prayer. Cf. 1Jn 5:14, 15.

29:14 I will be found by you. The Lord would answer their prayer by returning the Jews to their land, cf. Daniel's example and God's response (Da 9:4–27). Fulfillment would occur in the era of Ezra and Nehemiah, and beyond this in even fuller measure after the Second Advent of their Messiah (cf. Da 2:35, 45; 7:13, 14, 27; 12:1–3, 13).

29:15–19 Because you have said. Amazingly still rejecting God's true message, Jewish captives listened to false prophets among them (cf. vv. 8, 9, 21–23). This was the very sin which would cause God to send a further deportation to those still in Judah (586 B.C.).

29:17 like split-open figs. Cf. the principle of Jer 24.

29:21–23 Ahab ... Zedekiah. Two captive, false Israelite prophets, who had been misleading exiles in Babylon (v. 15), will stir up the wrath of their captor king, who will cast them into a furnace (as in Da 3). They aroused not only the Babylonian potentate's enmity, but also God's, because of prophecies against His Word and physical adultery (cf. 5:7).

29:24–32 The judgment against Shemaiah, the otherwise unknown prophet, who opposed Jeremiah, was similar to that experienced by Hananiah (cf. 28:15–17).

29:28 This referred to Jeremiah's letter mentioned in v. 5.

30:3 I will ... bring them back. This theme verse gives in capsule form the pledge of chaps. 30–33. God's restoration of the whole nation to their own land (cf. 29:10; Am 9:14, 15; Ro 11:26) has in view a final regathering never to be removed again (*see note on 16:15*), and not just a return in the time of Ezra and Nehemiah (vv. 8, 9; 31:31ff.; 32:39, 40; 33:8, 9, 15, 16). This verse is a summary of the prophecy given in vv. 4–9.

6 'Ask now, and see
If a male can give birth.
Why do I see every man
With his hands on his loins, [A]as
a woman in childbirth?
And *why* have all faces turned pale?
7 'Alas! for that [A]day is great,
There is [B]none like it;
And it is the time of Jacob's [C]distress,
But he will be [D]saved from it.

8 'It shall come about on that day,' declares the
LORD of hosts, 'that I will [A]break his yoke from
off [a]their neck and will tear off [a]their [B]bonds; and
strangers will no longer [C]make [b]them their slaves.
9 But they shall serve the LORD their God and [A]David
their king, whom I will raise up for them.

10 '[A]Fear not, O Jacob My servant,'
declares the LORD,
'And do not be dismayed, O Israel;
For behold, I will save you [B]from afar
And your [a]offspring from the
land of their captivity.
And Jacob will return and will
be [C]quiet and at ease,
And [D]no one will make him afraid.
11 'For [A]I am with you,' declares
the LORD, 'to save you;
For I will [B]destroy completely all the
nations where I have scattered you,
Only I will [C]not destroy
you completely.
But I will [D]chasten you justly
And will by no means leave
you unpunished.'
12 "For thus says the LORD,
'Your wound is incurable
And your [A]injury is serious.
13 'There is no one to plead your cause;
No healing for *your* sore,
[A]No recovery for you.
14 'All your [A]lovers have forgotten you,
They do not seek you;
For I have [B]wounded you with
the wound of an enemy,
With the [C]punishment of a [D]cruel one,
Because your [E]iniquity is great
And your [F]sins are numerous.
15 'Why do you cry out over your injury?
Your pain is incurable.
Because your iniquity is great
And your sins are numerous,
I have done these things to you.
16 'Therefore all who [A]devour
you will be devoured;
And all your adversaries, every one
of them, [B]will go into captivity;
And those who plunder you
will be for plunder,
And all who prey upon you
I will give for prey.
17 'For I will [a]restore you to [b,A]health
And I will heal you of your
wounds,' declares the LORD,
'Because they have called you
an [B]outcast, saying:
"It is Zion; no one [c]cares for her." '

RESTORATION OF JACOB

18 "Thus says the LORD,
'Behold, I will [A]restore the [a]fortunes
of the tents of Jacob
And [B]have compassion on
his dwelling places;
And the [C]city will be rebuilt on its ruin,
And the [D]palace will stand
on its rightful place.
19 'From them will proceed [A]thanksgiving
And the voice of those who [a,B]celebrate;
And I will [C]multiply them and
they will not be diminished;
I will also [D]honor them and they
will not be insignificant.
20 '[a]Their children also will be as formerly,
And [b]their congregation shall be
[A]established before Me;
And I will punish all [b]their oppressors.
21 '[a]Their [A]leader shall be one of them,
And [a]their ruler shall come
forth from [a]their midst;
And I will [B]bring him near and
he shall approach Me;
For [b]who would dare to risk his life to
[C]approach Me?' declares the LORD.

30:6 [A]Jer 4:31; 6:24; 22:23 30:7 [A]Is 2:12; Hos 1:11; Joel 2:11; Amos 5:18; Zeph 1:14 [B]Lam 1:12; Dan 9:12; 12:1 [C]Jer 2:27, 28; 14:8 [D]Jer 30:10; 50:19 30:8 [a]So Gr; Heb *your* [b]Lit *him their slave* [A]Is 9:4; Jer 2:20; Ezek 34:27 [B]Jer 27:2 [C]Ezek 34:27 30:9 [A]Is 55:3-5; Ezek 34:23, 24; 37:24, 25; Hos 3:5; Luke 1:69; Acts 2:30; 13:23, 34 30:10 [a]Lit *seed* [A]Is 41:13; 43:5; 44:2; Jer 46:27, 28 [B]Is 60:4; Jer 23:3, 8; 29:14 [C]Is 35:9; Jer 33:16; Hos 2:18 [D]Mic 4:4 30:11 [A]Jer 1:8, 19 [B]Jer 46:28; Amos 9:8 [C]Jer 4:27; 5:10, 18 [D]Ps 6:1; Jer 10:24 30:12 [A]2 Chr 36:16; Jer 15:18; 30:15 30:13 [A]Jer 14:19; 46:11 30:14 [A]Jer 22:20, 22; Lam 1:2 [B]Lam 2:4, 5 [C]Job 30:21 [D]Jer 6:23; 50:42 [E]Jer 32:30-35; 44:22 [F]Jer 5:6 30:16 [A]Jer 2:3; 8:16; 10:25 [B]Is 14:2; Joel 3:8 30:17 [a]Lit *cause to go up* [b]Or *healing* [c]Lit *is seeking* [A]Ex 15:26; Ps 107:20; Is 30:26; Jer 8:22; 33:6 [B]Is 11:12; 56:8; Jer 33:24 30:18 [a]Or *captivity* [A]Jer 30:3; 31:23 [B]Ps 102:13 [C]Jer 31:4, 38-40 [D]1 Chr 29:1, 19; Ps 48:3, 13; 122:7 30:19 [a]Or *dance* [A]Is 12:1; 35:10; 51:3; Jer 17:26; 33:11 [B]Ps 126:1, 2; Is 51:11; Jer 31:4; Zeph 3:14 [C]Jer 33:22 [D]Is 55:5; 60:9 30:20 [a]Lit *His* [b]Lit *his* [A]Is 54:14 30:21 [a]Lit *his* [b]Lit *who is he that gives his heart in pledge* [A]Jer 30:9; Ezek 34:23, 24; 37:24 [B]Num 16:5; Ps 65:4 [C]Ex 3:5; Jer 50:44

30:7 time of Jacob's distress. This period of unprecedented difficulty for Israel, as the verse defines, is set in a context of Israel's final restoration. It is best equated with the time of tribulation (cf. vv. 8, 9) just before Christ's Second Advent, mentioned elsewhere (Da 12:1; Mt 24:21, 22) and described in detail by Rev 6–19.

30:9 David their king. The Messiah, the greater David in David's dynasty, ultimately fulfills this promise (2Sa 7:16). He is the great king often promised as Israel's hope (23:5, 6; Is 9:7; Eze 37:24, 25; Da 2:35, 45; 7:13, 14, 27; Mt 25:34; 26:64; Lk 1:32; Rev 17:14; 19:16). No king of David's seed has held the scepter since the captivity. Zerubbabel, of David's line, never claimed the title of king (cf. Hag 2:2).

30:11 not destroy you completely. Israel will endure as a people until Messiah's kingdom (cf. Rom 11:1–29).

30:12–15 Judah had no reason to complain.

30:16–24 These absolute and extensive promises have yet to be fulfilled in history; they look forward to the reign of Christ, the greater David, in the millennial kingdom of the "latter days."

30:21 their ruler. This refers to the Messiah, the king of v. 9 and 23:5, 6, springing up from within Israel (cf. Is 11:1), able to approach God as a priest.

22 'You shall be [A]My people,
And I will be your God.' "

23 Behold, the [A]tempest of the LORD!
Wrath has gone forth,
A [a]sweeping tempest;
It will burst on the head of the wicked.
24 The [A]fierce anger of the LORD
will not turn back
Until He has performed and until
He has accomplished
The intent of His heart;
In the [B]latter days you will understand this.

ISRAEL'S MOURNING TURNED TO JOY

31 "At that time," declares the LORD, "I will be
the [A]God of all the [B]families of Israel, and they
shall be My people."

2 Thus says the LORD,
"The people who survived the sword
[A]Found grace in the wilderness—
Israel, when it went to [B]find its rest."
3 The LORD appeared to [a]him
from afar, *saying,*
"I have [A]loved you with an everlasting love;
Therefore I have drawn you
with [B]lovingkindness.
4 "[A]Again I will build you and
you will be rebuilt,
O virgin of Israel!
Again you will [a]take up your [B]tambourines,
And go forth to the dances of
the [C]merrymakers.
5 "Again you will [A]plant vineyards
On the [a]hills of Samaria;
The planters will plant
And will [b]enjoy *them.*
6 "For there will be a day when watchmen
On the hills of Ephraim call out,
'Arise, and [A]let us go up *to* Zion,
To the LORD our God.' "

7 For thus says the LORD,
"[A]Sing aloud with gladness for Jacob,
And shout among the [a,B]chief of the nations;
Proclaim, give praise and say,
'O LORD, [C]save Your people,
The [D]remnant of Israel.'
8 "Behold, I am [A]bringing them
from the north country,
And I will [B]gather them from the
remote parts of the earth,
Among them the [C]blind and the [D]lame,
The woman with child and she who
is in labor with child, together;
A great [a]company, they will return here.
9 "[A]With weeping they will come,
And by supplication I will lead them;
I will make them walk by
[B]streams of waters,
On a straight path in which
they will [C]not stumble;
For I am a [D]father to Israel,
And Ephraim is [E]My firstborn."

10 Hear the word of the LORD, O nations,
And declare in the [A]coastlands afar off,
And say, "He who scattered
Israel will [B]gather him
And keep him as a [C]shepherd
keeps his flock."
11 For the LORD has [A]ransomed Jacob
And redeemed him from the hand of
him who was [B]stronger than he.
12 "They will [A]come and shout for
joy on the [B]height of Zion,
And they will be [C]radiant over
the [a]bounty of the LORD—
Over the [D]grain and the new
wine and the oil,
And over the young of the
[E]flock and the herd;
And their life will be like a [F]watered garden,
And they will [G]never languish again.
13 "Then the virgin will rejoice in the [A]dance,
And the young men and the old, together,
For I will [B]turn their mourning into joy
And will comfort them and give
them [C]joy for their sorrow.
14 "I will [a]fill the soul of the priests
with [b]abundance,
And My people will be [A]satisfied with
My goodness," declares the LORD.

15 Thus says the LORD,
"[A]A voice is heard in [B]Ramah,
Lamentation *and* bitter weeping.
Rachel is weeping for her children;
She [C]refuses to be comforted
for her children,
Because [D]they are no more."

30:22 [A]Ex 6:7; Jer 32:38; Ezek 36:28; Hos 2:23; Zech 13:9 30:23 [a]Or *raging* [A]Jer 23:19 30:24 [A]Jer 4:8 [B]Jer 23:20 31:1 [A]Jer 30:22 [B]Gen 17:7, 8; Is 41:10; Rom 11:26-28 31:2 [A]Num 14:20 [B]Ex 33:14; Num 10:33; Deut 1:33; Josh 1:13 31:3 [a]Lit *me* [A]Deut 4:37; 7:8; Mal 1:2 [B]Ps 25:6 31:4 [a]Or *be adorned with* [A]Jer 24:6; 33:7 [B]Is 30:32 [C]Jer 30:19 31:5 [a]Or *mountains* [b]Lit *defile* [A]Ps 107:37; Is 65:21; Ezek 28:26; Amos 9:14 31:6 [A]Is 2:3; Jer 31:12; 50:4, 5; Mic 4:2 31:7 [a]Lit *head* [A]Ps 14:7; Jer 20:13 [B]Deut 28:13; Is 61:9 [C]Ps 28:9 [D]Is 37:31; Jer 23:3 31:8 [a]Or *assembly* [A]Jer 3:18; 23:8 [B]Deut 30:4; Is 43:6; Ezek 34:13 [C]Is 42:16 [D]Is 40:11; Ezek 34:16; Mic 4:6 31:9 [A]Ps 126:5; Jer 50:4 [B]Is 43:20; 49:10 [C]Is 63:13 [D]Is 64:8; Jer 3:4, 19 [E]Ex 4:22 31:10 [A]Is 66:19; Jer 25:22 [B]Jer 50:19 [C]Is 40:11; Ezek 34:12 31:11 [A]Is 44:23; 48:20; Jer 15:21; 50:34 [B]Ps 142:6 31:12 [a]Lit *goodness* [A]Jer 31:6, 7 [B]Ezek 17:23 [C]Is 2:2; Mic 4:1 [D]Hos 2:22; Joel 3:18 [E]Jer 31:24; 33:12, 13 [F]Is 58:11 [G]Is 35:10; 60:20; 65:19; John 16:22; Rev 21:4 31:13 [A]Judg 21:21; Ps 30:11; Zech 8:4, 5 [B]Is 61:3 [C]Is 51:11 31:14 [a]Lit *saturate* [b]Lit *fatness* [A]Jer 50:19 31:15 [A]Matt 2:18 [B]Josh 18:25; Judg 4:5; Is 10:29; Jer 40:1 [C]Gen 37:35; Ps 77:2 [D]Gen 5:24; 42:13, 36; Jer 10:20

31:1 At that time. Equated with the latter days in 30:24. In this chapter, prophecies of the restoration of the nation are continued.

31:2–14 Here are messianic kingdom conditions.

31:15 A voice … in Ramah. The reflection, for a moment, is on the distress of an Israelite mother for her children slain in the Babylonian invasion. This was a backdrop for the many contrasting promises of restoration to a joyful time (as vv. 12–14, 16, 17) in the messianic day. Matthew saw the same description of sadness as apt, in principle, to depict something of the similar weeping of Jewish mothers when King Herod had babies slain at Bethlehem in a bid to kill the Messiah as a child (Mt 2:17, 18).

16 Thus says the LORD,

"[A]Restrain your voice from weeping
And your eyes from tears;
For your [B]work will be rewarded,"
declares the LORD,
"And they will [C]return from
the land of the enemy.
17 "There is [A]hope for your future,"
declares the LORD,
"And *your* children will return
to their own territory.
18 "I have surely heard
Ephraim [A]grieving,
'You have [B]chastised me, and
I was chastised,
Like an untrained [C]calf;
[D]Bring me back that I may be restored,
For You are the LORD my God.
19 'For after I turned back, I [A]repented;
And after I was instructed, I
[B]smote on *my* thigh;
I was [C]ashamed and also humiliated
Because I bore the reproach
of my youth.'
20 "Is [A]Ephraim My dear son?
Is he a delightful child?
Indeed, as often as I have
spoken against him,
I certainly *still* remember him;
Therefore My [a,B]heart yearns for him;
I will surely [C]have mercy on
him," declares the LORD.

21 "Set up for yourself roadmarks,
Place for yourself guideposts;
[A]Direct your [a]mind to the highway,
The way by which you went.
[B]Return, O virgin of Israel,
Return to these your cities.
22 "How long will you go here and there,
O [A]faithless daughter?
For the LORD has created a new
thing in the earth—
A woman will encompass a man."

23 Thus says the LORD of hosts, the God of Israel, "Once again they will speak this word in the
land of Judah and in its cities when I [A]restore their
[a]fortunes,

'The LORD bless you, O [B]abode
of righteousness,
O [C]holy hill!'

24 Judah and all its cities will [A]dwell together in it,
the farmer and they who go about with flocks. 25 [A]For
I satisfy the weary ones and [a]refresh everyone who
languishes." 26 At this I [A]awoke and looked, and my
[B]sleep was pleasant to me.

A NEW COVENANT

27 "Behold, days are coming," declares the LORD,
"when I will [A]sow the house of Israel and the house
of Judah with the seed of man and with the seed
of beast. 28 As I have [A]watched over them to [B]pluck
up, to break down, to overthrow, to destroy and to
bring disaster, so I will watch over them to [C]build
and to plant," declares the LORD.

29 "In those days they will not say again,
'[A]The fathers have eaten sour grapes,
And the children's teeth are [a]set on edge.'

30 But [A]everyone will die for his own iniquity; each
man who eats the sour grapes, his teeth will be
[a]set on edge.
31 "[A]Behold, days are coming," declares the LORD,
"when I will make a [B]new covenant with the house
of Israel and with the house of Judah, 32 not like the
[A]covenant which I made with their fathers in the
day I [B]took them by the hand to bring them out of
the land of Egypt, My [C]covenant which they broke,
although I was a husband to them," declares the

31:16 [A]Is 25:8; 30:19 [B]Ruth 2:12; Heb 6:10 [C]Jer 30:3; Ezek 11:17 31:17 [A]Jer 29:11 31:18 [A]Jer 3:21 [B]Job 5:17; Ps 94:12 [C]Hos 4:16 [D]Ps 80:3, 7, 19; Jer 17:14; Lam 5:21; Acts 3:26 31:19 [A]Ezek 36:31; Zech 12:10 [B]Ezek 21:12; Luke 18:13 [C]Jer 3:25 31:20 [a]Lit *inward parts* [A]Hos 11:8 [B]Gen 43:30; Judg 10:16; Is 63:15; Hos 11:8 [C]Is 55:7; 57:18; Hos 14:4; Mic 7:18 31:21 [a]Lit *heart* [A]Jer 50:5 [B]Is 48:20; 52:11 31:22 [A]Jer 3:6; 49:4 31:23 [a]Or *captivity* [A]Jer 30:18; 32:44 [B]Is 1:26; Jer 50:7 [C]Ps 48:1; 87:1; Zech 8:3 31:24 [A]Jer 31:12; Ezek 36:10; Zech 8:4-8 31:25 [a]Lit *fill* [A]Ps 107:9; Jer 31:12, 14; Matt 5:6; John 4:14 31:26 [A]Zech 4:1 [B]Prov 3:24 31:27 [A]Ezek 36:9, 11; Hos 2:23 31:28 [A]Jer 44:27; Dan 9:14 [B]Jer 1:10; 18:7 [C]Jer 24:6 31:29 [a]Or *dull* [A]Lam 5:7; Ezek 18:2 31:30 [a]Or *dull* [A]Deut 24:16; Is 3:11; Ezek 18:4, 20 31:31 [A]Jer 31:31-34; Heb 8:8-12 [B]Jer 32:40; 33:14; Ezek 37:26; Luke 22:20; 1 Cor 11:25; 2 Cor 3:6; Heb 8:8-12; 10:16, 17 31:32 [A]Ex 19:5; 24:6-8; Deut 5:2, 3 [B]Deut 1:31; Is 63:12 [C]Jer 11:7, 8

31:18–20 I may be restored. Jeremiah wrote of Israel (the 10 tribes called Ephraim) as finally recognizing, in humility, the need for the Lord to move them to repentance and forgiveness. Cf. Ps 102:13–17 for the relation of Israel's restoration to their prayers; see also 24:6, 7; La 5:21; cf. Jn 6:44, 65.

31:22 faithless. *See note on 2:19.* **A woman will encompass a man.** Here is one of the most puzzling statements in Jeremiah. Some see the virgin birth of Christ (but "woman" means a woman, not a virgin, and "encompass" or "surround" does not suggest conceiving). Possibly it refers to the formerly virgin Israel (v. 21), who is now a disgraced, divorced wife (v. 22; 3:8). She will one day in the future re-embrace her former husband, the Lord, and He will receive her back, fully forgiven. That would be "a new thing in the earth."

31:26 my sleep was pleasant. The hope of Israel's restoration brought a moment of peace in Jeremiah's otherwise tumultuous ministry.

31:28 build and ... plant. The Lord repeated what He at first told Jeremiah in 1:10 regarding His two works of judging and blessing. The latter is in two images, architectural (building) and agricultural (planting).

31:29 eaten sour grapes. This was apparently a proverb among the exiles' children born in Babylon, to express that they suffered the consequences of their fathers' sins rather than their own (La 5:7; Eze 18:2, 3).

31:31–34 a new covenant. In contrast to the Mosaic Covenant under which Israel failed, God promised a New Covenant with a spiritual, divine dynamic by which those who know Him would participate in the blessings of salvation. The fulfillment was to individuals, yet also to Israel as a nation (v. 36; Ro 11:16–27). It is set 1) in the framework of a reestablishment in their land (e.g., chaps. 30–33 and in vv. 38–40) and 2) in the time after the ultimate difficulty (30:7). In principle, this covenant, also announced by Jesus Christ (Lk 22:20), begins to be exercised with spiritual aspects realized for Jewish and Gentile believers in the church era (1Co 11:25; Heb 8:7–13; 9:15; 10:14–17; 12:24; 13:20). It has already begun to take effect with "a remnant according to *God's* gracious choice" (Ro 11:5). It will be also realized by the people of Israel in the last days, including the regathering to their ancient land (chaps. 30–33). The streams of the Abrahamic, Davidic, and New Covenants find their confluence in the millennial kingdom ruled over by the Messiah.

LORD. 33 "But [A]this is the covenant which I will make
with the house of Israel after those days," declares
the LORD, "[B]I will put My law within them and on
their heart I will write it; and [C]I will be their God,
and they shall be My people. 34 They will [A]not teach
again, each man his neighbor and each man his
brother, saying, 'Know the LORD,' for they will all
[B]know Me, from the least of them to the greatest of
them," declares the LORD, "for I will [C]forgive their
iniquity, and their [D]sin I will remember no more."

35 Thus says the LORD,
Who [A]gives the sun for light by day
And the [a]fixed order of the moon
and the stars for light by night,
Who [B]stirs up the sea so
that its waves roar;
[C]The LORD of hosts is His name:
36 "[A]If [a]this fixed order departs
From before Me," declares the LORD,
"Then the offspring of Israel
also will [B]cease
From being a nation
before Me [b]forever."
37 Thus says the LORD,
"[A]If the heavens above can be measured
And the foundations of the earth
searched out below,
Then I will also [B]cast off all
the offspring of Israel
For all that they have done,"
declares the LORD.

38 "Behold, days are coming," declares the LORD,
"when the [A]city will be rebuilt for the LORD from
the [B]Tower of Hananel to the [C]Corner Gate. 39 The
[A]measuring line will go out farther straight ahead to
the hill Gareb; then it will turn to Goah. 40 And [A]the
whole valley of the dead bodies and of the ashes,
and all the fields as far as the brook [B]Kidron, to the
corner of the [C]Horse Gate toward the east, shall be
[D]holy to the LORD; it will not be plucked up or overthrown anymore forever."

JEREMIAH IMPRISONED

32 The word that came to Jeremiah from the
LORD in the [A]tenth year of Zedekiah king of
Judah, which was the eighteenth year of Nebuchadnezzar. 2 Now at that time the army of the king of
Babylon was besieging Jerusalem, and Jeremiah
the prophet was shut up in the [A]court of the guard,
which *was in* the house of the king of Judah, 3 because Zedekiah king of Judah had [A]shut him up,
saying, "Why do you [B]prophesy, saying, '[C]Thus says
the LORD, "Behold, I am about to [D]give this city into
the hand of the king of Babylon, and he will take it;
4 and Zedekiah king of Judah will [A]not escape out
of the hand of the Chaldeans, but he will surely be
given into the hand of the king of Babylon, and
he will [B]speak with him [a]face to face and see him
eye to eye; 5 and he will [A]take Zedekiah to Babylon,
and he will be there until I visit him," declares the
LORD. "If you fight against the Chaldeans, you will
[B]not succeed" '?"
6 And Jeremiah said, "The word of the LORD came
to me, saying, 7 'Behold, Hanamel the son of Shallum your uncle is coming to you, saying, "Buy for
yourself my field which is at [A]Anathoth, for you have
the [B]right of redemption to buy *it*." ' 8 Then Hanamel my uncle's son came to me in the [A]court of the
guard according to the word of the LORD and said
to me, 'Buy my field, please, that is at [B]Anathoth,
which is in the land of Benjamin; for you have the
right of possession and the redemption is yours;
buy *it* for yourself.' Then I knew that this was the
[C]word of the LORD.
9 "I bought the field which was at Anathoth from
Hanamel my uncle's son, and I [A]weighed out the silver for him, seventeen [B]shekels of silver. 10 I [a,A]signed
and [B]sealed the deed, and [C]called in witnesses, and
weighed out the silver on the scales. 11 Then I took
the deeds of purchase, both the sealed *copy containing* the [A]terms and conditions and the open *copy;*
12 and I gave the deed of purchase to [A]Baruch the
son of [B]Neriah, the son of Mahseiah, in the sight of
Hanamel my uncle's *son* and in the sight of the witnesses who signed the deed of purchase, before all

31:33 [A]Jer 32:40; Heb 10:16 [B]Ps 40:8; 2 Cor 3:3 [C]Jer 24:7; 30:22; 32:38 **31:34** [A]1 Thess 4:9; 1 John 2:27 [B]Is 11:9; 54:13; Jer 24:7; Hab 2:14; John 6:45; 1 John 2:20 [C]Jer 33:8; 50:20; Mic 7:18; Rom 11:27 [D]Is 43:25; Heb 10:17 **31:35** [a]Lit *statutes* [A]Gen 1:14-18; Deut 4:19; Ps 19:1-6; 136:7-9 [B]Is 51:15 [C]Jer 10:16; 32:18; 50:34 **31:36** [a]Lit *these statutes* [b]Lit *all the days* [A]Ps 89:36, 37; 148:6; Is 54:9, 10; Jer 33:20-26 [B]Amos 9:8, 9 **31:37** [A]Is 40:12; Jer 33:22 [B]Jer 33:24-26; Rom 11:2-5, 26, 27 **31:38** [A]Jer 30:18; 31:4 [B]Neh 3:1; 12:39; Zech 14:10 [C]2 Kin 14:13; 2 Chr 26:9 **31:39** [A]Zech 2:1 **31:40** [A]Jer 7:32; 8:2 [B]2 Sam 15:23; 2 Kin 23:6, 12; John 18:1 [C]2 Kin 11:16; 2 Chr 23:15; Neh 3:28 [D]Joel 3:17; Zech 14:20 **32:1** [A]2 Kin 25:1, 2; Jer 39:1, 2 **32:2** [A]Neh 3:25; Jer 33:1; 37:21; 38:6; 39:14 **32:3** [A]2 Kin 6:32 [B]Jer 26:8, 9 [C]Jer 21:3-7; 34:2, 3 [D]Jer 21:4-7; 32:28, 29; 34:2, 3 **32:4** [a]Lit *mouth to mouth* [A]2 Kin 25:4-7; Jer 37:17; 38:18, 23; 39:4-7 [B]Jer 39:5 **32:5** [A]Jer 27:22; 39:7; Ezek 12:12, 13 [B]Ezek 17:9, 10, 15 **32:7** [A]Jer 1:1; 11:21 [B]Lev 25:25; Ruth 4:3, 4 **32:8** [A]Jer 32:2; 33:1 [B]Jer 1:1; 32:7 [C]1 Sam 9:16, 17; 10:3-7; 1 Kin 22:25; Jer 32:25 **32:9** [A]Gen 23:16; Zech 11:12 [B]Gen 24:22; Ex 21:32; Neh 5:15; Ezek 4:10 **32:10** [a]Or *wrote...on the document* [A]Is 44:5; Jer 32:44 [B]Deut 32:34; Job 14:17 [C]Ruth 4:1, 9; Is 8:2 **32:11** [A]Luke 2:27 **32:12** [A]Jer 32:16; 36:4, 5, 32; 43:3; 45:1 [B]Jer 51:59

31:35–37 These verses emphasize the certainty with which Israel can expect God to fulfill the New Covenant (cf. 33:17–22, 25, 26).

31:38–40 The tower was in the NE corner of the city (cf. Ne 3:1; 12:39). When New Covenant promises are ultimately fulfilled to Israel in its regathering to its land, rebuilt Jerusalem will meet certain specifications. The "Corner Gate" is at the NW corner (2Ki 14:13; 2Ch 26:9). The "measuring line" marks out the area for rebuilding. It will point over the hill Gareb and then toward Goah; both places are impossible to identify today. The "valley of ... dead bodies" is the valley of Hinnom, a place of refuse and burning fires (cf. 7:31, and *see note there*). The "Horse Gate" was at the SE corner of the temple courts (2Ki 11:16; Ne 3:28).

32:1 tenth year. The time is 587 B.C., the tenth year in Zedekiah's reign (597–586 B.C.), the eighteenth of Nebuchadnezzar's rule, during Babylon's siege of Jerusalem.

32:2 army of ... Babylon was besieging. The siege, set up in the tenth month (Jan.) of 588 B.C., lasted at least 30 months to the fourth month (July) of 586 B.C. (39:1, 2). Cf. 34:1 and *see note there*. The events of the chapter occurred in this setting of Judah's imminent loss of its land, only about a year before Babylon's final takeover detailed in chaps. 39, 40, 52.

32:2–5 shut up in the court of the guard. Judah's final king put Jeremiah into prison on the charge of preaching treason, against nation and king, whereas Zedekiah savored positive talk to spark new morale to hold out.

32:8 the right of ... redemption. A man facing hardship could sell property, and the right to redeem it until the Jubilee year belonged to the closest blood relative. If a stranger had taken it due to unpaid debt, the relative could redeem it as a family possession (Lv 25:25). Levite land could be sold only to a Levite (Lv 25:32–34), such as Jeremiah. He did as the Lord told him (vv. 9–12).

the Jews who were sitting in the court of the guard. 13And I commanded Baruch in their presence, saying, 14'Thus says the LORD of hosts, the God of Israel, "Take these deeds, this sealed deed of purchase and this open deed, and put them in an earthenware jar, that they may [a]last a long time." 15For thus says the LORD of hosts, the God of Israel, "[A]Houses and fields and vineyards will again be bought in this land." '

JEREMIAH PRAYS AND GOD EXPLAINS

16"After I had given the deed of purchase to Baruch the son of Neriah, then I [A]prayed to the LORD, saying, 17'[A]Ah Lord [a]GOD! Behold, You have [B]made the heavens and the earth by Your great power and by Your outstretched arm! [C]Nothing is too difficult for You, 18who [A]shows lovingkindness to thousands, but [B]repays the iniquity of fathers into the bosom of their children after them, O [C]great and [D]mighty God. The [E]LORD of hosts is His name; 19[A]great in counsel and mighty in deed, whose [B]eyes are open to all the ways of the sons of men, [C]giving to everyone according to his ways and according to the fruit of his deeds; 20who has [A]set signs and wonders in the land of Egypt, *and* even to this day both in Israel and among mankind; and You have [B]made a name for Yourself, as at this day. 21You [A]brought Your people Israel out of the land of Egypt with signs and with wonders, and with a strong hand and with an outstretched arm and with great terror; 22and gave them this land, which You [A]swore to their forefathers to give them, a land flowing with milk and honey. 23They [A]came in and took possession of it, but they [B]did not obey Your voice or [C]walk in Your law; they have done nothing of all that You commanded them to do; therefore You have made [D]all this calamity come upon them. 24Behold, the [A]siege ramps have reached the city to take it; and the city is [B]given into the hand of the Chaldeans who fight against it, because of the [C]sword, the famine and the pestilence; and what You have spoken has [D]come to pass; and behold, You see *it*. 25You have said to me, O Lord [a]GOD, "Buy for yourself the field with money and call in witnesses"—although the city is given into the hand of the Chaldeans.' "

26Then the word of the LORD came to Jeremiah, saying, 27"Behold, I am the LORD, the [A]God of all flesh; is anything [B]too difficult for Me?" 28Therefore thus says the LORD, "Behold, I am about to [A]give this city into the hand of the Chaldeans and into the hand of Nebuchadnezzar king of Babylon, and he will take it. 29The Chaldeans who are fighting against this city will enter and [A]set this city on fire and burn it, with the [B]houses where *people* have offered incense to Baal on their roofs and poured out drink offerings to other gods to provoke Me to anger. 30Indeed the sons of Israel and the sons of Judah have been doing only [A]evil in My sight from their youth; for the sons of Israel have been only [B]provoking Me to anger by the work of their hands," declares the LORD. 31"Indeed this city has been to Me *a* [A]*provocation of* My anger and My wrath from the day that they built it, even to this day, so that it should be [B]removed from before My face, 32because of all the evil of the sons of Israel and the sons of Judah which they have done to provoke Me to anger—they, their [A]kings, their leaders, their priests, their prophets, the men of Judah and the inhabitants of Jerusalem. 33They have turned *their* back to Me and not *their* face; though *I* taught them, [a,A]teaching again and again, they would not listen [b]and receive instruction. 34But they [A]put their detestable things in the house which is called by My name, to defile it. 35They built the [A]high places of Baal that are in the valley of Ben-hinnom to cause their sons and their daughters to pass through *the fire* to [B]Molech, which I had not commanded them nor had it [a]entered My mind that they should do this abomination, to cause Judah to sin.

36"Now therefore thus says the LORD God of Israel concerning this city of which you say, 'It is [A]given into the hand of the king of Babylon by sword, by famine and by pestilence.' 37Behold, I will [A]gather them out of all the lands to which I have driven them in My anger, in My wrath and in great indignation; and I will bring them back to this place and [B]make them dwell in safety. 38They shall be [A]My people, and I will be their God; 39and I will [A]give them one heart and one way, that they may fear Me always, for their own [B]good and for *the good of* their children

32:14 [a]Lit *stand many days* 32:15 [A]Jer 30:18; 31:5, 12, 24; 32:37, 43, 44; 33:12, 13; Amos 9:14, 15; Zech 3:10 32:16 [A]Gen 32:9-12; Jer 12:1; Phil 4:6, 7 32:17 [a]Heb *YHWH*, usually rendered *LORD* [A]Jer 1:6; 4:10 [B]2 Kin 19:15; Ps 102:25; Is 40:26-29; Jer 27:5 [C]Gen 18:14; Jer 32:27; Zech 8:6; Matt 19:26; Mark 10:27; Luke 1:37; 18:27 32:18 [A]Ex 20:6; 34:6, 7; Deut 5:9, 10; 7:9, 10 [B]1 Kin 14:9, 10; 16:1-3; Matt 23:32-36 [C]Ps 145:3 [D]Ps 50:1; Is 9:6; Jer 20:11 [E]Jer 10:16; 31:35 32:19 [A]Is 9:6; 28:29 [B]Job 34:21; Jer 23:24 [C]Ps 62:12; Jer 17:10; 21:14; Matt 16:27; John 5:29 32:20 [A]Ps 78:43; 105:27 [B]Ex 9:16; Is 63:12, 14; Dan 9:15 32:21 [A]Ex 6:6; Deut 4:34; 7:19; 26:8; 2 Sam 7:23; 1 Chr 17:21; Ps 136:11 32:22 [A]Ex 3:8, 17; 13:5; Deut 1:8; Ps 105:9-11; Jer 11:5 32:23 [A]Ps 44:2, 3; 78:54, 55; Jer 2:7 [B]Neh 9:26; Jer 11:8; Dan 9:10-14 [C]Ezra 9:7; Jer 26:4; 44:10 [D]Lam 1:18; Dan 9:11, 12 32:24 [A]Jer 33:4; Ezek 21:22 [B]Jer 20:5; 21:4-7; 32:5 [C]Jer 14:12; 29:17, 18; 32:36; 34:17; Ezek 14:21 [D]Deut 4:26; Josh 23:15, 16; Zech 1:6 32:25 [a]Heb *YHWH*, usually rendered *LORD* 32:27 [A]Num 16:22; 27:16 [B]Jer 32:17; Matt 19:26 32:28 [A]2 Kin 25:11; 2 Chr 36:17-21; Jer 19:7-12; 32:3, 24, 36; 34:2, 3 32:29 [A]2 Chr 36:19; Jer 21:10; 37:8, 10; 39:8 [B]Jer 19:13; 44:17-19, 25; 52:13 32:30 [A]Deut 9:7-12; Is 63:10; Jer 2:7; 7:22-26 [B]Jer 8:19; 11:17; 25:7 32:31 [A]1 Kin 11:7, 8; 2 Kin 21:4-7, 16; Jer 5:9-11; 6:6, 7; Matt 23:37 [B]2 Kin 23:27; 24:3, 4; Jer 27:10 32:32 [A]Ezra 9:7; Is 1:4-6, 23; Jer 2:26; 44:17, 21; Dan 9:8 32:33 [a]Lit *rising up early and teaching* [b]Lit *to* [A]2 Chr 36:15, 16; Jer 7:13; 25:3; 26:5; 35:15; John 8:2 32:34 [A]2 Kin 21:1-7; Jer 7:30; 19:4-6; Ezek 8:5 32:35 [a]Lit *come up into My heart* [A]2 Chr 28:2, 3; 33:6; Jer 7:31; 19:5 [B]Lev 18:21; 20:2-5; 1 Kin 11:7; 2 Kin 23:10; Acts 7:43 32:36 [A]Jer 32:24 32:37 [A]Deut 30:3; Ps 106:47; Is 11:11-16; Jer 16:14, 15; 23:3, 8; Ezek 11:17; Hos 1:11; Amos 9:14, 15 [B]Jer 23:6; Ezek 34:25, 28; Zech 14:11 32:38 [A]Jer 24:7 32:39 [A]2 Chr 30:12; Jer 31:33; Ezek 11:19; John 17:21; Acts 4:32 [B]Deut 11:18-21; Ezek 37:25

32:14 Take these deeds. Title deeds to the land, kept for security reasons in a pottery jar, would attest in a future day to one's claim of possession. Men of Anathoth did return to Jerusalem from Babylon (Ezr 2:23). Also, some of the poor of the land, left by the Babylonians (chap. 39), could have included certain inhabitants of Anathoth. In a still future day, God will be able (vv. 17, 27) to make this land good to a resurrected Jeremiah and confirm to the right people that they are the prophet/priest's descendants.

32:16–25 With the immense sovereign power God possesses to do whatever He wishes in the present captivity and the future return, Jeremiah wondered why God had him redeem the field.

32:26–35 God reviewed Judah's sins and affirmed to Jeremiah that the Babylonians would prevail over Jerusalem ("this city" in v. 28, etc.).

32:36–41 However, one day God will restore Israel to the land and provide the blessing of salvation.

32:37 I will bring them back to this place. God pledged to restore Israelites to the very land of Israel (cf. v. 44). It is natural to expect His fulfillment of this blessing to be just as literal as the reverse—His scattering from the land (cf. v. 42).

32:38, 39 This speaks of spiritual salvation, i.e., the true knowledge and worship of God.

after them. 40 I will make an [A]everlasting covenant with them that I will [B]not turn away from them, to do them good; and I will [C]put the fear of Me in their hearts so that they will not turn away from Me. 41 I will [A]rejoice over them to do them good and will [a]faithfully [B]plant them in this land with [C]all My heart and with all My soul. 42 For thus says the LORD, '[A]Just as I brought all this great disaster on this people, so I am going to [B]bring on them all the good that I am promising them. 43 [A]Fields will be bought in this land of which you say, "[B]It is a desolation, without man or beast; it is given into the hand of the Chaldeans." 44 Men will buy fields for money, [a,A]sign and seal deeds, and call in witnesses in the [B]land of Benjamin, in the environs of Jerusalem, in the cities of Judah, in the cities of the hill country, in the cities of the lowland and in the cities of the [b]Negev; for I will [C]restore their [c]fortunes,' declares the LORD."

RESTORATION PROMISED

33 Then the word of the LORD came to Jeremiah the second time, while he was still [a,A]confined in the court of the guard, saying, 2 "Thus says [A]the LORD who made [a]*the earth,* the LORD who formed it to establish it, the [B]LORD is His name, 3 '[A]Call to Me and I will answer you, and I will tell you [B]great and mighty things, [C]which you do not know.' 4 For thus says the LORD God of Israel concerning the [A]houses of this city, and concerning the houses of the kings of Judah which are broken down *to make a defense* against the [B]siege ramps and against the sword, 5 'While *they* are coming to [A]fight with the Chaldeans and to fill them with the corpses of men whom I have slain in My anger and in My wrath, and I have [B]hidden My face from this city because of all their wickedness: 6 Behold, I will bring to it [A]health and healing, and I will heal them; and I will reveal to them an [B]abundance of peace and truth. 7 I will [A]restore the [a]fortunes of Judah and the fortunes of Israel and will [B]rebuild them as they were at first. 8 I will [A]cleanse them from all their iniquity by which they have sinned against Me, and I will pardon all their iniquities by which they have sinned against Me and by which they have transgressed against Me. 9 [a]It will be to Me a [A]name of joy, praise and glory before [B]all the nations of the earth which will hear of all the [C]good that I do for them, and they will [D]fear and tremble because of all the good and all the peace that I make for it.'

10 "Thus says the LORD, 'Yet again there will be heard in this place, of which you say, "It is a [A]waste, without man and without beast," *that is,* in the cities of Judah and in the streets of Jerusalem that are [B]desolate, without man and without inhabitant and without beast, 11 the voice of [A]joy and the voice of gladness, the voice of the bridegroom and the voice of the bride, the voice of those who say,

"[B]Give thanks to the LORD of hosts,
For the LORD is good,
For His lovingkindness is everlasting";

and of those who bring a [C]thank offering into the house of the LORD. For I will restore the [a]fortunes of the land as they were at first,' says the LORD.

12 "Thus says the LORD of hosts, 'There will again be in this place which is waste, [A]without man or beast, and in all its cities, a [a]habitation of shepherds who rest their [B]flocks. 13 In the [A]cities of the hill country, in the cities of the lowland, in the cities of the Negev, in the land of Benjamin, in the environs of Jerusalem and in the cities of Judah, the flocks will again [B]pass under the hands of the one who numbers them,' says the LORD.

THE DAVIDIC KINGDOM

14 'Behold, [A]days are coming,' declares the LORD, 'when I will [B]fulfill the good word which I have spoken concerning the house of Israel and the house of Judah. 15 In those days and at that time I will cause a [A]righteous Branch of David to spring forth; and He shall execute [B]justice and righteousness on the earth. 16 In those days [A]Judah will be saved and Jerusalem will dwell in safety; and this is *the name* by which she will be called: the [B]LORD is our righteousness.' 17 For thus says the LORD, '[a]David shall [A]never lack a man to sit on the throne of the house of Israel; 18 [a]and the [A]Levitical priests shall never lack a man before Me to offer burnt offerings, to burn grain offerings and to [B]prepare sacrifices [b]continually.' "

32:40 [A]Is 55:3; Jer 31:33, 34; 50:5; Ezek 37:26 [B]Deut 31:6, 8; Ezek 39:29 [C]Jer 24:7; 31:33 32:41 [a]Or *truly* [A]Deut 30:9; Is 62:5; 65:19 [B]Jer 24:6; 31:28; Amos 9:15 [C]Hos 2:19, 20 32:42 [A]Jer 31:28; Zech 8:14, 15 [B]Jer 33:14 32:43 [A]Jer 32:15, 25; Ezek 37:11-14 [B]Jer 33:10 32:44 [a]Or *write...on the document* [b]I.e. South country [c]Or *captivity* [A]Jer 32:10 [B]Jer 17:26; 33:13 [C]Jer 31:23; 33:7, 11, 26 33:1 [a]Lit *shut up* [A]Jer 32:2, 8; 37:21; 38:28 33:2 [a]Lit *it* [A]Jer 51:19 [B]Ex 3:15; 6:3; 15:3; Jer 10:16 33:3 [A]Ps 50:15; 91:15; Is 55:6, 7; Jer 29:12 [B]Jer 32:17, 27 [C]Is 48:6 33:4 [A]Is 32:13, 14 [B]Jer 32:24; Ezek 4:2; 21:22; Hab 1:10 33:5 [A]Jer 21:4-7; 32:5 [B]Is 8:17; Jer 21:10; Mic 3:4 33:6 [A]Jer 17:14; 30:17; Hos 6:1 [B]Is 66:12; Gal 5:22, 23 33:7 [a]Or *captivity* [A]Ps 85:1; Jer 30:18; 32:44; 33:26; Amos 9:14 [B]Is 1:26; Jer 30:18; 31:4, 38; Amos 9:14, 15 33:8 [A]Ps 51:2; Is 44:22; Jer 50:20; Ezek 36:25, 33; Mic 7:18, 19; Zech 13:1; Heb 9:11-14 33:9 [a]I.e. This city [A]Is 62:2, 4, 7; Jer 13:11 [B]Jer 3:17, 19; 4:2; 16:19 [C]Jer 24:6; 32:42 [D]Neh 6:16; Ps 40:3; Is 60:5; Hos 3:5 33:10 [A]Jer 32:43 [B]Jer 26:9; 34:22 33:11 [a]Or *captivity* [A]Is 35:10; 51:3, 11 [B]1 Chr 16:8, 34; 2 Chr 5:13; 7:3; Ezra 3:11; Ps 100:4, 5; 106:1; 107:1; 118:1; 136:1 [C]Lev 7:12, 13; Ps 107:22; 116:17; Jer 17:26; Heb 13:15 33:12 [a]Or *pasture* [A]Jer 32:43; 36:29; 51:62 [B]Is 65:10; Jer 31:12; Ezek 34:12-15; Zeph 2:6, 7 33:13 [A]Jer 17:26; 32:44 [B]Lev 27:32; Luke 15:4 33:14 [A]Jer 23:5 [B]Is 32:1, 2; Jer 29:10; 32:42; 33:9; Ezek 34:23-25; Hag 2:6-9 33:15 [A]Is 4:2; 11:1-5; Jer 23:5, 6; 30:9; Zech 3:8; 6:12, 13 [B]Ps 72:1-5 33:16 [A]Is 45:17, 22; Jer 23:6 [B]Is 45:24, 25; Jer 23:6; 1 Cor 1:30; 2 Cor 5:21; Phil 3:9 33:17 [a]Lit *There shall not be cut off for David* [A]2 Sam 7:16; 1 Kin 2:4; 8:25; 1 Chr 17:11-14; Ps 89:29-37 33:18 [a]Lit *there shall not be cut off for the Levitical priests* [b]Lit *all the days* [A]Num 3:5-10; Deut 18:1; 24:8; Josh 3:3; Ezek 44:15 [B]Ezra 3:5; Heb 13:15

32:40 an everlasting covenant. The ultimate fulfillment of a future in the land was not fulfilled in the Ezra/Nehemiah return. This occurs in the time when God gives the people of Israel a new heart in eternal salvation along with their return to the ancient land (cf. 33:8, 9, and Eze 36:26).

32:42–44 In the millennial kingdom, land will again be bought and sold in Israel.

33:3 Call .... will answer. God invited Jeremiah's prayer, which appeals to Him to fulfill the aspects of His promises which He guarantees He will attend to (as 29:11–14; Da 9:4–19; cf. Jn 15:7). His answer to the prayer was assured in vv. 4–26 here (cf. v. 14).

33:8 Again the Lord emphasized the individual spiritual salvation associated with the New Covenant restoration to the land.

33:11 Give thanks to the LORD. These are the words of Ps 136:1, actually used by the Jews at their return from Babylon (Ezr 3:11).

33:15 a righteous Branch. This is the Messiah King in David's lineage, as in 23:5, 6. He is the King whose reign immediately follows the second coming when He appears in power (Da 2:35, 45; 7:13, 14, 27; Mt 16:27, 28; 24:30; 26:64).

33:17–22 God promised to fulfill the Davidic (2Sa 7) and Priestly/Levitical (Nu 25:10–13) Covenants without exception. The promise was as certain as the sure appearance of night and day and the incalculable number of stars or sand grains (cf. 31:35–37; 33:25, 26).

19 The word of the LORD came to Jeremiah, saying, 20 "Thus says the LORD, 'If you can [A]break My covenant for the day and My covenant for the night, so that day and night will not be at their appointed time, 21 then [A]My covenant may also be broken with David My servant so that he will not have a son to reign on his throne, and with the Levitical priests, My ministers. 22 As the [A]host of heaven cannot be counted and the [B]sand of the sea cannot be measured, so I will [C]multiply the [a]descendants of David My servant and the [D]Levites who minister to Me.' "

23 And the word of the LORD came to Jeremiah, saying, 24 "Have you not observed what this people have spoken, saying, 'The [A]two families which the LORD chose, He has [B]rejected them'? Thus they [C]despise My people, no longer are they as a nation [a]in their sight. 25 Thus says the LORD, 'If My [A]covenant *for* day and night *stand* not, *and* the [a]fixed patterns of heaven and earth I have [B]not established, 26 then I would [A]reject the [a]descendants of Jacob and David My servant, [b]not taking from his [a]descendants [B]rulers over the [a]descendants of Abraham, Isaac and Jacob. But I will [C]restore their [c]fortunes and will have [D]mercy on them.' "

A PROPHECY AGAINST ZEDEKIAH

34 The word which came to Jeremiah from the LORD, when [A]Nebuchadnezzar king of Babylon and all his army, with [B]all the kingdoms of the earth that were under his dominion and all the peoples, were fighting against Jerusalem and against all its cities, saying, 2 "Thus says the LORD God of Israel, '[A]Go and speak to Zedekiah king of Judah and say to him: "Thus says the LORD, 'Behold, [B]I am giving this city into the hand of the king of Babylon, and [C]he will burn it with fire. 3 [A]You will not escape from his hand, for you will surely be captured and delivered into his hand; and you will [B]see the king of Babylon eye to eye, and he will speak with you [a]face to face, and you will go to Babylon.' " ' 4 Yet hear the word of the LORD, O Zedekiah king of Judah! Thus says the LORD concerning you, 'You will not die by the sword. 5 You will die in peace; and as *spices* were burned for your fathers, the former kings who were before you, so they will [A]burn *spices* for you; and [B]they will lament for you, "Alas, lord!" ' For I have spoken the word," declares the LORD.

6 Then Jeremiah the prophet spoke [A]all these words to Zedekiah king of Judah in Jerusalem 7 when the army of the king of Babylon was fighting against Jerusalem and against all the remaining cities of Judah, *that is,* [A]Lachish and [B]Azekah, for they *alone* remained as [C]fortified cities among the cities of Judah.

8 The word which came to Jeremiah from the LORD after King Zedekiah had [A]made a covenant with all the people who were in Jerusalem to [B]proclaim [a]release to them: 9 that each man should set free his male servant and each man his female servant, a [A]Hebrew man or a Hebrew woman; so that [B]no one should keep them, a Jew his brother, in bondage. 10 And all the [A]officials and all the people obeyed who had entered into the covenant that each man should set free his male servant and each man his female servant, so that no one should keep them any longer in bondage; they obeyed, and set *them free.* 11 But afterward they turned around and took back the male servants and the female servants whom they had set free, and brought them into subjection for male servants and for female servants.

12 Then the word of the LORD came to Jeremiah from the LORD, saying, 13 "Thus says the LORD God of Israel, 'I [A]made a covenant with your forefathers in the day that I [B]brought them out of the land of Egypt, from the house of bondage, saying, 14 "[A]At the end of seven years each of you shall set free his Hebrew brother who [a]has been sold to you and has served you six years, you shall send him out free from you; but your forefathers [B]did not obey Me or incline their ear to Me. 15 Although recently you *had* turned and [A]done what is right in My sight, each man proclaiming [a]release to his neighbor, and you had [B]made a covenant before Me [C]in the house which is called by My name. 16 Yet you [A]turned and [B]profaned My name, and each man [a]took back his male servant and each man his female servant whom you had set free according to their desire, and you brought them into subjection to be your male servants and female servants." '

17 "Therefore thus says the LORD, 'You have not obeyed Me in proclaiming [a]release each man to his brother and each man to his neighbor. Behold, I am

33:20 [A]Ps 89:37; 104:19-23; Is 54:9, 10; Jer 31:35-37; 33:25 33:21 [A]2 Sam 23:5; 2 Chr 7:18; 21:7 33:22 [a]Lit *seed* [A]Gen 15:5; Jer 31:37 [B]Gen 22:17 [C]Ezek 37:24-27 [D]Is 66:21; Jer 33:18 33:24 [a]Lit *to their faces* [A]Is 7:17; 11:13; Jer 3:7, 8, 10, 18; 33:26; Ezek 37:22 [B]Jer 30:17 [C]Neh 4:2-4; Esth 3:6, 8, 9; Ps 44:13, 14; 83:4 33:25 [a]Lit *statutes* [A]Gen 8:22; Jer 31:35, 36; 33:20 [B]Ps 74:16, 17 33:26 [a]Lit *seed* [b]Lit *from taking* [c]Or *captivity* [A]Jer 31:37 [B]Gen 49:10 [C]Jer 33:7 [D]Is 14:1; 54:8; Jer 31:20; Ezek 39:25; Hos 1:7; 2:23 34:1 [A]2 Kin 25:1; Jer 32:2; 39:1; 52:4 [B]Jer 1:15; 27:7; Dan 2:37, 38 34:2 [A]2 Chr 36:11, 12; Jer 22:1, 2; 37:1, 2 [B]Jer 21:10; 32:3; 34:22; 37:8-10 [C]Jer 32:29 34:3 [a]Lit *mouth to mouth* [A]2 Kin 25:4, 5; Jer 21:7; 32:4; 34:21 [B]2 Kin 25:6, 7; Jer 39:6, 7 34:5 [A]2 Chr 16:14; 21:19 [B]Jer 22:18 34:6 [A]1 Sam 3:18; 15:16-24 34:7 [A]Josh 10:3, 5; 2 Kin 14:19; 18:14; Is 36:2 [B]Josh 10:10; 2 Chr 11:9 [C]2 Chr 11:5-10 34:8 [a]Or *liberty* [A]2 Kin 11:17; 23:2, 3 [B]Ex 21:2; Lev 25:10, 39-46; Neh 5:1-13; Is 58:6; Jer 34:14, 17 34:9 [A]Gen 14:13; Ex 2:6 [B]Lev 25:39 34:10 [A]Jer 26:10, 16 34:13 [A]Ex 24:3, 7, 8; Deut 5:2, 3, 27; Jer 31:32 [B]Ex 20:2 34:14 [a]Or *has sold himself* [A]Ex 21:2; Deut 15:12; 1 Kin 9:22 [B]1 Sam 8:7, 8; 2 Kin 17:13, 14 34:15 [a]Or *liberty* [A]Jer 34:8 [B]2 Kin 23:3; Neh 10:29 [C]Jer 7:10f; 32:34 34:16 [a]Lit *caused them to return* [A]1 Sam 15:11; Jer 34:11; Ezek 3:20; 18:24 [B]Ex 20:7; Lev 19:12 34:17 [a]Or *liberty*

33:24 two families. Judah and Israel. **He has rejected them.** Many, even today, believe Israel as a nation has no future. In vv. 25, 26 God emphatically denies that notion (cf. 31:35, 36; Ps 74:16, 17; Ro 11:1, 2).

34:1 Nebuchadnezzar ... fighting. The siege began ca. Jan. 15, 588 B.C. (39:1), and ended ca. July 18, 586 (39:2; 52:5, 6). This chapter was set in Zedekiah's reign, during the siege of 588–586 B.C., and was an amplification of 32:1–5, the message that resulted in Jeremiah's incarceration. **against Jerusalem.** Babylon's destruction of Jerusalem began Aug. 14, 586 (2Ki 25:8, 9).

34:3 This prophecy about Zedekiah (cf. 32:1–5) was fulfilled as reported in 2Ki 25:6, 7; Jer 52:7–11.

34:8–10 a covenant ... to proclaim release. Zedekiah's pact to free slaves or servants met with initial compliance. The covenant followed the law of release (Lv 25:39–55; Dt 15:12–18) in hopes of courting God's favor and ending His judgment.

34:11 they turned around ... took back. Former slave masters treacherously went back on their agreement and recalled their servants. Some suggest that this treachery came when the Egyptian army approached and Babylon's forces withdrew temporarily (37:5, 11) and the inhabitants believed that danger was past.

34:12–16 Then the word ... came. God reminded the unfaithful Jews of His own covenant, when He freed Israelites from Egyptian bondage (cf. Ex 21:2; Dt 15:12–15). He had commanded that Hebrew slaves should serve only 6 years, then be set free in the seventh (vv. 13, 14).

34:17–22 You have not obeyed. Due to

[A]proclaiming a [a]release to you,' declares the LORD,
'to the [B]sword, to the pestilence and to the famine;
and I will make you a [C]terror to all the kingdoms
of the earth. 18 I will give the men who have [A]trans-
gressed My covenant, who have not fulfilled the
words of the covenant which they made before Me,
when they [B]cut the calf in two and passed between
its parts— 19 the [A]officials of Judah and the officials
of Jerusalem, the court officers and the priests and
all the people of the land who passed between the
parts of the calf— 20 I will give them into the hand
of their enemies and into the hand of those who
[A]seek their life. And their [B]dead bodies will be food
for the birds of the sky and the beasts of the earth.
21 [A]Zedekiah king of Judah and his officials I will give
into the hand of their enemies and into the hand
of those who seek their life, and into the hand of
the army of the king of Babylon which has [B]gone
away from you. 22 Behold, I am going to command,'
declares the LORD, 'and I will bring them back to
this city; and they will fight against it and [A]take it
and burn it with fire; and I will make the cities of
Judah a [B]desolation [C]without inhabitant.' "

THE RECHABITES' OBEDIENCE

35 The word which came to Jeremiah from the
LORD in the days of [A]Jehoiakim the son of Josiah, king of Judah, saying, 2 "Go to the house of the
[A]Rechabites and speak to them, and bring them into
the house of the LORD, into one of the [B]chambers,
and give them wine to drink." 3 Then I took Jaazaniah the son of Jeremiah, son of Habazziniah, and
his brothers and all his sons and the whole house
of the Rechabites, 4 and I brought them into the
house of the LORD, into the chamber of the sons of
Hanan the son of Igdaliah, the [A]man of God, which
was near the chamber of the officials, which was
above the chamber of Maaseiah the son of Shallum,
[B]the doorkeeper. 5 Then I set before the [a]men of the
house of the Rechabites pitchers full of wine and
cups; and I said to them, "[A]Drink wine!" 6 But they
said, "We will not drink wine, for [A]Jonadab the son
of [B]Rechab, our father, commanded us, saying, 'You
shall [C]not drink wine, you or your sons, forever. 7 You
shall not build a house, and you shall not sow seed
and you shall not plant a vineyard or own one; but
in [A]tents you shall dwell all your days, that you may
live [B]many days in the land where you [C]sojourn.'
8 We have [A]obeyed the voice of Jonadab the son of
Rechab, our father, in all that he commanded us, not
to drink wine all our days, we, our wives, our sons
or our daughters, 9 nor to build ourselves houses
to dwell in; and we [A]do not have vineyard or field
or seed. 10 We have only [A]dwelt in tents, and have
obeyed and have done according to all that [B]Jonadab
our father commanded us. 11 But when [A]Nebuchad-
nezzar king of Babylon came up against the land,
we said, 'Come and let us [B]go to Jerusalem before
the army of the Chaldeans and before the army of
the Arameans.' So we have dwelt in Jerusalem."

JUDAH REBUKED

12 Then the word of the LORD came to Jeremiah,
saying, 13 "Thus says the LORD of hosts, the God of
Israel, 'Go and say to the men of Judah and the inhabitants of Jerusalem, "[A]Will you not receive instruction
by listening to My words?" declares the LORD. 14 "The
[A]words of Jonadab the son of Rechab, which he commanded his sons not to drink wine, are observed.
So they do not drink *wine* to this day, for they have
obeyed their father's command. But I have spoken
to you [a,B]again and again; yet you have [C]not listened
to Me. 15 Also I have sent to you all My [A]servants the
prophets, sending *them* [a]again and again, saying:
'[B]Turn now every man from his evil way and amend
your deeds, and [C]do not go after other gods to worship them. Then you will [D]dwell in the land which I
have given to you and to your forefathers; but you
have not [E]inclined your ear or listened to Me. 16 Indeed, the sons of Jonadab the son of Rechab have
[A]observed the command of their father which he
commanded them, but this people has not listened
to Me.' " ' 17 Therefore thus says the LORD, the God
of hosts, the God of Israel, 'Behold, [A]I am bringing
on Judah and on all the inhabitants of Jerusalem all
the disaster that I have pronounced against them;
because I [B]spoke to them but they did not listen, and
I have called them but they did not answer.' "

34:17 [A]Lev 26:34, 35; Esth 7:10; Dan 6:24; Matt 7:2 [B]Jer 32:24; 38:2 [C]Deut 28:25; Jer 29:18 34:18 [A]Deut 17:2; Hos 6:7; 8:1; Rom 2:8 [B]Gen 15:10 34:19 [A]Jer 34:10; Ezek 22:27; Zeph 3:3, 4 34:20 [A]Jer 11:21; 21:7; 22:25 [B]Deut 28:26; 1 Sam 17:44, 46; 1 Kin 14:11; 16:4; Ps 79:2; Jer 7:33; 16:4; 19:7 34:21 [A]2 Kin 25:18-21; Jer 32:3, 4; 39:6; 52:10, 24-27; Ezek 17:16 [B]Jer 37:5-11 34:22 [A]Jer 34:2; 39:1, 2, 8; 52:7, 13 [B]Jer 4:7; 9:11 [C]Jer 33:10; 44:22 35:1 [A]2 Kin 23:34-36; 24:1; 2 Chr 36:5-7; Jer 1:3; 27:20; Dan 1:1 35:2 [A]2 Kin 10:15; 1 Chr 2:55 [B]1 Kin 6:5, 8; 1 Chr 9:26, 33 35:4 [A]Deut 33:1; Josh 14:6; 1 Kin 12:22; 2 Kin 1:9-13 [B]1 Chr 9:18f 35:5 [a]Lit *sons* [A]Amos 2:12 35:6 [A]2 Kin 10:15, 23 [B]1 Chr 2:55 [C]Lev 10:9; Num 6:2-4; Judg 13:7, 14; Luke 1:15 35:7 [A]Gen 25:27; Heb 11:9 [B]Ex 20:12; Eph 6:2, 3 [C]Gen 36:7 35:8 [A]Prov 1:8, 9; 4:1, 2, 10; 6:20; Eph 6:1; Col 3:20 35:9 [A]Ps 37:16; Jer 35:7; 1 Tim 6:6 35:10 [A]Jer 35:7 [B]Jer 35:6 35:11 [A]2 Kin 24:1, 2; Dan 1:1, 2 [B]Jer 4:5-7; 8:14 35:13 [A]Is 28:9-12; Jer 5:3; 6:8-10; 32:33 35:14 [a]Lit *rising early and speaking* [A]Jer 35:6-10 [B]2 Chr 36:15; Jer 7:13, 25; 11:7; 25:3, 4 [C]Is 30:9; 50:2 35:15 [a]Lit *rising early and speaking* [A]Jer 7:25; 25:4; 26:5; 29:19; 32:33 [B]Is 1:16, 17; Jer 4:1; 18:11; 25:5f; Ezek 18:30-32; Acts 26:20 [C]Deut 6:14; Jer 7:6; 13:10; 25:6 [D]Jer 7:7; 25:5, 6 [E]Jer 7:24, 26; 11:8; 17:23; 34:14 35:16 [A]Jer 35:14; Mal 1:6 35:17 [A]Josh 23:15; Jer 19:3, 15; 21:4-10; Mic 3:12 [B]Prov 1:24, 25; Is 65:12; 66:4; Jer 7:13, 26, 27; 26:5; Luke 13:34, 35; Rom 10:21

recent duplicity (v. 16), God promised only one kind of liberty to the offenders, liberty to judgment by sword, pestilence, and famine (v. 17).

34:18, 21 cut the calf in two. God will give the guilty over to death before the conqueror, for they denied the covenant ratified by blood (v. 21). In this custom, as in Ge 15:8–17, two parties laid out parts of a sacrifice on two sides, then walked between the parts. By that symbolic action, each pledged to fulfill his promise, agreeing in effect, "May my life (represented by the blood) be poured out if I fail to honor my part."

35:1–19 This chapter provided a description of the commitment to obedience by a group of people to their father, in contrast to the Jews' disobedience to God.

35:1 days of Jehoiakim. 609–597 B.C. This backed up to several years before 34:1, possibly for a thematic reason—to cite a case of obedience after the episode of treachery in chap. 34.

35:2 The Rechabites. These were a seminomadic Kenite group, related to Moses' father-in-law (Jdg 1:16; 4:11), descended from those in 1Ch 2:55. The originator of their rules was Jonadab (35:6, 14; 2Ki 10:15, 23). They derived their name from Rechab (v. 8) and were not of Jacob's seed, but "strangers" in Israel.

35:8 obeyed. What was commended here was not the father's specific commands about nomadic life, but the steadfast obedience of the sons. Their obedience was unreserved in all aspects, at all times, on the part of all, without exception; in all these respects Israel was lacking (v. 14).

35:13–17 The prophet indicted the Jews for flagrant disobedience.

[18] Then Jeremiah said to the house of the
Rechabites, "Thus says the LORD of hosts, the God
of Israel, 'Because you have [A]obeyed the command
of Jonadab your father, kept all his commands and
done according to all that he commanded you;
[19] therefore thus says the LORD of hosts, the God
of Israel, "Jonadab the son of Rechab [A]shall not lack
a man to [B]stand before Me [a]always." ' "

JEREMIAH'S SCROLL READ IN THE TEMPLE

36 In the [A]fourth year of Jehoiakim the son of
Josiah, king of Judah, this word came to Jeremiah from the LORD, saying, [2] "Take a [a,A]scroll and
write on it all the [B]words which I have spoken to
you concerning [C]Israel and concerning Judah, and
concerning all the [D]nations, from the [E]day I *first*
spoke to you, from the days of Josiah, even to this
day. [3] [A]Perhaps the house of Judah will hear all the
calamity which I plan to bring on them, in order
that every man will [B]turn from his evil way; then I
will [C]forgive their iniquity and their sin."
[4] Then Jeremiah called [A]Baruch the son of Neriah,
and Baruch wrote on a [a,B]scroll [b]at the dictation of
Jeremiah all the words of the LORD which He had
spoken to him. [5] Jeremiah commanded Baruch, saying, "I am [a,A]restricted; I cannot go into the house
of the LORD. [6] So you go and [A]read from the scroll
which you have [B]written [a]at my dictation the words
of the LORD [b]to the people in the LORD'S house on
a [C]fast day. And also you shall read them [b]to all
the people of Judah who come from their cities.
[7] [A]Perhaps their supplication will [a]come before the
LORD, and everyone will turn from his evil way, for
[B]great is the anger and the wrath that the LORD has
pronounced against this people." [8] Baruch the son
of Neriah did according to all that Jeremiah the
prophet commanded him, [A]reading from the book
the words of the LORD in the LORD'S house.
[9] Now in the [A]fifth year of Jehoiakim the son of
Josiah, king of Judah, in the [B]ninth month, all the
people in Jerusalem and all the people who [C]came
from the cities of Judah to Jerusalem proclaimed
a [D]fast before the LORD. [10] Then Baruch read from
the book the words of Jeremiah in the house of the
LORD in the [A]chamber of [B]Gemariah the son of Shaphan the [C]scribe, in the upper court, at the [D]entry of
the New Gate of the LORD'S house, to all the people.
[11] Now when [A]Micaiah the son of Gemariah, the son
of Shaphan, had heard all the words of the LORD from
the book, [12] he went down to the king's house, into the
scribe's chamber. And behold, all the officials were
sitting there—[A]Elishama the scribe, and [B]Delaiah the
son of Shemaiah, and [C]Elnathan the son of Achbor,
and Gemariah the son of Shaphan, and Zedekiah the
son of Hananiah, and all the *other* officials. [13] Micaiah
[A]declared to them all the words that he had heard
when Baruch read from the book to the people. [14] Then
all the officials sent [A]Jehudi the son of Nethaniah, the
son of Shelemiah, the son of Cushi, to Baruch, saying,
"Take in your hand the scroll from which you have
read to the people and come." So Baruch the son of
Neriah [B]took the scroll in his hand and went to them.
[15] They said to him, "Sit down, please, and read it to
us." So Baruch [A]read it to them. [16] When they had heard
all the words, they turned in [A]fear one to another and
said to Baruch, "We will surely [B]report all these words
to the king." [17] And they asked Baruch, saying, "Tell
us, please, [A]how did you write all these words? *Was
it* [a]at his dictation?" [18] Then Baruch said to them, "He
[A]dictated all these words to me, and I wrote them with
ink on the book." [19] Then the officials said to Baruch,
"Go, [A]hide yourself, you and Jeremiah, and do not let
anyone know where you are."

THE SCROLL IS BURNED

[20] So they went to the [A]king in the court, but they
had deposited the scroll in the chamber of [A]Elishama
the scribe, and they reported all the words to the
king. [21] Then the king sent Jehudi to get the scroll,
and he took it out of the chamber of Elishama the
scribe. And Jehudi [A]read it to the king as well as to

35:18 [A]Ex 20:12; Eph 6:1-3 35:19 [a]Lit *all the days* [A]1 Chr 2:55; Jer 33:17 [B]Jer 15:19; Luke 21:36 36:1 [A]2 Kin 24:1; 2 Chr 36:5-7; Jer 25:1, 3; 45:1; 46:2; Dan 1:1 36:2 [a]Lit *scroll of a book* [A]Ex 17:14; Is 8:1; Jer 36:6, 23, 28; Zech 5:1, 2 [B]Jer 1:9, 10; 30:2; Hab 2:2 [C]Jer 3:3-10; 23:13, 14; 32:30-32 [D]Jer 1:5, 10; 25:9-29; chs 47-51 [E]Jer 1:2, 3; 25:3 36:3 [A]Jer 26:3; 36:7; Ezek 12:3 [B]Deut 30:2, 8; 1 Sam 7:3; Is 55:7; Jer 18:8, 11; 35:15; Jon 3:8 [C]Jon 3:10; Mark 4:12; Acts 3:19 36:4 [a]Lit *scroll of a book* [b]Lit *from the mouth of* [A]Jer 32:12; 36:18; 43:3; 45:1 [B]Jer 36:14; Ezek 2:9 36:5 [a]Lit *shut up* [A]Jer 32:2; 33:1; 2 Cor 11:23 36:6 [a]Lit *from my mouth* [b]Lit *in the ears of,* and so throughout this context [A]Jer 36:8 [B]Jer 36:4 [C]Jer 36:9; Zech 8:19 36:7 [a]Lit *fall* [A]1 Kin 8:33; 2 Chr 33:12, 13; Jer 26:3; 36:3 [B]Deut 28:15; 31:16, 17; 2 Kin 22:13, 17; Jer 4:4; 21:5; Lam 4:11 36:8 [A]Jer 1:17; 36:6 36:9 [A]Jer 36:1 [B]Jer 36:22 [C]Jer 36:6 [D]Judg 20:26; 1 Sam 7:6; 2 Chr 20:3; Esth 4:16; Joel 1:14; 2:15; Jon 3:5 36:10 [A]Jer 35:4 [B]Jer 36:11, 25 [C]2 Sam 8:17; Jer 52:25 [D]Jer 26:10 36:11 [A]Jer 36:13 36:12 [A]Jer 36:20 [B]Jer 36:25 [C]Jer 26:22 36:13 [A]2 Kin 22:10 36:14 [A]Jer 36:21 [B]Jer 36:2; Ezek 2:7-10 36:15 [A]Jer 36:21 36:16 [A]Jer 36:24; Acts 24:25 [B]Jer 13:18; Amos 7:10, 11 36:17 [a]Lit *from his mouth,* and so throughout this context [A]John 9:10, 15, 26 36:18 [A]Jer 36:4 36:19 [A]1 Kin 17:3; 18:4, 10; Jer 26:20-24; 36:26 36:20 [A]Jer 36:12 36:21 [A]2 Kin 22:10; 2 Chr 34:18; Ezek 2:4, 5

35:18, 19 Because you have obeyed. God will bless the Rechabites not in spiritually saving them all, but in preserving a posterity in which some can have a place in His service. A Rechabite still has a role in Ne 3:14. Also, the title over Ps 71 in the LXX (Gr. translation of the OT) was addressed for use by the sons of Jonadab and the earliest captives.

36:1 fourth year of Jehoiakim. This chapter, like chap. 35, goes back several years earlier than chaps. 32–34, before or shortly after the first of 3 deportations from Jerusalem to Babylon in 605 B.C.

36:2 write on it. The command was to record in one volume all the messages since the outset of Jeremiah's ministry in 627 B.C. (1:2) up to 605/604 B.C., to be read to the people in the temple (v. 6.).

36:4 Baruch wrote. Jeremiah's recording secretary (cf. 32:12) wrote the prophet's messages (cf. 45:1), and penned them a second time after the first scroll was burned (cf. 36:32). He also read the messages in the temple (v. 10) and in the palace (v. 15). Later, Jehudi read a small part of the first scroll before King Jehoiakim (vv. 21–23).

36:5 restricted. The word means "confined, hindered, shut up," and is the same term used for imprisonment in 33:1 and 39:15. The fact that princes allowed Jeremiah to depart into hiding (v. 19) may indicate that he was curtailed in some ways without being in prison. There is no record of his being imprisoned in Jehoiakim's rule.

36:6 a fast day. Cf. v. 9. Here was a special fast day, appointed to avert the impending calamity, which would make the Jews more open to the message of the prophet (v. 7).

36:9 fifth year. This year (604 B.C.) was the next year after that of v. 1, which may suggest that it took some part of a year to repeat and record the long series of messages so far given (cf. v. 18). **ninth month.** Nov./ Dec. (cf. vv. 22, 23).

36:10 chamber. On the N side, above the wall overlooking the temple court, where the people gathered, Baruch read from a window or balcony.

36:17, 18 They asked if Baruch had written these words from memory or actual dictation from the inspired prophet. The latter was true. They were concerned it might be God's Word (cf. vv. 16, 25).

all the officials who stood beside the king. 22 Now
the king was sitting in the [A]winter house in the
[B]ninth month, with *a fire* burning in the brazier
before him. 23 When Jehudi had read three or four
columns, *the king* cut it with a scribe's knife and
[A]threw *it* into the fire that was in the brazier, until
all the scroll was consumed in the fire that was in
the brazier. 24 Yet the king and all his servants who
heard all these words were [A]not afraid, nor did they
[B]rend their garments. 25 Even though Elnathan and
Delaiah and Gemariah [A]pleaded with the king not to
burn the scroll, he would not listen to them. 26 And
the king commanded Jerahmeel the king's son, Seraiah the son of Azriel, and Shelemiah the son of
Abdeel to [A]seize Baruch the scribe and Jeremiah
the prophet, but the [B]LORD hid them.

THE SCROLL IS REPLACED

27 Then the word of the LORD came to Jeremiah
after the king had [A]burned the scroll and the words
which [B]Baruch had written at the dictation of Jeremiah, saying, 28 "[A]Take again another scroll and
write on it all the former words that were [B]on
the first scroll which Jehoiakim the king of Judah
burned. 29 And concerning Jehoiakim king of Judah you shall say, 'Thus says the LORD, "You have
[A]burned this scroll, saying, '[B]Why have you written
on it [a]that the [C]king of Babylon will certainly come
and destroy this land, and will make man and beast
to cease from it?' " 30 Therefore thus says the LORD
concerning Jehoiakim king of Judah, "He shall have
[A]no one to sit on the throne of David, and his [B]dead
body shall be cast out to the heat of the day and the
frost of the night. 31 I will also [A]punish him and his
[a]descendants and his servants for their iniquity, and
I will [B]bring on them and the inhabitants of Jerusalem and the men of Judah all the calamity that I
have declared to them—but they did not listen." ' "
32 Then Jeremiah took another scroll and gave
it to Baruch the son of Neriah, the scribe, and he
[A]wrote on it at the dictation of Jeremiah all the
words of the book which Jehoiakim king of Judah
had burned in the fire; and many [a]similar words
were added to them.

JEREMIAH WARNS AGAINST TRUST IN PHARAOH

37 Now [A]Zedekiah the son of Josiah whom Nebuchadnezzar king of Babylon had [B]made king
in the land of Judah, reigned as king in place of
[C]Coniah the son of Jehoiakim. 2 But [A]neither he nor
his servants nor the people of the land listened to
the words of the LORD which He spoke through
Jeremiah the prophet.
3 Yet [A]King Zedekiah sent Jehucal the son of Shelemiah, and [B]Zephaniah the son of Maaseiah, the
priest, to Jeremiah the prophet, saying, "[C]Please
pray to the LORD our God on our behalf." 4 Now
Jeremiah was *still* coming in and going out among
the people, for they had not *yet* [A]put him in the
prison. 5 Meanwhile, [A]Pharaoh's army had set out
from Egypt; and when the Chaldeans who had been
besieging Jerusalem heard the report about them,
they [B]lifted the *siege* from Jerusalem.
6 Then the word of the LORD came to Jeremiah the
prophet, saying, 7 "Thus says the LORD God of Israel,
'[A]Thus you are to say to the king of Judah, who sent
you to Me to inquire of Me: "Behold, [B]Pharaoh's army
which has come out for your assistance is going to
return to its own land of Egypt. 8 The Chaldeans will
also [A]return and fight against this city, and they will
capture it and burn it with fire." ' 9 Thus says the LORD,
'Do not [A]deceive yourselves, saying, "The Chaldeans
will surely go away from us," for they will not go. 10 For
[A]even if you had defeated the entire army of Chaldeans who were fighting against you, and there were
only wounded men left among them, each man in his
tent, they would rise up and [B]burn this city with fire.' "

JEREMIAH IMPRISONED

11 Now it happened when the army of the Chaldeans had lifted *the siege* from Jerusalem because of
Pharaoh's army, 12 that Jeremiah went out from Jerusalem to go to the land of Benjamin in order to [A]take
[a]possession of *some* property there among the people.
13 While he was at the [A]Gate of Benjamin, a captain of
the guard whose name was Irijah, the son of Shelemiah the son of Hananiah was there; and he [B]arrested
Jeremiah the prophet, saying, "You are [a]going over

36:22 [A]Judg 3:20; Amos 3:15 [B]Jer 36:9 36:23 [A]1 Kin 22:8, 27; Prov 1:30; Is 5:18, 19; 28:14, 22; Jer 36:29 36:24 [A]Ps 36:1; 64:5; Jer 36:16 [B]Gen 37:29, 34; 2 Sam 1:11; 1 Kin 21:27; 2 Kin 19:1, 2; 22:11, 19; Is 36:22; 37:1; Jon 3:6 36:25 [A]Gen 37:22, 26, 27; Acts 5:34-39 36:26 [A]1 Kin 19:1-3, 10, 14; Matt 23:34, 37 [B]Ps 91:1 36:27 [A]Jer 36:23 [B]Jer 36:4, 18 36:28 [A]Zech 1:5, 6 [B]Jer 36:4, 23 36:29 [a]Lit *saying* [A]Deut 29:19; Job 15:24, 25; Is 45:9 [B]Is 29:21; 30:10; Jer 26:9; 32:3 [C]Jer 25:9-11 36:30 [A]2 Kin 24:12-15; Jer 22:30 [B]Jer 22:19 36:31 [a]Lit *seed* [A]Jer 23:34 [B]Deut 28:15; Prov 29:1; Jer 19:15; 35:17 36:32 [a]Lit *like those* [A]Ex 4:15, 16; 34:1; Jer 36:4, 18, 23 37:1 [A]2 Kin 24:17; 1 Chr 3:15; 2 Chr 36:10 [B]Ezek 17:12-21 [C]2 Kin 24:12; 1 Chr 3:16; 2 Chr 36:9, 10; Jer 22:24, 28; 24:1; 52:31 37:2 [A]2 Kin 24:19, 20; 2 Chr 36:12-16; Prov 29:12 37:3 [A]Jer 21:1, 2 [B]Jer 29:25; 52:24 [C]1 Kin 13:6; Jer 2:27; 15:11; 21:1, 2; 42:1-4, 20; Acts 8:24 37:4 [A]Jer 32:2, 3; 37:15 37:5 [A]2 Kin 24:7; Jer 37:7; Ezek 17:15 [B]Jer 37:11 37:7 [A]2 Kin 22:18; Jer 21:1, 2; 37:3 [B]Is 30:1-3; 31:1-3; Jer 2:18, 36; Lam 4:17; Ezek 17:17 37:8 [A]Jer 34:22; 38:23; 39:2-8 37:9 [A]Jer 29:8; Obad 3; Matt 24:4, 5; Eph 5:6 37:10 [A]Lev 26:36-38; Is 30:17; Jer 21:4, 5 [B]Jer 37:8 37:12 [a]Or *part in a dividing* [A]Jer 32:8 37:13 [a]Lit *falling* [A]Jer 38:7; Zech 14:10 [B]Jer 18:18; 20:10; Luke 23:2; Acts 6:11; 24:5-9, 13

36:23 cut it. As often as Jehudi read "three or four columns," the king cut it up, doing so all the way through the whole scroll because he rejected the message (cf. v. 29). Jehoiakim is the king who sent men to Egypt (chap. 26) to bring back God's faithful prophet, Uriah, so that he could execute him.

36:24 not afraid. The king's servants were more hardened than the princes (v. 16).

36:26 the LORD hid them. God, who guides (cf. 1:8, 19; 10:23), gave Jeremiah and Baruch safety (cf. 36:19; Ps 32:8; Pr 3:5, 6).

36:27 Cf. Is 40:18; 55:11; Mt 5:18.

36:31 I will also punish him. Consequences followed Jehoiakim's defiance. In 598 B.C. he met his own death (22:18, 19; 2Ki 23:36; 2Ch 36:5). He had none to occupy the throne (v. 30). Jehoiachin or Jeconiah (Coniah in 22:24), his son, did succeed him, but with virtually no rule at all, lasting only 3 months and 10 days in 597 B.C. (22:24–30; 2Ch 36:9, 10). Babylon deported him for the rest of his life (cf. 52:31–34), and none of his descendants ruled (cf. 22:30, and *see note there*).

37:1 Zedekiah ... reigned. Zedekiah, an uncle of Jeconiah, was raised to the throne by Nebuchadnezzar in contempt for Jehoiakim and Jeconiah. His 11-year vassal rule was from 597–586 B.C. The message of the king to Jeremiah in this chapter is somewhat earlier than that in chap. 21, when Zedekiah was afraid of the Chaldean's (Babylonian's) defeating Egypt and returning to besiege Jerusalem (vv. 3, 5).

37:4 The prophet was no longer in the prison court as he had been (32:2; 33:1).

37:7–10 say to the king. Babylon, which temporarily ended the siege to deal with an Egyptian advance, would return and destroy Jerusalem.

37:12 Jeremiah went out. He returned to his hometown to claim the property he had purchased in 32:6–12.

37:13 Hananiah. Jeremiah had predicted his death (28:16), and thus the grandson took revenge with a false accusation (cf. 38:19; 52:15).

to the Chaldeans!" 14 But Jeremiah said, "[A]A lie! I am
not [a]going over to the Chaldeans"; yet he would not
listen to him. So Irijah arrested Jeremiah and brought
him to the officials. 15 Then the officials were [A]angry
at Jeremiah and beat him, and they [B]put him in jail
in the house of Jonathan the scribe, which they had
made into the prison. 16 For Jeremiah had come into
the [a,A]dungeon, that is, the vaulted cell; and Jeremiah
stayed there many days.
17 Now King Zedekiah sent and took him *out;* and
in his palace the king [A]secretly asked him and said,
"Is there a [B]word from the LORD?" And Jeremiah
said, "There is!" Then he said, "You will be [C]given
into the hand of the king of Babylon!" 18 Moreover
Jeremiah said to King Zedekiah, "[A]*In* what *way* have
I sinned against you, or against your servants, or
against this people, that you have put me in prison?
19 [A]Where then are your prophets who prophesied
to you, saying, 'The [B]king of Babylon will not come
against you or against this land'? 20 But now, please
listen, O my lord the king; please let my [A]petition
[a]come before you and do not make me return to
the house of Jonathan the scribe, that I may not die
there." 21 Then King Zedekiah gave commandment,
and they committed Jeremiah to the [A]court of the
guardhouse and gave him a loaf of [B]bread daily
from the bakers' street, until all the bread in the
city was [C]gone. So Jeremiah remained in the court
of the guardhouse.

JEREMIAH THROWN INTO THE CISTERN

38 Now Shephatiah the son of Mattan, and Gedaliah the son of Pashhur, and Jucal the [A]son
of Shelemiah, and [B]Pashhur the son of Malchijah
heard the words that Jeremiah was speaking to
all the people, saying, 2 "Thus says the LORD, 'He
who [A]stays in this city will die by the [B]sword and
by famine and by pestilence, but he who goes
out to the Chaldeans will live and have his *own*
[C]life as booty and stay alive.' 3 Thus says the LORD,
'This city will certainly be [A]given into the hand
of the army of the king of Babylon and he will
capture it.' " 4 Then the [A]officials said to the king,
"Now let this man be put to death, inasmuch as
he is [a,B]discouraging the men of war who are left
in this city and [b]all the people, by speaking such
words to them; for this man [C]is not seeking the
well-being of this people but rather their harm."
5 So King Zedekiah said, "Behold, he is in your
[a]hands; for the king [A]can *do* nothing against you."
6 Then they took Jeremiah and cast him into the
[A]cistern *of* Malchijah the king's son, which was
in the court of the guardhouse; and they let Jeremiah down with ropes. Now in the cistern there
was no water but only [B]mud, and Jeremiah sank
into the mud. 7 But [A]Ebed-melech the Ethiopian, [a]a
[B]eunuch, while he was in the king's palace, heard
that they had put Jeremiah into the cistern. Now
the king was sitting in the [C]Gate of Benjamin; 8 and
Ebed-melech went out from the king's palace and
spoke to the king, saying, 9 "My lord the king, these
men have acted wickedly in all that they have
done to Jeremiah the prophet whom they have
cast into the cistern; and he [a]will die right where
he is because of the famine, for there is [A]no more
bread in the city." 10 Then the king commanded
Ebed-melech the Ethiopian, saying, "Take thirty
men from here [a]under your authority and bring
up Jeremiah the prophet from the cistern before
he dies." 11 So Ebed-melech took the men under
his [a]authority and went into the king's palace to *a*
place beneath the storeroom and took from there
worn-out clothes and worn-out rags and let them
down by ropes into the cistern to Jeremiah. 12 Then
Ebed-melech the Ethiopian said to Jeremiah, "Now
put these worn-out clothes and rags under your
armpits under the ropes"; and Jeremiah did so.
13 So they pulled Jeremiah up with the ropes and
lifted him out of the cistern, and Jeremiah stayed
in the [A]court of the guardhouse.
14 Then King Zedekiah [A]sent and [a]had Jeremiah
the prophet brought to him at the third entrance
that is in the house of the LORD; and the king said
to Jeremiah, "I am going to [B]ask you something; do
not hide anything from me." 15 Then Jeremiah said

37:14 [a]Lit *falling* [A]Ps 27:12; 52:1, 2; Jer 40:4-6; Matt 5:11, 12 37:15 [A]Jer 18:23; 20:1-3; 26:16; Matt 21:35 [B]Gen 39:20; 2 Chr 16:10; 18:26; Jer 38:26; Acts 5:18 37:16 [a]Lit *house of the cistern-pit* [A]Jer 38:6 37:17 [A]1 Kin 14:1-4; Jer 38:5, 14-16, 24-27 [B]1 Kin 22:15, 16; 2 Kin 3:11, 12; Jer 15:11; 21:1, 2; 37:3 [C]Jer 21:7; 24:8; Ezek 12:12, 13; 17:19, 20 37:18 [A]1 Sam 24:9; 26:18; Dan 6:22; John 10:32; Acts 25:8, 11, 25 37:19 [A]Deut 32:37, 38; 2 Kin 3:13; Jer 2:28 [B]Jer 27:14; 28:1-4, 10-17 37:20 [a]Lit *fall* [A]Jer 36:7; 38:26 37:21 [A]Jer 32:2; 38:13, 28 [B]1 Kin 17:6; Job 5:20; Ps 33:18, 19; Is 33:16 [C]2 Kin 25:3; Jer 38:9; 52:6 38:1 [A]Jer 37:3 [B]Jer 21:1 38:2 [A]Jer 21:9 [B]Jer 34:17; 42:17 [C]Jer 21:9; 39:18; 45:5 38:3 [A]Jer 21:10; 32:3-5 38:4 [a]Lit *weakening the hands of* [b]Lit *the hands of all* [A]Jer 18:23; 26:11, 21; 36:12 [B]Ex 5:4; 1 Kin 18:17, 18; 21:20; Neh 6:9; Amos 7:10; Acts 16:20 [C]Jer 29:7 38:5 [a]Lit *hand* [A]2 Sam 3:39 38:6 [A]Jer 37:16, 21; Acts 16:24 [B]Ps 40:2; 69:2, 14, 15; Jer 38:22; Zech 9:11 38:7 [a]Or *an official* [A]Jer 39:16 [B]Jer 29:2; Acts 8:27 [C]Deut 21:19; Job 29:7; Jer 37:13; Amos 5:10 38:9 [a]M.T. reads *has died* [A]Jer 37:21; 52:6 38:10 [a]Lit *in your hand* 38:11 [a]Lit *hand* 38:13 [A]Neh 3:25; Jer 32:2; 37:21; 38:6; 39:14, 15; Acts 23:35; 24:27; 28:16, 30 38:14 [a]Lit *took Jeremiah the prophet to him* [A]Jer 21:1, 2; 37:17 [B]1 Sam 3:17, 18; 1 Kin 22:16; Jer 15:11; 42:2-5, 20

37:15 beat him. Jeremiah often absorbed blows, threats, or other mistreatment for proclaiming the truth from God (11:21; 20:2; 26:8; 36:26; 38:6, 25).

37:17 This showed Zedekiah's willful rejection. He knew Jeremiah spoke for God.

37:19 prophets. They were shown to be liars who said the "king of Babylon" would not come. He had come and would return.

37:21 bread. The king showed a measure of kindness by returning Jeremiah to "the court of the guardhouse" (cf. 32:2; 33:1), promising "bread" as long as it lasted in the siege (cf. 38:9). He remained there until Jerusalem was taken soon after the food was gone (38:28), with only a brief trip to a pit (38:6–13).

38:4 let this man be put to death. Cf. 26:11 and *see note there*. **he is discouraging the men of war.** They charged that Jeremiah's urging to submit to Babylon (v. 2) undermined the defenders' morale and will. By proclaiming Babylon's victory, he was viewed as a traitor to Judah.

38:5 the king can *do* nothing. This is a spineless evasion of courage and decency by a leader who rejected God's Word.

38:6 no water but only mud. The murderous princes (cf. v. 4) would let God's spokesman die of thirst, hunger, hypothermia, or suffocation if he sank too deeply into the bottom of the cistern. Cf. Ps 69:2, 14, a reference to Messiah.

38:7–13 Ebed-melech. An Ethiopian, Gentile stranger acted decisively to deliver Jeremiah from his own people who were seeking to kill him. Perhaps a keeper of the royal harem ("eunuch"), this man later received God's deliverance of his own life and His tribute for his faith (39:15–18).

38:14–23 I am going to ask you something. This is one of several queries as Zedekiah wanted to hear God's Word but rejected it. God's Word was surrender, and His answer for rejection was calamity for Jerusalem, capture of the king, and tragedy for his family plus others of the palace. For the fulfillment to Zedekiah, cf. 39:4–8.

to Zedekiah, "[A]If I tell you, will you not certainly
put me to death? Besides, if I give you advice, you
will not listen to me." 16 But King Zedekiah swore to
Jeremiah in [A]secret saying, "As the LORD lives, who
made this [a,B]life for us, surely I will not put you to
death nor will I give you over to the hand of [C]these
men who are seeking your [a]life."

INTERVIEW WITH ZEDEKIAH

17 Then Jeremiah said to Zedekiah, "Thus says the
LORD [A]God of hosts, the [B]God of Israel, 'If you will
indeed [C]go out to the officers of the king of Babylon,
then [a]you will live, this city will not be burned with
fire, and you and your household will [b]survive. 18 But
if you will [A]not go out to the officers of the king of
Babylon, then this city [B]will be given over to the
hand of the Chaldeans; and they will burn it with
fire, and [C]you yourself will not escape from their
hand.' " 19 Then King Zedekiah said to Jeremiah, "I
[A]dread the Jews who have [a,B]gone over to the Chaldeans, for they may give me over into their hand
and they will [C]abuse me." 20 But Jeremiah said, "They
will not give you over. Please [a,A]obey the LORD in
what I am saying to you, that it may go [B]well with
you and [b,C]you may live. 21 But if you keep refusing to go out, this is the word which the LORD has
shown me: 22 'Then behold, all of the [A]women who
have been left in the palace of the king of Judah are
going to be brought out to the [a]officers of the king
of Babylon; and those women will say,

"[b]Your close friends
Have misled and overpowered you;
While your feet were sunk in the mire,
They turned back."

23 They will also bring out all your wives and your
[A]sons to the Chaldeans, and [B]you yourself will not
escape from their hand, but will be seized by the
hand of the king of Babylon, and [B]this city will be
burned with fire.' "
24 Then Zedekiah said to Jeremiah, "Let no man
know about these words and you will not die. 25 But
if the [A]officials hear that I have talked with you and
come to you and say to you, 'Tell us now what you said
to the king and what the king said to you; do not hide
it from us and we will not put you to death,' 26 then
you are to say to them, 'I was [A]presenting my petition
before the king, not to make me return to the house of
Jonathan to die there.' " 27 Then all the officials came
to Jeremiah and questioned him. So he reported to
them in accordance with all these words which the
king had commanded; and they ceased speaking with
him, since the [a]conversation had not been overheard.
28 So Jeremiah [A]stayed in the court of the guardhouse
until the day that Jerusalem was captured.

JERUSALEM CAPTURED

39 [a]Now when Jerusalem was captured [b,A]in the
ninth year of Zedekiah king of Judah, in the
tenth month, Nebuchadnezzar king of Babylon and
all his army came to Jerusalem and laid siege to
it; 2 in the eleventh year of Zedekiah, in the fourth
month, in the ninth *day* of the month, the city *wall*
was [A]breached. 3 Then all the [A]officials of the king of
Babylon came in and sat down at the [B]Middle Gate:
Nergal-sar-ezer, Samgar-nebu, Sar-sekim the [a]Rab-sa-
ris, Nergal-sar-ezer *the* [b]Rab-mag, and all the rest of
the officials of the king of Babylon. 4 When Zedekiah
the king of Judah and all the men of war saw them,
they [A]fled and went out of the city at night by way of
the king's garden through the gate [B]between the two
walls; and he went out toward the [a]Arabah. 5 But the
army of the [A]Chaldeans pursued them and overtook
Zedekiah in the [B]plains of Jericho; and they seized
him and brought him up to Nebuchadnezzar king
of Babylon at [C]Riblah in the land of Hamath, and he
passed sentence on him. 6 Then the [A]king of Babylon
slew the sons of Zedekiah [B]before his eyes at Riblah;
the king of Babylon also slew all the [C]nobles of Judah.
7 He then [A]blinded Zedekiah's eyes and bound him
in [B]fetters of bronze to bring him to [C]Babylon. 8 The
Chaldeans also [A]burned with fire the king's palace and
the houses of the people, and they [B]broke down the
walls of Jerusalem. 9 As for the rest of the people who
were left in the city, the [a,A]deserters who had gone
over to him and [B]the rest of the people who remained,
[C]Nebuzaradan the [D]captain of the bodyguard carried
them into exile in Babylon. 10 But some of the [A]poorest
people who had nothing, [A]Nebuzaradan the captain
of the bodyguard left behind in the land of Judah,
and gave them vineyards and fields [a]at that time.

38:15 [A]Luke 22:67, 68 38:16 [a]Lit *soul* [A]Jer 37:17; John 3:2 [B]Num 16:22; 27:16; Is 42:5; 57:16; Zech 12:1; Acts 17:25, 28 [C]Jer 34:20; 38:4-6 38:17 [a]Lit *your soul* [b]Lit *live* [A]Ps 80:7, 14; Amos 5:27 [B]1 Chr 17:24; Ezek 8:4 [C]2 Kin 24:12; 25:27-30; Jer 21:8-10; 27:12, 17; 38:2; 39:3 38:18 [A]Jer 27:8 [B]2 Kin 25:4-10; Jer 24:8-10; 32:3-5; 37:8; 38:3 [C]Jer 32:4; 34:3 38:19 [a]Lit *fallen* [A]Is 51:12, 13; 57:11; John 12:42; 19:12, 13 [B]Jer 39:9 [C]2 Chr 30:10; Neh 4:1; Jer 38:22 38:20 [a]Lit *listen to the voice of* [b]Lit *your soul* [A]2 Chr 20:20; Jer 11:4, 8; 26:13; Dan 4:27; Acts 26:29 [B]Jer 7:23 [C]Gen 19:20; Is 55:3 38:22 [a]Or *princes* [b]Lit *The men of your peace* [A]Jer 6:12; 8:10; 43:6 38:23 [A]2 Kin 25:7; Jer 39:6; 41:10 [B]Jer 38:18 38:25 [A]Jer 38:4-6, 27 38:26 [A]Jer 37:20 38:27 [a]Lit *word* 38:28 [A]Ps 23:4; Jer 15:20, 21; 37:20, 21; 38:13; 39:13, 14 39:1 [a]Ch 38:28b in Heb [b]Ch 39:1 in Heb [A]2 Kin 25:1-12; Jer 52:4; Ezek 24:1, 2 39:2 [A]2 Kin 25:4; Jer 52:7 39:3 [a]I.e. chief official [b]I.e. title of a high official [A]Jer 38:17 [B]Jer 21:4 39:4 [a]I.e. Jordan valley [A]2 Kin 25:4; Is 30:16; Jer 52:7; Amos 2:14 [B]2 Chr 32:5 39:5 [A]Jer 32:4, 5; 38:18, 23; 52:8 [B]Josh 4:13; 5:10 [C]2 Kin 23:33; Jer 52:9, 26, 27 39:6 [A]2 Kin 25:7; Jer 52:10 [B]Deut 28:34 [C]Jer 21:7; 24:8-10; 34:19-21 39:7 [A]2 Kin 25:7; Jer 52:11; Ezek 12:13 [B]Judg 16:21 [C]Jer 32:5 39:8 [A]2 Kin 25:9; Jer 21:10; 38:18; 52:13 [B]2 Kin 25:10; Neh 1:3; Jer 52:14 39:9 [a]Lit *fallers who had fallen* [A]Jer 38:19; 52:15 [B]Jer 24:8 [C]2 Kin 25:11, 20; Jer 39:13; 40:1; 52:12-16, 26 [D]Gen 37:36 39:10 [a]Lit *on that day* [A]2 Kin 25:12; Jer 52:16

38:22 close friends have misled ... you. Palace women, taken over by Babylonians, heaped cutting ridicule on Zedekiah for listening to friends whose counsel failed him, who left him helpless as one with his feet stuck in mire.

38:27 these words ... the king ... commanded. Jeremiah did not fall into lying deception here. What he said was true, though he did not divulge all details of the conversation, to which the princes had no right.

39:1, 2 in the ninth year ... the eleventh year. Cf. 34:1, and *see note there*. Cf. 52:1–7; 2Ki 25:1–4. This siege of 30 months involved the enemy's surrounding the city walls, cutting off all entrances and exits, all food supplies, and as much water as possible, so that famine, thirst, and disease would eventually weaken the beleaguered city dwellers and they could be easily conquered.

39:3 sat down at the Middle Gate. This expressed full military occupation of the city, since this gate was between the upper city (Mt. Zion) and the lower city to the N.

39:5 Riblah in ... Hamath. Nebuchadnezzar's command headquarters were 230 mi. to the N of Jerusalem. **passed sentence.** He dealt with the king as a common criminal. The king had violated his oath (cf. 2Ch 36:13; Eze 17:13–19).

39:6–10 Cf. 52:12–16; 2Ki 25:8–12.

39:7 blinded Zedekiah's eyes. This reconciles 32:4 with Eze 12:13.

JEREMIAH SPARED

11 Now Nebuchadnezzar king of Babylon gave orders about [A]Jeremiah through Nebuzaradan the captain of the bodyguard, saying, 12 "Take him and [a]look after him, and [A]do nothing harmful to him, but rather deal with him just as he tells you." 13 So Nebuzaradan the captain of the bodyguard sent *word,* along with Nebushazban the [a]Rab-saris, and Nergal-sar-ezer the [b]Rab-mag, and all the leading officers of the king of Babylon; 14 they even sent and [A]took Jeremiah out of the court of the guardhouse and entrusted him to [B]Gedaliah, the son of [C]Ahikam, the son of Shaphan, to take him home. So he stayed among the people.

15 Now the word of the LORD had come to Jeremiah while he was [A]confined in the court of the guardhouse, saying, 16 "Go and speak to [A]Ebed-melech the Ethiopian, saying, 'Thus says the LORD of hosts, the God of Israel, "Behold, I am about to bring My words on this city [B]for disaster and not for [a]prosperity; and they will [C]take place before you on that day. 17 But I will [A]deliver you on that day," declares the LORD, "and you will not be given into the hand of the men whom you dread. 18 For I will certainly rescue you, and you will not fall by the sword; but you will have your *own* [A]life as booty, because you have [B]trusted in Me," declares the LORD.' "

JEREMIAH REMAINS IN JUDAH

40 The word which came to Jeremiah from the LORD after [A]Nebuzaradan captain of the bodyguard had released him from [B]Ramah, when he had taken him bound in [C]chains among all the exiles of Jerusalem and Judah who were being exiled to Babylon. 2 Now the captain of the bodyguard had taken Jeremiah and said to him, "The [A]LORD your God promised this calamity against this place; 3 and the LORD has brought *it* on and done just as He promised. Because you *people* [A]sinned against the LORD and did not listen to His voice, therefore this thing has happened to you. 4 But now, behold, I am [A]freeing you today from the chains which are on your hands. If [a]you would prefer to come with me to Babylon, come *along,* and I will [b]look after you; but if [c]you would prefer not to come with me to Babylon, [d]never mind. Look, the [B]whole land is before you; go wherever it seems good and right for you to go." 5 As [a]Jeremiah was still not going back, [b]*he said,* "Go on back then to [A]Gedaliah the son of Ahikam, the son of Shaphan, whom the king of Babylon has [B]appointed over the cities of Judah, and stay with him among the people; or else go anywhere it seems right for you to go." So the captain of the bodyguard gave him a [C]ration and a [D]gift and let him go. 6 Then Jeremiah went to [A]Mizpah to [B]Gedaliah the son of Ahikam and stayed with him among the people who were left in the land.

7 [A]Now all the [a]commanders of the forces that were in the field, they and their men, heard that the king of Babylon had appointed Gedaliah the son of Ahikam over the land and that he had put him in charge of the men, women and [b]children, those of the [B]poorest of the land who had not been exiled to Babylon. 8 So they came to Gedaliah at Mizpah, along with [A]Ishmael the son of Nethaniah, and [B]Johanan and Jonathan the sons of Kareah, and Seraiah the son of Tanhumeth, and the sons of Ephai the [C]Netophathite, and [D]Jezaniah the son of the [E]Maacathite, *both* they and their men. 9 Then Gedaliah the son of Ahikam, the son of Shaphan, [A]swore to them and to their men, saying, "[B]Do not be afraid of serving the Chaldeans; stay in the land and serve the king of Babylon, that it may go well with you. 10 Now as for me, behold, I am going to stay at Mizpah to [A]stand *for you* before the Chaldeans who come to us; but as for you, [B]gather in wine and [C]summer fruit and oil and put *them* in your *storage* vessels, and live in your cities that you have taken over." 11 Likewise, also all the Jews who were in [A]Moab and among the sons of [B]Ammon and in [C]Edom and who were in all the *other* countries, heard that the king of Babylon had left a remnant for Judah, and that he had appointed over them Gedaliah the son of Ahikam, the son of Shaphan. 12 Then all the Jews [A]returned from all the places to which they had been driven away and came to the land of Judah, to Gedaliah at Mizpah, and gathered in wine and summer fruit in great abundance.

13 Now Johanan the son of Kareah and all the commanders of the forces that were in the field came to Gedaliah at Mizpah 14 and said to him, "Are you well aware that Baalis the king of the sons of [A]Ammon has sent Ishmael the son of Nethaniah to take your life?" But Gedaliah the son of Ahikam did

39:11 [A]Job 5:15, 16; Jer 1:8; 15:20, 21; Acts 24:23 39:12 [a]Lit *set your eyes on* [A]Ps 105:14, 15; Prov 16:7; 21:1; 1 Pet 3:13 39:13 [a]I.e. chief official [b]I.e. title of a high official 39:14 [A]Jer 38:28; 40:1-6 [B]Jer 40:5 [C]2 Kin 22:12, 14; 2 Chr 34:20; Jer 26:24 39:15 [A]Jer 38:28 39:16 [a]Lit *good* [A]Jer 38:7 [B]Jer 21:10; Dan 9:12; Zech 1:6 [C]Ps 91:8 39:17 [A]Ps 41:1, 2; 50:15 39:18 [A]Jer 21:9; 38:2; 45:5 [B]Ps 34:22; Jer 17:7, 8 40:1 [A]Jer 39:9, 11 [B]Jer 31:15 [C]Acts 12:6, 7; 21:13; 28:20; Eph 6:20 40:2 [A]Lev 26:14-38; Deut 28:15-68; 29:24-28; 31:17; 32:19-25; Jer 22:8, 9 40:3 [A]Jer 50:7; Dan 9:11; Rom 2:5 40:4 [a]Lit *it is good in your eyes* [b]Lit *set my eyes on* [c]Lit *it is evil in your eyes* [d]Lit *refrain!* [A]Jer 39:11, 12 [B]Gen 13:9; 20:15; 47:6 40:5 [a]Lit *he* [b]I.e. Nebuzaradan [A]Jer 39:14 [B]2 Kin 25:23 [C]Jer 52:34 [D]2 Kin 8:7-9 40:6 [A]Judg 20:1; 21:1; 1 Sam 7:5; 2 Chr 16:6 [B]Jer 39:14 40:7 [a]Or *princes* [b]Lit *infants* [A]2 Kin 25:23 [B]Jer 39:10; 52:16 40:8 [A]Jer 40:14; 41:2 [B]Jer 40:13, 15; 42:1; 43:2 [C]2 Sam 23:28, 29; Ezra 2:22; Neh 7:26 [D]Jer 42:1 [E]Deut 3:14; Josh 12:5; 2 Sam 10:6, 8 40:9 [A]1 Sam 20:16, 17; 2 Kin 25:24 [B]Jer 27:11; 38:17-20 40:10 [A]Deut 1:38; 1 Kin 10:8; Jer 35:19 [B]Deut 16:13; Jer 39:10 [C]Is 16:9; Jer 40:12; 48:32 40:11 [A]Num 22:1; 25:1, 2; Is 16:4; Jer 9:26 [B]1 Sam 11:1; 12:12 [C]Gen 36:8; Is 11:14 40:12 [A]Jer 43:5 40:14 [A]1 Sam 11:1-3; 2 Sam 10:1-6; Jer 25:21; 41:10

39:11, 12 Jeremiah's prophecies were known to Nebuchadnezzar through defectors (v. 9; 38:19), and also through Jews taken to Babylon with Jeconiah (cf. 40:2).

39:14 took Jeremiah out of the court. This was given as a general summary, whereas 40:1–6 gave more detail concerning the prophet who was first carried to Ramah (40:1) with the other captives before being released (40:2–5). "Gedaliah" was a former supporter of Jeremiah (26:24) and chief among the defectors, loyal to Nebuchadnezzar, so he was made governor (40:5) over the remnant left in the land.

39:15–18 Cf. 38:7–13, and *see note there.*

40:2, 3 The pagan captain understood the judgment of God better than the leaders of Judah.

40:4, 5 The captain did exactly as Nebuchadnezzar had told him in 39:12.

40:5, 6 Jeremiah chose to go to Gedaliah, the newly appointed governor at Mizpah several mi. N of Jerusalem. Gedaliah was soon to be assassinated (cf. 41:1–3).

40:7 commanders ... in the field. The leaders of Judah's army scattered in fear.

40:9–12 God had tempered the severity of judgment by allowing a remnant to prosper.

40:13–16 Johanan. This man's fair warning to Gedaliah of Ishmael's death plot went unheeded.

not believe them. 15Then Johanan the son of Kareah
spoke secretly to Gedaliah in Mizpah, saying, "[A]Let
me go and kill Ishmael the son of Nethaniah, and not
a man will know! Why should he [B]take your life, so
that all the Jews who are gathered to you would be
scattered and the [C]remnant of Judah would perish?"
16But Gedaliah the son of Ahikam said to Johanan
the son of Kareah, "[A]Do not do this thing, for you
are telling a lie about Ishmael."

GEDALIAH IS MURDERED

41 [A]In the seventh month [B]Ishmael the son of
Nethaniah, the son of Elishama, of the royal
[a]family and *one* of the chief officers of the king,
along with ten men, came to Mizpah to [C]Gedaliah
the son of Ahikam. While they [D]were eating bread
together there in Mizpah, 2Ishmael the son of Nethaniah and the ten men who were with him arose
and [A]struck down Gedaliah the son of Ahikam, the
son of Shaphan, with the sword and [B]put to death
the one [C]whom the king of Babylon had appointed
over the land. 3Ishmael also struck down all the
Jews who were with him, *that is* with Gedaliah at
Mizpah, and the Chaldeans who were found there,
the men of war.
4Now it happened on the [a]next day after the killing of Gedaliah, when no one knew about *it,* 5that
eighty men [A]came from [B]Shechem, from [C]Shiloh,
and from [D]Samaria with [E]their beards shaved off
and their clothes torn and [a]their bodies [F]gashed,
having grain offerings and incense in their hands
to bring to the [G]house of the LORD. 6Then Ishmael
the son of Nethaniah went out from Mizpah to meet
them, [A]weeping as he went; and as he met them,
he said to them, "Come to Gedaliah the son of Ahikam!" 7Yet it turned out that as soon as they came
inside the city, Ishmael the son of Nethaniah and
the men that were with him [A]slaughtered them *and*
cast them into the cistern. 8But ten men who were
found among them said to Ishmael, "Do not put us
to death; for we have [A]stores of wheat, barley, oil and
honey hidden in the field." So he refrained and did
not put them to death along with their companions.
9Now as for the cistern where Ishmael had cast
all the corpses of the men whom he had struck
down [a]because of Gedaliah, it was the [A]one that
King Asa had made on [B]account of Baasha, king
of Israel; Ishmael the son of Nethaniah filled it
with the slain. 10Then Ishmael took captive all the
[A]remnant of the people who were in Mizpah, the
[B]king's daughters and all the people who were left
in Mizpah, whom Nebuzaradan the captain of the
bodyguard had put under the charge of Gedaliah the
son of Ahikam; thus Ishmael the son of Nethaniah
took them captive and proceeded to cross over to
the sons of [C]Ammon.

JOHANAN RESCUES THE PEOPLE

11But Johanan the son of Kareah and all the [A]com-
manders of the forces that were with him heard of
all the evil that Ishmael the son of Nethaniah had
done. 12So they took all the men and went to [A]fight
with Ishmael the son of Nethaniah and they found
him by the [B]great [a]pool that is in Gibeon. 13Now as
soon as all the people who were with Ishmael saw
Johanan the son of Kareah and the commanders
of the forces that were with him, they were glad.
14So all the people whom Ishmael had taken captive
from Mizpah turned around and came back, and
went to Johanan the son of Kareah. 15But Ishmael
the son of Nethaniah [A]escaped from Johanan with
eight men and went to the sons of Ammon. 16Then
Johanan the son of Kareah and all the commanders
of the forces that were with him took from Mizpah
[A]all the remnant of the people whom he had [a]re-
covered from Ishmael the son of Nethaniah, after
he had struck down Gedaliah the son of Ahikam,
that is, the men who were [b]soldiers, *the* women, *the*
[c]children, and *the* eunuchs, whom he had brought
back from Gibeon. 17And they went and stayed in
[a,A]Geruth Chimham, which is beside Bethlehem, in
order to [B]proceed into Egypt 18because of the Chaldeans; for they were [A]afraid of them, since Ishmael
the son of Nethaniah had struck down Gedaliah the
son of Ahikam, whom [B]the king of Babylon had appointed over the land.

WARNING AGAINST GOING TO EGYPT

42 Then all the [a]commanders of the forces, [A]Joha-
nan the son of Kareah, Jezaniah the son of Hoshaiah, and all the people [B]both small and great approached 2and said to Jeremiah the prophet, "Please
let our [A]petition [a]come before you, and [B]pray for us
to the LORD your God, *that is* for all this remnant;
because we are left *but* a [C]few out of many, as your
own eyes *now* see us, 3that the LORD your God may

40:15 [A]1 Sam 26:8 [B]2 Sam 21:17 [C]Jer 42:2 40:16 [A]Matt 10:16; 1 Cor 13:5 41:1 [a]Lit *seed* [A]2 Kin 25:25 [B]Jer 40:8, 14 [C]Jer 39:14; 40:5, 6 [D]Ps 41:9; Jer 40:13, 14 41:2 [A]2 Sam 3:27; 20:9, 10; 2 Kin 25:25; Ps 41:9; 109:5; John 13:18 [B]2 Kin 25:25 [C]Jer 40:5 41:4 [a]Or *second* 41:5 [a]Lit *having cut themselves* [A]2 Kin 10:13, 14 [B]Gen 33:18; 37:12; Judg 9:1; 1 Kin 12:1, 25 [C]Josh 18:1; Judg 18:31; 1 Sam 3:21; Ps 78:60 [D]1 Kin 16:24, 29 [E]Lev 19:27; Deut 14:1 [F]Deut 14:1; Jer 16:6 [G]1 Sam 1:7; 2 Kin 25:9 41:6 [A]2 Sam 3:16; Jer 50:4 41:7 [A]Ps 55:23; Is 59:7; Ezek 22:27; 33:24, 26 41:8 [A]Is 45:3 41:9 [a]Or *by the side of* [A]1 Kin 15:17-22; 2 Chr 16:1-6 [B]Judg 6:2; 1 Sam 13:6; 2 Sam 17:9; Heb 11:38 41:10 [A]Jer 40:11, 12 [B]Jer 43:6 [C]Neh 2:10, 19; 4:7; Jer 40:14 41:11 [A]Jer 40:7, 8, 13-16 41:12 [a]Lit *waters* [A]Gen 14:14-16; 1 Sam 30:1-8, 18, 20 [B]2 Sam 2:13 41:15 [A]1 Sam 30:17; 1 Kin 20:20; Job 21:30; Prov 28:17 41:16 [a]Lit *brought back* [b]Lit *men of war* [c]Lit *infants* [A]Jer 42:8; 43:4-7 41:17 [a]Or *the lodging place of Chimham* [A]2 Sam 19:37, 38, 40 [B]Jer 42:14 41:18 [A]Is 51:12, 13; 57:11; Jer 42:11, 16; 43:2, 3; Luke 12:4, 5 [B]Jer 40:5 42:1 [a]Or *princes* [A]Jer 40:8, 13; 41:11, 18 [B]Jer 6:13; 8:10; 42:8; 44:12; Acts 8:10 42:2 [a]Lit *fall* [A]Jer 36:7; 37:20 [B]Ex 8:28; 1 Sam 7:8; 12:19; 1 Kin 13:6; Is 37:4; Jer 37:3; 42:20; Acts 8:24; James 5:16 [C]Lev 26:22; Deut 28:62; Is 1:9; Lam 1:1

41:1–4 In the second month after the city of Jerusalem had been burned, the careless governor entertained Ishmael's group and invited a massacre.

41:5 eighty men. Most likely, this group had come in mourning over the destruction of Jerusalem, and so were led to slaughter. Ishmael did amazing damage with only 10 men (v. 1). Eventually they must have acquired more to do than what is described in v. 10.

41:9 Asa. He ruled Judah (ca. 911–873 B.C.). Cf. 1Ki 15:16–22.

41:12–15 went to fight with Ishmael. Johanan heard of Ishmael's murders and taking people captive, and brought men to stop him. They freed the captives (vv. 13, 14), but Ishmael and his men escaped (v. 15).

41:12 pool … Gibeon. Cf. 2Sa 2:13.

42:1, 2 Jeremiah. He probably was one carried off from Mizpah, freed, and dwelt with Johanan (41:16).

42:1–6 pray for us. The remnant in Judah asked Jeremiah to pray to God and find His

tell us the [A]way in which we should walk and the thing that we should do." 4 Then Jeremiah the prophet said to them, "I have heard *you*. Behold, I am going to [A]pray to the LORD your God in accordance with your words; and I will tell you the whole [a]message which the [B]LORD will answer you. I will [C]not keep back a word from you." 5 Then they said to Jeremiah, "May the [A]LORD be a true and faithful witness against us if we do not act in accordance with the whole [a]message with which the LORD your God will send you to us. 6 Whether *it is* [a]pleasant or [b]unpleasant, we will [A]listen to the voice of the LORD our God to whom we are sending you, so that it may go [B]well with us when we listen to the voice of the LORD our God."

7 Now at the [A]end of ten days the word of the LORD came to Jeremiah. 8 Then he called for Johanan the son of Kareah and all the [a]commanders of the forces that were with him, and for all the people both small and great, 9 and said to them, "Thus [A]says the LORD the God of Israel, to whom you sent me to present your petition before Him: 10 'If you will indeed stay in this land, then I will [A]build you up and not tear you down, and I will plant you and not uproot you; for I [a]will [B]relent concerning the calamity that I have inflicted on you. 11 [A]Do not be afraid of the king of Babylon, whom you are *now* fearing; do not be afraid of him,' declares the LORD, 'for [B]I am with you to save you and deliver you from his hand. 12 I will also show you compassion, so that [A]he will have compassion on you and restore you to your own soil. 13 But if you are going to say, "We will [A]not stay in this land," so as not to listen to the voice of the LORD your God, 14 saying, "No, but we will [A]go to the land of Egypt, where we will not see war or [B]hear the sound of a trumpet or hunger for bread, and we will stay there"; 15 then [a]in that case listen to the word of the LORD, O remnant of Judah. Thus says the LORD of hosts, the God of Israel, "If you really set your [b]mind to enter [A]Egypt and go in to reside there, 16 then the [A]sword, which you are afraid of, will overtake you there in the land of Egypt; and the famine, about which you are anxious, will follow closely after you there *in* Egypt, and you will die there. 17 So all the men who set their [a]mind to go to Egypt to reside there will die by the [A]sword, by famine and by pestilence; and they will [B]have no survivors or refugees from the calamity that I am going to bring on them." ' "

18 For thus says the LORD of hosts, the God of Israel, "As My [A]anger and wrath have been poured out on the inhabitants of Jerusalem, so My wrath will be poured out on you when you enter Egypt. And you will become a [B]curse, an object of horror, an imprecation and a reproach; and [C]you will see this place no more." 19 The LORD has spoken to you, O remnant of Judah, "Do not [A]go into Egypt!" You should clearly [B]understand that today I have [C]testified against you. 20 For you have *only* [a,A]deceived yourselves; for it is you who sent me to the LORD your God, saying, "Pray for us to the LORD our God; and whatever the LORD our God says, tell us so, and we will do it." 21 So I have [A]told you today, but you have [B]not [a]obeyed the LORD your God, even in whatever He has sent me to *tell* you. 22 Therefore you should now clearly understand that you will [A]die by the sword, by famine and by pestilence, in the [B]place where you wish to go to reside.

IN EGYPT JEREMIAH WARNS OF JUDGMENT

43 But as soon as Jeremiah, whom the LORD their God had sent, had [A]finished telling all the people all the words of the LORD their God—that is, all these words— 2 Azariah the [A]son of Hoshaiah, and Johanan the son of Kareah, and all the arrogant men said to Jeremiah, "You are [B]telling a lie! The LORD our God has not sent you to say, 'You are not to enter Egypt to reside there'; 3 but [A]Baruch the son of Neriah is inciting you against us to give us over into the hand of the Chaldeans, so they will put us to death or exile us to Babylon." 4 So [A]Johanan the son of Kareah and all the [a]commanders of the forces, and all the people, [B]did not obey the voice of the LORD to [C]stay in the land of Judah. 5 But Johanan the son of Kareah and all the [a]commanders of the forces took the [A]entire remnant of Judah who had returned from all the nations to which they had been driven away, in order to reside in the land of Judah— 6 the men, the women, the [a]children, the [A]king's daughters and [B]every person that Nebuzaradan the captain of the bodyguard had left with Gedaliah the son of Ahikam [b]and grandson of Shaphan, together with [C]Jeremiah the prophet and Baruch the son of Neriah— 7 and they entered the land of Egypt (for they did not obey the voice of the LORD) and went in as far as [A]Tahpanhes.

42:3 [A]Ps 86:11; Prov 3:6; Jer 6:16; Mic 4:2 **42:4** [a]Lit *word* [A]Ex 8:29; 1 Sam 12:23 [B]1 Kin 22:14; Jer 23:28 [C]1 Sam 3:17, 18; Ps 40:10; Acts 20:20 **42:5** [a]Lit *word* [A]Gen 31:50; Judg 11:10; Jer 43:2; Mic 1:2; Mal 2:14; 3:5 **42:6** [a]Lit *good* [b]Lit *evil* [A]Ex 24:7; Deut 5:27; Josh 24:24 [B]Deut 5:29, 33; 6:3; Jer 7:23 **42:7** [A]Ps 27:14; Is 30:18 **42:8** [a]Or *princes* **42:9** [A]2 Kin 19:4, 6, 20; 22:15 **42:10** [a]Or *shall have changed my mind about* [A]Jer 24:6; 31:28; 33:7; Ezek 36:36 [B]Jer 18:7, 8; Hos 11:8; Joel 2:13; Amos 7:3, 6; Jon 3:10; 4:2 **42:11** [A]Jer 1:8; 27:12, 17; 41:18 [B]Num 14:9; 2 Chr 32:7, 8; Ps 46:7, 11; 118:6; Is 8:9, 10; 43:2, 5; Jer 1:19; 15:20; Rom 8:31 **42:12** [A]Neh 1:11; Ps 106:46; Prov 16:7 **42:13** [A]Ex 5:2; Jer 44:16 **42:14** [A]Is 31:1; Jer 41:17 [B]Ex 16:3; Num 11:4; Jer 4:19, 21 **42:15** [a]Lit *now therefore* [b]Lit *face* [A]Deut 17:16; Jer 42:17; 44:12-14 **42:16** [A]Jer 44:13, 27; Ezek 11:8; Amos 9:1-4 **42:17** [a]Lit *face* [A]Jer 24:10; 38:2; 42:22; 44:13 [B]Jer 44:14, 28 **42:18** [A]2 Chr 36:16-19; Jer 7:20; 33:5; 39:1-9 [B]Deut 29:21; Is 65:15; Jer 18:16; 24:9; 29:18; 44:12 [C]Jer 22:10, 27 **42:19** [A]Deut 17:16; Is 30:1-7 [B]Ezek 2:5 [C]Neh 9:26, 29, 30 **42:20** [a]Or *acted errantly in your souls* [A]Jer 43:2; Ezek 14:3 **42:21** [a]Lit *listened to the voice of* [A]Deut 11:26; Jer 43:1; Ezek 2:7; Zech 7:11; Acts 20:26, 27 [B]Jer 43:4 **42:22** [A]Jer 43:11; Ezek 6:11 [B]Hos 9:6 **43:1** [A]Jer 26:8; 51:63 **43:2** [A]Jer 42:1 [B]2 Chr 36:13; Is 7:9; Jer 5:12, 13; 42:5 **43:3** [A]Jer 36:4, 10, 26, 32; 43:6; 45:1-3 **43:4** [a]Or *princes* [A]Jer 42:8 [B]2 Chr 25:16; Jer 42:5, 6; 44:5 [C]Ps 37:3; Jer 42:10-12 **43:5** [a]Or *princes* [A]Jer 40:11 **43:6** [a]Lit *infants* [b]Lit *the son* [A]Jer 41:10 [B]Jer 39:10; 40:7 [C]Eccl 9:1, 2; Lam 3:1 **43:7** [A]Jer 2:16; 44:1

will on what they should do. They promised to obey (v. 6).

42:7–12 After 10 days of prayer Jeremiah reported God's Word, telling them to remain in the land under God's protection (v. 10).

42:10 I will relent. By this God means "I am satisfied with the punishment inflicted if you do not add new offenses."

42:13–19 The prophet gave explicit warning (v. 19) not to go to Egypt where they would be exposed to corrupting paganism.

42:20 They were hypocrites who already desired Egypt.

43:1–7 as soon as Jeremiah ... had finished telling. The incorrigible, disobedient leaders accused him of deceit and forced Jeremiah and the remnant to go to Egypt, despite the fact that all his prophecies regarding Babylon had come to pass. In so doing, they went out of God's protection into His judgment, as all who are disobedient to His Word do.

43:3, 6 Baruch. The faithful recorder of chap. 36 was still with Jeremiah, kept safe as God promised him at least 20 years earlier (45:5; cf. 605 B.C. in v. 1).

43:7 Tahpanhes. A location in the eastern delta region of Egypt.

8 Then the word of the LORD came to Jeremiah
in [A]Tahpanhes, saying, 9 "Take *some* large stones
in your [a]hands and hide them in the mortar in
the [b]brick *terrace* which is at the entrance of
Pharaoh's [c]palace in Tahpanhes, in the sight of
[d]some *of the* Jews; 10 and say to them, 'Thus says
the LORD of hosts, the God of Israel, "Behold, I
am going to send and get [A]Nebuchadnezzar the
king of Babylon, [B]My servant, and I am going to
set his throne *right* over these stones that I have
hidden; and he will spread his [C]canopy over them.
11 He will also come and [A]strike the land of Egypt;
those who are *meant* for death *will be given over*
to death, and those for captivity to captivity, and
[B]those for the sword to the sword. 12 And [a]I shall
set fire to the temples of the [A]gods of Egypt, and
he will burn them and take them captive. So he
will [B]wrap himself with the land of Egypt as a
shepherd wraps himself with his garment, and
he will depart from there safely. 13 He will also
shatter the [a]obelisks of [b]Heliopolis, which is in
the land of Egypt; and the temples of the gods of
Egypt he will burn with fire." ' "

CONQUEST OF EGYPT PREDICTED

44 The word that came to Jeremiah for all the
Jews living in the land of Egypt, those who
were living in [A]Migdol, [B]Tahpanhes, [C]Memphis,
and the land of [D]Pathros, saying, 2 "Thus says the
LORD of hosts, the God of Israel, 'You yourselves
have seen all the calamity that I have brought on
Jerusalem and all the cities of Judah; and behold,
this day they are in [A]ruins and no one lives in them,
3 [A]because of their wickedness which they committed so as to [B]provoke Me to anger by continuing to
[C]burn [a]sacrifices *and* to [D]serve other gods whom
they had not known, *neither* they, you, nor your
fathers. 4 Yet I [A]sent you all My servants the prophets, [a]again and again, saying, "Oh, do not do this
[B]abominable thing which I hate." 5 But [A]they did
not listen or incline their ears to turn from their
wickedness, so as not to burn [a]sacrifices to other
gods. 6 Therefore My [A]wrath and My anger were
poured out and burned in the [B]cities of Judah and
in the streets of Jerusalem, so they have become a
ruin and a [C]desolation as it is this day. 7 Now then
thus says the LORD God of hosts, the God of Israel,
"Why are you [A]doing great harm to yourselves,
so as to [B]cut off from you man and woman, child
and infant, from among Judah, leaving yourselves
without remnant, 8 [A]provoking Me to anger with the
works of your hands, [B]burning [a]sacrifices to other
gods in the land of Egypt, where you are entering
to reside, so that you might be cut off and become
a [C]curse and a reproach among all the nations of
the earth? 9 Have you forgotten the [A]wickedness of
your fathers, the wickedness of the kings of Judah,
and the wickedness of their wives, your own wickedness, and the wickedness of your wives, which
they committed in the land of Judah and in the
streets of Jerusalem? 10 But they [A]have not become
[a]contrite even to this day, nor have they feared nor
[B]walked in My law or My statutes, which I have set
before you and before your fathers." '

11 "Therefore thus says the LORD of hosts, the
God of Israel, 'Behold, I am going to [A]set My face
against you for [a]woe, even to cut off all Judah.
12 And I will [A]take away the remnant of Judah who
have set their [a]mind on entering the land of Egypt
to reside there, and they will all [b,B]meet their end in
the land of Egypt; they will fall by the sword *and*
meet their end by famine. Both small and great
will die by the sword and famine; and they will
become a [C]curse, an object of horror, an imprecation and a reproach. 13 And I will [A]punish those
who live in the land of Egypt, as I have punished
Jerusalem, with the sword, with famine and with
pestilence. 14 So there will be [A]no refugees or survivors for the remnant of Judah who have entered
the land of Egypt to reside there and then to return
to the land of Judah, to which they are [a,B]longing
to return and live; for none will [C]return except *a*
few refugees.' "

15 Then [A]all the men who were aware that their
wives were burning [a]sacrifices to other gods, along
with all the women who were standing by, *as* a large
assembly, [b]including all the people who were living
in Pathros in the land of Egypt, responded to Jeremiah, saying, 16 "As for the [a,A]message that you have
spoken to us in the name of the LORD, [B]we are not

43:8 [A]Jer 2:16; 44:1; 46:14; Ezek 30:18 43:9 [a]Lit *hand* [b]Or *brickwork* [c]Lit *house* [d]Lit *men* 43:10 [A]Jer 25:9, 11 [B]Is 44:28; 45:1; Jer 25:9; 27:6 [C]Ps 18:11; 27:5; 31:20 43:11 [A]Is 19:1-25; Jer 25:15-19; 44:13; 46:1, 2, 13-26; Ezek 29:19, 20 [B]Jer 15:2 43:12 [a]Some ancient versions read *He will set* [A]Ex 12:12; Is 19:1; Jer 46:25; Ezek 30:13 [B]Ps 104:2; 109:18, 19; Is 49:18 43:13 [a]Or *stone pillars* [b]Heb *Beth-shemesh;* i.e. the house of the sun-god 44:1 [A]Ex 14:2; Jer 46:14 [B]Jer 43:7; Ezek 30:18 [C]Is 19:13; Jer 2:16; 46:14; Ezek 30:13, 16; Hos 9:6 [D]Is 11:11; Ezek 29:14; 30:14 44:2 [A]Is 6:11; Jer 4:7; 9:11; 34:22; Mic 3:12 44:3 [a]Or *incense* [A]Neh 9:33; Jer 2:17-19; 44:23; Ezek 8:17, 18; Dan 9:5 [B]Is 3:8; Jer 7:19; 32:30-32; 44:8 [C]Jer 19:4 [D]Deut 13:6; 29:26; 32:17 44:4 [a]Lit *rising early and sending* [A]Jer 7:13, 25; 25:4; 26:5; 29:19; 35:15; Zech 7:7 [B]Jer 16:18; 32:34, 35; Ezek 8:10 44:5 [a]Or *incense* [A]Jer 11:8, 10; 13:10 44:6 [A]Is 51:17-20; Jer 42:18; Ezek 8:18 [B]Jer 7:17, 34 [C]Jer 4:27; 34:22 44:7 [A]Num 16:38; Jer 26:19; Ezek 33:11; Hab 2:10 [B]Jer 3:24; 9:21; 51:22 44:8 [a]Or *incense* [A]2 Kin 17:15-17; Jer 25:6, 7; 44:3; 1 Cor 10:21, 22 [B]Jer 7:9; 11:12, 17; 44:3; Hos 4:13; Hab 1:16 [C]1 Kin 9:7, 8; 2 Chr 7:20; Jer 42:18 44:9 [A]Jer 7:9, 10, 17, 18; 44:17, 21 44:10 [a]Lit *crushed* [A]Jer 6:15; 8:12 [B]Jer 26:4; 32:23; 44:23 44:11 [a]Lit *evil* [A]Lev 17:10; 20:5, 6; 26:17; Jer 21:10; Amos 9:4 44:12 [a]Lit *face* [b]Lit *be finished* [A]Jer 42:15-18, 22 [B]Is 1:28; Jer 16:4; 44:7 [C]Is 65:15; Jer 18:16; 24:9; 26:6; 29:18; 42:18; Zech 8:13 44:13 [A]Jer 11:22; 44:27, 28 44:14 [a]Lit *lifting up their soul* [A]Jer 22:10; 44:27 [B]Jer 22:26, 27 [C]Is 4:2; 10:20; Jer 44:28; Rom 9:27 44:15 [a]Or *incense* [b]Lit *and* [A]Prov 11:21; Is 1:5; Jer 5:1-5 44:16 [a]Lit *word* [A]Jer 43:2 [B]Prov 1:24-27; Jer 11:8, 10; 13:10

43:9–13 Take … large stones. Stones, placed in the mortar of the brick pavement in the courtyard entrance of the Pharaoh's house, signaled the place where the conquering king of Babylon would bring devastation on Egypt and establish his throne. This was fulfilled in an invasion ca. 568/67 B.C.

43:12 as a shepherd wraps himself with his garment. A very simple and easy task describes how quickly and easily Nebuchadnezzar will conquer Egypt.

43:13 obelisks of Heliopolis. Heb. "house of the sun." This refers to a temple for the worship of the sun. Located N of Memphis, E of the Nile, these obelisks were said to be 60–100 ft. high.

44:1 The word that came. The unrelenting iniquity of the Jews called for yet another prophecy of judgment on them in Egypt.

44:2–6 The prophet summarized what had occurred in Judah as a basis for what he predicted coming on the refugees in Egypt.

44:7, 9, 10 Incredibly, after being spared death in Judah, they pursued it by their sin in Egypt.

44:11–14 Ironically, the Jews taken to Babylon were weaned from idolatry and restored to their land; those taken to Egypt for their obstinate idolatry perished there.

44:14 except *a few* refugees. A small number (v. 28) who fled before the arrival of Babylonian armies were spared.

44:15 wives. The idolatry apparently began with the women.

going to listen to you! 17 But rather we will certainly
[A]carry out every word that has proceeded from our
mouths, [a]by burning [b]sacrifices to the [B]queen of
heaven and pouring out drink offerings to her, just
as [C]we ourselves, our forefathers, our kings and our
princes did in the cities of Judah and in the streets
of Jerusalem; for *then* we had [D]plenty of [c]food and
were well off and saw no [d]misfortune. 18 But since we
stopped burning [a]sacrifices to the queen of heaven
and pouring out drink offerings to her, we have
[A]lacked everything and have [b]met our end by the
sword and by famine." 19 "And," *said the women,*
"when we were [A]burning [a]sacrifices to the queen
of heaven and [b]were pouring out drink offerings
to her, was it [B]without our husbands that we made
for her *sacrificial* cakes [c]in her image and poured
out drink offerings to her?"

CALAMITY FOR THE JEWS

20 Then Jeremiah said to all the people, to the
men and women—even to all the people who were
giving him *such* an answer—saying, 21 "As for the
[a,A]smoking sacrifices that you burned in the cities
of Judah and in the [B]streets of Jerusalem, you and
your forefathers, your kings and your princes, and
the people of the land, did not the LORD [C]remem-
ber them and did not *all this* come into His [b]mind?
22 So the LORD was [A]no longer able to endure *it,*
[B]because of the evil of your deeds, because of the
abominations which you have committed; thus
your land has become a [C]ruin, an object of horror
and a curse, without an inhabitant, as *it is* this day.
23 Because you have burned [a]sacrifices and have
sinned against the LORD and [A]not obeyed the voice
of the LORD or [B]walked in His law, His statutes or His
testimonies, therefore this [C]calamity has befallen
you, as *it has* this day."
24 Then Jeremiah said to all the people, including
all the women, "[A]Hear the word of the LORD, all Judah who are [B]in the land of Egypt, 25 thus says the
LORD of hosts, the God of Israel, as follows: 'As for
you and your wives, you have spoken with your
mouths and fulfilled *it* with your hands, saying,
"We will [A]certainly perform our vows that we have
vowed, to burn [a]sacrifices to the queen of heaven
and pour out drink offerings to her." [b,B]Go ahead
and confirm your vows, and certainly perform your
vows!' 26 [a]Nevertheless hear the word of the LORD,
all Judah who are living in the land of Egypt, 'Behold, I have [A]sworn by My great name,' says the
LORD, '[B]never shall My name be invoked again by
the mouth of any man of Judah in all the land of
Egypt, saying, "[C]As the Lord [b]GOD lives." 27 Behold,
I am watching over them [A]for harm and not for
good, and [B]all the men of Judah who are in the land
of Egypt will [a]meet their end by the sword and by
famine until they [b]are completely gone. 28 [A]Those
who escape the sword will return out of the land of
Egypt to the land of Judah [a,B]few in number. Then
all the remnant of Judah who have gone to the land
of Egypt to reside there will know [C]whose word
will stand, Mine or theirs. 29 This will be the [A]sign
to you,' declares the LORD, 'that I am going to punish you in this place, so that you may know that
[B]My words will surely stand against you for harm.'
30 Thus says the LORD, 'Behold, I am going to give
over [A]Pharaoh Hophra king of Egypt to the hand
of his enemies, to the hand of those who seek his
life, just as I gave over [B]Zedekiah king of Judah to
the hand of Nebuchadnezzar king of Babylon, *who*
was his enemy and was seeking his life.' "

MESSAGE TO BARUCH

45 *This is* the message which Jeremiah the
prophet spoke to [A]Baruch the son of Neriah, when he had [B]written down these words in
a book [a]at Jeremiah's dictation, in the [C]fourth year
of Jehoiakim the son of Josiah, king of Judah, saying: 2 "Thus says the LORD the God of Israel to you,
O Baruch: 3 'You said, "Ah, woe is me! For the LORD
has added sorrow to my pain; I am [A]weary with
my groaning and have found no rest." ' 4 Thus you
are to say to him, 'Thus says the LORD, "Behold,
[A]what I have built I am about to tear down, and
what I have planted I am about to uproot, that is,
the whole land." 5 But you, are you [A]seeking great
things for yourself? Do not seek *them;* for behold,
I am going to [B]bring disaster on all flesh,' declares
the LORD, 'but I will [C]give your life to you as booty
in all the places where you may go.' "

44:17 [a]*Or so as to burn* [b]*Or incense* [c]*Lit bread* [d]*Lit evil* [A]Num 30:12; Deut 23:23 [B]2 Kin 17:16; Jer 7:18 [C]Neh 9:34; Jer 32:32; 44:21 [D]Ex 16:3; Hos 2:5-9; Phil 3:19
44:18 [a]*Or incense* [b]*Lit been finished* [A]Num 11:5, 6; Jer 40:12; Mal 3:13-15 44:19 [a]*Or incense* [b]*Lit to pour* [c]*Lit to make an image of her* [A]Jer 7:18 [B]Num 30:6, 7; Jer 44:15
44:21 [a]*Or incense* [b]*Lit heart* [A]Ezek 8:10, 11 [B]Jer 11:13; 44:9, 17 [C]Ps 79:8; Is 64:9; Jer 14:10; Hos 7:2; Amos 8:7 44:22 [A]Is 7:13; 43:24; Mal 2:17 [B]Jer 4:4; 21:12; 30:14 [C]Gen 19:13; Ps 107:33, 34; Jer 25:11, 18, 38; 29:18; 42:18; 44:12 44:23 [a]*Or incense* [A]Jer 7:13-15; 40:3 [B]Jer 44:10; Ps 119:136, 150 [C]1 Kin 9:9; Neh 13:18; Jer 44:2; Dan 9:11, 12
44:24 [A]Jer 42:15; 44:16 [B]Jer 43:7; 44:15, 26 44:25 [a]*Or incense* [b]*Lit Surely cause to stand* [A]Jer 44:17; Matt 14:9; Acts 23:12 [B]Ezek 20:39 44:26 [a]*Lit Therefore* [b]Heb *YHWH*, usually rendered *LORD* [A]Gen 22:16; Deut 32:40, 41; Jer 22:5; Amos 6:8; Heb 6:13 [B]Ps 50:16; Ezek 20:39 [C]Is 48:1, 2; Jer 5:2 44:27 [a]*Lit be finished* [b]*Lit come to an end* [A]Jer 1:10; 31:28; 39:16 [B]2 Kin 21:14; Jer 44:14 44:28 [a]*Lit men of number* [A]Jer 44:14 [B]Is 10:19; 27:12, 13 [C]Ps 33:11; Is 14:27; 46:10, 11; Zech 1:6
44:29 [A]Is 7:11, 14; 8:18; Jer 44:30; Matt 24:15, 16, 32 [B]Prov 19:21; Is 40:8 44:30 [A]Jer 43:9-13; 46:25; Ezek 29:3; 30:21 [B]2 Kin 25:4-7; Jer 34:21; 39:5-7 45:1 [a]*Lit from the mouth of Jeremiah* [A]Jer 32:12, 16; 43:3, 6 [B]Jer 36:4, 18, 32 [C]2 Kin 24:1; 2 Chr 36:5-7; Jer 25:1; 36:1; 46:2; Dan 1:1 45:3 [A]Ps 6:6; 69:3; 2 Cor 4:1, 16; Gal 6:9
45:4 [A]Is 5:5; Jer 1:10; 11:17; 18:7-10; 31:28 45:5 [A]1 Kin 3:9, 11; 2 Kin 5:26; Matt 6:25, 32; Rom 12:16 [B]Is 66:16; Jer 25:31 [C]Jer 21:9; 38:2; 39:18

44:17–19 queen of heaven. *See note on 7:18.* This is a title Roman Catholicism erroneously attributes to Mary, the mother of Jesus, in a blending of Christianity with paganism. The Jews' twisted thinking credits the idol with the prosperity of precaptivity Judah, further mocking the goodness of God.

44:20–23 Jeremiah set the record straight, saying the idol was not the source of their prosperity, but it was the cause of their calamity.

44:24–28 Jeremiah repeated the doom stated in vv. 11–14.

44:29, 30 sign. The "sign" of punishment was described in v. 30 as the strangulation of Pharaoh Hophra in 570 B.C. by Amasis, which paved the way for Nebuchadnezzar's invasion in the 23rd year of his reign (568/67 B.C.).

45:1 fourth year of Jehoiakim. The year was 605 B.C. (chap. 36), when the recording of God's messages to Jeremiah was in view.

45:3 woe is me! Baruch felt anxiety as his own cherished plans of a bright future were apparently dashed; even death became a darkening peril (cf. v. 5). Also, he was possibly pressed by human questionings about God carrying through with such calamity (cf. v. 4). Jeremiah spoke to encourage him (v. 2).

45:4 say to him. God will judge this whole nation (the Jews).

45:5 are you seeking great things . . . ? Baruch had his expectations far too high, and that made the disasters harder to bear. It is enough that he be content just to live. Jeremiah, who once also complained, learned by his own suffering to encourage complainers.

DEFEAT OF PHARAOH FORETOLD

46 That which came as the word of the LORD
to Jeremiah the prophet [A]concerning the
nations.
2 To [A]Egypt, concerning the army of [B]Pharaoh
Neco king of Egypt, which was by the Euphrates
River at [C]Carchemish, which Nebuchadnezzar king
of Babylon defeated in the [D]fourth year of Jehoiakim
the son of Josiah, king of Judah:

3 "[A]Line up the shield and [a]buckler,
And draw near for the battle!
4 "Harness the horses,
And [a]mount the steeds,
And take your stand with helmets *on!*
[A]Polish the spears,
Put on the [B]scale-armor!
5 "Why have I seen *it?*
They are terrified,
They are [A]drawing back,
And their [B]mighty men are defeated
And have taken refuge in flight,
Without facing back;
[a,C]Terror is on every side!"
Declares the LORD.
6 Let not the [A]swift man flee,
Nor the mighty man escape;
In the north beside the river Euphrates
They have [B]stumbled and fallen.
7 Who is this that [A]rises like the Nile,
Like the rivers whose
waters surge about?
8 Egypt rises like the Nile,
Even like the rivers whose
waters surge about;
And He has said, "I will [A]rise
and cover *that* land;
I will surely [B]destroy the city
and its inhabitants."
9 Go up, you horses, and [a,A]drive
madly, you chariots,
That the mighty men may
[b]march forward:
Ethiopia and [c,B]Put, that handle the shield,
And the [d,C]Lydians, that handle
and bend the bow.
10 For [A]that day belongs to the
Lord [a]GOD of hosts,
A day of [B]vengeance, so as to
avenge Himself on His foes;
And the [C]sword will devour
and be satiated
And [b]drink its fill of their blood;
For there will be a [D]slaughter for
the Lord [a]GOD of hosts,
In the land of the north by
the river Euphrates.
11 Go [A]up to Gilead and obtain balm,
[B]O virgin daughter of Egypt!
In vain have you multiplied [a]remedies;
There is [C]no healing for you.
12 The nations have heard of your [A]shame,
And the earth is full of your
[B]cry *of distress;*
For one [C]warrior has stumbled
over [a]another,
And both of them have fallen
down together.

13 *This is* the [a]message which the LORD spoke to
Jeremiah the prophet about the [A]coming of Nebuchadnezzar king of Babylon to [B]smite the land
of Egypt:

14 "Declare in Egypt and proclaim in [A]Migdol,
Proclaim also in Memphis
and [B]Tahpanhes;
Say, 'Take your stand and
get yourself ready,
For the [C]sword has devoured
those around you.'
15 "Why have your [A]mighty ones
become prostrate?
They do not stand because the
LORD has [B]thrust them down.
16 "They have repeatedly [A]stumbled;
Indeed, they have fallen one
against another.
Then they said, 'Get up!
And [B]let us go back
To our own people and our native land
Away from the [a,C]sword
of the oppressor.'
17 "[a]They cried there, 'Pharaoh king
of Egypt *is but* [A]a big noise;
He has let the appointed time pass by!'

46:1 [A]Jer 1:10; 25:15-38 46:2 [A]Jer 46:14; Ezek chs 29-32 [B]2 Kin 18:21; 23:29, 33-35; Jer 25:19 [C]2 Chr 35:20; Is 10:9 [D]Jer 45:1 46:3 [a]I.e. small shield [A]Is 21:5; Jer 51:11; Joel 3:9; Nah 2:1; 3:14 46:4 [a]*Or go up, you horsemen* [A]Ezek 21:9-11 [B]1 Sam 17:5, 38; 2 Chr 26:14; Neh 4:16; Jer 51:3 46:5 [a]Heb *Magor-missabib;* i.e. Terror is on every side [A]Is 42:17; Jer 46:21 [B]Is 5:25; Ezek 39:18 [C]Jer 6:25; 20:3; 49:29 46:6 [A]Is 30:16 [B]Jer 46:12, 16; Dan 11:19 46:7 [A]Jer 47:2 46:8 [A]Is 37:24 [B]Is 10:13 46:9 [a]Lit *act like madmen* [b]Lit *go forth* [c]I.e. Libya (or Somaliland) [d]Heb *Ludim* [A]Jer 47:3; Nah 2:4 [B]Nah 3:9 [C]Is 66:19 46:10 [a]Heb *YHWH*, usually rendered *LORD* [b]Lit *be saturated with* [A]Joel 1:15 [B]Jer 50:15, 18 [C]Deut 32:42; Is 31:8; Jer 12:12 [D]Is 34:6; Zeph 1:7 46:11 [a]Lit *healings* [A]Jer 8:22 [B]Is 47:1; Jer 31:4, 21 [C]Jer 30:13; Mic 1:9; Nah 3:19 46:12 [a]Lit *warrior* [A]Jer 2:36; Nah 3:8-10 [B]Jer 14:2 [C]Is 19:2 46:13 [a]Lit *word* [A]Jer 43:10-13 [B]Is 19:1 46:14 [A]Jer 44:1 [B]Jer 43:8 [C]Is 1:20; Jer 2:30; 46:10; Nah 2:13 46:15 [A]Is 66:15, 16; Jer 46:5 [B]Ps 18:14, 39; 68:1, 2 46:16 [a]Lit *oppressing sword* [A]Lev 26:36, 37; Jer 46:6 [B]Jer 51:9 [C]Jer 50:16 46:17 [a]Some ancient versions read *Call the name of Pharaoh a big noise* [A]Ex 15:9, 10; 1 Kin 20:10, 11; Is 19:11-16

46:1 concerning the nations. Jeremiah had already proclaimed that all the nations at some time are to "drink the cup" of God's wrath (25:15–26). In chaps. 46–51 God selected certain nations and forecast their doom. Likely given to Jeremiah at different times, the prophecies were collected according to the nations, not the chronology.

46:2–26 To Egypt. Cf. Is 19, 20; Eze 29–32. Verses 2–12 depict Pharaoh Neco's overthrow by the Babylonians at Carchemish by the Euphrates River in 605 B.C., in which Egypt lost all its territory W of the river.

46:3–6 Here was a derisive call to Egypt to ready itself for defeat.

46:10 day belongs to the Lord. While this phrase, also rendered as "the day of the LORD," often refers to an eschatological judgment on earth (such as in Zep 1:7; Mal 4:5; 1Th 5:2; 2Pe 3:10), it also may refer to a historical day. In this case it refers to the Egyptian defeat (cf. La 2:22). *See note on Is 2:12.*

46:11 Gilead. *See note on 8:20–22.*

46:13–26 Babylon's invasion of Egypt, 15 or 16 years before the destruction of Jerusalem, is here detailed (601 B.C.; cf. v. 13). Having spent 13 years in a siege of Tyre, Nebuchadnezzar

18 “As I live,” declares the [A]King
Whose name is the LORD of hosts,
“Surely one shall come *who looms up*
like [B]Tabor among the mountains,
Or like [C]Carmel by the sea.
19 “Make your baggage ready for [A]exile,
O [B]daughter dwelling in Egypt,
For [C]Memphis will become a desolation;
It will even be burned down *and*
[a]bereft of inhabitants.
20 “Egypt is a pretty [A]heifer,
But a [a]horsefly is coming [B]from
the north—it is coming!
21 “Also her [A]mercenaries in her midst
Are like [a]fattened [B]calves,
For even they too have turned back
and have fled away together;
They did not stand *their ground*.
For the day of their calamity
has come upon them,
The time of their [C]punishment.
22 “Its sound moves along like a serpent;
For they move on [a]like an army
And come to her as
woodcutters with axes.
23 “They have cut down her [A]forest,”
declares the LORD;
“Surely it will no *more* be found,
Even though [a]they are *now* more
numerous than [B]locusts
And are without number.
24 “The daughter of Egypt has
been put to shame,
Given over to the [a]power of the
[A]people of the north.”

25 The LORD of hosts, the God of Israel, says, “Behold, I am going to punish Amon of [A]Thebes, and
[B]Pharaoh, and Egypt along with her [C]gods and her
kings, even Pharaoh and those who [D]trust in him.
26 I shall give them over to the [a]power of those who
are [A]seeking their lives, even into the hand of Nebuchadnezzar king of Babylon and into the hand of his
[b]officers. [B]Afterwards, however, it will be inhabited
as in the days of old,” declares the LORD.

27 “But as for you, O Jacob My
servant, [A]do not fear,
Nor be dismayed, O Israel!
For, see, I am going to [B]save
you from afar,
And your descendants from the
land of their captivity;
And Jacob will return and
be [C]undisturbed
And secure, with no one
making *him* tremble.
28 “O Jacob My servant, do not
fear,” declares the LORD,
“For [A]I am with you.
For I will make a full end of all the nations
Where I have driven you,
Yet I will [B]not make a full end of you;
But I will [C]correct you properly
And by no means leave you unpunished.”

PROPHECY AGAINST PHILISTIA

47 That which came as the word of the LORD to
Jeremiah the prophet concerning the [A]Phi-
listines, before Pharaoh [a]conquered [B]Gaza. 2 Thus
says the LORD:

“Behold, waters are going to
rise from [A]the north
And become an overflowing torrent,
And [B]overflow the land and
all its fullness,
The city and those who live in it;
And the men will [C]cry out,
And every inhabitant of the land will wail.
3 “Because of the noise of the [a,A]galloping
hoofs of his [b]stallions,
The tumult of his chariots, *and*
the rumbling of his wheels,
The fathers have not turned
back for *their* children,
Because of the limpness of *their* hands,
4 On account of the day that is coming
To [A]destroy all the Philistines,
To cut off from [B]Tyre and Sidon
Every ally that is left;
For the LORD is going to
destroy the Philistines,
The remnant of the coastland of [C]Caphtor.
5 “[A]Baldness has come upon Gaza;
[B]Ashkelon has been ruined.
O remnant of their valley,
How long will you [C]gash yourself?

46:18 [A]Jer 48:15; Mal 1:14 [B]Josh 19:22; Judg 4:6; Ps 89:12 [C]Josh 12:22; 1 Kin 18:42 46:19 [a]Lit *without* [A]Is 20:4 [B]Jer 48:18 [C]Jer 46:14; Ezek 30:13 46:20 [a]Or possibly *mosquito* [A]Hos 10:11 [B]Jer 1:14; 47:2 46:21 [a]Lit *of the stall* [A]2 Sam 10:6; 2 Kin 7:6; Jer 46:5 [B]Is 34:7 [C]Jer 48:44; Hos 9:7; Obad 13; Mic 7:4 46:22 [a]Or *in force* 46:23 [a]I.e. trees of the forest, the Egyptians [A]Jer 21:14 [B]Judg 6:5; 7:12; Joel 2:25 46:24 [a]Lit *hand* [A]Jer 1:15 46:25 [A]Ezek 30:14-16; Nah 3:8 [B]Jer 44:30 [C]Ex 12:12; Jer 43:12, 13; Ezek 30:13; Zeph 2:11 [D]Is 20:5 46:26 [a]Lit *hand* [b]Lit *servants* [A]Jer 44:30; Ezek 32:11 [B]Ezek 29:8-14 46:27 [A]Is 41:13, 14; Jer 30:10, 11 [B]Is 11:11; Jer 23:3, 4; 29:14; Mic 7:12 [C]Jer 23:6; 50:19 46:28 [A]Ps 46:7, 11; Is 8:10; 43:2; Jer 1:19 [B]Jer 4:27; Amos 9:8, 9 [C]Jer 10:24; Hab 3:2 47:1 [a]Lit *smote* [A]Jer 25:20; Zech 9:6 [B]Gen 10:19; 1 Kin 4:24; Jer 25:20; Amos 1:6; Zeph 2:4 47:2 [A]Is 14:31; Jer 1:14; 6:22; 46:20, 24 [B]Is 8:7, 8 [C]Is 15:2-5; Jer 46:12 47:3 [a]Lit *stamping of the* [b]Lit *mighty ones* [A]Judg 5:22; Jer 8:16; Nah 3:2 47:4 [A]Is 14:31 [B]Is 23:5; Jer 25:22; Joel 3:4; Amos 1:9, 10; Zech 9:2-4 [C]Gen 10:14; Deut 2:23; Amos 9:7 47:5 [A]Jer 48:37; Mic 1:16 [B]Judg 1:18; Jer 25:20; Amos 1:7, 8; Zeph 2:4, 7; Zech 9:5 [C]Jer 16:6; 41:5

was promised Egypt as a reward for humbling Tyre (cf. Eze 29:17–20).

46:18 Tabor ... Carmel. As those two mountains rise above the hills of Israel, so Nebuchadnezzar will be superior.

46:20, 21 a pretty heifer ... fattened calves. Fat and untamed, ready to kill.

46:26 Afterwards. Forty years after Nebuchadnezzar’s conquest of Egypt, it threw off the Babylonian yoke but never regained its former glory (Ezek 29:11–15).

46:27, 28 Jacob ... do not fear. Though Israel has been scattered to the nations, the nations will receive their judgments, and the Lord will restore Israel (repeated from 30:10, 11) from dispersion to its own land (as in Jer 23:5–8; 30–33). No matter what judgments fall on Israel, they will not be destroyed, as Paul reiterates in Ro 11:1, 2, 15, 25–27.

47:1–5 concerning the Philistines. Cf. Is 14:29–32; Eze 25:15–17; Am 1:6–8; Zep 2:4–7. Although Egypt’s Pharaoh Hophra conquered the Philistines (who lived on the coastal plain of Philistia) in Gaza and Phoenicia around

6 “Ah, [A]sword of the LORD,
How long will you not be quiet?
Withdraw into your sheath;
Be at rest and stay still.
7 “How can [a]it be quiet,
When the LORD has [A]given it an order?
Against Ashkelon and against
the seacoast—
There He has [B]assigned it.”

PROPHECY AGAINST MOAB

48 Concerning [A]Moab. Thus says the LORD of hosts, the God of Israel,

“Woe to [B]Nebo, for it has been destroyed;
[C]Kiriathaim has been put to shame,
it has been captured;
The lofty stronghold has been put
to shame and [a]shattered.
2 “There is praise for Moab no longer;
In [A]Heshbon they have devised
calamity against her:
‘Come and let us cut her off
from *being* a nation!’
You too, [a]Madmen, will be silenced;
The sword will follow after you.
3 “The sound of an outcry from [A]Horonaim,
‘Devastation and great destruction!’
4 “Moab is broken,
Her little ones have sounded
out a cry *of distress.*
5 “For by the ascent of [A]Luhith
They will ascend with continual weeping;
For at the descent of Horonaim
They have heard the [a]anguished
cry of destruction.
6 “[A]Flee, save your lives,
That you may be like a juniper
in the wilderness.
7 “For because of your [A]trust in your
own achievements and treasures,
Even you yourself will be captured;
And [B]Chemosh will go off into exile
Together with his priests and his princes.
8 “A destroyer will come to every city,
So that no city will escape;
The valley also will be ruined
And the [A]plateau will be destroyed,
As the LORD has said.
9 “Give [a,A]wings to Moab,
For she will [b]flee away;
And her cities will become a [B]desolation,
Without inhabitants in them.
10 “[A]Cursed be the one who does the
LORD’S work [B]negligently,
And cursed be the one who restrains
his [C]sword from blood.

11 “Moab has been [A]at ease since his youth;
He has also been [B]undisturbed,
like wine on [a]its dregs,
And he has not been [C]emptied
from vessel to vessel,
Nor has he gone into exile.
Therefore [b]he retains his flavor,
And his aroma has not changed.

12 Therefore behold, the days are coming,” declares
the LORD, “when I will send to him those who tip
vessels, and they will tip him over, and they will
empty his vessels and shatter [a]his jars. 13 And Moab
will be [A]ashamed of [B]Chemosh, as the house of Israel
was ashamed of [C]Bethel, their confidence.

14 “How can you say, ‘We are [A]mighty warriors,
And men valiant for battle’?
15 “Moab has been destroyed and [a]men
have gone up to [b]his cities;
His choicest [c,A]young men have also
gone down to the slaughter,”
Declares the [B]King, whose name
is the LORD of hosts.
16 “The disaster of Moab will [A]soon come,
And his calamity has swiftly hastened.
17 “Mourn for him, all you who *live* around him,
Even all of you who know his name;
Say, ‘How has the mighty
[a,A]scepter been broken,
A staff of splendor!’
18 “[A]Come down from your glory
And sit [a]on the parched ground,
O [B]daughter dwelling in [C]Dibon,

47:6 [A]Judg 7:20; Jer 12:12; Ezek 21:3-5 47:7 [a]Lit *you* [A]Is 10:6; Ezek 14:17 [B]Mic 6:9 48:1 [a]Or *dismayed* [A]Is 15:1; Ezek 25:9 [B]Num 32:3, 38; Jer 48:22 [C]Num 32:37; Jer 48:23; Ezek 25:9 48:2 [a]I.e. a city of Moab [A]Num 21:25; Jer 48:34, 45; 49:3 48:3 [A]Is 15:5; Jer 48:5, 34 48:5 [a]Lit *distresses of outcry* [A]Is 15:5 48:6 [A]Jer 51:6 48:7 [A]Ps 52:7; Is 59:4; Jer 9:23 [B]Num 21:29; 1 Kin 11:33; Jer 48:13, 46 48:8 [A]Josh 13:9, 17, 21 48:9 [a]Or *salt* [b]Or *fall in ruins* [A]Ps 11:1; Is 16:2; Jer 48:28 [B]Jer 44:22 48:10 [A]Jer 11:3 [B]1 Kin 20:39, 40, 42; 2 Kin 13:19 [C]Jer 47:6, 7 48:11 [a]Lit *his* [b]Lit *his flavor has stayed in him* [A]Jer 22:21; Ezek 16:49; Zech 1:15 [B]Zeph 1:12 [C]Nah 2:2 48:12 [a]Lit *their* 48:13 [A]Is 45:16; Jer 48:39 [B]Judg 11:24 [C]1 Kin 12:29; Hos 8:5, 6 48:14 [A]Ps 33:16; Is 10:13-16 48:15 [a]Lit *one has* [b]Lit *her* [c]I.e. warriors [A]Is 40:30, 31; Jer 50:27 [B]Jer 46:18; 51:57; Mal 1:14 48:16 [A]Is 13:22 48:17 [a]Or *rod* [A]Is 9:4; 14:5 48:18 [a]Lit *in thirst* [A]Is 47:1 [B]Jer 46:19 [C]Num 21:30; Josh 13:9, 17; Is 15:2; Jer 48:22

587 B.C. (v. 1), Babylon appears to be the conqueror in this scene (“from the north”), at the same time as the invasion of Judah (588–586 B.C.; cf. 39:1, 2).

47:6, 7 sword of the LORD. Cf. Jdg 7:18, 20.

48:1 Concerning Moab. Various sites of unknown location in Moab are to be destroyed (vv. 1–5). The judgment is framed in similar words or some of the same words as in other passages (Is 15:1–9; 16:6–14; 25:10–12; Eze 25:8–11; Am 2:1–3; Zep 2:8–11). Desolation overtook different parts of Moab at various times, but Babylon in 588–586 B.C. or 582–581 B.C. is likely the main destroyer (cf. 48:40). The Moabites were Lot’s descendants (cf. Ge 19:37), who lived E of the Dead Sea and often fought with Israel.

48:7 Chemosh. He was the leading god of Moab (cf. Nu 21:29; Jdg 11:24; 1Ki 11:7; 2Ki 23:13).

48:10 Cursed be the one. God’s aim to judge Moab was so intense that He pronounced a curse on whatever instrument (army) He would use should they carry it out “negligently,” i.e., “carelessly,” or “with slackness.”

48:11, 12 This winemaking imagery is vivid. In the production of sweet wine, the juice was left in a wineskin until the sediment or dregs settled onto the bottom. Then it was poured into another skin until more dregs were separated. This process continued until the dregs were all removed and a pure, sweet wine obtained. Moab was not taken from suffering to suffering so that her bitter dregs would be removed through the purging of pain. Thus the nation was settled into the thickness and bitterness of its own sin. Judgment from God was coming to smash them.

48:18–20 Dibon … Aroer. These places were on the Arnon River, but would be thirsty.

For the destroyer of Moab has
come up against you,
He has ruined your strongholds.
19 "Stand by the road and keep watch,
O inhabitant of [A]Aroer;
[B]Ask him who flees and
her who escapes
And say, 'What has happened?'
20 "Moab has been put to shame, for
it has been [a]shattered.
Wail and cry out;
Declare by the [A]Arnon
That Moab has been destroyed.

21 "Judgment has also come upon the plain, upon
Holon, [A]Jahzah and against [B]Mephaath, 22 against
Dibon, Nebo and Beth-diblathaim, 23 against Kiriathaim, Beth-gamul and [A]Beth-meon, 24 against [A]Ke-
rioth, Bozrah and all the cities of the land of Moab,
far and near. 25 The [A]horn of Moab has been cut off
and his [B]arm broken," declares the LORD. 26 "[A]Make
him drunk, for he has [a]become [B]arrogant toward
the LORD; so Moab will [b]wallow in his vomit, and he
also will become a laughingstock. 27 Now was not
Israel a [A]laughingstock to you? Or was he [a,B]caught
among thieves? For each time you speak about him
you [C]shake *your head in scorn.*

28 "Leave the cities and dwell
among the [A]crags,
O inhabitants of Moab,
And be like a [B]dove that nests
Beyond the mouth of the chasm.
29 "[A]We have heard of the pride of
Moab—he *is* very proud—
Of his haughtiness, his [B]pride, his
arrogance and [a]his self-exaltation.
30 "I know his [A]fury," declares the LORD,
"But it is futile;
His idle boasts have
accomplished nothing.
31 "Therefore I will [A]wail for Moab,
Even for all Moab will I cry out;
[a]I will moan for the men of [B]Kir-heres.
32 "More than the [A]weeping for [B]Jazer
I will weep for you, O vine of Sibmah!
Your tendrils stretched
across the sea,
They reached to the sea of Jazer;
Upon your summer fruits and
your grape harvest
The destroyer has fallen.
33 "So [A]gladness and joy are taken away
From the fruitful field, even
from the land of Moab.
And I have made the wine to [B]cease
from the wine presses;
No one will tread *them* with shouting,
The shouting will not be shouts *of joy.*

34 [A]From the outcry at Heshbon even to [B]Elealeh,
even to Jahaz they have [a]raised their voice, from
[C]Zoar even to Horonaim *and to* Eglath-shelishiyah;
for even the waters of Nimrim will become desolate.
35 I will make an end of Moab," declares the LORD,
"the one who offers *sacrifice* on the [A]high place and
the one who [a,B]burns incense to his gods.
36 "Therefore My [A]heart [a]wails for Moab like
flutes; My heart also [a]wails like flutes for the men of
Kir-heres. Therefore they have [B]lost the abundance it
produced. 37 For [A]every head is bald and every beard
cut short; there are gashes on all the hands and
[B]sackcloth on the loins. 38 On all the [A]housetops of
Moab and in its streets [a]there is lamentation everywhere; for I have broken Moab like an undesirable
[B]vessel," declares the LORD. 39 "How [a]shattered it is!
How they have wailed! How Moab has turned his
back—he is ashamed! So Moab will become a laughingstock and an [A]object of terror to all around him."

40 For thus says the LORD:
"Behold, one will [A]fly swiftly like an eagle
And [B]spread out his wings against Moab.
41 "Kerioth has been captured
And the strongholds have been seized,
So the [A]hearts of the mighty
men of Moab in that day
Will be like the heart of a
[B]woman in labor.
42 "Moab will be [A]destroyed
from *being* a people
Because he has [a]become [B]arrogant
toward the LORD.
43 "[A]Terror, pit and snare are
coming upon you,
O inhabitant of Moab," declares the LORD.
44 "The one who [A]flees from the terror
Will fall into the pit,
And the one who climbs up out of the pit
Will be caught in the snare;
For I shall bring upon her,
even upon Moab,
The year of their [B]punishment,"
declares the LORD.

48:19 [A]Deut 2:36; Josh 12:2 [B]1 Sam 4:13, 14, 16 48:20 [a]Or *dismayed* [A]Num 21:13 48:21 [A]Num 21:23; Is 15:4; Jer 48:34 [B]Josh 13:18 48:23 [A]Josh 13:17 48:24 [A]Jer 48:41; Amos 2:2 48:25 [A]Ps 75:10; Zech 1:19-21 [B]Job 22:9; Ps 10:15 48:26 [a]Or *magnified himself against* [b]Or *splash into* [A]Jer 25:15 [B]Ex 5:2; Jer 48:42; Dan 5:23 48:27 [a]Or *found* [A]Lam 2:15-17; Mic 7:8-10 [B]Jer 2:26 [C]Job 16:4; Jer 18:16 48:28 [A]Judg 6:2; Is 2:19; Jer 49:16; Obad 3 [B]Ps 55:6; Song 2:14 48:29 [a]Lit *elevation of his heart* [A]Is 16:6; Zeph 2:8 [B]Job 40:11, 12; Ps 138:6 48:30 [A]Is 37:28 48:31 [a]Another reading is *He* [A]Is 15:5; 16:7, 11 [B]2 Kin 3:25; Is 16:7, 11; Jer 48:36 48:32 [A]Is 16:8, 9 [B]Num 21:32 48:33 [A]Is 16:10; Jer 25:10; Joel 1:12 [B]Is 5:10; Hag 2:16 48:34 [a]Lit *given forth* [A]Is 15:4-6 [B]Num 32:3, 37 [C]Gen 13:10; 14:2; Is 15:5, 6 48:35 [a]Or *offers up in smoke* [A]Is 15:2; 16:12 [B]Jer 7:9; 11:13 48:36 [a]Lit *sounds* [A]Is 15:5; 16:11 [B]Is 15:7 48:37 [A]Is 15:2; Jer 16:6; 41:5; 47:5 [B]Gen 37:34; Is 15:3; 20:2 48:38 [a]Lit *all of it is lamentation* [A]Is 22:1 [B]Jer 19:10, 11; 22:28; 25:34 48:39 [a]Or *dismayed* [A]Ezek 26:16 48:40 [A]Deut 28:49; Jer 49:22; Hos 8:1; Hab 1:8 [B]Is 8:8 48:41 [A]Jer 49:22 [B]Is 13:8; 21:3; Jer 30:6; Mic 4:9, 10 48:42 [a]Or *magnified himself against* [A]Ps 83:4; Jer 48:2 [B]Is 37:23; Jer 48:26 48:43 [A]Is 24:17, 18; Lam 3:47 48:44 [A]1 Kin 19:17; Is 24:18; Amos 5:19 [B]Jer 46:21

48:24 Kerioth. Likely the city of Judas Iscariot. Cf. Jos 15:25.

48:25 horn ... has been cut off. An example of the OT use of "horn" as a symbol of military power, as an animal uses horns to hook, gouge, or ram. Moab is to be dehorned.

48:26 Here is a vivid picture of humiliation.

48:29 Suffering didn't come to humble Moab (*see note on vv. 11, 12*), so she remained proud.

45 “In the shadow of Heshbon
The fugitives stand without strength;
For a fire has gone forth from Heshbon
And a [A]flame from the midst of [B]Sihon,
And it has devoured the [C]forehead of Moab
And the scalps of the [a]riotous revelers.
46 “[A]Woe to you, Moab!
The people of [B]Chemosh have perished;
For your sons have been
taken away captive
And your daughters into captivity.
47 “Yet I will [A]restore the [a]fortunes of Moab
In the [b]latter days,” declares the LORD.

Thus far the judgment on Moab.

PROPHECY AGAINST AMMON

49 Concerning the sons of [A]Ammon. Thus says the LORD:

“Does Israel have no sons?
Or has he no heirs?
Why then has [a]Malcam taken
possession of Gad
And his people settled in its cities?
2 “Therefore behold, the days are
coming,” declares the LORD,
“That I will cause a [a,A]trumpet
blast of war to be heard
Against [B]Rabbah of the sons of Ammon;
And it will become a desolate heap,
And her [C]towns will be set on fire.
Then Israel will take [D]possession
of his possessors,”
Says the LORD.
3 “Wail, O [A]Heshbon, for [B]Ai
has been destroyed!
Cry out, O daughters of Rabbah,
[C]Gird yourselves with sackcloth
and lament,
And rush back and forth inside the walls;
For [a]Malcam will [D]go into exile
Together with his priests and his princes.
4 “How [A]boastful you are about the valleys!
Your valley is flowing *away*,
O [B]backsliding daughter
Who trusts in her [C]treasures, *saying*,
‘[D]Who will come against me?’
5 “Behold, I am going to bring
[A]terror upon you,”
Declares the Lord [a]GOD of hosts,
“From all *directions* around you;
And each of you will be
[B]driven out [b]headlong,
With no one to gather the
[C]fugitives together.
6 “But afterward I will [A]restore
The [a]fortunes of the sons of Ammon,”
Declares the LORD.

PROPHECY AGAINST EDOM

7 Concerning [A]Edom.
Thus says the LORD of hosts,
“Is there no longer any [B]wisdom in [C]Teman?
Has good counsel been lost to the prudent?
Has their wisdom decayed?
8 “Flee away, turn back, dwell in the depths,
O inhabitants of [A]Dedan,
For I [a]will bring the [B]disaster
of Esau upon him
At the time I [b]punish him.
9 “[A]If grape gatherers came to you,
Would they not leave gleanings?
If thieves *came* by night,
They would destroy *only* [a]until
they had enough.
10 “But I have [A]stripped Esau bare,
I have uncovered his hiding places
So that he will not be able
to conceal himself;
His [a]offspring has been destroyed
along with his [b]relatives
And his neighbors, and [B]he is no more.
11 “Leave your [a,A]orphans behind,
I will keep *them* alive;
And let your [B]widows trust in Me.”

48:45 [a]Lit *sons of tumult* [A]Num 21:28, 29 [B]Num 21:21, 26; Ps 135:11 [C]Num 24:17 48:46 [A]Num 21:29 [B]Judg 11:24; 1 Kin 11:7; Jer 48:7 48:47 [a]Or *captivity* [b]Lit *end of the days* [A]Jer 12:14-17; 49:6, 39 49:1 [a]In 1 Kin 11:5, 33 and Zeph 1:5, *Milcom* [A]Deut 23:3, 4; 2 Chr 20:1; Ezek 21:28-32; 25:2-10; Amos 1:13-15; Zeph 2:8-11 49:2 [a]Or *shout of* [A]Num 10:9; Jer 4:19 [B]Deut 3:11; 2 Sam 11:1; Ezek 21:20 [C]Josh 17:11, 16 [D]Is 14:2 49:3 [a]Cf v 1 [A]Jer 48:2 [B]Josh 7:2-5; 8:1-29; Ezra 2:28 [C]Is 32:11; Jer 48:37 [D]Jer 46:25; 48:7 49:4 [A]Jer 9:23 [B]Jer 31:22 [C]Ps 62:10; Ezek 28:4, 5; 1 Tim 6:17 [D]Jer 21:13 49:5 [a]Heb *YHWH*, usually rendered *LORD* [b]Lit *before him* [A]Jer 48:43f; 49:29 [B]Jer 16:16; 46:5 [C]Lam 4:15 49:6 [a]Or *captivity* [A]Jer 48:47; 49:39 49:7 [A]Gen 25:30; 32:3; Is 34:5, 6; Jer 25:21; Ezek 25:12; Amos 1:11; Obad 1-21 [B]Job 2:11; Jer 8:9 [C]Gen 36:11, 15, 34; Jer 49:20 49:8 [a]Or *brought* [b]Or *punished* [A]Is 21:13; Jer 25:23 [B]Jer 46:21; Mal 1:3, 4 49:9 [a]Lit *their sufficiency* [A]Obad 5 49:10 [a]Lit *seed* [b]Lit *brothers* [A]Jer 13:26 [B]Is 17:14 49:11 [a]Or *fatherless* [A]Ps 68:5; Hos 14:3 [B]Ps 68:5; Zech 7:10

48:47 **I will restore.** God will allow a remnant of Moab to return to the land (cf. 12:14–17; 46:26; 48:47; 49:6, 39) through their descendants in the messianic era (“the latter days”).

49:1–6 **Concerning the sons of Ammon.** Cf. Eze 25:1–7; Am 1:13–15; Zep 2:8–11. These people descended from Lot (cf. Ge 19:38) and lived N of Moab. Though Israel had people who were heirs to Transjordan, i.e., Gad, Reuben, and one half of Manasseh (cf. Jos 22:1–9), the Ammonites, whose god was Milcham or Molech, were chided for having usurped the area (v. 1), when the northern kingdom was taken captive by Shalmaneser.

49:2 **a trumpet blast of war.** Nebuchadnezzar defeated Ammon in the fifth year after the destruction of Jerusalem, around 582/81 B.C.

49:4 **valley is flowing.** Flowing with the blood of the slain. **backsliding.** *See note on Pr 14:14.*

49:6 **I will restore.** As with Moab (cf. 48:47 and *see note there*), God promised that captives would have an opportunity to return. This was partially fulfilled under Cyrus, but will be more fully in the coming kingdom of Messiah (cf. 48:47).

49:7–22 **Concerning Edom.** Cf. Is 21:11, 12; Eze 25:12–14; Am 1:11, 12; Ob 1. This prophecy is closely related to Obadiah. These people descended from Esau (cf. Ge 36:1–19) and lived S of the Dead Sea. Perpetual desolation is ahead for Edom (v. 13). God will make it bare (vv. 10, 18). The destroyer is probably Babylon in 588–586 B.C. or 582–581 B.C. as v. 19 has descriptions used of Babylon against Judah (lion, 4:7; flooding of the Jordan, 12:5). Also “swoop like an eagle” (v. 22) is used of Babylon (Hab 1:8). There is no prophecy of a future restoration.

49:8 **Esau.** He was cursed for his godlessness, and his punishment was perpetuated in his descendants (cf. Heb 12:11, 17).

49:9 *See note on Ob 5, 6.*

49:10 **he is no more.** Edom was politically extinct after the Roman conquest.

49:11 This was because no adult men will be left to care for them.

12 For thus says the LORD, "Behold, those [a]who
were not sentenced to drink the [A]cup will certainly
drink *it,* and are you the one who will be [B]completely
acquitted? You will not be acquitted, but you will
certainly drink *it.* 13 For I have [A]sworn by Myself,"
declares the LORD, "that [B]Bozrah will become an
[C]object of horror, a reproach, a ruin and a curse; and
all its cities will become perpetual ruins."

14 I have [A]heard a message from the LORD,
And an [B]envoy is sent among
the nations, *saying,*
"[C]Gather yourselves together
and come against her,
And rise up for battle!"
15 "For behold, I have made you
small among the nations,
Despised among men.
16 "As for the terror of you,
The arrogance of your heart
has deceived you,
O you who live in the clefts of [a]the [A]rock,
Who occupy the height of the hill.
Though you make your nest
as [B]high as an eagle's,
I will [C]bring you down from
there," declares the LORD.

17 "Edom will become an [A]object of horror; everyone who passes by it will be horrified and will [B]hiss
at all its wounds. 18 Like the [A]overthrow of Sodom
and Gomorrah with its neighbors," says the LORD,
"[B]no one will live there, nor will a son of man reside
in it. 19 [A]Behold, one will come up like a lion from
the [a,B]thickets of the Jordan against [b]a perennially
watered pasture; for in an instant I will make him
run away from it, and whoever is [C]chosen I shall
appoint over it. For who is [D]like Me, and who will
summon Me *into court?* And who then is the shepherd [E]who can stand against Me?"
20 Therefore hear the [A]plan of the LORD which
He has planned against Edom, and His purposes
which He has purposed against the inhabitants of
Teman: surely they will drag them off, *even* the little
ones of the flock; surely He will make their [a]pasture
[B]desolate because of them. 21 The [A]earth has quaked
at the noise of their downfall. There is an outcry!
The noise of it has been heard at the [a]Red Sea. 22 Behold, [a]He will mount up and [A]swoop like an eagle
and spread out His wings [b]against Bozrah; and the
[B]hearts of the mighty men of Edom in that day will
be like the heart of a woman in labor.

PROPHECY AGAINST DAMASCUS

23 Concerning [A]Damascus.
"[B]Hamath and [C]Arpad are put to shame,
For they have heard bad news;
They are [D]disheartened.
There is anxiety by the sea,
It [E]cannot be calmed.
24 "Damascus has become helpless;
She has turned away to flee,
And panic has gripped her;
[A]Distress and pangs have
taken hold of her
Like a woman in childbirth.
25 "How [a]the [A]city of praise has
not been deserted,
The town of My joy!
26 "Therefore, her [A]young men
will fall in her streets,
And all the men of war will be [a]silenced
in that day," declares the LORD of hosts.
27 "I will [A]set fire to the wall of Damascus,
And it will devour the [a]fortified
towers of [B]Ben-hadad."

PROPHECY AGAINST KEDAR AND HAZOR

28 Concerning [A]Kedar and the kingdoms of Hazor,
which Nebuchadnezzar king of Babylon defeated.
Thus says the LORD,

"Arise, go up to Kedar
And devastate the [a,B]men of the east.
29 "They will take away their
tents and their flocks;
They will carry off for themselves

49:12 [a]Lit *whose judgment was not to* [A]Jer 25:15 [B]Jer 25:28, 29; 1 Pet 4:17 49:13 [A]Gen 22:16; Is 45:23; Jer 44:26; Amos 6:8 [B]Gen 36:33; 1 Chr 1:44; Is 34:6; 63:1; Amos 1:12 [C]Is 34:9-15; Jer 18:16 49:14 [A]Obad 1-4 [B]Is 18:2; 30:4 [C]Jer 50:14 49:16 [a]Or *Sela* [A]2 Kin 14:7; Jer 48:28 [B]Job 39:27; Is 14:13-15 [C]Amos 9:2 49:17 [A]Jer 18:16; 49:13; 50:13; Ezek 35:7 [B]1 Kin 9:8; Jer 51:37 49:18 [A]Gen 19:24, 25; Deut 29:23; Jer 50:40; Amos 4:11; Zeph 2:9 [B]Job 18:15-18; Jer 49:33 49:19 [a]Lit *pride* [b]Or *an enduring habitation* [A]Jer 50:44 [B]Josh 3:15; Jer 12:5 [C]Num 16:5 [D]Ex 15:11; Is 46:9 [E]Job 41:10 49:20 [a]Or *habitation* [A]Is 14:24, 27; Jer 50:45 [B]Mal 1:3, 4 49:21 [a]Lit *Sea of Reeds* [A]Jer 50:46; Ezek 26:15, 18 49:22 [a]Or *one* [b]Or *over* [A]Jer 4:13; 48:40; Hos 8:1 [B]Is 13:8; Jer 30:6; 48:41 49:23 [A]Gen 14:15; 15:2; 2 Kin 5:12; 2 Chr 16:2; Is 7:8; 17:1; Amos 1:3; Acts 9:2 [B]Num 13:21; Is 10:9; Jer 39:5; Amos 6:2 [C]2 Kin 18:34; 19:13; Is 10:9 [D]Ex 15:15; Nah 2:10 [E]Is 57:20 49:24 [A]Is 13:8 49:25 [a]Or *deserted is the city of praise* [A]Jer 33:9; 51:41 49:26 [a]Or *destroyed* [A]Jer 11:22; 50:30; Amos 4:10 49:27 [a]Or *palaces* [A]Jer 43:12; Amos 1:3-5 [B]1 Kin 15:18-20; 2 Kin 13:3 49:28 [a]Lit *sons* [A]Gen 25:13; Ps 120:5; Is 21:16, 17; Jer 2:10; Ezek 27:21 [B]Job 1:3; Is 11:14

49:12 those ... not sentenced to drink ... will ... drink *it*. This refers to the Jews who had a covenant relation to God. What will happen to a nation that has no such pledge?

49:16, 17 Edom was situated in high and rugged mountains and thus convinced it was invincible. But the ruin will come and be irreversible.

49:19–21 These words are repeated in 50:44–46, where they refer to Babylon.

49:20 the little ones of the flock. The weakest of the Chaldeans shall drag them away captive.

49:23–27 Concerning Damascus. Cf. Is 17:1–3; Am 1:3–5. Hamath, a city on the Orontes River that marked the northern limit of Solomon's rule (2Ch 8:4), 110 mi. N of Damascus in southern Syria, and Arpad, 105 mi. SW of the modern Aleppo in Northern Syria, were to fall, as well as Damascus, Syria's capital. Nebuchadnezzar conquered them in 605 B.C.

49:25 city of praise ... My joy! Could be translated "the city of renown," famous due to its situation in a spacious oasis and its trade, as in Eze 27:18.

49:27 fortified towers of Ben-hadad. Here was the place where so many cruel evils against Israel were devised, thus the reason for its overthrow. The name is common among Syrian kings, meaning Son of Hadad, an idol, so it does not refer to the Ben-hadad of 2Ki 13:3 and Am 1:4.

49:28–33 Concerning Kedar ... Hazor. Cf. Is 21:13–17. These areas in the Arabian desert E of Judah were to be laid waste (as a different Hazor was a few mi. NW of the Sea of Galilee). Kedar was an Ishmaelite tribe (cf. Ge 25:13; Eze 27:21). The conqueror was Nebuchadnezzar in 599/98 B.C. as recounted in an ancient record, the Babylonian Chronicle. It was shortly after this that Babylon seized Jerusalem in 598/97 B.C.

Their tent [A]curtains, all their
goods and their [B]camels,
And they will call out to one another,
'[C]Terror on every side!'
30 "Run away, flee! Dwell in the depths,
O inhabitants of Hazor," declares the LORD;
"For [A]Nebuchadnezzar king of Babylon
has formed a plan against you
And devised a scheme against you.
31 "Arise, go up against a nation
which is [A]at ease,
Which lives securely," declares the LORD.
"It has [B]no gates or bars;
They [C]dwell alone.
32 "Their camels will become plunder,
And their many cattle for booty,
And I will [A]scatter to all the winds those
who [B]cut the corners *of their hair;*
And I will bring their disaster from
every side," declares the LORD.
33 "Hazor will become a [A]haunt of jackals,
A desolation forever;
No one will live there,
Nor will a son of man reside in it."

PROPHECY AGAINST ELAM

34 That which came as the word of the LORD to Jeremiah the prophet concerning [A]Elam, [B]at the beginning of the reign of Zedekiah king of Judah, saying:

35 "Thus says the LORD of hosts,
'Behold, I am going to [A]break
the bow of Elam,
The [a]finest of their might.
36 'I will bring upon Elam the [A]four winds
From the four ends of heaven,
And will [B]scatter them to all these winds;
And there will be no nation
To which the outcasts of Elam will not go.
37 'So I will [a]shatter Elam before their enemies
And before those who seek their lives;
And I will [A]bring calamity upon them,
Even My [B]fierce anger,' declares the LORD,
'And I will [C]send out the sword after them
Until I have consumed them.
38 'Then I will set My throne in Elam
And destroy [a]out of it king and princes,'
Declares the LORD.
39 'But it will come about in the last days
That I will [A]restore the [a]fortunes of Elam,' "
Declares the LORD.

PROPHECY AGAINST BABYLON

50 The word which the LORD spoke concerning
[A]Babylon, the land of the Chaldeans, through
Jeremiah the prophet:

2 "[A]Declare and proclaim among the nations.
Proclaim it and [B]lift up a standard.
Do not conceal *it but* say,
'[C]Babylon has been captured,
[D]Bel has been put to shame, [a]Marduk
has been [b]shattered;
Her [E]images have been put to shame,
her idols have been shattered.'

3 For a nation has come up against her out of the
[A]north; it will make her land [B]an object of horror,
and there will be [C]no inhabitant in it. Both man and
beast have wandered off, they have gone away!
4 "In those days and at that time," declares the
LORD, "the sons of Israel will come, *both* they and
the sons of Judah [A]as well; they will go along [B]weep-
ing as they go, and it will be [C]the LORD their God
they will seek. 5 They will [A]ask for the way to Zion,
turning their faces [a]in its direction; [b]they [c]will come
that they may join themselves to the LORD *in* an
[B]everlasting covenant that will not be forgotten.

6 "My people have become [A]lost sheep;
[B]Their shepherds have led them astray.
They have made them turn
aside *on* the [C]mountains;
They have gone along from
mountain to hill
And have forgotten their [D]resting place.

49:29 [A]Hab 3:7 [B]1 Chr 5:21 [C]Jer 46:5 49:30 [A]Jer 25:9; 27:6 49:31 [A]Judg 18:7; Is 47:8 [B]Is 42:11 [C]Num 23:9; Deut 33:28; Mic 7:14 49:32 [A]Ezek 5:10; 12:14, 15 [B]Jer 9:26; 25:23 49:33 [A]Is 13:20-22; Jer 9:11; 10:22; 51:37; Zeph 2:9, 13-15; Mal 1:3 49:34 [A]Gen 10:22; 14:1, 9; Is 11:11; Jer 25:25; Ezek 32:24; Dan 8:2 [B]2 Kin 24:17, 18; Jer 28:1 49:35 [a]Lit *first* [A]Ps 46:9; Is 22:6; Jer 51:56 49:36 [A]Dan 7:2; 8:8; Rev 7:1 [B]Jer 49:32; Ezek 5:10; Amos 9:9 49:37 [a]Or *dismay* [A]Jer 6:19 [B]Jer 30:24 [C]Jer 9:16; 48:2 49:38 [a]Or *from there* 49:39 [a]Or *captivity* [A]Jer 48:47 50:1 [A]Gen 10:10; 11:9; 2 Kin 17:24; Is 13:1; 47:1; Dan 1:1; Rev 14:8 50:2 [a]Heb *Merodach* [b]Or *dismayed* [A]Jer 4:16 [B]Jer 51:27 [C]Jer 51:31 [D]Is 46:1 [E]Jer 51:47 50:3 [A]Is 13:17; Jer 50:9; 51:11, 27 [B]Is 14:22, 23; Jer 50:13 [C]Jer 9:10, 11; Zeph 1:3 50:4 [A]Is 11:12, 13; Jer 3:18; 31:31; 33:7; Hos 1:11 [B]Ezra 3:12, 13; Ps 126:5; Jer 31:9 [C]Hos 3:5 50:5 [a]Lit *hither* [b]M.T. reads *come ye!* [c]Or *will have come* [A]Is 35:8; Jer 6:16 [B]Is 55:3; Jer 32:40; Heb 8:6-10 50:6 [A]Is 53:6; Ezek 34:15, 16; Matt 9:36; 10:6 [B]Jer 23:11-14 [C]Jer 13:16; Ezek 34:6 [D]Jer 33:12; 50:19

49:31 no gates or bars. These nomads were out of the way of contending powers in Asia and Africa.

49:34–39 concerning Elam. As in 25:25, Elam (200 mi. E of Babylon and W of the Tigris River) was to be subjugated. Babylon fulfilled this in 596 B.C. Later, Cyrus of Persia conquered Elam and incorporated Elamites into the Persian forces that conquered Babylon in 539 B.C. Its capital, Susa, was the residence of Darius and became the center of the Persian Empire (Ne 1:1; Da 8:2).

49:34 reign of Zedekiah. Jeremiah speaks of this judgment in 597 B.C.

49:35 break the bow. Elamites were famous archers (cf. Is 22:6).

49:39 I will restore. As with certain other peoples in this section of nations, God would allow Elamites to return to their homeland. In Ac 2:9, Elamites were among the group present at the Pentecost event. This has eschatological implications as well.

50:1 concerning Babylon. The subject of chaps. 50 and 51 (cf. Is 13:1–14:23; Hab 2:6–17). Judgment focuses on Media Persia's conquest of Babylon in 539 B.C. The prediction of elements of violent overthrow, which was not the case when Cyrus conquered since there was not even a battle, points to fulfillment near the coming of Messiah in glory when events more fully satisfy the description (cf. Rev 17, 18).

50:2 idols. First the idols of Babylon are discredited by Jeremiah's using an unusual word for idols, meaning in Hebrew "dung pellets."

50:3 no inhabitant. The far view in the v. 1 note cites this as not yet fulfilled in a sudden way (cf. 51:8). Media Persia came down from the N in 539 B.C., and armies in the years that followed gradually brought the past Babylon to complete desolation (cf. vv. 12, 13).

50:4–10 sons of Israel will come. Jeremiah predicted a return for exiled Israel and Judah (vv. 17–20, as chaps. 30–33) as the scattered and penitent people were given opportunity to escape Babylon's doom and return to Jerusalem and to the Lord in an eternal covenant (v. 5).

50:5 *in an everlasting covenant.* This is the New Covenant summarized in 31:31.

7 "All who came upon them
have devoured them;
And their adversaries have
said, '[A]We are not guilty,
Inasmuch as they have sinned
against the LORD *who is* the
[B]habitation of righteousness,
Even the LORD, the [C]hope of their fathers.'

8 "Wander away from the [A]midst of Babylon
And [a]go forth from the land
of the Chaldeans;
Be also like male goats [b]at
the head of the flock.
9 "For behold, I am going to [A]arouse
and bring up against Babylon
A horde of great nations from
the land of the north,
And they will draw up *their*
battle lines against her;
From there she will be taken captive.
Their arrows will be like [a]an expert warrior
Who does not return empty-handed.
10 "[a,A]Chaldea will become plunder;
All who plunder her will have
enough," declares the LORD.

11 "Because you are glad, because
you are jubilant,
O you who [A]pillage My heritage,
Because you skip about [a]like
a threshing [B]heifer
And neigh like [b]stallions,
12 Your [A]mother [a]will be greatly ashamed,
She who gave you birth
[a]will be humiliated.
Behold, *she will be* the least of the nations,
A [B]wilderness, a parched land and a desert.
13 "Because of the indignation of the
LORD she will [A]not be inhabited,
But she will be [B]completely desolate;
Everyone who passes by Babylon
[C]will be horrified
And will hiss because of all her wounds.
14 "Draw up your battle lines against
Babylon on every side,
All you who [a]bend the bow;
Shoot at her, do not be sparing
with *your* arrows,
For she has [A]sinned against the LORD.

15 "Raise your battle cry against
her on every side!
She has [A]given [a]herself up,
her pillars have fallen,
Her [B]walls have been torn down.
For this is the [C]vengeance of the LORD:
Take vengeance on her;
[D]As she has done *to others, so* do to her.
16 "Cut off the [A]sower from Babylon
And the one who wields the sickle
at the time of harvest;
From before [a]the [B]sword of the oppressor
[C]They will each turn back to his own people
And they will each flee to his own land.

17 "Israel is a [A]scattered [a]flock, the [B]lions have
driven *them* away. The first one *who* devoured him
was the [C]king of Assyria, and this last one *who* has
broken his bones is [D]Nebuchadnezzar king of Babylon. 18 Therefore thus says the LORD of hosts, the
God of Israel: 'Behold, I am going to punish the king
of Babylon and his land, just as I [A]punished the king
of Assyria. 19 And I will [A]bring Israel back to his
pasture and he will graze on Carmel and Bashan,
and his [a]desire will be satisfied in the [B]hill country
of Ephraim and Gilead. 20 In those days and at that
time,' declares the LORD, 'search will be made for
the iniquity of Israel, but [A]there will be none; and
for the sins of Judah, but they will not be found; for
I will pardon those [B]whom I leave as a remnant.'

21 "Against the land of [a]Merathaim,
go up against it,
And against the inhabitants of [b,A]Pekod.
Slay and [c]utterly destroy them,"
declares the LORD,
"And do according to all that I
have commanded you.
22 "The [A]noise of battle is in the land,
And great destruction.
23 "How the [A]hammer of the whole earth
Has been cut off and broken!
How Babylon has become
An object of horror among the nations!
24 "I [A]set a snare for you and you were
also [B]caught, O Babylon,
While you yourself were not aware;
You have been found and also seized
Because you have engaged in
[C]conflict with the LORD."

50:7 [A]Jer 2:3; Zech 11:5 [B]Jer 31:23; 40:2, 3 [C]Ps 22:4; Jer 14:8; 17:13 50:8 [a]Another reading is *let them go forth* [b]Or *in front of* [A]Is 48:20; Jer 51:6; Rev 18:4 50:9 [a]So some mss and versions; M.T. reads *a warrior who makes childless* [A]Jer 51:1 50:10 [a]Or *the Chaldeans* [A]Jer 51:24, 35; Ezek 11:24 50:11 [a]Another reading is *in the grass* [b]Lit *mighty ones* [A]Jer 12:14 [B]Jer 46:20 50:12 [a]Or *has become* [A]Jer 15:9 [B]Jer 22:6; 51:43 50:13 [A]Jer 34:22 [B]Jer 51:26 [C]Jer 18:16; 49:17 50:14 [a]Lit *tread* (in order to string) [A]Hab 2:8, 17 50:15 [a]Lit *her hand* [A]1 Chr 29:24; 2 Chr 30:8; Lam 5:6 [B]Jer 50:44; 51:58 [C]Jer 46:10 [D]Ps 137:8; Rev 18:6 50:16 [a]Or *the oppressing sword* [A]Joel 1:11 [B]Jer 25:38; 46:16 [C]Is 13:14 50:17 [a]Lit *sheep* [A]Joel 3:2 [B]Jer 2:15; 4:7 [C]2 Kin 15:19; 17:6; 18:9-13 [D]2 Kin 24:1, 10-12; 25:1-7 50:18 [A]Is 10:12; Ezek 31:3, 11, 12; Nah 3:7, 18, 19 50:19 [a]Lit *soul* [A]Is 65:10; Jer 31:10; 33:12; Ezek 34:13 [B]Jer 31:6 50:20 [A]Is 43:25; Jer 31:34; Mic 7:19 [B]Is 1:9 50:21 [a]Or *Double Rebellion* [b]Or *Punishment* [c]Lit *put under the ban* [A]Ezek 23:23 50:22 [A]Jer 4:19-21; 51:54-56 50:23 [A]Jer 51:20-24 50:24 [A]Jer 48:43, 44 [B]Jer 51:31; Dan 5:30, 31 [C]Job 9:4; 40:2, 9

50:11–16 Judgment on Babylon is the vengeance of God (v. 15) for her treatment of His people.

50:17–20 This section summarized the divine interpretation of Israel's history: 1) suffering and judgment on her (v. 17); 2) judgment on those who afflicted Israel (v. 18); 3) her return in peace and plenty (v. 19); and 4) the pardon of her iniquity (v. 20) under Messiah.

50:21 Merathaim ... Pekod. This was a dramatic play on words emphasizing cause and effect. The first means "double rebellion" and named a region in southern Babylon near the Persian Gulf; the latter, meaning "punishment," was also in southern Babylon on the E bank of the Tigris River.

50:23 hammer of the whole earth. The description was of Babylon's former conquering force, and God's breaking the "hammer" He had once used. The fact that God used Babylon as His executioner was no commendation of that nation (cf. Hab 1:6, 7).

25 The LORD has opened His armory
And has brought forth the
[A]weapons of His indignation,
For it is a [B]work of the Lord [a]GOD of hosts
In the land of the Chaldeans.
26 Come to her from the [a]farthest border;
[A]Open up her barns,
Pile her up like heaps
And [b,B]utterly destroy her,
Let nothing be left to her.
27 [A]Put all her young bulls to the sword;
Let them [B]go down to the slaughter!
Woe be upon them, for their
[C]day has come,
The time of their punishment.

28 There is a [A]sound of fugitives and
refugees from the land of Babylon,
To declare in Zion the [B]vengeance
of the LORD our God,
Vengeance for His [C]temple.

29 "Summon [a]many against Babylon,
All those who [b]bend the bow:
Encamp against her on every side,
Let there be no escape[c].
Repay her according to her work;
[A]According to all that she has
done, *so* do to her;
For she has become [B]arrogant
against the LORD,
Against the Holy One of Israel.
30 "Therefore her [A]young men
will fall in her streets,
And all her men of war will be [a,B]silenced
in that day," declares the LORD.
31 "Behold, [A]I am against you,
O [a]arrogant one,"
Declares the Lord [b]GOD of hosts,
"For your day has come,
The time [c]when I will punish you.
32 "The [a,A]arrogant one will stumble and fall
With no one to raise him up;
And I will [B]set fire to his cities
And it will devour all his environs."

33 Thus says the LORD of hosts,
"The sons of Israel are oppressed,
And the sons of Judah as well;
And [A]all who took them captive
have held them fast,
They have refused to let them go.
34 "Their [A]Redeemer is strong, [B]the
LORD of hosts is His name;
He will vigorously [C]plead their case
So that He may [D]bring
rest to [a]the earth,
But turmoil to the inhabitants of Babylon.
35 "A [A]sword against the Chaldeans,"
declares the LORD,
"And against the inhabitants of Babylon
And against her [B]officials
and her [C]wise men!
36 "A sword against the [A]oracle priests,
and they will become fools!
A sword against her [B]mighty men,
and they will be [a,C]shattered!
37 "A sword against [a]their [A]horses
and against [a]their chariots
And against all the [b,B]foreigners
who are in the midst of her,
And they will become [C]women!
A sword against her treasures,
and they will be plundered!
38 "A [a,A]drought on her waters, and
they will be dried up!
For it is a land of [B]idols,
And they are mad over fearsome idols.

39 "Therefore the [A]desert creatures will
live *there* along with the jackals;
The ostriches also will live in it,
And it will [B]never again be inhabited
Or dwelt in from generation
to generation.
40 "As when God overthrew [A]Sodom
And Gomorrah with its neighbors,"
declares the LORD,
"No man will live there,
Nor will *any* son of man reside in it.

41 "Behold, a people is coming
[A]from the north,
And a great nation and many kings
Will be aroused from the remote
parts of the earth.

50:25 [a]Heb *YHWH*, usually rendered *LORD* [A]Is 13:5 [B]Jer 50:15; 51:12, 25, 55 50:26 [a]Lit *end* [b]Lit *put under the ban* [A]Is 45:3; Jer 50:10 [B]Is 14:23 50:27 [A]Is 34:7 [B]Jer 48:10 [C]Ps 37:13; Jer 46:21; 48:44; Ezek 7:7 50:28 [A]Is 48:20 [B]Ps 149:6-9; Jer 50:15; 51:10 [C]Lam 1:10; 2:6, 7 50:29 [a]Another reading is *archers* [b]Lit *tread* (in order to string) [c]Some mss add *to her* [A]Ps 137:8; Jer 50:15; 51:56; 2 Thess 1:6 [B]Ex 10:3; Jer 49:16; Dan 4:37 50:30 [a]Or *made lifeless* or *destroyed* [A]Is 13:17, 18; Jer 9:21; 18:21; 49:26; 51:4 [B]Jer 51:57 50:31 [a]Lit *arrogance* [b]Heb *YHWH*, usually rendered *LORD* [c]Another reading is *of your punishment* [A]Jer 21:13; Nah 2:13 50:32 [a]Lit *arrogance* [A]Is 10:12-15 [B]Jer 21:14; 49:27 50:33 [A]Is 14:17; 58:6 50:34 [a]Or their *land* [A]Prov 23:11; Is 43:14; Jer 15:21; 31:11; Rev 18:8 [B]Is 47:4; Jer 32:18; 51:19 [C]Jer 51:36; Mic 7:9 [D]Is 14:3-7 50:35 [A]Jer 47:6; Hos 11:6 [B]Dan 5:1, 2 [C]Dan 5:7, 8 50:36 [a]Or *dismayed* [A]Is 44:25 [B]Jer 49:22 [C]Nah 3:13 50:37 [a]Lit *his* [b]Lit *mixed multitude* [A]Ps 20:7, 8; Jer 51:21, 22 [B]Jer 25:20; Ezek 30:5 [C]Jer 48:41; 51:30; Nah 3:13 50:38 [a]Another reading is *sword* [A]Is 44:27; Jer 51:32, 36; Rev 16:12 [B]Is 46:1, 6, 7 50:39 [A]Is 13:21; 34:14; Rev 18:2 [B]Is 13:20; Jer 25:12 50:40 [A]Gen 19:24, 25; Is 13:19; Jer 49:18; Luke 17:28-30; 2 Pet 2:6; Jude 7 50:41 [A]Is 13:2-5; Jer 6:22; 50:3, 9; 51:27, 28

50:28 Vengeance for His temple. This refers to their burning the temple in the destruction of Jerusalem (cf. 51:11).

50:29 Repay her. God aimed to bless Israel and curse all who curse her (cf. Ge 12:1–3, Abrahamic Covenant). The judgment on Babylon, as in Hab 2, was a repayment in view of Babylon's wrongs as God defends Israel's case (v. 34; 51:36, 56), particularly God's vengeance on her arrogance ("arrogant against the LORD" cf. vv. 31, 32).

50:34 Redeemer. The OT concept of kinsmen-redeemer included the protection of a relative's person and property, the avenging of a relative's murder, the purchase of alienated property, and even the marriage of his widow (cf. Lv 25:25; Nu 35:21; Ru 4:4).

50:35–38 The "sword" is mentioned 5 times (cf. Eze 21).

50:40 As when God overthrew Sodom. Cf. 50:1. What befell Sodom (cf. Ge 19) was sudden and total destruction, not like the Media Persia takeover, but like an example for the future devastation that will overtake the final Babylon (cf. Rev 17, 18).

50:41 from the north. Media Persia in 539 B.C.

50:41–46 Cf. 6:22–24; 49:19–21. The "lion" is Cyrus.

42 "They [A]seize *their* bow and javelin;
They are [B]cruel and have no mercy.
Their [C]voice roars like the sea;
And they ride on [D]horses,
[E]Marshalled like a man for the battle
Against you, O daughter of Babylon.
43 "The [A]king of Babylon has heard
the report about them,
And his hands hang limp;
[B]Distress has gripped him,
Agony like a woman in childbirth.

44 "[A]Behold, one will come up like a lion from
the [a]thicket of the Jordan to [b]a perennially watered
pasture; for in an instant I will make them run away
from it, and whoever is [B]chosen I will appoint over
it. For who is [C]like Me, and who will summon Me
into court? And who then is the shepherd who can
[D]stand before Me?" 45 Therefore hear the [A]plan of
the LORD which He has planned against Babylon,
and His purposes which He has purposed against
the land of the Chaldeans: [B]surely they will drag
them off, *even* the little ones of the flock; surely
He will make their [a]pasture desolate because of
them. 46 At the [a]shout, "Babylon has been seized!"
the [A]earth is shaken, and an [B]outcry is heard among
the nations.

BABYLON JUDGED FOR SINS AGAINST ISRAEL

51 Thus says the LORD:

"Behold, I am going to arouse
against Babylon
And against the inhabitants
of [a]Leb-kamai
[b]The [A]spirit of a destroyer.
2 "I will dispatch [a]foreigners to Babylon
that they may [A]winnow her
And may devastate her land;
For on every side they will
be opposed to her
In the day of *her* calamity.
3 "[a]Let not [b]him who [c,A]bends
his bow [c]bend *it,*
[a]Nor let him rise up in his [B]scale-armor;
So do not spare her young men;
Devote all her army to destruction.
4 "They will fall down [a]slain in the
land of the Chaldeans,
And [A]pierced through in their streets."
5 For [A]neither Israel nor Judah
has been [a]forsaken
By his God, the LORD of hosts,
Although their land is [B]full of guilt
[b]Before the Holy One of Israel.
6 [A]Flee from the midst of Babylon,
And each of you save his life!
Do not be [a,B]destroyed in her [b]punishment,
For this is the [C]LORD'S time of vengeance;
He is going to [D]render recompense to her.
7 Babylon has been a golden [A]cup
in the hand of the LORD,
Intoxicating all the earth.
The [B]nations have drunk of her wine;
Therefore the nations are [C]going mad.
8 Suddenly [A]Babylon has fallen
and been broken;
[B]Wail over her!
[C]Bring [a]balm for her pain;
Perhaps she may be healed.
9 We applied healing to Babylon,
but she was not healed;
Forsake her and [A]let us each
go to his own country,
For her judgment has [B]reached to heaven
And [a]towers up to the very skies.
10 The LORD has [A]brought [a]about
our vindication;
Come and let us [B]recount in Zion
The work of the LORD our God!

11 [A]Sharpen the arrows, fill the quivers!
The LORD has aroused the spirit
of the kings of the Medes,
Because His purpose is against
Babylon to destroy it;
For it is the [B]vengeance of the LORD,
vengeance for His temple.
12 [A]Lift up a [a]signal against the
walls of Babylon;
Post a strong guard,
Station [b]sentries,
Place men in ambush!
For the LORD has both [B]purposed
and performed
What He spoke concerning the
inhabitants of Babylon.
13 O you who [A]dwell by many waters,
Abundant in [B]treasures,
Your end has come,
The [a]measure of your [b,C]end.

50:42 [A]Jer 6:23 [B]Is 13:17, 18; 47:6 [C]Is 5:30 [D]Jer 8:16; 47:3; Hab 1:8 [E]Jer 50:9, 14; Joel 2:5 50:43 [A]Jer 51:31 [B]Jer 30:6; 49:24 50:44 [a]Lit *pride* [b]Or *an enduring habitation* [A]Jer 49:19-21 [B]Num 16:5 [C]Is 46:9 [D]Job 41:10; Jer 30:21 50:45 [a]Or *habitation* [A]Ps 33:11; Is 14:24; Jer 51:10, 11 [B]Jer 49:20 50:46 [a]Lit *voice* [A]Jer 10:10; 49:21; Ezek 26:18; 31:16 [B]Is 5:7; 15:5; Jer 46:12; 51:54; Ezek 27:28 51:1 [a]Cryptic name for Chaldea; or *the heart of those who rise up against Me* [b]Or *a destroying wind* [A]Jer 4:11, 12; 23:19; Hos 13:15 51:2 [a]Some versions read *winnowers* [A]Is 41:16; Jer 15:7; Matt 3:12 51:3 [a]M.T. reads *Against him who* [b]I.e. the Chaldean defender [c]Lit *tread(s)* (in order to string) [A]Jer 50:14, 29 [B]Jer 46:4 51:4 [a]Or *wounded* [A]Is 13:15; 14:19; Jer 49:26; 50:30, 37 51:5 [a]Lit *widowed* [b]Lit *From* [A]Is 54:7, 8; Jer 33:24-26 [B]Hos 4:1, 2 51:6 [a]Or *silenced* or *made lifeless* [b]Or *penalty for iniquity* [A]Jer 50:8, 28; Rev 18:4 [B]Num 16:26 [C]Jer 50:15 [D]Jer 25:14 51:7 [A]Jer 25:15; Hab 2:16; Rev 14:8; 17:4 [B]Rev 14:8; 18:3 [C]Jer 25:16 51:8 [a]Or *balsam resin* [A]Is 21:9; Jer 50:2; Rev 14:8; 18:2 [B]Is 13:6; Rev 18:9 [C]Jer 46:11 51:9 [a]Lit *is lifted* [A]Is 13:14; Jer 46:16; 50:16 [B]Ezra 9:6; Rev 18:5 51:10 [a]Lit *forth* [A]Ps 37:6; Mic 7:9 [B]Is 40:2; Jer 50:28 51:11 [A]Jer 46:4, 9; Joel 3:9, 10 [B]Jer 50:28 51:12 [a]Or *standard* [b]Or *watchmen* [A]Is 13:2; Jer 50:2; 51:27 [B]Jer 4:28; 23:20; 51:29 51:13 [a]Lit *cubit* [b]Lit *being cut off* [A]Rev 17:1 [B]Is 45:3 [C]Is 57:17; Hab 2:9-11

51:1–4 the day of . . . calamity. The coming of the northern invader is in view.

51:5 Here is a reminder that God will not utterly forget or destroy His people. Cf. Ro 11:1, 2, 29.

51:8 Suddenly . . . fallen. The focus was first on Babylon's sudden fall on one night in 539 B.C. (Da 5:30). The far view looks at the destruction of the final Babylon near the Second Advent when it will be absolutely sudden (Rev 18).

51:11 kings of the Medes. The aggressor was specifically identified (cf. v. 28) as the leader of the Medes, assisted by Persia (539 B.C.).

14 The [A]LORD of hosts has sworn by Himself:
"Surely I will fill you with a
[a]population like [B]locusts,
And they will cry out with [b]shouts
of victory over you."

15 *It is* [A]He who made the earth by His power,
Who established the world by His wisdom,
And by His understanding He
[B]stretched out the heavens.
16 When He utters His [A]voice, *there is* a
tumult of waters in the heavens,
And He causes the [B]clouds to ascend
from the end of the earth;
He makes lightning for the rain
And brings forth the [C]wind
from His storehouses.
17 [A]All mankind is stupid, devoid
of knowledge;
Every goldsmith is put to
shame by his [a]idols,
For his molten images are [B]deceitful,
And there is no breath in them.
18 They are [A]worthless, a work of mockery;
In the time of their punishment
they will perish.
19 The [A]portion of Jacob is not like these;
For the [a]Maker of all is He,
And of the [b]tribe of His inheritance;
The [B]LORD of hosts is His name.
20 *He says,* "You are My [a,A]war-club,
My weapon of war;
And with you I [B]shatter nations,
And with you I destroy kingdoms.
21 "With you I [A]shatter the
horse and his rider,
And with you I shatter the
[B]chariot and its rider,
22 And with you I shatter [A]man and woman,
And with you I shatter old
man and [B]youth,
And with you I shatter young
man and virgin,
23 And with you I shatter the
shepherd and his flock,
And with you I shatter the
farmer and his team,
And with you I shatter
governors and prefects.

24 "But I will repay Babylon and all the inhabitants of [A]Chaldea for [B]all their evil that they have
done in Zion before your eyes," declares the LORD.

25 "Behold, [A]I am against you,
[B]O destroying mountain,
Who destroys the whole earth,"
declares the LORD,
"And I will stretch out My
hand against you,
And roll you down from the crags,
And I will make you a [C]burnt
out mountain.
26 "They will not take from you
even a stone for a corner
Nor a stone for foundations,
But you will be [A]desolate forever,"
declares the LORD.

27 [A]Lift up a [a]signal in the land,
Blow a trumpet among the nations!
Consecrate the nations against her,
Summon against her the [B]kingdoms
of [C]Ararat, Minni and [D]Ashkenaz;
Appoint a marshal against her,
Bring up the [E]horses like
bristly locusts.
28 Consecrate the nations against her,
The kings of the Medes,
[a]Their governors and
all [a]their [b]prefects,
And every land of [c]their dominion.
29 So the [A]land quakes and writhes,
For the purposes of the LORD
against Babylon stand,
To make the land of Babylon
[a]A [B]desolation without inhabitants.
30 The [A]mighty men of Babylon
have ceased fighting,
They stay in the strongholds;
[B]Their strength is [a]exhausted,
They are becoming [B]*like* women;
Their dwelling places are set on fire,
The [C]bars of her *gates* are broken.
31 One [a,A]courier runs to meet [a]another,
And one [b,B]messenger to meet [b]another,
To tell the king of Babylon
That his city has been captured
from end *to end;*

51:14 [a]Or *mankind* [b]I.e. like the song of grape treaders [A]Jer 49:13 [B]Jer 51:27; Nah 3:15 51:15 [A]Gen 1:1; Jer 10:12-16; 51:15-19 [B]Job 9:8; Ps 146:5, 6; Jer 32:17; Acts 14:15; Rom 1:20 51:16 [A]Job 37:2-6; Ps 18:13 [B]Ps 135:7; Jer 10:13 [C]Jon 1:4 51:17 [a]Or *graven images* [A]Is 44:18-20; Jer 10:14 [B]Hab 2:18, 19 51:18 [A]Jer 18:15 51:19 [a]Lit *Fashioner* [b]Or *Scepter;* cf Num 24:17 [A]Ps 73:26; Jer 10:16 [B]Jer 50:34 51:20 [a]Lit *shatterer* [A]Is 10:5; 41:15, 16; Jer 50:23 [B]Is 8:9; 41:15, 16; Mic 4:12, 13 51:21 [A]Ex 15:1 [B]Ex 15:4; Is 43:17 51:22 [A]2 Chr 36:17; Is 13:15, 16 [B]Is 13:18 51:24 [A]Jer 50:10 [B]Jer 50:15, 29 51:25 [A]Jer 50:31 [B]Is 13:2; Zech 4:7 [C]Rev 8:8 51:26 [A]Is 13:19-22; Jer 50:13; 51:29 51:27 [a]Or *standard* [A]Is 13:2-5; 18:3; Jer 50:2; 51:12 [B]Jer 50:3, 9 [C]Gen 8:4; 2 Kin 19:37; Is 37:38 [D]Gen 10:3 [E]Jer 50:42 51:28 [a]Lit *Her* [b]I.e. lieutenant governors [c]Lit *his* 51:29 [a]Or *An object of horror* [A]Jer 8:16; 10:10; 50:46; Amos 8:8 [B]Is 13:19, 20; 47:11; Jer 50:13; 51:26, 43 51:30 [a]Lit *dried up* [A]Ps 76:5; Jer 50:15, 36, 37 [B]Is 13:7, 8; Nah 3:13 [C]Is 45:1, 2; Lam 2:9; Amos 1:5; Nah 3:13 51:31 [a]Lit *runner* [b]Lit *announcer* [A]2 Chr 30:6 [B]2 Sam 18:19-31

51:15–19 **He who made the earth.** God's almighty power and wisdom in creation are evidences of His superiority to all idols (vv. 17, 18), who along with their worshipers will all be destroyed by His mighty power (vv. 15, 16, 19), as in Babylon's case.

51:20–23 **You are My war-club.** Cyrus of Persia was God's war club. Ten times the phrase "with you" hits with the force of a hammer.

51:25 **destroying mountain.** Though Babylon existed on a plain, this phrase was meant as a portrayal of Babylon's looming greatness and power in devastating nations (cf. also 50:23, and *see note there*). **a burnt out mountain.** Babylon will be like a volcano that is extinct, never to be rebuilt (v. 26).

51:27 Here are listed the people N of Babylon who were conquered by the Medes early in the sixth century B.C. They assisted the Medes against Babylon.

51:31 **To tell the king of Babylon.** Couriers brought the report of the city's fall. Since Belshazzar was slain in the city on the night of the fall (Da 5:30), reference may be to runners speeding the news to his co-ruler Nabonidus, who was away from Babylon or possibly to Daniel, the third ruler in the kingdom (Da 5:29).

32 The fords also have been seized,
And they have burned the
marshes with fire,
And the men of war are terrified.

33 For thus says the LORD of
hosts, the God of Israel:
"The daughter of Babylon is
like a [A]threshing floor
At the time [a]it is stamped firm;
Yet in a little while the time of
[B]harvest will come for her."

34 "Nebuchadnezzar king of Babylon has
[A]devoured me *and* crushed me,
He has set me down *like* an [B]empty vessel;
He has [C]swallowed me like a monster,
He has filled his stomach
with my delicacies;
He has washed me away.
35 "May the [A]violence *done* to me and
to my flesh be upon Babylon,"
The [a]inhabitant of Zion will say;
And, "May my blood be upon the
inhabitants of Chaldea,"
Jerusalem will say.

36 Therefore thus says the LORD,

"Behold, I am going to [A]plead your case
And [B]exact full vengeance for you;
And [C]I will dry up her [a]sea
And make her fountain dry.
37 "[A]Babylon will become a heap *of*
ruins, a haunt of jackals,
An [B]object of horror and hissing,
without inhabitants.
38 "They will roar together
like [A]young lions,
They will growl like lions' cubs.
39 "When they become heated up, I
will serve *them* their banquet
And [A]make them drunk, that
they may become jubilant
And may [B]sleep a perpetual sleep
And not wake up," declares the LORD.
40 "I will bring them down like
[a]lambs [A]to the slaughter,
Like rams together with male goats.

41 "How [a,A]Sheshak has been captured,
And [B]the praise of the whole
earth been seized!
How Babylon has become an object
of horror among the nations!
42 "The [a,A]sea has come up over Babylon;
She has been engulfed with
its tumultuous waves.
43 "Her cities have become an
[A]object of horror,
A parched land and a desert,
A land in which [B]no man lives
And through which no son of man passes.
44 "[A]I will punish Bel in Babylon,
And I will make what he has swallowed
[B]come out of his mouth;
And the nations will no longer
[C]stream to him.
Even the [D]wall of Babylon has fallen down!

45 "[A]Come forth from her midst, My people,
And each of you [B]save yourselves
From the fierce anger of the LORD.
46 "Now [A]so that your heart
does not grow faint,
And you are not afraid at the [B]report
that *will be* heard in the land—
For the report will come [a]one year,
And after that [b]another report
in [b]another year,
And violence *will be* in the land
With [C]ruler against ruler—
47 Therefore behold, days are coming
When I will punish the [A]idols of Babylon;
And her whole land will be [B]put to shame
And all her slain will fall in her midst.
48 "Then [A]heaven and earth and
all that is in them
Will shout for joy over Babylon,
For [B]the destroyers will come
to her from the north,"
Declares the LORD.

49 [A]Indeed Babylon is to fall *for*
the slain of Israel,
As also for Babylon [B]the slain of
all the earth have fallen.
50 You [A]who have escaped the sword,
Depart! Do not stay!
[B]Remember the LORD from afar,
And let Jerusalem [a]come to your mind.
51 [A]We are ashamed because we
have heard reproach;
Disgrace has covered our faces,
For [B]aliens have entered
The holy places of the LORD'S house.

51:33 [a]Lit *of treading it* [A]Is 21:10; 41:15, 16; Mic 4:13 [B]Is 17:5; Hos 6:11; Joel 3:13; Rev 14:15 51:34 [A]Jer 50:17 [B]Is 24:1-3 [C]Job 20:15; Jer 51:44 51:35 [a]Lit *inhabitress* [A]Ps 137:8 51:36 [a]Or *broad river* [A]Ps 140:12 [B]Jer 51:6, 11; Rom 12:19 [C]Jer 50:38 51:37 [A]Rev 18:2 [B]Jer 25:9 51:38 [A]Jer 2:15 51:39 [A]Jer 25:27; 48:26; 51:57 [B]Ps 76:5 51:40 [a]Or *young rams* [A]Jer 48:15; 50:27 51:41 [a]Cryptic name for Babylon [A]Jer 25:26 [B]Jer 49:25 51:42 [a]Or *broad river* [A]Is 8:7, 8; Jer 51:55; Dan 9:26 51:43 [A]Jer 50:12 [B]Is 13:20; Jer 2:6 51:44 [A]Is 46:1; Jer 50:2 [B]Ezra 1:7, 8 [C]Is 2:2 [D]Jer 50:15; 51:58 51:45 [A]Is 48:20; Jer 50:8, 28; 51:6; Rev 18:4 [B]Gen 19:12-16; Acts 2:40 51:46 [a]Lit *in the* [b]Lit *the* [A]Is 43:5; Jer 46:27, 28 [B]2 Kin 19:7; Is 13:3-5 [C]Is 19:2 51:47 [A]Is 21:9; 46:1, 2; Jer 50:2; 51:52 [B]Jer 50:12, 35-37 51:48 [A]Is 44:23; 48:20; 49:13; Rev 18:20 [B]Jer 50:3 51:49 [A]Ps 137:8; Jer 50:29 [B]Rev 18:24 51:50 [a]Lit *come upon your heart* [A]Jer 44:28 [B]Deut 4:29-31; Ps 137:6 51:51 [A]Ps 44:15 [B]Ps 74:3-8; Lam 1:10

51:32 The method of capturing the city was to block off the Euphrates River and dry up the riverbed under the city wall, then march in. The "fire" was set to frighten and it did.

51:39 drunk. The allusion is possibly to Belshazzar's drunken feast, recorded in Da 5:1–4 (cf. v. 57).

51:41 Sheshak has been captured. This is another name for Babylon (cf. 25:26).

51:45–50 Again the Lord's people were warned to flee.

52 "Therefore behold, the days are
coming," declares the LORD,
"When I will punish her [A]idols,
And the mortally wounded will
groan throughout her land.
53 "Though Babylon should
[A]ascend to the heavens,
And though she should fortify
[a]her lofty stronghold,
From [B]Me destroyers will come
to her," declares the LORD.

54 The [A]sound of an outcry from Babylon,
And of great destruction from
the land of the Chaldeans!
55 For the LORD is going to destroy Babylon,
And He will make *her* loud
[a]noise vanish from her.
And their [A]waves will roar
like many waters;
The tumult of their voices [b]sounds forth.
56 For the [A]destroyer is coming
against her, against Babylon,
And her mighty men will be captured,
Their [B]bows are shattered;
For the LORD is a God of [C]recompense,
He will fully repay.
57 "I will [A]make her princes and
her wise men drunk,
Her governors, her prefects
and her mighty men,
That they may sleep a [B]perpetual
sleep and not wake up,"
[C]Declares the King, whose name
is the LORD of hosts.

58 Thus says the LORD of hosts,

"The broad [A]wall of Babylon will
be completely razed
And her high [B]gates will be set on fire;
So the peoples will [C]toil for nothing,
And the nations become
[D]exhausted *only* for fire."

59 The [a]message which Jeremiah the prophet
commanded Seraiah the son of [A]Neriah, the grandson of Mahseiah, when he went with [B]Zedekiah
the king of Judah to Babylon in the fourth year of
his reign. (Now Seraiah was quartermaster.) 60 So
Jeremiah [A]wrote in a single [a]scroll all the calamity
which would come upon Babylon, *that is,* all these
words which have been written concerning Babylon. 61 Then Jeremiah said to Seraiah, "As soon
as you come to Babylon, then see that you read all
these words aloud, 62 and say, 'You, O LORD, have
[a]promised concerning this place to [A]cut it off, so
that there will be [B]nothing dwelling in it, [b]whether
man or beast, but it will be a perpetual desolation.'
63 And as soon as you finish reading this [a]scroll, you
will tie a stone to it and [A]throw it into the middle
of the Euphrates, 64 and say, 'Just so shall Babylon
sink down and [A]not rise again because of the calamity that I am going to bring upon her; and they
will become [B]exhausted.' " [C]Thus far are the words
of Jeremiah.

THE FALL OF JERUSALEM

52 [A]Zedekiah was twenty-one years old when he
became king, and he reigned eleven years in
Jerusalem; and his mother's name was [a,B]Hamutal
the daughter of Jeremiah of [C]Libnah. 2 He did [A]evil
in the sight of the LORD like all that [B]Jehoiakim
had done. 3 For through the [A]anger of the LORD *this*
came about in Jerusalem and Judah until He cast
them out from His presence. And Zedekiah [B]rebelled
against the king of Babylon. 4 [A]Now it came about
in the ninth year of his reign, on the tenth *day* of
the tenth month, that Nebuchadnezzar king of Babylon came, he and all his army, against Jerusalem,
camped against it and built a [B]siege wall all around
[a]it. 5 [A]So the city was under siege until the eleventh
year of King Zedekiah. 6 On the ninth *day* of the
[A]fourth month the [B]famine was so severe in the city
that there was no food for the people of the land.
7 Then the city was [A]broken into, and all the [B]men
of war fled and went forth from the city at night by
way of the gate between the two walls which *was*
by the king's garden, though the Chaldeans were
[a,C]all around the city. And they went by way of the
Arabah. 8 But the army of the Chaldeans pursued
the king and [A]overtook Zedekiah in the [a]plains of
Jericho, and all his army was scattered from him.
9 Then they captured the king and [A]brought him up
to the king of Babylon at [B]Riblah in the land of [C]Ha-
math, and he [a]passed sentence on him. 10 The king

51:52 [A]Jer 50:38 51:53 [a]Lit *the height of her strength* [A]Gen 11:4; Job 20:6; Ps 139:8-10; Is 14:12-14; Jer 49:16; Amos 9:2; Obad 4 [B]Is 13:3 51:54 [A]Jer 48:3-5; 50:22, 46 51:55 [a]Or *voice* [b]Lit *is given* [A]Ps 18:4; 69:2; 124:2, 4, 5; Jer 51:42 51:56 [A]Jer 51:48, 53; Hab 2:8 [B]Ps 46:9; 76:3 [C]Deut 32:35; Ps 94:1, 2; Jer 51:6, 24 51:57 [A]Jer 25:27 [B]Ps 76:5, 6 [C]Jer 46:18; 48:15 51:58 [A]Jer 50:15 [B]Is 45:1, 2 [C]Hab 2:13 [D]Jer 9:5; 51:64; Lam 5:5 51:59 [a]Lit *word* [A]Jer 32:12; 36:4; 45:1 [B]Jer 28:1; 52:1 51:60 [a]Or *book* [A]Is 30:8; Jer 30:2, 3; 36:2, 4, 32 51:62 [a]Lit *spoken* [b]Lit *from man even to beast* [A]Is 13:19-22; 14:22, 23; Jer 50:3, 13, 39, 40 [B]Jer 51:43; Ezek 35:9 51:63 [a]Or *book* [A]Jer 19:10, 11; Rev 18:21 51:64 [A]Nah 1:8, 9 [B]Jer 51:58 [C]Job 31:40; Ps 72:20 52:1 [a]Another reading is *Hamital* [A]2 Kin 24:18; 2 Chr 36:11 [B]2 Kin 23:31; 24:18 [C]Josh 10:29; 2 Kin 8:22; Is 37:8 52:2 [A]1 Kin 14:22; 2 Kin 24:19; 2 Chr 36:12 [B]Jer 36:30, 31 52:3 [A]2 Kin 24:20; Is 3:1, 4, 5 [B]2 Chr 36:13; Ezek 17:12-16 52:4 [a]Lit *against it* [A]2 Kin 25:1; Jer 39:1; Ezek 24:1, 2; Zech 8:19 [B]Jer 32:24 52:5 [A]2 Kin 25:2 52:6 [A]Jer 39:2 [B]2 Kin 25:3; Is 3:1; Jer 38:9; Ezek 4:16; 5:16; 14:13 52:7 [a]Lit *against the city on every side* [A]2 Kin 25:4; Jer 39:2 [B]Jer 39:4-7; 51:32 [C]Ezek 33:21 52:8 [a]Lit *Arabah* [A]Jer 21:7; 32:4; 34:21; 37:17; 38:23 52:9 [a]Lit *spoke judgments with* [A]2 Kin 25:6; Jer 32:4; 39:5 [B]Num 34:11; Jer 39:5 [C]Num 13:21; Josh 13:5

51:58 toil for nothing. People from many nations enslaved in Babylon had built the wall for nothing.

51:59 Seraiah was quartermaster. This man looked after the comfort of the king. He may have been the brother of Baruch, Jeremiah's secretary (cf. 32:12).

51:60–63 This royal official carried the scroll (v. 60) to read (v. 61) in Babylon and then dramatically illustrated the coming destruction.

52:1–34 This chapter is almost identical to 2Ki 24:18–25:30, and it is a historical supplement detailing Jerusalem's fall (as chap. 39). It fittingly opens with her last king and his sin (597–586 B.C.). The purpose of this chapter is to show how accurate Jeremiah's prophecies were concerning Jerusalem and Judah.

52:1 Jeremiah. A different man from the author (cf. 1:1).

52:4–11 *See note on 34:1.* This narrative rehearses the account of the fall of Jerusalem. So crucial was this event that the OT records it 4 times (see also 39:1–14; 2Ki 25; 2Ch 36:11–21).

52:4 ninth year . . . tenth month. For vv. 4–6, *see notes on 34:1 and 39:1, 2.*

of Babylon [A]slaughtered the sons of Zedekiah before
his eyes, and he also slaughtered all the [a]princes
of Judah in Riblah. 11 Then he [A]blinded the eyes of
Zedekiah; and the king of Babylon bound him with
bronze fetters and brought him to Babylon and put
him in prison until the day of his death.
12 [A]Now on the tenth *day* of the fifth month, which
was the [B]nineteenth year of King Nebuchadnezzar,
king of Babylon, [C]Nebuzaradan the captain of the
bodyguard, [a]who was in the service of the king of
Babylon, came to Jerusalem. 13 He [A]burned the house
of the LORD, the [B]king's house and all the houses of Jerusalem; even every large house he burned with fire.
14 So all the army of the Chaldeans who *were* with the
captain of the guard [A]broke down all the walls around
Jerusalem. 15 Then Nebuzaradan the captain of the
guard [A]carried away into exile some of the poorest
of the people, the rest of the people who were left in
the city, the [a,B]deserters who had deserted to the king
of Babylon and the rest of the artisans. 16 But [A]Neb-
uzaradan the captain of the guard left some of the
poorest of the land to be vinedressers and [a]plowmen.
17 Now the bronze [A]pillars which belonged to the
house of the LORD and the [B]stands and the bronze
[C]sea, which were in the house of the LORD, the Chaldeans broke in pieces and carried all their bronze
to Babylon. 18 They also took away the [A]pots, the
shovels, the snuffers, the basins, the [a]pans and all
the bronze vessels which were used in *temple* service. 19 The captain of the guard also took away
the [A]bowls, the firepans, the basins, the pots, the
lampstands, the [a]pans and the drink offering bowls,
what was fine gold and what was fine silver. 20 The
two pillars, the one sea, and the twelve bronze bulls
that were under [a]the sea, *and* the stands, which King
Solomon had made for the house of the LORD—the
bronze of all these vessels was [A]beyond weight.
21 As for the pillars, the [A]height of each pillar *was*
eighteen [a]cubits, and [b]it *was* twelve cubits in [A]cir-
cumference and four fingers in thickness, *and* hollow. 22 Now a [A]capital of bronze was on it; and the
height of each capital was five cubits, with network
and [B]pomegranates upon the capital all around,
all of bronze. And the second pillar was like these,
including pomegranates. 23 There were ninety-six
[a]exposed pomegranates; all [A]the pomegranates
numbered a hundred on the network all around.
24 Then the captain of the guard took [A]Seraiah the
chief priest and [B]Zephaniah the second priest, with
the three [a,C]officers of the temple. 25 He also took
from the city one official who was overseer of the
men of war, and seven [a]of the [A]king's advisers who
were found in the city, and the scribe of the commander of the army who mustered the people of the
land, and sixty men of the people of the land who
were found in the midst of the city. 26 Nebuzaradan
the captain of the guard took them and [A]brought
them to the king of Babylon at Riblah. 27 Then the
king of Babylon [A]struck them down and put them
to death at Riblah in the land of Hamath. So Judah
was [B]led away into exile from its land.
28 These are the people whom [A]Nebuchadnezzar
carried away into exile: in the [a]seventh year 3,023
Jews; 29 in the eighteenth year of Nebuchadnezzar
832 persons from Jerusalem; 30 in the twenty-third
year of Nebuchadnezzar, [A]Nebuzaradan the captain

52:10 [a]Or *commanders* [A]2 Kin 25:7; Jer 22:30; 39:6 52:11 [A]Jer 39:7; Ezek 12:13 52:12 [a]Lit *stood before the king* [A]2 Kin 25:8-21; Zech 7:5; 8:19 [B]2 Kin 24:12; 25:8; Jer 52:29 [C]Jer 39:9 52:13 [A]1 Kin 9:8; 2 Kin 25:9; 2 Chr 36:19; Ps 74:6-8; 79:1; Is 64:10, 11; Lam 2:7; Mic 3:12 [B]Jer 39:8 52:14 [A]2 Kin 25:10; Neh 1:3 52:15 [a]Lit *fallers who had fallen* [A]2 Kin 25:11 [B]Jer 39:9 52:16 [a]Or *unpaid laborers* [A]2 Kin 25:12; Jer 39:10; 40:2-6 52:17 [A]1 Kin 7:15-22; 2 Kin 25:13; Jer 27:19-22; 52:20-23 [B]1 Kin 7:27-37 [C]1 Kin 7:23-26 52:18 [a]Or *spoons* for incense [A]Ex 27:3; 1 Kin 7:40, 45; 2 Kin 25:14 52:19 [a]Or *spoons* for incense [A]1 Kin 7:49, 50; 2 Kin 25:15 52:20 [a]So Gr and Syriac; Heb omits *the sea* [A]1 Kin 7:47; 2 Kin 25:16 52:21 [a]I.e. One cubit equals approx 18 in. [b]Lit *a line of 12 cubits would encircle it* [A]1 Kin 7:15; 2 Kin 25:17; 2 Chr 3:15 52:22 [A]1 Kin 7:16; 2 Kin 25:17 [B]1 Kin 7:20, 42 52:23 [a]Lit *windward* [A]1 Kin 7:20 52:24 [a]Lit *keepers of the door* [A]2 Kin 25:18; 1 Chr 6:14; Ezra 7:1 [B]2 Kin 25:18; Jer 21:1; 29:25, 29; 37:3 [C]1 Chr 9:19; Jer 35:4 52:25 [a]Lit *men of those seeing the king's face* [A]2 Kin 25:19; Esth 1:14 52:26 [A]2 Kin 25:20 52:27 [A]2 Kin 25:21; Ezek 8:11-18 [B]Is 6:11, 12; 27:10; 32:13, 14; Jer 13:19; 20:4; 25:9-11; 39:9; Ezek 33:28; Mic 4:10 52:28 [a]Or possibly *seventeenth* [A]2 Kin 24:2, 3, 12-16; 2 Chr 36:20; Ezra 2:1; Neh 7:6; Dan 1:1-3 52:30 [A]2 Kin 25:11; Jer 39:9

52:12 tenth *day*. The parallel phrase in 2Ki 25:8 reads "seventh day." Nebuzaradan (v. 12), "captain of the bodyguard," started from Riblah on the seventh day and arrived in Jerusalem on the tenth day. **nineteenth year.** 586 B.C.

52:18, 19 They also took. The conquerors plundered the magnificent Solomonic temple and took the articles to Babylon. First Kings 6–8 describes these articles. Later, Belshazzar would use some of these at his immoral banquet, gloating over victory he wrongly attributed to his gods (Da 5; cf. Da 1:2).

52:22 five. Second Kings 25:17 reads "three." There may have been two parts to the capitals, the lower part of two cubits and the upper part, carved ornately, of 3 cubits. The lower may be omitted in 2Ki 25:17 as belonging to the shaft of the pillar.

52:24–27 Babylon executed some Judean leaders as an act of power, of resentment over the 18-month resistance (cf. 52:4–6), and of intimidation to prevent future plots.

52:25 seven. Second Kings 25:19 reads "five."

52:28–30 carried away. The stages of deportation to Babylon are: 1) in 605 B.C. under Jehoiakim which marked the beginning of the 70 years of exile, 2) in 597 B.C. under Jehoiachin, 3) in 586 B.C. under Zedekiah, and 4) a mopping up campaign in 582–81 B.C. The number may include only males.

TIME LINE FOR JEREMIAH

722 B.C.	Israel is conquered by the Assyrians
640 B.C.	Josiah becomes king in Judah
627 B.C.	Jeremiah is called to prophesy
612 B.C.	Assyria falls to the Babylonians and Medes
609 B.C.	Jehoahaz's reign begins in Judah
608 B.C.	Joiakim's reign begins in Judah
605 B.C.	Nebuchadnezzar's reign begins in Babylon
598 B.C.	Jehoiachin becomes king in Judah
597 B.C.	Zedekiah becomes Judah's last king
586 B.C.	Jerusalem falls to the Babylonians
585 B.C.	Jeremiah is taken to Egypt

of the guard carried into exile 745 Jewish people;
there were 4,600 persons in all.
31 [A]Now it came about in the thirty-seventh year
of the exile of Jehoiachin king of Judah, in the
twelfth month, on the twenty-fifth of the month,
that [a]Evil-merodach king of Babylon, in the *first* year
of his reign, [b,B]showed favor to Jehoiachin king of
Judah and brought him out of prison. 32 [A]Then he
spoke kindly to him and set his throne above the
thrones of the kings who *were* with him in Babylon.
33 So [a]Jehoiachin [A]changed his prison clothes, and
[b,B]had his meals in [c]the king's presence regularly all
the days of his life. 34 For his allowance, a [A]regular
allowance was given him by the king of Babylon,
a daily portion all the days of his life until the day
of his death.

52:31 [a]Or *Awil-Marduk* ("Man of Marduk") [b]Lit *lifted up the head of* [A]2 Kin 25:27 [B]Gen 40:13, 20; Ps 3:3; 27:6 52:32 [A]2 Kin 25:28
52:33 [a]Lit *he* [b]Lit *ate* [c]Lit *his presence* [A]Gen 41:14, 42; 2 Kin 25:29 [B]2 Sam 9:7, 13; 1 Kin 2:7 52:34 [A]2 Sam 9:10; 2 Kin 25:30

52:31–34 exile of Jehoiachin. A captive since 597 B.C., he appears here in 561 B.C., after Nebuchadnezzar's death when Evil-merodach ruled Babylon. Though detained, the former king was kindly freed to enjoy previously denied privileges. The Lord did not forget the Davidic line even in exile.

52:31 twenty-fifth. Second Kings 25:27 reads "twenty-seventh." Probably the decree was on the 25th day and carried out on the 27th.

THE BOOK OF LAMENTATIONS

TITLE

"Lamentations" was derived from a translation of the title as found in the Latin Vulgate (Vg.) translation of the Greek OT, the Septuagint (LXX), and conveys the idea of "loud cries." The Hebrew exclamation *'ekah* ("How," which expresses "dismay"), used in 1:1; 2:1; 4:1, gives the book its Hebrew title. However, the rabbis began early to call the book "loud cries" or "lamentations" (cf. Jer 7:29). No other entire OT book contains only laments, as does this distressful dirge, marking the funeral of the once beautiful city of Jerusalem (cf. 2:15). This book keeps alive the memory of that fall and teaches all believers how to deal with suffering.

AUTHOR AND DATE

The author of Lamentations is not named within the book, but there are internal and historical indications that it was Jeremiah. The LXX introduces La 1:1, "And it came to pass, after Israel had been carried away captive . . . Jeremiah sat weeping [cf. 3:48, 49, etc.] . . . lamented . . . and said . . . ." God had told Jeremiah to have Judah lament (Jer 7:29), and Jeremiah also wrote laments for Josiah (2Ch 35:25).

Jeremiah wrote Lamentations as an eyewitness (cf. 1:13–15; 2:6, 9; 4:1–12), possibly with Baruch's secretarial help (cf. Jer 36:4; 45:1), during or soon after Jerusalem's fall in 586 B.C. It was mid-July when the city fell and mid-August when the temple was burned. Likely, Jeremiah saw the destruction of walls, towers, homes, palace, and temple; he wrote while the event remained painfully fresh in his memory, but before his forced departure to Egypt ca. 583 B.C. (cf. Jer 43:1–7). The language used in Lamentations closely parallels that used by Jeremiah in his much larger prophetic book (cf. 1:2 with Jer 30:14; 1:15 with Jer 8:21; 1:6 and 2:11 with Jer 9:1, 18; 2:22 with Jer 6:25; 4:21 with Jer 49:12).

BACKGROUND AND SETTING

The prophetic seeds of Jerusalem's destruction were sown through Joshua 800 years in advance (Jos 23:15, 16). Now, for over 40 years, Jeremiah had prophesied of coming judgment and been scorned by the people for preaching doom (ca. 645–605 B.C.). When that judgment came on the disbelieving people from Nebuchadnezzar and the Babylonian army, Jeremiah still responded with great sorrow and compassion toward his suffering and obstinate people. Lamentations relates closely to the book of Jeremiah, describing the anguish over Jerusalem's receiving God's judgment for unrepentant sins. In the book that bears his name, Jeremiah had predicted the calamity in chaps. 1–29. In Lamentations, he concentrates in more detail on the bitter suffering and heartbreak that was felt over Jerusalem's devastation (cf. Ps 46:4, 5). So critical was Jerusalem's destruction that the facts are recorded in 4 separate OT chapters: 2Ki 25; Jer 39:1–11; 52; and 2Ch 36:11–21.

All 154 verses have been recognized by the Jews as a part of their sacred canon. Along with Ruth, Esther, Song of Solomon, and Ecclesiastes, Lamentations is included among the OT books of the Megilloth, or "five scrolls," which were read in the synagogue on special occasions. Lamentations is read on the 9th of Ab (July/Aug.) to remember the date of Jerusalem's destruction by Nebuchadnezzar. Interestingly, this same date later marked the destruction of Herod's temple by the Romans in A.D. 70.

HISTORICAL AND THEOLOGICAL THEMES

The chief focus of Lamentations is on God's judgment in response to Judah's sin. This theme can be traced throughout the book (1:5, 8, 18, 20; 3:42; 4:6, 13, 22; 5:16). A second theme which surfaces is the hope found in God's compassion (as in 3:22–24, 31–33; cf. Ps 30:3–5). Though the book deals with disgrace, it turns to God's great faithfulness (3:22–25) and closes with grace as Jeremiah moves from lamentation to consolation (5:19–22).

God's sovereign judgment represents a third current in the book. His holiness was so offended by Judah's sin that He ultimately brought the destructive calamity. Babylon was chosen to be His human instrument of wrath (1:5, 12, 15; 2:1, 17; 3:37, 38; cf. Jer 50:23). Jeremiah mentions Babylon more than 150 times from Jer 20:4 to 52:34, but in Lamentations he never once explicitly names Babylon or its king, Nebuchadnezzar. Only the Lord is identified as the One who dealt with Judah's sin.

Fourth, because the sweeping judgment seemed to be the end of every hope of Israel's salvation and the fulfillment of God's promises (cf. 3:18), much of the book appears in the mode of prayer: 1) 1:11, which represents a wailing confession of sin (cf. v. 18); 2) 3:8, with its anguish when God "shuts out my prayer" (cf. 3:43–54; Jer 7:16); 3) 3:55–59, where Jeremiah cries to God for relief, or 3:60–66, where he seeks for recompense to the enemies (which Jer 50, 51 guarantees); and 4) 5:1–22, with its appeal to heaven for restored mercy (which Jer 30–33 assures), based on the confidence that God is faithful (3:23).

A fifth feature relates to Christ. Jeremiah's tears (3:48, 49) compare with Jesus' weeping over the same city of Jerusalem (Mt 23:37–39; Lk 19:41–44). Though God was the judge and executioner, it was a grief to Him to bring this destruction. The statement "In all their affliction, He [God] was afflicted" (Is 63:9) was true in principle. God will one day wipe away all tears (Is 25:8; Rev 7:17; 21:4) when sin shall be no more.

A sixth theme is an implied warning to all who read this book. If God did not hesitate to judge His beloved people (Dt 32:10), what will He do to the nations of the world who reject His Word?

INTERPRETIVE CHALLENGES

Certain details pose initial difficulties. Among them are: 1) imprecatory prayers for judgment on other sinners (1:21, 22; 3:64–66); 2) the reason for God shutting out prayer (3:8); and 3) the necessity of judgment that is so severe (cf. 1:1, 14; 3:8).

OUTLINE

In the first 4 chapters, each verse begins in an acrostic pattern, i.e., using the 22 letters of the Hebrew alphabet in sequence. Chapters 1, 2, and 4 have 22 verses corresponding to 22 letters, while chap. 3 employs each letter for 3 consecutive verses until there are 22 trios, or 66 verses. Chapter 5 is not written alphabetically, although it simulates the pattern in that it has 22 verses. An acrostic order, such as in Ps 119 (where all 22 Hebrew letters are used in series of 8 verses each), was used to aid memorization. The structure of the book ascends and descends from the great confession in 3:22–24, "Great is Your faithfulness," which is the literary center of the book.

OUTLINE

I. The First Lament: Jerusalem's Devastation (1:1–22)
- A. Jeremiah's Sorrow (1:1–11)
- B. Jerusalem's Sorrow (1:12–22)

II. The Second Lament: The Lord's Anger Explained (2:1–22)
- A. The Lord's Perspective (2:1–10)
- B. A Human Perspective (2:11–19)
- C. Jeremiah's Prayer (2:20–22)

III. The Third Lament: Jeremiah's Griefs Expressed (3:1–66)
- A. His Distress (3:1–20)
- B. His Hope (3:21–38)
- C. His Counsel/Prayer (3:39–66)

IV. The Fourth Lament: God's Wrath Detailed (4:1–22)
- A. For Jerusalem (4:1–20)
- B. For Edom (4:21, 22)

V. The Fifth Lament: The Remnant's Prayers (5:1–22)
- A. To Be Remembered by the Lord (5:1–18)
- B. To Be Restored by the Lord (5:19–22)

THE SORROWS OF ZION

1 How [A]lonely sits the city
That was [B]full of people!
She has become like a [C]widow
Who was *once* [D]great among the nations!
She who was a princess
among the [a]provinces
Has become a [E]forced laborer!
2 She [A]weeps bitterly in the night
And her tears are on her cheeks;
She has none to comfort her
Among all her [B]lovers.
All her friends have [C]dealt
treacherously with her;
They have become her enemies.
3 [A]Judah has gone into exile [a]under affliction
And [a]under [b]harsh servitude;
She dwells [B]among the nations,
But she has found no rest;
All [C]her pursuers have overtaken her
In the midst of [c]distress.
4 The roads [a]of Zion are in mourning
Because [A]no one comes to
the appointed feasts.
All her gates are [B]desolate;
Her priests are groaning,
Her [C]virgins are afflicted,
And she herself [b]is [D]bitter.
5 Her adversaries have become [a]her masters,
Her enemies [b]prosper;
For the LORD has [A]caused her grief
Because of the multitude of
her transgressions;
Her little ones have gone away
As captives before the adversary.
6 All her [A]majesty
Has departed from the daughter of Zion;
Her princes have become like deer
That have found no pasture;
And they have [a,B]fled without strength
Before the pursuer.
7 In the days of her affliction
and homelessness
[A]Jerusalem remembers all
her precious things
That were from the days of old,
When her people fell into the
hand of the adversary
And [B]no one helped her.
The adversaries saw her,
They [C]mocked at her [a]ruin.
8 Jerusalem sinned [A]greatly,
Therefore [B]she has become
an unclean thing.
All who honored her despise her
Because they have seen her nakedness;
Even [C]she herself groans and turns away.
9 Her [A]uncleanness was in her skirts;
She [a]did not consider her [B]future.
Therefore she has [b,C]fallen astonishingly;
[D]She has no comforter.
"[E]See, O LORD, my affliction,
For the enemy has [F]magnified himself!"
10 The adversary has stretched out his hand
Over all her precious things,
For she has seen the [A]nations
enter her sanctuary,
The ones whom You commanded
That they should [B]not enter
into Your congregation.
11 All her people groan [A]seeking bread;
They have given their precious
things for food
To [B]restore their [a]lives themselves.
"See, O LORD, and look,
For I am [C]despised."
12 "Is [A]it nothing to all you who pass this way?
Look and see if there is any
[a]pain like my [a]pain
Which was severely dealt out to me,
Which the [B]LORD inflicted on the
day of His [C]fierce anger.

1:1 [a]Or *districts* [A]Is 3:26 [B]Is 22:2 [C]Is 54:4 [D]1 Kin 4:21; Ezra 4:20; Jer 31:7 [E]2 Kin 23:35; Jer 40:9 1:2 [A]Ps 6:6; 77:2-6; Lam 1:16 [B]Jer 2:25; 3:1; 22:20-22 [C]Job 19:13, 14; Ps 31:11; Mic 7:5 1:3 [a]Or *by reason of* [b]Lit *great* [c]Or *narrow places* [A]Jer 13:19 [B]Lev 26:39; Deut 28:64-67 [C]2 Kin 25:4, 5 1:4 [a]Or *to* [b]Or *suffers bitterly* [A]Is 24:4-6; Lam 2:6, 7 [B]Jer 9:11; 10:22 [C]Lam 2:10, 21 [D]Joel 1:8-13 1:5 [a]Lit *head* [b]Or *are at ease* [A]Ps 90:7, 8; Ezek 8:17, 18; 9:9, 10 1:6 [a]Lit *gone* [A]Jer 13:18 [B]2 Kin 25:4, 5 1:7 [a]Lit *cessation* [A]Ps 42:4; 77:5-9 [B]Jer 37:7; Lam 4:17 [C]Ps 79:4; Jer 48:27 1:8 [A]Is 59:2-13; Lam 1:5, 20 [B]Lam 1:17 [C]Lam 1:11, 21, 22 1:9 [a]Lit *did not remember her latter end* [b]Lit *come down* [A]Jer 2:34; Ezek 24:13 [B]Deut 32:29; Is 47:7 [C]Is 3:8; Jer 13:17, 18 [D]Eccl 4:1; Jer 16:7 [E]Ps 25:18; 119:153 [F]Ps 74:23; Zeph 2:10 1:10 [A]Ps 74:4-8; Is 64:10, 11; Jer 51:51 [B]Deut 23:3 1:11 [a]Lit *soul* [A]Jer 38:9; 52:6 [B]1 Sam 30:12 [C]Jer 15:19 1:12 [a]Or *sorrow* [A]Jer 18:16; 48:27 [B]Jer 30:23, 24 [C]Is 13:13; Jer 4:8

1:1–22 How lonely sits the city. Jerusalem was lonely, its people mourning (v. 2), forsaken by formerly friendly nations (v. 2), in captivity (v. 3), uprooted from their land (v. 3), their temple violated (v. 10). The multitude of sins (vv. 5, 8) had brought this judgment from the righteous God (v. 18).

1:1 like a widow. Verses 1–11 vividly portray the city like a bereft and desolate woman, as often in other Scriptures (cf. Eze 16, 23; Mic 4:10, 13). **a forced laborer!** Judah was taken captive to serve as slaves in Babylon.

1:2 She has none to comfort her. This ominous theme is mentioned 4 other times (vv. 9, 16, 17, 21). **lovers ... friends ... have become her enemies.** This refers to the heathen nations allied to Judah, and their idols whom Judah "loved" (Jer 2:20–25). Some later joined as enemies against her (2Ki 24:2, 7; Ps 137:7).

1:3 exile. Ca. 586 B.C. as in Jer 39, 40, 52. There had been two deportations earlier, in 605 B.C. and 597 B.C. (cf. Introduction: Author and Date).

1:4 Zion. This represents the place where Jehovah dwells, the mount on which the temple was built. **appointed feasts.** Passover, Pentecost (Feast of Weeks), and Booths, or Tabernacles (cf. Ex 23; Lv 23). **priests are groaning.** These were among those left in Judah before fleeing to Egypt (Jer 43), or possibly exiles in Babylon who mourned from afar (cf. v. 3).

1:5 the multitude of her transgressions. This was the cause of the judgment (cf. Jer 40:3; Da 9:7, 16).

1:8 become an unclean thing. This could refer to either the vile, wretched estate of continued sin and its ruinous consequences through judgment, or to being "moved, removed," as the LXX and Vg. translate it. Probably the former is correct, as befits the third and fourth lines, i.e., a despised, shameful, naked condition in contrast to her former splendor (cf. v. 6b).

1:9 Her uncleanness was in her skirts. A graphic description of the flow of spiritual uncleanness reaching the bottom of her dress (cf. Lv 15:19–33).

1:10 enter her sanctuary. This was true of the Ammonites and Moabites (Dt 23:3; Ne 13:1, 2). If the heathen were not allowed to enter for worship, much less were they tolerated to loot and destroy. On a future day, the nations will come to worship (Zec 14:16).

1:11 See, O LORD. The description of the devastated widow ends with a plea for God's mercy.

1:12 all you who pass this way? Here was the pathetic appeal of Jerusalem for some compassion even from strangers!

13 “From on high He sent fire into my [A]bones,
And it [a]prevailed *over them*.
He has spread a [B]net for my feet;
He has turned me back;
He has made me [C]desolate,
[b]Faint all day long.
14 “The [A]yoke of my transgressions is bound;
By His hand they are knit together.
They have [B]come upon my neck;
He has made my strength [a]fail.
The Lord [C]has given me into the hands
Of *those against whom* I am
not able to stand.
15 “The [A]Lord has rejected all my strong men
In my midst;
He has called an appointed
[a]time against me
To crush my [B]young men;
The Lord has [C]trodden *as in* a wine press
The virgin daughter of Judah.
16 “For these things I [A]weep;
[a]My eyes run down with water;
Because far from me is a [B]comforter,
One who restores my soul.
My children are desolate
Because the enemy has prevailed.”
17 Zion [A]stretches out her hands;
There is no one to comfort her;
The LORD has [B]commanded
concerning Jacob
That the ones round about him
should be his adversaries;
[C]Jerusalem has become an unclean
thing among them.
18 “The LORD is [A]righteous;
For I have [B]rebelled against
His [a]command;
Hear now, all peoples,
And [C]behold my [b]pain;
[D]My virgins and my young men
Have gone into captivity.
19 “I [A]called to my lovers, *but*
they deceived me;
My [B]priests and my elders
perished in the city
While they sought food to [C]restore
[a]their strength themselves.
20 “See, O LORD, for I am in distress;
My [a,A]spirit is greatly troubled;
My heart is overturned within me,
For I have been very [B]rebellious.
In the street the sword [b]slays;
In the house it is like death.
21 “They have heard that I [A]groan;
There is no one to comfort me;
All my enemies have heard of my [a]calamity;
They are [B]glad that You have done *it*.
Oh, that You would bring the day
which You have proclaimed,
That they may become [C]like me.
22 “Let all their wickedness come before You;
And [A]deal with them as You
have dealt with me
For all my transgressions;
For my groans are many and
my heart is faint.”

GOD’S ANGER OVER ISRAEL

2 How the Lord has [A]covered
the daughter of Zion
With a cloud in His anger!
He has [B]cast from heaven to earth
The [C]glory of Israel,
And has not remembered His [D]footstool
In the day of His anger.
2 The Lord has [A]swallowed up;
He has not spared
All the habitations of Jacob.
In His wrath He has [B]thrown down
The strongholds of the daughter of Judah;
He has [C]brought *them* down to the ground;
He has [D]profaned the kingdom
and its princes.
3 In fierce anger He has cut off
[a]All the [A]strength of Israel;
He has [B]drawn back His right hand
From before the enemy.
And He has [C]burned in Jacob
like a flaming fire
Consuming round about.

1:13 [a]Or *descended, overthrew* [b]Or *Sick* [A]Job 30:30; Ps 22:14; Hab 3:16 [B]Job 19:6; Ps 66:11 [C]Jer 44:6 1:14 [a]Lit *stumble* [A]Prov 5:22; Is 47:6 [B]Jer 28:13, 14 [C]Jer 32:3, 5; Ezek 25:4, 7 1:15 [a]Or *feast* [A]Is 41:2; Jer 13:24; 37:10 [B]Jer 6:11; 18:21 [C]Mal 4:3 1:16 [a]Lit *My eye, my eye* [A]Jer 14:17; Lam 2:11, 18; 3:48, 49 [B]Ps 69:20; Eccl 4:1; Lam 1:2 1:17 [A]Is 1:15; Jer 4:31 [B]2 Kin 24:2-4; Jer 12:9 [C]Lam 1:8 1:18 [a]Lit *mouth* [b]Or *sorrow* [A]Ps 119:75; Jer 12:1 [B]1 Sam 12:14, 15; Jer 4:17 [C]Lam 1:12 [D]Deut 28:32, 41 1:19 [a]Lit *their soul* [A]Job 19:13-19; Lam 1:2 [B]Jer 14:15; Lam 2:20 [C]Lam 1:11 1:20 [a]Lit *inward parts are in ferment* [b]Lit *bereaves* [A]Is 16:11; Lam 2:11 [B]Jer 14:20 1:21 [a]Lit *evil* [A]Lam 1:4, 8, 22 [B]Ps 35:15; Jer 50:11; Lam 2:15 [C]Is 14:5, 6; 47:6, 11; Jer 30:16 1:22 [A]Neh 4:4, 5; Ps 137:7, 8 2:1 [A]Ezek 30:18 [B]Is 14:12-15; Ezek 28:14-16 [C]Is 64:11 [D]Ps 99:5; 132:7 2:2 [A]Ps 21:9; Lam 3:43 [B]Lam 2:5; Mic 5:11, 14 [C]Is 25:12; 26:5 [D]Ps 89:39, 40; Is 43:28 2:3 [a]Lit *Every horn* [A]Ps 75:5, 10; Jer 48:25 [B]Ps 74:11; Jer 21:4, 5 [C]Is 42:25; Jer 21:14

1:13 fire into my bones. This emphasizes the penetrating depth of the judgment. **turned me back.** God’s purpose was to bring repentance.

1:14 yoke of my transgressions … By His hand. Once the farmer had put the yoke on the animal’s neck, he would control it with the reins in his hands. So God, who has brought Jerusalem under yoke-bondage to Babylon, still controlled His people.

1:15 an appointed time against me. Not the usual assembly for a solemn feast; rather the army of Babylon for destruction. ***in a wine press.*** Speaks of forcing blood to burst forth like juice from crushed grapes. Comparable language is used in Rev 14:20 and 19:15 in regard to God’s final wrath.

1:17 unclean. This refers to a menstruous woman, shamed, separated from her husband and the temple (cf. vv. 8, 9 and Lv 15:19ff.).

1:18 The LORD is righteous .... have rebelled. The true sign of repentance was to justify God and condemn oneself.

1:21, 22 bring the day. A prayer that God will likewise bring other ungodly people into judgment, especially Babylon (3:64–66; 4:21, 22). Such prayers are acceptable against the enemies of God (cf. Ps 109:14, 15).

1:22 come before You. Cf. Rev 16:19.

2:1 How the Lord has. Much in La 2 depicts God’s judgment in vivid portrayals. He covered the Judeans with a cloud (v. 1), withdrew His hand of protection (v. 3), bent His bow and had slain with His arrows (v. 4), and stretched out a surveyor’s line to mark walls to be destroyed (v. 8). He will work a rebuilding of Jerusalem in the future kingdom (Zec 2:1–13). **The glory of Israel.** Likely refers to Mt. Zion and the temple (cf. Pss 48:2; 50:2; Is 60:13; 64:11; Eze 16:14; Da 11:45). **His footstool.** Refers to the ark of the covenant as indicated by 1Ch 28:2 and Pss 99:5; 132:7.

2:2 He has thrown down. The Lord had cast down the bastions of Judah’s defense, as He told Jeremiah He would do from the outset of his ministry (Jer 1:10).

4 He has bent His [A]bow like an enemy;
He has set His right hand like an adversary
And slain all that were
[B]pleasant to the eye;
In the tent of the daughter of Zion
He has [C]poured out His wrath like fire.
5 The Lord has become like an [A]enemy.
He has [B]swallowed up Israel;
He has swallowed up all its [C]palaces,
He has destroyed its strongholds
And [D]multiplied in the daughter of Judah
Mourning and moaning.
6 And He has violently treated His
[a]tabernacle like a garden *booth;*
He has [A]destroyed His appointed
[b]meeting place.
The LORD has [B]caused to be forgotten
The appointed feast and sabbath in Zion,
And He has [C]despised king and priest
In the indignation of His anger.
7 The Lord has [A]rejected His altar,
He has abandoned His sanctuary;
He [B]has delivered into the
hand of the enemy
The walls of her palaces.
They have made a [C]noise in
the house of the LORD
As in the day of an appointed feast.
8 The LORD [a]determined to destroy
The wall of the daughter of Zion.
He has [A]stretched out a line,
He has not restrained His
hand from [b]destroying,
And He has [B]caused rampart
and wall to lament;
They have languished together.
9 Her [A]gates have sunk into the ground,
He has destroyed and broken her bars.
Her king and her princes are
among the nations;
The [B]law is no more.
Also, her prophets find
[C]No vision from the LORD.
10 The elders of the daughter of Zion
[A]Sit on the ground, they [B]are silent.
They have thrown [C]dust on their heads;
They have girded themselves
with [D]sackcloth.
The [E]virgins of Jerusalem
Have bowed their heads to the ground.

11 My [A]eyes fail because of tears,
My [a,B]spirit is greatly troubled;
My [b,C]heart is poured out on the earth
[D]Because of the [c]destruction of the
daughter of my people,
When [E]little ones and infants faint
In the streets of the city.
12 They say to their mothers,
"[A]Where is grain and wine?"
As they faint like a wounded man
In the streets of the city,
As their [B]life is poured out
On their mothers' bosom.
13 How shall I admonish you?
To what [A]shall I compare you,
O daughter of Jerusalem?
To what shall I liken you as
I comfort you,
O [B]virgin daughter of Zion?
For your [a]ruin is as vast as the sea;
Who can [C]heal you?
14 Your [A]prophets have seen for you
False and foolish *visions;*
And they have not [B]exposed your iniquity
So as to restore you from captivity,
But they have [C]seen for you false
and misleading [a]oracles.
15 All who pass along the way
[A]Clap their hands *in derision* at you;
They [B]hiss and shake their heads
At the daughter of Jerusalem,
"Is this the city of which they said,
'[C]The perfection of beauty,
[D]A joy to all the earth'?"
16 All [A]your enemies
Have opened their mouths
wide against you;
They hiss and [B]gnash *their* teeth.
They say, "We have [C]swallowed *her* up!
Surely this is the [D]day for
which we waited;
We have reached *it,* we have seen *it.*"
17 The LORD has [A]done what He purposed;
He has accomplished His word
Which He commanded from days of old.
He has thrown down [B]without sparing,
And He has caused the enemy
to [C]rejoice over you;
He has [D]exalted the [a]might
of your adversaries.

2:4 [A]Job 6:4; 16:13; Lam 3:12, 13 [B]Ezek 24:25 [C]Is 42:25; Jer 7:20 2:5 [A]Jer 30:14 [B]Lam 2:2 [C]Jer 52:13; Lam 2:2 [D]Jer 9:17-20 2:6 [a]Lit *booth* [b]Or *feast* [A]Jer 52:13 [B]Jer 17:27; Lam 1:4; Zeph 3:18 [C]Lam 4:16 2:7 [A]Ps 78:59-61; Is 64:11; Ezek 7:20-22 [B]Jer 33:4, 5; 52:13 [C]Ps 74:3-8 2:8 [a]Lit *thought* [b]Lit *swallowing up* [A]2 Kin 21:13; Is 34:11; Amos 7:7-9 [B]Is 3:26; Jer 14:2 2:9 [A]Neh 1:3 [B]Hos 3:4 [C]Jer 14:14; 23:16; Ezek 7:26 2:10 [A]Job 2:13; Is 3:26; 47:1 [B]Amos 8:3 [C]Job 2:12; Ezek 27:30 [D]Is 15:3; Jon 3:6-8 [E]Lam 1:4 2:11 [a]Lit *inward parts are in ferment* [b]Lit *liver* [c]Lit *breaking* [A]Lam 1:16; 3:48, 51 [B]Jer 4:19 [C]Job 16:13 [D]Is 22:4; Lam 4:10 [E]Jer 44:7; Lam 2:19 2:12 [A]Jer 5:17 [B]Job 30:16; Ps 42:4; 62:8 2:13 [a]Lit *breaking* [A]Lam 1:12 [B]Is 37:22 [C]Jer 8:22; 30:12-15 2:14 [a]Lit *burdens* [A]Jer 23:25-29; 29:8, 9 [B]Is 58:1; Ezek 23:36; Mic 3:8 [C]Jer 23:36; Ezek 22:25, 28 2:15 [A]Job 27:23; Ezek 25:6 [B]Ps 22:7; Is 37:22; Jer 18:16; 19:8; Zeph 2:15 [C]Ps 50:2 [D]Ps 48:2 2:16 [A]Job 16:10; Ps 22:13; Lam 3:46 [B]Job 16:9; Ps 35:16; 37:12 [C]Ps 56:2; 124:3; Jer 51:34 [D]Obad 12-15 2:17 [a]Lit *horn* [A]Jer 4:28 [B]Lam 2:1, 2; Ezek 5:11; 7:8, 9; 8:18 [C]Ps 35:24, 26; 89:42; Is 14:29 [D]Deut 28:43, 44; Lam 1:5

2:6–11 Tragedy comes to everything and everyone through sin. The account mentions the temple or tabernacle where Israelites came to worship (v. 6), feasts and Sabbaths (v. 6), leaders such as the king and priests (v. 6), His altar and holy places (v. 7), city walls (v. 8), the law (v. 9), and children in the family (v. 11).

2:6, 7 Cf. 1:4.

2:7 noise ... house of the LORD ... day of an appointed feast. A shout of triumph in the captured temple resembled the joyous celebrations in the same place at the solemn feasts.

2:11, 12 This description of Babylon's invasion depicted the reality of a hungry child dying in its mother's arms as a result.

2:14 False and foolish *visions*. As Jer 23:16, 17 indicates, these lies spoke of peace and comfort, not judgment. Cf. Jer 23:30–40 to see how such lying led to destruction.

2:17 He has accomplished His word. The enemy that gloats in vv. 15, 16 should recognize that the destruction was the work of a sovereign God. This verse is the focal point of the chapter (cf. Jer 51:12).

18 Their [A]heart cried out to the Lord,
"O [B]wall of the daughter of Zion,
Let *your* [C]tears run down like
a river day and night;
Give yourself no relief,
Let [a]your eyes have no rest.
19 "Arise, cry aloud in the [A]night
At the beginning of
the night watches;
[B]Pour out your heart like water
Before the presence of the Lord;
Lift up your hands to Him
For the [C]life of your little ones
Who are [D]faint because of hunger
At the head of every street."
20 See, O LORD, and look!
With [A]whom have You dealt thus?
Should women [B]eat
their [a]offspring,
The little ones who were
[b]born healthy?
Should [C]priest and prophet be slain
In the sanctuary of the Lord?
21 On the ground in the streets
Lie [A]young and old;
My [B]virgins and my young men
Have fallen by the sword.
You have slain *them* in the
day of Your anger,
You have slaughtered,
[C]not sparing.
22 You called as in the day of
an appointed feast
My [A]terrors on every side;
And there was [B]no one who
escaped or survived
In the day of the LORD'S anger.
Those [C]whom I [a]bore and reared,
My enemy annihilated them.

JEREMIAH SHARES ISRAEL'S AFFLICTION

3 I am the man who has [A]seen affliction
Because of the rod of His wrath.
2 He has driven me and made me walk
In [A]darkness and not in light.
3 Surely against me He has [A]turned His hand
Repeatedly all the day.
4 He has caused my [A]flesh and
my skin to waste away,
He has [B]broken my bones.
5 He has [A]besieged and encompassed
me with [B]bitterness and hardship.
6 In [A]dark places He has made me dwell,
Like those who have long been dead.
7 He has [A]walled me in so that
I cannot go out;
He has made my [a,B]chain heavy.
8 Even when I cry out and call for help,
He [A]shuts out my prayer.
9 He has [A]blocked my ways
with hewn stone;
He has made my paths crooked.
10 He is to me like a bear lying in wait,
Like a lion in secret places.
11 He has turned aside my ways
and [A]torn me to pieces;
He has made me desolate.
12 He [A]bent His bow
And [B]set me as a target for the arrow.
13 He made the [a]arrows of His [A]quiver
To enter into my [b]inward parts.
14 I have become a [A]laughingstock
to all my people,
Their *mocking* [B]song all the day.
15 He has [A]filled me with bitterness,
He has made me drunk with wormwood.
16 He has [A]broken my teeth with [B]gravel;
He has made me cower in the [C]dust.

2:18 [a]Lit *the daughter of your eye* [A]Ps 119:145; Hos 7:14 [B]Lam 2:8; Hab 2:11 [C]Ps 119:136; Jer 9:1; Lam 1:2, 16; 3:48, 49 2:19 [A]Ps 42:3; Is 26:9 [B]1 Sam 1:15; Ps 42:4; 62:8 [C]Lam 2:11 [D]Is 51:20 2:20 [a]Lit *fruit* [b]Or *tenderly cared for* [A]Ex 32:11; Deut 9:26 [B]Jer 19:9; Lam 4:10 [C]Ps 78:64; Jer 14:15; 23:11, 12 2:21 [A]2 Chr 36:17; Jer 6:11 [B]Ps 78:62, 63 [C]Jer 13:14; Zech 11:6 2:22 [a]Lit *bore healthy* or, *tenderly cared for* [A]Ps 31:13; Is 24:17; Jer 6:25 [B]Jer 11:11 [C]Jer 16:2-4; 44:7 3:1 [A]Ps 88:7, 15, 16 3:2 [A]Job 30:26; Is 59:9; Jer 4:23 3:3 [A]Ps 38:2; Is 5:25 3:4 [A]Ps 31:9, 10; 38:2-8; 102:3-5 [B]Ps 51:8; Is 38:13 3:5 [A]Job 19:8 [B]Jer 23:15; Lam 3:19 3:6 [A]Ps 88:5, 6; 143:3 3:7 [a]Lit *bronze piece* [A]Job 3:23; 19:8 [B]Jer 40:4 3:8 [A]Job 30:20; Ps 22:2 3:9 [A]Is 63:17; Hos 2:6 3:11 [A]Job 16:12, 13; Jer 15:3; Hos 6:1 3:12 [A]Ps 7:12; Lam 2:4 [B]Job 6:4; 7:20; Ps 38:2 3:13 [a]Lit *sons* [b]Lit *kidneys* [A]Jer 5:16 3:14 [A]Ps 22:6, 7; 123:4; Jer 20:7 [B]Job 30:9; Lam 3:63 3:15 [A]Jer 9:15 3:16 [A]Ps 3:7; 58:6 [B]Prov 20:17 [C]Jer 6:26

2:18 wall of the daughter of Zion. The penetrated walls of Jerusalem cried out in anguish that they had been broached by the Babylonians.

2:20 See, O LORD, and look! The chapter closes by placing the issue before God. **women eat their offspring.** Hunger became so desperate in the 18-month siege that women resorted to the unbelievable—even eating their children (cf. 4:10; Lv 26:29; Dt 28:53, 56, 57; Jer 19:9).

2:21 the day of Your anger. This describes the complete slaughter, as does 2Ch 36:17.

3:1–20 the man who has seen affliction. Jeremiah's distress in such tragedy comes from God, referred to as "He" throughout this section. Even the righteous experience "the rod of His wrath."

3:8 He shuts out my prayer. Cf. v. 44. God's nonresponse to Jeremiah's prayers was not because Jeremiah was guilty of personal sin (cf. Ps 66:18); rather, it was due to Israel's perpetual sin without repentance (Jer 19:15). God's righteousness to judge that sin must pursue its course (Jer 7:16, and *see note there*; 11:14). Jeremiah knew that, yet prayed, wept (vv. 48–51), and longed to see repentance.

3:16 broken my teeth with gravel. This refers to the grit that often mixed with bread baked in ashes as was common in the E (cf. Pr 20:17).

OTHER LAMENTS
Job 3:3–26; 7:1–21; 10:1–22
Psalms (over 40), e.g., Pss 3; 120
Jeremiah 15:15–18; 17:14–18; 18:19–23
Ezekiel 19:1–14; 27:1–36; 32:1–21

17 My soul has been rejected [A]from peace;
I have forgotten [a]happiness.
18 So I say, "My strength has perished,
And *so has* my [A]hope from the LORD."

HOPE OF RELIEF IN GOD'S MERCY

19 Remember my affliction and my
[a]wandering, the [A]wormwood
and bitterness.
20 Surely [A]my soul remembers
And is [B]bowed down within me.
21 This I recall to my mind,
Therefore I have [A]hope.
22 The LORD'S [A]lovingkindnesses
[a]indeed never cease,
[B]For His compassions never fail.
23 *They* are new [A]every morning;
Great is [B]Your faithfulness.
24 "The LORD is my [A]portion,"
says my soul,
"Therefore I [B]have hope in Him."
25 The LORD is good to those
who [A]wait for Him,
To the [a]person who [B]seeks Him.
26 *It is* good that he [A]waits silently
For the salvation of the LORD.
27 *It is* good for a man that he should bear
The yoke in his youth.
28 Let him [A]sit alone and be silent
Since He has laid *it* on him.
29 Let him [a]put his mouth in the [A]dust,
Perhaps there is [B]hope.
30 Let him give his [A]cheek to [a]the smiter,
Let him be filled with reproach.
31 For the Lord will [A]not reject forever,
32 For if He causes grief,
Then He will have [A]compassion
According to His abundant lovingkindness.
33 For He [A]does not afflict [a]willingly
Or grieve the sons of men.
34 To crush under His feet
All the prisoners of the [a]land,
35 To [a]deprive a man of [A]justice
In the presence of the Most High,
36 To [a,A]defraud a man in his lawsuit—
Of these things the Lord does not [b]approve.
37 Who is [a]there who speaks and
it [A]comes to pass,
Unless the Lord has commanded *it?*
38 *Is it* not from the mouth of the Most High
That [a,A]both good and ill go forth?

39 Why should *any* living [a]mortal, or *any* man,
Offer [A]complaint [b]in view of his sins?
40 Let us [A]examine and probe our ways,
And let us return to the LORD.

3:17 [a]Lit *good* [A]Is 59:11; Jer 12:12 3:18 [A]Job 17:15; Ezek 37:11 3:19 [a]Or *bitterness* [A]Jer 9:15; Lam 3:5, 15 3:20 [A]Job 21:6 [B]Ps 42:5, 6, 11; 43:5; 44:25 3:21 [A]Ps 130:7 3:22 [a]Or *that we are not consumed* [A]Ps 78:38; Jer 3:12; 30:11 [B]Mal 3:6 3:23 [A]Is 33:2; Zeph 3:5 [B]Heb 10:23 3:24 [A]Ps 16:5; 73:26 [B]Ps 33:18 3:25 [a]Lit *soul* [A]Ps 27:14; Is 25:9 [B]Is 26:9 3:26 [A]Ps 37:7 3:28 [A]Jer 15:17 3:29 [a]Lit *give* [A]Job 16:15; 40:4 [B]Jer 31:17 3:30 [a]Lit *his* [A]Job 16:10; Is 50:6 3:31 [A]Ps 77:7; 94:14; Is 54:7-10 3:32 [A]Ps 78:38; 106:43-45; Hos 11:8 3:33 [a]Lit *from His heart* [A]Ps 119:67, 71, 75; Ezek 33:11; Heb 12:10 3:34 [a]Or *earth* 3:35 [a]Or *turn aside a man's case* [A]Ps 140:12; Prov 17:15 3:36 [a]Lit *make crooked* [b]Lit *see* [A]Jer 22:3; Hab 1:13 3:37 [a]Lit *this* [A]Ps 33:9-11 3:38 [a]Lit *the evil* things *and the good* [A]Job 2:10; Is 45:7; Jer 32:42 3:39 [a]Or *human being* [b]Or *on the basis of* [A]Jer 30:15; Mic 7:9; Heb 12:5, 6 3:40 [A]Ps 119:59; 139:23, 24; 2 Cor 13:5

3:21–33 The relentless sorrow over Judah's judgment drove Jeremiah to consider the grace, mercy, and compassion of God. The tone of his thinking changed dramatically.

3:21 This I recall. The prophet referred to what followed as he reviewed God's character.

3:22 lovingkindnesses. This Heb. word, used about 250 times in the OT, refers to God's gracious love. It is a comprehensive term that encompasses love, grace, mercy, goodness, forgiveness, truth, compassion, and faithfulness.

3:22–24 His compassions never fail. As bleak as the situation of judgment had become, God's covenant lovingkindness was always present (cf. vv. 31, 32), and His incredible faithfulness always endured so that Judah would not be destroyed forever (cf. Mal 3:6).

3:23 Great is Your faithfulness. The bedrock of faith is the reality that God keeps all His promises according to His truthful, faithful character.

3:27 The yoke in his youth. This speaks of the duty from God, including disciplinary training, that Jeremiah received in his youth (cf. Jer 1:6, 7).

3:29 mouth in the dust. A term which pictures submission.

3:30 give his cheek. The Lord Jesus did this (cf. Is 50:6; 1Pe 2:23).

3:33–47 God had a just basis for judgment.

3:38 This contrasted God's sovereign bestowal of judgment with blessing.

3:40, 41 return to the LORD. The solution to Judah's judgment was to repent, looking to God for relief and restoration.

BEYOND LAMENTATIONS—HOPE OF RESTORATION
1. Isaiah 35:1–10
2. Jeremiah 30:1–31:40
3. Ezekiel 37:1–28
4. Hosea 3:5; 14:1–9
5. Joel 3:18–21
6. Amos 9:11–15
7. Micah 7:14–20
8. Zephaniah 3:14–20
9. Zechariah 14:1–11
10. Malachi 4:1–6

8 [A]Slaves rule over us;
There is [B]no one to deliver
us from their hand.
9 We get our bread [a]at the [A]risk of our lives
[b]Because of the sword in the wilderness.
10 Our skin has become as [A]hot as an oven,
Because of [a]the burning heat of famine.
11 They ravished the [A]women in Zion,
The virgins in the cities of Judah.
12 Princes were hung by their hands;
[a,A]Elders were not respected.
13 Young men [a,A]worked at the grinding mill,
And youths [B]stumbled under
loads of wood.
14 Elders [a]are gone from the gate,
Young men from their [A]music.
15 The joy of our hearts has [A]ceased;
Our dancing has been turned
into mourning.
16 The [A]crown has fallen from our head;
[B]Woe to us, for we have sinned!
17 Because of this our [A]heart is faint,
Because of these things
our [B]eyes are dim;
18 Because of [A]Mount Zion
which lies desolate,
[B]Foxes prowl in it.

19 [A]You, O LORD, [a]rule forever;
Your [B]throne is from generation
to generation.
20 Why do You [A]forget us forever?
Why do You forsake us [a]so long?
21 [A]Restore us to You, O LORD, that
we may be restored;
Renew [B]our days as of old,
22 Unless [A]You have utterly rejected us
And are exceedingly [B]angry with us.

5:8 [A]Neh 5:15 [B]Ps 7:2; Zech 11:6 5:9 [a]Lit *with our soul* [b]Or *In the face of* [A]Jer 40:9-12 5:10 [a]Or *the ravages of hunger* [A]Job 30:30; Lam 4:8 5:11 [A]Is 13:16; Zech 14:2 5:12 [a]Lit *The faces of elders* [A]Is 47:6; Lam 4:16 5:13 [a]Lit *carry* [A]Judg 16:21 [B]Jer 7:18 5:14 [a]Lit *have ceased* [A]Is 24:8; Jer 7:34 5:15 [A]Jer 25:10; Amos 8:10 5:16 [A]Job 19:9; Ps 89:39; Jer 13:18 [B]Is 3:9-11 5:17 [A]Is 1:5 [B]Job 17:7; Lam 2:11 5:18 [A]Mic 3:12 [B]Neh 4:3 5:19 [a]Lit *sit* [A]Ps 102:12, 25-27 [B]Ps 45:6 5:20 [a]Lit *to length of days* [A]Ps 13:1; 44:24 5:21 [A]Ps 80:3; Jer 31:18 [B]Is 60:20-22 5:22 [A]Ps 60:1, 2; Jer 7:29 [B]Is 64:9

5:8–18 A list of horrors that had befallen Judah.

5:16 The crown has fallen. Israel lost its line of kings wearing the crown. The Davidic monarchy was temporarily over and will not be resumed until Christ comes as King (Jer 23:5–8; Eze 37:24–28; Rev 19:1–21).

5:19 Your throne is from generation to generation. Here is the high point of this chapter. Jeremiah was consoled by the fact that God always sits on His sovereign throne ruling over the universe from heaven (Pss 45:6; 93:2; 102:12; 103:19; Da 4:3, 34, 35).

5:21 Restore us to You. God must Himself initiate and enable any return to Him (cf. Ps 80:3, 7, 19; Jer 24:7; 31:18; Jn 6:44, 65). **Renew our days.** The intercessions of vv. 19–22 will yet be fulfilled in the New Covenant restoration of Israel (cf. Jer 30–33, and *see notes there*).

5:21, 22 This plea was not made with anger. The humble closing prayer sought God, who can never reject His people forever, to be faithful in restoring them (cf. Jer 31:35–37; 33:25, 26). In fact, their godly sorrow over sin was the beginning of that restoration, which would be completed by turning to God in faith and obedience.

THE BOOK OF

EZEKIEL

TITLE

The book has always been named for its author, Ezekiel (1:3; 24:24), who is nowhere else mentioned in Scripture. His name means "strengthened by God," which, indeed, he was for the prophetic ministry to which God called him (3:8, 9). Ezekiel uses visions, prophecies, parables, signs, and symbols to proclaim and dramatize the message of God to His exiled people.

AUTHOR AND DATE

If the "thirtieth year" of 1:1 refers to Ezekiel's age, he was 25 when taken captive and 30 when called into ministry. Thirty was the age when priests commenced their office, so it was a notable year for Ezekiel. His ministry began in 593/92 B.C. and extended at least 22 years until 571/70 B.C. (cf. 25:17). He was a contemporary of both Jeremiah (who was about 20 years older) and Daniel (who was the same age), whom he names in 14:14, 20; 28:3 as an already well-known prophet. Like Jeremiah (Jer 1:1) and Zechariah (cf. Zec 1:1 with Ne 12:16), Ezekiel was both a prophet and a priest (1:3). Because of his priestly background, he was particularly interested in and familiar with the temple details; so God used him to write much about them (8:1–11:25; 40:1–47:12).

Ezekiel and his wife (who is mentioned in 24:15–27) were among 10,000 Jews taken captive to Babylon in 597 B.C. (2Ki 24:11–18). They lived in Tel-abib (3:15) on the bank of the Chebar River, probably SE of Babylon. Ezekiel writes of his wife's death in exile (Eze 24:18), but the book does not mention Ezekiel's death, which rabbinical tradition suggests occurred at the hands of an Israelite prince whose idolatry he rebuked around 560 B.C.

The author received his call to prophesy in 593 B.C. (1:2), in Babylon ("the land of the Chaldeans"), during the fifth year of King Jehoiachin's captivity, which began in 597 B.C. Frequently, Ezekiel dates his prophecies from 597 B.C. (8:1; 20:1; 24:1; 26:1; 29:1; 30:20; 31:1; 32:1, 17; 33:21; 40:1). He also dates the message in 40:1 as 573/72, the 14th year after 586 B.C., i.e., Jerusalem's final fall. The last dated utterance of Ezekiel was in 571/70 B.C. (29:17).

Prophecies in chaps. 1–28 are in chronological order. In 29:1, the prophet regresses to a year earlier than in 26:1. But from 30:1 on (cf. 31:1; 32:1, 17), he is close to being strictly chronological.

BACKGROUND AND SETTING

From the historical perspective, Israel's united kingdom lasted more than 110 years (ca. 1043–931 B.C.), through the reigns of Saul, David, and Solomon. Then the divided kingdom, Israel (north) and Judah (south), extended from 931 B.C. to 722/21 B.C. Israel fell to Assyria in 722/21 B.C., leaving Judah, the surviving kingdom for 135 years, which fell to Babylon in 605–586 B.C.

In the more immediate setting, several features were strategic. Politically, Assyria's vaunted military might crumbled after 626 B.C., and the capital, Nineveh, was destroyed in 612 B.C. by the Babylonians and Medes (cf. Nahum). The neo-Babylonian Empire had flexed its muscles since Nabopolassar took the throne in 625 B.C., and Egypt, under Pharaoh Neco II, was determined to conquer what she could. Babylon smashed Assyria in 612–605 B.C., and registered a decisive victory against Egypt in 605 B.C. at Carchemish, leaving, according to the Babylonian Chronicle, no survivors. Also in 605 B.C., Babylon, led by Nebuchadnezzar, began the conquest of Jerusalem and the deportation of captives, among them Daniel (Da 1:2). In Dec., 598 B.C., he again besieged Jerusalem, and on Mar. 16, 597 B.C. he took possession. This time, he took captive Jehoiachin and a group of 10,000, including Ezekiel (2Ki 24:11–18). The final destruction of Jerusalem and the conquest of Judah, including the third deportation, came in 586 B.C.

Religiously, King Josiah (ca. 640–609 B.C.) had instituted reforms in Judah (cf. 2Ch 34). Tragically, despite his effort, idolatry had so dulled the Judeans that their awakening was only "skin deep" overall. The Egyptian army killed Josiah as it crossed Israel in 609 B.C., and the Jews plunged on in sin toward judgment under Jehoahaz (609 B.C.), Jehoiakim [Eliakim] (609–598 B.C.), Jehoiachin (598–597 B.C.), and Zedekiah (597–586 B.C.).

Domestically, Ezekiel and the 10,000 lived in exile in Babylonia (2Ki 24:14), more as colonists than captives, being permitted to farm tracts of land under somewhat favorable conditions (Jer 29). Ezekiel even had his own house (3:24; 20:1).

Prophetically, false prophets deceived the exiles with assurances of a speedy return to Judah (13:3, 16; Jer 29:1). From 593–585 B.C., Ezekiel warned that their beloved Jerusalem would be destroyed and their exile prolonged, so there was no hope of immediate return. In 585 B.C., an escapee from Jerusalem, who had evaded the Babylonians, reached Ezekiel with the first news that the city had fallen in 586 B.C., about 6 months earlier (33:21). That dashed the false hopes of any immediate deliverance for the exiles, so the remainder of Ezekiel's prophecies related to Israel's future restoration to its homeland and the final blessings of the messianic kingdom.

HISTORICAL AND THEOLOGICAL THEMES

The "glory of the Lord" is central to Ezekiel, appearing in 1:28; 3:12, 23; 10:4, 18; 11:23; 43:4, 5; 44:4. The book includes graphic descriptions of the disobedience of Israel and Judah, despite God's kindness (chap. 23; cf. chap. 16). It shows God's desire for Israel to bear fruit which He can bless; however, selfish indulgence had left Judah ready for judgment, like a torched vine (chap. 15). References are plentiful to Israel's idolatry and its consequences, such as Pelatiah dropping dead (11:13), a symbolic illustration of overall disaster for the people.

Many picturesque scenes illustrate spiritual principles. Among these are Ezekiel eating a scroll (chap. 2); the faces on 4 angels representing aspects of creation over which God rules (1:10); a "barbershop" scene (5:1–4); graffiti on temple walls reminding readers of what God really wants in His dwelling place, namely holiness and not ugliness (8:10); and sprinkled hot coals depicting judgment (10:2, 7).

Chief among the theological themes are God's holiness and sovereignty. These are conveyed by frequent contrast of His bright glory against the despicable backdrop of Judah's sins (1:26–28; often in chaps. 8–11; and 43:1–7). Closely related is God's purpose of glorious triumph so that all may "know that I am the LORD." This divine monogram, God's signature authenticating His acts, is mentioned more than 60 times, usually with a judgment (6:7; 7:4), but occasionally after the promised restoration (34:27; 36:11, 38; 39:28).

Another feature involves God's angels carrying out His program behind the scenes (1:5–25; 10:1–22). A further important theme is God's holding each individual accountable for pursuing righteousness (18:3–32).

Ezekiel also stresses sinfulness in Israel (2:3–7; 8:9, 10) and other nations (throughout chaps. 25–32). He deals with the necessity of God's wrath to deal with sin (7:1–8; 15:8); God's frustration of man's devices to escape from besieged Jerusalem (12:1–13; cf. Jer 39:4–7); and God's grace pledged in the Abrahamic Covenant (Ge 12:1–3) being fulfilled by restoring Abraham's people to the land of the covenant (chaps. 34, 36–48; cf. Ge 12:7). God promises to preserve a remnant of Israelites through whom He will fulfill His restoration promises and keep His inviolate Word.

INTERPRETIVE CHALLENGES

Ezekiel uses extensive symbolic language, as did Isaiah and Jeremiah. This raises the question as to whether certain portions of Ezekiel's writings are to be taken literally or figuratively, e.g., being bound with ropes, 3:25; whether the prophet was taken bodily to Jerusalem, 8:1–3; how individual judgment can be worked out in chap. 18 when the wicked elude death in 14:22, 23 and some of the godly die in an invasion, 21:3, 4; how God would permit a faithful prophet's wife to die (24:15–27); when some of the judgments on other nations will occur (chaps. 25–32); whether the temple in chaps. 40–46 will be a literal one and in what form; and how promises of Israel's future relate to God's program with the church. These issues will be treated in the study notes.

OUTLINE

The book can be largely divided into sections about condemnation/retribution and then consolation/restoration. A more detailed look divides the book into 4 sections. First, are prophecies on the ruin of Jerusalem (chaps. 1–24). Second, are prophecies of retribution on nearby nations (chaps. 25–32), with a glimpse at God's future restoration of Israel (28:25, 26). Thirdly, there is a transition chapter (33) which gives instruction concerning a last call for Israel to repent. Finally, the fourth division includes rich expectations involving God's future restoration of Israel (chaps. 34–48).

OUTLINE

I. Prophecies of Jerusalem's Ruin (1:1–24:27)

- A. Preparation and Commission of Ezekiel (1:1–3:27)
  1. Divine appearance to Ezekiel (1:1–28)
  2. Divine assignment to Ezekiel (2:1–3:27)
- B. Proclamation of Jerusalem's Condemnation (4:1–24:27)
  1. Signs of coming judgment (4:1–5:4)
  2. Messages concerning judgment (5:5–7:27)
  3. Visions concerning abomination in the city and temple (8:1–11:25)
  4. Explanations of judgment (12:1–24:27)

II. Prophecies of Retribution to the Nations (25:1–32:32)

- A. Ammon (25:1–7)
- B. Moab (25:8–11)

C. Edom (25:12–14)
D. Philistia (25:15–17)
E. Tyre (26:1–28:19)
F. Sidon (28:20–24)
1. Excursus: The Restoration of Israel (28:25, 26)
G. Egypt (29:1–32:32)

III. Provision for Israel's Repentance (33:1–33)

IV. Prophecies of Israel's Restoration (34:1–48:35)
A. Regathering of Israel to the Land (34:1–37:28)
1. Promise of a True Shepherd (34:1–31)
2. Punishment of the nations (35:1–36:7)
3. Purposes of restoration (36:8–38)
4. Pictures of restoration—dry bones and two sticks (37:1–28)
B. Removal of Israel's Enemies from the Land (38:1–39:29)
1. Invasion of Gog to plunder Israel (38:1–16)
2. Intervention of God to protect Israel (38:17–39:29)
C. Reinstatement of True Worship in Israel (40:1–46:24)
1. New temple (40:1–43:12)
2. New worship (43:13–46:24)
D. Redistribution of the Land in Israel (47:1–48:35)
1. Position of the river (47:1–12)
2. Portions for the tribes (47:13–48:35)

THE VISION OF FOUR FIGURES

1 Now it came about in the thirtieth year, on the
fifth *day* of the fourth month, while I was by the
[A]river Chebar among the exiles, the [B]heavens were
opened and I saw [a,C]visions of God. 2 (On the fifth of
the month [a]in the [A]fifth year of King Jehoiachin's
exile, 3 the [A]word of the LORD came expressly to
Ezekiel the priest, son of Buzi, in the [B]land of the
Chaldeans by the river Chebar; and there [C]the hand
of the LORD came upon him.)
4 As I looked, behold, a [A]storm wind was coming
from the north, a great cloud with fire flashing forth
continually and a bright light around it, and in its
midst something like [B]glowing metal in the midst
of the fire. 5 Within it there were figures resembling
[A]four living beings. And this was their appearance:
they had human [B]form. 6 Each of them had [A]four
faces and [B]four wings. 7 Their legs were straight and
[a]their feet were like a calf's hoof, and they gleamed
like [A]burnished bronze. 8 Under their wings on their
[A]four sides *were* human [B]hands. As for the faces and
wings of the four of them, 9 their wings touched one
another; *their faces* did [A]not turn when they moved,
each [B]went straight forward. 10 As for the [A]form of
their faces, *each* had the [B]face of a man; [a]all four had
the face of a lion on the right and the face of a bull on
the left, and [a]all four had the face of an eagle. 11 Such
were their faces. Their wings were spread out above;
each had two touching another *being*, and [A]two covering their bodies. 12 And [A]each went straight forward;
[B]wherever the spirit was about to go, they would go,
without turning as they went. 13 [a]In the midst of the
living beings there was something that looked like
burning coals of [A]fire, [b]like torches darting back and
forth among the living beings. The fire was bright,
and lightning was [c]flashing from the fire. 14 And the
living beings [A]ran to and fro like bolts of [B]lightning.
15 Now as I looked at the living beings, be-
hold, there was one [A]wheel on the earth beside
the living beings, [a]for *each of* the four of them.

1:1 [a]Some ancient mss and versions read *a vision* [A]Ezek 3:23; 10:15, 20 [B]Matt 3:16; Mark 1:10; Luke 3:21; Acts 7:56; 10:11; Rev 4:1; 19:11 [C]Ex 24:10; Num 12:6; Is 1:1; 6:1; Ezek 8:3; 11:24; 40:2; Dan 8:1, 2 1:2 [a]Lit *it was* [A]2 Kin 24:12-15; Ezek 8:1; 20:1 1:3 [A]2 Pet 1:21 [B]Ezek 12:13 [C]1 Kin 18:46; 2 Kin 3:15; Ezek 3:14, 22 1:4 [A]Is 21:1; Jer 23:19; Ezek 13:11, 13 [B]Ezek 1:27; 8:2 1:5 [A]Ezek 10:15, 17, 20; Rev 4:6-8 [B]Ezek 1:26 1:6 [A]Ezek 1:10; 10:14, 21 [B]Ezek 1:23 1:7 [a]Lit *the soles of their feet* [A]Dan 10:6; Rev 1:15 1:8 [A]Ezek 1:17; 10:11 [B]Ezek 10:8, 21 1:9 [A]Ezek 1:17 [B]Ezek 1:12; 10:22 1:10 [a]Lit *the four of them* [A]Rev 4:7 [B]Ezek 10:14 1:11 [A]Is 6:2; Ezek 1:23 1:12 [A]Ezek 1:9 [B]Ezek 1:20 1:13 [a]So with some ancient versions; Heb *as the likeness of the living beings* [b]Lit *like the appearance of* [c]Lit *coming out* [A]Ps 104:4; Rev 4:5 1:14 [A]Zech 4:10 [B]Matt 24:27; Luke 17:24 1:15 [a]Lit *for his four faces* [A]Ezek 1:19-21; 10:9

1:1 thirtieth year. Most likely this was Ezekiel's age, since the date relative to the king's reign is given in 1:2. Thirty was the age when a priest (cf. v. 3 with Nu 4) began his priestly duties. **river Chebar.** A major canal off of the Euphrates River, S of Babylon. **visions of God.** This scene has similarities to the visions of God's throne in Rev 4, 5, where the emphasis is also on a glimpse of that throne just before judgment is released in Rev 6–19.

1:2 fifth year. This is 593 B.C. The king, Ezekiel, and 10,000 others (2Ki 24:14) had been deported to Babylon in 597 B.C., Ezekiel at the age of 25.

1:3 word of the LORD ... hand of the LORD. As God prepared Isaiah (Is 6:5–13) and Jeremiah (Jer 1:4–19), so the Lord prepares Ezekiel to receive revelation and strengthens him for his high and arduous task to speak as His prophet. **Ezekiel the priest.** *See note on v. 1.*

1:4–14 The opening vision focuses on angels surrounding God's presence.

1:4 storm wind ... fire. Judgment on Judah in a further and totally devastating phase (beyond the 597 B.C. deportation) is to come out of the N, and did come from Babylon in 588–586 (as Jer 39, 40). Its terror is depicted by a fiery "storm wind" emblematic of God's judgments and the golden brightness signifying dazzling glory.

1:5 four living beings. Four angels, most likely the cherubs in 10:1–22, appearing in the erect posture and figure of man (note face, legs, feet, hands in vv. 6–8) emerge to serve God who judges. The number 4 may have respect to the 4 corners of the earth, implying that God's angels execute His commands everywhere.

1:6 four faces. *See note on v. 10.* **four wings.** Four wings instead of two symbolize speed in performing God's will (cf. v. 14).

1:7 legs. They were not bent like an animal's, but "straight" like pillars, showing strength. **calf's hoof.** This points to their stability and firm stance.

1:8 human hands. This is a symbol of their skillful service.

1:9 did not turn. They were able to move in any direction without needing to turn, giving swift access to do God's will. Apparently, all were in harmony as to the way they moved (v. 12).

1:10 faces. These symbols identify the angels as intelligent ("man"), powerful ("lion"), servile ("bull"), and swift ("eagle").

1:12 the spirit. This refers to the divine impulse by which God moved them to do His will (cf. 1:20).

1:13 like ... fire ... torches. Their appearance conveyed God's glory and pure, burning justice (cf. Is 6) which they assisted in carrying out even on Israel, who had for so long hardened themselves against His patience.

1:14 Intense, relentless motion signifies God's constant work of judgment.

1:15–25 This section looks at the glory of God's throne in heaven.

1:15 one wheel. This depicts God's judgment as a war machine (like a massive chariot) moving where He is to judge. The cherubim above the ark are called chariots in 1Ch 28:18.

DATES IN EZEKIEL

Event/Verse	Year	Month/Day	Date	Year
1. Call (1:2)	5	4/5	July 31	593
2. Temple tour (8:1)	6	6/5	Sept. 17	592
3. Elders' visit (20:1)	7	5/10	Aug. 17	591
4. Siege begins (24:1)	9	10/10	Jan. 15	588
5. Against Tyre (26:1)	11	?/1	?	587/586
6. Against Egypt (29:1)	10	10/12	Jan. 7	587
7. Against Tyre, Egypt (29:17)	27	1/1	April 26	571
8. Against Pharaoh (30:20)	11	1/7	April 29	587
9. Against Pharaoh (31:1)	11	3/1	June 21	587
10. Lament for Pharaoh (32:1)	12	12/1	March 3	585
11. Pharaoh to Sheol (32:17)	12	?/15	?	586/585
12. Refugee report on fall of Jerusalem (33:21)	12	10/5	Jan. 8	585
13. Vision of Future Temple Begins (40:1)	25	1/10	April 28	573

16 The [A]appearance of the wheels and their workmanship *was* like [a]sparkling [B]beryl, and all four
of them had the same form, their appearance and
workmanship *being* as if [b]one wheel were within
another. 17 Whenever they [a]moved, they [a]moved in
any of their four [b]directions without [A]turning as
they [a]moved. 18 As for their rims they were lofty
and awesome, and the rims of all four of them were
[A]full of eyes round about. 19 [A]Whenever the living
beings [a]moved, the wheels [a]moved with them. And
whenever the living beings [B]rose from the earth,
the wheels rose *also.* 20 [A]Wherever the spirit was
about to go, they would go in that direction[a]. And
the wheels rose close beside them; for the spirit of
the living [b]beings *was* in the wheels. 21 [A]Whenever
those went, these went; and whenever those stood
still, these stood still. And whenever those rose from
the earth, the wheels rose close beside them; for
the spirit of the living [a]beings *was* in the wheels.

VISION OF DIVINE GLORY

22 Now [A]over the heads of the living [a]beings *there*
was something like an expanse, like the awesome
gleam of [b]crystal, spread out over their heads. 23 Under the expanse their wings *were stretched out*
straight, one toward the other; each one also had
[A]two wings covering its body on the one side and
on the other. 24 I also heard the sound of their wings
like the [A]sound of abundant waters as they went, like
the [B]voice of [a]the Almighty, a sound of tumult like the
[C]sound of an army camp; whenever they stood still,
they dropped their wings. 25 And there came a voice
from above the [A]expanse that was over their heads;
whenever they stood still, they dropped their wings.
26 Now [A]above the expanse that was over their
heads there was something [B]resembling a throne,
like [a,C]lapis lazuli in appearance; and on that which
resembled a throne, high up, *was* a figure with the
appearance of a [D]man. 27 Then I [a]noticed from the
appearance of His loins and upward something
[A]like [b]glowing metal that looked like fire all around
within it, and from the appearance of His loins and
downward I saw something like fire; and *there was*
a radiance around Him. 28 As the appearance of
the [A]rainbow [a]in the clouds on a rainy day, so *was*
the appearance of the surrounding radiance. Such
was the appearance of the likeness of the [B]glory of
the LORD. And when I saw *it,* I [C]fell on my face and
heard a voice speaking.

THE PROPHET'S CALL

2 Then He said to me, "Son of man, [A]stand on
your feet that I may speak with you!" 2 As He
spoke to me the [A]Spirit entered me and set me on
my feet; and I heard *Him* speaking to me. 3 Then
He said to me, "Son of man, I am sending you to
the sons of Israel, to a rebellious people who have
[A]rebelled against Me; [B]they and their fathers have
transgressed against Me to this very day. 4 I am
sending you to them who are [a,A]stubborn and obstinate children, and you shall say to them, 'Thus says
the Lord [b]GOD.' 5 As for them, [A]whether they listen
or [a]not—for they are a rebellious house—they will
[B]know that a prophet has been among them. 6 And
you, son of man, [A]neither fear them nor fear their
words, though [B]thistles and thorns are with you and
you sit on scorpions; neither fear their words nor
be dismayed at their presence, for they are a rebellious house. 7 But you shall [A]speak My words to them
[B]whether they listen or [a]not, for they are rebellious.
8 "Now you, son of man, listen to what I am speaking to you; do not be rebellious like that rebellious
house. Open your mouth and [A]eat what I am giving
you." 9 Then I looked, and behold, a [A]hand was extended to me; and lo, a [a,B]scroll *was* in it. 10 When
He spread it out before me, it was written on the
front and back, and written on it were lamentations,
mourning and [A]woe.

1:16 [a]Lit *the look of beryl* [b]Lit *the wheel in the midst of the wheel* [A]Ezek 10:9-11 [B]Ezek 10:9; Dan 10:6 1:17 [a]Lit *went* [b]Lit *sides* [A]Ezek 1:9, 12; 10:11 1:18 [A]Ezek 10:12; Rev 4:6, 8 1:19 [a]Lit *went* [A]Ezek 10:16 [B]Ezek 10:19 1:20 [a]M.T. adds *the spirit to go* [b]M.T. reads *being* [A]Ezek 1:12 1:21 [a]M.T. reads *being* [A]Ezek 10:17 1:22 [a]So some ancient mss and versions; M.T. reads *being* [b]Or *ice* [A]Ezek 10:1 1:23 [A]Ezek 1:6, 11 1:24 [a]Heb *Shaddai* [A]Ezek 43:2; Rev 1:15; 19:6 [B]Ezek 10:5 [C]2 Kin 7:6; Dan 10:6 1:25 [A]Ezek 1:22; 10:1 1:26 [a]Heb *eben-sappir* [A]Ezek 1:22; 10:1 [B]Is 6:1; Ezek 10:1; Dan 7:9 [C]Ex 24:10; Is 54:11 [D]Ezek 43:6, 7; Rev 1:13 1:27 [a]Lit *saw* [b]Or *electrum* [A]Ezek 1:4; 8:2 1:28 [a]Lit *which occurs in* [A]Gen 9:13; Rev 4:3; 10:1 [B]Ex 24:16; Ezek 8:4; 11:22, 23; 43:4, 5 [C]Gen 17:3; Ezek 3:23; Dan 8:17; Rev 1:17 2:1 [A]Dan 10:11; Acts 9:6 2:2 [A]Ezek 3:24; Dan 8:18 2:3 [A]1 Sam 8:7, 8; Jer 3:25 [B]Ezek 20:18, 30 2:4 [a]Lit *the sons, stiff-faced and hard-hearted* [b]Heb *YHWH*, usually rendered *LORD* [A]Ps 95:8; Is 48:4; Jer 5:3; 6:15; Ezek 3:7 2:5 [a]Lit *forbear* [A]Ezek 2:7; 3:11, 27; Matt 10:12-15; Acts 13:46 [B]Ezek 33:33; Luke 10:10, 11; John 15:22 2:6 [A]Is 51:12; Jer 1:8, 17; Ezek 3:9 [B]2 Sam 23:6, 7; Ezek 28:24; Mic 7:4 2:7 [a]Lit *forbear* [A]Jer 1:7, 17; Ezek 3:10, 17 [B]Ezek 2:5 2:8 [A]Jer 15:16; Ezek 3:3; Rev 10:9 2:9 [a]Lit *scroll of a book* [A]Ezek 8:3 [B]Jer 36:2; Ezek 3:1; Rev 5:1-5; 10:8-11 2:10 [A]Is 3:11; Rev 8:13

1:16 as if one wheel were within another. This depicted the gigantic (v. 15, "on the earth" and "lofty," v. 18) energy of the complicated revolutions of God's massive judgment machinery bringing about His purposes with unerring certainty.

1:17 without turning. Cf. vv. 9, 12. The judgment machine moved where the angels went (cf. vv. 19, 20).

1:18 eyes. These may picture God's omniscience, i.e., perfect knowledge, given to these angelic servants so that they can act in judgment unerringly. God does nothing by blind impulse.

1:20 spirit. *See note on 1:12.*

1:24 sound of abundant waters. This imagery could have in mind a thunderous rush of heavy rain or the washing of surf on rocks (cf. 43:2; Rev 1:15; 14:2; 19:6).

1:25 voice. No doubt this is the "voice of the Almighty" (v. 24), since God's throne (v. 25) was "over their heads."

1:26 a throne. Cf. Ps 103:19; Rev 4:2–8. **a man.** The Godhead appears in the likeness of humanity, though God is a spirit (Jn 4:24). The Messiah, God incarnate, is the representative of the "fullness of Deity" (Col 2:9), so this can be a prelude to the incarnation of Messiah in His character as Savior and Judge (cf. Rev 19:11–16).

1:28 the glory of the LORD. That glory shines fully in the person of Jesus Christ (cf. 2Co 4:6), which is a constant theme in Ezekiel. **fell on my face.** John, in Rev 1:17, had the same reaction ("fell at His feet") to seeing the glory of the Lord.

2:1 Son of man. A term used over 90 times by Ezekiel to indicate his humanness.

2:2 the Spirit entered me. What God commands a servant to do (v. 1), He gives power to fulfill by His Spirit (cf. 3:14; Zec 4:6). This pictures the selective empowering by the Holy Spirit to enable an individual for special service to the Lord, which occurred frequently in the OT. For examples see 11:5; 37:1; Nu 24:2; Jdg 3:10; 6:34; 11:29; 13:25; 1Sa 10:10; 16:13, 14; 19:20; 2Ch 15:1; Lk 4:18.

2:5 The people cannot plead ignorance.

2:6 thistles and thorns ... scorpions. Cf. 3:7, 9; 22:29. These are figures of speech God used to describe the people of Judah, whose obstinate rejection of His Word was like the barbs of thorns and stings of scorpions to Ezekiel. The wicked were often so called (cf. 2Sa 23:6; SS 2:2; Is 9:18).

2:8 Open your mouth and eat. Ezekiel was to obey the command, not literally eating a scroll (vv. 9, 10), but in a spiritual sense by receiving God's message so that it became an inward passion. Cf. also 3:1–3, 10 and Jer 15:16.

2:10 written on the front and back. Scrolls were normally written on one side only, but

EZEKIEL'S COMMISSION

3 Then He said to me, "Son of man, eat what you
find; [A]eat this scroll, and go, speak to the house
of Israel." 2 So I [A]opened my mouth, and He fed me
this scroll. 3 He said to me, "Son of man, feed your
stomach and [A]fill your [a]body with this scroll which
I am giving you." Then I [B]ate it, and it was sweet as
[C]honey in my mouth.
4 Then He said to me, "Son of man, [a]go to the
house of Israel and speak with My words to them.
5 For [A]you are not being sent to a people of [a,B]unintel-
ligible speech or difficult language, *but* to the house
of Israel, 6 nor to many peoples of [a]unintelligible
speech or difficult language, whose words you cannot understand. [b]But I have sent you to them [c]who
should listen to you; 7 yet the house of Israel will not
be willing to listen to you, since they are [A]not willing to listen to Me. Surely the whole house of Israel
is [a]stubborn and obstinate. 8 Behold, I have made
your face as hard as their faces and your forehead
as hard as their foreheads. 9 Like [a]emery harder than
flint I have made your forehead. Do not be afraid
of them or be dismayed before them, though they
are a rebellious house." 10 Moreover, He said to me,
"Son of man, take into your heart all My [A]words
which I will speak to you and listen [a]closely. 11 [a]Go
to the exiles, to the sons of your people, and speak
to them and tell them, whether they listen or [b]not,
'Thus says the Lord [c]GOD.' "

12 Then the [A]Spirit lifted me up, and I heard a
great [B]rumbling sound behind me, "Blessed be the
glory of the LORD [a]in His place." 13 And I *heard* the
sound of the wings of the living beings touching one
another and the sound of the [A]wheels beside them,
even a great rumbling sound. 14 So the Spirit lifted
me up and took me away; and I went embittered
in the rage of my spirit, and [A]the hand of the LORD
was strong on me. 15 Then I came to the exiles who
lived beside the river Chebar at Tel-abib, and I sat
there [A]seven days where they were living, causing
consternation among them.
16 [A]At the end of seven days the word of the LORD
came to me, saying, 17 "Son of man, I have appointed
you a [A]watchman to the house of Israel; whenever
you hear a word from My mouth, [B]warn them from
Me. 18 When I say to the wicked, 'You will surely
die,' and you do not warn him or speak out to warn
the wicked from his wicked way that he may live,
that wicked man shall die in his iniquity, but his
[A]blood I will require at your hand. 19 Yet if you have
[A]warned the wicked and he does not turn from
his wickedness or from his wicked way, he shall
die in his iniquity; but you have [B]delivered yourself. 20 Again, [A]when a righteous man turns away
from his righteousness and commits iniquity, and
I place an [B]obstacle before him, he will die; since
you have not warned him, he shall die in his sin,
and his righteous deeds which he has done shall

3:1 [A]Ezek 2:9 3:2 [A]Jer 25:17 3:3 [a]Lit *inward parts* [A]Jer 6:11; 20:9 [B]Jer 15:16 [C]Ps 19:10; 119:103; Rev 10:9, 10 3:4 [a]Lit *go, come* 3:5 [a]Lit *deepness of lip and heaviness of tongue* [A]Jon 1:2; Acts 14:11; 26:17 [B]Is 28:11; 33:19 3:6 [a]Lit *deepness of lip and heaviness of tongue* [b]Or *If I had sent you to them, they would listen to you* [c]Lit *they* 3:7 [a]Lit *of a hard forehead and a stiff heart* [A]1 Sam 8:7 3:9 [a]Lit *corundum* 3:10 [a]Lit *with your ears* [A]Job 22:22; Ezek 2:8; 3:1-3 3:11 [a]Lit *Go, come* [b]Lit *forbear* [c]Heb *YHWH*, usually rendered *LORD* 3:12 [a]Or *from* [A]Ezek 3:14; 8:3; Acts 8:39 [B]Acts 2:2 3:13 [A]Ezek 1:15; 10:16, 17 3:14 [A]2 Kin 3:15 3:15 [A]Job 2:13 3:16 [A]Jer 42:7 3:17 [A]Is 52:8; 56:10; 62:6; Jer 6:17; Ezek 33:7-9 [B]2 Chr 19:10; Is 58:1; Hab 2:1 3:18 [A]Ezek 3:20; 33:6, 8 3:19 [A]2 Kin 17:13, 14; Ezek 33:3, 9 [B]Ezek 14:14, 20; Acts 18:6; 1 Tim 4:16 3:20 [A]Ps 125:5; Ezek 18:24; 33:18; Zeph 1:6 [B]Is 8:14; Jer 6:21; Ezek 14:3, 7-9

this judgment message was so full it required all the available space (cf. Zec 5:3; Rev 5:1) to chronicle the suffering and sorrow that sin had brought, as recorded in chaps. 2–32.

3:1–3 eat this scroll ... Then I ate. God's messenger must first internalize God's truth for himself, then preach it.

3:3 as honey. Even though the message was judgment on Israel, the scroll was sweet because it was God's Word (cf. Pss 19:10; 119:103) and because it vindicated God in holiness, righteousness, glory, and faithfulness, in which Jeremiah also delighted (Jer 15:16). Bitterness also was experienced by the prophet (3:14) in this message of judgment confronting Judah's rebellion (v. 9). The apostle John records a similar bittersweet experience with the Word of God in Rev 10:9, 10.

3:7 Cf. Jn 15:20.

3:8, 9 I have made your face ... hard. What God commands ("Do not be afraid") He gives sufficiency to do ("I have made"), so God will enable the prophet to live up to his name (which means "strengthened by God"). Cf. 2:2; 3:14, 24; Is 41:10; Jer 1:8, 17.

3:9 rebellious. It is sad to observe that the exile and affliction did not make the Jews more responsive to God; rather, they were hardened by their sufferings. God gave Ezekiel a "hardness" to surpass the people and sustain his ministry as prophet to the exiles.

3:12, 14 the Spirit lifted me up. This is a phrase used to describe the prophet being elevated to a heavenly vision, as in the experiences of 8:3 and 11:1.

3:14 embittered. *See note on 3:3.*

3:15 the exiles. Tel-abib was the main city for the Jewish captives, who may have included some of the 10 tribes taken long before in the conquering of the northern kingdom of Israel in 722 B.C., as 2Ki 17:6 may indicate ("Habor" is the same river as Chebar). **sat there seven days.** Ezekiel sat with the sorrowing people for 7 days, the usual period for manifesting deep grief (cf. Job 2:13). He identified with them in their suffering (cf. Ps 137:1), thus trying to win their trust when he spoke God's Word.

3:17 a watchman. This role was spiritually analogous to the role of watchmen on a city wall, vigilant to spot the approach of an enemy and warn the residents to muster a defense. The prophet gave timely warnings of approaching judgment. The work of a watchman is vividly set forth in 2Sa 18:24–27 and 2Ki 9:17–20. *See notes on 33:1–20.*

3:18–21 Cf. chap. 18, and *see notes there.*

3:18 the wicked ... him ... his. The emphasis of singular pronouns was on individuals. The ministries of Habakkuk (2:1), Jeremiah (6:17), and Isaiah (56:10) were more national than individual. Ezekiel's ministry was more personal, focused on individual responsibility to trust and obey God. Disobedience or obedience to God's messages was a matter of life or death; Eze 18:1–20 is particularly devoted to this emphasis. **do not warn ... die.** Men are not to assume that ignorance, even owing to the negligence of preachers, will be any excuse to save them from divine punishment. Cf. Ro 2:12. **that he may live.** This refers to physical death, not eternal damnation, though that would be a consequence for many. In the Pentateuch, God had commanded death for many violations of His law and warned that it could be a consequence of any kind of consistent sin (cf. Jos 1:16–18). The people of Israel had long abandoned that severe standard of purification, so God took execution back into His own hands, as in the destruction of Israel, Judah, and Jerusalem. On the other hand, God had also promised special protection and life to the obedient. Cf. 18:9–32; 33:11–16; Pr 4:4; 7:2; Am 5:4, 6.

3:18, 20 his blood I will require. Though each sinner is responsible for his own sin (cf. 18:1–20), the prophet who is negligent in his duty to proclaim the warning message becomes, in God's sight, a manslayer when God takes that person's life. The responsibility of the prophet is serious (cf. Jas 3:1), and he is responsible for that person's death in the sense of Ge 9:5. The apostle Paul had this passage (and Eze 33:6, 8) in view in Ac 18:6 and 20:26. Even for preachers today, there is such a warning in Heb 13:17. Certainly the consequence for such unfaithfulness on the preacher's part includes divine chastening and loss of eternal reward (cf. 1Co 4:1–5).

3:20 a righteous man. Here is a person who was obeying God by doing what was right, but fell into sin and God took his life in chastisement. The "obstacle" was a stone of judgment that kills. Ps 119:165 says: "Those who love Your law have great peace, and nothing causes them to stumble." The

not be remembered; but his blood I will require at
your hand. 21However, if you have [A]warned [a]the
righteous man that the righteous should not sin
and he does not sin, he shall surely live because
he took warning; and you have delivered yourself."
22The hand of the LORD was on me there, and He
said to me, "Get up, go out to the plain, and there
I will [A]speak to you." 23So I got up and went out to
the plain; and behold, the [A]glory of the LORD was
standing there, like the glory which [B]I saw by the
river Chebar, and I fell on my face. 24The [A]Spirit then
entered me and made me stand on my feet, and He
spoke with me and said to me, "Go, shut yourself up
in your house. 25As for you, son of man, they will
[A]put ropes on you and bind you with them so that
you cannot go out among them. 26Moreover, [A]I will
make your tongue stick to [a]the roof of your mouth
so that you will be mute and cannot be a man who
rebukes them, for they are a rebellious house. 27But
[A]when I speak to you, I will open your mouth and
you will say to them, 'Thus says the Lord [a]GOD.' He
who hears, let him hear; and he who refuses, let him
refuse; [B]for they are a rebellious house.

SIEGE OF JERUSALEM PREDICTED

4 "Now you son of man, [A]get yourself a brick, place
it before you and inscribe a city on it, Jerusalem.
2Then [A]lay siege against it, build a siege wall, [a]raise
up a ramp, pitch camps and place battering rams
against it all around. 3Then get yourself an iron plate
and set it up as an iron wall between you and the city,
and set your face toward it so that [A]it is under siege,
and besiege it. This is a [B]sign to the house of Israel.
4"As for you, lie down on your left side and lay the
iniquity of the house of Israel on it; you shall [A]bear
their iniquity for the number of days that you lie on

3:21 [a]Lit *him, the righteous* [A]Acts 20:31 3:22 [A]Acts 9:6 3:23 [A]Ezek 1:28; Acts 7:55 [B]Ezek 1:1 3:24 [A]Ezek 2:2 3:25 [A]Ezek 4:8 3:26 [a]Lit *your palate* [A]Luke 1:20, 22 3:27 [a]Heb *YHWH*, usually rendered *LORD* [A]Ezek 24:27; 33:22 [B]Ezek 12:2, 3 4:1 [A]Is 20:2; Jer 13:1; 18:2; 19:1 4:2 [a]Lit *cast* [A]Jer 6:6; Ezek 21:22 4:3 [A]Jer 39:1, 2; Ezek 5:2 [B]Is 8:18; 20:3; Ezek 12:6, 11; 24:24-27 4:4 [A]Lev 10:17; 16:22; Num 18:1

crushing stone always falls on the disobedient. Hebrews 12:9 says it is better to obey and "live." Cf. 1Co 11:30; Jas 1:21; 1Jn 5:16.

3:21 delivered yourself. The prophet had done his duty.

3:23 the glory of the LORD. See Introduction: Historical and Theological Themes.

3:24 shut yourself up in your house. He was to fulfill much of his ministry at home (8:1; 12:1–7), thereby limiting it to those who came to hear him there.

3:25 they will put ropes on you. These were not literal, but spiritual. On one hand, they could be the inner ropes of depressing influence which the rebellious Jews exerted on his spirit. Their perversity, like ropes, would repress his freedom in preaching. More likely, they imply the restraint that God placed on him by supernatural power, so that he could only go and speak where and when God chose (cf. vv. 26, 27).

3:26, 27 you will be mute. He was not to speak primarily, but to act out God's message. The prohibition was only partial, for on any occasion (v. 27) when God did open his mouth, as He often did in chaps. 5–7, he was to speak (3:22; 11:25; 12:10, 19, 23, 28). The end of such intermittent dumbness with regard to his own people closely synchronized with Ezekiel's receiving a refugee's report of Jerusalem's fall (24:25–27; 33:21, 22). He also spoke with regard to judgments on other nations (chaps. 25–32).

4:1–7:27 Here is the first series of prophecies given over a year's time, of Jerusalem's conquest by the Babylonians in 586 B.C.

4:1–3 inscribe … Jerusalem. Ezekiel's object lesson was to use a soft tile to create a miniature city layout of Jerusalem with walls and siege objects to illustrate Babylon's final coming siege of Jerusalem (588–586 B.C.).

4:4–6 lie … on your left side … right side. Lying on his side, likely facing N, illustrated God's applying judgment to Israel, and facing S pointed to judgment on Judah. It is not necessary to assume that Ezekiel was in the prone position all the time. It was doubtless part of each day, as his need for preparing food (v. 9) indicates.

4:4, 6 you shall bear their iniquity. Ezekiel's action was not to represent the time of Israel's sinning, but the time of its punishment.

EZEKIEL'S SIGN EXPERIENCES
(cf. Eze 24:24, 27)
1. Ezekiel was housebound, tied up, and mute (3:23–27).
2. Ezekiel used a brick and an iron plate as illustrations in his preaching (4:1–3).
3. Ezekiel had to lie on his left side for 390 days and his right side for 40 days (4:4–8).
4. Ezekiel had to eat in an unclean manner (4:9–17).
5. Ezekiel had to shave his head and beard (5:1–4).
6. Ezekiel had to pack his bags and dig through the wall of Jerusalem (12:1–14).
7. Ezekiel had to eat his bread with trembling and drink water with quivering (12:17–20).
8. Ezekiel brandished a sharp sword and struck his hands together (21:8–17).
9. Ezekiel portrayed Israel in the smelting furnace (22:17–22).
10. Ezekiel had to cook a pot of stew (24:1–14).
11. Ezekiel could not mourn at the death of his wife (24:15–24).
12. Ezekiel was mute for a season (24:25–27).
13. Ezekiel put two sticks together and they became one (37:15–28).

it. 5 For I have assigned you a number of days corresponding to the years of their iniquity, three hundred
and ninety days; thus [A]you shall bear the iniquity of
the house of Israel. 6 When you have completed these,
you shall lie down a second time, *but* on your right
side and bear the iniquity of the house of Judah; I
have assigned it to you for forty days, a day for [A]each
year. 7 Then you shall set your face toward the siege
of Jerusalem with your arm bared and [A]prophesy
against it. 8 Now behold, I will [A]put ropes on you so
that you cannot turn from one side to the other until
you have completed the days of your siege.

DEFILED BREAD

9 "But as for you, take wheat, barley, beans, lentils, millet and [A]spelt, put them in one vessel and
make them into bread for yourself; you shall eat
it according to the number of the days that you
lie on your side, three hundred and ninety days.
10 Your food which you eat *shall be* [A]twenty shekels
a day by weight; you shall eat it from time to time.
11 The water you drink shall be the sixth part of a hin
by measure; you shall drink it from time to time.
12 You shall eat it as a barley cake, having baked *it*
in their sight over human [A]dung." 13 Then the LORD
said, "Thus will the sons of Israel eat their bread
[A]unclean among the nations where I will banish
them." 14 But I said, "[A]Ah, Lord [a]GOD! Behold, I have
[B]never been defiled; for from my youth until now
I have never eaten what [C]died of itself or was torn
by beasts, nor has any [D]unclean meat ever entered
my mouth." 15 Then He said to me, "See, I will give
you cow's dung in place of human dung over which
you will prepare your bread." 16 Moreover, He said to
me, "Son of man, behold, I am going to [A]break the
staff of bread in Jerusalem, and they will eat bread
by [B]weight and with anxiety, and drink water by
[C]measure and in horror, 17 because bread and water
will be scarce; and they will be appalled with one
another and [A]waste away in their iniquity.

JERUSALEM'S DESOLATION FORETOLD

5 "As for you, son of man, take a [A]sharp sword;
take and [a]use it *as* a barber's razor on your head
and beard. Then take [B]scales for weighing and divide
[b]the hair. 2 One third you shall burn in the fire at the
center of the city, when the [A]days of the siege are
completed. Then you shall take one third and strike
it with the sword all around [a]the city, and one third
you shall scatter to the wind; and I will [B]unsheathe
a sword behind them. 3 Take also a few in number
from [a]them and bind them in the edges of your
robes. 4 Take again some of them and throw them
into the fire and burn them in the fire; from it a fire
will [a]spread to all the house of Israel.
5 "Thus says the Lord [a]GOD, 'This is [A]Jerusalem;
I have set her at the [B]center of the nations, with
lands around her. 6 But she has rebelled against
My ordinances more wickedly than the nations
and against My statutes [A]more than the lands
which surround her; for they have [B]rejected My
ordinances and have not walked [a]in My statutes.'
7 Therefore, thus says the Lord GOD, 'Because you
have [A]more turmoil than the nations which surround you *and* have not walked in My statutes,
nor observed My ordinances, nor observed the
ordinances of the nations which surround you,'
8 therefore, thus says the Lord GOD, 'Behold, I, even
I, am [A]against you, and I will [B]execute judgments
among you in the sight of the nations. 9 And because of all your abominations, I will do among you
what I have [A]not done, and the like of which I will
never do again. 10 Therefore, [A]fathers will eat *their*
sons among you, and sons will eat their fathers;
for I will execute judgments on you and [B]scatter all

4:5 [A]Num 14:34 4:6 [A]Num 14:34; Dan 9:24-26; 12:11, 12; Rev 11:2, 3 4:7 [A]Ezek 21:2 4:8 [A]Ezek 3:25 4:9 [A]Ex 9:32; Is 28:25 4:10 [A]Ezek 45:12 4:12 [A]Is 36:12 4:13 [A]Dan 1:8; Hos 9:3 4:14 [a]Heb *YHWH*, usually rendered *LORD* [A]Jer 1:6; Ezek 9:8; 20:49 [B]Acts 10:14 [C]Lev 17:15; 22:8; Ezek 44:31 [D]Deut 14:3; Is 65:4; 66:17 4:16 [A]Lev 26:26; Is 3:1; Ezek 5:16; 14:13 [B]Ezek 4:10, 11; 12:19 [C]Lam 5:4; Ezek 12:18, 19 4:17 [A]Lev 26:39; Ezek 24:23; 33:10 5:1 [a]Lit *make it pass over your head* [b]Lit *them* [A]Lev 21:5; Is 7:20; Ezek 44:20 [B]Dan 5:27 5:2 [a]Lit *it* [A]Jer 39:1, 2; Ezek 4:2-8 [B]Lev 26:33 5:3 [a]Lit *there* 5:4 [a]Lit *go out* 5:5 [a]Heb *YHWH*, usually rendered *LORD*, and so throughout the ch [A]Jer 6:6; Ezek 4:1 [B]Deut 4:6; Lam 1:1; Ezek 16:14 5:6 [a]Lit *in them, My statutes* [A]2 Kin 17:8-20; Ezek 16:47, 48, 51 [B]Neh 9:16, 17; Ps 78:10; Jer 11:10; Zech 7:11 5:7 [A]2 Kin 21:9-11; 2 Chr 33:9; Jer 2:10, 11 5:8 [A]Jer 21:5, 13; Ezek 15:7; 21:3; Zech 14:2 [B]Jer 24:9; Ezek 5:15; 11:9 5:9 [A]Dan 9:12; Amos 3:2; Matt 24:21 5:10 [A]Lev 26:29; Jer 19:9; Lam 4:10 [B]Ps 44:11; Ezek 5:2, 12; 6:8; 12:14; Amos 9:9; Zech 2:6; 7:14

4:5 three hundred and ninety. Each day symbolized a year (v. 6). Israel in the N was accountable during this span of time whose beginning and end are uncertain.

4:6 forty. Judah was also guilty, but the 40 cannot represent less guilt (cf. 23:11). It may extend the time beyond the 390 to 430, or they may run concurrently, but the exact timing is uncertain.

4:7 arm bared. A symbol for being ready for action, as a soldier would do (cf. Is 52:10).

4:8 I will put ropes on you. This was to symbolize the impossibility of the Jews being able to shake off their punishment.

4:9–13 make … bread. Scarcity of food in the 18-month siege especially made necessary the mixing of all kinds of grain for bread. The "twenty shekels" would be about 8 ounces, while "the sixth part of a hin" would be less than a quart. There would be minimums for daily rations. It must be noted that the command of v. 12 regarding "human dung" relates only to the fuel used to prepare the food. Bread was baked on hot stones (cf. 1Ki 19:6) heated by human waste because no other fuel was available. This was repulsive and polluting (cf. Dt 23:12–14) and the Lord calls it "bread unclean" (v. 13).

4:14, 15 never been defiled. Ezekiel, like Daniel, had convictions to be undefiled even in his food (cf. Da 1:8 and *see note there*). God permitted fuel of dried cow chips for cooking his food in gracious deference to His spokesman's sensitivity (cf. 44:31).

4:16, 17 They were soon to have neither bread nor water in any amount, and they were to grieve over the famine and their iniquity (cf. Lv 26:21–26).

5:1–4 a barber's razor. The sign in shaving his hair illustrated the severe humiliation to come at the hand of enemies, emphasizing calamities to three segments of Jerusalem due to the Babylonian conquest. Some were punished by fire, i.e., plague and famine (v. 12), others died by the enemy's sword, and some were dispersed and pursued by death (cf. v. 12). A small part of his hair clinging to his garment (v. 3) depicted a remaining remnant, some of whom were subject to further calamity (v. 4; cf. 6:8; Jer 41–44).

5:5 Jerusalem. Here the great city alone was not meant, but was used as a representative of the whole land which, despite its strategic opportunity and responsibility, rejected God (vv. 6, 7).

5:7 Instead of being a witness to the heathen nations, Israel had exceeded them in idolatrous practices. The nations maintained their familiar idols, while Israel defected from their true and living God. God's people were worse than the pagans in proportion to spiritual knowledge and privileges. The judgments of God are always relative to light and privilege granted. Since Ezekiel's people were unique in their disobedience, they were to be outstanding in their punishment.

5:8–10 The book of Lamentations reveals how literally these promises were realized when parents ate their children and sons ate

your remnant to every wind. 11 So as I live,' declares the Lord GOD, 'surely, because you have [A]defiled My sanctuary with all your [B]detestable idols and with all your abominations, therefore I will also withdraw, and My eye will have no pity and I will not spare. 12 One third of you will die by [A]plague or be consumed by famine among you, one third will fall by the sword around you, and one third I will [B]scatter to every wind, and I will [C]unsheathe a sword behind them.

13 'Thus My anger will be spent and I will [a]satisfy My wrath on them, and I will be [b,A]appeased; then they will know that I, the LORD, have [B]spoken in My zeal when I have spent My wrath upon them. 14 Moreover, I will make you a desolation and a [A]reproach among the nations which surround you, in the sight of all who pass by. 15 So [a]it will be a reproach, a reviling, a [A]warning and an object of horror to the nations who surround you when I [B]execute judgments against you in anger, wrath and raging rebukes. I, the LORD, have spoken. 16 When I send against them the [a]deadly arrows of famine which [b]were for the destruction of those whom I will send to destroy you, then I will also intensify the famine upon you and break the staff of bread. 17 Moreover, [A]I will send on you famine and wild beasts, and they will bereave you of children; [B]plague and bloodshed also will pass through you, and I will bring the sword on you. I, the LORD, have spoken.' "

IDOLATROUS WORSHIP DENOUNCED

6 And the word of the LORD came to me saying, 2 "Son of man, set your face toward the [A]mountains of Israel, and prophesy against them 3 and say, 'Mountains of Israel, listen to the word of the Lord [a]GOD! Thus says the Lord [a]GOD to the mountains, the hills, the ravines and the valleys: "Behold, I Myself am going to bring a sword on you, and [A]I will destroy your high places. 4 So your [A]altars will become desolate and your incense altars will be smashed; and I will make your slain fall in front of your idols. 5 I will also lay the dead bodies of the sons of Israel in front of their idols; and I will scatter your [A]bones around your altars. 6 In all your dwellings, [A]cities will become waste and the high places will be desolate, that your altars may become waste and [a]desolate, your [B]idols may be broken and brought to an end, your incense altars may be cut down, and your works may be blotted out. 7 The slain will fall among you, and you will know that I am the LORD.

8 "However, I will leave a [A]remnant, for you will have those who [B]escaped the sword among the nations when you are scattered among the countries. 9 Then those of you who escape will [A]remember Me among the nations to which they will be carried captive, how I have [a,B]been hurt by their adulterous hearts which turned away from Me, and by their eyes which played the harlot after their idols; and they will [C]loathe themselves in their own sight for the evils which they have committed, for all their abominations. 10 Then they will know that I am the LORD; I have not said in vain [a]that I would inflict this disaster on them." '

11 "Thus says the Lord [a]GOD, 'Clap your hand, [A]stamp your foot and say, "[B]Alas, because of all the evil abominations of the house of Israel, which will fall by [C]sword, famine and plague! 12 He who is [A]far off will die by the plague, and he who is near will fall by the sword, and he who remains and is besieged will die by the famine. Thus will I [B]spend My wrath on them. 13 Then you will know that I am the LORD, when their [A]slain are among their idols around their altars, on [B]every high hill, on all the tops of the mountains, under every green tree and under every leafy oak—the places where they offered soothing aroma to all their idols. 14 So throughout all their habitations I will [A]stretch out My hand against them and make the land more desolate and waste than the wilderness toward Diblah; thus they will know that I am the LORD." ' "

5:11 [A]Jer 7:9-11; Ezek 8:5, 6, 16 [B]Jer 16:18; Ezek 7:20 5:12 [A]Jer 15:2; 21:9; Ezek 5:17; 6:11, 12 [B]Ezek 5:2, 10; Amos 9:9; Zech 2:6 [C]Jer 43:10, 11; 44:27; Ezek 5:2; 12:14 5:13 [a]Lit *cause to rest* [b]Lit *comforted* [A]Is 1:24 [B]Is 59:17; Ezek 36:5, 6; 38:19 5:14 [A]Ps 74:3-10; 79:1-4; Ezek 22:4 5:15 [a]Ancient versions read *you* [A]Is 26:9; Jer 22:8, 9; 1 Cor 10:11 [B]Is 66:15, 16; Ezek 5:8; 25:17 5:16 [a]Lit *evil* [b]Or *are for destruction, which I will send* 5:17 [A]Lev 26:22; Rev 6:8 [B]Ezek 38:22 6:2 [A]Ezek 36:1 6:3 [a]Heb *YHWH*, usually rendered *LORD* [A]Lev 26:30 6:4 [A]Lev 26:30; 2 Chr 14:5; Is 27:9; Ezek 6:6 6:5 [A]2 Kin 23:14, 16, 20; Jer 8:1, 2 6:6 [a]So some ancient versions; Heb *bear their guilt* [A]Lev 26:31; Is 6:11; Ezek 5:14 [B]Ezek 6:4; Mic 1:7; Zech 13:2 6:8 [A]Is 6:13; Jer 30:11 [B]Jer 44:14, 28; Ezek 7:16; 14:22 6:9 [a]Lit *been broken*, or, *broken for Myself their* [A]Deut 4:29; 30:2; Jer 51:50 [B]Ps 78:40; Is 7:13; 43:24; Hos 11:8 [C]Job 42:6; Ezek 20:43; 36:31 6:10 [a]Lit *to do this evil to* 6:11 [a]Heb *YHWH*, usually rendered *LORD* [A]Ezek 25:6 [B]Ezek 9:4 [C]Ezek 5:12; 7:15 6:12 [A]Dan 9:7 [B]Lam 4:11, 22; Ezek 5:13 6:13 [A]Ezek 6:4-7 [B]1 Kin 14:23; 2 Kin 16:4; Is 57:5-7; Ezek 20:28; Hos 4:13 6:14 [A]Is 5:25; 9:12; Ezek 14:13; 20:33, 34

their fathers in the times of starvation. Down through the centuries had come the threats of Lv 26:29 and Dt 28:53, taken up by Jeremiah (Jer 19:9; La 2:22; 4:10; cf. Is 9:20), and sealed in the life of the disobedient nation. Even the remnant would be scattered and suffer.

5:11 as I live. Here was a solemn oath pledging the very existence of God for the fulfillment of the prophecy. It is found 16 times in this book. Their greatest sin was defiling the sanctuary, showing the height of their wickedness.

5:12 The 4 well known judgments (cf. vv. 2–4) of plague, famine, sword, and scattering were their judgment. They had no place to offer atoning blood, thus bearing their sins without relief.

5:13–15 Ezekiel's purpose was to impress on Israel's conscience God's intense hatred of idolatry and apostasy. "Anger" and "wrath" are repeated several times.

5:16 deadly arrows of famine. The evil arrows included hail, rain, mice, locusts, and mildew (cf. Dt 32:23, 24).

5:17 I, the LORD, have spoken. Cf. vv. 13, 15 for the same expression, which was God's personal signature on their doom.

6:3 says the Lord GOD to the mountains. God had the prophet do this because the people worshiped at idol altars in the "high places" (cf. Lv 26:30–33; Is 65:7; Jer 3:6; Hos 4:13; Mic 6:1, 2).

6:7 you will know that I am the LORD. This clause recurs in vv. 10, 13, 14 and 60 times elsewhere in the book. It shows that the essential reason for judgment is the violation of the character of God. This is repeatedly acknowledged in Lv 18–26, where the motive for all obedience to God's law is the fact that He is the Lord God.

6:8–10 The mass of people was rejected, but grace and mercy were given to a godly group in the nation. There never has been nor ever will be a complete end to Israel. The doctrine of the remnant can be studied in Is 1:9; 10:20; Jer 43:5; Zep 2:7; 3:13; Zec 10:9; Ro 9:6–13; 11:5.

6:14 Diblah. A reference to Diblathaim, a city on the eastern edge of Moab (Nu 33:46; Jer 48:22), near the desert E and S of the Dead Sea.

PUNISHMENT FOR WICKEDNESS FORETOLD

7 Moreover, the word of the LORD came to me
saying, 2 "And you, son of man, thus says the
Lord [a]GOD to the land of Israel, 'An [A]end! The end is
coming on the four corners of the land. 3 Now the end
is upon you, and I will send My anger against you; I
will judge you according to your ways and bring all
your abominations upon you. 4 For My eye will have
no pity on you, nor will I spare *you,* but I will [A]bring
your ways upon you, and your abominations will be
among you; then you will [B]know that I am the LORD!'
5 "Thus says the Lord [a]GOD, 'A [A]disaster, unique
disaster, behold it is coming! 6 An end is coming;
the end has come! It has [A]awakened against you;
behold, it has come! 7 Your doom has come to you,
O inhabitant of the land. The [A]time has come, the
[B]day is near—tumult rather than joyful shouting
on the mountains. 8 Now I will shortly [A]pour out
My wrath on you and spend My anger against you;
[B]judge you according to your ways and bring on you
all your abominations. 9 My eye will show no pity
nor will I spare. I will [a]repay you according to your
ways, while your abominations are in your midst;
then you will know that I, the LORD, do the smiting.
10 'Behold, the day! Behold, it is coming! *Your*
doom has gone forth; the [A]rod has budded, arrogance has blossomed. 11 Violence [a]has grown into
a rod of [A]wickedness. None of them *shall remain,*
none of their people, none of their [B]wealth, nor anything eminent among them. 12 The [A]time has come,
the day has arrived. Let not the [B]buyer rejoice nor
the seller mourn; for [C]wrath is against all their multitude. 13 Indeed, the seller will not [a,A]regain [b]what
he sold as long as [c]they *both* live; for the vision regarding all their multitude will not [d]be averted, nor
will any of them maintain his life by his iniquity.
14 'They have [A]blown the trumpet and made everything ready, but no one is going to the battle, for My
wrath is against all [a]their multitude. 15 The [A]sword is
outside and the plague and the famine are within.
He who is in the field will die by the sword; famine
and the plague will also consume those in the city.
16 Even when their survivors [A]escape, they will be
on the mountains like [B]doves of the valleys, all of
them [a,C]mourning, each over his own iniquity. 17 All
[A]hands will hang limp and all knees will [a]become *like*
water. 18 They will [A]gird themselves with sackcloth
and [B]shuddering will overwhelm them; and shame
will be on all faces and [C]baldness on all their heads.
19 They will [A]fling their silver into the streets and their
gold will become an abhorrent thing; their [B]silver
and their gold will not be able to deliver them in the
day of the wrath of the LORD. They cannot satisfy
their [a]appetite nor can they fill their stomachs, for
their iniquity has become an occasion of stumbling.

THE TEMPLE PROFANED

20 They transformed the beauty of His ornaments
into pride, and [A]they made the images of their
abominations *and* their detestable things with it;
therefore I will make it an abhorrent thing to them.
21 I will give it into the hands of the [A]foreigners as
plunder and to the wicked of the earth as spoil, and
they will profane it. 22 I will also turn My [A]face from
them, and they will profane My secret place; then
robbers will enter and profane it.
23 '[A]Make the chain, for the land is full of [a,B]bloody
crimes and the city is [C]full of violence. 24 Therefore,
I will bring the worst of the [A]nations, and they will
possess their houses. I will also make the [B]pride of
the strong ones cease, and their [C]holy places will
be profaned. 25 When anguish comes, they will seek
[A]peace, but there will be none. 26 [A]Disaster will come
upon disaster and [B]rumor will be *added* to rumor;
then they will seek a [C]vision from a prophet, but the
[D]law will be lost from the priest and [E]counsel from
the elders. 27 The king will mourn, the prince will be
[A]clothed with horror, and the hands of the people of
the land will [a]tremble. According to their conduct I
will deal with them, and by their judgments I will
judge them. And they will know that I am the LORD.' "

VISION OF ABOMINATIONS IN JERUSALEM

8 It came about in the sixth year, on the fifth *day*
of the sixth month, as I was sitting in my house
with the elders of Judah sitting before me, that the

7:2 [a]Heb *YHWH*, usually rendered *LORD* [A]Ezek 7:3, 5, 6; 11:13; Amos 8:2, 10 7:4 [A]Ezek 11:21; 22:31; Hos 9:7 [B]Ezek 6:7, 14; 7:27 7:5 [a]Heb *YHWH*, usually rendered *LORD* [A]2 Kin 21:12, 13; Nah 1:9 7:6 [A]Zech 13:7 7:7 [A]Ezek 7:12; 12:23-25, 28 [B]Is 22:5 7:8 [A]Is 42:25; Ezek 9:8; 14:19; Nah 1:6 [B]Ezek 7:3; 33:20; 36:19 7:9 [a]Lit *give* 7:10 [A]Ps 89:32; Is 10:5 7:11 [a]Lit *has risen* [A]Ps 73:8; 125:3; Is 59:6-8 [B]Zeph 1:18 7:12 [A]Ezek 7:5-7, 10; 1 Cor 7:29-31; James 5:8, 9 [B]Prov 20:14; 1 Cor 7:30 [C]Is 5:13, 14; Ezek 6:11, 12; 7:14 7:13 [a]Lit *return to* [b]Lit *thing sold,* i.e. his inherited land [c]Lit *their life among the living ones* [d]Lit *return* [A]Lev 25:24-28, 31 7:14 [a]Lit *her* [A]Num 10:9; Jer 4:5 7:15 [A]Jer 14:18; Ezek 5:12; 6:11, 12; 12:16 7:16 [a]Lit *moaning* [A]Ezra 9:15; Is 37:31; Ezek 6:8; 14:22 [B]Is 38:14 [C]Is 59:11; Nah 2:7 7:17 [a]Lit *run with water* [A]Is 13:7; Ezek 21:7; 22:14; Heb 12:12 7:18 [A]Is 15:3; Ezek 27:31; Amos 8:10 [B]Job 21:6; Ps 55:5 [C]Ezek 27:31 7:19 [a]Lit *soul* [A]Is 2:20; 30:22 [B]Prov 11:4; Zeph 1:18 7:20 [A]Jer 7:30 7:21 [A]2 Kin 24:13; Ps 74:2-8; Jer 52:13 7:22 [A]Jer 18:17; Ezek 39:23, 24 7:23 [a]Lit *judgment of blood* [A]Jer 27:2 [B]Ezek 9:9; Hos 4:2 [C]Ezek 8:17 7:24 [A]Ezek 21:31; 28:7 [B]Ezek 33:28 [C]2 Chr 7:20; Ezek 24:21 7:25 [A]Ezek 13:10, 16 7:26 [A]Is 47:11; Jer 4:20 [B]Ezek 21:7 [C]Jer 21:2; 37:17 [D]Ps 74:9; Ezek 22:26; Mic 3:6 [E]Jer 18:18; Ezek 11:2 7:27 [a]Lit *be terrified* [A]Job 8:22; Ps 35:26; 109:18, 29; Ezek 26:16

7:1–9 This lament declared that the entire land of Israel was ripe for judgment. God's patience had ended. The final destruction of Jerusalem by Nebuchadnezzar was in view (586 B.C.).

7:10 rod has budded. Verse 11 explains this. Violence had grown up into a rod of wickedness, which likely refers to Nebuchadnezzar, the instrument of God's vengeance (cf. Is 10:5; Jer 51:20).

7:12 buyer rejoice … seller mourn. Such matters of business were meaningless because the Chaldeans (Babylonians) took all the land and killed those they didn't take captive (v. 15), and the rest escaped (v. 16). Wealth was useless (vv. 19, 20).

7:13 seller will not regain what he sold. There was to be no Jubilee year in which all lands were returned to their original owners (cf. Lv 25).

7:17–22 This section described the mourning of the helpless and frightened people. In distress, they recognized the uselessness of the things in which they trusted. Their wealth provided nothing. Their "silver and … gold" (v. 19) and their "ornaments" (v. 20) were as useless as the idols they made with them.

7:22 My secret place. The Holy of Holies in the temple will be desecrated by pagans, that place where only once a year the High Priest could enter to make atonement in God's presence.

7:23 Make the chain. Ezekiel is to perform another emblematic act of captivity (cf. Jer 27:2; Na 3:10).

7:24 the worst of the nations. Babylonian pagans.

7:27 According to their conduct. Cf. Ge 18:25.

8:1 the sixth year. 592 B.C. (cf. 1:2) in Aug./Sep., a year and two months after the first

hand of the Lord [a]GOD fell on me there. 2 Then I looked, and behold, a likeness as the appearance of [a]a man; from His loins and downward *there was* the [A]appearance of fire, and from His loins and upward the appearance of brightness, like the appearance [B]of [b]glowing metal. 3 He stretched out the form of a hand and caught me by a lock of my head; and the [A]Spirit lifted me up between earth and heaven and brought me in the visions of God to Jerusalem, to the entrance of the [a]north gate of the inner *court,* where the seat of the idol of jealousy, which [B]provokes to jealousy, was *located.* 4 And behold, the [A]glory of the God of Israel *was* there, like the appearance which I saw in the plain.

5 Then He said to me, "Son of man, [A]raise your eyes now toward the north." So I raised my eyes toward the north, and behold, to the north of the altar gate *was* this [B]idol of jealousy at the entrance. 6 And He said to me, "Son of man, do you see what they are doing, the great [A]abominations which the house of Israel are committing here, so that I would be far from My sanctuary? But yet you will see still greater abominations."

7 Then He brought me to the entrance of the court, and when I looked, behold, a hole in the wall. 8 He said to me, "Son of man, now [A]dig through the wall." So I dug through the wall, and behold, an entrance. 9 And He said to me, "Go in and see the wicked abominations that they are committing here." 10 So I entered and looked, and behold, every form of creeping things and beasts *and* detestable things, with all the idols of the house of Israel, were carved on the wall all around. 11 Standing in front of them were [A]seventy [B]elders of the house of Israel, with Jaazaniah the son of Shaphan standing among them, each man with his [C]censer in his hand and the fragrance of the cloud of incense rising. 12 Then He said to me, "Son of man, do you see what the elders of the house of Israel are committing in the dark, each man in the room of his carved images? For they say, '[A]The LORD does not see us; the LORD has [B]forsaken the land.'" 13 And He said to me, "Yet you will see still greater abominations which they are committing."

14 Then He brought me to the entrance of the [A]gate of the LORD'S house which *was* toward the north; and behold, women were sitting there weeping for Tammuz. 15 He said to me, "Do you see *this,* son of man? Yet you will see still greater abominations than these."

16 Then He brought me into the inner court of the LORD'S house. And behold, at the entrance to the temple of the LORD, between the porch and the altar, *were* about twenty-five men with their [A]backs to the temple of the LORD and their faces toward the east; and [B]they were [a]prostrating themselves eastward toward the sun. 17 He said to me, "Do you see *this,* son of man? Is it too light a thing for the house of Judah to commit the abominations which they have committed here, that they have [A]filled the land with violence and [B]provoked Me repeatedly? For behold, they are putting the twig to their nose. 18 Therefore, I indeed will deal in wrath. My eye will have no pity nor will I spare; and [A]though they cry in My ears with a loud voice, yet I will not listen to them."

THE VISION OF SLAUGHTER

9 Then He cried out in my hearing with a loud [A]voice saying, "Draw near, [a]O executioners of the city, each with his destroying weapon in his hand." 2 Behold, six men came from the direction of the upper gate which faces north, each with his

8:1 [a]Heb *YHWH*, usually rendered *LORD* 8:2 [a]Lit *fire* [b]Or *electrum* [A]Ezek 1:27 [B]Ezek 1:4, 27 8:3 [a]Lit *facing north* [A]Ezek 3:12; 11:1 [B]Ex 20:4; Deut 32:16 8:4 [A]Ezek 1:28; 3:22, 23 8:5 [A]Jer 3:2; Zech 5:5 [B]Ps 78:58; Jer 7:30; 32:34; Ezek 8:3 8:6 [A]2 Kin 23:4, 5; Ezek 5:11; 8:9, 17 8:8 [A]Is 29:15 8:11 [A]Num 11:16, 25; Luke 10:1 [B]Jer 19:1 [C]Num 16:17, 35 8:12 [A]Ps 14:1; Is 29:15; Ezek 9:9 [B]Ps 10:11 8:14 [A]Ezek 44:4; 46:9 8:16 [a]I.e. worshiping [A]2 Chr 29:6; Jer 2:27; Ezek 23:39 [B]Deut 4:19; 17:3; Job 31:26-28; Jer 44:17 8:17 [A]Ezek 7:11, 23; 9:9; Amos 3:10; Mic 2:2 [B]Jer 7:18, 19; Ezek 16:26 8:18 [A]Is 1:15; Jer 11:11; Mic 3:4; Zech 7:13 9:1 [a]Lit *you who punish* [A]Is 6:8

vision (1:1). **the hand of the Lord.** This ushered the prophet into a series of visions (v. 3) stretching to the end of chap. 11.

8:2 a likeness. He saw the glory of the Lord (v. 4) as in 1:26–28.

8:3 the visions of God. Ezekiel 8–11 deals with details conveyed only to Ezekiel in visions. Ezekiel's trip to Jerusalem was in spirit only, while his body physically remained in his house. In visions, he went to Jerusalem, and in visions he returned to Babylon (11:24). After God finished the visions, Ezekiel told his home audience what he had seen. The visions are not a description of deeds done in the past in Israel, but a survey of Israel's current condition, as they existed at that very time. **the seat ... idol of jealousy.** God represents to Ezekiel the image of an idol (cf. Dt 4:16) in the entrance to the inner court of the temple. It is called "the idol of jealousy" because it provoked the Lord to jealousy (5:13; 16:38; 36:6; 38:19; Ex 20:5).

8:4 the glory of ... God. God was also there in glory, but was ignored while the people worshiped the idol (v. 6).

8:6 so that I would be far. Sin would expel the people from their land and God from His sanctuary.

8:7–12 This section describes "great abominations" (v. 6) of idolatry, namely a secret cult of idolatrous elders.

8:8 dug through the wall ... an entrance. This indicates the clandestine (cf. v. 12) secrecy of these idolaters, practicing their cult in hiding.

8:10 carved on the wall. The temple's walls are ugly with graffiti featuring creatures linked with Egyptian animal cults (cf. Ro 1:23) and other idols. Leaders of Israel, who should be worshiping the God of the temple, are offering incense to them (v. 11).

8:11 seventy elders. Obviously not the Sanhedrin, since it was not formed until after the restoration from Babylon, though the pattern had been suggested much earlier (cf. Ex 24:9, 10; Nu 11:16). These men were appointed to guard against idolatry! **Jaazaniah the son of Shaphan.** If he was the son of the Shaphan who read God's Word to Josiah (2Ki 22:8–11), we have some concept of the depth of sin to which the leaders had fallen. He is not to be confused with the man in 11:1, who had a different father.

8:14 weeping for Tammuz. Yet a greater abomination than the secret cult was Israel's engaging in the Babylonian worship of Tammuz or Dumuzi (Duzu), beloved of Ishtar, the god of spring vegetation. Vegetation burned in the summer, died in the winter, and came to life in the spring. The women mourned over the god's demise in July and longed for his revival. The fourth month of the Hebrew calendar still bears the name Tammuz. With the worship of this idol were connected the basest immoralities.

8:16 prostrating ... toward the sun. In the most sacred inner court where only priests could go (Joel 2:17), there was the crowning insult to God. Twenty-five men were worshiping the sun as an idol (cf. Dt 4:19; 2Ki 23:5, 11; Job 31:26; Jer 44:17). These 25 represent the 24 orders of priests plus the High Priest.

8:17 putting the twig to their nose. The meaning is uncertain, but it seems to have been some act of contempt toward God. The Gr. OT translators rendered it, "they are as mockers."

8:18 I ... will deal in wrath. God must judge intensely due to such horrible sins (cf. 24:9, 10).

9:1 executioners of the city. God summoned His servant angels to carry out His judgments. These angelic executioners (cf. Da 4:13, 17, 23) came equipped with weapons of destruction.

9:2 six men. Angels can appear like men when ministering on earth (cf. Ge 18:1; Da 9:20–23). **a certain man.** He was superior to

shattering weapon in his hand; and among them was [A]a certain man clothed in linen with a [a]writing case at his loins. And they went in and stood beside the bronze altar.

3 Then the [A]glory of the God of Israel went up from the cherub on which it had been, to the threshold of the [a]temple. And He called to the man clothed in linen at whose loins was the writing case. 4 The LORD said to him, "Go through the midst of the city, *even* through the midst of Jerusalem, and put a [A]mark on the foreheads of the men who [B]sigh and groan over all the abominations which are being committed in its midst." 5 But to the others He said in my hearing, "Go through the city after him and strike; do not let your eye have pity and do not spare. 6 [a]Utterly [A]slay old men, young men, maidens, little children, and women, but do not [B]touch any man on whom is the mark; and you shall [C]start from My sanctuary." So they started with the [b]elders who *were* before the [c]temple. 7 And He said to them, "[A]Defile the [a]temple and fill the courts with the slain. Go out!" Thus they went out and struck down *the people* in the city. 8 As they were striking *the people* and I *alone* was left, I [A]fell on my face and cried out [a]saying, "[B]Alas, Lord [b]GOD! Are You destroying the whole remnant of Israel [c]by pouring out Your wrath on Jerusalem?"

9 Then He said to me, "The iniquity of the house of Israel and Judah is very, very great, and the land is [A]filled with blood and the city is [B]full of perversion; for [C]they say, 'The LORD has forsaken the land, and the LORD does not see!' 10 But as for Me, [A]My eye will have no pity nor will I spare, but [B]I will bring their conduct upon their heads."

11 Then behold, the man clothed in linen at whose loins was the [a]writing case [b]reported, saying, "I have done just as You have commanded me."

VISION OF GOD'S GLORY DEPARTING FROM THE TEMPLE

10 Then I looked, and behold, in the [a,A]expanse that was over the heads of the cherubim something like a [B]sapphire stone, in appearance resembling a [C]throne, appeared above them. 2 And He spoke to the man clothed in linen and said, "Enter between the [A]whirling wheels under the [a]cherubim and fill your hands with [B]coals of fire from between the cherubim and scatter *them* over the city." And he entered in my sight.

3 Now the cherubim were standing on the right side of the [a]temple when the man entered, and the cloud filled the [A]inner court. 4 Then the [A]glory of the LORD went up from the cherub to the threshold of the temple, and the [B]temple was filled with the cloud and the court was filled with the [C]brightness of the glory of the LORD. 5 Moreover, the sound of the wings of the cherubim was heard as far as the outer court, like the [A]voice of [a]God Almighty when He speaks.

6 It came about when He commanded the man clothed in linen, saying, "Take fire from between the whirling wheels, from between the cherubim," he entered and stood beside a wheel. 7 Then the cherub stretched out his hand from between the cherubim to the fire which was between the cherubim, took *some* and put *it* into the hands of the one clothed in linen, who took *it* and went out. 8 The cherubim appeared to have the form of a man's hand under their wings.

9 Then I looked, and behold, [A]four wheels beside the cherubim, one wheel beside each cherub; and the appearance of the wheels *was* like the gleam of a [a,B]Tarshish stone. 10 As for their appearance, all four of them had the same likeness, as if one wheel were within another wheel. 11 When they

9:2 [a]Or *scribal inkhorn* [A]Lev 16:4 9:3 [a]Lit *house* [A]Ezek 10:4; 11:22, 23 9:4 [A]Ex 12:7, 13; Ezek 9:6; 2 Cor 1:22; 2 Tim 2:19; Rev 7:2, 3; 9:4; 14:1 [B]Ps 119:53, 136; Jer 13:17; Ezek 6:11; 21:6 9:6 [a]Lit *To destruction* [b]Or *old men* [c]Lit *house* [A]2 Chr 36:17 [B]Ex 12:23; Rev 9:4 [C]Jer 25:29; Amos 3:2; Luke 12:47 9:7 [a]Lit *house* [A]2 Chr 36:17; Ezek 7:20-22 9:8 [a]Lit *and said* [b]Heb *YHWH*, usually rendered *LORD* [c]Lit *by Your pouring* [A]1 Chr 21:16 [B]Ezek 11:13; Amos 7:2-6 9:9 [A]2 Kin 21:16; Jer 2:34; Ezek 7:23; 22:2, 3 [B]Ezek 22:29; Mic 3:1-3; 7:3 [C]Job 22:13; Ps 10:11; 94:7; Is 29:15; Ezek 8:12 9:10 [A]Is 65:6; Ezek 8:18; 24:14 [B]Ezek 7:4; 11:21; Hos 9:7 9:11 [a]Or *inkhorn* [b]Lit *brought back word* 10:1 [a]Or *firmament* [A]Ezek 1:22, 26 [B]Ex 24:10 [C]Rev 4:2, 3 10:2 [a]So with Gr; Heb *cherub* [A]Ezek 1:15-21; 10:13 [B]Ps 18:10-13; Is 6:6; Ezek 1:13; Rev 8:5 10:3 [a]Lit *house*, and so throughout the ch [A]Ezek 8:3, 16 10:4 [A]Ezek 9:3; 11:22, 23 [B]Ex 40:34, 35; Is 6:1-4 [C]Ezek 1:28 10:5 [a]Heb *El Shaddai* [A]Job 40:9; Ezek 1:24; Rev 10:3 10:9 [a]Perhaps, *beryl* [A]Ezek 1:15-17 [B]Dan 10:6; Rev 21:20

the others. Linen indicates high rank (cf. Da 10:5; 12:6). Perhaps this was the Angel of the Lord, the preincarnate Christ (*see note on Ex 3:2*). He had all the instruments of an oriental scribe to carry out His task (vv. 4, 11).

9:3 the glory . . . went up. The glory of God departs before the destruction of the city and temple. The gradual departure of God from His temple is depicted in stages: the glory resides in the temple's Most Holy Place, between the wings of the cherubs on each side of the ark of the covenant over the mercy seat, then leaves to the front door (9:3; 10:4), later to the E gate by the outer wall (10:18, 19), and finally to the Mt. of Olives to the E, having fully departed (11:22, 23). The glory will return in the future kingdom of Messiah (43:2–7).

9:4 a mark on the foreheads. Since God's departure removed all protection and gave the people over to destruction, it was necessary for the angelic scribe (Angel of the Lord) to mark for God's preservation the righteous who had been faithful to Him. Those left unmarked were subject to death in Babylon's siege (v. 5). The mark was the indication of God's elect, identified personally by the preincarnate Christ. He was marking the elect (cf. Ex 12:7). Malachi 3:16–18 indicates a similar idea. Cf. Rev 7:3; 9:4. The marked ones were penitent and were identified for protection. Here was a respite of grace for the remnant. The rest were to be killed (vv. 5–7).

9:8 Are You destroying . . . ? Ezekiel is fearfully aroused in prayer because the judgment on Jerusalem and Israel is so vast. God replies that pervasive sin demands thorough judgment (vv. 9, 10), yet comforts him by the report that the faithful had been marked to be spared (v. 11). Cf. Rom 11:1, 2, 25–27.

10:1 a throne. It rises above God's angelic servants, the same 4 as in chap. 1 (10:20, 22), and is the throne of 1:26–28 on which God sits (cf. 10:20). From it, He directs the operation of His war machine ("wheels," *see notes on 1:15, 16*) on Jerusalem (v. 2). The throne is like a sapphire shining forth representing God's glory and holiness (11:22).

10:2 fill . . . with coals. God specifies that the marking angel (9:2, 11) reach into the war machine and fill his hands with fiery coals in the presence of the angels of chap. 1. These coals picture the fires of judgment which God's angels are to "scatter" on Jerusalem. In Is 6, "a coal" was used for the purification of the prophet; here coals were for the destruction of the wicked (cf. Heb 12:29). Fire did destroy Jerusalem in 586 B.C.

10:3 cherubim. These were different from the cherubim of chap. 1 and here in v. 4.

10:4 This verse explains how the "cloud" of v. 3 "filled . . . the court." It repeats what is first described in 9:3.

10:6, 7 These verses picked up the action of the angelic scribe from v. 2.

10:7 cherub . . . put *it* into the hands. One of the 4 cherubim of 1:5ff. and v. 1 puts the fiery coals into the marking angel's hand.

10:9–17 wheels beside the cherubim. This whole section is similar to 1:4–21. Four wheels on God's chariot mingled with the 4 angels (cf. 1:15–21) coordinated with one another in

moved, they went [A]in *any of* their four [a]directions
without turning as they went; but they followed in
the direction which [b]they faced, without turning
as they went. 12 Their [A]whole body, their backs,
their hands, their wings and the [B]wheels were
full of eyes all around, the wheels belonging to
all four of them. 13 The wheels were called in my
hearing, the whirling wheels. 14 And [A]each one
had four faces. The first face *was* the face of a
cherub, the second face *was* the face of a man, the
third the face of a lion, and the fourth the face of
an eagle.
15 Then the cherubim rose up. They are the [A]living
beings that I saw by the river Chebar. 16 Now when
the cherubim moved, the wheels would go beside
them; also when the cherubim lifted up their wings
to rise from the ground, the wheels would not turn
from beside them. 17 When [a]the cherubim [A]stood
still, [a]the wheels would stand still; and when they
rose up, [a]the wheels would rise with them, for the
spirit of the living beings *was* in them.
18 Then the glory of the LORD departed from the
threshold of the temple and stood [A]over the cherubim. 19 When [A]the cherubim departed, they lifted
their wings and rose up from the earth in my sight
with the wheels beside them; and they stood still at
the entrance of the east gate of the LORD'S house,
and the glory of the God of Israel [a]hovered over
them.
20 These are the [A]living beings that I saw beneath
the God of Israel by [B]the river Chebar; so I knew that
they *were* cherubim. 21 [A]Each one had four faces and
each one four wings, and beneath their wings *was*
the form of human hands. 22 As for the likeness of
their faces, they were the same faces whose appearance I had seen by the river Chebar. Each one
went straight ahead.

EVIL RULERS TO BE JUDGED

11 Moreover, the [A]Spirit lifted me up and brought
me to the east gate of the LORD'S house which
faced eastward. And behold, *there were* twenty-five
men at the entrance of the gate, and among them
I saw Jaazaniah son of Azzur and [B]Pelatiah son of
Benaiah, leaders of the people. 2 He said to me, "Son
of man, these are the men who devise iniquity and
[A]give evil advice in this city, 3 who say, '*The time* is
not near to build houses. [a]This [A]*city* is the pot and
we are the flesh.' 4 Therefore, [A]prophesy against
them, son of man, prophesy!"
5 Then the Spirit of the LORD fell upon me, and He
said to me, "Say, 'Thus says the LORD, "So you think,
house of Israel, for [A]I know [a]your [B]thoughts. 6 You
have [A]multiplied your slain in this city, filling its
streets with [a]them." 7 Therefore, thus says the Lord
[a]GOD, "Your [A]slain whom you have laid in the midst
of [b]the city are the flesh and this *city* is the pot; but [c]I
will [B]bring you out of it. 8 You have [A]feared a sword;
so I will [B]bring a sword upon you," the Lord GOD
declares. 9 "And I will bring you out of the midst of
[a]the city and deliver you into the hands of [A]strang-
ers and [B]execute judgments against you. 10 You will
[A]fall by the sword. I will judge you to the [B]border of
Israel; so you shall know that I am the LORD. 11 This
city will [A]not be a pot for you, nor will you be flesh
in the midst of it, *but* I will judge you to the border
of Israel. 12 Thus you will know that I am the LORD;
for you have not walked in My statutes nor have you
[A]executed My ordinances, but have acted according
to the ordinances of the [B]nations around you." ' "
13 Now it came about as I prophesied, that [A]Pel-
atiah son of Benaiah died. Then I fell on my face
and cried out with a loud voice and said, "[B]Alas,
Lord GOD! Will You bring the remnant of Israel to
a complete end?"

10:11 [a]Lit *sides* [b]Lit *the head turned* [A]Ezek 1:17 10:12 [A]Rev 4:6, 8 [B]Ezek 1:18 10:14 [A]1 Kin 7:29, 36; Ezek 1:6, 10; 10:21; Rev 4:7 10:15 [A]Ezek 1:3, 5 10:17 [a]Lit *they* [A]Ezek 1:21 10:18 [A]Ps 18:10 10:19 [a]Lit *over them from above* [A]Ezek 11:22 10:20 [A]Ezek 1:5, 22, 26; 10:15 [B]Ezek 1:1 10:21 [A]Ezek 1:6, 8; 10:14; 41:18, 19 11:1 [A]Ezek 3:12, 14; 8:3; 11:24; 43:5 [B]Ezek 11:13 11:2 [A]Ps 2:1, 2; 52:2; Is 30:1; Jer 5:5; Mic 2:1 11:3 [a]Or *This is* [A]Jer 1:13; Ezek 11:7, 11; 24:3, 6 11:4 [A]Ezek 3:4, 17 11:5 [a]Lit *what comes up in your spirit* [A]Jer 11:20; 17:10 [B]Ezek 38:10 11:6 [a]Lit *the slain* [A]Is 1:15; Ezek 7:23; 22:2-6, 9, 12, 27 11:7 [a]Heb *YHWH*, usually rendered *LORD*, and so throughout the ch [b]Lit *it* [c]So with Gr; Heb *he will bring you out* [A]Ezek 24:3-13; Mic 3:2, 3 [B]2 Kin 25:18-22; Jer 52:24-27; Ezek 11:9 11:8 [A]Prov 10:24; Is 66:4 [B]Job 3:25; Is 24:17, 18 11:9 [a]Lit *it* [A]Deut 28:36, 49, 50; Ps 106:41 [B]Ezek 5:8; 16:41 11:10 [A]Jer 52:9, 10 [B]2 Kin 14:25 11:11 [A]Ezek 11:3, 7; 24:3, 6 11:12 [A]Ezek 18:8, 9 [B]Ezek 8:10, 14, 16 11:13 [A]Ezek 11:1 [B]Ezek 9:8

precision, and each with a different one of the cherubim. All looked so much alike that it was as if one wheel blended entirely with another (v. 10). As their appearance was so unified, their action was in unison, and instant (v. 11). The cherubim had bodies like men, and their chariot wheels were full of eyes, denoting full perception both to see the sinners and their fitting judgment. The color tarshish, or beryl, is a sparkling yellow or gold.

10:14 the face of a cherub. This description of one cherub in 1:10 indicates this was the face of an ox.

10:15 rose up. They were all ready to move in unison (vv. 16, 17) as the Shekinah glory of God departed (v. 18).

10:18, 19 glory ... departed. There were several stages: 9:3; 10:1, 3, 4; 10:18, 19; 11:22, 23. There was thus written over the entire structure, as well as Israel's spiritual life, "Ichabod" (the glory has departed). Cf. 1Sa 4:21; 10:18, 19.

11:1 twenty-five men. Ezekiel, though at the temple only in the vision (cf. 8:3, and *see note there*), saw because God, who was everywhere present and all-knowing, impressed specific details on him in the vision. The wicked leaders (cf. v. 2) were part of God's reason for the judgment (vv. 8, 10). Ezekiel was taken in spirit to the very place which the glory of God had left in 10:19 and was given a vision of "twenty-five men," who represented not priests, but influential leaders among the people who gave fatal advice to the people (v. 2). **Jaazaniah son of Azzur.** *See note on 8:11.*

11:3 pot ... flesh. Though this is obscure, it may be that the bad advice these leaders were giving was that the people should not be engaged in business as usual, "to build houses" or to take care of their comfort and futures, when they were about to be cooked like flesh in a pot over a blazing fire. The idea must have been that the people should get ready for battle, and be prepared to fight, not focusing on comfort, but survival. Jeremiah had told the people to surrender to the Babylonians and save their lives, rather than fight and be killed (cf. Jer 27:9–17). These false leaders, like the prophets and priests whom Jeremiah confronted for telling the people not to submit, scorned Jeremiah's words from God and would pay for it (v. 4). Cf. 24:1–14.

11:6 multiplied your slain. Leaders who misled Israel by inciting false expectations of a victorious defense, rather than peaceful surrender, were responsible for the deadly results. Many people died in resisting Babylon.

11:7 I will bring you out. The false leaders thought that unless they fought, they would all be in a boiling pot, i.e., the city. But here the Lord promised that some would be delivered from the city, only to die on Israel's border in the wilderness (vv. 8–11). This was literally fulfilled at Riblah (cf. 2Ki 25:18–21; Jer 52:24–27).

11:13 Pelatiah ... died. The death of one leader from v. 1 was a sign that God would indeed carry out His word. Apparently this leader did die suddenly at the time Ezekiel was shown the vision, so that the prophet feared that this death meant death for all Israelites (9:8).

PROMISE OF RESTORATION

14 Then the word of the LORD came to me, saying, 15 "Son of man, your brothers, your [a]relatives, [b]your fellow exiles and the whole house of Israel, all of them, *are those* to whom the inhabitants of Jerusalem have said, 'Go far from the LORD; this land has been given [A]us as a possession.' 16 Therefore say, 'Thus says the Lord GOD, "Though I had removed them far away among the nations and though I had scattered them among the countries, yet I was a [A]sanctuary for them a little while in the countries where they had gone." ' 17 Therefore say, 'Thus says the Lord GOD, "I will [A]gather you from the peoples and assemble you out of the countries among which you have been scattered, and I will give you the land of Israel." ' 18 When they come there, they will [A]remove all its [B]detestable things and all its abominations from it. 19 And I will [A]give them one heart, and put a new spirit within [a]them. And I will take the [B]heart of stone out of their flesh and give them a [C]heart of flesh, 20 that they may [A]walk in My statutes and keep My ordinances and do them. Then they will be [B]My people, and I shall be their God. 21 [a]But as for those whose hearts go after their [A]detestable things and abominations, I will [B]bring their conduct down on their heads," declares the Lord GOD.

22 Then the cherubim [A]lifted up their wings with the wheels beside them, and [B]the glory of the God of Israel [a]hovered over them. 23 The [A]glory of the LORD went up from the midst of the city and [B]stood over the mountain which is east of the city. 24 And the [A]Spirit lifted me up and brought me in a vision by the Spirit of God to the exiles [a]in Chaldea. So the vision that I had seen [b,B]left me. 25 Then I [A]told the exiles all the things that the LORD had shown me.

EZEKIEL PREPARES FOR EXILE

12 Then the word of the LORD came to me, saying, 2 "Son of man, you live in the [A]midst of the [B]rebellious house, who [C]have eyes to see but do not see, ears to hear but do not hear; for they are a rebellious house. 3 Therefore, son of man, prepare for yourself baggage for exile and go into exile by day in their sight; even go into exile from your place to another place in their sight. [A]Perhaps they will [a]understand though they are a rebellious house. 4 Bring your baggage out by day in their sight, as baggage for exile. Then you will go out [A]at evening in their sight, as those going into exile. 5 Dig a hole through the wall in their sight and [a]go out through it. 6 Load *the baggage* on *your* shoulder in their sight *and* carry *it* out in the dark. You shall [A]cover your face so that you cannot see the land, for I have set you as a [B]sign to the house of Israel."

7 I [A]did so, as I had been commanded. By day I [B]brought out my baggage like the baggage of an exile. Then in the evening I dug through the wall with my hands; I went out in the dark *and* carried *the baggage* on *my* shoulder in their sight.

8 In the morning the word of the LORD came to me, saying, 9 "Son of man, has not the house of Israel, the [A]rebellious house, said to you, '[B]What are you doing?' 10 Say to them, 'Thus says the Lord [a]GOD, "This [b,A]burden *concerns* the prince in Jerusalem as well as all the house of Israel who are [c]in it." ' 11 Say, 'I am [a]a [A]sign to you. As I have done, so it will be done to them; they will [B]go into exile, into captivity.' 12 The [A]prince who is among them will load *his baggage* on *his* shoulder in the dark and go out. [a]They will dig a hole through the wall to bring *it* out. He will cover his face so that he can not see the land with *his* eyes.

11:15 [a]Lit *brothers* [b]So with Gr and some ancient versions; Heb *the men of your redemption* [A]Ezek 33:24 11:16 [A]Ps 31:20; 90:1; 91:9; Is 8:14; Jer 29:7, 11 11:17 [A]Is 11:11-16; Jer 3:12, 18; 24:5; Ezek 20:41, 42; 28:25 11:18 [A]Ezek 37:23 [B]Ezek 5:11; 7:20 11:19 [a]So with Gr and many mss; Heb *you* [A]Jer 24:7; 32:39; Ezek 18:31; 36:26 [B]Zech 7:12; Rom 2:4, 5 [C]2 Cor 3:3 11:20 [A]Ps 105:45; Ezek 36:27 [B]Ezek 14:11 11:21 [a]Lit *And to the heart of their detestable things and their abomination their heart goes* [A]Jer 16:18; Ezek 11:18 [B]Ezek 9:10; 16:43 11:22 [a]Lit *over them from above* [A]Ezek 10:19 [B]Ezek 43:2 11:23 [A]Ezek 8:4 [B]Zech 14:4 11:24 [a]I.e. Babylonia [b]Lit *went up from* [A]Ezek 8:3; 11:1; 37:1; 2 Cor 12:2-4 [B]Acts 10:16 11:25 [A]Ezek 2:7; 3:4, 17, 27 12:2 [A]Is 6:5 [B]Ps 78:40; Is 1:23; Ezek 2:7, 8 [C]Is 6:9f; 43:8; Jer 5:21; Matt 13:13, 14; Mark 4:12; 8:18; Luke 8:10; John 9:39-41; 12:40; Acts 28:26f; Rom 11:8 12:3 [a]Or *see that they are* [A]Jer 26:3; 36:3, 7; Luke 20:13; 2 Tim 2:25 12:4 [A]2 Kin 25:4; Jer 39:4; Ezek 12:12 12:5 [a]Lit *bring it out* 12:6 [A]1 Sam 28:8; Ezek 12:12, 13 [B]Is 8:18; 20:3; Ezek 4:3; 12:11; 24:24 12:7 [A]Ezek 24:18; 37:7, 10 [B]Ezek 12:3-6 12:9 [A]Ezek 2:5-8; 12:1-3 [B]Ezek 17:12; 20:49; 24:19 12:10 [a]Heb *YHWH*, usually rendered *LORD*, and so throughout the ch [b]Or *oracle* [c]Lit *in their midst* [A]2 Kin 9:25; Is 13:1; Ezek 12:3-8 12:11 [a]Lit *your sign* [A]Ezek 12:6 [B]Jer 15:2; 52:15, 28-30; Ezek 12:3 12:12 [a]I.e. the king's attendants [A]2 Kin 25:4; Jer 39:4; 52:7; Ezek 12:6

11:14, 15 Ezekiel was told he had a new family, not the priests at Jerusalem to whom he was tied by blood, but his fellow exiles in Babylon, identified as those who were treated as outcasts. The priesthood was about to be ended, and he was to have a new family.

11:15 Go far from. The contemptuous words of those still left in Jerusalem at the carrying away of Jeconiah and the exiles indicated that they felt smugly secure and believed the land was their possession.

11:16 sanctuary. God was to be the protection and provision for those who had been scattered through all the 70 years until they were restored. The exiles may have cast off the Jews, but God had not (Is 8:14). This holds true for the future restoration of the Jews (vv. 17, 18).

11:19, 20 a new spirit. God pledged not only to restore Ezekiel's people to their ancient land, but to bring the New Covenant with its blessings. Cf. 36:25–28, and *see note on Jer 31:31–34*.

11:23 the mountain ... east. The glory of God moved to the Mt. of Olives to which the glorious Son of God will return at the Second Advent (cf. 43:1–5; Zec 14:4).

11:24 brought me in a vision. Again, Ezekiel has remained bodily in his Babylonian house, seen by his visitors (v. 25; 8:1). God, who supernaturally showed him a vision in Jerusalem, caused his sense of awareness to return to Chaldea, thus ending the vision state. Once the vision was completed, Ezekiel was able to tell his exiled countrymen what God had shown him (v. 25).

12:2 rebellious house. The message of Ezekiel was addressed to his fellow exiles who were as hardened as those still in Jerusalem. They were so intent on a quick return to Jerusalem that they would not accept his message of Jerusalem's destruction. Their rebellion is described in familiar terms (Dt 29:1–4; Is 6:9, 10; Jer 5:21; cf. Mt 13:13–15; Ac 28:26, 27).

12:3 prepare ... for exile. This dramatic object lesson by the prophet called for carrying belongings out in a stealthy way as an act that depicted baggage for exile, just the bare necessities. His countrymen carried out such baggage when they went into captivity, or sought to escape during Babylon's takeover of Jerusalem (vv. 7, 11). Some attempting to escape were caught as in a net, like King Zedekiah who was overtaken, blinded, and forced into exile (vv. 12, 13; 2Ki 24:18–25:7; Jer 39:4–7; 52:1–11). Verse 7 indicates that Ezekiel actually did what he was told.

12:5 This section depicts those in desperation trying to escape from their sun-dried brick homes.

12:6 cover your face. This was to avoid recognition.

12:10–13 the prince. This is a reference to King Zedekiah, who was always referred to by Ezekiel as prince, never king. Jehoiachin was regarded as the true king (cf. 17:13), because the Babylonians never deposed him formally. All the house of Israel, however, shared the calamity to fall on Zedekiah. How literally these prophecies were fulfilled can be seen from the account in 2Ki 25:1–7. The "net" and "snare" (v. 13) were the Babylonian army. He was taken captive to Babylon, but he never saw it because his eyes had been put out at Riblah.

13 I will also spread My [A]net over him, and he will be
caught in My snare. And I will bring him to Babylon
in the land of the Chaldeans; yet he will [B]not see it,
though he will die there. 14 I will [A]scatter to every
wind all who are around him, his helpers and all his
troops; and I will draw out a sword after them. 15 So
they will [A]know that I am the LORD when I scatter
them among the nations and spread them among
the countries. 16 But I will [a]spare a few of them from
the [A]sword, the famine and the pestilence that they
may tell all their abominations among the nations
where they go, and [b]may [B]know that I am the LORD."
17 Moreover, the word of the LORD came to me saying, 18 "Son of man, [A]eat your bread with trembling
and drink your water with quivering and anxiety.
19 Then say to the people of the land, 'Thus says the
Lord GOD concerning the inhabitants of Jerusalem
in the land of Israel, "They will eat their bread with
anxiety and drink their water with horror, because
[a]their land will be [b,A]stripped of its fullness on account of the violence of all who live in it. 20 The inhabited [A]cities will be laid waste and the [B]land will be
a desolation. So you will know that I am the LORD." ' "
21 Then the word of the LORD came to me, saying,
22 "Son of man, what is this [A]proverb you *people* have
concerning the land of Israel, saying, 'The [B]days
are long and every [C]vision fails'? 23 Therefore say
to them, 'Thus says the Lord GOD, "I will make this
proverb cease so that they will no longer use it as
a proverb in Israel." But tell them, "[A]The days draw
near as well as the [a]fulfillment of every vision. 24 For
there will no longer be any [a,A]false vision or flattering divination within the house of Israel. 25 For
I the LORD will speak, and whatever [A]word I speak
will be performed. It will no longer be delayed,
for in [B]your days, O [C]rebellious house, I will speak
the word and perform it," declares the Lord GOD.' "
26 Furthermore, the word of the LORD came to
me, saying, 27 "Son of man, behold, the house of Israel is saying, 'The vision that he sees is for [A]many
[a]years *from now,* and he prophesies of times far
off.' 28 Therefore say to them, 'Thus says the Lord
GOD, "None of My words will be delayed any longer. Whatever word I speak will be performed," ' "
declares the Lord GOD.

FALSE PROPHETS CONDEMNED

13 Then the word of the LORD came to me saying,
2 "Son of man, prophesy against the [A]proph-
ets of Israel who prophesy, and say to those who
prophesy from their own [a]inspiration, '[B]Listen to the
word of the LORD! 3 Thus says the Lord [a]GOD, "Woe
to the [A]foolish prophets who are following their
own spirit and have [B]seen nothing. 4 O Israel, your
prophets have been like foxes among ruins. 5 You
have not [A]gone up into the [B]breaches, nor did you
build the wall around the house of Israel to stand
in the battle on the [C]day of the LORD. 6 They see
[a,A]falsehood and lying divination who are saying,
'The LORD declares,' when the LORD has not sent
them; [B]yet they hope for the fulfillment of *their*
word. 7 [A]Did you not see a false vision and speak a
lying divination when you said, 'The LORD declares,'
but it is not I who have spoken?" ' "
8 Therefore, thus says the Lord GOD, "Because you
have spoken [a]falsehood and seen a lie, therefore behold, [A]I am against you," declares the Lord GOD. 9 "So
My hand will be against the [A]prophets who see false
visions and utter lying divinations. They will [a]have
no place in the council of My people, [B]nor will they
be written down in the register of the house of Israel,
nor will they enter the land of Israel, [b]that you may
know that I am the Lord GOD. 10 It is definitely because they have [A]misled My people by saying, '[B]Peace!'
when there is [C]no peace. And when anyone builds
a wall, behold, they plaster it over with whitewash;
11 *so* tell those who plaster *it* over with whitewash,
that it will fall. A [A]flooding rain will come, and you,
O hailstones, will fall; and a violent wind will break
out. 12 Behold, when the wall has fallen, will you not

12:13 [A]Is 24:17, 18; Ezek 17:20; 19:8; Hos 7:12 [B]Jer 39:7; 52:11 12:14 [A]2 Kin 25:4, 5; Ezek 5:2; 17:21 12:15 [A]Ezek 6:7, 14; 12:16, 20 12:16 [a]Lit *leave over* [b]Or *they will know* [A]Ezek 7:15; 14:21 [B]Jer 22:8, 9 12:18 [A]Lam 5:9; Ezek 4:16 12:19 [a]Lit *her* [b]Lit *desolate* [A]Jer 10:22; Ezek 6:6, 7, 14; Mic 7:13; Zech 7:14 12:20 [A]Is 3:26; Jer 4:7; Ezek 5:14 [B]Is 7:23, 24; Jer 25:9; Ezek 36:3 12:22 [A]Ezek 16:44; 18:2, 3 [B]Jer 5:12; Ezek 11:3; 12:27; Amos 6:3; 2 Pet 3:4 [C]Ezek 7:26 12:23 [a]Lit *word* [A]Ps 37:13; Joel 2:1; Zeph 1:14 12:24 [a]Lit *vain* [A]Jer 14:13-16; Ezek 13:6, 23; Zech 13:2-4 12:25 [A]Num 14:28-34; Is 14:24; Ezek 6:10; 12:28 [B]Jer 16:9; Hab 1:5 [C]Ezek 12:2 12:27 [a]Lit *days* [A]Ezek 12:22; Dan 10:14 13:2 [a]Lit *heart* [A]Is 9:15; Jer 37:19; Ezek 22:25, 28 [B]Is 1:10; Amos 7:16 13:3 [a]Heb *YHWH*, usually rendered *LORD*, and so throughout the ch [A]Lam 2:14; Hos 9:7; Zech 11:15 [B]Jer 23:28-32 13:5 [A]Ps 106:23; Jer 23:22; Ezek 22:30 [B]Is 58:12 [C]Is 13:6, 9; Ezek 7:19 13:6 [a]Lit *vanity* [A]Jer 29:8; Ezek 22:28 [B]Jer 28:15; 37:19 13:7 [A]Ezek 22:28 13:8 [a]Lit *vanity* [A]Ezek 5:8; 21:3; Nah 2:13 13:9 [a]Lit *not be in* [b]Or *and you will know* [A]Jer 20:3-6; 28:15-17 [B]Ps 69:28; 87:6; Jer 17:13; Dan 12:1 13:10 [A]Jer 23:32; 50:6 [B]Jer 6:14; 8:11; 14:13 [C]Ezek 7:25; 13:16 13:11 [A]Ezek 38:22

12:14–16 God's hand was to be with the enemy as His rod of correction, with only a few left.

12:22 this proverb. Delay had given the people the false impression that the stroke of judgment would never come. In fact, a saying had become popular, no doubt developed by false prophets who caused the people to reject Ezekiel's visions and prophecies (cf. v. 27) and gave "false vision or flattering divination" (vv. 23, 24).

12:25 in your days. The prophet is explicit about the present time for fulfillment, i.e., in their lifetime.

13:2 against the prophets. False prophets had long flourished in Judah and had been transported to Babylon as well. Here God directs Ezekiel to indict those false prophets for futile assurances of peace (as Jer 23) in vv. 1–16. Then His attention turns to lying prophetesses in vv. 17–23. The test of a prophet is found in Dt 13:1–5 and 18:21, 22.

13:2, 3 inspiration ... spirit. Spurious spokesmen prophesy subjectively out of their minds while claiming to have revelation and authority from the Lord (cf. v. 7).

13:4 like foxes. False prophets did not do anything helpful. Rather, like foxes, they were mischievous and destructive.

13:5 build the wall. The false prophets did nothing to shore up the spiritual defenses the people so needed in the face of judgment. The enemy had made "breaches" but the false prophets never encouraged the people to repent and return to the Lord. Those who would were called for in 22:30. The "day of the LORD" came in 586 B.C. when the theocracy fell. *See note on Is 2:12.*

13:9 A 3-fold judgment is given to the false prophets: 1) they would not be in the council of God's people; 2) their names would be wiped from the register of Israel (Ezr 2:62); and 3) they would never return to the land (cf. 20:38).

13:10, 11 builds a wall. False prophets had lulled the people into false security. Phony "peace" promises, while sin continued on the brink of God's judgment, was a way, so to speak, of erecting a defective "wall" and whitewashing it to make it look good. Such an unsafe "wall" was doomed to collapse (v. 11) when God would bring His storm, picturing the invaders' assault (v. 11).

13:11–16 These descriptions are all images belonging to the illustration of the wall, not meant to convey real wind, flood, and hail. The Babylonians were the actual destroyers of Israel's hypocritical false spirituality.

be asked, 'Where is the plaster with which you plastered *it?*' " 13 Therefore, thus says the Lord GOD, "I will
make a violent wind break out in My wrath. There will
also be in My anger a flooding rain and [A]hailstones
to consume *it* in wrath. 14 So I will tear down the wall
which you plastered over with whitewash and bring
it down to the ground, so that its [A]foundation is laid
bare; and when it falls, you will be [B]consumed in its
midst. And you will [C]know that I am the LORD. 15 Thus
I will spend My wrath on the wall and on those who
have plastered it over with whitewash; and I will say
to you, 'The wall [a]is gone and its plasterers are gone,
16 *along with* the prophets of Israel who prophesy
to Jerusalem, and who [A]see visions of peace for her
when there is [B]no peace,' declares the Lord GOD.

17 "Now you, son of man, set your face against
the daughters of your people who are [A]prophesy-
ing [B]from their own [a]inspiration. Prophesy against
them 18 and say, 'Thus says the Lord GOD, "Woe to
the women who sew *magic* bands on [a]all wrists
and make veils for the heads of *persons* of every
stature to [A]hunt down [b]lives! Will you hunt down
the [b]lives of My people, but preserve the [b]lives *of
others* for yourselves? 19 [A]For handfuls of barley
and fragments of bread, you have profaned Me to
My people to put to death [a]some who should not
die and to [B]keep [a]others alive who should not live,
by your lying to My people who listen to lies." ' "

20 Therefore, thus says the Lord GOD, "Behold, I am
against your *magic* bands by which you hunt [a]lives
there as [b]birds and I will tear them from your arms; and
I will let [a]them go, even those [a]lives whom you hunt as
[b]birds. 21 I will also tear off your veils and [A]deliver My
people from your hands, and they will no longer be
in your hands to be hunted; and you will know that I
am the LORD. 22 Because you [A]disheartened the righteous with falsehood when I did not cause him grief,
but have [a,B]encouraged the wicked not to [C]turn from
his wicked way *and* preserve his life, 23 therefore, you
women will no longer see [a,A]false visions or practice
divination, and I will [B]deliver My people out of your
hand. Thus you will [C]know that I am the LORD."

IDOLATROUS ELDERS CONDEMNED

14 Then some [A]elders of Israel came to me and
[B]sat down before me. 2 And the word of the
LORD came to me, saying, 3 "Son of man, these men
have [A]set up their idols in their hearts and have
[B]put right before their faces the stumbling block of
their iniquity. Should I be [C]consulted by them at all?
4 Therefore speak to them and tell them, 'Thus says
the Lord [a]GOD, "Any man of the house of Israel who
sets up his idols in his heart, puts right before his
face the stumbling block of his iniquity, and *then*
comes to the prophet, I the LORD will be brought
to give him an answer in [b]the matter in view of the
[A]multitude of his idols, 5 in order to lay hold of [a,A]the
hearts of the house of Israel who are [b,B]estranged
from Me through all their idols." '

6 "Therefore say to the house of Israel, 'Thus says
the Lord GOD, "[A]Repent and turn away from your
idols and turn your faces away from all your [B]abom-
inations. 7 For anyone of the house of Israel or of
the [A]immigrants who stay in Israel who separates
himself from Me, sets up his idols in his heart, puts
right before his face the stumbling block of his iniquity, and *then* comes to the prophet to inquire of Me
for himself, [B]I the LORD will be brought to answer
him in My own person. 8 I will [A]set My face against
that man and make him a [B]sign and [a]a proverb, and
I will cut him off from among My people. So you
will know that I am the LORD.

9 "But if the prophet is [a]prevailed upon to speak
a word, it is I, the LORD, who have [a]prevailed upon
that prophet, and I will stretch out My hand against
him and [A]destroy him from among My people Israel.
10 They will bear *the punishment of* their iniquity; as
the iniquity of the inquirer is, so the iniquity of the

13:13 [A]Ex 9:24, 25; Ps 18:12, 13; Is 30:30; Rev 11:19; 16:21 13:14 [A]Mic 1:6; Hab 3:13 [B]Jer 6:15; 14:15 [C]Ezek 13:9 13:15 [a]Lit *is not…are not* 13:16 [A]Jer 6:14; 8:11; Ezek 13:10 [B]Is 57:21 13:17 [a]Lit *heart* [A]Judg 4:4; 2 Kin 22:14; Luke 2:36; Acts 21:9 [B]Ezek 13:2; Rev 2:20 13:18 [a]Lit *all joints of the hand;* M.T. reads *of my hands* [b]Or *souls* [A]2 Pet 2:14 13:19 [a]Or *souls* [A]Prov 28:21; Mic 3:5 [B]Jer 23:14, 17 13:20 [a]Lit *souls* [b]Or *flying ones* 13:21 [A]Ps 91:3; 124:7 13:22 [a]Lit *strengthen the hands of* [A]Amos 5:12 [B]Jer 23:14; 34:16, 22 [C]Ezek 18:21, 27, 30-32; 33:14-16 13:23 [a]Lit *vanity* [A]Ezek 12:24; 13:6; Mic 3:6; Zech 13:3 [B]Ezek 13:21; 34:10 [C]Ezek 13:9, 21 14:1 [A]2 Kin 6:32; Ezek 8:1; 20:1 [B]Is 29:13; Ezek 33:31, 32 14:3 [A]Ezek 20:16 [B]Ezek 7:19; 14:4, 7; Zeph 1:3 [C]Is 1:15; Jer 11:11; Ezek 20:3, 31 14:4 [a]Heb *YHWH*, usually rendered *LORD*, and so throughout the ch [b]Lit *it* [A]1 Kin 21:20-24; 2 Kin 1:16; Is 66:4 14:5 [a]Lit *their* [b]Or *all estranged from Me through their idols* [A]Jer 17:10; Zech 7:12 [B]Is 1:4; Jer 2:11; Zech 11:8 14:6 [A]1 Sam 7:3; Neh 1:9; Is 2:20; 30:22; 55:6, 7; Ezek 18:30 [B]Ezek 8:6; 14:4 14:7 [A]Ex 12:48; 20:10 [B]Ezek 14:4 14:8 [a]Lit *proverbs* [A]Jer 44:11; Ezek 15:7 [B]Is 65:15; Ezek 5:15 14:9 [a]Or *enticed* [A]Jer 6:14, 15; 14:15

13:17–23 Although women are rebuked by Isaiah (3:16–4:1; 32:9–13) and Amos (4:1–3), this is the only OT text where false prophetesses are mentioned. Sorcery was practiced mainly by women. Jezebel is called a false prophetess in Rev 2:20.

13:18, 19 bands … veils … handfuls of barley … bread. Apparently, these sorceresses employed all these things in their divinations, hunting down souls for their advantage (v. 20).

13:22 with falsehood. Predators had saddened the righteous by a false message leading to calamity which involved great loss even for them (cf. 21:3, 4). They had encouraged the wicked to expect a bright future, and saw no need to repent to avoid death.

13:23 I will deliver My people. Certainly this was true in the restoration after the 70 years in Babylon, but will be fully true in Messiah's kingdom. God's true promise will bring an end to sorcery and false prophecy (cf. Mic 3:6, 7; Zec 13:1–6).

14:1–3 elders … came. These leaders came insincerely seeking God's counsel (v. 3; cf. Ps 66:18), as God reveals to the prophet, who thus saw through their facade and indicted them for determining to pursue their evil way and defy God's will. False prophets of chap. 13 were thriving, as the civil leaders and populace whom they represented set a welcoming climate and inclination for the delusions.

14:4 I the LORD will … answer. They received no verbal answer, but an answer directly from the Lord in the action of judgment.

14:6 turn away. The Lord answered the two-faced inquiry in only one way, by a call to repent. The seekers were turned away from Him to idols (v. 6b), and He must be turned away from them (v. 8a). The guilty, including both those back at Jerusalem and the exiles tolerating the same things, were to repent, turning away from idols to God.

14:8 The punishment echoed the warnings of Lv 20:3, 5, 6 and Dt 28:27.

14:9 prevailed upon. God will deceive (entice) a false prophet only in a qualified sense. When one willfully rejects His Word, He places a resulting cloud of darkness, or permits it to continue, hiding the truth so that the person is deceived by his own obstinate self-will. This fits with the same principle as when God gives up Israel to evil statutes (20:25, 26), counsel that they insist on as they spurn His Word (20:24, 26). When people refuse the truth, He lets them seek after their own inclinations and gives them over to falsehood (20:39). This is the wrath of abandonment noted in Ro 1:18–32 (cf. 1Ki 22:20–23; 2Th 2:11).

prophet will be, 11 in order that the house of Israel may no longer [A]stray from Me and no longer [B]defile themselves with all their transgressions. Thus they will be [C]My people, and I shall be their God," ' declares the Lord GOD."

THE CITY WILL NOT BE SPARED

12 Then the word of the LORD came to me saying, 13 "Son of man, if a country sins against Me by [A]committing unfaithfulness, and I stretch out My hand against it, [a]destroy its [B]supply of bread, send famine against it and cut off from it both man and beast, 14 even [A]*though* these three men, [B]Noah, [C]Daniel and [D]Job were in its midst, by their *own* righteousness they could *only* deliver [E]themselves," declares the Lord GOD. 15 "If I were to cause [A]wild beasts to pass through the land and they [a]depopulated it, and it became desolate so that no one would pass through it because of the beasts, 16 *though* these three men were in its midst, as I live," declares the Lord GOD, "they could not deliver either *their* sons or *their* daughters. [A]They alone would be delivered, but the country would be desolate. 17 Or *if* I should [A]bring a sword on that country and say, 'Let the sword pass through the country and [B]cut off man and beast from it,' 18 even *though* these three men were in its midst, as I live," declares the Lord GOD, "they could not deliver either *their* sons or *their* daughters, but they alone would be delivered. 19 Or *if* I should send a [A]plague against that country and pour out My wrath in blood on it to cut off man and beast from it, 20 even *though* Noah, Daniel and Job were in its midst, as I live," declares the Lord GOD, "they could not deliver either *their* son or *their* daughter. They would deliver only themselves by their righteousness."

21 For thus says the Lord GOD, "How much more when [A]I send My four [a]severe judgments against Jerusalem: sword, famine, wild beasts and plague to cut off man and beast from it! 22 Yet, behold, [a]survivors will be left in it who will be brought out, *both* sons and daughters. Behold, they are going to come forth to you and you will [A]see their conduct and actions; then you will be [B]comforted for the calamity which I have brought against Jerusalem for everything which I have brought upon it. 23 Then they will comfort you when you see their conduct and actions, for you will know that I have not done [A]in vain whatever I did [a]to it," declares the Lord GOD.

JERUSALEM LIKE A USELESS VINE

15 Then the word of the LORD came to me, saying, 2 "Son of man, how is the wood of the [A]vine *better* than any wood of a branch which is among the trees of the forest? 3 Can wood be taken from it to make [a]anything, or can *men* take a peg from it on which to hang any vessel? 4 [a]If it has been put into the [A]fire for fuel, *and* the fire has consumed both of its ends and its middle part has been charred, is it *then* useful for [b]anything? 5 Behold, while it is intact, it is not made into [a]anything. How much less, when the fire has consumed it and it is charred, can it still be made into [a]anything! 6 Therefore, thus says the Lord [a]GOD, 'As the wood of the vine among the trees of the forest, which I have given to the fire for fuel, so have I given up the inhabitants of Jerusalem; 7 and I [A]set My face against them. *Though* they have [B]come out of the fire, yet the fire will consume them. Then you will know that I am the LORD, when I set My face against them. 8 Thus I will make the land desolate, because they have [A]acted unfaithfully,' " declares the Lord GOD.

GOD'S GRACE TO UNFAITHFUL JERUSALEM

16 Then the word of the LORD came to me, saying, 2 "Son of man, [A]make known to Jerusalem her abominations 3 and say, 'Thus says the Lord [a]GOD

14:11 [A]Ezek 44:10, 15; 48:11 [B]Ezek 11:18; 37:23 [C]Ezek 11:20; 34:30; 36:28 14:13 [a]Lit *break the staff* [A]Ezek 15:8; 20:27 [B]Lev 26:26; Is 3:1; Ezek 4:16 14:14 [A]Jer 15:1 [B]Gen 6:8; 7:1; Heb 11:7 [C]Ezek 28:3; Dan 1:6; 9:21; 10:11 [D]Job 1:1, 5; 42:8, 9 [E]Ezek 16:18, 20; 18:20 14:15 [a]Lit *bereave of children* [A]Lev 26:22; Num 21:6; Ezek 5:17; 14:21 14:16 [A]Gen 19:29; Ezek 18:20 14:17 [A]Lev 26:25; Ezek 5:12; 21:3, 4 [B]Ezek 25:13; Zeph 1:3 14:19 [A]Jer 14:12; Ezek 5:12; 14:21 14:21 [a]Lit *evil* [A]Ezek 5:17; 33:27; Amos 4:6-10; Rev 6:8 14:22 [a]Lit *escaped ones* [A]Ezek 12:16; 36:20 [B]Ezek 16:54; 31:16; 32:31 14:23 [a]Or *in* [A]Jer 22:8, 9 15:2 [A]Ps 80:8-16; Is 5:1-7; Hos 10:1 15:3 [a]Lit *a work* 15:4 [a]Or *Behold* [b]Lit *a work* [A]Is 27:11; Ezek 15:6; 19:14 15:5 [a]Lit *a work* 15:6 [a]Heb *YHWH*, usually rendered *LORD*, and so throughout the ch 15:7 [A]Lev 26:17; Ps 34:16; Jer 21:10; Ezek 14:8 [B]1 Kin 19:17; Is 24:18; Amos 9:1-4 15:8 [A]Ezek 14:13; 17:20 16:2 [A]Is 58:1; Ezek 20:4; 22:2 16:3 [a]Heb *YHWH*, usually rendered *LORD*, and so throughout the ch

14:12 the word ... came. Ezekiel answered a deception that God would never judge the people of Judah, since some righteous were among them. God would honor the presence of the godly (vv. 14, 20).

14:13–20 My hand against. God promised 4 acts in His drama of judgment (cf. summary, v. 21). In none could the 3 heroes avert tragedy as advocates. These were: 1) famine; 2) wild beasts; 3) the sword; and 4) plague.

14:14–20 Noah, Daniel and Job. Jeremiah 7:16 and 15:1–4 provide a close parallel to this passage. According to Jeremiah, even Moses and Samuel, well known for their power in intercessory prayer, would not prevail to deliver Jerusalem and the people. The 3 OT heroes mentioned in this section exhibited power in intercession on behalf of others (cf. Ge 6:18; Job 42:7–10; Da 1, 2) at strategic points in redemptive history, and even they could not deliver anyone but themselves if they were there praying earnestly. Even the presence and prayers of the godly could not stop the coming judgment. Genesis 18:22–32 and Jer 5:1–4 provide rare exceptions to the principle that one man's righteousness is no protection for others.

14:22, 23 their conduct. An ungodly Jerusalem remnant, brought as captives to join exiled Jews in Babylon, were to be very wicked. Exiles already there, repulsed by this evil, were to realize God's justness in His severe judgment on Jerusalem.

15:1–3 Then the word ... came. Israel, often symbolized by a vine (17:6–10; Ge 49:22; Jer 2:21), had become useful for nothing. Failing to do the very thing God set her apart to do—bear fruit—she no longer served any purpose and was useless (v. 2). Other trees can be used for construction of certain things, but a fruitless vine is useless (v. 3). It has no value. In every age the people of God have their value in their fruitfulness.

15:4, 5 put into the fire. The burning of the fruitless vine symbolized judgment in the deportations of 605 B.C. and 597 B.C. leading up to the final conquest in 586 B.C. Isaiah made the same analogy in his prophecy (Is 5:1–7), saying Israel produced only useless sour berries.

15:6–8 Therefore. The prophet applies the symbol to Israel and predicts the desolation of the city and the land. In the time of the Great Tribulation, it will be so again (cf. Rev 14:18).

16:1–7 This section covers the period from Abraham entering Canaan (cf. Ge 12) through the exile in Egypt (cf. Ex 12).

16:1 the word. This longest chapter in Ezekiel is similar to chap. 23, in that both indict Judah as spiritually immoral (v. 2). The story of Israel's sin and unfaithfulness to the love of God is told in all its sordid, vile character. The chapter is so sad and indicting that some of the ancient rabbis did not allow it to be read in public.

16:3–5 Israel was like an abandoned child. In 16:4–14 we see the history of Israel from her conception to her glory under Solomon.

16:3 birth ... Amorite ... Hittite. Cf. 16:45. These names identify the residents of Canaan who occupied the land when Abraham migrated

to Jerusalem, "Your origin and your birth are from the land of the Canaanite, your father was an Amorite and your mother a Hittite. 4 As for your birth, [A]on the day you were born your navel cord was not cut, nor were you washed with water for cleansing; you were not rubbed with salt or even wrapped in cloths. 5 No eye looked with pity on you to do any of these things for you, to have compassion on you. Rather you were thrown out into the [a,A]open field, [b]for you were abhorred on the day you were born.

6 "When I passed by you and saw you squirming in your blood, I said to you *while you were* in your blood, 'Live!' Yes, I said to you *while you were* in your blood, 'Live!' 7 I [A]made you [a]numerous like plants of the field. Then you grew up, became tall and reached the age for fine ornaments; *your* breasts were formed and your hair had grown. Yet you were naked and bare.

8 "Then I passed by you and saw you, and behold, [a]you were at the time for love; so I [A]spread My skirt over you and covered your nakedness. I also [B]swore to you and [C]entered into a covenant with you so that you [D]became Mine," declares the Lord GOD. 9 "Then I bathed you with water, washed off your blood from you and [A]anointed you with oil. 10 I also clothed you with [A]embroidered cloth and put sandals of porpoise skin on your feet; and I wrapped you with fine linen and covered you with silk. 11 I adorned you with ornaments, put [A]bracelets on your hands and a [B]necklace around your neck. 12 I also put a [A]ring in your nostril, earrings in your ears and a [B]beautiful crown on your head. 13 Thus you were adorned with [A]gold and silver, and your dress was of fine linen, silk and embroidered cloth. You ate fine flour, honey and oil; so you were exceedingly beautiful and advanced to [B]royalty. 14 Then your [A]fame went forth among the nations on account of your beauty, for it was [B]perfect because of My splendor which I bestowed on you," declares the Lord GOD.

15 "But you [A]trusted in your beauty and [B]played the harlot because of your fame, and you poured out your harlotries on every passer-by [a]who might be *willing*. 16 You took some of your clothes, made for yourself high places of various colors and played the harlot on them, [a]which should never come about nor happen. 17 You also took your beautiful [a,A]jewels *made* of My gold and of My silver, which I had given you, and made for yourself male images that you might play the harlot with them. 18 Then you took your embroidered cloth and covered them, and offered My oil and My incense before them. 19 Also [A]My bread which I gave you, fine flour, oil and honey with which I fed you, [a]you would offer before them for a soothing aroma; so it happened," declares the Lord GOD. 20 "Moreover, you took your sons and daughters whom you had borne to [A]Me and [B]sacrificed them to [a]idols to be devoured. Were your harlotries so small a matter? 21 You slaughtered [A]My children and offered them up to [a]idols by [B]causing them to pass through *the fire*. 22 Besides all your abominations and harlotries you did not remember the days of [A]your youth, when you were naked and bare and squirming in your blood.

23 "Then it came about after all your wickedness ('Woe, woe to you!' declares the Lord GOD), 24 that you built yourself a [A]shrine and made yourself a [B]high place in every square. 25 You built yourself a high place at the top of [A]every street and made your beauty abominable, and you spread your legs to every passer-by to multiply your harlotry. 26 You also played the harlot with the Egyptians, your [a]lustful neighbors, and multiplied your harlotry to [A]make Me angry. 27 Behold now, I have stretched out My hand against you and diminished your rations. And I delivered you up to the desire of those who hate you, the [A]daughters of the Philistines, who are ashamed of your lewd conduct. 28 Moreover, you played the harlot with the [A]Assyrians because you

16:4 [A]Hos 2:3 16:5 [a]Lit *surface* [b]Lit *in the loathing of your soul* [A]Deut 32:10 16:7 [a]Lit *a myriad* [A]Ex 1:7; Deut 1:10 16:8 [a]Lit *your time was* [A]Ruth 3:9; Jer 2:2 [B]Gen 22:16-18 [C]Ex 24:7, 8 [D]Ex 19:5; Ezek 20:5; Hos 2:19, 20 16:9 [A]Ruth 3:3 16:10 [A]Ex 26:36; Ezek 16:13, 18; 26:16; 27:7, 16 16:11 [A]Gen 24:22, 47; Is 3:19; Ezek 23:42 [B]Gen 41:42; Prov 1:9 16:12 [A]Gen 24:47; Is 3:21 [B]Is 28:5; Jer 13:18; Ezek 16:14 16:13 [A]Ps 45:13, 14; Ezek 16:17 [B]1 Sam 10:1; 1 Kin 4:21 16:14 [A]1 Kin 10:1, 24 [B]Ps 50:2; Lam 2:15 16:15 [a]Lit *to whom it might be* [A]Ezek 16:25; 27:3 [B]Is 57:8; Jer 2:20 16:16 [a]Lit *things which had not happened nor will it be* 16:17 [a]Lit *articles of beauty* [A]Ezek 16:11, 12 16:19 [a]Lit *and you...offer it* [A]Hos 2:8 16:20 [a]Lit *them* [A]Ex 13:2, 12; Deut 29:11, 12 [B]Ps 106:37, 38; Jer 7:31; Ezek 20:31; 23:37 16:21 [a]Lit *them* [A]Ex 13:2 [B]2 Kin 17:17; Jer 19:5 16:22 [A]Jer 2:2 16:24 [A]Jer 11:13; Ezek 16:31, 39; 20:28, 29 [B]Ps 78:58; Is 57:7 16:25 [A]Prov 9:14 16:26 [a]Lit *great of flesh* [A]Jer 7:18, 19; Ezek 8:17 16:27 [A]Is 9:12; Ezek 16:57 16:28 [A]2 Kin 16:7, 10-18; 2 Chr 28:16, 20-23; Jer 2:18, 36; Ezek 23:12; Hos 10:6

there (cf. Ge 12:5, 6). Jerusalem had the same moral character as the rest of Canaan.

16:4, 5 Israel, in the day of its birth, was unwanted and uncared for.

16:6 **Live!** The time intended here is probably the patriarchal period of Abraham, Isaac, and Jacob, when God formed His people.

16:7 **numerous.** This refers more to the people than to the land. It seems to refer to the time of Israel's growth during the 430-year stay in Egypt; wild but flourishing and beautiful Israel was "naked," without the benefits of culture and civilization (Ge 46–Ex 12; cf. Ex 1:7, 9, 12).

16:8–14 This is best taken as the time from the Exodus (Ex 12ff.) through David's reign (1Ki 2).

16:8 **the time for love.** This refers to the marriageable state. Spreading his "skirt" was a custom of espousal (cf. Ru 3:9) and indicates that God entered into a covenant with the young nation at Mt. Sinai (cf. Ex 19:5–8). Making a covenant signifies marriage, the figure of God's relation to Israel (cf. Jer 2:2; 3:1ff.; Hos 2:2–23).

16:9–14 These gifts were marriage gifts customarily presented to a queen. The crowning may refer to the reigns of David and Solomon, when Jerusalem became the royal city. Israel was actually a small kingdom but with a great reputation (cf. 1Ki 10). This refers to the time from Joshua's conquest of Canaan (Jos 3ff.) through David's reign (cf. 1Ki 2) and into Solomon's time (before 1Ki 11).

16:14 **My splendor.** The nation was truly a trophy of God's grace (cf. Dt 7:6–8). The presence and glory of the Lord provided Jerusalem with her beauty and prominence.

16:15–34 Continuing the marriage metaphor, this section describes the spiritual harlotry of Israel from Solomon (cf. 1Ki 11:1) all the way to Ezekiel's time.

16:15–19 A general summary of the nation's idolatry as she gave herself to the religious practices of the Canaanites. Every gracious gift from God was devoted to idols.

16:20–22 **sons and daughters.** This refers to the sacrifices of children to pagan gods (cf. 20:25, 26, 31; 2Ki 16:3; 21:6; 23:10; 24:4). God had expressly forbidden this (cf. Dt 12:31; 18:10). Still, the children were first slain, then burned (cf. Jer 7:31; 19:5; 32:35; Mic 6:7) until Josiah's abolition of it. It had been reinstated in Ezekiel's day.

16:23–30 This section, partly woe and partly lament, spoke to Judah's obsession with idolatry and her being influenced by Egypt (v. 26), the Philistines (v. 27), Assyria (v. 28), and Chaldea, or Babylon (v. 29).

16:27 **ashamed.** The wickedness and gross evil of the Jews even scandalized pagan Philistines.

were not satisfied; you played the harlot with them
and still were not satisfied. 29 You also multiplied
your harlotry with the land of merchants, Chaldea,
yet even with this you were not satisfied." ' "
30 "How [A]languishing is your heart," declares the
Lord GOD, "while you do all these things, the actions of a [a,B]bold-faced harlot. 31 When you built your
shrine at the beginning of every street and made
your high place in every square, in [A]disdaining
money, you were not like a harlot. 32 You adulteress
wife, who takes strangers instead of her husband!
33 [a]Men give gifts to all harlots, but you [A]give your
gifts to all your lovers to bribe them to come to you
from every direction for your harlotries. 34 Thus you
are different from those women in your harlotries,
in that no one plays the harlot [a]as you do, because
you give money and no money is given you; thus
you are different."
35 Therefore, O harlot, hear the word of the LORD.
36 Thus says the Lord GOD, "Because your lewdness
was poured out and your nakedness uncovered
through your harlotries with your lovers and with
all your detestable [A]idols, and because of the blood
of your sons which you gave to [a]idols, 37 therefore,
behold, I will [A]gather all your lovers with whom you
took pleasure, even all those whom you loved *and*
all those whom you [B]hated. So I will gather them
against you from every direction and [C]expose your
nakedness to them that they may see all your nakedness. 38 Thus I will [A]judge you like women who
commit adultery or shed blood are judged; and I
will bring on you the blood of [B]wrath and jealousy.
39 I will also give you into [a]the hands of your lovers, and they will tear down your shrines, demolish your high places, [A]strip you of your clothing,
take away your [b]jewels, and will leave you naked
and bare. 40 They will [a]incite a [A]crowd against you
and they will stone you and cut you to pieces with
their swords. 41 They will [A]burn your houses with
fire and execute judgments on you in the sight of
many women. Then I will [B]stop you from playing
the harlot, and you will also no longer pay [a]your
lovers. 42 So I [A]will calm My fury against you and
My jealousy will depart from you, and I will be
pacified and angry [B]no more. 43 Because you have
[A]not remembered the days of your youth but [a]have
[B]enraged Me by all these things, behold, I in turn
will [C]bring your conduct down on your own head,"
declares the Lord GOD, "so that you will not commit
this lewdness on top of all your *other* abominations.
44 "Behold, everyone who quotes [A]proverbs will
quote *this* proverb concerning you, saying, '[a]Like
mother, [a]like daughter.' 45 You are the daughter of
your mother, who loathed her husband and children. You are also the [A]sister of your sisters, who
[B]loathed their husbands and children. Your mother
was a Hittite and your father an Amorite. 46 Now
your [A]older sister is Samaria, who lives [a]north of you
with her [b]daughters; and your younger sister, who
lives [c]south of you, is [B]Sodom with her [b]daughters.
47 Yet you have not merely walked in their ways or
done according to their abominations; but, as if that
were [A]too little, you acted [B]more corruptly in all your
conduct than they. 48 As I live," declares the Lord
GOD, "Sodom, your sister and her daughters have
[A]not done as you and your daughters have done.
49 Behold, this was the guilt of your sister Sodom:
she and her daughters had [A]arrogance, [B]abundant
food and [C]careless ease, but she did not [a]help the
[D]poor and needy. 50 Thus they were haughty and
committed [A]abominations before Me. Therefore I
[B]removed them [a]when I saw *it*. 51 Furthermore, Samaria did not commit half of your sins, for you have
multiplied your abominations more than they. Thus
you have made your sisters appear [A]righteous by
all your abominations which you have committed.
52 Also bear your disgrace in that you have [a]made
judgment favorable for your sisters. Because of
your sins in which you acted [A]more abominably
than they, they are more in the right than you. Yes,
be also ashamed and bear your disgrace, in that
you made your sisters appear righteous.
53 "Nevertheless, I will restore their captivity, the
captivity of Sodom and her daughters, the captivity of Samaria and her daughters, and [a]along with
them [b]your own captivity, 54 in order that you may
bear your humiliation and feel [A]ashamed for all that
you have done when you become [B]a consolation
to them. 55 Your sisters, Sodom with her daughters
and Samaria with her daughters, [a]will return to
their former state, and you with your daughters will
also return to your former state. 56 As *the name of*
your sister Sodom was not heard from your lips in
your day of pride, 57 before your [A]wickedness was
uncovered, [a]so now you have become the [B]reproach
of the daughters of [b]Edom and of all who are around

16:30 [a]Lit *domineering* [A]Prov 9:13; Is 1:3; Jer 4:22 [B]Is 3:9; Jer 3:3 16:31 [A]Is 52:3 16:33 [a]Lit *They* [A]Is 57:9; Ezek 16:41; Hos 8:9, 10 16:34 [a]Lit *after you* 16:36 [a]Lit *them* [A]Jer 19:5; Ezek 20:31; 23:37 16:37 [A]Jer 13:22, 26; Ezek 23:9, 22; Hos 2:3, 10; Nah 3:5, 6 [B]Ezek 23:17, 28 [C]Is 47:3 16:38 [A]Ezek 23:45 [B]Ps 79:3, 5; Jer 18:21; Ezek 23:25; Zeph 1:17 16:39 [a]Lit *their hands, and they* [b]Lit *articles of beauty* [A]Ezek 23:26; Hos 2:3 16:40 [a]Lit *bring up an assembly* [A]Ezek 23:47; Hab 1:6-10 16:41 [a]Lit *a harlot's hire* [A]2 Kin 25:9; Jer 39:8; 52:13 [B]Ezek 23:48 16:42 [A]2 Sam 24:25; Ezek 5:13; 21:17; Zech 6:8 [B]Is 40:1, 2; 54:9, 10; Ezek 39:29 16:43 [a]So with ancient versions; Heb *are angry against* [A]Ps 78:42; 106:13; Ezek 16:22 [B]Is 63:10; Ezek 6:9 [C]Ezek 11:21; 22:31 16:44 [a]Lit *Her* [A]1 Sam 24:13; Ezek 12:22, 23; 18:2, 3 16:45 [A]Ezek 23:2 [B]Is 1:4; Ezek 23:37-39; Zech 11:8 16:46 [a]Lit *on your left* [b]I.e. environs; so through v 55 [c]Lit *from your right* [A]Jer 3:8-11; Ezek 23:4 [B]Gen 13:10-13; 18:20; Ezek 16:48, 49, 53-56, 61 16:47 [A]1 Kin 16:31 [B]2 Kin 21:9; Ezek 5:6; 16:48, 51 16:48 [A]Matt 10:15; 11:23, 24 16:49 [a]Lit *grasp the hand of* [A]Gen 19:9; Ps 138:6; Is 3:9; Ezek 28:2, 9, 17 [B]Gen 13:10; Is 22:13; Amos 6:4-6 [C]Luke 12:16-20; 16:19 [D]Ezek 18:7, 12, 16 16:50 [a]Many ancient mss and versions read *as you have seen* [A]Gen 13:13; 18:20; 19:5 [B]Gen 19:24, 25 16:51 [A]Jer 3:8-11 16:52 [a]Lit *mediated for* [A]Ezek 16:47, 48, 51 16:53 [a]Lit *in their midst* [b]Lit *the captivity of your captivity* 16:54 [A]Jer 2:26 [B]Ezek 14:22, 23 16:55 [a]Heb includes *will return...state* after Sodom also 16:57 [a]Lit *as at the time of* [b]So with many mss and one version; M.T. *Aram* [A]Ezek 16:36, 37 [B]2 Kin 16:5-7; 2 Chr 28:5, 6, 18-23; Ezek 5:14, 15; 22:4

16:29 Chaldea. They even prostituted themselves with the Babylonians (cf. 2Ki 20:12–19).

16:31–34 It is wicked to solicit and then be paid for immorality. Israel engaged in far worse behavior—she solicited and even paid her idol consorts. This refers to the heavy tribute Israel had to pay to the godless nations.

16:35–40 I will … expose your nakedness. Public exposure of profligate women and the stoning of them were well-known customs in ancient Israel, making them a shameful spectacle.

16:42 By exacting the full penalty on Israel's sins in the destruction by Babylon, God's wrath was to be satisfied.

16:44, 45 Like mother, like daughter. Judah has followed in the pagan footsteps of her beginnings (cf. 16:3).

16:46–59 Judah is compared to Samaria and Sodom, whose judgment for sin was great. Judah was more corrupt (v. 47), multiplied Samaria's and Sodom's sin (v. 51), and committed more abominable sin (v. 52).

her, of the daughters of the Philistines—those surrounding *you* who despise you. 58 You have [A]borne
the penalty of your lewdness and abominations,"
the LORD declares. 59 For thus says the Lord GOD,
"I will also do with you as you have done, you who
have [A]despised the oath by breaking the covenant.

THE COVENANT REMEMBERED

60 "Nevertheless, I will remember My covenant
with you in the days of your youth, and I will establish an [A]everlasting covenant with you. 61 Then you
will [A]remember your ways and be ashamed when
you receive your sisters, *both* your older and your
younger; and I will give them to you as daughters,
but not because of your covenant. 62 Thus I will [A]es-
tablish My covenant with you, and you shall [B]know
that I am the LORD, 63 so that you may [A]remember
and be ashamed and [B]never open your mouth anymore because of your humiliation, when I have
[C]forgiven you for all that you have done," the Lord
GOD declares.

PARABLE OF TWO EAGLES AND A VINE

17 Now the word of the LORD came to me saying,
2 "Son of man, propound a riddle and speak a
[A]parable to the house of Israel, 3 [a]saying, 'Thus says
the Lord [b]GOD, "A great [A]eagle with [B]great wings,
long pinions and a full plumage of many colors
came to [C]Lebanon and took away the top of the cedar. 4 He plucked off the topmost of its young twigs
and brought it to a land of merchants; he set it in
a city of traders. 5 He also took some of the seed of
the land and planted it in [a,A]fertile soil. He [b]placed
it beside abundant waters; he set it *like* a [B]willow.
6 Then it sprouted and became a low, spreading
vine with its branches turned toward him, but its
roots remained under it. So it became a vine and
yielded shoots and sent out branches.

7 "But there was [a]another great eagle with great
wings and much plumage; and behold, this vine
bent its roots toward him and sent out its branches
toward him from the beds where it was [A]planted,
that he might water it. 8 It was planted in good
[a]soil beside abundant waters, that it might yield
branches and bear fruit *and* become a splendid
vine." ' 9 Say, 'Thus says the Lord GOD, "Will it thrive?
Will he not pull up its roots and cut off its fruit,
so that it withers—so that all its sprouting leaves
wither? And neither by great [a]strength nor by many
people can it be raised from its roots *again*. 10 Behold, though it is planted, will it thrive? Will it not
[A]completely wither as soon as the east wind strikes
it—wither on the beds where it grew?" ' "

ZEDEKIAH'S REBELLION

11 Moreover, the word of the LORD came to me,
saying, 12 "Say now to the [A]rebellious house, 'Do you
not [B]know what these things *mean?*' Say, 'Behold,
the [C]king of Babylon came to Jerusalem, took its
king and princes and brought them to him in Babylon. 13 He took one of the royal [a,A]family and made
a covenant with him, [b]putting him under [B]oath.
He also took away the [C]mighty of the land, 14 that
the kingdom might [A]be [a]in subjection, not exalting
itself, *but* keeping his covenant that it might continue. 15 But he [A]rebelled against him by sending his
envoys to Egypt that they might give him horses
and many [a]troops. Will he succeed? Will he who
does such things [B]escape? Can he indeed break the
covenant and escape? 16 As I live,' declares the Lord
GOD, 'Surely in the [a]country of the king who [b]put him
on the throne, whose oath he [A]despised and whose
covenant he broke, [c,B]in Babylon he shall die. 17 [A]Phar-
aoh with *his* mighty army and great company will
not [a]help him in the war, when they cast up ramps
and build siege walls to cut off many lives. 18 Now
he despised the oath by breaking the covenant, and

16:58 [A]Ezek 23:49 16:59 [A]Is 24:5; Ezek 17:19 16:60 [A]Is 55:3; Jer 32:38-41; Ezek 37:26 16:61 [A]Jer 50:4, 5; Ezek 6:9 16:62 [A]Ezek 20:37; 34:25; 37:26 [B]Jer 24:7; Ezek 20:43, 44 16:63 [A]Ezek 36:31, 32; Dan 9:7, 8 [B]Ps 39:9; Rom 3:19 [C]Ps 65:3; 78:38; 79:9 17:2 [A]Ezek 20:49; 24:3 17:3 [a]Lit *and you shall say* [b]Heb *YHWH*, usually rendered *LORD*, and so throughout the ch [A]Jer 48:40; Ezek 17:12; Hos 8:1 [B]Dan 4:22 [C]Jer 22:23 17:5 [a]Lit *a field of seed* [b]Lit *took* [A]Deut 8:7-9 [B]Is 44:4 17:7 [a]So with several ancient versions; M.T. *one* [A]Ezek 31:4 17:8 [a]Lit *field* 17:9 [a]Lit *arm* 17:10 [A]Ezek 19:14; Hos 13:15 17:12 [A]Ezek 2:3-5 [B]Ezek 12:9-11; 24:19 [C]2 Kin 24:11, 12, 15; Ezek 1:2; 17:3 17:13 [a]Lit *seed* [b]Lit *and caused him to enter into an oath* [A]2 Kin 24:17; Ezek 17:5 [B]2 Chr 36:13 [C]2 Kin 24:15, 16 17:14 [a]Lit *low* [A]Ezek 29:14 17:15 [a]Lit *people* [A]2 Kin 24:20; 2 Chr 36:13; Jer 52:3; Ezek 17:7 [B]Jer 34:3; 38:18, 23; Ezek 17:18 17:16 [a]Lit *place* [b]Lit *made him king* [c]Lit *with him in Babylon* [A]2 Kin 24:17, 20; Ezek 16:59; 17:13, 18, 19 [B]Jer 52:11; Ezek 12:13 17:17 [a]Lit *act with* [A]Is 36:6; Jer 37:5, 7; Ezek 29:6, 7

16:60 I will remember My covenant. God is gracious and He always finds a covenant basis on which He can exercise His grace. The Lord will remember the Abrahamic Covenant (cf. Ge 12:1ff.) made with Israel in her youth. Restoration will be by grace, not merit. **an everlasting covenant.** This is the New Covenant, which is unconditional, saving, and everlasting (cf. 37:26; Is 59:21; 61:8; Jer 31:31–34; Heb 8:6–13). The basis of God's grace will not be the Mosaic Covenant, which the Jews could never fulfill, even with the best intentions (cf. Ex 24:1ff.). When God establishes His eternal covenant, Israel will know that God is the Lord because of His grace.

16:63 have forgiven. This looks to the cross of Christ (cf. Is 53), by which God's just wrath on sin was satisfied so that He could grant grace to all who believe (cf. 2Co 5:21).

17:1 This chapter is dated about 588 B.C. (two years before the destruction of Jerusalem). The history of the period is in 2Ki 24; 2Ch 36; Jer 36, 37, 52.

17:3 A great eagle. The king of Babylon, in view here, took royal captives and others (vv. 4, 12, 13). **the cedar.** The kingdom of Judah.

17:4 topmost of its young twigs. This is Jehoiachin, the king, exiled in 597 B.C. (2Ki 24:11–16). Babylon is the "land of merchants" (16:29).

17:5, 6 seed. Those whom Babylon left in Judah in 597 B.C., who could prosper as a tributary to the conqueror, turned toward him (v. 6).

17:6 spreading vine. Refers to Zedekiah (ca. 597–586 B.C.), the youngest son of Josiah whom Nebuchadnezzar appointed king in Judah. The benevolent attitude of Nebuchadnezzar helped Zedekiah to prosper, and if he had remained faithful to his pledge to Nebuchadnezzar, Judah would have continued as a tributary kingdom. Instead, he began courting help from Egypt (2Ch 36:13), which Jeremiah protested (Jer 37:5–7).

17:7 another great eagle. Egypt is meant (v. 15), specifically Pharaoh Apries, a.k.a. Hophra (588–568 B.C.). Zedekiah turned to him to help revolt against Babylon.

17:9, 10 wither? Zedekiah's treachery would not prosper. The king was captured in the plains of Jericho (Jer 52:8). The dependence on Egypt would fail, and Judah would wither as the E wind (a picture of Babylon, cf. 13:11–13) blasted her.

17:11–21 putting him under oath. The parable is explained in detail. Babylon (v. 12) made Zedekiah a vassal subject to her, took captives, and left Judah weak (vv. 13, 14). Zedekiah broke the agreement (v. 15) in which he swore by the Lord to submit to Babylon (2Ch 36:13), and sought Egypt's help, thus he was taken to Babylon to live out his life (v. 16, 19; Jer 39:4–7). Egypt was to be no help to him (v. 17) or any protector of his army (v. 21).

behold, he [a,A]pledged his allegiance, yet did all these
things; he shall not escape.' " 19 Therefore, thus says
the Lord GOD, "As I live, surely My oath which he
despised and My covenant which he broke, I will
[a]inflict on his head. 20 I will spread My [A]net over
him, and he will be [B]caught in My snare. Then I will
bring him to Babylon and [C]enter into judgment with
him there *regarding* the unfaithful act which he has
committed against Me. 21 All the [a,A]choice men in all
his troops will fall by the sword, and the survivors
will be scattered to every wind; and you will know
that I, the LORD, have spoken."
22 Thus says the Lord GOD, "I will also take *a sprig*
from the lofty top of the cedar and set *it* out; I will
pluck from the topmost of its young twigs a tender
one and I will plant *it* on a [A]high and lofty mountain.
23 On the high mountain of Israel I will plant it, that
it may bring forth boughs and bear fruit and become
a stately [A]cedar. And birds of every [a]kind will [b]nest
under it; they will [b]nest in the shade of its branches.
24 All the [A]trees of the field will know that I am the
LORD; I bring down the high tree, exalt the low tree,
dry up the green tree and make the dry tree [B]flourish.
I am the LORD; I have spoken, and I will perform *it.*"

GOD DEALS JUSTLY WITH INDIVIDUALS

18 Then the word of the LORD came to me, saying, 2 "[A]What do you mean by using this proverb concerning the land of Israel, saying,

'[B]The fathers eat the sour grapes,
But the children's teeth [a]are set on edge'?

3 As I live," declares the Lord [a]GOD, "you are surely
not going to use this proverb in Israel anymore.
4 Behold, [A]all [a]souls are Mine; the [b]soul of the father
as well as the [b]soul of the son is Mine. The [c]soul
who [B]sins will die.
5 "But if a man is righteous and practices justice and righteousness, 6 and does not [A]eat at the
mountain *shrines* or [B]lift up his eyes to the idols of
the house of Israel, or [C]defile his neighbor's wife or
approach a woman during her menstrual period—
7 if a man does not oppress anyone, but [A]restores to
the debtor his pledge, [B]does not commit robbery,
but [C]gives his bread to the hungry and covers the
naked with clothing, 8 if he does not lend *money*
on [A]interest or take [B]increase, *if* he keeps his hand
from iniquity *and* [C]executes true justice between
man and man, 9 *if* he walks in [A]My statutes and My
ordinances so as to deal faithfully—[B]he is righteous
and will surely [C]live," declares the Lord GOD.
10 "Then he may [a]have a violent son who sheds
blood and who does any of these things to a brother
11 (though he himself did not do any of these things),
that is, he even eats at the mountain *shrines,* and
[A]defiles his neighbor's wife, 12 oppresses the [A]poor
and needy, [B]commits robbery, does not restore a
pledge, but lifts up his eyes to the idols *and* [C]com-
mits abomination, 13 he [A]lends *money* on interest
and takes increase; will he live? He will not live! He
has committed all these abominations, he will surely
be put to death; his [B]blood will be [a]on his own head.
14 "Now behold, he [a]has a son who has observed
all his father's sins which he committed, and [A]ob-
serving does not do likewise. 15 He does not eat at
the mountain *shrines* or lift up his eyes to the idols
of the house of Israel, or defile his neighbor's wife,
16 or oppress anyone, or retain a pledge, or commit
robbery, *but* he [A]gives his bread to the hungry and
covers the naked with clothing, 17 he keeps his hand

17:18 [a]Lit *gave his hand* [A]1 Chr 29:24 17:19 [a]Lit *give it* 17:20 [A]Ezek 12:13; 32:3 [B]Jer 39:5-7 [C]Jer 2:35; Ezek 20:35, 36 17:21 [a]So many ancient mss and versions; M.T. *fugitives* [A]2 Kin 25:5, 11; Ezek 5:2, 10, 12-14 17:22 [A]Ps 72:16; Ezek 20:40; 37:22 17:23 [a]Lit *wing* [b]Lit *dwell* [A]Ps 92:12 17:24 [A]Ps 96:12; Is 55:12 [B]Amos 9:11 18:2 [a]Lit *become dull* [A]Is 3:15 [B]Jer 31:29; Lam 5:7 18:3 [a]Heb *YHWH*, usually rendered *LORD*, and so throughout the ch 18:4 [a]Or *lives* [b]Or *life* [c]Or *person* [A]Num 16:22; 27:16; Is 42:5; 57:16 [B]Ezek 18:20; Rom 6:23 18:6 [A]Ezek 6:13; 18:15; 22:9 [B]Deut 4:19; Ezek 18:12, 15; 20:24; 33:25 [C]Ezek 18:15; 22:11 18:7 [A]Deut 24:13; Ezek 33:15; Amos 2:8 [B]Lev 19:13; Amos 3:10 [C]Deut 15:11; Ezek 18:16; Matt 25:35-40; Luke 3:11 18:8 [A]Ex 22:25; Deut 23:19, 20 [B]Lev 25:36 [C]Zech 7:9; 8:16 18:9 [A]Lev 18:5 [B]Rom 8:1 [C]Amos 5:4; Hab 2:4; Rom 1:17 18:10 [a]Lit *beget* 18:11 [A]1 Cor 6:9 18:12 [A]Amos 4:1; Zech 7:10 [B]Is 59:6, 7; Jer 22:3, 17; Ezek 7:23; 18:7, 16, 18 [C]2 Kin 21:11; Ezek 8:6, 17 18:13 [a]Lit *on him* [A]Ex 22:25 [B]Ezek 33:4, 5 18:14 [a]Lit *begets* [A]2 Chr 29:6-10; 34:21 18:16 [A]Job 31:16, 20; Ps 41:1; Is 58:7, 10; Ezek 18:7

17:22, 23 *a sprig* from the lofty top. This is messianic prophecy stating that God will provide the Messiah from the royal line of David ("the cedar") and establish Him in His kingdom (like a "mountain," cf. Da 2:35, 44, 45). He will be "*a sprig*" reigning in the height of success. "Sprig," or "branch," is a name for Messiah (cf. 34:23, 24; 37:24, 25; Is 4:2; Jer 23:5; 33:15; Zec 3:8; 6:12). Messiah will be "a tender one" (v. 22) growing into a "stately cedar" (v. 23). Under His kingdom rule, all nations will be blessed and Israel restored.

17:24 make the dry tree flourish. The Messiah would grow out of the dry tree left after humbling judgment, i.e., Judah's remnant from which He came of a lowly family (cf. Is 6:13), yet would prosper.

18:1–32 One of the foundational principles of Scripture is presented in this chapter (also taught in Dt 24:16; 2Ki 14:6): Judgment is according to individual faith and conduct. He had foretold national punishment, but the reason was individual sin (cf. 3:16–21; 14:12–20; 33:1–20).

18:2 eat the sour grapes. The people of Judah would not acknowledge their guilt worthy of judgment. Though they were themselves wicked and idolatrous, they blamed their forefathers for their state (cf. 2Ki 21:15). The rationalizing is expressed in a current proverb (cf. Jer 31:29) which means, in effect, "They sinned (eat the sour grapes); we inherit the bitterness" (teeth are set on edge).

18:3 not going to use this proverb. God rejected their blame shifting and evasion of responsibility.

18:4 The soul who sins will die. God played no favorites, but was fair in holding each individual accountable for his own sin. The death is physical death which, for many, results in eternal death.

18:5–18 Two scenarios are proposed to clarify the matter of personal guilt: 1) a righteous father of an unrighteous son (vv. 5–13); and 2) an unrighteous father of a righteous son (vv. 14–18).

18:5 if a man is righteous. The definition of "righteous" is given in specifics in vv. 6–9. Such behavior could only characterize a genuine believer who was "faithful" from the heart.

18:8 not lend *money* on interest. This refers to interest on loans (*see notes on Dt 23:19, 20; 24:10–13*).

18:9 he ... will surely live. The righteous do die physically for many reasons that do not contradict this principle, e.g., old age, martyrdom, or death in battle. While there are exceptions to "surely live" as to temporal life (cf. 21:3, 4), and sometimes the ungodly survive, unlike 18:13 (cf. 14:22, 23), there can be absolutely no exceptions in God's ultimate spiritual reckoning. In every case, the just die to live eternally and the unjust, who never possessed spiritual life, shall perish physically and eternally (Jn 5:28, 29; Rev 20:11–15). The just will live no matter what the character of his parents or children. For an explanation of Ex 20:5, 6, *see the note there.*

18:10–13 violent son. Could such a sinful son claim the merits of his father's righteousness and live? No! Each person is responsible for his own personal sin.

18:14–18 he will die for his iniquity. This part features an unrighteous father and a righteous son to make the same point. The righteous son shall "surely live" (v. 17).

from [a]the poor, does not take interest or increase, *but*
executes My ordinances, and walks in My statutes;
[A]he will not die for his father's iniquity, he will surely
live. 18 As for his father, because he practiced extortion, robbed *his* brother and did what was not good
among his people, behold, he will die for his iniquity.
19 "Yet you say, '[A]Why should the son not bear the
punishment for the father's iniquity?' When the son
has practiced [B]justice and righteousness and has
observed all My statutes and done them, he shall
surely live. 20 The person who [A]sins will die. The
[B]son will not bear the punishment for the father's
iniquity, nor will the father bear the punishment for
the son's iniquity; the [C]righteousness of the righteous will be upon himself, and the wickedness of
the wicked will be upon himself.
21 "But if the [A]wicked man turns from all his sins
which he has committed and observes all My statutes and practices justice and righteousness, he
shall surely live; he shall not die. 22 [A]All his transgressions which he has committed will not be remembered against him; because of his [B]righteous-
ness which he has practiced, he will live. 23 [A]Do
I have any pleasure in the death of the wicked,"
declares the Lord GOD, "[a]rather than that he should
[B]turn from his ways and live?
24 "But when a righteous man [A]turns away from
his righteousness, commits iniquity and does according to all the abominations that a wicked man
does, will he live? [B]All his righteous deeds which he
has done will not be remembered for his [C]treachery
which he has committed and his sin which he has
committed; for them he will die. 25 Yet you say, '[A]The
way of the Lord is not right.' Hear now, O house of
Israel! Is [B]My way not right? Is it not your ways
that are not right? 26 When a righteous man turns
away from his righteousness, commits iniquity
and dies because of it, for his iniquity which he
has committed he will die. 27 Again, when a wicked
man turns away [A]from his wickedness which he has
committed and practices justice and righteousness,
he will save his life. 28 Because he considered and
turned away from all his transgressions which he
had committed, he shall surely live; he shall not
die. 29 But the house of Israel says, 'The way of the
Lord is not right.' Are My ways not right, O house
of Israel? Is it not your ways that are not right?
30 "Therefore I will judge you, O house of Israel, each according to his conduct," declares the
Lord GOD. "[A]Repent and turn away from all your
transgressions, so that iniquity may not become a
stumbling block to you. 31 [A]Cast away from you all
your transgressions which you have committed
and make yourselves a [B]new heart and a new spirit!
For why will you die, O house of Israel? 32 For I have
[A]no pleasure in the death of anyone who dies," declares the Lord GOD. "Therefore, repent and live."

LAMENT FOR THE PRINCES OF ISRAEL

19 "As for you, take up a [A]lamentation for the
[B]princes of Israel 2 and say,

'[a]What was your mother?
A lioness among lions!
She lay down among young lions,
She reared her cubs.
3 'When she brought up one of her cubs,
He became a lion,
And he learned to tear *his* prey;
He devoured men.
4 'Then nations heard about him;
He was captured in their pit,
And they [A]brought him with hooks
To the land of Egypt.
5 'When she saw, as she waited,
That her hope was lost,
She took [a]another of her cubs
And made him a young lion.
6 'And he [A]walked about among the lions;
He became a young lion,

18:17 [a]So M.T.; Gr reads *iniquity* as in v 8 [A]Rom 2:7 18:19 [A]Ex 20:5; Jer 15:4; Ezek 18:2 [B]Ezek 18:9; 20:18-20; Zech 1:3-6 18:20 [A]2 Kin 14:6; 22:18-20; Ezek 18:4 [B]Deut 24:16; Jer 31:30 [C]1 Kin 8:32; Is 3:10, 11; Matt 16:27; Rom 2:6-9 18:21 [A]Ezek 18:27, 28; 33:12, 19 18:22 [A]Is 43:25; Jer 50:20; Ezek 18:24; 33:16; Mic 7:19 [B]Ps 18:20-24 18:23 [a]Lit *is it not* [A]Ezek 18:32; 33:11 [B]Ps 147:11; Mic 7:18 18:24 [A]1 Sam 15:11; 2 Chr 24:2, 17-22; Ezek 3:20; 18:26; 33:18 [B]Ezek 18:22; Gal 3:3, 4 [C]Prov 21:16; Ezek 17:20; 20:27 18:25 [A]Ezek 18:29; 33:17, 20; Mal 2:17; 3:13-15 [B]Gen 18:25; Jer 12:1; Zeph 3:5 18:27 [A]Is 1:18; 55:7 18:30 [A]Ezek 14:6; 33:11; Hos 12:6 18:31 [A]Is 1:16, 17; 55:7 [B]Ps 51:10; Ezek 11:19; 36:26 18:32 [A]Ezek 18:23; 33:11 19:1 [A]Ezek 2:10; 19:14 [B]2 Kin 23:29, 30, 34; 24:6, 12; 25:5-7 19:2 [a]Or *Why did your mother, a lioness, lie down among lions; among young lions rear her cubs?* 19:4 [A]2 Kin 23:34; 2 Chr 36:4, 6 19:5 [a]Lit *one* 19:6 [A]2 Kin 24:9; 2 Chr 36:9

18:19, 20 The prophet restated the principle of personal accountability.

18:19–29 Cf. 33:12–20.

18:21, 22 **if the wicked man turns.** The next case involves an unrighteous person turning to righteousness. He received a clean slate in forgiveness (v. 22), and spiritual life forever.

18:23 **Do I have … pleasure.** God takes no willful pleasure in the death of the unrighteous (cf. Jn 5:40; 1Ti 2:4; 2Pe 3:9).

18:24 **a righteous man turns.** The next scenario is a righteous man turning to a life of sin. His former, apparent righteousness was not genuine (cf. 1Jn 2:19), and God did not remember it as a valid expression of faith.

18:25–29 **Yet you say.** God applied the principle in summary to Israel's sin problem (cf. vv. 2–4). They, not He, must acknowledge their lack of equity (cf. vv. 25, 29).

18:30 **Therefore I will judge.** The conclusion is that the just God must judge each person for his own life. But He invites repentance, so that hope may replace ruin (cf. 33:10, 11).

18:31 **make …. new heart.** The key to life eternal and triumph over death is conversion. This involves repentance from sin (vv. 30, 31a) and receiving the new heart which God gives with a new spirit, wrought by the Holy Spirit (36:24–27; Jer 31:34; Jn 3:5–8).

18:32 **I have no pleasure.** The death of His saints is precious to God (Ps 116:15). By contrast, He has no such pleasure when a person dies without repentance. While God is sovereign in salvation, man is responsible for his own sin. **repent and live.** This was a call to repent and avoid physical and eternal death (cf. Pss 23:6; 73:24; Is 26:19–21; Da 12:2, 3, 13). Ezekiel was a preacher of repentance and of God's offer of mercy to the penitent.

19:1–14 **lamentation.** This is an elegy in typical lamentation meter (v. 14b), dealing with the captivity of Kings Jehoahaz (609 B.C.) and Jehoiachin (597 B.C.), and the collapse of the Davidic dynasty under Zedekiah (586 B.C.).

19:1 **the princes of Israel.** This refers to the kings of Judah just mentioned.

19:1–9 **What was your mother?** Judah is the "lioness," just as in v. 10 she is the "vine." Her cubs symbolize kings who were descendants of David exposed to the corrupting influences of heathen kings ("young lions").

19:3, 4 **one of her cubs.** This refers to Jehoahaz (Shallum), who ruled in 609 B.C. and was deposed by Egypt's Pharaoh Neco after reigning only 3 months (v. 4; 2Ki 23:32–34; 2Ch 36:2).

19:5–9 **another of her cubs.** This refers to Jehoiachin, who in 597 B.C. was carried to Babylon in a cage as in v. 9 (2Ki 24:6–15). Though he reigned only 3 months, he was oppressive and unjust. God used the pagan nations of Egypt and Babylon to judge these

He learned to tear *his* prey;
He devoured men.
7 ‘He [a]destroyed their [b]fortified towers
And laid waste their cities;
And the land and its fullness were appalled
Because of the sound of his roaring.
8 ‘Then [A]nations set against him
On every side from *their* provinces,
And they spread their net over him;
He was captured in their pit.
9 ‘[A]They put him in a cage with hooks
And [B]brought him to the king of Babylon;
They brought him in hunting nets
So that his voice would be heard no more
On the mountains of Israel.
10 ‘Your mother was [A]like a vine
in your [a]vineyard,
Planted by the waters;
It was fruitful and full of branches
Because of abundant waters.
11 ‘And it had [a,A]strong branches
fit for scepters of rulers,
And its [B]height was raised above the clouds
So that it was seen in its height
with the mass of its branches.
12 ‘But it was [A]plucked up in fury;
It was [B]cast down to the ground;
And the [C]east wind dried up its fruit.
Its [a,D]strong branch [b]was torn off
So that [c]it withered;
The fire consumed it.
13 ‘And now it is planted in the [A]wilderness,
In a dry and thirsty land.
14 ‘And [A]fire has gone out from *its* branch;
It has consumed its shoots *and* fruit,
So that there is not in it a [a]strong branch,
A scepter to rule.’ ”

This is a lamentation, and has become a lamentation.

GOD’S DEALINGS WITH ISRAEL REHEARSED

20 Now in the seventh year, in the fifth *month,* on
the tenth of the month, [a]certain of the [A]elders
of Israel came to inquire of the LORD, and sat before
me. 2 And the word of the LORD came to me saying,
3 “Son of man, speak to the elders of Israel and say
to them, ‘Thus says the Lord [a]GOD, “Do you come
to inquire of Me? As I live,” declares the Lord GOD,
“[A]I will not be inquired of by you.” ’ 4 Will you judge
them, will you judge them, son of man? [A]Make them
know the abominations of their fathers; 5 and say to
them, ‘Thus says the Lord GOD, “On the day when I
[A]chose Israel and [a]swore to the [b]descendants of the
house of Jacob and made Myself known to them in
the land of Egypt, when I [a]swore to them, saying, [B]I
am the LORD your God, 6 on that day I swore to them,
[A]to bring them out from the land of Egypt into a land
that I had [a]selected for them, [B]flowing with milk
and honey, which is [C]the glory of all lands. 7 I said to
them, ‘[A]Cast away, each of you, the detestable things
of his eyes, and [B]do not defile yourselves with the
idols of Egypt; [C]I am the LORD your God.’ 8 But they
[A]rebelled against Me and were not willing to listen
to Me; [a]they did not cast away the detestable things
of their eyes, nor did they forsake the [B]idols of Egypt.
Then I [b]resolved to [C]pour out My wrath on them,
to accomplish My anger against them in the midst
of the land of Egypt. 9 But I acted [A]for the sake of My
name, that it should [B]not be profaned in the sight
of the nations among whom they *lived,* in whose
sight I made Myself known to them by bringing
them out of the land of Egypt. 10 So I took them
out of the land of Egypt and brought them into
the [A]wilderness. 11 I gave them My [A]statutes and
informed them of My ordinances, by [B]which, if
a man [a]observes them, he will live. 12 Also I gave
them My sabbaths to be a [A]sign between Me and
them, that they might know that I am the LORD who
sanctifies them. 13 But the house of Israel [A]rebelled
against Me in the wilderness. They did not walk in
My statutes and they rejected My ordinances, [B]by
which, if a man [a]observes them, he will live; and My
[C]sabbaths they greatly profaned. Then I [b]resolved
to [D]pour out My wrath on them in the wilderness,
to annihilate them. 14 But I acted for the sake of My
name, that it should not be profaned in the sight of
the nations, before whose sight I had brought them
out. 15 Also [A]I swore to them in the wilderness that
I would not bring them into the land which I had
given them, flowing with milk and honey, which is

19:7 [a]So Targum; M.T. *knew* [b]Or *widows* **19:8** [A]2 Kin 24:11 **19:9** [A]2 Chr 36:6 [B]2 Kin 24:15 **19:10** [a]So with some ancient mss; M.T. *blood* [A]Ps 80:8-11 **19:11** [a]Lit *rods of strength* [A]Ps 80:15 [B]Ezek 31:3 **19:12** [a]Lit *rods of her strength* [b]So Gr; M.T. *they were* [c]So Gr; M.T. *they* [A]Jer 31:28 [B]Lam 2:1; Ezek 28:17 [C]Ezek 17:10; Hos 13:15 [D]Is 27:11; Ezek 19:11 **19:13** [A]2 Kin 24:12-16; Ezek 19:10; 20:35; Hos 2:3 **19:14** [a]Lit *rod of strength* [A]Ezek 15:4; 20:47, 48 **20:1** [a]Lit *men* [A]Ezek 8:1, 11, 12 **20:3** [a]Heb *YHWH*, usually rendered *LORD*, and so throughout the ch [A]Ezek 14:3 **20:4** [A]Ezek 16:2; 22:2; Matt 23:32 **20:5** [a]Lit *lifted up My hand,* and so throughout the ch [b]Lit *seed* [A]Ex 6:6-8 [B]Ex 6:2, 3 **20:6** [a]Lit *spied out* [A]Jer 32:22 [B]Ex 13:5; 33:3 [C]Ps 48:2 **20:7** [A]Ex 20:4, 5; 22:20 [B]Lev 18:3; Deut 29:16-18 [C]Ex 20:2 **20:8** [a]Lit *each one* [b]Lit *said* [A]Deut 9:7; Is 63:10 [B]Ex 32:1-9 [C]Ezek 5:13; 7:8; 20:13, 21 **20:9** [A]Ex 32:11-14; Ezek 20:14, 22; 36:21, 22 [B]Ezek 39:7 **20:10** [A]Ex 19:1 **20:11** [a]Lit *does* [A]Ex 20:1-23:33 [B]Lev 18:5; Ezek 20:13 **20:12** [A]Ex 31:13, 17; Ezek 20:20 **20:13** [a]Lit *does* [b]Lit *said* [A]Num 14:11, 12, 22; Ezek 20:8 [B]Lev 18:5 [C]Is 56:6; Ezek 20:21 [D]Ex 32:10; Deut 9:8; Ezek 20:8, 21 **20:15** [A]Num 14:30; Ps 95:11; 106:26

wicked kings. The Babylonians kept Jehoiachin imprisoned for 37 years, releasing him at the age of 55 (2Ki 25:27–30; Jer 52:31, 32).

19:10–14 Your mother was like a vine. Judah prospered as a luxuriant vine (v. 10), with strong power and eminence (v. 11). God plucked up the vine in judgment, desolating her (v. 12; cf. 13:11–13), exiling her (v. 13), and leaving no strong king (v. 14).

19:14 The blame for the catastrophe that came to Judah is laid on one ruler, King Zedekiah, who was responsible for the burning of Jerusalem because of his treachery (cf. Jer 38:20–23). The house of David ended in shame and, for nearly 2,600 years since, Israel has had no king of David’s line. When Messiah came, they rejected Him and preferred Caesar. Messiah still became their Savior and will return as their King.

20:1 the seventh year. Ca. 591 B.C.

20:3–44 elders . . . come to inquire. Cf. the similarity in 14:1–3. The prophet responds with a message from the Lord that gives a historical survey of Israel, featuring its uniform pattern of sin. Israel rebelled in Egypt (vv. 5–9), then in the wilderness trek (vv. 10–26), and the entry into the Land of Promise (vv. 27–32). Through all this, God kept delivering them to save His reputation (vv. 9, 14, 22). Yet sinful obstinacy finally led to His judging them (vv. 45–49). Verses 33–44 speak of His regathering Israel to their land in the future time of Christ’s Second Advent.

20:5 I swore. Cf. vv. 5, 6, 15, 23, 28, 42. God promised Israel deliverance from Egypt (cf. Ex 6:2–8).

the glory of all lands, 16 because they rejected My
ordinances, and as for My statutes, they did not walk
in them; they even profaned My sabbaths, for their
[A]heart continually went after their idols. 17 Yet My
eye spared them rather than destroying them, and I
did not cause their [A]annihilation in the wilderness.
18 "I said to their [a,A]children in the wilderness, '[B]Do
not walk in the statutes of your fathers or keep their
ordinances or defile yourselves with their idols. 19 [A]I
am the LORD your God; [B]walk in My statutes and keep
My ordinances and [a]observe them. 20 [A]Sanctify My
sabbaths; and they shall be a sign between Me and
you, that you may know that I am the LORD your God.'
21 But the [A]children rebelled against Me; they did not
walk in My statutes, nor were they careful to observe
My ordinances, by which, *if* a man observes them, he
will live; they profaned My sabbaths. So I [a]resolved to
pour out My wrath on them, to accomplish My anger
against them in the wilderness. 22 But I [A]withdrew My
hand and acted [B]for the sake of My name, that it should
not be profaned in the sight of the nations in whose
sight I had brought them out. 23 Also I swore to them
in the wilderness that I would [A]scatter them among
the nations and disperse them among the lands, 24 because they had not observed My ordinances, but had
rejected My statutes and had profaned My sabbaths,
and [A]their eyes were [a]on the idols of their fathers.
25 I also gave them statutes that were [A]not good and
ordinances by which they could not live; 26 and I pronounced them [A]unclean because of their gifts, in that
they [B]caused all [a]their firstborn to pass through *the*
fire so that I might make them desolate, in order that
they might [C]know that I am the LORD." '
27 "Therefore, son of man, [A]speak to the house of
Israel and say to them, 'Thus says the Lord GOD, "Yet
in this your fathers have [B]blasphemed Me by [C]acting
treacherously against Me. 28 When I had [A]brought
them into the land which I swore to give to them,
then they saw every [B]high hill and every leafy tree,
and they offered there their sacrifices and there they
presented the provocation of their offering. There
also they made their soothing aroma and there they
poured out their drink offerings. 29 Then I said to
them, 'What is the high place to which you go?' So
its name is called [a]Bamah to this day." ' 30 Therefore,
say to the house of Israel, 'Thus says the Lord GOD,
"Will you defile yourselves [a]after the manner of your
[A]fathers and play the harlot after their detestable
things? 31 [a]When you offer your gifts, when you [A]cause
your sons to pass through the fire, you are defiling
yourselves with all your idols to this day. And shall
I be inquired of by you, O house of Israel? As I live,"
declares the Lord GOD, "I will not be inquired of by
you. 32 What [A]comes [a]into your mind will not come
about, when you say: 'We will be like the nations,
like the tribes of the lands, [B]serving wood and stone.'

GOD WILL RESTORE ISRAEL TO HER LAND

33 "As I live," declares the Lord GOD, "surely with
a mighty hand and with an [A]outstretched arm and
with wrath poured out, I shall be [B]king over you.
34 I will [A]bring you out from the peoples and gather
you from the lands where you are scattered, with
a mighty hand and with an outstretched arm and
with [B]wrath poured out; 35 and I will bring you into
the [A]wilderness of the peoples, and there I will enter
into judgment with you face to face. 36 As I [A]entered
into judgment with your fathers in the [B]wilderness
of the land of Egypt, so I will enter into judgment
with you," declares the Lord GOD. 37 "I will make you
[A]pass under the rod, and I will bring you into the
bond of the covenant; 38 and I will [A]purge from you
the rebels and those who transgress against Me; I
will bring them out of the land where they sojourn,
but they will [B]not enter the [a]land of Israel. Thus you
will know that I am the LORD.
39 "As for you, O house of Israel," thus says the
Lord GOD, "[A]Go, serve everyone his idols; [a]but later
you will surely listen to Me, and My holy name you
will [B]profane no longer with your gifts and with
your idols. 40 For on My holy mountain, on the high

20:16 [A]Ezek 11:21; 14:3-7; 20:8 **20:17** [A]Jer 4:27; 5:18; Ezek 11:13 **20:18** [a]Lit *sons* [A]Num 14:31; Deut 4:3-6 [B]Zech 1:4 **20:19** [a]Lit *do* [A]Ex 6:7; 20:2 [B]Deut 5:32, 33; 6:1, 2; 8:1, 2; 11:1; 12:1 **20:20** [A]Jer 17:22 **20:21** [a]Lit *said* [A]Num 21:5; 25:1-3 **20:22** [A]Job 13:21; Ps 78:38; Ezek 20:17 [B]Is 48:9-11; Jer 14:7, 21; Ezek 20:9, 14 **20:23** [A]Lev 26:33; Deut 4:27; 28:64 **20:24** [a]Lit *after* [A]Ezek 6:9 **20:25** [A]Ps 81:12; Is 66:4; Rom 1:21-25, 28 **20:26** [a]Lit *that which opens the womb* [A]Lev 18:21; 20:2-5; Is 63:17; Ezek 20:30; Rom 11:8 [B]Jer 7:31; 19:4-9 [C]Ezek 6:7; 20:12, 20 **20:27** [A]Ezek 2:7; 3:4, 11, 27 [B]Num 15:30; Rom 2:24 [C]Ezek 18:24; 39:23, 26 **20:28** [A]Josh 23:3, 14; Neh 9:22-26; Ps 78:55; Jer 2:7 [B]1 Kin 14:23; Ps 78:58; Is 57:5-7; Jer 3:6; Ezek 6:13 **20:29** [a]Or *High Place* **20:30** [a]Lit *in the way of* [A]Judg 2:19; Jer 7:26; 16:12 **20:31** [a]Lit *In your lifting up* [A]Ps 106:37-39; Jer 7:31; Ezek 16:20; 20:26 **20:32** [a]Lit *upon your spirit* [A]Ezek 11:5 [B]Jer 2:25; 44:17 **20:33** [A]Jer 21:5 [B]Jer 51:57 **20:34** [A]Is 27:12, 13; Ezek 20:38; 34:16 [B]Jer 42:18; 44:6; Lam 2:4 **20:35** [A]Ezek 19:13; 20:36; Hos 2:14 **20:36** [A]Num 11:1-35; Ps 106:15; Ezek 20:13, 21; 1 Cor 10:5-10 [B]Deut 32:10 **20:37** [A]Lev 27:32; Jer 33:13 **20:38** [a]Lit *ground* or *soil* [A]Ezek 34:17-22; Amos 9:9, 10; Zech 13:8, 9; Mal 3:3; 4:1-3 [B]Num 14:29, 30; Ps 95:11; Ezek 13:9; 20:15, 16; Heb 4:3 **20:39** [a]Or *and afterwards, if you will not listen to Me, but* [A]Jer 44:25, 26 [B]Is 1:13-15; Ezek 23:38, 39; 43:7

20:25, 26 I ... gave them. God allowed the Jews to live in sin. Cf. v. 32, "We will be like the nations ...." Cf. Ps 81:11, 12; Ro 1:24–28. Like all human beings, the story of the Jews is one long history of rebellion.

20:34 Paul alludes to this in 2Co 6:17. God will someday rule over Israel in the glorious kingdom of Messiah, after the people have repented and been saved (cf. Zec 12–14).

20:35 wilderness of the peoples. Other lands where the scattered people of Israel live are pictured as a wilderness in which the Jews will suffer. This is analogous to God's bringing His people from Egypt through the wilderness long ago, before thrusting them into the Promised Land (v. 36).

20:37 pass under the rod. God used a shepherd figure here, apt since He was their Great Shepherd (34:11–13; Jer 23:5–8). As a shepherd, God brings His sheep home to their fold (cf. Jer 33:13), has them file in, separating sheep from goats (cf. Mt 25), passing under His shepherd's rod to be noted and checked for injury. He will bring them into the bond of the New Covenant by giving them His Spirit with life (36:24–27; 37:14; 39:29). This is Israel's final salvation (Ro 11:26–33).

20:38 I will purge from you the rebels. God will see that no rebel, no one without the renewing by His Spirit in salvation, will come back to Israel to have a part in the messianic kingdom. All whom He permits to return will serve Him (v. 40), in contrast to those who serve idols (v. 39). The purging takes place during the "time of Jacob's distress" (Jer 30:7), during the Great Tribulation (Mt 24:21).

20:39 If they persist in their stubborn idolatry, God will allow them to follow it to their doom. He would also rather have them as out-and-out idolaters rather than hypocritical patronizers of His worship as they had been (cf. Am 5:21–26).

20:40–42 all ... in the land. The promised regathering in Messiah's earthly kingdom is to the very same land—literal Palestine—from which they were scattered (v. 41), expressly the land given to their fathers (36:28; Ge 12:7). They will "all" be there, repentant (v. 43) and saved (Ro 11:26, 27), serving the Lord wholeheartedly, a united nation engaged in purified worship (cf. 27:22, 23; Is 11:13).

mountain of Israel," declares the Lord GOD, "there
the whole house of Israel, [A]all of them, will serve
Me in the land; there I will [B]accept them and there
I will [a]seek your contributions and the choicest of
your gifts, with all your holy things. 41 [a]As a soothing aroma I will accept you when I [A]bring you out
from the peoples and gather you from the lands
where you are scattered; and I will prove Myself
[B]holy among you in the sight of the nations. 42 And
[A]you will know that I am the LORD, [B]when I bring
you into the land of Israel, into the [C]land which I
swore to give to your forefathers. 43 There you will
[A]remember your ways and all your deeds with which
you have defiled yourselves; and you will [B]loathe
yourselves in your own [a]sight for all the evil things
that you have done. 44 Then [A]you will know that I
am the LORD when I have dealt with you [B]for My
name's sake, not according to your evil ways or according to your corrupt deeds, O house of Israel,"
declares the Lord GOD.' "

45 [a]Now the word of the LORD came to me, saying, 46 "Son of man, set your face toward [a]Teman,
and speak out against the [A]south and [B]prophesy
against the [C]forest [b]land of the Negev, 47 and say
to the forest of the Negev, 'Hear the word of the
LORD: thus says the Lord GOD, "Behold, I am about
to [A]kindle a fire in you, and it will consume every
[a]green tree in you, as well as every dry tree; the
blazing flame will not be quenched and [b,B]the whole
surface from south to north will be burned by it.
48 All flesh will see that I, the LORD, have kindled
it; it shall [A]not be quenched." ' " 49 Then I said, "Ah
Lord GOD! They are saying of me, 'Is he not *just*
speaking [A]parables?' "

PARABLE OF THE SWORD OF THE LORD

21 [a]And the word of the LORD came to me saying,
2 "Son of man, [A]set your face toward Jerusalem,
and [a,B]speak against the sanctuaries and prophesy

20:40 [a]Or *require* [A]Is 66:23; Ezek 37:22, 24 [B]Is 56:7; 60:7; Ezek 43:12, 27 20:41 [a]Lit *With* [A]Is 27:12, 13; Ezek 11:17; 28:25 [B]Is 5:16; Ezek 28:25; 36:23 20:42 [A]Ezek 36:23; 38:23 [B]Ezek 11:17; 34:13; 36:24 [C]Ezek 20:6, 15 20:43 [a]Lit *faces* [A]Ezek 6:9; 16:61, 63; Hos 5:15 [B]Jer 31:18; Ezek 36:31; Zech 12:10 20:44 [A]Ezek 24:24 [B]Ezek 36:22 20:45 [a]Ch 21:1 in Heb 20:46 [a]Or *the South* [b]Lit *of the field* [A]Jer 13:19; Ezek 21:4 [B]Ezek 21:2; Amos 7:16 [C]Is 30:6-11 20:47 [a]Lit *moist* [b]Or *all the faces* [A]Is 9:18, 19; Jer 21:14 [B]Is 13:8 20:48 [A]Jer 7:20; 17:27 20:49 [A]Ezek 17:2; Matt 13:13; John 16:25 21:1 [a]Ch 21:6 in Heb 21:2 [a]Lit *flow* [A]Ezek 20:46; 25:2; 28:21 [B]Job 29:22; Ezek 20:46

20:44 you will know. God purposed all of this great restoration so that repentant, renewed Israel knew that He is the Lord, a key theme, as in v. 38. Also, those of other nations will know by this who He is and render Him due reverence (v. 41; 36:23, 36).

20:46–48 speak out against the south. The S is Palestine, particularly Judah, usually invaded from the N. Though Babylonia was to the E (19:12), its army would swing W toward the Mediterranean Sea and then come S out of the N to invade Judah. The invader (Nebuchadnezzar in 586 B.C.) will overwhelm the land as a sweeping fire (cf. 15:1–8; 19:12; Zec 11:1–3), devouring trees indiscriminately, green or dry (cf. 21:3, 4). Palestine had much more "forest" in biblical times.

20:49 This demonstrates the elders' (v. 1) refusal to comprehend Ezekiel's clear message. To the unwilling heart, there was no understanding.

21:1–7 the word ... came. This is the sign of the sword against Jerusalem (vv. 1–17). God depicts His judgment in terms of a man

NATIONS AND CITIES UNDER JUDGMENT IN EZEKIEL

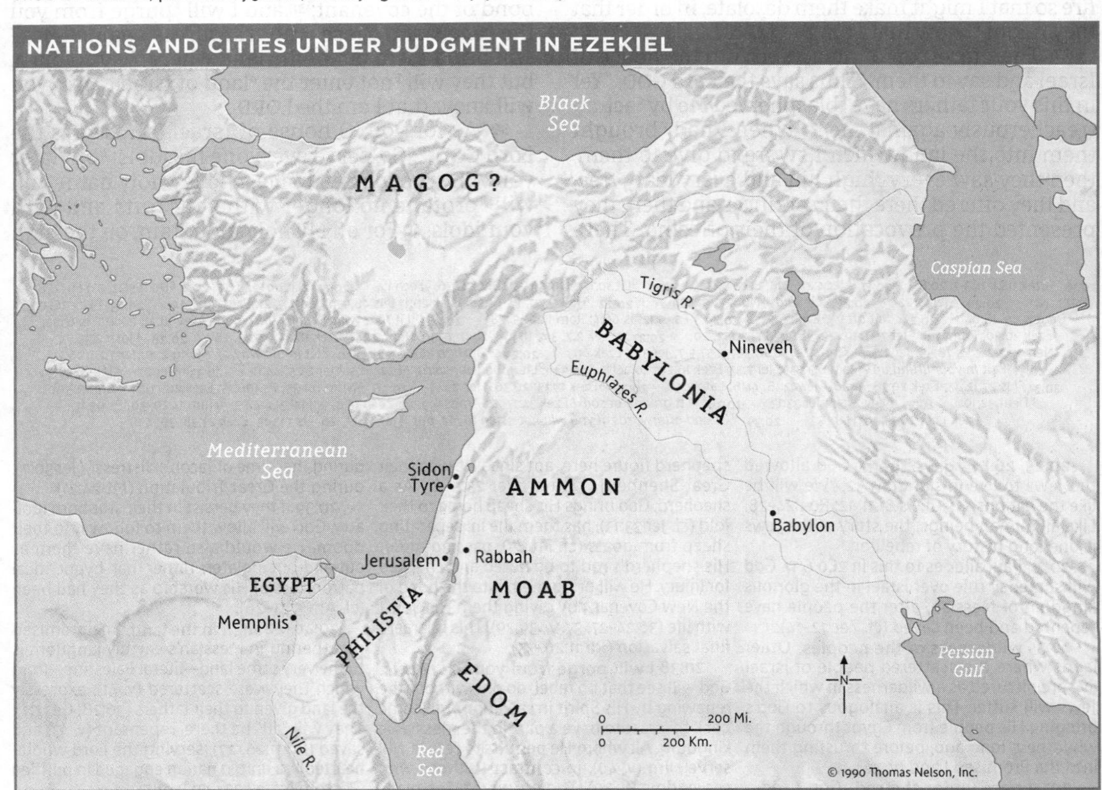

against the land of Israel; 3 and say to the land of Israel, 'Thus says the LORD, "Behold, [A]I am against you; and I will draw My sword out of its sheath and cut off from you the [B]righteous and the wicked. 4 Because I will cut off from you the righteous and the wicked, therefore My sword will go forth from its sheath against [A]all flesh from south *to* north. 5 Thus all flesh will know that I, the LORD, have drawn My sword out of its sheath. It will [A]not return *to its sheath* again." ' 6 As for you, son of man, groan with breaking [a]heart and bitter grief, groan in their sight. 7 And when they say to you, 'Why do you groan?' you shall say, 'Because of the [A]news that is coming; and [B]every heart will melt, all hands will be feeble, every spirit will [a]faint and all knees will [b]be weak as water. Behold, it comes and it will happen,' declares the Lord [c]GOD."

8 Again the word of the LORD came to me, saying, 9 "Son of man, prophesy and say, 'Thus says the LORD.' Say,

'[A]A sword, a sword sharpened
And also polished!
10 'Sharpened to make a [A]slaughter,
Polished [a]to flash like lightning!'

Or shall we rejoice, the [b]rod of My son [B]despising every tree? 11 It is given to be polished, that it may be handled; the sword is sharpened and polished, to give it into the hand of the slayer. 12 [A]Cry out and wail, son of man; for it is against My people, it is against all the [B]officials of Israel. They are delivered over to the sword with My people, therefore strike *your* thigh. 13 For *there is* a testing; and what if even the [a]rod which despises will be no more?" declares the Lord GOD.

14 "You therefore, son of man, prophesy and clap *your* hands together; and let the sword be [A]doubled the third time, the sword for the slain. It is the sword for the great one slain, which surrounds them, 15 that *their* [A]hearts may melt, and many [B]fall at all their [C]gates. I have given the glittering sword. Ah! It is made *for striking* like lightning, it is wrapped up *in readiness* for slaughter. 16 [a]Show yourself sharp, go to the right; set yourself; go to the left, wherever your [b]edge is appointed. 17 I will also clap My hands together, and I will [a,A]appease My wrath; I, the LORD, have spoken."

THE INSTRUMENT OF GOD'S JUDGMENT

18 The word of the LORD came to me saying, 19 "As for you, son of man, [a,A]make two ways for the sword of the king of Babylon to come; both of them will go out of one land. And [b]make a signpost; [c]make it at the head of the way to the city. 20 You shall [a]mark a way for the sword to come to [A]Rabbah of the sons of Ammon, and to Judah into [B]fortified Jerusalem. 21 For the king of Babylon stands at the [a]parting of the way, at the head of the two ways, to use [A]divination; he [B]shakes the arrows, he consults the [b,C]household idols, he looks at the liver. 22 Into his right hand came the divination, 'Jerusalem,' to [A]set battering rams, to open the mouth [a]for slaughter, to lift up the voice with a battle cry, to set battering rams against the gates, to cast up ramps, to build a siege wall. 23 And it will be to them like a false divination in their eyes; [A]they have *sworn* solemn oaths. But he [B]brings iniquity to remembrance, that they may be seized.

24 "Therefore, thus says the Lord GOD, 'Because you have made your iniquity to be remembered, in that your transgressions are uncovered, so that in all your deeds your sins appear—because you have come to remembrance, you will be seized with the hand. 25 And you, O slain, wicked one, the prince of Israel, whose [A]day has come, in the time of the [a]punishment of the end,' 26 thus says the Lord GOD, 'Remove the turban and take off the [A]crown; this *will* [a]no longer *be* the same. [B]Exalt that which is low and

21:3 [A]Jer 21:13; Ezek 5:8; Nah 2:13; 3:5 [B]Is 57:1 21:4 [A]Jer 12:12; Ezek 7:2; 20:47 21:5 [A]1 Sam 3:12; Jer 23:20; Ezek 21:30; Nah 1:9 21:6 [a]Lit *loins* 21:7 [a]Lit *be dim* [b]Lit *flow* [c]Heb *YHWH*, usually rendered *LORD*, and so throughout the ch [A]Ezek 7:26 [B]Is 13:7; Nah 2:10 21:9 [A]Deut 32:41 21:10 [a]Lit *lightning to be to her* [b]Or *scepter* [A]Is 34:5, 6 [B]Ps 110:5, 6; Ezek 20:47 21:12 [A]Ezek 21:6; Joel 1:13 [B]Ezek 21:25; 22:6 21:13 [a]Or *scepter* 21:14 [A]Lev 26:21, 24; 2 Kin 24:1, 10-16; 25:1 21:15 [A]Josh 2:11; 2 Sam 17:10; Ps 22:14; Ezek 21:7 [B]Is 59:10; Jer 13:16; 18:15 [C]Jer 17:27; Ezek 21:19 21:16 [a]Or *Unite yourself* [b]Lit *face* 21:17 [a]Lit *cause to rest* [A]Ezek 5:13 21:19 [a]Or *set for yourself* [b]Lit *cut out a hand* [c]Lit *cut it* [A]Jer 1:10; Ezek 4:1-3 21:20 [a]Lit *set* [A]Deut 3:11; Jer 49:2; Ezek 25:5; Amos 1:14 [B]Ps 48:12, 13; 125:1, 2 21:21 [a]Lit *mother* [b]Heb *teraphim* [A]Num 22:7; 23:23 [B]Prov 16:33 [C]Gen 31:19, 30; Judg 17:5; 18:17, 20 21:22 [a]Lit *in* [A]Ezek 4:2; 26:9 21:23 [A]Ezek 17:16, 18 [B]Num 5:15; Ezek 21:24; 29:16 21:25 [a]Or *iniquity* [A]Ps 37:13; Ezek 7:2, 3, 7 21:26 [a]Lit *not this* [A]Jer 13:18; Ezek 16:12 [B]Ps 75:7; Ezek 17:24

unsheathing his polished sword for deadly thrusts. God is the swordsman (vv. 3, 4), but Babylon is His sword (v. 19). The historical background for this prophecy is Nebuchadnezzar's 588 B.C. campaign to quell revolts in Judah, as well as Tyre and Ammon.

21:3, 4 the righteous and the wicked. In Babylon's indiscrimination as an invader, people in the army's path die, whether righteous or wicked. This occurs from N to S, through the whole span of Israel's land, tying in with the judgment pictured by fire (20:45–49). Trees green or dry (20:47) probably depict people whether righteous or wicked (21:3, 4; cf. Lk 23:31).

21:8–17 The sword (Babylon) was "sharpened."

21:10 the rod ... despising every tree. Cf. also v. 13. Possibly this affirmed that God's sword, so overwhelming in v. 10a, was to despise the Judean royal scepter (cf. Ge 49:9, 10), which was powerless to stop it and would soon pass away (vv. 25–27). God's judgment was too strong for this object made of (or partly of) wood, as it holds in contempt all such items of wood. "My son" may refer to Judah (cf. Ex 4:22, 23), or to the king as God's "son," such as was Solomon (1Ch 28:6).

21:11 the slayer. God is always the judge and executioner, no matter what He uses.

21:12 strike *your* thigh. Or it can be translated, "beat your breast." In either wording, it is an emphatic gesture of grief that the prophet acts out. This accompanies further symbols of grief in his "cry out and wail" (v. 12) and "clap" of hands (vv. 14, 17).

21:18–20 This imagery sees Babylon's army on the march coming to a crossroads. The sword is the king of Babylon, Nebuchadnezzar, who is faced with a decision. One sign points to Jerusalem and Judah, the other to Rabbah, the capital of Ammon. In 593 B.C. Ammon had conspired with Judah against Babylon. The king had to decide which place to attack, so he sought his gods through divination (v. 21).

21:21 the king ... stands ... to use divination. This means to "seek an omen," to gain guidance from superstitious devices (cf. Is 47:8–15). Three methods are available to Babylon's leader. He shook arrows and let them fall, then read a conclusion from the pattern. He looked at Teraphim (idols), or examined an animal liver to gain help from his gods. Actually, the true God controlled this superstition to achieve His will, the attack on Jerusalem and Judah. Later, Nebuchadnezzar attacked Rabbah in Ammon E of the Jordan (vv. 28–32).

21:22 All the paraphernalia of war were prepared.

21:23 false divination. The people of Jerusalem thought this superstitious decision was not a true divination and would fail. They were wrong (vv. 24, 25).

21:25 wicked ... prince. Zedekiah.

21:26 Remove ... turban ... crown. God, in the coming judgment on Judah in 588–586 B.C., removed the turban representing the

abase that which is high. 27 [A]A ruin, a ruin, a ruin, I will make it. This also will be no more until [B]He comes whose right it is, and I will give it *to Him.*'

28 "And you, son of man, prophesy and say, 'Thus says the Lord GOD concerning the sons of Ammon and concerning their [A]reproach,' and say: 'A sword, a sword is drawn, polished for the slaughter, to cause it [a]to [B]consume, that it may be like lightning— 29 while they see for you [A]false visions, while they divine lies for you—to place you on the necks of the wicked who are slain, whose day has come, in the [B]time of the [a]punishment of the end. 30 [A]Return *it* to its sheath. In the [B]place where you were created, in the land of your origin, I will judge you. 31 I will [A]pour out My indignation on you; I will [B]blow on you with the fire of My wrath, and I will give you into the hand of brutal men, [a,C]skilled in destruction. 32 You will be [a,A]fuel for the fire; your blood will be in the midst of the land. You will [B]not be remembered, for I, the LORD, have spoken.' "

THE SINS OF ISRAEL

22 Then the word of the LORD came to me, saying, 2 "And you, son of man, will you judge, will you judge the bloody city? Then cause her to know all her abominations. 3 You shall say, 'Thus says the Lord [a]GOD, "A city [A]shedding blood in her midst, so that her time will come, and that makes idols, contrary to her *interest,* for defilement! 4 You have become [A]guilty by [a]the blood which you have shed, and defiled by your idols which you have made. Thus you have brought your [b]day near and have come to your years; therefore I have made you a [B]reproach to the nations and a mocking to all the lands. 5 Those who are near and those who are far from you will mock you, you of ill repute, full of [A]turmoil.

6 "Behold, the [A]rulers of Israel, each according to his [a]power, have been in you for the purpose of shedding blood. 7 They have [A]treated father and mother lightly within you. The [B]alien they have oppressed in your midst; the [C]fatherless and the widow they have wronged in you. 8 You have [A]despised My holy things and [B]profaned My sabbaths. 9 Slanderous men have been in you for the purpose of shedding blood, and in you they have eaten at the mountain *shrines.* In your midst they have [A]committed acts of lewdness. 10 In you [a]they have [A]uncovered *their* fathers' nakedness; in you they have humbled her who was [B]unclean in her menstrual impurity. 11 One has committed abomination with his [A]neighbor's wife and another has lewdly defiled his [B]daughter-in-law. And another in you has [C]humbled his sister, his father's daughter. 12 In you they have [A]taken bribes to shed blood; you have taken [B]interest and profits, and you have injured your neighbors for gain by [C]oppression, and you have [D]forgotten Me," declares the Lord GOD.

13 "Behold, then, I smite My hand at your [A]dishonest gain which you have acquired and at [a]the bloodshed which is among you. 14 Can [A]your heart endure, or can your hands be strong in the days that I will deal with you? [B]I, the LORD, have spoken and will act. 15 I will [A]scatter you among the nations and I will disperse you through the lands, and I will [B]consume your uncleanness from you. 16 You will profane yourself in the sight of the nations, and you will [A]know that I am the LORD." ' "

17 And the word of the LORD came to me, saying, 18 "Son of man, the house of Israel has become [A]dross to Me; all of them are [B]bronze and tin and iron and lead in the [C]furnace; they are the dross of silver. 19 Therefore, thus says the Lord GOD, 'Because all of you have become dross, therefore,

21:27 [A]Hag 2:21, 22 [B]Ps 2:6; 72:7, 10; Jer 23:5, 6; Ezek 34:24; 37:24 21:28 [a]Lit *to finish* [A]Ezek 36:15; Zeph 2:8-10 [B]Is 31:8; Jer 12:12; 46:10, 14 21:29 [a]Or *iniquity* [A]Jer 27:9; Ezek 13:6-9; 22:28 [B]Ezek 21:25; 35:5 21:30 [A]Jer 47:6, 7 [B]Ezek 25:5 21:31 [a]Or *artisans of* [A]Ezek 14:19; 25:7; Nah 1:6 [B]Ps 18:15; Is 30:33; Ezek 22:20, 21; Hag 1:9 [C]Jer 4:7; 6:22, 23; 51:20-23; Hab 1:6, 10 21:32 [a]Lit *food* [A]Ezek 20:47, 48; Mal 4:1 [B]Ezek 25:10 22:3 [a]Heb *YHWH,* usually rendered *LORD,* and so throughout the ch [A]Ezek 22:6, 27; 23:37, 45 22:4 [a]Lit *your* [b]Lit *days* [A]2 Kin 21:16; Ezek 24:7, 8 [B]Ps 44:13, 14; Ezek 5:14, 15; 16:57 22:5 [A]Is 22:2 22:6 [a]Lit *arm* [A]Is 1:23; Ezek 22:27 22:7 [A]Ex 20:12; Lev 20:9; Deut 5:16; 27:16 [B]Ex 22:21f; 23:9; Deut 24:17; Jer 7:6; Zech 7:10 [C]Ex 22:22; Ezek 22:25; Mal 3:5 22:8 [A]Ezek 22:26 [B]Ezek 20:13, 21, 24; 23:38, 39 22:9 [A]Ezek 23:29; Hos 4:2, 10, 14 22:10 [a]Lit *he has* [A]Lev 18:8 [B]Lev 18:19; Ezek 18:6 22:11 [A]Ezek 18:11; 33:26 [B]Lev 18:15 [C]2 Sam 13:11-14 22:12 [A]Ex 23:8; Deut 16:19; 27:25; Mic 7:2, 3 [B]Lev 25:36; Deut 23:19 [C]Lev 19:13 [D]Ps 106:21; Ezek 23:35 22:13 [a]Lit *your* [A]Is 33:15; Amos 2:6-8; Mic 2:2 22:14 [A]Ezek 21:7 [B]Ezek 17:24 22:15 [A]Deut 4:27; Neh 1:8; Ezek 20:23; Zech 7:14 [B]Ezek 23:27, 48 22:16 [A]Ps 83:18; Ezek 6:7 22:18 [A]Ps 119:119; Is 1:22; Lam 4:1 [B]Jer 6:28-30 [C]Prov 17:3; Is 48:10

priestly leadership, and the crown picturing the succession of kings. Neither office was fully restored after the captivity. This marked the commencement of "the times of the Gentiles" (Lk 21:24).

21:27 until He comes. The 3-fold mention of "ruin" expresses the severest degree of unsettled and chaotic conditions. Israel was to experience severe instability and even the kingly privilege will not be Israel's again until the coming of the Messiah, "whose right it is" (cf. Ge 49:10). God will give the kingship to Him (cf. Jer 23:5–8), the greater "David" (Eze 37:24). His "right" is that perfect combination of priestly and royal offices (cf. Heb 5–7).

21:28–32 concerning the sons of Ammon. The Babylonian armies also were to conquer this people in 582/81 B.C. (cf. 25:1–7). Their "reproach" was the gleeful disdain they heaped on Jerusalem when the city fell, the temple was profaned, and Judeans were taken captive (25:3).

21:30 Return *it* to its sheath. This called for the Ammonites not to resist Babylon, which would be useless, for they would be slaughtered in their own land.

21:32 You will not be remembered. Israel had a future (v. 27), but God would not give Ammon mercy at the time and let the devastation occur. After this, they were further devastated by Judas Maccabeus' army, according to an ancient source (1 Macc. 5:6, 7). Later, according to Jeremiah 49:6, God permitted exiles to return to their land. Finally, they disappeared from the family of nations altogether.

22:2 the bloody city? Cf. vv. 3, 4, 6, 9, 12, 13. This refers to Jerusalem because of her judicial murders (vv. 6, 9, 23–27), her sacrifice of children, and her rebellion against Babylon (cf. 24:6).

22:4–13 become guilty. At least 17 kinds of sin appear in this indictment of Jerusalem's blood guiltiness, and more in vv. 25–29. The only restraint on their evil was their ability. They did all the evil they could, and shedding blood seemed to be the most popular.

22:5 Cf. Ro 2:24. God links His honor to the behavior of His people.

22:9 eaten at the mountain *shrines*. This meant idol worship which the passage clarifies (v. 4), i.e., eating meals at idol shrines, accompanied by sexual sins, such as those described in vv. 10, 11.

22:14–16 Ezekiel saw not only the punishment in the immediate future, but the worldwide dispersion of the Jews still going on today, which continues for the purging of Israel's sins.

22:16 you will know. After the defiling dispersion, when the sin has been purged, Israel will come to know the Lord. Many Jews do know Him now, but the nation will be saved in the future (cf. Zec 12–14; Ro 11:25–27).

22:17–22 bronze and tin and iron and lead. This pictures God's judgment of Jerusalem as a smelting furnace (cf. Is 1:22; Jer 6:28–30; Zec 13:9; Mal 3:2, 3) which burns away dross and impurities, resulting in purified metal. His wrath was the fire (v. 21; an apt term for

behold, I am going to gather you into the midst
of Jerusalem. 20 As they gather silver and bronze
and iron and lead and tin into the [A]furnace to blow
fire on it in order to melt *it,* so I will gather *you* in
My anger and in My wrath and I will lay you *there*
and melt you. 21 I will gather you and blow on you
with the fire of My wrath, and you will be melted
in the midst of it. 22 As silver is melted in the furnace, so you will be melted in the midst of it; and
you will know that I, the LORD, have [A]poured out
My wrath on you.' "

23 And the word of the LORD came to me, saying,
24 "Son of man, say to her, 'You are a land that is
[A]not cleansed or rained on in the day of indignation.' 25 There is a [A]conspiracy of her prophets in
her midst like a roaring lion tearing the prey. They
have [B]devoured lives; they have taken treasure and
precious things; they have made many [C]widows in
the midst of her. 26 Her [A]priests have done violence
to My law and have [B]profaned My holy things; they
have made no [C]distinction between the holy and
the profane, and they have not taught the difference between the [D]unclean and the clean; and they
hide their eyes from My sabbaths, and I am profaned among them. 27 Her princes within her are
like wolves tearing the prey, by shedding blood
and [A]destroying lives in order to get [B]dishonest
gain. 28 Her prophets have smeared whitewash
for them, seeing [A]false visions and divining lies
for them, saying, 'Thus says the Lord GOD,' when
the LORD has not spoken. 29 The people of the land
have practiced [A]oppression and committed robbery,
and they have wronged the poor and needy and
have [B]oppressed the sojourner without justice. 30 I
[A]searched for a man among them who would [B]build
up the wall and [C]stand in the gap before Me for the
land, so that I would not destroy it; but I found [a]no
one. 31 Thus I have poured out My [A]indignation on
them; I have consumed them with the fire of My
wrath; [B]their way I have brought upon their heads,"
declares the Lord GOD.

OHOLAH AND OHOLIBAH'S SIN AND ITS CONSEQUENCES

23 The word of the LORD came to me again, saying, 2 "Son of man, there were [A]two women, the
daughters of one mother; 3 and they played the harlot
in Egypt. They [A]played the harlot in their youth; there
their breasts were pressed and there their virgin
bosom was handled. 4 Their names were Oholah the
elder and Oholibah her sister. And they became Mine,
and they bore sons and daughters. And *as for* their
names, Samaria is Oholah and Jerusalem is Oholibah.

5 "Oholah played the harlot [a]while she was Mine;
and she lusted after her lovers, after the [A]Assyrians,
her neighbors, 6 who were clothed in purple, [A]gov-
ernors and officials, all of them desirable young
men, horsemen riding on horses. 7 She bestowed her
harlotries on them, all of whom *were* the choicest
[a]men of Assyria; and with all whom she lusted after,
with all their idols she [A]defiled herself. 8 She did not
forsake her harlotries [A]from *the time in* Egypt; for
in her youth [a]men had lain with her, and they handled her virgin bosom and poured out their [b]lust
on her. 9 Therefore, I gave her into the hand of her
[A]lovers, into the hand of the [a]Assyrians, after whom
she lusted. 10 They [A]uncovered her nakedness; they
took her sons and her daughters, but they slew her
with the sword. Thus she became a [a]byword among
women, and they executed judgments on her.

11 "Now her sister Oholibah saw *this,* yet she was
[A]more corrupt in her lust than she, and her harlotries were more than the harlotries of her sister. 12 She lusted after the [a,A]Assyrians, governors
and officials, the ones near, magnificently dressed,
horsemen riding on horses, all of them desirable
young men. 13 I saw that she had defiled herself;
they both took [a]the same way. 14 So she increased
her harlotries. And she saw men [A]portrayed on
the wall, images of the [B]Chaldeans portrayed with
vermilion, 15 girded with belts on their loins, with
flowing turbans on their heads, all of them looking like officers, [a]like the [b]Babylonians *in* Chaldea,

22:20 [A]Is 1:25 22:22 [A]Ezek 20:8, 33; Hos 5:10 22:24 [A]Is 9:13; Jer 2:30; Ezek 24:13; Zeph 3:2 22:25 [A]Jer 11:9; Hos 6:9 [B]Jer 2:34; Ezek 13:19; 22:27 [C]Jer 15:8; Ezek 22:7 22:26 [A]Jer 2:8, 26; Ezek 7:26 [B]1 Sam 2:12-17, 22; Ezek 22:8 [C]Lev 10:10; Ezek 44:23 [D]Hag 2:11-14 22:27 [A]Ezek 22:25 [B]Ezek 22:13 22:28 [A]Jer 23:25-32; Ezek 13:6 22:29 [A]Is 5:7; Ezek 9:9; 22:7; Amos 3:10 [B]Ex 23:9 22:30 [a]Lit *not* [A]Is 59:16; 63:5; Jer 5:1 [B]Ezek 13:5 [C]Ps 106:23; Jer 15:1 22:31 [A]Is 10:5; 13:5; 30:27; Ezek 22:20 [B]Ezek 7:3, 8, 9; 9:10; 16:43; Rom 2:8, 9 23:2 [A]Ezek 16:46 23:3 [A]Lev 17:7; Jer 3:9 23:5 [a]Lit *under Me* [A]2 Kin 15:19; 16:7; 17:3; Ezek 16:28; Hos 5:13; 8:9, 10 23:6 [A]Ezek 23:12, 13 23:7 [a]Lit *sons of Asshur* [A]Ezek 20:7; 22:3, 4; Hos 5:3; 6:10 23:8 [a]Lit *they* [b]Lit *harlotry* [A]Ex 32:4; 1 Kin 12:28; 2 Kin 10:29; 17:16; Ezek 23:3, 19 23:9 [a]Lit *sons of Asshur* [A]Ezek 16:37; 23:22 23:10 [a]Lit *name* [A]Ezek 16:37, 41 23:11 [A]Jer 3:8-11; Ezek 16:51 23:12 [a]Lit *sons of Asshur* [A]2 Kin 16:7 23:13 [a]Lit *one* 23:14 [A]Ezek 8:10 [B]Ezek 16:29 23:15 [a]Lit *the likeness of* [b]Lit *sons of Babel*

Babylon's fiery destruction of the city), and His people were to be refined (v. 20), with the sinful ones removed (cf. 21:13–22). Even in the ultimate day, God will follow this principle in purging His creation of sin (2Pe 3:9–14).

22:25–29 conspiracy. The whole nation was wicked. First, all leaders are indicted for their vicious sin: prophets, priests, princes, then the people in general.

22:30 I searched for a man. Ezekiel and Jeremiah were faithful, but apart from them God sought a man capable of advocacy for Israel when its sin had gone so far. But no one could lead the people to repentance and draw the nation back from the brink of the judgment that came in 586 B.C. (Jer 7:26, 34; 19:15). Only God's Messiah, God Himself, will have the character and the credentials sufficient to do what no man can do, intercede for Israel (cf. Is 59:16–19; 63:5; Rev 5). He was rejected by them in His earthly ministry, so the effects of this judgment continue today, until they turn to Him in faith (cf. Zec 12:10; 13:1).

23:2–4 two women. This chapter describes the spiritual infidelity of Israel and Judah, pictured as two sisters, to convey the gravity of sin in Judah. "One mother" refers to the united kingdom, while "two women" refers to the divided kingdom. Oholah, meaning "Her own tabernacle," as she had her separate dwelling-place apart from the temple, represents Samaria. In the northern kingdom, Jeroboam had set up worship, which God rejected. Oholibah, "My tabernacle is in her," represents Jerusalem, where God did establish worship.

23:5–10 Oholah played the harlot. The northern kingdom of Israel was a harlot, in a spiritual sense, by seeking union for fulfillment and security with idolatrous, young, wealthy, attractive Assyria. Assyria turned on her (v. 10), conquered her, and deported Israel in 722 B.C. (2Ki 17).

23:11–21 more corrupt. Cf. 16:47. The focus is Judah's (the southern kingdom) craving for Babylonian idolatry that alienated her from God. Judah learned nothing from Israel's punishment (v. 13).

23:12 Assyrians. Ahaz placed Judah under the protection of Assyria (2Ki 16:7–10), a political move denounced by Isaiah (Is 7:13–17).

23:14–16 Chaldeans. Judah was drawn to portraits of Babylonian men, done in brilliant colors, lusting for the Chaldean lifestyle. Social and political alliance led to spiritual defection.

the land of their birth. 16 [a]When she saw them she
[A]lusted after them and sent messengers to them in
Chaldea. 17 The [a,A]Babylonians came to her to the
bed of love and defiled her with their harlotry. And
when she had been defiled by them, [b]she became
disgusted with them. 18 She [A]uncovered her harlotries and uncovered her nakedness; then [a]I became
[B]disgusted with her, as [a]I had become disgusted with
her [C]sister. 19 Yet she multiplied her harlotries, remembering the days of her youth, when she played
the harlot in the land of Egypt. 20 She [A]lusted after
their paramours, whose flesh is *like* the flesh of
donkeys and whose issue is *like* the issue of horses.
21 Thus you longed for the [A]lewdness of your youth,
when [a]the Egyptians handled your bosom because
of the breasts of your youth.

22 "Therefore, O Oholibah, thus says the Lord [a]GOD,
'Behold I will arouse your lovers against you, from
whom [b]you were alienated, and I will bring them
against you from every side: 23 the [a,A]Babylonians
and all the [B]Chaldeans, [C]Pekod and Shoa and Koa,
and all the [b,D]Assyrians with them; desirable young
men, governors and officials all of them, officers
and [c]men of renown, all of them riding on horses.
24 They will come against you with weapons, [A]char-
iots and [a]wagons, and with a company of peoples.
They will set themselves against you on every side
with buckler and shield and helmet; and I will commit the [B]judgment to them, and they will judge you
according to their customs. 25 I will set My [A]jealousy
against you, that they may deal with you in wrath.
They will remove your nose and your ears; and your
[a]survivors will fall by the sword. They will take your
[B]sons and your daughters; and your [a]survivors will
be consumed by the fire. 26 They will also [A]strip you
of your clothes and take away your [B]beautiful jewels.
27 Thus [A]I will make your lewdness and your harlotry
brought from the land of Egypt to cease from you,
so that you will not lift up your eyes to them or remember Egypt anymore.' 28 For thus says the Lord
GOD, 'Behold, I will give you into the hand of those
whom you [A]hate, into the hand of those from whom
[a]you were alienated. 29 They will [A]deal with you in hatred, take all your property, and leave you naked and
bare. And the nakedness of your harlotries will be
uncovered, both your lewdness and your harlotries.
30 These things will be done to you because you have
[A]played the harlot with the nations, because you have
defiled yourself with their idols. 31 You have walked
in the way of your sister; therefore I will give [A]her
cup into your hand.' 32 Thus says the Lord GOD,

'You will [A]drink your sister's cup,
Which is deep and wide.
[a]You will be [B]laughed at and
held in derision;
It contains much.
33 'You will be filled with
[A]drunkenness and sorrow,
The cup of horror and desolation,
The cup of your sister Samaria.
34 'You will [A]drink it and drain it.
Then you will gnaw its fragments
And tear your breasts;

for I have spoken,' declares the Lord GOD. 35 Therefore,
thus says the Lord GOD, 'Because you have [A]forgot-
ten Me and [B]cast Me behind your back, bear now the
punishment of your lewdness and your harlotries.' "

36 Moreover, the LORD said to me, "Son of man, will
you [A]judge Oholah and Oholibah? Then [B]declare to
them their abominations. 37 For they have committed
adultery, and blood is on their hands. Thus they have
committed adultery with their idols and even caused
their sons, [A]whom they bore to Me, to pass through
the fire to [a]them as food. 38 Again, they have done
this to Me: they have [A]defiled My sanctuary on the
same day and have [B]profaned My sabbaths. 39 For
when they had slaughtered their children for their
idols, they entered My [A]sanctuary on the same day
to profane it; and lo, thus they did within My house.

40 "Furthermore, [a]they have even sent for men
who come from afar, to whom a messenger was
sent; and lo, they came—for whom you bathed,
[A]painted your eyes and [B]decorated yourselves with
ornaments; 41 and you sat on a splendid [A]couch with
a [B]table arranged before it on which you had set
My [C]incense and My [C]oil. 42 The sound of a [a,A]care-
free multitude was with her; and [B]drunkards were
brought from the wilderness with men of the [b]com-
mon sort. And they put [C]bracelets on [c]the hands of
the women and beautiful crowns on their heads.

23:16 [a]Lit *At the sight of her eyes* [A]Ezek 23:20; Matt 5:28 23:17 [a]Lit *sons of Babel* [b]Lit *her soul* [A]2 Kin 24:17 23:18 [a]Lit *My soul* [A]Jer 8:12; Ezek 21:24; 23:10 [B]Ps 78:59; 106:40; Jer 12:8 [C]Ezek 23:9; Amos 5:21 23:20 [A]Ezek 16:26; 17:15 23:21 [a]So two mss; M.T. *from Egypt* [A]Jer 3:9; Ezek 23:3 23:22 [a]Heb *YHWH*, usually rendered *LORD*, and so throughout the ch [b]Lit *your soul was alienated* 23:23 [a]Lit *sons of Babylon* [b]Lit *sons of Assyria* [c]Lit *the called ones* [A]2 Kin 20:14-17; Ezek 21:19; 23:14-17 [B]2 Kin 24:2; Job 1:17; Is 23:13 [C]Jer 50:21 [D]Gen 2:14; 25:18; Ezra 6:22 23:24 [a]Lit *wheels* [A]Jer 47:3; Ezek 26:10; Nah 2:3, 4 [B]Jer 39:5, 6; Ezek 16:38; 23:45 23:25 [a]Lit *remainder* [A]Ex 34:14; Ezek 5:13; 8:17, 18; Zeph 1:18 [B]Ezek 23:47; Hos 2:4 23:26 [A]Jer 13:22; Ezek 16:39; 23:29 [B]Is 3:18-23 23:27 [A]Ezek 16:41 23:28 [a]Lit *your soul was alienated* [A]Jer 21:7-10; 34:20; Ezek 16:37; 23:17, 22 23:29 [A]Deut 28:48; Ezek 23:25, 26, 45-47 23:30 [A]Ezek 6:9 23:31 [A]2 Kin 21:13; Jer 7:14, 15; Ezek 23:33 23:32 [a]Or *It will be for jesting and deriding because of its great size* [A]Ps 60:3; Is 51:17; Jer 25:15 [B]Ezek 5:14, 15; 16:57; 22:4, 5 23:33 [A]Jer 25:15, 16, 27; Hab 2:16 23:34 [A]Ps 75:8; Is 51:17 23:35 [A]Is 17:10; Jer 3:21; Ezek 22:12; Hos 8:14; 13:6 [B]1 Kin 14:9; Jer 2:27; 32:33 23:36 [A]Jer 1:10; Ezek 20:4; 22:2 [B]Is 58:1; Ezek 16:2; Mic 3:8 23:37 [a]I.e. idols [A]Ezek 16:20; 20:26 23:38 [A]2 Kin 21:4, 7; Ezek 5:11; 7:20 [B]Jer 17:27; Ezek 20:13, 24 23:39 [A]Jer 7:9-11 23:40 [a]Or *you* (women) [A]2 Kin 9:30; Jer 4:30 [B]Is 3:18-23; Ezek 16:13-16 23:41 [A]Esth 1:6; Is 57:7; Amos 6:4 [B]Is 65:11; Ezek 44:16 [C]Jer 44:17; Hos 2:8 23:42 [a]Lit *at ease* [b]Lit *multitude of mankind* [c]Lit *their hands* [A]Ezek 16:49; Amos 6:3-6 [B]Jer 51:7 [C]Gen 24:30; Ezek 16:11, 12

23:17 to the bed of love. The description portrays spiritual unfaithfulness graphically (v. 30).

23:19 Judah renewed her old sins from the days of Egypt, returning to her first degradation.

23:22–35 arouse your lovers. God's anger at Judah's sin prompted His bringing Babylonians and others to deal severely with her. The passage sets forth how Judah's companion nations were the instruments of her judgment.

23:23 Pekod and Shoa and Koa. Three different Aramean tribes.

23:25 remove your nose and your ears. Atrocities by Babylonians would include facial dismemberment, ancient punishment for an adulteress practiced in Egypt, Chaldea, and elsewhere.

23:32–34 drink your sister's cup. Judah was to experience the "cup" of God's judgment as Samaria had in 722 B.C. (cf. 23:46–49). Often the idea of "drinking a cup" is symbolic of receiving God's wrath (cf. Ps 75:8; Is 51:17–22; Jer 25:15–29; Mt 20:22).

23:36–42 The prophet detailed a shameful summary of God's case against the nation—a double arraignment calling for judgment.

43 "Then I said concerning her who was [A]worn
out by adulteries, '[a]Will they now commit adultery
with her when she is *thus?*' 44 [a]But they went in to
her as they would go in to a harlot. Thus they went
in to Oholah and to Oholibah, the lewd women.
45 But they, righteous men, will [A]judge them with
the judgment of adulteresses and with the judgment of women who shed blood, because they are
adulteresses and blood is on their hands.
46 "For thus says the Lord GOD, 'Bring up a company against them and give them over to [A]terror
and plunder. 47 The company will [A]stone them with
stones and cut them down with their swords; they
will slay their sons and their daughters and [B]burn
their houses with fire. 48 Thus I will make lewdness
cease from the land, that all women may be admonished and not commit [a]lewdness as you have done.
49 Your lewdness [a]will be [A]requited upon you, and
you will bear the penalty of *worshiping* your idols;
thus you will know that I am the Lord GOD.' "

PARABLE OF THE BOILING POT

24 And the word of the LORD came to me in
the ninth year, in the tenth month, on the
tenth of the month, saying, 2 "Son of man, write the
name of the day, this very day. The king of Babylon
[a]has [A]laid siege to Jerusalem this very day. 3 Speak a
[A]parable to the [B]rebellious house and say to them,
'Thus says the Lord [a]GOD,

"Put on the [C]pot, put *it* on and
also pour water in it;
4 [a,A]Put in it the pieces,
Every good piece, the thigh
and the shoulder;
Fill *it* with choice bones.
5 "Take the [A]choicest of the flock,
And also pile [a]wood under [b]the pot.
Make it boil vigorously.
Also seethe its bones in it."

6 'Therefore, thus says the Lord GOD,

"Woe to the [A]bloody city,
To the pot in which there is rust
And whose rust has not gone out of it!
Take out of it piece after piece,
[a]Without making a choice.
7 "For her blood is in her midst;
She placed it on the bare rock;
She did not [A]pour it on the ground
To cover it with dust.
8 "That it may [A]cause wrath to come
up to take vengeance,
I have put her blood on the bare rock,
That it may not be covered."

9 Therefore, thus says the Lord GOD,

"[A]Woe to the bloody city!
I also will make the pile great.
10 "Heap on the wood, kindle the fire,
[a]Boil the flesh well
And mix in the spices,
And let the bones be burned.
11 "Then [A]set it empty on its coals
So that it may be hot
And its bronze may [a]glow
And its [B]filthiness may be melted in it,
Its rust consumed.
12 "She has [A]wearied *Me* with toil,
Yet her great rust has not gone from her;
Let her rust *be* in the fire!
13 "In your filthiness is lewdness.
Because I *would* have cleansed you,
Yet you are [A]not clean,
You will not be cleansed from
your filthiness again
Until I have [a,B]spent My wrath on you.

14 I, the LORD, have spoken; it is [A]coming and I will
act. I will not relent, and I will not [B]pity and I will not
be sorry; [C]according to your ways and according to
your deeds [a]I will judge you," declares the Lord GOD.' "

DEATH OF EZEKIEL'S WIFE IS A SIGN

15 And the word of the LORD came to me saying,
16 "Son of man, behold, I am about to take from you
the [A]desire of your eyes with a [B]blow; but you shall
not [C]mourn and you shall not weep, and your [D]tears

23:43 [a]Or *Now they will commit adultery with her, and she with them* [A]Ezek 23:3 23:44 [a]Or *And* 23:45 [A]Ezek 16:38 23:46 [A]Jer 15:4; 24:9; 29:18 23:47 [A]Lev 20:10; Ezek 16:40 [B]Jer 39:8 23:48 [a]Lit *according to your lewdness* 23:49 [a]Lit *they will give* [A]Is 59:18; Ezek 7:4, 9; 9:10; 23:35 24:2 [a]Lit *leaned on* [A]2 Kin 25:1; Jer 39:1; 52:4 24:3 [a]Heb *YHWH*, usually rendered *LORD*, and so throughout the ch [A]Ps 78:2; Ezek 17:2; 20:49 [B]Is 1:2; 30:1, 9; Ezek 2:3, 6, 8 [C]Jer 1:13, 14; Ezek 11:3, 7, 11; 24:6 24:4 [a]Lit *Gather her pieces* [A]Mic 3:2, 3 24:5 [a]Lit *bones* [b]Lit *it* [A]Jer 39:6; 52:10, 24-27 24:6 [a]Lit *No lot has fallen on it* [A]2 Kin 24:3, 4; Ezek 22:2, 3, 27; Mic 7:2; Nah 3:1 24:7 [A]Lev 17:13; Deut 12:16 24:8 [A]Is 26:21 24:9 [A]Ezek 24:6; Hab 2:12 24:10 [a]Lit *Complete* 24:11 [a]Lit *become hot* [A]Jer 21:10; Mal 4:1 [B]Ezek 22:15; 23:27 24:12 [A]Jer 9:5 24:13 [a]Lit *caused to rest* [A]Jer 6:28-30; Ezek 22:24 [B]Ezek 5:13; 8:18 24:14 [a]So with several ancient mss and versions; M.T. *they* [A]Ps 33:9; Is 55:11 [B]Jer 13:14; Ezek 9:10 [C]Is 3:11; Ezek 18:30; 36:19 24:16 [A]Song 7:10; Ezek 24:18 [B]Job 23:2 [C]Jer 16:5; 22:10 [D]Jer 13:17

23:45 righteous men. This likely refers to the remnant of godly people in the nation who would affirm the justice of judgment.

24:1, 2 this very day. The time was Jan. 15, 588 B.C. (dating from 597 as in 1:2). The Babylonians began the 18-month siege of Jerusalem (Jer 39:1, 2; 52:4–12).

24:3–5 Speak a parable. The choice cuts of lamb picture God's flock being boiled in a pot, symbolizing Jerusalem in the heat of the siege. Cf. 11:3. Animal bones were frequently used for fuel.

24:6 Woe to the bloody city. Jerusalem's populace was guilty of bloody corruption, which was pictured by the boiled scum or rust in the pot (cf. 22:2).

24:7 her blood. The city's blood (a general symbol of sin) was blatantly open, not hidden, as depicted by exposure on top of a rock. When blood was not covered with dust, the law was violated (Lv 17:13). God's vengeance would come by Babylon's army.

24:9, 10 the pile great . . . bones be burned. Intensely provoked by sin, God wanted Ezekiel to picture the fire as furious judgment that kills the people.

24:11, 12 set it empty. After all pieces (people) were burned up, then the pot was heated empty. This portrayed the Lord's thorough follow-through by the besieger to totally destroy the city and the temple, with all its residue (cf. the treatment of a leprous house in Lv 14:34–45).

24:16–27 Ezekiel's wife died as a sign to Israel. All personal sorrow was eclipsed in the universal calamity. Just as Ezekiel was not to mourn the death of his wife (v. 17), so Israel was not to mourn the death of her families (vv. 19–24). Though the text emphasizes how precious his wife was, the "desire of [his] eyes" (v. 16), he was obedient and submitted to God's will. He became a heartbreaking sign to his people.

shall not come. 17 Groan silently; make [A]no mourning for the dead. Bind on your turban and put your
shoes on your feet, and do not cover *your* mustache
and [B]do not eat the bread of men." 18 So I spoke to
the people in the morning, and in the evening my
wife died. And in the morning I did as I was commanded. 19 The people said to me, "Will you not tell
us what these things that you are doing mean for
us?" 20 Then I said to them, "The word of the LORD
came to me saying, 21 'Speak to the house of Israel,
"Thus says the Lord GOD, 'Behold, I am about to
profane My sanctuary, the pride of your power, the
[A]desire of your eyes and the delight of your soul; and
your [B]sons and your daughters whom you have left
behind will fall by the sword. 22 You will do as I have
done; you will not cover *your* mustache and you will
not eat the bread of men. 23 Your turbans will be on
your heads and your shoes on your feet. You [A]will
not mourn and you will not weep, but [B]you will rot
away in your iniquities and you will groan [a]to one
another. 24 Thus Ezekiel will be a [A]sign to you; according to all that he has done you will do; when it
comes, then you will know that I am the Lord GOD.' "

25 'As for you, son of man, will *it* not be on the day
when I take from them their [A]stronghold, the joy of
their [a]pride, the desire of their eyes and [b]their heart's
delight, their sons and their daughters, 26 that on
that day he who [A]escapes will come to you with information for *your* ears? 27 On that day your [A]mouth
will be opened to him who escaped, and you will
speak and be mute no longer. Thus you will be a sign
to them, and they will know that I am the LORD.' "

JUDGMENT ON GENTILE NATIONS—AMMON

25 And the word of the LORD came to me saying, 2 "Son of man, set your face toward the
[A]sons of Ammon and prophesy against them, 3 and
say to the sons of Ammon, 'Hear the word of the
Lord [a]GOD! Thus says the Lord GOD, "Because you
said, '[A]Aha!' against My sanctuary when it was
profaned, and against the land of Israel when it
was made desolate, and against the house of Judah when they went into exile, 4 therefore, behold,
I am going to give you to the [A]sons of the east for
a possession, and they will set their encampments
among you and make their dwellings among you;
they will [B]eat your fruit and drink your milk. 5 I
will make [A]Rabbah a pasture for camels and the
sons of Ammon a resting place for flocks. Thus
you will know that I am the LORD." 6 For thus says
the Lord GOD, "Because you have [A]clapped your
hands and stamped your feet and [B]rejoiced with
all the scorn of your soul against the land of Israel, 7 therefore, behold, I have [A]stretched out My
hand against you and I will give you for [B]spoil
to the nations. And I will [C]cut you off from the
peoples and [D]make you perish from the lands; I
will destroy you. Thus you will [E]know that I am
the LORD."

MOAB

8 'Thus says the Lord GOD, "Because [A]Moab and
Seir say, 'Behold, the house of Judah is like all the
nations,' 9 therefore, behold, I am going to [a]de-
prive the flank of Moab of *its* cities, of its cities
which are on its [b]frontiers, the glory of the land,
[A]Beth-jeshimoth, [B]Baal-meon and [C]Kiriathaim,
10 and I will give it for a possession along with
the sons of Ammon to the [A]sons of the east, so
that the sons of Ammon will not be remembered
among the nations. 11 Thus I will execute judgments on Moab, and they will know that I am
the LORD."

24:17 [A]Lev 21:10-12 [B]Jer 16:7; Hos 9:4 24:21 [A]Ps 27:4; 84:1; Ezek 24:16 [B]Jer 6:11; 16:3, 4; Ezek 23:25, 47 24:23 [a]Lit *a man to his brother* [A]Job 27:15; Ps 78:64 [B]Lev 26:39; Ezek 33:10 24:24 [A]Ezek 4:3; Luke 11:29, 30 24:25 [a]Or *beauty* [b]Lit *the lifting up of their soul* [A]Ps 48:2; 50:2; Ezek 24:21 24:26 [A]1 Sam 4:12; Job 1:15-19 24:27 [A]Ezek 3:26; 33:22 25:2 [A]Jer 49:1-6; Amos 1:13-15; Zeph 2:9 25:3 [a]Heb *YHWH*, usually rendered *LORD*, and so throughout the ch [A]Ps 70:2, 3; Ezek 21:28; 25:6; 26:2; 36:2 25:4 [A]Judg 6:3, 33; 1 Kin 4:30 [B]Deut 28:33, 51; Is 1:7 25:5 [A]Deut 3:11; 2 Sam 12:26; Jer 49:2; Ezek 21:20 25:6 [A]Job 27:23; Nah 3:19 [B]Obad 12; Zeph 2:8, 10 25:7 [A]Ezek 25:13, 16; Zeph 1:4 [B]Is 33:4; Ezek 26:5 [C]Ezek 21:32 [D]Amos 1:14, 15 [E]Ezek 6:14 25:8 [A]Is 15:1; Jer 48:1; Amos 2:1, 2 25:9 [a]Lit *open* [b]Lit *end* [A]Num 33:49; Josh 12:3; 13:20 [B]Num 32:3, 38; Josh 13:17; 1 Chr 5:8; Jer 48:23 [C]Num 32:37; Josh 13:19; Jer 48:1, 23 25:10 [A]Ezek 25:4

24:25 on the day. This refers to the destruction of the temple.

24:26, 27 on that day. One who escaped the destruction of Jerusalem (586 B.C.) would come to Ezekiel in Babylon and report the story. From that day forward, he was to be silent until the captives arrived; then he could speak of Judah (cf. 3:26, 27). This was about a two-year period (cf. 33:21; Jer 52:5–7), when there was no need to preach judgment because it had come. He did speak of other nations (as recorded beginning in chap. 25).

25:1 the word of the LORD came. Ezekiel 25:1–32:32 proclaims judgments on 7 other nations, similar to the series in Jer 46–51. Four of them are singled out in this chapter for vindictive jealousy and hate toward Israel. After devoting chaps. 1-24 to calamity on His chosen nation, it is fitting that God should reveal His impartiality toward all sinners and give the prophet judgments to proclaim on Gentiles. Israel's sinful failure had profaned God's honor in the eyes of these peoples (36:21–23), but these nations had falsely assumed that when Israel was exiled, their God was defeated.

25:2, 3 toward the sons of Ammon. These people lived on the edge of the desert E of the Jordan River and N of Moab. They had joined Babylon against Judah about 600 B.C. (2Ki 24:2ff.). In 594 B.C., together with other nations, they tried to influence Judah to ally with them against Babylon (Jer 27:2ff.). Ezekiel 21:18–20 indicates that Babylon came after them. There is no record of an attack, so they must have surrendered (21:28; Zep 2:8–11). They were of incestuous origin (cf. Ge 19:37, 38) and often hostile toward Judah (cf. Jdg 10; 1Sa 11; 2Sa 10, 12; Jer 49:1–6; La 2:15; Am 1:13–15). God judged this people because of their enmity against Israel (vv. 3, 6). They expressed malicious pleasure at the dishonoring of the temple, desolation of the land, and dispersion of the inhabitants.

25:4 going to give you to the sons of the east. Perhaps this meant the coming of Babylon from the E which would devastate Ammon in either 588–86 B.C. or 582/81 B.C. Or it could refer to their land being occupied by the various nomadic tribes living beyond the Jordan.

25:5 Rabbah. This important Ammonite capital (cf. Am 1:14), now called Amman, is about 25 mi. NE of the upper tip of the Dead Sea, E of the Jordan River.

25:7 make you perish. Ammonites would be destroyed and eliminated from their land. Yet, Jer 49:6 assures a later return of a remnant of these scattered people.

25:8–11 Moab and Seir. The origin of these people is given in Ge 19:37, 38. Their land was the area S of the Arnon River along the lower region of the Dead Sea. Cf. Is 15, 16; Jer 48; Am 2:1–3. The Babylonians destroyed cities there in 582/81 B.C. The reason for judgment (v. 8) also included their gloating over Israel's fall, as well as their scorn in saying Israel was like all other people with no privileged position before God. Both Ammonites and Moabites became absorbed into the Arabian peoples.

25:8 Seir. Another name for the adjacent Edomite area (Ge 32:3; 36:20, 21, 30), dominated by Mt. Seir and a mountainous, extremely rugged, rocky country. Her judgments are given in 25:12–14.

EDOM

[12] 'Thus says the Lord GOD, "Because [A]Edom
has acted against the house of Judah by taking
vengeance, and has incurred grievous guilt, and
avenged themselves upon them," [13] therefore thus
says the Lord GOD, "I will also [A]stretch out My hand
against Edom and [B]cut off man and beast from it.
And I will lay it waste; from [C]Teman even to [D]Dedan
they will fall by the sword. [14] [A]I will lay My vengeance on Edom by the hand of My people Israel.
Therefore, they will act in Edom [B]according to My
anger and according to My wrath; thus they will
know My vengeance," declares the Lord GOD.

PHILISTIA

[15] 'Thus says the Lord GOD, "Because the Philistines have acted in [A]revenge and have taken vengeance with scorn of soul to destroy with everlasting enmity," [16] therefore thus says the Lord GOD,
"Behold, I will [A]stretch out My hand against the
Philistines, even cut off the [B]Cherethites and destroy the remnant of the seacoast. [17] I will execute
great vengeance on them with wrathful rebukes;
and they will [A]know that I am the LORD when I lay
My vengeance on them." ' "

JUDGMENT ON TYRE

26 Now in the eleventh year, on the first of the
month, the word of the LORD came to me
saying, [2] "Son of man, because [A]Tyre has said concerning Jerusalem, 'Aha, the [B]gateway of the peoples
is broken; it has [a,C]opened to me. I shall be filled,
now that she is laid waste,' [3] therefore thus says
the Lord [a]GOD, 'Behold, I am against you, O Tyre,
and I will bring up [A]many nations against you, as
the [B]sea brings up its waves. [4] They will [A]destroy
the walls of Tyre and break down her towers; and
I will scrape her debris from her and make her a
bare rock. [5] She will be a place for the spreading
of nets in the midst of the sea, for I have spoken,'
declares the Lord GOD, 'and she will become [A]spoil
for the nations. [6] Also her [A]daughters who are [a]on
the mainland will be slain by the sword, and they
will know that I am the LORD.' "
[7] For thus says the Lord GOD, "Behold, I will bring
upon Tyre from the north Nebuchadnezzar king of
Babylon, [A]king of kings, with horses, [B]chariots, cavalry
and [a]a great army. [8] He will slay your daughters [a]on
the mainland with the sword; and he will make [A]siege
walls against you, cast up a [B]ramp against you and
raise up a large shield against you. [9] The blow of his
battering rams he will direct against your walls, and
with his [a]axes he will break down your towers. [10] Because of the multitude of his [A]horses, the dust *raised*
by them will cover you; your walls will [B]shake at the
noise of cavalry and [a]wagons and chariots when he
[C]enters your gates as men enter a city that is breached.
[11] With the hoofs of his [A]horses he will trample all your
streets. He will slay your people with the sword; and
your strong pillars will [B]come down to the ground.
[12] Also they will make a spoil of your riches and a
prey of your [A]merchandise, [B]break down your walls
and destroy your [C]pleasant houses, and [a]throw your
stones and your timbers and your debris [D]into the

25:12 [A]2 Chr 28:17; Ps 137:7; Jer 49:7-22 25:13 [A]Jer 49:8, 13 [B]Ezek 29:8; Mal 1:3, 4 [C]Gen 36:34; Jer 49:7; Amos 1:12 [D]Jer 25:23; 49:8 25:14 [A]Is 11:14 [B]Ezek 35:11 25:15 [A]Is 14:29-31; Ezek 25:6, 12; Joel 3:4 25:16 [A]Jer 25:20; 47:1-7 [B]1 Sam 30:14; Zeph 2:5 25:17 [A]Ps 9:16 26:2 [a]Lit *turned* [A]2 Sam 5:11; Is 23:1; Jer 25:22 [B]Is 62:10 [C]Ezek 25:8; 35:10 26:3 [a]Heb *YHWH*, usually rendered *LORD*, and so throughout the ch [A]Mic 4:11 [B]Is 5:30; Jer 50:42; 51:42 26:4 [A]Is 23:11; Ezek 26:9; Amos 1:10 26:5 [A]Ezek 25:7; 29:19 26:6 [a]Lit *in the field* [A]Ezek 16:46, 53; 26:8 26:7 [a]Lit *an assembly, even many people* [A]Ezra 7:12; Is 10:8; Jer 52:32; Dan 2:37, 47 [B]Ezek 23:24; Nah 2:3, 4 26:8 [a]Lit *in the field* [A]Jer 52:4; Ezek 21:22 [B]Jer 32:24 26:9 [a]Lit *swords* 26:10 [a]Lit *wheels* [A]Jer 4:13; 47:3 [B]Ezek 26:15; 27:28 [C]Jer 39:3 26:11 [A]Is 5:28; Hab 1:8 [B]Is 26:5; Jer 43:13 26:12 [a]Lit *put* [A]Is 23:8, 18; Ezek 27:3-27; Zech 9:3 [B]Jer 52:14 [C]2 Chr 32:27; Amos 5:11 [D]Ezek 27:27, 32, 34; 28:8

25:12 Edom. Cf. chap. 35; Is 21:11, 12; Jer 49:7–22; Am 1:11, 12; Obadiah; Mal 1:3–5. These people lived S of Moab from the Dead Sea to the Gulf of Aqabah. These people had been almost annihilated by David (2Sa 8:14), but won back independence during the reign of Ahaz (ca. 735–715 B.C.). Their revenge was hostility to Israel constantly (cf. Ge 27:27–41; Is 34:5–7). The reason for judgment is Edom's disdain when the Israelites were devastated in 588–86 B.C. They acted like a cheering section for Babylon, "Raze it, raze it" (Ps 137:7; La 4:21, 22).

25:13, 14 against Edom … by the hand of My people Israel. The Arab tribe called Nabateans invaded Edom in 325 B.C.; but it was the Jewish forces of Judas Maccabeus in 164 B.C. and John Hyrcanus in 126 B.C. who fully subjugated Edom. Jews even compelled Edomites to submit to their religion. All 3 of these nations (Ammon, Moab, and Edom) have disappeared as separate nations into the Arab peoples.

25:13 Teman … Dedan. Reference is to key Edomite towns. Teman (Teima) was possibly 200 mi. E of the Dead Sea in the Arabian Desert in the northern expanse of Edom's territory. Dedan was maybe located 100 mi. S of Teman, yet far E of the Red Sea.

25:15–17 the Philistines. Cf. Is 14:29–32; Jer 47; Joel 3:4; Am 1:6–8; Ob 19; Zep 2:4–7; Zec 9:5. The reason for their judgment was perpetual enmity and vengefulness against Israel, which perpetuated the "old hatred" from as far back as Jdg 13–16. They constantly harassed and oppressed Israel until David broke their power during Saul's reign (1Sa 17). They repeatedly rose up and were subdued by Israel. Nebuchadnezzar invaded their land (Jer 47).

25:16 Cherethites. They originated in Crete and became part of the Philistine nation (*see note on 1Sa 30:14*), with some serving in David's bodyguard (2Sa 8:18; 15:18).

25:17 great vengeance. This was fulfilled at the time of Babylon's invasion of 588–86 B.C. or 582/81 B.C. (cf. Jer 25:20; 47:1–7).

26:1 the eleventh year. In 586 B.C., the 11th year of Jehoiachin's captivity, on the tenth day of the fifth month, Jerusalem was captured.

26:3, 4 I am against you, O Tyre. The judgment of this city covers 3 chaps. (26–28), indicating its importance to God. Cf. Is 23; Am 1:9, 10. Tyre was an ancient city of the Phoenicians, appearing for the first time in Jos 19:29. During the reigns of David and Solomon it had great influence. Hiram, its king, was a friend to David (2Sa 5:11), who helped him and Solomon in building operations (cf. 1Ki 5:1–12; 1Ch 14:1; 2Ch 2:3, 11). Later, Tyrians sold Jews into slavery (cf. Joel 3:4–8; Am 1:9, 10). God would move "many nations" to invade Tyre, the commercial center of the Mediterranean (cf. 27:3), in successive attacks pictured by wave following wave. Babylon (v. 7) besieged Tyre from 585–573 B.C.; later came Alexander's Grecian army in 332 B.C. Babylon had devastated the coastal city, but many Tyrians escaped to an island fortress which withstood attack. The later Grecian attackers "scraped" all the remaining "debris" and rubble and dumped it into the sea, building a causeway to the island nearly a half mile out. They also brought ships and overcame the fortress defenders in a devastating assault on Tyre. The predictions in chaps. 26–28 have been fulfilled with amazing literal accuracy.

26:5, 14 for the spreading of nets. Tyre became a fishing city, a place to spread fishing nets for centuries, until the Saracens finally destroyed what was left in the fourth century. Since then the once great center of Mediterranean commerce has been a nondescript village.

26:7–14 Here is a vivid description of the original devastation by Babylon's King Nebuchadnezzar called "king of kings" (v. 7) because so many other rulers were subject to him. God had given him universal rule (cf. Da 2:37). Verses 8 and 9 describe the siege, vv. 10–14, the devastation.

26:12 they will … spoil. After Nebuchadnezzar in v. 7 and "he" and "his" in vv. 8–11, "they" in v. 12 appears to broaden the reference to others among the "many nations" (v. 3). At

water. 13 So I will [a]silence the sound of your [A]songs,
and the sound of your [B]harps will be heard no more.
14 I will make you a bare rock; you will be a place for
the spreading of nets. You will be [A]built no more, for
I the [B]LORD have spoken," declares the Lord GOD.
15 Thus says the Lord GOD to Tyre, "Shall not the
[A]coastlands [B]shake at the sound of your fall when the
wounded groan, when the slaughter occurs in your
midst? 16 Then all the princes of the sea will [A]go down
from their thrones, remove their robes and strip off
their embroidered garments. They will [B]clothe themselves with [a]trembling; they will sit on the ground,
[C]tremble every moment and be appalled at you. 17 They
will take up a [A]lamentation over you and say to you,

'[B]How you have perished, O inhabited one,
From the seas, O renowned city,
Which was [C]mighty on the sea,
She and her inhabitants,
Who [a]imposed [b]her terror
On all her inhabitants!
18 'Now the [A]coastlands will tremble
On the day of your fall;
Yes, the coastlands which are by the sea
Will be terrified at your [B]passing.' "

19 For thus says the Lord GOD, "When I make you a
desolate city, like the cities which are not inhabited,
when I [A]bring up the deep over you and the great
waters cover you, 20 then I will bring you down with
those who [A]go down to the pit, to the people of old,
and I will make you dwell in the [B]lower parts of the
earth, like the ancient waste places, with those who
go down to the pit, so that you will not [a]be inhabited; but I will set [C]glory in the land of the living.
21 I will [a]bring [A]terrors on you and you will be no
more; though you will be sought, [B]you will never
be found again," declares the Lord GOD.

LAMENT OVER TYRE

27 Moreover, the word of the LORD came to me
saying, 2 "And you, son of man, [A]take up a lamentation over Tyre; 3 and say to Tyre, [A]who dwells at
the [a]entrance to the sea, [B]merchant of the peoples to
many coastlands, 'Thus says the Lord [b]GOD,

"O Tyre, you have said, 'I am
perfect in beauty.'
4 "Your borders are in the heart of the seas;
Your builders have perfected your beauty.
5 "They have [a]made all *your* planks
of fir trees from [A]Senir;
They have taken a cedar from
Lebanon to make a mast for you.
6 "Of [A]oaks from [B]Bashan they
have made your oars;
With ivory they have [a]inlaid your deck of
boxwood from the coastlands of [C]Cyprus.
7 "Your sail was of fine embroidered
linen from Egypt
So that it became your
[a]distinguishing mark;
Your [b]awning was [c,A]blue and purple
from the coastlands of [B]Elishah.
8 "The inhabitants of Sidon and
[A]Arvad were your rowers;
Your [B]wise men, O Tyre, were
[a]aboard; they were your pilots.
9 "The elders of [A]Gebal and her wise men
were with you repairing your seams;
All the ships of the sea and their
sailors were with you in order
to deal in your merchandise.

10 "[A]Persia and [A]Lud and [A]Put were in your army,
your men of war. They hung shield and helmet in
you; they set forth your splendor. 11 The sons of Arvad and your army were on your walls, *all* around,
and the [a]Gammadim were in your towers. They
hung their shields on your walls *all* around; they
perfected your beauty.
12 "Tarshish was your customer because of the
abundance of all *kinds* of wealth; with silver, iron,
tin and lead they paid for your wares. 13 [A]Javan, [A]Tu-
bal and [B]Meshech, they were your traders; with the
[C]lives of men and vessels of bronze they paid for

26:13 [a]Lit *cause to cease* [A]Is 23:16; 24:8, 9; Amos 6:5 [B]Is 5:12; Rev 18:22 26:14 [A]Deut 13:16; Job 12:14; Mal 1:4 [B]Is 14:27 26:15 [A]Ezek 26:18; 27:35 [B]Jer 49:21; Ezek 31:16 26:16 [a]Lit *tremblings* [A]Jon 3:6 [B]Job 8:22; Ps 35:26; Ezek 7:27; 1 Pet 5:5 [C]Ezek 32:10; Hos 11:10 26:17 [a]Lit *put* [b]Lit *their* [A]Ezek 19:1, 14; 27:2, 32; 32:2, 16 [B]Is 14:12; Jer 48:39; 50:23 [C]Ezek 27:3, 10, 11; 28:2 26:18 [A]Is 41:5; Ezek 26:15; 27:35 [B]Is 23:5-7, 10, 11 26:19 [A]Is 8:7, 8; Ezek 26:3 26:20 [a]Or *return* [A]Is 14:9, 10; Ezek 32:30 [B]Ps 88:6; Amos 9:2; Jon 2:2, 6 [C]Jer 33:9; Zech 2:8 26:21 [a]Lit *give you terrors* [A]Ezek 26:15, 16; 27:36 [B]Rev 18:21 27:2 [A]Jer 9:10, 17-20; Ezek 28:12 27:3 [a]Lit *entrances* [b]Heb *YHWH*, usually rendered *LORD*, and so throughout the ch [A]Ezek 28:2 [B]Is 23:3 27:5 [a]Lit *built* [A]Deut 3:9; 1 Chr 5:23; Song 4:8 27:6 [a]Lit *made* [A]Is 2:13; Zech 11:2 [B]Num 21:33; Is 2:13; Jer 22:20 [C]Gen 10:4; Is 23:1, 12; Jer 2:10 27:7 [a]Or *standard* [b]Lit *covering* [c]Or *violet* [A]Ex 25:4; Jer 10:9 [B]Gen 10:4 27:8 [a]Lit *in you* [A]Gen 10:18; 1 Chr 1:16; Ezek 27:11 [B]1 Kin 9:27 27:9 [A]Josh 13:5; 1 Kin 5:18 27:10 [A]Ezek 30:5; 38:5 27:11 [a]Or *valorous ones* 27:13 [A]Gen 10:2; Is 66:19; Ezek 27:19 [B]Gen 10:2; Ezek 38:2; 39:1 [C]Joel 3:3; Rev 18:13

this point, "they" are not only Babylonians, but also Alexander's army which later heaped debris from the ruins into the sea to advance to the island stronghold (cf. Zec 9:3, 4).

26:13 songs . . . harps. According to Is 23:16, Tyre was famous for musicians.

26:15–18 So important a center of commerce could not be destroyed without affecting all the nearby nations. All the nations around the Mediterranean would consider Tyre's fall a calamity. According to customs of mourning, rulers would descend from their thrones and disrobe.

26:19–21 Tyre's destruction is compared to a dead person placed in the grave.

27:1–11 a lamentation over Tyre. The whole chapter is a lamentation, describing Tyre as a great trade ship destroyed on the high seas. The proper names indicate the participants in commerce with Tyre.

27:5–9 fir trees from Senir. The area is the Amorite designation for Mt. Hermon, to the NE from the northern tip of the Sea of Galilee. Lesser known places were: Elishah (v. 7), believed to be in Cyprus; Arvad (v. 8), an island city off the Mediterranean coast N of Byblos; and Gebal (v. 9), a name also used for Byblos, N of today's Beirut.

27:10, 11 men of war. These places provided mercenary soldiers for the Phoenician army to defend Tyre.

27:11 Arvad. *See note on vv. 5–9.* **Gammadim.** People from a place often identified as northern Aram, or Syria.

27:12 Tarshish. This verse begins the description of the commercial glory of Tyre. Most likely this place refers to Tarshishah in southern Spain, a Phoenician colony famous for silver (Jer 10:9).

27:13 Javan, Tubal and Meshech. Javan was Ionia, a large area in Greece. The other two, in Asia Minor, may be the Tibarenoi and Moschoi mentioned by the writer Herodotus, or slave-trading cities called Tabal and Mushku by the Assyrians.

your merchandise. 14 Those from [A]Beth-togarmah gave horses and war horses and mules for your wares. 15 The sons of [A]Dedan were your traders. Many coastlands were [a]your market; [B]ivory tusks and ebony they brought as your payment. 16 [A]Aram was your customer because of the abundance of your [a]goods; they paid for your wares with [B]emeralds, purple, [C]embroidered work, fine linen, coral and rubies. 17 Judah and the land of Israel, they were your traders; with the wheat of [A]Minnith, [a]cakes, honey, oil and balm they paid for your merchandise. 18 [A]Damascus was your customer because of the abundance of your [a]goods, because of the abundance of all *kinds* of wealth, because of the wine of Helbon and white wool. 19 Vedan and Javan paid for your wares [a]from Uzal; wrought iron, cassia and [b]sweet cane were among your merchandise. 20 [A]Dedan traded with you in saddlecloths for riding. 21 [A]Arabia and all the princes of Kedar, they were [a]your customers for [B]lambs, rams and goats; for these they were your customers. 22 The traders of [A]Sheba and Raamah, they traded with you; they paid for your wares with the best of all *kinds* of [B]spices, and with all *kinds* of precious stones and gold. 23 Haran, Canneh, [A]Eden, the traders of Sheba, Asshur *and* Chilmad traded with you. 24 They traded with you in choice garments, in clothes of [a]blue and embroidered work, and in carpets of many colors *and* tightly wound cords, *which were* among your merchandise. 25 The [A]ships of Tarshish were [a]the carriers for your merchandise.

And you were filled and
were very [b]glorious
In the heart of the seas.

26 "Your rowers have brought you
Into [A]great waters;
The [B]east wind has broken you
In the heart of the seas.
27 "Your wealth, your wares,
your merchandise,
Your sailors and your pilots,
Your repairers of seams, your
dealers in merchandise
And all your men of war who are in you,
With all your company that
is in your midst,
Will fall into the heart of the seas
On the day of your overthrow.
28 "At the sound of the cry of your pilots
The pasture lands will [A]shake.
29 "All who handle the oar,
The [A]sailors *and* all the pilots of the sea
Will come down from their ships;
They will stand on the land,
30 And they will [A]make their
voice heard over you
And will cry bitterly.
They will [B]cast dust on their heads,
They will [C]wallow in ashes.
31 "Also they will make themselves
[A]bald for you
And [B]gird themselves with sackcloth;
And they will [C]weep for you
in bitterness of soul
With bitter mourning.
32 "Moreover, in their wailing they will
take up a [A]lamentation for you
And lament over you:
'Who is like Tyre,
Like her who is silent in the
midst of the sea?
33 'When your wares went out
from the seas,
You satisfied many peoples;
With the [A]abundance of your wealth
and your merchandise
You enriched the kings of earth.
34 '[a]Now that you are [A]broken by the seas
In the depths of the waters,
Your [B]merchandise and
all your company
Have fallen in the midst of you.
35 'All the [A]inhabitants of the coastlands
Are appalled at you,
And their kings are horribly afraid;
They are troubled in countenance.
36 'The merchants among the
peoples [A]hiss at you;
You have become [a]terrified
And you [B]will cease to be forever.' " ' "

27:14 [A]Gen 10:3; Ezek 38:6 27:15 [a]Lit *the market of your hand* [A]Jer 25:23; Ezek 25:13; 27:20 [B]1 Kin 10:22; Rev 18:12 27:16 [a]Lit *works* [A]Judg 10:6; Is 7:1-8; Ezek 16:57 [B]Ezek 28:13 [C]Ezek 16:13, 18 27:17 [a]Heb *pannag* [A]Judg 11:33 27:18 [a]Lit *works* [A]Gen 14:15; Is 7:8; Jer 49:23; Ezek 47:16-18 27:19 [a]Or *with yarn* [b]Or *calamus* 27:20 [A]Gen 25:3 27:21 [a]Lit *customers of your hand* [A]Is 21:13 [B]Is 60:7 27:22 [A]Gen 10:7; Is 60:6; Ezek 38:13 [B]Gen 43:11; 1 Kin 10:2 27:23 [A]2 Kin 19:12; Is 37:12; Amos 1:5 27:24 [a]Or *violet* 27:25 [a]Lit *your travelers* [b]Lit *honored* [A]Is 2:16 27:26 [A]Ezek 26:19 [B]Ps 48:7; Jer 18:17; Acts 27:14 27:28 [A]Ezek 26:10, 15, 18 27:29 [A]Rev 18:17-19 27:30 [A]Is 23:1-6; Ezek 26:17 [B]1 Sam 4:12; 2 Sam 1:2; Lam 2:10; Rev 18:19 [C]Jer 6:26; Jon 3:6 27:31 [A]Is 15:2; Ezek 29:18 [B]Is 22:12; Ezek 7:18 [C]Is 16:9; 22:4 27:32 [A]Ezek 26:17; 27:2; 28:12 27:33 [A]Ezek 27:12, 18; 28:4, 5 27:34 [a]Lit *The time* [A]Ezek 26:12; 27:26, 27 [B]Zech 9:3, 4 27:35 [A]Is 23:6; Ezek 26:16 27:36 [a]Lit *terrors* [A]Jer 18:16; 19:8; 49:17; 50:13; Zeph 2:15 [B]Ps 37:10, 36

27:14 **Beth-togarmah.** Beth-togarmah is identified with Armenia in NE Asia Minor, which is modern Turkey.

27:15 **Dedan.** Probably Rhodes.

27:17 **Minnith.** An Ammonite town (Jdg 11:33).

27:18 **Helbon.** Today it is called Halbun, 13 mi. N of Damascus.

27:19 **Vedan.** A Danite area is not meant; but translators are not sure which areas are designated by this and Javan. **cassia.** A perfume.

27:21 **Kedar.** Refers to nomadic Bedouin tribes.

27:22 **Sheba and Raamah.** These were cities in the SW extremity of Arabia (Ge 10:7; 1Ch 1:9).

27:23 **Haran, Canneh, Eden.** All were Mesopotamian towns; Canneh may have been in northern Syria, the Calneh of Am 6:2, or the Caino of Is 10:9. **Asshur *and* Chilmad.** These were also in Mesopotamia.

27:25 **ships of Tarshish.** The large cargo carrying sea ships that sailed across the Mediterranean.

27:26, 27 **The east wind has broken.** This pictures Tyre's fall aptly as a shipwreck on the seas. The sea, the place of her glory, will be her grave. "The east wind" is a picture of Babylon in its power from the E (cf. 13:11–13).

27:28–35 **the cry.** This maintains the metaphor of Tyre as a ship and turns particularly to men lamenting her ruin, for their livelihood has been tied to the commerce she represents. Verses 30–32 describe common actions signifying mourning.

27:36 There will be some who scorn with malicious joy.

TYRE'S KING OVERTHROWN

28 The word of the LORD came again to me,
saying, 2 "Son of man, say to the [a]leader of
Tyre, 'Thus says the Lord [b]GOD,

"Because your heart is lifted up
And you have said, '[A]I am a god,
I sit in the seat of [c]gods
In the heart of the seas';
Yet you are a [B]man and not God,
Although you make your heart
like the heart of God—
3 Behold, you are wiser than [A]Daniel;
There is no secret that is a match for you.
4 "By your wisdom and understanding
You have acquired [A]riches for yourself
And have acquired gold and
silver for your treasuries.
5 "By your great wisdom, by your [A]trade
You have increased your riches
And your [B]heart is lifted up
because of your riches—

6 Therefore thus says the Lord GOD,

'Because you have [A]made your heart
Like the heart of God,
7 Therefore, behold, I will bring
[A]strangers upon you,
The [B]most ruthless of the nations.
And they will draw their swords
Against the beauty of your wisdom
And defile your splendor.
8 'They will bring you down to the pit,
And you will die the [A]death of
those who are slain
In the heart of the seas.
9 'Will you still say, "I am a god,"
In the presence of your slayer,
Though you are a man and not God,
In the hands of those who wound you?
10 'You will die the death of the [A]uncircumcised
By the hand of strangers,
For I have spoken!' declares
the Lord GOD!" ' "

11 Again the word of the LORD came to me saying,
12 "Son of man, [A]take up a lamentation over the king
of Tyre and say to him, 'Thus says the Lord GOD,

"You [a]had the seal of perfection,
Full of wisdom and perfect in beauty.
13 "You were in [A]Eden, the garden of God;
[B]Every precious stone was your covering:
The [C]ruby, the topaz and the diamond;
The beryl, the onyx and the jasper;
The lapis lazuli, the turquoise
and the emerald;
And the gold, the workmanship of
your [a,D]settings and [b]sockets,
Was in you.
On the day that you were created
They were prepared.
14 "You were the [A]anointed
cherub who [a]covers,
And I placed you *there*.
You were on the holy [B]mountain of God;
You walked in the midst of
the [C]stones of fire.
15 "You were [A]blameless in your ways
From the day you were created
Until [B]unrighteousness was found in you.

28:2 [a]Or *ruler, prince* [b]Heb *YHWH*, usually rendered *LORD*, and so throughout the ch [c]Or *God* [A]Is 14:14; 47:8; Ezek 28:9; 2 Thess 2:4 [B]Ps 9:20; 82:6, 7; Is 31:3; Ezek 28:9 28:3 [A]Dan 1:20; 2:20-23, 28; 5:11, 12 28:4 [A]Ezek 27:33; Zech 9:2, 3 28:5 [A]Ezek 27:12; Hos 12:7, 8 [B]Job 31:24, 25; Ps 52:7; Ezek 28:2; Hos 13:6 28:6 [A]Ex 9:17; Ezek 28:2 28:7 [A]Ezek 26:7 [B]Ezek 30:11; 31:12; 32:12; Hab 1:6-8 28:8 [A]Ezek 27:26, 27, 34 28:10 [A]1 Sam 17:26, 36; Ezek 31:18; 32:30 28:12 [a]Lit were *the one sealing a pattern* [A]Ezek 19:1; 26:17; 27:2 28:13 [a]Or *tambourines* [b]Or *flutes* [A]Gen 2:8; Is 51:3; Ezek 31:8, 9, 16; 36:35 [B]Ezek 27:16, 22 [C]Ex 28:17-20 [D]Is 24:8; 30:32 28:14 [a]Or *guards* [A]Ex 25:17-20; 30:26; 40:9; Ezek 28:16 [B]Ezek 20:40; 28:16 [C]Ezek 28:13, 16; Rev 18:16 28:15 [A]Ezek 27:3, 4; 28:3-6, 12 [B]Ezek 28:17, 18

28:1–19 This section concerning the king of Tyre is similar to Is 14:3–23 referring to the king of Babylon. In both passages, some of the language best fits Satan. Most likely, both texts primarily describe the human king who is being used by Satan, much like Peter when Jesus said to him, "Get behind Me, Satan!" (Mt 16:23). The judgment can certainly apply to Satan also.

28:2 to the leader of Tyre. Since "leader," or "prince," is sometimes used to mean "the king" (37:24, 25), the "leader" in v. 2 is the "king" in v. 12, Itto-baal II. The prophet is dealing with the spirit of Tyre more than just the king. This prophecy is dated shortly before the siege of Tyre by Nebuchadnezzar (585–573 B.C.). **I am a god.** Many ancient kings claimed to be a god, and acted as if they were (v. 6). When this king claimed to be a god, he was displaying the same proud attitude as the serpent who promised Adam and Eve they could be like God (Ge 3:5).

28:3–5 wiser than Daniel. This is said in sarcastic derision of the leader's own exaggerated claims. Here is an indicator that Daniel, who had been captive for years in Babylon, had become well known.

28:6–10 strangers upon you ... strangers. The reference is to invading Babylonians, and later the Greeks (cf. chap. 26). God was the true executioner.

28:11–19 This lament over "the king of Tyre" reached behind to the real supernatural source of wickedness, Satan. Cf. Mt 16:21–23, where Peter was rebuked by the Lord, as under Satanic control and motivation.

28:12 the seal of perfection. The Lord led Ezekiel to address the king as the one to be judged, but clearly the power behind him was Satan. This phrase must be associated with Satan as one perfect in angelic beauty before he rebelled against God. But, it can also relate to "perfection" in the same context of Tyre's enterprise, topmost in its trade to the ancient world (27:3, 4, 11), glorious in her seafaring efforts (27:24), and the crowning city (Is 23:8), i.e., "perfect" as Jerusalem also is said to be (16:14; La 2:15). **Full of wisdom.** This referred to Satan's wisdom as an angel and to Tyre's wisdom (skill) in trade (cf. 27:8, 9; 28:4).

28:13 You were in Eden. This could be Satan in the Garden of Eden (Ge 3:1–15), or it might refer to Tyre's king in a beautiful environment, a kind of Eden. **Every precious stone.** This depicts Satan's rich investiture (Ge 2:12), and/or Tyre's king possessing every beautiful stone as Solomon had (1Ki 10:10). **workmanship of your settings.** This could refer both to Satan's once being in charge of heavenly praise and to Tyre's beautiful musical instruments used in celebration (26:13). **you were created.** Satan, however, is more likely to have such wealth and beauty, wisdom, and perfection at his creation than this earthly king would have at his birth.

28:14 anointed cherub. This refers to Satan in his exalted privilege as an angel guarding (i.e., covering) God's throne, as cherubim guarded Eden (Ge 3:24). Satan originally had continuous and unrestricted access to the glorious presence of God. **I placed you.** This was true of both Satan, by God's sovereign permission, and Tyre's king. **You were on the holy mountain.** A high privilege is meant, whether referring to Satan before God in His kingdom (mountain, cf. Da 2:35), or Tyre's monarch described in a picturesque analogy, as Assyria can be described as a cedar in Lebanon (31:3) to convey a picture of towering height.

28:15 blameless in your ways. This verse was not completely true of the king, but it was accurate of Satan before he sinned. **Until unrighteousness was found in you.** Satan's sin of pride (cf. Is 14:14; 1Ti 3:6) is in view here.

16 "By the [A]abundance of your trade
[a]You were internally [B]filled with violence,
And you sinned;
Therefore I have cast you as profane
From the mountain of God.
And I have destroyed you,
O [b]covering cherub,
From the midst of the stones of fire.
17 "Your heart was lifted up
because of your [A]beauty;
You [B]corrupted your wisdom by
reason of your splendor.
I cast you to the ground;
I put you before [C]kings,
That they may see you.
18 "By the multitude of your iniquities,
In the unrighteousness of your trade
You profaned your sanctuaries.
Therefore I have brought [A]fire
from the midst of you;
It has consumed you,
And I have turned you to
[B]ashes on the earth
In the eyes of all who see you.
19 "All who know you among the peoples
Are appalled at you;
You have become [a,A]terrified
And you will cease to be [B]forever." ' "

JUDGMENT OF SIDON

20 And the word of the LORD came to me saying,
21 "Son of man, [A]set your face toward [B]Sidon, prophesy against her 22 and say, 'Thus says the Lord GOD,

"Behold, I am against you, O Sidon,
And I will [a]be glorified in your midst.
Then they will know that I am the LORD
when I [A]execute judgments in her,
And I will manifest My holiness in her.
23 "For [A]I will send pestilence to her
And blood to her streets,
And the [B]wounded will [a]fall in her midst
By the sword upon her on every side;
Then they will know that I am the LORD.

24 And there will be no more for the house of Israel
a [A]prickling brier or a painful thorn from any round
about them who scorned them; then they will know
that I am the Lord GOD."

ISRAEL REGATHERED

25 'Thus says the Lord GOD, "When I [A]gather the
house of Israel from the peoples among whom they
are scattered, and will manifest My holiness in them
in the sight of the nations, then they will [B]live in their
[a]land which I gave to My servant Jacob. 26 They will
[A]live in it securely; and they will [B]build houses, plant
vineyards and live securely when I [C]execute judgments upon all who scorn them round about them.
Then they will know that I am the LORD their God." ' "

JUDGMENT OF EGYPT

29 In the [A]tenth year, in the tenth *month,* on
the twelfth of the month, the word of the
LORD came to me saying, 2 "Son of man, set your
face against [A]Pharaoh king of Egypt and prophesy
against him and against all [B]Egypt. 3 Speak and say,
'Thus says the Lord [a]GOD,

"Behold, I am against you,
Pharaoh king of Egypt,
The great [b,A]monster that lies in
the midst of his [c]rivers,
That [B]has said, 'My Nile is mine,
and I myself have made *it.*'
4 "I will put [A]hooks in your jaws
And make the fish of your [a]rivers
cling to your scales.
And I will bring you up out of
the midst of your [a]rivers,
And all the fish of your [a]rivers
will cling to your scales.

28:16 [a]Lit *They filled your midst* [b]Or *guardian* [A]Ezek 27:12 [B]Ezek 8:17; Hab 2:8, 17 28:17 [A]Ezek 27:3, 4; 28:7 [B]Is 19:11 [C]Ezek 26:16 28:18 [A]Amos 1:9, 10 [B]Mal 4:3 28:19 [a]Lit *terrors* [A]Ezek 26:21; 27:36 [B]Jer 51:64 28:21 [A]Ezek 6:2; 25:2 [B]Gen 10:15, 19; Is 23:2, 4; Ezek 27:8 28:22 [a]Or *glorify Myself* [A]Ezek 28:26; 30:19 28:23 [a]Or *be judged* [A]Ezek 38:22 [B]Jer 51:52 28:24 [A]Num 33:55; Josh 23:13; Is 55:13; Ezek 2:6 28:25 [a]Lit *ground* [A]Ps 106:47; Is 11:12, 13; Jer 32:37; Ezek 20:41; 34:13, 27 [B]Jer 23:8; 27:11 28:26 [A]Jer 23:6; Ezek 34:25-28; 38:8 [B]Jer 32:15, 43, 44; Amos 9:13, 14 [C]Ezek 25:11; 28:22 29:1 [A]Ezek 26:1; 29:17; 30:20 29:2 [A]Jer 44:30 [B]Is 19:1-17; Jer 46:2-26; Ezek 30:1-32:32 29:3 [a]Heb *YHWH*, usually rendered *LORD*, and so throughout the ch [b]Lit *tannim* [c]Or *Nile* [A]Is 27:1; Ezek 32:2 [B]Ezek 29:9; 30:12 29:4 [a]Or *Nile* [A]2 Kin 19:28; Ezek 38:4

28:16 The description transitions to feature the king of Tyre, describing his demise, as he followed the pattern of Satan himself.

28:17–19 I put you before kings. It would be difficult to relate this to Satan. The earthly king of Tyre, in his downfall, would be knocked or cast to the ground, cut down, and lie before the gaze of other kings. From Is 23:17 there is the implication of a revival under Persian rule (Ne 13:16). Two hundred and fifty years after Nebuchadnezzar, Tyre was strong enough to hold off Alexander for 7 years. The Romans made it a capital of the province. Gradually it disappeared, and its location is not prominent.

28:21 Sidon. Sidon (vv. 20–24) is a sister seaport to Tyre in Phoenicia, 23 mi. N. Even in the time of the judges (Jdg 10:6), the corrupting influence of this place had begun. It was the headquarters for Baal worship.

28:22, 23 judgments in her. God is to bring bloodshed and pestilence on people there, probably at the time He brings an invasion against Tyre.

28:24 no more .... prickling brier. This is a summary of the judgment scenarios so far revealed (chaps. 25–28). The enemies of Israel would be so devastated by God that 1) they would no longer be pestering Israel, and 2) they would see that the God who judges them is the true God of Israel.

28:25, 26 When I gather. In this brief excursus of hope, God promised to restore Israel to their land (cf. chaps. 34, 36–39; Is 65:21; Jer 30–33; Am 9:14, 15). This looks to Messiah's earthly kingdom.

29:1 the tenth year. 587 B.C. is the 10th year after Jehoiachin's deportation. It is a year and two days after Nebuchadnezzar had come to Jerusalem (24:1, 2; 2Ki 25:1) and 7 months before its destruction (2Ki 25:3–8). This is the first of 7 oracles against Egypt (cf. 29:17; 30:1; 30:20; 31:1; 32:1; 32:17).

29:2 against all Egypt. Cf. Is 19; Jer 46:1–26. Egypt was to fall, even though it could be pictured as a water monster (vv. 3–5), a towering tree like Assyria (31:3), a young lion (32:2), and a sea monster (32:2–8). The judgment looks ahead to 570 B.C. when the Greeks of Cyrene defeated Pharaoh (Apries) Hophra and 568/67 B.C. when Babylon conquered Egypt.

29:3 great monster. Most likely the crocodile is the figure used for the king. Crocodiles were worshiped by the Egyptians, and lived in their rivers. "Rahab" is a general term used for a monster which often symbolized Egypt. *See notes on Pss 87:4; 89:10; Is 30:7.*

29:4 fish of your rivers. This figuratively represents the people who followed Pharaoh and who were a part of God's judgment on Egypt as a whole (vv. 5, 6a).

5 "I will [A]abandon you to the wilderness,
you and all the fish of your [a]rivers;
You will fall on the [b]open field; you will
not be brought together or [c,B]gathered.
I have given you for [C]food to the beasts of
the earth and to the birds of the sky.
6 "Then all the inhabitants of Egypt
will know that I am the LORD,
Because they have been *only* a [A]staff
made of reed to the house of Israel.
7 "When they took hold of you
with the hand,
You [A]broke and tore all their [a]hands;
And when they leaned on you,
You broke and made all
their loins [b]quake."

8 'Therefore thus says the Lord GOD, "Behold, I will
[A]bring upon you a sword and I will cut off from you
man and beast. 9 The [A]land of Egypt will become a
desolation and waste. Then they will know that I
am the LORD.
Because [a]you [B]said, 'The Nile is mine, and I have
made *it*,' 10 therefore, behold, I am [A]against you and
against your [a]rivers, and I will make the land of Egypt
an utter waste and desolation, from Migdol *to* Syene
and even to the border of [b]Ethiopia. 11 A man's foot will
[A]not pass through it, and the foot of a beast will not
pass through it, and it will not be inhabited for forty
years. 12 So I will make the land of Egypt a desolation
in the [A]midst of desolated lands. And her cities, in the
midst of cities that are laid waste, will be desolate
forty years; and I will [B]scatter the Egyptians among
the nations and disperse them among the lands."
13 'For thus says the Lord GOD, "At the end of forty
years I will [A]gather the Egyptians from the peoples
[a]among whom they were scattered. 14 I will turn the
fortunes of Egypt and make them return to the land
of [A]Pathros, to the land of their origin, and there they
will be a lowly kingdom. 15 It will be the [A]lowest of
the kingdoms, and it will never again lift itself up
above the nations. And I will make them so small
that they will not [B]rule over the nations. 16 And it
will never again be the [A]confidence of the house
of Israel, [a,B]bringing to mind the iniquity of their
having turned [b]to Egypt. Then they will know that
I am the Lord GOD."'"
17 Now in the [A]twenty-seventh year, in the first
month, on the first of the month, the word of the
LORD came to me saying, 18 "Son of man, [A]Nebu-
chadnezzar king of Babylon made his army labor
[a]hard against Tyre; every head was made [B]bald
and every shoulder was rubbed bare. But he and
his army had no wages from Tyre for the labor that
he had [b]performed against it." 19 Therefore thus
says the Lord GOD, "Behold, I [A]will give the land of
Egypt to Nebuchadnezzar king of Babylon. And he
will carry off her [a,B]wealth and capture her spoil
and seize her plunder; and it will be wages for his
army. 20 I have given him the land of Egypt *for* his
labor which he [a,A]performed, because they acted for
Me," declares the Lord GOD.
21 "On that day I will make a [A]horn sprout for the
house of Israel, and I will [a,B]open your mouth in their
midst. Then they will know that I am the LORD."

LAMENT OVER EGYPT

30 The word of the LORD came again to me
saying, 2 "Son of man, prophesy and say,
'Thus says the Lord [a]GOD,

"[A]Wail, 'Alas for the day!'
3 "For the day is near,
Even [A]the day of the LORD is near;
It will be a day of [B]clouds,
A time *of doom* for the nations.

29:5 [a]Or *Nile* [b]Lit *faces of the field* [c]Or with several mss and Targum, *buried* [A]Ezek 32:4-6 [B]Jer 8:2; 25:33 [C]Jer 7:33; 34:20; Ezek 39:4 29:6 [A]2 Kin 18:21; Is 36:6 29:7 [a]So with some ancient versions; M.T. *shoulders* [b]Lit *stand* [A]2 Kin 18:21; Is 36:6; Ezek 17:15-17 29:8 [A]Jer 46:13; Ezek 14:17 29:9 [a]Lit *he* [A]Ezek 29:10-12; 30:7, 8, 13-19 [B]Prov 16:18; 18:12; Ezek 29:3 29:10 [a]Or *Nile* [b]Lit *Cush* [A]Ezek 13:8; 21:3; 26:3; 29:3 29:11 [A]Jer 43:11, 12; 46:19; Ezek 32:13 29:12 [A]Jer 25:15-19; 27:6-11; Ezek 30:7 [B]Jer 46:19; Ezek 30:23, 26 29:13 [a]Lit *where* [A]Is 19:22; Jer 46:26 29:14 [A]Is 11:11; Jer 44:1, 15; Ezek 30:14 29:15 [A]Ezek 17:6, 14; 30:13; Zech 10:11 [B]Ezek 31:2; 32:2; Nah 3:8-10 29:16 [a]Lit *causing to remember* [b]Lit *after them* [A]Is 20:5; 30:1-3; 31:1; 36:6; Ezek 17:15; 29:6, 7 [B]Is 64:9; Jer 14:10; Ezek 21:23; Hos 8:13 29:17 [A]Ezek 24:1; 26:1; 29:1; 30:20; 40:1 29:18 [a]Lit *a great labor* [b]Lit *labored* [A]Jer 25:9; 27:6; Ezek 26:7-12 [B]Jer 48:37; Ezek 27:31 29:19 [a]Or *multitude* [A]Ezek 30:10, 24, 25; 32:11 [B]Jer 43:10-13; Ezek 30:14 29:20 [a]Lit *labored* [A]Is 10:6, 7; 45:1-3; Jer 25:9 29:21 [a]Lit *give you an opening of the mouth* [A]1 Sam 2:10; Ps 92:10; 132:17 [B]Ezek 3:27; 24:27; 33:22; Amos 3:7, 8; Luke 21:15 30:2 [a]Heb *YHWH*, usually rendered *LORD*, and so throughout the ch [A]Is 13:6; 15:2; Ezek 21:12; Joel 1:5, 11, 13 30:3 [A]Ezek 7:19; 13:5; Joel 1:15; 2:1; Obad 15 [B]Ezek 30:18; 32:7; 34:12

29:6 a staff *made* of reed. The Israelites had depended on Egyptians in military alliances as people lean on a staff that gives way, failing them. Egypt had betrayed the confidence of Israel as God said they would (cf. Jer 17:5, 7). Because Israel never should have trusted Egypt does not lessen Egypt's judgment.

29:9 The Nile. The Nile River was the water supply for all Egypt's crops. *See note on v. 19.*

29:10 from Migdol *to* Syene. This covered the entirety of Egypt, since Migdol (Ex 14:2) was in the N and Syene *in* the southern border of "Ethiopia."

29:11, 12 not be inhabited for forty years. Although difficult to pinpoint, one possibility is that this period was when Babylon, under Nebuchadnezzar, reigned supreme in Egypt (vv. 19, 20), from ca. 568/67 B.C. to 525 B.C. until Cyrus gained Persian control.

29:13–16 I will gather the Egyptians. Egypt regained normalcy as is currently true, but never again reached the pinnacle of international prominence she once enjoyed.

29:17 the twenty-seventh year. This is 571/70 B.C. as counted from the captivity of Jehoiachin in 597 B.C., about 17 years after the prophecy in vv. 1–16.

29:18 labor … against Tyre. In ca. 585–573 B.C., Nebuchadnezzar besieged Tyre for 13 years before subduing the city (cf. Eze 26:1–28:19). Tyrians retreated to an island bastion out in the sea and survived, not giving Babylon full satisfaction in spoils ("wages") equal to such long struggle.

29:19 I will give the land of Egypt. To make up for Babylon's lack of sufficient reward from Tyre, God allowed a Babylonian conquest of Egypt in 568/67 B.C. Babylon's army had worked as an instrument which God used to bring down Egypt.

29:21 I will make a horn sprout. Cf. 23:25, 26. God caused Israel's power to return and restored her authority as the power in an animal's horn (cf. 1Sa 2:1). Though other nations subdued her, her latter end in messianic times will be blessed. **I will open your mouth.** Most likely this refers to the day when Ezekiel's writings would be understood by looking back at their fulfillment. His muteness had already ceased in 586/585 B.C. when Jerusalem fell (cf. 33:21, 22).

30:3 the day of the LORD is near. This is a common expression for God's judgment, especially His future judgment (cf. Joel 1:15; 2:1, 11; 3:14; Zec 14:1; 1Th 5:2; 2Th 2:2; 2Pe 3:10). God's judgment "day" for Egypt embraces a near fulfillment in Babylon's 568/67 invasion (v. 10; 32:11), as well as the distant day of the Lord in the future tribulation period when God calls all nations to judgment (Da 11:42, 43). *See note on Is 2:12.*

4 "A sword will come upon Egypt,
And anguish will be in [a]Ethiopia;
When the slain fall in Egypt,
They [A]take away her [b]wealth,
And her foundations are torn down.

5 [a]Ethiopia, Put, Lud, all [b,A]Arabia, [c]Libya and the
[d]people of the land [e]that is in league will fall with
them by the sword."

6 'Thus says the LORD,
"Indeed, those who support [A]Egypt will fall
And the pride of her power
will come down;
From Migdol *to* Syene
They will fall within her by the sword,"
Declares the Lord GOD.
7 "They will be desolate
In the [A]midst of the desolated lands;
And her cities will be
In the midst of the devastated cities.
8 "And they will [A]know that I am the LORD,
When I set a [B]fire in Egypt
And all her helpers are broken.

9 On that day [A]messengers will go forth from Me in
ships to frighten [B]secure [a]Ethiopia; and [C]anguish
will be on them as on the day of Egypt; for behold,
it comes!"
10 'Thus says the Lord GOD,

"[A]I will also make the [a]hordes of Egypt cease
By the hand of Nebuchadnezzar
king of Babylon.
11 "He and his people with him,
[A]The most ruthless of the nations,
Will be brought in to destroy the land;
And they will draw their
swords against Egypt
And fill the land with the slain.
12 "Moreover, I will make the [A]Nile canals dry
And [B]sell the land into the
hands of evil men.
And I will make the land desolate
And [a]all that is in it,
By the hand of strangers; I the
LORD have spoken."

13 'Thus says the Lord GOD,

"I will also [A]destroy the idols
And make the [a]images cease
from [b,B]Memphis.
And there will no longer be a
prince in the land of Egypt;
And I will put fear in the land of Egypt.
14 "I will make [A]Pathros desolate,
Set a fire in [B]Zoan
And execute judgments on [a,C]Thebes.
15 "I will pour out My wrath on [a]Sin,
The stronghold of Egypt;
I will also cut off the hordes of [b]Thebes.
16 "I will set a fire in Egypt;
[a]Sin will writhe in anguish,
[b]Thebes will be breached
And [c]Memphis *will have* [d]distresses daily.
17 "The young men of [a,A]On and of Pi-beseth
Will fall by the sword,
And [b]the women will go into captivity.
18 "In [A]Tehaphnehes the day will [a]be [B]dark
When I [C]break there the yoke bars of Egypt.
Then the pride of her power
will cease in her;
A cloud will cover her,
And her daughters will go into captivity.
19 "Thus I will [A]execute judgments on Egypt,
And they will know that I am the LORD." ' "

VICTORY FOR BABYLON

20 In the [A]eleventh year, in the first *month,* on the
seventh of the month, the word of the LORD came
to me saying, 21 "Son of man, I have [A]broken the
arm of Pharaoh king of Egypt; and, behold, it has
not been [B]bound up [a]for healing [b]or wrapped with
a bandage, that it may be strong to hold the sword.
22 Therefore thus says the Lord GOD, 'Behold, I am

30:4 [a]Lit *Cush* [b]Or *multitude* [A]Ezek 29:19 30:5 [a]Lit *Cush* [b]Or *the mixed people* [c]Or *Cub* [d]Lit *sons* [e]Lit *of the covenant* [A]Jer 25:20, 24 30:6 [A]Is 20:3-6 30:7 [A]Jer 25:18-26; Ezek 29:12 30:8 [A]Ps 58:11; Ezek 29:6, 9, 16 [B]Ezek 22:31; 30:14, 16; Amos 1:4, 7, 10, 12, 14 30:9 [a]Lit *Cush* [A]Is 18:1, 2 [B]Is 47:8; Ezek 38:11; 39:6 [C]Is 19:17; 23:5; Ezek 32:9, 10 30:10 [a]Or *people;* lit *crowd,* and so throughout the ch [A]Ezek 29:19 30:11 [A]Ezek 28:7 30:12 [a]Lit *her fullness* [A]Ezek 29:3, 9 [B]Is 19:4 30:13 [a]Or *futile ones* [b]Or *Noph* [A]Is 2:18 [B]Is 19:13; Jer 2:16; 44:1; 46:14; Ezek 30:16 30:14 [a]Or *No* [A]Is 11:11; Jer 44:1, 15; Ezek 29:14 [B]Ps 78:12, 43; Is 19:11, 13 [C]Jer 46:25; Ezek 30:15, 16; Nah 3:8 30:15 [a]Or *Pelusium* [b]Or *No* 30:16 [a]Or *Pelusium* [b]Or *No* [c]Or *Noph* [d]Or *adversaries* 30:17 [a]Or *Aven* [b]Lit *they* [A]Gen 41:45; 46:20 30:18 [a]So with many mss and ancient versions; M.T. *restrain* [A]Jer 43:8-13 [B]Ezek 30:3 [C]Lev 26:13; Is 10:27; Jer 27:2; 28:10, 13; 30:8; Ezek 34:27 30:19 [A]Ps 9:16; Ezek 5:8, 15; 25:11; 30:14 30:20 [A]Ezek 26:1; 29:1, 17; 31:1 30:21 [a]Lit *to give healing* [b]Lit *to put a bandage, to wrap it* [A]Ps 10:15; 37:17; Ezek 30:24 [B]Jer 30:13; 46:11

30:5 **Ethiopia, Put, Lud.** *See notes on 27:10, 11 and 29:10.* **Libya.** Or, Cub, an unidentified nation, along with the "people of the land that is in league." These also may have been mercenaries in Egypt's army, like the previous ones in this verse.

30:6 **Migdol *to* Syene.** *See note on 29:10.*

30:8 **helpers.** All Egypt's alliances and their arms will be useless in the day of God's judgment.

30:9 Apparently, the Egyptians will flee the horrors to Ethiopia and increase that nation's fear of its own inevitable judgment.

30:10, 11 Nebuchadnezzar was God's instrument.

30:12 **canals dry.** Apart from the Nile and its branches, Egypt was a barren desert. Her life depended on an annual inundation of the land by the flooding Nile.

30:14 **Pathros.** The large region S of Memphis. **Zoan.** This key city of the Nile Delta's eastern portion was called Tanis by Greeks.

30:15 **Sin.** The name referred to ancient Pelusium, a key city at the tip of the Nile's eastern arm near the Mediterranean Sea. Since "Thebes" and "Sin" were at opposite borders of Egypt and so many cities are named, the passage speaks of judgment on the entire land.

30:17 **Pi-beseth.** The city was on the NE branch of the Nile where cats were mummified in honor of the cat-headed goddess, Ugastet.

30:18 **Tehaphnehes.** This city, named after the Egyptian queen, was a residence of the pharaohs.

30:20 **the eleventh year.** Ca. 587 B.C., counted from the deportation of Judah in 597 B.C.

30:21 **I have broken the arm.** God figuratively depicted His act of taking power from Egypt through Nebuchadnezzar, resulting in defeat and dispersion (vv. 23, 26).

30:22 **break his arms.** Both the defeat of Pharaoh Hophra (cf. Jer 37:5ff.) and the earlier defeat of Pharaoh Neco at Carchemish (cf. 2Ki 24:7; Jer 46:2) are in view.

[A]against Pharaoh king of Egypt and will break his
arms, both the strong and the [B]broken; and I will
make the sword [C]fall from his hand. 23 I will [A]scat-
ter the Egyptians among the nations and disperse
them among the lands. 24 For I will [A]strengthen the
arms of the king of Babylon and put [B]My sword in
his hand; and I will break the arms of Pharaoh, so
that he will groan before him with the groanings of
a wounded man. 25 Thus I will strengthen the arms
of the king of Babylon, but the arms of Pharaoh will
fall. Then they will know that I am the LORD, when I
put My sword into the hand of the king of Babylon
and he [A]stretches it out against the land of Egypt.
26 When I scatter the Egyptians among the nations
and disperse them among the lands, then they will
know that I am the LORD.' "

PHARAOH WARNED OF ASSYRIA'S FATE

31 In the [A]eleventh year, in the third *month,* on
the first of the month, the word of the LORD
came to me saying, 2 "Son of man, say to Pharaoh
king of Egypt and to his [A]hordes,

'Whom are you like in your greatness?
3 'Behold, Assyria *was* a [A]cedar in Lebanon
With beautiful branches and forest shade,
And [a,B]very high,
And its top was among the [b]clouds.
4 'The [A]waters made it grow, the
[a]deep made it high.
With its rivers it continually [b]extended
all around its planting place,
And sent out its channels to all
the trees of the field.
5 'Therefore [A]its height was loftier
than all the trees of the field
And its boughs became many
and its branches long
Because of [B]many waters [a]as
it spread them out.
6 'All the [A]birds of the heavens
nested in its boughs,
And under its branches all the
beasts of the field gave birth,
And all great nations lived under its shade.
7 'So it was beautiful in its greatness,
in the length of its branches;
For its [a]roots extended to many waters.
8 'The [A]cedars in [B]God's garden
[a]could not match it;
The [b]cypresses [a]could not
compare with its boughs,
And the plane trees [c]could not
match its branches.
No tree in [B]God's garden [a]could
compare with it in its beauty.
9 'I made it beautiful with the
multitude of its branches,
And all the trees of [A]Eden, which were in
the [A]garden of God, were jealous of it.

10 'Therefore thus says the Lord [a]GOD, "Because
[b]it is high in stature and has set its top among the
[c]clouds, and its [A]heart is haughty in its loftiness,
11 therefore I will give it into the hand of a [a,A]despot of
the nations; he will thoroughly deal with it. According to its wickedness I have [B]driven it away. 12 [A]Alien
[B]tyrants of the nations have cut it down and left it;
on the [C]mountains and in all the valleys its branches
have fallen and its boughs have been broken in all
the ravines of the land. And all the peoples of the
earth have [D]gone down from its shade and left it.
13 On its ruin all the [A]birds of the heavens will dwell,
and all the beasts of the field will be on its *fallen*
branches 14 so that all the trees by the waters may not
be exalted in their stature, nor set their top among
the [a]clouds, nor their [b]well-watered mighty ones
stand *erect* in their height. For they have all been
given over to death, to the [A]earth beneath, among
the sons of men, with those who go down to the pit."
15 'Thus says the Lord GOD, "On the day when it
went down to Sheol I [A]caused lamentations; I closed
the [a]deep over it and held back its rivers. And *its*
many waters were stopped up, and I made Lebanon
[b]mourn for it, and all the trees of the field wilted
away on account of it. 16 I made the nations [A]quake
at the sound of its fall when I made it [B]go down to
Sheol with those who go down to the pit; and all the
[a]well-watered trees of Eden, the choicest and best
of [C]Lebanon, were [D]comforted in the earth beneath.

30:22 [A]Jer 46:25; Ezek 29:3 [B]2 Kin 24:7; Jer 37:7 [C]Jer 46:21 30:23 [A]Ezek 29:12; 30:17, 18, 26 30:24 [A]Neh 6:9; Is 45:1, 5; Ezek 30:10, 25; Zech 10:12 [B]Ezek 30:11, 25; Zeph 2:12 30:25 [A]Josh 8:18; 1 Chr 21:16; Is 5:25 31:1 [A]Jer 52:5, 6; Ezek 30:20; 32:1 31:2 [A]Ezek 29:19; 30:10; Nah 3:9 31:3 [a]Lit *high of stature* [b]So Gr; M.T. *thick boughs* [A]Is 10:33, 34; Ezek 17:3, 4, 22; 31:16; Dan 4:10, 20-23 [B]Is 10:33; Ezek 31:5, 10 31:4 [a]I.e. subterranean waters [b]Lit *was going* [A]Ezek 17:5, 8; Rev 17:1, 15 31:5 [a]Lit *in its sending forth* [A]Dan 4:11 [B]Ps 1:3; Ezek 17:5 31:6 [A]Ezek 17:23; 31:13; Dan 4:12, 21; Matt 13:32 31:7 [a]Lit *root was* 31:8 [a]Lit *did* [b]Or *Phoenician junipers* [c]Lit *were not like* [A]Ps 80:10; Ezek 31:3 [B]Gen 2:8, 9; 13:10; Is 51:3; Ezek 28:13; 31:16, 18 31:9 [A]Gen 2:8, 9; 13:10; Is 51:3; Ezek 28:13; 31:16, 18 31:10 [a]Heb *YHWH*, usually rendered *LORD*, and so throughout the ch [b]Lit *you are* [c]Or *thick boughs* [A]2 Chr 32:25; Is 10:12; 14:13, 14; Ezek 28:17; Dan 5:20 31:11 [a]Or *mighty one* [A]Ezek 30:10, 11; 32:11, 12; Dan 5:18, 19 [B]Deut 18:12; Nah 3:18 31:12 [A]Ezek 7:21; 28:7; 30:12; Hab 1:6 [B]Ezek 28:7; 30:11; 32:12 [C]Ezek 32:5; 35:8 [D]Ezek 31:17; Dan 4:14; Nah 3:17, 18 31:13 [A]Is 18:6; Ezek 29:5; 31:6; 32:4 31:14 [a]Or *thick boughs* [b]Lit *drinkers of water* [A]Num 16:30, 33; Ps 63:9; Ezek 26:20; 31:18; 32:24; Amos 9:2; Jon 2:2, 6; Eph 4:9 31:15 [a]I.e. subterranean waters [b]Lit *be darkened* [A]Ezek 32:7; Nah 2:10 31:16 [a]Lit *drinkers of water* [A]Ezek 26:15; 27:28; Hag 2:7 [B]Is 14:15; Ezek 32:18 [C]Is 14:8; Hab 2:17 [D]Ezek 14:22, 23; 32:31

30:26 People often don't learn that God is Lord until judgment falls.

31:1 the eleventh year. 587 B.C. Two months after the oracle of 30:20–26.

31:2–18 Whom are you like … ? Ezekiel filled this chapter with a metaphor/analogy comparing Egypt to a huge tree that dominates a forest to a king/nation that dominates the world (cf. 17:22–24; Da 4:1–12, 19–27). He reasoned that just as a strong tree like Assyria (v. 3) fell (ca. 609 B.C.), so will Egypt (ca. 568 B.C.). If the Egyptians tend to be proud and feel invincible, let them remember how powerful Assyria had fallen already.

31:3 cedar in Lebanon. The trees were as high as 80 ft. and were an example of supreme power and domination, particularly the great cedars which grew in the mountains N of Israel.

31:8, 9 God's garden … trees of Eden. (36:35; Ge 13:10; Is 51:3; Joel 2:3). Since Assyria was in the area of the Garden of Eden, Ezekiel used the ultimate of gardens as a point of relative reference by which to describe tree-like Assyria.

31:10 Because it is high in stature. Ezekiel shifted from the historical illustration of Assyria's pride and fall to the reality of Egypt. God was using Assyria to teach the nations the folly of earthly power and might.

31:14–16 the pit. The scene shifts from earth and the garden of God to the grave (cf. 32:18), as God again refers to the destruction of Assyria and all her allies ("all the trees," "all the well-watered trees").

17 They also [A]went down with it to Sheol to those who
were [B]slain by the sword; and those who were its
[a]strength lived [C]under its shade among the nations.
18 "To which among the trees of Eden are you
thus [a]equal in glory and greatness? Yet you will be
brought down with the trees of Eden to the earth
beneath; you will lie in the midst of the [A]uncircumcised, with those who were slain by the sword. [B]So
is Pharaoh and all his hordes!" ' declares the Lord
GOD."

LAMENT OVER PHARAOH AND EGYPT

32 In the [A]twelfth year, in the twelfth *month,* on
the first of the month, the word of the LORD
came to me saying, 2 "Son of man, take up a [A]lamentation over Pharaoh king of Egypt and say to him,

'You [a]compared yourself to a
young [B]lion of the nations,
Yet you are like the [C]monster in the seas;
And you [D]burst forth in your rivers
And muddied the waters with your feet
And [b]fouled their rivers.' "

3 Thus says the Lord [a]GOD,

"Now I will [A]spread My net over you
With a company of many peoples,
And they shall lift you up in My net.
4 "I will leave you on the land;
I will cast you on the [a]open field.
And I will cause all the [A]birds of
the heavens to dwell on you,
And I will satisfy the beasts of
the whole earth [b]with you.
5 "I will lay your flesh [A]on the mountains
And fill the valleys with your refuse.
6 "I will also make the land drink the
discharge of your [A]blood
As far as the mountains,
And the ravines will be full of you.
7 "And when *I* [A]extinguish you,
I will [B]cover the heavens and
darken their [C]stars;
I will cover the [D]sun with a cloud
And the moon will not give its light.
8 "All the shining [A]lights in the heavens
I will darken over you
And will set darkness on your land,"
Declares the Lord GOD.

9 "I will also [A]trouble the hearts of many peoples
when I [B]bring your destruction among the nations,
into lands which you have not known. 10 I will make
many peoples [A]appalled at you, and their kings will
be horribly afraid of you when I brandish My sword
before them; and [B]they will tremble every moment,
every man for his own life, on the day of your fall."
11 For [A]thus says the Lord GOD, "The sword of
the king of Babylon will come upon you. 12 By the
swords of the mighty ones I will cause your hordes
to fall; all of them are [A]tyrants of the nations,

And they will [B]devastate
the pride of Egypt,
And all its hordes will be destroyed.
13 "I will also destroy all its cattle
from beside many waters;
And [A]the foot of man will not
muddy them anymore
And the hoofs of beasts will
not muddy them.
14 "Then I will make their waters settle
And will cause their rivers to run like oil,"
Declares the Lord GOD.
15 "When I make the land of
Egypt a [A]desolation,
And the land is destitute of
that which filled it,
When I smite all those who live in it,
Then they shall [B]know that I am the LORD.

16 This is a [A]lamentation and they shall [a]chant it.
The daughters of the nations shall [a]chant it. Over
Egypt and over all her hordes they shall [a]chant it,"
declares the Lord GOD.
17 In the [A]twelfth year, on the [A]fifteenth of the
month, the word of the LORD came to me saying,
18 "Son of man, [A]wail for the hordes of Egypt and
[B]bring it down, her and the daughters of the powerful nations, to the [C]nether world, with those who
go down to the pit;

31:17 [a]Lit *arm* [A]Ps 9:17 [B]Ezek 32:20f [C]Ezek 31:3, 6; Dan 4:12 31:18 [a]Lit *like* [A]Jer 9:25, 26; Ezek 28:10; 32:19, 21 [B]Ps 52:7; Matt 13:19 32:1 [A]Ezek 30:20; 31:1; 32:17; 33:21 32:2 [a]Or *were like* [b]Lit *fouled by stamping* [A]Ezek 19:1; 27:2; 28:12; 32:16 [B]Jer 4:7; Ezek 19:2-6; Nah 2:11-13 [C]Is 27:1; Ezek 29:3 [D]Jer 46:7, 8 32:3 [a]Heb *YHWH*, usually rendered *LORD*, and so throughout the ch [A]Ezek 12:13 32:4 [a]Lit *surface of the field* [b]Lit *from* [A]Is 18:6 32:5 [A]Ezek 31:12 32:6 [A]Ex 7:17; Is 34:3, 7; Ezek 35:6; Rev 14:20 32:7 [A]Job 18:5, 6; Prov 13:9 [B]Ex 10:21-23; Is 34:4; Ezek 30:3, 18; 34:12 [C]Is 13:10 [D]Joel 2:2, 31; 3:15; Amos 8:9; Matt 24:29; Mark 13:24f; Luke 21:25; Rev 6:12; 8:12 32:8 [A]Gen 1:14 32:9 [A]Ezek 27:29-32; 28:19; Rev 18:10-15 [B]Ex 15:14-16 32:10 [A]Ezek 27:35 [B]Ezek 26:16 32:11 [A]Jer 46:26 32:12 [A]Ezek 28:7 [B]Ezek 28:19 32:13 [A]Ezek 29:11 32:15 [A]Ps 107:33, 34; Ezek 29:12, 19, 20 [B]Ex 7:5; 14:4, 18; Ps 9:16; 83:17, 18; Ezek 6:7; 30:19, 26 32:16 [a]Or *lament* [A]2 Sam 1:17; 3:33, 34; 2 Chr 35:25; Jer 9:17; Ezek 26:17; 32:2 32:17 [A]Ezek 31:1; 32:1; 33:21 32:18 [A]Is 16:9; Ezek 21:6; 32:2, 16; Mic 1:8 [B]Jer 1:10; Ezek 43:3; Hos 6:5 [C]Ezek 31:14, 16, 18; 32:24

31:18 To which ... are you thus equal ...? Egypt, like all the other great nations, including Assyria, will be felled by God.

32:1 the twelfth year. 585 B.C., 12 years from the deportation of Judah in 597 B.C.

32:2 a young lion. The picture describes Egypt's deadly energetic stalking power in her dealings with other nations. She was also violent like the crocodile, or "great monster" (cf. 29:3).

32:3–6 spread My net over you. God will entrap Egypt as a net ensnares a lion or crocodile, using "many peoples" (soldiers). Egyptians will fall, their corpses gorge birds and beasts, and their blood soaks the earth and waters.

32:7, 8 extinguish you. This is likely a reference to Pharaoh, whose life and power are extinguished, and all the rest of the leaders and people basking in his light are plunged into darkness.

32:11, 12 The sword of ... Babylon. This is the definite identification of the conqueror, as in 30:10 when Nebuchadnezzar is actually named (cf. 21:19; 29:19; Jer 46:26).

32:13, 14 With no men or beasts to stir up the mud in the Nile and its branches, the water will be clear and flow smoothly. Since the river was the center of all life, this pictures the devastation graphically.

32:17 the twelfth year. 585 B.C. reckoned from 597 B.C.

32:18 the powerful nations. All other countries which have been conquered. **the pit.** Refers to Sheol/grave (cf. 31:14–16).

19 'Whom do you surpass in beauty?
Go down and make your bed
with the [A]uncircumcised.'

20 They shall fall in the midst of those who are slain
by the sword. [a]She is given over to the sword; they
have [A]drawn her and all her hordes away. 21 The
[A]strong among the mighty ones shall speak of him
and his helpers from the midst of Sheol, 'They have
gone down, they lie still, the uncircumcised, slain
by the sword.'
22 "[A]Assyria is there and all her company; [a]her
graves are round about [b]her. All of them are slain,
fallen by the sword, 23 whose [A]graves are set in the
remotest parts of the pit and her company is round
about her grave. All of them are slain, fallen by the
sword, who [a]spread terror in the land of the living.
24 "[A]Elam is there and all her hordes around her
grave; all of them slain, fallen by the sword, who
went down uncircumcised to the [B]lower parts of
the earth, who instilled their terror in the [C]land of
the living and [D]bore their disgrace with those who
went down to the pit. 25 They have made a [A]bed for
her among the slain with all her hordes. Her graves
are around it, they are all uncircumcised, slain by
the sword (although their terror was [a]instilled in
the land of the living), and they bore their disgrace
with those who go down to the pit; [b]they were put
in the midst of the slain.
26 "[A]Meshech, [B]Tubal and all their hordes are
there; their graves [a]surround them. All of them
were slain by the sword [C]uncircumcised, though
they instilled their terror in the land of the living.
27 [A]Nor do they lie beside the fallen [a,B]heroes of the
uncircumcised, who went down to Sheol with their
weapons of war and whose swords were laid under
their heads; but the punishment for their [C]iniquity
rested on their bones, though the terror of *these*
[a]heroes *was once* in the land of the living. 28 But in
the midst of the uncircumcised you will be broken
and lie with those slain by the sword.

29 "There also is [A]Edom, its kings and all its
[a]princes, who [b]for *all* their might are laid with those
slain by the sword; they will lie with the uncircumcised and with those who go down to the pit.
30 "There also are the [a]chiefs of the [A]north, all of
them, and all the [B]Sidonians, who in spite of the
terror resulting from their might, in shame went
down with the slain. So they lay down uncircumcised with those slain by the sword and bore their
disgrace with those who go down to the pit.
31 "These Pharaoh will see, and he will be [A]com-
forted for all his hordes slain by the sword, *even*
Pharaoh and all his army," declares the Lord GOD.
32 "Though I instilled a terror of him in the land of
the living, yet he will be made to lie down among
the uncircumcised *along* with those slain by the
sword, *even* Pharaoh and all his hordes," declares
the Lord GOD.

THE WATCHMAN'S DUTY

33 And the word of the LORD came to me, saying, 2 "Son of man, speak to the [A]sons of your
people and say to them, 'If I bring a sword upon a
land, and the people of the land take one man from
among them and make him their watchman, 3 and
he sees the sword coming upon the land and [A]blows
on the trumpet and warns the people, 4 then he who
hears the sound of the trumpet and [A]does not take
warning, and a sword comes and takes him away,
his [B]blood will be on his *own* head. 5 He heard the
sound of the trumpet but did not take warning; his
blood will be on himself. But had he taken warning, he would have [A]delivered his life. 6 But if the
watchman sees the sword coming and does not
blow the trumpet and the people are not warned,
and a sword comes and takes a person from them,
he is [A]taken away [a]in his iniquity; but his [B]blood I
will require from the watchman's hand.'
7 "Now as for you, son of man, I have [a,A]appointed you
a watchman for the house of Israel; so you will hear
a [b]message from My mouth and give them [B]warning

32:19 [A]Jer 9:25, 26; Ezek 31:18; 32:21, 24, 29, 30 32:20 [a]Or *The sword is given* [A]Ps 28:3 32:21 [A]Is 14:9-12; Ezek 32:27 32:22 [a]Lit *his* [b]Lit *him* [A]Ezek 27:23; 31:3, 16 32:23 [a]Lit *gave,* and so throughout the ch [A]Is 14:15 32:24 [A]Gen 10:22; 14:1; Is 11:11; Jer 25:25; 49:34-39 [B]Ezek 26:20; 31:14, 18; 32:18 [C]Job 28:13; Ps 27:13; 52:5; 142:5; Is 38:11; Jer 11:19 [D]Ezek 16:52, 54; 32:25, 30 32:25 [a]Lit *given* [b]So with ancient versions; M.T. reads *he was* [A]Ps 139:8 32:26 [a]Lit *are around him* [A]Gen 10:2; Ezek 27:13; 38:2, 3; 39:1 [B]Gen 10:2; Is 66:19; Ezek 27:13; 38:2, 3; 39:1 [C]Ezek 32:19 32:27 [a]Or *mighty ones* [A]Is 14:18, 19 [B]Job 3:13-15; Ezek 32:21 [C]Job 20:11; Ps 109:18 32:29 [a]Or *leaders* [b]Or *in* [A]Is 34:5-15; Jer 49:7-22; Ezek 25:13; 35:9, 15 32:30 [a]Or *princes* [A]Jer 1:15; 25:26; Ezek 38:6, 15; 39:2 [B]Jer 25:22; Ezek 28:21-23 32:31 [A]Ezek 14:22; 31:16 33:2 [A]Ezek 3:11; 33:12, 17, 30; 37:18 33:3 [A]Neh 4:18-20; Is 58:1; Ezek 33:9; Hos 8:1; Joel 2:1 33:4 [A]2 Chr 25:16; Jer 6:17; Zech 1:4 [B]Ezek 18:13; 33:5, 9; Acts 18:6 33:5 [A]Ex 9:19-21; Heb 11:7 33:6 [a]Or *for,* and so throughout the ch [A]Ezek 18:20, 24; 33:8, 9 [B]Ezek 3:18, 20 33:7 [a]Or *given* [b]Lit *word* [A]Is 62:6; Ezek 3:17-21 [B]Jer 1:17; 26:2; Ezek 2:7, 8; Acts 5:20

32:19–21 The prophet followed Egypt and her people beyond the grave. The king of Egypt is addressed by the other nations in "Sheol," taunting him as he is on the same level with them. This shows that there is conscious existence and fixed destiny beyond death. See Lk 16:19–31.

32:22 Assyria is there. The slain of several nations are pictured in the afterlife: Assyria (vv. 22, 23), Elam (vv. 24, 25), Meshech and Tubal (vv. 26–28; cf. 38:1, 2, and *see notes there*), and Edom (vv. 29, 30). Although mighty for a time on earth, the fallen lie as defeated equals in death, all conquered by God and consigned to eternal hell (v. 21).

32:31, 32 Pharaoh ... comforted. A strange comfort coming from the recognition that he and his people were not alone in misery and doom.

33:1–33 the word ... came. This chapter is a transition between God's judgments against Jerusalem and the nations (chaps. 1–32), and Israel's bright future when she is restored to her land (chaps. 34–48). It provided God's instructions for national repentance, and is thus the preface to the prophecies of comfort and salvation which follow (chaps. 34–39).

33:2–20 speak to ... your people. This was given to prepare the exiles' minds to look on the awful calamity in Jerusalem as a just act by God (cf. 14:21–23). He had faithfully warned, but they did not pay heed. Ezekiel had been forbidden to speak to his people from 24:26, 27, until Jerusalem was captured. Meanwhile, he had spoken to the foreign nations (chaps. 25–32).

33:2–9 watchman. Such men as Jeremiah and Ezekiel (cf. 3:16–21) were spiritual watchmen (33:7–9), warning that God would bring a sword on His people so that they had opportunity to prepare and be safe. This analogy came from the custom of putting guards on the city wall watching for the approach of danger, then trumpeting the warning. For the function of a watchman, cf. 2Sa 18:24, 25; 2Ki 9:17; Jer 4:5; 6:1; Hos 8:1; Am 3:6; Hab 2:1.

33:4 his blood ... on his *own* head. Once the watchman did his duty, the responsibility passed to each person. *See the notes on chap. 18*, where each person is accountable for his own response to God's warnings, whether to die in judgment or to live as one who heeded and repented. Ezekiel had been a very faithful and obedient "watchman."

from Me. 8 When I say to the wicked, 'O wicked man,
you will [A]surely die,' and you do not speak to warn
the wicked from his way, that wicked man shall die
in his iniquity, but his blood I will require from your
hand. 9 But if you on your part warn a wicked man
to turn from his way and he [A]does not turn from
his way, he will die in his iniquity, but you have
[B]delivered your life.

10 "Now as for you, son of man, say to the house
of Israel, 'Thus you have spoken, saying, "Surely our
transgressions and our sins are upon us, and we are
[A]rotting away in them; [B]how then can we [a]survive?" '
11 Say to them, '[A]As I live!' declares the Lord [a]GOD,
'I take [B]no pleasure in the death of the wicked, but
rather that the wicked [C]turn from his way and live.
[D]Turn back, turn back from your evil ways! Why then
will you die, O house of Israel?' 12 And you, son of
man, say to [a]your fellow citizens, 'The [A]righteousness
of a righteous man will not deliver him in the day of
his transgression, and as for the wickedness of the
wicked, he will [B]not stumble because of it in the day
when he turns from his wickedness; whereas a righteous man will not be able to live [b]by his righteousness on the day when he commits sin.' 13 When I say
to the righteous he will surely live, and he *so* trusts in
his righteousness that he [A]commits iniquity, none of
his righteous deeds will be remembered; but in that
same iniquity of his which he has committed he will
die. 14 But when I say to the wicked, 'You will surely
die,' and he [A]turns from his sin and practices [B]jus-
tice and righteousness, 15 *if a* wicked man restores
a pledge, [A]pays back what he has taken by robbery,
walks by the [B]statutes [a]which ensure life without
committing iniquity, he shall surely live; he shall
not die. 16 [A]None of his sins that he has committed
will be remembered against him. He has practiced
justice and righteousness; he shall surely live.

17 "Yet [a]your fellow citizens say, 'The way of the
Lord is not right,' when it is their own way that
is not right. 18 When the righteous turns from his
righteousness and [A]commits iniquity, then he shall
die in [a]it. 19 But when the wicked turns from his
wickedness and practices justice and righteousness,
he will live by them. 20 Yet you say, '[A]The way of the
Lord is not right.' O house of Israel, I will judge each
of you according to his ways."

WORD OF JERUSALEM'S CAPTURE

21 Now [A]in the [B]twelfth year of our exile, on the
fifth of the tenth month, the [a]refugees from Jerusalem came to me, saying, "[C]The city has been [b]taken."
22 Now the [A]hand of the LORD had been upon me
in the evening, before the [a]refugees came. And He
[B]opened my mouth [b]at the time *they* came to me in
the morning; so my mouth was [C]opened and I was
no longer [c]speechless.

23 Then the word of the LORD came to me saying,
24 "Son of man, they who [A]live in these waste places in
the land of Israel are saying, '[B]Abraham was *only* one,
yet he possessed the land; so to [C]us who are many the
land has been given as a possession.' 25 Therefore say
to them, 'Thus says the Lord GOD, "You eat *meat* with
the [A]blood *in it,* lift up your eyes to your idols as you
shed blood. [B]Should you then possess the land? 26 You
[a,A]rely on your sword, you commit abominations and
each of you defiles his neighbor's wife. Should you
then possess the land?" ' 27 Thus you shall say to them,
'Thus says the Lord GOD, "As I live, surely those who
are in the waste places will [A]fall by the sword, and
whoever is in the [a]open field I will give to the beasts
to be devoured, and those who are in the strongholds
and in the [B]caves will die of pestilence. 28 I will [A]make
the land a desolation and a waste, and the [B]pride of
her power will cease; and the mountains of Israel will
be desolate so that no one will pass through. 29 Then
they will know that I am the LORD, when I make the
land a desolation and a waste because of all their
abominations which they have committed." '

33:8 [A]Is 3:11; Ezek 18:4, 13, 18, 20; 33:14 33:9 [A]Acts 13:40, 41, 46 [B]Ezek 3:19, 21; Acts 20:26 33:10 [a]Lit *live* [A]Lev 26:39; Ezek 4:17; 24:23 [B]Is 49:14; Ezek 37:11 33:11 [a]Heb *YHWH,* usually rendered *LORD*, and so throughout the ch [A]Is 49:18; Ezek 5:11 [B]Ezek 18:23, 32; Hos 11:8 [C]Jer 31:20; 1 Tim 2:4; 2 Pet 3:9 [D]Is 55:6, 7; Jer 3:22; Ezek 18:30, 31; Hos 14:1; Acts 3:19 33:12 [a]Lit *the sons of your people* [b]Lit *by it* [A]Ezek 3:18; 18:24; 33:20 [B]2 Chr 7:14; Ezek 18:21; 33:19 33:13 [A]Ezek 18:26; Heb 10:38; 2 Pet 2:20, 21 33:14 [A]Is 55:7; Jer 18:7, 8; Ezek 18:27; 33:8, 19; Hos 14:1, 4 [B]Mic 6:8 33:15 [a]Lit *of life* [A]Ex 22:1-4; Lev 6:4, 5; Luke 19:8 [B]Ps 119:59; 143:8; Ezek 20:11 33:16 [A]Is 1:18; 43:25; Ezek 18:22 33:17 [a]Lit *the sons of your people* 33:18 [a]Lit *them* [A]Ezek 3:20; 18:24; 33:12, 13 33:20 [A]Ezek 18:25 33:21 [a]Or *refugee* [b]Lit *smitten* [A]Ezek 31:1; 32:1, 17 [B]Jer 39:1, 2; 40:1; 52:4-7; Ezek 24:1, 2 [C]2 Kin 25:10; Jer 39:8 33:22 [a]Lit *refugee* [b]Lit *until he came* [c]Or *mute* [A]Ezek 1:3; 8:1; 37:1 [B]Ezek 3:26, 27; 24:27 [C]Luke 1:64 33:24 [A]Jer 39:10; 40:7; Ezek 33:27 [B]Is 51:2; Luke 3:8; Acts 7:5; Rom 4:12 [C]Ezek 11:15 33:25 [A]Lev 17:10, 12, 14; Deut 12:16, 23; 15:23 [B]Jer 7:9, 10 33:26 [a]Lit *stand* [A]Mic 2:1, 2; Zeph 3:3 33:27 [a]Lit *surface of the field* [A]Jer 15:2, 3; 42:22; Ezek 5:12 [B]1 Sam 13:6; Is 2:19 33:28 [A]Ezek 5:14; 6:14; Mic 7:13 [B]Ezek 7:24; 24:21; 30:6

33:8, 9 his blood I will require. A prophet who sounded the warning of repentance for sin was not to be judged (v. 9), but the one who failed to deliver the message was held accountable (v. 8). This referred to unfaithfulness on the part of the prophet for which he bore responsibility and was chastened by God. *See the notes on chap. 18 and Ac 20:26.*

33:10–11 how then can we survive? The Israelites reasoned that if they were liable to death in judgment that was inevitable, they were in a hopeless condition and had no future. God replied that He had no pleasure in seeing the wicked go into death for their sin, but desired them to repent and live (cf. 2Pe 3:9). The divine answer to the human question is "Repent and be saved!" (cf. 18:23, 30–32). Here was a blending of compassion with the demands of God's holiness. Repentance and forgiveness were offered to all.

33:12–20 *See notes on 18:19–29.* One of the basic principles of God's dealing with His people is presented here: judgment is according to personal faith and conduct. The discussion is not about eternal salvation and eternal death, but physical death in judgment for sin which, for believers, could not result in eternal death. The righteous behavior in v. 15 could only characterize a true believer, who was faithful from the heart. There is no distinction made as to the matter of who is a true believer in God. There is only a discussion of the issue of behavior as a factor in physical death. For those who were apostate idolaters, physical death would lead to eternal death. For believers who were lovers of the true God, their sin would lead only to physical punishment (cf. 1Co 11:28–31; 1Jn 5:16, 17). "Righteous" and "wicked" are terms describing behavior, not one's position before God. It is not the "righteousness of God" imputed as illustrated in the case of Abraham (Ge 15:6; Ro 4:3–5), but rather one's deeds that are in view (vv. 15–19).

33:17, 20 not right. They blamed God for their calamities when actually they were being judged for their sins.

33:21 The city has been taken. A fugitive or fugitives (the Heb. could be a collective noun) who escaped from Jerusalem reached Ezekiel with the report on Jan. 8, 585 B.C., almost 6 months after the fall on July 18, 586 (Jer 39:1, 2; 52:5–7). Ezekiel 24:1, 2 and 33:21 show a 36-month span from the outset of the siege on Jan. 15, 588, to the report in 33:21.

33:22 opened my mouth. God exercised control over the mouth of Ezekiel (*see note on 3:26, 27*).

33:23–29 There is no date attached to the prophecies from 33:23–39:29, but the first message after the fall of Jerusalem was a rebuke of Israel's carnal confidence. This prophecy was against the remnant of Judah who remained in the Land of Promise after the fall

30 "But as for you, son of man, [a]your fellow citizens who talk about you by the walls and in the doorways of the houses, speak to one another, each to his brother, saying, '[A]Come now and hear what the [b]message is which comes forth from the LORD.' 31 They come to you as people come, and sit before you *as* My people and hear your words, but they do not do them, for they do the lustful desires *expressed* by their [A]mouth, *and* their heart goes after their [B]gain. 32 Behold, you are to them like a sensual song by one who has a [A]beautiful voice and plays well on an instrument; for they hear your words but they do not practice them. 33 So when it [A]comes to pass—[a]as surely it will—then they will know that a prophet has been in their midst."

PROPHECY AGAINST THE SHEPHERDS OF ISRAEL

34 Then the word of the LORD came to me saying, 2 "Son of man, prophesy against the [A]shepherds of Israel. Prophesy and say to [a]those shepherds, 'Thus says the Lord [b]GOD, "Woe, shepherds of Israel who have been [c,B]feeding themselves! Should not the shepherds [c,C]feed the flock? 3 You [A]eat the fat and clothe yourselves with the wool, you [B]slaughter the fat *sheep* without [a]feeding the flock. 4 Those who are sickly you have not strengthened, the [a]diseased you have not healed, [A]the broken you have not bound up, the scattered you have not brought back, nor have you [B]sought for the lost; but with force and with severity you have dominated them. 5 They were [A]scattered for lack of a shepherd, and they became [B]food for every beast of the field and were scattered. 6 My flock [A]wandered through all the mountains and on every high hill; [B]My flock was scattered over all the surface of the earth, and there was [C]no one to search or seek *for them.*" ' "

7 Therefore, you shepherds, hear the word of the LORD: 8 "As I live," declares the Lord GOD, "surely because My flock has become a [A]prey, My flock has even become food for all the beasts of the field for lack of a shepherd, and My shepherds did not search for My flock, but *rather* the shepherds fed themselves and did not feed My flock; 9 therefore, you shepherds, hear the word of the LORD: 10 'Thus says the Lord GOD, "Behold, I am [A]against the shepherds, and I will demand My [a]sheep [b]from them and make them [B]cease from feeding [a]sheep. So the shepherds will not [c]feed themselves anymore, but I will [C]deliver My flock from their mouth, so that they will not be food for them." ' "

THE RESTORATION OF ISRAEL

11 For thus says the Lord GOD, "Behold, I Myself will [A]search for My sheep and seek them out. 12 [A]As a shepherd [a]cares for his herd in the day when he is among his scattered [b]sheep, so I will [a,B]care for My [b]sheep and will deliver them from all the places to which they were scattered on a [C]cloudy and gloomy day. 13 I will bring them out from the peoples and gather them from the countries and bring them to their own land; and I will [A]feed them on the mountains of Israel, by the [B]streams, and in all the inhabited places of the land. 14 I will feed them in a [A]good pasture, and their grazing ground will be on the mountain heights of Israel. There they will lie down on good grazing ground and feed in [a,B]rich pasture on the mountains of Israel. 15 I will [A]feed My flock and I will [a]lead them to rest," declares the Lord GOD. 16 "I will seek the lost, bring back the scattered, bind up the broken and strengthen the sick; but the [A]fat and the strong I will destroy. I will [B]feed them with judgment.

17 "As for you, My flock, thus says the Lord GOD, 'Behold, I will [A]judge between one [a]sheep and another, between the rams and the male goats. 18 Is it

33:30 [a]Lit *the sons of your people* [b]Lit *word* [A]Is 29:13; 58:2; Ezek 14:3; 20:3, 31 33:31 [A]Ps 78:36, 37; Is 29:13; 1 John 3:18 [B]Ezek 22:13, 27; Luke 12:15 33:32 [A]Mark 6:20 33:33 [a]Lit *behold, it is coming* [A]Jer 28:9; Ezek 33:29 34:2 [a]Lit *them, the shepherds* [b]Heb *YHWH*, usually rendered *LORD*, and so throughout the ch [c]Lit *pasturing, pasture* [A]Jer 2:8; 3:15; 10:21; 12:10 [B]Jer 23:1; Ezek 22:25; 34:8-10; Mic 3:1-3, 11 [C]Ps 78:71, 72; Is 40:11; Ezek 34:14, 15; John 10:11; 21:15-17 34:3 [a]Lit *pasturing* [A]Zech 11:16 [B]Ezek 22:25, 27 34:4 [a]Lit *sick* [A]Zech 11:16 [B]Matt 9:36; 10:6; 18:12, 13; Luke 15:4 34:5 [A]Num 27:17; 2 Chr 18:16; Jer 10:21; 23:2; 50:6, 7; Matt 9:36; Mark 6:34 [B]Ezek 34:8, 28 34:6 [A]Jer 40:11, 12; Ezek 7:16; 1 Pet 2:25 [B]John 10:16 [C]Ps 142:4 34:8 [A]Acts 20:29 34:10 [a]Or (a) *flock* [b]Lit *from their hand* [c]Lit *pasture,* and so throughout the ch [A]Jer 21:13; Ezek 5:8; 13:8; 34:2; Zech 10:3 [B]1 Sam 2:29, 30; Jer 52:24-27 [C]Ps 72:12-14; Ezek 13:23 34:11 [A]Ezek 11:17; 20:41 34:12 [a]Or *seek(s) out* [b]Or *flock* [A]Jer 31:10 [B]Is 40:11; 56:8; Jer 23:3; 31:8; Luke 19:10; John 10:16 [C]Jer 13:16; Ezek 30:3; Joel 2:2 34:13 [A]Ezek 34:23; 36:29, 30; Mic 7:14 [B]Is 30:25 34:14 [a]Lit *fat* [A]Ps 23:2; Jer 31:12-14, 25; John 10:9 [B]Ezek 28:25, 26; 36:29, 30 34:15 [a]Lit *cause them to lie down* [A]Ps 23:1, 2; Ezek 34:23 34:16 [A]Is 10:16 [B]Is 49:26 34:17 [a]Or *lamb* [A]Ezek 20:38; 34:20-22; Mal 4:1; Matt 25:32

of Jerusalem. Ezekiel warns the survivors that more judgment will come on them if they do not obey God. By some strange reasoning, they thought that if God had given the Land to Abraham when he was alone, it would be more securely theirs because they were many in number, a claim based on quantity rather than quality (v. 24). But judgment will come if they turn and reject God again (vv. 25–29).

33:30–33 Here was a message to exiles, who had no intention of obeying the prophet's messages. They liked to listen, but not apply the prophet's words. They finally knew by bitter experience that he had *spoken the truth of God.* The people appreciated the eloquence of Ezekiel, but not the reality of his message.

34:1 From this chapter on, Ezekiel's messages are mostly comforting, telling of God's grace and faithfulness to His covenant promises.

34:2 prophesy against the shepherds. The reference was to preexilic leaders such as kings, priests, and prophets, i.e., false ones who fleeced the flock for personal gain (vv. 3, 4) rather than fed or led righteously (as 22:25–28; Jer 14, 23; Zec 11). This stands in contrast to the Lord as Shepherd in Pss 23; 80:1; Is 40:11; Jer 31:10; Lk 15:4, 5; Jn 10:1ff.

34:5 food for every beast. The beast pictured nations that prey on Israel (cf. Da 7:3–7), though it could possibly include actual wild beasts, as in 14:21. Cf. 34:25, 28 and *see notes there.*

34:9, 10 This was no idle threat, as proven by the case of King Zedekiah (cf. Jer 52:10, 11).

34:11 I . . . will search. God, the true Shepherd, would search out and find His sheep in order to restore Israel to their land for the kingdom which the Messiah leads (vv. 12–14).

34:12 a cloudy and gloomy day. This refers to the "day of the LORD" judgment on Israel (cf. Jer 30:4–7).

34:12–14 Here is the promise of a literal regathering and restoration of the people of Israel to their own land from their worldwide dispersion. Since the scattering was literal, the regathering must also be literal. Once they are regathered in Messiah's kingdom, they will no longer want (vv. 15, 16).

34:15, 16 I will feed My flock. In contrast to self-indulgent leaders who took advantage of the sheep, God will meet the needs of His sheep (people). This is clearly reminiscent of Ps 23 and will be fulfilled by the Good Shepherd (Jn 10:1ff.), who will reign as Israel's Shepherd.

34:17–22 judge between. Once He has judged the leaders, God will also judge the abusive members of the flock as to their true spiritual state. This passage anticipates the judgment of the people given by Jesus Christ in Mt 25:31–46. The ungodly are known because they trample the poor. The Lord alone is able to sort out the true from the false

too [A]slight a thing for you that you should feed in the
good pasture, that you must tread down with your
feet the rest of your pastures? Or that you should
drink of the clear waters, that you must [a]foul the
rest with your feet? 19 As for My flock, they must
eat what you tread down with your feet and drink
what you [a]foul with your feet!' "
20 Therefore, thus says the Lord GOD to them,
"Behold, I, even I, will judge between the fat sheep
and the lean sheep. 21 Because you push with side
and with shoulder, and [A]thrust at all the [a]weak with
your horns until you have scattered them [b]abroad,
22 therefore, I will [A]deliver My flock, and they will
no longer be a prey; and I will judge between one
sheep and another.
23 "Then I will [A]set over them one [B]shepherd, My
servant [C]David, and he will feed them; he will feed
them himself and be their shepherd. 24 And I, the
LORD, will be their God, and My servant [A]David will
be prince among them; I the LORD have spoken.
25 "I will make a [A]covenant of peace with them and
[B]eliminate harmful beasts from the land so that they
may [C]live securely in the wilderness and sleep in the
woods. 26 I will make them and the places around My
hill a [A]blessing. And I will cause [B]showers to come
down in their season; they will be showers of [C]blessing.
27 Also the tree of the field will yield its fruit and the
earth will yield its increase, and they will be [A]secure
on their land. Then they will know that I am the LORD,
when I have [B]broken the bars of their yoke and have
delivered them from the hand of those who enslaved
them. 28 They will no longer be a prey to the nations,
and the beasts of the earth will not devour them; but
they will [A]live securely, and no one will make *them*
afraid. 29 I will establish for them a [A]renowned planting
place, and they will [B]not again be [a]victims of famine
in the land, and they will not [C]endure the insults of
the nations anymore. 30 Then they will know that [A]I,
the LORD their God, am with them, and that they, the
house of Israel, are My people," declares the Lord GOD.
31 "As for you, My [A]sheep, the [B]sheep of My pasture, you
are men, and I am your God," declares the Lord GOD.

PROPHECY AGAINST MOUNT SEIR

35 Moreover, the word of the LORD came to me
saying, 2 "Son of man, set your face against
[A]Mount Seir, and prophesy against it 3 and say to it,
'Thus says the Lord [a]GOD,

"Behold, I am against you, Mount Seir,
And I will [A]stretch out My hand against you
And make you a [B]desolation and a waste.
4 "I will [A]lay waste your cities
And you will become a desolation.
Then you will know that I am the LORD.

5 Because you have had everlasting [A]enmity and
have [a]delivered the sons of Israel to the power of
the sword at the time of their calamity, at the time
of the [b,B]punishment of the end, 6 therefore as I
live," declares the Lord GOD, "I will [a]give you over
to [A]bloodshed, and bloodshed will pursue you; since
you have not hated bloodshed, therefore bloodshed
will pursue you. 7 I will make Mount Seir a waste
and a desolation and I will cut off from it the one
who passes through and returns. 8 I will [A]fill its
mountains with its slain; on your hills and in your
valleys and in all your ravines those slain by the
sword will [a]fall. 9 I will make you an everlasting
[A]desolation and your cities will not be inhabited.
Then you will know that I am the LORD.
10 "Because you have [A]said, 'These two nations
and these two lands will be mine, and we will possess [a]them,' although the [B]LORD was there, 11 therefore as I live," declares the Lord GOD, "I will deal *with*
you [A]according to your anger and according to your
envy which you showed because of your hatred
against them; so I will [B]make Myself known among

34:18 [a]Lit *foul by trampling* [A]Num 16:9, 13; 2 Sam 7:19; Is 7:13 34:19 [a]Lit *foul by trampling* 34:21 [a]Or *sick* [b]Lit *to the outside* [A]Deut 33:17; Dan 8:4; Luke 13:14-16 34:22 [A]Ps 72:12-14; Jer 23:3; Ezek 34:10 34:23 [A]Rev 7:17 [B]Is 40:11; John 10:11 [C]Jer 30:9; Ezek 37:24 34:24 [A]Is 55:3; Jer 30:9; Ezek 37:24, 25; Hos 3:5 34:25 [A]Ezek 16:60; 20:37; 37:26 [B]Job 5:22, 23; Is 11:6-9 [C]Jer 33:16; Ezek 28:26; 34:27, 28 34:26 [A]Gen 12:2; Ezek 34:14 [B]Deut 11:13-15; 28:12 [C]Lev 25:21; Is 44:3 34:27 [A]Ezek 38:8, 11 [B]Lev 26:13; Is 52:2, 3; Jer 30:8 34:28 [A]Jer 30:10; Ezek 39:26 34:29 [a]Lit *those gathered* [A]Is 4:2; 60:21; 61:3 [B]Ezek 34:26, 27; 36:29 [C]Ezek 36:6, 15 34:30 [A]Ps 46:7, 11; Ezek 14:11; 36:28 34:31 [A]Ps 78:52; 80:1; Ezek 36:38 [B]Ps 100:3; Jer 23:1 35:2 [A]Gen 36:8; Ezek 25:12; 36:5 35:3 [a]Heb *YHWH*, usually rendered *LORD*, and so throughout the ch [A]Jer 6:12; 15:6; Ezek 25:13 [B]Jer 49:13, 17, 18; Ezek 35:7 35:4 [A]Ezek 6:6; 35:9; Mal 1:3, 4 35:5 [a]Lit *poured* [b]Or *iniquity* [A]Ps 137:7; Ezek 25:12, 15; 36:5; Amos 1:11; Obad 10 [B]Ezek 7:2; 21:25, 29 35:6 [a]Lit *prepare you for* [A]Is 63:2-6; Ezek 16:38; 32:6 35:8 [a]Lit *fall in them* [A]Is 34:5, 6; Ezek 31:12; 32:4, 5; 39:4, 5 35:9 [A]Jer 49:13; Ezek 25:13 35:10 [a]Lit *it* [A]Ps 83:4-12; Ezek 36:2, 5 [B]Ps 48:1-3; 132:13, 14; Is 12:6; Ezek 48:35; Zeph 3:15 35:11 [A]Ps 137:7; Ezek 25:14; Amos 1:11 [B]Ps 9:16; 73:17, 18

(cf. parables of Mt 13), and will do so in the final kingdom.

34:23 one shepherd . . . David. This refers to the greater One in David's dynasty (cf. 2Sa 7:12–16), the Messiah, who will be Israel's ultimate king over the millennial kingdom (37:24–26; Jer 30:9; Hos 3:5; Zec 14:9). The Lord in v. 24 is God the Father.

34:24 prince. The word can at times be used of the king himself (37:24–25; cf. 28:2, 12), as here.

34:25 covenant of peace. Refers to the New Covenant of Jer 31:31–34 (cf. 37:26) in full operation during the millennial kingdom. **harmful beasts.** This refers to actual animals that will be tamed in the kingdom, see Is 11:6–9; 35:9 and Hos 2:18.

34:26 My hill. A reference to Jerusalem and Zion in particular, where the Jews will come to worship the Lord. **showers of blessing.** Cf. the "times of refreshing" in Ac 3:19, 20, when the curses of Dt 28:15–68 are lifted.

34:27 The faithfulness of the land is also indicated in Am 9:13.

34:28, 29 no longer be a prey. God will stop other nations from subjugating the people of Israel.

34:30 I . . . their God. An oft-repeated OT theme (cf. Ge 17:7, 8). This speaks of the ultimate salvation of Israel as in Ro 11:25–27.

35:2 against Mount Seir. Cf. Is 21:11, 12; Jer 49:7–22; Am 1:11, 12; Obadiah. This is another name for Edom (cf. v. 15; Ge 32:3; 38:6), also threatened with judgment in 25:12–14 (*see notes there*). Edom was considered Israel's most inveterate and bitter enemy (cf. Ps 137:7; Mal 1:2–5) and was located E of the Arabah from the Dead Sea to the Gulf of Aqabah. The main cities were Teman and Petra, now in ruins.

35:3, 4 This prediction (cf. vv. 6–9) came to pass literally, first by Nebuchadnezzar and later in 126 B.C. by John Hyrcanus. There is no trace of Edomites now, though their desolate cities can be identified as predicted by Obadiah (Ob 18) and Jeremiah (Jer 49:13). Cf. vv. 6–9.

35:5 Because. God will judge Edom because of 1) her perpetual enmity against Israel since Esau's hatred of Jacob (Ge 25–28), and 2) Edom's spiteful bloodshed against the Israelites trying to escape the Babylonians in 586 B.C.

35:10 Because. A further reason for Edom's doom is her design to snatch control of the territory occupied by "two nations," i.e., Israel (N) and Judah (S). They plotted to take over these nations for their own gain (v. 12), but were prevented and destroyed because "the Lord was there."

35:11, 12 anger . . . envy . . . revilings. Here were more reasons for Edom's destruction.

them when I judge you. 12 Then you will know [a]that
I, the LORD, have heard all your revilings which you
have spoken against the mountains of Israel saying,
'They are laid desolate; they are [A]given to us for
food.' 13 And you have [a,A]spoken arrogantly against
Me and have multiplied your words against Me; [B]I
have heard *it*." 14 Thus says the Lord GOD, "As all the
[A]earth rejoices, I will make you a desolation. 15 As
you [A]rejoiced over the inheritance of the house of Israel because it was desolate, [B]so I will do to you. You
will be a [C]desolation, O Mount Seir, and all Edom,
all of it. Then they will know that I am the LORD." '

THE MOUNTAINS OF ISRAEL TO BE BLESSED

36 "And you, son of man, prophesy to the mountains of Israel and say, 'O mountains of Israel, hear the word of the LORD. 2 Thus says the Lord
[a]GOD, "Because the enemy has spoken against you,
'Aha!' and, 'The everlasting [b,A]heights have become
our possession,' 3 therefore prophesy and say, 'Thus
says the Lord GOD, "[a]For good reason they have
made you [A]desolate and crushed you from every
side, that you would become a possession of the
rest of the nations and you have been taken up in
the [b,B]talk and the whispering of the people." ' "
4 Therefore, O [A]mountains of Israel, hear the word
of the Lord GOD. Thus says the Lord GOD to the
mountains and to the hills, to the ravines and to the
valleys, to the desolate wastes and to the forsaken
cities which have become a [B]prey and a derision
to the rest of the nations which are round about,
5 therefore thus says the Lord GOD, "Surely in the
fire of My [A]jealousy I have spoken against the [B]rest
of the nations, and against all Edom, who [a]appro-
priated My land for themselves as a possession
with wholehearted [C]joy *and* with scorn of soul, to
drive it out for a prey." 6 Therefore prophesy concerning the land of Israel and say to the mountains
and to the hills, to the ravines and to the valleys,
"Thus says the Lord GOD, 'Behold, I have spoken
in My jealousy and in My wrath because you have
[A]endured the insults of the nations.' 7 Therefore
thus says the Lord GOD, 'I have [a]sworn that surely
the nations which are around you will themselves
endure their insults. 8 But you, O mountains of
Israel, you will [A]put forth your branches and bear
your fruit for My people Israel; for they will soon
come. 9 For, behold, I am for you, and I will [A]turn
to you, and you will be [B]cultivated and sown. 10 I
will multiply men on you, [A]all the house of Israel,
all of it; and the [B]cities will be inhabited and the
waste places will be rebuilt. 11 I will multiply on
you man and beast; and they will increase and be
fruitful; and I will cause you to be inhabited as you
were [A]formerly and will [a]treat you [B]better than at
the first. Thus you will know that I am the LORD.
12 Yes, I will cause [A]men—My people Israel—to walk
on you and possess you, so that you will become
their [B]inheritance and never again [C]bereave them
of children.'

13 "Thus says the Lord GOD, 'Because they say to
you, "You are a [A]devourer of men and have bereaved
your [a]nation of children," 14 therefore you will no
longer devour men and no longer bereave your
nation of children,' declares the Lord GOD. 15 I will
not let you hear [A]insults from the nations anymore,
nor will you bear [B]disgrace from the peoples any
longer, nor will you cause your nation to [C]stumble
any longer," declares the Lord GOD.' "

16 Then the word of the LORD came to me saying,
17 "Son of man, when the house of Israel was living in
their own land, they [A]defiled it by their ways and their
deeds; their way before Me was like [B]the uncleanness
of a woman in her impurity. 18 Therefore I [A]poured out
My wrath on them for the blood which they had shed
on the land, because they had defiled it with their idols.
19 Also I [A]scattered them among the nations and they
were dispersed throughout the lands. [B]According to
their ways and their deeds I judged them. 20 When they

35:12 [a]Or *that I am the LORD: I have heard* [A]Jer 50:7; Ezek 36:2 35:13 [a]Lit *made great with your mouth* [A]Is 10:13, 14; 36:20; Jer 48:26, 42; Dan 11:36 [B]Jer 7:11; 29:23 35:14 [A]Is 44:23; 49:13; Jer 51:48 35:15 [A]Jer 50:11; Lam 4:21 [B]Obad 15 [C]Is 34:5, 6; Ezek 35:3, 4 36:2 [a]Heb *YHWH*, usually rendered *LORD*, and so throughout the ch [b]Heb *Bamoth* [A]Deut 32:13; Ps 78:69; Is 58:14; Hab 3:19 36:3 [a]Lit *Because;* or *By the cause* [b]Lit *lip of the tongue* [A]Jer 2:15 [B]Ps 44:13, 14; Jer 18:16; Ezek 35:13 36:4 [A]Deut 11:11; Ezek 36:1, 6, 8 [B]Ezek 34:8, 28 36:5 [a]Lit *gave* [A]Ezek 5:13; 36:6; 38:19 [B]Jer 25:9, 15-29; Ezek 36:3 [C]Jer 50:11; Ezek 35:15; Mic 7:8 36:6 [A]Ps 74:10; 123:3, 4; Ezek 34:29 36:7 [a]Lit *lifted up My hand* 36:8 [A]Is 4:2; 27:6; Ezek 17:23; 34:26-29 36:9 [A]Lev 26:9 [B]Ezek 28:26; 34:14; 36:34 36:10 [A]Is 27:6; 49:17-23; Ezek 37:21, 22 [B]Jer 31:27, 28; 33:12; Ezek 36:33 36:11 [a]Lit *cause good* [A]Jer 30:18; Ezek 16:55; Mic 7:14 [B]Job 42:12; Is 51:3 36:12 [A]Ezek 34:13, 14 [B]Ezek 47:14 [C]Jer 15:7; Ezek 22:12, 27 36:13 [a]Or *nations,* and so throughout the ch [A]Num 13:32 36:15 [A]Is 60:14; Ezek 34:29; 36:7 [B]Ps 89:50; Is 54:4; Ezek 22:4 [C]Is 63:13; Jer 13:16; 18:15 36:17 [A]Jer 2:7 [B]Lev 15:19 36:18 [A]2 Chr 34:21, 25; Lam 2:4; 4:11; Ezek 22:20, 22 36:19 [A]Deut 28:64; Ezek 5:12; 22:15; Amos 9:9 [B]Ezek 24:14; 39:24; Rom 2:6

35:13 **you have spoken arrogantly against Me.** Still another reason for judgment was Edom's proud ambitions that were really against God (cf. v. 10, "although the LORD was there").

35:15 **As you rejoiced.** This final reason for doom was Edom's joy over Israel's calamity. **they will know.** The ultimate aim in Edom's judgment is that "all the earth" (v. 14) may know He is the Lord and see His glory. Sadly, sinners find this out only in their own destruction. Cf. Heb 10:31.

36:1 This chapter presents the prerequisite regeneration which Israel must experience before they can nationally enter into the promised blessings. This chapter must be understood to speak of a literal Israel, a literal land, and a literal regeneration, leading to a literal kingdom under Messiah. **prophesy to the mountains.** Cf. vv. 1, 4, 6, 8. Ezekiel addresses Israel's mountains, as symbolic of the whole nation. He promises: 1) to give these mountains again to dispersed Israel (v. 12); 2) to cause fruit to grow on them (v. 8); 3) to rebuild cities and to multiply people there (v. 10); and 4) to bless in a greater way than in the past (v. 11). This promise can only be fulfilled in future millennial blessing to Israel that she has not yet experienced, because it includes the salvation of the New Covenant (vv. 25–27, 29, 31, 33).

36:2–15 This section continues the prophecy against Edom from chap. 35.

36:2 **Because the enemy has spoken.** God will restore these areas to Israel which their enemies claim to possess (cf. Ge 12:7). They will pay for their spite against Israel.

36:7 **I have sworn.** God testifies, as a formal pledge, that He will bring a turnabout in which the nations that seized the land will be shamed.

36:8–15 Israel's land will be productive (vv. 8, 9), populated (vv. 10, 11), and peaceful (vv. 12–15). These features will be fully realized in the Messiah's kingdom. The return from Babylon was only a partial fulfillment and foreshadowing of the fullness to come in the future kingdom.

36:16–19 Ezekiel gives a backward look to underscore why Israel had suffered the past judgments by the Lord. It was because the Jews had "defiled" their land by their sins that the Lord purged it. He likened such a defilement to a menstrual condition (v. 17).

36:20 **they profaned My holy name.** Even in dispersion, Israelites tainted God's honor in the sight of the heathen, who concluded that the Lord of this exiled people was not powerful enough to keep them in their land.

came to the nations where they went, they [A]profaned
My holy name, because it was said of them, 'These
are the [B]people of the LORD; yet they have come out
of His land.' 21 But I had [a]concern for My [A]holy name,
which the house of Israel had profaned among the
nations where they went.

ISRAEL TO BE RENEWED FOR HIS NAME'S SAKE

22 "Therefore say to the house of Israel, 'Thus
says the Lord GOD, "It is [A]not for your sake, O house
of Israel, that I am about to act, but for My holy
name, which you have profaned among the nations where you went. 23 I will [A]vindicate the holiness of My great name which has been profaned
among the nations, which you have profaned in
their midst. Then the [B]nations will know that I am
the LORD," declares the Lord GOD, "when I prove
Myself holy among you in their sight. 24 For I will
[A]take you from the nations, gather you from all the
lands and bring you into your own land. 25 Then I
will [A]sprinkle clean water on you, and you will be
clean; I will cleanse you from all your [B]filthiness
and from all your [C]idols. 26 Moreover, I will give
you a [A]new heart and put a new spirit within you;
and I will remove the [B]heart of stone from your
flesh and give you a heart of flesh. 27 I will [A]put
My Spirit within you and cause you to walk in My
statutes, and you will be careful to observe My ordinances. 28 You will live in the land that I gave to
your forefathers; so you will be [A]My people, and I
will be your God. 29 Moreover, I will save you from
all your uncleanness; and I will call for the grain
and multiply it, and I [A]will not [a]bring a famine on
you. 30 I will [A]multiply the fruit of the tree and the
produce of the field, so that you will not receive
again the disgrace of famine among the nations.
31 Then you will [A]remember your evil ways and
your deeds that were not good, and you will loathe
yourselves in your own sight for your iniquities
and your abominations. 32 I am not doing *this* [A]for
your sake," declares the Lord GOD, "let it be known
to you. Be ashamed and confounded for your ways,
O house of Israel!"

33 'Thus says the Lord GOD, "On the day that I
cleanse you from all your iniquities, I will cause
the [A]cities to be inhabited, and the [B]waste places
will be rebuilt. 34 The desolate land will be cultivated instead of being a desolation in the sight
of everyone who passes by. 35 They will say, 'This
desolate land has become like the [A]garden of Eden;
and the waste, desolate and ruined cities are fortified *and* inhabited.' 36 Then the nations that are
left round about you will know that I, the LORD,
have rebuilt the ruined places *and* planted that
which was desolate; I, the LORD, have spoken and
[A]will do it."

37 'Thus says the Lord GOD, "This also I will let
the house of Israel ask Me to do for them: I will increase their men like a flock. 38 Like the [A]flock [a]for
sacrifices, like the flock at Jerusalem during her
appointed feasts, so will the waste cities be filled
with [B]flocks of men. Then they will know that I am
the LORD." ' "

36:20 [A]Is 52:5; Ezek 12:16; Rom 2:24 [B]Jer 33:24 36:21 [a]Lit *compassion* [A]Ps 74:18; Is 48:9; Ezek 20:44 36:22 [A]Deut 7:7, 8; 9:5, 6; Ezek 36:32 36:23 [A]Is 5:16; Ezek 20:41; 38:23; 39:7, 25 [B]Ps 102:15; 126:2 36:24 [A]Is 43:5, 6; Ezek 34:13; 37:21 36:25 [A]Num 19:17-19; Ps 51:7; Titus 3:5, 6; Heb 9:13, 19; 10:22 [B]Is 4:4; Zech 13:1 [C]Is 2:18, 20; Hos 14:3, 8 36:26 [A]Ps 51:10; Ezek 11:19; 18:31; John 3:3, 5; 2 Cor 5:17 [B]Ezek 11:19; Zech 7:12 36:27 [A]Is 44:3; 59:21; Ezek 37:14; 39:29; Joel 2:28, 29 36:28 [A]Ezek 14:11; 37:23, 27 36:29 [a]Lit *put* [A]Ezek 34:27, 29; Hos 2:21-23 36:30 [A]Lev 26:4; Ezek 34:27 36:31 [A]Ezek 16:61-63; 20:43 36:32 [A]Deut 9:5 36:33 [A]Ezek 36:10; Zech 8:7, 8 [B]Is 58:12 36:35 [A]Is 51:3; Ezek 31:9; Joel 2:3 36:36 [A]Ezek 17:24; 22:14; 37:14; Hos 14:4-9 36:38 [a]Lit *of holy things* [A]1 Kin 8:63; 2 Chr 35:7-9; John 2:14 [B]Ps 74:1; 100:3; Jer 23:1; John 10:7, 9, 16

36:21–23 for My holy name. Restoring Israel to the land that God pledged in covenant (Ge 12:7) will sanctify His great name, and move other peoples to "know that I am the LORD." This glory for God is the primary reason for Israel's restoration (cf. v. 32).

36:24 bring you into your own land. God assured Israel that He will bring them out of other lands back to the Promised Land (v. 24), the very land from which He scattered them (v. 20). It is the same "land that I gave to your forefathers" (v. 28), a land distinct from those of other nations (v. 36), and a land whose cities will be inhabited by those who return (vv. 33, 36, 38). The establishment of the modern state of Israel indicates this has initially begun.

36:25–27 I will cleanse you. Along with the physical reality of a return to the land, God pledged spiritual renewal: 1) cleansing from sin; 2) a new heart of the New Covenant (cf. Jer 31:31–34); 3) a new spirit or disposition inclined to worship Him; and 4) His Spirit dwelling in them, enabling them to walk in obedience to His Word. This has not happened, because Israel has not trusted Jesus Christ as Messiah and Savior, but it will before the kingdom of Messiah (cf. Zec 12–14; Ro 11:25–27; Rev 11:13).

36:25–31 This section is among the most glorious in all Scripture on the subject of Israel's restoration to the Lord and national salvation. This salvation is described in v. 25 as a cleansing that will wash away sin. Such washing was symbolized in the Mosaic rites of purification (cf. Nu 19:17–19; Ps 119:9; Is 4:4; Zec 13:1). For the concept of sprinkling in cleansing, see Ps 51:7, 10; Heb 9:13; 10:22. This is the washing Paul wrote of in Eph 5:26 and Tit 3:5. Jesus had this very promise in mind in Jn 3:5.

What was figuratively described in v. 25 is explained as literal in vv. 26, 27. The gift of the "new heart" signifies the new birth, which is regeneration by the Holy Spirit (cf. 11:18–20). The "heart" stands for the whole nature. The "spirit" indicates the governing power of the mind which directs thought and conduct. A "heart of stone" is stubborn and self-willed. A "heart of flesh" is pliable and responsive. The evil inclination is removed and a new nature replaces it. This is New Covenant character as in Jer 31:31–34.

The Lord will also give His "Spirit" to the faithful Jews (cf. 39:29; Is 44:3; 59:21; Joel 2:28, 29; Ac 2:16ff.). When Israel becomes the true people of God (v. 28), the judgment promise of Hosea 1:9 is nullified. All nature will experience the blessings of Israel's salvation (vv. 29, 30). When the Jews have experienced such grace, they will be even more repentant—a sign of true conversion (v. 31).

Ezekiel profoundly proclaims the doctrines of conversion and spiritual life. He includes forgiveness (v. 25), regeneration (v. 26), the indwelling Holy Spirit (v. 27), and the responsive obedience to God's law (v. 27). These are all clearly presented as he prophesies Israel's conversion. As a nation, they will truly know their God (v. 38), hate their sin (vv. 31, 32), and glorify their Savior (v. 32).

36:32 not . . . for your sake. God's glory and reputation among the nations, not Israel's, causes this restoration to be promised (cf. Ps 115:1; Ac 5:41; Ro 1:5; 3Jn 7).

36:35 the garden. Millennial conditions will be similar (not identical) to those in Eden (cf. 47:1–12; Is 35:1, 2; 55:13; Zec 8:12).

36:37 ask Me to do for them. God will sovereignly work this return/renewal, yet give Israelites the human privilege of praying for it to be realized. This prophecy was to stir up the people's prayers.

36:37, 38 increase their men. There will be an increase in the population during the Millennium. When the male population came to Jerusalem, they brought vast numbers of animals for sacrifice. That was small compared to future kingdom conditions.

VISION OF THE VALLEY OF DRY BONES

37 The [A]hand of the LORD was upon me, and He
[B]brought me out [a]by the Spirit of the LORD
and set me down in the middle of the [C]valley; and
it was full of bones. 2 He caused me to pass among
them round about, and behold, *there were* very
many on the surface of the valley; and lo, *they*
were very dry. 3 He said to me, "Son of man, [A]can
these bones live?" And I answered, "O Lord [a]GOD,
[B]You know." 4 Again He said to me, "[A]Prophesy over
these bones and say to them, 'O dry bones, [B]hear
the word of the LORD.' 5 Thus says the Lord GOD to
these bones, 'Behold, I will cause [a,A]breath to enter
you that you may come to life. 6 I will put sinews on
you, make flesh grow back on you, cover you with
skin and put breath in you that you may come alive;
and you will [A]know that I am the LORD.' "
7 So I prophesied [A]as I was commanded; and as
I prophesied, there was a [a]noise, and behold, a rattling; and the bones came together, bone to its bone.
8 And I looked, and behold, sinews were on them, and
flesh grew and skin covered them; but there was no
breath in them. 9 Then He said to me, "Prophesy to the
breath, prophesy, son of man, and say to the breath,
'Thus says the Lord GOD, "Come from the four winds,
O breath, and [A]breathe on these slain, that they [B]come
to life." ' " 10 So I prophesied as He commanded me,
and the [A]breath came into them, and they came to life
and stood on their feet, an [B]exceedingly great army.

THE VISION EXPLAINED

11 Then He said to me, "Son of man, these bones
are the [A]whole house of Israel; behold, they say, 'Our
[B]bones are dried up and our hope has perished. We
are [a]completely [C]cut off.' 12 Therefore prophesy and
say to them, 'Thus says the Lord GOD, "Behold, I will
open your graves and [A]cause you to come up out of
your graves, My people; and I will bring you into the
land of Israel. 13 Then you will know that I am the
LORD, when I have opened your graves and caused
you to come up out of your graves, My people. 14 I
will [A]put My [a]Spirit within you and you will come
to life, and I will place you on your own land. Then
you will know that I, the LORD, have spoken and
done it," declares the LORD.' "

REUNION OF JUDAH AND ISRAEL

15 The word of the LORD came again to me saying, 16 "And you, son of man, take for yourself [A]one
stick and write on it, 'For [B]Judah and for the sons
of Israel, his companions'; then take another stick
and write on it, 'For [C]Joseph, the stick of Ephraim

37:1 [a]Or *in* [A]Ezek 1:3; 33:22; 40:1 [B]Ezek 8:3; 11:24; 43:5; Acts 8:39 [C]Jer 7:32-8:2 37:3 [a]Heb *YHWH*, usually rendered *LORD*, and so throughout the ch [A]Ezek 26:19 [B]Deut 32:39; 1 Sam 2:6 37:4 [A]Ezek 37:9, 12 [B]Jer 22:29; Ezek 36:1 37:5 [a]Or *spirit*, and so throughout the ch [A]Gen 2:7; Ps 104:29, 30; Ezek 37:9, 10, 14 37:6 [A]Is 49:23; Ezek 35:9; 38:23; 39:6; Joel 2:27; 3:17 37:7 [a]Lit *voice; or thunder* [A]Jer 13:5-7 37:9 [A]Ps 104:30 [B]Hos 13:14 37:10 [A]Rev 11:11 [B]Jer 30:19; 33:22 37:11 [a]Lit *cut off to ourselves* [A]Jer 33:24; Ezek 36:10; 39:25 [B]Ps 141:7 [C]Ps 88:5; Lam 3:54 37:12 [A]Deut 32:39; 1 Sam 2:6; Is 26:19; 66:14; Hos 13:14 37:14 [a]Or *breath* [A]Is 32:15; Ezek 11:19; 36:27; 37:6, 9; 39:29; Joel 2:28, 29; Zech 12:10 37:16 [A]Num 17:2, 3 [B]2 Chr 10:17; 11:11-17; 15:9 [C]1 Kin 12:16-20; 2 Chr 10:19

37:1 brought me ... by the Spirit. 37:1–14 involves another vision. God does not change Ezekiel's location but gives him a vivid inward sense that he has been taken to a valley "full of bones." (For other visions, cf. 1:1–3:15; 8:1–11:24; 40:1–48:35.) This passage, part of a series of revelations received during the night before the messenger came with the news of the destruction of Jerusalem, was to ease the gloom of the people. **in the middle of the valley.** It no doubt represents the world area wherever Israelites were scattered (cf. v. 12).

37:2 very dry. This pictures the dead nation lifeless, scattered, and bleached, just as a dry tree (17:24) pictures a dead nation, to which only God can give life.

37:3 can these bones live? The many dry bones (v. 2) picture the nation Israel (v. 11) as apparently dead in their dispersion, and waiting for national resurrection. The people knew about the doctrine of individual resurrection, otherwise this prophecy would have had no meaning (cf. 1Ki 17; 2Ki 4; 13:21; Is 25:8; 26:19; Da 12:2; Hos 13:14).

37:4–6 Prophesy over these bones. Ezekiel is to proclaim God's pledge to reassemble Israelites from the world and restore the nation of Israel to life (v. 5) and give them His Spirit (v. 14) in true salvation and spiritual life. Clearly, God is promising the resurrection of the nation of Israel and its spiritual regeneration (cf. 36:25–27).

37:7–10 In the vision, Ezekiel did as he was told, and the dead bones became a living nation (v. 10).

37:11–13 This is the key to the interpretation of the vision. It is the resurrection and salvation of Israel.

37:14 I will put My Spirit within you. *See note on 36:25–27.* **done it.** God's reputation is at stake in the restoration and regeneration of Israel into the Land. He must do what He promised so all will know that He is Lord.

37:15–23 The vision ended and Ezekiel was given an object lesson which his people

THE VISIONS OF EZEKIEL

Vision	Reference	Significance
God	1:1–28	Ezekiel is called, commissioned, and empowered with an overwhelming vision of divine glory.
Abominations in the temple	8:1–18	Ezekiel is transported to Jerusalem where he sees pagan idols in the temple and Israelites worshiping these false gods. God reveals His anger to Ezekiel over such sinful behavior.
People slain in Jerusalem	9:1–11	Ezekiel witness a violent vision in which Israelites of all ages are judged and killed because of their rebelliousness and idolatry.
The temple and the cherubim	10:1–22	Ezekiel watches God's glory and the mysterious cherubim depart from the temple because of the sinfulness of the people.
25 wicked rulers	11:1–12	Ezekiel is transported to the East Gate where he sees 25 Israelite leaders plotting evil.
Valley of the dry bones	37:1–14	Ezekiel is transported to a valley where he sees dry, bleached bones come together, recover flesh, and come to life. This vision depicts God's power and promise to restore and revive a dead people.
The temple	40:1—43:12	Ezekiel sees a detailed vision of a new temple and the return of the Lord. This vision encourages the Israelites that God will return to bless His people.

and all the house of Israel, his companions.’ 17 Then
[A]join them for yourself one to another into one stick,
that they may become one in your hand. 18 When
the sons of your people speak to you saying, ‘Will
you not declare to us [A]what you mean by these?’
19 say to them, ‘Thus says the Lord GOD, “Behold, I
will take the stick of Joseph, which is in the hand of
Ephraim, and the tribes of Israel, his companions;
and I will put them with it, with the stick of Judah,
and make them one stick, and they will be one in
My hand.” ’ 20 The sticks on which you write will
be in your hand before their eyes. 21 Say to them,
‘Thus says the Lord GOD, “Behold, I will [A]take the
sons of Israel from among the nations where they
have gone, and I will gather them from every side
and bring them into their own land; 22 and I will
make them [A]one nation in the land, on the mountains of Israel; and [B]one king will be king for all of
them; and they will no longer be two nations and
no longer be divided into two kingdoms. 23 They
will [A]no longer defile themselves with their idols,
or with their detestable things, or with any of their
transgressions; but [B]I will deliver them from all
their [a]dwelling places in which they have sinned,
and will cleanse them. And they will be My people,
and I will be their God.

THE DAVIDIC KINGDOM

24 “My servant [A]David will be king over them,
and they will all have [B]one shepherd; and they will
walk in My ordinances and keep My statutes and
observe them. 25 They will live on the land that I
gave to Jacob My servant, in which your fathers
lived; and they will live on it, they, and their sons
and their sons’ sons, forever; and [A]David My servant
will be their prince forever. 26 I will make a [A]cov-
enant of peace with them; it will be an [B]everlasting
covenant with them. And I will [a]place them and
[C]multiply them, and will set My [D]sanctuary in their
midst forever. 27 My [A]dwelling place also will be with
them; and [B]I will be their God, and they will be My
people. 28 And the nations will know that I am the
LORD [A]who sanctifies Israel, when My sanctuary is
in their midst forever.” ’ ”

PROPHECY ABOUT GOG AND FUTURE INVASION OF ISRAEL

38 And the word of the LORD came to me saying,
2 “Son of man, set your face toward [A]Gog of
the land of [B]Magog, the [a]prince of [C]Rosh, [D]Meshech
and [D]Tubal, and prophesy against him 3 and say,
‘Thus says the Lord [a]GOD, “Behold, I am against
you, O Gog, [b]prince of Rosh, Meshech and Tubal.

37:17 [A]Is 11:13; Jer 50:4; Ezek 37:22-24; Hos 1:11; Zeph 3:9 37:18 [A]Ezek 12:9; 17:12; 20:49; 24:19 37:21 [A]Is 43:5, 6; Jer 29:14; Ezek 36:24; 39:27; Amos 9:14, 15 37:22 [A]Jer 3:18; 50:4, 5; Ezek 36:10 [B]Ezek 34:23, 24; 37:24 37:23 [a]Another reading is *backslidings* [A]Ezek 36:25 [B]Ezek 36:28, 29 37:24 [A]Jer 30:9; Ezek 34:24; 37:25; Hos 3:5 [B]Ps 78:71; Is 40:11; Ezek 34:23 37:25 [A]Is 11:1; Ezek 37:24; Zech 6:12 37:26 [a]Lit *give* [A]Ezek 16:62; 20:37; 34:25 [B]Ps 89:3, 4; Is 55:3; 59:21; Ezek 16:60 [C]Jer 30:19; Ezek 36:10, 11, 37 [D]Ezek 20:40; 43:7 37:27 [A]John 1:14; Rev 21:3 [B]Ezek 37:23; 2 Cor 6:16 37:28 [A]Ex 31:13; Ezek 20:12 38:2 [a]Or *chief prince of Meshech* [A]Ezek 38:3, 14, 16, 18; 39:1, 11; Rev 20:8 [B]Gen 10:2; Ezek 39:6; Rev 20:8 [C]Ezek 38:3; 39:1 [D]Ezek 27:13; 38:3; 39:1 38:3 [a]Heb *YHWH*, usually rendered *LORD*, and so throughout the ch [b]Or *chief prince of Meshech*

observed (vv. 18, 20). This drama of uniting two sticks offered a second illustration that God will not only regather Israelites to their land, but will for the first time since 931 B.C. (the end of Solomon’s reign, 1Ki 11:26–40) restore union between Israel and Judah (vv. 19, 21, 22) in the messianic reign (cf. Is 11:12, 13; Jer 3:18; Hos 1:11).

37:21–23 God made 3 promises that summarized His future plans for Israel: 1) restoration, v. 21; 2) unification, v. 22; and 3) purification, v. 23. These promises bring to fulfillment: 1) the Abrahamic Covenant (cf. Ge 12); 2) the Davidic Covenant (2Sa 7); and 3) the New Covenant (cf. Jer 31), respectively.

37:22 one king. This leader (cf. vv. 24, 25) is the Messiah-King-Shepherd often promised for David’s dynasty (34:23, 24; Jer 23:5–8; 30:9; Da 2:35, 45; 7:13, 14, 27), who is the one king of Zec 14:9 (cf. Mt 25:31, 34, 40).

37:23 cleanse them. This is provided by the provisions of the New Covenant (cf. 36:27; 37:14; Jer 31:31–34).

37:24, 25 David. This is to be understood as Jesus Christ the Messiah, descendant of David (cf. 2Sa 7:8–17; Is 7:14; 9:6, 7; Mic 5:2; Mt 1:1, 23; Lk 1:31–33).

37:25 land that I gave to Jacob. It is natural to see this physical land, so clarified, as the very land God gave to Abraham, Isaac, and Jacob (Ge 12:7; 26:24; 35:12).

37:26 covenant of peace. Cf. 34:25. This is the New Covenant in full force. Israel has never yet been in a state of perpetual salvation peace; this awaits fulfillment in the future kingdom of the Messiah who is the “Prince of Peace” (Is 9:6). **an everlasting covenant.** The everlasting nature of the Abrahamic (cf. Ge 17:7), Davidic (2Sa 23:5), and New (Jer 50:5) Covenants are joined together in the redeemed who experience the millennial kingdom “forever” (used 4 times in vv. 25–28). The Heb. word for “everlasting” may refer to a long time or eternity. It is also true that these covenants will continue to be fulfilled after the Millennium in the eternal state. **My sanctuary.** The Spirit of God begins to prepare for the great reality that God will have a sanctuary in the midst of His people and will dwell with them (cf. Zec 6:12, 13). God promised to dwell with man on earth (47:1–12). This has been God’s desire in all epochs: 1) before Moses (Ge 17:7, 8); 2) in the Mosaic era (Lv 26:11–13); 3) in the church era (1Co 3:16; 6:19); 4) in the Millennium (Eze 37:26–28); and 5) in eternity future (Rev 21:3).

37:27 Paul quotes this in 2Co 6:16.

38:1–39:29 These chapters tell of a coming northern confederacy of nations who will invade the Promised Land.

38:2 toward Gog. This name is found in 1Ch 5:4. The LXX used “Gog” to render names such as Agag (Nu 24:7) and Og (Dt 3:1), possibly showing that though it was a proper name, it came to be used as a general title for an enemy of God’s people. “Gog” most likely carries the idea “high” or “supreme one,” based on the comparison in Nu 24:7. It refers to a person, described as a “prince” from the land of Magog, who is the final Antichrist. *See note on Rev 20:8*, where Gog and Magog are referred to again. These titles are used there symbolically of the final world uprising against Jerusalem, its people and Messiah King. This attack comes not just from the N but the 4 corners of the world, as a world of sinners at the end of the 1,000 year kingdom come to fight the saints in the “beloved city” of Jerusalem. On that occasion, there is only one weapon used—divine fire. This is the climax to the last battle with Satan and his armies, whose eternal destiny is set. It is followed by the final judgment of all the ungodly before the Lord (Rev 20:11–15) and the creation of the eternal, sinless state (Rev 21:1). *See notes on chap. 39.* **Magog.** Some see this people as derived from Japheth (Ge 10:2), later called the Scythians. Others propose a people in SE Anatolia, later known as Asiatic people such as the Mongols and Huns. Others see Magog as an overall term for barbarians, N of Israel, around the Caspian and Black Seas. **prince of Rosh, Meshech and Tubal.** Should be translated “chief prince of Meshech and Tubal” because: 1) Rosh (more than 600 times) in the Heb. OT is an adjective, “chief,” often in references to the “chief priest” (2Ki 25:18); 2) most ancient versions took it to mean “chief” or “head”; and 3) in all places other than chaps. 38 and 39 where both Meshech and Tubal are mentioned, Rosh is not listed as a third people (27:13; 32:26; Ge 10:2; 1Ch 1:5). This is also descriptive of the Antichrist, who rises to world dominance in the coming time of tribulation (cf. Da 9:24–27; 11:36–45; Rev 13:1–17; 19:20). **Meshech and Tubal.** Two peoples were recognized in ancient Assyrian monuments: one called Mushki (Mushku) and the other Tubali (Tabal). Both were in Asia Minor, the area of Magog, modern-day Turkey. Summing up, a chief prince, who is the enemy of God’s people, will lead a coalition of nations against Jerusalem. The details of this enemy force and its destruction are given by Ezekiel in the rest of chaps. 38, 39.

4 I will turn you about and put hooks into your jaws,
and I will [A]bring you out, and all your army, [B]horses
and horsemen, all of them [a]splendidly attired, a great
company *with* buckler and shield, all of them wielding swords; 5 [A]Persia, [a,B]Ethiopia and [C]Put with them,
all of them *with* shield and helmet; 6 [A]Gomer with all
its troops; [B]Beth-togarmah *from* the remote parts of
the north with all its troops—many peoples with you.
7 "[A]Be prepared, and prepare yourself, you and all
your companies that are assembled about you, and
be a guard for them. 8 [A]After many days you will be
summoned; in the latter years you will come into the
land that is restored from the sword, *whose inhabitants* have been [B]gathered from many [a]nations to
the [C]mountains of Israel which had been a continual
waste; but [b]its people were brought out from the
[a]nations, and they are [D]living securely, all of them.
9 You will go up, you will come [A]like a storm; you
will be like a [B]cloud covering the land, you and all
your troops, and many peoples with you."
10 'Thus says the Lord GOD, "It will come about on
that day, that [a]thoughts will come into your mind
and you will [A]devise an evil plan, 11 and you will
say, 'I will go up against the land of [a,A]unwalled villages. I will go against those who are [B]at rest, that
live securely, all of them living without walls and
having no bars or gates, 12 to [A]capture spoil and to
seize plunder, to turn your hand against the waste
places which are *now* inhabited, and against the
people who are gathered from the nations, who
have acquired cattle and goods, who live at the
[a]center of the world.' 13 [A]Sheba and [B]Dedan and the
merchants of [C]Tarshish with all its [a]villages will
say to you, 'Have you come to capture spoil? Have
you assembled your company to seize plunder, to
carry away silver and gold, to take away cattle and
goods, to capture great [D]spoil?' " '
14 "Therefore prophesy, son of man, and say to
Gog, 'Thus says the Lord GOD, "On that day when
My people Israel are [A]living securely, will you not
know *it*? 15 [A]You will come from your place out of
the remote parts of the north, you and many peoples with you, all of them riding on horses, a great
assembly and a mighty army; 16 and you will come
up against My people Israel like a cloud to cover
the land. It shall come about in the last days that I
will bring you against My land, so that the nations
may [A]know Me when I am [B]sanctified through you
before their eyes, O Gog."
17 'Thus says the Lord GOD, "Are you the one of
whom I spoke in former days through My servants
the prophets of Israel, who [A]prophesied in those
days for *many* years that I would bring you against
them? 18 It will come about on that day, when Gog
comes against the land of Israel," declares the Lord
GOD, "that My fury will mount up in My [A]anger. 19 In
My [A]zeal and in My blazing wrath I declare *that* on
that day there will surely be a great [a,B]earthquake in

38:4 [a]Or *clothed in full armor* [A]Is 43:17 [B]Ezek 38:15; Dan 11:40 38:5 [a]Lit *Cush* [A]2 Chr 36:20; Ezra 1:1; Ezek 27:10; Dan 8:20 [B]Gen 10:6-8; Ezek 30:4, 5 [C]Ezek 27:10; 30:5 38:6 [A]Gen 10:2, 3 [B]Gen 10:3; Ezek 27:14 38:7 [A]Is 8:9 38:8 [a]Lit *peoples* [b]Lit *it was* [A]Is 24:22 [B]Is 11:11; Ezek 36:24; 37:21; 38:12; 39:27, 28 [C]Ezek 34:13; 36:1-8 [D]Ezek 38:11, 14; 39:26 38:9 [A]Is 5:28; 21:1; 25:4; 28:2; Jer 4:13 [B]Ezek 30:18; 38:16; Joel 2:2 38:10 [a]Lit *words* [A]Ps 36:4; Mic 2:1 38:11 [a]Or *open country* [A]Zech 2:4 [B]Jer 49:31 38:12 [a]Lit *navel* [A]Is 10:6; Ezek 29:19 38:13 [a]Or *young lions* [A]Ezek 27:22, 23 [B]Ezek 25:13; 27:15, 20 [C]Ezek 27:12 [D]Is 10:6; 33:23; Jer 15:13 38:14 [A]Jer 23:6; Ezek 38:8, 11; Zech 2:5, 8 38:15 [A]Ezek 39:2 38:16 [A]Ps 83:18; Ezek 36:23; 38:23 [B]Is 5:16; 8:13; 29:23; Ezek 28:22 38:17 [A]Is 5:26-29; 34:1-6; 63:1-6; 66:15, 16; Joel 3:9-14 38:18 [A]Ps 18:8, 15 38:19 [a]Or *shaking* [A]Deut 32:22; Ps 18:7, 8; Ezek 5:13; 36:5, 6; Nah 1:2; Heb 12:29 [B]Joel 3:16; Hag 2:6, 7, 21

38:4 I will bring you out. Just as God used Assyria (Is 8) and Babylon (21:19) as human invaders for His judgments, He aims to use this army. In this case, He brings the invader to Palestine so that He may visit judgment (v. 8) on the invader itself (38:18–23; 39:1–10). He thus uses the language of hooks in the jaws, as in judging Egypt (29:4). From the aggressors' perspective, they think that it is their plan only to seize the spoil which draws them to Palestine (vv. 11, 12).

38:5 Persia, Ethiopia and Put. The invasion involves a coalition of powers from the E and S of Palestine. Persia is modern Iran, Libya is in N Africa, W of Egypt; and Ethiopia is S of Egypt.

38:6 Gomer. Today the area is Armenia, which also was known as Cappadocia, having a people called Gomer in Assyrian inscriptions. **Beth-togarmah.** Today's eastern Turkey (*see note on 27:14*).

38:7, 8 This is the great time of Israel's cleansing, salvation, and spiritual life (cf. 39:22, 27, 28; Zec 12:10–13:9), getting them ready for Messiah's return and kingdom (Zec 14).

38:8 in the latter years. In the context of Israel's restoration (Eze 34–39), the invader will make its final bid for the land. **restored from the sword.** This refers to Israelites who have been returned to their land, after the sword had killed or scattered many of their people. The Heb. word for "restored" means "to return" (Ge 40:13; 41:13). **gathered.** This word also frequently refers to God's final regathering of Israel (37:21; Is 11:12; 43:5; Jer 32:37). It has begun historically and will continue until the latter days. In the final millennial kingdom, there will occur the full and spiritual regathering, when all Israel is saved to enter their promised kingdom (cf. Zec 12–14; Ro 11:25–27). **living securely.** This term occurs in several contexts devoted to the Israelites' blessed estate after God has brought them back to their land (28:26; 34:25, 28; 39:26; Jer 32:37; Zec 14:11).

38:9 You will go up. The time of the invasion is best understood as the end of the future tribulation period of 7 years. Israel will have been under a false peace in treaty with the Antichrist (Da 9:27; 11:22, 24), before he turns on them in the "abomination of desolation" (Mt 24:15; cf. Da 9:27). The false peace will end in hostility lasting to the completion of the 7 years (Zec 14:1–3). When this final war occurs (cf. Rev 16:12–16), Christ will ultimately conquer the beast, the false prophet, and all the ungodly forces (Rev 19:11–21) in order to establish His millennial kingdom (Rev 20:1–10).

38:10–13 This describes the peace in Israel during the period of Antichrist's short-lived treaty with them (Da 9:27) in the first half of Daniel's 70th week. References to "unwalled villages" refer to that period of 3 1/2 when Israel is secure under the protection of the world-ruling "prince that shall come," called Antichrist (cf. Da 9:27). After Antichrist turns on Israel, there is an escalation of hostility until the end of the 7-year time when this great force comes to plunder Jerusalem and the Promised Land (v. 12).

38:12 to capture spoil ... plunder. Antichrist takes over the world for his own power and possession. The wealth of his empire is described in Rev 18.

38:13 Dedan ... Tarshish. *See note on Jon 1:3.*

38:15 riding on horses. These could be actual horses used in war, if tribulation judgments (seals, trumpets, vials) in Rev 6–16 have dealt drastic blows to industries producing war vehicles and weaponry. Or, some see horses and weapons here (39:3, 9) being used symbolically to represent meaning which would be easy to grasp in Ezekiel's day, but which would be fulfilled in the future time with different war forms suitable to that time.

38:16 that the nations may know Me. The phrase, frequent in Ezekiel, is part of the theme to glorify God and show His sovereign power (cf. Introduction: Historical and Theological Themes). God is the victor, who will be "sanctified" by fire (cf. v. 19).

38:17 Are you the one ... ? *See notes on 38:2.* This refers to the general references to this time and the participants (cf. Joel 3:9–17; Am 5:11, 12; Zep 3:8). Even Daniel (Da 2:41–44) referred to this time at least 3 decades prior to Eze 38. The nature of the question presupposes that the previous generalities are now being particularized in the person of Gog.

38:18–23 My fury will mount up. God's patience will be exhausted with the repeated attempts to annihilate Israel since the "abomination" by Antichrist (Da 9:27; Mt 24:15), and He will employ a great earthquake in Israel; panic will seize the invading soldiers (v. 21),

the land of Israel. 20 [A]The fish of the sea, the
birds of the heavens, the beasts of the field, all
the creeping things that creep on the earth, and
all the men who are on the face of the earth will
shake at My presence; the [B]mountains also will be
thrown down, the steep pathways will [a]collapse
and every wall will fall to the ground. 21 I will call
for a [A]sword against [a]him on all My mountains,"
declares the Lord GOD. "[B]Every man's sword will
be against his brother. 22 With pestilence and with
blood I will enter into [A]judgment with him; and
I will rain on him and on his troops, and on the
many peoples who are with him, [a]a torrential rain,
with [B]hailstones, fire and brimstone. 23 I will magnify Myself, sanctify Myself, and [A]make Myself
known in the sight of many nations; and they will
know that I am the LORD." '

PROPHECY AGAINST GOG—INVADERS DESTROYED

39 "And [A]you, son of man, prophesy against Gog
and say, 'Thus says the Lord [a]GOD, "Behold,
I am against you, O Gog, [b]prince of Rosh, Meshech
and Tubal; 2 and I will turn you around, drive you
on, take you up from the remotest parts of the north
and bring you against the mountains of Israel. 3 I
will [A]strike your bow from your left hand and dash
down your arrows from your right hand. 4 You will
[A]fall on the mountains of Israel, you and all your
troops and the peoples who are with you; I will
give you as [B]food to every [a]kind of predatory bird
and beast of the field. 5 You will fall on the [a]open
field; for it is I who have spoken," declares the Lord
GOD. 6 "And I will send [A]fire upon Magog and those
who inhabit the [B]coastlands in safety; and they will
know that I am the LORD.

7 "My [A]holy name I will make known in the midst
of My people Israel; and I will not let My holy name
be [B]profaned anymore. And the [C]nations will know
that I am the LORD, the [D]Holy One in Israel. 8 Behold,
it is coming and it shall be done," declares the Lord
GOD. "That is the day of which I have spoken.

9 "Then those who inhabit the cities of Israel will
[A]go out and make [B]fires with the weapons and burn
them, both shields and bucklers, bows and arrows,
war clubs and spears, and for seven years they will
make fires of them. 10 They will not take wood from
the field or gather firewood from the forests, for
they will make fires with the weapons; and they
will take the spoil of those who despoiled them and
seize the [A]plunder of those who plundered them,"
declares the Lord GOD.

11 "On that day I will give Gog a burial ground
there in Israel, the valley of those who pass by
east of the sea, and it will block off those who
would pass by. So they will bury Gog there with
all his [a]horde, and they will call *it* the valley of
[b]Hamon-gog. 12 For seven months the house of
Israel will be burying them in order to [A]cleanse
the land. 13 Even all the people of the land will
bury *them;* and it will be [a]to their [A]renown *on* the
day that I [B]glorify Myself," declares the Lord GOD.
14 "They will set apart men who will constantly
pass through the land, [A]burying those who were
passing through, even those left on the surface
of the ground, in order to cleanse it. At the end
of seven months they will make a search. 15 As
those who pass through the land pass through
and anyone sees a man's bone, then he will [a]set
up a marker by it until the buriers have buried it
in the valley of [b]Hamon-gog. 16 And even *the* name
of *the* city will be Hamonah. So they will cleanse
the land." '

17 "As for you, son of man, thus says the Lord GOD,
'Speak to every [a]kind of [A]bird and to every [A]beast of
the field, "Assemble and come, gather from every
side to My sacrifice which I am going to [B]sacrifice
for you, as a great sacrifice on the mountains of Israel, that you may eat flesh and drink blood. 18 You
will [A]eat the flesh of mighty men and drink the
blood of the princes of the earth, as *though they
were* [B]rams, lambs, goats and [C]bulls, all of them
fatlings of [D]Bashan. 19 So you will eat fat until you
are glutted, and drink blood until you are drunk,
from My sacrifice which I have sacrificed for you.
20 You will be glutted at My table with [A]horses and
charioteers, with mighty men and all the men of
war," declares the Lord GOD.

38:20 [a]Lit *fall* [A]Jer 4:24, 25; Hos 4:3; Nah 1:4-6 [B]Zech 14:4 38:21 [a]I.e. Gog [A]Ezek 14:17 [B]Judg 7:22; 1 Sam 14:20; 2 Chr 20:23; Hag 2:22 38:22 [a]Lit *an overflowing* [A]Is 66:16; Jer 25:31 [B]Ps 11:6; 18:12-14; Is 28:17 38:23 [A]Ps 9:16; Ezek 37:28; 38:16 39:1 [a]Heb *YHWH,* usually rendered *LORD,* and so throughout the ch [b]Or *chief prince of Meshech* [A]Ezek 38:2 39:3 [A]Ps 76:3; Jer 21:4, 5; Ezek 30:21-24; Hos 1:5 39:4 [a]Lit *wing* [A]Is 14:24, 25; Ezek 39:17-20 [B]Ezek 29:5; 32:4, 5; 33:27 39:5 [a]Lit *face of the* 39:6 [A]Ezek 30:8, 16; 38:19, 22; Amos 1:4, 7, 10; Nah 1:6 [B]Ps 72:10; Is 66:19; Jer 25:22 39:7 [A]Ezek 36:20-22; 39:25 [B]Ex 20:7; Ezek 20:9, 14, 39 [C]Ezek 38:16, 23 [D]Is 12:6; 43:3, 14; 55:5; 60:9, 14 39:9 [A]Is 66:24; Mal 1:5 [B]Josh 11:6; Ps 46:9 39:10 [A]Is 14:2; 33:1; Mic 5:8; Hab 2:8 39:11 [a]Lit *crowd* [b]Or *the multitude of Gog* 39:12 [A]Deut 21:23; Ezek 39:14, 16 39:13 [a]Or *a memorial for them* [A]Jer 33:9; Zeph 3:19, 20 [B]Ezek 28:22 39:14 [A]Jer 14:16 39:15 [a]Lit *build* [b]Or *the multitude of Gog* 39:17 [a]Lit *wing* [A]Is 56:9; Jer 12:9; Ezek 39:4; Rev 19:17, 18 [B]Is 34:6, 7; Jer 46:10; Zeph 1:7 39:18 [A]Ezek 29:5; Rev 19:18 [B]Jer 51:40 [C]Jer 50:27 [D]Ps 22:12; Amos 4:1 39:20 [A]Ps 76:5, 6; Ezek 38:4; Hag 2:22; Rev 19:18

who will turn and use their weapons against one another (cf. 2Ch 20:22, 23). He will further decimate the ranks by pestilence, a deluge of rain, large hailstones, plus fire and brimstone. The descriptions here are identical to that of the last half of the 7-year tribulation in Rev 6:12–17; 11:19; 16:17–21; 19:11–21.

39:1–10 I am against you. This scene of the army's ruin adds detail to 38:18–23 such as: 1) the disarming of soldiers (v. 3); 2) their fall in death (vv. 4, 5); 3) the gorging of birds and beasts on the corpses (v. 4); 4) fire sent also on others besides the army (v. 6); and 5) burning of weapons by Israelites (vv. 9, 10).

39:9, 10 make fires with the weapons. There is enough equipment to provide fuel for 7 years.

39:9 seven years. A vast army (cf. "many," 38:15) would have much weaponry, requiring 7 years to burn. Since this is likely at the end of the time of tribulation, synonymous with the battle of Armageddon (Rev 16:16; 19:19–21), the burials would extend into the millennial kingdom.

39:11–16 give Gog a burial ground. Israelites moving E from the Mediterranean, with the sea to their backs and the Jezreel Valley before them, bury bodies. Further, people in the whole land help in the interment, which consumes 7 months. The description fits the time after Christ's Second Advent extending into the millennial era as those who go into His kingdom do the work (cf. Rev 20:1–10).

39:11, 16 Hamon-gog. Lit. "the multitude of Gog." In v. 16, a city in the area will be named Hamonah, "multitude" (cf. a similar idea in Joel 3:14).

39:17–20 Speak to … bird and … beast. God's word summons carrion birds and carnivorous animals to consume the fallen flesh as described in Rev 19:21.

39:17, 18 My sacrifice. Since God describes the feast by the imagery of a sacrificial meal, the warriors who fell (v. 19) are described figuratively in words such as rams and other animals used in sacrifice.

21 "And I will set My [A]glory among the nations;
and all the nations will see My judgment which I
have executed and My hand which I have laid on
them. 22 And the house of Israel will [A]know that I
am the LORD their God from that day onward. 23 The
nations will know that the house of Israel went into
exile for their [A]iniquity because they acted treacherously against Me, and I [B]hid My face from them; so
I gave them into the hand of their adversaries, and
all of them fell by the sword. 24 [A]According to their
uncleanness and according to their transgressions
I dealt with them, and I hid My face from them." ' "

ISRAEL RESTORED

25 Therefore thus says the Lord GOD, "Now I will
[a,A]restore the fortunes of Jacob and have mercy on
the whole [B]house of Israel; and I will be [C]jealous for
My holy name. 26 They will [a,A]forget their disgrace
and all their treachery which they [b]perpetrated
against Me, when they [B]live securely on their *own*
land with [C]no one to make *them* afraid. 27 When I
[A]bring them back from the peoples and gather them
from the lands of their enemies, then I shall be
[B]sanctified [a]through them in the sight of the many
nations. 28 Then they will know that I am the LORD
their God because I made them go into exile among
the nations, and then gathered them *again* to their
own land; and I will leave none of them there any
longer. 29 I will not hide My face from them any
longer, for I will have [A]poured out My Spirit on the
house of Israel," declares the Lord GOD.

VISION OF THE MAN WITH A MEASURING ROD

40 In the [A]twenty-fifth year of our exile, at the
beginning of the year, on the tenth of the
month, in the fourteenth year after the [B]city was
[a]taken, on that same day the [C]hand of the LORD was
upon me and He brought me there. 2 In the [A]visions
of God He brought me into the land of Israel and set
me on a very [B]high mountain, and on it [C]to the south
there was a [D]structure like a city. 3 So He brought me
there; and behold, there was a man whose appearance was like the appearance of [A]bronze, with a [B]line
of flax and a [C]measuring [a]rod in his hand; and he was
standing in the gateway. 4 The man said to me, "[A]Son
of man, [B]see with your eyes, hear with your ears, and
give attention to all that I am going to show you; for
you have been brought here in order to show *it* to
you. [C]Declare to the house of Israel all that you see."

MEASUREMENTS RELATING TO THE TEMPLE

5 And behold, there was a [A]wall on the outside of
the [a]temple all around, and in the man's hand was
a measuring rod of six cubits, *each of which was* a
cubit and a [b]handbreadth. So he measured the thickness of the [c]wall, one rod; and the height, one rod.

39:21 [A]Ex 9:16; Is 37:20; Ezek 36:23; 38:16, 23; 39:13 39:22 [A]Jer 24:7 39:23 [A]Jer 22:8, 9; 44:22; Ezek 36:18, 19 [B]Is 1:15; 59:2; Ezek 39:29 39:24 [A]2 Kin 17:7; Jer 2:17, 19; 4:18; Ezek 36:19 39:25 [a]Or *return the captivity* [A]Is 27:12, 13; Jer 33:7; Ezek 34:13 [B]Jer 31:1; Ezek 36:10; 37:21, 22; Hos 1:11 [C]Ex 20:5; Nah 1:2 39:26 [a]Another reading is *bear* [b]Lit *did treacherously* [A]Ezek 16:63; 20:43; 36:31 [B]1 Kin 4:25; Ezek 34:25-28 [C]Is 17:2; Mic 4:4 39:27 [a]Lit *in* [A]Ezek 36:24; 37:21 [B]Ezek 36:23; 38:16, 23 39:29 [A]Is 32:15; Ezek 36:27; 37:14; Joel 2:28 40:1 [a]Lit *struck* [A]Ezek 32:1, 17; 33:21 [B]2 Kin 25:1-7; Jer 39:1-9; 52:4-11; Ezek 33:21 [C]Ezek 1:3; 3:14, 22; 37:1 40:2 [A]Ezek 1:1; 8:3; Dan 7:1, 7 [B]Is 2:2, 3; Ezek 17:23; 20:40; 37:22; Mic 4:1; Rev 21:10 [C]Ps 48:2; Is 14:13 [D]1 Chr 28:12, 19 40:3 [a]Lit *reed*, and so throughout the ch [A]Ezek 1:7; Dan 10:6; Rev 1:15 [B]Ezek 47:3; Zech 2:1, 2 [C]Rev 11:1; 21:15 40:4 [A]Ezek 2:1, 3, 6, 8; 44:5 [B]Ezek 2:7, 8; 44:5 [C]Is 21:10; Jer 26:2; Acts 20:27 40:5 [a]Lit *house* [b]I.e. 20.4 in. or longer [c]Lit *building* [A]Is 26:1; Ezek 42:20

39:21–29 I will set My glory. God vanquishes Israel's foes to show His glory so that His enemies and Israel will all know that He is the Lord (vv. 6, 22). This is Israel's salvation spoken of in Zec 12:10–13:9 and Ro 11:25–27.

39:29 poured out My Spirit. God's provision of His Spirit at the Second Advent complements the regathering (cf. 36:27; 37:14; Joel 2:28). The Gog and Magog assault in Rev 20:7–9 at the end of the Millennium is another assault on Jerusalem patterned after certain images of the invasion here (chaps. 38, 39), but it is a distinct event one thousand years after the millennial kingdom begins. *See note on Rev 20:8, 9.*

40:1–48:35 Following this great battle at the end of the time of tribulation, this section provides explicit details concerning Christ's millennial reign which follows, giving more detail about the 1,000-year kingdom than all other OT prophecies put together. It is the "Holy of Holies" among millennial forecasts. As has been done with the previous 39 chapters, this concluding portion will also be approached in a literal, historical manner which best serves the interpreter in all Scripture. In many ways these chapters are the most important in the book since they form the crowning reality, the climax of Ezekiel's prophecy and Israel's restoration. The section includes: 1) the new temple (40:1–43:12); 2) the new worship (43:13–46:24); and 3) the new apportionment of the Land (47:1–48:35).

40:1 the twenty-fifth year. 573 B.C., in the first month of the ecclesiastical year, Nisan. The tenth day was the start of preparations for Passover.

40:2 In the visions of God He brought me. Ezekiel 40–48 narrates another vision, as did 1:1–3:27; 8–11; and 37:1–14. The characterization of the prophecy as a vision in no way detracts from its literal reality any more than Ezekiel's visions of Jerusalem's sins, idolatry, and destruction did. **into the land of Israel.** The vision pertains to Israel, as did chaps. 1–24, 33, 34–39. **a very high mountain.** The mountain is not named; however, it is most likely Mt. Zion (cf. 17:22; 20:40; Is 2:2; Micah 4:1), lifted up from its surroundings by a great earthquake (Zec 14:4, 5, 10). **structure like a city.** God will be explaining details relating to Israel's spiritual future (vv. 2, 4), so this must be the temple in particular and Jerusalem in general. This new and glorious temple will stand in contrast to the desecration and destruction of Solomon's temple (chaps. 8–11).

40:3 a man. An angel conducted a tour of all the details shown to the prophet, appearing in the form of a man (e.g., Ge 18; Eze 9), appearing like bright, gleaming bronze. He could be understood as the Angel of the Lord since he is called "LORD" (44:2, 5; *see note on Ex 3:2*). His "line of flax" was for larger measurements, the "rod" for shorter ones (cf. Rev 11:1; 21:15). In each case God measured what belongs to Him.

40:4 Declare ... all that you see. Ezekiel 1–24 refers to Israel's historical removal from her land; chaps. 25–32 to historical judgments against other nations; chap. 33 to a historical call to repentance and the fall of Jerusalem. So in chaps. 34–39, Israel's literal, future return to the same land as a reversal of the historical dispersion is the most natural way to interpret the chapters. Ezekiel 38, 39 describe a future, historical invasion of Israel and its aftermath during the time just before Messiah's return. Therefore, chaps. 40–48 would then be thought to continue the historical, prophetic pattern, describing the millennial conditions after Messiah comes and destroys the ungodly (Rev 19:11ff.), under which Israel will live and worship. Believing Gentiles will also be in the kingdom as sheep of the Great Shepherd (cf. Mt 25:31–46), while all unbelievers are destroyed. Ezekiel is to write down all the details.

40:5 a wall on the outside. This outer wall is later described as a separation of the holy areas (42:20). **the temple.** See 1Ki 6, 7 to compare with details of Solomon's temple. This could not be the heavenly temple since Ezekiel was taken to Israel to see it (v. 2). It could not be Zerubbabel's temple since the glory of God was not present then. It could not be the eternal temple since the Lord and the Lamb are its temple (cf. Rev 21:22). Therefore, it must be the earthly millennial temple built with all of the exquisite details that are yet to be outlined. **measuring rod of six cubits .... handbreadth.** The rod extended 6 royal (long) cubits of 21 in. for a total of 10.5 ft., each cubit being made up of a standard width of 18 in. and a handbreadth of 3 in.

6Then he went to the gate which faced [A]east, went up
its steps and measured the threshold of the gate, one
rod [a]in width; and the other threshold *was* one rod
[a]in width. 7The [A]guardroom *was* one rod long and
one rod wide; and *there were* five cubits between
the guardrooms. And the threshold of the gate by the
porch of the gate [a]facing inward *was* one rod. 8Then
he measured the porch of the gate [a]facing inward,
one rod. 9He measured the porch of the gate, eight
cubits; and its side pillars, two cubits. And the porch of
the gate was [a]faced inward. 10The guardrooms of the
gate toward the east *numbered* three on each side;
the three of them had the same measurement. The
side pillars also had the same measurement on each
side. 11And he measured the width of the [a]gateway,
ten cubits, and the length of the gate, thirteen cubits.
12*There was* a [a]barrier *wall* one cubit *wide* in front of
the guardrooms on each side; and the guardrooms
were six cubits *square* on each side. 13He measured
the gate from the roof of the one guardroom to the
roof of the other, a width of twenty-five cubits from
one door to *the* door opposite. 14He made the side pillars sixty cubits *high;* the gate *extended* round about
to the side pillar of the [A]courtyard. 15*From* the front
of the entrance gate to the front of the inner porch
of the gate *was* fifty cubits. 16*There were* [a,A]shuttered

40:6 [a]Or *in depth* [A]Ezek 8:16; 11:1; 40:20; 43:1 40:7 [a]Lit *from the house* [A]Ezek 40:10-16, 21, 29, 33, 36 40:8 [a]Lit *from the house* 40:9 [a]Lit *from the house* 40:11 [a]Lit *entrance of the gate* 40:12 [a]Lit *border* 40:14 [A]Ex 27:9; 1 Chr 28:6; Ps 100:4; Is 62:9; Ezek 8:7; 42:1 40:16 [a]Or *beveled inwards* [A]1 Kin 6:4; Ezek 41:16, 26

40:6, 7 the gate … east. The buildings of the E gate are first because this will be in the direct line of approach to the temple. Each opening was 10.5 ft. across. Chambers (rooms) in the wall are 10.5 x 10.5 ft. Precise measurements describe a literal temple, not a symbolic one.

40:8–16 The chambers described here are accommodations for the ministering priests and temple officers who care for the temple.

40:16 shuttered windows. Since they had no glass, these are lattices (cf. 41:16–26). **on *each* side pillar … palm tree ornaments.** These depict God's desire for fruit in Israel. Palms are symbols of beauty, salvation, and

EZEKIEL'S TEMPLE

Ezekiel's vision of a restored temple gave hope to the exiles in Babylon. They had heard of the temple's destruction in 586 B.C., but Ezekiel spoke of a more glorious temple than the one that had been destroyed. This glory of the new temple was not derived from gold or intricate carvings, but from the presence of the living God among His people (43:7).

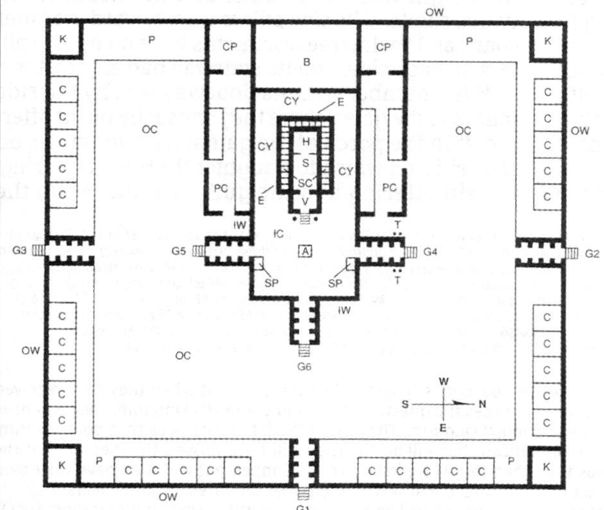

The Temple Complex

OW	Wall of outer court (40:5)
G1	Eastern outer gateway (40:6–16)
OC	Outer court (40:17)
C	Chambers in outer court (40:17)
P	Pavement (40:17, 18)
G2	Northern outer gateway (40:20–22)
G4	Northern inner gateway (40:23, 35–37)
G3	Southern outer gateway (40:24–26)
G5	Southern inner gateway (40:27–31)
IC	Inner court (40:32)
G6	Eastern inner gateway (40:32–34)
T	Tables for killing sacrifices (40:38)
SP	Chambers for singers and priests (40:44–46)
A	Altar (40:47; 43:13-27)
V	Vestibule of temple (40:48, 49)
S	Sanctuary or Holy Place (41:1, 2)
H	Most Holy Place (41:2, 4)
SC	Side chambers (41:5–7)
E	Elevation around temple (41:8)
CY	Separating courtyard (41:10)
B	Building at west end (41:12)
PC	Priest's chambers (42:1–14)
IW	Wall of inner court (42:10)
CP	Priest's cooking places (46:19, 20)
K	Kitchens (46:21–24)

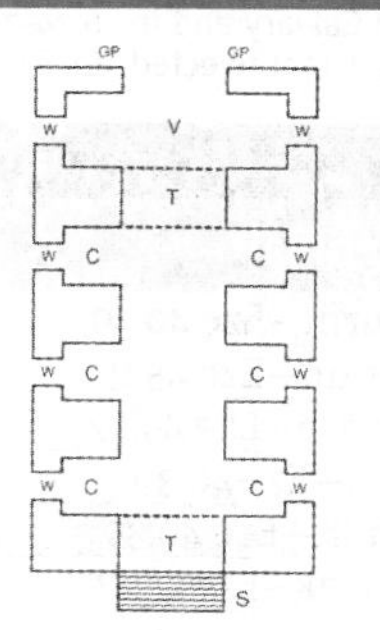

The Gateway

S	Steps (40:6)
T	Thresholds (40:6, 7)
C	Gate chambers (40:7, 10, 12)
W	Windows (40:16)
V	Vestibule (40:8, 9)
GP	Gateposts (40:10, 14)

windows *looking* toward the guardrooms, and toward their side pillars within the gate all around, and
likewise for the porches. And *there were* windows all
around inside; and on *each* side pillar *were* [B]palm
tree ornaments.
17 Then he brought me into the [A]outer court, and
behold, *there were* [B]chambers and a pavement made
for the court all around; thirty chambers [a]faced the
pavement. 18 The pavement (*that is,* the lower pavement) *was* by the [a]side of the gates, corresponding
to the length of the gates. 19 Then he measured the
width from the front of the [A]lower gate to the front
of the exterior of the inner court, a [B]hundred cubits
on the east and on the north.
20 *As for* the [A]gate of the outer court which faced the
north, he measured its length and its width. 21 [a]It had
three [A]guardrooms on each side; and its [B]side pillars
and its porches [b]had the same measurement as the
first gate. Its length *was* [C]fifty cubits and the width
[D]twenty-five cubits. 22 Its [A]windows and its porches
and its palm tree ornaments *had* the same measurements as the [B]gate which faced toward the east; and
[a]it was reached by seven [C]steps, and its [b]porch *was* in
front of them. 23 The inner court had a gate opposite
the gate on the north as well as *the gate* on the east;
and he measured a [A]hundred cubits from gate to gate.
24 Then he led me toward the south, and behold,
there was a [A]gate toward the south; and he measured its [B]side pillars and its porches according to
[a]those same measurements. 25 [a]The gate and its
porches had [A]windows all around like [b]those other
windows; the length *was* [B]fifty cubits and the width
twenty-five cubits. 26 *There were* seven [A]steps going
up to it, and its porches *were* in front of them; and it
had [B]palm tree ornaments on its side pillars, one on
each side. 27 The inner court had a gate toward the
[A]south; and he measured from gate to gate toward
the south, a [B]hundred cubits.
28 Then he brought me to the inner court by the
south gate; and he measured the south gate [A]accord-
ing to those same measurements. 29 Its [A]guardrooms
also, its side pillars and its [B]porches *were* according
to those same measurements. And [a]the gate and
its porches had [B]windows all around; it *was* [C]fifty
cubits long and twenty-five cubits wide. 30 *There
were* [A]porches all around, twenty-five cubits long
and five cubits wide. 31 Its porches *were* toward the
outer court; and [A]palm tree ornaments *were* on its
side pillars, and its stairway *had* eight [B]steps.
32 He brought me into the [A]inner court toward the
east. And he measured the gate [B]according to those
same measurements. 33 Its [A]guardrooms also, its
side pillars and its porches *were* according to those
same measurements. And [a]the gate and its porches
had [B]windows all around; it *was* [C]fifty cubits long
and twenty-five cubits wide. 34 Its [A]porches *were*
toward the outer court; and [A]palm tree ornaments
were on its side pillars, on each side, and its stairway *had* eight [B]steps.
35 Then he brought me to the [A]north gate; and
he measured *it* according to those same measurements, 36 *with* its [A]guardrooms, its side pillars and
its [B]porches. And [a]the gate had [B]windows all around;
the length *was* [C]fifty cubits and the width twenty-five cubits. 37 Its side pillars *were* toward the outer
court; and [A]palm tree ornaments *were* on its side pillars on each side, and its stairway had eight [B]steps.
38 A [A]chamber with its doorway was by the side
pillars at the gates; there they [B]rinse the burnt offering. 39 In the porch of the gate *were* two [A]tables on
each side, on which to slaughter the [B]burnt offering,
the sin offering and the guilt offering. 40 On the

40:16 [B]1 Kin 6:29, 32, 35; 2 Chr 3:5; Ezek 40:22, 26, 31, 34, 37; 41:18-20, 25, 26 40:17 [a]Lit *to* [A]Ezek 10:5; 42:1; 46:21; Rev 11:2 [B]2 Kin 23:11; 1 Chr 9:26; 23:28; 2 Chr 31:11; Ezek 40:38 40:18 [a]Lit *shoulder* 40:19 [A]Ezek 40:23, 27; 46:1, 2 [B]Ezek 40:23, 27 40:20 [A]Ezek 40:6 40:21 [a]Lit *Its guardrooms were three* [b]Lit *were* [A]Ezek 40:7 [B]Ezek 40:16, 30 [C]Ezek 40:15 [D]Ezek 40:13 40:22 [a]Lit *they were going up into it* [b]Or *porches* [A]Ezek 40:16 [B]Ezek 40:6 [C]Ezek 40:26, 31, 34, 37, 49 40:23 [A]Ezek 40:19, 27 40:24 [a]Lit *these measurements,* and so throughout the ch [A]Ezek 40:6, 20, 35; 46:9 [B]Ezek 40:21 40:25 [a]Lit *It* [b]Lit *these windows* [A]Ezek 40:16, 22, 29 [B]Ezek 40:21, 33 40:26 [A]Ezek 40:6, 22 [B]Ezek 40:16 40:27 [A]Ezek 40:23, 32 [B]Ezek 40:19 40:28 [A]Ezek 40:32, 35 40:29 [a]Lit *it* [A]Ezek 40:7, 10, 21 [B]Ezek 40:16, 22, 25 [C]Ezek 40:21 40:30 [A]Ezek 40:16, 21 40:31 [A]Ezek 40:16 [B]Ezek 40:22, 26, 34, 37 40:32 [A]Ezek 40:28-31, 35 [B]Ezek 40:28 40:33 [a]Lit *it* [A]Ezek 40:29 [B]Ezek 40:16 [C]Ezek 40:21 40:34 [A]Ezek 40:16 [B]Ezek 40:22, 37 40:35 [A]Ezek 40:27, 32; 44:4; 47:2 40:36 [a]Lit *it* [A]Ezek 40:7, 29 [B]Ezek 40:16 [C]Ezek 40:21 40:37 [A]Ezek 40:16 [B]Ezek 40:34 40:38 [A]1 Chr 28:12; Neh 13:5, 9; Jer 35:4; 36:10; Ezek 40:17; 41:10; 42:13 [B]2 Chr 4:6 40:39 [A]Ezek 40:42 [B]Lev 1:3-17; Ezek 46:2

triumph (cf. Zec 14:16ff.; Rev 7:9). Palms are on the inner court's side pillars as well (v. 31).

40:17 the outer court. This court is farthest out from the temple proper and enclosed by the outer walls.

40:17–37 Here is a further blueprint for the temple area, with more precise measurements. The numbers 5, 25, 50, and 100 are frequently used. The sanctuary formed a square of some 500 cubits.

40:38–47 This section describes "chambers" for the priests, and raises the question of sacrifices in the millennial kingdom. They will exist as vv. 39–43 indicate, but will be no more efficacious then than they were in OT times. No sacrifice before or after Christ saves. They only point to Him as the one true Lamb who takes away sin. The Lord's Supper is a memorial that looks back to Calvary and in no way diminishes the cross. Israel rejected their Messiah, but when they have received Him and are in His kingdom, they will have a memorial of sacrifices that point to Him. They will have missed the memorial of the Lord's Supper, but will then have their own memorial sacrifices for 1,000 years.

40:39 burnt … sin … guilt offering. For OT background see 1) Lv 1:1–17; 6:8–13; 2) Lv 4:1–35; 6:24–30; and 3) Lv 5:1–6:7; 7:1–10 respectively. Cf. Eze 43:18–27; 45:13–25; 46:1–15, 19–24.

MILLENNIAL SACRIFICES

Levitical	Millennial*
1. Burnt—Lv 1:3–17	1. Burnt—Eze 40:39
2. Grain—Lv 2:1–16	2. Grain—Eze 45:15
3. Peace—Lv 3:1–17	3. Peace—Eze 45:15
4. Sin—Lv 4:1–35	4. Sin—Eze 40:39
5. Guilt—Lv 5:1–6:7	5. Guilt—Eze 40:39
6. Drink—Lv 23:13, 37	6. Drink—Eze 45:17

**Is 56:7; 66:20–23; Jer 33:18 further confirm the burnt and grain offerings.*

outer [a]side, [b]as one went up to the [c]gateway toward the north, *were* two tables; and on the other [a]side of the porch of the gate *were* two tables. 41 Four [A]tables *were* on each side [a]next to the gate; *or,* eight tables on which they slaughter *sacrifices.* 42 For the burnt offering *there were* four [A]tables of [B]hewn stone, a cubit and a half long, a cubit and a half wide and one cubit high, on which they lay the instruments with which they slaughter the [A]burnt offering and the sacrifice. 43 The double [a]hooks, one handbreadth in length, were installed [b]in the house all around; and on the tables *was* the flesh of the offering.

44 From the outside to the [A]inner gate were [a,B]chambers for the [C]singers in the inner court, *one of* which was at the [b]side of the north gate, with [c]its front toward the south, and one at the [b]side of the [d]south gate facing toward the north. 45 He said to me, "This is the [A]chamber which faces toward the south, *intended* for the priests who [B]keep charge of the [a]temple; 46 but the [A]chamber which faces toward the north is for the priests who [B]keep charge of the altar. These are the [C]sons of Zadok, who from the sons of Levi [D]come near to the LORD to minister to Him." 47 He measured the court, a *perfect* square, a [A]hundred cubits long and a hundred cubits wide; and the altar was in front of the [a]temple.

48 Then he brought me to the [A]porch of the [a]temple and measured *each* side pillar of the porch, five cubits on each side; and the width of the gate was three cubits on each side. 49 The length of the porch *was* twenty cubits and the width eleven cubits; and at the [A]stairway by which it was ascended *were* [B]columns belonging to the side pillars, one on each side.

THE INNER TEMPLE

41 Then he [A]brought me to the [a,B]nave and measured the [C]side pillars; six cubits wide on each side *was* the width of the [b]side pillar. 2 The width of the entrance *was* ten cubits and the [a]sides of the entrance *were* five cubits on each side. And he measured [b]the length of the nave, [A]forty cubits, and the width, [A]twenty cubits. 3 Then he went [a,A]inside and measured each [B]side pillar of the doorway, two cubits, and the doorway, six cubits *high;* and the width of the doorway, seven cubits. 4 He measured its length, [A]twenty cubits, and the width, twenty cubits, before the [B]nave; and he said to me, "This is the [C]most holy *place.*"

5 Then he measured the wall of the [a]temple, six cubits; and the width of the [A]side chambers, four cubits, all around about the house on every side. 6 [A]The side chambers were in three stories, [a]one above another, and [b]thirty in each story; and [c]the side chambers [B]extended to the wall which *stood* on [d]their inward side all around, that they might be fastened, and not be fastened into the wall of the temple *itself.* 7 The side chambers surrounding the temple were wider at each successive story. Because the [A]structure surrounding the temple went upward by stages on all sides of the temple, therefore the width of the temple *increased* as it went higher; and thus one went up from the lowest *story* to the highest by way of the [a]second *story.* 8 I saw also that the house had a raised [a]platform all around; the foundations of the side chambers were a full rod of [A]six [b]long cubits *in height.* 9 The [a]thickness of the outer wall of the side chambers *was* five cubits. But the [A]free space between the side chambers belonging to the temple 10 and the *outer* [A]chambers *was* twenty cubits in width all around the temple on every side. 11 The [a]doorways of the [b]side chambers toward the [A]free space *consisted of* one doorway toward the north and another doorway toward the south; and the width of the [A]free space *was* five cubits all around.

12 The [A]building that *was* in front of the [B]separate area at the side toward the west *was* seventy cubits wide; and the wall of the building *was* five cubits [a]thick all around, and its length *was* ninety cubits.

13 Then he measured the temple, a [A]hundred cubits long; the [B]separate area with the [C]building and its walls *were* also a [A]hundred cubits long. 14 Also the width of the front of the temple and *that of* the separate [a]areas along the east *side totaled* a hundred cubits.

40:40 [a]Lit *shoulder* [b]Lit *to the one going up* [c]Lit *entrance of the gate* 40:41 [a]Lit *by the shoulder of* [A]Ezek 40:39, 40 40:42 [A]Ezek 40:39 [B]Ex 20:25 40:43 [a]Or *ledges* [b]Or *inside* 40:44 [a]Gr reads *in two chambers* [b]Lit *shoulder* [c]Lit *their* [d]So Gr; Heb reads *east* [A]Ezek 40:23, 27 [B]Ezek 40:17, 38 [C]1 Chr 6:31, 32; 16:41-43; 25:1-7 40:45 [a]Or *house* [A]Ezek 40:17, 38 [B]1 Chr 9:23; Ps 134:1 40:46 [A]Ezek 40:17, 38 [B]Lev 6:12, 13; Ezek 44:15 [C]1 Kin 2:35; Ezek 43:19; 48:11 [D]Lev 10:3; Num 16:5, 40; Ezek 42:13; 45:4 40:47 [a]Lit *house* [A]Ezek 40:19, 23, 27 40:48 [a]Lit *house* [A]1 Kin 6:3; 2 Chr 3:4 40:49 [A]Ezek 40:31, 34, 37 [B]1 Kin 7:15-22; 2 Chr 3:17; Jer 52:17-23; Rev 3:12 41:1 [a]I.e. the main inner hall [b]Lit *tent* [A]Ezek 40:2, 3, 17 [B]Ezek 41:21, 23 [C]Ezek 40:9; 41:3 41:2 [a]Lit *shoulders* [b]Lit *its length,* [A]1 Kin 6:2, 17; 2 Chr 3:3 41:3 [a]I.e. of the inner sanctuary [A]Ezek 40:16 [B]Ezek 41:1 41:4 [A]1 Kin 6:20 [B]1 Kin 6:5 [C]Ex 26:33, 34; 1 Kin 6:16; 7:50; 8:6; 2 Chr 5:7; Heb 9:3-8 41:5 [a]Lit *house,* and so throughout the ch [A]1 Kin 6:5; Ezek 41:6-11 41:6 [a]Lit *chamber upon chamber* [b]Lit *thirty times* [c]Lit *they were coming* [d]Lit *the inside of the side chambers* [A]1 Kin 6:5-10 [B]1 Kin 6:6, 10 41:7 [a]Lit *middle* [A]1 Kin 6:8 41:8 [a]Lit *height* [b]Or *to the joint* [A]Ezek 40:5 41:9 [a]Lit *width* [A]Ezek 41:11 41:10 [A]Ezek 40:17 41:11 [a]Lit *doorway* [b]Lit *side chamber* [A]Ezek 41:9 41:12 [a]Lit *wide* [A]Ezek 41:13, 15; 42:1 [B]Ezek 41:14; 42:10, 13 41:13 [A]Ezek 40:47 [B]Ezek 41:13-15; 42:1, 10, 13 [C]Ezek 41:12 41:14 [a]Lit *area*

40:41 tables on which they slaughter. Four tables are on either side of the inner court's N gate, used for commemorating the death of Christ by slaying burnt, sin, and guilt offerings.

40:44 singers. Provision is made for the praises of the redeemed in music.

40:46 sons of Zadok. Proper names tie the vision to historical reality, calling for literal interpretation. This Levitical family descended from Levi, Aaron, Eleazar, and Phinehas (1Ch 6:3–8). In accord with God's covenant with Phinehas (Nu 25:10–13), and because of Eli's unfaithfulness (cf. 1Sa 1, 2) and Zadok's faithfulness to David and Solomon (1Ki 1:32–40), Zadok's sons serve as priests in the millennial temple. Other references to sons of Zadok are in 43:19; 44:15 and 48:11.

40:47 measured the court. The court around the temple was a square, around the square temple (41:1). **the altar.** This is the bronze altar where offerings occur. Cf. 43:13–27.

40:48, 49 porch. This refers to the temple porch and is similar to that of Solomon's temple.

41:1 to the nave. Precise descriptions continue for the temple proper, its sanctuary or holy place (here called "nave"), and side chambers for priests' quarters (vv. 5–11). This chapter can be studied in the light of 1Ki 6, 7 to note differences from Solomon's temple.

41:4 the most holy *place*. The Holy of Holies, which the High Priest entered annually on the Day of Atonement (cf. Lv 16). These dimensions are identical to Solomon's (1Ki 6:20), and twice those of the tabernacle in the wilderness.

41:5–11 This section describes the "wall" and "side chambers."

41:12 building ... toward the west. Beyond the western end of the temple proper was a distinct building with space that serves the temple, possibly housing supplies.

41:13 measured the temple. Cf. 40:47. It was about 175 ft. square.

15 He measured the length of the [A]building [a]along
the front of the [B]separate area behind it, with a
[b,C]gallery on each side, a hundred cubits; *he* also
measured the inner nave and the porches of the
court. 16 The [A]thresholds, the [a,B]latticed windows
and the [b,C]galleries round about their [D]three stories,
opposite the threshold, were [E]paneled with wood all
around, and *from* the ground to the windows (but
the windows were covered), 17 over the entrance,
and to the inner house, and on the outside, and on
all the wall all around inside and outside, by measurement. 18 It was [a]carved with [A]cherubim and
[B]palm trees; and a palm tree was between cherub
and cherub, and every cherub had two faces, 19 a
[A]man's face toward the palm tree on one side and
a young [A]lion's face toward the palm tree on the
other side; they were [a]carved on all the house all
around. 20 From the ground to above the entrance
[A]cherubim and [A]palm trees were [a]carved, as well
as *on* the wall of the nave.
21 The [A]doorposts of the [B]nave were square; as
for the front of the sanctuary, the appearance of
one doorpost was like that of the other. 22 The [A]altar
was of wood, three cubits high and its length two
cubits; its corners, its [a]base and its [b]sides *were* of
wood. And he said to me, "This is the [B]table that is
before the LORD." 23 The [A]nave and the [B]sanctuary
each had a double [C]door. 24 Each of the doors had
two leaves, two [a,A]swinging leaves; two *leaves* for
one door and two leaves for the other. 25 Also there
were [a]carved on them, on the doors of the nave,
[A]cherubim and [A]palm trees like those [a]carved on the
walls; and *there was* a [b,B]threshold of wood on the
front of the porch outside. 26 *There were* [a,A]latticed
windows and [B]palm trees on one side and on the
other, on the sides of the [C]porch; thus *were* the [D]side
chambers of the house and the [b]thresholds.

CHAMBERS OF THE TEMPLE

42 Then he [A]brought me out into the [B]outer
court, the way [C]toward the north; and he
brought me to the [D]chamber which *was* opposite
the [E]separate area and opposite the [F]building toward
the north. 2 Along the length, *which was* a [A]hundred
cubits, *was* the north door; the width *was* fifty cubits. 3 Opposite the [A]twenty *cubits* which belonged to
the inner court, and opposite the [B]pavement which
belonged to the outer court, *was* [a,C]gallery corresponding to [a]gallery in three stories. 4 Before the
[A]chambers *was* an inner walk ten cubits wide, a way
of one *hundred* cubits; and their openings *were* on
the north. 5 Now the upper chambers *were* [a]smaller
because the [b,A]galleries took more *space* away from
them than from the lower and middle ones in the
building. 6 For they *were* in [A]three stories and had
no pillars like the pillars of the courts; therefore *the*
upper chambers were [a]set back from the ground
upward, more than the lower and middle ones. 7 As
for the [A]outer wall by the side of the chambers, toward the outer court facing the chambers, its length
was fifty cubits. 8 For the length of the chambers
which *were* in the outer court *was* fifty cubits; and
behold, *the length of those* facing the temple *was* a
[A]hundred cubits. 9 Below these chambers *was* the
[A]entrance on the east side, as one enters them from
the outer court.
10 In the [a]thickness of the [A]wall of the court toward the east, facing the [B]separate area and facing
the building, *there were* [C]chambers. 11 The [A]way in
front of them *was* like the appearance of the chambers which *were* on the north, according to their
length so was their width, and all their exits *were*
both according to their arrangements and openings.
12 Corresponding to the openings of the chambers
which were toward the south was an opening at
the head of the way, the way in front of the [A]wall
toward the east, as one enters them.
13 Then he said to me, "The north chambers *and*
the south chambers, which are opposite the [A]sep-
arate area, they are the [B]holy chambers where the
priests who are [C]near to the LORD shall eat the
[D]most holy things. There they shall lay the most
holy things, the grain offering, the sin offering and
the guilt offering; for the place is holy. 14 When the
priests enter, then they shall not go out into the
outer court from the sanctuary [a]without [A]laying
there their [B]garments in which they minister, for
they are holy. They shall put on other garments;
then they shall approach that which is for the people."
15 Now when he had finished measuring the inner
house, he brought me out by the way of the [A]gate
which faced toward the east and measured it all
around. 16 He measured on the east side with the

41:15 [a]Lit *to* [b]Or *passageway* [A]Ezek 41:12, 13; 42:1 [B]Ezek 41:14; 42:1, 10, 13 [C]Ezek 41:16; 42:3, 5 41:16 [a]Or *framed* [b]Or *passageways* [A]Is 6:4; Ezek 10:18; 40:6; 41:25 [B]1 Kin 6:4; Ezek 40:16, 25; 41:26 [C]Ezek 41:15 [D]Ezek 42:3 [E]1 Kin 6:15 41:18 [a]Lit *made* [A]1 Kin 6:29, 32, 35; 7:36; Ezek 41:20, 25 [B]2 Chr 3:5; Ezek 40:16 41:19 [a]Lit *made* [A]Ezek 1:10; 10:14 41:20 [a]Lit *made* [A]Ezek 41:18 41:21 [A]1 Kin 6:33; Ezek 40:9, 14, 16; 41:1 [B]Ezek 41:1 41:22 [a]Lit *length* [b]Lit *walls* [A]Ex 30:1-3; 1 Kin 6:20; Rev 8:3 [B]Ex 25:23, 30; Lev 24:6; Ezek 23:41; 44:16; Mal 1:7, 12 41:23 [A]Ezek 41:1 [B]Ezek 41:4 [C]1 Kin 6:31-35 41:24 [a]Or *turning* [A]1 Kin 6:34 41:25 [a]Lit *made* [b]Or *canopy of wood over* [A]Ezek 41:18 [B]Ezek 41:16 41:26 [a]Or *framed* [b]Or *canopies* [A]Ezek 41:16 [B]Ezek 40:16 [C]Ezek 40:9, 48 [D]Ezek 41:5 42:1 [A]Ezek 40:17, 28, 48; 41:1 [B]Ezek 40:17, 20 [C]Ezek 40:20 [D]Ezek 40:17; 42:4 [E]Ezek 41:12; 42:10, 13 [F]Ezek 41:12 42:2 [A]Ezek 41:13 42:3 [a]Or *passageway* [A]Ezek 41:10 [B]Ezek 40:17 [C]Ezek 41:15, 16; 42:5 42:4 [A]Ezek 46:19 42:5 [a]Lit *shorter* [b]Or *passageways* [A]Ezek 42:3 42:6 [a]Or *reduced* [A]Ezek 41:6 42:7 [A]Ezek 42:10, 12 42:8 [A]Ezek 41:13, 14 42:9 [A]Ezek 44:5; 46:19 42:10 [a]Lit *width* [A]Ezek 42:7 [B]Ezek 42:1, 13 [C]Ezek 40:17 42:11 [A]Ezek 42:4 42:12 [A]Ezek 42:7 42:13 [A]Ezek 42:1, 10 [B]Ex 29:31; Lev 7:6; 10:13, 14, 17 [C]Lev 10:3; Deut 21:5; Ezek 40:46 [D]Lev 6:25, 29; 14:13; Num 18:9, 10 42:14 [a]Lit *but there they shall lay* [A]Ezek 44:19 [B]Ex 29:4-9; Lev 8:7, 13; Is 61:10; Zech 3:4, 5 42:15 [A]Ezek 40:6; 43:1

41:15 gallery on each side. These were terraced buildings with decorations (vv. 18–20).

41:18 cherubim and palm trees. Figures of angels (cf. chaps. 1, 10) with palms between them (possibly to depict life and fruitfulness of God's servants) were on the walls of the temple proper and on the doors (v. 25). Each cherub (unlike that of chaps. 1, 10 which had 4 faces) had the face of a man and of a lion, possibly to represent the humanity and kingship of Messiah.

41:22 This was the altar of incense (cf. Ex 30:1–3; 1Ki 7:48).

42:3 gallery corresponding to gallery. Priestly rooms are described (vv. 3–12), situated along the S, N, and W walls of the sanctuary and Most Holy Place, in 3 stories. Priests eat the holy offerings (cf. Lv 2:3, 10; 6:9–11; 10:12) and dress there (vv. 13, 14).

42:15–20 out by the way of the gate. The angel measured the height and thickness of the outside wall (40:5); then the outer court (40:6–27); next the inner court with the chambers (40:28–42:14); finally, the extent of all the temple buildings outside. Measurements of the outer wall, 500 reeds each way, were approximately one mi. on each of the 4 sides. Much too large for Mt. Moriah, this scheme will require changes in the topography of Jerusalem, as Zechariah predicted (14:9–11).

measuring reed five hundred reeds by the [A]measuring reed. 17He measured on the north side five hundred reeds by the measuring reed. 18On the south side he measured five hundred reeds with the measuring reed. 19He turned to the west side *and* measured five hundred reeds with the measuring reed. 20He measured it [a]on the four sides; it had a [A]wall all around, the [B]length five hundred and the [B]width five hundred, to [C]divide between the holy and the profane.

VISION OF THE GLORY OF GOD FILLING THE TEMPLE

43 Then he led me to the [A]gate, the gate facing toward the east; 2and behold, the [A]glory of the God of Israel was coming from the way of the [B]east. And His [C]voice was like the sound of many waters; and the earth [D]shone with His glory. 3And *it was* like the appearance of the vision which I saw, like the [A]vision which I saw when [a]He came to [B]destroy the city. And the visions *were* like the vision which I saw by the [C]river Chebar; and I [D]fell on my face. 4And the glory of the LORD came into the house by the way of the gate facing toward the [A]east. 5And the [A]Spirit lifted me up and brought me into the inner court; and behold, the [B]glory of the LORD filled the house.

6Then I heard one speaking to me from the house, while a [A]man was standing beside me. 7He said to me, "Son of man, *this is* the place of My [A]throne and the place of the soles of My feet, where I will [B]dwell among the sons of Israel forever. And the house of Israel will not again defile My holy name, neither they nor their kings, by their harlotry and by the [a,C]corpses of their kings [b]when they die, 8by setting their threshold by My threshold and their door post beside My door post, with *only* the wall between Me and them. And they have [A]defiled My holy name by their abominations which they have committed. So I have consumed them in My anger. 9Now let them [A]put away their harlotry and the [a]corpses of their kings far from Me; and I will [B]dwell among them forever.

10"As for you, son of man, [a,A]describe the [b]temple to the house of Israel, that they may be [B]ashamed of their iniquities; and let them measure the [c,C]plan. 11If they are ashamed of all that they have done, make known to them the [a]design of the house, its structure, its [A]exits, its entrances, all its designs, all its statutes[b], and all its laws. And write *it* [B]in their sight, so that they may observe its whole [a]design and all its statutes and [C]do them. 12This is the [a]law of the house: its entire [b]area on the top of the [A]mountain all around *shall be* most holy. Behold, this is the [a]law of the house.

THE ALTAR OF SACRIFICE

13"And these are the measurements of the [A]altar by cubits (the [B]cubit being a cubit and a handbreadth): the [a]base *shall be* a cubit and the width a cubit, and its border on its edge round about one span; and this *shall be the height of* the [b]base of the altar. 14From the base on the ground to the lower [A]ledge *shall be* two cubits and the width one cubit; and from the smaller ledge to the larger ledge *shall be* four cubits and the width [a]one cubit. 15The [a]altar hearth *shall be* four cubits; and from the [a]altar hearth shall extend upwards four [A]horns. 16Now the [a]altar hearth *shall be* twelve *cubits* long by twelve wide, [A]square in its four sides. 17The ledge *shall be* fourteen *cubits* long by fourteen wide in its four sides, the border around it *shall be* half a cubit and its base *shall be* a cubit round about; and its [A]steps shall [a,B]face the east."

THE OFFERINGS

18And He said to me, "[A]Son of man, thus says the Lord [a]GOD, 'These are the statutes for the altar on the day it is built, to offer [B]burnt offerings on it and to [C]sprinkle blood on it. 19You shall give to the Levitical priests who are from the offspring of [A]Zadok, who draw [B]near to Me to minister to Me,'

42:16 [A]Ezek 40:3 42:20 [a]Lit *toward the four winds* [A]Is 60:18; Ezek 40:5; Zech 2:5 [B]Ezek 45:2; Rev 21:16 [C]Ezek 22:26; 44:23; 48:15 43:1 [A]Ezek 10:19; 40:6; 42:15; 43:4; 44:1; 46:1 43:2 [A]Is 6:3; Ezek 1:28; 3:23; 10:18, 19 [B]Ezek 11:23 [C]Ezek 1:24; Rev 1:15; 14:2 [D]Ezek 1:28; 10:4; Rev 18:1 43:3 [a]So with some mss and some ancient versions; M.T. *I* [A]Ezek 1:4-28 [B]Jer 1:10; Ezek 9:1, 5; 32:18 [C]Ezek 1:3; 10:20 [D]Ezek 1:28; 3:23 43:4 [A]Ezek 10:19; 11:23; 43:2 43:5 [A]Ezek 3:14; 8:3; 11:1, 24; 2 Cor 12:2-4 [B]Ezek 10:4 43:6 [A]Ezek 1:26; 40:3 43:7 [a]Or *monuments* as in Ugaritic [b]Or *in their high places* [A]Ps 47:8; Ezek 1:26 [B]Ezek 37:26, 28 [C]Lev 26:30; Ezek 6:5, 13 43:8 [A]Ezek 8:3, 16 43:9 [a]Or *monuments* as in Ugaritic [A]Ezek 18:30, 31 [B]Ezek 37:26-28; 43:7 43:10 [a]Lit *declare* [b]Lit *house* [c]Lit *perfection* or *pattern* [A]Ezek 40:4 [B]Ezek 16:61, 63; 43:11 [C]Ezek 28:12 43:11 [a]Or *form(s)* [b]M.T. repeats *and all its designs* after *statutes* [A]Ezek 44:5 [B]Ezek 12:3 [C]Ezek 11:20; 36:27 43:12 [a]Or *instruction for* [b]Lit *border* [A]Ezek 40:2 43:13 [a]Lit *lap* [b]Or *back* [A]Ex 27:1-8; 2 Chr 4:1 [B]Ezek 40:5; 41:8 43:14 [a]Lit *the* [A]Ezek 43:17, 20; 45:19 43:15 [a]Or *ariel* shall [A]Ex 27:2; Lev 9:9; 1 Kin 1:50; Ps 118:27 43:16 [a]Or *ariel* shall [A]Ex 27:1 43:17 [a]Or *be on the east side* [A]Ex 20:26 [B]Ezek 40:6 43:18 [a]Heb *YHWH*, usually rendered *LORD*, and so throughout the ch [A]Ezek 2:1 [B]Ex 40:29 [C]Lev 1:5, 11; Heb 9:21, 22 43:19 [A]1 Kin 2:35; Ezek 40:46; 44:15 [B]Num 16:5, 40

43:2 the glory of the God of Israel. In earlier chapters of this prophecy, emphasis was given to the departure of God's glory from the temple (see chaps. 8–11). Thus the Lord abandoned His people to destruction and dispersion. Here, in the millennial temple, the glory of God returns to dwell. His glory will be manifest in fullness in the future kingdom, after the Lord's Second Advent, which is also to be glorious (Mt 16:27; 25:31). Verses 1–12 describe God's glorious entrance into the sanctuary. **coming from ... the east.** The glory had been in the tabernacle (Ex 40:34, 35) and the temple (1Ki 8:10, 11), though not in Zerubbabel's temple. Here, the Lord returns to be Israel's King. The glory departed to the E from Israel (11:23) when God judged them, so the glory returns from the E when He has regathered them, and is restoring their worship.

43:3 like the vision. This vision appearance of God to Ezekiel is glorious, just as the vision in chaps. 8–11, which pictures His coming, by angels, to judge Jerusalem (cf. 9:3–11; 10:4–7). **like the vision ... by the river Chebar.** God's appearance is also glorious as in the vision of 1:3–28. **I fell on my face.** Just as in the other visions of God's glory (1:28; 9:8). Cf. Rev 1:12–17.

43:5 the glory ... filled the house. The future kingdom glory of God will fill His temple (Zec 2:5), as He filled the tabernacle (Ex 40:34) and later Solomon's temple (1Ki 8:11; Ps 29:9).

43:7 the place of My throne. The King of Glory (Ps 24:7–10) claims the millennial temple as His place to dwell. Cf. 1Ch 29:23; Zec 6:13. There will be human, unresurrected people in the kingdom, who entered when Christ returned and destroyed all the wicked. They will worship at this actual temple.

43:8, 9 The future temple will be most holy, protected from 1) harlotry such as the Israelites had engaged in (2Ki 23:7) and 2) defiling tombs of kings that Israel had allowed in the sacred temple area (20:18).

43:10–12 Here is the key to the entire vision of chaps. 40–48. These glorious future plans show how much Israel forfeited by their sins. Every detail should produce repentance in Ezekiel's hearers and readers.

43:13–27 the altar. The measurements of the altar of burnt offering are given in vv. 13–17, then the offerings are described (vv. 18–27). These offerings are not efficacious, nor were the OT sacrifices. They were all symbolic of death for sin. They do not take away sin (cf. Heb 10:4). They were prospective; these will be retrospective.

43:19 offspring of Zadok. Cf. 40:46 and 44:10, and *see notes there.* **a young bull for a sin offering.** Exact offerings, in language just

declares the Lord GOD, 'a [C]young bull for a [D]sin offering. 20 You shall take some of its blood and put
it on its four [A]horns and on the four corners of the
[B]ledge and on the border round about; thus you
shall [C]cleanse it and make atonement for it. 21 You
shall also take the bull for the sin offering, and it
shall be [A]burned in the appointed place of the house,
outside the sanctuary.
22 'On the second day you shall offer a [A]male goat
without blemish for a sin offering, and they shall
[B]cleanse the altar as they cleansed *it* with the bull.
23 When you have finished cleansing *it,* you shall
present a [A]young bull without blemish and a [B]ram
without blemish from the flock. 24 You shall present
them before the LORD, and the priests shall throw
[A]salt on them, and they shall offer them up as a
burnt offering to the LORD. 25 [A]For seven days you
shall prepare daily a goat for a sin offering; also a
young bull and a ram from the flock, without blemish, shall be prepared. 26 For seven days they shall
make atonement for the altar and purify it; so shall
they [a]consecrate it. 27 When they have completed the
days, it shall be that on the [A]eighth day and onward,
the priests shall [a]offer your burnt offerings on the
altar, and your [B]peace offerings; and I will [C]accept
you,' declares the Lord GOD."

GATE FOR THE PRINCE

44 Then He brought me back by the way of the
[A]outer gate of the sanctuary, which faces the
east; and it was shut. 2 The LORD said to me, "This
gate shall be shut; it shall not be opened, and no
one shall enter by it, for the [A]LORD God of Israel has
entered by it; therefore it shall be shut. 3 As for the
[A]prince, he shall sit in it as prince to [B]eat bread before the LORD; he shall [C]enter by way of the [D]porch
of the gate and shall go out [a]by the same way."
4 Then He brought me by way of the [A]north gate
to the front of the house; and I looked, and behold,
the [B]glory of the LORD filled the house of the LORD,
and I [C]fell on my face. 5 The LORD said to me, "Son
of man, [a,A]mark well, see with your eyes and hear
with your ears all that I say to you concerning all
the [B]statutes of the house of the LORD and concerning all its laws; and [a]mark well the entrance
of the house, with all exits of the sanctuary. 6 You
shall say to the [a,A]rebellious ones, to the house of
Israel, 'Thus says the Lord [b]GOD, "[B]Enough of all
your abominations, O house of Israel, 7 when you
brought in [A]foreigners, [B]uncircumcised in heart
and uncircumcised in flesh, to be in My sanctuary
to profane it, *even* My house, when you [C]offered
My food, the fat and the blood; for they [D]made My
covenant void—*this* in addition to all your abominations. 8 And you have not [A]kept charge of My holy
things yourselves, but you have set *foreigners* [a]to
keep charge of My sanctuary."
9 'Thus says the Lord GOD, "[A]No foreigner uncircumcised in heart and uncircumcised in flesh, of
all the foreigners who are among the sons of Israel,
shall enter My sanctuary. 10 But the Levites who
went far from Me when Israel went astray, who
[A]went astray from Me after their idols, shall [B]bear
the punishment for their iniquity. 11 Yet they shall

43:19 [C]Lev 4:3; Ezek 43:23; 45:18 [D]Ezek 45:19; Heb 7:27 43:20 [A]Lev 8:15; 9:9; Ezek 43:15 [B]Ezek 43:14, 17 [C]Lev 16:19; Ezek 43:22, 26 43:21 [A]Ex 29:14; Lev 4:12; Heb 13:11 43:22 [A]Ezek 43:25 [B]Ezek 43:20, 26 43:23 [A]Ex 29:1, 10; Ezek 45:18 [B]Ex 29:1 43:24 [A]Lev 2:13; Num 18:19; Mark 9:49, 50; Col 4:6 43:25 [A]Ex 29:35-37; Lev 8:33, 35 43:26 [a]Lit *fill its hands* 43:27 [a]Lit *make* [A]Lev 9:1 [B]Lev 3:1; 17:5 [C]Ezek 20:40 44:1 [A]Ezek 40:6, 17; 42:14 44:2 [A]Ezek 43:2-4 44:3 [a]Lit *by his way* [A]Ezek 34:24; 37:25 [B]Gen 31:54; Ex 24:9-11 [C]Ezek 46:2, 8-10 [D]Ezek 40:9 44:4 [A]Ezek 40:20, 40 [B]Is 6:3, 4; Ezek 1:28; 3:23; 43:4, 5; Hag 2:7 [C]Ezek 1:28; 43:3 44:5 [a]Lit *set your heart on* [A]Deut 32:46; Ezek 40:4 [B]Deut 12:32; Ezek 43:10, 11 44:6 [a]Lit *rebellion* [b]Heb *YHWH*, usually rendered *LORD*, and so throughout the ch [A]Ezek 2:5-7; 3:9 [B]Ezek 45:9; 1 Pet 4:3 44:7 [A]Ex 12:43-49 [B]Lev 26:41; Deut 10:16; Jer 4:4; 9:26 [C]Lev 22:25 [D]Gen 17:14 44:8 [a]Lit *as keepers of My charge in My* [A]Lev 22:2; Num 18:7 44:9 [A]Ezek 44:7; Joel 3:17; Zech 14:21 44:10 [A]2 Kin 23:8, 9; Ezek 22:26; 44:12 [B]Num 18:23

as definitive as the literal descriptions in Moses' day, are also just as literal here. They are of a memorial nature; they are not efficacious any more than OT sacrifices were. As OT sacrifices pointed forward to Christ's death, so these are tangible expressions, not competing with, but pointing back to the value of Christ's completely effective sacrifice, once for all (Heb 9:28; 10:10). God at that time endorsed OT offerings as tokens of forgiving and cleansing worshipers on the basis and credit of the great Lamb they pointed to, who alone could take away sins (Jn 1:29). The tangible expressions of worship, which the Israelites for so long failed to offer validly (cf. Is 1:11–15), will at last be offered acceptably, then with full understanding about the Lamb of God to whom they point. The bread and the cup, which believers today find meaningful, do not compete with Christ's cross but are tangible memorials of its glory. So will these sacrifices be.

43:24 salt. Cf. Lv 2:13. **burnt offering.** As the sin offering is a part of future millennial worship (v. 19), so there are other offerings also (cf. Lv 1–7). The burnt offering, denoting full consecration to God is one; the peace offering expressing gratitude for peace with God in covenant bonds is another (v. 27).

43:25 without blemish. Commemorative of Christ's unblemished perfection.

44:1, 2 the outer gate . . . was shut. The Lord has returned from the direction in which He departed (10:18, 19). It is kept closed, in honor of the Lord's glory having returned through it for the millennial worship and indicating that the Lord will not depart again as in chaps. 8–11 (cf. 43:1–5). This eastern gate of the temple should not be confused with the modern sealed eastern gate of the city (cf. 45:6–8).

44:3 the prince . . . shall sit in it. The designation "prince" is used at least 14 times in chaps. 44–47. He is not the Lord Jesus Christ, but someone distinct from Him (cf. "eat bread before the LORD"); he has sins for which he offers sacrifice (45:22), and fathers sons (46:16–18). He cannot enter by the E gate which the Lord used, but he is allowed to come in and go out by the gate's vestibule, and eat bread by the gateway. He cannot perform priestly duties (45:19) as Messiah will (cf. Ps 110:4; Zec 6:12, 13), and he must worship the Lord (46:2). Most likely "the prince" is one who is neither a priest nor the king, but rather one who administrates the kingdom, representing the King (the Lord Jesus Christ) on one hand, and also the princes (14:8, 9) who individually lead the 12 tribes. Possibly, he will be a descendant of David.

44:5–9 mark well the entrance. Since the Lord's glory fills the temple, it is sanctified (v. 4), and God is particular about what kind of people worship there. Sins of the past, as in chaps. 8–11, must not be repeated, and if they are they will exclude their perpetrators from the temple. Only the circumcised in heart may enter (Dt 30:6; Jer 4:4; Ro 2:25–29), whether of Israel or another nation (vv. 7, 9). Many other peoples than Jews will go into the kingdom in unresurrected bodies, because they have believed in Jesus Christ and were ready for His coming. They will escape His deadly judgment and populate and reproduce in the 1,000-year kingdom. Such circumcision pertains to a heart which is sincere about removing sin and being devoted to the Lord (cf. Jer 29:13). In the Millennium, a Jew with an uncircumcised heart will be considered a foreigner (v. 9). "Uncircumcised in flesh" refers to sinners and "foreigners" identifies rejecters of the true God.

44:10 Levites . . . shall bear the punishment for their iniquity. God makes distinctions. Levites in the line of those unfaithful in days before the judgment can minister in temple services, but they cannot make offerings or enter the Most Holy Place (vv. 11–14). Only Zadok's line can fulfill these ministries (vv. 15, 16). The reason for this is the value which God attaches to the faithfulness of Zadok in the past (1Sa 2:35; 2Sa 15:24ff.; 1Ki 1:32–40; 2:26–35). *See note on 40:46.*

be [A]ministers in My sanctuary, having [B]oversight
at the gates of the house and [C]ministering in the
house; they shall [D]slaughter the burnt offering and
the sacrifice for the people, and they shall [E]stand
before them to minister to them. 12 Because they
ministered to them [A]before their idols and became
a [B]stumbling block of iniquity to the house of Israel,
therefore I have [a,C]sworn against them," declares the
Lord GOD, "that they shall [D]bear *the punishment for*
their iniquity. 13 And they shall [A]not come near to Me
to serve as a priest to Me, nor come near to any of
My holy things, to the things that are most holy; but
they will [B]bear their shame and their abominations
which they have committed. 14 Yet I will [a]appoint
them [b]to [A]keep charge of the house, of all its service
and of all that shall be done in it.

ORDINANCES FOR THE LEVITES

15 "But the [A]Levitical priests, the sons of [B]Zadok,
who [C]kept charge of My sanctuary when the sons of
Israel [D]went astray from Me, shall come near to Me
to minister to Me; and they shall [E]stand before Me to
offer Me the [F]fat and the blood," declares the Lord
GOD. 16 "They shall [A]enter My sanctuary; they shall
come near to My [B]table to minister to Me and keep
My charge. 17 It shall be that when they enter at the
gates of the inner court, they shall be clothed with
[A]linen garments; and wool shall not [a]be on them
while they are ministering in the gates of the inner
court and in the house. 18 Linen [A]turbans shall be
on their heads and [B]linen undergarments shall be
on their loins; they shall not gird themselves with
anything which makes them sweat. 19 When they
go out into the outer court, into the outer court to
the people, they shall [A]put off their garments in
which they have been ministering and lay them
in the holy chambers; then they shall put on other
garments so that they will [B]not transmit holiness
to the people with their garments. 20 Also they shall
[A]not shave their heads, yet they shall not [B]let their
locks [a]grow long; they shall only trim *the hair of*
their heads. 21 [A]Nor shall any of the priests drink
wine when they enter the inner court. 22 And they
shall not [a]marry a widow or a [A]divorced woman
but shall [B]take virgins from the offspring of the
house of Israel, or a widow who is the widow of
a priest. 23 Moreover, they shall teach My people
the [A]*difference* between the holy and the profane,
and cause them to discern between the unclean
and the clean. 24 In a dispute [A]they shall take their
stand to judge; they shall judge it according to My
ordinances. They shall also keep My laws and My
statutes in all My [B]appointed feasts and [C]sanctify My
sabbaths. 25 [a,A]They shall not go to a dead person to
defile *themselves;* however, for father, for mother,
for son, for daughter, for brother, or for a sister who
has not had a husband, they may defile themselves.
26 After he is [A]cleansed, seven days shall [a]elapse for
him. 27 On the day that he goes into the sanctuary,
into the [A]inner court to minister in the sanctuary, he
shall offer his [B]sin offering," declares the Lord GOD.
28 "And it shall be with regard to an inheritance
for them, *that* [A]I am their inheritance; and you shall
give them no possession in Israel—I am their possession. 29 They shall [A]eat the grain offering, the sin
offering and the guilt offering; and every [a,B]devoted
thing in Israel shall be theirs. 30 The first of all the
[A]first fruits of every kind and every [a]contribution
of every kind, from all your [a]contributions, shall
be for the priests; you shall also give to the priest
the [B]first of your [b]dough to cause a [C]blessing to rest
on your house. 31 The priests shall not eat any bird
or beast that has [A]died a natural death or has been
torn to pieces.

THE LORD'S PORTION OF THE LAND

45 "And when you [A]divide by lot the land for
inheritance, you shall offer [a]an [B]allotment
to the LORD, a [C]holy portion of the land; the length
shall be the length of 25,000 [D]*cubits,* and the width
shall be [b]20,000. It shall be holy within all its boundary round about. 2 Out of this there shall be for the
holy place a square round about [A]five hundred by
five hundred *cubits,* and fifty cubits for its [a,B]open
space round about. 3 From this [a]area you shall measure a length of 25,000 *cubits* and a width of 10,000

44:11 [A]Num 3:5-37; 4:1-33; 18:2-7 [B]1 Chr 26:1-19 [C]Ezek 40:45; 44:14 [D]2 Chr 29:34; 30:17 [E]Num 16:9 44:12 [a]Lit *lifted up My hand* [A]2 Kin 16:10-16 [B]Ezek 14:3, 4 [C]Ezek 20:15, 23 [D]Ezek 44:10 44:13 [A]Num 18:3 [B]Ezek 16:61, 63; 39:26 44:14 [a]Lit *give* [b]Lit *keepers of the charge* [A]Num 18:4; 1 Chr 23:28-32; Ezek 44:11 44:15 [A]Jer 33:18-22 [B]Ezek 40:46; 43:19; 48:11 [C]Num 18:7; Ezek 40:45 [D]Ezek 44:10; 48:11 [E]Zech 3:1, 7 [F]Lev 3:16, 17; 17:5, 6; Ezek 44:7 44:16 [A]Num 18:5, 7, 8 [B]Ezek 41:22; Mal 1:7, 12 44:17 [a]Lit *come upon* [A]Ex 28:42, 43; 39:27-29; Rev 19:8 44:18 [A]Ex 28:40; Is 3:20; Ezek 24:17, 23 [B]Ex 28:42; Lev 16:4 44:19 [A]Lev 6:10; 16:4, 23, 24; Ezek 42:14 [B]Lev 6:27; Ezek 46:20 44:20 [a]Or *hang loose* [A]Lev 21:5 [B]Num 6:5 44:21 [A]Lev 10:9 44:22 [a]Lit *take as wives for themselves* [A]Lev 21:7, 14 [B]Lev 21:13 44:23 [A]Lev 10:10; Ezek 22:26; Hos 4:6; Mic 3:9-11; Zeph 3:4; Hag 2:11-13; Mal 2:6-8 44:24 [A]Deut 17:8, 9; 19:17; 21:5; 1 Chr 23:4; 2 Chr 19:8-10 [B]Lev 23:2, 4, 44 [C]Ezek 20:12, 20 44:25 [a]Lit *He* [A]Lev 21:1-4 44:26 [a]Lit *be counted* [A]Num 19:13-19 44:27 [A]Ezek 44:17 [B]Lev 5:3, 6; Num 6:9-11 44:28 [A]Num 18:20; Deut 10:9; 18:1, 2; Josh 13:33 44:29 [a]Or *dedicated* [A]Num 18:9, 14; Josh 13:14 [B]Lev 27:21, 28; Num 18:14 44:30 [a]Or *heave offering(s)* [b]Or *coarse meal* [A]Num 18:12, 13; 2 Chr 31:4-6, 10; Neh 10:35-37 [B]Num 15:20, 21 [C]Mal 3:10 44:31 [A]Lev 22:8; Deut 14:21; Ezek 4:14 45:1 [a]Or *a contribution* [b]Or with Gr *10,000* [A]Num 34:13; Josh 13:7; 14:3; Ezek 47:21; 48:29 [B]Ezek 48:8, 9 [C]Zech 14:20, 21 [D]Ezek 42:16; 45:2 45:2 [a]Or *pasture land* [A]Ezek 42:20 [B]Ezek 27:28 45:3 [a]Lit *measure*

44:16 My table. This is the altar of burnt offering (cf. 40:46; 41:22).

44:17–27 It shall be. Various standards govern priestly service, such as moderation (v. 20) and sobriety (v. 21). They will model holy behavior as they teach the people to live their lives set apart to God (vv. 23, 24). Minutia about dress (such as forbidding the uncleanness of sweat resulting from wearing wool), marriage (cf. Lv 21:14), contact with dead bodies, etc. point more naturally to a literal fulfillment than to a generalized blurring of details in a symbolical interpretation.

44:28–31 I am their possession. As the priests had no possession in the Land when it was originally apportioned, so in the future God will be their portion.

45:1–5 an allotment to the LORD. This sacred land, set apart at the heart (center) of Israel, is separate from allotments designated for various tribes, seven to the N and five to the S (cf. chap. 48). Though the whole earth is the Lord's (Ps 24:1), this area is meaningful to Him in a special sense, as providing for special purposes which 45:2–8 goes on to define. This holy rectangle (8.5 mi. by 3.3 mi.) (vv. 1, 3) corresponds to 48:8–22, which describes this portion as between Judah to the N and Benjamin to the S extending from the Mediterranean E to the eastern border. It is the area for the priestly homes (v. 4) particularly, but is also for the benefit of all worshipers.

45:2 for the holy place a square round. At the heart of the special allotment is the temple area (48:10), which serves all Israelite tribes, and also is the worship center for those of the whole world, who visit (Is 4:2, 3; Zec 14:16–19). It is one mi. square (cf. 42:15–20). As a center, not only for those in Palestine but for the world, the area is appropriately larger than past temples that served Israel.

cubits; and in it shall be the sanctuary, the most holy
place. 4 It shall be the holy portion of the land; it
shall be for the [A]priests, the ministers of the sanctuary, who [B]come near to minister to the LORD,
and it shall be a place for their houses and a holy
place for the sanctuary. 5 *An area* [A]25,000 *cubits* in
length and 10,000 in width shall be for the Levites,
the ministers of the house, *and* for their possession
[a]cities to dwell in.
6 "You shall give the [A]city possession of *an area*
5,000 *cubits* wide and 25,000 *cubits* long, alongside
the [a]allotment of the holy portion; it shall be for the
whole house of Israel.

PORTION FOR THE PRINCE

7 "The [A]prince shall have *land* on either side of
the holy [a]allotment and the [b]property of the city,
adjacent to the holy [a]allotment and the [b]property
of the city, on the west side toward the west and
on the east side toward the east, and in length
comparable to one of the portions, from the west
border to the east border. 8 This shall be his land
for a possession in Israel; so My princes shall no
longer [A]oppress My people, but they shall give *the
rest of* the land to the house of Israel [B]according
to their tribes."
9 'Thus says the Lord [a]GOD, "[A]Enough, you princes
of Israel; put away [B]violence and destruction, and
[C]practice justice and righteousness. Stop your
[D]expropriations from My people," declares the
Lord GOD.
10 "You shall have [A]just balances, a just [B]ephah
and a just [B]bath. 11 The ephah and the bath shall be
[a]the same quantity, so that the bath will contain a
tenth of a [A]homer and the ephah a tenth of a homer;
[b]their standard shall be according to the homer.
12 The [A]shekel shall be twenty [A]gerahs; twenty shekels, twenty-five shekels, *and* fifteen shekels shall be
your [a]maneh.
13 "This is the offering that you shall offer: a sixth
of an ephah from a homer of wheat; a sixth of an
ephah from a homer of barley; 14 and the prescribed
portion of oil (*namely,* the bath of oil), a tenth of
a bath from *each* kor (*which is* ten baths *or* a homer, for ten baths are a homer); 15 and one sheep
from *each* flock of two hundred from the watering
places of Israel—for a [A]grain offering, for a burnt
offering and for peace offerings, to [B]make atonement for them," declares the Lord GOD. 16 "[A]All the
people of the land shall [a]give to this offering for
the [B]prince in Israel. 17 It shall be the [A]prince's part
to provide the [B]burnt offerings, the grain offerings
and the drink offerings, at the [C]feasts, on the [D]new
moons and on the sabbaths, at all the appointed
feasts of the house of Israel; he shall provide the
sin offering, the grain offering, the burnt offering
and the [E]peace offerings, to make atonement for
the house of Israel."

45:4 [A]Ezek 48:10, 11 [B]Num 16:5; Ezek 40:45; 43:19 45:5 [a]So with Gr; M.T. *twenty chambers* [A]Ezek 48:13 45:6 [a]Or *contribution* [A]Ezek 48:15-18, 30-35 45:7 [a]Or *contribution* [b]Lit *possession* [A]Ezek 34:24; 37:24; 46:16-18; 48:21 45:8 [A]Is 11:3-5; Jer 23:5; Ezek 19:7; 22:27; 46:18 [B]Josh 11:23 45:9 [a]Heb *YHWH*, usually rendered *LORD*, and so throughout the ch [A]Ezek 44:6 [B]Jer 6:7; Ezek 7:11, 23; 8:17 [C]Jer 22:3; Zech 8:16 [D]Neh 5:1-5 45:10 [A]Lev 19:36; Deut 25:15; Prov 16:11; Amos 8:4-6; Mic 6:10, 11 [B]Is 5:10 45:11 [a]Lit *one* [b]Lit *its measure* [A]Is 5:10 45:12 [a]Or *mina* [A]Ex 30:13; Lev 27:25; Num 3:47 45:15 [A]Ezek 45:17 [B]Lev 1:4; 6:30 45:16 [a]Lit *be* [A]Ex 30:14, 15 [B]Is 16:1 45:17 [A]Ezek 46:4-12 [B]1 Kin 8:64; 1 Chr 16:2; 2 Chr 31:3 [C]Lev 23:1-44; Num 28:1-29:39 [D]Is 66:23 [E]1 Kin 8:63; Ezek 43:27

45:5 for the Levites. Distinct from the land devoted to temple and priestly homes is another portion for Levites, who assist in temple service. This portion is also about 8.5 x 3.3 mi. and lies N of the temple/priest allotment. Cf. 48:13, 14 for more details.

45:6 give the city possession. On the S of the central sanctuary plot is the city of Jerusalem with an area of about 8.5 x 1.65 mi. Cf. 48:15–20 for more details.

45:7 The prince shall have *land*. *See note on 44:3*. This administrator of the kingdom under Christ will have his territory in two parts, one to the W and the other to the E of the temple/priest and city portions in vv. 1–6. Cf. 48:21, 22 for more details.

45:8 My princes shall no longer oppress. God pledges a kingdom era free from civil leaders selfishly taking advantage of the people, i.e., seizing their land (cf. 22:27; Nu 36:7–9; 1Ki 21; Is 5:8; Hos 5:10; Mic 2:1, 2). The princes most likely are the leaders of each tribe. No one will be deprived of his possession under Messiah's rule.

45:9–12 The leaders of the land are urged to be thoroughly honest in their commercial dealings. This warning shows that there will be sin in the Millennium. The believing Jews who entered the 1,000-year reign of Christ on earth and inherited the promised kingdom will be fully human and capable of such sins. There also will be children who do not necessarily believe, as the final rebellion against King Messiah and His temple proves (cf. Rev 20:7–9).

45:10 balances. Relates to selling by weight. **ephah.** Relates to selling by dry volume. **bath.** Relates to selling by liquid volume.

45:11 ephah. About .75 bu. **bath.** About 6 gal. **homer.** In liquid volume about 60 gal. and in dry volume about 7.5 bu.

45:12 shekel. By weight about .4 oz. made up of 20 gerahs (.02 oz./each). Sixty shekels (20+25+15) equal a "maneh," or "mina," or about 24 oz. (1.5 lbs.).

45:13–17 Here are the offerings for Israel's prince (v. 16). Because of what the people will give him, he will provide for public sacrifices (v. 17).

45:13 They will give 1/60th of their grain.

45:14 kor. *See note on homer in 45:11.* They will give one percent of their oil.

45:15 They will give one lamb for every 200 in the flocks or one-half of one percent.

45:16, 17 prince. *See note on 44:3.*

45:17 feasts … new moons … sabbaths … appointed feasts. These will be discussed in notes on 45:18–46:15.

MILLENNIAL FEASTS

Levitical	Millennial
1. N/A	1. New Year—Eze 45:18–20
2. Passover—Lv 23:5	2. Passover—Eze 45:21–24
3. Unleavened Bread—Lv 23:6–8	3. Unleavened Bread—Eze 45:21–24
4. Pentecost—Lv 23:9–22	4. N/A
5. Trumpets—Lv 23:23–25	5. N/A
6. Atonement—Lv 23:26–32	6. N/A
7. Booths—Lv 23:33–44	7. Booths—Eze 45:25

18 'Thus says the Lord GOD, "In the [A]first *month,*
on the first of the month, you shall take a young bull
[B]without blemish and [C]cleanse the sanctuary. 19 The
priest shall take some of the blood from the sin
offering and put *it* on the door posts of the house,
on the [A]four corners of the [B]ledge of the altar and
on the posts of the gate of the inner court. 20 Thus
you shall do on the seventh *day* of the month for
everyone who goes [A]astray or is [a]naive; so you shall
make [B]atonement for the house.
21 "In the [A]first *month,* on the fourteenth day of
the month, you shall have the [B]Passover, a feast of
seven days; unleavened bread shall be eaten. 22 On
that day the prince shall provide for himself and
all the people of the land a [A]bull for a sin offering.
23 *During* the [A]seven days of the feast he shall provide as a [B]burnt offering to the LORD [C]seven bulls
and seven rams without blemish on every day of
the seven days, and a male goat daily for a sin offering. 24 He shall provide as a [A]grain offering an
ephah [a]with a bull, an ephah [a]with a ram and a hin
of oil [a]with an ephah. 25 In the [A]seventh *month,* on
the fifteenth day of the month, at the feast, he shall
provide like this, seven days [a]for the sin offering,
the burnt offering, the grain offering and the oil."

THE PRINCE'S OFFERINGS

46 'Thus says the Lord [a]GOD, "The [A]gate of the
[B]inner court facing east shall be [C]shut the six
[D]working days; but it shall be opened on the [E]sab-
bath day and opened on the day of the [F]new moon.
2 The [A]prince shall enter by way of the porch of the
gate from outside and stand by the [B]post of the gate.
Then the priests shall provide his burnt offering
and his peace offerings, and he shall worship at the
threshold of the gate and then go out; but the gate
shall not be [C]shut until the evening. 3 The [A]people of
the land shall also worship at the doorway of that
gate before the LORD on the sabbaths and on the
[B]new moons. 4 The [A]burnt offering which the prince
shall offer to the LORD on the sabbath day shall be
[B]six lambs without blemish and a ram without blemish; 5 and the [A]grain offering shall be an ephah [a]with
the ram, and the grain offering [a]with the lambs [b]as
much as he is [B]able to give, and a hin of oil [a]with an
ephah. 6 On the day of the [A]new moon *he shall offer*
a young bull without blemish, also six lambs and a
ram, *which* shall be without blemish. 7 And he shall
provide a [A]grain offering, an ephah [a]with the bull
and an ephah [a]with the ram, and [a]with the lambs as
[b]much as he is [B]able, and a hin of oil [a]with an ephah.
8 When the [A]prince enters, he shall go in by way of
the porch of the gate and go out [a]by the same way.
9 But when the people of the land come [A]before the
LORD at the appointed feasts, he who enters by way
of the north gate to worship shall go out by way of
the south gate. And he who enters by way of the
south gate shall go out by way of the north gate.
[a]No one shall return by way of the gate by which he
entered but shall go straight out. 10 When they go
in, the prince shall go in [A]among them; and when
they go out, [a]he shall go out.
11 "At the [A]festivals and the appointed feasts the
[B]grain offering shall be an ephah [a]with a bull and an
ephah [a]with a ram, and [a]with the lambs as [b]much as
one is able to give, and a hin of oil [a]with an ephah.

45:18 [A]Ex 12:2 [B]Lev 22:20; Heb 9:14 [C]Lev 16:16, 33; Ezek 43:22, 26 45:19 [A]Lev 16:18-20; Ezek 43:20 [B]Ezek 43:14, 17, 20 45:20 [a]Lit *simple* [A]Lev 4:27; Ps 19:12 [B]Lev 16:20; Ezek 45:15, 18 45:21 [A]Num 28:16f [B]Ex 12:1-24; Lev 23:5-8 45:22 [A]Lev 4:14 45:23 [A]Lev 23:8 [B]Num 28:16-25 [C]Num 23:1, 2; Job 42:8 45:24 [a]Lit *for* [A]Num 28:12-15; Ezek 46:5-7 45:25 [a]Lit *according to* [A]Lev 23:33-43; Num 29:12-38; 2 Chr 5:3; 7:8, 10 46:1 [a]Heb *YHWH*, usually rendered *LORD*, and so throughout the ch [A]Ezek 45:19 [B]Ezek 8:16; 10:3 [C]Ezek 44:1, 2 [D]Ex 20:9 [E]Is 66:23; Ezek 45:17 [F]Ezek 45:18; 46:3, 6 46:2 [A]Ezek 44:3; 46:8 [B]Ezek 45:19 [C]Ezek 46:12 46:3 [A]Luke 1:10 [B]Ezek 46:1 46:4 [A]Ezek 45:17 [B]Num 28:9 46:5 [a]Lit *for* [b]Lit *a gift of his hand* [A]Num 28:12; Ezek 45:24; 46:7, 11 [B]Ezek 46:7 46:6 [A]Ezek 46:1 46:7 [a]Lit *for* [b]Lit *his hand can reach* [A]Ezek 46:5 [B]Lev 14:21; Deut 16:17; Ezek 46:5 46:8 [a]Lit *by its way* [A]Ezek 44:3; 46:2 46:9 [a]Lit *He shall not* [A]Ex 34:23; Ps 84:7; Mic 6:6 46:10 [a]So with many mss and the ancient versions; M.T. *they* [A]2 Sam 6:14, 15; 1 Chr 29:20, 22; 2 Chr 6:3; 7:4; Ps 42:4 46:11 [a]Lit *for* [b]Lit *a gift of his hand* [A]Ezek 45:17 [B]Ezek 46:5, 7

45:18–25 The annual feasts for the nations are outlined. The millennial feasts include 3 of the 6 Levitical feasts: 1) Passover; 2) Unleavened Bread; and 3) Booths, or Tabernacles. Three Levitical feasts are not celebrated: 1) Pentecost; 2) Trumpets; and 3) Atonement. Most likely they are excluded because what they had looked forward to prophetically have been fulfilled and now serve no significant remembrance purpose such as Passover and Booths, or Tabernacle, will continue to provide.

45:18–20 atonement. The Day of Atonement is never mentioned, but God institutes a never-before-celebrated festival to start the "new year" with an emphasis on holiness in the temple. The first month, Abib, would be in Mar./Apr. The feast appears to last 7 days (v. 20). It indicates that there will be sin in the kingdom, committed by those who entered alive and their offspring.

45:21–24 Passover and Unleavened Bread are combined as in the NT and focus on remembering God's deliverance of the nation from Egypt and Christ's death providing deliverance from sin. They continue on into the Millennium as a week-long feast of remembrance, which will serve much the same purpose then as the bread and cup do now (cf. Ex 12–15 for details). The 3 annual pilgrimage feasts with required attendance under Mosaic legislation were: 1) Unleavened Bread, 2) Pentecost, and 3) Booths, or Tabernacles (cf. Ex 23:14–17; Nu 28:16–29:40; Dt 16:1–17). They have been modified with the 3 in 45:18–25. Pentecost is replaced by the new feast of vv. 18–20. There are also portion differences from the Mosaic law (cf. Nu 28:19–21), plus the millennial offerings are richer and more abundant, in general.

45:22, 23 the prince. *See note on 44:3.* Here he sacrifices for his own sin.

45:24 hin. About one gal.

45:25 The Feast of Booths, or Tabernacles, continues on into the Millennium as confirmed by Zec 14:16–21. This would be a remembrance of God's sustaining provision in the wilderness. The seventh month, Tishri, would be in Sep./Oct., and this feast will last for one week, as do the previous two. The prince ("he," v. 25) once again offers sacrifice.

46:1–15 This section further discusses offerings and deals with: 1) Sabbath and New Moon (vv. 1–8); 2) appointed feast days (9–11); 3) voluntary offerings (v. 12); and 4) daily sacrifices (vv. 13–15). Cf. Nu 28:1–15 for a summary of former Mosaic details.

46:1 The gate ... shall be shut. Shutting the gate 6 days seems to serve the purpose of giving special distinction to the Sabbath and New Moon, when it is open and in use. Israel largely failed and was judged in ancient times in regard to these days (Jer 17:22–27; cf. 2Ch 36:21). The Sabbath will be reinstated for a restored and regenerated Israel. Note here that modern-day sabbatarians fail to realize that the Sabbath consisted of far more than just rest from labor, but included specific sacrifices. It is inconsistent to take one part of the Sabbath observance and discard the others.

46:2 The prince. *See note on 44:3.* He appears 5 times (vv. 2, 4, 8, 10, 12) in regard to sacrifices. He is to be an example of spiritual integrity to the people (cf. v. 10).

46:6, 7 new moon. Israel's calendar was lunar, so the feasts were reckoned according to the phases of the moon.

46:8 When the prince enters. He does not normally use the eastern gate itself, which is for the Lord (44:2). Rather, he enters and exits by the gate's vestibule. However, v. 12 permits his use of the gate for freewill offerings.

46:9 the people. The people's entering and exiting for temple worship are to be done in an orderly flow to prevent congestion, since all will be present (cf. Dt 16:16).

46:10–12 the prince. He sets the example of worship for the people.

12 When the prince provides a [A]freewill offering,
a burnt offering, or peace offerings *as* a freewill
offering to the LORD, the gate facing east shall be
[B]opened for him. And he shall provide his burnt
offering and his peace offerings as he does on the
[C]sabbath day. Then he shall go out, and the gate
shall be shut after he goes out.
13 "And you shall provide a [A]lamb a year old without
blemish for a burnt offering to the LORD daily; [B]morn-
ing by morning you shall provide it. 14 Also you shall
provide a grain offering with it morning by morning, a
[A]sixth of an ephah and a third of a hin of oil to moisten
the fine flour, a grain offering to the LORD continually
by a perpetual [a]ordinance. 15 Thus they shall provide
the lamb, the grain offering and the oil, morning by
morning, for a [A]continual burnt offering."
16 'Thus says the Lord GOD, "If the prince gives
a [A]gift *out of* his inheritance to any of his sons, it
shall belong to his sons; it is their possession by
inheritance. 17 But if he gives a gift from his inheritance to one of his servants, it shall be his until the
[A]year of liberty; then it shall return to the prince.
His inheritance *shall be* only his sons'; it shall belong to them. 18 The prince shall [A]not take from the
people's inheritance, [a,B]thrusting them out of their
possession; he shall give his sons inheritance from
his own possession so that My people will not be
scattered, anyone from his possession." ' "

THE BOILING PLACES

19 Then he brought me through the [A]entrance,
which *was* at the side of the gate, into the holy
chambers for the priests, which faced north; and
behold, there *was* a place at the extreme rear toward
the west. 20 He said to me, "This is the place where
the priests shall boil the [A]guilt offering and the sin
offering *and* where they shall [B]bake the grain offering, in order that they may not bring *them* out into
the outer court to transmit holiness to the people."
21 Then he brought me out into the outer court and
led me across to the four corners of the court; and
behold, in every corner of the court *there was* a *small*
court. 22 In the four corners of the court *there were*
enclosed courts, forty *cubits* long and thirty wide;
these four in the corners *were* [a]the same size. 23 *There*
was a row *of masonry* round about in them, around
the four of them, and boiling places were made under the rows round about. 24 Then he said to me,
"These are the boiling [a]places where the ministers
of the house shall boil the sacrifices of the people."

WATER FROM THE TEMPLE

47 Then he brought me back to the [A]door of the
house; and behold, [B]water was flowing from
under the threshold of the house toward the east,
for the house faced east. And the water was flowing
down from under, from the right side of the house,
from south of the altar. 2 He brought me out by way
of the north gate and led me around [a]on the outside
to the outer gate by way of *the gate* that faces east.
And behold, water was trickling from the south side.
3 When the man went out toward the east with a line
in his hand, he measured a thousand cubits, and he
led me through the water, water *reaching* the ankles.
4 Again he measured a thousand and led me through
the water, water *reaching* the knees. Again he measured a thousand and led me through *the water,* water
reaching the loins. 5 Again he measured a thousand;
and it was a river that I could not ford, for the water
had risen, *enough* water to swim in, a [A]river that could
not be forded. 6 He said to me, "Son of man, have you
[A]seen *this?*" Then he brought me [a]back to the bank of
the river. 7 Now when I had returned, behold, on the
bank of the river there *were* very many [A]trees on the
one side and on the other. 8 Then he said to me, "These
waters go out toward the eastern region and go down
into the [A]Arabah; then they go toward the sea, being
made to flow into the [B]sea, and the waters *of the sea*
become [a]fresh. 9 It will come about that every living
creature which swarms in every place where the [a]river
goes, will live. And there will be very many fish, for
these waters go there and *the others* [b]become fresh;

46:12 [A]Lev 23:38; 2 Chr 29:31 [B]Ezek 44:3; 46:1, 2, 8 [C]Ezek 45:17 46:13 [A]Num 28:3-5 [B]Is 50:4 46:14 [a]Lit *statute* [A]Num 28:5 46:15 [A]Ex 29:42; Num 28:6 46:16 [A]2 Chr 21:3 46:17 [A]Lev 25:10 46:18 [a]Lit *oppressing* [A]Ezek 45:8 [B]1 Kin 21:19; Ezek 22:27; Mic 2:1, 2 46:19 [A]Ezek 42:9; 44:5 46:20 [A]2 Chr 35:13; Ezek 44:29 [B]Lev 2:4-7 46:22 [a]Lit *one measure* 46:24 [a]Lit *houses* 47:1 [A]Ezek 41:2, 23-25 [B]Ps 46:4; Is 30:25; 55:1; Jer 2:13; Joel 3:18; Zech 13:1; 14:8; Rev 22:1, 17 47:2 [a]Lit *by way of* 47:5 [A]Is 11:9; Hab 2:14 47:6 [a]Lit *and caused me to return* [A]Ezek 8:6; 40:4; 44:5 47:7 [A]Is 60:13, 21; 61:3; Ezek 47:12 47:8 [a]Lit *healed* [A]Deut 3:17; Is 35:6, 7; 41:17-19; 44:3 [B]Josh 3:16 47:9 [a]Lit *two rivers* [b]Lit *are healed*

46:13–15 daily. The testimony of the OT is that to remove the continual burnt offering meant an abolition of public worship (cf. Da 8:11–13; 11:31; 12:11).

46:16, 17 a gift. This explains inheritance laws governing the prince. A gift to one of his sons is permanent (v. 16), but a gift to a servant lasts only to the year of Jubilee, the 50th year (cf. Lv 25:10–13), and then returns to him (v. 17).

46:17 the year of liberty. The year of Jubilee.

46:18 The prince shall not take … inheritance. As in 45:8, 9, the prince is not to *confiscate others'* property to enlarge his own holdings, as often occurred in Israel's history when rulers became rich by making others poor (cf. 1Ki 21).

46:19–24 chambers. The priests' kitchen chambers are convenient for managing their parts of the offerings and cooking sacrificial meals for worshipers, possibly close to the inner E gate. The "ministers of the house" (v. 24) are not the priests, but temple servants.

47:1–12 This section reinforces the constant emphasis of the prophets that in the final kingdom amazing physical and geographical changes will occur on the earth, and especially the land of Israel. This chapter deals mainly with changes in the water.

47:1, 2 water was flowing … east. A stream of water flows up from underneath the temple (cf. Joel 3:18), going E to the Jordan, then curving S through the Dead Sea area (vv. 7, 8). Zechariah 14:8 refers to this stream as flowing from Jerusalem to the W (Mediterranean Sea) as well as to the E (Dead Sea). Its origin coincides with Christ's Second Advent arrival on the Mt. of Olives (cf. Zec 14:4; Ac 1:11), which will trigger a massive earthquake, thus creating a vast E-W valley running through Jerusalem and allowing for the water flow. *See note on Zec 14:3, 4.*

47:3–5 he measured. The escorting angel, wanting to reveal the size of the river, took Ezekiel, in the vision, to four different distances from the temple, where the stream was found to be at increasing depths until it was over his head. Cf. Is 35:1–7, where the prophet says "the desert will … blossom … like the crocus."

47:7 very many trees. Lush growth from the river.

47:8 waters … become fresh. The flow E, then S, runs into the Dead Sea and renders good the salty water (more than 6 times as salty as the sea) that formerly would not support life because of its high mineral content. The Dead Sea is transformed into a "living sea" of fresh water.

47:9 very many fish. These fish are said to be the same kinds in the Mediterranean (v. 10), probably referring to volume rather than species, since the river and the Dead Sea are fresh water.

so [A]everything will live where the river goes. 10 And
it will come about that [A]fishermen will stand beside it; from [B]Engedi to Eneglaim there will be a
place for the [C]spreading of nets. Their fish will be
according to their kinds, like the fish of the [D]Great
Sea, [E]very many. 11 But its swamps and marshes will
not become [a]fresh; they will be [b]left for [A]salt. 12 [A]By
the river on its bank, on one side and on the other,
will grow all *kinds of* [B]trees for food. Their [C]leaves
will not wither and their fruit will not fail. They will
bear every month because their water flows from
the sanctuary, and their fruit will be for food and
their [D]leaves for healing."

BOUNDARIES AND DIVISION OF THE LAND

13 Thus says the Lord [a]GOD, "This *shall be* the
[A]boundary by which you shall divide the land
for an inheritance among the twelve tribes of Israel; Joseph *shall have* two [B]portions. 14 You shall
divide it for an inheritance, each one [a]equally
with the other; for I [b,A]swore to give it to your
forefathers, and this land shall fall to you [c]as an
inheritance.
15 "This *shall be* the boundary of the land: on
the [A]north side, from the Great Sea *by* the way of
Hethlon, to the entrance of [a,B]Zedad; 16 [a,A]Hamath,
Berothah, Sibraim, which is between the border of
[B]Damascus and the border of Hamath; Hazer-hatti-
con, which is by the border of Hauran. 17 The boundary shall [a]extend from the sea *to* [A]Hazar-enan *at*
the border of Damascus, and on the north toward
the north is the border of Hamath. This is the north
side.
18 "The [A]east side, from between Hauran, Damascus, [B]Gilead and the land of Israel, *shall be* the [C]Jor-
dan; from the *north* border to the eastern sea you
shall measure. This is the east side.
19 "The [A]south side toward the south *shall extend*
from [B]Tamar as far as the waters of [C]Meribath-kadesh,
to the [D]brook *of Egypt and* to the [E]Great Sea. This is
the south side toward the south.
20 "The [A]west side *shall be* the Great Sea, from the
south border to a point opposite [a,B]Lebo-hamath.
This is the west side.
21 "So you shall divide this land among yourselves
according to the tribes of Israel. 22 You shall divide
it by [A]lot for an inheritance among yourselves and
among the [B]aliens who stay in your midst, who
bring forth sons in your midst. And they shall be
to you as the native-born among the sons of Israel; they shall be allotted an [C]inheritance with you
among the tribes of Israel. 23 And in the tribe with
which the alien stays, there you shall give *him* his
inheritance," declares the Lord GOD.

DIVISION OF THE LAND

48 "Now [A]these are the names of the tribes: from
the northern extremity, [a]beside the way of
Hethlon to [b]Lebo-hamath, *as far as* Hazar-enan *at*
the border of Damascus, toward the north [a]beside
Hamath, [c]running from east to west, [B]Dan, one *por-*
tion. 2 Beside the border of Dan, from the east side
to the west side, [A]Asher, one *portion.* 3 Beside the
border of Asher, from the east side to the west side,
[A]Naphtali, one *portion.* 4 Beside the border of Naphtali, from the east side to the west side, [A]Manasseh,
one *portion.* 5 Beside the border of Manasseh, from
the east side to the west side, [A]Ephraim, one *portion.*
6 Beside the border of Ephraim, from the east side
to the west side, [A]Reuben, one *portion.* 7 Beside the
border of Reuben, from the east side to the west
side, [A]Judah, one *portion.*
8 "And beside the border of Judah, from the east
side to the west side, shall be the [a]allotment which you
shall [b]set apart, 25,000 [c]*cubits* in width, and in length
like one of the portions, from the east side to the west
side; and the [A]sanctuary shall be in the middle of it.
9 The allotment that you shall set apart to the LORD
shall be 25,000 *cubits* in length and 10,000 in width.

47:9 [A]Is 12:3; 55:1; John 4:14; 7:37, 38 47:10 [A]Matt 4:19; 13:47; Luke 5:10 [B]Gen 14:7; Josh 15:62; 1 Sam 23:29; 24:1; 2 Chr 20:2 [C]Ezek 26:5, 14 [D]Num 34:6; Ps 104:25; Ezek 47:15; 48:28 [E]Luke 5:5-9; John 21:6 47:11 [a]Lit *healed* [b]Lit *given* [A]Deut 29:23 47:12 [A]Ezek 47:7; Rev 22:2 [B]Gen 2:9 [C]Ps 1:3; Jer 17:8 [D]Rev 22:2 47:13 [a]Heb *YHWH*, usually rendered *LORD*, and so throughout the ch [A]Num 34:2-12 [B]Gen 48:5; Ezek 48:4, 5 47:14 [a]Lit *like his brother* [b]Lit *lifted up My hand* [c]Lit *in* [A]Deut 1:8; Ezek 20:6 47:15 [a]Or *Hamath* [A]Num 34:7-9 [B]Num 34:8 47:16 [a]Or *Zedad* [A]Num 13:21; Is 10:9; Ezek 47:17, 20; 48:1; Zech 9:2 [B]Gen 14:15; Ezek 47:17, 18; 48:1 47:17 [a]Lit *be* [A]Num 34:9 47:18 [A]Num 34:10-12 [B]Gen 37:25; Jer 50:19 [C]Gen 13:10, 11 47:19 [A]Num 34:3-5 [B]Ezek 48:28 [C]Deut 32:51 [D]Num 34:5; 1 Kin 8:65; Is 27:12 [E]Ezek 47:10, 15 47:20 [a]Or *entrance of Hamath* [A]Num 34:6 [B]Judg 3:3; 2 Chr 7:8; Ezek 48:1; Amos 6:14 47:22 [A]Num 26:55, 56 [B]Is 14:1; 56:6, 7 [C]Acts 11:18; 15:9; Eph 2:12-14; 3:6; Col 3:11 48:1 [a]Lit *at the hand of* [b]Or *the entrance of Hamath* [c]Lit *and there shall be to it an east and west side* [A]Ex 1:1 [B]Josh 19:40-48 48:2 [A]Josh 19:24-31 48:3 [A]Josh 19:32-39 48:4 [A]Josh 13:29-31; 17:1-11 48:5 [A]Josh 16:5-9; 17:8-10, 14-18 48:6 [A]Josh 13:15-21 48:7 [A]Josh 15:1-63; 19:9 48:8 [a]Or *contribution*, and so throughout the ch [b]Lit *offer* [c]Or possibly *reeds*, and so throughout the ch [A]Is 12:6; 33:20-22; Ezek 45:3, 4

47:10 **Engedi.** The site is on the Dead Sea's W bank, about halfway along its length, near Masada. **Eneglaim.** Possibly it is Ein-Feska near Qumran at the northwestern extremity of the sea. Some argue for a site on the E bank, so that fishermen on both sides are in view.

47:11 **swamps and marshes.** This could supply salt for the temple offerings (cf. 43:24), as well as for food.

47:12 **all *kinds of* trees.** Cf. v. 7. The scene describes the blessing of returning to Eden-like abundance (Ge 2:8, 9, 16). **leaves … fruit.** Cf. v. 7. The fruit is for food, and the leaves serve a medicinal purpose, probably both in preventative and corrective senses. The fruit is perpetual, kept so by a continual and lavish supply of spring water from the temple.

47:13–23 **This *shall be* the boundary.** The picture is that of an enlarged Canaan for all to inhabit. The boundaries are substantially larger than those given to Moses in Nu 34:1–15. Israel, promised in God's covenant with Abraham (v. 14; Ge 12:7), has specific geographical limits within which Israel will finally occupy tribal areas which differ from the occupation in Joshua's day (cf. Jos 13–22). This is the complete fulfillment of the promise of the land in the Abrahamic Covenant.

47:13 **Joseph … two portions.** This is in keeping with the promise of Jacob to Joseph (Ge 48:5, 6, 22; 49:22–26).

47:15–20 The borders of the millennial Promised Land are described 1) to the N (vv. 15–17); 2) to the E (v. 18); 3) to the S (v. 19); and 4) to the W (v. 20).

47:22 **bring forth sons.** This reminds us that children will be born all through the 1,000-year rule of Messiah. Not all will believe and be saved, as evidenced by the final rebellion (cf. Rev 20:8, 9).

47:23 **alien.** This provision is in keeping with Lv 19:34.

48:1–7, 23–29 **the tribes.** The land pledged to each tribe within the total area described in 47:13–23 fulfills God's promises to actually restore Israel's people from around the world to the Promised Land just as they were actually scattered from it (28:25, 26; 34–37; 39:21–29; Jer 31:33). Dan is first mentioned. Though omitted from the 144,000 in Rev 7, probably because of severe idolatry, Dan is restored in grace.

48:8–22 **the allotment.** Already described in 45:1–8, this unique area includes land allotment for the sentry and the Zadokian priests (vv. 8–12); the Levites (vv. 13–14); the city (vv. 15–20); and the prince (vv. 21, 22).

PORTION FOR THE PRIESTS

10 The holy allotment shall be for these, *namely*
for the [A]priests, toward the north 25,000 *cubits in*
length, toward the west 10,000 in width, toward the
east 10,000 in width, and toward the south 25,000
in length; and the sanctuary of the LORD shall be
in its midst. 11 *It shall be* for the priests who are
sanctified of the [A]sons of Zadok, who have kept My
charge, who did not go astray when the sons of
Israel went astray as the [B]Levites went astray. 12 It
shall be an allotment to them from the allotment
of the land, a most holy place, by the border of the
Levites. 13 Alongside the border of the priests the
Levites *shall have* 25,000 *cubits* in length and 10,000
in width. The whole length *shall be* 25,000 *cubits*
and the width 10,000. 14 Moreover, they [A]shall not
sell or exchange any of it, or alienate this [a]choice
portion of land; for it is holy to the LORD.

15 "The remainder, 5,000 *cubits* in width and
25,000 [a]in length, shall be for [A]common use for
the city, for dwellings and for [b]open spaces; and the
city shall be in its midst. 16 These *shall be* its measurements: the north side 4,500 *cubits,* the south
side [A]4,500 *cubits,* the east side 4,500 *cubits,* and the
west side 4,500 *cubits.* 17 The city shall have [a]open
spaces: on the north 250 *cubits,* on the south 250
cubits, on the east 250 *cubits,* and on the west 250
cubits. 18 The remainder of the length alongside
the holy allotment shall be 10,000 *cubits* toward
the east and 10,000 toward the west; and it shall be
[a]alongside the holy allotment. And its produce shall
be food for the workers of the city. 19 The workers of
the city, out of all the tribes of Israel, shall cultivate
it. 20 The whole allotment *shall be* 25,000 by 25,000
cubits; you shall [a]set apart the holy allotment, a
[b]square, with the [c]property of the city.

PORTION FOR THE PRINCE

21 "The [A]remainder *shall be* for the prince, on the
one side and on the other of the holy allotment and
of the [a]property of the city; in front of the 25,000
cubits of the allotment toward the east border and
westward in front of the 25,000 toward the west
border, alongside the portions, *it shall be* for the
prince. And the holy allotment and the sanctuary of
the house shall be in the middle of it. 22 Exclusive of
the [a]property of the Levites and the [a]property of the
city, *which* are in the middle of that which belongs to
the prince, *everything* between the border of Judah
and the border of Benjamin shall be for the prince.

PORTION FOR OTHER TRIBES

23 "As for the rest of the tribes: from the east side
to the west side, [A]Benjamin, one *portion.* 24 Beside the
border of Benjamin, from the east side to the west
side, [A]Simeon, one *portion.* 25 Beside the border of
Simeon, from the east side to the west side, [A]Issachar,
one *portion.* 26 Beside the border of Issachar, from
the east side to the west side, [A]Zebulun, one *portion.*
27 Beside the border of Zebulun, from the east side
to the west side, [A]Gad, one *portion.* 28 And beside the
border of Gad, at the south side toward the south,
the border shall be from [A]Tamar to the waters of
Meribath-kadesh, to the brook *of Egypt,* to the [B]Great
Sea. 29 This is the [A]land which you shall divide by lot
to the tribes of Israel for an inheritance, and these
are their *several* portions," declares the Lord [a]GOD.

THE CITY GATES

30 "These are the exits of the city: on the [A]north
side, 4,500 *cubits* by measurement, 31 [a]shall be the
gates of the city, [b,A]named for the tribes of Israel,
three gates toward the north: the gate of Reuben,
one; the gate of Judah, one; the gate of Levi, one.
32 On the east side, 4,500 *cubits,* [a]shall be three gates:
the gate of Joseph, one; the gate of Benjamin, one;
the gate of Dan, one. 33 On the south side, 4,500 *cu-*
bits by measurement, [a]shall be three gates: the gate
of Simeon, one; the gate of Issachar, one; the gate
of Zebulun, one. 34 On the west side, 4,500 *cubits,*
shall be three gates: the gate of Gad, one; the gate of
Asher, one; the gate of Naphtali, one. 35 *The city shall*
be 18,000 *cubits* round about; and the [A]name of the
city from *that* day *shall be,* '[a]The [B]LORD is there.' "

48:10 [A]Ezek 44:28; 45:4 48:11 [A]Ezek 40:46; 44:15 [B]Ezek 44:10, 12 48:14 [a]Lit *first or first fruits* [A]Lev 25:32-34; 27:10, 28, 33 48:15 [a]Lit *in front* [b]Or *pasture land* [A]Ezek 42:20; 45:6 48:16 [A]Rev 21:16 48:17 [a]Or *pasture land* 48:18 [a]Or *exactly as* 48:20 [a]Lit *offer* [b]Lit *fourth* [c]Or *possession* 48:21 [a]Or *possession* [A]Ezek 34:24; 45:7; 48:22 48:22 [a]Or *possession* 48:23 [A]Josh 18:21-28 48:24 [A]Josh 19:1-9 48:25 [A]Josh 19:17-23 48:26 [A]Josh 19:10-16 48:27 [A]Josh 13:24-28 48:28 [A]Gen 14:7; 2 Chr 20:2; Ezek 47:19 [B]Ezek 47:10, 15, 19, 20 48:29 [a]Heb *YHWH,* usually rendered *LORD* [A]Ezek 47:13-20 48:30 [A]Ezek 48:32-34 48:31 [a]Lit *and* [b]Lit *according to the names of* [A]Rev 21:12, 13 48:32 [a]Lit *and* 48:33 [a]Lit *and* 48:35 [a]Heb *YHWH-shammah* [A]Jer 23:6; 33:16 [B]Is 12:6; 14:32; 24:23; Jer 3:17; 8:19; 14:9; Ezek 35:10; Joel 3:21; Zech 2:10; Rev 21:3; 22:3

48:30–35 These are the exits. Twelve city gates, 3 in each cardinal direction, bear the names of Israel's tribes, one on each gate.

48:30 on the north side, 4,500 *cubits.* All 4 sides when added together equal 18,000 cubits (cf. v. 16), which is nearly 6 mi. around. Josephus, a Jewish historian, reported in the first century A.D. that Jerusalem was approximately 4 mi. in perimeter.

48:35 the name. The city is called YHWH Shammah, "The LORD Is there." The departed glory of God (chaps. 8–11) has returned (44:1, 2), and His dwelling, the temple, is in the very center of the district given over to the Lord. With this final note, all of the unconditional promises which God had made to Israel in the Abrahamic Covenant (Ge 12); the Priestly Covenant (Nu 25); the Davidic Covenant (2Sa 7); and the New Covenant (Jer 31) have been fulfilled. So this final verse provides the consummation of Israel's history—the returned presence of God!

THE BOOK OF DANIEL

TITLE

According to Hebrew custom, the title is drawn from the prophet who throughout the book received revelations from God. Daniel bridges the entire 70 years of the Babylonian captivity (ca. 605–536 B.C.; cf. 1:1 and 9:1–3). Nine of the 12 chapters relate revelation through dreams/visions. Daniel was God's mouthpiece to the Gentile and Jewish world, declaring God's current and future plans. What Revelation is to the NT prophetically and apocalyptically, Daniel is to the OT.

AUTHOR AND DATE

Several verses indicate that the writer is Daniel (8:15, 27; 9:2; 10:2, 7; 12:4, 5), whose name means "God is my Judge." He wrote in the autobiographical first person from 7:2 on, and is to be distinguished from the other 3 Daniels of the OT (cf. 1Ch 3:1; Ezr 8:2; Ne 10:6). As a teenager, possibly about 15 years old, Daniel was kidnapped from his noble family in Judah and deported to Babylon to be brainwashed into Babylonian culture for the task of assisting in dealing with the imported Jews. There he spent the remainder of a long life (85 years or more). He made the most of the Exile, successfully exalting God by his character and service. He quickly rose to the role of statesman by official royal appointment and served as a confidante of kings as well as a prophet in two world empires, i.e., the Babylonian (2:48) and the Medo-Persian (6:1, 2). Christ confirmed Daniel as the author of this book (cf. Mt 24:15).

Daniel lived beyond the time described in Da 10:1 (ca. 536 B.C.). It seems most probable that he wrote the book shortly after this date but before ca. 530 B.C. Daniel 2:4b–7:28, which prophetically describes the course of Gentile world history, was originally and appropriately written in Aramaic, the contemporary language of international business. Ezekiel, Habakkuk, Jeremiah, and Zephaniah were Daniel's prophetic contemporaries.

BACKGROUND AND SETTING

The book begins in 605 B.C. when Babylon conquered Jerusalem and exiled Daniel, his 3 friends, and others. It continues to the eventual demise of Babylonian supremacy in 539 B.C., when Medo-Persian besiegers conquered Babylon (5:30, 31), and goes even beyond that to 536 B.C. (10:1). After Daniel was transported to Babylon, the Babylonian victors conquered Jerusalem in two further stages (597 B.C. and 586 B.C.). In both takeovers, they deported more Jewish captives. Daniel passionately remembered his home, particularly the temple at Jerusalem, almost 70 years after having been taken away from it (6:10).

Daniel's background is alluded to in part by Jeremiah, who names 3 of the last 5 kings in Judah before captivity (cf. Jer 1:1–3): Josiah (ca. 641–609 B.C.), Jehoiakim (ca. 609–597 B.C.) and Zedekiah (597–586 B.C.). Jehoahaz (ca. 609 B.C.) and Jehoiachin (ca. 598–597 B.C.) are not mentioned (cf. Jeremiah Introduction: Background and Setting). Daniel is also mentioned by Ezekiel (cf. 14:14, 20; 28:3) as being righteous and wise. He is alluded to by the writer of Hebrews as one of "… the prophets: who by faith … shut the mouths of lions" (Heb 11:32, 33).

The long-continued sin of the Judeans without national repentance eventually led to God's judgment for which Jeremiah, Habakkuk, and Zephaniah had given fair warning. Earlier, Isaiah and other faithful prophets of God had also trumpeted the danger. When Assyrian power had ebbed by 625 B.C., the Neo-Babylonians conquered: 1) Assyria with its capital Nineveh in 612 B.C.; 2) Egypt in the following years; and 3) Judah in 605 B.C. when they overthrew Jerusalem in the first of 3 steps (also 597 B.C., 586 B.C.). Daniel was one of the first groups of deportees, and Ezekiel followed in 597 B.C.

Israel of the northern kingdom had earlier fallen to Assyria in 722 B.C. With Judah's captivity, the judgment was complete. In Babylon, Daniel received God's word concerning successive stages of Gentile world domination through the centuries until the greatest Conqueror, Messiah, would put down all Gentile lordship. He then will defeat all foes and raise His covenant people to blessing in His glorious millennial kingdom.

HISTORICAL AND THEOLOGICAL THEMES

Daniel was written to encourage the exiled Jews by revealing God's program for them, both during and after the time of Gentile power in the world. Prominent above every other theme in the book is God's sovereign control over the affairs of all rulers and nations, and their final replacement with the True King. The key verses are 2:20–22, 44 (cf. 2:28, 37; 4:34–35; 6:25–27). God had not suffered defeat in allowing Israel's fall (Da 1), but was providentially working His sure purposes toward an eventual full display of His King, the exalted Christ. He sovereignly allowed Gentiles to dominate Israel, i.e., Babylon (605–539 B.C.), Medo-Persia (539–331 B.C.), Greece (331–146 B.C.), Rome (146 B.C.–A.D. 476), and all the way to the Second Advent of Christ. These stages in Gentile power are set forth in chaps. 2 and 7. This same theme also embraces Israel's experience both in defeat and finally in her kingdom blessing in chaps. 8–12 (cf. 2:35, 45; 7:27). A key aspect within the overarching theme of God's kingly control is Messiah's coming to rule the world in glory over all men (2:35, 45; 7:13, 14, 27). He is like a stone in chap. 2, and like a son of man in chap. 7. In addition, He is the Anointed One (Messiah) in chap. 9:26. Chapter 9 provides the chronological framework from Daniel's time to Christ's kingdom.

A second theme woven into the fabric of Daniel is the display of God's sovereign power through miracles. Daniel's era is one of 6 in the Bible with a major focus on miracles by which God accomplished His purposes. Other periods include: 1) the Creation and Flood (Ge 1–11); 2) the patriarchs and Moses (Ge 12–Dt); 3) Elijah and Elisha (1Ki 17–2Ki 13); 4) Jesus and the apostles (Gospels, Acts); and 5) the time of the Second Advent (Revelation). God, who has everlasting dominion and ability to work according to His will (4:34, 35), is capable of miracles, all of which would be lesser displays of power than was exhibited when He acted as Creator in Ge 1:1. Daniel chronicles the God-enabled recounting and interpreting of dreams which God used to reveal His will (chaps. 2, 4, 7). Other miracles included: 1) His writing on the wall and Daniel's interpreting it (chap. 5); 2) His protection of the 3 men in a blazing furnace (chap. 3); 3) His provision of safety for Daniel in a lions' den (chap. 6); and 4) supernatural prophecies (chaps. 2; 7; 8; 9:24–12:13).

INTERPRETIVE CHALLENGES

The main challenges center on interpreting passages about future tribulation and kingdom promises. Though the use of Imperial Aramaic and archeology have confirmed the early date of writing, some skeptical interpreters, unwilling to acknowledge supernatural prophecies that came to pass (there are over 100 in chap. 11 alone that were fulfilled), place these details in the intertestamental times. They see these prophecies, not as miraculously foretelling the future, but as simply the observations of a later writer, who is recording events of his own day. Thus, they date Daniel in the days of Antiochus IV Epiphanes (175–164 B.C., chap. 8; 11:21–45). According to this scheme, the expectation of the Stone and Son of Man (chaps. 2, 7) turned out to be a mistaken notion that did not actually come to pass, or the writer was being intentionally deceptive. Actually, a future 7-year judgment period (cf. 7:21, 22; 11:36–45; 12:1) and a literal 1,000-year kingdom (cf. Rev 20) after Christ's second coming when He will reign over Israelites and Gentiles (7:27) are taught. This will be an era before and distinct from the final, absolutely perfect, ultimate state, i.e., the new heaven and the new earth with its capital, the New Jerusalem (Rev 21, 22). The literal interpretation of prophecy, including Daniel, leads to the premillennial perspective.

Many other aspects of interpretation challenge readers: e.g., interpreting numbers (1:12, 20; 3:19; 9:24–27); identifying the one like a Son of Man (7:13, 14); determining whether to see Antiochus of the past or Antichrist of the far future in 8:19–23; explaining the "seventy weeks" in 9:24–27; and deciding whether Antiochus of 11:21–35 is still meant in 11:36–45, or whether it is the future Antichrist.

OUTLINE

I. The Personal Background of Daniel (1:1–21)
- A. Conquest of Jerusalem (1:1, 2)
- B. Conscription of Jews for Training (1:3–7)
- C. Courage of Four Men in Trial (1:8–16)
- D. Choice of Four Men for Royal Positions (1:17–21)

II. The Prophetic Course of Gentile Dominion (2:1–7:28)
- A. Dilemmas of Nebuchadnezzar (2:1–4:37)
- B. Debauchery and Demise of Belshazzar (5:1–31)
- C. Deliverance of Daniel (6:1–28)
- D. Dream of Daniel (7:1–28)

III. The Prophetic Course of Israel's Destiny (8:1–12:13)
- A. Prophecy of the Ram and Male Goat (8:1–27)
- B. Prophecy of the Seventy Weeks (9:1–27)
- C. Prophecy of Israel's Humiliation and Restoration (10:1–12:13)

THE CHOICE YOUNG MEN

1 In the third year of the reign of [A]Jehoiakim king of Judah, [B]Nebuchadnezzar king of Babylon came to Jerusalem and besieged it. 2 The [A]Lord gave Jehoiakim king of Judah into his hand, along with some of the [B]vessels of the house of God; and he brought them to the land of [C]Shinar, to the house of his [a]god, and he brought the vessels into the treasury of his [a,D]god.

3 Then the king [a]ordered Ashpenaz, the chief of his [b]officials, to bring in some of the sons of Israel, including some of the [c]royal [A]family and of the nobles, 4 youths in whom was [A]no defect, who were good-looking, showing [B]intelligence in every *branch of* wisdom, endowed with understanding and discerning knowledge, and who had ability for [a]serving in the king's [b]court; and *he ordered him* to teach them the [c]literature and [C]language of the [D]Chaldeans. 5 The king appointed for them a daily ration from the [A]king's choice food and from the wine which he drank, and *appointed* that they should be [a]educated three years, at the end of which they were to [b,B]enter the king's personal service. 6 Now among them from the sons of Judah were [A]Daniel, Hananiah, Mishael and Azariah. 7 Then the commander of the officials assigned *new* names to them; and to Daniel he assigned *the name* [A]Belteshazzar, to Hananiah [B]Shadrach, to Mishael [B]Meshach and to Azariah [B]Abed-nego.

DANIEL'S RESOLVE

8 But Daniel [a]made up his mind that he would not [A]defile himself with the [B]king's choice food or with the [C]wine which he drank; so he sought *permission* from the commander of the officials that he might not defile himself. 9 Now God granted Daniel [a,A]favor and compassion in the sight of the commander of the officials, 10 and the commander of the officials said to Daniel, "I am afraid of my lord the king, who has appointed your food and your drink; for why should he see your faces looking more haggard than the youths who are your own age? Then you would [a]make me forfeit my head to the king." 11 But Daniel said to the overseer whom the commander of the officials had appointed over Daniel, Hananiah, Mishael and Azariah, 12 "Please test your servants for ten days, and let us be [A]given some vegetables to eat and water to drink. 13 Then let our appearance be [a]observed in your presence and the appearance of the youths who are eating the king's choice food; and deal with your servants according to what you see."

14 So he listened to them in this matter and tested them for ten days. 15 At the end of ten days their appearance seemed [A]better and [a]they were fatter than all the youths who had been eating the king's choice food. 16 So the overseer continued to [a]withhold their choice food and the wine they were to drink, and kept [A]giving them vegetables.

17 As for these four youths, [A]God gave them knowledge and intelligence in every *branch of* [a]literature and wisdom; Daniel even understood all *kinds of* [B]visions and dreams.

18 Then at the end of the days which the king had [a]specified [b]for presenting them, the commander of the officials [c]presented them before Nebuchadnezzar. 19 The king talked with them, and out of them all not one was found like [A]Daniel, Hananiah, Mishael and Azariah; so they [a,B]entered the king's personal service. 20 As for every matter of [A]wisdom [a]and understanding about which the king consulted them, he found them [B]ten times [C]better than all the [b,D]magicians *and* conjurers who *were* in all his

1:1 [A]2 Kin 24:1; 2 Chr 36:5, 6 [B]Jer 25:1; 52:12, 28-30 1:2 [a]Or *gods* [A]Is 42:24; Dan 2:37, 38 [B]2 Chr 36:7; Jer 27:19, 20; Dan 5:2 [C]Gen 10:10; 11:2; Is 11:11; Zech 5:11 [D]Jer 50:2; 51:44 1:3 [a]Or *said to* [b]Or *eunuchs,* and so throughout the ch [c]Lit *seed of the* [A]2 Kin 24:15; Is 39:7 1:4 [a]Lit *standing* [b]Lit *palace* [c]Or *writing* [A]2 Sam 14:25 [B]Dan 1:17 [C]Is 36:11; Jer 5:15; Dan 2:4 [D]Dan 2:2, 4, 5, 10; 3:8; 4:7; 5:7, 11, 30; 9:1 1:5 [a]Or *reared* [b]Lit *stand before the king* [A]Dan 1:8 [B]1 Sam 16:22; Dan 1:19 1:6 [A]Ezek 14:14, 20; 28:3; Matt 24:15 1:7 [A]Dan 2:26; 4:8; 5:12 [B]Dan 2:49; 3:12 1:8 [a]Lit *set upon his heart* [A]Lev 11:47; Ezek 4:13, 14; Hos 9:3, 4 [B]Ps 141:4; Dan 1:5 [C]Deut 32:38; Dan 5:4 1:9 [a]Lit *lovingkindness* [A]Gen 39:21; 1 Kin 8:50; Job 5:15, 16; Ps 106:46; Prov 16:7 1:10 [a]Lit *make my head guilty* 1:12 [A]Dan 1:16 1:13 [a]Lit *seen* 1:15 [a]Lit *fat of flesh* [A]Ex 23:25; Prov 10:22 1:16 [a]Lit *take away* [A]Dan 1:12 1:17 [a]Or *writing* [A]1 Kin 3:12, 28; Job 32:8; Dan 1:20; 2:21, 23; Acts 7:22 [B]Dan 2:19; 7:1; 8:1 1:18 [a]Lit *said* [b]Lit *to bring them in* [c]Lit *brought in* 1:19 [a]Lit *stood before the king* [A]Dan 1:6, 7 [B]Gen 41:46; Dan 1:5 1:20 [a]Lit *of* [b]Or *soothsayer priests* [A]1 Kin 4:30, 31; Dan 1:17 [B]Gen 31:7; Num 14:22; Neh 4:12; Job 19:3 [C]Dan 2:27, 28, 46, 48 [D]Is 19:3; Dan 2:2; 4:18; 5:7

1:1 third year. 606–605 B.C. It was the third year by Babylonian dating, which did not count a king's initial (accession) year, but began with the following year. So the "third year" is in harmony with the same year labeled as "fourth" by the Judean system of dating (cf. Jer 46:2). **Jehoiakim.** Son of Josiah who ruled (ca. 609–597 B.C.) when Nebuchadnezzar first plundered Jerusalem. **Nebuchadnezzar.** Son of Nabopolassar who ruled Babylon (ca. 605–562 B.C.).

1:2 Shinar. A term for Babylon. **his god.** Bel or Marduk (same as Merodach). Babylonian religion recognized other gods too (cf. 1:7 and *see note there*). To conquer another nation's deities was thought to prove the superiority of the victor's god.

1:4 Qualifications for Jews to be trained in affairs of state included being: 1) *physically* free from bodily defects or handicap and handsome, i.e., a pleasing appearance in the public eye; 2) *mentally* sharp; and 3) *socially* poised and polished for representing the leadership. The ages of the trainees was most likely 14–17.

1:5 educated three years. Cf. 2:1 and *see note there.*

1:7 *new* names. A key factor in the "brainwashing" process of the Babylonian training was a name switch. This was to link the inductees to local gods rather than to support their former religious loyalty. Daniel means "God is my judge," but became Belteshazzar, or "Bel protect the king." Hananiah, "the Lord Is gracious," was changed to Shadrach, "command of Aku," another Babylonian god. Mishael, meaning "Who Is like the Lord?" was given the name Meshach, "Who Is what Aku is?" Finally, Azariah, "The Lord Is my helper," became Abed-nego, "servant of Nego," also called Nebo, a god of vegetation (cf. Is 46:1).

1:8 Daniel made up his mind. The pagan food and drink were devoted to idols. To indulge was to be understood as honoring these deities. Daniel "made up his mind" not to engage in compromise by being untrue to God's call of commitment (cf. Ex 34:14, 15). Also, foods that God's law prohibited (Lv 11) were items that pagans consumed; to partake entailed direct compromise (cf. Da 1:12). Moses took this stand (Heb 11:24–26), as did the psalmist (Ps 119:115), and Jesus (Heb 7:26). Cf. 2Co 6:14–18; 2 Tim 2:20.

1:9 God honored Daniel's trust and allegiance by sovereignly working favorably for him among the heathen leaders. In this instance, it prevented persecution and led to respect, whereas later on God permitted opposition against Daniel which also elevated him (Da 3, 6). One way or another, God honors those who honor Him (1Sa 2:30; 2Ch 16:9).

1:12 vegetables. This Heb. word appears in a plural form in the OT, only here and in v. 16. It might refer to wheat or barley, or it could be fresh vegetables.

1:15 fatter. Indicates healthiness.

1:20 ten times better. This probably uses the number qualitatively to signify fullness or completeness, i.e., they displayed incredible skill in answering, beyond the performance of other men who spoke without God's help. Compare this with "ten days" (vv. 12–15) which is quantitative, since it refers to an actual passage of time.

realm. 21 And Daniel [a]continued until the [A]first year
of Cyrus the king.

THE KING'S FORGOTTEN DREAM

2 Now in the second year of the reign of Nebuchadnezzar, Nebuchadnezzar [a,A]had dreams;
and his spirit was troubled and his [B]sleep [b]left him.
2 Then the king [a]gave orders to call in the [b,A]magi-
cians, the conjurers, the sorcerers and the [c]Chal-
deans to tell the king his dreams. So they came in
and stood before the king. 3 The king said to them,
"I [a,A]had a dream and my spirit [b]is anxious to [c]un-
derstand the dream."
4 Then the Chaldeans spoke to the king in [a,A]Aramaic:
"[B]O king, live forever! [C]Tell the dream to your servants,
and we will declare the interpretation." 5 The king
replied to the Chaldeans, "[a]The command from me
is firm: if you do not make known to me the dream
and its interpretation, you will be [b,A]torn limb from
limb and your houses will be made a rubbish heap.
6 But if you declare the dream and its interpretation,
you will receive from me [A]gifts and a reward and
great honor; therefore declare to me the dream and its
interpretation." 7 They answered a second time and
said, "Let the king [A]tell the dream to his servants,
and we will declare the interpretation." 8 The king
replied, "I know for certain that you are [a]bargaining
for time, inasmuch as you have seen that [b]the command from me is firm, 9 that if you do not make the
dream known to me, there is only [A]one [a]decree for
you. For you have agreed together to speak lying
and corrupt [b]words before me until the [c]situation
is changed; therefore tell me the dream, that I may
[B]know that you can declare to me its interpretation."
10 The Chaldeans answered [a]the king and said, "There
is not a man on earth who could declare the matter
[b]for the king, inasmuch as no great king or ruler
has *ever* asked anything like this of any [c,A]magician,
conjurer or Chaldean. 11 Moreover, the thing which
the king demands is [a]difficult, and there is no one else
who could declare it [b]to the king except [A]gods, whose
[B]dwelling place is not with *mortal* flesh."
12 Because of this the king became [A]indignant and
very furious and gave orders to destroy all the wise
men of Babylon. 13 So the [a]decree went forth that
the wise men should be slain; and they looked for
[A]Daniel and his friends to [b]kill *them*.
14 Then Daniel replied with discretion and discernment to [A]Arioch, the captain of the king's [a]body-
guard, who had gone forth to slay the wise men of
Babylon; 15 he said to Arioch, the king's commander,
"For what reason is the [a]decree from the king *so*
[b]urgent?" Then Arioch informed Daniel about the
matter. 16 So Daniel went in and requested of the
king that he would [a]give him time, in order that he
might declare the interpretation to the king.
17 Then Daniel went to his house and informed his
friends, [A]Hananiah, Mishael and Azariah, about the
matter, 18 so that they might [A]request compassion
from the God of heaven concerning this mystery, so
that Daniel and his friends would not be [B]destroyed
with the rest of the wise men of Babylon.

THE SECRET IS REVEALED TO DANIEL

19 Then the mystery was revealed to Daniel in
a night [A]vision. Then Daniel blessed the God of
heaven; 20 Daniel said,

"Let the name of God be [A]blessed
forever and ever,
For [B]wisdom and power belong to Him.
21 "It is He who [A]changes the
times and the epochs;
He [B]removes kings and [a]establishes kings;
He gives [C]wisdom to wise men
And knowledge to [b]men of understanding.
22 "It is He who [A]reveals the profound
and hidden things;
[B]He knows what is in the darkness,
And the [C]light dwells with Him.
23 "To You, O [A]God of my fathers, I
give thanks and praise,
For You have given me
[B]wisdom and power;

1:21 [a]Lit *was until* [A]Dan 6:28; 10:1 2:1 [a]Lit *dreamed dreams* [b]Lit *was gone upon him* [A]Gen 40:5-8; 41:1, 8; Job 33:15-17; Dan 2:3; 4:5 [B]Esth 6:1; Dan 6:18 2:2 [a]Lit *said to call* [b]Or *soothsayer priests* [c]Or *master astrologers*, and so throughout the ch [A]Gen 41:8; Ex 7:11; Is 47:12, 13; Dan 1:20; 2:10, 27; 4:6; 5:7 2:3 [a]Lit *dreamed* [b]Lit *was troubled* [c]Lit *know* [A]Gen 40:8; 41:15; Dan 4:5 2:4 [a]The text is in Aramaic from here through 7:28 [A]Ezra 4:7; Is 36:11 [B]Dan 3:9; 5:10 [C]Dan 2:7 2:5 [a]Another reading is *The word has gone from me* [b]Lit *made into limbs* [A]Ezra 6:11; Dan 2:12; 3:29 2:6 [A]Dan 2:48; 5:7, 16, 29 2:7 [A]Dan 2:4 2:8 [a]Lit *buying* [b]V 5, note 1 2:9 [a]Or *law* [b]Lit *word* [c]Lit *time* [A]Esth 4:11; Dan 3:15 [B]Is 41:23 2:10 [a]Lit *before the* [b]Lit *of* [c]Or *soothsayer priest* [A]Dan 2:2, 27 2:11 [a]Or *rare* [b]Lit *before* [A]Gen 41:39; Dan 5:11 [B]Ex 29:45; Is 57:15 2:12 [A]Ps 76:10; Dan 2:5; 3:13, 19 2:13 [a]Or *law* [b]Lit *be killed* [A]Dan 1:19, 20 2:14 [a]Or *executioners* [A]Dan 2:24 2:15 [a]Or *law* [b]Or *harsh* 2:16 [a]Or *appoint a time for him* 2:17 [A]Dan 1:6 2:18 [A]Esth 4:15, 16; Is 37:4; Jer 33:3; Ezek 36:37; Dan 2:23 [B]Gen 18:28; Mal 3:18 2:19 [A]Num 12:6; Job 33:15, 16; Dan 1:17; 7:2, 7, 13 2:20 [A]Ps 103:1, 2; 113:1, 2; 115:18; 145:1, 2, 21 [B]1 Chr 29:11, 12; Job 12:13, 16-22; Dan 2:21-23 2:21 [a]Or *sets up* [b]Lit *knowers* [A]Ps 31:15; Dan 2:9; 7:25 [B]Job 12:18; Ps 75:6, 7; Dan 4:17, 32 [C]1 Kin 3:9, 10; 4:29; James 1:5 2:22 [A]Job 12:22; Ps 25:14; Dan 2:19, 28 [B]Job 26:6; Ps 139:12; Is 45:7; Jer 23:24; Heb 4:13 [C]Ps 36:9; Dan 5:11, 14; James 1:17; 1 John 1:5 2:23 [A]Gen 31:42; Ex 3:15 [B]Dan 1:17; 2:21

1:21 first year. Cyrus of Persia conquered Babylon in 539 B.C. His third year, in 10:1, is the latest historical year that Daniel mentions (cf. Ezr 1:1–2:1).

2:1 second year. Promotion of the 4 Hebrews after 3 years (1:5, 18) agrees with the year of promotion after the dream in the "second year." *See note on 1:1.* **dreams.** In the time of revelation, God spoke through the interpretation of dreams that He induced (cf. v. 29).

2:2 Chaldeans. This could refer to all people native to Chaldea (1:4; 3:8), or, as here, to a special class of soothsayers who taught Chaldean culture.

2:4 Aramaic. This language, to which Daniel suddenly switches in v. 4b and retains through 7:28, was written with an alphabet like Hebrew, yet had distinctive differences. Aramaic was the popular language of the Babylonian, Assyrian, and Persian areas, and was useful in governmental and trade relations. Daniel 1:1–2:4a and 8:1–12:13 were written in Hebrew, possibly because the focus was more directly on Hebrew matters. Daniel 2:4b–7:28 switches to Aramaic because the subject matter is centered more on other nations and matters largely involving them.

2:5 The command ... is firm. The king shrewdly withheld the dream, though he remembered it, to test his experts. He was anxious for a straight interpretation, with no deception.

2:7 Let the king tell. The worldly men of human skill failed (cf. the magicians in Pharaoh's court, Ex 8:16–19, with Joseph, Ge 41:1ff.). Verses 8–13 show how impossible it is for humans to truly interpret dreams from God (cf. v. 27). But Daniel, who trusted God in prayer (v. 18), received His supernatural interpretation (vv. 19, 30). He gave credit to God in his prayer (vv. 20–23) and his testimony before Nebuchadnezzar (vv. 23, 45). Later the king, too, gave God the glory (v. 47).

2:20–23 This praise to God sums up the theme of the whole book, namely that God

Even now You have made known to
me what we [c]requested of You,
For You have made known to
us the king's matter."

24 Therefore, Daniel went in to Arioch, whom
the king had appointed to destroy the wise men
of Babylon; he went and spoke to him as follows:
"[A]Do not destroy the wise men of Babylon! Take
me [a]into the king's presence, and I will declare the
interpretation to the king."
25 Then Arioch hurriedly [A]brought Daniel [a]into the
king's presence and spoke to him as follows: "I have
found a man among the [b,B]exiles from Judah who can
make the interpretation known to the king!" 26 The
king said to Daniel, whose name was [A]Belteshazzar,
"Are you able to make known to me the dream which I
have seen and its interpretation?" 27 Daniel answered
before the king and said, "As for the mystery about
which the king has inquired, neither [A]wise men, conjurers, [a]magicians *nor* diviners are able to declare *it*
to the king. 28 However, there is a [A]God in heaven who
reveals mysteries, and He has made known to King
Nebuchadnezzar what will take place in the [a,B]latter
days. This was your dream and the [C]visions [b]in your
mind *while* on your bed. 29 As for you, O king, *while*
on your bed your thoughts [a]turned to what would
take place [b]in the future; and [A]He who reveals mysteries has made known to you what will take place.
30 But as for me, this mystery has not been revealed
to me for any [A]wisdom [a]residing in me more than *in*
any *other* living man, but for the purpose of making
the interpretation known to the king, and that you
may [b]understand the [B]thoughts of your [c]mind.

THE KING'S DREAM

31 "You, O king, were looking and behold, there
was a single great statue; that statue, which was
large and [a]of extraordinary splendor, was standing
in front of you, and its appearance was [A]awesome.
32 The [A]head of that statue *was made* of fine gold, its
breast and its arms of silver, its belly and its thighs
of bronze, 33 its legs of iron, its feet partly of iron
and partly of clay. 34 You [a]continued looking until
a [A]stone was cut out [B]without hands, and it struck
the statue on its feet of iron and clay and [C]crushed
them. 35 Then the iron, the clay, the bronze, the silver and the gold were crushed [a]all at the same time
and became [A]like chaff from the summer threshing
floors; and the wind carried them away so that [B]not
a trace of them was found. But the stone that struck
the statue became a great [C]mountain and filled the
whole earth.

THE INTERPRETATION—BABYLON THE FIRST KINGDOM

36 "This *was* the dream; now we will tell [A]its
interpretation before the king. 37 You, O king, are
the [A]king of kings, to whom the God of heaven has
given the [a]kingdom, the [B]power, the strength and
the glory; 38 and wherever the sons of men dwell,
or the [A]beasts of the field, or the birds of the sky,
He has given *them* into your hand and has caused
you to rule over them all. You are the head of gold.

MEDO-PERSIA AND GREECE

39 After you there will arise another kingdom inferior to you, then another third kingdom of bronze,
which will rule over all the earth.

2:23 [C]Ps 21:2, 4; Dan 2:18, 29, 30 2:24 [a]Lit *in before the king* [A]Dan 2:12, 13; Acts 27:24 2:25 [a]Lit *in before the king* [b]Lit *sons of the exile of* [A]Gen 41:14 [B]Dan 1:6; 5:13; 6:13 2:26 [A]Dan 1:7; 4:8; 5:12 2:27 [a]Or *soothsayer priests* [A]Dan 2:2, 10, 11; 5:7, 8 2:28 [a]Lit *end of the days* [b]Lit *of your head* [A]Gen 40:8; 41:16; Dan 2:22, 45 [B]Gen 49:1; Is 2:2; Dan 10:14; Mic 4:1 [C]Dan 4:5 2:29 [a]Lit *came up* [b]Lit *after this* [A]Dan 2:23, 47 2:30 [a]Lit *which is* [b]Lit *know* [c]Lit *heart* [A]Gen 41:16; Dan 1:17 [B]Ps 139:2; Amos 4:13 2:31 [a]Lit *its splendor was surpassing* [A]Hab 1:7 2:32 [A]Dan 2:38 2:34 [a]Lit *were* [A]Dan 2:45 [B]Dan 8:25; Zech 4:6 [C]Ps 2:9; Is 60:12 2:35 [a]Lit *like one* [A]Ps 1:4; Is 17:13; 41:15, 16; Hos 13:3 [B]Ps 37:10, 36 [C]Is 2:2; Mic 4:1 2:36 [A]Dan 2:24 2:37 [a]Or *sovereignty* [A]Is 47:5; Jer 27:6, 7; Ezek 26:7 [B]Ps 62:11 2:38 [A]Ps 50:10, 11; Dan 4:21, 22

is the One who controls all things and grants all wisdom and might.

2:28 God … reveals mysteries. Just as He did during Joseph's time in Egypt (cf. Ge 40:8; 41:16).

2:36–45 we will tell its interpretation. Five empires in succession would rule over Israel, here pictured by parts of a statue (body). In Da 7, the same empires are represented by 4 great beasts. These empires are Babylon, Medo-Persia, Greece, Rome, and the later revived Rome (cf. Introduction: Background and Setting), each one differentiated from the previous as indicated by the declining quality of the metal. A stone picturing Christ (Lk 20:18) at His second coming (as the Son of Man also does in Da 7:13, 14) will destroy the fourth empire in its final phase with catastrophic suddenness (2:34, 35, 44, 45). Christ's total shattering of Gentile power will result in the establishment of His millennial kingdom, the ultimate empire, and then continuing on eternally (2:44; 7:27).

2:39 inferior. This probably means "lower" (lit. "earthward") on the image of a man as

AN OVERVIEW OF DANIEL'S KINGDOMS		
I. Daniel 2/Daniel 7		
	A. Babylon	2:32, 37, 38; 7:4, 17
	B. Medo-Persia	2:32, 39; 7:5, 17
	C. Greece	2:32, 39; 7:6, 17
	D. Rome	2:33, 40; 7:7, 17, 23
	E. Revived Rome	2:33, 41–43; 7:7, 8, 11, 24, 25
	F. Millennium	2:34, 35, 44, 45; 7:13, 14, 26, 27
II. Daniel 8/Daniel 11		
	A. Medo-Persia	8:3–8, 20, 21; 10:20, 21; 11:2–35
	B. Greece	8:3–8, 20, 21; 10:20, 21; 11:2–35
	C. Revived Rome	8:9–12, 23–26; 11:36–45.

ROME

[40]Then there will be a [A]fourth kingdom as strong
as iron; inasmuch as iron crushes and shatters all
things, so, like iron that breaks in pieces, it will crush
and break all these in pieces. [41]In that you saw the
feet and toes, partly of potter's clay and partly of
iron, it will be a divided kingdom; but it will have
in it the toughness of iron, inasmuch as you saw the
iron mixed with [a]common clay. [42]*As* the toes of the
feet *were* partly of iron and partly of pottery, *so* some
of the kingdom will be strong and part of it will be
brittle. [43]And in that you saw the iron mixed with
[a]common clay, they will combine with one another
[b]in the seed of men; but they will not adhere to one
another, even as iron does not combine with pottery.

THE DIVINE KINGDOM

[44]In the days of those kings the [A]God of heaven
will [B]set up a [C]kingdom which will never be destroyed, and *that* kingdom will not be [a]left for

2:40 [A]Dan 7:23 2:41 [a]Lit *clay of mud* 2:43 [a]Lit *clay of mud* [b]Or *with* 2:44 [a]Or *passed on to* [A]Dan 2:28, 37 [B]Is 9:6, 7 [C]Ps 145:13; Ezek 37:25; Dan 4:3, 34; 6:26; 7:14, 27; Mic 4:7; Luke 1:32, 33

Daniel guides Nebuchadnezzar's thoughts downward on the body from his own empire (the head) to the one that would succeed it. Medo-Persia, though lacking the glory of Babylon (silver as compared to gold), was not inferior in strength to Babylon when its day of power came; it actually conquered Babylon (7:5). Also in the case of Greece, bronze is less glorious (valuable) than silver, but stronger. **rule over all the earth.** Alexander the Great became the ruler of the world, including Israel, from Europe to Egypt to India.

2:40 strong as iron. This metal fittingly represents the Roman Empire which would be characterized by the description predicted. It did have armies in iron armor known as the Iron Legions of Rome, and it had strength and invincibility.

2:41 toes. Ten toes represent the same kings as the 10 horns in 7:24. They will rule in the final time of the Gentile empire, which Christ destroys in violent abruptness at His second coming.

2:41–43 clay and ... iron. The iron in the 10 toes (kings) represents the Roman Empire in its revived form, prior to the second coming of Christ, as having iron-like strength for conquest (cf. Rev 13:4, 5). But the clay mixed in depicts that the union (federation) of kings and nations would have fatal flaws of human weakness, so that it is inherently vulnerable.

2:44 endure forever. God's kingdom ruled by Messiah is the final rule, never to be replaced. It has a millennial phase and an eternal future, but it is the same king who rules both.

ALEXANDER'S EMPIRE (323 B.C.)

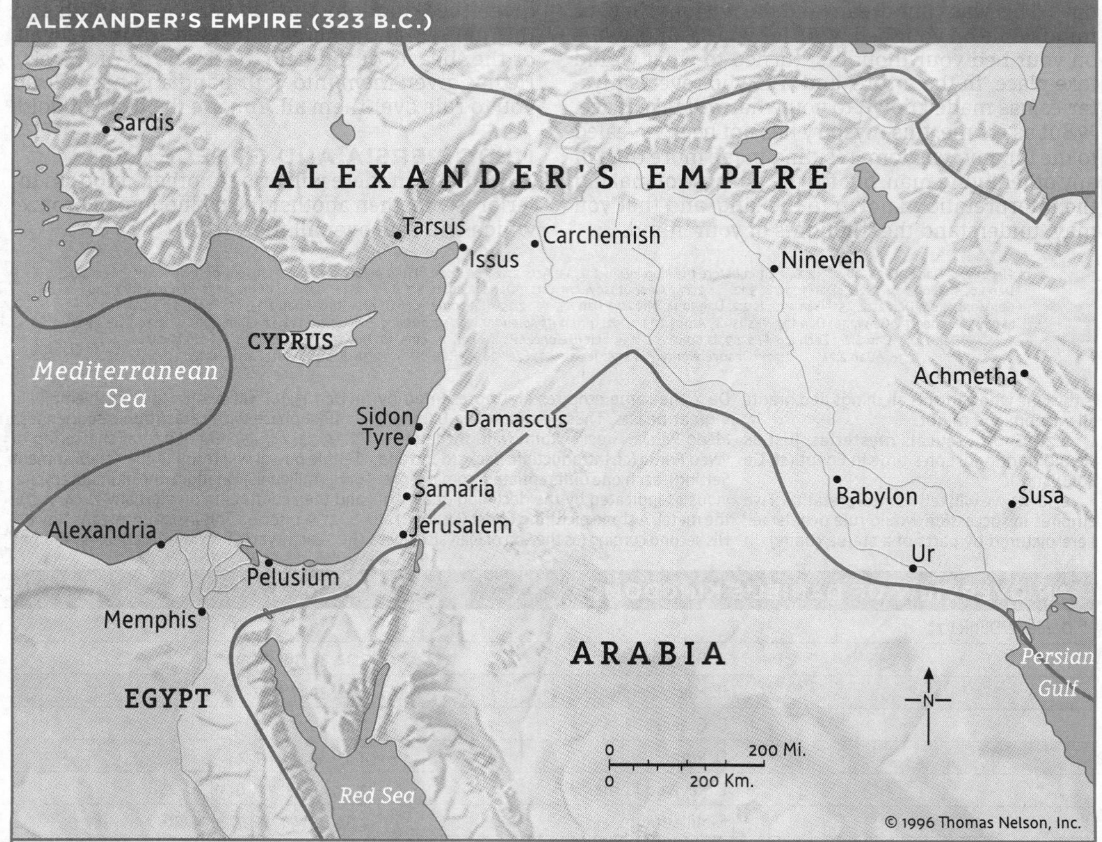

In 334 B.C. Alexander, son of Philip II of Macedon, began a military quest to destroy the Persian Empire. Moving from west to east, he was victorious in battle at Issus in 333 B.C. against the Persian Darius III. Moving south, Alexander defeated the Phoenicians at Tyre in 332 B.C., swept through Palestine, and conquered Egypt in 331 B.C. Reengaging Darius III near Nineveh, Alexander defeated him again. Alexander's campaigns continued east into India, securing vast territory for the Greek Empire. He died in Babylon in 323 B.C.

another people; it will [D]crush and put an end to all
these kingdoms, but it will itself endure forever.
45 Inasmuch as you saw that a [A]stone was cut out
of the mountain without hands and that it crushed
the iron, the bronze, the clay, the silver and the gold,
the [B]great God has made known to the king what
[C]will take place [a]in the future; so the dream is true
and its interpretation is trustworthy."

DANIEL PROMOTED

46 Then King Nebuchadnezzar fell on his face and
did [A]homage to Daniel, and gave orders to present
to him an offering and [a,B]fragrant incense. 47 The
king answered Daniel and said, "Surely [A]your God
is a [B]God of gods and a Lord of kings and a [C]revealer
of mysteries, since you have been able to reveal
this mystery." 48 Then the king [a,A]promoted Daniel
and gave him many great gifts, and he made him
ruler over the whole [B]province of Babylon and chief
[b]prefect over all the wise men of Babylon. 49 And
Daniel made request of the king, and he [A]appointed
[B]Shadrach, Meshach and Abed-nego over the administration of the province of Babylon, while Daniel
was at the king's [a,C]court.

THE KING'S GOLDEN IMAGE

3 Nebuchadnezzar the king made an [A]image of
gold, the height of which *was* sixty [a]cubits *and*
its width six [a]cubits; he set it up on the plain of Dura
in the [B]province of Babylon. 2 Then Nebuchadnezzar the king sent *word* to assemble the [A]satraps,
the prefects and the governors, the counselors, the
treasurers, the judges, the magistrates and all the
rulers of the provinces to come to the dedication
of the image that Nebuchadnezzar the king had set
up. 3 Then the satraps, the prefects and the governors, the counselors, the treasurers, the judges,
the magistrates and all the rulers of the provinces
were assembled for the dedication of the image that
Nebuchadnezzar the king had set up; and they stood
before the image that Nebuchadnezzar had set up.
4 Then the herald loudly proclaimed: "To you [a]the
command is given, [A]O peoples, nations and *men*
of every [b]language, 5 that at the moment you [A]hear
the sound of the horn, flute, [a]lyre, [b]trigon, [c]psaltery,
bagpipe and all kinds of music, you are to fall down
and worship the golden image that Nebuchadnezzar the king has set up. 6 But whoever does not fall
down and worship shall [a]immediately be [A]cast into
the midst of a [B]furnace of blazing fire." 7 Therefore
at that time, when all the peoples heard the sound
of the horn, flute, [a]lyre, trigon, psaltery, bagpipe
and all kinds of music, all the peoples, nations and
men of every [b]language fell down *and* worshiped
the golden image that Nebuchadnezzar the king
had set up.

WORSHIP OF THE IMAGE REFUSED

8 For this reason at that time certain [A]Chaldeans
came forward and [a,B]brought charges against the
Jews. 9 They responded and said to Nebuchadnezzar the king: "[A]O king, live forever! 10 You, O king,
have [A]made a decree that every man who hears the
sound of the horn, flute, [a]lyre, trigon, psaltery, and
bagpipe and all kinds of music, is to [B]fall down and
worship the golden image. 11 But whoever does not
fall down and worship shall be cast into the midst
of a furnace of blazing fire. 12 There are certain Jews
whom you have [A]appointed over the administration of the province of Babylon, *namely* Shadrach,
Meshach and Abed-nego. These men, O king, have
disregarded you; they do not serve your gods or
worship the golden image which you have set up."
13 Then Nebuchadnezzar in [A]rage and anger gave
orders to bring Shadrach, Meshach and Abed-nego; then these men were brought before the king.

2:44 [D]Ps 2:9; Is 60:12; Dan 2:34, 35 2:45 [a]Lit *after this* [A]Dan 2:34 [B]Deut 10:17; 2 Sam 7:22; Ps 48:1; Jer 32:18, 19; Dan 2:29; Mal 1:11 [C]Gen 41:28, 32 2:46 [a]Lit *sweet odors* [A]Dan 3:5, 7; Acts 10:25; 14:13; Rev 19:10; 22:8 [B]Lev 26:31; Ezra 6:10 2:47 [A]Dan 3:15; 4:25 [B]Deut 10:17; Ps 136:2, 3; Dan 11:36 [C]Dan 2:22, 30; Amos 3:7 2:48 [a]Lit *made great* [b]Lit *of the prefects* [A]Gen 41:39-43; Dan 2:6; 5:16, 29 [B]Dan 3:1, 12, 30 2:49 [a]Lit *gate* [A]Dan 3:12 [B]Dan 1:7 [C]Esth 2:19, 21; Amos 5:15 3:1 [a]I.e. One cubit equals approx 18 in. [A]1 Kin 12:28; Is 46:6; Jer 16:20; Dan 2:31; Hos 2:8; 8:4; Hab 2:19 [B]Dan 2:48; 3:30 3:2 [A]Dan 3:3, 27; 6:1-7 3:4 [a]Lit *they command* [b]Lit *tongue* [A]Dan 3:7; 4:1; 6:25 3:5 [a]Or *zither* [b]I.e. triangular lyre [c]Or *a type of harp* [A]Dan 3:7, 10, 15 3:6 [a]Or *in the same hour* [A]Dan 3:11, 15, 21; 6:7 [B]Jer 29:22; Ezek 22:18-22; Matt 13:42, 50; Rev 9:2; 14:11 3:7 [a]V 5, notes 1, 2, 3 [b]Lit *tongue* 3:8 [a]Lit *ate the pieces of* [A]Dan 2:2, 10; 4:7 [B]Ezra 4:12-16; Esth 3:8, 9; Dan 6:12, 13 3:9 [A]Dan 2:4; 5:10; 6:6, 21 3:10 [a]V 5, notes 1, 2, 3 [A]Esth 3:12-14; Dan 3:4-6; 6:12 [B]Dan 3:5, 7, 15 3:12 [A]Dan 2:49 3:13 [A]Dan 2:12; 3:19

2:45 stone … mountain. The stone is Messiah (cf. Ps 118:22, 23; Is 28:16; Ro 9:33; 1Pe 2:6; esp. Lk 20:18). The mountain pictures God's all-transcending government that looms over weak earthly powers (4:17, 25; Pss 47:8; 103:19; 145:13; Rev 17:9). Messiah is "cut out" of this sovereign realm by God, which accords with the Son of Man coming (7:13, 14); "without hands" denotes that the Messiah comes from God and is not of human origin or power (cf. the same idea in 8:25). The virgin birth and the resurrection, as well as the second coming, could be encompassed in this reference to supernatural origin.

3:1 image of gold. The statue, which the king arrogantly made, represented himself as an expression of his greatness and glory and reflected the dream where he was the head of gold (2:38). It was not necessarily made of solid gold, but more likely would have been overlaid with gold, like many objects found in the ruins of Babylon. The word for "image" usually means a human form. The height of the figure was about 90 ft. and the width 9 ft.; it would have been comparable in height to date palms found in that area. The self-deifying statue of the king need not have been grotesquely thin in proportion to the height since a massive base could have contributed to the height. This established the worship of Nebuchadnezzar and the nation under his power, in addition to the other gods.

3:2 Leaders attending the "summit conference" for Nebuchadnezzar's display are: satraps, or leaders over regions; prefects, or military chiefs; governors, or civil administrators; counselors, or lawyers; treasurers; judges, or government arbiters; magistrates, or judges in our sense today; rulers, or other civil leaders.

3:5 trigon. A smaller, portable version of the harp, most likely played with a plectrum (pick), yielding high tones. **psaltery.** Possibly an instrument plucked with the fingers rather than a plectrum (pick), yielding low tones.

3:6 furnace. Some ancient kilns were found to have been shaped like a vertical tunnel open only at the top, with a dome supported by columns. Charcoal normally served as fuel.

3:8 certain Chaldeans. These are most likely the priests of Bel-merodach who were envious of these young Jews, and sought their death.

3:12 they do not serve your gods or worship the golden image. Enemies of God's servants witnessed such a clear-cut testimony that they were in no doubt about their rejection of idolatry and unshakeable allegiance to the God of Israel.

3:13 these men. Daniel is not mentioned as being part of the refusal to worship witnessed by the Chaldeans. If present, he surely would have joined these others in faithfulness to God.

14 Nebuchadnezzar responded and said to them,
"Is it true, Shadrach, Meshach and Abed-nego, that
you do not serve [A]my gods or worship the golden
image that I have set up? 15 Now if you are ready, [a]at
the moment you hear the sound of the horn, flute,
[a]lyre, trigon, psaltery and bagpipe and all kinds of
music, to fall down and worship the image that I
have made, *very well.* But if you do not worship,
you will [b]immediately be [B]cast into the midst of a
furnace of blazing fire; and [C]what god is there who
can deliver you out of my hands?"
16 [A]Shadrach, Meshach and Abed-nego replied
to the king, "O Nebuchadnezzar, we do not need to
give you an answer concerning this matter. 17 [a]If it
be *so,* our [A]God whom we serve is able to deliver
us from the furnace of blazing fire; [b]and [B]He will
deliver us out of your hand, O king. 18 [A]But *even* if
He does not, [B]let it be known to you, O king, that
we are not going to serve your gods or worship the
golden image that you have set up."

DANIEL'S FRIENDS PROTECTED

19 Then Nebuchadnezzar was filled with [A]wrath,
and his facial expression was altered toward Shadrach, Meshach and Abed-nego. He answered [a]by
giving orders to heat the furnace seven times more
than it was usually heated. 20 He commanded certain valiant warriors who *were* in his army to tie
up Shadrach, Meshach and Abed-nego in order to
cast *them* into the furnace of blazing fire. 21 Then
these men were tied up in their [a,A]trousers, their
[b]coats, their caps and their *other* clothes, and were
cast into the midst of the furnace of blazing fire.
22 For this reason, because the king's [a]command
was [b,A]urgent and the furnace had been made extremely hot, the flame of the fire slew those men
who carried up Shadrach, Meshach and Abed-nego.
23 But these three men, Shadrach, Meshach and
Abed-nego, [A]fell into the midst of the furnace of
blazing fire *still* tied up.

24 Then Nebuchadnezzar the king was astounded
and stood up in haste; he said to his high officials,
"Was it not three men we cast bound into the midst
of the fire?" They replied to the king, "Certainly,
O king." 25 He said, "Look! I see four men loosed *and*
[A]walking *about* in the midst of the fire [a]without
harm, and the appearance of the fourth is like a son
of *the* [B]gods!" 26 Then Nebuchadnezzar came near to
the door of the furnace of blazing fire; he responded
and said, "Shadrach, Meshach and Abed-nego, come
out, you servants of the [A]Most High God, and come
here!" Then Shadrach, Meshach and Abed-nego
[B]came out of the midst of the fire. 27 The [A]satraps,
the prefects, the governors and the king's high officials gathered around *and* saw in regard to these
men that the [B]fire had no [a]effect on [b]the bodies of
these men nor was the hair of their head singed,
nor were their [c,C]trousers [d]damaged, nor had the
smell of fire *even* come upon them.
28 Nebuchadnezzar responded and said, "Blessed
be the [A]God of Shadrach, Meshach and Abed-nego,
who has [B]sent His angel and delivered His servants
who put their [C]trust in Him, [a]violating the king's
command, and yielded up their bodies so as [D]not
to serve or worship any god except their own God.
29 Therefore I [A]make a decree that any people, nation
or tongue that speaks anything offensive against
the God of [B]Shadrach, Meshach and Abed-nego shall
be torn limb from limb and their [C]houses reduced
to a rubbish heap, inasmuch as there is [D]no other
god who is able to deliver in this way." 30 Then the
king [A]caused Shadrach, Meshach and Abed-nego to
prosper in the province of Babylon.

THE KING ACKNOWLEDGES GOD

4 [a]Nebuchadnezzar the king to all the peoples,
nations, and *men of every* [b]language that live
in all the earth: "May your [c,A]peace abound! 2 It has
seemed good to me to declare the signs and wonders which the [A]Most High God has done for me.

3:14 [A]Is 46:1; Jer 50:2; Dan 3:1; 4:8 3:15 [a]V 5, notes 1, 2, 3 [b]Or *in the same hour* [A]Dan 3:5 [B]Dan 3:6 [C]Ex 5:2; Is 36:18-20; Dan 2:47 3:16 [A]Dan 1:7; 3:12 3:17 [a]Or *If our God…is able* [b]Or *then* [A]Job 5:19; Ps 27:1, 2; Is 26:3, 4; Jer 1:8; 15:20, 21 [B]1 Sam 17:37; Mic 7:7; 2 Cor 1:10 3:18 [A]Josh 24:15; 1 Kin 19:14, 18; Is 51:12, 13; Dan 3:28 [B]Heb 11:25 3:19 [a]Lit *and ordered to* [A]Esth 7:7; Dan 3:13 3:21 [a]Or *leggings* [b]Or *cloaks* [A]Dan 3:27 3:22 [a]Lit *word* [b]Or *harsh* [A]Ex 12:33; Dan 2:15 3:23 [A]Is 43:2 3:25 [a]Lit *there is no injury in them* [A]Ps 91:3-9; Is 43:2 [B]Jer 1:8, 19; 15:21 3:26 [A]Dan 3:17; 4:2 [B]Deut 4:20; 1 Kin 8:51; Jer 11:4 3:27 [a]Lit *power over* [b]Lit *their* [c]Or *cloaks* [d]Lit *changed* [A]Dan 3:2, 3 [B]Is 43:2; Heb 11:34 [C]Dan 3:21 3:28 [a]Lit *and changed the king's word* [A]Dan 2:47; 3:15-17 [B]Ps 34:7, 8; Is 37:36; Dan 3:25; 6:22; Acts 5:19; 12:7 [C]Ps 22:4, 5; 40:4; 84:12; Is 12:2; 26:3, 4; 50:10; Jer 17:7 [D]Dan 3:16-18 3:29 [A]Dan 6:26 [B]Dan 1:7, 19; 2:17, 49; 3:12 [C]Ezra 6:11; Dan 2:5 [D]Dan 2:47; 3:15 3:30 [A]Dan 2:49; 3:12 4:1 [a]Ch 3:31 in Aram [b]Lit *tongue* [c]Or *welfare or prosperity* [A]Ezra 4:17; Dan 6:25 4:2 [A]Dan 3:26; 4:17, 24, 25, 32, 34

3:15 what god … ? The king's challenge would return to embarrass him. The true God was able to deliver, just as He was able to reveal a dream and its meaning. Nebuchadnezzar had earlier called him "a God of gods" (2:47), but having let that fade from his attention, he soon would be shocked and humiliated when God took up his challenge (3:28, 29).

3:16 we do not need to … answer. The 3 men meant no disrespect. They did not have any defense, nor did they need to reconsider their commitment, since they stood fast for their God as the only true and living God. Their lives were in His hands as they indicated in vv. 17, 18 (cf. Is 43:1, 2).

3:19 seven times more. The king's fury at being defied to his face led him to cry for an intensification of the heat. He was not literally requiring the fire to be 7 times hotter as a gauge would indicate, or requiring 7 times as long to heat, or 7 times the amount of fuel (cf. v. 6, "immediately be cast"). The king in anger means "intensely hot," using "seven" figuratively to denote completeness (as Lv 26:18–28; Pr 6:31; 24:16), similar to "ten" in Da 1:20. Cf. "extremely hot" (3:22). A stone or brick furnace with an air draft could be made hotter by more fuel and air.

3:22 carried up. Refers to being taken upward on some kind of ramp to a spot near enough to the top to be thrown in (cf. v. 26). The fire was so hot it incinerated the king's men.

3:23 fell into the midst. A shaft directed them into the furnace bottom, on top of the fuel.

3:25 four men loosed. The king seemed only to have known that the fourth person was a heavenly being. He called him a "son of *the* gods" (a pagan reference to one who appeared supernatural) and an "angel" (v. 28). The fourth person could possibly have been the second person of the Godhead (Jesus Christ) in a pre-incarnate appearance (*see notes on Jos 5:13–15; Jdg 6:11*).

3:27 the fire had no effect. When God enacts a miracle, He supernaturally controls all details so that His power is unmistakable, and there is no other explanation.

3:28–30 The king was convinced and eager to add the God of these men to his panoply of deities. Soon he learned that God was not one of many, but the only God (Da 4).

4:1–3 Nebuchadnezzar's praise of God in 4:1–3 and 34b–37 is the theme that brackets the experience the king reiterates in the first person (vv. 4–34). He began and ended the narrative with praise, and in between told why he converted to such worship of the true God (cf. Ro 11:33).

3 "How great are His [A]signs
And how mighty are His wonders!
His [B]kingdom is an everlasting kingdom
And His dominion is from
generation to generation.

THE VISION OF A GREAT TREE

4 "[a]I, Nebuchadnezzar, was at ease in my house
and [A]flourishing in my palace. 5 I saw a [A]dream
and it made me fearful; and *these* fantasies *as I*
lay on my bed and the [B]visions [a]in my mind kept
alarming me. 6 So I gave orders to [A]bring into my
presence all the wise men of Babylon, that they
might make known to me the interpretation of the
dream. 7 Then the [a,A]magicians, the conjurers, the
[b]Chaldeans and the diviners came in and I related
the dream [c]to them, but they could not make its
[B]interpretation known to me. 8 But finally Daniel
came in before me, whose name is [A]Belteshazzar
according to the name of my god, and in whom is
[a,B]a spirit of the holy gods; and I related the dream
[b]to him, *saying,* 9 'O Belteshazzar, [A]chief of the magicians, since I know that [B]a spirit of the holy gods
is in you and [C]no mystery baffles you, [D]tell *me* the
visions of my dream which I have seen, along with
its interpretation.

10 'Now *these were* the [A]visions [a]in my mind *as*
I lay on my bed: I was looking, and behold, *there*
was a [B]tree in the midst of the [b]earth and its height
was great.

11 'The tree grew large and became strong
And its height [A]reached to the sky,
And it *was* visible to the end
of the whole earth.
12 'Its foliage *was* [A]beautiful and
its fruit abundant,
And in it *was* food for all.
The [B]beasts of the field found
[C]shade under it,
And the [D]birds of the sky
dwelt in its branches,
And all [a]living creatures fed
themselves from it.

13 'I was looking in the [A]visions [a]in my mind *as I*
lay on my bed, and behold, [B]an *angelic* watcher, a
[C]holy one, descended from heaven.

14 'He shouted out and
spoke as follows:
"[A]Chop down the tree and cut
off its branches,
Strip off its foliage and
scatter its fruit;
Let the [B]beasts flee from under it
And the birds from its branches.
15 "Yet [A]leave the stump [a]with its
roots in the ground,
But with a band of iron and
bronze *around it*
In the new grass of the field;
And let him be drenched with
the dew of heaven,
And let [b]him share with the beasts
in the grass of the earth.
16 "Let his [a]mind be changed
from *that of* a man
And let a beast's [a]mind
be given to him,
And let [A]seven [b]periods of
time pass over him.
17 "This sentence is by the decree
of the *angelic* watchers
And the decision is a command
of the holy ones,
In order that the living may [A]know
That the Most High is ruler over
the realm of mankind,
And [B]bestows it on whom
He wishes
And sets over it the [C]lowliest of men."

18 This is the dream *which* I, King Nebuchadnezzar, have seen. Now you, Belteshazzar, tell *me* its
interpretation, inasmuch as none of the [A]wise men
of my kingdom is able to make known to me the
interpretation; but you are able, for a [B]spirit of the
holy gods is in you.'

4:3 [A]Ps 77:19; 105:27; Is 25:1; Dan 6:27 [B]Dan 2:44; 4:34; 6:26 4:4 [a]Ch 4:1 in Aram [A]Ps 30:6; Is 47:7, 8 4:5 [a]Lit *of my head* [A]Dan 2:3 [B]Dan 2:1, 28; 4:10, 13 4:6 [A]Gen 41:8; Dan 2:2 4:7 [a]Or *soothsayer priests,* and so throughout the ch [b]Or *master astrologers* [c]Lit *before* [A]Gen 41:8; Dan 2:10, 27; 5:7 [B]Is 44:25; Jer 27:9, 10; Dan 2:7 4:8 [a]Or possibly *the Spirit of the holy God,* and so throughout the ch [b]Lit *before* [A]Dan 1:7; 2:26; 5:12 [B]Dan 4:9, 18; 5:11, 14 4:9 [A]Dan 1:20; 2:48; 5:11 [B]Gen 41:38; Dan 4:8 [C]Ezek 28:3; Dan 2:47 [D]Gen 41:15; Dan 2:4, 5 4:10 [a]Lit *of my head* [b]Or *land,* and so throughout the ch [A]Dan 4:5 [B]Ezek 31:3, 6 4:11 [A]Deut 9:1; Dan 4:21, 22 4:12 [a]Lit *flesh* [A]Ezek 31:7 [B]Jer 27:6; Ezek 31:6 [C]Lam 4:20 [D]Ezek 17:23; Matt 13:32; Luke 13:19 4:13 [a]Lit *of my head* [A]Dan 7:1 [B]Dan 4:17, 23 [C]Deut 33:2; Ps 89:7; Dan 8:13 4:14 [A]Ezek 31:10-14; Dan 4:23; Matt 3:10; 7:19; Luke 13:7-9 [B]Ezek 31:12, 13; Dan 4:12 4:15 [a]Lit *of* [b]Lit *his portion be with* [A]Job 14:7-9 4:16 [a]Lit *heart* [b]I.e. years [A]Dan 4:23, 25, 32 4:17 [A]Ps 9:16; 83:18; Dan 2:21; 5:21 [B]Jer 27:5-7; Dan 4:25; 5:18, 19 [C]1 Sam 2:8; Dan 11:21 4:18 [A]Gen 41:8, 15; Dan 4:7; 5:8, 15 [B]Dan 4:8, 9

4:6 wise men of Babylon. The king gave them another try (cf. 2:2–13), and they were again unable.

4:8 finally Daniel came. Daniel alone interpreted the tree vision (v. 10), enabled by God. **my god.** As the story began, he depicted himself still as a worshiper of Bel-merodach.

4:9 chief of the magicians. Here was the title the pagans gave him (cf. 5:11). **spirit.** The meaning here and in v. 18 (as well as 5:11, 14) is rightly translated by some versions as "the Spirit of the Holy God." Wording for the true God in the Heb. of Jos 24:19 is equivalent to the Aram. here (*see note on 2:4*). Some translators believe he meant "a spirit of the holy gods." This is unlikely, since no pagan worshipers claimed purity or holiness for their deities. In fact, just the opposite was believed. And since Nebuchadnezzar was rehearsing his conversion, he could genuinely identify the true Spirit of God.

4:10–17 a tree. This pictures Nebuchadnezzar after 605 B.C. (cf. 4:20–22). The creatures in v. 12 represent people under his rule (v. 22). The fall of the tree represents the coming time of God's judgment on him (cf. 4:23–25).

4:13 *angelic* watcher, a holy one. This was an angel (cf. v. 23), a servant of God, who controlled a nation's rise or fall (cf. Da 10:13). Angels often have roles administering God's judgment, as shown also in Ge 18, Is 37, and Rev 16.

4:15 stump. The basis (nucleus) of the kingdom, still in existence in v. 26 (cf. Is 6:13), will later sprout as in nature (Job 14:7–9). The band is a guarantee that God will protect what remains intact and preserve the king's rule (v. 26).

4:16 a beast's mind. Some form of the disease called lycanthropy, in which a person thinks he is an animal and lives wildly, caused him to eat grass, have thick and unkept nails, shaggy hair, and behave inhumanly. **seven periods of time.** (cf. also 4:23, 25, 32). Probably "years" are meant, not "months," which is used in v. 29. Daniel uses the same term clearly to mean "years" in 7:25.

DANIEL INTERPRETS THE VISION

19 "Then Daniel, whose name is Belteshazzar, was
appalled for a while as his [A]thoughts alarmed him. The
king responded and said, 'Belteshazzar, do not [B]let the
dream or its interpretation alarm you.' Belteshazzar
replied, '[C]My lord, *if only* the dream applied to those
who hate you and its interpretation to [D]your adversaries! 20 The [A]tree that you saw, which became large
and grew strong, whose height reached to the sky and
was visible to all the earth 21 and whose foliage *was*
beautiful and its fruit abundant, and in which *was*
food for all, under which the beasts of the field dwelt
and in whose branches the birds of the sky lodged—
22 it is [A]you, O king; for you have become great and
grown strong, and your [a]majesty has become great
and reached to the sky and your [B]dominion to the
end of the earth. 23 In that the king saw an *angelic*
watcher, a holy one, descending from heaven and
saying, "[A]Chop down the tree and destroy it; yet leave
the stump [a]with its roots in the ground, but with a
band of iron and bronze *around it* in the new grass
of the field, and let him be drenched with the dew of
heaven, and let [b]him share with the beasts of the field
until [B]seven [c]periods of time pass over him," 24 this is
the interpretation, O king, and this is the decree of the
Most High, which has [A]come upon my lord the king:
25 that you be [A]driven away from mankind and your
dwelling place be with the beasts of the field, and
you be given grass to eat like cattle and be drenched
with the dew of heaven; and seven [a]periods of time
will pass over you, until you recognize that the [B]Most
High is ruler over the realm of mankind and [C]bestows
it on whomever He wishes. 26 And in that it was commanded to [A]leave the stump [a]with the roots of the
tree, your kingdom will be [b]assured to you after you
recognize that *it is* [B]Heaven *that* rules. 27 Therefore,
O king, may my [A]advice be pleasing to you: [a,B]break
away now from your sins by *doing* righteousness and
from your iniquities by [C]showing mercy to *the* poor, in
case there may be a [D]prolonging of your prosperity.'

THE VISION FULFILLED

28 "All *this* [A]happened to Nebuchadnezzar the king.
29 [A]Twelve months later he was walking on the *roof
of* the royal palace of Babylon. 30 The king [a]reflected
and said, 'Is this not Babylon the [A]great, which I myself have built as a royal [b]residence by the might of
my power and for the glory of my majesty?' 31 While
the word *was* in the king's mouth, a voice [a]came from
heaven, *saying,* 'King Nebuchadnezzar, to you it is declared: [b]sovereignty has been removed from you, 32 and
[A]you will be driven away from mankind, and your
dwelling place *will be* with the beasts of the field. You
will be given grass to eat like cattle, and [B]seven [a]peri-
ods of time will pass over you until you recognize that
the [C]Most High is ruler over the realm of mankind and
bestows it on whomever He wishes.' 33 Immediately
the word concerning Nebuchadnezzar was fulfilled;
and he was [A]driven away from mankind and began
eating grass like cattle, and his body was drenched
with the dew of heaven until his hair had grown like
eagles' *feathers* and his nails like birds' *claws.*
34 "But at the end of [a]that period, I, Nebuchadnezzar, raised my eyes toward heaven and my [b]reason
returned to me, and I blessed the [A]Most High and
praised and honored [B]Him who lives forever;

For His dominion is an
[C]everlasting dominion,
And His kingdom *endures* from
generation to generation.
35 "[A]All the inhabitants of the earth
are accounted as nothing,
But [B]He does according to His
will in the host of heaven
And *among* the inhabitants of earth;
And [C]no one can [a]ward off His hand
Or say to Him, '[D]What have You done?'

36 At that time my [a,A]reason returned to me. And my
majesty and [B]splendor were [b]restored to me for the
glory of my kingdom, and my counselors and my
nobles began seeking me out; so I was reestablished
in my [c]sovereignty, and surpassing [C]greatness was
added to me. 37 Now I, Nebuchadnezzar, praise, exalt
and honor the King of [A]heaven, for [B]all His works are
[a]true and His ways [b]just, and He is able to humble
those who [C]walk in pride."

BELSHAZZAR'S FEAST

5 Belshazzar the king [a]held a great [A]feast for a
thousand of his nobles, and he was drinking
wine in the presence of the thousand. 2 When Belshazzar tasted the wine, he gave orders to bring the

4:19 [A]Jer 4:19; Dan 7:15, 28; 8:27; 10:16, 17 [B]1 Sam 3:17; Dan 4:4, 5 [C]2 Sam 18:31; Dan 4:24; 10:16 [D]2 Sam 18:32 4:20 [A]Dan 4:10-12 4:22 [a]Lit *greatness* [A]2 Sam 12:7; Dan 2:37, 38 [B]Jer 27:6, 7 4:23 [a]Lit *of* [b]Lit *his portion be with* [c]I.e. years [A]Dan 4:14, 15 [B]Dan 4:16 4:24 [A]Job 40:11, 12; Ps 107:40 4:25 [a]I.e. years [A]Dan 4:33; 5:21 [B]Ps 83:18; Jer 27:5; Dan 4:2, 17 [C]Dan 2:37; 4:17; 5:21 4:26 [a]Lit *of* [b]Lit *enduring* [A]Dan 4:15, 23 [B]Dan 2:18, 19, 28, 37, 44; 4:31 4:27 [a]Or *redeem now your sins* [A]Gen 41:33-37 [B]Prov 28:13; Is 55:6, 7; Ezek 18:7, 21, 22; Acts 8:22 [C]Ps 41:1-3; Is 58:6, 7, 10 [D]1 Kin 21:29; Jon 3:9 4:28 [A]Num 23:19; Zech 1:6 4:29 [A]2 Pet 3:9 4:30 [a]Lit *answered* [b]Lit *house* [A]Hab 2:4 4:31 [a]Lit *fell* [b]Or *kingdom* 4:32 [a]I.e. years [A]Dan 4:25 [B]Dan 4:16 [C]Dan 4:17 4:33 [A]Dan 4:25; 5:21 4:34 [a]Lit *the days* [b]Lit *knowledge* [A]Dan 4:2; 5:18, 21 [B]Ps 102:24-27; Dan 6:26; 12:7; Rev 4:10 [C]Ps 145:13; Jer 10:10; Dan 4:3; Mic 4:7; Luke 1:33 4:35 [a]Lit *strike against* [A]Ps 39:5; Is 40:15, 17 [B]Ps 33:11; 115:3; 135:6; Dan 6:27 [C]Job 42:2; Is 43:13 [D]Job 9:12; Is 45:9; Rom 9:20 4:36 [a]Lit *knowledge* [b]Lit *returning* [c]Or *kingdom* [A]2 Chr 33:12, 13; Dan 4:34 [B]Dan 2:31 [C]Prov 22:4; Dan 4:22 4:37 [a]Lit *truth* [b]Lit *justice* [A]Dan 4:26; 5:23 [B]Deut 32:4; Ps 33:4, 5; Is 5:16 [C]Ex 18:11; Job 40:11, 12; Dan 5:20 5:1 [a]Lit *made* [A]Esth 1:3; Is 22:12-14

4:19 appalled. Daniel's compassionate alarm at the coming calamity.

4:26 Heaven *that* rules. God is synonymous with His abode.

4:27 break away now from your sins. Daniel called for a recognition of sin and repentance (cf. Is 55:7). He was not presenting a works salvation, but treating the issue of sin exactly as Jesus did with the rich young ruler in Mt 19:16–23. The king failed to repent at this point (v. 30).

4:30 I myself have built. Nebuchadnezzar was known for his building projects, such as a 400 foot high mountain terraced with flowing water and hanging gardens for his wife (one of the 7 wonders of the ancient world) as a place for cool refreshment. For such pride, judgment fell (vv. 31–33).

4:34 raised my eyes. God's grace enables a person to do this (Jn 6:44, 65). "For those who honor Me I will honor" (1Sa 2:30); and "Though He [God] scoffs at the scoffers, yet He gives grace to the afflicted" (Pr 3:34). The praise of vv. 34b–37 and 1–3 came as a result (cf. Jer 9:23, 24).

5:1 Belshazzar. These events occurred in 539 B.C., over two decades after Nebuchadnezzar's death (ca. 563/2 B.C.). This king, whose name (similar to Daniel's, cf. 4:8) means "Bel, protect the king," is about to be conquered by the Medo-Persian army.

5:2 vessels. The celebration was designed to boost morale and break the feelings of

gold and silver [A]vessels which Nebuchadnezzar his
[a]father had taken out of the temple which *was* in
Jerusalem, so that the king and his nobles, his wives
and his concubines might drink from them. 3 Then
they brought the gold vessels that had been taken
out of the temple, the house of God which *was* in
Jerusalem; and the king and his nobles, his wives
and his concubines drank from them. 4 They [A]drank
the wine and praised the gods of [B]gold and silver,
of bronze, iron, wood and stone.
5 Suddenly the fingers of a man's hand emerged
and began writing opposite the lampstand on the
plaster of the wall of the king's palace, and the king
saw the [a]back of the hand that did the writing.
6 Then the king's [a,A]face grew pale and his thoughts
alarmed him, and his [B]hip joints went slack and his
[C]knees began knocking together. 7 The king called
aloud to bring in the [A]conjurers, the [a]Chaldeans
and the diviners. The king spoke and said to the
wise men of Babylon, "Any man who can read this
inscription and explain its interpretation to me
shall be [B]clothed with purple and *have* a [C]necklace
of gold around his neck, and have authority as
[b,D]third *ruler* in the kingdom." 8 Then all the king's
wise men came in, but [A]they could not read the
inscription or make known its interpretation to the
king. 9 Then King Belshazzar was greatly [A]alarmed,
his [a,B]face grew *even* paler, and his nobles were
perplexed.
10 The queen entered the banquet [a]hall because
of the words of the king and his nobles; the queen
spoke and said, "[A]O king, live forever! Do not let
your thoughts alarm you or your [b]face be pale.
11 There is a [A]man in your kingdom in whom is [a]a
[B]spirit of the holy gods; and in the days of your
father, illumination, insight and wisdom like the
wisdom of the gods were found in him. And King
Nebuchadnezzar, your father, your father [b,C]the king,
appointed him chief of the [c]magicians, conjurers,
[d]Chaldeans *and* diviners. 12 *This was* because an
[A]extraordinary spirit, knowledge and insight, interpretation of dreams, explanation of enigmas
and solving of difficult problems were found in
this Daniel, whom the king named [B]Belteshazzar.
Let Daniel now be summoned and he will declare
the interpretation."

DANIEL INTERPRETS HANDWRITING ON THE WALL

13 Then Daniel was brought in before the king. The
king spoke and said to Daniel, "Are you that Daniel
who is one of the [a,A]exiles from Judah, whom my
father the king [B]brought from Judah? 14 Now I have
heard about you that [a]a spirit of the gods is in you,
and that illumination, insight and extraordinary
wisdom have been found in you. 15 Just now the
[A]wise men *and* the conjurers were brought in before
me that they might read this inscription and make
its interpretation known to me, but they [B]could not
declare the interpretation of the [a]message. 16 But I
personally have heard about you, that you are able
to give interpretations and solve difficult problems.
Now if you are able to read the inscription and
make its [A]interpretation known to me, you will be
[B]clothed with purple and *wear* a necklace of gold
around your neck, and you will have authority as
the [a]third *ruler* in the kingdom."
17 Then Daniel answered and said before the king,
"[a]Keep your [A]gifts for yourself or give your rewards
to someone else; however, I will read the inscription
to the king and make the interpretation known to
him. 18 [a]O king, the [A]Most High God [B]granted [b]sover-
eignty, [C]grandeur, glory and majesty to Nebuchadnezzar your father. 19 Because of the grandeur which
He bestowed on him, all the peoples, nations and
men of every [a]language feared and trembled before
him; [A]whomever he wished he killed and whomever
he wished he spared alive; and whomever he wished
he elevated and whomever he wished he humbled.
20 But when his heart was [A]lifted up and his spirit
became so [a,B]proud that he behaved arrogantly, he
was [C]deposed from his royal throne and *his* glory
was taken away from him. 21 He was also [A]driven
away from [a]mankind, and his heart was made like
that of beasts, and his dwelling place *was* with
the [B]wild donkeys. He was given grass to eat like
cattle, and his body was drenched with the dew
of heaven until he recognized that the [C]Most High
God is ruler over the realm of mankind and *that*
He sets over it whomever He wishes. 22 Yet you, his
[a]son, Belshazzar, have [A]not humbled your heart,
[b]even though you knew all this, 23 but you have
[A]exalted yourself against the [B]Lord of heaven; and

5:2 [a]Or *forefather,* and so throughout the ch [A]2 Kin 24:13; 25:15; Ezra 1:7-11; Dan 1:2 5:4 [A]Is 42:8; Dan 5:23; Rev 9:20 [B]Ps 115:4; 135:15; Is 40:19, 20; Dan 3:1; Hab 2:19
5:5 [a]Or *palm* 5:6 [a]Lit *brightness changed for him* [A]Dan 5:9, 10; 7:28 [B]Ps 69:23 [C]Ezek 7:17; 21:7; Nah 2:10 5:7 [a]Or *master astrologers* [b]Or *a triumvir* [A]Is 44:25; 47:13; Dan 4:6, 7; 5:11, 15 [B]Gen 41:42-44; Dan 5:16, 29 [C]Ezek 16:11 [D]Dan 2:48; 5:16, 29; 6:2, 3 5:8 [A]Gen 41:8; Dan 2:27; 4:7; 5:15 5:9 [a]Lit *brightness was changing upon him* [A]Job 18:11; Is 21:2-4; Jer 6:24; Dan 2:1; 5:6 [B]Is 13:6-8 5:10 [a]Lit *house* [b]Lit *brightness be changed* [A]Dan 3:9; 6:6 5:11 [a]Or possibly *the Spirit of the holy God* [b]Or *O king* [c]Or *soothsayer priests* [d]Or *master astrologers* [A]Gen 41:11-15; Dan 2:47 [B]Dan 4:8, 9, 18; 5:14 [C]Dan 2:48 5:12 [A]Dan 5:14; 6:3 [B]Dan 1:7; 4:8
5:13 [a]Lit *sons of the exile* [A]Ezra 4:1; 6:16, 19, 20; Dan 2:25; 6:13 [B]Dan 1:1, 2 5:14 [a]Or possibly *the Spirit of God* 5:15 [a]Lit *word* [A]Dan 5:7 [B]Is 47:12f; Dan 5:8
5:16 [a]Or *triumvir* [A]Gen 40:8 [B]Dan 5:7, 29 5:17 [a]Lit *Let…be for* [A]2 Kin 5:16 5:18 [a]Lit *You, O king* [b]Or *the kingdom* [A]Dan 4:2; 5:21 [B]Dan 2:37, 38; 4:17 [C]Jer 25:9; 27:5-7 5:19 [a]Lit *tongue* [A]Dan 2:12, 13; 3:6; 11:3, 16, 36 5:20 [a]Lit *strong* [A]Ex 9:17; Job 15:25; Is 14:13-15; Dan 4:30, 31 [B]2 Kin 17:14; 2 Chr 36:13 [C]Job 40:11, 12; Jer 13:18 5:21 [a]Lit *the sons of man* [A]Job 30:3-7; Dan 4:32, 33 [B]Job 39:5-8 [C]Ex 9:14-16; Ps 83:17, 18; Ezek 17:24; Dan 4:17, 34, 35
5:22 [a]Or *descendant* [b]Lit *inasmuch as you* [A]Ex 10:3; 2 Chr 33:23; 36:12 5:23 [A]2 Kin 14:10; Is 2:12; 37:23; Jer 50:29; Dan 5:3, 4 [B]Dan 4:37

doom, because at this very time, armies of Medo-Persia (cf. v. 30) had Babylon helplessly under siege.

5:4 This exercise was a call for their deities to deliver them.

5:5 man's hand. Babylonian hands had taken God's vessels (mentioned twice) and held them in contempt to dishonor and challenge Him. Now the hand that controls all men, and which none can restrain, challenged them (4:35). God's answer to their challenge was clear, as in vv. 23–28.

5:7–9 they could not. Without God's help, the experts again failed (cf. chaps. 2, 4), but God's man Daniel would not.

5:10 the queen spoke. Possibly she was a surviving wife or a daughter of Nebuchadnezzar. If the latter, she was a wife of Nabonidus who co-ruled with Belshazzar (cf. "third *ruler*," v. 16). She, like Nebuchadnezzar in chap. 4, has confidence in Daniel (vv. 11, 12).

5:13 father. Used in the same sense of grandfather (cf. v. 18).

5:16 the third *ruler*. This trio included Daniel, along with Belshazzar, Nebuchadnezzar's grandson (ruled 553–539 B.C.), and Nabonidus (ruled 556–539 B.C.). The prizes turned out to be nonexistent in light of the city's conquest that very night (vv. 29, 30).

they have brought the vessels of His house before
you, and you and your nobles, your wives and your
concubines have been drinking wine from them;
and you have praised the [C]gods of silver and gold,
of bronze, iron, wood and stone, which do not see,
hear or understand. But the God [D]in whose hand
are your life-breath and all your [E]ways, you have
not glorified. 24 Then the [a,A]hand was sent from Him
and this inscription was written out.
25 "Now this is the inscription that was written out:

'[a]MENĒ, [a]MENĒ, [b]TEKĒL, [c]UPHARSIN.'

26 This is the interpretation of the [a]message:
'MENĒ'—God has numbered your kingdom and [A]put
an end to it. 27 'TEKĒL'—you have been [A]weighed
on the scales and found deficient. 28 'PERĒS'—your
kingdom has been divided and given over to the
[A]Medes and [a]Persians."
29 Then Belshazzar gave orders, and they [A]clothed
Daniel with purple and *put* a necklace of gold
around his neck, and issued a proclamation concerning him that he *now* had authority as the [a]third
ruler in the kingdom.
30 That same night [A]Belshazzar the Chaldean king
was [B]slain. 31 [a]So [A]Darius the Mede received the kingdom at about the age of sixty-two.

DANIEL SERVES DARIUS

6 [a]It seemed good to Darius to appoint 120 satraps over the kingdom, that they would be in
charge of the whole kingdom, 2 and over them three
commissioners (of whom [A]Daniel was one), that these
satraps might be accountable to them, and that the
king might not suffer [B]loss. 3 Then this Daniel began
distinguishing himself [a]among the commissioners
and satraps because [b]he possessed an [A]extraordinary
spirit, and the king planned to appoint him over the
[B]entire kingdom. 4 Then the commissioners and satraps began [A]trying to find a ground of accusation
against Daniel in regard to [a]government affairs; but
they could find [B]no ground of accusation or *evidence*
of corruption, inasmuch as he was faithful, and no
negligence or corruption was *to be* found in him.
5 Then these men said, "We will not find any ground
of accusation against this Daniel unless we find *it*
against him with regard to the [A]law of his God."
6 Then these commissioners and satraps came [a]by
agreement to the king and spoke to him as follows:
"King Darius, [A]live forever! 7 All the [A]commissioners
of the kingdom, the prefects and the satraps, the
high officials and the governors have [B]consulted
together that the king should establish a statute
and enforce an injunction that anyone who makes
a petition to any god or man besides you, O king,
for thirty days, shall [C]be cast into the lions' [a]den.
8 Now, O king, [A]establish the injunction and sign the
document so that it may not be changed, according
to the [B]law of the Medes and Persians, which [a]may
not be revoked." 9 Therefore King Darius [A]signed
the document, that is, the injunction.
10 Now when Daniel knew that the document
was signed, he entered his house (now in his roof
chamber he had windows open [A]toward Jerusalem);

5:23 [C]Ps 115:4-8; Is 37:19; Hab 2:18, 19 [D]Job 12:10 [E]Job 31:4; Ps 139:3; Prov 20:24; Jer 10:23 5:24 [a]Lit *palm of the hand* [A]Dan 5:5 5:25 [a]Or *a mina* (50 shekels) from verb "to number" [b]Or *a shekel* from verb "to weigh" [c]Or *and half-shekels* (sing: *perēs*) from verb "to divide" 5:26 [a]Lit *word* [A]Is 13:6, 17-19; Jer 50:41-43 5:27 [A]Job 31:6; Ps 62:9 5:28 [a]Aram: *Pāras* [A]Is 13:17; 21:2; 45:1, 2; Dan 5:31; 6:8, 28; Acts 2:9 5:29 [a]Or *triumvir* [A]Dan 5:7, 16 5:30 [A]Dan 5:1, 2 [B]Is 21:4-9; 47:9; Jer 51:11, 31, 39, 57 5:31 [a]Ch 6:1 in Aram [A]Dan 6:1; 9:1 6:1 [a]Ch 6:2 in Aram 6:2 [A]Dan 2:48, 49; 5:16, 29 [B]Ezra 4:22; Esth 7:4 6:3 [a]Lit *above* [b]Lit *there was in him* [A]Dan 5:12, 14; 9:23 [B]Gen 41:40; Esth 10:3 6:4 [a]Lit *the kingdom* [A]Gen 43:18; Judg 14:4; Jer 20:10; Dan 3:8; Luke 20:20 [B]Dan 6:22; Luke 20:26; 23:14, 15; Phil 2:15; 1 Pet 2:12; 3:16 6:5 [A]Acts 24:13-16, 20, 21 6:6 [a]Or *thronging* [A]Neh 2:3; Dan 2:4; 5:10; 6:21 6:7 [a]Or *pit,* and so throughout the ch [A]Dan 3:2, 27 [B]Ps 59:3; 62:4; 64:2-6; 83:1-3 [C]Ps 10:9; Dan 3:6; 6:16 6:8 [a]Lit *does not pass away* [A]Esth 3:12; 8:10; Is 10:1 [B]Esth 1:19; 8:8; Dan 6:12, 15 6:9 [A]Ps 118:9; 146:3 6:10 [A]1 Kin 8:44, 48, 49; Ps 5:7; Jon 2:4

5:25–29 MENĒ, MENĒ. This means "counted," or "appointed," and is doubled for stronger emphasis. TEKĒL means "weighed" or "assessed," by the God who weighs actions (1Sa 2:3; Ps 62:9). PERĒS denotes "divided," i.e., to the Medes and Persians. UPHARSIN in v. 25 is the plural of PERĒS, possibly emphasizing the parts in the division. The "U" prefix on PHARSIN has the idea of the English "and."

5:30 That same night. One ancient account alleged that Persia's General Ugbaru had troops dig a trench to divert and thus lower the waters of the Euphrates River. Since the river flowed through the city of Babylon, the lowered water enabled besiegers to unexpectedly invade via the waterway under the thick walls and reach the palace before the city was aware. The end then came quickly, as guards, Belshazzar, and others were slain on Oct. 16, 539 B.C.

5:31 Darius the Mede. Possibly Darius is not a name, but an honored title for Cyrus, who with his army entered Babylon Oct. 29, 539 B.C. It is used in inscriptions for at least 5 Persian rulers. History mentions no specific man named Darius the Mede. In 6:28 it is possible to translate, "Darius even ... Cyrus." A less likely possibility is that Darius is a second name for Gubaru, Cyrus' appointed king to head up the Babylonian sector of his empire. Gubaru (or Gobryas) is distinct from Ugbaru, the general, who died soon after conquering Babylon. As previously prophesied, Babylon met God's judgment (cf. Is 13; 47; Jer 50; 51; Hab 2:5–19).

6:1 satraps. Each is a provincial administrator under the king. Daniel's eminent appointment was to a post as "commissioner" (v. 2), assisting the king as his vice-regent.

6:2 not suffer loss. They were responsible to prevent loss from military revolts, tax evasion, or fraud.

6:3 an extraordinary spirit. Daniel, over 80, had enjoyed God's blessing throughout his life (cf. 1:20, 21; 2:49; 4:8; 5:12). **over the entire kingdom.** Daniel was the favorite of the king. He had experience, wisdom, a sense of history, leadership, a good reputation, ability, attitude, and revelation from the God of heaven. Apparently, God wanted him in the place of influence to encourage and assist in the Jews' return to Judah, since the return was made in Cyrus' first year (539–537 B.C.), right before the lions' den incident. From the record of Ezr 1 and 6, all the basic elements of the return appear: 1) the temple was to be rebuilt with the cost paid from Cyrus' treasury; 2) all Jews who visited could return, and those who stayed were urged to assist financially; and 3) the gold and silver vessels stolen from the temple by Nebuchadnezzar were to be taken back. To account for such favor toward the Jews, it is easy to think of Daniel not only influencing Cyrus to write such a decree, but even formulating it for him (cf. Pr 21:1).

6:4 accusation against Daniel. The jealous plot, not unlike the effort against Daniel's 3 friends in 3:8ff., was also similar to that by Joseph's brothers (cf. Ge 37:18–24).

6:7 besides you, O king. A deceptive stroke of the king's ego secured his injunction, which was designed to benefit Daniel's peers. Ancient kings were frequently worshiped as gods. Pagans had such inferior views of their gods that such homage was no problem.

6:8 law ... which may not be revoked. Once enacted, Medo-Persian law could not be changed, even by the king (cf. 6:12, 15; Est 1:19; 8:8).

6:10 toward Jerusalem. Daniel's uncompromising pattern of prayer toward God's temple conformed to Solomon's prayer that the Lord's people would do so (1Ki 8:44, 45). Three times a day was also the pattern established by David (Ps 55:16, 17).

and he continued [B]kneeling on his knees three times a day, [C]praying and [D]giving thanks before his God, [a]as he had been doing previously. 11 Then these men came [a,A]by agreement and found Daniel making petition and supplication before his God. 12 Then they approached and [A]spoke before the king about the king's injunction, "Did you not sign an injunction that any man who makes a petition to any god or man besides you, O king, for thirty days, is to be cast into the lions' den?" The king replied, "The statement is true, according to the [B]law of the Medes and Persians, which [a]may not be revoked." 13 Then they answered and spoke before the king, "[A]Daniel, who is one of the [a]exiles from Judah, pays [B]no attention to you, O king, or to the injunction which you signed, but keeps making his petition three times a day."

14 Then, as soon as the king heard this statement, he was deeply [A]distressed and set *his* mind on delivering Daniel; and even until sunset he kept exerting himself to rescue him. 15 Then these men came [a]by agreement to the king and said to the king, "Recognize, O king, that it is a [A]law of the Medes and Persians that no injunction or statute which the king establishes may be changed."

DANIEL IN THE LIONS' DEN

16 Then the king gave orders, and Daniel was brought in and [A]cast into the lions' den. The king spoke and said to Daniel, "[a,B]Your God whom you constantly serve will Himself deliver you." 17 A [A]stone was brought and laid over the mouth of the den; and the king sealed it with his own signet ring and with the signet rings of his nobles, so that nothing would be changed in regard to Daniel. 18 Then the king went off to his palace and spent the night [A]fasting, and no entertainment was brought before him; and his [B]sleep fled from him.

19 Then the king arose at dawn, at the break of day, and went in haste to the lions' den. 20 When he had come near the den to Daniel, he cried out with a troubled voice. The king spoke and said to Daniel, "Daniel, servant of the living God, has [A]your God, whom you constantly serve, been [B]able to deliver you from the lions?" 21 Then Daniel spoke [a]to the king, "[A]O king, live forever! 22 My God [A]sent His angel and [B]shut the lions' mouths and they have not harmed me, inasmuch as [a]I was found innocent before Him; and also [b]toward you, O king, I have committed no crime." 23 Then the king was very pleased and gave orders for Daniel to be taken up out of the den. So Daniel was taken up out of the den and [A]no injury whatever was found on him, because he had [B]trusted in his God. 24 The king then gave orders, and they brought those men who had [a]maliciously accused Daniel, and they [A]cast them, their [B]children and their wives into the lions' den; and they had not reached the bottom of the den before the lions overpowered them and crushed all their bones.

25 Then Darius the king wrote to all the [A]peoples, nations and *men of every* [a]language who were living in all the land: "[B]May your [b]peace abound! 26 [a]I [A]make a decree that in all the dominion of my kingdom men are to fear and tremble before the God of Daniel;

For He is the [B]living God and
  [C]enduring forever,
And [D]His kingdom is one which
  will not be destroyed,
And His dominion *will be* [b]forever.
27 "He delivers and rescues and
  performs [A]signs and wonders
In heaven and on earth,
Who has *also* delivered Daniel
  from the [a]power of the lions."

28 So this [A]Daniel enjoyed success in the reign of Darius and in the reign of [B]Cyrus the Persian.

VISION OF THE FOUR BEASTS

7 In the first year of Belshazzar king of Babylon Daniel saw a [A]dream and visions [a]in his mind *as he lay* on his bed; then he [B]wrote the dream down *and* related the [b]*following* summary of [c]it. 2 Daniel

6:10 [a]Or *because* [B]Ps 55:17; 95:6 [C]Dan 9:4-19 [D]Ps 34:1; Phil 4:6; 1 Thess 5:17, 18 6:11 [a]Or *thronging* [A]Ps 37:32, 33; Dan 6:6 6:12 [a]Lit *does not pass away* [A]Dan 3:8-12; Acts 16:19-21 [B]Esth 1:19; Dan 6:8, 15 6:13 [a]Lit *sons of the exile* [A]Dan 2:25; 5:13 [B]Esth 3:8; Dan 3:12; Acts 5:29 6:14 [A]Mark 6:26 6:15 [a]Or *thronging* [A]Esth 8:8; Ps 94:20, 21; Dan 6:8, 12 6:16 [a]Or *May your God...Himself deliver you* [A]2 Sam 3:39; Jer 38:5; Dan 6:7 [B]Job 5:19; Ps 37:39, 40; Is 41:10; Dan 3:17, 28; 6:20; 2 Cor 1:10 6:17 [A]Lam 3:53; Matt 27:66 6:18 [A]2 Sam 12:16, 17 [B]Esth 6:1; Ps 77:4; Dan 2:1 6:20 [A]Dan 6:16, 27 [B]Gen 18:14; Num 11:23; Jer 32:17; Dan 3:17 6:21 [a]Lit *with* [A]Dan 2:4; 6:6 6:22 [a]Lit *innocence was found for me* [b]Lit *before* [A]Num 20:16; Is 63:9; Dan 3:28; Acts 12:11; Heb 1:14 [B]Ps 91:11-13; 2 Tim 4:17; Heb 11:33 6:23 [A]Dan 3:25, 27 [B]1 Chr 5:20; 2 Chr 20:20; Ps 118:8, 9; Is 26:3; Dan 3:17, 28 6:24 [a]Lit *eaten the pieces of Daniel* [A]Deut 19:18, 19; Esth 7:10 [B]Deut 24:16; 2 Kin 14:6; Esth 9:10 6:25 [a]Lit *tongue* [b]Or *welfare or prosperity* [A]Ezra 1:1, 2; Esth 3:12; 8:9; Dan 4:1 [B]Ezra 4:17; 1 Pet 1:2 6:26 [a]Lit *From me a decree is made* [b]Lit *to the end* [A]Ezra 6:8-12; 7:13, 21; Dan 3:29 [B]Dan 4:34; 6:20; Hos 1:10; Rom 9:26 [C]Ps 93:1, 2; Mal 3:6 [D]Dan 2:44; 4:3; 7:14, 27; Luke 1:33 6:27 [a]Lit *hand* [A]Dan 4:2, 3 6:28 [A]Dan 1:21 [B]2 Chr 36:22, 23; Dan 10:1 7:1 [a]Lit *of his head* [b]Or *beginning* [c]Lit *words* [A]Job 33:14-16; Dan 1:17; 2:1, 26-28; 4:5-9; Joel 2:28 [B]Jer 36:4, 32

6:13 one of the exiles from Judah. Daniel had lived over 60 years in Babylon. His loyalty to the rulers was well known (5:13); in spite of that loyalty, his consistent faithfulness to God brought this threat.

6:14 He went from a self-styled god to a fool in one day.

6:16 lions' den. The word "den" is related to the Heb. term meaning "to dig," so it refers to an underground pit which likely had 1) a hole at the top from which to drop food into the pit, and 2) a door at the foot of a ramp or on a hillside through which the lions could enter.

6:22 His angel. In this miracle, the angel was possibly the same person as the fourth person in the fiery furnace (cf. 3:25 and *see note there*). **innocent before Him.** That is the supreme commendation of Daniel as blameless before God and unworthy of such a death.

6:23 no injury ... on him. God openly honored Daniel's faith for the purpose of showing His glory (cf. 3:26, 27). That is not always the case, as God may choose to be glorified by permitting a trusted servant to be martyred (cf. Daniel in Heb 11:33 with others in 11:35–38).

6:24 the king then gave orders. Like the sin of Achan (Jos 7:20–26), this sin against God, Darius, and Daniel cost the men and their families their lives. This judgment of God was also an important detail in the miracle, lest some critic suggest the lions were tame or toothless or not hungry.

6:25–27 Darius the king wrote. Impacted by Daniel and by the Lord, he expressed himself as if he had come to a point of personal trust in God for his salvation such as Nebuchadnezzar (cf. 4:1–3, 34–37). Daniel illustrated the evangelistic potency of a godly, uncompromising life. Cf. Mt 5:48.

7:1 first year. This represented a flashback to 553 B.C., 14 years before the feast of 5:1–3. Chapters 7, 8 occur after chap. 4, but before chap. 5. The dream of Da 7 moves far beyond Daniel's day to the coming of Israel's king to end all Gentile kingdoms and to establish His eternal kingdom (7:13, 14, 27; cf. 2:35, 45).

7:2 great sea. This superlative refers to the Mediterranean, much greater in size

[a]said, "I was [A]looking in my vision by night, and
behold, the [B]four winds of heaven were stirring up
the great sea. 3 And four great [A]beasts were coming
up from the sea, different from one another. 4 The
first *was* [A]like a lion and had *the* wings of an eagle.
I kept looking until its wings were plucked, and it
was lifted up from the ground and made to stand on
two feet like a man; a human [a]mind also was given
to it. 5 And behold, another beast, a second one, resembling a bear. And it was raised up on one side,
and three ribs *were* in its mouth between its teeth;
and thus they said to it, 'Arise, devour much meat!'
6 After this I kept looking, and behold, another one,
[A]like a leopard, which had on its [a]back four wings
of a bird; the beast also had [B]four heads, and dominion was given to it. 7 After this I kept looking
in the night visions, and behold, a [A]fourth beast,
dreadful and terrifying and extremely strong; and
it had large iron teeth. It devoured and crushed and
trampled down the remainder with its feet; and it
was different from all the beasts that were before it,
and it had [B]ten horns. 8 While I was contemplating
the horns, behold, [A]another horn, a little one, came
up among them, and three of the first horns were
pulled out by the roots before it; and behold, [a]this
horn possessed eyes like the eyes of a man and [B]a
mouth uttering great *boasts*.

THE ANCIENT OF DAYS REIGNS

9 "I kept looking
Until [A]thrones were set up,
And the Ancient of Days took *His* seat;
His [B]vesture *was* like white snow
And the [C]hair of His head like pure wool.
His [D]throne *was* [a]ablaze with flames,
Its [E]wheels *were* a burning fire.

10 "A river of [A]fire was flowing
And coming out from before Him;
[B]Thousands upon thousands
were attending Him,
And myriads upon myriads were
standing before Him;
The [C]court sat,
And [D]the books were opened.

11 Then I kept looking because of the sound of the
[a]boastful words which the horn was speaking; I
kept looking until the beast was slain, and its body
was destroyed and given to the [A]burning [b]fire. 12 As
for the rest of the beasts, their dominion was taken
away, but an extension of life was granted to them
for an appointed period of time.

THE SON OF MAN PRESENTED

13 "I kept looking in the night visions,
And behold, with the clouds of heaven
One like a [A]Son of Man was coming,
And He came up to the Ancient of Days
And was presented before Him.
14 "And to Him was given [A]dominion,
Glory and [a,B]a kingdom,
[C]That all the peoples, nations and
men of every [b]language
Might serve Him.
[D]His dominion is an everlasting dominion
Which will not pass away;
[E]And His kingdom is one
Which will not be destroyed.

THE VISION INTERPRETED

15 "As for me, Daniel, my spirit was distressed [a]within
me, and the [A]visions [b]in my mind kept [B]alarming me.

7:2 [a]Lit *spoke and said* [A]Dan 7:7, 13 [B]Rev 7:1 7:3 [A]Dan 7:17; Rev 13:1; 17:8 7:4 [a]Lit *heart* [A]Jer 4:7 7:6 [a]Or *sides* [A]Rev 13:2 [B]Dan 8:22 7:7 [A]Dan 7:19, 20, 23 [B]Rev 12:3; 13:1 7:8 [a]Lit *in this horn* were *eyes* [A]Dan 8:9 [B]Rev 13:5, 6 7:9 [a]Lit *flames of fire* [A]Rev 20:4 [B]Mark 9:3 [C]Rev 1:14 [D]Ezek 1:13, 26 [E]Ezek 10:2, 6 7:10 [A]Ps 18:8; 50:3; 97:3; Is 30:27, 33 [B]Deut 33:2; 1 Kin 22:19; Rev 5:11 [C]Ps 96:11-13; Dan 7:22, 26 [D]Dan 12:1; Rev 20:11-15 7:11 [a]Lit *great* [b]Lit *of the fire* [A]Rev 19:20; 20:10 7:13 [A]Matt 24:30; 26:64; Mark 13:26; 14:62; Luke 21:27; Rev 1:7, 13; 14:14 7:14 [a]Or *sovereignty* [b]Lit *tongue* [A]Dan 7:27; John 3:35; 1 Cor 15:27; Eph 1:20-22; Phil 2:9-11; Rev 1:6; 11:15 [B]Dan 2:37 [C]Ps 72:11; 102:22 [D]Mic 4:7; Luke 1:33 [E]Heb 12:28 7:15 [a]Lit *in the midst of its sheath* [b]Lit *of my head* [A]Dan 7:1 [B]Dan 4:19; 7:28

than other bodies of water in that area of the world. Here this "sea" is used to represent nations and peoples (cf. Da 7:3, 17; Rev 13:1).

7:3 four . . . beasts. These beasts represent the same empires as the individual parts of the image in chap. 2. Christ the King, the Son of Man from heaven (vv. 13, 14), corresponds to the Stone in 2:35, 45.

7:4 lion . . . wings. The vicious, powerful, swift king of beasts represents Babylon. Winged lions guarded the gates of the royal palaces of Babylon. Daniel's contemporaries, Jeremiah, Ezekiel, and Habakkuk, used animals to describe Nebuchadnezzar.

7:5 a bear. This is Medo-Persia, with the greater "side" being Persia and "ribs" referring to vanquished nations.

7:6 a leopard. This represents Greece with its fleetness in conquest under Alexander the Great (born in 356 B.C.). He ruled from Europe to Africa to India. The "four heads" represent the 4 generals who divided the kingdom after Alexander's death at age 33 (323 B.C.). They ruled Macedonia, Asia Minor, Syria, and Egypt (cf. 8:8).

7:7 fourth beast. No such animal exists; rather, this is a unique beast pointing to the Roman Empire, already represented by iron in 2:40, devastating in conquest. Roman dominion fell apart in A.D. 476, yet it lived on in a divided status (Europe), but will be revived and return to great unified strength near Christ's second coming. Then it will be comprised of the 10 parts under kings (vv. 7, 24), as well as an 11th king, the Antichrist (vv. 8, 24; 2Th 2:3–10; Rev 13:1–10).

7:8 another horn. This describes the rise of Antichrist (cf. v. 20). This beast is human ("eyes like .... man" and a "mouth uttering") and is proud (cf. Rev 13:5, 6).

7:9, 10 I kept looking. Daniel's vision flashes forward to the divine throne from which judgment will come on the fourth kingdom (cf. Rev 20:11–15).

7:11, 12 the beast was slain. Reference is to the fourth beast (i.e., the Roman sphere), headed up by the "little horn" or Antichrist (vv. 7, 24). He will be destroyed at Christ's second coming (cf. Rev 19:20; 20:10); cf. the smashing by the Stone, Da 2:35, 45.

7:12 rest of the beasts. These are the 3 earlier beasts (empires of chaps. 2, 7). Each successively lost its chief dominance when it was conquered in history. Yet each was amalgamated into the empire that gained ascendancy, and survived in its descendants. As the second advent draws near, all 3 empires in their descendants will be a part of the Roman phase in its final form (Rev 13:2). Survival will *not* be possible for the final and revived phase of the fourth empire after Christ's second coming, for catastrophic devastation (cf. 2:35) will utterly destroy it, and Christ's kingdom will replace it.

7:13, 14 Son of Man. The Messiah (cf. 9:26), Christ is meant; He often designated Himself by this phrase (Mt 16:27; 19:28; 26:64). "The clouds of heaven" are seen again in Rev 1:7. Here He is distinct from the Ancient of Days, or Eternal One, the Father, who will coronate Him for the kingdom (2:44). The picture of old age is not that of being feeble; rather, it highlights eternality and divine wisdom to judge (cf. 7:9, 10).

7:14 all the peoples, nations and . . . language. These distinctions are earthly and speak of the promise of an earthly kingdom, ruled by Christ, that merges into the eternal kingdom (cf. vv. 18, 27; Rev 20:1–4; 21; 22).

7:15 my spirit was distressed. Coming judgment made him sad, because it meant that history to its end would be a story of sin and judgment (cf. v. 28).

16 I approached one of those who were [A]standing by
and began asking him the [a]exact meaning of all this.
So he [B]told me and made known to me the interpretation of these things: 17 'These great beasts, which are
four *in number,* are four kings *who* will arise from
the earth. 18 But the [a,A]saints of the Highest One will
[B]receive the kingdom and possess the kingdom forever, [b]for all ages to come.'
19 "Then I desired to know the [a]exact meaning
of the [A]fourth beast, which was different from all
[b]the others, exceedingly dreadful, with its teeth of
iron and its claws of bronze, *and which* devoured,
crushed and trampled down the remainder with
its feet, 20 and *the meaning* of the ten horns that
were on its head and the other *horn* which came
up, and before which three *of them* fell, namely,
that horn which had eyes and a mouth uttering
great *boasts* and [a]which was larger in appearance
than its associates. 21 I kept looking, and that horn
was [A]waging war with the [a]saints and overpowering them 22 until the Ancient of Days came and
[A]judgment was [a]passed in favor of the [b]saints of the
Highest One, and the time arrived when the [b]saints
took possession of the kingdom.
23 "Thus he said: 'The fourth beast will be a fourth
kingdom on the earth, which will be different from
all the *other* kingdoms and will devour the whole
earth and tread it down and crush it. 24 As for the
[A]ten horns, out of this kingdom ten kings will arise;
and another will arise after them, and he will be
different from the previous ones and will subdue
three kings. 25 He will [A]speak [a]out against the [B]Most
High and [C]wear down the [b]saints of the Highest
One, and he will intend to make [D]alterations in
times and in law; and [c]they will be given into his
hand for a [d,E]time, [d]times, and half a [d]time. 26 But the
court will sit *for judgment,* and his dominion will
be [A]taken away, [a]annihilated and destroyed [b]for-
ever. 27 Then the [a,A]sovereignty, the dominion and
the greatness of *all* the kingdoms under the whole
heaven will be given to the people of the [b]saints of
the Highest One; His kingdom *will be* an [B]everlast-
ing kingdom, and all the dominions will [C]serve and
obey Him.'
28 "[a]At this point the revelation ended. As for me,
Daniel, my thoughts were [A]greatly alarming me and
my [b]face grew pale, but I [B]kept the matter [c]to myself."

VISION OF THE RAM AND GOAT

8 In the third year of the reign of Belshazzar the
king a vision appeared to me, [a]Daniel, subsequent to the one which appeared to me [b]previously.
2 I [A]looked in the vision, and while I was looking I
was in the citadel of [B]Susa, which is in the province
of [C]Elam; and I looked in the vision and I myself was
beside the Ulai [a]Canal. 3 Then I lifted my eyes and
looked, and behold, a [A]ram which had two horns
was standing in front of the [a]canal. Now the two
horns *were* [b]long, but one *was* [b]longer than the
other, with the [b]longer one coming up last. 4 I saw

7:16 [a]Lit *truth concerning* [A]Zech 1:9, 19; Rev 5:5; 7:13, 14 [B]Dan 8:16, 17; 9:22 7:18 [a]Lit *holy ones* [b]Lit *and unto the age of the ages* [A]Dan 7:22, 25, 27 [B]Ps 149:5-9; Is 60:12-14; Dan 7:14; Rev 2:26, 27; 20:4; 22:5 7:19 [a]Lit *truth concerning* [b]Lit *of them* [A]Dan 7:7, 8 7:20 [a]Lit *its appearance was larger* 7:21 [a]Lit *holy ones* [A]Rev 11:7; 13:7 7:22 [a]Lit *given for* [b]Lit *holy ones* [A]Dan 7:10; 1 Cor 6:2, 3 7:24 [A]Dan 7:7; Rev 17:12 7:25 [a]Lit *words* [b]Lit *holy ones* [c]I.e. the saints [d]I.e. year(s) [A]Dan 11:36; Rev 13:6 [B]Dan 3:26; 4:2, 17, 34 [C]Rev 13:7; 18:24 [D]Dan 2:21 [E]Dan 12:7; Rev 12:14 7:26 [a]Lit *to annihilate and to destroy* [b]Lit *to the end* [A]Rev 17:14; 19:2 7:27 [a]Or *kingdom* [b]Lit *holy ones* [A]Is 54:3; Dan 7:14, 18, 22; Rev 20:4 [B]Ps 145:13; Is 9:7; Dan 2:44; 4:34; 7:14; Luke 1:33; Rev 11:15; 22:5 [C]Ps 2:6-12; 22:27; 72:11; 86:9; Is 60:12; Rev 11:1 7:28 [a]Lit *To here the end of the word* [b]Lit *brightness was changing upon me* [c]Lit *in my heart* [A]Dan 4:19 [B]Luke 2:19, 51 8:1 [a]Lit *I, Daniel* [b]Lit *at the beginning* 8:2 [a]Or *river* [A]Num 12:6; Dan 7:2, 15; 8:3 [B]Neh 1:1; Esth 1:2; 2:8 [C]Gen 10:22; 14:1; Is 11:11; Jer 25:25; Ezek 32:24 8:3 [a]Or *river* [b]Lit *high(er)* [A]Dan 8:20

7:16 those who were standing by. Angels helped Daniel understand God's revelations (8:13–16; 9:22–27).

7:17 beasts ... four. These empires depicted by the lion, bear, leopard, and bizarre animal (vv. 3–7) are Babylon, Medo-Persia, Greece, and Rome. The "kings" are the most notable leaders over these empires, such as Nebuchadnezzar (2:37, 38), Cyrus, Alexander the Great, and finally the "little horn" (Antichrist).

7:18, 22, 27 saints. These who trusted God possess the kingdom headed up by the Son of Man, the Messiah, of vv. 13, 14. All serve Him in vv. 14 and 27, the latter verse clarifying that the one served is actually God the Most High. Just as the 4 Gentile empires have individuals as kings (cf. 2:38; 7:8; 8:8), so the final kingdom has Christ as King.

7:18 the Highest One. God is referred to in this book as above all gods (2:47; 3:29; 4:35), as He was for Melchizedek and Abraham (Ge 14:19, 20, 22) as well as Naaman (2Ki 5:17).

7:19 fourth beast ... different. This may refer to the empire's far greater diversity than previous empires, and its breadth of conquest (v. 24). It branches out into two great divisions (cf. "legs," 2:33), then near the end into 10 horns (a confederacy of 10 nations), and even an 11th horn (Antichrist's kingdom) lasting until Christ's second coming.

7:20 the other *horn*. The 11th horn (ruler and his realm) is small and less powerful before its big rise (v. 8). Early in the future tribulation period, it (he) grows to be "larger" or more powerful than any of the horns (rulers) in the group.

7:21 war with the saints. The final Antichrist will lead a great persecution of believers, especially in Israel (cf. Mt 24:15–22; 2Th 2:4; Rev 12:13–17; 13:6, 7).

7:22 Ancient of Days. Refers to God the Eternal One, who confers the messianic kingdom on the Son to rule at His second coming and following (7:13, 14). Judgment is against the Antichrist, Satan who empowers him (Rev 13:4; 20:1–3), and the unsaved who are not allowed into the kingdom at its outset, but are destroyed and await the final, Great White Throne resurrection and judgment (Rev 20:11–15). **saints took possession of the kingdom.** Believers enter the kingdom in its earthly, millennial phase (Rev 20:1–4) following Christ's second coming (Mt 25:34), having eternal life that continues into the eternal state (Rev 21, 22) after the thousand years.

7:24 another ... after them. The "little horn" (Antichrist) blasts his way to the zenith of world rule.

7:25 time, times, and half a time. This obviously refers to the 3 1/2 years which are the last half of the 7-year period of Antichrist's power (cf. 9:27), continuing on to Christ's second coming as the Judgment Stone (2:35, 45) and glorious Son of Man (7:13, 14). Cf. Rev 11:2, 3; 12:14; 13:5 for reference to this same period.

7:26 the court. God will have His court session to judge sinners and sin (vv. 9, 10). He will remove the Antichrist's rule and destroy him and his empire in eternal, conscious hell (Rev 19:20; 20:10).

7:27 the kingdoms ... given to ... the saints. God's kingdom in both earthly (Rev 20:4) and heavenly phases (Rev 21:27; 22:3, 4, 14).

8:1 third year. Ca. 551 B.C., two years after the dream of chap. 7 but before chap. 5. **previously.** Looks back to chap. 7.

8:2 Susa. This was a chief city of the Medo-Persian Empire, about 250 mi. E of Babylon. Since Daniel saw himself in a vision, he may not have been bodily in that place (cf. Ezekiel's vision of being at the Jerusalem temple, though bodily still with the elders in Babylon, Eze 8–11).

8:3–9 This imagery unfolded historically. The ram pictures the Medo-Persian Empire, as a whole, its two horns standing for the two entities (the Medes and the Persians) that merged into one. The history of this empire is briefly noted in v. 4, as it is seen conquering from the E to the W, S and N, under Cyrus, as predicted also by Isaiah 150 years earlier (Is 45:1–7). The longer horn, which appeared last, represents Persia. The goat (v. 5) represents Greece with its great horn Alexander, who with his army of 35,000, moved with such speed that he is pictured as not even touching the ground. The broken horn is Alexander

the ram [A]butting westward, northward, and southward, and no *other* beasts could stand before him
nor was there anyone to rescue from his [a]power,
but [B]he did as he pleased and magnified *himself.*
5 While I was observing, behold, a male goat was
coming from the west over the surface of the whole
earth without touching the ground; and the [a]goat
had a [A]conspicuous horn between his eyes. 6 He
came up to the ram that had the two horns, which I
had seen standing in front of the [a]canal, and rushed
at him in his mighty wrath. 7 I saw him come beside
the ram, and he was enraged at him; and he struck
the ram and shattered his two horns, and the ram
had no strength to withstand him. So he hurled him
to the ground and trampled on him, and there was
none to rescue the ram from his [a]power. 8 Then the
male goat magnified *himself* exceedingly. But as
soon as [A]he was mighty, the [B]large horn was broken;
and in its place there came up four conspicuous
horns toward the [C]four winds of heaven.

THE LITTLE HORN

9 Out of one of them came forth a rather [A]small
horn which grew exceedingly great toward the south,
toward the east, and toward the [a,B]Beautiful *Land.* 10 It
grew up to the host of heaven and caused some of the
host and some of the [A]stars to fall to the earth, and it
[B]trampled them down. 11 It even [A]magnified *itself* [a]to
be equal with the [b]Commander of the host; and it removed the [B]regular sacrifice from Him, and the place
of His sanctuary was thrown down. 12 And on account
of transgression the host will be given over *to the horn*
along with the regular sacrifice; and it will [A]fling truth
to the ground and perform *its will* and prosper. 13 Then
I heard a [A]holy one speaking, and another holy one
said to that particular one who was speaking, "[B]How
long will the vision *about* the regular sacrifice apply,
[a]while the transgression causes horror, so as to allow
both the holy place and the host [b]to be [C]trampled?"
14 He said to me, "For [A]2,300 evenings *and* mornings;
then the holy place will be [a]properly restored."

INTERPRETATION OF THE VISION

15 When [A]I, Daniel, had seen the vision, I sought [a]to
understand it; and behold, standing before me was
one [b]who looked like a [B]man. 16 And I heard the voice
of a man between *the banks of* Ulai, and he called out
and said, "[A]Gabriel, give this *man* an understanding
of the vision." 17 So he came near to where I was standing, and when he came I was frightened and [A]fell on
my face; but he said to me, "Son of man, understand
that the vision pertains to the [B]time of the end."
18 Now while he was talking with me, I [A]sank
into a deep sleep with my face to the ground; but
he [B]touched me and made me stand [a]upright. 19 He
said, "Behold, I am going to [A]let you know what will
occur at the final period of the indignation, for *it*
pertains to the appointed time of the end.

THE RAM'S IDENTITY

20 The [A]ram which you saw with the two horns
represents the kings of Media and Persia.

THE GOAT

21 The shaggy [a]goat *represents* the [b]kingdom of
Greece, and the large horn that is between his eyes
is the first king. 22 The [A]broken *horn* and the four
horns that arose in its place *represent* four kingdoms *which* will arise from *his* nation, although
not with his power.

8:4 [a]Lit *hand* [A]Deut 33:17; 1 Kin 22:11; Ezek 34:21 [B]Dan 11:3 8:5 [a]Lit *buck* [A]Dan 8:8, 21; 11:3 8:6 [a]Or *river* 8:7 [a]Lit *hand* 8:8 [A]2 Chr 26:16; Dan 5:20 [B]Dan 8:22 [C]Dan 7:2; Rev 7:1 8:9 [a]I.e. Israel [A]Dan 8:23 [B]Ps 48:2; Dan 11:16, 41 8:10 [A]Is 14:13; Jer 48:26; Rev 12:4 [B]Dan 7:7; 8:7 8:11 [a]Lit *up to the* [b]Or *Prince* [A]2 Kin 19:22, 23; 2 Chr 32:15-17; Is 37:23; Dan 8:25; 11:36, 37 [B]Ezek 46:14; Dan 11:31; 12:11 8:12 [A]Is 59:14 8:13 [a]Or possibly *and the transgression that horrifies* [b]Lit *as a trampling* [A]Dan 4:13, 23; 1 Pet 1:12 [B]Ps 74:10; 79:5; Is 6:11; Dan 12:6, 8; Rev 6:10 [C]Is 63:18; Jer 12:10; Luke 21:24; Heb 10:29; Rev 11:2 8:14 [a]Lit *vindicated* [A]Dan 7:25; 12:7, 11; Rev 11:2, 3; 12:14; 13:5 8:15 [a]Lit *understanding* [b]Lit *like the appearance of a man* [A]Dan 8:1 [B]Dan 7:13; 10:16, 18 8:16 [A]Dan 9:21; Luke 1:19, 26 8:17 [A]Ezek 1:28; 44:4; Dan 2:46; Rev 1:17 [B]Dan 8:19; 11:35, 40 8:18 [a]Lit *on my standing* [A]Dan 10:9; Luke 9:32 [B]Ezek 2:2; Dan 10:10, 16, 18 8:19 [A]Dan 8:15-17 8:20 [A]Dan 8:3 8:21 [a]Lit *buck* [b]Lit *king* 8:22 [A]Dan 8:8

in his death; the 4 horns are generals who became kings over 4 sectors of the Grecian empire after Alexander (cf. 7:6). The small horn is Antiochus Epiphanes, who rose from the third empire to rule the Syrian division in 175–164 B.C. and is the same king dominant in 11:21–35. Cf. 7:8, 24–26 where a similar "little horn" clearly represents the final Antichrist. The reason both are described as "little horns" is because one prefigures the other. A far more detailed summary will come later in 11:2–35.

8:9 Beautiful *Land.* Israel. Cf. 11:16, 41.

8:10 host of heaven. Picturesque language portrays Antiochus' persecution against Jewish people using the figure of stars (cf. Ge 12:3; 15:5; 22:17; Ex 12:41; Dt 1:10). When defeated, the "stars" (Jewish people) will fall under the tyrant's domination.

8:11 Commander. In addition to the desecration of the temple (cf. 1 Macc. 1:20–24, 41–50), Antiochus blasphemed Christ to whom ultimately the host of Jewish people sacrifice and to whom the sanctuary belongs. He is later the "Prince of princes" (v. 25).

8:13 holy one. Angels are in view here.

8:14 For 2,300 evenings *and* mornings. These are 2,300 evenings/mornings, with no "and" in between, which refers to 2,300 total units or days. Genesis 1:5 does use "and," i.e., "Evening and ... morning, one day." The period runs to about 6 1/3 years of sacrificing a lamb twice a day, morning and evening (Ex 29:38, 39). The prophecy was precise in identifying the time as that of Antiochus' persecution, ca. Sept. 6, 171 B.C. to Dec. 25, 165/4 B.C. After his death, Jews celebrated the cleansing of their holy place in the Feast of Lights, or Hanukkah, in celebration of the restoration led by Judas Maccabeus.

8:15 looked like a man. The word for man meaning "a mighty man" is the linguistic framework for "Gabriel," which means "mighty one of God." This is the first mention of an angel by name in the Bible.

8:16 voice of a man. God spoke with a human voice. **Ulai.** A river E of the Persian city of Susa.

8:17 frightened and fell. Loss of consciousness is a common reaction to heavenly visitation (cf. Eze 1; Is 6; Rev 1). **time of the end.** This term likely has a double sense of fulfillment. First, the "end" (as v. 19), "final" or "latter period" (vv. 19, 23), and "appointed time" (v. 19) refer to time late in the specific span that the historical prophecy has in view. That time is the period defined by the empires in these verses, Persia (Ram) and Greece (Goat), when the Grecian sector will be divided into 4 parts (v. 8). One of these, the Syrian under Seleucus (*see note on v. 22*), will eventually lead to Antiochus Epiphanes (175–164 B.C.) as the "little horn" meant in v. 9, who persecutes the people of Israel (v. 10) and defies God (v. 11). Cf. 11:21–35 and *see notes there*. Secondly, this "little horn" in v. 9, the Antichrist in the last days at the time of the eschatological fulfillment, sees Antiochus as a pattern of the Antichrist, who in many ways will be like him, though far greater in power, and will exercise his career in the end of the age just before Christ's return.

8:21 shaggy goat ... large horn. This is the third Gentile world power, the kingdom of Greece, and specifically Alexander the Great, the notable and "first king" after conquering Medo-Persia. Cf. 11:3.

8:22 broken *horn* and the four *horns*. Alexander died at age 33 in 323 B.C., leaving no heir ready to reign. So 4 men, after 22 years

23 "In the latter period of their [a]rule,
When the transgressors have
[b]run *their course,*
A king will arise,
[c]Insolent and skilled in [d]intrigue.
24 "His power will be mighty, but
not by his *own* power,
And he will [a,A]destroy to an
extraordinary degree
And prosper and perform *his will;*
He will [a]destroy mighty men
and [b]the holy people.
25 "And through his shrewdness
He will cause deceit to succeed
by his [a]influence;
And he will magnify *himself* in his heart,
And he will [b]destroy many
while *they are* [c]at ease.
He will even [d,A]oppose the Prince of princes,
But he will be broken [B]without
[a]human agency.
26 "The vision of the evenings and mornings
Which has been told is [A]true;
But [B]keep the vision secret,
For *it* pertains to many [C]days *in the future.*"

27 Then I, Daniel, was [a,A]exhausted and sick for days. Then I got up *again* and [B]carried on the king's business; but I was astounded at the vision, and there was none to [b]explain *it.*

DANIEL'S PRAYER FOR HIS PEOPLE

9 In the first year of [A]Darius the son of Ahasuerus,
of Median descent, who was made king over the
kingdom of the Chaldeans— 2 in the first year of his
reign, I, Daniel, observed in the books the number
of the years which was *revealed as* the word of the
LORD to [A]Jeremiah the prophet for the completion
of the desolations of Jerusalem, *namely,* [A]seventy
years. 3 So I [a]gave my attention to the Lord God to
seek *Him by* prayer and supplications, with fasting,
sackcloth and ashes. 4 I prayed to the LORD my God
and confessed and said, "Alas, O Lord, the [A]great
and awesome God, who [B]keeps His covenant and
lovingkindness for those who love Him and keep
His commandments, 5 [A]we have sinned, committed
iniquity, acted wickedly and [B]rebelled, even [C]turning
aside from Your commandments and ordinances.
6 Moreover, we have not [A]listened to Your servants
the prophets, who spoke in Your name to our kings,
our princes, our fathers and all the people of the land.
7 "[A]Righteousness belongs to You, O Lord, but to
us [a,B]open shame, as it is this day—to the men of
Judah, the inhabitants of Jerusalem and all Israel,
those who are nearby and those who are far away
in [C]all the countries to which You have driven them,
because of their unfaithful deeds which they have
committed against You. 8 [a]Open shame belongs to
us, O Lord, to our kings, our princes and our fathers, because we have sinned against You. 9 To the
Lord our God *belong* [A]compassion and forgiveness,
[a]for we have [B]rebelled against Him; 10 nor have we
obeyed the voice of the LORD our God, to walk in
His [a]teachings which He [A]set before us through
His servants the prophets. 11 Indeed [A]all Israel has
transgressed Your law and turned aside, not obeying Your voice; so the [B]curse has been poured out
on us, along with the oath which is written in the
law of Moses the servant of God, for we have sinned
against Him. 12 Thus He has [A]confirmed His words
which He had spoken against us and against our
[a,B]rulers who ruled us, to bring on us great calamity; for under the whole heaven there has [C]not been
done *anything* like what was done to Jerusalem. 13 As
it is written in the [A]law of Moses, all this calamity
has come on us; yet we have [B]not [a]sought the favor
of the LORD our God by [C]turning from our iniquity
and [b]giving attention to Your truth. 14 Therefore the

8:23 [a]Or *kingdom* [b]Lit *finished* [c]Lit *Strong of face* [d]Or *ambiguous speech* 8:24 [a]Or *corrupt* [b]Lit *people of the saints* [A]Dan 8:11-13; 11:36; 12:7 8:25 [a]Lit *hand* [b]Or *corrupt* [c]Or *secure* [d]Lit *stand against* [A]Dan 8:11 [B]Job 34:20; Dan 2:34, 45 8:26 [A]Dan 10:1 [B]Ezek 12:27; Dan 12:4, 9; Rev 22:10 [C]Dan 10:14 8:27 [a]Or *done in* [b]Lit *make me understand* [A]Dan 7:28; 8:17; Hab 3:16 [B]Dan 2:48 9:1 [A]Dan 5:31; 11:1 9:2 [A]2 Chr 36:21; Ezra 1:1; Jer 25:11, 12; 29:10; Zech 7:5 9:3 [a]Lit *set my face* 9:4 [A]Deut 7:21; Neh 9:32 [B]Deut 7:9 9:5 [A]1 Kin 8:48; Neh 9:33; Ps 106:6; Is 64:5-7; Jer 14:7 [B]Lam 1:18, 20 [C]Ps 119:176; Is 53:6; Dan 9:11 9:6 [A]2 Chr 36:16; Jer 44:4, 5 9:7 [a]Lit *the shame of face* [A]Jer 23:6; 33:16; Dan 9:18 [B]Ps 44:15; Jer 2:26, 27; 3:25 [C]Deut 4:27 9:8 [a]Lit *The shame of face* 9:9 [a]Or *though* [A]Neh 9:17; Ps 130:4 [B]Ps 106:43; Jer 14:7; Dan 9:5, 6 9:10 [a]Or *laws* [A]2 Kin 17:13-15; 18:12 9:11 [A]Is 1:3, 4; Jer 8:5-10 [B]Deut 27:15-26 9:12 [a]Lit *judges who judged us* [A]Is 44:26; Jer 44:2-6; Lam 2:17; Zech 1:6 [B]Job 12:17; Ps 82:2-7; 148:11 [C]Lam 1:12; 2:13; Ezek 5:9 9:13 [a]Lit *softened the face of* [b]Or *having insight into* [A]Lev 26:14-45; Deut 28:15-68; Dan 9:11 [B]Job 36:13; Is 9:13; Jer 2:30; 5:3 [C]Jer 31:18

of fighting, assumed rule over 4 Grecian sectors: 1) Cassander, Macedonia; 2) Lysimachus, Thrace, and Asia Minor; 3) Seleucus, Syria, and Babylonia; 4) Ptolemy, Egypt, and Arabia. These are the 4 referred to in "toward the four winds" (v. 8). The phrase "not with his power" indicates they did not have Alexander's power or direct family lineage.

8:23–25 A king will arise. The near fulfillment views Antiochus as the historical persecutor as in vv. 9–14. His career down to 164 B.C. was "in the latter period of their rule," that of the male goat in the Syrian territory. Rome conquered Greece by 146 B.C., only a few years later, and became the next dominant empire. Antiochus died, "broken without human agency," due to insanity and disease of the bowels. The far fulfillment sees Antiochus in vv. 23–25 as prophetically illustrating the final tribulation period and the Antichrist. In such a view, the king here is also the "little horn," as in 7:7; 8:9 and the willful king in 11:36–45.

8:25 Prince of princes. *See note on 8:11.*

8:26 keep the vision secret. Since he told it here, this did not mean to shut it up to secrecy but to preserve it as truth even if not to be fulfilled for a long time.

9:1 the first year. Ca. 539 B.C. **made king.** This may mean that Darius (a title, not a proper name, *see note on 5:31*) refers to Cyrus, who was made king by God's allowance (cf. Ps 75:6, 7). Since Cyrus was the first monarch of the Medo-Persian empire, this time note was also the first year after the death of Belshazzar, when Babylon fell.

9:2 seventy years. Daniel's study of "the books" (OT scrolls) focused on the years prophesied for the captivity by Jeremiah in Jer 25:11, 12 and 29:10. Since the end of that span was near, he prayed for God's next move on behalf of Israel. Cf. 2Ch 36:21, where it is indicated that the 70 years of exile were intended to restore the Sabbath rests that Israel had ignored for so many years (cf. Lv 25:4, 5; 26:34–43).

9:4–19 I prayed. Various aspects of the passage give rich instruction regarding prayer. True prayer is: in response to the Word (v. 2), characterized by fervency and self-denial (v. 3), identified unselfishly with God's people (v. 5), strengthened by confession (vv. 5–15), dependent on God's character (vv. 4, 7, 9, 15), and has as its goal God's glory (vv. 16–19).

9:11 the curse. This refers to the judgment that God brought, as promised, for Israel's disobedience in the land (Lv 26:21–42; Dt 28:15–68). This is in contrast to the blessings associated with faith and obedience (Lv 26:3–20; Dt 28:1–14). God had given the promise that even in a time of judgment, if Israel would confess their sin, He would bring blessing again (Lv 26:40–42).

LORD has [a,A]kept the calamity in store and brought
it on us; for the LORD our God is [B]righteous with
respect to all His deeds which He has done, but we
have not obeyed His voice.
15 "And now, O Lord our God, who have [A]brought
Your people out of the land of Egypt with a mighty
hand and have [B]made a name for Yourself, as it is
this day—we have sinned, we have been wicked.
16 O Lord, in accordance with all Your [a]righteous
acts, let now Your [A]anger and Your wrath turn away
from Your city Jerusalem, Your [B]holy mountain; for
because of our sins and the iniquities of our fathers,
Jerusalem and Your people *have become* a [C]reproach
to all those around us. 17 So now, our God, listen to
the prayer of Your servant and to his supplications,
and for [a]Your sake, O Lord, [A]let Your face shine on
Your [B]desolate sanctuary. 18 O my God, [A]incline Your
ear and hear! Open Your eyes and [B]see our desolations and the city which is [C]called by Your name; for
we are not [a,D]presenting our supplications before
You on account of [b]any merits of our own, but on
account of Your great compassion. 19 O Lord, hear!
O Lord, forgive! O Lord, listen and take action! For
Your own sake, O my God, [A]do not delay, because
Your city and Your people are called by Your name."

GABRIEL BRINGS AN ANSWER

20 Now while I was [A]speaking and praying, and
[B]confessing my sin and the sin of my people Israel,
and [a]presenting my supplication before the LORD
my God in behalf of the holy mountain of my God,
21 while I was still speaking in prayer, then the man
[A]Gabriel, whom I had seen in the vision [a]previously,
[b]came to me [c]in *my* extreme weariness about the
time of the [B]evening offering. 22 He gave *me* instruction and talked with me and said, "O Daniel, I have
now come forth to give you insight with [A]under-
standing. 23 At the [A]beginning of your supplications
the [a]command was issued, and I have come to tell
you, for you are [b,B]highly esteemed; so give heed to
the message and gain [C]understanding of the vision.

SEVENTY WEEKS AND THE MESSIAH

24 "Seventy [a,A]weeks have been decreed for your
people and your holy city, to [b]finish the transgression, to [c]make an end of sin, to [B]make atonement for
iniquity, to bring in [C]everlasting righteousness, to seal
up vision and [d]prophecy and to anoint the most holy
place. 25 So you are to know and discern *that* from the
issuing of a [a,A]decree to restore and rebuild Jerusalem
until [b,B]Messiah the [C]Prince *there will be* seven weeks
and sixty-two weeks; it will be built again, with [c]plaza
and moat, even in times of distress. 26 Then after the
sixty-two weeks the [a]Messiah will be [A]cut off and have
[b]nothing, and the people of the prince who is to come
will [B]destroy the city and the sanctuary. And [c]its end
will come with a [C]flood; even to the end [d]there will be
war; desolations are determined. 27 And he will make
a firm covenant with the many for one week, but in
the middle of the week he will put a stop to sacrifice
and grain offering; and on the wing of [a,A]abomina-
tions *will come* one who [b]makes desolate, even until a
[B]complete destruction, one that is decreed, is poured
out on the one who [b]makes desolate."

9:14 [a]Lit *watched over the evil* [A]Jer 31:28; 44:27 [B]Ps 51:14; Dan 9:7 9:15 [A]Deut 5:15 [B]Neh 9:10; Jer 32:20 9:16 [a]Lit *righteousnesses* [A]Jer 32:31, 32 [B]Ps 87:1-3; Dan 9:20; Joel 3:17; Zech 8:3 [C]Ezek 5:14 9:17 [a]Lit *the sake of the Lord* [A]Num 6:24-26; Ps 80:3, 7, 19 [B]Lam 5:18 9:18 [a]Lit *causing to fall* [b]Lit *our righteousnesses* [A]Is 37:17 [B]Ps 80:14 [C]Jer 7:10-12 [D]Jer 36:7 9:19 [A]Ps 44:23; 74:10, 11 9:20 [a]Lit *causing to fall* [A]Ps 145:18; Is 58:9; Dan 9:3; 10:12 [B]Is 6:5 9:21 [a]Lit *at the beginning* [b]Lit *was reaching;* or *touching* [c]Lit *wearied with weariness* [A]Dan 8:16; Luke 1:19, 26 [B]Ex 29:39; 1 Kin 18:36; Ezra 9:4 9:22 [A]Dan 8:16; 10:21; Zech 1:9 9:23 [a]Lit *word went out* [b]Lit *desirable;* or *precious* [A]Dan 10:12 [B]Dan 10:11, 19 [C]Matt 24:15 9:24 [a]Or *units of seven,* and so throughout the ch [b]Or *restrain* [c]Another reading is *seal up sins* [d]Lit *prophet* [A]Lev 25:8; Num 14:34; Ezek 4:5, 6 [B]2 Chr 29:24; Is 53:10; Rom 5:10 [C]Is 51:6, 8; 56:1; Jer 23:5, 6; Rom 3:21, 22 9:25 [a]Lit *word* [b]Or *an anointed one* [c]Or *streets* [A]Ezra 4:24; 6:1-15; Neh 2:1-8; 3:1 [B]John 1:41; 4:25 [C]Is 9:6; Dan 8:11, 25 9:26 [a]Or *anointed one* [b]Or *no one* [c]Or *his* [d]Or *war will be decreed for desolations* [A]Is 53:8; Mark 9:12; Luke 24:26 [B]Matt 24:2; Mark 13:2; Luke 19:43, 44 [C]Nah 1:8 9:27 [a]Or *detestable things* [b]Or *causes horror* [A]Dan 11:31; Matt 24:15; Mark 13:14; Luke 21:20 [B]Is 10:23; 28:22

9:16 Daniel prayed for restoration in 3 aspects. In effect he asked God to bring back "Your city" (vv. 16, 18), "Your desolate sanctuary" (v. 17), and "Your people" (v. 19). God's answer embraced all three (v. 24).

9:21 the man Gabriel. This angel, called a "man" because he appeared in the form of a man, appeared also in 8:16. Cf. the angel Michael in 10:13, 21; 12:1. **the evening offering.** This was the second lamb of two offered daily (cf. 8:14 and *see note there*), this one at 3 p.m., a common time for prayer (Ezr 9:5).

9:24–26 Seventy weeks … from … until. These are weeks of years, whereas weeks of days are described in a different way (10:2, 3). The time spans from the Persian Artaxerxes' decree to rebuild Jerusalem, ca. 445 B.C. (Ne 2:1–8), to the Messiah's kingdom. This panorama includes: 1) 7 weeks or 49 years, possibly closing Nehemiah's career in the rebuilding of Jerusalem as well as the end of the ministry of Malachi and the close of the OT; 2) 62 weeks or 434 more years for a total of 483 years to the first advent of Messiah. This was fulfilled at the triumphal entry on 10 Nisan, A.D. 30 (*see notes on Mt 21:1–9*). The Messiah will be "cut off," (a common reference to death); and 3) the final 7 years or 70th week of the time of Antichrist (cf. v. 27). Roman people, from whom the Antichrist will come, will "destroy the city" of Jerusalem and its temple in A.D. 70.

9:24 This highly complex and startlingly accurate prophecy answers Daniel's prayer, not with reference to near history, but by giving the future of Israel in the final end of the age. God promises 2 sets of 3 accomplishments each. First, those related to sin are: 1) **finish the transgression,** i.e., restrain sin and Israel's in particular in its long trend of apostasy, as in v. 11; 2) **make an end of sin,** i.e., to judge it with finality (cf. Heb 9:26); and 3) **make atonement for iniquity,** signifies to furnish the actual basis of covering sin by full atonement, the blood of the crucified Messiah who is "cut off" (v. 26), which affects the first two realities (cf. the fountain, Zec 13:1).

Second, those accomplishments related to righteousness are: 1) **bring in … righteousness,** the eternal righteousness of Daniel's people in their great change from centuries of apostasy; 2) **seal up vision,** i.e., no more revelation is needed, and God will bring these anticipations to completion by their fulfillment in Israel's blessing as a nation; and 3) **anoint the most holy *place*,** consecrate the Holy Place in a temple of the future that will be the center of worship in the millennial kingdom (cf. Eze 40–48). Clearly this must be understood to sweep to the end of Gentile power and the time of Antichrist right before Christ's return. Summing up, the first 3 are fulfilled in principle at Christ's first coming, in full at His return. The last 3 complete the plan at His Second Advent.

9:27 This is clearly the end of the age, the Second Advent judgment, because the bringing in of righteousness did not occur 7 years after the death of the Messiah, nor did the destruction of Jerusalem fit the 7-year period (occurring 37 years later). This is the future 7-year period which ends with sin's final judgment and Christ's reign of righteousness; i.e., the return of Christ and the establishment of His rule. These 7 years constitute the 70th week of Daniel. **he will make a firm covenant.** "He" is the last-mentioned prince (v. 26), leader of the Roman sphere (cf. chaps. 2 and 7), the Antichrist who comes in the latter days. The time is in the future tribulation period of "one week," i.e., the final 7 years of v. 24. He confirms (lit., causes to prevail) a 7 year covenant, his own pact with Israel for what will turn out actually to be for a shorter time. The leader in this covenant is the "little horn" of 7:7, 8, 20, 21, 24–26, and the evil leader of NT prophecy (Mk 13:14; 2Th

DANIEL IS TERRIFIED BY A VISION

10 In the third year of [A]Cyrus king of Persia a
[a]message was revealed to [B]Daniel, who was
named Belteshazzar; and the [a,C]message was true
and *one of* great [b]conflict, but he understood the
[a]message and had an [D]understanding of the vision.
2 In those days, I, Daniel, had been [A]mourning
for three entire weeks. 3 I [A]did not eat any [a]tasty
food, nor did meat or wine enter my mouth, nor
did I use any ointment at all until the entire three
weeks were completed. 4 On the twenty-fourth day
of the first month, while I was by the bank of the
great [A]river, that is, the [a]Tigris, 5 I lifted my eyes
and looked, and behold, there was a certain man
[A]dressed in linen, whose waist was [B]girded with *a
belt of* pure [C]gold of Uphaz. 6 His body also *was* like
[a]beryl, his face [b]had the appearance of lightning,
[A]his eyes were like flaming torches, his arms and
feet like the gleam of polished bronze, and the sound
of his words like the sound of a [c]tumult. 7 Now I,
Daniel, [A]alone saw the vision, while the [B]men who
were with me did not see the vision; nevertheless,
a great [C]dread fell on them, and they ran away to
hide themselves. 8 So I was [A]left alone and saw this
great vision; yet [B]no strength was left in me, for
my [a]natural color turned to [b]a deathly pallor, and
I retained no strength. 9 But I heard the sound of
his words; and as soon as I heard the sound of his
words, I [A]fell into a deep sleep on my face, with my
face to the ground.

DANIEL COMFORTED

10 Then behold, a hand [A]touched me and set
me trembling on my [a]hands and knees. 11 He said
to me, "O [A]Daniel, man of [a]high esteem, [B]under-
stand the words that I am about to tell you and
[c]stand [b]upright, for I have now been sent to
you." And when he had spoken this word to me, I
stood up [D]trembling. 12 Then he said to me, "[A]Do
not be afraid, Daniel, for from the first day that
you set your heart on understanding *this* and on
[B]humbling yourself before your God, your words
were heard, and I have come in response [C]to your
words. 13 But the prince of the kingdom of Persia
was [a]withstanding me for twenty-one days; then
behold, [A]Michael, one of the chief princes, came to
help me, for I had been left there with the kings of
Persia. 14 Now I have come to [A]give you an understanding of what will happen to your people in the
[a,B]latter days, for the vision pertains to [C]the days yet
future."
15 When he had spoken to me according to these
words, I [a]turned my face toward the ground and
became [A]speechless. 16 And behold, [a,A]one who resembled a human being was [B]touching my lips;
then I opened my mouth and spoke and said to him
who was standing before me, "O my lord, as a result
of the vision [b,C]anguish has come upon me, and I
have retained no strength. 17 For [A]how can such a
servant of my lord talk with such as my lord? As
for me, there remains just now [B]no strength in me,
nor has any breath been left in me."
18 Then *this* one with human appearance touched
me again and [A]strengthened me. 19 He said, "O man
of [a]high esteem, [A]do not be afraid. Peace [b]be with
you; take [B]courage and be courageous!" Now as
soon as he spoke to me, I received strength and
said, "May my lord speak, for you have [C]strength-
ened me." 20 Then he said, "Do you [a]understand
why I came to you? But I shall now return to fight
against the [b]prince of Persia; so I am going forth,
and behold, the [b,A]prince of [c]Greece is about to come.

10:1 [a]Lit *word* [b]Or *warfare* [A]Dan 1:21; 6:28 [B]Dan 1:7 [C]Dan 8:26 [D]Dan 1:17; 2:21 10:2 [A]Ezra 9:4, 5; Neh 1:4 10:3 [a]Lit *bread of desirability* [A]Dan 6:18 10:4 [a]Heb *Hiddekel* [A]Ezek 1:3; Dan 8:2 10:5 [A]Ezek 9:2; Dan 12:6, 7 [B]Rev 1:13; 15:6 [C]Jer 10:9 10:6 [a]Or *yellow serpentine* [b]Lit *like* [c]Or *roaring* [A]Rev 1:14; 2:18; 19:12 10:7 [A]2 Kin 6:17-20 [B]Acts 9:7 [C]Ezek 12:18 10:8 [a]Lit *splendor* [b]Lit *corruption* [A]Gen 32:24 [B]Dan 7:28; 8:27; Hab 3:16 10:9 [A]Gen 15:12; Job 4:13; Dan 8:18 10:10 [a]Lit *knees and the palms of my hands* [A]Jer 1:9; Dan 8:18 10:11 [a]Lit *desirability;* or *preciousness* [b]Lit *upon your standing* [A]Dan 10:19 [B]Dan 8:16, 17 [C]Ezek 2:1 [D]Job 4:14, 15 10:12 [A]Is 41:10, 14; Dan 10:19 [B]Dan 9:20-23; 10:2, 3 [C]Acts 10:30, 31 10:13 [a]Lit *standing opposite* [A]Dan 10:21; 12:1; Jude 9; Rev 12:7 10:14 [a]Lit *end of the days* [A]Dan 8:16; 9:22 [B]Deut 31:29; Dan 2:28 [C]Dan 8:26; 12:4, 9 10:15 [a]Lit *set* [A]Ezek 3:26; 24:27; Luke 1:20 10:16 [a]Lit *as a likeness of sons of man* [b]Lit *my pains have* [A]Dan 8:15 [B]Is 6:7; Jer 1:9 [C]Dan 7:15, 28; 8:17, 27; 10:8, 9 10:17 [A]Ex 24:10, 11; Is 6:1-5 [B]Dan 10:8 10:18 [A]Is 35:3, 4 10:19 [a]Lit *desirability;* or *preciousness* [b]Lit *to you* [A]Judg 6:23; Is 43:1; Dan 10:12 [B]Josh 1:6, 7, 9; Is 35:4 [C]Ps 138:3; 2 Cor 12:9 10:20 [a]Lit *know* [b]I.e. Satanic angel [c]Heb *Javan* [A]Dan 8:21; 11:2

2:3–10; Rev 13:1–10). That he is in the future, even after Christ's First Advent, is shown by 1) Mt 24:15; 2) by the time references that match (7:25; Rev 11:2, 3; 12:14; 13:5); and 3) by the end here extending to the Second Advent, matching the duration elsewhere mentioned in Daniel (2:35, 45; 7:15ff.; 12:1–3) and Rev 11:2; 12:14; 13:5. **middle of the week.** This is the halfway point of the 70th week of years, i.e., 7 years leading to Christ's second coming. The Antichrist will break his covenant with Israel (v. 27a), which has resumed its ancient sacrificial system. Three and a half years of tribulation remain, agreeing with the time in other Scriptures (7:25; Rev 11:2, 3; 12:14; 13:5; called "great tribulation," cf. Mt 24:21) as God's wrath intensifies. **abominations ... one who makes desolate.** The Antichrist will cause abomination against Jewish religion. This violation will desolate or ruin what Jews regard as sacred, namely their holy temple and the honoring of God's presence there (cf. 1Ki 9:3; 2Th 2:4). Jesus refers directly to this text in His Olivet discourse (Mt 24:15). *See note on 11:31.* **complete destruction.** God permits this tribulation under the Antichrist's persecutions and ultimately triumphs, achieving judgment of the sin and sinners in Israel (12:7) and in the world (cf. Jer 25:31). This includes the Antichrist (11:45; Rev 19:20), and all who deserve judgment (9:24; Mt 13:41–43).

10:1 third year. Ca. 536 B.C. Two years had passed since the first decree to let Israel return (cf. Ezr 1:1–2:1; 2:64–3:1).

10:6 His body ... like beryl. The messenger whom Daniel sees in a vision (vv. 1, 7) was distinct from the angel Michael, from whom he needed assistance (v. 13). The description of such glory has led some to see him as Christ in a pre-incarnate appearance (such as Jos 5:13–15; 6:2; Jdg 6:11–23). He is described almost identically to Christ (Rev 1:13, 14) and Daniel's reaction is similar to John's (Rev 1:17).

10:10 a hand touched me. Most likely this was Gabriel, who interpreted other revelations to Daniel (cf. 8:16) and spoke similarly of Daniel's being beloved in 9:20–23.

10:12 your words were heard. This was a great encouragement from God who was attentive to prayer and acted to answer it (cf. 9:20–27).

10:13 prince of ... Persia. The 3 week delay was due to an evil angel opposing Gabriel in heavenly warfare (cf. Rev 16:12–14). This angel was specially anointed with Persian power in an effort to thwart the work of God. This tells us that Satan engages in heavenly warfare to influence generations and nations against God and His people (cf. Eph 6:10ff.). **Michael.** This is the chief angel of heaven (cf. 10:21; 12:1; Jude 9; Rev 12:7). Michael remained to assure that the Jews would be free to return to their land.

10:14 the days yet *future.* This refers to the future plan of God for His people, extending from Daniel's time to that of the Antichrist.

10:19 I received strength. This was the third time (vv. 10, 16), showing the overwhelming trauma of divine presence and revelation.

10:20 prince of Greece. An evil angel contesting for the kingdom of Greece.

21 However, I will tell you what is inscribed in the
writing of [A]truth. Yet there is no one who [a]stands
firmly with me against these *forces* except [B]Michael
your prince.

CONFLICTS TO COME

11 "In the [A]first year of Darius the Mede, [a]I arose
to be [b]an encouragement and a protection for
him. 2 And now I will tell you the [A]truth. Behold,
three more kings are going to arise [a]in Persia. Then
a fourth will gain far more riches than all *of them;*
as soon as he becomes strong through his riches,
[b]he will arouse the whole *empire* against the realm
of [c,B]Greece. 3 And a [A]mighty king will arise, and he
will rule with great authority and [B]do as he pleases.
4 But as soon as he has arisen, his kingdom will
be broken up and parceled out [A]toward the [B]four
[a]points of the compass, though not to his *own* descendants, nor according to his authority which he
wielded, for his sovereignty will be [C]uprooted and
given to others besides [b]them.
5 "Then the [A]king of the South will grow strong,
[a]along with *one* of his princes [b]who will gain ascendancy over him and obtain dominion; his domain
will be a great dominion *indeed.* 6 After some years
they will form an alliance, and the daughter of the
king of the South will come to the [A]king of the North
to carry out [a]a peaceful arrangement. But she will
not retain her [b]position of power, nor will he remain
with his [c]power, but she will be given up, along with
those who brought her in and the one who sired
her as well as he who supported her in *those* times.
7 But one of the [a]descendants of her line will arise
in his place, and he will come against *their* army
and enter the [A]fortress of the king of the North, and
he will deal with them and display *great* strength.
8 Also their [A]gods with their [a]metal images *and* their
precious vessels of silver and gold he will take into
captivity to Egypt, and he on his part will [b]refrain
from *attacking* the king of the North for *some* years.
9 Then [a]the latter will enter the realm of the king of
the South, but will return to his *own* land.
10 "His sons will [a]mobilize and assemble a multitude of great forces; and one of them will keep on
coming and [A]overflow and pass through, that he
may [b]again wage war up to his *very* fortress. 11 The
[A]king of the South will be enraged and go forth and
fight [a]with the king of the North. Then the latter
will raise a great multitude, but *that* multitude will
be given into [b]the hand of the *former.* 12 When the
multitude is carried away, his heart will be lifted
up, and he will cause tens of thousands to fall; yet
he will not prevail. 13 For the king of the North will
again raise a greater multitude than the former, and
[a]after an [A]interval of some years he will [b]press on
with a great army and much equipment.
14 "Now in those times many will rise up against
the king of the South; the violent ones among your
people will also lift themselves up in order to fulfill
the vision, but they will [a]fall down. 15 Then the king
of the North will come, cast up a [A]siege ramp and
capture a well-fortified city; and the forces of the

10:21 [a]Lit *shows himself strong* [A]Dan 12:4 [B]Dan 10:13; Rev 12:7 11:1 [a]Lit *my standing up* was [b]Lit *for a strengthener* [A]Dan 5:31; 9:1 11:2 [a]Lit *for* [b]Or they *all will stir up the realm of Greece* [c]Heb *Javan* [A]Dan 8:26; 10:1, 21 [B]Dan 8:21; 10:20 11:3 [A]Dan 8:5, 21 [B]Dan 5:19; 8:4; 11:16, 36 11:4 [a]Lit *winds of the heaven* [b]I.e. his descendants [A]Dan 8:8, 22 [B]Jer 49:36; Ezek 37:9; Dan 7:2; 8:8; Zech 2:6; Rev 7:1 [C]Jer 12:15, 17; 18:7 11:5 [a]Lit *and* [b]Lit *and he* [A]Dan 11:9, 11, 14, 25, 40 11:6 [a]Or *an equitable agreement* [b]Lit *strength of arm* [c]Lit *arm* [A]Dan 11:7, 13, 15, 40 11:7 [a]Lit *branch of her roots* [A]Dan 11:19, 38, 39 11:8 [a]Lit *cast images* [b]Or *stand against the king* [A]Is 37:19; 46:1, 2; Jer 43:12, 13 11:9 [a]Lit *he will,* and so throughout the ch 11:10 [a]Or *wage war* [b]Or *return and wage* [A]Is 8:8; Jer 46:7, 8; 51:42; Dan 11:26, 40 11:11 [a]Lit *with him, with* [b]Lit *his hand* [A]Dan 11:5 11:13 [a]Lit *at the end of the times, years* [b]Or *keep on coming* [A]Dan 4:16; 12:7 11:14 [a]Lit *stumble,* and so throughout the ch 11:15 [A]Jer 6:6; Ezek 4:2; 17:17

10:21 writing of truth. God's plan of certain and true designs for men and nations, which He can reveal according to His discretion (11:2; Is 46:9–11). **except Michael.** The angel with Michael intended to handle the demons of Persia and Greece. This actually forms the heavenly basis for the earthly unfolding of history in 11:2–35.

11:1 first year. Ca. 539 B.C. (cf. 6:1ff.; 9:1). **an encouragement … protection for him.** The messenger of 10:10ff. continues to speak of assisting Michael (even as Michael had strengthened him in the battle with demons in 10:21), confirming Darius in his purpose of kindness to Israel in decreeing their return.

11:2–45 As in 8:3–26, this prophecy sweeps all the way from the history of spiritual conflict in Israel (11:2–35) to the tribulation (vv. 36–42) when Michael aids in fully delivering Israel (12:1). The detail of this history is so minute and accurate, so confirmed by history, that unbelieving critics have, without evidence, insisted that it was actually written 400 years later than Daniel, after it had happened, which would make the prophet a deceiver. The prophecy actually looks ahead from Daniel to the final Antichrist.

11:2–35 This section unfolds the near fulfillment of the Persian kingdom and the reign of Greece through Antiochus Epiphanes.

11:2 three more kings …. fourth. The 3 in the Persian sphere, after Cyrus (10:1), were Cambyses (ca. 530–522 B.C.), Psuedo-Smerdis (ca. 522 B.C.), and Darius I Hystaspes (ca. 522–486 B.C.). The fourth is Xerxes I, called Ahasuerus in Esther (486–465 B.C.). Kings after Xerxes are not included, probably because Xerxes' failed military campaign against the Greeks (481–479 B.C.) sounded the beginning of the end for Persia, which finally fell ca. 331 B.C. to Alexander the Great.

11:3 a mighty king. Alexander the Great (cf. 8:5).

11:4 After Alexander's death (ca. 323 B.C.), 4 who were not of his posterity took sectors of his wide empire (*see notes on 7:6; 8:3–9*). The king of the South (Egypt) and king of the North (Aram, or Syria) receive emphasis in v. 5 and after. As time moved on, other leaders ruled, crossing and recrossing Israel.

11:5, 6 king of the South … king of the North. King of the South represents the Ptolomies, the leaders of Egypt, contrasted often in vv. 5ff. with the king of the North, the Seleucids, leaders of Syria (v. 6). South and N are in relation to Israel, for which the angel Gabriel, speaking in this passage, is so concerned. Verses 5–20 cover almost 200 years of wars between these bordering powers.

11:6 form an alliance. Berenice, daughter of Egypt's Ptolemy II Philadelphus (285–246 B.C.), married Syria's King Antiochus II Theos (261–246 B.C.). The latter part of the verse refers to the political advantage they hoped the alliance would produce. Antiochus divorced his wife to marry Berenice. Later that divorced wife murdered Berenice, her baby son, and even Antiochus by poisoning him. Thus she brought her own son, Seleucus II Callinicus, to the throne.

11:7 descendants of her line. The murdered Berenice's brother stood in his father's place. His name was Ptolemy III Euergetes of Egypt (246–222 B.C.), and in reverse he conquered Syria, sacking their great treasure (v. 8).

11:9 the latter will enter. Syria's Callinicus attacked Egypt ca. 240 B.C. but retreated, soundly beaten.

11:10 His sons. Seleucus' sons (successors) kept up war against Egypt, as described in vv. 11–35.

11:11 king of the South. Ptolemy IV Philopator (222–203 B.C.) devastated the Syrian army under Antiochus III the Great (223–187 B.C.). Egypt's advantage would be brief (v. 12).

11:13–16 king of the North. Thirteen years later Antiochus returned with a great army, and in a series of strikes against Egypt brought Israel ("the Beautiful Land") into his control as far S as Gaza.

11:14 violent ones among your people. Violent Jews wanted Judean independence from Egypt, but failed in their revolt.

South will not stand *their ground,* not even [a]their
choicest troops, for there will be no strength to
make a stand. 16 But he who comes against him
will [A]do as he pleases, and [B]no one will *be able to*
withstand him; he will also stay *for a time* in the
[a,C]Beautiful Land, with destruction in his hand. 17 He
will [A]set his face to come with the power of his
whole kingdom, [a]bringing with him [b]a proposal
of peace which he will put into effect; he will also
give him the daughter of women to ruin it. But
she will not take a stand *for him* or be [c]on his side.
18 Then he will turn his face to the [A]coastlands and
capture many. But a commander will put a stop to
his scorn against him; moreover, he will [B]repay him
for his scorn. 19 So he will turn his face toward the
fortresses of his own land, but he will [A]stumble and
fall and be [B]found no more.

20 "Then in his place one will arise who will [A]send
an [a]oppressor through the [b]Jewel of *his* kingdom;
yet within a few days he will be shattered, though
not in anger nor in battle. 21 In his place a despicable
person will arise, on whom the honor of kingship
has not been conferred, but he will come in a time
of tranquility and [A]seize the kingdom by intrigue.
22 The overflowing [A]forces will be flooded away
before him and shattered, and also the prince of
the covenant. 23 After an alliance is made with him
he will practice deception, and he will go up and
gain power with a small *force of* people. 24 [a]In a
time of tranquility he will enter the [A]richest *parts*
of the [b]realm, and he will accomplish what his fathers never did, nor his [c]ancestors; he will distribute
plunder, booty and possessions among them, and
he will devise his schemes against strongholds,
but *only* for a time. 25 He will stir up his strength
and [a]courage against the [A]king of the South with a
large army; so the king of the South will mobilize
an extremely large and mighty army for war; but he
will not stand, for schemes will be devised against
him. 26 Those who eat his choice food will [a]destroy
him, and his army will [b,A]overflow, but many will
fall down slain. 27 As for both kings, their hearts
will be *intent* on [A]evil, and they will [B]speak lies *to
each other* at the same table; but it will not succeed, for the [C]end is still *to come* at the appointed
time. 28 Then he will return to his land with much
[a]plunder; but his heart will be *set* against the holy
covenant, and he will take action and *then* return
to his *own* land.

29 "At the appointed time he will return and come
into the South, but [a]this last time it will not turn out
the way it did before. 30 For ships of [a,A]Kittim will
come against him; therefore he will be disheartened and will return and become enraged at the
holy covenant and take action; so he will come back
and show regard for those who forsake the holy

11:15 [a]Lit *the people of its choice ones* 11:16 [a]I.e. Israel [A]Dan 5:19; 11:3, 36 [B]Josh 1:5 [C]Dan 8:9; 11:41 11:17 [a]Lit *and* [b]Lit *equitable things* [c]Lit *for him;* i.e. for her father [A]2 Kin 12:17; Ezek 4:3, 7 11:18 [A]Gen 10:5; Is 66:19; Jer 2:10; 31:10; Zeph 2:11 [B]Hos 12:14 11:19 [A]Ps 27:2; Jer 46:6 [B]Job 20:8; Ps 37:36; Ezek 26:21 11:20 [a]Or *exactor* of tribute [b]Lit *adornment;* i.e. probably Jerusalem and its temple [A]Is 60:17 11:21 [A]2 Sam 15:6 11:22 [A]Dan 9:26; 11:10 11:24 [a]Lit *Into tranquility and the richest...he will enter* [b]Or *province* [c]Lit *fathers' fathers* [A]Num 13:20; Neh 9:25; Ezek 34:14 11:25 [a]Lit *heart* [A]Dan 11:5 11:26 [a]Lit *break* [b]Or *be swept away, and many* [A]Dan 11:10, 40 11:27 [A]Ps 52:1; 64:6 [B]Ps 12:2; Jer 9:3-5; 41:1-3 [C]Dan 8:19; 11:35, 40; Hab 2:3 11:28 [a]Lit *possessions* 11:29 [a]Lit *it will not happen as the first and as the last* 11:30 [a]I.e. Cyprus [A]Gen 10:4; Num 24:24; Is 23:1, 12; Jer 2:10

11:16 he who comes against him. Antiochus III the Great took lasting dominion over Israel. **Beautiful Land.** Israel (cf. 8:9).

11:17 give ... the daughter. Antiochus, feeling pressure from Rome (fourth empire, 2:40; 7:7) to make peace with Egypt, offered his daughter Cleopatra to marry Ptolemy V Epiphanes (ca. 192 B.C.). The Syrian thus hoped his daughter would spy to help him to "ruin" or weaken Egypt and bring it under his power. Cleopatra, instead of helping her father, favored her Egyptian mate.

11:18 a commander. Antiochus had set his sights to conquer Greece, along the Mediterranean coastlands. But this brought him into conflict with Rome, so that a Roman, Lucius Scipio Asiaticus, repaid the Syrian aggression against Roman rights in the area with a resounding defeat (ca. 191–190 B.C.).

11:19 fall. Antiochus returned from defeat to his own land compelled by Rome to relinquish all his territory W of the Taurus and to repay the costs of war. He was likely killed by defenders of a Persian temple he tried to plunder at night in Elymais (to get money to pay reparations required by Rome).

11:20 an oppressor. Rome required Seleucus IV Philopator to render tribute, for Rome was increasingly powerful. The Syrian set out to tax his subjects heavily to raise the tribute. Soon, he died after being poisoned. The "Jewel of *his* kingdom" possibly refers to Israel ("the Beautiful Land") with its splendid temple.

11:21 a despicable person. In vv. 21–35, the most cruel king of the North was Seleucid, the Syrian persecutor of Israel named Antiochus IV Epiphanes (cf. 8:9–14, 23–25). He came to the throne when his brother Seleucus was murdered and a son of the dead king who might succeed him, Demetrius I Soter, was held hostage in Rome. In the vacuum, Antiochus seized power in Syria.

11:22 will be flooded away. Egypt's armies were swept away by Antiochus' invading forces as by a flood (cf. "flood" for military onslaught, 9:26). Israel's "prince of the covenant," Onias III, was murdered by his own defecting brother Menelaus at the request of Antiochus (171 B.C.).

11:23 an alliance. In an Egyptian struggle for the throne, Antiochus developed an alliance with Ptolemy VI Philometer over his rival Ptolemy VII Euergetes II (distinct from the leader in v. 7). By this alliance, Antiochus deceitfully plotted to gain greater power in Egypt. With a "small *force*," he conquered Memphis and the rest of Egypt all the way to Alexandria.

11:24 In a time of tranquility he will enter. Antiochus, under the guise of friendship, plundered the richest Egyptian places he could strike. To gain support, he gave lavish gifts, possibly battle spoils. **devise his schemes against strongholds.** He formed a scheme to take over Egypt.

11:25 his strength ... against the ... South. Antiochus attacked Philometer, who had become an enemy. The latter fell due to treachery by trusted supporters (v. 26a) and became Antiochus' captive.

11:26 Those who eat. Betraying counselors whom Philometer fed led him to attack Syria to secure his defeat and death for him and his men.

11:27 will speak lies. Antiochus feigned help to reinstate Ptolemy Philometer to Egypt's throne, occupied then by Ptolemy Euergetes. Both kings lied at the conference, and Antiochus set Philometer up as king at Memphis, whereas Euergetes reigned at Alexandria. The two Egyptians soon agreed on a joint rule, frustrating the Syrian.

11:28 against the holy covenant. En route N through Israel to Syria with riches, Antiochus met a revolt, as sources outside Scripture mention. He struck Jerusalem's temple, profaned the sacrificial system, massacred 80,000 men, took 40,000 prisoners, sold 40,000 as slaves, and squelched a Jewish bid to depose his own designated priest, Menelaus.

11:29 come into the south. Antiochus, for the third time, invaded Egypt against the joint rulership (ca. 168 B.C.); however, with much less success.

11:30 ships ... come against him. A Roman fleet from Cyprus sided with Egypt, thwarting Antiochus' attack. Backing down from engaging Rome in war, Antiochus left Egypt, taking out his rage on Israelites in his path. He opposed God's Mosaic Covenant that some Jews kept, despite Syrian policies and some Jewish compromise. Antiochus showed favors to Jewish apostates ("who forsake the holy covenant") as non-biblical writings attest.

covenant. 31Forces from him will arise, [A]desecrate
the sanctuary fortress, and do away with the regular sacrifice. And they will set up the [B]abomination
[a]of desolation. 32By [A]smooth *words* he will [a]turn to
godlessness those who act wickedly toward the covenant, but the people who know their God will display [B]strength and take action. 33[a,A]Those who have
insight among the people will give understanding to
the many; yet they will [B]fall by sword and by flame,
by captivity and by plunder for *many* days. 34Now
when they fall they will be granted a little help, and
many will [A]join with them in [B]hypocrisy. 35Some of
[a]those who have insight will fall, in order to [A]refine,
[B]purge and make them [b,C]pure until the [D]end time;
because *it is* still *to come* at the appointed time.
36"Then the king will [A]do as he pleases, and he
will exalt and [B]magnify himself above every god
and will [C]speak [a]monstrous things against the [D]God
of gods; and he will prosper until the [E]indignation
is finished, for that which is [F]decreed will be done.
37He will show no regard for the [a]gods of his fathers
or for the desire of women, nor will he show regard
for any *other* god; for he will magnify himself above
them all. 38But [a]instead he will honor a god of fortresses, a god whom his fathers did not know; he
will honor *him* with gold, silver, costly stones and
treasures. 39He will take action against the strongest
of fortresses with *the help of* a foreign god; he will
give great honor to [a]those who acknowledge *him*
and will cause them to rule over the many, and will
parcel out land for a price.
40"At the [A]end time the [B]king of the South will
collide with him, and the [C]king of the North will
[D]storm against him with chariots, with horsemen
and with many ships; and he will enter countries,
[E]overflow *them* and pass through. 41He will also
enter the [a,A]Beautiful Land, and many *countries* will
fall; but these will be rescued out of his hand: Edom,
[B]Moab and the foremost of the sons of [C]Ammon.
42Then he will stretch out his hand against *other*
countries, and the land of Egypt will not escape.
43But he will [a]gain control over the hidden treasures
of gold and silver and over all the precious things
of Egypt; and [A]Libyans and [B]Ethiopians *will follow*
at his [b]heels. 44But rumors from the East and from
the North will disturb him, and he will go forth with
great wrath to destroy and [a]annihilate many. 45He
will pitch the tents of his royal pavilion between the
seas and the beautiful [A]Holy Mountain; yet he will
come to his end, and no one will help him.

11:31 [a]Lit *that makes desolate;* or *that causes horror* [A]Dan 8:11-13; 12:11 [B]Dan 9:27; Matt 24:15; Mark 13:14 11:32 [a]Or *pollute those* [A]Dan 11:21, 34 [B]Mic 5:7-9; Zech 9:13-16; 10:3-6 11:33 [a]Or *Instructors of the people* [A]Mal 2:7 [B]Matt 24:9; John 16:2; Heb 11:36-38 11:34 [A]Matt 7:15; Acts 20:29, 30 [B]Dan 11:21, 32; Rom 16:18 11:35 [a]Or *the instructors* [b]Lit *white* [A]Deut 8:16; Prov 17:3; Dan 12:10; Zech 13:9; Mal 3:2, 3 [B]John 15:2 [C]Rev 7:14 [D]Dan 11:27 11:36 [a]Lit *extraordinary* [A]Dan 5:19; 11:3, 16 [B]Is 14:13; Dan 5:20; 8:11, 25; 2 Thess 2:4 [C]Rev 13:5, 6 [D]Deut 10:17; Ps 136:2; Dan 2:47 [E]Is 10:25; 26:20; Dan 8:19 [F]Dan 9:27 11:37 [a]Or *God* 11:38 [a]Lit *in his place* 11:39 [a]Lit *the one who acknowledges* 11:40 [A]Dan 11:27, 35; 12:4, 9 [B]Dan 11:11, 25 [C]Dan 11:7, 13, 15 [D]Is 5:28; Jer 4:13 [E]Dan 11:10, 26 11:41 [a]I.e. Palestine [A]Dan 8:9; 11:16 [B]Jer 48:47 [C]Jer 49:6 11:43 [a]Or *rule over* [b]Lit *footsteps* [A]2 Chr 12:3; Nah 3:9 [B]2 Chr 12:3; Ezek 30:4, 5; Nah 3:9 11:44 [a]Lit *devote to destruction* 11:45 [A]Is 11:9; 27:13; 65:25; 66:20; Dan 9:16, 20

11:31 desecrate the sanctuary. Antiochus' soldiers, no doubt working with apostate Jews, guarded the temple, halting all worship, while others attacked the city on the Sabbath and slaughtered men, women, and children. Soldiers desecrated Israel's temple, banned circumcision and daily sacrifices (1 Macc. 1:44–54), and sacrificed a pig on the altar. The Syrians on Chislev (Dec. 15, 167 B.C.) even imposed an idol statue in honor of the Olympian god Zeus into the temple. Jews called it "the abomination of desolation," i.e., emptying or ruining for Jewish worship. **abomination of desolation.** Antiochus' soldiers profaned God's temple by spreading sow's broth on the altar and banning daily sacrifices (cf. 8:14 and *see note there*) as described in 1 Macc. 1:44–54. Both Daniel and Jesus said this atrocity was only a preview of the abomination that would happen later under the final Antichrist (9:27; Mt 24:15).

11:32–34 Those who act wickedly. Compromisers (cf. v. 30) among the Jews were enticed by flattery to side with Antiochus and be corrupted (cf. 1 Macc. 1:11–15).

11:32 the people who know their God. Jews loyal to God (called Hasideans) stood on firm convictions, suffering death rather than compromising (v. 33; as also 1 Macc. 1:62, 63). Judas Maccabeus, helped by Rome, led them in a successful revolt.

11:33 give understanding to the many. Those who believe and know the truth will instruct others in the Scriptures, while also suffering continued persecution.

11:34 a little help. Many would fall away, and Jews committed to the covenant would have little help, humanly speaking. Some, fearing the faithful remnant's dealing with apostates, pretended loyalty.

11:35 to refine. Faced by persecution, some who remained true to God's "insight" (any true believers, 12:3) were to fall as martyrs. The gracious design of such suffering was to sanctify them. The persecution pattern continues until the final "end time" that God appointed, at Christ's second coming. Reference to this "end time" prepares for a transition in v. 36 to final tribulation times when the Antichrist, whom Antiochus prefigures, will be in power. **the end time … appointed time.** These two eschatological terms point to a forward leap across thousands of years of history from Antiochus to a future similar trial when the willful king (vv. 36–45) rules. The willful king is the "little horn," the Antichrist (7:7, 8, 20, 21, 24–26), the persecutor of 9:27 (*see note there*).

11:36–45 This section is the far fulfillment of God's prophetic plan. It summarizes details of Daniel's 70th week which are found nowhere else in Scripture. Antiochus Epiphanes, a type of Antichrist, is the perfect transition point to the actual Antichrist.

11:36 Then. This word points to the future "end time" mentioned in v. 35. Verses 36–45 discuss the career of the final Antichrist in the last 7 years before Christ's millennial kingdom. This willful king is the final Antichrist (*see notes on 7:8, 11, 12, 25; 9:27*; cf. Rev 13:4–7).

11:37 gods of his fathers. Pagan Gentiles have had traditional gods passed down from their fathers, but this king has no regard for any of them. His only god is power (v. 38, "god of fortresses"). **desire of women.** This could mean that Antichrist will be a homosexual; but it surely means he has no normal desire for or, interest in, women, e.g., as one who is celibate.

11:38 god of fortresses. The term for fortress is used 5 other times in this chapter (vv. 7, 10, 19, 31, 39) and each time means "a strong place." Power is to be his god, and he spends all his treasures to become powerful and to finance wars. With this power, he will attack every stronghold (v. 39).

11:40 king of … South … North. Here is the final N/S conflict. The S was Egypt in the earlier context. Here is the last great battle with the final army from the N retaliating against the attack of the final southern African power. Antichrist will not allow this without striking back and winning, defeating both as recorded in v. 41ff. The willful king, Antichrist, withstands onslaughts from both, and prevails, entering Israel ("the Beautiful Land") and, perhaps, committing at that time the abomination of desolation (9:23; Mt 24:15). With this victory, he will be established in power for a time.

11:44 rumors from … East and … North. Military bulletins alert the willful king, in his victories, of other sectors of the world deploying troops to the Palestinian theater (cf. Rev 9:16; 16:12).

11:45 his end. To face the latest threats, the willful king sets up his command post between the Mediterranean Sea and the Dead Sea (and/or Sea of Galilee) and the holy mountain of Jerusalem, his troops filling the land (cf. Zec 12:2, 3; 14:2, 3; Rev 19:17–21). No one is able to help him against God, who, by the return of Christ, brings him to his end (cf. Rev 19:20).

THE TIME OF THE END

12 "Now at that time [A]Michael, the great prince
who stands *guard* over the sons of your people,
will arise. And there will be a [B]time of distress [C]such
as never occurred since there was a nation until that
time; and at that time your people, everyone who is
found written in the [D]book, will be rescued. 2 [A]Many
of those who sleep in the dust of the ground will
awake, [B]these to everlasting life, but the others to
disgrace *and* everlasting [a]contempt. 3 [a]Those who
have [A]insight will [B]shine brightly like the brightness
of the [b]expanse of heaven, and those who [C]lead the
many to righteousness, like the stars forever and
ever. 4 But as for you, Daniel, [A]conceal these words
and [B]seal up the book until the [C]end of time; [D]many
will go back and forth, and knowledge will increase."
5 Then I, Daniel, looked and behold, two others
were standing, one on this bank of the river and
the other on that bank of the river. 6 And [A]one said
to the man [B]dressed in linen, who was above the
waters of the river, "[C]How long *will it be* until the
end of *these* wonders?" 7 I heard the man dressed
in linen, who was above the waters of the river,
[a]as he [A]raised his right hand and his left toward
heaven, and swore by [B]Him who lives forever that
it would be for a [b,C]time, [b]times, and half *a* [b]*time;*
and as soon as [c]they finish [D]shattering the [d]power of
the holy people, all these *events* will be completed.
8 As for me, I heard but could not understand; so I
said, "My lord, what *will be* the [a]outcome of these
events?" 9 He said, "Go *your way,* Daniel, for *these*
words are concealed and [A]sealed up until the end
time. 10 [A]Many will be purged, [a]purified and refined,
but the [B]wicked will act wickedly; and none of the
wicked will understand, but [b]those who [C]have insight will understand. 11 From the time that the regular sacrifice is abolished and the [a,A]abomination of
desolation is set up, *there will be* 1,290 days. 12 How
[A]blessed is he who keeps waiting and attains to the
[B]1,335 days! 13 But as for you, go *your way* to the
[a]end; then you will enter into [A]rest and rise *again*
for your [B]allotted portion at the end of the [b]age."

12:1 [A]Dan 10:13, 21; Rev 12:7 [B]Rev 7:14; 16:18 [C]Jer 30:7; Ezek 5:9; Dan 9:12; Matt 24:21; Mark 13:19 [D]Dan 7:10; 10:21 12:2 [a]Lit *abhorrence* [A]Is 26:19; Ezek 37:12-14 [B]Matt 25:46; John 5:28, 29 12:3 [a]Or *The instructors will* [b]Or *firmament* [A]Dan 11:33, 35; 12:10 [B]John 5:35 [C]Is 53:11; Dan 11:33 12:4 [A]Dan 8:26; 12:9 [B]Is 8:16; Dan 12:9; Rev 22:10 [C]Dan 8:17; 12:9, 13 [D]Is 11:9; 29:18, 19; Dan 11:33 12:6 [A]Dan 8:16; Zech 1:12, 13 [B]Ezek 9:2; Dan 10:5 [C]Dan 8:13; 12:8; Matt 24:3; Mark 13:4 12:7 [a]Lit *and* [b]I.e. year(s) [c]Lit *to finish* [d]Lit *hand* [A]Ezek 20:5; Rev 10:5, 6 [B]Dan 4:34 [C]Dan 7:25; Rev 12:14 [D]Dan 8:24; Luke 21:24 12:8 [a]Or *final end* 12:9 [A]Dan 12:4 12:10 [a]Lit *made white* [b]Or *the instructors will* [A]Zech 13:9 [B]Is 32:6, 7; Rev 22:11 [C]Dan 12:3; Hos 14:9; John 7:17; 8:47 12:11 [a]Or *horrible abomination* [A]Dan 9:27; 11:31; Matt 24:15; Mark 13:14 12:12 [A]Is 30:18 [B]Dan 8:14; Rev 11:2; 12:6; 13:5 12:13 [a]I.e. end of your life [b]Lit *days* [A]Is 57:2; Rev 14:13 [B]Ps 16:5

12:1 that time. This points back to 11:36–45, the time of the ascendancy of Antichrist during the final tribulation period. During that period, Michael the archangel (cf. Jude 9) of 10:13, 21 ministers with special attention to protecting Israel during that Gentile time (cf. Is 26:20, 21; Jer 30:7; Mt 24:21). "Your people" means Daniel's Israelite people, who can have hope, even in the distress of an unprecedented kind set for the Great Tribulation (Mt 24:21; cf. Rev 12:12–17; 13:7). "The book" is the book of the saved (Mal 3:16–4:3; Lk 10:20; Rev 13:8; 17:8; 20:12, 15; 21:27).

12:2 Many . . . these . . . others. Two groups will arise from death constituting the "many," meaning all, as in Jn 5:29. Those of faith will rise to eternal life, the rest of the unsaved to eternal torment. The souls of OT saints are already with the Lord; at that time, they will receive glorified bodies (cf. Rev 20:4–6).

12:3 have insight. Those having true knowledge, by faith in God's Word, not only leaders (as 11:33), but others (11:35; 12:10). To "shine" in glory is a privilege of all the saved (cf. the principle in 1Th 2:12; 1Pe 5:10). Any who influence others for righteousness shine like stars in varying capacities of light as their reward (as in 1Co 3:8). The faithfulness of the believer's witness will determine one's eternal capacity to reflect God's glory.

12:4 the end of time. Refers to the 70th week of tribulation (cf. 11:35, 40). **go back and forth.** This Heb. verb form always refers to the movement of a person searching for something. In the tribulation, people will search for answers to the devastation and discover increased knowledge through Daniel's preserved book.

12:5 two others. Two angels.

12:6 man . . . in linen. Cf. 10:5.

12:7 a time, times, and half *a* time. This answers the question of v. 6. Adding these (one, two, and one-half) come to the final 3 1/2 years of Daniel's 70th week (9:27), the time of trouble when the "little horn," or willful king, persecutes the saints (7:25; cf. 11:36–39 and Rev 12:14; the same span is described by other phrases in Rev 11:2, 3; 13:5).

12:10 Many . . . purified. Salvation will come to many Jews during the Great Tribulation (cf. Zec 13:8, 9, where the prophet speaks of one-third; Ro 11:26; Rev 11:13). The truly saved develop in godliness through trials. The unsaved pursue false values.

12:11 the regular sacrifice. This reference is to the end of daily temple sacrifice, previously allowed under a covenant which the Antichrist formed with Israel, which he later causes to cease in the middle of the final 7 years (9:27). Then, favorable relations give way to persecution. Even his abomination that desecrates the temple (as 9:27; Mt 24:1; Mk. 13:14; 2Th 2:3, 4) is accompanied with persecution. **will be 1,290 days.** From the intrusion of the abomination, there follow 1,290 days, including 1,260 which make up the last 3 1/2 years of the final 7 years (*see note on v. 7*), then 30 days more, possibly to allow for the judgment of the living subsequent to Christ's return (cf. Mt 24:29–31; 25:31–46), before millennial kingdom blessings begin.

12:12 blessed. This is in the kingdom (2:35, 45; 7:13, 14, 27) that gives blessedness after the subjugation to Gentile empires in chaps. 2, 7, 8. **to the 1,335 days!** Forty-five more days, even beyond the 1,290 days, allows for transition between Israel's time of being shattered (v. 7) and God's setting up of His kingdom (cf. 7:13, 14, 27).

12:13 go. Daniel's own career would soon involve death. **rise *again*.** In resurrection (cf. 12:2; Jn 5:28, 29). **at the end of the age.** The kingdom will ensue after the prophesied days of 9:24–27; 12:11, 12.

THE BOOK OF HOSEA

TITLE

The title is derived from the main character and author of the book. The meaning of his name, "salvation," is the same as that of Joshua (cf. Nu 13:8, 16) and Jesus (Mt 1:21). Hosea is the first of the 12 Minor Prophets. "Minor" refers to the brevity of the prophecies, as compared to the length of the works of Isaiah, Jeremiah, and Ezekiel.

AUTHOR AND DATE

The book of Hosea is the sole source of information about the author. Little is known about him, and even less about his father, Beeri (1:1). Hosea was probably a native of the northern kingdom of Israel, since he shows familiarity with the history, circumstances, and topography of the north (cf. 4:15; 5:1, 13; 6:8, 9; 10:5; 12:11, 12; 14:6). This would make him and Jonah the only writing prophets from the northern kingdom. Although he addressed both Israel (the northern kingdom) and Judah (the southern kingdom), he identified the king of Israel as "our king" (7:5).

Hosea had a lengthy period of ministry, prophesying ca. 755–710 B.C., during the reigns of Uzziah (790–739 B.C.), Jotham (750–731 B.C.), Ahaz (735–715 B.C.), and Hezekiah (715–686 B.C.) in Judah, and Jeroboam II (793–753 B.C.) in Israel (1:1). His long career spanned the last 6 kings of Israel from Zechariah (753–752 B.C.) to Hoshea (732–722 B.C.). The overthrow of Zechariah (the last of the dynasty of Jehu) in 752 B.C. is depicted as yet future (1:4). Thus he followed Amos' preaching in the north, and was a contemporary of Isaiah and Micah as well, both of whom prophesied in Judah. Second Kings 14–20 and 2 Chronicles 26–32 record the historical period of Hosea's ministry.

BACKGROUND AND SETTING

Hosea began his ministry to Israel (also called Ephraim, after its largest tribe) during the final days of Jeroboam II, under whose guidance Israel was enjoying both political peace and material prosperity as well as moral corruption and spiritual bankruptcy. Upon Jeroboam II's death (753 B.C.), however, anarchy prevailed and Israel declined rapidly. Until her overthrow by Assyria 30 years later, 4 of Israel's 6 kings were assassinated by their successors. Prophesying during the days surrounding the fall of Samaria, Hosea focuses on Israel's moral waywardness (cf. the book of Amos) and her breach of the covenantal relationship with the Lord, announcing that judgment was imminent.

Circumstances were not much better in the southern kingdom. Usurping the priestly function, Uzziah had been struck with leprosy (2Ch 26:16–21); Jotham condoned idolatrous practices, opening the way for Ahaz to encourage Baal worship (2Ch 27:1–28:4). Hezekiah's revival served only to slow Judah's acceleration toward a fate similar to that of her northern sister. Weak kings on both sides of the border repeatedly sought out alliances with their heathen neighbors (7:11; cf. 2Ki 15:19; 16:7) rather than seeking the Lord's help.

HISTORICAL AND THEOLOGICAL THEMES

The theme of Hosea is God's loyal love for His covenant people, Israel, in spite of their idolatry. Thus Hosea has been called the St. John (the apostle of love) of the OT. The Lord's true love for His people is unending and will tolerate no rival. Hosea's message contains much condemnation, both national and individual, but at the same time, he poignantly portrays the love of God toward His people with passionate emotion. Hosea was instructed by God to marry a certain woman and experience with her a domestic life which was a dramatization of the sin and unfaithfulness of Israel. The marital life of Hosea and his wife, Gomer, provide the rich metaphor which clarifies the themes of the book: sin, judgment, and forgiving love.

INTERPRETIVE CHALLENGES

That the faithless wife, Gomer, is symbolic of faithless Israel is without doubt; but questions remain. First, some suggest that the marital scenes in chaps. 1–3 should be taken only as allegory. However, there is nothing in the narrative, presented in simple prose, which would even question its literal occurrence.

Much of its impact would be lost if not literal. When nonliteral elements within the book are introduced, they are prefaced with "saw" (5:13; 9:10, 13), the normal Hebraic means of introducing nonliteral scenes. Furthermore, there is no account of a prophet ever making himself the subject of an allegory or parable.

Second, what are the moral implications of God's command for Hosea to marry a prostitute? It appears best to see Gomer as chaste at the time of marriage to Hosea, only later having become an immoral woman. The words "take yourself a wife of harlotry" are to be understood proleptically, i.e., looking to the future. An immoral woman could not serve as a picture of Israel coming out of Egypt (2:15; 9:10), who then later wandered away from God (11:1). Chapter 3 describes Hosea taking back his wife, who had been rejected because of adultery, a rejection that was unjustifiable if Hosea had married a prostitute with full knowledge of her character.

A third question arises concerning the relationship between chap. 1 and chap. 3 and whether the woman of chap. 3 is Gomer or another woman. There are a number of factors which suggest that the woman of chap. 3 is Gomer. In 1:2, God's command is to "Go, take"; in 3:1, however, His command is to "Go again, love," suggesting that Hosea's love was to be renewed to the same woman. Furthermore, within the analogy of chap. 1, Gomer represents Israel. As God renews His love toward faithless Israel, so Hosea is to renew his love toward faithless Gomer. For Hos. 3 to denote a different woman would confuse the analogy.

OUTLINE

I. Adulterous Wife and Faithful Husband (1:1–3:5)
- A. Hosea and Gomer (1:1–9)
- B. God and Israel (1:10–2:23)
- C. Both Parties Reconciled (3:1–5)

II. Adulterous Israel and Faithful Lord (4:1–14:9)
- A. Adulterous Israel Found Guilty (4:1–6:3)
- B. Adulterous Israel Put Away (6:4–10:15)
- C. Adulterous Israel Restored to the Lord (11:1–14:9)

HOSEA'S WIFE AND CHILDREN

1 The word of the LORD which came to [A]Hosea the
son of Beeri, during the days of [B]Uzziah, [C]Jotham,
[D]Ahaz *and* [E]Hezekiah, kings of Judah, and during the
days of [F]Jeroboam the son of Joash, king of Israel.
2 When the LORD first spoke through Hosea, the
LORD said to Hosea, "[A]Go, take to yourself a wife of
harlotry and *have* children of harlotry; for [B]the land
commits flagrant harlotry, [a]forsaking the LORD." 3 So
he went and took Gomer the daughter of Diblaim,
and she conceived and [A]bore him a son. 4 And the
LORD said to him, "Name him [A]Jezreel; for yet a little
while, and [B]I will [a]punish the house of Jehu for the
bloodshed of Jezreel, and [C]I will put an end to the
kingdom of the house of Israel. 5 On that day I will
[A]break the bow of Israel in the [B]valley of Jezreel."
6 Then she conceived again and gave birth to a
daughter. And [a]the LORD said to him, "Name her
[b]Lo-ruhamah, for I will no longer [A]have compassion
on the house of Israel, that I would ever forgive
them. 7 But I will have [A]compassion on the house
of Judah and [B]deliver them by the LORD their God,
and will not deliver them by [C]bow, sword, battle,
horses or horsemen."
8 When she had weaned Lo-ruhamah, she conceived and gave birth to a son. 9 And [a]the LORD said,
"Name him [b]Lo-ammi, for you are not My people
and I am not [c]your God."

10 [a]Yet the number of the sons of Israel
Will be like the [A]sand of the sea,
Which cannot be measured
or numbered;
And [B]in the place
Where it is said to them,
"You are [C]not My people,"
It will be said to them,
"*You are* the [D]sons of the living God."
11 And the [A]sons of Judah and the sons of
Israel will be [B]gathered together,
And they will appoint for
themselves [C]one leader,
And they will go up from the land,
For great will be the day of Jezreel.

ISRAEL'S UNFAITHFULNESS CONDEMNED

2 [a]Say to your brothers, "[b]Ammi," and to your
sisters, "[c]Ruhamah."

2 "Contend with your mother, [A]contend,
For she is [B]not my wife, and I
am not her husband;
And let her put away her
[C]harlotry from her face
And her adultery from
between her breasts,

1:1 [A]Rom 9:25 [B]2 Chr 26:1-23; Is 1:1; Amos 1:1 [C]2 Kin 15:5, 7, 32-38; 2 Chr 27:1-9 [D]2 Kin 16:1-20; 2 Chr 28:1-27; Is 1:1; 7:1-17; Mic 1:1 [E]2 Kin 18:1-20:21; 2 Chr 29:1-32:33; Mic 1:1 [F]2 Kin 13:13; 14:23-29; Amos 1:1 1:2 [a]Lit *from not following after* [A]Hos 3:1 [B]Deut 31:16; Jer 3:1; Ezek 23:3-21; Hos 2:5; 5:3 1:3 [A]Ezek 23:4 1:4 [a]Lit *visit the bloodshed of Jezreel on the house of Jehu* [A]Hos 2:22 [B]2 Kin 10:11 [C]2 Kin 15:8-10 1:5 [A]Jer 49:35; Ezek 39:3 [B]Josh 17:16; Judg 6:33 1:6 [a]Lit *He* [b]I.e. she has not obtained compassion [A]Hos 2:4 1:7 [A]2 Kin 19:29-35; Is 30:18 [B]Jer 25:5, 6; Zech 9:9, 10 [C]Ps 44:3-7; Zech 4:6 1:9 [a]Lit *He* [b]I.e. not my people [c]Lit *yours* 1:10 [a]Ch 2:1 in Heb [A]Gen 22:17; 32:12; Jer 33:22 [B]Rom 9:26 [C]Is 65:1; Hos 1:9 [D]Is 63:16; 64:8; John 1:12; 1 Pet 2:10 1:11 [A]Is 11:12 [B]Jer 23:5, 6; 50:4, 5; Ezek 37:21-24 [C]Jer 30:21; Hos 3:5 2:1 [a]Ch 2:3 in Heb [b]I.e. my people [c]I.e. she has obtained compassion 2:2 [A]Ezek 23:45; Hos 2:5; 4:5 [B]Is 50:1 [C]Jer 3:1, 9, 13

1:1 The word of the LORD. Cf. 6:5. This kind of introduction, expressing the prophet's divine authority and message source, appears also in Joel 1:1; Mic 1:1; Zep 1:1; Zec 1:1; Mal 1:1. Similar statements appear in Am 1:3; Ob 1; Jon 1:1; Hag 1:2.

1:2 wife of harlotry. See Introduction: Interpretive Challenges. **children of harlotry.** This points to the future unfaithfulness of their mother. The children were possibly not fathered by Hosea. That Hosea's marriage to Gomer was to depict God's marriage to Israel is clearly set forth and becomes the key to the theme of the book.

1:4 Jezreel. Meaning "God will scatter" (cf. Zec 10:9), the name is given to the child so named, as a prediction of judgment (cf. 2Ki 9:7–10:28). **I will punish the house of Jehu for the bloodshed of Jezreel.** It was at the city of Jezreel where Jehu slaughtered the house of Ahab (cf. 2Ki 9:7–10:28). **put an end.** Looks forward to the exile of Israel to Assyria in 722 B.C., from which she never returned.

1:5 break the bow. The bow was a common euphemism denoting military strength, the principal instrument of warfare in Israel. Fulfillment came in 722 B.C. when Assyria invaded. **the valley of Jezreel.** Jezreel, called Esdraelon, extends 10 mi. in breadth from the Jordan to the Mediterranean Sea, near Carmel; it was the great battlefield (see Rev 16:14–16) adjoining the Valley of Megiddo, which will become an avenue of blessing (cf. v. 11) when Christ returns in triumph.

1:6 Lo-ruhamah. Lit. "not pitied," this daughter is named to symbolize God bringing judgment on Israel, no longer extending His favor towards them.

1:7 I will have compassion on … Judah. God chose to intervene on behalf of Hezekiah when Jerusalem was besieged at the hands of the Assyrians in 701 B.C. (cf. 2Ki 19; Is 37).

1:9 Lo-ammi. The name means "not My people" and symbolizes God's rejection of Israel. **I am not your God.** Lit. "I am no longer 'I am' to you." The phrase gives the breaking of the covenant, a kind of divorce formula, in contrast to the covenant or marriage formula "I AM WHO I AM" given in Ex 3:14.

1:10–2:1 In spite of the waywardness of Israel, God preserved a remnant for Himself from both Israel and Judah. Speaking of millennial blessings, God promised national increase (cf. Is 54:1), national conversion and reunion (cf. Eze 37:15–23), national leadership (3:5), and national restoration (2:23).

1:10 number. A reaffirmation of the Abrahamic Covenant, not to be fulfilled in this generation but in the future (cf. Ge 22:17). **not My people.** Quoted by Paul in Ro 9:26.

1:11 one leader. Refers to Messiah (cf. 3:5). **day of Jezreel.** Here used positively in the sense of divine blessing (cf. 2:22).

2:2 Contend with your mother. Although the language is applicable to Gomer, it depicts a courtroom scene in which the Lord, as the plaintiff, brings charges against the defendant. Individual Israelites, depicted as the children, are commanded to bring charges against their mother, Israel, as a nation. The physical immorality of Gomer pictures the spiritual idolatry of Israel.

SIGNIFICANT NAMES

Names play a special part in interpreting the message of Hosea.

Name	Reference	Meaning
Jezreel	1:4	God Sows
Lo-ruhamah	1:6	Not Pitied
Lo-ammi	1:9	Not My People
Hosea	1:1; related also to *Joshua*, Nu 13:16, and *Jesus*, Mt 1:21	Yahweh Is Salvation

3 Or I will strip her [A]naked
And expose her as on the [B]day
when she was born.
I will also [C]make her like a wilderness,
Make her like desert land
And slay her with [D]thirst.
4 "Also, I will have no compassion
on her children,
Because they are [A]children of harlotry.
5 "For their mother has [A]played the harlot;
She who conceived them has
acted shamefully.
For she said, '[A]I will go after my lovers,
Who [B]give *me* my bread and my water,
My wool and my flax, my [C]oil and my drink.'
6 "Therefore, behold, I will [A]hedge
up [a]her way with [B]thorns,
And I will build [b]a wall against her so
that she cannot find her [C]paths.
7 "She will [A]pursue her lovers, but
she will not overtake them;
And she will seek them, but
will not find *them*.
Then she will say, '[B]I will go back
to my [C]first husband,
For it was [D]better for me then than now!'

8 "For she does [A]not know that it
was [B]I who gave her the grain,
the new wine and the oil,
And lavished on her silver and gold,
Which they [a]used for Baal.
9 "Therefore, I will [A]take back My
grain at [a]harvest time
And My new wine in its season.
I will also take away My wool and My flax
Given to cover her nakedness.
10 "And then I will [A]uncover her lewdness
In the sight of her lovers,
And no one will rescue her
out of My hand.
11 "I will also [A]put an end to all her gaiety,
Her [B]feasts, her [C]new moons, her sabbaths
And all her festal assemblies.
12 "I will [A]destroy her vines and fig trees,
Of which she said, 'These are my wages
Which my lovers have given me.'
And I will [B]make them a forest,
And the [C]beasts of the field
will devour them.
13 "I will punish her for the [A]days of the Baals
When she used to [a,B]offer
sacrifices to them
And [C]adorn herself with her
[b]earrings and jewelry,
And follow her lovers, so that she
[D]forgot Me," declares the LORD.

RESTORATION OF ISRAEL

14 "Therefore, behold, I will allure her,
[A]Bring her into the wilderness
And speak [a]kindly to her.
15 "Then I will give her her
[A]vineyards from there,
And [B]the valley of Achor
as a door of hope.
And she will [a,C]sing there as in
the days of her youth,
As in the [D]day when she came up
from the land of Egypt.
16 "It will come about in that day,"
declares the LORD,
"That you will call Me [a,A]Ishi
And will no longer call Me [b]Baali.
17 "For [A]I will remove the names of
the Baals from her mouth,
So that they will be [a]mentioned
by their names no more.
18 "In that day I will also make
a covenant for them
With the [A]beasts of the field,
The birds of the sky
And the creeping things of the ground.
And I will [a,B]abolish the bow, the
sword and war from the land,
And will make them [C]lie down in safety.

2:3 [A]Jer 13:22; Ezek 16:7, 22, 39 [B]Ezek 16:4 [C]Is 32:13, 14; Hos 13:15 [D]Jer 14:3; Amos 8:11-13 2:4 [A]Jer 13:14 2:5 [A]Is 1:21; Jer 2:25; 3:1, 2; Hos 3:1 [B]Jer 44:17, 18; Hos 2:12 [C]Hos 2:8 2:6 [a]So with some ancient versions; Heb *your* [b]Lit *her wall so that* [A]Job 19:8; Lam 3:7, 9 [B]Hos 9:6; 10:8 [C]Jer 18:15 2:7 [A]Hos 5:13 [B]Luke 15:17, 18 [C]Jer 2:2; 3:1; Ezek 16:8; 23:4 [D]Jer 14:22; Hos 13:6 2:8 [a]Or *made into the* [A]Is 1:3 [B]Ezek 16:19 2:9 [a]Lit *its time* [A]Hos 8:7; 9:2 2:10 [A]Ezek 16:37 2:11 [A]Jer 7:34; 16:9 [B]Hos 3:4; Amos 5:21; 8:10 [C]Is 1:13, 14 2:12 [A]Jer 5:17; 8:13 [B]Is 5:5; 7:23 [C]Hos 13:8 2:13 [a]Or *burn incense* [b]Or *nose rings* [A]Hos 4:13; 11:2 [B]Jer 7:9 [C]Ezek 16:12, 17; 23:40 [D]Hos 4:6; 8:14; 13:6 2:14 [a]Lit *upon her heart* [A]Ezek 20:33-38 2:15 [a]Or *give answer* [A]Ezek 28:25, 26 [B]Josh 7:26 [C]Jer 2:1-3; Ezek 16:8-14 [D]Hos 11:1; 12:9, 13; 13:4 2:16 [a]I.e. my husband [b]I.e. my master, or my Baal [A]Is 54:5; Hos 2:7 2:17 [a]Or *remembered* [A]Ex 23:13; Josh 23:7; Ps 16:4 2:18 [a]Lit *break* [A]Job 5:23; Is 11:6-9; Ezek 34:25 [B]Is 2:4; Ezek 39:1-10 [C]Lev 26:5; Jer 23:6; Ezek 34:25

2:5 I will go. Lit. "Let me go," it denotes strong desire and bent. Israel attributed her prosperity to the idols of her heathen neighbors, her "lovers" (cf. vv. 7, 10, 12). She would not be deterred from pursuing them.

2:8–13 God withheld rain and productivity to show Israel that the Canaanite god Baal was not the god of rain and fertility.

2:8 used for Baal. Baal (the Phoenician sun-god) worship, already present during the time of the judges (cf. Jdg 2:17; 3:3; 8:33), became established in Israel when King Ahab married Jezebel, who attempted to obliterate Israelite worship of the true God (cf. 1Ki 19). Offerings to Baal actually came from God's dowry to Israel (cf. Eze 16:10–14).

2:10 I will uncover her lewdness. God pledged to expose Israel's wickedness. The phrase is linked to being taken forcibly into captivity in Eze 16:37–40. **her lovers.** The idols were personified as if they could see, though they could offer no help.

2:11 feasts. Ever since the Exodus from Egypt, Israel had intermingled the worship of the Lord with the worship of false gods (cf. Am 5:26; Ac 7:43).

2:13 she forgot Me. Cf. 2Ki 17:7–18 for a detailed description of what their abandonment of God involved.

2:14 speak kindly to her. The phrase was used of wooing (Ge 34:3; Jdg 19:3; Ru 2:13). God will restore Israel to Himself.

2:15 valley of Achor. Lit. "valley of Trouble," near Jericho where Achan and his family were judged (Jos 7:24). This reference alerts Israel that her discipline and judgment would not last forever because there is a "door of hope."

2:16 Ishi … Baali. The former (lit. "husband") denotes affection and intimacy, while the latter (lit. "master") speaks of rulership.

2:17 In v. 13, Israel forgot her true God; God said she would forget her false gods. What the outward conformity to the Mosaic Covenant could not do, God does through a new, regenerated heart in the New Covenant (Jer 31:31–34; Zec 13:1, 2).

2:18 a covenant. This depicts a millennial scene (cf. Is 2:4; 11:6–9; Mic 4:3) when God's people become subject to God and creation becomes subject to them.

19 "I will [A]betroth you to Me forever;
Yes, I will betroth you to Me in
[B]righteousness and in justice,
In lovingkindness and in compassion,
20 And I will betroth you to
Me in faithfulness.
Then you will [A]know the LORD.
21 "It will come about in that day that [A]I
will respond," declares the LORD.
"I will respond to the heavens, and
they will respond to the earth,
22 And the [A]earth will respond to the grain,
to the new wine and to the oil,
And they will respond to [a]Jezreel.
23 "I will [A]sow her for Myself in the land.
[B]I will also have compassion on [a]her
who had not obtained compassion,
And [C]I will say to [b]those who
were [D]not My people,
'You are My people!'
And [c]they will say, '*You are* my God!' "

HOSEA'S SECOND SYMBOLIC MARRIAGE

3 Then the LORD said to me, "Go again, love a
[a]woman *who* is loved by *her* [b]husband, yet an
adulteress, even [A]as the LORD loves the sons of
Israel, though they turn to other gods and love
raisin [B]cakes." 2 So I [A]bought her for myself for fifteen *shekels* of silver and a homer and a [a]half of
barley. 3 Then I said to her, "You shall [A]stay with
me for many days. You shall not play the harlot,
nor shall you have a [a]man; so I will also be toward
you." 4 For the sons of Israel will remain for many
days [A]without king or prince, [B]without sacrifice or
sacred [C]pillar and without [D]ephod or [a,E]household
idols. 5 Afterward the sons of Israel will [A]return and
seek the LORD their God and [B]David their king; and
[C]they will come trembling to the LORD and to His
goodness in the last days.

GOD'S CONTROVERSY WITH ISRAEL

4 [A]Listen to the word of the
LORD, O sons of Israel,
For the LORD has a [B]case against
the inhabitants of the land,
Because there is [C]no [a]faithfulness
or [b]kindness
Or [D]knowledge of God in the land.
2 *There is* [A]swearing, [B]deception,
[C]murder, [D]stealing and [E]adultery.
They employ violence, so that
[F]bloodshed [a]follows bloodshed.
3 Therefore the land [A]mourns,
And everyone who lives in it languishes
Along with the beasts of the field
and the birds of the sky,
And also the fish of the sea [a]disappear.

4 Yet let no one [a,A]find fault, and
let none offer reproof;
For your people are like those who
[B]contend with the priest.
5 So you will [A]stumble by day,
And the prophet also will stumble
with you by night;
And I will destroy your [B]mother.
6 [A]My people are destroyed for
lack of knowledge.
Because you have [B]rejected knowledge,
I also will [C]reject you from
being My priest.
Since you have [D]forgotten
the [E]law of your God,
I also will forget your children.

2:19 [A]Is 62:4, 5 [B]Is 1:27; 54:6-8 2:20 [A]Jer 31:33, 34; Hos 6:6; 13:4 2:21 [A]Is 55:10; Zech 8:12; Mal 3:10, 11 2:22 [a]I.e. God sows [A]Jer 31:12; Joel 2:19 2:23 [a]Heb *Lo-ruhamah* [b]Heb *Lo-ammi* [C]Lit *he* [A]Jer 31:27 [B]Hos 1:6 [C]Rom 9:25; 1 Pet 2:10 [D]Hos 1:9 3:1 [a]I.e. Gomer [b]Lit *companion* [A]Jer 3:20 [B]2 Sam 6:19; 1 Chr 16:3; Song 2:5 3:2 [a]Heb *lethech* [A]Ruth 4:10 3:3 [a]Or *husband* [A]Deut 21:13 3:4 [a]Heb *teraphim* [A]Hos 10:3; 13:10, 11 [B]Dan 9:27; 11:31; 12:11; Hos 2:11 [C]Hos 10:1, 2 [D]Ex 28:4-12; 1 Sam 23:9-12 [E]Gen 31:19, 34; Judg 17:5; 18:14, 17; 1 Sam 15:23 3:5 [A]Jer 50:4, 5 [B]Jer 30:9; Ezek 34:24 [C]Is 2:2, 3; Jer 31:9 4:1 [a]Or *truth* [b]Or *loyalty* [A]Hos 5:1 [B]Hos 12:2; Mic 6:2 [C]Is 59:4; Jer 7:28 [D]Jer 4:22 4:2 [a]Lit *touches* [A]Deut 5:11; Hos 10:4 [B]Hos 7:3; 10:13; 11:12 [C]Gen 4:8; Hos 6:9 [D]Deut 5:19; Hos 7:1 [E]Deut 5:18; Hos 7:4 [F]Hos 6:8; 12:14 4:3 [a]Lit *are taken away* [A]Is 24:4; 33:9; Amos 5:16; Zeph 1:3 4:4 [a]Lit *contend* [A]Ezek 3:26; Amos 5:10, 13 [B]Deut 17:12 4:5 [A]Ezek 14:3, 7; Hos 5:5 [B]Jer 15:8; Hos 2:2, 5 4:6 [A]Is 5:13 [B]Hos 4:14; Mal 2:7, 8 [C]Zech 11:8, 9, 15-17 [D]Hos 2:13; 8:14; 13:6 [E]Hos 8:1, 12

2:19, 20 I will betroth you. Repeated 3 times, the term emphasizes the intensity of God's restoring love for the nation. In that day, Israel will no longer be thought of as a prostitute. Israel brings nothing to the marriage; God makes all the promises and provides all the dowry. These verses are recited by every orthodox Jew as he places the phylacteries on his hand and forehead (cf. Dt 11:18). The regeneration/conversion of the nation is much like that of an individual (cf. 2Co 5:16–19).

2:22, 23 A reversal of circumstances (cf. 1:4, 6, 9).

2:22 Jezreel. As in 1:11, used here in the positive sense of scattering seed to sow it.

2:23 Quoted by Paul in Ro 9:25.

3:1 Go again, love. Having been previously separated, Hosea was commanded to pursue his estranged wife Gomer (cf. Introduction: Interpretive Challenges), thereby illustrating God's unquenchable love for faithless Israel. **raisin cakes.** Eaten as a part of special occasions (cf. 2Sa 6:19), they may have been used in idolatrous ceremonies, possibly as an aphrodisiac (cf. SS 2:5).

3:2 bought her. Probably from a slave auction, Hosea purchased Gomer for 15 shekels of silver and 1 1/2 homers of barley. Together, the total may have equaled 30 pieces of silver, the price paid for a common slave (cf. Ex 21:32). Barley was the offering of one accused of adultery (Nu 5:15).

3:3–5 Gomer would not be allowed conjugal relations for "many days," with any man, including Hosea. As a further element of the picture of God's dealings with His covenant people during the present age, Israel would exist without her existing political and religious (both true and false) relations until Messiah returns at the Second Advent to set up His millennial reign (cf. Eze 40–48; Zec 12–14).

3:4 without ephod or household idols. Idolatrous items of priestly clothing and objects of worship.

3:5 David. Cf. 1:11. This must refer to Messiah during the Millennium, as "in the last days" specifies (cf. Is 55:3, 4; Jer 30:9; Eze 34:23, 24; 37:24, 25). The Jews did not seek after Christ at His first advent. This reference has the Davidic Covenant as its background (cf. 2Sa 7:12–17; Pss 39; 132).

4:1 the LORD has a case. Turning from the analogy of his own marriage, the prophet made the judicial charge in God's indictment against Israel.

4:2 Note the many infractions of the Ten Commandments (cf. Ex 20:3–17).

4:3 Sin plays havoc with lower creation and nature (cf. Joel 1:17–20; Ro 8:19–22).

4:4 let no one find fault. Rationalizing and denying their wrongs, the people protested their innocence, like those who would not humbly accept the decision of the priests (cf. Deut 17:8–13).

4:5 your mother. The Israelite nation of which the people are the children (cf. 2:2).

4:6 reject you from being My priest. Having rejected the Lord's instruction, Israel could

7 The more they [A]multiplied, the
more they sinned against Me;
I will [B]change their glory into shame.
8 They [A]feed on the [a]sin of My people
And [B]direct their desire
toward their iniquity.
9 And it will be, like people, [A]like priest;
So I will [B]punish them for their ways
And repay them for their deeds.
10 [A]They will eat, but not have enough;
They will [B]play the harlot, but not increase,
Because they have [a,C]stopped
giving heed to the LORD.

11 Harlotry, [A]wine and new wine take
away the [a]understanding.
12 My people [A]consult their wooden idol, and
their *diviner's* wand informs them;
For a spirit of harlotry has led *them* astray,
And they have played the harlot,
departing [a]from their God.
13 They offer sacrifices on the
[A]tops of the mountains
And [a,B]burn incense on the hills,
[C]Under oak, poplar and terebinth,
Because their shade is pleasant.
Therefore your daughters play the harlot
And your [b]brides commit adultery.
14 I will not punish your daughters
when they play the harlot
Or your [a]brides when they commit adultery,
For *the men* themselves go
apart with harlots
And offer sacrifices with [A]temple prostitutes;
So the people without
understanding are [b]ruined.

15 Though you, Israel, play the harlot,
Do not let Judah become guilty;
Also do not go to [A]Gilgal,
Or go up to Beth-aven
[B]And take the oath:
"As the LORD lives!"
16 Since Israel is [A]stubborn
Like a stubborn heifer,
[a]Can the LORD now [B]pasture them
Like a lamb in a large field?
17 Ephraim is joined to [A]idols;
[B]Let him alone.
18 Their liquor gone,
They play the harlot continually;
[A]Their [a]rulers dearly love shame.
19 [A]The wind wraps them in its wings,
And they will be ashamed
because of their sacrifices.

THE PEOPLE'S APOSTASY REBUKED

5 Hear this, O priests!
Give heed, O house of Israel!
Listen, O house of the king!
For the judgment applies to you,
For you have been a [A]snare at Mizpah
And a net spread out on Tabor.
2 The [A]revolters have [a,B]gone
deep in depravity,
But I will chastise all of them.
3 I [A]know Ephraim, and Israel is
not hidden from Me;
For now, O Ephraim, you have
played the harlot,
Israel has defiled itself.
4 Their deeds will not allow them
To return to their God.
For a [A]spirit of harlotry is within them,
And they [B]do not know the LORD.
5 Moreover, the [A]pride of Israel
testifies against him,
And Israel and Ephraim stumble
in their iniquity;
[B]Judah also has stumbled with them.

4:7 [A]Hos 10:1; 13:6 [B]Hab 2:16 4:8 [a]Or *sin offering* [A]Hos 10:13 [B]Is 56:11; Mic 3:11 4:9 [A]Is 24:2; Jer 5:31 [B]Hos 8:13; 9:9 4:10 [a]Lit *forsaken giving heed;* or *forsaken the LORD to practice* (v 11) *harlotry* [A]Lev 26:26; Is 65:13; Mic 6:14 [B]Hos 7:4 [C]Hos 9:17 4:11 [a]Lit *heart* [A]Prov 20:1; Is 5:12; 28:7 4:12 [a]Lit *from under* [A]Is 44:19; Jer 2:27 4:13 [a]Or *offer sacrifices* [b]Or *daughters-in-law* [A]Jer 3:6 [B]Hos 2:13; 11:2 [C]Is 1:29; Jer 2:20 4:14 [a]Or *daughters-in-law* [b]Lit *thrust down* [A]Deut 23:17 4:15 [A]Hos 9:15; 12:11 [B]Jer 5:2; 44:26; Amos 8:14 4:16 [a]Or *Now the LORD will pasture...field* [A]Ps 78:8 [B]Is 5:17; 7:25 4:17 [A]Hos 13:2 [B]Ps 81:12; Hos 4:4 4:18 [a]Lit *shields* [A]Mic 3:11 4:19 [A]Hos 12:1; 13:15 5:1 [A]Hos 9:8 5:2 [a]Or *waded deep in slaughter* [A]Hos 9:15 [B]Is 29:15; Hos 4:2; 6:9 5:3 [A]Amos 3:2; 5:12 5:4 [A]Hos 4:12 [B]Hos 4:6, 14 5:5 [A]Hos 7:10 [B]Ezek 23:31-35

no longer serve as His priest to the nations (cf. Ex 19:6; Jas 3:1).

4:7–10 Their position of power and glory, abused in succeeding generations by the eating of the sin offerings, would be turned to shame. Being no different from the people, the priests, who should have been faithful, would share their punishment (cf. Is 24:1–3).

4:11 Here is a moral truth applicable to all people and times. Verses 12, 13 are illustrations of the enslavement in Israel.

4:12 spirit of harlotry. A prevailing mindset and inclination to worldly spiritual immorality, i.e., idolatry (cf. 5:4).

4:13 Bereft of righteous teaching and understanding, they sacrificed to idols. Hilltops and groves of trees were favorite places for idolatrous worship (cf. Dt 12:2; Jer 2:20; Eze 6:13), including religious prostitution.

4:14 Although all who sin will be judged, God forbade punishing the adulteresses alone and leaving the men who patronized them to go free. The heaviest punishment would not be on the women who sin, but the fathers and husbands who set such a bad example by their engagement with prostitutes. **without understanding.** Cf. 4:6.

4:15 Gilgal. Between Jordan and Jericho in the area of Samaria, this was once a holy place to God (Jos 5:10–15; 1Sa 10:8; 15:21), afterwards desecrated by idol worship (cf. 9:15; 12:11; Am 4:4; 5:5). **Beth-aven.** Judah was to stay away from Israel's centers of false worship, including Beth-aven ("house of wickedness/deceit"). This was a deliberate substitution for the name Bethel ("house of God"), once sacred to God (Ge 28:17, 19), but made by Jeroboam a place to worship calves (cf. 1Ki 12:28–33; 13:1; Jer 48:13; Am 3:14; 7:13).

4:16 Because Israel was like a stubborn calf, God no longer attempted to corral her, abandoning her as a lamb in a vast wilderness.

4:17 Ephraim ... Let him alone. As the largest and most influential of the northern 10 tribes, Ephraim's name was often used as representative of the northern nation. This was an expression of God's wrath of abandonment. When sinners reject Him and are bent on fulfilling their wicked purposes, God removes restraining grace and turns them over to the results of their own perverse choices. This kind of wrath is that in Ro 1:18–32 (cf. Jdg 10:13; 2Ch 15:2; 24:20; Ps 81:11, 12).

5:1 Hosea addressed the priests, the people, and the royal family; the 3 imperatives demand attention. The religious and civil leaders had entrapped the people (cf. 6:9; 7:7). **Mizpah ... Tabor.** Mizpah of Gilead, lying E of the Jordan (Jdg 10:17; 11:29), and Tabor, SW of the Sea of Galilee, were likely places for false worship.

5:5 pride of Israel testifies against him. Israel's pride in idolatry provided self-incrimination (cf. 7:10).

6 They will [A]go with their flocks and herds
To seek the LORD, but they
will [B]not find *Him;*
He has [C]withdrawn from them.
7 They have [A]dealt treacherously
against the LORD,
For they have borne [a,B]illegitimate children.
Now the [C]new moon will devour
them with their [b]land.

8 [A]Blow the horn in [B]Gibeah,
The trumpet in Ramah.
Sound an alarm at Beth-aven:
"[C]Behind you, Benjamin!"
9 Ephraim will become a [A]desolation
in the [B]day of rebuke;
Among the tribes of Israel I
[C]declare what is sure.
10 The princes of Judah have become like
those who [A]move a boundary;
On them I will [B]pour out My
wrath [C]like water.
11 Ephraim is [A]oppressed,
crushed in judgment,
[B]Because he was determined to
[a]follow *man's* command.
12 Therefore I am like a [A]moth to Ephraim
And like rottenness to the house of Judah.
13 When Ephraim saw his sickness,
And Judah his [a]wound,
Then Ephraim went to [A]Assyria
And sent to [b,B]King Jareb.
But he is [C]unable to heal you,
Or to cure you of your [a]wound.
14 For I *will be* [A]like a lion to Ephraim
And like a young lion to the
house of Judah.
[B]I, even I, will tear to pieces and go away,
I will carry away, and there
will be [C]none to deliver.
15 I will go away *and* return to My place
Until they [a,A]acknowledge their
guilt and seek My face;
In their affliction they will
earnestly [B]seek Me.

THE RESPONSE TO GOD'S REBUKE

6 "[A]Come, let us return to the LORD.
For [B]He has torn *us,* but [C]He will heal us;
He has [a]wounded *us,* but He
will [D]bandage us.
2 "He will [A]revive us after two days;
He will [B]raise us up on the third day,
That we may live before Him.
3 "So let us [A]know, let us press
on to know the LORD.
His [B]going forth is as
certain as the dawn;
And He will come to us like the [C]rain,
Like the spring rain watering the earth."

4 What shall I do with you, O [A]Ephraim?
What shall I do with you, O Judah?
For your [a]loyalty is like a [B]morning cloud
And like the dew which
goes away early.
5 Therefore I have [A]hewn *them* in
pieces by the prophets;
I have slain them by the
[B]words of My mouth;
And the judgments on you are *like*
the light that goes forth.
6 For [A]I delight in loyalty
[B]rather than sacrifice,
And in the knowledge of God
rather than burnt offerings.
7 But [A]like [a]Adam they have
[B]transgressed the covenant;
There they have [C]dealt
treacherously against Me.
8 [A]Gilead is a city of wrongdoers,
Tracked with [B]bloody *footprints.*
9 And as [A]raiders wait for a man,
So a band of priests [B]murder
on the way to Shechem;
Surely they have committed [a,C]crime.

5:6 [A]Hos 8:13; Mic 6:6, 7 [B]Prov 1:28; Is 1:15; Jer 14:12 [C]Ezek 8:6 5:7 [a]Lit *strange* [b]Lit *portions* [A]Is 48:8; Jer 3:20; Hos 6:7 [B]Hos 2:4 [C]Is 1:14; Hos 2:11 5:8 [A]Joel 2:1 [B]Hos 9:9; 10:9 [C]Judg 5:14 5:9 [A]Is 28:1-4; Hos 9:11-17 [B]Is 37:3 [C]Is 46:10; Zech 1:6 5:10 [A]Deut 19:14; 27:17 [B]Ezek 7:8 [C]Ps 32:6; 93:3, 4 5:11 [a]Or with some ancient versions, *follow nothingness* [A]Deut 28:33 [B]Mic 6:16 5:12 [A]Ps 39:11; Is 51:8 5:13 [a]Or *ulcer* [b]Or *the avenging king* or *the great king* [A]Hos 7:11; 8:9; 12:1 [B]Hos 10:6 [C]Jer 30:12-15 5:14 [A]Ps 7:2; Hos 13:7, 8; Amos 3:4 [B]Ps 50:22 [C]Mic 5:8 5:15 [a]Or *bear their punishment* [A]Is 64:7-9; Jer 3:13, 14 [B]Ps 50:15; 78:34; Jer 2:27; Hos 3:5 6:1 [a]Lit *struck* [A]Jer 50:4, 5 [B]Deut 32:39; Hos 5:14 [C]Jer 30:17; Hos 14:4 [D]Is 30:26 6:2 [A]Ps 30:5 [B]1 Cor 15:4 6:3 [A]Is 2:3; Mic 4:2 [B]Ps 19:6; Mic 5:2 [C]Job 29:23; Ps 72:6; Joel 2:23 6:4 [a]Or *lovingkindness* [A]Hos 7:1; 11:8 [B]Ps 78:34-37; Hos 13:3 6:5 [A]1 Sam 15:32, 33; Jer 1:10; 5:14 [B]Jer 23:29 6:6 [A]Matt 9:13; 12:7 [B]Is 1:11 6:7 [a]Or *men* [A]Job 31:33 [B]Hos 8:1 [C]Hos 5:7 6:8 [A]Hos 12:11 [B]Hos 4:2 6:9 [a]Or *lewdness* [A]Hos 7:1 [B]Jer 7:9, 10; Hos 4:2 [C]Ezek 22:9; 23:27; Hos 2:10

5:6, 7 Her religious sacrifices and monthly festivals no longer brought divine favor, only judgment. God "has withdrawn from them." *See note on 4:17.*

5:8 The enemy was already upon them, and thus her watchmen were to sound the alarm (cf. Nu 10:9). **Gibeah … Ramah.** Located on Judah's northern border with Israel. **Beth-aven.** (Bethel) situated in southern Israel (cf. 4:15). All three were strategic defense cities. **Benjamin.** Used to refer to the whole southern kingdom.

5:10 move a boundary. Boundaries, marked by stones, could be easily moved at night. Moving them was tantamount to stealing land from a neighbor (cf. Dt 19:14; 27:17; Pr 22:28; 23:10). Worse, Israel's leaders were moving spiritual lines established by God (cf. v. 11).

5:12 moth … rottenness. God will be destructive to Israel.

5:13 King Jareb. "Jareb" means "warrior" and refers to the king of Assyria, to whom Israel (cf. 2Ki 15:19, 20) and later Judah (cf. 2Ki 16:5–9) turned for help.

5:14, 15 Foreign assistance would be of no value, since the Lord was orchestrating punishment at the hands of the Assyrians. He would remove Himself until "they acknowledge their guilt" and "seek My face" (cf. 3:5).

6:1–3 Coming with the beginning of Christ's millennial reign (cf. Zec 12:10–13:1; Is 43:1–6), Hosea records Israel's future words of repentance (cf. 5:15).

6:2 after two days … on the third day. Not a reference to the resurrection of Christ (illness, not death, is in the context), but to the quickness of healing and restoration (cf. the quickness with which the dry bones of Eze 37 respond). Numbers are used similarly elsewhere (e.g., Job 5:19; Pr 6:16; 30:15, 18; Am 1:3).

6:4–7 Because Israel's commitment to the Lord was fleeting and superficial, He had to send prophets with stern words (vv. 4, 5), calling for a covenantal loyalty befitting a marriage relationship (v. 6). But they violated the marriage vows (v. 7).

6:6 I delight in loyalty rather than sacrifice. Cf. Mt 9:13; 12:7.

6:7 Adam … covenant. A reference to the Mosaic Covenant (cf. 8:1; Ex 19:5, 6).

10 In the house of Israel I have
seen a [A]horrible thing;
Ephraim's [B]harlotry is there,
Israel has defiled itself.
11 Also, O Judah, there is a [A]harvest
appointed for you,
When I [B]restore the fortunes of My people.

EPHRAIM'S INIQUITY

7 When I [A]would heal Israel,
The iniquity of Ephraim is uncovered,
And the evil deeds of Samaria,
For they deal [B]falsely;
The thief enters in,
[C]Bandits raid outside,
2 And they do not [a]consider in their hearts
That I [A]remember all their wickedness.
Now their [B]deeds are all around them;
They are before My face.
3 [A]With their wickedness they
make the [B]king glad,
And the princes with their [C]lies.
4 They are [A]all adulterers,
Like an oven heated by the baker
Who ceases to stir up *the fire*
From the kneading of the dough
until it is leavened.
5 On the [a]day of our king, the princes
[A]became sick with the heat of wine;
He stretched out his hand with [B]scoffers,
6 For their hearts are like an [A]oven
As they approach their [a]plotting;
Their [b]anger [c]smolders all night,
In the morning it burns
like a flaming fire.
7 All of them are hot like an oven,
And they consume their [A]rulers;
All their kings have fallen.
[B]None of them calls on Me.

8 Ephraim [A]mixes himself
with the [a]nations;
Ephraim has become a cake not turned.
9 [A]Strangers devour his strength,
Yet he [B]does not know *it;*
Gray hairs also are sprinkled on him,
Yet he does not know *it.*
10 Though the [A]pride of Israel
testifies against him,
Yet [B]they have not returned
to the LORD their God,
Nor have they sought Him, for all this.
11 So [A]Ephraim has become like a
silly dove, [B]without [a]sense;
They call to [C]Egypt, they go to [D]Assyria.
12 When they go, I will [A]spread
My net over them;
I will bring them down like
the birds of the sky.
I will [B]chastise them in accordance with
the [a]proclamation to their assembly.
13 [A]Woe to them, for they have
[B]strayed from Me!
Destruction is theirs, for they
have rebelled against Me!
I [C]would redeem them, but they
speak lies against Me.
14 And [A]they do not cry to Me
from their heart
When they wail on their beds;
For the sake of grain and new wine
they [a,B]assemble themselves,
They [C]turn away from Me.
15 Although I trained *and*
strengthened their arms,
Yet they [A]devise evil against Me.
16 They turn, *but* not [a]upward,
They are like a [A]deceitful bow;
Their princes will fall by the sword
Because of the [b,B]insolence of their tongue.
This *will be* their [C]derision
in the land of Egypt.

ISRAEL REAPS THE WHIRLWIND

8 [A]*Put* the trumpet to your [a]lips!
[B]Like an eagle *the enemy comes*
[C]against the house of the LORD,
Because they have [D]transgressed
My covenant
And rebelled against My [E]law.

6:10 [A]Jer 5:30, 31; 23:14 [B]Hos 5:3 6:11 [A]Jer 51:33; Joel 3:13 [B]Zeph 2:7 7:1 [A]Ezek 24:13; Hos 6:4; 7:13; 11:8 [B]Hos 4:2 [C]Hos 6:9 7:2 [a]Lit *say to their heart* [A]Ps 25:7; Jer 14:10; 17:1; Hos 8:13; 9:9; Amos 8:7 [B]Jer 2:19; 4:18; Hos 4:9 7:3 [A]Rom 1:32 [B]Jer 28:1-4; Hos 7:5; Mic 7:3 [C]Hos 4:2; 11:12 7:4 [A]Jer 9:2; 23:10 7:5 [a]I.e. a festive occasion [A]Is 28:1, 7 [B]Is 28:14 7:6 [a]Lit *ambush* [b]So with some ancient versions; M.T. *baker* [C]Lit *sleeps* [A]Ps 21:9 7:7 [A]Hos 13:10 [B]Is 64:7 7:8 [a]Lit *peoples* [A]Ps 106:35 7:9 [A]Is 1:7; Hos 8:7 [B]Hos 4:6 7:10 [A]Hos 5:5 [B]Is 9:13 7:11 [a]Lit *heart* [A]Hos 11:11 [B]Hos 4:6, 11, 14; 5:4 [C]Hos 8:13; 9:3, 6 [D]Hos 5:13; 8:9; 12:1 7:12 [a]Lit *report* [A]Ezek 12:13 [B]Lev 26:14-39; Deut 28:15 7:13 [A]Hos 9:12 [B]Jer 14:10; Ezek 34:6; Hos 9:17 [C]Jer 51:9; Hos 7:1; Matt 23:37 7:14 [a]Or with Gr and many ancient mss *gash themselves* [A]Job 35:9-11; Hos 8:2; Zech 7:5 [B]Judg 9:27; Amos 2:8; Mic 2:11 [C]Hos 13:16 7:15 [A]Nah 1:9 7:16 [a]Or possibly *to the Most High* [b]Lit *indignation;* or *cursing* [A]Ps 78:57 [B]Ps 12:3, 4; 17:10; 73:9; Dan 7:25; Mal 3:13, 14 [C]Ezek 23:32; Hos 9:3, 6 8:1 [a]Lit *palate* [A]Jer 4:13; Hos 5:8 [B]Hab 1:8 [C]Deut 28:49 [D]Hos 6:7 [E]Hos 4:6

6:11 Lest Judah feel smug at her neighbor's demise, the prophet reminds them that they have a day of reckoning awaiting them (cf. Jer 51:13; Joel 2:1–3).

7:1 Samaria. As the capital, Samaria represents the northern kingdom.

7:4–7 The civil leaders' evil lust burned so passionately all night that the prophet repeatedly described it like a consuming oven (cf. vv. 4, 6, 7), so hot that the baker could forego stirring the fire during the entire night and still have adequate heat for baking the next morning.

7:7 All their kings have fallen. Four of Israel's final 6 kings were murdered by usurpers.

7:8, 9 At Israel's invitation, foreign nations made debilitating inroads into her national and religious life. This intrusion was making her like "a cake not turned," burned on one side and raw on the other. Payment for this foreign assistance would "devour" her strength (v. 9) and make her old and feeble without noticing it.

7:11, 12 Like a dove, reputed to lack good sense (cf. Mt 10:16), so Israel had sought assistance from Egypt and Assyria, rather than from the Lord, who would ultimately trap her (cf. 8:9, 10).

7:13 would redeem them. From Egypt and their other enemies.

7:14 wail on their beds ... assemble themselves. The former phrase may speak of appeals to pagan fertility gods upon beds of sacred prostitution, while the latter, if the marginal reading is correct, harkens to Elijah's encounter with the prophets of Baal on Mt. Carmel (cf. 1Ki 18:28).

8:1 Like an eagle. Lit. a "vulture," Assyria was ready to descend quickly upon Israel to devour her (cf. Dt 28:49). transgressed My covenant. *See note on 6:7.*

2 [A]They cry out to Me,
"My God, [B]we of Israel know You!"
3 Israel has rejected the good;
The enemy will pursue him.
4 [A]They have set up kings, but not by Me;
They have appointed princes,
but I did not know *it*.
With their [B]silver and gold they have
made idols for themselves,
That [a]they might be cut off.
5 [a]He has rejected your [A]calf,
O Samaria, *saying*,
"My anger burns against them!"
How long will they be incapable
of [B]innocence?
6 For from Israel is even this!
A [A]craftsman made it, so it is not God;
Surely the calf of Samaria will
be broken to [a]pieces.
7 For [A]they sow the wind
And they reap the [B]whirlwind.
The standing grain has no [a]heads;
It yields [C]no [b]grain.
Should it yield, strangers
would swallow it up.

8 Israel is [A]swallowed up;
They are now among the nations
Like a [B]vessel in which no one delights.
9 For they have gone up to [A]Assyria,
Like [B]a wild donkey all alone;
Ephraim has [C]hired [a]lovers.
10 Even though they hire *allies*
among the nations,
Now I will [A]gather them up;
And they will begin [B]to [a]diminish
Because of the burden of the
[C]king of princes.

11 Since Ephraim has [A]multiplied altars for sin,
They have become altars of sinning for him.
12 Though [A]I wrote for him ten
thousand *precepts* of My [B]law,
They are regarded as a strange thing.
13 As for My [A]sacrificial gifts,
They [B]sacrifice the flesh and eat *it*,
But the LORD has taken no
delight in them.
Now He will [C]remember their iniquity,
And [D]punish *them* for their sins;
They will return to [E]Egypt.
14 For Israel has [A]forgotten his
Maker and [B]built palaces;
And Judah has multiplied fortified cities,
But I will send a [C]fire on its cities that it
may consume its palatial dwellings.

EPHRAIM PUNISHED

9 [A]Do not rejoice, O Israel, [a]with
exultation like the [b]nations!
For you have [B]played the harlot,
[c]forsaking your God.
You have loved *harlots'* earnings
on [d]every threshing floor.
2 Threshing floor and wine press
will [A]not feed them,
And the new wine will fail [a]them.
3 They will not remain in [A]the LORD'S land,
But Ephraim will return to [B]Egypt,
And in [C]Assyria they will eat [D]unclean *food*.
4 They will not pour out drink
offerings of [A]wine to the LORD,
[B]Their sacrifices will not please Him.
Their bread will [a]*be* like [b]mourners' bread;
All who eat of it will be [C]defiled,
For their bread will be for
[c]themselves *alone;*
It will not enter the house of the LORD.
5 [A]What will you do on the day of
the appointed festival
And on the day of the [B]feast of the LORD?
6 For behold, they will go
because of destruction;
Egypt will gather them up,
[A]Memphis will bury them.
Weeds will take over their
treasures of silver;
[B]Thorns *will be* in their tents.

8:2 [A]Ps 78:34; Hos 7:14 [B]Titus 1:16 8:4 [a]Lit *he* [A]2 Kin 15:13, 17, 25; Hos 13:10, 11 [B]Hos 2:8; 13:1, 2 8:5 [a]Or *Your calf has rejected you* [A]Hos 10:5; 13:2 [B]Ps 19:13; Jer 13:27 8:6 [a]Or *splinters* [A]Hos 13:2 8:7 [a]Lit *growth* [b]Or *meal* [A]Prov 22:8 [B]Is 66:15; Nah 1:3 [C]Hos 2:9 8:8 [A]2 Kin 17:6; Jer 51:34 [B]Jer 22:28; 25:34 8:9 [a]Lit *loves* [A]Hos 7:11 [B]Jer 2:24 [C]Ezek 16:33, 34 8:10 [a]Or *suffer for awhile* [A]Ezek 16:37; 22:20 [B]Jer 42:2 [C]Is 10:8 8:11 [A]Hos 10:1 8:12 [A]Deut 4:6, 8 [B]Hos 4:6 8:13 [A]Hos 5:6 [B]Jer 6:20; 7:21 [C]Jer 14:10; Hos 7:2; Luke 12:2; 1 Cor 4:5 [D]Hos 4:9; 9:7 [E]Hos 9:3, 6 8:14 [A]Deut 32:18; Hos 2:13; 4:6; 13:6 [B]Is 9:9, 10 [C]Jer 17:27 9:1 [a]Lit *to* [b]Lit *peoples* [c]Lit *away from your God* [d]Lit *all threshing floors of grain* [A]Is 22:12, 13; Hos 10:5 [B]Hos 4:12 9:2 [a]Lit *her* [A]Hos 2:9 9:3 [A]Lev 25:23; Jer 2:7 [B]Hos 7:16; 8:13 [C]Hos 7:11 [D]Ezek 4:13 9:4 [a]Lit be *to them* [b]Or *bread of misfortune* [c]Lit *their appetite* [A]Ex 29:40 [B]Jer 6:20; Hos 8:13 [C]Hag 2:13, 14 9:5 [A]Is 10:3; Jer 5:31 [B]Hos 2:11; Joel 1:13 9:6 [A]Is 19:13; Jer 2:16; 44:1; 46:14, 19; Ezek 30:13, 16 [B]Is 5:6; 7:23; Hos 10:8

8:2 we … know You! Israel's syncretistic worship wherein she practiced idolatry while crying out to God.

8:5 He has rejected your calf. Calf worship was the national religion of the northern kingdom (cf. 1Ki 12:25–33; Ex 32).

8:7 sow the wind … reap the whirlwind. This indicates the escalating uselessness of all their false religion.

8:9 they have gone up to Assyria. As the context notes, this is not a reference to the captivity, but to the alliance she made with Assyria. "*Like* a wild donkey," Israel has stubbornly pursued foreign assistance rather than depending on the Lord.

8:12 Israel has been duly warned; she is without excuse (cf. 6:7; 8:1).

8:13 will return to Egypt. Recalling the place of Israel's former bondage, Hosea reminds them that Assyria will be their future "Egypt" (cf. 9:3; 11:5; Dt 28:68). A few Judean refugees actually did go to Egypt (cf. 2Ki 25:26). Isaiah used "Sodom" in a similar representative fashion (Is 1:9, 10).

8:14 Judah … fortified cities. Though less idolatrous than Israel, Judah showed lack of trust in God by trusting more in fortifications. Instead of drawing near to God, Judah multiplied human defenses (cf. Is 22:8; Jer 5:17).

9:1–17 Hosea enumerates the features of the Lord's banishment to Assyria: loss of joy (vv. 1, 2); exile (vv. 3–6); loss of spiritual discernment (vv. 7–9); declining birth rate (vv. 10–16); and abandonment by God (v. 17).

9:1, 2 threshing floor … wine press. These were the very places where sacred prostitution took place in an attempt to cause Baal to bring prosperity.

9:3 the LORD's land. Cf. Lv 25:23. **Egypt.** *See note on 8:13* (cf. 11:5).

9:4 mourners' bread … defiled. Food eaten on the occasion of mourning was considered unclean, defiling anyone eating it (cf. Dt 26:12–15).

9:6 Memphis. An ancient capital of Egypt known for its tombs and pyramids.

7 The days of [A]punishment have come,
The days of [B]retribution have come;
[a]Let Israel know *this!*
The prophet is a [C]fool,
The [b]inspired man is [D]demented,
Because of the grossness of your [E]iniquity,
And *because* your hostility is *so* great.
8 Ephraim *was* a watchman with
my God, a prophet;
Yet the snare of a bird catcher
is in all his ways,
And there is *only* hostility in
the house of his God.
9 They have gone [A]deep [a]in depravity
As in the days of [B]Gibeah;
He will [C]remember their iniquity,
He will punish their sins.

10 I found Israel like [A]grapes
in the wilderness;
I saw your forefathers as the [B]earliest
fruit on the fig tree in its first *season.*
But they came to [C]Baal-peor and
devoted themselves to [a,D]shame,
And they became as [E]detestable
as that which they loved.
11 As for Ephraim, their [A]glory
will fly away like a bird—
No birth, no pregnancy and
no conception!
12 Though they bring up their children,
Yet I will bereave them [a]until
not a man is left.
Yes, [A]woe to them indeed when
I depart from them!
13 Ephraim, as I have seen,
Is planted in a pleasant
meadow like [A]Tyre;
But Ephraim will bring out his
children for slaughter.
14 Give them, O LORD—what will You give?
Give them a [A]miscarrying
womb and dry breasts.

15 All their evil is at [A]Gilgal;
Indeed, I came to hate them there!
Because of the [B]wickedness of their deeds
I will drive them out of My house!
I will love them no more;
All their princes are [C]rebels.
16 [A]Ephraim is stricken, their root is dried up,
They will bear [B]no fruit.
Even though they bear children,
I will slay the [C]precious ones
of their womb.
17 My God will cast them away
Because they have [A]not listened to Him;
And they will be [B]wanderers
among the nations.

RETRIBUTION FOR ISRAEL'S SIN

10 Israel is a [a]luxuriant [A]vine;
He produces fruit for himself.
The more his fruit,
The more altars he [B]made;
The [b]richer his land,
The better [c]he made the *sacred* [C]pillars.
2 Their heart is [a,A]faithless;
Now they must bear their [B]guilt.
[b]The LORD will [C]break down their altars
And destroy their *sacred* pillars.

3 Surely now they will say, "We have [A]no king,
For we do not revere the LORD.
As for the king, what can he do for us?"
4 They speak *mere* words,
[a]With [A]worthless oaths they
make covenants;
And [B]judgment sprouts like poisonous
weeds in the furrows of the field.
5 The inhabitants of Samaria will fear
For the [a,A]calf of [B]Beth-aven.
Indeed, its people will mourn for it,
And its [C]idolatrous priests
[b]will cry out over it,
Over its [D]glory, since it has
departed from it.
6 The thing itself will be carried to [A]Assyria
As tribute to [a,B]King Jareb;
Ephraim will [b]be [C]seized with shame
And Israel will be ashamed
of its [D]own counsel.
7 Samaria will be [A]cut off *with* her king
Like a stick on the surface of the water.

9:7 [a]Or *Israel will know it* [b]Lit *man of the spirit* [A]Is 10:3; Jer 10:15; Mic 7:4; Luke 21:22 [B]Is 34:8; Jer 16:18; 25:14 [C]Lam 2:14; Ezek 13:3, 10 [D]Is 44:25 [E]Ezek 14:9, 10 9:9 [a]Lit *they have corrupted* [A]Is 31:6 [B]Judg 19:12, 16-30; Hos 10:9 [C]Hos 7:2; 8:13 9:10 [a]I.e. Baal [A]Mic 7:1 [B]Jer 24:2 [C]Num 25:1-5; Ps 106:28, 29 [D]Jer 11:13; Hos 4:18 [E]Ps 115:8; Ezek 20:8 9:11 [A]Hos 4:7; 10:5 9:12 [a]Lit *without a man* [A]Deut 31:17; Hos 7:13 9:13 [A]Ezek 26:1-21 9:14 [A]Hos 9:11 9:15 [A]Hos 4:15; 12:11 [B]Hos 4:9; 7:2; 12:2 [C]Is 1:23; Hos 5:2 9:16 [A]Hos 5:11 [B]Hos 8:7 [C]Ezek 24:21 9:17 [A]Hos 4:10 [B]Hos 7:13 10:1 [a]Or *degenerate* [b]Or *better* [c]Lit *they* [A]Is 5:1-7; Ezek 15:1-6 [B]Jer 2:28; Hos 8:11; 12:11 [C]1 Kin 14:23; Hos 3:4 10:2 [a]Lit *smooth* [b]Lit *He* [A]1 Kin 18:21; Zeph 1:5 [B]Hos 13:16 [C]Hos 10:8; Mic 5:13 10:3 [A]Ps 12:4; Is 5:19 10:4 [a]Or *Swearing falsely in making a covenant* [A]Ezek 17:13-19; Hos 4:2 [B]Deut 31:16, 17; 2 Kin 17:3, 4; Amos 5:7 10:5 [a]So with some ancient versions; Heb *calves* [b]Or who *used to rejoice over* [A]Hos 8:5, 6 [B]Hos 4:15; 5:8 [C]2 Kin 23:5 [D]Hos 9:11 10:6 [a]Or *the avenging king* or *the great king* [b]Lit *receive shame* [A]Hos 11:5 [B]Hos 5:13 [C]Hos 4:7 [D]Is 30:3; Jer 7:24 10:7 [A]Hos 13:11

9:7, 8 The prophets were God's inspired messengers and watchmen (cf. Eze 3:17; 33:1–7), yet Israel considered them fools and madmen.

9:9 Gibeah. Cf. 10:9. Israel's sin is likened to the gross evil of the men of Gibeah, a reference to their heinous rape of the concubine (Jdg 19:22–25), an infamous and unforgettable crime (cf. Jdg 19:30).

9:10 grapes in the wilderness. A rare and refreshing find (cf. Dt 32:10). **Baal-peor.** Prior to entering the Promised Land, Israel fell into worship of Baal at Baal-peor (Nu 25:3–18).

9:11–14 Reminiscent of the imprecatory psalms, Hosea prayed that God's blessing would be withdrawn, in the figure of withholding children, the ultimate earthly blessing.

9:15 Gilgal. As a center of idol worship (cf. 4:15), the place was representative of Israel's spiritual adultery; therefore, He had rejected them from intimate fellowship.

9:17 wanderers. God promised global dispersion for disobedience (cf. Lv 26:33; Dt 28:64, 65).

10:1 Agricultural prosperity had resulted in spiritual corruption (cf. Eze 16:10–19).

10:3, 4 The last 5 kings of Israel were usurpers. Impotent and unworthy of respect, they were incapable of enforcing the laws of the land.

10:5 the calf of Beth-aven. *See notes on 4:15; 8:5.*

8 Also the [A]high places of Aven, the
[B]sin of Israel, will be destroyed;
[C]Thorn and thistle will grow
on their altars;
Then they will [D]say to the mountains,
"Cover us!" And to the hills, "Fall on us!"
9 From the days of Gibeah you
have sinned, O Israel;
There they stand!
Will not the battle against the sons of
iniquity overtake them in Gibeah?
10 When it is My [A]desire, I will
[a,B]chastise them;
And [C]the peoples will be
gathered against them
When they are bound for
their double guilt.

11 Ephraim is a trained [A]heifer
that loves to thresh,
But I will [B]come over her fair
neck *with a yoke;*
I will harness Ephraim,
Judah will plow, Jacob will
harrow for himself.
12 [A]Sow with a view to righteousness,
Reap in accordance with [a]kindness;
[B]Break up your fallow ground,
For it is time to [C]seek the LORD
Until He [D]comes to [b,E]rain
righteousness on you.
13 You have [A]plowed wickedness,
you have reaped injustice,
You have eaten the fruit of [B]lies.
Because you have trusted in your way,
in your [C]numerous warriors,
14 Therefore a tumult will arise
among your people,
And all your [A]fortresses will be destroyed,
As Shalman destroyed Beth-arbel
on the day of battle,
When [B]mothers were dashed in
pieces with *their* children.
15 Thus it will be done to you at Bethel
because of your great wickedness.
At dawn the king of Israel will
be completely cut off.

GOD YEARNS OVER HIS PEOPLE

11 When Israel *was* a youth I loved him,
And [A]out of Egypt I [B]called My son.
2 The more [a,A]they called them,
The more they went from [a]them;
They kept [B]sacrificing to the Baals
And [C]burning incense to idols.
3 Yet it is I who taught Ephraim to walk,
[a]I [A]took them in My arms;
But they did not know that I [B]healed them.
4 I [A]led them with cords of a man,
with bonds of love,
And [B]I became to them as one who
lifts the yoke from their jaws;
And I bent down *and* [C]fed them.

5 [a]They will not return to the land of Egypt;
But Assyria—he will be [b]their king
Because they [A]refused to return *to Me.*
6 The [A]sword will whirl against [a]their cities,
And will demolish [a]their gate bars
And [B]consume *them* because
of their [C]counsels.
7 So My people are bent on [A]turning from Me.
Though [a]they call [b]them to *the One* on high,
None at all exalts *Him.*

8 [A]How can I give you up, O Ephraim?
How can I surrender you, O Israel?
How can I [a]make you like [B]Admah?
How can I treat you like [B]Zeboiim?
My heart is turned over within Me,
[b]All My compassions are kindled.
9 I will [A]not execute My fierce anger;
I will not destroy Ephraim [B]again.
For [C]I am God and not man, the
[D]Holy One in your midst,
And I will not come in [a]wrath.

10:8 [A]Hos 4:13 [B]1 Kin 12:28-30; 13:34 [C]Is 32:13; Hos 9:6; 10:2 [D]Is 2:19; Luke 23:30; Rev 6:16 10:10 [a]Or *bind* [A]Ezek 5:13 [B]Hos 4:9 [C]Jer 16:16 10:11 [A]Jer 50:11; Hos 4:16; Mic 4:13 [B]Jer 28:14 10:12 [a]Or *loyalty* [b]Or *teach* [A]Prov 11:18 [B]Jer 4:3 [C]Hos 12:6 [D]Hos 6:3 [E]Is 44:3; 45:8 10:13 [A]Job 4:8; Prov 22:8; Gal 6:7, 8 [B]Hos 4:2; 7:3; 11:12 [C]Ps 33:16 10:14 [A]Is 17:3 [B]Hos 13:16 11:1 [A]Hos 2:15; 12:9, 13; 13:4 [B]Ex 4:22, 23; Matt 2:15 11:2 [a]I.e. God's prophets [A]2 Kin 17:13-15 [B]Hos 2:13; 4:13 [C]Is 65:7; Jer 18:15 11:3 [a]So ancient versions; Heb *He...His* [A]Deut 1:31; 32:10, 11 [B]Ps 107:20; Jer 30:17 11:4 [A]Jer 31:2, 3 [B]Lev 26:13 [C]Ex 16:32; Ps 78:25 11:5 [a]Lit *He* [b]Lit *his* [A]Hos 7:16 11:6 [a]Lit *his* [A]Hos 13:16 [B]Lam 2:9 [C]Hos 4:16, 17 11:7 [a]I.e. God's prophets [b]Lit *him;* i.e. Israel [A]Jer 3:6, 7; 8:5 11:8 [a]Lit *give* [b]Lit *Together* [A]Hos 6:4; 7:1 [B]Gen 14:8; Deut 29:23 11:9 [a]Lit *excitement* [A]Deut 13:17 [B]Jer 26:3; 30:11 [C]Num 23:19 [D]Is 5:24; 12:6; 41:14, 16

10:8 Cover us! … Fall on us! The captivity would be so severe that the people would pray for the mountains and hills to fall on them, similar to the last days (cf. Lk 23:30; Rev 6:16).

10:10 double guilt. Israel would receive a double portion of judgment for her multiplied iniquity (cf. Is 40:2; Jer 16:18).

10:11 a trained heifer that loves to thresh. This was a far easier work than plowing, since cattle were not bound together under a yoke, but tread on the grain singly and were free to eat some of it, as the law required that they be unmuzzled (Dt 25:4; 1Co 9:9).

10:14 Shalman destroyed Beth-arbel. Shalman was probably Shalmaneser V, king of Assyria (727–722 B.C.), who played a role in Israel's demise (cf. 2Ki 17:3–6). Although the location of Beth-arbel is uncertain, the memory of the heinous crimes committed there was vividly etched into their minds.

10:15 king. Hoshea, ca. 732–722 B.C.

11:1 In tender words reminiscent of the Exodus from Egypt (cf. Ex 4:22, 23), the Lord reassured Israel of His intense love for her. His compassion for her was aroused (cf. Is 12:1; 40:1, 2; 49:13; Jer 31:10–14; Zec 1:12–17). See Mt 2:15 for Matthew's analogical use of this verse in relationship to Jesus Christ.

11:3, 4 The Lord's endearing word pictures are reflected in Ezekiel's touching descriptions of Israel's early years (cf. Eze 16).

11:5 will not return to … Egypt. *See note on 8:13.*

11:5–7 In spite of His tender care, Israel was ungrateful, demanding punishment (cf. Ro 1:21).

11:7 turning. *See note on Pr 14:14.*

11:8 Admah … Zeboiim. Because of the Lord's great love for Ephraim, it was painful to punish her as He did these two cities, which were destroyed with Sodom and Gomorrah (cf. Ge 10:19; 19:23–25; Dt 29:23).

11:9 I will not destroy Ephraim again. The destruction referred to that inflicted by Assyrian King Tiglath-pileser, who deprived Israel of Gilead, Galilee, and Naphtali (2Ki 15:29). Ultimately, it referred to the promise that after the long dispersion God would, in mercy, restore His people in the kingdom, never to be destroyed again.

10 They will [A]walk after the LORD,
He will [B]roar like a lion;
Indeed He will roar
And *His* sons will come
[C]trembling from the west.
11 They will come trembling like
birds from [A]Egypt
And like [B]doves from the land of [A]Assyria;
And I will [C]settle them in their
houses, declares the LORD.

12 [a]Ephraim surrounds Me with [A]lies
And the house of Israel with deceit;
Judah is also unruly against God,
Even against the Holy One who is faithful.

EPHRAIM REMINDED

12 [a]Ephraim feeds on [A]wind,
And pursues the [B]east wind continually;
He multiplies lies and violence.
Moreover, [b]he makes a
covenant with Assyria,
And oil is carried to Egypt.
2 The LORD also has a [A]dispute with Judah,
And will punish Jacob
[B]according to his ways;
He will repay him according to his deeds.
3 In the womb he [A]took his
brother by the heel,
And in his maturity he
[B]contended with God.
4 Yes, he wrestled with the
angel and prevailed;
He wept and [A]sought His favor.
He found Him at [B]Bethel
And there He spoke with us,
5 Even the LORD, the God of hosts,
The LORD is His [a,A]name.
6 Therefore, [A]return to your God,
[B]Observe [a]kindness and justice,
And [C]wait for your God continually.
7 A [a]merchant, in whose hands
are false [A]balances,
He loves to oppress.
8 And Ephraim said, "Surely I
have become [A]rich,
I have found wealth for myself;
In all my labors they will find in me
[B]No iniquity, which *would be* sin."
9 But I *have been* the LORD your
God since the land of Egypt;
I will make you [A]live in tents again,
As in the days of the appointed festival.
10 I have also spoken to the [A]prophets,
And I [a]gave numerous visions,
And through the prophets I gave [B]parables.
11 Is there iniquity *in* Gilead?
Surely they are worthless.
In Gilgal they sacrifice bulls,
Yes, [A]their altars are like the stone heaps
Beside the furrows of the field.

12 Now [A]Jacob fled to the [a]land of Aram,
And [B]Israel worked for a wife,
And for a wife he kept *sheep*.
13 But by a [A]prophet the LORD
brought Israel from Egypt,
And by a prophet he was kept.
14 [A]Ephraim has provoked to bitter anger;
So his Lord will leave his
[B]bloodguilt on him
And bring back his [C]reproach to him.

EPHRAIM'S IDOLATRY

13 [A]When Ephraim [a]spoke, *there*
was trembling.
He [B]exalted himself in Israel,
But through [C]Baal he [b]did wrong and died.
2 And now they sin more and more,
And make for themselves [A]molten images,
Idols [a,B]skillfully made from their silver,
All of them the [C]work of craftsmen.

11:10 [A]Hos 3:5; 6:1-3 [B]Is 31:4; Joel 3:16; Amos 1:2 [C]Is 66:2, 5 11:11 [A]Is 11:11 [B]Is 60:8; Hos 7:11 [C]Ezek 28:25, 26; 34:27, 28 11:12 [a]Ch 12:1 in Heb [A]Hos 4:2; 7:3 12:1 [a]Ch 12:2 in Heb [b]Lit *they make* [A]Jer 22:22 [B]Gen 41:6; Ezek 17:10 12:2 [A]Hos 4:1; Mic 6:2 [B]Hos 4:9; 7:2 12:3 [A]Gen 25:26 [B]Gen 32:28 12:4 [A]Gen 32:26 [B]Gen 28:13-19; 35:10-15 12:5 [a]Lit *memorial* [A]Ex 3:15 12:6 [a]Or *loyalty* [A]Hos 6:1-3; 10:12 [B]Mic 6:8 [C]Mic 7:7 12:7 [a]Or *Canaanite* [A]Prov 11:1; Amos 8:5; Mic 6:11 12:8 [A]Ps 62:10; Hos 13:6; Rev 3:17 [B]Hos 4:8; 14:1 12:9 [A]Lev 23:42 12:10 [a]Lit *multiplied the vision* [A]2 Kin 17:13; Jer 7:25 [B]Ezek 17:2; 20:49 12:11 [A]Hos 8:11; 10:1, 2 12:12 [a]Lit *field* [A]Gen 28:5 [B]Gen 29:20 12:13 [A]Ex 14:19-22; Is 63:11-14 12:14 [A]2 Kin 17:7-18 [B]Ezek 18:10-13 [C]Dan 11:18; Mic 6:16 13:1 [a]Or *spoke with trembling* [b]Or *became guilty* [A]Job 29:21, 22 [B]Judg 8:1; 12:1 [C]Hos 2:8-17; 11:2 13:2 [a]Or *according to their own understanding* [A]Is 46:6; Jer 10:4; Hos 2:8 [B]Is 44:17-20 [C]Hos 8:6

11:10 will roar like a lion. Though the Lord would, as a lion, roar against Israel in judgment (cf. Am 1:2), He would also roar for the purpose of calling, protecting, and blessing (cf. Joel 3:16). **from the west.** Returns from Assyrian and Babylonian captivities were from the E. This undoubtedly has reference to His return at the Second Advent to set up the millennial kingdom (cf. Is 11:11, 12), when He calls Israel from their worldwide dispersion and reverses the judgment of 9:17.

12:1 Israel's attempted alliances with heathen neighbors were of no worth. This prophecy was delivered at about the time of Israel's seeking the aid of the Egyptian king.

12:2 Jacob. Frequently used interchangeably with "Israel" (cf. 10:11; Ge 32:28).

12:3–6 He exhorted them to follow their father Jacob's persevering prayerfulness, which brought God's favor on him. As God is unchanging, He would show the same favor to Jacob's posterity as He did to Jacob, if, like him, they sought God.

12:7 merchant. Because the Canaanites were known as traders, the word "merchant" came to be used synonymously with "Canaanite" (cf. Eze 16:29; 17:4; Zep 1:11). Though she denied it (v. 8), Israel had become materialistic, filled with greed, and fond of dishonest gain.

12:9 At the annual Feast of Booths, or Tabernacles (Dt 16:13–15; cf. Nu 29:12–38), Israel dwelt in tents to commemorate her 40 years of wilderness wanderings. In captivity, she would be forced to live in them permanently.

12:10 I have also spoken. Here is an aggravation of their guilt. It was not through ignorance that they sinned, but in defiance of God's revealed Word.

12:11 heaps beside the furrows. As gathered and piled stones would dot a farmer's field, so Israel multiplied her stone altars across the land. "Gilgal" means "a heap of stones," so this is a play on words.

12:12–14 The reference to Jacob's wanderings to Syria and Israel's sojourn in Egypt should cause Ephraim to confess her pride, recognize her humble origins, and acknowledge that only by God's gracious power were they made a nation.

13:1 trembling. When Ephraim, the most powerful tribe, spoke early in Israel's history, it was with authority and produced fear. **died.** Because of his sins and in spite of being feared, Ephraim died, spiritually and now nationally.

13:2 kiss the calves! An act of devotion to their idols (cf. 1Ki 19:18).

They say of them, "Let the [b]men
who sacrifice kiss the [D]calves!"
3 Therefore they will be like
the [A]morning cloud
And like dew which [a]soon disappears,
Like [B]chaff which is blown away
from the threshing floor
And like [C]smoke from a [b]chimney.

4 Yet I *have been* the [A]LORD your God
Since the land of Egypt;
And you were not to know
[B]any god except Me,
For there is no savior [C]besides Me.
5 I [a,A]cared for you in the wilderness,
[B]In the land of drought.
6 As *they had* their pasture, they
became [A]satisfied,
And being satisfied, their
[B]heart became proud;
Therefore they [C]forgot Me.
7 So I will be [A]like a lion to them;
Like a [B]leopard I will [a]lie in
wait by the wayside.
8 I will encounter them [A]like a
bear robbed of her cubs,
And I will tear open [a]their chests;
There I will also [B]devour them like a lioness,
As a wild beast would tear them.

9 *It is* your destruction, O Israel,
[a]That *you are* [A]against Me, against your [B]help.
10 Where now is your [A]king
That he may save you in all your cities,
And your [B]judges of whom you [a]requested,
"Give me a king and princes"?
11 I [A]gave you a king in My anger
And [B]took him away in My wrath.

12 The iniquity of Ephraim is bound up;
His sin is [A]stored up.
13 The pains of [A]childbirth come upon him;
He is [B]not a wise son,
For [a]it is not the time that he should
[C]delay at the opening of the womb.
14 Shall I [A]ransom them from
the [a]power of Sheol?
Shall I redeem them from death?
[B]O Death, where are your thorns?
O Sheol, where is your sting?
[C]Compassion will be hidden from My sight.

15 Though he [A]flourishes among the [a]reeds,
An [B]east wind will come,
The wind of the LORD coming
up from the wilderness;
And his fountain will [C]become dry
And his spring will be dried up;
It will [D]plunder *his* treasury of
every precious article.
16 [a]Samaria will be held [A]guilty,
For she has [B]rebelled against her God.
[C]They will fall by the [D]sword,
Their little ones will be [E]dashed in pieces,
And their pregnant [F]women
will be ripped open.

ISRAEL'S FUTURE BLESSING

14 [a,A]Return, O Israel, to the LORD your God,
For you have stumbled [b]because
of your [B]iniquity.
2 Take words with you and
return to the LORD.
Say to Him, "[A]Take away all iniquity
And [a]receive *us* graciously,
That we may [B]present [b]the
fruit of our lips.
3 "Assyria will not save us,
We will [A]not ride on horses;
Nor will we say again, '[B]Our god,'
To the [C]work of our hands;
For in [D]You the [a]orphan finds mercy."

13:2 [b]Lit *sacrificers of* or, *(among) mankind* [D]Hos 8:5, 6; 10:5 13:3 [a]Lit *goes away early* [b]Lit *window* [A]Hos 6:4 [B]Ps 1:4; Is 17:13; Dan 2:35 [C]Ps 68:2 13:4 [A]Hos 12:9 [B]Ex 20:3; 2 Kin 18:35 [C]Is 43:11; 45:21, 22 13:5 [a]Or *knew* [A]Deut 2:7; 32:10 [B]Deut 8:15 13:6 [A]Deut 8:12, 14; 32:13-15; Jer 5:7 [B]Hos 7:14 [C]Hos 2:13; 4:6; 8:14 13:7 [a]Or *watch* [A]Lam 3:10; Hos 5:14 [B]Jer 5:6 13:8 [a]Lit *the enclosure of their heart* [A]2 Sam 17:8 [B]Ps 50:22 13:9 [a]Or *But in Me is your help* [A]Jer 2:17, 19; Mal 1:12, 13 [B]Deut 33:26, 29 13:10 [a]Lit *said* [A]2 Kin 17:4; Hos 8:4 [B]1 Sam 8:5, 6 13:11 [A]1 Sam 8:7; 10:17-24 [B]1 Sam 15:26; 1 Kin 14:7-10; Hos 10:7 13:12 [A]Deut 32:34, 35; Job 14:17; Rom 2:5 13:13 [a]Lit *it is the time that he should not tarry at the breaking forth of children* [A]Is 13:8; Mic 4:9, 10 [B]Deut 32:6; Hos 5:4 [C]Is 37:3; 66:9 13:14 [a]Lit *hand* [A]Ps 49:15; Ezek 37:12, 13 [B]1 Cor 15:55 [C]Jer 20:16; 31:35-37 13:15 [a]Or *brothers* [A]Gen 49:22; Hos 10:1 [B]Gen 41:6; Jer 4:11, 12; Ezek 17:10; 19:12 [C]Jer 51:36 [D]Jer 20:5 13:16 [a]Ch 14:1 in Heb [A]Hos 10:2 [B]Hos 7:14 [C]2 Kin 8:12 [D]Hos 11:6 [E]Hos 10:14 [F]2 Kin 15:16 14:1 [a]Ch 14:2 in Heb [b]Or *in* [A]Hos 6:1; 10:12; 12:6; Joel 2:13 [B]Hos 4:8; 5:5; 9:7 14:2 [a]Or *accept that which is good* [b]So with ancient versions; M.T. *our lips as bulls* [A]Mic 7:18, 19 [B]Ps 51:16, 17; Hos 6:6; Heb 13:15 14:3 [a]Or *fatherless* [A]Ps 33:17; Is 31:1 [B]Hos 8:6; 13:2 [C]Hos 4:12 [D]Ps 10:14; 68:5

13:4–6 Having entered into a marriage covenant with the Lord, Israel was to remain faithful to Him alone (cf. Ex 20:2, 3); yet she forgot Him.

13:7, 8 The lion, leopard, and bear are all native to Israel. Her Protector would now become to her as a wild beast, tearing and devouring (cf. Lv 26:21, 22; Dt 32:24; Eze 14:21).

13:12 bound up ... stored up. Israel's sins are all well-documented and safely preserved for the day of reckoning (cf. 7:2; Dt 32:34, 35; Job 14:17).

13:13 at the opening of the womb. This refers to the birth canal. Employing this figure of giving birth, the Lord likens Ephraim to an unwise child, unwilling to move through to birth. By long deferring a "new birth" with repentance, the nation was like a child remaining in the canal dangerously long and risking death (cf. 2Ki 19:3; Is 37:3; 66:9).

13:14 Placing the strong affirmation of deliverance so abruptly after a denunciation intensified the wonder of His unrequited love (cf. 11:8, 9; Lv 26:44). This can apply to God's restoration of Israel from Assyria, and in future times from all the lands of the dispersion, preserving them and bringing them back to their land for the kingdom of Messiah (Eze 37). It also speaks of the time of personal resurrection as in Da 12:2, 3. Repentant Israelites will be restored to the land and even raised from death to glory. Paul uses this text in 1Co 15:55 (quoting the LXX) to celebrate the future resurrection of the church. The Messiah's great victory over death and the grave is the firstfruits of the full harvest to come, when all believers will likewise experience the power of His resurrection.

13:15 east wind. Refers to Assyria.

13:16 The shocking atrocities mentioned were in keeping with brutalities characteristic of the Assyrians (cf. 2Ki 17:5; Is 13:6; Am 1:13; Na 3:10).

14:1, 2 Israel was invited to return, bringing words of repentance accompanied with obedience, repaying God's gracious acceptance of them with "fruit of our lips."

14:3 orphan. God repeatedly demanded mercy for the orphan (cf. Ex 22:22; Dt 10:18); consequently, Israel could expect to receive His compassion (cf. Lk 15:17–20).

4 I will [A]heal their apostasy,
I will [B]love them freely,
For My anger has [C]turned
away from them.
5 I will be like the [A]dew to Israel;
He will blossom like the [B]lily,
And he will [a]take root like *the*
cedars of [C]Lebanon.
6 His shoots will [a]sprout,
And his [b]beauty will be like
the [A]olive tree
And his fragrance like *the*
cedars of [B]Lebanon.
7 Those who [A]live in his shadow
Will [a]again raise [B]grain,
And they will blossom like the vine.
His renown *will be* like the
wine of Lebanon.

8 O Ephraim, what more have
I to do with [A]idols?
It is I who answer and look after [a]you.
I am like a luxuriant [B]cypress;
From [C]Me comes your fruit.

9 [A]Whoever is wise, let him
understand these things;
Whoever is discerning, let
him know them.
For the [B]ways of the LORD are right,
And the [C]righteous will walk in them,
But [D]transgressors will stumble in them.

14:4 [A]Is 57:18; Hos 6:1 [B]Zeph 3:17 [C]Is 12:1 14:5 [a]Lit *strike his roots* [A]Prov 19:12; Is 26:19 [B]Song 2:1; Matt 6:28 [C]Is 35:2 14:6 [a]Lit *go* [b]Or *splendor* [A]Jer 11:16 [B]Song 4:11 14:7 [a]Or *return, they will raise grain* [A]Ezek 17:23 [B]Hos 2:21, 22 14:8 [a]Lit *him* [A]Job 34:32; Hos 14:3 [B]Is 41:19 [C]Ezek 17:23 14:9 [A]Ps 107:43; Jer 9:12 [B]Ps 111:7, 8; Prov 10:29; Zeph 3:5 [C]Is 26:7 [D]Is 1:28

14:4–8 The ultimate fulfillment of these blessings must be millennial, since Israel has not repented and will not do so in the manner of vv. 2, 3 until the end of the Great Tribulation (cf. Zec 12:10–13:1). The Lord's love is beautifully presented in metaphors taken from the lily, the cedars of Lebanon, and the olive tree.

14:4 apostasy. *See note on Pr 14:14.*

14:7 renown ... like the wine of Lebanon. Their "renown" (lit. "remembrance") denotes worldwide fame and admiration.

14:8 The Lord, not idols, will care for Israel. He, not Israel, is the tree providing shelter and prosperity, the "luxuriant cypress" from whom her fruitfulness would come.

14:9 Representative of the theme of the book, Hosea's epilogue concludes the prophecy by presenting the reader with two ways of living (cf. Dt 30:19, 20; Ps 1). He appeals to all readers to be wise, to choose the Lord's way, for His ways are right (cf. Ps 107:43; Ecc 12:13, 14).

GOD'S LOVINGKINDNESS TO ISRAEL

	HOSEA and GOMER	GOD and ISRAEL
BETROTHAL	Hos 1:2	Assumed; Jer 2:2; Eze 16:8
ONE FLESH	Hos 1:3	Assumed; Jer 3:1; Eze 16:9–14
ADULTERY	Hos 2:2; 3:1	Hos 2:5; 4:12; Jer 3:6; 5:7; Eze 16:15–34
DIVORCE	Hos 3:1	Hos 2:2; Jer 3:8–10, 20; Eze 16:35–59
REMARRIAGE	Hos 3:3–5	Hos 1:10, 11; 2:14–23; 14:4–9; Jer 3:22–4:2; Eze 16:60–63

THE BOOK OF

JOEL

TITLE

The Greek Septuagint (LXX) and Latin Vulgate (Vg.) versions follow the Hebrew Masoretic Text (MT), titling this book after Joel the prophet, the recipient of the message from God (1:1). The name means "the Lord is God" and refers to at least a dozen men in the OT. Joel is referred to only once in the NT (Ac 2:16–21).

AUTHOR AND DATE

The author identified himself only as "Joel, the son of Pethuel" (1:1). The prophecy provides little else about the man. Even the name of his father is not mentioned elsewhere in the OT. Although he displayed a profound zeal for the temple sacrifices (1:9; 2:13–16), his familiarity with pastoral and agricultural life and his separation from the priests (1:13, 14; 2:17) suggest he was not a Levite. Extrabiblical tradition records that he was from the tribe of Reuben, from the town of Bethom or Beth-haram, located NE of the Dead Sea on the border of Reuben and Gad. The context of the prophecy, however, hints that he was a Judean from the Jerusalem vicinity, since the tone of a stranger is absent.

Dating the book relies solely on canonical position, historical allusions, and linguistic elements. Because of: 1) the lack of any mention of later world powers (Assyria, Babylon, or Persia); 2) the fact that Joel's style is like that of Hosea and Amos rather than of the post-Exilic prophets; and 3) the verbal parallels with other early prophets (Joel 3:16/Am 1:2; Joel 3:18/Am 9:13), a late ninth century B.C. date, during the reign of Joash (ca. 835–796 B.C.), seems most convincing. Nevertheless, while the date of the book cannot be known with certainty, the impact on its interpretation is minimal. The message of Joel is timeless, forming doctrine which could be repeated and applied in any age.

BACKGROUND AND SETTING

Tyre, Sidon, and Philistia had made frequent military incursions into Israel (3:2ff.). An extended drought and massive invasion of locusts had stripped every green thing from the land and brought severe economic devastation (1:7–20), leaving the southern kingdom weak. This physical disaster gives Joel the illustration for God's judgment. As the locusts were a judgment on sin, God's future judgments during the Day of the Lord will far exceed them. In that day, God will judge His enemies and bless the faithful. No mention is made of specific sins, nor is Judah rebuked for idolatry. Yet, possibly due to a calloused indifference, the prophet calls them to a bona fide repentance, admonishing them to "rend your heart and not your garments" (2:13).

HISTORICAL AND THEOLOGICAL THEMES

The theme of Joel is the Day of the Lord. It permeates all parts of Joel's message, making it the most sustained treatment in the entire OT (1:15; 2:1; 2:11; 2:31; 3:14). The phrase is employed 19 times by 8 different OT authors (Is 2:12; 13:6, 9; Eze 13:5; 30:3; Joel 1:15; 2:1, 11, 31; 3:14; Am 5:18 [2x], 20; Ob 15; Zep 1:7, 14 [2x]; Zec 14:1; Mal 4:5). The phrase does not have reference to a chronological time period, but to a general period of wrath and judgment uniquely belonging to the Lord. It is exclusively the day which unveils His character—mighty, powerful, and holy, thus terrifying His enemies. The Day of the Lord does not always refer to an eschatological event; on occasion it has a near historical fulfillment, as seen in Eze 13:5, where it speaks of the Babylonian conquest and destruction of Jerusalem. As is common in prophecy, the near fulfillment is a historic event upon which to comprehend the more distant, eschatological fulfillment.

The Day of the Lord is frequently associated with seismic disturbances (e.g., 2:1–11; 2:31; 3:16), violent weather (Eze 13:5ff.), clouds and thick darkness (e.g., 2:2; Zep 1:7ff.), cosmic upheaval (2:3, 30), and as a "great and very awesome" (2:11) day that would "come as destruction from the Almighty" (1:15). The latter half of Joel depicts time immediately prior to and subsequent to the Day of the Lord in terms of promise and hope. There will be a pouring out of the Spirit on all flesh, accompanied by prophetic utterances, dreams, visions (2:28, 29), as well as the coming of Elijah, an epiphany bringing restoration and hope (Mal 4:5, 6). As a result of the Day of the Lord there will be physical blessings, fruitfulness, and prosperity (2:21ff.; 3:16–21). It is a day when judgment is poured out on sinners that subsequently leads to blessings on the penitent, and reaffirmation of God's covenant with His people. *See note on 1Th 5:2.*

INTERPRETIVE CHALLENGES

It is preferable to view chap. 1 as describing an actual invasion of locusts that devastated the land. In chap. 2, a new level of description meets the interpreter. Here the prophet is projecting something beyond the locust plague of chap. 1, elevating the level of description to new heights, with increased intensity that is focused on the plague and the immediate necessity for true repentance. The prophet's choice of similes, such as "like the appearance of horses" (2:4) and "like mighty men" (2:7), suggests that he is still using the actual locusts to illustrate an invasion which can only be the massive overtaking of the final Day of the Lord.

A second issue confronting the interpreter is Peter's quotation from Joel 2:28–32 in Ac 2:16–21. Some have viewed the phenomena of Ac 2 and the destruction of Jerusalem in A.D. 70 as the fulfillment of the Joel passage, while others have reserved its fulfillment to the final Day of the Lord only—but clearly Joel is referring to the final terrible Day of the Lord. The pouring out of the Holy Spirit at Pentecost was not a fulfillment, but a preview and sample of the Spirit's power and work to be released fully and finally in the Messiah's kingdom after the Day of the Lord. *See note on Ac 2:16–21.*

OUTLINE

Following 1:1, the contents of the book are arranged under 3 basic categories. In the first section (1:2–20) the prophet describes the contemporary Day of the Lord. The land is suffering massive devastation caused by a locust plague and drought. The details of the calamity (1:2–12) are followed by a summons to communal penitence and reformation (1:13–20).

The second section (2:1–17) provides a transition from the historical plague of locusts described in chap. 1 to the eschatological Day of the Lord in 2:18–3:21. Employing the contemporary infestation of locusts as a backdrop, the prophet, with an increased level of intensity, paints a vivid and forceful picture of the impending visitation of the Lord (2:1–11) and, with powerful and explicit terminology, tenaciously renews the appeal for repentance (2:12–17).

In the third section (2:18–3:21), the Lord speaks directly, assuring His people of His presence among them (2:27; 3:17, 21). This portion of the book assumes that the repentance solicited (2:12–17) had occurred and describes the Lord's zealous response (2:18, 19a) to their prayer. Joel 2:18–20 forms the transition in the message from lamentation and woe to divine assurances of God's presence and the reversal of the calamities, with 2:19b, 20 introducing the essence and nature of that reversal. The Lord then gives 3 promises to assure the penitents of His presence: material restoration through the divine healing of their land (2:21–27), spiritual restoration through the divine outpouring of His Spirit (2:28–32), and national restoration through the divine judgment on the unrighteous (3:1–21).

OUTLINE

I. Day of the Lord Experienced: Historical (1:1–20)
- A. Source of the Message (1:1)
- B. Command to Contemplate the Devastation (1:2–4)
- C. Completeness of the Devastation (1:5–12)
- D. Call to Repent in Light of the Devastation (1:13–20)

II. Day of the Lord Illustrated: Transitional (2:1–17)
- A. Alarm Sounds (2:1)
- B. Army Invades (2:2–11)
- C. Admonition to Repent (2:12–17)

III. Day of the Lord Described: Eschatological (2:18–3:21)
- A. Introduction (2:18–20)
- B. Material Restoration (2:21–27)
- C. Spiritual Restoration (2:28–32)
- D. National Restoration (3:1–21)

THE DEVASTATION OF LOCUSTS

1 The [A]word of the LORD that came to [B]Joel, the son of Pethuel:

2 [A]Hear this, O [B]elders,
And listen, all inhabitants of the land.
[C]Has *anything like* this
happened in your days
Or in your fathers' days?
3 [A]Tell your sons about it,
And *let* your sons *tell* their sons,
And their sons the next generation.

4 What the [A]gnawing locust has left,
the swarming locust has eaten;
And what the [B]swarming locust has
left, the creeping locust has eaten;
And what the creeping locust has left,
the [C]stripping locust has eaten.
5 Awake, [A]drunkards, and weep;
And wail, all you wine drinkers,
On account of the sweet wine
That is [B]cut off from your mouth.
6 For a [A]nation has [a]invaded my land,
Mighty and without number;
[B]Its teeth are the teeth of a lion,
And it has the fangs of a lioness.
7 It has [A]made my vine a waste
And my fig tree [a]splinters.
It has stripped them bare
and cast *them* away;
Their branches have become white.

8 [A]Wail like a virgin [B]girded with sackcloth
For the bridegroom of her youth.
9 The [A]grain offering and the
drink offering are cut off
From the house of the LORD.
The [B]priests mourn,
The ministers of the LORD.
10 The field is [A]ruined,
[B]The land mourns;
For the grain is ruined,
The new wine dries up,
Fresh oil [a]fails.
11 [a],[A]Be ashamed, O farmers,
Wail, O vinedressers,
For the wheat and the barley;
Because the [B]harvest of the
field is destroyed.

1:1 [A]Jer 1:2; Ezek 1:3; Hos 1:1 [B]Acts 2:16 1:2 [A]Hos 4:1; 5:1 [B]Job 8:8; Joel 1:14 [C]Jer 30:7; Joel 2:2 1:3 [A]Ex 10:2; Ps 78:4 1:4 [A]Deut 28:38; Joel 2:25; Amos 4:9 [B]Nah 3:15, 16 [C]Is 33:4 1:5 [A]Joel 3:3 [B]Is 32:10 1:6 [a]Lit *come up against* [A]Joel 2:2, 11, 25 [B]Rev 9:8 1:7 [a]Or *a stump* [A]Is 5:6; Amos 4:9 1:8 [A]Is 22:12 [B]Joel 1:13; Amos 8:10 1:9 [A]Hos 9:4; Joel 1:13; 2:14 [B]Joel 2:17 1:10 [a]Lit *wastes away* [A]Is 24:4, 7 [B]Jer 12:11 1:11 [a]Or *The farmers are ashamed, The vinedressers wail* [A]Jer 14:4; Amos 5:16 [B]Is 17:11; Jer 9:12

1:1 The word of the LORD. This introductory phrase is commonly employed by the prophets to indicate that the message was divinely commissioned. Cf. Hos 1:1; Mic 1:1; Zep 1:1. Slightly varied forms are found in 1Sa 15:10; 2Sa 24:11; Jer 1:2; Eze 1:3; Jon 1:1; Zec 1:1; Mal 1:1. **LORD.** A distinctively Israelitish designation for God; the name speaks of intimacy and a relationship bonded metaphorically through the covenant likened to marriage and thus carries special significance to Israel (Ex 3:14). **Joel.** His name means "the Lord is God." **Pethuel.** His name means "openheartedness of/toward God" and is the only occurrence of this name in the Bible.

1:2–20 The prophet described the contemporary day of the Lord. The land was suffering massive devastation caused by a locust plague and drought. The details of the calamity (vv. 2–12) are followed by a summons to communal penitence and reformation (vv. 13–20).

1:2 Hear … listen. The gravity of the situation demanded the undivided focus of their senses, emphasizing the need to make a conscious, purposeful decision in the matter. The terminology was commonly used in "lawsuit" passages (cf. Is 1:2; Hos 4:1), intimating that Israel was found guilty and that the present judgment was her "sentence." **elders … all inhabitants.** The former term refers to the civil and religious leaders, who, in light of their position, were exhorted to lead by example the entire population toward repentance.

1:3 Tell … sons … next generation. The pedagogical importance of reciting the Lord's mighty acts to subsequent generations is heavily underscored by the 3-fold injunction (cf. Ex 10:1–6; Dt 4:9; 6:6, 7; 11:19; 32:7; Pss 78:5–7; 145:4–7; Pr 4:1ff.).

1:4 locust. The 4 kinds of locusts refer to their species or their stages of development. Cf. 2:25, where the writer mentions them in different order. The total destruction caused by their voracious appetites demands repentance (cf. Dt 28:38; Is 33:4; Am 7:1).

1:5–12 Total destruction affected all social and economic levels. Affected were the drunkards who delighted in the abundance of the vine (vv. 5–7), the priests who utilized the produce in the offerings (vv. 8–10), and the farmers who planted, cultivated, and reaped the harvest (vv. 11, 12). As if building toward a crescendo, the prophet noted in the first stanza that the luxuries of life were withdrawn. In the second, the elements needed to worship were interrupted. In the third, the essentials for living were snatched away. To lose the enjoyment of wine was one thing; to no longer be able to outwardly worship God was another; but to have nothing to eat was the sentence of death!

1:5 Awake … weep … wail. The drunkards were to awaken to the realization that their wine would be no more. They were to weep bitterly and to wail. The severity of the devastation called for public, communal mourning. **sweet wine.** The term can denote either freshly squeezed grape juice or newly fermented wine (cf. Is 49:26).

1:6, 7 my land … vine … fig tree. The possessive pronoun refers to the Lord. He is the owner of the land (cf. Lv 25:23; Nu 36:2; Eze 38:16), the vine, and the fig tree (cf. Hos 2:9). Instead of symbols of prosperity and peace (1Ki 4:25; Mic 4:4; Zec 3:10), the vine and fig tree had become visual reminders of divine judgment.

1:6 a nation. A literal invasion of locusts pictured the kind of destruction and judgment inflicted by human armies. **teeth of a lion.** Joel described these hostile, countless locusts as possessing the "fangs of a lioness," so able were they to devour anything in their path. They are occasionally used as symbolic of violence (Ge 49:9; Nu 23:24) and of the violent, awesome nature of God's judgment (Is 30:6; Hos 13:8).

1:8, 9 The metaphor is significant because the OT speaks of the Lord as the husband of Israel, His wife (Is 54:5–8; Jer 31:32). The covenantal offerings and libations could not be carried out; Israel, the wife of the Lord, was to repent, lest her relationship with the Lord became like that of the young widowed maiden.

1:8 Wail like a virgin. As with the drunkards, the religious leaders were to wail as a young maiden would upon the death of her youthful husband, wherein she exchanged the silky fabric of a wedding dress and the joy of a wedding feast for the scratchy, coarse clothing of goat's hair and the cry of a funeral dirge. The term "virgin" lacks the notion of virginity in many cases (e.g., Est 2:17; Eze 23:3), and when coupled together with the term "bridegroom," it points to a young maiden widowed shortly after marriage. **sackcloth.** Fabric generally made of goat's hair, usually black or dark in color (cf. Rev 6:12), and usually placed on the bare body around the hips (Ge 37:34; 1Ki 21:27), leaving the chest free for "beating" (Is 32:11, 12), was used in the ancient world to depict sorrow and penitence (Ne 9:1; Is 37:1; Mt 11:21). Because the prophets' message usually dealt with a call to repentance, it became the principal garment worn by prophets (Mt 3:4; Rev 11:3).

1:9 grain offering … drink offering are cut off. To cut off these offerings, sacrificed each morning and evening (Ex 29:38–42; Lv 23:13), was to cut off the people from the covenant. The gravity of the situation was deepened by the fact that it threatened the livelihood of the priests, who were given a portion of most sacrifices.

1:11 Be ashamed, O farmers. The primary emphasis of the Heb. term connotes a public disgrace, a physical state to which the guilty party has been forcibly brought.

12 The [A]vine dries up
And the fig tree [a]fails;
The [B]pomegranate, the [C]palm
also, and the [b,D]apple tree,
All the trees of the field dry up.
Indeed, [E]rejoicing dries up
From the sons of men.

13 [A]Gird yourselves *with sackcloth*
And lament, O priests;
[B]Wail, O ministers of the altar!
Come, [C]spend the night in sackcloth
O ministers of my God,
For the grain offering and
the drink offering
Are withheld from the house of your God.

STARVATION AND DROUGHT

14 [A]Consecrate a fast,
Proclaim a [B]solemn assembly;
Gather the elders
And all the inhabitants of the land
To the house of the LORD your God,
And [C]cry out to the LORD.
15 [A]Alas for the day!
For the [B]day of the LORD is near,
And it will come as [C]destruction
from the [a]Almighty.
16 Has not [A]food been cut off
before our eyes,
Gladness and [B]joy from the
house of our God?
17 The [a,A]seeds shrivel under their [b]clods;
The storehouses are desolate,
The barns are torn down,
For the grain is dried up.
18 How [A]the beasts groan!
The herds of cattle wander aimlessly
Because there is no pasture for them;
Even the flocks of sheep [a]suffer.
19 [A]To You, O LORD, I cry;
For [B]fire has devoured the
pastures of the wilderness
And the flame has burned up
all the trees of the field.
20 Even the beasts of the
field [a,A]pant for You;
For the [B]water brooks are dried up
And fire has devoured the
pastures of the wilderness.

THE TERRIBLE VISITATION

2 [A]Blow a trumpet in Zion,
And sound an alarm on My
holy mountain!
Let all the inhabitants of the land tremble,
For the [B]day of the LORD is coming;
Surely it is near,
2 A day of [A]darkness and gloom,
A day of clouds and thick darkness.
As the dawn is spread over
the mountains,
So there is a [B]great and mighty people;
There has [C]never been *anything* like it,
Nor will there be again after it
To the years of many generations.
3 A [A]fire consumes before them
And behind them a flame burns.
The land is [B]like the garden
of Eden before them
But a [C]desolate wilderness behind them,
And nothing at all escapes them.

1:12 [a]Lit *wastes away* [b]Or *apricot* [A]Joel 1:10; Hab 3:17 [B]Hag 2:19 [C]Song 7:8 [D]Song 2:3 [E]Is 16:10; 24:11; Jer 48:33 1:13 [A]Jer 4:8; Ezek 7:18 [B]Jer 9:10 [C]1 Kin 21:27 1:14 [A]Joel 2:15, 16 [B]Lev 23:36 [C]Jon 3:8 1:15 [a]Heb *Shaddai* [A]Is 13:9; Jer 30:7; Amos 5:16 [B]Joel 2:1, 11, 31 [C]Is 13:6; Ezek 7:2-12 1:16 [A]Is 3:7; Amos 4:6 [B]Deut 12:7; Ps 43:4 1:17 [a]Or *dried figs* [b]Or *shovels* [A]Is 17:10, 11 1:18 [a]Lit *bear punishment* [A]1 Kin 8:5; Jer 12:4; 14:5, 6; Hos 4:3 1:19 [A]Ps 50:15; Mic 7:7 [B]Jer 9:10; Amos 7:4 1:20 [a]Lit *long for* [A]Ps 104:21; 147:9; Joel 1:18 [B]1 Kin 17:7; 18:5 2:1 [A]Jer 4:5; Joel 2:15; Zeph 1:16 [B]Joel 1:15; 2:11, 31; 3:14; Obad 15; Zeph 1:14 2:2 [A]Joel 2:10, 31; Amos 5:18; Zeph 1:15 [B]Joel 1:6; 2:11, 25 [C]Lam 1:12; Dan 9:12; 12:1; Joel 1:2 2:3 [A]Ps 97:3; Is 9:18, 19 [B]Is 51:3; Ezek 36:35 [C]Ex 10:5, 15; Ps 105:34, 35; Zech 7:14

1:12 All the trees ... dry up. The picture was bleak, for even the deep roots of the trees could not withstand the torturous treatment administered by the locusts, especially when accompanied by an extended drought. **rejoicing dries up.** Human joy and delight had departed from all segments of society; none had escaped the grasp of the locusts. The joy that normally accompanied the time of harvest had been replaced with despair.

1:14 Consecrate a fast. The prophet called the priests to take action, first by example (v. 13) and then by proclamation (v. 14). As the official leaders, it was their duty to proclaim a public fast so that the entire nation could repent and petition the Lord to forgive and restore. Here they were admonished to "consecrate" a fast, denoting its urgent, sacred character. **Proclaim a solemn assembly.** Directives for calling an assembly, generally for festive purposes (cf. 2Ch 7:9; Neh 8:18), are given in Nu 10:3. Parallel in thought to "consecrate a fast," no work was permitted on such days (Lv 23:36; Nu 29:35; Dt 16:8).

1:15 the day of the LORD is near. See Introduction: Historical and Theological Themes. This is the first occurrence of the theme. Later in the book (2:18ff.; 3:1, 18–21), the day of the Lord (the occasion when God pours out His wrath on man) results in blessing and exoneration for God's people and judgment toward Gentiles (Is 13:6; Eze 30:3), but here Joel directs the warning toward his own people. The day of the Lord is speedily approaching; unless sinners repent, dire consequences await them. **destruction from the Almighty.** The Heb. term "destruction" forms a powerful play on words with the "Almighty." The notion of invincible strength is foremost; destruction at the hand of omnipotent God is coming.

1:17, 18 seeds shrivel ... beasts groan. From the spiritual realm to the physical realm, all was in shambles. Though innocent, in judgment even the animals suffered (cf. Ro 8:18–22) the loss of food.

1:19 To You, O LORD, I cry. As the first to call to repentance, the prophet had to be the first to heed the warning. He had to lead by example and motivate the people to respond. In the midst of proclaiming judgment, God's prophets often led in intercessory prayer for mercy and forgiveness (cf. Ex 32:11–14; Jer 42:1–4; Da 9:1–19; Am 7:1–6).

2:1–17 With an increased level of intensity, Joel utilized the metaphor of the locust plague and drought as a backdrop from which to launch an intensified call to repent in view of the coming invasion of Judah and the day of the Lord, present and future.

2:1 Blow a trumpet. In the ancient world, horns were used to gather people for special occasions or to warn of danger (Ex 19:13, 16, 19; 20:18; Nu 10:1–10; Is 27:13; Am 3:6; Zep 1:14–16; Zec 9:14; 1Th 4:16). The term here refers to a ram's horn. **day of the LORD.** *See note on 1:15.*

2:2–11 In dramatic and vivid language, Joel compared the drought and locusts to fire, horses, and an invading army.

2:2 darkness and gloom ... clouds and thick darkness. These features describe the blackness of a locust invasion, so thick that it blots out the sun with its deadly living cloud of insects. Such terms are also often common figures for misery and calamity in the OT (Is 8:22; 60:2; Jer 13:16; Am 5:18, 20; Zep 1:15) and past visitations of the Lord (Ex 10:12ff.; 19:16–19; 24:16; Dt 4:12; 5:22, 23).

4 Their [A]appearance is like the
appearance of horses;
And like war horses, so they run.
5 [a]With a [A]noise as of chariots
They leap on the tops of the mountains,
Like the [b]crackling of a [B]flame of
fire consuming the stubble,
Like a mighty people arranged for battle.
6 Before them the people are in [A]anguish;
All [B]faces [a]turn pale.
7 They run like mighty men,
They climb the wall like soldiers;
And they each [A]march [a]in line,
Nor do they deviate from their paths.
8 They do not crowd each other,
They march everyone in his path;
When they [a]burst through the [b]defenses,
They do not break ranks.
9 They rush on the city,
They run on the wall;
They climb into the [A]houses,
They [B]enter through the windows like a thief.
10 Before them the earth [A]quakes,
The heavens tremble,

2:4 [A]Rev 9:7 2:5 [a]Lit *Like the noise of chariots* [b]Lit *noise* [A]Rev 9:9 [B]Is 5:24; 30:30 2:6 [a]Or *become flushed* [A]Is 13:8; Nah 2:10 [B]Jer 30:6 2:7 [a]Lit *in his ways* [A]Prov 30:27 2:8 [a]Lit *fall* [b]Lit *weapon,* probably *javelin* 2:9 [A]Ex 10:6 [B]Jer 9:21; John 10:1 2:10 [A]Ps 18:7; Joel 3:16; Nah 1:5

2:4 Their appearance is like … horses. The resemblance of the locust's head to that of a horse is striking, so much so that the prophet reiterates the word "appearance." Horses were not used for agricultural purposes in ancient times, but were the most feared military equipment (Ex 15:1ff., 19; Dt 20:1; Jos 11:4). The simile continues with "as of chariots" (v. 5); "like a mighty people" (v. 5); "like mighty men" (v. 7); and "like soldiers" (v. 7).

2:10 earth quakes … sun and the moon grow dark. The ground trembles as dust flies along with the growing devastation. Earthquakes and cosmic disruptions are well attested elsewhere as signs accompanying divine appearances (Jdg 5:4; Ps 18:7; Jer 4:23–26; Na 1:5, 6; Mt 24:7). Joel later refers to these signs (cf. 2:31; 3:15).

DAY OF THE LORD

SEVENTEEN EXPLICIT MENTIONS OF "DAY OF THE LORD" IN THE OLD TESTAMENT
1. Obadiah 15
2. Joel 1:15
3. Joel 2:1
4. Joel 2:11
5. Joel 2:31
6. Joel 3:14
7. Amos 5:18
8. Amos 5:18
9. Amos 5:20
10. Isaiah 13:6
11. Isaiah 13:9
12. Zephaniah 1:7
13. Zephaniah 1:14
14. Zephaniah 1:14
15. Ezekiel 13:5
16. Ezekiel 30:3
17. Malachi 4:5

FOUR EXPLICIT MENTIONS OF "DAY OF THE LORD" IN THE NEW TESTAMENT
1. Acts 2:20
2. 1 Thessalonians 5:2
3. 2 Thessalonians 2:2
4. 2 Peter 3:10

The [B]sun and the moon grow dark
And the stars lose their brightness.
11 The LORD [A]utters His voice
before [B]His army;
Surely His camp is very great,
For [C]strong is he who carries
out His word.
The [D]day of the LORD is indeed
great and very awesome,
And [E]who can endure it?
12 "Yet even now," declares the LORD,
"[A]Return to Me with all your heart,
And with [B]fasting, weeping
and mourning;
13 And [A]rend your heart and
not [B]your garments."
Now return to the LORD your God,
For He is [C]gracious and compassionate,
Slow to anger, abounding
in lovingkindness
And [D]relenting of evil.
14 Who knows [A]whether He will
not turn and relent
And leave a [B]blessing behind Him,
Even [C]a grain offering and
a drink offering
For the LORD your God?
15 [A]Blow a trumpet in Zion,
[B]Consecrate a fast, proclaim
a solemn assembly,
16 Gather the people, [A]sanctify
the congregation,
Assemble the elders,
Gather the children and the
nursing infants.
Let the [B]bridegroom come
out of his room
And the bride out of her *bridal* chamber.
17 Let the priests, the LORD'S ministers,
Weep [A]between the porch and the altar,
And let them say, "[B]Spare
Your people, O LORD,
And do not make Your
inheritance a [C]reproach,
A byword among the nations.
Why should they among the peoples say,
'[D]Where is their God?' "

DELIVERANCE PROMISED

18 Then the LORD [a]will be [A]zealous for His land
And [b]will have [B]pity on His people.
19 The LORD [a]will answer and
say to His people,
"Behold, I am going to [A]send you
grain, new wine and oil,
And you will be satisfied *in full* with [b]them;
And I will [B]never again make you a
reproach among the nations.
20 "But I will remove the [A]northern
army far from you,
And I will drive it into a parched
and desolate land,
And its vanguard into the [B]eastern sea,
And its rear guard into the [C]western sea.
And its [D]stench will arise and its
foul smell will come up,
For it has done great things."

21 [A]Do not fear, O land, rejoice and be glad,
For the LORD has done [B]great things.
22 Do not fear, beasts of the field,
For the [A]pastures of the wilderness
have turned green,
For the tree has borne its fruit,
The fig tree and the vine
have yielded [a]in full.
23 So rejoice, O [A]sons of Zion,
And [B]be glad in the LORD your God;
For He has [C]given you [a]the early
rain for *your* vindication.
And He has poured down for you the rain,
The [b]early and [c,D]latter rain [d]as before.
24 The threshing floors will be full of grain,
And the vats will [A]overflow with
the new wine and oil.
25 "Then I will make up to you for the years
That the swarming [A]locust has eaten,
The creeping locust, the stripping
locust and the gnawing locust,
My great army which I sent among you.
26 "You will have plenty to [A]eat and be satisfied
And [B]praise the name of the LORD your God,
Who has [C]dealt wondrously with you;
Then My people will [D]never
be put to shame.

2:10 [B]Is 13:10; 34:4; Jer 4:23; Ezek 32:7, 8; Joel 2:31; 3:15; Matt 24:29; Rev 8:12 2:11 [A]Ps 46:6; Is 13:4; Jer 25:30; Joel 3:16 [B]Joel 2:25 [C]Jer 50:34; Rev 18:8 [D]Jer 30:7; Joel 1:15; 2:1, 31; 3:14; Zeph 1:14, 15; Rev 6:17 [E]Ezek 22:14; Mal 3:2 2:12 [A]Deut 4:29; Jer 4:1, 2; Ezek 33:11; Hos 12:6 [B]Dan 9:3 2:13 [A]Ps 34:18; 51:17; Is 57:15 [B]Gen 37:34; 2 Sam 1:11; Job 1:20; Jer 41:5 [C]Ex 34:6 [D]Jer 18:8; 42:10; Amos 7:3, 6 2:14 [A]Jer 26:3; Jon 3:9 [B]Hag 2:19 [C]Joel 1:9, 13 2:15 [A]Num 10:3; 2 Kin 10:20 [B]Joel 1:14 2:16 [A]1 Sam 16:5; 2 Chr 29:5 [B]Ps 19:5 2:17 [A]2 Chr 8:12; Ezek 8:16 [B]Ex 32:11, 12; Is 37:20; Amos 7:2, 5 [C]Ps 44:13; 74:10 [D]Ps 42:10; 79:10; 115:2 2:18 [a]Or *was zealous* [b]Or *had pity* [A]Zech 1:14; 8:2 [B]Is 60:10; 63:9, 15 2:19 [a]Or *answered and said* [b]Lit *it* [A]Jer 31:12; Hos 2:21, 22; Joel 1:10; Mal 3:10 [B]Ezek 34:29; 36:15 2:20 [A]Jer 1:14, 15 [B]Zech 14:8 [C]Deut 11:24 [D]Is 34:3; Amos 4:10 2:21 [A]Is 54:4; Jer 30:10; Zeph 3:16, 17 [B]Ps 126:3; Joel 2:26 2:22 [a]Lit *their wealth* [A]Ps 65:12, 13 2:23 [a]I.e. autumn; or possibly *the teacher for righteousness* [b]I.e. autumn [c]I.e. spring [d]So with ancient versions; Heb *in the first* [A]Ps 149:2 [B]Is 12:2-6 [C]Deut 11:14; Is 41:16; Jer 5:24; Hab 3:18; Zech 10:7 [D]Lev 26:4; Hos 6:3; Zech 10:1 2:24 [A]Lev 26:10; Amos 9:13; Mal 3:10 2:25 [A]Joel 1:4-7; 2:2-11 2:26 [A]Lev 26:5; Deut 11:15; Is 62:9 [B]Deut 12:7; Ps 67:5-7 [C]Ps 126:2, 3; Is 25:1 [D]Is 45:17

2:12–14 Even in the midst of judgment, opportunity to repent was given. If they would demonstrate genuine repentance, the Lord stood ready to forgive and bless.

2:16 From oldest to youngest they were to come. The situation is so grave that even the groom and bride were exhorted to assemble (cf. Dt 24:5); consummation of the marriage could wait.

2:18–3:21 With the advent of v. 18, the text makes a decisive transition, devoting the remainder of the book to restoration. It assumes an interval of time between v. 17 and v. 18 during which Israel repented. As a result of her repentance, the 3 major concerns of 1:1–2:17 are answered by the Lord: physical restoration (2:21–27), spiritual restoration (2:28–32), and national restoration (3:1–21).

2:20 northern *army*. Although some have viewed this as a reference to the locusts, it is more likely referring to a military invasion by a country coming down from the N of Israel (cf. Eze 38:6, 15; 39:2). That future army will be driven into the eastern sea (Dead Sea) and the western sea (Mediterranean Sea).

2:21–24 Reminiscent of 1:18–20, the former situation had been reversed. The animals were admonished to be afraid no longer.

2:23, 24 early and latter rain. The early rains came in Oct.-Dec. to prepare the seed-bed and assist germination, while the latter rains came in Mar.-May to provide ample moisture for the grain and fruit crops to be rich and full.

27 "Thus you will [A]know that I am
in the midst of Israel,
And that I am the LORD your God,
And there is [B]no other;
And My people will never be [C]put to shame.

THE PROMISE OF THE SPIRIT

28 "[a,A]It will come about after this
That I will [B]pour out My Spirit
on all [b,C]mankind;
And your sons and daughters will prophesy,
Your old men will dream dreams,
Your young men will see visions.
29 "Even on the [A]male and female servants
I will pour out My Spirit in those days.

THE DAY OF THE LORD

30 "I will [A]display wonders in the
sky and on the earth,
Blood, fire and columns of smoke.
31 "The [A]sun will be turned into darkness
And the moon into blood
Before the [B]great and awesome
day of the LORD comes.
32 "And it will come about that [A]whoever
calls on the name of the LORD
Will be delivered;
For [B]on Mount Zion and in Jerusalem
There will be those who [C]escape,
As the LORD has said,
Even among the [D]survivors
whom the LORD calls.

THE NATIONS WILL BE JUDGED

3 "[a]For behold, [A]in those days and at that time,
When I [B]restore the fortunes of
Judah and Jerusalem,
2 I will [A]gather all the nations
And bring them down to the
[B]valley of [a]Jehoshaphat.
Then I will [C]enter into judgment
with them there
On behalf of My people and
My inheritance, Israel,
Whom they have [D]scattered
among the nations;
And they have [E]divided up My land.
3 "They have also [A]cast
lots for My people,
[a,B]Traded a boy for a harlot
And sold a girl for wine that
they may drink.

4 Moreover, what are you to Me, O [A]Tyre, Sidon and
all the regions of [B]Philistia? Are you rendering Me a
recompense? But if you do recompense Me, swiftly
and speedily I will [C]return your recompense on your
head. 5 Since you have [A]taken My silver and My gold,
brought My precious [a]treasures to your temples,
6 and sold the [A]sons of Judah and Jerusalem to the
[a]Greeks in order to remove them far from their territory, 7 behold, I am going to [A]arouse them from the
place where you have sold them, and return your
recompense on your head. 8 Also I will [A]sell your
sons and your daughters into the hand of the sons
of Judah, and they will sell them to the [B]Sabeans, to
a distant nation," for the LORD has spoken.

9 [A]Proclaim this among the nations:
[B]Prepare a war; [C]rouse the mighty men!
Let all the soldiers draw near,
let them come up!
10 [A]Beat your plowshares into swords
And your pruning hooks into spears;
[B]Let the weak say, "I am a mighty man."
11 [a,A]Hasten and come, all you
surrounding nations,
And gather yourselves there.
Bring down, O LORD,
Your [B]mighty ones.

2:27 [A]Lev 26:11, 12; Joel 3:17, 21 [B]Is 45:5, 6 [C]Is 49:23 2:28 [a]Ch 3:1 in Heb [b]Lit *flesh* [A]Acts 2:17-21 [B]Is 32:15; 44:3; Ezek 39:29; Zech 12:10 [C]Is 40:5; 49:26 2:29 [A]1 Cor 12:13; Gal 3:28 2:30 [A]Matt 24:29; Mark 13:24, 25; Luke 21:11, 25, 26; Acts 2:19 2:31 [A]Is 13:10; 34:4; Joel 2:10; 3:15; Matt 24:29; Mark 13:24; Luke 21:25; Acts 2:20; Rev 6:12, 13 [B]Is 13:9; Zeph 1:14-16; Mal 4:1, 5 2:32 [A]Jer 33:3; Acts 2:21; Rom 10:13 [B]Is 46:13; Rom 11:26 [C]Is 4:2; Obad 17 [D]Is 11:11; Jer 31:7; Mic 4:7; Rom 9:27 3:1 [a]Ch 4:1 in Heb [A]Jer 30:3; Ezek 38:14 [B]Jer 16:15 3:2 [a]I.e. YHWH judges [A]Is 66:18; Mic 4:12; Zech 14:2 [B]Joel 3:12, 14 [C]Is 66:16; Jer 25:31; Ezek 38:22 [D]Jer 50:17; Ezek 34:6 [E]Ezek 35:10; 36:1-5 3:3 [a]Lit *Given* [A]Obad 11; Nah 3:10 [B]Amos 2:6 3:4 [A]Is 23:1-18; Amos 1:9, 10; Zech 9:2-4; Matt 11:21, 22; Luke 10:13, 14 [B]Is 14:29-31; Jer 47:1-7; Ezek 25:15-17; Amos 1:6-8; Zech 9:5-7 [C]Is 34:8; 59:18 3:5 [a]Lit *goodly things* [A]2 Kin 12:18; 2 Chr 21:16, 17 3:6 [a]Lit *sons of Javan* [A]Ezek 27:13 3:7 [A]Is 43:5, 6; Jer 23:8; Zech 9:13 3:8 [A]Is 14:2; 60:14 [B]Job 1:15; Ps 72:10; Ezek 38:13 3:9 [A]Jer 51:27 [B]Jer 6:4; Ezek 38:7; Mic 3:5 [C]Is 8:9, 10; Jer 46:3, 4; Zech 14:2, 3 3:10 [A]Is 2:4; Mic 4:3 [B]Zech 12:8 3:11 [a]Or *Lend aid* [A]Ezek 38:15, 16 [B]Is 13:3

2:27 I am in the midst of Israel. This return promised a reversal of the Lord's departure (cf. Eze 8–11).

2:28–32 See Introduction: Interpretive Challenges; *see notes on Ac 2:16–21.*

2:28 after this. The abundance of material blessings would be followed by the outpouring of spiritual blessings. When coupled with the other temporal phrases within the passage ("in those days" [v. 29] and "before the great and awesome day of the LORD comes" [v. 31]), the term points to a Second Advent fulfillment time frame. **all mankind.** Since the context is "your sons and daughters," "all mankind" best refers to the house of Israel only. The nations are the recipients of God's wrath, not the effusion of His Spirit (cf. 3:2, 9ff.).

2:30, 31 Before ... day of the LORD. Unmistakable heavenly phenomena will signal the imminent arrival of God's wrath in the day of the Lord (cf. v. 10; *see note on 1:15*).

2:32 whoever calls. Quoted by Paul in Ro 10:13. **survivors.** In spite of the nation's sin, God promised to fulfill His unconditional covenants (Noahic, Abrahamic, Davidic, and New). A future remnant of Jews will inherit God's promised blessings (cf. Is 10:20–22; 11:11, 16; Jer 31:7; Mic 2:12; Zep 3:13; Ro 9:27).

3:1–21 Joel notes the national restoration of Israel, in which the people will be regathered to Israel (Is 11:15, 16; Mt 24:31).

3:2 gather all the nations. The nations of the world will be gathered to Jerusalem to the battle of Armageddon (Zec 12:3; 14:2; Rev 16:16; 19:11–21). **valley of Jehoshaphat.** The name means "Yahweh judges" (cf. 3:12, 14) and although the exact location is unknown, other prophets spoke of this judgment as occurring near Jerusalem (Eze 38, 39; Da 11:45; Zec 9:14ff.; 12:1ff.). This judgment of the nations includes the event of Mt 25:31–46.

3:5, 6 The exact historical event referred to here is uncertain. Slave trading was a common practice among the Phoenicians and Philistines.

3:6 the Greeks. Although not prominent militarily, the Greeks were active in commerce on the Mediterranean in the 9th century B.C.

3:7, 8 The reversal of fortunes will be startling. The victims themselves will be called upon to be the instruments and avengers of the Lord's wrath (cf. Is 11:12–14; Zec 12:8).

3:8 Sabeans. Trading merchants who lived in Arabia (1Ki 10; Jer 6:20).

3:9–17 Joel resumes the theme of vv. 1–3, the gathering of the nations to the earthly courtroom, the valley of Jehoshaphat. The sentence has been handed down and the Judge orders His agents to ready the scene for the execution.

12 Let the nations be aroused
And come up to the [A]valley
of [a]Jehoshaphat,
For there I will sit to [B]judge
All the surrounding nations.
13 [A]Put in the sickle, for the [B]harvest is ripe.
Come, [C]tread, for the [D]wine
press is full;
The vats overflow, for their
[E]wickedness is great.
14 [A]Multitudes, multitudes in the
[B]valley of [a]decision!
For the [C]day of the LORD is near
in the valley of [a]decision.
15 The [A]sun and moon grow dark
And the stars lose their brightness.
16 The LORD [A]roars from Zion
And [B]utters His voice from Jerusalem,
And the [C]heavens and the earth tremble.
But the LORD is a [D]refuge for His people
And a [E]stronghold to the sons of Israel.
17 Then you will [A]know that I am
the LORD your God,
Dwelling in Zion, My [B]holy mountain.
So Jerusalem will be [C]holy,
And [D]strangers will pass
through it no more.

JUDAH WILL BE BLESSED

18 And in that day
The [A]mountains will drip
with [a]sweet wine,
And the hills will [B]flow with milk,
And all the [C]brooks of Judah
will flow with water;
And a [D]spring will go out from
the house of the LORD
To water the valley of [b]Shittim.
19 Egypt will become a waste,
And Edom will become a
desolate wilderness,
Because of the [A]violence [a]done
to the sons of Judah,
In whose land they have
shed innocent blood.
20 But Judah will be [A]inhabited forever
And Jerusalem for all generations.
21 And I will [A]avenge their blood
which I have not avenged,
For the LORD dwells in Zion.

3:12 [a]I.e. YHWH judges [A]Joel 3:2, 14 [B]Ps 7:6; 96:13; 98:9; Is 2:4; 3:13 3:13 [A]Rev 14:14-19 [B]Jer 51:33; Hos 6:11 [C]Rev 14:19, 20; 19:15 [D]Is 63:3; Lam 1:15 [E]Gen 18:20 3:14 [a]I.e. God's verdict [A]Is 34:2-8 [B]Joel 3:2, 12 [C]Joel 1:15; 2:1, 11, 31 3:15 [A]Joel 2:10, 31 3:16 [A]Hos 11:10; Amos 1:2 [B]Joel 2:11 [C]Ezek 38:19; Joel 2:10; Hag 2:6 [D]Ps 61:3; Is 33:16; Jer 17:17 [E]Jer 16:19; Nah 1:7 3:17 [A]Joel 2:27 [B]Is 11:9; 56:7; Ezek 20:40 [C]Is 4:3; Obad 17 [D]Is 52:1; Nah 1:15 3:18 [a]Lit *freshly pressed out grape juice* [b]Or *acacias* [A]Amos 9:13 [B]Ex 3:8 [C]Is 30:25; 35:6 [D]Ezek 47:1-12 3:19 [a]Lit *of the sons* [A]Obad 10 3:20 [A]Ezek 37:25; Amos 9:15 3:21 [A]Is 4:4

3:14 valley of decision. This location is the same as the valley of Jehoshaphat where the sentence of judgment will be carried out (cf. 3:2, 12). *See note on 3:2.*

3:15, 16 sun … moon … stars. Cf. 2:10, 30, 31. These are signs that precede the coming eschatological day of the Lord at the end of the Great Tribulation (cf. Mt 24:29, 30).

3:17 Zion, My holy mountain. This will be the earthly location of God's presence in the millennial temple (cf. Eze 40–48) at Jerusalem. **will pass through it no more.** God has promised a future time when His glory in Judah will not be eclipsed. This time of ultimate peace and prosperity will be experienced after Christ conquers the world and sets up His millennial kingdom on earth (cf. Eze 37:24–28; Mt 24, 25; Rev 19).

3:18 valley of Shittim. Known for its acacia trees, the valley was situated on the northern shores of the Dead Sea and served as the final stopover for Israel prior to her entrance into the Promised Land (Nu 25:1; Jos 2:1; 3:1). This valley is also the place to which the millennial river will flow (Eze 47:1–12; Zec 14:8).

3:20 Judah … forever. This is in reference to Christ's millennial kingdom on earth, which is yet to be fulfilled.

THE BOOK OF

AMOS

TITLE

As with each of the Minor Prophets, the title comes from the name of the prophet to whom God gave His message (1:1). Amos' name means "burden" or "burden-bearer." He is not to be confused with Amoz ("stout, strong"), the father of Isaiah (Is 1:1).

AUTHOR AND DATE

Amos was from Tekoa, a small village 10 mi. S of Jerusalem. He was the only prophet to give his occupation before declaring his divine commission. He was not of priestly or noble descent, but worked as a "sheepherder" (1:1; cf. 2Ki 3:4) and a "grower of sycamore figs" (7:14) and was a contemporary of Jonah (2Ki 14:25), Hosea (Hos 1:1), and Isaiah (Is 1:1). The date of writing is mid-eighth century B.C., during the reigns of Uzziah, king of Judah (ca. 790–739 B.C.) and Jeroboam II, king of Israel (ca. 793–753 B.C.), two years before a memorable earthquake (1:1; cf. Zec 14:5).

BACKGROUND AND SETTING

Amos was a Judean prophet called to deliver a message primarily to the northern tribes of Israel (7:15). Politically, it was a time of prosperity under the long and secure reign of Jeroboam II who, following the example of his father Joash (2Ki 13:25), significantly "restored the border of Israel" (2Ki 14:25). It was also a time of peace with both Judah (cf. 5:5) and her more distant neighbors; the ever-present menace of Assyria was subdued, possibly because of Nineveh's repentance at the preaching of Jonah (Jon 3:10). Spiritually, however, it was a time of rampant corruption and moral decay (4:1; 5:10–13; 2Ki 14:24).

HISTORICAL AND THEOLOGICAL THEMES

Amos addresses Israel's two primary sins: 1) an absence of true worship, and 2) a lack of justice. In the midst of their ritualistic performance of worship, they were not pursuing the Lord with their hearts (4:4, 5; 5:4–6) nor following His standard of justice with their neighbors (5:10–13; 6:12). This apostasy, evidenced by continual, willful rejection of the prophetic message of Amos, is promised divine judgment. Because of His covenant, however, the Lord will not abandon Israel altogether, but will bring future restoration to the righteous remnant (9:7–15).

INTERPRETIVE CHALLENGES

In 9:11, the Lord promised that He "will raise up the fallen booth of David." At the Jerusalem Council, convened to discuss whether Gentiles should be allowed into the church without requiring circumcision, James quotes this passage (Ac 15:15, 16) to support Peter's report of how God had taken "from among the Gentiles a people for His name" (Ac 15:14). Some have thus concluded that the passage was fulfilled in Jesus, the greater Son of David, through whom the dynasty of David was reestablished. The Acts reference, however, is best seen as an illustration of Amos' words and not the fulfillment. The temporal allusions to a future time ("In that day," 9:11), when Israel will "possess the remnant of Edom and all the nations" (9:12), when the Lord will "plant them on their land, and they will not again be rooted out from their land which I have given them" (9:15), all make it clear that the prophet is speaking of Messiah's return at the Second Advent to sit upon the throne of David (cf. Is 9:7), not the establishment of the church by the apostles.

OUTLINE

I. Judgments Against the Nations (1:1–2:16)

A. Introduction (1:1, 2)
B. Against Israel's Enemies (1:3–2:3)
C. Against Judah (2:4, 5)
D. Against Israel (2:6–16)

II. Condemnations Against Israel (3:1–6:14)
- A. Sin of Irresponsibility (3:1–15)
- B. Sin of Idolatry (4:1–13)
- C. Sin of Moral/Ethical Decay (5:1–6:14)

III. Visions of Judgment and Restoration (7:1–9:15)
- A. The Lord Will Spare (7:1–6)
  1. Vision of locusts (7:1–3)
  2. Vision of fire (7:4–6)
- B. The Lord Will No Longer Spare (7:7–9:10)
  1. Vision of the plumb line (7:7–9)
  2. Historical interlude (7:10–17)
  3. Vision of the fruit basket (8:1–14)
  4. Vision of the altar (9:1–10)
- C. The Lord Will Restore (9:11–15)

JUDGMENT ON NEIGHBOR NATIONS

1 The words of Amos, who was among the [A]sheep-
herders from [B]Tekoa, which he [a]envisioned in
visions concerning Israel in the days of [C]Uzziah king
of Judah, and in the days of [D]Jeroboam son of Joash,
king of Israel, two years before the [E]earthquake.

2 He said,
"The [A]LORD roars from Zion
And from Jerusalem He utters His voice;
And the shepherds' [B]pasture
grounds mourn,
And the [a,C]summit of Carmel dries up."

3 Thus says the LORD,
"For [A]three transgressions of
[B]Damascus and for four
I will not [a]revoke its *punishment,*
Because they threshed Gilead with
implements of sharp iron.
4 "So I will send fire upon the house of Hazael
And it will consume the
citadels of [A]Ben-hadad.
5 "I will also [A]break the *gate* bar of Damascus,
And cut off the inhabitant from
the [a]valley of Aven,
And him who holds the scepter,
from Beth-eden;
So the people of Aram will go exiled to [B]Kir,"
Says the LORD.

6 Thus says the LORD,
"For three transgressions of
[A]Gaza and for four
I will not revoke its *punishment,*
Because they deported an entire population
To [B]deliver *it* up to Edom.
7 "So I will send fire upon the wall of Gaza
And it will consume her citadels.
8 "I will also cut off the inhabitant
from [A]Ashdod,
And him who holds the scepter,
from [B]Ashkelon;
I will even [a]unleash My [b]power upon Ekron,
And the remnant of the
[C]Philistines will perish,"
Says the Lord [c]GOD.

AMOS: PLACES JUDGED BY GOD

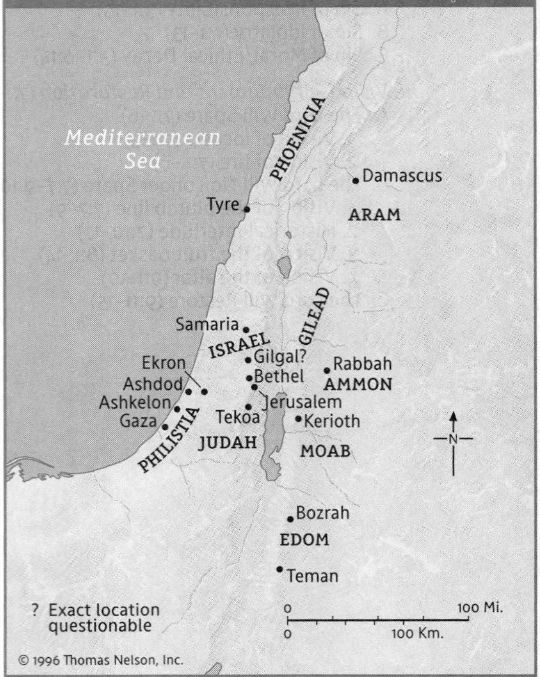

Although Amos was a simple shepherd, God had given him knowledge of lands and nations beyond the Judean pastures where he tended his sheep. Because God had placed prophetic messages on his lips, he knew of the tragic futures of cities as far away as the Syrian city of Damascus (1:5), but also as close as the Philistine city of Gaza (1:6). His pronouncements of doom encompassed the Phoenicians in the seacoast town of Tyre and the Edomites in the arid lands of the south.

1:1 [a]Lit *saw concerning* [A]Amos 7:14 [B]2 Sam 14:2; Jer 6:1 [C]2 Chr 26:1-23; Is 1:1 [D]2 Kin 14:23-29; Hos 1:1; Amos 7:10, 11 [E]Zech 14:5 1:2 [a]Lit *head* [A]Is 42:13; Jer 25:30; Joel 3:16 [B]Jer 12:4; Joel 1:18, 19 [C]Amos 9:3 1:3 [a]Lit *cause it to turn back,* and so throughout the ch [A]Amos 2:1, 4, 6 [B]Is 8:4; 17:1-3; Jer 49:23-27; Zech 9:1 1:4 [A]1 Kin 20:1; 2 Kin 6:24 1:5 [a]Possibly, *Baalbek* [A]Jer 51:30; Lam 2:9 [B]2 Kin 16:9; Amos 9:7 1:6 [A]1 Sam 6:17; Jer 47:1, 5; Zeph 2:4 [B]Ezek 35:5; Obad 11 1:8 [a]Lit *cause to return* [b]Lit *hand* [c]Heb *YHWH,* usually rendered *LORD* [A]2 Chr 26:6; Amos 3:9; Zech 9:6 [B]Jer 47:5; Zeph 2:4 [C]Is 14:29-31; Jer 47:1-7; Ezek 25:16; Joel 3:4-8; Zeph 2:4-7; Zech 9:5-7

1:1 the earthquake. Mentioned by Zechariah (14:5), Josephus (*Antiquities,* IX:10:4) connects it with Uzziah's sin of usurping the role of a priest (2Ch 26:16–23). An earthquake of severe magnitude occurred ca. 755 B.C.

1:2 roars. In Joel 3:16, the Lord "roars" against the nations; here His wrath was directed primarily toward Israel (cf. Jer 25:30). Amos, a shepherd, courageously warned the flock of God's pasture that they were in imminent danger from a roaring lion who turned out to be the ultimate Shepherd of the flock (cf. 3:8). **Carmel.** Known for its bountiful trees and lush gardens, "Carmel" means "fertility" or "garden land" and refers to the mountain range that runs E to W in northern Israel and juts out into the Mediterranean Sea (cf. 9:3).

1:3–2:3 Amos began with Israel's enemies, and thereby gained an initial hearing. When he turned to God's judgment on Israel, the leaders tried to silence him (cf. 7:10–17).

1:3 For three transgressions ... for four. This rhetorical device is repeated in each of the 8 messages, differing from a similar pattern used elsewhere. These are specific mathematical enumerations (e.g., Pr 30:18, 21, 29), emphasizing that each nation was being visited for an incalculable number of infractions. With 3, the cup of iniquity was full; with 4 it overflowed. This judgment was to fall on Syria, whose capital is Damascus. **threshed Gilead.** Large threshing sleds which, when dragged over grain, would both thresh the grain and cut the straw. Gilead, located in the northeastern, Golan Heights region of Israel, was vulnerable to Syria's cruel attacks (cf. 2Ki 13:7; 18:12).

1:4 Ben-hadad. Apparently a throne name, meaning "son of (the god) Hadad." Ben-hadad II was a son of Syrian king Hazael (841–801 B.C.).

1:5 valley of Aven. Meaning "valley of wickedness," it may refer to Baalbek, the center of sun worship, located N of Damascus. **Beth-eden.** "House of pleasure." It was located in eastern Syria across the Euphrates. **Kir.** Apparently the original home of the Syrians. It was a region to which they were later exiled (2Ki 16:9). Its exact location is unknown.

1:6 Gaza. Philistia's most prominent merchant city, ideally situated between Egypt and Israel, here used to refer to the Philistine nation. **deported an entire population.** Cf. Jer 13:19. Possibly during the reign of Jehoram (2Ch 21:16, 17; Joel 3:3), ca. 853–841 B.C.

1:7, 8 Four of the 5 major cities of Philistia. The fifth, Gath, was not mentioned because it had been destroyed earlier by Uzziah (2Ch 26:6).

9 Thus says the LORD,
"For three transgressions of
[A]Tyre and for four
I will not revoke its *punishment,*
Because they delivered up an
entire population to Edom
And did not remember *the*
covenant of [a,B]brotherhood.
10 "So I will [A]send fire upon
the wall of Tyre
And it will consume her citadels."

11 Thus says the LORD,
"For three transgressions of
[A]Edom and for four
I will not revoke its *punishment,*
Because he [B]pursued his
brother with the sword,
While he [a]stifled his compassion;
His anger also [C]tore continually,
And he maintained his fury forever.
12 "So I will send fire upon [A]Teman
And it will consume the
citadels of Bozrah."

13 Thus says the LORD,
"For three transgressions of the
sons of [A]Ammon and for four
I will not revoke its *punishment,*
Because they [B]ripped open the
pregnant women of Gilead
In order to [C]enlarge their borders.
14 "So I will kindle a fire on the
wall of [A]Rabbah
And it will consume her citadels
Amid [a,B]war cries on the day of battle,
And a [C]storm on the day of tempest.
15 "Their [A]king will go into exile,
He and his princes together,"
says the LORD.

JUDGMENT ON JUDAH AND ISRAEL

2 Thus says the LORD,
"For three transgressions of
[A]Moab and for four
I will not [a]revoke its *punishment,*
Because he [B]burned the bones of
the king of Edom to lime.
2 "So I will send fire upon Moab
And it will consume the citadels of [A]Kerioth;
And Moab will die amid [B]tumult,
With [a]war cries and the sound of a trumpet.
3 "I will also cut off the [a,A]judge
from her midst
And slay all her [B]princes with
him," says the LORD.

4 Thus says the LORD,
"For three transgressions of
[A]Judah and for four
I will not revoke its *punishment,*
Because they [B]rejected the law of the LORD
And have not kept His statutes;
Their [a,C]lies also have led them astray,
Those after which their [D]fathers walked.
5 "So I will [A]send fire upon Judah
And it will consume the
citadels of Jerusalem."

6 Thus says the LORD,
"For three transgressions of
[A]Israel and for four
I will not revoke its *punishment,*
Because they [B]sell the righteous for money
And the needy for a pair of sandals.
7 "These who [a]pant after the *very* dust of
the earth on the head of the [A]helpless
Also [B]turn aside the way of the humble;
And a [C]man and his father
[b]resort to the same [c]girl
In order to profane My holy name.

1:9 [a]Lit *brothers* [A]Is 23:1-18; Jer 25:22; Ezek 26:2-4; Joel 3:4-8; Zech 9:1-4; Matt 11:21, 22; Luke 10:13, 14 [B]1 Kin 9:11-14 1:10 [A]Zech 9:4 1:11 [a]Lit *corrupted* [A]Is 34:5, 6; 63:1-6; Jer 49:7-22; Ezek 25:12-14; 35:1-15; Obad 1-14; Mal 1:2-5 [B]Num 20:14-21; 2 Chr 28:17; Obad 10-12 [C]Is 57:16; Mic 7:18 1:12 [A]Jer 49:7, 20; Obad 9 1:13 [A]Jer 49:1-6; Ezek 21:28-32; 25:2-7; Zeph 2:8, 9 [B]2 Kin 15:16; Hos 13:16 [C]Is 5:8; Ezek 35:10 1:14 [a]Or *shouts* [A]Deut 3:11; 1 Chr 20:1; Jer 49:2 [B]Ezek 21:22; Amos 2:2 [C]Is 29:6; 30:30 1:15 [A]Jer 49:3 2:1 [a]Lit *cause it to turn back,* and so throughout the ch [A]Is 15:1-16:14; 25:10-12; Jer 48:1-47; Ezek 25:8-11; Zeph 2:8, 9 [B]2 Kin 3:26, 27 2:2 [a]Or *shouts* [A]Jer 48:24, 41 [B]Jer 48:45 2:3 [a]Or *executive officer* [A]Ps 2:10; 141:6; Amos 5:7, 12; 6:12 [B]Job 12:21; Is 40:23 2:4 [a]Or *false gods* [A]2 Kin 17:19; Hos 12:2; Amos 3:2 [B]Judg 2:17-20; 2 Kin 22:11-17; Jer 6:19; 8:9 [C]Is 9:15, 16; 28:15; Jer 16:19; Hab 2:18 [D]Jer 9:14; 16:11, 12; Ezek 20:18, 24, 30 2:5 [A]Jer 17:27; 21:10; Hos 8:14 2:6 [A]2 Kin 18:11, 12 [B]Joel 3:3; Amos 5:11, 12; 8:6 2:7 [a]Or *trample* or, *snap at the head of the helpless on the dust* [b]Lit *go* [c]Possibly a harlot, or a temple prostitute [A]Amos 8:4; Mic 2:2, 9 [B]Amos 5:12 [C]Hos 4:14

1:9 covenant of brotherhood. A longstanding brotherly relationship existed between Phoenicia and Israel, beginning with King Hiram's assistance to David in building his house and Solomon in the building of the temple (2Sa 5:11; 1Ki 5:1–12; 9:11–14), and later cemented through the marriage of Jezebel to Ahab (1Ki 16:31). No king of Israel ever made war against Phoenicia, especially the two major cities, Tyre and Sidon.

1:10 Tyre. Alexander the Great conquered this stronghold ca. 330 B.C. (cf. Eze 26:1–18).

1:11 pursued ... stifled his compassion. More than mere fighting, Edom pursued his brother, stifling any feelings of compassion. *See notes on Obadiah* for a more complete description of Edom's judgment.

1:12 Teman. The grandson of Esau (Ge 36:11), after whom this town in northern Edom was named. **Bozrah.** A fortress city of northern Edom, about 35 mi. N of Petra.

1:13 sons of Ammon. Descendants of Ben-ammi, the son of Lot and his younger daughter (Ge 19:34–38). **ripped open the pregnant women.** Such inhumane treatment in wartime was not an uncommon practice (cf. 2Ki 8:12; 15:16; Hos 13:16).

1:14 Rabbah. Situated E of the Jordan River, this was the capital city.

2:1 Moab. Descendants of Lot and his elder daughter (Ge 19:37). **burned the bones.** This event, where vengeance didn't stop at death, is not recorded elsewhere in Scripture.

2:2 Kerioth. An important Moabite city, either as a capital or center of worship.

2:3 judge. Possibly denoting the king, who was often so designated (2Ki 15:5; Da 9:12).

2:4 Judah. With the judgments against the nations finished, the prophet proceeded to address Judah, moving ever closer to his ultimate target of Israel. **rejected the law of the LORD.** The nations were judged because they had sinned against the law of God, which was written in the heart and conscience (cf. Ro 2:14, 15). Judah and Israel were judged because they sinned against God's revealed, written law.

2:5 fire upon Judah. The Babylonian King Nebuchadnezzar fulfilled this judgment, ca. 605–586 B.C. (cf. 2Ki 24, 25).

2:6, 7 Greed, so all-consuming that for insignificant debts they would sell another into slavery (cf. Mt 18:23–35), was accompanied by uncontained sexual passion. Care for the poor is a prominent OT theme (e.g., Pr 14:31; 17:5) and sexual purity is mandated repeatedly. Violations of both are an affront to God's holy name.

2:7 resort to the same girl. In the context of oppressing the helpless, the reference was probably to a slave girl (cf. Ex 21:7–11).

8 "On garments [A]taken as pledges they
stretch out beside [B]every altar,
And in the house of their God
they [C]drink the wine of those
who have been fined.

9 "Yet it was I who destroyed the
[A]Amorite before them,
[a]Though his [B]height *was* like
the height of cedars
And he *was* strong as the oaks;
I even destroyed his [C]fruit above
and his root below.
10 "It was I who [A]brought you up
from the land of Egypt,
And I led you in the wilderness
[B]forty years
[a]That you might take possession
of the land of the [C]Amorite.
11 "Then I [A]raised up some of your
sons to be prophets
And some of your young
men to be [B]Nazirites.
Is this not so, O sons of Israel?"
declares the LORD.
12 "But you made the Nazirites drink wine,
And you commanded the prophets
saying, 'You [A]shall not prophesy!'
13 "Behold, I am [a,A]weighted
down beneath you
As a wagon [b]is weighted down
when filled with sheaves.
14 "[a,A]Flight will perish from the swift,
And the stalwart will not
strengthen his power,
Nor the [B]mighty man save his [b]life.
15 "He who [A]grasps the bow will
not stand *his ground,*
The swift of foot will not escape,
Nor will he who rides the
[B]horse save his [a]life.
16 "Even the [a]bravest among the
warriors will [A]flee naked in that
day," declares the LORD.

ALL THE TRIBES ARE GUILTY

3 Hear this word which the LORD has spoken
against you, sons of Israel, against the entire
[a,A]family which [b]He brought up from the land of
Egypt:

2 "[A]You only have I [a]chosen among
all the families of the earth;
Therefore I will [b,B]punish you
for all your iniquities."
3 Do two men walk together unless they
have made an [a]appointment?
4 Does a [A]lion roar in the forest
when he has no prey?
Does a young lion [a]growl from his den
unless he has captured *something?*
5 Does a bird fall into a trap on the
ground when there is no [a]bait in it?
Does a trap spring up from the earth
when it captures nothing at all?
6 If a [A]trumpet is blown in a city
will not the people tremble?
If a [B]calamity occurs in a city
has not the LORD done it?
7 [a]Surely the Lord [b]GOD does nothing
Unless He [A]reveals His secret counsel
To His servants the prophets.
8 A [A]lion has roared! Who will not fear?
The [B]Lord [a]GOD has spoken!
[C]Who can but prophesy?

9 Proclaim on the citadels in [A]Ashdod and on the
citadels in the land of Egypt and say, "Assemble
yourselves on the [B]mountains of Samaria and see
the great tumults within her and *the* [C]oppressions in
her midst. 10 But they [A]do not know how to do what
is right," declares the LORD, "these who [B]hoard up
[a]violence and devastation in their citadels."
11 Therefore, thus says the Lord GOD,

"An [A]enemy, even one
surrounding the land,
Will pull down your [a]strength from you
And your [B]citadels will be looted."

2:8 [A]Ex 22:26 [B]Amos 3:14 [C]Amos 4:1; 6:6 2:9 [a]Lit *Whose height* [A]Num 21:23-25; Josh 10:12 [B]Num 13:32 [C]Ezek 17:9; Mal 4:1 2:10 [a]Lit *To possess* [A]Ex 12:51; 20:2; Amos 3:1; 9:7 [B]Deut 2:7 [C]Ex 3:8 2:11 [A]Deut 18:18; Jer 7:25 [B]Num 6:2, 3; Judg 13:5 2:12 [A]Is 30:10; Jer 11:21; Amos 7:13, 16; Mic 2:6 2:13 [a]Or *tottering* [b]Or *totters* [A]Is 1:14 2:14 [a]Or *A place of refuge* [b]Lit *soul* [A]Is 30:16, 17 [B]Ps 33:16; Jer 9:23 2:15 [a]Lit *soul* [A]Jer 51:56; Ezek 39:3 [B]Is 31:3 2:16 [a]Lit *stout of heart* [A]Judg 4:17 3:1 [a]I.e. nation [b]Lit *I* [A]Jer 8:3; 13:11 3:2 [a]Lit *known* [b]Lit *visit* [A]Gen 18:19; Ex 19:5, 6; Deut 4:32-37; 7:6 [B]Jer 14:10; Ezek 20:36; Dan 9:12; Rom 2:9 3:3 [a]Or *agreement* 3:4 [a]Lit *give his voice* [A]Ps 104:21; Hos 5:14; 11:10 3:5 [a]Or *striker-bar set* 3:6 [A]Jer 4:5, 19, 21; 6:1; Hos 5:8; Zeph 1:16 [B]Is 14:24-27; 45:7 3:7 [a]Or *For* [b]Heb *YHWH* [A]Gen 6:13; 18:17; Jer 23:22; Dan 9:22; John 15:15 3:8 [a]Heb *YHWH*, usually rendered *LORD*, and so throughout the ch [A]Amos 1:2 [B]Jon 1:1-3; 3:1-3 [C]Jer 20:9; Acts 4:20 3:9 [A]1 Sam 5:1 [B]Amos 4:1; 6:1 [C]Amos 5:11; 8:6 3:10 [a]I.e. the booty from violence [A]Ps 14:4; Jer 4:22; Amos 5:7; 6:12 [B]Hab 2:8-10; Zeph 1:9; Zech 5:3, 4 3:11 [a]Or *stronghold* [A]Amos 6:14 [B]Amos 2:5

2:8 garments taken as pledges. Outer garments used to secure a loan were to be returned before sunset (Ex 22:25–27; Dt 24:12, 13); instead, they used them to engage in idolatrous acts.

2:9 Amorite. The pre-Conquest inhabitants of Canaan, whom God defeated for the Jews (cf. Jos 10:12–15). Their giant stature was said to make the spies look like grasshoppers (Nu 13:32, 33).

2:11 Nazirites. See Nu 6:1–21.

2:14–16 Neither personal strength nor military armament was sufficient to prevent the Lord's hand of judgment by the Assyrians ca. 722 B.C. (cf. 2Ki 17).

3:1 the entire family. The primary recipient of these messages was Israel; Judah was not excluded.

3:2 You only have I chosen. God's sovereign choice of Israel did not exempt her from punishment for disobedience.

3:3–8 The Lord posed a series of questions to show that, as some things are certain in nature, surely nothing happens in Israel that is outside His sovereignty. Certain actions have certain results! The Lord had spoken a word, and therefore the prophet was to speak, and the people were to listen with trembling. Instead, they tried to silence the prophet (cf. 2:12; 7:12, 13).

3:7 Judgment is coming, but the Lord graciously warned the nation in advance through His prophets (e.g., Noah, Ge 6; Abraham, Ge 18).

3:9 The heathen nations, such as the Philistines and Egyptians, were rhetorically summoned to witness God's judgment. If they condemn Israel, how much more will a righteous God?

3:11 An enemy. The Assyrians who captured and deported Israel in 722 B.C.

12 Thus says the LORD,

"Just as the shepherd [a,A]snatches
from the lion's mouth a couple
of legs or a piece of an ear,
So will the sons of Israel dwelling in
Samaria be [b]snatched away—
With *the* [B]corner of a bed and
the [c,C]cover of a couch!
13 "Hear and [A]testify against
the house of Jacob,"
Declares the Lord GOD, the God of hosts.
14 "For on the day that I punish
Israel's transgressions,
I will also punish the altars of [A]Bethel;
The horns of the altar will be cut off
And they will fall to the ground.
15 "I will also smite the [a,A]winter house
together with the [B]summer house;
The houses of [b,C]ivory will also perish
And the [D]great houses will
come to an end,"
Declares the LORD.

"YET YOU HAVE NOT RETURNED TO ME"

4 Hear this word, you cows of [A]Bashan who
are on the [B]mountain of Samaria,
Who [C]oppress the poor, who
crush the needy,
Who say to [a]your husbands, "Bring
now, that we may [D]drink!"
2 The Lord [a]GOD has [A]sworn
by His [B]holiness,
"Behold, the days are coming upon you
When [b]they will take you away
with [C]meat hooks,
And the last of you with [D]fish hooks.
3 "You will [A]go out *through*
breaches *in the walls,*
Each one straight before her,
And you [a]will be cast to Harmon,"
declares the LORD.

4 "Enter Bethel and transgress;
In Gilgal multiply transgression!
[A]Bring your sacrifices
every morning,
Your tithes every three days.
5 "[a]Offer a [A]thank offering also from
that which is leavened,
And proclaim [B]freewill offerings,
make them known.
For so you [C]love *to do,*
you sons of Israel,"
Declares the Lord GOD.

6 "But I gave you also [A]cleanness
of teeth in all your cities
And lack of bread in all your places,
Yet you have [B]not returned to
Me," declares the LORD.
7 "Furthermore, I [A]withheld
the rain from you
While *there were* still three
months until harvest.
Then I would send rain on one city
And on [B]another city I would
not send rain;
One part would be rained on,
While the part not rained
on would dry up.
8 "So two or three cities would stagger
to another city to drink [A]water,
But would [B]not be satisfied;
Yet you have [C]not returned to
Me," declares the LORD.
9 "I [A]smote you with scorching
wind and mildew;
And the [B]caterpillar was devouring
Your many gardens and vineyards,
fig trees and olive trees;
Yet you have [C]not returned to
Me," declares the LORD.
10 "I sent a [A]plague among you after
the manner of Egypt;
I [B]slew your young men by the sword
along with your [C]captured horses,
And I made the [D]stench of your
camp rise up in your nostrils;
Yet you have [E]not returned to
Me," declares the LORD.

3:12 [a]Or *delivers* [b]Or *delivered* [c]Lit *damask* [A]1 Sam 17:34-37 [B]Ps 132:3 [C]Esth 1:6; 7:8; Amos 6:4 3:13 [A]Ezek 2:7 3:14 [A]2 Kin 23:15; Hos 10:5-8, 14, 15; Amos 4:4; 5:5, 6; 7:10, 13 3:15 [a]Or *autumn* [b]I.e. ivory inlay [A]Jer 36:22 [B]Judg 3:20 [C]1 Kin 22:39; Ps 45:8 [D]Amos 2:5; 6:11 4:1 [a]Lit *their lords* [A]Ps 22:12; Ezek 39:18 [B]Amos 3:9; 6:1 [C]Amos 5:11; 8:6 [D]Amos 2:8; 6:6 4:2 [a]Heb *YHWH*, usually rendered *LORD*, and so throughout the ch [b]Lit *he* [A]Amos 6:8; 8:7 [B]Ps 89:35 [C]Is 37:29; Ezek 38:4 [D]Jer 16:16; Ezek 29:4; Hab 1:15 4:3 [a]So Gr; M.T. reads *will cast* [A]Jer 52:7 4:4 [A]Num 28:3; Amos 5:21, 22 4:5 [a]Lit *Offer up in smoke* [A]Lev 7:13 [B]Lev 22:18-21 [C]Jer 7:9, 10; Hos 9:1, 10 4:6 [A]Is 3:1; Jer 14:18 [B]Is 9:13; Jer 5:3; Hag 2:17 4:7 [A]Deut 11:17; 2 Chr 7:13; Is 5:6 [B]Ex 9:4, 26; 10:22, 23 4:8 [A]1 Kin 18:5; Jer 14:4 [B]Ezek 4:16, 17; Hag 1:6 [C]Jer 3:7 4:9 [A]Deut 28:22; Hag 2:17 [B]Joel 1:4, 7; Amos 7:1, 2 [C]Jer 3:10 4:10 [A]Ex 9:3; Lev 26:25; Deut 28:27, 60; Ps 78:50 [B]Jer 11:22; 18:21; 48:15 [C]2 Kin 13:3, 7 [D]Joel 2:20 [E]Is 9:13

3:12 The Lord gives a vivid description of the small remnant left in Israel after the Assyrian invasion.

3:13 Hear and testify. As in v. 9, the heathen nations were once again called upon to witness and testify.

3:14 Bethel. The principal place of idol worship in Israel (cf. 1Ki 12:25–33).

4:1 cows of Bashan. A description of the women of Samaria who lived luxurious lives (cf. Is 3:16–26; 32:9–13; Jer 4:30). Bashan was a fertile region below Mt. Hermon E of the Jordan River known for its lush pastures. Under Jeroboam II, Israel was enjoying great prosperity.

4:3 *through* breaches *in the walls* … to Harmon. Captives will be led out of the city through breaches in the walls, depicting massive overthrow. The location of Harmon is unknown.

4:4, 5 With poignant sarcasm, Amos indicted Israel for idolatrous sacrifices and ritualistic religion.

4:4 Bethel … Gilgal. Bethel, the place of Jacob's dream (Ge 28), and Gilgal, where Israel was circumcised before surrounding Jericho (Jos 5:1–9), were sacred to Israel.

4:5 offering … leavened. Though prohibited from most offerings, leaven was required as a part of the thank offering (Lv 7:11–15).

4:6–11 Past warnings were futile, a fact repeatedly emphasized by "Yet you have not returned to Me" (vv. 6, 8, 9, 10, 11).

4:6 cleanness of teeth. Amos employed this euphemism to depict the absence of food during famine and drought sent by God to warn Israel, which he described in vv. 6–9 (cf. Dt 28:22, 23, 24, 47, 48; Lv 26:18).

11 "I overthrew you, as [A]God overthrew
Sodom and Gomorrah,
And you were like a [B]firebrand
snatched from a blaze;
Yet you have [C]not returned to
Me," declares the LORD.
12 "Therefore thus I will do to you, O Israel;
Because I will do this to you,
Prepare to [A]meet your God, O Israel."
13 For behold, He who [A]forms mountains
and [B]creates the wind
And [C]declares to man what
are His thoughts,
He who [D]makes dawn into darkness
And [E]treads on the high places of the earth,
[F]The LORD God of hosts is His name.

"SEEK ME THAT YOU MAY LIVE"

5 Hear this word which I take up for
you as a [A]dirge, O house of Israel:
2 She has fallen, she will [A]not rise again—
The [B]virgin Israel.
She *lies* neglected on her land;
There is [C]none to raise her up.

3 For thus says the Lord [a]GOD,

"The city which goes forth a thousand *strong*
Will have a [A]hundred left,
And the one which goes forth
a hundred *strong*
Will have [B]ten left to the house of Israel."

4 For thus says the LORD to the house of Israel,

"[A]Seek Me [B]that you may live.
5 "But do not [a]resort to [A]Bethel
And do not come to [B]Gilgal,
Nor cross over to [C]Beersheba;
For Gilgal will certainly go into captivity
And Bethel will [b]come to trouble.
6 "[A]Seek the LORD that you may live,
Or He will break forth like a
[B]fire, [a]O house of Joseph,
And it will consume with none
to quench *it* for Bethel,
7 *For* those who turn [A]justice
into wormwood
And [a]cast righteousness
down to the earth."

8 He who made the [A]Pleiades and Orion
And [B]changes deep darkness
into morning,
[a]Who also [C]darkens day *into* night,
Who [D]calls for the waters of the sea
And pours them out on the
surface of the earth,
The [E]LORD is His name.
9 It is He who [A]flashes forth *with*
destruction upon the strong,
So that [B]destruction comes
upon the fortress.

10 They hate him who [A]reproves in the [a]gate,
And they [B]abhor him who
speaks *with* integrity.
11 Therefore because you [a]impose
heavy rent on the poor
And exact a tribute of grain from them,
Though you have built [A]houses
of well-hewn stone,
Yet you will not live in them;
You have planted pleasant vineyards,
yet you will [B]not drink their wine.
12 For I know your transgressions are
many and your sins are great,
You who [A]distress the righteous
and accept bribes
And [a]turn aside the poor in the [b]gate.
13 Therefore at [a]such a time the
prudent person [A]keeps silent,
for it is an evil time.

14 Seek good and not evil, that you may live;
And thus may the LORD God
of hosts be with you,
[A]Just as you have said!
15 [A]Hate evil, love good,
And establish justice in the [a]gate!
Perhaps the LORD God of hosts
[B]May be gracious to the [C]remnant of Joseph.

4:11 [A]Gen 19:24, 25; Deut 29:23; Is 13:19 [B]Zech 3:2 [C]Jer 23:14 4:12 [A]Is 32:11; 64:2; Jer 5:22 4:13 [A]Job 38:4-7; Ps 65:6; Is 40:12 [B]Ps 135:7; Jer 10:13 [C]Dan 2:28, 30 [D]Jer 13:16; Joel 2:2; Amos 5:8 [E]Mic 1:3 [F]Is 47:4; Jer 10:16; Amos 5:8, 27; 9:6 5:1 [A]Jer 7:29; 9:10, 17; Ezek 19:1 5:2 [A]Amos 8:14 [B]Jer 14:17 [C]Is 51:18; Jer 50:32 5:3 [a]Heb *YHWH*, usually rendered *LORD*, and so throughout the ch [A]Is 6:13 [B]Amos 6:9 5:4 [A]Deut 4:29; 32:46, 47; Jer 29:13 [B]Is 55:3 5:5 [a]Lit *seek* [b]Or *become iniquity* [A]1 Kin 12:28, 29; Amos 3:14; 4:4; 7:10, 13 [B]1 Sam 7:16; 11:14 [C]Gen 21:31-33; Amos 8:14 5:6 [a]Or *in the house* [A]Is 55:3, 6, 7; Amos 5:14 [B]Deut 4:24 5:7 [a]Lit *they have put down* [A]Amos 2:3; 5:12; 6:12 5:8 [a]Lit *And He darkened* [A]Job 9:9; 38:31 [B]Job 12:22; 38:12; Is 42:16 [C]Ps 104:20 [D]Ps 104:6-9; Amos 9:6 [E]Amos 4:13 5:9 [A]Is 29:5; Amos 2:14 [B]Mic 5:11 5:10 [a]I.e. the place where court was held [A]Is 29:21; Amos 5:15 [B]1 Kin 22:8; Is 59:15; Jer 17:16-18 5:11 [a]Another reading is *trample upon* [A]Amos 3:15; 6:11 [B]Mic 6:15 5:12 [a]Lit *they turn* [b]I.e. the place where court was held [A]Is 1:23; 5:23; Amos 2:6 5:13 [a]Lit *that time* [A]Eccl 3:7; Hos 4:4 5:14 [A]Mic 3:11 5:15 [a]I.e. the place where court was held [A]Ps 97:10; Rom 12:9 [B]Joel 2:14 [C]Mic 5:3, 7, 8

4:11 firebrand snatched from a blaze. Only because of God's mercy was Israel saved from extinction (cf. Zec 3:2; Jude 23).

4:12 Prepare to meet your God. The general concept was first used of Israel's preparation to receive the covenant at Sinai (Ex 19:11, 15); here she was implored to prepare for His judgment.

4:13 This is the God whom they were to be prepared to face. He is the Lord God Almighty.

5:1, 2 A funeral dirge was taken up for Israel, likened to a young woman who had died.

5:3 Many were to be killed in battle or taken captive; only a handful would return (cf. 3:12; Is 6:11–13).

5:5 Bethel ... Gilgal. *See note on 4:4.* **Beersheba.** Located in southern Judah, 50 mi. SW of Jerusalem, Beersheba had a rich Israelite history (cf. Ge 21:33; 26:23; 1Sa 8:1–3; 1Ki 19:3–7). Apparently, people from the N crossed over the border to worship there (cf. 8:14).

5:6 house of Joseph. Refers to the northern kingdom, since Ephraim and Manasseh, sons of Joseph, were two of its largest tribes.

5:7 justice into wormwood. Justice was so perverted that it was like wormwood, an herb known for its bitter taste (cf. Rev 8:11).

5:8 Pleiades and Orion. Pleiades, part of the constellation Taurus, and Orion depict God's creative power and wisdom (cf. Job 9:9; 38:31–35). Israel was guilty of worshiping the stars (cf. v. 26) instead of their Creator.

5:10–13 The fabric of justice had been destroyed, causing pervasive corruption "in the gate," the place where justice was administered (cf. v. 15; Dt 21:19; Jos 20:4).

16 Therefore thus says the LORD God of hosts, the Lord,

"There is [A]wailing in all the plazas,
And in all the streets they say, 'Alas! Alas!'
They also call the [B]farmer to mourning
And [a,C]professional mourners
to lamentation.
17 "And in all the [A]vineyards *there is* wailing,
Because I will pass through the
midst of you," says the LORD.

18 Alas, you who are longing for
the [A]day of the LORD,
For what purpose *will* the day
of the LORD *be* to you?
It *will be* [B]darkness and not light;
19 As when a man [A]flees from a lion
And a bear meets him,
[a]Or goes home, leans his hand
against the wall
And a snake bites him.
20 *Will* not the day of the LORD *be*
[A]darkness instead of light,
Even gloom with no brightness in it?

21 "I hate, I [A]reject your festivals,
Nor do I [a,B]delight in your
solemn assemblies.
22 "Even though you [A]offer up to Me burnt
offerings and your grain offerings,
I will not accept *them;*
And I will not *even* look at the [B]peace
offerings of your fatlings.
23 "Take away from Me the
noise of your songs;
I will not even listen to the
sound of your harps.
24 "But let [A]justice roll down like waters
And righteousness like an
ever-flowing stream.

25 "[a,A]Did you present Me with sacrifices and grain
offerings in the wilderness for forty years, O house
of Israel? 26 [A]You also carried along [a]Sikkuth your
king and [b]Kiyyun, your images, [c]the star of your
gods which you made for yourselves. 27 Therefore,
I will make you go into exile beyond Damascus,"
says the LORD, whose name is the God of hosts.

"THOSE AT EASE IN ZION"

6 [A]Woe to those who are at ease in Zion
And to those who *feel* secure in
the mountain of Samaria,
The [B]distinguished men of the
foremost of nations,
To whom the house of Israel comes.
2 Go over to [A]Calneh and look,
And go from there to
[B]Hamath the great,
Then go down to [C]Gath
of the Philistines.
Are [a]they better than these kingdoms,
Or is their territory greater
than yours?
3 Do you [A]put off the day of calamity,
And would you [B]bring near
the seat of violence?

5:16 [a]Lit *those who know lamentation* [A]Jer 9:10, 18-20; Amos 8:3 [B]Joel 1:11 [C]2 Chr 35:25; Jer 9:17 5:17 [A]Is 16:10; Jer 48:33 5:18 [A]Is 5:19; Jer 30:7; Joel 1:15; 2:1, 11, 31 [B]Is 5:30; Joel 2:2 5:19 [a]Or *Then* [A]Job 20:24; Is 24:17, 18; Jer 15:2, 3; 48:44 5:20 [A]Is 13:10; Zeph 1:15 5:21 [a]Lit *like to smell* [A]Is 1:11-16; 66:3; Amos 4:4, 5; 8:10 [B]Lev 26:31; Jer 14:12; Hos 5:6 5:22 [A]Is 66:3; Mic 6:6, 7 [B]Lev 7:11-15; Amos 4:5 5:24 [A]Jer 22:3; Ezek 45:9; Mic 6:8 5:25 [a]Or *You presented Me with the sacrifices and a grain offering* [A]Deut 32:17; Josh 24:14; Neh 9:18-21; Acts 7:42, 43 5:26 [a]Or *Sakkuth (Saturn)* or *shrine of your Moloch* [b]Or *Kaiwan (Saturn)* or *stands of* [c]Or *your star gods* [A]Acts 7:43 6:1 [A]Is 32:9-11; Zeph 1:12; Luke 6:24 [B]Ex 19:5; Amos 3:2 6:2 [a]Or *you* [A]Gen 10:10; Is 10:9 [B]1 Kin 8:65; 2 Kin 18:34; Is 10:9 [C]1 Sam 5:8; 2 Chr 26:6 6:3 [A]Is 56:12; Amos 9:10 [B]Amos 3:10

5:16, 17 Looking back at the accusations made earlier, Amos pictured the people mourning as the Lord passed through their midst, executing His sentence of judgment (cf. Ex 11:3ff.).

5:18–20 Even the wicked wanted the day of the Lord to come, mistakenly thinking that it would bring victory instead of judgment (cf. Zep 1:14–18).

5:21–24 When performed with a corrupt heart, even the savored festivals and offerings were despised by the Lord (cf. Lv 26:27, 31; Ps 51:16, 17, 19).

5:25, 26 In addition to worshiping the Lord in the wilderness, Israel also worshiped other gods, carrying along "Sikkuth (or 'tabernacle') your king (or 'Molech') and Kiyyun, your images." Molech worship included the astrological worship of Saturn and the host of heaven and the actual sacrificing of children (2Ki 17:16, 17). Warned against Molech worship (Dt 18:9–13), Israel nevertheless pursued all facets of it, continuing with Solomon (1Ki 11:7) and his descendants (1Ki 12:28; 2Ki 17:16, 17; Jer 32:35) until Josiah (2Ki 23:10). Stephen recited Am 5:25–27 when he recounted the sins of Israel in Ac 7:42, 43.

5:27 Assyria conquered Damascus in 732 B.C., then overtook Israel in 722 B.C.

6:1, 2 The two capitals of Judah and Israel, Zion and Samaria, were invited to look around. If Calneh (possibly the Calno of Is 10:9) and Hamath (Syria) and Gath (Philistia) could not put off judgment, how could they?

THE PRESERVATION OF A REMNANT

In the eighth century B.C., Amos prophesied Israel's doom (8:1, 2), but he also declared the possibility of deliverance for the "remnant of Joseph" (5:15). Throughout history God has always preserved a remnant of His people.

People or Group	Reference
Noah and family in the flood	Ge 7:1
Joseph in Egypt during the famine	Ge 45:7
Israel in their homeland	Dt 4:27–31
7,000 who had not worshiped Baal	1Ki 19:18
Portion of Judah after captivity	Is 10:20–23
Remnant of Zion	Mic 2:12, 13
The church, both Jews and Gentiles	Ro 9:22–27

4 Those who recline on beds of ivory
And sprawl on their [A]couches,
And [B]eat lambs from the flock
And calves from the midst of the stall,
5 Who improvise to the sound of the harp,
And like David have [a]composed
[A]songs for themselves,
6 Who [A]drink wine from [a]sacrificial bowls
While they anoint themselves
with the finest of oils,
Yet they have not [B]grieved
over the ruin of Joseph.
7 Therefore, they will now [A]go into
exile at the head of the exiles,
And the [B]sprawlers' [a]banqueting
will [b]pass away.

8 The Lord [a]GOD has [A]sworn by Himself,
the LORD God of hosts has declared:
"I [B]loathe the arrogance of Jacob,
And [b]detest his [C]citadels;
Therefore I will [D]deliver up *the*
city and [c]all it contains."

9 And it will be, if [A]ten men are left in one house, they
will die. 10 Then one's [a]uncle, or his [b,A]undertaker, will
lift him up to carry out *his* bones from the house,
and he will say to the one who is in the innermost
part of the house, "Is anyone else with you?" And
that one will say, "No one." Then he will [c]answer,
"[B]Keep quiet. For [d]the name of the LORD is [C]not to
be mentioned." 11 For behold, the LORD is going to
[A]command that the [B]great house be smashed to
pieces and the small house to fragments.

12 Do horses run on rocks?
Or does one plow [a]them with oxen?
Yet you have turned [A]justice into poison
And the fruit of righteousness
into [b]wormwood,
13 You who rejoice in [a,A]Lodebar,
[b]And say, "Have we not [B]by our *own*
strength taken [c]Karnaim for ourselves?"
14 "For behold, [A]I am going to raise
up a nation against you,
O house of Israel," declares
the LORD God of hosts,
"And they will afflict you from
the [B]entrance of Hamath
To the [B]brook of the Arabah."

WARNING THROUGH VISIONS

7 Thus the Lord [a]GOD showed me, and behold, He
was forming a [A]locust-swarm [b]when the spring
crop began to sprout. And behold, the spring crop
was after the king's [c]mowing. 2 And it came about,
[a]when it had [A]finished eating the vegetation of the
land, that I said,

"[B]Lord GOD, please pardon!
[b]How can Jacob stand,
For he is [C]small?"
3 The LORD [a,A]changed His mind about this.
"It shall not be," said the LORD.

6:4 [A]Amos 3:12 [B]Ezek 34:2, 3 6:5 [a]Or *invented musical instruments* [A]1 Chr 15:16; 23:5; Is 5:12 6:6 [a]Lit *sprinkling basins* [A]Amos 2:8; 4:1 [B]Ezek 9:4 6:7 [a]Or *cultic feasts* [b]Lit *turn aside* [A]Amos 7:11, 17 [B]1 Kin 20:16-21; Dan 5:4-6, 30 6:8 [a]Heb *YHWH*, usually rendered *LORD* [b]Lit *hate* [c]Lit *its fullness* [A]Gen 22:16; Jer 22:5; 51:14; Amos 4:2; 8:7 [B]Lev 26:30; Deut 32:19; Ps 106:40; Amos 5:21 [C]Amos 3:10, 11 [D]Hos 11:6 6:9 [A]Amos 5:3 6:10 [a]Or *beloved one* [b]Lit *one who burns him* [c]Lit *say* [d]Lit *not to make mention of the name of* [A]1 Sam 31:12 [B]Amos 5:13; 8:3 [C]Jer 44:26; Ezek 20:39 6:11 [A]Is 55:11 [B]2 Kin 25:9; Amos 3:15; 5:11 6:12 [a]Another reading is *the sea with oxen* [b]I.e. bitterness [A]1 Kin 21:7-13; Is 59:13, 14; Hos 10:4; Amos 5:7, 11, 12 6:13 [a]Lit *a thing of nothing* [b]Lit *Who* [c]Lit *a pair of horns* [A]Job 8:14, 15; Ps 2:2-4; Luke 12:19, 20 [B]Ps 75:4, 5; Is 28:14, 15 6:14 [A]Jer 5:15 [B]Num 34:7, 8; 1 Kin 8:65; 2 Kin 14:25 7:1 [a]Heb *YHWH*, usually rendered *LORD*, and so throughout the ch [b]Lit *at the beginning of the coming up of* [c]Or *shearings* [A]Joel 1:4; Amos 4:9; Nah 3:15 7:2 [a]Lit *if* [b]Lit *As who* [A]Ex 10:15 [B]Jer 14:7, 20, 21; Ezek 9:8; 11:13 [C]Is 37:4; Jer 42:2 7:3 [a]Or *relented* [A]Deut 32:36; Jer 26:19; Hos 11:8; Amos 5:15; Jon 3:10

6:6 drink wine from sacrificial bowls. These large bowls, usually used for sacrificial purposes, here typify the excesses of their lifestyle.

6:8 sworn by Himself. Cf. Ge 22:16; Heb 6:13, 14.

6:9, 10 The judgment was so comprehensive that even small remnants were sought out and killed.

6:10 undertaker. Lit. "one who burns him." This could refer to cremation, demanded by the excessive number killed and because of fear of epidemics. With rare exceptions (cf. 1Sa 31:12), corpses were buried in ancient Israel. **name of the LORD is not to be mentioned.** Previously welcomed as a friend, the Lord came in judgment as a foe; survivors would not want to invoke His name out of fear.

6:12 Israel's exercise of justice was as absurd as running horses on rocks or plowing rocks with oxen.

6:13 Lodebar ... Karnaim. These were, apparently, two Syrian sites captured by Jeroboam II (cf. 2Ki 14:25). "Lodebar" means "nothing" and sarcastically points out that Israel's "great" gain will amount to nothing. "Karnaim" means "horns," which symbolizes the strength of an animal. Israel foolishly believed they had conquered in their own strength.

6:14 a nation. Assyria in 722 B.C. **entrance of Hamath ... brook of the Arabah.** These represent the northern and southern perimeters of the kingdom as reestablished by Jeroboam II (cf. 2Ki 14:25).

7:1–9:10 Amos introduced 5 visions, with a historical interlude (7:10–17). The first two depict the Lord's commitment to spare a remnant, while the last 3 announce the inevitability of judgment.

7:1–3 The first vision, symbolizing God's action, saw a swarm of locusts devouring the people's portion of the later cuttings, after the king had taken the first cutting (cf. Joel 1:2–12).

7:3 The LORD changed His mind. Much like He did at Abraham's pleading over Sodom in Ge 18:22, 23.

FIVE VISIONS OF AMOS
1. Vision of Locusts (7:1–3)
2. Vision of Fire (7:4–6)
3. Vision of the Plumb Line (7:7–9)
4. Vision of the Summer Fruit (8:1–14)
5. Vision of the Lord (9:1–10)

4 Thus the Lord GOD showed me, and behold,
the Lord GOD was calling to contend *with them* by
[A]fire, and it consumed the great deep and began to
consume the [a]farm land. 5 Then I said,

"[A]Lord GOD, please stop!
[B]How can Jacob stand, for he is small?"
6 The LORD [a,A]changed His mind about this.
"This too shall not be," said the Lord GOD.

7 Thus He showed me, and behold, the Lord was
standing [a]by a [b]vertical wall with a plumb line in
His hand. 8 The LORD said to me, "[A]What do you see,
Amos?" And I said, "A plumb line." Then the Lord said,

"Behold I am about to put a [B]plumb line
In the midst of My people Israel.
I will [a,C]spare them no longer.
9 "The [A]high places of Isaac will be desolated
And the [B]sanctuaries of Israel laid waste.
Then I will [C]rise up against the house
of Jeroboam with the sword."

AMOS ACCUSED, ANSWERS

10 Then Amaziah, the [A]priest of Bethel, sent *word*
to [B]Jeroboam king of Israel, saying, "Amos has [C]con-
spired against you in the midst of the house of Israel;
the land is unable to endure all his words. 11 For thus
Amos says, 'Jeroboam will die by the sword and Israel
will certainly go from its land into exile.' " 12 Then
Amaziah said to Amos, "[A]Go, you seer, flee away to the
land of Judah and there eat bread and there do your
prophesying! 13 But [A]no longer prophesy at Bethel, for
it is a [B]sanctuary of the king and a royal [a]residence."
14 Then Amos replied to Amaziah, "I am not a
prophet, nor am I the [A]son of a prophet; for I am a
herdsman and a [a]grower of sycamore figs. 15 But the
LORD took me from [a]following the flock and the LORD
said to me, 'Go [A]prophesy to My people Israel.' 16 Now
hear the word of the LORD: you are saying, 'You [A]shall
not prophesy against Israel [B]nor shall you [a]speak
against the house of Isaac.' 17 Therefore, thus says the
LORD, 'Your [A]wife will become a harlot in the city, your
[B]sons and your daughters will fall by the sword, your
land will be parceled up by a *measuring* line and you
yourself will die [a]upon [C]unclean soil. Moreover, Israel
will certainly go from its land into exile.' "

BASKET OF FRUIT AND ISRAEL'S CAPTIVITY

8 Thus the Lord [a]GOD showed me, and behold, *there*
was a basket of summer fruit. 2 He said, "What
do you see, Amos?" And [A]I said, "A basket of summer
fruit." Then the LORD said to me, "The [B]end has come
for My people Israel. I will [a,C]spare them no longer.
3 [a]The [A]songs of the palace will turn to [B]wailing in that
day," declares the Lord GOD. "Many *will be* the [C]corpses;
in every place [b]they will cast them forth [c]in silence."
4 Hear this, you who [a,A]trample the needy, to do
away with the humble of the land, 5 saying,

"When will the [A]new moon [a]be over,
So that we may sell grain,
And the [B]sabbath, that we may
open the wheat *market,*
To make the [b]bushel smaller
and the shekel bigger,
And to [c]cheat with [c]dishonest scales,
6 So as to [A]buy the helpless for [a]money
And the needy for a pair of sandals,
And *that* we may sell the
refuse of the wheat?"

7 The LORD has [A]sworn by the [B]pride of Jacob,
"Indeed, I will [C]never forget
any of their deeds.
8 "Because of this will not the land [A]quake
And everyone who dwells in it [B]mourn?
Indeed, all of it will [C]rise up like the Nile,
And it will be tossed about
And subside like the Nile of Egypt.
9 "It will come about in that day,"
declares the Lord GOD,
"That I will make the [A]sun go down at noon
And [B]make the earth dark
in [a]broad daylight.

7:4 [a]Lit *portion* [A]Deut 32:22; Is 66:15, 16; Amos 2:5 7:5 [A]Ps 85:4; Joel 2:17 [B]Amos 7:2 7:6 [a]Or *relented* [A]Ps 106:45; Amos 7:3; Jon 3:10 7:7 [a]Or *upon* [b]Lit *wall of a plumb line* 7:8 [a]Lit *pass him by* [A]Jer 1:11; Amos 8:2 [B]2 Kin 21:13; Is 28:17; 34:11; Lam 2:8 [C]Jer 15:6; Ezek 7:4-9; Amos 8:2 7:9 [A]Gen 46:1; Hos 10:8; Mic 1:5 [B]Lev 26:31; Is 63:18; Jer 51:51; Amos 7:13 [C]2 Kin 15:8-10; Amos 7:11 7:10 [A]1 Kin 12:31, 32; 13:33 [B]2 Kin 14:23, 24 [C]Jer 26:8-11; 38:4 7:12 [A]Matt 8:34 7:13 [a]Lit *house* [A]Amos 2:12; Acts 4:18 [B]1 Kin 12:29, 32; Amos 7:9 7:14 [a]Or *nipper* [A]1 Kin 20:35; 2 Kin 2:3, 5; 4:38; 2 Chr 19:2 7:15 [a]Lit *behind* [A]Jer 1:7; Ezek 2:3, 4 7:16 [a]Lit *flow* [A]Amos 2:12; 7:13 [B]Deut 32:2; Ezek 20:46; 21:2 7:17 [a]Or *in an unclean land* [A]Hos 4:13, 14 [B]Jer 14:16 [C]2 Kin 17:6; Ezek 4:13; Hos 9:3 8:1 [a]Heb *YHWH*, usually rendered *LORD*, and so throughout the ch 8:2 [a]Lit *pass him by* [A]Jer 24:3 [B]Ezek 7:2, 3, 6 [C]Amos 7:8 8:3 [a]Or *They will howl the palace songs* [b]Lit *he has thrown* [c]Or *hush!* [A]Amos 5:23; 6:4, 5; 8:10 [B]Amos 5:16 [C]Amos 6:8-10 8:4 [a]Or *snap at* [A]Ps 14:4; Prov 30:14; Amos 2:7; 5:11, 12 8:5 [a]Lit *pass by* [b]Lit *ephah* [c]Lit *balances of deception* [A]Num 28:11; 2 Kin 4:23 [B]Ex 31:13-17; Neh 13:15 [C]Hos 12:7; Mic 6:11 8:6 [a]Lit *silver* [A]Amos 2:6 8:7 [A]Amos 4:2 [B]Deut 33:26, 29; Ps 68:34; Amos 6:8 [C]Ps 10:11; Hos 7:2; 8:13 8:8 [A]Ps 18:7; 60:2; Is 5:25 [B]Hos 4:3 [C]Jer 46:7, 8; Amos 9:5 8:9 [a]Lit *a day of light* [A]Job 5:14; Is 13:10; Jer 15:9; Mic 3:6 [B]Is 59:9, 10; Amos 4:13; 5:8

7:4–6 Under the figure of fire, the second vision concerns a devastating drought, causing the underground water supplies to dry up and the fields to be consumed (cf. Dt 32:22). Amos again pleaded Israel's cause (cf. vv. 2, 3).

7:7–9 The true spiritual nature of Israel was here tested (and found wanting) by God's plumb line of righteousness in this third of 5 visions. The sword of judgment was to come from Assyria.

7:10–17 The words of Amos cut deep into the heart of Israel's leadership, causing them to accuse him of conspiracy against the king (cf. Jer 26:11; 37:11–13; 38:1–6).

7:11 Amos says. This most likely refers to v. 9.

7:17 go ... into exile. To Assyria ca. 722 B.C.

8:1 summer fruit. In this fourth vision, as fruit was fully ripened by the summer's sun, so Israel was ripe for judgment.

8:5 new moon. Based on a lunar calendar, Israel would celebrate the day with a festival. Like the Sabbath, no work was to be done (1Sa 20:5, 6; 2Ki 4:23; Eze 46:3). The merchants' eagerness for the day to end revealed their appetite for greed. **bushel smaller ... shekel bigger.** By dishonest weighing, the merchant decreased the actual amount received and increased the cost of the merchandise. *See note on Pr 11:1* for other passages on dishonest measures.

8:6 refuse of the wheat. This denotes the chaff, which was mixed into the good wheat to cheat the buyer.

8:7 pride of Jacob. As surely as the nation was filled with pride, so the Lord would not forget her works (cf. 6:8).

8:8 tossed about and subside like the Nile of Egypt. Like the Nile, which annually provided water and rich soil deposits for farmers by greatly overflowing its banks, so judgment would overflow the land.

8:9 the sun go down at noon. Probably referring to the total eclipse of the sun ca. 763 B.C. as a picture of God's coming judgment.

10 "Then I will [A]turn your festivals
into mourning
And all your songs into [a]lamentation;
And I will bring [B]sackcloth
on everyone's loins
And baldness on every head.
And I will make it [C]like *a time of*
mourning for an only son,
And the end of it will be like a bitter day.

11 "Behold, days are coming,"
declares the Lord GOD,
"When I will send a famine on the land,
Not a famine for bread or a thirst for water,
But rather [A]for hearing the
words of the LORD.
12 "People will stagger from sea to sea
And from the north even to the east;
They will go to and fro to [A]seek
the word of the LORD,
But they will not find *it*.
13 "In that day the beautiful [A]virgins
And the young men will [B]faint from thirst.
14 "*As for* those who swear by
the [a][A]guilt of Samaria,
Who say, 'As your god lives, O [B]Dan,'
And, 'As the way of [C]Beersheba lives,'
They will fall and [D]not rise again."

GOD'S JUDGMENT UNAVOIDABLE

9 I saw the Lord standing beside the [A]altar, and
He said,

"Smite the capitals so that the
[B]thresholds will shake,
And [C]break them on the heads of them all!
Then I will [D]slay the rest of
them with the sword;
They will [E]not have a fugitive who will flee,
Or a refugee who will escape.
2 "Though they dig into [A]Sheol,
From there will My hand take them;
And though they [B]ascend to heaven,
From there will I bring them down.
3 "Though they hide on the
summit of Carmel,
I will [A]search them out and
take them from there;
And though they [B]conceal themselves
from My sight on the floor of the sea,
From there I will command the
[C]serpent and it will bite them.
4 "And though they go into [A]captivity
before their enemies,
From there I will command the
sword that it slay them,
And I will [B]set My eyes against them
for evil and not for good."

5 The Lord [a]GOD of hosts,
The One who [A]touches the
land so that it melts,
And [B]all those who dwell in it mourn,
And all of it rises up like the Nile
And subsides like the Nile of Egypt;
6 The One who builds His [a][A]upper
chambers in the heavens
And has founded His vaulted
dome over the earth,
He who [B]calls for the waters of the sea
And [C]pours them out on the
face of the earth,
[D]The LORD is His name.

7 "Are you not as the sons of [A]Ethiopia to Me,
O sons of Israel?" declares the LORD.
"Have I not brought up Israel
from the land of Egypt,
And the [B]Philistines from Caphtor
and the [C]Arameans from [D]Kir?
8 "Behold, the [A]eyes of the Lord GOD
are on the sinful kingdom,
And I will [B]destroy it from
the face of the earth;
Nevertheless, I will [C]not totally
destroy the house of Jacob,"
Declares the LORD.
9 "For behold, I am commanding,
And I will [A]shake the house of
Israel among all nations
As *grain* is shaken in a sieve,
But not a [a]kernel will fall to the ground.
10 "All the [A]sinners of My people
will die by the sword,
Those who say, '[B]The calamity will
not overtake or confront us.'

8:10 [a]Or *a dirge* [A]Job 20:23; Amos 5:21 [B]Is 15:2, 3; Jer 48:37; Ezek 7:18; 27:31 [C]Jer 6:26; Zech 12:10 8:11 [A]1 Sam 3:1; 2 Chr 15:3; Ps 74:9; Ezek 7:26; Mic 3:6 8:12 [A]Ezek 20:3, 31 8:13 [A]Lam 1:18; 2:21 [B]Is 41:17; Hos 2:3 8:14 [a]Or *Ashimah* [A]Hos 8:5 [B]1 Kin 12:28, 29 [C]Amos 5:5 [D]Amos 5:2 9:1 [A]Amos 3:14 [B]Zeph 2:14 [C]Ps 68:21; Hab 3:13 [D]Amos 7:17 [E]Jer 11:11 9:2 [A]Ps 139:8 [B]Jer 51:53; Obad 4 9:3 [A]Jer 16:16 [B]Job 34:22; Ps 139:9, 10 [C]Is 27:1 9:4 [A]Lev 26:33 [B]Lev 17:10; Jer 21:10; 39:16; 44:11 9:5 [a]Heb *YHWH*, usually rendered *LORD*, and so throughout the ch [A]Ps 104:32; 144:5; Is 64:1; Mic 1:4 [B]Amos 8:8 9:6 [a]Or *stairs* [A]Ps 104:3, 13 [B]Amos 5:8 [C]Ps 104:6 [D]Amos 4:13 9:7 [A]2 Chr 14:9, 12; Is 20:4; 43:3 [B]Deut 2:23; Jer 47:4 [C]Amos 1:5 [D]2 Kin 16:9; Is 22:6 9:8 [A]Jer 44:27; Amos 9:4 [B]Amos 7:17; 9:10 [C]Jer 5:10; 30:11; 31:35, 36; Joel 2:32; Amos 3:12; Obad 17 9:9 [a]Or *pebble* [A]Is 30:28; Luke 22:31 9:10 [A]Is 33:14; Zech 13:8 [B]Amos 6:3

8:10 sackcloth. *See note on Joel 1:8.*

8:11, 12 During prosperity, the nation rejected the prophets (cf. 7:10–17); in captivity no word from the Lord could be found (cf. 1Sa 28:6ff.).

8:14 Samaria ... Dan. Jeroboam I built altars at both locations in an effort to keep Israel from going to Jerusalem to worship (1Ki 12:26–29). **Beersheba.** *See note on 5:5.*

9:1 The fifth vision opens with the Lord standing beside the altar in Bethel, commanding that the temple be torn down, thus falling upon the worshipers. He would spare none.

9:2–4 Desperate to escape, none will successfully hide from the hand of judgment. Righteous David found solace in the omnipresence of God (Ps 139:7–10; cf. Jer 23:23, 24); the wicked find only His wrath (cf. Rev 20:13).

9:3 Carmel. A mountainous region, rising 1800 feet above the Mediterranean, known for its many caves and forests. *See note on 1:2.*

9:5–9 Lest anyone question the Lord's power, they are reminded of His omnipotence revealed in creation and in His sovereign rulership of the nations. Other nations have been transplanted from their homelands; why not Israel?

9:5 the Nile. *See note on 8:8.*

9:7 Kir. *See note on 1:5.*

9:9 shake ... among all nations. Only the chaff was to be punished; His remnant was to be preserved to inherit the blessings spoken of in the following verses.

THE RESTORATION OF ISRAEL

11 "In that day I will [A]raise up the
fallen [a,B]booth of David,
And wall up its [C]breaches;
I will also raise up its ruins
And rebuild it as in
the [D]days of old;
12 [A]That they may possess the
remnant of [B]Edom
And all the [a]nations who are
[C]called by My name,"
Declares the LORD who does this.

13 "Behold, days are coming,"
declares the LORD,
"When the [A]plowman will
overtake the reaper
And the treader of grapes
him who sows seed;
When the [B]mountains will
drip sweet [C]wine
And all the hills will be dissolved.
14 "Also I will [A]restore the [a]captivity
of My people Israel,
And they will [B]rebuild the ruined
cities and live *in them;*
They will also [C]plant vineyards
and drink their wine,
And make gardens and eat their fruit.
15 "I will also plant them on their land,
And [A]they will not again be
rooted out from their land
Which I have given them,"
Says the LORD your God.

9:11 [a]Or *shelter* or *tabernacle* [A]Acts 15:16-18 [B]Is 16:5 [C]Ps 80:12 [D]Is 63:11; Jer 46:26 9:12 [a]Or *Gentiles* [A]Obad 19 [B]Num 24:18; Is 11:14 [C]Is 43:7 9:13 [A]Lev 26:5 [B]Joel 3:18 [C]Gen 49:11 9:14 [a]Or *fortunes* [A]Ps 53:6; Is 60:4; Jer 30:3, 18 [B]Is 61:4; 65:21 [C]Jer 24:6; 31:28 9:15 [A]Is 60:21; Ezek 34:28; 37:25

9:11–15 Millennial blessings await the final faithful remnant, when Messiah personally reigns over all nations in Jerusalem upon the throne of David, and the Jews are never again pulled up from their divinely inherited land.

9:11 booth of David. A reference to the dynasty of David (cf. Introduction: Interpretive Challenges). God will "raise up" and "rebuild" this tabernacle on earth for Christ to rule in His millennial kingdom (cf. Zec 14:9–11). The apostles used this passage to illustrate that Gentiles could thus be a part of God's redemption. *See notes on Ac 15:13–18.*

9:13, 14 Prosperity, in hyperbolic fashion, is here described (cf. Lv 26:5; Joel 3:18; contra. Is 5). Fruitfulness is so enormous that planting and reaping seasons overlap. This prosperity will encourage massive repatriation (cf. Is 11:15, 16) and reconstruction (cf. Zec 2:1–5).

9:15 they will not again be rooted out from their land. The ultimate fulfillment of God's land promise to Abraham (cf. Ge 12:7; 15:7; 17:8) will occur during Christ's millennial reign on earth (cf. Joel 2:26, 27).

THE ULTIMATE RESTORATION OF ISRAEL
1. Is 27; 42–44; 65; 66
2. Jer 30–33
3. Eze 36; 37; 40–48
4. Da 9:20–27; 12:1–3
5. Hos 2:14–23; 14:4–7
6. Joel 3:18–21
7. Am 9:11–15
8. Ob 17, 21
9. Mic 7:14–20
10. Zep 3:14–20
11. Hag 2:20–23
12. Zec 13; 14
13. Mal 4:1–3

THE
BOOK OF

OBADIAH

TITLE

The book is named after the prophet who received the vision (1:1). Obadiah means "servant of the Lord" and occurs 20 times in the OT, referring to many other OT individuals. Obadiah is the shortest book in the OT and is not quoted in the NT.

AUTHOR AND DATE

Nothing is known for certain about the author. Other OT references to men of this name do not appear to be referring to this prophet. His frequent mentions of Jerusalem, Judah, and Zion suggest that he belonged to the southern kingdom (cf. vv. 10–12, 17, 21). Obadiah was probably a contemporary of Elijah and Elisha.

The date of writing is equally difficult to determine, though we know it is tied to the Edomite assault on Jerusalem described in vv. 10–14. Obadiah apparently wrote shortly after the attack. There were 4 significant invasions of Jerusalem in OT history: 1) by Shishak, king of Egypt, ca. 925 B.C. during the reign of Rehoboam (1Ki 14:25, 26; 2Ch 12); 2) by the Philistines and Arabians between 848–841 B.C. during the reign of Jehoram of Judah (2Ch 21:8–20); 3) by Jehoash, king of Israel, ca. 790 B.C. (2Ki 14; 2Ch 25); and 4) by Nebuchadnezzar, king of Babylon, in the fall of Jerusalem in 586 B.C. Of these 4, only the second and the fourth are possible fits with historical data. Number two is preferable, since Obadiah's description does not indicate the total destruction of the city, which took place under Nebuchadnezzar's attack. Also, although the Edomites were involved in Nebuchadnezzar's destruction of Jerusalem (Ps 137; La 4:21), it is significant that Obadiah does not mention the Babylonians by name (as with all the other prophets who wrote about Jerusalem's fall), nor is there any reference to the destruction of the temple or the deportation of the people; in fact, the captives appear to have been taken to the SW, not E to Babylon (cf. v. 20).

BACKGROUND AND SETTING

The Edomites trace their origin to Esau, the firstborn (twin) son of Isaac and Rebekah (Ge 25:24–26), who struggled with Jacob even while in the womb (Ge 25:22). Esau's name means "hairy," because he was "all over like a hairy garment" (Ge 25:25). He is also called Edom, meaning "red," owing to the sale of his birthright in exchange for some red stew (Ge 25:30). He showed a disregard for the covenant promises by marrying two Canaanite women (Ge 26:34) and later the daughter of Ishmael (Ge 28:9). He loved the out-of-doors and, after having his father's blessing stolen from him by Jacob, was destined to remain a man of the open spaces (Ge 25:27; 27:38–40). Esau settled in a region of mostly rugged mountains S of the Dead Sea (Ge 33:16; 36:8, 9; Dt 2:4, 5) called Edom (Gr., "Idumea"), the 4-mi. wide area which stretches approximately 100 mi. S to the Gulf of Aqabah. The famed King's Highway, an essential caravan route linking North Africa with Europe and Asia, passes along the eastern plateau (Nu 20:17). The struggle and birth of Jacob and Esau (Ge 25) form the ultimate background to the prophecy of Ge 25:23, "two nations are in your womb." Their respective descendants, Israel and Edom, were perpetual enemies. When Israel came out from Egypt, Edom denied their brother Jacob passage through their land, located S of the Dead Sea (Nu 20:14–21). Nevertheless, Israel was instructed by God to be kind to Edom (Dt 23:7, 8). Obadiah, having received a vision from God, was sent to describe their crimes and to pronounce total destruction upon Edom because of their treatment of Israel.

The Edomites opposed Saul (ca. 1043–1011 B.C.) and were subdued under David (ca. 1011–971 B.C.) and Solomon (ca. 971–931 B.C.). They fought against Jehoshaphat (ca. 873–848 B.C.) and successfully rebelled against Jehoram (ca. 853–841 B.C.). They were again conquered by Judah under Amaziah (ca. 796–767 B.C.), but they regained their freedom during the reign of Ahaz (ca. 735–715 B.C.). Edom was later controlled by Assyria and Babylon; and in the fifth century B.C. the Edomites were forced by the Nabateans to leave their territory. They moved to the area of southern Israel and became known as Idumeans. Herod the Great, an Idumean, became king of Judea under Rome in 37 B.C. In a sense, the enmity between Esau and Jacob was continued in Herod's attempt to murder Jesus. The Idumeans participated in the rebellion of Jerusalem against Rome and were defeated along with the Jews by Titus in A.D. 70. Ironically, the Edomites applauded the destruction of Jerusalem in 586 B.C. (cf. Ps 137:7) but died trying to defend it in A.D. 70. After that time they were never heard of again. As Obadiah predicted, they would be "cut off forever" (v. 10); and there would be "no survivor of the house of Esau" (v. 18).

HISTORICAL AND THEOLOGICAL THEMES

Obadiah is a case study of the curses/blessings in Ge 12:1–3, with two interrelated themes: 1) the judgment of Edom by God for cursing Israel. This was apparently told to Judah, thereby providing reassurance that the Lord would bring judgment upon Edom for her pride and for her participation in Judah's downfall; 2) Judah's restoration. This would even include the territory of the Edomites (vv. 19–21; Is 11:14). Obadiah's blessing for Judah includes the near fulfillment of Edom's demise (vv. 1–14), and the far fulfillment of the nations' judgment and Israel's final possession of Edom (vv. 15–21).

INTERPRETIVE CHALLENGES

The striking similarity between Ob 1–9 and Jer 49:7–22 brings up the question: Who borrowed from whom? Assuming there was not a third common source, it appears that Jeremiah borrowed, where appropriate, from Obadiah, since the shared verses form one unit in Obadiah, while in Jeremiah they are scattered among other verses.

OUTLINE

I. God's Judgment on Edom (1–14)
- A. Edom's Punishment (1–9)
- B. Edom's Crimes (10–14)

II. God's Judgment on the Nations (15, 16)

III. God's Restoration of Israel (17–21)

EDOM WILL BE HUMBLED

1 The vision of Obadiah.
Thus says the Lord [a]GOD concerning [A]Edom—

[B]We have heard a report from the LORD,
And an [C]envoy has been sent
among the nations *saying,*
"[D]Arise and let us go against
her for battle"—
2 "Behold, I will make you [A]small
among the nations;
You are greatly despised.
3 "The [A]arrogance of your heart
has deceived you,
You who live in the clefts of [a]the [B]rock,
In the loftiness of your dwelling place,
Who say in your heart,
'[C]Who will bring me down to earth?'
4 "Though you [A]build high like the eagle,
Though you set your nest
among the [B]stars,
From there I will bring you
down," declares the LORD.
5 "If [A]thieves came to you,
If [a]robbers by night—
O how you will be ruined!—
Would they not steal *only* [b]until
they had enough?
If grape gatherers came to you,
[B]Would they not leave *some* gleanings?
6 "O how Esau will be [A]ransacked,
And his hidden treasures searched out!
7 "All the [A]men [a]allied with you
Will send you forth to the border,
And the men at peace with you
Will deceive you and overpower you.
They who eat your [B]bread
Will set an ambush for you.
(There is [C]no understanding [b]in him.)
8 "Will I not on that day,"
declares the LORD,
"[A]Destroy wise men from Edom
And understanding from the
mountain of Esau?
9 "Then your [A]mighty men will
be dismayed, O [B]Teman,
So that everyone may be [C]cut off from
the mountain of Esau by slaughter.

10 "Because of [A]violence to
your brother Jacob,
[a]You will be covered *with* shame,
[B]And you will be cut off forever.
11 "On the day that you [A]stood aloof,
On the day that strangers
carried off his wealth,
And foreigners entered his gate
And [B]cast lots for Jerusalem—
[C]You too were as one of them.
12 "[A]Do not [a]gloat over your
brother's day,
The day of his misfortune.
And [B]do not rejoice over
the sons of Judah
In the day of their destruction;
Yes, [C]do not [b]boast
In the day of *their* distress.
13 "Do not enter the gate of My people
In the [A]day of their disaster.
Yes, you, do not [a]gloat
over their calamity
In the day of their disaster.
And do not [B]loot their wealth
In the day of their disaster.
14 "Do not [A]stand at the fork of the road
To cut down their fugitives;
And do not imprison their survivors
In the day of their distress.

1:1 [a]Heb *YHWH*, usually rendered *LORD* [A]Ps 137:7; Is 21:11, 12; 34:1-17; 63:1-6; Jer 49:7-22; Ezek 25:12-14; 35:15; Joel 3:19; Amos 1:11, 12; Mal 1:4 [B]Jer 49:14-16; Obad 1-4 [C]Is 18:2; 30:4 [D]Jer 6:4, 5 1:2 [A]Num 24:18; Is 23:9 1:3 [a]Or *Sela* [A]Is 16:6; Jer 49:16 [B]2 Kin 14:7; 2 Chr 25:11f [C]Is 14:13-15; Rev 18:7 1:4 [A]Job 20:6, 7; Hab 2:9 [B]Is 14:12-15 1:5 [a]Lit *devastators of* the *night* [b]Lit *their sufficiency* [A]Jer 49:9 [B]Deut 24:21 1:6 [A]Jer 49:10 1:7 [a]Lit *of your covenant* [b]I.e. in Esau; or *of it* [A]Jer 30:14 [B]Ps 41:9 [C]Is 19:11; Jer 49:7 1:8 [A]Job 5:12-14; Is 29:14 1:9 [A]Jer 49:22 [B]Gen 36:11; 1 Chr 1:45; Job 2:11; Jer 49:7; Ezek 25:13; Amos 1:12; Hab 3:3 [C]Is 34:5-8; 63:1-3; Obad 5 1:10 [a]Lit *Shame will cover you* [A]Gen 27:41; Ezek 25:12; Joel 3:19; Amos 1:11 [B]Ezek 35:9 1:11 [A]Ps 83:5, 6; 137:7; Amos 1:6, 9 [B]Joel 3:3; Nah 3:10 [C]Ezek 35:10 1:12 [a]Lit *look on* [b]Lit *make your mouth large* [A]Mic 4:11; 7:10 [B]Prov 17:5; Ezek 35:15; 36:5 [C]Ps 31:18; Ezek 35:12 1:13 [a]Lit *look on* [A]Ezek 35:5 [B]Ezek 35:10; 36:2, 3 1:14 [A]Is 16:3, 4

1 The vision. The prophetic word often came from God in the form of a vision (cf. Hab 1:1). **Thus says the Lord GOD.** Although the background of the prophet is obscure, the source of his message is not. It was supernaturally given by God, and was not motivated by unholy vengeance. **Edom.** Descendants of Esau (Ge 25:30; 36:1ff.), the Edomites settled in the region S of the Dead Sea. See Introduction: Background and Setting. **Arise ... go against her.** The prophet heard of a God-ordained international plot to overthrow Edom. The selfish motives of Edom's enemies were divinely controlled by the Lord's "envoy" to serve His sovereign purposes (cf. Ps 104:4).

3 the clefts of the rock. Dwelling in difficult mountain terrain, Edom's imposing, impregnable capital city of Petra was virtually inaccessible, giving her a sense of security and self-sufficiency. Deep, terrifying gorges emanating from peaks reaching 5,700 ft. surrounded her like a fortress, generating a proud, false sense of security.

3, 4 Who will bring me down .... will bring you down. Edom's pride was answered decisively by the Sovereign Ruler (cf. Mt 23:12). The calamity against Edom, though brought about by her enemies, was truly God's judgment of her pride (cf. Pr 16:18; 1Co 10:12).

5 robbers by night. Because of the rugged terrain and very narrow access through the gorges, predatory attack could only come at night.

5, 6 Edom's attackers, by divine judgment, would not stop where normal thieves would when they have enough. Instead, they would leave nothing.

7 Those conspiring against Edom (v. 1) were her allies ("men allied with you"), her neighbors ("men at peace with you"), and even the outlying tribes who benefited from Edom's prosperity ("*They who eat your bread*").

8 wise men. Edom was known for her wise men and sages (Jer 49:7). Her location on the King's Highway provided her with intellectual stimulation with India, Europe, and North Africa.

9 Teman. A name derived from a descendant of Esau (Ge 36:11), it refers to a region in the northern part of Edom which was the home of Job's friend, Eliphaz (Job 4:1).

10 violence to ... Jacob. Edom's opposition is in view, which began as Israel approached the land (cf. Nu 20:14–21) and continued to Habakkuk's day. "Slaughter" (v. 9) and shame for Edom will be just retribution for Edom's violence and slaughter against her brother's people.

11–14 The charge of v. 10 is here amplified: 1) they "stood aloof," withholding assistance (v. 11); 2) they rejoiced over Judah's downfall (v. 12; cf. Pss 83:4–6; 137:4–6); 3) they plundered the city (v. 13); and 4) they prevented the escape of her fugitives (v. 14).

THE DAY OF THE LORD AND THE FUTURE

15 "For the [A]day of the LORD draws
near on all the nations.
[B]As you have done, it will be done to you.
Your [C]dealings will return
on your own head.
16 "Because just as you [A]drank on
[B]My holy mountain,
All the nations [C]will drink continually.
They will drink and [a]swallow
And become as if they had never existed.
17 "But on Mount [A]Zion there will
be those who escape,
And it will be holy.
And the house of Jacob will
[B]possess their possessions.
18 "Then the house of Jacob will be a [A]fire
And the house of Joseph a flame;
But the house of Esau *will be* as stubble.
And they will set [a]them on fire
and consume [a]them,
So that there will be [B]no survivor
of the house of Esau,"
For the LORD has spoken.
19 Then *those of* the [a]Negev will
[A]possess the mountain of Esau,
And *those of* the [b]Shephelah
the [B]Philistine *plain;*
Also, [C]possess the territory of Ephraim
and the territory of Samaria,
And Benjamin *will possess* Gilead.
20 And the exiles of this host
of the sons of Israel,
Who are *among* the Canaanites
as far as [A]Zarephath,
And the exiles of Jerusalem
who are in Sepharad
Will possess the [B]cities of the Negev.
21 The [A]deliverers will ascend Mount Zion
To judge the mountain of Esau,
And the [B]kingdom will be the LORD'S.

1:15 [A]Ezek 30:3; Joel 1:15; 2:1, 11, 31; Amos 5:18, 20 [B]Jer 50:29; 51:56; Hab 2:8 [C]Ezek 35:11 1:16 [a]Or *stagger* [A]Jer 49:12 [B]Joel 3:17 [C]Is 51:22, 23; Jer 25:15, 16 1:17 [A]Is 4:2, 3 [B]Is 14:1, 2; Amos 9:11-15 1:18 [a]I.e. the people of Esau [A]Is 5:24; 9:18, 19; Zech 12:6 [B]Jer 11:23; Amos 1:8 1:19 [a]I.e. South country [b]I.e. the foothills [A]Is 11:14; Amos 9:12 [B]Is 11:14 [C]Jer 31:5; 32:44 1:20 [A]1 Kin 17:9; Luke 4:26 [B]Jer 32:44; 33:13 1:21 [A]Neh 9:27 [B]Ps 22:28; 47:7-9; 67:4; Zech 14:9; Rev 11:15

15 day of the LORD. God's near judgment of Edom in history (vv. 1–14) was a preview of His far judgment on all nations (vv. 15, 16) who refuse to bow to His sovereignty (cf. discussion of "Day of the Lord" in Introduction to Joel).

16 My holy mountain. Zion, referring to Jerusalem (cf. v. 17). **drink and swallow.** Compare Zec 12:2, where the Lord will make His people as a "cup that causes reeling" from which His enemies will be made to drink. This refers to the cup of God's wrath. Judah drank temporarily of judgment, Edom will drink "continually."

17 A reversal of Judah's plight in vv. 10–14 will come about when Messiah intercedes and establishes His millennial kingdom and holiness prevails.

18–20 Those of Judah who remain (v. 14) will be divinely empowered to "consume" (v. 18) and completely wipe out the "house of Esau" (cf. Is 11:14; 34:5–17). When Messiah sets up His kingdom, the boundaries of the Davidic and Solomonic kingdoms will once again expand to include that promised to Jacob in his dream at Bethel (Ge 28:14) which reaffirmed God's promise to Abraham (cf. Ge 12). This would include the S (mountains of Esau); the W (Philistia); the N (Ephraim … Samaria); and the E (Gilead).

18 house of Jacob … house of Joseph. Representatives of Abraham's descendants.

20 Canaanites. Those peoples who occupied the land before the Exodus. **Zarephath.** Also known as Sarepta (cf. Lk 4:26), this town was located on the Phoenician coast between Tyre and Sidon. **Sepharad.** Not mentioned elsewhere in the Bible, the location is uncertain. Most rabbis identify it with Spain; others have suggested Sparta or Sardis.

21 deliverers will ascend … to judge. Just as the Lord raised up judges to deliver His people (cf. Ne 9:27), so will He establish similar leaders to help rule in the millennial kingdom (cf. 1Co 6:2; Rev 20:4). **the kingdom will be the LORD's.** When the nations are judged in the day of the Lord, He will then set up His millennial kingdom, a theocracy in which He rules His people directly on earth (Zec 14:4–9; Rev 11:15).

GOD'S JUDGMENT ON EDOM
More than any other nation mentioned in the OT, Edom is the supreme object of God's wrath.
• Pss 83:5–18; 137:7
• Is 11:14; 21:11, 12; 34:5; 63:1–6
• Jer 49:7–22
• La 4:21, 22
• Eze 25:12–14; 35:1–15
• Joel 3:19
• Am 1:11, 12; 9:11, 12
• Mal 1:2–5

THE BOOK OF

JONAH

TITLE

Following the lead of the Hebrew Masoretic text (MT), the title of the book is derived from the principal character, Jonah (meaning "dove"), the son of Amittai (1:1). Both the Septuagint (LXX) and the Latin Vulgate (Vg.) ascribe the same name.

AUTHOR AND DATE

The book makes no direct claim regarding authorship. Throughout the book, Jonah is repeatedly referred to in the third person, causing some to search for another author. It was not an uncommon OT practice, however, to write in the third person (e.g., Ex 11:3; 1Sa 12:11). Furthermore, the autobiographical information revealed within its pages clearly points to Jonah as the author. The firsthand accounts of such unusual events and experiences would be best recounted from the hand of Jonah himself. Nor should the introductory verse suggest otherwise, since other prophets such as Hosea, Joel, Micah, Zephaniah, Haggai, and Zechariah have similar openings.

According to 2Ki 14:25, Jonah came from Gath-hepher near Nazareth. The context places him during the long and prosperous reign of Jeroboam II (ca. 793–753 B.C.), making him a prophet to the northern tribes just prior to Amos during the first half of the eighth century B.C., ca. 760 B.C. The Pharisees were wrong when they said "no prophet arises out of Galilee" (Jn 7:52), because Jonah was a Galilean. An unverifiable Jewish tradition says Jonah was the son of the widow of Zarephath whom Elijah raised from the dead (1Ki 17:8–24).

BACKGROUND AND SETTING

As a prophet to the 10 northern tribes of Israel, Jonah shares a background and setting with Amos. The nation enjoyed a time of relative peace and prosperity. Both Syria and Assyria were weak, allowing Jeroboam II to enlarge the northern borders of Israel to where they had been in the days of David and Solomon (2Ki 14:23–27). Spiritually, however, it was a time of poverty; religion was ritualistic and increasingly idolatrous, and justice had become perverted. Peacetime and wealth had made her bankrupt spiritually, morally, and ethically (cf. 2Ki 14:24; Am 4:1ff.; 5:10–13). As a result, God was to punish her by bringing destruction and captivity from the Assyrians in 722 B.C. Nineveh's repentance may have been aided by the two plagues (765 and 759 B.C.) and a solar eclipse (763 B.C.), preparing them for Jonah's judgment message.

HISTORICAL AND THEOLOGICAL THEMES

Jonah, though a prophet of Israel, is not remembered for his ministry in Israel which could explain why the Pharisees erringly claimed in Jesus' day that no prophet had come from Galilee (cf. Jn 7:52). Rather, the book relates the account of his call to preach repentance to Nineveh and his refusal to go. Nineveh, the capital of Assyria and infamous for its cruelty, was a historical nemesis of Israel and Judah. The focus of this book is on that Gentile city, which was founded by Nimrod, great-grandson of Noah (Ge 10:6–12). Perhaps the largest city in the ancient world (1:2; 3:2, 3; 4:11), it was nevertheless destroyed about 150 years after the repentance of the generation in the time of Jonah's visit (612 B.C.), as Nahum prophesied (Na 1:1ff.). Israel's political distaste for Assyria, coupled with a sense of spiritual superiority as the recipient of God's covenant blessing, produced a recalcitrant attitude in Jonah toward God's request for missionary service. Jonah was sent to Nineveh in part to shame Israel by the fact that a pagan city repented at the preaching of a stranger, whereas Israel would not repent though preached to by many prophets. He was soon to learn that God's love and mercy extends to all of His creatures (4:2, 10, 11), not just His covenant people (cf. Ge 9:27; 12:3; Lv 19:33, 34; 1Sa 2:10; Is 2:2; Joel 2:28–32).

The book of Jonah reveals God's sovereign rule over man and all creation. Creation came into being through Him (1:9) and responds to His every command (1:4, 17; 2:10; 4:6, 7; cf. Mk 4:41). Jesus employed the repentance of the Ninevites to rebuke the Pharisees, thereby illustrating the hardness of the Pharisees' hearts and their unwillingness to repent (Mt 12:38–41; Lk 11:29–32). The heathen city of Nineveh repented at the preaching of a reluctant prophet, but the Pharisees would not repent at the preaching of the greatest of all prophets, in spite of overwhelming evidence that He was actually their Lord and Messiah. Jonah is a picture of Israel, who was chosen and commissioned by God to be His witness (Is 43:10–12; 44:8), who rebelled against His will (Ex 32:1–4; Jdg 2:11–19; Eze 6:1–5; Mk 7:6–9), but who has been miraculously preserved by God through centuries of exile and dispersion to finally preach His truth (Jer 30:11; 31:35–37; Hos 3:3–5; Rev 7:1–8; 14:1–3).

INTERPRETIVE CHALLENGES

The primary challenge is whether the book is to be interpreted as historical narrative or as allegory/parable. The grand scale of the miracles, such as being kept alive 3 days and nights in a big fish, has led some skeptics and critics to deny their historical validity and substitute spiritual lessons, either to the constituent parts (allegory) or to the book as a whole (parable). But however grandiose and miraculous the events may have been, the narrative must be viewed as historical. Centered on a historically identifiable OT prophet who lived in the eighth century B.C., the account of whom has been recorded in narrative form, there is no alternative but to understand Jonah as historical. Furthermore, Jesus did not teach the story of Jonah as a parable but as an actual account firmly rooted in history (Mt 12:38–41; 16:4; Lk 11:29–32).

OUTLINE

I. Running from God's Will (1:1–17)
- A. The Commission of Jonah (1:1, 2)
- B. The Flight of Jonah (1:3)
- C. The Pursuit of Jonah (1:4–16)
- D. The Preservation of Jonah (1:17)

II. Submitting to God's Will (2:1–10)
- A. The Helplessness of Jonah (2:1–3)
- B. The Prayer of Jonah (2:4–7)
- C. The Repentance of Jonah (2:8, 9)
- D. The Deliverance of Jonah (2:10)

III. Fulfilling God's Will (3:1–10)
- A. The Commission Renewed (3:1, 2)
- B. The Prophet Obeys (3:3, 4)
- C. The City Repents (3:5–9)
- D. The Lord Relents (3:10)

IV. Questioning God's Will (4:1–11)
- A. The Prophet Displeased (4:1–5)
- B. The Prophet Rebuked (4:6–11)

JONAH'S DISOBEDIENCE

1 The word of the LORD came to [A]Jonah the son of
Amittai saying, 2 "Arise, go to [A]Nineveh the great
city and [B]cry against it, for their [C]wickedness has
come up before Me." 3 But Jonah rose up to flee to
[A]Tarshish [B]from the presence of the LORD. So he
went down to [C]Joppa, found a ship which was going to Tarshish, paid the fare and went down into
it to go with them to Tarshish from the presence
of the LORD.
4 The [A]LORD hurled a great wind on the sea and
there was a great storm on the sea so that the ship
was about to [a]break up. 5 Then the sailors became
afraid and every man cried to [A]his god, and they
[B]threw the [a]cargo which was in the ship into the
sea to lighten *it* [b]for them. But Jonah had gone below into the hold of the ship, lain down and fallen
sound asleep. 6 So the captain approached him and
said, "How is it that you are sleeping? Get up, [A]call
on your god. Perhaps *your* [B]god will be concerned
about us so that we will not perish."
7 Each man said to his mate, "Come, let us [A]cast lots
so we may [a]learn on whose account this calamity *has*
struck us." So they cast lots and the [B]lot fell on Jonah.
8 Then they said to him, "[A]Tell us, now! On whose
account *has* this calamity *struck* us? What is your
[B]occupation? And where do you come from? What
is your country? From what people are you?" 9 He
said to them, "I am a [A]Hebrew, and I [B]fear the LORD
[C]God of heaven who [D]made the sea and the dry land."
10 Then the men became extremely frightened and
they said to him, "[a]How could you do this?" For the
men knew that he was [A]fleeing from the presence of
the LORD, because he had told them. 11 So they said
to him, "What should we do to you that the sea may
become calm [a]for us?"—for the sea was becoming

1:1 [A]2 Kin 14:25; Matt 12:39-41; 16:4; Luke 11:29, 30, 32 1:2 [A]Gen 10:11; 2 Kin 19:36; Is 37:37; Nah 1:1; Zeph 2:13 [B]Is 58:1 [C]Gen 18:20; Hos 7:2 1:3 [A]Is 23:1, 6, 10; Jer 10:9 [B]Gen 4:16; Ps 139:7, 9, 10 [C]Josh 19:46; 2 Chr 2:16; Ezra 3:7; Acts 9:36, 43 1:4 [a]Lit *be broken* [A]Ps 107:23-28; 135:6, 7 1:5 [a]Lit *vessels* [b]Lit *from upon them* [A]1 Kin 18:26 [B]Acts 27:18, 19, 38 1:6 [A]Ps 107:28 [B]2 Sam 12:22; Amos 5:15; Jon 3:9 1:7 [a]Lit *know* [A]Josh 7:14-18; 1 Sam 10:20, 21; 14:41, 42; Acts 1:23-26 [B]Num 32:23; Prov 16:33 1:8 [A]Josh 7:19; 1 Sam 14:43 [B]Gen 47:3; 1 Sam 30:13 1:9 [A]Gen 14:13; Ex 1:15; 2:13 [B]2 Kin 17:25, 28, 32, 33 [C]Ezra 1:2; Neh 1:4; Ps 136:26; Dan 2:18 [D]Neh 9:6; Ps 95:5; 146:6 1:10 [a]Lit *What is this you have done* [A]Job 27:22; Jon 1:3 1:11 [a]Lit *from upon us*

1:1 Jonah the son of Amittai. Jonah's name is Heb. for "dove," while that of his father means "truthful" or "loyal."

1:2 Arise, go to Nineveh. While other prophets prophesied against Gentile nations, this is the only case of a prophet actually being sent to a foreign nation to deliver God's message against them. This was for the salvation of that city and for the shame and jealousy of Israel, as well as a rebuke to the reluctance of the Jews to bring Gentiles to the true God. Nineveh, which dates back to Nimrod (Ge 10:11), was located on the banks of the Tigris River approximately 500 mi. NE of Israel. It was always one of Assyria's royal cities and for many years served as the capital. The name Nineveh is thought to derive from "ninus," i.e., Nimrod, and means the residence of Nimrod or "nunu" (Akkadian for "fish"). The people worshiped the fish goddess Nanshe (the daughter of Ea, the goddess of fresh water) and Dagon the fish god who was represented as half man and half fish. **the great city.** Nineveh was great both in size (3:3) and in power, exerting significant influence over the Middle East until her destruction by Nebuchadnezzar in 612 B.C. It was possibly the largest city in the world at this time. According to historians, magnificent walls almost 8 mi. long enveloped the inner city, with the rest of the city/district occupying an area with a circumference of some 60 miles. Its population could have approached 600,000 (cf. 4:11). **their wickedness has come up before Me.** Nineveh was the center of idolatrous worship of Assur and Ishtar. A century later, Nahum pronounced doom upon Assyria for her evil ways and cruelty (Na 3), which was carried out by Nebuchadnezzar in 612 B.C.

1:3 But Jonah rose up to flee to Tarshish. This is the only recorded instance of a prophet refusing God's commission (cf. Jer 20:7–9). The location of Tarshish, known for its wealth (Ps 72:10; Jer 10:9; Eze 27:12, 25), is uncertain. The Gr. historian Herodotus identified it with Tartessus, a merchant city in southern Spain. The prophet went as far W in the opposite direction as possible, showing his reluctance to bring salvation blessing to Gentiles. **from the presence of the LORD.** While no one can escape from the Lord's omnipresence (Ps 139:7–12), it is thought that the prophet was attempting to flee His manifest presence in the temple at Jerusalem (cf. Ge 4:16; Jon 2:4). **Joppa.** Joppa (today Jaffa), located on the Mediterranean coast near the border of Judah and Samaria, was also the location of Peter's vision in preparation for his visit to Cornelius, a Gentile (Ac 10).

1:4 a great wind. This is not an ordinary storm, but an extreme one sent ("hurled") from God. Sailors, accustomed to storms, were afraid of this one (v. 5), a fear which served God's purpose (cf. Ps 104:4).

1:7 cast lots. The last resort is to ascertain whose guilt has caused such divine anger. God could reveal His will by controlling the lots, which He did. This method of discernment by casting lots, the exact procedure of which is not known, was not forbidden in Israel (cf. Pr 16:33; Jos 7:14ff.; 15:1; 1Sa 14:36–45; Ac 1:26).

1:9 I am a Hebrew. Jonah identified himself by the name that Israelites used among Gentiles (cf. 1Sa 4:6, 9; 14:11). **the LORD God of heaven.** This title, in use from earliest times (Ge 24:3, 7), may have been specifically chosen by Jonah to express the sovereignty of the Lord in contrast to Baal, who was a sky god (cf. 1Ki 18:24). Spoken to sailors who were most likely from Phoenicia, the center of Baal worship, the title bears significant weight, especially when coupled with the phrase "who made the sea and the dry land." This was the appropriate identification when introducing the true and living God to pagans who didn't have Scripture, but whose reason led them to recognize the fact that there had to be a Creator (cf. Ro 1:18–23). To begin with creation, as in Ac 14:14–17 and 17:23b–29, was the proper starting point. To evangelize Jews, one can begin with the OT Scripture.

1:11, 12 Unwilling to go to Nineveh and feeling guilty, Jonah was willing to sacrifice himself in an effort to save the lives of others. Apparently, he would rather have died than go to Nineveh.

TEN MIRACLES IN JONAH

1. 1:4	"the LORD hurled a great wind on the sea"
2. 1:7	"the lot fell on Jonah"
3. 1:15	"the sea stopped its raging"
4. 1:17	"the LORD appointed a great fish"
5. 1:17	"to swallow Jonah (alive)"
6. 2:10	"the LORD commanded the fish ... it vomited Jonah up onto the dry land"
7. 3:10	"God saw their deeds ... they turned from their wicked way"
8. 4:6	"the LORD God appointed a plant"
9. 4:7	"God appointed a worm"
10. 4:8	"God appointed a scorching east wind"

increasingly stormy. 12 He said to them, “Pick me up
and throw me into the sea. Then the sea will become
calm [a]for you, for I know that [A]on account of me this
great storm *has come* upon you.” 13 However, the men
[a]rowed *desperately* to return to land but they could
not, for the sea was becoming *even* stormier against
them. 14 Then they called on the [A]LORD and said, “We
earnestly pray, O LORD, do not let us perish on account
of this man’s life and do not put innocent blood on
us; for [B]You, O LORD, have done as You have pleased.”
15 So they picked up Jonah, threw him into the
sea, and the sea [A]stopped its raging. 16 Then the
men feared the LORD greatly, and they offered a
sacrifice to the LORD and made [A]vows.
17 [a]And the LORD appointed a great fish to swallow Jonah, and Jonah was in the [A]stomach of the
fish three days and three nights.

JONAH’S PRAYER

2 [a]Then Jonah prayed to the LORD his God [A]from
the stomach of the fish, 2 and he said,

“I [A]called out of my distress to the LORD,
And He answered me.
I cried for help from the [a]depth of [B]Sheol;
You heard my voice.
3 “For You had [A]cast me into the deep,
Into the heart of the seas,
And the current [a]engulfed me.
All Your [B]breakers and billows
passed over me.
4 “So I said, ‘I have been [A]expelled
from [a]Your sight.
Nevertheless I will look again
[B]toward Your holy temple.’
5 “[A]Water encompassed me to
the [a]point of death.
The great [B]deep [b]engulfed me,
Weeds were wrapped around my head.
6 “I [A]descended to the roots of the mountains.
The earth with its [B]bars *was*
around me forever,
But You have [C]brought up my life
from [a]the pit, O LORD my God.
7 “While [a]I was [A]fainting away,
I [B]remembered the LORD,
And my [C]prayer came to You,
Into [D]Your holy temple.
8 “Those who [A]regard [a]vain idols
Forsake their faithfulness,
9 But I will [A]sacrifice to You
With the voice of thanksgiving.
That which I have vowed I will [B]pay.
[C]Salvation is from the LORD.”

10 Then the LORD commanded the [A]fish, and it
vomited Jonah up onto the dry land.

NINEVEH REPENTS

3 Now the word of the LORD came to Jonah the
second time, saying, 2 “Arise, go to [A]Nineveh
the great city and [B]proclaim to it the proclamation
which I am going to tell you.” 3 So Jonah arose and
went to Nineveh according to the word of the LORD.
Now Nineveh was [a]an [A]exceedingly great city, a
three days’ walk. 4 Then Jonah began to go through
the city one day’s walk; and he [A]cried out and said,
“Yet forty days and Nineveh will be overthrown.”
5 Then the people of Nineveh believed in God;
and they called a [A]fast and put on sackcloth from

1:12 [a]Lit *from upon you* [A]2 Sam 24:17; 1 Chr 21:17 1:13 [a]Lit *dug their oars into the water* 1:14 [A]Ps 107:28; Jon 1:16 [B]Ps 115:3; 135:6; Dan 4:34, 35 1:15 [A]Ps 65:7; 93:3, 4; 107:29 1:16 [A]Ps 50:14; 66:13, 14 1:17 [a]Ch 2:1 in Heb [A]Matt 12:40; 16:4 2:1 [a]Ch 2:2 in Heb [A]Job 13:15; Ps 130:1, 2; Lam 3:53-56 2:2 [a]Lit *belly* [A]1 Sam 30:6; Ps 18:4-6; 22:24; 120:1 [B]Ps 18:5, 6; 86:13; 88:1-7 2:3 [a]Lit *surrounded* [A]Ps 69:1, 2, 14, 15; Lam 3:54 [B]Ps 42:7 2:4 [a]Lit *before Your eyes* [A]Ps 31:22; Jer 7:15 [B]1 Kin 8:38; 2 Chr 6:38; Ps 5:7 2:5 [a]Lit *soul* [b]Lit *surrounded* [A]Lam 3:54 [B]Ps 69:1, 2 2:6 [a]Or *corruption* [A]Ps 18:5; 116:3 [B]Is 38:10; Matt 16:18 [C]Job 33:28; Ps 16:10; 30:3; Is 38:17 2:7 [a]Lit *my soul…within me* [A]Ps 142:3 [B]Ps 77:10, 11; 143:5 [C]2 Chr 30:27; Ps 18:6 [D]Ps 11:4; 65:4; Jon 2:4; Mic 1:2; Hab 2:20 2:8 [a]Lit *empty vanities* [A]2 Kin 17:15; Ps 31:6; Jer 10:8 2:9 [A]Ps 50:14, 23; Jer 33:11; Hos 14:2 [B]Job 22:27; Eccl 5:4, 5 [C]Ps 3:8; Is 45:17 2:10 [A]Jon 1:17 3:2 [A]Zeph 2:13 [B]Jer 1:17; Ezek 2:7 3:3 [a]Lit *a great city to God* [A]Jon 1:2; 4:11 3:4 [A]Matt 12:41; Luke 11:32 3:5 [A]Dan 9:3; Joel 1:14

1:13, 14 Heathen sailors had more concern for one man than Jonah had for tens of thousands in Nineveh. The storm, Jonah’s words, and the lots all indicated to the sailors that the Lord was involved; thus they offered sacrifices to Him and made vows, indicating Jonah had told them more about God than is recorded here.

1:15 **the sea stopped.** This was similar to Christ’s quieting the storm on the Sea of Galilee (cf. Mt 8:23–27).

1:17 **a great fish.** The species of fish is uncertain; the Heb. word for whale is not here employed. God sovereignly prepared (lit. “appointed”) a great fish to rescue Jonah. Apparently, Jonah sank into the depth of the sea before the fish swallowed him (cf. 2:3, 5, 6). **three days and three nights.** *See note on Mt 12:40.*

2:1–9 Jonah acknowledged God’s sovereignty (vv. 1–3) and submitted to it (vv. 4–9).

2:2 **from the depth of Sheol.** The phrase does not necessarily indicate that Jonah actually died. “Sheol” frequently has a hyperbolic meaning in contexts where it denotes a catastrophic condition near death (Ps 30:3). Later Jonah expressed praise for his deliverance “from the pit” (v. 6), speaking of his escape from certain death.

2:3 In describing his watery experience, Jonah acknowledged that his circumstances were judgment from the Lord.

2:4 **I have been expelled from Your sight.** In 1:3, Jonah ran from the Lord’s presence; here he realizes that the Lord has temporarily expelled him.

2:5 **point of death.** Lit. “soul.” This describes Jonah’s total person—both physically and spiritually (cf. v. 7).

2:9 **I have vowed.** Jonah found himself in the same position as the mariners: offering sacrifices and making vows (cf. 1:16). In light of 3:1–4, Jonah’s vow could well have been to carry out God’s ministry will for him by preaching in Nineveh (Pss 50:14; 66:13, 14).

2:10 **the LORD commanded.** Just as God calls the stars by name (Is 40:26; cf. Ps 147:4), so He speaks to His creation in the animal world (cf. Nu 22:28–30). Most likely, Jonah was vomited upon the shore near Joppa.

3:1, 2 Gracious in giving Jonah a second chance, God again commissioned him to go to Nineveh. Jonah is the only prophet actually sent by God to preach repentance in a foreign land.

3:3 **an exceedingly great city, a three days’ walk.** Lit. “a great city to God,” the text emphasizes not only its size (cf. 1:2) but its importance (cf. 4:11). A metropolitan city the size of Nineveh, with a circumference of about 60 mi., would require 3 days just to get around it. These dimensions are confirmed by historians. Stopping to preach would only add to the time requirement.

3:4 **Yet forty days.** The time frame may harken back to Moses’ supplication for 40 days and nights at Sinai (Dt 9:18, 25). Jonah’s message, while short, accomplishes God’s intended purpose.

3:5 **the people … believed in God.** Jonah’s experience with the fish (2:1–10), in light of the Ninevites’ pagan beliefs (*see note on 1:2*), certainly gained him an instant hearing. From the divine side, this wholesale repentance was a miraculous work of God. Pagan sailors and a pagan city responded to the reluctant prophet, showing the power of God in spite of the weakness of His servant.

the greatest to the least of them. 6 When the word
reached the king of Nineveh, he arose from his
throne, laid aside his robe from him, [A]covered *him-*
self with sackcloth and sat on the [a]ashes. 7 He issued
a [A]proclamation and it said, "In Nineveh by the
decree of the king and his nobles: Do not let man,
beast, herd, or flock taste a thing. Do not let them
eat or drink water. 8 But both man and beast must
be covered with sackcloth; and let [a]men [A]call on God
earnestly that each may [B]turn from his wicked way
and from the violence which is in [b]his hands. 9 [A]Who
knows, God may turn and relent and withdraw His
burning anger so that we will not perish."
10 When God saw their deeds, that they [A]turned
from their wicked way, then [B]God relented concerning the calamity which He had declared He would
[a]bring upon them. And He did not do *it*.

JONAH'S DISPLEASURE REBUKED

4 But it greatly displeased Jonah and he became
[A]angry. 2 He [A]prayed to the LORD and said,
"Please LORD, was not this [a]what I said while I
was still in my *own* country? Therefore [b]in order
to forestall this I [B]fled to Tarshish, for I knew that
You are a [C]gracious and compassionate God, slow
to anger and abundant in lovingkindness, and one
who relents concerning calamity. 3 Therefore now,
O LORD, please [A]take my [a]life from me, for death is
[B]better to me than life." 4 The LORD said, "Do you
have good reason to be angry?"
5 Then Jonah went out from the city and sat east
of [a]it. There he made a shelter for himself and [A]sat
under it in the shade until he could see what would
happen in the city. 6 So the LORD God appointed
a [a]plant and it grew up over Jonah to be a shade
over his head to deliver him from his discomfort.
And Jonah was [b]extremely happy about the [a]plant.
7 But God appointed a worm when dawn came the
next day and it attacked the plant and it [A]withered.
8 When the sun came up God appointed a scorching
[A]east wind, and the [B]sun beat down on Jonah's head
so that he became faint and begged with *all* his
soul to die, saying, "[C]Death is better to me than life."
9 Then God said to Jonah, "Do you have good reason to be angry about the plant?" And he said, "I
have good reason to be angry, even to death." 10 Then
the LORD said, "You had compassion on the plant
for which you did not work and *which* you did not
cause to grow, which [a]came up overnight and perished [b]overnight. 11 Should I not [A]have compassion
on Nineveh, the great city in which there are more
than 120,000 persons who do not [B]know *the differ-*
ence between their right and left hand, as well as
many [C]animals?"

3:6 [a]Or *dust* [A]Esth 4:1-4; Jer 6:26; Ezek 27:30, 31 3:7 [A]2 Chr 20:3; Ezra 8:21; Jon 3:5 3:8 [a]Lit *them* [b]Lit *their* [A]Ps 130:1; Jon 1:6, 14 [B]Is 1:16-19; 55:6, 7; Jer 18:11 3:9 [A]2 Sam 12:22; Joel 2:14 3:10 [a]Lit *do* [A]1 Kin 21:27-29; Jer 31:18 [B]Ex 32:14; Jer 18:8; Amos 7:3, 6 4:1 [A]Jon 4:4, 9; Matt 20:15; Luke 15:28 4:2 [a]Lit *my word* [b]Lit *I was beforehand in fleeing* [A]Jer 20:7 [B]Jon 1:3 [C]Ex 34:6; Num 14:18; Ps 86:5, 15; Joel 2:13 4:3 [a]Lit *soul* [A]1 Kin 19:4; Job 6:8, 9 [B]Job 7:15, 16; Eccl 7:1 4:5 [a]Lit *the city* [A]1 Kin 19:9, 13 4:6 [a]Probably a castor oil plant, and so in vv 7, 9 and 10 [b]Lit *greatly* 4:7 [A]Joel 1:12 4:8 [A]Ezek 19:12; Hos 13:15 [B]Ps 121:6; Is 49:10 [C]Jon 4:3 4:10 [a]Lit *was a son of a night* [b]Lit *a son of a night* 4:11 [A]Jon 3:10 [B]Deut 1:39; Is 7:16 [C]Ps 36:6

3:6 The king of Nineveh, thought to be either Adad-nirari III (ca. 810–783 B.C.) or Assurdan III (ca. 772–755 B.C.), exchanged his royal robes for sackcloth and ashes (cf. Job 42:6; Is 58:5). Reports of Jonah's miraculous fish experience may have preceded him to Nineveh, accounting for the swift and widespread receptivity of his message (cf. 1:2). It is generally believed that acid from the fish's stomach would have bleached Jonah's face, thus validating the experience.

3:7–9 man, beast. It was a Persian custom to use animals in mourning ceremonies.

3:10 God saw ... God relented. *See notes on 2Sa 24:16; Jer 42:10* (cf. Jer 18:7, 8). The Ninevites truly repented.

4:1, 2 Jonah, because of his rejection of Gentiles and distaste for their participation in salvation, was displeased at God's demonstration of mercy towards the Ninevites, thereby displaying the real reason for his original flight to Tarshish. From the very beginning, Jonah had clearly understood the gracious character of God (cf. 1Ti 2:4; 2Pe 3:9). He had received pardon, but he didn't want Nineveh to know God's mercy (cf. a similar attitude in Lk 15:25ff.).

4:3 death is better ... than life. Perhaps Jonah was expressing the reality of breaking his vow (2:9) to God a second time (cf. Nu 30:2; Ecc 5:1–6).

4:6 a plant. The identity is uncertain, but it possibly could be the fast-growing castor oil plant, which in hot climates grows rapidly to give shade with its large leaves.

4:8 scorching east wind. A hot, scorching wind, normally called "sirocco," blowing off the Arabian desert. The shelter Jonah made for himself (v. 5) would not exclude this agent of God's sovereignty.

4:10, 11 God's love for the people of Nineveh, whom He had created, is far different from Jonah's indifference to their damnation and greater than Jonah's warped concern for a wild plant for which he had done nothing. God was ready to spare Sodom for 10 righteous; how much more a city which includes 120,000 small children, identified as those who cannot discern the right hand from the left (cf. Ge 18:22, 23). With that many 3- or 4-year-old children, it is reasonable to expect a total population in excess of 600,000.

THE
BOOK OF

MICAH

TITLE

The name of the book is derived from the prophet who, having received the word of the Lord, was commissioned to proclaim it. Micah, whose name is shared by others in the OT (e.g., Jdg 17:1; 2Ch 13:2; Jer 36:11), is a shortened form of Micaiah (or Michaiah) and means "Who is like the Lord?" In 7:18, Micah uses a play on his own name, saying "Who is a God like You?"

AUTHOR AND DATE

The first verse establishes Micah as the author. Beyond that, little is known about him. His parentage is not given, but his name suggests a godly heritage. He traces his roots to the town of Moresheth (1:1, 14), located in the foothills of Judah, approximately 25 mi. SW of Jerusalem, on the border of Judah and Philistia, near Gath. From a productive agricultural area, he was like Amos, a country resident removed from the national politics and religion, yet chosen by God (3:8) to deliver a message of judgment to the princes and people of Jerusalem.

Micah places his prophecy during the reigns of Jotham (750–731 B.C.), Ahaz (731–715 B.C.), and Hezekiah (715–686 B.C.). His indictments of social injustices and religious corruption renew the theme of Amos (mid-eighth century B.C.) and his contemporaries, Hosea in the N (ca. 755–710 B.C.) and Isaiah in in the S (ca. 739–690 B.C.). This fits that which is known about the character of Ahaz (2Ki 16:10–18) and his son Hezekiah prior to his sweeping spiritual reformations (2Ch 29; 31:1). His references to the imminent fall of Samaria (1:6) clearly position him before 722 B.C., at approximately 735–710 B.C.

BACKGROUND AND SETTING

Because the northern kingdom was about to fall to Assyria during Micah's ministry in 722 B.C., Micah dates his message with the mention of Judean kings only. While Israel was an occasional recipient of his words (cf. 1:5–7), his primary attention was directed toward the southern kingdom in which he lived. The economic prosperity and the absence of international crises which marked the days of Jeroboam II (793–753 B.C.), during which the borders of Judah and Israel rivaled those of David and Solomon (cf. 2Ki 14:23–27), were slipping away. Syria and Israel invaded Judah, taking the wicked Ahaz temporarily captive (cf. 2Ch 28:5–16; Is 7:1, 2). After Assyria had overthrown Syria and Israel, the good king Hezekiah withdrew his allegiance to Assyria, causing Sennacherib to besiege Jerusalem in 701 B.C. (cf. 2Ki 18, 19; 2Ch 32). The Lord then sent His angel to deliver Judah (2Ch 32:21). Hezekiah was used by God to lead Judah back to true worship.

After the prosperous reign of Uzziah, who died in 739 B.C., his son Jotham continued the same policies, but failed to remove the centers of idolatry. Outward prosperity was only a facade masking rampant social corruption and religious syncretism. Worship of the Canaanite fertility god Baal was increasingly integrated with the OT sacrificial system, reaching epidemic proportions under the reign of Ahaz (cf. 2Ch 28:1–4). When Samaria fell, thousands of refugees swarmed into Judah, bringing their religious syncretism with them. But while Micah (like Hosea) addressed this issue, it was the disintegration of personal and social values to which he delivered his most stinging rebukes and stern warnings (e.g., 7:5, 6). Assyria was the dominant power and a constant threat to Judah, so Micah's prediction that Babylon, then under Assyrian rule, would conquer Judah (4:10) seemed remote. Thus, as the prophet Amos was to Israel, Micah was to Judah.

HISTORICAL AND THEOLOGICAL THEMES

Primarily, Micah proclaimed a message of judgment to a people persistently pursuing evil. Similar to other prophets (cf. Hos 4:1; Am 3:1), Micah presented his message in lawsuit/courtroom terminology (1:2; 6:1, 2). The prophecy is arranged in 3 oracles or cycles, each beginning with the admonition to "hear" (1:2; 3:1; 6:1). Within each oracle, he moves from doom to hope—doom because they have broken God's law given at Sinai; hope because of God's unchanging covenant with their forefathers (7:20). One-third of the book targets the sins of his people; another third looks at the punishment of God to come; and another third promises hope for the faithful after the judgment. Thus, the theme of the inevitability of divine judgment for sin is coupled together with God's immutable commitment to His covenant promises. The combination of God's 1) absolute consistency in judging sin and 2) unbending commitment to His covenant through the remnant of His people provides the hearers with a clear disclosure of the character of the Sovereign of the universe. Through divine intervention, He will bring about both judgment on sinners and blessing on those who repent.

INTERPRETIVE CHALLENGES

The verbal similarity between Mic 4:1–3 and Is 2:2–4 raises the question of who quoted whom. Interpreters are divided, with no clear-cut answers on either side. Because the two prophets lived in close proximity to each other, prophesying during the same period, this similarity is understandable. God gave the same message through two preachers. The introductory phrase, "in the last days" (4:1), removes these verses from any post-Exilic fulfillment and requires an eschatological timeframe surrounding the Second Advent of Christ and the beginning of the Millennium.

Apart from Is 2:2–4, three other passages from Micah are quoted elsewhere in Scripture. Micah 3:12 is quoted in Jer 26:18, thereby saving Jeremiah's life from King Jehoiakim's death sentence. Micah 5:2 is quoted by the chief priests and scribes (Mt 2:6) in response to Herod's query about the birthplace of the Messiah. Micah 7:6 is employed by Jesus in Mt 10:35, 36 when commissioning His disciples.

OUTLINE

I. Superscription (1:1)

II. God Gathers to Judge and Deliver (1:2–2:13)
- A. Samaria and Judah Punished (1:2–16)
- B. Oppressors Judged (2:1–5)
- C. False Prophets Renounced (2:6–11)
- D. Promise of Deliverance (2:12, 13)

III. God Judges Rulers and Comes to Deliver (3:1–5:15)
- A. The Contemporary Leaders are Guilty (3:1–12)
- B. The Coming Leader Will Deliver and Restore (4:1–5:15)

IV. God Brings Indictments and Ultimate Deliverance (6:1–7:20)
- A. Messages of Reproof and Lament (6:1–7:6)
- B. Messages of Confidence and Victory (7:7–20)

DESTRUCTION IN ISRAEL AND JUDAH

1 The [A]word of the LORD which came *to* [B]Micah of Moresheth in the days of [C]Jotham, [D]Ahaz *and* [E]Hezekiah, kings of Judah, which he saw concerning Samaria and Jerusalem.

2 Hear, O peoples, all of [a]you;
[A]Listen, O earth and [b]all it contains,
And let the Lord [c]GOD be a
[B]witness against you,
The Lord from His holy temple.
3 For behold, the LORD is [A]coming
forth from His place.
He will come down and [B]tread on
the high places of the [a]earth.
4 [A]The mountains will melt under Him
And the valleys will be split,
Like wax before the fire,
Like water poured down a steep place.
5 All this is for the rebellion of Jacob
And for the sins of the house of Israel.
What is the [A]rebellion of Jacob?
Is it not [B]Samaria?
What is the [C]high [a]place of Judah?
Is it not Jerusalem?
6 For I will make Samaria a [A]heap of
ruins [a]in the open country,
[B]Planting places for a vineyard.
I will [C]pour her stones down into the valley
And will [D]lay bare her foundations.
7 All of her [A]idols will be smashed,
All of her earnings will be
burned with fire
And all of her images I will make desolate,
For she collected *them* from
a [B]harlot's earnings,
And to the earnings of a harlot
they will return.
8 Because of this I must lament and wail,
I must go [A]barefoot and naked;
I must make a lament like the [B]jackals
And a mourning like the ostriches.
9 For her [a,A]wound is incurable,
For [B]it has come to Judah;
It has reached the [C]gate of my people,
Even to Jerusalem.
10 [A]Tell it not in Gath,
Weep not at all.
At [a]Beth-le-aphrah roll
yourself in the dust.
11 [a]Go on your way, inhabitant of [b]Shaphir,
in [A]shameful nakedness.
The inhabitant of [c,B]Zaanan
does not [d]escape.
The lamentation of [e]Beth-ezel: "He
will take from you its [f]support."
12 For the inhabitant of [a]Maroth
Becomes weak [A]waiting for good,
Because a calamity has come
down from the LORD
To the [B]gate of Jerusalem.
13 Harness the chariot to the team of horses,
O inhabitant of [A]Lachish—
She was the beginning of sin
To the daughter of Zion—
Because in you were found
The [B]rebellious acts of Israel.
14 Therefore you will give parting [A]gifts
On behalf of Moresheth-gath;
The houses of [B]Achzib *will*
become a [C]deception
To the kings of Israel.
15 Moreover, I will bring on you
The one who takes possession,
O inhabitant of [a,A]Mareshah.
The glory of Israel will enter [B]Adullam.

1:1 [A]2 Pet 1:21 [B]Jer 26:18 [C]2 Kin 15:5, 32-38; 2 Chr 27:1-9; Is 1:1; Hos 1:1 [D]2 Kin 16:1-20; 2 Chr 28:1-27; Is 7:1-12 [E]2 Kin 18:1-20; 2 Chr 29:1-31 1:2 [a]Lit *them* [b]Lit *its fullness* [c]Heb *YHWH*, usually rendered *LORD* [A]Jer 6:19; 22:29 [B]Is 50:7 1:3 [a]Or *land* [A]Is 26:21 [B]Amos 4:13 1:4 [A]Ps 97:5; Is 64:1, 2; Nah 1:5 1:5 [a]Lit *places* [A]Jer 2:19 [B]Is 7:9; Amos 8:14 [C]2 Chr 34:3, 4 1:6 [a]Lit *of the field* [A]2 Kin 19:25; Mic 3:12 [B]Jer 31:5; Amos 5:11 [C]Lam 4:1 [D]Ezek 13:14 1:7 [A]Deut 9:21; 2 Chr 34:7 [B]Deut 23:18; Is 23:17 1:8 [A]Is 32:11 [B]Is 13:21, 22 1:9 [a]Lit *wounds* [A]Is 3:26; Jer 30:12, 15 [B]2 Kin 18:13; Is 8:7, 8 [C]Mic 1:12 1:10 [a]I.e. house of dust [A]2 Sam 1:20 1:11 [a]I.e. Go into captivity [b]I.e. pleasantness [c]I.e. going out [d]Lit *go out* [e]I.e. house of removal [f]Lit *standing place* [A]Ezek 23:29 [B]Josh 15:37 1:12 [a]I.e. bitterness [A]Is 59:9-11; Jer 14:19 [B]Mic 1:9 1:13 [A]Josh 10:3; 2 Kin 14:19; Is 36:2 [B]Mic 1:5 1:14 [A]2 Kin 16:8 [B]Josh 15:44 [C]Jer 15:18 1:15 [a]I.e. possession [A]Josh 15:44 [B]Josh 12:15; 15:35; 2 Sam 23:13

1:1 Moresheth. Located SW of Jerusalem, near the Philistine city of Gath (cf. 1:14).

1:2–7 The prophet summons all the nations (v. 2) of the world into court to hear charges against Samaria and Judah (vv. 5–7; cf. Is 3:13, 14). Their destruction was to be a warning example to the nations, prefiguring God's judgment on all who sin against Him. As an omnipotent Conqueror, the Sovereign over all creation is assured of victory (vv. 3, 4).

1:2 His holy temple. Context points to God's heavenly throne (cf. Ps 11:4; Is 6:1, 4).

1:3, 4 high places ... mountains. These could refer to key military positions, so crucial to Israel's defense, or to the pagan places of worship in the land (cf. v. 5). When fortifications disappeared like melted wax, people were gripped by the terrifying reality that they were to answer to the Judge of all the earth (Ge 18:25; Am 4:12, 13).

1:3 the LORD is coming ... down. A warning of impending divine judgment by One who sits in the ultimate High Place.

1:5 Samaria ... Jerusalem. The two capitals of Israel and Judah, here representative of their respective nations.

1:6, 7 The Lord spoke directly of the fall of Samaria at the hands of the Assyrians (ca. 722 B.C.).

1:7 a harlot's earnings. Centers of idolatry were financed primarily through payments of money, food, and clothing (cf. Ge 38:17, 18; Eze 16:10, 11; Hos 2:8, 9; 3:1) to cultic prostitutes, who were strictly forbidden in Israel (Dt 23:17, 18). Precious gold and silver, taken from Israel's temples, was used by the Assyrian invaders for their own idol worship.

1:8–16 The judgment was so grave that even the prophet lamented as he traced the enemy's irreversible (v. 9) invasion.

1:9 the gate of my people. Assyria, under Sennacherib, came close to toppling Judah in 701 B.C. (cf. 2Ki 18:13–27). It is best to see "my" in reference to Micah, not God, contra. some translations.

1:10–15 Eleven towns W of Jerusalem are mentioned, some with a play on words.

1:10 Tell it not in Gath. Reflective of David's dirge at Saul's death (cf. 2Sa 1:20), Micah admonished them not to tell the Philistines, lest they would be glad and rejoice. Micah, because of the location of his upbringing, knew how they would react.

1:11 Zaanan does not escape. These inhabitants, in danger and fear, would not go out to console their neighbors who had been overrun.

1:12 calamity has come down. This points to the Lord as the source of judgment (cf. vv. 3, 4).

1:13 Lachish ... sin to the daughter of Zion. Located SW of Jerusalem, Lachish was a key military fortress whose "sin" was dependence on military might.

1:14 give parting gifts. As parting gifts were given to brides (cf. 1Ki 9:16), this was a symbol of the departure of Moresheth-gath into captivity.

1:15 glory of Israel ... Adullam. The people of Israel (i.e., her "glory"; cf. Hos 9:11–13) were to flee to the caves, as David did to the cave at Adullam (2 Sam 23:13).

16 Make yourself [A]bald and cut off your hair,
Because of the children of your delight;
Extend your baldness like the eagle,
For they will [B]go from you into exile.

WOE TO OPPRESSORS

2 Woe to those who [A]scheme iniquity,
Who work out evil on their beds!
[a,B]When morning comes, they do it,
For it is in the [C]power of their hands.
2 They [A]covet fields and then [B]seize *them,*
And houses, and take *them* away.
They [a,C]rob a man and his house,
A man and his inheritance.

3 Therefore thus says the LORD,

"Behold, I am [A]planning against
this [B]family a calamity
From which you [C]cannot
remove your necks;
And you will not walk [D]haughtily,
For it will be an [E]evil time.
4 "On that day they will [A]take up
against you a [a]taunt
And [b,B]utter a bitter lamentation *and* say,
'We are completely [C]destroyed!
He exchanges the portion of my people;
How He removes it from me!
To the apostate He [D]apportions our fields.'
5 "Therefore you will have no one
[a,A]stretching a measuring line
For you by lot in the assembly of the LORD.

6 '[A]Do not [a]speak out,' *so* they [a]speak out.
But if [b]they do [B]not [a]speak out
concerning these things,
[C]Reproaches will not be turned back.
7 "Is it being said, O house of Jacob:
'Is the Spirit of the LORD [A]impatient?
Are these His doings?'
Do not My words [B]do good
To the one [C]walking uprightly?
8 "[a]Recently My people have
arisen as an [A]enemy—
You [B]strip the [b]robe off the garment
From [C]unsuspecting passers-by,
From those returned from war.
9 "The women of My people you [A]evict,
Each *one* from her pleasant house.
From her children you take
My [B]splendor forever.
10 "Arise and go,
For this is no place [A]of rest
Because of the [B]uncleanness that
brings on destruction,
A painful destruction.
11 "If a man walking after wind and [A]falsehood
Had told lies *and said,*
'I will [a]speak out to you concerning
[B]wine and liquor,'
He would be [b]spokesman to [C]this people.

12 "I will surely [A]assemble all of you, Jacob,
I will surely gather the [B]remnant of Israel.
I will put them together like sheep in the fold;
Like a flock in the midst of its pasture
They will be noisy with men.
13 "The breaker goes up before them;
They break out, pass through
the gate and go out by it.
So their king goes on before them,
And the LORD at their head."

RULERS DENOUNCED

3 And I said,

"[A]Hear now, heads of Jacob
And rulers of the house of Israel.
Is it not for you to [B]know justice?

1:16 [A]Is 22:12 [B]2 Kin 17:6; Amos 7:11, 17 2:1 [a]Lit *In the light of the morning* [A]Ps 36:4; Is 32:7; Nah 1:11 [B]Hos 7:6, 7 [C]Gen 31:29; Deut 28:32; Prov 3:27 2:2 [a]Lit *oppress* [A]Jer 22:17; Amos 8:4 [B]Is 5:8 [C]1 Kin 21:1-15 2:3 [A]Deut 28:48; Jer 18:11 [B]Jer 8:3; Amos 3:1, 2 [C]Lam 1:14; 5:5 [D]Is 2:11, 12 [E]Amos 5:13 2:4 [a]Or *proverb* [b]Lit *lament* [A]Hab 2:6 [B]Jer 9:10, 17-21; Mic 1:8 [C]Is 6:11; 24:3; Jer 4:13 [D]Jer 6:12; 8:10 2:5 [a]Lit *casting* [A]Num 34:13, 16-29; Deut 32:8; Josh 18:4, 10 2:6 [a]Lit *flow* [b]I.e. God's prophets [A]Is 30:10; Amos 2:12; 7:16 [B]Is 29:10; Mic 3:6 [C]Mic 6:16 2:7 [A]Is 50:2; 59:1 [B]Ps 119:65, 68, 116; Jer 15:16 [C]Ps 15:2; 84:11 2:8 [a]Lit *And yesterday* [b]Or *ornaments* [A]Jer 12:8 [B]Mic 3:2, 3; 7:2, 3 [C]Ps 120:6, 7 2:9 [A]Jer 10:20 [B]Ezek 39:21; Hab 2:14 2:10 [A]Deut 12:9 [B]Ps 106:38 2:11 [a]Lit *flow* [b]Lit *one who flows* oracles [A]Jer 5:31 [B]Is 28:7 [C]Is 30:10, 11 2:12 [A]Mic 4:6, 7 [B]Mic 5:7, 8; 7:18 3:1 [A]Is 1:10; Mic 3:9 [B]Ps 82:1-5; Jer 5:5

1:16 Make yourself bald. Priests were forbidden to make themselves bald (Lv 21:5), nor were the people to imitate the heathen practice of doing so (Dt 14:1). But here it would be acceptable as a sign of deep mourning (Ezr 9:3; Job 1:20; Is 22:12; Eze 7:18).

2:1–11 As chapter 1 denounced sin against God; chapter 2 denounces sin against man. In vv. 1–5, Micah decried the corrupt practices of the affluent; in vv. 6–11 he attacked the false prophets and those who would silence the true prophets.

2:1, 2 The courtroom scene continues, with the accusations being read against the affluent: they had violated the tenth commandment (Ex 20:17; cf. 22:26; 23:4–9). The poor, unable to defend themselves, were at the mercy of the wealthy.

2:2 his inheritance. Property in Israel was ultimately to be permanent (Lv 25:10, 13; Nu 36:1–12; cf. 1Ki 21).

2:3–5 As a result of sin, God would allow foreign invaders to divide their land; none of them would have the inheritance apportioned to them. As the rich took from the poor, so God would take back that which He gave as judgment on the nation.

2:6–11 False prophets, commanding Micah to cease prophesying, would certainly not prophesy against the people's evildoing; they would not confront them with the divine standard of holiness. Rather, their false message (v. 7) had stopped the mouths of the true prophets and had permitted the rulers to engage in social atrocities (vv. 8, 9), leading the people to destruction (v. 10). They didn't want true prophecies; therefore, they got what they wanted (cf. Is 30:10). It is best to understand that Micah speaks in v. 6 and God in vv. 7–11.

2:6 Do not speak out. The true prophet was accused of childish babbling, when the real babblers were the false prophets (cf. v. 11).

2:7 Spirit of the LORD. God responded to the evil prophets that their message affirming sin in the nation was inconsistent with the Holy Spirit and His true message to Micah (cf. 3:8). God's words do reward the righteous, but they also rebuke those engaging in evil deeds.

2:9 women of My people. Most likely a reference to widows.

2:11 The people accepted any "prophet" who would tailor his message to their greed, wealth, and prosperity.

2:12, 13 Messiah will make ready the way, removing the obstacles which might hinder His remnant's deliverance and return at the Second Advent (cf. Is 11:15, 16; 52:12).

2:12 remnant. Cf. 4:7; 5:7, 8; 7:18. *See note on Is 10:20.*

3:1–4 In beginning the second oracle, Micah first addressed Israel's corrupt rulers, as in 2:1, 2, who should be aware of injustice. Yet their conduct toward the poor was like the

2 "You who hate good and love evil,
Who [A]tear off their skin from them
And their flesh from their bones,
3 Who [A]eat the flesh of my people,
Strip off their skin from them,
Break their bones
And [B]chop *them* up as for the pot
And as meat in a kettle."
4 Then they will [A]cry out to the LORD,
But He will not answer them.
Instead, He will [B]hide His face
from them at that time
Because they have [C]practiced evil deeds.

5 Thus says the LORD concerning the prophets
who [A]lead my people astray;

When they have *something* to
bite with their teeth,
They [B]cry, "Peace,"
But against him who puts
nothing in their mouths
They declare holy war.
6 Therefore *it will be* [A]night for
you—without vision,
And darkness for you—without divination.
The [B]sun will go down on the prophets,
And the day will become dark over them.
7 The seers will be [A]ashamed
And the [B]diviners will be embarrassed.
Indeed, they will all [C]cover *their* [a]mouths
Because there is [D]no answer from God.
8 On the other hand [A]I am
filled with power—
With the Spirit of the LORD—
And with justice and courage
To [B]make known to Jacob
his rebellious act,
Even to Israel his sin.
9 Now hear this, [A]heads of
the house of Jacob
And rulers of the house of Israel,
Who [B]abhor justice
And twist everything that is straight,
10 Who [A]build Zion with bloodshed
And Jerusalem with violent injustice.
11 Her leaders pronounce
[A]judgment for a bribe,
Her [B]priests instruct for a price
And her prophets divine for money.
Yet they lean on the LORD saying,
"[C]Is not the LORD in our midst?
Calamity will not come upon us."
12 Therefore, on account of you
[A]Zion will be plowed as a field,
[B]Jerusalem will become a heap of ruins,
And the [C]mountain of the [a]temple *will
become* high places of a forest.

PEACEFUL LATTER DAYS

4 And it will come about in the [A]last days
That the [B]mountain of the
house of the LORD
Will be established [a]as the
chief of the mountains.
It will be raised above the hills,
And the [C]peoples will stream to it.
2 [A]Many nations will come and say,
"[B]Come and let us go up to the
mountain of the LORD
And to the house of the God of Jacob,
That [C]He may teach us about His ways
And that we may walk in His paths."
For [D]from Zion will go forth the law,
Even the word of the LORD from Jerusalem.
3 And He will [A]judge between many peoples
And render decisions for
mighty, [a]distant nations.
Then they will hammer their
swords [B]into plowshares
And their spears into pruning hooks;
Nation will not lift up sword against nation,
And never again will they [b]train for war.
4 Each of them will [A]sit under his vine
And under his fig tree,
With [B]no one to make *them* afraid,
For the [C]mouth of the LORD
of hosts has spoken.

3:2 [A]Ps 53:4; Ezek 22:27; Mic 2:8; 7:2, 3 3:3 [A]Ps 14:4; 27:2; Zeph 3:3 [B]Ezek 11:3, 6, 7 3:4 [A]Ps 18:41; Prov 1:28; Is 1:15; Jer 11:11 [B]Deut 31:17; Is 59:2 [C]Is 3:11; Mic 7:13 3:5 [A]Is 3:12; 9:15, 16; Jer 14:14, 15 [B]Jer 6:14 3:6 [A]Is 8:20-22; 29:10-12 [B]Is 59:10 3:7 [a]Lit *mustache* [A]Zech 13:4 [B]Is 44:25; 47:12-14 [C]Mic 7:16 [D]1 Sam 28:6; Mic 3:4 3:8 [A]Is 61:1, 2; Jer 1:18 [B]Is 58:1 3:9 [A]Mic 1:1 [B]Ps 58:1, 2; Is 1:23 3:10 [A]Jer 22:13, 17; Hab 2:12 3:11 [A]Is 1:23; Mic 7:3 [B]Jer 6:13 [C]Is 48:2 3:12 [a]Lit *house* [A]Jer 26:18 [B]Ps 79:1; Jer 9:11 [C]Mic 4:1 4:1 [a]Lit *on* [A]Is 2:2-4; Dan 2:28; 10:14; Hos 3:5 [B]Ezek 43:12; Mic 3:12; Zech 8:3 [C]Ps 22:27; 86:9; Jer 3:17 4:2 [A]Zech 2:11; 14:16 [B]Is 2:3; Jer 31:6 [C]Ps 25:8, 9, 12; Is 54:13 [D]Is 42:1-4; Zech 14:8, 9 4:3 [a]Lit *at a distance* [b]Lit *learn* [A]Is 2:4; 11:3-5 [B]Joel 3:10 4:4 [A]1 Kin 4:25; Zech 3:10 [B]Lev 26:6; Jer 30:10 [C]Is 1:20; 40:5

butchering of animals (vv. 2, 3). Therefore, when judgment came and they cried for help, God didn't answer (v. 4).

3:5–7 False prophets (cf. 2:6–11) also stood guilty before the Judge because they misled the people, prophesying peace when they were fed, but predicting war when they were not (v. 5). Like the rulers, they too were motivated by greed. Therefore, having blinded others, they would be struck with blindness and silence (vv. 6, 7).

3:8 Micah, in contrast to the false prophets, spoke by the power of God's Holy Spirit (cf. 2:7). Therefore his message was authoritative and true.

3:9–12 All ruling classes are guilty: rulers judged for reward (vv. 9–11a), priests taught for hire (v. 11b), and prophets divined for money (v. 11c). All the while, they were self-deceived into thinking the Lord would give them favor because they identified themselves with Him. Consequently, the nation would be destroyed (fulfilled by Nebuchadnezzar in 586 B.C.).

3:12 Cf. Jer 26:18.

4:1–3 Cf. Is 2:2–4.

4:1 In a reversal of 3:12, Micah shifted from impending judgment to prophecies of the future millennial kingdom ("the last days") in which Mt. Zion (v. 2), the center of Messiah's coming earthly kingdom, shall be raised both spiritually and physically (cf. Zec 14:9, 10). This discussion continues to 5:15.

4:2 Many nations. People throughout the earth, not just Israel, will come as a spontaneous "stream" (cf. v. 1) to worship the Lord in Jerusalem during the Millennium (cf. Zec 8:20–23).

4:3 hammer their swords into plowshares. Because the Almighty One is ruling in Jerusalem with a rod of iron (cf. Rev 2:27; 12:5; 19:15), and because of the unprecedented fruitfulness of the land (cf. Am 9:13), military hardware will no longer be needed.

4:4 under his vine ... fig tree. Once employed as a description of the peaceful era of Solomon (cf. 1Ki 4:25), this phrase looks forward to greater peace and prosperity in the Millennium (cf. Zec 3:10).

5 Though all the peoples walk
Each in the [A]name of his god,
As for us, [B]we will walk
In the name of the [C]LORD our
God forever and ever.

6 "In that day," declares the LORD,
"I will assemble the [A]lame
And [B]gather the outcasts,
Even those whom I have afflicted.
7 "I will make the lame a [A]remnant
And the outcasts a strong nation,
And the [B]LORD will reign over
them in Mount Zion
From now on and forever.
8 "As for you, [a,A]tower of the flock,
[b]Hill of the daughter of Zion,
To you it will come—
Even the [B]former dominion will come,
The kingdom of the daughter of Jerusalem.

9 "Now, why do you [A]cry out loudly?
Is there no king among you,
Or has your [B]counselor perished,
That agony has gripped you like
a woman in childbirth?
10 "[A]Writhe and labor to give birth,
Daughter of Zion,
Like a woman in childbirth;
For now you will [B]go out of the city,
Dwell in the field,
And go to Babylon.
[C]There you will be rescued;
[D]There the LORD will redeem you
From the hand of your enemies.
11 "And now [A]many nations have
been assembled against you
Who say, 'Let her be polluted,
And let our eyes [a]gloat over Zion.'
12 "But they do not [A]know the
thoughts of the LORD,
And they do not understand His purpose;
For He has gathered them like
sheaves to the threshing floor.
13 "Arise and [A]thresh, daughter of Zion,
For your horn I will make iron
And your hoofs I will make bronze,
That you may [B]pulverize many peoples,
That you may [C]devote to the
LORD their unjust gain
And their wealth to the Lord of all the earth.

BIRTH OF THE KING IN BETHLEHEM

5 "[a]Now muster yourselves in troops,
daughter of troops;
[b]They have laid siege against us;
With a rod they will [A]smite the
judge of Israel on the cheek.
2 "[a]But as for [A]you, Bethlehem Ephrathah,
Too little to be among the clans of Judah,
From [B]you One will go forth for
Me to be [C]ruler in Israel.
[b]His goings forth are [D]from long ago,
From the days of eternity."
3 Therefore He will [A]give them
up until the time
When she [B]who is in labor has borne a child.
Then the [C]remainder of His brethren
Will return to the sons of Israel.
4 And He will arise and [A]shepherd *His flock*
In the strength of the LORD,
In the majesty of the name
of the LORD His God.
And they will [a]remain,
Because [b]at that time He will be great
To the [B]ends of the earth.

4:5 [A]2 Kin 17:29 [B]Zech 10:12 [C]Josh 24:15; Is 26:8, 13 4:6 [A]Zeph 3:19 [B]Ps 147:2; Ezek 34:13, 16; 37:21 4:7 [A]Mic 5:7, 8; 7:18 [B]Is 24:23 4:8 [a]Heb *Migdal-eder* [b]Heb *Ophel of* [A]Ps 48:3, 12; 61:3; Mic 2:12 [B]Is 1:26; Zech 9:10 4:9 [A]Jer 8:19 [B]Is 3:1-3 4:10 [A]Mic 5:3 [B]2 Kin 20:18; Hos 2:14 [C]Is 43:14; 45:13; Mic 7:8-12 [D]Is 48:20; 52:9-12 4:11 [a]Lit *look on* [A]Is 5:25-30; 17:12-14 4:12 [A]Ps 147:19, 20 4:13 [A]Is 41:15 [B]Jer 51:20-23 [C]Is 60:9 5:1 [a]Ch 4:14 in Heb [b]Lit *He has* [A]1 Kin 22:24; Job 16:10; Lam 3:30 5:2 [a]Ch 5:1 in Heb [b]Or *His appearances are from long ago, from days of old* [A]Gen 35:19; 48:7; Ruth 4:11; Matt 2:6 [B]Is 11:1; Luke 2:4; John 7:42 [C]Jer 30:21; Zech 9:9 [D]Ps 102:25; Prov 8:22, 23 5:3 [A]Hos 11:8; Mic 4:10; 7:13 [B]Mic 4:9, 10 [C]Is 10:20-22; Mic 5:7, 8 5:4 [a]Or *live* in safety [b]Lit *now* [A]Is 40:11; 49:9; Ezek 34:13-15, 23, 24; Mic 7:14 [B]Is 45:22; 52:10

4:5 Even if all others were walking after other gods at the present, the godly remnant of Israel would no longer pursue other gods but would walk after the true God in the millennial kingdom (cf. Jos 24:15).

4:6–8 Micah continued to describe the wonderful conditions of the coming earthly kingdom of Messiah. Repeating the figure of sheep (cf. 2:12, 13), the "tower of the flock" depicted the city of Jerusalem, the future dwelling place of Messiah, as watching over the people.

4:7 forever. The Heb. term does not always mean "without end," but signifies a long, indefinite period of time, the length of which is always determined by the context. Here it refers to the 1,000-year reign of Messiah on earth (cf. Rev 20).

4:9, 10 Judah will be taken captive to Babylon (vv. 9, 10a), but the Lord will release them from there (v. 10b), by the edict of Persian king Cyrus (ca. 538 B.C.), allowing them to return to Jerusalem (cf. Ezr 1:2–4).

4:11–13 Micah switched again to the time of the Second Advent. The gathering of "many nations" and "many peoples" depicts that future battle of Armageddon (Zec 12; 14). In that day, the Lord will empower His people (cf. 5:7–9; Is 11:14; Zec 14:14).

4:13 horn ... iron ... hoofs ... bronze. Using the figurative language of an animal with metal features, the Lord looked to a day when Israel will permanently defeat their enemies.

5:1 smite the judge of Israel. A reference to the capture of King Zedekiah at the hands of Babylon in 586 B.C. (cf. 2Ki 24, 25).

5:2–4 This passage looked forward to Christ's First Advent (5:2), an intervening time (5:3a), and beyond to the Second Advent (5:3b, 4).

5:2 Bethlehem Ephrathah. The town S of Jerusalem which was the birthplace of David and later Jesus Christ (1Sa 16; Mt 2:5; Lk 2:4–7). The name Bethlehem means "house of bread" because the area was a grain-producing region in OT times. The name Ephrathah ("fruitful") differentiates it from the Galilean town by the same name. The town, known for her many vineyards and olive orchards, was small in size but not in honor. **from long ago, From the days of eternity.** This speaks of eternal God's incarnation in the person of Jesus Christ. It points to His millennial reign as King of kings (cf. Is 9:6).

5:3 give them *up*. A reference to the interval between Messiah's rejection at His First Advent and His Second Advent, during the times of the Gentiles when Israel rejects Christ and is under the domination of enemies. Regathering of the "remainder of His brethren" did not occur at the First Advent but is slated for the Second Advent (cf. Is 10:20–22; 11:11–16). Nor can "return" speak of Gentiles, since it cannot be said that they "returned" to the Lord. Rather, the context of 5:3, 4 is millennial and cannot be made to fit the First Advent. Thus, "she who is in labor" must denote the nation of Israel (cf. Rev 12:1–6).

5:4 The millennial rule of Christ, sitting upon the throne of David (cf. Is 6:13).

5 This One [A]will be *our* peace.

When the [B]Assyrian invades our land,
When he tramples on our [a]citadels,
Then we will raise against him
Seven shepherds and eight
leaders of men.
6 They will [A]shepherd the land of
Assyria with the sword,
The land of [B]Nimrod at its entrances;
And He will [C]deliver *us* from the Assyrian
When he attacks our land
And when he tramples our territory.

7 Then the [A]remnant of Jacob
Will be among many peoples
Like [B]dew from the LORD,
Like [C]showers on vegetation
Which do not wait for man
Or delay for the sons of men.
8 The remnant of Jacob
Will be among the nations,
Among many peoples
[A]Like a lion among the beasts of the forest,
Like a young lion among flocks of sheep,
Which, if he passes through,
[B]Tramples down and [C]tears,
And there is [D]none to rescue.
9 Your hand will be [A]lifted up
against your adversaries,
And all your enemies will be cut off.

10 "It will be in that day," declares the LORD,
"[A]That I will cut off your [B]horses
from among you
And destroy your chariots.
11 "I will also cut off the [A]cities of your land
And tear down all your [B]fortifications.
12 "I will cut off [A]sorceries from your hand,
And you will have fortune-tellers no more.
13 "[A]I will cut off your carved images
And your *sacred* pillars
from among you,
So that you will no longer bow down
To the work of your hands.
14 "I will root out your [a,A]Asherim
from among you
And destroy your cities.
15 "And I will [A]execute vengeance
in anger and wrath
On the nations which have not obeyed."

GOD'S INDICTMENT OF HIS PEOPLE

6 Hear now what the LORD is saying,
"Arise, plead your case [a]before
the mountains,
And let the hills hear your voice.
2 "Listen, you mountains, to the
indictment of the LORD,
And you enduring [A]foundations
of the earth,
Because the [B]LORD has a case
against His people;
Even with Israel He will dispute.
3 "[A]My people, [B]what have I done to you,
And [C]how have I wearied
you? Answer Me.
4 "Indeed, I [A]brought you up
from the land of Egypt
And [B]ransomed you from
the house of slavery,
And I sent before you [C]Moses,
Aaron and [D]Miriam.
5 "My people, remember now
What [A]Balak king of Moab counseled
And what Balaam son of
Beor answered him,
And from [B]Shittim to [C]Gilgal,
So [a]that you might know the
[D]righteous acts of the LORD."

5:5 [a]Or *palaces* [A]Is 9:6; Luke 2:14; Eph 2:14; Col 1:20 [B]Is 8:7, 8; 10:24-27 5:6 [A]Nah 2:11-13; Zeph 2:13 [B]Gen 10:8-11 [C]Is 14:25; 37:36, 37 5:7 [A]Mic 2:12; 4:7; 5:3; 7:18 [B]Deut 32:2; Ps 110:3; Hos 14:5 [C]Ps 72:6; Is 44:3 5:8 [A]Gen 49:9; Num 24:9 [B]Ps 44:5; Is 41:15, 16; Mic 4:13; Zech 10:5 [C]Hos 5:14 [D]Ps 50:22 5:9 [A]Ps 10:12; 21:8; Is 26:11 5:10 [A]Zech 9:10 [B]Deut 17:16; Is 2:7; Hos 14:3 5:11 [A]Is 1:7; 6:11 [B]Is 2:12-17; Hos 10:14; Amos 5:9 5:12 [A]Deut 18:10-12; Is 2:6; 8:19 5:13 [A]Is 2:18; 17:8; Ezek 6:9 5:14 [a]I.e. wooden symbols of a female deity [A]Ex 34:13; Is 17:8; 27:9 5:15 [A]Is 1:24; 65:12 6:1 [a]Lit *with* 6:2 [A]2 Sam 22:16; Ps 104:5 [B]Is 1:18; Hos 4:1; 12:2 6:3 [A]Ps 50:7 [B]Jer 2:5 [C]Is 43:22, 23 6:4 [A]Ex 12:51; 20:2 [B]Deut 7:8 [C]Ex 4:10-16; Ps 77:20 [D]Ex 15:20 6:5 [a]Lit *to know* [A]Num 22:5, 6 [B]Num 25:1; Josh 2:1; 3:1 [C]Josh 4:19; 5:9, 10 [D]1 Sam 12:7; Is 1:27

5:5, 6 Assyrian. Assyria, God's instrument against Israel (722 B.C.) and Judah (Sennacherib's siege in 701 B.C.) is here used as a representative of enemy nations in opposition to the Lord.

5:5 Seven ... eight. An idiom for a full and sufficient number of leaders, more than enough for the task (cf. Ecc 11:2).

5:6 Nimrod. A reference to Assyria (cf. Ge 10:11) that could possibly also include Babylon (cf. Ge 10:10).

5:7–9 Israel's presence in the midst of many peoples would be to some a source of blessing (cf. Zec 8:22, 23); to others, she would be like a lion—a source of fear and destruction (cf. Is 11:14; Zec 12:2, 3, 6; 14:14).

5:9 all your enemies. This absolute and complete peace has never yet been experienced by Israel. This points to the millennial kingdom when the Prince of Peace shall reign, having conquered the nations (cf. v.15).

5:10 in that day. The future kingdom is in view. Israel had been forbidden the use of cavalry (Dt 17:16), lest they trust in earthly forces, rather than God (1Ki 10:26, 28). God will remove all implements in which they trust so the people, stripped of all human resources, rest only on Him. War instruments will have no place in that time of peace.

5:11–14 cut off the cities ... fortifications. Continuing the thought from v. 10, fortified cities were designed for defense; their strength tempted people to put their trust in them rather than in God alone (cf. 1:13; Ps 27:1; Hos 10:13, 14). People will live in peace in unwalled villages (Eze 38:11). The cities are also associated with centers of pagan worship (v. 14; cf. Dt 16:21), the worship of Asherah (Canaanite goddess of fertility and war). All forms of self-reliance in war and idolatrous worship will be removed so that the nation must rely solely on Christ their King for deliverance and worship Him alone.

6:1 Micah opens this third cycle of oracles (6:1–7:20) with a dramatic courtroom motif moving back and forth between 3 speakers: the Lord pleading His case, the people responding under conviction, and the prophet as the lawyer for the plaintiff.

6:1, 2 The Lord commanded Micah (v. 1), as His advocate, to plead His case before the mountains and hills, which were to act as witnesses against His people (cf. Dt 4:25, 26; Is 1:2). The mountains and hills were present at Sinai when the Lord made His covenant with Israel and when the Ten Commandments were written and placed in the ark of the covenant as a permanent witness (cf. Dt 31:26).

6:3–5 This was the Lord's appeal. With tenderness and emotion, the divine Plaintiff recalled His many gracious acts toward them, almost to the point of assuming the tone of a defendant. Noting their trek from bondage in

WHAT GOD REQUIRES OF MAN

6 [A]With what shall I come to the LORD
And bow myself before the God on high?
Shall I come to Him with [B]burnt offerings,
With yearling calves?
7 Does the LORD take delight in
[A]thousands of rams,
In ten thousand rivers of oil?
Shall I present my [B]firstborn
for my rebellious acts,
The fruit of my body for
the sin of my soul?
8 He has [A]told you, O man, what is good;
And [B]what does the LORD require of you
But to [C]do justice, to [D]love [a]kindness,
And to walk [b,E]humbly with your God?

9 The voice of the LORD will
call to the city—
And it is sound wisdom to
fear Your name:
"Hear, O tribe. Who has
appointed [a]its time?
10 "Is there yet a man in the wicked house,
Along with treasures of [A]wickedness
And a [a,B]short measure *that is* cursed?
11 "Can I justify wicked [A]scales
And a bag of deceptive weights?
12 "For the rich men of *the* [a]city
are full of [A]violence,
Her residents speak [B]lies,
And their [C]tongue is deceitful
in their mouth.
13 "So also I will make *you* [A]sick,
striking you down,
[B]Desolating *you* because of your sins.
14 "You will eat, but you will [A]not be satisfied,
And your [a]vileness will be in your midst.
You will *try to* remove *for safekeeping,*
But you will [B]not preserve *anything,*
And what you do preserve I
will give to the sword.
15 "You will sow but you will [A]not reap.
You will tread the olive but will
not anoint yourself with oil;
And the grapes, but you will
[B]not drink wine.
16 "The statutes of [A]Omri
And all the works of the house
of [B]Ahab are observed;
And in their devices you [C]walk.
Therefore I will give you
up for [D]destruction
And [a]your inhabitants for [E]derision,
And you will bear the [F]reproach
of My people."

THE PROPHET ACKNOWLEDGES

7 Woe is me! For I am
Like the fruit pickers, like the
[A]grape gatherers.
There is not a cluster of grapes to eat,
Or a [B]first-ripe fig *which* [a]I crave.
2 The [a]godly person has [A]perished
from the land,
And there is no upright
person among men.
All of them lie in wait for [B]bloodshed;
Each of them hunts the other with a [C]net.
3 Concerning evil, both hands do it [A]well.
The prince asks, also the
judge, for a [B]bribe,
And a great man speaks the
desire of his soul;
So they weave it together.
4 The best of them is like a [A]briar,
The most upright like a [B]thorn hedge.
The day when you post your watchmen,
Your [C]punishment will come.
Then their [D]confusion will occur.
5 Do not [A]trust in a neighbor;
Do not have confidence in a friend.
From her who lies in your bosom
Guard [a]your lips.

6:6 [A]Ps 40:6-8 [B]Ps 51:16, 17 6:7 [A]Ps 50:9; Is 1:1; 40:16 [B]Lev 18:21; 20:1-5; 2 Kin 16:3; Jer 7:31 6:8 [a]Or *loyalty* [b]Or *circumspectly* [A]Deut 30:15 [B]Deut 10:12 [C]Is 56:1; Jer 22:3 [D]Hos 6:6 [E]Is 57:15; 66:2 6:9 [a]Lit *it* 6:10 [a]Lit *shrunken ephah* [A]Jer 5:26, 27; Amos 3:10 [B]Ezek 45:9, 10; Amos 8:5 6:11 [A]Lev 19:36; Hos 12:7 6:12 [a]Lit *her* [A]Is 1:23; 5:7; Amos 6:3, 4; Mic 2:1, 2 [B]Jer 9:2-6, 8; Hos 7:13; Amos 2:4 [C]Is 3:8 6:13 [A]Mic 1:9 [B]Is 1:7; 6:11 6:14 [a]Or possibly *garbage* or *excreta* [A]Is 9:20 [B]Is 30:6 6:15 [A]Deut 28:38-40; Jer 12:13 [B]Amos 5:11; Zeph 1:13 6:16 [a]Lit *her* [A]1 Kin 16:25, 26 [B]1 Kin 16:29-33 [C]Jer 7:24 [D]Jer 18:16; Mic 6:13 [E]Jer 19:8; 25:9, 18; 29:18 [F]Ps 44:13; Jer 51:51; Hos 12:14 7:1 [a]Lit *my soul* [A]Is 24:13 [B]Is 28:4; Hos 9:10 7:2 [a]Or *loyal* [A]Is 57:1 [B]Is 59:7; Mic 3:10 [C]Jer 5:26; Hos 5:1 7:3 [A]Prov 4:16, 17 [B]Amos 5:12; Mic 3:11 7:4 [A]Ezek 2:6; 28:24 [B]Nah 1:10 [C]Is 10:3; Hos 9:7 [D]Is 22:5 7:5 [a]Lit *openings of your mouth* [A]Jer 9:4

Egypt to their own homeland, God had provided leadership (v. 4), reversed the attempts of Balaam to curse the people (v. 5a; cf. Nu 22–24), and miraculously parted the Jordan River (v. 5b) so they could cross over from Shittim, located E of the Jordan, to Gilgal on the W side near Jericho. God had faithfully kept all His promises to them.

6:6, 7 Micah, as though speaking on behalf of the people, asked rhetorically how, in light of God's faithfulness toward them, they could continue their hypocrisy by being outwardly religious but inwardly sinful.

6:8 Micah's terse response (v. 8) indicated they should have known the answer to the rhetorical question. Spiritual blindness had led them to offer everything except the one thing He wanted—a spiritual commitment of the heart from which right behavior would ensue (cf. Dt 10:12–19; Mt 22:37–39). This theme is often represented in the OT (cf. 1Sa 15:22; Is 1:11–20; Jer 7:21–23; Hos 6:6; Am 5:15).

6:9–16 The Lord was sending judgment; God Himself had appointed the time and instrument to punish His people. The Lord spoke, noting that their corrupt deeds perpetrated on the poor were still continuing, in spite of His warnings and discipline (vv. 10–12). Therefore, a severe judgment was coming (vv. 13–15); it would happen to them just as it did to their northern neighbor, Israel (v. 16), when led by the counsel of wicked kings.

6:9 Hear, O tribe. Listen for the description of the coming punishment (cf. vv. 13–15; Is 10:5, 24).

6:16 statutes of Omri. Ca. 885–874 B.C. He was the founder of Samaria and of Ahab's wicked house as well as a supporter of Jeroboam's superstitions (cf. 1Ki 16:16–28). **works of the house of Ahab.** Cf. 1Ki 21:25, 26 (ca. 874–853 B.C.).

7:1–6 Micah lamented the circumstances of his day. In his vain search for an upright person (cf. v. 2), he compared himself to the vinedresser who enters his vineyard late in the season and finds no fruit. The leaders conspired together to get what they wanted (v. 3). No one could be trusted (vv. 5, 6). Christ used v. 6 as an illustration when He commissioned the twelve (Mt 10:1, 35, 36).

7:1 Woe is me! Micah sounded like Isaiah (cf. Is 6:5).

6 For [A]son treats father contemptuously,
Daughter rises up against her mother,
Daughter-in-law against her mother-in-law;
[B]A man's enemies are the men
of his own household.

GOD IS THE SOURCE OF SALVATION AND LIGHT

7 But as for me, I will [A]watch
expectantly for the LORD;
I will [B]wait for the God of my salvation.
My [C]God will hear me.
8 [A]Do not rejoice over me, O [B]my enemy.
Though I fall I will [C]rise;
Though I dwell in darkness, the
LORD is a [D]light for me.

9 I will bear the indignation of the LORD
Because I have sinned against Him,
Until He [A]pleads my case and
executes justice for me.
He will bring me out to the [B]light,
And I will see His [a,C]righteousness.
10 Then my enemy will see,
And shame will cover her
who [A]said to me,
"Where is the LORD your God?"
My eyes will look on her;
[a]At that time she will [b]be [B]trampled down
Like mire of the streets.
11 *It will be* a day for [A]building your walls.
On that day will your boundary
be extended.
12 It *will be* a day when [a]they will [A]come to you
From Assyria and the cities of Egypt,
From Egypt even to the [b]Euphrates,
Even from sea to sea and
mountain to mountain.
13 And the earth will become [A]desolate
because of her inhabitants,
On account of the [B]fruit of their deeds.

14 [A]Shepherd Your people with Your [B]scepter,
The flock of Your [a]possession
Which dwells by itself in the woodland,
In the midst of [b]a fruitful field.
Let them feed in [C]Bashan and Gilead
[D]As in the days of old.
15 "As in the days when you came
out from the land of Egypt,
I will show [a,A]you miracles."
16 Nations [A]will see and be ashamed
Of all their might.
They will [B]put *their* hand on *their* mouth,
Their ears will be deaf.
17 They will [A]lick the dust like a serpent,
Like [B]reptiles of the earth.
They will come [C]trembling out
of their [a]fortresses;
To the LORD our God they
will come in [D]dread
And they will be afraid before You.
18 Who is a God like You, who
[A]pardons iniquity
And passes over the rebellious act of
the [B]remnant of His [a]possession?

7:6 [A]Matt 10:21, 35; Luke 12:53 [B]Matt 10:36 7:7 [A]Hab 2:1 [B]Ps 130:5; Is 25:9 [C]Ps 4:3 7:8 [A]Prov 24:17; Obad 12 [B]Mic 7:10 [C]Amos 9:11 [D]Is 9:2 7:9 [a]I.e. right dealing [A]Jer 50:34 [B]Ps 37:6; Is 42:7, 16 [C]Is 46:13; 56:1 7:10 [a]Lit *Now* [b]Lit *become a trampled* place [A]Joel 2:17 [B]Is 51:23; Zech 10:5 7:11 [A]Is 54:11; Amos 9:11 7:12 [a]Lit *he* [b]Lit *River* [A]Is 19:23-25; 60:4, 9 7:13 [A]Jer 25:11; Mic 6:13 [B]Is 3:10, 11; Mic 3:4 7:14 [a]Or *inheritance* [b]Or *Carmel* [A]Ps 95:7; Is 40:11; 49:10; Mic 5:4 [B]Lev 27:32; Ps 23:4 [C]Jer 50:19 [D]Amos 9:11 7:15 [a]Lit *him* [A]Ex 3:20; 34:10; Ps 78:12 7:16 [A]Is 26:11 [B]Mic 3:7 7:17 [a]Lit *fastnesses* [A]Ps 72:9; Is 49:23 [B]Deut 32:24 [C]Ps 18:45 [D]Is 25:3; 59:19 7:18 [a]Or *inheritance* [A]Ex 34:7, 9; Is 43:25 [B]Mic 2:12; 4:7; 5:7, 8

7:7 In spite of his dire circumstances, Micah, as a watchman (cf. v. 4), would intently look for evidence of God's working, trusting God to act in His own time and way (cf. Hab 3:16–19).

7:8–10 Israel confessed her faith in the Lord, warning her enemies that she will rise again (vv. 8, 10). She confessed her sin, acknowledging the justice of God's punishment and anticipating His restoration.

7:10 Where is the LORD your God? Cf. Ps 42:3, 10; Mt 27:43.

7:11–13 Micah again spoke, recounting the many blessings awaiting the faithful remnant in Messiah's millennial rule. It would include unprecedented expansion (cf. Zec 2:1–5) and massive infusion of immigrants (cf. Is 11:15, 16). For those who defied Messiah's millennial rulership, their land would become desolate (v. 13; cf. Zec 14:16–19).

7:14–17 Micah petitioned the Lord (v. 14) to shepherd, feed, and protect His people like a flock (cf. Ps 23). The Lord answered, reiterating that He would demonstrate His presence and power among them as He did in the Exodus from Egypt (v. 15). As a result (cf. v. 10), the vaunted pride and power of the nations would be rendered powerless (cf. Jos 2:9–11) and, having been humbled (v. 17), they would no longer listen to or engage in the taunting of His people (v. 16b; cf. Ge 12:3; Is 52:15).

7:15 miracles. These miracles will be fulfilled in God's judgment on the earth which precedes the Second Advent of Messiah (cf. Rev 6–19).

7:18–20 In response to the gracious, forgiving character displayed toward Israel by their Master, the repentant remnant of the people extolled His incomparable grace and mercy (cf. Ps 130:3, 4).

7:18 Who is a God like You ... ? Micah began this final section with a play on words involving his name. See Introduction: Title.

GOD'S FORGIVENESS OF SIN
1. God removes our sins as far as the E is from the W (Ps 103:12)
2. God completely cleanses us from the stain of our sins (Is 1:18)
3. God throws our sins behind His back (Is 38:17)
4. God remembers our sins no more (Jer 31:34)
5. God treads our sins underfoot (Mic 7:19)
6. God casts our sins into the depths of the sea (Mic 7:19)

He does not [C]retain His anger forever,
Because He [D]delights in
[b]unchanging love.
19 He will again have compassion on us;
[A]He will tread our iniquities
under foot.
Yes, You will [B]cast all [a]their sins
Into the depths of the sea.
20 You will give [a,A]truth to Jacob
And [b]unchanging love to Abraham,
Which You [B]swore to our forefathers
From the days of old.

7:18 [b]Or *lovingkindness* [C]Ps 103:8, 9, 13 [D]Jer 32:41 7:19 [a]Several ancient versions read *our* [A]Jer 50:20 [B]Is 38:17; 43:25; Jer 31:34 7:20 [a]Or *faithfulness* [b]Or *lovingkindness* [A]Gen 24:27; 32:10 [B]Deut 7:8, 12

7:20 swore to our forefathers. In spite of Israel's unfaithfulness to God, the Lord intends to fulfill His unconditional promises in the Abrahamic Covenant made with Abraham and confirmed with Isaac and Jacob (cf. Ge 12, 15, 17, 22, 26, 28, 35). When enacted in conjunction with the Davidic Covenant, Israel will again be restored as a people and a nation to the land originally promised to Abraham. Jesus Christ, the ultimate descendant of David, will rule from Jerusalem over the world as King of kings and Lord of lords (cf. Rev 17:14; 19:16).

THE
BOOK OF
NAHUM

TITLE

The book's title is taken from the prophet-of-God's oracle against Nineveh, the capital of Assyria. Nahum means "comfort" or "consolation" and is a short form of Nehemiah ("comfort of Yahweh"). Nahum is not quoted in the NT, although there may be an allusion to Na 1:15 in Ro 10:15 (cf. Is 52:7).

AUTHOR AND DATE

The significance of the writing prophets was not their personal lives; it was their message. Thus, background information about the prophet from within the prophecy is rare. Occasionally, one of the historical books will shed additional light. In the case of Nahum, nothing is provided except that he was an Elkoshite (1:1), referring either to his birthplace or his place of ministry. Attempts to identify the location of Elkosh have been unsuccessful. Suggestions include Al Qosh, situated in northern Iraq (thus Nahum would have been a descendant of the exiles taken to Assyria in 722 B.C.), Capernaum ("town of Nahum"), or a location in southern Judah (cf. 1:15). His birthplace or locale is not significant to the interpretation of the book.

With no mention of any kings in the introduction, the date of Nahum's prophecy must be implied by historical data. The message of judgment against Nineveh portrays a nation of strength, intimating a time not only prior to her fall in 612 B.C. but probably before the death of Ashurbanipal in 626 B.C., after which Assyria's power fell rapidly. Nahum's mention of the fall of No-amon, also called Thebes (3:8–10), in 663 B.C. (at the hands of Ashurbanipal) appears to be fresh in their minds, and there is no mention of the rekindling that occurred ten years later, suggesting a mid-seventh century B.C. date during the reign of Manasseh (ca. 695–642 B.C.; cf. 2Ki 21:1–18).

BACKGROUND AND SETTING

A century after Nineveh repented at the preaching of Jonah, she returned to idolatry, violence, and arrogance (3:1–4). Assyria was at the height of her power, having recovered from Sennacherib's defeat (701 B.C.) at Jerusalem (cf. Is 37:36–38). Her borders extended all the way into Egypt. Esarhaddon had recently transplanted conquered peoples into Samaria and Galilee in 670 B.C. (cf. 2Ki 17:24; Ezr 4:2), leaving Syria and Israel very weak. But God brought Nineveh down under the rising power of Babylon's king Nabopolassar and his son, Nebuchadnezzar (ca. 612 B.C.). Assyria's demise turned out just as God had prophesied.

HISTORICAL AND THEOLOGICAL THEMES

Nahum forms a sequel to the book of Jonah, who prophesied over a century earlier. Jonah recounts the remission of God's promised judgment toward Nineveh, while Nahum depicts the later execution of God's judgment. Nineveh was proud of her invulnerable city, with her walls reaching 100 ft. high and with a moat 150 ft. wide and 60 ft. deep; but Nahum established the fact that the sovereign God (1:2–5) would bring vengeance upon those who violated His law (1:8, 14; 3:5–7). The same God had a retributive judgment against evil which is also redemptive, bestowing His loving-kindnesses upon the faithful (cf. 1:7, 12, 13, 15; 2:2). The prophecy brought comfort to Judah and all who feared the cruel Assyrians. Nahum said Nineveh would end "with an overflowing flood" (1:8); and it happened when the Tigris River overflowed to destroy enough of the walls to let the Babylonians through. Nahum also predicted that the city would be hidden (3:11). After its destruction in 612 B.C., the site was not rediscovered until A.D. 1842.

INTERPRETIVE CHALLENGES

Apart from the uncertain identity of Elkosh (cf. Introduction: Author and Date), the prophecy presents no real interpretive difficulties. The book is a straightforward prophetic announcement of judgment against Assyria and her capital Nineveh for cruel atrocities and idolatrous practices.

OUTLINE

I. Superscription (1:1)

II. Destruction of Nineveh Declared (1:2–15)
- A. God's Power Illustrated (1:2–8)
- B. God's Punishment Stated (1:9–15)

III. Destruction of Nineveh Detailed (2:1–13)
- A. The City is Assaulted (2:1–10)
- B. The City is Discredited (2:11–13)

IV. Destruction of Nineveh Demanded (3:1–19)
- A. The First Charge (3:1–3)
- B. The Second Charge (3:4–7)
- C. The Third Charge (3:8–19)

GOD IS AWESOME

1 The [a,A]oracle of [B]Nineveh. The book of the vision of Nahum the Elkoshite.

2 A [A]jealous and avenging God is the LORD;
The LORD is [B]avenging and [a]wrathful.
The LORD takes [C]vengeance
on His adversaries,
And He reserves wrath for His enemies.
3 The LORD is [A]slow to anger
and great in power,
And the LORD will by no means
leave *the guilty* unpunished.
In [B]whirlwind and storm is His way,
And [C]clouds are the dust beneath His feet.
4 He [A]rebukes the sea and makes it dry;
He dries up all the rivers.
[B]Bashan and Carmel wither;
The blossoms of Lebanon wither.
5 Mountains [A]quake because of Him
And the hills [B]dissolve;
Indeed the earth is [C]upheaved
by His presence,
The [D]world and all the inhabitants in it.
6 [A]Who can stand before His indignation?
Who can endure the [B]burning of His anger?
His [C]wrath is poured out like fire
And the [D]rocks are broken up by Him.
7 The LORD is [A]good,
A stronghold in the day of trouble,
And [B]He knows those who
take refuge in Him.
8 But with an [A]overflowing flood
He will make a complete end of [a]its site,
And will pursue His enemies into [B]darkness.

9 Whatever you [A]devise against the LORD,
He will make a [B]complete end of it.
Distress will not rise up twice.
10 Like tangled [A]thorns,
And like those who are [B]drunken
with their drink,
They are [C]consumed
As stubble completely withered.
11 From you has gone forth
One who [A]plotted evil against the LORD,
A [a,B]wicked counselor.

12 Thus says the LORD,

"Though they are at full *strength*
and likewise many,
Even so, they will be [A]cut off and pass away.
Though I have afflicted you,
I will afflict you [B]no longer.
13 "So now, I will [A]break his yoke
bar from upon you,
And I will tear off your shackles."

14 The LORD has issued a command
concerning [a]you:
"[b]Your name will [A]no longer be perpetuated.
I will cut off [c,B]idol and [d]image
From the house of your gods.

1:1 [a]Or *burden* [A]Is 13:1; 19:1; Jer 23:33, 34; Hab 1:1; Zech 9:1; Mal 1:1 [B]2 Kin 19:36; Jon 1:2; Nah 2:8; Zeph 2:13 1:2 [a]Lit *a possessor of wrath* [A]Ex 20:5; Josh 24:19 [B]Deut 32:35, 41 [C]Ps 94:1 1:3 [A]Ex 34:6, 7; Neh 9:17; Ps 103:8 [B]Ex 19:16; Is 29:6 [C]Ps 104:3; Is 19:1 1:4 [A]Josh 3:15, 16; Ps 106:9; Is 50:2; Matt 8:26 [B]Is 33:9 1:5 [A]Ex 19:18; 2 Sam 22:8; Ps 18:7 [B]Mic 1:4 [C]Is 24:1, 20 [D]Ps 98:7 1:6 [A]Jer 10:10; Mal 3:2 [B]Is 13:13 [C]Is 66:15 [D]1 Kin 19:11 1:7 [A]Ps 25:8; 37:39, 40; Jer 33:11 [B]Ps 1:6; John 10:14; 2 Tim 2:19 1:8 [a]I.e. Nineveh's [A]Is 28:2, 17f; Amos 8:8 [B]Is 13:9, 10 1:9 [A]Ps 2:1; Nah 1:11 [B]Is 28:22 1:10 [A]2 Sam 23:6; Mic 7:4 [B]Is 56:12; Nah 3:11 [C]Is 5:24; 10:17; Mal 4:1 1:11 [a]Or *worthless;* Heb *Belial* [A]Is 10:7-11; Nah 1:9 [B]Ezek 11:2 1:12 [A]Is 10:16-19, 33, 34 [B]Lam 3:31, 32 1:13 [A]Is 9:4; 10:27; Jer 2:20 1:14 [a]I.e. the king of Nineveh [b]Lit *No more of your name will be sown* [c]Or *a graven image* [d]Lit *cast* metal *image* [A]Job 18:17; Ps 109:13; Is 14:22 [B]Is 46:1, 2; Mic 5:13, 14

1:1 oracle. The prophecy is a message of doom. Nahum was only the messenger of this divine oracle of judgment on Nineveh.

1:2–15 The destruction of Nineveh was announced.

1:2–8 Nahum, defining God's power in general, establishes the fact that He is omnipotent, a holy and jealous God who will punish the wicked and avenge His own.

1:2 jealous. This attribute, often used of God's burning zeal for His wife, Israel, emphasizes His passionate reaction against anyone guilty of spiritual adultery. Possibly the captivity of the 10 northern tribes (722 B.C.) or the invasion of Sennacherib (701 B.C.) is in view here.

1:3 slow to anger. The jealousy of v. 2 should not suggest that God is quick to anger; rather He is longsuffering (cf. Ex 34:6; Nu 14:18). God had extended His forbearance to Nineveh at least a century earlier in response to their repentance at Jonah's preaching (cf. Jon 3:10; 4:2). But although patient, His justice will eventually punish the wicked. **whirlwind ... storm ... clouds.** These figures frequently describe the Lord's appearances (theophanies), often in judgment (cf. Ex 19:9, 16; Ps 83:15; Is 29:6; Joel 2:2; 1Th 4:17). Nature is the theater in which His power and majesty is showcased.

1:4 His mighty power is revealed when He rebukes the sea, as in the crossing of the Red Sea (Ex 14:15–25) and when He withholds His rain from the fertile valleys and coastal highlands. **Bashan ... Carmel ... Lebanon.** Bashan, located below Mt. Hermon, E of the Jordan, was known for her lush pastures (Mic 7:14). Carmel, along the coast of Canaan, became synonymous with fruitfulness (SS 7:5). Lebanon was renowned for her beautiful cedars (1Ki 5:14–18). Yet, they too would wither before the infinite strength of the omnipotent Judge.

1:5 The violent shaking of the earth provides another evidence of the Lord's awesome power, as even that which seems to be most stable trembles.

1:6 This series of rhetorical questions summarizes vv. 2–5; His power and resolve to spew His wrath on Nineveh is irresistible, melting all opposition before it.

1:7 In contrast to v. 6, Nahum eased the fury by adding that God was compassionate, a stronghold or fortress (cf. Ps 46:1) to those who put their hope in Him (cf. Is 33:2–4; 37:3–7, 29–38). The verse foreshadowed the vindication of Judah in vv. 12b, 13, 15; 2:2.

1:8 flood ... darkness. Nahum described Nineveh's judgment metaphorically as an engulfing flood and darkness from which none can escape.

1:9–15 Having established God's power and sovereign right to judge generally, Nahum announced specifically God's judgment upon Nineveh, interweaving expressions of blessing and hope for Israel within the oracles of doom upon the wicked nation. The sovereign Judge not only punishes (vv. 9–12a, 14) but also saves (vv. 12b, 13, 15).

1:9 Whatever you devise. All Assyrian attempts to foil God's judgment would end in futility (cf. Ps 2). Their affliction of His people would not be allowed to occur again (cf. v. 12). Their end was determined.

1:11 wicked counselor. The phrase, lit. "counselor of Belial," suggests Satanic influence on the leadership, identified as the king of Assyria (cf. 3:18). Specific reference could be to Ashurbanipal (669–633 B.C.) or more likely to Sennacherib (705–681 B.C.), who invaded Judah in 701 B.C. and of whom Isaiah speaks in similar language (Is 10:7).

1:12 Thus says the LORD. Used as a common prophetic formula introducing God's unequivocal message, it occurs only here in the book. Verse 12a is related in the third person, denoting the enemy, while in v. 12b the chosen people of God are spoken of in the second person. The safety of a walled city and massive numbers ("many") would not be a sufficient defense. "Even so" harkens back to vv. 7–10.

1:12b, 13 I will afflict you no longer. Judah was to be no longer afflicted by Assyria.

1:14 Three judgments were pronounced. First, the king of Assyria, representing the nation, would become destitute of descendants.

I will prepare your [C]grave,
For you are contemptible."

15 [a]Behold, [A]on the mountains the feet
of him who brings good news,
Who announces peace!
[B]Celebrate your feasts, O Judah;
Pay your vows.
For [C]never again will the [b]wicked
one pass through you;
He is [D]cut off completely.

THE OVERTHROW OF NINEVEH

2 [a]The one who [A]scatters has
come up against [b]you.
Man the fortress, watch the road;
[c]Strengthen your back, [d]summon
all *your* strength.

2 For the LORD will restore the
[A]splendor of Jacob
[B]Like the splendor of Israel,
Even though devastators
have devastated them
And [C]destroyed their vine branches.

3 The shields of [a]his mighty
men are *colored* red,
The warriors are dressed in [A]scarlet,
The chariots are *enveloped*
in [b]flashing steel
[c]When he is prepared *to march,*
And the cypress [B]*spears* are brandished.

4 The [A]chariots race madly in the streets,
They rush wildly in the [a]squares,
Their appearance is like torches,
They dash to and fro like lightning flashes.

1:14 [C]Ezek 32:22, 23 1:15 [a]Ch 2:1 in Heb [b]Or *worthless one;* Heb *Belial* [A]Is 40:9; 52:7; Rom 10:15 [B]Lev 23:2, 4 [C]Is 52:1; Joel 3:17 [D]Is 29:7, 8 2:1 [a]Ch 2:2 in Heb [b]Lit *your face* [c]Lit *Make strong your loins* [d]Lit *strengthen power greatly* [A]Jer 51:20-23 2:2 [A]Is 60:15 [B]Ezek 37:21-23 [C]Ps 80:12, 13 2:3 [a]I.e. those attacking Nineveh [b]Lit *fire of steel* [c]Lit *On the day of his preparation* [A]Ezek 23:14, 15 [B]Job 39:23 2:4 [a]Lit *broad places* [A]Is 66:15; Jer 4:13; Ezek 26:10; Nah 3:2, 3

Second, the gods by which they received their authority would be destroyed. Third, the king would be put to death (cf. the fall of Nineveh in 612 B.C.).

1:15 mountains … feet. The verse echoes Is 52:7, where it refers to those who announced the deliverance from Babylon. The theme of good tidings and peace reverberates throughout the message of the NT (cf. Lk 2:10; Is 61:1 with Lk 4:16–21; Ro 10:15; Eph 2:14–18). **feasts.** During a siege, people were prevented from going up to Jerusalem to celebrate her annual feasts (cf. Nu 28, 29). With the destruction of Assyria, Judah was called upon to celebrate her feasts and to pay the vows made while under siege (cf. Ps 116:14, 17, 18).

2:1–13 Nineveh's fall in 612 B.C. at the hands of Nebuchadnezzar of Babylon, though still future in Nahum's day, is described vividly in present tense terms.

2:1 scatters. Assyria had made a practice of dispersing captives to many nations; now she would receive similar judgment. **Man … watch … Strengthen.** The prophet, with irony and satire, ordered the Assyrians to prepare for the coming invasion from Babylon.

2:2 splendor of Jacob … Israel. This is not a reference to the southern and northern tribes, since the northern tribes had been overrun by Assyria almost a century earlier; but these are titles of honor for Judah, remembering the day when Jacob received God's blessing at Peniel (Ge 32:27, 28) and had his name changed to Israel. Together, they signify the nation's restoration to the promised position. **devastators have devastated them.** Assyria had repeatedly "devastated" the land, destroying its fruitful vineyards and economic lifeblood.

2:3 shields … *colored* red. Shields were either overlaid with copper, whose reflections of sunshine would make the army appear larger and strike terror in the enemy, or they were covered with hide that was dyed red, so as to extinguish fiery arrows and to minimize the sight of blood. "Scarlet" clothing would have similar benefits. ***spears* are brandished.** Warriors, denoting their eagerness and readiness for battle, would wave their weapons.

2:4 Confusion reigned in Nineveh, where battle preparations were hurriedly made.

GOD'S JUDGMENT AGAINST ASSYRIA/NINEVEH
IN RETROSPECT—Fulfilled
1. Jer 50:17, 18
2. Eze 32:22, 23
IN PROSPECT—Prophesied
1. Is 10:5
2. Is 10:24–27
3. Is 14:24, 25
4. Is 30:31–33
5. Is 31:8, 9
6. Mic 5:5, 6
7. Na 1:1
8. Na 2:8
9. Na 3:7, 18
10. Zep 2:13–15

5 He remembers his [A]nobles;
They [B]stumble in their march,
They hurry to her wall,
And the [a]mantelet is set up.
6 The gates of the rivers are opened
And the palace is dissolved.
7 It is fixed:
She is stripped, she is carried away,
And her handmaids are [A]moaning
like the sound of doves,
[B]Beating on their [a]breasts.

8 Though Nineveh *was* like a pool of
water throughout her days,
Now they are fleeing;
"Stop, stop,"
But [A]no one turns back.
9 Plunder the silver!
Plunder the [A]gold!
For there is no limit to the treasure—
Wealth from every kind of
desirable object.
10 She is [A]emptied! Yes, she is
desolate and waste!
[B]Hearts are melting and knees knocking!
Also anguish is in [a]the whole body
And all their [C]faces are grown pale!
11 Where is the den of the lions
And the feeding place
of the [A]young lions,
Where the lion, lioness and
lion's cub prowled,
With nothing to disturb *them?*
12 The lion tore enough for his cubs,
[a]Killed *enough* for his lionesses,
And filled his lairs with prey
And his dens with torn flesh.

13 "Behold, [A]I am against you," declares the LORD
of hosts. "I will [B]burn up her chariots in smoke, a
sword will devour your young lions; I will [C]cut off
your prey from the land, and no longer will the
voice of your messengers be heard."

NINEVEH'S COMPLETE RUIN

3 [A]Woe to the bloody city, completely
full of lies *and* pillage;
Her prey never departs.
2 The [A]noise of the whip,
The noise of the rattling
of the wheel,
Galloping horses
And [a]bounding chariots!
3 Horsemen charging,
Swords flashing, [A]spears gleaming,
[B]Many slain, a mass of corpses,
And [a,C]countless dead bodies—
They stumble over
[b]the dead bodies!
4 *All* because of the [A]many
harlotries of the harlot,
The charming one, the
[B]mistress of sorceries,
Who [C]sells nations by her harlotries
And families by her sorceries.
5 "Behold, [A]I am against you,"
declares the LORD of hosts;
"And I will [a,B]lift up your skirts
over your face,
And [C]show to the nations
your nakedness
And to the kingdoms your disgrace.
6 "I will [A]throw [a]filth on you
And [B]make you vile,
And set you up as a [C]spectacle.

2:5 [a]Lit *covering* used in a siege [A]Nah 3:18 [B]Jer 46:12 2:7 [a]Lit *hearts* [A]Is 38:14; 59:11 [B]Is 32:12 2:8 [A]Jer 46:5; 47:3 2:9 [A]Rev 18:12, 16 2:10 [a]Lit *all the loin* [A]Is 24:1; 34:10-13; Nah 2:2 [B]Ps 22:14; Is 13:7, 8; Ezek 21:7 [C]Joel 2:6 2:11 [A]Is 5:29 2:12 [a]Lit *Strangled* 2:13 [A]Jer 21:13; Ezek 5:8; Nah 3:5 [B]Josh 11:6, 9; Ps 46:9 [C]Is 49:24, 25; Nah 3:1 3:1 [A]Ezek 24:6, 9 3:2 [a]Lit *skipping* [A]Job 39:22-25; Jer 47:3; Nah 2:3, 4 3:3 [a]Lit *there is no end to* [b]Lit *their* [A]Hab 3:11 [B]Is 34:3; 66:16 [C]Is 37:36; Ezek 39:4 3:4 [A]Is 23:17; Ezek 16:25-29; Rev 17:1, 2 [B]Is 47:9, 12, 13 [C]Rev 18:3 3:5 [a]Lit *uncover your* [A]Jer 50:31; Ezek 26:3; Nah 2:13 [B]Is 47:2, 3; Jer 13:26 [C]Ezek 16:37 3:6 [a]Lit *detestable things* [A]Job 9:31 [B]Job 30:8; Mal 2:9 [C]Is 14:16; Jer 51:37

2:5 They hurry to her wall. This may continue the thought of v. 4, depicting Nineveh's royalty and military leaders dashing to one of her many defense towers which, according to the Greek historian Diodorus Siculus, numbered 1,500 and reached a height of 200 ft. It is also possible that the latter part of the verse is a description of the attackers preparing to erect a "mantelet," a small fortress-type box in which soldiers rode for protection as they advanced to the wall.

2:6 gates of the rivers. Nineveh, lying at the confluence of 3 rivers (the Tigris and two smaller rivers), constructed dams to minimize the damage of seasonal flooding to her walls. The latter part of v. 6 suggests that these dam gates were opened, causing the walls to be dissolved and the palace to be taken (cf. Introduction: Historical and Theological Themes; 1:8).

2:7 she is carried away. The goddess of Nineveh, probably Ishtar, was taken by her attackers to demonstrate the superiority of their gods (cf. 1Sa 4:1–11). The temple prostitutes ("handmaids") mourned the fate of their goddess.

2:8 pool of water. Though Nineveh was like an oasis in the desert that attracted many people, they fled from the devastation.

2:9 Plunder. Spoils abounded in Nineveh, but it was her turn to be plundered.

2:10 Hearts are melting. The great city of Nineveh, lying in ruin, evoked fear and terror in those who observed it (cf. Da 5:6).

2:11–13 Where is . . . ? Archeologists have found a carving from a palace showing an Assyrian king on a lion hunt. Nahum rhetorically asks where Nineveh has gone. No longer describing Nineveh's fall, the prophet taunted her, ridiculing her fall from power and glory. Like a pride of lions, with plenty to eat and in fear of no enemy, Nineveh ruthlessly "tore" her prey. She herself will become prey for another nation, under the sovereign direction of God. "I am against you" should be the most feared words a nation could receive from God.

2:13 burn up her chariots. Nineveh, known for burning the captured cities, would receive the same fate. **your messengers.** The voice of the messengers who carried the edicts of the mighty king of Assyria to the captured nations would become mute.

3:1–19 The prophet Nahum, asserting that the destruction of Nineveh was justly deserved, makes 3 charges against her (vv. 1, 4, 8–10), followed by the consequences (vv. 2, 3, 5–7, 11–19).

3:1 bloody city. The first accusation was a charge well documented in history. Assyria proved to be an unusually cruel, bloodthirsty nation. **lies.** Assyria employed falsehood and treachery to subdue her enemies (cf. 2Ki 18:28–32). **pillage.** See 2:11, 12. Preying upon her victims, she filled her cities with the goods of other nations.

3:2, 3 These verses reach back to the scene portrayed in 2:3–5. Assyria was so overrun that she is filled with corpses, causing the defenders to stumble over them.

3:4 The second charge against Nineveh was spiritual and moral harlotry. The nation was likened to a beautiful prostitute who seduced the nations with her illicit enticements.

3:5, 6 Nineveh would be publicly exposed, resulting in shame and humiliation.

7 "And it will come about that
all who see you
Will [a]shrink from you and say,
'Nineveh is devastated!
[A]Who will grieve for her?'
Where will I seek comforters for you?"

8 Are you better than [a,A]No-amon,
Which was situated by the
[B]waters of the Nile,
With water surrounding her,
Whose rampart *was* [b]the sea,
Whose wall *consisted* of [b]the sea?
9 [A]Ethiopia was *her* might,
And Egypt too, without limits.
[B]Put and [C]Lubim were among [a]her helpers.
10 Yet she [A]became an exile,
She went into captivity;
Also her [B]small children were
dashed to pieces
[C]At the head of every street;
They [D]cast lots for her honorable men,
And all her great men were
bound with fetters.
11 You too will become [A]drunk,
You will be [B]hidden.
You too will search for a refuge
from the enemy.
12 All your fortifications are [A]fig
trees with [a,B]ripe fruit—
When shaken, they fall into
the eater's mouth.
13 Behold, your people are
[A]women in your midst!
The gates of your land are [B]opened
wide to your enemies;
Fire consumes your gate bars.
14 [A]Draw for yourself water for the siege!
[B]Strengthen your fortifications!
Go into the clay and tread the mortar!
Take hold of the brick mold!
15 There [A]fire will consume you,
The sword will cut you down;
It will [B]consume you as the locust *does.*

Multiply yourself like the creeping locust,
Multiply yourself like the
swarming locust.
16 You have increased your [A]traders
more than the stars of heaven—
The creeping locust [a]strips
and flies away.
17 Your [a,A]guardsmen are like
the swarming locust.
Your [B]marshals are like hordes
of grasshoppers
Settling in the stone walls on a cold day.
The sun rises and they flee,
And the place where they
are is not known.
18 Your shepherds are [A]sleeping,
O [B]king of Assyria;
Your [C]nobles are lying down.
Your people are [D]scattered
on the mountains
And there is no one to regather *them.*
19 There is [A]no relief for your breakdown,
Your [B]wound is incurable.
All who hear [a]about you
Will [C]clap *their* hands over you,
For on whom has not your evil
passed continually?

3:7 [a]Lit *flee* [A]Is 51:19; Jer 15:5 3:8 [a]I.e. the city of Amon: Thebes [b]I.e. the Nile [A]Jer 46:25; Ezek 30:14-16 [B]Is 19:6-8 3:9 [a]Lit *your* [A]Is 20:5 [B]Jer 46:9; Ezek 27:10; 30:5; 38:5 [C]2 Chr 12:3; 16:8 3:10 [A]Is 19:4; 20:4 [B]Ps 137:9; Is 13:16; Hos 13:16 [C]Lam 2:19 [D]Joel 3:3; Obad 11 3:11 [A]Is 49:26; Jer 25:27; Nah 1:10 [B]Is 2:10, 19; Hos 10:8 3:12 [a]Lit *first fruits* [A]Rev 6:13 [B]Is 28:4 3:13 [A]Is 19:16; Jer 50:37; 51:30 [B]Is 45:1, 2; Nah 2:6 3:14 [A]2 Chr 32:3, 4 [B]Nah 2:1 3:15 [A]Is 66:15, 16; Nah 2:13; 3:13 [B]Joel 1:4 3:16 [a]I.e. strips vegetation; or *molts* [A]Is 23:8 3:17 [a]Or *officials* [A]Rev 9:7 [B]Jer 51:27 3:18 [A]Ps 76:5, 6; Is 56:10; Jer 51:57 [B]Jer 50:18 [C]Nah 2:5 [D]1 Kin 22:17; Is 13:14 3:19 [a]Lit *your report* [A]Jer 46:11; Mic 1:9 [B]Jer 30:12 [C]Job 27:23; Lam 2:15

3:7 Nineveh is devastated! Instead of mourning, there would be rejoicing at her fall. None would be found to comfort her; she would bear her misery alone.

3:8–10 Nahum sets forth the third and final charge against Nineveh: they hadn't learned from No-amon. Also known as Thebes, No-amon was the great capital of southern Egypt, 400 mi. S of Cairo. One of the most magnificent ancient civilizations of the world, it was renowned for its 100 gates, a temple measuring 330 ft. long and 170 ft. wide, and its network of canals. It fell to Ashurbanipal of Assyria in 663 B.C. Like No-amon by the Nile, Nineveh was situated by the Tigris River, enjoying the security of conquered nations around her. However, her end would be like that of No-amon.

3:9 Ethiopia … Egypt … Put … Lubim. No-amon was well protected on all sides, nestled between lower Egypt on the N and Ethiopia on the S. The location of Put is best identified in the general vicinity of North Africa. Josephus says that Put, the third son of Ham (Ge 10:6), was the founder of Libya. Lubim has been identified with the area of modern Libya as well.

3:11 drunk. As predicted (cf. 1:10), Nineveh would be made to drink of God's wrath, making her drunk and defenseless to His judgment.

3:12, 13 Nahum employed a series of metaphors to emphasize that Nineveh's strong defenses would be easily overrun. Their walls would be like ripe fruit that falls at the slightest shaking and their battle forces like weak women.

3:14, 15 The prophet taunted the people with sarcasm, urging them to prepare for battle, to fortify the city's defenses, only to be destroyed. As the locust leaves nothing, stripping all the foliage, so there would be nothing left of Nineveh (cf. Am 7:1).

3:16 increased your traders. Nineveh had increased her traders, or merchants, bringing immense wealth, which is just more to destroy.

3:17 locust. Not only was Nineveh's commercial strength gone (v. 16), but her governing resources disappeared as well. After camping for the night within the massive walls of this great citadel, the locusts, depicting Assyria's leadership, flew away with the first rays of warm sunshine in search of food.

3:18, 19 The destiny of Nineveh was certain. She had received the death blow; she would not recover. And all who hear of it would rejoice. Assyria had devastated the nations with her atrocities and cruelties; the news of her downfall brought happiness and mirth among the nations.

3:18 sleeping … lying down. The Assyrian leaders and army, described in terms of exhaustion and sleep, were dead; the people were scattered. There were none left to help against the invasion of the Babylonians, to whom they fell in 612 B.C.

THE BOOK OF HABAKKUK

TITLE

This prophetic book takes its name from its author and possibly means "one who embraces" (1:1; 3:1). By the end of the prophecy, this name becomes appropriate as the prophet clings to God regardless of his confusion about God's plans for His people.

AUTHOR AND DATE

As with many of the Minor Prophets, nothing is known about the prophet except that which can be inferred from the book. In the case of Habakkuk, internal information is virtually nonexistent, making conclusions about his identity and life conjectural. His simple introduction as "Habakkuk the prophet" may imply that he needed no introduction since he was a well-known prophet of his day. It is certain that he was a contemporary of Jeremiah, Ezekiel, Daniel, and Zephaniah.

The mention of the Chaldeans (1:6) suggests a late seventh century B.C. date, shortly before Nebuchadnezzar commenced his military march through Nineveh (612 B.C.), Haran (609 B.C.), and Carchemish (605 B.C.), on his way to Jerusalem (605 B.C.). Habakkuk's bitter lament (1:2–4) may reflect a time period shortly after the death of Josiah (609 B.C.), days in which the godly king's reforms (cf. 2Ki 23) were quickly overturned by his successor, Jehoiakim (Jer 22:13–19).

BACKGROUND AND SETTING

Habakkuk prophesied during the final days of the Assyrian Empire and the beginning of Babylonia's world rulership under Nabopolassar and his son Nebuchadnezzar. When Nabopolassar ascended to power in 626 B.C., he immediately began to expand his influence to the N and W. Under the leadership of his son, the Babylonian army overthrew Nineveh in 612 B.C., forcing the Assyrian nobility to take refuge first in Haran and then Carchemish. Nebuchadnezzar pursued them, overrunning Haran in 609 B.C. and Carchemish in 605 B.C.

The Egyptian king Neco, traveling through Judah in 609 B.C. to assist the fleeing Assyrian king, was opposed by King Josiah at Megiddo (2Ch 35:20–24). Josiah was killed in the ensuing battle, leaving his throne to a succession of 3 sons and a grandson. Earlier, as a result of discovering the Book of the Law in the temple (622 B.C.), Josiah had instituted significant spiritual reforms in Judah (2Ki 22, 23), abolishing many of the idolatrous practices of his father Amon (2Ki 21:20–22) and grandfather Manasseh (2Ki 21:11–13). Upon his death, however, the nation quickly reverted to her evil ways (cf. Jer 22:13–19), causing Habakkuk to question God's silence and apparent lack of punitive action (1:2–4) to purge His covenant people.

HISTORICAL AND THEOLOGICAL THEMES

The opening verses reveal a historical situation similar to the days of Amos and Micah. Justice had essentially disappeared from the Land; violence and wickedness were pervasive, existing unchecked. In the midst of these dark days, the prophet cried out for divine intervention (1:2–4). God's response, that He was sending the Chaldeans to judge Judah (1:5–11), creates an even greater theological dilemma for Habakkuk: Why didn't God purge His people and restore their righteousness? How could God use the Chaldeans to judge a people more righteous than they (1:12–2:1)? God's answer that He would also judge the Chaldeans also (2:2–20) did not fully satisfy the prophet's theological quandary; in fact, it only intensified it. In Habakkuk's mind, the issue crying for resolution is no longer God's righteous response toward evil (or lack thereof), but the vindication of God's character and covenant with His people (1:13). Like Job, the prophet argued with God, and through that experience he achieved a deeper understanding of God's sovereign character and a firmer faith in Him (cf. Job 42:5, 6; Is 55:8, 9). Ultimately, Habakkuk realized that God was not to be worshiped merely because of the temporal blessings He bestowed, but for His own sake (3:17–19).

INTERPRETIVE CHALLENGES

The queries of the prophet represent some of the most fundamental questions in all of life, with the answers providing crucial foundation stones on which to build a proper understanding of God's character and His sovereign ways in history. The core of his message lies in the call to trust God (2:4), "the righteous shall live by his faith." The NT references ascribe unusual importance theologically to Habakkuk. The writer of Hebrews quotes Hab 2:4 to amplify the believer's need to remain strong and faithful in the midst of affliction and trials (Heb 10:38). The apostle Paul, on the other hand, employs the verse twice (Ro 1:17; Gal 3:11) to accentuate the doctrine of justification by faith. There need not be any interpretive conflict, however, for the emphasis in both Habakkuk and the NT references goes beyond the act of faith to include the continuity of faith. Faith is not a one-time act, but a way of life. The true believer, declared righteous by God, will habitually persevere in faith throughout all his life (cf. Col 1:22, 23; Heb 3:12–14). He will trust the sovereign God who only does what is right.

OUTLINE

I. Superscription (1:1)

II. The Prophet's Perplexities (1:2–2:20)
- A. His First Complaint (1:2–4)
- B. God's First Response (1:5–11)
- C. His Second Complaint (1:12–2:1)
- D. God's Second Response (2:2–20)

III. The Prophet's Prayer (3:1–19)
- A. Petition for God's Mercy (3:1, 2)
- B. Praise of God's Power (3:3–15)
- C. Promise of God's Sufficiency (3:16–19)

CHALDEANS USED TO PUNISH JUDAH

1 The [a,A]oracle which Habakkuk the prophet saw.

2 [A]How long, O LORD, will I call for help,
And You will not hear?
I cry out to You, "Violence!"
Yet You do [B]not save.
3 Why do You make me [A]see iniquity,
And cause *me* to look on wickedness?
Yes, [B]destruction and violence
are before me;
[C]Strife exists and contention arises.
4 Therefore the [A]law is [a]ignored
And justice [b]is never upheld.
For the wicked [B]surround the righteous;
Therefore justice comes out [C]perverted.

5 "[A]Look among the nations! Observe!
Be astonished! [B]Wonder!
Because *I am* doing [C]something
in your days—
You would not believe if [a]you were told.
6 "For behold, I am [A]raising up the Chaldeans,
That [a]fierce and impetuous people
Who march [b]throughout the earth
To [c,B]seize dwelling places
which are not theirs.
7 "They are dreaded and [A]feared;
Their [B]justice and [a]authority
[b]originate with themselves.
8 "Their [A]horses are swifter than leopards
And [a]keener than [B]wolves in the evening.
Their [b]horsemen come galloping,
Their horsemen come from afar;
They fly like an [C]eagle swooping
down to devour.
9 "All of them come for violence.
[a]Their horde of [A]faces *moves* forward.
They collect captives like sand.
10 "They [A]mock at kings
And rulers are a laughing matter to them.
They [B]laugh at every fortress
And [C]heap up rubble to capture it.
11 "Then they will sweep through
like the [A]wind and pass on.
But they will be held [B]guilty,
They whose [C]strength is their god."

12 Are You not from [A]everlasting,
O LORD, my God, my Holy One?
We will not die.
You, O LORD, have [B]appointed
them to judge;
And You, O [C]Rock, have established
them to correct.
13 *Your* eyes are too [A]pure to [a]approve evil,
And You can not look on
wickedness *with favor.*
Why do You [B]look with favor
On those who deal [C]treacherously?

1:1 [a]Or *burden* [A]Is 13:1; Nah 1:1 1:2 [A]Ps 13:1, 2; 22:1, 2 [B]Jer 14:9 1:3 [A]Ps 55:9-11; Jer 20:18 [B]Jer 20:8 [C]Jer 15:10 1:4 [a]Or *ineffective;* lit *numbed* [b]Lit *never goes forth* [A]Ps 58:1, 2; 119:126; Is 59:12-14 [B]Ps 22:12; Is 1:21-23 [C]Is 5:20; Ezek 9:9 1:5 [a]Lit *it* [A]Acts 13:41 [B]Is 29:9 [C]Is 29:14; Ezek 12:22-28 1:6 [a]Lit *bitter* [b]Lit *the breadth of* [c]Lit *take possession of* [A]2 Kin 24:2; Jer 4:11-13 [B]Jer 8:10 1:7 [a]Lit *eminence* [b]Lit *proceeds from* [A]Is 18:2, 7 [B]Jer 39:5-9 1:8 [a]Or *more eager* to attack [b]Or *steeds paw* the ground [A]Jer 4:13 [B]Zeph 3:3 [C]Ezek 17:3; Hos 8:1 1:9 [a]Or *The eagerness of their faces* [A]2 Kin 12:17; Dan 11:17 1:10 [A]2 Chr 36:6, 10; Is 37:13 [B]Is 10:9; 14:16 [C]Jer 32:24; Ezek 26:8 1:11 [A]Jer 4:11, 12 [B]Jer 2:3 [C]Dan 4:30; Hab 1:16 1:12 [A]Deut 33:27; Ps 90:2; Mal 3:6 [B]Is 10:5, 6; Mal 3:5 [C]Deut 32:4 1:13 [a]Lit *look at* [A]Ps 11:4-6; 34:15, 16 [B]Jer 12:1, 2 [C]Is 24:16

1:1 oracle. A weighty oracle of judgment (cf. 1:5–11; 2:2–20) is often depicted by this term when employed by the prophets to announce God's wrath against sin (e.g., Is 13:1; 15:1; 17:1; 19:1; Na 1:1; Zec 9:1; 12:1; Mal 1:1). **saw.** God's message to Habakkuk took the form of a vision.

1:2–4 In Habakkuk's first complaint, he perceived that God appeared indifferent to Judah's sin. Jealous for His righteousness and knowing that a breach of the covenant required judgment (cf. Dt 28), Habakkuk questioned God's wisdom, expressing bewilderment at His seeming inactivity in the face of blatant violation of His law. The Jews had sinned by violence and injustice and should have been punished by the same.

1:2 How long . . . will I call. The phrase, reflecting the prophet's impatience, is frequently used by the psalmist to express similar thoughts of perplexity (cf. Pss 13:1, 2; 62:3; Jer 14:9; Mt 27:46).

1:2, 3 Violence . . . iniquity . . . wickedness . . . destruction. Judah's society is defined with 4 terms denoting malicious wickedness by which one morally and ethically oppresses his neighbor, resulting in contention and strife.

1:2 Yet You do not save. The prophet wanted a cleansing, purging, chastening, and revival among the people that would return them to righteousness.

1:4 law is ignored. Lit. the "law is chilled, numbed" (cf. Ge 45:26; Ps 77:2). It had no respect, was given no authority. As hands rendered useless by cold, the impact and effectiveness of the law were paralyzed by the corruption of Judah's leaders (cf. Ecc 8:11).

1:5–11 In response to Habakkuk's perplexity and pleading, God broke His silence, informing him that He was not indifferent to Judah's sin; but rather than revival, He was sending the "dreaded and feared" judgment (v. 7).

1:5 Look . . . Observe . . . Be astonished! The series of commands is plural, indicating that the wider community of Judah and Jerusalem was to take note of this imminent invasion. Paul quotes this text in Ac 13:41.

1:6–8 The Chaldeans (Babylonians) would come at the behest of the divine Commander. He is the Sovereign who brings this people of ruthless character and conduct to invade Judah. The Chaldeans are described as self-assured, self-sufficient, self-deified, and deadly (cf. Jer 51:20).

1:8 wolves in the evening. These were wolves who had suffered hunger all day long and were forced to prowl into the night for food. Like wolves, Babylon's army displayed extraordinary stamina and an undaunted eagerness to attack for the purpose of devouring the spoils of victory.

1:10 Whether it be royal authority or physical obstacles, the Babylonian army marched forward with nothing but scorn for those in their path. **heap up rubble.** Rubble and dirt piled up against the fortress or city wall as a ramp to gain entry.

1:11 strength is their god. Though the Chaldeans were God's instruments of judgment, their self-sufficiency and self-adulation planted the seeds for their own destruction (described in 2:2–20), as they stood guilty of idolatry and blasphemy before the sovereign Lord.

1:12–2:1 Habakkuk, in his reaction to the perplexing revelation (vv. 5–11), declared his confidence in the Lord (v. 12), then unveiled his second complaint, namely, how could the Lord use a wicked nation (the Chaldeans) to judge a nation (Judah) more righteous than they (vv. 13–17)? The prophet ended by expressing his determination to wait for an answer (2:1).

1:12 O LORD, my God, my Holy One. Although the prophet could not fully comprehend the sovereign workings of his righteous God, he expressed his complete faith and trust. As he rehearsed the unchangeable character of God as eternal, sovereign, and holy, he became assured that Judah would not be completely destroyed (cf. Jer 31:35–40; 33:23–26). Under the faithful hand of God, he realized that the Chaldeans were coming to correct, not annihilate. **O Rock.** A title for God which expresses His immovable and unshakable character (cf. Pss 18:2, 31, 46; 31:2, 3; 62:2, 6, 7; 78:16, 20, 35).

1:13 eyes are too pure. In spite of the prophet's expressions of faith and trust, he found himself in even further perplexity. The essence of Habakkuk's next quandary is expressed in this verse: If God is too pure to behold evil, then how can He use the wicked to devour a person more righteous than they? Would not God's use of the Chaldeans result in even greater damage to His righteous character?

Why are You [D]silent when the
wicked [E]swallow up
Those more righteous than they?
14 *Why* have You made men like
the fish of the sea,
Like creeping things without
a ruler over them?
15 *The Chaldeans* [A]bring all of
them up with a hook,
[B]Drag them away with their net,
And gather them together
in their fishing net.
Therefore they rejoice and are glad.
16 Therefore they offer a
sacrifice to their net
And [a]burn incense to
their fishing net;
Because through [A]these things
their [b]catch is [c]large,
And their food is [d]plentiful.
17 Will they therefore empty their [A]net
And continually [B]slay nations
without sparing?

GOD ANSWERS THE PROPHET

2 I will [A]stand on my guard post
And station myself on the rampart;
And I will [B]keep watch to see
[C]what He will speak to me,
And how I may reply [a]when
I am reproved.

2 Then the LORD answered me and said,
"[A]Record the vision
And inscribe *it* on tablets,
That [a]the one who [b]reads it may run.
3 "For the vision is yet for the
[A]appointed time;
It [a]hastens toward the goal
and it will not [b]fail.
Though it tarries, [B]wait for it;
For it will certainly come,
it [C]will not delay.

4 "Behold, as for the [A]proud one,
His soul is not right within him;
But the [B]righteous will live by his [a]faith.
5 "Furthermore, [A]wine betrays
the [B]haughty man,
So that he does not [C]stay at home.
He [D]enlarges his appetite like Sheol,
And he is like death, never satisfied.
He also gathers to himself all nations
And collects to himself all peoples.

6 "Will not all of these [A]take up a
taunt-song against him,
Even mockery *and* insinuations
against him
And say, '[B]Woe to him who
increases what is not his—
For how long—
And makes himself [a]rich with loans?'

1:13 [D]Ps 50:21 [E]Ps 35:25 1:15 [A]Jer 16:16; Amos 4:2 [B]Ps 10:9 1:16 [a]Or *sacrifice* [b]Lit *portion* [c]Lit *fat;* or *plentiful* [d]Lit *the fat portion* [A]Jer 44:17
1:17 [A]Is 19:8 [B]Is 14:5, 6 2:1 [a]Lit *upon my reproof* [A]Is 21:8 [B]Ps 5:3 [C]Ps 85:8 2:2 [a]Or *one may read it fluently* [b]Or *is to proclaim it* [A]Deut 27:8; Rom 15:4; Rev 1:19 2:3 [a]Lit *pants* [b]Or *lie* [A]Dan 8:17, 19; 10:14 [B]Ps 27:14 [C]Ezek 12:25; Heb 10:37 2:4 [a]Or *faithfulness* [A]Ps 49:18; Is 13:11 [B]Rom 1:17; Gal 3:11; Heb 10:38
2:5 [A]Prov 20:1 [B]Prov 21:24 [C]2 Kin 14:10 [D]Prov 27:20; 30:16; Is 5:11-15 2:6 [a]Lit *heavy* [A]Is 14:4-10; Jer 50:13 [B]Job 20:15-29; Hab 2:12

1:14–17 Lest God had forgotten just how wicked the Chaldeans were, Habakkuk drew attention to their evil character and behavior. Life was cheap to the Chaldeans. In the face of their ruthless tactics of war, other societies were "like the fish of the sea, like creeping things without a ruler." In light of their reputation (vv. 6–10), how could God have unleashed this ruthless force upon another helpless people?

1:16 sacrifice ... burn incense to their fishing net. If that is not enough, the prophet added that they attributed their gain to their own military might rather than to the true God.

1:17 empty their net. How long will the aggressor (the Chaldeans) be permitted to pursue injustice and engage in such wickedness? Can God tolerate it indefinitely?

2:1 stand on my guard post. Comparing himself to a watchman (cf. Eze 3, 33), standing as a sentinel upon the city walls, Habakkuk prepared to wait for God's answer and to ponder his reply.

2:2–20 In response to Habakkuk's second complaint (1:12–2:1), the Lord announced that He would judge the Chaldeans as well for their wickedness. His reply included: 1) the instructions to write it down, as a reminder that it would surely occur (vv. 2, 3); 2) a description of the character of the wicked in comparison to the righteous (vv. 4, 5); and 3) the pronouncement of 5 woes describing the Chaldeans' demise (vv. 6–20).

2:2, 3 Record the vision. Habakkuk was to record the vision to preserve it for posterity, so that all who read it would know of the certainty of its fulfillment (cf. similar language in Da 12:4, 9). The prophecy had lasting relevance and thus had to be preserved. Although a period of time would occur before its fulfillment, all were to know that it would occur at God's "appointed time" (cf. Is 13; Jer 50, 51). Babylon would fall to the Medo-Persian kingdom of Cyrus ca. 539 B.C. (cf. Da 5).

2:2 That the one who reads it may run. Perhaps referring 1) to clarity of form, so even the one who runs by it may easily absorb its meaning, or 2) to clarity of content, so that the courier could easily transmit the message to others.

2:4 the proud one. While the context makes this an obvious reference to the Chaldeans, the passage introduces the marks which distinguish all wicked from all righteous, regardless of ethnic origin. Two opposing characteristics are here contrasted. The proud trusts in himself; the just lives by his faith. **the righteous will live by his faith.** In contrast to the proud, the righteous will be truly preserved through his faithfulness to God. This is the core of God's message to/through Habakkuk. Both the aspect of justification by faith, as noted by Paul's usage in Ro 1:17 and Gal 3:11, as well as the aspect of sanctification by faith, as employed by the writer of Hebrews (10:38), reflect the essence of Habakkuk; no conflict exists. The emphasis in both Habakkuk and the NT references goes beyond the act of faith to include the continuity of faith. Faith is not a one-time act, but a way of life. The true believer, declared righteous by God, will persevere in faith as the pattern of his life (cf. Col 1:22, 23; Heb 3:12–14).

2:5 The diatribe against the Chaldeans served as the basis for the denunciations described in vv. 6–20. They were proud and greedy. Like Sheol and death (cf. Pr 1:12; 27:20; 30:15, 16), they were never satisfied but always wanted more.

2:6–20 Five woes, in the form of a taunt song, were pronounced upon the Chaldeans in anticipation of their eventual judgment. Presented in 5 stanzas of 3 verses each, the 5 woes were directed at 5 different classes of evildoers.

2:6–8 The first woe charged extortion, i.e., plundering nations under threat of great bodily harm for the purpose of making themselves rich. As a result, they were to become plunder for those nations who remained.

2:6 all of these. A reference to all the nations who suffered at the hands of the Babylonians. **Woe.** An interjection often used in prophetic literature to introduce a judicial indictment or a sentence of judgment (Is 5:8, 11, 18, 20–22; Jer 22:13; 23:1; Am 5:18; 6:1). **loans.** The Babylonians exacted heavy taxation of conquered nations. Such action often accompanied loans with excessive interest made to the poor (cf. Dt 24:10–13; 2Ki 4:1–7; Ne 5:1–13).

7 “Will not [a]your creditors [A]rise up suddenly,
And those who [b]collect from you awaken?
Indeed, you will become
plunder for them.
8 “Because you have [A]looted many nations,
All the remainder of the
peoples will loot you—
Because of human bloodshed and
violence [a]done to the land,
To the town and all its inhabitants.

9 “Woe to him who gets [A]evil
gain for his house
To [B]put his nest on high,
To be delivered from the
hand of calamity!
10 “You have devised a [A]shameful
thing for your house
By cutting off many peoples;
So you are [B]sinning against yourself.
11 “Surely the [A]stone will cry
out from the wall,
And the rafter will answer it
from the [a]framework.

12 “Woe to him who [A]builds a
city with bloodshed
And founds a town with [a]violence!
13 “Is it not indeed from the LORD of hosts
That peoples [A]toil for fire,
And nations grow weary for nothing?
14 “For the earth will be [A]filled
With the knowledge of the
glory of the LORD,
As the waters cover the sea.

15 “Woe to you who make [a]your
neighbors drink,
Who mix in your venom even
to make *them* drunk
So as to look on their nakedness!
16 “You will be filled with disgrace
rather than honor.
Now you yourself [A]drink and
[a]expose your *own* nakedness.
The [B]cup in the LORD’S right hand
will come around to you,
And [C]utter disgrace *will come*
upon your glory.
17 “For the [A]violence [a]done to Lebanon
will [b]overwhelm you,
And the devastation of *its* beasts
[c]by which you terrified them,
[B]Because of human bloodshed and
[C]violence [d]done to the land,
To the town and all its inhabitants.

18 “What [A]profit is the [a]idol when
its maker has carved it,
Or [b]an image, a [B]teacher of falsehood?
For *its* maker [C]trusts in his
own handiwork
When he fashions speechless idols.
19 “Woe to him who [A]says to a
piece of wood, ‘[B]Awake!’
To a mute stone, ‘Arise!’
And that is *your* teacher?
Behold, it is overlaid with [C]gold and silver,
And there is [D]no breath at all inside it.
20 “But the [A]LORD is in His holy temple.
[a]Let all the earth [B]be silent before Him.”

2:7 [a]Lit *those who bite you* [b]Lit *violently shake you* [A]Prov 29:1 2:8 [a]Lit *of the land* [A]Is 33:1; Jer 27:7; Zech 2:8 2:9 [A]Jer 22:13; Ezek 22:27 [B]Jer 49:16 2:10 [A]2 Kin 9:26; Nah 1:14; Hab 2:16 [B]Jer 26:19 2:11 [a]Lit *wood* [A]Josh 24:27; Luke 19:40 2:12 [a]Or *injustice* [A]Mic 3:10; Nah 3:1 2:13 [A]Is 50:11; Jer 51:58 2:14 [A]Ps 22:27; Is 11:9; Zech 14:9 2:15 [a]Lit *his neighbor* 2:16 [a]Lit *show yourself uncircumcised;* or *stagger;* so DSS and ancient versions [A]Lam 4:21 [B]Jer 25:15, 17 [C]Nah 3:6 2:17 [a]Lit *of Lebanon* [b]Lit *cover* [c]Lit which *terrified them* [d]Lit *of the land* [A]Joel 3:19; Zech 11:1 [B]Ps 55:23; Hab 2:8 [C]Jer 51:35; Hab 2:8 2:18 [a]Or *a graven image* [b]Lit a *cast* metal *image* [A]Is 42:17; 44:9; Jer 2:27, 28 [B]Jer 10:8, 14; Zech 10:2 [C]Ps 115:4, 8 2:19 [A]Jer 2:27, 28; 10:3 [B]1 Kin 18:26-29 [C]Ps 135:15-18; Jer 10:4, 9, 14 [D]Ps 135:17 2:20 [a]Lit *Hush before Him, all the earth* [A]Mic 1:2 [B]Zeph 1:7; Zech 2:13

2:7 your creditors. The survivor nations, from whom taxation was extorted (cf. v. 8).

2:9–11 The second charge, of premeditated exploitation borne out of covetousness, was a continuation of vv. 6–8. The walls of their houses, built with stones and timbers taken from others, testified against them (v. 11).

2:9 put his nest on high. Wanting to protect themselves from any recriminations their enemies might seek to shower upon them, the Chaldeans had sought to make their cities impregnable and inaccessible to the enemy (cf. Is 14:13, 14).

2:10 You have devised a shameful thing. The Chaldean leaders, by counseling to kill, shamed themselves and harmed their souls.

2:12–14 The third woe accuses them of being ruthless despots, building luxurious palaces by means of bloodshed and forced labor. Like a fire that burns everything given to it, their labors would all be futile, having no lasting value (v. 13; cf. Mic 3:10).

2:14 filled. In contrast to the self-exaltation of the Chaldeans, whose efforts come to naught, God promised that the whole earth would recognize His glory at the establishment of His millennial kingdom (cf. Nu 14:21; Ps 72:19; Is 6:3; 11:9).

2:15–17 The fourth charge is debauchery, wherein Babylon forced others to become intoxicated and poisoned, making them behave shamefully and become easy prey. As a result, they too would be forced to drink the cup of God’s wrath and exposed to public shame (cf. Jer 49:12).

2:16 nakedness. This word refers to “foreskin,” expressing in Heb. thought the greatest contempt, the sign of being an alien from God. *See note on Jer 4:4.* **cup in the LORD’s right hand.** A metaphor referring to divine retribution, served up by His powerful right hand (cf. Ps 21:8). What the Chaldeans did to others would also be done to them (vv. 7, 8). **disgrace *will come* upon your glory.** Carrying out the metaphor of drunkenness, here is a reference to the humiliation of “shameful spewing.” The very thing in which they gloried would become the object of their shame. While the Lord’s glory would be “as the waters cover the sea” (v. 14), Babylon’s glory would be covered with shame.

2:17 violence. The reference may be to the ruthless exploitation of trees and animals, providing building materials, firewood, and food, which often accompanied military campaigns. Lebanon’s beautiful cedars were plundered for selfish purposes (cf. Is 14:7, 8; 37:24). It also includes the slaughter of men. Verse 17b suggests that it may symbolize Israel and her inhabitants, whom Nebuchadnezzar conquered (cf. 2Ki 14:9; Jer 22:6, 23; Eze 17:3).

2:18–20 The fifth accusation is idolatry, exposing the folly of following other gods (cf. Is 41:24; 44:9). The destruction of the Chaldeans would demonstrate the superiority of the Lord over all gods.

2:19 Awake! … Arise! Compare the sarcasm with that of Elijah’s words to the prophets of Baal on Mt. Carmel (1Ki 18:27; cf. Jer 2:27).

2:20 holy temple. A reference to heaven, from where the Lord rules (Ps 11:4) and answers the prayers of those who seek Him (1Ki 8:28–30; Ps 73:17). **be silent.** In contrast to the silence of the idols (v. 19), the living, Sovereign Ruler of the universe calls all the earth to be silent before Him. None can assert his independence from Him; all the earth must worship in humble submission (cf. Ps 46:10; Is 52:15).

GOD'S DELIVERANCE OF HIS PEOPLE

3 A prayer of Habakkuk the prophet, according to [a]Shigionoth.

2 LORD, I have [A]heard [a]the report
about You *and* [b]I [B]fear.
O LORD, [C]revive [D]Your work in
the midst of the years,
In the midst of the years make it known;
In wrath remember [c,E]mercy.

3 God comes from [A]Teman,
And the Holy One from Mount [B]Paran.
Selah
His [C]splendor covers the heavens,
And the [D]earth is full of His praise.
4 *His* [A]radiance is like the sunlight;
He has rays *flashing* from His hand,
And there is the hiding of His [B]power.
5 Before Him goes [A]pestilence,
And [B]plague comes [a]after Him.
6 He stood and surveyed the earth;
He looked and [A]startled the nations.
Yes, the perpetual mountains
were shattered,
The ancient hills [a]collapsed.
His ways are [B]everlasting.
7 I saw the tents of Cushan
under [A]distress,
The tent curtains of the land of
[B]Midian were trembling.

8 Did the LORD rage against the [A]rivers,
Or *was* Your anger against the rivers,
Or *was* Your wrath against the [B]sea,
That You [C]rode on Your horses,
On Your [D]chariots of salvation?
9 Your [A]bow was made bare,
The rods of [a]chastisement were sworn.
Selah
You [B]cleaved the earth with rivers.
10 The mountains saw
You *and* quaked;
The downpour of waters swept by.
The deep [A]uttered forth its voice,
It lifted high its hands.

3:1 [a]I.e. a highly emotional poetic form 3:2 [a]Or *Your report* [b]Or *I stand in awe of Your work, O LORD; In the midst of the years revive it,* [c]Or *compassion* [A]Job 42:5 [B]Ps 119:120; Jer 10:7 [C]Ps 71:20; 85:6 [D]Ps 44:1-8; Hab 1:5 [E]Num 14:19; 2 Sam 24:15-17; Is 54:8 3:3 [A]Jer 49:7; Amos 1:12; Obad 9 [B]Gen 21:21; Deut 33:2 [C]Ps 113:4; 148:13 [D]Ps 48:10 3:4 [A]Ps 18:12 [B]Job 26:14 3:5 [a]Lit *at His feet* [A]Ex 12:29, 30; Num 16:46-49 [B]Num 11:1-3; Ps 18:12, 13 3:6 [a]Lit *bowed; or sank down* [A]Job 21:18; Ps 35:5 [B]Hab 1:12 3:7 [A]Ex 15:14-16 [B]Num 31:7, 8; Judg 7:24, 25; 8:12 3:8 [A]Ex 7:19, 20; Josh 3:16; Is 50:2 [B]Ex 14:16, 21; Ps 114:3, 5 [C]Deut 33:26; Ps 18:10; Hab 3:15 [D]Ps 68:17 3:9 [a]Lit *word* [A]Ps 7:12, 13; Hab 3:11 [B]Ps 78:16; 105:41 3:10 [A]Ps 93:3; 98:7, 8

3:1–19 The reference to "Habakkuk the prophet" (cf. 1:1) marks a transition. The argumentative tone of the previous chapters, in which he cried for divine interference, is transformed into a plea for God's mercy (v. 2), a review of God's power (vv. 3–15), and a chorus of praise for God's sustaining grace and sufficiency (vv. 16–19). But while the tone changes, a strong, thematic connection remains. Having been informed of God's plan of judgment, Habakkuk returns to the matter of Judah's judgment, pleading for mercy.

3:1 Shigionoth. The precise meaning is unknown (its singular form occurs in the heading to Ps 7). In light of the musical notation at the end of chap. 3, it is thought that it has a musical-liturgical significance, and that this chapter was sung.

3:2 the report about You. A reference back to 1:5–11 and 2:2–20, where the Lord informed Habakkuk of His plans for judging Judah and the Chaldeans. **revive Your work.** Knowledge of the severity of God's judgment struck Habakkuk with fear. As though God's power had not been used in a long time, the prophet asked the Lord to "revive" (lit. "to quicken"), to repeat His mighty saving works on behalf of His people, Israel. **In the midst of the years.** In the midst of His punishment of Judah at the hand of the Chaldeans, the prophet begged that God would remember mercy.

3:3–15 Employing figures from God's past intervention on Israel's behalf, taken from the deliverance of His people from Egypt and the conquest of Canaan, Habakkuk painted a picture of their future redemption. The Exodus from Egypt is often used as an analogy of the future redemption of Israel at the beginning of the Millennium (cf. Is 11:16).

3:3 Teman … Mount Paran. Teman, named after a grandson of Esau, was an Edomite city (Am 1:12; Ob 9). Mount Paran was located in the Sinai peninsula. Both allude to the theater in which God displayed great power when He brought Israel into the land of Canaan (cf. Dt 33:2; Jdg 5:4).

3:3, 4 The Shekinah glory, which protected and led Israel from Egypt through the wilderness (cf. Ex 40:34–38), was the physical manifestation of His presence. Like the sun, He spread His radiance throughout the heavens and the earth.

3:5 pestilence … plague. Recalling the judgment attending Israel's disobedience to the covenant given at Sinai (Ex 5:3; Nu 14:12; Dt 28:21, 22; 32:24), Habakkuk accentuated the sovereign agency of God's judgments. Both were a part of the divine entourage.

3:6, 7 The entire universe responds in fear at the approach of Almighty God (cf. Ex 15:14). As at the Creation (Is 40:12), the earth and its inhabitants are at His disposal.

3:7 Cushan … Midian. Probably referring to one people living in the Sinai peninsula region (cf. Ex 2:16–22; 18:1–5; Nu 12:1, where Moses' wife was identified as being both Midianite and Cushite).

3:8–15 With rhetorical vividness, Habakkuk addressed the Lord directly, rehearsing His judicial actions against anything that opposes His will.

3:8 Your horses … Your chariots. Symbolic descriptions of God defeating the enemy (cf. 3:11, 15).

3:9 rods of chastisement were sworn. The Lord's arrows were commissioned under divine oaths (cf. Jer 47:6, 7).

OTHER PSALMS OF THE BIBLE	
1. "The Song of Deliverance"	Exodus 15:1–18
2. "The Song of Moses"	Deuteronomy 32:1–43
3. "The Song of Deborah"	Judges 5:1–31
4. "The Song of Hannah"	1 Samuel 2:1–10
5. "The Song of the Women"	1 Samuel 18:6, 7
6. "The Song of David"	2 Samuel 22:1–51
7. "The Song of Hezekiah"	Isaiah 38:9–20
8. "The Song of Jonah"	Jonah 2:1–9
9. "The Song of Habakkuk"	Habakkuk 3:1–19
10. "The Song of Mary"	Luke 1:46–55

11 [A]Sun *and* moon stood in their places;
They went away at the [B]light
of Your arrows,
At the radiance of Your gleaming spear.
12 In indignation You [A]marched
through the earth;
In anger You [a,B]trampled the nations.
13 You went forth for the [A]salvation
of Your people,
For the salvation of Your [B]anointed.
You struck the [C]head of the
house of the evil
To lay him open from [a]thigh to neck.
Selah
14 You pierced with his [A]own [a]spears
The head of his [b]throngs.
They [B]stormed in to scatter [c]us;
Their exultation *was* like those
Who [C]devour the oppressed in secret.
15 You [A]trampled on the sea
with Your horses,
On the [B]surge of many waters.

16 I heard and my [a]inward parts [A]trembled,
At the sound my lips quivered.
Decay enters my [B]bones,
And in my place I tremble.
Because I must [C]wait quietly
for the day of distress,
[b]For the [D]people to arise *who*
will invade us.
17 Though the [A]fig tree should not blossom
And there be no [a]fruit on the vines,
Though the yield of the [B]olive should fail
And the fields produce no food,
Though the [C]flock should be
cut off from the fold
And there be [D]no cattle in the stalls,
18 Yet I will [A]exult in the LORD,
I will [B]rejoice in the [C]God of my salvation.
19 The Lord [a]GOD is my [A]strength,
And [B]He has made my feet like hinds' *feet*,
And makes me walk on my [C]high places.

For the choir director, on my stringed instruments.

3:11 [A]Josh 10:12-14 [B]Ps 18:14 3:12 [a]Or *thresh* [A]Ps 68:7 [B]Is 41:15; Jer 51:33; Mic 4:13 3:13 [a]Lit *foundation* [A]Ex 15:2; 2 Sam 5:20; Ps 68:19, 20 [B]Ps 20:6; 28:8 [C]Ps 68:21; 110:6 3:14 [a]Lit *shafts* [b]Or *warriors* or *villagers* [c]Lit *me* [A]Judg 7:22 [B]Dan 11:40; Zech 9:14 [C]Ps 10:8; 64:2-5 3:15 [A]Ps 77:19; Hab 3:8 [B]Ex 15:8 3:16 [a]Lit *belly* [b]Or *To come upon the people* who *will* [A]Dan 10:8; Hab 3:2 [B]Job 30:17, 30; Jer 23:9 [C]Luke 21:19 [D]Jer 5:15 3:17 [a]Lit *produce* [A]Joel 1:10-12; Amos 4:9; 2 Cor 4:8, 9 [B]Mic 6:15 [C]Joel 1:18 [D]Jer 5:17 3:18 [A]Ex 15:1, 2; Job 13:15; Is 61:10; Rom 5:2, 3 [B]Ps 46:1-5; Phil 4:4 [C]Ps 25:5; 27:1; Is 12:2 3:19 [a]Heb *YHWH*, usually rendered *LORD* [A]Ps 18:32, 33; 27:1; 46:1; Is 45:24 [B]2 Sam 22:34 [C]Deut 33:29

3:11 Sun *and* moon stood in their places. As prominent symbols of God's created order, the sun and moon are subservient to His beckoning. The imagery is reminiscent of Israel's victory over the Amorites at Gibeon (Jos 10:12–14).

3:12 trampled. Lit. "threshed," the term is often used to depict military invasions and the execution of judgment (cf. Jdg 8:7; 2Ki 13:7; Is 21:10; 25:10; Da 7:23; Am 1:3).

3:13 salvation of Your anointed. Both the parallelism with v. 13a ("Your people") and the numerous contextual allusions to the Exodus make this a likely reference to Moses and the chosen people of Israel, who, as God's anointed, achieved victory over Pharaoh and the armies of Egypt (cf. Ps 105:15). Ultimately, it foreshadows a subsequent, future deliverance in anticipation of the Messiah (cf. Ps 132:10–12) promised in the Davidic Covenant (cf. 2Sa 7:11–16). **struck the head of the house of the evil.** Possible reference to either the pharaoh of the Exodus, whose firstborn was slain, or to the king of the Chaldeans, whose house was built by unjust gain (2:9–11).

3:14 They stormed in to scatter. A possible reference to the pursuit of fleeing Israel at the Red Sea by Pharaoh's army (Ex 14:5–9). Like the poor, Israel appeared to be easy prey for the pursuing Egyptians.

3:15 You trampled on the sea. Another reference to God's miraculous, protective intervention on behalf of Israel at the Red Sea. The historical event demonstrates His sovereign rulership of the universe and provides assurance to the troubled prophet that the Lord could be counted on to save His people once more.

3:16–19 Habakkuk ended the prophecy with renewed commitment and affirmation of faith, expressing unwavering confidence in God.

3:16 wait quietly. The Lord had answered his prayer (v. 1); the Lord would vindicate His righteousness and ultimately restore a truly repentant people (cf. 2:4). While the answer satisfied Habakkuk, the thought of a Chaldean invasion of his people has also left him physically exhausted and overwhelmed (cf. Jer 4:19). Nevertheless, the prophet could "wait quietly for the day of distress" because he knew the Lord would judge righteously.

3:17, 18 I will exult in the LORD. If everything that was normal and predictable collapsed, the prophet would still rejoice. Obedience to the covenant was a requisite element to the enjoyment of agricultural and pastoral prosperity (Dt 28:1–14). Though disobedience would initiate the covenant curses (Dt 28:31–34, 49–51), the prophet affirmed his commitment to the Lord; his longing and joyful desire was for God Himself.

3:19 The Lord GOD is my strength. God's response to Habakkuk's perplexities not only promised divine wrath but also provided assurance of divine favor and hope. Security and hope were not based on temporal blessings but on the Lord Himself. This is the essence of 2:4: "the righteous will live by his faith." **like hinds' *feet*.** As the sure-footed hind, or deer, scaled the precipitous mountain heights without slipping, so Habakkuk's faith in the Lord enabled him to endure the hardships of the imminent invasion, and all of his perplexing questions. **For the choir director.** Habakkuk 3 possibly served as a psalm for temple worship (cf. 3:1).

THE BOOK OF ZEPHANIAH

TITLE

As with each of the 12 Minor Prophets, the prophecy bears the name of its author, which is generally thought to mean "the Lord hides" (cf. 2:3).

AUTHOR AND DATE

Little is known about the author, Zephaniah. Three other OT individuals share his name. He traces his genealogy back 4 generations to King Hezekiah (ca. 715–686 B.C.), standing alone among the prophets descended from royal blood (1:1). Royal genealogy would have given him the ear of Judah's king, Josiah, during whose reign he preached.

The prophet himself dates his message during the reign of Josiah (640–609 B.C.). The moral and spiritual conditions detailed in the book (cf. 1:4–6; 3:1–7) seem to place the prophecy prior to Josiah's reforms, when Judah was still languishing in idolatry and wickedness. It was in 628 B.C. that Josiah tore down all the altars to Baal, burned the bones of false prophets, and broke the carved idols (2Ch 34:3–7); and in 622 B.C. the Book of the Law was found (2Ch 34:8–35:19). Consequently, Zephaniah most likely prophesied from 635–625 B.C., and was a contemporary of Jeremiah.

BACKGROUND AND SETTING

Politically, the imminent transfer of Assyrian world power to the Babylonians weakened Nineveh's hold on Judah, bringing an element of independence to Judah for the first time in 50 years. King Josiah's desire to retain this newfound freedom from taxation and subservience undoubtedly led him to interfere later with Egypt's attempt to interdict the fleeing king of Nineveh in 609 B.C. (cf. 2Ch 35:20–27). Spiritually, the reigns of Hezekiah's son Manasseh (ca. 695–642 B.C.), extending over 4 decades, and his grandson Amon (ca. 642–640 B.C.), lasting only two years, were marked by wickedness and apostasy (2Ki 21; 2Ch 33). The early years of Josiah's reign were also characterized by the evil from his father (2Ki 23:4). In 622 B.C., however, while repairing the house of the Lord, Hilkiah the High Priest found the Book of the Law (2Ki 22:8). Upon reading it, Josiah initiated extensive reforms (2Ki 23). It was during the early years of Josiah's reign, prior to the great revival, that this 11th hour prophet, Zephaniah, prophesied and no doubt had an influence on the sweeping reforms Josiah brought to the nation. But the evil kings before Josiah (55 years) had had such an effect on Judah that it never recovered. Josiah's reforms were too late and didn't outlast his life.

HISTORICAL AND THEOLOGICAL THEMES

Zephaniah's message on the Day of the Lord warned Judah that the final days were near, through divine judgment at the hands of Nebuchadnezzar, ca. 605–586 B.C. (1:4–13). Yet, it also looks beyond to the far fulfillment in the judgments of Daniel's 70th week (1:18; 3:8). The expression "Day of the Lord" is described as a day that is near (1:7), and as a day of wrath, trouble, distress, devastation, desolation, darkness, gloominess, clouds, thick darkness, trumpet, and alarm (1:15, 16, 18). Yet even within these oracles of divine wrath, the prophet exhorted the people to seek the Lord, offering a shelter in the midst of judgment (2:3), and proclaiming the promise of eventual salvation for His believing remnant (2:7; 3:9–20).

INTERPRETIVE CHALLENGES

The book presents an unambiguous denunciation of sin and warning of imminent judgment on Judah. Some have referred the phrase "I will give to the peoples purified lips" (3:9) to the restoration of a universal language, similar to the days prior to confusion of languages at the Tower of Babel (Ge 11:1–9). They point out that the same Hebrew word translated "lips" is also used in Ge 11:7. It is better, however, to understand the passage as pointing to a purification of heart and life. This is confirmed by the context (cf. 3:13) and corroborated by the fact that the word "language" is most commonly translated "lip," as here. When combined with "pure," the reference to speech speaks of inward cleansing from sin (Is 6:5) manifested in speech (cf. Mt 12:34), including the removal of the names of false gods from their lips (Hos 2:17). It does not imply a one world language.

OUTLINE

I. Superscription (1:1)

II. The Lord's Judgment (1:2–3:8)
- A. On the Whole Earth (1:2, 3)
- B. On Judah (1:4–2:3)
- C. On the Surrounding Nations (2:4–15)
  1. Philistia (2:4–7)
  2. Moab/Ammon (2:8–11)
  3. Ethiopia (2:12)
  4. Assyria (2:13–15)
- D. On Jerusalem (3:1–7)
- E. On All Nations (3:8)

III. The Lord's Blessing (3:9–20)
- A. For the Nations (3:9, 10)
- B. For Judah (3:11–20)

DAY OF JUDGMENT ON JUDAH

1 The word of the LORD which came to Zephaniah son of Cushi, son of Gedaliah, son of Amariah, son of Hezekiah, in the days of [A]Josiah son of [B]Amon, king of Judah:

2 "I will completely [A]remove all *things*
From the face of the [a]earth,"
declares the LORD.
3 "I will remove [A]man and beast;
I will remove the [B]birds of the sky
And the fish of the sea,
And the [a,C]ruins along with the wicked;
And I will cut off man from the face
of the [b]earth," declares the LORD.
4 "So I will [A]stretch out My
hand against Judah
And against all the inhabitants
of Jerusalem.
And I will [B]cut off the remnant
of Baal from this place,
And the names of the [C]idolatrous
priests along with the priests.
5 "And those who bow down on the
[A]housetops to the host of heaven,
And those who bow down *and* [B]swear to
the LORD and *yet* swear by [a,C]Milcom,
6 And those who have [A]turned back
from following the LORD,
And those who have [B]not sought
the LORD or inquired of Him."
7 [a,A]Be silent before the Lord [b]GOD!
For the [B]day of the LORD is near,
For the LORD has prepared a [C]sacrifice,
He has [D]consecrated His guests.
8 "Then it will come about on the
day of the LORD'S sacrifice
That I will [A]punish the princes,
the king's sons
And all who clothe themselves
with [B]foreign garments.
9 "And I will punish on that day all who
leap on the *temple* threshold,
Who fill the house of their [a]lord
with [A]violence and deceit.
10 "On that day," declares the LORD,
"There will be the sound of a
cry from the [A]Fish Gate,
A wail from the [a,B]Second Quarter,
And a loud crash from the [C]hills.
11 "Wail, O inhabitants of the [a]Mortar,
For all the [b]people of [A]Canaan
will be silenced;
All who weigh out [B]silver
will be cut off.
12 "It will come about at that time
That I will [A]search Jerusalem
with lamps,
And I will punish the men
Who are [a,B]stagnant in spirit,
Who say in their hearts,
'The LORD will [C]not do good or evil!'

1:1 [A]2 Kin 22:1, 2; 2 Chr 34:1-33; Jer 1:2; 22:11 [B]2 Kin 21:18-26; 2 Chr 33:20-25 1:2 [a]Lit *ground* [A]Gen 6:7; Jer 7:20; Ezek 33:27, 28 1:3 [a]Or *stumbling blocks* [b]Lit *ground* [A]Is 6:11, 12 [B]Jer 4:25; 9:10 [C]Ezek 7:19; 14:3, 4, 8 1:4 [A]Jer 6:12; Ezek 6:14 [B]Mic 5:13 [C]2 Kin 23:5; Hos 10:5 1:5 [a]Or *their king;* M.T. *Malcam,* probably a variant spelling of Milcom [A]2 Kin 23:12; Jer 19:13 [B]Jer 5:2, 7; 7:9, 10 [C]1 Kin 11:5, 33; Jer 49:1 1:6 [A]Is 1:4; Hos 7:10 [B]Is 9:13 1:7 [a]Lit *Hush* [b]Heb *YHWH,* usually rendered *LORD* [A]Hab 2:20; Zech 2:13 [B]Zeph 1:14 [C]Is 34:6; Jer 46:10 [D]1 Sam 16:5; Is 13:3 1:8 [A]Is 24:21; Hab 1:10 [B]Is 2:6 1:9 [a]Or *Lord* [A]Jer 5:27; Amos 3:10 1:10 [a]I.e. a district of Jerusalem [A]2 Chr 33:14; Neh 3:3; 12:39 [B]2 Chr 34:22 [C]Ezek 6:13 1:11 [a]I.e. a district of Jerusalem [b]Or *merchant people will* [A]Zeph 2:5; Zech 14:21 [B]Job 27:16, 17; Hos 9:6 1:12 [a]Lit *thickening on their lees* [A]Jer 16:16, 17; Ezek 9:4-11; Amos 9:1-3 [B]Jer 48:11; Amos 6:1 [C]Ezek 8:12; 9:9

1:1 Hezekiah … Josiah. Zephaniah traced his royal lineage back to his great-great-grandfather Hezekiah (ca. 715–686 B.C.) and placed his ministry contemporaneous with Josiah (ca. 640–609 B.C.).

1:2, 3 The prophet began by noting the far fulfillment of the day of the Lord, when even animal and physical creation will be affected by His judgment of the earth (cf. Ge 3:17–19; Ex 12:29; Jos 7:24, 25; Ro 8:22).

1:2 face of the earth. Generally translated "ground," the term is used in reference to the whole earth (1:18). The phraseology is reminiscent of the Noahic Flood (Ge 6:7, 17; 7:21–23).

1:3 Comparisons with the Genesis Flood continue with "man and beast" and "birds of the sky" (Ge 6:7; 7:23). The prophet also alluded to the creation, pairing man and beast (sixth day of creation) and birds with fish (fifth day of creation). **ruins.** An alternate translation is "stumbling blocks." Whatever alienates man from God will be removed.

1:4–9 The Lord narrowed His words of judgment to specifically focus on Judah, specifying the causes of judgment as apostasy and idolatry (vv. 4–6), as always coupled with moral and ethical corruption (vv. 7–9).

1:4 cut off the remnant of Baal. The worship of Baal, the Canaanite god of fertility, was a constant source of temptation to Israel (cf. Nu 25:1–5; Jdg 2:13), as people tried worshiping him alongside the worship of the Lord (Jer 7:9; 23:25–29). This mix became a primary cause for judgment (2Ki 17:16–20; Jer 11:13–17; Hos 2:8) which would forever excise the worship of Baal from Israel.

1:5 bow down … to the host of heaven. Astrology was also a prominent part of Israel's idolatrous practices; they worshiped the host of heaven from as early as the Exodus (cf. Dt 4:19; Am 5:25, 26; Ac 7:40–43). God warned them repeatedly, but they rebelled (2Ki 23:5, 6; Jer 7:17, 18; 8:2; 44:17–25). Altars were often erected on housetop roofs to provide a clear view of the sky (Jer 8:2; 19:13; 32:29). **swear by Milcom.** Judah's syncretistic worship was reflected in swearing by the Lord and, at the same time, by Milcom, who may be either the Ammonite deity of 1Ki 11:5, 33, or Molech, the worship of whom included child sacrifice, astrology, and temple prostitution (cf. Lv 18:21; Am 5:25, 26; Ac 7:40–43).

1:6 Zephaniah lastly mentioned those who had at first heeded calls to repentance but later had willfully turned away.

1:7 Be silent. In view of the just judgment, there was no defense to be spoken, and in view of the devastation, only shocked and mute wonder (cf. Hab 2:20; Zec 2:13). **day of the LORD.** *See notes on Joel 1:15.* **prepared a sacrifice … consecrated His guests.** God's judgment on Israel was viewed as His sacrifice. The guests were the dreaded Babylonians, who as "priests" were invited to slay the sacrifice, i.e., Judah (cf. Is 13:3; 34:6; Jer 46:10; Eze 39:17; Hab 1:6; Rev 19:17, 18).

1:8 the princes … king's sons. Judgment began with the royal house. Lacking commitment to God's covenant, they had adopted the customs and idolatrous practices of the heathen. Since Josiah was only 8 years old when he assumed rulership (ca. 640 B.C.), the reference would not be to his sons, but to the princes of the royal house or to the children of the king who would be ruling when the prophecy was fulfilled (cf. 2Ki 25:7; Jer 39:6).

1:9 leap on the *temple* threshold. Lit. "leap." Perhaps this describes a pagan practice (cf. 1Sa 5:5) now adapted by the Israelites.

1:10, 11 The merchants, made wealthy from dishonest gain (cf. v. 9), were singled out to depict the anguish of the coming judgment. The Fish Gate, known today as the Damascus Gate, is located on the N side. The Second Quarter was a district within the city walls. "Mortar" was a name applied to the Valley of Siloam from its shape; it was a district where merchants carried on business.

1:12 I will search. None would escape the punishment of the Lord (Am 9:1–4). **stagnant in spirit.** See marginal note. With this term referring to a thickened crust which forms on wine when left undisturbed for a long period of time, the prophet described the people's indifference and slothfulness toward God. Their indifference led them to regard God as morally indifferent.

13 "Moreover, their wealth will
become [A]plunder
And their houses desolate;
Yes, [B]they will build houses
but not inhabit *them,*
And plant vineyards but not
drink their wine."

14 Near is the [A]great [B]day of the LORD,
Near and coming very quickly;
Listen, the day of the LORD!
[a]In it the warrior [C]cries out bitterly.
15 A day of wrath is that day,
A day of [A]trouble and distress,
A day of destruction and desolation,
A day of [B]darkness and gloom,
A day of clouds and thick darkness,
16 A day of [A]trumpet and battle cry
Against the [B]fortified cities
And the high corner towers.
17 I will bring [A]distress on men
So that they will walk [B]like the blind,
Because they have sinned
against the LORD;
And their [C]blood will be
poured out like dust
And their [D]flesh like dung.
18 Neither their [A]silver nor their gold
Will be able to deliver them
On the day of the LORD'S wrath;
And [B]all the earth will be devoured
In the fire of His jealousy,
For He will [C]make a complete end,
Indeed a terrifying one,
Of all the inhabitants of the earth.

JUDGMENTS ON JUDAH'S ENEMIES

2 Gather yourselves together, yes, [A]gather,
O nation [B]without [a]shame,
2 Before the decree [a]takes effect—
The day passes [A]like the chaff—
Before the [B]burning anger of the
LORD comes upon you,
Before the [C]day of the LORD'S
anger comes upon you.
3 [A]Seek the LORD,
All you [B]humble of the [a]earth
Who have carried out His [b]ordinances;
[C]Seek righteousness, seek humility.
Perhaps you will be [D]hidden
In the day of the LORD'S anger.

4 For [A]Gaza will be abandoned
And Ashkelon a desolation;
[A]Ashdod will be driven out at noon
And [A]Ekron will be uprooted.
5 Woe to the inhabitants of the seacoast,
The nation of the [a,A]Cherethites!
The word of the LORD is [B]against you,
O [C]Canaan, land of the Philistines;
And I will [D]destroy you
So that there will be [E]no inhabitant.

1:13 [A]Jer 15:13; 17:3 [B]Amos 5:11; Mic 6:15 1:14 [a]Lit *There* [A]Jer 30:7; Joel 2:11; Mal 4:5 [B]Ezek 7:7, 12; 30:3; Joel 1:15; 3:14; Zeph 1:7 [C]Ezek 7:16-18 1:15 [A]Is 22:5 [B]Joel 2:2, 31; Amos 5:18-20 1:16 [A]Is 27:13; Jer 4:19 [B]Is 2:12-15 1:17 [A]Jer 10:18 [B]Deut 28:29 [C]Ezek 24:7, 8 [D]Jer 8:2; 9:22 1:18 [A]Ezek 7:19 [B]Zeph 3:8 [C]Gen 6:7; Ezek 7:5-7 2:1 [a]Or *longing* [A]2 Chr 20:4; Joel 1:14 [B]Jer 3:3; 6:15 2:2 [a]Lit *is born* [A]Is 17:13; Hos 13:3 [B]Lam 4:11; Nah 1:6 [C]Zeph 1:18 2:3 [a]Or *land* [b]Or *justice* [A]Ps 105:4; Amos 5:6 [B]Ps 22:26; Is 11:4 [C]Amos 5:14, 15 [D]Ps 57:1; Is 26:20 2:4 [A]Amos 1:7, 8; Zech 9:5-7 2:5 [a]I.e. a segment of the Philistines with roots in Crete [A]Ezek 25:16 [B]Amos 3:1 [C]Zeph 1:11 [D]Is 14:29, 30 [E]Zeph 3:6

1:14–18 Zephaniah vividly described the day of the Lord in staccato fashion, rehearsing the ominous conditions characterizing that day. This section seems to point to the near fulfillment when Babylon subdued Judah (vv. 4–13), as well as a far fulfillment which will involve the whole earth (v. 18).

1:16 **day of trumpet and battle cry.** In accordance with God's instructions, a trumpet was fashioned for the purpose of sounding an alarm (Nu 10:1–10).

1:17, 18 As though worthless, their blood and flesh were discarded as dust. Their silver and gold, corruptly gained (cf. vv. 9–13), would be of no avail to protect them from the wrath of holy God (cf. Jer 46:28).

1:17 **walk like the blind.** As blind men, they would grope unsuccessfully for escape routes (Dt 28:29).

1:18 **all the earth.** The discussion expands to include the whole earth as in vv. 2, 3.

2:1–3 With the announcement of coming judgment, God mercifully invited His people to repent. They were to assemble to entreat the favor of the Lord and avert His wrath (cf. Joel 2:16).

2:1 **nation without shame.** No longer sensitive to God's call to repentance through His many prophets, Judah had sunk to shamelessness.

2:3 **Perhaps you will be hidden.** Even the humble, those who had followed the law of the Lord, were encouraged to continue to manifest fruits of repentance, so they would be sheltered in the day of His judgment (Is 26:20).

2:4–15 God used the heathen nations to punish His people, but He would not permit those nations to go unpunished. To illustrate this, 4 representative nations were chosen from the 4 points of the compass.

2:4–7 The first nation to be judged was Philistia, to the W of Israel. Judgment was to come swiftly and unexpectedly, even at noonday when it was least expected. Of the 5 Philistine cities, only Gath was omitted (cf. Am 1:6–8).

2:5 **Cherethites.** Occasionally a synonym for Philistia, this term represented a branch from Crete *(see note on Eze 25:16)*. David's bodyguard was comprised of both Cherethites and Pelethites (2Sa 8:18; 1Ki 1:38, 44). *See note on 1Sa 30:14.*

"DAY OF THE LORD" FULFILLMENTS

Near	Far
Obadiah 1–14	Obadiah 15–21
Joel 1:15; 2:1, 11	Joel 2:31 (3:1); 3:14
Amos 5:18–20	———
———	Isaiah 2:12
Isaiah 13:6	Isaiah 13:9
Zephaniah 1:7	Zephaniah 1:18
Ezekiel 13:5; 20:3	———
———	Zechariah 14:1
———	Malachi 4:5

6 So the seacoast will be [A]pastures,
With [a]caves for shepherds
and folds for flocks.
7 And the coast will be
For the [A]remnant of the house of Judah,
They will [B]pasture on it.
In the houses of Ashkelon they
will lie down at evening;
For the LORD their God will [C]care for them
And [D]restore their fortune.

8 "I have heard the [a,A]taunting of Moab
And the [B]revilings of the sons of Ammon,
With which they have [b]taunted My people
And [c,C]become arrogant
against their territory.
9 "Therefore, as I live," declares
the LORD of hosts,
The God of Israel,
"Surely [A]Moab will be like [B]Sodom
And the sons of [C]Ammon like [D]Gomorrah—
A place possessed by nettles and salt pits,
And a perpetual desolation.
The remnant of My people
will [E]plunder them
And the remainder of My nation
will inherit them."

10 This they will have in return for their [A]pride, because
they have [a,B]taunted and [b]become arrogant against
the people of the LORD of hosts. 11 The LORD will be
[A]terrifying to them, for He will [a]starve [B]all the gods of
the earth; and all the [C]coastlands of the nations will
[D]bow down to Him, everyone from his *own* place.

12 "You also, O [A]Ethiopians, will
be slain by My sword."
13 And He will [A]stretch out His
hand against the north
And destroy [B]Assyria,
And He will make [C]Nineveh a desolation,
Parched like the wilderness.
14 Flocks will lie down in her midst,
[a]All beasts which range in herds;
Both the [b,A]pelican and the hedgehog
Will lodge in [c]the tops of her pillars;
[d]Birds will sing in the window,
Desolation *will be* on the threshold;
For He has laid bare the cedar work.
15 This is the [A]exultant city
Which [B]dwells securely,
Who says in her heart,
"[C]I am, and there is no one besides me."
How she has become a [D]desolation,
A resting place for beasts!
[E]Everyone who passes by her will hiss
And wave his hand *in contempt*.

WOE TO JERUSALEM AND THE NATIONS

3 Woe to her who is [A]rebellious and [B]defiled,
The [C]tyrannical city!
2 She [A]heeded no voice,
She [B]accepted no instruction.
She did not [C]trust in the LORD,
She did not [D]draw near to her God.
3 Her [A]princes within her are roaring lions,
Her judges are [B]wolves at evening;
They leave nothing for the morning.
4 Her prophets are [A]reckless,
treacherous men;
Her [B]priests have profaned the sanctuary.
They have done violence to the law.
5 The LORD is [A]righteous [B]within her;
He will [C]do no injustice.
[D]Every morning He brings
His justice to light;
He does not fail.
But the unjust [E]knows no shame.
6 "I have cut off nations;
Their corner towers are in ruins.
I have made their streets [A]desolate,

2:6 [a]Or *meadows* or *wells* [A]Is 5:17; 7:25 2:7 [A]Is 11:16 [B]Is 32:14 [C]Ex 4:31; Ps 80:14 [D]Jer 32:44; Zeph 3:20 2:8 [a]Lit *reproach* [b]Lit *reproached* [c]Lit *made* themselves *great* [A]Ezek 25:8 [B]Ezek 25:3 [C]Amos 1:13 2:9 [A]Is 15:1-9; Jer 48:1-47; Amos 2:1-3 [B]Gen 19:24 [C]Jer 49:1-6; Ezek 25:1-10 [D]Deut 29:23 [E]Is 11:14 2:10 [a]Lit *reproached* [b]Lit *made* themselves *great* [A]Is 16:6 [B]Zeph 2:8 2:11 [a]Lit *make lean* [A]Joel 2:11 [B]Zeph 1:4 [C]Is 24:15 [D]Ps 72:8-11; Zeph 3:9 2:12 [A]Is 18:1-7; 20:4, 5; Ezek 30:4-9 2:13 [A]Is 14:26; Zeph 1:4 [B]Is 10:16; Mic 5:6 [C]Nah 3:7 2:14 [a]Or *All* kinds of *beasts in crowds;* lit *Every* kind of *beast of a nation* [b]Or *owl* or *jackdaw* [c]Lit *her capitals* [d]Lit *A voice* [A]Is 14:23; 34:11 2:15 [A]Is 22:2 [B]Is 32:9, 11; 47:8 [C]Is 47:8; Ezek 28:2, 9 [D]Is 32:14 [E]Jer 18:16; 19:8 3:1 [A]Jer 5:23 [B]Ezek 23:30 [C]Jer 6:6 3:2 [A]Jer 7:23-28 [B]Jer 2:30; 5:3; 2 Tim 3:16 [C]Ps 78:22; Jer 13:25 [D]Ps 73:28 3:3 [A]Ezek 22:27 [B]Jer 5:6; Hab 1:8 3:4 [A]Judg 9:4 [B]Ezek 22:26; Mal 2:7, 8 3:5 [A]Deut 32:4 [B]Zeph 3:15, 17 [C]Ps 92:15 [D]Job 7:18 [E]Zeph 2:1 3:6 [A]Jer 9:12; Zech 7:14; Matt 23:38

2:7 restore their fortune. The Lord would initiate the physical return of Israel's exiles to occupy the land vacated by judgment on Philistia.

2:8–11 To the E, the descendants of Lot by his daughters through incest, Moab and Ammon (Ge 19:30–38), are mentioned. They had reproached and reviled God's people, incurring divine wrath (cf. Ge 12:3). Like Sodom and Gomorrah in the days of their ancestor Lot, they too would come to ruin and desolation.

2:11 all the coastlands of the nations will bow down to Him. The final fulfillment of these predictions is yet future, depicting the Millennium when all the gods of the nations will be reduced to nothing and the Lord Himself will be worshiped universally (Is 66:18–21; Zec 14:16; Mal 1:11).

2:12 Ethiopia lay to the S of Israel. She would be judged by His sword, fulfilled in Nebuchadnezzar's invasion and conquest of Egypt (Eze 30:24, 25).

2:13–15 Assyria, located NE of Israel, would be desolated as well. Nineveh fell, shortly after this prophecy, to the Babylonians in 612 B.C. Famed for her irrigation system, she would be left dry.

2:15 In language similar to that of the king of Babylon (Is 14:13, 14; 47:8) and the prince of Tyre (Eze 28:2), Assyria had claimed for herself divine attributes. For this she would be brought to ruin.

3:1–7 After pronouncing judgment on the nations, the prophet returned to again pronounce woe upon Jerusalem. Because of that city's favored position among the nations (cf. Ex 19:5), more was expected.

3:2 She accepted no instruction. Jerusalem was soon to learn that to reject God's correction leads to destruction (Pr 5:23). **She did not draw near to her God.** The Lord had taken up residence in that city, making Him easily accessible (Dt 4:7), yet they had refused to draw near to Him in proper worship.

3:3–5 Four classes of leadership were singled out for condemnation: The political leaders, i.e., the 1) princes and 2) judges; who are both likened to ravenous wolves, endlessly searching for more prey (cf. 1:8, 9). The spiritual leaders, i.e., the 3) prophets and 4) priests, were unfaithful to the Lord whom they claimed to represent. By contrast, the Lord never failed to manifest a faithful standard of justice and righteousness.

3:6, 7 The desolations brought by the Lord on surrounding nations were to serve as warnings to Judah, meant to turn His people

With no one passing by;
Their [B]cities are laid waste,
Without a man, [C]without an inhabitant.
7 "I said, 'Surely you will revere Me,
[A]Accept instruction.'
So her dwelling will [B]not be cut off
According to all that I have
appointed concerning her.
But they were eager to [C]corrupt
all their deeds.

8 "Therefore [A]wait for Me," declares the LORD,
"For the day when I rise up as a witness.
Indeed, My decision is to [B]gather nations,
To assemble kingdoms,
To pour out on them My indignation,
All My burning anger;
For [C]all the earth will be devoured
By the fire of My zeal.
9 "For then I will [a]give to the
peoples [A]purified lips,
That all of them may [B]call on
the name of the LORD,
To serve Him [b]shoulder to shoulder.
10 "From beyond the rivers of [A]Ethiopia
My [a]worshipers, [b]My dispersed ones,
Will [B]bring My offerings.
11 "In that day you will [A]feel no shame
Because of all your deeds
By which you have rebelled against Me;
For then I will remove from your midst
Your [B]proud, exulting ones,
And you will never again be haughty
On My [C]holy mountain.

A REMNANT OF ISRAEL

12 "But I will leave among you
A [A]humble and lowly people,
And they will [B]take refuge in
the name of the LORD.
13 "The [A]remnant of Israel will [B]do no wrong
And [C]tell no lies,
Nor will a deceitful tongue
Be found in their mouths;
For they will [D]feed and lie down
With no one to make them tremble."

14 Shout for joy, O daughter of Zion!
[A]Shout *in triumph,* O Israel!
Rejoice and exult with all *your* heart,
O daughter of Jerusalem!
15 The LORD has taken away [A]*His*
judgments against you,
He has cleared away your enemies.
The King of Israel, the LORD,
is [B]in your midst;
You will [C]fear disaster no more.
16 [A]In that day it will be said to Jerusalem:
"[B]Do not be afraid, O Zion;
[C]Do not let your hands fall limp.
17 "The LORD your God is [A]in your midst,
A [a,B]victorious warrior.
He will [C]exult over you with joy,
He will [b]be quiet in His love,
He will rejoice over you with shouts of joy.
18 "I will gather those who [A]grieve
about the appointed feasts—
They [a]came from you, *O Zion;*
The reproach *of exile* is a burden on [b]them.

3:6 [B]Lev 26:31; Is 6:11 [C]Zeph 2:5 3:7 [A]Job 36:10; Ps 32:8; 1 Tim 1:5 [B]Jer 7:7 [C]Hos 9:9 3:8 [A]Ps 27:14; Is 30:18; Hab 2:3 [B]Ezek 38:14-23; Joel 3:2 [C]Zeph 1:18 3:9 [a]Lit *change* [b]Lit *with one shoulder* [A]Is 19:18; 57:19 [B]Ps 22:27; 86:9; Hab 2:14; Zeph 2:11 3:10 [a]Or *suppliants* [b]Lit *the daughter of My dispersed ones* [A]Ps 68:31; Is 18:1 [B]Is 60:6, 7 3:11 [A]Is 45:17; 54:4; Joel 2:26, 27 [B]Is 2:12; 5:15 [C]Is 11:9; 56:7; Ezek 20:40 3:12 [A]Is 14:30 [B]Is 14:32; 50:10; Nah 1:7; Zech 13:8, 9 3:13 [A]Is 10:20-22; Mic 4:7; Zeph 2:7 [B]Ps 119:3; Jer 31:33; Zeph 3:5 [C]Zech 8:3, 16; Rev 14:5 [D]Ezek 34:13-15 3:14 [A]Zech 9:9 3:15 [A]Ps 19:9; John 5:30; Rev 18:20 [B]Ezek 37:26-28; Zeph 3:5 [C]Is 54:14 3:16 [A]Is 25:9 [B]Is 35:3, 4 [C]Job 4:3; Heb 12:12 3:17 [a]Lit *A warrior who saves* [b]Or with some ancient versions, *renew* you *in* [A]Zeph 3:5, 15 [B]Is 63:1 [C]Is 62:5 3:18 [a]Lit *were* [b]Lit *her* [A]Ps 42:2-4; Ezek 9:4

back to Him. But instead, enticed by the fruits of corruption, the people rose early to zealously and deliberately pursue the way of sin.

3:8 The prophet transitions from the historical invasion of Judah by Babylon to the future day of the Lord. He speaks of the Great Tribulation, when the Lord will gather all the nations for judgment (cf. Joel 3:1, 2, 12–17; Zec 12:2, 3; 14:2; Mt 24:21). The faithful remnant, presumably the meek of 2:1–3, are exhorted to wait in trust for Him to carry out His judgment.

3:9–20 The final section unveils the blessings of restoration for God's people and the nations.

3:9 purified lips. See Introduction: Interpretive Challenges. A remnant of the nations, converted to the Lord, will worship Him in righteousness and truth (Zec 8:20–23; 14:16). Pure speech will come from purified hearts (cf. Lk 6:45).

3:10 They will return from distant places (cf. Is 11:11, 15, 16; 27:13).

3:11–13 The Lord will purge the proud and ungodly from among them (Zec 13:1–6), leaving a meek and humble people. Material prosperity and peace will accompany them as well, allowing them to enjoy the rich blessings of God undisturbed (Joel 3:18–20; Mic 4:4).

3:14–20 The messianic era of millennial blessing and restoration is described.

3:15–17 The basis for rejoicing in v. 14 is that Israel's day of judgment is past, and her King is residing in her midst. His departure just prior to Nebuchadnezzar's destruction of the temple is graphically depicted in Eze 8–11; but He will return as Lord and Messiah, a fact so glorious that it is repeated in v. 17.

3:17 As a bridegroom rejoices over his bride (cf. Is 62:4), the Lord will exult over His people with gladness and song, resting in quiet ecstasy over His people in whom is all His delight (cf. Dt 30:9; Is 54).

3:18 those who grieve about the appointed feasts. Unable to celebrate the appointed feasts (cf. Ex 23:14–17) while in exile,

GOD'S "I WILLS" OF RESTORATION

Zephaniah 3:18–20	
1. I will gather	3:18
2. I will deal	3:19
3. I will save	3:19
4. I will turn	3:19
5. I will bring you in	3:20
6. I will give you	3:20

19 "Behold, I am going to deal
at that time
With all your [A]oppressors,
I will save the [B]lame
And gather the outcast,
And I will turn their [C]shame
into [D]praise and renown
In all the earth.

20 "At that time I will [A]bring you in,
Even at the time when I
gather you together;
Indeed, I will give you [B]renown and praise
Among all the peoples of the earth,
When I [C]restore your fortunes
before your eyes,"
Says the LORD.

3:19 [A]Is 60:14 [B]Ezek 34:16; Mic 4:6 [C]Ezek 16:27, 57 [D]Is 60:18; 62:7; Zech 8:23 3:20 [A]Ezek 37:12, 21 [B]Deut 26:18, 19; Is 56:5; 66:22 [C]Jer 29:14; Joel 3:1; Zeph 2:7

the godly remnant sorrowed. But the Lord will remove their sorrow, giving them praise and fame (v. 19).

3:19, 20 at that time. The time of the return of the King, Messiah, when the Jews will be regathered and become a source of blessing to the world, fulfilling Israel's original destiny (Dt 26:18, 19; Is 62:7).

THE BOOK OF HAGGAI

TITLE

The prophecy bears the name of its author. Because his name means "festal one," it is suggested that Haggai was born on a feast day. Haggai is the second shortest book in the OT (Obadiah is shorter) and is quoted by the NT once (cf. Heb 12:26).

AUTHOR AND DATE

Little is known about Haggai apart from this short prophecy. He is mentioned briefly in Ezr 5:1 and 6:14, on both occasions in conjunction with the prophet Zechariah. The lists of refugees in Ezra mention nothing of Haggai; there are no indications of his parentage or tribal ancestry. Nor does history provide any record of his occupation. He is the only person in the OT with the name, although similar names occur (cf. Ge 46:16; Nu 26:15; 2Sa 3:4; 1Ch 6:30). Furthermore, Hag 2:3 may suggest that he too had seen the glory of Solomon's temple before it was destroyed, making him at least 70 years of age when writing his prophecy.

There is no ambiguity or controversy about the date of the prophecy. The occasion of each of his 4 prophecies is clearly specified (1:1; 2:1; 2:10; 2:20), occurring within a 4-month span of time in the second year (ca. 520 B.C.) of Persian king Darius Hystaspes (ca. 521–486 B.C.). Haggai most likely had returned to Jerusalem from Babylon with Zerubbabel 18 years earlier in 538 B.C.

BACKGROUND AND SETTING

In 538 B.C., as a result of the proclamation of Cyrus the Persian (cf. Ezr 1:1–4), Israel was allowed to return from Babylon to her homeland under the civil leadership of Zerubbabel and the spiritual guidance of Joshua the High Priest (cf. Ezr 3:2). About 50,000 Jews returned. In 536 B.C., they began to rebuild the temple (cf. Ezr 3:1–4:5) but opposition from neighbors and indifference by the Jews caused the work to be abandoned (cf. Ezr 4:1–24). Sixteen years later Haggai and Zechariah were commissioned by the Lord to stir up the people to 1) not only rebuild the temple, but also to 2) reorder their spiritual priorities (cf. Ezr 5:1–6:22). As a result, the temple was completed 4 years later (ca. 516 B.C.; cf. Ezr 6:15).

HISTORICAL AND THEOLOGICAL THEMES

The primary theme is the rebuilding of God's temple, which had been lying in ruins since its destruction by Nebuchadnezzar in 586 B.C. By means of 5 messages from the Lord, Haggai exhorted the people to renew their efforts to build the house of the Lord. He motivated them by noting that the drought and crop failures were caused by misplaced spiritual priorities (1:9–11).

But to Haggai, the rebuilding of the temple was not an end in itself. The temple represented God's dwelling place, His manifest presence with His chosen people. The destruction of the temple by Nebuchadnezzar followed the departure of God's dwelling glory (cf. Eze 8–11); to the prophet, the rebuilding of the temple invited the return of God's presence to their midst. Using the historical situation as a springboard, Haggai reveled in the supreme glory of the ultimate messianic temple yet to come (2:7), encouraging them with the promise of even greater peace (2:9), prosperity (2:19), divine rulership (2:21, 22), and national blessing (2:23) during the Millennium.

INTERPRETIVE CHALLENGES

The most prominent interpretive ambiguity within the prophecy is the phrase "the wealth of all nations" (2:7). Although many translations exist, there are essentially only two interpretations. Pointing to "The silver is Mine and the gold is Mine" (2:8), as well as to Is 60:5 and Zec 14:14, some contend that it refers to Jerusalem, to which the wealth of other nations will be brought during the Millennium (cf. Is 60:11; 61:6). It seems preferable, however, to see a reference here to the Messiah, a Deliverer for whom all the nations ultimately long. Not only is this interpretation supported by the ancient rabbis and the early church, the mention of "glory" in the latter part of the verse suggests a personal reference to the Messiah (cf. Is 40:5; 60:1; Lk 2:32).

OUTLINE

		Year	Month	Day
I. Rebuke for Disobedience	1:1–11	2	6	1
II. Remnant Responds and Rebuilds	1:12–15	2	6	24
III. Return of God's Glory	2:1–9	2	7	21
IV. Religious Questions	2:10–19	2	9	24
V. Reign of the Lord	2:20–23	2	9	24

HAGGAI BEGINS TEMPLE BUILDING

1 In the [A]second year of Darius the king, on the
first day of the sixth month, the word of the
LORD came by the prophet [B]Haggai to [C]Zerubba-
bel the son of Shealtiel, [D]governor of Judah, and
to [E]Joshua the son of Jehozadak, the high priest,
saying, 2 "Thus says the LORD of [a]hosts, 'This people says, "The time has not come, *even* the time
for the house of the LORD to be rebuilt." ' " 3 Then
the word of the LORD came by Haggai the prophet,
saying, 4 "Is it time for you yourselves to dwell in
your paneled houses while this house [A]*lies* desolate?" 5 Now therefore, thus says the LORD of hosts,
"[a]Consider your ways! 6 You have [A]sown much, but
[a]harvest little; *you* eat, but *there is* not *enough* to
be satisfied; *you* drink, but *there is* [b]not *enough* to
become drunk; *you* put on clothing, but no one is
warm *enough;* and he who earns, earns wages *to*
put into a purse with holes."
7 Thus says the LORD of hosts, "[a]Consider your
ways! 8 Go up to the [a]mountains, bring wood and
[A]rebuild the [b]temple, that I may be [B]pleased with
it and be [C]glorified," says the LORD. 9 "[A]*You* look
for much, but behold, *it comes* to little; when you
bring *it* home, I [B]blow it *away.* Why?" declares the
LORD of hosts, "Because of My house which [C]*lies*
desolate, while each of you runs to his own house.
10 Therefore, because of you the [A]sky has withheld
[a]its dew and the earth has withheld its produce. 11 I
called for a [A]drought on the land, on the mountains,
on the grain, on the new wine, on the oil, on what
the ground produces, on [B]men, on cattle, and on
[C]all the labor of [a]your hands."
12 Then [A]Zerubbabel the son of Shealtiel, and
[B]Joshua the son of Jehozadak, the high priest, with
all the remnant of the people, [C]obeyed the voice
of the LORD their God and the words of Haggai
the prophet, as the LORD their God had sent him.
And the people [a,D]showed reverence for the LORD.
13 Then Haggai, the [A]messenger of the LORD, spoke
[a]by the commission of the LORD to the people
saying, " '[B]I am with you,' declares the LORD." 14 So
the LORD stirred up the spirit of [A]Zerubbabel the
son of Shealtiel, [A]governor of Judah, and the spirit
of Joshua the son of Jehozadak, the high priest,
and the spirit of all the [B]remnant of the people;
and they came and [C]worked on the house of the
LORD of hosts, their God, 15 on the twenty-fourth
day of the sixth month in the second year of Darius the king.

1:1 [A]Ezra 4:24 [B]Ezra 5:1; 6:14; Hag 1:3, 12, 13; 2:1, 10, 20 [C]Ezra 2:2; Neh 7:7; Hag 1:12, 14; Zech 4:6; Matt 1:12, 13 [D]1 Kin 10:15; Ezra 5:3 [E]Zech 6:11 1:2 [a]Lit *hosts, saying* 1:4 [A]Jer 33:10, 12; Hag 1:9 1:5 [a]Lit *Set your heart on* 1:6 [a]Lit *bring in* [b]Lit *not becoming drunk* [A]Deut 28:38-40; Hos 8:7; Hag 1:9, 10; 2:16, 17 1:7 [a]Lit *Set your heart on* 1:8 [a]Lit *mountain* [b]Lit *house* [A]1 Kin 6:1 [B]Ps 132:13, 14 [C]Hag 2:7, 9 1:9 [A]Prov 27:20; Eccl 1:8 [B]Is 40:7 [C]Hag 1:4 1:10 [a]Lit *from dew* [A]Deut 28:23, 24; 1 Kin 17:1; Joel 1:18-20 1:11 [a]Lit *the palms* [A]Jer 14:2-6; Mal 3:9, 11 [B]Deut 28:22 [C]Hag 2:17 1:12 [a]Lit *feared before* [A]Hag 1:1 [B]Hag 1:14; 2:2 [C]Is 1:19; 1 Thess 2:13 [D]Deut 31:12, 13; Ps 112:1; Is 50:10 1:13 [a]Or *the message* [A]Is 44:26; Ezek 3:17; Mal 2:7; 3:1 [B]Ps 46:11; Is 41:10; 43:2 1:14 [A]Hag 1:1; 2:2, 21 [B]Hag 1:12 [C]Ezra 5:2; Neh 4:6

1:1–11 Discouraged by the opposition of her neighbors (Ezr 4:1–5, 24), the people had wrongly concluded that it was not yet time for them to rebuild the temple (v. 2). With a biting query, the Lord reminded them that it was not right for them to live in paneled houses while the temple lay in ruins (v. 4) and urged them to consider carefully the consequences of their indifference (vv. 5–11).

1:1 second year of Darius the king. Not to be confused with Darius the Mede (cf. Da 5:31), Darius I (Hystaspes) became king of Persia in 521 B.C., having ascended to the throne after the death of Cambyses. As an officer of Cambyses and the great-grandson of Cyrus the Great's brother, Darius retained the loyalty of the Persian army and thereby defeated other contenders for the throne. He reigned until his death in 486 B.C. **first day ... sixth month.** The first day of the month of Elul corresponds to Aug. 29, 520 B.C. **Zerubbabel.** Zerubbabel was the grandson of Jehoiachin (Jeconiah in Mt 1:12; cf. 1Ch 3:17, 19) and thus he was in the Davidic line. Though it is highly questionable *if* he is to be identified with Sheshbazzar (Ezr 1:8, 11; 5:14, 16), his role as civil leader (Ezr 2:2) and overseer of the temple rebuilding project (Zec 4:6–10) is certain. He reestablished the Davidic throne, even though it will not again be occupied until the time of Messiah (cf. Pss 2; 110). **Joshua ... the high priest.** Spelled Jeshua in Ezr 3:2, Joshua was a descendant of Zadok (1Ch 6:15) and the religious leader of the exilic community that returned to Jerusalem. He reestablished the high-priestly line of Aaron through Eleazar. **Jehozadak.** One of Nebuchadnezzar's captives (cf. 1Ch 6:15).

1:2 This people says. Haggai begins his message by quoting a popular expression of the people, saying it was not time to build the temple. Though propelled by the hostile opposition of their neighbors (Ezr 4:1–5, 24) and the lack of economic prosperity (cf. vv. 9–11), the roots of their reluctance lay ultimately in their selfish indifference to the Lord. God's displeasure is noted in His reference to them as "This people" and not "My people." They wanted their wealth for themselves, not a temple.

1:4 this house *lies* desolate. Cf. Ezr 3:1–13 for the start of the second temple. Selfish indulgence, revealed by the prophet's rhetorical query, demonstrated their hypocrisy and misplaced priorities. Walls and ceilings overlaid with cedar were common in wealthy residences (cf. 1Ki 7:3, 7; Jer 22:14).

1:6 Using 5 pairs of poetic contrasts, each concluding essentially the same thing, Haggai painted a vivid picture of their economic and social distress. Their selfish lack of concern for God's house had only caused them more hardship (cf. Mt 6:33). This was Solomon's message in Ecclesiastes, restated, "All is vanity."

1:8 Go up ... bring wood ... rebuild. Three imperatives give the remedy for their trouble. The long captivity of 70 years had let the forests grow so there was ample wood. They were to use it to rebuild the house of the Lord, and therein He would be glorified. By putting God first, He would then be honored in their worship, and they would be blessed in the secondary matters of life. Compare this pitiful project (Ezr 3:12; Hag 2:3) to the opulence of Solomon's first temple (cf. 1Ch 28, 29; 2Ch 2–6).

1:9 runs to his own house. Because the Jews were zealous to pursue their own interests, the prophet drew a contrast between the one who eagerly ran to care for "his own house," while disregarding God's house ("My house").

1:10, 11 Economic catastrophe, resulting from God's withholding of the summer dew, was the price for their disobedience (cf. Dt 7:13). Grain, wine, and oil were the primary crops of the land. Cattle also languished because of the absence of spiritual health (cf. Joel 1:18–20).

1:12–15 Haggai's second message came 23 days after the first one (v. 15), around Sep. 21, 520 B.C. The Lord's call to "Consider your ways" (vv. 5, 7) caused the people to respond in repentance and obedience (v. 12). This new message "I am with you" further stirred the Jews to action (vv. 13, 14).

1:12, 14 the remnant of the people. The exiles who returned from Babylon took the message to heart. Realizing that the words of the prophet were from the Lord, they "obeyed" and "showed reverence," knowing that God was present.

1:13 I am with you. The people were oppressed by hostilities from without and famine from within. The Lord responded to their genuine repentance and obedience, assuring them of His presence with them. This should have evoked a memory of God's Word to Joshua and the returning people centuries before (cf. Jos 1:5).

1:14 stirred up the spirit. The Lord energized the leaders and the people through His Word to carry on the work of rebuilding the temple. God had sovereignly moved in the heart of Cyrus 16 years earlier (cf. 2Ch 36:22, 23; Ezr 1:1–3). The people's response of repentance and obedience allowed God's Spirit to energize them for the task.

THE BUILDERS ENCOURAGED

2 On the twenty-first of the seventh month, the
word of the LORD came by [A]Haggai the prophet
saying, 2 "Speak now to [A]Zerubbabel the son of Shealtiel, [A]governor of Judah, and to [A]Joshua the son of
Jehozadak, the high priest, and to the [B]remnant of
the people saying, 3 'Who is [A]left among you who saw
this [a]temple in its [B]former glory? And how do you
see it now? Does it not [b]seem to you like nothing [c]in
comparison? 4 But now [a,A]take courage, Zerubbabel,'
declares the LORD, 'take courage also, Joshua son
of Jehozadak, the high priest, and all you people
of the land take courage,' declares the LORD, 'and
work; for [B]I am with you,' declares the LORD of hosts.
5 'As for the [a,A]promise which I [b]made you when you
came out of Egypt, [c]My [B]Spirit is abiding in your
midst; [C]do not fear!' 6 For thus says the LORD of
hosts, '[A]Once more [a]in a [B]little while, I am going to
[C]shake the heavens and the earth, the sea also and
the dry land. 7 I will shake [A]all the nations; and [a]they
will come with the [B]wealth of all nations, and I will
[C]fill this house with glory,' says the LORD of hosts.

2:1 [A]Hag 1:1 2:2 [A]Hag 1:1 [B]Hag 1:12 2:3 [a]Lit *house* [b]Lit *in your eyes* [c]Lit *like it* [A]Ezra 3:12 [B]Hag 2:9 2:4 [a]Lit *be strong* [A]Deut 31:23; 1 Chr 22:13; 28:20; Zech 8:9; Eph 6:10 [B]2 Sam 5:10; Acts 7:9 2:5 [a]Lit *word* [b]Lit *cut with* [c]Or *while...was standing* [A]Ex 19:4-6; 29:45, 46; 33:12-14; 34:8-10 [B]Neh 9:20; Is 63:11, 14 [C]Is 41:10, 13; Zech 8:13 2:6 [a]Lit *it is a little* [A]Heb 12:26 [B]Is 10:25; 29:17 [C]Hag 2:21 2:7 [a]Or *the desire of all nations will come* [A]Dan 2:44; Joel 3:9, 16 [B]Is 60:4-9 [C]1 Kin 8:11; Is 60:7

2:1–9 With building operations in full swing, the Lord gave a strong message of encouragement, especially to the elderly among them who had seen Solomon's temple. Though the temple of Solomon was of greater magnificence, the Lord urged the people to be courageous, assuring them of His presence (v. 4), His faithfulness to His covenant promises (v. 5), and promises of a greater, more glorious temple in the future (vv. 6–9).

2:1 twenty-first ... seventh month. This day in the month of Tishri corresponds to Oct. 17, 520 B.C. Leviticus 23:39–44 indicates that this was the final day of the Feast of Booths, or Tabernacles, a feast to celebrate God's provision for Israel during her 40 years of wilderness wanderings and give thanks for a bountiful harvest. On this occasion the Lord gave Haggai the third message.

2:2 The first message was directed toward the leaders, Zerubbabel and Joshua (*see notes on 1:1*). Here the prophet includes the remainder of the exiles who returned from Babylon.

2:3 you who saw. Some remained, perhaps even Haggai, who had seen the temple of Solomon before its destruction (cf. Ezr 3:12, 13). With 3 rhetorical questions, the Lord through His prophet Haggai drew attention to the fact that this temple was inferior to Solomon's temple (cf. Ezr 3:8–13), which caused many to be discouraged by its lack of splendor.

2:4 take courage. To counteract the discouragement, the Lord repeated the command to "take courage" and to "work," assuring them of God's presence. This was the second reminder from the Lord, "I am with you" (cf. 1:13).

2:5 Spoken at the close of the feast commemorating God's provision during the wilderness wanderings, His covenant commitment and the promise that His Spirit would be with them as "when you came out of Egypt" would be most reassuring (ca. 1445 B.C.). He had not forgotten them over the last 9 centuries (Ex 33:14). **My Spirit.** The third Person of the Triune Godhead (cf. Nu 11:16, 17).

2:6, 7 I will shake. The shaking of the cosmic bodies and the nations goes beyond the historical removal of kingdoms and the establishment of others, such as the defeat of Persia by Greece (Da 7). Rather, the text looks to the cataclysm in the universe described in Rev 6–19, the subjugation of the nations by the Messiah, and the setting up of His kingdom which will never be destroyed (cf. Da 2:44; 7:27; Zec 14:16–21; Mt 25:32; Lk 21:26; Heb 12:26; Rev 19:19–21).

2:7 wealth of all nations. See Introduction: Interpretive Challenges. While some view the phrase as referring to Jerusalem (e.g., Ezr 6:3–9), it seems preferable to see a reference here to the Messiah, the Deliverer for whom all the nations ultimately long. **I will fill this house with glory.** There is no Scripture to indicate that God's glory ever did come to Zerubbabel's temple, as the first temple was filled with the Shekinah glory (cf. 1Ki 8:10, 11; 2Ch 5:13, 14). However, His glory will fill the millennial temple (Eze 43:5). This glorification cannot refer to Christ's physical presence in Herod's temple, for the events of vv. 6–9 cannot be accounted for historically. The context speaks of the establishment of His earthly, Davidic, millennial kingdom and His presence in the temple during that kingdom.

THE TEMPLES OF THE BIBLE

Identification	Date	Description	References
The Tabernacle (mobile Temple)	about 1444 B.C.	Detailed plan received by Moses from the Lord Constructed by divinely appointed artisans Desecrated by Nadab and Abihu	Ex 25–30; 35:30–40:38; Lv 10:1–7
Solomon's Temple	966–586 B.C.	Planned by David Constructed by Solomon Destroyed by Nebuchadnezzar	2Sa 7:1–29; 1Ki 8:1–66; Jer 32:28–44
Zerubbabel's Temple	516–169 B.C.	Envisioned by Zerubbabel Constructed by Zerubbabel and the elders of the Jews Desecrated by Antiochus Epiphanes	Ezr 3:1–8; 4:1–14; 6:1–22
Herod's Temple	19 B.C.–A.D. 70	Zerubbabel's temple restored by Herod the Great Destroyed by the Romans	Mk 13:2, 14–23; Lk 1:11–20; 2:22–38; 2:42–51; 4:21–24; Ac 21:27–33
The Present Temple	Present Age	Found in the heart of the believer The body of the believer is the Lord's only temple until the Messiah returns	1Co 6:19, 20; 2Co 6:16–18
The Temple of Revelation 11	Tribulation Period	To be constructed during the tribulation by the Antichrist To be desecrated and destroyed	Da 9:2; Mt 24:15; 2Th 2:4; Rev 17:18
Ezekiel's (Millennial) Temple	Millennium	Envisioned by the prophet Ezekiel To be built by the Messiah during His millennial reign	Eze 40:1–42:20; Zec 6:12, 13
The Eternal Temple of His Presence	The Eternal Kingdom	The greatest temple of all ("The Lord God the Almighty and the Lamb are its temple") A spiritual temple	Rev 21:22; 22:1–21

The temple (Gr. hieron) is a place of worship, a sacred or holy space built primarily for the national worship of God.

8 'The [A]silver is Mine and the gold is Mine,' declares
the LORD of hosts. 9 'The latter [A]glory of this house
will be greater than the [B]former,' says the LORD of
hosts, 'and in this place I will give [C]peace,' declares
the LORD of hosts."

10 On the [A]twenty-fourth of the ninth *month,* in
the second year of Darius, the word of the LORD
came to Haggai the prophet, saying, 11 "Thus says
the LORD of hosts, '[A]Ask now the priests *for* a [a]rul-
ing: 12 If a man carries [A]holy meat in the [a]fold of
his garment, and touches bread with [b]this fold,
or cooked food, wine, oil, or any *other* food, will
it become holy?' " And the priests answered, "No."
13 Then Haggai said, "[A]If one who is unclean from a
[a]corpse touches any of these, will *the latter* become
unclean?" And the priests answered, "It will become
unclean." 14 Then Haggai said, " '[A]So is this people.
And so is this nation before Me,' declares the LORD,
'and so is every work of their hands; and what they
offer there is unclean. 15 But now, do [a,A]consider from
this day [b]onward: before one [B]stone was placed on
another in the temple of the LORD, 16 [a]from that time
when one came to a *grain* heap of twenty *measures,*
there would be only ten; and *when* one came to the
wine vat to draw fifty [b]measures, there would be
only twenty. 17 I smote you *and* every work of your
hands with [A]blasting wind, mildew and hail; [a]yet
you *did* not *come back* to Me,' declares the LORD.
18 'Do [a,A]consider from this day [b]onward, from the
[B]twenty-fourth day of the ninth *month;* from the
day when the temple of the LORD was [C]founded,
[a]consider: 19 Is the seed still in the barn? Even including the vine, the fig tree, the pomegranate and
the olive tree, it has not borne *fruit.* Yet from this
day on I will [A]bless *you.*' "

20 Then the word of the LORD came a second time
to Haggai on the [A]twenty-fourth *day* of the month,
saying, 21 "Speak to [A]Zerubbabel governor of Judah,
saying, 'I am going to [B]shake the heavens and the
earth. 22 I will [A]overthrow the thrones of kingdoms
and destroy the [B]power of the kingdoms of the [a]na-
tions; and I will [C]overthrow the chariots and their
riders, and the [D]horses and their riders will go down,
[E]everyone by the sword of another.' 23 'On that day,'
declares the LORD of hosts, 'I will take you, Zerubbabel, son of Shealtiel, My servant,' declares the
LORD, 'and I will make you like a [a,A]signet *ring,* for
[B]I have chosen you,' " declares the LORD of hosts.

2:8 [A]1 Chr 29:14, 16; Is 60:17 2:9 [A]Zech 2:5 [B]Hag 2:3 [C]Is 9:6, 7; 66:12 2:10 [A]Hag 2:20 2:11 [a]Lit *law* [A]Deut 17:8-11; Mal 2:7 2:12 [a]Lit *wing* [b]Lit *his wing* [A]Ex 29:37; Lev 6:27, 29; 7:6; Ezek 44:19; Matt 23:19 2:13 [a]Lit *soul* [A]Lev 22:4-6; Num 19:22 2:14 [A]Prov 15:8; Is 1:11-15 2:15 [a]Lit *set your heart* [b]Or *backward* [A]Hag 1:5, 7; 2:18 [B]Ezra 3:10; 4:24 2:16 [a]Lit *since they were* [b]Or *troughs full* 2:17 [a]Or *but what did we have in common?* [A]Deut 28:22; 1 Kin 8:37; Amos 4:9 2:18 [a]Lit *set your heart* [b]Or *backward* [A]Deut 32:29; Hag 2:15 [B]Hag 2:10 [C]Ezra 5:1, 2; Zech 8:9, 12 2:19 [A]Ps 128:1-6; Jer 31:12, 14; Mal 3:10 2:20 [A]Hag 2:10 2:21 [A]Ezra 5:2; Hag 1:1; Zech 4:6-10 [B]Hag 2:6; Heb 12:26, 27 2:22 [a]Or *Gentiles* [A]Ezek 26:16; Zeph 3:8 [B]Mic 7:16 [C]Ps 46:9; Ezek 39:20; Mic 5:10 [D]Amos 2:15 [E]Judg 7:22; 2 Chr 20:23 2:23 [a]Or *seal* [A]Song 8:6; Jer 22:24 [B]Is 42:1; 43:10

2:8 silver . . . gold. Economically destitute, the people were reassured that He is the possessor of all things (cf. Ps 50:12).

2:9 The latter glory of this house. The Jews viewed the temple in Jerusalem as one temple existing in different forms at different times. The rebuilt temple was considered a continuation of Solomon's temple (cf. v. 3). However, the eschatological glory of the millennial temple, i.e., the latter temple, will far surpass even the grandeur of Solomon's temple (the former temple). Cf. Eze 40–48 for the detailed description of the millennial temple. **I will give peace.** This peace is not limited to that peace which He gives to believers (e.g., Ro 5:1), but looks ahead to that ultimate peace when He returns to rule as the Prince of Peace upon the throne of David in Jerusalem (Is 9:6, 7; Zec 6:13; Ac 2:30).

2:10–19 The fourth message of Haggai occurred 2 months after the third, on the 24th day of the month of Chislev, corresponding to Dec. 18, 520 B.C. Only one month earlier, Zechariah began his prophetic ministry (Zec 1:1). The message sought to demonstrate that while their disobedience caused God's blessings to be withheld, their obedience would cause His blessings to be released.

2:11–14 To provide an analogy or object lesson for the people, two questions were asked of the priests relative to ceremonial law. The first question was intended to show that ceremonial cleanness cannot be transferred (v. 12), while the second question showed that ceremonial uncleanness can be transferred (v. 13). Haggai then applied the lesson (v. 14). Even though the people had been bringing their offerings while neglecting the rebuilding of the temple, their offerings had not been acceptable. Their sin had caused their sacrifices to be contaminated and ineffectual. And their good works, their offerings, could not transmit cleanness. In other words, sin is contagious; righteousness is not (cf. 1Sa 15:22; Hos 6:6).

2:15–18 The Lord called the people to again consider their situation prior to the resumption of the temple building. In those days, the farmer found less than expected (cf. 1:6, 9–11).

2:16 ten . . . twenty. Between 50 to 60 percent of the expected harvest had been lost.

2:19 Yet from this day on I will bless *you.* As a result of their obedience, God promised to bless them from that day forth (cf. v. 10).

2:20–23 The fifth message to Zerubbabel the governor of Judah (v. 20) came on the same day as the fourth, and he returned to the theme of vv. 6–9 and the millennial reign of the Messiah. Once again, it depicted the overthrow of the kingdoms of the world and the establishment of the messianic kingdom (cf. Da 2:44; 7:27). As the events predicted did not transpire historically, the promise pertains to the royal line through whom the Messiah would come. It looked to the ultimate day when Messiah reigns on earth (cf. Ps 2; Rev 19, 20).

2:23 On that day. The day of Messiah's triumph (cf. Zec 12–14). **My servant.** A distinctly Davidic and messianic title (cf. 2Sa 3:18; 1Ki 11:34; Is 42:1–9; Eze 37:24, 25). **signet *ring.*** The signet ring was a symbol of honor, authority, and power (cf. SS 8:6). It corresponded to a king's scepter which was used to seal letters and decrees (cf. 1Ki 21:8; Est 8:8; Da 6:17). Zerubbabel, as God's signet ring, stands as the official representative of the Davidic dynasty and represents the resumption of the messianic line interrupted by the Exile. Just as Pharaoh gave Joseph his signet ring and made him second in the kingdom (Ge 41:41–43), so God will do for the Davidic line of kings. The pre-Exilic signet of Jehoiachin was removed by God (Jer 22:24) and renewed here in his grandson, Zerubbabel, who reestablished the Davidic line of kings, which would culminate in the millennial reign of Christ. *See note on Ezr 2:2.*

THE
BOOK OF
ZECHARIAH

TITLE

The universal tradition of both Jews and Christians endorses the prophet Zechariah as author. His name, common to more than 29 OT men, means "The Lord remembers." This book is second only to Isaiah in the breadth of the prophets' writings about Messiah.

AUTHOR AND DATE

Like Jeremiah and Ezekiel, Zechariah was also a priest (Ne 12:12–16). According to tradition, he was a member of the Great Synagogue, a council of 120 originated by Nehemiah and presided over by Ezra. This council later developed into the ruling elders of the nation, called the Sanhedrin. He was born in Babylon and joined his grandfather, Iddo, in the group of exiles who first returned to Jerusalem under the leadership of Zerubbabel and Joshua the High Priest (cf. Ne 12:4). Because he is occasionally mentioned as the son of his grandfather (cf. Ezr 5:1; 6:14; Ne 12:16), it is thought that his father, Berechiah, died at an early age before he could succeed his father into the priesthood.

Zechariah's opening words are dated from 520 B.C., the second year of Darius I (cf. 1:1). The Persian emperor Cyrus had died and was succeeded by Cambyses (ca. 530–521 B.C.) who conquered Egypt. He had no son, he killed himself, and Darius rose to the throne by quelling a revolution. He was a contemporary of Haggai, and began his prophesying 2 months after him (cf. Haggai Introduction). He is called a young man in 2:4, suggesting that Zechariah was younger than Haggai. The length of his ministry is uncertain; the last dated prophecy (7:1) came approximately two years after the first, making them identical in time with Haggai's prophecy (520–518 B.C.). Chapters 9–14 are generally thought to come from a later period of his ministry. Differences in style and references to Greece indicate a date of ca. 480–470 B.C., after Darius I (ca. 521–486 B.C.) and during Xerxes' reign (ca. 486–464 B.C.), the king who made Esther queen of Persia. According to Mt 23:35, he was murdered between the temple and the altar, a fate similar to an earlier Zechariah (cf. 2Ch 24:20, 21), who had been stoned to death.

BACKGROUND AND SETTING

The historical background and setting of Zechariah are the same as that of his contemporary, Haggai (cf. Haggai Introduction). In 538 B.C., Cyrus the Persian freed the captives from Israel to resettle their homeland (cf. Ezr 1:1–4) and about 50,000 returned from Babylon. They immediately began to rebuild the temple (cf. Ezr 3:1–4:5), but opposition from neighbors, followed by indifference from within, caused the work to be abandoned (cf. Ezr 4:24). Sixteen years later (cf. Ezr 5:1, 2), Zechariah and Haggai were commissioned by the Lord to stir up the people to rebuild the temple. As a result, the temple was completed 4 years later in 516 B.C. (Ezr 6:15).

HISTORICAL AND THEOLOGICAL THEMES

Zechariah joined Haggai in rousing the people from their indifference, challenging them to resume the building of the temple. Haggai's primary purpose was to rebuild the temple; his preaching has a tone of rebuke for the people's indifference, sin, and lack of trust in God. He was used to start the revival, while Zechariah was used to keep it going strong with a more positive emphasis, calling the people to repentance and reassuring them regarding future blessings. Zechariah sought to encourage the people to build the temple in view of the promise that someday Messiah would come to inhabit it. The people were not just building for the present, but with the future hope of Messiah in mind. He encouraged the people, still downtrodden by the Gentile powers (1:8–12), with the reality that the Lord remembers His covenant promises to them and that He would restore and bless them. Thus the name of the book (which means "The Lord remembers") contains in seed form the theme of the prophecy.

This "apocalypse of the OT" as it is often called, relates both to Zechariah's immediate audience as well as to the future. This is borne out in the structure of the prophecy itself, since in each of the 3 major sections (chaps. 1–6, 7, 8, 9–14), the prophet begins historically and then moves forward to the time of the Second Advent, when Messiah returns to His temple to set up His earthly kingdom. The prophet reminded the people that Messiah had both an immediate and long-term commitment to His people. Thus the prophet's words were "gracious words, comforting words" (1:13), both to the exiles of Zechariah's day as well as to the remnant of God's chosen people in that future day.

This book is the most messianic, apocalyptic, and eschatological in the OT. Primarily, it is a prophecy about Jesus Christ, focusing on His coming glory as a means to comfort Israel (cf. 1:13, 17). While the book is filled with visions, prophecies, signs, celestial visitors, and the voice of God, it is also practical, dealing with issues like repentance, divine care, salvation, and holy living. Prophecy was soon to be silent for more than 400 years until John the Baptist, so God used Zechariah to bring a rich, abundant outburst of promise for the future to sustain the faithful remnant through those silent years.

INTERPRETIVE CHALLENGES

While there are numerous challenges to the reader, two passages within the prophecy present notable interpretive difficulty. In 11:8, the Good Shepherd "annihilated the three shepherds in one month." The presence of the definite article points to familiarity, so that the Jews would have understood the identity of these shepherds without further reference. It is not so easy for modern readers to understand. Numerous alternatives concerning their identity have been suggested. One of the oldest views, and probably the correct one, identifies them as three orders of leaders: the priests, elders, and scribes of Israel. During His earthly ministry, Jesus also confronted the hypocrisy of Israel's religious leaders (cf. Mt 23), disowning them with scathing denunciations, followed by destruction of the whole nation in A.D. 70. Since His coming, the Jewish people have had no other prophet, priest, or king.

Considerable discussion also surrounds the identity of the individual who possessed "wounds between your arms" (13:6). Some have identified him with Christ, the wounds supposedly referring to His crucifixion. But Christ could neither have denied that He was a prophet, nor could He have claimed that He was a farmer, or that He was wounded in the house of His friends. Obviously, it is a reference to a false prophet (cf. vv. 4, 5) who was wounded in his idolatrous worship. The zeal for the Lord will be so great in the kingdom of Messiah that idolaters will make every attempt to hide their true identity, but their scars will be the telltale evidence of their iniquity.

OUTLINE

I. Call to Repentance (1:1–6)

II. Eight Night Visions of Zechariah (1:7–6:15)
- A. Man Among the Myrtle Trees (1:7–17)
- B. Four Horns and Four Craftsmen (1:18–21)
- C. Man with Measuring Line (2:1–13)
- D. Cleansing of High Priest (3:1–10)
- E. Gold Lampstand and Two Olive Trees (4:1–14)
- F. Flying Scroll (5:1–4)
- G. Woman in Ephah (5:5–11)
- H. Four Chariots (6:1–8)
- I. Appendix: Coronation of Joshua the High Priest (6:9–15)

III. Four Messages of Zechariah (7:1–8:23)
- A. Question about Fasting (7:1–3)
- B. Four Responses (7:4–8:23)
  1. Rebuke for wrong motives (7:4–7)
  2. Repentance required (7:8–14)
  3. Restoration of favor (8:1–17)
  4. Fasts become feasts (8:18–23)

IV. Two Burdens of Zechariah (9:1–14:21)
- A. Messiah's Rejection at First Advent (9:1–11:17)
- B. Messiah's Acceptance at Second Advent (12:1–14:21)

A CALL TO REPENTANCE

1 In the eighth month of the second year of [A]Da-
rius, the word of the LORD came to [B]Zechariah
the prophet, the son of Berechiah, the son of [C]Iddo
saying, 2 "The LORD was very [A]angry with your fathers. 3 Therefore say to them, 'Thus says the LORD
of hosts, "[A]Return to Me," declares the LORD of hosts,
"that I may return to you," says the LORD of hosts.
4 "Do not be [A]like your fathers, to whom the [B]former
prophets proclaimed, saying, 'Thus says the LORD of
hosts, "[C]Return now from your evil ways and from
your evil deeds." ' But they did [D]not listen or give
heed to Me," declares the LORD. 5 "Your [A]fathers,
where are they? And the [B]prophets, do they live
forever? 6 But did not My words and My statutes,
which I commanded My servants the prophets,
[A]overtake your fathers? Then they repented and
said, '[B]As the LORD of hosts purposed to do to us
in accordance with our ways and our deeds, so He
has dealt with us.' " ' "

PATROL OF THE EARTH

7 On the twenty-fourth day of the eleventh month,
which is the month Shebat, in the second year of
Darius, the word of the LORD came to Zechariah
the prophet, the son of Berechiah, the son of Iddo,
as follows: 8 I saw at night, and behold, a man
was riding on a [A]red horse, and he was standing
among the [B]myrtle trees which were in the ravine,
with red, sorrel and [C]white horses behind him.

1:1 [A]Ezra 4:24; 6:15; Hag 1:15; 2:10; Zech 1:7; 7:1 [B]Ezra 5:1; 6:14; Zech 7:1; Matt 23:35; Luke 11:51 [C]Neh 12:4, 16 1:2 [A]2 Chr 36:16; Jer 44:6; Ezek 8:18; Zech 1:15 1:3 [A]Is 31:6; 44:22; Mal 3:7 1:4 [A]Ps 78:8; 106:6, 7 [B]2 Chr 24:19; 36:15 [C]Is 1:16-19; Jer 4:1; Ezek 33:11 [D]Jer 6:17; 11:7, 8 1:5 [A]Lam 5:7 [B]John 8:52 1:6 [A]Jer 12:16, 17; 44:28, 29; Amos 9:10 [B]Lam 2:17 1:8 [A]Zech 6:2; Rev 6:4 [B]Neh 8:15; Is 41:19; 55:13; Zech 1:10, 11 [C]Zech 6:3; Rev 6:2

1:1–6 The opening 6 verses provide an introduction to the entire prophecy in which the prophet calls upon the people to repent and never again repeat the past sins of their fathers (cf. 1Co 10:11).

1:1 **eighth month of the second year of Darius.** Ca. Oct./Nov. 520 B.C. See Introduction: Author and Date. Zechariah began his ministry two months after the start of Haggai's ministry (cf. Hag 1:1) and the resumption of the rebuilding of the temple (cf. Hag 1:12–15). Most OT prophets who dated their prophecies did so according to the reign of a king in Israel, Judah, or both. Haggai and Zechariah date their prophecies according to the reign of the Gentile king, indicating that the times of the Gentiles (Lk 21:24) had begun. **Zechariah.** See Introduction: Author and Date.

1:2 **The LORD was very angry.** This actually means "to break out in long-controlled indignation," reminding the people of the severity of God's wrath and the necessity of His judgment on their past sins in pre-Exilic times.

1:3 **the LORD of hosts.** This frequently used name for God shows His might as the commander of the hosts, whether they are the armies of Israel (cf. 2Ch 26:11), the armies of the heathen nations (cf. Jdg 4:2), or the heavenly inhabitants (cf. 1Ki 22:19). **Return to Me.** Though primarily a book of consolation, the prophet begins with a call to repentance, to preclude any false security on the part of Israel, i.e., thinking that God would bless His chosen people regardless of their spiritual condition. This expresses the ongoing desire of God (cf. Ge 17:7; Lv 26:12; Eze 37:27; 2Co 6:16; Jas 4:8; Rev 21:3), and the constant condition for blessing.

1:4 **Do not be like your fathers.** The disobedient, obstinate behavior of their fathers was not so much directed toward the prophets, but at God Himself. The people were well aware of their fathers' sins (cf. Ezr 9:7) and could look around them and see the results. History should have taught them to repent. **the former prophets.** A reference to the pre-Exilic prophets who all preached the same message of repentance before the Exile, e.g., Isaiah and Jeremiah. Cf. "My servants" (v. 6).

1:5 While both their fathers and the former prophets were dead, the legacy of their fathers' failure to heed the prophets' warnings was vividly before them, exemplified by the city of Jerusalem and the temple lying in ruins, needing to be rebuilt.

1:6 God's Word accomplishes all which He designs (Is 55:10, 11), in blessing and in judgment. His warnings, so precisely fulfilled, overtook and destroyed their fathers, who recognized God's hand in the judgment (cf. La 2:17; Ezr 9:6ff.). The Exile was positive proof that God punishes those who sin and reject His warnings. **they repented.** Cf. Da 9:1–19.

1:7–6:15 God gave Zechariah these visions for the comfort of the post-Exilic remnant of Israel who had been commissioned to return from Persia to the land promised to Abraham (cf. Ge 12). They were to rebuild the temple (cf. 1 and 2Ch) and to anticipate the day of Messiah's return, when all of God's promises to Israel would finally, fully, and ultimately be fulfilled. Some portions of the visions have been fulfilled, but the large number await the Second Advent of Jesus Christ. The following summary will help to distinguish the contribution of individual visions and clarify the whole. Vision 1—Man among the myrtle trees (1:7–17), God promises prosperity to Israel. Vision 2—Four horns and four craftsmen (1:18–21), God judges the nations who attacked Israel. Vision 3—Man with a measuring line (2:1–13), God rebuilds Jerusalem. Vision 4—Cleansing of the High Priest (3:1–10), God purifies both High Priest and people. Vision 5—Golden lampstand and two olive trees (4:1–14), God rebuilds the temple. Vision 6—Flying scroll (5:1–4), God removes imparted sin/idolatry. Vision 7—Woman in basket (5:5–11), God removes the system of false religion. Vision 8—Four chariots (6:1–8), God brings peace and rest to Israel. Appendix—Coronation of the High Priest (6:9–15), Messiah assumes the office of both King and Priest.

1:7–17 This is the first of 8 night visions which Zechariah saw in a single night. It summarized all the other 7 by giving the general theme, leaving the details to the other visions. Reassuring words are provided to the exiles by revealing God's purpose for the future of His chosen people.

1:7 **the twenty-fourth day of the eleventh month.** Ca. Jan./Feb. 519 B.C. Approximately 3 months after Zechariah's opening call to repentance.

1:8 **I saw at night.** This is the first vision revealing God's plan for Jerusalem, which begins with the sight of "a man ... riding on a red horse." The man is identified as the Angel of the Lord (cf. v. 11). The other riders report to Him, indicating His authority over them. Because of the strength of horses, they became symbols of war. Red is often the symbol of blood, hence judgment (cf.

ZECHARIAH'S VISIONS

Vision	Significance
Man and horses among the myrtle trees (1:8)	The Lord will again be merciful to Jerusalem (1:14, 16, 17)
Four horns, four craftsmen (1:18–20)	Those who scattered Judah are cast out (1:21)
Man with measuring line (2:1)	God will be a protective wall of fire around Jerusalem (2:3–5)
Cleansing of Joshua (3:4)	The Servant, the Branch, comes to save (3:8, 9)
Golden lampstand and olive trees (4:2, 3)	The Lord empowers Israel by His Spirit (4:6)
Flying scroll (5:1)	Dishonesty is cursed (5:3)
Woman in the basket (5:6, 7)	Wickedness will be removed (5:9)
Four chariots (6:1)	The spirits of heaven execute judgment on the whole earth (6:5, 7)

9 Then I said, "My [A]lord, what are these?" And the
[B]angel who was speaking with me said to me, "I will
show you what these are." 10 And the man who was
standing among the myrtle trees answered and
said, "These are those whom the LORD has sent to
[a,A]patrol the earth." 11 So they answered the angel
of the LORD who was [A]standing among the myrtle
trees and said, "We have [a]patrolled the earth, and
behold, [B]all the earth is [b]peaceful and quiet."
12 Then the angel of the LORD said, "O LORD of
hosts, [A]how long will You [B]have no compassion for
Jerusalem and the cities of Judah, with which You
have been [C]indignant these [D]seventy years?" 13 The
LORD answered the [A]angel who was speaking with
me with [a]gracious words, [B]comforting words. 14 So
the angel who was speaking with me said to me,
"[A]Proclaim, saying, 'Thus says the LORD of hosts,
"I am [B]exceedingly jealous for Jerusalem and Zion.
15 But I am very [A]angry with the nations who are
[B]at ease; for while I was only a little angry, they
[a,C]furthered the disaster." 16 Therefore thus says the
LORD, "I will [A]return to Jerusalem with compassion;
My [B]house will be built in it," declares the LORD of
hosts, "and a measuring [C]line will be stretched over
Jerusalem." ' 17 Again, proclaim, saying, 'Thus says
the LORD of hosts, "My [A]cities will again overflow
with prosperity, and the LORD will again [B]comfort
Zion and again [C]choose Jerusalem." ' "
18 [a]Then I lifted up my eyes and looked, and behold, *there were* four horns. 19 So I said to the angel
who was speaking with me, "What are these?" And
he answered me, "These are the [A]horns which have
scattered Judah, Israel and Jerusalem." 20 Then the
LORD showed me four [A]craftsmen. 21 I said, "What
are these coming to do?" And he said, "These are
the [A]horns which have scattered Judah so that no
man lifts up his head; but these *craftsmen* have
come to terrify them, to [B]throw down the horns of
the nations who have lifted up *their* horns against
the land of Judah in order to scatter it."

1:9 [A]Zech 1:19; 4:4, 5, 13; 6:4 [B]Zech 2:3; 5:5 1:10 [a]Lit *walk about through* [A]Job 1:7; Zech 1:11; 4:10; 6:5-8 1:11 [a]Lit *walked about through* [b]Lit *sitting* [A]Zech 1:8, 10 [B]Is 14:7 1:12 [A]Ps 74:10; Jer 12:4; Hab 1:2 [B]Ps 102:13; Jer 30:18 [C]Ps 102:10; Jer 15:17 [D]Jer 25:11; 29:10; Dan 9:2; Zech 7:5 1:13 [a]Lit *good* [A]Zech 1:9; 4:1 [B]Is 40:1, 2; 57:18 1:14 [A]Is 40:2, 6; Zech 1:17 [B]Zech 8:2 1:15 [a]Lit *helped for evil* [A]Zech 1:2 [B]Ps 123:4; Jer 48:11 [C]Amos 1:11 1:16 [A]Is 54:8-10; Zech 2:10, 11 [B]Ezra 6:14, 15; Zech 4:9 [C]Jer 31:39; Zech 2:2, 4 1:17 [A]Is 44:26; 61:4 [B]Is 51:3 [C]Zech 2:12 1:18 [a]Ch 2:1 in Heb 1:19 [A]1 Kin 22:11; Ps 75:4, 5; Amos 6:13 mg 1:20 [A]Is 44:12; 54:16 1:21 [A]Zech 1:19 [B]Ps 75:10

Is 63:1–4; Rev 6:3ff.). **among the myrtle trees ... in the ravine.** Myrtle trees were associated with booth-making at the Feast of Booths, or Tabernacles (Lv 23:33–44; Ne 8:15), and with messianic blessing (cf. Is 41:19; 55:13), and thereby possibly speak of restoration and blessing. Their location in the ravine has been thought to refer to a low place where such shrubs would flourish. Because of the lowliness (these shrubs would never exceed 8 ft. in height), commonness, fragrance (from white blossoms), and abundance in flourishing places, it is best to see these as representing Israel, God's people. They are the lowly and yet enriched people. Their lowliness in the ravine could also refer to Israel's current humiliation. **red, sorrel, and white.** Presumably these other horses had riders as well. The colors may speak of the work of the riders: red speaking of bloodshed and judgment (cf. Is 63:1, 2), white speaking of victory (cf. Rev 19:11), and sorrel or a brownish color is possibly a combination of the others. A similar picture is found in Rev 6:1–8. These horses are about to gain a victorious judgment. Since they are messengers of vengeance, they likely represent angels, so frequently employed as God's instruments of judgment.

1:9 the angel who was speaking with me. This interpreting angel (1:13, 14, 19; 2:3; 3:1; 4:1) is to be distinguished from the Angel of the Lord (vv. 11, 12).

1:10 patrol. A symbolic military description of angelic movement patrolling and reconnoitering on a global scale. The purpose is to ascertain the state of the enemy and to respond to God's will in engaging that enemy triumphantly.

1:11 the angel of the LORD. Elsewhere the Angel of the Lord is frequently identified with the pre-incarnate Lord Himself (e.g., Ge 16:11, 13; 18:1, 2, 13, 17; 22:11–18; Ex 3:2, 4; Jos 5:13; 6:2; Jdg 6:12, 14; 13:21, 22). In v. 13, this Angel is called Lord, and is the divine Commander-in-Chief of this angelic army. **all the earth is peaceful and quiet.** In contrast to the difficulties facing the exiles, without temple or city walls, the heathen nations were superficially at rest, occupied with their own selfish interests (cf. v. 15). This was generally the condition in the second year of Darius. The contrast makes the plight of Israel all the more distressing and the hope for the fulfillment of Hag 2:7, 22 more intense.

1:12 The Angel of the Lord interceded to God the Father on behalf of Israel, pleading for the withdrawal of God's chastening hand. The "seventy years" refers to God's words to Jeremiah concerning the length of Judah's exile (Jer 25:11, 12; 29:10).

1:13 gracious ... comforting words. The content of these words is given in vv. 14–17: God still loved Jerusalem (v. 14), He was angry with the nations who afflicted them (v. 15), and He will bring prosperity to Jerusalem (vv. 16, 17).

1:14 I am exceedingly jealous for Jerusalem. God first described Himself as jealous when making His covenant with Israel (Ex 20:5; 34:14). This same jealousy had been experienced by Israel in punishment (cf. Dt 29:18–28; Eze 5:13). That same jealous love is expressed emphatically in the city's defense.

1:15 Moved by His great love for His people, the Lord acted in anger (cf. v. 2) against the nations which mistreated His people. Although they were His instrument of judgment against Israel, they had exceeded God's instructions in meting out punishment. They did not understand that God's intention was to punish for a time and then show compassion (cf. Is 54:7, 8).

1:16, 17 Not only would the temple be rebuilt, which at that time had only foundations (cf. Hag 2:18), but the city itself would again expand due to the prosperity (cf. Is 40:9, 10). The wall was completed 75 years later. God would again comfort Jerusalem (cf. Is 40:1, 2; 51:3, 12) and would again choose it as the place of His earthly throne (cf. Ps 132:13). This will be fulfilled in the millennial kingdom of Messiah (cf. Rev 20). Given the fact that the returning Jews lost sight of their priorities (cf. Hag 1:1–12), this message reaffirmed God's plan. It should be noted that the millennial kingdom will provide the presence of God in Jerusalem (Eze 48:35), a glorious temple (Eze 40–48), a rebuilt Jerusalem (Jer 31:38–40), the nations punished (Mt 25:31–46), the prosperity of Judah's cities (Is 60:4–9), the blessedness of the people (Zec 9:17), and the comfort of Zion (Is 14:1).

1:18–21 The second of 8 night visions adds details to the judgment of the nations who persecuted His Israel, building upon God's promise to comfort His people (1:13, 17).

1:18 four horns. Horns were symbols of power and pride (cf. Pss 75:10; 89:17; 92:10; Da 7:24; 8:20, 21; Mic 4:13). In the context of judgment, each symbolizes either a nation or the head of that nation (cf. Da 7:21, 24; 8:3; Rev 17:12). Here the horns represent nations that attacked God's people (vv. 19, 21), referring either to Egypt, Assyria, Babylonia, and Medo-Persia or perhaps, more likely, to the 4 world empires of Da 2, 7: Babylonia, Medo-Persia, Greece, and Rome, all of which oppressed Israel.

1:20 four craftsmen. The word is literally the term for stoneworkers, metal workers, and woodworkers—those who shape material with hammers and chisels. These "hammers" represent the nations which overthrow the 4 horns (v. 18). As with the 4 beasts of Da 7, each empire is overthrown by the subsequent one, the last being replaced by Messiah's kingdom (cf. Da 2:44; 7:9–14, 21, 22). Babylon was hammered in a night attack by the Medo-Persians (539 B.C.). With the victory of Alexander over Darius in 333 B.C. at Issus, the Greeks hammered the Medo-Persian "horn." In the second century B.C., the Roman hammer fell, and one by one the nations fell (Israel in 63 B.C.). The Roman Empire, revived in the last days, according to Daniel, will be hammered by the returning Messiah (cf. Da 2:34, 35, 45).

GOD'S FAVOR TO ZION

2 [a]Then I lifted up my eyes and looked, and behold, *there was* a man with a [A]measuring line
in his hand. 2 So I said, "Where are you going?" And
he said to me, "To [A]measure Jerusalem, to see how
wide it is and how long it is." 3 And behold, the [A]an-
gel who was speaking with me was going out, and
another angel was coming out to meet him, 4 and
said to him, "Run, speak to that [A]young man, saying, '[B]Jerusalem will be inhabited [a,C]without walls
because of the [D]multitude of men and cattle within
it. 5 For I,' declares the LORD, 'will be a [A]wall of fire
[a]around her, and I will be the [B]glory in her midst.' "
6 "[a]Ho there! [A]Flee from the land of the north,"
declares the LORD, "for I have [B]dispersed you as
the four winds of the heavens," declares the LORD.
7 "Ho, Zion! [A]Escape, you who are living with the
daughter of Babylon." 8 For thus says the LORD of
hosts, "After [a,A]glory He has sent me against the
nations which plunder you, for he who touches
you, touches the [b,B]apple of His eye. 9 For behold, I
will [A]wave My hand over them so that they will be
[B]plunder for their slaves. Then you will know that
the LORD of hosts has sent Me. 10 [A]Sing for joy and
be glad, O daughter of Zion; for behold I am coming
and I will [B]dwell in your midst," declares the LORD.
11 "[A]Many nations will join themselves to the LORD
in that day and will become My people. Then I will
[B]dwell in your midst, and you will [C]know that the
LORD of hosts has sent Me to you. 12 The LORD will
[a,A]possess Judah as His portion in the holy land, and
will again [B]choose Jerusalem.
13 "[a,A]Be silent, all flesh, before the LORD; for He
is [B]aroused from His holy habitation."

JOSHUA, THE HIGH PRIEST

3 Then he showed me [A]Joshua the high priest
standing before the angel of the LORD, and
[a,B]Satan standing at his right hand to accuse him.
2 The LORD said to Satan, "[A]The LORD rebuke you,
Satan! Indeed, the LORD who has [B]chosen Jerusalem rebuke you! Is this not a [C]brand plucked
from the fire?" 3 Now Joshua was clothed with
[A]filthy garments and standing before the angel.

2:1 [a]Ch 2:5 in Heb [A]Jer 31:39; Ezek 40:3; 47:3; Zech 1:16 2:2 [A]Jer 31:39; Ezek 40:3; Rev 21:15-17 2:3 [A]Zech 1:9 2:4 [a]Lit like *unwalled villages;* or like *open country* [A]Jer 1:6; Dan 1:4; 1 Tim 4:12 [B]Zech 1:17; 8:4 [C]Ezek 38:11 [D]Is 49:20; Jer 30:19; 33:22 2:5 [a]Lit *to her* [A]Is 4:5; 26:1; 60:18 [B]Hag 2:9; Zech 2:10, 11 2:6 [a]Lit *Ho! Ho!* [A]Jer 3:18 [B]Jer 31:10; Ezek 11:16 2:7 [A]Is 48:20; Jer 51:6 2:8 [a]Or *the glory* [b]Lit *pupil* [A]Is 60:7-9 [B]Deut 32:10; Ps 17:8 2:9 [A]Is 19:16 [B]Is 14:2 2:10 [A]Is 65:18, 19; Zech 9:9 [B]Zech 2:5; 8:3 2:11 [A]Mic 4:2 [B]Zech 2:5, 10 [C]Zech 2:9 2:12 [a]Or *inherit* [A]Deut 32:9; Ps 33:12; Jer 10:16 [B]2 Chr 6:6; Ps 132:13, 14; Zech 1:17 2:13 [a]Lit *Hush* [A]Hab 2:20; Zeph 1:7 [B]Ps 78:65; Is 51:9 3:1 [a]Or the *Adversary* or *Accuser* [A]Ezra 5:2; Hag 1:1; Zech 6:11 [B]1 Chr 21:1; Job 1:6; Ps 109:6; Rev 12:10 3:2 [A]Mark 9:25; Jude 9 [B]Zech 2:12 [C]Amos 4:11; Jude 23 3:3 [A]Ezra 9:15; Is 4:4; 64:6

2:1–13 The third vision reveals a man with a measuring line. Like the second vision, it also builds on God's promise to comfort His people (1:13, 17). The restoration of Jerusalem after the return from Babylon is only a foretaste of the future messianic kingdom, for the language of the vision cannot be fulfilled historically. Its scope extends beyond the time of Zechariah to the rule of the Messiah on earth.

2:1 a man with a measuring line. The restoration and rebuilding of Jerusalem are symbolized. It is very possible that the surveyor is the Angel of the Lord (cf. 1:11; 6:12; Eze 40:2, 3), who is laying out the future dimensions of the city.

2:3 angel . . . was speaking with me. This is the instructing angel of 1:9.

2:4 The news was so wonderful that it was to be heralded immediately. An angel arrived to explain that Jerusalem will become so large that it will extend beyond any walls (cf. Is 49:19, 20; Eze 38:11). The conditions here described have at no time been true historically (cf. Ne 7:4; 11:1, 2); full realization must be assigned to a future earthly kingdom (cf. Is 49:19, 20). A counterfeit of this unwalled safety will exist under Antichrist in the time of tribulation (*see notes on Eze 38:8–12*).

2:5 a wall of fire around her. Though without walls, Jerusalem will dwell securely because of divine protection. The phrase is reminiscent of the pillar of fire at the Exodus (cf. Ex 13:21; 2Ki 6:15–17; Is 4:5, 6). **I will be the glory in her midst.** More than protection, the glory depicts the Messiah's blessing and personal presence in His earthly kingdom (cf. Is 4:2–6; 40:5; 60:17, 18; Eze 42:1–7).

2:6–9 The prophet turned from the distant future (vv. 4, 5) to the present, summoning those Israelites still in Babylon (referred to as the land of the north, cf. v. 7, because of the direction from which it invaded Israel) to flee before God poured out His judgment on it. This also implied a future call to leave a future Babylon (cf. Rev 17:3–5; 18:1–8).

2:6 I have dispersed you. According to 2Ki 17:6, they were scattered from the Gozan River, 200 mi. W of Nineveh, to Media, 300 mi. E. Some had even taken refuge in Moab, Ammon, Edom, and Egypt (cf. Jer 40:11, 12; 43:7).

2:8 After glory He has sent Me. The Messiah is sent by the "LORD of hosts" (v. 9) to procure His glory and to vindicate Him in the nations who have spoiled Israel. **the apple of His eye.** *See note on Dt 32:10.* Harming God's chosen people is like striking the pupil of God's eye.

2:10–13 The language is once again messianic, describing the personal presence of the Messiah, dwelling on the throne of David in Jerusalem during the Millennium.

2:11, 12 Echoing the promise to Abraham (Ge 12:3), many nations will join themselves to the Lord (cf. 6:15; 8:20–23; Is 2:2–4; 56:6, 7; 60:3). But this will not alter God's choice of His people, they will still be "His portion in the holy land" (cf. Dt 32:9).

2:12 holy land. Used only here, the expression is made not because it is the Promised Land, but because it will be the site of Messiah's earthly throne when the land has been cleansed. A holy land is appropriate and expected for its holy Lord (Is 6:1–5).

2:13 His holy habitation. God's dwelling in heaven (cf. Pss 15:1; 24:3).

3:1–10 The fourth night vision emphasizes Israel's cleansing and restoration as a priestly nation. The vision itself is given in vv. 1–5, followed by the explanation and significance in vv. 6–10. The revealer was most likely God Himself.

3:1 The scene is invested with a judicial character as Joshua, the High Priest of the restoration who came back in the first group with Zerubbabel (cf. Ezr 3:2; 5:2; Hag 1:1), was accused by Satan, who was standing at the right side, the place of accusation under the law (cf. Ps 109:6). That Joshua was representative of the nation is evident from: 1) the emphasis on the nation in these visions; 2) the fact that the rebuke in v. 2 is based on God's choice of Jerusalem, not Joshua; 3) the identification in v. 8 of Joshua and his fellow priests as symbolic of future Israel; and 4) its application to the land in v. 9. **Satan.** This could also be translated "adversary" and thus the person's identity would be unknown. However, because the activity of accusation is so in keeping with Satan (cf. Job 1, 2; Rev 12:10), his identification is preferable. The malicious adversary stands in the presence of the Lord to proclaim Israel's sins and their unworthiness of God's favor. The situation is crucial: if Joshua is vindicated, Israel is accepted; if Joshua is rejected, Israel is rejected. The entire plan of God for the nation was revealed in the outcome. Israel's hopes would either be destroyed or confirmed.

3:2 The LORD said. The Angel of the Lord is identified as the Lord, thus verifying this "messenger" as deity. *See notes on 1:11; Jdg 6:11.* And the message was crucial in confirming that 1) God had not cast off the Jews, but was consistent with His covenants with them in Abraham and David, and 2) His election takes their side against Satan's accusations. God will do this rebuking, as reported in Rev 20:10. *See note on Jude 9.* **chosen Jerusalem.** God's favor rested on Israel above any nation on earth (cf. Dt 7:6–11). He snatched them from potential disappearance in their captivity, like pulling a stick out of the fire just before it is torched (cf. Am 4:11). Thus, God confirmed His purposes for Israel, sweeping from Zechariah's time to the consummation of human history (cf. Rev 12:3–17).

3:3 filthy garments. Employing the most loathsome, vile term for filth, the phrase pictures the habitual condition of defilement of the priesthood and the people (cf. Is 4:4; 64:6), which became the basis of Satan's accusation

4 He spoke and said to those who were standing
before him, saying, "[A]Remove the filthy garments
from him." Again he said to him, "See, I have [B]taken
your iniquity away from you and [a]will [C]clothe you
with festal robes." 5 Then I said, "Let them put a clean
[A]turban on his head." So they put a clean turban on
his head and clothed him with garments, while the
angel of the LORD was standing by.
6 And the angel of the LORD admonished Joshua,
saying, 7 "Thus says the LORD of hosts, 'If you will
[A]walk in My ways and if you will perform My service, then you will also [B]govern My house and also
have charge of My [C]courts, and I will grant you [a]free
access among these who are standing *here*.

THE BRANCH

8 Now listen, Joshua the high priest, you and your
friends who are sitting in front of you—indeed they
are men who are a [A]symbol, for behold, I am going
to bring in My servant the [a,B]Branch. 9 For behold, the
stone that I have set before Joshua; on one stone are
[A]seven eyes. Behold, I will engrave an inscription on
it,' declares the LORD of hosts, 'and I will [B]remove the
iniquity of that land in one day. 10 In that day,' declares
the LORD of hosts, 'every one of you will invite his
neighbor to *sit* under *his* [A]vine and under *his* fig tree.' "

THE GOLDEN LAMPSTAND AND OLIVE TREES

4 Then [A]the angel who was speaking with me
returned and [B]roused me, as a man who is awakened from his sleep. 2 He said to me, "[A]What do you
see?" And I said, "I see, and behold, a [B]lampstand all
of gold with its bowl on the top of it, and its [C]seven
lamps on it with seven spouts belonging to each of
the lamps which are on the top of it; 3 also [A]two olive
trees by it, one on the right side of the bowl and
the other on its left side." 4 Then I said to the angel
who was speaking with me saying, "What are these,
[A]my lord?" 5 So [A]the angel who was speaking with
me answered and said to me, "[B]Do you not know
what these are?" And I said, "No, my lord." 6 Then
he [a]said to me, "This is the word of the LORD to
[A]Zerubbabel saying, '[B]Not by might nor by power,
but by My [C]Spirit,' says the LORD of hosts. 7 'What
are you, O great [A]mountain? Before Zerubbabel *you
will become* a plain; and he will bring forth the top
stone with [B]shouts of "Grace, grace to it!" ' "

3:4 [a]Lit *to clothe* [A]Is 43:25; Ezek 36:25 [B]Mic 7:18, 19; Zech 3:9 [C]Is 52:1; 61:10 3:5 [A]Job 29:14; Is 3:23 3:7 [a]Lit *goings* [A]1 Kin 3:14 [B]Deut 17:9, 12 [C]Is 62:9 3:8 [a]Lit *Sprout* [A]Is 8:18; 20:3; Ezek 12:11 [B]Is 11:1; 53:2; Jer 23:5; 33:15; Zech 6:12 3:9 [A]Zech 4:10 [B]Jer 31:34; 50:20; Zech 3:4 3:10 [A]1 Kin 4:25; Is 36:16; Mic 4:4 4:1 [A]Zech 1:9 [B]1 Kin 19:5-7; Jer 31:26 4:2 [A]Jer 1:13; Zech 5:2 [B]Ex 25:31, 37; Jer 52:19 [C]Rev 4:5 4:3 [A]Zech 4:11; Rev 11:4 4:4 [A]Zech 1:9; 4:5, 13; 6:4 4:5 [A]Zech 1:9; 4:1 [B]Zech 4:13 4:6 [a]Lit *said to me, saying* [A]Ezra 5:2; Hag 2:4, 5 [B]Is 11:2-4; 30:1; Hos 1:7 [C]2 Chr 32:7, 8; Eph 6:17 4:7 [A]Ps 114:4, 6; Is 40:4; Jer 51:25; Nah 1:5; Zech 14:4, 5 [B]Ezra 3:10, 11; Ps 84:11

that the nation is morally impure and unworthy of God's protection and blessing.

3:4 The removal of filthy garments by the angels ("who were standing before him") depicted the promised future forensic justification, the salvation of the nation (cf. v. 9; 12:10–13:1; Ro 11:25–27). The High Priest was symbolically clothed with rich robes, which spoke of righteousness imputed (cf. Is 61:10) and the restoration of Israel to her original calling (cf. Ex 19:6; Is 61:6; Ro 11:1, 2).

3:5 a clean turban. The turban, part of the High Priest's dress, was inscribed with the words: "Holy to the LORD" (Ex 28:36, 37; 39:30, 31). Zechariah joined the scene, calling for this because it strongly symbolized that Israel's priestly place with God was restored.

3:6, 7 Although God will keep His promise to justify Israel, reinstate the nation as His priestly people to serve in His house, keep His courts, and have complete access to His presence—all based on His sovereign, electing love and not by merit or works of man—that will not be fulfilled until Israel is faithful to the Lord. It awaits the fulfillment of 12:10–13:1.

3:8 men who are a symbol. The companion priests sitting before Joshua were symbols of future Israel, foreshadowing the coming Messiah. **My servant the Branch.** Two messianic phrases are here combined. "My Servant" is used by earlier prophets to depict the Messiah (Is 42:1; 49:3, 5; 52:13; 53:11; Eze 34:23, 24) and speaks of His complete obedience and His humble estate. "Branch" also points to the Messiah (cf. 6:12, 13; Is 4:2; Jer 23:5; 33:15) and denotes His rise from humble beginnings (Is 11:1; Jer 23:5, 6) and His fruitfulness (6:12; Is 11:1).

3:9 the stone. Here is another reference to Messiah. In Ps 118:22, 23; Is 8:13–15; 28:16; Da 2:35, 45; Mt 21:42; Eph 2:19–22; 1Pe 2:6–8, He is a rejected stone, a stone of stumbling, a stone of refuge, a destroying stone, and a foundation stone. Here He is the precious foundation stone, with "seven eyes" symbolic of His omniscience and infinite intelligence (cf. 4:10; Is 11:2; Col 2:3; Rev 5:6). The engraving may be a reference to the cornerstone of the temple building, on which will be engraved an inscription attesting to the Divine Builder and the purpose for which the building was erected. As such, it is closely tied to the removal of "the iniquity of that land in one day," symbolized by the removal of filthy garments in v. 4. The phrase looks to the future day when there will be cleansing and forgiveness for the nation as a whole (12:10–13:1; Ro 11:25–27), made possible through Christ's redemptive provision at Calvary.

3:10 invite his neighbor to *sit* under. A common expression in Israel for peace and prosperity (cf. 1Ki 4:25; Mic 4:4), here depicting the peace during the millennial rule of Messiah.

4:1–14 The fourth vision focused on Joshua the High Priest and, by extension, the cleansing and restoration of the nation to her divinely appointed role as priest. This fifth vision focuses on the civil leader Zerubbabel, a descendant of David, to encourage him in the work of rebuilding the temple. The faithful completion of the work would then enable Israel to again bear light of God's grace (testimony) to the world.

4:1 as a man who is awakened. Once again the interpreting angel comes to awaken the prophet out of spiritual exhaustion from the holy trauma of the previous vision. Cf. Da 10:9.

4:2 seven spouts belonging to each of the lamps. The lampstand is the 7-branched kind used in the tabernacle, with the addition of a bowl on the top of it in order to maintain an abundant supply of oil and spouts to carry the oil to keep the 7 lamps burning. The picture is of an abundant supply.

4:3 two olive trees. Olive oil was used in those days to fuel the lamps. The two olive trees supply oil to the bowl. The graphic picture is of limitless oil, supplied automatically without human agency, flowing from the trees down to the bowl, down to the lamps.

4:4 What are these. Zechariah wanted to know the meaning of the two olive trees. Because of Zechariah's priestly background, his query surprised the interpreting angel (v. 5). His question goes unanswered until later (v. 14).

4:6 This is the word of the LORD to Zerubbabel. The purpose of the vision was to encourage Zerubbabel to complete the temple rebuilding, to assure him of divine enablement for that venture and the endless supply for the future glory of Messiah's kingdom and temple. The lampstand pictured Israel fully supplied by God to be His light then and in the future. It must be noted that the church has temporarily taken this role presently (cf. Eph 5:8, 9; Rev 1:12, 13, 20), until Israel's salvation and restoration to covenant blessing and usefulness. Cf. Ro 11:11–24. **Not by might ... power, but by My Spirit.** Neither human might, wealth, or physical stamina would be sufficient to complete the work. Only an abundant supply of the power of the Holy Spirit, pictured by the "bowl" (v. 2) would enable him to carry out the task, and enable Israel in the Messiah's kingdom to be a light again to the world by the operation of the Spirit (cf. Eze 36:24).

4:7 What are you, O great mountain? Because the outcome is guaranteed (vv. 6, 9), any mountain-like opposition will be leveled by God to become like a flat surface. No obstacle will be able to stop the completion of the temple in Zerubbabel's time or in the final kingdom of Messiah (cf. Eze 40–48). **the top stone.** The final stone of the building will be put into place, signifying its completion.

8 Also the word of the LORD came to me, saying,
9 "The hands of Zerubbabel have [A]laid the foundation of this house, and his hands will [B]finish *it*. Then
you will know that the LORD of hosts has sent me
to [a]you. 10 For who has despised the day of [A]small
things? [a]But these [B]seven will be glad when they see
the [b,C]plumb line in the hand of Zerubbabel—*these
are* the [D]eyes of the LORD which [E]range to and fro
throughout the earth."
11 Then I said to him, "What are these [A]two olive
trees on the right of the lampstand and on its left?"
12 And I answered the second time and said to him,
"What are the two olive [a]branches which are beside
the two golden pipes, which empty the golden *oil* from
themselves?" 13 So he answered me, saying, "[A]Do you
not know what these are?" And I said, "No, [B]my lord."
14 Then he said, "These are the two [a,A]anointed ones
who are [B]standing by the [C]Lord of the whole earth."

THE FLYING SCROLL

5 Then I lifted up my eyes again and looked, and
behold, *there was* a flying [A]scroll. 2 And he said
to me, "[A]What do you see?" And I answered, "I see a
flying scroll; its length is twenty [a]cubits and its width
ten cubits." 3 Then he said to me, "This is the [A]curse
that is going forth over the face of the whole [a]land;
surely everyone who [B]steals will be purged away according to [b]the writing on one side, and everyone who
[C]swears will be purged away according to [b]the writing
on the other side. 4 I will [A]make it go forth," declares
the LORD of hosts, "and it will [B]enter the house of the
[C]thief and the house of the one who swears falsely
by My name; and it will spend the night within that
house and [D]consume it with its timber and stones."
5 Then [A]the angel who was speaking with me went
out and said to me, "Lift up now your eyes and see
what this is going forth." 6 I said, "What is it?" And
he said, "This is the [a,A]ephah going forth." Again
he said, "This is their [b]appearance in all the [c]land
7 (and behold, a lead cover was lifted up); and this is
a woman sitting inside the ephah." 8 Then he said,
"This is [A]Wickedness!" And he threw her down into
the middle of the ephah and cast the lead weight on
its [a]opening. 9 Then I lifted up my eyes and looked,
and there two women were coming out with the
wind in their wings; and they had wings like the
wings of a [A]stork, and they lifted up the ephah between the earth and the heavens. 10 I said to the
angel who was speaking with me, "Where are they
taking the ephah?" 11 Then he said to me, "To build a
[a]temple for her in the land of [A]Shinar; and when it is
prepared, she will be set there on her own pedestal."

4:9 [a]Lit *you* (plural) [A]Ezra 3:8-10; 5:16; Hag 2:18 [B]Ezra 6:14, 15; Zech 6:12, 13 4:10 [a]Or *But they will rejoice when they see…Zerubbabel. These seven are the eyes of the LORD* [b]Lit *plummet stone* [A]Neh 4:2-4; Amos 7:2, 5; Hag 2:3 [B]Zech 3:9; Rev 8:2 [C]Amos 7:7, 8 [D]2 Chr 16:9; Prov 15:3; Jer 16:17 [E]Zech 1:10; Rev 5:6 4:11 [A]Zech 4:3; Rev 11:4 4:12 [a]Or *clusters* 4:13 [A]Zech 4:5 [B]Zech 4:4, 5 4:14 [a]Lit *sons of fresh oil* [A]Ex 29:7; 40:15; 1 Sam 16:1, 12, 13; Is 61:1-3; Dan 9:24-26 [B]Zech 3:1-7 [C]Mic 4:13 5:1 [A]Jer 36:2; Ezek 2:9; Rev 5:1 5:2 [a]I.e. One cubit equals approx 18 in. [A]Zech 4:2 5:3 [a]Or *earth* [b]Lit *it* [A]Is 24:6; 43:28; Jer 26:6 [B]Ex 20:15; Lev 19:11; Mal 3:8, 9 [C]Lev 19:12; Is 48:1; Jer 5:2; Zech 5:4 5:4 [A]Mal 3:5 [B]Hos 4:2, 3 [C]Jer 2:26 [D]Lev 14:34, 35; Job 18:15 5:5 [A]Zech 1:9 5:6 [a]I.e. Approx one bu [b]Lit *eye;* some ancient versions read *iniquity* [c]Or *earth* [A]Lev 19:36; Amos 8:5 5:8 [a]Lit *mouth* [A]Hos 12:7; Amos 8:5; Mic 6:11 5:9 [A]Lev 11:13, 19; Ps 104:17; Jer 8:7 5:11 [a]Lit *house* [A]Gen 10:10; 11:2; 14:1; Is 11:11; Dan 1:2

Grace, grace to it! This blessing signifying shouts of joy and thanksgiving came to pass (cf. Ezr 3:11–13) over the completion of the temple. Contrast this attitude with that of the people seeing the unfinished temple (Hag 2:3).

4:9 me. This is the Angel of the Lord (*see note on 1:11*), the Protector, Deliverer, Defender of Israel, sent to bring this to fulfillment. In the future, He will come as Messiah to set up worship in the temple in His kingdom.

4:10 the day of small things. Though the rebuilding of a temple smaller than Solomon's may have been discouraging to some (cf. Ezr 3:12; Hag 2:3), the Lord announced that His pleasure was upon this work, and that His omniscient care was watching over and taking pleasure in its completion. He said in effect, "Don't despise what God is pleased with." This was only a picture of the glorious restoration when Messiah comes to reign. That temple will make all others pale by comparison (cf. Eze 40–48).

4:14 These are the two anointed ones. The two olive trees (vv. 3, 11) represent the kingly and priestly offices in Israel through which the blessing of God was to flow. The two olive branches (v. 12) are the two men who occupied the supreme positions in those offices at that time: Zerubbabel, as a descendant of David, and Joshua, the High Priest, a descendant of Eleazar. Together, they foreshadow the Messiah, in whom these two offices are combined (cf. 6:13; Ps 110) and who is the true source of blessing to make Israel the light to the nations (cf. Is 60:1–3). They had positions of responsibility in service to "the Lord of the whole earth," a millennial term that points to the final kingdom (cf. Mic 5:4).

5:1–4 This sixth vision of the flying scroll depicts the Word of God which has been disobeyed by Israel and the entire world. It calls for God's righteous judgment of the sinner according to His standard, clearly set forth in His Word.

5:1, 2 This flying scroll, unfurled for all to read both sides, measured 30 ft. long and 15 ft. wide (a cubit being 18 in.), exactly the size of the Holy Place in the tabernacle. The scroll represents, then, a divine standard by which man is to be measured.

5:3 curse. The scroll, symbolizing the law of God, is a figure for a curse or punishment on all who disobeyed it and for blessing on all who obeyed it (cf. Dt 27:26; 28:15–68). A similar picture is presented in Rev 5:1–9; 10:1–11. **everyone who steals … everyone who swears.** Written on both sides, the scroll probably contained the Ten Commandments, not just two. The two singled out, the third and eighth, are most likely representative of all commands of God's law for which Israel was guilty of violations (cf. Jas 2:10). It has an immediate message to those of Zechariah's time that God will root out and destroy the sinners who reject His Word; but it also has a future message for Israel and the world prior to Messiah's kingdom (cf. Eze 20:33–38; Mt 25:31–46).

5:4 There is no escape from the judgment of God. His Word will enter the place of sinners and remain there until it has accomplished its purpose (Is 55:10, 11), which will be particularly true in the kingdom. The promise of the land in Dt 30:1–10 will be fulfilled in the future day, as will consuming judgment (cf. Rev 6–19).

5:5–11 The previous vision dealt with the purging of sinners from the land. This seventh vision of a woman in a basket continues the theme, focusing on the removal of the whole sinful system from Israel, which will happen before the kingdom comes (cf. Eze 20:38).

5:5, 6 The wicked system is represented as a basket with a woman held captive inside under a lead cover. An ephah (basket) was smaller than a bushel, holding about 5 gallons. Like the flying scroll (cf. vv. 1–4), this was obviously enlarged for the purpose of the vision. The people of Israel are seen as pieces of grain, perhaps indicating that the wickedness is particularly materialistic. This was a sin that Israel picked up in Babylon, and it has influenced them through the centuries until removed by the Messiah in the last days. This secular commercialism is central to the final world system (cf. Rev 18).

5:7, 8 woman. Inside the basket was sitting a woman, personifying this final wickedness (cf. Rev 17:3–5), which is not dormant, since the lead cover is required to restrain it in the basket (cf. 2Th 2:6–8).

5:9 two women … wind in their wings. Since storks are unclean birds (Lv 11:19; Dt 14:18) these must be agents of evil, demonic forces, protective of the wicked secularism, who set up the final system of evil. God allows them to set up the world system that the Lord destroys when He returns (cf. Rev 19:11–16).

5:11 Shinar. The destination of the women bearing the basket was Shinar, an older word designating Babylon (cf. Ge 10:10). The older word is used possibly to recall the Tower of Babel as a symbol of opposition against

THE FOUR CHARIOTS

6 Now I lifted up my eyes again and looked, and
behold, [A]four chariots were coming forth from
between the two mountains; and the mountains
were bronze mountains. 2 With the first chariot *were*
[A]red horses, with the second chariot [B]black horses,
3 with the third chariot [A]white horses, and with the
fourth chariot strong [B]dappled horses. 4 Then I spoke
and said to the angel who was speaking with me,
"[A]What are these, my lord?" 5 The angel replied to
me, "These are the [A]four spirits of heaven, going
forth after standing before the Lord of all the earth,
6 with one of which the black horses are going forth
to the [A]north country; and the white ones go forth
after them, while the dappled ones go forth to the
[B]south country. 7 When the strong ones went out, they
[a]were eager to go to [b,A]patrol the earth." And He said,
"Go, [b]patrol the earth." So they [c]patrolled the earth.
8 Then He cried out to me and spoke to me saying,
"See, those who are going to the land of the north
have [a,A]appeased My wrath in the land of the north."
9 The [A]word of the LORD also came to me, saying,
10 "[A]Take *an offering* from the exiles, from Heldai,
Tobijah and Jedaiah; and you go the same day and
enter the house of Josiah the son of Zephaniah,
where they have arrived from Babylon.

THE SYMBOLIC CROWNS

11 Take silver and gold, make an *ornate* [A]crown
and set *it* on the head of [B]Joshua the son of Jehozadak, the high priest. 12 Then say to him, 'Thus says
the LORD of hosts, "Behold, a man whose name is
[a,A]Branch, for He will [b,B]branch out from where He
is; and He will [C]build the temple of the LORD. 13 Yes,
it is He who will build the temple of the LORD,
and He who will [A]bear the honor and sit and [B]rule
on His throne. Thus, He will be a [C]priest on His
throne, and the counsel of peace will be between
the two [a]offices." ' 14 Now the [A]crown will become
a reminder in the temple of the LORD to Helem,
Tobijah, Jedaiah and [a]Hen the son of Zephaniah.
15 [A]Those who are far off will come and [a]build
the temple of the LORD." Then you will [B]know
that the LORD of hosts has sent me to you. And it
will take place if you completely [C]obey the LORD
your God.

6:1 [A]Dan 7:3; 8:22; Zech 1:18; 6:5 6:2 [A]Zech 1:8; Rev 6:4 [B]Rev 6:5 6:3 [A]Rev 6:2 [B]Rev 6:8 6:4 [A]Zech 1:9 6:5 [A]Jer 49:36; Ezek 37:9; Dan 7:2; 11:4; Matt 24:31; Rev 7:1 6:6 [A]Jer 1:14, 15; 4:6; 6:1; 25:9; 46:10; Ezek 1:4 [B]Is 43:6; Dan 11:5 6:7 [a]Lit *sought to go* [b]Lit *walk about through* [c]Lit *walked about through* [A]Zech 1:10 6:8 [a]Lit *caused My spirit to rest in* [A]Ezek 5:13; 24:13; Zech 1:15 6:9 [A]Zech 1:1; 7:1; 8:1 6:10 [A]Ezra 7:14-16; 8:26-30; Jer 28:6 6:11 [A]2 Sam 12:30; Ps 21:3; Song 3:11 [B]Ezra 3:2; Hag 1:1; Zech 3:1 6:12 [a]Lit *Sprout* [b]Lit *sprout up* [A]Is 4:2; 11:1; Jer 23:5; 33:15; Zech 3:8 [B]Is 53:2 [C]Ezra 3:8, 10; Amos 9:11; Zech 4:6-9 6:13 [a]Lit *of them* [A]Is 9:6; 11:10; 22:24; 49:5, 6 [B]Is 9:7 [C]Ps 110:1, 4 6:14 [a]I.e. Josiah [A]Zech 6:11 6:15 [a]Lit *build in* [A]Is 56:6-8; 60:10 [B]Zech 2:9-11; 4:9 [C]Is 58:10-14; Jer 7:23; Zech 3:7

God (cf. Ge 11:2). There it will be placed in a "temple" and set on a base or pedestal as an idol. Again the vision is unmistakably looking forward to the final Babylon of Rev 17, 18 at the second coming of Christ (cf. Mal 4:1–3).

6:1–8 The eighth and final vision completes the cycle and connects with the first vision. It pictures 4 chariots with the horses introduced in the first vision (1:8), symbolizing God's angelic agents (cf. v. 5) swiftly carrying out His judgment on the nations just prior to the establishment of the messianic kingdom.

6:1 two mountains ... bronze. Representing the reality of God's judgment on the nations who attack Israel, the two mountains are probably Mt. Zion and the Mt. of Olives, where the Lord will return and judge (cf. Joel 3:2, 12, 14; Zec 14:4). This valley, called Jehoshaphat ("Jehovah judges") could refer to the Kidron Valley between these two mountains. Jews, Christians, and even Muslims have long taught that the last judgment will be there. The bronze has a symbolic relationship to judgment as in the case of the bronze serpent (Nu 21:9) and/or the bronze altar (Ex 27:2), where sin was dealt with by God.

6:2, 3 The judgment scene is further dramatized by these chariots and horses. For the significance of the horses' colors, *see note on 1:8*. The addition of "black" horses may represent famine and death. The "sorrel" horse has been replaced with "dappled" (i.e., spotted) horses. A similar picture is found in Rev 6:1–8, where the horsemen of the apocalypse appear in judgment imagery, riding forth in vengeance on the nations.

6:5 four spirits of heaven. This imagery represents divine angelic agents sent out to execute judgment on behalf of the "Lord of all the earth," a millennial title designating the universal rule of the Messiah in the kingdom age (cf. 4:14; Mic 4:13).

6:6, 7 going ... to patrol the earth. These angelic judgment carriers unleash catastrophic judgment on the earth (cf. Rev 6:1–19:16 for similarities). Nothing is said about going E and W because of the sea and the desert. Israel's enemies came from the N (Assyria, Babylon, Seleucids, and Romans) and the S (Egyptians). This N, S exit leads to a worldwide unleashing of judgment on the nations all over the earth (cf. Mt 25:31–46).

6:8 appeased My wrath. As a result of God's judgment of His enemies, His wrath can rest. God has been avenged by this action, particularly in regard to the power from the N being judged finally. This likely refers to the final Babylon (cf. Rev 17, 18). Until this judgment is done and God's wrath rests, the kingdom can't be established (Rev 19, 20) with the Messiah on His throne.

6:9–15 Joshua served as an illustration of the Messiah in this passage in that Zechariah's crowning of Joshua, the High Priest, was a miniature, advance illustration of the future coronation of Messiah, the Branch, who will unite the two offices of priest and king (v. 13). This appendix supplements visions 4 and 5 (3:1–10; 4:1–14) and culminates the series of 8 visions with the climax of history—the coronation of the Lord Jesus Christ.

6:10 *offering* from the exiles. Jewish exiles who remained in Babylon, but who had come bearing gifts for the building of the temple are identified. Zechariah was told to meet them that same day and receive their gifts.

6:11 an *ornate* crown. Zechariah was to make not a High Priest's crown or turban, but an ornate crown, one constructed of many circlets, a majestic crown (like the one on the returning Messiah in Rev 19:12). This crown was to be set on the head of the High Priest, Joshua. In the OT, the kingly and priestly offices were kept rigidly distinct. The office of king belonged only to the house of David, while the office of priest was only for the house of Levi. Uzziah's mingling of the two brought about his death (cf. 2Ch 26:16–23). But here this act is ordered by God to depict the coming King/Priest Messiah.

6:12 name is Branch. Though the crown was placed on the head of Joshua, the High Priest (v. 11), the act was a symbol of that future crowning of Messiah, the Branch (cf. 3:8). In Messiah, the offices of king and priest will be united.

6:12–15 In this brief section, 8 facts are given about Messiah, the Branch: 1) He will come from Israel (v. 12); 2) He will build the millennial temple (vv. 12b, 13a); 3) He will be glorious (v. 13); 4) He will be king and priest (v. 13); 5) He makes peace (v. 13); 6) He opens the kingdom to Gentiles (v. 15a); 7) He will corroborate God's Word (v. 15b); and 8) He demands obedience (v. 15c). This, as always, is the essential matter. After Israel believes, the Messiah will come to set up His kingdom (cf. 12:10–13:1; 14:9–21). Faith and cleansing must come first.

6:12, 13 He will build the temple. The building of the restoration temple was promised to Zerubbabel (cf. 4:9, 10). The building of this temple, promised to Messiah, points to the construction of the millennial temple (cf. Is 2:2–4; Eze 40–43; Hag 2:6–9).

6:14 The crown was not to be kept by Joshua, but was to serve as both a memorial to the devotion of the men who came from Babylon and, more importantly, as a reminder of the coming of Messiah and the ultimate hope of Israel. **Helem ... Hen.** Helem is apparently another name of Heldai, and Hen another name for Josiah the son of Zephaniah (see v. 10).

HEARTS LIKE FLINT

7 In the fourth year of King Darius, the word of the LORD came to Zechariah on the fourth *day* of the ninth month, *which is* [A]Chislev. 2 Now *the town of* Bethel had sent Sharezer and Regemmelech and [a]their men to [b,A]seek the favor of the LORD, 3 speaking to the [A]priests who belong to the house of the LORD of hosts, and to the prophets, saying, "Shall I weep in the [B]fifth month [a]and abstain, as I have done these many years?" 4 Then the word of the LORD of hosts came to me, saying, 5 "Say to all the people of the land and to the priests, 'When you fasted and mourned in the fifth and seventh months [a]these [A]seventy years, was it actually for [B]Me that you fasted? 6 When you eat and drink, [a]do you not eat for yourselves and do you not drink for yourselves? 7 Are not *these* the words which the LORD [A]proclaimed by the former prophets, when Jerusalem was inhabited and [a,B]prosperous along with its cities around it, and the [b,C]Negev and the [c]foothills were inhabited?' "

8 Then the word of the LORD came to Zechariah saying, 9 "Thus has the LORD of hosts said, '[A]Dispense true justice and practice [B]kindness and compassion each to his brother; 10 and [A]do not oppress the widow or the [a]orphan, the [b]stranger or the poor; and do [B]not devise evil in your hearts against one another.' 11 But they [A]refused to pay attention and [a,B]turned a stubborn shoulder and [b,C]stopped their ears from hearing. 12 They made their [A]hearts *like* [a,B]flint [b]so that they could not hear the law and the [C]words which the LORD of hosts had sent by His Spirit through the [D]former prophets; therefore great [E]wrath came from the LORD of hosts. 13 And just as [A]He called and they would not listen, so [B]they called and I would not listen," says the LORD of hosts; 14 "but I [a,A]scattered them with a [B]storm wind among all the nations whom they have not known. Thus the land is [C]desolated behind them [b]so that [D]no one went back and forth, for they [E]made the pleasant land desolate."

THE COMING PEACE AND PROSPERITY OF ZION

8 Then the word of the LORD of hosts came, saying, 2 "Thus says the LORD of hosts, 'I am [A]exceedingly jealous for Zion, yes, with great wrath I am jealous for her.' 3 Thus says the LORD, 'I will return to Zion and will [A]dwell in the midst of Jerusalem. Then Jerusalem will be called the City of

7:1 [A]Neh 1:1 7:2 [a]Lit *his* [b]Lit *soften the face of* [A]1 Kin 13:6; Jer 26:19; Zech 8:21 7:3 [a]Lit *abstaining;* or *dedicating myself* [A]Ezra 3:10-12 [B]Zech 8:19 7:5 [a]Lit *and these* [A]Zech 1:12 [B]Is 1:11, 12; 58:5 7:6 [a]Lit *is it not you who eat and you who drink* 7:7 [a]Or *at ease* [b]I.e. South country [c]Heb *Shephelah* [A]Is 1:16-20; Jer 7:5, 23; Zech 1:4 [B]Jer 22:21 [C]Jer 13:19; 32:44 7:9 [A]Ezek 18:8; 45:9; Zech 8:16 [B]2 Sam 9:7; Job 6:14; Mic 6:8 7:10 [a]Or *fatherless* [b]Or *resident alien* [A]Ex 22:22; Ps 72:4; Jer 7:6 [B]Ps 21:11; Mic 2:1; Zech 8:17 7:11 [a]Lit *gave* [b]Lit *made heavy* [A]Jer 5:3; 8:5; 11:10 [B]Jer 7:26; 17:23 [C]Ps 58:4; Jer 5:21 7:12 [a]Lit *corundum* [b]Lit *from hearing* [A]2 Chr 36:13; Ezek 2:4; 3:7-9 [B]Jer 17:1; Ezek 3:9 [C]Zech 7:7 [D]Neh 9:30 [E]2 Chr 36:16; Dan 9:11, 12 7:13 [A]Jer 11:10, 14; 14:12 [B]Prov 1:24-28; Is 1:15 7:14 [a]Lit *stormed them away upon all* [b]Lit *from passing and from returning* [A]Deut 4:27; 28:64 [B]Jer 23:19 [C]Jer 44:6 [D]Is 60:15 [E]Jer 12:10 8:2 [A]Zech 1:14 8:3 [A]Zech 2:10, 11

7:1–8:23 As a result of the night visions which described the future of Israel, including the subjugation of her enemies, the final regathering to the Land, her cleansing, restoration, and the coming of Messiah and His kingdom, the Jews were greatly encouraged and comforted. The temple was more than half done, all obstacles to the construction were removed by the decree of Darius confirming the decree of Cyrus (cf. Ezr 6:1–14), and all was going very well. This gave rise to a question by the delegation from Bethel. The question involved the continuation of a national fast to mourn the fall of Jerusalem and the destruction of the temple. Though Jerusalem had no walls yet and there were many ruins (cf. Hag 1:4), now that the temple was being finished, they were sent to inquire of the Lord and the priests whether they needed to continue the fast. The question is answered negatively in chap. 7 with two messages and positively in chap. 8 with two messages. Each of the 4 messages was given to impress upon the people the need to live righteously. As with chaps. 1–6, the prophet began historically and then moved prophetically to the time of the Second Advent of Christ.

7:1 the fourth year of King Darius. Nov./Dec. 518 B.C., two years after Zechariah's first message (cf. 1:1) and the night visions (cf. 1:7), and two years before the temple was completed.

7:2 Bethel. The town of Bethel was 12 mi. N of Jerusalem. Since the return from Babylon, the Jews had rebuilt and reinhabited Bethel (cf. Ezr 2:28; Ne 7:32).

7:3 weep in the fifth month and abstain. The Day of Atonement was the only annual fast required by God's law (Lv 23:27), and other occasional fasts were called for by God (cf. Joel 1:12, 14). The fall of Jerusalem was remembered by 4 fasts (cf. 2Ki 25; Jer 39:1–4; 41; 52:13), in the fourth, fifth, seventh, and tenth months (*see note on 8:19*). Because the temple was burned in the fifth month (July–Aug.), that fast was considered the most serious, and thus the delegation uses it as the test case (cf. 2Ki 25:8; Jer 52:12). They had kept this wailing and fasting for "many years," but it seemed only a wearisome ritual in light of the present prosperity.

7:5 seventh months. This fast mourned the death of Gedaliah, the governor appointed by Nebuchadnezzar (2Ki 25:22–26; Jer 41) after the fall of Jerusalem in 586 B.C.

7:5, 6 was it actually for Me that you fasted? Zechariah pointed out that they were not fasting out of genuine sorrow and repentance, but out of self-pity (cf. Is 1:10–15; 58:3–9).

7:7 words … the LORD proclaimed. The important matter is not ritual, but obedience. It is obedience to God's Word that brought in the past great joy, peace, and prosperity to Israel, and that covered the land during the time of David and Solomon. If the present generation in Zechariah's time substitutes ritual for obedience, they too will lose the joy, peace, and prosperity they were enjoying. **Negev … foothills.** A reference to the area S of Beersheba and the Mediterranean coastal plain, encompassing the land from S to W.

7:8–14 This is the second of the 4 messages in answer to the question (v. 3). Harkening back to his opening call (1:4) and to the warnings of earlier prophets (cf. Is 1:11–17; 58:1–7; Am 5:10–15), the prophet alerts the delegation to produce the fruits of righteousness that demonstrate obedience to God's Word (vv. 9, 10) and to revisit the actions of their fathers who deliberately rejected God's Word (vv. 11, 12a) which activated the fury of God against them (v. 12b). Cf. Dt 28:15–68; 2Ch 36:14–16.

7:12 by His Spirit. The Holy Spirit served a vital function in the revelation and inspiration of God's Word through human authors (cf. 1Co 2:10; 2Pe 1:21).

7:13 I would not listen. This reflects a severe form of God's wrath by which He abandons disobedient sinners. *See note on 11:9;* cf. Jdg 10:13, 14; 16:18–21; Pr 1:24–31; Hos 4:17; Mt 15:14; Ro 1:18–32.

7:14 I scattered them. This refers to the captivity and dispersion of the people and the desolation of the land in their absence (cf. Dt 30:3–10).

8:1–23 Continuing his response to the delegation from Bethel, Zechariah contrasted Israel's past judgment with the promised future restoration. In light of past captivity, the nation was to repent and live righteously; in light of promised future blessings, Israel is to repent and live righteously. The last two messages (vv. 1–17 and 18–23) look positively to the future, when Israel will be brought to a place of special blessing and fasts will become feasts.

8:2 jealous. *See note on 1:14.* This very strong language expresses the idea that God can't bear the estrangement from His chosen people brought about by their sin, nor can He always tolerate the enemies of Israel. His love for Israel is so great that He will come in full presence to Israel again and dwell with His people. Ezekiel had the vision of God leaving Jerusalem (Eze 8–11) and of His presence returning (43:1–5). **Zion.** The mountain on which ancient Jerusalem was built, which became a name for the city.

8:3 City of Truth. A city which is characterized by truth, both in word and in deed (vv. 8, 16) because it is ruled over by Messiah who is characterized by truth (Jn 14:6). **the Holy Mountain.** Zion is holy because the King who lives there is holy (Is 6:3).

[B]Truth, and the mountain of the LORD of hosts *will*
be called the Holy Mountain.' 4 Thus says the LORD
of hosts, '[A]Old men and old women will again sit in
the [a]streets of Jerusalem, each man with his staff
in his hand because of [b]age. 5 And the [a]streets of
the city will be filled with [A]boys and girls playing
in its [a]streets.' 6 Thus says the LORD of hosts, 'If it
is [a,A]too difficult in the sight of the remnant of this
people in those days, will it also be [a,B]too difficult in
My sight?' declares the LORD of hosts. 7 Thus says
the LORD of hosts, 'Behold, I am going to save My
people from the land of the [a,A]east and from the land
of the [b]west; 8 and I will [A]bring them *back* and they
will [B]live in the midst of Jerusalem; and they shall
be [C]My people, and I will be their God in [a]truth and
righteousness.'
9 "Thus says the LORD of hosts, 'Let your hands
be [A]strong, you who are listening in these days
to these words from the mouth of the [B]prophets,
those who *spoke* in the day that the foundation
of the house of the LORD of hosts was laid, to the
end that the temple might be built. 10 For before
those days there was [A]no wage for man or any
wage for animal; and for him who went out or
came in there was no [a,B]peace because of [b]his enemies, and I [C]set all men one against another. 11 But
now I will [A]not [a]treat the remnant of this people
as in the former days,' declares the LORD of hosts.

8:3 [B]Zech 8:16, 19 8:4 [a]Or *squares* [b]Lit *the multitude of days* [A]Is 65:20 8:5 [a]Or *squares* [A]Jer 30:19, 20; 31:12, 13 8:6 [a]Or *wonderful* [A]Ps 118:23; 126:1-3 [B]Jer 32:17, 27 8:7 [a]Lit *rising* [b]Lit *setting sun* [A]Ps 107:3; Is 11:11; 27:12, 13; 43:5 8:8 [a]Or *faithfulness* [A]Zeph 3:20; Zech 10:10 [B]Jer 3:17; Ezek 37:25 [C]Ezek 11:20; 36:28; Zech 2:11 8:9 [A]1 Chr 22:13; Is 35:4; Hag 2:4 [B]Ezra 5:1; 6:14 8:10 [a]Or *safety* [b]Lit *the adversary* [A]Hag 2:15-19 [B]2 Chr 15:5 [C]Is 19:2; Amos 3:6; 9:4 8:11 [a]Lit *be to the* [A]Ps 103:9; Is 12:1; Hag 2:19

8:4, 5 The most defenseless of society will live in tranquility, peace, and security (cf. Is 65:20–22).

8:6 Men tend to limit God (cf. Ps 78:19, 20, 41), but nothing is too hard for the Lord (cf. Ge 18:14; Jer 32:17, 27). "Just because they seem too difficult for you," the Lord asks, in effect, "Must they be too hard for Me?"

8:7, 8 east … west. The context assures that this return speaks of a worldwide regathering at the Second Advent of Christ. The return from Babylon cannot be in view also, since Israel had not been scattered to the W until the diaspora engineered by the Romans in the first century A.D.

8:8 *See note on Zec 1:3.* This refers to Israel's national conversion, spoken of in 12:10–13:1, and by Jeremiah (32:38–41) and Paul (Ro 11:25–27).

8:9–17 The practical results of vv. 1–8 were laid out for the people. In view of such a glorious future, the people were exhorted to renew their energy toward the building of the temple and toward righteous living.

8:9 the prophets. This refers to Haggai and Zechariah for sure; possibly there were non-writing prophets also.

8:10, 11 Zechariah recalled the immediate years prior to 520 B.C., described in Hag 1:6–11, when their hassles and intrigues with the Samaritans and their love of ease and comfort developed indifference toward building the temple, resulting in divine punishment. But, since they had begun again to build the temple, God would not treat the people as He had those described in v. 10.

OTHER NAMES FOR JERUSALEM
Lit. "The city of peace"
· The city of our God (Ps 48:1)
· The city of the great King (Ps 48:2)
· The city of the LORD of hosts (Ps 48:8)
· Salem (Ps 76:2)
· Zion (Ps 76:2)
· The city of righteousness (Is 1:26)
· The faithful city (Is 1:26)
· Ariel, i.e., Lion of God (Is 29:1)
· The holy city (Is 52:1)
· City of the LORD (Is 60:14)
· "My delight is in her" (Is 62:4)
· The Throne of the LORD (Jer 3:17)
· The LORD is our righteousness (Jer 33:16)
· The perfection of beauty (La 2:15)
· The joy to all the whole earth (La 2:15)
· The LORD is there [YHWH Shammah] (Eze 48:35)
· City of Truth (Zec 8:3)
· The Holy Mountain (Zec 8:3)

12 'For *there will be* [A]peace for the seed: the vine will
yield its fruit, the land will yield its produce and the
heavens will give their [B]dew; and I will cause the
remnant of this people to inherit [C]all these *things*.
13 It will come about that just as you were a [A]curse
among the nations, O house of Judah and house
of Israel, so I will save you that you may become a
[B]blessing. Do not fear; let your [C]hands be strong.'
14 "For thus says the LORD of hosts, 'Just as I [A]pur-
posed to do harm to you when your fathers provoked Me to wrath,' says the LORD of hosts, 'and I
have not [B]relented, 15 so I have again purposed in
these days to [A]do good to Jerusalem and to the house
of Judah. [B]Do not fear! 16 These are the things which
you should do: speak the [A]truth to one another;
[B]judge with truth and judgment for peace in your
[a]gates. 17 Also let none of you [A]devise evil in your
heart against another, and do not love [a,B]perjury;
for all these are what I [C]hate,' declares the LORD."
18 Then the word of the LORD of hosts came to
me, saying, 19 "Thus says the LORD of hosts, 'The
fast of the [A]fourth, the fast of the [B]fifth, the fast of
the [C]seventh and the fast of the [D]tenth *months* will
become [E]joy, gladness, and [a]cheerful feasts for the
house of Judah; so [F]love truth and peace.'
20 "Thus says the LORD of hosts, '*It will* yet *be* that
[A]peoples will come, even the inhabitants of many
cities. 21 The inhabitants of one will go to another,
saying, "Let us go at once to [A]entreat the favor of
the LORD, and to seek the LORD of hosts; [a]I will also
go." 22 So [A]many peoples and mighty nations will
come to seek the LORD of hosts in Jerusalem and
to [B]entreat the favor of the LORD.' 23 Thus says the
LORD of hosts, 'In those days ten men from all the
[a]nations will [b,A]grasp the [c]garment of a Jew, saying,
"Let us go with you, for we have heard that God is
with you." ' "

PROPHECIES AGAINST NEIGHBORING NATIONS

9 The [a]burden of the word of the LORD is against
the land of Hadrach, with [A]Damascus as its resting place (for the eyes of men, especially of all the
tribes of Israel, are toward the LORD),

2 And [A]Hamath also, which borders on it;
[B]Tyre and [C]Sidon, [a]though
[b]they are [B]very wise.
3 For Tyre built herself a [A]fortress
And [B]piled up silver like dust,
And [C]gold like the mire of the streets.
4 Behold, the Lord will [A]dispossess her
And cast her wealth into the sea;
And she will be [B]consumed with fire.

8:12 [A]Lev 26:3-6 [B]Gen 27:28; Deut 33:13, 28; Hos 13:3 [C]Is 61:7; Obad 17 8:13 [A]Jer 29:18; Dan 9:11 [B]Ps 72:17; Is 19:24, 25; Ezek 34:26; Zech 14:11 [C]Zech 8:9 8:14 [A]Jer 31:28 [B]Jer 4:28; Ezek 24:14 8:15 [A]Jer 29:11; Mic 7:18-20 [B]Zech 8:13 8:16 [a]I.e. the place where court was held [A]Ps 15:2; Prov 12:17-19; Zech 8:3; Eph 4:25 [B]Is 9:7; 11:4, 5; Zech 7:9 8:17 [a]Lit *false oath* [A]Prov 3:29; Jer 4:14; Zech 7:10 [B]Zech 5:4; Mal 3:5 [C]Prov 6:16-19; Hab 1:13 8:19 [a]Or *goodly* [A]2 Kin 25:3, 4; Jer 39:2 [B]Zech 7:3, 5 [C]2 Kin 25:25; Zech 7:5 [D]Jer 52:4 [E]Ps 30:11; Is 12:1 [F]Zech 8:16; Luke 1:74, 75 8:20 [A]Ps 117:1; Jer 16:19; Mic 4:2, 3; Zech 2:11; 14:16 8:21 [a]Or *let me go too* [A]Zech 7:2 8:22 [A]Is 2:2, 3; 25:7; 49:6, 22, 23; 60:3-12 [B]Zech 8:21 8:23 [a]Lit *languages of the nations* [b]Lit *grasp, and they will grasp* [c]Or *corner of the garment* [A]Is 45:14, 24; 60:14 9:1 [a]Or *oracle* [A]Is 17:1; Jer 49:23-27; Amos 1:3-5 9:2 [a]Or *because* [b]I.e. they think they are [A]Jer 49:23 [B]Ezek 28:2-5, 12 [C]Ezek 28:21 9:3 [A]Josh 19:29; 2 Sam 24:7 [B]Job 27:16; Ezek 27:33; 28:4, 5 [C]1 Kin 10:21, 27 9:4 [A]Ezek 26:3-5 [B]Ezek 28:18

8:12, 13 The richness and comprehensiveness of these promises of prosperity look beyond the historical moment to the time when Messiah reigns in His millennial kingdom. This will be a reversal of Dt 28:15–68 and Jer 24:9; 25:18; 29:22.

8:14, 15 The sorrows of past judgment became the pledges of future blessings (cf. Jer 32:42).

8:16, 17 As always, the promised blessings are connected with obedience to God's righteous standards. Such obedience can only be brought about by the power of the Spirit in the life of one who has been transformed by God's grace through faith. These standards are reminiscent of Pss 15:1–5; 24:4; Pr 6:20–22.

8:18, 19 The fourth and final response to the delegation from Bethel notes how national days of fasting and mourning will be transformed into joyous feasts. This was really the answer to the original question in 7:3. Turn the fasts into feasts of joy in light of the promised blessings of God.

8:19 In addition to the fasts of the fifth and seventh months (*see notes on 7:3, 5*), two additional fasts were held. In the fourth month they commemorated the breaching of the wall of Jerusalem (2Ki 25:3; Jer 39:2–4) and in the tenth month they remembered the beginning of the final siege of Jerusalem which began in 588 B.C. (2Ki 25:1; Jer 39:1).

8:20–22 Israel restored in millennial glory will be the means of blessing to all the world (cf. Is 2:2–4; Mic 4:1–5). Gentiles from around the world will make a pilgrimage to Jerusalem to entreat the Lord. This signifies salvation of people from all over the world during the kingdom, fulfilling Ps 122.

8:23 In those days. In the days in which the messianic kingdom on earth is inaugurated (*see note on Joel 3:18*), the Jews will truly be God's messengers as originally intended, and will bring multitudes to Christ. The 10 to 1 ratio represents a vast number of Gentiles who will come (cf. Ge 31:7; Lv 26:26; Nu 14:22; 1Sa 1:8; Ne 4:12). The Messiah, in the midst of millennial Israel, will be the attraction of the world. People, seeing the Jews so blessed in their kingdom, will demand to go and meet the Savior King.

9:1–14:21 Employing the phrase "in that day," Zechariah places primary focus in his final two undated oracles on: 1) the downfall of the nation; 2) the salvation of Israel; and 3) the establishment of the Messiah as King. The first oracle (9:1–11:17) deals with the first and third features and ends with prophecies of the rejection of Christ at His first coming; the second oracle (12:1–14:21) deals with the second and third culminating with the kingdom of Messiah Christ.

9:1–8 This oracle features a series of judgments announced against the nations surrounding Israel (vv. 1–7), with deliverance promised for His people (v. 8). Most understand this to be a prophecy of the famous Greek conqueror, Alexander the Great's victories, given approximately 200 years before he marched through Israel. He provides an analogy of Christ returning to judge the nations and save Israel at the end of the Great Tribulation (cf. Mt 24:21).

9:1 burden. A heavy, burdensome message (i.e., oracle), the prediction of a threatening event, in this case the judgment of the nations. **Hadrach.** The location is uncertain. Possibly it is ancient Hatarika, a city mentioned in the annals of Assyrian Kings, in the vicinity of Hamath. The old Jewish tradition made it a compound name, *Had* meaning sharp and *rach* meaning soft. The sharp/soft land could be a reference to the dual Medo-Persian kingdom. Media was thought to be the sharp side because of its powerful conquerors like Cyrus, and Persia the soft side because of its debauchery. The cities in vv. 1, 2 were major cities under Medo-Persian power. **Damascus.** This city was to be the main target of the judgment of God through Alexander upon the capital of Syria, one of Israel's worst enemies from ca. 900–722 B.C. **the eyes of men . . . are toward the LORD.** God's judgment through Alexander the Great would be visible to all mankind, especially Israel.

9:2 Hamath. A major city, 125 mi. N of Damascus on the Orontes River. Alexander conquered these cities of the Syrian interior under Medo-Persian control, then turned to the coast moving S, conquering the cities of the Phoenicians and Philistines on the way to Egypt. **Tyre and Sidon . . . are very wise.** These Phoenician cities on the Mediterranean coast were known for their skill and wisdom (cf. Eze 28:12–15) and Satanic influence (Eze 28:11–19).

9:3, 4 Tyre. This city was occupying an island one-half mile offshore, and thought itself to be invincible (cf. Is 23:1–4). With walls 150 ft. high in some places, it was such

5 Ashkelon will see *it* and be afraid.
Gaza too will writhe in great pain;
Also Ekron, for her expectation
has been confounded.
Moreover, the king will perish from Gaza,
And Ashkelon will not be inhabited.
6 And a [a]mongrel race will dwell in [A]Ashdod,
And I will cut off the pride
of the Philistines.
7 And I will remove their blood
from their mouth
And their detestable things
from between their teeth.
Then they also will be a
remnant for our God,
And be like a [a]clan in Judah,
And Ekron like a Jebusite.
8 But I will camp around My house
[a]because of an army,
Because of [A]him who passes
by and returns;
And [B]no oppressor will pass
over them anymore,
For now I have seen with My eyes.
9 [A]Rejoice greatly, O daughter of Zion!
Shout *in triumph,* O daughter
of Jerusalem!
Behold, your [B]king is coming to you;
He is [a,C]just and [D]endowed with salvation,
[E]Humble, and mounted on a donkey,
Even on a [F]colt, the [b]foal of a donkey.
10 I will [A]cut off the chariot from Ephraim
And the [B]horse from Jerusalem;
And the [C]bow of war will be cut off.
And He will speak [D]peace to the nations;
And His [E]dominion will be
from sea to sea,
And from the [a]River to the
ends of the earth.

DELIVERANCE OF JUDAH AND EPHRAIM

11 As for you also, because of the [A]blood
of *My* covenant with you,
I have set your [B]prisoners free
from the [a]waterless pit.
12 Return to the [a,A]stronghold,
O prisoners [b]who have the [B]hope;
This very day I am declaring that
I will restore [C]double to you.
13 For I will [A]bend Judah [a]as My bow,
I will fill the bow with Ephraim.
And I will stir up your sons, O Zion,
against your sons, O [B]Greece;
And I will make you like a
[C]warrior's sword.
14 Then the LORD will appear [A]over them,
And His [B]arrow will go forth
like lightning;
And the Lord [a]GOD will blow the [C]trumpet,
And will march in the [D]storm
winds of the south.

9:6 [a]Lit *bastard will* [A]Amos 1:8; Zeph 2:4 9:7 [a]Or *chief* 9:8 [a]Or *as a guard, so that none will go back and forth* [A]Is 52:1 [B]Is 54:14; 60:18 9:9 [a]Or *vindicated and victorious* [b]Lit *son of a female donkey* [A]Zeph 3:14, 15; Zech 2:10 [B]Ps 110:1; Is 9:6, 7; Jer 23:5, 6; Matt 21:5; John 12:15 [C]Zeph 3:5 [D]Is 43:3, 11 [E]Is 57:15 [F]Judg 10:4; Is 30:6 9:10 [a]I.e. Euphrates [A]Hos 1:7 [B]Mic 5:10 [C]Hos 2:18 [D]Is 57:19; Mic 4:2-4 [E]Ps 72:8; Is 60:12 9:11 [a]Lit *cistern in which there is no water* [A]Ex 24:8; Heb 10:2 [B]Is 24:22; 51:14 9:12 [a]Or *Stronghold* [b]Lit *of the hope* [A]Jer 16:19; Joel 3:16 [B]Jer 14:8; 17:13; Heb 6:18, 19 [C]Is 61:7 9:13 [a]Lit *for Me* [A]Jer 51:20 [B]Joel 3:6 [C]Ps 45:3 9:14 [a]Heb *YHWH*, usually rendered *LORD* [A]Is 31:5; Zech 2:5 [B]Ps 18:14; Hab 3:11 [C]Is 27:13 [D]Is 21:1; 66:15

an impregnable city that the Assyrian Shalmaneser besieged it for 5 years and failed to conquer it. Nebuchadnezzar tried for 13 years unsuccessfully. But Alexander, God's judgment instrument, using the rubble of the mainland city destroyed by Nebuchadnezzar, built a causeway out to the island and destroyed it in 7 months (ca. 334–332 B.C.).

9:5, 6 The cities of Philistia were terrified at the swiftness with which Alexander the Great's army was able to conquer Tyre. Then, Alexander marched S, conquering all these Philistine cities and killing their national pride.

9:7 This judgment put an end to idolatry for many Philistines who turned to the God of Israel. In the imagery of this verse, the nation is seen as a man with blood in his mouth (from eating sacrifices to idols) and abominations (the other defiled food of idol worship) which are removed. The picture is of conversion to worship the true God. **like a Jebusite.** These ancient inhabitants of Jerusalem were conquered by David (cf. 2Sa 5:6–11) and amalgamated into Israel. So it will be with these Philistines.

9:8 This is the pledge of God's protection of Jerusalem from Alexander. It came true when, on his way S, Alexander treated Jerusalem with kindness. After having subjugated Egypt, he returned through Israel again without doing Israel harm. **no oppressor will pass over them anymore.** The supernatural and lasting protection here promised must anticipate the Second Advent of Messiah, whose coming is the subject through the rest of this message. The transition from Alexander to Christ can be understood in this way: if God can use a pagan king to judge the nations and save Israel, how much more will He use His righteous Messiah? So v. 8 bridges to the final judgment and deliverance of Messiah.

9:9, 10 The two advents of Christ are here compressed as though they were one as in Is 61:1–3 (cf. Lk 4:16, 21). Actually, v. 9 refers to His first coming and v. 10 is His second. OT prophets didn't see the great time period between the two comings. The church age was a "mystery" hidden from them (cf. Eph 3:1–9; Col 1:27).

9:9 king … mounted on a donkey. Unlike Alexander the Great, this King comes riding on a donkey (cf. Jer 17:25). This was fulfilled at Christ's triumphal entry (Mt 21:1–5; Jn 12:12–16). The Jews should have been looking for someone from the line of David (cf. 2Sa 7; 1Ch 17). Four elements in this verse describe Messiah's character: 1) He is King; 2) He is just; 3) He brings salvation; and 4) He is humble.

9:10–15 Zechariah moves to the Second Advent of Christ and the establishment of His universal kingdom (*see notes on 9:9, 10; 11:15, 16*). Not characterized by bloodshed, Messiah's rule will be a kingdom of peace in which weapons of warfare will be destroyed or converted to peaceful uses (cf. Is 2:4; 9:5–7; 11:1–10; Mic 5:2, 10–15), and peace spreads from the Euphrates River (the terminus of civilization) to the world.

9:10 Ephraim. This is another name for Israel, used often in the OT for the northern kingdom and occasionally for the whole nation.

9:11 blood of *My* covenant. Why is Israel to be so blessed? It is not because of her faithfulness through the centuries, but because of God's unfailing devotion to His covenant of blood made with Abraham (Ge 15:1–10), which is in force as long as God lives. **from the waterless pit.** Prisoners in ancient times were often kept in dry wells or pits, as Joseph was (Ge 37:24, 28). The exiles of Israel, pictured as being in a dry well of captivity, suffering, and despair, will be freed because of His unbreakable covenant with them. They are thus called "prisoners who have the hope" (v. 12) who are to receive "double" blessing (cf. Is 61:7).

9:13–15 Reminiscent of the Exodus (Ex 19:16–19; Hab 3:3–15), the Lord will protect and empower them (cf. Is 11:11–16; Zec 12:6, 8). The initial historical fulfillment of this prophecy came when the Maccabees defeated the Greeks ca. 167 B.C.; the final, complete fulfillment will occur at His Second Advent. The Maccabean triumph is only a pledge and a preview of final triumph over all enemies.

15 [A]The LORD of hosts will defend them.
And they will [B]devour and trample
on the [C]sling stones;
And they will drink *and* be
[D]boisterous as with wine;
And they will be filled like
a *sacrificial* basin,
Drenched like the [E]corners of the altar.
16 And the LORD their God will
[A]save them in that day
As the flock of His people;
For *they are as* the stones of a [B]crown,
[a]Sparkling in His land.
17 For what [a,A]comeliness and
[B]beauty *will be* [b]theirs!
Grain will make the young men
flourish, and new wine the virgins.

GOD WILL BLESS JUDAH AND EPHRAIM

10 Ask [A]rain from the LORD at the
time of the spring rain—
The LORD who [B]makes the [a]storm clouds;
And He will give them [C]showers of rain,
vegetation in the field to *each* man.
2 For the [A]teraphim speak [a]iniquity,
And the [B]diviners see [b]lying visions
And tell [C]false dreams;
They comfort in vain.
Therefore *the people* [c]wander like [D]sheep,
They are afflicted, because
there is no shepherd.
3 "My [A]anger is kindled against the shepherds,
And I will punish the [a]male goats;
For the LORD of hosts has [B]visited
His flock, the house of Judah,
And will make them like His
majestic horse in battle.
4 "From [a]them will come the [A]cornerstone,
From [a]them the tent peg,
From [a]them the bow of [B]battle,
From [a]them every [b]ruler, *all*
of them together.
5 "They will be as mighty men,
[A]Treading down *the enemy* in the
mire of the streets in battle;
And they will fight, for the
LORD *will be* with them;
And the [B]riders on horses
will be put to shame.
6 "I will [A]strengthen the house of Judah,
And I will [B]save the house of Joseph,
And I will [a,C]bring them back,
Because I have had [D]compassion on them;
And they will be as though I
had [E]not rejected them,
For I am the LORD their God
and I will [F]answer them.
7 "Ephraim will be like a mighty man,
And their heart will be glad as if *from* wine;
Indeed, their [A]children will
see *it* and be glad,
[a]Their heart will rejoice in the LORD.
8 "I will [A]whistle for them to
gather them together,
For I have redeemed them;
And they will be as [B]numerous
as they [a,C]were before.

9:15 [A]Is 37:35; Zech 12:8 [B]Zech 12:6 [C]Job 41:28 [D]Ps 78:65 [E]Ex 27:2 9:16 [a]Or *Displayed over* [A]Jer 31:10, 11 [B]Is 62:3 9:17 [a]Lit *goodness* [b]Lit *his* [A]Jer 31:12, 14 [B]Ps 27:4; Is 33:17 10:1 [a]Or *thunderbolts* [A]Joel 2:23 [B]Jer 10:13 [C]Is 30:23 10:2 [a]Or *futility* [b]Lit *a lie* [c]Lit *journey* [A]Ezek 21:21; Hos 3:4 [B]Jer 27:9 [C]Jer 23:32 [D]Ezek 34:5, 8; Matt 9:36; Mark 6:34 10:3 [a]I.e. leaders [A]Jer 25:34-36 [B]Ezek 34:12 10:4 [a]Lit *him* [b]Or *oppressor* [A]Luke 20:17; Eph 2:20; 1 Pet 2:6 [B]Jer 51:20; Zech 9:10 10:5 [A]2 Sam 22:43 [B]Amos 2:15; Hag 2:22 10:6 [a]Or *make them dwell* [A]Zech 10:12 [B]Zech 8:7; 9:16 [C]Zech 8:8 [D]Is 54:8; Zech 1:16 [E]Is 54:4 [F]Zech 13:9 10:7 [a]Or *Let their heart rejoice* [A]Is 54:13; Ezek 37:25 10:8 [a]Lit *were numerous* [A]Is 5:26; 7:18, 19 [B]Jer 33:22; Rev 7:9 [C]Jer 30:20; Ezek 36:11

9:15 trample on … sling stones. This may mean the Jews will easily subdue their enemies as David did Goliath (1Sa 17). Or better, it could mean they will contemptuously tread on the harmless missiles cast at them by their enemies. This could depict the futility of Armageddon when the armies of the God-hating world gather in Israel and are destroyed by the Messiah (cf. Rev 16:12–16; 19:11–16). The bloodshed of the godless will be visible in that day, from one end of the land to the other, like blood splattered on the corners of the altar of sacrifice from basins which caught it when the animal was slain (cf. Rev 14:20). **drink … be boisterous.** This describes Israel's excitement and exuberance over their victory.

9:16, 17 Abundant prosperity, such as the world has never seen, results in excessive rejoicing, and praise results from God "saving" His people, Israel (cf. Dt 33:28; Ps 4:7, 8).

10:1 Ask rain from the LORD. In light of the promised blessings of 9:17, the prophet encourages the people to request these blessings from the Lord, with confidence. There will be literal rain and spring rain (Apr./May) in the kingdom (cf. Is 35:1–7) making the land flourish, but the promise here extends to refer to spiritual blessings (cf Hos 6:1–3). The "spring rain" of spiritual grace and goodness from God will bring refreshment to people's souls (cf. Is 44:3).

10:2 teraphim … diviners. In contrast to God who provides abundance, idols or household gods (cf. Ge 31:19, 34) and demonic fortunetellers left Israel as sheep without a shepherd (cf. Eze 34:6–10). God will judge them all for that false leadership (v. 3). The implication of these words is that a similar deception will occur in the end times. The NT confirms this (cf. Mt 24:5, 11, 22–28; 2Th 1:8–12).

10:3 majestic horse. Though like sheep, Israel will become like an invincible majestic warhorse when strengthened by the Lord to conquer His foes (12:8).

10:4 cornerstone. A frequently used messianic title (cf. Is 28:16; Eph 2:20; 1Pe 2:6–8). Christ is the foundation on which His kingdom rests. **tent peg.** This may refer to a peg attached to the tent's center pole on which utensils and valuables were hung. Messiah is the peg in the midst of His kingdom, for all the glory of the kingdom will hang on Him (cf. 6:13; Is 22:23–24). **bow of battle … ruler.** Another reference to the Messiah (cf. 9:13; Rev 19:11–16), under whose authority every ruler will be sanctioned.

10:5 the LORD *will be* with them. The prophet pictured foot soldiers overpowering the cavalry (cf. 12:1–9) in battle. This analogy was to illustrate the power of God's people when He is "with them."

10:6 house of Judah … Joseph. Both the southern and northern kingdoms of Israel will be restored to a position of blessing, as the whole nation is restored in millennial blessing (cf. Jer 32:37). **I am the LORD their God.** The reason for Israel's restoration was because of God, the covenant keeper, who gave a strong reiteration of His continuing, unconditional commitment to them. The curses of Dt 28:15–68 expressed in the Assyrian and Babylonian deportations did not abrogate God's promised blessings to Israel or transfer them to another people. Even after they had crucified the Messiah, Peter told them they were still able to receive the promise (cf. Ac 2:39) because the Abrahamic Covenant was still in place and they were the people of God's promise (Ac 3:25).

10:7 The joy of the restored nation of Israel at the beginning of the Millennium is likened to those who have been drinking wine (cf. Is 66:10–14; Zep 3:14–20).

10:8 I will whistle for them. The prophecy summarized what had been said, namely the Messiah's call for Israel to be redeemed and

9 "When I [a]scatter them among the peoples,
They will [A]remember Me in far countries,
And they with their children
will live and come back.
10 "I will [A]bring them back from
the land of Egypt
And gather them from Assyria;
And I will bring them into the
land of [B]Gilead and Lebanon
[a]Until [C]no *room* can be found for them.
11 "And they will pass through
the [A]sea *of* distress
And He will strike the waves in the sea,
So that all the depths of the
[B]Nile will dry up;
And the pride of [C]Assyria
will be brought down
And the scepter of [D]Egypt will depart.
12 "And I will [A]strengthen them in the LORD,
And in His name [B]they will
walk," declares the LORD.

THE DOOMED FLOCK

11 Open your doors, O Lebanon,
That a [A]fire may feed on your [B]cedars.
2 Wail, O [a]cypress, for the cedar has fallen,
Because the glorious *trees*
have been destroyed;
Wail, O oaks of Bashan,
For the [b]impenetrable forest
has come down.
3 There is a sound of the
shepherds' [A]wail,
For their glory is ruined;
There is a [B]sound of the
young lions' roar,
For the [a]pride of the Jordan
is ruined.

4 Thus says the LORD my God, "Pasture the flock
doomed to [A]slaughter. 5 Those who buy them slay
them and [a]go [A]unpunished, and *each of* those who
sell them says, 'Blessed be the LORD, for [B]I have
become rich!' And their [C]own shepherds have no
pity on them. 6 For I will [A]no longer have pity on
the inhabitants of the land," declares the LORD;
"but behold, I will [B]cause the men to [a]fall, each into
another's [b]power and into the [b]power of his king;
and they will strike the land, and I will [C]not deliver
them from their [b]power."
7 So I [A]pastured the flock *doomed* to slaughter, [a]hence
the [B]afflicted of the flock. And I took for myself two
[C]staffs: the one I called [b,D]Favor and the other I called
[c,E]Union; so I pastured the flock. 8 Then I annihilated
the three shepherds in [A]one month, for my soul was
impatient with them, and their soul also [a]was weary

10:9 [a]Lit *sow* [A]1 Kin 8:47, 48; Ezek 6:9 10:10 [a]Lit *And* [A]Is 11:11 [B]Jer 50:19 [C]Is 49:19, 20 10:11 [A]Is 51:9, 10 [B]Is 19:5-7 [C]Zeph 2:13 [D]Ezek 30:13 10:12 [A]Zech 10:6 [B]Mic 4:5 11:1 [A]Jer 22:6, 7 [B]Ezek 31:3 11:2 [a]Or *juniper* [b]Another reading is *forest of the vintage* 11:3 [a]Or *jungle* [A]Jer 25:34-36 [B]Jer 2:15; 50:44 11:4 [A]Ps 44:22; Zech 11:7 11:5 [a]Lit *are not held guilty* [A]Jer 50:7 [B]Hos 12:8; 1 Tim 6:9 [C]Ezek 34:2, 3 11:6 [a]Lit *find* [b]Lit *hand* [A]Jer 13:14 [B]Is 9:19-21; Mic 7:2-6; Zech 14:13 [C]Ps 50:22; Mic 5:8 11:7 [a]Another reading is *for the sheep dealers* [b]Or *Pleasantness* [c]Or *Cords* [A]Zech 11:4 [B]Jer 39:10; Zeph 3:12 [C]Ezek 37:16 [D]Ps 27:4; 90:17; Zech 11:10 [E]Ps 133:1; Ezek 37:16-23; Zech 11:14 11:8 [a]Or *detested* [A]Hos 5:7

for them to regather in His land (cf. Is 5:26). As in Egypt (cf. Ex 1:8–22), those of Israel who are protected by God because of their faith in Messiah will survive the Tribulation and enter the Millennium to multiply greatly (cf. 2:4; Is 54:1–3).

10:9, 10 Another summary is given stating that, as God had previously scattered them all over the world (A.D. 70), He would bring them back to populate His messianic kingdom (cf. Is 11:11, 12; 49:20–22).

10:11 Similar to Israel crossing the Red Sea, God will remove both geographical and political obstacles to Israel's return for the Kingdom of Messiah. Assyria and Egypt, traditional enemies of Israel, symbolize any nation that would try to withstand God from fulfilling His will (cf. Is 11:11, 12).

10:12 **in His name they will walk.** The people of Israel will be the messengers of their Messiah in the millennial kingdom. This is the complete spiritual restoration spoken of by Ezekiel (cf. Eze 36:21–38; 37:1–14, 22–28).

11:1–17 In stark contrast to chaps. 9, 10, in which Messiah is pictured as a wonderful Shepherd, this passage presents an ugly picture of the rejection of the Messiah, the true Shepherd. The prophet turns from the glories of the accepted Messiah at His second coming to the national apostasy and rejection of Messiah at His first coming.

11:1–3 As a fire sweeping down to ravage the whole land of Israel, Zechariah described a fire of judgment that would consume the ungodly as a conflagration consumes trees. The devastation is not limited to spiritual judgment only, but includes the death of people as the land of Israel is judged. The language is the book's most poetic. "Lebanon," "Bashan," and "Jordan" represent the whole land as judgment sweeps from top to bottom covering the entire nation from the north, inland, and down the Jordan Valley to the southern border.

11:2 **Wail, O cypress.** If the mighty cedars have fallen, surely the more vulnerable smaller trees will be unable to stand. **oaks of Bashan.** The poem moves from Lebanon, on the northern border of Israel, to Bashan, E of the Sea of Galilee, known for its oaks and lush pastures (cf. Am 4:1; Mic 7:14).

11:3 **shepherds' wail.** The shepherds lament the loss of their pastures, and the young lions their homes and food. Both are poetic figures of the misery that will occur in the land under the ravaging judgment. As the chapter unfolds, it becomes clear that this most likely prophesies the destruction of Jerusalem in A.D. 70 and the subsequent devastation of the whole land, which resulted in the dissolution of the Jewish state.

11:4–14 The cause for the calamity of vv. 1–3 is here given: the rejection of the true Shepherd. God used the prophet Zechariah as an actor playing the part of a shepherd to illustrate the true Shepherd, Jesus Christ, and the rejection He encountered. Instructions given in vv. 4–6 are enacted in vv. 7–14.

11:4–6 The Lord God said that His people were to be treated like sheep fattened for the slaughter, whose shepherds have no pity, but are only interested in money for the meat. Thus God will serve up His sheep for slaughter without pity. With God's pity (cf. Hos 1:6) and protection withdrawn, they will be given over to their Roman "neighbors" and to their "King" Caesar (cf. Jn 19:14, 15), who will ultimately lead them to their destruction in A.D. 70 by the Roman army (cf. Jn 11:47–50). Over one million Jews were slaughtered in that assault, and almost half a million in subsequent Roman attacks in Israel.

11:7–14 Here is the record of Zechariah playing a dramatic role to act out the rejection of Christ that will lead to the judgment of Israel outlined in vv. 1–3.

11:7 **I pastured the flock.** The prophet did feed the truth of God to his people as a picture of what Messiah would do when He came. **the afflicted of the flock.** Only the poor responded when Jesus came to feed the flock (cf. Mt 11:5; 1Co 1:26). They were the lowly who would not follow the pride of the priest, scribes, and Pharisees, but believed on Jesus. **Favor … Union.** The prophet's symbolic act called for him to take "two staffs." Eastern shepherds often carried two sticks, a rod to ward off wild beasts and a staff to guide and retrieve wayward sheep (cf. Ps 23:4). The staff speaks of Christ the Good Shepherd who expressed the love and grace of God by tenderly leading and protecting His people (Mk 6:34), while the rod speaks of His unifying ministry, binding together the scattered house of Israel into one fold (cf. v. 14; Mt 15:24).

11:8 **annihilated the three shepherds.** Though difficult to identify, one of the oldest interpretations is that this refers to the priests, elders, and scribes of Israel (see Introduction: Interpretive Challenges). Jesus bestowed grace and unity upon the populace,

of me. 9 Then I said, "I will not pasture you. What is
to [A]die, [a]let it die, and what is to be annihilated, [b]let
it be annihilated; and [c]let those who are left eat one
another's flesh." 10 I took my staff [a,A]Favor and cut it in
pieces, to [b,B]break my covenant which I had made with
all the peoples. 11 So it was [a]broken on that day, and
[b]thus the [A]afflicted of the flock who were watching me
realized that it was the word of the LORD. 12 I said to
them, "If it is good in your sight, give *me* my [A]wages;
but if not, [a]never mind!" So they weighed out [B]thirty
shekels of silver as my wages. 13 Then the LORD said
to me, "Throw it to the [A]potter, *that* magnificent price
at which I was valued by them." So I took the thirty
shekels of silver and threw them to the potter in the
house of the LORD. 14 Then I cut in pieces my second
staff [a,A]Union, to [B]break the brotherhood between
Judah and Israel.

15 The LORD said to me, "Take again for yourself
the equipment of a [a,A]foolish shepherd. 16 For behold,
I am going to raise up a shepherd in the land who
will [A]not care for the perishing, seek the scattered,
heal the broken, or sustain the one standing, but
will [B]devour the flesh of the fat *sheep* and tear off
their hoofs.

17 "[A]Woe to the worthless shepherd
Who leaves the flock!
A [B]sword will be on his arm
And on his right eye!
His [C]arm will be totally withered
And his right eye will be [a]blind."

JERUSALEM TO BE ATTACKED

12 The [a]burden of the word of the LORD concerning Israel.

Thus declares the LORD who [A]stretches out the
heavens, [B]lays the foundation of the earth, and
[C]forms the spirit of man within him, 2 "Behold, I
am going to make Jerusalem a [A]cup [a]that causes
reeling to all the peoples around; and when the
siege is against Jerusalem, it will also be against
[B]Judah. 3 It will come about in that day that I will
make Jerusalem a heavy [A]stone for all the peoples;
all who lift it will be [B]severely [a]injured. And all the
[C]nations of the earth will be gathered against it.
4 In that day," declares the LORD, "I will strike every
horse with bewilderment and his rider with madness. But I will [a]watch over the house of Judah, while
I strike every horse of the peoples with blindness.

11:9 [a]Or *will die* [b]Or *will be annihilated* [c]Or *those...will eat* [A]Jer 15:2 11:10 [a]Or *Pleasantness* [b]Or *annul* [A]Zech 11:7 [B]Ps 89:39; Jer 14:21 11:11 [a]Or *annulled* [b]Another reading is *the sheep dealers who* [A]Zeph 3:12 11:12 [a]Lit *cease* [A]1 Kin 5:6; Mal 3:5 [B]Gen 37:28; Ex 21:32; Matt 26:15; 27:9, 10 11:13 [A]Matt 27:3-10; Acts 1:18, 19 11:14 [a]Or *Cords* [A]Zech 11:7 [B]Is 9:21; Zech 11:6 11:15 [a]Or *useless* [A]Is 6:10-12; Zech 11:17 11:16 [A]Jer 23:2 [B]Ezek 34:2-6 11:17 [a]Lit *completely dimmed* [A]Jer 23:1; Zech 10:2; 11:15 [B]Jer 50:35-37 [C]Ezek 30:21, 22 12:1 [a]Or *oracle* [A]Is 42:5; 44:24; Jer 51:15 [B]Job 26:7; Ps 102:25, 26; Heb 1:10-12 [C]Is 57:16; Heb 12:9 12:2 [a]Lit *of reeling* [A]Ps 75:8; Is 51:22, 23 [B]Zech 14:14 12:3 [a]Lit *scratched* [A]Dan 2:34, 35, 44, 45 [B]Matt 21:44 [C]Zech 14:2 12:4 [a]Lit *open My eyes*

but confronted the hypocrisy of these religious leaders, and because they rejected Him all 3 offices were obliterated in a short time. God ended the traditional offices of the mediators and in their place brought a new priesthood of believers (cf. 1Pe 2:5, 9; Rev 1:6; 5:10; 20:6). **my soul was impatient with them.** Lit. it means "My soul was short with them," referring to the limits of God's patience toward the unrepentant.

11:9 one another's flesh. *See note on 7:13.* In this drama, Zechariah played the unnatural role of a shepherd who abandons his sheep and stops teaching and protecting them. Those who refused to believe were to be given over to pursue their own desires and left exposed to deadly enemies. In the Roman siege of A.D. 70, some of the starving inhabitants did resort to cannibalism (cf. Jer 19:9).

11:10 break my covenant. Apparently, this refers to God's promise to restrain the nations from decimating Israel if she would consistently obey (Dt 28:1–14). God set aside His kind and gracious protection and His providential care for His people, allowing Rome to invade and destroy Israel (cf. Lk 19:41–44; 21:24).

11:11 The believing remnant of Christ's day knew God's Word was being fulfilled. They knew judgment was coming, but avoided the long-term consequences by faith in Christ.

11:12 thirty *shekels* of silver. Zechariah carried on the drama by symbolically picturing Jesus asking those He came to shepherd what they felt He was worth to them. In a mocking response, the leaders offered 30 silver pieces, which was the amount of compensation paid for a slave gored by an ox (cf. Ex 21:32). This is exactly what Judas Iscariot was paid to betray the Great Shepherd (Mt 26:14–16). The Jews of Jesus' day who offered that amount were saying He was worth no more than a common slave.

11:13 The prophet received further instruction in acting out the drama that pictures the rejection of Christ, namely to throw the 30 pieces into the temple. This was fulfilled when Judas Iscariot, laden with guilt, went back and threw the blood money on the temple floor. The priests gathered the money and used it to buy a field from a potter (cf. Mt 27:3–10). **magnificent price.** This ultimate sarcasm from God greeted the ultimate insult from humanity.

11:14 The breaking of the first staff (v. 10) preceded the Jews' rejection of the Shepherd, while the breaking of this rod once symbolizing the nation's unity (v. 7) followed His rejection, being fulfilled in the Roman breakup of the Jewish commonwealth. Josephus recorded that in the Roman conquering, the internal dissension among the people in their conflicting parties set Jew against Jew so that they struck each other as cruelly as the Romans struck them.

11:15, 16 With the removal of the true Shepherd, the drama called for the prophet to play a foolish shepherd, who depicted the Antichrist of Daniel's 70th week (cf. 2Th 2:3; Jn 5:43; Da 9:27). Zechariah's prophecy jumped from the first century A.D. to the last days before the second coming, omitting the present mystery of the church age (*see notes on 9:9, 10; 9:10–15*). This foolish (wicked) shepherd had a broken staff or club which he used to beat stubborn sheep into submission, something clearly inappropriate for a shepherd who thoughtfully and tenderly cared for his sheep. God permitted this wicked shepherd to arise, to destroy the sheep. Because they did not choose the Good Shepherd, Israel will receive a foolish one who will do absolutely the opposite of what is expected of shepherds, he will destroy the sheep (v. 16). This is exactly what Antichrist does (cf. Da 9:27; Mt 24:15–22).

11:17 his arm ... right eye. Zechariah condemned the worthless shepherd, noting that his strength ("arm") and his intelligence ("eye") would be taken away from him (cf. Da 7:9–14, 24–27; 8:23–25; 2Th 2:8; Rev 19:20; 20:10).

12:1–14:21 The second and final burden of Zechariah presents the familiar theme of Israel's ultimate deliverance and salvation. In contrast to initial judgment, he now encourages God's covenant people with a description of her restoration and blessing in the millennial kingdom, as true to His character and Zechariah's name, "the Lord remembers."

12:1 burden ... concerning Israel. *See note on 9:1.* The prophecy described a future siege against the nation, indicating that there would be significant devastation before there was repentance and conversion in Israel (cf. 14:1, 2). **stretches ... lays ... forms.** The God who performed the work of creation will ultimately do the work of consummation.

12:2 cup that causes reeling. Jerusalem is pictured as a large basin from which the nations will figuratively drink with eagerness, only to find themselves becoming intoxicated, disoriented, and thus easy prey for divine judgment at the end of Daniel's 70th week in the battle of Armageddon when nations gather to attack Jerusalem (cf. Eze 38:1–6, 14–16; Da 11:40–44; Rev 9:13–16; 14:20; 16:12–16).

12:3 will be severely injured. Like lifting a heavy weight, Jerusalem will "seriously injure" (lit.) any people that try to gain victory over it. This is due to divine intervention (cf. vv. 4, 5).

12:4 Horses, ancient symbols of strength, emphasize God's superior power over Israel's enemies. Confusion, madness, and blindness are noted as curses on Israel in Dt 28:28; here they are promised to Israel's enemies.

5 Then the clans of Judah will say in their hearts,
'[a]A strong support for us are the inhabitants of
Jerusalem through the LORD of hosts, their God.'
6 "In that day I will make the clans of Judah like a
[A]firepot among pieces of wood and a flaming torch
among sheaves, so they will consume on the right
hand and on the left all the surrounding peoples,
while the [B]inhabitants of Jerusalem again dwell on
their own sites in Jerusalem. 7 The LORD also will
[A]save the tents of Judah first, so that the glory of
the house of [B]David and the glory of the inhabitants
of Jerusalem will not be magnified above Judah.
8 In that day the LORD will [A]defend the inhabitants
of Jerusalem, and the one who [a,B]is feeble among
them in that day will be like David, and the house of
David *will be* like [C]God, like the [D]angel of the LORD
before them. 9 And in that day I will [a,A]set about to
destroy all the nations that come against Jerusalem.
10 "I will [A]pour out on the house of David and on
the inhabitants of Jerusalem, [a]the Spirit of grace and
of supplication, so that they will look on Me whom
they have [B]pierced; and they will mourn for Him,
as one [C]mourns for an only son, and they will weep
bitterly over Him like the bitter weeping over a firstborn. 11 In that day there will be great [A]mourning
in Jerusalem, like the mourning of Hadadrimmon
in the [a]plain of [b]Megiddo. 12 The land will mourn,
every family by itself; the family of the house of
David by itself and their wives by themselves; the
family of the house of Nathan by itself and their
wives by themselves; 13 the family of the house of
Levi by itself and their wives by themselves; the
family of the Shimeites by itself and their wives
by themselves; 14 all the families that remain, every family by itself and their wives by themselves.

FALSE PROPHETS ASHAMED

13 "In that day a [A]fountain will be opened for
the house of David and for the inhabitants of
Jerusalem, for [B]sin and for [C]impurity.
2 "It will come about in that day," declares the LORD
of hosts, "that I will [A]cut off the names of the idols
from the land, and they will no longer be remembered; and I will also remove the [B]prophets and the
[C]unclean spirit from the land. 3 And if anyone still
[A]prophesies, then his father and mother who gave
birth to him will say to him, 'You shall [B]not live, for
you have spoken [C]falsely in the name of the LORD';
and his [D]father and mother who gave birth to him will
pierce him through when he prophesies. 4 Also it will
come about in that day that the prophets will each be
[A]ashamed of his vision when he prophesies, and they
will not put on a [B]hairy robe in order to deceive; 5 but
he will say, 'I am [A]not a prophet; I am a tiller of the
ground, for a man [a]sold me as a slave in my youth.'
6 And one will say to him, 'What are these wounds
[A]between your [a]arms?' Then he will say, '*Those* with
which I was wounded in the house of [b]my friends.'

12:5 [a]Lit *My strength is* 12:6 [A]Is 10:17, 18; Obad 18; Zech 11:1 [B]Zech 2:4; 8:3-5 12:7 [A]Jer 30:18 [B]Amos 9:11 12:8 [a]Or *stumbles* [A]Joel 3:16; Zech 9:14, 15 [B]Lev 26:8; Josh 23:10; Mic 7:8 [C]Ps 8:5; 82:6 [D]Ex 14:19; 33:2 12:9 [a]Lit *seek to* [A]Zech 14:2, 3 12:10 [a]Or *a spirit* [A]Is 44:3; Ezek 39:29; Joel 2:28, 29 [B]John 19:37; Rev 1:7 [C]Jer 6:26; Amos 8:10 12:11 [a]I.e. broad valley [b]Heb *Megiddon* [A]Matt 24:30; Rev 1:7 13:1 [A]Jer 2:13; 17:13 [B]Ps 51:2, 7; Is 1:16-18; John 1:29 [C]Num 19:17; Is 4:4; Ezek 36:25 13:2 [A]Ex 23:13; Hos 2:17 [B]Jer 23:14, 15 [C]1 Kin 22:22; Ezek 36:25, 29 13:3 [A]Jer 23:34 [B]Deut 18:20; Ezek 14:9 [C]Jer 23:25 [D]Deut 13:6-11; Matt 10:37 13:4 [A]Jer 6:15; 8:9; Mic 3:7 [B]2 Kin 1:8; Is 20:2; Matt 3:4 13:5 [a]Lit *caused another to buy me* [A]Amos 7:14 13:6 [a]Lit *hands* [b]Lit *those who love me* [A]2 Kin 9:24

12:5 Knowing that God had chosen Jerusalem as the city of His special affection will give confidence to the "clans" (leaders) all over the land (cf. Ps 46:5). This verse has overtones indicating the saving faith of the Jews in that day, since they are claiming to have trust in God.

12:6 Two similes describe the operation of God's power: a "firepot" used to carry hot coals to start a wood fire and a "torch" used to light dry grain. Thus will the power of God devour the armies that attack Israel in the latter days.

12:7 **Judah first.** God will first deliver the defenseless country people before the well-fortified capital, demonstrating that the battle was not won by military might or strategy.

12:8 The Lord will make the feeble like David, the greatest soldier in Israel's history (cf. 1Sa 18:7). And the "house of David," like the "angel of the LORD," are most likely references to the Messiah Himself, who will be the strength of His people.

12:9 *See note on 12:2* for important cross references.

12:10 **I will pour.** God, in His own perfect time and by His own power, will sovereignly act to save Israel. This was prophesied by other prophets (cf. Eze 39:29; Joel 2:28–32), and by the apostle Paul (cf. Ro 11:25–27). **Spirit of grace and of supplication.** The Holy Spirit is so identified because He brings saving grace and because that grace produces sorrow that will result in repentant prayer to God for forgiveness (cf. Mt 5:4; Heb 10:29). **look on Me whom they have pierced.** Israel's repentance will come because they look to Jesus, the One whom they rejected and crucified (cf. Is 53:5; Jn 19:37), in faith at the Second Advent (Ro 11:25–27). When God says they pierced "Me," He is certainly affirming the incarnation of deity—Jesus was God. *See note on Jn 10:30.*

12:11 **Hadadrimmon ... Megiddo.** The bitter mourning of that day is likened to the death of righteous king Josiah at Hadadrimmon in the Megiddo plain (cf. 2Ch 35:20–24), located NW of Jerusalem (cf. Jas 4:8, 9).

12:12–14 The royal (David and his son Nathan) and priestly (Levi and his grandson Shimei) lines, who in the past had set an evil example, were foremost in their contrition and mourning (cf. Nu 3:17–21; 2Sa 5:14). It is possible that Is 53:1–9 comprises the content of their confession. This mourning and deep penitence is not some corporate emotion, but each person individually is brought to sorrow and faith in the Lord Jesus Christ. *See note on Rev 11:13.*

13:1 **house of David ... inhabitants of Jerusalem.** The totality of cleansing is noted by its effect on both royalty and commoners. **a fountain ... for sin and for impurity.** A symbolic reference to the means of cleansing and purification through the atoning death of the pierced One (cf. 1Jn 1:7). This has direct reference to the New Covenant of Jer 31:31–34; Eze 36:25–32; Ro 11:26–29. So the storm that broke upon Israel for the crime of Calvary and has raged with unmitigated fury for long, tragic centuries will suddenly end, and salvation will turn sin into righteousness in the gladness and glory of the kingdom of Messiah Jesus.

13:2–6 When Christ returns and cleanses Israel from her defilement, He is also going to cleanse the nation from the deception of false prophets and their demonic religion.

13:2 **unclean spirit.** The agents of idolatry are false prophets, but the spiritual power behind it is demonic. The wicked spirits who energize false prophets are unclean because they hate God and holiness and drive their victims into moral impurities and false religion (cf. Dt 32:17; 1Ki 22:19–23; Ps 106:34–39; 1Co 10:20).

13:3 Because of the salvation of God which has cleansed God's people and made them love Him and His truth, hatred of false prophecy will overrule normal human feelings, causing even a father and mother to put their own apostate child to death (cf. Dt 13:6–9, 12–15; Dt 18:18–22). This is a stern reminder of how God feels about and will eventually treat those preachers who misrepresent the truth.

13:4, 5 **a hairy robe.** Because of these stern measures, false prophets will cease wearing the traditional clothing of a prophet (cf. 2Ki 1:8; Mt 3:4). They will adopt a clandestine approach to propagating their demon-inspired lies (cf. Jer 22:22; Mic 3:7), and lie if they are asked whether they are prophets, claiming to be farmers.

13:6 **wounds between your arms.** The phrase cannot refer to Messiah, but is a continuation of the false prophet's behavior in vv. 4, 5. When the false prophet denies any association with pagan practices, others will challenge him to explain the suspicious wounds on his body. False prophets would cut themselves to arouse prophetic ecstasy in idolatrous rites (cf. Lv 19:28; Dt 14:1; 1Ki 18:28; Jer 16:6; 48:37), but they will claim the scars represent some attack they suffered from friends. See Introduction: Interpretive Challenges.

7 "Awake, O [A]sword, against My [B]Shepherd,
And against the man, My [C]Associate,"
Declares the LORD of hosts.
"[D]Strike the Shepherd that the
sheep may be scattered;
And I will [E]turn My hand
[a]against the little ones.
8 "It will come about in all the land,"
Declares the LORD,
"That [A]two parts in it will be
cut off *and* perish;
But the third will be left in it.
9 "And I will bring the third part
through the [A]fire,
Refine them as silver is refined,
And test them as gold is tested.
They will [B]call on My name,
And I will [C]answer them;
I will say, 'They are [D]My people,'
And they will say, 'The LORD is my God.' "

GOD WILL BATTLE JERUSALEM'S FOES

14 Behold, a [A]day is coming for the LORD when
[B]the spoil taken from you will be divided
among you. 2 For I will [A]gather all the nations against
Jerusalem to battle, and the city will be captured, the
[B]houses plundered, the women ravished and half of
the city exiled, but the rest of the people will not be
cut off from the city. 3 Then the LORD will go forth
and [A]fight against those nations, as [a]when He fights
on a day of battle. 4 In that day His feet will [A]stand on
the Mount of Olives, which is in front of Jerusalem
on the east; and the Mount of Olives will be [B]split in
its middle from east to west by a very large valley,
so that half of the mountain will move toward the
north and the other half toward the south. 5 You will
flee by the valley of My mountains, for the valley of
the mountains will reach to Azel; yes, you will flee
just as you fled before the [A]earthquake in the days
of Uzziah king of Judah. [B]Then the LORD, my God,
will come, *and* all the holy ones with [a]Him!
6 In that day there will be [A]no light; the [a]lumi-
naries will dwindle. 7 For it will be [A]a unique day
which is [B]known to the LORD, neither day nor night,
but it will come about that at [C]evening time there
will be light.
8 And in that day [A]living waters will flow out of
Jerusalem, half of them toward the eastern sea and

13:7 [a]Or *upon* [A]Jer 47:6; Ezek 21:3-5 [B]Is 40:11; Ezek 34:23, 24; 37:24; Mic 5:2, 4 [C]Ps 2:2; Jer 23:5, 6 [D]Is 53:4, 5, 10; Matt 26:31; Mark 14:27 [E]Is 1:25 13:8 [A]Is 6:13; Ezek 5:2-4, 12 13:9 [A]Is 48:10; Mal 3:3 [B]Ps 34:15-17; 50:15; Zech 12:10 [C]Is 58:9; 65:24; Jer 29:11-13; Zech 10:6 [D]Hos 2:23 14:1 [A]Is 13:6, 9; Joel 2:1; Mal 4:1 [B]Zech 14:14 14:2 [A]Zech 12:2, 3 [B]Is 13:16 14:3 [a]Lit *His day of fighting* [A]Zech 9:14, 15 14:4 [A]Ezek 11:23 [B]Is 64:1, 2; Ezek 47:1-10; Mic 1:3, 4; Hab 3:6; Zech 4:7; 14:8 14:5 [a]So the versions; Heb *You* [A]Is 29:6; Amos 1:1 [B]Ps 96:13; Is 66:15, 16; Matt 16:27; 25:31 14:6 [a]Lit *glorious ones will congeal* [A]Is 13:10; Jer 4:23; Ezek 32:7, 8; Joel 2:30, 31; Acts 2:16, 19 14:7 [A]Jer 30:7; Amos 8:9 [B]Is 45:21; Acts 15:18 [C]Is 58:10; Rev 22:5 14:8 [A]Ezek 47:1-12; Joel 3:18; John 7:38; Rev 22:1, 2

13:7–9 Zechariah turned from the false prophets wounded in "friends" ' houses to the true prophet wounded in the house of His friends, Israel. He compressed events of both the First (13:7) and Second (13:8, 9) Advents into this brief section. It spoke of Christ's crucifixion (v. 7) and the Jewish remnant at His second coming (vv. 8, 9).

13:7 My Shepherd ... My Associate. God spoke of the True Shepherd, that mighty Man who is His intimate associate, thus He identified Christ as His co-equal, affirming the deity of Christ (cf. Jn 1:1; 10:30; 14:9). **Strike the Shepherd.** In 11:17, it was the worthless shepherd who was to be struck; now it is the Good Shepherd (cf. 12:10) whose death was designed by God from before the foundation of the world (cf. Is 53:10; Ac 2:23; 1Pe 1:18–20). **sheep ... scattered.** *See notes on Mt 26:31; Mk 14:27,* where Jesus applies this prophecy to the disciples who defected from Him after His arrest (Mt 26:56; Mk 14:50), including Peter's denial (Mt 26:33–35, 69–75). **the little ones.** The same as the "afflicted of the flock" (11:7). The reference is to the remnant of believers, among the Jews, who were faithful to the Messiah after His crucifixion. Turning God's hand "against" them could mean they would suffer persecution, which they did (cf. Jn 15:18, 20; 16:2; Jas 1:1), or it could be translated "upon" and refer to God's protection of the faithful.

13:8 two parts ... third. Only a portion of the people of Israel will remain faithful to Christ and be alive in the end. The spiritual survivors will be the remnant who look upon Christ in repentance at His return (cf. 12:10–13:1), which will include those who make up the 144,000 (cf. Rev 7:4). These will be the sheep of the sheep-goat judgment after Christ's return who enter the kingdom alive (cf. Is 35:10; Jer 30:11; Mt 25:31–46).

13:9 they will say. From the midst of their fiery refinement, the elect remnant of Israel will see Jesus Christ, their Messiah, and call on Him as their Savior and Lord. Israel will thus be saved and restored to covenant relationship with the Lord.

14:1–21 Chapter 14 is an amplification of 13:8, 9. Prior to Israel's national conversion (cf. 12:10–13:1), the Jews will make a pact with a false messiah (cf. Da 9:27), known as the foolish shepherd (cf. 11:15–17) or Antichrist. In the middle of that 7-year covenant, Antichrist will break his treaty with Israel and require the worship of him alone (Da 9:24–27; Mt 24:15; 2Th 2:3, 4). When Israel refuses, the armies of the world will gather to do battle, climaxing in a great siege of Jerusalem and the Battle of Armageddon (Rev 19). Following the Lord's victory at that battle (cf. Rev 19:11–16) will come the full restoration of Israel as anticipated in Hos 14:4–7; Joel 3:18–21; Am 9:13–15; Mic 4:1–3; Zep 3:14–20.

14:1 a day is coming for the LORD. The "Day of the Lord" is a technical term for God's wrath unleashed against sinners. Here, Zechariah is looking at the day of the Lord when His wrath is unleashed against the whole world of sinners, which results in the establishment of the Lord's millennial reign on earth. *See note on Is 2:12* and Introduction to Joel: Historical and Theological Themes. **spoil ... divided among you.** Jerusalem will be so overcome by the enemy that the spoil will be leisurely divided in the midst of the city, illustrating how completely Jerusalem will be overthrown. This atrocity then triggers the wrath of God against the world in the day of the Lord.

14:2 I will gather all the nations. God Himself will gather the nations, using them to purge, refine, and judge (cf. Rev 16:13, 14, 16). Their presence results in an unprecedented time of national calamity. This is the climax of "the time of Jacob's distress" (Jer 30:5–7).

14:3, 4 His feet will stand on the Mount of Olives. To prevent the eradication of His remnant, the Lord will personally intervene to fight against the gathered nations. Just as He fought for His people in the past, so He will do in the future as the ultimate Warrior-King. Jesus will literally return to the Mt. of Olives, located E of the Kidron Valley, just as the angels announced at His ascension (cf. Ac 1:11). When He does, there will be a tremendous topographical upheaval (perhaps an earthquake), a phenomenon not uncommon when God announces His coming in judgment (cf. Mic 1:2–4; Na 1:5; Rev 16:18–21). The reaction of people is given in Rev 6:15–17.

14:4 the Mount of Olives will be split in its middle. A valley running E and W will be created as the mountain is pulled northward and southward (cf. Mic 1:2–4; Na 1:5; Rev 16:18, 19).

14:5 Azel. It is best understood as a place E of Jerusalem, marking the eastern end of the newly created valley. Though exact identification is unknown, it is possibly the Valley of Jehoshaphat or Valley of Decision (cf. Joel 3:12, 14) which will be for judgment of the nations and for the escape of the half who were not captured (v. 2). **all the holy ones with Him.** This term could refer to angels, Jewish believers, or Gentile Christians together (cf. Rev 19:14).

14:6, 7 As these Jews are fleeing through this newly created valley, the lights in the world will go out (cf. Is 13:9, 10; 24:23; Joel 2:10; 3:14–16; Mt 24:29, 30; Rev 6:12–14) and be replaced by the light of Christ's glory (cf. Is 60:19, 20). Only the Lord knows the fullness of the plan for that day—when the lights go out and are lit again in the millennial kingdom (cf. Is 30:26; Mal 4:2).

14:8 The highest elevation of the temple mount in Jerusalem is more than 300 ft. lower than the Mt. of Olives, but the topographical

the other half toward the western sea; it will be in
summer as well as in winter.

GOD WILL BE KING OVER ALL

9 And the LORD will be [A]king over all the earth;
in that day the LORD will be *the only* [B]one, and His
name *the only* one.
10 All the land will be changed into a plain from
[A]Geba to [B]Rimmon south of Jerusalem; but [a]Jeru-
salem will [C]rise and [D]remain on its site from [E]Ben-
jamin's Gate as far as the place of the First Gate to
the [F]Corner Gate, and from the [G]Tower of Hananel
to the king's wine presses. 11 [a]People will live in it,
and there will [A]no longer be a curse, for Jerusalem
will [B]dwell in security.
12 Now this will be the plague with which the
LORD will strike all the peoples who have gone to
war against Jerusalem; their flesh will [A]rot while they
stand on their feet, and their eyes will rot in their
sockets, and their tongue will rot in their mouth. 13 It
will come about in that day that a great panic from
the LORD will [a]fall on them; and they will [A]seize one
another's hand, and the hand of one will [b]be lifted
against the hand of another. 14 [A]Judah also will fight at
Jerusalem; and the [B]wealth of all the surrounding nations will be gathered, gold and silver and garments
in great abundance. 15 So also like this [A]plague will
be the plague on the horse, the mule, the camel, the
donkey and all the cattle that will be in those camps.
16 Then it will come about that any who are left
of all the nations that went against Jerusalem will
[A]go up from year to year to worship the King, the
LORD of hosts, and to celebrate the [B]Feast of Booths.
17 And it will be that whichever of the families of
the earth does not go up to Jerusalem to worship
the [A]King, the LORD of hosts, there will be [B]no rain
on them. 18 If the family of Egypt does not go up or
enter, then no *rain will fall* on them; it will be the
[A]plague with which the LORD smites the nations
who do not go up to celebrate the Feast of Booths.
19 This will be the [a]punishment of Egypt, and the
[a]punishment of all the nations who do not go up
to celebrate the Feast of Booths.
20 In that day there will *be inscribed* on the bells
of the horses,

"[A]HOLY TO THE LORD."

And the [B]cooking pots in the LORD'S house will be
like the bowls before the altar. 21 Every cooking pot in
Jerusalem and in Judah will be [A]holy to the LORD of
hosts; and all who sacrifice will come and take of them
and boil in them. And there will no longer be a [a,B]Ca-
naanite in the house of the LORD of hosts in that day.

14:9 [A]Is 2:2-4; 45:23; Zech 9:9; 14:16, 17 [B]Deut 6:4; Is 45:21-24 14:10 [a]Lit *it* [A]1 Kin 15:22 [B]Josh 15:32; Judg 20:45, 47 [C]Is 2:2; Amos 9:11 [D]Jer 30:18; Zech 12:6 [E]Jer 37:13; 38:7 [F]2 Kin 14:13 [G]Jer 31:38 14:11 [a]Lit *They* [A]Zech 8:13; Rev 22:3 [B]Jer 23:5, 6; Ezek 34:25-28 14:12 [A]Lev 26:16; Deut 28:21, 22 14:13 [a]Lit *be among* [b]Lit *rise up against* [A]Zech 11:6 14:14 [A]Zech 12:2, 5 [B]Is 23:18; Zech 14:1 14:15 [A]Zech 14:12 14:16 [A]Is 60:6-9; 66:18-21, 23 [B]Lev 23:34-44 14:17 [A]Zech 14:9, 16 [B]Jer 14:3-6; Amos 4:7 14:18 [A]Zech 14:12, 15 14:19 [a]Lit *sin* 14:20 [A]Ex 28:36-38 [B]Ezek 46:20 14:21 [a]Or *merchant* [A]Neh 8:10; Rom 14:6, 7; 1 Cor 10:31 [B]Zeph 1:11

alterations described in vv. 4, 10 will allow the spring to flow toward the Dead Sea (E) and the Mediterranean Sea (W) (*see notes on Eze 47:1–12*). It will not dry up in summer, as most Palestinian streams do, but will flow all year, making the desert "blossom like the crocus" (Is 35:1).

14:9 LORD will be *the only* one ... His name *the only* one. Cf. Rev 11:15. There will be only one religion in the entire world during the millennial reign of Christ. Ruling with a rod of iron (cf. Rev 19:15), Christ will have done away with all false religions spawned by Satan. This will be the ultimate fulfillment of the Abrahamic Covenant, providing a Jewish people, the nation of Israel, and the land given to Abraham; the Davidic Covenant which promised a king from the tribe of Judah and the line of David; and the New Covenant which held out the hope of spiritual redemption for Jew and Gentile. All of this will be fulfilled in and by the Lord Jesus Christ.

14:10 All the land ... into a plain. The term "plain" pictures the Jordan Valley, extending from Mt. Hermon (elevation 9,100 ft.) to the Gulf of Aqabah. Here the entire land, from Geba, 6 mi. to the N, to Rimmon in the S, would be leveled to become like the well-watered and fertile lowlands of the Jordan Valley (cf. Ge 13:10), causing Jerusalem to be exalted above like a solitaire diamond on a ring. Jerusalem, having been rebuilt according to these dimensions, will be exalted in both place and purpose, the prominent royal city containing the temple of God and the throne of Jesus Christ (cf. Eze 40–48). The locations of these landmarks would be the equivalent of meaning "all Jerusalem, E to W and N to S."

14:11 dwell in security. Jerusalem, the city of peace, has been fought over more frequently than any other city on earth, and prayed for over the millennia (Ps 122:6–9). As promised by God (2Sa 7:10–17; Ps 2:6; Eze 37:24–28; Joel 3:16, 17), she will know permanent righteousness and with it peace, rest, and safety.

14:12–15 The prophet, one final time, cycles back over the judgment that precedes the kingdom. God will strike the heathen forces gathered against Israel (vv. 1–3) with a supernatural plague similar to His judgment of the Assyrian army (Is 37:36), causing a panic so great that they begin to attack one another (cf. Jdg 7:22; 1Sa 14:15–20; 2Ch 20:23), aiding in the escape of the half (cf. vv. 2, 5). God will enable His people to fight (cf. Is 11:13, 14). Then He will send a widespread plague that even extends to their animals, preventing their use for military endeavors or escape. This depicts the thwarting of their efforts as God ultimately destroys them by the Messiah (Rev 19:11–16).

14:16–19 This very important passage reveals that some Gentiles will go into the millennial kingdom alive along with the redeemed Jews. A converted remnant from those heathen nations will make annual pilgrimages to Jerusalem to worship the Lord and to celebrate the Feast of Booths, or Tabernacles, during the Millennium. Commemorating the time when God "tabernacled" with Israel in the wilderness, the feast represented the last of the 3 major pilgrimage festivals (Lv 23:34–36), marked the final harvest of the year's crops, and provided a time of rejoicing. In the Millennium, it will celebrate Messiah's presence again dwelling among His people and the joyful restoration of Israel, including the ingathering of the nations. Those who refuse to go will experience drought and plague. Tragically, as the thousand years go on, there will be many people from all over the world who will reject Christ as Savior and King, joining in a final war against Him, only to be destroyed and cast into hell forever (cf. Rev 20:7–15).

14:16 Feast of Booths. The historical background can be found in Lv 23:33–36; Nu 29:12–38; Dt 16:13–17. In addition to the Feast of Booths, or Tabernacles, two other feasts will be celebrated in the Millennium, i.e., 1) Feast of the New Year (Eze 45:18–20) and 2) Passover (Eze 45:21–25). These feasts are no more efficacious than were the feasts of the Mosaic era or the Lord's Supper in the church age. They all provided a symbolic anticipation or remembrance of Christ's unique and once-for-all sacrifice at Calvary.

14:17 no rain. Drought is a dreaded punishment (cf. 1Ki 17:1–7; 2Ch 7:13, 14; Jas 5:17, 18) since it deprives the people of life-sustaining water.

14:20, 21 Just as the High Priest, whose turban was engraved with the phrase "HOLY TO THE LORD," was set apart for the service of the Lord (cf. Zec 3:5; also Ex 28:36; 39:30), so even mundane and ordinary things like the bells that decorate horses and common pots and pans will be as holy as the High Priest and the altar bowls used in sacrifices. There will be no need for distinctions between holy and secular. Everything will be set apart to the service of the Lord in the Messiah's glorious kingdom.

14:21 Canaanite. This identification is used as a figure for the morally and spiritually unclean persons who will be excluded from entering the millennial temple. Before Israel conquered the Promised Land, the vile Canaanites inhabited it; thus the term became proverbial in Israel for a morally degenerate, ceremonially unclean person.

THE
BOOK OF
MALACHI

TITLE

The title is derived from the prophecy's author, Malachi. With this last work in the Minor Prophets, God closes the OT canon historically and prophetically.

AUTHOR AND DATE

Some have suggested that the book was written anonymously, noting that the name, meaning "my messenger" or "the Lord's messenger," could be a title rather than a proper name. It is pointed out that the name occurs nowhere else in the OT, nor is any background material provided about the author. However, since all other prophetic books have historically identified their author in the introductory heading, this suggests that Malachi was indeed the name of the last OT writing prophet in Israel. Jewish tradition identifies him as a member of the Great Synagogue that collected and preserved the Scriptures.

Looking solely at internal evidence, the date of the prophecy points to the late fifth century B.C., most likely during Nehemiah's return to Persia ca. 433–424 B.C. (cf. Ne 5:14; 13:6). Sacrifices were being made at the second temple (1:7–10; 3:8), which was finished in 516 B.C. (cf. Ezr 6:13–15). Many years had passed since then, as the priests had increasingly become complacent and corrupt (1:6–2:9). Malachi's reference to "governor" (1:8) speaks of the time of Persian dominance in Judah when Nehemiah was revisiting Persia (Ne 13:6), while his emphasis on the law (4:4) coincides with a similar focus by Ezra and Nehemiah (cf. Ezr 7:14, 25, 26; Ne 8:18). They shared other concerns as well, such as marriages to foreign wives (2:11–15; cf. Ezr 9, 10; Ne 13:23–27), withholding of tithes (3:8–10; cf. Ne 13:10–14), and social injustice (3:5; cf. Ne 5:1–13). Nehemiah came to Jerusalem in 445 B.C. to rebuild the wall, and returned to Persia in 433 B.C. He later returned to Israel (ca. 424 B.C.) to deal with the sins Malachi described (Ne 13:6). So it is likely that Malachi was written during the period of Nehemiah's absence, almost a century after Haggai and Zechariah began to prophesy. Similar to Rev 2, 3, in which Christ writes what He thinks about the conditions of the churches, here God writes through Malachi to impress upon Israel His thoughts about the nation.

BACKGROUND AND SETTING

Only 50,000 exiles had returned to Judah from Babylon (538–536 B.C.). The temple had been rebuilt under the leadership of Zerubbabel (516 B.C.) and the sacrificial system renewed. Ezra had returned in 458 B.C., followed by Nehemiah in 445 B.C. After being back in the land of Israel for only a century, the ritual of the Jews' religious routine led to hard-heartedness toward God's great love for them and to widespread departure from His law by both people and priest. Malachi rebuked and condemned these abuses, forcefully indicting the people and calling them to repentance. When Nehemiah returned from Persia the second time (ca. 424 B.C.), he vigorously rebuked them for these abuses in the temple and priesthood, for the violation of the Sabbath rest, and for the unlawful divorce of their Jewish wives so they could marry Gentile women (cf. Ne 13).

As over two millennia of OT history since Abraham concluded, none of the glorious promises of the Abrahamic, Davidic, and New Covenants had been fulfilled in their ultimate sense. Although there had been a few high points in Israel's history, e.g., Joshua, David, and Josiah, the Jews had seemingly lost all opportunity to receive God's favor since less than 100 years after returning from captivity, they had already sunk to a depth of sin that exceeded the former iniquities which brought on the Assyrian and Babylonian deportations. Beyond this, the long-anticipated Messiah had not arrived and did not seem to be in sight.

So, Malachi wrote the capstone prophecy of the OT in which he delivered God's message of judgment on Israel for their continuing sin and God's promise that one day in the future, when the Jews would repent, Messiah would be revealed and God's covenant promises would be fulfilled. There were over 400 years of divine silence, with only Malachi's words ringing condemnation in their ears, before another prophet arrived with a message from God. That was John the Baptist preaching, "Repent, for the kingdom of heaven is at hand!" (Mt 3:2). Messiah had come.

HISTORICAL AND THEOLOGICAL THEMES

The Lord repeatedly referred to His covenant with Israel (cf. 2:4, 5, 8, 10, 14; 3:1), reminding them, from His opening words, of their unfaithfulness to His love/marriage relationship with them (cf. 1:2–5). God's love for His people pervades the book. Apparently the promises by the former prophets of the coming Messiah who would bring final deliverance and age-long blessings, and the encouragement from the recent promises (ca. 500 B.C.) of Haggai and Zechariah, had only made the people and their leaders more resolute in their complacency. They thought that this love relationship could be maintained by formal ritual alone, no matter how they lived. In a penetrating rebuke of both priests (1:6–2:9) and people (2:10–16), the prophet reminds them that the Lord's coming, which they were seeking (3:1), would be in judgment to refine, purify, and purge (3:2, 3). The Lord not only wanted outward compliance with the law, but an inward acceptance as well (cf. Mt 23:23). The prophet assaults the corruption, wickedness, and false security by directing his judgments at their hypocrisy, infidelity, compromise, divorce, false worship, and arrogance.

Malachi set forth his prophecy in the form of a dispute, employing the question-and-answer method. The Lord's accusations against His people were frequently met by cynical questions from the people (1:2, 6, 7; 2:17; 3:7, 8, 13). At other times, the prophet presented himself as God's advocate in a lawsuit, posing rhetorical questions to the people based on their defiant criticisms (1:6, 8, 9; 2:10, 15; 3:2).

Malachi indicted the priests and the people on at least 6 counts of willful sin: 1) repudiating God's love (1:2–5); 2) refusing God His due honor (1:6–2:9); 3) rejecting God's faithfulness (2:10–16); 4) redefining God's righteousness (2:17–3:6); 5) robbing God's riches (3:7–12); and 6) reviling God's grace (3:13–15). There are 3 interludes in which Malachi rendered God's judgment: 1) to the priests (2:1–9); 2) to the nation (3:1–6); and 3) to the remnant (3:16–4:6).

INTERPRETIVE CHALLENGES

The meaning of Elijah being sent "before the coming of the great and terrible day of the LORD" (4:5) has been debated. Was this fulfilled in John the Baptist or is it yet future? Will Elijah be reincarnated? It seems best to view Malachi's prophecy as a reference to John the Baptist and not to a literally returned Elijah. Not only did the angel announce that John the Baptist would go "before Him in the spirit and power of Elijah" (Lk 1:17), but John the Baptist himself said he was not Elijah (Jn 1:21). Thus John was like Elijah, internally in "spirit and power" and externally in rugged independence and nonconformity. If the Jews would receive the Messiah, then he would be the Elijah spoken of (cf. Mt 11:14; 17:9–13); if they refused the King, then another Elijah-like prophet would be sent in the future, perhaps as one of the two witnesses (cf. Rev 11:1–19).

OUTLINE

I. The Denunciation of Israel's Sins (1:1–2:16)

- A. Reminder of God's Love for Israel (1:1–5)
- B. Rebuke of the Priests (1:6–2:9)
    1. Contempt for God's altar (1:6–14)
    2. Contempt for God's glory (2:1–3)
    3. Contempt for God's law (2:4–9)
- C. Rebuke of the People (2:10–16)

II. The Declaration of Israel's Judgment and Blessing (2:17–4:6)

- A. Coming of a Messenger (2:17–3:5)
- B. Challenge to Repent (3:6–12)
- C. Criticism by Israel Against the Lord (3:13–15)
- D. Consolation to the Faithful Remnant (3:16–4:6)

GOD'S LOVE FOR JACOB

1 The [a,A]oracle of the word of the LORD to [B]Israel
through [b]Malachi.
2 "I have [A]loved you," says the LORD. But you say,
"How have You loved us?" "*Was* not Esau Jacob's
brother?" declares the LORD. "Yet I [B]have loved Jacob; 3 but I have hated Esau, and I have [A]made his
mountains a desolation and *appointed* his inheritance for the jackals of the wilderness." 4 Though
Edom says, "We have been [A]beaten down, but we
will [a,B]return and build up the ruins"; thus says the
LORD of hosts, "They may [C]build, but I will tear
down; and *men* will call them the [b]wicked territory, and the people [c]toward whom the LORD is
indignant [D]forever." 5 Your eyes will see this and
you will say, "[A]The LORD [a]be magnified beyond the
[b]border of Israel!"

SIN OF THE PRIESTS

6 " 'A son [A]honors *his* father, and a servant his
master. Then if I am a [B]father, where is My honor?
And if I am a master, where is My [a]respect?' says
the LORD of hosts to you, O [C]priests who despise
My name. But you say, 'How have we despised Your
name?' 7 *You* are presenting [A]defiled [a,B]food upon My
altar. But you say, 'How have we defiled You?' In that
you say, 'The [C]table of the LORD is to be despised.'
8 But when you present the [A]blind for sacrifice, is it
not evil? And when you present the lame and sick,
is it not evil? [a]Why not offer it to your [B]governor?

1:1 [a]Lit *burden* [b]Or *My messenger* [A]Is 13:1; Nah 1:1; Hab 1:1; Zech 9:1 [B]Mal 2:11 1:2 [A]Deut 4:37; 7:8; 23:5; Is 41:8, 9; Jer 31:3; John 15:12 [B]Rom 9:13 1:3 [A]Jer 49:10, 16-18; Ezek 35:3, 4, 7, 8, 15 1:4 [a]Or *rebuild the ruins* [b]Lit *border of wickedness* [c]Or *whom the LORD has cursed* [A]Jer 5:17 [B]Is 9:9, 10 [C]Amos 3:15; 5:11; 6:11 [D]Ezek 35:9; Obad 10 1:5 [a]Or *will be great* [b]Or *territory* [A]Ps 35:27; Mic 5:4 1:6 [a]Lit *fear* [A]Ex 20:12; Prov 30:11, 17 [B]Deut 1:31; Is 1:2; Jer 3:4; Mal 2:10 [C]Zeph 3:4; Mal 2:1-9 1:7 [a]Lit *bread* [A]Mal 1:8, 13 [B]Lev 3:11; 21:6, 8 [C]Mal 1:12 1:8 [a]Lit *Offer it, please* [A]Lev 22:22; Deut 15:21 [B]Hag 1:1

1:1–2:16 In the first of two major sections (cf. 2:17–4:6), Malachi delivered God's message which denounced sin among the people of Israel.

1:1 oracle. This term refers to the sentence pronounced by the prophet. *See notes on Is 13:1; Na 1:1; Hab 1:1; Zec 9:1; 12:1.*

1:2 I have loved you. The great privilege of Israel as God's beloved people is forcefully presented by comparing the nation with Edom. In response to the affirmation of the Lord's love for them, the people, looking only at what they had lost since the captivity and how feeble their nation was, incredulously expressed doubt about God's love and insolently challenged it. Nevertheless, God reaffirmed His love to them, recalling His covenant choice of Jacob over Esau, father of the Edomites (cf. Ge 25:23). In this closing book of the OT, God's electing love toward Israel, sovereign, undeserved, and persistent (cf. Ro 9:13), is boldly and explicitly reiterated by the Lord Himself and illustrated by His choice of Jacob and his offspring. Unconditionally, and completely apart from any consideration of human merit, God elected Jacob and his descendants to become His heirs of promise (cf. Ro 9:6–29). No one should conclude that God does not love His people because He afflicted them, but rather He loves them because He elected them.

1:3 I have hated Esau. While Genesis mentions no divine hatred toward Esau, Obadiah's prophecy over 1,000 years later (see Ob 1–21) indicated that the Lord's hatred was against Esau's idolatrous descendants. In the same way, the Lord's love for Jacob refers to his descendants who were His sovereignly elected people through whom the world's Redeemer would come. Nor does the love/hate language signify a comparative love in which He loved Jacob more and Esau less. Rather, the context here speaks of love as "choosing for intimate fellowship" and hate as "not choosing for intimate fellowship" in the realm of redemption. *See notes on Ro 9:6–13.* **made his mountains a desolation … inheritance.** A reference to Edom's (later called Idumea) destruction, first by Nebuchadnezzar and later by neighboring people, e.g., Egypt, Ammon, and Moab, as well as at the hands of the Nabateans. See Introduction to Obadiah: Background and Setting; Historical and Theological Themes.

1:4, 5 Though the Edomites would attempt to rebuild their ruins, God would negate their efforts. Israel, on the other hand, is restored; and though complete restoration has been delayed, it will come and the nation will bear witness to God's gracious rulership, both within as well as beyond her borders (cf. Ge 12:3; Mal 1:11).

1:6–2:9 Affirming the unconditional love of the Lord (vv. 2–5) did not absolve guilt, thus Malachi delivered an opening indictment against the priests, the nation's spiritual leaders, pointing out how they were showing contempt for God's sacrifices (vv. 6–14), His glory (2:1–3), and His law (2:4–9).

1:6 priests. He addressed the priests first because they should be leaders in righteous devotion to God, but were foremost in despising His name, though their question was tantamount to a denial of their wicked attitude toward God (cf. Lk 6:46).

1:7 defiled food. That the reference here is to animal sacrifices is evident from v. 8. The priests were offering ceremonially unclean or blemished (cf. v. 13) sacrifices, strictly forbidden by the Lord (cf. Lv 22:20–25; Dt 15:21), and again hypocritically questioning such an indictment. They had only contempt for the Lord as indicated by the offerings brought to the Lord of "blind," "lame" and "sick" animals (v. 8). **table of the LORD.** This refers to the altar for sacrifices (cf. Eze 41:22).

1:8 offer it to your governor. The priests had the audacity to offer God what their governor, as a form of taxation, would never have

OLD TESTAMENT NAMES FOR GOD	
1. Elohim, "God," i.e., His power and might	Ge 1:1; Ps 19:1
2. El-Elyon, "The most high God"	Ge 14:17–20; Is 14:13, 14
3. El-Olam, "The everlasting God"	Is 40:28–31
4. El-Roi, "The strong one who sees"	Ge 16:13
5. El-Shaddai, "God Almighty"	Ge 17:1; Ps 91:1
6. Adonai, "Lord," i.e., the Lordship of God	Mal 1:6
7. Jehovah (Yahweh), "The LORD," i.e., God's eternal nature	Ge 2:4
8. Jehovah-Jireh, "The LORD will provide"	Ge 22:13, 14
9. Jehovah-Maccaddeshem, "The LORD your sanctifier"	Ex 31:13
10. Jehovah-Nissi, "The LORD our banner"	Ex 17:15
11. Jehovah-Rapha, "The LORD our healer"	Ex 15:26
12. Jehovah-Rohi, "The LORD my shepherd"	Ps 23:1
13. Jehovah-Sabbaoth, "The LORD of Hosts"	Is 6:1–3
14. Jehovah-Shalom, "The LORD is peace"	Jdg 6:24
15. Jehovah-Shammah, "The LORD who is present"	Eze 48:35
16. Jehovah-Tsidkenu, "The LORD our righteousness"	Jer 23:6

Would he be pleased with you? Or would he receive you kindly?" says the LORD of hosts. 9 "But now [a]will you not [A]entreat God's favor, that He may be gracious to us? [b]With such an offering on your part, will He [B]receive any of you kindly?" says the LORD of hosts. 10 "Oh that there were one among you who would [A]shut the [a]gates, that you might not uselessly kindle *fire on* My altar! I am not pleased with you," says the LORD of hosts, "[B]nor will I accept an offering from [b]you. 11 For from the [A]rising of the sun even to its setting, [B]My name *will be* [C]great among the nations, and in every place [D]incense is going to be offered to My name, and a grain offering *that is* pure; for My name *will be* [E]great among the nations," says the LORD of hosts. 12 "But you are [A]profaning it, in that you say, 'The table of the Lord is defiled, and as for its fruit, its food is to be despised.' 13 You also say, '[a]My, how [A]tiresome it is!' And you disdainfully sniff at it," says the LORD of hosts, "and you bring what was taken by [B]robbery and *what is* [C]lame or sick; so you bring the offering! Should I [D]receive that from your hand?" says the LORD. 14 "But cursed be the [A]swindler who has a male in his flock and vows it, but sacrifices a [B]blemished animal to the Lord, for I am a great [C]King," says the LORD of hosts, "and My name is [a,D]feared among the [b]nations."

PRIESTS TO BE DISCIPLINED

2 "And now this commandment is for you, O priests. 2 If you do [A]not listen, and if you do not take it to heart to give honor to My name," says the LORD of hosts, "then I will send the [B]curse upon you and I will curse your blessings; and indeed, I have [C]cursed them *already,* because you are not taking *it* to heart. 3 Behold, I am going to [A]rebuke your [a]offspring, and I will [B]spread [b]refuse on your faces, the [b]refuse of your [C]feasts; and you will be taken away [c]with it. 4 Then you will know that I have sent this commandment to you, [a]that My [A]covenant may [b]continue with Levi," says the LORD of hosts. 5 "My covenant with him was *one of* life and [A]peace, and I gave them to him *as an object of* [a]reverence; so he [b,B]revered Me and stood in awe of My name. 6 [a,A]True instruction was in his mouth and unrighteousness was not found on his lips; he walked [B]with Me in peace and uprightness, and he [C]turned many back from iniquity. 7 For the lips of a priest should preserve [A]knowledge, and [a]men should [B]seek [b]instruction from his mouth; for he is the [C]messenger of the LORD of hosts. 8 But as for you, you have turned aside from the way; you have caused many to [A]stumble [a]by the instruction; you have [b,B]corrupted the covenant of Levi," says the LORD of hosts.

1:9 [a]Lit *entreat, please* [b]Lit *This has been from your hand* [A]Jer 27:18; Joel 2:12-14 [B]Amos 5:22 1:10 [a]Or *doors* [b]Lit *your hand* [A]Is 1:13 [B]Jer 14:10, 12; Hos 5:6 1:11 [A]Is 45:6 [B]Ps 111:9 [C]Is 66:18, 19 [D]Is 60:6 [E]Is 12:4, 5; 54:5; Jer 10:6, 7 1:12 [A]Mal 1:7 1:13 [a]Lit *Behold* it is *weariness* [A]Is 43:22 [B]Lev 6:4; Is 61:8 [C]Mal 1:8 [D]Mal 1:10 1:14 [a]Or *revered* [b]Or *Gentiles* [A]Acts 5:1-4 [B]Lev 22:18-20 [C]Zech 14:9 [D]Zeph 2:11 2:2 [A]Lev 26:14, 15; Deut 28:15 [B]Deut 28:16-20 [C]Mal 3:9 2:3 [a]Lit *seed* [b]Or *vomit* [c]Lit *to* [A]Lev 26:16; Deut 28:38 [B]Nah 3:6 [C]Ex 29:14 2:4 [a]Or *to be My covenant with* [b]Lit *be* [A]Num 3:11-13, 45; 18:21; Neh 13:29; Mal 3:1 2:5 [a]Or *fear* [b]Or *feared* [A]Num 25:12 [B]Num 25:7, 8, 13 2:6 [a]Or *Law of truth* [A]Ps 119:142, 151, 160 [B]Deut 33:8, 9; Ps 37:37 [C]Jer 23:22 2:7 [a]Lit *they* [b]Or *law* [A]Lev 10:11; Neh 8:7 [B]Num 27:21; Deut 17:8-11; Jer 18:18; Ezek 7:26 [C]Hag 1:13 2:8 [a]Or *in the law* [b]Or *violated* [A]Jer 18:15 [B]Num 25:12, 13; Neh 13:29; Ezek 44:10

accepted from them. They were more fearful of the governor's rejection than of God's. This would have been during the time that Nehemiah was back in Persia (cf. Ne 13:6), when he would have relinquished the office for some time.

1:9 The invitation to repent is best taken as irony. How could they expect God to extend His grace when they were insulting Him with unacceptable sacrifices?

1:10 shut the gates. God, speaking in the first person, desired for someone to shut the temple doors, thereby preventing the useless, insincere presentation of sacrifices (cf. Is 1:11–15). It would be better to stop all sacrifices than to offer insincere offerings.

1:11 from the rising of the sun even to its setting. The phrase is a way of referring to the whole earth (cf. Pss 50:1; 103:12; Is 45:6; 59:19; Zec 8:7), as the subsequent phrase, "in every place," indicates (cf. 1:5). Although no indication is given as to the time when such worship of God will fill the earth, this cannot be a reference to any historic Jewish worship outside the borders of Israel. Malachi's zeal for Israel's sacrifices, coupled with his negative attitude toward foreigners and their gods (vv. 2–5; 2:11), points to the millennial era, when they will worship in the rebuilt temple, and incense plus offerings will be present (cf. Eze 40–48). At that time, and not until that time, the Lord will receive pure worship throughout the world, and His name will be honored everywhere (cf. Is 2:2–4; 19:19–21; 24:14–16; 45:22–24; 66:18–21; Mic 4:1–3; Zec 8:20–23; 14:16–19).

1:12, 13 The reproof of vv. 7, 8 is repeated. The exacting requirements of the sacrifices wearied the priests. They did not literally say the Lord's table (the place of offerings) is contemptible, but they virtually said so by refusing to lead the people to reverence and to offer the Lord their best; thus their attitude and actions were profaning the altar and insulting to the Lord (cf. Is 43:22–24; Mic 6:3), so He rejected their offerings.

1:14 a blemished animal. Instead of the unblemished male animal (cf. Lv 22:19), which was considered more valuable and which he had vowed to voluntarily give, the offerer suddenly substituted a blemished female. The fact that it was voluntary makes it that much more incongruous (cf. Ac 5:1–5). **a great King.** If such presentations are unacceptable to their governor (v. 8), how much more to the King of the universe? Cf. Ps 48:2; Mt 5:35.

2:2 I will send the curse. Failing to render glory to God would result in a curse being sent upon them. This is a fundamental OT theme: blessing for obedience, cursing for disobedience (cf. 1:14; Dt 27:15–26; 28:15–68). **your blessings.** These were not restricted to material blessings only (cf. Nu 18:21) but referred to all the benefits of God's gracious hand (cf. v. 5), including the blessings pronounced by the priests over the people (cf. Nu 6:23–27).

2:3 refuse. This very graphic language shows how God viewed unfaithful priests as worthy of the most unthinkable disgrace. As the internal waste of the sacrificial animal was normally carried outside the camp and burned (cf. Ex 29:14; Lv 4:11, 12; 8:17; 16:27), so the priests would be discarded and suffer humiliation and loss of office. The Lord's purpose in such a warning was to shake them out of their complacency.

2:4, 5 My covenant . . . with Levi. The relationship of God to the priesthood was clearly set forth in the Levitic covenant (Nu 3:44–48; 18:8–24; Dt 33:8–11). The covenant was one of mutual responsibility, in which God expected reverence for Himself in exchange for life and peace for the priests. Verbally similar to the covenant made with Phinehas relating to the lineage of the High Priest (cf. Nu 25:10–13), this covenant was made with Aaron of Levi's line and his descendants. The Jewish priests of Malachi's day had deceived themselves by claiming the privileges of the covenant, while neglecting the conditions of it, as if God was bound to bless them even while they rejected the obligation to serve Him.

2:4 Then you will know. The priests will know the price of disobedience by bitter experience with the consequences.

2:6 Aaron, unlike the priests of Malachi's time, feared and reverenced God. Aaron also fulfilled this responsibility and lived the godliness he taught (Lv 8, 9). *See note on vv. 4, 5.*

2:7 The priests were the messengers of God in Israel. Not only were they to represent the people to God, but they were also responsible to represent God to the people by teaching the law of Moses to the nation (cf. Lv 10:9–11; Dt 33:10; Ezr 7:10; Hos 4:6).

2:8, 9 The priests of Malachi's day had made a radical departure from God's standard, originally given to Levi, causing others to stumble by their bad example and false interpretation of the law. Consequently, the worst shame and degradation fell upon them (cf. v. 3; Ne 13:29).

9 "So [A]I also have made you despised and [B]abased
[a]before all the people, just as you are not keeping My
ways but are showing [C]partiality in the [b]instruction.

SIN IN THE FAMILY

10 "Do we not all have [A]one father? [B]Has not one
God created us? Why do we deal [C]treacherously each
against his brother so as to profane the [D]covenant
of our fathers? 11 Judah has dealt [A]treacherously, and
an abomination has been committed in Israel and
in Jerusalem; for Judah has [B]profaned the sanctuary
of the LORD [a]which He loves and has married the
daughter of a foreign god. 12 *As* for the man who
does this, may the [A]LORD cut off from the tents of
Jacob *everyone* who awakes and answers, or who
[B]presents [a]an offering to the LORD of hosts.
13 "This is [a]another thing you do: you cover the
altar of the LORD with tears, with weeping and with
groaning, because He [A]no longer regards the [b]offer-
ing or accepts *it with* favor from your hand. 14 Yet you
say, 'For what reason?' Because the LORD has been
a witness between you and the [A]wife of your youth,
against whom you have dealt [B]treacherously, though
she is your companion and your wife by covenant.
15 [a]But not one has [A]done *so* who has a remnant of the
Spirit. And [b]what did *that* one *do* while he was seeking a [B]godly [c]offspring? Take heed then to your spirit,
and let no one deal [C]treacherously against the wife
of your youth. 16 For [a]I hate [b,A]divorce," says the LORD,
the God of Israel, "and [c]him who covers his garment
with [d,B]wrong," says the LORD of hosts. "So take heed
to your spirit, that you do not deal treacherously."
17 You have [A]wearied the LORD with your words.
Yet you say, "How have we wearied *Him?*" In that
you say, "[B]Everyone who does evil is good in the
sight of the LORD, and He [C]delights in them," or,
"[D]Where is the God of [E]justice?"

THE PURIFIER

3 "[A]Behold, I am going to send [B]My [a]messenger,
and he will [b,C]clear the way before Me. And the
Lord, whom you seek, will suddenly come to His
temple; [c]and the [a,D]messenger of the covenant, in
whom you delight, behold, He is coming," says the

2:9 [a]Lit *to* [b]Or *law* [A]Nah 3:6 [B]Ezek 7:26 [C]Deut 1:17; Mic 3:11 2:10 [A]Is 63:16; 64:8; Jer 31:9; 1 Cor 8:6; Eph 4:6 [B]Acts 17:24f [C]Jer 9:4, 5 [D]Ex 19:4-6; 24:3, 7, 8 2:11 [a]Or *in that He has loved and married* [A]Jer 3:7-9 [B]Ezra 9:1, 2 2:12 [a]Or *a grain offering* [A]Ezek 24:21; Hos 9:12 [B]Mal 1:10, 13 2:13 [a]Lit *second* [b]Or *grain offering* [A]Jer 11:14; 14:12 2:14 [A]Is 54:6 [B]Jer 9:2; Mal 3:5 2:15 [a]Or *Did He not make one, although He had the remnant* [b]Or *why one? He sought a godly offspring* [c]Lit *seed* [A]Gen 2:24; Matt 19:4, 5 [B]Ruth 4:12; 1 Sam 2:20 [C]Ex 20:14; Lev 20:10 2:16 [a]Lit *He hates* [b]Lit *sending away* [c]Lit *he covers* [d]Or *violence* [A]Deut 24:1; Matt 5:31; 19:6-8 [B]Ps 73:6; Is 59:6 2:17 [A]Is 43:22, 24 [B]Is 5:20; Zeph 1:12 [C]Job 9:24 [D]2 Pet 3:4 [E]Is 5:19; Jer 17:15 3:1 [a]Or *angel* [b]Or *prepare* [c]Or *even* [A]Matt 11:10, 14; Mark 1:2; Luke 1:76; 7:27 [B]Hag 1:13; John 1:6, 7 [C]Is 40:3 [D]Is 63:9

2:10–16 Israel's spiritual leaders committed grievous sins (1:6–2:9), leading the people to do the same. They too were violating the requirements of God's law by profaning the institution of the Levitical priesthood, marrying foreign wives (vv. 10–12), and divorcing the wives of their youth (vv. 13–16).

2:10 one father. Though God is Father of all through creation (cf. Ac 17:29; Eph 3:14, 15), the primary focus is directed to God as the Father of Israel as His covenant people (see "father" in 1:6, where this indictment began; also cf. Jer 2:27).

2:10, 11 deal treacherously. This key phrase (vv. 10, 11, 14, 15, 16) refers to the violation of God's will by divorcing Jewish wives and marrying foreign women. God is the Father who gave life to Israel (cf. Is 43:1; 60:21), yet they had, through intermarriage with idol worshipers, introduced division by violating the covenant He made with their fathers to ensure the maintenance of a separated people (cf. Ex 19:5; 24:8; 34:14–16; Lv 20:24, 26; Dt 7:1–4).

2:11 married the daughter of a foreign god. A worshiper of an idol was considered to be its child (Jer 2:27). The prophets often mixed the ideas of adultery and idolatry or physical and spiritual adultery. Unless they became true proselytes to Judaism, pagan women led their husbands into idolatry and thereby contaminated Israelite worship (cf. Jdg 3:5–7). Those Jews who married them profaned God's temple and the covenant community. Solomon's violation of this law had opened the door for idolatry to enter Judah (1Ki 11:1–6). Both Ezra (Ezr 9:2–15) and Nehemiah (Ne 13:23–29) faced this sinful problem.

2:12 cut off. This common term was generally used for death. Their adulterous actions of divorce and intermarriage disqualified them from participation in the rights and privileges of the community of Israel, so their offerings to God would be rejected. **who awakes and answers.** A proverbial expression referring to two classes of people: "the active watcher" who "awakens" people to reality and "the passive hearer" who "answers." This proverb apparently came from nomadic people who had guards around their tents to stay awake and make others aware of danger. This signified judgment so that everyone who sins in this gross, idolatrous way would be exterminated.

2:13 cover the altar ... with tears. Weeping and wailing would achieve nothing because sin had shut the door of access to God. They had violated their marriage vows and the separation from idols as God required. This double disloyalty made their offerings a hypocritical mockery. Since lay people had no access to the altars but the priests did, it was clearly their guilt which was foremost, and their hypocrisy so unacceptable to God.

2:14 your wife by covenant. The prophet accentuated the iniquity by mentioning the legally binding nature of the marriage contract, a covenant made before God as witness (cf. Ge 31:50; Pr 2:17). Wives were married young, sometimes before 15 years of age (cf. Pr 5:18; Is 54:6).

2:15 Noting God's original institution of marriage (Ge 2:24), in which He made two into one, Malachi reminded them that God provided only one woman for one man. Though He had the life-giving power of the Spirit, and could have made Adam a number of wives, He created only one—to raise up a "godly offspring." Polygamy, divorce, and marriage to idolatrous women are destructive to obtaining the godly remnant in the line of the promised Messiah. Only when both parents remain faithful to their marriage vows can the children be given the security which provides the basis for godly living. Because this foundational divine institution of marriage was being threatened, Malachi urged that no husband act in a treacherous way toward his wife. For polygamy *see note on 1Ki 11:1–6.*

2:16 I hate divorce. The Lord emphasized what He had been saying by this emphatic declaration. In fact, God sees this unwarranted divorce as a gross act of sin which, like blood splattered from a murder victim on the killer, leaves evidence of the evil deed. For discussion of divorce, which God actually commanded the Jews to do by separating from these idolatrous wives, *see notes on Ezr 10:9–18* and the Ezra Introduction: Interpretive Challenges. Though God hates divorce, there are times when it is the lesser of the evils and would prevent a future and even greater spiritual catastrophe. *See notes on Mt 5:32; 19:3–12; 1Co 7:10–16.*

2:17–4:6 The denunciation of Israel's sins was followed by a declaration of the judgment on the unrepentant and subsequent blessing on the faithful remnant. Verse 17 is the introduction to the rest of the book. These faithless, disobedient priests and people had worn out God's patience by their skepticism and self-justification, so judgment is on the way.

2:17 wearied the LORD. Disillusionment followed the rebuilding of the temple. The presence of God had not come to the new temple. They began to live in indifference to God. Calloused and lacking in spiritual discernment, the people persisted in cynical expressions of innocence. They had rejected all intention of taking right and wrong seriously. So deeply gripped by complacent self-righteousness, they had the gall to insolently question the Lord, implying that He seemed to favor the wicked and was unconcerned about the righteous. The prophet faced them with imminent judgment, telling them God was coming, but to refine and purify (cf. 3:1, 5).

3:1 My messenger. It was a custom of the Near Eastern kings to send messengers before them to remove obstacles to their visit. Employing a wordplay on the name of Malachi, ("the Lord's messenger"), the Lord Himself announced He was sending one who would

LORD of hosts. 2 "But who can [A]endure the day of His
coming? And who can stand when He appears? For
He is like a [B]refiner's fire and like [a]fullers' soap. 3 He
will sit as a smelter and purifier of silver, and He will
[A]purify the sons of Levi and refine them like gold
and silver, so that they may [B]present to the LORD
[a]offerings in righteousness. 4 Then the [a]offering of
Judah and Jerusalem will be [A]pleasing to the LORD
as in the [B]days of old and as in former years.
5 "Then I will draw near to you for judgment;
and I will be a swift witness against the [A]sorcerers
and against the [B]adulterers and against those who
[C]swear falsely, and against those who oppress the
[D]wage earner in his wages, the [E]widow and the
[a]orphan, and those who turn aside the [b,F]alien and
do not [c]fear Me," says the LORD of hosts. 6 "For [a]I,
the LORD, [A]do not change; therefore you, O sons of
Jacob, [b]are not consumed.
7 "From the [A]days of your fathers you have turned
aside from My statutes and have not kept *them*.
[B]Return to Me, and I will return to you," says the
LORD of hosts. "But you say, 'How shall we return?'

YOU HAVE ROBBED GOD

8 "Will a man [a]rob God? Yet you are robbing Me!
But you say, 'How have we robbed You?' In [A]tithes
and [b]offerings. 9 You are [A]cursed with a curse, for
you are [a]robbing Me, the whole nation *of you!*
10 [A]Bring the whole tithe into the storehouse, so
that there may be [a]food in My house, and test Me
now in this," says the LORD of hosts, "if I will not
[B]open for you the windows of heaven and [C]pour
out for you a blessing until [b,D]it overflows. 11 Then I
will rebuke the [A]devourer for you, so that it will not
[a]destroy the fruits of the ground; nor will your vine
in the field cast *its grapes,*" says the LORD of hosts.

3:2 [a]Lit *laundrymen's* [A]Is 33:14; Ezek 22:14; Rev 6:17 [B]Zech 13:9; Matt 3:10-12; 1 Cor 3:13-15 3:3 [a]Or *grain offerings* [A]Is 1:25; Dan 12:10 [B]Ps 4:5; 51:19 3:4 [a]Or *grain offering* [A]Ps 51:17-19 [B]2 Chr 7:1-3, 12 3:5 [a]Or *fatherless* [b]Or *sojourner* [c]Or *revere* [A]Deut 18:10; Jer 27:9, 10 [B]Ezek 22:9-11 [C]Jer 5:2; 7:9; Zech 5:4 [D]Lev 19:13 [E]Ex 22:22-24 [F]Deut 27:19 3:6 [a]Or *I am the LORD; I do not* [b]Or *have not come to an end* [A]Num 23:19; James 1:17 3:7 [A]Jer 7:25, 26; 16:11, 12 [B]Zech 1:3 3:8 [a]Or *defraud* [b]Or *heave offerings* [A]Neh 13:11, 12 3:9 [a]Or *defrauding* [A]Mal 2:2 3:10 [a]Lit *prey* [b]Or *there is not room enough* [A]Lev 27:30; Num 18:21-24; Deut 12:6; 14:22-29; Neh 13:12 [B]Ps 78:23-29 [C]Ezek 34:26 [D]Lev 26:3-5 3:11 [a]Lit *ruin* [A]Joel 1:4; 2:25

"clear the way before Me." This is the voice of one "calling" in the wilderness (Is 40:3) and the Elijah of 4:5 who comes before the Lord. The NT clearly identifies him as John the Baptist (cf. Mt 3:3; 11:10, 14; 17:12ff.; Mk 1:2; Lk 1:17; 7:26, 27; Jn 1:23). **will suddenly come.** To come "suddenly" does not mean immediately, but instantaneously and unannounced. It usually refers to a calamitous event (cf. Is 47:11; 48:3; Jer 4:20, etc.). When all the preparations are completed, the Lord will come, not to Zerubbabel's temple, nor in partial fulfillment to Herod's temple (*see notes on Jn 2:13–24*), but finally to that millennial temple which Ezekiel describes in Eze 40–48. The unexpected coming of Christ, partially fulfilled at His First Advent, will be accomplished in full at His Second Coming (cf. Mt 24:40–42). **messenger of the covenant.** Probably not the messenger just mentioned. Rather, because this Messenger "will come to His temple," it is most likely a reference to the Lord Himself, the One who has the authority to reward or judge His people on the basis of their faithfulness to His covenant with them. The title may reflect earlier OT references to His "angel," which is lit. "messenger" (cf. Ex 23:20–23; 32:34; Is 63:9). **in whom you delight.** This is likely sarcastic. These sinful people were not delighting in God then, nor would they when He came in judgment on their hypocritical worship and cleansed the temple (cf. Jn 2:13–25). All the ungodly will be destroyed at His return (cf. Rev 19:11ff.).

3:2 refiner's fire … fullers' soap. Instead of bringing rewards, His coming is likened to two purifying agents—fire to burn off dross and alkali to whiten—an indication of the true condition of their hearts. The fire will burn off the dross of iniquity; the soap will wash out the stain of sin. His coming will be one in which He removes all impurities. No one will escape this cleansing. Importantly, He will come purifying and cleansing, but not necessarily destroying (cf. Is 1:25; 48:10; Jer 6:29, 30; Eze 22:17–22).

3:3 purify the sons of Levi. Since the Levitical priests were instrumental in leading the nation astray and a new group of pure priests was required for the work of the millennial temple (cf. Eze 44–45:8), the cleansing of the nation would begin with them (cf. Eze 9:6). Then they can "present to the LORD" what is righteous as called for in the millennial sacrifices (cf. Eze 45:9–46:24). **offerings in righteousness.** Given from cleansed hearts in a right condition before God, their offerings will be "in righteousness." These millennial sacrifices will be a memorial for the redeemed nation of Israel, commemorating Christ's sacrifice at Calvary. *See notes on Eze 44–46.*

3:4 the days of old. Only after the priesthood is purged and when the people are cleansed will they be able to offer what pleases the Lord as in the days of Solomon (2Ch 7:8–10); Hezekiah (2Ch 30:26); Josiah (2Ch 35:18); and Ezra (Ne 8:7).

3:5 What is a refining process for the remnant of repentant Jews who acknowledge their Messiah (cf. Zec 12–14; Ro 11:25–27), preparing them to enter the kingdom and worship in the millennial temple, will be for others utter destruction. All the iniquitous behavior in this verse is evidence that these are people who "do not fear" God. In 2:17, they asked a question, and here is the answer, "I will draw near to you for judgment." Occult practices were clearly forbidden (cf. Ex 22:18; Dt 18:10–12), but continued into NT times (cf. Ac 8:9). Adultery also violated God's law (2:16), as did perjury (cf. Ex 20:16; Lv 19:12; Dt 19:16–20), extortion, and oppression.

3:6–12 These verses form a parenthesis between two messages concerning God's justice and judgment. What the Jews have labeled as God's injustice is not God's being unrighteous or unfair, but His being mercifully patient. A genuine call of repentance is then issued (v. 7) and the fruit of it described (v. 10).

3:6, 7 Contrary to God's having become unjust and thus not acting on behalf of Israel, in light of their history of rebellion, Israel's existence was due only to the Lord's unchanging character and unswerving commitment to His covenant promise with the patriarchs (cf. Nu 23:19; 1Sa 15:29; Jas 1:17 in general; Jer 31:35–37; 33:14–22 in particular). They may experience God's goodness again, and be blessed—if they repent. In view of the Lord's coming to refine and purify, Malachi presents a powerful challenge to repent (cf. Zec 1:3). Yet, apparently unwilling to admit the sins on their part needing repentance (also cf. v. 8b), the invitation to return is met with another cynical query, asking how they can return when, from their perspective, they haven't left—God has. The truth was, God hasn't changed and neither have they; He was as righteous as ever and they as unrighteous.

3:8–12 In answer to their query about how they have deviated from God's way and need to return, the prophet picked an illustration of their spiritual defection that is very visible and undeniable. The Lord pointed out that they had not brought the required tithes and offerings, those used to fund the theocracy by sustaining the Levites (cf. Lv 27:30–33; Nu 18:8–28; Dt 12:18; Ne 13:10), the national religious festivals (Dt 12:6–17; 14:22–27), and the poor (Dt 14:28, 29). But in not paying their taxes, and so robbing God, they had robbed themselves, for God had withheld His blessing. On believers' responsibility to pay taxes, *see notes on Mt 22:21; Ro 13:1–7*. On NT freewill giving, *see 1Co 16:1, 2; 2Co 8, 9.*

3:8, 9 you are robbing Me. Here was a glaring, widespread sin; they had stolen from God what was rightfully His by divine law.

3:10–12 test Me. Contrary to the normal biblical pattern, the people were invited to put God to the test (cf. Is 7:11, 12; 1Ki 18:20–46). If they would honor Him by reversing their robbery and in a show of true repentance bring what He required, He would shower them with excessive abundance (cf. Pr 11:24, 25), protect them from locusts ("the devourer"), and they would be the delight of the nations (cf. Is 62:4). *See notes on Lk 6:38; 2Co 9:6–10.*

3:10 the whole tithe. *See note on vv. 8–12.* When tithes were unpaid, the priests were deprived and had to give up their ministry and to begin farming. The nation's religious life was hindered, and the poor and strangers suffered (cf. Ne 13:10–11). But, the real iniquity was that such disobedience was robbing God, who was the true King of the theocracy of

12 "[A]All the nations will call you blessed, for you
shall be a [B]delightful land," says the LORD of hosts.
13 "Your words have been [a]arrogant against Me,"
says the LORD. "Yet you say, 'What have we spoken
against You?' 14 You have said, 'It is [A]vain to serve
God; and what [B]profit is it that we have kept His
charge, and that we have walked in mourning before the LORD of hosts? 15 So now we [A]call the arrogant blessed; not only are the doers of wickedness
built up but they also test God and [B]escape.' "

THE BOOK OF REMEMBRANCE

16 Then those who [a]feared the LORD spoke to one
another, and the LORD [A]gave attention and heard
it, and a [B]book of remembrance was written before
Him for those who [a]fear the LORD and who esteem
His name. 17 "They will be [A]Mine," says the LORD of
hosts, "on the [B]day that I [a]prepare *My* [b,C]own possession, and I will [c]spare them as a man [c,D]spares
his own son who serves him." 18 So you will again
[A]distinguish between the righteous and the wicked,

3:12 [A]Is 61:9 [B]Is 62:4 3:13 [a]Lit *strong* 3:14 [A]Jer 2:25; 18:12 [B]Is 58:3 3:15 [A]Is 2:22; Mal 4:1 [B]Jer 7:10 3:16 [a]Or *revere(d)* [A]Ps 34:15; Jer 31:18-20 [B]Is 4:3; Dan 12:1 3:17 [a]Lit *make* [b]Or *special treasure* [c]Or *have (has) compassion on* [A]Is 43:1 [B]Is 4:2 [C]Ex 19:5; Deut 7:6; Is 43:21; 1 Pet 2:9 [D]Ps 103:13 3:18 [A]Gen 18:25; Amos 5:15

Israel. **storehouse.** A room in the temple to store the tithes of crops and animals brought by the people (cf. 2Ch 31:11; Ne 10:38, 39; 12:44; 13:12). This was the temple treasury. One of Nehemiah's tasks was to ensure that the supplies needed for support of the temple ministry did not fail as it had during his absence (cf. Ne 13:10–13).

3:13 These sinful priests and people had not just questioned God (2:17), violated God's covenant (2:11), disobeyed His laws (2:9), defiled His altar (1:7, 12) and despised His name (1:6), but had openly spoken against Him. In spite of what was promised (vv. 10–12), the people complained that obedience to God's law brought no rewards (v. 14). Only the proud and wicked prospered, they said (v. 15).

3:14 walked in mourning. The people pretended to grieve for their sins, walking around in sackcloth or even with blackened faces to convey apparent sorrow (cf. Is 58:5; Joel 2:13; Mt 6:16–18), then complained that all that religious activity was useless.

3:15 test God. The proud and wicked, with apparent impunity, put God to the test by seeing how far they could go in doing evil (cf. Ps 73:2–14). In v. 10, God invited His people to see how far He would go in blessing.

3:16–4:6 Malachi ended with an encouraging word for the faithful remnant.

3:16 book of remembrance. In the hearts of the true and righteous worshipers who loved and served God in Israel, all the talk of judgment produced fear that they, too, might be swept away when God's wrath came. To encourage the godly remnant, Malachi noted how the Lord had not forgotten those "who fear the LORD and who esteem His name." The book may be a reference to the "book of life" in which the names of God's children are recorded (e.g., Ex 32:32–34; Ne 13:14; Ps 69:28; Da 12:1). The Persians had a custom of recording in a book all acts of a person that should be rewarded in the future (e.g., Est 6:1, 2). The psalmist knew of such a book as well (Ps 56:8).

3:17 Mine . . . *My* own possession. "Mine" is emphatic in the Hebrew. The godly remnant will belong to Him and will be His special treasure, or "possession" (cf. same word in Ex 19:5; Dt 7:6; 14:2; 26:18; Ps 135:4). In the midst of judgment, He will spare them (cf. Ps 103:13).

3:18 The distinction between the godly and ungodly will be evident for all when the

ROMAN CONTROL OF ISRAEL AT THE TIME OF CHRIST

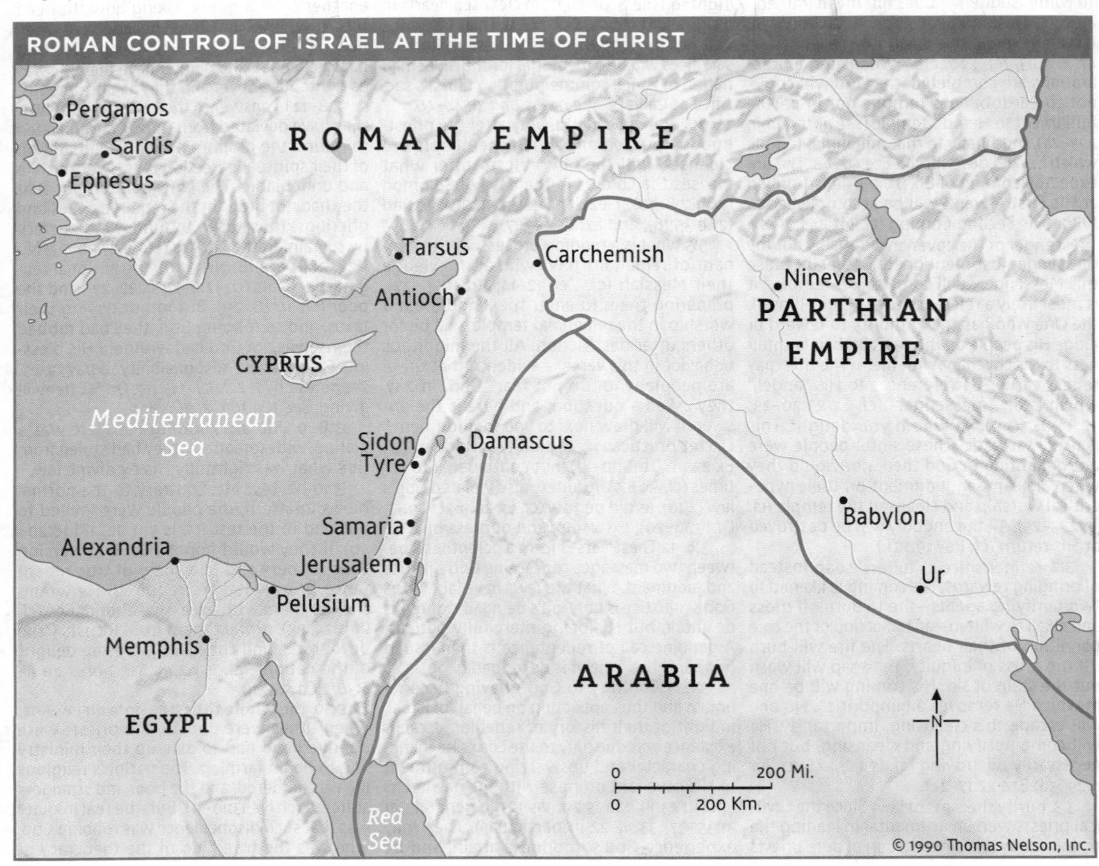

between one who serves God and one who does
not serve Him.

FINAL ADMONITION

4 "[a]For behold, the day is coming, [A]burning like
a furnace; and all the arrogant and every evildoer will be [B]chaff; and the day that is coming will
[C]set them ablaze," says the LORD of hosts, "so that it
will leave them neither root nor branch." 2 "But for
you who [a]fear My name, the [A]sun of righteousness
will rise with [B]healing in its wings; and you will go
forth and [C]skip about like calves from the stall. 3 You
will [A]tread down the wicked, for they will be [B]ashes
under the soles of your feet [C]on the day [a]which I am
preparing," says the LORD of hosts.
4 "[a,A]Remember the law of Moses My servant, *even*
the statutes and ordinances which I commanded
him in Horeb for all Israel.
5 "Behold, I am going to send you [A]Elijah the
prophet before the coming of the great and terrible day of the LORD. 6 He will [a,A]restore the hearts
of the fathers to *their* children and the hearts of the
children to their fathers, so that I will not come and
[B]smite the land with a [b]curse."

4:1 [a]Ch 3:19 in Heb [A]Ps 21:9; Nah 1:5, 6; Mal 3:2, 3; 2 Pet 3:7 [B]Is 5:24; Obad 18 [C]Is 9:18, 19 4:2 [a]Or *revere* [A]2 Sam 23:4; Is 30:26; 60:1 [B]Jer 30:17; 33:6 [C]Is 35:6 4:3 [a]Or *when I act* [A]Job 40:12; Is 26:6; Mic 5:8 [B]Ezek 28:18 [C]Mal 3:17 4:4 [a]Ch 3:22 in Heb [A]Deut 4:23; 8:11, 19 4:5 [A]Matt 11:14; 17:10-13; Mark 9:11-13; Luke 1:17; John 1:21 4:6 [a]Or *turn* [b]Or *ban of destruction* [A]Luke 1:17 [B]Is 11:4; Rev 19:15

righteous Lord is present, ruling from the throne of David in Jerusalem.

4:1 **the day is coming.** The first 3 verses continue the thought of the closing verses of the previous chapter, elaborating on God's punishment of the wicked and His deliverance of the godly (cf. 3:1–5). This eschatological reference to the day of the Lord (cf. Is 13:6; Joel 2:11, 31; Zep 1:14) is injected 4 times into the prophet's final words (3:17; 4:1, 3, 5). It anticipated the return of the Lord Jesus in judgment (cf. Rev 19:11–21). **burning like a furnace.** Adding to the imagery of a refining fire (3:2), Malachi spoke of God's judgment as a destructive fire that swiftly and totally consumes with excessive heat (cf. with the proud of 3:15). The destruction of the roots, normally protected by their subsurface location, provides a vivid, proverbial picture of its totality. All who refuse to repent will be cast into the fire of hell (cf. Rev 20:11–15).

4:2 **sun of righteousness.** While the wicked will be devoured by the heat of His wrath, those who fear Him will feel His warmth with healing in His "light" (cf. Is 30:26; 60:1, 3). The reference is to the Messiah, "the LORD our righteousness" (Ps 84:11; Jer 23:5, 6; 1Co 1:30). **healing.** The reference should not be limited to the physical recovery from the harm done by the wicked (cf. 3:5). This sickness is inextricably linked with sin, with healing coming only through the suffering of the Servant (cf. Ps 103:3; Is 53:5; 57:18, 19; 1Pe 2:24). **like calves from the stall.** Calves, when confined to a stall for extended periods of time, leap for sheer joy when turned loose into the sunlight. The picture is one of a joyful, vigorous, and carefree life.

4:3 **ashes under . . . your feet.** The destruction of the wicked is appreciated by those who suffered at their hand. Ashes were often poured on foot trails to provide a more solid pathway during wet weather. Here the wicked are compared to ashes, which the righteous will tread down as a result of the fire of God's judgment (cf. v. 1). The prophet desires, as should all believers, that there be far-reaching repentance, and if not, destruction of the impenitent is inescapable.

4:4 Both the Law and the Prophets play a part in preparing for the arrival of the day of the Lord. First, the people were to remember what was given at Sinai (Horeb), the law of Moses primarily focusing on the obligations to obedience at the time of entering into that covenant (Ex 24:1ff.; Jos 8:32; 23:6; 1Ki 2:3).

4:5 **Elijah.** The mention of Elijah was to announce the Messiah's arrival (see Introduction: Interpretive Challenges). John the Baptist was a type of Elijah at Christ's First Advent (cf. Lk 1:17). Moses and Elijah appeared together at the Mt. of Transfiguration (cf. Mt 17:1–4) and may be the two witnesses in the Great Tribulation (cf. Rev 11:1–3). Most likely, this will be an Elijah-like person, as John the Baptist was Elijah-like (*see note on 3:1*). In that day, his task will be to preach reconciliation to God so that souls can believe and be spared God's curse. He will be effective (v. 6).

4:6 **restore . . . hearts.** The very opposite of what occurred at Christ's first coming (cf. Mt 10:34–36) anticipates a general societal repentance (cf. Mt 25:31–46; Rev 7:9–17; 20:4–6), so that complete destruction might be averted. The earth will be restored to Edenic wonder, the curse reversed, the kingdom established with Messiah reigning, and the righteous Jews and Gentiles entering it. **curse.** Not the normal word for curse, this word refers to the practice of devoting things or persons irrevocably to God, often by total destruction. Cities of Canaan were put under the "curse," and thus the people were to be exterminated (cf. Dt 13:12–18; 20:16ff.). Its use here suggests that God would make a whole burnt offering of the earth if there was not a repentant remnant.

INTRODUCTION TO THE

INTERTESTAMENTAL PERIOD

Over 400 years separated the final events (Ne 13:4–30) and final prophecy (Mal 1:1–4:6) recorded in the Old Testament (ca. 424 B.C.) from the beginning actions (Lk 1:5–25) narrated in the New Testament (ca. 6 B.C.). Because there was no prophetic word from God during this time, this period is sometimes called "the four hundred silent years." However, the history of these years followed the pattern predicted in Daniel (Da 2:24, 45; 7:1–28; 8:1–27; 11:1–35) with exact precision. Though the voice of God was silent, the hand of God was actively directing the course of events during these centuries.

JEWISH HISTORY

As predicted by Daniel, control of the land of Israel passed from the empire of Medo-Persia to Greece and then to Rome (Da 2:39, 40; 7:5–7). For about 200 years, the Persian Empire ruled the Jews (539–332 B.C.). The Persians allowed the Jews to return, rebuild, and worship at the temple in Jerusalem (2Ch 36:22, 23; Ezr 1:1–4). For about 100 years after the close of the Old Testament canon, Judea continued to be a Persian territory under the governor of Syria with the High Priest exercising a measure of civil authority. The Jews were allowed to observe their religious tenets without any official governmental interference.

Between 334 B.C. and 331 B.C., Alexander the Great defeated the Persian king, Darius III, in 3 decisive battles that gave him control of the lands of the Persian Empire. The land of Israel thus passed into Greek control in 332 B.C. (Da 8:5–7, 20, 21; 11:3). Alexander permitted the Jews in Judea to observe their laws and granted them an exemption from taxes during their sabbatical years. However, Alexander sought to bring Greek culture, called "Hellenism," to the lands he had conquered. He wished to create a world united by Greek language and thinking. This policy, carried on by Alexander's successors, was as dangerous to the religion of Israel as the cult of Baal had been, because the Greek way of life was attractive, sophisticated, and humanly appealing, but utterly ungodly.

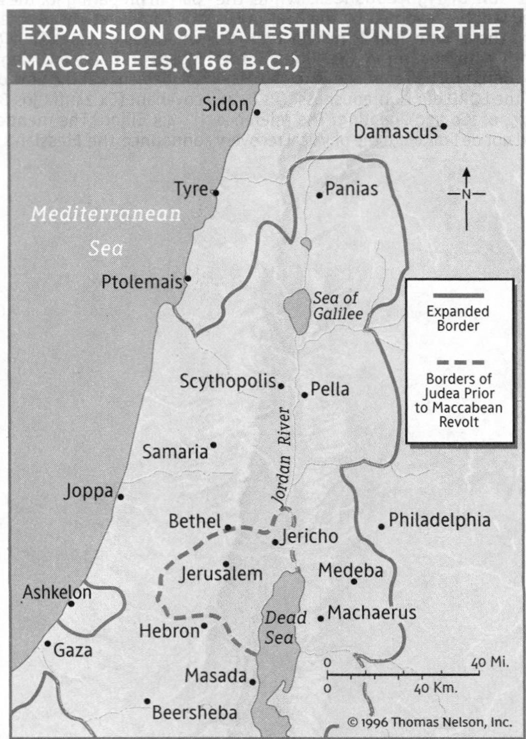

Upon Alexander's death in 323 B.C., a struggle ensued among his generals as his empire was divided (Da 8:22; 11:4). Ptolemy I Sater, founder of the Ptolemies of Egypt, took control of Israel, even though an agreement in 301 B.C. assigned it to Seleucus I Nicator, founder of the Seleucids of Syria. This caused continuing contention between the Seleucid and Ptolemaic dynasties (Da 11:5). The Ptolemies ruled Judea from 301 B.C. to 198 B.C. (Da 11:6–12). Under the Ptolemies, the Jews had comparative religious freedom in a setting of economic oppression.

In 198 B.C., Antiochus III the Great defeated Ptolemy V Epiphanes and took control of Israel (Da 11:13–16). Judea was under Seleucid rule until 143 B.C. (Da 11:17–35). Early Seleucid toleration of Jewish religious practices came to an end in the reign of Antiochus IV Epiphanes (175–164 B.C.). Antiochus desecrated and plundered the temple of Jerusalem in 170 B.C. In 167 B.C., Antiochus ordered Hellenization in Palestine and forbade the Jews from keeping their laws, observing the Sabbath, keeping festivals, offering sacrifices, and circumcising their children. Copies of the Torah were ordered destroyed, idolatrous altars were set up, plus the Jews were commanded by Antiochus to offer unclean sacrifices and to eat swine's flesh. Antiochus was the first pagan monarch to persecute the Jews for their faith (Da 8:9–14, 23–25; 11:21–35).

An aged priest, Mattathias, and his 5 sons led the Jewish resistance against Antiochus and his Seleucid successors. This was known as the Maccabean Revolt because Judas Maccabeus (lit. "Hammer") was the first leader among the 5 sons. After a 24-year war (166–142 B.C.), the Jews were able to gain their independence from Syria because of the growing Roman pressure on the Seleucids. The descendants of Mattathias founded the Hasmonean dynasty, a name derived from Hashmon, an ancestor of the Maccabees.

The Hasmoneans took over the office of High Priest, although they did not belong to the line of Zadok (Nu 25:10–13; Eze 40:46; 48:11). Quickly, the Hasmoneans began to follow Hellenistic ways, the very practices they had at first resisted. The Greek influence continued in Palestine from 142 B.C. to 63 B.C. through this native dynasty.

The Hasmonean dynasty ended in 63 B.C. when Pompey, a general of Rome, intervened in a clash between two claimants to the High Priesthood, Aristobolus II and Hyrcanus II. The land thus passed into Roman control (Da 2:40; 7:7). Continuing unrest led the Romans to make Herod the Great king of Judea. He was an Idumean by birth, a Jewish proselyte, and thoroughly Greco-Roman in outlook. He ruled Palestine from 37 B.C. to 4 B.C. and was the "king of the Jews" when Jesus was born (Mt 2:1, 2).

JEWISH DEVELOPMENTS

Diaspora. The dispersion of Israel began in the two exiles, i.e., Israel in Assyria (2Ki 17:23) and Judah in Babylon (2Ki 25:21). The majority of Israelites did not return to Judea after the exile and so became colonists, no longer captives, in the Persian Empire. The geographical movement of Israelites continued in the Greek and Roman Empires so that by the first century A.D., Jews were found throughout the Mediterranean basin and Mesopotamia. The majority of Israelites lived outside of the land during the later Intertestamental Period.

Scribes and Rabbis. Believing the Exile had come because of a lack of knowledge of and obedience to the Torah, the Israelite exiles devoted themselves to the study of the Old Testament. The scribes became experts in and were considered authorities on the interpretation of the Scriptures during the Intertestamental Period. The rabbis were the teachers who passed on the scribal understanding of the Scriptures to the people of Israel.

Synagogue. With the destruction of the temple in 586 B.C., the synagogue became the place of education and worship for the Jews in exile. Since the majority of Jews did not return to Palestine after the Exile, synagogues continued to function in the Diaspora and also became established in Palestine, even after the reconstruction of the temple by Zerubbabel in 516 B.C.

Septuagint. With the emphasis placed on using the Greek language from ca. 330 B.C. on, the Jews of the Diaspora became predominately Greek-speakers. According to Jewish legend, in ca. 250 B.C., Ptolemy Philadelphus brought together 72 scholars who translated the Old Testament into Greek in 72 days. Thus, the Latin word for 70, "Septuagint" (LXX), was the name attached to this translation. Probably translated over the period from 250 B.C. to 125 B.C. in Alexandria, Egypt, the Septuagint was the most important and widely used Greek translation of the Old Testament.

Pharisees. This religious party probably began as the "holy ones" associated with the Maccabees in the endeavor to rid the land of Hellenistic elements. When the Maccabees turned themselves to Hellenism once it was in power, these holy ones "separated" (the possible source of the name, Pharisee) from the official religious establishment of Judea. The Pharisees interpreted the law strictly in accordance with a developing oral tradition and sought to make their understanding binding upon all Jews. Though few in number, the Pharisees enjoyed the favor of the majority of the people in Israel.

Sadducees. Probably from the name "Zadok," the high priestly line, these Hellenized, aristocratic Jews became the guardians of the temple policy and practices. The Sadducees rejected the Old Testament as Scripture, except for the Torah, as well as any teaching they believed was not found in the Torah (the first 5 books of the OT), e.g., the resurrection from the dead (Ac 23:6–8).

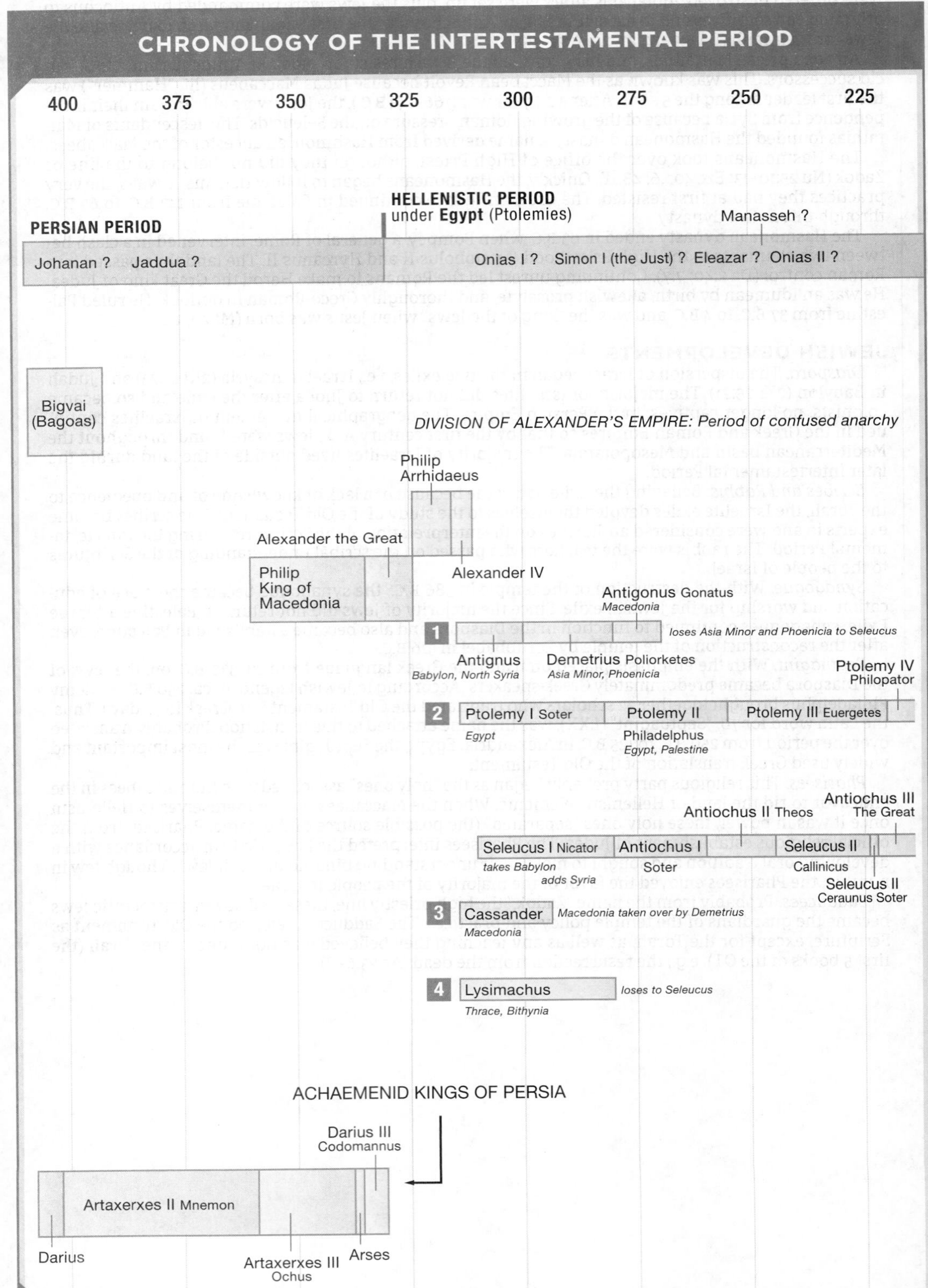
CHRONOLOGY OF THE INTERTESTAMENTAL PERIOD
400
375
350
325
300
275
250
225
HELLENISTIC PERIOD
under Egypt (Ptolemies)
PERSIAN PERIOD
Manasseh ?
Johanan ?
Jaddua ?
Onias I ?
Simon I (the Just) ?
Eleazar ?
Onias II ?
Bigvai (Bagoas)
DIVISION OF ALEXANDER'S EMPIRE: Period of confused anarchy
Philip Arrhidaeus
Alexander the Great
Philip King of Macedonia
Alexander IV
Antigonus Gonatus
Macedonia
1
loses Asia Minor and Phoenicia to Seleucus
Antignus
Babylon, North Syria
Demetrius Poliorketes
Asia Minor, Phoenicia
Ptolemy IV
Philopator
2
Ptolemy I Soter
Egypt
Ptolemy II
Philadelphus
Egypt, Palestine
Ptolemy III Euergetes
Antiochus III
The Great
Antiochus II Theos
Seleucus I Nicator
takes Babylon
adds Syria
Antiochus I
Soter
Seleucus II
Callinicus
Seleucus II
Ceraunus Soter
3
Cassander
Macedonia
Macedonia taken over by Demetrius
4
Lysimachus
Thrace, Bithynia
loses to Seleucus
ACHAEMENID KINGS OF PERSIA
Darius III
Codomannus
Artaxerxes II Mnemon
Darius
Artaxerxes III
Ochus
Arses

CHRONOLOGY OF THE INTERTESTAMENTAL PERIOD

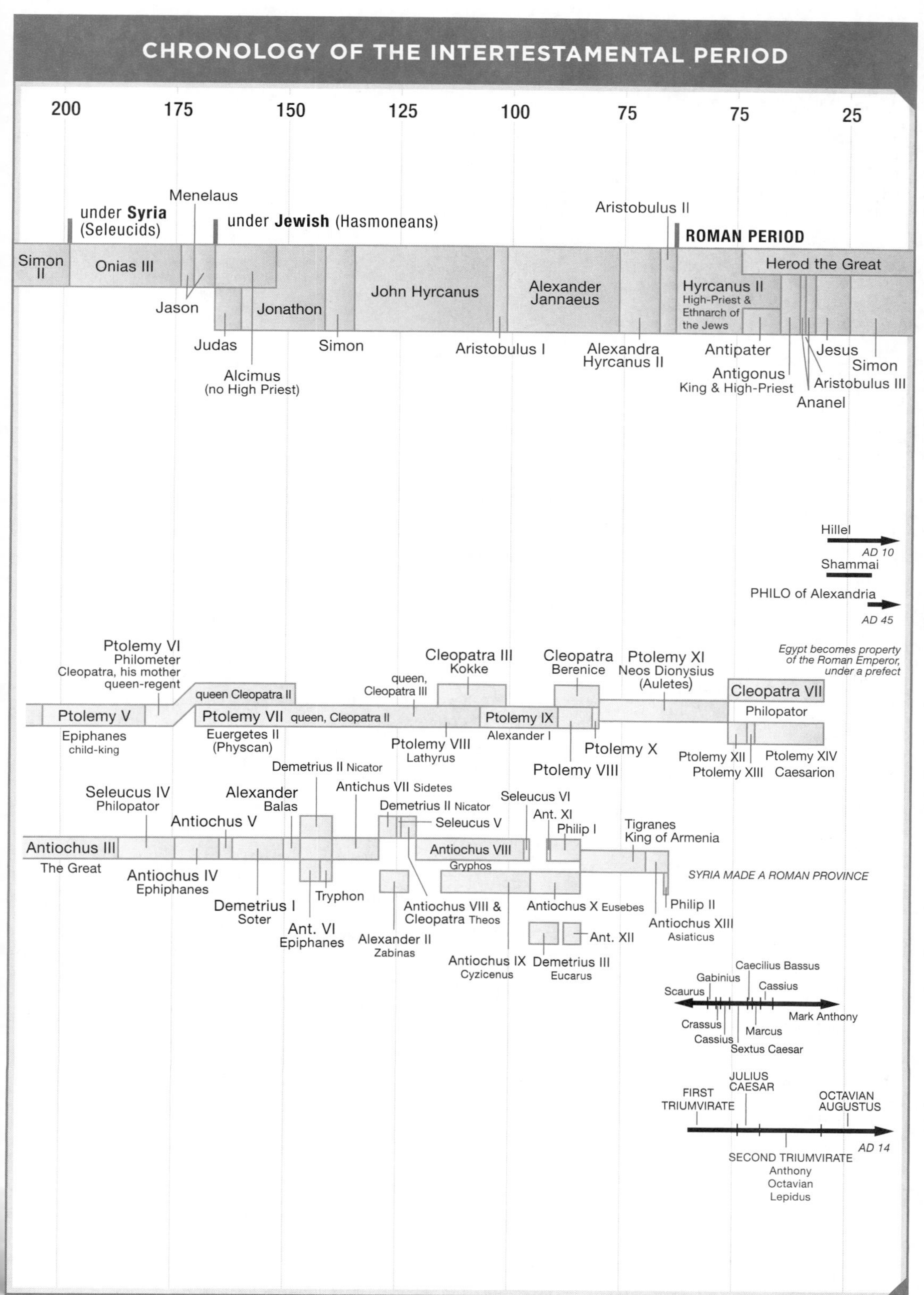

200
175
150
125
100
75
75
25
under Syria (Seleucids)
under Jewish (Hasmoneans)
ROMAN PERIOD
Menelaus
Aristobulus II
Simon II
Onias III
Jason
Jonathon
John Hyrcanus
Alexander Jannaeus
Hyrcanus II High-Priest & Ethnarch of the Jews
Herod the Great
Judas
Simon
Aristobulus I
Alexandra Hyrcanus II
Antipater
Jesus
Simon
Alcimus (no High Priest)
Antigonus King & High-Priest
Aristobulus III
Ananel
Hillel
AD 10
Shammai
PHILO of Alexandria
AD 45
Ptolemy VI Philometer
Cleopatra, his mother queen-regent
queen Cleopatra II
Cleopatra III Kokke
queen, Cleopatra III
Cleopatra Berenice
Ptolemy XI Neos Dionysius (Auletes)
Egypt becomes property of the Roman Emperor, under a prefect
Cleopatra VII Philopator
Ptolemy V Epiphanes child-king
Ptolemy VII queen, Cleopatra II
Euergetes II (Physcan)
Ptolemy IX Alexander I
Ptolemy VIII Lathyrus
Ptolemy X
Ptolemy VIII
Ptolemy XII
Ptolemy XIII
Ptolemy XIV Caesarion
Demetrius II Nicator
Antichus VII Sidetes
Seleucus IV Philopator
Alexander Balas
Demetrius II Nicator
Seleucus VI
Antiochus V
Seleucus V
Ant. XI
Philip I
Tigranes King of Armenia
Antiochus III The Great
Antiochus VIII Gryphos
Antiochus IV Ephiphanes
SYRIA MADE A ROMAN PROVINCE
Tryphon
Demetrius I Soter
Antiochus VIII & Cleopatra Theos
Antiochus X Eusebes
Philip II
Ant. VI Epiphanes
Antiochus XIII Asiaticus
Ant. XII
Alexander II Zabinas
Antiochus IX Cyzicenus
Demetrius III Eucarus
Caecilius Bassus
Gabinius
Scaurus
Cassius
Mark Anthony
Crassus
Cassius
Marcus
Sextus Caesar
JULIUS CAESAR
FIRST TRIUMVIRATE
OCTAVIAN AUGUSTUS
AD 14
SECOND TRIUMVIRATE Anthony Octavian Lepidus

THE NEW TESTAMENT

INTRODUCTION TO THE

GOSPELS

The English word "gospel" derives from the Anglo-Saxon word *godspell,* which can mean either "a story about God," or "a good story." The latter meaning is in harmony with the Greek word translated "gospel," *euangellion,* which means "good news." In secular Greek, *euangellion* referred to a good report about an important event. The 4 Gospels are the good news about the most significant events in all of history—the life, sacrificial death, and resurrection of Jesus of Nazareth.

The Gospels are not biographies in the modern sense of the word, since they do not intend to present a complete life of Jesus (cf. Jn 20:30; 21:25). Apart from the birth narratives, they give little information about the first 30 years of Jesus' life. While Jesus' public ministry lasted over 3 years, the Gospels focus much of their attention on the last week of His life (cf. Jn 12–20). Though they are completely accurate historically, and present important biographical details of Jesus' life, the primary purposes of the Gospels are theological and apologetic (Jn 20:31). They provide authoritative answers to questions about Jesus' life and ministry, and they strengthen believers' assurance regarding the reality of their faith (Lk 1:4).

Although many spurious gospels were written, the church from earliest times has accepted only Matthew, Mark, Luke, and John as inspired Scripture. While each gospel has its unique perspective (see the discussion of the "Synoptic Problem" in the Introduction to Mark: Interpretive Challenges), Matthew, Mark, and Luke, when compared to John, share a common point of view. Because of that, they are known as the synoptic (from a Greek word meaning "to see together," or "to share a common point of view") gospels. Matthew, Mark, and Luke, for example, focus on Christ's Galilean ministry, while John focuses on His ministry in Judea. The Synoptic Gospels contain numerous parables, while John records none. John and the Synoptic Gospels record only two common events (Jesus' walking on the water, and the feeding of the 5,000) prior to Passion Week. These differences between John and the Synoptic Gospels, however, are not contradictory, but complementary.

As already noted, each gospel writer wrote from a unique perspective, for a different audience. As a result, each gospel contains distinctive elements. Taken together, the 4 gospels form a complete testimony about Jesus Christ.

Matthew wrote primarily to a Jewish audience, presenting Jesus of Nazareth as Israel's long-awaited Messiah and rightful King. His genealogy, unlike Luke's, focuses on Jesus' royal descent from Israel's greatest king, David. Interspersed throughout Matthew are OT quotes presenting various aspects of Jesus' life and ministry as the fulfillment of OT messianic prophecy. Matthew alone uses the phrase "kingdom of heaven," avoiding the parallel phrase "kingdom of God" because of the unbiblical connotations it had in first-century Jewish thought. Matthew wrote his gospel, then, to strengthen the faith of Jewish Christians, and it provides a useful apologetic tool for Jewish evangelism.

Mark targeted a Gentile audience, especially a Roman one (see Introduction to Mark: Background and Setting). Mark is the gospel of action; the frequent use of "immediately" and "then" keeps his narrative moving rapidly along. Jesus appears in Mark as the Servant (cf. Mk 10:45) who came to suffer for the sins of many. Mark's fast-paced approach would especially appeal to the practical, action-oriented Romans.

Luke addressed a broader Gentile audience. As an educated Greek (see Introduction to Luke: Author and Date), Luke wrote using the most sophisticated literary Greek of any NT writer. He was a careful researcher (Lk 1:1–4) and an accurate historian. Luke portrays Jesus as the Son of Man (a title appearing 26 times), the answer to the needs and hopes of the human race, who came to seek and save lost sinners (Lk 9:56; 19:10).

John, the last gospel written, emphasizes the deity of Jesus Christ (e.g., 5:18; 8:58; 10:30–33; 14:9). John wrote to strengthen the faith of believers and to appeal to unbelievers to come to faith in Christ. The apostle clearly stated his purpose for writing in 20:31: "... these have been written so that you may believe that Jesus is the Christ, the Son of God, and that believing you may have life in His name."

Taken together, the 4 gospels weave a complete portrait of the God-Man, Jesus of Nazareth. In Him were blended perfect humanity and deity, making Him the only sacrifice for the sins of the world, and the worthy Lord of those who believe.

THE ROMAN EMPIRE IN THE NEW TESTAMENT

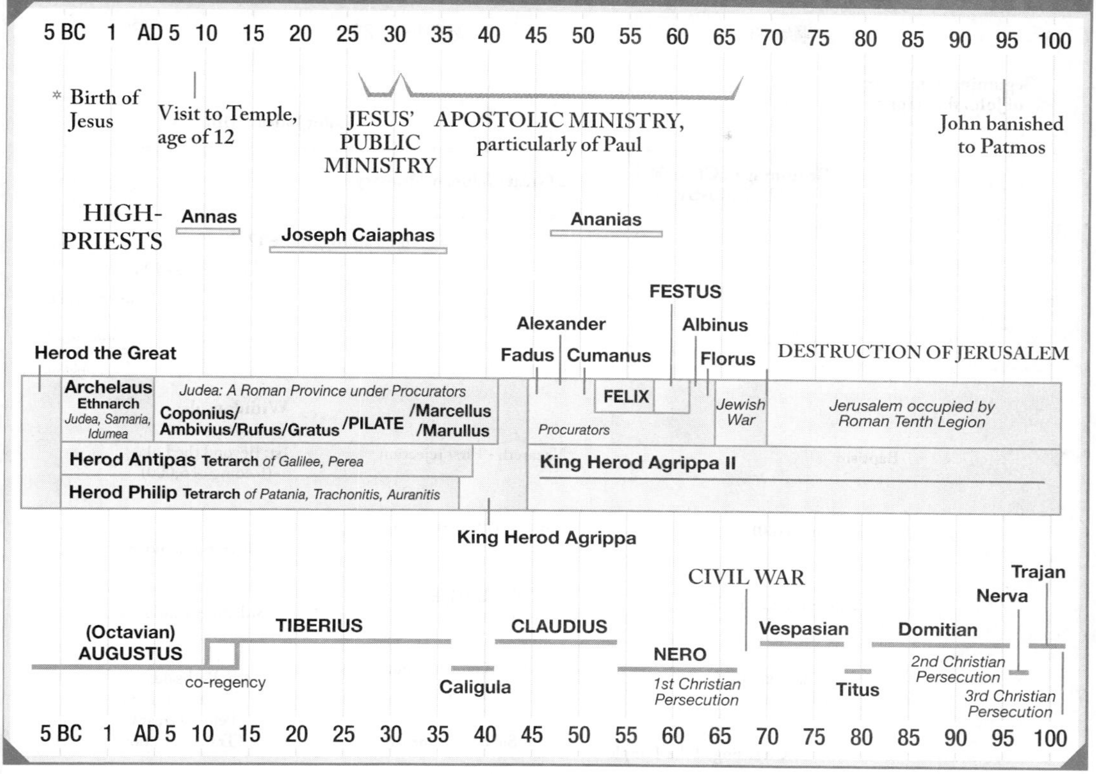

5 BC 1 AD 5 10 15 20 25 30 35 40 45 50 55 60 65 70 75 80 85 90 95 100

* Birth of Jesus

Visit to Temple, age of 12

JESUS' PUBLIC MINISTRY

APOSTOLIC MINISTRY, particularly of Paul

John banished to Patmos

HIGH-PRIESTS

Annas

Joseph Caiaphas

Ananias

FESTUS

Alexander

Albinus

Herod the Great

Fadus

Cumanus

Florus

DESTRUCTION OF JERUSALEM

Archelaus Ethnarch *Judea, Samaria, Idumea*

Judea: A Roman Province under Procurators

Coponius/ Ambivius/Rufus/Gratus /PILATE /Marcellus /Marullus

FELIX

Procurators

Jewish War

Jerusalem occupied by Roman Tenth Legion

Herod Antipas Tetrarch *of Galilee, Perea*

King Herod Agrippa II

Herod Philip Tetrarch *of Patania, Trachonitis, Auranitis*

King Herod Agrippa

CIVIL WAR

Trajan

Nerva

(Octavian) AUGUSTUS

TIBERIUS

CLAUDIUS

Vespasian

Domitian

NERO

co-regency

Caligula

1st Christian Persecution

Titus

2nd Christian Persecution

3rd Christian Persecution

5 BC 1 AD 5 10 15 20 25 30 35 40 45 50 55 60 65 70 75 80 85 90 95 100

THE MINISTRIES OF THE APOSTLES

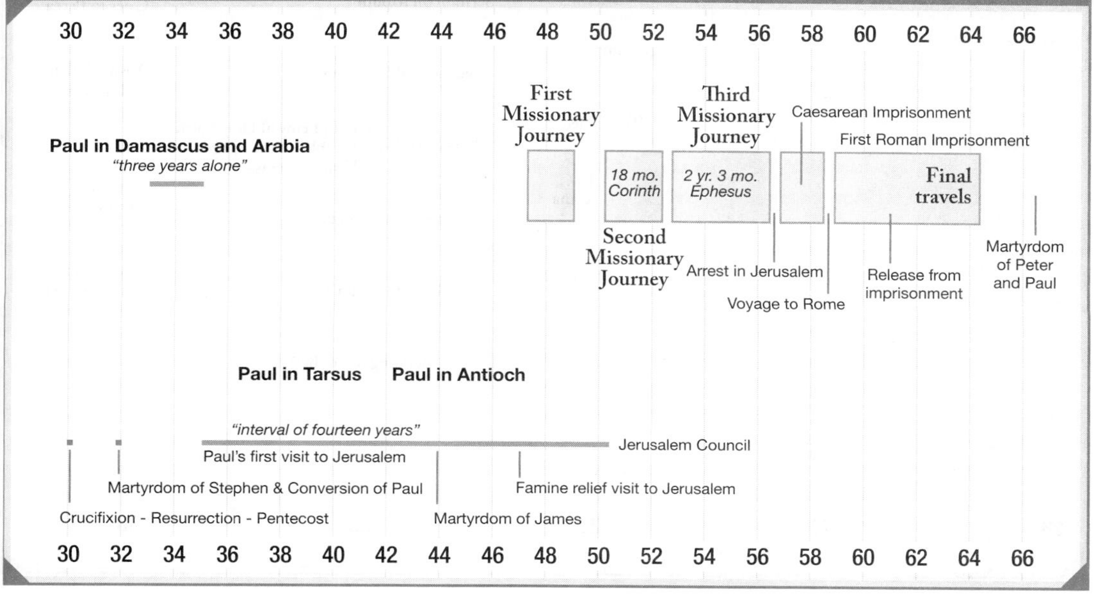

30 32 34 36 38 40 42 44 46 48 50 52 54 56 58 60 62 64 66

First Missionary Journey

Third Missionary Journey

Caesarean Imprisonment

Paul in Damascus and Arabia

"three years alone"

First Roman Imprisonment

18 mo. Corinth

2 yr. 3 mo. Ephesus

Final travels

Second Missionary Journey

Arrest in Jerusalem

Voyage to Rome

Release from imprisonment

Martyrdom of Peter and Paul

Paul in Tarsus

Paul in Antioch

"interval of fourteen years"

Jerusalem Council

Paul's first visit to Jerusalem

Martyrdom of Stephen & Conversion of Paul

Famine relief visit to Jerusalem

Crucifixion - Resurrection - Pentecost

Martyrdom of James

30 32 34 36 38 40 42 44 46 48 50 52 54 56 58 60 62 64 66

THE MINISTRY OF JESUS CHRIST

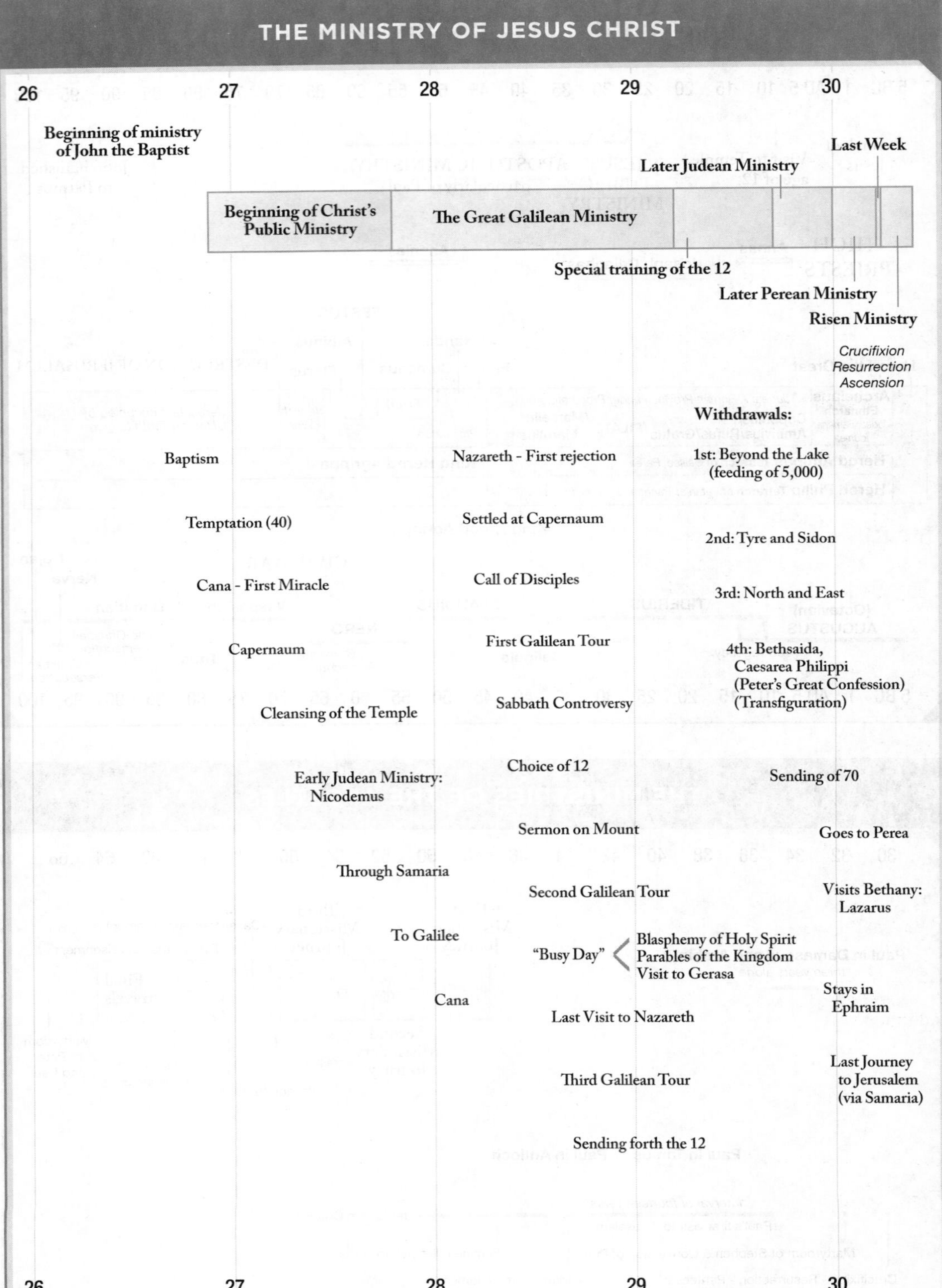
26
27
28
29
30
Beginning of ministry of John the Baptist
Last Week
Later Judean Ministry
Beginning of Christ's Public Ministry
The Great Galilean Ministry
Special training of the 12
Later Perean Ministry
Risen Ministry
Crucifixion
Resurrection
Ascension
Withdrawals:
Baptism
Nazareth - First rejection
1st: Beyond the Lake (feeding of 5,000)
Temptation (40)
Settled at Capernaum
2nd: Tyre and Sidon
Cana - First Miracle
Call of Disciples
3rd: North and East
Capernaum
First Galilean Tour
4th: Bethsaida, Caesarea Philippi (Peter's Great Confession) (Transfiguration)
Cleansing of the Temple
Sabbath Controversy
Choice of 12
Early Judean Ministry: Nicodemus
Sending of 70
Sermon on Mount
Goes to Perea
Through Samaria
Second Galilean Tour
Visits Bethany: Lazarus
To Galilee
"Busy Day"
Blasphemy of Holy Spirit
Parables of the Kingdom
Visit to Gerasa
Stays in Ephraim
Cana
Last Visit to Nazareth
Last Journey to Jerusalem (via Samaria)
Third Galilean Tour
Sending forth the 12
26
27
28
29
30

A HARMONY OF THE GOSPELS

INTRODUCTIONS TO JESUS CHRIST

	Matt.	Mark	Luke	John
(1) Luke's Introduction			1:1–4	
(2) Pre-fleshly state of Christ				1:1–18
(3) Genealogy of Jesus Christ	1:1–17		3:23–38	

BIRTH, INFANCY, AND ADOLESCENCE OF JESUS AND JOHN THE BAPTIST

	Matt.	Mark	Luke	John
(1) Announcement of Birth of John			1:5–25	
(2) Announcement of Birth of Jesus to the Virgin			1:26–38	
(3) Song of Elizabeth to Mary			1:39–45	
(4) Mary's Song of Praise			1:46–56	
(5) Birth, Infancy, and Purpose for Future of John the Baptist			1:57–80	
(6) Announcement of Jesus' Birth to Joseph	1:18–23			
(7) Birth of Jesus Christ	1:24, 25		2:1–7	
(8) Proclamation by the Angels			2:8–14	
(9) The Visit of Homage by Shepherds			2:15–20	
(10) Jesus' Circumcision			2:21	
(11) First Temple Visit with Acknowledgments by Simeon and Anna			2:22–38	
(12) Visit of the Wise Men	2:1–12			
(13) Flight into Egypt and Massacre of Innocents	2:13–18			
(14) From Egypt to Nazareth with Jesus	2:19–23		2:39	
(15) Childhood of Jesus			2:40	
(16) Jesus, 12 Years Old, Visits the Temple			2:41–50	
(17) 18-Year Account of Jesus' Adolescence and Adulthood			2:51, 52	

TRUTHS ABOUT JOHN THE BAPTIST

	Matt.	Mark	Luke	John
(1) John's Ministry Begins	3:1	1:1–4	3:1, 2	
(2) Man and Message	3:2–12	1:2–8	3:3–14	
(3) His Picture of Jesus	3:11, 12	1:7, 8	3:15–18	
(4) His Courage	14:4–12		3:19, 20	

BEGINNING OF JESUS' MINISTRY

	Matt.	Mark	Luke	John
(1) Jesus Baptized	3:13–17	1:9–11	3:21–22	
(2) Jesus Tempted	4:1–11	1:12, 13	4:1–13	
(3) John's Testimony				1:19–34
(4) Calls First Disciples				1:35–51
(5) The First Miracle				2:1–11
(6) First Stay in Capernaum				2:12
(7) First Cleansing of the Temple				2:13–22
(8) Received at Jerusalem				2:23–25
(9) Teaches Nicodemus about Second Birth				3:1–21
(10) Co-ministry with John				3:22–36
(11) Leaves for Galilee	4:12	1:14	4:14	4:1–4
(12) Samaritan Woman at Jacob's Well				4:5–42
(13) Returns to Galilee		1:15	4:15	4:43–45

THE GALILEAN MINISTRY OF JESUS

	Matt.	Mark	Luke	John
(1) Healing of the Nobleman's Son				4:46–54
(2) Rejected at Nazareth			4:16–30	
(3) Moved to Capernaum	4:13–17			
(4) Four Become Fishers of Men	4:18–22	1:16–20	5:1–11	
(5) Demoniac Healed on the Sabbath Day		1:21–28	4:31–37	
(6) Peter's Mother-in-Law Cured, Plus Others	8:14–17	1:29–34	4:38–41	
(7) First Preaching Tour of Galilee	4:23–25	1:35–39	4:42–44	
(8) Leper Healed and Response Recorded	8:1–4	1:40–45	5:12–16	
(9) Paralytic Healed	9:1–8	2:1–12	5:17–26	
(10) Matthew's Call and Reception Held	9:9–13	2:13–17	5:27–32	
(11) Disciples Defended via a Parable	9:14–17	2:18–22	5:33–39	
(12) Goes to Jerusalem for Second Passover; Heals Lame Man				5:1–47
(13) Plucked Grain Precipitates Sabbath Controversy	12:1–8	2:23–28	6:1–5	
(14) Withered Hand Healed Causes Another Sabbath Controversy	12:9–14	3:1–6	6:6–11	
(15) Multitudes Healed	12:15–21	3:7–12	6:17–19	
(16) Twelve Apostles Selected After a Night of Prayer		3:13–19	6:12–16	
(17) Sermon on the Mount	5:1–7:29		6:20–49	
(18) Centurion's Servant Healed	8:5–13		7:1–10	
(19) Raises Widow's Son from Dead			7:11–17	
(20) Jesus Allays John's Doubts	11:2–19		7:18–35	
(21) Woes Upon the Privileged		11:20–30		
(22) A Sinful Woman Anoints Jesus			7:36–50	
(23) Another Tour of Galilee			8:1–3	
(24) Jesus Accused of Blasphemy	12:22–37	3:20–30		
(25) Jesus' Answer to a Demand for a Sign	12:38–45			
(26) Mother, Brothers Seek Audience	12:46–50	3:31–35	8:19–21	
(27) Famous Parables of Sower, Seed, Tares, Mustard Seed, Leaven, Treasure, Pearl, Dragnet, Lamp Told	13:1–52	4:1–34	8:4–18	
(28) Sea Made Serene	8:23–27	4:35–41	8:22–25	
(29) Gadarene Demoniac Healed	8:28–34	5:1–20	8:26–39	
(30) Jairus's Daughter Raised and Woman with Hemorrhage Healed	9:18–26	5:21–43	8:40–56	

	Matt.	Mark	Luke	John
(31) Two Blind Men's Sight Restored	9:27–31			
(32) Mute Demoniac Healed	9:32–34			
(33) Nazareth's Second Rejection of Christ	13:53–58	6:1–6		
(34) Twelve Sent Out	9:35–11:1	6:7–13	9:1–6	
(35) Fearful Herod Beheads John	14:1–12	6:14–29	9:7–9	
(36) Return of Twelve, Jesus Withdraws, 5,000 Fed	14:13–21	6:30–44	9:10–17	6:1–14
(37) Walks on the Water	14:22–33	6:45–52		6:15–21
(38) Sick of Gennesaret Healed	14:34–36	6:53–56		
(39) Peak of Popularity Passes in Galilee				6:22–71; 7:1
(40) Traditions Attacked	15:1–20	7:1–23		
(41) Aborted Retirement in Phoenicia: Syrophoenician Healed	15:21–28	7:24–30		
(42) Afflicted Healed	15:29–31	7:31–37		
(43) 4,000 Fed	15:32–39	8:1–9		
(44) Pharisees Increase Attack	16:1–4	8:10–13		
(45) Disciples' Carelessness Condemned; Blind Man Healed	16:5–12	8:14–26		
(46) Peter Confesses Jesus Is the Christ	16:13–20	8:27–30	9:18–21	
(47) Jesus Foretells His Death	16:21–26	8:31–38	9:22–25	
(48) Kingdom Promised	16:27, 28	9:1	9:26, 27	
(49) The Transfiguration	17:1–13	9:2–13	9:28–36	
(50) Epileptic Healed	17:14–21	9:14–29	9:37–42	
(51) Again Tells of Death, Resurrection	17:22, 23	9:30–32	9:43–45	
(52) Taxes Paid	17:24–27			
(53) Disciples Contend About Greatness; Jesus Defines; also Patience, Loyalty, Forgiveness	18:1–35	9:33–50	9:46–50	
(54) Jesus Rejects Brothers' Advice				7:2–9
(55) Galilee Departure and Samaritan Rejection	19:1		9:51–56	7:10
(56) Cost of Discipleship	8:18–22		9:57–62	

LAST JUDEAN AND PEREAN MINISTRY OF JESUS

	Matt.	Mark	Luke	John
(1) Feast of Tabernacles				7:11–52
(2) Forgiveness of Adulteress				7:53–8:11
(3) Christ—the Light of the World				8:12–20
(4) Pharisees Can't Meet the Prophecy Thus Try to Destroy the Prophet				8:12–59
(5) The Service of the Seventy			10:1–24	
(6) Lawyer Hears the Story of the Good Samaritan			10:25–37	
(7) The Hospitality of Martha and Mary			10:38–42	
(8) Another Lesson on Prayer			11:1–13	
(9) Accused of Connection with Beelzebub			11:14–36	
(10) Judgment Against Lawyers and Pharisees			11:37–54	
(11) Jesus Deals with Hypocrisy, Covetousness, Worry, and Alertness			12:1–59	
(12) Repent or Perish			13:1–5	
(13) Barren Fig Tree			13:6–9	
(14) Crippled Woman Healed on Sabbath			13:10–17	
(15) Parables of Mustard Seed and Leaven			13:18–21	
(16) Man Born Blind Healed; Following Consequences				9:1–41
(17) Parable of the Good Shepherd				10:1–21
(18) Feast of Dedication				10:22–39
(19) Withdrawal Beyond Jordan				10:40–42

	Matt.	Mark	Luke	John
(20) Begins Teaching Return to Jerusalem with Special Words About Herod			13:22–35	
(21) Meal with a Pharisee Ruler Occasions Healing Man with Dropsy; Parables of Ox, Best Places, and Great Supper			14:1–24	
(22) Demands of Discipleship			14:25–35	
(23) Parables of Lost Sheep, Coin, Son			15:1–32	
(24) Parables of Unjust Steward, Rich Man and Lazarus			16:1–31	
(25) Lessons on Service, Faith, Influence			17:1–10	
(26) Resurrection of Lazarus				11:1–44
(27) Reaction to It: Withdrawal of Jesus				11:45–54
(28) Begins Last Journey to Jerusalem via Samaria and Galilee			17:11	
(29) Heals Ten Lepers			17:12–19	
(30) Lessons on the Coming Kingdom			17:20–37	
(31) Parables: Persistent Widow, Pharisee and Tax Collector			18:1–14	
(32) Doctrine on Divorce	19:1–12	10:1–12		
(33) Jesus Blesses Children: Objections	19:13–15	10:13–16	18:15–17	
(34) Rich Young Ruler	19:16–30	10:17–31	18:18–30	
(35) Laborers of the 11th Hour	20:1–16			
(36) Foretells Death and Resurrection	20:17–19	10:32–34	18:31–34	
(37) Ambition of James and John	20:20–28	10:35–45		
(38) Blind Bartimaeus Healed	20:29–34	10:46–52	18:35–43	
(39) Interview with Zacchaeus			19:1–10	
(40) Parable: the Minas			19:11–27	
(41) Returns to Home of Mary and Martha				11:55–12:1
(42) Plot to Kill Lazarus				12:9–11

JESUS' FINAL WEEK OF WORK AT JERUSALEM

	Matt.	Mark	Luke	John
(1) Triumphal Entry	21:1–9	11:1–11	19:28–44	12:12–19
(2) Fig Tree Cursed and Temple Cleansed	21:10–19	11:12–18	19:45–48	
(3) The Attraction of Sacrifice				12:20–50
(4) Withered Fig Tree Testifies	21:20–22	11:19–26		
(5) Sanhedrin Challenges Jesus. Answered by Parables: Two Sons, Wicked Vinedressers, and Marriage Feast	21:23–22:14	11:27–12:12	20:1–19	
(6) Tribute to Caesar	22:15–22	12:13–17	20:20–26	
(7) Sadducees Question the Resurrection	22:23–33	12:18–27	20:27–40	
(8) Pharisees Question Commandments	22:34–40	12:28–34		
(9) Jesus and David	22:41–46	12:35–37	20:41–44	
(10) Jesus' Last Sermon	23:1–39	12:38–40	20:45–47	
(11) Widow's Mite		12:41–44	21:1–4	
(12) Jesus Tells of the Future	24:1–51	13:1–37	21:5–36	
(13) Parables: Ten Virgins, Talents, The Day of Judgment	25:1–46			
(14) Jesus Tells Date of Crucifixion	26:1–5	14:1, 2	21:37, 38; 22:1, 2	
(15) Anointing by Mary at Simon's Feast	26:6–13	14:3–9		12:2–8
(16) Judas Contracts the Betrayal	26:14–16	14:10, 11	22:3–6	
(17) Preparation for the Passover	26:17–19	14:12–16	22:7–13	
(18) Passover Eaten, Jealousy Rebuked	26:20	14:17	22:14–16, 24–30	
(19) Feet Washed				13:1–20
(20) Judas Revealed, Defects	26:21–25	14:18–21	22:21–23	13:21–30

	Matt.	Mark	Luke	John
(21) Jesus Warns About Further Desertion; Cries of Loyalty	26:31-35	14:27-31	22:31-38	13:31-38
(22) Institution of the Lord's Supper	26:26-29	14:22-25	22:17-20	
(23) Last Speech to the Apostles and Intercessory Prayer				14:1-17:26
(24) The Grief of Gethsemane	26:30, 36-46	14:26, 32-42	22:39-46	18:1
(25) Betrayal, Arrest, Desertion	26:47-56	14:43-52	22:47-53	18:2-12
(26) First Examined by Annas				18:13-14, 19-23
(27) Trial by Caiaphas and Council; Following Indignities	26:57, 59-68	14:53, 55-65	22:54a, 63-65	18:24
(28) Peter's Triple Denial	26:58, 69-75	14:54, 66-72	22:54b-62	18:15-18, 25-27
(29) Condemnation by the Council	27:1	15:1a	22:66-71	
(30) Suicide of Judas	27:3-10			
(31) First Appearance Before Pilate	27:2, 11-14	15:1b-5	23:1-7	18:28-38
(32) Jesus Before Herod			23:6-12	
(33) Second Appearance Before Pilate	27:15-26	15:6-15	23:13-25	18:39-19:16a
(34) Mockery by Roman Soldiers	27:27-30	15:16-19		
(35) Led to Golgotha	27:31-34	15:20-23	23:26-33a	19:16b, 17
(36) Six Events of First Three Hours on Cross	27:35-44	15:24-32	23:33b-43	19:18-27
(37) Last Three Hours on Cross	27:45-50	15:33-37	23:44-46	19:28-30
(38) Events Attending Jesus' Death	27:51-56	15:38-41	23:45, 47-49	
(39) Burial of Jesus	27:57-60	15:42-46	23:50-54	19:31-42
(40) Tomb Sealed and Women Watch	27:61-66	15:47	23:55, 56	

THE RESURRECTION THROUGH THE ASCENSION

	Matt.	Mark	Luke	John
(1) Women Visit the Tomb	28:1-8	16:1-8	24:1-11	
(2) Peter and John See the Empty Tomb			24:12	20:1-10
(3) Jesus' Appearance to Mary Magdalene		16:9-11		20:11-18
(4) Jesus' Appearance to the Other Women	28:9, 10			
(5) Guards' Report of the Resurrection	28:11-15			
(6) Jesus' Appearance to Two Disciples on Way to Emmaus		16:12, 13	24:13-35	
(7) Jesus' Appearance to Ten Disciples Without Thomas			24:36-43	20:19-25
(8) Appearance to Disciples with Thomas				20:26-31
(9) Jesus' Appearance to Seven Disciples by Sea of Galilee				21:1-25
(10) Great Commission	28:16-20	16:14-18	24:44-49	
(11) The Ascension		16:19, 20	24:50-53	

PROPHECIES OF THE MESSIAH FULFILLED IN

JESUS CHRIST

Presented Here in Their Order of Fulfillment

Prophetic Scripture	Subject	Fulfilled
Ge 3:15 "And I will put enmity between you and the woman, and between your seed and her Seed; He shall bruise your head, and you shall bruise His heel."	seed of a woman	Gal 4:4 "But when the fullness of the time had come, God sent forth His Son, born of a woman, born under the law."
Ge 12:3 "I will bless those who bless you, and I will curse him who curses you; and in you all the families of the earth shall be blessed."	descendant of Abraham	Mt 1:1 "The book of the genealogy of Jesus Christ, the Son of David, the Son of Abraham."
Ge 17:19 "Then God said, 'No, Sarah your wife shall bear you a son, and you shall call his name Isaac; I will establish My covenant with him for an everlasting covenant, and with his descendants after him.'"	descendant of Isaac	Lk 3:34 "the son of Jacob, the son of Isaac, the son of Abraham, the son of Terah, the son of Nahor."
Nu 24:17 "I see Him, but not now; I behold Him, but not near; a Star shall come out of Jacob; a Scepter shall rise out of Israel, and batter the brow of Moab, and destroy all the sons of tumult."	descendant of Jacob	Mt 1:2 "Abraham begot Isaac, Isaac begot Jacob, and Jacob begot Judah and his brothers."
Ge 49:10 "The scepter shall not depart from Judah, nor a lawgiver from between his feet, until Shiloh comes; and to Him shall be the obedience of the people."	from the tribe of Judah	Lk 3:33 "the son of Amminadab, the son of Ram, the son of Hezron, the son of Perez, the son of Judah."
Is 9:7 "Of the increase of His government and peace there will be no end, upon the throne of David and over His kingdom, to order it and establish it with judgment and justice from that time forward, even forever. The zeal of the LORD of hosts will perform this."	heir to the throne of David	Lk 1:32, 33 "He will be great, and will be called the Son of the Highest; and the Lord God will give Him the throne of His father David. And He will reign over the house of Jacob forever, and of His kingdom there will be no end."

Prophetic Scripture	Subject	Fulfilled
Ps 45:6, 7; 102:25–27 "Your throne, O God, is forever and ever; a scepter of righteousness is the scepter of Your kingdom. You love righteousness, and hate wickedness; therefore God, Your God, has anointed You with the oil of gladness more than Your companions." "Of old You laid the foundation of the earth, and the heavens are the work of Your hands. They will perish, but You will endure; yes, they will all grow old like a garment; like a cloak You will change them, and they will be changed. But You are the same, and Your years will have no end."	anointed and eternal	Heb 1:8–12 "But to the Son He says: 'Your throne, O God, is forever and ever; a scepter of righteousness is the scepter of Your kingdom. You have loved righteousness and hated lawlessness; therefore God, Your God, has anointed You with the oil of gladness more than Your companions.' And: 'You, LORD, in the beginning laid the foundation of the earth, and the heavens are the work of Your hands. They will perish, but You remain; and they will all grow old like a garment; like a cloak You will fold them up, and they will be changed. But You are the same, and Your years will not fail.'"
Mic 5:2 "But you, Bethlehem, Ephrathah, though you are little among the thousands of Judah, yet out of you shall come forth to Me the One to be Ruler in Israel, whose goings forth are from of old, from everlasting."	born in Bethlehem	Lk 2:4, 5, 7 "And Joseph also went up from Galilee, out of the city of Nazareth, into Judea, to the city of David, which is called Bethlehem, because he was of the house and lineage of David, to be registered with Mary, his betrothed wife, who was with child. . . . And she brought forth her firstborn Son, and wrapped Him in swaddling cloths, and laid Him in a manger, because there was no room for them in the inn."
Da 9:25 "Know therefore and understand, that from the going forth of the command to restore and build Jerusalem until Messiah the Prince, there shall be seven weeks, and sixty-two weeks; the street shall be built again, and the wall, even in troublesome times."	time for His birth	Lk 2:1, 2 "And it came to pass in those days that a decree went out from Caesar Augustus that all the world should be registered. This census first took place while Quirinius was governing Syria."
Is 7:14 "Therefore the Lord Himself will give you a sign: behold, the virgin shall conceive and bear a Son, and shall call His name Immanuel."	to be born of a virgin	Lk 1:26, 27, 30, 31 "Now in the sixth month the angel Gabriel was sent by God to a city of Galilee named Nazareth, to a virgin betrothed to a man whose name was Joseph, of the house of David. The virgin's name was Mary. . . . Then the angel said to her, 'Do not be afraid, Mary, for you have found favor with God. And behold, you will conceive in your womb and bring forth a Son, and shall call His name JESUS.'"
Jer 31:15 "Thus says the LORD: 'A voice was heard in Ramah, lamentation, and bitter weeping, Rachel weeping for her children, refusing to be comforted for her children, because they are no more.'"	slaughter of children	Mt 2:16–18 "Then Herod, when he saw that he was deceived by the wise men, was exceedingly angry; and he sent forth and put to death all the male children who were in Bethlehem and in all its districts, from two years old and under, according to the time which he had determined from the wise men. Then was fulfilled what was spoken by Jeremiah the prophet, saying: 'A voice was heard in Ramah, lamentation, weeping, and great mourning, Rachel weeping for her children, refusing to be comforted, because they are no more.'"

Prophetic Scripture	Subject	Fulfilled
Hos 11:1 "When Israel was a child, I loved him, and out of Egypt I called My son."	flight to Egypt	Mt 2:14, 15 "When he arose, he took the young Child and His mother by night and departed for Egypt, and was there until the death of Herod, that it might be fulfilled which was spoken by the Lord through the prophet, saying, 'Out of Egypt I called My Son.'"
Is 40:3–5 "The voice of one crying in the wilderness: 'Prepare the way of the LORD; make straight in the desert a highway for our God. Every valley shall be exalted, and every mountain and hill brought low; the crooked places shall be made straight and the rough places smooth; the glory of the LORD shall be revealed, and all flesh shall see it together; for the mouth of the LORD has spoken.'"	the way prepared	Lk 3:3–6 "And he went into all the region around the Jordan, preaching a baptism of repentance for the remission of sins, as it is written in the book of the words of Isaiah the prophet, saying: 'The voice of one crying in the wilderness: "Prepare the way of the LORD; make His paths straight. Every valley shall be filled and every mountain and hill brought low; the crooked places shall be made straight and the rough ways smooth; and all flesh shall see the salvation of God."'"
Mal 3:1 "'Behold, I send My messenger, and he will prepare the way before Me. And the Lord, whom you seek, will suddenly come to His temple, even the Messenger of the covenant, in whom you delight. Behold, He is coming,' says the LORD of hosts."	preceded by a forerunner	Lk 7:24, 27 "When the messengers of John had departed, He began to speak to the multitudes concerning John: 'What did you go out into the wilderness to see? A reed shaken by the wind? . . . This is he of whom it is written: "Behold, I send My messenger before Your face, who will prepare Your way before You."'"
Mal. 4:5, 6 "Behold, I will send you Elijah the prophet before the coming of the great and dreadful day of the LORD. And he will turn the hearts of the fathers to the children, and the hearts of the children to their fathers, lest I come and strike the earth with a curse."	preceded by Elijah	Mt 11:13, 14 "For all the prophets and the law prophesied until John. And if you are willing to receive it, he is Elijah who is to come."
Ps 2:7 "I will declare the decree: the LORD has said to Me, 'You are My Son, today I have begotten You.'"	declared the Son of God	Mt 3:17 "And suddenly a voice came from heaven, saying, 'This is My beloved Son, in whom I am well pleased.'"
Is 9:1, 2 "Nevertheless the gloom will not be upon her who is distressed, as when at first He lightly esteemed the land of Zebulun and the land of Naphtali, and afterward more heavily oppressed her, by the way of the sea, beyond the Jordan, in Galilee of the Gentiles. The people who walked in darkness have seen a great light; those who dwelt in the land of the shadow of death, upon them a light has shined."	Galilean ministry	Mt 4:13–16 "And leaving Nazareth, He came and dwelt in Capernaum, which is by the sea, in the regions of Zebulun and Naphtali, that it might be fulfilled which was spoken by Isaiah the prophet, saying: 'The land of Zebulun and the land of Naphtali, by the way of the sea, beyond the Jordan, Galilee of the Gentiles: The people who sat in darkness have seen a great light, and upon those who sat in the region and shadow of death light has dawned.'"

Prophetic Scripture	Subject	Fulfilled
Ps 78:2–4 "I will open my mouth in a parable; I will utter dark sayings of old, which we have heard and known, and our fathers have told us. We will not hide them from their children, telling to the generation to come the praises of the LORD, and His strength and His wonderful works that He has done."	speaks in parables	Mt 13:34, 35 "All these things Jesus spoke to the multitude in parables; and without a parable He did not speak to them, that it might be fulfilled which was spoken by the prophet, saying: 'I will open My mouth in parables; I will utter things kept secret from the foundation of the world.'"
Dt 18:15 "The LORD your God will raise up for you a Prophet like me from your midst, from your brethren. Him you shall hear."	a prophet	Ac 3:20, 22 "And that He may send Jesus Christ, who was preached to you before, . . . For Moses truly said to the fathers, 'The LORD your God will raise up for you a Prophet like me from your brethren. Him you shall hear in all things, whatever He says to you.'"
Is 61:1, 2 "The Spirit of the Lord GOD is upon Me, because the LORD has anointed Me to preach good tidings to the poor; He has sent Me to heal the brokenhearted, to proclaim liberty to the captives, and the opening of the prison to those who are bound; to proclaim the acceptable year of the LORD, and the day of vengeance of our God; to comfort all who mourn."	to bind up the brokenhearted	Lk 4:18, 19 "The Spirit of the LORD is upon Me, because He has anointed Me to preach the gospel to the poor; He has sent Me to heal the brokenhearted, to proclaim liberty to the captives, and recovery of sight to the blind, to set at liberty those who are oppressed; to proclaim the acceptable year of the LORD."
Is 53:3 "He is despised and rejected by men, a Man of sorrows and acquainted with grief. And we hid, as it were, our faces from Him; He was despised, and we did not esteem Him."	rejected by His own people, the Jews	Jn 1:11 "He came to His own, and His own did not receive Him." Luke 23:18 "And they all cried out at once, saying, 'Away with this Man, and release to us Barabbas.'"
Ps 110:4 "The LORD has sworn and will not relent, 'You are a priest forever according to the order of Melchizedek.'"	priest after order of Melchizedek	Heb 5:5, 6 "So also Christ did not glorify Himself to become High Priest, but it was He who said to Him: 'You are My Son, today I have begotten You.' As He also says in another place: 'You are a priest forever according to the order of Melchizedek.'"
Zec 9:9 "Rejoice greatly, O daughter of Zion! Shout, O daughter of Jerusalem! Behold, your King is coming to you; He is just and having salvation, lowly and riding on a donkey, a colt, the foal of a donkey."	triumphal entry	Mk 11:7, 9, 11 "Then they brought the colt to Jesus and threw their clothes on it, and He sat on it. . . . Then those who went before and those who followed cried out, saying: 'Hosanna! Blessed is He who comes in the name of the LORD!' . . . And Jesus went into Jerusalem and into the temple. So when He had looked around at all things, as the hour was already late, He went out to Bethany with the twelve."

Prophetic Scripture	Subject	Fulfilled
Ps 8:2 "Out of the mouth of babes and nursing infants You have ordained strength, because of Your enemies, that You may silence the enemy and the avenger."	adored by infants	Mt 21:15, 16 "But when the chief priests and scribes saw the wonderful things that He did, and the children crying out in the temple and saying, 'Hosanna to the Son of David!' they were indignant and said to Him, 'Do You hear what these are saying?' And Jesus said to them, 'Yes. Have you never read, "Out of the mouth of babes and nursing infants You have perfected praise"?' "
Is 53:1 "Who has believed our report? And to whom has the arm of the LORD been revealed?"	not believed	Jn 12:37, 38 "But although He had done so many signs before them, they did not believe in Him, that the word of Isaiah the prophet might be fulfilled, which he spoke: 'Lord, who has believed our report? And to whom has the arm of the LORD been revealed?' "
Ps 41:9 "Even my own familiar friend in whom I trusted, who ate my bread, has lifted up his heel against me."	betrayed by a close friend	Lk 22:47, 48 "And while He was still speaking, behold, a multitude; and he who was called Judas, one of the twelve, went before them and drew near to Jesus to kiss Him. But Jesus said to him, 'Judas, are you betraying the Son of Man with a kiss?' "
Zec 11:12 "Then I said to them, 'If it is agreeable to you, give me my wages; and if not, refrain.' So they weighed out for my wages thirty pieces of silver."	betrayed for thirty pieces of silver	Mt 26:14, 15 "Then one of the twelve, called Judas Iscariot, went to the chief priests and said, 'What are you willing to give me if I deliver Him to you?' And they counted out to him thirty pieces of silver."
Ps 35:11 "Fierce witnesses rise up; they ask me things that I do not know."	accused by false witnesses	Mk 14:57, 58 "Then some rose up and bore false witness against Him, saying, 'We heard Him say, "I will destroy this temple made with hands, and within three days I will build another made without hands." ' "
Is 53:7 "He was oppressed and He was afflicted, yet He opened not His mouth; He was led as a lamb to the slaughter, and as a sheep before its shearers is silent, so He opened not His mouth."	silent to accusations	Mk 15:4, 5 "Then Pilate asked Him again, saying, 'Do You answer nothing? See how many things they testify against You!' But Jesus still answered nothing, so that Pilate marveled."
Is 50:6 "I gave My back to those who struck Me, and My cheeks to those who plucked out the beard; I did not hide My face from shame and spitting."	spat on and struck	Mt 26:67 "Then they spat in His face and beat Him; and others struck Him with the palms of their hands."

Prophetic Scripture	Subject	Fulfilled
Ps 35:19 "Let them not rejoice over me who are wrongfully my enemies; nor let them wink with the eye who hate me without a cause."	hated without reason	Jn 15:24, 25 "If I had not done among them the works which no one else did, they would have no sin; but now they have seen and also hated both Me and My Father. But this happened that the word might be fulfilled which is written in their law, 'They hated Me without a cause.'"
Is 53:5 "But He was wounded for our transgressions, He was bruised for our iniquities; the chastisement for our peace was upon Him, and by His stripes we are healed."	vicarious sacrifice	Ro 5:6, 8 "For when we were still without strength, in due time Christ died for the ungodly. . . . But God demonstrates His own love toward us, in that while we were still sinners, Christ died for us."
Is 53:12 "Therefore I will divide Him a portion with the great, and He shall divide the spoil with the strong. Because He poured out His soul unto death, and He was numbered with the transgressors, and He bore the sin of many, and made intercession for the transgressors."	crucified with malefactors	Mk 15:27, 28 "With Him they also crucified two robbers, one on His right and the other on His left. So the Scripture was fulfilled which says, 'And He was numbered with the transgressors.'"
Zec 12:10 "And I will pour on the house of David and on the inhabitants of Jerusalem the Spirit of grace and supplication; then they will look on Me whom they pierced. Yes, they will mourn for Him as one mourns for his only son, and grieve for Him as one grieves for a firstborn."	pierced through hands and feet	Jn 20:27 "Then He said to Thomas, 'Reach your finger here, and look at My hands; and reach your hand here, and put it into My side. Do not be unbelieving, but believing.'"
Ps 22:7, 8 "All those who see Me ridicule Me; they shoot out the lip, they shake the head, saying, 'He trusted in the LORD, let Him rescue Him; let Him deliver Him, since He delights in Him!'"	sneered and mocked	Lk 23:35 "And the people stood looking on. But even the rulers with them sneered, saying, 'He saved others; let Him save Himself if He is the Christ, the chosen of God.'"
Ps 69:9 "Because zeal for Your house has eaten me up, and the reproaches of those who reproach You have fallen on me."	was reproached	Ro 15:3 "For even Christ did not please Himself; but as it is written, 'The reproaches of those who reproached You fell on Me.'"
Ps 109:4 "In return for my love they are my accusers, but I give myself to prayer."	prayer for His enemies	Lk 23:34 "Then Jesus said, 'Father, forgive them, for they do not know what they do.' And they divided His garments and cast lots."

Prophetic Scripture	Subject	Fulfilled
Ps 22:17, 18 "I can count all My bones. They look and stare at Me. They divide My garments among them, and for My clothing they cast lots."	soldiers gambled for His clothing	Mt 27:35, 36 "Then they crucified Him, and divided His garments, casting lots, that it might be fulfilled which was spoken by the prophet: 'They divided My garments among them, and for My clothing they cast lots.' Sitting down, they kept watch over Him there."
Ps 22:1 "My God, My God, why have You forsaken Me? Why are You so far from helping Me, and from the words of My groaning?"	forsaken by God	Mt 27:46 "And about the ninth hour Jesus cried out with a loud voice, saying, 'Eli, Eli, lama sabachthani?' that is, 'My God, My God, why have You forsaken Me?'"
Ps 34:20 "He guards all his bones, not one of them is broken."	no bones broken	Jn 19:32, 33, 36 "Then the soldiers came and broke the legs of the first and of the other who was crucified with Him. But when they came to Jesus and saw that He was already dead, they did not break His legs. . . . For these things were done that the Scripture should be fulfilled, 'Not one of His bones shall be broken.'"
Zec 12:10 "And I will pour on the house of David and on the inhabitants of Jerusalem the Spirit of grace and supplication; then they will look on Me whom they have pierced. Yes, they will mourn for Him as one mourns for his only son, and grieve for Him as one grieves for a firstborn."	His side pierced	Jn 19:34 "But one of the soldiers pierced His side with a spear, and immediately blood and water came out."
Is 53:9 "And they made His grave with the wicked—but with the rich at His death, because He had done no violence, nor was any deceit in His mouth."	buried with the rich	Mt 27:57–60 "Now when evening had come, there came a rich man from Arimathea, named Joseph, who himself had also become a disciple of Jesus. This man went to Pilate and asked for the body of Jesus. Then Pilate commanded the body to be given to him. When Joseph had taken the body, he wrapped it in a clean linen cloth, and laid it in his new tomb which he had hewn out of the rock; and he rolled a large stone against the door of the tomb, and departed."
Ps 16:10 "For You will not leave my soul in Sheol, nor will You allow Your Holy One to see corruption." Ps 49:15 "But God will redeem my soul from the power of the grave, for He shall receive me. Selah"	to be resurrected	Mk 16:6, 7 "But he said to them, 'Do not be alarmed. You seek Jesus of Nazareth, who was crucified. He is risen! He is not here. See the place where they laid Him. But go, tell His disciples—and Peter—that He is going before you into Galilee; there you will see Him, as He said to you.'"

Prophetic Scripture	Subject	Fulfilled
Ps 68:18 "You have ascended on high. You have led captivity captive; You have received gifts among men; even from the rebellious, that the LORD God might dwell there."	His ascension to God's right hand	Mk 16:19 "So then, after the Lord had spoken to them, He was received up into heaven, and sat down at the right hand of God." 1Co 15:4 "And that He was buried, and that He rose again the third day according to the Scriptures." Eph 4:8 "Therefore He says: 'When He ascended on high, He led captivity captive, and gave gifts to men.'"

A BRIEF OVERVIEW OF CHRIST'S LIFE

6 B.C.	Birth of Christ
	Death of Herod the Great
1 B.C.	
A.D. 1	
	Growth and Early Life
A.D. 5	
	First Passover in Jerusalem
A.D. 10	
A.D. 15	
	Adolescence and Early Manhood
A.D. 20	
A.D. 25	
	Baptism of Christ
	Ministry, Death and Resurrection
A.D. 30	

A BRIEF OVERVIEW OF CHRIST'S MINISTRY

26
Winter
Spring
Summer
Fall

27
Winter
Spring
Summer
Fall

28
Winter
Spring
Summer
Fall

29
Winter
Spring
Summer
Fall

30
Winter
Spring
Summer
Fall

Public Ministry of John
Baptism of Christ
The Temptation

End of John's Ministry and Beginning of Christ's
First Passover in His Public Ministry
Nicodemus' interview with Christ
Challenge of a spiritual harvest

Disciples called
Second Passover (not mentioned in gospels)
Ministry in Galilee
Feast of the Tabernacles; Sabbath controversies
Sermon on the Mount
First Public Rejection; parabolic Ministry begun
Final Galilean campaign
Third Passover
The Bread of Life
Ministry around Galilee
Lesson of Messiahship learned and confirmed
Feast of Tabernacles
Later Judean Ministry
Feast of Dedication
Ministry in and around Perea
Passion Week
Resurrection and Ascension

THE PASSOVERS OF CHRIST'S MINISTRY

A.D. 27	First Passover of Christ's Ministry
A.D. 28	Second Passover of Christ's Ministry
A.D. 29	Third Passover of Christ's Ministry
A.D. 30	Crucifixion of Christ

CHRIST'S PASSION WEEK

Day	Events
Sunday (a.m. / p.m.)	Crowds Visit Jesus and Lazarus in Bethany
Monday (a.m. / p.m.)	Triumphal Entry
Tuesday (a.m. / p.m.)	Cursing of the Fig Tree Request of some Greeks Cleansing the Temple
Wednesday (a.m. / p.m.)	Withered Fig Tree Official Challenge of Christ's Authority The Olivet Discourse
Thursday (a.m. / p.m.)	The Last Supper The Upper Room Discourse Betrayal and Arrest; Trial
Friday (a.m. / p.m.)	Crucifixion Burial
Saturday (a.m. / p.m.)	
Sunday (a.m. / p.m.)	Postresurrection Appearances

THE GOSPEL ACCORDING TO MATTHEW

TITLE

Matthew, meaning "gift of the Lord," was the other name of Levi (9:9), the tax collector who left everything to follow Christ (Lk 5:27, 28). Matthew was one of the 12 apostles (10:3; Mk 3:18; Lk 6:15; Ac 1:13). In his own list of the 12, he explicitly calls himself a "tax collector" (10:3). Nowhere else in Scripture is the name Matthew associated with "tax collector"; the other evangelists always employ his former name, Levi, when speaking of his sinful past. This is evidence of humility on Matthew's part. As with the other 3 gospels, this work is known by the name of its author.

AUTHOR AND DATE

The canonicity and Matthean authorship of this gospel were unchallenged in the early church. Eusebius (ca. A.D. 265–339) quotes Origen (ca. A.D. 185–254):

Among the four Gospels, which are the only indisputable ones in the Church of God under heaven, I have learned by tradition that the first was written by Matthew, who was once a publican, but afterwards an apostle of Jesus Christ, and it was prepared for the converts from Judaism (*Ecclesiastical History*, 6:25).

It is clear that this gospel was written at a relatively early date—prior to the destruction of the temple in A.D. 70. Some scholars have proposed a date as early as A.D. 50. For a further discussion of some of the issues related to the authorship and dating of this gospel, especially "The Synoptic Problem," see Introduction to Mark: Interpretive Challenges.

BACKGROUND AND SETTING

The Jewish flavor of Matthew's gospel is remarkable. This is evident even in the opening genealogy, which Matthew traces back only as far as Abraham. In contrast, Luke, aiming to show Christ as the Redeemer of humanity, goes all the way back to Adam. Matthew's purpose is somewhat narrower: to demonstrate that Christ is the King and Messiah of Israel. This gospel quotes more than 60 times from OT prophetic passages, emphasizing how Christ is the fulfillment of all those promises.

The probability that Matthew's audience was predominantly Jewish is further evident from several facts: Matthew usually cites Jewish custom without explaining it, in contrast to the other gospels (cf. Mk 7:3; Jn 19:40). He constantly refers to Christ as "the Son of David" (1:1; 9:27; 12:23; 15:22; 20:30; 21:9, 15; 22:42, 45). Matthew even guards Jewish sensibilities regarding the name of God, referring to "the kingdom of heaven," where the other evangelists speak of "the kingdom of God." All the book's major themes are rooted in the OT and set in light of Israel's messianic expectations.

Matthew's use of Greek may suggest that he was writing as a Palestinian Jew to Hellenistic Jews elsewhere. He wrote as an eyewitness of many of the events he described, giving firsthand testimony about the words and works of Jesus of Nazareth.

His purpose is clear: to demonstrate that Jesus is the Jewish nation's long-awaited Messiah. His voluminous quoting of the OT is specifically designed to show the tie between the Messiah of promise and the Christ of history. This purpose is never out of focus for Matthew, and he even adduces many incidental details from the OT prophecies as proofs of Jesus' messianic claims (e.g., 2:17, 18; 4:13–15; 13:35; 21:4, 5; 27:9, 10).

HISTORICAL AND THEOLOGICAL THEMES

Since Matthew is concerned with setting forth Jesus as Messiah, the King of the Jews, an interest in the OT kingdom promises runs throughout this gospel. Matthew's signature phrase "the kingdom of heaven" occurs 32 times in this book (and nowhere else in all of Scripture).

The opening genealogy is designed to document Christ's credentials as Israel's king, and the rest of the book completes this theme. Matthew shows that Christ is the heir of the kingly line. He demonstrates that He is the fulfillment of dozens of OT prophecies regarding the king who would come. He offers evidence after evidence to establish Christ's kingly prerogative. All other historical and theological themes in the book revolve around this one.

Matthew records 5 major discourses: the Sermon on the Mount (chaps. 5–7); the commissioning of the apostles (chap. 10); the parables about the kingdom (chap. 13); a discourse about the childlikeness of the believer (chap. 18); and the discourse on His second coming (chaps. 24, 25). Each discourse ends with a variation of this phrase: "when Jesus had finished these words" (7:28; 11:1; 13:53; 19:1; 26:1). That becomes a motif signaling a new narrative portion. A long opening section (chaps. 1–4) and a short conclusion (28:16–20) bracket the rest of the gospel, which naturally divides into 5 sections, each with a discourse and a narrative section. Some have seen a parallel between these 5 sections and the 5 books of Moses in the OT.

The conflict between Christ and Pharisaism is another common theme in Matthew's gospel. But Matthew is keen to show the error of the Pharisees for the benefit of his Jewish audience—not for personal or self-aggrandizing reasons. Matthew omits, for example, the parable of the Pharisee and the tax collector, even though that parable would have put him in a favorable light.

Matthew also mentions the Sadducees more than any of the other gospels. Both Pharisees and Sadducees are regularly portrayed negatively, and held up as warning beacons. Their doctrine is a leaven that must be avoided (16:11, 12). Although these groups were doctrinally at odds with one another, they were united in their hatred of Christ. To Matthew, they epitomized all in Israel who rejected Christ as King.

The rejection of Israel's Messiah is another constant theme in this gospel. In no other gospel are the attacks against Jesus portrayed as strongly as here. From the flight into Egypt to the scene at the cross, Matthew paints a more vivid portrayal of Christ's rejection than any of the other evangelists. In Matthew's account of the crucifixion, for example, no thief repents, and no friends or loved ones are seen at the foot of the cross. In His death, He is forsaken even by God (27:46). The shadow of rejection is never lifted from the story.

Yet Matthew portrays Him as a victorious King who will one day return "on the clouds of the sky with power and great glory" (24:30).

INTERPRETIVE CHALLENGES

As noted above, Matthew groups his narrative material around 5 great discourses. He makes no attempt to follow a strict chronology, and a comparison of the gospels reveals that Matthew freely places things out of order. He is dealing with themes and broad concepts, not laying out a timeline.

The prophetic passages present a particular interpretive challenge. Jesus' Olivet discourse, for example, contains some details that evoke images of the violent destruction of Jerusalem in A.D. 70. Jesus' words in 24:34 have led some to conclude that all these things were fulfilled—albeit not literally—in the Roman conquest of that era. This is the view known as "preterism." But this is a serious interpretive blunder, forcing the interpreter to read into these passages spiritualized, allegorical meanings unwarranted by normal exegetical methods. The grammatical-historical hermeneutical approach to these passages is the approach to follow, and it yields a consistently futuristic interpretation of crucial prophecies.

For a discussion of the Synoptic Problem, see Introduction to Mark: Interpretive Challenges.

OUTLINE

I. (Prologue) The King's Advent (1:1–4:25)

- A. His Birth (1:1–2:23)
  1. His ancestry (1:1–17)
  2. His arrival (1:18–25)
  3. His adoration (2:1–12)
  4. His adversaries (2:13–23)
- B. His Entry into Public Ministry (3:1–4:25)
  1. His forerunner (3:1–12)
  2. His baptism (3:13–17)
  3. His temptation (4:1–11)
  4. His earliest ministry (4:12–25)

II. The King's Authority (5:1–9:38)
  A. Discourse 1: The Sermon on the Mount (5:1–7:29)
    1. Righteousness and happiness (5:1–12)
    2. Righteousness and discipleship (5:13–16)
    3. Righteousness and the Scriptures (5:17–20)
    4. Righteousness and morality (5:21–48)
    5. Righteousness and practical religion (6:1–18)
    6. Righteousness and mundane things (6:19–34)
    7. Righteousness and human relations (7:1–12)
    8. Righteousness and salvation (7:13–29)
  B. Narrative 1: The Authenticating Miracles (8:1–9:38)
    1. A leper cleansed (8:1–4)
    2. The centurion's servant healed (8:5–13)
    3. Peter's mother-in-law healed (8:14, 15)
    4. Multitudes healed (8:16–22)
    5. The winds and sea rebuked (8:23–27)
    6. Two demoniacs delivered (8:28–34)
    7. A paralytic pardoned and healed (9:1–8)
    8. A tax collector called (9:9–13)
    9. A question answered (9:14–17)
    10. A girl raised from the dead (9:18–26)
    11. Two blind men given sight (9:27–31)
    12. A mute speaks (9:32–34)
    13. Multitudes viewed with compassion (9:35–38)

III. The King's Agenda (10:1–12:50)
  A. Discourse 2: The Commissioning of the Twelve (10:1–42)
    1. The Master's men (10:1–4)
    2. The sending of the disciples (10:5–23)
    3. Hallmarks of discipleship (10:24–42)
  B. Narrative 2: The Mission of the King (11:1–12:50)
    1. Jesus' identity affirmed for John's disciples (11:1–19)
    2. Woes pronounced on the impenitent (11:20–24)
    3. Rest offered to the weary (11:25–30)
    4. Lordship asserted over the Sabbath (12:1–13)
    5. Opposition fomented by the Jewish leaders (12:14–45)
    6. Eternal relationships defined by spiritual ancestry (12:46–50)

IV. The King's Adversaries (13:1–17:27)
  A. Discourse 3: The Kingdom Parables (13:1–52)
    1. The soils (13:1–23)
    2. The wheat and tares (13:24–30, 34–43)
    3. The mustard seed (13:31, 32)
    4. The leaven (13:33)
    5. The hidden treasure (13:44)
    6. The pearl of great price (13:45, 46)
    7. The dragnet (13:47–50)
    8. The householder (13:51, 52)
  B. Narrative 3: The Kingdom Conflict (13:53–17:27)
    1. Nazareth rejects the King (13:53–58)
    2. Herod murders John the Baptist (14:1–12)
    3. Jesus feeds the 5,000 (14:13–21)
    4. Jesus walks on water (14:22–33)
    5. Multitudes seek healing (14:34–36)
    6. The Scribes and Pharisees challenge Jesus (15:1–20)
    7. A Canaanite woman believes (15:21–28)
    8. Jesus heals multitudes (15:29–31)
    9. Jesus feeds the 4,000 (15:32–39)
    10. The Pharisees and Sadducees seek a sign (16:1–12)
    11. Peter confesses Christ (16:13–20)
    12. Jesus predicts His death (16:21–28)

13. Jesus reveals His glory (17:1–13)
14. Jesus heals a child (17:14–21)
15. Jesus foretells His betrayal (17:22, 23)
16. Jesus pays the temple tax (17:24–27)

V. The King's Administration (18:1–23:39)

A. Discourse 4: The Childlikeness of the Believer (18:1–35)
   1. A call for childlike faith (18:1–6)
   2. A warning against offenses (18:7–9)
   3. A parable about a lost sheep (18:10–14)
   4. A pattern for church discipline (18:15–20)
   5. A lesson about forgiveness (18:21–35)

B. Narrative 4: The Jerusalem Ministry (19:1–23:39)
   1. Some kingly lessons (19:1–20:28)
      a. On divorce (19:1–10)
      b. On celibacy (19:11, 12)
      c. On children (19:13–15)
      d. On surrender (19:16–22)
      e. On who may be saved (19:23–30)
      f. On equality in the kingdom (20:1–16)
      g. On His death (20:17–19)
      h. On true greatness (20:20–28)
   2. Some kingly deeds (20:29–21:27)
      a. He heals two blind men (20:29–34)
      b. He receives adoration (21:1–11)
      c. He cleanses the temple (21:12–17)
      d. He curses a fig tree (21:18–22)
      e. He answers a challenge (21:23–27)
   3. Some kingly parables (21:28–22:14)
      a. The two sons (21:28–32)
      b. The wicked vine-growers (21:33–46)
      c. The wedding feast (22:1–14)
   4. Some kingly answers (22:15–46)
      a. The Herodians: on paying taxes (22:15–22)
      b. The Sadducees: on the resurrection (22:23–33)
      c. The Scribes: on the first and great commandment (22:34–40)
      d. The Pharisees: on David's greater Son (22:41–46)
   5. Some kingly pronouncements (23:1–39)
      a. Woe to the scribes and Pharisees (23:1–36)
      b. Woe to Jerusalem (23:37–39)

VI. The King's Atonement (24:1–28:15)

A. Discourse 5: The Olivet Discourse (24:1–25:46)
   1. The destruction of the temple (24:1, 2)
   2. The signs of the times (24:3–31)
   3. The parable of the fig tree (24:32–35)
   4. The lesson of Noah (24:36–44)
   5. The parable of the two slaves (24:45–51)
   6. The parable of the ten virgins (25:1–13)
   7. The parable of the talents (25:14–30)
   8. The judgment of the nations (25:31–46)

B. Narrative 5: The Crucifixion and Resurrection (26:1–28:15)
   1. The plot to kill the King (26:1–5)
   2. Mary's anointing (26:6–13)
   3. Judas' betrayal (26:14–16)
   4. The Passover (26:17–30)
   5. The prophecy of Peter's denial (26:31–35)
   6. Jesus' agony (26:36–46)
   7. Jesus' arrest (26:47–56)
   8. The trial before the Sanhedrin (26:57–68)
   9. Peter's denial (26:69–75)
   10. Judas' suicide (27:1–10)
   11. The trial before Pilate (27:11–26)
   12. The soldiers' mocking (27:27–31)

13. The crucifixion (27:32–56)
14. The burial (27:57–66)
15. The resurrection (28:1–15)

VII. (Epilogue) The King's Assignment (28:16–20)

THE GENEALOGY OF JESUS THE MESSIAH

1 The [a]record of the genealogy of [b]Jesus [c]the Messiah, [A]the son of David, [B]the son of Abraham:
2 Abraham [a]was the father of Isaac, [b]Isaac the
father of Jacob, and Jacob the father of [c]Judah and
his brothers. 3 Judah was the father of Perez and
Zerah by Tamar, [A]Perez was the father of Hezron,
and Hezron the father of [a]Ram. 4 Ram was the father
of Amminadab, Amminadab the father of Nahshon,
and Nahshon the father of Salmon. 5 Salmon was
the father of Boaz by Rahab, Boaz was the father of
Obed by Ruth, and Obed the father of Jesse. 6 Jesse
was the father of David the king.

David [A]was the father of Solomon by [a]Bathsheba
who had been the wife of Uriah. 7 Solomon [A]was the
father of Rehoboam, Rehoboam the father of Abijah,
and Abijah the father of [a]Asa. 8 Asa was the father
of Jehoshaphat, Jehoshaphat the father of [a]Joram,
and Joram the father of Uzziah. 9 Uzziah was the
father of [a]Jotham, Jotham the father of Ahaz, and
Ahaz the father of Hezekiah. 10 Hezekiah was the
father of Manasseh, Manasseh the father of [a]Amon,
and Amon the [A]father of Josiah. 11 Josiah became the
father of [a]Jeconiah and his brothers, at the time of
the [A]deportation to Babylon.

12 After the [A]deportation to Babylon: Jeconiah
became the father of [a]Shealtiel, and Shealtiel the
father of Zerubbabel. 13 Zerubbabel was the father
of [a]Abihud, Abihud the father of Eliakim, and Eliakim the father of Azor. 14 Azor was the father of
Zadok, Zadok the father of Achim, and Achim the
father of Eliud. 15 Eliud was the father of Eleazar,
Eleazar the father of Matthan, and Matthan the father of Jacob. 16 Jacob was the father of Joseph the
husband of Mary, by whom Jesus was born, [A]who
is called [a]the Messiah.

17 So all the generations from Abraham to David are fourteen generations; from David to the
[A]deportation to Babylon, fourteen generations; and
from the [A]deportation to Babylon to [a]the Messiah,
fourteen generations.

CONCEPTION AND BIRTH OF JESUS

18 Now the birth of Jesus [a]Christ was as follows:
when His [A]mother Mary had been [b]betrothed to
Joseph, before they came together she was [B]found
to be with child by the Holy Spirit. 19 And Joseph
her husband, being a righteous man and not
wanting to disgrace her, planned [a,A]to send her
away secretly. 20 But when he had considered this,
behold, an angel of the Lord appeared to him in a
dream, saying, "[A]Joseph, son of David, do not be
afraid to take Mary as your wife; for [a]the Child who
has been [b]conceived in her is of the Holy Spirit.

1:1 [a]Lit *book* [b]Heb *Yeshua (Joshua)*, meaning *The LORD saves* [c]Gr *Christos (Christ)*, Gr for *Messiah*, which means *Anointed One* [A]2 Sam 7:12-16; Ps 89:3f; 132:11; Is 9:6f; 11:1; Matt 9:27; Luke 1:32, 69; John 7:42; Acts 13:23; Rom 1:3; Rev 22:16 [B]Matt 1:1-6: *Luke 3:32-34;* Gen 22:18; Gal 3:16 1:2 [a]Lit *fathered*, and throughout the genealogy [b]Lit *and...*, and throughout the genealogy [c]Gr *Judas;* names of people in the Old Testament are given in their Old Testament form 1:3 [a]Gr *Aram* [A]Ruth 4:18-22; 1 Chr 2:1-15; Matt 1:3-6 1:6 [a]Lit *her of Uriah* [A]2 Sam 11:27; 12:24 1:7 [a]Gr *Asaph* [A]1 Chr 3:10ff 1:8 [a]Also Gr for *Jehoram* in 2 Kin 8:16; cf 1 Chr 3:11 1:9 [a]Gr *Joatham* 1:10 [a]Gr *Amos* [A]1 Chr 3:14 1:11 [a]*Jehoiachin* in 2 Kin 24:15 [A]2 Kin 24:14f; Jer 27:20; Matt 1:17 1:12 [a]Gr *Salathiel* [A]2 Kin 24:14f; Jer 27:20; Matt 1:17 1:13 [a]Gr *Abioud*, usually spelled *Abiud* 1:16 [a]Gr *Christos (Christ)* [A]Matt 27:17, 22; Luke 2:11; John 4:25 1:17 [a]Gr *Christos (Christ)* [A]2 Kin 24:14f; Jer 27:20; Matt 1:11, 12 1:18 [a]I.e. The Messiah [b]The first stage of marriage in Jewish culture, usually lasting for a year before the wedding night, more legal than an engagement [A]Matt 12:46; Luke 1:27 [B]Luke 1:35 1:19 [a]Or *to divorce her* [A]Deut 22:20-24; 24:1-4; John 8:4, 5 1:20 [a]Lit *that which* [b]Lit *begotten* [A]Luke 2:4

1:1 record of the genealogy of Jesus the Messiah. This phrase is viewed by some as Matthew's title for the entire gospel. The Gr. phrase translated "book of the genealogy" is exactly the same phrase used in Ge 5:1 in the LXX. **Jesus.** The Hebrew *Jeshua* means "the Lord is Salvation." **son of David.** A messianic title used as such in only the Synoptic G ospels (*see notes on 22:42, 45*). **son of Abraham.** Takes His royal lineage all the way back to the nation's inception in the Abrahamic Covenant (Ge 12:1–3).

1:2 For a comparison of this genealogy and the one given by Luke, *see note on Lk 3:23–38.*

1:3 Tamar. It is unusual for women to be named in genealogies. Matthew names 5: "Tamar" was a Canaanite woman who posed as a prostitute to seduce Judah (Ge 38:13–30). "Rahab" (v. 5) was a Gentile and a prostitute (Jos 2:1). "Ruth" (v. 5) was a Moabite woman (Ru 1:3) and a worshiper of idols. "Bathsheba" ("wife of Uriah," v. 6) committed adultery with David (2Sa 11). And "Mary" (v. 16) bore the stigma of pregnancy outside of wedlock. Each of these women is an object lesson about the workings of divine grace.

1:5, 6 Salmon was the father of Boaz by Rahab .... Jesse was the father of David the king. This is not an exhaustive genealogy. Several additional generations must have elapsed between Rahab (in Joshua's time) and David (v. 6)—nearly 4 centuries later. Matthew's genealogy (like most of the biblical ones) sometimes skips over several generations between well known characters in order to abbreviate the listing.

1:8 Joram the father of Uzziah. Cf. 1Ch 3:10–12. Matthew skips over Ahaziah, Joash, and Amaziah, going directly from Joram to Uzziah (Azariah)—using a kind of genealogical shorthand. He seems to do this intentionally in order to make a symmetrical 3-fold division in v. 17.

1:11 Josiah became the father of Jeconiah. Again, Matthew skips a generation between Josiah and Jeconiah (cf. 1Ch 3:14–16). Jeconiah is also called Jehoiachin (2Ki 24:6; 2Ch 36:8) and sometimes Coniah (Jer 22:24). Jeconiah's presence in this genealogy presents an interesting dilemma. A curse on him forbade any of his descendants from the throne of David forever (Jer 22:30). Since Jesus was heir through Joseph to the royal line of descent, but not an actual son of Joseph and thus not a physical descendant through this line, the curse bypassed Him.

1:12 Shealtiel the father of Zerubbabel. See 1Ch 3:17–19, where Zerubbabel is said to be the offspring of Pedaiah, Shealtiel's brother. Elsewhere in the OT, Zerubbabel is always called the son of Shealtiel (e.g., Hag 1:1; Ezr 3:2; Ne 12:1). Possibly Shealtiel adopted his nephew (*see note on Hag 2:23*). Zerubbabel is the last character in Matthew's list who appears in any of the OT genealogies.

1:16 Joseph the husband of Mary, by whom Jesus was born. The pronoun "whom" is sing., referring to Mary alone. The unusual way in which this final entry is phrased underscores the fact that Jesus was not Joseph's literal offspring. The genealogy nonetheless establishes His claim to the throne of David as Joseph's legal heir.

1:17 fourteen generations. The significance of the number 14 is not clear, but Matthew's attention to numbers—a distinctly Hebrew characteristic—is evident throughout the gospel. The systematic ordering may be an aid for memorization. Note that Matthew counts Jeconiah in both the third and fourth groups, representing both the last generation before the Babylonian captivity and the first generation after.

1:18 betrothed. Jewish betrothal was as binding as modern marriage. A divorce was necessary to terminate the betrothal (v. 19) and the betrothed couple were regarded legally as husband and wife (v. 19)—although physical union had not yet taken place. *See note on Lk 2:5.* **with child by the Holy Spirit.** See vv. 20, 23; Lk 1:26–35.

1:19 Joseph .... righteous man ... planned to send her away secretly. Stoning was the legal prescription for this sort of adultery (Dt 22:23, 24). Joseph's righteousness meant he was also merciful; thus he did not intend to "disgrace" Mary. The phrase "a righteous man" is a Hebraism suggesting that he was a true believer in God who had thereby been declared righteous, and who carefully obeyed the law (see Ge 6:9). To "send her away" would be to obtain a legal divorce (19:8, 9; Dt 24:1), which according to the Jewish custom was necessary in order to dissolve a betrothal (*see note on v. 18*).

1:20 an angel of the Lord. This is one of

21 She will bear a Son; and [A]you shall call His name
Jesus, for [a]He [B]will save His people from their sins."
22 Now all this [a]took place to fulfill what was [A]spoken
by the Lord through the prophet: 23 "[A]BEHOLD, THE
VIRGIN SHALL BE WITH [B]CHILD AND SHALL BEAR A
SON, AND THEY SHALL CALL HIS NAME [a]IMMANUEL,"
which translated means, "[C]GOD WITH US." 24 And
Joseph [a]awoke from his sleep and did as the angel
of the Lord commanded him, and took *Mary* as his
wife, 25 [a]but kept her a virgin until she [A]gave birth
to a Son; and [B]he called His name Jesus.

THE VISIT OF THE MAGI

2 Now after Jesus was [A]born in Bethlehem of Judea
in the days of [B]Herod the king, [a]magi from the
east arrived in Jerusalem, saying, 2 "Where is He
who has been born [A]King of the Jews? For we saw
[B]His star in the east and have come to worship Him."
3 When Herod the king heard *this,* he was troubled,
and all Jerusalem with him. 4 Gathering together
all the chief priests and scribes of the people, he
inquired of them where the [a]Messiah was to be
born. 5 They said to him, "[A]In Bethlehem of Judea;
for this is what has been written [a]by the prophet:

6 '[A]AND YOU, BETHLEHEM, LAND OF JUDAH,
ARE BY NO MEANS LEAST AMONG
THE LEADERS OF JUDAH;
FOR OUT OF YOU SHALL COME
FORTH A RULER
WHO WILL [B]SHEPHERD MY PEOPLE ISRAEL.' "

7 Then Herod secretly called the magi and determined from them [a]the exact time [A]the star appeared.
8 And he sent them to Bethlehem and said, "Go and
search carefully for the Child; and when you have
found *Him,* report to me, so that I too may come and
worship Him." 9 After hearing the king, they went
their way; and the star, which they had seen in the
east, went on before them until it came and stood
over *the place* where the Child was. 10 When they
saw the star, they rejoiced exceedingly with great
joy. 11 After coming into the house they saw the Child
with [A]Mary His mother; and they [a]fell to the ground
and [B]worshiped Him. Then, opening their treasures,
they presented to Him gifts of gold, frankincense,
and myrrh. 12 And having been [A]warned *by God* [B]in
a dream not to return to Herod, the magi left for
their own country by another way.

THE FLIGHT TO EGYPT

13 Now when they had gone, behold, an [A]angel of
the Lord *[B]appeared to Joseph in a dream and said,
"Get up! Take the Child and His mother and flee to
Egypt, and remain there until I tell you; for Herod
is going to search for the Child to destroy Him."

1:21 [a]Lit *He Himself* [A]Luke 1:31; 2:21 [B]Luke 2:11; John 1:29; Acts 4:12; 5:31; 13:23, 38, 39; Col 1:20-23 1:22 [a]Lit *has happened* [A]Luke 24:44; Rom 1:2-4 1:23 [a]Or *Emmanuel* [A]Is 7:14 [B]Is 9:6, 7 [C]Is 8:10 1:24 [a]Lit *got up* 1:25 [a]Lit *and was not knowing her* [A]Luke 2:7 [B]Matt 1:21; Luke 2:21 2:1 [a]A caste of wise men specializing in astronomy, astrology, and natural science [A]Mic 5:2; Luke 2:4-7 [B]Luke 1:5 2:2 [A]Jer 23:5; 30:9; Zech 9:9; Matt 27:11; Luke 19:38; 23:38; John 1:49 [B]Num 24:17 2:4 [a]Gr *Christos (Christ)* 2:5 [a]Or *through* [A]John 7:42 2:6 [A]Mic 5:2; John 7:42 [B]John 21:16 2:7 [a]Lit *the time of the appearing star* [A]Num 24:17 2:11 [a]Lit *prostrated;* i.e. face down in a prone position to indicate worship [A]Matt 1:18; 12:46 [B]Matt 14:33 2:12 [A]Matt 2:13, 19, 22; Luke 2:26; Acts 10:22; Heb 8:5; 11:7 [B]Job 33:15, 16; Matt 1:20 2:13 [A]Acts 5:19; 10:7; 12:7-11 [B]Matt 2:12, 19

only a few such angelic visitations in the NT, most of which are associated with Christ's birth. For others, see 28:2; Ac 5:19; 8:26; 10:3; 12:7–10; 27:23; Rev 1:1. **in a dream.** As if to underscore the supernatural character of Christ's advent, Matthew's narrative of the event describes 5 such revelatory dreams: v. 20; 2:12, 13, 19, 22. Here the angel told Joseph he was to take Mary into his own home.

1:21 Jesus. See v. 25; Lk 1:31. The name actually means "Savior" (*see note on v. 1*).

1:22 to fulfill. Matthew points out fulfillments of OT prophecies no less than a dozen times (cf. 2:15, 17, 23; 4:14; 8:17; 12:17; 13:14, 35; 21:4; 26:54–56; 27:9, 35). He quotes from the OT more than 60 times, more frequently than any other NT writer, except Paul in Romans.

1:23 virgin. Scholars sometimes dispute whether the Hebrew term in Is 7:14 means "virgin" or "maiden." Matthew is quoting here from the LXX which uses the unambiguous Gr. term for "virgin" (*see note on Is 7:14*). Thus Matthew, writing under the Spirit's inspiration, ends all doubt about the meaning of the word in Is 7:14. **Immanuel.** Cf. Is 8:8, 10.

1:24 took *Mary* as his wife. *See note on Lk 2:5.*

2:1 Bethlehem. A small village on the southern outskirts of Jerusalem. Hebrew scholars in Jesus' day clearly expected Bethlehem to be the birthplace of the Messiah (cf. Mic 5:2; Jn 7:42). **in the days of Herod the king.** This refers to Herod the Great, the first of several important rulers from the Herodian dynasty who are named in Scripture. This Herod, founder of the famous line, ruled from 37–4 B.C. He is thought to have been Idumean, a descendant of the Edomites, offspring of Esau. Herod was ruthless and cunning. He loved opulence and grand building projects, and many of the most magnificent ruins that can be seen in modern Israel date back to the days of Herod the Great. His most famous project was the rebuilding of the temple at Jerusalem (*see note on 24:1*). That project alone took several decades and was not completed until long after Herod's death (cf. Jn 2:20). *See note on v. 22.* **magi from the east.** The number of wise men is not given. The traditional notion that there were 3 stems from the number of gifts they brought. These were not kings, but Magi, magicians or astrologers—possibly Zoroastrian wise men from Persia whose knowledge of the Hebrew Scriptures could be traced back to the time of Daniel (cf. Da 5:11). **saying.** This present participle conveys the idea of continuous action. It suggests they went around the city questioning everyone they met.

2:2 star. This could not have been a supernova or a conjunction of planets, as some modern theories suggest, because of the way the star moved and settled over one place (cf. v. 9). It is more likely a supernatural reality similar to the Shekinah that guided the Israelites in the days of Moses (Ex 13:21).

2:4 chief priests. These were the temple hierarchy. They were mostly Sadducees (*see note on 3:7*). **scribes.** Primarily Pharisees, i.e., authorities on Jewish law. Sometimes they are referred to as "lawyers" (*see note on Lk 10:25*). They were professional scholars whose specialty was explaining the application of the law. They knew exactly where the Messiah was to be born (v. 5), but lacked the faith to accompany the Magi to the place where He was.

2:6 This ancient prophecy from Mic 5:2 was written in the eighth century B.C. The original prophecy, not quoted in full by Matthew, declared the deity of Israel's Messiah: "From you One will go forth for Me to be ruler in Israel. His goings forth are from long ago, from the days of eternity." A ruler who will shepherd My people Israel. This portion of Matthew's quote actually seems to be a reference to God's words to David when Israel's kingdom was originally established (2Sa 5:2; 1Ch 11:2). The Gr. word for "ruler" evokes the image of strong, even stern, leadership. "Shepherd" emphasizes tender care. Christ's rule involves both (cf. Rev 12:5).

2:8 that I too may come and worship Him. Herod actually wanted to kill the Child (vv. 13–18), whom he saw as a potential threat to his throne.

2:11 into the house. By the time the wise men arrived, Mary and Joseph were situated in a house, not a stable (cf. Lk 2:7). **the Child with Mary His mother.** Whenever Matthew mentions Mary in connection with her Child, Christ is always given first place (cf. vv. 13, 14, 20, 21). **gold, frankincense, and myrrh.** Gifts suitable for a king (cf. Is 60:6). The fact that Gentiles would offer such worship had prophetic significance as well (Ps 72:10).

2:12, 13 in a dream. *See note on 1:20.*

14 So [a]Joseph got up and took the Child and His
mother while it was still night, and left for Egypt.
15 He [a]remained there until the death of Herod. *This*
was to fulfill what had been spoken by the Lord
through the prophet: "[A]Out of Egypt I called [B]My
Son."

HEROD SLAUGHTERS BABIES

16 Then when Herod saw that he had been tricked
by [A]the magi, he became very enraged, and sent and
[B]slew all the male children who were in Bethlehem
and all its vicinity, from two years old and under, according to the time which he had determined from
the magi. 17 Then what had been spoken through
Jeremiah the prophet was fulfilled:

18 "[A]A voice was heard in Ramah,
Weeping and great mourning,
Rachel weeping for her children;
And she refused to be comforted,
Because they were no more."

19 But when Herod died, behold, an angel of the
Lord *[A]appeared in a dream to Joseph in Egypt,
and said, 20 "Get up, take the Child and His mother,
and go into the land of Israel; for those who sought
the Child's life are dead." 21 So [a]Joseph got up, took
the Child and His mother, and came into the land
of Israel. 22 But when he heard that Archelaus was
reigning over Judea in place of his father Herod, he
was afraid to go there. Then after being [A]warned
by God in a dream, he left for the regions of Galilee,
23 and came and lived in a city called [A]Nazareth. *This*
was to fulfill what was spoken through the prophets:
"He shall be called a [B]Nazarene."

THE PREACHING OF JOHN THE BAPTIST

3 Now [A]in those days [B]John the Baptist *[a]came,
[b]preaching in the [C]wilderness of Judea, saying, 2 "[A]Repent, for [B]the kingdom of heaven [a]is at
hand." 3 For this is the [A]one referred to [a]by Isaiah
the prophet when he said,

"[B]The voice of one [b]crying
in the wilderness,
'[C]Make ready the way of the Lord,
Make His paths straight!' "

4 Now John himself had [a][A]a garment of camel's hair
and a leather belt around his waist; and his food
was [B]locusts and wild honey. 5 Then Jerusalem [A]was
going out to him, and all Judea and all [B]the district
around the Jordan; 6 and they were being [A]bap-
tized by him in the Jordan River, as they confessed
their sins.

2:14 [a]Lit *he* 2:15 [a]Lit *was* [A]Hos 11:1; Num 24:8 [B]Ex 4:22f 2:16 [A]Matt 2:1 [B]Is 59:7 2:18 [A]Jer 31:15 2:19 [A]Matt 1:20; 2:12, 13, 22 2:21 [a]Lit *he* 2:22 [A]Matt 2:12, 13, 19 2:23 [A]Luke 1:26; 2:39; John 1:45, 46 [B]Mark 1:24; John 18:5, 7; 19:19 3:1 [a]Or *arrived*, or *appeared* [b]Or *proclaiming as a herald* [A]Matt 3:1-12: *Mark 1:3-8; Luke 3:2-17;* John 1:6-8, 19-28 [B]Matt 11:11-14; 16:14 [C]Josh 15:61; Judg 1:16 3:2 [a]Lit *has come near* [A]Matt 4:17 [B]Dan 2:44; Matt 4:17, 23; 6:10; 10:7; Mark 1:15; Luke 10:9f; 11:20; 21:31 3:3 [a]Or *through* [b]Or *shouting* [A]Luke 1:17, 76 [B]Is 40:3 [C]John 1:23 3:4 [a]Lit *his garment* [A]2 Kin 1:8; Zech 13:4; Matt 11:8; Mark 1:6 [B]Lev 11:22 3:5 [A]Mark 1:5 [B]Luke 3:3 3:6 [A]Matt 3:11, 13-16; Mark 1:5; John 1:25, 26; 3:23; Acts 1:5; 2:38-41; 10:37

2:15 the death of Herod. Recent scholarship sets this date at 4 B.C. It is probable that the stay in Egypt was very brief—perhaps no more than a few weeks. Out of Egypt. This quotation is from Hos 11:1 (*see note there*), which speaks of God's leading Israel out of Egypt in the Exodus. Matthew suggests that Israel's sojourn in Egypt was a pictorial prophecy, rather than a specific verbal one such as v. 6; cf. 1:23. These are called "types" and all are always fulfilled in Christ, and identified clearly by the NT writers. Another example of a type is found in Jn 3:14. *See note on v. 17.*

2:16 slew all the male children. Herod's act is all the more heinous in light of his full knowledge that the Lord's Anointed One was the target of his murderous plot.

2:17 fulfilled. *See note on v. 15.* Again, this prophecy is in the form of a type. Verse 18 quotes Jer 31:15 (*see note there*), which speaks of all Israel's mourning at the time of the Babylonian captivity (ca. 586 B.C.). That wailing prefigured the wailing over Herod's massacre.

2:19 in a dream. *See note on 1:20.*

2:22 Archelaus. Herod's kingdom was divided 3 ways and given to his sons: Archelaus ruled Judea, Samaria, and Idumea; Herod Philip II ruled the regions N of Galilee (Lk 3:1); and Herod Antipas ruled Galilee and Perea (Lk 3:1). History records that Archelaus was so brutal and ineffective that he was deposed by Rome after a short reign and replaced with a governor appointed by Rome. Pontius Pilate was the fifth governor of Judea. Herod Antipas is the main Herod in the gospel accounts. He was the one who had John the Baptist put to death (14:1–12), and examined Christ on the eve of the crucifixion (Lk 23:7–12).

2:23 He shall be called a Nazarene. Nazareth, an obscure town 70 mi. N of Jerusalem, was a place of lowly reputation, and nowhere mentioned in the OT. Some have suggested that "Nazarene" is a reference to the Heb. word for branch in Is 11:1. Others point out that Matthew's statement that "prophets" had made this prediction may be a reference to verbal prophecies nowhere recorded in the OT. A still more likely explanation is that Matthew is using "Nazarene" as a synonym for someone who is despised or detestable—for that was how people from the region were often characterized (cf. Jn 1:46). If that is the case, the prophecies Matthew has in mind would include Ps 22:6–8; Is 49:7; 53:3.

3:1 John the Baptist. Cf. Mk 1:2–14; Lk 1:5–25, 57–80; 3:3–20; Jn 1:6–8, 19–39. **the wilderness of Judea.** The region to the immediate W of the Dead Sea—an utterly barren desert. The Jewish sect of the Essenes had significant communities in this region. But there is no biblical evidence to suggest that John was in any way connected with that sect. John seems to have preached near the northern end of this region, close by where the Jordan flows into the Dead Sea (v. 6). This was a full day's journey from Jerusalem and seems an odd location to announce the arrival of a King. But it is perfectly in keeping with God's ways (1Co 1:26–29).

3:2 Repent. This is no mere academic change of mind, nor mere regret or remorse. John the Baptist spoke of repentance as a radical turning from sin that inevitably became manifest in the fruit of righteousness (v. 8). Jesus' first sermon began with the same imperative (4:17). For a discussion of the nature of repentance, *see notes on 2Co 7:8–11.* **the kingdom of heaven.** This is an expression unique to Matthew's gospel. Matthew uses the word "heaven" as a euphemism for God's name—to accommodate his Jewish readers' sensitivities (cf. 23:22). Throughout the rest of Scripture, the kingdom is called "the kingdom of God." Both expressions refer to the sphere of God's dominion over those who belong to Him. The kingdom is now manifest in heaven's spiritual rule over the hearts of believers (Lk 17:21); and one day it will be established in a literal earthly kingdom (Rev 20:4–6). **is at hand.** In one sense the kingdom is a present reality, but in its fullest sense it awaits a yet-future fulfillment.

3:3 referred to by Isaiah the prophet. John's mission had long ago been described in Is 40:3–5 (*see notes there*). All 4 of the Gospels cite this passage as a prophecy pointing to John the Baptist (*see note on Lk 3:6*).

3:4 a garment of camel's hair and a leather belt. Practical and long-wearing clothes, but far from comfortable or fashionable. John evokes the image of Elijah (2Ki 1:8)—and the Israelites were expecting Elijah before the day of the Lord (Mal 4:5). **locusts.** These were an allowed food (Lv 11:22).

3:6 baptized. The symbolism of John's baptism likely had its roots in OT purification rituals (cf. Lv 15:13). Baptism had also long been administered to Gentile proselytes coming

7 But when he saw many of the [A]Pharisees and
[B]Sadducees coming for baptism, he said to them,
"You [C]brood of vipers, who warned you to flee
from [D]the wrath to come? 8 [A]Therefore bear fruit
[B]in keeping with repentance; 9 and do not suppose that you can say to yourselves, '[A]We have
Abraham for our father'; for I say to you that
from these stones God is able to raise up children to Abraham. 10 The [A]axe is already laid at the
root of the trees; therefore [B]every tree that does
not bear good fruit is cut down and thrown into
the fire.

11 "As for me, [A]I baptize you [a]with water for repentance, but He who is coming after me is mightier than I, and I am not fit to remove His sandals;
[B]He will baptize you [a]with the Holy Spirit and fire.
12 His [A]winnowing fork is in His hand, and He will
thoroughly clear His threshing floor; and He will
[B]gather His wheat into the barn, but He will burn
up the [C]chaff with [D]unquenchable fire."

THE BAPTISM OF JESUS

13 [A]Then Jesus *arrived [B]from Galilee at the Jordan
coming to John, to be baptized by him. 14 But John
tried to prevent Him, saying, "I have need to be baptized by You, and do You come to me?" 15 But Jesus
answering said to him, "Permit *it* at this time; for in
this way it is fitting for us [A]to fulfill all righteousness."
Then he *permitted Him. 16 After being baptized, Jesus
came up immediately from the water; and behold,
the heavens were opened, and [a,A]he saw the Spirit of
God descending as a dove *and* [b]lighting on Him, 17 and
behold, a voice out of the heavens said, "[A]This is [a]My
beloved Son, in whom I am well-pleased."

THE TEMPTATION OF JESUS

4 [A]Then Jesus was led up by the Spirit into the
wilderness [B]to be tempted by the devil. 2 And
after He had [A]fasted forty days and forty nights, He
[a]then became hungry. 3 And [A]the tempter came and
said to Him, "If You are the [B]Son of God, command

3:7 [A]Matt 16:1ff; 23:13, 15 [B]Matt 22:23; Acts 4:1; 5:17; 23:6ff [C]Matt 12:34; 23:33 [D]1 Thess 1:10 3:8 [A]Luke 3:8; Eph 5:8, 9 [B]Acts 26:20 3:9 [A]Luke 3:8; 16:24; John 8:33, 39, 53; Acts 13:26; Rom 4:1; 9:7, 8; Gal 3:29 3:10 [A]Luke 3:9 [B]Ps 92:12-14; Matt 7:19; John 15:2 3:11 [a]The Gr here can be translated *in, with* or *by* [A]Mark 1:4, 8; Luke 3:16; John 1:26f; Acts 1:5; 8:36, 38; 11:16 [B]John 1:33; Acts 2:3, 4; Titus 3:5 3:12 [A]Is 30:24; 41:16; Jer 15:7; 51:2; Luke 3:17 [B]Matt 13:30 [C]Ps 1:4 [D]Is 66:24; Jer 7:20; Matt 13:41, 42; Mark 9:43, 48 3:13 [A]Matt 3:13-17: *Mark 1:9-11; Luke 3:21, 22;* John 1:31-34 [B]Matt 2:22 3:15 [A]Ps 40:7, 8; John 4:34; 8:29 3:16 [a]Or *He* [b]Lit *coming upon Him* [A]Mark 1:10; Luke 3:22; John 1:32; Acts 7:56 3:17 [a]Or *My Son, the Beloved* [A]Ps 2:7; Is 42:1; Matt 12:18; 17:5; Mark 9:7; Luke 9:35; John 12:28 4:1 [A]Matt 4:1-11: *Mark 1:12, 13; Luke 4:1-13* [B]Heb 4:15; James 1:14 4:2 [a]Lit *later became;* or *afterward became* [A]Ex 34:28; 1 Kin 19:8 4:3 [A]1 Thess 3:5 [B]Matt 14:33; 26:63; Mark 3:11; 5:7; Luke 1:35; 4:41; John 1:34, 49; Acts 9:20

into Judaism. The baptism of John thus powerfully and dramatically symbolized repentance. Jews accepting John's baptism were admitting they had been as Gentiles and needed to become the people of God genuinely, inwardly (an amazing admission, given their hatred of Gentiles). The people were repenting in anticipation of the Messiah's arrival. The meaning of John's baptism differs somewhat from Christian baptism (cf. Ac 18:25). Actually, Christian baptism altered the significance of the ritual, symbolizing the believer's identification with Christ in His death, burial, and resurrection (Ro 6:3–5; Col 2:12).

3:7 Pharisees and Sadducees. *See note on Jn 3:1.* The Pharisees were a small (about 6,000), legalistic sect of the Jews who were known for their rigid adherence to the ceremonial fine points of the law. Their name means "separated ones." Jesus' interaction with the Pharisees was usually adversarial. He rebuked them for using human tradition to nullify Scripture (15:3–9), and especially for rank hypocrisy (15:7, 8; 22:18; 23:13, 23, 25, 29; Lk 12:1). The Sadducees were known for their denial of things supernatural. They denied the resurrection of the dead (22:23) and the existence of angels (Ac 23:8). Unlike the Pharisees, they rejected human tradition and scorned legalism. They accepted only the Pentateuch as authoritative. They tended to be wealthy, aristocratic members of the priestly tribe, and in the days of Herod their sect controlled the temple (*see note on 2:4*), though they were fewer in number than the Pharisees. Pharisees and Sadducees had little in common. Pharisees were ritualists; Sadducees were rationalists. Pharisees were legalists; Sadducees were liberals. Pharisees were separatists; Sadducees were compromisers and political opportunists. Yet they united together in their opposition to Christ (22:15, 16, 23, 34, 35). John publicly addressed them as deadly snakes. **the wrath to come.** *See note on Lk 3:7.* John's preaching echoed the familiar OT theme of promised wrath in the Day of the Lord (e.g., Eze 7:19; Zep 1:18; see Introduction to Joel: Historical and Theological Themes). This must have been a particularly stinging rebuke to the Jewish leaders, who imagined that divine wrath was reserved only for non-Jews.

3:8 fruit in keeping with repentance. *See note on v. 2.* Repentance itself is not a work, but works are its inevitable fruit. Repentance and faith are inextricably linked in Scripture. Repentance means turning from one's sin, and faith is turning to God (cf. 1Th. 1:9). They are like opposite sides of the same coin. That is why both are linked to conversion (Mk 1:15; Ac 3:19; 20:21). Note that the works John demanded to see were "fruit" of repentance. But repentance itself is no more a "work" than faith is (*see note on 2Ti 2:25*).

3:9 Abraham for our father. See Jn 8:39–44. They believed that merely being descendants of Abraham, members of God's chosen race, made them spiritually secure. But Abraham's real descendants are those who share his faith (cf. Ro 4:16). And "those who are of faith ... are sons of Abraham" (Gal 3:7, 29). *See note on Lk 3:8.*

3:10 the axe is ... laid at the root. Irreversible judgment was imminent (*see note on 11:3*).

3:11 Three types of baptism are referred to here: 1) **with water for repentance.** John's baptism symbolized cleansing (*see note on v. 6*); 2) **with the Holy Spirit.** All believers in Christ are Spirit-baptized (1Co 12:13); and 3) **with ... fire.** Because fire is used throughout this context as a means of judgment (vv. 10, 12), this must speak of a baptism of judgment upon the unrepentant.

3:12 winnowing fork. A tool for tossing grain into the wind so that the chaff is blown away.

3:14 John tried to prevent Him. John's baptism symbolized repentance, and John saw this as inappropriate for the One he knew was the spotless Lamb of God (cf. Jn 1:29).

3:15 it is fitting for us to fulfill all righteousness. Christ was here identifying Himself with sinners. He will ultimately bear their sins; His perfect righteousness will be imputed to them (2Co 5:21). This act of baptism was a necessary part of the righteousness He secured for sinners. This first public event of His ministry is also rich in meaning: 1) it pictured His death and resurrection (cf. Lk 12:50); 2) it therefore prefigured the significance of Christian baptism (*see note on v. 6*); 3) it marked His first public identification with those whose sins He would bear (Is 53:11; 1Pe 3:18); and 4) it was a public affirmation of His messiahship by testimony directly from heaven (*see note on v. 17*).

3:16, 17 Jesus ... the Spirit of God .... voice out of the heavens. Here all 3 Persons of the Trinity are clearly delineated. *See note on Lk 3:22.* The Father's command to hear His Son and the Spirit's vindication and empowerment (*see note on 12:31*) officially inaugurated Christ's ministry.

3:17 My beloved Son, in whom I am well-pleased. This heavenly pronouncement combines language from Ps 2:7 and Is 42:1—prophecies that would have been well known to those with messianic expectations. Cf. 17:5; Mk 1:11; 9:7; Lk 3:22; 9:35.

4:1 led up by the Spirit ... to be tempted by the devil. God Himself is never the agent of temptation (Jas 1:13), but here—as in the book of Job—God uses even satanic tempting to serve His sovereign purposes. Christ was tempted in all points (Heb 4:15; 1Jn 2:16); Satan tempted Him with "the lust of the flesh" (vv. 2, 3); "the lust of the eyes" (vv. 8, 9); and "the pride of life" (vv. 5, 6).

4:2 forty days and forty nights. Similarly, Moses was without food or drink on Sinai for "forty days and forty nights" (Dt 9:9), and Elijah also fasted that long (1Ki 19:8). *See note on 12:40.*

4:3 If You are the Son of God. The conditional "if" carries the meaning of "since" in this context. There was no doubt in Satan's mind who Jesus was; but Satan's design was to get Him to violate the plan of God and employ the divine power that He had set aside in His humiliation (cf. Php 2:7).

that these stones become bread." 4 But He answered
and said, "It is written, '[A]MAN SHALL NOT LIVE ON
BREAD ALONE, BUT ON EVERY WORD THAT PROCEEDS
OUT OF THE MOUTH OF GOD.' "
5 Then the devil *took Him into [A]the holy city
and had Him stand on the pinnacle of the temple,
6 and *said to Him, "If You are the Son of God, throw
Yourself down; for it is written,

> '[A]HE WILL COMMAND HIS ANGELS
> CONCERNING YOU';

and

> 'ON *their* HANDS THEY WILL
> BEAR YOU UP,
> SO THAT YOU WILL NOT STRIKE YOUR
> FOOT AGAINST A STONE.' "

7 Jesus said to him, "[a]On the other hand, it is written, '[A]YOU SHALL NOT PUT THE LORD YOUR GOD TO
THE TEST.' "
8 [A]Again, the devil *took Him to a very high
mountain and *showed Him all the kingdoms of
the world and their glory; 9 and he said to Him,
"[A]All these things I will give You, if You fall down
and [a]worship me." 10 Then Jesus *said to him, "Go,
Satan! For it is written, '[A]YOU SHALL WORSHIP THE
LORD YOUR GOD, AND [a]SERVE HIM ONLY.' " 11 Then
the devil *left Him; and behold, [A]angels came and
began to minister to Him.

JESUS BEGINS HIS MINISTRY

12 Now when Jesus heard that [A]John had been
taken into custody, [B]He withdrew into Galilee; 13 and
leaving Nazareth, He came and [A]settled in Capernaum, which is by the sea, in the region of Zebulun
and Naphtali. 14 *This was* to fulfill what was spoken
through Isaiah the prophet:

> 15 "[A]THE LAND OF ZEBULUN AND
> THE LAND OF NAPHTALI,
> [a]BY THE WAY OF THE SEA, BEYOND THE
> JORDAN, GALILEE OF THE [b]GENTILES—
> 16 [A]THE PEOPLE WHO WERE SITTING IN
> DARKNESS SAW A GREAT LIGHT,
> AND THOSE WHO WERE SITTING IN THE
> LAND AND SHADOW OF DEATH,
> UPON THEM A LIGHT DAWNED."

17 [A]From that time Jesus began to [a]preach and say,
"[B]Repent, for the kingdom of heaven is at hand."

THE FIRST DISCIPLES

18 [A]Now as Jesus was walking by [B]the Sea of Galilee, He saw two brothers, [C]Simon who was called
Peter, and Andrew his brother, casting a net into
the sea; for they were fishermen. 19 And He *said
to them, "[a]Follow Me, and I will make you fishers
of men." 20 Immediately they left their nets and
followed Him. 21 Going on from there He saw two
other brothers, [a,A]James the *son* of Zebedee, and
[b]John his brother, in the boat with Zebedee their

4:4 [A]Deut 8:3 4:5 [A]Neh 11:1, 18; Dan 9:24; Matt 27:53 4:6 [A]Ps 91:11, 12 4:7 [a]Lit *Again* [A]Deut 6:16 4:8 [A]Matt 16:26; 1 John 2:15-17 4:9 [a]Lit *prostrate Yourself* [A]1 Cor 10:20f 4:10 [a]Or *fulfill religious duty to Him* [A]Deut 6:13; 10:20 4:11 [A]Matt 26:53; Luke 22:43; Heb 1:14 4:12 [A]Matt 14:3; Mark 1:14; Luke 3:20; John 3:24 [B]Mark 1:14; Luke 4:14; John 1:43; 2:11 4:13 [A]Matt 11:23; Mark 1:21; 2:1; Luke 4:23, 31; John 2:12; 4:46f 4:15 [a]Or *Toward the sea* [b]Lit *nations*, usually non-Jewish [A]Is 9:1 4:16 [A]Is 9:2; 60:1-3; Luke 2:32 4:17 [a]Or *proclaim* [A]Mark 1:14, 15 [B]Matt 3:2 4:18 [A]Matt 4:18-22: *Mark 1:16-20;* Luke 5:2-11; John 1:40-42 [B]Matt 15:29; Mark 7:31; Luke 5:1; John 6:1 [C]Matt 10:2; 16:18; John 1:40-42 4:19 [a]Lit *Come here after Me* 4:21 [a]Or *Jacob;* James is the Eng form of Jacob [b]Gr *Joannes*, Heb *Johanan* [A]Matt 10:2; 20:20

4:4 It is written. All 3 of Jesus' replies to the Devil were taken from Deuteronomy. This one, from Dt 8:3, states that God allowed Israel to hunger, so that He might feed them with manna and teach them to trust Him to provide for them. So the verse is directly applicable to Jesus' circumstances and a fitting reply to Satan's temptation. **every word that proceeds out of the mouth of God.** A more important source of sustenance than food, it nurtures our spiritual needs in a way that benefits us eternally, rather than merely providing temporal relief from physical hunger.

4:5 pinnacle of the temple. This was probably a roof with a portico at the SE corner of the temple complex, where a massive retaining wall reached from a level well above the temple mount, deep into the Kidron Valley. According to the Jewish historian Josephus, this was a drop of nearly 450 ft.

4:6 for it is written . . . You will not strike Your foot against a stone. Note that Satan also quoted Scripture (Ps 91:11, 12)—but utterly twisted its meaning, employing a passage about *trusting* God to justify *testing* Him.

4:7 it is written. Christ replied with another verse from Israel's wilderness experience (Dt 6:16)—recalling the experience at Massah, where the grumbling Israelites put the Lord to the test, angrily demanding that Moses produce water where there was none (Ex 17:2–7).

4:9 I will give You. Satan is the "ruler of this world" (Jn 12:31; 14:30; 16:11), and the "god of this world" (2Co 4:4). The whole world lies in his power (1Jn 5:19). This is illustrated in Da 10:13 (*see note there*), where demonic power controlled the kingdom of Persia, so that a demon is called the prince of the kingdom of Persia.

4:10 For it is written. Here Christ was citing and paraphrasing Dt 6:13, 14. Again, these relate to the Israelites' wilderness experiences. Christ, like them, was led into the wilderness to be tested (cf. Dt 8:2). Unlike them, He withstood every aspect of the test.

4:11 angels came and *began* to minister to Him. Psalm 91:11, 12—the verse Satan tried to twist—was thus fulfilled in God's way, and in God's perfect timing.

4:12 John had been taken into custody. John was imprisoned for his bold rebuke of Herod Antipas. See 14:3, 4.

4:13 leaving Nazareth. Some time elapsed between vv. 12 and 13. Jesus' stay in Nazareth ended abruptly when He was violently rejected by the people of Nazareth, who tried to murder Him (see Lk 4:16–30). **Capernaum.** He settled in this important town on the trade route at the N end of the Sea of Galilee. Capernaum was the home of Peter and Andrew (v. 18), James and John (v. 21), and Matthew (9:9). A comparison of the gospels reveals that Christ had already ministered extensively in Capernaum (*see note on Lk 4:23*).

4:15 Galilee of the Gentiles. This name was used even in Isaiah's time because Galilee lay on the route through which all Gentiles passed in and out of Israel. In Jesus' time, the region of Galilee had become an important center of Roman occupation. The prophecy cited by Matthew is from Is 9:1, 2. See Is 42:6, 7.

4:17 From that time Jesus began to preach. This marks the beginning of His public ministry. Note that His message was an exact echo of what John the Baptist preached. **Repent, for the kingdom of heaven is at hand.** *See note on 3:2.* The opening word of this first sermon sets the tone for Jesus' entire earthly ministry (cf. Lk 5:32). Repentance was a constant motif in all His public preaching. And in His closing charge to the apostles, He commanded them to preach repentance as well (Lk 24:47).

4:18 two brothers. Jesus had encountered Peter and Andrew before, near Bethabara, in the Jordan region, where Andrew (and perhaps Peter as well) had become a disciple of John the Baptist (Jn 1:35–42). They left John to follow Jesus for a time before returning to fishing in Capernaum. Perhaps they had returned to Capernaum during Jesus' earlier ministry here (*see note on Lk 4:23*). Here He called them to follow Him in long-term discipleship.

4:21 James the *son* of Zebedee. This James is easy to distinguish from the other men named James in the NT, because he is never mentioned in Scripture apart from

father, mending their nets; and He called them.
22 Immediately they left the boat and their father,
and followed Him.

MINISTRY IN GALILEE

23 Jesus was going [A]throughout all Galilee,
[B]teaching in their synagogues and [C]proclaiming
the [a]gospel of the kingdom, and [D]healing every
kind of disease and every kind of sickness among
the people.
24 The news about Him spread [A]throughout all
Syria; and they brought to Him all who were ill,
those suffering with various diseases and pains,
[B]demoniacs, [a,C]epileptics, [D]paralytics; and He healed
them. 25 Large crowds [A]followed Him from Galilee
and [B]*the* Decapolis and Jerusalem and Judea and
from [C]beyond the Jordan.

THE SERMON ON THE MOUNT; THE BEATITUDES

5 [A]When Jesus saw the crowds, He went up on [B]the
[a]mountain; and after He sat down, His disciples
came to Him. 2 [A]He opened His mouth and *began*
to teach them, saying,
3 "[a,A]Blessed are the [b]poor in spirit, for [B]theirs is
the kingdom of heaven.
4 "Blessed are [A]those who mourn, for they shall
be comforted.
5 "Blessed are [A]the [a]gentle, for they shall inherit
the earth.
6 "Blessed are [A]those who hunger and thirst for
righteousness, for they shall be satisfied.
7 "Blessed are [A]the merciful, for they shall receive mercy.
8 "Blessed are [A]the pure in heart, for [B]they shall
see God.
9 "Blessed are the peacemakers, for [A]they shall
be called sons of God.
10 "Blessed are those who have been [A]persecuted
for the sake of righteousness, for [B]theirs is the kingdom of heaven.
11 "Blessed are you when *people* [A]insult you and
persecute you, and falsely say all kinds of evil
against you because of Me. 12 Rejoice and be glad, for
your reward in heaven is great; for [A]in the same way
they persecuted the prophets who were before you.

DISCIPLES AND THE WORLD

13 "You are the salt of the earth; but [A]if the salt
has become tasteless, how [a]can it be made salty
again? It is no longer good for anything, except to
be thrown out and trampled under foot by men.

4:23 [a]Or *good news* [A]Mark 1:39; Luke 4:14, 44 [B]Matt 9:35; 13:54; Mark 1:21; 6:2; 10:1; Luke 4:15; 6:6; 13:10; John 6:59; 18:20 [C]Matt 3:2; 9:35; 24:14; Mark 1:14; Luke 4:43; 8:1; 16:16; Acts 20:25; 28:31 [D]Matt 8:16; 9:35; 14:14; 15:30; 19:2; 21:14; Mark 1:34; 3:10; Luke 4:40; 7:21; Acts 10:38 4:24 [a]Lit *moonstruck* [A]Mark 7:26; Luke 2:2; Acts 15:23; 18:18; 20:3; 21:3; Gal 1:21 [B]Matt 8:16, 28, 33; 9:32; 12:22; 15:22; Mark 1:32; 5:15, 16, 18; Luke 8:36; John 10:21 [C]Matt 17:15 [D]Matt 8:6; 9:2, 6; Mark 2:3-5, 9; Luke 5:24 4:25 [A]Mark 3:7, 8; Luke 6:17 [B]Mark 5:20; 7:31 [C]Matt 4:15 5:1 [a]Or *hill* [A]Matt ch 5-7; Luke 6:20-49 [B]Mark 3:13; Luke 6:17; 9:28; John 6:3, 15 5:2 [A]Matt 13:35; Acts 8:35; 10:34; 18:14 5:3 [a]I.e. fortunate or prosperous, and so through v 11 [b]I.e. those who are not spiritually arrogant [A]Matt 5:3-12: *Luke 6:20-23* [B]Matt 5:10; 19:14; 25:34; Mark 10:14; Luke 6:20; 22:29f 5:4 [A]Is 61:2; John 16:20; Rev 7:17 5:5 [a]Or *humble, meek* [A]Ps 37:11 5:6 [A]Is 55:1, 2; John 4:14; 6:48ff; 7:37 5:7 [A]Prov 11:17; Matt 6:14, 15; 18:33-35 5:8 [A]Ps 24:4 [B]Heb 12:14; 1 John 3:2; Rev 22:4 5:9 [A]Matt 5:45; Luke 6:35; Rom 8:14 5:10 [A]1 Pet 3:14 [B]Matt 5:3; 19:14; 25:34; Mark 10:14; Luke 6:20; 22:29f 5:11 [A]1 Pet 4:14 5:12 [A]2 Chr 36:16; Matt 23:37; Acts 7:52; 1 Thess 2:15; Heb 11:33ff; James 5:10 5:13 [a]Lit *will* [A]Mark 9:50; Luke 14:34f

his brother John. His martyrdom by Herod Agrippa I marked the beginning of a time of severe persecution in the early church (Ac 12:2). For information on others named James, *see note on 10:2*; Introduction to James: Author and Date.

4:23 teaching ... proclaiming the gospel ... healing. The 3 main aspects of Christ's public ministry.

4:24 Syria. The area immediately NE of Galilee.

4:25 Decapolis. A confederation of 10 Hellenized cities S of Galilee and mostly E of the Jordan. The league of cities was formed shortly after Pompey's invasion of Israel (ca. 64 B.C.) to preserve Gr. culture in the Semitic region. These cities were naturally Gentile strongholds.

5:1–7:29 The Sermon on the Mount introduces a series of 5 important discourses recorded in Matthew (see Introduction: Historical and Theological Themes). This sermon is a masterful exposition of the law and a potent assault on Pharisaic legalism, closing with a call to true faith and salvation (7:13–29). Christ expounded the full meaning of the law, showing that its demands were humanly impossible (cf. 5:48). This is the proper use of the law with respect to salvation: it closes off every possible avenue of human merit and leaves sinners dependent on nothing but divine grace for salvation (cf. Ro 3:19, 20; Gal 3:23, 24). Christ plumbed the depth of the law, showing that its true demands went far beyond the surface meaning of the words (5:28, 39, 44) and set a standard that is higher than the most diligent students of the law had heretofore realized (5:20). *See note on Lk 6:17–49.*

5:1 He sat down. This was the normal posture for rabbis while teaching (cf. 13:1, 2; 26:55; Mk 4:1; 9:35; Lk 5:3; Jn 6:3; 8:2). *See note on Lk 4:20.*

5:3 Blessed. The word lit. means "happy, fortunate, blissful." Here it speaks of more than a surface emotion. Jesus was describing the divinely bestowed well-being that belongs only to the faithful. The Beatitudes demonstrate that the way to heavenly blessedness is antithetical to the worldly path normally followed in pursuit of happiness. The worldly idea is that happiness is found in riches, merriment, abundance, leisure, and such things. The real truth is the very opposite. The Beatitudes give Jesus' description of the character of true faith. **poor in spirit.** The opposite of self-sufficiency. This speaks of the deep humility of recognizing one's utter spiritual bankruptcy apart from God. It describes those who are acutely conscious of their own lostness and hopelessness apart from divine grace (cf. 9:12; Lk 18:13). *See note on 19:17.* **theirs is the kingdom of heaven.** *See note on 3:2.* Notice that the truth of salvation by grace is clearly presupposed in this opening verse of the Sermon on the Mount. Jesus was teaching that the kingdom is a gracious gift to those who sense their own poverty of spirit.

5:4 those who mourn. This speaks of mourning over sin, the godly sorrow that produces repentance leading to salvation without regret (2Co 7:10). The "comfort" is the comfort of forgiveness and salvation (cf. Is 40:1, 2).

5:5 the gentle. Gentleness or meekness is the opposite of being out of control. It is not weakness, but supreme self-control empowered by the Spirit (cf. Gal 5:23). The statement that the meek "shall inherit the earth" is quoted from Ps 37:11.

5:6 hunger and thirst for righteousness. This is the opposite of the self-righteousness of the Pharisees. It speaks of those who seek God's righteousness rather than attempting to establish a righteousness of their own (Ro 10:3; Php 3:9). What they seek will fill them, i.e., it will satisfy their hunger and thirst for a right relationship with God.

5:7 they shall receive mercy. The converse is also true. Cf. Jas 2:13.

5:8 see God. Not only with the perception of faith, but in the glory of heaven. Cf. Heb 12:14; Rev 22:3, 4.

5:9 peacemakers. See vv. 44, 45 for more on this quality.

5:10 persecuted. Cf. Jas 5:10, 11; 1Pe 4:12–14. *See note on Lk 6:22.*

5:13 salt ... tasteless, how can it be made salty *again?* Salt is both a preservative and a flavor enhancer. No doubt its use as a preservative is what Jesus had mostly in view here. Pure salt cannot lose its flavor or effectiveness, but the salt that is common in the Dead Sea area is contaminated with gypsum and other minerals and may have a flat taste or be ineffective as a preservative. Such mineral salts were useful for little more than keeping footpaths free of vegetation.

14 "You are [A]the light of the world. A city set on a
[a]hill cannot be hidden; 15 [A]nor does *anyone* light a
lamp and put it under a [a]basket, but on the lampstand, and it gives light to all who are in the house.
16 Let your light shine before men in such a way that
they may [A]see your good works, and [B]glorify your
Father who is in heaven.

17 "Do not think that I came to abolish the [A]Law
or the Prophets; I did not come to abolish but to
fulfill. 18 For truly I say to you, [A]until heaven and
earth pass away, not [a]the smallest letter or stroke
shall pass from the Law until all is accomplished.
19 Whoever then annuls one of the least of these
commandments, and teaches [a]others *to do* the same,
shall be called least [A]in the kingdom of heaven; but
whoever [b]keeps and teaches *them*, he shall be called
great in the kingdom of heaven.

20 "For I say to you that unless your [A]righteous-
ness surpasses *that* of the scribes and Pharisees,
you will not enter the kingdom of heaven.

PERSONAL RELATIONSHIPS

21 "[A]You have heard that [a]the ancients were told,
'[B]YOU SHALL NOT COMMIT MURDER' and 'Whoever
commits murder shall be [b]liable to [C]the court.' 22 But
I say to you that everyone who is angry with his
brother shall be [a]guilty before [A]the court; and whoever says to his brother, '[b]You good-for-nothing,'
shall be [a]guilty before [c,B]the supreme court; and
whoever says, 'You fool,' shall be [a]guilty *enough
to go* into the [d,C]fiery hell. 23 Therefore if you are
[A]presenting your [a]offering at the altar, and there
remember that your brother has something against
you, 24 leave your [a]offering there before the altar and
go; first be [A]reconciled to your brother, and then
come and present your [a]offering. 25 [A]Make friends
quickly with your opponent at law while you are
with him on the way, so that your opponent may
not hand you over to the judge, and the judge to
the officer, and you be thrown into prison. 26 Truly
I say to you, [A]you will not come out of there until
you have paid up the last [a]cent.

27 "[A]You have heard that it was said, '[B]YOU SHALL
NOT COMMIT ADULTERY'; 28 but I say to you that everyone who looks at a woman [A]with lust for her
has already committed adultery with her in his
heart. 29 [A]If your right eye makes you [a]stumble,
tear it out and throw it from you; for it is better for you [b]to lose one of the parts of your body,
[c]than for your whole body to be thrown into [d,B]hell.

5:14 [a]Or *mountain* [A]Prov 4:18; John 8:12; 9:5; 12:36 5:15 [a]Or *peck-measure* [A]Mark 4:21; Luke 8:16; 11:33; Phil 2:15 5:16 [A]1 Pet 2:12 [B]Matt 9:8 5:17 [A]Matt 7:12 5:18 [a]Lit *one iota* (Heb yodh) or *one projection of a letter* (serif) [A]Matt 24:35; Luke 16:17 5:19 [a]Gr *anthropoi* [b]Lit *does* [A]Matt 11:11 5:20 [A]Luke 18:11, 12 5:21 [a]Lit *it was said to the ancients* [b]Or *guilty before* [A]Matt 5:27, 33, 38, 43 [B]Ex 20:13; Deut 5:17 [C]Deut 16:18; 2 Chr 19:5f 5:22 [a]Or *liable to* [b]Or *empty-head;* Gr *Raka (Raca)* fr Aram *reqa* [c]Lit *the Sanhedrin* [d]Lit *Gehenna of fire* [A]Deut 16:18; 2 Chr 19:5f [B]Matt 10:17; 26:59; Mark 13:9; 14:55; 15:1; Luke 22:66; John 11:47; Acts 4:15; 5:21; 6:12; 22:30; 23:1; 24:20 [C]Matt 5:29f; 10:28; 18:9; 23:15, 33; Mark 9:43ff; Luke 12:5; James 3:6 5:23 [a]Or *gift* [A]Matt 5:24 5:24 [a]Or *gift* [A]Rom 12:17, 18 5:25 [A]Prov 25:8f; Luke 12:58 5:26 [a]Lit *quadrans* (equaling two mites); i.e. 1/64 of a daily wage [A]Luke 12:59 5:27 [A]Matt 5:21, 33, 38, 43 [B]Ex 20:14; Deut 5:18 5:28 [A]2 Sam 11:2-5; Job 31:1; Matt 15:19; James 1:14, 15 5:29 [a]I.e. sin [b]Lit *that one…be lost* [c]Lit *not your whole body* [d]Gr *Gehenna* [A]Matt 18:9; Mark 9:47 [B]Matt 5:22

5:16 light shine. A godly life gives convincing testimony of the saving power of God. That brings Him glory. Cf. 1Pe 2:12.

5:17 Do not think … abolish the Law or the Prophets. Jesus was neither giving a new law nor modifying the old, but rather explaining the true significance of the moral content of Moses' law and the rest of the OT. "The Law and the Prophets" speaks of the entirety of the OT Scriptures, not the rabbinical interpretations of them. **fulfill.** This speaks of fulfillment in the same sense that prophecy is fulfilled. Christ was indicating that He is the fulfillment of the law in all its aspects. He fulfilled the moral law by keeping it perfectly. He fulfilled the ceremonial law by being the embodiment of everything the law's types and symbols pointed to. And He fulfilled the judicial law by personifying God's perfect justice (cf. 12:18, 20).

5:18 until heaven and earth pass away … until all is accomplished. Here Christ was affirming the utter inerrancy and absolute authority of the OT as the Word of God—down to the smallest stroke or letter. Again (*see note on v. 17*), this suggests that the NT should not be seen as supplanting and abrogating the OT, but as fulfilling and explicating it. For example, all the ceremonial requirements of the Mosaic law were fulfilled in Christ and are no longer to be observed by Christians (Col 2:16, 17). Yet not the smallest letter or stroke is thereby erased; the underlying truths of those Scriptures remain—and in fact the mysteries behind them are now revealed in the brighter light of the gospel. **smallest letter or stroke.** The phrase "smallest letter" refers to the smallest Heb. letter, the *yohd,* which is a meager stroke of the pen, like an accent mark or an apostrophe. The "stroke" is a tiny extension on a Heb. letter, like the serif in modern typefaces.

5:19 shall be called least … shall be called great. The consequence of practicing or teaching disobedience of any of God's Word is to be called least in the kingdom of heaven (see note on Jas 2:10). Determining rank in the kingdom of heaven is entirely God's prerogative (cf. Mt 20:23), and Jesus declares that He will hold those in lowest esteem who hold His Word in low esteem. There is no impunity for believers who disobey, discredit, or belittle God's law (see note on 2Co 5:10). That Jesus does not refer to loss of salvation is clear from the fact that, though offenders will be called least, they will still be in the kingdom of heaven. The positive result is that whoever keeps and teaches God's Word, he shall be called great in the kingdom of heaven. Here again Jesus mentions the two aspects of doing and teaching. Kingdom citizens are to uphold every part of God's law both in their living and in their teaching.

5:20 unless your righteousness surpasses *that* of the scribes and Pharisees. On the one hand, Jesus was calling His disciples to a deeper, more radical holiness than that of the Pharisees. Pharisaism had a tendency to soften the law's demands by focusing only on external obedience. In the verses that follow, Jesus unpacks the full moral significance of the law, and shows that the righteousness the law calls for actually involves an internal conformity to the spirit of the law, rather than mere external compliance to the letter. **will not enter the kingdom of heaven.** On the other hand, this sets up an impossible barrier to works-salvation. Scripture teaches repeatedly that sinners are capable of nothing but a flawed and imperfect righteousness (e.g., Is 64:6). Therefore, the only righteousness by which sinners may be justified is the perfect righteousness of God that is imputed to those who believe (Ge 15:6; Ro 4:5).

5:21, 22 You have heard … But I say to you. See vv. 27, 31, 33, 38, 43. The quotes are from Ex 20:13; Dt 5:17. Jesus was not altering the terms of the law in any of these passages. Rather, He was correcting what they had "heard"—the rabbinical understanding of the law (*see note on v. 38*).

5:22 You good-for-nothing. Lit. "Empty-headed." Jesus suggested here that the verbal abuse stems from the same sinful motives (anger and hatred) that ultimately lead to murder. The internal attitude is what the law actually prohibits, and therefore an abusive insult carries the same kind of moral guilt as an act of murder. **hell.** A reference to the Hinnom Valley, SW of Jerusalem. Ahaz and Manasseh permitted human sacrifices there during their reigns (2Ch 28:3; 33:6), and therefore it was called "the valley of Slaughter" (Jer 19:6). In Jesus' day, it was a garbage dump where fires burned continually and was thus an apt symbol of eternal fire.

5:25 Make friends quickly. Jesus calls for reconciliation to be sought eagerly, aggressively, quickly—even if it involves self-sacrifice. It is better to be wronged than to allow a dispute between brethren to be a cause for dishonoring Christ (1Co 6:7). **opponent.** This speaks of one's adversary in a law case. **prison.** Debtor's prison, where the person could work to earn back what he had defrauded.

5:27 Quoted from Ex 20:14; Dt 5:18.

5:29 tear it out and throw it from you.

30 [A]If your right hand makes you [a]stumble, cut it off
and throw it from you; for it is better for you [b]to
lose one of the parts of your body, [c]than for your
whole body to go into [d,B]hell.
31 "It was said, '[A]WHOEVER SENDS HIS WIFE AWAY,
LET HIM GIVE HER A CERTIFICATE OF DIVORCE'; 32 [A]but I
say to you that everyone who [a]divorces his wife, except for *the* reason of unchastity, makes her commit
adultery; and whoever marries a [b]divorced woman
commits adultery.
33 "Again, [A]you have heard that [a]the ancients
were told, '[b,B]YOU SHALL NOT [c]MAKE FALSE VOWS,
BUT SHALL FULFILL YOUR [d]VOWS TO THE LORD.' 34 But
I say to you, [A]make no oath at all, either by heaven,
for it is [B]the throne of God, 35 or by the earth, for it
is the [A]footstool of His feet, or [a]by Jerusalem, for
it is [B]THE CITY OF THE GREAT KING. 36 Nor shall you
make an oath by your head, for you cannot make
one hair white or black. 37 But let your statement
be, 'Yes, yes' *or* 'No, no'; anything beyond these is
[a]of [A]evil.
38 "[A]You have heard that it was said, '[B]AN EYE FOR
AN EYE, AND A TOOTH FOR A TOOTH.' 39 But I say to
you, do not resist an evil person; but [A]whoever slaps
you on your right cheek, turn the other to him also.
40 If anyone wants to sue you and take your [a]shirt,
let him have your [b]coat also. 41 Whoever [a]forces you
to go one mile, go with him two. 42 [A]Give to him who
asks of you, and do not turn away from him who
wants to borrow from you.
43 "[A]You have heard that it was said, '[B]YOU SHALL
LOVE YOUR NEIGHBOR [C]and hate your enemy.' 44 But
I say to you, [A]love your enemies and pray for those
who persecute you, 45 so that you may [a]be [A]sons of
your Father who is in heaven; for He causes His sun
to rise on *the* evil and *the* good, and sends rain on
the righteous and *the* unrighteous. 46 For [A]if you
love those who love you, what reward do you have?
Do not even the tax collectors do the same? 47 If
you greet only your brothers, what more are you
doing *than others?* Do not even the Gentiles do the
same? 48 Therefore [a,A]you are to be perfect, as your
heavenly Father is perfect.

GIVING TO THE POOR AND PRAYER

6 "Beware of practicing your righteousness before men [A]to be noticed by them; otherwise you
have no reward with your Father who is in heaven.

5:30 [a]I.e. sin [b]Lit *that one...be lost* [c]Lit *not your whole body* [d]Gr *Gehenna* [A]Matt 18:8; Mark 9:43 [B]Matt 5:22 5:31 [A]Deut 24:1, 3; Jer 3:1; Matt 19:7; Mark 10:4 5:32 [a]Or *sends away* [b]Or *sent away* [A]Matt 19:9; Mark 10:11f; Luke 16:18; 1 Cor 7:11f 5:33 [a]Lit *it was said to the ancients* [b]*you* and *your* are singular here [c]Or *break your vows* [d]Lit *oaths* [A]Matt 5:21, 27, 38, 43; 23:16ff [B]Lev 19:12; Num 30:2; Deut 23:21, 23 5:34 [A]James 5:12 [B]Is 66:1; Matt 23:22 5:35 [a]Or *toward* [A]Is 66:1; Acts 7:49 [B]Ps 48:2 5:37 [a]Or *from the evil one* [A]Matt 6:13; 13:19, 38; John 17:15; 2 Thess 3:3; 1 John 2:13f; 3:12; 5:18f 5:38 [A]Matt 5:21, 27, 33, 43 [B]Ex 21:24; Lev 24:20; Deut 19:21 5:39 [A]Matt 5:39-42: *Luke 6:29, 30;* 1 Cor 6:7 5:40 [a]Lit *tunic;* i.e. a garment worn next to the body [b]Lit *cloak;* i.e. an outer garment 5:41 [a]Lit *will force* 5:42 [A]Deut 15:7-11; Luke 6:34f; 1 Tim 6:18 5:43 [A]Matt 5:21, 27, 33, 38 [B]Lev 19:18 [C]Deut 23:3-6 5:44 [A]Luke 6:27f; 23:34; Acts 7:60; Rom 12:20 5:45 [a]Or *show yourselves to be* [A]Matt 5:9; Luke 6:35; Acts 14:17 5:46 [A]Luke 6:32 5:48 [a]Lit *you shall be* [A]Lev 19:2; Deut 18:13; 2 Cor 7:1; Phil 3:12-15 6:1 [A]Matt 6:5, 16; 23:5

Jesus was not advocating self-mutilation (for this would not in fact cure lust, which is actually a problem of the heart). He was using this graphic hyperbole to demonstrate the seriousness of sins of lust and evil desire. The point is that it would be "better" (v. 30) to lose a member of one's own body than to bear the eternal consequences of the guilt from such a sin. Sin must be dealt with drastically because of its deadly effects.

5:31 It was said. *See note on Dt 24:1–4.* The rabbis had taken liberty with what Scripture actually said. They referred to Dt 24:1–4 as if it were given merely to regulate the paperwork when one sought divorce (*see note on 19:7*). Thus, they had wrongly concluded that men could divorce their wives for anything that displeased them, as long as they gave "a certificate of divorce." But Moses provided this as a concession to protect the woman who was divorced (*see notes on 19:7–9*), not to justify or legalize divorce under all circumstances.

5:32 except for … unchastity. *See note on 19:9.* Divorce was allowed in cases of adultery. Luke 16:18 must be understood in the light of this verse. **makes her commit adultery.** The assumption is that divorced people will remarry. If the divorce was not for sexual immorality, any remarriage is adultery, because God does not acknowledge the divorce. For more on divorce, *see note on 1Co 7:15.*

5:33 You shall not make false vows. This expresses teaching from Lv 19:12; Nu 30:2; Dt 23:21, 23.

5:34 make no oath at all. Cf. Jas 5:12. This should not be taken as a universal condemnation of oaths in all circumstances. God Himself confirmed a promise with an oath (Heb 6:13–18; cf. Ac 2:30). Christ Himself spoke under oath (26:63, 64). And the law prescribed oaths in certain circumstances (e.g., Nu 5:19, 21; 30:2, 3). What Christ is forbidding here is the flippant, profane, or careless use of oaths in everyday speech. In that culture, such oaths were often employed for deceptive purposes. To make the person being victimized believe the truth was being told, the Jews would swear by "heaven," "earth," "Jerusalem," or their own "heads" (vv. 34–36), not by God, hoping to avoid divine judgment for their lie. But it all was in God's creation, so it drew Him in and produced guilt before Him, exactly as if the oath were made in His name. Jesus suggested that all our speech should be as if we were under an oath to tell the truth (v. 37).

5:38 An eye for an eye. The law did establish this standard as a principle for limiting retribution to that which was just (Ex 21:24; Lv 24:20; Dt 19:21). Its design was to ensure that the punishment in civil cases fit the crime. It was never meant to sanction acts of personal retaliation. So again (*see notes on vv. 17, 18*) Jesus made no alteration to the true meaning of the law. He was merely explaining and affirming the law's true meaning.

5:39 do not resist an evil person. Like v. 38, this deals only with matters of personal retaliation, not criminal offenses or acts of military aggression. Jesus applied this principle of nonretaliation to affronts against one's dignity (v. 39), lawsuits to gain one's personal assets (v. 40), infringements on one's liberty (v. 41), and violations of property rights (v. 42). He was calling for a full surrender of all personal rights.

5:41 forces. The word speaks of coercion. The NT picture of this is when Roman soldiers forced Simon the Cyrene to carry Jesus' cross (27:32).

5:43 love your neighbor **and hate your enemy.** The first half of this is found in Moses' law (Lv 19:18). The second part was found in how the scribes and Pharisees explained and applied that OT command. Jesus' application was exactly the opposite, resulting in a much higher standard: love for one's neighbors should extend even to those neighbors who are enemies (v. 44). Again, this was no innovation, since even the OT taught that God's people should do good to their enemies (Pr 25:21).

5:44, 45 love your enemies … that you may be sons of your Father. This plainly teaches that God's love extends even to His enemies. This universal love of God is manifest in blessings which God bestows on all indiscriminately. Theologians refer to this as common grace. This must be distinguished from the everlasting love God has for the elect (Jer 31:3), but it is a sincere goodwill nonetheless (cf. Ps 145:9).

5:46 tax collectors. Disloyal Israelites hired by the Romans to tax other Jews for personal profit. They became symbols for the worst kind of people. Cf. 9:10, 11; 11:19; 18:17; 21:31; Mk 2:14–16; Lk 5:30; 7:25, 29, 34; 18:11–13. Matthew had been one of them (*see notes on 9:9; Mk 2:15*).

5:48 you are to be perfect. Christ sets an unattainable standard. This sums up what the law itself demanded (Jas 2:10). Though this standard is impossible to meet, God could not lower it without compromising His own perfection. He who is perfect could not set an imperfect standard of righteousness. The marvelous truth of the gospel is that Christ has met this standard on our behalf (*see note on 2Co 5:21*).

6:1–18 Here Christ expands the thought

2 "So when you [a]give to the poor, do not sound
a trumpet before you, as the hypocrites do in the
synagogues and in the streets, so that they [A]may be
honored by men. [B]Truly I say to you, they have their
reward in full. 3 But when you [a]give to the poor, do
not let your left hand know what your right hand
is doing, 4 so that your [a]giving will be in secret;
and [A]your Father who sees *what is done* in secret
will reward you.
5 "When you pray, you are not to be like the hypocrites; for they love to [A]stand and pray in the synagogues and on the street corners [a,B]so that they may
be seen by men. [C]Truly I say to you, they have their
reward in full. 6 But you, when you pray, [A]go into
your inner room, close your door and pray to your
Father who is in secret, and [B]your Father who sees
what is done in secret will reward you.
7 "And when you are praying, do not use meaningless repetition as the Gentiles do, for they suppose
that they will be heard for their [A]many words. 8 So
do not be like them; for [A]your Father knows what
you need before you ask Him.
9 "[A]Pray, then, in this way:

'Our Father who is in heaven,
Hallowed be Your name.
10 '[A]Your kingdom come.
[B]Your will be done,
On earth as it is in heaven.
11 '[A]Give us this day [a]our daily bread.
12 'And [A]forgive us our debts, as we
also have forgiven our debtors.
13 'And do not lead us into temptation,
but [A]deliver us from [a,B]evil.
[b][For Yours is the kingdom
and the power and the
glory forever. Amen.']

14 [A]For if you forgive [a]others for their transgressions,
your heavenly Father will also forgive you. 15 But [A]if
you do not forgive [a]others, then your Father will not
forgive your transgressions.

FASTING; THE TRUE TREASURE; WEALTH (MAMMON)

16 "[A]Whenever you fast, do not put on a gloomy
face as the hypocrites *do,* for they [a]neglect their appearance so that they will be noticed by men when
they are fasting. [B]Truly I say to you, they have their
reward in full. 17 But you, when you fast, [A]anoint
your head and wash your face 18 so that your fasting will not be noticed by men, but by your Father
who is in secret; and your [A]Father who sees *what
is done* in secret will reward you.
19 "[A]Do not store up for yourselves treasures on
earth, where moth and rust destroy, and where
thieves break in and steal. 20 But store up for yourselves [A]treasures in heaven, where neither moth
nor rust destroys, and where thieves do not break
in or steal; 21 for [A]where your treasure is, there your
heart will be also.
22 "[A]The eye is the lamp of the body; so then if
your eye is [a]clear, your whole body will be full of
light. 23 But if [A]your eye is [a]bad, your whole body

6:2 [a]Or *give alms* [A]Matt 6:5, 16; 23:5 [B]Matt 6:5, 16; Luke 6:24 6:3 [a]Or *give alms* 6:4 [a]Or *alms* [A]Jer 17:10; Matt 6:6, 18; Heb 4:13 6:5 [a]Lit *to be apparent to men* [A]Mark 11:25; Luke 18:11, 13 [B]Matt 6:1, 16 [C]Matt 6:2, 16; Luke 6:24 6:6 [A]Is 26:20; Matt 26:36-39; Acts 9:40 [B]Matt 6:4, 18 6:7 [A]1 Kin 18:26f 6:8 [A]Ps 38:9; 69:17-19; Matt 6:32; Luke 12:30 6:9 [A]Matt 6:9-13: *Luke 11:2-4* 6:10 [A]Matt 3:2; 4:17 [B]Matt 26:42; Luke 22:42; Acts 21:14 6:11 [a]Or *our bread for tomorrow* [A]Prov 30:8; Is 33:16; Luke 11:3 6:12 [A]Ex 34:7; Ps 32:1; 130:4; Matt 9:2; 26:28; Eph 1:7; 1 John 1:7-9 6:13 [a]Or *the evil one* [b]This clause not found in early mss [A]John 17:15; 1 Cor 10:13; 2 Thess 3:3; 2 Tim 4:18; 2 Pet 2:9; 1 John 5:18 [B]Matt 5:37 6:14 [a]Gr *anthropoi* [A]Matt 7:2; Mark 11:25f; Eph 4:32; Col 3:13 6:15 [a]Gr *anthropoi* [A]Matt 18:35 6:16 [a]Lit *distort their faces,* i.e. discolor their faces with makeup [A]Is 58:5 [B]Matt 6:2 6:17 [A]Ruth 3:3; 2 Sam 12:20 6:18 [A]Matt 6:4, 6 6:19 [A]Prov 23:4; Matt 19:21; Luke 12:21, 33; 18:22; 1 Tim 6:9, 10; Heb 13:5; James 5:2 6:20 [A]Matt 19:21; Luke 12:33; 1 Tim 6:19 6:21 [A]Luke 12:34 6:22 [a]Or *healthy;* or *sincere* [A]Matt 6:22, 23: *Luke 11:34, 35* 6:23 [a]Or *evil* [A]Matt 20:15; Mark 7:22

of 5:20, showing how the Pharisees' righteousness was deficient by exposing their hypocrisy in the matters of giving to the poor (vv. 1–4); prayer (vv. 5–15); and fasting (vv. 16–18). All of these acts are supposed to be worship rendered to God, never displays of self-righteousness to gain the admiration of others.

6:2 hypocrites. This word had its origins in Gr. theater, describing a character who wore a mask. The term, as used in the NT, normally described an unregenerate person who was self-deceived. **they have their reward.** Cf. vv. 5, 16. Their reward is that they were seen by men, nothing more. God does not reward hypocrisy, but He does punish it (cf. 23:13–23).

6:4 sees . . . in secret. Cf. vv. 6, 18; Jer 17:10; Heb 4:13. God is omniscient.

6:7 meaningless repetition. Prayers are not to be merely recited, nor are our words to be repeated thoughtlessly, or as if they were automatic formulas. But this is not a prohibition against importunity (*see notes on Lk 11:1–8*).

6:9 in this way. Cf. Lk 11:2–4. The prayer is a model, not merely a liturgy. It is notable for its brevity, simplicity, and comprehensiveness. Of the 6 petitions, 3 are directed to God (vv. 9, 10) and 3 toward human needs (vv. 11–13).

6:10 Your will be done. All prayer, first of all, willingly submits to God's purposes, plans, and glory. *See note on 26:39.*

6:12 forgive us our debts. The parallel passage (Lk 11:4) uses a word that means "sins," so that in context, spiritual debts are intended. Sinners are debtors to God for their violations of His laws (*see notes on 18:23–27*). This request is the heart of the prayer; it is what Jesus stressed in the words that immediately follow the prayer (vv. 14, 15; cf. Mk 11:25).

6:13 do not lead us into temptation. Cf. Lk 22:40. God does not tempt men (Jas 1:13), but He will subject them to trials that may expose them to Satan's assaults, as in the case of Job and Peter (Lk 22:31, 32). This petition reflects the believing one's desire to avoid the dangers of sin altogether. God knows what one's need is before one asks (v. 8), and He promises that no one will be subjected to testing beyond what can be endured. He also promises a way of escape—often through endurance (1Co 10:13). But still, the proper attitude for the believer is the one expressed in this petition.

6:15 then your Father will not forgive your transgressions. This is not to suggest that God will withdraw justification from those who have already received the free pardon He extends to all believers. Forgiveness in that sense—a permanent and complete acquittal from the guilt and ultimate penalty of sin—belongs to all who are in Christ (cf. Jn 5:24; Ro 8:1; Eph 1:7). Yet, Scripture also teaches that God chastens His children who disobey (Heb 12:5–7). Believers are to confess their sins in order to obtain a day-to-day cleansing (1Jn 1:9). This sort of forgiveness is a simple washing from the worldly defilements of sin, not a repeat of the wholesale cleansing from sin's corruption that comes with justification. It is like a washing of the feet rather than a bath (cf. Jn 13:10). Forgiveness in this latter sense is what God threatens to withhold from Christians who refuse to forgive others (cf. 18:23–35).

6:16, 17 Whenever you fast. This indicates that fasting is assumed to be a normal part of one's spiritual life (cf. 1Co 7:5). Fasting is associated with sadness (9:14, 15), prayer (17:21), charity (Is 58:3–6), and seeking the Lord's will (Ac 13:2, 3; 14:23).

6:20 treasures. Don't amass earthly wealth. Jesus commends the use of financial assets for purposes which are heavenly and eternal. *See notes on Lk 16:1–9.*

6:22, 23 This is an argument from the lesser to the greater. The analogy is simple. If your eye is bad, no light can come in, and you are left with darkness because of that malady. How much worse when the problem is not merely

will be full of darkness. If then the light that is in
you is darkness, how great is the darkness!
24 "[A]No one can serve two masters; for either he
will hate the one and love the other, or he will be
devoted to one and despise the other. You cannot
serve God and [a,B]wealth.

THE CURE FOR ANXIETY

25 "[A]For this reason I say to you, [a]do not be [B]worried
about your [b]life, *as to* what you will eat or what you
will drink; nor for your body, *as to* what you will put
on. Is not life more than food, and the body more than
clothing? 26 [A]Look at the birds of the [a]air, that they
do not sow, nor reap nor gather into barns, and *yet*
your heavenly Father feeds them. Are you not worth
much more than they? 27 And who of you by being
[A]worried can [B]add a *single* [a]hour to his [b]life? 28 And
why are you [A]worried about clothing? Observe how
the lilies of the field grow; they do not toil nor do they
spin, 29 yet I say to you that not even [A]Solomon in all
his glory clothed himself like one of these. 30 But if
God so clothes the [A]grass of the field, which is *alive*
today and tomorrow is thrown into the furnace, *will*
He not much more *clothe* you? [B]You of little faith! 31 Do
not [A]worry then, saying, 'What will we eat?' or 'What
will we drink?' or 'What will we wear for clothing?'
32 For the Gentiles eagerly seek all these things; for
[A]your heavenly Father knows that you need all these
things. 33 But [a]seek first [b]His kingdom and His righteousness, and [A]all these things will be [c]added to you.
34 "So do not [A]worry about tomorrow; for tomorrow will [a]care for itself. [b]Each day has enough trouble of its own.

JUDGING OTHERS

7 "[A]Do not judge so that you will not be judged. 2 For
in the way you judge, you will be judged; and
[a,A]by your standard of measure, it will be measured
to you. 3 Why do you [A]look at the speck that is in your
brother's eye, but do not notice the log that is in your
own eye? 4 [A]Or how [a]can you say to your brother, 'Let
me take the speck out of your eye,' and behold, the
log is in your own eye? 5 You hypocrite, first take
the log out of your own eye, and then you will see
clearly to take the speck out of your brother's eye.
6 "[A]Do not give what is holy to dogs, and do not
throw your pearls before swine, or they will trample
them under their feet, and turn and tear you to pieces.

PRAYER AND THE GOLDEN RULE

7 "[a,A]Ask, and [B]it will be given to you; [b]seek, and you
will find; [c]knock, and it will be opened to you. 8 For
everyone who asks receives, and he who seeks finds,
and to him who knocks it will be opened. 9 Or what
man is there among you [a]who, when his son asks
for a loaf, [b]will give him a stone? 10 Or [a]if he asks for
a fish, he will not give him a snake, will he? 11 If you
then, being evil, know how to give good gifts to your
children, [A]how much more will your Father who is
in heaven give what is good to those who ask Him!
12 "In everything, [A]therefore, [a]treat people the
same way you want [b]them to treat you, for [B]this is
the Law and the Prophets.

THE NARROW AND WIDE GATES

13 "[A]Enter through the narrow gate; for the gate is
wide and the way is broad that leads to destruction,

6:24 [a]Gr *mamonas,* for Aram *mamon* (mammon); i.e. wealth, etc., personified as an object of worship [A]1 Kin 18:21; Luke 16:13; Gal 1:10; James 4:4 [B]Luke 16:9, 11, 13 6:25 [a]Or *stop being worried* [b]Lit *soul* [A]Matt 6:25-33: *Luke 12:22-31* [B]Matt 6:27, 28, 31, 34; Luke 10:41; 12:11, 22; Phil 4:6; 1 Pet 5:7 6:26 [a]Lit *heaven* [A]Job 35:11; 38:41; Ps 104:27, 28; Matt 10:29ff; Luke 12:24 6:27 [a]Lit *cubit* (approx 18 in.) [b]Or *height* [A]Matt 6:25, 28, 31, 34; Luke 10:41; 12:11, 22; Phil 4:6; 1 Pet 5:7 [B]Ps 39:5 6:28 [A]Matt 6:25, 27, 31, 34; Luke 10:41; 12:11, 22; Phil 4:6; 1 Pet 5:7 6:29 [A]1 Kin 10:4-7; 2 Chr 9:4-6, 20-22 6:30 [A]James 1:10, 11; 1 Pet 1:24 [B]Matt 8:26; 14:31; 16:8 6:31 [A]Matt 6:25, 27, 28, 34; Luke 10:41; 12:11, 22; Phil 4:6; 1 Pet 5:7 6:32 [A]Matt 6:8; Phil 4:19 6:33 [a]Or *continually seek* [b]Or *the kingdom* [c]Or *provided* [A]Matt 19:28; Mark 10:29f; Luke 18:29f; 1 Tim 4:8 6:34 [a]Lit *worry about itself* [b]Lit *Sufficient for the day is its evils* [A]Matt 6:25, 27, 28, 31; Luke 10:41; 12:11, 22; Phil 4:6; 1 Pet 5:7 7:1 [A]Matt 7:1-5: *Luke 6:37f, 41f;* Rom 14:10, 13 7:2 [a]Lit *by what measure you measure* [A]Mark 4:24; Luke 6:38 7:3 [A]Rom 2:1 7:4 [a]Lit *will* [A]Luke 6:42 7:6 [A]Matt 15:26 7:7 [a]Or *Keep asking* [b]Or *keep seeking* [c]Or *keep knocking* [A]Matt 7:7-11: *Luke 11:9-13* [B]Matt 18:19; 21:22; Mark 11:24; John 14:13; 15:7, 16; 16:23f; James 1:5f; 1 John 3:22; 5:14f 7:9 [a]Lit *whom his son will ask* [b]Lit *he will not give him a stone, will he?* 7:10 [a]Lit *also will ask* 7:11 [A]Ps 84:11; Is 63:7; Rom 8:32; James 1:17 7:12 [a]Lit *you, too, do so for them* [b]Lit *people;* Gr *anthropoi* [A]Luke 6:31 [B]Matt 22:40; Rom 13:8ff; Gal 5:14 7:13 [A]Luke 13:24

related to external perception, but an internal corruption of one's whole nature, so that the darkness actually emanates from within and affects one's whole being. Jesus was indicting them for their superficial earthly religion that left their hearts dark. *See note on Lk 11:34.*

6:24 wealth. Earthly, material treasures, especially money. *See note on Lk 16:13.*

6:26 your heavenly Father feeds them. Obviously this in no way advocates a sinful kind of idleness (Pr 19:15). Birds are not idle, either. But it is God who provides them with food to eat.

6:29 Solomon in all his glory. The glory and pageantry of Solomon's kingdom was famous worldwide. Cf. 2Ch 9.

6:30 You of little faith! Cf. 8:26; 14:31; 16:8; 17:20. This was the Lord's recurring rebuke of the weak disciples.

6:32 Gentiles. I.e., those outside the people of promise and outside the blessing of God. Cf. Eph 4:17–19.

6:33 His kingdom. This is the same as the kingdom of heaven. *See note on 3:2.* It refers to the sphere of salvation. Jesus was urging them to seek salvation—and with it would come the full care and provision of God. Cf. Ro 8:32; Php 4:19; 1Pe 5:7.

7:1 Do not judge. As the context reveals, this does not prohibit all types of judging (v. 16). There is a righteous kind of judgment we are supposed to exercise with careful discernment (Jn 7:24). Censorious, hypocritical, self-righteous, or other kinds of unfair judgments are forbidden; but in order to fulfill the commandments that follow, it is necessary to discern dogs and swine (v. 6) from one's own brethren (vv. 3–5).

7:6 Do not give what is holy to dogs. This principle is why Jesus Himself did not do miracles for unbelievers (13:58). This is to be done in respect for what is holy, not merely out of contempt for the dogs and swine. Nothing here contradicts the principle of 5:44. That verse governs personal dealings with one's enemies (*see note there*); this principle governs how one handles the gospel in the face of those who hate the truth.

7:11 you … being evil. Jesus presupposes the doctrine of human depravity (*see note on Ro 1:18–3:20*). **how much more.** If earthly fathers give what their sons need (vv. 9, 10), will not God give to His sons what they ask (vv. 7, 8)? *See note on Jas 1:17.*

7:12 same way you want them to treat you. Versions of the "Golden Rule" existed before Christ, in the rabbinic writings and even in Hinduism and Buddhism. All of them cast the rule as a negative command, such as Rabbi Hillel's version, "What is hateful to yourself do not to someone else." Jesus made it a positive command, enriching its meaning and underscoring that this one imperative aptly summarizes the whole gist of the ethical principles contained in the Law and the Prophets.

7:13–29 This closing section of the Sermon on the Mount is a gospel application. Here are two gates, two ways, two destinations, and two groups of people (vv. 13, 14); two kinds of trees and two kinds of fruit (vv. 17–20); two groups at the judgment (vv. 21–23); and two kinds of builders, building on two kinds of foundations (vv. 24–28). Christ is drawing the line as clearly as possible between the way that leads to destruction and the way that leads to life.

7:13, 14 Both the narrow gate and the wide gate are assumed to provide the entrance to God's kingdom. Two ways are offered to people.

and there are many who enter through it. 14 For the
gate is small and the way is narrow that leads to
life, and there are few who find it.

A TREE AND ITS FRUIT

15 "Beware of the [A]false prophets, who come to
you in sheep's clothing, but inwardly are [B]raven-
ous wolves. 16 You will [a,A]know them by their fruits.
[b]Grapes are not gathered from thorn *bushes* nor
figs from thistles, are they? 17 So [A]every good tree
bears good fruit, but the bad tree bears bad fruit.
18 A good tree cannot produce bad fruit, nor can a
bad tree produce good fruit. 19 [A]Every tree that does
not bear good fruit is cut down and thrown into the
fire. 20 So then, you will [a]know them [A]by their fruits.
21 "[A]Not everyone who says to Me, 'Lord, Lord,' will
enter the kingdom of heaven, but he who does the
will of My Father who is in heaven *will enter.* 22 [A]Many
will say to Me on [B]that day, 'Lord, Lord, did we not
prophesy in Your name, and in Your name cast out
demons, and in Your name perform many [a]miracles?'
23 And then I will declare to them, 'I never knew you;
[A]DEPART FROM ME, YOU WHO PRACTICE LAWLESSNESS.'

THE TWO FOUNDATIONS

24 "Therefore [A]everyone who hears these words
of Mine and [a]acts on them, [b]may be compared to a
wise man who built his house on the rock. 25 And the
rain fell, and the [a]floods came, and the winds blew
and slammed against that house; and *yet* it did not
fall, for it had been founded on the rock. 26 Everyone
who hears these words of Mine and does not [a]act
on them, will be like a foolish man who built his
house on the sand. 27 The rain fell, and the [a]floods
came, and the winds blew and slammed against that
house; and it fell—and great was its fall."
28 [a,A]When Jesus had finished these words, [B]the
crowds were amazed at His teaching; 29 for He was
teaching them as *one* having authority, and not as
their scribes.

JESUS CLEANSES A LEPER; THE CENTURION'S FAITH

8 When [a]Jesus came down from the mountain,
[b]large crowds followed Him. 2 And [A]a leper came
to Him and [a,B]bowed down before Him, and said,
"Lord, if You are willing, You can make me clean."
3 Jesus stretched out His hand and touched him,
saying, "I am willing; be cleansed." And immediately
his [A]leprosy was cleansed. 4 And Jesus *said to him,
"[A]See that you tell no one; but [B]go, [C]show yourself
to the priest and present the [a]offering that Moses
commanded, as a testimony to them."
5 And [A]when [a]Jesus entered Capernaum, a centurion came to Him, imploring Him, 6 and saying,
"[a]Lord, my [b]servant is [c]lying [A]paralyzed at home,
fearfully tormented." 7 Jesus *said to him, "I will
come and heal him." 8 But the centurion said, "[a]Lord,
I am not worthy for You to come under my roof, but
just [b]say the word, and my [c]servant will be healed.
9 For I also am a man under [A]authority, with soldiers under me; and I say to this one, 'Go!' and he

7:15 [A]Matt 24:11, 24; Mark 13:22; Luke 6:26; Acts 13:6; 2 Pet 2:1; 1 John 4:1; Rev 16:13; 19:20; 20:10 [B]Ezek 22:27; John 10:12; Acts 20:29 7:16 [a]Or *recognize* [b]Lit *They do not gather* [A]Matt 7:20; 12:33; Luke 6:44; James 3:12 7:17 [A]Matt 12:33, 35 7:19 [A]Matt 3:10; Luke 3:9; 13:7; John 15:2, 6 7:20 [a]Or *recognize* [A]Matt 7:16; 12:33; Luke 6:44; James 3:12 7:21 [A]Luke 6:46 7:22 [a]Or *works of power* [A]Matt 25:11f; Luke 13:25ff [B]Matt 10:15 7:23 [A]Ps 6:8; Matt 25:41; Luke 13:27 7:24 [a]Lit *does* [b]Lit *will* [A]Matt 7:24-27: *Luke 6:47-49;* Matt 16:18; James 1:22-25 7:25 [a]Lit *rivers* 7:26 [a]Lit *do* 7:27 [a]Lit *rivers* 7:28 [a]Lit *And it happened when* [A]Matt 11:1; 13:53; 19:1; 26:1 [B]Matt 13:54; 22:33; Mark 1:22; 6:2; 11:18; Luke 4:32; John 7:46 8:1 [a]Lit *He* [b]Lit *many* 8:2 [a]Or *worshiped* [A]Matt 8:2-4: *Mark 1:40-44; Luke 5:12-14* [B]Matt 9:18; 15:25; 18:26; 20:20; John 9:38; Acts 10:25 8:3 [A]Matt 11:5; Luke 4:27 8:4 [a]Lit *gift* [A]Matt 9:30; 12:16; 17:9; Mark 1:44; 3:12; 5:43; 7:36; 8:30; 9:9; Luke 4:41; 8:56; 9:21 [B]Mark 1:44; Luke 5:14; 17:14 [C]Lev 13:49; 14:2ff 8:5 [a]Lit *He* [A]Matt 8:5-13: *Luke 7:1-10* 8:6 [a]Or *Sir* [b]Lit *boy* [c]Lit *thrown down* [A]Matt 4:24 8:8 [a]Or *Sir* [b]Lit *say with a word* [c]Lit *boy* 8:9 [A]Mark 1:27; Luke 9:1

The narrow gate is by faith, only through Christ, constricted and precise. It represents true salvation in God's way that leads to life eternal. The wide gate includes all religions of works and self-righteousness, with no single way (cf. Ac 4:12), but it leads to hell, not heaven.

7:14 way is narrow. Christ continually emphasized the difficulty of following Him (10:38; 16:24, 25; Jn 15:18, 19; 16:1–3; cf. Ac 14:22). Salvation is by grace alone, but is not easy. It calls for knowledge of the truth, repentance, submission to Christ as Lord, and a willingness to obey His will and Word. *See notes on 19:16–28.*

7:15 false prophets. These deceive not by disguising themselves as sheep, but by impersonating true shepherds. They promote the wide gate and the wide way. **sheep's clothing.** This may refer to the woolen attire that was the characteristic garb of a shepherd.

7:16 You will know them by their fruits. *See note on 3:8.* False doctrine cannot restrain the flesh, so false prophets manifest wickedness. Cf. 2Pe 2:12–22.

7:21 Not everyone who says . . . but he who does. The barrenness of this sort of faith demonstrates its real character (cf. v. 20)—the faith that says but does not do is really unbelief. Jesus was not suggesting that works are meritorious for salvation, but that true faith will not fail to produce the fruit of good works. This is precisely the point of Jas 1:22–25; 2:26.

7:22 did we not prophesy . . . cast out demons . . . perform many miracles? Note that far from being totally devoid of works of any kind, these people were claiming to have done some remarkable signs and wonders. In fact, their whole confidence was in these works—further proof that these works, spectacular as they might have appeared, could not have been authentic. No one so bereft of genuine faith could possibly produce true good works. A bad tree cannot bear good fruit (v. 18).

7:23 lawlessness. All sin is lawlessness (1Jn 3:4), i.e., rebellion against the law of God (cf. 13:41).

7:24–27 The house represents a religious life; the rain represents divine judgment. Only the house built on the foundation of obedience to God's Word stands, which calls for repentance, rejection of salvation by works, and trust in God's grace to save through His merciful provision. *See notes on Jas 1:22–25.*

7:29 not as their scribes. The scribes quoted others to establish the authority of their teachings; Jesus was His own authority (28:18). This matter of authority was a major issue between Jesus and the Jews, who felt their authority challenged. *See note on 21:23.* Cf. Mk 1:22; 11:28–33; Lk 4:32; 20:2–8; Jn 12:49, 50; 14:10.

8:1 down from the mountain. Cf. 5:1.

8:2 if You are willing. He had no doubt about Christ's power, only His will (cf. Mk 1:40–45).

8:4 tell no one. Publicity over such miracles might hinder Christ's mission and divert public attention from His message. Mark records that this is precisely what happened. In this man's exuberance over the miracle, he disobeyed; as a result, Christ had to move His ministry away from the city and into the desert regions (Mk 1:45). **the offering that Moses commanded.** A sacrifice of two birds, one of which was killed and the other set free (Lv 14:4–7). **as a testimony to them.** I.e., the priests.

8:5 Capernaum. *See note on 4:13.* **centurion.** A Roman military officer who commanded (cf. v. 9) 100 men. Luke indicates that the centurion appealed to Jesus through intermediaries (Lk 7:3–6)—because of his own sense of unworthiness (v. 8; cf. Lk 7:7). Matthew makes no mention of the intermediaries.

8:8 I am not worthy for You to come under my roof. Jewish tradition held that a person who entered a Gentile's house was ceremonially defiled (cf. Jn 18:28). The centurion, undoubtedly familiar with this law, felt unworthy of having Jesus suffer such an inconvenience for his sake. He also had faith enough to know that Christ could heal by merely speaking a word (*see note on v. 10*).

goes, and to another, 'Come!' and he comes, and to
my slave, 'Do this!' and he does *it*." 10 Now when
Jesus heard *this*, He marveled and said to those who
were following, "Truly I say to you, I have not found
such great faith [a]with anyone in Israel. 11 I say to
you that many [A]will come from east and west, and
[a]recline *at the table* with Abraham, Isaac and Jacob
in the kingdom of heaven; 12 but [A]the sons of the
kingdom will be cast out into [B]the outer darkness;
in that place [C]there will be weeping and gnashing
of teeth." 13 And Jesus said to the centurion, "Go; [a]it
shall be done for you [A]as you have believed." And
the [b]servant was healed that *very* [c]moment.

PETER'S MOTHER-IN-LAW AND MANY OTHERS HEALED

14 [A]When Jesus came into Peter's [a]home, He saw
his mother-in-law lying sick in bed with a fever. 15 He
touched her hand, and the fever left her; and she got
up and [a]waited on Him. 16 When evening came, they
brought to Him many [A]who were demon-possessed;
and He cast out the spirits with a word, and [B]healed
all who were ill. 17 *This was* to fulfill what was spoken through Isaiah the prophet: "[A]HE HIMSELF TOOK
OUR INFIRMITIES AND [a]CARRIED AWAY OUR DISEASES."

DISCIPLESHIP TESTED

18 Now when Jesus saw a crowd around Him, [A]He
gave orders to depart to the other side *of the sea*.
19 [A]Then a scribe came and said to Him, "Teacher, I
will follow You wherever You go." 20 Jesus *said to
him, "The foxes have holes and the birds of the [a]air
have [b]nests, but [A]the Son of Man has nowhere to lay
His head." 21 Another of the disciples said to Him,
"Lord, permit me first to go and bury my father."
22 But Jesus *said to him, "[A]Follow Me, and allow
the dead to bury their own dead."
23 [A]When He got into the boat, His disciples followed Him. 24 And behold, there arose [a]a great storm
on the sea, so that the boat was being covered with
the waves; but Jesus Himself was asleep. 25 And
they came to *Him* and woke Him, saying, "[A]Save *us*,
Lord; we are perishing!" 26 He *said to them, "Why
are you [a]afraid, [A]you men of little faith?" Then He
got up and rebuked the winds and the sea, and [b]it
became perfectly calm. 27 The men were amazed,
and said, "What kind of a man is this, that even the
winds and the sea obey Him?"

JESUS CASTS OUT DEMONS

28 [A]When He came to the other side into the
country of the Gadarenes, two men who were
[B]demon-possessed met Him as they were coming
out of the tombs. *They were* so extremely violent
that no one could pass by that way. 29 And they
cried out, saying, "[a,A]What business do we have
with each other, Son of God? Have You come here
to torment us before [b]the time?" 30 Now there was

8:10 [a]One early ms reads *not even in Israel* 8:11 [a]Or *dine* [A]Is 49:12; 59:19; Mal 1:11; Luke 13:29 8:12 [A]Matt 13:38 [B]Matt 22:13; 25:30 [C]Matt 13:42, 50; 22:13; 24:51; 25:30; Luke 13:28 8:13 [a]Or *let it be done;* i.e. a command [b]Lit *boy* [c]Lit *hour* [A]Matt 9:22, 29 8:14 [a]Or *house* [A]Matt 8:14-16: *Mark 1:29-34; Luke 4:38-41* 8:15 [a]Or *served* 8:16 [A]Matt 4:24 [B]Matt 4:23; 8:33 8:17 [a]Or *removed* [A]Is 53:4 8:18 [A]Mark 4:35; Luke 8:22 8:19 [A]Matt 8:19-22: *Luke 9:57-60* 8:20 [a]Or *sky* [b]Or *roosting places* [A]Dan 7:13; Matt 9:6; 12:8, 32, 40; 13:41; 16:13, 27f; 17:9; 19:28; 26:64; Mark 8:38; Luke 12:8; 18:8; 21:36; John 1:51; 3:13f; 6:27; 12:34; Acts 7:56 8:22 [A]Matt 9:9; Mark 2:14; Luke 9:59, 60; John 1:43; 21:19 8:23 [A]Matt 8:23-27: *Mark 4:36-41; Luke 8:22-25* 8:24 [a]Lit *a shaking* 8:25 [A]Matt 8:2; 9:18 8:26 [a]Or *cowardly* [b]Lit *a great calm occurred* [A]Matt 6:30; 14:31; 16:8; 17:20 8:28 [A]Matt 8:28-34: *Mark 5:1-17; Luke 8:26-37* [B]Matt 4:24 8:29 [a]Lit *What is to us and to you* (a Heb idiom) [b]I.e. the appointed time of judgment [A]Judg 11:12; 2 Sam 16:10; 19:22; 1 Kin 17:18; 2 Kin 3:13; 2 Chr 35:21; Mark 1:24; 5:7; Luke 4:34; 8:28; John 2:4

8:10 I have not found such great faith with anyone in Israel. This centurion understood Jesus' absolute authority (vv. 8, 9). Even some of Jesus' own disciples did not see things so clearly (cf. v. 26).

8:11 many ... from east and west. Gentiles, in the kingdom with Abraham, will enjoy salvation and the blessing of God (cf. Is 49:8–12; 59:19; Mal 1:11; Lk 13:28, 29).

8:12 sons of the kingdom. The Hebrew nation, physical heirs of Abraham. **will be cast out.** This was exactly opposite to the rabbinical understanding, which suggested that the kingdom would feature a great feast in the company of Abraham and the Messiah—open to Jews only. **weeping and gnashing.** *See note on 22:13.* Cf. 24:51; 25:30; Lk 13:28. This expression describes the eternal agonies of those in hell.

8:13 as you have believed. Sometimes faith was involved in the Lord's healings (in this case not by the one being healed, as in 9:2; 15:28); other times it was not a factor (vv. 14–16; Lk 22:51).

8:16 demon-possessed. This means "demonized," or under the internal control of a demon. All of the cases of demonization dealt with by Christ involved the actual indwelling of demons who utterly controlled the bodies of their victims, even to the point of speaking through them (Mk 5:5–9), causing derangement (Jn 10:20), violence (Lk 8:29), or rendering them mute (Mk 9:17–22).

8:17 spoken through Isaiah the prophet. *See note on healing and the atonement at Is 53:4, 5.* Matthew was citing that passage here. Christ bore both the guilt and the curse of sin (cf. Gal 3:13). Both physical healing and ultimate victory over death are guaranteed by Christ's atoning work, but these will not be fully realized until the very end (1Co 15:26).

8:18 the other side. The eastern shore of the lake.

8:19 a scribe. As a scribe, this man was breaking with his fellow scribes by publicly declaring his willingness to follow Jesus. Nonetheless, Jesus evidently knew that he had not counted the cost in terms of suffering and inconvenience.

8:20 Son of Man. *See notes on Mk 2:10; Jn 1:51.* This is the name Jesus used for Himself more than any other. It is used 83 times in the Gospels, always by Jesus Himself. It was a messianic title (Da 7:13, 14), with an obvious reference to the humanity and the humility of Christ. Yet, it also speaks of His everlasting glory, as Da 7:13, 14 shows (cf. 24:27; Ac 7:56).

8:21 permit me first to go and bury my father. This does not mean that the man's father was already dead. The phrase, "I must bury my father" was a common figure of speech meaning, "Let me wait until I receive my inheritance."

8:22 allow the dead to bury their own dead. Let the world (the spiritually dead) take care of mundane things.

8:24 there arose a great storm. The Sea of Galilee is more than 690 ft. below sea level. To the N, Mt. Hermon rises 9,200 ft., and from May to Oct. strong winds often sweep through the narrow surrounding gorges into this valley, causing extremely sudden and violent storms. **Jesus ... was asleep.** Just before the disciples saw one of the most awesome displays of His deity, they were given a touching picture of His humanity. He was so weary that not even the violent tossing of the boat awakened Him—even though the disciples feared they would drown (v. 25).

8:26 you men of little faith. *See note on 6:30.* **calm.** Cf. Pss 65:7; 89:9.

8:27 the winds and the sea obey Him. This was convincing proof of His deity (cf. Pss 29:3, 4; 89:9; 93:4; 107:25–29).

8:28 country of the Gadarenes. This refers to a small town on the lake opposite Tiberius, perhaps where the modern village of Khersa (Kursi) is located. Some ancient tombs are there, and the shoreline descends steeply into the water, exactly matching the description of the terrain in this account. **two men ... demon-possessed.** Mk 5:2 and Lk 8:27 mention only one of the men. Evidently one was more dominant than the other.

8:29 to torment us before the time? Evidently, even the demons not only recognized the deity of Jesus, but also knew there was a divinely appointed time for their judgment and He would be their judge. Their eschatology was factually correct, but it is one thing to know the truth, and quite another thing to love it (cf. Jas 2:19).

8:30 herd of many swine. Mk 5:13 adds that there were 2,000 in this herd. Such a

a herd of many swine feeding at a distance from
them. 31 The demons *began* to entreat Him, saying, "If You *are going to* cast us out, send us into
the herd of swine." 32 And He said to them, "Go!"
And they came out and went into the swine, and
the whole herd rushed down the steep bank into
the sea and perished in the waters. 33 The herdsmen ran away, and went to the city and reported
everything, [a]including what had happened to the
[A]demoniacs. 34 And behold, the whole city came
out to meet Jesus; and when they saw Him, [A]they
implored Him to leave their region.

A PARALYTIC HEALED

9 Getting into a boat, Jesus crossed over *the sea*
and came to [A]His own city.
2 [A]And they brought to Him a [B]paralytic lying on
a bed. Seeing their faith, Jesus said to the paralytic,
"[C]Take courage, [a]son; [D]your sins are forgiven." 3 And
some of the scribes said [a]to themselves, "This *fellow*
[A]blasphemes." 4 And Jesus [A]knowing their thoughts
said, "Why are you thinking evil in your hearts?
5 Which is easier, to say, '[A]Your sins are forgiven,'
or to say, 'Get up, and walk'? 6 But so that you may
know that [A]the Son of Man has authority on earth
to forgive sins"—then He *said to the [B]paralytic, "Get
up, pick up your bed and go home." 7 And he got up
and [a]went home. 8 But when the crowds saw *this*,
they were [a]awestruck, and [A]glorified God, who had
given such authority to men.

MATTHEW CALLED

9 [A]As Jesus went on from there, He saw a man
called [B]Matthew, sitting in the tax collector's booth;
and He *said to him, "[C]Follow Me!" And he got up
and followed Him.
10 Then it happened that as [a]Jesus was reclining
at the table in the house, behold, many tax collectors and [b]sinners came and were dining with Jesus
and His disciples. 11 When the Pharisees saw *this*,
they said to His disciples, "[A]Why is your Teacher
eating with the tax collectors and sinners?" 12 But
when Jesus heard *this*, He said, "*It is* not [A]those who
are healthy who need a physician, but those who
are sick. 13 But go and learn [a,A]what this means: '[B]I
DESIRE [b]COMPASSION, [c]AND NOT SACRIFICE,' for [C]I did
not come to call the righteous, but sinners."

THE QUESTION ABOUT FASTING

14 Then the disciples of John *came to Him, asking, "Why do we and [A]the Pharisees fast, but Your
disciples do not fast?" 15 And Jesus said to them, "The
[a]attendants of the bridegroom cannot mourn as
long as the bridegroom is with them, can they? But
the days will come when the bridegroom is taken
away from them, and then they will fast. 16 But no
one puts [a]a patch of unshrunk cloth on an old garment; for [b]the patch pulls away from the garment,
and a worse tear results. 17 Nor do *people* put new
wine into old wineskins; otherwise the wineskins
burst, and the wine pours out and the wineskins are

8:33 [a]Lit *and the things of* [A]Matt 4:24 8:34 [A]Amos 7:12; Acts 16:39 9:1 [A]Matt 4:13; Mark 5:21 9:2 [a]Lit *child* [A]Matt 9:2-8: *Mark 2:3-12; Luke 5:18-26* [B]Matt 4:24; 9:6 [C]Matt 9:22; 14:27; Mark 6:50; 10:49; John 16:33; Acts 23:11 [D]Mark 2:5, 9; Luke 5:20, 23; 7:48 9:3 [a]Lit *among* [A]Mark 3:28, 29 9:4 [A]Matt 12:25; Luke 6:8; 9:47 9:5 [A]Matt 9:2, 6; Mark 2:5, 9; Luke 5:20, 23; 7:48 9:6 [A]Matt 8:20; John 5:27 [B]Matt 4:24; 9:2 9:7 [a]Or *departed* 9:8 [a]Lit *afraid* [A]Matt 5:16; 15:31; Mark 2:12; Luke 2:20; 5:25, 26; 7:16; 13:13; 17:15; 23:47; John 15:8; Acts 4:21; 11:18; 21:20; 2 Cor 9:13; Gal 1:24 9:9 [A]Matt 9:9-17: *Mark 2:14-22; Luke 5:27-38* [B]Matt 10:3; Mark 2:14; 3:18; Luke 6:15; Acts 1:13 [C]Matt 8:22 9:10 [a]Lit *He* [b]I.e. irreligious Jews 9:11 [A]Matt 11:19; Mark 2:16; Luke 5:30; 15:2 9:12 [A]Mark 2:17; Luke 5:31 9:13 [a]Lit *what is* [b]Or *mercy* [c]I.e. more than [A]Matt 12:7 [B]Hos 6:6 [C]Mark 2:17; Luke 5:32; 1 Tim 1:15 9:14 [A]Luke 18:12 9:15 [a]Lit *sons of the wedding place* 9:16 [a]Lit *that which is put on* [b]Lit *that which fills up*

large herd of unclean animals suggests that Gentiles dominated the region. It also suggests that the number of demons was large (cf. Mk 5:9).

8:31 The demons *began* to entreat Him. Luke 8:31 relates they pleaded not to be sent into the abyss, meaning the pit, the underworld, the prison of bound demons who disobeyed (*see notes on 2Pe 2:4; Jude 6*). They knew Jesus had the power and authority to send them there if He desired.

8:34 implored Him to leave. Perhaps they were concerned with the financial impact from the loss of the pigs. More likely, they were all ungodly people frightened to be in the presence of such spiritual power (cf. Mk 5:14, 15).

9:1 His own city. Capernaum (*see note on 4:13*). Jesus had left there to get away from the crowds for a time (8:18).

9:2 your sins are forgiven. The fact that the man was brought on a bed indicates that his paralysis was severe. Jesus' words of forgiveness may indicate that the paralysis was a direct consequence of the man's own sin. Cf. Jn 9:1–3; *see notes on Lk 5:20–26*.

9:3 This *fellow* blasphemes. This would be a true judgment about anyone but God incarnate, for only the One who has been sinned against has the prerogative to forgive. Jesus' words to the man were therefore an unequivocal claim of divine authority.

9:4 knowing their thoughts. Cf. 12:25; Jn 2:24. Though the Lord Jesus humbled Himself (Php 2:4–8) and set aside the independent use of His divine prerogatives in incarnation (Jn 5:30), He was still fully God and, therefore, omniscient. See Mk 13:32; Lk 2:52.

9:5 Which is easier. It is certainly easier to claim the power to pronounce absolution from sin than to demonstrate the power to heal. Christ actually proved His power to forgive by instantly healing the man of his paralysis. If He could do the apparently harder, He could also do what seemed easier. The actual forgiving of the sins was in reality the more difficult task, however, because it ultimately required Him to sacrifice His life.

9:9 sitting in the tax collector's booth. Matthew's own humility is seen here. He did not disguise his past or make any excuse for it. Whereas Mk 2:14 and Lk 5:27 employ his former name, Levi, Matthew himself used the name by which he was known after becoming a disciple (cf. Mk 3:18; Lk 6:15). Tax collectors were among the most despised persons in this society. The money they collected was often partly extorted for personal gain (cf. Lk 19:8) and partly a tax for Rome, which made them not only thieves, but also traitors to the Jewish nation (*see notes on 5:46; Mk 2:15*).

9:11 tax collectors. *See note on 5:46*.

9:12 healthy . . . sick. The Pharisees thought they were well—religiously pure and whole. The outcasts knew they were not. Salvation can't come to the self-righteous.

9:13 go and learn what this means. This phrase was commonly used as a rebuke for those who did not know something they should have known. The verse Jesus cites is Hos 6:6 (cf. 1Sa 15:22; Mic 6:6–8), which emphasizes the absolute priority of the law's moral standards over the ceremonial requirements. The Pharisees tended to focus on the outward, ritual, and ceremonial aspects of God's law—to the neglect of its inward, eternal, and moral precepts. In doing so, they became harsh, judgmental, and self-righteously scornful of others. Jesus repeated this same criticism in 12:7.

9:14 disciples of John. Luke implies that the Pharisees asked this question (*see note on Lk 5:33*; cf. Mk 2:18–20). Evidently, some Pharisees were still present when John's disciples came. Both groups together may have asked this question. **the Pharisees fast.** Cf. Lk 18:12.

9:15 then they will fast. *See note on 6:16, 17*. Using the analogy of a wedding party, Jesus answered that as long as Christ was present with them there was too much joy for fasting, which was connected to seasons of sorrow and intense prayer.

9:16 unshrunk cloth on an old garment. That new cloth does not work on old material is analogous to trying to patch New Covenant truth onto old Mosaic ceremonial forms.

9:17 new wine into old wineskins. Animal skins were used for fermentation of wine because of their elasticity. As the wine fermented, pressure built up, stretching the wineskin.

ruined; but they put new wine into fresh wineskins, and both are preserved."

MIRACLES OF HEALING

18 [A]While He was saying these things to them, [a]a *synagogue* [b]official came and [c,B]bowed down before Him, and said, "My daughter has just died; but come and lay Your hand on her, and she will live." 19 Jesus got up and *began* to follow him, and *so did* His disciples.

20 And a woman who had been suffering from a hemorrhage for twelve years, came up behind Him and touched [A]the [a]fringe of His [b]cloak; 21 for she was saying [a]to herself, "If I only [A]touch His garment, I will

9:18 [a]Or *one* [b]Lit *ruler* [c]Or *worshiped* [A]Matt 9:18-26; *Mark 5:22-43; Luke 8:41-56* [B]Matt 8:2 9:20 [a]I.e. tassel fringe with a blue cord [b]Or *outer garment* [A]Num 15:38; Deut 22:12; Matt 14:36; 23:5 9:21 [a]Lit *in herself* [A]Matt 14:36; Mark 3:10; Luke 6:19

A previously stretched skin lacked elasticity and would rupture, ruining both wine and wineskin. Jesus used this as an illustration to teach that the forms of old rituals, such as the ceremonial fastings practiced by the Pharisees and John's disciples, were not fit for the new wine of the New Covenant era (cf. Col 2:17). In both analogies (vv. 16, 17), the Lord was saying that what the Pharisees did in fasting or any other ritual had no part with the gospel.

9:18 official. Jairus (Mk 5:22; Lk 8:41) was a ruler of the synagogue.

9:20 hemorrhage for twelve years. This woman's affliction not only was serious physically but also left her permanently unclean

The Parables of Jesus	Matthew	Mark	Luke
1. Lamp Under a Basket	5:14–16	4:21, 22	8:16, 17; 11:33–36
2. A Wise Man Builds on Rock and a Foolish Man Builds on Sand	7:24–27		6:47–49
3. Unshrunk (New) Cloth on an Old Garment	9:16	2:21	5:36
4. New Wine in Old Wineskins	9:17	2:22	5:37, 38
5. The Sower	13:3–23	4:2–20	8:4–15
6. The Tares (Weeds)	13:24–30		
7. The Mustard Seed	13:31, 32	4:30–32	13:18, 19
8. The Leaven	13:33		13:20, 21
9. The Hidden Treasure	13:44		
10. The Pearl of Great Price	13:45, 46		
11. The Dragnet	13:47–50		
12. The Lost Sheep	18:12–14		15:3–7
13. The Unforgiving Servant	18:23–35		
14. The Workers in the Vineyard	20:1–16		
15. The Two Sons	21:28–32		
16. The Wicked Vine-growers	21:33–45	12:1–12	20:9–19
17. The Wedding Feast	22:2–14		
18. The Fig Tree	24:32–44	13:28–32	21:29–33
19. The Wise and Foolish Virgins	25:1–13		
20. The Talents	25:14–30		
21. The Growing Seed		4:26–29	
22. The Absent Householder		13:33–37	
23. The Creditor and Two Debtors			7:41–43
24. The Good Samaritan			10:30–37
25. A Friend in Need			11:5–13
26. The Rich Fool			12:16–21
27. The Watchful Servants			12:35–40
28. The Faithful Servant and the Evil Servant			12:42–48
29. The Barren Fig Tree			13:6–9
30. The Great Supper			14:16–24
31. Building a Tower and a King Making War			14:25–35
32. The Lost Coin			15:8–10
33. The Lost Son			15:11–32
34. The Unrighteous Steward			16:1–13
35. The Rich Man and Lazarus			16:19–31
36. Unprofitable Servants			17:7–10
37. The Persistent Widow			18:1–8
38. The Pharisee and the Tax Collector			18:9–14
39. The Minas			19:11–27

[b]get well." 22 But Jesus turning and seeing her said, "Daughter, [A]take courage; [B]your faith has [c]made you well." [b]At once the woman was [c]made well.

23 When Jesus came into the [a]official's house, and saw [A]the flute-players and the crowd in noisy disorder, 24 He said, "Leave; for the girl [A]has not died, but is asleep." And they *began* laughing at Him. 25 But [A]when the crowd had been sent out, He entered and [B]took her by the hand, and the girl [a]got up. 26 [A]This news spread throughout all that land.

27 As Jesus went on from there, two blind men followed Him, crying out, "Have mercy on us, [A]Son of David!" 28 When He entered the house, the blind men came up to Him, and Jesus *said to them, "Do you believe that I am able to do this?" They *said to Him, "Yes, Lord." 29 Then He touched their eyes, saying, "[a]It shall be done to you [A]according to your faith." 30 And their eyes were opened. And Jesus [A]sternly warned them: "See that no one knows *about this!*" 31 But they went out and [A]spread the news about Him throughout all that land.

32 As they were going out, [A]a mute, [B]demon-possessed man [a]was brought to Him. 33 After the demon was cast out, the mute man spoke; and the crowds were amazed, *and were* saying, "[A]Nothing like this has [a]ever been seen in Israel." 34 But the Pharisees were saying, "He [A]casts out the demons by the ruler of the demons."

35 Jesus was going through all the cities and villages, [A]teaching in their synagogues and proclaiming the gospel of the kingdom, and healing every kind of disease and every kind of sickness.

36 [A]Seeing the [a]people, He felt compassion for them, [B]because they were [b]distressed and [c]dispirited like sheep [d]without a shepherd. 37 Then He *said to His disciples, "[A]The harvest is plentiful, but the workers are few. 38 Therefore beseech the Lord of the harvest to send out workers into His harvest."

THE TWELVE DISCIPLES; INSTRUCTIONS FOR SERVICE

10 Jesus [A]summoned His twelve disciples and gave them authority over unclean spirits, to cast them out, and to [B]heal every kind of disease and every kind of sickness.

2 [A]Now the names of the twelve apostles are these: The first, [B]Simon, who is called Peter, and [B]Andrew his brother; and [a,C]James the son of Zebedee, and [b]John his brother; 3 [A]Philip and [a]Bartholomew; [B]Thomas and [C]Matthew the tax collector; [b,D]James the son of Alphaeus, and [E]Thaddaeus;

9:21 [b]Lit *be saved* 9:22 [a]Lit *saved you* [b]Lit *from that hour* [c]Lit *saved* [A]Matt 9:2 [B]Matt 9:29; 15:28; Mark 5:34; 10:52; Luke 7:50; 8:48; 17:19; 18:42 9:23 [a]Lit *ruler's* [A]2 Chr 35:25; Jer 9:17; 16:6; Ezek 24:17 9:24 [A]John 11:13; Acts 20:10 9:25 [a]Or *was raised up* [A]Acts 9:40 [B]Mark 9:27 9:26 [A]Matt 4:24; 9:31; 14:1; Mark 1:28, 45; Luke 4:14, 37; 5:15; 7:17 9:27 [A]Matt 1:1; 12:23; 15:22; 20:30, 31; 21:9, 15; 22:42; Mark 10:47, 48; 12:35; Luke 18:38, 39; 20:41f 9:29 [a]Or *Let it be done;* Gr command [A]Matt 8:13; 9:22 9:30 [A]Matt 8:4 9:31 [A]Matt 4:24; 9:26; 14:1; Mark 1:28, 45; Luke 4:14, 37; 5:15; 7:17 9:32 [a]Lit *they brought* [A]Matt 12:22, 24 [B]Matt 4:24 9:33 [a]Lit *ever appeared* [A]Mark 2:12 9:34 [A]Matt 12:24; Mark 3:22; Luke 11:15; John 7:20f 9:35 [A]Matt 4:23; Mark 1:14 9:36 [a]Lit *crowds* [b]Or *harassed* [c]Lit *thrown down* [d]Lit *not having* [A]Matt 14:14; 15:32; Mark 6:34; 8:2 [B]Num 27:17; Ezek 34:5; Zech 10:2; Mark 6:34 9:37 [A]Luke 10:2 10:1 [A]Mark 3:13-15; 6:7 [B]Matt 9:35; Luke 9:1 10:2 [a]Or *Jacob;* James is the Eng form of Jacob [b]Gr *Joannes,* Heb *Johanan* [A]Matt 10:2-4: *Mark 3:16-19; Luke 6:14-16; Acts 1:13* [B]Matt 4:18 [C]Matt 4:21 10:3 [a]I.e. son of Talmai (Aram) [b]Or *Jacob* [A]John 1:43ff [B]John 11:16; 14:5; 20:24ff; 21:2 [C]Matt 9:9 [D]Mark 15:40 [E]Mark 3:18; Luke 6:16; Acts 1:13

for ceremonial reasons (cf. Lv 15:25–27). This meant she would have been shunned by all, including her own family, and excluded from both synagogue and temple. **the fringe of His cloak.** Cf. 14:36. Probably one of the tassels that were sown to the corners of a garment in order to remind the wearer to obey God's commandments (Nu 15:38–40; Dt 22:12).

9:22 made you well. Lit. "saved you."

9:23 flute-players ... crowd in noisy disorder. Typical fixtures at a time of mourning in that culture (cf. 2Ch 35:25). The crowd at a funeral usually included professional mourners, women whose task it was to wail plaintively, while reciting the name of the departed one, as well as any other loved ones who had died recently. The result was a noisy, chaotic din.

9:24 asleep. Jesus was not saying that her death was a misdiagnosis. This was a prophecy that she would live again. He made a similar comment about Lazarus' death (Jn 11:11)—and then had to explain to the disciples that he was speaking metaphorically (Jn 11:14). Sleep is a designation for death in the NT (cf. 1Co 11:30; 15:51; 1Th. 5:10). **they *began* laughing at Him.** How quickly their paid act of mourning turned to derision!

9:27 Son of David. Cf. 1:1; 12:23; 21:9, 15. A messianic title (*see note on 1:1*). See 20:29–34 for a remarkably similar, but separate, account.

9:29 according to your faith. *See note on 8:13.*

9:30 See that no one knows. *See note on 8:4.*

9:34 the ruler of the demons. The Pharisees had seen enough of Jesus' power to know it was God's power. But, in their willful unbelief, they said His was the power of Satan. *See note on 12:24*; cf. 25:41; Mk 3:22; Lk 11:15.

9:35 every ... disease and ... sickness. Jesus banished illness in an unprecedented healing display, giving impressive evidence of His deity, and making the Jews' rejection all the more heinous. *See note on 12:15.*

9:36 He felt compassion for them. Here the humanity of Christ allowed expression of His attitude toward sinners in terms of human passion. He was moved with compassion. Whereas God, who is immutable, is not subject to the rise and fall and change of emotions (Nu 23:19), Christ, who was fully human with all the faculties of humanity, was on occasion moved to literal tears over the plight of sinners (Lk 19:41; *see note on Lk 13:34*). God Himself expressed similar compassion through the prophets (Ex 33:19; Ps 86:15; Jer 9:1; 13:17; 14:17). **they were distressed and dispirited.** The people's spiritual needs were even more desperate than the need for physical healing. Meeting that need would require more laborers (v. 37).

9:37 harvest. Cf. Lk 10:1, 2. The Lord spoke of the spiritual harvest of souls for salvation.

9:38 Therefore beseech. Jesus affirmed the fact that believers' prayers participate in the fulfillment of God's plans.

10:1, 2 disciples ... apostles. "Disciple" means "student," one who is being taught by another. "Apostle" refers to a qualified representative who is sent on a mission. The two terms emphasize different aspects of their calling.

10:1 gave them authority. *See note on 2Co 12:12.* Jesus delegated His power and authority to the apostles to show clearly that He and His kingdom were sovereign over the physical and spiritual realms, the effects of sin, and the efforts of Satan. This was an unheard of display of power, never before seen in all redemptive history, to announce Messiah's arrival and authenticate Him plus His apostles who preached His gospel. This power was a preview of the power Christ will exhibit in His earthly kingdom, when Satan will be bound (Rev 20) and the curse on physical life curtailed (Is 65:20–25).

10:2 the names of the twelve apostles. The 12 are always listed in a similar order (cf. Mk 3:16–19; Lk 6:13–16; Ac 1:13). Peter is always named first. The list contains 3 groups of 4. The 3 subgroups are always listed in the same order, and the first name in each subgroup is always the same, though there is some variation in the order within the subgroups—but Judas Iscariot is always named last. **Peter ... Andrew ... James ... John.** The first subgroup of 4 are the most familiar to us. These two sets of brothers, all fishermen, represent an inner circle of disciples often seen closest to Jesus (*see note on 17:1*).

10:3 James the son of Alphaeus. There are 4 men in the NT named James: 1) the Apostle James, brother of John (*see note on 4:21*); 2) the disciple mentioned here, also called "James the Less" (Mk 15:40); 3) James, father of Judas (not Iscariot, Lk 6:16); and 4) James, the Lord's half-brother (Mk 6:3; Gal 1:19), who wrote the epistle that bears the name. He also played a leading role in the early Jerusalem Church (Ac 12:17; 15:13; Gal 1:19). **Thaddaeus.** Elsewhere he is called Judas, son of James (Lk 6:16; Ac 1:13).

4 Simon the [a]Zealot, and [A]Judas Iscariot, the one
who betrayed Him.
5 [A]These twelve Jesus sent out after instructing
them: "Do not [a]go [b]in *the* way of *the* Gentiles, and do
not enter *any* city of the [B]Samaritans; 6 but rather
go to [A]the lost sheep of the house of Israel. 7 And as
you go, [a]preach, saying, '[A]The kingdom of heaven [b]is
at hand.' 8 Heal *the* sick, raise *the* dead, cleanse *the*
lepers, cast out demons. Freely you received, freely
give. 9 [A]Do not acquire gold, or silver, or copper
for your money belts, 10 or a [a]bag for *your* journey,
or even two [b]coats, or sandals, or a staff; for [A]the
worker is worthy of his [c]support. 11 And whatever
city or village you enter, inquire who is worthy in
it, and stay [a]at his house until you leave *that city.*
12 As you enter the [a]house, [A]give it your [b]greeting. 13 If
the house is worthy, [a]give it your *blessing of* peace.
But if it is not worthy, [b]take back your *blessing of*
peace. 14 Whoever does not receive you, nor heed
your words, as you go out of that house or that city,
[A]shake the dust off your feet. 15 Truly I say to you, [A]it
will be more tolerable for *the* land of [B]Sodom and
Gomorrah in [C]the day of judgment than for that city.

A HARD ROAD BEFORE THEM

16 "[A]Behold, I send you out as sheep in the midst
of wolves; so [a]be [B]shrewd as serpents and [C]innocent
as doves. 17 But beware of men, for they will hand
you over to *the* [A]courts and scourge you [B]in their
synagogues; 18 and you will even be brought before
governors and kings for My sake, as a testimony to
them and to the Gentiles. 19 [A]But when they hand
you over, [B]do not worry about how or what you are
to say; for it will be given you in that hour what you
are to say. 20 For [A]it is not you who speak, but *it is*
the Spirit of your Father who speaks in you.
21 "[A]Brother will betray brother to death, and a
father *his* child; and [B]children will rise up against
parents and [a]cause them to be put to death. 22 [A]You
will be hated by all because of My name, but [B]it is the
one who has endured to the end who will be saved.
23 "But whenever they [A]persecute you in [a]one city,
flee to [b]the next; for truly I say to you, you will not
finish *going through* the cities of Israel [B]until the
Son of Man comes.

THE MEANING OF DISCIPLESHIP

24 "[A]A [a]disciple is not above his teacher, nor a slave
above his master. 25 It is enough for the disciple that
he become like his teacher, and the slave like his
master. [A]If they have called the head of the house
[a,B]Beelzebul, how much more *will they malign* the
members of his household!
26 "Therefore do not [A]fear them, [B]for there is nothing concealed that will not be revealed, or hidden
that will not be known. 27 [A]What I tell you in the
darkness, speak in the light; and what you hear
whispered in *your* ear, proclaim [B]upon the housetops. 28 Do not fear those who kill the body but are
unable to kill the soul; but rather [A]fear Him who is

10:4 [a]Or *Cananaean* [A]Matt 26:14; Luke 22:3; John 6:71; 13:2, 26 10:5 [a]Or *go off* [b]Or *on the road of* (Gr *hodos: way* or *road*) [A]Mark 6:7; Luke 9:2 [B]2 Kin 17:24ff; Luke 9:52; 10:33; 17:16; John 4:9, 39f; 8:48; Acts 8:25 10:6 [A]Matt 15:24 10:7 [a]Or *proclaim* [b]Lit *has come near* [A]Matt 3:2 10:9 [A]Matt 10:9-15: *Mark 6:8-11; Luke 9:3-5; 10:4-12;* Luke 22:35 10:10 [a]Or *knapsack*, or *beggar's bag* [b]Or *inner garments* [c]Lit *nourishment* [A]1 Cor 9:14; 1 Tim 5:18 10:11 [a]Lit *there until* 10:12 [a]Or *household* [b]I.e. the familiar Heb blessing, "Peace be to this house!" [A]1 Sam 25:6; Ps 122:7, 8 10:13 [a]Lit *your peace is to come upon it* [b]Lit *your peace is to return to you* 10:14 [A]Acts 13:51 10:15 [A]Matt 11:22, 24 [B]Matt 11:24; 2 Pet 2:6; Jude 7 [C]Matt 7:22; 11:22, 24; 12:36; Acts 17:31; 1 Thess 5:4; Heb 10:25; 2 Pet 2:9; 3:7; 1 John 4:17; Jude 6 10:16 [a]Or *show yourselves to be* [A]Luke 10:3 [B]Gen 3:1; Matt 24:25; Rom 16:19 [C]Hos 7:11 10:17 [A]Matt 5:22 [B]Matt 23:34; Mark 13:9; Luke 12:11; Acts 5:40; 22:19; 26:11 10:19 [A]Matt 10:19-22: *Mark 13:11-13; Luke 21:12-17* [B]Matt 6:25; Luke 12:11, 12 10:20 [A]Luke 12:12; Acts 4:8; 13:9; 2 Cor 13:3 10:21 [a]Lit *put them to death* [A]Matt 10:35, 36; Mark 13:12 [B]Mic 7:6 10:22 [A]Matt 24:9; Luke 21:17; John 15:18ff [B]Matt 24:13; Mark 13:13 10:23 [a]Lit *this* [b]Lit *the other* [A]Matt 23:34 [B]Matt 16:27f 10:24 [a]Or *student* [A]Luke 6:40; John 13:16; 15:20 10:25 [a]Or *Beezebul:* ruler of demons [A]Matt 9:34 [B]2 Kin 1:2; Matt 12:24, 27; Mark 3:22; Luke 11:15, 18, 19 10:26 [A]Matt 10:26-33: *Luke 12:2-9* [B]Mark 4:22; Luke 8:17; 12:2; 1 Cor 4:5 10:27 [A]Luke 12:3 [B]Matt 24:17; Acts 5:20 10:28 [A]Heb 10:31

10:4 Simon the Zealot. The better manuscripts read "Cananaean"—a term for the party of the Zealots, a group determined to overthrow Roman domination in Israel. Simon was probably a member of the Zealot party before coming to Christ. *See note on Mk 3:18.*

10:5–11:1 This is the second of 5 major discourses recorded in Matthew (see Introduction: Historical and Theological Themes).

10:5 Do not go in *the* way of *the* Gentiles. Christ did not forbid the disciples to preach to Gentiles or Samaritans if they encountered them on the way, but they were to take the message first to the covenant people, in the regions nearby (cf. Ro 1:16).

10:6 lost sheep of the house of Israel. Cf. 15:24; Jer 50:6. Jesus narrowed this priority even more when He said the gospel was only for those who knew they were spiritually sick (9:13) and needed a physician (Lk 5:31, 32).

10:7 at hand. *See note on 3:2.*

10:8 Freely you received, freely give. Jesus was giving them great power, to heal the sick and raise the dead. If they sold these gifts for money, they could have made quite a fortune. But that would have obscured the message of grace Christ sent them to preach. So He forbade them to charge money for their ministry. Yet they were permitted to accept support to meet their basic needs, for a workman is worthy of such support (v. 10).

10:9, 10 *See note on Lk 9:3.* The restrictions on what they were to carry were unique for this mission. See Lk 22:36 where, on a later mission, Christ gave completely different instructions. The point here was to teach them to trust the Lord to supply their needs through the generosity of the people to whom they ministered, and to teach those who received the blessing of their ministry to support the servants of Christ. Cf. 1Ti 5:18.

10:13 peace. This is equivalent to the Heb. "shalom" and refers to prosperity, well-being, or blessing.

10:14 heed your words. The priority was to preach that the King had come and His kingdom was near. The message was the main thing. The signs and wonders were to authenticate it. **shake the dust off your feet.** It was common for Jews to shake the dust off their feet—as an expression of disdain—when returning from Gentile regions. Paul and Barnabas also did this when expelled from Antioch (Ac 13:51). This was a visible protest, signifying that they regarded the place as no better than a pagan land.

10:15 Sodom and Gomorrah. Those cities and the entire surrounding region were judged without warning, and with the utmost severity. *See notes on Ge 19:1–29.*

10:16 wolves. Used to describe false prophets who persecute the true ones and seek to destroy the Church (cf. 7:15; Lk 10:3; Ac 20:29). *See note on Lk 10:3.*

10:17 hand you over. This is a technical word, in this context, used for delivering a prisoner for punishment. Persecution of believers has often been the official policy of governments. Such persecutions give opportunity for testifying to the truth of the gospel. Cf. Jn 16:1–4; 2Ti 4:16.

10:19 do not worry. *See note on Lk 12:11.*

10:21–23 These verses clearly have an eschatological significance that goes beyond the disciples' immediate mission. The persecutions He describes seem to belong to the tribulation period that precedes Christ's second coming, alluded to in v. 23.

10:22 one who has endured to the end. *See note on 24:13.*

10:24 not above. If the Teacher (Christ) suffers, so will His pupils. If they attack the Master (Christ) with blasphemies, so will they curse the servants. This was the promise of persecution. Cf. Jn 15:20.

10:25 Beelzebul. The Philistine deity associated with satanic idolatry. The name came to be used for Satan, the prince of demons (*see notes on 2Ki 1:2; Lk 11:15*).

10:28 fear Him. God is the one who destroys in hell. Cf. Lk 12:5. Persecutors can only harm the body.

able to destroy both soul and body in [a,B]hell. 29 [A]Are
not two sparrows sold for a [a]cent? And *yet* not one
of them will fall to the ground apart from your
Father. 30 But [A]the very hairs of your head are all
numbered. 31 So do not fear; [A]you are more valuable
than many sparrows.
32 "Therefore [A]everyone who [a]confesses Me before
men, I will also confess [b]him before My Father who is
in heaven. 33 But [A]whoever [a]denies Me before men, I
will also deny him before My Father who is in heaven.
34 "[A]Do not think that I came to [a]bring peace
on the earth; I did not come to bring peace, but a
sword. 35 For I came to [A]SET A MAN AGAINST HIS FA-
THER, AND A DAUGHTER AGAINST HER MOTHER, AND
A DAUGHTER-IN-LAW AGAINST HER MOTHER-IN-LAW;
36 and [A]A MAN'S ENEMIES WILL BE THE MEMBERS OF
HIS HOUSEHOLD.
37 "[A]He who loves father or mother more than
Me is not worthy of Me; and he who loves son or
daughter more than Me is not worthy of Me. 38 And
[A]he who does not take his cross and follow after
Me is not worthy of Me. 39 [A]He who has found his
[a]life will lose it, and he who has lost his [a]life for My
sake will find it.

THE REWARD OF SERVICE

40 "[A]He who receives you receives Me, and [B]he
who receives Me receives Him who sent Me. 41 [A]He
who receives a prophet in *the* name of a prophet
shall receive a prophet's reward; and he who receives a righteous man in the name of a righteous
man shall receive a righteous man's reward. 42 And
[A]whoever in the name of a disciple gives to one of
these [a]little ones even a cup of cold water to drink,
truly I say to you, he shall not lose his reward."

JOHN'S QUESTIONS

11 [A]When Jesus had finished [a]giving instructions
to His twelve disciples, He departed from there
[B]to teach and [b]preach in their cities.
2 [A]Now when [B]John, [a]while imprisoned, heard of
the works of Christ, he sent *word* by his disciples
3 and said to Him, "Are You [A]the [a]Expected One, or
shall we look for someone else?" 4 Jesus answered
and said to them, "Go and report to John what you
hear and see: 5 [A]*the* BLIND RECEIVE SIGHT and *the*
lame walk, *the* lepers are cleansed and *the* deaf
hear, *the* dead are raised up, and *the* [B]POOR HAVE
THE [a]GOSPEL PREACHED TO THEM. 6 And blessed is
he [a]who [A]does not [b]take offense at Me."

JESUS' TRIBUTE TO JOHN

7 As these men were going *away,* Jesus began
to speak to the crowds about John, "What did you
go out into [A]the wilderness to see? A reed shaken
by the wind? 8 [a]But what did you go out to see? A
man dressed in soft *clothing?* Those who wear soft
clothing are in kings' [b]palaces! 9 [a]But what did you
go out to see? [A]A prophet? Yes, I tell you, and one
who is more than a prophet. 10 This is the one about
whom it [a]is written,

'[A]BEHOLD, I SEND MY MESSENGER
[b]AHEAD OF YOU,
WHO WILL PREPARE YOUR
WAY BEFORE YOU.'

10:28 [a]Gr *Gehenna* [B]Matt 5:22; Luke 12:5 10:29 [a]Gr *assarion*, the smallest copper coin [A]Luke 12:6 10:30 [A]1 Sam 14:45; 2 Sam 14:11; 1 Kin 1:52; Luke 21:18; Acts 27:34 10:31 [A]Matt 12:12 10:32 [a]Lit *will confess in Me* [b]Lit *in him* [A]Luke 12:8; Rev 3:5 10:33 [a]Lit *will deny* [A]Mark 8:38; Luke 9:26; 2 Tim 2:12 10:34 [a]Lit *cast* [A]Matt 10:34, 35: *Luke 12:51-53* 10:35 [A]Mic 7:6; Matt 10:21; Luke 12:53 10:36 [A]Mic 7:6; Matt 10:21 10:37 [A]Deut 33:9; Luke 14:26 10:38 [A]Matt 16:24; Mark 8:34; Luke 9:23; 14:27 10:39 [a]Or *soul* [A]Matt 16:25; Mark 8:35; Luke 9:24; 17:33; John 12:25 10:40 [A]Matt 18:5; Luke 10:16; John 13:20; Gal 4:14 [B]Mark 9:37; Luke 9:48; John 12:44 10:41 [A]Matt 25:44, 45 10:42 [a]I.e. humble [A]Matt 25:40; Mark 9:41 11:1 [a]Or *commanding* [b]Or *proclaim* [A]Matt 7:28 [B]Matt 9:35; Luke 23:5 11:2 [a]Lit *in prison* [A]Matt 11:2-19: *Luke 7:18-35;* Matt 4:12 [B]Matt 14:3; Mark 6:17; Luke 9:7ff 11:3 [a]Lit *Coming One* [A]Ps 118:26; Matt 11:10; John 6:14; 11:27; Heb 10:37 11:5 [a]Or *good news* [A]Is 35:5f; Matt 8:3; 12:13 [B]Is 61:1; Luke 4:18 11:6 [a]Lit *whoever* [b]Or *stumble over Me* [A]Matt 5:29; 13:57; 24:10; 26:31; Mark 6:3; John 6:61; 16:1 11:7 [A]Matt 3:1 11:8 [a]Or *Well then,* [b]Lit *houses* 11:9 [a]Or *Well then,* [A]Matt 14:5; 21:26; Luke 1:76; 20:6 11:10 [a]Lit *has been written* [b]Lit *before your face* [A]Mal 3:1; Mark 1:2

10:29 apart from your Father. Not merely "without His knowledge"; Jesus was teaching that God providentially controls the timing and circumstances of such insignificant events as the death of a sparrow. Even the number of hairs on our heads is controlled by His sovereign will (v. 30). In other words, divine providence governs even the smallest details and even the most mundane matters. These are very powerful affirmations of the sovereignty of God.

10:32 confesses Me. The person who acknowledges Christ as Lord in life or in death, if necessary, is the one whom the Lord will acknowledge before God as His own. *See note on 2Ti 2:10–13.*

10:33 *See note on Lk 12:9.*

10:34 not ... peace, but a sword. Though the ultimate end of the gospel is peace with God (Jn 14:27; Ro 8:6), the immediate result of the gospel is frequently conflict. Conversion to Christ can result in strained family relationships (vv. 35, 36), persecution, and even martyrdom. Following Christ presupposes a willingness to endure such hardships (vv. 32, 33, 37–39). Though He is called "Prince of Peace" (Is 9:6), Christ will have no one deluded into thinking that He calls believers to a life devoid of all conflict.

10:35, 36 Quoted from Mic 7:6.

10:38 take his cross. Here is Jesus' first mention of the word "cross" to His disciples (*see note on 16:21*). To them it would have evoked a picture of a violent, degrading death (*see note on 27:31*). He was demanding total commitment from them—even unto physical death—and making this call to full surrender a part of the message they were to proclaim to others. This same call to life-or-death devotion to Christ is repeated in 16:24; Mk 8:34; Lk 9:23; 14:27. For those who come to Christ with self-renouncing faith, there will be true and eternal life (v. 39).

10:40 He who receives you receives Me. Christ lives in His people. They also come in His name as His ambassadors (2Co 5:20). Therefore, how they are treated is how He is treated (cf. 18:5; 25:45; Lk 9:48).

10:41 in *the* name of a prophet ... in the name of a righteous man. This expands on the principle of v. 40. To welcome Christ's emissaries is tantamount to welcoming Him (cf. 25:40).

10:42 little ones. Believers. *See notes on 18:3–10; 25:40.*

11:1 in their cities. I.e., in Galilee. Meanwhile, the disciples were also ministering in the Jewish towns in and around Galilee (10:5, 6).

11:3 Are You the Expected One, or shall we look for someone else? John the Baptist had introduced Christ as One who would bring a fierce judgment and "burn up the chaff with unquenchable fire" (3:12). He was understandably confused by the turn of events: he was imprisoned, and Christ was carrying on a ministry of healing, not judgment, in Galilee, far from Jerusalem, the city of the King—and not finding a completely warm reception there (cf. 8:34). John wondered if he had misunderstood Jesus' agenda. It would be wrong to interpret this as a wavering of his faith (v. 7).

11:4 report to John. He sent John's disciples back as eyewitnesses of many miracles. Evidently, He performed these miracles in their presence just so that they could report back to John that they had personally seen proof that He was indeed the Messiah (cf. Is 29:18, 19; 35:5–10). Note, however, that He offered no further explanation to John, knowing exactly how strong John's faith was (cf. 1Co 10:13).

11:10 Quoted from Mal 3:1.

11 Truly I say to you, among those born of women there
has not arisen *anyone* greater than John the Baptist!
Yet the one who is [a]least in the kingdom of heaven is
greater than he. 12 [A]From the days of John the Baptist
until now the kingdom of heaven [a]suffers violence,
and violent men [b]take it by force. 13 For all the prophets
and the Law prophesied until John. 14 And if you are
willing to accept *it,* John himself is [A]Elijah who [a]was
to come. 15 [A]He who has ears to hear, [a]let him hear.
16 "But to what shall I compare this generation?
It is like children sitting in the market places, who
call out to the other *children,* 17 and say, 'We played
the flute for you, and you did not dance; we sang
a dirge, and you did not [a]mourn.' 18 For John came
neither [A]eating nor [B]drinking, and they say, '[C]He
has a demon!' 19 The Son of Man came eating and
drinking, and they say, 'Behold, a gluttonous man
and a [a]drunkard, [A]a friend of tax collectors and
[b]sinners!' Yet wisdom is vindicated by her deeds."

THE UNREPENTING CITIES

20 Then He began to denounce the cities in which
most of His [a,A]miracles were done, because they did
not repent. 21 "[A]Woe to you, Chorazin! Woe to you,
[B]Bethsaida! For if the [a]miracles had occurred in [C]Tyre
and [C]Sidon which occurred in you, they would have
repented long ago in [b,D]sackcloth and ashes. 22 Nevertheless I say to you, [A]it will be more tolerable for Tyre
and Sidon in [B]*the* day of judgment than for you. 23 And
you, [A]Capernaum, will not be exalted to heaven, will
you? You will [B]descend to [C]Hades; for if the [a]miracles
had occurred in [D]Sodom which occurred in you, it
would have remained to this day. 24 Nevertheless I
say to you that [A]it will be more tolerable for the land
of [B]Sodom in *the* day of judgment, than for you."

COME TO ME

25 [A]At that [a]time Jesus said, "I praise You, [B]Father,
Lord of heaven and earth, that [C]You have hidden
these things from *the* wise and intelligent and have
revealed them to infants. 26 Yes, [A]Father, for this way
was well-pleasing in Your sight. 27 [A]All things have
been handed over to Me by My Father; and no one
knows the Son except the Father; nor does anyone
know the Father [B]except the Son, and anyone to
whom the Son wills to reveal *Him.*
28 "[A]Come to Me, all [a]who are weary and heavy-lad-
en, and I will give you rest. 29 Take My yoke upon
you and [A]learn from Me, for I am gentle and humble
in heart, and [B]YOU WILL FIND REST FOR YOUR SOULS.
30 For [A]My yoke is [a]easy and My burden is light."

SABBATH QUESTIONS

12 [A]At that [a]time Jesus went through the grainfields on the Sabbath, and His disciples became hungry and began to [B]pick the heads *of grain*
and eat. 2 But when the Pharisees saw *this,* they said
to Him, "Look, Your disciples do what [A]is not lawful

11:11 [a]Or *less* 11:12 [a]Or *is forcibly entered* [b]Or *seize it for themselves* [A]Luke 16:16 11:14 [a]Or *is going to come* [A]Mal 4:5; Matt 17:10-13; Mark 9:11-13; Luke 1:17; John 1:21 11:15 [a]Or *hear!* Or *listen!* [A]Matt 13:9, 43; Mark 4:9, 23; Luke 8:8; 14:35; Rev 2:7, 11, 17, 29; 3:6, 13, 22; 13:9 11:17 [a]Lit *beat the breast* 11:18 [A]Matt 3:4 [B]Luke 1:15 [C]Matt 9:34; John 7:20; 8:48f, 52; 10:20 11:19 [a]Or *wine-drinker* [b]I.e. irreligious Jews [A]Matt 9:11; Luke 5:29-32; 15:2 11:20 [a]Or *works of power* [A]Luke 10:13-15 11:21 [a]Or *works of power* [b]I.e. symbols of mourning [A]Matt 11:21-23: *Luke 10:13-15* [B]Mark 6:45; 8:22; Luke 9:10; John 1:44; 12:21 [C]Matt 11:22; 15:21; Mark 3:8; 7:24, 31; Luke 4:26; 6:17; Acts 12:20; 27:3 [D]Rev 11:3 11:22 [A]Matt 10:15; 11:24 [B]Matt 10:15; 12:36; Rev 20:11, 12 11:23 [a]Or *works of power* [A]Matt 4:13 [B]Is 14:13, 15; Ezek 26:20; 31:14; 32:18, 24 [C]Matt 16:18; Luke 10:15; 16:23; Acts 2:27, 31; Rev 1:18; 6:8; 20:13f [D]Matt 10:15 11:24 [A]Matt 10:15; 11:22 [B]Matt 10:15 11:25 [a]Or *occasion* [A]Matt 11:25-27: *Luke 10:21, 22* [B]Luke 22:42; 23:34; John 11:41; 12:27, 28 [C]Ps 8:2; 1 Cor 1:26ff 11:26 [A]Luke 22:42; 23:34; John 11:41; 12:27, 28 11:27 [A]Matt 28:18; John 3:35; 13:3; 17:2 [B]John 7:29; 10:15; 17:25 11:28 [a]Or *who work to exhaustion* [A]Jer 31:25; John 7:37 11:29 [A]John 13:15; Eph 4:20; Phil 2:5; 1 Pet 2:21; 1 John 2:6 [B]Jer 6:16 11:30 [a]Or *comfortable,* or *pleasant* [A]1 John 5:3 12:1 [a]Or *occasion* [A]Matt 12:1-8: *Mark 2:23-28; Luke 6:1-5* [B]Deut 23:25 12:2 [A]Matt 12:10; Luke 13:14; 14:3; John 5:10; 7:23; 9:16

11:11 least … is greater than he. John was greater than the OT prophets because he actually saw with his eyes and personally participated in the fulfillment of what they only prophesied (vv. 10, 13; cf. 1Pe 1:10, 11). But all believers after the cross are greater still, because they participate in the full understanding and experience of something John merely foresaw in shadowy form—the actual atoning work of Christ.

11:12 the kingdom of heaven suffers violence. From the time he began his preaching ministry, John the Baptist evoked a strong reaction. Having been imprisoned already, John ultimately fell victim to Herod's savagery. But the kingdom can never be subdued or opposed by human violence. Notice that where Matthew says, "the violent take it by force," Luke has, "everyone forcing his way into it" (Lk 16:16). So the sense of this verse may be rendered this way: "The kingdom presses ahead relentlessly, and only the relentless press their way into it." Thus again Christ is magnifying the difficulty of entering the kingdom (*see notes on 7:13, 14*).

11:14 John himself is Elijah. I.e., he is the fulfillment of Mal 4:5, 6 (see 17:12, 13). The Jews were aware that Elijah had not died (cf. 2Ki 2:11). This does not suggest that John was Elijah returned. In fact, John himself denied that he was Elijah (Jn 1:21); yet he came in the spirit and power of Elijah (Lk 1:17). If they had believed, John would have been the fulfillment of the Elijah prophecies. *See notes on Mk 9:13; Rev 11:5, 6.*

11:16 like children. *See note on Lk 7:32.*

11:19 eating and drinking. *See note on Lk 7:34.*

11:21 Woe to you, Chorazin! … Bethsaida! Both were cities very close to Capernaum, near the northern shore of the Sea of Galilee. **Tyre … Sidon.** Phoenician cities on the shore of the Mediterranean. The prophecy about the destruction of Tyre and Sidon in Eze 26–28 was fulfilled in precise detail.

11:22, 24 more tolerable. This indicates that there will be degrees of punishment in hell for the ungodly (*see notes on 10:15; Mk 6:11; Lk 12:47, 48; Heb 10:29*).

11:23 Capernaum … exalted … descend. Capernaum, chosen by Jesus to be His headquarters, faced an even greater condemnation. Curiously, there is no record that the people of that city ever mocked or ridiculed Jesus, ran Him out of town, or threatened His life. Yet the sin of that city—indifference to Christ—was worse than Sodom's gross wickedness (cf. 10:15).

11:25 wise and intelligent … infants. There is sarcasm in these words as the Jewish leaders are ironically identified as wise and intelligent and the followers of Christ as the infants (cf. 18:3–10)—yet God has revealed to those followers the truth of the Messiah and His gospel. Cf. 13:10–17.

11:26 this way was well-pleasing in Your sight. Cf. Lk 10:21, 22. This is a powerful affirmation of the sovereignty of God over all the affairs of men; and in the verse that follows, Christ claimed that the task of executing the divine will had been committed to Him—a claim that would be utterly blasphemous if Jesus were anything less than sovereign God Himself.

11:28–30 Come to Me, all who are weary and heavy-laden. There is an echo of the first beatitude (5:3) in this passage. Note that this is an open invitation to all who hear—but phrased in such a way that the only ones who will respond to the invitation are those who are burdened by their own spiritual bankruptcy and the weight of trying to save themselves by keeping the law. The stubbornness of humanity's sinful rebellion is such that without a sovereignly bestowed spiritual awakening, all sinners refuse to acknowledge the depth of their spiritual poverty. That is why, as Jesus says in v. 27, our salvation is the sovereign work of God. But the truth of divine election in v. 27 is not incompatible with the free offer to all in vv. 28–30.

11:29 you will find rest. I.e., from the endless, fruitless effort to save oneself by the works of the law (cf. Heb 4:1–3, 6, 9–11). This speaks of a permanent respite in the grace of God which is apart from works (v. 30).

12:2 not lawful to do on a Sabbath. Actually, no law prohibited the plucking of grain in order to eat on the Sabbath. Gleaning handfuls of grain from a neighbor's field to satisfy

to do on a Sabbath." 3 But He said to them, "Have you
not read what David did when he became hungry,
he and his companions, 4 how he entered the house
of God, and [A]they ate the [a]consecrated bread, which
was not lawful for him to eat nor for those with him,
but for the priests alone? 5 Or have you not read
in the Law, that on the Sabbath the priests in the
temple [a]break the Sabbath and are innocent? 6 But I
say to you that something [A]greater than the temple
is here. 7 But if you had known what this [a]means,
'[A]I DESIRE [b]COMPASSION, AND NOT A SACRIFICE,' you
would not have condemned the innocent.

LORD OF THE SABBATH

8 For [A]the Son of Man is Lord of the Sabbath."
9 [A]Departing from there, He went into their synagogue. 10 And a man *was there* whose hand was
withered. And they questioned [a]Jesus, asking, "[A]Is it
lawful to heal on the Sabbath?"—so that they might
accuse Him. 11 And He said to them, "[A]What man [a]is
there among you who [b]has a sheep, and if it falls
into a pit on the Sabbath, will he not take hold of
it and lift it out? 12 [A]How much more valuable then
is a man than a sheep! So then, it is lawful to do
[a]good on the Sabbath." 13 Then He *said to the man,
"Stretch out your hand!" [A]He stretched it out, and
it was restored to [a]normal, like the other. 14 But the
Pharisees went out and [a,A]conspired against Him,
as to how they might destroy Him.
15 But Jesus, [a]aware of *this*, withdrew from there.
Many followed Him, and [A]He healed them all, 16 and
[A]warned them not to [a]tell who He was. 17 *This was* to
fulfill what was spoken through Isaiah the prophet:

18 "[A]BEHOLD, MY [a]SERVANT WHOM
I [b]HAVE CHOSEN;
[B]MY BELOVED IN WHOM MY
SOUL [c]IS WELL-PLEASED;
[C]I WILL PUT MY SPIRIT UPON HIM,
[A]AND HE SHALL PROCLAIM [d]JUSTICE
TO THE [e]GENTILES.
19 "[A]HE WILL NOT QUARREL, NOR CRY OUT;
NOR WILL ANYONE HEAR HIS
VOICE IN THE STREETS.
20 "[A]A BATTERED REED HE WILL NOT BREAK OFF,
AND A SMOLDERING WICK HE
WILL NOT PUT OUT,
UNTIL HE [a]LEADS [b]JUSTICE TO VICTORY.
21 "[A]AND IN HIS NAME THE
[a]GENTILES WILL HOPE."

THE PHARISEES REBUKED

22 [A]Then a [B]demon-possessed man *who was* blind
and mute was brought to [a]Jesus, and He healed
him, so that the mute man spoke and saw. 23 All the
crowds were amazed, and were saying, "This man
cannot be the [A]Son of David, can he?" 24 But when the
Pharisees heard *this*, they said, "This man [A]casts out
demons only by [a]Beelzebul the ruler of the demons."
25 [A]And [B]knowing their thoughts Jesus said to them,
"[a]Any kingdom divided against itself is laid waste;
and [a]any city or house divided against itself will

12:4 [a]Or *showbread*; lit *loaves of presentation* [A]1 Sam 21:6 12:5 [a]Or *profane* 12:6 [A]2 Chr 6:18; Is 66:1, 2; Matt 12:41, 42 12:7 [a]Lit *is* [b]Or *mercy* [A]Hos 6:6; Matt 9:13 12:8 [A]Matt 8:20; 12:32, 40 12:9 [A]Matt 12:9-14: *Mark 3:1-6; Luke 6:6-11* 12:10 [a]Lit *Him* [A]Matt 12:2; Luke 13:14; 14:3; John 5:10; 7:23; 9:16 12:11 [a]Lit *will be from you* [b]Lit *will have* [A]Luke 14:5 12:12 [a]Lit *well* [A]Matt 10:31; Luke 14:1-6 12:13 [a]Lit *health* [A]Matt 8:3; Acts 28:8 12:14 [a]Lit *took counsel* [A]Matt 26:4; Mark 14:1; Luke 22:2; John 7:30, 44; 8:59; 10:31, 39; 11:53 12:15 [a]Lit *knowing* [A]Matt 4:23 12:16 [a]Lit *make Him known* [A]Matt 8:4; 9:30; 17:9 12:18 [a]Lit *Child* [b]Lit *chose* [c]Or *took pleasure* [d]Or *judgment* [e]Or *nations* [A]Is 42:1 [B]Matt 3:17; 17:5 [C]Luke 4:18; John 3:34 12:19 [A]Is 42:2 12:20 [a]Or *puts forth* [b]Or *judgment* [A]Is 42:3 12:21 [a]Or *nations* [A]Rom 15:12 12:22 [a]Lit *Him* [A]Matt 12:22, 24: *Luke 11:14, 15;* Matt 9:32, 34 [B]Matt 4:24; 2 Thess 2:9 12:23 [A]Matt 9:27 12:24 [a]Or *Beezebul;* i.e. ruler of demons [A]Matt 9:34 12:25 [a]Lit *Every* [A]Matt 12:25-29: *Mark 3:23-27; Luke 11:17-22* [B]Matt 9:4

one's immediate hunger was explicitly permitted (Dt 23:25). What was prohibited was labor for the sake of profit. Thus a farmer could not harvest for profit on the Sabbath, but an individual could glean enough grain to eat.

12:3 He said. Jesus' answer in vv. 3–8 points out that the Sabbath laws do not restrict deeds of necessity (vv. 3, 4); service to God (vv. 5, 6); or acts of mercy (vv. 7, 8). He reaffirmed that the Sabbath was made for man's benefit and God's glory. It was never intended to be a yoke of bondage to the people of God (Mk 2:27). *See note on Lk 6:9.*

12:4 the consecrated bread. The consecrated bread of the Presence, 12 loaves baked fresh each Sabbath, which was usually eaten by the priests only (Lv 24:5–9). God was not offended by David's act, done to satisfy a legitimate need when his men were weak with hunger (1Sa 21:4–6). *See notes on Mk 2:26; Lk 6:3.*

12:5 break the Sabbath and are innocent? I.e., the priests have to do their work on the Sabbath, proving that some aspects of the Sabbath restrictions are not inviolable moral absolutes, but rather precepts pertaining to the ceremonial features of the law.

12:6 greater than the temple. This was a straightforward claim of deity. The Lord Jesus was God incarnate—God dwelling in human flesh—far superior to a building which God merely visited.

12:7 compassion, and not a sacrifice. Quoted from Hos 6:6. *See note on 9:13.*

12:8 the Son of Man is Lord of the Sabbath. Christ has the prerogative to rule over not only their man-made sabbatarian rules, but also over the Sabbath itself—which was designed for worshiping God. Again, this was an inescapable claim of deity—and as such it prompted the Pharisees' violent outrage (v. 14).

12:10 Is it lawful to heal on the Sabbath? Jewish tradition prohibited the practice of medicine on the Sabbath, except in life-threatening situations. But no actual law in the OT forbade the giving of medicine, healing, or any other acts of mercy on the Sabbath. It is always lawful to do good.

12:15 He healed them all. *See note on 9:35.* In all of OT history there was never a time or a person who exhibited such extensive healing power. Physical healings were very rare in the OT. Christ chose to display His deity by healing, raising the dead, and liberating people from demons. That not only showed the Messiah's power over the physical and spiritual realms, but also demonstrated the compassion of God toward those affected by sin. *See note on Jn 11:35.*

12:16 warned them not to tell who He was. *See note on 8:4.* Here Christ seems concerned about the potential zealotry of those who would try to press Him into the conquering-hero mold that the rabbinical experts had made out of messianic prophecy (*see note on v. 18*).

12:18 Behold, My Servant. Verses 18–21 are quoted from Is 42:1–4, to demonstrate that (contrary to the typical first-century rabbinical expectations) the Messiah would not arrive with political agendas, military campaigns, and great fanfare, but with gentleness and meekness—declaring righteousness even "to the Gentiles."

12:19 not quarrel, nor cry out. The Messiah would not try to stir up a revolution or force His way into power.

12:20 battered reed … smoldering wick. The reed was used by shepherds to fashion a small musical instrument. Once cracked or worn, it was useless. A smoldering wick was also useless for giving light. These represent people who are deemed useless by the world. Christ's work was to restore and rekindle such people, not to "break" them. This speaks of His tender compassion toward the lowliest of the lost. He came not to gather the strong for a revolution, but to show mercy to the weak. Cf. 1Co 1:26–29.

12:23 Son of David. *See note on 1:1.*

12:24 Beelzebul. *See note on 10:25.* After all the displays of Jesus' deity, the Pharisees declared that He was from Satan—exactly opposite the truth, and they knew it (*see note on v. 31*; cf. 9:34; Mk 3:22; Lk 11:15).

not stand. 26 If [A]Satan casts out Satan, he [a]is divided
against himself; how then will his kingdom stand?
27 If I [A]by [a]Beelzebul cast out demons, [B]by whom do
your sons cast *them* out? For this reason they will be
your judges. 28 But [A]if I cast out demons by the Spirit
of God, then the kingdom of God has come upon you.
29 Or how can anyone enter the strong man's house
and carry off his property, unless he first binds the
strong *man?* And then he will plunder his house.

THE UNPARDONABLE SIN

30 [A]He who is not with Me is against Me; and he
who does not gather with Me scatters.
31 "[A]Therefore I say to you, any sin and blasphemy
shall be forgiven people, but blasphemy against the
Spirit shall not be forgiven. 32 [A]Whoever [a]speaks a word
against the Son of Man, it shall be forgiven him; but
whoever [a]speaks against the Holy Spirit, it shall not be
forgiven him, either in [B]this age or in the *age* to come.

WORDS REVEAL CHARACTER

33 "Either make the tree good and its fruit good,
or make the tree bad and its fruit bad; for [A]the tree
is known by its fruit. 34 [A]You brood of vipers, how
can you, being evil, speak [a]what is good? [B]For the
mouth speaks out of that which fills the heart.
35 [A]The good man brings out of *his* good treasure
[a]what is good; and the evil man brings out of *his*
evil treasure [b]what is evil. 36 But I tell you that every
[a]careless word that people [b]speak, they shall give
an accounting for it in [A]the day of judgment. 37 For
[a]by your words you will be justified, and [a]by your
words you will be condemned."

THE DESIRE FOR SIGNS

38 Then some of the scribes and Pharisees said to
Him, "Teacher, [A]we want to see a [a]sign from You."
39 But He answered and said to them, "[A]An evil and
adulterous generation craves for a [a]sign; and *yet* no
[a]sign will be given to it but the [a]sign of Jonah the
prophet; 40 for just as [A]JONAH WAS THREE DAYS AND
THREE NIGHTS IN THE BELLY OF THE SEA MONSTER, so
will [B]the Son of Man be [C]three days and three nights
in the heart of the earth. 41 [A]The men of Nineveh
will stand up with this generation at the judgment,
and will condemn it because [B]they repented at the
preaching of Jonah; and behold, [C]something greater
than Jonah is here. 42 [A]*The* Queen of *the* South will
rise up with this generation at the judgment and
will condemn it, because she came from the ends
of the earth to hear the wisdom of Solomon; and
behold, [B]something greater than Solomon is here.
43 "[A]Now when the unclean spirit goes out of a
man, it passes through waterless places seeking
rest, and does not find *it.* 44 Then it says, 'I will return to my house from which I came'; and when
it comes, it finds *it* unoccupied, swept, and put in
order. 45 Then it goes and takes along with it seven
other spirits more wicked than itself, and they go
in and live there; and [A]the last state of that man

12:26 [a]Lit *was* [A]Matt 4:10; 13:19 12:27 [a]V 24, note 1 [A]Matt 9:34 [B]Acts 19:13 12:28 [A]1 John 3:8 12:30 [A]Mark 9:40; Luke 9:50; 11:23 12:31 [A]Matt 12:31, 32: *Mark 3:28-30;* Luke 12:10 12:32 [a]Lit *will speak* [A]Luke 12:10 [B]Matt 13:22, 39; Mark 10:30; Luke 16:8; 18:30; 20:34, 35; Eph 1:21; 1 Tim 6:17; 2 Tim 4:10; Titus 2:12; Heb 6:5 12:33 [A]Matt 7:16-18; Luke 6:43, 44; John 15:4-7 12:34 [a]Lit *good things* [A]Matt 3:7; 23:33; Luke 3:7 [B]1 Sam 24:13; Is 32:6; Matt 12:34, 35: *Luke 6:45;* Matt 15:18; Eph 4:29; James 3:2-12 12:35 [a]Lit *good things* [b]Lit *evil things* [A]Prov 10:20, 21; 25:11, 12; Matt 13:52; Col 4:6 12:36 [a]Or *useless* [b]Lit *will speak* [A]Matt 10:15 12:37 [a]Or *in accordance with* 12:38 [a]I.e. attesting miracle [A]Matt 16:1; Mark 8:11, 12; Luke 11:16; John 2:18; 6:30; 1 Cor 1:22 12:39 [a]I.e. attesting miracle [A]Matt 12:39-42: *Luke 11:29-32;* Matt 16:4 12:40 [A]Jon 1:17 [B]Matt 8:20 [C]Matt 16:21 12:41 [A]Jon 1:2 [B]Jon 3:5 [C]Matt 12:6, 42 12:42 [A]1 Kin 10:1; 2 Chr 9:1 [B]Matt 12:6, 41 12:43 [A]Matt 12:43-45: *Luke 11:24-26* 12:45 [A]Mark 5:9; Luke 11:26; Heb 6:4-8; 2 Pet 2:20

12:28 kingdom of God has come. That was precisely true. The King was in their midst, displaying His sovereign power. He showed it by demonstrating His ability to bind Satan and his demons (v. 29).

12:31 blasphemy against the Spirit. The sin He was confronting was the Pharisees' deliberate rejection of that which they knew to be of God (cf. Jn 11:48; Ac 4:16). They could not deny the reality of what the Holy Spirit had done through Him, so they attributed to Satan a work that they knew was of God (v. 24; Mk 3:22).

12:32 it shall be forgiven him. Someone never exposed to Christ's divine power and presence might reject Him in ignorance and be forgiven—assuming the unbelief gives way to genuine repentance. Even a Pharisee such as Saul of Tarsus could be forgiven for speaking against Jesus or persecuting His followers—because his unbelief stemmed from ignorance (1Ti 1:13). But those who know His claims are true and reject Him anyway sin "against the Holy Spirit"—because it is the Holy Spirit who testifies of Christ and makes His truth known to us (Jn 15:26; 16:14, 15). No forgiveness was possible for these Pharisees who witnessed His miracles firsthand, knew the truth of His claims, and still blasphemed the Holy Spirit—because they had already rejected the fullest possible revelation. *See notes on Heb 6:4–6; 10:29.*

12:36 every careless word. The most seemingly insignificant sin—even a slip of the tongue—carries the full potential of all hell's evil (cf. Jas 3:6). No infraction against God's holiness is therefore a trifling thing, and each person will ultimately give account of every such indiscretion. There is no truer indication of a bad tree than the bad fruit of speech (vv. 33, 35). The poisonous snakes were known by their poisonous mouths revealing evil hearts (v. 34; cf. Lk 6:45). Every person is judged by his words, because they reveal the state of his heart.

12:38 we want to see a sign from You. They were hoping for a sign of astronomical proportions (Lk 11:16). Instead, He gives them a "sign" from Scripture. *See notes on 16:1; 21:21.*

12:39 An evil and adulterous generation. This speaks of spiritual adultery—unfaithfulness to God (cf. Jer 5:7, 8).

12:40 three days and three nights. Quoted from Jon 1:17. This sort of expression was a common way of underscoring the prophetic significance of a period of time. An expression like "forty days and forty nights" (*see note on 4:2*) may in some cases simply refer to a period of time longer than a month. "Three days and three nights" was an emphatic way of saying "three days," and by Jewish reckoning this would be an apt way of expressing a period of time that includes parts of 3 days. Thus, if Christ was crucified on a Friday, and His resurrection occurred on the first day of the week, by Hebrew reckoning this would qualify as 3 days and 3 nights. All sorts of elaborate schemes have been devised to suggest that Christ might have died on a Wednesday or Thursday, just to accommodate the extreme literal meaning of these words. But the original meaning would not have required that sort of wooden interpretation. *See note on Lk 13:32.*

12:41 men of Nineveh ... repented. *See Jon 3:5–10.* The revival in Nineveh under Jonah's preaching was one of the most extraordinary spiritual revivals the world has ever seen. Some have suggested that the repentance of the Ninevites stopped short of saving faith, because the city reverted within one generation to its old pagan ways (cf. Na 3:7, 8). From Jesus' words here, however, it is clear that the revival under Jonah represented authentic saving conversions. Only eternity will reveal how many souls from that one generation were swept into the kingdom as a result of the revival.

12:42 Queen of *the* South. See 1Ki 10:1–13. The queen of Sheba came to see Solomon's glory (*see note on 6:29*) and in the process encountered the glory of Solomon's God (1Ki 10:9).

12:45 the last state of that man becomes worse than the first. The problem is that the evil spirit found the house "unoccupied" (v. 44). This is the description of someone who attempts moral reform without ever being indwelt by the Holy Spirit. Reform apart from regeneration is never effective and eventually reverts back to prereform behavior.

becomes worse than the first. That is the way it will
also be with this evil generation."

CHANGED RELATIONSHIPS

46 [A]While He was still speaking to the crowds,
behold, His [B]mother and [C]brothers were standing
outside, seeking to speak to Him. 47 Someone said
to Him, "Behold, Your mother and Your brothers are
standing outside seeking to speak to You."[a] 48 But
[a]Jesus answered the one who was telling Him and
said, "Who is My mother and who are My brothers?"
49 And stretching out His hand toward His disciples,
He said, "Behold My mother and My brothers! 50 For
whoever does the will of My Father who is in heaven,
he is My brother and sister and mother."

JESUS TEACHES IN PARABLES

13 That day Jesus went out of [A]the house and was
sitting [B]by the sea. 2 And [a]large crowds gathered to Him, so [A]He got into a boat and sat down,
and the whole crowd was standing on the beach.
3 And He spoke many things to them in [A]parables,
saying, "Behold, the sower went out to sow; 4 and
as he sowed, some *seeds* fell beside the road, and
the birds came and ate them up. 5 Others fell on the
rocky places, where they did not have much soil;
and immediately they sprang up, because they had
no depth of soil. 6 But when the sun had risen, they
were scorched; and because they had no root, they
withered away. 7 Others fell [a]among the thorns, and
the thorns came up and choked them out. 8 And others fell on the good soil and *yielded a crop, some
a [A]hundredfold, some sixty, and some thirty. 9 [A]He
who has ears, [a]let him hear."

AN EXPLANATION

10 And the disciples came and said to Him, "Why
do You speak to them in parables?" 11 [a]Jesus answered them, "[A]To you it has been granted to know
the mysteries of the kingdom of heaven, but to them
it has not been granted. 12 [A]For whoever has, to him
more shall be given, and he will have an abundance;
but whoever does not have, even what he has shall
be taken away from him. 13 Therefore I speak to
them in parables; because while [A]seeing they do
not see, and while hearing they do not hear, nor
do they understand. 14 [a]In their case the prophecy
of Isaiah is being fulfilled, which says,

'[b,A]YOU WILL KEEP ON HEARING, [c]BUT
WILL NOT UNDERSTAND;
[d]YOU WILL KEEP ON SEEING, BUT
WILL NOT PERCEIVE;
15 [A]FOR THE HEART OF THIS PEOPLE
HAS BECOME DULL,
WITH THEIR EARS THEY SCARCELY HEAR,
AND THEY HAVE CLOSED THEIR EYES,
OTHERWISE THEY WOULD SEE
WITH THEIR EYES,
HEAR WITH THEIR EARS,
AND UNDERSTAND WITH THEIR
HEART AND RETURN,
AND I WOULD HEAL THEM.'

16 [A]But blessed are your eyes, because they see; and
your ears, because they hear. 17 For truly I say to you
that [A]many prophets and righteous men desired
to see what you see, and did not see *it*, and to hear
what you hear, and did not hear *it*.

12:46 [A]Matt 12:46-50: *Mark 3:31-35; Luke 8:19-21* [B]Matt 1:18; 2:11ff; 13:55; Luke 1:43; 2:33f, 48, 51; John 2:1, 5, 12; 19:25f; Acts 1:14 [C]Matt 13:55; Mark 6:3; John 2:12; 7:3, 5, 10; Acts 1:14; 1 Cor 9:5; Gal 1:19 12:47 [a]This verse is not found in early mss 12:48 [a]Lit *He* 13:1 [A]Matt 9:28; 13:36 [B]Matt 13:1-15: *Mark 4:1-12; Luke 8:4-10;* Mark 2:13 13:2 [a]Lit *Many* [A]Luke 5:3 13:3 [A]Matt 13:10ff; Mark 4:2ff 13:7 [a]Lit *upon* 13:8 [A]Gen 26:12; Matt 13:23 13:9 [a]Or *hear! Or listen!* [A]Matt 11:15; Rev 2:7, 11, 17, 29; 3:6, 13, 22 13:11 [a]Lit *He* [A]Matt 19:11; 20:23; John 6:65; 1 Cor 2:10; Col 1:27; 1 John 2:20, 27 13:12 [A]Matt 25:29; Mark 4:25; Luke 8:18; 19:26 13:13 [A]Deut 29:4; Is 42:19, 20; Jer 5:21; Ezek 12:2 13:14 [a]Lit *For them* [b]Lit *With a hearing you will hear* [c]Lit *and* [d]Lit *Seeing you will see* [A]Is 6:9; Mark 4:12; Luke 8:10; John 12:40; Acts 28:26, 27; Rom 10:16; 11:8 13:15 [A]Is 6:10; Ps 119:70; Zech 7:11; Luke 19:42; John 8:43, 44; 2 Tim 4:4; Heb 5:11 13:16 [A]Matt 13:16, 17: *Luke 10:23, 24;* Matt 16:17; John 20:29 13:17 [A]John 8:56; Heb 11:13; 1 Pet 1:10-12

12:46 brothers. These are actual siblings (half-brothers) of Jesus. Matthew explicitly connects them with Mary, indicating that they were not cousins or Joseph's sons from a previous marriage, as some of the church fathers imagined. They are mentioned in all the Gospels (Mk 3:31; Lk 8:19–21; Jn 7:3–5). Matthew and Mark give the names of 4 of Jesus' brothers, and mention that He had sisters as well (13:55; Mk 6:3).

12:48, 49 Jesus was not repudiating His earthly family (cf. Jn 19:26, 27). Rather, He was emphasizing the supremacy and eternality of spiritual relationships (cf. 10:37). After all, even His own family needed Him as Savior (cf. Jn 7:5).

12:50 does the will of My Father. This is not salvation by works. Doing the will of God is the evidence of salvation by grace. *See notes on 7:21–27.*

13:1–52 This is the third of 5 discourses featured in Matthew (see Introduction: Historical and Theological Themes).

13:3 parables. Parables were a common form of teaching in Judaism. The Gr. term for "parable" appears 45 times in the LXX. A parable is a long analogy, often cast in the form of a story. Before this point in His ministry, Jesus had employed many graphic analogies (cf. 5:13–16), but their meaning was fairly clear in the context of His teaching. Parables required more explanation (cf. v. 36) and Jesus employed them to obscure the truth from unbelievers while making it clearer to His disciples (vv. 11, 12). For the remainder of His Galilean ministry, He did not speak to the multitudes except in parables (v. 34). Jesus' veiling the truth from unbelievers this way was both an act of judgment and an act of mercy. It was "judgment" because it kept them in the darkness that they loved (cf. Jn 3:19), but it was "mercy" because they had already rejected the light, so any exposure to more truth would only increase their condemnation. *See note on v. 13.*

13:4 beside the road. The fields were bordered by paths beaten hard by foot traffic and baking sun.

13:5 rocky places. Very shallow soil atop a layer of bedrock. From the top it looks fertile, but there is no depth to sustain a root system or reach water (v. 21).

13:7 thorns. Weeds, the roots of which were still in the ground after plowing had been done.

13:11 To you it has been granted. Here Jesus clearly affirms that the ability to comprehend spiritual truth is a gracious gift of God, sovereignly bestowed on the elect (v. 11). The reprobate ones, on the other hand, are passed over. They reap the natural consequence of their own unbelief and rebellion—spiritual blindness (v. 13). **the mysteries of the kingdom of heaven.** "Mysteries" are those truths which have been hidden from all ages in the past and revealed in the NT. *See notes on 1Co 2:7; 4:1; Eph 3:4, 5.* Many specific doctrines of the NT are identified as "mysteries" (e.g., Ro 11:25; 1Co 15:51; Eph 5:32; 6:19; Col 1:26, 27; 2Th 2:7; 1Ti 3:9, 16).

13:13 because while seeing they do not see. Here Matthew seems to suggest that their own unbelief is the cause of their spiritual blindness. Luke 8:10, however, emphasizes God's initiative in obscuring the truth from these unbelievers ("to the rest *it is* in parables, so that SEEING THEY MAY NOT SEE, AND HEARING THEY MAY NOT UNDERSTAND"—cf. Is 6:9). Both things are true, of course. Yet we are not to think that God blinds them because He somehow delights in their destruction (cf. Eze 33:11; *see note on 23:37*). This judicial blinding may be viewed as an act of mercy, lest their condemnation be increased (*see note on v. 3*).

13:14, 15 Quoted from Is 6:9, 10 (*see notes there*).

13:17 many ... desired to see. Cf. Jn 8:56; 1Pe 1:9–12.

THE SOWER EXPLAINED

18 "[A]Hear then the parable of the sower. 19 When
anyone hears [A]the [a]word of the kingdom and does
not understand it, [B]the evil *one* comes and snatches
away what has been sown in his heart. This is the
one on whom seed was sown beside the road. 20 The
one on whom seed was sown on the rocky places,
this is the man who hears the word and immediately receives it with joy; 21 yet he has no *firm* root in
himself, but is *only* temporary, and when affliction
or persecution arises because of the [a]word, immediately he [b,A]falls away. 22 And the one on whom seed
was sown among the thorns, this is the man who
hears the word, and the worry of [A]the [a]world and
the [B]deceitfulness of wealth choke the word, and it
becomes unfruitful. 23 And the one on whom seed
was sown on the good soil, this is the man who
hears the word and understands it; who indeed
bears fruit and brings forth, some [A]a hundredfold,
some sixty, and some thirty."

TARES AMONG WHEAT

24 Jesus presented another parable to them, saying, "[A]The kingdom of heaven [a]may be compared
to a man who sowed good seed in his field. 25 But
while his men were sleeping, his enemy came and
sowed [a]tares among the wheat, and went away.
26 But when the [a]wheat sprouted and bore grain,
then the tares became evident also. 27 The slaves of
the landowner came and said to him, 'Sir, did you
not sow good seed in your field? [a]How then does it
have tares?' 28 And he said to them, 'An [a]enemy has
done this!' The slaves *said to him, 'Do you want us,
then, to go and gather them up?' 29 But he *said, 'No;
for while you are gathering up the tares, you may
uproot the wheat with them. 30 Allow both to grow
together until the harvest; and in the time of the
harvest I will say to the reapers, "First gather up
the tares and bind them in bundles to burn them
up; but [A]gather the wheat into my barn." ' "

THE MUSTARD SEED

31 He presented another parable to them, saying,
"[A]The kingdom of heaven is like [B]a mustard seed,
which a man took and sowed in his field; 32 and
this is smaller than all *other* seeds, but when it is
full grown, it is larger than the garden plants and
becomes a tree, so that [A]THE BIRDS OF THE [a]AIR come
and NEST IN ITS BRANCHES."

THE LEAVEN

33 He spoke another parable to them, "[A]The kingdom of heaven is like leaven, which a woman took
and hid in [B]three [a]pecks of flour until it was all
leavened."

34 All these things Jesus spoke to the crowds in
parables, and He did not speak to them [A]without
a parable. 35 *This was* to fulfill what was spoken
through the prophet:

"[A]I WILL OPEN MY MOUTH IN PARABLES;
I WILL UTTER THINGS HIDDEN SINCE
THE FOUNDATION OF THE WORLD."

THE TARES EXPLAINED

36 Then He left the crowds and went into [A]the
house. And His disciples came to Him and said,
"[B]Explain to us the parable of the [a]tares of the field."
37 And He said, "The one who sows the good seed is
[A]the Son of Man, 38 and the field is the world; and *as
for* the good seed, these are [A]the sons of the kingdom; and the tares are [B]the sons of [C]the evil *one;*
39 and the enemy who sowed them is the devil, and
the harvest is [A]the [a]end of the age; and the reapers
are angels. 40 So just as the tares are gathered up
and burned with fire, so shall it be at [A]the [a]end of the

13:18 [A]Matt 13:18-23: *Mark 4:13-20; Luke 8:11-15* 13:19 [a]I.e. message [A]Matt 4:23 [B]Matt 5:37 13:21 [a]I.e. message [b]Lit *is caused to stumble* [A]Matt 11:6 13:22 [a]Or *age* [A]Matt 12:32; 13:39; Mark 4:19; Rom 12:2; 1 Cor 1:20; 2:6, 8; 3:18; 2 Cor 4:4; Gal 1:4; Eph 2:2 [B]Matt 19:23; 1 Tim 6:9, 10, 17 13:23 [A]Matt 13:8 13:24 [a]Lit *was compared to* [A]Matt 13:31, 33, 45, 47; 18:23; 20:1; 22:2; 25:1; Mark 4:26-30; Luke 13:18, 20 13:25 [a]Or *darnel*, a weed resembling wheat 13:26 [a]Lit *grass* 13:27 [a]Lit *From where* 13:28 [a]Lit *enemy man* 13:30 [A]Matt 3:12 13:31 [A]Matt 13:31, 32: *Mark 4:30-32; Luke 13:18, 19;* Matt 13:24 [B]Matt 17:20; Luke 17:6 13:32 [a]Or *sky* [A]Ezek 17:23; Ps 104:12; Ezek 31:6; Dan 4:12 13:33 [a]Gr *sata* [A]Matt 13:33: *Luke 13:21;* Matt 13:24 [B]Gen 18:6; Judg 6:19; 1 Sam 1:24 13:34 [A]Mark 4:34; John 10:6; 16:25 13:35 [A]Ps 78:2 13:36 [a]Or *darnel*, a weed resembling wheat [A]Matt 13:1 [B]Matt 15:15 13:37 [A]Matt 8:20 13:38 [A]Matt 8:12 [B]John 8:44; Acts 13:10; 1 John 3:10 [C]Matt 5:37 13:39 [a]Or *consummation* [A]Matt 12:32; 13:22, 40, 49; 24:3; 28:20; 1 Cor 10:11; Heb 9:26 13:40 [a]Or *consummation* [A]Matt 12:32; 13:22, 39, 49; 24:3; 28:20; 1 Cor 10:11; Heb 9:26

13:19 word of the kingdom. The message of how to enter God's kingdom, the sphere of salvation, i.e., the gospel (cf. "word of reconciliation" in 2Co 5:19). **evil *one*.** Satan. Cf. 1Jn 5:19. The gospel never penetrates these souls, so it disappears from the surface of their understanding—seen as the enemy snatching it away.

13:20 rocky places. Some people make an emotional, superficial commitment to salvation in Christ, but it is not real. They remain interested only until there is a sacrificial price to pay, and then abandon Christ. *See note on 1Jn 2:19.*

13:22 seed was sown among the thorns. These people make superficial commitments without a true repentance. They can't break with the love of money and the world (Jas 4:4; 1Jn 2:15–17; *see notes on 19:16–21*).

13:23 the good soil. As there were 3 soils with no fruit, thus no salvation, there are 3 kinds of good soil with fruit. Not all believers are equally fruitful, but all are fruitful (cf. 7:16; Jn 15:8).

13:25 tares. Probably darnel, a type of weed that can hardly be distinguished from wheat until the head matures. In an agricultural setting, sowing darnel in someone else's wheat field was a way for enemies to destroy someone's livelihood catastrophically. It pictures Satan's efforts to deceive the church by mingling his children with God's, in some cases making it impossible for believers to discern the true from the false. The parable is explained in vv. 36–43.

13:32 a tree, so that the birds of the air **come and** nest in its branches. Palestinian mustard plants are large shrubs, sometimes up to 15 ft. high—certainly large enough for birds to lodge in. This is undoubtedly a reference to several OT passages, including Eze 17:23; 31:6; Da 4:21—passages which prophesied the inclusion of Gentiles in the kingdom.

13:33 The kingdom of heaven is like leaven. Here the kingdom is pictured as yeast, multiplying quietly and permeating all that it contacts. The lesson is the same as the parable of the mustard seed. Some interpreters suggest that since leaven is nearly always a symbol of evil in Scripture (*see note on Mk 8:15*), it must carry that connotation here as well. They make the leaven some evil influence inside the kingdom. But that twists Jesus' actual words and violates the context, in which Jesus is repeatedly describing that kingdom itself as the pervading influence.

13:34 He did not speak to them without a parable. For the rest of His Galilean ministry, all Jesus' public teaching consisted only of parables.

13:35 spoken through the prophet. The "prophet" in this case was the psalmist. See Ps 78:2.

13:37 The one who sows. The true sower of salvation seed is the Lord Himself. He alone can give the power in the heart to transform. He is the One who saves sinners, even through the preaching and witnessing of believers (Ro 10:14).

age. 41 [A]The Son of Man [B]will send forth His angels,
and they will gather out of His kingdom [a]all [C]stum-
bling blocks, and those who commit lawlessness,
42 and [A]will throw them into the furnace of fire; in
that place [B]there will be weeping and gnashing of
teeth. 43 [A]Then THE RIGHTEOUS WILL SHINE FORTH AS
THE SUN in the kingdom of their Father. [B]He who
has ears, [a]let him hear.

HIDDEN TREASURE

44 "[A]The kingdom of heaven is like a treasure hidden in the field, which a man found and hid *again;*
and from joy over it he goes and [B]sells all that he
has and buys that field.

A COSTLY PEARL

45 "Again, [A]the kingdom of heaven is like a merchant seeking fine pearls, 46 and upon finding one
pearl of great value, he went and sold all that he
had and bought it.

A DRAGNET

47 "Again, [A]the kingdom of heaven is like a dragnet
cast into the sea, and gathering *fish* of every kind;
48 and when it was filled, they drew it up on the
beach; and they sat down and gathered the good
fish into containers, but the bad they threw away.
49 So it will be at [A]the [a]end of the age; the angels will
come forth and [b]take out the wicked from among
the righteous, 50 and [A]will throw them into the furnace of fire; in that place [B]there will be weeping and
gnashing of teeth.
51 "Have you understood all these things?" They
*said to Him, "Yes." 52 And [a]Jesus said to them,
"Therefore every scribe who has become a disciple of the kingdom of heaven is like a head of a
household, who brings out of his treasure things
new and old."

JESUS REVISITS NAZARETH

53 [A]When Jesus had finished these parables, He
departed from there. 54 [A]He came to [a]His hometown
and [B]*began* teaching them in their synagogue, so
that [C]they were astonished, and said, "Where *did*
this man *get* this wisdom and *these* [b]miraculous
powers? 55 Is not this the carpenter's son? Is not
[A]His mother called Mary, and His [A]brothers, James
and Joseph and Simon and Judas? 56 And [A]His sisters, are they not all with us? Where then *did* this
man *get* all these things?" 57 And they took [A]offense
at Him. But Jesus said to them, "[B]A prophet is not
without honor except in his [a]hometown and in his
own household." 58 And He did not do many [a]mir-
acles there because of their unbelief.

JOHN THE BAPTIST BEHEADED

14 [A]At that [a]time [B]Herod the tetrarch heard the
news about Jesus, 2 and said to his servants,
"[A]This is John the Baptist; [a]he has risen from the
dead, and that is why miraculous powers are at
work in him."
3 For when [A]Herod had John arrested, he bound
him and put him [B]in prison because of [C]Herodias,
the wife of his brother Philip. 4 For John had been
saying to him, "[A]It is not lawful for you to have her."
5 Although Herod wanted to put him to death, he
feared the crowd, because they regarded [a]John as
[A]a prophet.
6 But when Herod's birthday came, the daughter of [A]Herodias danced [a]before *them* and pleased
[B]Herod, 7 so *much* that he promised with an oath
to give her whatever she asked. 8 Having been

13:41 [a]Or *everything that is offensive* [A]Matt 8:20 [B]Matt 24:31 [C]Zeph 1:3 13:42 [A]Matt 13:50 [B]Matt 8:12 13:43 [a]Or *hear!* Or *listen!* [A]Dan 12:3 [B]Matt 11:15 13:44 [A]Matt 13:24 [B]Matt 13:46 13:45 [A]Matt 13:24 13:47 [A]Matt 13:44 13:49 [a]Or *consummation* [b]Or *separate* [A]Matt 13:39, 40 13:50 [A]Matt 13:42 [B]Matt 8:12 13:52 [a]Lit *He* 13:53 [A]Matt 7:28 13:54 [a]Or *His own part of the country* [b]Or *miracles* [A]Matt 13:54-58: *Mark 6:1-6* [B]Matt 4:23 [C]Matt 7:28 13:55 [A]Matt 12:46 13:56 [A]Mark 6:3 13:57 [a]Or *own part of the country* [A]Matt 11:6 [B]Mark 6:4; Luke 4:24; John 4:44 13:58 [a]Or *works of power* 14:1 [a]Or *occasion* [A]Matt 14:1-12: *Mark 6:14-29;* Matt 14:1, 2: *Luke 9:7-9* [B]Mark 8:15; Luke 3:1, 19; 8:3; 13:31; 23:7f, 11f, 15; Acts 4:27; 12:1 14:2 [a]Or *he, himself* [A]Matt 16:14; Mark 6:14; Luke 9:7 14:3 [A]Matt 14:1-12: *Mark 6:14-29;* Mark 8:15; Luke 3:1, 19; 8:3; 13:31; 23:7f, 11f, 15; Acts 4:27; 12:1 [B]Matt 4:12; 11:2 [C]Matt 14:6; Mark 6:17, 19, 22; Luke 3:19f 14:4 [A]Lev 18:16; 20:21 14:5 [a]Lit *him* [A]Matt 11:9 14:6 [a]Lit *in the midst* [A]Matt 14:3; Mark 6:17, 19, 22; Luke 3:19 [B]Matt 14:1-12: *Mark 6:14-29;* Mark 8:15; Luke 3:1, 19; 8:3; 13:31; 23:7f, 11f, 15; Acts 4:27; 12:1

13:43 shine forth as the sun. Cf. Da 12:3. Believers already shine in that they possess the Spirit of Christ and the glorious message of the gospel (5:16; 2Co 4:3–7). We will shine even more in the glory of Christ's kingdom and eternal heaven (Ro 8:16–23; Php 3:20, 21; Rev 19:7–9).

13:44–46 These two parables have identical meanings. Both picture salvation as something hidden from most people (*see note on v. 11*), but so valuable that people who have it revealed to them are willing to give up all they have to possess it.

13:47 dragnet. Some fishing was done with a large weighted net dragged along the bottom of the lake. When pulled in, it contained an assortment that had to be separated. In a similar way the visible kingdom, the sphere of those who claim to be believers, is full of both good and bad and will be sorted in the judgment.

13:49 angels. They serve God in judgment (cf. v. 41; 2Th 1:7–10).

13:52 brings out of his treasure things new and old. The disciples were not to spurn the old for the sake of the new. Rather, the new insights they gleaned from Jesus' parables were to be understood in light of the old truths, and vice versa.

13:54 His hometown. I.e., Nazareth.

13:55 His brothers. *See note on 12:46.* The fact that Joseph does not actually appear in any of these accounts suggests that he was no longer living.

13:57 A prophet … without honor … in his hometown. This is an ancient proverb paralleling the modern saying, "familiarity breeds contempt." They knew Jesus too well as a boy and a young man from their own town—and they concluded that He was nothing special. Verse 58 gives the sad result (cf. Mk 6:4).

13:58 He did not do many miracles there. *See note on Mk 6:5.*

14:1–12 The record of the murder of John the Baptist is also in Mk 6:14–29; cf. Lk 9:7–9.

14:1 Herod. *See note on 2:22.* This was Herod Antipas, ruler of Galilee. **tetrarch.** One of 4 rulers of a divided region. After the death of Herod the Great, Israel had been divided among his sons. Elsewhere, Matthew refers to Herod as "king" (v. 9), because that was the title by which he was known among the Galileans.

14:3 Herodias, the wife of his brother Philip. Herodias was the daughter of Aristobulus, another son of Herod the Great; so when she married Philip, she was marrying her own father's brother. What precipitated the arrest of John the Baptist was that Herod Antipas (another of Herodias' uncles) talked Herodias into leaving her husband (his brother) in order to marry him (Mk 6:17)—thus compounding the incest, as well as violating Lv 18:16. John was outraged that a ruler in Israel would commit such a sin openly, so he rebuked Herod severely (v. 4). For this, he was imprisoned and later killed (Mk 6:14–29).

14:6 the daughter of Herodias. Salome, daughter of Herodias and Philip. According to Josephus, the Jewish historian, she married yet another son (her own father's brother and her mother's uncle) of Herod the Great, thus further tangling the web of incest in that family.

14:8 prompted by her mother. *See note on v. 6.*

prompted by her mother, she *said, "Give me here
on a platter the head of John the Baptist." 9 Although
he was grieved, the king commanded *it* to be given
because of his oaths, and because of [a]his dinner
guests. 10 He sent and had John beheaded in the
prison. 11 And his head was brought on a platter and
given to the girl, and she brought it to her mother.
12 His disciples came and took away the body and
buried [a]it; and they went and reported to Jesus.

FIVE THOUSAND FED

13 [A]Now when Jesus heard *about John,* He withdrew from there in a boat to a secluded place by
Himself; and when the [a]people heard *of this,* they
followed Him on foot from the cities. 14 When He
went [a]ashore, He [A]saw a large crowd, and felt compassion for them and [B]healed their sick.
15 When it was evening, the disciples came to
Him and said, "This place is desolate and the hour
is already [a]late; so send the crowds away, that they
may go into the villages and buy food for themselves." 16 But Jesus said to them, "They do not need
to go away; you give them *something* to eat!" 17 They
*said to Him, "We have here only [A]five loaves and
two fish." 18 And He said, "Bring them here to Me."
19 Ordering the [a]people to [b]sit down on the grass, He
took the five loaves and the two fish, and looking up
toward heaven, He [A]blessed *the food,* and breaking
the loaves He gave them to the disciples, and the
disciples *gave them* to the crowds, 20 and they all
ate and were satisfied. They picked up what was
left over of the broken pieces, twelve full [A]baskets.
21 There were about five thousand men who ate,
besides women and children.

JESUS WALKS ON THE WATER

22 [A]Immediately He [a]made the disciples get into
the boat and go ahead of Him to the other side, while
He sent the crowds away. 23 After He had sent the
crowds away, [A]He went up on the mountain by Himself to pray; and when it was evening, He was there
alone. 24 But the boat was already [a]a long distance
from the land, [b]battered by the waves; for the wind
was [c,A]contrary. 25 And in [A]the [a]fourth watch of the
night He came to them, walking on the sea. 26 When
the disciples saw Him walking on the sea, they were
terrified, and said, "It is [A]a ghost!" And they cried
out [a]in fear. 27 But immediately Jesus spoke to them,
saying, "[A]Take courage, it is I; [B]do not be afraid."
28 Peter said to Him, "Lord, if it is You, command
me to come to You on the water." 29 And He said,
"Come!" And Peter got out of the boat, and walked
on the water and came toward Jesus. 30 But seeing
the wind, he became frightened, and beginning to
sink, he cried out, "Lord, save me!" 31 Immediately
Jesus stretched out His hand and took hold of him,
and *said to him, "[A]You of little faith, why did you
doubt?" 32 When they got into the boat, the wind
stopped. 33 And those who were in the boat worshiped Him, saying, "You are certainly [A]God's Son!"
34 [A]When they had crossed over, they came to
land at [B]Gennesaret. 35 And when the men of that
place [a]recognized Him, they sent *word* into all that
surrounding district and brought to Him all who
were sick; 36 and they implored Him that they might
just touch [A]the fringe of His cloak; and as many as
[B]touched *it* were cured.

TRADITION AND COMMANDMENT

15 [A]Then some Pharisees and scribes *came to
Jesus [B]from Jerusalem and said, 2 "Why do
Your disciples break the tradition of the elders?
For they [A]do not wash their hands when they eat
bread." 3 And He answered and said to them, "Why
do you yourselves transgress the commandment of
God for the sake of your tradition? 4 For God said,
'[A]HONOR YOUR FATHER AND MOTHER,' and, '[B]HE WHO
SPEAKS EVIL OF FATHER OR MOTHER IS TO [a]BE PUT TO
DEATH.' 5 But you say, 'Whoever says to *his* father or
mother, "Whatever I have that would help you has
been [a]given *to God,*" 6 he is not to honor his father or
his mother[a].' And *by this* you invalidated the word of
God for the sake of your tradition. 7 You hypocrites,
rightly did Isaiah prophesy of you:

14:9 [a]Lit *those who reclined* at the table *with him* 14:12 [a]Lit *him* 14:13 [a]Lit *the crowds* [A]Matt 14:13-21: *Mark 6:32-44; Luke 9:10-17; John 6:1-13;* Matt 15:32-38 14:14 [a]Lit *out* [A]Matt 9:36 [B]Matt 4:23 14:15 [a]Lit *past* 14:17 [A]Matt 16:9 14:19 [a]Lit *crowds* [b]Lit *recline* [A]1 Sam 9:13; Matt 15:36; 26:26; Mark 6:41; 8:7; 14:22; Luke 24:30; Acts 27:35; Rom 14:6 14:20 [A]Matt 16:9; Mark 6:43; 8:19; Luke 9:17; John 6:13 14:22 [a]Lit *compelled* [A]Matt 14:22-33: *Mark 6:45-51; John 6:15-21* 14:23 [A]Mark 6:46; Luke 6:12; 9:28; John 6:15 14:24 [a]Lit *many stadia from;* a stadion was about 600 feet or about 182 meters [b]Lit *tormented* [c]Or *adverse* [A]Acts 27:4 14:25 [a]I.e. 3-6 a.m. [A]Matt 24:43; Mark 13:35 14:26 [a]Lit *from* [A]Luke 24:37 14:27 [A]Matt 9:2 [B]Matt 17:7; 28:5, 10; Mark 6:50; Luke 1:13, 30; 2:10; 5:10; 12:32; John 6:20; Rev 1:17 14:31 [A]Matt 6:30; 8:26; 16:8 14:33 [A]Matt 4:3 14:34 [A]Matt 14:34-36: *Mark 6:53-56;* John 6:24, 25 [B]Mark 6:53; Luke 5:1 14:35 [a]Or *knew* 14:36 [A]Matt 9:20 [B]Matt 9:21; Mark 3:10; 6:56; 8:22; Luke 6:19 15:1 [A]Matt 15:1-20: *Mark 7:1-23* [B]Mark 3:22; 7:1; John 1:19; Acts 25:7 15:2 [A]Luke 11:38 15:4 [a]Lit *die the death* [A]Ex 20:12; Deut 5:16 [B]Ex 21:17; Lev 20:9 15:5 [a]Lit *a gift;* i.e. an offering 15:6 [a]I.e. by supporting them with it

14:9 because of his oaths. A promise made with a certain oath was considered sacred and inviolable (*see note on 5:34*)—especially when made by a ruling monarch. Herod was widely known for his duplicity, so it was not honesty that he was concerned about, but rather the appearance of things. He did not want to be embarrassed in front of his dinner guests.

14:12 buried it. In a cave (Mk 6:29).

14:13 people . . . followed Him on foot. They traveled great distances over land to reach the secluded spot where He had come by boat.

14:14 felt compassion. *See note on 9:36.*

14:16 give them *something* to eat! Jesus knew they did not have enough food to feed the crowd. He wanted the disciples to state it plainly so the record would be clear that a miracle by His power occurred (vv. 17, 18). See 16:9, 10.

14:24 battered by the waves. *See notes on 8:24, 27.*

14:25 fourth watch. 3:00–6:00 a.m.

14:33 You are certainly God's Son! Cf. 27:43, 54.

14:34 Gennesaret. A town on the NW shore of the Sea of Galilee.

14:36 the fringe of His cloak. *See note on 9:20.*

15:2 tradition of the elders. This was a body of extrabiblical law that had existed only in oral form and only since the time of the Babylonian captivity. Later it was committed to writing in the *Mishna* near the end of the second century. The law of Moses contained no commandment about washing one's hands before eating—except for priests who were required to wash before eating holy offerings (Lv 22:6, 7).

15:3 transgress. The nature of this sin is identified in vv. 4–6 as dishonoring one's parents in a cleverly devised way. The commandments of God were clear (quoted from Ex 20:12; 21:17; Dt 5:16); but to circumvent them, some people claimed they could not financially assist their parents because they had dedicated a certain sum of money to God, who was greater than their parents. The rabbis had approved this exception to the commandments of Moses and thus in effect nullified God's law (v. 6).

15:6 invalidated the word of God . . . your tradition. *See note on Mk 7:13.*

8 '[A]THIS PEOPLE HONORS ME WITH THEIR LIPS,
BUT THEIR HEART IS FAR AWAY FROM ME.
9 'BUT IN VAIN DO THEY WORSHIP ME,
TEACHING AS [A]DOCTRINES THE
PRECEPTS OF MEN.' "

10 After Jesus called the crowd to Him, He said to
them, "Hear and understand. 11 [A]*It is* not what enters into the mouth *that* defiles the man, but what
proceeds out of the mouth, this defiles the man."
12 Then the disciples *came and *said to Him, "Do
You know that the Pharisees were [a]offended when
they heard this statement?" 13 But He answered and
said, "[A]Every plant which My heavenly Father did
not plant shall be uprooted. 14 Let them alone; [A]they
are blind guides [a]of the blind. And [B]if a blind man
guides a blind man, both will fall into a pit."

THE HEART OF MAN

15 Peter [a]said to Him, "[A]Explain the parable to us."
16 [a]Jesus said, "Are you still lacking in understanding
also? 17 Do you not understand that everything that
goes into the mouth passes into the stomach, and is
[a]eliminated? 18 But [A]the things that proceed out of the
mouth come from the heart, and those defile the man.
19 [A]For out of the heart come evil thoughts, murders,
adulteries, [a]fornications, thefts, false witness, slanders.
20 These are the things which defile the man; but to
eat with unwashed hands does not defile the man."

THE SYROPHOENICIAN WOMAN

21 [A]Jesus went away from there, and withdrew
into the district of [B]Tyre and [B]Sidon. 22 And a Canaanite woman from that region came out and *began* to
cry out, saying, "Have mercy on me, Lord, [A]Son of
David; my daughter is cruelly [B]demon-possessed."
23 But He did not answer her a word. And His disciples came and implored Him, saying, "Send her
away, because she keeps shouting [a]at us." 24 But
He answered and said, "I was sent only to [A]the lost
sheep of the house of Israel." 25 But she came and
[A]*began* [a]to bow down before Him, saying, "Lord,
help me!" 26 And He answered and said, "It is not
[a]good to take the children's bread and throw it to the
dogs." 27 But she said, "Yes, Lord; [a]but even the dogs
feed on the crumbs which fall from their masters'
table." 28 Then Jesus said to her, "O woman, [A]your
faith is great; it shall be done for you as you wish."
And her daughter was healed [a]at once.

HEALING CROWDS

29 [A]Departing from there, Jesus went along by [B]the
Sea of Galilee, and having gone up on the mountain,
He was sitting there. 30 And [a]large crowds came to
Him, bringing with them *those who were* lame, crippled, blind, mute, and many others, and they laid
them down at His feet; and [A]He healed them. 31 So
the crowd marveled as they saw the mute speaking,
the crippled [a]restored, and the lame walking, and the
blind seeing; and they [A]glorified the God of Israel.

FOUR THOUSAND FED

32 [A]And Jesus called His disciples to Him, and
said, "[B]I feel compassion for the [a]people, because
they [b]have remained with Me now three days and
have nothing to eat; and I do not want to send them
away hungry, for they might faint on the way." 33 The
disciples *said to Him, "Where would we get so
many loaves in *this* desolate place to satisfy such
a large crowd?" 34 And Jesus *said to them, "How
many loaves do you have?" And they said, "Seven,
and a few small fish." 35 And He directed the [a]people
to [b]sit down on the ground; 36 and He took the seven
loaves and the fish; and [A]giving thanks, He broke
them and started giving them to the disciples, and
the disciples *gave them* to the people. 37 And they all
ate and were satisfied, and they picked up what was
left over of the broken pieces, seven large [A]baskets
full. 38 And those who ate were four thousand men,
besides women and children.
39 And sending away the crowds, Jesus got into
[A]the boat and came to the region of [B]Magadan.

15:8 [A]Is 29:13 15:9 [A]Col 2:22 15:11 [A]Matt 15:18; Acts 10:14, 15; 1 Tim 4:3 15:12 [a]Lit *caused to stumble* 15:13 [A]Is 60:21; 61:3; John 15:2; 1 Cor 3:9 15:14 [a]Later mss add *of the blind* [A]Matt 23:16, 24 [B]Luke 6:39 15:15 [a]Lit *answered and said* [A]Matt 13:36 15:16 [a]Lit *and He* 15:17 [a]Lit *thrown out into the latrine* 15:18 [A]Matt 12:34; Mark 7:20 15:19 [a]I.e. sexual immorality [A]Gal 5:19ff 15:21 [A]Matt 15:21-28: *Mark 7:24-30* [B]Matt 11:21 15:22 [A]Matt 9:27 [B]Matt 4:24 15:23 [a]Lit *behind us* 15:24 [A]Matt 10:6 15:25 [a]Or *worshiped* [A]Matt 8:2 15:26 [a]Or *proper* 15:27 [a]Lit *for* 15:28 [a]Lit *from that hour* [A]Matt 9:22 15:29 [A]Matt 15:29-31: *Mark 7:31-37* [B]Matt 4:18 15:30 [a]Lit *many* [A]Matt 4:23 15:31 [a]Or *healthy* [A]Matt 9:8 15:32 [a]Lit *crowd* [b]Lit *are remaining* [A]Matt 15:32-39: *Mark 8:1-10;* Matt 14:13-21 [B]Matt 9:36 15:35 [a]Lit *crowd* [b]Lit *recline* 15:36 [A]Matt 14:19; 26:27; Luke 22:17, 19; John 6:11, 23; Acts 27:35; Rom 14:6 15:37 [A]Matt 16:10; Mark 8:8, 20; Acts 9:25 15:39 [A]Mark 3:9 [B]Mark 8:10

15:8, 9 Quoted from Is 29:13.

15:11 what proceeds out of the mouth … defiles the man. People might defile themselves ceremonially (under the Old Covenant) by eating something unclean, but they would defile themselves morally by saying something sinful (cf. Jas 3:6). Here Jesus clearly distinguished between the law's ceremonial requirements and its inviolable moral standard. Ceremonial defilement could be dealt with through ceremonial means. But moral defilement corrupts a person's soul.

15:14 Let them alone. This severe judgment is a form of God's wrath. It signifies abandonment by God and is described as "giving them over" in Ro 1:18–32 (*see notes there*). Cf. Hos 4:17.

15:15 the parable. I.e., v. 11. The "parable" is not at all hard to understand, but it was hard for even the disciples to accept. Years later, Peter still found it hard to accept that all foods are clean (Ac 10:14).

15:22 Son of David. *See note on 1:1.*

15:24 lost sheep of the house of Israel. *See note on 10:6.*

15:26 the children's bread. The lost sheep of the house of Israel must be fed before the "little dogs" (*see note on 10:5*). Christ employed a word here that speaks of a family pet. His words with this woman are not to be understood as harsh or unfeeling. In fact, He was tenderly drawing from her an expression of her faith in v. 27.

15:29 went along by the Sea of Galilee. He actually traveled N from Tyre to Sidon and then cut a wide path around the eastern shore of Galilee to Decapolis (Mk 7:31), a primarily Gentile region. He may have taken this route to avoid the territory ruled by Herod Antipas (cf. 14:1, 2). The events that follow must have occurred in Decapolis (*see note on 4:25*).

15:33 Where would we get so many loaves … ? No wonder our Lord called them men of little faith (8:26; 14:31; 16:8; 17:20), when they asked a question like that in the light of the recent feeding of the 5,000 (14:13–21).

15:34 *See note on 14:16.* Again the Lord had them confess for the record how little food they had in comparison to the size of the crowd. This made clear that the feeding was miraculous evidence of His deity.

15:38 four thousand. Christ ended His ministry in Galilee with the feeding of the 5,000 (14:13–21). Here, He ended His ministry in the Gentile regions by feeding the 4,000. He later would end His Jerusalem ministry with a meal in the upper room with His disciples.

PHARISEES TEST JESUS

16 [A]The [B]Pharisees and Sadducees came up, and
testing Jesus, they [C]asked Him to show them a
[a]sign from heaven. 2 But He replied to them, "[a,A]When
it is evening, you say, '*It will be* fair weather, for
the sky is red.' 3 And in the morning, '*There will be*
a storm today, for the sky is red and threatening.'
[A]Do you know how to discern the [a]appearance of
the sky, but cannot *discern* the signs of the times?
4 [A]An evil and adulterous generation seeks after a
[a]sign; and a [a]sign will not be given it, except the
sign of Jonah." And He left them and went away.
5 And the disciples came to the other side *of the*
sea, but they had forgotten to bring *any* bread. 6 And
Jesus said to them, "Watch out and [A]beware of the
[a]leaven of the [B]Pharisees and Sadducees." 7 They
began to discuss *this* among themselves, saying,
"*He said that* because we did not bring *any* bread."
8 But Jesus, aware of this, said, "[A]You men of little
faith, why do you discuss among yourselves that
you have no bread? 9 Do you not yet understand
or remember [A]the five loaves of the five thousand,
and how many baskets *full* you picked up? 10 Or [A]the
seven loaves of the four thousand, and how many
large baskets *full* you picked up? 11 How is it that
you do not understand that I did not speak to you
concerning bread? But [A]beware of the [a]leaven of the
[B]Pharisees and Sadducees." 12 Then they understood
that He did not say to beware of the leaven of bread,
but of the teaching of the [A]Pharisees and Sadducees.

PETER'S CONFESSION OF CHRIST

13 [A]Now when Jesus came into the district of [B]Caes-
area Philippi, He was asking His disciples, "Who do
people say that [C]the Son of Man is?" 14 And they said,
"Some *say* [A]John the Baptist; and others, [a,B]Elijah;
but still others, [b]Jeremiah, or one of the prophets."
15 He *said to them, "But who do you say that I am?"
16 Simon Peter answered, "You are [a,A]the Christ, [B]the
Son of [C]the living God." 17 And Jesus said to him,
"Blessed are you, [A]Simon [a]Barjona, because [B]flesh
and blood did not reveal *this* to you, but My Father

16:1 [a]Or *attesting miracle* [A]Matt 16:1-12: *Mark 8:11-21* [B]Matt 3:7; 16:6, 11, 12 [C]Matt 12:38; Luke 11:16 16:2 [a]Early mss do not contain the rest of v 2 and v 3 [A]Luke 12:54f 16:3 [a]Lit *face* [A]Luke 12:56 16:4 [a]Or *attesting miracle* [A]Matt 12:39; Luke 11:29 16:6 [a]Or *yeast* [A]Mark 8:15; Luke 12:1 [B]Matt 3:7 16:8 [A]Matt 6:30; 8:26; 14:31 16:9 [A]Matt 14:17-21 16:10 [A]Matt 15:34-38 16:11 [a]Or *yeast* [A]Matt 16:6; Mark 8:15; Luke 12:1 [B]Matt 3:7; 16:6, 12 16:12 [A]Matt 3:7; 5:20 16:13 [A]Matt 16:13-16: *Mark 8:27-29; Luke 9:18-20* [B]Mark 8:27 [C]Matt 8:20; 16:27, 28 16:14 [a]Gr *Elias* [b]Gr *Jeremias* [A]Matt 14:2 [B]Matt 17:10; Mark 6:15; Luke 9:8; John 1:21 16:16 [a]I.e. the Messiah [A]Matt 1:16; 16:20; John 11:27 [B]Matt 4:3 [C]Ps 42:2; Matt 26:63; Acts 14:15; Rom 9:26; 2 Cor 3:3; 6:16; 1 Thess 1:9; 1 Tim 3:15; 4:10; Heb 3:12; 9:14; 10:31; 12:22; Rev 7:2 16:17 [a]I.e. son of Jonah [A]John 1:42; 21:15-17 [B]1 Cor 15:50; Gal 1:16; Eph 6:12; Heb 2:14

16:1 a sign from heaven. *See note on 12:38.* This time Jesus rebuked them for being so concerned with heavenly signs that they could not even interpret the signs of the times all around them. Then He referred them to the same sign He gave them before, the sign of the prophet Jonah (v. 4; cf. 12:39).

16:2, 3 As primitive as their method of predicting the weather was, their ability to discern spiritual matters was worse. They had the long-promised and long-awaited Messiah in their midst and refused to acknowledge Him.

16:6 the leaven of the Pharisees and Sadducees. When Jesus warned of this dangerous influence, the disciples thought He was talking about bread. Again, He reminded them of the fact that the Lord provided plenty of bread, so they didn't need the bread the Pharisees were offering. How soon they forgot the miracles. *See note on 13:33.*

16:12 the teaching of the Pharisees and Sadducees. Here the leaven of the Pharisees is their "teaching." In Lk 12:1 it is their "hypocrisy." The two things are inextricably linked. The most sinister influence of the Jewish leaders was a pragmatic doctrine that made room for hypocrisy. They were too concerned with externals and ceremonies and the way things appeared, and not concerned enough with matters of the heart. Jesus rebuked them for their hypocrisy again and again. *See note on 23:25.*

16:13 Caesarea Philippi. A district about 25 mi. N of Galilee, at the base of Mt. Hermon. This was different from the city of Caesarea built by Herod the Great on the Mediterranean coast.

16:16 the living God. An OT name for Jehovah (e.g., Dt 5:26; Jos 3:10; 1Sa 17:26, 36; 2Ki 19:4, 16; Pss 42:2; 84:2; Da 6:26; Hos 1:10) as contrasted with the dead, dumb idols (Jer 10:8; 18:15; 1Co 12:2).

16:17 flesh and blood did not reveal *this* to you. Christ's messianic claims had always been subtle allusions to OT prophecies, combined with miraculous works that substantiated those claims. Never before had He explicitly taught Peter and the apostles the fullness of His identity. God the Father had opened Peter's eyes to the full significance of those claims, and revealed to him who Jesus really was. In

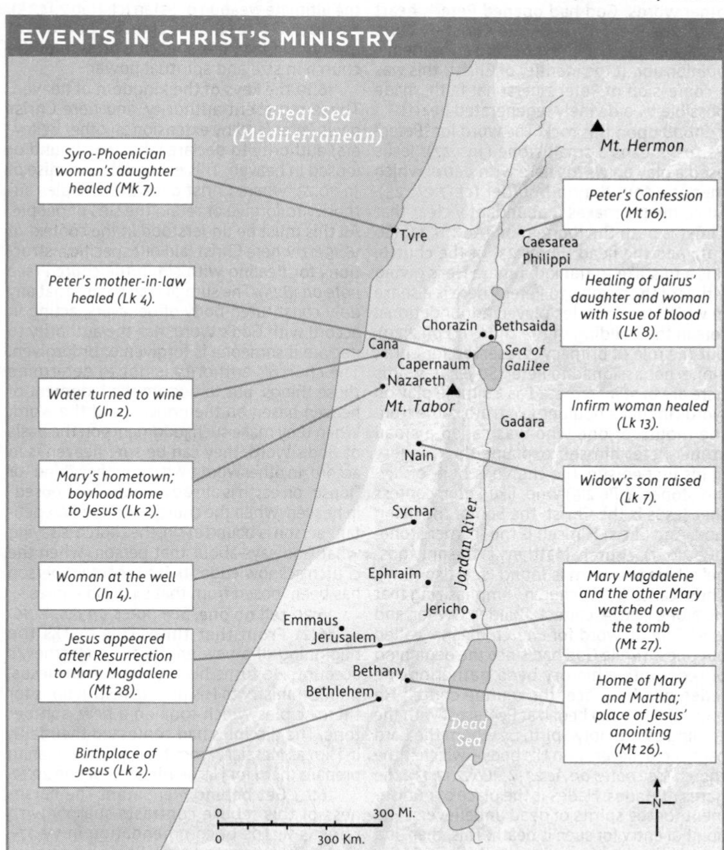

who is in heaven. 18 I also say to you that you are
[a,A]Peter, and upon this [b]rock I will build My church;
and the gates of [B]Hades will not overpower it. 19 I
will give you [A]the keys of the kingdom of heaven;
and [B]whatever you bind on earth [a]shall have been
bound in heaven, and whatever you loose on earth
[b]shall have been loosed in heaven." 20 [A]Then He
[a]warned the disciples that they should tell no one
that He was [b,B]the Christ.

JESUS FORETELLS HIS DEATH

21 [A]From that time [a]Jesus began to show His disciples that He must go to Jerusalem, and [B]suffer
many things from the elders and chief priests and
scribes, and be killed, and be raised up on the third
day. 22 Peter took Him aside and began to rebuke
Him, saying, "[a]God forbid *it,* Lord! This shall never
[b]happen to You." 23 But He turned and said to Peter,
"Get behind Me, [A]Satan! You are a stumbling block
to Me; for you are not setting your mind on [a]God's
interests, but man's."

DISCIPLESHIP IS COSTLY

24 Then Jesus said to His disciples, "If anyone
wishes to come after Me, he must deny himself, and
[A]take up his cross and follow Me. 25 For [A]whoever
wishes to save his [a]life will lose it; but whoever loses
his [a]life for My sake will find it. 26 For what will it
profit a man if he gains the whole world and forfeits
his soul? Or what will a man give in exchange for
his soul? 27 For the [A]Son of Man [B]is going to come in
the glory of His Father with His angels, and [C]WILL
THEN [a]REPAY EVERY MAN ACCORDING TO HIS [b]DEEDS.
28 "Truly I say to you, there are some of those who
are standing here who will not taste death until
they see the [A]Son of Man [B]coming in His kingdom."

THE TRANSFIGURATION

17 [A]Six days later Jesus *took with Him [B]Peter and
[a]James and John his brother, and *led them up
on a high mountain by themselves. 2 And He was
transfigured before them; and His face shone like
the sun, and His garments became as white as light.

16:18 [a]Gr *Petros,* a stone [b]Gr *petra,* large rock; bed-rock [A]Matt 4:18 [B]Matt 11:23 16:19 [a]Gr *estai dedemenon,* fut. pft. pass. [b]Gr *estai lelumenon,* fut. pft. pass. [A]Is 22:22; Rev 1:18; 3:7 [B]Matt 18:18; John 20:23 16:20 [a]Or *strictly admonished* [b]I.e. the Messiah [A]Matt 8:4; Mark 8:30; Luke 9:21 [B]Matt 1:16; 16:16; John 11:27 16:21 [a]Two early mss read *Jesus Christ* [A]Matt 16:21-28: *Mark 8:31-9:1; Luke 9:22-27* [B]Matt 12:40; 17:9, 12, 22f; 20:18f; 27:63; Mark 9:12, 31; Luke 17:25; 18:32; 24:7; John 2:19 16:22 [a]Lit (God be) *merciful to You* [b]Lit *be* 16:23 [a]Lit *the things of God* [A]Matt 4:10 16:24 [A]Matt 10:38; Luke 14:27 16:25 [a]Or *soul* [A]Matt 10:39 16:27 [a]Or *recompense* [b]Lit *doing* [A]Matt 8:20 [B]Matt 10:23; 24:3, 27, 37, 39; 26:64; Mark 8:38; 13:26; Luke 21:27; John 21:22; Acts 1:11; 1 Cor 15:23; 1 Thess 1:10; 4:16; 2 Thess 1:7, 10; 2:1, 8; James 5:7f; 2 Pet 1:16; 3:4, 12; 1 John 2:28; Rev 1:7 [C]Ps 62:12; Prov 24:12; Rom 2:6; 14:12; 1 Cor 3:13; 2 Cor 5:10; Eph 6:8; Col 3:25; Rev 2:23; 20:12; 22:12 16:28 [A]Matt 8:20 [B]Matt 10:23; 24:3, 27, 37, 39; 26:64; Mark 8:38; 13:26; Luke 21:27; John 21:22; Acts 1:11; 1 Cor 15:23; 1 Thess 1:10; 4:16; 2 Thess 1:7, 10; 2:1, 8; James 5:7f; 2 Pet 1:16; 3:4, 12; 1 John 2:28; Rev 1:7 17:1 [a]Or *Jacob* [A]Matt 17:1-8: *Mark 9:2-8; Luke 9:28-36* [B]Matt 26:37; Mark 5:37; 13:3

other words, God had opened Peter's heart to this deeper knowledge of Christ by faith. Peter was not merely expressing an academic opinion about the identity of Christ; this was a confession of Peter's personal faith, made possible by a divinely regenerated heart.

16:18 upon this rock. The word for "Peter," *Petros,* means a small stone (Jn 1:42). Jesus used a play on words here with *petra,* which means a foundation boulder (cf. 7:24, 25). Since the NT makes it abundantly clear that Christ is both the foundation (Ac 4:11, 12; 1Co 3:11), and the head (Eph 5:23) of the church, it is a mistake to think that here He is giving either of those roles to Peter. There is a sense in which the apostles played a foundational role in the building of the church (Eph 2:20), but the role of primacy is reserved for Christ alone, not assigned to Peter. So Jesus' words here are best interpreted as a simple play on words in that a boulder-like truth came from the mouth of one who was called a small stone. Peter himself explains the imagery in his first epistle: the church is built of "living stones" (1Pe 2:5) who, like Peter, confess that Jesus is the Christ, the Son of the living God. And Christ Himself is the "corner stone" (1Pe 2:6, 7). **church.** Matthew is the only gospel where this term is found (see also 18:17). Christ called it "My church," emphasizing that He alone is its Architect, Builder, Owner, and Lord. The Gr. word for church means "called out ones." While God had since the beginning of redemptive history been gathering the redeemed by grace, the unique church He promised to build began at Pentecost with the coming of the Holy Spirit, by whom the Lord baptized believers into His body—which is the church (*see notes on Ac 2:1–4; 1Co 12:12, 13*). **the gates of Hades.** Hades is the place of punishment for the spirits of dead unbelievers. The point of entry for such is death. This, then, is a Jewish phrase referring to death. Even death, the ultimate weapon of Satan (cf. Heb 2:14, 15), has no power to stop the church. The blood of martyrs, in fact, has sped the growth of the church in size and spiritual power.

16:19 the keys of the kingdom of heaven. These represent authority, and here Christ gives Peter (and by extension all other believers) authority to declare what was bound or loosed in heaven. This echoed the promise of Jn 20:23, where Christ gave the disciples authority to forgive or retain the sins of people. All this must be understood in the context of 18:15–17, where Christ laid out specific instructions for dealing with sin in the church (*see note on 18:15*). The sum of it all means that any duly constituted body of believers, acting in accord with God's Word, has the authority to declare if someone is forgiven or unforgiven. The church's authority is not to determine these things, but to declare the judgment of heaven based on the principles of the Word. When they make such judgments on the basis of God's Word, they can be sure heaven is in accord. In other words, whatever they "bind" or "loose" on earth is already "bound" or "loosed" in heaven. When the church says the unrepentant person is bound in sin, the church is saying what God says about that person. When the church acknowledges that a repentant person has been loosed from that sin, God agrees.

16:20 tell no one. *See notes on 8:4; 12:16.*

16:21 From that time. This marks the beginning of a new emphasis in Matthew's account. He turns his attention from Jesus' public ministry to His private instructions for the disciples which took on a new, somber tone. The disciples had confessed their faith in Him as Messiah. From then on, He began to prepare them for His death. *See note on 20:19.*

16:23 Get behind Me, Satan! The harshness of this rebuke contrasts sharply with Christ's words of commendation in vv. 17–19. Jesus suggested that Peter was being a mouthpiece for Satan. Jesus' death was part of God's sovereign plan (Ac 2:23; 4:27, 28). "The LORD was pleased to crush Him" (Is 53:10). Christ had come with the express purpose of dying as an atonement for sin (Jn 12:27). And those who would thwart His mission were doing Satan's work.

16:24 take up his cross. *See note on 10:38.*

16:26 exchange. At the judgment when he faces the disastrous hell of remorse and suffering for his lost soul, with what will he buy it back from perdition? Nothing.

16:27 is going to come ... will then repay. There is coming a time of rewards in the future for believers (1Co 4:5; 2Co 5:8–10; Rev 22:12). Here, however, the Lord was concerned with the reward of the ungodly—final and eternal judgment (Ro 2:5–11; 2Th 1:6–10).

16:28 some ... standing. In all 3 of the Synoptic Gospels, this promise is made immediately prior to the Transfiguration (Mk 9:1–8; Lk 9:27–36). Furthermore the word for "kingdom" can be translated "royal splendor." Therefore, it seems most natural to interpret this promise as a reference to the Transfiguration, which "some" of the disciples—Peter, James, and John would witness only 6 days later (*see note on 17:1*).

17:1 Six days later. The precise reference to the amount of time elapsed is unusual for Matthew. It seems he is carefully drawing the connection between Jesus' promise in 16:28 and the event that immediately follows. Mark agrees on the figure of 6 days (Mk 9:2), but Luke, probably counting the day of Peter's confession and the day of Christ's Transfiguration separately at the start and end of this time period, says it was "some eight days" (Lk 9:28). **Peter and James and John.** These 3, in the inner circle closest to Christ (*see note on 10:2*), are often seen alone together with Jesus (26:37; Mk 5:37; 13:3).

17:2 transfigured. Christ underwent a dramatic change in appearance, so the disciples could behold Him in His glory.

3 And behold, Moses and Elijah appeared to them,
talking with Him. 4 Peter said to Jesus, "Lord, it is
good for us to be here; if You wish, [A]I will make three
[a]tabernacles here, one for You, and one for Moses,
and one for Elijah." 5 While he was still speaking, a
bright cloud overshadowed them, and behold, [A]a
voice out of the cloud said, "[B]This is My beloved
Son, with whom I am well-pleased; listen to Him!"
6 When the disciples heard *this,* they fell [a]face down
to the ground and were terrified. 7 And Jesus came
to *them* and touched them and said, "Get up, and
[A]do not be afraid." 8 And lifting up their eyes, they
saw no one except Jesus Himself alone.
9 [A]As they were coming down from the mountain,
Jesus commanded them, saying, "[B]Tell the vision to no
one until [C]the Son of Man has [D]risen from the dead."
10 And His disciples asked Him, "Why then do the
scribes say that [A]Elijah must come first?" 11 And He
answered and said, "Elijah is coming and will restore
all things; 12 but I say to you that Elijah already came,
and they did not recognize him, but did [a]to him whatever they wished. So also [A]the Son of Man is going to
suffer [b]at their hands." 13 Then the disciples understood
that He had spoken to them about John the Baptist.

THE DEMONIAC

14 [A]When they came to the crowd, a man came
up to Jesus, falling on his knees before Him and
saying, 15 "[a]Lord, have mercy on my son, for he is a
[b,A]lunatic and is very ill; for he often falls into the
fire and often into the water. 16 I brought him to
Your disciples, and they could not cure him." 17 And
Jesus answered and said, "You unbelieving and
perverted generation, how long shall I be with you?
How long shall I put up with you? Bring him here
to Me." 18 And Jesus rebuked him, and the demon
came out of him, and the boy was cured [a]at once.
19 Then the disciples came to Jesus privately and
said, "Why could we not drive it out?" 20 And He
*said to them, "Because of the littleness of your faith;
for truly I say to you, [A]if you have faith [a]the size of [B]a
mustard seed, you will say to [C]this mountain, 'Move
from here to there,' and it will move; and [D]nothing
will be impossible to you. 21 [[a,A]But this kind does
not go out except by prayer and fasting."]
22 [A]And while they were gathering together in
Galilee, Jesus said to them, "The Son of Man is going
to be [a]delivered into the hands of men; 23 and [A]they
will kill Him, and He will be raised on the third day."
And they were deeply grieved.

THE TRIBUTE MONEY

24 When they came to Capernaum, those who collected [A]the [a]two-drachma *tax* came to Peter and said,
"Does your teacher not pay [A]the [a]two-drachma *tax?*"
25 He *said, "Yes." And when he came into the house,
Jesus spoke to him first, saying, "What do you think,
Simon? From whom do the kings of the earth collect
[A]customs or [B]poll-tax, from their sons or from strangers?" 26 When Peter said, "From strangers," Jesus
said to him, "Then the sons are [a]exempt. 27 However,
so that we do not [a,A]offend them, go to the sea and
throw in a hook, and take the first fish that comes
up; and when you open its mouth, you will find [b]a
shekel. Take that and give it to them for you and Me."

RANK IN THE KINGDOM

18 [A]At that [a]time the disciples came to Jesus and
said, "[B]Who then is greatest in the kingdom
of heaven?" 2 And He called a child to Himself and

17:4 [a]Or *sacred tents* [A]Mark 9:5; Luke 9:33 17:5 [A]Mark 1:11; Luke 3:22; 2 Pet 1:17f [B]Is 42:1; Matt 3:17; 12:18 17:6 [a]Lit *on their faces* 17:7 [A]Matt 14:27 17:9 [A]Matt 17:9-13: *Mark 9:9-13* [B]Matt 8:4 [C]Matt 8:20; 17:12, 22 [D]Matt 16:21 17:10 [A]Mal 4:5; Matt 11:14; 16:14 17:12 [a]Lit *in him;* or *in his case* [b]Lit *by them* [A]Matt 8:20; 17:9, 22 17:14 [A]Matt 17:14-19: *Mark 9:14-28;* Matt 17:14-18: *Luke 9:37-42* 17:15 [a]Or *Sir* [b]Or moonstruck; Gr *seleniazo* [A]Matt 4:24 17:18 [a]Lit *from that hour* 17:20 [a]Lit *as* [A]Matt 21:21f; Mark 11:23f; Luke 17:6 [B]Matt 13:31; Luke 17:6 [C]Matt 17:9; 1 Cor 13:2 [D]Mark 9:23; John 11:40 17:21 [a]Early mss do not contain this v [A]Mark 9:29 17:22 [a]Or *betrayed* [A]Matt 17:22, 23: *Mark 9:30-32; Luke 9:44, 45* 17:23 [A]Matt 16:21; 17:9 17:24 [a]Equivalent to two denarii or two days' wages, paid as a temple tax [A]Ex 30:13; 38:26 17:25 [A]Rom 13:7 [B]Matt 22:17, 19 17:26 [a]Or *free* 17:27 [a]Lit *cause them to stumble* [b]Lit *standard coin,* which was a shekel [A]Matt 5:29, 30; 18:6, 8, 9; Mark 9:42, 43, 45, 47; Luke 17:2; John 6:61; 1 Cor 8:13 18:1 [a]Lit *hour* [A]Matt 18:1-5: *Mark 9:33-37; Luke 9:46-48* [B]Luke 22:24

17:3 **Moses and Elijah.** Representing the Law and the prophets respectively, both of which had foretold Christ's death, and that is what Luke says the 3 of them were discussing (Lk 9:31).

17:4 **three tabernacles.** This is undoubtedly a reference to the booths that were used to celebrate the Feast of Tabernacles, when the Israelites dwelt in booths for 7 days (Lv 23:34–42). Peter was expressing a wish to stay in that place.

17:5 **listen to Him!** Peter erred in placing Moses and Elijah on the same level as Christ. Christ was the very one to whom Elijah and Moses had pointed. The voice of the Father (v. 5) interrupted while Peter "was still speaking." The words were the same as those spoken from heaven at Christ's baptism (3:17).

17:6 **fell face down.** A common response to the realization that the Holy God of the universe is present. Cf. Is 6:5; Eze 1:28; Rev 1:17.

17:9 **Tell the vision to no one.** *See notes on 8:4 and 12:16.*

17:10 **Why ... Elijah must come first?** Because it was so prophesied by Mal 4:5, 6. *See note on 11:14.*

17:12 **Elijah already came.** *See note on 11:14.* The Jewish leaders had failed to recognize John the Baptist (though the disciples did, v. 13). John came in the spirit and power of Elijah—and the Jewish leaders had killed him. The Messiah was "going to suffer" similarly.

17:17 **You unbelieving and perverted generation.** Verse 20 indicates that the Lord was referring to the disciples and their weak faith (*see note on 15:33*).

17:19 **Why could we not drive it out?** When Christ sent the disciples out (10:6–8), He explicitly commissioned them to do these kinds of miracles. Less than a year later, they failed where they had once succeeded. Christ's explanation for their failure was that their faith was deficient (v. 20). The deficiency did not consist in a lack of confidence; they were surprised that they could not cast out this demon. The problem probably lay in a failure to make God—rather than their own gifts—the object of their confidence (*see note on v. 20*).

17:20 **faith the size of a mustard seed.** True faith, by Christ's definition, always involves surrender to the will of God. What He was teaching here is nothing like positive-thinking psychology. He was saying that both the source and the object of all genuine faith—even the weak, mustard-seed variety—is God. And "nothing will be impossible with God" (Lk 1:37). *See also note on 21:21.* **nothing will be impossible.** Here, Christ assumes the qualifying thought that is explicitly added by 1Jn 5:14: what we ask for must be "according to His will."

17:21 **except by prayer and fasting.** Again, this suggests that the underlying problem was the disciples' failure to make God the object of their faith (*see notes on vv. 19, 20*). But this verse is not found in the best manuscripts.

17:22 **going to be delivered.** By Judas Iscariot. *See notes on 26:47, 50.*

17:24 **the two-drachma *tax*.** A half-shekel tax (equivalent to about two days' wages) collected annually from every male over 20, for the upkeep of the temple (Ex 30:13, 14; 2Ch 24:9). As kings did not tax their own sons, technically, Jesus, as God's Son, was exempt from the tax (v. 26). But to avoid offense, He paid on behalf of Himself and Peter (v. 27). Cf. Ro 13:1–7; Tit 3:1; 1Pe 2:13–17.

18:1–35 This is the fourth of 5 discourses around which Matthew frames his narrative (see Introduction: Historical and Theological Themes). This section's theme is the childlikeness of the believer.

set him [a]before them, 3 and said, "Truly I say to you,
unless you [a]are converted and [A]become like children,
you will not enter the kingdom of heaven. 4 Whoever then humbles himself as this child, he is the
greatest in the kingdom of heaven. 5 And whoever
receives one such child in My name receives Me;
6 but [A]whoever [B]causes one of these little ones who
believe in Me to stumble, it [a]would be better for him
to have a [b]heavy millstone hung around his neck,
and to be drowned in the depth of the sea.

STUMBLING BLOCKS

7 "Woe to the world because of *its* stumbling
blocks! For [A]it is inevitable that stumbling blocks
come; but woe to that man through whom the stumbling block comes!
8 "[A]If your hand or your foot causes you to stumble, cut it off and throw it from you; it is better for
you to enter life crippled or lame, than [a]to have two
hands or two feet and be cast into the eternal fire.
9 [A]If your eye causes you to stumble, pluck it out and
throw it from you. It is better for you to enter life
with one eye, than [a]to have two eyes and be cast
into the [b,B]fiery hell.
10 "See that you do not despise one of these little
ones, for I say to you that [A]their angels in heaven
continually see the face of My Father who is in
heaven. 11 [[a,A]For the Son of Man has come to save
that which was lost.]

NINETY-NINE PLUS ONE

12 "What do you think? [A]If any man has a hundred
sheep, and one of them has gone astray, does he
not leave the ninety-nine on the mountains and
go and search for the one that is straying? 13 If
it turns out that he finds it, truly I say to you, he
rejoices over it more than over the ninety-nine
which have not gone astray. 14 So it is not *the* will
[a]of your Father who is in heaven that one of these
little ones perish.

DISCIPLINE AND PRAYER

15 "[A]If your brother sins[a], go and [b]show him his
fault [c]in private; if he listens to you, you have won
your brother. 16 But if he does not listen *to you,* take
one or two more with you, so that [A]BY THE MOUTH
OF TWO OR THREE WITNESSES EVERY [a]FACT MAY BE
CONFIRMED. 17 If he refuses to listen to them, [A]tell
it to the church; and if he refuses to listen even to
the church, [B]let him be to you as [a]a Gentile and [a]a
tax collector. 18 Truly I say to you, [A]whatever you
[a]bind on earth [b]shall have been bound in heaven;
and whatever you [c]loose on earth [b]shall have been
loosed in heaven.
19 "Again I say to you, that if two of you agree on
earth about anything that they may ask, [A]it shall
be done for them [a]by My Father who is in heaven.
20 For where two or three have gathered together
in My name, [A]I am there in their midst."

FORGIVENESS

21 Then Peter came and said to Him, "Lord, [A]how
often shall my brother sin against me and I forgive
him? Up to [B]seven times?" 22 Jesus *said to him, "I
do not say to you, up to seven times, but up to [A]sev-
enty times seven.

18:2 [a]Lit *in their midst* 18:3 [a]Lit *are turned* [A]Matt 19:14; Mark 10:15; Luke 18:17; 1 Cor 14:20; 1 Pet 2:2 18:6 [a]Lit *is better* [b]Lit *millstone turned by a donkey* [A]Mark 9:42; Luke 17:2; 1 Cor 8:12 [B]Matt 17:27 18:7 [A]Luke 17:1; 1 Cor 11:19; 1 Tim 4:1 18:8 [a]Lit *having;* Gr part. [A]Matt 5:30; Mark 9:43 18:9 [a]Lit *having;* Gr part. [b]Lit *Gehenna of fire* [A]Matt 5:29; Mark 9:47 [B]Matt 5:22 18:10 [A]Luke 1:19; Acts 12:15; Rev 8:2 18:11 [a]Early mss do not contain this v [A]Luke 19:10 18:12 [A]Matt 18:12-14: *Luke 15:4-7* 18:14 [a]Lit *before* 18:15 [a]Late mss add *against you* [b]Or *reprove* [c]Lit *between you and him alone* [A]Lev 19:17; Luke 17:3; Gal 6:1; 2 Thess 3:15; James 5:19 18:16 [a]Lit *word* [A]Deut 19:15; John 8:17; 2 Cor 13:1; 1 Tim 5:19; Heb 10:28 18:17 [a]Lit *the* [A]1 Cor 6:1ff [B]2 Thess 3:6, 14f 18:18 [a]Or *forbid* [b]Gr fut. pft. pass. [c]Or *permit* [A]Matt 16:19; John 20:23 18:19 [a]Lit *from* [A]Matt 7:7 18:20 [A]Matt 28:20 18:21 [A]Matt 18:15 [B]Luke 17:4 18:22 [A]Gen 4:24

18:3 become like children. This is how Jesus characterized conversion. Like the Beatitudes, it pictures faith as the simple, helpless, trusting dependence of those who have no resources of their own. Like children, they have no achievements and no accomplishments to offer or commend themselves with.

18:5 whoever receives. *See note on 10:41.* **one such child.** This speaks not of literal children, but children in the sense described in vv. 3, 4 (those who have humbled themselves like children), i.e., true believers (v. 6). *See notes on 10:42; 19:14.*

18:6 millstone. A stone used for grinding grain. Lit. "the millstone of an ass"—a stone so large it took a donkey to turn it.

18:7 Woe to the world. It is expected that those in the world will cause Christians to be offended, stumble and sin, and they will be judged for it. But it should not be that fellow believers lead others into sin, directly or indirectly. One would be better off dead. Cf. Ro 14:13, 19, 21; 15:2; 1Co 8:13.

18:8, 9 cut it off … pluck it out. *See note on 5:29.*

18:10 do not despise. I.e., spurn or belittle another believer by treating him or her unkindly or indifferently. **their angels.** This does not suggest that each believer has a personal guardian angel. Rather, the pronoun is collective and refers to the fact that believers are served by angels in general. These angels are pictured "continually" watching the face of God so as to hear His command to them to help a believer when needed. It is extremely serious to treat any fellow believer with contempt since God and the holy angels are so concerned for their well-being.

18:14 perish. The word here can (and does in this context) refer to spiritual devastation rather than utter eternal destruction. This does not suggest that God's children ever could perish in the ultimate sense (cf. Jn 10:28).

18:15 The prescription for church discipline in vv. 15–17 must be read in light of the parable of the lost sheep in vv. 12–14. The goal of this process is restoration. If successful, "you have won your brother." Step 1 is to "show him his fault" privately.

18:16 if he does not listen. I.e., if he remains impenitent, follow step 2: "take one or two more with you," to fulfill the principle of Dt 19:15.

18:17 tell it to the church. If he still refuses to repent, step 3 requires that the matter be reported to the whole assembly (v. 17)—so that all may lovingly pursue the sinning brother's reconciliation. But failing that, step 4 means that the offender must be excommunicated, regarded by the church as "a Gentile and a tax collector" (*see note on 5:46*). The idea is not merely to punish the offender, or to shun him completely, but to remove him as a detrimental influence from the fellowship of the church, and henceforth to regard him as an evangelistic prospect rather than as a brother. Ultimately, the sin for which he is excommunicated is a hard-hearted impenitence.

18:18 bind on earth … bound in heaven. *See note on 16:19.*

18:19 if two of you agree on earth. This promise applies to the issue of discipline discussed in vv. 15–17. The "two of you" spoken of here harks back to the two or three witnesses involved in step two of the discipline process (*see note on v. 15*).

18:20 two or three. Jewish tradition requires at least 10 men (a *minyan*) to constitute a synagogue or even hold public prayer. Here, Christ promised to be present in the midst of an even smaller flock—"two or three witnesses" gathered in His name for the purpose of discipline (*see note on v. 15*).

18:21 Up to seven times? Peter thought he was being magnanimous. The rabbis, citing several verses from Amos (1:3, 6, 9, 11, 13) taught that since God forgave Israel's enemies only 3 times, it was presumptuous and unnecessary to forgive anyone more than 3 times.

18:22 seventy times seven. Innumerable times. *See note on Lk 17:4.*

23 "For this reason [A]the kingdom of heaven [a]may be
compared to a king who wished to [B]settle accounts
with his slaves. 24 When he had begun to settle *them,*
one who owed him [a]ten thousand talents was brought
to him. 25 But since he [a,A]did not have *the means* to
repay, his lord commanded him [B]to be sold, along
with his wife and children and all that he had, and repayment to be made. 26 So the slave fell *to the ground*
and [A]prostrated himself before him, saying, 'Have
patience with me and I will repay you everything.'
27 And the lord of that slave felt compassion and
released him and [A]forgave him the [a]debt. 28 But that
slave went out and found one of his fellow slaves who
owed him a hundred [a]denarii; and he seized him and
began to choke *him,* saying, 'Pay back what you owe.'
29 So his fellow slave fell *to the ground* and *began* to
plead with him, saying, 'Have patience with me and I
will repay you.' 30 But he was unwilling [a]and went and
threw him in prison until he should pay back what
was owed. 31 So when his fellow slaves saw what had
happened, they were deeply grieved and came and
reported to their lord all that had happened. 32 Then
summoning him, his lord *said to him, 'You wicked
slave, I forgave you all that debt because you pleaded
with me. 33 [A]Should you not also have had mercy on
your fellow slave, in the same way that I had mercy
on you?' 34 And his lord, moved with anger, handed
him over to the torturers until he should repay all
that was owed him. 35 [A]My heavenly Father will also
do the same to you, if each of you does not forgive
his brother from [a]your heart."

CONCERNING DIVORCE

19 [A]When Jesus had finished these words, He departed from Galilee and [B]came into the region
of Judea beyond the Jordan; 2 and [a]large crowds
followed Him, and [A]He healed them there.
3 *Some* Pharisees came to [a]Jesus, testing Him and
asking, "[A]Is it lawful *for a man* to [b]divorce his wife
for any reason at all?" 4 And He answered and said,
"Have you not read [A]that He who created *them* from
the beginning MADE THEM MALE AND FEMALE, 5 and
said, '[A]FOR THIS REASON A MAN SHALL LEAVE HIS FA-
THER AND MOTHER AND BE JOINED TO HIS WIFE, AND
[B]THE TWO SHALL BECOME ONE FLESH'? 6 So they are
no longer two, but one flesh. What therefore God
has joined together, let no man separate." 7 They
*said to Him, "[A]Why then did Moses command to
GIVE HER A CERTIFICATE OF DIVORCE AND SEND *her*
AWAY?" 8 He *said to them, "Because of your hardness of heart Moses permitted you to [a]divorce your
wives; but from the beginning it has not been this
way. 9 And I say to you, [A]whoever [a]divorces his wife,
except for [b]immorality, and marries another woman
[c]commits adultery[d]."
10 The disciples *said to Him, "If the relationship
of the man with his wife is like this, it is better not
to marry." 11 But He said to them, "[A]Not all men *can*
accept this statement, but [B]*only* those to whom it has
been given. 12 For there are eunuchs who were born
that way from their mother's womb; and there are
eunuchs who were made eunuchs by men; and there
are *also* eunuchs who made themselves eunuchs

18:23 [a]Lit *was compared to* [A]Matt 13:24 [B]Matt 25:19 18:24 [a]A talent was worth more than fifteen years' wages of a laborer 18:25 [a]Or *was unable to* [A]Luke 7:42 [B]Ex 21:2; Lev 25:39; 2 Kin 4:1; Neh 5:5 18:26 [A]Matt 8:2 18:27 [a]Or *loan* [A]Luke 7:42 18:28 [a]The denarius was a day's wages 18:30 [a]Lit *but* 18:33 [A]Matt 6:12; Eph 4:32 18:35 [a]Lit *your hearts* [A]Matt 6:14 19:1 [A]Matt 7:28 [B]Matt 19:1-9: *Mark 10:1-12* 19:2 [a]Lit *many* [A]Matt 4:23 19:3 [a]Lit *Him* [b]Or *send away* [A]Matt 5:31 19:4 [A]Gen 1:27; 5:2 19:5 [A]Gen 2:24; Eph 5:31 [B]1 Cor 6:16 19:7 [A]Deut 24:1-4; Matt 5:31 19:8 [a]Or *send away* 19:9 [a]Or *sends away* [b]Lit *fornication* [c]Some early mss read *makes her commit adultery* [d]Some early mss add *and he who marries a divorced woman commits adultery* [A]Matt 5:32 19:11 [A]1 Cor 7:7ff [B]Matt 13:11

18:23 slaves. Due to the large amounts of money involved, it is likely these "slaves" would have been provincial governors who owed the king the money from taxation.

18:24 ten thousand talents. This represents an incomprehensible amount of money. The talent was the largest denomination of currency, and "ten thousand" in common parlance signified an infinite number.

18:25 commanded him to be sold. A way to recover some of this loss was for the king to sell the family members into slavery.

18:27 forgave him. Picturing the generous, compassionate forgiveness of God to a pleading sinner who owes Him an unpayable debt. Cf. Col 2:14.

18:28 a hundred denarii. About 3 months' wages. This was not a negligible amount by normal standards, but it was a pittance in comparison to what the slave had been forgiven.

18:29 Have patience .... will repay you. Cf. v. 26. The forgiven man heard the same pleading he had given before his master, but was utterly without compassion (v. 30).

18:31 fellow slaves ... grieved. A lack of forgiveness is offensive to fellow believers. Most of all it offends God, who chastens His unforgiving children severely (vv. 32–34). *See notes on v. 34*; cf. 6:15.

18:34 his lord, moved with anger. Because He is holy and just, God is always angry at sin, including the sins of His children (cf. Heb 12:5–11). **torturers.** Not executioners. This pictures severe discipline, not final condemnation. **all that was owed him.** The original debt was unpayable and the man was still without resources. So it seems unlikely that the slave was saddled once again with the same debt he had already been forgiven. Rather, what he now owed his master would be exacted in chastening by his master until he was willing to forgive others.

19:1 the region of Judea beyond the Jordan. Perea was the name of the region just E of the Jordan River. It was not technically part of Judea, but the territory ruled by Herod the Great had included both regions, and it was commonly referred to this way. Christ's ministry in Perea lasted only a few months. It was from here that He would make His final journey to Jerusalem just prior to the Passion Week (20:17–19).

19:3 Is it lawful. A hotly debated difference of opinion existed between the Rabbis Shammai and Hillel (both near-contemporaries of Christ). The Shammaites interpreted the law rigidly, and permitted a man to divorce his wife only if she was guilty of sexual immorality. **for any reason at all?** The Hillelites took a wholly pragmatic approach, and permitted a man to divorce his wife indiscriminately.

19:4 Quoted from Ge 1:27; 5:2.

19:5 Quoted from Ge 2:24 (*see note there*).

19:7 Why then did Moses command to give her a certificate of divorce ... ? The Pharisees misrepresented Dt 24:1–4. It was not a "command" for divorce, but a limitation on remarriage in the event of a divorce. While recognizing the legitimacy of divorce when a man "has found some indecency" (Dt 24:1) in his wife (sexual sin, by Jesus' interpretation in v. 9), Moses did not "command" divorce. *See note on Dt 24:1–4.*

19:8 Because of your hardness of heart. The phrase underscores the truth that divorce is only a last-resort response to hard-hearted sexual immorality (v. 9). **Moses permitted you to divorce.** The stress is certainly on the word "permitted." Thus Jesus clearly sides with the Shammai school of interpretation (*see note on v. 3*).

19:9 immorality. This is a term that encompasses all sorts of sexual sins. Both here and in 5:32, Jesus includes this "exception clause," clearly permitting the innocent party in such a divorce to remarry without incurring the stigma of one who "commits adultery." *See notes on 5:31, 32.*

19:10 it is better not to marry. The disciples correctly understood the binding nature of marriage, and that Jesus was setting a very high standard, permitting divorce only in the most extreme of circumstances.

19:12 let him accept *it*. Since all cannot handle it (v. 11), Christ is not enjoining celibacy here. Rather, He makes it entirely a matter of personal choice—except for those who are physically unable to marry, either through natural causes or because of the violence of other men. Still others may find there are

for the sake of the kingdom of heaven. He who is
able to accept *this,* let him accept *it.*"

JESUS BLESSES LITTLE CHILDREN

13 [A]Then *some* children were brought to Him so
that He might lay His hands on them and pray; and
the disciples rebuked them. 14 But Jesus said, "[a,A]Let
the children alone, and do not hinder them from
coming to Me; for [B]the kingdom of heaven belongs
to such as these." 15 After laying His hands on them,
He departed from there.

THE RICH YOUNG RULER

16 [A]And someone came to Him and said, "Teacher,
what good thing shall I do that I may obtain [B]eternal
life?" 17 And He said to him, "Why are you asking Me
about what is good? There is *only* One who is good;
but [A]if you wish to enter into life, keep the commandments." 18 *Then* he *said to Him, "Which ones?" And
Jesus said, "[A]YOU SHALL NOT COMMIT MURDER; YOU
SHALL NOT COMMIT ADULTERY; YOU SHALL NOT STEAL;
YOU SHALL NOT BEAR FALSE WITNESS; 19 [A]HONOR YOUR
FATHER AND MOTHER; and [B]YOU SHALL LOVE YOUR
NEIGHBOR AS YOURSELF." 20 The young man *said to
Him, "All these things I have kept; what am I still
lacking?" 21 Jesus said to him, "If you wish to be
[a]complete, go *and* [A]sell your possessions and give
to *the* poor, and you will have [B]treasure in heaven;
and come, follow Me." 22 But when the young man
heard this statement, he went away grieving; for
he was one who owned much property.
23 And Jesus said to His disciples, "Truly I say to
you, [A]it is hard for a rich man to enter the kingdom
of heaven. 24 Again I say to you, [A]it is easier for a
camel to go through the eye of a needle, than for
a rich man to enter the kingdom of God." 25 When
the disciples heard *this,* they were very astonished
and said, "Then who can be saved?" 26 And looking
at *them* Jesus said to them, "[A]With people this is
impossible, but with God all things are possible."

THE DISCIPLES' REWARD

27 Then Peter said to Him, "Behold, we have left
everything and followed You; what then will there
be for us?" 28 And Jesus said to them, "Truly I say
to you, that you who have followed Me, in the regeneration when [A]the Son of Man will sit on [a]His
glorious throne, [B]you also shall sit upon twelve
thrones, judging the twelve tribes of Israel. 29 And
[A]everyone who has left houses or brothers or sisters or father or mother [a]or children or farms for
My name's sake, will receive [b]many times as much,

19:13 [A]Matt 19:13-15: *Mark 10:13-16; Luke 18:15-17* 19:14 [a]Or *Permit the children* [A]Matt 18:3; Mark 10:15; Luke 18:17; 1 Cor 14:20; 1 Pet 2:2 [B]Matt 5:3 19:16 [A]Matt 19:16-29: *Mark 10:17-30; Luke 18:18-30;* Luke 10:25-28 [B]Matt 25:46 19:17 [A]Lev 18:5; Neh 9:29; Ezek 20:21 19:18 [A]Ex 20:13-16; Deut 5:17-20 19:19 [A]Ex 20:12; Deut 5:16 [B]Lev 19:18 19:21 [a]Or *perfect* [A]Luke 12:33; 16:9; Acts 2:45; 4:34f [B]Matt 6:20 19:23 [A]Matt 13:22; Mark 10:23f; Luke 18:24 19:24 [A]Mark 10:25; Luke 18:25 19:26 [A]Gen 18:14; Job 42:2; Jer 32:17; Zech 8:6; Mark 10:27; Luke 1:37; 18:27 19:28 [a]Lit *the throne of His glory* [A]Matt 25:31 [B]Luke 22:30; Rev 3:21; 4:4; 11:16; 20:4 19:29 [a]One early ms adds *or wife* [b]One early ms reads *a hundred times* [A]Matt 6:33; Mark 10:29f; Luke 18:29f

pragmatic reasons not to marry for the good of the kingdom (*see notes on 1Co 7:7–9*). But in no way did Christ suggest that celibacy is superior to marriage (cf. Ge 2:18; 1Ti 4:3).

19:14 such as these. These children were too young to have exercised personal faith. See Lk 18:15, where Luke refers to them as "babies." Therefore, it is all the more significant that Christ used them as an illustration of those who make up "the kingdom of heaven" (cf. 18:1–4). Mk 10:16 also says He "blessed them." God often shows a special mercy to those who because of age or mental deficiency are incapable of either faith or willful unbelief (cf. Jon 4:11). They are called "innocent" in Jer 19:4. This does not mean they are free from the inherited guilt and moral corruption of Adam's sin (*see notes on Ro 5:12–19*), but rather that they are not culpable in the same sense as those whose sins are premeditated and deliberate. Jesus' words here suggest that God's mercy is graciously extended to infants so that those who die are sovereignly regenerated and granted entrance into the kingdom—not because they are deserving of heaven, but because God in His grace chooses to redeem them. *See notes on 2Sa 12:23; Mk 10:14.*

19:16 Teacher. This is not necessarily a recognition of Christ's deity. The young man simply meant that Christ was righteous and a teacher from God who apparently had eternal life and might know how he could get it.

19:17 Why are you asking Me about what is good? There is *only* One who is good. Jesus was not disclaiming His own deity, but rather teaching the young man that all but God are sinners. This young man's most serious spiritual defect was his reluctance to confess his own utter spiritual bankruptcy. *See note on 5:3;* cf. Lk 18:11. **if you wish to enter into life, keep the commandments.** This, of course, is law, not gospel. Before showing him the way to life, Jesus wanted to impress on the young man both the high standard required by God and the absolute futility of seeking salvation by his own merit. This should have elicited a response about the impossibility of keeping the law perfectly (like the disciples' response in v. 25), but instead the young man confidently declared that he qualified for heaven under those terms.

19:18, 19 These are 5 of the 6 commandments that make up the second table of the Ten Commandments—all dealing with human relationships (cf. Ex 20:12–16; Dt 5:16–20). *See note on 22:40.* Christ omitted the tenth commandment, which deals with covetousness, and added Lv 19:18, the summation of the second half of the Decalogue. Cf. Ro 13:1–10.

19:20 I have kept. The self-righteous young man would not admit to his own sin. *See note on 9:13.*

19:21 go *and* sell your possessions and give to *the* poor. Again, Jesus was not setting forth terms for salvation, but rather exposing the young man's true heart. His refusal to obey here revealed two things: 1) he was not blameless as far as the law was concerned, because he was guilty of loving himself and his possessions more than his neighbors (cf. v. 19); and 2) he lacked true faith, which involves a willingness to surrender all at Christ's bidding (16:24). Jesus was not teaching salvation by philanthropy; but He was demanding that this young man give Him first place. The young man failed the test (v. 22). **come, follow Me.** This was the answer to the young man's question in v. 16. It was a call to faith. It is likely that the young man never even heard or contemplated it, though, because his own love of his possessions was such a stumbling block that he had already rejected Jesus' claim to lordship over his life. Thus he walked away in unbelief.

19:24 camel . . . eye of a needle. I.e., it is impossible. Jesus was underscoring the impossibility of anyone's being saved by merit. Since wealth was deemed proof of God's approval, and those who had it could give more alms, it was commonly thought that rich people were the most likely candidates for heaven (*see note on Mk 10:25*). Jesus destroyed that notion, and along with it, the notion that anyone can merit enough divine favor to gain entrance into heaven. *See note on v. 25.*

19:25 Then who can be saved? This was the right question to ask; it showed that they understood Jesus' message (*see note on v. 17*). Salvation is possible only through divine grace (v. 26). *See notes on Ro 3:9–20; Gal 3:10–13; Php 3:4–9.*

19:27 we have left everything and followed You. Peter points out that they had already done what Christ demanded of the rich young ruler (v. 21). They had embarked on the life of faith with Christ. Note that Jesus did not rebuke Peter for his expectation of reward (cf. Rev 22:12).

19:28 regeneration. Here the term does not carry its normal theological meaning of personal regeneration (cf. Tit 3:5). Instead, Jesus was speaking of "the period of restoration of all things about which God spoke by the mouth of His holy prophets from ancient time" (Ac 3:21). This is a reference to the earthly kingdom described in Rev 20:1–15, when believers will sit with Christ on His throne (Rev 3:21). **judging.** Governing. Cf. 1Co 6:2, 3.

and will inherit eternal life. 30 [A]But many *who are*
first will be last; and *the* last, first.

LABORERS IN THE VINEYARD

20 "For [A]the kingdom of heaven is like [a]a landowner who went out early in the morning
to hire laborers for his [B]vineyard. 2 When he had
agreed with the laborers for a [a]denarius for the
day, he sent them into his vineyard. 3 And he went
out about the [a]third hour and saw others standing
idle in the market place; 4 and to those he said, 'You
also go into the vineyard, and whatever is right I
will give you.' And *so* they went. 5 Again he went out
about the [a]sixth and the ninth hour, and did [b]the
same thing. 6 And about the [a]eleventh *hour* he went
out and found others standing *around;* and he *said
to them, 'Why have you been standing here idle all
day long?' 7 They *said to him, 'Because no one hired
us.' He *said to them, 'You go into the vineyard too.'
8 "When [A]evening came, the [a]owner of the vineyard *said to his [B]foreman, 'Call the laborers and
pay them their wages, beginning with the last *group*
to the first.' 9 When those *hired* about the eleventh
hour came, each one received a [a]denarius. 10 When
those *hired* first came, they thought that they would
receive more; [a]but each of them also received a
denarius. 11 When they received it, they grumbled
at the landowner, 12 saying, 'These last men have
worked *only* one hour, and you have made them
equal to us who have borne the burden and the
[A]scorching heat of the day.' 13 But he answered and
said to one of them, '[A]Friend, I am doing you no
wrong; did you not agree with me for a denarius?
14 Take what is yours and go, but I wish to give to
this last man the same as to you. 15 Is it not lawful
for me to do what I wish with what is my own? Or
is your [A]eye [a]envious because I am [b]generous?' 16 So
[A]the last shall be first, and the first last."

DEATH, RESURRECTION FORETOLD

17 [A]As Jesus was about to go up to Jerusalem, He
took the twelve *disciples* aside by themselves, and
on the way He said to them, 18 "Behold, we are going up to Jerusalem; and the Son of Man [A]will be
[a]delivered to the chief priests and scribes, and they
will condemn Him to death, 19 and [A]will hand Him
over to the Gentiles to mock and scourge and crucify
Him, and on [B]the third day He will be raised up."

PREFERMENT ASKED

20 [A]Then the mother of [B]the sons of Zebedee came
to [a]Jesus with her sons, [C]bowing down and making
a request of Him. 21 And He said to her, "What do
you wish?" She *said to Him, "Command that in
Your kingdom these two sons of mine [A]may sit one
on Your right and one on Your left." 22 But Jesus
answered, "You do not know what you are asking.
Are you able [A]to drink the cup that I am about to
drink?" They *said to Him, "We are able." 23 He *said
to them, "[A]My cup you shall drink; but to sit on My
right and on *My* left, this is not Mine to give, [B]but
it is for those for whom it has been [C]prepared by
My Father."
24 And hearing *this,* the ten became indignant
with the two brothers. 25 [A]But Jesus called them to
Himself and said, "You know that the rulers of the
Gentiles lord it over them, and *their* great men exercise authority over them. 26 It is not this way among
you, [A]but whoever wishes to become great among
you shall be your servant, 27 and whoever wishes

19:30 [A]Matt 20:16; Mark 10:31; Luke 13:30 20:1 [a]Lit *a man, a landowner* [A]Matt 13:24 [B]Matt 21:28, 33 20:2 [a]The denarius was a day's wages 20:3 [a]I.e. 9 a.m. 20:5 [a]I.e. noon and 3 p.m. [b]Lit *similarly* 20:6 [a]I.e. 5 p.m. 20:8 [a]Or *lord* [A]Lev 19:13; Deut 24:15 [B]Luke 8:3 20:9 [a]The denarius was a day's wages 20:10 [a]Lit *each one a denarius* 20:12 [A]Jon 4:8; Luke 12:55; James 1:11 20:13 [A]Matt 22:12; 26:50 20:15 [a]Lit *evil* [b]Lit *good* [A]Deut 15:9; Matt 6:23; Mark 7:22 20:16 [A]Matt 19:30; Mark 10:31; Luke 13:30 20:17 [A]Matt 20:17-19: *Mark 10:32-34; Luke 18:31-33* 20:18 [a]Or *betrayed* [A]Matt 16:21 20:19 [A]Matt 27:2; Acts 2:23; 3:13; 4:27; 21:11 [B]Matt 16:21; 17:23; Luke 18:32f 20:20 [a]Lit *Him* [A]Matt 20:20-28: *Mark 10:35-45* [B]Matt 4:21; 10:2 [C]Matt 8:2 20:21 [A]Matt 19:28 20:22 [A]Is 51:17, 22; Jer 49:12; Matt 26:39, 42; Luke 22:42; John 18:11 20:23 [A]Acts 12:2; Rev 1:9 [B]Matt 13:11 [C]Matt 25:34 20:25 [A]Matt 20:25-28: *Luke 22:25-27* 20:26 [A]Matt 23:11; Mark 9:35; 10:43; Luke 22:26

19:30 **first … last … first.** This statement means that everyone ends up the same, a truth that is explained by the parable that follows (*see note on 20:16*).

20:1 **hire laborers.** This was typical during harvest. Day laborers stood in the marketplace from dawn, hoping to be hired for the day's work. The workday began at 6:00 a.m. and went to 6:00 p.m.

20:2 **a denarius for the day.** A fair wage for a full day's labor (*see note on 22:19*).

20:3 **third hour.** 9:00 a.m. They were standing *idle because no* one had hired them (v. 7).

20:4 **whatever is right.** So eager to work, these men did not even negotiate a specific wage.

20:6 **eleventh *hour*.** I.e., 5:00 p.m. Desperate for work, they had waited nearly "all day." They would take whatever they could get.

20:8 **last … to the first.** This is the clue that opens the parable (*see note on v. 16*).

20:13 **I am doing you no wrong.** Everyone received a full day's wage, to their shock (vv. 9–11). The man was acting graciously to those whom he overpaid. This was no slight against those whom he paid a full wage for a full day's work. That was precisely what they agreed to in the beginning. But it was his privilege to extend the same generosity to all (v. 15; cf. Ro 9:15).

20:16 **last shall be first … first last.** In other words, everyone finishes in a dead heat. No matter how long each of the workers worked, they each received a full day's wage. Similarly, the thief on the cross will enjoy the full blessings of heaven alongside those who have labored their whole lives for Christ. Such is the grace of God (*see note on 19:30*).

20:17 **go up to Jerusalem.** Thus began His final journey to the cross.

20:19 **scourge and crucify.** This was the third time Jesus told the disciples of His death (*see note on 16:21*; cf. 17:22, 23)—plus 3 of the disciples had overheard Jesus discussing His death with Moses and Elijah at the Transfiguration (Lk 9:31). This time, however, He added more details.

20:20 **mother of the sons of Zebedee.** Mk 10:35 says James and John themselves raised the question of v. 21. There is no contradiction. It is possible either that the 3 of them asked together, or perhaps even more likely that they had discussed it among themselves beforehand, and each posed the question to Jesus privately.

20:21 **Command … these two sons of mine.** Probably playing off the words of Jesus in 19:28, James and John had enlisted their mother to convey their proud, self-seeking request to Jesus. This was a recurring matter among the disciples (cf. 18:1, 4; 23:11; Mk 9:34; Lk 9:46; 22:24, 26), right up to the table at the Last Supper.

20:22 **You do not know what you are asking.** The greatest glory goes to those who suffer the most for Christ. **the cup that I am about to drink?** The cup of God's wrath (*see notes on 26:39; Mk 14:36; Lk 22:42; Jn 18:11*).

20:23 **My cup you shall drink.** James was beheaded (Ac 12:2) and John tortured and exiled to Patmos (Rev 1:9) for the sake of Christ. **for whom it has been prepared.** God alone has chosen.

20:24 **became indignant.** Jealous displeasure, no doubt. They all would have petitioned Jesus for the exalted, favored positions, given the opportunity. *See note on v. 21.*

20:25–28 In this rich text, the Lord was teaching the disciples that the style of greatness and leadership for believers is different. The Gentile leaders dominate in dictatorial fashion, using carnal power and authority.

to be first among you shall be your slave; 28 just as
[A]the Son of Man [B]did not come to be served, but
to serve, and to give His [a]life a ransom for many."

SIGHT FOR THE BLIND

29 [A]As they were leaving Jericho, a large crowd
followed Him. 30 And two blind men sitting by the
road, hearing that Jesus was passing by, cried out,
"Lord, [A]have mercy on us, [B]Son of David!" 31 The
crowd sternly told them to be quiet, but they cried
out all the more, "Lord, [A]Son of David, have mercy
on us!" 32 And Jesus stopped and called them, and
said, "What do you want Me to do for you?" 33 They
*said to Him, "Lord, *we want* our eyes to be opened."
34 Moved with compassion, Jesus touched their eyes;
and immediately they regained their sight and followed Him.

THE TRIUMPHAL ENTRY

21 [A]When they had approached Jerusalem and
had come to Bethphage, at [B]the Mount of Olives, then Jesus sent two disciples, 2 saying to them,
"Go into the village opposite you, and immediately
you will find a donkey tied *there* and a colt with
her; untie them and bring them to Me. 3 If anyone
says anything to you, you shall say, 'The Lord has
need of them,' and immediately he will send them."
4 [A]This [a]took place to fulfill what was spoken through
the prophet:

5 "[A]SAY TO THE DAUGHTER OF ZION,
'BEHOLD YOUR KING IS COMING TO YOU,
GENTLE, AND MOUNTED ON A DONKEY,
EVEN ON A COLT, THE FOAL OF
A BEAST OF BURDEN.' "

6 The disciples went and did just as Jesus had instructed them, 7 and brought the donkey and the
colt, and laid their coats on them; and He sat on [a]the
coats. 8 Most of the crowd [A]spread their coats in the
road, and others were cutting branches from the trees
and spreading them in the road. 9 The crowds going
ahead of Him, and those who followed, were shouting,

"Hosanna to the [A]Son of David;
[B]BLESSED IS HE WHO COMES IN
THE NAME OF THE LORD;
Hosanna [C]in the highest!"

10 When He had entered Jerusalem, all the city was
stirred, saying, "Who is this?" 11 And the crowds were
saying, "This is [A]the prophet Jesus, from [B]Nazareth
in Galilee."

CLEANSING THE TEMPLE

12 [A]And Jesus entered the temple and drove out all
those who were buying and selling in the temple,
and overturned the tables of the [B]money changers
and the seats of those who were selling [C]doves.

20:28 [a]Or *soul* [A]Matt 8:20 [B]Matt 26:28; John 13:13ff; 2 Cor 8:9; Phil 2:7; 1 Tim 2:6; Titus 2:14; Heb 9:28; Rev 1:5 20:29 [A]Matt 20:29-34: *Mark 10:46-52; Luke 18:35-43;* Matt 9:27-31 20:30 [A]Matt 9:27 [B]Matt 20:31 20:31 [A]Matt 9:27 21:1 [A]Matt 21:1-9: *Mark 11:1-10; Luke 19:29-38* [B]Matt 24:3; 26:30; Mark 11:1; 13:3; 14:26; Luke 19:29, 37; 21:37; 22:39; John 8:1; Acts 1:12 21:4 [a]Lit *has happened* [A]Matt 21:4-9: *Mark 11:7-10; Luke 19:35-38; John 12:12-15* 21:5 [A]Is 62:11; Zech 9:9 21:7 [a]Lit *them* 21:8 [A]2 Kin 9:13 21:9 [A]Matt 9:27 [B]Ps 118:26 [C]Luke 2:14 21:11 [A]Matt 21:26; Mark 6:15; Luke 7:16, 39; 13:33; 24:19; John 1:21, 25; 4:19; 6:14; 7:40; 9:17; Acts 3:22f; 7:37 [B]Matt 2:23 21:12 [A]Matt 21:12-16: *Mark 11:15-18; Luke 19:45-47;* Matt 21:12, 13: *John 2:13-16* [B]Ex 30:13 [C]Lev 1:14; 5:7; 12:8

Believers are to do the opposite—they lead by being servants and giving themselves away for others, as Jesus did.

20:28 to give His life a ransom for many. The word translated "for" means "in the place of," underscoring the substitutionary nature of Christ's sacrifice. A "ransom" is a price paid to redeem a slave or a prisoner. Redemption does not involve a price paid to Satan. Rather, the ransom is offered to God—to satisfy His justice and wrath against sin. The price paid was Christ's own life—as a blood atonement (cf. Lv 17:11; Heb 9:22). This, then, is the meaning of the cross: Christ subjected Himself to the divine punishment against sin on our behalf (cf. Is 53:4, 5; *see note on 2Co 5:21*). Suffering the brunt of divine wrath in the place of sinners was the "cup" He spoke of having to drink (v. 22).

20:29 leaving Jericho. *See note on v. 30.*

20:30 two blind men. Mark 10:46 and Lk 18:35 mention only one blind man, and Luke says this encounter took place as Christ was approaching Jericho rather than when He was leaving (v. 29). The difficulties are fairly simple to reconcile: there were two blind men, but Bartimaeus (Mk 10:46) was the spokesman of the two and was, therefore, the sole focus of both Luke's and Mark's accounts (*see note on 8:28*). It is also a fact that there were two Jerichos—one the mound of the ancient city (the ruins of which may still be seen today), and the other, the inhabited city of Jericho, close by. Jesus may have been going out of old Jericho and entering new Jericho. Or it may also be that the events are telescoped for us, so that Christ first encountered the blind men on His way into the city, but the healing took place as He was departing. **Son of David.** *See note on 1:1.*

21:1 Bethphage. A small town near Bethany, on the SE slope of the Mt. of Olives. It is mentioned nowhere else in Scripture except in connection with Christ's triumphal entry (Mk 11:1; Lk 19:29).

21:3 If anyone says anything to you. Mark recorded that this was in fact exactly what happened (Mk 11:5, 6). Having just arrived in Bethphage (v. 1), Jesus would have had no opportunity to make arrangements for the use of these animals. Yet He knew precisely the location of the animals and the disposition of the owners. Such detailed foreknowledge reveals His divine omniscience.

21:5 a colt, the foal of a beast of burden. An exact quotation from Zec 9:9 (cf. Is 62:11). The precise fulfillment of this messianic prophecy would not have escaped the Jewish multitudes, who responded with titles and accolades fit only for the Messiah (*see note on v. 9*).

21:7 the donkey and the colt. Matthew is the only gospel writer who mentions the mare donkey. But all mention the young age of the donkey (Jn 12:14), or state that no man had ever sat on him (Mk 11:2; Lk 19:30). The mare was brought along, possibly to induce the colt to cooperate. **He sat.** I.e., on the clothes. Christ rode on the young colt (Mk 11:7).

21:8 spread their coats in the road. Spreading one's garments on the street was an ancient act of homage reserved for high royalty (cf. 2Ki 9:13), suggesting that they recognized His claim to be King of the Jews.

21:9 Hosanna. This transliterates the Heb. expression which is translated "Save now" in Ps 118:25. Blessed is He. This is an exact quotation from v. 26 of the same psalm. This, along with the messianic title "Son of David," make it clear that the crowd was acknowledging Christ's messianic claim (*see note on 1:1*). The date of this entry was Monday, 10 Nisan, A.D. 30, exactly 483 years after the decree of Artaxerxes mentioned in Da 9:24–26 (*see note there*).

21:12 drove out. This was the second time Jesus had cleansed the temple. Jn 2:14–16 describes a similar incident at the beginning of Christ's public ministry. There are distinct differences in the two incidents. In the first cleansing, temple officials confronted Christ immediately afterward (*see note on v. 23*; cf. Jn 2:18); none of the accounts of this second cleansing mention any such confrontation. Instead, the Synoptics all describe how Jesus addressed all present (v. 13) and even made the incident an occasion for public teaching (Mk 11:17; Lk 19:46, 47). **those who were buying and selling.** He regarded both merchants and customers guilty of desecrating the temple. Items being bought and sold included "doves" and other animals for sacrifice (cf. Jn 2:14). **money changers.** Currency-exchange agents, present in droves, were needed because Roman coins and other forms of currency were deemed unacceptable for temple offerings. Evidently, both merchants and money changers were charging such excessive rates that the temple

13 And He *said to them, "It is written, '[A]MY HOUSE SHALL BE CALLED A HOUSE OF PRAYER'; but you are making it a [B]ROBBERS' [a]DEN."

14 And *the* blind and *the* lame came to Him in the temple, and [A]He healed them. 15 But when the chief priests and the scribes saw the wonderful things that He had done, and the children who were shouting in the temple, "Hosanna to the [A]Son of David," they became indignant 16 and said to Him, "Do You hear what these *children* are saying?" And Jesus *said to them, "Yes; have you never read, '[A]OUT OF THE MOUTH OF INFANTS AND NURSING BABIES YOU HAVE PREPARED PRAISE FOR YOURSELF'?" 17 And He left them and went out of the city to [A]Bethany, and spent the night there.

THE BARREN FIG TREE

18 [A]Now in the morning, when He was returning to the city, He became hungry. 19 Seeing a lone [A]fig tree by the road, He came to it and found nothing on it except leaves only; and He *said to it, "No longer shall there ever be *any* fruit from you." And at once the fig tree withered.

20 Seeing *this,* the disciples were amazed and asked, "How did the fig tree wither *all* at once?" 21 And Jesus answered and said to them, "Truly I say to you, [A]if you have faith and do not doubt, you will not only do what was done to the fig tree, but even if you say to this mountain, 'Be taken up and cast into the sea,' it will happen. 22 And [A]all things you ask in prayer, believing, you will receive."

AUTHORITY CHALLENGED

23 [A]When He entered the temple, the chief priests and the elders of the people came to Him [B]while He was teaching, and said, "By what authority are You doing these things, and who gave You this authority?" 24 Jesus said to them, "I will also ask you one [a]thing, which if you tell Me, I will also tell you by what authority I do these things. 25 The baptism of John was from what *source,* from heaven or from men?" And they *began* reasoning among themselves, saying, "If we say, 'From heaven,' He will say to us, 'Then why did you not believe him?' 26 But if we say, 'From men,' we fear the [a]people; for they all regard John as [A]a prophet." 27 And answering Jesus, they said, "We do not know." He also said to them, "Neither will I tell you by what authority I do these things.

PARABLE OF TWO SONS

28 "But what do you think? A man had two [a]sons, and he came to the first and said, '[b]Son, go work today in the [A]vineyard.' 29 And he answered, 'I will not'; but afterward he regretted it and went. 30 The man came to the second and said the same thing; and he answered, 'I *will,* sir'; but he did not go. 31 Which of the two did the will of his father?" They *said, "The first." Jesus *said to them, "Truly I say to you that [A]the tax collectors and prostitutes [a]will get into the kingdom of God before you. 32 For John came to you in the way of righteousness and you did not believe him; but [A]the tax collectors and prostitutes did believe him; and you, seeing *this,* did not even feel remorse afterward so as to believe him.

21:13 [a]Lit *cave* [A]Is 56:7 [B]Jer 7:11 21:14 [A]Matt 4:23 21:15 [A]Matt 9:27 21:16 [A]Ps 8:2; Matt 11:25 21:17 [A]Matt 26:6; Mark 11:1, 11, 12; 14:3; Luke 19:29; 24:50; John 11:1, 18; 12:1 21:18 [A]Matt 21:18-22: *Mark 11:12-14, 20-24* 21:19 [A]Luke 13:6-9 21:21 [A]Matt 17:20; Mark 11:23; Luke 17:6; James 1:6 21:22 [A]Matt 7:7 21:23 [A]Matt 21:23-27: *Mark 11:27-33; Luke 20:1-8* [B]Matt 26:55 21:24 [a]Lit *word* 21:26 [a]Lit *crowd* [A]Matt 11:9; Mark 6:20 21:28 [a]Lit *children* [b]Lit *Child* [A]Matt 20:1; 21:33 21:31 [a]Lit *are getting into* [A]Luke 7:29, 37-50 21:32 [A]Luke 3:12; 7:29f

marketplace took on the atmosphere of a thieves' den (v. 13). This kind of commerce took place in the court of the Gentiles, a large area covering several acres on the temple mount.

21:13 It is written. Jesus conflates two OT prophecies, Is 56:7 ("My house will be called a house of prayer for all the peoples") and Jer 7:11 ("Has this house, which is called by My name, become a den of robbers in your sight?").

21:15 children. Lit. "boys." The crowd in Jerusalem for the Passover would have included a large number of 12-year-olds, who were there to celebrate their first Passover, just as Jesus Himself had done.

21:16 Yes; have you never read. Jesus' reply to the "indignant" chief priests and scribes amounted to an inescapable assertion of His deity. In quoting from Ps 8:2, He was claiming the right to receive worship as God.

21:19 at once. This is a relative term; the tree may have died at once, but Mk 11:14, 20 (*see notes there*) suggested that the withering was not visible until the following day. Jesus' cursing of the tree was a purposeful divine object lesson, not an impetuous act of frustration. The fig tree is often employed in Scripture as a symbol of Israel (Hos 9:10; Joel 1:7)—and the barren fig tree often symbolizes divine judgment on Israel because of her spiritual fruitlessness (*see note on 3:8*) despite an abundance of spiritual advantages (Jer 8:13; Joel 1:12). Jesus' act therefore illustrates God's judgment against earthly Israel for shameful fruitlessness, exemplified in the rejection of their Messiah. One of Christ's parables taught a similar lesson (Lk 13:6–9).

21:21 if you have faith and do not doubt. This presupposes that the thing requested is actually God's will (*see note on 17:20*)—for only God-given faith is so doubt-free (cf. Mk 9:24). **it will happen.** A miracle on such a cosmic scale was precisely what the scribes and Pharisees wanted Christ to do, but He always declined (*see note on 12:38*). Here, He was speaking figuratively about the immeasurable power of God, unleashed in the lives of those with true faith.

21:23 these things. I.e., both His public teaching and miracles. They may have also had in mind His act of cleansing the temple on the day before (*see note on v. 12*). **who gave You this authority?** They were forced to acknowledge that He had some source of indisputable authority. His miracles were too obvious and too numerous to be fraudulent. Even His teaching was with such force and clarity that it was obvious to all that there was authority in His words (*see note on 7:29*).

21:25 The baptism of John was from what *source* . . . ? Jesus caught the Jewish leaders in their own trap. They had no doubt hoped that He would answer by asserting that His authority came directly from God (as He had many times before—cf. Jn 5:19–23; 10:18). They then accused Him of blasphemy and used the charge as an excuse to kill Him—as they had also attempted to do before (Jn 5:18; 10:31–33). Here, however, He asked a question that placed them in an impossible dilemma, because John was widely revered by the people. They could not affirm John's ministry without condemning themselves. And if they denied John's legitimacy, they feared the response of the people (v. 26). In effect, Jesus exposed their own lack of any authority to examine Him. *See note on Lk 20:5.*

21:31 Which of the two did the will of his father? Jesus forced them to testify against themselves. The point of the parable was that doing is more important than saying (cf. 7:21–27; Jas 1:22). They had to acknowledge this, yet in doing so they condemned themselves. The idea that repentant tax collectors and harlots would enter the kingdom before outwardly religious hypocrites was a recurring theme in His ministry (*see note on 5:20*), and this infuriated the Jewish leaders.

21:32 the way of righteousness. I.e., the repentance and faith that results in the imputation of God's righteousness (*see note on Ro 3:21*). **tax collectors and prostitutes.** *See notes on 5:46; 9:9; Mk 2:15.* The pariahs of Jewish society, most publicly despised by the chief priests and elders, had found salvation, while the self-righteous leaders had not. Cf. Ro 10:3.

PARABLE OF THE LANDOWNER

33 "Listen to another parable. [A]There was a [a]land-
owner who [B]PLANTED A [C]VINEYARD AND PUT A WALL
AROUND IT AND DUG A WINE PRESS IN IT, AND BUILT
A TOWER, and rented it out to [b]vine-growers and
[D]went on a journey. 34 When the [a]harvest time approached, he [A]sent his slaves to the vine-growers
to receive his produce. 35 The vine-growers took his
slaves and beat one, and killed another, and stoned
a third. 36 Again he [A]sent another group of slaves
larger than the first; and they did the same thing
to them. 37 But afterward he sent his son to them,
saying, 'They will respect my son.' 38 But when the
vine-growers saw the son, they said among themselves, 'This is the heir; come, let us kill him and
seize his inheritance.' 39 They took him, and threw
him out of the vineyard and killed him. 40 Therefore
when the [a]owner of the vineyard comes, what will
he do to those vine-growers?" 41 They *said to Him,
"He will bring those wretches to a wretched end,
and [A]will rent out the vineyard to other vine-growers who will pay him the proceeds at the *proper*
seasons."
42 Jesus *said to them, "Did you never read in
the Scriptures,

'[A]THE STONE WHICH THE BUILDERS REJECTED,
THIS BECAME THE CHIEF CORNER *stone;*
THIS CAME ABOUT FROM THE LORD,
AND IT IS MARVELOUS IN OUR EYES'?

43 Therefore I say to you, the kingdom of God will
be taken away from you and given to a [a]people,
producing the fruit of it. 44 And [A]he who falls on this
stone will be broken to pieces; but on whomever it
falls, it will scatter him like dust."
45 When the chief priests and the Pharisees heard
His parables, they understood that He was speaking
about them. 46 When they sought to seize Him, they
[A]feared the [a]people, because they considered Him
to be a [B]prophet.

PARABLE OF THE MARRIAGE FEAST

22 Jesus spoke to them again in parables, saying,
2 "[A]The kingdom of heaven [a]may be compared to [b]a king who [c]gave a [B]wedding feast for
his son. 3 And he [A]sent out his slaves to call those
who had been invited to the wedding feast, and
they were unwilling to come. 4 Again he [A]sent out
other slaves saying, 'Tell those who have been invited, "Behold, I have prepared my dinner; my oxen
and my fattened livestock are *all* butchered and
everything is ready; come to the wedding feast." '
5 But they paid no attention and went their way,
one to his own [a]farm, another to his business, 6 and
the rest seized his slaves and mistreated them and
killed them. 7 But the king was enraged, and he sent
his armies and destroyed those murderers and
set their city on fire. 8 Then he *said to his slaves,
'The wedding is ready, but those who were invited
were not worthy. 9 Go therefore to [A]the main highways, and as many as you find *there,* invite to the
wedding feast.' 10 Those slaves went out into the
streets and gathered together all they found, both
evil and good; and the wedding hall was filled with
[a]dinner guests.

21:33 [a]Lit *a man, head of a household* [b]Or *tenant farmers,* also vv 34, 35, 38, 40 [A]Matt 21:33-46: *Mark 12:1-12; Luke 20:9-19* [B]Is 5:1, 2 [C]Matt 20:1; 21:28 [D]Matt 25:14
21:34 [a]Lit *the fruit season* [A]Matt 22:3 21:36 [A]Matt 22:4 21:40 [a]Lit *lord* 21:41 [A]Matt 8:11f; Acts 13:46; 18:6; 28:28 21:42 [A]Ps 118:22f; Acts 4:11; Rom 9:33; 1 Pet 2:7 21:43 [a]Lit *nation* 21:44 [A]Is 8:14, 15 21:46 [a]Lit *crowds* [A]Matt 21:26 [B]Matt 21:11 22:2 [a]Lit *was compared to* [b]Lit *a man, a king* [c]Lit *made* [A]Matt 13:24; 22:2-14; Luke 14:16-24 [B]Luke 12:36; John 2:2 22:3 [A]Matt 21:34
22:4 [A]Matt 21:36 22:5 [a]Or *field* 22:9 [A]Ezek 21:21; Obad 14 22:10 [a]Lit *those reclining* at the table

21:33 a vineyard .... wine press. See Is 5:2. Jesus was clearly alluding to this OT passage, which would have been familiar to the Jewish leaders. The "vineyard" is a common symbol for the Jewish nation in Scripture. Here the landowner, representing God, developed the vineyard with great care, then leased it to "vine-growers," representing the Jewish leaders.

21:34 his slaves. I.e., the OT prophets.

21:35 beat one ... killed another ... stoned a third. Matthew often blends and simplifies details (*see notes on v. 19; 8:28; 20:30*). From Mark's account we learn that in Jesus' telling of this story, 3 different slaves came individually. The tenants "beat" the first one, "wounded" the second, and "killed" the third (Mk 12:2–5). This corresponds to the Jewish rulers' treatment of many of the OT prophets (1Ki 22:24; 2Ch 24:20, 21; 36:15, 16; Ne 9:26; Jer 2:30).

21:37 my son. This person represents the Lord Jesus Christ, whom they killed (vv. 38, 39) and thereby incurred divine judgment (v. 41).

21:41 rent out the vineyard to other vine-growers. Again the Jewish leaders pronounced their own judgment (*see note on v. 31*). Their verdict against the evil vine-growers was also Christ's judgment against them (v. 43). The kingdom and all the spiritual advantages given to Israel would now be given to "other vine-growers," symbolizing the church (v. 43), which consists primarily of Gentiles (cf. Ro 11:11).

21:42 the stone ... rejected. This refers to His crucifixion; and the restoration of "the chief corner stone" anticipates His resurrection. the chief corner *stone.* To the superficial eye, this quotation from Ps 118:22, 23 is irrelevant to the parable that precedes it. But it is taken from a messianic psalm. Jesus cited it to suggest that the Son who was killed and thrown out of the vineyard was also "the chief corner stone" in God's redemptive plan.

21:43 a people, producing the fruit of it. The church. *See note on v. 41.* Peter spoke of the church as "a holy nation" (1Pe 2:9).

21:44 this stone. Christ is "a stone to strike and a rock to stumble over" to unbelievers (Is 8:14; 1Pe 2:8). And the prophet Daniel pictured Him as a great stone "cut out of the mountain without hands," which falls on the kingdoms of the world and crushes them (Da 2:44, 45). Whether a ceramic vessel "falls on" a rock, or the rock "falls" on the vessel, the result is the same. The saying suggests that both enmity and apathy are wrong responses to Christ, and those guilty of either are in danger of judgment.

21:45 they understood that He was speaking about them. By evoking so much familiar messianic imagery (vv. 42–44), Christ made His meaning inescapable to the chief priests and Pharisees.

22:2 a king who gave a wedding feast for his son. Jesus told a similar, but different, parable in Lk 14:16–23. Here, the banquet was a wedding feast for the king's own son, making the apathy (v. 5) and rejection (v. 6) of those invited much more of a personal slight against the king. Also, here they actually mistreated and killed the king's messengers—an unthinkable affront to the king's goodness.

22:4 Again he sent out other slaves. This illustrates God's patience and forbearance with those who deliberately spurn Him. He continues to extend the invitation even after His goodness has been ignored or rebuffed.

22:7 the king was enraged. His vast patience finally exhausted, He judges them. **set their city on fire.** The judgment Jesus described anticipated the destruction of Jerusalem in A.D. 70. Even the massive stone temple was destroyed by fire and reduced to rubble in that conflagration. *See notes on 23:36; 24:2; Lk 19:43.*

22:9 as many as you find ... invite to the wedding feast. This illustrates the free offer of the gospel, which is extended to all indiscriminately (cf. Rev 22:17).

11 “But when the king came in to look over the
dinner guests, he saw [A]a man there who was not
dressed in wedding clothes, 12 and he *said to him,
‘[A]Friend, how did you come in here without wedding clothes?’ And the man was speechless. 13 Then
the king said to the servants, ‘Bind him hand and
foot, and throw him into [A]the outer darkness; in
that place there will be weeping and gnashing of
teeth.’ 14 For many are [a,A]called, but few *are* [A]chosen.”

TRIBUTE TO CAESAR

15 [A]Then the Pharisees went and [a]plotted together
how they might trap Him [b]in what He said. 16 And
they *sent their disciples to Him, along with the
[A]Herodians, saying, “Teacher, we know that You
are truthful and teach the way of God in truth, and
[a]defer to no one; for You are not partial to any. 17 Tell
us then, what do You think? Is it [a]lawful to give a
[A]poll-tax to [B]Caesar, or not?” 18 But Jesus perceived
their [a]malice, and said, “Why are you testing Me,
you hypocrites? 19 Show Me the [A]coin *used* for the
poll-tax.” And they brought Him a [a]denarius. 20 And
He *said to them, “Whose likeness and inscription
is this?” 21 They *said to Him, “Caesar’s.” Then He
*said to them, “[A]Then render to Caesar the things
that are Caesar’s; and to God the things that are
God’s.” 22 And hearing *this,* they were amazed, and
[A]leaving Him, they went away.

JESUS ANSWERS THE SADDUCEES

23 [A]On that day *some* [B]Sadducees (who say [C]there
is no resurrection) came to Jesus and questioned
Him, 24 asking, “Teacher, Moses said, ‘[A]IF A MAN DIES
HAVING NO CHILDREN, HIS BROTHER AS NEXT OF KIN
SHALL MARRY HIS WIFE, AND RAISE UP CHILDREN FOR
HIS BROTHER.’ 25 Now there were seven brothers with
us; and the first married and died, and having no
children left his wife to his brother; 26 so also the
second, and the third, down to the seventh. 27 Last
of all, the woman died. 28 In the resurrection, therefore, whose wife of the seven will she be? For they
all had *married* her.”

29 But Jesus answered and said to them, “You are
mistaken, [A]not [a]understanding the Scriptures nor the
power of God. 30 For in the resurrection they neither
[A]marry nor are given in marriage, but are like angels

22:11 [A]2 Kin 10:22; Zech 3:3, 4 22:12 [A]Matt 20:13; 26:50 22:13 [A]Matt 8:12; 25:30; Luke 13:28 22:14 [a]Or *invited* [A]Matt 24:22; 2 Pet 1:10; Rev 17:14 22:15 [a]Lit *took counsel* [b]Lit *in word* [A]Matt 22:15-22: *Mark 12:13-17; Luke 20:20-26* 22:16 [a]Lit *it is not a concern to You about anyone;* i.e. You do not seek anyone’s favor [A]Mark 3:6; 8:15; 12:13 22:17 [a]Or *permissible* [A]Matt 17:25 [B]Luke 2:1; 3:1 22:18 [a]Or *wickedness* 22:19 [a]The denarius was a day’s wages [A]Matt 17:25 22:21 [A]Mark 12:17; Luke 20:25; Rom 13:7 22:22 [A]Mark 12:12 22:23 [A]Matt 22:23-33: *Mark 12:18-27; Luke 20:27-40* [B]Matt 3:7 [C]Acts 23:8 22:24 [A]Deut 25:5 22:29 [a]Or *knowing* [A]John 20:9 22:30 [A]Matt 24:38; Luke 17:27

22:11 wedding clothes. All without exception were invited to the banquet, so this man is not to be viewed as a common party-crasher. In fact, all the guests were rounded up hastily from “the streets” and therefore none could be expected to come with proper attire. That means the wedding garments were supplied by the king himself. So this man’s lack of a proper garment indicates he had purposely rejected the king’s own gracious provision. His affront to the king was actually a greater insult than those who refused to come at all, because he committed his impertinence in the very presence of the king. The imagery seems to represent those who identify with the kingdom externally, profess to be Christians, belong to the church in a visible sense—yet spurn the garment of righteousness Christ offers (cf. Is 61:10) by seeking to establish a righteousness of their own (cf. Ro 10:3; Php 3:8, 9). Ashamed to admit their own spiritual poverty (*see note on 5:3*), they refuse the better garment the King graciously offers—and thus they are guilty of a horrible sin against His goodness.

22:12 the man was speechless. I.e., he had no excuse.

22:13 outer darkness. This would describe the darkness farthest from the light, i.e., outer darkness. **weeping and gnashing of teeth.** This speaks of inconsolable grief and unremitting torment. Jesus commonly used the phrases in this verse to describe hell (cf. 13:42, 50; 24:51).

22:14 many are called, but few *are* chosen. The call spoken of here is sometimes referred to as the “general call” (or the “external” call)—a summons to repentance and faith that is inherent in the gospel message. This call extends to all who hear the gospel. “Many” hear it; “few” respond (see the many-few comparison in 7:13, 14). Those who respond are the “chosen,” the elect. In the Pauline writings, the word “call” usually refers to God’s irresistible calling extended to the elect alone (Ro 8:30)—known as the “effectual call” (or the “internal” call). The effectual call is the supernatural drawing of God which Jesus speaks of in Jn 6:44. Here a general call is in view, and this call extends to all who hear the gospel—this call is the great “whosoever will” of the gospel (cf. Rev 22:17). Here, then, is the proper balance between human responsibility and divine sovereignty: the “called” who reject the invitation do so willingly, and therefore their exclusion from the kingdom is perfectly just. The “chosen” enter the kingdom only because of the grace of God in choosing and drawing them.

22:16 Herodians. A party of the Jews who supported the Roman-backed Herodian dynasty. The Herodians were not a religious party, like the Pharisees, but a political party, probably consisting largely of Sadducees (including the rulers of the temple). By contrast, the Pharisees hated Roman rule and the Herodian influence. The fact that these groups would conspire together to entrap Jesus reveals how seriously both groups viewed Him as a threat. Herod himself wanted Jesus dead (Lk 13:31), and the Pharisees were already plotting to kill Him as well (Jn 11:53). So they joined efforts to seek their common goal.

22:17 Is it lawful to give a poll-tax to Caesar, or not? At issue was an annual fee of one denarius (*see note on v. 19*) per person. Such taxes were part of the heavy taxation Rome assessed. Since these funds were used to finance the occupying armies, all Roman taxes were hated by the people. But the poll tax was the most hated of all because it suggested that Rome owned even the people, while they viewed themselves and their nation as possessions of God. It was therefore significant that they questioned Christ about the poll tax in particular. If He answered no to their question, the Herodians would charge Him with treason against Rome. If He said yes, the Pharisees would accuse Him of disloyalty to the Jewish nation, and He would lose the support of the crowds.

22:19 denarius. *See note on Mk 12:16.* A silver coin, the value of a day’s wage for a Roman soldier. The coins were minted under the emperor’s authority since only he could issue gold or silver coins. The “denarius” of Jesus’ day was minted by Tiberius. One side bore an image of his face; the other featured an engraving of him sitting on his throne in priestly robes. The Jews considered such images idolatry, forbidden by the second commandment (Ex 20:4), which made this tax and these coins doubly offensive.

22:21 Caesar’s ... God’s. Caesar’s image is stamped on the coin; God’s image is stamped on the person (Gen 1:26, 27). The Christian must “render” obedience to Caesar in Caesar’s realm (Ro 13:1–7; 1Pe 2:13–17), but “the things that are God’s” are things that do not belong to Caesar and should be given only to God. Christ thus acknowledged Caesar’s right to assess and collect taxes, and He made it the duty of Christians to pay them. But He did not suggest (as some suppose) that Caesar had sole or ultimate authority in the social or political realms. Ultimately, all things are God’s (Ro 11:36; 2Co 5:18; Rev 4:11)—including the realm in which Caesar or any other earthly ruler exercises authority.

22:23 no resurrection. *See note on 3:7.*

22:24 his brother ... shall marry his wife. This refers to the law of levirate marriage, found in Dt 25:5–10 (*see note there*). This was a provision to ensure that family lines were kept intact and widows were cared for.

22:30 like angels in heaven. The Sadducees did not believe in angels (*see note on 3:7*)—so here Jesus was exposing another of their false beliefs. Angels are deathless creatures who do not propagate and therefore have no need for marriage. “In the resurrection,” the saints will have those same characteristics.

in heaven. 31 But regarding the resurrection of the
dead, have you not read what was spoken to you by
God: 32 '[A]I AM THE GOD OF ABRAHAM, AND THE GOD
OF ISAAC, AND THE GOD OF JACOB'? He is not the God
of the dead but of the living." 33 When the crowds
heard *this,* [A]they were astonished at His teaching.
34 [A]But when the Pharisees heard that Jesus had
silenced [B]the Sadducees, they gathered themselves
together. 35 One of them, [a,A]a lawyer, asked Him *a*
question, testing Him, 36 "Teacher, which is the great
commandment in the Law?" 37 And He said to him,
" '[A]YOU SHALL LOVE THE LORD YOUR GOD WITH ALL
YOUR HEART, AND WITH ALL YOUR SOUL, AND WITH ALL
YOUR MIND.' 38 This is the great and [a]foremost commandment. 39 The second is like it, '[A]YOU SHALL LOVE
YOUR NEIGHBOR AS YOURSELF.' 40 [A]On these two commandments depend the whole Law and the Prophets."
41 [A]Now while the Pharisees were gathered together, Jesus asked them a question: 42 "What do you
think about [a]the Christ, whose son is He?" They *said
to Him, "[A]*The son* of David." 43 He *said to them, "Then
how does David [a,A]in the Spirit call Him 'Lord,' saying,

44 '[A]THE LORD SAID TO MY LORD,
"SIT AT MY RIGHT HAND,
UNTIL I PUT YOUR ENEMIES
BENEATH YOUR FEET" '?

45 If David then calls Him 'Lord,' how is He his son?"
46 [A]No one was able to answer Him a word, nor did
anyone dare from that day on to ask Him [a]another
question.

PHARISAISM EXPOSED

23 [A]Then Jesus spoke to the crowds and to His
disciples, 2 saying: "[A]The scribes and the Pharisees have seated themselves in the chair of Moses;
3 therefore all that they tell you, do and observe, but
do not do according to their deeds; for they say *things*
and do not do *them.* 4 [A]They tie up heavy burdens and
lay them on men's shoulders, but they themselves are
unwilling to move them with *so much as* a finger.
5 But they do all their deeds [A]to be noticed by men;
for they [B]broaden their [a]phylacteries and lengthen
[C]the tassels *of their garments.* 6 They [A]love the place
of honor at banquets and the chief seats in the synagogues, 7 and respectful greetings in the market
places, and being called [A]Rabbi by men. 8 But [A]do not
be called [B]Rabbi; for One is your Teacher, and you are
all brothers. 9 Do not call *anyone* on earth your father;
for [A]One is your Father, He who is in heaven. 10 Do
not be called [a]leaders; for One is your Leader, *that is,*
Christ. 11 [A]But the greatest among you shall be your
servant. 12 [A]Whoever exalts himself shall be humbled;
and whoever humbles himself shall be exalted.

22:32 [A]Ex 3:6 22:33 [A]Matt 7:28 22:34 [A]Matt 22:34-40: *Mark 12:28-31;* Luke 10:25-37 [B]Matt 3:7 22:35 [a]I.e. an expert in the Mosaic Law [A]Luke 7:30; 10:25; 11:45, 46, 52; 14:3; Titus 3:13 22:37 [A]Deut 6:5 22:38 [a]Or *first* 22:39 [A]Lev 19:18; Matt 19:19; Gal 5:14 22:40 [A]Matt 7:12 22:41 [A]Matt 22:41-46: *Mark 12:35-37; Luke 20:41-44* 22:42 [a]I.e. the Messiah [A]Matt 9:27 22:43 [a]Or *by inspiration* [A]2 Sam 23:2; Rev 1:10; 4:2 22:44 [A]Ps 110:1; Matt 26:64; Mark 16:19; Acts 2:34f; 1 Cor 15:25; Heb 1:13; 10:13 22:46 [a]Lit *any longer* [A]Mark 12:34; Luke 14:6; 20:40 23:1 [A]Matt 23:1-7: *Mark 12:38, 39; Luke 20:45, 46* 23:2 [A]Deut 33:3f; Ezra 7:6, 25; Neh 8:4 23:4 [A]Luke 11:46; Acts 15:10 23:5 [a]I.e. small cases containing Scripture texts worn on the left arm and forehead for religious purposes [A]Matt 6:1, 5, 16 [B]Ex 13:9; Deut 6:8; 11:18 [C]Matt 9:20 23:6 [A]Luke 11:43; 14:7; 20:46 23:7 [A]Matt 23:8; 26:25, 49; Mark 9:5; 10:51; 11:21; John 1:38, 49; 3:2, 26; 4:31; 6:25; 9:2; 11:8; 20:16 23:8 [A]James 3:1 [B]Matt 23:7; 26:25, 49; Mark 9:5; 10:51; 11:21; 14:45; John 1:38, 49; 3:2, 26; 4:31; 6:25; 9:2; 11:8; 20:16 23:9 [A]Matt 6:9; 7:11 23:10 [a]Or *teachers* 23:11 [A]Matt 20:26 23:12 [A]Luke 14:11; 18:14

22:32 not the God of the dead. Jesus' argument (taken from the Pentateuch, because the Sadducees recognized only Moses' authority—*see note on 3:7*) was based on the emphatic present tense "I am" of Ex 3:6. This subtle but effective argument utterly silenced the Sadducees (v. 34). *See note on Mk 12:26.*

22:35 a lawyer. A scribe whose specialty was interpreting the law. *See notes on 2:4; Lk 10:25.*

22:36 *See note on Mk 12:28.*

22:37 heart ... soul ... mind. Mark 12:30 adds "strength." The quote is from Dt 6:5, part of the *shema,* (Heb. for "hear"—Dt 6:4). That verse says "heart ... soul ... strength." Some LXX manuscripts added "mind." The use of the various terms is not meant to delineate distinct human faculties, but to underscore the completeness of the kind of love that is called for.

22:39 love your neighbor as yourself. This is a quotation from Lv 19:18. Contrary to some contemporary interpretations, it is not a mandate for self-love. Rather, it contains in different words the very same idea as the Golden Rule (*see note on 7:12*). It prompts believers to measure their love for others by what they wish for themselves.

22:40 the whole Law and the Prophets. I.e., the whole OT. Thus Jesus subsumes man's whole moral duty under two categories: love for God, and love for one's neighbors. These same two categories differentiate the first 4 commandments of the Decalogue from the final 6.

22:42 What do you think ... ? A phrase often used by Christ to introduce a question designed to test someone (v. 17; 17:25; 18:12; 21:28; 26:66). Here, the Pharisees, Herodians, Sadducees, and scribes had all put Him to the test. He also had a test for them. ***The son of David.*** *See note on 1:1.* "Son of David" was the most common messianic title in the usage of Jesus' day. Their answer reflected their conviction that the Messiah would be no more than a man, and Jesus' reply was another assertion of His deity. *See note on v. 45.*

22:43 in the Spirit. I.e., under the inspiration of the Holy Spirit (cf. Mk 12:36).

22:44 Quoted from Ps 110:1.

22:45 David then calls Him "Lord." David would not have addressed a merely human descendant as "Lord." Here Jesus was not disputing whether "Son of David" was an appropriate title for the Messiah; after all, the title is based on what is revealed about the Messiah in the OT (Is 11:1; Jer 23:5) and it is used as a messianic title in 1:1 (*see note there*). But Jesus was pointing out that the title "son of David" did not begin to sum up all that is true about the Messiah who is also "son of God" (Lk 22:70). The inescapable implication is that Jesus was declaring His deity.

23:2 chair of Moses. The expression is equivalent to a university's "chair of philosophy." To "sit in the chair of Moses" was to have the highest authority to instruct people in the law. The expression here may be translated, "[they] have seated themselves in Moses' seat"—stressing the fact that this was an imaginary authority they claimed for themselves. There was a legitimate sense in which the priests and Levites had authority to decide matters of the law (Dt 17:9), but the scribes and Pharisees had gone beyond any legitimate authority and were adding human tradition to the Word of God (15:3–9). For that Jesus condemned them (vv. 8–36).

23:3 observe ... do not do. I.e., insofar as it accords with the Word of God. The Pharisees were prone to bind "heavy burdens" (v. 4) of extrabiblical traditions and put them on others' shoulders. Jesus explicitly condemned that sort of legalism.

23:5 phylacteries. Leather boxes containing a parchment on which is written in 4 columns (Ex 13:1–10, 11–16; Dt 6:4–9; 11:13–21). These are worn by men during prayer—one on the middle of the forehead and one on the left arm just above the elbow. The use of phylacteries was based on an overly literal interpretation of passages like Ex 13:9, 10; Dt 6:8. Evidently, the Pharisees would broaden the leather straps by which the phylacteries were bound to their arms and foreheads, in order to make the phylacteries more prominent. ***the tassels of their garments.*** Jesus Himself wore them (*see note on 9:20*), so it was not the tassels themselves that He condemned, only the mentality that would lengthen the tassels to make it appear that one was especially spiritual.

23:8–10 Rabbi ... father ... leaders. Here Jesus condemns pride and pretense, not titles per se. Paul repeatedly speaks of "leaders" in the church, and even refers to himself as the Corinthians' "father" (1Co 4:15). Obviously, this does not forbid the showing of respect, either (cf. 1Th. 5:11, 12; 1Ti 5:1). Christ is merely forbidding the use of such names as spiritual titles, or in an ostentatious sense that accords undue spiritual authority to a human being, as

EIGHT WOES

13 "[A]But woe to you, scribes and Pharisees, hypocrites, [B]because you shut off the kingdom of heaven
[a]from [b]people; for you do not enter in yourselves,
nor do you allow those who are entering to go in.
14 [[a]Woe to you, scribes and Pharisees, hypocrites,
because [A]you devour widows' houses, and for a
pretense you make long prayers; therefore you will
receive greater condemnation.]
15 "Woe to you, scribes and Pharisees, hypocrites,
because you travel around on sea and land to make
one [a,A]proselyte; and when he becomes one, you
make him twice as much a son of [b,B]hell as yourselves.
16 "Woe to you, [A]blind guides, who say, '[B]Who-
ever swears by the [a]temple, *that* is nothing; but
whoever swears by the gold of the [a]temple is obligated.' 17 You fools and blind men! [A]Which is [a]more
important, the gold or the [b]temple that sanctified
the gold? 18 And, 'Whoever swears by the altar, *that*
is nothing, but whoever swears by the [a]offering on
it, he is obligated.' 19 You blind men, [A]which is [a]more
important, the [b]offering, or the altar that sanctifies
the [b]offering? 20 Therefore, [a]whoever swears by the
altar, swears *both* by [b]the altar and by everything
on it. 21 And [a]whoever swears by the [b]temple, swears
both by [c]the temple and by Him who [A]dwells within
it. 22 And [a]whoever swears by heaven, [A]swears *both*
by the throne of God and by Him who sits upon it.
23 "[A]Woe to you, scribes and Pharisees, hypocrites!
For you tithe mint and dill and [a]cummin, and have
neglected the weightier provisions of the law: justice and mercy and faithfulness; but these are the
things you should have done without neglecting
the others. 24 You [A]blind guides, who strain out a
gnat and swallow a camel!
25 "Woe to you, scribes and Pharisees, hypocrites!
For [A]you clean the outside of the cup and of the dish,
but inside they are full [a]of robbery and self-indulgence. 26 You blind Pharisee, first [A]clean the inside
of the cup and of the dish, so that the outside of it
may become clean also.
27 "[A]Woe to you, scribes and Pharisees, hypocrites!
For you are like whitewashed tombs which on the
outside appear beautiful, but inside they are full of
dead men's bones and all uncleanness. 28 So you, too,
outwardly appear righteous to men, but inwardly
you are full of hypocrisy and lawlessness.
29 "[A]Woe to you, scribes and Pharisees, hypocrites!
For you build the tombs of the prophets and adorn
the monuments of the righteous, 30 and say, 'If we
had been *living* in the days of our fathers, we would
not have been partners with them in *shedding* the
blood of the prophets.' 31 So you testify against yourselves, that you [A]are [a]sons of those who murdered
the prophets. 32 Fill up, then, the measure *of the
guilt* of your fathers. 33 You serpents, [A]you brood of
vipers, how [a]will you escape the [b]sentence of [c,B]hell?
34 "[A]Therefore, behold, [B]I am sending you prophets
and wise men and scribes; some of them you will kill
and crucify, and some of them you will [C]scourge in
your synagogues, and [D]persecute from city to city,
35 so that upon you may fall *the guilt of* all the righteous blood shed on earth, from the blood of righteous [A]Abel to the blood of Zechariah, the [B]son of
Berechiah, whom [C]you murdered between the [a]temple

23:13 [a]Lit *in front of* [b]Gr *anthropoi* [A]Matt 23:15, 16, 23, 25, 27, 29 [B]Luke 11:52 23:14 [a]This v not found in early mss [A]Mark 12:40; Luke 20:47 23:15 [a]Or *convert* [b]Gr *Gehenna* [A]Acts 2:10; 6:5; 13:43 [B]Matt 5:22 23:16 [a]Or *sanctuary* [A]Matt 15:14; 23:24 [B]Matt 5:33-35 23:17 [a]Lit *greater* [b]Or *sanctuary* [A]Ex 30:29 23:18 [a]Or *gift* 23:19 [a]Lit *greater* [b]Or *gift* [A]Ex 29:37 23:20 [a]Lit *he who* [b]Lit *it* 23:21 [a]Lit *he who* [b]Or *sanctuary* [c]Lit *it* [A]1 Kin 8:13; Ps 26:8; 132:14 23:22 [a]Lit *he who* [A]Is 66:1; Matt 5:34 23:23 [a]Similar to caraway seeds [A]Matt 23:13; Luke 11:42 23:24 [A]Matt 23:16 23:25 [a]Or *as a result of* [A]Mark 7:4; Luke 11:39f 23:26 [A]Mark 7:4; Luke 11:39f 23:27 [A]Luke 11:44; Acts 23:3 23:29 [A]Luke 11:47f 23:31 [a]Or *descendants* [A]Matt 23:34, 37; Acts 7:51f 23:33 [a]Lit *would* [b]Or *judgment* [c]Gr *Gehenna* [A]Matt 3:7; Luke 3:7 [B]Matt 5:22 23:34 [A]Matt 23:34-36; Luke 11:49-51 [B]2 Chr 36:15, 16 [C]Matt 10:17 [D]Matt 10:23 23:35 [a]Or *sanctuary* [A]Gen 4:8ff; Heb 11:4 [B]Zech 1:1 [C]2 Chr 24:21

if he were the source of truth rather than God.

23:13 nor do you allow. The Pharisees, having shunned God's righteousness, were seeking to establish a righteousness of their own (Ro 10:3)—and teaching others to do so as well. Their legalism and self-righteousness effectively obscured the narrow gate by which the kingdom must be entered (*see notes on 7:13, 14*).

23:14 This verse does not appear in the earliest available manuscripts of Matthew, but does appear in Mark. *See notes on Mk 12:40.*

23:15 proselyte. A Gentile convert to Judaism. *See Ac 6:5.* **a son of hell.** I.e., someone whose eternal destination is hell.

23:16 *that* is nothing. This was an arbitrary distinction the Pharisees had made, which gave them a sanctimonious justification for lying with impunity. If someone swore "by the temple" (or the altar, v. 18; or heaven, v. 22), his oath was not considered binding, but if he swore "by the gold of the temple," he could not break his word without being subject to the penalties of Jewish law. Our Lord makes it clear that swearing by those things is tantamount to swearing by God Himself. *See note on 5:34.*

23:23 tithe mint and dill and cummin. Garden herbs, not really the kind of farm produce that the tithe was designed to cover (Lv 27:30). But the Pharisees fastidiously weighed out a tenth of every herb, perhaps even counting individual dill seeds. Jesus' point, however, was not to condemn their observance of the law's fine points. The problem was that they "neglected the weightier provisions" of justice and mercy and faith—the moral principles underlying all the laws. They were satisfied with their focus on the incidentals and externals but willfully resisted the spiritual meaning of the law. He told them they should have concentrated on those larger issues "without neglecting the others."

23:24 strain out a gnat and swallow a camel! Some Pharisees would strain their beverages through a fine cloth to make sure they did not inadvertently swallow a gnat—the smallest of unclean animals (Lv 11:23). The camel was the largest of all the unclean animals (Lv 11:4).

23:25 you clean the outside. The Pharisees' focus on external issues lay at the heart of their error. Who would want to drink from a cup that had been washed on the outside but was still filthy inside? Yet the Pharisees lived their lives as if external appearance were more important than internal reality. That was the very essence of their hypocrisy, and Jesus rebuked them for it repeatedly (*see notes on 5:20; 16:12*).

23:27 whitewashed tombs. Tombs were regularly whitewashed to make them stand out. Accidentally touching or stepping on a grave caused ceremonial uncleanness (Nu 19:16). A freshly whitewashed tomb would be brilliantly white and clean-looking—and sometimes spectacularly ornate. But the inside was full of defilement and decay. Contrast Jesus' words here and in Lk 11:44.

23:30 we would not have been partners. A ridiculous claim to self-righteousness when they were already plotting the murder of the Messiah (cf. Jn 11:47–53).

23:34 prophets and wise men and scribes. I.e., the disciples, as well as the prophets, evangelists, and pastors who followed them (cf. Eph 4:11).

23:35 Abel ... Zechariah. The first and last OT martyrs, respectively. **son of Berechiah.** (Zec 1:1). The OT does not record how he died. However, the death of another Zechariah, son of Jehoiada, is recorded in 2Ch 24:20, 21. He was stoned in the court of the temple, exactly as Jesus describes here. All the best manuscripts of Matthew contain the phrase "Zechariah, son of Berechiah" (though it does not appear in Lk 11:51). Some have suggested that the Zechariah in 2Ch 24 was actually a grandson of Jehoiada, and that his father's

and the altar. 36 Truly I say to you, all these things will
come upon [A]this generation.

LAMENT OVER JERUSALEM

37 "[A]Jerusalem, Jerusalem, who [B]kills the prophets
and stones those who are sent to her! How often I
wanted to gather your children together, [C]the way
a hen gathers her chicks under her wings, and you
were unwilling. 38 Behold, [A]your house is being left
to you desolate! 39 For I say to you, from now on you
will not see Me until you say, '[A]BLESSED IS HE WHO
COMES IN THE NAME OF THE LORD!' "

SIGNS OF CHRIST'S RETURN

24 [A]Jesus [B]came out from the temple and was
going away [a]when His disciples came up to
point out the temple buildings to Him. 2 And He
said to them, "Do you not see all these things? Truly
I say to you, [A]not one stone here will be left upon
another, which will not be torn down."
3 As He was sitting on [A]the Mount of Olives, the
disciples came to Him privately, saying, "Tell us,
when will these things happen, and what *will be* the
sign of [B]Your coming, and of the [a]end of the age?"
4 And Jesus answered and said to them, "[A]See to it
that no one misleads you. 5 For [A]many will come in
My name, saying, 'I am the [a]Christ,' and will mislead
many. 6 You will be hearing of [A]wars and rumors
of wars. See that you are not frightened, for *those
things* must take place, but *that* is not yet the end.
7 For [A]nation will rise against nation, and kingdom
against kingdom, and in various places there will
be [B]famines and earthquakes. 8 [A]But all these things
are *merely* the beginning of birth pangs.
9 "[A]Then they will deliver you to tribulation, and
will kill you, and [B]you will be hated by all nations

23:36 [A]Matt 10:23; 24:34 23:37 [A]Matt 23:37-39: *Luke 13:34, 35* [B]Matt 5:12 [C]Ruth 2:12 23:38 [A]1 Kin 9:7f; Jer 22:5 23:39 [A]Ps 118:26; Matt 21:9 24:1 [a]Lit *and* [A]Matt 24:1-51: *Mark 13; Luke 21:5-36* [B]Matt 21:23 24:2 [A]Luke 19:44 24:3 [a]Or *consummation* [A]Matt 21:1 [B]Matt 16:27f; 24:27, 37, 39 24:4 [A]Jer 29:8 24:5 [a]I.e. the Messiah [A]Matt 24:11, 24; Acts 5:36f; 1 John 2:18; 4:3 24:6 [A]Rev 6:4 24:7 [A]2 Chr 15:6; Is 19:2; Rev 6:8, 12 [B]Acts 11:28; Rev 6:5, 6 24:8 [A]Matt 24:8-20: *Luke 21:12-24* 24:9 [A]Matt 10:17; John 16:2 [B]Matt 10:22; John 15:18ff

name was also Berechiah. But there is no difficulty if we simply take Jesus' words at face value and accept His infallible testimony that Zechariah the prophet was martyred between the temple and the altar, in a way very similar to how the earlier Zechariah was killed.

23:36 this generation. Historically, this was the generation that experienced the utter destruction of Jerusalem and the burning of the temple in A.D. 70. Jesus' lament over Jerusalem and His removal of the blessing of God from the temple (vv. 37, 38) strongly suggest that the sacking of Jerusalem in A.D. 70 was the judgment He was speaking about. *See notes on 22:7; 24:2; Lk 19:43.*

23:37 I wanted … you were unwilling. God is utterly sovereign and therefore fully capable of bringing to pass whatever He desires (cf. Is 46:10)—including the salvation of whomever He chooses (Eph 1:4, 5). Yet, He sometimes expresses a wish for that which He does not sovereignly bring to pass (cf. Ge 6:6; Dt 5:29; Ps 81:13; Is 48:18). Such expressions in no way suggest a limitation on the sovereignty of God or imply any actual change in Him (Nu 23:19). But these statements do reveal essential aspects of the divine character: He is full of compassion, sincerely good to all, desirous of good, not evil—and therefore not delighting in the destruction of the wicked (Eze 18:32; 33:11). While affirming God's sovereignty, one must understand His pleas for the repentance of the reprobate as well-meant appeals—and His goodness toward the wicked as a genuine mercy designed to provoke them to repentance (Ro 2:4). The emotion displayed by Christ here (and in all similar passages, such as Lk 19:41) is obviously a deep, sincere passion. All Christ's feelings must be in perfect harmony with the divine will (cf. Jn 8:29)—and therefore these lamentations should not be thought of as mere exhibitions of His humanity.

23:38 your house is being left to you desolate! A few days earlier, Christ had referred to the temple as His Father's "house" (21:13). But the blessing and glory of God were being removed from Israel (see 1Sa 4:21). When Christ "came out from the temple" (24:1), the glory of God went with Him. Ezekiel 11:23 described Ezekiel's vision of the departure of the Shekinah glory in his day. The glory left the temple and stood on the Mt. of Olives (*see notes on 24:3; Lk 19:29*), exactly the same route Christ followed here (cf. 24:3).

23:39 you will not see Me. Christ's public teaching ministry was over. He withdrew from national Israel until the time yet future when they will recognize Him as Messiah (Ro 11:23–26). Then Christ quoted from Ps 118:26.

24:1–25:46 This is the last of the 5 discourses Matthew features (see Introduction: Historical and Theological Themes). It is known as the Olivet Discourse, and it contains some of the most important prophetic material in all of Scripture.

24:1 the temple buildings. This temple was begun by Herod the Great in 20 B.C. (*see note on 2:1*) and was still under construction when the Romans destroyed it in A.D. 70 (*see note on v. 2*). At the time of Jesus' ministry, the temple was one of the most impressive structures in the world, made of massive blocks of stone bedecked with gold ornamentation. Some of the stones in the temple complex measured 40x12x12 ft. and were expertly quarried to fit perfectly against one another. The temple buildings were made of gleaming white marble, and the whole eastern wall of the large main structure was covered with gold plates that reflected the morning sun, making a spectacle that was visible for miles. The entire temple mount had been enlarged by Herod's engineers, by means of large retaining walls and vaulted chambers on the S side and SE corner. By this means the large courtyard area atop the temple mount was effectively doubled. The whole temple complex was magnificent by any standard. The disciples' conversation here may have been prompted by Jesus' words in 23:38. They were undoubtedly wondering how a site so spectacular could be left "desolate."

24:2 not one stone here … left upon another. These words were literally fulfilled in A.D. 70. Titus, the Roman general, built large wooden scaffolds around the walls of the temple buildings, piled them high with wood and other flammable items, and set them ablaze. The heat from the fires was so intense that the stones crumbled. The rubble was then sifted to retrieve the melted gold, and the remaining ruins were "thrown down" into the Kidron Valley. *See notes on 22:7; Lk 19:43.*

24:3 Mount of Olives. The hill directly opposite the temple, across the Kidron Valley to the E (*see note on Lk 19:29*). This spot affords the best panoramic view of Jerusalem. At the base of this mountain is Gethsemane (*see note on 26:36*). **what *will be* the sign of Your coming …?** Luke 19:11 records that the disciples still "supposed that the kingdom of God was going to appear immediately." The destruction of the temple (v. 2) did not fit the eschatological scheme they envisioned, so they asked for clarification. Jesus addressed their questions in reverse order, describing the prophetic sign of His coming (actually a series of signs) in vv. 4–35 and then addressing their question about the timing of these events beginning in v. 36. When they asked about His coming (Gr., *parousia;* lit. "presence"), they did not envision a second coming in the far-off future. They were speaking of His coming in triumph as Messiah, an event which they no doubt anticipated would occur presently. Even if they were conscious of His approaching death, which He had plainly prophesied to them on repeated occasions (*see note on 20:19*), they could not have anticipated His ascension to heaven and the long intervening church age. However, when Jesus used the term *parousia* in His discourse, He used it in the technical sense as a reference to His second coming.

24:6 not yet the end. False prophets, as well as wars and rumors of wars, characterize the whole of the present age, but will escalate toward the end (cf. 2Ti 3:13).

24:8 birth pangs. Famines, earthquakes, and conflicts have always characterized life in a fallen world; but by calling these things "the beginning" of labor pains, He indicated that things will get notably and remarkably worse at the end of the era as these unique tribulations signal the soon arrival of Messiah to judge sinful humanity and set up His millennial kingdom. Cf. 1Th. 5:3; Rev 6:1–17; 8:1–9:21; 16:1–21; *see note on v. 14.*

24:9 deliver you. *See note on 10:17.*

because of My name. 10 At that time many will [a,A]fall away and will [b]betray one another and hate one another. 11 Many [A]false prophets will arise and will mislead many. 12 Because lawlessness is increased, [a]most people's love will grow cold. 13 [A]But the one who endures to the end, he will be saved. 14 This [A]gospel of the kingdom [B]shall be preached in the whole [a,C]world as a testimony to all the nations, and then the end will come.

PERILOUS TIMES

15 "Therefore when you see the [A]ABOMINATION OF DESOLATION which was spoken of through Daniel the prophet, standing in [B]the holy place ([C]let the reader understand), 16 then those who are in Judea must flee to the mountains. 17 [a]Whoever is on [A]the housetop must not go down to get the things out that are in his house. 18 [a]Whoever is in the field must not turn back to get his cloak. 19 But [A]woe to those who are pregnant and to those who are nursing babies in those days! 20 But pray that your flight will not be in the winter, or on a Sabbath. 21 For then there will be a [A]great tribulation, such as has not occurred since the beginning of the world until now, nor ever will. 22 Unless those days had been cut short, no [a]life would have been saved; but for [A]the sake of the [b]elect those days will be cut short. 23 [A]Then if anyone says to you, 'Behold, here is the [a]Christ,' or '[b]There *He is,*' do not believe *him.* 24 For false Christs and [A]false prophets will arise and will [a]show great [b,B]signs and wonders, so as to mislead, if possible, even [C]the [c]elect. 25 Behold, I have told you in advance. 26 So if they say to you, 'Behold, He is in the wilderness,' do not go out, *or,* 'Behold, He is in the inner rooms,' do not believe *them.* 27 [A]For just as the lightning comes from the east and flashes even to the west, so will the [B]coming of the [C]Son of Man be. 28 [A]Wherever the corpse is, there the [a]vultures will gather.

THE GLORIOUS RETURN

29 "But immediately after the [A]tribulation of those days [B]THE SUN WILL BE DARKENED, AND THE MOON WILL NOT GIVE ITS LIGHT, AND [C]THE STARS WILL FALL from [a]the sky, and the powers of [a]the heavens will be shaken. 30 And then [A]the sign of the Son of Man

24:10 [a]Lit *be caused to stumble* [b]Or *hand over* [A]Matt 11:6 24:11 [A]Matt 7:15; 24:24 24:12 [a]Lit *the love of many* 24:13 [A]Matt 10:22 24:14 [a]Lit *inhabited earth* [A]Matt 4:23 [B]Rom 10:18; Col 1:6, 23 [C]Luke 2:1; 4:5; Acts 11:28; 17:6, 31; 19:27; Rom 10:18; Heb 1:6; 2:5; Rev 3:10; 16:14 24:15 [A]Dan 9:27; 11:31; 12:11 [B]Mark 13:14; Luke 21:20; John 11:48; Acts 6:13f; 21:28 [C]Mark 13:14; Rev 1:3 24:17 [a]Lit *He who* [A]1 Sam 9:25; 2 Sam 11:2; Matt 10:27; Luke 5:19; 12:3; 17:31; Acts 10:9 24:18 [a]Lit *He who* 24:19 [A]Luke 23:29 24:21 [A]Dan 12:1; Joel 2:2; Matt 24:29 24:22 [a]Lit *flesh* [b]Or *chosen ones* [A]Matt 22:14; 24:24, 31; Luke 18:7 24:23 [a]I.e. Messiah [b]Lit *here* [A]Luke 17:23f 24:24 [a]Lit *give* [b]Or *attesting miracles* [c]Or *chosen ones* [A]Matt 7:15; 24:11 [B]John 4:48; 2 Thess 2:9 [C]Matt 22:14; 24:22, 31; Luke 18:7 24:27 [A]Luke 17:24 [B]Matt 24:3, 37, 39 [C]Matt 8:20 24:28 [a]Or *eagles* [A]Job 39:30; Ezek 39:17; Hab 1:8; Luke 17:37 24:29 [a]Or *heaven* [A]Matt 24:21 [B]Is 13:10; 24:23; Ezek 32:7; Joel 2:10, 31; 3:15f; Amos 5:20; 8:9; Zeph 1:15; Matt 24:29-35; Acts 2:20; Rev 6:12-17; 8:12 [C]Is 34:4; Rev 6:13 24:30 [A]Matt 24:3; Rev 1:7

24:10 many will fall away. Lit. "cause to stumble"—suggesting professing believers who fall away—and even turn against "one another" in shocking acts of spiritual treachery. Those who fall away in such a manner give evidence that they never were true believers at all (*see note on v. 13*).

24:13 endures to the end ... be saved. Cf. 10:22. The ones who persevere are the same ones who are saved—not the ones whose love grows cold (v. 12). This does not suggest that our perseverance secures our salvation. Scripture everywhere teaches precisely the opposite: God, as part of His saving work, secures our perseverance. True believers "are protected by the power of God through faith for ... salvation" (1Pe 1:5). The guarantee of our perseverance is built into the New Covenant promise. God says: "I will put the fear of Me in their hearts so that they will not turn away from Me" (Jer 32:40). Those who do fall away from Christ give conclusive proof that they were never truly believers to begin with (1Jn 2:19). To say that God secures our perseverance is not to say that we are passive in the process, however. He keeps us "through faith" (1Pe 1:5)—our faith. Scripture sometimes calls us to hold fast to our faith (Heb 10:23; Rev 3:11) or warns us against falling away (Heb 10:26–29). Such admonitions do not negate the many promises that true believers will persevere (Jn 10:28, 29; Ro 8:38, 39; 1Co 1:8, 9; Php 1:6). Rather, the warnings and pleas are among the means God uses to secure our perseverance in the faith. Notice that the warnings and the promises often appear side by side. For example, when Jude urges believers, "keep yourselves in the love of God" (Jude 21), he immediately points them to God, "who is able to keep you from stumbling" (Jude 24).

24:14 preached in the whole world. Despite all the tribulations that would come—the deception of false teachers, the wars, persecutions, natural disasters, defections from Christ, and all the obstacles to the spread of the gospel—the message ultimately penetrates every part of the globe. God is never without a witness, and He will proclaim the gospel from heaven itself if necessary (cf. Rev 14:6). **then the end will come.** "The end" refers to the final, excruciating birth pangs (*see note on v. 8*). This is how Christ characterizes the time of Great Tribulation described in the verses that follow.

24:15 abomination of desolation. *See notes on Da 9:27; 11:31.* This phrase originally referred to the desecration of the temple by Antiochus Epiphanes, king of Syria in the second century B.C. Antiochus invaded Jerusalem in 168 B.C., made the altar into a shrine to Zeus, and even sacrificed pigs on it. However, Jesus clearly was looking toward a yet-future "abomination of desolation." Some suggest that this prophecy was fulfilled in A.D. 70 when Titus invaded Jerusalem and destroyed the temple (*see note on v. 2*). However, the Apostle Paul saw a still-future fulfillment (2Th 2:3, 4), as did John (Rev 13:14, 15)—when the Antichrist sets up an image in the temple during the future tribulation. Christ's words here therefore look beyond the events of A.D. 70 to a time of even greater global cataclysm that will immediately precede His coming (cf. vv. 29–31).

24:16 the mountains. Probably a reference to the region SE of Jerusalem, particularly the Dead Sea area, where there are many caves and places of refuge. David hid from Saul in this area (1Sa 23:29). This would also include the hills of Moab and Edom.

24:21 great tribulation. The words "such as has not occurred" and "nor ever will"—along with the description that follows—identify this as the yet-future time in which God's wrath shall be poured out upon the earth (*see note on Rev 7:14*). Jesus' descriptions of the cataclysms that follow closely resemble the outpouring of divine wrath described in the bowl judgments of Rev 16 and His subsequent appearing in Rev 19 (*see note on v. 30*).

24:22 those days had been cut short. If the afflictions of this time were to continue, "no life would have been saved," i.e., no one would survive. But "for the sake of the elect" (so that redeemed people do not suffer more than they can bear) the time is "cut short"—i.e., held short of total destruction. Both Da 7:25 and Rev 12:14 (*see notes there*) suggest that the actual length of time the Beast will be permitted to terrorize the world is fixed at 3 1/2 years.

24:24 to mislead, if possible, even the elect. This clearly implies that such deception is not possible (Jn 10:4, 5).

24:26 do not believe *them*. No one should consider the claims of self-styled messiahs because all of them are false. When Christ returns, no one will miss it (vv. 27, 28).

24:28 there the vultures will gather. The location of a carcass is visible from great distances because of the circling carrion birds overhead (cf. Job 39:27–30). Similarly, Christ's return will be clearly evident to all near and far. The same point is made by the lightning in v. 27. The vulture-dead body imagery here also speaks of the judgment that will accompany His return (Rev 19:21).

24:29 the sun will be darkened. Such phenomena are a common feature of day of the Lord prophecy (see Is 13:9, 10; Eze 32:7, 8; Joel 2:10, 31; 3:15; Am 8:9). The ultimate fulfillment of these prophecies takes place during the time of the Beast's reign (Rev 6:12, 13; 8:12).

24:30 the sign of the Son of Man. I.e., the Son of Man Himself is the sign. The events described here precisely parallel the description in Da 7:13; Rev 19:11–21. **all the tribes of the**

will appear in the sky, and then all the tribes of the earth will mourn, and they will see [B]the SON OF MAN COMING ON THE CLOUDS OF THE SKY with power and great glory. 31 And [A]He will send forth His angels with [B]A GREAT TRUMPET and THEY WILL GATHER TOGETHER His [a,C]elect from [D]the four winds, from one end of the sky to the other.

PARABLE OF THE FIG TREE

32 "Now learn the parable from the fig tree: when its branch has already become tender and puts forth its leaves, you know that summer is near; 33 so, you too, when you see all these things, [a]recognize that [b]He is near, *right* [A]at the [c]door. 34 Truly I say to you, [A]this [a]generation will not pass away until all these things take place. 35 [A]Heaven and earth will pass away, but My words will not pass away.

36 "But [A]of that day and hour no one knows, not even the angels of heaven, nor the Son, but the Father alone. 37 For [a]the [A]coming of the Son of Man will be [B]just like the days of Noah. 38 For as in those days before the flood they were eating and drinking, [A]marrying and giving in marriage, until the day that [B]Noah entered the ark, 39 and they did not [a]understand until the flood came and took them all away; so will the [A]coming of the Son of Man be. 40 Then there will be two men in the field; one [a]will be taken and one [a]will be left. 41 [A]Two women *will be* grinding at the [a,B]mill; one [b]will be taken and one [b]will be left.

BE READY FOR HIS COMING

42 "Therefore [A]be on the alert, for you do not know which day your Lord is coming. 43 But [a]be sure of this, that [A]if the head of the house had known [B]at what time of the night the thief was coming, he would have been on the alert and would not have allowed his house to be [b]broken into. 44 For this reason [A]you also must be ready; for [B]the Son of Man is coming at an hour when you do not think *He will.*

45 "[A]Who then is the [B]faithful and [C]sensible slave whom his [a]master [D]put in charge of his household to give them their food at the proper time? 46 Blessed is that slave whom his [a]master finds so doing when he comes. 47 Truly I say to you that [A]he will put him in charge of all his possessions. 48 But if that evil slave says in his heart, 'My [a]master [b]is not coming for a long time,' 49 and begins to beat his fellow slaves and eat and drink with drunkards; 50 the [a]master of that slave will come on a day when he does not expect *him* and at an hour which he does not know, 51 and will [a]cut him in pieces and [b]assign him a place with the hypocrites; in that place there will be [A]weeping and gnashing of teeth.

PARABLE OF TEN VIRGINS

25 "Then [A]the kingdom of heaven will be comparable to ten virgins, who took their [B]lamps and went out to meet the bridegroom. 2 Five of them were foolish, and five were [A]prudent. 3 For when the foolish took their lamps, they took no oil with

24:30 [B]Dan 7:13; Matt 16:27; 24:3, 37, 39 24:31 [a]Or *chosen ones* [A]Matt 13:41 [B]Ex 19:16; Deut 30:4; Is 27:13; Zech 9:14; 1 Cor 15:52; 1 Thess 4:16; Heb 12:19; Rev 8:2; 11:15 [C]Matt 24:22 [D]Dan 7:2; Zech 2:6; Rev 7:1 24:33 [a]Or *know* [b]Or *it* [c]Lit *doors* [A]James 5:9; Rev 3:20 24:34 [a]Or *race* [A]Matt 10:23; 16:28; 23:36 24:35 [A]Matt 5:18; Mark 13:31; Luke 21:33 24:36 [A]Mark 13:32; Acts 1:7 24:37 [a]Lit *just as...were the days* [A]Matt 16:27; 24:3, 30, 39 [B]Gen 6:5; 7:6-23; Luke 17:26f 24:38 [A]Matt 22:30 [B]Gen 7:7 24:39 [a]Lit *know* [A]Matt 16:27; 24:3, 30, 37 24:40 [a]Lit *is* 24:41 [a]I.e. handmill [b]Lit *is* [A]Luke 17:35 [B]Ex 11:5; Deut 24:6; Is 47:2 24:42 [A]Matt 24:43, 44; 25:10, 13; Luke 12:39f; 21:36 24:43 [a]Lit *know this* [b]Lit *dug through* [A]Matt 24:42, 44; 25:10, 13; Luke 12:39f; 21:36 [B]Matt 14:25; Mark 6:48; 13:35; Luke 12:38 24:44 [A]Matt 24:42, 43; 25:10, 13; Luke 12:39f; 21:36 [B]Matt 24:27 24:45 [a]Or *lord* [A]Matt 24:45-51: *Luke 12:42-46* [B]Matt 25:21, 23; Luke 16:10 [C]Matt 7:24; 10:16; 25:2ff [D]Matt 25:21, 23 24:46 [a]Or *lord* 24:47 [A]Matt 25:21, 23 24:48 [a]Or *lord* [b]Lit *lingers* 24:50 [a]Or *lord* 24:51 [a]Or *severely scourge him* [b]Lit *appoint his portion* [A]Matt 8:12 25:1 [A]Matt 13:24 [B]John 18:3; Acts 20:8; Rev 4:5; 8:10 25:2 [A]Matt 7:24; 10:16; 25:2ff

earth will mourn. I.e., over their own rebellion. Israel in particular will mourn over their rejection of the Messiah (cf. Zech 12:10–12).

24:31 from one end of the sky to the other. All the "elect" from heaven and earth are gathered and assembled before Christ. This is the culmination of world history, ushering in the millennial reign of Christ (cf. Rev 20:4).

24:32 parable from the fig tree. When the fig branch "puts forth its leaves," only a short time remains until summer. Likewise, when the final labor pains begin (*see note on v. 14*), Christ's return "is near, right at the door" (v. 33).

24:34 this generation. This cannot refer to the generation living at the time of Christ, for "all these things"—the abomination of desolation (v. 15), the persecutions and judgments (vv. 17–22), the false prophets (vv. 23–26), the signs in the heavens (vv. 27–29), Christ's final return (v. 30), and the gathering of the elect (v. 31)—did not "take place" in their lifetime. It seems best to interpret Christ's words as a reference to the generation alive at the time when those final hard labor pains begin (*see note on v. 14*). This would fit with the lesson of the fig tree, which stresses the short span of time in which these things will occur (*see note on v. 32*).

24:35 Heaven and earth will pass away. Cf. Is 24:18–20. *See notes on 2Pe 3:10–13.*

24:36 day and hour. *See note on Mk 13:32.* The disciples wanted to fix the precise time, but this was not for them to know (Ac 1:7). Christ's emphasis instead is on faithfulness, watchfulness, stewardship, expectancy, and preparedness. These are the lessons He taught in the parables that immediately follow.

24:37 like the days of Noah. Jesus' emphasis here is not so much on the extreme wickedness of Noah's day (Ge 6:5), but on the people's preoccupation with mundane matters of everyday life ("eating and drinking, marrying and giving in marriage"—v. 38), when judgment fell suddenly. They had received warnings, in the form of Noah's preaching (2Pe 2:5)—and the ark itself, which was a testimony to the judgment that was to come. But they were unconcerned about such matters and therefore were swept away unexpectedly in the midst of their daily activities.

24:40, 41 one will be taken. I.e., taken in judgment (cf. v. 39) just as in Noah's day ("took them"; v. 39). This is clearly not a reference to the catching away of believers described in 1Th. 4:16, 17.

24:43 the thief. As no one knows what hour the thief will come, no one knows the hour of the Lord's return or the day of the Lord that accompanies His coming (cf. 1Th. 5:2; 2Pe 3:10). But the believer is to be ready at all times.

24:44 at an hour when you do not think *He will*. The parables that follow teach Christ's followers to be ready in case He comes sooner than anticipated (vv. 43–51); and also to be prepared in case He delays longer than expected (25:1–13).

24:45–51 The evil slave represents an unbeliever who refuses to take seriously the promise of Christ's return (cf. 2Pe 3:4). Though he is an unbeliever (as demonstrated by his punishment—*see note on 22:13*), he is nonetheless accountable to Christ for the stewardship of his time. Jesus was teaching that every person in the world holds his life, natural abilities, wealth, and possessions in trust from God and must give account of how these things are used.

24:51 weeping and gnashing of teeth. *See note on 22:13.*

25:1–13 The parable of the 10 virgins is given to underscore the importance of being ready for Christ's return in any event—even if He delays longer than expected. For when He does return, there will be no second chances for the unprepared (vv. 11, 12).

25:1 ten virgins. I.e., bridesmaids. The wedding would begin at the bride's house when the bridegroom arrived to observe the wedding ritual. Then a procession would follow as the bridegroom took the bride to his house for the completion of festivities. For a night wedding, "lamps," which were actually torches, were needed for the procession.

them, 4 but the [A]prudent took oil in flasks along
with their lamps. 5 Now while the bridegroom was
delaying, they all got drowsy and *began* to sleep.
6 But at midnight there was a shout, 'Behold, the
bridegroom! Come out to meet *him*.' 7 Then all those
virgins rose and trimmed their lamps. 8 The foolish said to the prudent, 'Give us some of your oil,
for our lamps are going out.' 9 But the [A]prudent
answered, 'No, there will not be enough for us and
you *too;* go instead to the dealers and buy *some*
for yourselves.' 10 And while they were going away
to make the purchase, the bridegroom came, and
those who were [A]ready went in with him to [B]the
wedding feast; and [C]the door was shut. 11 Later the
other virgins also came, saying, '[A]Lord, lord, open
up for us.' 12 But he answered, 'Truly I say to you, I
do not know you.' 13 [A]Be on the alert then, for you
do not know the day nor the hour.

PARABLE OF THE TALENTS

14 "[A]For *it is* just like a man [B]*about* to go on a journey, who called his own slaves and entrusted his
possessions to them. 15 To one he gave five [a,A]talents,
to another, two, and to another, one, each according to his own ability; and he [B]went on his journey.
16 Immediately the one who had received the five
[A]talents went and traded with them, and gained five
more talents. 17 In the same manner the one who
had received the two *talents* gained two more. 18 But
he who received the one *talent* went away, and dug
a hole in the ground and hid his [a]master's money.
19 "Now after a long time the master of those
slaves *came and *[A]settled accounts with them.
20 The one who had received the five [A]talents came
up and brought five more talents, saying, 'Master,
you entrusted five talents to me. See, I have gained
five more talents.' 21 His master said to him, 'Well
done, good and [A]faithful slave. You were faithful
with a few things, I will [B]put you in charge of many
things; enter into the joy of your [a]master.'
22 "Also the one who *had received* the two [A]talents
came up and said, 'Master, you entrusted two talents
to me. See, I have gained two more talents.' 23 His
master said to him, 'Well done, good and [A]faithful
slave. You were faithful with a few things, I will
put you in charge of many things; enter into the
joy of your master.'
24 "And the one also who had received the one
[A]talent came up and said, 'Master, I knew you to be
a hard man, reaping where you did not sow and
gathering where you scattered no *seed*. 25 And I
was afraid, and went away and hid your talent in
the ground. See, you have what is yours.'
26 "But his master answered and said to him, 'You
wicked, lazy slave, you knew that I reap where I
did not sow and gather where I scattered no *seed*.
27 Then you ought to have put my money [a]in the
bank, and on my arrival I would have received my
money back with interest. 28 Therefore take away
the talent from him, and give it to the one who has
the ten talents.'
29 "[A]For to everyone who has, *more* shall be given,
and he will have an abundance; but from the one
who does not have, even what he does have shall
be taken away. 30 Throw out the worthless slave
into [A]the outer darkness; in that place there will be
weeping and gnashing of teeth.

THE JUDGMENT

31 "But when [A]the Son of Man comes in His glory,
and all the angels with Him, then [B]He will sit on His
glorious throne. 32 All the nations will be [A]gathered
before Him; and He will separate them from one
another, [B]as the shepherd separates the sheep from
the goats; 33 and He will put the sheep [A]on His right,
and the goats [B]on the left.

25:4 [A]Matt 7:24; 10:16; 25:2ff 25:9 [A]Matt 7:24; 10:16; 25:2ff 25:10 [A]Matt 24:42ff [B]Luke 12:35f [C]Matt 7:21ff; Luke 13:25 25:11 [A]Matt 7:21ff; Luke 13:25 25:13 [A]Matt 24:42ff 25:14 [A]Matt 25:14-30: *Luke 19:12-27* [B]Matt 21:33 25:15 [a]A talent was worth about fifteen years' wages of a laborer [A]Matt 18:24; Luke 19:13 [B]Matt 21:33 25:16 [A]Matt 18:24; Luke 19:13 25:18 [a]*Or lord's* 25:19 [A]Matt 18:23 25:20 [A]Matt 18:24; Luke 19:13 25:21 [a]*Or lord* [A]Matt 24:45, 47; 25:23 [B]Luke 12:44; 22:29; Rev 3:21; 21:7 25:22 [A]Matt 18:24; Luke 19:13 25:23 [A]Matt 24:45, 47; 25:21 25:24 [A]Matt 18:24; Luke 19:13 25:27 [a]Lit *to the bankers* 25:29 [A]Matt 13:12; Mark 4:25; Luke 8:18; John 15:2 25:30 [A]Matt 8:12; 22:13; Luke 13:28 25:31 [A]Matt 16:27f; 1 Thess 4:16; 2 Thess 1:7; Heb 9:28; Jude 14; Rev 1:7 [B]Matt 19:28 25:32 [A]Matt 13:49; 2 Cor 5:10 [B]Ezek 34:17, 20 25:33 [A]1 Kin 2:19; Ps 45:9 [B]Eccl 10:2

25:14–30 The parable of the talents illustrates the tragedy of wasted opportunity. The man who goes on the journey represents Christ, and the slaves represent professing believers given different levels of responsibility. Faithfulness is what he demands of them (*see note on v. 23*), but the parable suggests that all who are faithful will be fruitful to some degree. The fruitless person is unmasked as a hypocrite and utterly destroyed (v. 30).

25:15 **talents.** A talent was a measure of weight, not a specific coin, so that a talent of gold was more valuable than a talent of silver. A talent of silver (the word translated "money" in v. 18 is lit. silver) was a considerable sum of money. The modern meaning of the word "talent," denoting a natural ability, stems from the fact that this parable is erroneously applied to the stewardship of one's natural gifts.

25:23 **the joy of your master.** Both the man with 5 talents and the man with two received exactly the same reward, indicating that the reward is based on faithfulness, not results.

25:24 **a hard man.** His characterization of the master maligns the man as a cruel and ruthless opportunist, "reaping and gathering" what he had no right to claim as his own. This slothful servant does not represent a genuine believer, for it is obvious that this man had no true knowledge of the master.

25:26 **you knew that I reap where I did not sow.** In repeating the slave's charge against him, the master was not acknowledging that it was true. He was allowing the man's own words to condemn him. If the slave really believed the master to be the kind of man he portrayed, that was all the more reason for him not to be slothful. His accusation against the master—even if it had been true—did not justify his own laziness.

25:29 **to everyone who has, *more* shall be given.** See 13:12. The recipients of divine grace inherit immeasurable blessings in addition to eternal life and the favor of God (cf. Ro 8:32). But those who despise the riches of God's goodness, forbearance, and longsuffering (Ro 2:4), burying them in the ground and clinging instead to the paltry and transient goods of this world, will ultimately lose everything they have (cf. 6:19; Jn 12:25).

25:30 **outer darkness ... weeping and gnashing of teeth.** *See note on 22:13.*

25:31 **He will sit on His glorious throne.** This speaks of the earthly reign of Christ described in Rev 20:4–6. The judgment described here in vv. 32–46 is different from the Great White Throne judgment of Rev 20:11–15. This judgment precedes Christ's millennial reign, and the subjects seem to be only those who are alive at His coming. This is sometimes referred to as the judgment of the nations, but His verdicts address individuals in the nations, not the nations as a whole (cf. v. 46).

25:32, 33 **sheep.** I.e., believers (10:16; Ps 79:13; Eze 34). They are given the place on "His right"—the place of favor. **goats.** These represent unbelievers, consigned to the place of dishonor and rejection.

34 "Then the King will say to those on His right,
'Come, you who are blessed of My Father, [A]inherit
the kingdom prepared for you [B]from the foundation
of the world. 35 For [A]I was hungry, and you gave
Me *something* to eat; I was thirsty, and you gave
Me *something* to drink; [B]I was a stranger, and you
invited Me in; 36 [A]naked, and you clothed Me; I was
sick, and you [B]visited Me; [C]I was in prison, and you
came to Me.' 37 Then the righteous will answer Him,
'Lord, when did we see You hungry, and feed You,
or thirsty, and give You *something* to drink? 38 And
when did we see You a stranger, and invite You in,
or naked, and clothe You? 39 When did we see You
sick, or in prison, and come to You?' 40 [A]The King
will answer and say to them, 'Truly I say to you, [B]to
the extent that you did it to one of these brothers
of Mine, *even* the least *of them,* you did it to Me.'
41 "Then He will also say to those on His left, '[A]Depart from Me, accursed ones, into the [B]eternal fire
which has been prepared for [C]the devil and his angels; 42 for I was hungry, and you gave Me *nothing* to
eat; I was thirsty, and you gave Me nothing to drink;
43 I was a stranger, and you did not invite Me in; naked, and you did not clothe Me; sick, and in prison,
and you did not visit Me.' 44 Then they themselves
also will answer, 'Lord, when did we see You hungry, or thirsty, or a stranger, or naked, or sick, or in
prison, and did not [a]take care of You?' 45 Then He will
answer them, 'Truly I say to you, to the extent that
you did not do it to one of the least of these, you did
not do it to Me.' 46 These will go away into [A]eternal
punishment, but the righteous into [B]eternal life."

THE PLOT TO KILL JESUS

26 [A]When Jesus had finished all these words, He
said to His disciples, 2 "[A]You know that after
two days [B]the Passover is coming, and the Son of
Man is *to be* [C]handed over for crucifixion."
3 [A]Then the chief priests and the elders of the
people were gathered together in [B]the court of the
high priest, named [C]Caiaphas; 4 and they [A]plotted
together to seize Jesus by stealth and kill Him. 5 But
they were saying, "Not during the festival, [A]otherwise a riot might occur among the people."

THE PRECIOUS OINTMENT

6 [A]Now when Jesus was in [B]Bethany, at the home
of Simon the leper, 7 [A]a woman came to Him with an
alabaster vial of very costly perfume, and she poured
it on His head as He reclined *at the table.* 8 But the disciples were indignant when they saw *this,* and said,
"Why this waste? 9 For this *perfume* might have been
sold for a high price and *the money* given to the poor."
10 But Jesus, aware of this, said to them, "Why do you

25:34 [A]Matt 5:3; 19:29; Luke 12:32; 1 Cor 6:9; 15:50; Gal 5:21; James 2:5 [B]Matt 13:35; Luke 11:50; John 17:24; Eph 1:4; Heb 4:3; 9:26; 1 Pet 1:20; Rev 13:8; 17:8 25:35 [A]Is 58:7; Ezek 18:7, 16; James 2:15, 16 [B]Job 31:32; Heb 13:2 25:36 [A]Is 58:7; Ezek 18:7, 16; James 2:15, 16 [B]James 1:27 [C]2 Tim 1:16f 25:40 [A]Matt 25:34; Luke 19:38; Rev 17:14; 19:16 [B]Prov 19:17; Matt 10:42; Heb 6:10 25:41 [A]Matt 7:23 [B]Mark 9:48; Luke 16:24; Jude 7 [C]Matt 4:10; Rev 12:9 25:44 [a]Or *serve* 25:46 [A]Dan 12:2; John 5:29; Acts 24:15 [B]Matt 19:29; John 3:15f, 36; 5:24; 6:27, 40, 47, 54; 17:2f; Acts 13:46, 48; Rom 2:7; 5:21; 6:23; Gal 6:8; 1 John 5:11 26:1 [A]Matt 7:28 26:2 [A]Matt 26:2-5: *Mark 14:1, 2; Luke 22:1, 2* [B]John 11:55; 13:1 [C]Matt 10:4 26:3 [A]John 11:47 [B]Matt 26:58, 69; 27:27; Mark 14:54, 66; 15:16; Luke 22:55; John 18:15 [C]Matt 26:57; Luke 3:2; John 11:49; 18:13, 14, 24, 28; Acts 4:6 26:4 [A]Matt 12:14 26:5 [A]Matt 27:24 26:6 [A]Matt 26:6-13: *Mark 14:3-9;* Luke 7:37-39; John 12:1-8 [B]Matt 21:17 26:7 [A]Luke 7:37f

25:34 prepared for you. This terminology underscores that their salvation is a gracious gift of God, not something merited by the deeds described in vv. 35, 36. Before "the foundation of the world," they were chosen by God and ordained to be holy (Eph 1:4)—predestined to be conformed to Christ's image (Ro 8:29). So the good deeds commended in vv. 35, 36 are the fruit, not the root of their salvation. The deeds are not the basis for their entrance into the kingdom, but merely manifestations of God's grace in their lives. They are the objective criteria for judgment, because they are the evidence of saving faith (cf. Jas 2:14–26).

25:40 one of these brothers of Mine. This refers in particular to other disciples. Some would apply this to national Israel; others to needy people in general. But here Christ is specifically commending "those on His right" (v. 34) for the way they received His emissaries. *See note on 18:5.*

25:46 eternal punishment ... eternal life. The same Gr. word is used in both instances. The punishment of the wicked is as never-ending as the bliss of the righteous. The wicked are not given a second chance, nor are they annihilated. The punishment of the wicked dead is described throughout Scripture as "eternal fire" (v. 41); "unquenchable fire" (3:12); "disgrace and everlasting contempt" (Da 12:2); a place where "their worm does not die, and the fire is not quenched" (Mk 9:44–49); a place of "torments" and "flame" (Lk 16:23, 24); "eternal destruction" (2Th 1:9); a place of torment with "fire and brimstone" where "the smoke of their torment goes up forever and ever" (Rev 14:10, 11); and a "lake of fire and brimstone" where the wicked are "tormented day and night forever and ever" (Rev 20:10). Here Jesus indicates that the punishment itself is everlasting—not merely the smoke and flames. The wicked are forever subject to the fury and the wrath of God. They consciously suffer shame and contempt and the assaults of an accusing conscience—along with the fiery wrath of an offended deity—for all of eternity. Even hell will acknowledge the perfect justice of God (Ps 76:10); those who are there will know that their punishment is just and that they alone are to blame (cf. Dt 32:3–5).

26:2 Passover. This was God's chosen time for Christ to die. He was the antitype to which the Passover Lamb had always referred. Christ had always avoided His enemies' plots to kill Him (Lk 4:29, 30; Jn 5:18; 10:39), but now it was His time (*see note on v. 5*). The true Lamb of God would take away the sin of the world (Jn 1:29).

26:3 Caiaphas. Caiaphas served as High Priest from A.D. 18 to 36, an unusually long tenure for anyone in that role. His longevity suggests he had a close relationship with both Rome and the Herodian dynasty. He was son-in-law to his predecessor, Annas (Jn 18:13; *see note on Lk 3:2*). He controlled the temple and no doubt personally profited from the corrupt merchandising that was taking place there (*see note on 21:12*). His enmity against Jesus seems intensely personal and especially malevolent; every time he appears in Scripture, he is seeking Jesus' destruction.

26:5 Not during the festival. The Jewish leaders, who had been eager to kill Him for so long, decided to postpone their plot until a more politically opportune time. But they could not; God's chosen time had come (*see notes on vv. 2, 18, 54*).

26:6 Simon the leper. Simon was almost certainly someone whom Jesus had healed of leprosy, for lepers were deemed unclean and therefore not permitted to socialize or even live in cities. *See note on Lv 13:2* for a discussion on leprosy.

26:7 an alabaster vial of very costly perfume. Mark sets the value at "over three hundred denarii" (*see note on Mk 14:5*), nearly a year's wages—very costly indeed. Even the expensive flask was broken (Mk 14:3), making the act that much more costly. "Alabaster" was a fine variety of marble, quarried in Egypt, which could be carved into delicate containers for storing costly perfumes. John tells us this woman was Mary, sister of Martha and Lazarus (Jn 12:3); thus Martha and Mary were evidently serving the meal for Simon the leper. Matthew and Mark mention that she anointed His head. John adds that she anointed His feet and wiped them with her hair. A similar act of worship is related in Lk 7:36–38, but the differences in timing, location, and other details make it clear that the two occasions were different.

26:8 the disciples were indignant. John says Judas was the spokesman who voiced the complaint, and that he did it for hypocritical reasons (Jn 12:4–6). Evidently the other disciples, being undiscerning, were quick to voice sympathy with Judas' protest.

bother the woman? For she has done a good deed to
Me. 11 For you always have [A]the poor with you; but
you do not always have Me. 12 For when she poured
this perfume on My body, she did it [A]to prepare Me
for burial. 13 Truly I say to you, [A]wherever this gospel
is preached in the whole world, what this woman
has done will also be spoken of in memory of her."

JUDAS'S BARGAIN

14 [A]Then one of the twelve, named [B]Judas Iscariot, went to the chief priests 15 and said, "What are
you willing to give me [a]to [b,A]betray Him to you?"
And [B]they weighed out thirty [c]pieces of silver to
him. 16 From then on he *began* looking for a good
opportunity to [a]betray [b]Jesus.
17 [A]Now on the first *day* of [B]Unleavened Bread the
disciples came to Jesus and asked, "Where do You
want us to prepare for You to eat the Passover?"
18 And He said, "Go into the city to [A]a certain man,
and say to him, 'The Teacher says, "[B]My time is near;
I *am to* keep the Passover at your house with My disciples." ' " 19 The disciples did as Jesus had directed
them; and they prepared the Passover.

THE LAST PASSOVER

20 [A]Now when evening came, Jesus was reclining
at the table with the twelve disciples. 21 As they were
eating, He said, "[A]Truly I say to you that one of you
will betray Me." 22 Being deeply grieved, they [a]each
one began to say to Him, "Surely not I, Lord?" 23 And
He answered, "[A]He who dipped his hand with Me in
the bowl is the one who will betray Me. 24 The Son
of Man *is to* go, [A]just as it is written of Him; but woe
to that man by whom the Son of Man is betrayed!
[B]It would have been good [a]for that man if he had
not been born." 25 And [A]Judas, who was betraying
Him, said, "Surely it is not I, [B]Rabbi?" Jesus *said to
him, "[C]You have said *it* yourself."

THE LORD'S SUPPER INSTITUTED

26 [A]While they were eating, Jesus took *some* bread,
and [a,B]after a blessing, He broke *it* and gave *it* to the
disciples, and said, "Take, eat; this is My body." 27 And
when He had taken a cup and given thanks, He gave
it to them, saying, "Drink from it, all of you; 28 for
[A]this is My blood of the covenant, which is poured
out for [B]many for forgiveness of sins. 29 But I say
to you, I will not drink of this fruit of the vine from
now on until that day when I drink it new with you
in My Father's kingdom."
30 [A]After singing a hymn, they went out to [B]the
Mount of Olives.
31 Then Jesus *said to them, "You will all [a,A]fall
away because of Me this night, for it is written, '[B]I
WILL STRIKE DOWN THE SHEPHERD, AND THE SHEEP
OF THE FLOCK SHALL BE [C]SCATTERED.' 32 But after I
have been raised, [A]I will go ahead of you to Galilee."
33 But Peter said to Him, "*Even* though all may [a]fall
away because of You, I will never fall away." 34 Jesus
said to him, "[A]Truly I say to you that [B]this *very* night,

26:11 [A]Deut 15:11; Mark 14:7; John 12:8 26:12 [A]John 19:40 26:13 [A]Mark 14:9 26:14 [A]Matt 26:14-16: *Mark 14:10, 11; Luke 22:3-6* [B]Matt 10:4; 26:25, 47; 27:3; John 6:71; 12:4; 13:26; Acts 1:16 26:15 [a]Lit *and I will* [b]Or *deliver* [c]I.e. silver shekels [A]Matt 10:4 [B]Ex 21:32; Zech 11:12 26:16 [a]Or *deliver* [b]Lit *Him* 26:17 [A]Matt 26:17-19: *Mark 14:12-16; Luke 22:7-13* [B]Ex 12:18-20 26:18 [A]Mark 14:13; Luke 22:10 [B]John 7:6, 8 26:20 [A]Matt 26:20-24: *Mark 14:17-21* 26:21 [A]Luke 22:21-23; John 13:21f 26:22 [a]Or *one after another* 26:23 [A]Ps 41:9; John 13:18, 26 26:24 [a]Lit *for him if that man had not been born* [A]Matt 26:31, 54, 56; Mark 9:12; Luke 24:25-27, 46; Acts 17:2f; 26:22f; 1 Cor 15:3; 1 Pet 1:10f [B]Matt 18:7; Mark 14:21 26:25 [A]Matt 26:14 [B]Matt 23:7; 26:49 [C]Matt 26:64; 27:11; Luke 22:70 26:26 [a]Lit *having blessed* [A]Matt 26:26-29: *Mark 14:22-25; Luke 22:17-20; 1 Cor 11:23-25;* 1 Cor 10:16 [B]Matt 14:19 26:28 [A]Ex 24:8; Heb 9:20 [B]Matt 20:28 26:30 [A]Matt 26:30-35: *Mark 14:26-31; Luke 22:31-34* [B]Matt 21:1 26:31 [a]Or *stumble* [A]Matt 11:6 [B]Zech 13:7 [C]John 16:32 26:32 [A]Matt 28:7, 10, 16; Mark 16:7 26:33 [a]Or *stumble* 26:34 [A]Matt 26:75; John 13:38 [B]Mark 14:30

26:11 **For you always have the poor with you.** Jesus certainly was not disparaging ministry to the poor—especially so soon after the lesson of the sheep and goats judgment (cf. 25:35, 36). However, He revealed here that there is a higher priority than any other earthly ministry, and that is worship rendered to Him. This would be an utter blasphemy for anyone less than God, so yet again He was implicitly affirming His deity (*see notes on 8:27; 12:6, 8; 21:16; 22:42, 45*).

26:12 **she did it to prepare Me for burial.** This does not necessarily mean that Mary was consciously aware of the significance of her act. It is doubtful that she knew of His approaching death, or at least how close it was. But this was an act of pure worship, her heart having been moved by God to perform a sacrificial and symbolic act, the full significance of which she probably did not know.

26:13 **in memory of her.** This promise was guaranteed by the inclusion of this story in the NT.

26:15 **thirty pieces of silver.** The price of a slave (Ex 21:32).

26:17 **the first *day* of Unleavened Bread.** The Passover lambs were killed (Mk 14:12) on 14 Nisan (Mar./Apr.). That evening, the Passover meal was eaten. The Feast of Unleavened Bread followed immediately after Passover, from 15–21 Nisan. The entire time was often referred to either as "Passover" (Lk 22:1), or as the Feast of Unleavened Bread. Therefore the first day refers to 14 Nisan. See Introduction to John: Interpretive Challenges; *see note on Jn 19:14.*

26:18 **a certain man.** Mark 14:13 and Lk 22:10 say they would be able to identify the man because he would be "carrying a pitcher of water," a chore normally reserved for women. He was evidently someone they did not know, probably a servant of whoever owned the house with an "upper room," where the Passover meal was to be eaten (Mk 14:15; Lk 22:12). Jesus had evidently made these arrangements clandestinely, in order to prevent His premature betrayal. Had Judas known ahead of time where the meal was to be eaten, he would surely have alerted the chief priests and elders (see vv. 14–16). But none of these things were to happen until the "time" was "near." All of this reveals how Jesus Himself was sovereignly in control of the details of His own crucifixion (*see notes on vv. 5, 54*).

26:20 **was reclining.** *See note on Mk 14:18;* cf. Jn 13:25.

26:26 **Take, eat; this is My body.** Jesus thus transformed the last Passover into the first observance of the Lord's Supper. He is the central antitype in both ceremonies, being represented symbolically by both the paschal lamb of the Passover and the elements in the communion service. His statement, "this is My body" could not possibly have been taken in any literal sense by the disciples present that evening. *See note on Lk 22:19.*

26:28 **My blood of the covenant.** Covenants were ratified with the blood of a sacrifice (Ge 8:20; 15:9, 10). Jesus' words here echo Moses' pronouncement in Ex 24:8. The blood of the New Covenant is not an animal's blood, but Christ's own blood, shed for the remission of sins. *See notes on Jer 31:31–34; Heb 8:1–10:18; 8:6.*

26:29 **My Father's kingdom.** I.e., the earthly millennial kingdom (see Lk 22:18, 29, 30).

26:30 **After singing a hymn.** Probably Ps 118. The Talmud designated Pss 113–118 as the Hallel (praise psalms) of Egypt. These psalms were sung at Passover (*see notes on Pss 113–118*).

26:31 **fall away.** See v. 56. The Gr. word is the same word Jesus used in 24:10, describing the falling away and spiritual treachery that would occur in the last days. Here, however, Jesus spoke of something less than full and final apostasy. In a moment of fleshly fear they disowned Christ (v. 34), but He prayed that their faith would not fail (Lk 22:32; Jn 17:9–11), and that prayer was answered. The verse Jesus quotes here is Zec 13:7 (*see note there*).

26:32 **I will go ahead of you to Galilee.** *See note on 28:7.*

26:34 **before a rooster crows.** Mark adds "twice." The rooster would begin crowing about 3:00 a.m. (cf. Mk 13:35). Though Peter and all the disciples insisted that they would never deny Christ (vv. 33, 35), they were only a few hours away from fulfilling this prophecy (vv. 74, 75; Mk 14:66–72).

before a rooster crows, you will deny Me three times."
35 Peter *said to Him, "[A]Even if I have to die with
You, I will not deny You." All the disciples said the
same thing too.

THE GARDEN OF GETHSEMANE

36 [A]Then Jesus *came with them to a place called
[B]Gethsemane, and *said to His disciples, "Sit here
while I go over there and pray." 37 And He took with
Him [A]Peter and the two sons of Zebedee, and began to be grieved and distressed. 38 Then He *said
to them, "[A]My soul is deeply grieved, to the point
of death; remain here and [B]keep watch with Me."
39 And He went a little beyond *them,* and fell on
His face and prayed, saying, "My Father, if it is possible, let [A]this cup pass from Me; [B]yet not as I will, but
as You will." 40 And He *came to the disciples and
*found them sleeping, and *said to Peter, "So, you *men*
could not [A]keep watch with Me for one hour? 41 [A]Keep
watching and praying that you may not enter into
temptation; [B]the spirit is willing, but the flesh is weak."
42 He went away again a second time and prayed,
saying, "My Father, if this [A]cannot pass away unless
I drink it, [B]Your will be done." 43 Again He came and
found them sleeping, for their eyes were heavy.
44 And He left them again, and went away and
prayed a third time, saying the same thing once
more. 45 Then He *came to the disciples and *said to
them, "[a]Are you still sleeping and resting? Behold,
[A]the hour is at hand and the Son of Man is being betrayed into the hands of sinners. 46 Get up, let us be
going; behold, the one who betrays Me is at hand!"

JESUS' BETRAYAL AND ARREST

47 [A]While He was still speaking, behold, [B]Judas,
one of the twelve, came up [a]accompanied by a large
crowd with swords and clubs, *who came* from the
chief priests and elders of the people. 48 Now he
who was betraying Him gave them a sign, saying, "Whomever I kiss, He is the one; seize Him."
49 Immediately Judas went to Jesus and said, "Hail,
[A]Rabbi!" and kissed Him. 50 And Jesus said to him,
"[A]Friend, *do* what you have come for." Then they
came and laid hands on Jesus and seized Him.
51 And behold, [A]one of those who were with Jesus
[a]reached and drew out his [B]sword, and struck the
[A]slave of the high priest and [b]cut off his ear. 52 Then
Jesus *said to him, "Put your sword back into its
place; for [A]all those who take up the sword shall
perish by the sword. 53 Or do you think that I cannot appeal to My Father, and He will at once put at
My disposal more than twelve [a,A]legions of [B]angels?
54 How then will [A]the Scriptures be fulfilled, *which
say* that it must happen this way?"
55 At that time Jesus said to the crowds, "Have
you come out with swords and clubs to arrest Me
as *you would* against a robber? [A]Every day I used
to sit in the temple teaching and you did not seize
Me. 56 But all this has taken place to fulfill [A]the Scriptures of the prophets." Then all the disciples left Him
and fled.

JESUS BEFORE CAIAPHAS

57 [A]Those who had seized Jesus led Him away to
[B]Caiaphas, the high priest, where the scribes and

26:35 [A]John 13:37 26:36 [A]Matt 26:36-46: *Mark 14:32-42; Luke 22:40-46* [B]Mark 14:32; Luke 22:39; John 18:1 26:37 [A]Matt 4:21; 17:1; Mark 5:37 26:38 [A]John 12:27 [B]Matt 26:40, 41 26:39 [A]Matt 20:22 [B]Matt 26:42; Mark 14:36; Luke 22:42; John 6:38 26:40 [A]Matt 26:38 26:41 [A]Matt 26:38 [B]Mark 14:38 26:42 [A]Matt 20:22 [B]Matt 26:39; Mark 14:36; Luke 22:42; John 6:38 26:45 [a]Or *Keep on sleeping therefore* [A]Mark 14:41; John 12:27; 13:1 26:47 [a]Lit *and with him* [A]Matt 26:47-56: *Mark 14:43-50; Luke 22:47-53; John 18:3-11* [B]Matt 26:14 26:49 [A]Matt 23:7; 26:25 26:50 [A]Matt 20:13; 22:12 26:51 [a]Lit *extended the hand* [b]Lit *took off* [A]Mark 14:47; Luke 22:50; John 18:10 [B]Luke 22:38 26:52 [A]Gen 9:6; Rev 13:10 26:53 [a]A legion equaled 6,000 troops [A]Mark 5:9, 15; Luke 8:30 [B]Matt 4:11 26:54 [A]Matt 26:24 26:55 [A]Mark 12:35; 14:49; Luke 4:20; 19:47; 20:1; 21:37; John 7:14, 28; 8:2, 20; 18:20 26:56 [A]Matt 26:24 26:57 [A]Matt 26:57-68: *Mark 14:53-65; John 18:12f, 19-24* [B]Matt 26:3

26:36 Gethsemane. Lit. "oil press." This was a frequent meeting place for Christ and His disciples (Jn 18:2), just across the Kidron Valley from Jerusalem (Jn 18:1). A garden of ancient olive trees is there to this day. Judas' familiarity with Jesus' patterns enabled him to find Jesus there—even though Christ had not previously announced His intentions.

26:38 grieved, to the point of death. His anguish had nothing to do with fear of men or the physical torments of the cross. He was sorrowful because within hours the full cup of divine fury against sin would be His to drink (*see note on v. 39*).

26:39 this cup. Cf. v. 42. A cup is often the symbol of divine wrath against sin in the OT (Is 51:17, 22; Jer 25:15–17, 27–29; La 4:21, 22; Eze 23:31–34; Hab 2:16). The next day Christ would "bear the sins of many" (Heb 9:28)—and the fullness of divine wrath would fall on Him (Is 53:10, 11; 2Co 5:21). This was the price of the sin He bore, and He paid it in full. His cry of anguish in 27:46 reflects the extreme bitterness of the cup of wrath He was given. **not as I will, but as You will.** This implies no conflict between the Persons of the Godhead. Rather, it graphically reveals how Christ in His humanity voluntarily surrendered His will to the will of the Father in all things—precisely so that there would be no conflict between the divine will and His desires. See Jn 4:34; 6:38; 8:29; Php 2:8. *See note on Jn 5:30.*

26:41 the flesh is weak. The tenderness of this plea is touching. Christ Himself was well acquainted with the feeling of human infirmities (Heb 4:15)—yet without sin. At that very moment He was locked in a struggle against human passions which, while not sinful in themselves, must be subjugated to the divine will if sin was to be avoided. *See note on v. 39.*

26:47 Judas, one of the twelve. See v. 14. All 4 evangelists refer to Judas this way (Mk 14:10, 43; Lk 22:47; Jn 6:71). Only once (Jn 20:24) is another disciple so described. The gospel writers seem to use the expression to underscore the insidiousness of Judas' crime—especially here, in the midst of the betrayal.

26:48, 49 *See notes on Mk 14:44, 45.*

26:50 Friend. Not the usual Gr. word for "friend," but another word meaning "comrade."

26:51 one of those. John identifies the swordsman as Peter and the victim as Malchus (Jn 18:10). Clearly, Peter was not aiming for the ear, but for the head. Only Luke mentions that Jesus healed Malchus' ear (*see note on Lk 22:51*).

26:52 perish by the sword. Peter's action was vigilantism. No matter how unjust the arrest of Jesus, Peter had no right to take the law into his own hands in order to stop it. Jesus' reply was a restatement of the Ge 9:6 principle: "Whoever sheds man's blood, by man his blood shall be shed," an affirmation that capital punishment is an appropriate penalty for murder.

26:53 more than twelve legions. A Roman legion was composed of 6,000 soldiers, so this would represent more than 72,000 angels. In 2Ki 19:35 a single angel killed more than 185,000 men in a single night, so this many angels would make a formidable army. *See note on Lk 2:13.*

26:54 Scriptures be fulfilled. God Himself had foreordained the very minutest details of how Jesus would die (Ac 2:23; 4:27, 28). Dying was Christ's consummate act of submission to the Father's will (*see note on v. 39*). Jesus Himself was in absolute control (Jn 10:17, 18). Yet it was not Jesus alone, but everyone around Him—His enemies included—who fulfilled precisely the details of the OT prophecies. These events display His divine sovereignty. *See notes on v. 2; 1:22; 5:18; 27:50.*

26:57 Caiaphas, the high priest. *See note on v. 3.* From Jn 18:13, we learn that Christ was taken first to Annas (former High Priest and father-in-law to Caiaphas). He then was sent

the elders were gathered together. 58 But [A]Peter was
following Him at a distance as far as the [B]courtyard
of the high priest, and entered in, and sat down with
the [a,C]officers to see the outcome.
59 Now the chief priests and the whole [a,A]Council
kept trying to obtain false testimony against Jesus,
so that they might put Him to death. 60 They did
not find *any,* even though many false witnesses
came forward. But later on [A]two came forward,
61 and said, "This man stated, '[A]I am able to destroy the [a]temple of God and to rebuild it [b]in three
days.' " 62 The high priest stood up and said to Him,
"Do You not answer? What is it that these men are
testifying against You?" 63 But [A]Jesus kept silent.
[B]And the high priest said to Him, "I [a,C]adjure You
by [D]the living God, that You tell us whether You are
[b]the Christ, [E]the Son of God." 64 Jesus *said to him,
"[A]You have said it *yourself;* nevertheless I tell you,
[a]hereafter you will see [B]THE SON OF MAN SITTING
AT THE RIGHT HAND OF POWER, and [C]COMING ON THE
CLOUDS OF HEAVEN."
65 Then the high priest [A]tore his [a]robes and said,
"He has blasphemed! What further need do we have
of witnesses? Behold, you have now heard the blasphemy; 66 what do you think?" They answered, "[A]He
deserves death!"
67 [A]Then they [B]spat in His face and beat Him with
their fists; and others [a]slapped Him, 68 and said,
"[A]Prophesy to us, You [a]Christ; who is the one who
hit You?"

PETER'S DENIALS

69 [A]Now Peter was sitting outside in the [B]court-
yard, and a servant-girl came to him and said, "You
too were with Jesus the Galilean." 70 But he denied
it before them all, saying, "I do not know what
you are talking about." 71 When he had gone out
to the gateway, another *servant-girl* saw him and

26:58 [a]Or *servants* [A]John 18:15 [B]Matt 26:3 [C]Matt 5:25; John 7:32, 45f; 19:6; Acts 5:22, 26 26:59 [a]Or *Sanhedrin* [A]Matt 5:22 26:60 [A]Deut 19:15 26:61 [a]Or *sanctuary* [b]Or *after* [A]Matt 27:40; Mark 14:58; 15:29; John 2:19; Acts 6:14 26:63 [a]Or *charge You under oath* [b]I.e. the Messiah [A]Matt 27:12, 14; John 19:9 [B]Matt 26:63-66: *Luke 22:67-71* [C]Lev 5:1 [D]Matt 16:16 [E]Matt 4:3 26:64 [a]Or *from now on* [A]Matt 26:25 [B]Ps 110:1; Mark 14:62 [C]Dan 7:13; Matt 16:27f 26:65 [a]Or *outer garments* [A]Num 14:6; Mark 14:63; Acts 14:14 26:66 [A]Lev 24:16; John 19:7 26:67 [a]Or *beat Him with rods* [A]Is 50:6; Matt 26:67, 68: *Luke 22:63-65; John 18:22* [B]Matt 27:30; Mark 10:34 26:68 [a]I.e. the Messiah [A]Mark 14:65; Luke 22:64 26:69 [A]Matt 26:69-75: *Mark 14:66-72; Luke 22:55-62; John 18:16-18, 25-27* [B]Matt 26:3

bound to Caiaphas' house (Jn 18:24). The conspiracy was well planned, so that "the scribes and the elders" (the Sanhedrin, *see note on v. 59*) were already "gathered" at Caiaphas' house and ready to try Jesus. The time was sometime between midnight and the first rooster's crowing (v. 74). Such a hearing was illegal on several counts: criminal trials were not to be held at night (*see note on 27:1*); and trials in capital cases could only be held at the temple and only in public. *See note on 27:2* for a fuller chronology of the events leading up to the crucifixion.

26:59 the whole Council. *See note on Jn 3:1.* The great Sanhedrin was the Supreme Court of Israel, consisting of 71 members, presided over by the High Priest. They met daily in the temple to hold court, except on the Sabbath and other holy days. Technically, they did not have the power to administer capital punishment (Jn 18:31), but in the case of Stephen, for example, this was no deterrent to his stoning (cf. Ac 6:12–14; 7:58–60). Roman governors evidently sometimes ignored such incidents as a matter of political expediency. In Jesus' case, the men who were trying Him were the same ones who had conspired against Him (cf. Jn 11:47–50).

26:60 did not find *any*. Even though many were willing to perjure themselves, the Sanhedrin could not find a charge that had enough credibility to indict Jesus. Evidently the "false witnesses" could not agree between themselves.

26:61 destroy the temple of God. See Jn 2:19–21. The witnesses' account was a distortion of Jesus' meaning. Mark 14:58 gives a fuller account of their testimony.

26:63 adjure You. *See note on 5:34.* Caiaphas was trying to break Jesus' silence (v. 62) by placing Him under oath. The oath was supposed to make Him legally obligated to reply. Jesus' answer (v. 64) implies acceptance of the oath.

26:64 The imagery was taken from Ps 110:1 and Da 7:13.

26:65 the high priest tore his robes. Normally, this was an expression of deep grief (2Ki 19:1; Job 1:20; Jer 36:24). The High Priest was forbidden to tear his clothes (Lv 10:6; 21:10)—but the Talmud made an exception for High Priests who witnessed a blasphemy. But Caiaphas' supposed grief was as phony as the charge of blasphemy against Jesus; he was gloating over having found something to base his charges on (v. 67).

JESUS' TRIAL, JUDGMENT, AND CRUCIFIXION

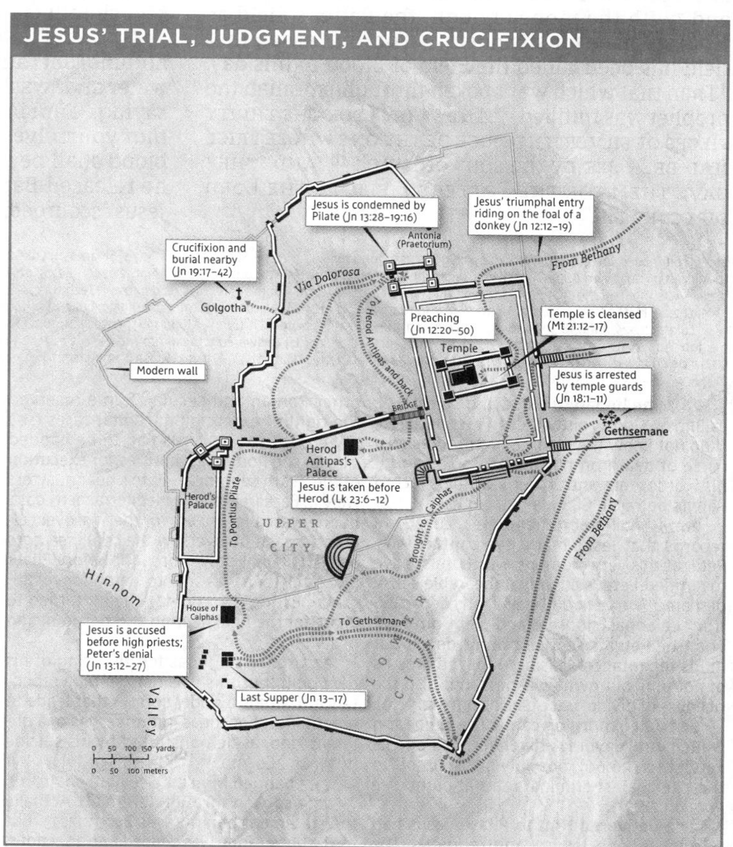

*said to those who were there, "This man was with
Jesus of Nazareth." 72 And again he denied *it* with
an oath, "I do not know the man." 73 A little later
the bystanders came up and said to Peter, "Surely
you too are *one* of them; [A]for even the way you talk
[a]gives you away." 74 Then he began to curse and
swear, "I do not know the man!" And immediately a
rooster crowed. 75 And Peter remembered the word
which Jesus had said, "[A]Before a rooster crows, you
will deny Me three times." And he went out and
wept bitterly.

JUDAS'S REMORSE

27 [A]Now when morning came, all the chief
priests and the elders of the people conferred
together against Jesus to put Him to death; 2 and
they bound Him, and led Him away and [A]delivered
Him to [B]Pilate the governor.
3 Then when [A]Judas, who had betrayed Him, saw
that He had been condemned, he felt remorse and
returned [B]the thirty [a]pieces of silver to the chief
priests and elders, 4 saying, "I have sinned by betraying innocent blood." But they said, "What is that to
us? [A]See *to that* yourself!" 5 And he threw the pieces
of silver into [A]the temple sanctuary and departed;
and [B]he went away and hanged himself. 6 The chief
priests took the pieces of silver and said, "It is not
lawful to put them into the temple treasury, since it
is the price of blood." 7 And they conferred together
and [a]with the money bought the Potter's Field as
a burial place for strangers. 8 [A]For this reason that
field has been called the Field of Blood to this day.
9 Then that which was spoken through Jeremiah the
prophet was fulfilled: "[A]AND [a]THEY TOOK THE THIRTY
PIECES OF SILVER, THE PRICE OF THE ONE WHOSE PRICE
HAD BEEN SET by the sons of Israel; 10 [A]AND [a]THEY
GAVE THEM FOR THE POTTER'S FIELD, AS THE LORD
DIRECTED ME."

JESUS BEFORE PILATE

11 [A]Now Jesus stood before the governor, and the
governor questioned Him, saying, "Are You the
[B]King of the Jews?" And Jesus said to him, "[C]*It is as*
you say." 12 And while He was being accused by the
chief priests and elders, [A]He did not answer. 13 Then
Pilate *said to Him, "Do You not hear how many
things they testify against You?" 14 And [A]He did not
answer him with regard to even a *single* [a]charge,
so the governor was quite amazed.
15 [A]Now at *the* feast the governor was accustomed
to release for the [a]people *any* one prisoner whom
they wanted. 16 At that time they were holding a
notorious prisoner, called Barabbas. 17 So when
the people gathered together, Pilate said to them,
"Whom do you want me to release for you? Barabbas, or Jesus [A]who is called Christ?" 18 For he knew
that because of envy they had handed Him over.
19 [A]While he was sitting on the judgment seat, his
wife sent him *a message,* saying, "Have nothing to
do with that [B]righteous Man; for [a]last night I suffered
greatly [C]in a dream because of Him." 20 But the chief
priests and the elders persuaded the crowds to [A]ask
for Barabbas and to put Jesus to death. 21 But the governor [a]said to them, "Which of the two do you want
me to release for you?" And they said, "Barabbas."
22 Pilate *said to them, "Then what shall I do with Jesus
[A]who is called Christ?" They all *said, "[a]Crucify Him!"
23 And he said, "Why, what evil has He done?" But they
kept shouting all the more, saying, "[a]Crucify Him!"
24 When Pilate saw that he was accomplishing
nothing, but rather that [A]a riot was starting, he took
water and [B]washed his hands in front of the crowd,
saying, "I am innocent of [C]this Man's blood; [D]see *to*
that yourselves." 25 And all the people said, "[A]His
blood shall be on us and on our children!" 26 Then
he released Barabbas [a]for them; but after having
Jesus [A]scourged, he handed Him over to be crucified.

26:73 [a]Lit *makes you evident* [A]Mark 14:70; Luke 22:59; John 18:26 26:75 [A]Matt 26:34 27:1 [A]Mark 15:1; Luke 22:66; John 18:28 27:2 [A]Matt 20:19 [B]Luke 3:1; 13:1; 23:12; Acts 3:13; 4:27; 1 Tim 6:13 27:3 [a]Or *silver shekels* [A]Matt 26:14 [B]Matt 26:15 27:4 [A]Matt 27:24 27:5 [A]Matt 26:61; Luke 1:9, 21 [B]Acts 1:18 27:7 [a]Lit *from them* 27:8 [A]Acts 1:19 27:9 [a]Or *I took;* cf Zech 11:13 [A]Zech 11:12 27:10 [a]Some early mss read *I gave* [A]Zech 11:13 27:11 [A]Matt 27:11-14: *Mark 15:2-5; Luke 23:2, 3; John 18:29-38* [B]Matt 2:2 [C]Matt 26:25 27:12 [A]Matt 26:63; John 19:9 27:14 [a]Lit *word* [A]Matt 27:12; Mark 15:5; Luke 23:9; John 19:9 27:15 [a]Lit *crowd* [A]Matt 27:15-26: *Mark 15:6-15; Luke 23:17-25;* John 18:39-19:16 27:17 [A]Matt 1:16; 27:22 27:19 [a]Lit *today* [A]John 19:13; Acts 12:21; 18:12, 16f; 25:6, 10, 17 [B]Matt 27:24 [C]Gen 20:6; 31:11; Num 12:6; Job 33:15; Matt 1:20; 2:12f, 19, 22 27:20 [A]Acts 3:14 27:21 [a]Lit *answered and said to them* 27:22 [a]Lit *Let Him be crucified* [A]Matt 1:16 27:23 [a]Lit *Let Him be crucified* 27:24 [A]Matt 26:5 [B]Deut 21:6-8 [C]Matt 27:19 [D]Matt 27:4 27:25 [A]Josh 2:19; Acts 5:28 27:26 [a]Or *to them* [A]Mark 15:15; Luke 23:16; John 19:1

26:74 he began to curse and swear. I.e., calling on God as his witness, Peter declared, "I do not know the man!" and pronounced a curse of death on himself at God's hand if his words were untrue. All 4 Gospels record Peter's betrayal. Cf. vv. 31–35.

26:75 And Peter remembered. Luke 22:61 records that Jesus made eye contact with Peter at this very moment, which must have magnified Peter's already unbearable sense of shame. "He went out"—evidently departing from Caiaphas' house—"and wept bitterly." The true Peter is seen not in his denial but in his repentance. This account reminds us of not only our own weakness, but also the richness of divine grace (see also Jn 21:15–19).

27:1 when morning came. The Sanhedrin waited until daybreak to render their official verdict (cf. 26:66), possibly a token nod to the rule against criminal trials at night (*see note on 26:57*).

27:2 delivered Him to Pilate. Jesus had two trials, one Jewish and religious, the other Roman and secular. Rome reserved the right of execution in capital cases (*see note on 26:59*), so Jesus had to be handed over to the Roman authorities for execution of the death sentence. Pilate's headquarters were in Caesarea, on the Mediterranean coast, but he was in Jerusalem for the Passover celebrations, so he oversaw the trial (*see note on Mk 15:1*). Christ was brought before Pilate (vv. 2–14), then was sent to Herod for yet another hearing (Lk 23:6–12), then returned to Pilate for the final hearing and pronouncing of sentence (vv. 15–26).

27:3 remorse. Judas felt the sting of his own guilt, but this was not genuine repentance. There is a godly sorrow that leads to repentance, but Judas' remorse was of a different kind, as demonstrated by his suicide (v. 5). Cf. 2Co 7:10.

27:5 hanged himself. *See note on Ac 1:18.*

27:9 spoken through Jeremiah. Actually the statement paraphrases Zec 11:12, 13. But the Hebrew canon was divided into 3 sections, Law, Writings, and Prophets (cf. Lk 24:44). Jeremiah came first in the order of prophetic books, so the Prophets were sometimes collectively referred to by his name.

27:11 *It is as* you say. These words were probably spoken immediately after the dialogue Jn 18:34–36 reports.

27:25 His blood shall be on us. The Jews accepted the blame for the execution of Jesus and did not hold the Romans responsible. Cf. 21:38, 39.

27:26 scourged. The whip used for scourging consisted of several strands of leather attached to a wooden handle. Each strand had a bit of metal or bone attached to the end. The victim was bound to a post by the wrists, high over his head, so that the flesh of the back would be taut. An expert at wielding the scourge could literally tear the flesh from the back, lacerating muscles, and sometimes even exposing the kidneys or other internal organs. Scourging alone was fatal in some cases.

JESUS IS MOCKED

27 [A]Then the soldiers of the governor took Jesus
into [B]the [a]Praetorium and gathered the whole *Roman* [b,C]cohort around Him. 28 They stripped Him and
[A]put a scarlet robe on Him. 29 [A]And after twisting
together a crown of thorns, they put it on His head,
and a [a]reed in His right hand; and they knelt down
before Him and mocked Him, saying, "[B]Hail, King
of the Jews!" 30 [A]They spat on Him, and took the
reed and *began* to beat Him on the head. 31 [A]After
they had mocked Him, they took the *scarlet* robe
off Him and put His *own* garments back on Him,
and led Him away to crucify Him.

32 [A]As they were coming out, they found a man
of [B]Cyrene named Simon, [a]whom they pressed into
service to bear His cross.

THE CRUCIFIXION

33 [A]And when they came to a place called [B]Golgo-
tha, which means Place of a Skull, 34 [A]they gave Him
[B]wine to drink mixed with gall; and after tasting *it,*
He was unwilling to drink.

35 And when they had crucified Him, [A]they divided
up His garments among themselves by casting [a]lots.
36 And sitting down, they *began* to [A]keep watch over
Him there. 37 And above His head they put up the
charge against Him [a]which read,

"[A]THIS IS JESUS THE KING OF THE JEWS."

38 At that time two robbers *were crucified with
Him, one on the right and one on the left. 39 And
those passing by were [a]hurling abuse at Him, [A]wag-
ging their heads 40 and saying, "[A]You who *are going to* destroy the temple and rebuild it in three
days, save Yourself! [B]If You are the Son of God, come
down from the cross." 41 In the same way the chief
priests also, along with the scribes and elders, were
mocking *Him* and saying, 42 "[A]He saved others; [a]He
cannot save Himself. [B]He is the King of Israel; let
Him now come down from the cross, and we will
believe in Him. 43 [A]HE TRUSTS IN GOD; LET GOD RES-
CUE *Him* now, IF HE [a]DELIGHTS IN HIM; for He said,
'I am the Son of God.' " 44 [A]The robbers who had
been crucified with Him were also insulting Him
with the same words.

45 [A]Now from the [a]sixth hour darkness [b]fell upon
all the land until the [c]ninth hour. 46 About the ninth
hour Jesus cried out with a loud voice, saying, "[A]ELI,
ELI, LAMA SABACHTHANI?" that is, "MY GOD, MY GOD,

27:27 [a]I.e. the governor's official residence [b]Or *battalion* [A]Matt 27:27-31: *Mark 15:16-20* [B]Matt 26:3; John 18:28, 33; 19:9 [C]Acts 10:1 27:28 [A]Mark 15:17; John 19:2 27:29 [a]Or *staff;* i.e. to mimic a king's scepter [A]Mark 15:17; John 19:2 [B]Mark 15:18; John 19:3 27:30 [A]Matt 26:67; Mark 10:34; 14:65; 15:19 27:31 [A]Mark 15:20 27:32 [a]Lit *this one* [A]Matt 27:32: *Mark 15:21; Luke 23:26;* John 19:17 [B]Acts 2:10; 6:9; 11:20; 13:1 27:33 [A]Matt 27:34-44: *Mark 15:22-32; Luke 23:33-43; John 19:17-24* [B]Luke 23:33; John 19:17 27:34 [A]Ps 69:21 [B]Mark 15:23 27:35 [a]Lit *a lot* [A]Ps 22:18 27:36 [A]Matt 27:54 27:37 [a]Lit *written* [A]Mark 15:26; Luke 23:38; John 19:19 27:39 [a]Or *blaspheming* [A]Job 16:4; Ps 22:7; 109:25; Lam 2:15; Mark 15:29 27:40 [A]Matt 26:61; John 2:19 [B]Matt 27:42 27:42 [a]Or *can He not save Himself?* [A]Mark 15:31; Luke 23:35 [B]Matt 27:37; Luke 23:37; John 1:49; 12:13 27:43 [a]Or *takes pleasure in;* or *cares for him* [A]Ps 22:8 27:44 [A]Luke 23:39-43 27:45 [a]I.e. 12 noon [b]Or *occurred* [c]I.e. 3 p.m. [A]Matt 27:45-56: *Mark 15:33-41; Luke 23:44-49* 27:46 [A]Ps 22:1

27:27 **Praetorium.** Pilate's residence in Jerusalem. It was probably located in the Antonia Fortress, adjacent to the NW corner of the temple. "The soldiers of the governor" were part of a "cohort"—about 600 soldiers—assigned to serve the governor (Pilate) during his stay in Jerusalem.

27:28 **scarlet robe.** Mark 15:17 and Jn 19:2 say "purple," suggesting that the robe may have been something between royal purple, and "scarlet," the closest thing they could find to the traditional garb of royalty. The word for "robe" refers to a military cloak undoubtedly belonging to one of the soldiers.

27:29 **a reed in His right hand.** To imitate a scepter they purposely chose something flimsy-looking.

27:30 **They spat on Him.** See Is 50:6. **beat Him on the head.** A reed long enough to make a mock scepter would be firm enough to be extremely painful, about like a broom handle. Jn 19:3 says they hit Him with their fists as well.

27:31 **to crucify Him.** Crucifixion was a form of punishment that had been passed down to the Romans from the Persians, Phoenicians, and Carthaginians. Roman crucifixion was a lingering doom—by design. Roman executioners had perfected the art of slow torture while keeping the victim alive. Some victims even lingered until they were eaten alive by birds of prey or wild beasts. Most hung on the cross for days before dying of exhaustion, dehydration, traumatic fever, or—most likely—suffocation. When the legs would no longer support the weight of the body, the diaphragm was constricted in a way that made breathing impossible. That is why breaking the legs would hasten death (Jn 19:31–33), but this was unnecessary in Jesus' case. The hands were usually nailed through the wrists, and the feet through the instep or the Achilles tendon (sometimes using one nail for both feet). None of these wounds would be fatal, but their pain would become unbearable as the hours dragged on. The most notable feature of crucifixion was the stigma of disgrace that was attached to it (Gal 3:13; 5:11; Heb 12:2). One indignity was the humiliation of carrying one's own cross, which might weigh as much as 200 pounds. Normally a quaternion, 4 soldiers, would escort the prisoner through the crowds to the place of crucifixion. A placard bearing the indictment would be hung around the person's neck.

27:32 **Cyrene.** A city in N Africa. Evidently the scourging had so weakened Jesus that He was unable to carry the cross. This is another touching picture of His humanity, beset with all human weaknesses except sin (Heb 4:15).

27:33 **Place of a Skull.** "Golgotha" may have been a skull-shaped hill, or it may have been so named because as a place of crucifixion, it accumulated skulls. None of the gospels mention a hill.

27:34 **wine ... mixed with gall.** "Gall" simply refers to something bitter. Mark 15:23 identifies it as myrrh, a narcotic. The Jews had a custom, based on Pr 31:6, of administering a pain-deadening medication mixed with wine to victims of crucifixion, in order to deaden the pain. Tasting what it was, Christ, though thirsty, "was unwilling to drink," lest it dull His senses before He completed His work. The lessening of physical pain would probably not have diminished the efficacy of His atoning work (*see notes on 26:38, 39*). But He needed His full mental faculties for the hours yet to come. It was necessary for Him to be awake and fully conscious, for example, to minister to the dying thief (Lk 23:43).

27:35 **divided up His garments.** The garments of the victim were the customary spoils of the executioners. John 19:23, 24 gives a fuller account. This action was foretold in Ps 22:18.

27:37 **the charge.** For a reconciliation of the differences between the various accounts of this inscription, *see note on Lk 23:38* (cf. Mk 15:26). The fact that the placard was placed "above His head" suggests that this cross was in the familiar shape with an upright protruding above the transom, and not the T-shaped cross that was also sometimes used.

27:38 **robbers.** This word denotes a rebel and brigand who plunders as he steals. Mere thieves were not usually crucified. These were probably cohorts of Barabbas.

27:40 **destroy the temple and rebuild it in three days.** See 26:61. They had missed His point. "He was speaking of the temple of His body" (Jn 2:21). He would not "come down from the cross," but it was not because He was powerless to do so (Jn 10:18). The proof that He was the Son of God came "in three days" (*see note on 12:40*), when He returned with "the temple" (i.e., His body) rebuilt.

27:42 **we will believe in Him.** *See notes on 12:38; 16:1.*

27:45 **from the sixth hour ... until the ninth hour.** From noon until 3:00 p.m. The crucifixion began at 9:00 a.m. (*see notes on Mk 15:25; Lk 23:44*).

27:46 **Eli, Eli, lama sabachthani.** "Eli" is Heb.; the rest Aram. (Mk 15:34 gives the entire wail in Aramaic.) This cry is a fulfillment of Ps

WHY HAVE YOU FORSAKEN ME?" 47 And some of those
who were standing there, when they heard it, *began*
saying, "This man is calling for Elijah." 48 [A]Immedi-
ately one of them ran, and taking a sponge, he filled
it with sour wine and put it on a reed, and gave
Him a drink. 49 But the rest *of them* said, "[a]Let us
see whether Elijah will come to save Him[b]." 50 And
Jesus [A]cried out again with a loud voice, and yielded
up His spirit. 51 [A]And behold, [B]the [a]veil of the temple
was torn in two from top to bottom; and [C]the earth
shook and the rocks were split. 52 The tombs were
opened, and many bodies of the [a]saints who had
[A]fallen asleep were raised; 53 and coming out of the
tombs after His resurrection they entered [A]the holy
city and appeared to many. 54 [A]Now the centurion,
and those who were with him [B]keeping guard over
Jesus, when they saw [C]the earthquake and the things
that were happening, became very frightened and
said, "Truly this was [a,D]the Son of God!"

55 [A]Many women were there looking on from a
distance, who had followed Jesus from Galilee while
[a,B]ministering to Him. 56 Among them was [A]Mary
Magdalene, and Mary the mother of James and
Joseph, and [B]the mother of the sons of Zebedee.

JESUS IS BURIED

57 [A]When it was evening, there came a rich man
from Arimathea, named Joseph, who himself had
also become a disciple of Jesus. 58 This man went to
Pilate and asked for the body of Jesus. Then Pilate
ordered it to be given *to him*. 59 And Joseph took the
body and wrapped it in a clean linen cloth, 60 and
laid it in his own new tomb, which he had hewn out
in the rock; and he rolled [A]a large stone against the
entrance of the tomb and went away. 61 And [A]Mary
Magdalene was there, and the other Mary, sitting
opposite the grave.

62 Now on the next day, [a]the day after [A]the preparation, the chief priests and the Pharisees gathered
together with Pilate, 63 and said, "Sir, we remember
that when He was still alive that deceiver said, '[A]Af-
ter three days I *am to* rise again.' 64 Therefore, give
orders for the grave to be made secure until the
third day, otherwise His disciples may come and
steal Him away and say to the people, 'He has risen
from the dead,' and the last deception will be worse
than the first." 65 Pilate said to them, "You have a
[A]guard; go, make it *as* secure as you know how."
66 And they went and made the grave secure, and
along with [A]the guard they set a [B]seal on [C]the stone.

JESUS IS RISEN!

28 [A]Now after the Sabbath, as it began to dawn
toward the first *day* of the week, [B]Mary Magdalene and the other Mary came to look at the grave.
2 And behold, a severe earthquake had occurred, for
[A]an angel of the Lord descended from heaven and
came and rolled away [B]the stone and sat upon it.
3 And [A]his appearance was like lightning, and his
clothing as white as snow. 4 The guards shook for fear
of him and became like dead men. 5 The angel said to
the women, "[a,A]Do not be afraid; for I know that you

27:48 [A]Ps 69:21; Mark 15:36; Luke 23:36; John 19:29 27:49 [a]Lit *Permit that we see* [b]Some early mss read *And another took a spear and pierced His side, and there came out water and blood* (cf John 19:34) 27:50 [A]Mark 15:37; Luke 23:46; John 19:30 27:51 [a]Or *curtain* [A]Matt 27:51-56: *Mark 15:38-41;* Luke 23:47-49 [B]Ex 26:31ff; Mark 15:38; Luke 23:45; Heb 9:3 [C]Matt 27:54 27:52 [a]Or *holy ones* [A]Acts 7:60 27:53 [A]Matt 4:5 27:54 [a]Or *a son of God* or *a son of a god* [A]Mark 15:39; Luke 23:47 [B]Matt 27:36 [C]Matt 27:51 [D]Matt 4:3; 27:43 27:55 [a]Or *caring for Him* [A]Mark 15:40f; Luke 23:49; John 19:25 [B]Mark 15:41; Luke 8:2, 3 27:56 [A]Matt 28:1; Mark 15:40, 47; 16:9; Luke 8:2; John 19:25; 20:1, 18 [B]Matt 20:20 27:57 [A]Matt 27:57-61: *Mark 15:42-47; Luke 23:50-56; John 19:38-42* 27:60 [A]Matt 27:66; 28:2; Mark 16:4 27:61 [A]Matt 27:56; 28:1 27:62 [a]Lit *which is after* [A]Mark 15:42; Luke 23:54; John 19:14, 31, 42 27:63 [A]Matt 16:21; 17:23; 20:19; Mark 8:31; 9:31; 10:34; Luke 9:22; 18:31-33 27:65 [A]Matt 27:66; 28:11 27:66 [A]Matt 27:65; 28:11 [B]Dan 6:17 [C]Matt 27:60; 28:2; Mark 16:4 28:1 [A]Matt 28:1-8: *Mark 16:1-8; Luke 24:1-10;* John 20:1-8 [B]Matt 27:56, 61 28:2 [A]Luke 24:4; John 20:12 [B]Matt 27:66; Mark 16:4 28:3 [A]Dan 7:9; 10:6; Mark 9:3; John 20:12; Acts 1:10 28:5 [a]Or *Stop being afraid* [A]Matt 14:27; 28:10; Rev 1:17

22:1, one of many striking parallels between that psalm and the specific events of the crucifixion (*see notes on Ps 22*). Christ at that moment was experiencing the abandonment and despair that resulted from the outpouring of divine wrath on Him as sin-bearer (*see note on 26:39*).

27:50 yielded up His spirit. A voluntary act. See Jn 10:18. *See note on 26:54.*

27:51 the veil of the temple. I.e., the curtain that blocked the entrance to the Most Holy Place (Ex 26:33; Heb 9:3). The tearing of the veil signified that the way into God's presence was now open to all through a new and living way (Heb 10:19–22). The fact that it tore "from top to bottom" showed that no man had split the veil. God did it.

27:52 bodies of the saints ... were raised. Matthew alone mentions this miracle. Nothing more is said about these people, which would be unlikely if they remained on earth for long. Evidently, these people were given glorified bodies; they appeared "to many" (v. 53), enough to establish the reality of the miracle; and then they no doubt ascended to glory—a kind of foretaste of 1Th. 4:16.

27:54 the centurion. *See note on 8:5.* **those ... with him.** These were probably men under his charge. Mark 15:39 says the centurion was the one who uttered the words of confession, but he evidently spoke for his men as well. Their fear speaks of an awareness of their sin, and the word "truly" suggests a certainty and conviction that bespeaks genuine faith. These men represent an answer to Jesus' prayer in Lk 23:34. Their response contrasts sharply with the mocking taunts of vv. 39–44.

27:56 Mary Magdalene. She had been delivered from 7 demons (Lk 8:2); the other "Mary" ("wife of Clopas," Jn 19:25—a variant of Alphaeus) was the mother of the apostle known as "James the Less" (Mk 15:40; *see note on 10:2*). **the mother of the sons of Zebedee.** Salome (Mk 15:40), mother of James and John. From Jn 19:26, we learn that Mary, the mother of Jesus, was also present at the cross—possibly standing apart from these 3, who were "looking on from a distance" (v. 55), as if they could not bear to watch His sufferings, but neither could they bear to leave Him.

27:57 Arimathea. A town about 15–20 mi. NW of Jerusalem. **Joseph.** Mark 15:43 and Luke 23:50, 51 identify him as a member of the Sanhedrin (*see note on 26:59*), though Luke says "he had not consented to their plan and action" in condemning Christ. Joseph and Nicodemus (Jn 19:39), both being prominent Jewish leaders, buried Christ in Joseph's own "new tomb" (v. 60), thus fulfilling exactly the prophecy of Is 53:9.

27:62 the next day. The Sabbath. **the day after the preparation.** This was on Friday.

28:1 it began to dawn toward the first *day* of the week. Sabbath officially ended with sundown on Saturday. At that time the women could purchase and prepare spices (Lk 24:1). The event described here occurred the next morning, at dawn on Sunday, the first day of the week. **other Mary.** The mother of James the Less (*see note on 27:56*).

28:2 a severe earthquake. The second earthquake associated with Christ's death (27:51). This one may have been confined to the immediate area around the grave, when "an angel" supernaturally "rolled away the stone"—not to let Jesus out, for if He could rise from the dead, He would need no help escaping an earthly tomb, but to let the women and the apostles in (v. 6).

28:4 became like dead men. This suggests that they were not merely paralyzed with fear, but completely unconscious, totally traumatized by what they had seen. The word translated "shook" has the same root as the word for "earthquake" in v. 2. The sudden appearance of this angel, at the same time the women arrived, was their first clue that anything extraordinary was happening.

are looking for Jesus who has been crucified. 6 He
is not here, for He has risen, [A]just as He said. Come,
see the place where He was lying. 7 Go quickly and
tell His disciples that He has risen from the dead;
and behold, He is going ahead of you [A]into Galilee,
there you will see Him; behold, I have told you."
8 And they left the tomb quickly with fear and
great joy and ran to report it to His disciples. 9 And
behold, Jesus met them [a]and greeted them. And
they came up and took hold of His feet and worshiped Him. 10 Then Jesus *said to them, "[a,A]Do not
be afraid; go and take word to [B]My brethren to leave
[C]for Galilee, and there they will see Me."
11 Now while they were on their way, some of [A]the
guard came into the city and reported to the chief
priests all that had happened. 12 And when they had
assembled with the elders and consulted together,
they gave a large sum of money to the soldiers,
13 and said, "You are to say, 'His disciples came by
night and stole Him away while we were asleep.'
14 And if this should come to [A]the governor's ears,
we will win him over and [a]keep you out of trouble."
15 And they took the money and did as they had
been instructed; and this story was widely [A]spread
among the Jews, *and is* [B]to this day.

THE GREAT COMMISSION

16 But the eleven disciples proceeded [A]to Galilee, to the mountain which Jesus had designated.
17 When they saw Him, they worshiped *Him;* but
[A]some were doubtful. 18 And Jesus came up and
spoke to them, saying, "[A]All authority has been
given to Me in heaven and on earth. 19 [a,A]Go therefore
and [B]make disciples of [C]all the nations, [D]baptizing
them in the name of the Father and the Son and the
Holy Spirit, 20 teaching them to observe all that I
commanded you; and lo, [A]I am with you [a]always,
even to [B]the end of the age."

28:6 [A]Matt 12:40; 16:21; 27:63 28:7 [A]Matt 26:32; 28:10, 16; Mark 16:7 28:9 [a]Lit *saying hello* 28:10 [a]Or *Stop being afraid* [A]Matt 14:27; 28:5 [B]John 20:17; Rom 8:29; Heb 2:11f, 17 [C]Matt 26:32; 28:7, 16 28:11 [A]Matt 27:65, 66 28:14 [a]Lit *make you free from care* [A]Matt 27:2 28:15 [A]Matt 9:31; Mark 1:45 [B]Matt 27:8 28:16 [A]Matt 26:32; 28:7, 10; Mark 15:41; 16:7 28:17 [A]Mark 16:11 28:18 [A]Dan 7:13f; Matt 11:27; 26:64; Rom 14:9; Eph 1:20-22; Phil 2:9f; Col 2:10; 1 Pet 3:22 28:19 [a]Or *Having gone;* Gr aorist part. [A]Mark 16:15f [B]Matt 13:52; Acts 1:8; 14:21 [C]Matt 25:32; Luke 24:47 [D]Acts 2:38; 8:16; Rom 6:3; 1 Cor 1:13, 15ff; Gal 3:27 28:20 [a]Lit *all the days* [A]Matt 18:20; Acts 18:10 [B]Matt 13:39

28:6 Come, see the place where He was lying. *See note on Lk 24:4* for the order of these events as gleaned from all 4 Gospels.

28:7 there you will see Him. See vv. 10, 16; 26:32; Jn 21:1–14. This does not mean they would not see Him until then. He was seen by the apostles several times before they saw Him in Galilee (Lk 24:15, 34, 36; Jn 20:19, 26). But His supreme post-resurrection appearance was in Galilee, where "He appeared to more than five hundred brethren at once" (1Co 15:6). *See note on v. 16.*

28:9 Jesus met them. For a summary of Christ's postresurrection appearances, *see note on Lk 24:34.*

28:10 My brethren. I.e., the disciples.

28:11 reported to the chief priests. The Jewish leaders' determination to cover up what had occurred reveals the obstinacy of unbelief in the face of evidence (Lk 16:31).

28:12 a large sum of money. Lit. "silver" (cf. 26:15). The bribery was necessary because the soldiers' story, if true, could cost them their lives—since they were charged with guard duty under Pilate's personal orders (27:65). The Jewish leaders also promised to cover for the soldiers if the false story they spread leaked back to Pilate (v. 14).

28:13 while we were asleep. The story was obviously bogus, and not a very good cover-up. They could not possibly know what had happened while they were asleep.

28:16 the eleven disciples. This does not mean that only the 11 were present. The fact that some were "doubtful" (v. 17) strongly suggests that more than the 11 were present. It is likely that Christ arranged this meeting in Galilee because that was where most of His followers were. This seems the most likely location for the massive gathering of disciples Paul describes in 1Co 15:6 (*see note on v. 7*).

28:17 but some were doubtful. That simple phrase is one of countless testimonies to the integrity of Scripture. The transparent honesty of a statement like this shows that Matthew was not attempting to exclude or cover up facts that might lessen the perfection of such a glorious moment.

28:18 All authority. See 11:27; Jn 3:35. Absolute sovereign authority—lordship over all—is handed to Christ, "in heaven and on earth." This is clear proof of His deity. The time of His humiliation was at an end, and God had exalted Him above all (Php 2:9–11).

28:19 therefore. I.e., on the basis of His authority, the disciples were sent to "make disciples of all the nations." The sweeping scope of their commission is consummate with His unlimited authority. in the name of the Father … Son … Holy Spirit. The formula is a strong affirmation of trinitarianism.

28:20 teaching them to observe all that I commanded you. The kind of evangelism called for in this commission does not end with the conversion of the unbeliever. I am with you. There's a touching echo of the beginning of Matthew's gospel here. Immanuel, which is translated, "GOD WITH US" (1:23), remains "with" us "even to the end of the age"—i.e., until He returns bodily to judge the world and establish His earthly kingdom.

THE GOSPEL ACCORDING TO MARK

TITLE

Mark, for whom this gospel is named, was a close companion of the apostle Peter and a recurring character in the book of Acts, where he is known as "John who was also called Mark" (Ac 12:12, 25; 15:37, 39). It was to John Mark's mother's home in Jerusalem that Peter went when released from prison (Ac 12:12).

John Mark was a cousin of Barnabas (Col 4:10), who accompanied Paul and Barnabas on Paul's first missionary journey (Ac 12:25; 13:5). But he deserted them along the way in Perga and returned to Jerusalem (Ac 13:13). When Barnabas wanted Paul to take John Mark on the second missionary journey, Paul refused. The friction which resulted between Paul and Barnabas led to their separation (Ac 15:38–40).

But John Mark's earlier vacillation evidently gave way to great strength and maturity, and in time he proved himself even to the apostle Paul. When Paul wrote the Colossians, he instructed them that if John Mark came, they were to welcome him (Col 4:10). Paul even listed Mark as a fellow worker (Phm 24). Later, Paul told Timothy to "Pick up Mark and bring him with you, for he is useful to me for service" (2Ti 4:11).

John Mark's restoration to useful ministry may have been, in part, due to the ministry of Peter. Peter's close relationship with Mark is evident from his description of him as "my son, Mark" (1Pe 5:13). Peter, of course, was no stranger to failure himself, and his influence on the younger man was no doubt instrumental in helping him out of the instability of his youth and into the strength and maturity he would need for the work to which God had called him.

AUTHOR AND DATE

Unlike the Epistles, the Gospels do not name their authors. The early church fathers, however, unanimously affirm that Mark wrote this second gospel. Papias, bishop of Hieropolis, writing about A.D. 140, noted:

And the presbyter [the Apostle John] said this:

Mark having become the interpreter of Peter, wrote down accurately whatsoever he remembered. It was not, however, in exact order that he related the sayings or deeds of Christ. For he neither heard the Lord nor accompanied Him. But afterwards, as I said, he accompanied Peter, who accommodated his instructions to the necessities [of his hearers], but with no intention of giving a regular narrative of the Lord's sayings. Wherefore Mark made no mistake in thus writing some things as he remembered them. For of one thing he took especial care, not to omit anything he had heard, and not to put anything fictitious into the statements. [*From the Exposition of the Oracles of the Lord* (6)]

Justin Martyr, writing about A.D. 150, referred to the Gospel of Mark as "the memoirs of Peter," and suggested that Mark committed his gospel to writing while in Italy. This agrees with the uniform voice of early tradition, which regarded this gospel as having been written in Rome, for the benefit of Roman Christians. Irenaeus, writing about A.D. 185, called Mark "the disciple and interpreter of Peter," and recorded that the second gospel consisted of what Peter preached about Christ. The testimony of the church fathers differs as to whether this gospel was written before or after Peter's death (ca. A.D. 67–68).

Evangelical scholars have suggested dates for the writing of Mark's gospel ranging from A.D. 50 to 70. A date before the destruction of Jerusalem and the temple in A.D. 70 is required by the comment of Jesus in 13:2. Luke's gospel was clearly written before Acts (Ac 1:1–3). The date of the writing of Acts can probably be fixed at about A.D. 63, because that is shortly after the narrative ends (see Introduction to Acts: Author and Date). It is therefore likely, though not certain, that Mark was written at an early date, probably sometime in the 50s.

BACKGROUND AND SETTING

Whereas Matthew was written to a Jewish audience, Mark seems to have targeted Roman believers, particularly Gentiles. When employing Aramaic terms, Mark translated them for his readers (3:17; 5:41; 7:11, 34; 10:46; 14:36; 15:22, 34). On the other hand, in some places he used Latin expressions instead of their Greek equivalents (5:9; 6:27; 12:15, 42; 15:16, 39). He also reckoned time according to the Roman system (6:48; 13:35) and carefully explained Jewish customs (7:3, 4; 14:12; 15:42). Mark omitted Jewish elements, such as the genealogies found in Matthew and Luke. This gospel also makes fewer references to the OT, and includes less material that would be of particular interest to Jewish readers—such as that which is critical of the Pharisees and Sadducees (Sadducees are mentioned only once, in 12:18). When mentioning Simon of Cyrene (15:21), Mark identifies him as the father of Rufus, a prominent member of the church at Rome (Ro 16:13). All of this supports the traditional view that Mark was written for a Gentile audience initially at Rome.

HISTORICAL AND THEOLOGICAL THEMES

Mark presents Jesus as the suffering Servant of the Lord (10:45). His focus is on the deeds of Jesus more than His teaching, particularly emphasizing service and sacrifice. Mark omits the lengthy discourses found in the other Gospels, often relating only brief excerpts to give the gist of Jesus' teaching. Mark also omits any account of Jesus' ancestry and birth, beginning where Jesus' public ministry began, with His baptism by John in the wilderness.

Mark demonstrated the humanity of Christ more clearly than any of the other evangelists, emphasizing Christ's human emotions (1:41; 3:5; 6:34; 8:12; 9:36), His human limitations (4:38; 11:12; 13:32), and other small details that highlight the human side of the Son of God (e.g., 7:33, 34; 8:12; 9:36; 10:13–16).

INTERPRETIVE CHALLENGES

Three significant questions confront the interpreter of Mark: 1) What is the relationship of Mark to Luke and Matthew? (*see below, "The Synoptic Problem"*); 2) How should one interpret the eschatological passages? (*see notes on chaps. 4, 13*); and 3) Were the last 12 verses of chap. 16 originally part of Mark's gospel? (*see note on 16:9–20*).

THE SYNOPTIC PROBLEM

Even a cursory reading of Matthew, Mark, and Luke reveals both striking similarities (cf. 2:3–12; Mt 9:2–8; Lk 5:18–26) and significant differences, as each views the life, ministry, and teaching of Jesus. The question of how to explain those similarities and differences is known as the "Synoptic Problem" (*syn* means "together"; *optic* means "seeing").

The modern solution—even among evangelicals—has been to assume that some form of literary dependence exists between the Synoptic Gospels. The most commonly accepted theory to explain such an alleged literary dependence is known as the "Two-Source" theory. According to that hypothesis, Mark was the first gospel written, and Matthew and Luke then used Mark as a source in writing their gospels. Proponents of this view imagine a non-existent, second source, labeled Q (from the German word *Quelle*, "source"), and argue that this allegedly is the source of the material in Matthew and Luke that does not appear in Mark. They advance several lines of evidence to support their scenario.

First, most of Mark is paralleled in Matthew and Luke. Since it is much shorter than Matthew and Luke, the latter must be expansions of Mark. Second, the 3 gospels follow the same general chronological outline, but when either Matthew or Luke departs from Mark's chronology, the other agrees with Mark. Put another way, Matthew and Luke do not both depart from Mark's chronology in the same places. That, it is argued, shows that Matthew and Luke used Mark for their historical framework. Third, in passages common to all 3 gospels, Matthew's and Luke's wording seldom agrees when it differs from Mark's. Proponents of the "Two-Source" theory see that as confirmation that Matthew and Luke used Mark's gospel as a source.

But those arguments do not prove that Matthew and Luke used Mark's gospel as a source. In fact, the weight of evidence is strongly against such a theory:

1) The nearly unanimous testimony of the church until the nineteenth century was that Matthew was the first gospel written. Such an impressive body of evidence cannot be ignored.

2) Why would Matthew, an apostle and eyewitness to the events of Christ's life, depend on Mark (who was not an eyewitness)—even for the account of his own conversion?

3) A significant statistical analysis of the Synoptic Gospels has revealed that the parallels between them are far less extensive and the differences more significant than is commonly acknowledged. The differences, in particular, argue against literary dependence between the Gospel writers.

4) Since the gospels record actual historical events, it would be surprising if they did not follow the same general historical sequence. For example, the fact that 3 books on American history all had the Revolutionary War, the Civil War, World War I, World War II, the Vietnam War, and the Gulf War in the same chronological order would not prove that the authors had read each others' books. General agreement in content does not prove literary dependency.

5) The passages in which Matthew and Luke agree against Mark (see argument 3 in favor of the "Two-Source" theory) amount to about one-sixth of Matthew and one-sixth of Luke. If they used Mark's gospel as a source, there is no satisfactory explanation for why Matthew and Luke would so often both change Mark's wording in the same way.

6) The "Two-Source" theory cannot account for the important section in Mark's gospel (6:45–8:26) which Luke omits. That omission suggests Luke had not seen Mark's gospel when he wrote.

7) There is no historical or manuscript evidence that the *Q* document ever existed; it is purely a fabrication of modern skepticism and a way to possibly deny the verbal inspiration of the Gospels.

8) Any theory of literary dependence between the gospel writers overlooks the significance of their personal contacts with one another. Mark and Luke were both companions of Paul (cf. Phm 24); the early church (including Matthew) met for a time in the home of Mark's mother (Ac 12:12); and Luke could easily have met Matthew during Paul's two-year imprisonment at Caesarea (*see note on Ac 27:1*). Such contacts make theories of mutual literary dependence unnecessary.

The simplest solution to the Synoptic Problem is that no such problem exists! Because critics cannot prove literary dependence between the gospel writers, there is no need to explain it. The traditional view that the gospel writers were inspired by God and wrote independently of one another—except that all 3 were moved by the same Holy Spirit (2Pe 1:21)—remains the only plausible view.

As the reader compares the various viewpoints in the Gospels, it becomes clear how well they harmonize and lead to a more complete picture of the whole event or message. The accounts are not contradictory, but complementary, revealing a fuller understanding when brought together. Apparent difficulties are dealt with in the notes of each gospel.

OUTLINE

I. Prologue: In the Wilderness (1:1–13)
- A. John's Message (1:1–8)
- B. Jesus' Baptism (1:9–11)
- C. Jesus' Temptation (1:12, 13)

II. Beginning His Ministry: In Galilee and the Surrounding Regions (1:14–7:23)
- A. He Announces His Message (1:14, 15)
- B. He Calls His Disciples (1:16–20)
- C. He Ministers in Capernaum (1:21–34)
- D. He Reaches Out to Galilee (1:35–45)
- E. He Defends His Ministry (2:1–3:6)
- F. He Ministers to Multitudes (3:7–12)
- G. He Commissions the Twelve (3:13–19)
- H. He Rebukes the Scribes and Pharisees (3:20–30)
- I. He Identifies His Spiritual Family (3:31–35)
- J. He Preaches in Parables (4:1–34)
  1. The sower (4:1–9)
  2. The reason for parables (4:10–12)
  3. The parable of the sower explained (4:13–20)
  4. The lamp (4:21–25)
  5. The seed (4:26–29)
  6. The mustard seed (4:30–34)
- K. He Demonstrates His Power (4:35–5:43)
  1. Calming the waves (4:35–41)
  2. Casting out unclean spirits (5:1–20)
  3. Healing the sick (5:21–34)
  4. Raising the dead (5:35–43)
- L. He Returns to His Hometown (6:1–6)
- M. He Sends out His Disciples (6:7–13)
- N. He Gains a Powerful Enemy (6:14–29)
- O. He Regroups with the Disciples (6:30–32)
- P. He Feeds the Five Thousand (6:33–44)
- Q. He Walks on Water (6:45–52)
- R. He Heals Many People (6:53–56)
- S. He Answers the Pharisees (7:1–23)

III. Broadening His Ministry: In Various Gentile Regions (7:24–9:50)
- A. Tyre and Sidon: He Delivers a Gentile Woman's Daughter (7:24–30)
- B. Decapolis: He Heals a Deaf-Mute (7:31–37)
- C. The Eastern Shore of Galilee: He Feeds the Four Thousand (8:1–9)
- D. Dalmanutha: He Disputes with the Pharisees (8:10–12)
- E. The Other Side of the Lake: He Rebukes the Disciples (8:13–21)
- F. Bethsaida: He Heals a Blind Man (8:22–26)
- G. Caesarea Philippi and Capernaum: He Instructs the Disciples (8:27–9:50)
  1. Peter confesses Jesus as Christ (8:27–30)
  2. He predicts His death (8:31–33)
  3. He explains the cost of discipleship (8:34–38)
  4. He reveals His glory (9:1–10)
  5. He clarifies Elijah's role (9:11–13)
  6. He casts out a stubborn spirit (9:14–29)
  7. He again predicts His death and resurrection (9:30–32)
  8. He defines kingdom greatness (9:33–37)
  9. He identifies true spiritual fruit (9:38–41)
  10. He warns would-be stumbling blocks (9:42–50)

IV. Concluding His Ministry: The Road to Jerusalem (10:1–52)
- A. He Teaches on Divorce (10:1–12)
- B. He Blesses the Children (10:13–16)
- C. He Confronts the Rich Young Ruler (10:17–27)
- D. He Confirms the Disciples' Rewards (10:28–31)
- E. He Prepares the Disciples for His Death (10:32–34)
- F. He Challenges the Disciples to Humble Service (10:35–45)
- G. He Heals a Blind Man (10:46–52)

V. Consummating His Ministry: Jerusalem (11:1–16:20)
- A. Triumphal Entry (11:1–11)
- B. Purification (11:12–19)
  - 1. Cursing the fig tree (11:12–14)
  - 2. Cleansing the temple (11:15–19)
- C. Teaching in Public and in Private (11:20–13:37)
  - 1. Publicly: in the temple (11:20–12:44)
    - a. Prelude: the lesson of the cursed fig tree (11:20–26)
    - b. Concerning His authority (11:27–33)
    - c. Concerning His rejection (12:1–12)
    - d. Concerning paying taxes (12:13–17)
    - e. Concerning the resurrection (12:18–27)
    - f. Concerning the greatest commandment (12:28–34)
    - g. Concerning the Messiah's true sonship (12:35–37)
    - h. Concerning the scribes (12:38–40)
    - i. Concerning true giving (12:41–44)
  - 2. Privately: on the Mount of Olives (13:1–37)
    - a. The disciples' question about the end times (13:1)
    - b. The Lord's answer (13:2–37)
- D. Arrangements for Betrayal (14:1, 2, 10, 11)
- E. Anointing, the Last Supper, Betrayal, Arrest, Trial (Jewish Phase) (14:3–9; 12–72)
  - 1. The anointing: Bethany (14:3–9)
  - 2. The Last Supper: Jerusalem (14:12–31)
  - 3. The prayer: Gethsemane (14:32–42)
  - 4. The betrayal: Gethsemane (14:43–52)
  - 5. The Jewish trial: Caiaphas' house (14:53–72)
- F. Trial (Roman Phase), Crucifixion (15:1–41)
  - 1. The Roman trial: Pilate's Praetorium (15:1–15)
  - 2. The crucifixion: Golgotha (15:16–41)
- G. Burial in Joseph of Arimathea's Tomb (15:42–47)
- H. Resurrection (16:1–8)
- I. Postscript (16:9–20)

PREACHING OF JOHN THE BAPTIST

1 The beginning of the gospel of Jesus Christ, [A]the
Son of God.
2 [A]As it is written in Isaiah the prophet:

"[B]Behold, I send My messenger
[a]ahead of You,
Who will prepare Your way;
3 [A]The voice of one crying in
the wilderness,
'Make ready the way
of the Lord,
Make His paths straight.' "

4 John the Baptist appeared in the wilderness
[a,A]preaching a baptism of repentance for the [B]for-
giveness of sins. 5 And all the country of Judea was
going out to him, and all the people of Jerusalem;
and they were being baptized by him in the Jordan
River, confessing their sins. 6 John was clothed with
camel's hair and *wore* [A]a leather belt around his
waist, and [a]his diet was locusts and wild honey.
7 And he was [a]preaching, and saying, "After me One
is coming who is mightier than I, and I am not fit to
stoop down and untie the thong of His sandals. 8 I
baptized you [a]with water; but He will baptize you
[a]with the Holy Spirit."

THE BAPTISM OF JESUS

9 [A]In those days Jesus [B]came from Nazareth in
Galilee and was baptized by John in the Jordan.
10 Immediately coming up out of the water, He saw
the heavens [a]opening, and the Spirit like a dove
descending upon Him; 11 and a voice came out of
the heavens: "[A]You are My beloved Son, in You I
am well-pleased."

1:1 [A]Matt 4:3 1:2 [a]Lit *before your face* [A]Mark 1:2-8: *Matt 3:1-11; Luke 3:2-16* [B]Mal 3:1; Matt 11:10; Luke 7:27 1:3 [A]Is 40:3; Matt 3:3; Luke 3:4; John 1:23 1:4 [a]Or *proclaiming* [A]Acts 13:24 [B]Luke 1:77 1:6 [a]Lit *he was eating* [A]2 Kin 1:8 1:7 [a]Or *proclaiming* 1:8 [a]The Gr here can be translated *in, with* or *by* 1:9 [A]Mark 1:9-11: *Matt 3:13-17; Luke 3:21, 22* [B]Matt 2:23; Luke 2:51 1:10 [a]Or *being parted* 1:11 [A]Ps 2:7; Is 42:1; Matt 3:17; 12:18; Mark 9:7; Luke 3:22

1:1 The beginning ... the Son of God. This is best viewed as Mark's title for his gospel. The historical record of the gospel message began with John the Baptist (cf. Mt 11:12; Lk 16:16; Ac 1:22; 10:37; 13:24). **gospel.** The good news about the life, death, and resurrection of Jesus Christ, of which the 4 Gospels are written records (see Introduction to the Gospels). **Jesus Christ.** "Jesus" is the Gr. form of the Heb. name *Joshua* ("the Lord is salvation"); "Christ" ("anointed one") is the Gr. equivalent of the Heb. word *Messiah.* "Jesus" is the Lord's human name (cf. Mt 1:21; Lk 1:31); "Christ" signifies His office as ruler of God's coming kingdom (Da 9:25, 26). **Son of God.** An affirmation of Jesus' deity, stressing His unique relationship to the Father (cf. 3:11; 5:7; 9:7; 13:32; 15:39; *see note on Jn 1:34*).

1:2 it is written. A phrase commonly used in the NT to introduce OT quotes (cf. 7:6; 9:13; 14:21, 27; Mt 2:5; 4:4, 6, 7; Lk 2:23; 3:4; Jn 6:45; 12:14; Ac 1:20; 7:42; Ro 3:4; 8:36; 1Co 1:31; 9:9; 2Co 8:15; 9:9; Gal 3:10; 4:22; Heb 10:7; 1Pe 1:16). **in Isaiah the prophet.** Mark's quote is actually from two OT passages (Is 40:3; Mal 3:1), which probably explains the reading "the Prophets" found in some manuscripts. The Gospels all introduce John the Baptist's ministry by quoting Is 40:3 (cf. Mt 3:3; Lk 3:4; Jn 1:23). My messenger. John was the divinely promised messenger, sent to prepare the way for the Messiah. In ancient times, a king's envoys would travel ahead of him, making sure the roads were safe and fit for him to travel on, as well as announcing his arrival.

1:4 John. A common Jewish name in NT times, it is the Gr. equivalent of the Heb. name "Johanan" (cf. 2Ki 25:23; 1Ch 3:15; Jer 40:8), meaning "the Lord is gracious." John's name was given by the angel Gabriel to his father Zacharias, during his time of priestly service in the temple (Lk 1:13). His mother, Elizabeth, also a descendant of Aaron (Lk 1:5), was a relative of Mary the mother of Jesus (Lk 1:36). As the last OT prophet and the divinely ordained forerunner of the Messiah (*see note on v. 2*), John was the culmination of OT history and prophecy (Lk 16:16) as well as the beginning of the historical record of the gospel of Jesus Christ. Not surprisingly, Jesus designated John as the greatest man who had lived until his time (Mt 11:11). **baptism.** Being the distinctive mark of John's ministry, his baptism differed from the ritual Jewish washings in that it was a one-time act. The Jews performed a similar one-time washing of Gentile proselytes, symbolizing their embracing of the true faith. That Jews would participate in such a rite was a startling admission that they, although members of God's covenant people, needed to come to God through repentance and faith just like Gentiles. **in the wilderness.** The desolate, arid region between Jerusalem and the Dead Sea (*see note on Mt 3:1*). **baptism of repentance.** A baptism resulting from true repentance. John's ministry was to call Israel to repentance in preparation for the coming of Messiah. Baptism did not produce repentance, but was its result (cf. Mt 3:7, 8). Far more than a mere change of mind or remorse, repentance involves a turning from sin to God (cf. 1Th 1:9), which results in righteous living. Genuine repentance is a work of God in the human heart (Ac 11:18). For a discussion of the nature of repentance, *see notes on 2Co 7:9–12.* **for the forgiveness of sins.** John's rite of baptism did not produce forgiveness of sin (*see notes on Ac 2:38; 22:16*); it was only the outward confession and illustration of the true repentance that results in forgiveness (cf. Lk 24:47; Ac 3:19; 5:31; 2Co 7:10).

1:5 all the country of Judea ... all the people of Jerusalem. After centuries without a prophetic voice in Israel (Malachi had prophesied more than 400 years earlier), John's ministry generated an intense amount of interest. **Judea.** The southernmost division of Israel (Samaria and Galilee being the others) in Jesus' day. It extended from about Bethel in the N to Beersheba in the S, and from the Mediterranean Sea in the W to the Dead Sea and Jordan River in the E. Included within Judea was the city of Jerusalem. **Jordan River.** Palestine's major river, flowing through the Jordan Rift Valley from Lake Hula (drained in modern times), N of the Sea of Galilee, S to the Dead Sea. According to tradition, John began his baptizing ministry at the fords near Jericho. **confessing.** To confess one's sins, as they were being baptized, is to agree with God about them. John baptized no one who did not confess and repent of his sins.

1:6 camel's hair ... leather belt. The traditional clothes of a wilderness dweller which were sturdy, but neither fashionable nor comfortable. John's clothing would have reminded his audience of Elijah (cf. 2Ki 1:8), whom they expected to come before Messiah (Mal 4:5; cf. Mt 17:10–13). **locusts and wild honey.** The OT dietary regulations permitted the eating of "locusts" (Lv 11:21, 22). "Wild honey" could often be found in the wilderness (Dt 32:13; 1Sa 14:25–27). John's austere diet was in keeping with his status as a lifelong Nazirite (cf. Lk 1:15; for Nazirite, *see notes on Nu 6:2–13*).

1:7 preaching. Better translated "proclaiming," John was Jesus' herald, sent to announce His coming (*see note on v. 4*). **not fit to stoop down and untie the thong of His sandals.** The most menial task a slave could perform. John vividly expressed his humility.

1:8 baptize you with the Holy Spirit. This takes place when a person comes to faith in Christ (*see notes on Ac 1:5; 8:16, 17; 1Co 12:13*).

1:9 In those days. At some unspecified time during John's baptizing ministry at the Jordan. **Nazareth.** An obscure village (not mentioned in the OT, or by Josephus, or in the Talmud) about 70 mi. N of Jerusalem, which did not enjoy a favorable reputation (cf. Jn 1:46). Jesus had apparently been living there before His public appearance to Israel. **baptized by John.** Over John's objections (cf. Mt 3:14), who saw no need for the sinless Lamb of God (Jn 1:29) to participate in a baptism of repentance (*see notes on vv. 4, 5;* for an explanation of why Jesus was baptized, *see note on Mt 3:15*).

1:10 Immediately. In keeping with his fast-paced narrative style (see Introduction to the Gospels), Mark used this adverb more than the other 3 gospel writers combined. This first occurrence sets the stage for the audible and visible signs that followed Jesus' baptism. **the Spirit like a dove descending upon Him.** This was most likely symbolic of Jesus' empowerment for ministry (Is 61:1). *See note on Mt 3:16, 17.*

1:11 The Father's pronouncement would have reminded the audience of the messianic prophecies of Ps 2:7; Is 42:1.

12 [A]Immediately the Spirit *impelled Him *to go*
out into the wilderness. 13 And He was in the wilderness forty days being tempted by [A]Satan; and
He was with the wild beasts, and the angels were
ministering to Him.

JESUS PREACHES IN GALILEE

14 [A]Now after John had been [a]taken into custody,
Jesus came into Galilee, [b,B]preaching the gospel of
God, 15 and saying, "[A]The time is fulfilled, and the
kingdom of God [a]is at hand; [B]repent and [b]believe
in the gospel."
16 [A]As He was going along by the Sea of Galilee,
He saw Simon and Andrew, the brother of Simon,
casting a net in the sea; for they were fishermen.
17 And Jesus said to them, "Follow Me, and I will
make you become fishers of men." 18 Immediately
they left their nets and followed Him. 19 Going on
a little farther, He saw [a]James the son of Zebedee,
and John his brother, who were also in the boat
mending the nets. 20 Immediately He called them;
and they left their father Zebedee in the boat with
the hired servants, and went away [a]to follow Him.
21 [A]They *went into Capernaum; and immediately
on the Sabbath [B]He entered the synagogue and *began* to teach. 22 [A]They were amazed at His teaching;
for He was teaching them as *one* having authority, and not as the scribes. 23 Just then there was
a man in their synagogue with an unclean spirit;
and he cried out, 24 saying, "[A]What [a]business do we
have with each other, Jesus [b]of [B]Nazareth? Have You
come to destroy us? I know who You are—[C]the Holy
One of God!" 25 And Jesus rebuked him, saying, "Be
quiet, and come out of him!" 26 Throwing him into

1:12 [A]Mark 1:12, 13: *Matt 4:1-11; Luke 4:1-13* 1:13 [A]Matt 4:10 1:14 [a]Lit *delivered up* [b]Or *proclaiming* [A]Matt 4:12 [B]Matt 4:23 1:15 [a]Lit *has come near* [b]Or *put your trust in* [A]Gal 4:4; Eph 1:10; 1 Tim 2:6; Titus 1:3 [B]Matt 3:2; Acts 20:21 1:16 [A]Mark 1:16-20: *Matt 4:18-22;* Luke 5:2-11; John 1:40-42 1:19 [a]Or *Jacob* 1:20 [a]Lit *after Him* 1:21 [A]Mark 1:21-28: *Luke 4:31-37* [B]Matt 4:23; Mark 1:39; 10:1 1:22 [A]Matt 7:28 1:24 [a]Lit *What to us and to You* (a Heb idiom) [b]Lit *the Nazarene* [A]Matt 8:29 [B]Matt 2:23; Mark 10:47; 14:67; 16:6; Luke 4:34; 24:19; Acts 24:5 [C]Luke 1:35; 4:34; John 6:69; Acts 3:14

1:12 **Immediately.** *See note on v. 10*. Jesus' temptation came right after His baptism. **the Spirit impelled Him.** Compelled by the Spirit, Jesus confronted Satan and took the first step toward overthrowing his evil kingdom (cf. 1Jn 3:8). Though God tempts no one (Jas 1:13), He sometimes sovereignly permits Satan to tempt His people (e.g., Job; Lk 22:31, 32). **the wilderness.** The exact location of Jesus' encounter with Satan is unknown. It most likely would have been the same wilderness where John lived and ministered (*see note on v. 4*), the desolate region farther S, or the arid Arabian desert across the Jordan.

1:13 **forty days.** Perhaps reminiscent of Israel's 40 years of wandering in the wilderness (Nu 14:33; 32:13). Matthew and Luke add that Jesus went without food during this time. Moses (twice, Dt 9:9, 18) and Elijah (1Ki 19:8) also fasted for that length of time. **Satan.** From a Heb. word meaning "adversary." Since He had no fallen nature, Jesus' temptation was not an internal emotional or psychological struggle, but an external attack by a personal being. **wild beasts.** A detail unique to Mark's account, stressing Jesus' loneliness and complete isolation from other people. **angels were ministering to Him.** Cf. Ps 91:11, 12. The tense of this Gr. verb, "to minister," suggests the angels ministered to Jesus throughout His temptation.

1:14 **John had been taken into custody.** He was incarcerated for rebuking Herod Antipas over his incestuous marriage to his niece, Herodias (*see notes on 6:17–27*). **Jesus came into Galilee.** From Judea (Mt 4:12; Lk 4:13; Jn 4:3). Mark, along with Matthew and Luke, passes directly from the temptation to the beginning of the Galilean ministry, skipping Jesus' intervening ministry in Judea (Jn 2:13–4:4). Galilee was the northernmost region of Israel, and the most heavily populated. **the gospel of God.** The good news of salvation both about God and from Him (*see note on Ro 1:1*; cf. Ro 15:16; 1Th 2:2, 8, 9; 1Ti 1:11; 1Pe 4:17).

1:15 **The time is fulfilled.** Not time in a chronological sense, but the time for decisive action on God's part. With the arrival of the King, a new era in God's dealings with men had come. *See note on Gal 4:4*. **the kingdom of God.** God's sovereign rule over the sphere of salvation; at present in the hearts of His people (Lk 17:21), and in the future, in a literal, earthly kingdom (Rev 20:4–6). **at hand.** Because the King was present. **repent and believe.** Repentance (*see note on v. 4*) and faith (*see note on Ro 1:16*) are man's required responses to God's gracious offer of salvation (cf. Ac 20:21).

1:16 **Sea of Galilee.** Also known as the Sea of Chinnereth (Nu 34:11), the Lake of Gennesaret (Lk 5:1), and the Sea of Tiberias (Jn 6:1). A large, freshwater lake about 13 mi. long and 7 mi. wide, and about 690 ft. below sea level (making it the lowest body of fresh water on earth), the Sea of Galilee was home to a thriving fishing industry. **Simon and Andrew.** The first of two sets of brothers Jesus called to follow Him. Like James and John, they were fishermen. Since Andrew had been a follower of John the Baptist (Jn 1:40), it is possible that Peter had been as well. They had evidently returned to their fishing business after John's arrest (*see note on v. 14*). They had already met and spent time with Jesus (*see note on Mt 4:18*), but were here called to follow Him permanently. **net.** A rope forming a circle about 9 ft. in diameter with a net attached. It could be thrown by hand into the water, then hauled in by means of the length of weighted rope attached to it.

1:17 **Follow Me.** Used frequently in the Gospels in reference to discipleship (2:14; 8:34; 10:21; Mt 4:19; 8:22; 9:9; 10:38; 16:24; 19:21; Lk 9:23, 59, 61; 18:22; Jn 1:43; 10:27; 12:26). **fishers of men.** Evangelism was the primary purpose for which Jesus called the apostles, and it remains the central mission for His people (cf. Mt 28:19, 20; Ac 1:8).

1:18 **followed Him.** I.e., became His permanent disciples (*see note on v. 16*).

1:19 **James ... John.** The second set of fishermen brothers called by Jesus (*see note on v. 16*). Their mother and Jesus' mother may have been sisters (cf. 15:40; Mt 27:55, 56 with Jn 19:25). If so, they were Jesus' cousins.

1:20 **hired servants.** This indicates that Zebedee's fishing business was a prosperous one and that he was a man of importance (cf. Jn 18:15).

1:21 **Capernaum.** A prosperous fishing village on the NW shore of the Sea of Galilee, Capernaum was a more important city than Nazareth; it contained a Roman garrison and was located on a major road. Jesus made the city His headquarters (cf. 2:1) after His rejection at Nazareth (Mt 4:13; Lk 4:16–31). **synagogue.** The place where Jewish people gathered for worship ("synagogue" is a transliteration of a Gr. word meaning "to gather together"). Synagogues originated in the Babylonian captivity after the 586 B.C. destruction of the temple by Nebuchadnezzar. They served as places of worship and instruction. Jesus frequently taught in the synagogues (cf. v. 39; 3:1; 6:2), as did Paul (cf. Ac 13:5; 14:1; 17:1). **teach.** Mark frequently mentions Jesus' teaching ministry (cf. 2:13; 4:1, 2; 6:2, 6, 34; 10:1; 11:17; 12:35; 14:49).

1:22 **authority.** Jesus' authoritative teaching, as the spoken Word of God, was in sharp contrast to that of the scribes (experts in the OT Scriptures), who based their authority largely on that of other rabbis. Jesus' direct, personal, and forceful teaching was so foreign to their experience that those who heard Him were "amazed" (cf. Titus 2:15).

1:23 **man ... cried out.** Satan and his demon hosts opposed Jesus' work throughout His ministry, culminating in the cross. Jesus always triumphed over their futile efforts (cf. Col 2:15), convincingly demonstrating His ultimate victory by His resurrection. **unclean spirit.** I.e., morally impure. The term is used interchangeably in the NT with "demon." *See note on 5:2*.

1:24 **What business do we have with each other ... ?** Or, possibly, "Why do You interfere with us?" The demon was acutely aware that he and Jesus belonged to two radically different kingdoms, and thus had nothing in common. That the demon used the plural pronoun "we" indicates he spoke for all the demons. **Nazareth.** *See note on v. 9*. **the Holy One of God.** Cf. Ps 16:10; Da 9:24; Lk 4:34; Ac 2:27; 3:14; 4:27; Rev 3:7. Amazingly, the demon affirmed Jesus' sinlessness and deity—truths which many in Israel denied, and still deny.

1:25 **Be quiet.** Jesus wanted no testimony to the truth from the demonic realm to fuel charges that He was in league with Satan (cf. 3:22; Ac 16:16–18).

convulsions, the unclean spirit cried out with a loud
voice and came out of him. 27 They were all [A]amazed,
so that they debated among themselves, saying,
"What is this? A new teaching with authority! He
commands even the unclean spirits, and they obey
Him." 28 Immediately the news about Him spread everywhere into all the surrounding district of Galilee.

CROWDS HEALED

29 [A]And immediately after they came [B]out of the
synagogue, they came into the house of Simon and
Andrew, with [a]James and John. 30 Now Simon's
mother-in-law was lying sick with a fever; and immediately they *spoke to [a]Jesus about her. 31 And
He came to her and raised her up, taking her by the
hand, and the fever left her, and she [a]waited on them.
32 [A]When evening came, [B]after the sun had set,
they *began* bringing to Him all who were ill and
those who were [C]demon-possessed. 33 And the whole
[A]city had gathered at the door. 34 And He [A]healed
many who were ill with various diseases, and cast
out many demons; and He was not permitting the
demons to speak, because they knew who He was.
35 [A]In the early morning, while it was still dark,
Jesus got up, left *the house,* and went away to a
secluded place, and [B]was praying there. 36 Simon
and his companions searched for Him; 37 they found
Him, and *said to Him, "Everyone is looking for You."
38 He *said to them, "Let us go somewhere else to the
towns nearby, so that I may [a]preach there also; for
that is what I came for." 39 [A]And He went into their
synagogues throughout all Galilee, [a]preaching and
casting out the demons.
40 [A]And a leper *came to Jesus, beseeching Him
and [B]falling on his knees before Him, and saying, "If
You are willing, You can make me clean." 41 Moved
with compassion, Jesus stretched out His hand and
touched him, and *said to him, "I am willing; be
cleansed." 42 Immediately the leprosy left him and
he was cleansed. 43 And He sternly warned him and
immediately sent him away, 44 and He *said to him,
"[A]See that you say nothing to anyone; but [A]go, show
yourself to the priest and [B]offer for your cleansing
what Moses commanded, as a testimony to them."
45 But he went out and began to [A]proclaim it freely
and to [A]spread the news around, to such an extent
that [a]Jesus could no longer publicly enter a city, but
[b]stayed out in unpopulated areas; and [B]they were
coming to Him from everywhere.

THE PARALYTIC HEALED

2 When He had come back to Capernaum several days afterward, it was heard that He was
at home. 2 And [A]many were gathered together, so
that there was no longer room, not even near the
door; and He was speaking the word to them. 3 [A]And
they *came, bringing to Him a [B]paralytic, carried
by four men. 4 Being unable to [a]get to Him because

1:27 [A]Mark 10:24, 32; 16:5, 6 1:29 [a]*Or Jacob* [A]Mark 1:29-31: *Matt 8:14, 15; Luke 4:38, 39* [B]Mark 1:21, 23 1:30 [a]Lit *Him* 1:31 [a]*Or served* 1:32 [A]Mark 1:32-34: *Matt 8:16, 17; Luke 4:40, 41* [B]Matt 8:16; Luke 4:40 [C]Matt 4:24 1:33 [A]Mark 1:21 1:34 [A]Matt 4:23 1:35 [A]Mark 1:35-38: *Luke 4:42, 43* [B]Matt 14:23; Luke 5:16 1:38 [a]*Or proclaim* 1:39 [a]*Or proclaiming* [A]Matt 4:23; 9:35; Mark 1:23; 3:1 1:40 [A]Mark 1:40-44: *Matt 8:2-4; Luke 5:12-14* [B]Matt 8:2; Mark 10:17; Luke 5:12 1:44 [A]Matt 8:4 [B]Lev 14:1-32 1:45 [a]Lit *He* [b]Lit *was* [A]Matt 28:15; Luke 5:15 [B]Mark 2:2, 13; 3:7; Luke 5:17; John 6:2 2:2 [A]Mark 1:45; 2:13 2:3 [A]Mark 2:3-12: *Matt 9:2-8; Luke 5:18-26* [B]Matt 4:24 2:4 [a]Lit *bring to*

1:27 with authority. *See note on v. 22.* Jesus had absolute authority in His actions as well as His words (Mt 28:18).

1:29 the house of Simon and Andrew. Originally from Bethsaida (Jn 1:44), the two brothers had moved to Capernaum when Jesus established His headquarters there (*see note on v. 21*). **James and John.** Only Mark mentions their presence at the healing of Peter's mother-in-law.

1:30 Simon's mother-in-law. Paul also affirmed that Peter was married (1Co 9:5). That his mother-in-law was living with Peter and his wife may indicate that her husband was dead. **a fever.** That she was too ill to get out of bed, coupled with Luke's description of her fever as a "high fever" (Lk 4:38), suggests her illness was serious, even life-threatening.

1:32 after the sun had set. Marking the close of the Sabbath and the easing of the restrictions associated with it. Specifically, rabbinic law prohibited carrying any burdens (such as stretchers) on the Sabbath. **they *began* bringing.** The report of Jesus' healing of the demon-possessed man in the synagogue and Peter's mother-in-law created a sensation in Capernaum and aroused the hopes of other sufferers.

1:34 not permitting the demons to speak. *See notes on v. 25; 3:11, 12.* **they knew who He was.** The demons' theology is absolutely orthodox (Jas 2:19); but though they know the truth, they reject it and God, who is its source.

1:36 Simon and his companions. The first instance in the gospels of Peter's assuming of leadership. Those with Peter are not revealed, though Andrew, James, and John were likely among them.

1:37 Finding Jesus after a diligent search (v. 36), Peter and the others excitedly implored Him to return to Capernaum and capitalize on the excitement generated by the previous night's healings.

1:39 throughout all Galilee. Mark's terse statement summarizes a preaching tour that must have lasted for weeks, or even months (cf. Mt 4:23, 24).

1:40–45 Mark relates one of Jesus' many healings during the Galilean ministry summarized in v. 39. The leper's healing emphasizes Jesus' miraculous power over disease, since leprosy was one of the most dreaded diseases of antiquity.

1:40 leper. Lepers were considered ceremonially unclean, and were outcasts from society (Lv 13:11). While the OT term for leprosy included other skin diseases (*see note on Lv 13:2*), this man may have actually had true leprosy (Hansen's Disease), or else his cure would not have created such a sensation (v. 45).

1:41 compassion. Only Mark records Jesus' emotional reaction to the leper's desperate plight. The Gr. word appears only in the Synoptic Gospels and (apart from parables) is used only in reference to Jesus. **touched him.** Unlike rabbis, who avoided lepers lest they become ceremonially defiled, Jesus expressed His compassion with a physical gesture.

1:44 say nothing to anyone. The ensuing publicity would hinder Jesus' ability to minister (as in fact happened, cf. v. 45) and divert attention away from His message. Cf. 3:12; 5:43; 7:36; *see note on Mt 8:4.* **go, show yourself to the priest.** The "priest" was the one on duty at the temple. Jesus commanded the healed leper to observe the OT regulations concerning cleansed lepers (Lv 14:1–32). Until the required offerings had been made, the man remained ceremonially unclean. **a testimony to them.** The priest's acceptance of the man's offering would be public affirmation of his cure and cleansing.

1:45 proclaim it freely. Only Mark records the cleansed leper's disobedience, although Luke hints at it (Lk 5:15). **no longer publicly enter a city.** The result of the leper's disobedience was that Jesus could no longer enter a city without being mobbed by those seeking to be cured of diseases. Jesus' ministry of teaching in that area thus came to a halt. **unpopulated areas.** Jesus kept to the relatively uninhabited regions to allow the excitement over His cure of the leper to die down. Luke also notes that He used His time in the wilderness for prayer (Lk 5:16).

2:1 He was at home. This was likely Peter's home, where Jesus had taken up temporary residence (cf. Mt 4:13).

2:2 the word. The good news of the gospel, that salvation is by grace alone, through faith alone, for the forgiveness of sins.

2:3 a paralytic. Since he was lying on a bed, the man's paralysis was severe—perhaps he was a quadriplegic.

2:4 they removed the roof. Most homes in Israel had flat roofs used for relaxation in the cool of the day and for sleeping on hot nights. And there was usually an external stairway that extended to the roof. Often, as here, the

of the crowd, they [A]removed the roof [b]above Him;
and when they had dug an opening, they let down
the pallet on which the [B]paralytic was lying. 5 And
Jesus seeing their faith *said to the paralytic, "[a]Son,
[A]your sins are forgiven." 6 But some of the scribes
were sitting there and reasoning in their hearts,
7 "Why does this man speak that way? He is blaspheming; [A]who can forgive sins [a]but God alone?"
8 Immediately Jesus, aware [a]in His spirit that they
were reasoning that way within themselves, *said

2:4 [b]Lit *where He was* [A]Luke 5:19 [B]Matt 4:24 2:5 [a]Lit *child* [A]Matt 9:2 2:7 [a]Lit *if not one, God* [A]Is 43:25 2:8 [a]Lit *by*

roof was made of slabs of burnt or dried clay that were placed on supporting beams which stretched from wall to wall. The builder then spread a uniform coat of fresh, wet clay over those slabs of hardened clay to serve as a seal against the rain. The paralytic's friends took him up to the top of such a house and dug out the top coat of clay, removing several of the slabs until they made enough room to lower him down into Jesus' presence. **the paralytic.** *See note on v. 3.*

2:5 Jesus seeing their faith. The aggressive, persistent effort of the paralytic's friends was visible evidence of their faith in Christ to heal. **Son, your sins are forgiven.** Many Jews in that day believed that all disease and affliction was a direct result of one's sins. This paralytic may have believed that as well; thus he would have welcomed forgiveness of his sins before healing. The Gr. verb for "are forgiven" refers to sending or driving away (cf. Ps 103:12; Jer 31:34; Mic 7:19). Thus Jesus dismissed the man's sin and freed him from the guilt of it (*see note on Mt 9:2*).

2:6 the scribes. *See note on Mt 2:4*; cf. 1:22.

2:7 this man ... blaspheming. The scribes were correct in saying that only God can forgive sins (cf. Is 43:25), but incorrect in saying Jesus blasphemed. They refused to recognize Jesus' power as coming from God, much less that He Himself was God.

2:8 in His spirit. This can also be translated, "by His spirit." This is not the Holy

THE MIRACLES OF JESUS

Miracle	Matthew	Mark	Luke	John
1. Cleansing a Leper	8:2	1:40	5:12	
2. Healing a Centurion's Servant (of paralysis)	8:5		7:1	
3. Healing Peter's Mother-in-Law	8:14	1:30	4:38	
4. Healing the Sick at Evening	8:16	1:32	4:40	
5. Stilling the Storm	8:23	4:35	8:22	
6. Demons Entering a Herd of Swine	8:28	5:1	8:26	
7. Healing a Paralytic	9:2	2:3	5:18	
8. Raising the Official's Daughter	9:18, 23	5:22, 35	8:40, 49	
9. Healing the Hemorrhaging Woman	9:20	5:25	8:43	
10. Healing Two Blind Men	9:27			
11. Curing a Demon-Possessed, Mute Man	9:32			
12. Healing a Man's Withered Hand	12:9	3:1	6:6	
13. Curing a Demon-Possessed, Blind and Mute Man	12:22		11:14	
14. Feeding the 5,000	14:13	6:30	9:10	6:1
15. Walking on the Sea	14:25	6:48		6:19
16. Healing the Canaanite Woman's Daughter	15:21	7:24		
17. Feeding the 4,000	15:32	8:1		
18. Healing the Lunatic Boy	17:14	9:17	9:38	
19. Two-drachma Tax in the Fish's Mouth	17:24			
20. Healing Two Blind Men	20:30	10:46	18:35	
21. Withering the Fig Tree	21:18	11:12		
22. Casting Out an Unclean Spirit		1:23	4:33	
23. Healing a Deaf-Mute Man		7:31		
24. Healing a Blind Man at Bethsaida		8:22		
25. Escape from the Hostile Multitude			4:30	
26. Catch of Fish			5:1	
27. Raising of a Widow's Son at Nain			7:11	
28. Healing the Afflicted, Bent Woman			13:11	
29. Healing the Man with Dropsy			14:1	
30. Cleansing the Ten Lepers			17:11	
31. Restoring a Servant's Ear			22:51	
32. Turning Water into Wine				2:1
33. Healing the Royal Official's Son (of fever)				4:46
34. Healing an Afflicted Man at Bethesda				5:1
35. Healing the Man Born Blind				9:1
36. Raising of Lazarus				11:43
37. Second Catch of Fish				21:1

to them, "Why are you reasoning about these things
in your hearts? 9Which is easier, to say to the [A]par-
alytic, 'Your sins are forgiven'; or to say, 'Get up,
and pick up your pallet and walk'? 10But so that
you may know that the Son of Man has authority
on earth to forgive sins"—He *said to the paralytic,
11"I say to you, get up, pick up your pallet and go
home." 12And he got up and immediately picked up
the pallet and went out in the sight of everyone, so
that they were all amazed and [A]were glorifying God,
saying, "[B]We have never seen anything like this."

13And He went out again by the seashore; and
[A]all the [a]people were coming to Him, and He was
teaching them.

LEVI (MATTHEW) CALLED

14[A]As He passed by, He saw [a,B]Levi the *son* of Alphaeus sitting in the tax booth, and He *said to him,
"[C]Follow Me!" And he got up and followed Him.

15And it *[a]happened that He was reclining *at the*
table in his house, and many tax collectors and [b]sin-
ners [c]were dining with Jesus and His disciples; for
there were many of them, and they were following
Him. 16When [A]the scribes of the Pharisees saw that
He was eating with the sinners and tax collectors,
they said to His disciples, "[B]Why is He eating and
drinking with tax collectors and [a]sinners?" 17And
hearing *this,* Jesus *said to them, "[A]*It is* not those who
are healthy who need a physician, but those who are
sick; I did not come to call the righteous, but sinners."

18[A]John's disciples and the Pharisees were fasting;
and they *came and *said to Him, "Why do John's
disciples and the disciples of the Pharisees fast,
but Your disciples do not fast?" 19And Jesus said
to them, "While the bridegroom is with them, [a]the
attendants of the bridegroom cannot fast, can they?
So long as they have the bridegroom with them,
they cannot fast. 20But the [A]days will come when
the bridegroom is taken away from them, and then
they will fast in that day.

21"No one sews [a]a patch of unshrunk cloth on an
old garment; otherwise [b]the patch pulls away from
it, the new from the old, and a worse tear results.
22No one puts new wine into old wineskins; otherwise the wine will burst the skins, and the wine is
lost and the skins *as well;* but *one puts* new wine
into fresh wineskins."

QUESTION OF THE SABBATH

23[A]And it happened that He was passing through
the grainfields on the Sabbath, and His disciples
began to make their way along while [B]picking the

2:9 [A]Matt 4:24 2:12 [A]Matt 9:8 [B]Matt 9:33 2:13 [a]Lit *crowd* [A]Mark 1:45 2:14 [a]also called *Matthew* [A]Mark 2:14-17: *Matt 9:9-13; Luke 5:27-32* [B]Matt 9:9 [C]Matt 8:22 2:15 [a]Lit *happens* [b]I.e. irreligious Jews [c]Lit *were reclining with* 2:16 [a]I.e. irreligious Jews [A]Luke 5:30; Acts 23:9 [B]Matt 9:11 2:17 [A]Matt 9:12, 13; Luke 5:31, 32 2:18 [A]Mark 2:18-22: *Matt 9:14-17; Luke 5:33-38* 2:19 [a]Lit *sons of the bridal-chamber* 2:20 [A]Matt 9:15; Luke 17:22 2:21 [a]Lit *that which is put on* [b]Lit *that which fills up* 2:23 [A]Mark 2:23-28: *Matt 12:1-8; Luke 6:1-5* [B]Deut 23:25

Spirit, but the omniscient mind of the Savior.

2:9 Which is easier . . . ? It is much easier to say, "Your sins are forgiven you." No human can prove that such a thing actually occurred since it is invisible. Commanding a paralytic to walk would be more difficult to say convincingly, however, because the actions of the paralytic would immediately verify the effect of the command (*see note on Mt 9:5*).

2:10 But so that you may know. Jesus' power to heal the paralytic's physical infirmities proved the veracity of His claim and power to forgive sins. **Son of Man.** Jesus used this term for Himself to emphasize His humiliation (*see notes on 14:62; Mt 8:20*). It appears 14 times in Mark (v. 10, 28; 8:31, 38; 9:9, 12, 31; 10:33, 45; 13:26; 14:21, 41, 62).

2:14 Levi the *son* of Alphaeus. One of the 12, more commonly known as Matthew (see Introduction to Matthew: Title). **tax booth.** Matthew was a publican, a tax collector, a despised profession in Palestine because such men were viewed as traitors. Tax collectors were Jews who had bought tax franchises from the Roman government. Any amount they collected over what Rome required they were allowed to keep. Thus many tax collectors became wealthy at the expense of their own people (*see notes on Mt 5:46; 9:9*). **he got up and followed Him.** This simple action of Matthew signified his conversion. Because his response was so immediate, it is likely Matthew was already convicted of his sin and recognized his need of forgiveness.

2:15 dining. This can also be translated, "reclining at table," a common posture for eating when guests were present. According to Lk 5:29, this was a feast that Matthew gave in Jesus' honor. **tax collectors.** There were two categories of tax collectors: 1) *gabbai* collected general taxes on land and property, and on income, referred to as poll or registration taxes; 2) *mokhes* collected a wide variety of use taxes, similar to our import duties, business license fees, and toll fees. There were two categories of *mokhes:* great *mokhes* hired others to collect taxes for them; small *mokhes* did their own assessing and collecting. Matthew was a small *mokhe.* It is likely representatives of both classes attended Matthew's feast. All of them were considered both religious and social outcasts. **sinners.** A term the Jews used to describe people who had no respect for the Mosaic law or rabbinic traditions, and were therefore the most vile and worthless of people. **dining with.** Lit. "were reclining with." Jesus' willingness to associate with tax collectors and sinners by sharing in the feast with them deeply offended the scribes and Pharisees.

2:16 scribes of the Pharisees. This phrase indicates that not all scribes were Pharisees (regarding scribes, *see note on Mt 2:4*). Pharisees were a legalistic sect of Jews known for their strict devotion to the ceremonial law (*see note on Mt 3:7*).

2:17 I did not come to call the righteous. In the parallel passage, Lk 5:32, sinners are called "to repentance." The repentant person—the one who recognizes he is a sinner and who turns from his sin—is the object of Jesus' call. The person who is sinful but thinks he is righteous refuses to acknowledge his need to repent of his sin. *See notes on Mt 9:12, 13; Jn 9:39–41.*

2:18 John's disciples. Those followers of John the Baptist who did not transfer their allegiance to Jesus (cf. Jn 3:30; Ac 19:1–7). At this time John was in prison (Mt 4:12). Their question indicates they were observing the Pharisaic traditions (cf. Mt 9:14). **the Pharisees.** *See note on v. 16.* The association of John's disciples with the Pharisees indicates that both groups were disturbed about the problem raised by Jesus' association with tax collectors and sinners (cf. v. 15). **fasting.** The twice-a-week fast was a major expression of orthodox Judaism during Jesus' day (cf. Lk 18:9–14). Yet, the OT prescribed only one fast, and that on the Day of Atonement (Lv 16:29, 31).

2:19 attendants of the bridegroom cannot fast. In Jesus' illustration, the "attendants of the bridegroom" were the friends the bridegroom selected to carry out the festivities. That certainly was not a time to fast, which was usually associated with mourning or times of great spiritual need. Jesus' point was that the ritual practiced by John's disciples and the Pharisees was out of touch with reality. There was no reason for Jesus' followers to mourn and fast while enjoying the unique reality that He was with them.

2:20 taken away from them. This refers to a sudden removal or being snatched away violently—an obvious reference to Jesus' capture and crucifixion. **then they will fast.** An appropriate time for mourning was to be at the crucifixion of Jesus.

2:21, 22 Jesus offered two parables to illustrate that His new and internal gospel of repentance from and forgiveness of sin could not be connected to or contained in the old and external traditions of self-righteousness and ritual (*see note on Mt 9:17*).

2:22 fresh wineskins. Newly made and unused wineskins provided the necessary strength and elasticity to hold up as wine fermented.

2:23 grainfields. The roads in first-century Israel were primarily major arteries; so once travelers left those main roads they walked

heads *of grain.* 24 The Pharisees were saying to Him,
"Look, [A]why are they doing what is not lawful on
the Sabbath?" 25 And He *said to them, "Have you
never read what David did when he was in need and
he and his companions became hungry; 26 how he
entered the house of God in the time of [A]Abiathar *the*
high priest, and ate the [a]consecrated bread, which
[B]is not lawful for *anyone* to eat except the priests,
and he also gave it to those who were with him?"
27 Jesus said to them, "[A]The Sabbath [a]was made [b]for
man, and [B]not man [b]for the Sabbath. 28 So the Son
of Man is Lord even of the Sabbath."

JESUS HEALS ON THE SABBATH

3 [A]He [B]entered again into a synagogue; and a man
was there whose hand was withered. 2 [A]They
were watching Him *to see* if He would heal him on
the Sabbath, [B]so that they might accuse Him. 3 He
*said to the man with the withered hand, "[a]Get up
and come forward!" 4 And He *said to them, "Is it
lawful to do good or to do harm on the Sabbath,
to save a life or to kill?" But they kept silent. 5 After
[A]looking around at them with anger, grieved at their
hardness of heart, He *said to the man, "Stretch out
your hand." And he stretched it out, and his hand
was restored. 6 The Pharisees went out and immediately *began* [a]conspiring with the [A]Herodians against
Him, *as to* how they might destroy Him.
7 [A]Jesus withdrew to the sea with His disciples;
and [B]a great multitude from Galilee followed; and
also from Judea, 8 and from Jerusalem, and from
[A]Idumea, and beyond the Jordan, and the vicinity
of [B]Tyre and Sidon, a great number of people heard
of all that He was doing and came to Him. 9 [A]And
He told His disciples that a boat should stand ready
for Him because of the crowd, so that they would

2:24 [A]Matt 12:2 2:26 [a]Or *showbread;* lit *loaves of presentation* [A]1 Sam 21:1; 2 Sam 8:17; 1 Chr 24:6 [B]Lev 24:9 2:27 [a]Or *came into being* [b]Lit *because for the sake of* [A]Ex 23:12; Deut 5:14 [B]Col 2:16 3:1 [A]Mark 3:1-6: *Matt 12:9-14; Luke 6:6-11* [B]Mark 1:21, 39 3:2 [A]Luke 6:7; 14:1; 20:20 [B]Matt 12:10; Luke 6:7; 11:54 3:3 [a]Lit *Arise into the midst* 3:5 [A]Luke 6:10 3:6 [a]Lit *giving counsel* [A]Matt 22:16; Mark 12:13 3:7 [A]Mark 3:7-12: *Matt 12:15, 16; Luke 6:17-19* [B]Matt 4:25; Luke 6:17 3:8 [A]Josh 15:1, 21; Ezek 35:15; 36:5 [B]Matt 11:21 3:9 [A]Mark 4:1; Luke 5:1-3

along wide paths that bordered and traversed pastures and grainfields. **on the Sabbath.** "Sabbath" transliterates a Heb. word that refers to a ceasing of activity or rest. In honor of the day when God rested from His creation of the world (Ge 2:3), the Lord declared the seventh day of the week to be a special time of rest and remembrance for His people, which He incorporated into the Ten Commandments (*see note on Ex 20:8*). But hundreds of years of rabbinical teaching had added numerous unbearable and arbitrary restrictions to God's original requirement, one of which forbade any travel beyond 3,000 ft. of one's home (cf. Nu 35:5; Jos 3:4). **picking the heads *of grain*.** Travelers who did not take enough food for their journey were permitted by Mosaic law to pick enough grain to satisfy their hunger (Dt 23:24, 25; *see note on Mt 12:2*).

2:24 **what is not lawful on the Sabbath.** Rabbinical tradition had interpreted the rubbing of grain in the hands (cf. Lk 6:1) as a form of threshing and had forbidden it. Reaping for profit on the Sabbath was forbidden by Mosaic law (Ex 34:21), but that was obviously not the situation here (*see note on Mt 12:2*). Actually the Pharisees' charge was itself sinful since they were holding their tradition on a par with God's Word (*see notes on Mt 15:2–9*).

2:25 **He said to them, "Have you never read . . . ?"** Jesus' sarcasm pointed out the main fault of the Pharisees, who claimed to be experts and guardians of Scripture, yet were ignorant of what it actually taught (cf. Ro 2:17–24). **what David did.** David and his companions were fleeing for their lives from Saul when they arrived at Nob, where the tabernacle was located at that time. Because they were hungry, they asked for food (cf. 1Sa 21:1–6).

2:26 **in the time of Abiathar *the* high priest.** The phrase "in the time" can mean "during the lifetime." According to 1Sa 21:1, Ahimelech was the priest who gave the bread to David. Abiathar was Ahimelech's son, who later was the High Priest during David's reign. Since Ahimelech died shortly after this incident (cf. 1Sa 22:19, 20), it is likely that Mark simply added this designation to identify the well known companion of David who later became the High Priest, along with Zadok (2Sa 15:35). **the consecrated bread.** Twelve loaves of unleavened bread (representing the 12 tribes of Israel) were placed on the table in the sanctuary and at the end of the week replaced with fresh ones. The old loaves were to be eaten only by the priests. While it was not normally lawful for David and his companions to eat this consecrated bread, neither did God want them to starve, so nowhere does Scripture condemn them for eating (*see note on Mt 12:4*).

2:27 **The Sabbath was made for man.** God instituted the Sabbath to benefit man by giving him a day to rest from his labors and to be a blessing to him. The Pharisees turned it into a burden and made man a slave to their myriad of man-made regulations.

2:28 **Lord even of the Sabbath.** Jesus claimed He was greater than the Sabbath, and thus was God. Based on that authority, Jesus could in fact reject the Pharisaic regulations concerning the Sabbath and restore God's original intention for Sabbath observance to be a blessing not a burden.

3:1–6 This is the last of the 5 conflict episodes which began in 2:1 (2:1–11; 13–17; 18–22; 23–28), and as such it gives a sense of climax to the growing antagonism between Jesus and the Jewish leaders. In this encounter, Jesus gave the Pharisees a living illustration of scriptural Sabbath observance and His sovereign authority over both man and the Sabbath.

3:1 **synagogue.** The Jews' local places of assembly and worship (*see note on 1:21*). **hand was withered.** This describes a condition of paralysis or deformity from an accident, a disease, or a congenital defect.

3:2 **accuse.** The Pharisees were not open to learning from Jesus, but only looked for an opportunity to charge Him with a violation of the Sabbath, an accusation they could bring before the Sanhedrin.

3:4 Jesus countered the Pharisees with a question that elevated the issue at hand from a legal to a moral problem. **Is it lawful.** A reference to the Mosaic law. Jesus was forcing the Pharisees to examine their tradition regarding the Sabbath to see if it was consistent with God's OT law. **to do good . . . harm . . . to save . . . kill.** Christ used a device common in the Middle East—He framed the issue in terms of clear-cut extremes. The obvious implication is that failure to do good or save a life was wrong and not in keeping with God's original intention for the Sabbath (*see notes on 2:27; Mt 12:10*). **But they kept silent.** The Pharisees refused to answer Jesus' question, and by so doing implied that their Sabbath views and practices were false.

3:5 **anger.** Definite displeasure with human sin reveals a healthy, moral nature. Jesus' reaction was consistent with His divine nature and proved that He is the righteous Son of God. This kind of holy indignation with sinful attitudes and practices was to be more fully demonstrated when Jesus cleansed the temple (cf. 11:15–18; Mt 21:12, 13; Lk 19:45–48). **their hardness of heart.** This phrase refers to an inability to understand because of a rebellious attitude (Ps 95:8; Heb 3:8, 15). The Pharisees' hearts were becoming more and more obstinate and unresponsive to the truth (cf. 16:14; Ro 9:18).

3:6 **the Pharisees . . . *began* conspiring.** They absolutely refused to be persuaded by anything Jesus said and did (cf. Jn 3:19), but were instead determined to kill Him. The Gr. word for "conspiring" includes the notion of carrying out a decision already made—the Pharisees were simply discussing how to implement theirs. **Herodians.** This secular political party, which took its name from Herod Antipas and was strong in its support for Rome, opposed the Pharisees on nearly every issue, but were willing to join forces with them because both desperately wanted to destroy Jesus. *See note on Mt 22:16.*

3:8 In spite of His conflicts with the Pharisees, Jesus remained very popular with the ordinary people. Mark is the only gospel writer who at this point in Jesus' ministry noted that the masses came from all parts of Israel to see and hear Him. **Idumea.** An area SE of Judea, mentioned only here in the NT and populated by many Edomites (originally descendants of Esau, *see note on Ge 36:43*). By this time it had become mostly Jewish in population and was considered a part of Judea. **beyond the Jordan.** The region E of the Jordan River, also called Perea, and ruled by Herod Antipas. Its population contained a

not crowd Him; 10 for He had [A]healed many, with
the result that all those who had [B]afflictions pressed
around Him in order to [C]touch Him. 11 Whenever the
unclean spirits saw Him, they would fall down before Him and shout, "You are [A]the Son of God!" 12 And
He [A]earnestly warned them not to [a]tell who He was.

THE TWELVE ARE CHOSEN

13 And He *went up on [A]the mountain and *[B]sum-
moned those whom He Himself wanted, and they
came to Him. 14 And He appointed twelve, so that
they would be with Him and that He *could* send
them out to preach, 15 and to have authority to cast
out the demons. 16 And He appointed the twelve:
[A]Simon (to whom He gave the name Peter), 17 and
[a]James, the *son* of Zebedee, and John the brother
of [a]James (to them He gave the name Boanerges,
which means, "Sons of Thunder"); 18 and Andrew,
and Philip, and Bartholomew, and Matthew, and
Thomas, and [a]James the son of Alphaeus, and Thaddaeus, and Simon the [b]Zealot; 19 and Judas Iscariot,
who betrayed Him.
20 And He *came [a,A]home, and the [B]crowd *gathered again, [C]to such an extent that they could not
even eat [b]a meal. 21 When [A]His own [a]people heard *of
this,* they went out to take custody of Him; for they
were saying, "[B]He has lost His senses." 22 The scribes
who came down [A]from Jerusalem were saying, "He
is possessed by [a,B]Beelzebul," and "[C]He casts out the
demons by the ruler of the demons." 23 [A]And He
called them to Himself and began speaking to them
in [B]parables, "How can [C]Satan cast out Satan? 24 If
a kingdom is divided against itself, that kingdom
cannot stand. 25 If a house is divided against itself,
that house will not be able to stand. 26 If [A]Satan has
risen up against himself and is divided, he cannot
stand, but [a]he is finished! 27 [A]But no one can enter
the strong man's house and plunder his property
unless he first binds the strong man, and then he
will plunder his house.
28 "[A]Truly I say to you, all sins shall be forgiven
the sons of men, and whatever blasphemies they
utter; 29 but [A]whoever blasphemes against the Holy
Spirit never has forgiveness, but is guilty of an
eternal sin"— 30 because they were saying, "He has
an unclean spirit."
31 [A]Then His mother and His brothers *arrived,
and standing outside they sent *word* to Him and

3:10 [A]Matt 4:23 [B]Mark 5:29, 34; Luke 7:21 [C]Matt 9:21; 14:36; Mark 6:56; 8:22 3:11 [A]Matt 4:3 3:12 [a]Lit *make Him known* [A]Matt 8:4 3:13 [A]Matt 5:1; Luke 6:12 [B]Matt 10:1; Mark 6:7; Luke 9:1 3:16 [A]Mark 3:16-19: *Matt 10:2-4; Luke 6:14-16;* Acts 1:13 3:17 [a]Or *Jacob* 3:18 [a]Or *Jacob* [b]Or *Cananaean* 3:20 [a]Lit *into a house* [b]Lit *bread* [A]Mark 2:1; 7:17; 9:28 [B]Mark 1:45; 3:7 [C]Mark 6:31 3:21 [a]Or *kinsmen* [A]Mark 3:31f [B]John 10:20; Acts 26:24 3:22 [a]Or *Beezebul;* others read *Beelzebub* [A]Matt 15:1 [B]Matt 10:25; 11:18 [C]Matt 9:34 3:23 [A]Mark 3:23-27: *Matt 12:25-29; Luke 11:17-22* [B]Matt 13:3ff; Mark 4:2ff [C]Matt 4:10 3:26 [a]Lit *he has an end* [A]Matt 4:10 3:27 [A]Is 49:24, 25 3:28 [A]Mark 3:28-30: *Matt 12:31, 32; Luke 12:10* 3:29 [A]Luke 12:10 3:31 [A]Mark 3:31-35: *Matt 12:46-50; Luke 8:19-21*

large number of Jews. **Tyre and Sidon.** Two Phoenician cities on the Mediterranean coast, N of Galilee. Phoenicia as a whole was often designated by these cities (cf. Jer 47:4; Joel 3:4; Mt 11:21; Ac 12:20).

3:10 afflictions. Lit. "a whip, a lash," sometimes translated "plagues," or "scourges." This metaphorically describes various painful, agonizing, physical ailments and illnesses.

3:11 unclean spirits. This refers to demons (*see note on 1:23;* cf. Lk 4:41). **saw Him.** The tense of the Gr. verb means there were many times when demons looked at Jesus and contemplated the truth of His character and identity. **You are the Son of God!** Cf. 1:24. The demons unhesitatingly affirmed the uniqueness of Jesus' nature, which Mark saw as clear proof of Jesus' deity.

3:12 warned ... not to tell who He was. Jesus always rebuked demons for their testimonies about Him. He wanted His teaching and actions, not the impure words of demons, to proclaim who He was (*see note on 1:25;* cf. Ac 16:16–18).

3:13 summoned those whom He Himself wanted. The Gr. verb "summoned" stresses that Jesus acted in His own sovereign interest when He chose the 12 disciples (cf. Jn 15:16).

3:14 appointed twelve. Christ, by an explicit act of His will, formed a distinct group of 12 men who were among His followers (*see note on Mt 10:1*). This new group constituted the foundation of His church (cf. Eph 2:20).

3:15 have authority. This word is sometimes rendered "power." Along with the main task of preaching, Jesus gave the 12 the right to expel demons (cf. Lk 9:1).

3:16–19 A list of the 12 (*see notes on Mt 10:2–4*).

3:16 Peter. From this point on (except in 14:37), Mark uses this name for Simon, though this is not when the designation was first given (cf. Jn 1:42), nor does it mark the complete replacement of the name Simon (cf. Ac 15:14). The name means "stone," and describes Peter's character and activities, namely his position as a foundation rock in the building of the church (cf. Mt 16:18; Eph 2:20).

3:17 Sons of Thunder. Mark defines the Aram. term "Boanerges" for his Gentile readers. This name for the two brothers probably referred to their intense, outspoken personalities (cf. 9:38; Lk 9:54).

3:18 Thaddaeus. The only name that is not the same in all the NT lists of the 12 (cf. Mt 10:2–4; Lk 6:14–16; Ac 1:13). Luke and Acts call him "Judas *the son* of James," and Jn 14:22 refers to him as "Judas (not Iscariot)." **the Zealot.** This does not indicate that this Simon was a native of Cana. Rather, the word is derived from the Aram. which means "to be zealous" and was used for those who were zealous for the law. Luke uses the word transliterated from the Gr. term that meant "the Zealot" (Lk 6:15; *see note on Mt 10:4*).

3:19 Iscariot. This Heb. term means "man of Kerioth," as in Kerioth-hezron, S of Hebron (Jos 15:25).

3:20 came home. This refers to Jesus' return to Capernaum (cf. 2:1).

3:21 His own people. In Gr., this expression was used in various ways to describe someone's friends or close associates. In the strictest sense, it meant family, which is probably the best understanding here. **take custody of Him.** Mark used this same term elsewhere to mean the arrest of a person (6:17; 12:12; 14:1, 44, 46, 51). Jesus' relatives evidently heard the report of v. 20 and came to Capernaum to restrain Him from His many activities and bring Him under their care and control, all supposedly for His own good. **lost His senses.** Jesus' family could only explain His unconventional lifestyle, with its willingness for others always to impose on Him, by saying He was irrational or had lost His mind.

3:22 scribes. Jewish scholars, also called lawyers, (mostly Pharisees) who were experts on the law and its application (*see note on Mt 2:4*). **Beelzebul.** Satan (*see note on Lk 11:15*).

3:23 parables. Jesus answered the scribes by making an analogy between well known facts and the truths He expounded (*see note on Mt 13:3*).

3:26 he is finished! An expression used only in Mark which refers to Satan's ultimate doom as head of the demonic world system. *See notes on Rev 20:1–10.*

3:27 enter the strong man's house and plunder his property. One must be stronger than Satan in order to enter his domain ("strong man's house"), bind him (restrain his action), and free ("plunder") people ("his property") from his control. Only Jesus had such power over the devil. Cf. Ro 16:20; Heb 2:14, 15.

3:28 Truly I say to you. Mark's first use of this expression, which occurs throughout the Gospels, was employed as a formula that always introduced truthful and authoritative words from Jesus (cf. 6:11; 8:12; 9:1, 41; 10:15, 29; 11:23; 12:43; 13:30; 14:9, 18, 25, 30).

3:29 whoever blasphemes ... never has forgiveness. Whenever someone deliberately and disrespectfully slanders the person and ministry of the Holy Spirit in pointing to the Lordship and redemption of Jesus Christ, he completely negates and forfeits any possibility of present or future forgiveness of sins (*see note on Mt 12:31*), because he has wholly rejected the only basis of God's salvation.

3:31 His mother and His brothers. Jesus' earthly family (*see notes on v. 21; Mt 12:46*). The narrative that left off at v. 21 resumes here.

called Him. 32 A crowd was sitting around Him,
and they *said to Him, "Behold, Your mother and
Your brothers are outside looking for You." 33 Answering them, He *said, "Who are My mother and
My brothers?" 34 Looking about at those who were
sitting around Him, He *said, "[A]Behold My mother
and My brothers! 35 For whoever [A]does the will of
God, he is My brother and sister and mother."

PARABLE OF THE SOWER AND SOILS

4 [A]He began to teach again [B]by the sea. And such
a very large crowd gathered to Him that [C]He
got into a boat in the sea and sat down; and the
whole crowd was by the sea on the land. 2 And He
was teaching them many things in [A]parables, and
was saying to them in His teaching, 3 "Listen *to this!*
Behold, the sower went out to sow; 4 as he was sowing, some *seed* fell beside the road, and the birds
came and ate it up. 5 Other *seed* fell on the rocky
ground where it did not have much soil; and immediately it sprang up because it had no depth of
soil. 6 And after the sun had risen, it was scorched;
and because it had no root, it withered away. 7 Other
seed fell among the thorns, and the thorns came up
and choked it, and it yielded no crop. 8 Other *seeds*
fell into the good soil, and as they grew up and increased, they yielded a crop and produced thirty,
sixty, and a hundredfold." 9 And He was saying, "[A]He
who has ears to hear, [a]let him hear."

10 As soon as He was alone, [a]His followers, along
with the twelve, *began* asking Him *about* the parables. 11 And He was saying to them, "To you has
been given the mystery of the kingdom of God, but
[A]those who are outside get everything [B]in parables,
12 so that [A]WHILE SEEING, THEY MAY SEE AND NOT
PERCEIVE, AND WHILE HEARING, THEY MAY HEAR AND
NOT UNDERSTAND, OTHERWISE THEY MIGHT RETURN
AND BE FORGIVEN."

EXPLANATION

13 [A]And He *said to them, "Do you not understand this parable? How will you understand all
the parables? 14 The sower sows the word. 15 These
are the ones who are beside the road where the
word is sown; and when they hear, immediately
[A]Satan comes and takes away the word which has
been sown in them. 16 In a similar way these are
the ones on whom seed was sown on the rocky
places, who, when they hear the word, immediately
receive it with joy; 17 and they have no *firm* root in
themselves, but are *only* temporary; then, when
affliction or persecution arises because of the word,
immediately they [a]fall away. 18 And others are the
ones on whom seed was sown among the thorns;
these are the ones who have heard the word, 19 but
the worries of [A]the [a]world, and the [B]deceitfulness
of riches, and the desires for other things enter
in and choke the word, and it becomes unfruitful.

3:34 [A]Matt 12:49 3:35 [A]Eph 6:6; Heb 10:36; 1 Pet 4:2; 1 John 2:17 4:1 [A]Mark 4:1-12: *Matt 13:1-15; Luke 8:4-10* [B]Mark 2:13; 3:7 [C]Luke 5:1-3 4:2 [A]Matt 13:3ff; Mark 3:23; 4:2ff 4:9 [a]Or *hear!;* or *listen!* [A]Matt 11:15; Mark 4:23; Rev 2:7, 11, 17, 29 4:10 [a]Lit *those about Him* 4:11 [A]1 Cor 5:12f; Col 4:5; 1 Thess 4:12; 1 Tim 3:7 [B]Mark 3:23; 4:2 4:12 [A]Is 6:9f; 43:8; Jer 5:21; Ezek 12:2; Matt 13:14; Luke 8:10; John 12:40; Rom 11:8 4:13 [A]Mark 4:13-20: *Matt 13:18-23; Luke 8:11-15* 4:15 [A]Matt 4:10f; 1 Pet 5:8; Rev 20:2, 3, 7-10 4:17 [a]Lit *are caused to stumble* 4:19 [a]Or *age* [A]Matt 13:22; Rom 12:2; Eph 2:2; 6:12 [B]Prov 23:4; 1 Tim 6:9, 10, 17

3:35 Jesus made a decisive and comprehensive statement on true Christian discipleship. Such discipleship involves a spiritual relationship that transcends the physical family and is open to all who are empowered by the Spirit of God to come to Christ in repentance and faith and enabled to live a life of obedience to God's Word.

4:1 sat. The typical rabbinical position for teaching; and more practically, Jesus may have sat because of the rocking of the boat in the water.

4:2 parables. A common method of teaching in Judaism, which Jesus employed to conceal the truth from unbelievers while explaining it to His disciples (cf. v. 11; *see note on Mt 13:3*).

4:3–8 This parable depicts the teaching of the gospel throughout the world and the various responses of people to it. Some will reject it; some will accept it for a brief time but then fall away; yet some will believe and will lead others to believe.

4:4 beside the road. Either a road near a field's edge or a path that traversed a field, both of which were hard surfaces due to constant foot traffic.

4:5 rocky *ground*. Beds of solid rock, usually limestone, lying under the surface of good soil. They are a little too deep for the plow to reach, and too shallow to allow a plant to reach water and develop a decent root system in the small amount of soil that covers them.

4:7 thorns. Tough, thistle-bearing weeds that use up the available space, light, and water which good plants need.

4:8 produced .... hundredfold. An average ratio of harvested grain to what had been sown was 8 to 1, with a 10 to 1 ratio considered exceptional. The yields Jesus refers to are like an unbelievable harvest.

4:9 He who has ears to hear, let him hear. On the surface, this is a call for the listener to be attentive and discern the meaning of His analogy. Yet more than human understanding is necessary to interpret the parable—only those who have been redeemed will have the true meaning explained to them by the divine Teacher.

4:11 mystery ... parables. A "mystery" in the NT refers to something previously hidden and unknown but revealed in the NT (*see notes on 1Co 2:7; Eph 3:4–6*). In context, the subject of the mystery is the kingdom of heaven (*see note on Mt 3:2*), which Jesus communicates in the form of parables. Thus the mystery is revealed to those who believe, yet it remains concealed to those who reject Christ and His gospel (*see note on Mt 13:11*). **but those who are outside.** Those who are not followers of Christ.

4:12 so that. *See note on Mt 13:13.* Unlike Matthew, which specifically quotes Is 6:9, 10, Mark quotes Jesus as giving the substance of what Isaiah wrote in that text. otherwise they might return. The implication is that unbelievers do not want to turn from sin (*see notes on Mt 13:3, 13*).

4:13 all the parables. Understanding the parable of the sower was to be key in the disciples' ability to discern the meaning of Jesus' other parables of the kingdom (vv. 21–34).

4:14–20 Jesus' explanation of the parable of the sower, who is in fact Jesus Himself (cf. Mt 13:37) and anyone who proclaims the gospel.

4:14 the word. Luke 8:11 says it is the "word of God," and Mt 13:19 calls it the "word of the kingdom." It is the salvation gospel (*see note on Mt 13:19*).

4:16 receive it with joy. An enthusiastic, emotional, yet superficial response to the gospel that does not take into account the cost involved.

4:17 no *firm* root. Because the person's heart is hard, like the rocky ground (*see note on v. 5*), the gospel never takes root in the individual's soul and never transforms his life—there is only a temporary, surface change. **affliction or persecution.** Not the routine difficulties and troubles of life, but specifically the suffering, trials, and persecutions which result from one's association with God's Word. **fall away.** The Gr. word also means "to cause offense," from which comes the Eng. word "scandalize." All those meanings are appropriate since the superficial believer is offended, stumbles, and falls away when his faith is put to the test (cf. Jn 8:31; 1Jn 2:19).

4:19 worries of the world. Lit. "the distractions of the age." A preoccupation with the temporal issues of this present age blinds a person to any serious consideration of the gospel (cf. Jas 4:4; 1Jn 2:15, 16). **deceitfulness of riches.** Not only can money and material possessions not satisfy the desires of the heart or bring the lasting happiness they deceptively promise, but they also blind those who pursue them to eternal, spiritual concerns (1Ti 6:9, 10).

20And those are the ones on whom seed was sown
on the good soil; and they hear the word and accept
it and [A]bear fruit, thirty, sixty, and a hundredfold."
21And He was saying to them, "[A]A lamp is not
brought to be put under a [a]basket, is it, or under a
bed? Is it not *brought* to be put on the lampstand?
22[A]For nothing is hidden, except to be revealed; nor
has *anything* been secret, but that it would come to
light. 23[A]If anyone has ears to hear, let him hear."
24And He was saying to them, "Take care what you
listen to. [a,A]By your standard of measure it will be
measured to you; and more will be given you besides. 25[A]For whoever has, to him *more* shall be
given; and whoever does not have, even what he
has shall be taken away from him."

PARABLE OF THE SEED

26And He was saying, "The kingdom of God is
like a man who casts seed upon the soil; 27and he
goes to bed at night and gets up by day, and the
seed sprouts and grows—how, he himself does
not know. 28The soil produces crops by itself;
first the blade, then the head, then the mature
grain in the head. 29But when the crop permits,
he immediately [a,A]puts in the sickle, because the
harvest has come."

PARABLE OF THE MUSTARD SEED

30[A]And He said, "How shall we [a,B]picture the kingdom of God, or by what parable shall we present it?
31*It is* like a mustard seed, which, when sown upon
the soil, though it is smaller than all the seeds that
are upon the soil, 32yet when it is sown, it grows
up and becomes larger than all the garden plants
and forms large branches; so that [A]THE BIRDS OF
THE [a]AIR can NEST UNDER ITS SHADE."
33With many such parables He was speaking the
word to them, so far as they were able to hear it;
34and He did not speak to them [A]without a parable;
but He was [B]explaining everything privately to His
own disciples.

JESUS STILLS THE SEA

35[A]On that day, when evening came, He *said to
them, "Let us go over to the other side." 36[a]Leaving
the crowd, they *took Him along with them [A]in the
boat, just as He was; and other boats were with
Him. 37And there *arose a fierce gale of wind, and
the waves were breaking over the boat so much
that the boat was already filling up. 38Jesus Himself was in the stern, asleep on the cushion; and
they *woke Him and *said to Him, "Teacher, do You
not care that we are perishing?" 39And He got up

4:20 [A]John 15:2ff; Rom 7:4 4:21 [a]Or *peck-measure* [A]Matt 5:15; Luke 8:16; 11:33 4:22 [A]Matt 10:26; Luke 8:17; 12:2 4:23 [A]Matt 11:15; 13:9, 43; Mark 4:9; Luke 8:8; 14:35; Rev 3:6, 13, 22; 13:9 4:24 [a]Lit *By what measure you measure* [A]Matt 7:2; Luke 6:38 4:25 [A]Matt 13:12; 25:29; Luke 8:18; 19:26 4:29 [a]Lit *sends forth* [A]Joel 3:13 4:30 [a]Lit *compare* [A]Mark 4:30-32: *Matt 13:31, 32; Luke 13:18, 19* [B]Matt 13:24 4:32 [a]Or *sky* [A]Ezek 17:23; Ps 104:12; Ezek 31:6; Dan 4:12 4:34 [A]Matt 13:34; John 10:6; 16:25 [B]Luke 24:27 4:35 [A]Mark 4:35-41: *Matt 8:18, 23-27; Luke 8:22, 25* 4:36 [a]Or *Sending away* [A]Mark 3:9; 4:1; 5:2, 21

4:20 hear … accept … bear fruit. Three Gr. present participles mark continuing action. Believers, in contrast to unbelievers, hear God's Word because God allows them to hear it. They "accept" it—they understand and obey it because God opens their mind and heart and transforms their lives. The result is that they produce spiritual fruit.

4:21 lamp. This refers to a very small clay bowl made with a spout to hold a wick and containing a few ounces of oil that served as the fuel. **the lampstand.** In common homes, this was simply a shelf protruding from the wall. Wealthier homes might have separate, ornate stands (cf. Rev 1:12).

4:22 nothing is hidden … revealed. The purpose in keeping something hidden is so that one day it can be revealed. Jesus' teaching was never intended to be just for an inner circle of followers. It would be the responsibility of the disciples to communicate the gospel of the kingdom to the world at large (cf. Mt 28:19, 20).

4:24 By your standard of measure. The spiritual results which the disciples realized were to be based on the amount of effort they put forth; they would reap as they had sown. **more will be given.** The one who has learned spiritual truth and applied it diligently will receive even more truth to faithfully apply.

4:26–29 This parable is recorded only by Mark and complements the parable of the sower by explaining in more depth the results of spiritual growth accomplished in good soil.

4:26 kingdom of God. *See note on 1:15.*

4:29 puts in the sickle, because the harvest has come. When the grain is ripe, the sower of the seed must harvest the crop. There are two possible interpretations of this unexplained parable. It could be referring to the entire scope of the kingdom, from the time Jesus sowed the gospel message until the final harvest in the future. His disciples would continue the work of presenting the gospel that would eventually yield a harvest. The better interpretation pictures the gospel working in lives. After the gospel is presented, the Word of God works in the individual heart, sometimes slowly, until the time when God reaps the harvest in that individual and saves him.

4:30–32 This parable of the mustard seed pictures the kingdom of God beginning with a small influence and then becoming worldwide in its scope.

4:31 a mustard seed. A reference to the common black mustard plant. The leaves were used as a vegetable and the seed as a condiment. It also had medicinal benefits. **smaller than all.** The mustard seed is not the smallest of all seeds in existence, but it was in comparison to all the other seeds the Jews sowed in Israel.

4:32 birds of the air. While not a tree in the truest sense of the word, the mustard shrub has been known to grow as large as 15 ft. high and to have the properties of a tree, such as having branches large enough for birds to nest in. The tree represents the sphere of salvation, which would grow so large that it would provide shelter, protection, and benefit to people (*see note on Mt 13:32*). Even unbelievers have been blessed by association with the gospel and the power of God in salvation. Christians have been a benediction to the world. *See note on 1Co 7:14.*

4:33, 34 This conclusion to Mark's account of Jesus' parables highlights Mark's recording only representative samples of all the parables Jesus taught.

4:34 He did not speak to them without a parable. On that particular day, Jesus spoke to the larger crowd only in parables. This method of teaching left unbelievers with riddles and kept them from being forced to believe or disbelieve Him—they could make no decision to follow Him since they did not understand what He taught.

4:35–41 This account demonstrates Jesus' unlimited power over the natural world.

4:35 the other side. Jesus and His disciples were on the western shore of the Sea of Galilee. To escape the crowds for a brief respite, Jesus wanted to go to the eastern shore, which had no large cities and therefore fewer people.

4:37 fierce gale of wind. Wind is a common occurrence on that lake, about 690 ft. below sea level and surrounded by hills. The Gr. word can also mean "whirlwind." In this case, it was a storm so severe that it took on the properties of a hurricane (*see note on Mt 8:24*). The disciples, used to being on the lake in the wind, thought this storm would drown them (v. 38).

4:38 Jesus … was … asleep. Jesus was so exhausted from a full day of healing and preaching, even that storm could not wake Him up (*see note on Mt 8:24*).

4:39 Hush, be still. Lit. "be silent, be muzzled." Storms normally subside gradually, but when the Creator gave the order, the natural elements of this storm ceased immediately.

and [A]rebuked the wind and said to the sea, "Hush,
be still." And the wind died down and [a]it became
perfectly calm. 40 And He said to them, "Why are
you [a]afraid? [A]Do you still have no faith?" 41 They
became very much afraid and said to one another,
"Who then is this, that even the wind and the sea
obey Him?"

THE GERASENE DEMONIAC

5 [A]They came to the other side of the sea, into the
country of the Gerasenes. 2 When He got out
of [A]the boat, immediately a man from the tombs
[B]with an unclean spirit met Him, 3 and he had his
dwelling among the tombs. And no one was able
to bind him anymore, even with a chain; 4 because
he had often been bound with shackles and chains,
and the chains had been torn apart by him and the
shackles broken in pieces, and no one was strong
enough to subdue him. 5 Constantly, night and day,
he was screaming among the tombs and in the
mountains, and gashing himself with stones. 6 Seeing Jesus from a distance, he ran up and bowed
down before Him; 7 and shouting with a loud voice,
he *said, "[a,A]What business do we have with each
other, Jesus, [B]Son of [C]the Most High God? I implore
You by God, do not torment me!" 8 For He had been
saying to him, "Come out of the man, you unclean
spirit!" 9 And He was asking him, "What is your
name?" And he *said to Him, "My name is [A]Legion;
for we are many." 10 And he *began* to implore Him
earnestly not to send them out of the country. 11 Now
there was a large herd of swine feeding [a]nearby
on the mountain. 12 *The demons* implored Him,
saying, "Send us into the swine so that we may
enter them." 13 Jesus gave them permission. And
coming out, the unclean spirits entered the swine;
and the herd rushed down the steep bank into the
sea, about two thousand *of them;* and they were
drowned in the sea.

14 Their herdsmen ran away and reported it in
the city and in the country. And *the people* came to
see what it was that had happened. 15 They *came
to Jesus and *observed the man who had been [A]de-
mon-possessed sitting down, [B]clothed and [C]in his
right mind, the very man who had had the "[D]legion";
and they became frightened. 16 Those who had seen
it described to them how it had happened to the
[A]demon-possessed man, and *all* about the swine.
17 And they began to [A]implore Him to leave their
region. 18 [A]As He was getting into the boat, the man
who had been [B]demon-possessed was imploring
Him that he might [a]accompany Him. 19 And He did
not let him, but He *said to him, "[A]Go home to your
people and report to them [a]what great things the

4:39 [a]Lit *a great calm occurred* [A]Ps 65:7; 89:9; 107:29; Matt 8:26; Luke 8:24 4:40 [a]Or *cowardly* [A]Matt 14:31; Luke 8:25 5:1 [A]Mark 5:1-17: *Matt 8:28-34; Luke 8:26-37* 5:2 [A]Mark 3:9; 4:1, 36; 5:21 [B]Mark 1:23 5:7 [a]Lit *What to me and to you* (a Heb idiom) [A]Matt 8:29 [B]Matt 4:3 [C]Luke 8:28; Acts 16:17; Heb 7:1 5:9 [A]Matt 26:53; Mark 5:15; Luke 8:30 5:11 [a]Lit *there* 5:15 [A]Matt 4:24; Mark 5:16, 18 [B]Luke 8:27 [C]Luke 8:35 [D]Mark 5:9 5:16 [A]Matt 4:24; Mark 5:15 5:17 [A]Matt 8:34; Acts 16:39 5:18 [a]Lit *be with Him* [A]Mark 5:18-20: *Luke 8:38, 39* [B]Matt 4:24; Mark 5:15, 16 5:19 [a]Or *everything that* [A]Luke 8:39

4:41 they became … afraid. This was not fear of being harmed by the storm, but a reverence for the supernatural power Jesus had just displayed. The only thing more terrifying than having a storm outside the boat was having God in the boat! **Who then is this … ?** This statement betrayed the disciples' wonder at the true identity of Jesus.

5:1 the other side of the sea. The eastern shore of the Sea of Galilee (cf. Lk 8:26). **the country of the Gerasenes.** This word most likely refers to the small town of Gersa (or Khersa, Kursi; *see note on Mt 8:28*) which was located midway on the eastern shore. "Country of" refers to the general region that included Gersa and was under the jurisdiction of the city of Gadara, which was located some 6 mi. SE of the Sea of Galilee.

5:2 a man from the tombs. Mark mentions only one of the demon-possessed men, who was probably the more prominent of the two (cf. Mt 8:28). The "tombs"—common dwelling places for the demented of that day—were burial chambers carved out of rock hillsides on the outskirts of town. If the man and his possible companion were Jews, for whom touching dead bodies was a great defilement, living in such an area was an added torment. **unclean spirit.** This refers to the demon who was controlling the man. Such spirits in themselves were morally filthy and caused much harm for those whom they possessed (*see notes on 1:32–34*; cf. Lk 4:33, 36; 7:21; 8:2).

5:3 no one was able to bind him. Multiple negatives are used in the Gr. text to emphasize the man's tremendous strength.

5:4 shackles and chains. "Shackles" (probably metal or perhaps, in part, cord or rope) were used to restrain the feet and "chains" were metal restraints for the rest of the body.

5:5 screaming … gashing himself with stones. "Screaming" describes a continual unearthly scream uttered with intense emotion. The "stones" likely were rocks made of flint with sharp, jagged edges.

5:7 What business do we have with each other … ? A common expression of protest (*see note on 1:24*). **Son of the Most High God.** The demons knew that Jesus was deity, the God-Man. "Most High God" was an ancient title used by both Jews and Gentiles to identify the one, true, and living God of Israel and distinguish Him from all false idol gods (cf. Ge 14:18–20; Nu 24:16; Dt 32:8; Pss 18:13; 21:7; Is 14:14; Da 3:26; Lk 1:32; Heb 7:1). **I implore You … do not torment me!** *See note on Mt 8:29.* Mark adds "I implore you," which shows the demon tried to have Jesus soften the severity of his inevitable fate. Cf. Jas 2:19.

5:9 What is your name? Most likely, Jesus asked this in view of the demon's appeal not to be tormented. However, He did not need to know the demon's name in order to expel him. Rather, Jesus posed the question to bring the reality and complexity of this case into the open. **Legion.** A Lat. term, by then common to Jews and Greeks, that defined a Roman military unit of 6,000 infantrymen. Such a name denotes that the man was controlled by an extremely large number of militant evil spirits, a truth reiterated by the expression "for we are many."

5:10 he *began* to implore Him earnestly. The demon understood that Jesus had all power over him and addressed Him with an intense desire that his request be granted. **not to send them out of the country.** *See note on v. 1.* The demons wanted to remain in the same area where they had been exercising their evil powers.

5:11 swine. Pigs were unclean animals to the Jews, so the people tending this herd were either Gentiles or Jews unconcerned about the law (*see note on Mt 8:30*).

5:13 Jesus gave them permission. According to His sovereign purposes Jesus allowed the demons to enter the pigs and destroy them—the text offers no other explanation (cf. Dt 29:29; Ro 9:20). By doing this, Jesus gave the man a graphic, visible, and powerful lesson on the immensity of the evil from which he had been delivered.

5:15 sitting. The man's restful condition was a strong contrast with his former restless, agitated state. **in his right mind.** He was no longer under the frenzied, screaming control of the demons.

5:16 Those … described … about the swine. "Those" may refer to both the 12 and the men who tended the pigs. They wanted people to know what had happened to the man and the pigs, and the relationship between the two events.

5:17 implore Him to leave their region. The residents of the region became frightened and resentful toward Jesus because of what had happened. They may have been concerned about the disruption of their normal routine and the loss of property, and they wanted Jesus and His powers to leave the area so no more such financial losses would occur. More compelling, however, was the reality that they were ungodly people frightened by Christ's display of spiritual power (*see note on Mt 8:34*).

5:19 report to them … the Lord has done. Jesus was referring to Himself as God who controlled both the natural and the supernatural worlds (cf. Lk 8:39).

Lord has done for you, and *how* He had mercy on
you." 20 And he went away and began to [A]proclaim
in [B]Decapolis [a]what great things Jesus had done for
him; and everyone was amazed.

MIRACLES AND HEALING

21 [A]When Jesus had crossed over again in [B]the boat
to the other side, a large crowd gathered around
Him; and so He [a]stayed [C]by the seashore. 22 [A]One of
[B]the synagogue [a]officials named Jairus *came up,
and on seeing Him, *fell at His feet 23 and *implored
Him earnestly, saying, "My little daughter is at the
point of death; *please* come and [A]lay Your hands on
her, so that she will [a]get well and live." 24 And He
went off with him; and a large crowd was following
Him and pressing in on Him.

25 A woman who had had a hemorrhage for
twelve years, 26 and had endured much at the hands
of many physicians, and had spent all that she had
and was not helped at all, but rather had grown
worse— 27 after hearing about Jesus, she came up
in the crowd behind *Him* and touched His [a]cloak.
28 For she [a]thought, "If I just touch His garments, I
will [b]get well." 29 Immediately the flow of her blood
was dried up; and she felt in her body that she was
healed of her [A]affliction. 30 Immediately Jesus, perceiving in Himself that [A]the power *proceeding* from
Him had gone forth, turned around in the crowd
and said, "Who touched My garments?" 31 And His
disciples said to Him, "You see the crowd pressing
in on You, and You say, 'Who touched Me?' " 32 And
He looked around to see the woman who had done
this. 33 But the woman fearing and trembling, aware
of what had happened to her, came and fell down
before Him and told Him the whole truth. 34 And He
said to her, "Daughter, [A]your faith has [a]made you
well; [B]go in peace and be healed of your [C]affliction."

35 While He was still speaking, they *came from
the *house of* the [A]synagogue official, saying, "Your
daughter has died; why trouble the Teacher anymore?" 36 But Jesus, overhearing what was being
spoken, *said to the [A]synagogue official, "[B]Do not be
afraid *any longer,* only [a]believe." 37 And He allowed
no one to accompany Him, except [A]Peter and [a]James
and John the brother of [a]James. 38 They *came to
the house of the [A]synagogue official; and He *saw a
commotion, and *people* loudly weeping and wailing.
39 And entering in, He *said to them, "Why make a
commotion and weep? The child has not died, but
is asleep." 40 They *began* laughing at Him. But putting them all out, He *took along the child's father
and mother and His own companions, and *entered
the room where the child was. 41 Taking the child
by the hand, He *said to her, "Talitha kum!" (which
translated means, "Little girl, [A]I say to you, get up!").
42 Immediately the girl got up and *began* to walk,
for she was twelve years old. And immediately they
were completely astounded. 43 And He [A]gave them

5:20 [a]Or *everything that* [A]Ps 66:16 [B]Matt 4:25; Mark 7:31 5:21 [a]Lit *was* [A]Matt 9:1; Luke 8:40 [B]Mark 4:36 [C]Mark 4:1 5:22 [a]Or *rulers* [A]Mark 5:22-43: *Matt 9:18-26; Luke 8:41-56* [B]Matt 9:18; Mark 5:35, 36, 38; Luke 8:49; 13:14; Acts 13:15; 18:8, 17 5:23 [a]Lit *be saved* [A]Mark 6:5; 7:32; 8:23; 16:18; Luke 4:40; 13:13; Acts 6:6; 9:17; 28:8 5:27 [a]Or *outer garment* 5:28 [a]Lit *was saying* [b]Lit *be saved* 5:29 [A]Mark 3:10; 5:34 5:30 [A]Luke 5:17 5:34 [a]Lit *saved you* [A]Matt 9:22 [B]Luke 7:50; 8:48; Acts 16:36; James 2:16 [C]Mark 3:10; 5:29 5:35 [A]Mark 5:22 5:36 [a]Or *keep on believing* [A]Mark 5:22 [B]Luke 8:50 5:37 [a]Or *Jacob;* James is the Eng form of Jacob [A]Matt 17:1; 26:37 5:38 [A]Mark 5:22 5:41 [A]Luke 7:14; Acts 9:40 5:43 [A]Matt 8:4

5:20 Decapolis. A league of 10 Greek-influenced (Hellenized) cities E of the Jordan River (*see note on Mt 4:25*).

5:21 the other side. Jesus and the disciples returned to the NW shore of the Sea of Galilee.

5:22 One of the synagogue officials. These officials presided over the elders of local synagogues. Those elder groups, made up of lay officials, were in charge of arranging the services and overseeing other synagogue affairs.

5:25 hemorrhage. Denotes a chronic internal bleeding, perhaps from a tumor or other disease (*see note on Mt 9:20*).

5:26 endured much ... many physicians. In NT times, it was common practice in difficult medical cases for people to consult many different doctors and receive a variety of treatments. The supposed cures were often conflicting, abusive, and many times made the ailment worse, not better. Luke, the physician, in Lk 8:43 suggested the woman was not helped because her condition was incurable.

5:28 If I just touch His garments. The woman's faith in Jesus' healing powers was so great that she believed even indirect contact with Him through His garments (*see note on Mt 9:20*) would be enough to produce a cure.

5:29 flow of her blood. The source of her bleeding, with the analogy being to the origin of a spring.

5:30 power *proceeding* from Him had gone forth. Christ's "power," His inherent ability to minister and work supernaturally, proceeded from Him under the conscious control of His sovereign will. **Who touched My garments?** Jesus asked this question, not out of ignorance, but so He might draw the woman out of the crowd and allow her to praise God for what had happened.

5:34 your faith has made you well. Jesus' public statement concerning the woman's faith (expressed in vv. 28, 33) and its results. The form of the Gr. verb translated "has made you well," which can also be rendered "has made you whole," indicates that her healing was complete. It is the same Gr. word often translated "to save" (*see note on Mt 9:22*) and is the normal NT word for saving from sin, which strongly suggests that the woman's faith also led to spiritual salvation.

5:36 only believe. The verb is a command for present, continuous action urging Jairus to maintain the faith he had initially demonstrated in coming to Jesus. Christ knew there was no other proper response to Jairus' helpless situation, and He was confident of faith's outcome (cf. Lk 8:50).

5:37 Peter and James and John. This is the first time Mark gives special status to these 3 disciples. Scripture never explains why these men were sometimes allowed to witness things that the other disciples were excluded from (cf. 9:2; 14:33), but the trio did constitute an inner circle within the 12. Even the Gr. grammar implies this inner grouping by placing their 3 names under one definite article.

5:38 weeping and wailing. In that culture, a sure sign that a death had occurred. Because burial followed soon after death, it was the people's only opportunity to mourn publicly. The wailing was especially loud and mostly from paid mourners (*see note on Mt 9:23*).

5:39 has not died, but is asleep. With this figurative expression, Jesus meant that the girl was not dead in the normal sense, because her condition was temporary and would be reversed (*see note on Mt 9:24*; cf. Jn 11:11–14; Ac 7:60; 13:36; 1Co 11:30; 15:6, 18, 20, 51; 1Th 4:13, 14).

5:40 laughing at Him. This could more literally be translated, "laughed Him to scorn," or "were laughing in His face." They understood Jesus' words literally and thought they were absurd, so "laughing" most likely refers to repeated bursts of laughter aimed at humiliating the Lord. This reaction, although shallow and irreverent, indicates the people were convinced of the irreversible nature of the girl's death and underscores the reality of the miracle Jesus was about to do. **putting them all out.** This was an emphatic, forceful expulsion which showed Christ's authority and was done because the disbelieving mourners had disqualified themselves from witnessing the girl's resurrection.

5:41 Talitha kum! Mark is the only gospel writer who recorded Jesus' original Aram. words. "Talitha" is a feminine form of "lamb," or "youth." "Kum" is an imperative meaning "arise." As in other such instances, Jesus addressed the person of the one being raised, not just the dead body (cf. Lk 7:14; Jn 11:43).

5:43 no one should know about this. Knowledge of the miracle could not be completely withheld, but Christ did not want news of it to spread until after He had left the area, because

strict orders that no one should know about this, and He said that *something* should be given her to eat.

TEACHING AT NAZARETH

6 [A]Jesus went out from there and *came into
[a,B]His hometown; and His disciples *followed
Him. 2 When the Sabbath came, He began [A]to teach
in the synagogue; and the [B]many listeners were
astonished, saying, "Where did this man *get* these
things, and what is *this* wisdom given to Him,
and such [a]miracles as these performed by His
hands? 3 Is not this [A]the carpenter, [B]the son of
Mary, and brother of [a]James and Joses and Judas
and Simon? Are not [C]His sisters here with us?" And
they took [D]offense at Him. 4 Jesus said to them,
"[A]A prophet is not without honor except in [a,B]his
hometown and among his *own* relatives and in
his *own* household." 5 And He could do no [a]mira-
cle there except that He [A]laid His hands on a few
sick people and healed them. 6 And He wondered
at their unbelief.

[A]And He was going around the villages teaching.

THE TWELVE SENT OUT

7 [A]And [B]He *summoned the twelve and began to
send them out [C]in pairs, and gave them authority over
the unclean spirits; 8 [A]and He instructed them that they
should take nothing for *their* journey, except a mere
staff—no bread, no [a]bag, no money in their belt— 9 but
[a]*to* wear sandals; and *He added,* "Do not put on two
[b]tunics." 10 And He said to them, "Wherever you enter
a house, stay there until you [a]leave town. 11 Any place
that does not receive you or listen to you, as you go out
from there, [A]shake the dust [a]off the soles of your feet
for a testimony against them." 12 [A]They went out and
[a]preached that *men* should repent. 13 And they were
casting out many demons and [A]were anointing with
oil many sick people and healing them.

6:1 [a]Or *His own part of the country* [A]Mark 6:1-6: *Matt 13:54-58* [B]Matt 13:54, 57; Luke 4:16, 23 6:2 [a]Or *works of power* [A]Matt 4:23; Mark 10:1 [B]Matt 7:28 6:3 [a]Or *Jacob* [A]Matt 13:55 [B]Matt 12:46 [C]Matt 13:56 [D]Matt 11:6 6:4 [a]Or *his own part of the country* [A]Matt 13:57; John 4:44 [B]Mark 6:1 6:5 [a]Or *work of power* [A]Mark 5:23 6:6 [A]Matt 9:35; Mark 1:39; 10:1; Luke 13:22 6:7 [A]Mark 6:7-11: *Matt 10:1, 9-14; Luke 9:1, 3-5;* Luke 10:4-11 [B]Matt 10:1, 5; Mark 3:13; Luke 9:1 [C]Luke 10:1 6:8 [a]Or *knapsack* or *beggar's bag* [A]Matt 10:10 6:9 [a]Lit *being shod with* [b]Or *inner garments* 6:10 [a]Lit *go out from there* 6:11 [a]Lit *under your feet* [A]Matt 10:14; Acts 13:51 6:12 [a]Or *proclaimed as a herald* [A]Matt 11:1; Luke 9:6 6:13 [A]James 5:14

He knew such news might cause His many Jewish opponents in Galilee to seek Him out and kill Him prematurely. He also wanted to be known for bringing the gospel, not as simply a miracle-worker. Jesus was no doubt concerned that the girl and her parents not be made the center of undue curiosity and sensationalism.

6:1 His hometown. Nazareth, Jesus' hometown (*see note on Mt 2:23*). **His disciples.** This was not a private, family visit for Jesus, but a time for ministry.

6:2 Sabbath. *See note on 2:23.* This implies that no public teaching was done until the Sabbath. **teach in the synagogue.** *See note on 1:21.* **astonished.** The same word as used in 1:22 (*see note there*); however, here the people's initial reaction gave way to skepticism and a critical attitude toward Jesus.

6:3 carpenter. The people of Nazareth still thought of Jesus as one who carried on His father's trade (cf. Mt 13:55) as a craftsman who worked in wood and other hard materials (e.g., stones, bricks). The common earthly position of Jesus and His family caused the townspeople to stumble—they refused to see Him as higher than themselves and found it impossible to accept Him as the Son of God and Messiah. **son of Mary.** Only here is Jesus called this. The normal Jewish practice was to identify a son by his father's (Joseph's) name. Perhaps that was not done here because Joseph was already dead, or because Christ's audience was recalling the rumors concerning Jesus' illegitimate birth (cf. Jn 8:41; 9:29)—a man was called the son of his mother if his father was unknown—and were purposely insulting Him with this title as a reference to illegitimacy. **brother of James and Joses and Judas and Simon.** *See note on Mt 12:46.* These were actual half-brothers of Jesus. "James" was later the leader in the Jerusalem church (cf. Ac 12:17; 15:13; 21:18; 1Co 15:7; Gal 1:19; 2:9, 12) and wrote the epistle of James. "Judas" (Heb. name "Judah") wrote the epistle of Jude. Nothing more is known of the other two. **His sisters.** Actual half-sisters whose names are never given in the NT. Nothing is known of them, not even if they became believers as the other family members did. **they took offense at Him.** The Eng. term "scandalize" comes from the Gr. verb translated "were offended," which essentially means "to stumble," or "become ensnared," and fall into a sin (*see note on 4:17*). The residents of Nazareth were deeply offended at Jesus' posturing Himself as some great teacher because of His ordinary background, His limited formal education, and His lack of an officially sanctioned religious position.

6:4 *See note on Mt 13:57.* Jesus called Himself a prophet, in accord with one of His roles (cf. v. 15; 8:28; Mt 21:11, 46; Lk 7:16; 24:19; Jn 6:14; 7:40; 9:17). ***own* household.** His own family (cf. Jn 7:5; Ac 1:14).

6:5 He could do no miracle there. Cf. Mt 13:58. This is not to suggest that His power was somehow diminished by their unbelief. It may suggest that because of their unbelief people were not coming to Him for healing or miracles the way they did in Capernaum and Jerusalem. Or, more importantly it may signify that Christ limited His ministry both as an act of mercy, so that the exposure to greater light would not result in a worse hardening that would only subject them to greater condemnation, and a judgment on their unbelief. He had the power to do more miracles, but not the will, because they rejected Him. Miracles belonged among those who were ready to believe.

6:6 He wondered at their unbelief. "Wondered" means Jesus was completely astonished and amazed at Nazareth's reaction to Him, His teaching, and His miracles. He was not surprised at the fact of the people's unbelief, but at how they could reject Him while claiming to know all about Him. Faith should have been the response in that town in Galilee, the region where Christ did so many miracles and so much teaching. **around the villages.** The outcome of Jesus' visit to Nazareth was that He left there and made a teaching tour of other places in Galilee, concluding near where He started (cf. Mt 9:35).

6:7 the twelve. *See notes on 3:16–19; Mt 10:2–4.* The 12 disciples were by then a divinely commissioned, recognized group. **send them out.** The form of this Gr. verb indicates that Jesus individually commissioned each pair to go out as His representatives. **in pairs.** This was a prudent practice (cf. Ecc 4:9–12) employed by Jewish alms collectors, by John the Baptist (Lk 7:19), by Jesus on other occasions (11:1; 14:13; Lk 10:1), and by the early church (Ac 13:2, 3; 15:39–41; 19:22). The practice gave the disciples mutual help and encouragement and met the legal requirement for an authentic testimony (Dt 19:15). **unclean spirits.** *See notes on 1:23; 5:2.*

6:8 staff. The walking stick, a universal companion of travelers in those days, which also provided potential protection from criminals and wild animals. **no bag.** They were not to carry the usual leather traveling bag or food sack.

6:9 *to* wear sandals. Ordinary footwear consisting of leather or wood soles bound on by straps around the ankle and instep. "Sandals" were necessary protection for the feet in view of the hot, rough terrain of Israel. **not put on two tunics.** "Tunics" were standard garments of clothing. Men of comparative wealth would wear two, but Jesus wanted the disciples to identify with common people and travel with just minimum clothing.

6:10 The disciples were to carefully select where they stayed (cf. Mt 10:11), but once there, the sole focus was to be on ministry. Contentment with their first host and his accommodations would be a testimony to others while the disciples ministered (cf. 1Ti 6:6).

6:11 shake the dust off. A symbolic act that signified complete renunciation of further fellowship with those who rejected them (*see note on Mt 10:14*). When the disciples made this gesture, it would show that the people had rejected Jesus and the gospel, and were hence rejected by the disciples and by the Lord.

6:12, 13 preached ... casting out many demons. Cf. v. 7. They were heralds of the gospel and had repeated success in expelling evil spirits from people. This demonstrated Christ's power over the supernatural world and confirmed His claim to being God.

6:12 repent. *See notes on 1:15; Mt 3:2.*

6:13 anointing with oil ... sick. In Jesus' day olive oil was often used medicinally (cf.

JOHN'S FATE RECALLED

14 [A]And King Herod heard *of it,* for His name had
become well known; and *people* were saying, "[B]John
the Baptist has risen from the dead, and that is why
these miraculous powers are at work in Him." 15 But
others were saying, "He is [A]Elijah." And others were
saying, "*He is* [B]a prophet, like one of the prophets *of
old.*" 16 But when Herod heard *of it,* he kept saying,
"John, whom I beheaded, has risen!"
17 For Herod himself had sent and had John arrested and bound in prison on account of [A]Hero-
dias, the wife of his brother Philip, because he had
married her. 18 For John had been saying to Herod,
"[A]It is not lawful for you to have your brother's
wife." 19 [A]Herodias had a grudge against him and
wanted to put him to death and could not *do so;*
20 for [A]Herod was afraid of John, knowing that he
was a righteous and holy man, and he kept him
safe. And when he heard him, he was very perplexed; [a]but he [b]used to enjoy listening to him. 21 A
strategic day came when Herod on his birthday
[A]gave a banquet for his lords and [a]military commanders and the leading men [B]of Galilee; 22 and
when the daughter of [A]Herodias herself came in
and danced, she pleased Herod and [a]his dinner
guests; and the king said to the girl, "Ask me for
whatever you want and I will give it to you." 23 And
he swore to her, "Whatever you ask of me, I will
give it to you; up to [A]half of my kingdom." 24 And
she went out and said to her mother, "What shall I
ask for?" And she said, "The head of John the Baptist." 25 Immediately she came in a hurry to the king
and asked, saying, "I want you to give me at once
the head of John the Baptist on a platter." 26 And
although the king was very sorry, *yet* because of
his oaths and because of [a]his dinner guests, he
was unwilling to refuse her. 27 Immediately the
king sent an executioner and commanded *him*
to bring *back* his head. And he went and had him
beheaded in the prison, 28 and brought his head
on a platter, and gave it to the girl; and the girl
gave it to her mother. 29 When his disciples heard
about this, they came and took away his body and
laid it in a tomb.
30 [A]The [B]apostles *gathered together with Jesus;
and they reported to Him all that they had done
and taught. 31 And He *said to them, "Come away
by yourselves to a secluded place and rest a while."
(For there were many *people* coming and going, and
[A]they did not even have time to eat.) 32 [A]They went
away in [B]the boat to a secluded place by themselves.

FIVE THOUSAND FED

33 *The people* saw them going, and many recognized *them* and ran there together on foot
from all the cities, and got there ahead of them.

6:14 [A]Mark 6:14-29: *Matt 14:1-12;* Mark 6:14-16: *Luke 9:7-9* [B]Matt 14:2; Luke 9:19 6:15 [A]Matt 16:14; Mark 8:28 [B]Matt 21:11 6:17 [A]Matt 14:3; Luke 3:19 6:18 [A]Matt 14:4 6:19 [A]Matt 14:3 6:20 [a]Lit *and* [b]Lit *was hearing him gladly* [A]Matt 21:26 6:21 [a]I.e. chiliarchs, in command of a thousand troops [A]Esth 1:3; 2:18 [B]Luke 3:1 6:22 [a]Lit *those who reclined at the table with him* [A]Matt 14:3 6:23 [A]Esth 5:3, 6; 7:2 6:26 [a]Lit *those reclining at the table* 6:30 [A]Luke 9:10 [B]Matt 10:2; Mark 3:14; Luke 6:13; 9:10; 17:5; 22:14; 24:10; Acts 1:2, 26 6:31 [A]Mark 3:20 6:32 [A]Mark 6:32-44: *Matt 14:13-21; Luke 9:10-17; John 6:5-13;* Mark 8:2-9 [B]Mark 3:9; 4:36; 6:45

Lk 10:34). But here it represented the power and presence of the Holy Spirit and was used symbolically in relation to supernatural healing (cf. Is 11:2; Zec 4:1–6; Mt 25:2–4; Rev 1:4, 12). As a well known healing agent, the oil was an appropriate, tangible medium the people could identify with as the disciples ministered to the sick among them.

6:14 **King Herod heard.** *See note on Mt 14:1.* The context indicates Herod heard some exciting news centering on Jesus and resulting from the disciples' recent preaching and miracle working in Galilee. **John the Baptist.** The forerunner of Christ (*see notes on 1:4–7; Mt 3:1, 4, 6*).

6:15 **He is Elijah.** This identification of Jesus, which probably had been discussed repeatedly among the Jews, was based on the Jewish expectation that the prophet Elijah would return prior to Messiah's coming (*see notes on Mal 4:5; Mt 11:14; Lk 1:17*). **a prophet . . . one of the prophets.** Some saw Jesus as the fulfillment of Dt 18:15, the messianic prophecy that looked to the One who, like Moses, would lead His people. Others were willing to identify Jesus only as a great prophet, or one who was resuming the suspended line of OT prophets. These and the other opinions, although misplaced, show that the people still thought Jesus was special or somehow supernatural.

6:16 **John . . . has risen!** By this excited, guilt-laden confession, Herod showed that he could not forget the evil he had done in beheading John the Baptist and that his conscience had led him to the eerie fear that John was back from the dead (cf. Mt 14:1, 2; Lk 9:7–9).

6:17 **John . . . bound in prison.** Herod kept him fettered while imprisoned, probably at Machaerus, near the NE shore of the Dead Sea. Herod's intention was to protect John from the plots of Herodias (cf. v. 20). **Herodias.** Herod's niece, the daughter of his half-brother Aristobulus. **Philip.** Herod Philip II, another half-brother to Herod Antipas (the Herod in this passage). Therefore, Philip was also an uncle to Herodias (*see note on Mt 14:3*).

6:18 **John had been saying . . . "It is not lawful."** The tense of the Gr. verb and Mark's wording imply that John had repeatedly rebuked Herod Antipas in private confrontation that his marriage to Herodias was contrary to Mosaic law (*see note on Mt 14:3*; cf. Mt 3:7–10).

6:20 **he was very perplexed.** This indicates that Herod's interaction with John left him in great internal conflict—a moral struggle between his lust for Herodias and the prodding of his guilty conscience.

6:21 **lords.** This term may also be translated "nobles," or "great ones." These were men who held high civil offices under Herod. **military commanders.** High-ranking military officials (Gr. *chiliarchs*) who each commanded 1,000 men. **leading men of Galilee.** The key social leaders of the region.

6:22 **daughter of Herodias.** Salome, her daughter by Philip (*see note on Mt 14:6*). **danced.** Refers to a solo dance with highly suggestive hand and body movements, comparable to a modern striptease. It was unusual and almost unprecedented that Salome would have performed in this way before Herod's guests (cf. Est 1:11, 12).

6:23 **up to half of my kingdom.** This was an exaggeration designed to enhance his previous statement of generosity. As a Roman tetrarch, Herod actually had no "kingdom" to give.

6:26 **because of his oaths.** Herod, as a monarch, felt bound because oaths were considered sacred and unbreakable (*see notes on Mt 5:34; 14:9*).

6:27 **executioner.** Originally meant spy or scout, but came to describe a staff member of a Roman tribune. They served as couriers and bodyguards as well as executioners. Herod had adopted the custom of surrounding himself with such men.

6:31 **by yourselves.** Jesus' invitation for a retreat into the desert was restricted to the 12. He knew they needed rest and privacy after their tiring ministry expedition and the continuing press of the people.

6:32 **went away in the boat . . . by themselves.** The disciples obeyed Jesus' proposal, departing from His headquarters in Capernaum using the same boat as in 5:2.

6:33 **ran there . . . on foot.** The direction (toward the NE shore of the lake) and speed of the boat, along with the immediate lack of other available boats, caused the crowd to follow by land. **got there ahead of them.** Contained only in Mark's account, this does not necessarily mean everyone arrived before the boat, because the land distance was probably 8 mi., twice as far as the 4 mi. the boat had to travel. Rather, those young and eager in the crowd were able to outrun both the rest and the boat (probably because it encountered no wind or a contrary wind) and actually arrive at the shore before the boat (cf. Mt 14:13, 14; Lk 9:11; Jn 6:3, 5).

34 When Jesus went [a]ashore, He [A]saw a large crowd,
and He felt compassion for them because [B]they
were like sheep without a shepherd; and He began
to teach them many things. 35 When it was already
quite late, His disciples came to Him and said, "[a]This
place is desolate and it is already quite late; 36 send
them away so that they may go into the surrounding countryside and villages and buy themselves
[a]something to eat." 37 But He answered them, "You
give them *something* to eat!" [A]And they *said to Him,
"Shall we go and spend two hundred [a,B]denarii on
bread and give them *something* to eat?" 38 And He
*said to them, "How many loaves do you have? Go
look!" And when they found out, they *said, "Five,
and two fish." 39 And He commanded them all to
[a]sit down by groups on the green grass. 40 They [a]sat
down in groups of hundreds and of fifties. 41 And He
took the five loaves and the two fish, and looking
up toward heaven, He [A]blessed *the food* and broke
the loaves and He kept giving *them* to the disciples
to set before them; and He divided up the two fish
among them all. 42 They all ate and were satisfied,
43 and they picked up twelve full [A]baskets of the
broken pieces, and also of the fish. 44 There were
[A]five thousand men who ate the loaves.

JESUS WALKS ON THE WATER

45 [A]Immediately Jesus made His disciples get into
[B]the boat and go ahead of *Him* to the other side to
[C]Bethsaida, while He Himself was sending the crowd
away. 46 After [A]bidding them farewell, He left [B]for
the mountain to pray.
47 When it was evening, the boat was in the middle of the sea, and He was alone on the land. 48 Seeing them [a]straining at the oars, for the wind was
against them, at about the [b,A]fourth watch of the
night He *came to them, walking on the sea; and
He intended to pass by them. 49 But when they saw
Him walking on the sea, they supposed that it was
a ghost, and cried out; 50 for they all saw Him and
were [a]terrified. But immediately He spoke with
them and *said to them, "[A]Take courage; it is I, [B]do
not be afraid." 51 Then He got into [A]the boat with
them, and the wind stopped; and they were utterly
astonished, 52 for [A]they [a]had not gained any insight
from the *incident of* the loaves, but [b]their heart
[B]was hardened.

HEALING AT GENNESARET

53 [A]When they had crossed over they came to land
at Gennesaret, and moored to the shore. 54 When
they got out of the boat, immediately *the people*
recognized Him, 55 and ran about that whole country
and began to carry here and there on their pallets
those who were sick, to [a]the place they heard He
was. 56 Wherever He entered villages, or cities, or
countryside, they were laying the sick in the market places, and imploring Him that they might just
[A]touch [B]the fringe of His cloak; and as many as
touched it were being cured.

6:34 [a]Lit *out* [A]Matt 9:36 [B]Num 27:17; 1 Kin 22:17; 2 Chr 18:16; Zech 10:2 6:35 [a]Lit *The* 6:36 [a]Lit *what they may eat* 6:37 [a]The denarius was equivalent to one day's wage [A]John 6:7 [B]Matt 18:28; Luke 7:41 6:39 [a]Lit *recline* 6:40 [a]Lit *reclined* 6:41 [A]Matt 14:19 6:43 [A]Matt 14:20 6:44 [A]Matt 14:21 6:45 [A]Mark 6:45-51: *Matt 14:22-32; John 6:15-21* [B]Mark 6:32 [C]Matt 11:21; Mark 8:22 6:46 [A]Acts 18:18, 21; 2 Cor 2:13 [B]Matt 14:23 6:48 [a]Lit *harassed in rowing* [b]I.e. 3-6 a.m. [A]Matt 24:43; Mark 13:35 6:50 [a]*Or troubled* [A]Matt 9:2 [B]Matt 14:27 6:51 [A]Mark 6:32 6:52 [a]Lit *had not understood on the basis of* [b]*Or their mind was closed, made dull, or insensible* [A]Mark 8:17ff [B]Rom 11:7 6:53 [A]Mark 6:53-56: *Matt 14:34-36; John 6:24, 25* 6:55 [a]Lit *where they were hearing that He was* 6:56 [A]Mark 3:10 [B]Matt 9:20; Num 15:37-40

6:34 felt compassion. *See note on Mt 9:36.* **sheep without a shepherd.** An OT picture (cf. Nu 27:17; 1Ki 22:17; 2Ch 18:16; Eze 34:5) used to describe the people as helpless and starving, lacking in spiritual guidance and protection, and exposed to the perils of sin and spiritual destruction.

6:37 two hundred denarii. A single denarius (*see note on Mt 22:19*) was equivalent to a day's pay for the day laborer (cf. Mt 20:2). "Two hundred" would therefore equal 8 months' wages and be quite beyond the disciples' (or any average person's) means.

6:38 loaves. Lit. "bread-cakes," or "rolls."

6:39 green grass. This detail indicates it was the spring rainy season, before the hot summer would have turned the grass dry and brown.

6:40 in groups of hundreds and of fifties. A symmetrical seating arrangement, possibly 50 semi-circles of 100 people each, with the semi-circles one behind the other in ranks. Such an arrangement was familiar to the Jews during their festivals, and it made food distribution more convenient.

6:41 looking up toward heaven. A typical prayer posture for Jesus (cf. 7:34; Lk 24:35; Jn 11:41; 17:1). Heaven was universally regarded as the Father's dwelling place (Mt 6:9).

6:42 all ate and were satisfied. The hunger of everyone in the crowd was completely satisfied (cf. Jn 6:11).

6:43 twelve full baskets. The "baskets," apparently the same ones used to bring the food, were small wicker containers like the ones the Jews used to carry food.

6:44 five thousand men. The Gr. word for "men" means strictly males, so the numerical estimate did not include women and children (cf. Mt 14:21). The women and children were traditionally seated separately from the men for meals. When everyone was added, there could have been at least 20,000.

6:45 the boat. *See note on v. 32.* **go ahead of *Him*.** The implication is that Jesus was to rejoin the disciples later. **Bethsaida.** A town on the N side of the Sea of Galilee and E of Capernaum (cf. Mt 11:21).

6:46 the mountain. The entire E side of the Sea of Galilee is mountainous with steep slopes leading up to a plateau. Up one of the slopes was a good place to pray, away from the crowd (cf. Jn 6:15).

6:47 middle of the sea. Normally in traveling across the northern end of the lake they would have been within one or two mi. of shore. But on that occasion, the wind had carried the boat several mi. S, closer to the center of the lake (cf. Mt 14:24).

6:48 fourth watch. 3:00 a.m. to 6:00 a.m. **walking on the sea.** The verb's tense depicts a steady progress, unhindered by the waves. **intended to pass by them.** The more literal rendering, "desired to come alongside of," indicates Jesus' intention here. He wanted to test the disciples' faith, so He deliberately changed course and came parallel to the boat to see if they would recognize Him and His supernatural powers and invite Him aboard.

6:49 a ghost. An apparition or imaginary creature. The Gr. term gives us the English "phantom." Because of the impossibility of such an act and their fatigue and fear in the stormy conditions, the 12, even though each one saw Him, did not at first believe the figure was actually Jesus.

6:50 Take courage. This command, always linked in the Gospels to a situation of fear and apprehension (cf. 10:49; Mt 9:2, 22; 14:27; Lk 8:48; Jn 16:33; Ac 23:11), urged the disciples to have a continuing attitude of courage. **it is I.** Lit. "I AM." This statement clearly identified the figure as the Lord Jesus, not some phantom. It also echoed the OT self-revelation of God (cf. Ex 3:14).

6:52 not gained any insight ... loaves. An explanation of the disciples' overwhelming astonishment at what had just happened. Because they misunderstood the real significance of that afternoon's miracle, they could not grasp Jesus' supernatural character as displayed in His power over the lake. **their heart was hardened.** Cf. 8:17. The disciples' minds were impenetrable, so that they could not perceive what Christ was saying (cf. 4:11, 12). This phrase conveys or alludes to rebellion, not just ignorance (*see note on 3:5*).

6:53 Gennesaret. *See note on Mt 14:34.*

6:56 market places. Open spaces, usually just inside city walls or near city centers, where people congregated for various

FOLLOWERS OF TRADITION

7 [A]The Pharisees and some of the scribes gathered around Him when they had come [B]from
Jerusalem, 2 and had seen that some of His disciples
were eating their bread with [A]impure hands, that
is, unwashed. 3 (For the Pharisees and all the Jews
do not eat unless they [a]carefully wash their hands,
thus observing the [A]traditions of the elders; 4 and
when they come from the market place, they do
not eat unless they [a]cleanse themselves; and there
are many other things which they have received
in order to observe, such as the [b]washing of [A]cups
and pitchers and copper pots.) 5 The Pharisees and
the scribes *asked Him, "Why do Your disciples
not walk according to the [A]tradition of the elders,
but eat their bread with [B]impure hands?" 6 And He
said to them, "Rightly did Isaiah prophesy of you
hypocrites, as it is written:

'[A]THIS PEOPLE HONORS ME WITH THEIR LIPS,
BUT THEIR HEART IS FAR AWAY FROM ME.
7 'BUT IN VAIN DO THEY WORSHIP ME,
TEACHING AS DOCTRINES THE
PRECEPTS OF MEN.'

8 Neglecting the commandment of God, you hold
to the [A]tradition of men."
9 He was also saying to them, "You are experts
at setting aside the commandment of God in order
to keep your [A]tradition. 10 For Moses said, '[A]HONOR
YOUR FATHER AND YOUR MOTHER'; and, '[B]HE WHO
SPEAKS EVIL OF FATHER OR MOTHER, IS TO [a]BE PUT
TO DEATH'; 11 but you say, 'If a man says to *his* father
or *his* mother, whatever I have that would help you
is [A]Corban (that is to say, [a]given *to God*),' 12 you no
longer permit him to do anything for *his* father or
his mother; 13 *thus* invalidating the word of God by
your [A]tradition which you have handed down; and
you do many things such as that."

THE HEART OF MAN

14 After He called the crowd to Him again, He *began* saying to them, "Listen to Me, all of you, and understand: 15 there is nothing outside the man which
can defile him if it goes into him; but the things
which proceed out of the man are what defile the
man. 16 [[a]If anyone has ears to hear, let him hear."]
17 When he had left the crowd *and* entered [A]the
house, [B]His disciples questioned Him about the parable. 18 And He *said to them, "Are you so lacking
in understanding also? Do you not understand that
whatever goes into the man from outside cannot
defile him, 19 because it does not go into his heart,
but into his stomach, and [a]is eliminated?" (*Thus He*
declared [A]all foods [B]clean.) 20 And He was saying,
"[A]That which proceeds out of the man, that is what
defiles the man. 21 For from within, out of the heart
of men, proceed the evil thoughts, [a]fornications,

7:1 [A]Mark 7:1-23: *Matt 15:1-20* [B]Matt 15:1 7:2 [A]Matt 15:2; Mark 7:5; Luke 11:38; Acts 10:14, 28; 11:8; Rom 14:14; Heb 10:29; Rev 21:27 7:3 [a]Lit *with the fist* [A]Mark 7:5, 8, 9, 13; Gal 1:14 7:4 [a]Or *sprinkle* [b]Lit *baptizing* [A]Matt 23:25 7:5 [A]Mark 7:3, 8, 9, 13; Gal 1:14 [B]Mark 7:2 7:6 [A]Is 29:13 7:7 [A]Is 29:13 7:8 [A]Mark 7:3, 5, 9, 13; Gal 1:14 7:9 [A]Mark 7:3, 5, 8, 13; Gal 1:14 7:10 [a]Lit *die the death* [A]Ex 20:12; Deut 5:16 [B]Ex 21:17; Lev 20:9 7:11 [a]Or *a gift*, i.e. *an offering* [A]Lev 1:2; Matt 27:6 7:13 [A]Mark 7:3, 5, 8, 9; Gal 1:14 7:16 [a]Early mss do not contain this verse 7:17 [A]Mark 2:1; 3:20; 9:28 [B]Matt 15:15 7:19 [a]Lit *goes out into the latrine* [A]Rom 14:1-12; Col 2:16 [B]Luke 11:41; Acts 10:15; 11:9 7:20 [A]Matt 15:18; Mark 7:23 7:21 [a]I.e. acts of sexual immorality

business and social purposes. Here the term might indicate its original meaning of any place where people generally assembled. The people brought the sick to such locations because Jesus was more likely to pass by. **fringe of His cloak.** *See note on 5:28.*

7:1 Pharisees ... come from Jerusalem. This delegation of leading representatives of Judaism came from Jerusalem probably at the request of the Galilean Pharisees. **scribes.** *See notes on 3:22; Mt 2:4.*

7:2 impure. The disciples of Jesus were being accused of eating with hands that had not been ceremonially cleansed, and thus had not been separated from the defilement associated with their having touched anything profane.

7:3 wash. This washing had nothing to do with cleaning dirty hands but with a ceremonial rinsing. The ceremony involved someone pouring water out of a jar onto another's hands, whose fingers must be pointing up. As long as the water dripped off at the wrist, the person could proceed to the next step. He then had water poured over both hands with the fingers pointing down. Then each hand was to be rubbed with the fist of the other hand. **traditions of the elders.** This body of extrabiblical laws and interpretations of Scripture had in actuality supplanted Scripture as the highest religious authority in Judaism (*see note on Mt 15:2*).

7:4 market place. *See note on 6:56.*

7:5 Why do Your disciples not ... ? The Pharisees and scribes went to the disciples' Master for an explanation of the disciples' allegedly disgraceful conduct. In reality they were accusing Jesus of teaching His disciples to disobey the traditions of the elders. **impure hands.** *See note on v. 3.*

7:6 did Isaiah prophesy. Isaiah 29:13 is quoted almost word for word from the Gr. translation of the OT (LXX). Isaiah's prophecy perfectly fit the actions of the Pharisees and scribes (*see note on Is 29:13*). **hypocrites.** Spiritual phonies (*see note on Mt 6:2*). They followed the traditions of men because such teaching required only mechanical and thoughtless conformity without a pure heart.

7:8 commandment of God ... tradition of men. Jesus first accused them of abandoning all the commandments contained in God's Word. Then He charged them with substituting God's standard with a humanly designed standard. *See note on Mt 15:2.*

7:10 Moses said. Quoted from Ex 20:12 (the fifth commandment) and Ex 21:17. Both refer specifically to the duty of honoring one's parents, which includes treating them with respect, love, reverence, dignity, and assisting them financially. The second quotation indicates how seriously God regards this obligation.

7:11 Corban. A Heb. term meaning "given to God." It refers to any gift or sacrifice of money or goods an individual vowed to dedicate specifically to God. As a result of such dedication, the money or goods could be used only for sacred purposes.

7:13 invalidating the word of God by your tradition. "Invalidating" means "to deprive of authority" or "to cancel." The "tradition" in question allowed any individual to call all his possessions "Corban" (*see note on v. 11*). If a son became angry with his parents, he could declare his money and property "Corban." Since Scripture teaches that any vow made to God could not be violated (Nu 30:2), his possessions could not be used for anything but service to God and not as a resource of financial assistance for his parents. But Jesus condemned this practice by showing that the Pharisees and scribes were guilty of canceling out God's Word (and His command to honor one's parents) through their tradition.

7:16 This verse does not occur in the best manuscripts.

7:18 defile him. *See note on v. 2.*

7:19 Since food is merely physical, no one who eats it will defile his heart or inner person, which is spiritual. Physical pollution, no matter how corrupt, cannot cause spiritual or moral pollution. Neither can external ceremonies and rituals cleanse a person spiritually. ***Thus He* declared all foods clean.** By overturning the tradition of handwashing, Jesus in effect removed the restrictions regarding dietary laws. This comment by Mark had the advantage of hindsight as he looked back on the event, and was no doubt influenced by Peter's (see Introduction: Author and Date) own experience in Joppa (*see note on Ac 10:15*).

7:20 That which proceeds out of the man. A person's defiled heart is expressed in both what he says and what he does (*see note on Mt 15:11*; cf. 12:34–37). **defiles.** *See note on v. 2.*

7:21 fornications. Lit. illicit sexual activity.

thefts, murders, adulteries, 22 deeds of coveting *and*
wickedness, *as well as* deceit, sensuality, [a,A]envy,
slander, [b]pride *and* foolishness. 23 All these evil
things proceed from within and defile the man."

THE SYROPHOENICIAN WOMAN

24 [A]Jesus got up and went away from there to
the region of [B]Tyre[a]. And when He had entered
a house, He wanted no one to know *of it;* [b]yet He
could not escape notice. 25 But after hearing of Him,
a woman whose little daughter had an unclean
spirit immediately came and fell at His feet. 26 Now
the woman was a [a]Gentile, of the Syrophoenician
race. And she kept asking Him to cast the demon
out of her daughter. 27 And He was saying to her,
"Let the children be satisfied first, for it is not [a]good
to take the children's bread and throw it to the
dogs." 28 But she answered and *said to Him, "Yes,
Lord, *but* even the dogs under the table feed on
the children's crumbs." 29 And He said to her, "Because of this [a]answer go; the demon has gone out
of your daughter." 30 And going back to her home,
she found the child [a]lying on the bed, the demon
having left.

31 [A]Again He went out from the region of [B]Tyre,
and came through Sidon to [C]the Sea of Galilee,
within the region of [D]Decapolis. 32 They *brought
to Him one who was deaf and spoke with difficulty,
and they *implored Him to [A]lay His hand on him.
33 [A]Jesus took him aside from the crowd, by himself, and put His fingers into his ears, and after
[A]spitting, He touched his tongue *with the saliva;*
34 and looking up to heaven with a deep [A]sigh, He
*said to him, "Ephphatha!" that is, "Be opened!"
35 And his ears were opened, and the [a]impediment
of his tongue [b]was removed, and he *began* speaking plainly. 36 And [A]He gave them orders not to tell
anyone; but the more He ordered them, the more
widely they [B]continued to proclaim it. 37 They were
utterly astonished, saying, "He has done all things
well; He makes even the deaf to hear and the mute
to speak."

FOUR THOUSAND FED

8 In those days, when there was again a large
crowd and they had nothing to eat, [A]Jesus called
His disciples and *said to them, 2 "[A]I feel compassion
for the [a]people because they have remained with Me
now three days and have nothing to eat. 3 If I send
them away hungry to their homes, they will faint
on the way; and some of them have come from a
great distance." 4 And His disciples answered Him,
"Where will anyone be able *to find enough* [a]bread
here in *this* desolate place to satisfy these people?"
5 And He was asking them, "How many loaves do
you have?" And they said, "Seven." 6 And He *directed the [a]people to [b]sit down on the ground; and
taking the seven loaves, He gave thanks and broke
them, and started giving them to His disciples to
[c]serve to them, and they served them to the [a]people.
7 They also had a few small fish; and [A]after He had
blessed them, He ordered these to be [a]served as well.
8 And they ate and were satisfied; and they picked
up seven large [A]baskets full of what was left over

7:22 [a]Lit *an evil eye* [b]Or *arrogance* [A]Matt 6:23; 20:15 7:24 [a]Two early mss add *and Sidon* [b]Lit *and* [A]Mark 7:24-30: *Matt 15:21-28* [B]Matt 11:21; Mark 7:31 7:26 [a]Lit *Greek* 7:27 [a]Or *proper* 7:29 [a]Lit *word* 7:30 [a]Lit *thrown* 7:31 [A]Mark 7:31-37: *Matt 15:29-31* [B]Matt 11:21; Mark 7:24 [C]Matt 4:18 [D]Matt 4:25; Mark 5:20 7:32 [A]Mark 5:23 7:33 [A]Mark 8:23 7:34 [A]Mark 8:12 7:35 [a]Or *bond* [b]Lit *was loosed* 7:36 [A]Matt 8:4 [B]Mark 1:45 8:1 [A]Mark 8:1-9: *Matt 15:32-39;* Mark 6:34-44 8:2 [a]Lit *crowd* [A]Matt 9:36; Mark 6:34 8:4 [a]Lit *loaves* 8:6 [a]Lit *crowd* [b]Lit *recline* [c]Lit *set before* 8:7 [a]Lit *set before them* [A]Matt 14:19 8:8 [A]Matt 15:37; Mark 8:20

7:22 sensuality. Lit. unrestrained, shameless behavior.

7:24 Tyre. *See note on 3:8.* **wanted no one to know.** Jesus did not seek a public ministry in the area. It is likely He wanted time to rest from the pressure of the Jewish leaders and an opportunity to further prepare the disciples for His coming crucifixion and their ministry.

7:25 unclean spirit. A demon (*see note on 1:23;* cf. Mt 15:22).

7:26 Gentile. A non-Jew in both her language and religion (*see note on Ro 1:14*). **Syrophoenician.** The region of Phoenicia at that time was part of the province of Syria. Matthew 15:22 adds that she was a descendant of the Canaanites.

7:27 first. The illustration Jesus gave was in essence a test of the woman's faith. Jesus' "first" responsibility was to preach the gospel to the children of Israel (cf. Ro 1:16; 15:8). But that also implied there would come a time when Gentiles would be the recipients of God's blessings. **the children's bread and throw it to the dogs.** "The children's bread" refers to God's blessings offered to the Jews. This picture indicates that the "dogs" (Gentiles) had a place in the household of God, but not the prominent one (*see note on Mt 15:26*). **dogs.** This reference is to dogs that were kept as pets. Jesus was referring to the Gentiles, but He did not use the derisive term the Jews usually employed for them that described mangy, vicious mongrels.

7:28 Yes, Lord. Indicative of the woman's humble faith and worshipful attitude. She knew she was sinful and undeserving of any of God's blessing. Her response was characterized by a complete absence of pride and self-reliance, which Jesus answered by granting her request (vv. 29, 30).

7:31 went out from the region of Tyre ... Sidon ... Sea of Galilee. Jesus traveled 20 mi. N from Tyre and passed through Sidon, which was deep into Gentile territory. From there He went E, crossed the Jordan, and traveled S along the eastern shore of the Sea of Galilee. **Decapolis.** *See note on 5:20.*

7:33 put His fingers into his ears. Because the man could not hear, Jesus used His own form of sign language to tell him that He was about to heal the man's deafness. **after spitting, He touched his tongue.** Also a form of sign language in which Jesus offered the man hope for a restored speech.

7:34 Ephphatha. An Aram. word that Mark immediately defines.

7:36 not to tell anyone. Although Jesus ministered to Gentiles as the need arose, His intention was not to have a public ministry among them. *See note on 1:44.*

8:1–9 While all 4 Gospels record the feeding of the 5,000, only Matthew (15:32–38) and Mark record the feeding of the 4,000.

8:1 a large crowd. Probably because of the widespread report of Jesus' healing of the deaf and mute man (7:36).

8:2 I feel compassion. Only here and in the parallel passage (Mt 15:32) did Jesus use this word of Himself. When He fed the 5,000, Jesus expressed "compassion" for the people's lost spiritual condition (6:34); here, He expressed "compassion" for people's physical needs (cf. Mt 6:8, 32). Jesus could empathize with their hunger, having experienced it Himself (Mt 4:2). **remained with Me now three days.** This reflects the crowd's eagerness to hear Jesus' teaching and experience His healings (cf. Mt 15:30). That they were with Him for that time before the miraculous feeding distinguishes this event from the earlier feeding of the 5,000, in which the crowd gathered, ate, and dispersed in one day (Mt 14:14, 15, 22, 23).

8:4 bread ... to satisfy these people. Some find the disciples' question incredible in light of the earlier feeding of the 5,000. But it was consistent with their spiritual dullness and lack of understanding (cf. vv. 14–21; 6:52). **in *this* desolate place.** The Decapolis (*see note on 5:20*) region was not as heavily populated as Galilee.

8:5 loaves. Flat cakes of bread which could easily be broken into smaller pieces.

8:8 seven large baskets. Not the same baskets mentioned in the feeding of the 5,000 (6:43). Those were small baskets, commonly used by the Jewish people to hold one or two meals when traveling. The word here refers to large baskets (large enough to hold a man, Ac 9:25) used by Gentiles. What was done with the leftover food is not mentioned. It

of the broken pieces. 9 About four thousand were
there; and He sent them away. 10 And immediately
He entered the boat with His disciples and came to
the district of [A]Dalmanutha.
11 [A]The Pharisees came out and began to argue
with Him, [B]seeking from Him a [a]sign from heaven,
[b]to test Him. 12 [A]Sighing deeply [a]in His spirit, He
*said, "Why does this generation seek for a [b]sign?
Truly I say to you, [c,B]no [b]sign will be given to this
generation." 13 Leaving them, He again embarked
and went away to the other side.
14 And they had forgotten to take bread, and
did not have more than one loaf in the boat with
them. 15 And He was giving orders to them, saying,
"[A]Watch out! Beware of the leaven of the Pharisees
and the leaven of [B]Herod." 16 They *began* to discuss
with one another *the fact* that they had no bread.
17 And Jesus, aware of this, *said to them, "Why
do you discuss *the fact* that you have no bread?
[A]Do you not yet see or understand? Do you have
a [a]hardened heart? 18 [A]HAVING EYES, DO YOU NOT
SEE? AND HAVING EARS, DO YOU NOT HEAR? And do
you not remember, 19 when I broke [A]the five loaves
for the five thousand, how many [B]baskets full of
broken pieces you picked up?" They *said to Him,
"Twelve." 20 "When *I broke* [A]the seven for the four
thousand, how many large [B]baskets full of broken
pieces did you pick up?" And they *said to Him,
"Seven." 21 And He was saying to them, "[A]Do you
not yet understand?"
22 And they *came to [A]Bethsaida. And they
*brought a blind man to Jesus and *implored Him to
[B]touch him. 23 Taking the blind man by the hand, He
[A]brought him out of the village; and after [A]spitting
on his eyes and [B]laying His hands on him, He asked
him, "Do you see anything?" 24 And he [a]looked up
and said, "I see men, for [b]I see *them* like trees, walking around." 25 Then again He laid His hands on his
eyes; and he looked intently and was restored, and
began to see everything clearly. 26 And He sent him
to his home, saying, "Do not even enter [A]the village."

PETER'S CONFESSION OF CHRIST

27 [A]Jesus went out, along with His disciples, to
the villages of [B]Caesarea Philippi; and on the way
He questioned His disciples, saying to them, "Who
do people say that I am?" 28 [A]They told Him, saying,
"John the Baptist; and others *say* Elijah; but others,
one of the prophets." 29 And He *continued* by questioning them, "But who do you say that I am?" [A]Peter
*answered and *said to Him, "You are [a]the Christ."
30 And [A]He [a]warned them to tell no one about Him.
31 [A]And He began to teach them that [B]the Son of
Man must suffer many things and be rejected by
the elders and the chief priests and the scribes,
and be killed, and after three days rise again.

8:10 [A]Matt 15:39 8:11 [a]Or *attesting miracle* [b]Lit *testing Him* [A]Mark 8:11-21: *Matt 16:1-12* [B]Matt 12:38 8:12 [a]Or *to Himself* [b]Or *attesting miracle* [c]Lit *if a sign shall be given* [A]Mark 7:34 [B]Matt 12:39 8:15 [A]Matt 16:6; Luke 12:1 [B]Matt 14:1; 22:16 8:17 [a]Or *dull, insensible* [A]Mark 6:52 8:18 [A]Jer 5:21; Ezek 12:2; Mark 4:12 8:19 [A]Mark 6:41-44 [B]Matt 14:20 8:20 [A]Mark 8:6-9 [B]Mark 8:8 8:21 [A]Mark 6:52 8:22 [A]Matt 11:21; Mark 6:45 [B]Mark 3:10 8:23 [A]Mark 7:33 [B]Mark 5:23 8:24 [a]Or *gained sight* [b]Or *they look to me* 8:26 [A]Mark 8:23 8:27 [A]Mark 8:27-29: *Matt 16:13-16; Luke 9:18-20* [B]Matt 16:13 8:28 [A]Mark 6:14; Luke 9:7, 8 8:29 [a]I.e. the Messiah [A]John 6:68, 69 8:30 [a]Or *strictly admonished* [A]Matt 8:4; 16:20; Luke 9:21 8:31 [A]Mark 8:31-9:1: *Matt 16:21-28; Luke 9:22-27* [B]Matt 16:21

was likely given back to the people to sustain them on their trip home, since the disciples evidently did not take it with them (cf. v. 14).

8:9 four thousand. The number of the men only, not including the women and children (Mt 15:38). This could indicate at least 16,000 people.

8:10 Dalmanutha. This location is not mentioned in any secular literature and only mentioned here in the NT. The location is unknown, but clearly in the region near Magdala (cf. Mt 15:39, Magadan). Recent archeological work in the area, when the water level of Galilee was at an all-time low, revealed several heretofore unknown anchorages. One small harbor has been found between Magdala and Capernaum which may be Dalmanutha.

8:11 Pharisees. *See notes on 2:16; Mt 3:7.* **sign from heaven.** The skeptical Pharisees demanded further miraculous proof of Jesus' messianic claims. Not content with the countless miracles He had performed on earth, they demanded some sort of astronomical miracle. Having already given them more than enough proof, Jesus refused to accommodate their spiritual blindness. The supreme sign verifying His claim to be Son of God and Messiah was to be His resurrection (Mt 12:39, 40).

8:13 the other side. To the NE shore, where Bethsaida (Julias) was located (v. 22).

8:15 leaven of the Pharisees and ... Herod. "Leaven" in the NT is an illustration of influence (*see note on Mt 13:33*) and most often symbolizes the evil influence of sin. The "leaven" of the Pharisees included both their false teaching (Mt 16:12) and their hypocritical behavior (Lk 12:1); the "leaven" of Herod Antipas was his immoral, corrupt conduct (cf. 6:17–29). The Pharisees and the Herodians were allied against Christ (3:6).

8:17 Why do you discuss ... no bread? Jesus' question rebuked the disciples for completely missing His point (*see note on v. 15*). He was concerned with spiritual truth, not mundane physical matters. **hardened heart.** I.e., they were rebellious, spiritually insensitive, and unable to understand spiritual truth (*see notes on 3:5; 6:52*).

8:18–21 Jesus' 5 questions further rebuked the disciples for their hardness of heart, and also reminded them of His ability to provide anything they might lack.

8:21 Do you not yet understand? An appeal based on the questions He had just asked. Matthew's parallel account reveals that the disciples finally understood His point (Mt 16:12).

8:22–26 The second of Jesus' two miracles recorded only in Mark (cf. 7:31–37). It is also the first of two healings of blind men recorded in Mark (cf. 10:46–52).

8:22 Bethsaida. *See note on 6:45, for the other Bethsaida.* This is Bethsaida-julias, several mi. N of the Sea of Galilee and E of the Jordan River.

8:23 spitting on his eyes. This action and Jesus' touching his eyes with His hands (v. 25) were apparently meant to reassure the blind man (who would naturally depend on his other senses, such as touch) that Jesus would heal his eyes (cf. 7:33; Jn 9:6).

8:26 Do not even enter the village. Jesus led the blind man out of town before healing him (v. 23), probably to avoid publicity and the mob scene that would otherwise result. Unlike others in the past (cf. 1:45; 7:36), he apparently obeyed.

8:27 Caesarea Philippi. A city about 25 mi. N of Bethsaida near Mt. Hermon, not to be confused with the Caesarea located on the Mediterranean coast about 60 mi. NW of Jerusalem.

8:28 Elijah. *See notes on 6:15; Mal 4:5; Mt 11:14; Lk 1:17.*

8:29 But who do you say that I am? After they reported the prevailing erroneous views about Jesus (v. 28), He asked the disciples to give their own evaluation of who He was. The answer every person gives to this question will determine his or her eternal destiny. **You are the Christ.** Peter unhesitatingly replied on behalf of the 12 (cf. Mt 14:28; 15:15; 17:4; 19:27; 26:33; Jn 6:68; 13:36), clearly and unequivocally affirming that they believed Jesus to be the Messiah.

8:30 tell no one. Jesus' messianic mission cannot be understood apart from the cross, which the disciples did not yet understand (cf. vv. 31–33; 9:30–32). For them to have proclaimed Jesus as Messiah at this point would have only furthered the misunderstanding that the Messiah was to be a political-military deliverer. The fallout was that the Jewish people, desperate to be rid of the yoke of Rome, would seek to make Jesus king by force (Jn 6:15; cf. 12:12–19).

8:31–10:52 In this section, as they traveled to Jerusalem, Jesus prepared the disciples for His death.

8:31 Son of Man. *See note on 2:10.* **must suffer many things.** Jesus' sufferings and death were inevitable because they were divinely ordained (Ac 2:22, 23; 4:27, 28), though, humanly speaking, caused by His rejection

32 And He was stating the matter [A]plainly. And Peter took Him aside and began to rebuke Him. 33 But
turning around and seeing His disciples, He rebuked
Peter and *said, "Get behind Me, [A]Satan; for you are
not setting your mind on [a]God's interests, but man's."
34 And He summoned the crowd with His disciples,
and said to them, "If anyone wishes to come after
Me, he must deny himself, and [A]take up his cross and
follow Me. 35 For [A]whoever wishes to save his [a]life will
lose it, but whoever loses his [a]life for My sake and the
gospel's will save it. 36 For what does it profit a man
to gain the whole world, and forfeit his soul? 37 For
what will a man give in exchange for his soul? 38 For
[A]whoever is ashamed of Me and My words in this
adulterous and sinful generation, [B]the Son of Man
will also be ashamed of him when He [C]comes in the
glory of His Father with the holy angels."

THE TRANSFIGURATION

9 And Jesus was saying to them, "[A]Truly I say to
you, there are some of those who are standing
here who will not taste death until they see the
kingdom of God after it has come with power."
2 [A]Six days later, Jesus *took with Him [B]Peter
and [a]James and John, and *brought them up on a
high mountain by themselves. And He was transfigured before them; 3 and [A]His garments became
radiant and exceedingly white, as no launderer on
earth can whiten them. 4 Elijah appeared to them
along with Moses; and they were talking with Jesus.
5 Peter *said to Jesus, "[A]Rabbi, it is good for us to
be here; [B]let us make three [a]tabernacles, one for
You, and one for Moses, and one for Elijah." 6 For
he did not know what to answer; for they became
terrified. 7 Then a cloud [a]formed, overshadowing
them, and [A]a voice [a]came out of the cloud, "[B]This is
My beloved Son, [b]listen to Him!" 8 All at once they
looked around and saw no one with them anymore,
except Jesus alone.
9 [A]As they were coming down from the mountain,
He [B]gave them orders not to relate to anyone what
they had seen, [a]until the Son of Man rose from the

8:32 [A]John 10:24; 11:14; 16:25, 29; 18:20 8:33 [a]Lit *the things of God* [A]Matt 4:10 8:34 [A]Matt 10:38; Luke 14:27 8:35 [a]Or *soul* [A]Matt 10:39; Luke 17:33; John 12:25 8:38 [A]Matt 10:33; Luke 9:26; Heb 11:16 [B]Matt 8:20 [C]Matt 16:27; Mark 13:26; Luke 9:26 9:1 [A]Matt 16:28; Mark 13:26; Luke 9:27 9:2 [a]Or *Jacob* [A]Mark 9:2-8: *Matt 17:1-8; Luke 9:28-36* [B]Mark 5:37 9:3 [A]Matt 28:3 9:5 [a]Or *sacred tents* [A]Matt 23:7 [B]Matt 17:4; Luke 9:33 9:7 [a]Or *occurred* [b]Or *give constant heed* [A]2 Pet 1:17f [B]Matt 3:17; Mark 1:11; Luke 3:22 9:9 [a]Lit *except when* [A]Mark 9:9-13: *Matt 17:9-13* [B]Matt 8:4; Mark 5:43; 7:36; 8:30

from the Jewish leaders. *See notes on Ps 118:22; Is 53:3*; cf. 12:10; Mt 21:42. **elders.** *See note on 7:3.* **chief priests.** Members of the Sanhedrin and representatives of the 24 orders of ordinary priests (cf. Lk 1:8). **scribes.** Experts in the OT law (*see note on Mt 2:4*). **after three days.** In keeping with the sign of Jonah (Mt 12:40). **rise again.** Jesus always mentioned His resurrection in connection with His death (cf. 9:31; 10:34; Mt 16:21; 17:23; 20:19; Lk 9:22; 18:33), making it all the more incomprehensible that the disciples were so slow to understand.

8:32 stating the matter plainly. I.e., not in parables or allusions (cf. Jn 16:29). **Peter ... began to rebuke Him.** The disciples still could not comprehend a dying Messiah (*see note on v. 30*). Peter, as usual (*see note on v. 29*) expressed the thoughts of the rest of the 12 (cf. v. 33). His brash outburst expressed not only presumption and misunderstanding, but also deep love for Jesus.

8:33 Get behind Me, Satan. In a startling turnaround, Peter, who had just been praised for being God's spokesman (Mt 16:17–19), was then condemned as Satan's mouthpiece. Yet Jesus' sacrificial death was God's plan (Ac 2:22, 23; 4:27, 28) and whoever opposed it was, wittingly or not, advocating Satan's work.

8:34 deny himself. No one who is unwilling to deny himself can legitimately claim to be a disciple of Jesus Christ. **take up his cross.** This reveals the extent of self-denial—to the point of death, if necessary. The extent of desperation on the part of the penitent sinner who is aware he can't save himself reaches the place where nothing is held back (cf. Mt 19:21, 22). **and follow Me.** *See notes on 1:17; Mt 10:38.*

8:35 loses his life ... will save it. This paradoxical saying reveals an important spiritual truth: those who pursue a life of ease, comfort, and acceptance by the world will not find eternal life. On the other hand, those who give up their lives (*see note on v. 34*) for the sake of Christ and the gospel will find it. Cf. Jn 12:25.

8:36, 37 soul. The real person, who will live forever in heaven or hell. To have all that the world has to offer yet not have Christ is to be eternally bankrupt; all the world's goods will not compensate for losing one's soul eternally. *See note on Mt 16:26.*

8:38 ashamed of Me and My words. Those who reject the demands of discipleship prove themselves to be ashamed of Jesus Christ and the truth He taught, thus not redeemed from sin at all. **Son of Man.** *See note on 2:10.* **when He comes.** Mark's first reference to Jesus' second coming, an event later described in detail in the Olivet Discourse (13:1–37).

9:1 Truly I say to you. A solemn statement appearing only in the Gospels and always spoken by Jesus. It introduces topics of utmost significance (*see note on 3:28*). **not taste death until they see the kingdom.** The event Jesus had in mind has been variously interpreted as His resurrection and ascension, the coming of the Spirit at Pentecost, the spread of Christianity, or the destruction of Jerusalem in A.D. 70. The most accurate interpretation, however, is to connect Christ's promise with the Transfiguration in the context (vv. 2–8), which provided a foretaste of His second coming glory. That all 3 synoptic Gospels place this promise immediately before the Transfiguration supports this view, as does the fact that "kingdom" can refer to royal splendor.

9:2 Six days later. Matthew and Mark place the Transfiguration "six days" after Jesus' promise (v. 1); Luke, no doubt including the day the promise was made and the day of the Transfiguration itself, describes the interval as "some eight days" (Lk 9:28). **Peter and James and John.** *See note on 5:37.* As the inner circle of Jesus' disciples, these 3 were sometimes allowed to witness events that the other disciples were not (cf. 14:33). **a high mountain.** Most likely Mt. Hermon (about 9,200 ft. above sea level), the highest mountain in the vicinity of Caesarea Philippi (cf. 8:27). **transfigured.** From a Gr. word meaning "to change in form," or "to be transformed." In some inexplicable way, Jesus manifested some of His divine glory to the 3 disciples (cf. 2Pe 1:16).

9:3 radiant and exceedingly white. The divine glory emanating from Jesus made even His clothing radiate brilliant white light. Light is often associated with God's visible presence (cf. Ps 104:2; Da 7:9; 1Ti 6:16; Rev 1:14; 21:23).

9:4 Elijah ... with Moses. Symbolic of the Prophets and the Law, the two great divisions of the OT. The order, "Elijah," then "Moses," is unique to Mark (who reverses the order in v. 5). **talking with Jesus.** The subject was His coming death (Lk 9:31).

9:5 Rabbi. Lit. "my master." A title of esteem and honor given by the Jews to respected teachers. In the NT, it is also used of John the Baptist (Jn 3:26). **let us make three tabernacles.** So as to make the 3 illustrious figures' stay permanent. It is also possible that Peter's suggestion reflected his belief that the millennial kingdom was about to be inaugurated (cf. Zec 14:16).

9:7 a cloud ... overshadowing them. This is the glory cloud, Shekinah, which throughout the OT was symbolic of God's presence (*see note on Rev 1:7*; cf. Ex 13:21; 33:18–23; 40:34, 35; Nu 9:15; 14:14; Dt 1:33). **a voice came out of the cloud.** The Father's voice from the cloud cut off Peter's fumbling words (Mt 17:5; Lk 9:34). **This is My beloved Son.** The Father repeated the affirmation of His love for the Son first given at Jesus' baptism (1:11). The parallel accounts of the Transfiguration (Mt 17:5; Lk 9:35) also record these words, as does Peter (2Pe 1:17). **listen to Him!** Jesus, the One to whom the Law and Prophets pointed (cf. Dt 18:15), is the One whom the disciples are to listen to and obey (cf. Heb 1:1, 2).

9:9 gave them orders not to relate to anyone. *See note on 8:30.* **until the Son of Man rose from the dead.** This looks to the time when the true nature of Jesus' messianic mission became evident to all—that He came to conquer sin and death, not the Romans. **Son of Man.** *See note on 2:10.*

dead. 10 They [a]seized upon [b]that statement, discussing with one another [c]what rising from the dead
meant. 11 They asked Him, saying, "*Why is it* that the
scribes say that [A]Elijah must come first?" 12 And He
said to them, "Elijah does first come and restore all
things. And *yet* how is it written of [A]the Son of Man
that [B]He will suffer many things and be treated with
contempt? 13 But I say to you that Elijah has [a]indeed
come, and they did to him whatever they wished,
just as it is written of him."

ALL THINGS POSSIBLE

14 [A]When they came *back* to the disciples, they
saw a large crowd around them, and *some* scribes
arguing with them. 15 Immediately, when the entire
crowd saw Him, they were [A]amazed and *began* running up to greet Him. 16 And He asked them, "What
are you discussing with them?" 17 And one of the
crowd answered Him, "Teacher, I brought You my
son, possessed with a spirit which makes him mute;
18 and [a]whenever it seizes him, it [b]slams him *to the*
ground and he foams *at the mouth,* and grinds his
teeth and [c]stiffens out. I told Your disciples to cast it
out, and they could not *do it.*" 19 And He *answered
them and *said, "O unbelieving generation, how
long shall I be with you? How long shall I put up
with you? Bring him to Me!" 20 They brought [a]the
boy to Him. When he saw Him, immediately the
spirit threw him into a convulsion, and falling to
the ground, he *began* rolling around and foaming *at the mouth.* 21 And He asked his father, "How
long has this been happening to him?" And he said,
"From childhood. 22 It has often thrown him both
into the fire and into the water to destroy him. But
if You can do anything, take pity on us and help us!"
23 And Jesus said to him, " 'If You can?' [A]All things
are possible to him who believes." 24 Immediately
the boy's father cried out and said, "I do believe;
help my unbelief." 25 When Jesus saw that [A]a crowd
was [a]rapidly gathering, He rebuked the unclean
spirit, saying to it, "You deaf and mute spirit, I [b]com-
mand you, come out of him and do not enter him
[c]again." 26 After crying out and throwing him into
terrible convulsions, it came out; and *the boy* became so much like a corpse that most *of them* said,
"He is dead!" 27 But Jesus took him by the hand and
raised him; and he got up. 28 When He came [A]into
the house, His disciples *began* questioning Him
privately, "Why could we not drive it out?" 29 And
He said to them, "This kind cannot come out by
anything but prayer."

DEATH AND RESURRECTION FORETOLD

30 [A]From there they went out and *began* to go
through Galilee, and He did not want anyone to

9:10 [a]Or *kept to themselves* [b]Lit *the statement* [c]Lit *what was the rising from the dead* 9:11 [A]Mal 4:5; Matt 11:14 9:12 [A]Mark 9:31 [B]Matt 16:21; 26:24 9:13 [a]Lit *also* 9:14 [A]Mark 9:14-28: *Matt 17:14-19; Luke 9:37-42* 9:15 [A]Mark 14:33; 16:5, 6 9:18 [a]Or *wherever* [b]Or *tears him* [c]Or *withers away* 9:20 [a]Lit *him* 9:23 [A]Matt 17:20; John 11:40 9:25 [a]Or *running together* [b]Or *I Myself command* [c]Or *from now on* [A]Mark 9:15 9:28 [A]Mark 2:1; 7:17 9:30 [A]Mark 9:30-32: *Matt 17:22, 23; Luke 9:43-45*

9:10 discussing ... what rising from the dead meant. Like most of the Jewish people (the Sadducees being notable exceptions), the disciples believed in a future resurrection (cf. Jn 11:24). What confused them was Jesus' implication that His own resurrection was imminent, and thus so was His death. The disciples' confusion provides further evidence that they still did not understand Jesus' messianic mission (*see notes on v. 9; 8:30*).

9:11 Elijah must come first. Cf. 8:28, 29. The scribes' teaching in this case was not based on rabbinical tradition, but on the OT (Mal 3:1; 4:5). Malachi's prediction was well known among the Jews of Jesus' day, and the disciples were no doubt trying to figure out how to harmonize it with the appearance of Elijah they had just witnessed. The scribes and Pharisees also no doubt argued that Jesus could not be the Messiah based on the fact that Elijah had not yet appeared. Confused, the 3 disciples asked Jesus for His interpretation.

9:12 Elijah does first come. Jesus affirmed the correctness of the scribal interpretation of Mal 3:1; 4:5, which must have puzzled the disciples even more. **Son of Man.** *See note on 2:10.* **suffer ... be treated with contempt.** Jesus pointed out that the prophecies about Elijah in no way precluded the suffering and death of Messiah, for that, too, was predicted in the OT (e.g., Pss 22; 69:20, 21; Is 53; *see note on Ro 1:2*).

9:13 Elijah has indeed come. Jesus directly addressed the disciples' question: the prophecies of Elijah's coming had been fulfilled in John the Baptist. Though certainly not a reincarnation of Elijah (cf. Jn 1:21), John came in the "spirit and power of Elijah," and would have fulfilled prophecies if they had believed (*see notes on Mt 11:14; Lk 1:17*). Because they did reject both John the Baptist and Jesus, there will be another who will come in the spirit and power of Elijah before the second coming of Christ (*see notes on Mt 11:14; Rev 11:5, 6*). **they did to him.** The Jewish leaders rejected John the Baptist (Mt 21:25; Lk 7:33), and Herod killed him (6:17–29). **as it is written of him.** No specific OT prophecies predicted that Messiah's forerunner would die. Therefore, this statement is best understood as having been fulfilled typically. The fate intended for Elijah (1Ki 19:1, 2) had befallen the Baptist. *See notes on Mt 11:11–14.*

9:14 the disciples. The 9 who had remained behind.

9:17 spirit which makes him mute. The boy had a demonically induced inability to speak, a detail found only in Mark's account.

9:18 they could not. The disciples' failure is surprising, in light of the power granted them by Jesus (3:15; 6:13).

9:19 O unbelieving generation. Cf. Ps 95:10. The word "generation" indicates that Jesus' exasperation was not merely with the father, or the 9 disciples, but also with the unbelieving scribes, who were no doubt gloating over the disciples' failure (cf. v. 14), and with unbelieving Israel in general.

9:22 to destroy him. This demon was an especially violent and dangerous one. Open fires and unfenced bodies of water were common in first-century Israel, providing ample opportunity for the demon's attempts to destroy the child. The father's statement added to the pathos of the situation. The boy himself was probably disfigured from burn scars, and possibly further ostracized because of them. His situation also created a hardship for his family, who would have had to watch the boy constantly to protect him from harm.

9:23 All things are possible. The issue was not His lack of power, but the father's lack of faith. Though Jesus often healed apart from the faith of those involved, here He chose to emphasize the power of faith (cf. Mt 17:20; Lk 17:6). Jesus healed multitudes, but many, if not most, did not believe in Him. Cf. Lk 17:15–19.

9:24 I do believe; help my unbelief. Admitting the imperfection of his faith, mixed as it was with doubt, the desperate father pleaded with Jesus to help him to have the greater faith the Lord demanded of him.

9:25 a crowd was rapidly gathering. Noting the growing crowd, Jesus acted without further delay, perhaps to spare the boy and his anguished father any further embarrassment. Also, the Lord did not perform miracles to satisfy thrill seekers (cf. 8:11; Lk 23:8, 9). **I command you.** Jesus' absolute authority over demons is well attested in the NT (e.g., 1:32–34; 5:1–13; Lk 4:33–35). His healings demonstrated His deity by power over the natural world. His authority over demons demonstrated His deity by power over the supernatural world.

9:29 This kind. Some demons are more powerful and obstinate, and thus more resistant to being cast out, than others (cf. Mt 12:45). *See notes on Da 10:10–21.* **anything but prayer.** Perhaps overconfident from their earlier successes (cf. 6:13), the disciples became enamored with their own gifts and neglected to draw on divine power.

9:30 go through Galilee. Leaving the region around Caesarea Philippi, Jesus and the disciples began the journey to Jerusalem that would result in His crucifixion several months

know *about it.* 31 For He was teaching His disciples
and telling them, "[A]The Son of Man is to be [a]deliv-
ered into the hands of men, and they will kill Him;
and when He has been killed, He will rise three
days later." 32 But [A]they [a]did not understand *this*
statement, and they were afraid to ask Him.
33 [A]They came to Capernaum; and when He [a]was
in [B]the house, He *began* to question them, "What
were you discussing on the way?" 34 But they kept
silent, for on the way [A]they had discussed with one
another which *of them was* the greatest. 35 Sitting
down, He called the twelve and *said to them, "[A]If
anyone wants to be first, [a]he shall be last of all and
servant of all." 36 Taking a child, He set him [a]before
them, and taking him in His arms, He said to them,
37 "[A]Whoever receives [a]one child like this in My name
receives Me; and whoever receives Me does not receive Me, but Him who sent Me."

DIRE WARNINGS

38 [A]John said to Him, "Teacher, we saw someone
casting out demons in Your name, and [B]we tried to
prevent him because he was not following us." 39 But
Jesus said, "Do not hinder him, for there is no one who
will perform a miracle in My name, and be able soon
afterward to speak evil of Me. 40 [A]For he who is not
against us is [a]for us. 41 For [A]whoever gives you a cup of
water to drink [a]because of your name as *followers* of
Christ, truly I say to you, he will not lose his reward.
42 "[A]Whoever causes one of these [a]little ones who
believe to stumble, it [b]would be better for him if,
with a heavy millstone hung around his neck, he
[c]had been cast into the sea. 43 [A]If your hand causes
you to stumble, cut it off; it is better for you to enter
life crippled, than, having your two hands, to go
into [a,B]hell, into the [C]unquenchable fire, 44 [[a]where
THEIR WORM DOES NOT DIE, AND THE FIRE IS NOT
QUENCHED.] 45 If your foot causes you to stumble, cut
it off; it is better for you to enter life lame, than, having your two feet, to be cast into [a,A]hell, 46 [[a]where
THEIR WORM DOES NOT DIE, AND THE FIRE IS NOT
QUENCHED.] 47 [A]If your eye causes you to stumble,
throw it out; it is better for you to enter the kingdom of God with one eye, than, having two eyes, to
be cast into [a,B]hell, 48 [A]where THEIR WORM DOES NOT
DIE, AND [B]THE FIRE IS NOT QUENCHED.
49 "For everyone will be salted with fire. 50 Salt is
good; but [A]if the salt becomes unsalty, with what will
you [a]make it salty *again?* [B]Have salt in yourselves,
and [C]be at peace with one another."

9:31 [a]Or *betrayed* [A]Matt 16:21; Mark 8:31; 9:12 9:32 [a]Lit *were not knowing* [A]Luke 2:50; 9:45; 18:34; John 12:16 9:33 [a]Lit *had come* [A]Mark 9:33-37: *Matt 18:1-5; Luke 9:46-48* [B]Mark 3:19 9:34 [A]Matt 18:4; Mark 9:50; Luke 22:24 9:35 [a]Or *let him be* [A]Matt 20:26; 23:11; Mark 10:43, 44; Luke 22:26 9:36 [a]Lit *in their midst* 9:37 [a]Lit *one of such children* [A]Matt 10:40; Luke 10:16; John 13:20 9:38 [A]Mark 9:38-40: *Luke 9:49, 50* [B]Num 11:27-29 9:40 [a]Or *on our side* [A]Matt 12:30; Luke 11:23 9:41 [a]Lit *in a name that you are Christ's* [A]Matt 10:42 9:42 [a]I.e. humble [b]Lit *is better for him if a millstone turned by a donkey is hung* [c]Lit *has been thrown* [A]Matt 18:6; Luke 17:2; 1 Cor 8:12 9:43 [a]Gr *Gehenna* [A]Matt 5:30; 18:8 [B]Matt 5:22 [C]Matt 3:12; 25:41 9:44 [a]Vv 44 and 46, which are identical to v 48, are not found in the early mss 9:45 [a]Gr *Gehenna* [A]Matt 5:22 9:46 [a]V. 44, see note [a] 9:47 [a]Gr *Gehenna* [A]Matt 5:29; 18:9 [B]Matt 5:22 9:48 [A]Is 66:24 [B]Matt 3:12; 25:41 9:50 [a]Lit *season it* [A]Matt 5:13; Luke 14:34f [B]Col 4:6 [C]Mark 9:34; Rom 12:18; 2 Cor 13:11; 1 Thess 5:13

later. Their immediate destination was Capernaum (v. 33). **did not want anyone to know.** Jesus continued to seek seclusion so He could prepare the disciples for His death (cf. 7:24).

9:31 Son of Man. *See note on 2:10.*

9:31, 32 Jesus continued His teaching about His upcoming death and resurrection—a subject the disciples still did not understand (*see notes on v. 10; 8:30–33*).

9:33 Capernaum. *See note on 1:21.* **the house.** The use of the definite article suggests this to be the house Jesus habitually stayed in when in Capernaum. Whether it was Peter's house (cf. 1:29) or someone else's is not known.

9:34 they kept silent. Convicted and embarrassed, the disciples were speechless. **which *of them was* the greatest.** A dispute possibly triggered by the privilege granted Peter, James, and John to witness the Transfiguration. The disciples' quarrel highlights their failure to apply Jesus' explicit teaching on humility (e.g., Mt 5:3), and the example of His own suffering and death (vv. 31, 32; 8:30–33). It also prompted them to ask Jesus to settle the issue, which He did—though not as they had expected.

9:35 Sitting down. Rabbis usually sat down to teach (cf. Mt 15:29; Lk 4:20; 5:3; Jn 8:2). **If anyone wants to be first.** As the disciples undeniably did (v. 34; cf. 10:35–37). **last of all and servant of all.** The disciples' concept of greatness and leadership, drawn from their culture, needed to be completely reversed. Not those who lord their position over others are great in God's kingdom, but those who humbly serve others (cf. 10:31, 43–45; Mt 19:30–20:16; 23:11, 12; Lk 13:30; 14:8–11; 18:14; 22:24–27).

9:36 a child. The Gr. word indicates an infant or toddler. If the house they were in was Peter's (*see note on v. 33*), this may have been one of his children. The child became in Jesus' masterful teaching an example of believers who have humbled themselves and become like trusting children.

9:37 Whoever receives one child like this in My name. Not actual children, but true believers—those who have humbled themselves like little children (*see note on v. 36*).

9:38 John said. The only recorded instance in the Synoptic Gospels in which he alone speaks. In light of Jesus' rebuke (vv. 35–37), John's conscience troubled him about an earlier incident he had been involved in. It is clear that the unnamed exorcist was not a fraud because he actually was casting out demons. He was apparently a true believer in Jesus; John and the others opposed him because he was not openly and officially allied with Jesus, as they were.

9:39, 40 Jesus ordered them not to hinder the exorcist, making the logical point that someone sincerely acting in His name would not soon turn against Him. There is no neutral ground regarding Jesus Christ; those who are "not against" Him are on His side, but by the same token, "He who is not with Me is against Me; and he who does not gather with Me scatters" (Mt 12:30).

9:41 your name as *followers* of Christ. Jesus considered acts of kindness done to His followers to have been done to Him (cf. Mt 25:37–40). **truly I say to you.** *See note on 3:28.* **his reward.** That is, his unique place and service in the eternal kingdom.

9:42 Whoever causes . . . to stumble. The word translated "to stumble" lit. means "to cause to fall." To entice, trap, or lead a believer into sin is a very serious matter. **little ones who believe.** *See note on v. 37.* **millstone.** This refers to a large, upper millstone so heavy that it had to be turned by a donkey (*see note on Mt 18:6*). Even such a horrifying death (a Gentile form of execution) is preferable to leading a Christian into sin.

9:43 cut it off. *See note on Mt 5:29.* Jesus' words are to be taken figuratively; no amount of self-mutilation can deal with sin, which is an issue of the heart. The Lord is emphasizing the seriousness of sin and the need to do whatever is necessary to deal with it. **life.** The contrast of "life" with "hell" indicates that Jesus was referring to eternal life. **hell.** The Gr. word refers to the Valley of Hinnom near Jerusalem, a garbage dump where fires constantly burned, furnishing a graphic symbol of eternal torment (*see note on Mt 5:22*). **the unquenchable fire.** *See note on Mt 25:46.* That the punishment of hell lasts for eternity is the unmistakable teaching of Scripture (cf. Da 12:2; Mt 25:41; 2Th 1:9; Rev 14:10, 11; 20:10).

9:44, 46 The better Gr. manuscripts omit these verses, which merely repeat the quote from Is 66:24 found in v. 48.

9:47 kingdom of God. *See note on 1:15.*

9:49 The meaning of this difficult verse seems to be that believers are purified through suffering and persecution. The link between salt and fire seems to lie in the OT sacrifices, which were accompanied by salt (Lv 2:13).

9:50 Salt is good. Salt was an essential item in first-century Palestine. In a hot climate, without refrigeration, salt was the practical means of preserving food. **Have salt in yourselves.** The work of the Word (Col 3:16) and the Spirit (Gal 5:22, 23) produce godly character, enabling a person to act as a preservative in society. Cf. Mt 5:13. **be at peace with one another.** Cf. Mt 5:9; Ro 12:18; 2Co 13:11; 1Th 5:13; Jas 3:18.

JESUS' TEACHING ABOUT DIVORCE

10 [A]Getting up, He *went from there to the region of Judea and beyond the Jordan; crowds
*gathered around Him again, and, [B]according to
His custom, He once more *began* to teach them.
2 *Some* Pharisees came up to Jesus, testing Him,
and *began* to question Him whether it was lawful
for a man to [a]divorce a wife. 3 And He answered
and said to them, "What did Moses command you?"
4 They said, "[A]Moses permitted *a man* TO WRITE A
CERTIFICATE OF DIVORCE AND [a]SEND *her* AWAY." 5 But
Jesus said to them, "[a,A]Because of your hardness of
heart he wrote you this commandment. 6 But [A]from
the beginning of creation, *God* [B]MADE THEM MALE
AND FEMALE. 7 [A]FOR THIS REASON A MAN SHALL LEAVE
HIS FATHER AND MOTHER[a], 8 [A]AND THE TWO SHALL
BECOME ONE FLESH; so they are no longer two, but
one flesh. 9 What therefore God has joined together,
let no man separate."
10 In the house the disciples *began* questioning Him about this again. 11 And He *said to them,
"[A]Whoever [a]divorces his wife and marries another
woman commits adultery against her; 12 and [A]if she
herself [a]divorces her husband and marries another
man, she is committing adultery."

JESUS BLESSES LITTLE CHILDREN

13 [A]And they were bringing children to Him so
that He might touch them; but the disciples rebuked them. 14 But when Jesus saw this, He was
indignant and said to them, "Permit the children
to come to Me; do not hinder them; [A]for the kingdom of God belongs to such as these. 15 Truly I say
to you, [A]whoever does not receive the kingdom of
God like a child will not enter it *at all*." 16 And He
[A]took them in His arms and *began* blessing them,
laying His hands on them.

THE RICH YOUNG RULER

17 [A]As He was setting out on a journey, a man ran
up to Him and [B]knelt before Him, and asked Him,
"Good Teacher, what shall I do to [C]inherit eternal

10:1 [A]Mark 10:1-12: *Matt 19:1-9* [B]Matt 4:23; 26:55; Mark 1:21; 2:13; 4:2; 6:2, 6, 34; 12:35; 14:49 10:2 [a]Or *send away* 10:4 [a]Or *divorce* her [A]Deut 24:1, 3; Matt 5:31 10:5 [a]Or *With reference to* [A]Matt 19:8 10:6 [A]Mark 13:19; 2 Pet 3:4 [B]Gen 1:27; 5:2 10:7 [a]Many late mss add *and shall cling to his wife* [A]Gen 2:24 10:8 [A]Gen 2:24 10:11 [a]Or *sends away* [A]Matt 5:32 10:12 [a]Or *sends away* [A]1 Cor 7:11, 13 10:13 [A]Mark 10:13-16: *Matt 19:13-15; Luke 18:15-17* 10:14 [A]Matt 5:3 10:15 [A]Matt 18:3; 19:14; Luke 18:17; 1 Cor 14:20; 1 Pet 2:2 10:16 [A]Mark 9:36 10:17 [A]Mark 10:17-31: *Matt 19:16-30; Luke 18:18-30* [B]Mark 1:40 [C]Matt 25:34; Luke 10:25; 18:18; Acts 20:32; Eph 1:18; 1 Pet 1:4

10:1 beyond the Jordan. This region was known as Perea. Jesus was to minister there until leaving for Jerusalem shortly before Passion Week (*see note on Mt 19:1*). **Jordan.** *See note on 1:5.*

10:2 Pharisees. *See note on 2:16.* **came … testing Him.** The Pharisees hoped to publicly discredit Jesus' ministry. The resulting loss of popularity, they hoped, would make it easier for them to destroy Him. Also, Perea (*see note on v. 1*) was ruled by Herod Antipas—who had imprisoned John the Baptist for his views on divorce and remarriage (6:17, 18). The Pharisees no doubt hoped a similar fate would befall Jesus. **whether it was lawful … to divorce.** The Pharisees attempted to entrap Jesus with a volatile issue in first-century Judaism: divorce. There were two schools of thought, one allowing divorce for virtually any reason, the other denying divorce except on grounds of adultery (*see note on Mt 19:3*). The Pharisees undoubtedly expected Jesus to take one side, in which case He would lose the support of the other faction.

10:3 What did Moses command you? Jesus set the proper ground rules for the discussion. The issue was not rabbinical interpretations, but the teaching of Scripture.

10:4 permitted. The Mosaic law, as the Pharisees were forced to concede, nowhere commanded divorce. The passage in question, Dt 24:1–4, recognized the reality of divorce and sought to protect the wife's rights and reputation and also regulated remarriage. **certificate of divorce.** In this document, the husband was required to state the reason for the divorce, thus protecting the wife's reputation (if she were, in fact, innocent of wrongdoing). It also served as her formal release from the marriage, and affirmed her right to remarry (assuming she was not guilty of immorality). The liberal wing of the Pharisees had misconstrued Dt 24 to be teaching that divorce was "permitted" for any cause whatsoever (citing as legitimate grounds such trivial events as the wife's ruining dinner or the husband's simply finding a more desirable woman), providing the proper legal paperwork was done. They thus magnified a detail, mentioned merely in passing, into the main emphasis of the passage.

10:5 your hardness of heart. *See notes on 3:5; 6:52.* This refers to the flagrant, unrepentant pursuit of sexual immorality—divorce was to be a last resort in dealing with such hard-heartedness. The Pharisees mistook God's gracious provision in permitting divorce (under certain circumstances) for His ordaining of it.

10:6 from the beginning. Divorce formed no part of God's original plan for marriage, which was that one man be married to one woman for life (Ge 2:24). **male and female.** Lit. "a male and a female," Adam and Eve. Mark quoted from Ge 1:27; 5:2.

10:7, 8 Jesus took the issue beyond mere rabbinical quibbling over the technicalities of divorce to God's design for marriage. The passage Christ quotes (Ge 2:24) presents 3 reasons for the inviolability of marriage: 1) God created only two humans (*see note on v. 6*), not a group of males and females who could configure as they pleased or switch partners as it suited them; 2) the word translated "become one" lit. means "to be joined" or "to glue," thus reflecting the strength of the marriage bond; 3) in God's eyes a married couple is "one flesh," forming an indivisible union, manifesting that oneness in a child.

10:9 What therefore God has joined together. Jesus added a fourth reason for the inviolability of marriage (*see note on vv. 7, 8*): God ordains marriages, and thus they are not to be broken by man.

10:11, 12 Remarriage after a divorce—except for legitimate biblical grounds—proliferates adultery. The innocent party—one whose spouse has committed prolonged, hard-hearted, unrepentant adultery—may remarry without being guilty of adultery, as may a believer whose unbelieving spouse has chosen to leave the marriage (*see note on 1Co 7:15*).

10:13 children. *See note on 9:36.* **that He might touch them.** I.e., lay His hands on them and pray for them (Mt 19:13). Jewish parents commonly sought the blessing of prominent rabbis for their children.

10:14 do not hinder them. Jesus rebuked the disciples for their attempt to prevent the children from seeing Him (v. 13). They were not the ones to decide who had access to Jesus (cf. Mt 15:23). **for the kingdom of God belongs to such as these.** Most, if not all, of these children would have been too young to exercise personal faith. Jesus' words imply that God graciously extends salvation to those too young or too mentally impaired to exercise faith (*see note on Mt 19:14*). **kingdom of God.** *See note on 1:15.*

10:15 Truly I say to you. *See note on 3:28.* **like a child.** With humble, trusting dependence, and the recognition of having achieved nothing of value or virtue.

10:16 blessing them. *See note on v. 13.*

10:17 a man. The other Synoptic Gospels reveal that he was young (Mt 19:20), and a "ruler," probably in the synagogue (Lk 18:18). He was also wealthy (v. 22). **what shall I do.** Steeped in the legalism of his day, the young man naturally thought in terms of some religious deed that would guarantee him eternal life. His lack of understanding about the true nature of salvation, however, does not mean he was insincere. **eternal life.** More than just eternal existence, it is a different quality of life. Eternal life is in Christ alone (*see notes on Jn 3:15, 16*; cf. Jn 10:28; 17:2, 3; Ro 6:23; 1Jn 5:11, 13, 20). Those who possess it have "passed out of death into life" (Jn 5:24; 1Jn 3:14; cf. Eph 2:1–3); they have died to sin and are alive to God (Ro 6:11); they have the very life of Christ in them (2Co 4:11; Gal 2:20); and enjoy a relationship with Jesus Christ that will never end (Jn 17:3).

life?" 18 And Jesus said to him, "Why do you call Me
good? No one is good except God alone. 19 You know
the commandments, '[A]DO NOT MURDER, DO NOT COM-
MIT ADULTERY, DO NOT STEAL, DO NOT BEAR FALSE
WITNESS, Do not defraud, HONOR YOUR FATHER AND
MOTHER.' " 20 And he said to Him, "Teacher, I have
kept [A]all these things from my youth up." 21 Looking
at him, Jesus felt a love for him and said to him, "One
thing you lack: go and sell all you possess and give
to the poor, and you will have [A]treasure in heaven;
and come, follow Me." 22 But at these words [a]he was
saddened, and he went away grieving, for he was
one who owned much property.
23 And Jesus, looking around, *said to His disciples, "[A]How hard it will be for those who are
wealthy to enter the kingdom of God!" 24 The
disciples [A]were amazed at His words. But Jesus
*answered again and *said to them, "Children,
how hard it is to enter the kingdom of God! 25 [A]It
is easier for a camel to go through the eye of a
needle than for a rich man to enter the kingdom
of God." 26 They were even more astonished and
said to Him, "[a]Then who can be saved?" 27 Looking
at them, Jesus *said, "[A]With people it is impossible, but not with God; for all things are possible
with God."
28 [A]Peter began to say to Him, "Behold, we have
left everything and followed You." 29 Jesus said,
"Truly I say to you, [A]there is no one who has left
house or brothers or sisters or mother or father or
children or farms, for My sake and for the gospel's
sake, 30 [a]but that he will receive a hundred times as
much now in [b]the present age, houses and brothers
and sisters and mothers and children and farms,
along with persecutions; and in [A]the age to come,
eternal life. 31 But [A]many *who are* first will be last,
and the last, first."

JESUS' SUFFERINGS FORETOLD

32 [A]They were on the road going up to Jerusalem,
and Jesus was walking on ahead of them; and they
[B]were amazed, and those who followed were fearful.
And again He took the twelve aside and began to tell
them what was going to happen to Him, 33 *saying,*

10:19 [A]Ex 20:12-16; Deut 5:16-20 10:20 [A]Matt 19:20 10:21 [A]Matt 6:20 10:22 [a]Or *he became gloomy* 10:23 [A]Matt 19:23 10:24 [A]Mark 1:27 10:25 [A]Matt 19:24 10:26 [a]Lit *And* 10:27 [A]Matt 19:26 10:28 [A]Matt 4:20-22 10:29 [A]Matt 6:33; 19:29; Luke 18:29f 10:30 [a]Lit *if not* [b]Lit *this time* [A]Matt 12:32 10:31 [A]Matt 19:30; 20:16; Luke 13:30 10:32 [A]Mark 10:32-34; *Matt 20:17-19; Luke 18:31-33* [B]Mark 1:27

10:18 Why do you call Me good? Jesus challenged the ruler to think through the implications of ascribing to Him the title "good." Since only God is intrinsically good, was he prepared to acknowledge Jesus' deity? By this query Jesus did not deny His deity; on the contrary, He affirmed it.

10:19 Quoted from Ex 20:12–16. **Do not defraud.** This was not the wording of any of the Ten Commandments, and is unique to Mark's account. It seems to be a paraphrase for the command against coveting.

10:20 I have kept all these things. His answer was no doubt sincere, but superficial and untrue. He, like Paul (Php 3:6), may have been blameless in terms of external actions, but not in terms of internal attitudes and motives (cf. Mt 5:21–48).

10:21 Jesus felt a love for him. I.e., felt great compassion for this sincere truth-seeker who was so hopelessly lost. God does love the unsaved (*see notes on Mt 5:43–48*). **sell all you possess.** Jesus was not making either philanthropy or poverty a requirement for salvation, but exposing the young man's heart. He was not blameless, as he maintained (v. 20), since he loved his possessions more than his neighbors (cf. Lv 19:18). More importantly, he refused to obey Christ's direct command, choosing to serve riches instead of God (Mt 6:24). The issue was to determine whether he would submit to the Lordship of Christ no matter what He asked of him. So, as he would not acknowledge his sin and repent, neither would he submit to the Sovereign Savior. Such unwillingness on both counts kept him from the eternal life he sought. **treasure in heaven.** Salvation and all its benefits, given by the Father who dwells there, both in this life and the life to come (cf. Mt 13:44–46).

10:22 went away grieving. It was purely a worldly disappointment based on the fact that he didn't receive the eternal life he sought because the price of sacrifice was too high. He loved his wealth (cf. 8:36, 37).

10:23 How hard … for those who are wealthy. *See note on v. 27.* "Hard" in this context means impossible (cf. v. 25). "Wealth" tends to breed self-sufficiency and a false sense of security, leading those who have it to imagine they do not need divine resources (see Lk 16:13; contra. Lk 19:2; cf. 1Ti 6:9, 17, 18).

10:24 amazed. *See note on v. 26.*

10:25 camel … eye of a needle. The Persians expressed impossibility by saying it would be easier to put an elephant through the eye of a needle. This was a Jewish colloquial adaptation of that expression denoting impossibility (the largest animal in the region was a camel). Many improbable interpretations have arisen that attempt to soften this phrase, e.g., that "needle" referred to a tiny gate in the Jerusalem city wall that camels could enter only with difficulty (but there is no evidence that such a gate ever existed, and if it had, any sensible camel driver would have simply found a larger gate); or that a copyist's error resulted in *kamelos* (camel) being substituted for *kamilos* (a large rope or cable) (but a large rope could no more go through the eye of a needle than a camel could, and it is extremely unlikely that the text of all 3 Synoptic Gospels would have been changed in exactly the same way). Jesus' use of this illustration was to explicitly say that salvation by human effort is impossible; it is wholly by God's grace. The Jews believed that with alms a man purchased salvation (as recorded in the Talmud), so the more wealth one had, the more alms he could give, the more sacrifices and offerings he could offer, thus purchasing redemption. The disciples' question (v. 26) makes it clear that they understood what Jesus meant—that not even the rich could buy salvation. *See note on Mt 19:24.*

10:26 Then who can be saved? Jesus' teaching ran counter to the prevailing rabbinical teaching, which gave the wealthy a clear advantage for salvation. Jesus' emphatic teaching that even the rich could not be saved by their own efforts left the bewildered disciples wondering what chance the poor stood. *See notes on Ro 3:9–20; Gal 3:10–13; Php 3:4–9.*

10:27 With people it is impossible, but not with God. It is impossible for anyone to be saved by his own efforts (*see note on v. 25*) since salvation is entirely a gracious, sovereign work of God. *See notes on Ro 3:21–28; 8:28–30; Gal 3:6–9; 26–29.*

10:28 we have left everything. Peter noted that the 12 had done what the Lord had asked the rich young ruler to do (cf. v. 21) and had come to Him on His terms. Would that self-abandoning faith, Peter asked, qualify them for a place in the kingdom?

10:29 Truly I say to you. *See note on 3:28.*

10:30 in the present age … the age to come. Following Jesus brings rewards in this present age and when Messiah's glorious kingdom comes. **with persecutions.** Great trials often accompany great blessings (*see notes on Ro 8:17; Php 1:29; 2Ti 3:12*). **eternal life.** *See note on v. 17.*

10:31 Believers will share equally in the blessings of heaven—a truth illustrated by the parable of Mt 19:30–20:16 (*see notes there*).

10:32 going up to Jerusalem. From Perea (*see note on v. 1*), via Jericho (v. 46). This is the first mention of Jerusalem as Jesus' destination. Because of the elevation of Jerusalem (about 2,550 ft. above sea level), travelers always spoke of going up to the city, regardless of where in Israel they started. **amazed.** At Jesus' resolute determination to go to Jerusalem (cf. Lk 9:51) despite the cruel death that awaited Him there (cf. vv. 32–34). **those who followed.** The Gr. syntax makes it clear that this was a group distinct from the 12, probably pilgrims en route to Jerusalem for Passover. They were afraid because they realized something significant was about to happen that they did not understand. **the twelve.** *See note on 3:14.*

10:32–34 The third and last prediction of His death and resurrection that Jesus made to the 12 is given (cf. 8:31; 9:31). This is also the most detailed of the 3 predictions, specifically mentioning that He would be mocked (15:17–20; Lk 23:11, 35–39), scourged (15:15), and spat upon (14:65; 15:19).

"Behold, we are going up to Jerusalem, and [A]the Son
of Man will be [a]delivered to the chief priests and
the scribes; and they will condemn Him to death
and will [b]hand Him over to the Gentiles. 34 They will
mock Him and [A]spit on Him, and scourge Him and
kill *Him,* and three days later He will rise again."
35 [a,A]James and John, the two sons of Zebedee,
*came up to Jesus, saying, "Teacher, we want You to
do for us whatever we ask of You." 36 And He said to
them, "What do you want Me to do for you?" 37 They
said to Him, "[a]Grant that we [A]may sit, one on Your
right and one on *Your* left, in Your glory." 38 But
Jesus said to them, "You do not know what you are
asking. Are you able [A]to drink the cup that I drink,
or [B]to be baptized with the baptism with which I am
baptized?" 39 They said to Him, "We are able." And
Jesus said to them, "The cup that I drink [A]you shall
drink; and you shall be baptized with the baptism
with which I am baptized. 40 But to sit on My right
or on *My* left, this is not Mine to give; [A]but it is for
those for whom it has been prepared."
41 [A]Hearing *this,* the ten began to feel indignant
with [a]James and John. 42 Calling them to Himself,
Jesus *said to them, "You know that those who are
recognized as rulers of the Gentiles lord it over
them; and their great men exercise authority over
them. 43 But it is not this way among you, [A]but
whoever wishes to become great among you shall
be your servant; 44 and whoever wishes to be first
among you shall be slave of all. 45 For even the Son
of Man [A]did not come to be served, but to serve, and
to give His [a]life a ransom for many."

BARTIMAEUS RECEIVES HIS SIGHT

46 [A]Then they *came to Jericho. And [B]as He was
leaving Jericho with His disciples and a large crowd,
a blind beggar *named* Bartimaeus, the son of Timaeus, was sitting by the road. 47 When he heard
that it was Jesus the [A]Nazarene, he began to cry out
and say, "Jesus, [B]Son of David, have mercy on me!"
48 Many were sternly telling him to be quiet, but he
kept crying out all the more, "[A]Son of David, have
mercy on me!" 49 And Jesus stopped and said, "Call
him *here.*" So they *called the blind man, saying to
him, "[A]Take courage, stand up! He is calling for you."
50 Throwing aside his cloak, he jumped up and came
to Jesus. 51 And answering him, Jesus said, "What
do you want Me to do for you?" And the blind man
said to Him, "[a,A]Rabboni, *I want* to regain my sight!"
52 And Jesus said to him, "Go; [A]your faith has [a]made
you well." Immediately he regained his sight and
began following Him on the road.

THE TRIUMPHAL ENTRY

11 [A]As they *approached Jerusalem, at Bethphage
and [B]Bethany, near [C]the Mount of Olives, He

10:33 [a]Or *betrayed* [b]Or *betray* [A]Mark 8:31; 9:12 10:34 [A]Matt 16:21; 26:67; 27:30; Mark 9:31; 14:65 10:35 [a]Or *Jacob* [A]Mark 10:35-45: *Matt 20:20-28* 10:37 [a]Lit *Give to us* [A]Matt 19:28 10:38 [A]Matt 20:22 [B]Luke 12:50 10:39 [A]Acts 12:2; Rev 1:9 10:40 [A]Matt 13:11 10:41 [a]Or *Jacob* [A]Mark 10:42-45; Luke 22:25-27 10:43 [A]Matt 20:26; 23:11; Mark 9:35; Luke 22:26 10:45 [a]Or *soul* [A]Matt 20:28 10:46 [A]Mark 10:46-52: *Matt 20:29-34; Luke 18:35-43* [B]Luke 18:35; 19:1 10:47 [A]Mark 1:24 [B]Matt 9:27 10:48 [A]Matt 9:27 10:49 [A]Matt 9:2 10:51 [a]I.e. My Master [A]Matt 23:7; John 20:16 10:52 [a]Lit *saved you* [A]Matt 9:22 11:1 [A]Mark 11:1-10: *Matt 21:1-9; Luke 19:29-38* [B]Matt 21:17 [C]Matt 21:1

10:35–45 This incident reveals yet again the disciples' failure to grasp Jesus' teaching on humility (*see notes on 9:34; Mt 20:21*). Ignoring the Lord's repeated instruction that He was going to Jerusalem to die (*see note on vv. 32–34*), the disciples still thought the physical manifestation of the kingdom was about to appear and were busy maneuvering for the places of prominence in it (cf. Mt 18:1).

10:35 James and John, the two sons of Zebedee. *See note on 1:19.* Matthew reveals that their mother accompanied them and spoke first (Mt 20:20, 21), after which James and John reiterated her request. If she was Jesus' aunt, the 3 undoubtedly hoped to capitalize on the family ties.

10:37 sit … on Your right … *Your* left. In the places of highest prominence and honor beside the throne. **in Your glory.** In the glorious majesty of His kingdom (cf. Mt 20:21).

10:38 the cup … the baptism. Endure suffering and death as Jesus would (cf. vv. 32–34; *see note on Mt 20:22*).

10:39 James and John would suffer like their Master (cf. Ac 12:2; Rev 1:9), but that in itself would not earn them the honors they desired.

10:40 not Mine to give. Honors in the kingdom are bestowed not on the basis of selfish ambition, but of divine sovereign will.

10:41 the ten began to feel indignant. Not righteous indignation, since they, too, had been guilty in the past of such self-serving conduct (9:33, 34) and would be so in the future (Lk 22:24). The rest of the disciples resented James and John for their attempt to gain an advantage over the others in pursuing the honor they all wanted.

10:42 lord it over them … exercise authority. These parallel phrases convey the sense of autocratic, domineering authority.

10:43 not this way among you. There is no place in the church for domineering leaders (cf. 9:35; Mt 23:8–12; 1Pe 5:3–6; 3Jn 9, 10).

10:45 Son of Man. *See note on 2:10.* **did not come to be served.** Jesus was the supreme example of servant leadership (cf. Jn 13:13–15). The King of kings and Lord of Lords (Rev 19:16) relinquished His privileges (Php 2:5–8) and gave His life as a selfless sacrifice in serving others. **ransom for many.** *See note on Mt 20:28.* "Ransom" refers to the price paid to free a slave or a prisoner; "for" means "in place of." Christ's substitutionary death on behalf of those who would put their faith in Him is the most glorious, blessed truth in all of Scripture (cf. Ro 8:1–3; 1Co 6:20; Gal 3:13; 4:5; Eph 1:7; Titus 2:14; 1Pe 1:18, 19). The ransom was not paid to Satan, as some erroneous theories of the atonement teach. Satan is presented in Scripture as a foe to be defeated, not a ruler to be placated. The ransom price was paid to God to satisfy His justice and holy wrath against sin. In paying it, Christ "bore our sins in His body on the cross" (1Pe 2:24). *See notes on 2Co 5:21.*

10:46–52 The second of two healings of blind men recorded in Mark (cf. 8:22–26).

10:46 Jericho. A city located about 15 mi. NE of Jerusalem and 5 mi. from the Jordan River. The route from Perea to Jerusalem passed through it. This is the only recorded visit of Jesus to Jericho. **as He was leaving.** Mark and Matthew state that the healing took place as Jesus was leaving Jericho, Luke as He was entering the city. Mark and Matthew may be referring to the ancient walled city, just N of the NT city, while Luke refers to NT Jericho. Or Luke's words may simply mean Jesus was in the vicinity of Jericho when the healing took place. *See note on Mt 20:30.* **blind beggar.** Matthew notes that there were two blind beggars, whereas Mark and Luke focus on the more vocal of them (cf. Mt 8:28 with 5:2; Lk 8:27). Since they were unable to work, blind people commonly made their living by begging (cf. Jn 9:8). These men had staked out a good site on the main road to Jerusalem. **son of Timaeus.** The translation of "Bartimaeus"; the Aram. prefix "bar" means "son of."

10:47 the Nazarene. *See note on 1:9.* **Son of David.** A common messianic title, used as such only in the synoptic gospels (*see note on Mt 1:1*).

10:49 Jesus … said, "Call him *here*." Thus implicitly rebuking those trying to silence him (v. 48).

10:51 Rabboni. An intensified form of "rabbi" (*see note on 9:5*).

10:52 your faith has made you well. Lit. "saved you." Bartimaeus' physical and spiritual eyes were likely opened at the same time. The outward healing reflected the inner wellness of salvation.

11:1–11 This passage, traditionally called Jesus' triumphal entry (more accurately, it was Jesus' coronation as the true King), was His last major public appearance before His crucifixion. The importance of this event is indicated by the fact that this is only the second time all 4 gospels include the same event (cf. Mt 21:1–11; Lk 19:29–44; Jn 12:12–19).

11:1 approached Jerusalem. A general transition statement marking the end of the

*sent two of His disciples, 2 and *said to them, "Go
into the village opposite you, and immediately as
you enter it, you will find a colt tied *there,* on which
no one yet has ever sat; untie it and bring it *here.* 3 If
anyone says to you, 'Why are you doing this?' you
say, 'The Lord has need of it'; and immediately he
[a]will send it back here." 4 They went away and found
a colt tied at the door, outside in the street; and they
*untied it. 5 Some of the bystanders were saying
to them, "What are you doing, untying the colt?"
6 They spoke to them just as Jesus had told *them,*
and they gave them permission. 7 [A]They *brought
the colt to Jesus and put their coats on it; and He
sat on it. 8 And many spread their coats in the road,
and others *spread* leafy branches which they had
cut from the fields. 9 Those who went in front and
those who followed were shouting:

"Hosanna!
[A]BLESSED IS HE WHO COMES IN
THE NAME OF THE LORD;
10 Blessed *is* the coming kingdom
of our father David;
Hosanna [A]in the highest!"

11:3 [a]Lit *sends* 11:7 [A]Mark 11:7-10: *Matt 21:4-9; Luke 19:35-38; John 12:12-15* 11:9 [A]Ps 118:26; Matt 21:9 11:10 [A]Matt 21:9

narrative in chap. 10. It also indicates the beginning of the final phase of Christ's 3-year ministry. **Bethphage.** A small town just E of Jerusalem whose name lit. means "house of unripe figs" (*see note on Mt 21:1*). **Bethany.** The hometown of Mary, Martha, and Lazarus (Jn 11:1) on the eastern slope of the Mt. of Olives, two mi. E of Jerusalem. **Mount of Olives.** This mountain stood between Bethany and Jerusalem (*see note on Mt 24:3*).

11:2 the village opposite you. Most likely Bethphage. "Opposite" implies that it was somewhat off the main road. **colt.** According to usage of this word in Gr. papyri (ordinary written documents dating from NT times that were made of papyrus reed), this was most likely a young donkey—a definition also in harmony with other Scripture usage (*see note on Mt 21:5*; cf. Ge 49:11; Jdg 10:4; 12:14; Zec 9:9). **no one yet has ever sat.** The Jews regarded animals that had never been ridden as especially suited for holy purposes (cf. Nu 19:2; Dt 21:3; 1Sa 6:7).

11:3 If anyone says to you. Because of its very nature, Jesus anticipated the disciples' action would be challenged (v. 5). **Lord.** Even though he does not use "Lord" with this meaning in the rest of his gospel, Mark was referring to Jesus. In Luke and John this appears often as a name for Jesus. People in the area knew Christ and the disciples well, so the owner would have understood the reference.

11:8 spread their coats. Such action was part of the ancient practice of welcoming a new king (*see note on Mt 21:8*). **branches.** Palm branches which symbolized joy and salvation and pictured future royal tribute to Christ (Rev 7:9). The crowd was greatly excited and filled with praise for the Messiah who taught with such authority, healed the sick, and raised the dead (Lazarus; cf. Jn 12:12–18).

11:9 Hosanna! Originally a Heb. prayer meaning "save now." On that occasion it probably served simply as an acclamation of welcome. Blessed is He who comes. *See note on Mt 21:9.* This phrase is part (Ps 118:26) of the Hallel (the Heb. word for "praise"), comprised of Pss 113–118, which was sung at all the Jewish religious festivals, most notably at the Passover. "He who comes" was not an OT messianic title, but definitely had come to carry such implications for the Jews (cf. Mt 11:3; Lk 7:19; Jn 3:31; 6:14; 11:27; Heb 10:37).

11:10 the coming kingdom of our father David. This tribute, recorded only by Mark, acknowledges Jesus as bringing in the messianic kingdom promised to David's Son. The crowd paraphrased the quote from Ps 118:26 (v. 9) in anticipation that Jesus was fulfilling prophecy by bringing in the kingdom.

EVENTS OF HOLY WEEK

The Gospel writers devoted much of their material to the events leading up to the crucifixion of Jesus. The final week of His earthly ministry began with the triumphal entry into Jerusalem and the "Hosannas" from the crowd that changed to cries of "Crucify Him" before the week was over. Jesus apparently spent most of the week teaching in the temple area during the day. His evenings were spent in the home of Mary, Martha, and Lazarus in Bethany. Significant events during this week included the plot of the Sanhedrin, Jesus' betrayal and arrest, the trials of Jesus, His journey to Golgotha down the Jerusalem street known today as the Via Dolorosa ("Way of Suffering"), and the Resurrection. After His resurrection, Jesus ministered another 40 days before His ascension.

Day	Event	Biblical Reference
Sunday	The triumphal entry into Jerusalem	Mark 11:1–11
Monday	Cleanses the temple in Jerusalem	Mark 11:15–19
Tuesday	The Sanhedrin challenges Jesus' authority Jesus foretells the destruction of Jerusalem and His return Mary anoints Jesus at Bethany Judas bargains with the Jewish rulers to betray Jesus	Luke 20:1–8 Matthew 24:25 John 12:2–8 Luke 22:3–6
Thursday	Jesus eats the Passover meal with His disciples and institutes the Memorial Supper Prays in Gethsemane for His disciples	John 13:1–30 Mark 14:22–26 John 17
Friday	His betrayal and arrest in the garden of Gethsemane Jesus questioned by Annas, the former high priest Condemned by the high priest and the Sanhedrin Peter denies Jesus three times Jesus is formally condemned by the Sanhedrin Judas commits suicide The trial of Jesus before Pilate Jesus' appearance before Herod Antipas Formally sentenced to death by Pilate Jesus is mocked and crucified between two thieves The veil of the temple is torn as Jesus dies His burial in the tomb of Joseph of Arimathea	Mark 14:43–50 John 18:12–24 Mark 14:53–65 John 18:15–27 Luke 22:66–71 Matthew 27:3–10 Luke 23:1–5 Luke 23:6–12 Luke 23:13–25 Mark 15:16–27 Matthew 27:51–56 John 19:31–42
Sunday	Jesus is raised from the dead	Luke 24:1–9

11 [A]Jesus entered Jerusalem *and came* into the
temple; and after looking around at everything,
[B]He left for Bethany with the twelve, since it was
already late.
12 [A]On the next day, when they had left Bethany,
He became hungry. 13 Seeing at a distance a fig tree
in leaf, He went *to see* if perhaps He would find
anything on it; and when He came to it, He found
nothing but leaves, for it was not the season for figs.
14 He said to it, "May no one ever eat fruit from you
again!" And His disciples were listening.

JESUS DRIVES MONEY CHANGERS FROM THE TEMPLE

15 [A]Then they *came to Jerusalem. And He entered
the temple and began to drive out those who were
buying and selling in the temple, and overturned
the tables of the money changers and the seats of
those who were selling [a]doves; 16 and He would not
permit anyone to carry [a]merchandise through the
temple. 17 And He *began* to teach and say to them,
"Is it not written, '[A]MY HOUSE SHALL BE CALLED A
HOUSE OF PRAYER FOR ALL THE NATIONS'? [B]But you
have made it a ROBBERS' [a]DEN." 18 The chief priests
and the scribes heard *this,* and [A]*began* seeking how
to destroy Him; for they were afraid of Him, for
[B]the whole crowd was astonished at His teaching.
19 [A]When evening came, [a]they would go out of
the city.
20 [A]As they were passing by in the morning, they
saw the fig tree withered from the roots *up.* 21 Being
reminded, Peter *said to Him, "[A]Rabbi, look, the fig
tree which You cursed has withered." 22 And Jesus *answered saying to them, "[A]Have faith in God. 23 [A]Truly
I say to you, whoever says to this mountain, 'Be taken
up and cast into the sea,' and does not doubt in his

11:11 [A]Matt 21:12 [B]Matt 21:17 11:12 [A]Mark 11:12-14, 20-24: *Matt 21:18-22* 11:15 [a]Lit *the doves* [A]Mark 11:15-18: *Matt 21:12-16; Luke 19:45-47;* John 2:13-16 11:16 [a]Lit *a vessel;* i.e. a receptacle or implement of any kind 11:17 [a]Lit *cave* [A]Is 56:7 [B]Jer 7:11 11:18 [A]Matt 21:46; Mark 12:12; Luke 20:19; John 7:1 [B]Matt 7:28 11:19 [a]I.e. Jesus and His disciples [A]Matt 21:17; Mark 11:11; Luke 21:37 11:20 [A]Mark 11:12-14, 20-24: *Matt 21:19-22* 11:21 [A]Matt 23:7 11:22 [A]Matt 17:20; 21:21f 11:23 [A]Matt 17:20; 1 Cor 13:2

11:11 temple. Not a reference limited to the inner, sacred sanctuary, but the entire area of courts and buildings. **looking around at everything.** A description distinctive to Mark, quite possibly based on one of Peter's eyewitness memories. Christ acted as one who had the authority to inspect temple conditions, and His observation missed nothing. **He left for Bethany.** Nearby "Bethany" was a relatively safe place to avoid sudden, premature arrest by the Jewish leaders.

11:12 the next day. Matthew 21:18 says this was "in the morning," probably before 6:00 a.m. **Bethany.** *See note on v. 1.*

11:13 fig tree in leaf. Fig trees were common as a source of food. Three years were required from planting until fruit bearing. After that, a tree could be harvested twice a year, usually yielding much fruit. The figs normally grew with the leaves. This tree had leaves but, strangely, no fruit. That this tree was along the side of the road (cf. Mt 21:19) implies it was public property. It was also apparently in good soil because its foliage was ahead of season and ahead of the surrounding fig trees. The abundance of leaves held out promise that the tree might also be ahead of schedule with its fruit. **not the season for figs.** The next normal fig season was in June, more than a month away. This phrase, unique to Mark, emphasizes the unusual nature of this fig tree.

11:14 May no one ever eat fruit from you again! Jesus' direct address to the tree personified it and condemned it for not providing what its appearance promised. This incident was not the acting out of the parable of the fig tree (Lk 13:6–9), which was a warning against spiritual fruitlessness. Here, Jesus cursed the tree for its misleading appearance that suggested great productivity without providing it. It should have been full of fruit, but was barren. The fig tree was frequently an OT type of the Jewish nation (Hos 9:10; Na 3:12; Zec 3:10), and in this instance Jesus used the tree by the road as a divine object lesson concerning Israel's spiritual hypocrisy and fruitlessness (*see note on Mt 21:19*; cf. Is 5:1–7).

11:15–19 *See note on Mt 21:12.* Although Jesus had cleansed the temple 3 years earlier (Jn 2:14–16), it had become more corrupt and profane than ever and thus He was compelled to again offer clear testimony to God's holiness and to His judgment against spiritual desecration and false religion. Even as God sent His prophets repeatedly throughout the OT to warn His people of their sin and idolatry, Christ never stopped declaring God's will to a rebellious people, no matter how often they rejected it. With this temple cleansing, Jesus showed vividly that He was on a divine mission as the Son of God.

11:15 temple. *See note on v. 11.* The large Court of the Gentiles was the setting for the events that followed. **buying and selling.** Animals were needed by the Jews for their sacrificial temple offerings, and it was more convenient for the worshipers to buy them there rather than bring the animals from a distance and risk that they would not pass the High Priest's inspection. The sellers either belonged to the High Priestly hierarchy or paid a large fee to temple authorities for the privilege of selling. Whichever was the case, the High Priest's family benefited monetarily. **money changers.** They were in the court to exchange Greek and Roman coins for Jewish or Tyrian coins which pilgrims (every Jewish male 20 and older) had to use for the annual half-shekel payment for temple religious services (*see note on Mt 21:12*). A fee as high as 10 or 12 percent was assessed for this exchange service. **those who were selling doves.** These birds were so often used for sacrifice that Mark makes separate mention of their sellers. Doves were the normal offering of the poor (Lv 5:7) and were also required for other purposes (Lv 12:6; 14:22; 15:14, 29).

11:16 not permit anyone to carry merchandise. Jesus did not want people to continue the practice of using the court as a shortcut through which to carry utensils and containers with merchandise to other parts of Jerusalem because such a practice revealed great irreverence for the temple—and ultimately for God Himself.

11:17 Jesus defended Himself by appealing to Scripture (*see note on Mt 21:13*) after His actions had caused a crowd to gather. **a house of prayer for all the nations.** The true purpose for God's temple. Only Mark includes "for all the nations" from Isaiah's text (56:7), probably because he was mainly addressing Gentiles. The Court of the Gentiles was the only part of the temple they were permitted to use for prayer and worship of God, and the Jews had frustrated that worship by turning it into a place of greedy business. **a robbers' den.** Using Jeremiah's phrase (Jer 7:11), Jesus described the religious leaders as robbers who found refuge in the temple, comparable to how highwaymen took refuge in caves with other robbers. The temple had become a place where God's people, instead of being able to worship undisturbed, were extorted and their extortioners were protected.

11:18 chief priests and the scribes. Here Mark uses this combination for the first time. These men were among those who comprised the principal leadership in the Sanhedrin (*see notes on Mt 2:4; 26:59*). **seeking how to destroy Him.** *See note on 3:6.* The leaders had continuing discussions on how to kill Jesus. **astonished at His teaching.** *See note on 1:22.*

11:19 go out of the city. Jesus' practice during the first 3 days of Passion Week was not to leave Jerusalem until sunset, when the crowds dispersed and the city gates were about to be closed.

11:20 in the morning. *See note on v. 12.* **withered from the roots *up.*** The tree blight that prevented fruit (v. 14) had spread upward through the tree and killed it. Matthew described the event in a more compact fashion, but his account still allows the same time frame as Mark's (*see note on Mt 21:19*).

11:21 Rabbi. *See note on 9:5.*

11:22 Have faith in God. A gentle rebuke for the disciples' lack of faith in the power of His word. Such faith believes in God's revealed truth, His power, and seeks to do His will (cf. 1Jn 5:14; *see note on Mt 21:21*).

11:23 this mountain ... into the sea. This expression was related to a common metaphor of that day, "rooter up of mountains," which was used in Jewish literature of great rabbis and spiritual leaders who could solve difficult problems and seemingly do the impossible. Obviously, Jesus did not literally uproot mountains; in fact, He refused to do such spectacular miracles for the unbelieving Jewish leaders (*see note on Mt 12:38*). Jesus' point is that if believers sincerely trust in God and truly realize the

heart, but believes that what he says is going to happen, it will be *granted* him. 24 Therefore I say to you,
[A]all things for which you pray and ask, believe that
you have received them, and they will be *granted* you.
25 Whenever you [A]stand praying, [B]forgive, if you have
anything against anyone, so that your Father who is
in heaven will also forgive you your transgressions.
26 [[a,A]But if you do not forgive, neither will your Father who is in heaven forgive your transgressions."]

JESUS' AUTHORITY QUESTIONED

27 They *came again to Jerusalem. [A]And as He
was walking in the temple, the chief priests and the
scribes and the elders *came to Him, 28 and *began*
saying to Him, "By what authority are You doing
these things, or who gave You this authority to do
these things?" 29 And Jesus said to them, "I will ask
you one question, and you answer Me, and *then* I
will tell you by what authority I do these things.
30 Was the baptism of John from heaven, or from
men? Answer Me." 31 They *began* reasoning among
themselves, saying, "If we say, 'From heaven,' He
will say, 'Then why did you not believe him?' 32 But
[a]shall we say, 'From men'?"—they were afraid of the
people, for everyone considered John to have been
a real prophet. 33 Answering Jesus, they *said, "We
do not know." And Jesus *said to them, "Nor [a]will I
tell you by what authority I do these things."

PARABLE OF THE VINE-GROWERS

12 [A]And He began to speak to them in parables: "[B]A man [C]PLANTED A VINEYARD AND
PUT A [a]WALL AROUND IT, AND DUG A VAT UNDER THE
WINE PRESS AND BUILT A TOWER, and rented it out
to [b]vine-growers and went on a journey. 2 At the
harvest time he sent a slave to the vine-growers, in
order to receive *some* of the produce of the vineyard
from the vine-growers. 3 They took him, and beat
him and sent him away empty-handed. 4 Again he
sent them another slave, and they wounded him in
the head, and treated him shamefully. 5 And he sent
another, and that one they killed; and *so with* many
others, beating some and killing others. 6 He had
one more *to send,* a beloved son; he sent him last *of
all* to them, saying, 'They will respect my son.' 7 But
those vine-growers said to one another, 'This is the
heir; come, let us kill him, and the inheritance will
be ours!' 8 They took him, and killed him and threw
him out of the vineyard. 9 What will the [a]owner
of the vineyard do? He will come and destroy the

11:24 [A]Matt 7:7f 11:25 [A]Matt 6:5 [B]Matt 6:14 11:26 [a]Early mss do not contain this v [A]Matt 6:15; 18:35 11:27 [A]Mark 11:27-33: *Matt 21:23-27; Luke 20:1-8* 11:32 [a]Or *if we say* 11:33 [a]Lit *do I tell* 12:1 [a]Or *fence* [b]Or *tenant farmers,* also vv 2, 7, 9 [A]Mark 3:23; 4:2ff [B]Mark 12:1-12: *Matt 21:33-46; Luke 20:9-19* [C]Is 5:1, 2 12:9 [a]Lit *lord*

unlimited power that is available through such faith in Him, they will see His mighty powers at work (cf. Jn 14:13, 14; *see note on Mt 21:21*).

11:24 all things for which you pray. This places no limits on a believer's prayers, as long as they are according to God's will and purpose (*see note on Mt 17:20*). This therefore means that man's faith and prayer are not inconsistent with God's sovereignty. And it is not the believer's responsibility to figure out how that can be true, but simply to be faithful and obedient to the clear teaching on prayer, as Jesus gives it in this passage. God's will is being unfolded through all of redemptive history, by means of the prayers of His people—as His saving purpose is coming to pass through the faith of those who hear the gospel and repent. Cf. Jas 5:16.

11:25 stand praying. The traditional Jewish prayer posture (cf. 1Sa 1:26; 1Ki 8:14, 22; Ne 9:4; Mt 6:5; Lk 18:11, 13). Kneeling or lying with one's face on the ground was used during extraordinary circumstances or for extremely urgent requests (cf. 1Ki 8:54; Ezr 9:5; Da 6:10; Mt 26:39; Ac 7:60). **anything against anyone.** An all-inclusive statement that includes both sins and simple dislikes, which cause the believer to hold something against another person. "Anyone" incorporates believers and unbelievers. **forgive.** Jesus states the believer's ongoing duty to have a forgiving attitude. Successful prayer requires forgiveness as well as faith. *See notes on Eph 4:32.*

11:26 *See notes on Mt 6:15; 18:21–34.* This is the only occurrence in Mark of "transgressions," a term that denotes a falling aside or departing from the path of truth and uprightness.

11:27 temple. Again this was the Court of the Gentiles; this time more specifically Solomon's porch or the royal porch on the S side of the court (cf. v. 11; Jn 10:23; Ac 5:12). **chief priests.** *See note on Mt 2:4.* The group that met Jesus might well have included Caiaphas and Annas, who served concurrently for several years (Lk 3:2). Because of the importance of this confrontation, the captain of the temple, the second highest official, may also have been present.

11:28 By what authority. The leaders wanted to know what credentials Jesus—an untrained, unrecognized, seemingly self-appointed rabbi—claimed that would authorize Him to do what He was doing. They had recovered from the initial shock of the previous day's events, and had become aggressive in demanding an explanation (*see note on Mt 21:23*; cf. Jn 2:18). **these things.** Primarily a reference to His actions in cleansing the temple. But the undefined, vague nature of this expression leaves open the inclusion of everything Jesus had been doing and teaching during His public ministry.

11:30 baptism of John. *See notes on 1:4; Mt 21:25.* Jesus put them on the defensive and made their evaluation of John's authority a test case for their evaluation of His own authority. **from heaven, or from men?** Jesus gave the Jewish leaders only those two alternatives in judging the source of John's authority, and by implication, His own authority. Christ was in effect forcing the men to carry out their roles as religious guides for the people and to go on record with an evaluation of both John's and His ministries (*see note on Mt 21:25*). **Answer Me.** This challenge by Jesus is only in Mark's account. It implies that the Jews did not have the courage to answer His question honestly.

12:1–12 Jesus taught this parable to confront the chief priests and elders and reveal their hypocritical character.

12:1 them. The chief priests, scribes, and elders (cf. 11:27). **parables.** *See notes on 4:2, 11.* **vineyard.** A common sight in that region. The hillsides of Israel were covered with grape vineyards, the backbone of the economy. Here it is a symbol for Israel (cf. Ps 80:8–16; Is 5:1–7; Jer 2:21). Jesus uses Is 5:1, 2 as the basis for this imagery (*see note on Mt 21:33*). **a wall.** Lit. "a fence." It may have been a stone wall or a hedge of briars built for protection. **vat.** Located under the winepress. The grapes were squeezed in the press, and the juice ran through a trough into this lower basin, where it could be collected into wineskins or jars. **tower.** This structure had a 3-fold purpose: 1) it served as a lookout post; 2) it provided shelter for the workers; and 3) it was used for storage of seed and tools. **rented it out to vine-growers.** Jesus added to the picture from Is 5:1, 2. The owner makes an agreement with men he believes are reliable caretakers, who are to pay a certain percentage of the proceeds to him as rent. The rest of the profit belonged to them for their work in cultivating the crop. The "vine-growers" represent the Jewish leaders.

12:2 *harvest* time. This usually occurred for the first time in the fifth year after the initial planting (cf. Lv 19:23–25). **slave.** All the servants, or slaves, in the parable represent the OT prophets.

12:6 a beloved son. The son represents Jesus Christ (*see note on Mt 21:37*).

12:7 the inheritance will be ours! The vine-growers were greedy; because they wanted the entire harvest and the vineyard for themselves and would stop at nothing to achieve that end, they plotted to kill the owner's son. Because Jesus had achieved such a following, the Jewish leaders believed the only way to maintain their position and power over the people was to kill Him (cf. Jn 11:48).

12:9 destroy the vine-growers. The owner of the vineyard will execute the vine-growers, thus serving as a prophecy of the destruction of Jerusalem (A.D. 70) and the nation of Israel. According to Matthew, this verdict was echoed by the chief priests, scribes, and elders (*see note on Mt 21:41*). **give the vineyard**

vine-growers, and will give the vineyard to others.
10 Have you not even read this Scripture:

> '[A]THE STONE WHICH THE BUILDERS REJECTED,
> THIS BECAME THE CHIEF CORNER *stone;*
> 11 [A]THIS CAME ABOUT FROM THE LORD,
> AND IT IS MARVELOUS IN OUR EYES'?"

12 [A]And they were seeking to seize Him, and *yet*
they feared the [a]people, for they understood that
He spoke the parable against them. And *so* [B]they
left Him and went away.

JESUS ANSWERS THE PHARISEES, SADDUCEES AND SCRIBES

13 [A]Then they *sent some of the Pharisees and
[B]Herodians to Him in order to [C]trap Him in a statement. 14 They *came and *said to Him, "Teacher, we
know that You are truthful and [a]defer to no one; for
You are not partial to any, but teach the way of God
in truth. Is it [b]lawful to pay a poll-tax to Caesar, or
not? 15 Shall we pay or shall we not pay?" But He,
knowing their hypocrisy, said to them, "Why are
you testing Me? Bring Me a [a]denarius to look at."
16 They brought *one.* And He *said to them, "Whose
likeness and inscription is this?" And they said to
Him, "Caesar's." 17 And Jesus said to them, "[A]Render
to Caesar the things that are Caesar's, and to God
the things that are God's." And they [a]were amazed
at Him.
18 [A]*Some* Sadducees (who say that there is no resurrection) *came to Jesus, and *began* questioning
Him, saying, 19 "Teacher, Moses wrote for us that
[A]IF A MAN'S BROTHER DIES and leaves behind a wife
AND LEAVES NO CHILD, HIS BROTHER SHOULD [a]MARRY
THE WIFE AND RAISE UP CHILDREN TO HIS BROTHER.
20 There were seven brothers; and the first took a
wife, and died leaving no children. 21 The second
one [a]married her, and died leaving behind no children; and the third likewise; 22 and *so* [a]all seven
left no children. Last of all the woman died also.
23 In the resurrection, [a]when they rise again, which
one's wife will she be? For [b]all seven had married
her." 24 Jesus said to them, "Is this not the reason
you are mistaken, that you do not [a]understand the
Scriptures or the power of God? 25 For when they
rise from the dead, they neither marry nor are
given in marriage, but are like angels in heaven.

12:10 [A]Ps 118:22 12:11 [A]Ps 118:23 12:12 [a]Lit *crowd* [A]Mark 11:18 [B]Matt 22:22 12:13 [A]Mark 12:13-17: *Matt 22:15-22; Luke 20:20-26* [B]Matt 22:16 [C]Luke 11:54 12:14 [a]Lit *it is not a concern to You about anyone;* i.e. You do not seek anyone's favor [b]Or *permissible* 12:15 [a]The denarius was a day's wages 12:17 [a]Or *were greatly marveling* [A]Matt 22:21 12:18 [A]Mark 12:18-27: *Matt 22:23-33; Luke 20:27-38;* Acts 23:8 12:19 [a]Lit *take* [A]Deut 25:5 12:21 [a]Lit *took* 12:22 [a]Lit *the seven* 12:23 [a]Early mss do not contain *when they rise again* [b]Lit *the seven* 12:24 [a]Or *know*

to others. This was fulfilled in the establishment of Christ's church and its leaders, who were mostly Gentiles.

12:10, 11 This messianic prophecy is a quotation of Ps 118:22, 23 from the LXX. Jesus continued His teaching in the form of a parable, but here His kingdom is seen as a building instead of a vineyard. The point is that the rejected son and the rejected stone represent Christ.

12:10 The stone which the builders rejected. Builders typically rejected stones until they found one perfectly straight in lines that could serve as the cornerstone, which was critical to the symmetry and stability of the building. In Jesus' metaphor, He Himself is the stone the builders (the Jewish religious leaders) rejected (crucified). But the resurrected Christ is the cornerstone (cf. Ac 4:10–12; 1Pe 2:6, 7; *see note on Mt 21:42*).

12:12 against them. The chief priests, scribes, and elders were completely aware that Christ was condemning their actions, but it only aroused their hatred, not their repentance.

12:13–17 The second of a series of questions that the Jewish religious leaders hoped would trap Jesus into declaring Himself an insurrectionist (cf. 11:28). This one concerns the controversial issue of paying taxes to Rome.

12:13 Pharisees and Herodians. Matthew indicates that disciples of the Pharisees accompanied the Herodians. The Pharisees may have hoped that Jesus would not recognize them and be caught off-guard by their seemingly sincere question. The Herodians were a political party of Jews who backed Herod Antipas, who in turn was only a puppet of Rome (*see note on Mt 22:16*).

12:14 not partial to any. This speaks of impartiality, or showing no favoritism. While this was flattery on the part of the Pharisees and Herodians, it was nonetheless true that Jesus would not be swayed by a person's power, prestige, or position. **poll-tax to Caesar.** The Gr. word for "poll-tax" was borrowed from the Lat. word that gives us the Eng. "census." The Romans counted all the citizens and made each one pay an annual poll tax of one denarius (*see note on Mt 22:17*).

12:15 hypocrisy. The Pharisees and Herodians, using feigned interest in His teaching, attempted to hide their true intention to trap Jesus. But He perceived their true motives (cf. Jn 2:25). **Why are you testing Me?** Jesus' response exposed the true motive of the Pharisees and Herodians and revealed their hypocrisy. **denarius.** This small silver coin, minted by the Roman emperor, was the equivalent of a day's wage for a common laborer or soldier (*see note on Mt 22:19*).

12:16 likeness. On one side of the denarius was likely the image of the current emperor, Tiberius, though at that time it could have also been Augustus, since both coins were in circulation. Tiberius is most likely because the response was "Caesar's," indicating the current ruler rather than the past one. **inscription.** If the coin was minted by Tiberius, it would have read, "Tiberius Caesar Augustus, the son of the Divine Augustus" on one side and "Chief Priest" on the other. *See note on Mt 22:19.*

12:17 Render to Caesar. The Gr. word for "render" means "to pay or give back," which implies a debt. All who lived within the realm of Caesar were obligated to return to him the tax that was owed him. It was not optional. Thus Jesus declared that all citizens are under divine obligation to pay taxes to whatever government is over them (cf. Ro 13:1–7; 1Pe 2:13–17; *see note on Mt 22:21*).

12:18 Sadducees. The most wealthy, influential, and aristocratic of all the Jewish sects. All the High Priests, chief priests, and the majority of the Sanhedrin (*see note on Mt 26:59*) were Sadducees. They ignored the oral law, traditions, and scribal laws of the Pharisees, viewing only the Pentateuch as authoritative (*see note on Mt 3:7*). **who say that there is no resurrection.** The most distinctive aspect of the Sadducees' theology, which they adopted because of their allegiance to the Pentateuch and their belief that Moses did not teach a literal resurrection from the dead. With such a disregard for the future, the Sadducees lived for the moment and whatever profit they could make. Since they controlled the temple businesses, they were extremely upset when Jesus cleansed the temple of the money changers because He cut into their profits (11:15–18)—the reason they also wanted to discredit Jesus in front of the people.

12:19 The Sadducees were summarizing Dt 25:5, 6, which refers to the custom of a levirate marriage (marriage to a dead husband's brother). God placed it in the law of Moses to preserve tribal names, families, and inheritances (*see note on Mt 22:24*). **Moses wrote.** The Sadducees appealed to Moses because they were fully aware of Jesus' high regard for Scripture, and therefore believed He would not contest the validity of the levirate marriage.

12:24 the power of God. Their ignorance of the Scriptures extended to their lack of understanding regarding the miracles God performed throughout the OT. Such knowledge would have enabled them to believe in God's power to raise the dead.

12:25 neither marry. Marriage was designed by God for companionship and the perpetuation of the human race on the earth. Jesus was emphasizing the fact that in heaven there will be no exclusive or sexual relationships. Believers will experience an entirely new existence in which they will have perfect spiritual relationships with everyone else. **like angels.** Believers will be like angels in that they will be spiritual, eternal beings who will not die (cf. 1Co 15:39–44, 48, 49; *see note on Mt 22:30*).

26 But [a]regarding the fact that the dead rise again,
have you not read in the book of Moses, [A]in the
passage about *the burning* bush, how God spoke
to him, saying, '[B]I AM THE GOD OF ABRAHAM, AND
THE GOD OF ISAAC, AND THE GOD OF JACOB'? 27 [A]He
is not the God [a]of the dead, but of the living; you
are greatly mistaken."
28 [A]One of the scribes came and heard them arguing, and [B]recognizing that He had answered them
well, asked Him, "What commandment is the [a]fore-
most of all?" 29 Jesus answered, "The foremost is,
'[A]HEAR, O ISRAEL! THE LORD OUR GOD IS ONE LORD;
30 [A]AND YOU SHALL LOVE THE LORD YOUR GOD WITH
ALL YOUR HEART, AND WITH ALL YOUR SOUL, AND
WITH ALL YOUR MIND, AND WITH ALL YOUR STRENGTH.'
31 The second is this, '[A]YOU SHALL LOVE YOUR NEIGH-
BOR AS YOURSELF.' There is no other commandment
greater than these." 32 The scribe said to Him, "Right,
Teacher; You have truly stated that [A]HE IS ONE, AND
THERE IS NO ONE ELSE BESIDES HIM; 33 [A]AND TO LOVE
HIM WITH ALL THE HEART AND WITH ALL THE UN-
DERSTANDING AND WITH ALL THE STRENGTH, AND TO
LOVE ONE'S NEIGHBOR AS HIMSELF, [B]is much more
than all burnt offerings and sacrifices." 34 When
Jesus saw that he had answered intelligently, He
said to him, "You are not far from the kingdom of
God." [A]After that, no one would venture to ask Him
any more questions.
35 [A]And Jesus *began* to say, as He [B]taught in the
temple, "How *is it that* the scribes say that [a]the
Christ is the [C]son of David? 36 David himself said
[a]in the Holy Spirit,

'[A]THE LORD SAID TO MY LORD,
"SIT AT MY RIGHT HAND,
UNTIL I PUT YOUR ENEMIES
BENEATH YOUR FEET." '

37 David himself calls Him 'Lord'; so in what sense
is He his son?" And [A]the large crowd [a]enjoyed listening to Him.
38 [A]In His teaching He was saying: "Beware of
the scribes who like to walk around in long robes,
and *like* [B]respectful greetings in the market places,
39 and chief seats in the synagogues and places of
honor at banquets, 40 [A]who devour widows' houses,
and for appearance's sake offer long prayers; these
will receive greater condemnation."

12:26 [a]Lit *concerning the dead, that they rise* [A]Luke 20:37; Rom 11:2 [B]Ex 3:6 12:27 [a]Or *of corpses* [A]Matt 22:32; Luke 20:38 12:28 [a]Or *first* [A]Mark 12:28-34: *Matt 22:34-40; Luke 10:25-28; 20:39f* [B]Matt 22:34; Luke 20:39 12:29 [A]Deut 6:4 12:30 [A]Deut 6:5 12:31 [A]Lev 19:18 12:32 [A]Deut 4:35 12:33 [A]Deut 6:5 [B]1 Sam 15:22; Hos 6:6; Mic 6:6-8; Matt 9:13; 12:7 12:34 [A]Matt 22:46 12:35 [a]I.e. the Messiah [A]Mark 12:35-37: *Matt 22:41-46; Luke 20:41-44* [B]Matt 26:55; Mark 10:1 [C]Matt 9:27 12:36 [a]Or *by* [A]Ps 110:1 12:37 [a]Lit *was gladly hearing Him* [A]John 12:9 12:38 [A]Mark 12:38-40: *Matt 23:1-7; Luke 20:45-47* [B]Matt 23:7; Luke 11:43 12:40 [A]Luke 20:47

12:26 **book of Moses.** The Pentateuch—the first 5 books of the OT. Jesus appealed to the only Scriptures the Sadducees held as completely authoritative. ***passage* about *the burning* bush.** A reference to Ex 3:1–4:17 where God first appeared to Moses at the bush. **how God spoke to him, saying, 'I am.'** By keying on the emphatic present tense of Ex 3:6, "I am … the God of Abraham, the God of Isaac, and the God of Jacob," Jesus was underscoring the personal and perpetual covenantal relationship God established with the 3 patriarchs. Even though all 3 were dead when God spoke to Moses, God was still their God just as much as when they were alive on earth—and more so in that they were experiencing eternal fellowship with Him in heaven (*see note on Mt 22:32*).

12:27 **you are greatly mistaken.** Jesus accused the Sadducees of making a complete error in teaching that there is no resurrection.

12:28 **scribes.** *See note on 1:22.* **What commandment is the foremost … ?** The rabbis had determined that there were 613 commandments contained in the Pentateuch, one for each letter of the Ten Commandments. Of the 613 commandments, 248 were seen as affirmative and 365 as negative. Those laws were also divided into heavy and light categories, with the heavy laws being more binding than the light ones. The scribes and rabbis, however, had been unable to agree on which were heavy and which were light. This orientation to the law led the Pharisees to think Jesus had devised His own theory. So the Pharisees asked this particular question to get Jesus to incriminate Himself by revealing His unorthodox and unilateral beliefs.

12:29 Hear, O Israel! By quoting the first part of the Shema (Dt 6:4, 5), which is Heb. for "hear," Jesus confirmed the practice of every pious Jew who recited the entire Shema (Nu 15:37–41; Dt 6:4–9; 11:13–21) every morning and evening.

12:30 love the **LORD**. Taken from Dt 10:12; 30:6, Jesus used God's own Word from the Pentateuch to answer the question, indicating the orthodox nature of His theology. *See note on Mt 22:37.*

12:31 **The second.** Jesus took the Pharisees' question one step further by identifying the second greatest commandment because it was critical to an understanding of the complete duty of love. This commandment, also from the books of Moses (Lv 19:18) is of the same nature and character as the first. Genuine love for God is followed in importance by a genuine love for people (*see note on Mt 22:39*). neighbor. Cf. Lk 10:29–37.

12:32, 33 **The scribe said.** The scribe's response reveals he understood OT teaching that moral concerns took precedence over ceremonial practices (cf. 1Sa 15:22; Is 1:11–15; Hos 6:6; Mic 6:6–8).

12:33 **burnt offerings.** Sacrifices that were completely consumed on the altar (cf. Lv 1:1–17; 6:8–13).

12:34 **not far from the kingdom.** Jesus both complimented and challenged the scribe. Jesus acknowledged the scribe's insight regarding the importance of love. Yet by stating that the scribe was "not far" from the kingdom, He emphasized that he was not in the kingdom. He understood the requirements of love he needed only to love and obey the One who alone could grant him entrance to the kingdom.

12:35 Jesus' question exposed the Jewish religious leaders' ineptness as teachers and their ignorance of what the OT taught regarding the true nature of the Messiah. **temple.** *See note on 11:11.* **Christ.** This is a translation of the OT Heb. word "Messiah," which means "anointed one" and refers to the King whom God had promised. **son of David.** The common messianic title that was standard scribal teaching. The religious leaders were convinced that the Messiah would be no more than a man, thus they deemed such a title appropriate (*see notes on 10:47; Mt 22:42*).

12:36 **David himself said in the Holy Spirit.** David used his own words, yet he wrote under the inspiration of the Holy Spirit (cf. 2Sa 23:2). **The LORD said to my LORD.** In this quote from the Heb. text (Ps 110:1), the first word for "Lord" is *Yahweh,* which is God's covenant name. The second word for "Lord" is a different word that the Jews used as a title for God. Here David pictures God speaking to the Messiah, whom David calls his Lord. The religious leaders of Jesus' day recognized this psalm as messianic.

12:37 **David himself calls Him 'Lord.'** Jesus interpreted Ps 110:1 for the Pharisees. David would not have called one of his descendants "Lord." Thus the Messiah is more than the "Son of David"—He is also the "Son of God." Jesus was proclaiming the Messiah's deity, and thus His own (cf. Ro 1:3; 2Ti 2:8; *see note on Mt 22:45*). **large crowd.** The multitude of people who observed this confrontation between Jesus and the religious leaders.

12:38 **Beware.** This means "to see" or "to watch." It carries the idea of guarding against the evil influence of the scribes. **long robes.** A long, flowing cloak that essentially trumpeted the wearer as a devout and noted scholar. **greetings.** Accolades for those holding titles of honor.

12:39 **chief seats in the synagogues.** The bench in the synagogue nearest the chest where the sacred scrolls were housed—an area reserved for leaders and people of renown (*see note on Jas 2:3*).

12:40 **devour widows' houses.** Jesus exposed the greedy, unscrupulous practice of the scribes. Scribes often served as estate planners for widows, which gave them the opportunity to convince distraught widows that they would be serving God by supporting the temple or the scribe's own holy work. In either case, the

THE WIDOW'S MITE

41[A]And He sat down opposite [B]the treasury, and
began observing how the people were [c]putting
[a]money into the treasury; and many rich people
were putting in large sums. 42A poor widow came
and put in two [a]small copper coins, which amount
to a [b]cent. 43Calling His disciples to Him, He said
to them, "Truly I say to you, this poor widow put
in more than all [a]the contributors to the treasury;
44for they all put in out of their [a]surplus, but she,
out of her poverty, put in all she owned, [b]all she
had [A]to live on."

THINGS TO COME

13 [A]As He was going out of the temple, one of His
disciples *said to Him, "Teacher, behold [a]what
wonderful stones and [a]what wonderful buildings!"
2And Jesus said to him, "Do you see these great
buildings? [A]Not one stone will be left upon another
which will not be torn down."
3As He was sitting on [A]the Mount of Olives opposite the temple, [B]Peter and [a]James and John and
Andrew were questioning Him privately, 4"Tell us,
when will these things be, and what *will be* the [a]sign
when all these things are going to be fulfilled?" 5And
Jesus began to say to them, "See to it that no one
misleads you. 6Many will come in My name, saying,
'[A]I am *He!*' and will mislead many. 7When you hear
of wars and rumors of wars, do not be frightened;
those things must take place; but *that is* not yet the
end. 8For nation will rise up against nation, and
kingdom against kingdom; there will be earthquakes
in various places; there will *also* be famines. These
things are *merely* the beginning of birth pangs.
9"But [a]be on your guard; for they will [A]deliver you
to *the* [b]courts, and you will be flogged [A]in *the* synagogues, and you will stand before governors and
kings for My sake, as a testimony to them. 10[A]The
gospel must first be preached to all the nations.
11[A]When they [a]arrest you and hand you over, do not
worry beforehand about what you are to say, but
say whatever is given you in that hour; for it is not
you who speak, but *it is* the Holy Spirit. 12Brother
will betray brother to death, and a father *his* child;

12:41 [a]I.e. copper coins [A]Mark 12:41-44: *Luke 21:1-4* [B]John 8:20 [C]2 Kin 12:9 12:42 [a]Gr *lepta* [b]Gr *quadrans;* i.e. 1/64 of a denarius 12:43 [a]Lit *those who were putting in* 12:44 [a]Or *abundance* [b]Lit *her whole livelihood* [A]Luke 8:43; 15:12, 30; 21:4 13:1 [a]Lit *how great* [A]Mark 13:1-37: *Matt 24; Luke 21:5-36* 13:2 [A]Luke 19:44 13:3 [a]Or *Jacob* [A]Matt 21:1 [B]Matt 17:1 13:4 [a]Or *attesting miracle* 13:6 [A]John 8:24 13:9 [a]Lit *look to yourselves* [b]Or *Sanhedrin* or *Council* [A]Matt 10:17 13:10 [A]Matt 24:14 13:11 [a]Lit *lead* [A]Mark 13:11-13: *Matt 10:19-22; Luke 21:12-17*

scribe benefited monetarily and effectively robbed the widow of her husband's legacy to her. **long prayers.** The Pharisees attempted to flaunt their piety by praying for long periods. Their motive was not devotion to God, but a desire to be revered by the people.

12:41 treasury. This refers to the 13 trumpet-shaped receptacles on the walls in the court of the women where offerings and donations to the temple were placed.

12:42 two small copper coins. A small copper coin was the smallest denomination in use. It was worth about an eighth of a cent. **a cent.** For the benefit of his Roman audience (see Introduction: Background and Setting), Mark related the "small copper coin" to this smallest denomination of Roman coinage. A "cent" was equal to 1/64 of a denarius, and a denarius was the equivalent of a day's wage.

12:43 Truly I say to you. *See note on 3:28.*

12:44 all she had to live on. This meant she would not be able to eat until she earned more. The religious system at the temple was thoroughly corrupt. It was literally devouring widows' houses (cf. v. 40).

13:1–37 This great sermon by Jesus is commonly known as the Olivet Discourse because Jesus delivered it on the Mt. of Olives just E of the temple across the Kidron Valley. Jesus' prediction of the coming destruction of the temple prompted a question from the disciples about the character of the end times. The remainder of the passage (vv. 5–37) is His response to their question as He describes His second coming at the end of the present age.

13:1 what wonderful stones and what wonderful buildings! *See note on Mt 24:1.* This unidentified disciple was admiring the magnificence and beauty of the temple and the surrounding buildings and was encouraging a like response from Jesus. It is likely that he could not comprehend how such an awesome structure could be left "desolate" (cf. Mt 23:38).

13:2 Jesus said. In response to the disciple's admiration, Jesus again predicted that the temple would be destroyed. About 40 years later, in A.D. 70, the Romans ransacked Jerusalem, killed a million Jews, and demolished the temple. **Not one stone.** The only stones left undisturbed were huge foundation stones that were not actually a part of the temple edifice but formed footings for the retaining wall under the entire temple mount. These can be viewed today in the "Rabbi's Tunnel" which runs N-S along the western wall. It is a portion of the western side of the retaining wall that today is called the Wailing Wall. More of that retaining wall, including the steps used to ascend and descend from the temple mount, has also been uncovered on the southern side.

13:3 Mount of Olives. *See note on 11:1.* **Peter and James and John and Andrew were questioning Him privately.** These 4 disciples were asking on behalf of all the 12.

13:4 The disciples were speculating that Jesus would imminently usher in the kingdom, so they asked a twofold question: 1) When would the temple be destroyed and the kingdom begin? and 2) What event would herald the beginning of the kingdom? **when will these things be . . . ?** "When" implies immediacy. The disciples thought that Jesus was about to usher in the kingdom of God at any time (cf. Lk 19:11), at least by the end of the Passover season. "These things" refers to the desolation and destruction of the temple (cf. Mt 23:38; 24:2) **the sign.** The disciples probably expected some miraculous occurrence—such as complete darkness, brilliant light, or an angel from heaven—to announce the coming millennial kingdom (*see note on Mt 24:3*). All of those things will occur at that time (*see notes on vv. 24–27*).

13:5 See to it. This Gr. word was often used as it is here with the idea of "keep your eyes open," or "beware."

13:6 I am *He!* Many false prophets will come forward claiming to be messiahs and deliverers, offering themselves as the solution to the world's problems. Some will even claim to be Christ Himself. The number of false christs will increase as the end nears (cf. Mt 24:23, 24).

13:7 the end. The consummation of the present age (*see note on Mt 24:6*).

13:8 the beginning of birth pangs. The Lord was referring to the pain a woman experiences in childbirth. Birth pains signal the end of pregnancy—they are infrequent at first and gradually increase just before the child is born. Likewise, the signs of vv. 6–8 will be infrequent, relatively speaking, in the beginning and will escalate to massive and tragic proportions just prior to Christ's second coming (cf. 1Th 5:3; *see note on Mt 24:8*).

13:9 courts. The Gr. word is lit. "sanhedrins." These were local, Jewish courts attached to the synagogues which tried charges of heresy and normal infractions of the law. The historian Josephus says that each city's court was composed of 7 judges (*Antiquities,* 4.8.14), and the *Mishnah* records that there were 23 judges in every city with more than 100 Jewish men ("Sanhedrin" I.6). These "courts" were like smaller versions of the great Sanhedrin that convened in Jerusalem (*see note on Mt 26:59*). **flogged.** These local courts usually administered 39 stripes so as not to violate Dt 25:2, 3. The recipient of the punishment was stripped bare to the waist. He received 13 lashings to his chest and 26 to his back (*see note on 2Co 11:24*). **in *the* synagogues.** The "synagogues" were the places for Jewish assembly and worship. When the "courts" convened, they typically met in the "synagogue."

13:10 first be preached to all the nations. Before the end (*see note on v. 7*), there will be a worldwide proclamation of the gospel. This may even refer to the occasion when an angel will supernaturally proclaim the gospel throughout the world before God pours out His judgment at the end of the Tribulation (Rev 14:6–8; *see note on Mt 24:14*).

13:11 what you are to say. Although the persecution will be terrifying, Christians are not to be anxious in anticipation of those events.

and children will rise up against parents and [a]have them put to death. 13 [A]You will be hated by all because of My name, but the one who endures to the end, he will be saved.

14 "But [A]when you see the [B]ABOMINATION OF DESOLATION standing where it should not be (let the reader understand), then those who are in Judea must flee to the mountains. 15 [A]The one who is on the housetop must not go down, or go in to get anything out of his house; 16 and the one who is in the field must not turn back to get his coat. 17 But woe to those who are pregnant and to those who are nursing babies in those days! 18 But pray that it may not happen in the winter. 19 For those days will be a *time of* tribulation such as has not occurred [A]since the beginning of the creation which God created until now, and never will. 20 Unless the Lord had shortened *those* days, no [a]life would have been saved; but for the sake of the [b]elect, whom He chose, He shortened the days. 21 And then if anyone says to you, 'Behold, here is [a]the Christ'; or, 'Behold, *He is* there'; do not believe *him;* 22 for false Christs and [A]false prophets will arise, and will show [a,B]signs and [B]wonders, in order to lead astray, if possible, the elect. 23 But take heed; behold, I have told you everything in advance.

THE RETURN OF CHRIST

24 "But in those days, after that tribulation, [A]THE SUN WILL BE DARKENED AND THE MOON WILL NOT GIVE ITS LIGHT, 25 [A]AND THE STARS WILL BE FALLING from heaven, and the powers that are in [a]the heavens will be shaken. 26 Then they will see [A]THE SON OF MAN [B]COMING IN CLOUDS with great power and glory. 27 And then He will send forth the angels, and [A]will gather together His [a]elect from the four winds, [B]from the farthest end of the earth to the farthest end of heaven.

13:12 [a]Lit *put them to death* 13:13 [A]Matt 10:22; John 15:21 13:14 [A]Matt 24:15f [B]Dan 9:27; 11:31; 12:11 13:15 [A]Luke 17:31 13:19 [A]Dan 12:1; Mark 10:6 13:20 [a]Lit *flesh* [b]Or *chosen ones* 13:21 [a]I.e. the Messiah 13:22 [a]Or *attesting miracles* [A]Matt 7:15 [B]Matt 24:24; John 4:48 13:24 [A]Is 13:10; Ezek 32:7; Joel 2:10, 31; 3:15; Rev 6:12 13:25 [a]Or *heaven* [A]Is 34:4; Rev 6:13 13:26 [A]Dan 7:13; Rev 1:7 [B]Matt 16:27; Mark 8:38 13:27 [a]Or *chosen ones* [A]Deut 30:4 [B]Zech 2:6

for it is not you who speak. Rather than being fearful, believers can remain calm and depend on the Holy Spirit, who will give them the appropriate and effective words to say in defense of their faith in Christ. *See note on Lk 12:11.*

13:13 endures to the end, he will be saved. *See note on Mt 24:13.* This endurance does not produce salvation; it is Spirit-empowered perseverance and proof of the reality of salvation in the one who endures. Christ will eventually deliver such believers out of the present evil system into God's eternal kingdom (cf. Mt 10:22).

13:14 the abomination of desolation. This first referred to the desecration of the temple by Antiochus Epiphanes, the king of Syria, in the second century B.C. when he sacrificed a pig on the temple altar. That event was similar in character to what Jesus refers to here, i.e., the Antichrist's ultimate desecration when he sets up an image of himself in the temple during the tribulation (*see notes on Da 9:27; 11:31; Mt 24:15; 2Th 2:4*). **standing where it should not be.** Matthew 24:15 indicates the location as the "holy place." On the only other occasion where this phrase from Matthew appears in the NT, it clearly refers to the temple (Ac 21:28). This specifically implies that the temple will be rebuilt in the future and that the daily sacrificial system will be reinstated. "Standing" indicates that the abomination of desolation will be continuous, actually lasting for 3 1/2 years (Da 12:11; cf. Rev 12:6). **let the reader understand.** This indicates that Jesus was not issuing these warnings to the disciples or to others of their generation who would not experience this event, but to believers in the end times. Those who will read these truths will be prepared and "understand" the trials they are enduring. **flee to the mountains.** The Gr. word for "flee" is related to the Eng. word "fugitive," a person who is on the run to escape danger. Jesus warns those who live in Judea to escape the holocaust by taking refuge in the mountains (*see note on Mt 24:16*).

13:15 not go down. So urgent will be the need to flee that if a person happens to be on the roof of his house (*see note on 2:4*) when he hears the news, he is to run down the outside stairway and leave town without going inside his house to retrieve any belongings.

13:16 coat. The Gr. word refers to the outer cloak. Jesus warns those working in the fields not to take the time to retrieve their cloaks that may be at home or some distance away at the entrance to the field.

13:17 pregnant and ... nursing babies. Jesus certainly felt compassion for those women who will be hindered from fleeing quickly because they carry children. But He may have been warning them about atrocities that could include unborn children being slashed in the wombs and tiny infants being crushed (cf. Hos 13:16).

13:18 in the winter. This refers to the rainy season in Israel, when streams could become impassable and it would be difficult to glean food from barren fields.

13:19 tribulation such as has not occurred. This reveals that the tribulation Jesus was referring to is in the future and that it will be the greatest that has ever occurred. It will be of long duration and characterized by severe pressure and continual anguish. This is the Great Tribulation at the end of the age (cf. Rev 7:14; *see note on Mt 24:21*).

13:20 shortened. Lit. "mutilated" or "amputated." Jesus was referring to the determination of God to cut short or limit the period of time to only 3 1/2 years (cf. Da 7:25; Rev 12:14; *see note on Mt 24:22*). **sake of the elect.** The "elect" could refer to the nation of Israel (cf. Is 45:4), or those who become Christians during the Tribulation (Rev 17:14). In either case, God cuts short the days for their benefit.

13:21 Behold, here is the Christ. Satan will cause false christs to appear in an attempt to deceive the elect into leaving their places of refuge. False teachers will claim that Christ is in their midst or is back in Jerusalem or elsewhere in Judea.

13:22 signs and wonders. Satanic inspired pseudo-miracles employed to support their claims to be the true Christ (cf. 2Th 2:9).

13:23 take heed. Jesus issues a prophetic warning to be on guard. He has told the elect refugees of the future all that they need to know to avoid being misled and deceived by Satan's emissaries.

13:24 in those days, after that tribulation. "Those days" describes the events of vv. 6–23 and, thus, "that tribulation" refers to the Great Tribulation Jesus just spoke of. This also means that what He was about to describe (vv. 24–27) will occur immediately at the end of the future tribulation period (cf. Mt 24:29). **the sun will be darkened.** The sun will go black as the universe begins to disintegrate prior to the return of Christ (*see notes on Mt 24:29; Ac 2:20; Rev 6:12*).

13:25 stars will be falling. Heavenly bodies will careen at random through space (cf. Rev 6:13, 14; 8:10–13; 16:8, 17–20). **powers ... in the heavens.** All the forces of energy that hold everything in space constant, and which Christ controls, He will allow to become random and chaotic (cf. Is 13:6–16; 34:1–5; 2Pe 3:10–12).

13:26 Son of Man. *See note on 2:10.* **coming in clouds with great power and glory.** Jesus will return to earth in the same manner in which He left it (cf. Ac 1:9–11; cf. Da 7:13, 14; Rev 1:7). The psalmist said that God uses "clouds" as His chariot (Ps 104:3), and Is 19:1 pictures the Lord riding on a cloud. Although these "clouds" could be natural, they more likely describe the supernatural "glory cloud" that represented God's presence in OT Israel (*see note on Rev 1:7*). While Christ possesses "great power and glory," His return will be accompanied with visible manifestations of that power and glory (cf. Rev 6:15–17; 11:15–19; 16:17–21; 19:11–16)—He will redeem the elect, restore the devastated earth, and establish His rule on earth.

13:27 angels. A number of angels return with Christ (cf. 8:38; Mt 16:27; *see following note*). **gather ... His elect.** Angels are God's gatherers—they gather unbelievers for judgment (Mt 13:41, 49, 50), and they gather the elect for glory. The "elect" will include the 144,000 Jewish witnesses (*see note on Rev 7:4*), their converts (Rev 7:9), and the converts of the angelic preachers (*see note on Rev 14:6*). They will also include the OT saints, gathered out of their graves and united with their redeemed spirits (Da 12:1–3). **from the four winds.** A colloquial expression meaning "from everywhere," and similar to the expression "from the four corners of the world."

28 "Now learn the parable from the fig tree: when
its branch has already become tender and puts forth
its leaves, you know that summer is near. 29 Even
so, you too, when you see these things happening,
[a]recognize that [b]He is near, *right* at the [c]door. 30 Truly
I say to you, this [a]generation will not pass away until
all these things take place. 31 Heaven and earth will
pass away, but My words will not pass away. 32 [A]But
of that day or hour no one knows, not even the angels in heaven, nor the Son, but the Father *alone*.
33 "Take heed, [A]keep on the alert; for you do not
know when the *appointed* time [a]will come. 34 [A]*It is*
like a man away on a journey, *who* upon leaving his
house and [a]putting his slaves in charge, *assigning* to
each one his task, also commanded the doorkeeper
to stay on the alert. 35 Therefore, [A]be on the alert—for
you do not know when the [a]master of the house is
coming, whether in the evening, at midnight, or
[B]when the rooster crows, or [C]in the morning— 36 in
case he should come suddenly and find you [A]asleep.
37 What I say to you I say to all, '[A]Be on the alert!' "

DEATH PLOT AND ANOINTING

14 [A]Now [B]the Passover and Unleavened Bread
were two days away; and the chief priests
and the scribes [C]were seeking how to seize Him by
stealth and kill *Him;* 2 for they were saying, "Not
during the festival, otherwise there might be a riot
of the people."
3 [A]While He was in [B]Bethany at the home of Simon
the leper, and reclining *at the table,* there came a
woman with an alabaster vial of very [C]costly perfume of pure [a]nard; *and* she broke the vial and
poured it over His head. 4 But some were indignantly
remarking to one another, "Why has this perfume
been wasted? 5 For this perfume might have been
sold for over three hundred [a]denarii, and *the money*
given to the poor." And they were scolding her. 6 But

13:29 [a]Or *know* [b]Or *it* [c]Lit *doors* 13:30 [a]Or *race* 13:32 [A]Matt 24:36; Acts 1:7 13:33 [a]Lit *is* [A]Eph 6:18; Col 4:2 13:34 [a]Lit *giving the authority to* [A]Luke 12:36-38 13:35 [a]Lit *lord* [A]Matt 24:42; Mark 13:37 [B]Mark 14:30 [C]Matt 14:25; Mark 6:48 13:36 [A]Rom 13:11 13:37 [A]Matt 24:42; Mark 13:35 14:1 [A]Mark 14:1, 2: *Matt 26:2-5; Luke 22:1, 2* [B]Ex 12:1-27; Mark 14:12; John 11:55; 13:1 [C]Matt 12:14 14:3 [a]An aromatic oil extracted from an East Indian plant [A]Mark 14:3-9: *Matt 26:6-13;* Luke 7:37-39; John 12:1-8 [B]Matt 21:17 [C]Matt 26:6f; John 12:3 14:5 [a]The denarius was equivalent to a day's wages

None of the elect on earth or in heaven will miss entering the kingdom.

13:28 **the parable.** *See note on 4:2.* **fig tree.** *See note on 11:13.*

13:29 Just as the fig tree's buds turning into leaves was a sign of the nearness of summer, the events Jesus described as birth pains (vv. 6–23) are to be a clear indication of the return of Christ (*see note on Mt 24:32*). **these things.** The events of vv. 6–23. **He is near.** Luke 21:31 says, "The kingdom of God is near." That is consistent with the questions the disciples initially asked Jesus (v. 4), which was about the signs that would herald the establishment of the kingdom.

13:30 **Truly I say to you.** *See note on 3:28.* **this generation.** The generation of people living during the end times that witnesses the signs and events leading to the return of Christ (*see note on Mt 24:34*).

13:31 **Heaven and earth will pass away.** The universe as we know it will be dramatically altered after the thousand-year reign of Christ (*see notes on 2Pe 3:10–13*). **My words will not pass away.** It is impossible for God's Word to be negated, destroyed, or altered in any way (cf. Ps 19:9; Mt 5:18; Lk 16:17; Jn 10:35).

13:32 **that day or hour.** The exact day and time of Christ's return (*see note on Mt 24:36*). **no one knows.** The time of Christ's return will not be revealed in advance to any man. At this time, it was known only to God the Father. **angels.** While all the angelic beings enjoy intimacy with God, hover around His throne to do His bidding (Is 6:2–7), and continually behold Him (Mt 18:10), they have no knowledge of the time of Christ's return. **nor the Son.** When Jesus spoke these words to the disciples, even He had no knowledge of the date and time of His return. Although Jesus was fully God (Jn 1:1, 14), when He became a man, He voluntarily restricted the use of certain divine attributes (Php 2:6–8). He did not manifest them unless directed by the Father (Jn 4:34; 5:30; 6:38). He demonstrated His omniscience on several occasions (cf. Jn 2:25; 13:3), but He voluntarily restricted that omniscience to only those things God wanted Him to know during the days of His humanity (Jn 15:15). Such was the case regarding the knowledge of the date and time of His return. After He was resurrected, Jesus resumed His full divine knowledge (cf. Mt 28:18; Ac 1:7).

13:33 **keep on the alert.** Christ sounded a warning for believers to be on guard (*see note on v. 5*). Even believers do not have in themselves sufficient resources to be alert to spiritual dangers that can so easily surprise them.

13:34 **doorkeeper.** In Jesus' day, this individual guarded the outer gate of the house, so as to be ready to let the returning master in upon his arrival. All Christ's disciples are to be like doorkeepers, always remaining alert and vigilant for their Master's return.

13:35 **in the evening ... or in the morning.** The normal expressions designating the 4 three-hour watches of the night from 6:00 p.m. to 6:00 a.m. Their names identify the ends of the three-hour periods rather than the periods' beginnings.

14:1 **the Passover.** Friday of Passover which would have begun on Thursday at sunset. The Passover commemorated the "passing over" of the homes of the Israelites by the angel of death, who killed the firstborn of Egypt (Ex 12:1–13:16). The Passover began on the 14th day of Nisan (the first month of the Jewish calendar) with the slaying of the Passover lamb, and continued into the early hours of the 15th (*see notes on Ex 12:6; Mt 26:2*). **Unleavened Bread.** This feast commemorated the departure of the Israelites from Egypt (Ex 23:15). It began immediately after the Passover and lasted from Nisan 15–21. Unleavened bread refers to the type of bread the Israelites were to take with them in their escape which represented the absence of the leaven of sin in their lives and household (*see notes on Ex 12:14; Lv 23:6–8*). **two days away.** In the context of Mt 26:2, Jesus predicted His crucifixion was to take place in "two days," which would be Friday, since when He was speaking it was Wednesday evening. Mark's time line here is the same as Matthew's (*see note on Mt 26:2*). **chief priests.** *See note on 8:31.* **scribes.** *See note on Mt 2:4.*

14:2 **Not during the festival.** Because the Passover had to be celebrated in Jerusalem, the city would have been overflowing—perhaps as many as two million people were there. Since many would have been from Galilee—an area where Jesus had many followers—and the religious leaders did not want to start a riot, they determined to wait until after the Passover season when the crowds would be diminished (*see note on Mt 26:5*).

14:3–9 The incident recorded here had occurred the previous Saturday (cf. Jn 12:1). It is Mark's account of the anointing of Jesus by Mary in preparation for His crucifixion (cf. Mt 26:6–13; Jn 12:2–8).

14:3 **Bethany.** *See note on 11:1.* **Simon the leper.** This man is mentioned in the NT only in connection with this narrative. Since a leper was an outcast in Jewish society, he was probably miraculously cleansed of his leprosy by Jesus, and may have planned this meal for Jesus in gratitude (*see notes on Lv 13; Mt 26:6*). **a woman.** John 12:3 identifies her as Mary, the sister of Martha and Lazarus, who were also present at this meal. **alabaster vial.** This long-necked bottle was made out of a special variety of marble, a material which proved to be the best container for preserving expensive perfumes and oils (*see note on Mt 26:7*). **pure nard.** This oil was derived from the nard plant, which was native to India. That it was pure meant it was genuine and unadulterated, which is what made it so costly. **broke the vial.** She may have simply broken the neck of the bottle so that she could pour out the contents more quickly, an expression of her sincere and total devotion to the Lord.

14:4 **some were indignantly *remarking*.** John 12:4, 5 says that Judas was the instigator, and Mt 26:8 indicates that all the disciples, following Judas' lead, were angry with Mary's waste of a very valuable commodity.

14:5 **three hundred denarii.** Since a denarius was a day's wage for a common laborer, it represented almost a year's work for such a person. **given to the poor.** While 11 of the disciples would have agreed to this use of the money, the fact is the poor may never have seen it. Since Judas was in reality a thief masquerading as the treasurer of the 12, he could have embezzled all of it (Jn 12:6).

Jesus said, "Let her alone; why do you bother her?
She has done a good deed to Me. 7 For you always
have [A]the poor with you, and whenever you wish
you can do good to them; but you do not always
have Me. 8 She has done what she could; [A]she has
anointed My body beforehand for the burial. 9 Truly
I say to you, [A]wherever the gospel is preached in
the whole world, what this woman has done will
also be spoken of in memory of her."
10 [A]Then Judas Iscariot, [B]who was one of the
twelve, went off to the chief priests in order to [a]be-
tray Him to them. 11 They were glad when they heard
this, and promised to give him money. And he *began*
seeking how to betray Him at an opportune time.

THE LAST PASSOVER

12 [A]On the first day of [B]Unleavened Bread, when
[a]the Passover *lamb* was being [C]sacrificed, His disciples *said to Him, "Where do You want us to go and
prepare for You to eat the Passover?" 13 And He *sent
two of His disciples and *said to them, "Go into the
city, and a man will meet you carrying a pitcher of
water; follow him; 14 and wherever he enters, say to
the owner of the house, 'The Teacher says, "Where
is My [A]guest room in which I may eat the Passover
with My disciples?"' 15 And he himself will show you
a large upper room furnished *and* ready; prepare
for us there." 16 The disciples went out and came to
the city, and found *it* just as He had told them; and
they prepared the Passover.
17 [A]When it was evening He *came with the twelve.
18 As they were reclining *at the table* and eating, Jesus
said, "Truly I say to you that one of you will [a]betray
Me—[b]one who is eating with Me." 19 They began to be
grieved and to say to Him one by one, "Surely not I?"
20 And He said to them, "*It is* one of the twelve, [a]one
who dips with Me in the bowl. 21 For the Son of Man *is
to* go just as it is written of Him; but woe to that man
[a]by whom the Son of Man is betrayed! *It would have
been* good [b]for that man if he had not been born."

THE LORD'S SUPPER

22 [A]While they were eating, He took *some* bread,
and [a]after a [B]blessing He broke *it,* and gave *it* to

14:7 [A]Deut 15:11; Matt 26:11; John 12:8 14:8 [A]John 19:40 14:9 [A]Matt 26:13 14:10 [a]Or *hand Him over* [A]Mark 14:10, 11: *Matt 26:14-16; Luke 22:3-6* [B]John 6:71
14:12 [a]Lit *they were sacrificing* [A]Mark 14:12-16: *Matt 26:17-19; Luke 22:7-13* [B]Matt 26:17 [C]Deut 16:5; Mark 14:1; Luke 22:7; 1 Cor 5:7 14:14 [A]Luke 22:11 14:17 [A]Mark 14:17-21: *Matt 26:20-24; Luke 22:14, 21-23;* John 13:18ff 14:18 [a]Or *deliver Me over* [b]Or *the one* 14:20 [a]Or *the one* 14:21 [a]Or *through* [b]Lit *for him if that man had not been born* 14:22 [a]Lit *having blessed* [A]Mark 14:22-25: *Matt 26:26-29; Luke 22:17-20; 1 Cor 11:23-25;* Mark 10:16 [B]Matt 14:19

14:7 you always have the poor with you. Opportunities to minister to the poor are "always" available, but Jesus would be in their presence for only a limited time. This was not a time for meeting the needs of the poor and the sick—it was a time for sacrificial worship of the One who would soon suffer and be crucified (*see note on Mt 26:11;* cf. 2:19).

14:8 anointed My body . . . for the burial. Mary did so probably without ever realizing what she was doing. Her anointing of Jesus became a symbol that anticipated His death and burial (*see note on Mt 26:12*).

14:9 Truly I say to you. *See note on 3:28.* **gospel.** *See note on 1:1.*

14:10 Judas Iscariot. Standing in sharp contrast to the love and devotion of Mary was the hatred and treachery of Judas. This disciple, who is understandably referred to last in the lists of the 12, was the son of Simon, who was also called "Iscariot." The name "Iscariot" means "man of Kerioth," which was a small town in Judea about 23 mi. S of Jerusalem (cf. 3:19). Thus Judas was not a Galilean like the other disciples. It is clear that Judas never had any spiritual interest in Jesus—he was attracted to Him because he expected Jesus to become a powerful religious and political leader. He saw great potential for power, wealth, and prestige through his association with Him. But Jesus knew what Judas was like from the start, and that is why He chose him as one of the 12. He was the one who would betray Him so that the Scripture and God's plan of salvation would be fulfilled (Pss 41:9; 55:12–15, 20, 21; Zec 11:12, 13; Jn 6:64, 70, 71; 13:18; 17:12). **the twelve.** *See note on 3:14.* **chief priests.** *See note on 8:31.*

14:11 money. Matthew says the amount Judas agreed to as blood money was 30 pieces of silver (*see note on Mt 26:15*). **seeking how to betray . . . opportune time.** "Seeking" is better translated "began to seek." Judas was looking for a suitable occasion to carry out his evil plan, which would be when Jesus was away from the crowds (Lk 22:6).

14:12 Unleavened Bread. Passover and the Feast of Unleavened Bread were so closely associated that both terms were used interchangeably to refer to the 8-day celebration that began with the Passover. Although Unleavened Bread is used here, Mark's clear intention is the preparation for Passover (*see notes on v. 1; Mt 26:17*). **the Passover *lamb* was being sacrificed.** The lambs were killed on 14 Nisan at twilight (Ex 12:6), a Heb. term meaning "between the two evenings," or between 3:00 and 5:00 p.m. After the lamb was slaughtered and some of its blood sprinkled on the altar, the lamb was taken home, roasted whole, and eaten in the evening meal with unleavened bread, bitter herbs, *charoseth* (a paste made of crushed apples, dates, pomegranates, and nuts, into which they dipped bread), and wine.

14:13 two of His disciples. Peter and John (Lk 22:8). Only two people were allowed to accompany a lamb to the sacrifice. **man . . . carrying a pitcher of water.** This is the only way that Jesus identified the man. But he stood out because it was uncommon for a man to carry a pitcher of water—women usually performed that chore (*see note on Mt 26:18*).

14:14 guest room. The word is translated "inn" in Lk 2:7. It typically referred to a place where a traveler could spend the night—a place of lodging or a guest room in someone's home, as was the case here (cf. Mt 26:18).

14:15 large upper room. This indicates the room was located upstairs, and may have been a roof chamber built on top of the house. **prepare.** Peter and John were to prepare the Passover meal for Jesus and the other disciples.

14:17 evening. The Passover meal was to be eaten at night after sunset, but had to be completed before midnight (Ex 12:8–14). **with the twelve.** Peter and John may have rejoined Jesus and the other disciples and led them to the upper room. This may also be a general reference to the 12, meaning that Jesus came with the other 10 disciples to meet Peter and John.

14:18 reclining . . . eating. The order of the Passover meal was: 1) drinking a cup of red wine mixed with water (cf. Lk 22:17); 2) the ceremonial washing of hands symbolizing the need for spiritual and moral cleansing; 3) eating the bitter herbs, symbolic of the bondage in Egypt; 4) drinking the second cup of wine, at which time the head of the household explained the meaning of Passover; 5) singing of the Hallel (Pss 113–118)—at this point they sang the first two; 6) the lamb was brought out, and the head of the household distributed pieces of it with the unleavened bread; 7) drinking the third cup of wine (*see notes on 1Co 10:16*).

14:20 dips with Me in the bowl. There were likely several dishes around the table—Judas was probably one of several sitting near Jesus and thus would have dipped in the same bowl with Him.

14:21 Son of Man. *See note on 2:10.* **as it is written.** Jesus was no victim—His betrayal by Judas was prophesied in the OT (Ps 22; Is 53), and was part of God's predetermined plan to provide salvation (Ac 2:23). **good . . . if he had not been born.** Cf. Jn 8:21–24; 16:8–11. This is because the terror Judas would experience in hell would be so great. The severest punishment is reserved for Judas and others like him (Heb 10:29). This is one of the strongest statements in Scripture on human responsibility for believing in Jesus Christ, coupled with the consequences of such unbelief.

14:22–25 At this point in the narrative, it appears that Judas had gone (Jn 13:23–30) and Jesus was alone with the faithful 11 disciples (*see note on Lk 22:21*). Then it was that He transformed the Passover of the Old Covenant into the Lord's Supper of the New Covenant, creating a new memorial feast to remember God's deliverance from sin.

14:22 While they were eating. There is no indication from any of the gospel accounts as to which part of the meal they were eating, but it is likely that this occurred just prior to eating the roasted lamb or concurrently with

them, and said, "Take *it;* this is My body." 23 And
when He had taken a cup *and* given thanks, He gave
it to them, and they all drank from it. 24 And He said
to them, "This is My [A]blood of the [B]covenant, which
is poured out for many. 25 Truly I say to you, I will
never again drink of the fruit of the vine until that
day when I drink it new in the kingdom of God."
26 [A]After singing a hymn, they went out to [B]the
Mount of Olives.
27 [A]And Jesus *said to them, "You will all [a]fall
away, because it is written, '[B]I WILL STRIKE DOWN
THE SHEPHERD, AND THE SHEEP SHALL BE SCAT-
TERED.' 28 But after I have been raised, [A]I will go
ahead of you to Galilee." 29 But Peter said to Him,
"*Even* though all may [a]fall away, yet I will not."
30 And Jesus *said to him, "Truly I say to you, that
[a,A]this very night, before [B]a rooster crows twice, you
yourself will deny Me three times." 31 But *Peter* kept
saying insistently, "*Even* if I have to die with You,
I will not deny You!" And they all were saying the
same thing also.

JESUS IN GETHSEMANE

32 [A]They *came to a place named Gethsemane;
and He *said to His disciples, "Sit here until I have
prayed." 33 And He *took with Him Peter and [a]James
and John, and began to be very [A]distressed and troubled. 34 And He *said to them, "[A]My soul is deeply
grieved to the point of death; remain here and keep
watch." 35 And He went a little beyond *them,* and
fell to the ground and *began* to pray that if it were
possible, [A]the hour might [a]pass Him by. 36 And He
was saying, "[A]Abba! Father! All things are possible
for You; remove this cup from Me; [B]yet not what I
will, but what You will." 37 And He *came and *found
them sleeping, and *said to Peter, "Simon, are you
asleep? Could you not keep watch for one hour?
38 [A]Keep watching and praying that you may not
come into temptation; the spirit is willing, but the
flesh is weak." 39 Again He went away and prayed,
saying the same [a]words. 40 And again He came and
found them sleeping, for their eyes were very heavy;
and they did not know what to answer Him. 41 And

14:24 [A]Ex 24:8 [B]Jer 31:31-34 14:26 [A]Matt 26:30 [B]Matt 21:1 14:27 [a]Or *stumble* [A]Mark 14:27-31: *Matt 26:31-35* [B]Zech 13:7 14:28 [A]Matt 28:16 14:29 [a]Or *stumble* 14:30 [a]Lit *today, on this night* [A]Matt 26:34 [B]Mark 14:68, 72; John 13:38 14:32 [A]Mark 14:32-42: *Matt 26:36-46; Luke 22:40-46* 14:33 [a]Or *Jacob* [A]Mark 9:15; 16:5, 6 14:34 [A]Matt 26:38; John 12:27 14:35 [a]Lit *pass from Him* [A]Matt 26:45; Mark 14:41 14:36 [A]Rom 8:15; Gal 4:6 [B]Matt 26:39 14:38 [A]Matt 26:41 14:39 [a]Lit *word*

it. It is significant that Jesus established the truth of the New Covenant while in the midst of eating the Passover. **this is My body.** Jesus gave new meaning to eating the bread. The unleavened bread symbolized the severing of the Israelites from the old life in Egypt. It represented a separation from worldliness, sin, and false religion and the beginning of a new life of holiness and godliness. From then on in the Lord's Supper, the bread would symbolize Christ's body, which He sacrificed for the salvation of men (*see note on Mt 26:26*).

14:23 a cup. The third cup of wine in the ceremony (*see note on 1Co 10:16*).

14:24 My blood of the covenant. The shedding of blood in a sacrifice was always God's requirement in establishing any covenant (cf. Ge 8:20; 15:10; Ex 24:5–8). Here, Christ's blood needed to be shed for the remission of sins (Heb 9:22; 1Pe 1:19; *see note on Mt 26:28*). **for many.** This lit. means "for the benefit of many." The "many" are all who believe, both Jew and Gentile. *See note on 10:45;* cf. Mt 20:28.

14:25 Truly I say to you. *See note on 3:28.* **I will never again drink.** Jesus declared that this would be the last Passover, and that He would not even drink wine with them again, since this was His last meal. Until the inauguration of the millennial kingdom, believers are to share this memorial meal (*see notes on 1Co 11:23–34*). **drink it new.** This served as an assurance to them of Jesus' return and His establishment of His earthly, millennial kingdom. It possibly implies that the communion service will continue to be observed in the millennial kingdom, as a memorial to the cross. It more probably indicates that Jesus would not have another Passover with them until the kingdom (*see notes on Eze 45:18–25; 45:21–24*). It is also true that in the kingdom, commemorative sacrifices from the Old Covenant will be restored (Eze 43–45) which will have meaning never understood before the cross of Christ to which they pointed. **kingdom of God.** The earthly millennial kingdom is in view.

14:26 singing a hymn. Probably Ps 118, the last psalm of the traditional Hallel sung at Passover (*see note on Mt 26:30*). **Mount of Olives.** *See note on 11:1.*

14:27 fall away. *See note on 4:17; Mt 26:31.* This refers to the disciples' temporary falling away from their loyalty to Jesus. **it is written.** Quoted from Zec 13:7.

14:28 to Galilee. Jesus' promise to meet the disciples in His postresurrection form (cf. 16:7; Mt 28:16, 17; *see note on Mt 28:7*).

14:30 Truly I say to you. *See note on 3:28.* **before a rooster crows twice.** In Jewish reckoning of time, "cock crow" was the third watch of the night, ending at 3:00 a.m., which was when roosters typically began to crow (*see note on 13:35*). Mark, alone of the gospels, indicates that the cock crowed two times (v. 72; *see note on Mt 26:34*).

14:32 Gethsemane. The name means "oil press," and referred to a garden filled with olive trees on a slope of the Mt. of Olives. Jesus frequented this spot with the disciples when He wanted to get away from the crowds to pray (cf. Jn 18:1, 2; *see note on Mt 26:36*).

14:33 Peter and James and John. *See note on 5:37.* Jesus likely had them accompany Him into the garden because they were the leaders of the 12 and had to learn an important lesson to pass on to the others (vv. 34–42). **troubled.** The Gr. word refers to a feeling of terrified amazement. In the face of the dreadful prospect of bearing God's full fury against sin, Jesus was in the grip of terror (*see note on Mt 26:38*).

14:34 to the point of death. Jesus' sorrow was so severe that it threatened to cause His death at that moment. It is possible for a person to die from sheer anguish (cf. Lk 22:44; *see note on Mt 26:38*).

14:35 if … possible. Jesus was not asking God if He had the power to let the cup pass from Him, but if it were possible in God's plan. Christ was to soon partake of this cup in the cross as God's only sacrifice for sin (cf. Ac 4:12). **the hour.** The time of His sacrificial death as decreed by God. It included everything from the betrayal (v. 41) to Jesus' trials, the mockery, and His crucifixion.

14:36 Abba! An endearing, intimate Aram. term that is essentially equivalent to the Eng. word "Daddy" (cf. Ro 8:15; Gal 4:6). **All things are possible.** Jesus knew that it was in the scope of God's power and omniscience to provide an alternate plan of salvation, if He desired (*see note on v. 35*). **cup.** This was the cup of divine wrath referred to in the OT (Ps 75:8; Is 51:17; Jer 49:12). Christ was to endure the fury of God over sin, Satan, the power of death, and the guilt of iniquity (*see notes on Mt 26:39; Lk 22:42; Jn 18:11*). **not what I will, but what You will.** This reveals Jesus' total resolution and resignation to do the will of God. He came into the world to do God's will, and that remained His commitment while here (*see notes on Mt 26:39;* cf. Jn 6:38–40).

14:37 Simon. Jesus' use of "Simon" may have implied that Peter was not living up to the significance and meaning of his new name, "Peter" (*see note on Mt 16:18*). **one hour.** This suggests that Jesus had spent an hour praying, a duration in which Peter had been unable to stay awake.

14:38 watching. This Gr. word means "to keep alert." Jesus was encouraging Peter, James, and John to discern when they were under spiritual attack. They were not to let their self-confidence lull them to sleep spiritually. **the flesh is weak.** Because willing spirits are still attached to unredeemed flesh, believers are not always able to practice the righteousness they desire to do (cf. Ro 7:15–23; *see note on Mt 26:41*).

14:41 Are you still sleeping and resting? The 3 disciples remained indifferent not only to the needs of Christ at that moment, but their need of strength and watchfulness for the impending temptation that all 11 would face. The disciples needed to learn that spiritual victory goes to those who are alert in prayer and depend on God, and that self-confidence and spiritual unpreparedness lead to spiritual disaster. **Son of Man.** *See note on 2:10.*

He *came the third time, and *said to them, "[a]Are
you still sleeping and resting? It is enough; [A]the
hour has come; behold, the Son of Man is being [b]be-
trayed into the hands of sinners. 42 Get up, let us be
going; behold, the one who betrays Me is at hand!"

BETRAYAL AND ARREST

43 [A]Immediately while He was still speaking, Judas, one of the twelve, *came up [a]accompanied by
a crowd with swords and clubs, *who were* from the
chief priests and the scribes and the elders. 44 Now
he who was betraying Him had given them a signal,
saying, "Whomever I kiss, He is the one; seize Him
and lead Him away [a]under guard." 45 After coming,
Judas immediately went to Him, saying, "[A]Rabbi!"
and kissed Him. 46 They laid hands on Him and
seized Him. 47 But one of those who stood by drew
his sword, and struck the slave of the high priest
and [a]cut off his ear. 48 And Jesus said to them, "Have
you come out with swords and clubs to arrest Me,
as *you would* against a robber? 49 Every day I was
with you [A]in the temple teaching, and you did not
seize Me; but *this has taken place* to fulfill the Scriptures." 50 And they all left Him and fled.

51 A young man was following Him, wearing *nothing but* a linen sheet over *his* naked *body;* and they
*seized him. 52 But he [a]pulled free of the linen sheet
and escaped naked.

JESUS BEFORE HIS ACCUSERS

53 [A]They led Jesus away to the high priest; and
all the chief priests and the elders and the scribes
*gathered together. 54 Peter had followed Him at
a distance, [A]right into [B]the courtyard of the high
priest; and he was sitting with the [a]officers and
[C]warming himself at the [b]fire. 55 Now the chief
priests and the whole [a,A]Council kept trying to obtain
testimony against Jesus to put Him to death, and
they were not finding any. 56 For many were giving
false testimony against Him, but their testimony

14:41 [a]Or *Keep on sleeping therefore* [b]Or *delivered* [A]Mark 14:35 14:43 [a]Lit *and with him* [A]Mark 14:43-50: *Matt 26:47-56; Luke 22:47-53; John 18:3-11* 14:44 [a]Lit *safely* 14:45 [A]Matt 23:7 14:47 [a]Lit *took off* 14:49 [A]Mark 12:35; Luke 19:47; 21:37 14:52 [a]Lit *left behind* 14:53 [A]Mark 14:53-65: *Matt 26:57-68; John 18:12f, 19-24* 14:54 [a]Or *servants* [b]Lit *light* [A]Mark 14:68 [B]Matt 26:3 [C]Mark 14:67; John 18:18 14:55 [a]Or *Sanhedrin* [A]Matt 5:22

14:43 **Judas, one of the twelve.** *See notes on 3:19; Mt 26:47.* All the gospel writers refer to him this way (vv. 10, 20; Mt 26:14, 47; Lk 22:47; Jn 6:71); and in so doing, they display remarkable restraint in describing and evaluating Judas. Especially in this context, such a simple description actually heightens the evil of his crime more than any series of derogatory epithets or negative criticisms could do. It also points out the precise fulfillment of Jesus' announcement in vv. 18–20. **a crowd with swords and clubs.** This "crowd" was a carefully selected group whose sole purpose was arresting Jesus so He could be put to death. A cohort (600 men at full strength) of Roman soldiers (Jn 18:3, 12) was in this crowd because the Jewish leaders (cf. Lk 22:52) who organized the throng needed permission from Rome to carry out the death penalty and feared the crowds. The "swords" were the regular small hand weapons of the Romans, and the wood "clubs" were ordinary weapons carried by the Jewish temple police. **chief priests … scribes … elders.** Although 3 distinct sections of the Sanhedrin (as indicated by the Gr. definite article with each), they were acting in unity. These Jewish leaders had evidently for some time (*see notes on 3:6; 11:18*) hoped to accuse Jesus of rebellion against Rome. Then, His execution could be blamed on the Romans, and the leaders could escape potential reprisals from those Jews who admired Jesus. The Sanhedrin likely had hurried to Pontius Pilate, the Roman governor, to ask immediate use of his soldiers; or perhaps acted on a prearranged agreement for troop use on short notice. Whatever the case, the leaders procured the assistance of the Roman military from Fort Antonia in Jerusalem.

14:44 **kiss.** In addition to being a special act of respect and affection, this kind of kiss was a sign of homage in Middle East culture. Out of the varieties of this kiss (on the feet, on the back of the hand, on the palm, on the hem of the garment), Judas chose the embrace and the kiss on the cheek—the one that showed the closest love and affection, normally reserved for one with whom a person had a close, intimate relationship (such as a pupil for his teacher). Judas could not have chosen a more despicable way to identify Jesus, because he perverted its usual meaning so treacherously and hypocritically.

14:45 **Rabbi!** "My master" (*see note on 9:5*). **kissed Him.** "Kissed" is an intensified form of the verb for "kiss" in v. 44, and it denotes a fervent, continuous expression of affection (cf. Lk 7:38, 45; 15:20; Ac 20:37). It was with intensity that Judas pretended to love Christ. The act was likely prolonged enough so the crowd had time to identify Jesus.

14:47 **one of those who stood by.** Simon Peter (Jn 18:10), one of the two disciples who brought a weapon (Lk 22:38). Mark and the other synoptic writers do not identify Peter explicitly, perhaps because they wrote earlier than John, during the time when Peter would still have been in danger of Jewish revenge. **the slave of the high priest.** Malchus (Jn 18:10). He was neither a soldier nor temple policeman, but rather was a high-ranking personal slave of Caiaphas, the High Priest, probably sent along to observe Judas and report on the events of the evening.

14:48 **as … against a robber.** Jesus expressed a righteous resentment toward the crowd's actions and attitudes. "Robber" was normally a highwayman or armed bandit who would resist arrest. The setting which the crowd orchestrated was completely inconsistent with His well known ministry as a religious teacher.

14:49 **temple.** *See note on 11:11.* This was the most public place in Jerusalem. **to fulfill the Scriptures.** Entirely apart from the crowd's sinful intentions against Jesus, God was sovereignly using them to fulfill prophecy (cf. Is 53:7–9, 12) and accomplish His gracious purposes (*see note on Mt 26:54*).

14:50 **left Him.** The disciples found no comfort in Jesus' reference to Scripture, but instead their faith in Him collapsed as they realized He would not resist arrest and that they also might be captured.

14:51 **A young man.** This perhaps was Mark himself. If the mob under Judas' guidance had first gone to Mark's mother's house in search of Jesus—possibly where the last Passover was observed by Jesus and the 12—Mark could have heard the noise, suspected what was happening, and hurried to follow the multitude. **a linen sheet.** Either a loose-fitting linen sleeping garment or a sheet Mark had hastily wrapped around himself after being roused from bed.

14:52 **escaped naked.** Mark escaped capture and ran, but in so doing his covering came off or was pulled off, and he left with nothing at all on, or nothing more than undergarments.

14:53–15:15 Mark's account of Jesus' trials, like that of all the gospels, makes it clear that Christ was tried in two general phases: first, before the religious authorities (the Jewish Sanhedrin), and second, before the secular political authorities (Rome, represented by governor Pontius Pilate). Each of these phases had 3 parts: preliminary interrogation, formal arraignment, and formal sentencing. Mark, like the other gospel writers, did not include a comprehensive account of all the details and stages. A complete picture requires the material from all 4 Gospels being combined.

14:53 **high priest.** Caiaphas, the leader of the Sanhedrin (*see notes on Mt 26:3, 57;* cf. Jn 18:24). He was the official High Priest in A.D. 18–36. **chief priests … elders … scribes.** *See note on v. 43.* The entire Sanhedrin, the whole hierarchy, was out in force.

14:54 **courtyard of the high priest.** A quadrangle in the center of the High Priest's residence.

14:55 **Council.** The Sanhedrin (*see note on Mt 26:59*).

14:56 Because Jesus was innocent, the Jewish leaders could not convict Him except by relying on perjured testimony and perverted justice. The Jews were intent on doing whatever was necessary, even if they had to violate every biblical and rabbinical rule. **many were giving false testimony against Him.** There was no lack of people to come forward at the Sanhedrin's invitation to consciously present false, lying testimony. **was not consistent.** The testimonies were grossly inconsistent. The law, however, required exact agreement between two witnesses (Dt 17:6; 19:15).

was not consistent. 57 Some stood up and *began* to
give false testimony against Him, saying, 58 "We
heard Him say, '[A]I will destroy this [a]temple made
with hands, and in three days I will build another
made without hands.' " 59 Not even in this respect
was their testimony consistent. 60 The high priest
stood up *and came* forward and questioned Jesus,
saying, "Do You not answer? [a]What is it that these
men are testifying against You?" 61 [A]But He kept
silent and did not answer. [B]Again the high priest
was questioning Him, and [a]saying to Him, "Are
You [b]the Christ, the Son of the Blessed *One?*" 62 And
Jesus said, "I am; and you shall see [A]THE SON OF
MAN SITTING AT THE RIGHT HAND OF POWER, and
[B]COMING WITH THE CLOUDS OF HEAVEN." 63 [A]Tearing
his clothes, the high priest *said, "What further
need do we have of witnesses? 64 You have heard
the [A]blasphemy; how does it seem to you?" And
they all condemned Him to be deserving of death.
65 Some began to [A]spit at Him, and [a,B]to blindfold
Him, and to beat Him with their fists, and to say to
Him, "[C]Prophesy!" And the officers [b]received Him
with [c]slaps *in the face.*

PETER'S DENIALS

66 [A]As Peter was below in [B]the courtyard, one of
the servant-girls of the high priest *came, 67 and
seeing Peter [A]warming himself, she looked at him
and *said, "You also were with Jesus the [B]Nazarene."
68 But he denied *it,* saying, "I neither know nor understand what you are talking about." And he [A]went
out onto the [a]porch.[b] 69 The servant-girl saw him,
and began once more to say to the bystanders, "This
is *one* of them!" 70 But again [A]he denied it. And after
a little while the bystanders were again saying to
Peter, "Surely you are *one* of them, [B]for you are a
Galilean too." 71 But he began to [a]curse and swear,
"I do not know this man you are talking about!"
72 Immediately a rooster crowed a second time.
And Peter remembered how Jesus had made the
remark to him, "Before [A]a rooster crows twice, you
will deny Me three times." [a]And he began to weep.

JESUS BEFORE PILATE

15 [A]Early in the morning the chief priests with
the elders and scribes and the whole [a,B]Council,
immediately held a consultation; and binding Jesus,

14:58 [a]Or *sanctuary* [A]Matt 26:61; Mark 15:29; John 2:19 14:60 [a]Or *what do these testify?* 14:61 [a]Lit *says* [b]I.e. the Messiah [A]Matt 26:63 [B]Mark 14:61-63: *Matt 26:63ff; Luke 22:67-71* 14:62 [A]Ps 110:1; Mark 13:26 [B]Dan 7:13 14:63 [A]Num 14:6; Matt 26:65; Acts 14:14 14:64 [A]Lev 24:16 14:65 [a]Or *cover over His face* [b]Or *treated* [c]Or *blows with rods* [A]Matt 26:67; Mark 10:34 [B]Esth 7:8 [C]Matt 26:68; Luke 22:64 14:66 [A]Mark 14:66-72: *Matt 26:69-75; Luke 22:56-62; John 18:16-18, 25-27* [B]Mark 14:54 14:67 [A]Mark 14:54 [B]Mark 1:24 14:68 [a]Or *forecourt, gateway* [b]Later mss add *and a rooster crowed* [A]Mark 14:54 14:70 [A]Mark 14:68 [B]Matt 26:73; Luke 22:59 14:71 [a]Or *put himself under a curse* 14:72 [a]Or *Thinking of this, he began weeping* or *Rushing out, he began weeping* [A]Mark 14:30, 68 15:1 [a]Or *Sanhedrin* [A]Matt 27:1 [B]Matt 5:22

14:57, 58 false testimony. The witnesses maliciously garbled and misrepresented Jesus' statements. Quite possibly they blended His figurative statement regarding His death and resurrection in Jn 2:19–22 with His prediction of a literal destruction of the temple in 13:2. Their charge claimed He was disloyal to the present order of religion and worship (by replacing the current temple), and that He was blaspheming God (by saying He would so quickly rebuild the temple without hands).

14:58 I will destroy this temple made with hands. This refers to the material sanctuary in Jerusalem. Jesus boldly made this assertion in front of the temple the Jews revered, but His words were not fully understood (*see notes on 14:57, 58; Jn 2:19, 20*).

14:60 Caiaphas attempted to salvage the tense situation when the continued false charges were failing to establish a case or elicit a response from the Lord. The High Priest could not understand how Jesus could remain silent and not offer any defense.

14:61 kept silent. The silence of innocence, integrity, and faith in God. An answer by Jesus would have given all the false testimonies and illegal proceedings an appearance of legitimacy. **Christ.** This term refers to Jesus' claim to be the promised Messiah (*see note on Mt 1:1*). **Son of the Blessed *One*.** This refers to Jesus' claim to deity. This is the only NT use of the expression, and it is an example of Jewish wording that avoided using God's name (*see note on Jn 8:58*). Jesus' acceptance of messiahship and deity (cf. Lk 4:18–21; Jn 4:25, 26; 5:17, 18; 8:58) had always brought vigorous opposition from the Jewish leaders (Jn 5:19–47; 8:16–19; 10:29–39). Clearly, the High Priest was asking this question in hopes that Jesus would affirm it and open Himself to the formal charge of blasphemy.

14:62 I am. An explicit, unambiguous declaration that Jesus was and is both the Messiah and the Son of God. Son of Man. *See notes on 2:10; Mt 8:20.* Jesus used this commonly acknowledged messianic title of Himself more than 80 times in the gospels, here in a reference to Ps 110:1 and Da 7:13 (cf. Rev 1:13; 14:14). right hand of Power. Cf. 10:37; Ac 2:33; 7:55; Heb 2:9; Rev 12:5. Jesus' glorified position is next to the throne of God (the "Power" is another reference to God). clouds. *See note on 13:26*; cf. Mt 24:30; 26:64; Lk 21:27; Ac 1:9–11; Rev 1:7; 14:14.

14:63 Tearing his clothes. A ceremonial, and in this case contrived, display of grief and indignation over the presumed dishonoring of God's name by Jesus (cf. Gen 37:29; Lv 10:6; Job 1:20; Ac 14:14; *see note on Mt 26:65*). **further need ... of witnesses.** A rhetorical question that expressed relief that the tense and embarrassing situation was finally over. Because Jesus had allegedly incriminated Himself in the eyes of the Sanhedrin, they would not need to summon any more lying witnesses.

14:64 blasphemy. *See note on 2:7*; cf. 3:29. Strictly speaking, Jesus' words were not "blasphemy," or defiant irreverence of God (Lv 24:10–23), but Caiaphas regarded them as such because Jesus claimed for Himself equal power and prerogative with God.

14:65 spit at Him ... beat Him. For the Jews, to "spit" in another's face was the grossest, most hateful form of personal insult (cf. Nu 12:14; Dt 25:9). Their brutal cruelty reached a climax and revealed the great depravity of their hearts when they "beat Him," or hit Him with clenched fists. **Prophesy!** They jeeringly and disrespectfully ordered Jesus to use the prophetic powers He claimed to have—even in the frivolous manner of telling them who struck Him (Mt 26:68).

14:66 below. The apartments around it were higher than the courtyard itself. **one of the servant-girls.** Female slave, or maid, in the household of the High Priest. She might have been the same gatekeeper (cf. Jn 18:15, 16) who admitted Peter, and who being curious and suspicious of him, wanted a closer look.

14:67 the Nazarene. Their reference to Jesus' hometown communicates a feeling of contempt, in keeping with the views of the Jewish leaders and the poor reputation Nazareth generally had (cf. Jn 1:46).

14:68 the porch. Used only here in the NT, this term denotes "the forecourt," or "entryway," a covered archway of the courtyard, opening onto the street.

14:70 Galilean. Frequently used as a derisive label by people in Jerusalem toward their northern neighbors. It strongly suggested that natives of Galilee were deemed unsophisticated and uneducated (cf. Ac 4:13).

14:72 a rooster crowed. This reference brings to mind Jesus' prediction in v. 30 (*see note there*) and Mt 26:34. Amid all the accusations being hurled at him, Peter either did not hear the rooster's crowing, or failed to realize its significance. When the rooster crowed the second time, Jesus looked at Peter (Lk 22:61), triggering Peter's memory and bringing conviction of his denials (cf. v. 72).

15:1 Early in the morning. At daybreak, probably between 5:00 and 6:00 a.m. Having illegally decided Jesus' guilt during the night (14:53–65; Jn 18:13–24), the Sanhedrin formally convened after daybreak to pronounce a sentence. **chief priests.** *See note on Mt 2:4.* **elders and scribes.** *See notes on 14:43; Mt 2:4.* **the whole Council.** The entire Sanhedrin (*see notes on 14:43, 53; Mt 26:59*). **a consultation.** This meeting is described

they led Him away and delivered Him to Pilate.
2 [A]Pilate questioned Him, "Are You the King of the
Jews?" And He *answered him, "*It is as* you say."
3 The chief priests *began* to accuse Him [a]harshly.
4 Then Pilate questioned Him again, saying, "Do
You not answer? See how many charges they bring
against You!" 5 But Jesus [A]made no further answer;
so Pilate was amazed.
6 [A]Now at *the* feast he used to release for them
any one prisoner whom they requested. 7 The man
named Barabbas had been imprisoned with the in-
surrectionists who had committed murder in the
insurrection. 8 The crowd went up and began asking
him *to do* as he had been accustomed to do for them.
9 Pilate answered them, saying, "Do you want me
to release for you the King of the Jews?" 10 For he
was aware that the chief priests had handed Him
over because of envy. 11 But the chief priests stirred
up the crowd [A]*to ask* him to release Barabbas for
them instead. 12 Answering again, Pilate said to
them, "Then what shall I do with Him whom you
call the King of the Jews?" 13 They shouted [a]back,
"Crucify Him!" 14 But Pilate said to them, "Why, what
evil has He done?" But they shouted all the more,
"Crucify Him!" 15 Wishing to satisfy the crowd, Pilate
released Barabbas for them, and after having Jesus
[A]scourged, he handed Him over to be crucified.

JESUS IS MOCKED

16 [A]The soldiers took Him away into [B]the [a]palace
(that is, the Praetorium), and they *called together
the whole *Roman* [b,C]cohort. 17 They *dressed Him up
in purple, and after twisting a crown of thorns, they
put it on Him; 18 and they began to acclaim Him, "Hail,
King of the Jews!" 19 They kept beating His head with a
[a]reed, and spitting on Him, and kneeling and bowing
before Him. 20 After they had mocked Him, they took
the purple robe off Him and put His *own* garments
on Him. And they *led Him out to crucify Him.
21 [A]They *pressed into service a passer-by coming
from the country, Simon of Cyrene (the father of
Alexander and [B]Rufus), to bear His cross.

THE CRUCIFIXION

22 [A]Then they *brought Him to the place [B]Gol-
gotha, which is translated, Place of a Skull. 23 They
tried to give Him [A]wine mixed with myrrh; but He
did not take it. 24 And they *crucified Him, and *[A]di-
vided up His garments among themselves, casting
[a]lots for them *to decide* [b]what each man should take.

15:2 [A]Mark 15:2-5: *Matt 27:11-14; Luke 23:2, 3; John 18:29-38* 15:3 [a]Or *of many things* 15:5 [A]Matt 27:12 15:6 [A]Mark 15:6-15: *Matt 27:15-26; Luke 23:18-25; John 18:39-19:16* 15:11 [A]Acts 3:14 15:13 [a]Or *again* 15:15 [A]Matt 27:26 15:16 [a]Or *court* [b]Or *battalion* [A]Mark 15:16-20: *Matt 27:27-31* [B]Matt 26:3; 27:27 [C]Acts 10:1 15:19 [a]Or *staff* (made of a reed) 15:21 [A]Mark 15:21: *Matt 27:32; Luke 23:26* [B]Rom 16:13 15:22 [A]Mark 15:22-32: *Matt 27:33-44; Luke 23:33-43; John 19:17-24* [B]Luke 23:33; John 19:17 15:23 [A]Matt 27:34 15:24 [a]Lit *a lot upon* [b]Lit *who should take what* [A]Ps 22:18; John 19:24

in Lk 22:66–71. It amounted to little more than reiterating the charges earlier made against Jesus and affirming His guilty verdict. **Pilate.** Roman procurator (governor) of Judea from A.D. 26–36. His official residence was at Caesarea, but he was in Jerusalem for Passover.

15:2 Pilate questioned Him. John records (Jn 18:30) that the Jewish leaders demanded that Pilate simply agree to the death sentence they had already pronounced on Jesus (14:64). Pilate refused, and the Jewish leaders then presented their false charges against Jesus (Lk 23:2). Having heard those charges, Pilate then questioned Him. **Are You the King of the Jews?** The only charge Pilate took seriously was that Jesus claimed to be a king, thus making Him guilty of rebellion against Rome. Pilate's question reveals that he had already been informed of this charge (Lk 23:2). ***It is as* you say.** Jesus' answer acknowledged that He was the rightful king of Israel, but implied that Pilate's concept of what that meant differed from His (cf. Jn 18:34–37).

15:4 Do You not answer? Pilate was amazed at Jesus' silence, since accused prisoners predictably and vehemently denied the charges against them. Jesus may have remained silent in fulfillment of prophecy (Is 42:1, 2; 53:7), because Pilate had already pronounced him innocent (Lk 23:4; Jn 18:38), or both.

15:6 at *the* feast. The Passover. **used to.** Ancient secular sources indicate that Roman governors occasionally granted amnesty at the request of their subjects. Assuming that the people would ask for their king (whom they had so acknowledged earlier in the week; 11:1–10) to be freed, Pilate undoubtedly saw this annual custom as the way out of his dilemma regarding Jesus.

15:7 Barabbas. A robber (Jn 18:40) and murderer (Lk 23:18, 19) in some way involved as an anti-Roman insurrectionist. Whether his involvement was motivated by political conviction or personal greed is not known. It is impossible to identify the specific insurrection in question, but such uprisings were common in Jesus' day and were precursors of the wholesale revolt of A.D. 66–70.

15:10 because of envy. Pilate realized that the Jewish authorities had not handed Jesus over to him out of loyalty to Rome. He saw through their deceit to the underlying reason—their jealousy over Jesus' popularity with the people.

15:13 Crucify. *See note on v. 15.*

15:15 scourged. With a whip (known as a *flagellum*) consisting of a wooden handle to which metal-tipped leather thongs were attached. Being scourged with a *flagellum* was a fearful ordeal, ripping the flesh down to the bone, causing severe bleeding. It was a beating from which prisoners often died. **crucified.** *See note on Mt 27:31.* Crucifixion, the common Roman method of execution for slaves and foreigners, was described by the Roman writer Cicero as "the cruelest and most hideous punishment possible."

15:16 Praetorium. The governor's official residence in Jerusalem, probably located in the Fortress Antonia complex. **whole *Roman* cohort.** The Roman cohort, consisting of 600 men, was stationed in Jerusalem. All the soldiers who were not on duty at that time gathered to mock Jesus.

15:17 dressed Him up in purple ... crown of thorns. "Purple" was the color traditionally worn by royalty; the "crown of thorns" was in mockery of a royal crown. The callous soldiers decided to hold a mock coronation of Jesus as king of the Jews.

15:18 Hail, King of the Jews! The greeting was a parody of that given to Caesar.

15:19 a reed. An imitation of a royal scepter.

15:21 Condemned prisoners were required to carry the heavy crossbeam of their cross to the execution site. Exhausted from a sleepless night and severely wounded and weakened by His scourging, Jesus was unable to continue. The Roman guards conscripted Simon, apparently at random, to carry Jesus' crossbeam the rest of the way. Simon, from the North African city of Cyrene, was on his way into Jerusalem. The identification of him as "the father of Alexander and Rufus" (cf. Ro 16:13) is evidence of Mark's connection with the church at Rome (see Introduction: Background and Setting).

15:22 Golgotha ... Place of a Skull. "Golgotha" is an Aram. word meaning "skull," which Mark translated for his readers (see Introduction: Background and Setting). Although the exact site is unknown, today two locations in Jerusalem are considered as possibilities: 1) Gordon's Calvary (named for the man who discovered it in modern times) to the N; and 2) the traditional site to the W at the Church of the Holy Sepulchre, a tradition dating to the fourth century.

15:23 wine mixed with myrrh. To temporarily deaden the pain (*see note on Mt 27:34*), the Romans allowed this drink to be administered to victims of crucifixion, probably not out of compassion, but to keep them from struggling while being crucified.

15:24 crucified. *See note on v. 15.* None of the gospel accounts give a detailed description of the actual crucifixion process. **divided up His garments.** This was in fulfillment of Ps 22:18. The executioners customarily divided the victim's clothes among themselves.

25 It was the [a,A]third hour [b]when they crucified Him.
26 The inscription of the charge against Him [a]read,

"[A]THE KING OF THE JEWS."

27 They *crucified two robbers with Him, one on
His right and one on His left. 28 [[a]And the Scripture
was fulfilled which says, "And He was numbered
with transgressors."] 29 Those passing by were [a]hurl-
ing abuse at Him, [A]wagging their heads, and saying,
"Ha! You who *are going to* [B]destroy the temple and
rebuild it in three days, 30 save Yourself, and come
down from the cross!" 31 In the same way the chief
priests also, along with the scribes, were mocking
Him among themselves and saying, "[A]He saved
others; [a]He cannot save Himself. 32 Let *this* Christ,
[A]the King of Israel, now come down from the cross,
so that we may see and believe!" [B]Those who were
crucified with Him were also insulting Him.
33 [A]When the [a,B]sixth hour came, darkness [b]fell
over the whole land until the [c,B]ninth hour. 34 At the
[A]ninth hour Jesus cried out with a loud voice, "[B]ELOI,
ELOI, LAMA SABACHTHANI?" which is translated,
"MY GOD, MY GOD, WHY HAVE YOU FORSAKEN ME?"
35 When some of the bystanders heard it, they *began*
saying, "Behold, He is calling for Elijah." 36 Someone ran and filled a sponge with sour wine, put it
on a reed, and gave Him a drink, saying, "[a]Let us
see whether Elijah will come to take Him down."
37 [A]And Jesus uttered a loud cry, and breathed His
last. 38 [A]And the veil of the temple was torn in two
from top to bottom. 39 [A]When the centurion, who
was standing [a]right in front of Him, saw [b]the way
He breathed His last, he said, "Truly this man was
[c]the Son of God!"
40 [A]There were also *some* women looking on from
a distance, among whom *were* Mary Magdalene,
and Mary the mother of [a]James [B]the [b]Less and Joses,
and [C]Salome. 41 When He was in Galilee, they used
to follow Him and [a,A]minister to Him; and *there*
were many other women who came up with Him
to Jerusalem.

15:25 [a]I.e. 9 a.m. [b]Lit *and* [A]Mark 15:33 15:26 [a]Lit *had been inscribed* [A]Matt 27:37 15:28 [a]Early mss do not contain this v 15:29 [a]Or *blaspheming* [A]Ps 22:7; 109:25; Matt 27:39 [B]Mark 14:58; John 2:19 15:31 [a]Or *can He not save Himself?* [A]Matt 27:42; Luke 23:35 15:32 [A]Matt 27:42; Mark 15:26 [B]Matt 27:44; Mark 15:27; Luke 23:39-43 15:33 [a]I.e. noon [b]Or *occurred* [c]I.e. 3 p.m. [A]Mark 15:33-41: *Matt 27:45-56; Luke 23:44-49* [B]Matt 27:45f; Mark 15:25; Luke 23:44 15:34 [A]Matt 27:45f; Mark 15:25; Luke 23:44 [B]Ps 22:1; Matt 27:46 15:36 [a]Lit *Permit that we see;* or *Hold off, let us see* 15:37 [A]Matt 27:50; Luke 23:46; John 19:30 15:38 [A]Ex 26:31-33; Matt 27:51; Luke 23:45 15:39 [a]Or *opposite Him* [b]Lit *that He thus* [c]Or *a son of God* or *son of a god* [A]Matt 27:54; Mark 15:45; Luke 23:47 15:40 [a]Or *Jacob* [b]Lit *little* (either in stature or age) [A]Mark 15:40, 41: *Matt 27:55f;* Luke 23:49; John 19:25 [B]Luke 19:3 [C]Mark 16:1 15:41 [a]Or *wait on* [A]Matt 27:55f

15:25 third hour. The crucifixion occurred at 9:00 a.m. based on the Jewish method of reckoning time. John notes that it was "about the sixth hour" when Pilate sentenced Jesus to be crucified (Jn 19:14). John apparently used the Roman method of reckoning time, which counted the hours from midnight. Thus John's "sixth hour" would have been about 6:00 a.m.

15:26 inscription of the charge. The crime for which a condemned man was executed was written on a wooden board, which was fastened to the cross above his head. Jesus' inscription was written in Lat., Heb., and Gr. (Jn 19:20). *See note on Mt 27:37.* **THE KING OF THE JEWS.** Since Pilate had repeatedly declared Jesus to be innocent of any crime (Lk 23:4, 14, 15, 22), he ordered this inscription written for Him. While Pilate's intent was probably neither to mock nor to honor Jesus, he certainly intended it as an affront to the Jewish authorities, who had given him so much trouble. When the outraged Jewish leaders demanded the wording be changed, Pilate bluntly refused (*see note on Jn 19:22*). A comparison of all 4 gospel accounts reveals that the full inscription read THIS IS JESUS OF NAZARETH, THE KING OF THE JEWS. *See note on Lk 23:38.*

15:27 two robbers. They were probably involved with Barabbas in the rebellion (*see note on v. 7*), since robbery itself was not a capital offense under Roman law.

15:28 By placing Jesus' cross between the two robbers (v. 27), Pilate may have intended to further insult the Jews, implying that their king was nothing but a common criminal. God intended it, however, as a fulfillment of prophecy (cf. Is 53:12).

15:29 wagging their heads. A gesture of contempt and derision (cf. 2Ki 19:21; Pss 22:7; 44:14; 109:25; Jer 18:16; La 2:15). **You who *are going to* destroy the temple and rebuild it in three days.** The passersby repeated the false charge made during Jesus' trial before Caiaphas (14:58). The charge was a misunderstanding of Jesus' words in Jn 2:19–21.

15:32 Christ. *See note on 1:1.* **come down from the cross.** A final demand for a miracle by the unbelieving Jewish authorities (cf. 8:11). Their claim that they would then see and believe was false, since they later refused to believe the even greater miracle of Christ's resurrection. **Those who were crucified with Him.** The two robbers joined in the reviling of Jesus, though one later repented (Lk 23:40–43).

15:33 sixth hour. Noon, by Jewish reckoning, at the halfway point of Jesus' 6 hours on the cross (*see note on v. 25*). **darkness.** A mark of divine judgment (cf. Is 5:30; 13:10, 11; Joel 2:1, 2; Am 5:20; Zep 1:14, 15; Mt 8:12; 22:13; 25:30). The geographical extent of the darkness is not known, although the writings of the church fathers hint that it extended beyond Israel (regionally). **ninth hour.** I.e., 3:00 p.m.

15:34 Eloi ... sabachthani? The Aram. words of Ps 22:1. Matthew, who also recorded this cry, gave the Heb. words (Mt 27:46). **why have You forsaken Me?** Jesus felt keenly His abandonment by the Father, resulting from God's wrath being poured out on Him as the substitute for sinners (*see notes on 2Co 5:21*).

15:35 Elijah. Further mockery which in effect meant, "Let the forerunner come and save this so-called Messiah" (*see note on Lk 1:17*).

15:36 sour wine. Cheap wine commonly consumed by soldiers and workers. It may have been an act of mercy, or merely intended to prolong His suffering. **a reed.** A hyssop branch (Jn 19:29).

15:37 uttered a loud cry. Demonstrating amazing strength in light of the intense suffering He had endured, His shout reveals that His life did not slowly ebb away, but that He voluntarily gave it up (Jn 10:17, 18). For the words of Christ's cry, see Lk 23:46.

15:38 the veil of the temple was torn in two. The massive curtain separating the Holy of Holies from the rest of the sanctuary (Ex 26:31–33; 40:20, 21; Lv 16:2; Heb 9:3). This rending signified that the way into God's presence was open by the death of His Son.

15:39 centurion. The Roman officer in charge of the crucifixion. Centurions, considered the backbone of the Roman army, commanded 100 soldiers. **saw the way He breathed His last.** The centurion had seen many crucified victims die, but none like Jesus. The strength He possessed at His death, as evidenced by His loud cry (v. 37), was unheard of for a victim of crucifixion. That, coupled with the earthquake that coincided with Christ's death (Mt 27:51–54), convinced the centurion that Jesus "was the Son of God." According to tradition, this man actually became a believer (*see note on Mt 27:54*).

15:40 Some of these women had earlier been at the foot of the cross (Jn 19:25–27). By then, unable to watch Jesus' suffering at such close range, they were "looking on from a distance." Their sympathetic loyalty was in sharp contrast to the disciples who, except for John, were nowhere to be found. **Mary Magdalene.** She was from the village of Magdala, on the W shore of the Sea of Galilee, hence her name. Luke notes that Jesus had cast 7 demons out of her (Lk 8:2). She is usually named first when the women who followed Jesus are listed, which may suggest that she was their leader. **Mary the mother of James the Less and Joses.** She is distinguished from the other Marys by the name of her sons. "James the Less" (called "James the son of Alphaeus" in Mt 10:3) was one of the 12. **Salome.** The wife of Zebedee (Mt 27:56), and the mother of James and John (*see note on 10:35*).

15:41 many other women. They had been with Jesus since the days of His Galilean ministry, traveling with Him and the disciples, caring for their needs (cf. Lk 8:2, 3).

JESUS IS BURIED

42 [A]When evening had already come, because it
was [B]the preparation day, that is, the day before
the Sabbath, 43 Joseph of Arimathea came, a [A]prom-
inent member of the Council, who himself was
[B]waiting for the kingdom of God; and he [C]gathered
up courage and went in before Pilate, and asked
for the body of Jesus. 44 Pilate wondered if He was
dead by this time, and summoning the centurion,
he questioned him as to whether He was already
dead. 45 And ascertaining this from [A]the centurion,
he granted the body to Joseph. 46 Joseph bought a
linen cloth, took Him down, wrapped Him in the
linen cloth and laid Him in a tomb which had been
hewn out in the rock; and he rolled a stone against
the entrance of the tomb. 47 [A]Mary Magdalene and
Mary the *mother* of Joses were looking on *to see*
where He was laid.

THE RESURRECTION

16 [A]When the Sabbath was over, [B]Mary Magdalene,
and Mary the *mother* of [a]James, and Salome,
[C]bought spices, so that they might come and anoint
Him. 2 Very early on the first day of the week, they
*came to the tomb when the sun had risen. 3 They
were saying to one another, "Who will roll away
[A]the stone for us from the entrance of the tomb?"
4 Looking up, they *saw that the stone had been rolled
away, [a]although it was extremely large. 5 [A]Entering
the tomb, they saw a young man sitting at the right,
wearing a white robe; and they [B]were amazed. 6 And
he *said to them, "[A]Do not be amazed; you are looking
for Jesus the [B]Nazarene, who has been crucified. [C]He
has risen; He is not here; behold, *here is* the place
where they laid Him. 7 But go, tell His disciples and
Peter, '[A]He is going ahead of you to Galilee; there you
will see Him, just as He told you.' " 8 They went out

15:42 [A]Mark 15:42-47: *Matt 27:57-61; Luke 23:50-56; John 19:38-42* [B]Matt 27:62 15:43 [A]Matt 27:57; Luke 23:50, 51; Acts 13:50; 17:12 [B]Matt 27:57; Luke 2:25, 38; 23:51; John 19:38 [C]John 19:38 15:45 [A]Mark 15:39 15:47 [A]Matt 27:56; Mark 15:40; 16:1 16:1 [a]Or *Jacob* [A]Mark 16:1-8: *Matt 28:1-8; Luke 24:1-10;* John 20:1-8 [B]Mark 15:47 [C]Luke 23:56; John 19:39f 16:3 [A]Matt 27:60; Mark 15:46; 16:4 16:4 [a]Lit *for* 16:5 [A]John 20:11, 12 [B]Mark 9:15 16:6 [A]Mark 9:15 [B]Mark 1:24 [C]Matt 28:6; Luke 24:6 16:7 [A]Matt 26:32; Mark 14:28

15:42 preparation day. Friday, the day before the Sabbath (Saturday).

15:43 Joseph of Arimathea. "Arimathea," known in the OT as Ramah, or Ramathaim-zophim (the birthplace of Samuel, 1Sa 1:1, 19; 2:11), was located about 15–20 mi. NW of Jerusalem. Joseph was a prominent member of the "council" (or the Sanhedrin, *see note on 14:43*), who had opposed Jesus' condemnation (Lk 23:51). **kingdom of God.** *See note on 1:15.* **gathered up courage.** Pilate would not likely have been pleased to see a member of the Sanhedrin, after that group had forced him to crucify an innocent man. Further, Joseph's public identification with Jesus would enrage the other members of the Sanhedrin. **asked for the body of Jesus.** Though prisoners sentenced to death forfeited the right to burial under Roman law, their bodies were usually granted to relatives who asked for them, but Jesus' mother was emotionally exhausted from the ordeal. There is no evidence that His brothers and sisters were in Jerusalem, and His closest friends, the disciples, had fled (except for John, who had Mary to take care of; Jn 19:26, 27). In the absence of those closest to Jesus, Joseph courageously asked Pilate for Jesus' body.

15:44 Pilate wondered. Victims of crucifixion often lingered for days, hence Pilate's surprise that Jesus was dead after only 6 hours. Before granting Jesus' body to Joseph, Pilate checked with the "centurion" in charge of the crucifixion (*see note on v. 39*) to verify that Jesus was really dead.

15:45 he granted the body to Joseph. Having received confirmation from the centurion that Jesus was dead, Pilate granted Jesus' body to Joseph. By that act, the Romans officially pronounced Jesus dead.

15:46 wrapped Him in the linen cloth. The Jews did not embalm corpses, but wrapped them in perfumed burial cloths (*see note on 16:1*). Nicodemus, another prominent member of the Sanhedrin (cf. Jn 7:50), assisted Joseph in caring for the body of Jesus (Jn 19:39, 40). These men, who had kept their allegiance to Jesus secret during His lifetime, then came forward publicly to bury Him, while the disciples, who had openly followed Jesus, hid (Jn 20:19). **tomb … hewn out in the rock.** This "tomb" was located near Golgotha (Jn 19:42). Matthew adds that it was Joseph's own (Mt 27:60), while Luke and John note that no one as yet had been buried in it (Lk 23:53; Jn 19:41).

16:1 Sabbath was over. The Sabbath officially ended at sundown on Saturday, after which the women were able to purchase spices. **Mary Magdalene, and Mary the *mother* of James, and Salome.** *See note on Mt 27:56.* Luke mentions that Joanna and other women were also there (Lk 24:10; cf. 15:41). **spices.** The women bought more spices in addition to those prepared earlier (cf. Lk 23:56; Jn 19:39, 40). **anoint.** Unlike the Egyptians, the Jewish people did not embalm their dead. Anointing was an act of love, to offset the stench of a decaying body. That the women came to anoint Jesus' body on the third day after His burial showed that they, like the disciples, were not expecting Him to rise from the dead (cf. 8:31; 9:31; 10:34).

16:2 when the sun had risen. John 20:1 says that Mary Magdalene arrived at the tomb while it was still dark. She may have gone on ahead of the other women, or the whole party may have set out together while it was still dark and arrived at the tomb after sunrise.

16:3 Who will roll away the stone … ? Only Mark records this discussion on the way to the tomb. The women realized they had no men with them to move the heavy stone (v. 4) away from the entrance to the tomb. Since they had last visited the tomb on Friday evening, they did not know it had been sealed and a guard posted, which took place on Saturday (Mt 27:62–66).

16:4 the stone had been rolled away. This was not to let Jesus out, but to let the witnesses in. The earthquake when the angel rolled away the stone (Mt 28:2) may have affected only the area around the tomb, since the women apparently did not feel it.

16:5 Entering the tomb. The outer chamber, separated from the burial chamber by a small doorway. **young man … wearing a white robe.** The angel, having rolled away the stone (Mt 28:2), had then entered the burial chamber. Luke records that there were two angels in the tomb; Matthew and Mark focus on the one who spoke (for similar instances, *see note on 10:46*).

16:6 Jesus the Nazarene, who has been crucified. *See note on Mt 2:23.* The inspired account leaves no doubt about who had been in the tomb. The idea of some unbelievers that the women went to the wrong tomb is ludicrous. **He has risen.** Christ's resurrection is one of the central truths of the Christian faith (1Co 15:4) and the only plausible explanation for the empty tomb. Even the Jewish leaders did not deny the reality of the empty tomb, but concocted the story that the disciples had stolen Jesus' body (Mt 28:11–15). The idea that the fearful (Jn 20:19), doubting (vv. 11, 13; Lk 24:10, 11) disciples somehow overpowered the Roman guard detachment and stole Jesus' body is absurd. That they did it while the guards were asleep is even more preposterous. Surely, in moving the heavy stone from the mouth of the tomb, the disciples would have awakened at least one of the soldiers. And in any case, how could the guards have known what happened while they were asleep? Many other theories have been sinfully invented over the centuries to explain away the empty tomb, all of them equally futile.

16:7 and Peter. Peter was not singled out as the leader of the disciples, but to be reassured that, despite his denials of Christ, he was still one of them. **He is going ahead of you to Galilee … as He told you.** *See note on 14:28.* The disciples' lack of faith made them slow to act on these words; they did not leave for Galilee (Mt 28:7, 16) until after Jesus repeatedly appeared to them in Jerusalem (cf. Lk 24:13–32; Jn 20:19–31).

16:8 afraid. They were overwhelmed by the frightening appearance of the angel and the awesome mystery of the Resurrection.

and fled from the tomb, for trembling and astonishment had gripped them; and they said nothing
to anyone, for they were afraid.
9 [[a]Now after He had risen early on the first day
of the week, He first appeared to [A]Mary Magdalene,
from whom He had cast out seven demons. 10 [A]She
went and reported to those who had been with Him,
while they were mourning and weeping. 11 When
they heard that He was alive and had been seen by
her, [A]they refused to believe it.
12 After that, [A]He appeared in a different form [B]to
two of them while they were walking along on their
way to the country. 13 They went away and reported
it to the others, but they [A]did not believe them either.

THE DISCIPLES COMMISSIONED

14 Afterward [A]He appeared [B]to the eleven themselves as they were reclining *at the table;* and He
reproached them for their [C]unbelief and hardness
of heart, because they had not believed those who
had seen Him after He had risen. 15 And He said to
them, "[A]Go into all the world and preach the gospel
to all creation. 16 [A]He who has believed and has been
baptized shall be saved; but he who has disbelieved
shall be condemned. 17 These [a]signs will accompany
those who have believed: [A]in My name they will cast
out demons, they will [B]speak with new tongues;
18 they will [A]pick up serpents, and if they drink any
deadly *poison,* it will not hurt them; they will [B]lay
hands on the sick, and they will recover."
19 So then, when the Lord Jesus had [A]spoken to them,
He [B]was received up into heaven and [C]sat down at the
right hand of God. 20 And they went out and preached
everywhere, while the Lord worked with them, and
confirmed the word by the [a]signs that followed.]

[[b]*And they promptly reported all these instructions to Peter and his companions. And after that, Jesus Himself sent out through them from east to west the sacred and imperishable proclamation of eternal salvation.*]

16:9 [a]Later mss add vv 9-20 [A]Matt 27:56; John 20:14 16:10 [A]John 20:18 16:11 [A]Matt 28:17; Mark 16:13, 14; Luke 24:11, 41; John 20:25 16:12 [A]Mark 16:14; John 21:1, 14 [B]Luke 24:13-35 16:13 [A]Matt 28:17; Mark 16:11, 14; Luke 24:11, 41; John 20:25 16:14 [A]Mark 16:12; John 21:1, 14 [B]Luke 24:36; John 20:19, 26; 1 Cor 15:5 [C]Matt 28:17; Mark 16:11, 13; Luke 24:11, 41; John 20:25 16:15 [A]Matt 28:19; Acts 1:8 16:16 [A]John 3:18, 36; Acts 16:31 16:17 [a]Or *attesting miracles* [A]Mark 9:38; Luke 10:17; Acts 5:16; 8:7; 16:18; 19:12 [B]Acts 2:4; 10:46; 19:6; 1 Cor 12:10, 28, 30; 13:1; 14:2 16:18 [A]Luke 10:19; Acts 28:3-5 [B]Mark 5:23 16:19 [A]Acts 1:3 [B]Luke 9:51; 24:51; John 6:62; 20:17; Acts 1:2, 9-11; 1 Tim 3:16 [C]Ps 110:1; Luke 22:69; Acts 7:55f; Rom 8:34; Eph 1:20; Col 3:1; Heb 1:3; 8:1; 10:12; 12:2; 1 Pet 3:22 16:20 [a]Or *attesting miracles* [b]A few late mss and versions contain this paragraph, usually after v 8; a few have it at the end of ch

16:9–20 The external evidence strongly suggests these verses were not originally part of Mark's gospel. While the majority of Gr. manuscripts contain these verses, the earliest and most reliable do not. A shorter ending also existed, but it is not included in the text. Further, some that include the passage note that it was missing from older Gr. manuscripts, while others have scribal marks indicating the passage was considered spurious. The fourth-century church fathers Eusebius and Jerome noted that almost all Gr. manuscripts available to them lacked vv. 9–20. The internal evidence from this passage also weighs heavily against Mark's authorship. The transition between vv. 8 and 9 is abrupt and awkward. The Gr. particle translated "now" that begins v. 9 implies continuity with the preceding narrative. What follows, however, does not continue the story of the women referred to in v. 8, but describes Christ's appearance to Mary Magdalene (cf. Jn 20:11–18). The masculine participle in v. 9 expects "he" as its antecedent, yet the subject of v. 8 is the women. Although she had just been mentioned 3 times (v. 1; 15:40, 47), v. 9 introduces Mary Magdalene as if for the first time. Further, if Mark wrote v. 9, it is strange that he would only now note that Jesus had cast 7 demons out of her. The angel spoke of Jesus' appearing to His followers in Galilee, yet the appearances described in vv. 9–20 are all in the Jerusalem area. Finally, the presence in these verses of a significant number of Gr. words used nowhere else in Mark argues that Mark did not write them. Verses 9–20 represent an early (they were known to the second-century fathers Irenaeus, Tatian, and, possibly, Justin Martyr) attempt to complete Mark's gospel. While for the most part summarizing truths taught elsewhere in Scripture, vv. 9–20 should always be compared with the rest of Scripture, and no doctrines should be formulated based solely on them. In spite of all these considerations of the likely unreliability of this section, it is possible to be wrong on the issue, and thus, it is good to consider the meaning of this passage and leave it in the text, just as with Jn 7:53–8:11.

16:9 He had risen early on the first day of the week. That is, early Sunday morning. **Mary Magdalene.** *See note on 15:40.*

16:12, 13 This incident is related in Lk 24:13–32.

16:14 the eleven. The 12 minus Judas, who had committed suicide (Mt 27:3–10). **unbelief and hardness of heart.** In not believing the witnesses of the resurrection (vv. 12, 13; cf. Lk 24:10, 11).

16:15, 16 Similar to Matthew's account of the Great Commission, with the added contrast of those who have been baptized (believers) with those who refuse to believe and are condemned. Even if v. 16 is a genuine part of Mark's gospel, it does not teach that baptism saves, since the lost are condemned for unbelief, not for not being baptized (*see note on Ac 2:38*).

16:17, 18 These signs were promised to the apostolic community (Mt 10:1; 2Co 12:12), not all believers in all ages (cf. 1Co 12:29, 30). All (with the exception of drinking poison) were experienced by some in the apostolic church and reported in Scripture (e.g., Ac 28:5), but not afterward (cf. v. 20).

16:19 right hand of God. The place of honor Jesus assumed after His ascension (*see note on Ac 2:33*).

16:20 confirmed the word by the signs. *See notes on Ac 2:22; 2Co 12:12; Heb 2:4.*

THE GOSPEL
ACCORDING TO

LUKE

TITLE

As with the other 3 gospels, the title is derived from the author's name. According to tradition, Luke was a Gentile. The apostle Paul seems to confirm this, distinguishing Luke from those who were "from the circumcision" (Col 4:11, 14). That would make Luke the only Gentile to pen any books of Scripture. He is responsible for a significant portion of the NT, having written both this gospel and the book of Acts (see Author and Date).

Very little is known about Luke. He almost never included personal details about himself, and nothing definite is known about his background or his conversion. Both Eusebius and Jerome identified him as a native of Antioch (which may explain why so much of the book of Acts centers on Antioch—cf. Ac 11:19–27; 13:1–3; 14:26; 15:22, 23, 30–35; 18:22, 23). Luke was a frequent companion of the apostle Paul, at least from the time of Paul's Macedonian vision (Ac 16:9, 10) right up to the time of Paul's martyrdom (2Ti 4:11).

The apostle Paul referred to Luke as a physician (Col 4:14). Luke's interest in medical phenomena is evident in the high profile he gave to Jesus' healing ministry (e.g., 4:38–40; 5:15–25; 6:17–19; 7:11–15; 8:43–47, 49–56; 9:2, 6, 11; 13:11–13; 14:2–4; 17:12–14; 22:50, 51). In Luke's day, physicians did not have a unique vocabulary of technical terminology; so when Luke discusses healings and other medical issues, his language is not markedly different from that of the other gospel writers.

AUTHOR AND DATE

The Gospel of Luke and the book of Acts clearly were written by the same individual (cf. 1:1–4; Ac 1:1). Although he never identified himself by name, it is clear from his use of "we" in many sections of Acts that he was a close companion of the apostle Paul (Ac 16:10–17; 20:5–15; 21:1–18; 27:1–28:16). Luke is the only person, among the colleagues Paul mentions in his own epistles (Col 4:14; 2Ti 4:11; Phm 24), who fits the profile of the author of these books. That accords perfectly with the earliest tradition of the church which unanimously attributed this gospel to Luke.

Luke and Acts appear to have been written at about the same time—Luke first, then Acts. Combined, they make a 2-volume work addressed to "Theophilus" (1:3; Ac 1:1; see Background and Setting) giving a sweeping history of the founding of Christianity, from the birth of Christ to Paul's imprisonment under house arrest in Rome (Ac 28:30, 31).

The book of Acts ends with Paul still in Rome, which leads to the conclusion that Luke wrote these books from Rome during Paul's imprisonment there (ca. A.D. 60–62). Luke records Jesus' prophecy of the destruction of Jerusalem in A.D. 70 (19:42–44; 21:20–24) but makes no mention of the fulfillment of that prophecy, either here or in Acts. Luke made it a point to record such prophetic fulfillments (cf. Ac 11:28), so it is extremely unlikely he wrote these books after the Roman invasion of Jerusalem. Acts also includes no mention of the great persecution that began under Nero in A.D. 64. In addition, many scholars set the date of James' martyrdom at A.D. 62, and if that was before Luke completed his history, he certainly would have mentioned it. So, the most likely date for this gospel is A.D. 60 or 61.

BACKGROUND AND SETTING

Luke dedicated his works to "most excellent Theophilus" (lit. "lover of God"—1:3; cf. Ac 1:1). This designation, which may be a nickname or a pseudonym, is accompanied by a formal address ("most excellent")—possibly signifying that "Theophilus" was a well known Roman dignitary, perhaps one of those who had turned to Christ in "Caesar's household" (Php 4:22).

It is almost certain, however, that Luke envisioned a much broader audience for his work than this one man. The dedications at the outset of Luke and Acts are like the formal dedication in a modern book. They are not like the address of an epistle.

Luke expressly stated that his knowledge of the events recorded in his gospel came from the reports of those who were eyewitnesses (1:1, 2)—strongly implying that he himself was not an eyewitness. It is clear from his prologue that his aim was to give an ordered account of the events of Jesus' life, but this does not mean he always followed a strict chronological order in all instances (e.g., *see note on 3:20*).

By acknowledging that he had compiled his account from various extant sources (*see note on 1:1*), Luke was not disclaiming divine inspiration for his work. The process of inspiration never bypasses or overrides the personalities, vocabularies, and styles of the human authors of Scripture. The unique traits of the human authors are always indelibly stamped on all the books of Scripture. Luke's research is no exception to this rule. The research itself was orchestrated by divine Providence. And in his writing, Luke was moved by the Spirit of God (2Pe 1:21). Therefore, his account is infallibly true (*see note on 1:3*).

HISTORICAL AND THEOLOGICAL THEMES

Luke's style is that of a scholarly, well-read author (*see note on 1:1–4*). He wrote as a meticulous historian, often giving details that helped identify the historical context of the events he described (1:5; 2:1, 2; 3:1, 2; 13:1–4).

His account of the nativity is the fullest in all the gospel records—and (like the rest of Luke's work) more polished in its literary style. He included in the birth narrative a series of praise psalms (1:46–55; 1:68–79; 2:14; 2:29–32, 34, 35). He alone reported the unusual circumstances surrounding the birth of John the Baptist, the annunciation to Mary, the manger, the shepherds, and Simeon and Anna (2:25–38).

A running theme in Luke's gospel is Jesus' compassion for Gentiles, Samaritans, women, children, tax collectors, sinners, and others often regarded as outcasts in Israel. Every time he mentions a tax collector (3:12; 5:27; 7:29; 15:1; 18:10–13; 19:2), it is in a positive sense. Yet, Luke did not ignore the salvation of those who were rich and respectable—e.g., 23:50–53. From the outset of Jesus' public ministry (4:18) to the Lord's final words on the cross (23:40–43), Luke underscored this theme of Christ's ministry to the pariahs of society. Again and again he showed how the Great Physician ministered to those most aware of their need (cf. 5:31, 32; 15:4–7, 31, 32; 19:10).

The high profile Luke accords to women is particularly significant. From the nativity account, where Mary, Elizabeth, and Anna are given prominence (chaps. 1; 2), to the events of resurrection morning, where women again are major characters (24:1, 10), Luke emphasized the central role of women in the life and ministry of our Lord (e.g., 7:12–15, 37–50; 8:2, 3, 43–48; 10:38–42; 13:11–13; 21:2–4; 23:27–29, 49, 55, 56).

Several other recurring themes form threads through Luke's gospel. Examples of these are human fear in the presence of God (*see note on 1:12*); forgiveness (3:3; 5:20–25; 6:37; 7:41–50; 11:4; 12:10; 17:3, 4; 23:34; 24:47); joy (*see note on 1:14*); wonder at the mysteries of divine truth (*see note on 2:18*); the role of the Holy Spirit (1:15, 35, 41, 67; 2:25–27; 3:16, 22; 4:1, 14, 18; 10:21; 11:13; 12:10, 12); the temple in Jerusalem (1:9–22; 2:27–38, 46–49; 4:9–13; 18:10–14; 19:45–48; 20:1–21:6; 21:37, 38; 24:53); and Jesus' prayers (*see note on 6:12*).

Starting with 9:51, Luke devoted 10 chapters of his narrative to a travelogue of Jesus' final journey to Jerusalem. Much of the material in this section is unique to Luke. This is the heart of Luke's gospel, and it features a theme Luke stressed throughout: Jesus' relentless progression toward the cross. This was the very purpose for which Christ had come to earth (cf. 9:22, 23; 17:25; 18:31–33; 24:25, 26, 46), and He would not be deterred. The saving of sinners was His whole mission (19:10).

INTERPRETIVE CHALLENGES

Luke, like Mark, and in contrast to Matthew, appears to target a Gentile readership (for a discussion of the Synoptic Problem, see Introduction to Mark: Interpretive Challenges). He identified locations that would have been familiar to all Jews (e.g., 4:31; 23:51; 24:13), suggesting that his audience went beyond those who already had knowledge of Palestinian geography. He usually preferred Greek terminology over Hebraisms (e.g., "The Skull" instead of "Golgotha" in 23:33). The other Gospels all use occasional Semitic terms such as "Abba" (Mk 14:36), "rabbi" (Mt 23:7, 8; Jn 1:38, 49), and "hosanna" (Mt 21:9; Mk 11:9, 10; Jn 12:13)—but Luke either omitted them or used Greek equivalents.

Luke quoted the OT more sparingly than Matthew, and when citing OT passages, he nearly always employed the LXX, a Greek translation of the Hebrew Scriptures. Furthermore, most of Luke's OT citations are allusions rather than direct quotations, and many of them appear in Jesus' words rather than Luke's narration (2:23, 24; 3:4–6; 4:4, 8, 10–12, 18, 19; 7:27; 10:27; 18:20; 19:46; 20:17, 18, 37, 42, 43; 22:37).

Luke, more than any of the other gospel writers, highlighted the universal scope of the gospel invitation. He portrayed Jesus as the Son of Man, rejected by Israel, and then offered to the world. As noted above (see Historical and Theological Themes), Luke repeatedly related accounts of Gentiles, Samaritans, and other outcasts who found grace in Jesus' eyes. This emphasis is precisely what we would expect from a close companion of the "apostle of Gentiles" (Ro 11:13).

Yet some critics have claimed to see a wide gap between Luke's theology and that of Paul. It is true that Luke's gospel is practically devoid of terminology that is uniquely Pauline. Luke wrote with his own style. Yet the underlying theology is perfectly in harmony with that of the apostle's. The centerpiece of Paul's doctrine was justification by faith (*see note on Ro 3:24*). Luke also highlighted and illustrated justification by faith in many of the incidents and parables he related, chiefly the account of the Pharisee and the publican (18:9–14); the familiar story of the Prodigal Son (15:11–32); the incident at Simon's house (7:36–50); and the salvation of Zacchaeus (19:1–10).

OUTLINE

I. The Prelude to Christ's Ministry (1:1–4:13)
- A. Preamble (1:1–4)
- B. The Birth of Jesus (1:5–2:38)
  1. The annunciation to Zacharias (1:5–25)
  2. The annunciation to Mary (1:26–38)

3. The visitation (1:39–45)
4. The Magnificat (1:46–56)
5. The birth of the forerunner (1:57–80)
6. The nativity (2:1–38)

C. The Boyhood of Jesus (2:39–52)
1. In Nazareth (2:39, 40)
2. In the temple (2:41–50)
3. In His family (2:51, 52)

D. The Baptism of Jesus (3:1–4:13)
1. The preaching of John the Baptist (3:1–20)
2. The testimony of heaven (3:21, 22)
3. The genealogy of the Son of Man (3:23–38)
4. The temptation of the Son of God (4:1–13)

II. The Ministry in Galilee (4:14–9:50)

A. The Commencement of His Ministry (4:14–44)
1. Nazareth (4:14–30)
2. Capernaum (4:31–42)
   a. A demon cast out (4:31–37)
   b. Multitudes healed (4:38–42)
3. The cities of Galilee (4:43, 44)

B. The Calling of His Disciples (5:1–6:16)
1. Four fishermen (5:1–26)
   a. Fishing for men (5:1–11)
   b. Healing infirmities (5:12–16)
   c. Pardoning sins (5:17–26)
2. Levi (5:27–6:11)
   a. The gospel: not for the righteous, but for sinners (5:27–32)
   b. The wineskins: not old, but new (5:33–39)
   c. The Sabbath: not for bondage, but for doing good (6:1–11)
3. The twelve (6:12–16)

C. The Continuation of His Work (6:17–9:50)
1. Preaching on the plateau (6:17–49)
   a. Beatitudes (6:17–23)
   b. Woes (6:24–26)
   c. Commandments (6:27–49)
2. Ministering in the cities (7:1–8:25)
   a. He heals a centurion's servant (7:1–10)
   b. He raises a widow's son (7:11–17)
   c. He encourages John the Baptist's disciples (7:18–35)
   d. He forgives a sinful woman (7:36–50)
   e. He gathers loving disciples (8:1–3)
   f. He teaches the multitudes with parables (8:4–21)
   g. He stills the winds and waves (8:22–25)
3. Traveling in Galilee (8:26–9:50)
   a. He delivers a demoniac (8:26–39)
   b. He heals a woman (8:40–48)
   c. He raises a girl (8:49–56)
   d. He sends out the Twelve (9:1–6)
   e. He confounds Herod (9:7–9)
   f. He feeds the multitude (9:10–17)
   g. He predicts His crucifixion (9:18–26)
   h. He unveils His glory (9:27–36)
   i. He casts out an unclean spirit (9:37–42)
   j. He instructs His disciples (9:43–50)

III. The Journey to Jerusalem (9:51–19:27)

A. Samaria (9:51–10:37)
1. A village turns Him away (9:51–56)
2. He turns away the half-hearted (9:57–62)
3. He sends out the seventy (10:1–24)
4. He gives the parable of the Good Samaritan (10:25–37)

B. Bethany and Judea (10:38–13:35)
1. Mary and Martha (10:38–42)
2. The Lord's prayer (11:1–4)
3. The importance of persistence (11:5–13)
4. The impossibility of neutrality (11:14–36)

5. Woes upon Pharisees and lawyers (11:37–54)
6. Lessons along the way (12:1–59)
    a. Against hypocrisy (12:1–12)
    b. Against worldly materialism (12:13–21)
    c. Against worry (12:22–34)
    d. Against unfaithfulness (12:35–48)
    e. Against love of ease (12:49–53)
    f. Against unpreparedness (12:54–56)
    g. Against division (12:57–59)
7. Questions answered (13:1–30)
    a. About the justice of God (13:1–9)
    b. About the Sabbath (13:10–17)
    c. About the kingdom (13:18–21)
    d. About the few who are saved (13:22–30)
8. Christ's lament (13:31–35)

C. Perea (14:1–19:27)
1. Guest of a Pharisee (14:1–24)
    a. He tests them about the Sabbath (14:1–6)
    b. He teaches them about humility (14:7–14)
    c. He tells them about the heavenly banquet (14:15–24)
2. Teacher of multitudes (14:25–18:34)
    a. The cost of discipleship (14:25–35)
    b. The parable of the lost sheep (15:1–7)
    c. The parable of the lost coin (15:8–10)
    d. The parable of the lost son (15:11–32)
    e. The parable of the unrighteous steward (16:1–18)
    f. The rich man and Lazarus (16:19–31)
    g. A lesson about forgiveness (17:1–4)
    h. A lesson about faithfulness (17:5–10)
    i. A lesson about thankfulness (17:11–19)
    j. A lesson about readiness (17:20–37)
    k. The parable of the persistent widow (18:1–8)
    l. The parable of the Pharisee and the tax collector (18:9–14)
    m. A lesson about childlikeness (18:15–17)
    n. A lesson about commitment (18:18–30)
    o. A lesson about the plan of redemption (18:31–34)
3. Friend of sinners (18:35–19:10)
    a. He opens blind eyes (18:35–43)
    b. He seeks and saves the lost (19:1–10)
4. Judge of all the earth (19:11–27)
    a. The end of a long journey (19:11)
    b. The parable of the minas (19:12–27)

IV. The Passion Week (19:28–23:56)

A. Sunday (19:28–44)
1. The triumphal entry (19:28–40)
2. Christ weeps over the city (19:41–44)

B. Tuesday (19:45–48)
1. He cleanses the temple (19:45, 46)
2. He teaches the Passover crowds (19:47, 48)

C. Wednesday (20:1–22:6)
1. He contends with the Jewish rulers (20:1–8)
2. He teaches the Passover crowds (20:9–21:38)
    a. The parable of the wicked vine-growers (20:9–19)
    b. An answer to the Pharisees about paying taxes (20:20–26)
    c. An answer to the Sadducees about the resurrection (20:27–40)
    d. A question for the scribes about messianic prophecy (20:41–47)
    e. The lesson of the widow's coins (21:1–4)
    f. A prophecy about the destruction of Jerusalem (21:5–24)
    g. Some signs of the times (21:25–38)
3. The plot against Jesus (22:1, 2)
4. Judas joins the conspiracy (22:3–6)

D. Thursday (22:7–53)
1. Preparation for Passover (22:7–13)
2. The Lord's Supper (22:14–38)
    a. The New Covenant instituted (22:14–22)
    b. Disputes among the disciples (22:23–30)

c. Peter's denial predicted (22:31–34)
d. God's provision promised (22:35–38)
3. The agony in the garden (22:39–46)
4. Jesus' arrest (22:47–53)

E. Friday (22:54–23:55)
1. Peter's denial (22:54–62)
2. Jesus mocked and beaten (22:63–65)
3. The trial before the Sanhedrin (22:66–71)
4. The trial before Pilate (23:1–25)
a. The indictment (23:1–5)
b. The hearing before Herod (23:6–12)
c. Pilate's verdict (23:13–25)
5. The crucifixion (23:26–49)
6. The burial (23:50–55)

F. The Sabbath (23:56)

V. The Consummation of Christ's Ministry (24:1–53)
A. The Resurrection (24:1–12)
B. The Road to Emmaus (24:13–45)
C. The Ascension (24:46–53)

INTRODUCTION

1 Inasmuch as many have undertaken to compile
an account of the things [a,A]accomplished among
us, 2 just as they were handed down to us by those
who [A]from the beginning [a]were [B]eyewitnesses and
[b,C]servants of [D]the [c]word, 3 it seemed fitting for me
as well, [A]having [a]investigated everything carefully
from the beginning, to write *it* out for you [B]in consecutive order, [C]most excellent [D]Theophilus; 4 so that
you may know the exact truth about the things you
have been [a,A]taught.

BIRTH OF JOHN THE BAPTIST FORETOLD

5 [A]In the days of Herod, king of Judea, there was a
priest named [a]Zacharias, of the [B]division of [b]Abijah;
and he had a wife [c]from the daughters of Aaron, and
her name was Elizabeth. 6 They were both [A]righteous
in the sight of God, walking [B]blamelessly in all the
commandments and requirements of the Lord. 7 But
they had no child, because Elizabeth was barren,
and they were both advanced in [a]years.
8 Now it happened *that* while [A]he was performing his priestly service before God in the *appointed*
order of his division, 9 according to the custom of
the priestly office, he was chosen by lot [A]to enter
the temple of the Lord and burn incense. 10 And
the whole multitude of the people were in prayer
[A]outside at the hour of the incense offering. 11 And
[A]an angel of the Lord appeared to him, standing to
the right of the altar of incense. 12 Zacharias was
troubled when he saw *the angel,* and [A]fear [a]gripped
him. 13 But the angel said to him, "[A]Do not be afraid,
Zacharias, for your petition has been heard, and
your wife Elizabeth will bear you a son, and [B]you
will [a]give him the name John. 14 You will have joy

1:1 [a]Or *on which there is full conviction* [A]Rom 4:21; 14:5; Col 2:2; 4:12; 1 Thess 1:5; 2 Tim 4:17; Heb 6:11; 10:22 1:2 [a]Lit *became* [b]Or *ministers* [c]I.e. gospel [A]John 15:27; Acts 1:21f [B]2 Pet 1:16; 1 John 1:1 [C]Acts 26:16; 1 Cor 4:1; Heb 2:3 [D]Mark 4:14; 16:20; Acts 8:4; 14:25; 16:6; 17:11 1:3 [a]Or *followed* [A]1 Tim 4:6 [B]Acts 11:4; 18:23 [C]Acts 23:26; 24:3; 26:25 [D]Acts 1:1 1:4 [a]Or *orally instructed in* [A]Acts 18:25; Rom 2:18; 1 Cor 14:19; Gal 6:6 1:5 [a]I.e. Zechariah [b]Gr *Abia* [c]I.e. of priestly descent [A]Matt 2:1 [B]1 Chr 24:10 1:6 [A]Gen 7:1; Acts 2:25; 8:21 [B]Phil 2:15; 3:6; 1 Thess 3:13 1:7 [a]Lit *days* 1:8 [A]1 Chr 24:19; 2 Chr 8:14; 31:2 1:9 [A]Ex 30:7f 1:10 [A]Lev 16:17 1:11 [A]Luke 2:9; Acts 5:19 1:12 [a]Or *fell upon* [A]Luke 2:9 1:13 [a]Lit *call his name* [A]Matt 14:27; Luke 1:30 [B]Luke 1:60, 63

1:1–4 These 4 verses make a single sentence, written in the polished style of a Gr. literary classic. It was common for Gr. historical works to begin with such a prologue. After this formal prologue, however, Luke shifted into a simpler style of narrative, probably patterned after the familiar style of the LXX.

1:1 **many.** Although Luke wrote direct divine revelation inspired by the Holy Spirit, he acknowledged the works of others (*see note on v. 2*) who had set down in writing events from Christ's life. All those sources have been long lost, except for the inspired Gospels. Since Matthew and Mark were most likely written before Luke, it has been suggested that either one or both of those may have been among Luke's sources when he did his research. It is also known that he was personally acquainted with many firsthand witnesses to the events of Christ's life. And it is possible that some of his sources were word-of-mouth reports. About 60 percent of the material in Mark is repeated in Luke, and Luke seems to follow Mark's order of events closely (see Introduction to Mark: Interpretive Challenges, the Synoptic Problem). **compile an account.** Luke proposed to narrate the ministry of Christ in an authoritative, logical, and factual order (though not always strictly chronological—v. 3). **the things accomplished.** I.e., the OT messianic promises fulfilled in Christ. **among us.** I.e., in our generation. This phrase does not mean Luke was personally an eyewitness to the life of Christ (*see note on v. 2*).

1:2 **eyewitnesses and servants of the word.** Luke's primary sources were the apostles themselves, who delivered facts about Jesus' life and teaching—both orally and by means of recorded memoirs in written documents made available to Luke. In any case, Luke made no pretense of *being an* eyewitness himself, but explained that these were facts supported by careful research (*see note on v. 3*).

1:3 **having investigated ... carefully.** Lit. "having traced out carefully." Luke's gospel was the result of painstaking investigation. Luke, more than anyone else in the early church, had the abilities and the opportunity to consult with eye-witnesses of Jesus' ministry and consolidate their accounts. He spent more than two years during Paul's imprisonment at Caesarea (Ac 24:26, 27), during which time he would have been able to meet and interview many of the apostles and other eyewitnesses of Jesus' ministry. We know, for example, that he met Philip (Ac 21:8), who was undoubtedly one of Luke's sources. In his travels, he may also have encountered the apostle John. Joanna, wife of Herod's steward, is mentioned only in Luke's Gospel (*see note on 8:3*; cf. 24:10), so she must have been a personal acquaintance of his. Luke also related details about Herod's dealings with Christ not found in the other Gospels (13:31–33; 23:7–12). No doubt it was from Joanna (or someone in a similar position) that Luke learned those facts. However, his understanding was perfect because of the divine revelation he received from the Holy Spirit (2Ti 3:16, 17; 2Pe 1:19–21). **from the beginning.** This could mean from the beginning of Christ's earthly life. However, the word can mean from above (Jn 3:31; 19:11; Jas 3:15). From the beginning in v. 2 uses a different Gr. word, *archē*—so it is best to understand that Luke was saying he used earthly sources for his material, but was given heavenly guidance as he did his research and writing. It is clear that he regarded his account as authoritative (*see note on v. 4*). **in consecutive order.** Luke's account is predominantly ordered chronologically, but he does not follow such an arrangement slavishly. **most excellent.** This was a title used to address governors (Ac 23:26; 24:3; 26:25). This sort of language was reserved for the highest dignitaries, suggesting that "Theophilus" was such a person.

1:4 **the exact truth.** Note the implicit claim of authority. Though Luke drew from other sources (v. 3), he regarded the reliability and authority of his gospel as superior to uninspired sources. **taught.** Theophilus had been schooled in the apostolic tradition, possibly even by the apostle Paul himself. Yet the written Scripture by means of this gospel sealed the certainty of what he had heard.

1:5 **Herod.** Herod the Great. *See note on Mt 2:1.* **Zacharias.** Lit. "Jehovah has remembered." **the division of Abijah.** The temple priesthood was organized into 24 divisions, with each division serving twice a year for one week (1Ch 24:4–19); Abijah's was the 8th division (1Ch 24:10). **daughters of Aaron.** I.e., both husband and wife were from the priestly tribe.

1:6 **both righteous in the sight of God.** I.e., they were believers, justified in God's sight. There is a clear echo of Pauline theology in this expression. See Introduction: Interpretive Challenges.

1:7 **barren ... advanced in years.** This was seen by many as a sign of divine disfavor. *See note on v. 25.*

1:8 **in the *appointed* order of his division.** I.e., his division was on duty for one of their two annual stints (*see note on v. 5*).

1:9 **chosen by lot to ... burn incense.** A high honor (Ex 30:7, 8; 2Ch 29:11). Because of the large number of priests, most would never be chosen for such a duty, and no one was permitted to serve in this capacity twice. Zacharias no doubt regarded this as the supreme moment in a lifetime of priestly service. The incense was kept burning perpetually, just in front of the veil that divided the holy place from the most holy place. The lone priest would offer the incense every morning and every evening, while the rest of the priests and worshipers stood outside the holy place in prayer (v. 10).

1:12 **fear.** The normal response—and an appropriate one (12:5)—when someone is confronted by a divine visitation or a mighty work of God (Jdg 6:22; 13:22; Mk 16:5; *see note on Rev. 1:17*). Luke seems especially to take note of this; he often reports fear in the presence of God and His works (cf. vv. 30, 65; 2:9, 10; 5:10, 26; 7:16; 8:25, 37, 50; 9:34, 45; 23:40).

1:13 **your petition.** Probably a prayer for children to be in his home (*see note on v. 7*; cf. v. 25). **John.** Lit. "Jehovah has shown grace."

1:14 **joy and gladness.** The hallmarks of the messianic kingdom (Is 25:9; Pss 14:7; 48:11). The motif of joy runs through Luke's gospel (cf. vv. 44, 47, 58; 2:10; 6:23; 8:13; 10:17–21; 13:17; 15:5–10, 22–32; 19:6, 37; 24:52).

and gladness, and many will rejoice at his birth.
15 For he will be great in the sight of the Lord; and
he will [A]drink no wine or liquor, and he will be filled
with the Holy Spirit [a]while yet in his mother's womb.
16 And he will [A]turn many of the sons of Israel back
to the Lord their God. 17 It is he who will [A]go *as a
forerunner* before Him in the spirit and power of
[B]Elijah, [C]TO TURN THE HEARTS OF THE FATHERS BACK
TO THE CHILDREN, and the disobedient to the attitude of the righteous, so as to [A]make ready a people
prepared for the Lord."

18 Zacharias said to the angel, "How will I know
this *for certain?* For [A]I am an old man and my wife is
advanced in [a]years." 19 The angel answered and said
to him, "I am [A]Gabriel, who [a,B]stands in the presence
of God, and I have been sent to speak to you and to
bring you this good news. 20 And behold, you shall be
silent and unable to speak until the day when these
things take place, because you did not believe my
words, which will be fulfilled in their proper time."

21 The people were waiting for Zacharias, and
were wondering at his delay in the temple. 22 But
when he came out, he was unable to speak to them;
and they realized that he had seen a vision in the
temple; and he [A]kept [a]making signs to them, and
remained mute. 23 When the days of his priestly
service were ended, he went back home.

24 After these days Elizabeth his wife became
pregnant, and she [a]kept herself in seclusion for
five months, saying, 25 "This is the way the Lord has
dealt with me in the days when He looked *with favor*
upon *me*, to [A]take away my disgrace among men."

JESUS' BIRTH FORETOLD

26 Now in the sixth month the angel [A]Gabriel was
sent from God to a city in Galilee called [B]Nazareth, 27 to
[A]a virgin [a]engaged to a man whose name was Joseph,
[B]of the [b]descendants of David; and the virgin's name
was [c]Mary. 28 And coming in, he said to her, "Greetings,
[a]favored one! The Lord [b]*is* with you." 29 But she [A]was
very perplexed at *this* statement, and kept pondering
what kind of salutation this was. 30 The angel said
to her, "[A]Do not be afraid, Mary; for you have found
favor with God. 31 And behold, you will conceive in
your womb and bear a son, and you [A]shall name Him
Jesus. 32 He will be great and will be called the Son of
[A]the Most High; and the Lord God will give Him [B]the
throne of His father David; 33 [A]and He will reign over
the house of Jacob forever, [B]and His kingdom will have
no end." 34 Mary said to the angel, "How [a]can this be,
since I [b]am a virgin?" 35 The angel answered and said
to her, "[A]The Holy Spirit will come upon you, and the
power of [B]the Most High will overshadow you; and for
that reason [C]the [a]holy Child shall be called [D]the Son of

1:15 [a]Lit *from* [A]Num 6:3; Judg 13:4; Matt 11:18; Luke 7:33 1:16 [A]Matt 3:2, 6; Luke 3:3 1:17 [A]Luke 1:76 [B]Matt 11:14 [C]Mal 4:6 1:18 [a]Lit *days* [A]Gen 17:17 1:19 [a]Lit *stand beside* [A]Dan 8:16; 9:21; Luke 1:26 [B]Matt 18:10 1:22 [a]Or *beckoning to* or *nodding to* [A]Luke 1:62 1:24 [a]Lit *was hidden* 1:25 [A]Gen 30:23; Is 4:1; 25:8 1:26 [A]Luke 1:19 [B]Matt 2:23 1:27 [a]Or *betrothed;* i.e. the first stage of marriage in Jewish culture, usually lasting for a year before the wedding night. More legal than engagement [b]Lit *house* [c]Gr *Mariam;* i.e. Heb Miriam; so throughout Luke [A]Matt 1:18 [B]Matt 1:16, 20; Luke 2:4 1:28 [a]Or *woman richly blessed* [b]Or *be* 1:29 [A]Luke 1:12 1:30 [A]Matt 14:27; Luke 1:13 1:31 [A]Is 7:14; Matt 1:21, 25; Luke 2:21 1:32 [A]Mark 5:7; Luke 1:35, 76; 6:35; Acts 7:48 [B]2 Sam 7:12, 13, 16; Is 9:7 1:33 [A]Matt 1:1 [B]2 Sam 7:13, 16; Ps 89:36, 37; Dan 2:44; 7:14, 18, 27; Matt 28:18 1:34 [a]Lit *will* [b]Lit *know no man* 1:35 [a]Lit *the holy thing begotten* [A]Matt 1:18 [B]Luke 1:32 [C]Mark 1:24 [D]Matt 4:3; John 1:34, 49; 20:31

1:15 drink no wine or liquor. This was a key element of the Nazirite vow (Nu 6:1–21) and would probably have been understood as such by Zacharias. Usually such a vow was temporary, but Samson (Jdg 16:17) and Samuel (1Sa 1:11) were subject to it from birth. The language here is reminiscent of the angel's instructions to Samson's parents (Jdg 13:4–7). However, no mention is made here of any restriction on the cutting of John's hair. Luke may have simply omitted that detail to avoid weighing his Gentile audience down with the details of Jewish law. **while yet in his mother's womb.** Reminiscent of Jeremiah (Jer 1:5). This illustrates God's sovereignty in salvation.

1:17 in the spirit and power of Elijah. Elijah, like John the Baptist, was known for his bold, uncompromising stand for the Word of God—even in the face of a ruthless monarch (cf. 1Ki 18:17–24; Mk 6:15). The final two verses of the OT (Mal 4:5, 6) had promised the return of Elijah before the day of the Lord. *See notes on Mt 3:4; 11:14; Mk 9:11, 12.* **to turn the hearts.** Quoted from Mal 4:6, showing that John the Baptist fulfilled that prophecy. **make ready.** Possibly an allusion to Is 40:3–5 (*see notes on 3:4; Mt 3:3*).

1:18 How will I know this ... ? Abraham also asked for a sign under similar circumstances (Ge 15:8). The sign given Zacharias was also a mild rebuke for doubting (v. 20).

1:19 Gabriel. Lit. "strong man of God." Gabriel also appears in Da 8:16; 9:21 (*see notes there*). He is one of only two holy angels whose names are given in Scripture, the other being Michael (Da 10:13, 21; Jude 9; Rev 12:7).

1:21 wondering at his delay. Zacharias was only supposed to offer incense, then come out to pronounce the familiar blessing of Nu 6:23–27 on the people who were waiting in the temple court. The conversation with the angel would have taken additional time.

1:23 the days of his priestly service. A week. *See note on v. 5.* **went back home.** In the hill country of Judea (v. 39).

1:24 kept herself in seclusion. Probably an act of devotion out of deep gratitude to the Lord.

1:25 my disgrace. Childlessness carried a reproach in a culture where blessings were tied to birthrights and family lines. Barrenness could occasionally be a sign of divine disfavor (Lv 20:20, 21), but it was not always so (cf. Ge 30:23; 1Sa 1:5–10). Still, it carried a social stigma that could be humiliating.

1:26 in the sixth month. I.e., Elizabeth's sixth month of pregnancy. **Nazareth.** *See note on Mt 2:23.*

1:27 a virgin. The importance of the virgin birth cannot be overstated. A right view of the incarnation hinges on the truth that Jesus was virgin-born. Both Luke and Matthew expressly state that Mary was a virgin when Jesus was conceived (*see note on Mt 1:23*). The Holy Spirit wrought the conception through supernatural means (*see notes on v. 35; Mt 1:18*). The nature of Christ's conception testifies of both His deity and His sinlessness. **engaged.** *See notes on Mt 1:18, 19.*

1:28 favored one! Lit. "full of grace"—a term used of all believers in Eph 1:6, where it is translated "bestowed." This portrays Mary as a recipient, not a dispenser, of divine grace.

1:30 Do not be afraid. The same thing Gabriel had said to Zacharias (v. 13). *See note on v. 12.*

1:31 Jesus. *See notes on Mt 1:1, 21.*

1:32 He will be great. This same promise was made of John the Baptist. However, the subsequent title is what set Jesus apart. **the Son of the Most High.** Cf. v. 76, where John the Baptist is called "the prophet of the Most High." The Gr. term Luke uses for "Most High" is the one employed in the LXX to translate the Heb., "The Most High God." Since a son bears his father's qualities, calling a person someone else's "son" was a way of signifying equality. Here the angel was telling Mary that her Son would be equal to the Most High God. **His father David.** *See note on Mt 9:27.* Jesus was David's physical descendant through Mary's line. David's "throne" was emblematic of the messianic kingdom (cf. 2Sa 7:13–16; Ps 89:26–29).

1:33 over the house of Jacob forever. This emphasizes both the Jewish character of the millennial kingdom and the eternal permanence of Christ's rule over all. *See notes on Is 9:7; Da 2:44.*

1:34 I am a virgin. Mary understood that the angel was speaking of an immediate conception, and she and Joseph were still in the midst of the long betrothal, or engagement period (*see note on Mt 1:18*), before the actual marriage and consummation. Her question was borne out of wonder, not doubt, nor disbelief, so the angel did not rebuke her as he had Zacharias (v. 20).

1:35 The Holy Spirit will come upon you. This was a creative act of the Holy Spirit, not the sort of divine-human cohabitation sometimes seen in pagan mythology.

God. 36 And behold, even your relative Elizabeth has
also conceived a son in her old age; and [a]she who
was called barren is now in her sixth month. 37 For
[a,A]nothing will be impossible with God." 38 And Mary
said, "Behold, the [a]bondslave of the Lord; may it be
done to me according to your word." And the angel
departed from her.

MARY VISITS ELIZABETH

39 Now [a]at this time Mary arose and went in a hurry
to [A]the hill country, to a city of Judah, 40 and entered
the house of Zacharias and greeted Elizabeth. 41 When
Elizabeth heard Mary's greeting, the baby leaped in
her womb; and Elizabeth was [A]filled with the Holy
Spirit. 42 And she cried out with a loud voice and said,
"Blessed *are* you among women, and blessed *is* the
fruit of your womb! 43 And [a]how has it *happened* to me,
that the mother of [A]my Lord would come to me? 44 For
behold, when the sound of your greeting reached
my ears, the baby leaped in my womb for joy. 45 And
[A]blessed *is* she who [a]believed that there would be a fulfillment of what had been spoken to her [b]by the Lord."

THE MAGNIFICAT

46 And Mary said:

"[A]My soul [a,B]exalts the Lord,
47 And [A]my spirit has rejoiced
in [B]God my Savior.
48 "For [A]He has had regard for the
humble state of His [a]bondslave;
For behold, from this time on all
generations will count me [B]blessed.
49 "For the Mighty One has done
great things for me;
And holy is His name.
50 "[A]AND HIS MERCY IS [a]UPON GENERATION
AFTER GENERATION
TOWARD THOSE WHO FEAR HIM.
51 "[A]He has done [a]mighty deeds with His arm;
He has scattered *those who were* proud
in the [b]thoughts of their heart.
52 "He has brought down rulers
from *their* thrones,
And has [A]exalted those who were humble.
53 "[A]HE HAS FILLED THE HUNGRY
WITH GOOD THINGS;
And sent away the rich empty-handed.
54 "He has given help to Israel His servant,
[a]In remembrance of His mercy,
55 [A]As He spoke to our fathers,
[B]To Abraham and his [a]descendants forever."

56 And Mary stayed with her about three months,
and *then* returned to her home.

JOHN IS BORN

57 Now the time [a]had come for Elizabeth to give
birth, and she gave birth to a son. 58 Her neighbors
and her relatives heard that the Lord had [a,A]dis-
played His great mercy toward her; and they were
rejoicing with her.
59 And it happened that on [A]the eighth day they
came to circumcise the child, and they were going
to call him Zacharias, [a]after his father. 60 But his
mother answered and said, "No indeed; but [A]he shall

1:36 [a]Lit *this is the sixth month to her who* 1:37 [a]Lit *not any word* [A]Gen 18:14; Jer 32:17; Matt 19:26 1:38 [a]I.e. female slave 1:39 [a]Lit *in these days* [A]Josh 20:7; 21:11; Luke 1:65 1:41 [A]Luke 1:67; Acts 2:4; 4:8; 9:17 1:43 [a]Lit *from where this to me* [A]Luke 2:11 1:45 [a]Or *believed, because there will be* [b]Lit *from* [A]Luke 1:20, 48 1:46 [a]Lit *makes great* [A]Luke 1:46-53: *1 Sam 2:1-10* [B]Ps 34:2f 1:47 [A]Ps 35:9; Hab 3:18 [B]1 Tim 1:1; 2:3; Titus 1:3; 2:10; 3:4; Jude 25 1:48 [a]I.e. female slave [A]Ps 138:6 [B]Luke 1:45 1:50 [a]Lit *unto generations and generations* [A]Ps 103:17 1:51 [a]Lit *might* [b]Lit *thought, attitude* [A]Ps 98:1; 118:15 1:52 [A]Job 5:11 1:53 [A]Ps 107:9 1:54 [a]Lit *So as to remember* 1:55 [a]Lit *seed* [A]Gen 17:19; Ps 132:11; Gal 3:16 [B]Gen 17:7 1:57 [a]Lit *was fulfilled* 1:58 [a]Lit *magnified* [A]Gen 19:19 1:59 [a]Lit *after the name of* [A]Gen 17:12; Lev 12:3; Luke 2:21; Phil 3:5 1:60 [A]Luke 1:13, 63

1:36 your relative Elizabeth. It seems most reasonable to regard the genealogy of 3:23–38 as Mary's (*see note on 3:23*). This would make her a direct descendant of David (*see note on v. 32*). Yet, Elizabeth was a descendant of Aaron (*see note on v. 5*). Therefore, Mary must have been related to Elizabeth through her mother, who would have been of Aaronic descent. Thus, Mary was a descendant of David through her father.

1:38 may it be done to me according to your word. Mary was in an extremely embarrassing and difficult position. Betrothed to Joseph, she faced the stigma of unwed motherhood. Joseph would obviously have known that the child was not his. She knew she would be accused of adultery—an offense punishable by stoning (Dt 22:13–21; cf. Jn 8:3–5). Yet she willingly and graciously submitted to the will of God.

1:41 filled with the Holy Spirit. I.e., controlled by the Holy Spirit, who undoubtedly guided Elizabeth's remarkable expression of praise. *See notes on vv. 43, 44, 67.*

1:43 the mother of my Lord. This expression is not in praise of Mary, but in praise of the Child whom she bore. It was a profound expression of Elizabeth's confidence that Mary's Child would be the long-hoped-for Messiah—the one whom even David called "Lord" (cf. 20:44). Elizabeth's grasp of the situation was extraordinary, considering the aura of mystery that overshadowed all these events (cf. 2:19). She greeted Mary not with skepticism but with joy. She understood the response of the child in her own womb. And she seemed to comprehend the immense importance of the Child whom Mary was carrying. All of this must be attributed to the illuminating work of the Spirit (v. 41).

1:44 the baby leaped in my womb for joy. The infant, like his mother, was Spirit-filled (cf. vv. 15, 41). His response, like that of Elizabeth, was supernaturally prompted by the Spirit of God (*see note on v. 41*).

1:46–55 Mary's *Magnificat* (the first word in the Latin translation; *see notes on vv. 68–79; 2:29–32*) is filled with OT allusions and quotations. It reveals that Mary's heart and mind were saturated with the Word of God. It contains repeated echoes of Hannah's prayers, e.g., 1Sa 1:11; 2:1–10. These verses also contain numerous allusions to the law, the psalms, and the prophets. The entire passage is a point-by-point reciting of the covenant promises of God.

1:47 my Savior. Mary referred to God as "Savior," indicating both that she recognized her own need of a Savior, and that she knew the true God as her Savior. Nothing here or anywhere else in Scripture indicates Mary thought of herself as "immaculate" (free from the taint of original sin). Quite the opposite is true; she employed language typical of someone whose only hope for salvation is divine grace. Nothing in this passage lends support to the notion that Mary herself ought to be an object of adoration.

1:48 humble state. The quality of Mary that shines most clearly through this passage is a deep sense of humility.

1:56 about three months. Mary arrived in the sixth month of Elizabeth's pregnancy (v. 26), so she evidently stayed until John the Baptist was born. **her home.** At this point Mary was still betrothed to Joseph, not yet living in his house (cf. Mt 1:24).

1:59 the eighth day. In accord with God's commandment (Ge 17:12; Lv 12:1–3; cf. Php 3:5), it had become customary to name a child at circumcision. The ritual brought together family and friends, who in this case, pressured the parents to name the baby "after his father"—probably intending this as a gesture of respect to Zacharias.

1:60 No indeed. Elizabeth had learned from Zacharias in writing (v. 63), everything Gabriel had said to him.

be called John." 61 And they said to her, "There is
no one among your relatives who is called by that
name." 62 And they [A]made signs to his father, as to
what he wanted him called. 63 And he asked for a
tablet and wrote as follows, "[A]His name is John."
And they were all astonished. 64 [A]And at once his
mouth was opened and his tongue *loosed,* and he
began to speak in praise of God. 65 Fear came on all
those living around them; and all these matters were
being talked about in all [A]the hill country of Judea.
66 All who heard them kept them in mind, saying,
"What then will this child *turn out to* be?" For [A]the
hand of the Lord was certainly with him.

ZACHARIAS'S PROPHECY

67 And his father Zacharias [A]was filled with the
Holy Spirit, and [B]prophesied, saying:

68 "[A]Blessed *be* the Lord God of Israel,
For He has visited us and accomplished
[B]redemption for His people,
69 And has raised up a [A]horn
of salvation for us
In the house of David [B]His servant—
70 [A]As He spoke by the mouth of His
holy prophets [B]from of old—
71 [a,A]Salvation [B]FROM OUR ENEMIES,
And FROM THE HAND OF ALL WHO HATE US;
72 [A]To show mercy toward our fathers,
[B]And to remember His holy covenant,
73 [A]The oath which He swore to
Abraham our father,
74 To grant us that we, being rescued
from the hand of our enemies,
Might serve Him without fear,
75 [A]In holiness and righteousness
before Him all our days.
76 "And you, child, will be called the
[A]prophet of [B]the Most High;
For you will go on [C]BEFORE THE
LORD TO [D]PREPARE HIS WAYS;
77 To give to His people *the*
knowledge of salvation
[a]By [A]the forgiveness of their sins,
78 Because of the tender mercy of our God,
With which [A]the Sunrise from
on high will visit us,
79 [A]TO SHINE UPON THOSE WHO SIT IN
DARKNESS AND THE SHADOW OF DEATH,
To guide our feet into the [B]way of peace."

80 [A]And the child continued to grow and to become strong in spirit, and he lived in the deserts
until the day of his public appearance to Israel.

JESUS' BIRTH IN BETHLEHEM

2 Now in those days a decree went out from
[A]Caesar Augustus, that a census be taken of
[B]all [a]the inhabited earth. 2 [a]This was the first cen-
sus taken while [b]Quirinius was governor of [A]Syria.

1:62 [A]Luke 1:22 1:63 [A]Luke 1:13, 60 1:64 [A]Luke 1:20 1:65 [A]Luke 1:39 1:66 [A]Acts 11:21 1:67 [A]Luke 1:41; Acts 2:4, 8; 9:17 [B]Joel 2:28 1:68 [A]1 Kin 1:48; Ps 41:13; 72:18; 106:48 [B]Luke 1:71; 2:38; Heb 9:12 1:69 [A]1 Sam 2:1, 10; Ps 18:2; 89:17; 132:17; Ezek 29:21 [B]Matt 1:1 1:70 [A]Rom 1:2 [B]Acts 3:21 1:71 [a]Or *Deliverance* [A]Luke 1:68 [B]Ps 106:10 1:72 [A]Mic 7:20 [B]Ps 105:8f, 42; 106:45 1:73 [A]Gen 22:16ff; Heb 6:13 1:75 [A]Eph 4:24 1:76 [A]Matt 11:9 [B]Luke 1:32 [C]Mal 3:1; Matt 11:10; Mark 1:2; Luke 7:27 [D]Luke 1:17 1:77 [a]Or *Consisting in* [A]Jer 31:34; Mark 1:4 1:78 [A]Mal 4:2; Eph 5:14; 2 Pet 1:19 1:79 [A]Is 9:2 [B]Is 59:8; Matt 4:16 1:80 [A]Luke 2:40 2:1 [a]I.e. the Roman empire [A]Matt 22:17; Luke 3:1 [B]Matt 24:14 2:2 [a]Or *This took place as a first census* [b]Gr *Kyrenios* [A]Matt 4:24

1:62 made signs to his father. The priests conducting the circumcision ceremony appear to have assumed that since he could not speak he was also deaf.

1:65 Fear. *See note on v. 12.* **all the hill country of Judea.** I.e., Jerusalem and the surrounding area. John the Baptist's reputation began to spread from the time of his birth (v. 66).

1:67 filled with the Holy Spirit. *See note on v. 41.* In every case where someone was Spirit-filled in Luke's nativity account, the result was Spirit-directed worship. Cf. Eph 5:18–20.

1:68–79 This passage is known as the *Benedictus* (the first word of v. 68 in the Latin translation; *see notes on vv. 46–55; 2:29–32*). Like Mary's *Magnificat,* it is liberally sprinkled with OT quotations and allusions. When Zacharias was struck mute in the temple (v. 20), he was supposed to deliver a benediction (*see note on v. 21*). So it is fitting that when his speech was restored, the first words out of his mouth were this inspired benediction.

1:69 horn of salvation. A common expression in the OT (2Sa 22:3; Ps 18:2; cf. 1Sa 2:1). The horn is a symbol of strength (Dt 33:17). These words were clearly not meant to exalt John the Baptist. Since both Zacharias and Elizabeth were Levites (*see note on v. 5*), the One raised up "in the house of David" could not be John, but spoke of Someone greater than he (Jn 1:26, 27). Verses 76–79 speak of John's role.

1:72 His holy covenant. I.e., the Abrahamic Covenant (v. 73), with its promise of salvation by grace. *See note on Ge 12:1–3.*

1:76 the prophet of the Most High. *See note on v. 32.*

1:77 the forgiveness of their sins. Forgiveness of sins is the heart of salvation. God saves sinners from separation from Him and from eternal hell only by atoning for and forgiving their sins. *See notes on Ro 4:6–8; 2 Cor. 5:19; Eph 1:7; Heb 9:22.*

1:78 Sunrise. A messianic reference (cf. Is 9:2; 60:1–3; Mal 4:2; 2Pe 1:19; Rev 22:16).

1:80 lived in the deserts. Several groups of ascetics inhabited the wilderness regions E of Jerusalem. One was the famous Qumran community, source of the Dead Sea Scrolls. John's parents, already old when he was born, might have given him over to the care of someone with ties to such a community. In a similar way, Hannah consecrated Samuel to the Lord by entrusting him to Eli (1Sa 1:22–28). However, there is nothing concrete in Scripture to suggest that John was part of any such group. On the contrary, he is painted as a solitary figure, in the spirit of Elijah. *See note on v. 17.*

2:1 Caesar Augustus. Caius Octavius, grand-nephew, adopted son, and primary heir to Julius Caesar. Before and after Julius' death in 44 B.C., the Roman government was constantly torn by power struggles. Octavius ascended to undisputed supremacy in 31 B.C. by defeating his last remaining rival, Antony, in a military battle at Actium. In 29 B.C., the Roman senate declared Octavius Rome's first emperor. Two years later they honored him with the title "Augustus" ("exalted one"—a term signifying religious veneration). Rome's republican government was effectively abolished, and Augustus was given supreme military power. He reigned until his death at age 76 (A.D. 14). Under his rule, the Roman Empire dominated the Mediterranean region, ushering in a period of great prosperity and relative peace (the *Pax Romana*). He ordered "all the inhabited earth" (i.e., the world of the Roman Empire) to be counted. This was not merely a one-time census; the decree actually established a cycle of enrollments that were to occur every 14 years. Israel had previously been excluded from the Roman census, because Jews were exempt from serving in the Roman army, and the census was designed primarily to register young men for military service (as well as account for all Roman citizens). This new, universal census was ostensibly to number each nation by family and tribe (hence Joseph, a Judean, had to return to his ancestral home to register—*see note on v. 3*). Property and income values were not recorded in this registration. But soon the names and population statistics gathered in this census were used for the levying of poll taxes (*see note on Mt 22:17*), and the Jews came to regard the census itself as a distasteful symbol of Roman oppression. *See note on v. 2.*

2:2 Quirinius was governor of Syria. Fixing a precise date for this census is problematic. Publius Sulpicius Quirinius is known to have governed Syria during A.D. 6–9. A well known census was taken in Palestine in A.D. 6.

3 And everyone was on his way to register for the
census, each to his own city. 4 Joseph also went up
from Galilee, from the city of Nazareth, to Judea, to
the city of David which is called Bethlehem, because
[A]he was of the house and family of David, 5 in order
to register along with Mary, who was engaged to
him, and was with child. 6 While they were there, the
days were completed for her to give birth. 7 And she
[A]gave birth to her firstborn son; and she wrapped
Him in cloths, and laid Him in a [a]manger, because
there was no room for them in the inn.
8 In the same region there were *some* shepherds
staying out in the fields and keeping watch over their
flock by night. 9 And [A]an angel of the Lord suddenly
[B]stood before them, and the glory of the Lord shone
around them; and they were terribly frightened. 10 But
the angel said to them, "[A]Do not be afraid; for behold,
I bring you good news of great joy which will be for
all the people; 11 for today in the city of David there
has been born for you a [A]Savior, who is [a,B]Christ [C]the
Lord. 12 [A]This *will be* a sign for you: you will find a
baby wrapped in cloths and lying in a [a]manger."
13 And suddenly there appeared with the angel a multitude of the heavenly host praising God and saying,

14 "[A]Glory to God in the highest,
And on earth peace among men
[a,B]with whom He is pleased."

15 When the angels had gone away from them
into heaven, the shepherds *began* saying to one
another, "Let us go straight to Bethlehem then, and
see this thing that has happened which the Lord has
made known to us." 16 So they came in a hurry and
found their way to Mary and Joseph, and the baby
as He lay in the [a]manger. 17 When they had seen this,
they made known the statement which had been
told them about this Child. 18 And all who heard it
wondered at the things which were told them by the
shepherds. 19 But Mary [A]treasured all these things,
pondering them in her heart. 20 The shepherds went
back, [A]glorifying and praising God for all that they
had heard and seen, just as had been told them.

JESUS PRESENTED AT THE TEMPLE

21 And when [A]eight days had passed, [a]before His
circumcision, [B]His name was *then* called Jesus, the
name given by the angel before He was conceived
in the womb.

2:4 [A]Luke 1:27 2:7 [a]Or *feeding trough* [A]Matt 1:25 2:9 [A]Luke 1:11; Acts 5:19 [B]Luke 24:4; Acts 12:7 2:10 [A]Matt 14:27 2:11 [a]I.e. Messiah [A]Matt 1:21; John 4:42; Acts 5:31 [B]Matt 1:16; 16:16, 20; John 11:27 [C]Luke 1:43; Acts 2:36; 10:36 2:12 [a]Or *feeding trough* [A]1 Sam 2:34; 2 Kin 19:29; 20:8f; Is 7:11, 14 2:14 [a]Lit *of good pleasure;* or *of good will* [A]Matt 21:9; Luke 19:38 [B]Luke 3:22; Eph 1:9; Phil 2:13 2:16 [a]Or *feeding trough* 2:19 [A]Luke 2:51 2:20 [A]Matt 9:8 2:21 [a]Lit *so as to circumcise Him* [A]Gen 17:12; Lev 12:3; Luke 1:59 [B]Matt 1:21, 25; Luke 1:31

Josephus records that it sparked a violent Jewish revolt (mentioned by Luke, quoting Gamaliel, in Ac 5:37). Quirinius was responsible for administering that census, and he also played a major role in quelling the subsequent rebellion. However, that cannot be the census Luke has in mind here, because it occurred about a decade after the death of Herod (*see note on Mt 2:1*)—much too late to fit Luke's chronology (cf. 1:5). In light of Luke's meticulous care as a historian, it would be unreasonable to charge him with such an obvious anachronism. Indeed, archeology has vindicated Luke. A fragment of stone discovered at Tivoli (near Rome) in A.D. 1764 contains an inscription in honor of a Roman official who, it states, was twice governor of Syria and Phoenicia during the reign of Augustus. The name of the official is not on the fragment, but among his accomplishments are listed details that, as far as is known, can fit no one other than Quirinius. Thus, he must have served as governor in Syria twice. He was probably military governor at the same time that history records Varus was civil governor there. With regard to the dating of the census, some ancient records found in Egypt mention a worldwide census ordered in 8 B.C. That date is not without problems, either. It is generally thought by scholars that 6 B.C. is the earliest possible date for Christ's birth. Evidently, the census was ordered by Caesar Augustus in 8 B.C. but was not actually carried out in Palestine until 2–4 years later, perhaps because of political difficulties between Rome and Herod. Therefore, the precise year of Christ's birth cannot be known with certainty, but it was probably no earlier than 6 B.C. and certainly no later than 4 B.C. Luke's readers, familiar with the political history of that era, would no doubt have been able to discern a very precise date from the information he gave.

2:3 own city. I.e., the place of tribal origin.

2:4 Nazareth ... Bethlehem. Both Joseph and Mary were descendants of David and therefore went to their tribal home in Judea to be registered. This was a difficult trek of more than 70 mi. through mountainous terrain—a particularly grueling journey for Mary, on the verge of delivery. Perhaps she and Joseph were conscious that a birth in Bethlehem would fulfill the prophecy in Mic 5:2.

2:5 engaged. *See note on Mt 1:18.* Matthew 1:24 indicates that when the angel told Joseph about Mary's pregnancy, he "took her as his wife"—i.e., he took her into his home. But they did not consummate their marriage until after the birth of Jesus (Mt 1:25). Therefore, technically, they were still betrothed.

2:7 firstborn. Mary had other children subsequent to this. *See note on Mt 12:46.* **cloths.** Strips of cloth were used to bind a baby tightly. It kept the baby from injuring sensitive facial skin and eyes with its own (often sharp) fingernails, and was believed to strengthen the limbs. This is still the custom in some Eastern cultures. The absence of such cloths was a sign of poverty or lack of parental care (Eze 16:4). **manger.** A feeding trough for animals. This is the source of the notion that Christ was born in a stable, something nowhere stated in Scripture. Ancient tradition held that He was born in a cave (possibly one used as a shelter for animals). But no actual description of the location is given. **no room for them in the inn.** Possibly because many were returning to this ancient town to register in the census.

2:8 shepherds. Bethlehem was nearby Jerusalem, and many of the sheep used in the temple sacrifices came from there. The surrounding hills were prime grazing land, and shepherds worked in the area day and night, all year round. Therefore it is not possible to draw any conclusion about the time of year by the fact that shepherds were living out in the fields.

2:10 Do not be afraid. *See note on 1:12*; cf. 1:65.

2:11 city of David. I.e., Bethlehem, the town where David was born—not the City of David, which was on the southern slope of Mt. Zion (cf. 2Sa 5:7–9). **a Savior.** This is one of only two places in the Gospels where Christ is referred to as "Savior"—the other being Jn 4:42, where the men of Sychar confessed Him as "Savior of the world." **Christ.** "Christ" is the Gr. equivalent of "Messiah" (*see note on Mt 1:1*). **Lord.** The Gr. word can mean "master"—but it is also the word used to translate the covenant name of God. Here (and in most of its NT occurrences), it is used in the latter sense, as a title of deity.

2:13 host. A term used to describe an army encampment. Christ also used military imagery to describe the angels in Mt 26:53 (*see note there*). Revelation 5:11 suggests that the number of the angelic host may be too large for the human mind to fathom. Note that here the heavenly army brought a message of peace (v. 14).

2:14 the highest. I.e., heaven. **peace.** This is not to be taken as a universal declaration of peace toward all humanity. Rather, peace with God is a corollary of justification (*see note on Ro 5:1*). **among men with whom He is pleased.** God's peace is a gracious gift to those who are the objects of His pleasure.

2:18 all who heard it wondered. Wonderment at the mysteries of Christ's words and works is one of the threads that runs through Luke's gospel. Cf. vv. 19, 33, 47, 48; 1:21, 63, 4:22, 36; 5:9; 8:25; 9:43–45; 11:14; 20:26; 24:12, 41. *See note on v. 20.*

2:20 praising God. Luke often reports this response. Cf. v. 28; 1:64; 5:25, 26; 7:16; 13:13, 17:15–18; 18:43; 19:37–40; 23:47; 24:52, 53.

2:21 eight days. *See note on 1:59.*

22 [A]And when the days for their purification according to the law of Moses were completed, they
brought Him up to Jerusalem to present Him to the
Lord 23 (as it is written in the Law of the Lord, "[A]EV-
ERY *firstborn* MALE THAT OPENS THE WOMB SHALL BE
CALLED HOLY TO THE LORD"), 24 and to offer a sacrifice
according to what was said in the Law of the Lord,
"[A]A PAIR OF TURTLEDOVES OR TWO YOUNG PIGEONS."
25 And there was a man in Jerusalem whose name
was Simeon; and this man was [A]righteous and devout, [B]looking for the consolation of Israel; and
the Holy Spirit was upon him. 26 And [A]it had been
revealed to him by the Holy Spirit that he would
not [B]see death before he had seen the Lord's [a]Christ.
27 And he came in the Spirit into the temple; and
when the parents brought in the child Jesus, [a,A]to
carry out for Him the custom of the Law, 28 then he
took Him into his arms, and blessed God, and said,

29 "Now Lord, You are releasing Your
bond-servant to depart in peace,
[A]According to Your word;
30 For my eyes have [A]seen Your salvation,
31 Which You have prepared in the
presence of all peoples,
32 [A]A LIGHT [a]OF REVELATION TO THE GENTILES,
And the glory of Your people Israel."

33 And His father and [A]mother were amazed at the
things which were being said about Him. 34 And Simeon blessed them and said to Mary [A]His mother, "Behold, this *Child* is appointed for [B]the fall and [a]rise of
many in Israel, and for a sign to be opposed— 35 and
a sword will pierce even your own soul—to the end
that thoughts from many hearts may be revealed."
36 And there was a [A]prophetess, [a]Anna the daughter
of Phanuel, of [B]the tribe of Asher. She was advanced

2:22 [A]Lev 12:6-8 2:23 [A]Ex 13:2, 12; Num 3:13; 8:17 2:24 [A]Lev 5:11; 12:8 2:25 [A]Luke 1:6 [B]Mark 15:43; Luke 2:38; 23:51 2:26 [a]I.e. Messiah [A]Matt 2:12 [B]Ps 89:48; John 8:51; Heb 11:5 2:27 [a]Lit *to do for Him according to* [A]Luke 2:22 2:29 [A]Luke 2:26 2:30 [A]Ps 119:166, 174; Is 52:10; Luke 3:6 2:32 [a]Or *for* [A]Is 9:2; 42:6; 49:6, 9; 51:4; 60:1-3; Matt 4:16; Acts 13:47; 26:23 2:33 [A]Matt 12:46 2:34 [a]Or *resurrection* [A]Matt 12:46 [B]Matt 21:44; 1 Cor 1:23; 2 Cor 2:16; 1 Pet 2:8 2:36 [a]Or *Hannah* [A]Luke 2:38; Acts 21:9 [B]Josh 19:24

2:22 purification. A woman who bore a son was ceremonially unclean for 40 days (twice that if she bore a daughter—Lv 12:2–5). After that she was to offer a yearling lamb and a dove or pigeon (Lv 12:6). If poor, she could offer two doves or pigeons (Lv 12:8). Mary's offering indicates that she and Joseph were poor (v. 24). **to Jerusalem.** A journey of about 6 mi. from Bethlehem. **to present Him to the Lord.** The dedication of the firstborn son was also required by Moses' law (v. 23, cf. Ex 13:2, 12–15).

2:24 A pair of turtledoves. *See note on v. 22.* Quoted from Lv 12:8.

2:25 Simeon. He is mentioned nowhere else in Scripture. **the consolation of Israel.** A messianic title, evidently derived from verses like Is 25:9; 40:1, 2; 66:1–11.

2:26 it had been revealed to him. It is significant that with messianic expectation running so high (cf. 3:15), and with the many OT prophecies that spoke of His coming, still only a handful of people realized the significance of Christ's birth. Most of them, including Simeon, received some angelic message or other special revelation to make the fulfillment of the OT prophecies clear.

2:29–32 Simeon's psalm is known as the *Nunc Dimittis,* from the first two words of the Latin translation (*see notes on 1:46–55; 1:68–79*). It is the fourth of 5 psalms of praise Luke included in his birth narrative (see Introduction: Historical and Theological Themes). It is a touching expression of Simeon's extraordinary faith.

2:30 Your salvation. I.e., the One who would redeem His people from their sins.

2:31 all peoples. I.e., all nations, tongues, and tribes (cf. Rev 7:9)—both Israel and the Gentiles (v. 32).

2:34 fall and rise of many in Israel. To those who reject Him, He is a stone of stumbling (1Pe 2:8); those who receive Him are raised up (Eph 2:6). Cf. Is 8:14, 15; Hos 14:9; 1Co 1:23, 24. **sign to be opposed.** This was synecdoche. Simeon mentioned only the verbal insults hurled at Christ, but the expression actually embraced more than that—Israel's rejection, and hatred, and crucifixion of the Messiah. *See note on v. 35.*

2:35 a sword. This was undoubtedly a reference to the personal grief Mary would endure when she watched her own Son die in agony (Jn 19:25). **that thoughts from many hearts may be revealed.** The rejection of the Messiah (*see note on v. 34*) would reveal the appalling truth about the apostate state of the Jews.

2:36 a prophetess. This refers to a woman who spoke God's Word. She was a teacher of the OT, not a source of revelation. The OT mentions only 3 women who prophesied: Miriam (Ex 15:20); Deborah (Jdg 4:4);

NEW TESTAMENT WOMEN

Mary, the virgin mother of Jesus, has a place of honor among the women of the New Testament. She is an enduring example of faith, humility, and service (Lk 1:26–56). Other notable women of the New Testament include the following:

Name	Description	Biblical Reference
Anna	Recognized Jesus as the long-awaited Messiah	Lk 2:36–38
Bernice	Sister of Agrippa before whom Paul made his defense	Ac 25:13
Candace	A queen of Ethiopia	Ac 8:27
Chloe	Woman who knew of divisions in the church at Corinth	1Co 1:11
Claudia	Christian of Rome	2Ti 4:21
Damaris	Woman of Athens converted under Paul's ministry	Ac 17:34
Dorcas (Tabitha)	Christian in Joppa who was raised from the dead by Peter	Ac 9:36–41
Drusilla	Wife of Felix, governor of Judea	Ac 24:24
Elizabeth	Mother of John the Baptist	Lk 1:5, 13
Eunice	Mother of Timothy	2Ti 1:5
Herodias	Queen who demanded the execution of John the Baptist	Mt 14:3–10
Joanna	Provided for the material needs of Jesus	Lk 8:3
Lois	Grandmother of Timothy	2Ti 1:5
Lydia	Converted under Paul's ministry in Philippi	Ac 16:14
Martha and Mary	Sisters of Lazarus; friends of Jesus	Lk 10:38–42
Mary Magdalene	Woman from whom Jesus cast out demons	Mt 27:56–61; Mk 16:9
Phoebe	A servant, perhaps a deaconess, in the church at Cenchrea	Ro 16:1, 2
Priscilla	Wife of Aquila; laborer with Paul at Corinth and Ephesus	Ac 18:2, 18, 19
Salome	Mother of Jesus' disciples James and John	Mt 20:20–24
Sapphira	Held back goods from the early Christian community	Ac 5:1
Susanna	Provided for the material needs of Jesus	Lk 8:3

in [b]years [c]and had lived with *her* husband seven
years after her [c]marriage, 37 and then as a widow
to the age of eighty-four. She never left the temple,
serving night and day with [A]fastings and prayers.
38 At that very [a]moment she came up and *began* giving thanks to God, and continued to speak of Him
to all those who were [A]looking for the redemption
of Jerusalem.

RETURN TO NAZARETH

39 When they had performed everything according to the Law of the Lord, they returned to Galilee,
to [A]their own city of Nazareth. 40 [A]The Child continued to grow and become strong, [a]increasing in
wisdom; and the grace of God was upon Him.

VISIT TO JERUSALEM

41 Now His parents went to Jerusalem every year
at [A]the Feast of the Passover. 42 And when He became twelve, they went up *there* according to the
custom of the Feast; 43 and as they were returning,
after spending the [A]full number of days, the boy
Jesus stayed behind in Jerusalem. But His parents
were unaware of it, 44 but supposed Him to be in
the caravan, and went a day's journey; and they
began looking for Him among their relatives and
acquaintances. 45 When they did not find Him, they
returned to Jerusalem looking for Him. 46 Then, after three days they found Him in the temple, sitting
in the midst of the teachers, both listening to them
and asking them questions. 47 And all who heard
Him [A]were amazed at His understanding and His
answers. 48 When they saw Him, they were astonished; and [A]His mother said to Him, "[a]Son, why
have You treated us this way? Behold, [B]Your father
and I [b]have been anxiously looking for You." 49 And
He said to them, "Why is it that you were looking
for Me? Did you not know that [A]I had to be in My
Father's [a]*house?*" 50 But [A]they did not understand
the statement which He [a]had made to them. 51 And
He went down with them and came to [A]Nazareth,
and He continued in subjection to them; and [B]His
mother [C]treasured all *these* [a]things in her heart.
52 And Jesus kept increasing in wisdom and [a]stat-
ure, and in [A]favor with God and men.

JOHN THE BAPTIST PREACHES

3 Now in the fifteenth year of the reign of Tiberius Caesar, when [A]Pontius Pilate was governor
of Judea, and [B]Herod was tetrarch of Galilee, and

2:36 [b]Lit *days* [c]Lit *virginity* [C]1 Tim 5:9 2:37 [A]Luke 5:33; Acts 13:3; 14:23; 1 Tim 5:5 2:38 [a]Lit *hour* [A]Luke 1:68; 2:25 2:39 [A]Matt 2:23; Luke 1:26; 2:51; 4:16 2:40 [a]Lit *becoming full of* [A]Luke 1:80; 2:52 2:41 [A]Ex 12:11; 23:15; Deut 16:1-6 2:43 [A]Ex 12:15 2:47 [A]Matt 7:28; 13:54; 22:33; Mark 1:22; 6:2; 11:18; Luke 4:32; John 7:15 2:48 [a]Or *Child* [b]Lit *are looking* [A]Matt 12:46 [B]Luke 2:49; 3:23; 4:22 2:49 [a]Or *affairs;* lit *in the things of My Father* [A]John 4:34; 5:36 2:50 [a]Lit *had spoken* [A]Mark 9:32; Luke 9:45; 18:34 2:51 [a]Lit *words* [A]Luke 2:39 [B]Matt 12:46 [C]Luke 2:19 2:52 [a]Or *age* [A]Luke 2:40 3:1 [A]Matt 27:2 [B]Matt 14:1

Huldah (2Ki 22:14; 2Ch 34:22). One other, the "prophetess" Noadiah, was evidently a false prophet, grouped by Nehemiah with his enemies. Isaiah 8:3 refers to the prophet's wife as a "prophetess"—but there is no evidence Isaiah's wife prophesied. Perhaps she is so-called because the child she bore was given a name that was prophetic (Is 8:3, 4). This use of the title for Isaiah's wife also shows that the title does not necessarily indicate an ongoing revelatory prophetic ministry. Rabbinical tradition also regarded Sarah, Hannah, Abigail, and Esther as prophetesses (apparently to make an even 7 with Miriam, Deborah, and Huldah). In the NT, the daughters of Philip prophesied (*see note on Ac 21:9*).

2:37 never left the temple. Anna evidently had her living quarters on the temple grounds. There would have been several such dwelling places for priests in the outer court, and Anna must have been allowed to live there permanently because of her unusual status as a prophetess.

2:39 they returned to Galilee. Luke omitted the visit of the Magi and the flight into Egypt (Mt 2:1–18). The theme of early rejection, so prominent in Matthew (see Introduction to Matthew: Historical and Theological Themes), was not where Luke focused his attention.

2:41 Feast of the Passover. *See note on Ex 23:14–19.* Passover was a one-day feast, followed immediately by the week-long Feast of Unleavened Bread (*see note on Mt 26:17*).

2:43 Jesus stayed behind. In stark contrast to the apocryphal gospels' spurious tales of youthful miracles and supernatural exploits, this lone biblical insight into the youth of Jesus portrays Him as a typical boy in a typical family. His lingering was neither mischievous nor disobedient; it was owing to a simple mistaken presumption on His parents' part (v. 44) that He was left behind.

2:44 in the caravan. Obviously, Joseph and Mary were traveling with a large caravan of friends and relatives from Nazareth. No doubt hundreds of people from their community went together to the feast. Men and women in such a group might have been separated by some distance, and it appears each parent thought He was with the other.

2:46 three days. This probably does not mean they searched Jerusalem for 3 days. They apparently realized He was missing at the end of a full day's travel. That required another full day's journey back to Jerusalem, and the better part of another day was spent seeking Him. **listening to them and asking them questions.** The boy Jesus was utterly respectful, taking the role of the student. But even at that young age, His questions showed a wisdom that put the teachers to shame.

2:48 why have You treated us this way? Mary's words convey a tone of exasperation and rebuke—normal for any mother under such circumstances, but misplaced in this case. Jesus was not hiding from them or defying their authority. In fact, He had done precisely what any child should do under such circumstances (being left by His parents)—He went to a safe, public place, in the presence of trusted adults, where His parents could be expected to come looking for Him (v. 49). **Your father.** I.e., Joseph, who was legally His father.

2:49 My Father's *house*. Contrasting with Mary's "your father" in v. 48. His reply was in no sense insolent, but reveals a genuine amazement that they did not know where to look for Him. This also reveals that even at so young an age, He had a clear consciousness of His identity and mission.

2:51 continued in subjection. Jesus' relationship with His Heavenly Father did not override or nullify His duty to His earthly parents. His obedience to the fifth commandment was an essential part of the perfect legal obedience He rendered on our behalf (Heb 4:4; 5:8, 9). He had to fulfill all righteousness (*see note on Mt 3:15*).

2:52 And Jesus kept increasing. Jesus did not cease being God or divest Himself of divine attributes in order to become man. Rather, He took on a human nature (an addition, not a subtraction), and submitted the use of His divine attributes to the will of the Father (Jn 5:19, 30; 8:28; Php 2:5–8). Therefore, there were times when His omniscience was on display (Mt 9:4; Jn 2:24, 25; 4:17, 18; 11:11–14; 16:30) and other times when it was veiled by His humanity in accordance with the Father's will (Mk 13:32). Christ was therefore subject to the normal process of human growth, intellectually, physically, spiritually, and socially. *See note on Mk 13:32.*

3:1 fifteenth year of the reign of Tiberius. Because of the way Tiberius came to power, this date is hard to fix precisely. When the Roman Senate declared Augustus emperor (*see note on 2:1*), they did so on condition that his power would end with his death, rather than passing to his heirs. The idea was that the senate, rather than the emperor himself, was to choose the heir to the throne. However, Augustus circumvented that difficulty by appointing a co-regent, on whom he planned gradually to confer the imperial powers. When he outlived his first choice for successor, Augustus next selected his son-in-law, Tiberius, whom he adopted and made his heir in A.D. 4 (Augustus disliked Tiberius but hoped to pass power to his grandsons through him). Tiberius was made co-regent in A.D. 11, then automatically became sole ruler

his brother Philip was tetrarch of the region of Ituraea and Trachonitis, and Lysanias was tetrarch
of Abilene, 2 in the high priesthood of [A]Annas and
[B]Caiaphas, [C]the word of God came to John, the son
of Zacharias, in the wilderness. 3 And he came into
all [A]the district around the Jordan, preaching a baptism of repentance for the forgiveness of sins; 4 as
it is written in the book of the words of Isaiah the
prophet,

"[A]THE VOICE OF ONE CRYING IN
THE WILDERNESS,
'MAKE READY THE WAY OF THE LORD,
MAKE HIS PATHS STRAIGHT.
5 '[A]EVERY RAVINE WILL BE FILLED,
AND EVERY MOUNTAIN AND HILL
WILL BE [a]BROUGHT LOW;
THE CROOKED WILL BECOME STRAIGHT,
AND THE ROUGH ROADS SMOOTH;
6 [A]AND ALL [a]FLESH WILL [B]SEE THE
SALVATION OF GOD.' "

7 So he *began* saying to the crowds who were
going out to be baptized by him, "[A]You brood of
vipers, who warned you to flee from the wrath to
come? 8 Therefore bear fruits in keeping with repentance, and [A]do not begin to say [a]to yourselves, '[B]We
have Abraham for our father,' for I say to you that
from these stones God is able to raise up children
to Abraham. 9 Indeed the axe is already laid at the
root of the trees; so [A]every tree that does not bear
good fruit is cut down and thrown into the fire."
10 And the crowds were questioning him, saying,
"[A]Then what shall we do?" 11 And he would answer
and say to them, "The man who has two tunics is to
[A]share with him who has none; and he who has food
is to do likewise." 12 And *some* [A]tax collectors also
came to be baptized, and they said to him, "Teacher,
what shall we do?" 13 And he said to them, "[a]Collect no
more than what you have been ordered to." 14 *Some*
soldiers were questioning him, saying, "And *what
about* us, what shall we do?" And he said to them,
"Do not take money from anyone by force, or [A]accuse
anyone falsely, and [B]be content with your wages."
15 Now while the people were in a state of expectation and all were [a]wondering in their hearts about
John, [A]as to whether he was [b]the Christ, 16 [A]John answered and said to them all, "As for me, I baptize you
with water; but One is coming who is mightier than I,
and I am not fit to untie the thong of His sandals; He
will baptize you [a]with the Holy Spirit and fire. 17 His
[A]winnowing fork is in His hand to thoroughly clear His
threshing floor, and to gather the wheat into His barn;
but He will burn up the chaff with [B]unquenchable fire."
18 So with many other exhortations he preached
the gospel to the people. 19 But when [A]Herod the
tetrarch was reprimanded by him because of [A]He-
rodias, his brother's wife, and because of all the
wicked things which [B]Herod had done, 20 Herod also
added this to them all: [A]he locked John up in prison.

3:2 [A]John 18:13, 24; Acts 4:6 [B]Matt 26:3 [C]Luke 3:3-10: *Matt 3:1-10; Mark 1:3-5* 3:3 [A]Matt 3:5 3:4 [A]Is 40:3 3:5 [a]Or *leveled* [A]Is 40:4 3:6 [a]Or *mankind* [A]Is 40:5 [B]Luke 2:30 3:7 [A]Matt 12:34; 23:33 3:8 [a]Or *in* [A]Luke 5:21; 13:25, 26; 14:9 [B]John 8:33 3:9 [A]Matt 7:19; Luke 13:6-9 3:10 [A]Luke 3:12, 14; Acts 2:37, 38 3:11 [A]Is 58:7; 1 Tim 6:17, 18; James 2:14-20 3:12 [A]Luke 7:29 3:13 [a]Or *Exact* 3:14 [A]Ex 20:16; 23:1 [B]Phil 4:11 3:15 [a]Or *reasoning* or *debating* [b]I.e. the Messiah [A]John 1:19f 3:16 [a]The Gr here can be translated *in, with* or *by* [A]Luke 3:16, 17: *Matt 3:11, 12; Mark 1:7, 8* 3:17 [A]Is 30:24 [B]Mark 9:43, 48 3:19 [A]Matt 14:3; Mark 6:17 [B]Matt 14:1; Luke 3:1 3:20 [A]John 3:24

at the death of Augustus on Aug. 19, A.D. 14. If Luke's chronology is dated from Tiberius' appointment to the co-regency, the 15th year would be A.D. 25 or 26. If Luke was reckoning from the death of Augustus, this date would fall between Aug. 19, A.D. 28 and Aug. 18, A.D. 29. One other fact complicates the setting of a precise date: the Jews reckoned a ruler's term from the Jewish New Year following accession, so if Luke was using the Jewish system, the actual dates could be slightly later. The earlier date of A.D. 25–26 seems to fit the chronology of Christ's life best. **Pontius Pilate ... Herod ... Philip.** *See note on Mt 2:22.* **Lysanias.** Ruler of the area NW of Damascus. History is virtually silent about him.

3:2 **high priesthood of Annas and Caiaphas.** *See note on Ac 4:6.* According to Josephus, Annas served as High Priest A.D. 6–15, when he was deposed by Roman officials. He nonetheless retained *de facto* power, as seen in the fact that his successors included 5 of his sons and Caiaphas, a son-in-law (*see note on Mt 26:3*). Caiaphas was the actual High Priest during the time Luke describes, but Annas still controlled the office. This is seen clearly in the fact that Christ was taken to Annas first after His arrest, then to Caiaphas (*see note on Mt 26:57*). **wilderness.** *See note on Mt 3:1.*

3:3 **baptism of repentance.** *See note on Mt 3:6.* **for the forgiveness of sins.** I.e., to symbolize and testify of the forgiveness already received upon repentance (*see note on Ac 2:38*).

3:4 Make His paths straight. Quoted from Is 40:3–5 (*see notes there*). A monarch traveling in wilderness regions would have a crew of workmen go ahead to make sure the road was clear of debris, obstructions, potholes, and other hazards that made the journey difficult. In a spiritual sense, John was calling the people of Israel to prepare their hearts for the coming of their Messiah.

3:6 all flesh. I.e., Gentiles as well as Jews (*see note on 2:31*). All 4 Gospels quote Is 40:3 (Mt 3:3; Mk 1:3; Jn 1:23). Only Luke adds vv. 5, 6—thus using a familiar text from Isaiah to stress his theme of the universal scope of the gospel (see Introduction: Interpretive Challenges).

3:7 **the wrath to come.** Possibly a reference to the coming destruction of Jerusalem. But this certainly also looks beyond any earthly calamity to the eschatological outpouring of divine wrath in the day of the Lord, and especially the final judgment, where divine wrath will be the just fruit of all the unrepentant (cf. Ro 1:18; 1Th 1:10; Heb 10:27). *See note on Mt 3:7.*

3:8 **stones.** Cf. 19:40. The imagery may echo OT verses such as Eze 11:19; 36:26; God can sovereignly turn a heart of stone into a believing heart. He can raise up children to Abraham from inanimate objects if He chooses—or even from stony-hearted Gentiles (cf. Gal 3:29). **children to Abraham.** Abraham's true children are not merely physical descendants, but those who follow his faith, believing God's Word the way he did (Ro 4:11–16; 9:8; Gal 3:7). To trust one's physical ancestry is to shift the focus of faith away from God Himself—and that is spiritually fatal (cf. Jn 8:39–44).

3:9 **axe ... at the root.** *See note on Mt 3:10.*

3:11 **two tunics.** Shirtlike garments. Only one could be worn at a time. John was still stressing the imminence of the coming judgment. This was not a time to hoard one's surplus goods.

3:12 **tax collectors.** *See note on Mt 5:46.*

3:14 **soldiers.** These were most likely members of the forces of Herod Antipas, stationed at Perea, perhaps, along with Judean police. **Do not take money ... by force.** Here and in v. 13, John demanded integrity and high character in the practical matters of everyday life, not a monastic lifestyle or a mystical asceticism. Cf. Jas 1:27.

3:16 **baptize.** *See note on Mt 3:11.* **thong of His sandals.** Unfastening the sandal thong was the lowliest slave's task, preliminary to washing the feet (*see note on Jn 13:4, 5*).

3:17 **winnowing fork.** *See note on Mt 3:12.*

3:19 **reprimanded ... because of Herodias.** *See note on Mt 14:3.*

3:20 **locked John up in prison.** This event actually occurred much later during Jesus' ministry (Mt 14:1–12; Jn 3:22–24). But Luke organized his material on John the Baptist topically rather than chronologically (see Introduction: Background and Setting).

JESUS IS BAPTIZED

21 [A]Now when all the people were baptized, Jesus was also baptized, and while He was [B]praying, heaven was opened, 22 and the Holy Spirit descended upon Him in bodily form like a dove, and a voice came out of heaven, "[A]You are My beloved Son, in You I am well-pleased."

GENEALOGY OF JESUS

23 [A]When He began His ministry, Jesus Himself was about thirty years of age, being, [a]as was supposed, the son of [B]Joseph, [b]the son of [c]Eli, 24 the son of Matthat, the son of Levi, the son of Melchi, the son of Jannai, the son of Joseph, 25 the son of Mattathias, the son of Amos, the son of Nahum, the son of [a]Hesli, the son of Naggai, 26 the son of Maath, the son of Mattathias, the son of Semein, the son of Josech, the son of Joda, 27 the son of Joanan, the son of Rhesa, [A]the son of Zerubbabel, the son of [a]Shealtiel, the son of Neri, 28 the son of Melchi, the son of Addi, the son of Cosam, the son of Elmadam, the son of Er, 29 the son of [a]Joshua, the son of Eliezer, the son of Jorim, the son of Matthat, the son of Levi, 30 the son of Simeon, the son of [a]Judah, the son of Joseph, the son of Jonam, the son of Eliakim, 31 the son of Melea, the son of Menna, the son of Mattatha, the son of Nathan, the son of David, 32 [A]the son of Jesse, the son of Obed, the son of Boaz, the son of [a]Salmon, the son of [b]Nahshon, 33 the son of Amminadab, the son of Admin, the son of [a]Ram, the son of Hezron, the son of Perez, the son of Judah, 34 the son of Jacob, the son of Isaac, [A]the son of Abraham, the son of Terah, the son of Nahor, 35 the son of Serug, the son of [a]Reu, the son of Peleg, the son of [b]Heber, the son of Shelah, 36 the son of Cainan, the son of Arphaxad, the son of Shem, [A]the son of Noah, the son of Lamech, 37 the son of Methuselah, the son of Enoch, the son of Jared, the son of Mahalaleel, the son of Cainan, 38 the son of Enosh, the son of Seth, the son of Adam, the son of God.

THE TEMPTATION OF JESUS

4 [A]Jesus, full of the Holy Spirit, [B]returned from the Jordan and was led around [a]by the Spirit in the wilderness 2 for [A]forty days, being tempted by the devil. And He ate nothing during those days, and when they had ended, He became hungry. 3 And the devil said to Him, "If You are the Son of God, tell this stone to become bread." 4 And Jesus answered him, "It is written, '[A]MAN SHALL NOT LIVE ON BREAD ALONE.' "

5 [A]And he led Him up and showed Him all the kingdoms of [a,B]the world in a moment of time. 6 And the devil said to Him, "I will give You all this domain and [a]its glory; [A]for it has been handed over to me, and I give it to whomever I wish. 7 Therefore if You [a]worship before me, it shall all be Yours." 8 Jesus answered him, "It is written, '[A]YOU SHALL WORSHIP THE LORD YOUR GOD AND SERVE HIM ONLY.' "

9 [A]And he led Him to Jerusalem and had Him stand on the pinnacle of the temple, and said to Him, "If You are the Son of God, throw Yourself down from here; 10 for it is written,

> '[A]HE WILL COMMAND HIS ANGELS
> CONCERNING YOU TO GUARD YOU,'

11 and,

> '[A]ON *their* HANDS THEY WILL BEAR YOU UP,
> SO THAT YOU WILL NOT STRIKE YOUR
> FOOT AGAINST A STONE.' "

12 And Jesus answered and said to him, "It is said, '[A]YOU SHALL NOT PUT THE LORD YOUR GOD TO THE TEST.' "

13 When the devil had finished every temptation, he left Him until an opportune time.

3:21 [A]Luke 3:21, 22: *Matt 3:13-17; Mark 1:9-11* [B]Matt 14:23; Luke 5:16; 9:18, 28f 3:22 [A]Ps 2:7; Is 42:1; Matt 3:17; 17:5; Mark 1:11; Luke 9:35; 2 Pet 1:17 3:23 [a]Lit *as it was being thought* [b]Lit *of Eli*, and so throughout the genealogy [c]Also spelled *Heli* [A]Matt 4:17; Acts 1:1 [B]Luke 3:23-27: *Matt 1:16* 3:25 [a]Also spelled *Esli* 3:27 [a]Gr *Salathiel;* names of people in the Old Testament are given in their Old Testament form through v 38 [A]Matt 1:12 3:29 [a]Gr *Jesus* 3:30 [a]Gr *Judas* 3:32 [a]Gr *Sala* [b]Gr *Naasson* [A]Luke 3:32-34: *Matt 1:1-6* 3:33 [a]Gr *Arni* 3:34 [A]Luke 3:34-36: *Gen 11:26-30; 1 Chr 1:24-27* 3:35 [a]Gr *Ragau* [b]Gr *Eber* 3:36 [A]Luke 3:36-38: *Gen 5:3-32; 1 Chr 1:1-4* 4:1 [a]Or *under the influence of;* lit *in* [A]Luke 4:1-13: *Matt 4:1-11; Mark 1:12, 13* [B]Luke 3:3 4:2 [A]Ex 34:28; 1 Kin 19:8 4:4 [A]Deut 8:3 4:5 [a]Lit *the inhabited earth* [A]Matt 4:8-10 [B]Matt 24:14 4:6 [a]Lit *their* (referring to the kingdoms in v 5) [A]1 John 5:19 4:7 [a]Or *bow down before* 4:8 [A]Deut 6:13; 10:20; Matt 4:10 4:9 [A]Matt 4:5-7 4:10 [A]Ps 91:11 4:11 [A]Ps 91:12 4:12 [A]Deut 6:16

3:21 baptized. *See note on Mt 3:15.* **while He was praying.** Luke alone notes that Jesus was praying. Prayer is one of Luke's themes (see Introduction: Historical and Theological Themes).

3:22 Holy Spirit. *See note on Mt 3:16, 17.* All 3 persons of the Trinity are distinguishable in this verse, a strong proof against the heresy of modalism, which suggests that God is one Person who manifests Himself in 3 distinct modes, one at a time. **in bodily form.** I.e., physical and visible to all (cf. Mt 3:16; Jn 1:32). **like a dove.** A picture of gentleness (Mt 10:16). **My beloved Son.** *See note on Mt 3:17.*

3:23–38 Luke's genealogy moves backward, from Jesus to Adam; Matthew's moves forward, from Abraham to Joseph. Luke's entire section from Joseph to David differs starkly from that given by Matthew. The two genealogies are easily reconciled if Luke's is seen as Mary's genealogy, and Matthew's version represents Joseph's. Thus the royal line is passed through Jesus' legal father, and His physical descent from David is established by Mary's lineage. Luke, unlike Matthew (*see note on Mt 1:3*), includes no women in his genealogy—even Mary herself. Joseph was "the son of Eli" by marriage (Eli having no sons of his own), and thus is named here in v. 23 as the representative of Mary's generation. Moses himself established precedent for this sort of substitution in Nu 27:1–11; 36:1–12. The men listed from Eli (v. 23) to Rhesa (v. 27) are found nowhere else in Scripture. Zerubbabel and Shealtiel (v. 27) are the only two names here that correspond to names in Matthew's genealogy between David and Jesus. For an explanation *see notes on Hag 2:23; Mt 1:12.*

3:23 about thirty years of age. Luke was probably not fixing an exact age. Rather, this was an approximation, 30 being a customary age for entering into the office of prophet (Eze 1:1); priest (Nu 4:3, 35, 39, 43, 47), or king (Ge 41:46; 2Sa 5:4). **as was supposed.** Luke had already established the fact of the virgin birth (1:34, 35); here he made clear once again that Joseph was not Jesus' true father.

4:1 led … by the Spirit. *See note on Mt 4:1.*

4:2 forty days … tempted. Evidently, the temptation of Christ encompassed the full 40 days of His fast (*see note on Mt 4:2*). Both Matthew and Luke give a condensed recounting of only 3 specific temptations. Luke reverses the order of the last two temptations in Matthew's account. Luke occasionally ordered material logically, rather than chronologically (see Introduction: Background and Setting; *see note on 1:3*). Luke may have had some purpose for doing so here—perhaps to end his account of Jesus' temptation at the temple in Jerusalem (cf. v. 9), a very important location in Luke's narrative (see Introduction: Historical and Theological Themes).

4:3–13 *See notes on Mt 4:3–10.*

4:4 Jesus quoted Dt 8:3.

4:8 Jesus quoted Dt 6:13.

4:10, 11 Satan quoted Ps 91:11, 12.

4:12 Jesus quoted Dt 6:16.

4:13 until an opportune time. Satan's temptations did not end here for Christ,

JESUS' PUBLIC MINISTRY

14 And [A]Jesus returned to Galilee in the power of
the Spirit, and [B]news about Him spread through all
the surrounding district. 15 And He *began* [A]teaching
in their synagogues and was praised by all.
16 And He came to [A]Nazareth, where He had been
brought up; and as was His custom, [B]He entered the
synagogue on the Sabbath, and [C]stood up to read.
17 And the [a]book of the prophet Isaiah was handed
to Him. And He opened the [a]book and found the
place where it was written,

18 "[A]THE SPIRIT OF THE LORD IS UPON ME,
BECAUSE HE ANOINTED ME TO PREACH
THE GOSPEL TO THE POOR.
HE HAS SENT ME TO PROCLAIM
RELEASE TO THE CAPTIVES,
AND RECOVERY OF SIGHT TO THE BLIND,
TO SET FREE THOSE WHO ARE OPPRESSED,
19 [A]TO PROCLAIM THE FAVORABLE
YEAR OF THE LORD."

20 And He [A]closed the [a]book, gave it back to the attendant and [B]sat down; and the eyes of all in the
synagogue were fixed on Him. 21 And He began to
say to them, "Today this Scripture has been fulfilled in your [a]hearing." 22 And all were [a]speaking
well of Him, and wondering at the [b]gracious words
which [c]were falling from His lips; and they were
saying, "[A]Is this not Joseph's son?" 23 And He said to
them, "No doubt you will quote this proverb to Me,
'Physician, heal yourself! Whatever we heard was
done [A]at Capernaum, do here in [B]your hometown
as well.' " 24 And He said, "Truly I say to you, [A]no
prophet is welcome in his hometown. 25 But I say
to you in truth, there were many widows in Israel
[A]in the days of Elijah, when the sky was shut up for
three years and six months, when a great famine
came over all the land; 26 and yet Elijah was sent to
none of them, but [A]only to [a]Zarephath, *in the land* of
[B]Sidon, to a woman who was a widow. 27 And there
were many lepers in Israel in the time of Elisha
the prophet; and none of them was cleansed, but
[A]only Naaman the Syrian." 28 And all *the people* in
the synagogue were filled with rage as they heard
these things; 29 and they got up and [A]drove Him out
of the city, and led Him to the brow of the hill on
which their city had been built, in order to throw
Him down the cliff. 30 But [A]passing through their
midst, He went His way.
31 And [A]He came down to [B]Capernaum, a city of
Galilee, and He was teaching them on the Sabbath;
32 and [A]they were amazed at His teaching, for [B]His
[a]message was with authority. 33 In the synagogue
there was a man [a]possessed by the spirit of an unclean demon, and he cried out with a loud voice,
34 "Let us alone! [a,A]What business do we have with
each other, Jesus [b]of [B]Nazareth? Have You come to
destroy us? I know who You are—[B]the Holy One of
God!" 35 But Jesus [A]rebuked him, saying, "Be quiet
and come out of him!" And when the demon had
thrown him down in the midst *of the people,* he
came out of him without doing him any harm.
36 And amazement came upon them all, and they
began talking with one another saying, "What is
[a]this message? For [A]with authority and power He

4:14 [A]Matt 4:12 [B]Matt 9:26; Luke 4:37 4:15 [A]Matt 4:23 4:16 [A]Luke 2:39, 51 [B]Matt 13:54; Mark 6:1f [C]Acts 13:14-16 4:17 [a]Or *scroll* 4:18 [A]Is 61:1; Matt 11:5; 12:18; John 3:34 4:19 [A]Is 61:2; Lev 25:10 4:20 [a]Or *scroll* [A]Luke 4:17 [B]Matt 26:55 4:21 [a]Lit *ears* 4:22 [a]Or *testifying* [b]Or *words of grace* [c]Lit *were proceeding out of His mouth* [A]Matt 13:55; Mark 6:3; John 6:42 4:23 [A]Matt 4:13; Mark 1:21ff; 2:1ff; Luke 4:35ff; John 4:46ff [B]Mark 6:1; Luke 2:39, 51; 4:16 4:24 [A]Matt 13:57; Mark 6:4; John 4:44 4:25 [A]1 Kin 17:1; 18:1; James 5:17 4:26 [a]Gr *Sarepta* [A]1 Kin 17:9 [B]Matt 11:21 4:27 [A]2 Kin 5:1-14 4:29 [A]Num 15:35; Acts 7:58; Heb 13:12 4:30 [A]John 10:39 4:31 [A]Luke 4:31-37: *Mark 1:21-28* [B]Matt 4:13; Luke 4:23 4:32 [a]Lit *word* [A]Matt 7:28 [B]Luke 4:36; John 7:46 4:33 [a]Lit *having a spirit* 4:34 [a]Lit *What to us and to you* (a Heb idiom) [b]Lit *the Nazarene* [A]Matt 8:29 [B]Mark 1:24 4:35 [A]Matt 8:26; Mark 4:39; Luke 4:39, 41; 8:24 4:36 [a]Or *this word, that with authority...come out?* [A]Luke 4:32

but persisted throughout His ministry (cf. Heb 4:15), and culminated in Gethsemane (22:39–46).

4:14 returned to Galilee. The synoptic gospels are largely silent about Jesus' ministry between His baptism and His return to Galilee, but John recorded a fairly extensive ministry in Jerusalem and Judea (Jn 2:12–4:1). Because of this, news of Him quickly spread.

4:15 synagogues. *See note on Mk 1:21.*

4:16 He came to Nazareth. Luke acknowledged in v. 23 (*see note there*) that Christ had already ministered in Capernaum. Yet Luke purposely situated this episode at the beginning of his account of Christ's public ministry. Here is an example of Luke's ordering things logically rather than chronologically (see Introduction: Background and Setting; see note on 1:3). **As was His custom.** Nazareth was His hometown, so He would have been well known to all who regularly attended this synagogue.

4:18 He anointed Me. I.e., the Spirit Himself was the anointing (vv. 1, 14).

4:19 the favorable year of the LORD. Or, "the year of the Lord's favor." The passage Christ read was Is 61:1, 2. He stopped in the middle of v. 2. The rest of the verse prophesies judgment in the day of God's vengeance. Since that part of the verse pertains to the second advent, He did not read it.

4:20 sat down. It was customary for a teacher to stand respectfully during the reading of the Scriptures (v. 16), and sit humbly to teach. *See note on Mt 5:1.*

4:21 this Scripture has been fulfilled. This was an unambiguous claim that He was the Messiah who fulfilled the prophecy. They correctly understood His meaning but could not accept such lofty claims from One whom they knew so well as the carpenter's son (v. 22; cf. Mt 13:55).

4:23 Capernaum. Obviously, Christ had already gained a reputation for His miraculous works in Capernaum. Scripture gives few details about that first year of public ministry. Most of what we know about those months is found in John's gospel, and it suggests Christ ministered mostly in Judea. However, Jn 2:12 mentions a brief visit to Capernaum, with no other details. John 4:46–54 describes how while Christ was at Cana, He healed a royal official's son who lay sick in Capernaum. We also know that Christ had already gathered some of His disciples, who were men from the N shore of the Sea of Galilee (Jn 1:35–42; *see note on Mt 4:18*). He might have visited there more than once during that first year of ministry. In any case, He had been there long enough to do miracles, and His fame had spread throughout Galilee (cf. v. 14).

4:25–27 Both the widow of Zarephath (1Ki 17:8–24) and Naaman the Syrian (2Ki 5) were Gentiles. Both lived during times of widespread unbelief in Israel. Jesus' point was that God bypassed all the widows and lepers in Israel, yet showed grace to two Gentiles. God's concern for Gentiles and outcasts is one of the thematic threads that runs through Luke's gospel (see Introduction: Historical and Theological Themes).

4:28 filled with rage. This is Luke's first mention of hostile opposition to Christ's ministry. What seems to have sparked the Nazarenes' fury was Christ's suggestion that divine grace might be withheld from them yet extended to Gentiles.

4:30 passing through their midst. The implication is that this was a miraculous escape—the first of several similar incidents in which He escaped a premature death at the hands of a mob (cf. Jn 7:30; 8:59; 10:39).

4:32 authority. *See note on Mt 7:29.*

4:33 demon. *See note on Mt 8:16.*

4:34 Holy One of God. Demons always recognized Christ immediately (cf. v. 41; 8:28; Mt 8:29; Mk 1:24; 3:11; 5:7)

commands the unclean spirits and they come out."
37 And [A]the report about Him was spreading into
every locality in the surrounding district.

MANY ARE HEALED

38 [A]Then He got up and *left* the synagogue, and
entered Simon's home. Now Simon's mother-in-law
was [B]suffering from a high fever, and they asked
Him [a]to help her. 39 And standing over her, He [A]re-
buked the fever, and it left her; and she immediately
got up and [a]waited on them.
40 [A]While [B]the sun was setting, all those who had
any *who were* sick with various diseases brought
them to Him; and [C]laying His hands on each one of
them, He was [D]healing them. 41 Demons also were
coming out of many, shouting, "You are [A]the Son of
God!" But [B]rebuking them, He would [C]not allow them
to speak, because they knew Him to be [a]the Christ.
42 [A]When day came, Jesus left and went to a secluded place; and the crowds were searching for
Him, and came to Him and tried to keep Him from
going away from them. 43 But He said to them, "I
must preach the kingdom of God to the other cities
also, [A]for I was sent for this purpose."
44 So He kept on preaching in the synagogues
[A]of [a]Judea.

THE FIRST DISCIPLES

5 [A]Now it happened that while the crowd was
pressing around Him and listening to the word
of God, He was standing by [B]the lake of Gennesaret; 2 and He saw two boats lying at the edge of
the lake; but the fishermen had gotten out of them
and were washing their nets. 3 And [A]He got into
one of the boats, which was Simon's, and asked
him to put out a little way from the land. And He
sat down and *began* teaching the [a]people from the
boat. 4 When He had finished speaking, He said to
Simon, "Put out into the deep water and [A]let down
your nets for a catch." 5 Simon answered and said,
"[A]Master, [B]we worked hard all night and caught
nothing, but [a]I will do as You say *and* let down the
nets." 6 When they had done this, [A]they enclosed
a great quantity of fish, and their nets *began* to
break; 7 so they signaled to their partners in the
other boat for them to come and help them. And
they came and filled both of the boats, so that they
began to sink. 8 But when Simon Peter saw *that,* he
fell down at Jesus' [a]feet, saying, "Go away from me
Lord, for I am a sinful man!" 9 For amazement had
seized him and all his companions because of the
catch of fish which they had taken; 10 and so also
were [a]James and John, sons of Zebedee, who were
partners with Simon. And Jesus said to Simon, "[A]Do
not fear, from now on you will be [B]catching men."
11 When they had brought their boats to land, [A]they
left everything and followed Him.

THE LEPER AND THE PARALYTIC

12 [A]While He was in one of the cities, behold, *there*
was a man [a]covered with leprosy; and when he saw
Jesus, he fell on his face and implored Him, saying,
"Lord, if You are willing, You can make me clean."
13 And He stretched out His hand and touched him,
saying, "I am willing; be cleansed." And immediately
the leprosy left him. 14 And He ordered him to tell
no one, "But go and [A]show yourself to the priest
and make an offering for your cleansing, just as
Moses commanded, as a testimony to them." 15 But
[A]the news about Him was spreading even farther,
and large crowds were gathering to hear *Him* and
to be healed of their sicknesses. 16 But Jesus Himself
would *often* slip away [a]to the [b]wilderness and [A]pray.
17 [a]One day He was teaching; and [A]there were
some Pharisees and [B]teachers of the law sitting
there, who had [C]come from every village of Galilee
and Judea and *from* Jerusalem; and [D]the power of
the Lord was *present* for Him to perform healing.

4:37 [A]Luke 4:14 4:38 [a]Lit *about her* [A]Luke 4:38, 39: *Matt 8:14, 15; Mark 1:29-31* [B]Matt 4:24 4:39 [a]Or *served* [A]Luke 4:35, 41 4:40 [A]Luke 4:40, 41: *Matt 8:16, 17; Mark 1:32-34* [B]Mark 1:32 [C]Mark 5:23 [D]Matt 4:23 4:41 [a]I.e. the Messiah [A]Matt 4:3 [B]Luke 4:35 [C]Matt 8:16; Mark 1:34 4:42 [A]Luke 4:42, 43: *Mark 1:35-38* 4:43 [A]Mark 1:38 4:44 [a]I.e. the country of the Jews (including Galilee) [A]Matt 4:23 5:1 [A]Matt 4:18-22; Mark 1:16-20; Luke 5:1-11; John 1:40-42 [B]Num 34:11; Deut 3:17; Josh 12:3; 13:27; Matt 4:18 5:3 [a]Lit *crowds* [A]Matt 13:2; Mark 3:9, 10; 4:1 5:4 [A]John 21:6 5:5 [a]Lit *upon Your word* [A]Luke 8:24; 9:33, 49; 17:13 [B]John 21:3 5:6 [A]John 21:6 5:8 [a]Lit *knees* 5:10 [a]Or *Jacob* [A]Matt 14:27 [B]2 Tim 2:26 5:11 [A]Matt 4:20, 22; 19:29; Mark 1:18, 20; Luke 5:28 5:12 [a]Lit *full of* [A]Luke 5:12-14: *Matt 8:2-4; Mark 1:40-44* 5:14 [A]Lev 13:49; 14:2ff 5:15 [A]Matt 9:26 5:16 [a]Lit *in* [b]Or *deserted places* [A]Matt 14:23; Mark 1:35; Luke 6:12 5:17 [a]Lit *On one of the days* [A]Matt 15:1 [B]Luke 2:46 [C]Mark 1:45 [D]Mark 5:30; Luke 6:19; 8:46

4:38 Simon's mother-in-law. Peter was married (cf. 1Co 9:5), though no details about his wife are given anywhere in Scripture. **a high fever.** Matthew 8:14, 15 and Mk 1:30, 31 also report this miracle. But only Luke, the physician, remarks that the fever was "high," and makes note of the means Jesus used to heal her (v. 39).

4:40 the sun was setting. Signifying the end of the Sabbath. As soon as they were free to travel, the multitudes came.

4:41 You are the Son of God! *See note on v. 34.*

4:43 kingdom of God. This term, so prominent throughout the remainder of Luke's gospel, is introduced here for the first time. *See note on Mt 3:2.*

5:1 lake of Gennesaret. I.e., the Sea of Galilee, sometimes also called the Sea of Tiberias (Jn 6:1; 21:1). It is actually a large freshwater lake, over 690 ft. below sea level, and serves as the main source of water and commerce for the Galilee region.

5:2 washing their nets. Having fished all night with nothing to show for their labor (cf. v. 5), they were drying and mending their nets for another night's work.

5:3 He sat. *See notes on 4:20; Mt 5:1.*

5:4 let down your nets. Normally, the fish that were netted in shallow water at night would migrate during the daylight hours to waters too deep to reach easily with nets, which is why Peter fished at night. Peter no doubt thought Jesus' directive made no sense, but he obeyed anyway, and was rewarded for his obedience (v. 6).

5:8 Go away from me. The remarkable catch of fish was clearly a miracle, astonishing to all the fishermen in Capernaum (v. 9). Peter immediately realized he was in the presence of the Holy One exercising His divine power, and he was stricken with shame over his own sin. Cf. Ex 20:19; 33:20; Jdg 13:22; Job 42:5, 6. *See note on Is 6:5.*

5:11 left everything and followed Him. *See note on Mt 4:18.* Luke gave a more detailed account of the second call of these disciples.

5:12 covered with leprosy. Luke's emphasis suggests this was an extremely serious case of leprosy. *See note on Mk 1:40.*

5:13 immediately. One of the characteristics of Jesus' healings was immediate and total wholeness. Cf. 17:14; Mt 8:13; Mk 5:29; Jn 5:9.

5:14 tell no one. *See note on Mt 8:4.* **show yourself to the priest.** I.e., in accordance with the law governing leprosy (Lv 13:1–46).

5:17 Pharisees. *See note on Mt 3:7.* **teachers of the law.** I.e., scribes. *See note on Mt 2:4.* These Jewish leaders came from as far away as Jerusalem. His reputation had spread, and already the scribes and Pharisees were watching Him critically.

18 [A]And *some* men *were* carrying on a [a]bed a man
who was paralyzed; and they were trying to bring
him in and to set him down in front of Him. 19 But
not finding any *way* to bring him in because of the
crowd, they went up on [A]the roof and let him down
[B]through the tiles with his stretcher, into the middle
of the crowd, in front of Jesus. 20 Seeing their faith,
He said, "[a]Friend, [A]your sins are forgiven you." 21 The
scribes and the Pharisees [A]began to reason, saying,
"[B]Who is this *man* who speaks blasphemies? [C]Who
can forgive sins, but God alone?" 22 But Jesus, [a]aware
of their reasonings, answered and said to them, "Why
are you reasoning in your hearts? 23 Which is easier,
to say, 'Your sins have been forgiven you,' or to say,
'Get up and walk'? 24 But, so that you may know that
the Son of Man has authority on earth to forgive
sins,"—He said to the [A]paralytic—"I say to you, get up,
and pick up your stretcher and go home." 25 Immediately he got up before them, and picked up what
he had been lying on, and went home [A]glorifying
God. 26 [a]They were all struck with astonishment and
began [A]glorifying God; and they were filled [B]with
fear, saying, "We have seen remarkable things today."

CALL OF LEVI (MATTHEW)

27 [A]After that He went out and noticed a tax collector named [a,B]Levi sitting in the tax booth, and He
said to him, "Follow Me." 28 And he [A]left everything
behind, and got up and *began* to follow Him.
29 And [A]Levi gave a big reception for Him in his
house; and there was a great crowd of [B]tax collectors
and other *people* who were reclining *at the table*
with them. 30 [A]The Pharisees and their scribes *began*
grumbling at His disciples, saying, "Why do you
eat and drink with the tax collectors and [a]sinners?"
31 And Jesus answered and said to them, "[A]*It is* not
those who are well who need a physician, but those
who are sick. 32 I have not come to call the righteous
but sinners to repentance."
33 And they said to Him, "[A]The disciples of John often fast and offer prayers, the *disciples* of the Pharisees also do [a]the same, but Yours eat and drink."
34 And Jesus said to them, "You cannot make the
[a]attendants of the bridegroom fast while the bridegroom is with them, can you? 35 [A]But *the* days will
come; and when the bridegroom is taken away from
them, then they will fast in those days." 36 And He
was also telling them a parable: "No one tears a
piece of cloth from a new garment and puts it on an
old garment; otherwise he will both tear the new,
and the piece from the new will not match the old.
37 And no one puts new wine into old wineskins;
otherwise the new wine will burst the skins and
it will be spilled out, and the skins will be ruined.
38 But new wine must be put into fresh wineskins.
39 And no one, after drinking old *wine* wishes for
new; for he says, 'The old is good *enough.*' "

JESUS IS LORD OF THE SABBATH

6 [A]Now it happened that He was passing through
some grainfields on a Sabbath; and His disciples
[B]were picking the heads of grain, rubbing them in
their hands, and eating *the grain.* 2 But some of the
Pharisees said, "Why do you do what [A]is not lawful
on the Sabbath?" 3 And Jesus answering them said,
"Have you not even read [A]what David did when he
was hungry, he and those who were with him, 4 how
he entered the house of God, and took and ate the
[a]consecrated bread which [A]is not lawful for any
to eat except the priests alone, and gave it to his
companions?" 5 And He was saying to them, "The
Son of Man is Lord of the Sabbath."

5:18 [a]Or *stretcher* [A]Luke 5:18-26: *Matt 9:2-8; Mark 2:3-12* 5:19 [A]Matt 24:17 [B]Mark 2:4 5:20 [a]Lit *Man* [A]Matt 9:2 5:21 [A]Luke 3:8 [B]Luke 7:49 [C]Is 43:25 5:22 [a]Or *perceiving* 5:24 [A]Matt 4:24 5:25 [A]Matt 9:8 5:26 [a]Lit *Astonishment took them all* [A]Matt 9:8 [B]Luke 1:65; 7:16 5:27 [a]Also called *Matthew* [A]Luke 5:27-39: *Matt 9:9-17; Mark 2:14-22* [B]Matt 9:9 5:28 [A]Luke 5:11 5:29 [A]Matt 9:9 [B]Luke 15:1 5:30 [a]I.e. irreligious Jews [A]Mark 2:16; Luke 15:2; Acts 23:9 5:31 [A]Matt 9:12, 13; Mark 2:17 5:33 [a]Or *likewise* [A]Matt 9:14; Mark 2:18 5:34 [a]Lit *sons of the bridal-chamber* 5:35 [A]Matt 9:15; Mark 2:20; Luke 17:22 6:1 [A]Luke 6:1-5: *Matt 12:1-8; Mark 2:23-28* [B]Deut 23:25 6:2 [A]Matt 12:2 6:3 [A]1 Sam 21:6 6:4 [a]Or *showbread; lit loaves of presentation* [A]Lev 24:9

5:19 through the tiles. This appears to have been a home with roof tiles which, when removed, gave access to lower the man between the roof beams. The extreme measures they took to lay this man before Jesus indicate that the crowds following Him were very large. With the press of people around Jesus, it would have been impossible for men carrying a paralytic to get close enough to Him, even if they waited until He left the house.

5:20 your sins are forgiven. Christ ignored the paralysis and addressed the man's greater need first. *See note on Mt 9:2.* In doing so He asserted a prerogative that was God's alone (v. 21; cf. 7:49). His subsequent healing of the man's paralysis was proof that He had the authority to forgive sins as well.

5:21 blasphemies. Their assessment would have been correct if He were not God incarnate. *See note on Mt 9:3.*

5:22 aware of their reasonings. I.e., by means of His omniscience. Cf. Mt 9:4; Jn 5:24, 25.

5:23 Which is easier . . . ? *See note on Mt 9:5.*

5:24 that you may know. His ability to heal anyone and everyone at will—totally and immediately (v. 25)—was incontrovertible proof of His deity. As God, He had all authority to forgive sins. This was a decisive moment and should have ended once and for all the Pharisees' opposition. Instead, they began to try to discredit Him by charging Him with violating their Sabbath rules (*see notes on 6:2–11*).

5:26 remarkable things. The response is curiously noncommittal—not void of wonder and amazement, but utterly void of true faith.

5:27 Levi. Matthew's name prior to his conversion. *See notes on Mt 9:9, 11.*

5:28 left everything. Cf. v. 11; 9:59–62. This implies an irreversible action.

5:29 a great crowd of tax collectors. Levi's immediate response was to introduce his former comrades to Christ.

5:30 eat and drink. Consorting with outcasts on any level—even merely speaking to them—was bad enough. Eating and drinking with them implied a level of friendship that was abhorrent to the Pharisees (cf. 7:34; 15:2; 19:7).

5:31 who are well. I.e., those who think they are whole don't seek healing. *See note on Mt 9:12.*

5:33 often fast. Jesus did fast on at least one occasion (Mt 4:2)—but privately, in accordance with His own teaching (cf. Mt 6:16–18). The law also prescribed a fast on the Day of Atonement (Lv 16:29–31; 23:27)—but all other fasts were supposed to be voluntary, for specific reasons such as penitence and earnest prayer. The fact that these Pharisees raised this question shows that they thought of fasting as a public exercise to display one's own spirituality. Yet, the OT also rebuked hypocritical fasting (Is 58:3–6). *See notes on Mt 6:16, 17; 9:15.*

5:36–38 *See notes on Mt 9:16, 17.*

5:39 The old is good *enough*. Those who had acquired a taste for Old Covenant ceremonies and Pharisaic traditions were loath to give them up for the new wine of Jesus' teaching. Luke alone adds this saying.

6:2 not lawful. *See note on Mt 12:2.*

6:3 Have you not . . . read. A rebuke, suggesting that they were culpable for their ignorance of so basic a truth (cf. Mt 12:5; 19:4; 21:16, 42; 22:31). **what David did.** *See notes on 1Sa 21:1–6.*

6:4 the consecrated bread. *See note on Mt 12:4.*

6:5 Lord of the Sabbath. *See note on Mt 12:8.*

6 [A]On another Sabbath He entered [B]the synagogue and was teaching; and there was a man there
[a]whose right hand was withered. 7 The scribes and
the Pharisees [A]were watching Him closely *to see* if
He healed on the Sabbath, so that they might find
reason to accuse Him. 8 But He [A]knew [a]what they
were thinking, and He said to the man with the
withered hand, "Get up and [b]come forward!" And
he got up and [c]came forward. 9 And Jesus said to
them, "I ask you, is it lawful to do good or to do
harm on the Sabbath, to save a life or to destroy
it?" 10 After [A]looking around at them all, He said to
him, "Stretch out your hand!" And he did *so;* and
his hand was restored. 11 But they themselves were
filled with [a]rage, and discussed together what they
might do to Jesus.

CHOOSING THE TWELVE

12 It was [a]at this time that He went off to [A]the
mountain to [B]pray, and He spent the whole night in
prayer to God. 13 And when day came, [A]He called His
disciples to Him and chose twelve of them, whom
He also named as [B]apostles: 14 Simon, whom He also
named Peter, and Andrew his brother; and [a]James
and John; and Philip and Bartholomew; 15 and [A]Mat-
thew and Thomas; James *the son* of Alphaeus, and
Simon who was called the Zealot; 16 Judas *the son*
of James, and Judas Iscariot, who became a traitor.
17 Jesus [A]came down with them and stood on a
level place; and *there was* [B]a large crowd of His
disciples, and a great throng of people from all Judea and Jerusalem and the coastal region of [C]Tyre
and Sidon, 18 who had come to hear Him and to be

6:6 [a]Lit *and his* [A]Luke 6:6-11: *Matt 12:9-14; Mark 3:1-6;* Luke 6:1 [B]Matt 4:23 6:7 [A]Mark 3:2 6:8 [a]Lit *their thoughts* [b]Lit *stand into the middle* [c]Lit *stood* [A]Matt 9:4 6:10 [A]Mark 3:5 6:11 [a]Lit *folly* 6:12 [a]Lit *in these days* [A]Matt 5:1 [B]Matt 14:23; Luke 5:16; 9:18, 28 6:13 [A]Luke 6:13-16: *Matt 10:2-4; Mark 3:16-19; Acts 1:13* [B]Mark 6:30 6:14 [a]Or *Jacob,* also vv 15 and 16 6:15 [A]Matt 9:9 6:17 [A]Luke 6:12 [B]Matt 4:25; Mark 3:7, 8 [C]Matt 11:21

6:7 ***to see* if He healed on the Sabbath.** The scribes and Pharisees spotted the man with the withered hand (v. 6) and, with Christ present, they immediately knew that this would be an occasion for the man's healing. In stark contrast to all other so-called healers, Christ was not selective. He healed all who came to Him (v. 19; cf. 4:40; Mt 8:16).

6:8 knew what they were thinking. Cf. 5:22. *See note on Mt 9:4.* **come forward.** Jesus purposely did this miracle openly, before all, as if to demonstrate His contempt for the Pharisees' man-made regulations.

6:9 to do good. The Sabbath laws forbade labor for profit, frivolous diversions, and things extraneous to worship. Activity per se was not unlawful. Good works were especially appropriate on the Sabbath—particularly deeds of charity, mercy, and worship. Works necessary for the preservation of life were also permitted. To corrupt the Sabbath to forbid such works was a perversion of God's design. *See notes on Mt 12:2, 3.* **to do harm.** Refusal to do good is tantamount to doing evil (Jas 4:17).

6:10 looking around at them. I.e., giving them a chance to respond to the question of v. 9. Evidently no one did.

6:11 filled with rage. A curious response in the face of so glorious a miracle. Such irrational hatred was their response to having been publicly humiliated—something they hated worse than anything (cf. Mt 23:6, 7). They were unable to answer His reasoning (vv. 9, 10). And furthermore, by healing the man only with a command, He had performed no actual "work" that they could charge Him with. Desperately seeking a reason to accuse Him (v. 7), they could find none. Their response was blind fury.

6:12 spent the whole night in prayer. Luke frequently shows Jesus praying—and particularly before major events in His ministry. Cf. 3:21; 5:16; 9:18, 28, 29; 11:1; 22:32, 40–46.

6:13 He called His disciples. *See notes on Mt 10:1–4.* Christ had many disciples. At one point He sent 70 out in pairs to proclaim the gospel (10:1). But on this occasion, He chose 12 and specifically commissioned them as apostles, i.e., "sent ones," with a special authority to deliver His message on His behalf (cf. Ac 1:21, 22).

6:17–49 The Sermon on the Plateau. The similarity to the Sermon on the Mount (*see notes on Mt 5:1–7:29*) is remarkable. It is possible, of course, that Jesus simply preached the same sermon on more than one occasion. (It is evident that He often used the same material more than once—e.g., 12:58, 59; cf. Mt 5:25, 26.) It appears more likely, however, that these are variant accounts of the same event. Luke's version is abbreviated somewhat, because he omitted sections from the sermon that are uniquely Jewish (particularly Christ's exposition of the law). Aside from that, the two sermons follow exactly the same flow of thought, beginning with the Beatitudes and ending with the parable about building on the rock. Differences in wording between the two accounts are undoubtedly owing to the fact that the sermon was originally delivered in Aramaic. Luke and Matthew translate into Gr. with slight variances. Of course, both translations are equally inspired and authoritative.

6:17 a level place. Elsewhere it says "on the mountain" (Mt 5:1). These harmonize easily if Luke is referring to either a plateau or a level place on the mountainside. Indeed, there is such a place at the site near Capernaum where tradition says this sermon was delivered. **Tyre and Sidon.** *See notes on Mt 11:21; Mk 3:8.*

6:18 unclean spirits. Another name for demons, used 10 times in the Gospels.

THE TWELVE APOSTLES

Matthew 10:2–4	Mark 3:16–19	Luke 6:14–16	Acts 1:13
Simon Peter	Simon Peter	Simon Peter	Simon Peter
Andrew	James	Andrew	John
James	John	James	James
John	Andrew	John	Andrew
Philip	Philip	Philip	Philip
Bartholomew	Bartholomew	Bartholomew	Thomas
Thomas	Matthew	Matthew	Bartholomew
Matthew	Thomas	Thomas	Matthew
James (of Alphaeus)	James (of Alphaeus)	James (of Alphaeus)	James (of Alphaeus)
Thaddaeus	Thaddaeus	Simon (the Zealot)	Simon (the Zealot)
Simon (the Canaanite)	Simon (the Canaanite)	Judas (of James)	Judas (of James)
Judas Iscariot	Judas Iscariot	Judas Iscariot	

Matthew and Mark have the name Thaddaeus while Luke, in his two lists (Luke 6 and Acts 1), has Judas (of James). Some think Judas may have been his original name and that it was changed later to Thaddaeus in order to avoid the stigma attached to the name of Judas Iscariot.

"The Canaanite" is a transliteration that probably represents an Aramaic word meaning "Zealous."

healed of their diseases; and those who were troubled with unclean spirits were being cured. 19 And
all the [a]people were trying to [A]touch Him, for [B]power
was coming from Him and healing *them* all.

THE BEATITUDES

20 And turning His gaze toward His disciples,
He *began* to say, "[A]Blessed *are* [a]you *who are* poor,
for [B]yours is the kingdom of God. 21 Blessed *are*
[a]you who hunger now, for you shall be satisfied.
Blessed *are* you who weep now, for you shall laugh.
22 [A]Blessed are you when men hate you, and [B]os-
tracize you, and insult you, and scorn your name
as evil, for the sake of the Son of Man. 23 Be glad in
that day and [A]leap *for joy*, for behold, your reward is
great in heaven. For [B]in the same way their fathers
used to [a]treat the prophets. 24 But woe to [A]you who
are rich, for [B]you are receiving your comfort in full.
25 Woe to you who [a]are well-fed now, for you shall
be hungry. Woe *to you* who laugh now, for you shall
mourn and weep. 26 Woe *to you* when all men speak
well of you, for their fathers used to [a]treat the [A]false
prophets in the same way.
27 "But I say to you who hear, [A]love your enemies, do good to those who hate you, 28 bless those
who curse you, [A]pray for those who [a]mistreat you.
29 [A]Whoever hits you on the cheek, offer him the
other also; and whoever takes away your [a]coat, do
not withhold your [b]shirt from him either. 30 Give to
everyone who asks of you, and whoever takes away
what is yours, do not demand it back. 31 [a,A]Treat others the same way you want [b]them to treat you. 32 [A]If
you love those who love you, what credit is *that* to
you? For even sinners love those who love them.
33 If you do good to those who do good to you, what
credit is *that* to you? For even sinners do the same.
34 [A]If you lend to those from whom you expect to
receive, what credit is *that* to you? Even sinners lend
to sinners in order to receive back the same *amount*.
35 But [A]love your enemies, and do good, and lend,
[a]expecting nothing in return; and your reward will
be great, and you will be [B]sons of [C]the Most High;
for He Himself is kind to ungrateful and evil *men*.
36 [a]Be merciful, just as your Father is merciful.
37 "[A]Do not judge, and you will not be judged; and
do not condemn, and you will not be condemned;
[a,B]pardon, and you will be pardoned. 38 Give, and it
will be given to you. They will [a]pour [A]into your lap
a [B]good measure—pressed down, shaken together,
and running over. For by your standard of measure
it will be measured to you in return."
39 And He also spoke a parable to them: "[A]A blind
man cannot guide a blind man, can he? Will they
not both fall into a pit? 40 [A]A [a]pupil is not above
his teacher; but everyone, after he has been fully
trained, will [b]be like his teacher. 41 Why do you look
at the speck that is in your brother's eye, but do not
notice the log that is in your own eye? 42 Or how can
you say to your brother, 'Brother, let me take out the
speck that is in your eye,' when you yourself do not
see the log that is in your own eye? You hypocrite,
first take the log out of your own eye, and then you
will see clearly to take out the speck that is in your
brother's eye. 43 [A]For there is no good tree which
produces bad fruit, nor, [a]on the other hand, a bad
tree which produces good fruit. 44 [A]For each tree is
known by its own fruit. For men do not gather figs
from thorns, nor do they pick grapes from a briar
bush. 45 [A]The good man out of the good [a]treasure of
his heart brings forth what is good; and the evil *man*
out of the evil *treasure* brings forth what is evil; [B]for
his mouth speaks from [b]that which fills his heart.

BUILDERS AND FOUNDATIONS

46 "[A]Why do you call Me, 'Lord, Lord,' and do not
do what I say? 47 [A]Everyone who comes to Me and
hears My words and [a]acts on them, I will show
you whom he is like: 48 he is like a man building a
house, who [a]dug deep and laid a foundation on the
rock; and when a flood occurred, the [b]torrent burst
against that house and could not shake it, because
it had been well built. 49 But the one who has heard

6:19 [a]Lit *crowd* [A]Matt 9:21; 14:36; Mark 3:10 [B]Luke 5:17 6:20 [a]Lit *the* [A]Luke 6:20-23: *Matt 5:3-12* [B]Matt 5:3 6:21 [a]Lit *the* 6:22 [A]1 Pet 4:14 [B]John 9:22; 16:2 6:23 [a]Lit *do to* [A]Mal 4 [B]2 Chr 36:16; Acts 7:52 6:24 [A]Luke 16:25; James 5:1 [B]Matt 6:2 6:25 [a]Lit *having been filled* 6:26 [a]Lit *do to* [A]Matt 7:15 6:27 [A]Matt 5:44; Luke 6:35 6:28 [a]Or *revile* [A]Matt 5:44; Luke 6:35 6:29 [a]I.e. outer garment [b]Or *tunic;* i.e. garment worn next to body [A]Luke 6:29, 30: *Matt 5:39-42* 6:31 [a]Lit *Do to* [b]Lit *people* [A]Matt 7:12 6:32 [A]Matt 5:46 6:34 [A]Matt 5:42 6:35 [a]Or *not despairing at all* [A]Luke 6:27 [B]Matt 5:9 [C]Luke 1:32 6:36 [a]Or *Become* 6:37 [a]Lit *release* [A]Luke 6:37-42: *Matt 7:1-5* [B]Matt 6:14; Luke 23:16; Acts 3:13 6:38 [a]Lit *give* [A]Mark 4:24 [B]Ps 79:12; Is 65:6, 7; Jer 32:18 6:39 [A]Matt 15:14 6:40 [a]Or *disciple* [b]Or *reach his teacher's level* [A]Matt 10:24; John 13:16; 15:20 6:43 [a]Lit *again* [A]Luke 6:43, 44: *Matt 7:16, 18, 20* 6:44 [A]Matt 7:16; 12:33 6:45 [a]Or *treasury, storehouse* [b]Lit *the abundance of* [A]Matt 12:35 [B]Matt 12:34 6:46 [A]Mal 1:6; Matt 7:21 6:47 [a]Lit *does* [A]Luke 6:47-49: *Matt 7:24-27;* James 1:22ff 6:48 [a]Lit *dug and went deep* [b]Lit *river*

6:19 power was coming from Him. Cf. 8:45, 46; *see note on Mk 5:30.*

6:20–25 Luke's account of the Beatitudes is abbreviated (cf. Mt 5:3–12). He lists only 4, and balances them with 4 parallel woes.

6:20 you *who are* poor. Christ's concern for the poor and outcasts is one of Luke's favorite themes (see Introduction: Historical and Theological Themes). Luke used a personal pronoun ("you") where Mt 5:3 employed a definite article ("the"); Luke was underscoring the tender, personal sense of Christ's words. A comparison of the two passages reveals that Christ was dealing with something more significant than mere material poverty and wealth, however. The poverty spoken of here refers primarily to a sense of one's own spiritual impoverishment.

6:21 you who hunger. No mere craving for food, but a hunger and thirst for righteousness (*see note on Mt 5:6*).

6:22 for the sake of the Son of Man. Persecution per se is not something to be sought. But when evil is spoken against a Christian falsely and for Christ's sake (Mt 5:11), such persecution carries with it the blessing of God.

6:29 offer … the other also. *See notes on Mt 5:39.*

6:31 *See note on Mt 7:12.*

6:35 sons of the Most High. I.e., God's children should bear the indelible stamp of His moral character. Since He is loving, gracious, and generous—even to those who are His enemies—we should be like Him. *See note on Mt 5:44, 45;* cf. Eph 5:1, 2.

6:37 Do not judge. This forbids hypocrisy and a condemning spirit rising from self-righteousness. It does not condemn true discernment. *See note on Mt 7:1.* **you will be pardoned.** *See note on Mt 6:15.*

6:38 will pour into your lap. A long robe was used to carry the overflow of grain. Cf. Ps 79:12; Is 65:6; Jer 32:18.

6:41 speck … log. The humor of the imagery was no doubt intentional. Christ often employed hyperbole to paint comical images (cf. 18:25; Mt 23:24).

6:46 you call Me, 'Lord, Lord.' It is not sufficient to give lip service to Christ's lordship. Genuine faith produces obedience. A tree is known by its fruits (v. 44). *See notes on Mt 7:21–23.*

6:47–49 *See note on Mt 7:24–28.*

and has not acted *accordingly,* is like a man who
built a house on the ground without any foundation;
and the [a]torrent burst against it and immediately
it collapsed, and the ruin of that house was great."

JESUS HEALS A CENTURION'S SERVANT

7 [A]When He had completed all His discourse in the
hearing of the people, [B]He went to Capernaum.
2 And a centurion's slave, [a]who was highly regarded by him, was sick and about to die. 3 When
he heard about Jesus, [A]he sent some [a]Jewish elders
asking Him to come and [b]save the life of his slave.
4 When they came to Jesus, they earnestly implored
Him, saying, "He is worthy for You to grant this to
him; 5 for he loves our nation and it was he who built
us our synagogue." 6 Now Jesus *started* on His way
with them; and when He was not far from the house,
the centurion sent friends, saying to Him, "[a]Lord, do
not trouble Yourself further, for I am not worthy for
You to come under my roof; 7 for this reason I did
not even consider myself worthy to come to You, but
just [a]say the word, and my [b]servant will be healed.
8 For I also am a man placed under authority, with
soldiers under me; and I say to this one, 'Go!' and
he goes, and to another, 'Come!' and he comes, and
to my slave, 'Do this!' and he does it." 9 Now when
Jesus heard this, He marveled at him, and turned
and said to the crowd that was following Him, "I say
to you, [A]not even in Israel have I found such great
faith." 10 When those who had been sent returned
to the house, they found the slave in good health.
11 Soon afterwards He went to a city called Nain;
and His disciples were going along with Him,
[a]accompanied by a large crowd. 12 Now as He approached the gate of the city, [a]a dead man was being
carried out, the [b]only son of his mother, and she
was a widow; and a sizeable crowd from the city
was with her. 13 When [A]the Lord saw her, He felt
compassion for her, and said to her, "[a]Do not weep."
14 And He came up and touched the coffin; and the
bearers came to a halt. And He said, "Young man, I
say to you, arise!" 15 The [a]dead man sat up and began
to speak. And *Jesus* gave him back to his mother.
16 [A]Fear gripped them all, and they *began* [B]glorifying
God, saying, "A great [C]prophet has arisen among us!"
and, "God has [a]visited His people!" 17 [A]This report
concerning Him went out all over Judea and in all
the surrounding district.

A DEPUTATION FROM JOHN

18 [A]The disciples of John reported to him about
all these things. 19 Summoning [a]two of his disciples,
John sent them to [A]the Lord, saying, "Are You the [b]Ex-
pected One, or do we look for someone else?" 20 When
the men came to Him, they said, "John the Baptist has
sent us to You, to ask, 'Are You the [a]Expected One, or
do we look for someone else?'" 21 At that [a]very time
He [A]cured many *people* of diseases and [B]afflictions
and evil spirits; and He gave sight to many *who were*
blind. 22 And He answered and said to them, "Go
and report to John what you have seen and heard:
the [A]BLIND RECEIVE SIGHT, *the* lame walk, *the* lepers
are cleansed, and *the* deaf hear, *the* dead are raised
up, *the* [B]POOR HAVE THE GOSPEL PREACHED TO THEM.
23 Blessed is he [a]who does not take offense at Me."
24 When the messengers of John had left, He began to speak to the crowds about John, "What did
you go out into the wilderness to see? A reed shaken
by the wind? 25 [a]But what did you go out to see?
A man dressed in soft [b]clothing? Those who are
splendidly clothed and live in luxury are *found* in
royal palaces! 26 But what did you go out to see? A
prophet? Yes, I say to you, and one who is more than
a prophet. 27 This is the one about whom it is written,

'[A]BEHOLD, I SEND MY MESSENGER
[a]AHEAD OF YOU,
WHO WILL PREPARE YOUR
WAY BEFORE YOU.'

6:49 [a]Lit *river* 7:1 [A]Matt 7:28 [B]Luke 7:1-10: *Matt 8:5-13* 7:2 [a]Lit *to whom he was honorable* 7:3 [a]Lit *elders of the Jews* [b]Lit *bring safely through, rescue* [A]Matt 8:5 7:6 [a]Or *Sir* 7:7 [a]Lit *say with a word* [b]Or *boy* 7:9 [A]Matt 8:10; Luke 7:50 7:11 [a]Lit *and* 7:12 [a]Lit *one who had died* [b]Or *only begotten* 7:13 [a]Or *Stop weeping* [A]Luke 7:19; 10:1; 11:1, 39; 12:42; 13:15; 17:5, 6; 18:6; 19:8; 22:61; 24:34; John 4:1; 6:23; 11:2 7:15 [a]Or *corpse* 7:16 [a]Or *cared for* [A]Luke 5:26 [B]Matt 9:8 [C]Matt 21:11; Luke 7:39 7:17 [A]Matt 9:26 7:18 [A]Luke 7:18-35: *Matt 11:2-19* 7:19 [a]Lit *a certain two* [b]Lit *Coming One* [A]Luke 7:13; 10:1; 11:1, 39; 12:42; 13:15; 17:5, 6; 18:6; 19:8; 22:61; 24:34; John 4:1; 6:23; 11:2 7:20 [a]Lit *Coming One* 7:21 [a]Lit *hour* [A]Matt 4:23 [B]Mark 3:10 7:22 [A]Is 35:5 [B]Is 61:1 7:23 [a]Lit *whoever* 7:25 [a]Or *Well then, what* [b]Or *garments* 7:27 [a]Lit *before Your face* [A]Mal 3:1; Matt 11:10; Mark 1:2

7:2 centurion's slave. *See note on Mt 8:5.* The centurion's tender concern for a lowly slave was contrary to the reputation Roman army officers had acquired in Israel. Yet, this is one of 3 centurions featured in the NT who gave evidence of genuine faith (*see note on Mt 27:54;* cf. Ac 10).

7:3 Jewish elders. Matthew 8:5–13 does not mention that the centurion appealed to Jesus through these intermediaries. It is a measure of the respect this man had in the community that Jewish elders would be willing to bring his cause to Jesus. He loved the Jewish nation and was somehow personally responsible for the building of the local synagogue (v. 5). He obviously was being drawn to Christ by God Himself (cf. Jn 6:44, 65). Like all men under conviction, he deeply sensed his own unworthiness (*see note on 5:8*), and that is why he used intermediaries rather than speaking to Jesus personally (vv. 6, 7).

7:6 not worthy. *See note on Mt 8:8.*

7:11 Nain. A small town SE of Nazareth.

7:12 only son. *See note on 9:38.*

7:14 touched the coffin. A ceremonially defiling act, normally. Jesus graphically illustrated how impervious He was to such defilements. When He touched the coffin, its defilement did not taint Him; rather, His power immediately dispelled the presence of all death and defilement (*see notes on v. 39; 8:44*). This was the first of 3 times Jesus raised people from the dead (cf. 8:49–56; Jn 11:20–44). Verse 22 implies that Christ also raised others who are not specifically mentioned.

7:18 The disciples of John. John the Baptist evidently kept apprised of Christ's ministry—even after his imprisonment—through disciples who acted as messengers for him. Cf. Ac 19:1–7.

7:19 Are You the Expected One . . . ? John was not the sort of man who vacillated (v. 24). We are not to think that his faith was failing or that he had lost confidence in Christ. But with so many unexpected turns of events—John in prison, Christ encountering unbelief and hostility—John wanted reassurance from Christ Himself. That is precisely what Jesus gave him (vv. 22, 23). *See notes on Mt 11:3–11.*

7:22 Go and report to John. Verses 22, 23 are quoted from Is 35:5, 6; 61:1. These were messianic promises. (Is 61:1 is from the same passage Jesus read in the Nazareth synagogue—*see note on 4:19*). John's disciples were to report that Jesus was doing precisely what Scripture foretold of the Messiah (v. 21)—even though the scheme of prophetic fulfillment was not unfolding quite the way John the Baptist had envisioned it.

7:23 he who does not take offense at Me. This was not meant as a rebuke for John the Baptist, but as encouragement for him (cf. v. 28).

7:27 Quoted from Mal 3:1.

28 I say to you, among those born of women there is no one greater than John; yet he who is [a]least in the kingdom of God is greater than he." 29 When all the people and the tax collectors heard *this,* they [a]acknowledged [A]God's justice, [B]having been baptized with [C]the baptism of John. 30 But the Pharisees and the [a,A]lawyers rejected God's purpose for themselves, not having been baptized by [b]John.

31 "To what then shall I compare the men of this generation, and what are they like? 32 They are like children who sit in the market place and call to one another, and they say, 'We played the flute for you, and you did not dance; we sang a dirge, and you did not weep.' 33 For John the Baptist has come [A]eating no bread and drinking no wine, and you say, 'He has a demon!' 34 The Son of Man has come eating and drinking, and you say, 'Behold, a gluttonous man and a [a]drunkard, a friend of tax collectors and [b]sinners!' 35 Yet wisdom [A]is vindicated by all her children."

36 Now one of the Pharisees was requesting Him to [a]dine with him, and He entered the Pharisee's house and reclined *at the table.* 37 [A]And there was a woman in the city who was a [a]sinner; and when she learned that He was reclining *at the table* in the Pharisee's house, she brought an alabaster vial of perfume, 38 and standing behind *Him* at His feet, weeping, she began to wet His feet with her tears, and kept wiping them with the hair of her head, and kissing His feet and anointing them with the perfume. 39 Now when the Pharisee who had invited Him saw this, he said to himself, "If this man were [A]a prophet He would know who and what sort of person this woman is who is touching Him, that she is a [a]sinner."

PARABLE OF TWO DEBTORS

40 And Jesus answered him, "Simon, I have something to say to you." And he [a]replied, "Say it, Teacher." 41 "A moneylender had two debtors: one owed five hundred [a,A]denarii, and the other fifty. 42 When they [A]were unable to repay, he graciously forgave them both. So which of them will love him more?" 43 Simon answered and said, "I suppose the one whom he forgave more." And He said to him, "You have judged correctly." 44 Turning toward the woman, He said to Simon, "Do you see this woman? I entered your house; you [A]gave Me no water for My feet, but she has wet My feet with her tears and wiped them with her hair. 45 You [A]gave Me no kiss; but she, since the time I came in, has not ceased to kiss My feet. 46 [A]You did not anoint My head with oil, but she anointed My feet with perfume. 47 For this reason I say to you, her sins, which are many, have been forgiven, for she loved much; but he who is forgiven little, loves little." 48 Then He said to her, "[A]Your sins have been forgiven." 49 Those who were reclining *at the table* with Him began to say [a]to themselves, "[A]Who is this *man* who even forgives sins?" 50 And He said to the woman, "[A]Your faith has saved you; [B]go in peace."

7:28 [a]Or *less* 7:29 [a]Or *justified God* [A]Luke 7:35 [B]Matt 21:32; Luke 3:12 [C]Acts 18:25; 19:3 7:30 [a]I.e. experts in the Mosaic Law [b]Lit *him* [A]Matt 22:35 7:33 [A]Luke 1:15 7:34 [a]Or *wine-drinker* [b]I.e. irreligious Jews 7:35 [A]Luke 7:29 7:36 [a]Lit *eat* 7:37 [a]I.e. an immoral woman [A]Luke 7:37-39: *Matt 26:6-13; Mark 14:3-9; John 12:1-8* 7:39 [a]I.e. an immoral woman [A]Luke 7:16; John 4:19 7:40 [a]Lit *says* 7:41 [a]The denarius was equivalent to a day's wages [A]Matt 18:28; Mark 6:37 7:42 [A]Matt 18:25 7:44 [A]Gen 18:4; 19:2; 43:24; Judg 19:21; 1 Tim 5:10 7:45 [A]2 Sam 15:5 7:46 [A]2 Sam 12:20; Ps 23:5; Eccl 9:8; Dan 10:3 7:48 [A]Matt 9:2; Mark 2:5, 9; Luke 5:20, 23 7:49 [a]Or *among* [A]Luke 5:21 7:50 [A]Matt 9:22; Luke 17:19; 18:42 [B]Mark 5:34; Luke 8:48

7:28 *See note on Mt 11:11.*

7:29 acknowledged God's justice. The common people and the outcast tax collectors who heard John the Baptist's preaching acknowledged that what he required by way of repentance was from God and was righteous.

7:30 lawyers. *See note on 10:25.* **rejected God's purpose.** John's call to repentance was an expression of the will of God. By refusing repentance, they rejected not just John the Baptist, but also God Himself.

7:32 like children. Christ used strong derision to rebuke the Pharisees. He suggested they were behaving childishly, determined not to be pleased, whether invited to "dance" (a reference to Christ's joyous style of ministry, "eating and drinking" with sinners—v. 34), or urged to "weep" (a reference to John the Baptist's call to repentance, and John's more austere manner of ministry—v. 33).

7:34 eating and drinking. I.e., living an ordinary life. This passage explains why John's style of ministry differed so dramatically from Jesus' approach, although their message was the same (*see note on Mt 4:17*). The different methods took away all the Pharisees' excuses. The very thing they had professed to want to see in Jesus—rigid abstinence and a Spartan lifestyle—was what characterized the ministry of John the Baptist, yet they had already rejected him, too. The real problem lay in the corruption of their own hearts, but they would not acknowledge that. **friend of ... sinners.** *See notes on 5:30–33; 15:2.*

7:35 wisdom is vindicated by all her children. I.e., true wisdom is vindicated by its consequences—what it produces. Cf. Jas 2:14–17.

7:36 one of the Pharisees. His name was Simon (v. 40). He does not appear to have been sympathetic to Jesus (cf. vv. 44–46). Undoubtedly, his motive was either to entrap Jesus, or to find some reason to accuse Him (cf. 6:7).

7:37 an alabaster vial. *See note on Mt 26:7.* This is similar in many ways to the events described in Mt 26:6–13; Mk 14:3–9; Jn 12:2–8, but it is clearly a different incident. That took place in Bethany, near Jerusalem, during the Passion Week. In the anointing at Bethany it was Mary, sister of Martha and Lazarus, who anointed Jesus. This incident takes place in Galilee and involves "a woman ... who was a sinner"—i.e., a prostitute. There is no reason to identify this woman with Mary Magdalene, as some have done (*see note on 8:2*).

7:38 standing behind *Him* at His feet. He was reclining at a low table, as was the custom. It would have been shocking to all for a woman of such low reputation to come to a Pharisee's house. Such dinners involving dignitaries were often open to spectators—but no one would have expected a prostitute to attend. Her coming took great courage, and reveals the desperation with which she sought forgiveness. Her "weeping" was an expression of deep repentance.

7:39 what sort of ... woman. The Pharisees showed nothing but contempt for sinners. Simon was convinced that if Jesus knew her character, He would have sent her away, for her touching Him was presumed to convey ceremonial uncleanness. *See notes on v. 14; 8:44.*

7:40 Jesus answered. Jesus knew Simon's thoughts (cf. 5:22; *see note on Mt 9:4*)—demonstrating to Simon that He was indeed a Prophet.

7:41 denarii. Each denarius was worth a day's labor (*see note on Mt 22:19*), so this was a large sum—about two years' full wages.

7:44 no water for My feet. A glaring oversight. Washing a guest's feet was an essential formality (*see note on Jn 13:4, 5*). Not to offer a guest water for the washing of feet was tantamount to an insult—as it would be in modern Western culture if one did not offer to take a guest's coat.

7:47 for she loved much. This is not to suggest that she was forgiven because she loved much. The parable (vv. 41–43) pictured a forgiveness that was unconditional, and love was the result. Therefore to make the woman's love the reason for her forgiveness would be to distort the lesson Jesus is teaching here. "For" here has the sense of "wherefore." And her faith (v. 50), not the act of anointing Jesus' feet, was the instrument by which she laid hold of His forgiveness.

7:49 forgives sins. *See notes on 5:20, 21; Mt 9:1–3; Mk 2:7.*

7:50 Your faith has saved you. Not all whom Jesus healed were saved, but those who exhibited true faith were (cf. 17:19; 18:42; Mt 9:22; *see note on Mk 5:34*).

MINISTERING WOMEN

8 Soon afterwards, He *began* going around from one city and village to another, [A]proclaiming and preaching the kingdom of God. The twelve were with Him, 2 and *also* [A]some women who had been healed of evil spirits and sicknesses: [B]Mary who was called Magdalene, from whom seven demons had gone out, 3 and Joanna the wife of Chuza, [A]Herod's [B]steward, and Susanna, and many others who were contributing to their support out of their private means.

PARABLE OF THE SOWER

4 [A]When a large crowd was coming together, and those from the various cities were journeying to Him, He spoke by way of a parable: 5 "The sower went out to sow his seed; and as he sowed, some fell beside the road, and it was trampled under foot and the birds of the [a]air ate it up. 6 Other *seed* fell on rocky *soil,* and as soon as it grew up, it withered away, because it had no moisture. 7 Other *seed* fell among the thorns; and the thorns grew up with it and choked it out. 8 Other *seed* fell into the good soil, and grew up, and produced a crop a hundred times as great." As He said these things, He would call out, "[A]He who has ears to hear, [a]let him hear."

9 [A]His disciples *began* questioning Him as to what this parable meant. 10 And He said, "[A]To you it has been granted to know the mysteries of the kingdom of God, but to the rest *it is* in parables, so that [B]SEEING THEY MAY NOT SEE, AND HEARING THEY MAY NOT UNDERSTAND.

11 "Now the parable is this: [A]the seed is the word of God. 12 Those beside the road are those who have heard; then the devil comes and takes away the word from their heart, so that they will not believe and be saved. 13 Those on the rocky *soil are* those who, when they hear, receive the word with joy; and these have no *firm* root; [a]they believe for a while, and in time of temptation fall away. 14 The *seed* which fell among the thorns, these are the ones who have heard, and as they go on their way they are choked with worries and riches and pleasures of *this* life, and bring no fruit to maturity. 15 But the *seed* in the good soil, these are the ones who have heard the word in an honest and good heart, and hold it fast, and bear fruit with [a]perseverance.

PARABLE OF THE LAMP

16 "Now [A]no one after lighting a lamp covers it over with a container, or puts it under a bed; but he puts it on a lampstand, so that those who come in may see the light. 17 [A]For nothing is hidden that will not become evident, nor *anything* secret that will not be known and come to light. 18 So take care how you listen; [A]for whoever has, to him *more* shall be given; and whoever does not have, even what he [a]thinks he has shall be taken away from him."

19 [A]And His mother and brothers came to Him, and they were unable to get to Him because of the crowd. 20 And it was reported to Him, "Your mother and Your brothers are standing outside, wishing to see You." 21 But He answered and said to them, "My mother and My brothers are these [A]who hear the word of God and do it."

8:1 [A]Matt 4:23 8:2 [A]Matt 27:55; Mark 15:40, 41; Luke 23:49, 55 [B]Matt 27:56; Mark 16:9 8:3 [A]Matt 14:1 [B]Matt 20:8 8:4 [A]Luke 8:4-8: *Matt 13:2-9; Mark 4:1-9* 8:5 [a]Lit *heaven* 8:8 [a]Or *hear!* Or *listen!* [A]Matt 11:15; Mark 7:16; Luke 14:35; Rev 2:7, 11, 17, 29; 3:6, 13, 22; 13:9 8:9 [A]Luke 8:9-15: *Matt 13:10-23; Mark 4:10-20* 8:10 [A]Matt 13:11 [B]Is 6:9; Matt 13:14; Acts 28:26 8:11 [A]1 Pet 1:23 8:13 [a]Lit *who believe* 8:15 [a]Or *steadfastness* 8:16 [A]Matt 5:15; Mark 4:21; Luke 11:33 8:17 [A]Matt 10:26; Mark 4:22; Luke 12:2 8:18 [a]Or *seems to have* [A]Matt 13:12; 25:29; Luke 19:26 8:19 [A]Luke 8:19-21: *Matt 12:46-50; Mark 3:31-35* 8:21 [A]Luke 11:28

8:2 some women. Rabbis normally did not have women as disciples. **Mary ... called Magdalene.** Her name probably derives from the Galilean town of Magdala. Some believe she is the woman described in 7:37–50, but it seems highly unlikely that Luke would introduce her here by name for the first time if she were the main figure in the account he just completed. Also, while it is clear that she had suffered at the hands of "demons," there is no reason whatsoever to think that she had ever been a prostitute.

8:3 Joanna. This woman is also mentioned in 24:10, but nowhere else in Scripture. It is possible that she was a source for some of the details Luke recounts about Herod (cf. 23:8, 12). *See note on 1:3.* **Susanna.** Aside from this reference, she is nowhere mentioned in Scripture. She is probably someone Luke knew personally. **out of their private means.** It was a Jewish custom for disciples to support rabbis in this way. Cf. 10:7; 1Co 9:4–11; Gal 6:6; 1Ti 5:17, 18.

8:4 spoke by .... parable. This marked a significant turning point in Jesus' ministry. *See notes on Mt 13:3, 34.*

8:5 to sow his seed. Seed was sown by hand over plowed soil. In throwing seed toward the edges of a field, the sower would naturally throw some that landed or was blown onto the hard beaten path on the edges of the field, where it could not penetrate the soil and grow (*see notes on Mt 13:4, 19*). This could refer to the hard, obstinate Jewish leaders.

8:6 on rocky *soil*. I.e., very shallow soil with a layer of rock lying just below the surface. *See notes on Mt 13:5, 20.* This could refer to the fickle mob that followed Jesus only for His miracles.

8:7 thorns. *See notes on Mt 13:7, 22.* This could refer to the materialists to whom earthly wealth was more important than spiritual riches.

8:8 a hundred times. Luke simplified the parable. Matthew 13:8 and Mark 4:8 described 3 levels of fruitfulness. "A hundred times" simply speaks of inconceivable abundance (cf. Ge 26:12). **He who has ears.** All 3 of the Synoptics include this admonition with the parable of the sower (cf. Mt 13:9; 4:9). Jesus often said this to stress particularly important statements cast in mysterious language (cf. 14:35; Mt 11:15; 13:43; Mk 4:23).

8:10 mysteries. *See notes on Mt 13:11, 13.* seeing they may not see. This quotation from Is 6:9 describes God's act of judicially blinding unbelievers.

8:13 they believe for a while. I.e., with a nominal, nonsaving faith. *See note on Mt 13:20.*

8:15 heard ... hold ... bear fruit. This constitutes evidence of true salvation. "Heard" is a reference to understanding and believing (Jn 8:31, 47). "Hold" refers to ongoing obedience (11:28; *see note on Jn 14:21–24*). "Fruit" is good works (Mt 7:16–20; Jas 2:14–26).

8:16 under a bed. The fact that Christ taught mysteries in parables was not to suggest that His message was meant for elite disciples or that it should be kept secret. A lamp is not lit to be hidden, but must be put on a lampstand, where its light will reach furthest. Still, only those with eyes to see will see it.

8:17 nothing is hidden that will not become evident. All truth will be manifest in the judgment. Cf. 12:2, 3; 1Co 4:5; 1Ti 5:24, 25. God's ultimate purpose is not to hide the truth, but to make it known.

8:18 take care how you listen. One's response to the light in this life is crucial, because at the throne of judgment there will be no opportunity to embrace truth that was formerly spurned (Rev 20:11–15). Those who scorn the light of the gospel now will have all light removed from them in eternity. Cf. 19:26; Mt 25:29.

8:19 brothers. *See notes on Mt 12:46–49.*

8:20, 21 *See notes on Mk 3:31, 35.*

JESUS STILLS THE SEA

22 [A]Now on one of *those* days Jesus and His disciples got into a boat, and He said to them, "Let us go over to the other side of [B]the lake." So they launched out. 23 But as they were sailing along He fell asleep; and a fierce gale of wind descended on [A]the lake, and they *began* to be swamped and to be in danger. 24 They came to Jesus and woke Him up, saying, "[A]Master, Master, we are perishing!" And He got up and [B]rebuked the wind and the surging waves, and they stopped, and [a]it became calm. 25 And He said to them, "Where is your faith?" They were fearful and amazed, saying to one another, "Who then is this, that He commands even the winds and the water, and they obey Him?"

THE DEMONIAC CURED

26 [A]Then they sailed to the country of the Gerasenes, which is opposite Galilee. 27 And when He came out onto the land, He was met by a man from the city who was possessed with demons; and who had not put on any clothing for a long time, and was not living in a house, but in the tombs. 28 Seeing Jesus, he cried out and fell before Him, and said in a loud voice, "[a,A]What business do we have with each other, Jesus, Son of [B]the Most High God? I beg You, do not torment me." 29 For He had commanded the unclean spirit to come out of the man. For it had seized him many times; and he was bound with chains and shackles and kept under guard, and *yet* he would break his bonds and be driven by the demon into the desert. 30 And Jesus asked him, "What is your name?" And he said, "[A]Legion"; for many demons had entered him. 31 They were imploring Him not to command them to go away into [A]the abyss.

32 Now there was a herd of many swine feeding there on the mountain; and *the demons* implored Him to permit them to enter [a]the swine. And He gave them permission. 33 And the demons came out of the man and entered the swine; and the herd rushed down the steep bank into [A]the lake and was drowned.

34 When the herdsmen saw what had happened, they ran away and reported it in the city and *out* in the country. 35 *The people* went out to see what had happened; and they came to Jesus, and found the man from whom the demons had gone out, sitting down [A]at the feet of Jesus, clothed and in his right mind; and they became frightened. 36 Those who had seen it reported to them how the man who was [A]demon-possessed had been [a]made well. 37 And all the people of the country of the Gerasenes and the surrounding district asked Him to leave them, for they were gripped with great fear; and He got into a boat and returned. 38 [A]But the man from whom the demons had gone out was begging Him that he might [a]accompany Him; but He sent him away, saying, 39 "Return to your house and describe what great things God has done for you." So he went away, proclaiming throughout the whole city what great things Jesus had done for him.

MIRACLES OF HEALING

40 [A]And as Jesus returned, the [a]people welcomed Him, for they had all been waiting for Him. 41 [A]And there came a man named Jairus, and he was an [a,B]official of the synagogue; and he fell at Jesus' feet, and *began* to implore Him to come to his house; 42 for he had an [a]only daughter, about twelve years old, and she was dying. But as He went, the crowds were pressing against Him.

43 And a woman who had a hemorrhage for twelve years, and could not be healed by anyone, 44 came up behind Him and touched the fringe of His [a]cloak, and immediately her hemorrhage stopped. 45 And Jesus said, "Who is the one who touched Me?" And while they were all denying it, Peter said, "[A]Master, the [a]people are crowding and pressing in on You." 46 But Jesus said, "Someone did touch Me, for I was aware that [A]power had gone out of Me." 47 When the woman saw that she had not escaped notice, she came trembling and fell down before Him, and declared in the presence of all the people the reason why she had touched Him, and how she had been immediately healed. 48 And He said to her, "Daughter, [A]your faith has [a]made you well; [B]go in peace."

49 While He was still speaking, someone *came from *the house of* [A]the synagogue official, saying, "Your daughter has died; do not trouble the Teacher anymore." 50 But when Jesus heard *this,* He answered him, "[A]Do not be afraid *any longer;* only believe, and she will be [a]made well." 51 When He came to the house, He did not allow anyone to enter with Him, except Peter and John and James, and the girl's father and mother. 52 Now they were all weeping and [A]lamenting for her; but He said, "Stop weeping, for she has not died, but [B]is asleep." 53 And they *began* laughing at Him, knowing that she had died. 54 He, however, took her by the hand

8:22 [A]Luke 8:22-25: *Matt 8:23-27; Mark 4:36-41* [B]Luke 5:1f; 8:23 8:23 [A]Luke 5:1f; 8:22 8:24 [a]Lit *a calm occurred* [A]Luke 5:5 [B]Luke 4:39 8:26 [A]Luke 8:26-37: *Matt 8:28-34; Mark 5:1-17* 8:28 [a]Lit *What to me and to you* (a Heb idiom) [A]Matt 8:29 [B]Mark 5:7 8:30 [A]Matt 26:53 8:31 [A]Rom 10:7; Rev 9:1f, 11; 11:7; 17:8; 20:1, 3 8:32 [a]Lit *them* 8:33 [A]Luke 5:1f; 8:22 8:35 [A]Luke 10:39 8:36 [a]Or *saved* [A]Matt 4:24 8:38 [a]Lit *be with* [A]Luke 8:38, 39: *Mark 5:18-20* 8:40 [a]Lit *crowd* [A]Matt 9:1; Mark 5:21 8:41 [a]Lit *ruler* [A]Luke 8:41-56: *Matt 9:18-26; Mark 5:22-43* [B]Mark 5:22; Luke 8:49 8:42 [a]Or *only begotten* 8:44 [a]Or *outer garment* 8:45 [a]Lit *crowds* [A]Luke 5:5 8:46 [A]Luke 5:17 8:48 [a]Or *saved you* [A]Matt 9:22 [B]Mark 5:34; Luke 7:50 8:49 [A]Luke 8:41 8:50 [a]Or *saved* [A]Mark 5:36 8:52 [A]Matt 11:17; Luke 23:27 [B]John 11:13

8:22–25 *See notes on Mt 8:24–27.*

8:26–38 *See notes on Mt 8:28–34.*

8:27 a man. Matthew reveals there were actually two men. Only one did the talking. *See note on Mt 8:28.*

8:30 Legion. *See notes on Mt 8:30; Mk 5:9.*

8:31 the abyss. *See note on Mt 8:31.*

8:41 an official of the synagogue. *See note on 13:14.* Jesus had once cast a demon out of a man in Jairus' synagogue (4:33–37).

8:42 only daughter. *See note on 9:38.* **pressing.** Lit. "choked," i.e., they almost crushed Him.

8:43 a hemorrhage. *See note on Mt 9:20.*

8:44 came up behind Him and touched. Because of her affliction, she would normally render anyone she touched unclean. The effect here was precisely the opposite. *See notes on 7:14, 39.* **fringe.** *See note on Mt 9:20.*

8:46 power had gone out of Me. *See note on Mk 5:30.*

8:50 only believe. Though not all Jesus' healings required faith (cf. 22:51), at times He required it.

8:51 Peter and John and James. *See notes on 9:28; Mt 10:2; 17:1.*

8:52 she has not died. *See notes on Mt 9:23, 24.*

and called, saying, "Child, arise!" 55 And her spirit returned, and she got up immediately; and He gave orders for *something* to be given her to eat. 56 Her parents were amazed; but He [A]instructed them to tell no one what had happened.

MINISTRY OF THE TWELVE

9 [A]And He called the twelve together, and gave them power and authority over all the demons and to heal diseases. 2 And He sent them out to [A]proclaim the kingdom of God and to perform healing. 3 And He said to them, "[A]Take nothing for *your* journey, [B]neither a staff, nor a [a]bag, nor bread, nor money; and do not *even* have [b]two tunics apiece. 4 Whatever house you enter, stay there [a]until you leave that city. 5 And as for those who do not receive you, as you go out from that city, [A]shake the dust off your feet as a testimony against them." 6 Departing, they *began* going [a]throughout the villages, [A]preaching the gospel and healing everywhere.

7 [A]Now [B]Herod the tetrarch heard of all that was happening; and he was greatly perplexed, because it was said by some that [C]John had risen from the dead, 8 and by some that [A]Elijah had appeared, and by others that one of the prophets of old had risen again. 9 Herod said, "I myself had John beheaded; but who is this man about whom I hear such things?" And [A]he kept trying to see Him.

10 [A]When the apostles returned, they gave an account to Him of all that they had done. [B]Taking them with Him, He withdrew by Himself to a city called [C]Bethsaida. 11 But the crowds were aware of this and followed Him; and welcoming them, He *began* speaking to them about the kingdom of God and curing those who had need of healing.

FIVE THOUSAND FED

12 Now the day [a]was ending, and the twelve came and said to Him, "Send the crowd away, that they may go into the surrounding villages and countryside and find lodging and get [b]something to eat; for here we are in a desolate place." 13 But He said to them, "You give them *something* to eat!" And they said, "We have no more than five loaves and two fish, unless perhaps we go and buy food for all these people." 14 (For there were about five thousand men.) And He said to His disciples, "Have them [a]sit down *to eat* [A]in groups of about fifty each." 15 They did so, and had them all [a]sit down. 16 Then He took the five loaves and the two fish, and looking up to heaven, He blessed them, and broke *them*, and kept giving *them* to the disciples to set before the [a]people. 17 And they all ate and were satisfied; and [a]the broken pieces which they had left over were picked up, twelve [A]baskets *full*.

18 [A]And it happened that while He was [B]praying alone, the disciples were with Him, and He questioned them, saying, "Who do the [a]people say that I am?" 19 They answered and said, "John the Baptist, and others *say* Elijah; but others, that one of the prophets of old has risen again." 20 And He said to them, "But who do you say that I am?" And Peter answered and said, "[A]The [a]Christ of God." 21 But He [a,A]warned them and instructed *them* not to tell this to anyone, 22 [A]saying, "[B]The Son of Man must suffer many things and be rejected by the elders and chief priests and scribes, and be killed and be raised up on the third day."

23 And He was saying to *them* all, "[A]If anyone wishes to come after Me, he must deny himself, and take up his cross daily and follow Me. 24 For [A]whoever wishes to save his [a]life will lose it, but whoever loses his [a]life for My sake, he is the one who will save it. 25 For what is a man profited if he gains the whole world, and [A]loses or forfeits himself? 26 [A]For whoever is ashamed of Me and My words, the Son of Man will be ashamed of him when He comes in His glory, and *the glory* of the Father and of the

8:56 [A]Matt 8:4 9:1 [A]Matt 10:5; Mark 6:7 9:2 [A]Matt 10:7 9:3 [a]Or *knapsack or beggar's bag* [b]Or *inner garments* [A]Luke 9:3-5: *Matt 10:9-15; Mark 6:8-11;* Luke 10:4-12; 22:35 [B]Matt 10:10; Mark 6:8; Luke 22:35f 9:4 [a]Lit *and leave from there* 9:5 [A]Luke 10:11; Acts 13:51 9:6 [a]Or *from village to village* [A]Mark 6:12; Luke 8:1 9:7 [A]Luke 9:7-9: *Matt 14:1, 2;* Mark 6:14f [B]Matt 14:1; Luke 3:1; 13:31; 23:7 [C]Matt 14:2 9:8 [A]Matt 16:14 9:9 [A]Luke 23:8 9:10 [A]Mark 6:30 [B]Luke 9:10-17: *Matt 14:13-21; Mark 6:32-44; John 6:5-13* [C]Matt 11:21 9:12 [a]Lit *began to decline* [b]Lit *provisions* 9:14 [a]Lit *recline* [A]Mark 6:39 9:15 [a]Lit *recline* 9:16 [a]Lit *crowd* 9:17 [a]Lit *that which was left over to them of the broken pieces was* [A]Matt 14:20 9:18 [a]Lit *crowds* [A]Luke 9:18-20: *Matt 16:13-16; Mark 8:27-29* [B]Matt 14:23; Luke 6:12; 9:28 9:20 [a]I.e. Messiah [A]John 6:68f 9:21 [a]Or *strictly admonished* [A]Matt 8:4; 16:20; Mark 8:30 9:22 [A]Luke 9:22-27: *Matt 16:21-28; Mark 8:31-9:1* [B]Matt 16:21; Luke 9:44 9:23 [A]Matt 10:38; Luke 14:27 9:24 [a]Or *soul* [A]Matt 10:39; Luke 17:33; John 12:25 9:25 [A]Heb 10:34 9:26 [A]Matt 10:33; Luke 12:9

8:56 tell no one. *See note on Mt 8:4.*

9:1–6 *See notes on Mt 10:1–42.*

9:3 Take nothing. Slight differences between Matthew, Mark, and Luke have troubled some. Matthew 10:9, 10 and this text say the disciples were not to take staffs (*see note there*); but Mk 6:8 prohibited everything "except a ... staff." Mark 6:9 also instructed them to "wear sandals"; but in Mt 10:10 sandals were included in the things they were not to carry. Actually, however, what Mt 10:10 and this verse prohibited was the packing of extra staffs and sandals. The disciples were not to be carrying baggage for the journey, but merely to go with the clothes on their backs.

9:7 Herod the tetrarch. *See note on Mt 14:1.* News of Christ reached to the highest levels of government. **John had risen from the dead.** Of course, this was not true, but Herod himself nonetheless seemed gripped by guilty fear (cf. Mk 6:16).

9:8 Elijah. *See note on 1:17.*

9:9 kept trying to see Him. Only Luke gives this detail. *See notes on 1:3; 8:3.*

9:10 withdrew. They were trying to get some rest and a break from the crowds. Cf. Mk 6:31, 32. **Bethsaida.** *See note on Mk 8:22.* Bethsaida Julias is on the N shore and to the E of Galilee, where the Jordan River enters the lake.

9:12–17 Aside from the resurrection, the feeding of the 5,000 is the only miracle of Jesus recorded in all 4 Gospels (cf. Mt 14:15–21; Mk 6:35–44; Jn 6:4–13).

9:14 about five thousand men. Counting women and children, the actual size of the crowd may have been closer to 20,000.

9:17 baskets. *See notes on Mk 6:43; 8:8.*

9:18–21 *See notes on Mt 16:13–20.*

9:19 John the Baptist ... Elijah ... one of the prophets of old. Cf. vv. 7, 8. Such rumors were apparently quite common. *See notes on 1:17; Mt 11:14; Mk 9:13; Rev 11:5, 6.*

9:20 The Christ of God. I.e., the Messiah promised in the OT (Da 9:25, 26). *See note on Mt 16:16.*

9:21 not to tell this to anyone. *See notes on Mt 8:4; 12:16.*

9:22 The Son of Man must suffer. This pronouncement signified a great turning point in Jesus' ministry. *See note on Mt 16:21.*

9:23 cross. *See note on Mt 10:38.* Self-denial was a common thread in Christ's teaching to His disciples (cf. 14:26, 27; Mt 10:38; 16:24; Mk 8:34; Jn 12:24–26). The kind of self-denial He sought was not a reclusive asceticism (*see note on 7:34*), but a willingness to obey His commandments, serve one another, and suffer—perhaps even die—for His sake.

9:24 whoever loses his life for My sake. Aside from the command "follow Me," this saying is repeated more times in the gospels than any other saying of Christ. Cf. 17:33; Mt 10:39; 16:25; Mk 8:35; Jn 12:25. *See note on 14:11.*

9:26 whoever is ashamed of Me. I.e., unbelievers. Cf. Mt 10:33; Ro 9:33; 10:11; 2Ti 2:12. *See note on 12:9.*

holy angels. 27 But I say to you truthfully, [A]there are some of those standing here who will not taste death until they see the kingdom of God."

THE TRANSFIGURATION

28 [A]Some eight days after these sayings, He took along [B]Peter and John and James, and [C]went up on the mountain [D]to pray. 29 And while He was [A]praying, the appearance of His face [B]became different, and His clothing *became* white *and* [a]gleaming. 30 And behold, two men were talking with Him; and they were Moses and Elijah, 31 who, appearing in [a]glory, were speaking of His [A]departure which He was about to accomplish at Jerusalem. 32 Now Peter and his companions [A]had been overcome with sleep; but when they were fully awake, they saw His glory and the two men standing with Him. 33 And as [a]these were leaving Him, Peter said to Jesus, "[A]Master, it is good for us to be here; [B]let us make three [b]tabernacles: one for You, and one for Moses, and one for Elijah"—[C]not realizing what he was saying. 34 While he was saying this, a cloud [a]formed and *began* to overshadow them; and they were afraid as they entered the cloud. 35 Then [A]a voice came out of the cloud, saying, "[B]This is My Son, *My* Chosen One; listen to Him!" 36 And when the voice [a]had spoken, Jesus was found alone. And [A]they kept silent, and reported to no one in those days any of the things which they had seen.

37 [A]On the next day, when they came down from the mountain, a large crowd met Him. 38 And a man from the crowd shouted, saying, "Teacher, I beg You to look at my son, for he is my [a]only *boy,* 39 and a spirit seizes him, and he suddenly screams, and it throws him into a convulsion with foaming *at the mouth;* and only with difficulty does it leave him, mauling him *as it leaves.* 40 I begged Your disciples to cast it out, and they could not." 41 And Jesus answered and said, "You unbelieving and perverted generation, how long shall I be with you and put up with you? Bring your son here." 42 While he was still approaching, the demon [a]slammed him *to the ground* and threw him into a convulsion. But Jesus rebuked the unclean spirit, and healed the boy and gave him back to his father. 43 And they were all amazed at the [a,A]greatness of God.

[B]But while everyone was marveling at all that He was doing, He said to His disciples, 44 "Let these words sink into your ears; [A]for the Son of Man is going to be [a]delivered into the hands of men." 45 But [A]they [a]did not understand this statement, and it was concealed from them so that they would not perceive it; and they were afraid to ask Him about this statement.

THE TEST OF GREATNESS

46 [A]An argument [a]started among them as to which of them might be the greatest. 47 But Jesus, [A]knowing [a]what they were thinking in their heart, took a child and stood him by His side, 48 and said to them, "[A]Whoever receives this child in My name receives Me, and whoever receives Me receives Him who sent Me; [B]for the one who is least among all of you, this is the one who is great."

49 [A]John answered and said, "[B]Master, we saw someone casting out demons in Your name; and we tried to prevent him because he does not follow

9:27 [A]Matt 16:28 9:28 [A]Luke 9:28-36: *Matt 17:1-8; Mark 9:2-8* [B]Matt 17:1 [C]Matt 5:1 [D]Luke 3:21; 5:16; 6:12; 9:18 9:29 [a]Lit *flashing like lightning* [A]Luke 3:21; 5:16; 6:12; 9:18 [B]Mark 16:12 9:31 [a]Or *splendor* [A]2 Pet 1:15 9:32 [A]Matt 26:43; Mark 14:40 9:33 [a]Lit *they* [b]Or *sacred tents* [A]Luke 5:5; 9:49 [B]Matt 17:4; Mark 9:5 [C]Mark 9:6 9:34 [a]Lit *occurred* 9:35 [A]2 Pet 1:17f [B]Is 42:1; Matt 3:17; 12:18; Mark 1:11; Luke 3:22 9:36 [a]Lit *occurred* [A]Matt 17:9; Mark 9:9f 9:37 [A]Luke 9:37-42: *Matt 17:14-18; Mark 9:14-27* 9:38 [a]Or *only begotten* 9:42 [a]Or *tore him* 9:43 [a]Or *majesty* [A]2 Pet 1:16 [B]Luke 9:43-45: *Matt 17:22f; Mark 9:30-32* 9:44 [a]Or *betrayed* [A]Luke 9:22 9:45 [a]Lit *were not knowing* [A]Mark 9:32 9:46 [a]Lit *entered in* [A]Luke 9:46-48: *Matt 18:1-5; Mark 9:33-37;* Luke 22:24 9:47 [a]Lit *the reasoning;* or *argument* [A]Matt 9:4 9:48 [A]Matt 10:40; Luke 10:16; John 13:20 [B]Luke 22:26 9:49 [A]Luke 9:49, 50: *Mark 9:38-40* [B]Luke 5:5; 9:33

9:27 see the kingdom. *See note on Mt 16:28.*

9:28 Some eight days. A common expression signifying about a week (cf. Jn 20:26). *See note on Mt 17:1.* **after these sayings.** This expression ties the promise of seeing the kingdom (v. 27) to the events that follow (*see note on Mt 16:28*). **Peter and John and James.** These 3 alone were permitted to witness the raising of Jairus' daughter (8:51), the Transfiguration (cf. Mt 17:1), and Christ's agony in the garden (Mk 14:33). **the mountain.** The traditional site, Mt. Tabor, is unlikely. Jesus and the disciples had been in "the district of Caesarea Philippi" (Mt 16:13), and Tabor is nowhere near there. Besides, Tabor had evidently been the site of pagan worship (Hos 5:1), and in Jesus' day, an army garrison had their fortress at the top. The actual location of the Transfiguration is nowhere identified, but Mt. Hermon (7,000 ft higher than Tabor, and closer to Caesarea Philippi) is believed by many to be the place.

9:29 while He was praying. *See note on 3:21.* As at His baptism, while He was praying, the Father's voice came from heaven (cf. Introduction: Historical and Theological Themes). **gleaming.** Lit. "emitting light." This word is used only here in the NT. It suggests a brilliant flashing light, similar to lightning.

9:30 Moses and Elijah. *See note on Mt 17:3.*

9:31 His departure. Peter uses the same term to speak of his own death (2Pe 1:15). Only Luke mentions the subject matter of their conversation and the fact that Peter, James, and John had fallen asleep (v. 32). Cf. 22:45.

9:32 saw His glory. Cf. Ex 33:18–23.

9:33 three tabernacles. *See note on Mt 17:4.*

9:34 a cloud. Matthew 17:5 says "a bright cloud," i.e., enveloping the glory of God—similar to the pillar of cloud that led the Israelites in the OT (Ex 14:19, 20). The brightness of this cloud and the sleepiness of the disciples (v. 32) suggest that this event may have occurred at night.

9:35 This is My Son. *See note on Mt 3:17.*

9:38 my only *boy*. Cf. 7:12; 8:42. The son of the widow of Nain was her only child; and Jairus' daughter was his only child. Luke alone mentions these details.

9:39 a spirit seizes him. This was no mere case of epilepsy; it was plainly demon possession. There's no reason to think Luke, a physician, was merely accommodating the understanding of his readers. Besides, Jesus healed the boy by rebuking the demon (v. 42; cf. Mk 9:25).

9:40 they could not. *See notes on Mt 17:19–21.*

9:41 unbelieving and perverted generation. *See note on Mt 17:17.*

9:44 going to be delivered. *See note on Mt 17:22.*

9:45 concealed from them. I.e., in accord with God's sovereign design. Cf. 24:45.

9:46 be the greatest. *See note on Mt 20:21.*

9:48 Whoever receives this child. *See note on Mt 18:5.* **one who is least ... is the one who is great.** The way to preeminence in Christ's kingdom is by sacrifice and self-denial. *See note on v. 23.*

9:49 because he does not follow along with us. It is ironic that John, who came to be known as "the apostle of love," would be the one to raise this objection (*see note on v. 54*). John came to see that only legitimate tests of another person's ministry are the test of doctrine (1Jn 4:1–3; 2Jn 7–11) and the test of fruit (1Jn 2:4–6, 29; 3:4–12; 4:5, 20; cf. Mt 7:16). This man would have passed both tests, but John was inclined to reject him because of his group affiliation. That is the error of sectarianism.

along with us." 50 But Jesus said to him, "Do not hinder *him;* [A]for he who is not against you is [a]for you."
51 When the days were approaching for [A]His [a]as-
cension, He [b]was determined [B]to go to Jerusalem;
52 and He sent messengers on ahead of Him, and
they went and entered a village of the [A]Samaritans
to [a]make arrangements for Him. 53 But they did not
receive Him, [A]because [a]He was traveling toward
Jerusalem. 54 When His disciples [A]James and John
saw *this,* they said, "Lord, do You want us to [B]com-
mand fire to come down from heaven and consume
them?" 55 But He turned and rebuked them, [[a]and
said, "You do not know what kind of spirit you are
of; 56 for the Son of Man did not come to destroy
men's lives, but to save them."] And they went on
to another village.

EXACTING DISCIPLESHIP

57 [A]As they were going along the road, [B]someone
said to Him, "I will follow You wherever You go."
58 And Jesus said to him, "The foxes have holes and
the birds of the [a]air *have* [b]nests, but [A]the Son of
Man has nowhere to lay His head." 59 And He said
to another, "[A]Follow Me." But he said, "Lord, permit
me first to go and bury my father." 60 But He said
to him, "Allow the dead to bury their own dead;
but as for you, go and [A]proclaim everywhere the
kingdom of God." 61 Another also said, "I will follow
You, Lord; but [A]first permit me to say good-bye to
those at home." 62 But Jesus said to him, "[A]No one,
after putting his hand to the plow and looking back,
is fit for the kingdom of God."

THE SEVENTY SENT OUT

10 Now after this [A]the Lord appointed [a]seventy
[B]others, and sent them [C]in pairs ahead of Him
to every city and place where He Himself was going
to come. 2 And He was saying to them, "[A]The harvest is plentiful, but the laborers are few; therefore
beseech the Lord of the harvest to send out laborers
into His harvest. 3 Go; [A]behold, I send you out as
lambs in the midst of wolves. 4 [A]Carry no money
belt, no [a]bag, no shoes; and greet no one on the way.
5 Whatever house you enter, first say, 'Peace *be* to this
house.' 6 If a [a]man of peace is there, your peace will
rest on him; but if not, it will return to you. 7 Stay
in [a]that house, eating and drinking [b]what they give
you; for [A]the laborer is worthy of his wages. Do
not keep moving from house to house. 8 Whatever
city you enter and they receive you, [A]eat what is
set before you; 9 and heal those in it who are sick,
and say to them, '[A]The kingdom of God has come

9:50 [a]Or *on your side* [A]Matt 12:30; Luke 11:23 9:51 [a]Lit *taking up* [b]Lit *set His face* [A]Mark 16:19 [B]Luke 13:22; 17:11; 18:31; 19:11, 28 9:52 [a]Or *prepare* [A]Matt 10:5; Luke 10:33; 17:16; John 4:4 9:53 [a]Lit *His face was proceeding toward* [A]John 4:9 9:54 [A]Mark 3:17 [B]2 Kin 1:9-16 9:55 [a]Early mss do not contain bracketed portion 9:57 [A]Luke 9:51 [B]Luke 9:57-60: *Matt 8:19-22* 9:58 [a]Or *sky* [b]Or *roosting-places* [A]Matt 8:20 9:59 [A]Matt 8:22 9:60 [A]Matt 4:23 9:61 [A]1 Kin 19:20 9:62 [A]Phil 3:13 10:1 [a]Some mss read *seventy-two* [A]Luke 7:13 [B]Luke 9:1f, 52 [C]Mark 6:7 10:2 [A]Matt 9:37, 38; John 4:35 10:3 [A]Matt 10:16 10:4 [a]Or *knapsack or beggar's bag* [A]Matt 10:9-14; Mark 6:8-11; Luke 9:3-5; 10:4-12 10:6 [a]Lit *son of peace;* i.e. a person inclined toward peace 10:7 [a]Lit *the house itself* [b]Lit *the things from them* [A]Matt 10:10; 1 Cor 9:14; 1 Tim 5:18 10:8 [A]1 Cor 10:27 10:9 [A]Matt 3:2; 10:7; Luke 10:11

9:50 he who is not against you is for you. Contrast this with 11:23. There is no middle ground and no neutrality. Here Christ gave a test of outward conduct to use for measuring others. In 11:23, He gave a test of the inward life that is to be applied to oneself.

9:51 was determined to go to Jerusalem. This begins a major section of Luke's gospel. From here to 19:27, Christ's face was set toward Jerusalem (*see note on v. 53*), and Luke's narrative is a travelogue of that long journey to the cross. This was a dramatic turning point in Christ's ministry. After this, Galilee was no longer His base of operation. Although 17:11–37 describes a return visit to Galilee, Luke included everything between this point and that short Galilean sojourn as part of the journey to Jerusalem. We know from a comparison of the Gospels that, during this period of Christ's ministry, He made short visits to Jerusalem to celebrate feasts (*see notes on 13:22; 17:11*). Nonetheless, those brief visits were only interludes in this period of ministry that would culminate in a final journey to Jerusalem for the purpose of dying there. Thus Luke underscored this turning point in Christ's ministry more dramatically than any of the other Gospels, by showing Christ's determination to complete His mission of going to the cross. *See note on 12:50.*

9:52 Samaritans. These people were descendants of Jewish mixed marriages from the days of captivity. They were rivals of the Jewish nation and had devised their own worship, a hybrid of Judaism and paganism, with a temple of their own on Mt. Gerizim. They were considered unclean by the Jews and were so hated that most Jewish travelers from Galilee to Judah took the longer route E of the Jordan to avoid traveling through Samaria. *See note on Jn 4:4.*

9:53 because He was traveling toward Jerusalem. Traveling to Jerusalem for worship implied rejection of the rituals on Mt. Gerizim and a contempt for Samaritan worship (*see note on v. 52*). This was a strong point of contention between Jews and Samaritans (cf. Jn 4:20–22).

9:54 James and John. Jesus nicknamed these brothers "Boanerges"—Sons of Thunder (Mk 3:17)—a fitting title, apparently. This was John's second sin against charity in such a short time (*see note on v. 49*). It is interesting to note that several years later, the apostle John journeyed through Samaria once again with Peter, this time preaching the gospel in Samaritan villages (Ac 8:25).

9:55 rebuked them. Christ's response to the Samaritans exemplifies the attitude the church ought to have with regard to all forms of religious persecution. The Samaritans' worship was pagan at heart, plainly wrong (*see note on Jn 4:22*). Compounding that was their intolerance. Yet, the Lord would not retaliate with force against them. Nor did He even revile them verbally. He had come to save, not to destroy, and so His response was grace rather than destructive fury. Nonetheless, Christ's words of disapproval here must not be taken as condemnation of Elijah's actions in 1Ki 18:38–40 or 2Ki 1:10–12. Elijah was commissioned to a special ministry as prophet in a theocracy, and it was his God-ordained task to confront an evil monarch (Ahab) who was attempting to usurp God's authority. Elijah was specifically authorized to measure out the reprisal of God's wrath. Elijah acted with an authority comparable to that of modern civil authorities (cf. Ro 13:4)—not in a capacity that parallels that of ministers of the gospel.

9:59, 60 *See notes on Mt 8:21, 22.*

9:62 looking back. A plowman looking back cuts a crooked furrow.

10:1 seventy others. The commissioning of the 70 is recorded only in Luke. Moses also appointed 70 elders as his representatives (Nu 11:16, 24, 25). The 12 disciples had been sent into Galilee (9:1–6); the 70 were sent into every city and place where He was about to go—i.e., into Judea, and possibly Perea (*see note on Mt 19:1*). **in pairs.** As the 12 had been sent (Mk 6:7; cf. Ecc 4:9, 11; Ac 13:2; 15:27, 39, 40; 19:22; Rev 11:3).

10:3 lambs in the midst of wolves. I.e., they would face hostility (cf. Eze 2:3–6; Jn 15:20) and spiritual danger (cf. Mt 7:15; Jn 10:12).

10:4 no money belt, no bag, no shoes. I.e., travel without luggage. This does not mean they would be barefoot. *See note on 9:3.* **greet no one.** A greeting in that culture was an elaborate ceremony, involving many formalities, perhaps even a meal, and long delays (*see note on 11:43*). A person on an extremely urgent mission could be excused from such formalities without being thought rude. Everything in Jesus' instructions speaks of the shortness of time and the great urgency of the task.

10:7 Do not keep moving from house to house. I.e., for lodging (*see note on Mk 6:10*). They were to establish headquarters in a village and not waste time moving around or seeking more comfortable housing.

near to you.’ 10 But whatever city you enter and they
do not receive you, go out into its streets and say,
11 ‘[A]Even the dust of your city which clings to our
feet we wipe off *in protest* against you; yet [a]be sure
of this, that [B]the kingdom of God has come near.’
12 I say to you, [A]it will be more tolerable in that day
for [B]Sodom than for that city.
13 “[A]Woe to you, [B]Chorazin! Woe to you, [B]Bethsaida!
For if the [a]miracles had been performed in [B]Tyre
and Sidon which occurred in you, they would have
repented long ago, sitting in [b,C]sackcloth and ashes.
14 But it will be more tolerable for [A]Tyre and Sidon
in the judgment than for you. 15 And you, [A]Caper-
naum, will not be exalted to heaven, will you? You
will be brought down to Hades!
16 “[A]The one who listens to you listens to Me, and
[B]the one who rejects you rejects Me; and he who
rejects Me rejects the One who sent Me.”

THE HAPPY RESULTS

17 The [a]seventy returned with joy, saying, “Lord,
even [A]the demons are subject to us in Your name.”
18 And He said to them, “I was watching [A]Satan fall
from heaven like lightning. 19 Behold, I have given
you authority to [A]tread on serpents and scorpions,
and over all the power of the enemy, and nothing
will injure you. 20 Nevertheless do not rejoice in this,
that the spirits are subject to you, but rejoice that
[A]your names are recorded in heaven.”
21 [A]At that very [a]time He rejoiced greatly in the
Holy Spirit, and said, “I [b]praise You, O Father, Lord of
heaven and earth, that You have hidden these things
from *the* wise and intelligent and have revealed them
to infants. Yes, Father, for this way was well-pleasing
in Your sight. 22 [A]All things have been handed over to
Me by My Father, and [B]no one knows who the Son is
except the Father, and who the Father is except the
Son, and anyone to whom the Son wills to reveal *Him.*”
23 [A]Turning to the disciples, He said privately,
“Blessed *are* the eyes which see the things you see,
24 for I say to you, that many prophets and kings
wished to see the things which you see, and did not
see *them,* and to hear the things which you hear,
and did not hear *them.*”
25 [A]And a [a,B]lawyer stood up and put Him to the
test, saying, “Teacher, what shall I do to inherit
eternal life?” 26 And He said to him, “What is written in the Law? [a]How does it read to you?” 27 And he
answered, “[A]YOU SHALL LOVE THE LORD YOUR GOD
WITH ALL YOUR HEART, AND WITH ALL YOUR SOUL,
AND WITH ALL YOUR STRENGTH, AND WITH ALL YOUR
MIND; AND YOUR NEIGHBOR AS YOURSELF.” 28 And
He said to him, “You have answered correctly; [A]DO
THIS AND YOU WILL LIVE.” 29 But wishing [A]to justify
himself, he said to Jesus, “And who is my neighbor?”

THE GOOD SAMARITAN

30 Jesus replied and said, “A man was [A]going down
from Jerusalem to Jericho, and fell among robbers,
and they stripped him and [a]beat him, and went away
leaving him half dead. 31 And by chance a priest was
going down on that road, and when he saw him, he
passed by on the other side. 32 Likewise a Levite also,
when he came to the place and saw him, passed by

10:11 [a]Lit *know* [A]Matt 10:14; Mark 6:11; Luke 9:5; Acts 13:51 [B]Matt 3:2; 10:7; Luke 10:9 10:12 [A]Gen 19:24-28; Matt 10:15; 11:24 [B]Matt 10:15 10:13 [a]Or *works of power* [b]I.e. symbols of mourning [A]Luke 10:13-15: *Matt 11:21-23* [B]Is 23:1-18; Ezek 26:1-28:26; Joel 3:4-8; Matt 11:21 [C]Rev 11:3 10:14 [A]Matt 11:21 10:15 [A]Is 14:13-15; Matt 4:13; 11:23 10:16 [A]Matt 10:40; Mark 9:37; Luke 9:48; John 13:20; Gal 4:14 [B]John 12:48; 1 Thess 4:8 10:17 [a]Some mss read *seventy-two* [A]Mark 16:17 10:18 [A]Matt 4:10 10:19 [A]Ps 91:13; Mark 16:18 10:20 [A]Ex 32:32; Ps 69:28; Is 4:3; Ezek 13:9; Dan 12:1; Phil 4:3; Heb 12:23; Rev 3:5; 13:8; 17:8; 20:12, 15; 21:27 10:21 [a]Lit *hour* [b]Or *acknowledge to You* [A]Luke 10:21, 22: *Matt 11:25-27* 10:22 [A]John 3:35 [B]John 10:15 10:23 [A]Luke 10:23, 24: *Matt 13:16, 17* 10:25 [a]I.e. an expert in the Mosaic Law [A]Luke 10:25-28: *Matt 22:34-40; Mark 12:28-31;* Matt 19:16-19 [B]Matt 22:35 10:26 [a]Lit *How do you read?* 10:27 [A]Deut 6:5; Lev 19:18 10:28 [A]Lev 18:5; Ezek 20:11; Matt 19:17 10:29 [A]Luke 16:15 10:30 [a]Lit *laid blows upon* [A]Luke 18:31; 19:28

10:11, 12 *See notes on Mt 10:14, 15.*

10:13–15 *See notes on Mt 11:21, 23.*

10:16 These words elevate the office of a faithful minister of Christ, and magnify the guilt and the condemnation of those who reject the message.

10:17 **returned with joy.** How long the mission lasted is not recorded. It may have been several weeks. The 70 probably did not return all at once, but this dialogue appears to have occurred after they had all reassembled.

10:18 **I was watching Satan fall.** In this context, it appears Jesus' meaning was, "Don't be so surprised that the demons are subject to you; I saw their commander cast out of heaven, so it is no wonder if his minions are cast out on earth. After all, I am the source of the authority that makes them subject to you" (v. 19). He may also have intended a subtle reminder and warning against pride—the reason for Satan's fall (cf. 1Ti 3:6). For discussions of Satan's fall, *see notes on Is 14:12–14; Eze 28:12–15.*

10:19 **serpents and scorpions.** Cf. Ps 91:13; Eze 2:6. These appear to be figurative terms for demonic powers (cf. Ro 16:20).

10:20 **do not rejoice in this.** Rather than being so enthralled with extraordinary manifestations such as power over demons and the ability to work miracles, they should have realized that the greatest wonder of all is the reality of salvation—the whole point of the gospel message and the central issue to which all the miracles pointed. **that your names are recorded in heaven.** Cf. Php 4:3; Heb 12:23; Rev 21:27. By contrast, unbelievers are "written down, because they have forsaken … the LORD" (Jer 17:13).

10:21, 22 *See notes on Mt 11:25, 26.*

10:25 **lawyer.** I.e., a scribe who was supposedly an expert in the law of God. Aside from one usage of this word in Mt 22:35 (*see note there*), Luke is the only one of the gospel writers who uses it (11:45, 46). **what shall I do to inherit eternal life?** The same question is raised by several inquirers (18:18–23; Mt 19:16–22; Jn 3:1–15).

10:27 **he answered.** The lawyer summed up the requirements of the law (Lv 19:18; Dt 6:5) exactly as Christ did on another occasion (*see notes on Mt 22:37–40*).

10:28 do this and you will live. Cf. Lv 18:5; Eze 20:11. "Do and live" is the promise of the law. But since no sinner can obey perfectly, the impossible demands of the law are meant to drive us to seek divine mercy (Gal 3:10–13, 22–25). This man should have responded with a confession of his own guilt, rather than self-justification (v. 29).

10:29 **wishing to justify himself.** This reveals the man's self-righteous character. **who is my neighbor?** The prevailing opinion among scribes and Pharisees was that one's neighbors were the righteous alone. According to them, the wicked—including rank sinners (such as tax collectors and prostitutes), Gentiles, and especially Samaritans—were to be hated because they were the enemies of God. They cited Ps 139:21, 22 to justify their position. As that passage suggests, hatred of evil is the natural corollary of loving righteousness. But the truly righteous person's "hatred" for sinners is not a malevolent enmity. It is a righteous abhorrence of all that is base and corrupt—not a spiteful, personal loathing of individuals. Godly hatred is marked by a broken-hearted grieving over the condition of the sinner. And as Jesus taught here and elsewhere (6:27–36; Mt 5:44–48), it is also tempered by a genuine love. The Pharisees had elevated hostility toward the wicked to the status of a virtue, in effect nullifying the second Great Commandment. Jesus' answer to this lawyer demolished the pharisaical excuse for hating one's enemies.

10:30 **down from Jerusalem to Jericho.** A rocky, winding, treacherous descent of about 3,300 feet in 17 miles. That stretch of road was notorious for being beset with thieves and danger.

10:32 **Levite.** These were from the tribe of Levi, but not descendants of Aaron. They assisted the priests in the work of the temple.

on the other side. 33But a [A]Samaritan, who was on a
journey, came upon him; and when he saw him, he
felt compassion, 34and came to him and bandaged
up his wounds, pouring oil and wine on *them;* and
he put him on his own beast, and brought him to an
inn and took care of him. 35On the next day he took
out two [a]denarii and gave them to the innkeeper
and said, 'Take care of him; and whatever more you
spend, when I return I will repay you.' 36Which of
these three do you think proved to be a neighbor to
the man who fell into the robbers' *hands?*" 37And
he said, "The one who showed mercy toward him."
Then Jesus said to him, "Go and do [a]the same."

MARTHA AND MARY

38Now as they were traveling along, He entered a
village; and a woman named [A]Martha welcomed Him
into her home. 39She had a sister called [A]Mary, who
was [B]seated at the Lord's feet, listening to His word.
40But [A]Martha was distracted with [a]all her preparations; and she came up *to Him* and said, "Lord, do You
not care that my sister has left me to do all the serving alone? Then tell her to help me." 41But the Lord
answered and said to her, "[A]Martha, Martha, you are
[B]worried and bothered about so many things; 42[A]but
only one thing is necessary, for [B]Mary has chosen the
good part, which shall not be taken away from her."

INSTRUCTION ABOUT PRAYER

11 It happened that while [a]Jesus was praying in a
certain place, after He had finished, one of His
disciples said to Him, "Lord, teach us to pray just
as John also taught his disciples." 2And He said to
them, "[A]When you pray, say:

'[a]Father, hallowed be Your name.
Your kingdom come.
3 'Give us [A]each day our [a]daily bread.
4 'And forgive us our sins,
For we ourselves also forgive
everyone who [A]is indebted to us.
And lead us not into temptation.' "

5Then He said to them, "[a]Suppose one of you has a
friend, and goes to him at midnight and says to him,
'Friend, lend me three loaves; 6for a friend of mine
has come to me from a journey, and I have nothing
to set before him'; 7and from inside he answers and
says, 'Do not bother me; the door has already been
shut and my children [a]and I are in bed; I cannot get
up and give you *anything.*' 8I tell you, even though
he will not get up and give him *anything* because
he is his friend, yet [A]because of his [a]persistence
he will get up and give him as much as he needs.
9"So I say to you, [a,A]ask, and it will be given to
you; [b]seek, and you will find; [c]knock, and it will be
opened to you. 10For everyone who asks, receives;
and he who seeks, finds; and to him who knocks, it
will be opened. 11Now [a]suppose one of you fathers
is asked by his son for a [b]fish; he will not give him
a snake instead of a fish, will he? 12Or *if* he is asked
for an egg, he will not give him a scorpion, will he?
13[A]If you then, being evil, know how to give good
gifts to your children, how much more will *your*
[a]heavenly Father give the Holy Spirit to those who
ask Him?"

PHARISEES' BLASPHEMY

14[A]And He was casting out a demon, and it was
mute; when the demon had gone out, the mute man
spoke; and the crowds were amazed. 15But some
of them said, "He casts out demons [A]by [B]Beelzebul,
the ruler of the demons." 16Others, [a]to test *Him,*
[A]were demanding of Him a [b]sign from heaven.

10:33 [A]Matt 10:5; Luke 9:52 10:35 [a]The denarius was equivalent to a day's wages 10:37 [a]Or *likewise* 10:38 [A]Luke 10:40f; John 11:1, 5, 19ff, 30, 39; 12:2 10:39 [A]Luke 10:42; John 11:1f, 19f, 28, 31f, 45; 12:3 [B]Luke 8:35; Acts 22:3 10:40 [a]Lit *much service* [A]Luke 10:38, 41; John 11:1, 5, 19ff, 30, 39; 12:2 10:41 [A]Luke 10:38, 40; John 11:1, 5, 19ff, 30, 39; 12:2 [B]Matt 6:25 10:42 [A]Ps 27:4; John 6:27 [B]Luke 10:39; John 11:1f, 19f, 28, 31f, 45; 12:3 11:1 [a]Lit *He* 11:2 [a]Later mss add phrases from Matt 6:9-13 to make the two passages closely similar [A]Luke 11:2-4: *Matt 6:9-13* 11:3 [a]Or *bread for the coming day* or *needful bread* [A]Acts 17:11 11:4 [A]Luke 13:4 mg 11:5 [a]Lit *Which one of you will have* 11:7 [a]Lit *with me* 11:8 [a]Lit *shamelessness* [A]Luke 18:1-5 11:9 [a]Or *keep asking* [b]Or *keep seeking* [c]Or *keep knocking* [A]Luke 11:9-13: *Matt 7:7-11* 11:11 [a]Lit *which of you, a son, will ask the father* [b]Two early mss insert *loaf, he will not give him a stone, will he, or for a* 11:13 [a]Lit *Father from heaven* [A]Matt 7:11; Luke 18:7f 11:14 [A]Luke 11:14, 15: *Matt 12:22, 24;* Matt 9:32-34 11:15 [A]Matt 9:34 [B]Matt 10:25 11:16 [a]Lit *testing* [b]Or *attesting miracle* [A]Matt 12:38; 16:1; Mark 8:11

10:33 Samaritan. For a Samaritan to travel this road was unusual. The Samaritan himself was risking not only the thieves, but also the hostility of other travelers.

10:34 oil and wine. Probably carried by most travelers in small amounts as a kind of first-aid kit. The wine was antiseptic; the oil soothing and healing.

10:35 two denarii. I.e., two days' wages (*see notes on Mt 20:2; 22:19*). Probably more than enough to permit the man to stay until he recovered.

10:36 neighbor to the man. Jesus reversed the lawyer's original question (v. 29). The lawyer assumed it was up to others to prove themselves neighbor to him (*see note on v. 29*). Jesus' reply makes it clear that each has a responsibility to be a neighbor—especially to those who are in need.

10:38 a village. Bethany, two mi. E of the temple in Jerusalem, on the E slope of the Mt. of Olives. This was the home of Mary, Martha, and Lazarus (cf. Jn 11:1).

10:40 distracted. Lit. "dragging all around." The expression implies that Martha was in a tumult. **with all her preparations.** Martha was evidently fussing about with details that were unnecessarily elaborate.

10:42 one thing ... good part. Jesus was not speaking of the number of dishes to be served. The one thing necessary was exemplified by Mary, i.e., an attitude of worship and meditation, listening with an open mind and heart to Jesus' words.

11:1 Lord, teach us to pray. Rabbis often composed prayers for their disciples to recite. Having seen Jesus pray many times, they knew of His love for prayer, and they knew prayer was not just the reciting of words (*see note on Mt 6:7*).

11:2 Father. Virtually the same prayer was given as a model on two separate occasions by Christ, first in the Sermon on the Mount (*see notes on Mt 6:9-13*), and then here, in response to a direct question. That accounts for minor variations between the two versions. **Your name.** God's name represents all His character and attributes. Cf. Pss 8:1, 9; 9:10; 22:22; 52:9; 115:1.

11:4 sins. *See note on Mt 6:12.*

11:7 my children and I are in bed. The one-room houses that were common in Israel had a common sleeping area shared by the whole family. If one person arose and lit a lamp to get bread, all would be awakened.

11:8 persistence. The word can even mean "impudence." It conveys the ideas of urgency, audacity, earnestness, boldness, and relentlessness—like the persistent asking of a desperate beggar.

11:13 being evil. I.e., by nature. *See note on Mt 7:11.*

11:14 it was mute. I.e., the demon.

11:15 Beelzebul. Originally, this referred to Baal-zebul ("Baal, the prince"), chief god of the Philistine city of Ekron; the Israelites disdainfully referred to him as Baal-zebub ("Lord of Flies"). *See note on 2Ki 1:2.*

11:16 a sign from heaven. I.e., a miraculous

17 [A]But He knew their thoughts and said to them,
"[a]Any kingdom divided against itself is laid waste;
and a house *divided* against [b]itself falls. 18 If [A]Satan
also is divided against himself, how will his kingdom stand? For you say that I cast out demons by
[B]Beelzebul. 19 And if I by [A]Beelzebul cast out demons, by whom do your sons cast them out? So
they will be your judges. 20 But if I cast out demons
by the [A]finger of God, then [B]the kingdom of God
has come upon you. 21 When [a]a strong *man*, fully
armed, guards his own house, his possessions are
[b]undisturbed. 22 But when someone stronger than
he attacks him and overpowers him, he takes away
from him all his armor on which he had relied and
distributes his plunder. 23 [A]He who is not with Me
is against Me; and he who does not gather with
Me, scatters.
24 "[A]When the unclean spirit goes out of [a]a man,
it passes through waterless places seeking rest, and
not finding any, it says, 'I will return to my house
from which I came.' 25 And when it comes, it finds
it swept and put in order. 26 Then it goes and takes
along seven other spirits more evil than itself, and
they go in and live there; and the last state of that
man becomes worse than the first."
27 While [a]Jesus was saying these things, one of
the women in the crowd raised her voice and said
to Him, "[A]Blessed is the womb that bore You and
the breasts at which You nursed." 28 But He said,
"On the contrary, blessed are [A]those who hear the
word of God and observe it."

THE SIGN OF JONAH

29 As the crowds were increasing, He began to
say, "[A]This generation is a wicked generation; it
[B]seeks for a [a]sign, and *yet* no [a]sign will be given
to it but the [a]sign of Jonah. 30 For just as [A]Jonah
became a [a]sign to the Ninevites, so will the Son
of Man be to this generation. 31 The [A]Queen of the
South will rise up with the men of this generation
at the judgment and condemn them, because she
came from the ends of the earth to hear the wisdom of Solomon; and behold, something greater
than Solomon is here. 32 The men of Nineveh will
stand up with this generation at the judgment and
condemn it, because [A]they repented at the preaching of Jonah; and behold, something greater than
Jonah is here.
33 "[A]No one, after lighting a lamp, puts it away in
a cellar nor under a basket, but on the lampstand, so
that those who enter may see the light. 34 [A]The eye
is the lamp of your body; when your eye is [a]clear,
your whole body also is full of light; but when it
is [b]bad, your body also is full of darkness. 35 Then
watch out that the light in you is not darkness. 36 If
therefore your whole body is full of light, with no
dark part in it, it will be wholly illumined, as when
the lamp illumines you with its rays."

WOES UPON THE PHARISEES

37 Now when He had spoken, a Pharisee *asked
Him to have lunch with him; and He went in, and
reclined *at the table*. 38 When the Pharisee saw it, he

11:17 [a]Lit *every* [b]Lit *a house* [A]Luke 11:17-22: *Matt 12:25-29; Mark 3:23-27* 11:18 [A]Matt 4:10 [B]Matt 10:25 11:19 [A]Matt 10:25 11:20 [A]Ex 8:19 [B]Matt 3:2 11:21 [a]Lit *the* [b]Lit *in peace* 11:23 [A]Matt 12:30; Mark 9:40 11:24 [a]Lit *the* [A]Luke 11:24-26: *Matt 12:43-45* 11:27 [a]Lit *He* [A]Luke 23:29 11:28 [A]Luke 8:21 11:29 [a]Or *attesting miracle* [A]Luke 11:29-32: *Matt 12:39-42;* Matt 16:4; Mark 8:12 [B]Matt 12:38; Luke 11:16 11:30 [a]Or *attesting miracle* [A]Jon 3:4 11:31 [A]1 Kin 10:1-10; 2 Chr 9:1-12 11:32 [A]Jon 3:5 11:33 [A]Matt 5:15; Mark 4:21; Luke 8:16 11:34 [a]Or *healthy* [b]Or *evil* [A]Luke 11:34, 35: *Matt 6:22, 23*

work of cosmological proportions, like the rearranging of the constellations, or something far greater than the casting out of a demon, which they had just witnessed. *See note on Mt 12:38.*

11:17 He knew their thoughts. Jesus was God with full omniscience if He used it (*see notes on 2:52; Mk 13:32; Jn 2:23–25*). **kingdom divided against itself.** This may have been a subtle jab at the Jewish nation, a kingdom divided in the time of Jeroboam, and still marked by various kinds of bitter internal strife and factionalism, right up to the destruction of Jerusalem in A.D. 70.

11:19 by whom do your sons cast them out? There were Jewish exorcists who claimed power to cast out demons (Ac 19:13–15). Jesus' point was that if such exorcisms could be done via satanic power, the Pharisaical exorcists must be suspect as well. And, in fact, the evidence in Ac 19 suggests that the sons of Sceva were charlatans who employed fraud and trickery to fabricate phony exorcisms. **your judges.** I.e., witnesses against you. This seems to suggest that the fraudulent exorcisms (which had their approval) stood as a testimony against the Pharisees themselves, who disapproved of Christ's genuine exorcisms.

11:20 by the finger of God. In Ex 8:19 the phony magicians of Egypt were forced to confess that Moses' miracles were genuine works of God, not mere trickery such as they had performed. Here Jesus made a similar comparison between His exorcisms and the work of the Jewish exorcists. **the kingdom of God has come.** *See note on Mt 12:28.*

11:21 a strong *man*. I.e., Satan.

11:22 someone stronger than he. I.e., Christ. **distributes his plunder.** Probably a reference to Is 53:12. When a demon is defeated by the power of Christ, the soul vacated by the power of darkness is taken over by Christ. Cf. vv. 24–26.

11:23 He who is not with Me is against Me. *See note on 9:50.*

11:24 unclean spirit goes out. Christ was characterizing the work of the phony exorcists (*see note on v. 19*). What appears to be a true exorcism is merely a temporary respite, after which the demon returns with 7 others (v. 26).

11:26 worse than the first. *See note on Mt 12:45.*

11:28 On the contrary. This has the sense of, "Yes, but rather...." While not denying the blessedness of Mary, Christ did not countenance any tendency to elevate Mary as an object of veneration. Mary's relationship to Him as His physical mother did not confer on her any greater honor than the blessedness of those who hear and obey the Word of God. *See note on 1:47.*

11:29 it seeks for a sign. *See note on v. 16.* Jesus always declined to give signs on demand. Evidences were not the means by which He appealed to unbelievers. *See note on 16:31.*

11:30 Jonah became a sign. I.e., a sign of judgment to come. Jonah's emergence from the fish's belly pictured Christ's resurrection. Jesus clearly regarded Jonah's account as historically accurate. *See notes on Mt 12:39, 40.*

11:31, 32 *See notes on Mt 12:41, 42.*

11:33 *See note on 8:16.*

11:34 the lamp of your body. This is a different metaphor from the one in v. 33. There the lamp speaks of the Word of God; here the eye is the "lamp"—i.e., the source of light—for the body. *See note on Mt 6:22, 23.* **when your eye ... is bad.** The problem was their perception, not a lack of light. They did not need a sign; they needed hearts to believe the great display of divine power they had already seen.

11:38 He had not first ceremonially washed. The Pharisee was concerned with ceremony, not hygiene. The Gr. word for "washed" refers to a ceremonial ablution. Nothing in the law commanded such washings, but the Pharisees practiced them, believing the ritual cleansed them of any accidental ceremonial defilement. *See notes on Mk 7:2, 3.*

was surprised that He had not first [a,A]ceremonially
washed before the [b]meal. 39 But [A]the Lord said to
him, "Now [B]you Pharisees clean the outside of the
cup and of the platter; but [a]inside of you, you are
full of robbery and wickedness. 40 [A]You foolish ones,
did not He who made the outside make the inside
also? 41 But [A]give that which is within as charity,
and [a]then all things are [B]clean for you.
42 "[A]But woe to you Pharisees! For you [B]pay tithe
of mint and rue and every *kind of* garden herb,
and *yet* disregard justice and the love of God; but
these are the things you should have done without
neglecting the others. 43 Woe to you Pharisees! For
you [A]love the chief seats in the synagogues and the
respectful greetings in the market places. 44 [A]Woe
to you! For you are like [a]concealed tombs, and the
people who walk over *them* are unaware *of it*."
45 One of the [a,A]lawyers *said to Him in reply,
"Teacher, when You say this, You insult us too." 46 But
He said, "Woe to you [A]lawyers as well! For [B]you
weigh men down with burdens hard to bear, [a]while
you yourselves will not even touch the burdens
with one of your fingers. 47 [A]Woe to you! For you
build the [a]tombs of the prophets, and *it was* your
fathers *who* killed them. 48 So you are witnesses
and approve the deeds of your fathers; because
it was they who killed them, and you build *their*
tombs. 49 For this reason also [A]the wisdom of God
said, '[B]I will send to them prophets and apostles,
and *some* of them they will kill and *some* they will
[a]persecute, 50 so that the blood of all the prophets,
shed [A]since the foundation of the world, may be
[a]charged against this generation, 51 from [A]the blood
of Abel to [B]the blood of Zechariah, who was killed
between the altar and the house *of God;* yes, I tell
you, it shall be [a]charged against this generation.'
52 Woe to you [a,A]lawyers! For you have taken away
the key of knowledge; [B]you yourselves did not enter, and you hindered those who were entering."
53 When He left there, the scribes and the Pharisees began to be very hostile and to question Him
closely on many subjects, 54 [A]plotting against Him
[B]to catch [a]*Him* in something He might say.

GOD KNOWS AND CARES

12 Under these circumstances, after [a]so many
thousands of [b]people had gathered together
that they were stepping on one another, He began
saying to His disciples first *of all*, "[A]Beware of the
leaven of the Pharisees, which is hypocrisy. 2 [A]But
there is nothing covered up that will not be revealed,
and hidden that will not be known. 3 Accordingly,
whatever you have said in the dark will be heard in
the light, and what you have [a]whispered in the inner rooms will be proclaimed upon [A]the housetops.
4 "I say to you, [A]My friends, do not be afraid of
those who kill the body and after that have no more
that they can do. 5 But I will [a]warn you whom to
fear: [A]fear the One who, after He has killed, has authority to cast into [b,B]hell; yes, I tell you, fear Him!
6 Are not [A]five sparrows sold for two [a]cents? *Yet* not
one of them is forgotten before God. 7 [A]Indeed, the
very hairs of your head are all numbered. Do not
fear; you are more valuable than many sparrows.
8 "And I say to you, everyone who [A]confesses Me
before men, the Son of Man will confess him also
before the angels of God; 9 but [A]he who denies Me
before men will be denied [B]before the angels of
God. 10 [A]And everyone who [a]speaks a word against
the Son of Man, it will be forgiven him; but he who

11:38 [a]Lit *baptized* [b]Or *lunch* [A]Matt 15:2; Mark 7:3f 11:39 [a]Lit *your inside is full* [A]Luke 7:13 [B]Matt 23:25f 11:40 [A]Luke 12:20; 1 Cor 15:36 11:41 [a]Lit *behold* [A]Luke 12:33; 16:9 [B]Mark 7:19; Titus 1:15 11:42 [A]Matt 23:23 [B]Lev 27:30; Luke 18:12 11:43 [A]Matt 23:6f; Mark 12:38f; Luke 14:7; 20:46 11:44 [a]Or *indistinct, unseen* [A]Matt 23:27 11:45 [a]I.e. experts in the Mosaic Law [A]Matt 22:35; Luke 11:46, 52 11:46 [a]Lit *and* [A]Matt 22:35; Luke 11:45, 52 [B]Matt 23:4 11:47 [a]Or *monuments to* [A]Matt 23:29ff 11:49 [a]Or *drive out* [A]1 Cor 1:24, 30; Col 2:3 [B]Matt 23:34-36 11:50 [a]Or *required of* [A]Matt 25:34 11:51 [a]Or *required of* [A]Gen 4:8 [B]2 Chr 24:20, 21 11:52 [a]I.e. experts in the Mosaic Law [A]Matt 22:35; Luke 11:45, 46 [B]Matt 23:13 11:54 [a]Lit *something out of His mouth* [A]Mark 3:2; Luke 20:20; Acts 23:21 [B]Mark 12:13 12:1 [a]Lit *myriads* [b]Lit *the crowd* [A]Matt 16:6, 11f; Mark 8:15 12:2 [A]Luke 12:2-9: *Matt 10:26-33;* Matt 10:26; Mark 4:22; Luke 8:17 12:3 [a]Lit *spoken in the ear* [A]Matt 10:27; 24:17 12:4 [A]John 15:13-15 12:5 [a]Or *show* [b]Gr *Gehenna* [A]Heb 10:31 [B]Matt 5:22 12:6 [a]Gr *assaria,* the smallest of copper coins [A]Matt 10:29 12:7 [A]Matt 10:30 12:8 [A]Matt 10:32; Luke 15:10; Rom 10:9 12:9 [A]Matt 10:33; Luke 9:26 [B]Luke 15:10 12:10 [a]Lit *will speak* [A]Matt 12:31, 32; Mark 3:28-30

11:39 full of robbery and wickedness. I.e., they were preoccupied with external ceremonies but overlooked the more important issue of internal morality. *See note on Mt 23:25.*

11:40 foolish ones. I.e., persons who lack understanding. This was the truth and not the sort of coarse name-calling Christ forbade in Mt 5:22.

11:41 give that which is within as charity. This contrasts inner virtues with external ceremonies. Alms are to be given not for show, but as an expression of a faithful heart (cf. Mt 6:1–4)—and the true almsgiving is not the external act, but one's attitude before God.

11:42 tithe. *See note on Mt 23:23.*

11:43 greetings. These were ostentatious ceremonies that were more or less elaborate depending on the rank of the person being greeted.

11:44 concealed tombs. Hidden sources of defilement. They had carefully concealed their own inward corruption, but it still was a source of defilement. *See note on Mt 23:27.*

11:45 lawyers. I.e., scribes. *See note on 10:25.*

11:46 burdens. *See note on Mt 23:3.*

11:47 you build the tombs of the prophets. They thought they were honoring those prophets, but in reality they had more in common with those who killed the prophets (v. 48). *See note on Mt 23:30.*

11:49 the wisdom of God said. There is no OT source for this quotation. Christ is prophetically announcing the coming judgment of God, not quoting a previously written source, but giving them a direct warning from God.

11:49–51 *See notes on Mt 23:34–36.*

11:52 the key of knowledge. They had locked up the truth of the Scriptures and thrown away the key by imposing their faulty interpretations and human traditions on God's Word. *See note on Mt 23:13.*

11:54 to catch. The same word is used in Gr. literature for the hunting of animals.

12:1 many thousands. The Gr. word is the same from which we get the word "myriads." **leaven.** *See notes on Mt 16:12; Mk 8:15.*

12:2, 3 *See notes on 8:17; Mk 4:22.*

12:5 fear Him! *See note on Mt 10:28.*

12:6 two cents. Gr., *assariōn,* a Roman coin equal to a 16th of a denarius. One assarius would be less than an hour's wage. **not one of them is forgotten before God.** Divine providence governs even the most inconsequential details of God's creation. He cares for all that He created, regardless of how insignificant. *See note on Mt 10:29.*

12:8 before the angels of God. I.e., in the day of judgment. Cf. Mt 25:31–34; Jude 24. *See note on Mt 10:32.*

12:9 he who denies Me before men. This describes a soul-damning denial of Christ—not the sort of temporary wavering Peter was guilty of (22:56–62)—but the sin of those who through fear, shame, neglect, delay, or love of the world reject all evidence and revelation and decline to confess Christ as Savior and King, until it is too late.

12:10 blasphemes against the Holy Spirit. *See notes on Mt 12:31, 32.* This was not a sin of ignorance, but a deliberate, willful, settled hostility toward Christ—exemplified by the Pharisees in Mt 12, who attributed to Satan the work of Christ (cf. 11:15).

blasphemes against the Holy Spirit, it will not be
forgiven him. 11 When they bring you before [A]the
synagogues and the rulers and the authorities, do
not [B]worry about how or what you are to speak
in your defense, or what you are to say; 12 for [A]the
Holy Spirit will teach you in that very hour what
you ought to say."

COVETOUSNESS DENOUNCED

13 Someone [a]in the crowd said to Him, "Teacher,
tell my brother to divide the *family* inheritance with
me." 14 But He said to him, "[A]Man, who appointed
Me a judge or arbitrator over you?" 15 Then He said
to them, "[A]Beware, and be on your guard against
every form of greed; for not *even* when one has an
abundance does his life consist of his possessions."
16 And He told them a parable, saying, "The land of
a rich man was very productive. 17 And he began
reasoning to himself, saying, 'What shall I do, since
I have no place to store my crops?' 18 Then he said,
'This is what I will do: I will tear down my barns
and build larger ones, and there I will store all my
grain and my goods. 19 And I will say to my soul,
"Soul, [A]you have many goods laid up for many years
to come; take your ease, eat, drink *and* be merry." '
20 But God said to him, '[A]You fool! This *very* night
[a,B]your soul is required of you; and [C]*now* who will
own what you have prepared?' 21 So is the man who
[A]stores up treasure for himself, and is not rich toward God."

22 And He said to His disciples, "[A]For this reason I say to you, [a]do not worry about *your* [b]life,
as to what you will eat; nor for your body, *as to*
what you will put on. 23 For life is more than food,
and the body more than clothing. 24 Consider the
[A]ravens, for they neither sow nor reap; they have
no storeroom nor [B]barn, and *yet* God feeds them;
how much more valuable you are than the birds!
25 And which of you by worrying can add a *single*
[a,A]hour to his [b]life's span? 26 If then you cannot do
even a very little thing, why do you worry about
other matters? 27 Consider the lilies, how they
grow: they neither toil nor spin; but I tell you,
not even [A]Solomon in all his glory clothed himself
like one of these. 28 But if God so clothes the grass
in the field, which is *alive* today and tomorrow
is thrown into the furnace, how much more *will
He clothe* you? [A]You men of little faith! 29 And
do not seek what you will eat and what you will
drink, and do not [A]keep worrying. 30 For [a]all these
things the nations of the world eagerly seek; but
your Father knows that you need these things.
31 But seek His kingdom, and [A]these things will
be added to you. 32 [A]Do not be afraid, [B]little flock,
for [C]your Father has chosen gladly to give you the
kingdom.

33 "[A]Sell your possessions and give to charity;
make yourselves money belts which do not wear
out, [B]an unfailing treasure in heaven, where no thief
comes near nor moth destroys. 34 For [A]where your
treasure is, there your heart will be also.

BE IN READINESS

35 "[a,A]Be dressed in [B]readiness, and *keep* your
lamps lit. 36 Be like men who are waiting for their
master when he returns from the wedding feast, so
that they may immediately open *the door* to him
when he comes and knocks. 37 Blessed are those
slaves whom the master will find [A]on the alert when
he comes; truly I say to you, that [B]he will gird himself *to serve,* and have them recline *at the table,*
and will come up and wait on them. 38 [A]Whether he
comes in the [a]second watch, or even in the [b]third,
and finds *them* so, blessed are those *slaves.*

12:11 [A]Matt 10:17 [B]Matt 6:25; 10:19; Mark 13:11; Luke 12:22; 21:14 12:12 [A]Matt 10:20; Luke 21:15 12:13 [a]Lit *out of* 12:14 [A]Mic 6:8; Rom 2:1, 3; 9:20 12:15 [A]1 Tim 6:6-10 12:19 [A]Eccl 11:9 12:20 [a]Lit *they are demanding your soul from you* [A]Jer 17:11; Luke 11:40 [B]Job 27:8 [C]Ps 39:6 12:21 [A]Luke 12:33 12:22 [a]Or *stop being worried* [b]Lit *soul* [A]Luke 12:22-31: *Matt 6:25-33* 12:24 [A]Job 38:41 [B]Luke 12:18 12:25 [a]Lit *cubit* (approx 18 in.) [b]Or *height* [A]Ps 39:5 12:27 [A]1 Kin 10:4-7; 2 Chr 9:3-6 12:28 [A]Matt 6:30 12:29 [A]Matt 6:31 12:30 [a]Or *these things all the nations of the world* 12:31 [A]Matt 6:33 12:32 [A]Matt 14:27 [B]John 21:15-17 [C]Eph 1:5, 9 12:33 [A]Matt 19:21; Luke 11:41; 18:22 [B]Matt 6:20; Luke 12:21 12:34 [A]Matt 6:21 12:35 [a]Lit *Let your loins be girded* [A]Matt 25:1ff [B]Eph 6:14; 1 Pet 1:13 12:37 [A]Matt 24:42 [B]Luke 17:8; John 13:4 12:38 [a]I.e. 9 p.m. to midnight [b]I.e. midnight to 3 a.m. [A]Matt 24:43

12:11 do not worry. I.e., do not be anxious. This does not suggest that ministers and teachers should forego preparation in their normal spiritual duties. To cite this passage and others like it (21:12–15; Mt 10:19) to justify the neglect of study and meditation is to twist the meaning of Scripture. This verse is meant as a comfort for those under life-threatening persecution, not an excuse for laziness in ministry. The exact same expression is used in v. 22, speaking of concern for one's material necessities. In neither context was Jesus condemning legitimate toil and preparation. He was promising the Holy Spirit's aid for times of persecution when there can be no preparation. *See note on Mk 13:11.*

12:13 tell my brother to divide the *family* inheritance. "The right of the firstborn" was a double portion of the inheritance (Dt 21:17). Perhaps this man wanted an equal share. In any case, Jesus seemed unconcerned about the implied injustice, and refused the man's request to arbitrate the family dispute.

12:14 who appointed Me a judge . . . ? One of Christ's roles is that of Judge of all the earth (Jn 5:22), but He did not come to be an arbiter of petty earthly disputes. Settling an inheritance dispute was a matter for civil authorities.

12:22–31 *See notes on Mt 6:26–33.*

12:22 do not worry. *See note on v. 11.*

12:32 has chosen gladly. *See note on 2:14.* Christ stressed the Father's tender care over His little flock as an antidote to anxiety (vv. 22–30).

12:33 Sell your possessions and give to charity. Those who amassed earthly possessions, falsely thinking their security lay in material resources (vv. 16–20), needed to lay up treasure in heaven instead. *See note on Mt 6:20.* Believers in the early church did sell their goods to meet the basic needs of poorer brethren (Ac 2:44, 45; 4:32–37). But this commandment is not to be twisted into an absolute prohibition of all earthly possessions. In fact, Peter's words to Ananias in Ac 5:4 make it clear that the selling of one's possessions was optional. money belts which do not wear out. These belts that do not wear out (so as to lose the money) are defined as "treasure in the heavens that does not fail." The surest place to put one's money is in such a belt—in heaven, where it is safe from thieves and decay as well.

12:34 your heart will be also. Where one puts his money reveals the priorities of his heart. Cf. 16:1–13; Mt 6:21.

12:35 dressed. Speaks of preparedness. Long, flowing robes would be tucked into the belt to allow freedom to work. Cf. Ex 12:11; 1Pe 1:13.

12:36 when he returns. The servants were responsible to meet him with burning torches.

12:37 on the alert. The key here is readiness at all times for Christ's return. *See note on Mt 25:1–13.* gird himself. I.e., he will take the servant's role and wait on them. This remarkable statement pictures Christ, at His return, ministering as a servant to believers.

12:38 second watch. 9:00 p.m. to midnight. third. Midnight to 3:00 a.m.

39“[A]But [a]be sure of this, that if the head of the
house had known at what hour the thief was coming, he would not have allowed his house to be
[b,B]broken into. 40[A]You too, be ready; for the Son of
Man is coming at an hour that you do not [a]expect.”
41Peter said, “Lord, are You addressing this parable to us, or [A]to everyone *else* as well?” 42And [A]the
Lord said, “[B]Who then is the faithful and sensible
[C]steward, whom his master will put in charge of his
[a]servants, to give them their rations at the proper
time? 43Blessed is that [A]slave whom his [a]master
finds so doing when he comes. 44Truly I say to
you that he will put him in charge of all his possessions. 45But if that slave says in his heart, ‘My
master [a]will be a long time in coming,’ and begins
to beat the slaves, *both* men and women, and to
eat and drink and get drunk; 46the master of that
slave will come on a day when he does not expect
him and at an hour he does not know, and will cut
him in pieces, and assign him a place with the unbelievers. 47And that slave who knew his master’s
will and did not get ready or act in accord with his
will, will [A]receive many lashes, 48but the one who
did not [A]know *it,* and committed deeds worthy of
[a]a flogging, will receive but few. [B]From everyone
who has been given much, much will be required;
and to whom they entrusted much, of him they will
ask all the more.

CHRIST DIVIDES MEN

49“I [a]have come to cast fire upon the earth; and
[b]how I wish it were already kindled! 50But I have
a [A]baptism to [a]undergo, and how distressed I am
until it is accomplished! 51[A]Do you suppose that I
came to grant peace on earth? I tell you, no, but
rather division; 52for from now on five *members*
in one household will be divided, three against
two and two against three. 53They will be divided,
[A]father against son and son against father, mother
against daughter and daughter against mother,
mother-in-law against daughter-in-law and daughter-in-law against mother-in-law.”
54And He was also saying to the crowds, “[A]When
you see a cloud rising in the west, immediately you
say, ‘A shower is coming,’ and so it turns out. 55And
when *you see* a south wind blowing, you say, ‘It
will be a [A]hot day,’ and it turns out *that way.* 56You
hypocrites! [A]You know how to analyze the appearance of the earth and the sky, but [a]why do you not
analyze this present time?
57“And [A]why do you not even on your own initiative judge what is right? 58For [A]while you are
going with your opponent to appear before the
magistrate, on *your* way *there* make an effort to
[a]settle with him, so that he may not drag you before the judge, and the judge turn you over to the
officer, and the officer throw you into prison. 59I
say to you, you will not get out of there until you
have paid the very last [a,A]cent.”

CALL TO REPENT

13 Now on the same occasion there were some
present who reported to Him about the Galileans whose blood [A]Pilate had [a]mixed with their
sacrifices. 2And Jesus said to them, “[A]Do you suppose that these Galileans were *greater* sinners than
all *other* Galileans because they suffered this *fate?*
3I tell you, no, but unless you [a]repent, you will all

12:39 [a]Lit *know* [b]Lit *dug through* [A]Luke 12:39, 40: *Matt 24:43, 44* [B]Matt 6:19 12:40 [a]Lit *think, suppose* [A]Mark 13:33; Luke 21:36 12:41 [A]Luke 12:47, 48 12:42 [a]Lit *service* [A]Luke 7:13 [B]Luke 12:42-46: *Matt 24:45-51* [C]Matt 24:45; Luke 16:1ff 12:43 [a]Or *lord* [A]Luke 12:42 12:45 [a]Lit *is delaying to come* 12:47 [A]Deut 25:2; James 4:17 12:48 [a]Lit *blows* [A]Lev 5:17; Num 15:29f [B]Matt 13:12 12:49 [a]Or *came* [b]Lit *what do I wish if...?* 12:50 [a]Lit *be baptized with* [A]Mark 10:38 12:51 [A]Luke 12:51-53: *Matt 10:34-36* 12:53 [A]Mic 7:6; Matt 10:21 12:54 [A]Matt 16:2f 12:55 [A]Matt 20:12 12:56 [a]Lit *how* [A]Matt 16:3 12:57 [A]Luke 21:30 12:58 [a]Lit *be released from him* [A]Luke 12:58, 59: *Matt 5:25, 26* 12:59 [a]Gr *lepton;* i.e. 1/128 of a denarius [A]Mark 12:42 13:1 [a]I.e. shed along with [A]Matt 27 13:2 [A]John 9:2f 13:3 [a]Or *are repentant*

12:40 an hour that you do not expect. Cf. 21:34; Mt 24:36, 42–44; 1Th 5:2–4; 2Pe 3:10; Rev 3:3; 16:15.

12:42 Christ did not directly answer Peter’s question (v. 41), but implied that these truths apply to unbelievers—most of all those to whom much has been committed (v. 48). **steward.** *See note on 16:1.*

12:43 Blessed is that slave. The faithful steward pictures the genuine believer, who manages well the spiritual riches God has put in his care for the benefit of others, and the careful management of the master’s estate. Faithful expression of the duty of such spiritual stewardship will result in honor and reward (v. 44).

12:45 to beat the slaves. This wicked steward’s unfaithfulness and cruel behavior illustrates the evil of an unbelieving heart.

12:46 cut him in pieces. I.e., utterly destroy him. This speaks of the severity of final judgment of unbelievers.

12:47, 48 The degree of punishment is commensurate with the extent to which the unfaithful behavior was willful. Note that ignorance is nonetheless no excuse (v. 48). That there will be varying degrees of punishment in hell is clearly taught in Mt 10:15; 11:22, 24; Mk 6:11; Heb 10:29 (*see notes there*).

12:49 fire. I.e., judgment. *See note on Mt 3:11.* For the connection between fire and judgment, see Is 66:15; Joel 2:30; Am 1:7, 10–14; 2:2, 5; Mal 3:2, 5; 1Co 3:13; 2Th 1:7, 8.

12:50 a baptism. A baptism of suffering. Christ was referring to His death. Christian baptism symbolizes identification with Him in death, burial, and resurrection. **distressed.** *See note on Mt 26:38.* **until it is accomplished.** Though distressed about His coming passion, it was nonetheless the work He came to do, and He set His face steadfastly to accomplish it (*see note on 9:51;* cf. Jn 12:23–27).

12:51 I tell you, no. *See note on Mt 10:34.*

12:54–56 *See note on Mt 16:2, 3.*

12:58 on *your* way ... make an effort to settle. *See note on Mt 5:25.*

12:59 cent. *See notes on 21:2; Mk 12:42.*

13:1 Galileans whose blood Pilate had mixed with their sacrifices. This incident is in keeping with what was known about the character of Pilate. Evidently, some worshipers from Galilee were condemned by Rome—perhaps because they were seditious zealots (*see note on Mt 10:4*)—and were sought out and killed in the temple by Roman authorities while in the process of offering a sacrifice. Such a killing would have been the grossest sort of blasphemy. Incidents like this inflamed the Jews’ hatred of Rome and finally led to rebellion, and the destruction of Jerusalem in A.D. 70.

13:2 *greater* sinners. It was the belief of many that disaster and sudden death always signified divine displeasure over particular sins (cf. Job 4:7). Those who suffered in uncommon ways were therefore assumed to be guilty of some more severe immorality (cf. Jn 9:2).

13:3 unless you repent. Jesus did not deny the connection between catastrophe and human evil, for all such afflictions ultimately stem from the curse of humanity’s fallenness (Ge 3:17–19). Furthermore, specific calamities may indeed be the fruit of certain iniquities (Pr 24:16). But Christ challenged the people’s notion that they were morally superior to those who suffered in such catastrophes. He called all to repent, for all were in danger of sudden destruction. No one is guaranteed time to prepare for death, so now is the time for repentance for all (cf. 2 Cor. 6:2). **you will all likewise perish.** These words prophetically warned of the approaching judgment of Israel, which culminated in the catastrophic destruction of Jerusalem in A.D. 70. Thousands in Jerusalem were killed by the Romans. *See note on Mt 23:36.*

likewise perish. 4 Or do you suppose that those eighteen on whom the tower in [A]Siloam fell and killed
them were *worse* [a,B]culprits than all the men who
live in Jerusalem? 5 I tell you, no, but unless you
repent, you will all likewise perish."
6 And He *began* telling this parable: "A man had
[A]a fig tree which had been planted in his vineyard;
and he came looking for fruit on it and did not find
any. 7 And he said to the vineyard-keeper, 'Behold,
for three years I have come looking for fruit on
this fig tree [a]without finding any. [A]Cut it down!
Why does it even use up the ground?' 8 And he
answered and said to him, 'Let it alone, sir, for this
year too, until I dig around it and put in fertilizer;
9 and if it bears fruit next year, *fine;* but if not, cut
it down.' "

HEALING ON THE SABBATH

10 And He was [A]teaching in one of the synagogues
on the Sabbath. 11 And there was a woman who
for eighteen years had had [A]a sickness caused by
a spirit; and she was bent double, and could not
straighten up at all. 12 When Jesus saw her, He called
her over and said to her, "Woman, you are freed
from your sickness." 13 And He [A]laid His hands on
her; and immediately she was made erect again
and *began* [B]glorifying God. 14 But [A]the synagogue
official, indignant because Jesus [B]had healed on the
Sabbath, *began* saying to the crowd in response,
"[C]There are six days in which work should be done;
so come during them and get healed, and not on
the Sabbath day." 15 But [A]the Lord answered him
and said, "You hypocrites, [B]does not each of you
on the Sabbath untie his ox or his donkey from the
stall and lead him away to water *him?* 16 And this
woman, [A]a daughter of Abraham as she is, whom
[B]Satan has bound for eighteen long years, should
she not have been released from this bond on the
Sabbath day?" 17 As He said this, all His opponents
were being humiliated; and [A]the entire crowd was
rejoicing over all the glorious things being done
by Him.

PARABLES OF MUSTARD SEED AND LEAVEN

18 So [A]He was saying, "[B]What is the kingdom of
God like, and to what shall I compare it? 19 It is like
a mustard seed, which a man took and threw into
his own garden; and it grew and became a tree, and
[A]THE BIRDS OF THE [a]AIR NESTED IN ITS BRANCHES."
20 And again He said, "[A]To what shall I compare
the kingdom of God? 21 [A]It is like leaven, which a
woman took and hid in [B]three [a]pecks of flour until
it was all leavened."

TEACHING IN THE VILLAGES

22 And He was passing through from one city and
village to another, teaching, and [A]proceeding on
His way to Jerusalem. 23 And someone said to Him,
"Lord, are there *just* a few who are being saved?"

13:4 [a]Lit *debtors* [A]Neh 3:15; Is 8:6; John 9:7, 11 [B]Matt 6:12; Luke 11:4 13:6 [A]Matt 21:19 13:7 [a]Lit *and I do not find* [A]Matt 3:10; 7:19; Luke 3:9 13:10 [A]Matt 4:23 13:11 [A]Luke 13:16 13:13 [A]Mark 5:23 [B]Matt 9:8 13:14 [A]Mark 5:22 [B]Matt 12:2; Luke 14:3 [C]Ex 20:9; Deut 5:13 13:15 [A]Luke 7:13 [B]Luke 14:5 13:16 [A]Luke 19:9 [B]Matt 4:10; Luke 13:11 13:17 [A]Luke 18:43 13:18 [A]Luke 13:18, 19: *Matt 13:31, 32; Mark 4:30-32* [B]Matt 13:24; Luke 13:20 13:19 [a]Or *sky* [A]Ezek 17:23 13:20 [A]Matt 13:24; Luke 13:18 13:21 [a]Gr *sata* [A]Luke 13:20, 21: *Matt 13:33* [B]Matt 13:33 13:22 [A]Luke 9:51

13:4 Siloam. An area at the S end of the lower city of Jerusalem, where there was a well-known pool (cf. Jn 9:7, 11). Evidently, one of the towers guarding the aqueduct collapsed, perhaps while under construction, killing some people. Again, the question in the minds of people was regarding the connection between calamity and iniquity ("*worse* culprits"). Jesus responded by saying that such a calamity was not God's way to single out an especially evil group for death, but as a means of warning to all sinners. Calamitous judgment was eventually coming to all if they did not repent.

13:6 fig tree. Often used as a symbol for Israel (*see notes on Mt 21:19; Mk 11:14*). In this case, however, the parable's lesson about fruitlessness applies equally to the whole nation, and to each individual soul.

13:8 Let it alone ... this year. This illustrates both the intercession of Christ and the extreme patience and graciousness of the Father.

13:10 synagogues. *See note on Mk 1:21.* **the Sabbath.** The Pharisees' Sabbath traditions were the issue that most frequently provoked controversy in Jesus' ministry. Cf. 6:5–11; 14:1–5; Mt 12:2–10; Mk 2:23–3:4.

13:11 had a sickness caused by a spirit. This suggests that her physical ailment, which left her unable to stand erect, was caused by an evil spirit. However, Christ did not have to confront and drive out a demon, but simply declared her loosed (v. 12), so her case appears somewhat different from other cases of demonic possession He often encountered (cf. 11:14; *see note on v. 16*).

13:12 He called her over. The healing was unsolicited; He took the initiative (cf. 7:12–14). Furthermore, no special faith was required on her part or anyone else's. Jesus sometimes called for faith, but not always (cf. 8:48; Mk 5:34).

13:14 official. An eminent layman whose responsibilities included conducting meetings, caring for the building, and supervising the teaching in the synagogue (cf. 8:41; Mt 9:18; Mk 5:38).

13:15 untie his ox. Nothing in Scripture forbade either the watering of an ox or the healing of the sick (*see notes on 6:9; Mt 12:2, 3, 10*). Their Sabbath traditions actually placed a higher value on animals than on people in distress—and therefore corrupted the whole purpose of the Sabbath (Mk 2:27).

13:16 a daughter of Abraham. She was a Jewess. **whom Satan has bound.** Job's physical ailments and other disasters were also inflicted by Satan, with divine permission. This woman had apparently been permitted to suffer, not because of any evil she had done, but so that the glory of God might be manifest in her (cf. Jn 9:3).

13:19, 21 *See notes on Mt 13:32, 33.*

13:22 from one city and village to another. Luke's geographical points of reference are often vague; the readers he had in mind were probably largely unfamiliar with Palestinian geography anyway. Matthew 19:1; Mark 10:1; and John 10:40 all say that Christ moved His ministry to the region E of the Jordan, known as Perea. That move probably took place at about this point in Luke's narrative. Therefore the cities and villages He traveled through may have included places in both Judea and Perea. **proceeding ... to Jerusalem.** During His ministry in Judea to Perea, Christ actually went to Jerusalem on more than one occasion—at least once for the Feast of Tabernacles (Jn 7:11–8:59), another time for the Feast of Dedication (Jn 9:1–10:39), and another time when He raised Lazarus. Luke's focus was on Christ's constant progression toward His final trek to Jerusalem for the express purpose of dying there—and he therefore described all Christ's traveling as one long trek toward Jerusalem. *See notes on 9:51; 17:11.*

13:23 are there *just* a few who are being saved? That question may have been prompted by a number of factors. The great multitudes that had once followed Christ were subsiding to a faithful few (cf. Jn 6:66). Great crowds still came to hear (14:25), but committed followers were increasingly scarce. Moreover, Christ's messages often seemed designed to discourage the half-hearted (*see note on 14:33*). And He Himself had stated that the way is so narrow that few find it (Mt 7:14). This contradicted the Jewish belief that all Jews, except for tax collectors and other notorious sinners, would be saved. Christ's reply once again underscored the difficulty of entering at the narrow gate. After the resurrection, only 120 disciples gathered in the upper room in Jerusalem (Ac 1:15), and only about 500 in Galilee (1Co 15:6; *see notes on 24:34; Mt 28:16*).

And He said to them, 24 "[A]Strive to enter through the narrow door; for many, I tell you, will seek to enter and will not be able. 25 Once the head of the house gets up and [A]shuts the door, and you begin to stand outside and knock on the door, saying, '[B]Lord, open up to us!' then He will answer and say to you, '[C]I do not know where you are from.' 26 Then you will [A]begin to say, 'We ate and drank in Your presence, and You taught in our streets'; 27 and He will say, 'I tell you, [A]I do not know where you are from; [B]DEPART FROM ME, ALL YOU EVILDOERS.' 28 [A]In that place there will be weeping and gnashing of teeth when you see Abraham and Isaac and Jacob and all the prophets in the kingdom of God, but yourselves being thrown out. 29 And they [A]will come from east and west and from north and south, and will recline *at the table* in the kingdom of God. 30 And behold, [A]*some* are last who will be first and *some* are first who will be last."

31 Just at that time some Pharisees approached, saying to Him, "Go away, leave here, for [A]Herod wants to kill You." 32 And He said to them, "Go and tell that fox, 'Behold, I cast out demons and perform cures today and tomorrow, and the third *day* I [a,A]reach My goal.' 33 Nevertheless [A]I must journey on today and tomorrow and the next *day;* for it cannot be that a [B]prophet would perish outside of Jerusalem. 34 [A]O Jerusalem, Jerusalem, *the city* that kills the prophets and stones those sent to her! How often I wanted to gather your children together, [B]just as a hen *gathers* her brood under her wings, and you would not *have it!* 35 Behold, your house is left to you *desolate;* and I say to you, you will not see Me until *the time* comes when you say, '[A]BLESSED IS HE WHO COMES IN THE NAME OF THE LORD!' "

JESUS HEALS ON THE SABBATH

14 It happened that when He went into the house of one of the [a]leaders of the Pharisees on *the* Sabbath to eat bread, [A]they were watching Him closely. 2 And [a]there in front of Him was a man suffering from dropsy. 3 And Jesus answered and spoke to the [a,A]lawyers and Pharisees, saying, "[B]Is it lawful to heal on the Sabbath, or not?" 4 But they kept silent. And He took hold of him and healed him, and sent him away. 5 And He said to them, "[a,A]Which one of

13:24 [A]Matt 7:13 13:25 [A]Matt 25:10 [B]Matt 7:22; 25:11 [C]Matt 7:23; 25:12; Luke 13:27 13:26 [A]Luke 3:8 13:27 [A]Luke 13:25 [B]Ps 6:8; Matt 25:41 13:28 [A]Matt 8:12; 22:13; 25:30 13:29 [A]Matt 8:11 13:30 [A]Matt 19:30; 20:16; Mark 10:31 13:31 [A]Matt 14:1; Luke 3:1; 9:7; 23:7 13:32 [a]Or *am perfected* [A]Heb 2:10; 5:9; 7:28 13:33 [A]John 11:9 [B]Matt 21:11 13:34 [A]Luke 13:34, 35: *Matt 23:37-39;* Luke 19:41 [B]Matt 23:37 13:35 [A]Ps 118:26; Matt 21:9; Luke 19:38 14:1 [a]I.e. members of the Sanhedrin [A]Mark 3:2 14:2 [a]Lit *behold* 14:3 [a]I.e. experts in Mosaic Law [A]Matt 22:35 [B]Matt 12:2; Luke 13:14 14:5 [a]Lit *Whose son of you...will fall* [A]Matt 12:11; Luke 13:15

13:24 Strive. This signifies a great struggle against conflict. Christ was not suggesting that anyone could *merit* heaven by striving for it. No matter how rigorously they labored, sinners could never save themselves. Salvation is solely by grace, not by works (Eph 2:8, 9). But entering the narrow gate is nonetheless difficult because of its cost in terms of human pride, because of the sinner's natural love for sin, and because of the world's and Satan's opposition to the truth. *See notes on 16:16; Mt 11:12.* **many ... will seek to enter.** I.e., at the judgment, when many will protest that they deserve entrance into heaven (cf. Mt 7:21–23).

13:25 I do not know ... you. Cf. Mt 7:23; 25:12. Clearly, no relationship ever existed, though they had deluded themselves into thinking they knew the owner of the house (v. 26). Despite their protests, He repeated His denial emphatically in v. 27.

13:28 weeping and gnashing of teeth. *See note on Mt 22:13.*

13:29 they will come. By including people from the 4 corners of the earth, Jesus made it clear that even Gentiles would be invited to the heavenly banquet table. This was contrary to prevailing rabbinical thought, but perfectly consistent with the OT Scriptures (Ps 107:3; Is 66:18, 19; Mal 1:11). *See notes on 2:31; Mk 13:27.*

13:30 last ... first ... first ... last. *See note on Mt 20:16.* In this context the saying seems to contrast Jews ("the first") and Gentiles ("the last"). *See note on 14:11.*

13:31 leave here. Herod Antipas ruled Galilee and Perea (*see note on Mt 2:22*). Christ was probably either approaching Perea or ministering there already (*see note on v. 22*). The Pharisees—no friends of Herod themselves—may have warned Christ because they hoped the threat of violence from Herod would either silence Him—or drive Him back to Judea, where the Sanhedrin would have jurisdiction over Him.

13:32 that fox. Some have suggested that Jesus' use of this expression is hard to reconcile with Ex 22:28; Ecc 10:20; and Ac 23:5. However, those verses apply to everyday discourse. Prophets, speaking as mouthpieces of God, and with divine authority, were often commissioned to rebuke leaders publicly (cf. Is 1:23; Eze 22:27; Hos 7:3–7; Zep 3:3). Since Jesus spoke with perfect divine authority, He had every right to speak of Herod in such terms. Rabbinical writings often used "the fox" to signify someone who was both crafty and worthless. The Pharisees, who trembled at Herod's power, must have been astonished at Christ's boldness. **today and tomorrow, and the third *day*.** This expression signified only that Christ was on His own divine timetable; it was not meant to lay out a literal 3-day schedule. Expressions like this were common in Semitic usage, and seldom were employed in a literal sense to specify precise intervals of time. *See note on Mt 12:40.* **reach My goal.** I.e., by death, in the finishing of His work. Cf. Jn 17:4, 5; 19:30; Heb 2:10. Herod was threatening to kill Him, but no one could kill Christ before His time (Jn 10:17, 18).

13:33 it cannot be. Not all prophets who were martyred died in Jerusalem, of course. John the Baptist, for example, was beheaded by Herod, probably at Herod's palace in Machaerus. This saying was probably a familiar proverb, like the adage in 4:24; Mt 13:57. The statement is full of irony, noting that most of the OT prophets were martyred at the hands of the Jewish people, not by foreign enemies. Luke's inclusion of this saying underscores his theme in this section of his gospel—Jesus' relentless journey to Jerusalem for the purpose of dying (*see note on 9:51*).

13:34 O Jerusalem, Jerusalem. There is great tenderness in these words, as seen in the imagery of a hen with chickens. This outpouring of divine compassion foreshadows His weeping over the city as He approached it for the final time (19:41). Clearly, these are deep and sincere emotions (*see note on Mt 9:36*). **I wanted ... you would not.** Lit. "I willed, but you willed not." Christ's repeated expressions of grief over the plight of Jerusalem do not diminish the reality of His absolute sovereignty over all that happens. Nor should the truth of divine sovereignty be used to depreciate the sincerity of His compassion. *See note on Mt 23:37.*

13:35 This account of Luke's clearly falls at an earlier point in Christ's ministry than the parallel account in Mt 23:37–39, which took place in the temple during Christ's final days in Jerusalem. The wording of the two laments is nonetheless virtually identical. Here Christ delivers prophetically the same message He would later pronounce as a final judgment. Blessed. Quotation from Ps 118:26.

14:1 Sabbath. *See note on 13:10.* Luke shows Christ healing on the Sabbath more frequently than any of the other Gospels. Christ seems to have favored the Sabbath as a day for doing acts of mercy. **watching Him closely.** Evidently, the Pharisee had less than honorable motives for inviting Him to a meal.

14:2 dropsy. A condition where fluid is retained in the tissues and cavities of the body—often caused by kidney or liver ailments, including cancer.

14:3 lawyers. I.e., scribes. *See note on 10:25.* **Is it lawful.** He had repeatedly defended Sabbath healings, and His arguments consistently silenced the nay-sayers (cf. 6:9, 10; 13:14–17). Here and in 6:9, He questioned the scribes about the legality of healing on the Sabbath beforehand—and still they could give no cogent reasons why they believed healing was a violation of Sabbath laws (cf. v. 6).

14:5 an ox. Cf. 13:15; Mt 12:11, 12. Common humanitarianism (not to mention economic necessity) taught them that it was right

you will have a son or an ox fall into a well, and will
not immediately pull him out on a Sabbath day?"
6 [A]And they could make no reply to this.

PARABLE OF THE GUESTS

7 And He *began* speaking a parable to the invited
guests when He noticed how [A]they had been picking
out the places of honor *at the table,* saying to them,
8 "When you are invited by someone to a wedding
feast, [A]do not [a]take the place of honor, for someone
more distinguished than you may have been invited
by him, 9 and he who invited you both will come
and say to you, 'Give *your* place to this man,' and
then [A]in disgrace you [a]proceed to occupy the last
place. 10 But when you are invited, go and recline at
the last place, so that when the one who has invited
you comes, he may say to you, 'Friend, [A]move up
higher'; then you will have honor in the sight of
all who [a]are at the table with you. 11 [A]For everyone
who exalts himself will be humbled, and he who
humbles himself will be exalted."
12 And He also went on to say to the one who
had invited Him, "When you give a luncheon or a
dinner, do not invite your friends or your brothers
or your relatives or rich neighbors, otherwise they
may also invite you in return and *that* will be your
repayment. 13 But when you give a [a]reception, invite
the poor, *the* crippled, *the* lame, *the* blind, 14 and you
will be blessed, since they [a]do not have *the means*
to repay you; for you will be repaid at [A]the resurrection of the righteous."
15 When one of those who were reclining *at the table* with Him heard this, he said to Him, "[A]Blessed is
everyone who will eat bread in the kingdom of God!"

PARABLE OF THE DINNER

16 But He said to him, "[A]A man was giving a big
dinner, and he invited many; 17 and at the dinner hour
he sent his slave to say to those who had been invited,
'Come; for everything is ready now.' 18 But they all alike
began to make excuses. The first one said to him, 'I
have bought a [a]piece of land and I need to go out and
look at it; [b]please consider me excused.' 19 Another one
said, 'I have bought five yoke of oxen, and I am going to
try them out; [a]please consider me excused.' 20 Another
one said, '[A]I have married a wife, and for that reason I
cannot come.' 21 And the slave came *back* and reported
this to his master. Then the head of the household
became angry and said to his slave, 'Go out at once
into the streets and lanes of the city and bring in here
the poor and crippled and blind and lame.' 22 And the
slave said, 'Master, what you commanded has been
done, and still there is room.' 23 And the master said
to the slave, 'Go out into the highways and along the
hedges, and compel *them* to come in, so that my house
may be filled. 24 For I tell you, none of those men who
were invited shall taste of my dinner.' "

DISCIPLESHIP TESTED

25 Now [a]large crowds were going along with
Him; and He turned and said to them, 26 "[A]If anyone comes to Me, and does not [a]hate his own father

14:6 [A]Matt 22:46; Luke 20:40 14:7 [A]Matt 23:6 14:8 [a]Lit *recline at* [A]Prov 25:6, 7 14:9 [a]Lit *begin* [A]Luke 3:8 14:10 [a]Lit *recline* at the table [A]Prov 25:6, 7 14:11 [A]2 Sam 22:28; Prov 29:23; Matt 23:12; Luke 1:52; 18:14; James 4:10 14:13 [a]Or *banquet* 14:14 [a]Or *are unable to* [A]John 5:29; Acts 24:15; Rev 20:4, 5 14:15 [A]Rev 19:9 14:16 [A]Luke 14:16-24: *Matt 22:2-14* 14:18 [a]Or *field* [b]Lit *I request you* 14:19 [a]Lit *I request you* 14:20 [A]Deut 24:5; 1 Cor 7:33 14:25 [a]Lit *many* 14:26 [a]I.e. by comparison of his love for Me [A]Matt 10:37

to show mercy to animals on the Sabbath. Should not the same principles be applied in showing mercy to suffering people?

14:7 places of honor. I.e., the best seats at the table. Cf. 11:43; Mt 23:6.

14:11 who exalts himself will be humbled. Jesus favored this sort of paradoxical play on words (cf. 9:24; 13:30; 17:33; 18:14; Mt 23:11, 12). This comment made the point of vv. 8–10 clear. The point of this whole lesson closely parallels Pr 25:6, 7.

14:12 do not invite your friends or your brothers. Clearly, this is not to be taken as an absolute prohibition against inviting friends or relatives to a meal. Christ employed similar hyperbole in v. 26. Such language is common in Semitic discourse and is used for emphasis. His point here is that inviting one's friends and relatives cannot be classified as a spiritual act of true charity. It may also be a rebuke against those prone to reserve their hospitality for "rich neighbors" who they know will feel obligated to return the favor. Cf. Dt 14:28, 29.

14:14 repaid at the resurrection. I.e., with treasure in heaven (cf. 18:22).

14:15 everyone who will eat bread in the kingdom. The man probably held the common view that only Jews would be invited to the heavenly feast (*see note on Mt 8:12*). Perhaps this was an idle or pious saying, made without much serious reflection. Christ replied with a parable that pictures the inclusion of Gentiles.

14:16 a big dinner. This parable, similar in many ways to the one in Mt 22:2–14, and making the same point, is nonetheless distinct. That parable was told on a different occasion, and some key details differ. **invited many.** Apparently, no one declined the invitation. The man evidently had every reason to expect that all who were invited would attend.

14:17 those who had been invited. Guests for a wedding, which could last a full week, were preinvited and given a general idea of the time. When all the many preparations were finally ready, the preinvited guests were notified that the event would commence. The preinvited guests refer to the people of Israel, who by the OT had been told to be ready for the arrival of the Messiah.

14:18 excuses. All the excuses smack of insincerity. One does not purchase property without seeing it first. And since the purchase was already complete, there was no urgency. The land would still be there after the banquet. Likewise (v. 19), one does not purchase oxen without first testing them. The man who had recently married (v. 20) was excused from business travel, or serving in the military (Dt 24:5), but there was no legitimate reason for newlyweds to avoid such a social engagement.

14:21 the poor and crippled and blind and lame. I.e., people the Pharisees tended to regard as unclean or unworthy. The religious leaders condemned Jesus for His associations with prostitutes and tax collectors (cf. 5:29, 30; 15:1; Mt 9:10, 11; 11:19; 21:31, 32; Mk 2:15, 16).

14:22 still there is room. God is more willing to save sinners than sinners are to be saved.

14:23 into the highways and along the hedges. This evidently represents the Gentile regions. **compel *them* to come in.** I.e., not by force or violence, but by earnest persuasion.

14:24 none of those men who were invited. I.e., those who refused. Having spurned the invitation, Israel was shut out of the banquet. The master's judgment against them was to seal their own decision. Most of them were killed by divine judgment at the hands of the Romans in A.D. 70. *See notes on Mt 22:7; 23:36; 24:2.*

14:25 large crowds. Christ's aim was not to gather appreciative crowds, but to make true disciples (*see note on 13:23*). He never adapted His message to majority preferences, but always plainly declared the high cost of discipleship. Here He made several bold demands that would discourage the halfhearted.

14:26 hate. A similar statement in Mt 10:37 is the key to understanding this difficult command. The "hatred" called for here is actually a lesser love. Jesus was calling His disciples to cultivate such a devotion to Him that their attachment to everything else—including their own lives—would seem like hatred by comparison. See 16:13; Ge 29:30, 31 for similar usages of the word "hate."

and mother and wife and children and brothers and sisters, yes, and even his own life, he cannot be My disciple. 27 Whoever does not [A]carry his own cross and come after Me cannot be My disciple. 28 For which one of you, when he wants to build a tower, does not first sit down and calculate the cost to see if he has enough to complete it? 29 Otherwise, when he has laid a foundation and is not able to finish, all who observe it begin to ridicule him, 30 saying, 'This man began to build and was not able to finish.' 31 Or what king, when he sets out to meet another king in battle, will not first sit down and [A]consider whether he is strong enough with ten thousand *men* to encounter the one coming against him with twenty thousand? 32 Or else, while the other is still far away, he sends [a]a delegation and asks for terms of peace. 33 So then, none of you can be My disciple who [A]does not give up all his own possessions.

34 "Therefore, salt is good; but [A]if even salt has become tasteless, with what will it be seasoned? 35 It is useless either for the soil or for the manure pile; it is thrown out. [A]He who has ears to hear, [a]let him hear."

THE LOST SHEEP

15 Now all the [A]tax collectors and the [a]sinners were coming near Him to listen to Him. 2 Both the Pharisees and the scribes *began* to grumble, saying, "This man receives sinners and [A]eats with them."

3 So He told them this parable, saying, 4 "[A]What man among you, if he has a hundred sheep and has lost one of them, does not leave the ninety-nine in the [a]open pasture and go after the one which is lost until he finds it? 5 When he has found it, he lays it on his shoulders, rejoicing. 6 And when he comes home, he calls together his friends and his neighbors, saying to them, 'Rejoice with me, for I have found my sheep which was lost!' 7 I tell you that in the same way, there will be *more* joy in heaven over one sinner who repents than over ninety-nine righteous persons who need no repentance.

THE LOST COIN

8 "Or what woman, if she has ten [a]silver coins and loses one coin, does not light a lamp and sweep the house and search carefully until she finds it? 9 When she has found it, she calls together her friends and neighbors, saying, 'Rejoice with me, for I have found the coin which I had lost!' 10 In the same way, I tell you, there is joy [A]in the presence of the angels of God over one sinner who repents."

THE PRODIGAL SON

11 And He said, "A man had two sons. 12 The younger of them said to his father, 'Father, give me [A]the share of the estate that falls to me.' So he divided his [a,B]wealth between them. 13 And not many days later, the younger son gathered everything together and went on a journey into a distant country, and there he squandered his estate with loose living. 14 Now when he had spent everything, a severe famine occurred in that country, and he began to be

14:27 [A]Matt 10:38; 16:24; Mark 8:34; Luke 9:23 14:31 [A]Prov 20:18 14:32 [a]Or *an embassy* 14:33 [A]Phil 3:7; Heb 11:26 14:34 [A]Matt 5:13; Mark 9:50 14:35 [a]Or *hear!* Or *listen!* [A]Matt 11:15 15:1 [a]I.e. irreligious Jews [A]Luke 5:29 15:2 [A]Matt 9:11 15:4 [a]Lit *wilderness* [A]Luke 15:4-7: *Matt 18:12-14* 15:8 [a]Gr *drachmas*, one drachma was a day's wages 15:10 [A]Matt 10:32; Luke 15:7 15:12 [a]Lit *living* [A]Deut 21:17 [B]Mark 12:44; Luke 15:30

14:27 carry his own cross. I.e., willingly. This parallels the idea of hating one's own life in v. 26. *See notes on 9:23; Mt 10:38*; cf. Mk 8:34.

14:28 calculate the cost. The multitudes were positive but uncommitted. Far from making it easy for them to respond positively, He set the cost of discipleship as high as possible (vv. 26, 27, 33)—and encouraged them to do a careful inventory before declaring their willingness to follow. Cf. 9:57–62.

14:33 give up all. Only those willing to carefully assess the cost (vv. 28–32) and invest all they had in His kingdom were worthy to enter. This speaks of something far more than mere abandonment of one's material possessions; it is an absolute, unconditional surrender. His disciples were permitted to retain no privileges and make no demands. They were to safeguard no cherished sins; treasure no earthly possessions; and cling to no secret self-indulgences. Their commitment to Him must be without reservation. *See notes on 9:23–26.*

14:34 salt is good. *See notes on Mt 5:13; Mk 9:50.* Christ employed this same imagery on at least 3 different occasions in His ministry.

15:1 the tax collectors and the sinners. *See notes on 14:21; Mt 5:46; 21:32.* Despite the difficulties of Christ's message (14:25–35), the outcasts of society were drawn to Him, while the religious leaders grew more and more determined to kill Him. Cf. 1Co 1:26–29.

15:2 *began* to grumble. Lit. "murmured greatly"—i.e., through the crowds. Their grumbling prompted 3 parables designed to illustrate the joy of God over the repentance of sinners. **This man receives sinners.** This phrase is the key to the trilogy of parables that follow. Christ was not ashamed to be known as a "friend of tax collectors and sinners" (7:34).

15:4 go after the one which is lost. The first two parables both picture God as taking the initiative in seeking sinners. The rabbis taught that God would receive sinners who sought His forgiveness earnestly enough, but here God is the One seeking the sinner (*see note on 19:10*). The shepherd in the Middle East was responsible for every sheep. He was obligated to his master to see that none was lost, killed, or injured (cf. Mt 18:11–14).

15:5 lays it on his shoulders. The picture of a loving shepherd. Cf. Jn 10:11; Ps 24:1. **rejoicing.** Joy over the return of the lost is the most prominent feature in all 3 parables (vv. 7, 10, 32).

15:7 joy in heaven. A reference to the joy of God Himself. There was complaining on earth, among the Pharisees (v. 2); but there was great joy with God and among the angels (v. 10). **persons who need no repentance.** I.e., those who think themselves righteous (cf. 5:32; 16:15; 18:9).

15:8 silver coins. The drachma was a Greek coin roughly equivalent in value to the Roman denarius (*see note on Mt 22:19*). **light a lamp.** The typical one-room house had no windows. **sweep the house.** This illustrates the thoroughness of the search.

15:11, 12 The parable of the prodigal son is the most familiar and beloved of all Christ's parables. It is one of the longest and most detailed parables. And unlike most parables, it has more than one lesson. The prodigal is an example of sound repentance. The elder brother illustrates the wickedness of the Pharisees' self-righteousness, prejudice, and indifference toward repenting sinners. And the father pictures God, eager to forgive, and longing for the return of the sinner. The main feature, however, as in the other two parables in this chapter, is the joy of God, the celebrations that fill heaven when a sinner repents.

15:12 give me the share of the estate that falls to me. A shocking request, tantamount to saying he wished his father were dead. He was not entitled to any inheritance while his father still lived. Yet the father graciously fulfilled the request, giving him his full share, which would have been one-third of the entire estate—because the right of the firstborn (Dt 21:17) gave the elder brother a double portion. This act pictures all sinners (related to God the Father by creation) who waste their potential privileges and refuse any relationship with Him, choosing instead a life of sinful self-indulgence.

15:13 gathered everything together. The prodigal son evidently took his share in liquid assets, and left, abandoning his father, and heading into a life of iniquity. **loose living.** Not merely wasteful extravagance, but also wanton immorality (v. 30). The Gr. word for "loose" means "dissolute," or "wasteful," and conveys the idea of an utterly debauched lifestyle.

impoverished. 15 So he went and [a]hired himself out
to one of the citizens of that country, and he sent him
into his fields to feed swine. 16 And he would have
gladly filled his stomach with the [a]pods that the
swine were eating, and no one was giving *anything*
to him. 17 But when he came to [a]his senses, he said,
'How many of my father's hired men have more than
enough bread, but I am dying here with hunger! 18 I
will get up and go to my father, and will say to him,
"Father, I have sinned against heaven, and [a]in your
sight; 19 I am no longer worthy to be called your son;
make me as one of your hired men." ' 20 So he got up
and came to [a]his father. But while he was still a long
way off, his father saw him and felt compassion *for*
him, and ran and [b,A]embraced him and kissed him.
21 And the son said to him, 'Father, I have sinned
against heaven and in your sight; I am no longer
worthy to be called your son.' 22 But the father said
to his slaves, 'Quickly bring out [A]the best robe and
put it on him, and [B]put a ring on his hand and sandals on his feet; 23 and bring the fattened calf, kill it,
and let us eat and celebrate; 24 for this son of mine
was [A]dead and has come to life again; he was lost
and has been found.' And they began to celebrate.
25 "Now his older son was in the field, and when
he came and approached the house, he heard music
and dancing. 26 And he summoned one of the servants and *began* inquiring what these things could
be. 27 And he said to him, 'Your brother has come,
and your father has killed the fattened calf because
he has received him back safe and sound.' 28 But he
became angry and was not willing to go in; and
his father came out and *began* pleading with him.
29 But he answered and said to his father, 'Look! For
so many years I have been serving you and I have
never [a]neglected a command of yours; and *yet* you
have never given me a young goat, so that I might
celebrate with my friends; 30 but when this son of
yours came, who has devoured your [a,A]wealth with
prostitutes, you killed the fattened calf for him.'
31 And he said to him, 'Son, you [a]have always been
with me, and all that is mine is yours. 32 But we had
to celebrate and rejoice, for this brother of yours
was [A]dead and *has begun* to live, and *was* lost and
has been found.' "

THE UNRIGHTEOUS STEWARD

16 Now He was also saying to the disciples,
"There was a rich man who had a manager,
and this *manager* was [a]reported to him as [A]squan-
dering his possessions. 2 And he called him and
said to him, 'What is this I hear about you? Give an

15:15 [a]Lit *was joined to* 15:16 [a]I.e. of the carob tree 15:17 [a]Lit *himself* 15:18 [a]Lit *before you* 15:20 [a]Lit *his own* [b]Lit *fell on his neck* [A]Gen 45:14; 46:29; Acts 20:37 15:22 [A]Zech 3:4; Rev 6:11 [B]Gen 41:42 15:24 [A]Matt 8:22; Luke 9:60; 15:32; Rom 11:15; Eph 2:1, 5; 5:14; Col 2:13; 1 Tim 5:6 15:29 [a]Or *disobeyed* 15:30 [a]Lit *living* [A]Prov 29:3; Luke 15:12 15:31 [a]Lit *are always with me* 15:32 [A]Luke 15:24 16:1 [a]Or *accused* [A]Luke 15:13

15:15 to feed swine. This was the worst sort of degradation imaginable for Jesus' Jewish audience; swine were the worst sort of unclean animals.

15:16 would have gladly filled his stomach with the pods. I.e., carob pods, used to feed swine but virtually undigestible for humans. In other words, the only reason he did not eat the same food as the swine is that he could not. **no one was giving *anything* to him.** He could not even eke out a living by begging. His situation could hardly have been more desperate. Thus he symbolizes the estranged sinner who is helpless in despair.

15:17 came to his senses. When his incessant sinning had left him utterly bankrupt and hungry, he was able to think more clearly. In that condition, he was a candidate for salvation (*see notes on Mt 5:3–6*).

15:18 will say to him. He carefully contemplated what he would say and counted the cost of his repentance (v. 19). **sinned against heaven.** A euphemism, meaning he had sinned against God. He not only realized the futility of his situation, but he also understood the gravity of his transgressions against the father.

15:20 his father saw him. Clearly, the father had been waiting and looking for his son's return. **ran.** The father's eagerness and joy at his son's return is unmistakable. This is the magnificent attribute of God that sets Him apart from all the false gods invented by men and demons. He is not indifferent or hostile, but a Savior by nature, longing to see sinners repent and rejoicing when they do. *See notes on 1Ti 2:4; 4:10.* From Ge 3:8 to Rev 22:17, from the fall to the consummation, God has been and will be seeking to save sinners, and rejoicing each time one repents and is converted.

15:21 Note that the son did not get to finish his rehearsed words of repentance before the father interrupted to grant forgiveness. This pictures God's eagerness to forgive.

15:22 the father said. Without a single word of rebuke for the past, the father pours out his love for the son, and expresses his joy that what was lost had been found. Each of the father's gifts said something unique about his acceptance of the son: **robe.** Reserved for the guest of honor. **ring.** A symbol of authority. **sandals.** These were not usually worn by slaves, and therefore signified his full restoration to sonship.

15:23 the fattened calf. Reserved only for the most special of occasions—a sacrifice or a feast of great celebration. All this (vv. 22, 23) symbolizes the lavishness of salvation's blessings (cf. Eph 1:3; 2:4–7).

15:25 older son. He symbolizes the Pharisee, the hypocritical religious person, who stays close to the place of the Father (the temple) but has no sense of sin, no real love for the Father (so as to share in His joy), and no interest in repenting sinners.

15:28 he became angry. This parallels the complaining done by the scribes and Pharisees (v. 2).

15:29 I have never neglected a command of yours. Unlikely, given the boy's obvious contempt for his father, shown by his refusal to participate in the father's great joy. This statement reveals the telltale problem with all religious hypocrites. They will not recognize their sin and repent (*see notes on Mt 9:12, 13; 19:16–20*). The elder son's comment reeks of the same spirit as the words of the Pharisee in 18:11. **you have never given me a young goat.** All those years of service to the father appear to have been motivated too much by concern for what he could get for himself. This son's self-righteous behavior was more socially acceptable than the younger brother's debauchery, but it was equally dishonoring to the father—and called for repentance.

15:30 this son of yours. An expression of deep contempt (cf. "this tax collector" in 18:11). He could not bring himself to refer to him as "my brother."

15:31 all that is mine is yours. The inheritance had already been distributed (v. 12). Everything the father had was literally in the elder son's possession. Yet the elder son was begrudging even the love the father showed to the prodigal son. The Pharisees and scribes had easy access to all the riches of God's truth. They spent their lives dealing with Scripture and public worship—but they never really possessed any of the treasures enjoyed by the repentant sinner.

15:32 we had to celebrate and rejoice. This summarizes the point of all 3 parables. **brother of yours.** *See note on v. 30.*

16:1 manager. A manager was a trusted servant, usually someone born in the household, who was chief of the management and distribution of household provisions. He provided food for all the other servants, thus managing his master's resources for the well-being of others. He acted as an agent for his master, with full authority to transact business in the master's name. **squandering his possessions.** His prodigality is a thread that ties this parable to the preceding one. Like the younger son in the earlier parable, this manager was guilty of wasting the resources available to him. Unlike the prodigal, however, he had enough sense to make sure that his wastefulness did not leave him friendless and unprovided for in the future.

16:2 you can no longer be manager. By announcing his intention to fire the man, the owner acted unwisely, and it cost him even

accounting of your management, for you can no longer be manager.' 3 The manager said to himself, 'What shall I do, since my [a]master is taking the management away from me? I am not strong enough to dig; I am ashamed to beg. 4 I know what I shall do, so that when I am removed from the management people will welcome me into their homes.' 5 And he summoned each one of his [a]master's debtors, and he *began* saying to the first, 'How much do you owe my master?' 6 And he said, 'A hundred [a]measures of oil.' And he said to him, 'Take your bill, and sit down quickly and write fifty.' 7 Then he said to another, 'And how much do you owe?' And he said, 'A hundred [a]measures of wheat.' He *said to him, 'Take your bill, and write eighty.' 8 And his [a]master praised the unrighteous manager because he had acted shrewdly; for the sons of [A]this age are more shrewd in relation to their own [b]kind than the [B]sons of light. 9 And I say to you, [A]make friends for yourselves by means of the [a,B]wealth of unrighteousness, so that when it fails, [C]they will receive you into the eternal dwellings.

10 "[A]He who is faithful in a very little thing is faithful also in much; and he who is unrighteous in a very little thing is unrighteous also in much. 11 Therefore if you have not been faithful in the *use of* unrighteous [a,A]wealth, who will entrust the true *riches* to you? 12 And if you have not been faithful in *the use of* that which is another's, who will give you that which is your own? 13 [A]No [a]servant can serve two masters; for either he will hate the one and love the other, or else he will be devoted to one and despise the other. You cannot serve God and [b,B]wealth."

14 Now the Pharisees, who were [A]lovers of money, were listening to all these things and [B]were scoffing at Him. 15 And He said to them, "You are those who [A]justify yourselves [a]in the sight of men, but [B]God knows your hearts; for that which is highly esteemed among men is detestable [a]in the sight of God.

16 "[A]The Law and the Prophets *were proclaimed* until John; since that time [B]the gospel of the kingdom of God [a]has been preached, and everyone is forcing his way into it. 17 [A]But it is easier for heaven and earth to pass away than for one [a]stroke of a letter of the Law to fail.

18 "[A]Everyone who [a]divorces his wife and marries another commits adultery, and he who marries one who is [b]divorced from a husband commits adultery.

16:3 [a]Or *lord* 16:5 [a]Or *lord's* 16:6 [a]Gr *baths,* a Heb unit of measure equaling about 7 1/2 gal. 16:7 [a]Gr *kors,* one kor equals between 10 and 12 bu 16:8 [a]Or *lord* [b]Lit *generation* [A]Matt 12:32; Luke 20:34 [B]John 12:36; Eph 5:8; 1 Thess 5:5 16:9 [a]Gr *mamonas,* for Aram *mamon* (mammon); i.e. wealth, etc., personified as an object of worship [A]Matt 19:21; Luke 11:41; 12:33 [B]Matt 6:24; Luke 16:11, 13 [C]Luke 16:4 16:10 [A]Matt 25:21, 23 16:11 [a]Gr *mamonas,* for Aram *mamon* (mammon); i.e. wealth, etc., personified as an object of worship [A]Luke 16:9 16:13 [a]Or *house-servant* [b]Gr *mamonas,* for Aram *mamon* (mammon); i.e. wealth, etc., personified as an object of worship [A]Matt 6:24 [B]Luke 16:9 16:14 [A]2 Tim 3:2 [B]Luke 23:35 16:15 [a]Lit *before* [A]Luke 10:29; 18:9, 14 [B]1 Sam 16:7; Prov 21:2; Acts 1:24; Rom 8:27 16:16 [a]Lit *is preached* [A]Matt 11:12f [B]Matt 4:23 16:17 [a]I.e. projection of a letter (serif) [A]Matt 5:18 16:18 [a]Or *sends away* [b]Or *sent away* [A]Matt 5:32; 1 Cor 7:10, 11

more. Evidently, he thought the man guilty of incompetence, rather than fraud. That would explain his reaction in v. 8.

16:3 not strong enough to dig. I.e., he did not consider himself fit for physical labor.

16:4 know what I shall do. Cleverly, he arranged to give large discounts to his master's debtors, which they would eagerly agree to pay. **welcome me into their homes.** By reducing their debts to his master, he gained their indebtedness to him. They would thus be obligated to take him into their homes when he was put out of his master's home.

16:6 quickly. This was a secret transaction, unauthorized by the master. The borrower was guilty of deliberate complicity in the man's fraud.

16:8 his master praised the unrighteous manager. Outwitted, he applauded the man's cunning. His admiration for the evil steward's criminal genius shows that he, too, was a wicked man. It is the natural tendency of fallen hearts to admire a villain's craftiness (Ps 49:18). Note that all the characters in this parable are unjust, unscrupulous, and corrupt. **more shrewd.** I.e., most unbelievers are wiser in the ways of the world than some believers ("sons of light," cf. Jn 12:36; Eph 5:18) are toward the things of God.

16:9 wealth of unrighteousness. I.e., money. The unrighteous manager used his master's money to buy earthly friends; believers are to use their Master's money in a way that will accrue friends for eternity—by investing in the kingdom gospel that brings sinners to salvation, so that when they arrive in heaven ("eternal dwellings"), those sinners will be there to welcome them. Christ did not commend the man's dishonesty; He pointedly called him "unrighteous" (v. 8). He only used him as an illustration to show that even the most wicked sons of this world are shrewd enough to provide for themselves against coming evil. Believers ought to be more shrewd, because they are concerned with eternal matters, not just earthly ones. Cf. 12:33; Mt 6:19–21.

16:10 He who is faithful. Probably a common proverb. Cf. 19:17; Mt 25:21.

16:11 true *riches*. Faithful use of one's earthly wealth is repeatedly tied to the accumulation of treasure in heaven (cf. 12:33; 18:22; Mt 6:19–21).

16:12 that which is another's. This refers to God, and the believer's stewardship of His money, which believers only manage as stewards.

16:13 You cannot serve God and wealth. Many of the Pharisees taught that devotion to money and devotion to God were perfectly compatible (v. 14). This went hand-in-hand with the commonly held notion that earthly riches signified divine blessing. Rich people were therefore regarded as God's favorites (*see note on Mt 19:24*). While not condemning wealth per se, Christ denounced both love of wealth and devotion to mammon. On the love of money, *see notes on 1Ti 6:9, 10, 17–19*.

16:15 justify yourselves. The Pharisees' belief was that their own goodness was what justified them (cf. Ro 10:3). This is the very definition of "self-righteousness." But, as Jesus suggested, their righteousness was flawed, being an external veneer only. That might be enough to justify them before men, but not before God, because He knew their hearts. He repeatedly exposed their habit of seeking the approval of people (cf. Mt 6:2, 5, 16; 23:28).

16:16 until John. John the Baptist's ministry marked the turning point of redemptive history. Prior to that, the great truths of Christ and His kingdom were veiled in the types and shadows of the law, and promised in the writings of the prophets (cf. 1Pe 1:10–12). But John the Baptist introduced the King Himself (*see note on Mt 11:11*). The Pharisees, who thought of themselves as experts in the Law and the Prophets, missed the significance of the very One to whom the Law and the Prophets pointed. **everyone is forcing his way into it.** Cf. Jer 29:13. While the Pharisees were busy opposing Christ, sinners were entering His kingdom in droves. The language of this expression speaks of violent force—probably signifying the zeal with which sinners were seeking with all of their heart to enter the kingdom (*see notes on 13:24; Is 55:6, 7; Mt 11:12*).

16:17 than for one stroke of a letter of the Law to fail. Lest anyone think the statement in v. 16 meant He was declaring the law and the prophets annulled, He added this (*see note on Mt 5:18*). The great moral principles of the law, the eternal truths contained in the law's types and symbols, and the promises recorded by the prophets all remain in force and are not abrogated by the kingdom message.

16:18 commits adultery. I.e., if the divorce had no legitimate grounds. Luke gave an abbreviated record of Jesus' teaching on divorce, stressing only the main issue. Matthew's fuller account makes it clear that He permitted divorce in cases where one's spouse was guilty of adultery. *See notes on Mt 5:31, 32; 19:3–9.* This countered the rabbis' doctrine, which permitted men to divorce their wives easily, and for almost any cause (Mt 19:3).

THE RICH MAN AND LAZARUS

19 "Now there was a rich man, and he habitually
dressed in purple and fine linen, joyously living in
splendor every day. 20 And a poor man named Lazarus [A]was laid at his gate, covered with sores, 21 and
longing to be fed with the *crumbs* which were falling
from the rich man's table; besides, even the dogs
were coming and licking his sores. 22 Now the poor
man died and was carried away by the angels to
[A]Abraham's bosom; and the rich man also died and
was buried. 23 In [A]Hades he lifted up his eyes, being
in torment, and *saw Abraham far away and Lazarus
in his bosom. 24 And he cried out and said, '[A]Father
Abraham, have mercy on me, and send Lazarus so
that he may dip the tip of his finger in water and
cool off my tongue, for I am in agony in [B]this flame.'
25 But Abraham said, 'Child, remember that [A]during
your life you received your good things, and likewise
Lazarus bad things; but now he is being comforted
here, and you are in agony. 26 And [a]besides all this,
between us and you there is a great chasm fixed, so
that those who wish to come over from here to you
will not be able, and *that* none may cross over from
there to us.' 27 And he said, 'Then I beg you, father,
that you send him to my father's house— 28 for I have
five brothers—in order that he may [A]warn them, so
that they will not also come to this place of torment.'
29 But Abraham *said, 'They have [A]Moses and the
Prophets; let them hear them.' 30 But he said, 'No, [A]fa-
ther Abraham, but if someone goes to them from the
dead, they will repent!' 31 But he said to him, 'If they
do not listen to Moses and the Prophets, they will not
be persuaded even if someone rises from the dead.' "

INSTRUCTIONS

17 He said to His disciples, "[A]It is inevitable
that [a]stumbling blocks come, but woe to him
through whom they come! 2 [A]It [a]would be better for
him if a millstone were hung around his neck and
he were thrown into the sea, than that he would
cause one of these little ones to stumble. 3 [a]Be on
your guard! [A]If your brother sins, rebuke him; and
if he repents, forgive him. 4 And if he sins against
you [A]seven times a day, and returns to you seven
times, saying, 'I repent,' [a]forgive him."
5 [A]The apostles said to [B]the Lord, "Increase our
faith!" 6 And [A]the Lord said, "If you [a]had faith like
[B]a mustard seed, you would say to this [C]mulberry
tree, 'Be uprooted and be planted in the sea'; and
it would [b]obey you.
7 "Which of you, having a slave plowing or tending
sheep, will say to him when he has come in from the
field, 'Come immediately and [a]sit down to eat'? 8 But
will he not say to him, '[A]Prepare something for me
to eat, and *properly* [a]clothe yourself and serve me
while I eat and drink; and [b]afterward you [c]may eat

16:20 [A]Acts 3:2 16:22 [A]John 1:18; 13:23 16:23 [A]Matt 11:23 16:24 [A]Luke 3:8; 16:30; 19:9 [B]Matt 25:41 16:25 [A]Luke 6:24 16:26 [a]Lit *in all these things* 16:28 [A]Acts 2:40; 8:25; 10:42; 18:5; 20:21ff; 23:11; 28:23; Gal 5:3; Eph 4:17; 1 Thess 2:11; 4:6 16:29 [A]Luke 4:17; John 5:45-47; Acts 15:21 16:30 [A]Luke 3:8; 16:24; 19:9 17:1 [a]Or *temptations to sin* [A]Matt 18:7; 1 Cor 11:19; 1 Tim 4:1 17:2 [a]Lit *is* [A]Matt 18:6; Mark 9:42; 1 Cor 8:12 17:3 [a]Lit *Take heed to yourselves* [A]Matt 18:15 17:4 [a]Lit *you shall forgive* [A]Matt 18:21f 17:5 [A]Mark 6:30 [B]Luke 7:13 17:6 [a]Lit *have* [b]Lit *have obeyed* [A]Luke 7:13 [B]Matt 13:31; 17:20; Mark 4:31; Luke 13:19 [C]Luke 19:4 17:7 [a]Lit *recline* 17:8 [a]Lit *gird* [b]Lit *after these things* [c]Lit *will* [A]Luke 12:37

16:20 Lazarus. Clearly not the Lazarus in Jn 11 (who died at a later time). This beggar was the only character in any of Jesus' parables ever given a name. Some therefore have speculated that this was no imaginary tale, but an actual incident that really took place. Either way, Christ employs it in the same fashion as all His parables, to teach a lesson, in this case for the benefit of the Pharisees. The rich man in the parable is sometimes called *Dives,* after the Latin word for "rich."

16:21 The mention of crumbs, sores, and dogs all made this poor man appear odious in the eyes of the Pharisees. They were inclined to see all such things as proof of divine disfavor. They would have viewed such a person as not only unclean, but also despised by God.

16:22 Abraham's bosom. This same expression (found only here in Scripture) was used in the Talmud as a figure for heaven. The idea was that Lazarus was given a place of high honor, reclining next to Abraham at the heavenly banquet.

16:23 In Hades. The suggestion that a rich man would be excluded from heaven would have scandalized the Pharisees (*see note on Mt 19:24*); especially galling was the idea that a beggar who ate scraps from his table was granted the place of honor next to Abraham. "Hades" was the Gr. term for the abode of the dead. In the LXX, it was used to translate the Heb. *Sheol,* which referred to the realm of the dead in general, without necessarily distinguishing between righteous or unrighteous souls. However, in NT usage, "Hades" always refers to the place of the wicked prior to final judgment in hell. The imagery Jesus used paralleled the common rabbinical idea that Sheol had two parts, one for the souls of the righteous and the other for the souls of the wicked—separated by an impassable gulf. But there is no reason to suppose, as some do, that "Abraham's bosom" spoke of a temporary prison for the souls of OT saints, who were brought to heaven only after He had actually atoned for their sins. Scripture consistently teaches that the spirits of the righteous dead go immediately into the presence of God (cf. 23:43; 2Co 5:8; Php 1:23). And the presence of Moses and Elijah on the Mount of Transfiguration (9:30) belies the notion that they were confined in a compartment of Sheol until Christ finished His work.

16:24 I am in agony. Christ pictured Hades as a place where the unspeakable torment of hell had already begun. Among the miseries featured here are unquenchable flame (*see note on Mt 25:46*); an accusing conscience fed by undying memories of lost opportunity (v. 25); and permanent, irreversible separation from God and everything good (v. 26).

16:27 send him to my father's house. The rich man retained a condescending attitude toward Lazarus even in hell, repeatedly asking Abraham to "send" Lazarus to wait on him (cf. v. 24). The flames of hell do not atone for sin or purge hardened sinners from their depravity (cf. Rev 22:11).

16:29 They have Moses and the Prophets. I.e., the OT Scriptures.

16:31 they will not be persuaded. This speaks powerfully of the singular sufficiency of Scripture to overcome unbelief. The gospel itself is the power of God unto salvation (Ro 1:16). Since unbelief is at heart a moral, rather than an intellectual, problem, no amount of evidences will ever turn unbelief to faith. But the revealed Word of God has inherent power to do so (cf. Jn 6:63; Heb 4:12; Jas 1:18; 1Pe 1:23).

17:1 stumbling blocks. Lit. "snares." *See note on Mt 18:7.*

17:2 a millstone. Lit. "the millstone of a donkey." *See note on Mt 18:6.* **little ones.** Believers; God's children who are under His care. *See note on Mt 18:5.*

17:3 rebuke him. It is the Christian's duty to deal straightforwardly with a brother or sister in sin. *See note on Mt 18:15.*

17:4 seven times a day. I.e., no matter how many times he sins and repents. *See notes on Mt 18:21, 22.* The number 7 was not to set a limit on the number of times to forgive (cf. Ps 119:164), but precisely the opposite. Christ meant that forgiveness should be granted unendingly (cf. Eph 4:32; Col 3:13).

17:5 Increase our faith! Lit. "Give us more faith." They felt inadequate in the face of the high standard He set for them.

17:6 faith like a mustard seed. *See note on Mt 17:20.*

17:7–10 The point of this parable was that a slave, or servant, should expect no special reward for doing what was his duty in the first place. The demanding standards Christ set (vv. 1–4) may have seemed too high to the disciples, but they represented only the minimal duties for a servant of Christ. Those who obey are not to think their obedience is meritorious.

and drink'? 9He does not thank the slave because
he did the things which were commanded, does he?
10So you too, when you do all the things which are
commanded you, say, 'We are unworthy slaves; we
have done *only* that which we ought to have done.' "

TEN LEPERS CLEANSED

11While He was [A]on the way to Jerusalem, [B]He
was passing [a]between Samaria and Galilee. 12As He
entered a village, ten leprous men who [A]stood at a
distance met Him; 13and they raised their voices,
saying, "Jesus, [A]Master, have mercy on us!" 14When
He saw them, He said to them, "[A]Go and show yourselves to the priests." And as they were going, they
were cleansed. 15Now one of them, when he saw
that he had been healed, turned back, [A]glorifying
God with a loud voice, 16and he fell on his face at
His feet, giving thanks to Him. And he was a [A]Sa-
maritan. 17Then Jesus answered and said, "Were
there not ten cleansed? But the nine—where are
they? 18[a]Was no one found who returned to [A]give
glory to God, except this foreigner?" 19And He said
to him, "Stand up and go; [A]your faith [a]has made
you well."

20Now having been questioned by the Pharisees
[A]as to when the kingdom of God was coming, He
answered them and said, "The kingdom of God is
not coming with [a,B]signs to be observed; 21nor will
[A]they say, 'Look, here *it is!*' or, 'There *it is!*' For behold,
the kingdom of God is [a]in your midst."

SECOND COMING FORETOLD

22And He said to the disciples, "[A]The days will
come when you will long to see one of the days
of the Son of Man, and you will not see it. 23[A]They
will say to you, 'Look there! Look here!' Do not go
away, and do not run after *them.* 24[A]For just like
the lightning, when it flashes out of one part [a]of
the sky, shines to the other part [a]of the sky, so will
the Son of Man be in His day. 25[A]But first He must
suffer many things and be rejected by this generation. 26[A]And just as it happened [B]in the days
of Noah, so it will be also in the days of the Son
of Man: 27they were eating, they were drinking,
they were marrying, they were being given in
marriage, until the day that Noah entered the ark,
and the flood came and destroyed them all. 28[a]It
was the same as happened in [A]the days of Lot: they
were eating, they were drinking, they were buying,
they were selling, they were planting, they were
building; 29but on the day that Lot went out from
Sodom it rained fire and [a]brimstone from heaven
and destroyed them all. 30It will be [a]just the same
on the day that the Son of Man [A]is revealed. 31On
that day, the one who is [A]on the housetop and
whose goods are in the house must not go down

17:11 [a]Lit *through the middle of;* or *along the borders of* [A]Luke 9:51 [B]Luke 9:52ff; John 4:3f 17:12 [A]Lev 13:45f 17:13 [A]Luke 5:5 17:14 [A]Lev 14:1-32; Matt 8:4; Luke 5:14 17:15 [A]Matt 9:8 17:16 [A]Matt 10:5 17:18 [a]Lit *Were there not found those who* [A]Matt 9:8 17:19 [a]Lit *has saved you* [A]Matt 9:22; Luke 18:42 17:20 [a]Lit *observation* [A]Luke 19:11; Acts 1:6 [B]Luke 14:1 17:21 [a]Or *within you* [A]Luke 17:23 17:22 [A]Matt 9:15; Mark 2:20; Luke 5:35 17:23 [A]Matt 24:23; Mark 13:21; Luke 21:8 17:24 [a]Lit *under heaven* [A]Matt 24:27 17:25 [A]Matt 16:21; Luke 9:22 17:26 [A]Luke 17:26, 27: *Matt 24:37-39* [B]Gen 6:5-8; 7 17:28 [a]Lit *In the same way as* [A]Gen 19 17:29 [a]I.e. burning sulfur 17:30 [a]Lit *according to the same things* [A]Matt 16:27; 1 Cor 1:7; Col 3:4; 2 Thess 1:7; 1 Pet 1:7; 4:13; 1 John 2:28 17:31 [A]Matt 24:17, 18; Mark 13:15f; Luke 21:21

17:10 unworthy slaves. I.e., not worthy of any special honor.

17:11 to Jerusalem … passing between Samaria and Galilee. Luke did not explain the reason for such a circuitous route, but a comparison of the Gospels yields several clues. It appears that time elapsed between v. 10 and v. 11. The raising of Lazarus at Bethany, near Jerusalem (Jn 11), appears to fit into this time frame. John 11:54 states that after raising Lazarus, to avoid the authorities who were seeking to kill Him, Christ went to "a city called Ephraim"—N of Jerusalem near the border of Samaria. From there He apparently traveled N through Samaria and Galilee one more time, possibly to join friends and family from Galilee who would be making a pilgrimage to Jerusalem for the Passover. From there He would have traveled S by the conventional route, which would have brought Him through Jericho (18:35) to Jerusalem. *See notes on 9:51; 13:22.*

17:12 leprous men. These men were ceremonially defiled and forced to live outside the village (Lv 13:46; Nu 5:2, 3). They were legally required to stand at a distance, and thus their communication with Christ was by shouting. For a description of leprosy, *see note on Lv 13:2.*

17:13 have mercy on us! Cf. 16:24; 18:38, 39; Mt 9:27; 15:22; 17:15; 20:31; Mk 10:47, 48. This was a common plea from those desiring healing.

17:14 show yourselves to the priests. I.e., to be declared clean (Lv 13:2, 3; 14:2–32). **as they were going.** The healing was sudden and immediately visible, but occurred after they obeyed His command.

17:15 one of them … turned back. His response was reminiscent of the conduct of Naaman (2Ki 5:15). The others, eager to be declared clean so that they could return to normal life in society, evidently continued on to the priest, forgetting to give thanks.

17:16 he was a Samaritan. Jesus' sending the lepers to show themselves to the priest suggests that they were Jewish. This Samaritan had been permitted to associate with them when all were ceremonially unclean, but in their healing, they did not share his deep gratitude.

17:18 this foreigner. Evidently Jesus did not view Samaritans as anything more or less than other Gentiles. *See note on Jn 4:4.*

17:19 made you well. Lit. "saved you" (cf. Mt 9:22; *see note on Mk 5:34*).

17:20 when the kingdom of God was coming. They may have asked the question mockingly, having already concluded that He was not the Messiah. **not coming with signs to be observed.** The Pharisees believed that the Messiah's triumph would be immediate. They were looking for Him to come, overthrow Rome, and set up the millennial kingdom. Christ's program was altogether different. He was inaugurating an era in which the kingdom would be manifest in the rule of God in men's hearts through faith in the Savior (v. 21; cf. Ro 14:17). That kingdom was neither confined to a particular geographical location nor visible to human eyes. It would come quietly, invisibly, and without the normal pomp and splendor associated with the arrival of a king. Jesus did not suggest that the OT promises of an earthly kingdom were hereby nullified. Rather, that earthly, visible manifestation of the kingdom is yet to come (Rev 20:1–6).

17:21 in your midst. I.e., within people's hearts. The pronoun could hardly refer to the Pharisees in general.

17:22 The days will come. This introduces a brief discourse that has some similarities to the Olivet Discourse of Mt 24, 25. **you will long to see one of the days of the Son of Man.** I.e., desire to have Him physically present. This suggests a longing for His return to set things right (cf. Rev 6:9–11; 22:20).

17:23, 24 *See note on Mt 24:26.*

17:25 must suffer. I.e., because it was the sovereign plan of God for Him to die as a substitute for sinners. Cf. 9:22; 18:31–33; 24:25, 26; Mt 16:21; Mk 8:31.

17:26, 27 *See note on Mt 24:37.*

17:28 in the days of Lot. I.e., judgment came suddenly, destroying people in the midst of their everyday activities (Ge 19:24, 25). None of the things Jesus cited with regard to Noah's day or Lot's day were inherently sinful. But people were so absorbed in the things of this life that they were utterly unprepared when the time of judgment came.

17:31 housetop. The typical house had a flat roof with an external stairway. The danger would be so great that those on the roofs should flee, without going into the house to retrieve anything.

to take them out; and likewise the one who is in
the field must not turn back. 32 [A]Remember Lot's
wife. 33 [A]Whoever seeks to keep his [a]life will lose
it, and whoever loses *his life* will preserve it. 34 I
tell you, on that night there will be two in one
bed; one will be taken and the other will be left.
35 [A]There will be two women grinding at the same
place; one will be taken and the other will be left.
36 [[a,A]Two men will be in the field; one will be taken
and the other will be left."] 37 And answering they
*said to Him, "Where, Lord?" And He said to them,
"[A]Where the body *is,* there also the [a]vultures will
be gathered."

PARABLES ON PRAYER

18 Now He was telling them a parable to show
that at all times they [A]ought to pray and not
to [B]lose heart, 2 saying, "In a certain city there was
a judge who did not fear God and did not [A]respect
man. 3 There was a widow in that city, and she kept
coming to him, saying, '[a]Give me legal protection
from my opponent.' 4 For a while he was unwilling;
but afterward he said to himself, 'Even though I
do not fear God nor [A]respect man, 5 yet [A]because
this widow bothers me, I will [a]give her legal protection, otherwise by continually coming she will
[b,B]wear me out.' " 6 And [A]the Lord said, "Hear what
the unrighteous judge *said; 7 now, will not God
[A]bring about justice for His [B]elect who cry to Him
day and night, [a]and will He [C]delay long over them?
8 I tell you that He will bring about justice for them
quickly. However, when the Son of Man comes, [A]will
He find [a]faith on the earth?"

THE PHARISEE AND THE PUBLICAN

9 And He also told this parable to some people
who [A]trusted in themselves that they were righteous, and [B]viewed others with contempt: 10 "Two
men [A]went up into the temple to pray, one a Pharisee
and the other a tax collector. 11 The Pharisee [A]stood
and was praying this to himself: 'God, I thank You
that I am not like other people: swindlers, unjust,
adulterers, or even like this tax collector. 12 I [A]fast
twice a week; I [B]pay tithes of all that I get.' 13 But the
tax collector, [A]standing some distance away, [B]was
even unwilling to lift up his eyes to heaven, but
[C]was beating his breast, saying, 'God, be [a]merciful
to me, the sinner!' 14 I tell you, this man went to his
house justified rather than the other; [A]for everyone
who exalts himself will be humbled, but he who
humbles himself will be exalted."
15 [A]And they were bringing even their babies to
Him so that He would touch them, but when the
disciples saw it, they *began* rebuking them. 16 But
Jesus called for them, saying, "Permit the children
to come to Me, and do not hinder them, for the
kingdom of God belongs to such as these. 17 Truly I
say to you, [A]whoever does not receive the kingdom
of God like a child will not enter it *at all.*"

THE RICH YOUNG RULER

18 [A]A ruler questioned Him, saying, "Good Teacher,
what shall I do to inherit eternal life?" 19 And Jesus
said to him, "Why do you call Me good? No one is
good except God alone. 20 You know the commandments, '[A]DO NOT COMMIT ADULTERY, DO NOT MURDER,
DO NOT STEAL, DO NOT BEAR FALSE WITNESS, HONOR

17:32 [A]Gen 19:26 17:33 [a]Or *soul* [A]Matt 10:39 17:35 [A]Matt 24:41 17:36 [a]Early mss do not contain this v [A]Matt 24:40 17:37 [a]Or *eagles* [A]Matt 24:28 18:1 [A]Luke 11:5-10 [B]2 Cor 4:1 18:2 [A]Luke 18:4; 20:13; Heb 12:9 18:3 [a]Lit *Do me justice* 18:4 [A]Luke 18:2; 20:13; Heb 12:9 18:5 [a]Lit *do her justice* [b]Lit *hit me under the eye* [A]Luke 11:8 [B]1 Cor 9:27 18:6 [A]Luke 7:13 18:7 [a]Or *and yet He is very patient toward them* [A]Rev 6:10 [B]Matt 24:22; Rom 8:33; Col 3:12; 2 Tim 2:10; Titus 1:1 [C]2 Pet 3:9 18:8 [a]Lit *the faith* [A]Luke 17:26ff 18:9 [A]Luke 16:15 [B]Rom 14:3, 10 18:10 [A]1 Kin 10:5; 2 Kin 20:5, 8; Acts 3:1 18:11 [A]Matt 6:5; Mark 11:25; Luke 22:41 18:12 [A]Matt 9:14 [B]Luke 11:42 18:13 [a]Or *propitious* [A]Matt 6:5; Mark 11:25; Luke 22:41 [B]Ezra 9:6 [C]Luke 23:48 18:14 [A]Matt 23:12; Luke 14:11 18:15 [A]Luke 18:15-17: *Matt 19:13-15; Mark 10:13-16* 18:17 [A]Matt 18:3; 19:14; Mark 10:15; 1 Cor 14:20; 1 Pet 2:2 18:18 [A]Luke 18:18-30: *Matt 19:16-29; Mark 10:17-30;* Luke 10:25-28 18:20 [A]Ex 20:12-16; Deut 5:16-20

17:32 Lot's wife was destroyed on the very threshold of deliverance. Her attachment to Sodom was so powerful that she delayed and looked back; she was overwhelmed by oncoming judgment, just before reaching the place of safety (Ge 19:26).

17:33 *See note on 14:11.*

17:34–36 *See note on Mt 24:40, 41.*

17:37 *See note on Mt 24:28.*

18:1 **all times . . . pray.** A common theme in Paul's epistles (see Introduction: Interpretive Challenges). Cf. Ro 1:9; 12:12; Eph 6:18; 1Th 5:17; 2Th 1:11. **not to lose heart.** I.e., in light of the afflictions and hardships of life, and the evidence of approaching judgment (described in the preceding discourse).

18:2 **did not fear God and did not respect man.** This man was thoroughly wicked. Christ described him as "unrighteous" (v. 6)—like the manager in 16:8. The judge is not given as a symbol of God, but rather in contrast to Him. If such an unrighteous man would respond to persistent pleas, would not God, who is not only just, but also loving and merciful, do so more readily?

18:5 **wear me out.** Lit. "hit under the eye." What the judge would not do out of compassion for the widow or reverence for God, he would do out of sheer frustration with her incessant pleading.

18:6 **Hear what the unrighteous judge said.** I.e., listen to the point of the story, namely, that God, who always does right and is filled with compassion for believers who suffer, will certainly respond to His beloved ones who cry for His help (v. 7).

18:8 **quickly.** He may delay long, but He does so for good reason (cf. 2Pe 3:8, 9) and when He acts, His vengeance is swift. **will He find faith.** This suggests that when He returns, the true faith will be comparatively rare—as in the days of Noah (17:26), when only 8 souls were saved. The period before His return will be marked by persecution, apostasy, and unbelief (Mt 24:9–13, 24).

18:9 This parable is rich with truth about the doctrine of justification by faith. It illustrates perfectly how a sinner who is utterly devoid of personal righteousness may be declared righteous before God instantaneously through an act of repentant faith. The parable is addressed to Pharisees who trusted their own righteousness (vv. 10, 11). Such confidence in one's inherent righteousness is a damning hope (cf. Ro 10:3; Php 3:9), because human righteousness—even the righteousness of the most fastidious Pharisee—falls short of the divine standard (Mt 5:48). Scripture consistently teaches that sinners are justified when God's perfect righteousness is imputed to their account (cf. Ge 15:6; Ro 4:4, 5; 2Co 5:21; Php 3:4–9)—and it was only on that basis that this tax collector (or anyone else) could be saved.

18:12 **fast twice a week.** I.e., more than is required by any biblical standard (*see note on 5:33*). By exalting his own works, the Pharisee revealed that his entire hope lay in his not being as bad as someone else. He lacked any sense of his own unworthiness and sin. Cf. vv. 18–21; Mt 19:17–20. *See note on 17:7–10.*

18:13 The tax collector's humility is notable in everything about his posture and behavior. Here was a man who had been made to face the reality of his own sin, and his only response was abject humility and repentance. He contrasts with the Pharisee in virtually every detail. **God, be merciful.** He had no hope but the mercy of God. This is the point to which the law aims to bring every sinner (cf. Ro 3:19, 20; 7:13; Gal 3:22–24).

18:14 **justified.** I.e., reckoned righteous before God by means of an imputed righteousness (*see note on v. 9*).

18:17 **like a child.** *See note on Mt 18:3.*

18:18–30 *See notes on Mt 19:16–30; Mk 10:17–31.*

18:20 Quoted from Ex 20:12–16; Dt 5:16–20.

YOUR FATHER AND MOTHER.' " 21 And he said, "All
these things I have kept from *my* youth." 22 When
Jesus heard *this,* He said to him, "One thing you still
lack; [A]sell all that you possess and distribute it to the
poor, and you shall have [B]treasure in heaven; and
come, follow Me." 23 But when he had heard these
things, he became very sad, for he was extremely
rich. 24 And Jesus looked at him and said, "[A]How hard
it is for those who are wealthy to enter the kingdom
of God! 25 For [A]it is easier for a camel to [a]go through
the eye of a needle than for a rich man to enter the
kingdom of God." 26 They who heard it said, "Then
who can be saved?" 27 But He said, "[A]The things that
are impossible with people are possible with God."
28 Peter said, "Behold, [A]we have left [a]our own *homes*
and followed You." 29 And He said to them, "Truly I
say to you, [A]there is no one who has left house or wife
or brothers or parents or children, for the sake of the
kingdom of God, 30 who will not receive many times as
much at this time and in [A]the age to come, eternal life."
31 [A]Then He took the twelve aside and said to
them, "Behold, [B]we are going up to Jerusalem, and
[C]all things which are written through the prophets
about the Son of Man will be accomplished. 32 [A]For
He will be [a]handed over to the Gentiles, and will be
mocked and mistreated and spit upon, 33 and after
they have scourged Him, they will kill Him; and the
third day He will rise again." 34 But [A]the disciples
understood none of these things, and *the meaning*
of this statement was hidden from them, and they
did not comprehend the things that were said.

BARTIMAEUS RECEIVES SIGHT

35 [A]As [a,B]Jesus was approaching Jericho, a blind
man was sitting by the road begging. 36 Now hearing
a crowd going by, he *began* to inquire what this was.
37 They told him that Jesus of Nazareth was passing
by. 38 And he called out, saying, "Jesus, [A]Son of David,
have mercy on me!" 39 Those who led the way were
sternly telling him to be quiet; but he kept crying
out all the more, "[A]Son of David, have mercy on
me!" 40 And Jesus stopped and commanded that
he be brought to Him; and when he came near,
He questioned him, 41 "What do you want Me to do
for you?" And he said, "Lord, *I want* to regain my
sight!" 42 And Jesus said to him, "[a]Receive your sight;
[A]your faith has [b]made you well." 43 Immediately he
regained his sight and *began* following Him, [A]glo-
rifying God; and when [B]all the people saw it, they
gave praise to God.

ZACCHEUS CONVERTED

19 He [A]entered Jericho and was passing through.
2 And there was a man called by the name
of Zaccheus; he was a chief tax collector and he
was rich. 3 Zaccheus was trying to see who Jesus
was, and was unable because of the crowd, for
he was small in stature. 4 So he ran on ahead and
climbed up into a [a,A]sycamore tree in order to see
Him, for He was about to pass through that way.
5 When Jesus came to the place, He looked up and
said to him, "Zaccheus, hurry and come down, for
today I must stay at your house." 6 And he hurried
and came down and received Him [a]gladly. 7 When
they saw it, they all *began* to grumble, saying,
"He has gone [a]to be the guest of a man who is a
sinner." 8 Zaccheus stopped and said to [A]the Lord,
"Behold, Lord, half of my possessions I [a]will give
to the poor, and if I have [B]defrauded anyone of
anything, I [a]will give back [C]four times as much."

18:22 [A]Matt 19:21; Luke 12:33 [B]Matt 6:20 18:24 [A]Matt 19:23; Mark 10:23f 18:25 [a]Lit *enter* [A]Matt 19:24; Mark 10:25 18:27 [A]Matt 19:26 18:28 [a]Lit *our own things* [A]Luke 5:11 18:29 [A]Matt 6:33; 19:29; Mark 10:29f 18:30 [A]Matt 12:32 18:31 [A]Luke 18:31-33: *Matt 20:17-19; Mark 10:32-34* [B]Luke 9:51 [C]Ps 22; Is 53 18:32 [a]Or *betrayed* [A]Matt 16:21 18:34 [A]Mark 9:32; Luke 9:45 18:35 [a]Lit *He* [A]Luke 18:35-43: *Matt 20:29-34; Mark 10:46-52* [B]Matt 20:29; Mark 10:46; Luke 19:1 18:38 [A]Matt 9:27; Luke 18:39 18:39 [A]Luke 18:38 18:42 [a]Lit *Regain your sight* [b]Lit *saved you* [A]Matt 9:22 18:43 [A]Matt 9:8 [B]Luke 9:43; 13:17; 19:37 19:1 [A]Luke 18:35 19:4 [a]I.e. fig-mulberry [A]1 Kin 10:27; 1 Chr 27:28; 2 Chr 1:15; 9:27; Ps 78:47; Is 9:10; Luke 17:6 19:6 [a]Lit *rejoicing* 19:7 [a]Or *to find lodging* 19:8 [a]Lit *am giving* [A]Luke 7:13 [B]Luke 3:14 [C]Ex 22:1; Lev 6:5; Num 5:7; 2 Sam 12:6

18:31 all things … written through the prophets. E.g., Pss 22; 69; Is 53; Da 9:26; Zec 13:7.

18:32 handed over to the Gentiles. Each prophecy of His death (cf. 9:22, 44; 12:50; 13:32, 33; 17:25) was more explicit than the last. This is His first mention of being turned over to the Gentiles.

18:33 He will rise again. Christ had predicted His resurrection on the third day before (9:22). But the disciples missed the import of these words, and when He actually did rise, they were surprised by it (24:6).

18:34 they did not comprehend. The whole matter of Christ's death and resurrection was not grasped by the 12. The reason may have been that they were enamored with other ideas about the Messiah and how His earthly rule would operate (cf. Mt 16:22; 17:10; Ac 1:6).

18:35 Jericho. *See note on Mk 10:46.* **blind man.** There were actually two blind men. One probably spoke for both of them. *See note on Mt 20:30.*

18:38 Son of David. An affirmation that he recognized Jesus as Messiah and King. *See note on Mt 9:27.*

18:42 made you well. Lit. "saved you" (cf. Mt 9:22; *see note on Mk 5:34*).

19:2 chief tax collector. *See note on Mt 5:46.* Zaccheus probably oversaw a large tax district, and had other tax collectors working for him. Jericho alone was a prosperous trading center, so it is certain that Zaccheus was a wealthy man. It is striking to note that only a chapter earlier, Luke recorded the account of the rich young ruler, and Jesus' statement about "how hard it is for those who are wealthy to enter the kingdom of God" (18:24). Here Jesus demonstrates that with God, nothing is impossible (cf. 18:27).

19:3 the crowd. Christ was probably traveling with a large entourage of pilgrims to the Passover in Jerusalem. But "the crowd" apparently refers to people in Jericho who lined the street to see Him pass through. They had undoubtedly heard about the recent raising of Lazarus in Bethany, less than 15 mi. away (Jn 11). That, combined with His fame as a healer and teacher, stirred the entire city when word arrived that He was coming.

19:4 sycamore tree. A sturdy tree with low, spreading branches. A small person could get out on a limb and hang over the road. This was an undignified position for someone of Zaccheus' rank, but he was desperate to see Christ.

19:5 I must stay at your house. This was worded as a mandate, not a request. It is the only place in all the Gospels where Jesus invited Himself to be someone's guest (cf. Is 65:1).

19:6 gladly. Such a despicable sinner as a typical tax collector (*see note on Mt 5:46*) might have been distressed at the prospect of a visit from the perfect, sinless Son of God. But Zaccheus' heart was prepared.

19:7 they all *began* to grumble. Both the religious elite and the common people hated Zaccheus. They did not understand, and in their blind pride refused to see, what possible righteous purpose Jesus had in visiting such a notorious sinner. But He had come to seek and to save the lost (v. 10). *See note on 15:2.*

19:8 I will give back four times as much. Zaccheus' willingness to make restitution was proof that his conversion was genuine. It was the fruit, not the condition, of his salvation. The law required a penalty of one-fifth as restitution for money acquired by fraud (Lv 6:5; Nu 5:6, 7), so Zaccheus was doing more

9 And Jesus said to him, "Today salvation has come to this house, because he, too, is [A]a son of Abraham. 10 For [A]the Son of Man has come to seek and to save that which was lost."

PARABLE OF MONEY USAGE

11 While they were listening to these things, Jesus went on to tell a parable, because [A]He was near Jerusalem, and they supposed that [B]the kingdom of God was going to appear immediately. 12 So He said, "[A]A nobleman went to a distant country to receive a kingdom for himself, and *then* return. 13 And he called ten of his slaves, and gave them ten [a]minas and said to them, 'Do business *with this* [b]until I come *back*.' 14 But his citizens hated him and sent [a]a delegation after him, saying, 'We do not want this man to reign over us.' 15 When he returned, after receiving the kingdom, he ordered that these slaves, to whom he had given the money, be called to him so that he might know what business they had done. 16 The first appeared, saying, '[a]Master, your [b]mina has made ten minas more.' 17 And he said to him, 'Well done, good slave, because you have been [A]faithful in a very little thing, you are to be in authority over ten cities.' 18 The second came, saying, 'Your [a]mina, [b]master, has made five minas.' 19 And he said to him also, 'And you are to be over five cities.' 20 Another came, saying, 'Master, here is your mina, which I kept put away in a handkerchief; 21 for I was afraid of you, because you are an exacting man; you take up what you did not lay down and reap what you did not sow.' 22 He *said to him, '[a]By your own words I will judge you, you worthless slave. Did you know that I am an exacting man, taking up what I did not lay down and reaping what I did not sow? 23 Then why did you not put my money in the bank, and having come, I would have collected it with interest?' 24 Then he said to the bystanders, 'Take the mina away from him and give it to the one who has the ten minas.' 25 And they said to him, 'Master, he has ten minas *already*.' 26 '[A]I tell you that to everyone who has, more shall be given, but from the one who does not have, even what he does have shall be taken away. 27 But [A]these enemies of mine, who did not want me to reign over them, bring them here and [B]slay them in my presence.' "

TRIUMPHAL ENTRY

28 After He had said these things, He [A]was going on ahead, [B]going up to Jerusalem.

29 [A]When He approached Bethphage and [B]Bethany, near the [a]mount that is called [C]Olivet, He sent two of the disciples, 30 saying, "Go into the village ahead of *you;* there, as you enter, you will find a colt tied on

19:9 [A]Luke 3:8; 13:16; Rom 4:16; Gal 3:7 19:10 [A]Matt 18:11 19:11 [A]Luke 9:51 [B]Luke 17:20 19:12 [A]Luke 19:12-27: *Matt 25:14-30* 19:13 [a]A mina is equal to about 100 days' wages [b]Lit *while I am coming* 19:14 [a]Or *an embassy* 19:16 [a]Lit *Lord* [b]V 13, note 1 19:17 [A]Luke 16:10 19:18 [a]V 13, note 1 [b]Lit *lord* 19:22 [a]Lit *Out of your own mouth* 19:26 [A]Matt 13:12; Mark 4:25; Luke 8:18 19:27 [A]Luke 19:14 [B]Matt 22:7; Luke 20:16 19:28 [A]Mark 10:32 [B]Luke 9:51 19:29 [a]Or *hill...Olive Grove;* Mount of Olives [A]Luke 19:29-38: *Matt 21:1-9; Mark 11:1-10* [B]Matt 21:17 [C]Luke 21:37; Acts 1:12

than was required. The law required 4-fold restitution only when an animal was stolen and killed (Ex 22:1). If the animal was found alive, only two-fold restitution was required (Ex 22:4). But Zaccheus judged his own crime severely, acknowledging that he was as guilty as the lowest common robber. Since much of his wealth had probably been acquired fraudulently, this was a costly commitment. On top of that, he gave half his goods to the poor. But Zaccheus had just found incomprehensible spiritual riches and did not mind the loss of material wealth (*see notes on 14:28; Mt 13:44–46*). He stands in stark contrast with the rich young ruler in 18:18–24.

19:9 **a son of Abraham.** A Jew by race for whom Christ came as Savior (cf. Mt 1:21; 10:6; 15:24; Jn 4:22).

19:10 **the Son of Man.** *See note on Mt 8:20.* **to seek and to save that which was lost.** The main theme of Luke's gospel. Cf. 5:31, 32; 15:4–7, 32; *see notes on 1Ti 2:4; 4:10.*

19:11 **they supposed.** The disciples still mistakenly assumed that Christ would establish His kingdom on earth at Jerusalem (*see note on 17:20*).

19:12 **a distant country.** Kings in Roman provinces like Galilee and Perea actually went to Rome to receive their kingdoms. The entire Herodian dynasty was dependent on Rome for ruling power, and Herod the Great himself had gone to Rome to be given his kingdom. This parable illustrates Christ, who would soon depart to receive His kingdom, and will one day return to rule. It is similar to the parable of the talents (Mt 25:14–30) but there are significant differences (*see note on v. 13*). That parable was told during the Olivet Discourse (*see note on Mt 24:1–25:46*); this one was told on the road from Jericho up to Jerusalem (cf. v. 28).

19:13 **minas.** A Gr. measure of money (*see note on 15:8*), equal to slightly more than 3 months' salary. The mina was one-sixtieth of a talent, meaning that the 10 servants in this parable had been given a considerably smaller sum to account for than any of the 3 servants in the parable of the talents (Mt 25:14–30).

19:14 **sent a delegation after him.** This was precisely what had happened to Archelaus (*see note on Mt 2:22*), son of Herod the Great, when he went to Rome to be made tetrarch of Judea. A delegation of Jews traveled to Rome with a protest to Caesar Augustus (*see note on 2:1*). He refused their complaint and made Archelaus king anyway. Archelaus subsequently built his palace in Jericho, not far from where Jesus told this parable. Archelaus' rule was so inept and despotic that Rome quickly replaced him with a succession of procurators, of whom Pontius Pilate was the fifth. With this parable Jesus warned that the Jews were about to do the same thing, in a spiritual sense, to their true Messiah.

19:15–27 *See notes on Mt 25:14–30.*

19:15 **When he returned.** This pictured Christ's return to earth. The full manifestation of His kingdom on earth awaits that time. *See note on 17:20.*

19:17 **faithful in a very little.** *See note on v. 13.* Those with relatively small gifts and opportunities are just as responsible to use them faithfully as those who are given much more. **over ten cities.** The reward is incomparably greater than the 10 minas warranted. Note also that the rewards were apportioned according to the servants' diligence: the one who gained 10 minas was given 10 cities, the one who gained 5 minas, 5 cities (v. 19), and so on.

19:21 **I was afraid of you.** A craven fear, not borne out of love or reverence, but tainted with contempt for the master (*see note on Mt 25:24*). Had he had any true regard for the master, a righteous "fear" would have provoked diligence rather than sloth.

19:22 **Did you know.** *See note on Mt 25:26.* This did not suggest that what the man "knew" about the master was true. However, even the knowledge he claimed to have was enough to condemn him. Thus will it be with the wicked in the day of judgment.

19:26 *See note on Mt 25:29.*

19:27 **these enemies of mine.** These illustrated the Jews who actively opposed him. **slay them in my presence.** This spoke of harsh, violent judgment and may be a reference to the destruction of Jerusalem (*see note on Mt 24:2*).

19:28 **up to Jerusalem.** The road from Jericho to Jerusalem was a steep ascent, rising some 3,300 feet in about 17 miles. This represented the last leg of the long journey that began in 9:51 (*see note there*).

19:29 **Bethphage.** *See note on Mt 21:1.* **Bethany.** Jesus often stayed there during His visits to Jerusalem. *See note on 10:38.* **mount ... called Olivet.** The main peak of a ridge running N to S, located E of the Kidron Valley adjacent to the temple. Olivet derived its name from the dense olive groves that once covered it. *See note on Mt 24:3.*

19:30–36 *See notes on Mt 21:1–8; Mk 11:1–8.*

19:30 **colt.** The other Gospels say this was a donkey colt (cf. Zec 9:9), and Mt reveals that the mare was brought along as well (*see note on Mt 21:7*). **on which no one yet has ever sat.** *See note on Mk 11:2.*

which no one yet has ever sat; untie it and bring it
here. 31 If anyone asks you, 'Why are you untying it?'
you shall say, 'The Lord has need of it.' " 32 So those
who were sent went away and found it just as He
had told them. 33 As they were untying the colt, its
[a]owners said to them, "Why are you untying the
colt?" 34 They said, "The Lord has need of it." 35 They
brought it to Jesus, [A]and they threw their coats on
the colt and put Jesus *on it.* 36 As He was going, they
were spreading their coats on the road. 37 As soon
as He was approaching, near the descent of [A]the
Mount of Olives, the whole crowd of the disciples
began to [B]praise God [a]joyfully with a loud voice for
all the [b]miracles which they had seen, 38 shouting:

"[A]BLESSED IS THE [B]KING WHO COMES
IN THE NAME OF THE LORD;
Peace in heaven and [C]glory
in the highest!"

39 [A]Some of the Pharisees [a]in the crowd said to
Him, "Teacher, rebuke Your disciples." 40 But Jesus
answered, "I tell you, if these become silent, [A]the
stones will cry out!"
41 When He approached *Jerusalem,* He saw the
city and [A]wept over it, 42 saying, "If you had known
in this day, even you, the things which make for
peace! But now they have been hidden from your
eyes. 43 For the days will come upon you [a]when
your enemies will [A]throw up a [b]barricade against
you, and [B]surround you and hem you in on every
side, 44 and they will level you to the ground and
your children within you, and [A]they will not leave
in you one stone upon another, because you did not
recognize [B]the time of your visitation."

TRADERS DRIVEN FROM THE TEMPLE

45 [A]Jesus entered the temple and began to drive
out those who were selling, 46 saying to them, "It
is written, '[A]AND MY HOUSE SHALL BE A HOUSE OF
PRAYER,' [B]but you have made it a ROBBERS' [a]DEN."
47 And [A]He was teaching daily in the temple; but
the chief priests and the scribes and the leading
men among the people [B]were trying to destroy
Him, 48 and they could not find [a]anything that they
might do, for all the people were hanging on to
[b]every word He said.

JESUS' AUTHORITY QUESTIONED

20 [A]On one of the days while [B]He was teaching
the people in the temple and [C]preaching the
gospel, the chief priests and the scribes with the
elders [D]confronted *Him,* 2 and they spoke, saying
to Him, "Tell us by what authority You are doing
these things, or who is the one who gave You this
authority?" 3 Jesus answered and said to them, "I
will also ask you a [a]question, and you tell Me: 4 Was
the baptism of John from heaven or from men?"
5 They reasoned among themselves, saying, "If we
say, 'From heaven,' He will say, 'Why did you not

19:33 [a]Lit *lords* 19:35 [A]Luke 19:35-38: *Matt 21:4-9; Mark 11:7-10; John 12:12-15* 19:37 [a]Lit *rejoicing* [b]Or *works of power* [A]Matt 21:1; Luke 19:29 [B]Luke 18:43 19:38 [A]Ps 118:26 [B]Matt 2:2; 25:34 [C]Matt 21:9; Luke 2:14 19:39 [a]Lit *from* [A]Matt 21:15f 19:40 [A]Hab 2:11 19:41 [A]Luke 13:34, 35 19:43 [a]Lit *and* [b]I.e. a dirt wall or mound for siege purposes [A]Eccl 9:14; Is 29:3; 37:33; Jer 6:6; Ezek 4:2; 26:8 [B]Luke 21:20 19:44 [A]Matt 24:2; Mark 13:2; Luke 21:6 [B]1 Pet 2:12 19:45 [A]Luke 19:45, 46: *Matt 21:12, 13; Mark 11:15-17;* John 2:13-16 19:46 [a]Lit *cave* [A]Is 56:7; Jer 7:11; Matt 21:13; Mark 11:17 [B]Jer 7:11 19:47 [A]Matt 26:55; Luke 21:37 [B]Luke 20:19 19:48 [a]Lit *what they would do* [b]Lit *Him, listening* 20:1 [A]Luke 20:1-8: *Matt 21:23-27; Mark 11:27-33* [B]Matt 26:55 [C]Luke 8:1 [D]Acts 4:1; 6:12 20:3 [a]Lit *word*

19:36 spreading their coats. *See notes on Mt 21:8; Mk 11:8.* Luke omits the cutting of palm branches mentioned by Matthew and Mark.

19:37 the whole crowd of the disciples. Doubtless many in the crowd were not true disciples. **miracles.** John 12:17, 18 specifically mentions that news of the raising of Lazarus had provoked many in the crowd to come to see Him.

19:38 Blessed is the King. Quoting Ps 118:26, they hailed Jesus as Messiah. *See note on Mt 21:9.* **Peace in heaven.** Only Luke reported this phrase. It is reminiscent of the angels' message in 2:14.

19:39 rebuke Your disciples. The Pharisees were offended by people offering Him such worshipful praise. They wanted Him to stop them.

19:40 the stones will cry out! This was a strong claim of deity, and perhaps a reference to the words of Hab 2:11. Scripture often speaks of inanimate nature praising God. Cf. Pss 96:11; 98:7–9; 114:7; Is 55:12. Cf. also the words of John the Baptist in Mt 3:9; note the fulfillment of Jesus' words in Mt 27:51.

19:41, 42 Only Luke recorded the weeping of Jesus over the city of Jerusalem. Christ grieved over Jerusalem on at least two other occasions (13:34; Mt 23:37). The timing of this lament may seem incongruous with the triumphal entry, but it reveals that Jesus knew the true superficiality of the peoples' hearts, and His mood was anything but giddy as He rode into the city. The same crowd would soon cry for His death (23:21).

19:43 surround you and hem you in. Cf. 21:20. This is precisely the method used by Titus when he laid siege to Jerusalem in A.D. 70. He surrounded the city on Apr. 9, cutting off all supplies, and trapping thousands of people who had been in Jerusalem for the Passover and Feast of Unleavened Bread (just completed). The Romans systematically built embankments around the city, gradually starving the city's inhabitants. The Romans held the city in this manner through the summer, defeating various sections of the city one by one. The final overthrow of the city occurred in early Sept.

19:44 they will level you. This was literally fulfilled. The Romans utterly demolished the city, temple, residences, and people. Men, women, and children were brutally slaughtered by the tens of thousands. The few survivors were carried off to become victims of the Roman circus games and gladiatorial bouts. **because you did not recognize the time of your visitation.** I.e., Jerusalem's utter destruction was divine judgment for their failure to recognize and embrace their Messiah when He visited them (cf. 20:13–16; Jn 1:10, 11).

19:45, 46 This was the second time Jesus had driven the sellers out of the temple, and is a different incident from the one described in Jn 2:14–16. He quotes from Is 56:7. *See note on Mt 21:12.*

19:47 chief priests. *See note on Mt 2:4.* The rulers of the temple. **scribes.** Mostly Pharisees, experts in the law and traditions. **leading men among the people.** Prominent Jewish laymen with influence in temple affairs. By bringing His ministry to the temple, Christ had walked into the very heart of the opposition against Him. **trying to destroy Him.** I.e., kill Him (cf. 22:2; Mt 26:3, 4; Jn 5:16–18; 7:1, 19, 25).

20:1 one of the days. Probably Wednesday of Passion Week. The triumphal entry was on Monday, and the cleansing of the temple on Tuesday. The events in this chapter best fit Wednesday in the chronology of that week. This chapter features a series of carefully coordinated attacks on Christ by the Jewish leaders. **chief priests . . . scribes . . . elders.** *See note on 19:47.* Each of these groups played a unique role in the various attacks that follow. Each was also represented in the Sanhedrin, the Jewish council (*see note on Mt 26:59*)—suggesting that the council had met to orchestrate the attack against Jesus. Their attacks came in the form of a series of questions designed to entrap Him (*see notes on vv. 2, 22, 33*).

20:2–8 *See notes on Mt 21:23, 25.*

20:2 This was the first in a series of questions designed to entrap Jesus. This question was raised by the chief priests, scribes, and elders—evidently representatives of the Sanhedrin. *See notes on vv. 22, 33.*

20:5 Why did you not believe him? John had clearly testified that Jesus was the Messiah. If John was a prophet whose words were true, they ought to believe his testimony about

believe him?' 6But if we say, 'From men,' all the people will stone us to death, for they are convinced that John was a [A]prophet." 7So they answered that they did not know where *it came* from. 8And Jesus said to them, "Nor [a]will I tell you by what authority I do these things."

PARABLE OF THE VINE-GROWERS

9[A]And He began to tell the people this parable: "A man planted a vineyard and rented it out to [a]vine-growers, and went on a journey for a long time. 10At the *harvest* time he sent a slave to the vine-growers, so that they would give him *some* of the produce of the vineyard; but the vine-growers beat him and sent him away empty-handed. 11And he proceeded to send another slave; and they beat him also and treated him shamefully and sent him away empty-handed. 12And he proceeded to send a third; and this one also they wounded and cast out. 13The [a]owner of the vineyard said, 'What shall I do? I will send my beloved son; perhaps they will [A]respect him.' 14But when the vine-growers saw him, they reasoned with one another, saying, 'This is the heir; let us kill him so that the inheritance will be ours.' 15So they threw him out of the vineyard and killed him. What, then, will the [a]owner of the vineyard do to them? 16He will come and [A]destroy these vine-growers and will give the vineyard to others." When they heard it, they said, "[B]May it never be!" 17But [a]Jesus looked at them and said, "What then is this that is written:

> '[A]THE STONE WHICH THE BUILDERS REJECTED,
> THIS BECAME [B]THE CHIEF CORNER *stone*'?

18[A]Everyone who falls on that stone will be broken to pieces; but on whomever it falls, it will scatter him like dust."

TRIBUTE TO CAESAR

19The scribes and the chief priests [A]tried to lay hands on Him that very hour, and they feared the people; for they understood that He spoke this parable against them. 20[A]So they watched Him, and sent spies who [a]pretended to be righteous, in order [B]that they might [b]catch Him in some statement, so that they *could* deliver Him to the rule and the authority of [C]the governor. 21They questioned Him, saying, "Teacher, we know that You speak and teach correctly, and You [a]are not partial to any, but teach the way of God in truth. 22Is it [a]lawful for us [A]to pay taxes to Caesar, or not?" 23But He detected their trickery and said to them, 24"Show Me a [a]denarius. Whose [b]likeness and inscription does it have?" They said, "Caesar's." 25And He said to them, "Then [A]render to Caesar the things that are Caesar's, and to God the things that are God's." 26And they were unable to [a,A]catch Him in a saying in the presence of the people; and being amazed at His answer, they became silent.

IS THERE A RESURRECTION?

27[A]Now there came to Him some of the [B]Sadducees (who say that there is no resurrection), 28and they questioned Him, saying, "Teacher, Moses wrote for us that [A]IF A MAN'S BROTHER DIES, having a wife, AND HE IS CHILDLESS, HIS BROTHER SHOULD [a]MARRY THE WIFE AND RAISE UP CHILDREN TO HIS BROTHER. 29Now there were seven brothers; and the first took a wife and died childless; 30and the second 31and the third [a]married her; and in the same way [b]all seven [c]died, leaving no children. 32Finally the woman died also. 33In the resurrection therefore, which one's wife will she be? For [a]all seven [b]had married her."

34Jesus said to them, "The sons of [A]this age marry and are given in marriage, 35but those who are

20:6 [A]Matt 11:9; Luke 7:29, 30 20:8 [a]Lit *do I tell* 20:9 [a]Or *tenant farmers,* also vv 10, 14, 16 [A]Luke 20:9-19: *Matt 21:33-46; Mark 12:1-12* 20:13 [a]Lit *lord* [A]Luke 18:2 20:15 [a]Lit *lord* 20:16 [A]Matt 21:41; Mark 12:9; Luke 19:27 [B]Rom 3:4, 6, 31; 6:2, 15; 7:7, 13; 9:14; 11:1, 11; 1 Cor 6:15; Gal 2:17; 3:21; 6:14 20:17 [a]Lit *He* [A]Ps 118:22 [B]Eph 2:20; 1 Pet 2:6 20:18 [A]Matt 21:44 20:19 [A]Luke 19:47 20:20 [a]Lit *falsely represented themselves* [b]Lit *take hold of His word* [A]Luke 20:20-26: *Matt 22:15-22; Mark 12:13-17;* Mark 3:2 [B]Luke 11:54; 20:26 [C]Matt 27:2 20:21 [a]Lit *do not receive a face* 20:22 [a]Or *permissible* [A]Matt 17:25; Luke 23:2 20:24 [a]The denarius was a day's wages [b]Lit *image* 20:25 [A]Matt 22:21; Mark 12:17 20:26 [a]Lit *catch His statement* [A]Luke 11:54 20:27 [A]Luke 20:27-40: *Matt 22:23-33; Mark 12:18-27* [B]Acts 23:8 20:28 [a]Lit *take* [A]Deut 25:5 20:31 [a]Lit *took* [b]Lit *the seven also* [c]Lit *left no children, and died* 20:33 [a]Lit *the* [b]Lit *had her as wife* 20:34 [A]Matt 12:32; Luke 16:8

Christ. On the other hand, it would have been political folly for the Pharisees to attack the legitimacy of John the Baptist or deny his authority as a prophet of God. John was enormously popular with the people, and a martyr at the hands of the despised Herod. For the Pharisees to question John's authority was to attack a national hero, and they knew better than that. So they pleaded ignorance (v. 7).

20:8 Nor will I tell you. Jesus exposed the hypocrisy of the question, unmasking their evil motives. He wasted no truth on them (cf. Mt 7:6).

20:9–19 *See notes on Mt 21:33–45; Mk 12:1–12.*

20:9 the people. Luke alone noted the parable was addressed to all the people, not just the Jewish leaders.

20:13 beloved son. Both Luke and Mark recorded this expression, which makes clear that the son in the parable is an illustration of Christ (*see note on Mt 21:37*).

20:16 destroy these vine-growers. This probably pictures the destruction of Jerusalem (*see note on 19:43*). **give the vineyard to others.** *See note on 21:24.* **May it never be!** Only Luke recorded this hostile reaction from the crowd. The response suggests that they grasped the meaning of the parable.

20:17 Quoted from Ps 118:22.

20:18 Everyone who falls ... on whomever it falls. *See note on Mt 21:44.* The expression was a quotation from Is 8:13–15, which speaks of Jehovah. Like so many other OT passages applied to Christ, it proves that He was Jehovah incarnate.

20:20 spies. The fact that the Jewish leaders resorted to such tactics is a measure of their desperation. They could not find any legitimate reason to accuse Him (cf. 6:7; 11:53, 54; Mt 22:15; 26:59, 60). **the governor.** I.e., Pilate, who was in town for the coming Passover and Feast of Unleavened Bread (*see note on Mt 27:2*).

20:21–26 *See notes on Mt 22:16–21; Mark 12:13–17.*

20:22 This was the second in a series of questions designed to entrap Jesus. This question was raised by the Pharisees and Herodians (Mk 12:13). *See notes on vv. 2, 33.*

20:24 Whose likeness ... ? The image on the denarius was one of the main reasons the Jews chafed at the poll tax. They claimed it was a violation of the commandment against graven images, and since Caesar pretended to a position tantamount to deity, the paying of the tax was unlawful worship—and in the minds of many, tantamount to gross idolatry. *See notes on Mt 22:19; Mk 12:16.*

20:25 render to Caesar. Christ thus recognized that all citizens have duties to the secular state, as well as duties to God—and He recognized a legitimate distinction between the two (*see notes on Mt 22:21; Mk 12:17*).

20:27–38 *See notes on Mt 22:23–32; Mk 12:18–27.*

20:27 Sadducees. *See note on Mt 3:7.*

20:28 his brother should marry the wife. According to the law of levirate marriage outlined in Dt 25:5 (*see note on Mt 22:24*).

20:33 This was the third in a series of questions designed to entrap Jesus. This question was raised by the Sadducees (v. 27). *See*

considered worthy to attain to [A]that age and the
resurrection from the dead, neither marry nor are
given in marriage; 36 for they cannot even die anymore, because they are like angels, and are [A]sons of
God, being sons of the resurrection. 37 But that the
dead are raised, even Moses showed, in [A]the *passage*
about the burning bush, where he calls the Lord
[B]THE GOD OF ABRAHAM, AND THE GOD OF ISAAC, AND
THE GOD OF JACOB. 38 [A]Now He is not the God of the
dead but of the living; for [B]all live to Him." 39 Some
of the scribes answered and said, "Teacher, You have
spoken well." 40 For [A]they did not have courage to
question Him any longer about anything.
41 [A]Then He said to them, "How *is it that* they say
[a]the Christ is [B]David's son? 42 For David himself says
in the book of Psalms,

'[A]THE LORD SAID TO MY LORD,
"SIT AT MY RIGHT HAND,
43 [A]UNTIL I MAKE YOUR ENEMIES A
FOOTSTOOL FOR YOUR FEET." '

44 Therefore David calls Him 'Lord,' and how is He
his son?"
45 [A]And while all the people were listening, He said
to the disciples, 46 "Beware of the scribes, [A]who like to
walk around in long robes, and love respectful greetings in the market places, and chief seats in the synagogues and places of honor at banquets, 47 who devour
widows' houses, and for appearance's sake offer long
prayers. These will receive greater condemnation."

THE WIDOW'S GIFT

21 [A]And He looked up and saw the rich putting
their gifts into the treasury. 2 And He saw a
poor widow putting [a]in [A]two [b]small copper coins.
3 And He said, "Truly I say to you, this poor widow
put in more than all *of them;* 4 for they all out of
their [a]surplus put into the [b]offering; but she out
of her poverty put in all [c]that she had [A]to live on."
5 [A]And while some were talking about the temple,
that it was adorned with beautiful stones and votive
gifts, He said, 6 "*As for* these things which you are
looking at, the days will come in which [A]there will
not be left one stone upon another which will not
be torn down."
7 They questioned Him, saying, "Teacher, when
therefore will these things happen? And what *will*
be the [a]sign when these things are about to take
place?" 8 And He said, "See to it that you are not
misled; for many will come in My name, saying, '[A]I
am *He*,' and, 'The time is near.' [B]Do not go after them.
9 When you hear of wars and disturbances, do not
be terrified; for these things must take place first,
but the end *does* not *follow* immediately."

THINGS TO COME

10 Then He continued by saying to them, "Nation
will rise against nation and kingdom against kingdom, 11 and there will be great earthquakes, and in
various places plagues and famines; and there will
be terrors and great [a]signs from heaven.
12 "But before all these things, [A]they will lay their
hands on you and will persecute you, delivering you
to the synagogues and prisons, [a]bringing you before
kings and governors for My name's sake. 13 [A]It will
lead to [a]an opportunity for your testimony. 14 [A]So
make up your minds not to prepare beforehand to
defend yourselves; 15 for [A]I will give you [a]utterance
and wisdom which none of your opponents will be
able to resist or refute. 16 But you will be betrayed
even by parents and brothers and relatives and

20:35 [A]Matt 12:32; Luke 16:8 20:36 [A]Rom 8:16f; 1 John 3:1, 2 20:37 [A]Mark 12:26 [B]Ex 3:6 20:38 [A]Matt 22:32; Mark 12:27 [B]Rom 14:8 20:40 [A]Matt 22:46; Luke 14:6 20:41 [a]I.e. the Messiah [A]Luke 20:41-44: *Matt 22:41-46; Mark 12:35-37* [B]Matt 9:27 20:42 [A]Ps 110:1 20:43 [A]Ps 110:1 20:45 [A]Luke 20:45-47: *Matt 23:1-7; Mark 12:38-40* 20:46 [A]Luke 11:43; 14:7 21:1 [A]Luke 21:1-4: *Mark 12:41-44* 21:2 [a]Lit *there* [b]Gr *lepta* [A]Mark 12:42 21:4 [a]Or *abundance* [b]Lit *gifts* [c]Lit *the living that she had* [A]Mark 12:44 21:5 [A]Luke 21:5-36: *Matt 24; Mark 13* 21:6 [A]Luke 19:44 21:7 [a]Or *attesting miracle* 21:8 [A]John 8:24 [B]Luke 17:23 21:11 [a]Or *attesting miracles* 21:12 [a]Lit *being brought* [A]Luke 21:12-17: *Matt 10:19-22; Mark 13:11-13* 21:13 [a]Lit *a testimony for you* [A]Phil 1:12 21:14 [A]Luke 12:11 21:15 [a]Lit *a mouth* [A]Luke 12:12

notes on vv. 2, 22. Matthew 22:34–40 and Mark 12:28–34 recorded one last question raised by a scribe. Luke omitted it from his record.

20:36 like angels. I.e., like the angels in that they do not procreate (*see note on Mt 22:30*).

20:37 *passage about the burning* bush. Ex 3:1–4:17. In that passage God identified Himself to Moses as the God of Abraham, Isaac, and Jacob—using the present tense. He didn't say He *was* their God, but "I AM" their God, indicating that their existence had not ended with their deaths.

20:38 all live to Him. Only Luke records this phrase. All people—whether departed from their earthly bodies or not—are still living, and will live forever. No one is annihilated in death (cf. Jn 5:28–30).

20:39 Teacher, You have spoken well. Christ had given a powerful argument for the resurrection of the dead, and on that subject, the Pharisees agreed with Him against the Sadducees. This scribe, in spite of his hatred for Christ, was pleased with the answer He had given.

20:40 not have courage to question Him. The more questions Jesus answered the clearer it became that His understanding and authority were vastly superior to that of the scribes and Pharisees. Cf. Mt 22:46; Mk 12:34.

20:41–44 After the Jewish leaders gave up questioning Him, Christ turned the tables and posed a question to them. *See notes on Mt 22:42–45; Mk 12:35–37.*

20:42 Quoted from Ps 110:1.

20:45–47 *See notes on Mk 12:38–40.*

21:1 the treasury. Thirteen chests with funnel-shaped openings stood in the court of the women. Each was labeled for a specific use, and donations were given accordingly.

21:2 poor widow. The Gr. expression signifies extreme poverty. This woman was desperately poor, and more fit to be a recipient of charity than a donor. **copper coins.** The smallest copper coins in use in the region were worth about one-eighth of a cent, but they were all this woman had to live on (v. 4). *See note on Mk 12:42.*

21:3 put in more. I.e., more in proportion to her means, and therefore more in the sight of God.

21:4 The religious system was literally devouring widows' houses (cf. 10:47).

21:5 beautiful stones. *See notes on Mt 24:1; Mk 13:1.* **votive gifts.** Wealthy people gave gifts of gold sculptures, golden plaques, and other treasures to the temple. Herod had donated a golden vine with clusters of golden grapes nearly 6 feet tall. The gifts were displayed on the walls and suspended in the portico. They constituted an unimaginable collection of wealth. All of these riches were looted by the Romans when the temple was destroyed (v. 6).

21:6–17 *See notes on Mt 24:2–10; Mk 13:2–11.*

21:8 Do not go after them. Cf. 17:23. *See note on Mt 24:26.*

21:9 the end. *See notes on Mt 24:6, 14.*

21:11 signs from heaven. The cross references in Mt 24:7 and Mk 13:8 omit this phrase. Cf. v. 25. *See note on Mk 13:25.*

21:13 an opportunity for your testimony. Trials are always opportunities (Jas 1:2–4), and persecution is often an opportunity to magnify one's testimony.

21:14 not to prepare beforehand. *See note on 12:11.*

friends, and they will put *some* of you to death, 17 and you will be hated by all because of My name. 18 Yet [A]not a hair of your head will perish. 19 [A]By your endurance you will gain your [a]lives.

20 "But when you see Jerusalem [A]surrounded by armies, then [a]recognize that her desolation is near. 21 Then those who are in Judea must flee to the mountains, and those who are in the midst of [a]the city must leave, and [A]those who are in the country must not enter [a]the city; 22 because these are [A]days of vengeance, so that all things which are written will be fulfilled. 23 Woe to those who are pregnant and to those who are nursing babies in those days; for [A]there will be great distress upon the [a]land and wrath to this people; 24 and they will fall by [A]the edge of the sword, and will be led captive into all the nations; and [B]Jerusalem will be [C]trampled under foot by the Gentiles until [D]the times of the Gentiles are fulfilled.

THE RETURN OF CHRIST

25 "There will be [a]signs in sun and moon and stars, and on the earth dismay among nations, in perplexity at the roaring of the sea and the waves, 26 men fainting from fear and the expectation of the things which are coming upon the [a]world; for the powers of [b]the heavens will be shaken. 27 [A]Then they will see [B]THE SON OF MAN COMING IN A CLOUD with power and great glory. 28 But when these things begin to take place, straighten up and lift up your heads, because [A]your redemption is drawing near."

29 Then He told them a parable: "Behold the fig tree and all the trees; 30 as soon as they put forth *leaves,* you see it and [A]know for yourselves that summer is now near. 31 So you also, when you see these things happening, [a]recognize that [A]the kingdom of God is near. 32 Truly I say to you, this [a]generation will not pass away until all things take place. 33 [A]Heaven and earth will pass away, but My words will not pass away.

34 "[A]Be on guard, so that your hearts will not be weighted down with dissipation and drunkenness and the worries of life, and that day will not come on you suddenly like a trap; 35 for it will come upon all those who dwell on the face of all the earth. 36 But [A]keep on the alert at all times, praying that you may have strength to escape all these things that are about to take place, and to [B]stand before the Son of Man."

37 Now [a]during the day He was [A]teaching in the temple, but [b,B]at evening He would go out and spend the night on [c,C]the mount that is called [d]Olivet. 38 And all the people would get up [A]early in the morning *to come* to Him in the temple to listen to Him.

PREPARING THE PASSOVER

22 [A]Now the Feast of Unleavened Bread, which is called the [B]Passover, was approaching. 2 The chief priests and the scribes [A]were seeking how they might put Him to death; for they were afraid of the people.

3 [A]And [B]Satan entered into Judas who was called Iscariot, [a]belonging to the number of the twelve. 4 And he went away and discussed with the chief priests and [A]officers how he might betray Him to them. 5 They were glad and agreed to give him money. 6 So he consented, and *began* seeking a good opportunity to betray Him to them [a]apart from the crowd.

21:18 [A]Matt 10:30; Luke 12:7 21:19 [a]Lit *souls* [A]Matt 10:22; 24:13; Rom 2:7; 5:3f; Heb 10:36; James 1:3; 2 Pet 1:6 21:20 [a]Lit *know* [A]Luke 19:43 21:21 [a]Lit *her* [A]Luke 17:31 21:22 [A]Is 63:4; Dan 9:24-27; Hos 9:7 21:23 [a]Or *earth* [A]Dan 8:19; 1 Cor 7:26 21:24 [A]Gen 34:26; Ex 17:13; Heb 11:34 [B]Is 63:18; Dan 8:13 [C]Rev 11:2 [D]Rom 11:25 21:25 [a]Or *attesting miracles* 21:26 [a]Lit *inhabited earth* [b]Or *heaven* 21:27 [A]Matt 16:27; 24:30; 26:64; Mark 13:26 [B]Dan 7:13; Rev 1:7 21:28 [A]Luke 18:7 21:30 [A]Luke 12:57 21:31 [a]Lit *know* [A]Matt 3:2 21:32 [a]Or *race* 21:33 [A]Matt 5:18; Luke 16:17 21:34 [A]Matt 24:42-44; Mark 4:19; Luke 12:40, 45; 1 Thess 5:2ff 21:36 [A]Mark 13:33; Luke 12:40 [B]Luke 1:19; Rev 7:9; 8:2; 11:4 21:37 [a]Lit *days* [b]Lit *nights* [c]Or *the hill* [d]Or *Olive Grove* [A]Matt 26:55; Luke 19:47 [B]Mark 11:19 [C]Matt 21:1 21:38 [A]John 8:2 22:1 [A]Luke 22:1, 2: *Matt 26:2-5; Mark 14:1, 2;* Ex 12:1-27 [B]John 11:55; 13:1 22:2 [A]Matt 12:14 22:3 [a]Lit *being of* [A]Luke 22:3-6: *Matt 26:14-16; Mark 14:10, 11* [B]Matt 4:10; John 13:2, 27 22:4 [A]1 Chr 9:11; Neh 11:11; Luke 22:52; Acts 4:1; 5:24, 26 22:6 [a]Or *without a disturbance*

21:18 not a hair. Cf. v. 16. This was not a promise for the preservation of their physical lives, but a guarantee that they would suffer no eternal loss. God Himself sovereignly preserves His own. *See note on Jn 10:28, 29.*

21:19 The true sense of this verse seems to be, "By your endurance you will gain your lives," referring to the final aspect of salvation, namely, glorification. *See note on Mt 24:13.*

21:20 Jerusalem surrounded by armies. *See note on 19:43.* A comparison with Mt 24:15, 16 and Mk 13:14 suggests that this sign is closely associated with "the abomination of desolation" (*see notes on Mt 24:15; Da 9:27; 11:31*). This sign of Jerusalem under siege was previewed in A.D. 70, but awaits its fulfillment in the future.

21:21 the mountains. *See notes on Mt 24:16; Mk 13:14.*

21:22 vengeance. I.e., God's righteous retribution against sin.

21:23 pregnant ... nursing. *See note on Mk 13:17.*

21:24 the times of the Gentiles. This expression is unique to Luke. It identifies the era from Israel's captivity (ca. 586 B.C. to Babylon; cf. 2Ki 25) to her restoration in the kingdom (Rev 20:1–6). It has been a time during which, in accord with God's purpose, Gentiles have dominated or threatened Jerusalem. The era has also been marked by vast spiritual privileges for the Gentile nations (cf. Is 66:12; Mal 1:11; Mt 24:14; Mk 13:10).

21:25 There will be signs. The celestial signs and wonders described here immediately precede the return of Christ. *See note on Mt 24:29.*

21:27 coming. Quoted from Da 7:13. *See notes on Mt 24:30, 31; Mk 13:26, 27.* Cf. 2Th 1:7–10; Rev 19:11–16.

21:28 lift up your heads. The dreadful tribulations and signs that mark the last days are a cause of great expectation, joy, and triumph for the true believer. **redemption.** I.e., the final fullness of redemption, when the redeemed are reunited with Christ forever.

21:29–33 *See notes on Mt 24:32–36; Mk 13:29–32.*

21:34 that day. I.e., the day of His return. *See note on Mt 24:37.* When Christ mentions His return, He invariably enjoins watchfulness (cf. 12:37–40; Mt 25:13; Mk 13:33–37).

21:36 at all times, praying. *See note on 18:1.*

21:37 during the day. I.e., during the days of that final week in Jerusalem.

22:1 which is called the Passover. *See note on Mt 26:17.* Passover was a single day, followed immediately by the Feast of the Unleavened Bread (Lv 23:5, 6). The whole season could be referred to by either name (cf. v. 7).

22:2 chief priests and the scribes. *See notes on 19:47; 20:1.* **For they were afraid of the people.** They were therefore plotting secretly, hoping to eliminate Him after the Passover season, when Jerusalem would not be filled with so many people (cf. v. 6; Mt 26:4, 5; Mk 14:1, 2). But these events occurred according to God's timetable, not theirs (*see note on Mt 26:2*).

22:3 Satan entered. I.e., Judas was possessed by Satan himself. Satan evidently gained direct control over Judas on two occasions—once just before Judas arranged his betrayal with the chief priests, and again during the Last Supper (Jn 13:27), immediately before the betrayal was actually carried out.

22:4 officers. I.e., the temple guard, a security force consisting of Levites.

22:5 agreed to give him money. Matthew 26:15 says 30 pieces of silver, the price of a slave (Ex 21:32).

7 [A]Then came the *first* day of Unleavened Bread
on which [B]the Passover *lamb* had to be sacrificed.
8 And Jesus sent [A]Peter and John, saying, "Go and
prepare the Passover for us, so that we may eat it."
9 They said to Him, "Where do You want us to prepare it?" 10 And He said to them, "When you have
entered the city, a man will meet you carrying a
pitcher of water; follow him into the house that
he enters. 11 And you shall say to the owner of the
house, 'The Teacher says to you, "Where is the guest
room in which I may eat the Passover with My disciples?"' 12 And he will show you a large, furnished
upper room; prepare it there." 13 And they left and
found *everything* just as He had told them; and they
prepared the Passover.

THE LORD'S SUPPER

14 [A]When the hour had come, He reclined *at the
table,* and [B]the apostles with Him. 15 And He said
to them, "I have earnestly desired to eat this Passover with you before I suffer; 16 for I say to you, I
shall never again eat it [A]until it is fulfilled in the
kingdom of God." 17 [A]And when He had taken a cup
and [B]given thanks, He said, "Take this and share
it among yourselves; 18 for [A]I say to you, I will not
drink of the fruit of the vine from now on until the
kingdom of God comes." 19 And when He had taken
some bread *and* [A]given thanks, He broke it and gave
it to them, saying, "This is My body which is given
for you; do this in remembrance of Me." 20 And in
the same way *He took* the cup after they had eaten,
saying, "This cup which is [A]poured out for you is
the [B]new covenant in My blood. 21 [A]But behold, the
hand of the one betraying Me is with [a]Mine on the
table. 22 For indeed, the Son of Man is going [A]as it
has been determined; but woe to that man by whom
He is betrayed!" 23 And they began to discuss among
themselves which one of them it might be who was
going to do this thing.

WHO IS GREATEST

24 And there arose also [A]a dispute among them *as
to* which one of them was regarded to be greatest.
25 [A]And He said to them, "The kings of the Gentiles
lord it over them; and those who have authority
over them are called 'Benefactors.' 26 But *it is* not
this way with you, [A]but the one who is the greatest
among you must become like [B]the youngest, and

22:7 [A]Luke 22:7-13: *Matt 26:17-19; Mark 14:12-16* [B]Mark 14:12 22:8 [A]Acts 3:1, 11; 4:13, 19; 8:14; Gal 2:9 22:14 [A]Matt 26:20; Mark 14:17 [B]Mark 6:30 22:16 [A]Luke 14:15; 22:18, 30; Rev 19:9 22:17 [A]Luke 22:17-20: *Matt 26:26-29; Mark 14:22-25; 1 Cor 11:23-25;* 1 Cor 10:16 [B]Matt 14:19 22:18 [A]Matt 26:29; Mark 14:25 22:19 [A]Matt 14:19 22:20 [A]Matt 26:28; Mark 14:24 [B]Ex 24:8; Jer 31:31; 1 Cor 11:25; 2 Cor 3:6; Heb 8:8, 13; 9:15 22:21 [a]Lit *Me* [A]Luke 22:21-23: *Matt 26:21-24; Mark 14:18-21;* Ps 41:9; John 13:18, 21, 22, 26 22:22 [A]Acts 2:23; 4:28; 10:42; 17:31 22:24 [A]Mark 9:34; Luke 9:46 22:25 [A]Luke 22:25-27: *Matt 20:25-28; Mark 10:42-45* 22:26 [A]Matt 23:11; Mark 9:35; Luke 9:48 [B]1 Pet 5:5

22:7 day of Unleavened Bread. I.e., the first day of the feast season (*see note on Mt 26:17*). The people from Galilee celebrated the Passover on Thursday evening (see Introduction to John: Interpretive Challenges), so the lambs were killed in the afternoon of that day. The disciples and Jesus ate the Passover meal that evening, after sundown (when Passover officially began). Judeans would follow this same sequence one day later on Friday.

22:8 Peter and John. Identified only by Luke. **Go and prepare.** This was no small task. They had to take the paschal lamb to be sacrificed, and make preparations for a meal for 13 (v. 14). But preliminary arrangements for the meal had apparently been made personally by Jesus Himself, and the owner of the upper room was taking care of many of those details for them. *See note on Mt 26:18.*

22:10 a man ... carrying ... water. Probably part of his work to prepare for the meal. Normally carrying water was woman's work, so a man carrying a pitcher would stand out. It is unlikely that the water pitcher was any sort of prearranged signal. Christ's knowledge of what the man would be doing at the precise moment the disciples arrived appears to be a manifestation of His divine omniscience.

22:12 a large, furnished upper room. One of many such rooms for rent in Jerusalem that were maintained for the express purpose of providing pilgrims a place to celebrate feasts. The furnishings undoubtedly included everything necessary to prepare and serve a meal.

22:14 the hour had come. I.e., sundown, marking the official beginning of Passover (*see note on v. 7*).

22:15 earnestly desired. Cf. Jn 13:1. Jesus wanted to prepare them for what was coming.

22:16 fulfilled. Christ's death on the following day fulfilled the symbolism of the Passover meal. Passover was both a memorial of the deliverance from Egypt, and a prophetic type of the sacrifice of Christ.

22:17 when He had taken a cup. Luke mentions two cups (cf. v. 20). The Passover seder involved the sharing of 4 cups of diluted red wine. This cup was the first of the 4 (the cup of thanksgiving) and was preliminary to the institution of the Lord's Supper (*see note on 1Co 10:16*). It represented the end of His time of eating and drinking with the disciples, particularly partaking of the Passover (v. 18; cf. 5:34, 35; Mt 9:15; 26:29; *see note on Mk 14:25*).

22:19 This is My body. I.e., it represented His body (cf. the words of 8:11, "the seed is the word of God"—and also v. 20). Such metaphorical language was a typical Hebraism. No eucharistic miracle of transubstantiation was implied, nor could the disciples have missed the symbolic intent of His statement, for His actual body—yet unbroken—was before their very eyes. *See note on Mt 26:26.* **do this.** Thus He established the observance as an ordinance for worship (*see notes on 1Co 11:23–26*). **remembrance of Me.** Passover had looked forward to the sacrifice of Christ; He transformed the seder into an altogether different ceremony, which looks back in remembrance at His atoning death.

22:20 *took* the cup. This is the third (the cup of blessing) of the 4 cups in the Passover celebration (*see note on 1Co 10:16*). **after they had eaten.** Cf. 1Co 11:25. These two verses are virtually identical in form. Paul stated that he had received his information about this event from the Lord Himself (1Co 11:23). **This cup ... is the new covenant.** Clearly, the cup only represented the New Covenant (*see note on v. 19*).

22:21 the hand ... betraying Me. Luke recounted the details of the Lord's Supper topically, not chronologically (see Introduction: Background and Setting; see *note on 1:3*). Matthew and Mark placed Jesus' warning about the betrayer prior to the giving of the bread and cup; Luke put it afterward. Only Jn 13:30 records Judas' departure, but John says nothing about the bread and cup. So it is difficult to tell by comparison whether Judas left before or after the institution of the Lord's Supper. But Luke's words here seem to imply that Judas actually shared in that event. If so, his presence at that time makes his hypocrisy and crime all the more despicable (cf. 1Co 11:27–30).

22:22 as it has been determined. Every detail of the crucifixion of Christ was under the sovereign control of God and in accord with His eternal purposes. Cf. Ac 2:23; 4:26–28. **but woe.** The fact that Judas' betrayal was part of God's plan does not free him from the guilt of a crime he entered into willfully. God's sovereignty is never a legitimate excuse for human guilt.

22:24 a dispute. Cf. 9:46; Mt 20:20–24. This dispute may have prompted the episode where Christ washed their feet (Jn 13:1–20). It reveals how large an issue this was in the minds of the disciples, and how far they were from grasping all that He had taught them.

22:25 Benefactors. Cf. Mt 20:25. This title was used by the heathen rulers of both Egypt and Syria, though it was rarely a fitting description. The intent was to portray themselves as champions of their people, but it had a very condescending ring to it—especially when so many "benefactors" were actually ruthless tyrants.

22:26 leader like the servant. Cf. Mt 20:26–28. This is an apparent reference to the washing of their feet (*see note on v. 24*). Christ Himself had modeled such servitude throughout His ministry (v. 27; cf. Php 2:5–8).

the leader like the servant. 27 For [A]who is greater,
the one who reclines *at the table* or the one who
serves? Is it not the one who reclines *at the table?*
But [B]I am among you as the one who serves.
28 "You are those who have stood by Me in My
[A]trials; 29 and just as My Father has granted Me
a [A]kingdom, I grant you 30 that you may [A]eat and
drink at My table in My [B]kingdom, and [C]you will
sit on thrones judging the twelve tribes of Israel.
31 "Simon, Simon, behold, [A]Satan has [a]demanded
permission to [B]sift you like wheat; 32 but I [A]have
prayed for you, that your faith may not fail; and
you, when once you have turned again, [B]strengthen
your brothers." 33 [A]But he said to Him, "Lord, with
You I am ready to go both to prison and to death!"
34 And He said, "I say to you, Peter, the rooster will
not crow today until you have denied three times
that you know Me."
35 And He said to them, "[A]When I sent you out
without money belt and bag and sandals, you did
not lack anything, did you?" They said, "*No,* nothing."
36 And He said to them, "But now, [a]whoever has a
money belt is to take it along, likewise also a bag,
and [a]whoever has no sword is to sell his [b]coat and
buy one. 37 For I tell you that this which is written
must be fulfilled in Me, '[A]AND HE WAS NUMBERED
WITH TRANSGRESSORS'; for [B]that which refers to
Me has *its* [a]fulfillment." 38 They said, "Lord, look,
here are two [A]swords." And He said to them, "It is
enough."

THE GARDEN OF GETHSEMANE

39 [A]And He came out and proceeded [B]as was His
custom to [C]the Mount of Olives; and the disciples
also followed Him. 40 [A]When He arrived at the place,
He said to them, "[B]Pray that you may not enter into
temptation." 41 And He withdrew from them about
a stone's throw, and He [A]knelt down and *began* to
pray, 42 saying, "Father, if You are willing, remove
this [A]cup from Me; [B]yet not My will, but Yours be
done." 43 [a]Now an [A]angel from heaven appeared to
Him, strengthening Him. 44 And [A]being in agony
He was praying very fervently; and His sweat became like drops of blood, falling down upon the
ground. 45 When He rose from prayer, He came to
the disciples and found them sleeping from sorrow,
46 and said to them, "Why are you sleeping? Get up
and [A]pray that you may not enter into temptation."

22:27 [A]Luke 12:37 [B]Matt 20:28; John 13:12-15 22:28 [A]Heb 2:18; 4:15 22:29 [A]Matt 5:3; 2 Tim 2:12 22:30 [A]Luke 22:16 [B]Matt 5:3; 2 Tim 2:12 [C]Matt 19:28 22:31 [a]Or *obtained by asking* [A]Job 1:6-12; 2:1-6; Matt 4:10 [B]Amos 9:9 22:32 [A]John 17:9, 15 [B]John 21:15-17 22:33 [A]Luke 22:33, 34: *Matt 26:33-35; Mark 14:29-31; John 13:37, 38* 22:35 [A]Matt 10:9f; Mark 6:8; Luke 9:3ff; 10:4 22:36 [a]Lit *he who* [b]Or *outer garment* 22:37 [a]Lit *end* [A]Is 53:12 [B]John 17:4; 19:30 22:38 [A]Luke 22:36, 49 22:39 [A]Matt 26:30; Mark 14:26; John 18:1 [B]Luke 21:37 [C]Matt 21:1 22:40 [A]Luke 22:40-46: *Matt 26:36-46; Mark 14:32-42* [B]Matt 6:13; Luke 22:46 22:41 [A]Matt 26:39; Mark 14:35; Luke 18:11 22:42 [A]Matt 20:22 [B]Matt 26:39 22:43 [a]Most early mss do not contain vv 43 and 44 [A]Matt 4:11 22:44 [A]Heb 5:7 22:46 [A]Luke 22:40

22:28 My trials. Christ's entire life and ministry were filled with temptations (4:1–13); hardships (9:58); sorrows (19:41); and agonies (v. 44)—not to mention the sufferings of the cross which He knew were yet to come.

22:29 a kingdom, I grant you. Christ confirmed the disciples' expectation of an earthly kingdom yet to come. It would not come in the timing or the manner that they hoped, but He affirmed the promise that such a kingdom would indeed be established, and that they would have a principal role in it (v. 30; cf. Mt 19:28).

22:30 judging the twelve tribes of Israel. The language identifies this as a millennial promise. *See note on Rev 20:4.*

22:31 Simon, Simon. The repetition of the name (cf. 10:41; Ac 9:4) implied an earnest and somber tone of warning. Christ Himself had given Simon the name Peter (6:14), but here He reverted to his old name, perhaps to intensify His rebuke about Peter's fleshly overconfidence. The context also suggests that Peter may have been one of the more vocal participants in the dispute of v. 24. Satan has demanded *permission*. Though addressed specifically to Peter, this warning embraced the other disciples as well. sift you like wheat. The imagery is apt. It suggests that such trials, though unsettling and undesirable, have a necessary refining effect.

22:32 I have prayed for you. The pronoun "you" is singular (*see note on v. 31*). Although it is clear that Jesus prayed for all of them (Jn 17:6–19), He personally assured Peter of His prayers and of Peter's ultimate victory, even encouraging Peter to be an encourager to the others. that your faith may not fail. Peter himself failed miserably, but his faith was never overthrown (cf. Jn 21:18, 19).

22:34 you have denied. This prediction of Peter's denial evidently took place in the upper room (cf. Jn 13:38). Matthew 26:34 and Mark 14:30 record a second, nearly identical incident, which took place on the Mt. of Olives on the way to Gethsemane (cf. Mt 26:30; Mk 14:26).

22:35 When I sent you. Cf. 9:3; 10:4.

22:36 But now. When Christ sent them out before, He had sovereignly arranged for their needs to be met. Henceforth they were to use normal means to provide for their own support and protection. The money bag, knapsack, and sword were figurative expressions for such means (the sword being emblematic of protection, not aggression). But they mistakenly took His words literally (v. 38).

22:37 Quoted from Is 53:12.

22:38 two swords. These were short, daggerlike instruments—more like knives than swords. There was nothing unusual about the carrying of such weapons in that culture. They had many practical uses besides violence against other people. It is enough. I.e., enough of such talk (cf. v. 51).

22:39 Mount of Olives. *See notes on 19:29; Mt 24:3.* the disciples also followed Him. Matthew 26:36, 37 and Mark 14:32, 33 give more details. He left most of the disciples at the entrance to Gethsemane, and took Peter, James, and John inside with Him to pray.

22:40 the place. Gethsemane. *See notes on Mt 26:36; Mk 14:32.* Pray. He had already warned them—and Peter in particular—that an egregious trial was imminent (v. 31). Sadly, that warning, as well as His imploring them to pray, went unheeded.

22:41 about a stone's throw. I.e., within earshot. His prayer was partly for their benefit (cf. Jn 11:41, 42).

22:42 this cup. I.e., the cup of divine wrath (cf. Is 51:17, 22; Jer 25:15–17, 27–29; La 4:21, 22; Eze 23:31–34; Hab 2:16). not My will. Cf. Mt 26:39; Jn 4:34; 5:30; 6:38; 8:29. This does not imply that there was any conflict between the will of the Father and the will of the Son. It was a perfectly normal expression of His humanity that He shrank from the cup of divine wrath (*see note on Mt 26:39*). But even though the cup was abhorrent to Him, He willingly took it, because it was the will of the Father. In this prayer He was consciously, deliberately, and voluntarily subjugating all His human desires to the Father's perfect will. Thus there was neither conflict between Father and Son, nor between the deity of Christ and His human desires.

22:43, 44 The facts in these verses are related only by Luke, the physician.

22:44 like drops of blood. This suggests a dangerous condition known as *hematidrosis,* the effusion of blood in one's perspiration. It can be caused by extreme anguish or physical strain. Subcutaneous capillaries dilate and burst, mingling blood with sweat. Christ Himself stated that His distress had brought Him to the threshold of death (*see notes on Mt 26:38; Mk 14:34;* cf. Heb 12:3, 4).

22:45 sleeping from sorrow. Cf. 9:32. The emotional strain was wearing on the disciples as well as Christ. Their response, however, was to capitulate to fleshly cravings. Thus they gratified their immediate desire for sleep, rather than staying awake to pray for strength, as Christ had commanded them (v. 40). All the reasons for their subsequent failure are found in their behavior in the garden.

22:46 Get up and pray. A tender appeal to the disciples, who in their weakness were disobeying Him at a critical moment. He may have been summoning them to a standing posture, to help overcome their drowsiness. Matthew 26:43 and Mark 14:40 reveal that He again found them sleeping at least one more time.

JESUS BETRAYED BY JUDAS

47[A]While He was still speaking, behold, a crowd
came, and the one called Judas, one of the twelve,
was preceding them; and he approached Jesus to
kiss Him. 48But Jesus said to him, "Judas, are you
betraying the Son of Man with a kiss?" 49When
those who were around Him saw what was going
to happen, they said, "Lord, shall we strike with
the [A]sword?" 50And one of them struck the slave
of the high priest and cut off his right ear. 51But
Jesus answered and said, "[a]Stop! No more of this."
And He touched his ear and healed him. 52Then
Jesus said to the chief priests and [A]officers of the
temple and elders who had come against Him,
"Have you come out with swords and clubs [B]as
you would against a robber? 53While I was with
you daily in the temple, you did not lay hands
on Me; but [a]this hour and the power of darkness
are yours."

JESUS' ARREST

54[A]Having arrested Him, they led Him *away* and
brought Him to the house of the high priest; but
[B]Peter was following at a distance. 55[A]After they had
kindled a fire in the middle of [B]the courtyard and
had sat down together, Peter was sitting among
them. 56And a servant-girl, seeing him as he sat
in the firelight and looking intently at him, said,
"This man was with Him too." 57But he denied *it,*
saying, "Woman, I do not know Him." 58A little
later, [A]another saw him and said, "You are *one* of
them too!" But Peter said, "Man, I am not!" 59After
about an hour had passed, another man *began* to
insist, saying, "Certainly this man also was with
Him, [A]for he is a Galilean too." 60But Peter said,
"Man, I do not know what you are talking about."
Immediately, while he was still speaking, a rooster
crowed. 61[A]The Lord turned and looked at Peter.
And Peter remembered the word of the Lord, how
He had told him, "[B]Before a rooster crows today,
you will deny Me three times." 62And he went out
and wept bitterly.

63[A]Now the men who were holding [a]Jesus in custody were mocking Him and beating Him, 64and
they blindfolded Him and were asking Him, saying,
"[A]Prophesy, who is the one who hit You?" 65And
they were saying many other things against Him,
[A]blaspheming.

JESUS BEFORE THE SANHEDRIN

66[A]When it was day, [B]the [a]Council of elders of the
people assembled, both chief priests and scribes,
and they led Him away to their [C]council *chamber,*
saying, 67"[A]If You are the [a]Christ, tell us." But He said
to them, "If I tell you, you will not believe; 68and if
I ask a question, you will not answer. 69[A]But from
now on [B]THE SON OF MAN WILL BE SEATED AT THE
RIGHT HAND of the power OF GOD." 70And they all
said, "Are You [A]the Son of God, then?" And He said to
them, "[a,B]Yes, I am." 71Then they said, "What further
need do we have of testimony? For we have heard
it ourselves from His own mouth."

22:47 [A]Luke 22:47-53: *Matt 26:47-56; Mark 14:43-50; John 18:3-11* 22:49 [A]Luke 22:38 22:51 [a]Or "*Let Me at least do this," and He touched* 22:52 [A]Luke 22:4 [B]Luke 22:37 22:53 [a]Lit *this is your hour and power of darkness* 22:54 [A]Matt 26:57; Mark 14:53 [B]Matt 26:58; Mark 14:54; John 18:15 22:55 [A]Luke 22:55-62: *Matt 26:69-75; Mark 14:66-72; John 18:16-18, 25-27* [B]Matt 26:3 22:58 [A]John 18:26 22:59 [A]Matt 26:73; Mark 14:70 22:61 [A]Luke 7:13 [B]Luke 22:34 22:63 [a]Lit *Him* [A]Matt 26:67f; Mark 14:65; John 18:22f 22:64 [A]Matt 26:68; Mark 14:65 22:65 [A]Matt 27:39 22:66 [a]Or *Sanhedrin* [A]Matt 27:1f; Mark 15:1; John 18:28 [B]Acts 22:5 [C]Matt 5:22 22:67 [a]I.e. Messiah [A]Luke 22:67-71: *Matt 26:63-66; Mark 14:61-63; John 18:19-21* 22:69 [A]Matt 26:64; Mark 14:62; 16:19 [B]Ps 110:1 22:70 [a]Lit *You say that I am* [A]Matt 4:3 [B]Matt 26:64; 27:11; Luke 23:3

22:47 a crowd. These were heavily armed representatives of the Sanhedrin (Mt 26:47; Mk 14:43), accompanied by a Roman cohort with lanterns, torches, and weapons (Jn 18:3). **kiss.** A typical greeting, but this was the prearranged signal by which Judas would identify Christ for the soldiers (cf. Mt 26:48, 49; *see note on Mk 14:44*).

22:50 cut off his right ear. All 4 Gospels record this incident. Only John reveals that the swordsman was Peter and the victim was named Malchus (Jn 18:10). And only Luke, the physician, records the subsequent healing (v. 51).

22:51 touched his ear and healed him. This is the only instance in all of Scripture where Christ healed a flesh wound. The miracle is also unique in that Christ healed an enemy, unasked, and without any evidence of faith in the recipient. It is also remarkable that such a dramatic miracle had no effect whatsoever on the hearts of those men. Neither had the explosive power of Jesus' words, which knocked them to the ground (Jn 18:6). They carried on with the arrest as if nothing peculiar had happened (v. 54).

22:53 this hour ... darkness are yours. I.e., nighttime, the hour of darkness. They had not the courage to confront Jesus in the presence of the crowds at the temple, where He had openly taught each day. Their skulking tactics betrayed the truth about their hearts. Nighttime was a fitting hour for the servants of the power of darkness (Satan) to be afoot (cf. Jn 3:20, 21; Eph 5:8, 12–15; 1Th 5:5–7).

22:54 house of the high priest. I.e., Caiaphas' house. *See note on Mt 26:57.* **Peter was following at a distance.** All 4 Gospels record this fact. John indicates that another disciple—presumably himself—also followed (Jn 18:15).

22:56 a servant-girl. All 4 Gospels mention her. She appears to have been the doorkeeper of Annas' house (cf. Mt 26:69; Mk 14:66; Jn 18:17).

22:57 But he denied *it*. John 18:13–18 says this first denial took place while Jesus was being examined by Annas, father-in-law to Caiaphas (*see note on 3:2*). Both accounts mention a fire in the courtyard (v. 55; Jn 18:18) so it may be that the houses of Annas and Caiaphas shared a common courtyard. Only John mentions the examination by Annas, so the other Gospels describe Peter's 3-fold denial as an incident that took place in the porch and courtyard of Caiaphas' house.

22:58 another saw him. "Another" is a masculine pronoun in the Gr., indicating a man. Mark 14:69 says this second challenge to Peter came from the same servant-girl who first recognized him (v. 56). The supposed discrepancy is easily reconciled when it is remembered that Peter was among several bystanders, and many of them questioned him at once (Mt 26:73). He responded with his second denial.

22:59 he is a Galilean. They knew because of his accent (Mt 26:73).

22:61 The Lord turned and looked at Peter. Luke alone records that Jesus made eye contact with Peter. The verb used suggests an intent, fixed look. The fact that He could see Peter suggests that the men holding Jesus had already brought Him into the courtyard to beat Him (v. 63). **Peter remembered.** *See note on Mt 26:75.*

22:63 mocking Him and beating Him. Luke includes no details about Caiaphas' first interrogation of Jesus, recorded in Mt 26:59–68; Mk 14:55–65. The beating described here evidently took place after that first examination, before the Sanhedrin could assemble for its official hearing (v. 66).

22:66 When it was day. Criminal trials were not deemed legal if held at night, so the Sanhedrin dutifully waited until daybreak to render the verdict they had already agreed on anyway (cf. Mt 26:66; Mk 14:64).

22:67 If You are the Christ. The Sanhedrin subjected Him to the same set of questions He had been asked in the nighttime trial, and the answers He gave were substantially the same (cf. vv. 67–71; Mt 26:63–66; Mk 14:61–64).

JESUS BEFORE PILATE

23 Then the whole body of them got up and
[A]brought Him before Pilate. 2 [A]And they began to accuse Him, saying, "We found this man
[B]misleading our nation and [C]forbidding to pay taxes
to Caesar, and saying that He Himself is [a]Christ, a
King." 3 So Pilate asked Him, saying, "Are You the
King of the Jews?" And He answered him and said,
"[A]*It is as* you say." 4 Then Pilate said to the chief
priests and the crowds, "[A]I find no guilt in this man."
5 But they kept on insisting, saying, "He stirs up the
people, teaching all over Judea, [A]starting from Galilee even as far as this place."

6 When Pilate heard it, he asked whether the man
was a Galilean. 7 And when he learned that He belonged to Herod's jurisdiction, he sent Him to [A]Herod,
who himself also was in Jerusalem [a]at that time.

JESUS BEFORE HEROD

8 Now Herod was very glad when he saw Jesus;
for [A]he had wanted to see Him for a long time, because he had been hearing about Him and was hoping to see some [a]sign performed by Him. 9 And he
questioned Him [a]at some length; but [A]He answered
him nothing. 10 And the chief priests and the scribes
were standing there, accusing Him vehemently.
11 And Herod with his soldiers, after treating Him
with contempt and mocking Him, [A]dressed Him in
a gorgeous robe and sent Him back to Pilate. 12 Now
[A]Herod and Pilate became friends with one another
that very day; for before they had been enemies
with each other.

PILATE SEEKS JESUS' RELEASE

13 Pilate summoned the chief priests and the [A]rulers
and the people, 14 and said to them, "You brought this
man to me as one who [A]incites the people to rebellion,
and behold, having examined Him before you, I [B]have
found no guilt in this man regarding the charges
which you make against Him. 15 No, nor has [A]Herod,
for he sent Him back to us; and behold, nothing deserving death has been done by Him. 16 Therefore I
will [A]punish Him and release Him." 17 [[a]Now he was
obliged to release to them at the feast one prisoner.]

18 But they cried out all together, saying, "[A]Away
with this man, and release for us Barabbas!" 19 (He
was one who had been thrown into prison for an
insurrection made in the city, and for murder.) 20 Pilate, wanting to release Jesus, addressed them again,
21 but they kept on calling out, saying, "Crucify, crucify Him!" 22 And he said to them the third time,
"Why, what evil has this man done? I have found
in Him no guilt *demanding* death; therefore I will
[A]punish Him and release Him." 23 But they were
insistent, with loud voices asking that He be crucified. And their voices *began* to prevail. 24 And Pilate
pronounced sentence that their demand be granted.
25 And he released the man they were asking for
who had been thrown into prison for insurrection
and murder, but he delivered Jesus to their will.

SIMON BEARS THE CROSS

26 [A]When they led Him away, they seized a man,
Simon of [B]Cyrene, coming in from the country, and
placed on him the cross to carry behind Jesus.

23:1 [A]Matt 27:2; Mark 15:1; John 18:28 23:2 [a]I.e. Messiah [A]Luke 23:2, 3: *Matt 27:11-14; Mark 15:2-5; John 18:29-37* [B]Luke 23:14 [C]Luke 20:22; John 18:33ff; 19:12; Acts 17:7 23:3 [A]Luke 22:70 23:4 [A]Matt 27:23; Mark 15:14; Luke 23:14, 22; John 18:38; 19:4, 6 23:5 [A]Matt 4:12 23:7 [a]Lit *in these days* [A]Matt 14:1; Mark 6:14; Luke 3:1; 9:7; 13:31 23:8 [a]Or *attesting miracle* [A]Luke 9:9 23:9 [a]Lit *in many words* [A]Matt 27:12, 14; Mark 15:5; John 19:9 23:11 [A]Matt 27:28 23:12 [A]Acts 4:27 23:13 [A]Luke 23:35; John 7:26, 48; 12:42; Acts 3:17; 4:5, 8; 13:27 23:14 [A]Luke 23:2 [B]Luke 23:4 23:15 [A]Luke 9:9 23:16 [A]Matt 27:26; Mark 15:15; Luke 23:22; John 19:1; Acts 16:37 23:17 [a]Early mss do not contain this v 23:18 [A]Luke 23:18-25: *Matt 27:15-26; Mark 15:6-15;* John 18:39-19:16 23:22 [A]Luke 23:16 23:26 [A]Luke 23:26: *Matt 27:32; Mark 15:21;* John 19:17 [B]Matt 27:32

23:1 the whole body of them. I.e., the entire Sanhedrin, some 70 men. At least one member of the council, Joseph of Arimathea, dissented from the decision to condemn Christ (vv. 50–52). **brought Him before Pilate.** *See note on Mt 27:2.*

23:2 forbidding to pay taxes to Caesar. This was a deliberate lie. Members of the Sanhedrin had publicly questioned Jesus on this very issue (hoping to discredit Him before the Jews), and He expressly upheld Caesar's right to demand taxes (20:20–25). **saying that He … is Christ, a King.** This was innuendo, implying that He was seditious against Rome—another untrue charge.

23:3 *It is as* you say. John 18:33–37 gives a fuller account of Jesus' reply to this question.

23:4 no guilt. Despite the Jewish leaders' desperate attempts to accuse Him, Pilate was satisfied that Jesus was no insurrectionist, but the ferocity of the people made him afraid to exonerate Jesus. He was relieved to hear that Jesus was a Galilean, because that gave him an excuse to send Him to Herod (vv. 5, 6).

23:7 Herod's jurisdiction. *See note on 13:31.* **sent Him to Herod.** Herod had come to Jerusalem for the feasts, and Pilate seized the opportunity to free himself from a political dilemma by sending Jesus to his rival. *See note on v. 12.*

23:8 had wanted to see Him. Herod's interest in Christ was fueled by the fact that Christ reminded him of his late nemesis, John the Baptist (cf. 9:7–9). At one time Herod had apparently threatened to kill Jesus (13:31–33), but with Christ in Judea rather than Galilee and Perea (where Herod ruled), the king's concern seems to have been nothing more than an eager curiosity.

23:9 answered him nothing. It is significant that in all Jesus' various interrogations, Herod was the only one to whom He refused to speak. Cf. Mt 7:6. Herod had summarily rejected the truth when he heard it from John the Baptist, so it would have been pointless for Jesus to answer him. Cf. Is 53:7; Pss 38:13, 14; 39:1, 2, 9; 1Pe 2:23.

23:11 his soldiers. I.e., his security force. **treating Him with contempt.** Herod made Christ and the charges against Him as an occasion for a joke for Pilate's amusement (v. 12). **a gorgeous robe.** Probably not the same robe mentioned in Mt 27:28, which was a military cloak. This was an elegant king's garment, probably one that Herod was prepared to discard.

23:12 friends. Based on their common unjust and cowardly treatment of Jesus.

23:13 summoned. Pilate intended to declare Christ not guilty (v. 14), and it was his intention to make the verdict as public as possible. He undoubtedly expected that it would put an end to the whole matter.

23:14, 15 Pilate and Herod concurred in the verdict (cf. 1Ti 6:13).

23:16 I will punish Him. Cf. v. 22. Though Pilate found Him innocent of any wrongdoing, he was prepared to scourge Him merely to pacify the Jews. But even that punishment, severe as it was (*see note on Mt 27:26*), could not quench their thirst for His blood.

23:17 he was obliged. I.e., because it was a longstanding Jewish custom (Jn 18:39), traditionally honored by the Romans.

23:18 Barabbas. *See note on Mk 15:7.*

23:21 crucify Him! Crucifixion was the most painful and disgraceful form of execution the Romans employed. *See note on Mt 27:31.*

23:22 the third time. Pilate repeatedly gave powerful testimony to the innocence of Christ (vv. 4, 14, 15). In doing so, he not only condemned the Jews, who demanded Jesus' death, but also himself, because he handed the Savior over without cause.

23:24 Pilate pronounced sentence. Pilate's response reveals his lack of principle. His desire to please the Jews for political reasons (to save himself from Rome's displeasure) ultimately overcame his desire to set Jesus free (cf. v. 20). John 18:39–19:16 gives a much more detailed account of Pilate's decision to hand Jesus over.

23:26 Simon of Cyrene. All 3 Synoptic Gospels mention Simon. *See notes on Mt 27:32; Mk 15:21.*

27 And following Him was a large crowd of the
people, and of women who were [a,A]mourning and
lamenting Him. 28 But Jesus turning to them said,
"Daughters of Jerusalem, stop weeping for Me, but
weep for yourselves and for your children. 29 For
behold, the days are coming when they will say,
'[A]Blessed are the barren, and the wombs that never
bore, and the breasts that never nursed.' 30 Then
they will begin TO [A]SAY TO THE MOUNTAINS, 'FALL
ON US,' AND TO THE HILLS, 'COVER US.' 31 For if they
do these things [a]when the tree is green, what will
happen [b]when it is dry?"
32 [A]Two others also, who were criminals, were
being led away to be put to death with Him.

THE CRUCIFIXION

33 [A]When they came to the place called [a]The Skull,
there they crucified Him and the criminals, one on
the right and the other on the left. 34 [a]But Jesus was
saying, "[A]Father, forgive them; for they do not know
what they are doing." [B]And they cast lots, dividing
up His garments among themselves. 35 And the people stood by, looking on. And even the [A]rulers were
sneering at Him, saying, "He saved others; [B]let Him
save Himself if this is the [a]Christ of God, His Chosen
One." 36 The soldiers also mocked Him, coming up
to Him, [A]offering Him sour wine, 37 and saying, "[A]If
You are the King of the Jews, save Yourself!" 38 Now
there was also an inscription above Him,

"[A]THIS IS THE KING OF THE JEWS."

39 [A]One of the criminals who were hanged *there*
was [a]hurling abuse at Him, saying, "Are You not
the [b]Christ? [B]Save Yourself and us!" 40 But the other
answered, and rebuking him said, "Do you not even
fear God, since you are under the same sentence
of condemnation? 41 And we indeed *are suffering*
justly, for we are receiving [a]what we deserve for
our deeds; but this man has done nothing wrong."
42 And he was saying, "Jesus, remember me when
You come [a]in Your kingdom!" 43 And He said to him,
"Truly I say to you, today you shall be with Me in
[A]Paradise."
44 [A]It was now about [a,B]the sixth hour, and darkness [b]fell over the whole land until [c]the ninth
hour, 45 [a]because the sun was obscured; and [A]the
veil of the temple was torn [b]in two. 46 And Jesus,
[A]crying out with a loud voice, said, "Father, [B]INTO
YOUR HANDS I COMMIT MY SPIRIT." Having said
this, He breathed His last. 47 [A]Now when the centurion saw what had happened, he *began* [B]praising

23:27 [a]Lit *beating the breast* [A]Luke 8:52 23:29 [A]Matt 24:19; Luke 11:27; 21:23 23:30 [A]Hos 10:8; Is 2:19, 20; Rev 6:16 23:31 [a]Lit *in the green tree* [b]Lit *in the dry* 23:32 [A]Matt 27:38; Mark 15:27; John 19:18 23:33 [a]In Lat *Calvarius;* or *Calvary* [A]Luke 23:33-43: *Matt 27:33-44; Mark 15:22-32; John 19:17-24* 23:34 [a]Some early mss do not contain *But Jesus was saying…doing* [A]Matt 11:25; Luke 22:42 [B]Ps 22:18; John 19:24 23:35 [a]I.e. Messiah [A]Luke 23:13 [B]Matt 27:43 23:36 [A]Matt 27:48 23:37 [A]Matt 27:43 23:38 [A]Matt 27:37; Mark 15:26; John 19:19 23:39 [a]Or *blaspheming* [b]I.e. Messiah [A]Luke 23:39-43: *Matt 27:44; Mark 15:32* [B]Luke 23:35, 37 23:41 [a]Lit *things worthy of what we have done* 23:42 [a]Or *into* 23:43 [A]2 Cor 12:4; Rev 2:7 23:44 [a]I.e. noon [b]Or *occurred* [c]I.e. 3 p.m. [A]Luke 23:44-49: *Matt 27:45-56; Mark 15:33-41* [B]John 19:14 23:45 [a]Lit *the sun failing* [b]Lit *in the middle* [A]Ex 26:31-33; Matt 27:51 23:46 [A]Matt 27:50; Mark 15:37; John 19:30 [B]Ps 31:5 23:47 [A]Matt 27:54; Mark 15:39 [B]Matt 9:8

23:28 Daughters of Jerusalem. There is nothing to suggest that these women were Christ's disciples. They may have been professional mourners, obligatory at Jewish funerals (*see note on Mt 9:23*), and probably present at high-profile executions as well. **weep for yourselves.** Christ's reply to them was a prophetic warning. Only Luke recorded this incident.

23:29 Blessed are the barren. I.e., a time is coming when those who have no children to mourn will be considered blessed.

23:30 to say. Quoted from Hos 10:8. Cf. Rev 6:16, 17; 9:6.

23:31 tree is green … dry. This was probably a common proverb. Jesus' meaning seems to be this: if the Romans would perpetrate such atrocities on Jesus (the "green" wood—young, strong, and a source of life), what would they do to the Jewish nation (the "dry" wood—old, barren, and ripe for judgment)?

23:32 Two others … criminals. *See notes on Mt 27:38; Mk 15:27.*

23:33 The Skull. The Latin equivalent of *Golgotha. See notes on Mt 27:33; Mk 15:22.* **crucified.** *See note on Mt 27:31.*

23:34 forgive them. I.e., His tormentors, both Jews and Romans (cf. Ac 7:60). Some of the fruit of this prayer can be in the salvation of thousands of people in Jerusalem at Pentecost (Ac 2:41). **they do not know what they are doing.** I.e., they were not aware of the full scope of their wickedness. They did not recognize Him as the true Messiah (Ac 13:27, 28). They were blind to the light of divine truth, "for if they had understood it, they would not have crucified the Lord of glory" (1Co 2:8). Still, their ignorance certainly did not mean that they deserved forgiveness; rather, their spiritual blindness itself was a manifestation of their guilt (Jn 3:19). But Christ's prayer while they were in the very act of mocking Him is an expression of the boundless compassion of divine grace. **cast lots.** *See notes on Mt 27:35; Mk 15:24.*

23:35 sneering. Cf. Ps 22:6, 7, 16–18.

22:36 sour wine. Cf. Ps 69:21; *see note on Mt 27:34.*

23:38 an inscription. All 4 gospel writers mentioned the inscription, but each reported a slightly different variation. Both Luke and John (19:20) said that the inscription was written in Greek, Latin, and Hebrew, so the varying reports in the Gospels may simply reflect variant ways the inscription was translated on the placard itself. It is even more likely that all 4 evangelists simply reported the substance of the inscription elliptically, with each one omitting different parts of the full inscription. All 4 concurred with Mark that the inscription said THE KING OF THE JEWS (Mt 27:37; Mk 15:26; Jn 19:19). Luke added "THIS IS" at the beginning, and Matthew started with "THIS IS JESUS." John's version began, "JESUS OF NAZARETH." Putting them all together, the full inscription would read "THIS IS JESUS OF NAZARETH, THE KING OF THE JEWS."

23:39 One of the criminals. Matthew 27:44 and Mark 15:32 report that both criminals were mocking Christ along with the crowd. As the hours wore on, however, this criminal's conscience was smitten, and he repented. When the impenitent thief resumed his mocking (v. 39), this thief rebuked him and refused to participate again.

23:41 this man has done nothing wrong. Cf. vv. 4, 15, 22. Even the thief testified of His innocence.

23:42 Jesus, remember me. The penitent thief's prayer reflected his belief that the soul lives on after death; that Christ had a right to rule over a kingdom of the souls of men; and that He would soon enter that kingdom despite His impending death. His request to be remembered was a plea for mercy, which also reveals that the thief understood he had no hope but divine grace, and that the dispensing of that grace lay in Jesus' power. All of this demonstrates true faith on the part of the dying thief, and Christ graciously affirmed the man's salvation (v. 43).

23:43 Paradise. The only other places this word is used in the NT are 2Co 12:4 and Rev 2:7. The word suggests a garden (it is the word used of Eden in the LXX), but in all 3 NT uses it speaks of heaven.

23:44 sixth hour … until the ninth hour. From noon to 3:00 p.m. Luke was using the Jewish method of reckoning time. *See notes on Mt 27:45; Mk 15:25.* **darkness.** *See note on Mk 15:33.* This could not have been caused by an eclipse, because the Jews used a lunar calendar, and Passover always fell on the full moon, making a solar eclipse out of the question. This was a supernatural darkness.

23:45 the veil. *See note on Mt 27:51.*

23:46 into Your hands. This quotes Ps 31:5, and the manner of His death accords with Jn 10:18. Normally, victims of crucifixion died much slower deaths. He, being in control, simply yielded up His soul (Jn 10:18; 19:30), committing it to God. Thus He "offered Himself without blemish to God" (Heb 9:14).

23:47 the centurion. *See note on Mt 27:54.* **this man was innocent.** Matthew 27:54 and Mark 15:39 say the centurion stated, "This

God, saying, "Certainly this man was [a]innocent."
48 And all the crowds who came together for this
spectacle, when they observed what had happened,
began to return, [a,A]beating their breasts. 49 [A]And all
His acquaintances and [A]the women who accompanied Him from Galilee were standing at a distance,
seeing these things.

JESUS IS BURIED

50 [A]And a man named Joseph, who was a [B]mem-
ber of the Council, a good and righteous man 51 (he
had not consented to their plan and action), *a man*
from Arimathea, a city of the Jews, who was [A]wait-
ing for the kingdom of God; 52 this man went to
Pilate and asked for the body of Jesus. 53 And he
took it down and wrapped it in a linen cloth, and
laid Him in a tomb cut into the rock, where no
one had ever lain. 54 It was [A]the [a]preparation day,
and the Sabbath was about to [b]begin. 55 Now [A]the
women who had come with Him out of Galilee followed, and saw the tomb and how His body was
laid. 56 Then they returned and [A]prepared spices
and perfumes.

And [B]on the Sabbath they rested according to
the commandment.

THE RESURRECTION

24 [A]But on the first day of the week, at early dawn,
they came to the tomb bringing the spices
which they had prepared. 2 And they found the stone
rolled away from the tomb, 3 but when they entered,
they did not find the body of [A]the Lord Jesus. 4 While
they were perplexed about this, behold, [A]two men
suddenly [B]stood near them in dazzling clothing; 5 and
as *the women* were terrified and bowed their faces
to the ground, *the men* said to them, "Why do you
seek the living One among the dead? 6 He is not here,
but He [A]has [a]risen. Remember how He spoke to you
[B]while He was still in Galilee, 7 saying that [A]the Son of
Man must be delivered into the hands of sinful men,
and be crucified, and the third day rise again." 8 And
[A]they remembered His words, 9 and returned from
the tomb and reported all these things to the eleven
and to all the rest. 10 Now they were [A]Mary Magdalene
and Joanna and Mary the *mother* of James; also the
other women with them were telling these things to
[B]the apostles. 11 But these words appeared [a]to them as
nonsense, and they [A]would not believe them. 12 But Peter got up and [A]ran to the tomb; stooping and looking
in, he *saw the linen wrappings [a]only; and he went
away [B]to his home, marveling at what had happened.

23:47 [a]Lit *righteous* 23:48 [a]I.e. as a traditional sign of mourning or contrition [A]Luke 8:52; 18:13 23:49 [A]Matt 27:55f; Mark 15:40f; Luke 8:2; John 19:25 23:50 [A]Luke 23:50-56: *Matt 27:57-61; Mark 15:42-47; John 19:38-42* [B]Mark 15:43 23:51 [A]Mark 15:43; Luke 2:25 23:54 [a]I.e. preparation for the Sabbath [b]Lit *dawn* [A]Matt 27:62; Mark 15:42 23:55 [A]Luke 23:49 23:56 [A]Mark 16:1; Luke 24:1 [B]Ex 20:10f; Deut 5:14 24:1 [A]Luke 24:1-10: *Matt 28:1-8; Mark 16:1-8;* John 20:1-8 24:3 [A]Luke 7:13; Acts 1:21 24:4 [A]John 20:12 [B]Luke 2:9; Acts 12:7 24:6 [a]Or *been raised* [A]Mark 16:6 [B]Matt 17:22f; Mark 9:30f; Luke 9:44; 24:44 24:7 [A]Matt 16:21; Luke 24:46 24:8 [A]John 2:22 24:10 [A]Matt 27:56 [B]Mark 6:30 24:11 [a]Lit *in their sight* [A]Mark 16:11 24:12 [a]Or *by themselves* [A]John 20:3-6 [B]John 20:10

[man] was the Son of God." Luke may be giving an equivalent expression; or, more likely, the centurion said both things.

23:48 beating their breasts. Luke alone records this expression of remorse and anguish (cf. 18:13).

23:49 the women ... from Galilee. Matthew 27:56 and Mark 15:40, 41 (*see notes there*) report that this included Mary Magdalene (*see note on 8:2*); Mary, mother of James (the less) and Joses; Salome, mother of James and John, and many others. The same women were present at His burial (v. 55; Mt 27:61; Mk 15:47) and His resurrection (24:1; Mt 28:1; Mk 16:1)—so they were eyewitnesses to all the crucial events of the gospel (cf. 1Co 15:3, 4).

23:50 Joseph. *See notes on Mt 27:57; Mk 15:43; Jn 19:38.* All 4 evangelists mentioned him; Mark and Luke identified him as a member of the Sanhedrin; only Luke noted that he dissented from the council's verdict against Jesus (v. 51).

23:51 waiting for the kingdom of God. I.e., he believed Jesus' claims. John 19:38 refers to him as a secret disciple.

23:53 a tomb cut into the rock. Joseph, a wealthy man, undoubtedly had the tomb built for his own family. It had remained unused. Christ's burial there was a wonderful fulfillment of Is 53:9.

23:54 the preparation day. I.e., Friday, the day before the Sabbath.

23:55 saw ... how His body was laid. According to Jn 19:39, Nicodemus brought a hundred pounds of spices and aloes (probably obtained while Joseph was negotiating with Pilate for Jesus' body), and he and Joseph wrapped the body with linen and the spices. These women, from Galilee, were probably unfamiliar with Joseph and Nicodemus, who were Judeans. After all, both men were associated with the Jewish leaders who orchestrated the conspiracy against Jesus (v. 50; Jn 3:1). So the women were determined to prepare Jesus' body for burial themselves. So they returned (i.e., went to their homes) to prepare their own spices and perfumes (v. 56). They had to have Jesus' body placed in the tomb before sunset, when the Sabbath began, so they were not able to finish preparing the body. Mark 16:1 says they purchased more spices "when the Sabbath was over," i.e., after sundown Saturday. Then they returned Sunday morning with the spices (24:1), expecting to finish the task that had been interrupted by the Sabbath.

24:1 bringing the spices. *See note on 23:55.* The women were not expecting to find Jesus risen from the dead; their only plan was to finish anointing His body for burial. *See note on Mk 16:1.*

24:2 the stone rolled away. Matthew 28:2–4 records that an earthquake occurred and an angel rolled the stone away. The Roman guards fainted with fear. Mark, Luke, and John make no mention of the guards, so it appears they fled when they awoke to find the empty tomb. The women must have arrived shortly after.

24:4 two men. These were angels. Only Luke mentioned them both (*see note on Mk 16:5*). Mark was concerned only with the one who spoke for the duo. Such minor differences in the gospel accounts are all reconcilable. Here's a summary of the events of the resurrection, assembled from all 4 evangelists' accounts: finding the stone rolled away, the women entered the tomb, but found it empty (v. 3). While they were still in the tomb, the angels suddenly appeared (v. 4; Mk 16:5). The angel who spoke reminded them of Jesus' promises (vv. 6–8), then sent them to find Peter and the disciples to report that Jesus was risen (Mt 28:7, 8; Mk 16:7, 8). The women did as they were told (vv. 9–11). The disciples were skeptical at first (v. 11), but ran to where the tomb was, John arriving first (Jn 20:4), but Peter actually entering the tomb first (Jn 20:6). They saw the linen wrappings intact but empty, proof that Jesus was risen (v. 12; Jn 20:6–8). They left immediately (v. 12; Jn 20:10). Meanwhile, Mary Magdalene returned to the tomb, and was standing outside weeping when Christ suddenly appeared to her (Jn 20:11–18). That was His first appearance (Mk 16:9). Sometime soon after that, He met the other women on the road and appeared to them as well (Mt 28:9, 10). Later that day He appeared to two of the disciples on the road to Emmaus (vv. 13–32), and to Peter (v. 34). For a chronological listing of all His post-resurrection appearances, *see note on v. 34.*

24:6 how He spoke to you ... in Galilee. *See notes on 9:22; 18:31–33.*

24:9 all the rest. I.e., other disciples, mostly from Galilee, who were in Jerusalem for the Passover.

24:10 Mary Magdalene. *See note on 8:2.* She was the first to see Jesus alive (Mk 16:9; Jn 20:11–18). *See note on v. 4.* **Joanna.** Her husband was Herod's steward. *See note on 8:3.* **Mary the *mother* of James.** *See note on Mt 27:56.* **The other women.** They are never explicitly identified (cf. 23:49, 55).

24:11 nonsense. I.e., idle tales.

24:12 Peter ... ran. John ran with Peter, but reached the tomb first (Jn 20:4). **Linen wrappings.** I.e., the empty shell of wrappings that had contained the body.

THE ROAD TO EMMAUS

13 And behold, [A]two of them were going that
very day to a village named Emmaus, which was
[a]about seven miles from Jerusalem. 14 And they
were talking with each other about all these things
which had taken place. 15 While they were talking
and discussing, Jesus Himself approached and *began* traveling with them. 16 But [A]their eyes were
prevented from recognizing Him. 17 And He said
to them, "What are these words that you are exchanging with one another as you are walking?"
And they stood still, looking sad. 18 One *of them,*
named Cleopas, answered and said to Him, "Are
You [a]the only one visiting Jerusalem and unaware
of the things which have happened here in these
days?" 19 And He said to them, "What things?" And
they said to Him, "The things about [A]Jesus the Nazarene, who was a [B]prophet mighty in deed and word
in the sight of God and all the people, 20 and how
the chief priests and our [A]rulers delivered Him to
the sentence of death, and crucified Him. 21 But we
were hoping that it was He who was going to [A]re-
deem Israel. Indeed, besides all this, it is the third
day since these things happened. 22 But also some
women among us amazed us. [A]When they were at
the tomb early in the morning, 23 and did not find
His body, they came, saying that they had also seen a
vision of angels who said that He was alive. 24 Some
of those who were with us went to the tomb and
found it just exactly as the women also had said;
but Him they did not see." 25 And He said to them,
"O foolish men and slow of heart to believe in all that
[A]the prophets have spoken! 26 [A]Was it not necessary
for the [a]Christ to suffer these things and to enter
into His glory?" 27 Then beginning [a]with [A]Moses
and [a]with all the [B]prophets, He explained to them
the things concerning Himself in all the Scriptures.
28 And they approached the village where they
were going, and [A]He acted as though He were going
farther. 29 But they urged Him, saying, "Stay with
us, for it is *getting* toward evening, and the day [a]is
now nearly over." So He went in to stay with them.
30 When He had reclined *at the table* with them, He
took the bread and [A]blessed *it,* and breaking *it,* He
began giving *it* to them. 31 Then their [A]eyes were
opened and they recognized Him; and He vanished
from [a]their sight. 32 They said to one another, "[a]Were
not our hearts burning within us while He was
speaking to us on the road, while He [A]was [b]explain-
ing the Scriptures to us?" 33 And they got up that
very hour and returned to Jerusalem, and [A]found
gathered together the eleven and [B]those who were
with them, 34 saying, "[A]The Lord has really risen and
[B]has appeared to Simon." 35 They *began* to relate
[a]their experiences on the road and how [A]He was
recognized by them in the breaking of the bread.

24:13 [a]Lit *60 stadia;* one stadion was about 600 ft [A]Mark 16:12 24:16 [A]Luke 24:31; John 20:14; 21:4 24:18 [a]Or *visiting Jerusalem alone* 24:19 [A]Mark 1:24 [B]Matt 21:11 24:20 [A]Luke 23:13 24:21 [A]Luke 1:68 24:22 [A]Luke 24:1ff 24:25 [A]Matt 26:24 24:26 [a]I.e. Messiah [A]Luke 24:7, 44ff; Heb 2:10; 1 Pet 1:11 24:27 [a]Lit *from* [A]Gen 3:15; 12:3; Num 21:9 [John 3:14]; Deut 18:15 [John 1:45]; John 5:46 [B]2 Sam 7:12-16; Is 7:14 [Matt 1:23]; Is 9:1f [Matt 4:15f]; Is 42:1 [Matt 12:18ff]; Is 53:4 [Matt 8:17; Luke 22:37]; Dan 7:13 [Matt 24:30]; Mic 5:2 [Matt 2:6]; Zech 9:9 [Matt 21:5]; Acts 13:27 24:28 [A]Mark 6:48 24:29 [a]Lit *has now declined* 24:30 [A]Matt 14:19 24:31 [a]Lit *them* [A]Luke 24:16 24:32 [a]Lit *Was not our heart* [b]Lit *opening* [A]Luke 24:45 24:33 [A]Mark 16:13 [B]Acts 1:14 24:34 [A]Luke 24:6 [B]1 Cor 15:5 24:35 [a]Lit *the things* [A]Luke 24:30f

24:13 two of them. These evidently were not any of the 11 disciples. According to v. 18, one was named Cleopas. **Emmaus.** Mentioned nowhere else in Scripture. Its exact location is not known, but tradition says it is a town known as Kubeibeh, 7 mi. NW of Jerusalem.

24:16 their eyes were prevented. I.e., they were kept by God from recognizing Him.

24:18 Are You the only one visiting Jerusalem. The crucifixion of Jesus was already such a well known event around Jerusalem that they were shocked that He seemed not to know about it.

24:21 But we were hoping. They had been looking for an immediate earthly kingdom. With Jesus crucified, they were probably struggling with doubt about whether He was the Messiah who would reign. But they still regarded Him as a true prophet (v. 19). **The third day.** There may have been a glimmer of hope in these words. They had heard rumors of His resurrection already (vv. 22–24). Perhaps Cleopas recalled the Lord's promises of 9:22; 18:33. More likely, however, it seems this was his way of expressing surprise that this Stranger did not yet know the news everyone else in Jerusalem had been discussing for the past 3 days.

24:24 Some of those who were with us. I.e., Peter and John (*see note on v. 12*). **But Him they did not see.** This was true. Evidently, Cleopas and his companion had not heard about the appearance to Mary Magdalene (*see note on v. 4*).

24:26 Was it not necessary . . . ? OT prophecies spoke often of a suffering servant of Jehovah (*see note on v. 27*).

24:27 Moses . . . all the prophets. Verse 44 gives the 3-fold division; this expression is merely a shortened way to say the same thing. **in all the Scriptures.** In the inscrutable wisdom of divine providence, the substance of Christ's exposition of the OT messianic prophecies was not recorded. But the gist of what He expounded would have undoubtedly included an explanation of the OT sacrificial system, which was full of types and symbols that spoke of His sufferings and death. He also would have pointed them to the major prophetic passages which spoke of the crucifixion, such as Pss 16:9–11; 22; 69; Is 52:14–53:12; Zec 12:10; 13:7. And He would have pointed out the true meaning of passages like Ge 3:15; Nu 21:6–9; Ps 16:10; Jer 23:5, 6; Da 9:26—and a host of other key messianic prophecies, particularly those that spoke of His death and resurrection.

24:30 took the bread. A simple expression, meaning to share a meal (v. 35).

24:31 their eyes were opened. I.e., by God. They had been sovereignly kept from recognizing Him until this point (cf. v. 16). His resurrection body was glorified, and altered from its previous appearance (see John's description in Rev 1:13–16), and this surely explains why even Mary did not recognize Him at first (cf. Jn 20:14–16). But in this case, God actively intervened to keep them from recognizing Him until it was time for Him to depart. **He vanished from their sight.** His resurrection body, though real and tangible (Jn 20:27)—and even capable of ingesting earthly food (vv. 42, 43)—nonetheless possessed certain properties that indicate it was glorified, altered in a mysterious way (cf. 1Co 15:35–54; Php 3:21). Christ could appear and disappear bodily, as seen in this text. His body could pass through solid objects—such as the grave clothes (*see note on v. 12*), or the walls and doors of a closed room (Jn 20:19, 26). He could apparently travel great distances in a moment, for by the time these disciples returned to Jerusalem, Christ had already appeared to Peter (v. 34). The fact that He ascended into heaven bodily demonstrated that His resurrection body was already fit for heaven. Yet it was His body, the same one that was missing from the tomb, even retaining identifying features such as the nail-wounds (Jn 20:25–27). He was no ghost or phantom.

24:34 appeared to Simon. Cf. 1Co 15:5–8. Scripture describes at least 10 distinct appearances of Christ between the resurrection and ascension. He appeared to: 1) Mary Magdalene at the tomb (Mk 16:9; Jn 20:11–18); 2) to the women on the road (Mt 28:9, 10); 3) to the disciples on the road to Emmaus (vv. 13–32); 4) to Peter (v. 34); 5) to 10 of the 11 disciples, Thomas being absent (vv. 36–43; Mk 16:14; Jn 20:19–25); 6) to the 11 disciples (with Thomas present) 8 days later (Jn 20:26–31); 7) to 7 disciples by the shore of the Sea of Galilee (Jn 21:1–25); 8) to more than 500 disciples, probably on a mountain in Galilee (1Co 15:6; *see note on Mt 28:16*); 9) to James (1Co 15:7); and 10) to the apostles when He ascended into heaven (Ac 1:3–11). After His ascension, He appeared to Paul (1Co 15:8). The next time He appears it will be in glory (Mt 24:30).

OTHER APPEARANCES

36 While they were telling these things, [A]He Himself stood in their midst and *said to them, "Peace
be to you." 37 But they were startled and frightened
and thought that they were seeing [A]a spirit. 38 And
He said to them, "Why are you troubled, and why
do doubts arise in your [a]hearts? 39 [A]See My hands
and My feet, that it is I Myself; [B]touch Me and see,
for a spirit does not have flesh and bones as you
see that I have." 40 And when He had said this, He
showed them His hands and His feet. 41 While they
still [a,A]could not believe *it* because of their joy and
amazement, He said to them, "[B]Have you anything
here to eat?" 42 They gave Him a piece of a broiled
fish; 43 and He took it and [A]ate *it* before them.
44 Now He said to them, "[A]These are My words
which I spoke to you while I was still with you, that
all things which are written about Me in the [B]Law
of Moses and the Prophets and [C]the Psalms must
be fulfilled." 45 Then He [A]opened their [a]minds to
understand the Scriptures, 46 and He said to them,
"[A]Thus it is written, that the [a]Christ would suffer
and [B]rise again from the dead the third day, 47 and
that [A]repentance [a]for forgiveness of sins would be
proclaimed [b]in His name to [B]all the nations, beginning from Jerusalem. 48 You are [A]witnesses of
these things. 49 And behold, [A]I am sending forth
the promise of My Father upon you; but [B]you are
to stay in the city until you are clothed with power
from on high."

THE ASCENSION

50 And He led them out as far as [A]Bethany, and
He lifted up His hands and blessed them. 51 While
He was blessing them, He parted from them and
was carried up into heaven. 52 And they, after worshiping Him, returned to Jerusalem with great joy,
53 and were continually in the temple [a]praising God.

24:36 [A]Mark 16:14 24:37 [A]Matt 14:26; Mark 6:49 24:38 [a]Lit *heart* 24:39 [A]John 20:20, 27 [B]John 20:27; 1 John 1:1 24:41 [a]Lit *were disbelieving* [A]Luke 24:11 [B]John 21:5 24:43 [A]Acts 10:41 24:44 [A]Luke 9:22, 44f; 18:31-34; 22:37 [B]Luke 24:27 [C]Ps 2:7ff [Acts 13:33]; Ps 16:10 [Acts 2:27]; Ps 22:1-18 [Matt 27:34-46]; Ps 69:1-21 [John 19:28ff]; Ps 72; 110:1 [Matt 22:43f]; Ps 118:22f [Matt 21:42] 24:45 [a]Lit *mind* [A]Luke 24:32; Acts 16:14; 1 John 5:20 24:46 [a]I.e. Messiah [A]Luke 24:26, 44 [B]Luke 24:7 24:47 [a]Later mss read *and forgiveness* [b]Or *on the basis of* [A]Acts 5:31; 10:43; 13:38; 26:18 [B]Matt 28:19 24:48 [A]Acts 1:8, 22; 2:32; 3:15; 4:33; 5:32; 10:39, 41; 13:31; 1 Pet 5:1 24:49 [A]John 14:26 [B]Acts 1:4 24:50 [A]Matt 21:17; Acts 1:12 24:53 [a]Lit *blessing*

24:36 He Himself stood in their midst. The doors were closed and locked (Jn 20:19). *See note on v. 31.*

24:39 See My hands and My feet. He was showing them the nail wounds to prove it was really Him. Cf. Jn 20:27.

24:41–43 *See note on v. 31.* Cf. Ac 10:41.

24:44 the Law of Moses and the Prophets and the Psalms. I.e., the whole OT. *See note on v. 27.*

24:45 opened their minds. He undoubtedly taught them from the OT, as He had on the road to Emmaus (*see note on v. 27*). But the gist of the expression also seems to convey a supernatural opening of their minds to receive the truths He unfolded. Whereas their understanding was once dull (9:45), they finally saw clearly (cf. Ps 119:18; Is 29:18, 19; 2Co 3:14–16).

24:46–53 This section contains several ideas that are echoed in the opening of Acts, including Christ's suffering and resurrection (v. 46; Ac 1:3); the message of repentance and remission of sins (v. 47; Ac 2:38); the disciples as His witnesses (v. 48; Ac 1:8); the Promise of the Father (v. 49; Ac 1:4); tarrying in Jerusalem (v. 49; Ac 1:4) and the beginning of gospel outreach there (v. 47; Ac 1:8); power from on high (v. 49; Ac 1:8); Christ's ascension (v. 51; Ac 1:9–11); the disciples' return to Jerusalem (v. 52; Ac 1:12); and their meeting in the temple (v. 53; Ac 2:46).

24:46 it is written. I.e., in the OT. *See note on v. 27.*

24:47 This was the Great Commission (cf. Mt 28:19, 20; Mk 16:15).

24:49 the promise of My Father. I.e., the Holy Spirit (Jn 14:26; 15:26; cf. Joel 2:28, 29; Ac 2:1–4).

24:50 Bethany. *See notes on 19:29; Mk 11:1.*

24:51 carried up into heaven. I.e., visibly. Before when the resurrected Christ left them, He simply vanished (v. 31). This time they saw Him ascend. Cf. Ac 1:9–11.

24:52 after worshiping Him. I.e., a formal act of worship. Now that He had opened their understanding (*see note on v. 45*), they perceived the full truth of His deity, unclouded by the darkness of confusion or doubt. Cf. Mt 28:9; Jn 20:28; contra. Mt 28:17.

24:53 in the temple. This became the first meeting-place of the church (Ac 2:46; 5:21, 42). There were rooms around the porticoes of the outer court available for such meetings.

THE GOSPEL ACCORDING TO JOHN

TITLE

The title of the Fourth Gospel continues the pattern of the other Gospels, being identified originally as "According to John." Like the others, "The Gospel" was added later.

AUTHOR AND DATE

Although the author's name does not appear in the gospel, early church tradition strongly and consistently identified him as the apostle John. The early church father Irenaeus (ca. A.D. 130–200) was a disciple of Polycarp (ca. A.D. 70–160), who was a disciple of the apostle John, and he testified on Polycarp's authority that John wrote the gospel during his residence at Ephesus in Asia Minor when he was advanced in age (*Against Heresies* 2.22.5; 3.1.1). Subsequent to Irenaeus, all the church fathers assumed John to be the gospel's author. Clement of Alexandria (ca. A.D. 150–215) wrote that John, aware of the facts set forth in the other Gospels and being moved by the Holy Spirit, composed a "spiritual gospel" (see Eusebius' *Ecclesiastical History* 6.14.7).

Reinforcing early church tradition are significant internal characteristics of the gospel. While the Synoptic Gospels (Matthew, Mark, Luke) identify the apostle John by name approximately 20 times (including parallels), he is not directly mentioned by name in the Gospel of John. Instead, the author prefers to identify himself as the disciple "whom Jesus loved" (13:23; 19:26; 20:2; 21:7, 20). The absence of any mention of John's name directly is remarkable when one considers the important part played by other named disciples in this gospel. Yet, the recurring designation of himself as the disciple "whom Jesus loved," a deliberate avoidance by John of his personal name, reflects his humility and celebrates his relation to his Lord Jesus. No mention of his name was necessary since his original readers clearly understood that he was the gospel's author. Also, through a process of elimination based primarily on analyzing the material in chaps. 20, 21, this disciple "whom Jesus loved" narrows down to the apostle John (e.g., 21:24; cf. 21:2). Since the gospel's author is exacting in mentioning the names of other characters in the book, if the author had been someone other than John the apostle, he would not have omitted John's name.

The gospel's anonymity strongly reinforces the arguments favoring John's authorship, for only someone of his well-known and preeminent authority as an apostle would be able to write a gospel that differed so markedly in form and substance from the other gospels and have it receive unanimous acceptance in the early church. In contrast, apocryphal gospels produced from the mid-second century onward were falsely ascribed to apostles or other famous persons closely associated with Jesus, yet universally rejected by the church.

John and James, his older brother (Ac 12:2), were known as "the sons of Zebedee" (Mt 10:2–4), and Jesus gave them the name "Sons of Thunder" (Mk 3:17). John was an apostle (Lk 6:12–16) and one of the 3 most intimate associates of Jesus (along with Peter and James—cf. Mt 17:1; 26:37), being an eyewitness to and participant in Jesus' earthly ministry (1Jn 1:1–4). After Christ's ascension, John became a "pillar" in the Jerusalem church (Gal 2:9). He ministered with Peter (Ac 3:1; 4:13; 8:14) until he went to Ephesus (tradition says before the destruction of Jerusalem), from where he wrote this gospel and from where the Romans exiled him to Patmos (Rev 1:9). Besides the gospel that bears his name, John also authored 1–3 John and the Book of Revelation (Rev 1:1).

Because the writings of some church fathers indicate that John was actively writing in his old age and that he was already aware of the Synoptic Gospels, many date the gospel sometime after their composition, but prior to John's writing of 1–3 John or Revelation. John wrote his gospel ca. A.D. 80–90, about 50 years after he witnessed Jesus' earthly ministry.

BACKGROUND AND SETTING

Strategic to John's background and setting is the fact that according to tradition John was aware of the Synoptic Gospels. Apparently, he wrote his gospel in order to make a unique contribution to the record of the Lord's life ("a spiritual gospel") and, in part, to be supplementary as well as complementary to Matthew, Mark, and Luke.

The gospel's unique characteristics reinforce this purpose: first, John supplied a large amount of unique material not recorded in the other gospels. Second, he often supplied information that helps the understanding of the events in the Synoptics. For example, while the Synoptics begin with Jesus' ministry in Galilee, they imply that Jesus had a ministry prior to that (e.g., Mt 4:12; Mk 1:14). John supplies the answer with information on Jesus' prior ministry in Judea (chap. 3) and Samaria (chap. 4). In Mk 6:45, after the feeding of the 5,000, Jesus compelled His disciples to cross the Sea of Galilee to Bethsaida. John recorded the reason. The people were about to make Jesus king because of His miraculous multiplying of food, and He was avoiding their ill-motivated efforts (6:26). Third, John is the most theological of the Gospels, containing, for example, a heavily theological prologue (1:1–18), larger amounts of didactic and discourse material in proportion to narrative (e.g., 3:13–17), and the largest amount of teaching on the Holy Spirit (e.g., 14:16, 17, 26; 16:7–14). Although John was aware of the Synoptics and fashioned his gospel with them in mind, he did not depend upon them for information. Rather, under the inspiration of the Holy Spirit, he utilized his own memory as an eyewitness in composing the gospel (1:14; 19:35; 21:24).

John's Gospel is the second (cf. Lk 1:1–4) that contains a precise statement regarding the author's purpose (20:30, 31). He declares, "these have been written so that you may believe that Jesus is the Christ, the Son of God, and that believing you may have life in His name" (20:31). The primary purposes, therefore, are two-fold: evangelistic and apologetic. Reinforcing the evangelistic purpose is the fact that the word "believe" occurs approximately 100 times in the gospel (the Synoptics use the term less than half as much). John composed his gospel to provide reasons for saving faith in his readers and, as a result, to assure them that they would receive the divine gift of eternal life (1:12).

The apologetic purpose is closely related to the evangelistic purpose. John wrote to convince his readers of Jesus' true identity as the incarnate God-Man whose divine and human natures were perfectly united into one person who was the prophesied Christ ("Messiah") and Savior of the world (e.g., 1:41; 3:16; 4:25, 26; 8:58). He organized his whole gospel around 8 "signs" or proofs that reinforce Jesus' true identity leading to faith. The first half of his work centers around 7 miraculous signs selected to reveal Christ's person and engender belief: 1) water made into wine (2:1–11); 2) the healing of the royal official's son (4:46–54); 3) the healing of the lame man (5:1–18); 4) the feeding of a multitude (6:1–15); 5) walking on water (6:16–21); 6) healing of the blind man (9:1–41); and 7) the raising of Lazarus (11:1–57). The eighth sign is the miraculous catch of fish (21:6–11) after Jesus' resurrection.

HISTORICAL AND THEOLOGICAL THEMES

In accordance with John's evangelistic and apologetic purposes, the overall message of the Gospel is found in 20:31: "Jesus is the Christ, the Son of God." The book, therefore, centers on the person and work of Christ. Three predominant words ("signs," "believe," and "life") in 20:30, 31 receive constant reemphasis throughout the gospel to enforce the theme of salvation in Him, which is first set forth in the prologue (1:1–18; cf. 1Jn 1:1–4) and re-expressed throughout the gospel in varying ways (e.g., 6:35, 48; 8:12; 10:7, 9; 10:11–14; 11:25; 14:6; 17:3). In addition, John provides the record of how men responded to Jesus Christ and the salvation that He offered. Summing up, the gospel focuses on: 1) Jesus as the Word, the Messiah, and Son of God; 2) who brings the gift of salvation to mankind; 3) who either accept or reject the offer.

John also presents certain contrastive subthemes that reinforce his main theme. He uses dualism (life and death, light and darkness, love and hate, from above and from below) to convey vital information about the person and work of Christ and the need to believe in Him (e.g., 1:4, 5, 12, 13; 3:16–21; 12:44–46; 15:17–20).

There are also 7 emphatic "I AM" statements which identify Jesus as God and Messiah (6:35; 8:12; 10:7, 9; 10:11, 14; 11:25; 14:6; 15:1, 5).

INTERPRETIVE CHALLENGES

Because John composed his record in a clear and simple style, one might tend to underestimate the depth of this gospel. Since John's gospel is a "spiritual" gospel (see Authorship and Date), the truths he conveys are profound. The reader must prayerfully and meticulously explore the book, in order to discover the vast richness of the spiritual treasures that the apostle, under the guidance of the Holy Spirit (14:26; 16:13), has lovingly deposited in his gospel.

The chronological reckoning between John's Gospel and the Synoptics presents a challenge, especially in relation to the time of the Last Supper (13:2). While the Synoptics portray the disciples and the Lord at the Last Supper as eating the Passover meal on Thursday evening (Nisan 14) and Jesus being crucified on Friday, John's Gospel states that the Jews did not enter into the Praetorium "so that they would not be defiled, but might eat the Passover" (18:28). So, the disciples had eaten the Passover on Thursday evening, but the Jews had not. In fact, John (19:14) states that Jesus' trial and crucifixion were on the day of Preparation for the Passover and not after the eating of the Passover, so that with the trial and crucifixion on Friday, Christ was actually sacrificed at the same time the Passover lambs were being slain (19:14). The question is, "Why did the disciples eat the Passover meal on Thursday?"

The answer lies in a difference among the Jews in the way they reckoned the beginning and ending of days. From Josephus, the Mishna, and other ancient Jewish sources, we learn that the Jews in northern Israel calculated days from sunrise to sunrise. That area included the region of Galilee, where Jesus and all the disciples, except Judas, had grown up. Apparently most, if not all, of the Pharisees used that system of reckoning. But Jews in the southern part, which centered in Jerusalem, calculated days from sunset to sunset. Because all the priests necessarily lived in or near Jerusalem, as did most of the Sadducees, those groups followed the southern scheme.

That variation doubtlessly caused confusion at times, but it also had some practical benefits. During Passover time, for instance, it allowed for the feast to be celebrated legitimately on two adjoining days, thereby permitting the temple sacrifices to be made over a total period of four hours rather than two. That separation of days may also have had the effect of reducing both regional and religious clashes between the two groups.

On that basis the seeming contradictions in the Gospel accounts are easily explained. Being Galileans, Jesus and the disciples considered Passover day to have started at sunrise on Thursday and to end at sunrise on Friday. The Jewish leaders who arrested and tried Jesus, being mostly priests and Sadducees, considered Passover day to begin at sunset on Thursday and end at sunset on Friday. By that variation, predetermined by God's sovereign provision, Jesus could thereby legitimately celebrate the last Passover meal with His disciples and yet still be sacrificed on Passover day.

Once again one can see how God sovereignly and marvelously provides for the precise fulfillment of His redemptive plan. Jesus was anything but a victim of men's wicked schemes, much less of blind circumstance. Every word He spoke and every action He took were divinely directed and secured. Even the words and actions by others against Him were divinely controlled. See, e.g., 11:49–52; 19:11.

OUTLINE

I. The Incarnation of the Son of God (1:1–18)
- A. His Eternality (1:1, 2)
- B. His Preincarnate Work (1:3–5)
- C. His Forerunner (1:6–8)
- D. His Rejection (1:9–11)
- E. His Reception (1:12, 13)
- F. His Deity (1:14–18)

II. The Presentation of the Son of God (1:19–4:54)
- A. Presentation by John the Baptist (1:19–34)
  - 1. To the religious leaders (1:19–28)
  - 2. At Christ's baptism (1:29–34)
- B. Presentation to John's Disciples (1:35–51)
  - 1. Andrew and Peter (1:35–42)
  - 2. Philip and Nathanael (1:43–51)
- C. Presentation in Galilee (2:1–12)
  - 1. First sign: water to wine (2:1–10)
  - 2. Disciples believe (2:11, 12)
- D. Presentation in Judea (2:13–3:36)
  - 1. Cleansing the temple (2:13–25)
  - 2. Teaching Nicodemus (3:1–21)
  - 3. Preaching by John the Baptist (3:22–36)
- E. Presentation in Samaria (4:1–42)
  - 1. Witness to the Samaritan woman (4:1–26)
  - 2. Witness to the disciples (4:27–38)
  - 3. Witness to the Samaritans (4:39–42)
- F. Presentation in Galilee (4:43–54)
  - 1. Reception by the Galileans (4:43–45)
  - 2. Second sign: healing the royal official's son (4:46–54)

III. The Opposition to the Son of God (5:1–12:50)
- A. Opposition at the Feast in Jerusalem (5:1–47)
  - 1. Third sign: healing the paralytic (5:1–9)
  - 2. Rejection by the Jews (5:10–47)
- B. Opposition During Passover (6:1–71)
  - 1. Fourth sign: feeding the 5,000 (6:1–14)
  - 2. Fifth sign: walking on water (6:15–21)
  - 3. Bread of Life discourse (6:22–71)
- C. Opposition at the Feast of Booths (7:1–10:21)
  - 1. The opposition (7:1–8:59)
  - 2. Sixth sign (9:1–10:21)
- D. Opposition at the Feast of Dedication (10:22–42)
- E. Opposition at Bethany (11:1–12:11)
  - 1. Seventh sign: raising of Lazarus (11:1–44)
  - 2. Pharisees plot to kill Christ (11:45–57)
  - 3. Mary anointing Christ (12:1–11)
- F. Opposition in Jerusalem (12:12–50)
  - 1. The triumphal entry (12:12–22)
  - 2. The discourse on faith and rejection (12:23–50)

IV. The Preparation of the Disciples by the Son of God (13:1–17:26)
- A. In the Upper Room (13:1–14:31)
  - 1. Washing feet (13:1–20)
  - 2. Announcing the betrayal (13:21–30)
  - 3. Discourse on Christ's departure (13:31–14:31)
- B. On the Way to the Garden (15:1–17:26)
  - 1. Instructing the disciples (15:1–16:33)
  - 2. Interceding with the Father (17:1–26)

V. The Execution of the Son of God (18:1–19:37)
- A. The Rejection of Christ (18:1–19:16)
  - 1. His arrest (18:1–11)
  - 2. His trials (18:12–19:16)
- B. The Crucifixion of Christ (19:17–37)

VI. The Resurrection of the Son of God (19:38–21:23)
- A. The Burial of Christ (19:38–42)
- B. The Resurrection of Christ (20:1–10)
- C. The Appearances of Christ (20:11–21:23)
  - 1. To Mary Magdalene (20:11–18)
  - 2. To the disciples without Thomas (20:19–25)
  - 3. To the disciples with Thomas (20:26–29)
  - 4. Statement of purpose for the Gospel (20:30, 31)
  - 5. To the disciples (21:1–14)
  - 6. To Peter (21:15–23)

VII. Conclusion (21:24, 25)

THE DEITY OF JESUS CHRIST

1 [A]In the beginning was [B]the Word, and the Word
was [C]with God, and [D]the Word was God. 2 [a]He was
in the beginning with God. 3 [A]All things came into
being through Him, and apart from Him nothing
came into being that has come into being. 4 [A]In Him
was life, and the life was [B]the Light of men. 5 [A]The
Light shines in the darkness, and the darkness did
not [a]comprehend it.

THE WITNESS JOHN

6 There [a]came a man sent from God, whose name
was [A]John. 7 [a]He came [b,A]as a witness, to testify about
the Light, [B]so that all might believe through him.
8 [a,A]He was not the Light, but *he came* to testify about
the Light.
9 There was [A]the true Light [a]which, coming into
the world, enlightens every man. 10 He was in the
world, and [A]the world was made through Him, and the

1:1 [A]Gen 1:1; Col 1:17; 1 John 1:1 [B]John 1:14; Rev 19:13 [C]John 17:5; 1 John 1:2 [D]Phil 2:6 1:2 [a]Lit *This one* 1:3 [A]John 1:10; 1 Cor 8:6; Col 1:16; Heb 1:2 1:4 [A]John 5:26; 11:25; 14:6 [B]John 8:12; 9:5; 12:46 1:5 [a]Or *overpower* [A]John 3:19 1:6 [a]Or *came into being* [A]Matt 3:1 1:7 [a]Lit *This one* [b]Lit *for testimony* [A]John 1:15, 19, 32; 3:26; 5:33 [B]John 1:12; Acts 19:4; Gal 3:26 1:8 [a]Lit *That one* [A]John 1:20 1:9 [a]Or *which enlightens every person coming into the world* [A]1 John 2:8 1:10 [A]1 Cor 8:6; Col 1:16; Heb 1:2

1:1–18 These verses constitute the prologue which introduces many of the major themes that John will treat, especially the main theme that "Jesus is the Christ, the Son of God" (vv. 12–14, 18; cf. 20:31). Several key words repeated throughout the gospel (e.g., life, light, witness, glory) appear here. The remainder of the gospel develops the theme of the prologue as to how the eternal "Word" of God, Jesus the Messiah and Son of God, became flesh and ministered among men so that all who believe in Him would be saved. Although John wrote the prologue with the simplest vocabulary in the NT, the truths which the prologue conveys are the most profound. Six basic truths about Christ as the Son of God are featured in the prologue: 1) the eternal Christ (vv. 1–3); 2) the incarnate Christ (vv. 4, 5); 3) the forerunner of Christ (vv. 6–8); 4) the unrecognized Christ (vv. 9–11); 5) the omnipotent Christ (vv. 12, 13); and 6) the glorious Christ (vv. 14–18).

1:1 In the beginning. In contrast to 1Jn 1:1 where John used a similar phrase ("from the beginning") to refer to the starting point of Jesus' ministry and gospel preaching, this phrase parallels Ge 1:1 where the same phrase is used. John used the phrase in an absolute sense to refer to the beginning of the time-space-material universe. **was.** The verb highlights the eternal preexistence of the Word, i.e., Jesus Christ. Before the universe began, the Second Person of the Trinity always existed; i.e., He always was (cf. 8:58). This word is used in contrast with the verb "came into being" in v. 3 which indicates a beginning in time. Because of John's theme that Jesus Christ is the eternal God, the Second Person of the Trinity, he did not include a genealogy as Matthew and Luke did. While in terms of Jesus' humanity, He had a human genealogy; in terms of His deity, He has no genealogy. **the Word.** John borrowed the use of the term "Word" not only from the vocabulary of the OT but also from Gr. philosophy, in which the term was essentially impersonal, signifying the rational principle of "divine reason," "mind," or even "wisdom." John, however, imbued the term entirely with OT and Christian meaning (e.g., Ge 1:3 where God's Word brought the world into being; Pss 33:6; 107:20; Pr 8:27 where God's Word is His powerful self-expression in creation, wisdom, revelation, and salvation) and made it refer to a person, i.e., Jesus Christ. Greek philosophical usage, therefore, is not the exclusive background of John's thought. Strategically, the term "Word" serves as a bridge-word to reach not only Jews but also the unsaved Greeks. John chose this concept because both Jews and Greeks were familiar with it. **the Word was with God.** The Word, as the Second Person of the Trinity, was in intimate fellowship with God the Father throughout all eternity. Yet, although the Word enjoyed the splendors of heaven and eternity with the Father (Is 6:1–13; cf. 12:41; 17:5), He willingly gave up His heavenly status, taking the form of a man, and became subject to the death of the cross (*see notes on Php 2:6–8*). **was God.** The Gr. construction emphasizes that the Word had all the essence or attributes of deity, i.e., Jesus the Messiah was fully God (cf. Col 2:9). Even in His incarnation when He emptied Himself, He did not cease to be God but took on a genuine human nature/body and voluntarily refrained from the independent exercise of the attributes of deity.

1:3 All things came into being through Him. Jesus Christ was God the Father's agent involved in creating everything in the universe (Col 1:16, 17; Heb 1:2).

1:4, 5 life . . . Light . . . darkness. John introduces the reader to contrastive themes that occur throughout the gospel. "Life" and "light" are qualities of the Word that are shared not only among the Godhead (5:26) but also by those who respond to the gospel message regarding Jesus Christ (8:12; 9:5; 10:28; 11:25; 14:6). John uses the word "life" about 36 times in his gospel, far more than any other NT book. It refers not only in a broad sense to physical and temporal life that the Son imparted to the created world through His involvement as the agent of creation (v. 3), but especially to spiritual and eternal life imparted as a gift through belief in Him (3:15; 17:3; Eph 2:5). In Scripture "light" and "darkness" are very familiar symbols. Intellectually, "light" refers to biblical truth, while "darkness" refers to error or falsehood (cf. Ps 119:105; Pr 6:23). Morally, "light" refers to holiness or purity (1Jn 1:5), while "darkness" refers to sin or wrongdoing (3:19; 12:35, 46; Ro 13:11–14; 1Th 5:4–7; 1Jn 1:6; 2:8–11). "Darkness" has special significance in relationship to Satan (and his demonic cohorts) who rules the present spiritually dark world (1Jn 5:19) as the "prince of the power of the air" promoting spiritual darkness and rebellion against God (Eph 2:2). John uses the term "darkness" 14 times (8 in the gospel and 6 in 1 John) out of its 17 occurrences in the NT, making it almost an exclusive Johannine word. In John, "light" and "life" have their special significance in relationship to the Lord Jesus Christ, the Word (v. 9; 9:5; 1Jn 1:5–7; 5:12, 20).

1:5 comprehend. The better meaning of this term in context is "overcome." Darkness is not able to overcome or conquer the light. Just as a single candle can overcome a room filled with darkness, so also the powers of darkness are overcome by the person and work of the Son through His death on the cross (cf. 19:11a).

1:6 sent from God. As forerunner to Jesus, John was to bear witness to Him as the Messiah and Son of God. With John's ministry, the "400 silent years" between the end of the OT and the beginning of the NT period, during which God had given no revelation, ended. **John.** The name "John" always refers to John the Baptist in this gospel, never to the apostle John. The writer of this Gospel calls him merely "John" without using the phrase "the Baptist," unlike the other gospels which use the additional description to identify him (Mt 3:1; Mk 6:14; Lk 7:20). Moreover, John the apostle (or, son of Zebedee) never identified himself directly by name in the gospel even though he was one of the 3 most intimate associates of Jesus (Mt 17:1). Such silence argues strongly that John the apostle authored the gospel and that his readers knew full well that he composed the gospel that bears his name. For more on John the Baptist, cf. Mt 3:1–6; Mk 1:2–6; Lk 1:5–25, 57–80.

1:7 witness, to testify. The terms "witness" or "to testify" receive special attention in this gospel, reflecting the courtroom language of the OT where the truth of a matter was to be established on the basis of multiple witnesses (8:17, 18; cf. Dt 17:6; 19:15). Not only did John the Baptist witness regarding Jesus as Messiah and Son of God (vv. 19–34; 3:27–30; 5:35), but there were other witnesses: 1) the Samaritan woman (4:29); 2) the works of Jesus (10:25); 3) the Father (5:32–37); 4) the OT (5:39, 40); 5) the crowd (12:17); and 6) the Holy Spirit (15:26, 27). **that all might believe through him.** "Him" refers not to Christ but to John as the agent who witnessed to Christ. The purpose of his testimony was to produce faith in Jesus Christ as the Savior of the world.

1:8 He was not the Light. While John the Baptist was the agent of belief, Jesus Christ is the object of belief. Although John's person and ministry were vitally important (Mt 11:11), he was merely the forerunner who announced the coming of the Messiah. Many years after John's ministry and death, some still failed to understand John's subordinate role to Jesus (Ac 19:1–3).

1:9 the true Light . . . coming into the world. This phrase highlights the incarnation of Jesus Christ (v. 14; 3:16). **enlightens every man.** Through God's sovereign power, every man has enough light to be responsible. God has planted His knowledge in man through general revelation in creation and conscience. The result of general revelation, however, does not produce salvation but either leads to the complete light of Jesus Christ or produces condemnation in those who reject such "light" (*see notes on Ro 1:19, 20; 2:12–16*). The coming of Jesus Christ was the fulfillment and embodiment

world did not know Him. 11 He came to His [a]own, and those who were His own did not receive Him. 12 But as many as received Him, to them He gave the right to become [A]children of God, *even* [B]to those who believe in His name, 13 [A]who were [a]born, not of [b]blood nor of the will of the flesh nor of the will of man, but of God.

THE WORD MADE FLESH

14 And [A]the Word [B]became flesh, and [a,C]dwelt among us, and [D]we saw His glory, glory as of [b]the only begotten from the Father, full of [E]grace and [F]truth. 15 John *[A]testified about Him and cried out, saying, "This was He of whom I said, '[B]He who comes after me [a]has a higher rank than I, [C]for He existed before me.' " 16 For of His [A]fullness [a]we have all received, and [b]grace upon grace. 17 For [A]the Law was given through Moses; [B]grace and [C]truth [a]were realized through Jesus Christ. 18 [A]No one has seen God at any time; [B]the only begotten God who is [C]in the bosom of the Father, [D]He has explained *Him*.

THE TESTIMONY OF JOHN

19 This is [A]the testimony of John, when [B]the Jews sent to him priests and Levites [C]from Jerusalem to

1:11 [a]Or *own things, possessions, domain* 1:12 [A]John 11:52; Gal 3:26 [B]John 1:7; 3:18; 1 John 3:23; 5:13 1:13 [a]Or *begotten* [b]Lit *bloods* [A]John 3:5f; James 1:18; 1 Pet 1:23; 1 John 2:29; 3:9 1:14 [a]Or *tabernacled;* i.e. lived temporarily [b]Or *unique, only one of His kind* [A]Rev 19:13 [B]Rom 1:3; Gal 4:4; Phil 2:7f; 1 Tim 3:16; Heb 2:14; 1 John 1:1f; 4:2; 2 John 7 [C]Rev 21:3 [D]Luke 9:32; John 2:11; 17:22, 24; 2 Pet 1:16f; 1 John 1:1 [E]John 1:17; Rom 5:21; 6:14 [F]John 8:32; 14:6; 18:37 1:15 [a]Lit *has become before me* [A]John 1:7 [B]Matt 3:11; John 1:27, 30 [C]John 1:30 1:16 [a]Lit *we all received* [b]Lit *grace for grace* [A]Eph 1:23; 3:19; 4:13; Col 1:19; 2:9 1:17 [a]Lit *came to be* [A]John 7:19 [B]John 1:14; Rom 5:21; 6:14 [C]John 8:32; 14:6; 18:37 1:18 [A]Ex 33:20; John 6:46; Col 1:15; 1 Tim 6:16; 1 John 4:12 [B]John 3:16, 18; 1 John 4:9 [C]Luke 16:22; John 13:23 [D]John 3:11 1:19 [A]John 1:7 [B]John 2:18, 20; 5:10, 15f, 18; 6:41, 52; 7:1, 11, 13, 15, 35; 8:22, 48, 52, 57; 9:18, 22; 10:24, 31, 33 [C]Matt 15:1

of the light that God had placed inside the heart of man. **the world.** The basic sense of this Gr. word meaning "an ornament" is illustrated by the word "adornment" (1Pe 3:3). While the NT uses it a total of 185 times, John had a particular fondness for this term, using it 78 times in his gospel, 24 times in 1–3 John and 3 times in Revelation. John gives it several shades of meaning: 1) the physical created universe (v. 9; cf. v. 3; 21:24, 25); 2) humanity in general (3:16; 6:33, 51; 12:19); and 3) the invisible spiritual system of evil dominated by Satan and all that it offers in opposition to God, His Word, and His people (3:19; 4:42; 7:7; 14:17, 22, 27, 30; 15:18, 19; 16:8, 20, 33; 17:6, 9, 14; cf. 1Co 1:21; 2Pe 1:4; 1Jn 5:19). The latter concept is the significant new use that the term acquires in the NT and that predominates in John. Thus, in the majority of times that John uses the word, it has decidedly negative overtones.

1:11 His own … His own. The first usage of "His own" most likely refers to the world of mankind in general, while the second refers to the Jewish nation. As Creator, the world belongs to the Word as His property, but the world did not even recognize Him due to spiritual blindness (cf. also v. 10). John used the second occurrence of "His own" in a narrower sense to refer to Jesus' own physical lineage, the Jews. Although they possessed the Scriptures that testified of His person and coming, they still did not accept Him (Is 65:2, 3; Jer 7:25). This theme of Jewish rejection of their promised Messiah receives special attention in John's Gospel (12:37–41).

1:12, 13 These verses stand in contrast to vv. 10, 11. John softens the sweeping rejection of Messiah by stressing a believing remnant. This previews the book since the first 12 chapters stress the rejection of Christ, while chaps. 13–21 focus on the believing remnant who received Him.

1:12 as many as received Him … to those who believe in His name. The second phrase describes the first. To receive Him who is the Word of God means to acknowledge His claims, place one's faith in Him, and thereby yield allegiance to Him. **gave.** The term emphasizes the grace of God involved in the gift of salvation (cf. Eph 2:8–10). **the right.** Those who receive Jesus, the Word, receive full authority to claim the exalted title of "children of God." **His name.** Denotes the character of the person himself. *See note on 14:13, 14.*

1:13 of God. The divine side of salvation: ultimately, it is not a man's will that produces salvation but God's will (cf. 3:6–8; Tit 3:5; 1Jn 2:29).

1:14 the Word became flesh. While Christ as God was uncreated and eternal (*see notes on v. 1*), the word "became" emphasizes Christ's taking on humanity (cf. Heb 1:1–3; 2:14–18). This reality is surely the most profound ever because it indicates that the Infinite became finite; the Eternal was conformed to time; the Invisible became visible; the supernatural One reduced Himself to the natural. In the incarnation, however, the Word did not cease to be God but became God in human flesh, i.e., undiminished deity in human form as a man (1Ti 3:16). **dwelt.** Meaning "to pitch a tabernacle," or "live in a tent." The term recalls to mind the OT tabernacle where God met with Israel before the temple was constructed (Ex 25:8). It was called the "tent of meeting" (Ex 33:7; "tabernacle of witness"—LXX) where "the LORD used to speak to Moses face to face, just as a man speaks to his friend" (Ex 33:11). In the NT, God chose to dwell among His people in a far more personal way through becoming a man. In the OT, when the tabernacle was completed, God's Shekinah presence filled the entire structure (Ex 40:34; cf. 1Ki 8:10). When the Word became flesh, the glorious presence of deity was embodied in Him (cf. Col 2:9). **we saw His glory.** Although His deity may have been veiled in human flesh, glimpses exist in the Gospels of His divine majesty. The disciples saw glimpses of His glory on the Mount of Transfiguration (Mt 17:1–8). The reference to Christ's glory, however, was not only visible but also spiritual. They saw Him display the attributes or characteristics of God (grace, goodness, mercy, wisdom, truth, etc.; cf. Ex 33:18–23). **glory as of … the Father.** Jesus as God displayed the same essential glory as the Father. They are one in essential nature (cf. 5:17–30; 8:19; 10:30). **only begotten.** The term "only begotten" is a mistranslation of the Gr. word. The word does not come from the term meaning "beget" but instead has the idea of "the only beloved one." It, therefore, has the idea of singular uniqueness, of being beloved like no other. By this word, John emphasized the exclusive character of the relationship between the Father and the Son in the Godhead (cf. 3:16, 18; 1Jn 4:9). It does not connote origin but rather unique prominence; e.g., it was used of Isaac (Heb 11:17) who was Abraham's second son (Ishmael being the first; cf. Ge 16:15 with Ge 21:2, 3). **full of grace and truth.** John probably had Ex 33, 34 in mind. On that occasion, Moses requested that God display His glory to him. The Lord replied to Moses that He would make all His "goodness" pass before him, and then as He passed by God declared "The LORD … compassionate and gracious, slow to anger, and abounding in lovingkindness and truth" (Ex 33:18, 19; 34:5–7). These attributes of God's glory emphasize the goodness of God's character, especially in relationship to salvation. Jesus as Yahweh of the OT (8:58; "I am") displayed the same divine attributes when He tabernacled among men in the NT era (Col 2:9).

1:15 John the Baptist's testimony corroborates John the apostle's statement regarding the eternality of the Incarnate Word (cf. v. 14).

1:16 grace upon grace. This phrase emphasizes the superabundance of grace that has been displayed by God toward mankind, especially believers (Eph 1:5–8; 2:7).

1:17, 18 Corroborating the truth of v. 14, these verses draw a closing contrast to the prologue. The law, given by Moses, was not a display of God's grace, but God's demand for holiness. God designed the law as a means to demonstrate the unrighteousness of man in order to show the need for a Savior, Jesus Christ (Ro 3:19, 20; Gal 3:10–14, 21–26). Furthermore, the law revealed only a part of truth and was preparatory in nature. The reality or full truth toward which the law pointed came through the person of Jesus Christ.

1:18 who is in the bosom of the Father. This term denotes the mutual intimacy, love and knowledge existing in the Godhead (see 13:23; Lk 16:22, 23). **explained.** Theologians derived the term "exegesis" or "to interpret" from this word. John meant that all that Jesus is and does interprets and explains who God is and what He does (14:8–10).

1:19–37 In these verses, John presented the first of many witnesses to prove that Jesus is the Messiah and Son of God, thus reinforcing his main theme (20:30, 31). The testimony of John the Baptist was given on 3 different days to 3 different groups (cf. vv. 29, 35, 36). Each time, he spoke of Christ in a different way and emphasized distinct aspects regarding Him. The events in these verses took place in A.D. 26/27, just a few months after John's baptism of Jesus (cf. Mt 3:13–17; Lk 3:21, 22).

1:19 John. John, born into a priestly family, belonged to the tribe of Levi (Lk 1:5). He began his ministry in the Jordan Valley when

ask him, "Who are you?" 20 And he confessed and
did not deny, but confessed, "[A]I am not [a]the Christ."
21 They asked him, "What then? Are you [A]Elijah?" And
he *said, "I am not." "Are you [B]the Prophet?" And he
answered, "No." 22 Then they said to him, "Who are
you, so that we may give an answer to those who
sent us? What do you say about yourself?" 23 He said,
"I am [A]A VOICE OF ONE CRYING IN THE WILDERNESS,
'MAKE STRAIGHT THE WAY OF THE LORD,' as Isaiah
the prophet said."
24 Now they had been sent from the Pharisees.
25 They asked him, and said to him, "Why then are
you baptizing, if you are not the [a]Christ, nor Elijah,
nor [A]the Prophet?" 26 John answered them saying, "[A]I
baptize [a]in water, *but* among you stands One whom
you do not know. 27 *It is* [A]He who comes after me, the
[B]thong of whose sandal I am not worthy to untie."
28 These things took place in Bethany [A]beyond the
Jordan, where John was baptizing.
29 The next day he *saw Jesus coming to him and
*said, "Behold, [A]the Lamb of God who [B]takes away
the sin of the world! 30 This is He on behalf of whom
I said, '[A]After me comes a Man who [a]has a higher
rank than I, [B]for He existed before me.' 31 I did not
recognize [a]Him, but so that He might be manifested
to Israel, I came baptizing [b]in water." 32 John [A]testi-
fied saying, "[B]I have seen the Spirit descending as
a dove out of heaven, and He remained upon Him.
33 I did not recognize [a]Him, but He who sent me to
baptize [b]in water said to me, 'He upon whom you
see the Spirit descending and remaining upon Him,
[A]this is the One who baptizes [b]in the Holy Spirit.'
34 I myself have seen, and have testified that this
is [A]the Son of God."

1:20 [a]I.e. the Messiah [A]Luke 3:15f; John 3:28 1:21 [A]Matt 11:14; 16:14 [B]Deut 18:15, 18; Matt 21:11; John 1:25 1:23 [A]Is 40:3; Matt 3:3; Mark 1:3; Luke 3:4 1:25 [a]I.e. Messiah [A]Deut 18:15, 18; Matt 21:11; John 1:21 1:26 [a]The Gr here can be translated *in, with* or *by* [A]Matt 3:11; Mark 1:8; Luke 3:16; Acts 1:5 1:27 [A]Matt 3:11; John 1:30 [B]Matt 3:11; Mark 1:7; Luke 3:16 1:28 [A]John 3:26; 10:40 1:29 [A]Is 53:7; John 1:36; Acts 8:32; 1 Pet 1:19; Rev 5:6, 8, 12f; 6:1 [B]Matt 1:21; 1 John 3:5 1:30 [a]Lit *has become before me* [A]Matt 3:11; John 1:27 [B]John 1:15 1:31 [a]I.e. as the Messiah [b]The Gr here can be translated *in, with* or *by* 1:32 [A]John 1:7 [B]Matt 3:16; Mark 1:10; Luke 3:22 1:33 [a]I.e. as the Messiah [b]The Gr here can be translated *in, with* or *by* [A]Matt 3:11; Mark 1:8; Luke 3:16; Acts 1:5 1:34 [A]Matt 4:3; John 1:49

he was approximately 29 or 30 years old and boldly proclaimed the need for spiritual repentance and preparation for the coming of the Messiah. He was the cousin of Jesus Christ and served as His prophetic forerunner (Mt 3:3; Lk 1:5–25, 36). **the Jews … from Jerusalem.** This may refer to the Sanhedrin, the main governing body of the Jewish nation. The Sanhedrin was controlled by the family of the High Priest, and thus the envoys would naturally be priests and Levites who would be interested in John's ministry, both his message and his baptism.

1:20 I am not the Christ. Some thought that John was the Messiah (Lk 3:15–17). **Christ.** The term "Christ" is the Gr. equivalent of the Heb. term for "Messiah."

1:21 Are you Elijah? Malachi 4:5 (*see note there*) promises that the prophet Elijah will return before Messiah establishes His earthly kingdom. If John was the forerunner of Messiah, was he Elijah, they asked? The angel announcing John's birth said that John would go before Jesus "in the spirit and power of Elijah" (Lk 1:17), thus indicating that someone other than literal Elijah could fulfill the prophecy. God sent John who was like Elijah, i.e., one who had the same type of ministry, the same power and similar personality (2Ki 1:8; cf. Mt 3:4). If they had received Jesus as Messiah, John would have fulfilled that prophecy (*see notes on Mt 11:14; Mk 9:13; Lk 1:17; Rev 11:5, 6*). **Are you the Prophet?** This is a reference to Dt 18:15–18, which predicted God would raise up a great prophet like Moses who would function as His voice. While some in John's time interpreted this prophecy as referring to another forerunner of Messiah, the NT (Ac 3:22, 23; 7:37) applies the passage to Jesus.

1:23 John quoted and applied Is 40:3 to himself (cf. Mt 3:3; Mk 1:3; Lk 3:4). In the original context of Is 40:3, the prophet heard a voice calling for the leveling of a path. This call was a prophetic picture that foreshadowed the final and greatest return of Israel to their God from spiritual darkness and alienation through the spiritual redemption accomplished by the Messiah (cf. Ro 11:25–27). In humility, John compared himself to a voice rather than a person, thus focusing the attention exclusively upon Christ (cf. Lk 17:10).

1:25 baptizing. Since John had identified himself as a mere voice (v. 23), the question arose as to his authority for baptizing. The OT associated the coming of Messiah with repentance and spiritual cleansing (Eze 36, 37; Zec 13:1). John focused attention on his position as forerunner of Messiah, who used traditional proselyte baptism as a symbol of the need to recognize those Jews who were outside God's saving covenant like Gentiles. They too needed spiritual cleansing and preparation (repentance—Mt 3:11; Mk 1:4; Lk 3:7, 8) for Messiah's advent. *See notes on Mt 3:6, 11, 16, 17* for an explanation of the significance of John's baptism.

1:27 John the Baptist's words here continue a theme of the preeminence of Messiah in the prologue (vv. 6–8, 15) and demonstrate extraordinary humility. Each time John had opportunity to focus on himself in these encounters, he instead shifted the focus onto Messiah. John went so far as to state that he, unlike a slave that was required to remove his master's shoes, was not even worthy of performing this action in relationship to Messiah.

1:28 Bethany. Some translations render this word as "Bethabara." Some feel that John incorrectly identified Bethany as the place of these events. The solution is that two Bethanys existed, i.e., one near Jerusalem where Mary, Martha, and Lazarus lived (11:1) and one "beyond the Jordan" near the region of Galilee. Since John took great pains to identify the other Bethany's close proximity to Jerusalem, he most likely was referring here to that other town with the same name.

1:29–34 This portion deals with John's witness to a second group of Jews on the second day (see vv. 19–28 for the first group and day) regarding Jesus. This section forms something of a bridge. It continues the theme of John the Baptist's witness but also introduces a lengthy list of titles applied to Jesus: Lamb of God (vv. 29, 36), Rabbi (vv. 38, 49), Messiah/Christ (v. 41), Son of God (vv. 34, 49), King of Israel (v. 49), Son of Man (v. 51), and "Him of whom Moses in the Law, and *also* the Prophets wrote" (v. 45).

1:29 The next day. This phrase probably refers to the day after John's response to the Jerusalem delegation. It also initiates a sequence of days (v. 43; 2:1) that culminated in the miracle at Cana (2:1–11). **the Lamb of God.** The use of a lamb for sacrifice was very familiar to Jews. A lamb was used as a sacrifice during Passover (Ex 12:1–36); a lamb was led to the slaughter in the prophecies of Isaiah (Is 53:7); a lamb was offered in the daily sacrifices of Israel (Lv 14:12–21; cf. Heb 10:5–7). John the Baptist used this expression as a reference to the ultimate sacrifice of Jesus on the cross to atone for the sins of the world, a theme which John the apostle carries throughout his writings (19:36; cf. Rev 5:1–6; 7:17; 17:14) and that appears in other NT writings (e.g., 1Pe 1:19). **sin of the world.** *See note on v. 9*; cf. 3:16; 6:33, 51. In this context "world" has the connotation of humanity in general, not specifically every person. The use of the singular "sin" in conjunction with "of the world" indicates that Jesus' sacrifice for sin potentially reaches all human beings without distinction (cf. 1Jn 2:2). John makes clear, however, that its efficacious effect is only for those who receive Christ (vv. 11, 12). For discussion of the relation of Christ's death to the world, *see note on 2Co 5:19*.

1:31 I did not recognize Him. Although John was Jesus' cousin, he did not know Jesus as the "Coming One" or "Messiah" (v. 30).

1:32 the Spirit descending. God had previously communicated to John that this sign was to indicate the promised Messiah (v. 33), so when John witnessed this act, he was able to identify the Messiah as Jesus (cf. Mt 3:16; Mk 1:10; Lk 3:22).

1:34 the Son of God. Although, in a limited sense, believers can be called "sons of God" (e.g., Mt 5:9; Ro 8:14), John uses this phrase with the full force as a title that points to the unique oneness and intimacy that Jesus sustains to the Father as "Son." The term carries the idea of the deity of Jesus as Messiah (v. 49; 5:16–30; cf. 2Sa 7:14; Ps 2:7; *see notes on Heb 1:1–9*).

JESUS' PUBLIC MINISTRY, FIRST CONVERTS

35 Again [A]the next day John was standing [a]with two of his disciples, 36 and he looked at Jesus as He walked, and *said, "Behold, [A]the Lamb of God!" 37 The two disciples heard him speak, and they followed Jesus. 38 And Jesus turned and saw them following, and *said to them, "What do you seek?" They said to Him, "[A]Rabbi (which translated means Teacher), where are You staying?" 39 He *said to them, "Come, and you will see." So they came and saw where He was staying; and they stayed with Him that day, for it was about the [a]tenth hour. 40 [A]One of the two who heard John *speak* and followed Him, was Andrew, Simon Peter's brother. 41 He *found first his own brother Simon and *said to him, "We have found the [A]Messiah" (which translated means [a]Christ). 42 He brought him to Jesus. Jesus looked at him and said, "You are Simon the son of [a,A]John; you shall be called [B]Cephas" (which is translated [b,C]Peter).

43 [A]The next day He purposed to go into [B]Galilee, and He *found [C]Philip. And Jesus *said to him, "[D]Follow Me." 44 Now [A]Philip was from [B]Bethsaida, of the city of Andrew and Peter. 45 [A]Philip *found [B]Nathanael and *said to him, "We have found Him of whom [C]Moses in the Law and *also* [C]the Prophets wrote—Jesus of [D]Nazareth, [E]the son of Joseph." 46 Nathanael said to him, "[A]Can any good thing come out of Nazareth?" [B]Philip *said to him, "Come and see." 47 Jesus saw Nathanael coming to Him, and *said of him, "Behold, an [A]Israelite indeed, in whom there is no deceit!" 48 Nathanael *said to Him, "How do You know me?" Jesus answered and said to him, "Before [A]Philip called you, when you were under the fig tree, I saw you." 49 Nathanael answered Him, "[A]Rabbi, You are [B]the Son of God; You are the [C]King of Israel." 50 Jesus answered and said to him, "Because I said to you that I saw you under the fig tree, do you believe? You will see greater things than these." 51 And He *said to him, "Truly, truly, I

1:35 [a]Lit *and* [A]John 1:29 1:36 [A]John 1:29 1:38 [A]Matt 23:7f; John 1:49 1:39 [a]Perhaps 10 a.m. (Roman time) 1:40 [A]Matt 4:18-22; Mark 1:16-20; Luke 5:2-11; John 1:40-42 1:41 [a]Gr *Anointed One* [A]Dan 9:25; John 4:25 1:42 [a]Gr *Joannes* [b]I.e. Rock or Stone [A]Matt 16:17; John 21:15-17 [B]1 Cor 1:12; 3:22; 9:5; 15:5; Gal 1:18; 2:9, 11, 14 [C]Matt 16:18 1:43 [A]John 1:29, 35 [B]Matt 4:12; John 1:28; 2:11 [C]Matt 10:3; John 1:44-48; 6:5, 7; 12:21f; 14:8f [D]Matt 8:22 1:44 [A]Matt 10:3; John 1:44-48; 6:5, 7; 12:21f; 14:8f [B]Matt 11:21 1:45 [A]Matt 10:3; John 1:44-48; 6:5, 7; 12:21f; 14:8f [B]John 1:46-49; 21:2 [C]Luke 24:27 [D]Matt 2:23 [E]Luke 2:48; 3:23; 4:22; John 6:42 1:46 [A]John 7:41, 52 [B]Matt 10:3; John 1:44-48; 6:5, 7; 12:21f; 14:8f 1:47 [A]Rom 9:4 1:48 [A]Matt 10:3; John 1:44-48; 6:5, 7; 12:21f; 14:8f 1:49 [A]John 1:38 [B]John 1:34 [C]Matt 2:2; 27:42; Mark 15:32; John 12:13

1:35–51 This portion deals with John's witness to a third group, i.e., some of John's disciples, on the third day (see vv. 19–28, 29–34 for the first and second groups) regarding Jesus. Consistent with John's humility (v. 27), he focuses the attention of his own disciples onto Jesus (v. 37).

1:37 they followed Jesus. Although the verb "follow" usually means "to follow as a disciple" in the writing of the apostle (v. 43; 8:12; 12:26; 21:19, 20, 22), it may also have a neutral sense (11:31). The "following" here does not necessarily mean that they became permanent disciples at this time. The implication may be that they went after Jesus to examine Him more closely because of John's testimony. This event constituted a preliminary exposure of John the Baptist's disciples to Jesus (e.g., Andrew; 1:40). They eventually dedicated their lives to Him as true disciples and apostles when Jesus called them to permanent service after these events (Mt 4:18–22; 9:9; Mk 1:16–20). At this point in the narrative, John the Baptist fades from the scene, and the attention focuses upon the ministry of Christ.

1:39 the tenth hour. The Jews divided the daylight period of the day into 12 hours (starting at sunrise, approximately 6:00 a.m.). This would make the time about 4:00 p.m. *See note on Mk 15:25.* This would make the time about 10:00 a.m. John mentions the precise time most likely to emphasize that he was the other disciple of John the Baptist who was with Andrew (v. 40). As an eyewitness to these events occurring on 3 successive days, John's first meeting with Jesus was so life-changing that he remembered the exact hour when he first met the Lord.

1:41 Messiah. The term "Messiah" is a transliteration of a Heb. or Aram. verbal adjective that means "Anointed One." It comes from a verb that means "to anoint" someone as an action involved in consecrating that person to a particular office or function. While the term at first applied to the king of Israel ("the LORD's anointed"—1Sa 16:6), the High Priest ("the anointed priest," Lv 4:3) and, in one passage, the patriarchs ("My anointed ones," Ps 105:15), the term eventually came to point above all to the prophesied "Coming One" or "Messiah" in His role as prophet, priest, and king. The term "Christ," a Gr. word (verbal adjective) that comes from a verb meaning "to anoint," is used in translating the Heb. term, so that the terms "Messiah" or "Christ" are titles and not personal names of Jesus.

1:42 Jesus looked at him. Jesus knows hearts thoroughly (vv. 43–51) and not only sees into them (vv. 47, 48) but also transforms a person into what He wants him to become. **you shall be called Cephas.** Up to this time, Peter had been known as "Simon the son of John" ("Jonah" in some translations; the name "Jonah" in Aram. means "John"; cf. 21:15–17; Mt 16:17). The term "Cephas" means "rock" in Aram, which is translated "Peter" in Greek. Jesus' assignment of the name "Cephas" or "Peter" to Simon occurred at the outset of his ministry (cf. Mt 16:18; Mk 3:16). The statement not only is predictive of what Peter would be called but also declarative of how Jesus would transform his character and use him in relationship to the foundation of the church (cf. 21:18, 19; Mt 16:16–18; Ac 2:14–4:32).

1:43–51 This section introduces the fourth day since the beginning of John the Baptist's witness (cf. vv. 19, 29, 35).

1:44 Bethsaida, of the city of Andrew and Peter. While Mk 1:21, 29 locates Peter's house in Capernaum, John relates that he was from Bethsaida. Resolution centers in the fact that Peter (and Andrew) most likely grew up in Bethsaida and later relocated to Capernaum in the same way that Jesus was consistently identified with His hometown of Nazareth, though He lived elsewhere later (Mt 2:23; 4:13; Mk 1:9; Lk 1:26).

1:45 Him of whom Moses in the Law and *also* the Prophets wrote. This phrase encapsulates the stance of John's whole gospel: Jesus is the fulfillment of OT Scripture (cf. v. 21; 5:39; Dt 18:15–19; Lk 24:44–47; Ac 10:43; 18:28; 26:22, 23; Ro 1:2; 1Co 15:3; 1Pe 1:10, 11; Rev 19:10).

1:46 Can any good thing come out of Nazareth? Nathanael was from Cana (21:2), another town in Galilee. While Galileans were despised by Judeans, Galileans themselves despised people from Nazareth. In light of 7:52, Nathanael's scorn may have centered in the fact that Nazareth was an insignificant village without seeming prophetic importance (cf., however, Mt 2:23). Later, some would contemptuously refer to Christians as the "sect of the Nazarenes" (Ac 24:5).

1:47 no deceit. Jesus' point was that Nathanael's bluntness revealed that he was an Israelite without duplicitous motives who was willing to examine for himself the claims being made about Jesus. The term reveals an honest, seeking heart. The reference here may be an allusion to Ge 27:35 where Jacob, in contrast to the sincere Nathanael, was known for his trickery. The meaning may be that the employment of trickery characterized not only Jacob but also his descendants. In Jesus' mind, an honest and sincere Israelite had become an exception rather than the rule (cf. 2:23–25).

1:48 I saw you. A brief glimpse of Jesus' supernatural knowledge. Not only was Jesus' brief summary of Nathanael accurate (v. 47), but He also revealed information that could only be known by Nathanael himself. Perhaps Nathanael had some significant or outstanding experience of communion with God at the location, and he was able to recognize Jesus' allusion to it. At any rate, Jesus had knowledge of this event not available to men.

1:49 the Son of God ... the King of Israel. Jesus' display of supernatural knowledge and Philip's witness removed Nathanael's doubts, so John added the witness of Nathanael to this section. The use of "the" with "Son of God" most likely indicates that the expression is to be understood as bearing its full significance (cf. v. 34; 11:27). For Nathanael, here was One who could not be described merely in human terms.

1:51 Truly, truly. Cf. 5:19, 24, 25. A phrase used frequently for emphasizing the importance and truth of the coming statement. **heavens opened and the angels of God ascending and descending.** In light of the context of v. 47,

say to you, you will see [A]the heavens opened and
[B]the angels of God ascending and descending on
[C]the Son of Man."

MIRACLE AT CANA

2 On [A]the third day there was a wedding in [B]Cana
of Galilee, and the [C]mother of Jesus was there;
2 and both Jesus and His [A]disciples were invited to
the wedding. 3 When the wine ran out, the mother of
Jesus *said to Him, "They have no wine." 4 And Jesus
*said to her, "[A]Woman, [a,B]what does that have to do
with us? [C]My hour has not yet come." 5 His [A]mother
*said to the servants, "Whatever He says to you, do
it." 6 Now there were six stone waterpots set there
[A]for the Jewish custom of purification, containing
[a]twenty or thirty gallons each. 7 Jesus *said to them,
"Fill the waterpots with water." So they filled them
up to the brim. 8 And He *said to them, "Draw *some*
out now and take it to the [a]headwaiter." So they took
it *to him*. 9 When the headwaiter tasted the water
[A]which had become wine, and did not know where
it came from (but the servants who had drawn
the water knew), the headwaiter *called the bridegroom, 10 and *said to him, "Every man serves the
good wine first, and when *the people* [A]have [a]drunk
freely, *then he serves* the poorer *wine; but* you have
kept the good wine until now." 11 This beginning of
His [a,A]signs Jesus did in Cana of [B]Galilee, and manifested His [C]glory, and His disciples believed in Him.
12 After this He went down to [A]Capernaum, He and
His [B]mother and *His* [B]brothers and His [C]disciples;
and they stayed there a few days.

1:51 [A]Ezek 1:1; Matt 3:16; Luke 3:21; Acts 7:56; 10:11; Rev 19:11 [B]Gen 28:12 [C]Matt 8:20 2:1 [A]John 1:29, 35, 43 [B]John 2:11; 4:46; 21:2 [C]Matt 12:46 2:2 [A]John 1:40-49; 2:12, 17, 22; 3:22; 4:2, 8, 27; 6:8, 12, 16, 22, 24, 60f, 66; 7:3; 8:31 2:4 [a]Lit *what to Me and to you* (a Hebrew idiom) [A]John 19:26 [B]Matt 8:29 [C]John 7:6, 8, 30; 8:20 2:5 [A]Matt 12:46 2:6 [a]Lit *two or three measures* [A]Mark 7:3f; John 3:25 2:8 [a]Or *steward* 2:9 [A]John 4:46 2:10 [a]Or *have become drunk* [A]Matt 24:49; Luke 12:45; Acts 2:15; 1 Cor 11:21; Eph 5:18; 1 Thess 5:7; Rev 17:2, 6 2:11 [a]Or *attesting miracles;* i.e. one which points to the supernatural power of God in redeeming grace [A]John 2:23; 3:2; 4:54; 6:2, 14, 26, 30; 7:31; 9:16; 10:41; 11:47; 12:18, 37; 20:30 [B]John 1:43 [C]John 1:14 2:12 [A]Matt 4:13 [B]Matt 12:46 [C]John 2:2

this verse most likely refers to Ge 28:12 where Jacob dreamed about a ladder from heaven. Jesus' point to Nathanael was that just like Jacob experienced supernatural or heaven-sent revelation, Nathanael and the other disciples would experience supernatural communication confirming who Jesus was. Moreover, the term "Son of Man" replaced the ladder in Jacob's dream, signifying that Jesus was the means of access between God and man. **Son of Man.** *See note on Mt 8:20.* This is Jesus' favorite self-designation, for it was mostly spoken by Jesus who used it over 80 times. In the NT, it refers only to Jesus and appears mostly in the Gospels (cf. Ac 7:56). In the Fourth Gospel, the expression occurs 13 times and is most commonly associated with the themes of crucifixion and suffering (3:14; 8:28) and revelation (6:27, 53) but also with eschatological authority (5:27). While the term at times may refer merely to a human being or as a substitute for "I" (6:27; cf. 6:20), it especially takes on an eschatological significance referring to Da 7:13, 14 where the "Son of Man" or Messiah comes in glory to receive the kingdom from the "Ancient of Days" (i.e., the Father).

2:1–11 John relates the first great sign performed by Jesus to demonstrate His deity, the turning of water into wine. Only God can create from nothing. John identifies 8 miracles in his gospel that constitute "signs" or confirmation of who Jesus is. Each of the 8 miracles were different; no two were alike (cf. v. 11).

2:1 On the third day. This phrase has reference to the last narrated event, i.e., the calling of Philip and Nathanael (1:43). **wedding.** Such a wedding celebration in Jewish culture could last for a week. Financial responsibility lay with the groom (vv. 9, 10). To run out of wine for the guests would have been an embarrassment to the groom and may have even opened him to a potential lawsuit from the relatives of the bride. **Cana of Galilee.** Cana was the home of Nathanael (21:2). Its exact location is unknown. A probable location is Khirbet Qana, a village now in ruins approximately 9 mi. N of Nazareth.

2:2 both Jesus and His disciples were invited. The fact that Jesus, His mother, and His disciples all attended the wedding suggests that the wedding may have been for a relative or close family friend. The disciples who accompanied Him are the 5 mentioned in chap. 1: Andrew, Simon Peter, Philip, Nathanael, and the unnamed disciple (1:35) who was surely John, who also witnessed this miracle.

2:3 wine. The wine served was subject to fermentation. In the ancient world, however, to quench thirst without inducing drunkenness, wine was diluted with water to between one-third and one-tenth of its strength. Due to the climate and circumstances, even "new wine," or "sweet wine," fermented quickly and had an inebriating effect if not mixed (Ac 2:13). Because of a lack of water purification process, wine mixed with water was also safer to drink than water alone. While the Bible condemns drunkenness, it does not necessarily condemn the consumption of wine (Ps 104:15; Pr 20:1; *see notes on Eph 5:18*).

2:4 Woman. The term is not necessarily impolite, but it does have the effect of distancing Jesus from His mother and her request. Perhaps it has the equivalent of "ma'am." **what does that have to do with us?** The expression, common in Semitic idiom (Jdg 11:12; 2Sa 16:10), always distances the two parties, the speaker's tone conveying some degree of reproach. Jesus' tone was not rude, but abrupt. The phrase asks what is shared in common between the parties. The thrust of Jesus' comment was that He had entered into the purpose for His mission on earth, so that He subordinated all activities to the fulfillment of that mission. Mary had to recognize Him not so much as a son whom she raised but as the promised Messiah and Son of God. Cf. Mk 3:31–35. **My hour has not yet come.** The phrase constantly refers to Jesus' death and exaltation (7:30; 8:20; 12:23, 27; 13:1; 17:1). He was on a divine schedule decreed by God before the foundation of the world. Since the prophets characterized the messianic age as a time when wine would flow liberally (Jer 31:12; Hos 14:7; Am 9:13, 14), Jesus was likely referring to the fact that the necessity of the cross must come before the blessings of the millennial age.

2:6 Jewish custom of purification. The 6 water jars were made of stone because stone was more impervious than earthenware and did not contract uncleanness. Also, this made them more suitable to ceremonial washing (cf. Mk 7:3, 4).

2:11 signs. John used the word "signs" here to refer to significant displays of power that pointed beyond themselves to the deeper divine realities that could be perceived by the eyes of faith. By this word, John emphasized that miracles were not merely displays of power but had a significance beyond the mere acts themselves.

2:12 After this. The phrase "after this" (or similar wording such as "after these things") is a frequent connective between narratives in this gospel (e.g., 3:22; 5:1, 14; 6:1; 7:1; 11:7, 11; 19:28, 38). John placed this verse here as a transition to explain Jesus' movement from Cana in Galilee to Capernaum and eventual

THE EIGHT SIGNS	
Turns water into wine (Jn 2:1–12)	Jesus is the source of life.
Heals a royal official's son (Jn 4:46–54)	Jesus is master over distance.
Heals a lame man at the pool of Bethesda (Jn 5:1–17)	Jesus is master over time.
Feeds 5,000 (Jn 6:1–14)	Jesus is the bread of life.
Walks on water, stills a storm (Jn 6:15–21)	Jesus is master over nature.
Heals a man blind from birth (Jn 9:1–41)	Jesus is the light of the world.
Raises Lazarus from the dead (Jn 11:17–45)	Jesus has power over death.
Causes abundant catch of fish (Jn 21:6)	Jesus is master over the animal world.

FIRST PASSOVER—CLEANSING THE TEMPLE

13 [A]The Passover of the Jews was near, and Jesus
[B]went up to Jerusalem. 14 [A]And He found in the temple those who were selling oxen and sheep and
doves, and the money changers seated *at their ta-*
bles. 15 And He made a scourge of cords, and drove
them all out of the temple, with the sheep and the
oxen; and He poured out the coins of the money
changers and overturned their tables; 16 and to
those who were selling [A]the doves He said, "Take
these things away; stop making [B]My Father's house
a [a]place of business." 17 His [A]disciples remembered
that it was written, "[B]ZEAL FOR YOUR HOUSE WILL
CONSUME ME." 18 [A]The Jews then said to Him, "[B]What
sign do You show us [a]as your authority for doing
these things?" 19 Jesus answered them, "[A]Destroy this
[a]temple, and in three days I will raise it up." 20 [A]The
Jews then said, "It took [B]forty-six years to build this
[a]temple, and will You raise it up in three days?" 21 But
He was speaking of [A]the [a]temple of His body. 22 So
when He was raised from the dead, His [A]disciples
[B]remembered that He said this; and they believed
[C]the Scripture and the word which Jesus had spoken.

2:13 [A]Deut 16:1-6; John 5:1; 6:4; 11:55 [B]Luke 2:41; John 2:23 2:14 [A]John 2:14-16: *Matt 21:12ff; Mark 11:15, 17; Luke 19:45f;* Mal 3:1ff 2:16 [a]Lit *house* [A]Matt 21:12 [B]Luke 2:49 2:17 [A]John 2:2 [B]Ps 69:9 2:18 [a]Lit *that You do these* [A]John 1:19 [B]Matt 12:38 2:19 [a]Or *sanctuary* [A]Matt 26:61; 27:40; Mark 14:58; 15:29; Acts 6:14 2:20 [a]Or *sanctuary* [A]John 1:19 [B]Ezra 5:16 2:21 [a]Or *sanctuary* [A]1 Cor 6:19 2:22 [A]John 2:2 [B]Luke 24:8; John 2:17; 12:16; 14:26 [C]Ps 16:10; Luke 24:26f; John 20:9; Acts 13:33

arrival at Jerusalem for the Passover celebration. Capernaum was on the NW shore of Galilee about 16 mi. NE of Cana.

2:13–25 John used this section where Jesus cleansed the temple in righteous indignation to reinforce his main theme that He was the promised Messiah and Son of God. In this section, he highlighted 3 attributes of Jesus that confirm His deity: 1) His passion for reverence (vv. 13–17); 2) His power of resurrection (vv. 18–22); and 3) His perception of reality (vv. 23–25).

2:13–17 The first way John demonstrated Christ's deity in the narrative of the temple cleansing was to show His passion for reverence. God alone exercises the right to regulate His worship.

2:13 Passover of the Jews. This is the first of 3 Passovers which John mentions (v. 13; 6:4; 11:55). Jews selected the lamb on the tenth of the month, and celebrated Passover on the 14th day of the lunar month of Nisan (full moon at the end of Mar. or beginning of Apr.). They slaughtered the lamb between 3:00 and 6:00 p.m. on the night of the feast. Passover commemorates the deliverance of the Jews from slavery in Egypt when the angel of death "passed over" Jewish homes in Egypt whose "doorposts" were sprinkled with blood (Ex 12:23–27). **Jesus went up to Jerusalem.** Jesus' journeying to Jerusalem for the Passover was a standard annual procedure for every devout Jewish male over 12 years old (Ex 23:14–17). Jewish pilgrims crowded into Jerusalem for this greatest of Jewish feasts.

2:14 those who were selling . . . the money changers. During the celebration of Passover, worshipers came from all over Israel and the Roman Empire to Jerusalem. Because many traveled large distances, it was inconvenient to bring their sacrificial animals with them. Opportunistic merchants, seeing a chance to provide a service and probably eyeing considerable profit during this time, set up areas in the outer courts of the temple in order for travelers to buy animals. The money changers were needed because the temple tax, paid annually by every conscientious Jewish male 20 years of age or older (Ex 30:13, 14; Mt 17:24–27), had to be in Jewish or Tyrian coinage (because of its high purity of silver). Those coming from foreign lands would need to exchange their money into the proper coinage for the tax. The money changers charged a high fee for the exchange. With such a large group of travelers and because of the seasonal nature of the celebration, both the animal dealers and money exchangers exploited the situation for monetary gain ("robbers' den"; Mt 21:13). Religion had become crass and materialistic.

2:15 As John recorded this cleansing of the temple at the beginning of Jesus' ministry, the Synoptic Gospels record a temple cleansing at the end of Jesus' ministry during the final Passover week before Jesus' crucifixion (Mt 21:12–17; Mk 11:15–18; Lk 19:45, 46). The historical circumstances and literary contexts of the two temple cleansings differ so widely that attempts to equate the two are unsuccessful. Furthermore, that two cleansings occurred is entirely consistent with the overall context of Jesus' ministry, for the Jewish nation as a whole never recognized Jesus' authority as Messiah (Mt 23:37–39). Instead, they rejected His message as well as His person, making such repeated cleansing of the temple highly probable (as well as necessary). **drove *them* all out of the temple.** When the holiness of God and His worship was at stake, Jesus took fast and furious action. The "all" indicates that He drove not only men out but also animals. Yet, although His physical action was forceful, it was not cruel. The moderation of His actions is seen in the fact that no riotous uproar occurred; otherwise the specially large contingent of Roman troops in Jerusalem at that time because of the Passover crowds, stationed in the Antonia Fortress overlooking the temple, would have swiftly reacted. Although the primary reference is to the actions of the Messiah in the millennial kingdom, Jesus' actions in cleansing the temple were an initial fulfillment of Mal 3:1–3 (and Zec 14:20, 21) that speak of Messiah's purifying the religious worship of His people.

2:16 stop making. The force of the Gr. imperative indicates that Jesus made a strong demand that they stop their current practice. God's holiness demands holiness in worship. **My Father's.** John gave a subtle hint of Jesus' divine Sonship as well as His messiahship with the recording of this phrase (see 5:17, 18). **house a place of business.** Jesus may have intended a play on words. The word "business" pictures a trading house filled with wares.

2:17 Quoted from Ps 69:9 to indicate that Jesus would not tolerate irreverence toward God. When David wrote this psalm, he was being persecuted because of his zeal toward God's house and his defense of God's honor. The disciples were afraid that Jesus' actions would precipitate the same type of persecution. Paul quotes the latter half of Ps 69:9 in Ro 15:3 ("THE REPROACHES OF THOSE WHO REPROACHED YOU FELL ON ME"), clearly indicating the messianic nature that the psalm had for the early church.

2:18–22 The second way John demonstrated Christ's deity in the account of the temple cleansing was to show His power over death through resurrection. Only God has this right.

2:18 The Jews. Most likely the temple authorities or representatives of the Sanhedrin (cf. 1:19). **sign.** The Jews demanded that Jesus show some type of miraculous sign that would indicate His authority for the actions that He had just taken in regulating the activities of the temple. Their demand of a sign reveals that they had not grasped the significance of Jesus' rebuke that centered in their need for proper attitudes and holiness in worship. Such an action itself constituted a "sign" of Jesus' person and authority. Moreover, they were requesting from Jesus a crass display of miracles on demand, further displaying their unbelief.

2:19 At His trial, the authorities charged Jesus (Mk 14:58; cf. Mk 15:29) with making a threatening statement against the temple, revealing that they did not understand Jesus' response here. Once again John's gospel supplements the other gospels at this point by indicating that Jesus enigmatically referred to His resurrection. As with His usage of parables, Jesus' cryptic statement most likely was designed to reveal the truth to His disciples but conceal its meaning from unbelievers who questioned Him (Mt 13:10, 11). Only after His resurrection, however, did the disciples understand the real significance of this statement (v. 22; cf. Mt 12:40). Importantly, through the death and resurrection of Christ, temple worship in Jerusalem was destroyed (cf. 4:21) and reinstituted in the hearts of those who were built into a spiritual temple called the church (Eph 2:19–22).

2:20 forty-six years to build this temple. This was not a reference to the Solomonic temple, since it had been destroyed during the Babylonian conquest in 586 B.C. When the captives returned from Babylon, Zerubbabel and Jeshua began rebuilding the temple (Ezr 1–4). Encouraged by the prophets Haggai and Zechariah (Ezr 5:1–6:18), the Jews completed the work in 516 B.C. In 20/19 B.C. Herod the Great began a reconstruction and expansion. Workers completed the main part of the project in 10 years, but other parts were still being constructed even at the time Jesus cleansed the temple. Interestingly, the finishing touches on the whole enterprise were still being made at its destruction by the Romans along with Jerusalem in A.D. 70. The famous "Wailing Wall" is built on part of the Herodian temple foundation.

23 Now when He was in Jerusalem at [A]the Passover, during the feast, many believed in His name,
[B]observing His signs which He was doing. 24 But
Jesus, on His part, was not entrusting Himself to
them, for [A]He knew all men, 25 and because He did
not need anyone to testify concerning man, [A]for He
Himself knew what was in man.

THE NEW BIRTH

3 Now there was a man of the Pharisees, named
[A]Nicodemus, a [B]ruler of the Jews; 2 this man
came to Jesus by night and said to Him, "[A]Rabbi, we
know that You have come from God *as* a teacher;
for no one can do these [a,B]signs that You do unless
[C]God is with him." 3 Jesus answered and said to him,
"Truly, truly, I say to you, unless one [A]is born [a]again
he cannot see [B]the kingdom of God."
4 Nicodemus *said to Him, "How can a man be
born when he is old? He cannot enter a second time
into his mother's womb and be born, can he?" 5 Jesus
answered, "Truly, truly, I say to you, unless one is
born of [A]water and the Spirit he cannot enter into
[B]the kingdom of God. 6 [A]That which is born of the
flesh is flesh, and that which is born of the Spirit
is spirit. 7 Do not be amazed that I said to you, 'You
must be born [a]again.' 8 [A]The wind blows where it

2:23 [A]John 2:13 [B]John 2:11 2:24 [A]Acts 1:24; 15:8 2:25 [A]Matt 9:4; John 1:42, 47; 6:61, 64; 13:11 3:1 [A]John 7:50; 19:39 [B]Luke 23:13; John 7:26, 48 3:2 [a]Or *attesting miracles* [A]Matt 23:7; John 3:26 [B]John 2:11 [C]John 9:33; 10:38; 14:10f; Acts 2:22; 10:38 3:3 [a]Or *from above* [A]2 Cor 5:17; 1 Pet 1:23 [B]Matt 19:24; 21:31; Mark 9:47; 10:14f; John 3:5 3:5 [A]Ezek 36:25-27; Eph 5:26; Titus 3:5 [B]Matt 19:24; 21:31; Mark 9:47; 10:14f; John 3:3 3:6 [A]John 1:13; 1 Cor 15:50 3:7 [a]Or *from above* 3:8 [A]Ps 135:7; Eccl 11:5; Ezek 37:9

2:23–25 The third way John demonstrated Christ's deity in the account of the temple cleansing was to show His perception of reality. Only God truly knows the hearts of men.

2:23, 24 many believed in His name .... But Jesus ... was not entrusting Himself to them. John based these two phrases on the same Gr. verb for "believe." This verse subtly reveals the true nature of belief from a biblical standpoint. Because of what they knew of Jesus from His miraculous signs, many came to believe in Him. However, Jesus made it His habit not to wholeheartedly "entrust" or "commit" Himself to them because He knew their hearts. Verse 24 indicates that Jesus looked for genuine conversion rather than enthusiasm for the spectacular. The latter verse also leaves a subtle doubt as to the genuineness of the conversion of some (cf. 8:31, 32). This emphatic contrast between vv. 23, 24 in terms of type of trust, therefore, reveals that, lit., "belief into His name" involved much more than intellectual assent. It called for whole-hearted commitment of one's life as Jesus' disciple (cf. Mt 10:37; 16:24–26).

3:1–21 The story of Jesus and Nicodemus reinforces John's themes that Jesus is the Messiah and Son of God (apologetic) and that He came to offer salvation to men (evangelistic). John 2:23, 24 actually serves as the introduction to Nicodemus' story, since chap. 3 constitutes tangible evidence of Jesus' ability to know men's hearts and thereby also demonstrates Jesus' deity. Jesus also presented God's plan of salvation to Nicodemus, showing that He was God's messenger, whose redemptive work brings about the promised salvation to His people (v. 14). The chapter may be divided into two sections: 1) Jesus' dialogue with Nicodemus (vv. 1–10); and 2) Jesus' discourse on God's plan of salvation (vv. 11–21).

3:1–10 This section on Jesus' dialogue with Nicodemus may be divided into 3 sections: 1) Nicodemus' inquiry of Jesus (vv. 1–3); 2) Jesus' insight into Nicodemus (vv. 4–8); and 3) Jesus' indictment of Nicodemus (vv. 9, 10).

3:1 Pharisees. *See note on Mt 3:7.* The word "Pharisee" most likely comes from a Heb. word meaning "to separate" and therefore probably means "separated ones." They were not separatists in the sense of isolationists but in the puritanical sense, i.e., they were highly zealous for ritual and religious purity according to the Mosaic law as well as their own traditions that they added to the OT legislation. Although their origin is unknown, they seem to have arisen as an offshoot from the "Hasidim" or "pious ones" during the Maccabean era. They were generally from the Jewish middle class and mostly consisted of laity (business men) rather than priests or Levites. They represented the orthodox core of Judaism and very strongly influenced the common people of Israel. According to Josephus, 6,000 existed at the time of Herod the Great. Jesus condemned them for their hyper concentration on externalizing religion (rules and regulations) rather than inward spiritual transformation (vv. 3, 7). **Nicodemus.** Although Nicodemus was a Pharisee, his name was Gr. in origin and means "victor over the people." He was a prominent Pharisee and member of the Sanhedrin ("a ruler of the Jews"). Nothing is known about his family background. He eventually came to believe in Jesus (7:50–52), risking his own life and reputation by helping to give Jesus' body a decent burial (19:38–42). **a ruler of the Jews.** This is a reference to the Sanhedrin (*see note on Mt 26:59*), the main ruling body of the Jews in Israel during the Greco-Roman Period. It was the Jewish "supreme court" or ruling council of the time and arose most likely during the Persian period. In NT times, the Sanhedrin was composed of the High Priest (president), chief priests, elders (family heads), and scribes for a total of 71 people. The method of appointment was both hereditary and political. It executed both civil and criminal jurisdiction according to Jewish law. However, capital punishment cases required the sanction of the Roman procurator (18:30–32). After A.D. 70 and the destruction of Jerusalem, the Sanhedrin was abolished and replaced by the Beth Din (court of Judgment) that was composed of scribes whose decisions had only moral and religious authority.

3:2 came to Jesus by night. While some have thought that Nicodemus' visit at night was somehow figurative of the spiritual darkness of his heart (cf. 1:5; 9:4; 11:10; 13:30) or that he decided to come at this time because he could take more time with Jesus and be unhurried in conversation, perhaps the most logical explanation lies in the fact that, as a ruler of the Jews, Nicodemus was afraid of the implications of associating openly in conversation with Jesus. He chose night in order to have a clandestine meeting with Jesus rather than risk disfavor with his fellow Pharisees among whom Jesus was generally unpopular.

3:3 born again. The phrase lit. means "born from above." Jesus answered a question that Nicodemus does not even ask. He read Nicodemus' heart and came to the very core of his problem, i.e., the need for spiritual transformation or regeneration produced by the Holy Spirit. New birth is an act of God whereby eternal life is imparted to the believer (2Co 5:17; Tit 3:5; 1Pe 1:3; 1Jn 2:29; 3:9; 4:7; 5:1, 4, 18). Chapter 1:12, 13 indicates that "born again" also carries the idea "to become children of God" through trust in the name of the incarnate Word. **cannot see the kingdom of God.** In context, this is primarily a reference to participation in the millennial kingdom at the end of the age, fervently anticipated by the Pharisees and other Jews. Since the Pharisees were supernaturalists, they naturally and eagerly expected the coming of the prophesied resurrection of the saints and institution of the messianic kingdom (Is 11:1–16; Da 12:2). Their problem was that they thought that mere physical lineage and keeping of religious externals qualified them for entrance into the kingdom rather than the needed spiritual transformation which Jesus emphasized (cf. 8:33–39; Gal 6:15). The coming of the kingdom at the end of the age can be described as the "regeneration" of the world (Mt 19:28), but regeneration of the individual is required before the end of the world in order to enter the kingdom.

3:4 A teacher himself, Nicodemus understood the rabbinical method of using figurative language to teach spiritual truth, and he was merely picking up Jesus' symbolism.

3:5 born of water and the Spirit. Jesus referred not to literal water here, but to the need for "cleansing" (e.g., Eze 36:24–27). When water is used figuratively in the OT, it habitually refers to renewal or spiritual cleansing, especially when used in conjunction with "spirit" (Nu 19:17–19; Ps 51:9, 10; Is 32:15; 44:3–5; 55:1–3; Jer 2:13; Joel 2:28, 29). Thus, Jesus made reference to the spiritual washing or purification of the soul, accomplished by the Holy Spirit through the Word of God at the moment of salvation (cf. Eph 5:26; Tit 3:5), required for belonging to His kingdom.

3:8 The wind blows where it wishes. Jesus' point was that just as the wind cannot be controlled or understood by human beings, but its effects can be witnessed, so also it is with the Holy Spirit. He cannot be controlled or understood, but the proof of His work is apparent. Where the Spirit works, there is undeniable and unmistakable evidence.

wishes and you hear the sound of it, but do not know where it comes from and where it is going; so is everyone who is born of the Spirit."

9 Nicodemus said to Him, "How can these things be?" 10 Jesus answered and said to him, "Are you [A]the teacher of Israel and do not understand these things? 11 Truly, truly, I say to you, [A]we speak of what we know and [B]testify of what we have seen, and [B]you do not accept our testimony. 12 If I told you earthly things and you do not believe, how will you believe if I tell you heavenly things? 13 [A]No one has ascended into heaven, but [B]He who descended from heaven: [C]the Son of Man. 14 As [A]Moses lifted up the serpent in the wilderness, even so must [B]the Son of Man [C]be lifted up; 15 so that whoever [a]believes will [A]in Him have eternal life.

16 "For God so [A]loved the world, that He [B]gave His [a,C]only begotten Son, that whoever [D]believes in Him shall not perish, but have eternal life. 17 For God [A]did not send the Son into the world [B]to judge the world, but that the world might be saved through Him. 18 [A]He who believes in Him is not judged; he who does not believe has been judged already, because he has not believed in the name of [B]the [a]only begotten Son of God. 19 This is the judgment, that [A]the Light has come into the world, and men loved the darkness rather than the Light, for [B]their deeds were evil. 20 [A]For everyone who does evil hates the Light, and does not come to the Light for fear that his deeds will be exposed. 21 But he who [A]practices the truth comes to the Light, so that his deeds may be manifested as having been wrought in God."

JOHN'S LAST TESTIMONY

22 After these things Jesus and His [A]disciples came into the land of Judea, and there He was spending time with them and [B]baptizing. 23 John also was baptizing in Aenon near Salim, because there was much water there; and *people* were coming and were being baptized— 24 for [A]John had not yet been thrown into prison.

25 Therefore there arose a discussion on the part of John's disciples with a Jew about [A]purification.

3:10 [A]Luke 2:46; 5:17; Acts 5:34 3:11 [A]John 1:18; 7:16f; 8:26, 28; 12:49; 14:24 [B]John 3:32 3:13 [A]Deut 30:12; Prov 30:4; Acts 2:34; Rom 10:6; Eph 4:9 [B]John 3:31; 6:38, 42 [C]Matt 8:20 3:14 [A]Num 21:9 [B]Matt 8:20 [C]John 8:28; 12:34 3:15 [a]Or *believes in Him will have eternal life* [A]John 20:31; 1 John 5:11-13 3:16 [a]Or *unique,* only one of His kind [A]Rom 5:8; Eph 2:4; 2 Thess 2:16; 1 John 4:10; Rev 1:5 [B]Rom 8:32; 1 John 4:9 [C]John 1:18; 3:18; 1 John 4:9 [D]John 3:36; 6:40; 11:25f 3:17 [A]John 3:34; 5:36, 38; 6:29, 38, 57; 7:29; 8:42; 10:36; 11:42; 17:3, 8, 18, 21, 23, 25; 20:21 [B]Luke 19:10; John 8:15; 12:47; 1 John 4:14 3:18 [a]Or *unique,* only one of His kind [A]Mark 16:16; John 5:24 [B]John 1:18; 1 John 4:9 3:19 [A]John 1:4; 8:12; 9:5; 12:46 [B]John 7:7 3:20 [A]John 3:20, 21; Eph 5:11, 13 3:21 [A]1 John 1:6 3:22 [A]John 2:2 [B]John 4:1, 2 3:24 [A]Matt 4:12; 14:3; Mark 6:17; Luke 3:20 3:25 [A]John 2:6

3:10 the teacher. The use of the definite article "the" indicates that Nicodemus was a renowned master-teacher in the nation of Israel, an established religious authority *par excellence.* He enjoyed a high standing among the rabbis or teachers of his day. Jesus' reply emphasized the spiritual bankruptcy of the nation at that time, since even one of the greatest of Jewish teachers did not recognize this teaching on spiritual cleansing and transformation based clearly in the OT (cf. v. 5). The net effect is to show that externals of religion may have a deadening effect on one's spiritual perception.

3:11–21 The focus of these verses turns away from Nicodemus and centers on Jesus' discourse regarding the true meaning of salvation. The key word in these verses is "believe," used 7 times. The new birth must be appropriated by an act of faith. While vv. 1–10 center on the divine initiative in salvation, vv. 11–21 emphasize the human reaction to the work of God in regeneration. In vv. 11–21, the section may be divided into 3 parts: 1) the problem of unbelief (vv. 11, 12); 2) the answer to unbelief (vv. 13–17); and 3) the results of unbelief (vv. 18–21).

3:11, 12 Jesus focused on the idea that unbelief is the cause of ignorance. At heart, Nicodemus' failure to understand Jesus' words centered not so much in his intellect, but in his failure to believe Jesus' witness.

3:11 you do not accept our testimony. The plural "you" here refers back to the "we" of v. 2, where Nicodemus was speaking as a representative of his nation Israel ("we know"). Jesus replied in v. 11 with "you" indicating that Nicodemus' unbelief was typical of the nation as a collective whole.

3:13 No one has ascended into heaven. This verse contradicts other religious systems' claims to special revelation from God. Jesus insisted that no one has ascended to heaven in such a way as to return and talk about heavenly things (cf. 2Co 12:1–4). Only He had His permanent abode in heaven prior to His incarnation and, therefore, only He has the true knowledge regarding heavenly wisdom (cf. Pr 30:4).

3:14 so must the Son of Man be lifted up. Cf. 8:28; 12:32, 34; 18:31, 32. This is a veiled prediction of Jesus' death on the cross. Jesus referred to the story of Nu 21:5–9 where the Israelite people who looked at the serpent lifted up by Moses were healed. The point of this illustration or analogy is in the "lifted up." Just as Moses lifted up the snake on the pole so that all who looked upon it might live physically, those who look to Christ, who was "lifted up" on the cross, will live spiritually and eternally.

3:15 eternal life. This is the first of 17 references to "eternal life" in John's Gospel. The same Gr. phrase is translated in some versions as "everlasting life." The two expressions appear in the NT nearly 50 times. Eternal life refers not only to eternal quantity but divine quality of life. It means lit. "life of the age to come" and refers therefore to resurrection and heavenly existence in perfect glory and holiness. This life for believers in the Lord Jesus is experienced before heaven is reached. This "eternal life" is in essence nothing less than participation in the eternal life of the Living Word, Jesus Christ. It is the life of God in every believer, yet not fully manifest until the resurrection (Ro 8:19–23; Php 3:20, 21).

3:16 For God so loved the world. The Son's mission is bound up in the supreme love of God for the evil, sinful "world" of humanity (cf. 6:32, 51; 12:47; *see notes on 1:9; Mt 5:44, 45*) that is in rebellion against Him. The word "so" emphasizes the intensity or greatness of His love. The Father gave His unique and beloved Son to die on behalf of sinful men (*see note on 2Co 5:21*). **eternal life.** *See note on v. 15*; cf. 17:3; 1Jn 5:20.

3:18 believed in the name. This phrase (lit. "to believe into the name") means more than mere intellectual assent to the claims of the gospel. It includes trust and commitment to Christ as Lord and Savior which results in receiving a new nature (v. 7) which produces a change in heart and obedience to the Lord (*see note on 2:23, 24*).

3:22–36 This section constitutes John the Baptist's last testimony in this gospel regarding Christ. As his ministry faded away, Jesus' ministry moved to the forefront. In spite of the fact that John the Baptist received widespread fame in Israel and was generally accepted by the common people of the land as well as those who were social outcasts, his testimony regarding Jesus was rejected, especially by the leaders of Israel (cf. Mt 3:5–10; Lk 7:29).

3:22 into the land of Judea. While the previous episode with Nicodemus took place in Jerusalem (2:23), which was part of Judea, the phrase here means that Jesus went out into the rural areas of that region. **baptizing.** Chapter 4:2 specifically says that Jesus did not personally baptize but that His disciples carried on this work.

3:23 Aenon near Salim. The exact location of this reference is disputed. The phrase may refer to either Salim near Shechem or Salim that is 6 mi. S of Beth-shean. Both are in the region of Samaria. Aenon is a transliterated Heb. word meaning "springs," and both of these possible sites have plenty of water ("much water there").

3:24 John had not yet been thrown into prison. This provides another indication that John supplemented the Synoptic Gospels by providing additional information that helps further understanding of the movements of John the Baptist and Jesus (see Introduction). In Matthew and Mark, Christ's temptation is followed by John's imprisonment. With this phrase, John the apostle fills in the slot between Jesus' baptism and temptation and the Baptist's imprisonment.

3:25 there arose a discussion. The discussion probably concerned the relation of the baptismal ministries of John and Jesus to the Jews' purification practices alluded to in 2:6. The real underlying impetus, however, centered in the concern of John's disciples that Jesus was in competition with him.

3:25–36 This section may be divided into

26 And they came to John and said to him, "[A]Rabbi,
He who was with you [B]beyond the Jordan, to whom
you [C]have testified, behold, He is baptizing and all
are coming to Him." 27 John answered and said,
"[A]A man can receive nothing unless it [B]has been
given him from heaven. 28 You yourselves [a]are my
witnesses that I said, '[A]I am not the [b]Christ,' but, 'I
have been sent ahead of Him.' 29 He who has the
bride is [A]the bridegroom; but the friend of the bridegroom, who stands and hears him, rejoices greatly
because of the bridegroom's voice. So this [B]joy of
mine has been made full. 30 He must increase, but
I must decrease.
31 "[A]He who comes from above is above all, [B]he
who is of the earth is from the earth and speaks of
the earth. [A]He who comes from heaven is above all.
32 What He has seen and heard, of that He [A]testifies;
and [A]no one receives His testimony. 33 He who has
received His testimony [A]has set his seal to *this,* that
God is true. 34 For He whom God has [A]sent speaks
the words of God; [a,B]for He gives the Spirit without measure. 35 [A]The Father loves the Son and [B]has
given all things into His hand. 36 He who [A]believes
in the Son has eternal life; but he who [B]does not
[a]obey the Son will not see life, but the wrath of God
abides on him."

JESUS GOES TO GALILEE

4 Therefore when [A]the Lord knew that the Phar-
isees had heard that Jesus was making and
[B]baptizing more disciples than John 2 (although
[A]Jesus Himself was not baptizing, but His [B]disciples
were), 3 He left [A]Judea and went away [B]again into
Galilee. 4 And He had to pass through [A]Samaria.

3:26 [A]Matt 23:7; John 3:2 [B]John 1:28 [C]John 1:7 3:27 [A]1 Cor 4:7; Heb 5:4 [B]James 1:17 3:28 [a]Lit *testify for me* [b]I.e. Messiah [A]John 1:20, 23 3:29 [A]Matt 9:15; 25:1 [B]John 15:11; 16:24; 17:13; Phil 2:2; 1 John 1:4; 2 John 12 3:31 [A]Matt 28:18; John 3:13; 8:23 [B]1 Cor 15:47; 1 John 4:5 3:32 [A]John 3:11 3:33 [A]John 6:27; Rom 4:11; 15:28; 1 Cor 9:2; 2 Cor 1:22; Eph 1:13; 4:30; 2 Tim 2:19; Rev 7:3-8 3:34 [a]Lit *because He does not give the Spirit by measure* [A]John 3:17 [B]Matt 12:18; Luke 4:18; Acts 1:2; 10:38 3:35 [A]Matt 28:18; John 5:20; 17:2 [B]Matt 11:27; Luke 10:22 3:36 [a]Or *believe* [A]John 3:16 [B]Acts 14:2; Heb 3:18 4:1 [A]Luke 7:13 [B]John 3:22, 26; 1 Cor 1:17 4:2 [A]John 3:22, 26; 1 Cor 1:17 [B]John 2:2 4:3 [A]John 3:22 [B]John 2:11f 4:4 [A]Luke 9:52

3 parts which highlight the significance of what was occurring in relationship to John's and Jesus' ministry: 1) John the Baptist constituted the end of the old age (vv. 25–29); 2) the transition to Jesus' ministry (v. 30); and 3) Jesus' ministry as constituting the beginning of the new age (vv. 31–36). Instead of jealousy, John exhibited humble faithfulness to the superiority of Jesus' person and ministry.

3:26 all are coming to Him. The potential conflict between John and Jesus was heightened by the fact that both were engaged in ministry in close proximity to each other. Because baptism is mentioned in v. 22, Jesus may have been close to Jericho near the fords of the Jordan, while John was a short distance N baptizing at Aenon. John's followers were especially disturbed by the fact that so many were flocking to Jesus whereas formerly they had come to John.

3:27 given him from heaven. This verse emphasizes God's sovereign authority in granting ministry opportunity (cf. 1Co 4:7; 15:10).

3:29 bridegroom . . . friend of the bridegroom. John conveyed his understanding of his own role through the use of a parable. The "friend of the bridegroom" was the ancient equivalent of the best man who organized the details and presided over the Judean wedding (Galilean weddings were somewhat different). This friend found his greatest joy in watching the ceremony proceed without problems. Most likely, John was also alluding to OT passages where faithful Israel is depicted as the bride of the Lord (Is 62:4, 5; Jer 2:2; Hos 2:16–20).

3:31–36 In these verses, John the Baptist gave 5 reasons for Christ's superiority to him: 1) Christ had a heavenly origin (v. 31); 2) Christ knew what was true by firsthand experience (v. 32); 3) Christ's testimony always agreed with God (v. 33); 4) Christ experienced the Holy Spirit in an unlimited manner (v. 34); and 5) Christ was supreme because the Father sovereignly had granted that status to Him (v. 35).

3:31, 32 above all. These verses bring together several of the themes from the entire chapter. From the immediate context, John explained why Jesus the incarnate Word must become greater, i.e., He alone is "from above" (heavenly origin) and therefore "above all." The Gr. term "above all" recalls v. 3 (see marginal note) where the new birth "from above" can only be experienced by faith in the One who is "from above." In contrast, all others are "of the earth," signifying finitude and limitation. In the immediate context, John the Baptist had to become less (v. 30) because he was "from the earth" and belonged to the earth. Although he called for repentance and baptism, John could not reveal heaven's counsel like Jesus, the God-Man.

3:34 the Spirit without measure. God gave the Spirit to the Son without limits (1:32, 33; Is 11:2; 42:1; 61:1).

3:36 This constitutes a fitting climax to the chapter. John the Baptist laid out two alternatives, genuine faith and defiant disobedience, thereby bringing to the forefront the threat of looming judgment. As John faded from the forefront, he offered an invitation to faith in the Son and clearly expressed the ultimate consequence of failure to believe, i.e., "the wrath of God."

4:1–26 The story of the Samaritan woman reinforces John's main theme that Jesus is the Messiah and Son of God. The thrust of these verses is not so much her conversion, but that Jesus is Messiah (v. 26). While her conversion is clearly implied, the apostle's focus centers on Jesus' declaration foretold in the Scriptures (v. 25). Important also is the fact that this chapter demonstrates Jesus' love and understanding of people. His love for mankind involved no boundaries, for He lovingly and compassionately reached out to a woman who was a social outcast. In contrast to the limitations of human love, Christ exhibits the character of divine love that is indiscriminate and all-encompassing (3:16).

4:3 He left Judea. John the Baptist and Jesus had official scrutiny focused on them because of their distinctive message regarding repentance and the kingdom. Most likely, Jesus wanted to avoid any possible trouble with John's disciples who were troubled with His growing popularity and, since the Pharisees were also focusing on His growing influence, Jesus decided to leave Judea and travel N in order to avoid any conflict.

4:4 He had to pass through. Several roads led from Judea to Galilee: one near the seacoast; another through the region of Perea; and one through the heart of Samaria. Even with the strong antipathy between Jews and Samaritans, the Jewish historian Josephus relates that the custom of Judeans at the time of the great festivals was to travel through the country of the Samaritans because it was the shorter route. Although the verb "had to" may possibly refer to the fact that Jesus wanted to save time and needless steps, because of the gospel's emphasis on the Lord's consciousness of fulfilling His Father's plan (2:4; 7:30; 8:20; 12:23; 13:1; 14:31), the apostle may have been highlighting divine, spiritual necessity, i.e., Jesus had an appointment with divine destiny in meeting the Samaritan woman, to whom He would reveal His messiahship. **Samaria.** When the nation of Israel split politically after Solomon's rule, King Omri named the capital of the northern kingdom of Israel "Samaria" (1Ki 16:24). The name eventually referred to the entire district and sometimes to the entire northern kingdom, which had been taken captive (capital, Samaria) by Assyria in 722 B.C. (2Ki 17:1–6). While Assyria led most of the populace of the 10 northern tribes away (into the region which today is northern Iraq), it left a sizable population of Jews in the northern Samaritan region and transported many non-Jews into Samaria. These groups intermingled to form a mixed race through intermarriage. Eventually, tension developed between the Jews who returned from captivity and the Samaritans. The Samaritans withdrew from the worship of Yahweh at Jerusalem and established their worship at Mt. Gerizim in Samaria (vv. 20–22). Samaritans regarded only the Pentateuch as authoritative. As a result of this history, Jews repudiated Samaritans and considered them heretical. Intense ethnic and cultural tensions raged historically between the two groups so that both avoided contact as much as possible (v. 9; Ezr 4:1–24; Ne 4:1–6; Lk 10:25–37). *See note on 2Ki 17:24.*

5 So He *came to a city of [A]Samaria called Sychar,
near [B]the parcel of ground that [C]Jacob gave to his
son Joseph; 6 and Jacob's well was there. So Jesus,
being wearied from His journey, was sitting thus
by the well. It was about [a]the sixth hour.

THE WOMAN OF SAMARIA

7 There *came a woman of Samaria to draw water. Jesus *said to her, "Give Me a drink." 8 For His
[A]disciples had gone away into [B]the city to buy food.
9 Therefore the [A]Samaritan woman *said to Him,
"How is it that You, being a Jew, ask me for a drink
since I am a Samaritan woman?" (For [B]Jews have no
dealings with Samaritans.) 10 Jesus answered and
said to her, "If you knew the gift of God, and who it
is who says to you, 'Give Me a drink,' you would have
asked Him, and He would have given you [A]living
water." 11 She *said to Him, "[a]Sir, You have nothing to
draw with and the well is deep; where then do You
get that [A]living water? 12 You are not greater than
our father Jacob, are You, who [A]gave us the well,
and drank of it himself and his sons and his cattle?"
13 Jesus answered and said to her, "Everyone who
drinks of this water will thirst again; 14 but whoever
drinks of the water that I will give him [A]shall never
thirst; but the water that I will give him will become
in him a well of water springing up to [B]eternal life."
15 The woman *said to Him, "[a]Sir, [A]give me this
water, so I will not be thirsty nor come all the way
here to draw." 16 He *said to her, "Go, call your husband and come here." 17 The woman answered and
said, "I have no husband." Jesus *said to her, "You
have correctly said, 'I have no husband'; 18 for you
have had five husbands, and the one whom you
now have is not your husband; this you have said
truly." 19 The woman *said to Him, "[a]Sir, I perceive
that You are [A]a prophet. 20 [A]Our fathers worshiped
in [B]this mountain, and you *people* say that [C]in Jerusalem is the place where men ought to worship."
21 Jesus *said to her, "Woman, believe Me, [A]an hour
is coming when [B]neither in this mountain nor in
Jerusalem will you worship the Father. 22 [A]You worship what you do not know; we worship what we
know, for [B]salvation is from the Jews. 23 But [A]an hour
is coming, and now is, when the true worshipers
will worship the Father [B]in spirit and truth; for

4:5 [A]Luke 9:52 [B]Gen 33:19; Josh 24:32 [C]Gen 48:22; John 4:12 4:6 [a]Perhaps 6 p.m. Roman time or noon Jewish time 4:8 [A]John 2:2 [B]John 4:5, 39 4:9 [A]Luke 9:52 [B]Ezra 4:3-6, 11ff; Matt 10:5; John 8:48; Acts 10:28 4:10 [A]Jer 2:13; John 4:14; 7:37f; Rev 7:17; 21:6; 22:1, 17 4:11 [a]Or *Lord* [A]Jer 2:13; John 4:14; 7:37f; Rev 7:17; 21:6; 22:1, 17 4:12 [A]John 4:6 4:14 [A]John 6:35; 7:38 [B]Matt 25:46; John 6:27 4:15 [a]Or *Lord* [A]John 6:35 4:19 [a]Or *Lord* [A]Matt 21:11; Luke 7:16, 39; 24:19; John 6:14; 7:40; 9:17 4:20 [A]Gen 33:20; John 4:12 [B]Deut 11:29; Josh 8:33 [C]Luke 9:53 4:21 [A]John 4:23; 5:25, 28; 16:2, 32 [B]Mal 1:11; 1 Tim 2:8 4:22 [A]2 Kin 17:28-41 [B]Is 2:3; Rom 3:1f; 9:4f 4:23 [A]John 4:21; 5:25, 28; 16:2, 32 [B]Phil 3:3

4:5, 6 These verses refer back to Ge 48:22 where Jacob bequeathed a section of land to Joseph which he had purchased from the "sons of Hamor" (cf. Ge 33:19). When the Jews returned from Egypt, they buried Joseph's bones in that land at Shechem. This area became the inheritance of Joseph's descendants. The precise location of "Jacob's well" has been set by a firm tradition among Jews, Samaritans, Muslims, and Christians and lies today in the shadow of the crypt of an unfinished Orthodox church. The term used here for "well" denotes a running spring, while in vv. 11, 12 John used another term for "well" that means "cistern" or "dug-out-well" indicating that the well was both dug out and fed by an underground spring. This spring is still active today.

4:5 Sychar. This town is probably identified with the modern village of Askar on the shoulder of Mt. Ebal, opposite Mt. Gerizim. A continuous line of tradition identifies Jacob's well as lying about a half mile S of Askar.

4:6 wearied from His journey. Since the Word became flesh (1:14), He also suffered from physical limitations in His humanity (Heb 2:10–14). the sixth hour. Based on the Jewish reckoning of time, calculated from sunrise at about 6:00 a.m., the time was about noon.

4:7 came a woman of Samaria to draw water. Women generally came in groups to collect water, either earlier or later in the day to avoid the sun's heat. If the Samaritan woman alone came at 12:00 p.m. (*see note on v. 6*), this may indicate that her public shame (vv. 16–19) caused her to be isolated from other women. Give Me a drink. For a Jewish man to speak to a woman in public, let alone to ask from her, a Samaritan, a drink was a definite breach of rigid social custom as well as a marked departure from the social animosity that existed between the two groups. Further, a "rabbi" and religious leader did not hold conversations with women of ill-repute (v. 18).

4:8 to buy food. This verse indicates that since Jesus and His disciples were willing to purchase food from Samaritans, they did not follow some of the self-imposed regulations of stricter Jews, who would have been unwilling to eat food handled by outcast Samaritans.

4:10 living water. The OT is the background for this term, which has important metaphorical significance. In Jer 2:13, Yahweh decries the disobedient Jews for rejecting Him, the "fountain of living waters." The OT prophets looked forward to a time when "living waters will flow out of Jerusalem" (Eze 47:9; Zec 14:8). The OT metaphor spoke of the knowledge of God and His grace which provides cleansing, spiritual life, and the transforming power of the Holy Spirit (cf. Is 1:16–18; 12:3; 44:3; Eze 36:25–27). John applies these themes to Jesus Christ as the living water which is symbolic of eternal life mediated by the Holy Spirit from Him (cf. v. 14; 6:35; 7:37–39). Jesus used the woman's need for physical water to sustain life in this arid region in order to serve as an object lesson for her need for spiritual transformation.

4:15 The woman, like Nicodemus (3:4), did not realize that Jesus was talking about her spiritual needs. Instead, in her mind, she wanted such water in order to avoid her frequent trips to Jacob's well.

4:16 call your husband. Since the woman failed to understand the nature of the living water He offered (v. 15), Jesus abruptly turned the dialogue to focus sharply on her real spiritual need for conversion and cleansing from sin. His intimate knowledge of her morally depraved life not only indicated His supernatural ability, but also focused on her spiritual condition.

4:18 not your husband. She was living conjugally with a man who Jesus said was not her husband. By such an explicit statement, our Lord rejected the notion that when two people live together it constitutes marriage. Biblically, marriage is always restricted to a public, formal, official, and recognized covenant.

4:19 You are a prophet. His knowledge of her life indicated He had supernatural inspiration.

4:20 in this mountain. Both Jews and Samaritans recognized that God had commanded their forefathers to identify a special place for worshiping Him (Dt 12:5). The Jews, recognizing the entire Hebrew canon, chose Jerusalem (2Sa 7:5–13; 2Ch 6:6). The Samaritans, recognizing only the Pentateuch, noted that the first place Abraham built an altar to God was at Shechem (Ge 12:6, 7), which was overlooked by Mt. Gerizim, where the Israelites had shouted the blessings promised by God before they entered the Promised Land (Dt 11:29, 30). As a result, they chose Mt. Gerizim for the place of their temple.

4:21 neither in this mountain nor in Jerusalem. There was no reason to debate locations, since both places would be obsolete soon, and neither would have any role to play in the lives of those who genuinely worship God. Jerusalem would even be destroyed with its temple (A.D. 70).

4:22 you do not know. The Samaritans did not know God. They did not have the full revelation of Him, and thus could not worship in truth. The Jews did have the full revelation of God in the OT; thus they knew the God they worshiped, because salvation's truth came first to them (*see note on Lk 19:9*) and through them to the world (cf. Ro 3:2; 9:4, 5).

4:23 hour. This refers to Jesus' death, resurrection, and ascension to God, having completed redemption. true worshipers. Jesus'

such people the Father seeks to be His worshipers.
24 God is [a]spirit, and those who worship Him must
worship [A]in spirit and truth." 25 The woman *said
to Him, "I know that [A]Messiah is coming ([B]He who
is called Christ); when that One comes, He will declare all things to us." 26 Jesus *said to her, "[A]I who
speak to you am *He*."
27 At this point His [A]disciples came, and they
were amazed that He had been speaking with a
woman, yet no one said, "What do You seek?" or,
"Why do You speak with her?" 28 So the woman left
her waterpot, and went into the city and *said to
the men, 29 "Come, see a man [A]who told me all the
things that I *have* done; [B]this is not [a]the Christ, is
it?" 30 They went out of the city, and were coming
to Him.
31 Meanwhile the disciples were urging Him, saying, "[A]Rabbi, eat." 32 But He said to them, "I have food
to eat that you do not know about." 33 So the [A]disci-
ples were saying to one another, "No one brought
Him *anything* to eat, did he?" 34 Jesus *said to them,
"My food is to [A]do the will of Him who sent Me and
to [B]accomplish His work. 35 Do you not say, 'There
are yet four months, and *then* comes the harvest'?
Behold, I say to you, lift up your eyes and look on
the fields, that they are white [A]for harvest. 36 Already
he who reaps is receiving [A]wages and is gathering
[B]fruit for [C]life eternal; so that he who sows and he
who reaps may rejoice together. 37 For in this *case*
the saying is true, '[A]One sows and another reaps.'
38 I sent you to reap that for which you have not
labored; others have labored and you have entered
into their labor."

THE SAMARITANS

39 From [A]that city many of the Samaritans believed in Him because of the word of the woman
who testified, "[B]He told me all the things that I *have*
done." 40 So when the Samaritans came to Jesus,
they were asking Him to stay with them; and He
stayed there two days. 41 Many more believed because of His word; 42 and they were saying to the
woman, "It is no longer because of what you said
that we believe, for we have heard for ourselves
and know that this One is indeed [A]the Savior of
the world."

4:24 [a]Or *Spirit* [A]Phil 3:3 4:25 [A]Dan 9:25; John 1:41 [B]Matt 1:16; 27:17, 22; Luke 2:11 4:26 [A]John 8:24, 28, 58; 9:37; 13:19 4:27 [A]John 4:8 4:29 [a]I.e. the Messiah [A]John 4:17f [B]Matt 12:23; John 7:26, 31 4:31 [A]Matt 23:7; 26:25, 49; Mark 9:5; 11:21; 14:45; John 1:38, 49; 3:2, 26; 6:25; 9:2; 11:8 4:33 [A]Luke 6:13-16; John 1:40-49; 2:2 4:34 [A]John 5:30; 6:38 [B]John 5:36; 17:4; 19:28, 30 4:35 [A]Matt 9:37, 38; Luke 10:2 4:36 [A]Prov 11:18; 1 Cor 9:17f [B]Rom 1:13 [C]Matt 19:29; John 3:36; 4:14; 5:24; Rom 2:7; 6:23 4:37 [A]Job 31:8; Mic 6:15 4:39 [A]John 4:5, 30 [B]John 4:29 4:42 [A]Matt 1:21; Luke 2:11; John 1:29; Acts 5:31; 13:23; 1 Tim 4:10; 1 John 4:14

point is that in light of His coming as Messiah and Savior, worshipers will be identified, not by a particular shrine or location, but by their worship of the Father through the Son. With Christ's coming, previous distinctions between true and false worshipers based on locations disappeared. True worshipers are all those everywhere who worship God through the Son, from the heart (cf. Php 3:3).

4:24 God is spirit. This verse represents the classical statement on the nature of God as Spirit. The phrase means that God is invisible (Col 1:15; 1Ti 1:17; Heb 11:27), as opposed to the physical or material nature of man (1:18; 3:6). The word order of this phrase puts an emphasis on "spirit," and the statement is essentially emphatic. Man could never comprehend the invisible God unless He revealed Himself, as He did in Scripture and the Incarnation. **must worship.** Jesus is not speaking of a desirable element in worship but that which is absolutely necessary. **in spirit and truth.** The word "spirit" does not refer to the Holy Spirit, but to the human spirit. Jesus' point here is that a person must worship not simply by external conformity to religious rituals and places (outwardly), but inwardly ("in spirit") with the proper heart attitude. The reference to "truth" refers to worship of God consistent with the revealed Scripture and centered on the "Word made flesh" who ultimately revealed His Father (14:6).

4:25 Messiah. The Samaritans also anticipated Messiah's coming.

4:26 I who speak to you am *He*. Jesus forthrightly declared Himself to be Messiah, though His habit was to avoid such declarations to His own Jewish people who had such crassly political and militaristic views regarding Messiah (cf. 10:24; Mk 9:41). The "He" in this translation is not in the original Gr. for Jesus lit. said "I who speak to you am." The usage of "I am" is similar to 8:58 (*see notes there*). This claim constitutes the main point of the story regarding the Samaritan woman.

4:27–42 These verses reinforce Jesus' acknowledgment that He was Messiah by offering proof for His claim. John gave 5 genuine, but subtle, proofs that Jesus was truly Messiah and Son of God, which reinforced his main theme of 20:31: 1) proof from His immediate control of everything (v. 27); 2) proof from His impact on the woman (vv. 28–30); 3) proof from His intimacy with the Father (vv. 31–34); 4) proof from His insight into men's souls (vv. 35–38); and 5) proof from His impression on the Samaritans (vv. 39–42).

4:27 At this point. Had the disciples arrived earlier, they would have interrupted and destroyed the conversation, and if they had arrived any later, she would have gone and they would not have heard His declaration of messiahship. This feature subtly reveals Jesus' divine control over the situation that was occurring.

4:28–31 to the men. Jesus had such an impact on the woman that she was eager to share the news among the townspeople whom she had previously avoided because of her reputation. Her witness and candor regarding her own life so impressed them that they came to see Jesus for themselves.

4:32, 33 I have food. Just like the Samaritan woman's misunderstanding of Jesus' words regarding literal water (v. 15), Jesus' own disciples thought only of literal food. John commonly used such misunderstanding to advance the argument of his gospel (e.g., 2:20; 3:3).

4:34 My food is to do the will of Him who sent Me. Most likely Jesus echoed Dt 8:3 where Moses stated, "man does not live by bread alone; but man lives by everything that proceeds out of the mouth of the LORD" (cf. Mt 4:4; Lk 4:4). When He talked with the Samaritan woman, Jesus was performing the will of the Father and thereby received greater sustenance and satisfaction than any mere physical food could offer Him (5:23, 24; 8:29; 17:4). Obedience to and dependence upon God's will summed up Jesus' whole life (Eph 5:17). God's will for Him to finish is explained in 6:38–40 (*see note on 6:40*).

4:35 four months, and *then* comes the harvest. The event probably happened in Dec. or Jan., which was 4 months before the normal spring harvest (mid-Apr.). Crops were planted in Nov., and by Dec. or Jan. the grain would be sprouting up in vibrant green color. Jesus used the fact that they were surrounded by crops growing in the field and waiting to be harvested as an object lesson to illustrate His urgency about reaching the lost which the "harvest" symbolized. Jesus points out the Samaritan woman and people of Sychar ("lift up your eyes") who were at that moment coming upon the scene (v. 30) looking like a ripened "harvest" that urgently needed "gathering," i.e., evangelizing. **white for harvest.** Their white clothing seen above the growing grain may have looked like white heads on the stalks, an indication of readiness for harvest. Jesus knew the hearts of all (2:24), so He was able to state their readiness for salvation (cf. vv. 39–41).

4:36–38 The Lord's call to His disciples to do the work of evangelism contains promises of reward ("wages"), fruit that brings eternal joy (v. 36), and the mutual partnership of shared privilege (vv. 37, 38).

4:42 Savior of the world. This phrase occurs also in 1Jn 4:14. The verse constitutes the climax to the story of the woman of Samaria. The Samaritans themselves became another in a series of witnesses in John's gospel that demonstrated the identity of Jesus as the Messiah and Son of God. This episode represents the first instance of cross-cultural evangelism (Ac 1:8).

43 After [A]the two days He went forth from there
into Galilee. 44 For Jesus Himself testified that [A]a
prophet has no honor in his own country. 45 So when
He came to Galilee, the Galileans received Him, [A]hav-
ing seen all the things that He did in Jerusalem at
the feast; for they themselves also went to the feast.

HEALING A NOBLEMAN'S SON

46 Therefore He came again to [A]Cana of Galilee
[B]where He had made the water wine. And there was
a royal official whose son was sick at [C]Capernaum.
47 When he heard that Jesus had come [A]out of Judea
into Galilee, he went to Him and was imploring *Him*
to come down and heal his son; for he was at the
point of death. 48 So Jesus said to him, "Unless you
people see [a,A]signs and [A]wonders, you *simply* will
not believe." 49 The royal official *said to Him, "[a]Sir,
come down before my child dies." 50 Jesus *said to
him, "[A]Go; your son lives." The man believed the
word that Jesus spoke to him and started off. 51 As
he was now going down, *his* slaves met him, saying
that his [a]son was living. 52 So he inquired of them the
hour when he began to get better. Then they said to
him, "Yesterday at the [a]seventh hour the fever left
him." 53 So the father knew that *it was* at that hour
in which Jesus said to him, "Your son lives"; and he
himself believed and [A]his whole household. 54 This
is again a [A]second [a]sign that Jesus performed when
He had [B]come out of Judea into Galilee.

THE HEALING AT BETHESDA

5 After these things there was [A]a feast of the Jews,
and Jesus went up to Jerusalem.
2 Now there is in Jerusalem by [A]the sheep *gate* a
pool, which is called [B]in [a]Hebrew [b]Bethesda, having
five porticoes. 3 In these lay a multitude of those
who were sick, blind, lame, and withered, [[a]waiting
for the moving of the waters; 4 for an angel of the

4:43 [A]John 4:40 4:44 [A]Matt 13:57; Mark 6:4; Luke 4:24 4:45 [A]John 2:23 4:46 [A]John 2:1 [B]John 2:9 [C]Luke 4:23; John 2:12 4:47 [A]John 4:3, 54 4:48 [a]Or *attesting miracles* [A]Dan 4:2f; 6:27; Matt 24:24; Mark 13:22; Acts 2:19, 22, 43; 4:30; 5:12; 6:8; 7:36; 14:3; 15:12; Rom 15:19; 1 Cor 1:22; 2 Cor 12:12; 2 Thess 2:9; Heb 2:4 4:49 [a]Or *Lord* 4:50 [A]Matt 8:13 4:51 [a]Or *boy* 4:52 [a]Perhaps 7 p.m. Roman time or 1 p.m. Jewish time 4:53 [A]Acts 11:14 4:54 [a]Or *attesting miracle* [A]John 2:11 [B]John 4:45f 5:1 [A]Deut 16:1; John 2:13 5:2 [a]I.e. Jewish Aramaic [b]Some early mss read *Bethsaida* or *Bethzatha* [A]Neh 3:1, 32; 12:39 [B]John 19:13, 17, 20; 20:16; Acts 21:40; Rev 9:11; 16:16 5:3 [a]Early mss do not contain the remainder of v 3, nor v 4

4:43–54 The episode of Jesus' healing of the official's son constitutes the second major "sign" of 8 which John used to reinforce Jesus' true identity for producing belief in his readers (v. 54). In this episode, Jesus chided the official's unbelief in needing a miraculous sign in order to trust in Christ (v. 48). While some believe that this story is the same as the healing of the centurion's servant (Mt 8:5–13; Lk 7:2–10), sufficient differences exist to demonstrate that it is different from the synoptic account; e.g., 1) no evidence exists that the official's son was a Gentile; 2) the official's son, not his servant, was healed; and 3) Jesus was far more negative regarding the official's faith (v. 48) than the centurion's (Mt 8:10). One may divide this section into 3 parts: 1) Jesus contemplating unbelief (vv. 43–45); 2) Jesus confronting unbelief (vv. 46–49); and 3) Jesus conquering unbelief (vv. 50–54).

4:43 **went ... into Galilee.** After two days in Samaria, Jesus traveled to Galilee, resuming the trip that began in v. 3.

4:44 **a prophet has no honor in his own country.** This proverb (also in Mt 13:57; Mk 6:4) contrasts the believing response of the Samaritans (v. 39) with the characteristic unbelief of Jesus' own people in Galilee (and Judea) whose reticent faith depended so much on Jesus' performance of miracles (v. 48). While in Samaria, Jesus had enjoyed His first unqualified and unopposed success. His own people's hearts were not open to Him, but exhibited reluctance and hardness.

4:45 **the Galileans received Him.** The apostle may have meant these words as irony especially in light of the surrounding context of vv. 44, 48. The reception was likely that of curiosity seekers whose appetite centered more on seeing miracles than believing in Jesus as Messiah—as it had been at "the feast" (*see notes on 2:23–25*).

4:46 **Cana of Galilee.** The deep irony of the statement in v. 45 increases with the fact that Jesus had only recently performed a miracle in Cana at the wedding. Instead of responding in belief, the people wanted more (*see note on v. 48*). The basis of their welcome was extremely crass. **royal official.** This term most likely designated someone officially attached to the service of King Herod Antipas, tetrarch of Galilee from 4 B.C. to A.D. 39. **sick at Capernaum.** Capernaum was approximately 16 mi. NE of Cana.

4:47 **imploring *Him*.** The language here indicates that he repeatedly begged Jesus to heal his son. His approach to Jesus was out of desperation, but he had little appreciation of who Jesus was. In light of v. 46, apparently the nobleman's motivation centered in Jesus' reputation as a miracle worker rather than as Messiah.

4:48 **Unless you *people* see signs and wonders.** The "you" is plural. Jesus addresses these words to the Galileans as a whole and not just to the royal official (*see notes on vv. 45, 46*). The response of the Galileans was fundamentally flawed because it disregarded the person of Christ and centered in the need for a constant display of miraculous signs. Such an attitude represents the deepest state of unbelief.

4:50 **your son lives.** Jesus met the demands of Galilean unbelief by healing the official's son, revealing not only His sympathy, but His marvelous graciousness in spite of such a faithless demand for miracles.

4:52 **the seventh hour.** About 1:00 p.m. reckoning from sunrise. *See note on v. 6.*

4:53 **at that hour.** The time when the official's son improved corresponded precisely with the time that he had spoken with Jesus. This served to strengthen the official's faith and, as a result, the "whole household" believed.

5:1–7:52 This section evidences the shift from reservation and hesitation about Jesus as Messiah (3:26; 4:1–3) to outright rejection (7:52). The opposition started with controversy regarding Jesus' healing on the Sabbath (vv. 1–18), intensified in chap. 6 with many of His disciples abandoning Him (6:66), and finally hardened in chap. 7 into official opposition against Him with the religious authorities' unsuccessful attempt to arrest Him (7:20–52). Accordingly, the theme of this section is the rejection of Jesus as Messiah.

5:1–18 Although opposition to Jesus smoldered beneath the surface (e.g., 2:13–20), the story of Jesus' healing at the Pool of Bethesda highlights the beginning of open hostility toward Him in Jerusalem. The passage may be divided into 3 parts: 1) the miracle performed (vv. 1–9); 2) the Master persecuted (vv. 10–16); and 3) the murder planned (vv. 16–18).

5:1 **a feast of the Jews.** John repeatedly tied his narrative to various Jewish feasts, (2:13—Passover; 6:4—Passover; 7:2—Booths, or Tabernacles; 10:22—Hanukkah or Feast of Dedication; and 11:55—Passover), but this reference is the only instance when he did not identify the particular feast occurring at the time.

5:2 **sheep *gate*.** is a reference to the gate identified in Ne 3:1, 32; 12:39. It was a small opening in the N wall of the city, just W of the NE corner. **there is .... pool.** Some have suggested that John wrote his gospel before the destruction of Jerusalem in A.D. 70, because his usage of "is" here implies that the pool still existed. However, John frequently used what is known as a "historical present" to refer to past events, so this argument carries little weight. For more on the date of writing, see Introduction: Author and Date. **Bethesda.** "Bethesda" is the Gr. transliteration of a Heb. (or Aram.) name meaning "house of outpouring."

5:3a **lay.** It was a custom at that time for people with infirmities to gather at this pool. Intermittent springs may have fed the pool and caused the disturbance of the water (v. 7). Some ancient witnesses indicate that the waters of the pool were red with minerals, and thus thought to have medicinal value.

5:3b, 4 The statement in the latter half of v. 3, "waiting for the moving of the waters," along with v. 4 are not original to the gospel. The earliest and best Gr. manuscripts, as well as the early versions, exclude the reading. The presence of words or expressions unfamiliar to John's writings also militate against its inclusion.

Lord went down at certain seasons into the pool and
stirred up the water; whoever then first, after the
stirring up of the water, stepped in was made well
from whatever disease with which he was afflicted.]
5 A man was there who had been [a]ill for thirty-eight
years. 6 When Jesus saw him lying *there,* and knew
that he had already been a long time *in that condition,* He *said to him, "Do you wish to get well?" 7 The
sick man answered Him, "Sir, I have no man to put
me into the pool when [A]the water is stirred up, but
while I am coming, another steps down before me."
8 Jesus *said to him, "[A]Get up, pick up your pallet
and walk." 9 Immediately the man became well, and
picked up his pallet and *began* to walk.

[A]Now it was the Sabbath on that day. 10 So [A]the
Jews were saying to the man who was cured, "It is
the Sabbath, and [B]it is not permissible for you to
carry your pallet." 11 But he answered them, "He who
made me well was the one who said to me, 'Pick
up your pallet and walk.' " 12 They asked him, "Who
is the man who said to you, 'Pick up *your pallet*
and walk'?" 13 But the man who was healed did not
know who it was, for Jesus had slipped away while
there was a crowd in *that* place. 14 Afterward Jesus
*found him in the temple and said to him, "Behold,
you have become well; do not [A]sin anymore, [B]so
that nothing worse happens to you." 15 The man
went away, and told [A]the Jews that it was Jesus
who had made him well. 16 For this reason [A]the
Jews were persecuting Jesus, because He was doing
these things on the Sabbath. 17 But He answered
them, "My Father is working until now, and I Myself
am working."

JESUS' EQUALITY WITH GOD

18 For this reason therefore [A]the Jews [B]were seeking all the more to kill Him, because He not only
was breaking the Sabbath, but also was calling God
His own Father, [C]making Himself equal with God.

19 Therefore Jesus answered and was saying to
them, "Truly, truly, I say to you, [A]the Son can do nothing of Himself, unless *it is* something He sees the
Father doing; for whatever [a]the Father does, these
things the Son also does in like manner. 20 [A]For the
Father loves the Son, and shows Him all things that
He Himself is doing; and *the Father* will show Him
[B]greater works than these, so that you will marvel.
21 For just as the Father raises the dead and [A]gives
them life, even so [B]the Son also gives life to whom
He wishes. 22 For not even the Father judges anyone, but [A]He has given all judgment to the Son, 23 so
that all will honor the Son even as they honor the
Father. [A]He who does not honor the Son does not
honor the Father who sent Him.

5:5 [a]Lit *in his sickness* 5:7 [A]John 5:4 5:8 [A]Matt 9:6; Mark 2:11; Luke 5:24 5:9 [A]John 9:14 5:10 [A]John 1:19; 5:15, 16, 18 [B]Neh 13:19; Jer 17:21f; Matt 12:2; Luke 6:2; John 7:23; 9:16 5:14 [A]Mark 2:5; John 8:11 [B]Ezra 9:14 5:15 [A]John 1:19; 5:16, 18 5:16 [A]John 1:19; 5:10, 15, 18 5:18 [A]John 1:19; 5:15, 16 [B]John 5:16; 7:1 [C]John 10:33; 19:7 5:19 [a]Lit *that One* [A]Matt 26:39; John 5:30; 6:38; 8:28; 12:49; 14:10 5:20 [A]Matt 3:17; John 3:35; 2 Pet 1:17 [B]John 14:12 5:21 [A]Rom 4:17; 8:11 [B]John 11:25 5:22 [A]John 5:27; 9:39; Acts 10:42; 17:31 5:23 [A]Luke 10:16; 1 John 2:23

5:5 thirty-eight years. John included this figure to emphasize the gravity of the debilitating disease that afflicted the individual. Since his sickness had been witnessed by many people for almost 4 decades, when Jesus cured him everyone knew the genuineness of the healing (cf. v. 9).

5:6 knew. The word implies supernatural knowledge of the man's situation (1:47, 48; 4:17). Jesus picked the man out from among many sick people. The sovereign initiative was His, and no reason is given as to His choice.

5:8 Get up, pick up ... walk. In the same way that He spoke the world into being at creation, (Ge 1:3), Jesus' spoken words had the power to cure (cf. 1:3; 8:58; Ge 1:1; Col 1:16; Heb 1:2). **pallet.** The "pallet" or "mat" was normally made of straw and was light enough so that it could be carried on the shoulder of a well person who assisted the infirm (cf. Mk 2:3).

5:9 picked up his pallet and *began* to walk. This phrase emphasizes the completeness of the cure (cf. v. 5).

5:10, 11 The OT had forbidden work on the Sabbath but did not stipulate what "work" was specifically indicated (Ex 20:8–11). The assumption in Scripture seems to be that "work" was one's customary employment, but rabbinical opinion had developed oral tradition beyond the OT which stipulated 39 activities forbidden (Mishnah *Shabbath* 7:2; 10:5), including carrying anything from one domain to another. Thus, the man had broken oral tradition, not OT law (*see notes on v. 16*).

5:10 it is not permissible. The phrase reveals that the Judaism during Jesus' time had degenerated into pious hypocrisy. Such hypocrisy especially enraged the Lord Jesus (cf. Mt 22, 23), who used this incident to set up a confrontation with Jewish hyperlegalism and identified the need for national repentance.

5:14 do not sin anymore, so that nothing worse happens to you. The basic thrust of Jesus' comments here indicates that sin has its inevitable consequences (cf. Gal 6:7, 8). Although Scripture makes clear that not all disease is a consequence of sin (cf. 9:1–3; Lk 13:1–5), illness at times may be directly tied into one's moral turpitude (cf. 1Co 11:29, 30; Jas 5:15). Jesus may specifically have chosen this man in order to highlight this point.

5:16 persecuting. The verb tense means that the Jews repeatedly persecuted Jesus, i.e., continued hostile activity. This was not an isolated incident of their hatred toward Him because of His healings on the Sabbath (cf. Mk 3:1–6). **on the Sabbath.** Jesus did not break God's law since in it there was no prohibition of doing good on that day (Mk 2:27). However, Jesus disregarded the oral law of the Jews that had developed, i.e., "the tradition of the elders" (cf. also Mt 15:1–9). Most likely, Jesus deliberately practiced such healing on the Sabbath to provoke a confrontation with their religious hypocrisy that blinded them to the true worship of God (see vv. 17–47 for the main reason for Jesus' confrontation; *see notes on vv. 10, 11*).

5:17–47 These verses reveal the ultimate reason Jesus confronted the Jews' religious hypocrisy, i.e., the opportunity to declare who He was. This section is Christ's own personal statement of His deity. As such, it is one of the greatest Christological discourses in Scripture. Herein Jesus makes 5 claims to equality with God: 1) He is equal with God in His person (vv. 17, 18); 2) He is equal with God in His works (vv. 19, 20); 3) He is equal with God in His power and sovereignty (v. 21); 4) He is equal with God in His judgment (v. 22); and 5) He is equal with God in His honor (v. 23).

5:17 Jesus' point is that whether He broke the Sabbath or not, God was working continuously and, since Jesus Himself worked continuously, He also must be God. Furthermore, God does not need a day of rest for He never wearies (Is 40:28). For Jesus' self-defense to be valid, the same factors that apply to God must also apply to Him. Jesus is Lord of the Sabbath (Mt 12:8)! Interestingly, even the rabbis admitted that God's work had not ceased after the Sabbath because He sustains the universe.

5:18 This verse confirms that the Jews instantly grasped the implications of His remarks that He was God (*see notes on v. 17*).

5:19 Truly, truly. Cf. vv. 24, 25; 1:51. This is an emphatic way of saying "I'm telling you the truth." In response to Jewish hostility at the implications of His assertions of equality with God, Jesus became even more fearless, forceful, and emphatic. Jesus essentially tied His activities of healing on the Sabbath directly to the Father. The Son never took independent action that set Him against the Father because the Son only did those things that were coincident with and coextensive with all that the Father does. Jesus thus implied that the only One who could do what the Father does must be as great as the Father.

5:20 greater works. This refers to the powerful work of raising the dead. God has that power (cf. 1Ki 17:17–24; 2Ki 4:32–37; 5:7), and so does the Lord Jesus (vv. 21–29; 11:25–44; 14:19; 20:1–18).

5:23 honor the Son. This verse gives the reason that God entrusted all judgment to

24 "Truly, truly, I say to you, he who hears My
word, and [A]believes Him who sent Me, has eternal
life, and [B]does not come into judgment, but has
[C]passed out of death into life.

TWO RESURRECTIONS

25 Truly, truly, I say to you, [A]an hour is coming and
now is, when [B]the dead will hear the voice of the Son
of God, and those who [C]hear will live. 26 For just as
the Father has life in Himself, even so He [A]gave to
the Son also to have life in Himself; 27 and He gave
Him authority to [A]execute judgment, because He
is [a]*the* Son of Man. 28 Do not marvel at this; for [A]an
hour is coming, in which [B]all who are in the tombs
will hear His voice, 29 and will come forth; [A]those
who did the good *deeds* to a resurrection of life,
those who committed the evil *deeds* to a resurrection of judgment.

30 "[A]I can do nothing on My own initiative. As I
hear, I judge; and [B]My judgment is just, because I
do not seek My own will, but [C]the will of Him who
sent Me.

31 "[A]If I *alone* testify about Myself, My testimony
is not [a]true. 32 There is [A]another who testifies of
Me, and I know that the testimony which He gives
about Me is true.

WITNESS OF JOHN

33 You have sent to John, and he [A]has testified to
the truth. 34 But [A]the testimony which I receive is
not from man, but I say these things so that you
may be saved. 35 He was [A]the lamp that was burning
and was shining and you [B]were willing to rejoice
for [a]a while in his light.

WITNESS OF WORKS

36 But the testimony which I have is greater than
the testimony of John; for [A]the works which the Father
has given Me [B]to accomplish—the very works that I
do—testify about Me, that the Father [C]has sent Me.

WITNESS OF THE FATHER

37 And the Father who sent Me, [A]He has testified of
Me. You have neither heard His voice at any time nor
seen His form. 38 You do not have [A]His word abiding
in you, for you do not believe Him whom He [B]sent.

WITNESS OF THE SCRIPTURE

39 [a,A]You search the Scriptures because you think
that in them you have eternal life; it is [B]these that
testify about Me; 40 and you are unwilling to come
to Me so that you may have life. 41 [A]I do not receive
glory from men; 42 but I know you, that you do not

5:24 [A]John 3:18; 12:44; 20:31; 1 John 5:13 [B]John 3:18 [C]1 John 3:14 5:25 [A]John 4:21, 23; 5:28 [B]Luke 15:24 [C]John 6:60; 8:43, 47; 9:27 5:26 [A]John 1:4; 6:57 5:27 [a]Or *a son of man* [A]John 9:39; Acts 10:42; 17:31 5:28 [A]John 4:21 [B]John 11:24; 1 Cor 15:52 5:29 [A]Dan 12:2; Matt 25:46; Acts 24:15 5:30 [A]John 5:19 [B]John 8:16 [C]John 4:34; 6:38 5:31 [a]I.e. admissible as legal evidence [A]John 8:14 5:32 [A]John 5:37 5:33 [A]John 1:7, 15, 19, 32; 3:26-30 5:34 [A]John 5:32; 1 John 5:9 5:35 [a]Lit *an hour* [A]2 Sam 21:17; 2 Pet 1:19 [B]Mark 1:5 5:36 [A]Matt 11:4; John 2:23; 10:25, 38; 14:11; 15:24 [B]John 4:34 [C]John 3:17 5:37 [A]Matt 3:17; Mark 1:11; Luke 3:22; 24:27; John 8:18; 1 John 5:9 5:38 [A]1 John 2:14 [B]John 3:17 5:39 [a]Or (a command) *Search the Scriptures!* [A]John 7:52; Rom 2:17ff [B]Luke 24:25, 27; Acts 13:27 5:41 [A]John 5:44; 7:18; 1 Thess 2:6

the Son (v. 22), i.e., so that all men should honor the Son just as they honor the Father. This verse goes far beyond making Jesus a mere ambassador who is acting in the name of a monarch, but gives Him full and complete equality with the Father (cf. Php 2:9–11). **honor the Father.** Jesus turned the tables on the Jewish accusation against Him of blasphemy. Instead, Jesus affirmed that the only way anyone can honor the Father is through receiving the Son. Therefore, the Jews were the ones who actually blasphemed the Father by rejection of His Son.

5:24 passed out of death into life. This develops the truth of v. 21: Jesus gives life to whomever He desires. The people who receive that life are here identified as those who hear the Word and believe in the Father and the Son. They are the people who have eternal life and never will be condemned (Ro 8:1; Col 1:13).

5:25–29 The theme of these verses is resurrection. Jesus related that all men, saved and unsaved, will be literally and physically resurrected from the dead. However, only the saved experience a spiritual ("born again"), as well as physical, resurrection unto eternal life. The unsaved will be resurrected unto judgment and eternal punishment through separation from God (i.e., the second death; cf. Rev 20:6, 14; 21:8). These verses also constitute proof of the deity of Jesus Christ since the Son has resurrection power (vv. 25, 26), and the Father has granted Him the status of Judge of all mankind (v. 27). In the light of other Scripture, it is clear that Jesus speaks generally about resurrection, but not about one general resurrection (*see notes on Da 12:2; 1Co 15:23; 1Th 4:16*).

5:25 hour is coming and now is. Cf. 4:23. This phrase reveals an already/not yet tension regarding the resurrection. Those who are born again are already "spiritually" resurrected ("now is"; Eph 2:1; Col 2:13), and yet a future physical resurrection still awaits them ("hour is coming"; 1Co 15:35–54; Php 3:20, 21).

5:26 He gave to the Son. The Son from all eternity had the right to grant life (1:4). The distinction involves Jesus' deity versus His incarnation. In becoming a man, Jesus voluntarily set aside the independent exercise of His divine attributes and prerogatives (Php 2:6–11). Jesus here affirmed that even in His humanity, the Father granted Him "life-giving" power, i.e., the power of resurrection (*see note on v. 20*).

5:27 authority. Cf. 17:2; *see note on Mt 28:18.*

5:29 those who did the good ... evil *deeds*. Jesus was not teaching justification by works (see 6:29). In the context, the "good" is believing on the Son so as to receive a new nature that produces good works (3:21; Jas 2:14–20), while the "evil" done is to reject the Son (the unsaved) and hate the light, which has the result of evil deeds (3:18, 19). In essence, works merely evidence one's nature as saved or unsaved (*see notes on Ro 2:5–10*), but human works never determine one's salvation.

5:30 the will of Him who sent Me. In summarizing all He has said from v. 19 on about His equality with God, Jesus claimed that the judgment He exercised was because everything He did was dependent upon the Father's word and will (cf. vv. 19, 20).

5:32–47 The background of these verses is Dt 17:6; 19:15, where witnesses were to establish the truthfulness of a matter (*see note on 1:7*). Jesus Himself emphasized the familiar theme of witnesses who testify to the identity of the Son: 1) John the Baptist (vv. 32–35); 2) Jesus' works (vv. 35, 36); 3) the Father (vv. 37, 38); and 4) the OT Scriptures (vv. 39–47).

5:36 the very works that I do. Cf. 10:25. The miracles of Jesus were witness to His deity and messiahship. Such miracles are the major signs recorded by John in this gospel, so as to fulfill his purpose in 20:30, 31 (see Introduction: Historical and Theological Themes).

5:37 Father ... has testified. Cf. Mt 3:17; Mk 1:11; Lk 3:22.

5:39 You search. Although the verb "search" could also be understood as a command (i.e., "Search the Scriptures!"), most prefer this translation as an indicative. The verb implies diligent scrutiny in investigating the Scriptures to find "eternal life." However, Jesus points out that with all their fastidious effort, they miserably failed in their understanding of the true way to eternal life through the Son of God (*see notes on Mt 19:16–25*; cf. 14:6; 2Ti 3:15). **testify about Me.** Cf. v. 45. Christ is the main theme of Scripture. *See note on 1:45.*

5:40 unwilling. They searched for eternal life, but were not willing to trust its only source (cf. v. 24; 1:11; 3:19).

5:41 glory from men. If Jesus agreed to be the kind of Messiah the Jews wanted, providing miracles and food along with political and military power, He would receive honor and glory from them. But He sought only to please God (vv. 19ff.).

have the love of God in yourselves. 43 I have come in
My Father's name, and you do not receive Me; [A]if another comes in his own name, you will receive him.
44 How can you believe, when you [A]receive [a]glory
from one another and you do not seek [B]the [a]glory
that is from [C]the *one and* only God? 45 Do not think
that I will accuse you before the Father; the one who
accuses you is [A]Moses, in whom you have set your
hope. 46 For if you believed Moses, you would believe
Me, for [A]he wrote about Me. 47 But [A]if you do not believe his writings, how will you believe My words?"

FIVE THOUSAND FED

6 After these things [A]Jesus went away to the other
side of [B]the Sea of Galilee (or [C]Tiberias). 2 A large
crowd followed Him, because they saw the [a,A]signs
which He was performing on those who were sick.
3 Then [A]Jesus went up on the mountain, and there
He sat down with His disciples. 4 Now [A]the Passover,
the feast of the Jews, was near. 5 Therefore Jesus,
lifting up His eyes and seeing that a large crowd
was coming to Him, *said to [A]Philip, "Where are we
to buy bread, so that these may eat?" 6 This He was
saying to [A]test him, for He Himself knew what He
was intending to do. 7 [A]Philip answered Him, "[B]Two
hundred [a]denarii worth of bread is not sufficient
for them, for everyone to receive a little." 8 One of
His [A]disciples, [B]Andrew, Simon Peter's brother, *said
to Him, 9 "There is a lad here who has five barley
loaves and two [A]fish, but what are these for so many
people?" 10 Jesus said, "Have the people [a]sit down."
Now there was [A]much grass in the place. So the men
[a]sat down, in number about [B]five thousand. 11 Jesus
then took the loaves, and [A]having given thanks, He
distributed to those who were seated; likewise also
of the [B]fish as much as they wanted. 12 When they
were filled, He *said to His [A]disciples, "Gather up the
leftover fragments so that nothing will be lost." 13 So
they gathered them up, and filled twelve [A]baskets
with fragments from the five barley loaves which
were left over by those who had eaten. 14 Therefore
when the people saw the [a]sign which He had performed, they said, "This is truly the [A]Prophet who
is to come into the world."

5:43 [A]Matt 24:5 5:44 [a]Or *honor* or *fame* [A]John 5:41 [B]Rom 2:29 [C]John 17:3; 1 Tim 1:17 5:45 [A]John 9:28; Rom 2:17ff 5:46 [A]Luke 24:27 5:47 [A]Luke 16:29, 31
6:1 [A]John 6:1-13: *Matt 14:13-21; Mark 6:32-44; Luke 9:10-17* [B]Matt 4:18; Luke 5:1 [C]John 6:23; 21:1 6:2 [a]Or *attesting miracles* [A]John 2:11, 23; 3:2; 6:14, 30; 11:47; 12:18, 37; 20:30
6:3 [A]Matt 5:1; Mark 3:13; Luke 6:12; 9:28; John 6:15 6:4 [A]Deut 16:1; John 2:13 6:5 [A]John 1:43 6:6 [A]2 Cor 13:5; Rev 2:2 6:7 [a]The denarius was equivalent to a day's wages [A]John 1:43 [B]Mark 6:37 6:8 [A]John 2:2 [B]John 1:40 6:9 [A]John 6:11; 21:9, 10, 13 6:10 [a]Lit *recline(d)* [A]Mark 6:39 [B]Matt 14:21
6:11 [A]Matt 15:36; John 6:23 [B]John 6:9; 21:9, 10, 13 6:12 [A]John 2:2 6:13 [A]Matt 14:20 6:14 [a]Or *attesting miracle* [A]Matt 11:3; 21:11; John 1:21

5:43 you will receive him. The Jewish historian, Josephus, records that a string of messianic pretenders arose in the years before A.D. 70. This verse contrasts the Jewish rejection of their true Messiah because they did not love or know God (v. 42), with their willing acceptance of charlatans.

5:46 Moses ... for he wrote about Me. Jesus does not mention any specific passage in the 5 books of Moses, although there are many (e.g., Dt 18:15; cf. 1:21; 4:19; 6:14; 7:40, 52).

6:1–14 The story of the feeding of the 5,000 is the fourth sign John employed to demonstrate that Jesus is the Messiah and Son of God. It is the only miracle recorded in all 4 Gospels (Mt 14:13–23; Mk 6:30–46; Lk 9:10–17). Since John most likely wrote to supplement and provide additional information not recorded in the Synoptics (see Introduction: Background and Setting), his recording of this miracle emphasized its strategic importance in two ways: 1) it demonstrated the creative power of Christ more clearly than any other miracle, and 2) it decisively supported John's purposes of demonstrating the deity of Jesus Christ while also serving to set the stage for Jesus' discourse on the "bread of life" (vv. 22–40). Interestingly, both creative miracles of Jesus, the water into wine (2:1–10) and the multiplying of bread (vv. 1–14) speak of the main elements in the Lord's supper or communion (v. 53).

6:1 After these things. A large gap of time may exist between chaps. 5 and 6. If the feast in 5:1 is Booths, or Tabernacles, then at least 6 months passed (Oct. to Apr.). If the feast of 5:1 is Passover, then a year passed between these chapters. **the Sea of Galilee.** Chapter 6 is very close to the same structure as chap. 5 since both occur around a Jewish feast and both lead to a discourse of Jesus' deity. While chap. 5 takes place in the S around Judea and Jerusalem, chap. 6 takes place in the N around Galilee. The result of both chapters is the same: He is rejected not only in the southern but also in the northern regions. *See note on 21:1.*

6:2 they saw the signs. The crowds followed not out of belief, but out of curiosity concerning the miracles that He performed (v. 26). However, in spite of the crowd's crass motivations, Jesus, having compassion on them, healed their sick and fed them (cf. Mt 13:14; Mk 6:34).

6:7 Two hundred denarii. Since one denarius was a day's pay for a common laborer, 200 denarii would be approximately 8 months' wages. The crowd, however, was so large that such a significant amount was still inadequate to feed them.

6:10 five thousand. The number of men was 5,000, not including women and children, who probably brought the total up to 20,000.

6:14 the Prophet. The crowd referred to "the Prophet" of Dt 18:15. Sadly, these comments, coming right after Jesus healed and fed them, indicate that the people desired a

THE "I AM" STATEMENTS
Twenty-three times in all we find our Lord's meaningful "I AM" (*ego eimi*, Gr.) in the Greek text of this Gospel (Jn 4:26; 6:20, 35, 41, 48, 51; 8:12, 18, 24, 28, 58; 10:7, 9, 11, 14; 11:25; 13:19; 14:6; 15:1, 5; 18:5, 6, 8). In several of these, He joins His "I AM" with seven tremendous metaphors which are expressive of His saving relationship toward the world.
"I AM the Bread of life" (Jn 6:35, 41, 48, 51).
"I AM the Light of the world" (Jn 8:12).
"I AM the Door of the sheep" (Jn 10:7, 9).
"I AM the Good Shepherd" (Jn 10:11, 14).
"I AM the Resurrection and the Life" (Jn 11:25).
"I AM the Way, the Truth, and the Life" (Jn 14:6).
"I AM the true Vine" (Jn 15:1, 5).

JESUS WALKS ON THE WATER

15 So Jesus, perceiving that they were [a]intending
to come and take Him by force [A]to make Him king,
[B]withdrew again to [C]the mountain by Himself alone.
16 Now when evening came, His [A]disciples went
down to the sea, 17 and after getting into a boat,
they *started to* cross the sea [A]to Capernaum. It had
already become dark, and Jesus had not yet come
to them. 18 The sea *began* to be stirred up because
a strong wind was blowing. 19 Then, when they had
rowed about [a]three or four miles, they *saw Jesus
walking on the sea and drawing near to the boat;
and they were frightened. 20 But He *said to them,
"It is I; [a,A]do not be afraid." 21 So they were willing
to receive Him into the boat, and immediately the
boat was at the land to which they were going.
22 The next day [A]the crowd that stood on the
other side of the sea saw that there was no other
small boat there, except one, and that Jesus [B]had
not entered with His disciples into the boat, but
that His disciples had gone away alone. 23 There
came other small boats from [A]Tiberias near to the
place where they ate the bread after the [B]Lord [C]had
given thanks. 24 So when the crowd saw that Jesus
was not there, nor His disciples, they themselves
got into the small boats, and [A]came to Capernaum
seeking Jesus. 25 When they found Him on the other
side of the sea, they said to Him, "[A]Rabbi, when did
You get here?"

WORDS TO THE PEOPLE

26 Jesus answered them and said, "Truly, truly, I
say to you, you [A]seek Me, not because you saw [B]signs,
but because you ate of the loaves and were filled.
27 Do not [A]work for the food which perishes, but for
the food which endures to [B]eternal life, which [C]the
Son of Man will give to you, for on Him the Father,
God, [D]has set His seal." 28 Therefore they said to
Him, "What shall we do, so that we may work the
works of God?" 29 Jesus answered and said to them,
"This is [A]the work of God, that you believe in Him
whom He [B]has sent." 30 So they said to Him, "[A]What
then do You do for a [B]sign, so that we may see, and
believe You? What work do You perform? 31 [A]Our
fathers ate the manna in the wilderness; as it is
written, '[B]HE GAVE THEM BREAD OUT OF HEAVEN TO

6:15 [a]Or *about* [A]John 18:36f [B]John 6:15-21: *Matt 14:22-33; Mark 6:45-51* [C]John 6:3 6:16 [A]John 2:2 6:17 [A]Mark 6:45; John 6:24, 59 6:19 [a]Lit *25 or 30 stadia* 6:20 [a]Or *stop being afraid* [A]Matt 14:27 6:22 [A]John 6:2 [B]John 6:15ff 6:23 [A]John 6:1 [B]Luke 7:13 [C]John 6:11 6:24 [A]Matt 14:34; Mark 6:53; John 6:17, 59 6:25 [A]Matt 23:7 6:26 [A]John 6:24 [B]John 6:2, 14, 30 6:27 [A]Is 55:2 [B]John 3:15f; 4:14; 6:40, 47, 54; 10:28; 17:2f [C]Matt 8:20; John 6:53, 62 [D]John 3:33 6:29 [A]1 Thess 1:3; James 2:22; 1 John 3:23; Rev 2:26 [B]John 3:17 6:30 [A]Matt 12:38 [B]John 6:2, 14, 26 6:31 [A]Ex 16:4, 15, 21; Num 11:8; John 6:49, 58 [B]Ps 78:24; Ex 16:4, 15; Neh 9:15; Ps 105:40

Messiah who met their physical, rather than spiritual, needs. Apparently, no recognition existed for the need of spiritual repentance and preparation for the kingdom (Mt 4:17). They wanted an earthly, political Messiah to meet all their needs and to deliver them from Roman oppression. Their reaction typifies many who want a "Christ" that makes no demands of them (cf. Mt 10:34–39; 16:24–26), but of whom they can make their selfish personal requests.

6:15 take Him by force to make Him king. John supplemented the information in Matthew and Mark by indicating that the reason Jesus dismissed the disciples and withdrew from the crowd into a mountain alone was because of His supernatural knowledge of their intention to make Him king in light of His healing and feeding of them. The crowd, incited by mob enthusiasm, was ready to proceed with crassly political intentions that would have jeopardized God's will.

6:16–21 The story of Jesus' walking on the water constituted the fifth sign in John's gospel designed to demonstrate the writer's purpose that Jesus is the Messiah and Son of God (20:30, 31). The miracle demonstrates Jesus' deity by His sovereignty over the laws of nature.

6:17 to Capernaum. Matthew 14:22 and Mark 6:45 indicate that as soon as Jesus had fed the multitudes, He immediately dismissed His disciples to travel W toward Capernaum (vv. 16, 17).

6:18 a strong wind was blowing. The Sea of Galilee is almost 700 ft. below sea level. Cooler air from the northern mountains and southeastern tablelands rushes down into the lake and displaces the warm moist air, causing violent churning of the water.

6:19, 20 Jesus walking on the sea. The Synoptics reveal that in fear and the darkness, they thought He was a ghost (Mt 14:26; Mk 6:49). The Son of God, who made the world, was in control of its forces, and, in this case, He suspended the law of gravity. The act was not frivolous on Jesus' part, for it constituted a dramatic object lesson to the disciples of Jesus' true identity as the sovereign Lord of all creation (cf. 1:3).

6:21 immediately the boat was at the land. This wording indicates that another miracle occurred besides walking on the water, i.e., the boat miraculously and instantly arrived at its precise destination as soon as Jesus stepped into the boat.

6:22–58 Jesus' famous discourse on the bread of life. The key theme is v. 35, i.e., "I am the bread of life," which is the first of 7 emphatic "I AM" statements of Jesus in this gospel (8:12; 10:7, 9; 10:11, 14; 11:25; 14:6; 15:1, 5). This analogy of Jesus as "the bread" of life reinforces John's theme of Jesus as the Messiah and Son of God (20:30, 31). Although John records Jesus' miracles to establish His deity, he moves quickly to Jesus' discourse on the spiritual realities of His person in order to define correctly who Jesus Christ was, i.e., not merely a wonder-worker, but the Son of God who came to save mankind from sin (3:16). This discourse took place in the synagogue at Capernaum (v. 59).

6:22, 23 These verses indicate that the crowds who witnessed Jesus' healings and His feeding of the multitudes were still at the original site of these miracles (E of the lake) and, out of heightened curiosity, desired to find Jesus once again. Other boats loaded with people from Tiberias (on the NW shore of the lake) also heard of the miracles and sought Him out.

6:26 because you ate. This phrase emphasizes Jesus' point that the crowds which followed Him were motivated by superficial desire for food rather than any understanding of the true spiritual significance of Jesus' person and mission (8:14–21; Mk 6:52).

6:27 food which perishes. Jesus rebuked the crowd for purely materialistic notions of the messianic kingdom (cf. v. 26; 4:15). Although Messiah's kingdom would be literal and physical someday, the people failed to see the overriding spiritual character and blessing of "eternal life" given immediately to those who believe the witness of God to His Son. **food which endures to eternal life.** The continuing discourse indicates that this was a reference to Jesus Himself (v. 35).

6:28 works of God. They thought Jesus was saying that God required them to do some works to earn everlasting life, which they thought they would be able to do.

6:29 the work of God, that you believe. The crowd misunderstood Jesus' prohibition in v. 27 ("Do not work") which prompted Jesus to remind them that an exclusive focus on material blessings is wrong. The only work God desired was faith or trust in Jesus as Messiah and Son of God (cf. Mal 3:1). The "work" that God requires is to believe in His Son (cf. 5:24).

6:30 What work do You perform? The question demonstrated the obtuseness, the spiritual blindness of the crowd, and their shallow, selfish curiosity. The feeding of 20,000 (v. 10) was a sufficient enough sign to demonstrate Christ's deity (cf. Lk 16:31).

6:31 Our fathers ate the manna. The crowd's logic appeared to be that Jesus' miraculous feeding was a small miracle compared to what Moses did. In order for them to believe in Him, they would need to see Him feed the nation of Israel on the same scale that God did when He sent manna and fed the entire nation of Israel during their wilderness wanderings for 40 years (Ex 16:11–36). They were demanding that Jesus outdo Moses if they were to believe in Him. They quoted from Ps 78:24.

EAT.' " 32 Jesus then said to them, "Truly, truly, I say
to you, it is not Moses who has given you the bread
out of heaven, but it is My Father who gives you the
true bread out of heaven. 33 For the bread of God is
[a]that which [A]comes down out of heaven, and gives
life to the world." 34 Then they said to Him, "Lord,
always [A]give us this bread."
35 Jesus said to them, "[A]I am the bread of life;
he who comes to Me will not hunger, and he who
believes in Me [B]will never thirst. 36 But [A]I said to
you that you have seen Me, and yet do not believe.
37 [A]All that the Father gives Me will come to Me, and
the one who comes to Me I will certainly not cast
out. 38 For [A]I have come down from heaven, [B]not to
do My own will, but [C]the will of Him who [D]sent Me.
39 This is the will of Him who sent Me, that of [A]all
that He has given Me I [B]lose nothing, but [C]raise it up
on the last day. 40 For this is the will of My Father,
that everyone who [A]beholds the Son and [B]believes
in Him will have eternal life, and I Myself will [C]raise
him up on the last day."

WORDS TO THE JEWS

41 [A]Therefore the Jews were grumbling about
Him, because He said, "I am the bread that [B]came
down out of heaven." 42 They were saying, "[A]Is not
this Jesus, the son of Joseph, whose father and
mother [B]we know? How does He now say, '[C]I have
come down out of heaven'?" 43 Jesus answered and
said to them, "Do not grumble among yourselves.
44 No one can come to Me unless the Father who
sent Me [A]draws him; and I will [B]raise him up on
the last day. 45 It is written [A]in the prophets, '[B]AND
THEY SHALL ALL BE [C]TAUGHT OF GOD.' Everyone who
has heard and learned from the Father, comes to
Me. 46 [A]Not that anyone has seen the Father, except
the One who is from God; He has seen the Father.
47 Truly, truly, I say to you, he who believes [A]has
eternal life. 48 [A]I am the bread of life. 49 [A]Your fathers ate the manna in the wilderness, and they
died. 50 This is the bread which [A]comes down out
of heaven, so that one may eat of it and [B]not die.
51 [A]I am the living bread that [B]came down out of

6:33 [a]Or *He who comes* [A]John 6:41, 50 6:34 [A]John 4:15 6:35 [A]John 6:48, 51 [B]John 4:14 6:36 [A]John 6:26 6:37 [A]John 6:39; 17:2, 24 6:38 [A]John 3:13 [B]Matt 26:39 [C]John 4:34; 5:30 [D]John 6:29 6:39 [A]John 6:37; 17:2, 24 [B]John 17:12; 18:9 [C]Matt 10:15; John 6:40, 44, 54; 11:24 6:40 [A]John 12:45; 14:17, 19 [B]John 3:16 [C]Matt 10:15; John 6:39, 44, 54; 11:24 6:41 [A]John 1:19; 6:52 [B]John 6:33, 51, 58 6:42 [A]Luke 4:22 [B]John 7:27f [C]John 6:38, 62 6:44 [A]Jer 31:3; Hos 11:4; John 6:65; 12:32 [B]John 6:39 6:45 [A]Acts 7:42; 13:40; Heb 8:11 [B]Is 54:13; Jer 31:34 [C]Phil 3:15; 1 Thess 4:9; 1 John 2:27 6:46 [A]John 1:18 6:47 [A]John 3:36; 5:24; 6:51, 58; 11:26 6:48 [A]John 6:35, 51 6:49 [A]John 6:31, 58 6:50 [A]John 6:33 [B]John 3:36; 5:24; 6:47, 51, 58; 11:26 6:51 [A]John 6:35, 48 [B]John 6:41, 58

6:32 true bread out of heaven. The manna God gave was temporary and perished and was only a meager shadow of what God offered them in the true bread, Jesus Christ, who gives spiritual and eternal life to mankind ("world").

6:33 bread of God. This phrase is synonymous with the phrase "bread out of heaven" (v. 32).

6:34 Lord, always give us this bread. This statement once again demonstrated the blindness of the crowd, for they were thinking of some physical bread and failed to understand the spiritual implication that Jesus was that "bread" (cf. 4:15).

6:35 I am the bread of life. The obtuseness in v. 34 prompted Jesus to speak very plainly that He was referring to Himself.

6:37 All that the Father gives Me will come to Me. This verse emphasizes the sovereign will of God in the selection of those who come to Him for salvation (cf. vv. 44, 65; 17:6, 12, 24). The Father has predestined those who would be saved (*see notes on Ro 8:29, 30; Eph 1:3–6; 1Pe 1:2*). The absolute sovereignty of God is the basis of Jesus' confidence in the success of His mission (*see note on v. 40*; cf. Php 1:6). The security of salvation rests in the sovereignty of God, for God is the guarantee that "all" He has chosen will come to Him for salvation. The idea of "gives Me" is that every person chosen by God and drawn by God (v. 44) must be seen as a gift of the Father's love to the Son. The Son receives each "love gift" (v. 37), holds on to each (v. 39), and will raise each to eternal glory (vv. 39, 40). No one chosen will be lost (*see notes on Ro 8:31–39*). This saving purpose is the Father's will which the Son will not fail to do perfectly (v. 38; cf. 4:34; 10:28, 29; 17:6, 12, 24).

6:40 everyone who beholds the Son and believes in Him. This verse emphasizes human responsibility in salvation. Although God is sovereign, He works through faith, so that a person must believe in Jesus as the Messiah and Son of God who alone offers the only way of salvation (cf. 14:6). However, even faith is a gift of God (Ro 12:3; Eph 2:8, 9). Intellectually harmonizing the sovereignty of God and the responsibility of man is impossible humanly, but perfectly resolved in the infinite mind of God.

6:41–50 This section constitutes the beginning of the crowd's reaction to Jesus' discourse on the bread of life and may be divided into 3 sections: 1) the murmuring reaction of the crowd (vv. 41, 42); 2) Jesus' rebuke of the crowd for their reaction (vv. 43–46); and 3) Jesus' reiteration of His message to the crowd (vv. 47–51).

6:41 the Jews. In this gospel, the term "Jews" is often associated with hostility toward Christ. It is used ironically to indicate the incongruity of their rising hostility toward their Messiah. Since they hardened their hearts, God judicially hardened their hearts also (cf. 12:37–40; Is 6:10; 53:1; Mt 13:10–15). In the Tribulation, Israel will turn to Jesus as their true Messiah and be saved (Ro 11:25–27; Rev 1:7; 7:1–8; cf. Zec 12:10–14). **grumbling.** The reaction of the synagogue crowds to Jesus' statements was the same as the Jews in the wilderness who grumbled against God both before and after the manna was given to them (Ex 16:2, 8, 9; Nu 11:4–6). **because He said, "I am the bread ... out of heaven."** The Jews' anger centered in two things: 1) that Jesus said He was the bread and 2) that He came down from heaven. Both the Jews in Jerusalem (5:18) and the Galileans reacted negatively when Jesus placed Himself equal with God.

6:42 whose father and mother we know? On the human level, they knew Jesus as a fellow Galilean. These words are reminiscent of Jesus' words in 4:44, "a prophet has no honor in his own country." Their hostility sprang from the root of unbelief. Jesus' death was impending because hostility had resulted everywhere He went.

6:44 draws him. Cf. v. 65. The combination of v. 37a and v. 44 indicate that the divine drawing activity which Jesus referred to cannot be reduced to what theologians call "prevenient grace," i.e., that somehow the power to come to Christ is allegedly dispensed to all of mankind, thus enabling everyone to accept or reject the gospel according to their own will alone. Scripture indicates that no "free will" exists in man's nature, for man is enslaved to sin (total depravity) and unable to believe apart from God's empowerment (Ro 3:1–19; Eph 2:1–3; 2Co 4:4; 2Ti 1:9). While "whosoever will" may come to the Father, only those whom the Father gives the ability to will toward Him will actually come to Him. The drawing here is selective and efficacious (producing the desired effect) upon those whom God has sovereignly chosen for salvation, i.e., those whom God has chosen will believe because God has sovereignly determined that result from eternity past (Eph 1:9–11).

6:45 Jesus paraphrased Is 54:13 to support the point that if someone comes to faith and repentance to God, it is because they have been taught, and hence drawn, by God. The "drawing" and "learning" are just different aspects of God's sovereign direction in the person's life. Those taught by God to grasp the truth are also drawn by God the Father to embrace the Son.

6:49, 50 Jesus contrasted the earthly and heavenly bread. The manna that was given in the wilderness, although sent from heaven to help sustain the Israelites for their physical needs, could not impart eternal life nor meet their spiritual needs as could the "bread of life" (v. 48) that came down from heaven in the person of Jesus the Messiah. The proof of this contrast centers in the irrefutable fact that all the fathers died who ate the wilderness manna.

6:51–59 This section may be divided into 3 divisions: 1) Jesus' pronouncement (v. 51); 2) the crowd's perplexity (v. 52); and 3) Jesus' promises (vv. 53–59).

6:51 This pronouncement exactly reiterates

heaven; if anyone eats of this bread, [C]he will live
forever; and the bread also which I will give [D]for
the life of the world is [E]My flesh."
52 [A]Then the Jews [B]*began* to argue with one another, saying, "How can this man give us *His* flesh
to eat?" 53 So Jesus said to them, "Truly, truly, I say
to you, unless you eat the flesh of [A]the Son of Man
and drink His blood, you have no life in yourselves.
54 He who eats My flesh and drinks My blood has
eternal life, and I will [A]raise him up on the last day.
55 For My flesh is true food, and My blood is true
drink. 56 He who eats My flesh and drinks My blood
[A]abides in Me, and I in him. 57 As the [A]living Father
[B]sent Me, and I live because of the Father, so he who
eats Me, he also will live because of Me. 58 This is
the bread which [A]came down out of heaven; not as
[B]the fathers ate and died; he who eats this bread
[C]will live forever."

WORDS TO THE DISCIPLES

59 These things He said [A]in the synagogue as He
taught [B]in Capernaum.
60 Therefore many of His [A]disciples, when they
heard *this* said, "[B]This is a difficult statement; who
can listen to it?" 61 But Jesus, [A]conscious that His
disciples grumbled at this, said to them, "Does this
[B]cause you to stumble? 62 *What* then if you see [A]the
Son of Man [B]ascending to where He was before?
63 [A]It is the Spirit who gives life; the flesh profits
nothing; [B]the words that I have spoken to you are
spirit and are life. 64 But there are [A]some of you
who do not believe." For Jesus [B]knew from the beginning who they were who did not believe, and
[C]who it was that would [a]betray Him. 65 And He was
saying, "For this reason I have [A]said to you, that no
one can come to Me unless [B]it has been granted
him from the Father."

PETER'S CONFESSION OF FAITH

66 As a result of this many of His [A]disciples [B]with-
drew and were not walking with Him anymore.
67 So Jesus said to [A]the twelve, "You do not want to
go away also, do you?" 68 [A]Simon Peter answered
Him, "Lord, to whom shall we go? You have [B]words
of eternal life. 69 We have believed and have come
to know that You are [A]the Holy One of God." 70 Jesus
answered them, "[A]Did I Myself not choose you, [B]the
twelve, and *yet* one of you is [C]a devil?" 71 Now He
meant Judas [A]*the son* of Simon Iscariot, for he, [B]one
of [C]the twelve, [a]was going to betray Him.

6:51 [C]John 3:36; 5:24; 6:47, 58; 11:26 [D]John 1:29; 3:14f; Heb 10:10; 1 John 4:10 [E]John 6:53-56 6:52 [A]John 1:19; 6:41 [B]John 9:16; 10:19 6:53 [A]Matt 8:20; John 6:27, 62 6:54 [A]John 6:39 6:56 [A]John 15:4f; 17:23; 1 John 2:24; 3:24; 4:15f 6:57 [A]Matt 16:16; John 5:26 [B]John 3:17; 6:29, 38 6:58 [A]John 6:33, 41, 51 [B]John 6:31, 49 [C]John 3:36; 5:24; 6:47, 51; 11:26 6:59 [A]Matt 4:23 [B]John 6:24 6:60 [A]John 2:2; 6:66; 7:3 [B]John 6:52 6:61 [A]John 6:64 [B]Matt 11:6 6:62 [A]Matt 8:20; John 6:27, 53 [B]Mark 16:19; John 3:13 6:63 [A]2 Cor 3:6 [B]John 6:68 6:64 [a]Or *hand Him over* [A]John 6:60, 66 [B]John 2:25 [C]Matt 10:4; John 6:71; 13:11 6:65 [A]John 6:37, 44 [B]Matt 13:11; John 3:27 6:66 [A]John 2:2; 7:3 [B]John 6:60, 64 6:67 [A]Matt 10:2; John 2:2; 6:70f; 20:24 6:68 [A]Matt 16:16 [B]John 6:63; 12:49f; 17:8 6:69 [A]Mark 1:24; 8:29; Luke 9:20 6:70 [A]John 15:16, 19 [B]Matt 10:2; John 2:2; 6:71; 20:24 [C]John 8:44; 13:2, 27; 17:12 6:71 [a]Or *was intending to* [A]John 12:4; 13:2, 26 [B]Mark 14:10 [C]Matt 10:2; John 2:2; 6:70; 20:24

vv. 33, 35, 47, 48. **bread ... is My flesh.** Jesus refers here prophetically to His impending sacrifice upon the cross (cf. 2Co 5:21; 1Pe 2:24). Jesus voluntarily laid down His life for evil, sinful mankind (10:18; 1Jn 2:2).

6:52 argue. Once again the perplexity of the Jews indicates that they failed to understand the spiritual truth behind Jesus' illustration. Every time Jesus had given them a veiled saying or physical illustration, the Jews failed to see its spiritual significance (e.g., 3:4; 4:15). The Mosaic law prohibited the drinking of blood or the eating of meat with blood still in it (Lv 17:10–14; Dt 12:16; Ac 15:29). The Jews, unable to go beyond the mere physical perspective, were perplexed and angered.

6:53–58 eat ... drink. Jesus' point was an analogy that has spiritual, rather than literal, significance: just as eating and drinking are necessary for physical life, so also is belief in His sacrificial death on the cross necessary for eternal life. The eating of His flesh and drinking of His blood metaphorically symbolize the need for accepting Jesus' cross work. For the Jews, however, a crucified Messiah was unthinkable (cf. Ac 17:1–3). Once again, the Jews, in their willful and judicial blindness, could not see the real spiritual significance and truth behind Jesus' statements. Moreover, Jesus' reference here to eating and drinking was not referring to the ordinance of communion for two significant reasons: 1) communion had not been instituted yet, and 2) if Jesus was referring to communion, then the passage would teach that anyone partaking of communion would receive eternal life.

6:60–71 These verses constitute the reaction of Jesus' disciples to His sermon on the "bread of life." As with the crowds' response in Jerusalem (chap. 5) and in Galilee (chap. 6), the response of many of His disciples was unbelief and rejection of Him. John lists two groups and their reactions: 1) the false disciples' reaction of unbelief (vv. 60–66), and 2) the true disciples' reaction of belief (vv. 67–71). After this sermon, only a small nucleus of disciples remained (v. 67).

6:61 His disciples grumbled. Many of Jesus' disciples had the same reaction as the Jews in v. 41 and of the first generation of Israelites to manna, i.e., they grumbled (Ex 16:2).

6:64 Jesus knew. Reminiscent of John's words in 2:23–25, Jesus knew the hearts of men, including those disciples who followed Him. He supernaturally knew that many did not believe in Him as Messiah and Son of God so He did not entrust Himself to them. These false disciples were simply attracted to the physical phenomena (e.g., miracles and food), and failed to understand the true significance of Jesus' teaching (v. 61).

6:65 I have said. *See notes on vv. 37, 44.* Although men and women are commanded to believe and will be held accountable for unbelief, genuine faith is never exclusively a matter of human decision. Once again, in the face of unbelief, Jesus reiterated God's sovereignty involved in selection for salvation.

6:66 disciples ... were not walking with Him anymore. The language indicates that the abandonment was decisive and final (cf. 1Pe 2:6–8; 1Jn 2:19).

6:69 We have believed. Peter's words were somewhat pretentious in that he implied that the true disciples somehow had superior insight and, as a result, came to belief through that insight.

6:70 Did I Myself not choose you, the twelve. In response to Peter's words that the disciples had come to believe in Jesus, He reminds them that He sovereignly chose them (vv. 37, 44, 65). Jesus would not allow even a whisper of human pretension in God's sovereign selection. **a devil.** The word "devil" means "slanderer" or "false accuser." The idea perhaps is better rendered "one of you is the devil." This meaning is clear from 13:2, 27; Mk 8:33; Lk 22:3. The supreme adversary of God so operates behind fallen human beings that his malice becomes theirs (cf. Mt 16:23). Jesus supernaturally knew the source and identified it precisely. This clearly fixes the character of Judas, not as a well-intentioned but misguided man trying to force Jesus to exert His power and set up His kingdom (as some suggest), but as a tool of Satan doing unmitigated wickedness (*see notes on 13:21–30*).

6:71 Iscariot. The word most likely is from a Heb. word meaning "man of Kerioth," the name of a village in Judah. As with the other 3 Gospels, as soon as he was named, he became identified as the betrayer.

JESUS TEACHES AT THE FEAST

7 After these things Jesus [A]was walking in Galilee,
for He was unwilling to walk in Judea because
[B]the Jews [C]were seeking to kill Him. 2 Now the feast
of the Jews, [A]the Feast of Booths, was near. 3 Therefore His [A]brothers said to Him, "Leave here and go
into Judea, so that Your [B]disciples also may see
Your works which You are doing. 4 For no one does
anything in secret [a]when he himself seeks to be
known publicly. If You do these things, show Yourself to the world." 5 For not even His [A]brothers were
believing in Him. 6 So Jesus *said to them, "[A]My
time is not yet here, but your time is always opportune. 7 [A]The world cannot hate you, but it hates
Me because I testify of it, that [B]its deeds are evil.
8 Go up to the feast yourselves; I do not go up to
this feast because [A]My time has not yet fully come."
9 Having said these things to them, He stayed
in Galilee.
10 But when His [A]brothers had gone up to the
feast, then He Himself also went up, not publicly,
but as if, in secret. 11 [A]So the Jews [B]were seeking
Him at the feast and were saying, "Where is He?"
12 There was much grumbling among the crowds
concerning Him; [A]some were saying, "He is a good
man"; others were saying, "No, on the contrary, He
leads the people astray." 13 Yet no one was speaking
openly of Him for [A]fear of the Jews.
14 But when it was now the midst of the feast
Jesus went up into the temple, and *began to* [A]teach.

7:1 [A]John 4:3; 6:1; 11:54 [B]John 1:19; 7:11, 13, 15, 35 [C]John 5:18; 7:19; 8:37, 40; 11:53 7:2 [A]Lev 23:34; Deut 16:13, 16; Zech 14:16-19 7:3 [A]Matt 12:46; Mark 3:21; John 7:5, 10 [B]John 6:60 7:4 [a]Lit *and* 7:5 [A]Matt 12:46; Mark 3:21; John 7:3, 10 7:6 [A]Matt 26:18; John 2:4; 7:8, 30 7:7 [A]John 15:18f [B]John 3:19f 7:8 [A]John 7:6 7:10 [A]Matt 12:46; Mark 3:21; John 7:3, 5 7:11 [A]John 7:13, 15, 35 [B]John 11:56 7:12 [A]John 7:40-43 7:13 [A]John 9:22; 12:42; 19:38; 20:19 7:14 [A]Matt 26:55; John 7:28

7:1–8:59 The main thrust of this section can be summarized as "high intensity hatred" since the smoldering dislike of Jesus in chaps. 5, 6 erupted into a blazing inferno. The culmination of this hatred occurs in 11:45–57 where the Jewish authorities plot to kill the Son of God, culminating ultimately in His crucifixion. Both chapters deal with Jesus at the Feast of Booths, or Tabernacles, in Jerusalem. Especially noteworthy is the fact that two major themes associated with Tabernacles, i.e., water and light, come to prominence in these two chapters (vv. 37–39; 8:12). At the next Passover following this celebration of Tabernacles, Jesus was crucified. The central truth that dominates this whole passage is that Jesus was on a divine timetable. His life was not random, but operated according to God's sovereign and perfect timing and direction.

7:1–13 This section has two parts: 1) Jesus' avoidance of the wrong time in God's sovereign plan (vv. 1–9), and 2) Jesus' perfect obedience to the right time in God's sovereign plan (vv. 10–13).

7:1 **After these things.** A 6-month gap most likely took place between chaps. 6 and 7. While chap. 6 occurred around Passover (6:4—Apr.), chap. 7 occurs at the Feast of Booths, or Tabernacles (Oct.). John wrote nothing about those months since his purpose was not to present an exhaustive chronology of Christ's life, but to portray Him as the Messiah and Son of God and show how men reacted to Him. **walking in Galilee.** Chapter 6 indicates Jesus spent two days with the multitude of 20,000 people (6:22), but He spent 7 months teaching His 12 disciples who believed in Him. This phrase subtly highlights the great importance of discipleship, for Jesus concentrated great lengths of time upon training His future spiritual leaders.

7:2 **Feast of Booths.** *See note on 5:1.* The Feast of Booths, or Tabernacles, was associated in the OT with the ingathering of the harvest of grapes and olives (Ex 23:16; Lv 23:33–36, 39–43; Dt 16:13–15), while grain was reaped between Apr. and June. The feast occurred for 7 days from the 15th to the 21st of Tishri (Sep.-Oct.). *According to Josephus, this feast was the most popular of the 3 principal Jewish feasts (Passover, Pentecost, and Booths, or Tabernacles).* People living in rural areas built makeshift structures of light branches and leaves to live in for the week (hence, "booths" or "tabernacles"; cf. Lv 23:42) while town dwellers put up similar structures on their flat roofs or in their courtyards. The feast was known for water-drawing and lamp-lighting rites to which Jesus makes reference ("If anyone is thirsty, let him come to Me and drink"—vv. 37, 38 and "I am the Light of the world"—8:12).

7:3 **His brothers.** Matthew 13:55 lists Jesus' brothers as "James and Joseph and Simon and Judas." James authored the NT epistle that bears his name and became the leader of the Jerusalem church and Judas (or Jude) wrote the epistle that also bears his name. Because of Jesus' virgin birth, they were only the half-brothers of Jesus since Mary, not Joseph, was Jesus' only human parent (cf. Mt 1:16, 18, 23; Lk 1:35).

7:4 **to be *known* publicly ….show Yourself to the world.** Jesus' brothers wanted Him to put on a display of His miracles. Although the text does not clearly state their motivation, perhaps they made the request for two reasons: 1) they wanted to see the miracles for themselves to determine their genuineness, and 2) they may have had similar crass political motives as did the people, namely that He would become their social and political Messiah. Jerusalem's acceptance of Him was to be the acid test for them as to whether His own family would believe in Him as Messiah.

7:5 As with the crowds in Jerusalem and Galilee, even His own brothers did not believe in Jesus at first. They did not become His followers until after the resurrection (Ac 1:14; 1Co 15:7).

7:6 **My time is not yet here.** This recalls the response to Jesus' mother at the wedding in Cana (see 2:4). It also reveals the first reason why Jesus would not go to the feast: it was not in God's perfect timing. The sentence reveals Jesus' complete dependence on and commitment to the Father's sovereign timetable for His life (cf. 8:20; Ac 1:7; 17:26). Furthermore, Jesus never committed Himself to being motivated by unbelief, even that of His own half-brothers. **your time is always opportune.** Because Jesus' brothers did not believe in Him, they were of the world and, therefore, knew nothing of God or His purposes. Because of unbelief, they did not listen to His word, did not recognize God's schedule, and could not perceive the incarnate Word before them. As a result, any time would do for them, preferably that moment.

7:7 **The world cannot hate you.** The world cannot hate Jesus' brothers because they belonged to the world, and the world loves its own (cf. 15:18, 19). The evil world system and all who reject the Word and Son of God lie in the control of the evil one himself (1Jn 5:19). **I testify of it, that its deeds are evil.** A true born-again believer who is living a life for God's glory should experience the hatred and antagonism of the world (cf. 15:18–25; 16:1–3; 2Ti 3:12).

7:8 **My time has not yet fully come.** This reveals the second reason why Jesus would not go to the feast in Jerusalem. The Jews could not kill Him before God's perfect timing and plan was ready (cf. Gal 4:4). Jesus' commitment to God's timetable would not permit any deviance from what God had decreed.

7:10 **in secret.** The assumption is that the Father had directed Jesus to permit Him to go to Jerusalem. The secrecy of His journey indicates His maximum discretion which was the complete opposite of what His brothers had demanded of Him (cf. v. 4).

7:11 **the Jews were seeking Him.** The contrast between the phrase "the Jews" in this verse and "the crowds" in v. 12 indicates that the term "Jews" designates the hostile Jewish authorities in Judea who were headquartered in Jerusalem. The search for Jesus was certainly hostile in intent.

7:12, 13 **grumbling among the crowds.** The crowds, made up of Judeans, Galileans, and Diaspora (scattered) Jews, expressed various opinions regarding Christ. The spectrum ranged from superficial acceptance ("He is a good man") to cynical rejection ("He leads the people astray"). The Jewish Talmud reveals that the latter view of deception became the predominant opinion of many Jews (Babylonian Talmud *Sanhedrin* 43a).

7:14–24 The increasing hostility to Jesus did not prevent His teaching ministry. Instead, Jesus relentlessly set forth His claims regarding His identity and mission. In the midst of the Feast of Tabernacles, when Jews from all over Israel had migrated into Jerusalem, Jesus once again began to teach. In this section, Jesus set forth the justification of His ministry and taught with authority as God's Son. In this passage, 5 reasons are set forth as to why Jesus' claims regarding Himself are true: 1) His supernatural knowledge originated from the Father Himself (vv. 15, 16); 2) His teaching and knowledge could be confirmed by testing (v. 17); 3) His actions demonstrated His selflessness (v. 18); 4) His impact on the world was startling (vv. 19, 20); and 5) His deeds demonstrated His identity as the Son of God (vv. 21–24).

7:14 **midst of the feast.** Jesus may have

15 [A]The Jews then were astonished, saying, "How has
this man [B]become learned, having never been educated?" 16 So Jesus answered them and said, "[A]My
teaching is not Mine, but His who sent Me. 17 [A]If
anyone is willing to do His will, he will know of the
teaching, whether it is of God or *whether* I speak
from Myself. 18 He who speaks from himself [A]seeks
his own glory; but He who is seeking the glory of
the One who sent Him, He is true, and there is no
unrighteousness in Him.

19 "[A]Did not Moses give you the Law, and *yet*
none of you carries out the Law? Why do you [B]seek
to kill Me?" 20 The crowd answered, "[A]You have a
demon! Who seeks to kill You?" 21 Jesus answered
them, "I did [A]one [a]deed, and you all marvel. 22 For
this reason [A]Moses has given you circumcision
(not because it is from Moses, but from [B]the fathers), and on *the* Sabbath you circumcise a man.
23 [A]If a man receives circumcision on *the* Sabbath
so that the Law of Moses will not be broken, are
you angry with Me because I made an entire man
well on *the* Sabbath? 24 Do not [A]judge according to appearance, but [a]judge with righteous
judgment."

25 So some of the people of Jerusalem were saying, "Is this not the man whom they are seeking to
kill? 26 Look, He is speaking publicly, and they are
saying nothing to Him. [A]The rulers do not really
know that this is [a]the Christ, do they? 27 However,
[A]we know where this man is from; but whenever the
Christ may come, no one knows where He is from."
28 Then Jesus cried out in the temple, [A]teaching and
saying, "[B]You both know Me and know where I am
from; and [C]I have not come of Myself, but He who
sent Me is true, whom you do not know. 29 [A]I know
Him, because [B]I am from Him, and [C]He sent Me."

7:15 [A]John 1:19; 7:11, 13, 35 [B]Acts 26:24 7:16 [A]John 3:11 7:17 [A]Ps 25:9, 14; Prov 3:32; Dan 12:10; John 3:21; 8:43f 7:18 [A]John 5:41; 8:50, 54; 12:43 7:19 [A]John 1:17 [B]Mark 11:18; John 7:1 7:20 [A]Matt 11:18; John 8:48f, 52; 10:20 7:21 [a]Or *work* [A]John 5:2-9, 16; 7:23 7:22 [A]Lev 12:3 [B]Gen 17:10ff; 21:4; Acts 7:8 7:23 [A]Matt 12:2; John 5:9, 10 7:24 [a]Lit *judge the righteous judgment* [A]Lev 19:15; Is 11:3; Zech 7:9; John 8:15 7:26 [a]I.e. the Messiah [A]Luke 23:13; John 3:1 7:27 [A]John 6:42; 7:41f; 9:29 7:28 [A]John 7:14 [B]John 6:42; 7:14f; 9:29 [C]John 8:42 7:29 [A]Matt 11:27; John 8:55; 17:25 [B]John 6:46 [C]John 3:17

waited until the middle of the feast in order to prevent a premature "triumphal entry" that some may have forced upon Him for political motivations. **into the temple, and *began to* teach.** Jesus taught according to the custom of the teachers or rabbis of His day. Prominent rabbis would enter the temple environs and expound on the OT to crowds who sat around them.

7:15 astonished. Jesus' knowledge of Scripture was supernatural. The people were amazed that someone who had never studied at any great rabbinical centers or under any great rabbis could display such profound mastery of Scripture. Both the content and manner of Jesus' teachings were qualitatively different from any other teacher.

7:16 His who sent Me. The qualitative difference of Jesus' teaching was found in its source, i.e., the Father gave it to Him (8:26, 40, 46, 47; 12:49, 50). It originated from God the Father Himself, in contrast to rabbis who received it from man (Gal 1:12). While rabbis relied on the authority of others (a long chain of human tradition), Jesus' authority centered in Himself (cf. Mt 7:28, 29; Ac 4:13).

7:17 If anyone is willing to do His will, he will know. Those who are fundamentally committed to doing the will of God will be guided by Him in the affirmation of His truth. God's truth is self-authenticating through the teaching ministry of the Holy Spirit (cf. 16:13; 1Jn 2:20, 27).

7:18 He who is seeking the glory of the One who sent Him. While other saviors and messiahs acted for their own selfish interests, thereby revealing their falseness, Jesus Christ as God's Son came solely to glorify the Father and accomplish the Father's will (2Co 2:17; Php 2:5–11; Heb 10:7).

7:19, 20 kill Me. If Jesus were another religious fake, the world never would have reacted in such hatred. Since the evil world system loves its own, its hatred toward Him demonstrates that He came from God (15:18, 19).

7:21 one deed. The context makes clear (vv. 22, 23) that Jesus was referencing the healing of the paralytic that evoked the beginning of persecution against Him by the Jewish authorities because it took place on the Sabbath (see 5:1–16).

7:22 but from the fathers. The patriarchal period during the time of Abraham when God instituted the sign of circumcision (Ge 17:10–12), which was later included as part of the Mosaic covenant at Sinai (Ex 4:26; 12:44, 45). This observation not only depreciated the Jewish esteem for Moses, but even more importantly showed that this rite was antecedent to the Mosaic law and took precedence over it (Gal 3:17). Furthermore, circumcision antedates the Sabbath law also.

7:23 on *the* Sabbath. The law required that circumcision occur on the eighth day (Lv 12:1–3). If a child was born on the Sabbath, then the eighth day would fall again on the subsequent Sabbath, when the Jews would circumcise the child. Jesus' point was that the Jews broke their own Sabbath law with the circumcision of the child. Their hypocrisy is evident. **I made an entire man well.** Jesus used an argument of the lesser to the greater. If ceremonial cleansing of one part of the body is permitted on the Sabbath through the act of circumcision (the less), how much more so should the actual healing of the entire body be permitted on the Sabbath (the greater).

7:24 with righteous judgment. While Jesus forbade harsh, censorious judgment that self-righteous legalism promotes (Mt 7:1), He demanded the exercise of moral and theological discernment.

7:25–36 In this section, John once again reiterated the claims of Jesus to His identity as the Messiah and Son of God. He focused on His divine origin and citizenship. While some believed in Him at this time (v. 31), the religious leaders became even more angry at Him and nefariously planned to seize Him (v. 32). Jesus confronted the people with 3 dilemmas recorded in these verses: 1) the problem of dense confusion (vv. 25–29); 2) the problem of divided conviction (vv. 30–32); and 3) the problem of delayed conversion (vv. 33–36). These 3 problems left Jerusalem in a state of utter despair.

7:26 He is speaking publicly. What surprised the masses was that in spite of the ominous threat from the religious authorities (vv. 20, 32), Jesus boldly proclaimed His identity. **The rulers do not really know.** The question indicates the crowds and the rulers were in great confusion and uncertainty as to who Jesus was and what to do about Him. They did not really have any firm convictions regarding Jesus' identity, for their question reveals their doubt and unbelief. They were also perplexed at the religious leaders' failure to arrest and silence Him if He really were a fraud. Such dense confusion caused the crowd to wonder if the religious authorities in private concluded that He was indeed the Christ. Mass confusion among all groups reigned regarding Jesus. **Christ.** *See notes on 1:20, 41.*

7:27 no one knows where He is from. Only information regarding Messiah's birthplace was revealed in Scripture (Mic 5:2; Mt 2:5, 6). Beyond that, a tradition had developed in Jewish circles that Messiah would appear suddenly to the people, based on a misinterpretation of Is 53:8 and Mal 3:1. In light of this, the meaning of this phrase most likely is that the identity of the Messiah would be wholly unknown until He suddenly appeared in Israel and accomplished Israel's redemption. In contrast, Jesus had lived His life in Nazareth and was known (at least superficially) to the people (v. 28).

7:28 cried out. Jesus gave the greatest publicity to this important teaching by voicing it loudly (cf. v. 37; 1:15; 12:44). **You both know Me and know where I am from.** These words stand in antithesis with 8:19 where Jesus told His enemies that they neither knew Him nor the Father, thus indicating a deep irony and sarcasm on Jesus' part here. Jesus' point is that contrary to what they thought, they really had no true understanding of who He was. They knew Him in the earthly sense, but not in the spiritual sense, because they didn't know God either. **whom you do not know.** Although they thought that they were acutely perceptive and spiritually oriented, their rejection of Jesus revealed their spiritual bankruptcy (Ro 2:17–19).

30 So they [A]were seeking to seize Him; and no man
laid his hand on Him, because His [B]hour had not yet
come. 31 But [A]many of the crowd believed in Him;
and they were saying, "[B]When [a]the Christ comes,
He will not perform more [b,C]signs than those which
this man has, will He?"
32 The Pharisees heard the crowd muttering these
things about Him, and the chief priests and the Pharisees sent [A]officers to [B]seize Him. 33 Therefore Jesus
said, "[A]For a little while longer I am with you, then
[B]I go to Him who sent Me. 34 [A]You will seek Me, and
will not find Me; and where I am, you cannot come."
35 [A]The Jews then said to one another, "[B]Where does
this man intend to go that we will not find Him? He
is not intending to go to [C]the Dispersion among [D]the
Greeks, and teach the Greeks, is He? 36 What is this
statement that He said, '[A]You will seek Me, and will
not find Me; and where I am, you cannot come'?"
37 Now on [A]the last day, the great *day* of the feast,
Jesus stood and cried out, saying, "[a,B]If anyone is
thirsty, [b]let him come to Me and drink. 38 He who
believes in Me, [A]as the Scripture said, 'From [a]his
innermost being will flow rivers of [B]living water.' "
39 But this He spoke [A]of the Spirit, whom those who
believed in Him were to receive; for [B]the Spirit was
not yet *given*, because Jesus was not yet [C]glorified.

DIVISION OF PEOPLE OVER JESUS

40 *Some* of the people therefore, when they heard
these words, were saying, "This certainly is [A]the
Prophet." 41 Others were saying, "This is [a]the Christ."
Still others were saying, "[A]Surely [a]the Christ is not
going to come from Galilee, is He? 42 Has not the
Scripture said that the Christ comes from [A]the descendants of David, and from Bethlehem, the village
where David was?" 43 So [A]a division occurred in the
crowd because of Him. 44 [A]Some of them wanted to
seize Him, but no one laid hands on Him.
45 The [A]officers then came to the chief priests
and Pharisees, and they said to them, "Why did you
not bring Him?" 46 The [A]officers answered, "[B]Never
has a man spoken the way this man speaks." 47 The
Pharisees then answered them, "[A]You have not also
been led astray, have you? 48 [A]No one of [B]the rulers

7:30 [A]Matt 21:46; John 7:32, 44; 10:39 [B]John 7:6; 8:20 7:31 [a]I.e. the Messiah [b]Or *attesting miracles* [A]John 2:23; 8:30; 10:42; 11:45; 12:11, 42 [B]John 7:26 [C]John 2:11 7:32 [A]Matt 26:58; John 7:45f [B]Matt 12:14 7:33 [A]John 12:35; 13:33; 14:19; 16:16-19 [B]John 14:12, 28; 16:5, 10, 17, 28; 20:17 7:34 [A]John 7:36; 8:21; 13:33 7:35 [A]John 7:1 [B]John 8:22 [C]Ps 147:2; Is 11:12; 56:8; Zeph 3:10; James 1:1; 1 Pet 1:1 [D]John 12:20; Acts 14:1; 17:4; 18:4; Rom 1:16 7:36 [A]John 7:34; 8:21; 13:33 7:37 [a]Vv 37-38 may also be read: *If anyone is thirsty,...let him come..., he who believes in me as...* [b]Or *let him keep coming to Me and let him keep drinking* [A]Lev 23:36; Num 29:35; Neh 8:18 [B]John 4:10, 14; 6:35 7:38 [a]Lit *out of his belly* [A]Is 44:3; 55:1; 58:11 [B]John 4:10 7:39 [A]Joel 2:28; John 1:33 [B]John 20:22; Acts 1:4f; 2:4, 33; 19:2 [C]John 12:16, 23; 13:31f; 16:14; 17:1 7:40 [A]Matt 21:11; John 1:21 7:41 [a]I.e. the Messiah [A]John 1:46; 7:52 7:42 [A]Ps 89:4; Mic 5:2; Matt 1:1; 2:5f; Luke 2:4ff 7:43 [A]John 9:16; 10:19 7:44 [A]John 7:30 7:45 [A]John 7:32 7:46 [A]John 7:32 [B]Matt 7:28 7:47 [A]John 7:12 7:48 [A]John 12:42 [B]Luke 23:13; John 7:26

7:30 His hour had not yet come. This reveals the reason why they could not seize Him, i.e., God's sovereign timetable and plan for Jesus would not allow it.

7:31 many ... believed. Divided conviction existed among the people regarding Jesus. While some wanted to seize Him, a small remnant of genuine believers existed among the crowds. The question here anticipates a negative answer, i.e., the Messiah could do no greater kinds of miracles than those Jesus had done.

7:32 the chief priests and the Pharisees. *See note on 3:1.* The Pharisees and chief priests historically did not have harmonious relationships with each other. Most of the chief priests were Sadducees, who were political and religious opponents to the Pharisees. John repeatedly links these two groups in his gospel (see also v. 45; 11:47, 57; 18:3) in order to emphasize that their cooperation stemmed from their mutual hatred of Jesus. Both were alarmed at the faith of those indicated in v. 31 and, in order to avoid any veneration of Jesus as Messiah, attempted unsuccessfully to arrest Him (v. 30). **officers.** Temple guards who functioned as a kind of police force composed of Levites who were in charge of maintaining order in the temple environs. They could also be used by the Sanhedrin in areas outside the temple environs in religious disputes that did not affect Roman policy.

7:34 where I am, you cannot come. Jesus referred here to His return to His heavenly origin with His Father after His crucifixion and resurrection (see 17:15).

7:35, 36 John again highlights the ignorance of the Jews regarding Jesus' words. The words were spoken to mock Jesus.

7:35 teach the Greeks. The phrase "teach the Greeks" probably had reference to Jewish proselytes, i.e., Gentiles. John may have been citing this phrase with ironic force since the gospel eventually went to the Gentiles because of Jewish blindness and rejection of their Messiah. *See notes on Ro 11:7–11.*

7:37–52 This section catalogues the different reactions of people to Jesus' claims. These reactions have become universal patterns for reactions to Him through the ages. This section may be divided into the claim of Christ (vv. 37–39) and the reactions to Christ (vv. 40–52). The reactions may be subdivided into 5 sections: 1) the reaction of the convinced (vv. 40–41a); 2) the reaction of the contrary (vv. 41b–42); 3) the reaction of the hostile (vv. 43, 44); 4) the reaction of the confused (vv. 45, 46); and 5) the reaction of the religious authorities (vv. 47–52).

7:37 on the last day. This suggests that this occasion occurred on a different day than the controversy in vv. 11–36. **If anyone is thirsty.** A tradition grew up in the few centuries before Jesus that on the 7 days of the Feast of Booths, or Tabernacles, a golden container filled with water from the pool of Siloam was carried in procession by the High Priest back to the temple. As the procession came to the Water Gate on the S side of the inner temple court, 3 trumpet blasts were made to mark the joy of the occasion and the people recited Is 12:3, "you will joyously draw water from the springs of salvation." At the temple, while onlookers watched, the priests would march around the altar with the water container while the temple choir sang the Hallel (Pss 113–118). The water was offered in sacrifice to God at the time of the morning sacrifice. The use of the water symbolized the blessing of adequate rainfall for crops. Jesus used this event as an object lesson and opportunity to make a very public invitation on the last day of the feast for His people to accept Him as the living water. His words recall Is 55:1. **thirsty ... come ... drink.** These 3 words summarize the gospel invitation. A recognition of need leads to an approach to the source of provision, followed by receiving what is needed. The thirsty, needy soul feels the craving to come to the Savior and drink, i.e., receive the salvation that He offers.

7:38 living water. The water-pouring rite was also associated within Jewish tradition as a foreshadowing of the eschatological rivers of living water foreseen in Eze 47:1–9 and Zec 13:1. The significance of Jesus' invitation centers in the fact that He was the fulfillment of all the Feast of Booths, or Tabernacles, anticipated, i.e., He was the One who provided the living water that gives eternal life to man (cf. 4:10, 11).

7:39 He spoke of the Spirit. The impartation of the Holy Spirit is the source of spiritual and eternal life. *See note on 16:7.*

7:41 from Galilee. This betrays the people's great ignorance, because Jesus was born in Bethlehem of Judea not Galilee (Mic 5:2 cf. Mt 2:6; Lk 2:4). They did not even bother to investigate His true birthplace, showing their lack of interest in messianic credentials.

7:43 division. See Mt 10:34–36; Lk 12:51–53.

7:44 *See notes on vv. 8, 30.*

7:45 The officers. The officers failed in their attempt to arrest Jesus when they were confronted with His person and powerful teaching. Since they were religiously trained, Jesus' words struck at their very heart. For their identity, *see notes on v. 32.*

7:47, 48 The Pharisees mocked the officers, not on professional (as police officers) but religious grounds (as Levites). In essence, they accused them of being seduced by a deceiver (i.e., Jesus) in contrast to the Pharisees themselves who arrogantly and self-righteously felt that in their wisdom and knowledge no one could ever deceive them.

or Pharisees has believed in Him, has he? 49 But this crowd which does not know the Law is accursed." 50 [A]Nicodemus (he who came to Him before, being one of them) *said to them, 51 "[A]Our Law does not judge a man unless it first hears from him and knows what he is doing, does it?" 52 They answered him, "[A]You are not also from Galilee, are you? Search, and see that no prophet arises out of Galilee." 53 [[a]Everyone went to his home.

THE ADULTEROUS WOMAN

8 But Jesus went to [A]the Mount of Olives. 2 Early in the morning He came again into the temple, and all the people were coming to Him; and [A]He sat down and *began* to teach them. 3 The scribes and the Pharisees *brought a woman caught in adultery, and having set her in the center *of the court,* 4 they *said to Him, "Teacher, this woman has been caught in adultery, in the very act. 5 Now in the Law [A]Moses commanded us to stone such women; what then do You say?" 6 They were saying this, [A]testing Him, [B]so that they might have grounds for accusing Him. But Jesus stooped down and with His finger wrote on the ground. 7 But when they persisted in asking Him, [A]He straightened up, and said to them, "[B]He who is without sin among you, let him *be the* [C]first to throw a stone at her." 8 Again He stooped down and wrote on the ground. 9 When they heard it, they *began* to go out one by one, beginning with the older ones, and He was left alone, and the woman, where she was, in the center *of the court.* 10 [A]Straightening up, Jesus said to her, "Woman, where are they? Did no one condemn you?" 11 She said, "No one, [a]Lord." And Jesus said, "[A]I do not condemn you, either. Go. From now on [B]sin no more."]

JESUS IS THE LIGHT OF THE WORLD

12 Then Jesus again spoke to them, saying, "[A]I am the Light of the world; [B]he who follows Me will not walk in the darkness, but will have the Light of life." 13 So the Pharisees said to Him, "[A]You are testifying about Yourself; Your testimony is not [a]true." 14 Jesus answered and said to them, "[A]Even if I testify about Myself, My testimony is [a]true, for I know [B]where I came from and where I am going; but [C]you do not know where I come from or where

7:50 [A]John 3:1; 19:39 7:51 [A]Ex 23:1; Deut 17:6; 19:15; Prov 18:13; Acts 23:3 7:52 [A]John 1:46; 7:41 7:53 [a]Later mss add the story of the adulterous woman, numbering it as John 7:53-8:11 8:1 [A]Matt 21:1 8:2 [A]Matt 26:55; John 8:20 8:5 [A]Lev 20:10; Deut 22:22f 8:6 [A]Matt 16:1; 19:3; 22:18, 35; Mark 8:11; 10:2; 12:15; Luke 10:25; 11:16 [B]Mark 3:2 8:7 [A]John 8:10 [B]Matt 7:1; Rom 2:1 [C]Deut 17:7 8:10 [A]John 8:7 8:11 [a]Or *Sir* [A]John 3:17 [B]John 5:14 8:12 [A]John 1:4; 9:5; 12:35 [B]Matt 5:14 8:13 [a]Or *valid* [A]John 5:31 8:14 [a]Or *valid* [A]John 18:37; Rev 1:5; 3:14 [B]John 8:42; 13:3; 16:28 [C]John 7:28; 9:29

7:49 crowd. The Pharisees condescendingly labeled the people as a "crowd." The rabbis viewed the common people (or, people of the land) as ignorant and impious in contrast to themselves. This ignorance was not only because of their ignorance of Scripture, but especially the common people's failure to follow the Pharisees' oral traditions. **accursed.** The people were considered damned because they did not belong to the elite group or follow their beliefs regarding the law.

7:50–52 Nicodemus' (see 3:10) mind had not closed regarding Christ's claims, so that while not defending Jesus directly, he did raise a procedural point in Jesus' favor.

7:51 Our Law does not judge. No explicit OT text can be cited that makes Nicodemus' point. Most likely he referred to rabbinical traditions contained in their oral law.

7:52 no prophet arises out of Galilee. The real ignorance lay with the arrogant Pharisees who did not carefully search out the facts as to where Jesus was actually born. While they accused the crowds of ignorance, they too were really as ignorant (v. 42). Furthermore, the prophet Jonah did come from Galilee.

7:53–8:11 This section dealing with the adulteress most likely was not a part of the original contents of John. It has been incorporated into various manuscripts at different places in the gospel (e.g., after vv. 36, 44, 52, or 21:25), while one manuscript places it after Lk 21:38. External manuscript evidence representing a great variety of textual traditions is decidedly against its inclusion, for the earliest and best manuscripts exclude it. Many manuscripts mark the passage to indicate doubt as to its inclusion. Significant early versions exclude it. No Gr. church father comments on the passage until the twelfth century. The vocabulary and style of the section also are different from the rest of the gospel, and the section interrupts the sequence of v. 52 with 8:12ff. Many, however, do think that it has all the earmarks of historical veracity, perhaps being a piece of oral tradition that circulated in parts of the western church, so that a few comments are in order. In spite of all these considerations of the likely unreliability of this section, it is possible to be wrong on the issue, and thus it is good to consider the meaning of this passage and leave it in the text, just as with Mk 16:9–20.

8:6 testing Him . . . accusing Him. If Jesus rejected the law of Moses (Lv 20:10; Dt 22:22), His credibility would be gone. If He held to Mosaic law, His reputation for compassion and forgiveness would have been questioned.

8:7 He who is without sin. This directly refers to Dt 13:9; 17:7, where the witnesses of a crime are to start the execution. Only those who were not guilty of the same sin could participate.

8:8 Cf. v. 6. This seems to have been a delaying device, giving them time to think.

8:11 sin no more. Actually, "Leave your life of sin" (cf. 3:17; 12:47; Mt 9:1–8; Mk 2:13–17).

8:12–21 Excluding the story of the adulterous woman in 7:53–8:11, this verse attaches itself well to 7:52. The word "again" indicates that Jesus spoke once more to the people at this same Feast of Booths, or Tabernacles (see 7:2, 10). While Jesus first used the water-drawing rite (7:37–39) as a metaphor to portray the ultimate spiritual truth of Himself as Messiah who fulfills all that the feast anticipated, He then turned to another rite that traditionally occurred at the feast: the lighting ceremony. During Tabernacles, 4 large lamps in the temple's court of women were lit and an exuberant nightly celebration took place under their light with people dancing through the night and holding burning torches in their hands while singing songs and praises. The levitical orchestras also played. Jesus took this opportunity of the lighting celebration to portray another spiritual analogy for the people: "I am the Light of the world."

8:12 I am the Light of the world. This is the second "I am" statement (see 6:35). John has already used the "light" metaphor for Jesus (1:4). Jesus' metaphor here is steeped in OT allusions (Ex 13:21, 22; 14:19–25; Pss 27:1; 119:105; Pr 6:23; Eze 1:4, 13, 26–28; Hab 3:3, 4). The phrase highlights Jesus' role as Messiah and Son of God (Ps 27:1; Mal 4:2). The OT indicates that the coming age of Messiah would be a time when the Lord would be a light for His people (Is 60:19–22; cf. Rev 21:23, 24) as well as for the whole earth (Is 42:6; 49:6). Zechariah 14:5b–8 has an emphasis on God as the light of the world who gives living waters to His people. This latter passage probably formed the liturgical readings for the Feast of Tabernacles. For further significance of Jesus as the "light," *see notes on 1:4, 5; 1Jn 1:5.* **he who follows Me.** The word "follows" conveys the idea of someone who gives himself completely to the person followed. No half-hearted followers exist in Jesus' mind (cf. Mt 8:18–22; 10:38, 39). A veiled reference exists here to the Jews, following the pillar of cloud and fire that led them during the Exodus (Ex 13:21).

8:13 You are testifying about Yourself. The Jews mockingly brought up Jesus' own words from 5:31. However, Jesus' words there and here are reconciled by the fact that OT law required not one but multiple witnesses to establish the truth of a matter (Dt 17:6). Jesus was not alone in His witness that pointed to Him as Messiah, for many had already testified concerning this truth (*see note on 1:7*).

8:14–18 These verses give 3 reasons why Jesus' witness was true: 1) Jesus knew His origin and destiny, while the Jews were ignorant even of basic spiritual truths, making their judgment limited and superficial (vv. 14,

I am going. 15 [A]You judge [a]according to the flesh; [B]I am not judging anyone. 16 But even [A]if I do judge, My judgment is true; for I am not alone *in it,* but I and the Father who sent Me. 17 Even in [A]your law it has been written that the testimony of [B]two men is [a]true. 18 I am He who testifies about Myself, and [A]the Father who sent Me testifies about Me." 19 So they were saying to Him, "Where is Your Father?" Jesus answered, "You know neither Me nor My Father; [A]if you knew Me, you would know My Father also." 20 These words He spoke in [A]the treasury, as [B]He taught in the temple; and no one seized Him, because [C]His hour had not yet come.

21 Then He said again to them, "I go away, and [A]you will seek Me, and [B]will die in your sin; where I am going, you cannot come." 22 So [A]the Jews were saying, "Surely He will not kill Himself, will He, since He says, '[B]Where I am going, you cannot come'?" 23 And He was saying to them, "[A]You are from below, I am from above; [B]you are of this world, [C]I am not of this world. 24 Therefore I said to you that you [A]will die in your sins; for unless you believe that [a,B]I am *He,* [A]you will die in your sins." 25 So they were saying to Him, "Who are You?" Jesus said to them, "[a]What have I been saying to you *from* the beginning? 26 I have many things to speak and to judge concerning you, but [A]He who sent Me is true; and [B]the things which I heard from Him, these I speak to the world." 27 They did not realize that He had been speaking to them about the Father. 28 So Jesus said, "When you [A]lift up the Son of Man, then you will know that [a,B]I am *He,* and [C]I do nothing on My own initiative, but I speak these things as the Father taught Me. 29 And He who sent Me is with Me; [A]He [a]has not left Me alone, for [B]I always do the things that are pleasing to Him." 30 As He spoke these things, [A]many came to believe in Him.

THE TRUTH WILL MAKE YOU FREE

31 So Jesus was saying to those Jews who had believed Him, "[A]If you continue in My word, *then* you are truly [B]disciples of Mine; 32 and [A]you will know the truth, and [B]the truth will make you free." 33 They answered Him, "[A]We are Abraham's descendants

8:15 [a]I.e. by a carnal standard [A]1 Sam 16:7; John 7:24 [B]John 3:17 8:16 [A]John 5:30 8:17 [a]I.e. valid or admissible [A]Deut 17:6; 19:15 [B]Matt 18:16 8:18 [A]John 5:37; 1 John 5:9 8:19 [A]John 7:28; 8:55; 14:7, 9; 16:3 8:20 [A]Mark 12:41, 43; Luke 21:1 [B]John 7:14; 8:2 [C]John 7:30 8:21 [A]John 7:34 [B]John 8:24 8:22 [A]John 1:19; 8:48, 52, 57 [B]John 7:35 8:23 [A]John 3:31 [B]1 John 4:5 [C]John 17:14, 16 8:24 [a]Most authorities associate this with Ex 3:14, *I AM WHO I AM* [A]John 8:21 [B]Matt 24:5; Mark 13:6; Luke 21:8; John 4:26; 8:28, 58; 13:19 8:25 [a]Or *That which I have been saying to you from the beginning* 8:26 [A]John 3:33; 7:28 [B]John 8:40; 12:49; 15:15 8:28 [a]Lit *I AM* (v 24 note) [A]John 3:14; 12:32 [B]Matt 24:5; Mark 13:6; Luke 21:8; John 4:26; 8:24, 58; 13:19 [C]John 3:11; 5:19 8:29 [a]Or *did not leave* [A]John 8:16; 16:32 [B]John 4:34 8:30 [A]John 7:31 8:31 [A]John 15:7; 2 John 9 [B]John 2:2 8:32 [A]John 1:14, 17 [B]John 8:36; Rom 8:2; 2 Cor 3:17; Gal 5:1, 13; James 2:12; 1 Pet 2:16 8:33 [A]Matt 3:9; Luke 3:8; John 8:37, 39

15); 2) the intimate union of the Son with the Father guaranteed the truth of the Son's witness (v. 16); and 3) the Father and Son witnessed harmoniously together regarding the identity of the Son (vv. 17, 18).

8:17 in your law it has been written. Cf. Dt 17:6; 19:15. *See notes on 1:7.*

8:19 Where is your Father? The Jews, as was their habit (e.g., 3:4; 4:11; 6:52), once again thought merely on human terms in asking about Jesus' paternity.

8:21–30 Jesus revealed the consequence of the rejection of Him as Messiah and Son of God, i.e., spiritual death (v. 24; cf. Heb 10:26–31). These verses reveal 4 ways that ensure people will die in their sins and, as a result, experience spiritual death: 1) being self-righteous (vv. 20–22); 2) being earthbound (vv. 23, 24); 3) being unbelieving (v. 24); and 4) being willfully ignorant (vv. 25–29). The Jews who rejected Jesus displayed all 4 of these characteristics.

8:21 Jesus repeated His message of 7:33, 34 but with more ominous overtones regarding the consequences of rejecting Him. **I go away.** By means of His impending death, resurrection, and ascension to the Father.

8:22 Surely He will not kill Himself. The Jews spoke either in confusion (*see notes on 7:34, 35*) or, perhaps more likely, in mockery of Christ. Jewish tradition condemned suicide as a particularly heinous sin that resulted in permanent banishment to the worst part of Hades (Josephus, *Jewish Wars* iii.viii.5 [iii.375]). God did deliver Him to be killed (Ac 2:23); thus, as God, He gave up His own life (10:18).

8:23 You are from below. The contrast here is between the realm of God and that of the fallen, sinful world (i.e., "from below"). The world in this context is the invisible spiritual system of evil dominated by Satan and all that it offers in opposition to God, His Word, and His people (*see notes on 1:9; 1Jn 5:19*). Jesus declared that His opponents' true kinship was with Satan and his realm. By this domination, they were spiritually blinded (see 2Co 4:4; Eph 2:1–3).

8:24 unless you believe. Jesus emphasized that the fatal, unforgivable, and eternal sin is failure to believe in Him as Messiah and Son of God. In truth, all other sins can be forgiven if this one is repented of. *See notes on 16:8, 9.* **I am *He*.** The word *"He"* is not part of the original statement. Jesus' words were not constructed normally but were influenced by OT Heb. usage. It is an absolute usage meaning "I AM" and has immense theological significance. The reference may be to both Ex 3:14 where the Lord declared His name as "I AM" and to Is 40–55 where the phrase "I am" occurs repeatedly (especially 43:10, 13, 25; 46:4; 48:12). In this, Jesus referred to Himself as the God (Yahweh—the Lord) of the OT, and directly claimed full deity for Himself, prompting the Jews' question of v. 25. *See note on v. 58.*

8:25 Who are You? The Jews were willfully ignorant because chaps. 1–8 demonstrate that multiple witnesses testified to Jesus' identity, and Jesus Himself in words and actions persistently proved throughout His ministry on earth that He was the Son of God and Messiah. ***from* the beginning.** The start of Jesus' ministry among the Jews.

8:28 When you lift up the Son of Man. Jesus' impending crucifixion. **you will know that I am *He*.** Having refused to accept Him by faith and having nailed Him to the cross, they would one day awaken to the terrifying realization that this One whom they despised was the One whom they should have worshiped (cf. Php 2:9–11; Rev 1:7). Many Jews believed on Christ after His death and ascension, realizing that the One whom they rejected was truly the Messiah (Ac 2:36, 37, 41).

8:31–36 These verses are a pivotal passage in understanding genuine salvation and true discipleship. John emphasized these realities by stressing truth and freedom. The focus in the passage is upon those who were exercising the beginnings of faith in Jesus as Messiah and Son of God. Jesus desired them to move on in their faith. Saving faith is not fickle but firm and settled. Such maturity expresses itself in full commitment to the truth in Jesus Christ resulting in genuine freedom. The passage has 3 features: 1) the progress of freedom (vv. 31, 32); 2) the pretense of freedom (vv. 33, 34); and 3) the promise of freedom (vv. 35, 36).

8:31 who had believed Him. The first step in the progress toward true discipleship is belief in Jesus Christ as Messiah and Son of God. **If you continue in My word, *then* you are truly disciples of Mine.** This reveals the second step in the progress toward true discipleship. Perseverance in obedience to Scripture (cf. Mt 28:19, 20) is the fruit or evidence of genuine faith (see Eph 2:10). The word "continue" means to habitually abide in Jesus' words. A genuine believer holds fast, obeys, and practices Jesus' teaching. The one who continues in His teaching has both the Father and the Son (2Jn 9; cf. Heb 3:14; Rev 2:26). Real disciples are both learners (the basic meaning of the word) and faithful followers.

8:32 the truth. "Truth" here has reference not only to the facts surrounding Jesus as the Messiah and Son of God but also to the teaching that He brought. A genuinely saved and obedient follower of the Lord Jesus will know divine truth and both freedom from sin (v. 34) and the search for reality. This divine truth comes not merely by intellectual assent (1Co 2:14) but saving commitment to Christ (cf. Tit 1:1, 2).

8:33 never yet been enslaved to anyone. Because the Jews had often been in political subjection to many nations (Egypt, Assyria, Babylon, Greece, Syria, and Rome), they must

and have never yet been enslaved to anyone; how
is it that You say, 'You will become free'?"
34 Jesus answered them, "Truly, truly, I say to
you, [A]everyone who commits sin is the slave of
sin. 35 [A]The slave does not remain in the house forever; [B]the son does remain forever. 36 So if the Son
[A]makes you free, you will be free indeed. 37 I know
that you are [A]Abraham's descendants; yet [B]you seek
to kill Me, because My word [a]has no place in you. 38 I
speak the things which I have seen [a]with *My* Father;
therefore you also do the things which you heard
from [A]*your* father."
39 They answered and said to Him, "Abraham is
[A]our father." Jesus *said to them, "[B]If you are Abraham's children, do the deeds of Abraham. 40 But
as it is, [A]you are seeking to kill Me, a man who has
[B]told you the truth, which I heard from God; this
Abraham did not do. 41 You are doing the deeds of
[A]your father." They said to Him, "We were not born
of fornication; [B]we have one Father: God." 42 Jesus
said to them, "If God were your Father, [A]you would
love Me, [B]for I proceeded forth and have come from
God, for I have [C]not even come on My own initiative, but [a,D]He sent Me. 43 Why do you not understand [a,A]what I am saying? *It is* because you cannot
[B]hear My word. 44 [A]You are of [B]*your* father the devil,
and [C]you want to do the desires of your father. [D]He
was a murderer from the beginning, and does not
stand in the truth because [E]there is no truth in him.
Whenever he speaks [a]a lie, he [F]speaks from his own
nature, for he is a liar and the father of [b]lies. 45 But
because [A]I speak the truth, you do not believe Me.
46 Which one of you convicts Me of sin? If [A]I speak
truth, why do you not believe Me? 47 [A]He who is of
God hears the words of God; for this reason you do
not hear *them,* because you are not of God."
48 [A]The Jews answered and said to Him, "Do we
not say rightly that You are a [B]Samaritan and [C]have
a demon?" 49 Jesus answered, "I do not [A]have a demon; but I honor My Father, and you dishonor Me.
50 But [A]I do not seek My glory; there is One who seeks
and judges. 51 Truly, truly, I say to you, if anyone
[A]keeps My word he will never [B]see death." 52 [A]The
Jews said to Him, "Now we know that You [B]have
a demon. Abraham died, and the prophets *also;*
and You say, 'If anyone [C]keeps My word, he will
never [D]taste of death.' 53 Surely You [A]are not greater
than our father Abraham, who died? The prophets
died too; whom do You make Yourself out *to be?*"
54 Jesus answered, "[A]If I glorify Myself, My glory is
nothing; [B]it is My Father who glorifies Me, of whom
you say, 'He is our God'; 55 and [A]you have not come
to know Him, [B]but I know Him; and if I say that I
do not know Him, I will be [C]a liar like you, [B]but I
do know Him and [D]keep His word. 56 [A]Your father
Abraham [B]rejoiced [a]to see My day, and he saw *it* and

8:34 [A]Rom 6:16; 2 Pet 2:19 8:35 [A]Gen 21:10; Gal 4:30 [B]Luke 15:31 8:36 [A]John 8:32 8:37 [a]Or *makes no progress* [A]Matt 3:9; John 8:39 [B]John 7:1; 8:40 8:38 [a]Or *in the presence of* [A]John 8:41, 44 8:39 [A]Matt 3:9; John 8:37 [B]Rom 9:7; Gal 3:7 8:40 [A]John 7:1; 8:37 [B]John 8:26 8:41 [A]John 8:38, 44 [B]Deut 32:6; Is 63:16; 64:8 8:42 [a]Lit *that One* [A]1 John 5:1 [B]John 13:3; 16:28, 30; 17:8 [C]John 7:28 [D]John 3:17 8:43 [a]Or *My way of speaking* [A]John 8:33, 39, 41 [B]John 5:25 8:44 [a]Lit *the lie* [b]Lit *it* [A]1 John 3:8 [B]John 8:38, 41 [C]John 7:17 [D]Gen 3:4; 1 John 3:8, 15 [E]1 John 2:4 [F]Matt 12:34 8:45 [A]John 18:37 8:46 [A]John 18:37 8:47 [A]1 John 4:6 8:48 [A]John 1:19 [B]Matt 10:5; John 4:9 [C]John 7:20 8:49 [A]John 7:20 8:50 [A]John 5:41; 8:54 8:51 [A]John 8:55; 14:23; 15:20; 17:6 [B]Matt 16:28; Luke 2:26; John 8:52; Heb 2:9; 11:5 8:52 [A]John 1:19 [B]John 7:20 [C]John 8:55; 14:23; 15:20; 17:6 [D]John 8:51 8:53 [A]John 4:12 8:54 [A]John 8:50 [B]John 7:39 8:55 [A]John 8:19; 15:21 [B]John 7:29 [C]John 8:44 [D]John 8:51; 15:10 8:56 [a]Lit *in order that he might see* [A]John 8:37, 39 [B]Matt 13:17; Heb 11:13

have been referring to their inward sense of freedom.

8:34 Truly, truly. *See note on 1:51.* **everyone who commits sin.** The kind of slavery that Jesus had in mind was not physical slavery but slavery to sin (cf. Ro 6:17, 18). The idea of "commits sin" means to practice sin habitually (1Jn 3:4, 8, 9). The ultimate bondage is not political or economic enslavement, but spiritual bondage to sin and rebellion against God. Thus, this also explains why Jesus would not let Himself be reduced to merely a political Messiah (6:14, 15).

8:35, 36 The notion of slavery in v. 34 moves to the status of slaves. While the Jews thought of themselves only as free sons of Abraham, in reality, they were slaves of sin. The genuine son in the context is Christ Himself, who sets the slaves free from sin. Those whom Jesus Christ liberates from the tyranny of sin and the bondage of legalism are really free (Ro 8:2; Gal 5:1).

8:39 If you are Abraham's children. The construction of this phrase indicates that Jesus was denying that mere physical lineage was sufficient for salvation (see Php 3:4–9). The sense would be "if you are Abraham's children, but you are not, then you would act like Abraham did." Just as children inherit genetic characteristics from their parents, so also those who are truly Abraham's offspring will act like Abraham, i.e., imitate Abraham's faith and obedience (see Ro 4:16; Gal 3:6–9; Heb 11:8–19; Jas 2:21–24). **deeds of Abraham.** Abraham's faith was demonstrated through his obedience to God (Jas 2:21–24). Jesus' point was that the conduct of the unbelieving Jews was diametrically opposed by the conduct of Abraham, who lived a life of obedience to all that God had commanded. Their conduct toward Jesus demonstrated that their real father was Satan (vv. 41, 44).

8:41 We were not born of fornication. The Jews may well have been referring to the controversy surrounding Jesus' birth. The Jews knew the story about Mary's betrothal and that Joseph was not Jesus' real father; thus they implied that Jesus' birth was illegitimate (see Mt 1:18–25; Lk 1:26–38).

8:42 If God were your Father, you would love Me. The construction here (as in v. 39) denies that God is truly their Father. Although the OT calls Israel His "firstborn son" (Ex 4:22) and affirms that God is Israel's father by creation and separation (Jer 31:9), the unbelief of the Jews toward Jesus demonstrated that God was not their Father spiritually. Jesus stressed that the explicit criterion verifying the claim to be a child of God is love for His Son, Jesus. Since God is love, those who love His Son also demonstrate His nature (1Jn 4:7–11; 5:1).

8:44 *your* father the devil. Sonship is predicated on conduct. A son will manifest his father's characteristics (cf. Eph 5:1, 2). Since the Jews exhibited the patterns of Satan in their hostility toward Jesus and their failure to believe in Him as Messiah, their paternity was the exact opposite of their claims, i.e., they belonged to Satan. **He was a murderer from the beginning.** Jesus' words refer to the fall when Satan tempted Adam and Eve and successfully killed their spiritual life (Ge 2:17; 3:17–24; Ro 5:12; Heb 2:14). Some think that the reference may also refer to Cain's murder of Abel (Ge 4:1–9; 1Jn 3:12).

8:46 convicts Me of sin. Although the Jews argued that Jesus was guilty of sin (5:18), the sense here is that the perfect holiness of Christ was demonstrated, not by the Jews' silence at Jesus' question here, but by the assurance of His direct consciousness of the purity of His whole life. Only a perfectly holy One who has the closest and most intimate communion with the Father could speak such words. The Jews could martial no convincing evidence that could convict Him of sin in the heavenly court.

8:48 You are a Samaritan. Since the Jews could not attack Jesus' personal life and conduct (v. 46), they tried an *ad hominem* attack of personal abuse toward Him. The reference to Jesus as a "Samaritan" probably centers in the fact that the Samaritans, like Jesus, questioned the Jews' exclusive right to be called Abraham's children (see vv. 33, 39).

8:51 never see death. Heeding Jesus' teaching and following Him results in eternal life (6:63, 68). Physical death cannot extinguish such life (see 5:24; 6:40, 47; 11:25, 26).

8:52 Abraham died. Jesus' assertion that anyone who keeps His word will never die (v. 51) prompted the Jews to offer a retort that once again revealed their thinking on strictly a literal and earthly level (see 3:4; 4:15).

8:56 Hebrews 11:13 indicates that Abraham saw Christ's day ("having seen them ... from a distance"; *see note there*). Abraham particularly saw in the continuing seed of Isaac

was glad." 57 [A]So the Jews said to Him, "You are not
yet fifty years old, and have You seen Abraham?"
58 Jesus said to them, "Truly, truly, I say to you, before Abraham [a]was born, [A]I am." 59 Therefore they
[A]picked up stones to throw at Him, but Jesus [a,B]hid
Himself and went out of the temple.

HEALING THE MAN BORN BLIND

9 As He passed by, He saw a man blind from
birth. 2 And His disciples asked Him, "[A]Rabbi,
who sinned, [B]this man or his [C]parents, that he
would be born blind?" 3 Jesus answered, "*It was*
neither *that* this man sinned, nor his parents; but *it*
was so [A]that the works of God might be displayed in
him. 4 We must work the works of Him who sent Me
[A]as long as it is day; night is coming when no one
can work. 5 While I am in the world, I am [A]the Light
of the world." 6 When He had said this, He [A]spat
on the ground, and made clay of the spittle, and
applied the clay to his eyes, 7 and said to him, "Go,
wash in [A]the pool of Siloam" (which is translated,
Sent). So he went away and [B]washed, and [C]came
back seeing. 8 Therefore the neighbors, and those
who previously saw him as a beggar, were saying, "Is not this the one who used to [A]sit and beg?"
9 Others were saying, "This is he," *still* others were
saying, "No, but he is like him." [a]He kept saying, "I
am the one." 10 So they were saying to him, "How
then were your eyes opened?" 11 He answered, "The
man who is called Jesus made clay, and anointed
my eyes, and said to me, 'Go to [A]Siloam and wash';
so I went away and washed, and I received sight."
12 They said to him, "Where is He?" He *said, "I do
not know."

CONTROVERSY OVER THE MAN

13 They *brought to the Pharisees the man who
was formerly blind. 14 [A]Now it was a Sabbath on the
day when Jesus made the clay and opened his eyes.
15 [A]Then the Pharisees also were asking him again
how he received his sight. And he said to them, "He
applied clay to my eyes, and I washed, and I see."
16 Therefore some of the Pharisees were saying,
"This man is not from God, because He [A]does not
keep the Sabbath." But others were saying, "How
can a man who is a sinner perform such [a,B]signs?"
And [C]there was a division among them. 17 So they
*said to the blind man [A]again, "What do you say
about Him, since He opened your eyes?" And he
said, "He is a [B]prophet."

8:57 [A]John 1:19 8:58 [a]Lit *came into being* [A]Ex 3:14; John 1:1; 17:5, 24 8:59 [a]Lit *was hidden* [A]Matt 12:14; John 10:31; 11:8 [B]John 12:36 9:2 [A]Matt 23:7 [B]Luke 13:2; John 9:34; Acts 28:4 [C]Ex 20:5 9:3 [A]John 11:4 9:4 [A]John 7:33; 11:9; 12:35; Gal 6:10 9:5 [A]Matt 5:14; John 1:4; 8:12; 12:46 9:6 [A]Mark 7:33; 8:23 9:7 [A]Neh 3:15; Is 8:6; Luke 13:4; John 9:11 [B]2 Kin 5:13f [C]Is 29:18; 35:5; 42:7; Matt 11:5; John 11:37 9:8 [A]Acts 3:2, 10 9:9 [a]Lit *That one* 9:11 [A]John 9:7 9:14 [A]John 5:9 9:15 [A]John 9:10 9:16 [a]Or *attesting miracles* [A]Matt 12:2; Luke 13:14; John 5:10; 7:23 [B]John 2:11 [C]John 6:52; 7:12, 43; 10:19 9:17 [A]John 9:15 [B]Deut 18:15; Matt 21:11

the beginning of God's fulfilling the covenant (Ge 12:1–3; 15:1–21; 17:1–8; cf. 22:8) that would culminate in Christ.

8:58 Truly, truly. *See note on 1:51.* **I am.** *See note on 6:22–58.* Here Jesus declared Himself to be Yahweh, i.e., the Lord of the OT. Basic to the expression are such passages as Ex 3:14; Dt 32:39; Is 41:4; 43:10 where God declared Himself to be the eternally preexistent God who revealed Himself in the OT to the Jews. *See also notes on vv. 24, 28.*

8:59 they picked up stones. The Jews understood Jesus' claim and followed Lv 24:16, which indicates that any man who falsely claims to be God should be stoned. **hid Himself and went out of the temple.** Jesus repeatedly escaped arrest and death because His hour had not yet come (*see notes on 7:8, 30*). The verse most likely indicates escape by miraculous means.

9:1–13 Jesus performed a miracle by recreating the eyes of a man who was born with congenital blindness (v. 1). Four features highlight this healing: 1) the problem that precipitated the healing (v. 1); 2) the purpose for the man's being born blind (vv. 2–5); 3) the power that healed him (vv. 6, 7); and 4) the perplexity of the people who saw the healing (vv. 8–13).

9:2 who sinned. While sin may be a cause of suffering, as clearly indicated in Scripture (see 5:14; Nu 12; 1Co 11:30; Jas 5:15), it is not always the case necessarily (see Job; 2Co 12:7; Gal 4:13). The disciples assumed, like most Jews of their day, that sin was the primary, if not exclusive, cause of all suffering. In this instance, however, Jesus made it clear that personal sin was not the reason for the blindness (see v. 3).

9:3 Jesus did not deny the general connection between sin and suffering, but He refuted the idea that personal acts of sin were the direct cause. God's sovereignty and purposes play a part in such matters, as is clear from Job 1, 2.

9:4 as long as it is day. Jesus meant as long as He was still on earth with His disciples. The phrase does not mean that Jesus somehow stopped being the light of the world once He ascended but that the light shone most brightly among men when He was on the earth doing the Father's will (cf. 8:12). **night is coming.** *See notes on 1:4, 5; 1Jn 1:5–7.* The darkness has special reference to the period when Jesus was taken from His disciples during His crucifixion (v. 5).

9:5 I am the Light of the world. *See note on 8:12*; cf. 1:5, 9; 3:19; 12:35, 46. Not only was Jesus spiritually the light of the world, but He would also provide the means of physical light for this blind man.

9:6 made clay of the spittle. As He had done when He originally made human beings out of the dust of the ground (Ge 2:7), Jesus may have used the clay to fashion a new pair of eyes.

9:7 wash in the pool of Siloam. The term "Siloam" is Heb. for "Sent." The pool of Siloam was SE of the original City of David. Its water source was through a channel (Hezekiah's tunnel) that carried water to it from the spring of Gihon in the Kidron Valley. It may be identified with the "lower pool" or "old pool" mentioned in Is 22:9, 11. Water for the water-pouring rites at the Feast of Booths, or Tabernacles was drawn from this pool (*see notes on 7:37–39*).

9:8, 9 In ancient times, such severe physical deformities as congenital blindness sentenced a person to begging as the only means of support (see Ac 3:1–7). The drastic change in the healed man caused many to faithlessly believe that he was not the person born blind.

9:13–34 This section in the story of the healing of the blind man reveals some key characteristics of willful unbelief: 1) unbelief sets false standards; 2) unbelief always wants more evidence but never has enough; 3) unbelief does biased research on a purely subjective basis; 4) unbelief rejects the facts; and 5) unbelief is self-centered. John included this section on the dialogue of the Pharisees with the blind man most likely for two reasons: 1) the dialogue carefully demonstrates the character of willful and fixed unbelief, and 2) the story confirms the first great schism between the synagogue and Christ's new followers. The blind man was the first known person thrown out of the synagogue because he chose to follow Christ (see 16:1–3).

9:13 They. This has reference to the blind man's "neighbors, and those who previously saw him as a beggar" (v. 8). **to the Pharisees.** The people brought the blind man to the Pharisees most likely because the miracle had happened on the Sabbath (v. 14), and they were aware that the Pharisees reacted negatively to those who violated the Sabbath (cf. 5:1–15). The people also wanted advice from their local synagogue and religious leaders.

9:16 not from God. The reasoning may have been that since Jesus violated their interpretation of the Sabbath law, He could not be the promised Prophet of God (Dt 13:1–5). **a division.** Earlier the crowds were divided in opinion regarding Jesus (7:40–43); here the authorities also became divided.

9:17 He is a prophet. While the blind man saw clearly that Jesus was more than a mere man, the sighted but obstinate Pharisees were spiritually blind to that truth (see v. 39). Blindness in the Bible is a metaphor for spiritual darkness, i.e., inability to discern God or His truth (2Co 4:3–6; Col 1:12–14).

18 [A]The Jews then did not believe *it* of him, that he
had been blind and had received sight, until they
called the parents of the very one who had received
his sight, 19 and questioned them, saying, "Is this
your son, who you say was born blind? Then how
does he now see?" 20 His parents answered them
and said, "We know that this is our son, and that
he was born blind; 21 but how he now sees, we do
not know; or who opened his eyes, we do not know.
Ask him; he is of age, he will speak for himself."
22 His parents said this because they [A]were afraid
of the Jews; for the Jews [B]had already agreed that
if anyone confessed Him to be [a]Christ, [C]he was to
be put out of the synagogue. 23 For this reason his
parents said, "[A]He is of age; ask him."
24 So a second time they called the man who had
been blind, and said to him, "[A]Give glory to God;
we know that [B]this man is a sinner." 25 He then answered, "Whether He is a sinner, I do not know; one
thing I do know, that though I was blind, now I see."
26 So they said to him, "What did He do to you? How
did He open your eyes?" 27 He answered them, "[A]I
told you already and you did not [B]listen; why do you
want to hear *it* again? You do not want to become
His disciples too, do you?" 28 They reviled him and
said, "You are His disciple, but [A]we are disciples of
Moses. 29 We know that God has spoken to Moses, but
as for this man, [A]we do not know where He is from."
30 The man answered and said to them, "Well, here
is an amazing thing, that you do not know where
He is from, and *yet* He opened my eyes. 31 We know
that [A]God does not hear sinners; but if anyone is
God-fearing and does His will, He hears him. 32 [a]Since
the beginning of time it has never been heard that
anyone opened the eyes of a person born blind. 33 [A]If
this man were not from God, He could do nothing."
34 They answered him, "[A]You were born entirely in
sins, and are you teaching us?" So they [B]put him out.

JESUS AFFIRMS HIS DEITY

35 Jesus heard that they had [A]put him out, and finding him, He said, "Do you believe in the [B]Son of Man?"
36 He answered, "[A]Who is He, [a]Lord, that I may believe
in Him?" 37 Jesus said to him, "You have both seen
Him, and [A]He is the one who is talking with you."
38 And he said, "Lord, I believe." And he [A]worshiped
Him. 39 And Jesus said, "[A]For judgment I came into
this world, so that [B]those who do not see may see, and
that [C]those who see may become blind." 40 Those of the
Pharisees who were with Him heard these things and
said to Him, "[A]We are not blind too, are we?" 41 Jesus
said to them, "[A]If you were blind, you would have no
sin; but [a]since you say, '[B]We see,' your sin remains.

PARABLE OF THE GOOD SHEPHERD

10 "Truly, truly, I say to you, he who does not
enter by the door into the fold of the sheep,
but climbs up some other way, he is [A]a thief and a

9:18 [A]John 1:19; 9:22 9:22 [a]I.e. the Messiah [A]John 7:13 [B]John 7:45-52 [C]Luke 6:22; John 12:42; 16:2 9:23 [A]John 9:21 9:24 [A]Josh 7:19; Ezra 10:11; Rev 11:13 [B]John 9:16 9:27 [A]John 9:15 [B]John 5:25 9:28 [A]John 5:45; Rom 2:17 9:29 [A]John 8:14 9:31 [A]Job 27:8f; 35:13; Ps 34:15f; 66:18; 145:19; Prov 15:29; 28:9; Is 1:15; James 5:16ff 9:32 [a]Lit *From the age it was not heard* 9:33 [A]John 3:2; 9:16 9:34 [A]John 9:2 [B]John 9:22, 35; 3 John 10 9:35 [A]John 9:22, 34; 3 John 10 [B]Matt 4:3 9:36 [a]Or *Sir* [A]Rom 10:14 9:37 [A]John 4:26 9:38 [A]Matt 8:2 9:39 [A]John 3:19; 5:22, 27 [B]Luke 4:18 [C]Matt 13:13; 15:14 9:40 [A]Rom 2:19 9:41 [a]Lit *now* [A]John 15:22, 24 [B]Prov 26:12 10:1 [A]John 10:8

9:18 called the parents. While neighbors may have been mistaken about the man's identity, the parents would know if this was their own son. The authorities considered the witness of the healed man worthless.

9:24 Give glory to God. This means that the authorities wanted the man to own up and admit the truth that Jesus was a sinner because He violated their traditions and threatened their influence (cf. Jos 7:19). **we know that this man is a sinner.** Enough unanimity existed among the religious authorities to conclude that Jesus was a sinner (cf. 8:46). Because of this already predetermined opinion, they refused to accept any of the testimony that a miracle had actually taken place.

9:27 In order to forcefully emphasize their hypocrisy, the healed man resorted to biting sarcasm when he suggested they desired to be Jesus' disciples.

9:28 You are His disciple, but we are disciples of Moses. At this point, the meeting degenerated into a shouting match of insults. The healed man's wit had exposed the bias of his inquisitors. As far as the authorities were concerned, the conflict between Jesus and Moses was irreconcilable. If the healed man defended Jesus, then such defense could only mean that he was Jesus' disciple.

9:30 The healed man demonstrated more spiritual insight and common sense than all of the religious authorities combined who sat in judgment of Jesus and him. His penetrating wit focused in on their intractable unbelief. His logic was that such an extraordinary miracle could only indicate that Jesus was from God, for the Jews believed that God responds in proportion to the righteousness of the one praying (see Job 27:9; 35:13; Pss 66:18; 109:7; Pr 15:29; Is 1:15; cf. 14:13, 14; 16:23–27; 1Jn 3:21, 22). The greatness of the miracle could only indicate that Jesus was actually from God.

9:34 are you teaching us? The Pharisees were incensed with the man, and their anger prevented them from seeing the penetrating insight that the uneducated, healed man had demonstrated. The phrase also revealed their ignorance of Scripture, for the OT indicated that the coming messianic age would be evidenced by restoration of sight to the blind (Is 29:18; 35:5; 42:7; cf. Mt 11:4, 5; Lk 4:18, 19).

9:35–41 While vv. 1–34 dealt with Jesus' restoration of physical sight in the blind man, vv. 35–41 featured Jesus bringing spiritual "sight" to him.

9:35 Do you believe . . . ? Jesus invited the man to put his trust in Him as the One who revealed God to man. Jesus placed great emphasis on public acknowledgment of who He was and confession of faith in Him (Mt 10:32; Lk 12:8). **Son of Man.** Cf. 1:51; 3:13, 14; 5:27; 6:27, 53, 62; 8:28.

9:36 Lord. The word here should be understood not as an indication that he understood Jesus' deity, but as meaning "sir." See also v. 38. Since the blind man had never seen Jesus (v. 7) nor met Him since he went to wash in the pool, he did not recognize Jesus at first as the One who healed him.

9:39 For judgment. Not that His purpose was to condemn, but rather to save (12:47; Lk 19:10); saving some, nevertheless, involves condemning others (*see notes on 3:16, 18*). The last part of this verse is taken from Is 6:10; 42:19 (cf. Mk 4:12). **those who do not see.** Those people who know they are in spiritual darkness. **those who see.** Refers in an ironic way to those who think they are in the light, but are not (cf. Mk 2:17; Lk 5:31).

9:40 not blind too, are we? Apparently, Jesus found (v. 35) the man in a public place, where the Pharisees were present listening.

9:41 your sin remains. Jesus had particular reference to the sin of unbelief and rejection of Him as Messiah and Son of God. If they knew their lostness and darkness and cried out for spiritual light, they would no longer be guilty of the sin of unbelief in Christ. But satisfied that their darkness was light, and continuing in rejection of Christ, their sin remained. *See note on Mt 6:22, 23.*

10:1–39 Jesus' discourse on Himself as the "Good Shepherd" flowed directly from chap. 9, as Jesus continued to talk to the very same people. The problem of chap. 9 was that Israel was led by false shepherds who drew them astray from the true knowledge and kingdom of Messiah (9:39–41). In chap. 10, Jesus declared Himself to be the "Good Shepherd" who was appointed by His Father as Savior and King, in contrast to the false shepherds of Israel who were self-appointed and self-righteous (Ps 23:1; Is 40:11; Jer 3:15; cf. Is 56:9–12; Jer 23:1–4; 25:32–38; Eze 34:1–31; Zec 11:16).

10:1 fold of the sheep. Jesus spoke in vv. 1–30 using a sustained metaphor based on

robber. 2 But he who enters by the door is [A]a shepherd of the sheep. 3 To him the doorkeeper opens,
and the sheep hear [A]his voice, and he calls his own
sheep by name and [B]leads them out. 4 When he puts
forth all his own, he goes ahead of them, and the
sheep follow him because they know [A]his voice. 5 A
stranger they simply will not follow, but will flee
from him, because they do not know [A]the voice of
strangers." 6 This [A]figure of speech Jesus spoke to
them, but they did not understand what those things
were which He had been saying to them.

7 So Jesus said to them again, "Truly, truly, I say
to you, I am [A]the door of the sheep. 8 All who came
before Me are [A]thieves and robbers, but the sheep
did not hear them. 9 [A]I am the door; if anyone enters through Me, he will be saved, and will go in
and out and find pasture. 10 The thief comes only
to steal and kill and destroy; I came that they [A]may
have life, and [a]have *it* abundantly.

11 "[A]I am the good shepherd; the good shepherd
[B]lays down His life for the sheep. 12 He who is a
hired hand, and not a [A]shepherd, who is not the
owner of the sheep, sees the wolf coming, and
leaves the sheep and flees, and the wolf snatches
them and scatters *them*. 13 *He flees* because he is a
hired hand and is not concerned about the sheep.
14 [A]I am the good shepherd, and [B]I know My own
and My own know Me, 15 even as [A]the Father knows
Me and I know the Father; and [B]I lay down My life
for the sheep. 16 I have [A]other sheep, which are not
of this fold; I must bring them also, and they will
hear My voice; and they will become [B]one flock
with [C]one shepherd. 17 For this reason the Father
loves Me, because I [A]lay down My life so that I may
take it again. 18 [A]No one has taken it away from
Me, but I [B]lay it down on My own initiative. I have
authority to lay it down, and I have authority to
take it up again. [C]This commandment I received
from My Father."

19 [A]A division occurred again among the Jews because of these words. 20 Many of them were saying,
"He [A]has a demon and [B]is insane. Why do you listen
to Him?" 21 Others were saying, "These are not the
sayings of one [A]demon-possessed. [B]A demon cannot
open the eyes of the blind, can he?"

JESUS ASSERTS HIS DEITY

22 At that time the Feast of the Dedication took
place at Jerusalem; 23 it was winter, and Jesus was
walking in the temple in the portico of [A]Solomon.

10:2 [A]John 10:11f 10:3 [A]John 10:4f, 16, 27 [B]John 10:9 10:4 [A]John 10:5, 16, 27 10:5 [A]John 10:4, 16, 27 10:6 [A]John 16:25, 29; 2 Pet 2:22 10:7 [A]John 10:1f, 9 10:8 [A]Jer 23:1f; Ezek 34:2ff; John 10:1 10:9 [A]John 10:1f, 9 10:10 [a]Or *have abundance* [A]John 5:40 10:11 [A]Is 40:11; Ezek 34:11-16, 23; John 10:14; Heb 13:20; 1 Pet 5:4; Rev 7:17 [B]John 10:15, 17, 18; 15:13; 1 John 3:16 10:12 [A]John 10:2 10:14 [A]John 10:11 [B]John 10:27 10:15 [A]Matt 11:27; Luke 10:22 [B]John 10:11, 17, 18 10:16 [A]Is 56:8 [B]John 11:52; 17:20f; Eph 2:13-18; 1 Pet 2:25 [C]Ezek 34:23; 37:24 10:17 [A]John 10:11, 15, 18 10:18 [A]Matt 26:53; John 2:19; 5:26 [B]John 10:11, 15, 17 [C]John 14:31; 15:10; Phil 2:8; Heb 5:8 10:19 [A]John 7:43; 9:16 10:20 [A]John 7:20 [B]Mark 3:21 10:21 [A]Matt 4:24 [B]Ex 4:11; John 9:32f 10:23 [A]Acts 3:11; 5:12

first-century sheep ranching. The sheep were kept in a pen, which had a gate through which the sheep entered and left. The shepherd engaged a "doorkeeper" (v. 3) or "hired hand" (v. 12) as an undershepherd to guard the gate. The shepherd entered through that gate. He whose interest was stealing or wounding the sheep would choose another way to attempt entrance. The words of Eze 34 most likely form the background to Jesus' teaching since God decried the false shepherds of Israel (i.e., the spiritual leaders of the nation) for not caring properly for the flock of Israel (i.e., the nation). The Gospels themselves contain extensive sheep/shepherd imagery (see Mt 9:36; Mk 6:34; 14:27; Lk 15:1–7).

10:3 the doorkeeper. The doorkeeper was a hired undershepherd who recognized the true shepherd of the flock, opened the gate for Him, assisted the shepherd in caring for the flock, and especially guarded them at night. **the sheep hear his voice.** Near Eastern shepherds stand at different locations outside the sheep pen, sounding out their own unique calls which their sheep recognize. As a result, the sheep gather around the shepherd. **he calls his own sheep by name.** This shepherd goes even further by calling each sheep by its own special name. Jesus' point is that He comes to the fold of Israel and calls out His own sheep individually to come into His own messianic fold. The assumption is that they are already in some way His sheep even before He calls them by name (see vv. 25–27; 6:37, 39, 44, 64, 65; 17:6, 9, 24; 18:9).

10:4, 5 Unlike Western shepherds who drive the sheep from the side or behind, often using sheep dogs, Near Eastern shepherds lead their flocks, their voice calling them to move on. This draws a remarkable picture of the master/disciple relationship. NT spiritual leadership is always by example, i.e., a call to imitate conduct (cf. 1Ti 4:12; 1Pe 5:1–3).

10:6 figure of speech. This phrase conveys the idea that something cryptic or enigmatic is intended in it. It occurs again in 16:25, 29, but not in the Synoptics. Having given the illustration (vv. 1–5), Jesus then began to draw salient spiritual truth from it.

10:7–10 I am the door. This is the third of 7 "I am" statements of Jesus (see 6:35; 8:12). Here, He changes the metaphor slightly. While in vv. 1–5 He was the shepherd, here He is the gate. While in vv. 1–5, the shepherd led the sheep out of the sheep fold, here He is the entrance to the fold (v. 9) that leads to proper pasture. This section echoes Jesus' words in 14:6 that He is the only way to the Father. His point is that He serves as the sole means to approach the Father and partake of God's promised salvation. As some Near Eastern shepherds slept in the gateway to guard the sheep, Jesus here pictures Himself as the gate.

10:9, 10 These two verses are a proverbial way of insisting that belief in Jesus as the Messiah and Son of God is the only way of being "saved" from sin and hell and receiving eternal life. Only Jesus Christ is the one true source for the knowledge of God and the one basis for spiritual security.

10:11–18 Jesus picked up another expression from vv. 1–5, i.e., He is the "good shepherd" in contrast to the present evil leadership of Israel (9:40, 41). This is the fourth of 7 "I am" statements of Jesus (see vv. 7, 9; 6:35; 8:12). The term "good" has the idea of "noble" and stands in contrast to the "hired hand" who cares only for self-interest.

10:11 lays down His life for the sheep. This is a reference to Jesus' substitutionary death for sinners on the cross. Cf. v. 15; 6:51; 11:50, 51; 17:19; 18:14.

10:12 sees the wolf coming ... flees. The hired hand likely represents religious leaders who perform their duty in good times but who never display sacrificial care for the sheep in times of danger. They stand in contrast to Jesus, who laid down His life for His flock (see 15:13).

10:16 not of this fold. This refers to Gentiles who will respond to His voice and become a part of the church (cf. Ro 1:16). Jesus' death was not only for Jews (*see notes on vv. 1, 3*), but also for non-Jews whom He will make into one new body, the church (*see notes on 11:51, 52*; cf. Eph 2:11–22).

10:17, 18 take it again. Jesus repeated this phrase twice in these two verses, indicating that His sacrificial death was not the end. His resurrection followed in demonstration of His messiahship and deity (Ro 1:4). His death and resurrection resulted in His ultimate glorification (12:23; 17:5) and the outpouring of the Holy Spirit (7:37–39; cf. Ac 2:16–39).

10:19–21 The Jews once again had a mixed reaction to Jesus' words (see 7:12, 13). While some charged Him with demon possession (see 7:20; 8:48; cf. Mt 12:22–32), others concluded His works and words were a demonstration of God's sanction upon Him.

10:22, 23 Feast of the Dedication. The Jewish celebration of Hanukkah, which celebrates the Israelite victory over the Syrian leader Antiochus Epiphanes, who persecuted Israel. In ca. 170 B.C. he conquered Jerusalem and desecrated the Jewish temple by setting up a pagan altar to displace the altar of God. Under the leadership of an old priest named Mattathias (his family name was called the Hasmoneans), the Jews fought guerrilla warfare (known as the

24 [A]The Jews then gathered around Him, and were
saying to Him, "How long [a]will You keep us in suspense? If You are [b]the Christ, tell us [B]plainly." 25 Jesus
answered them, "[A]I told you, and you do not believe;
[B]the works that I do in My Father's name, these testify of Me. 26 But you do not believe because [A]you are
not of My sheep. 27 My sheep [A]hear My voice, and [B]I
know them, and they follow Me; 28 and I give [A]eter-
nal life to them, and they will never perish; and [B]no
one will snatch them out of My hand. 29 [a]My Father,
who has given *them* to Me, is greater than all; and
no one is able to snatch *them* out of the Father's
hand. 30 [A]I and the Father are [a]one."
31 The Jews [A]picked up stones again to stone Him.
32 Jesus answered them, "I showed you many good
works from the Father; for which of them are you
stoning Me?" 33 The Jews answered Him, "For a good
work we do not stone You, but for [A]blasphemy; and
because You, being a man, [B]make Yourself out *to be*
God." 34 Jesus answered them, "Has it not been written in [A]your [B]Law, '[C]I SAID, YOU ARE GODS'? 35 If he
called them gods, to whom the word of God came
(and the Scripture cannot be broken), 36 do you say
of Him, whom the Father [A]sanctified and [B]sent into
the world, 'You are blaspheming,' because I said, '[C]I
am the Son of God'? 37 [A]If I do not do the works of My
Father, do not believe Me; 38 but if I do them, though
you do not believe Me, believe [A]the works, so that
you may [a]know and understand that [B]the Father is in
Me, and I in the Father." 39 Therefore [A]they were seeking again to seize Him, and [B]He eluded their grasp.
40 And He went away [A]again beyond the Jordan
to the place where John was first baptizing, and He
was staying there. 41 Many came to Him and were
saying, "While John performed no [A]sign, yet [B]every-
thing John said about this man was true." 42 [A]Many
believed in Him there.

THE DEATH AND RESURRECTION OF LAZARUS

11 Now a certain man was sick, Lazarus of [A]Beth-
any, the village of Mary and her sister [B]Martha.
2 It was the Mary who [A]anointed [B]the Lord with
ointment, and wiped His feet with her hair, whose

10:24 [a]Lit *do You lift up our soul* [b]I.e. the Messiah [A]John 1:19; 10:31, 33 [B]Luke 22:67; John 16:25 10:25 [A]John 8:56, 58 [B]John 5:36; 10:38 10:26 [A]John 8:47 10:27 [A]John 10:4, 16 [B]John 10:14 10:28 [A]John 17:2f; 1 John 2:25; 5:11 [B]John 6:37, 39 10:29 [a]One early ms reads *What My Father has given Me is greater than all* 10:30 [a]Or *a unity;* or *one essence* [A]John 17:21ff 10:31 [A]John 8:59 10:33 [A]Lev 24:16 [B]John 5:18 10:34 [A]John 8:17 [B]John 12:34; 15:25; Rom 3:19; 1 Cor 14:21 [C]Ps 82:6 10:36 [A]Jer 1:5; John 6:69 [B]John 3:17 [C]John 5:17f; 10:30 10:37 [A]John 10:25; 15:24 10:38 [a]Lit *know and continue knowing* [A]John 10:25; 14:11 [B]John 14:10f, 20; 17:21, 23 10:39 [A]John 7:30 [B]Luke 4:30; John 8:59 10:40 [A]John 1:28 10:41 [A]John 2:11 [B]John 1:27, 30, 34; 3:27-30 10:42 [A]John 7:31 11:1 [A]Matt 21:17; John 11:18 [B]Luke 10:38; John 11:5, 19ff 11:2 [A]Luke 7:38; John 12:3 [B]Luke 7:13; John 11:3, 21, 32; 13:13f

Maccabean Revolt—166–142 B.C.) against Syria and freed the temple and the land from Syrian dominance until 63 B.C. when Rome (Pompey) took control of the region. It was in 164 B.C., on 25 Chislev (Dec. approximately), that the Jews liberated the temple and rededicated it. The celebration is also known as the "Feast of Lights" because of the lighting of lamps and candles in Jewish homes to commemorate the event. it was winter. John indicated by this phrase that the cold weather drove Jesus to walk on the eastern side of the temple in the sheltered area of Solomon's porch, which after the resurrection became the regular gathering place of Christians where they would proclaim the gospel (see Ac 3:11; 5:12).

10:24 tell us plainly. In light of the context of vv. 31–39, the Jews were not seeking merely for clarity and understanding regarding who Jesus was, but rather wanted Him to declare openly that He was Messiah in order to justify attacking Him.

10:26, 27 This clearly indicates that God has chosen His sheep, and it is they who believe and follow (*see notes on vv. 3, 16*; cf. 6:37–40, 44, 65).

10:28, 29 The security of Jesus' sheep rests with Him as the good shepherd, who has the power to keep them safe. Neither thieves and robbers (vv. 1, 8) nor the wolf (v. 12) can harm them. Verse 29 makes clear that the Father ultimately stands behind the sheep's security, for no one is able to steal from God, who is in sovereign control of all things (Col 3:3). *See notes on Ro 8:31–39*. No stronger passage in the OT or NT exists for the absolute, eternal security of every true Christian.

10:30 I and the Father are one. Both Father and Son are committed to the perfect protection and preservation of Jesus' sheep. The sentence, stressing the united purpose and action of both in the security and safety of the flock, presupposes unity of nature and essence (see 5:17–23; 17:22).

10:31 For the third time John records that the Jews attempted to stone Jesus (see 5:18; 8:59). Jesus' assertion (v. 30) that He was One with the Father affirmed His claim to deity and caused the Jews to seek His execution (v. 33). Although the OT permitted stoning in certain instances (e.g., Lv 24:16), the Romans reserved the right of capital punishment for themselves (18:31). Nevertheless, out-of-control Jews attempted a mob action in lieu of legal proceedings (see Ac 7:54–60).

10:33 make Yourself out *to be* God. There was no doubt in the minds of those Jews that Jesus was claiming to be God (cf. 5:18).

10:34–36 Quoted from Ps 82:6 where God calls some unjust judges "gods" and pronounces calamity against them. Jesus' argument is that this psalm proves that the word "god" can be legitimately used to refer to others than God Himself. His reasoning is that if there are others whom God can address as "god" or "sons of the Most High," why then should the Jews object to Jesus' statement that He is "the Son of God" (v. 36)?

10:35 Scripture cannot be broken. An affirmation of the absolute accuracy and authority of Scripture (*see notes on Mt 5:17–19*).

10:38 believe the works. Jesus did not expect to be believed merely on His own assertions. Since He did the same things that the Father does (*see notes on 5:19*), His enemies should consider this in their evaluation of Him. The implication is, however, that they were so ignorant of God that they could not recognize the works of the Father or the One whom the Father sent (see also 14:10, 11).

10:40 He went away again beyond the Jordan. Because of the increasing hostility (see v. 39), Jesus went from the region of Judea into the unpopulated area across the Jordan. to the place where John was first baptizing. Cf. Mt 3:1–6; Mk 1:2–6; Lk 3:3–6. This is probably a reference to either Perea or Batanea, the general area in the tetrarchy of Philip in the E and NE of the Sea of Galilee. The statement is ironic, since the area where John first began became the last area in which Jesus stayed before He left for Jerusalem and crucifixion. The people remembered John's testimony to Christ and affirmed their faith in Him (vv. 41, 42).

11:1–12:50 The previous passage (10:40–42) marked the end of John's treatment of Jesus' public ministry. At that point, He began to move into seclusion and minister to His own disciples and those who loved Him as He prepared to face death. Israel had her day of opportunity; the sun was setting and the night was coming. These two chapters form the transition to chaps. 13–21 which record the passion of Christ, i.e., the events surrounding the cross.

11:1–57 As chap. 11 begins, Jesus stands in the shadow of facing the cross. The little time that He had in the area beyond the Jordan (cf. Mt 19:1–20:34; Mk 10:1–52; Lk 17:11–19:28) would soon come to an end. John picked up the story (vv. 55–57) after He moved back into the area of Jerusalem, and His death on the cross was only a few days away. In those last few days before His death, the scene in John's gospel changes from hatred and rejection (10:39) to an unmistakable and blessed witness of the glory of Christ. All the rejection and hatred could not dim His glory as displayed through the resurrection of Lazarus. That miracle evidences His glory in 3 ways: 1) it pointed to His deity; 2) it strengthened the faith of the disciples; and 3) it led directly to the cross (12:23). The chapter can be divided as follows: 1) the preparation for the miracle (vv. 1–16); 2) the arrival of Jesus (vv. 17–36); 3) the miracle itself (vv. 37–44); and 4) the results of the miracle (vv. 45–57).

11:1 Lazarus. The resurrection of Lazarus is the climactic and most dramatic sign in this gospel and the capstone of His public ministry. Six miracles have already been

brother Lazarus was sick. 3 So the sisters sent *word*
to Him, saying, "[A]Lord, behold, [B]he whom You love
is sick." 4 But when Jesus heard *this,* He said, "This
sickness is not to end in death, but for [A]the glory
of God, so that the Son of God may be glorified by
it." 5 Now Jesus loved [A]Martha and her sister and
Lazarus. 6 So when He heard that he was sick, He
then stayed two days *longer* in the place where
He was. 7 Then after this He *said to the disciples,
"[A]Let us go to Judea again." 8 The disciples *said to
Him, "[A]Rabbi, the Jews were just now seeking [B]to
stone You, and are You going there again?" 9 Jesus
answered, "[A]Are there not twelve hours in the day?
If anyone walks in the day, he does not stumble, because he sees the light of this world. 10 But if anyone
walks in the night, he stumbles, because the light is
not in him." 11 This He said, and after that He *said
to them, "Our [A]friend Lazarus [B]has fallen asleep; but
I go, so that I may awaken him out of sleep." 12 The
disciples then said to Him, "Lord, if he has fallen
asleep, he will [a]recover." 13 Now [A]Jesus had spoken
of his death, but they thought that He was speaking of [a]literal sleep. 14 So Jesus then said to them
plainly, "Lazarus is dead, 15 and I am glad for your
sakes that I was not there, so that you may believe;
but let us go to him." 16 [A]Therefore Thomas, who is
called [a,B]Didymus, said to *his* fellow disciples, "Let
us also go, so that we may die with Him."
17 So when Jesus came, He found that he had already been in the tomb [A]four days. 18 Now [A]Beth-
any was near Jerusalem, about [a]two miles off;
19 and many of [A]the Jews had come to [B]Martha and
Mary, [C]to console them concerning *their* brother.
20 [A]Martha therefore, when she heard that Jesus
was coming, went to meet Him, but [A]Mary [a]stayed
at the house. 21 Martha then said to Jesus, "[A]Lord,
[B]if You had been here, my brother would not have
died. 22 Even now I know that [A]whatever You ask of
God, God will give You." 23 Jesus *said to her, "Your
brother will rise again." 24 Martha *said to Him, "[A]I
know that he will rise again in the resurrection
on the last day." 25 Jesus said to her, "[A]I am the resurrection and the life; he who believes in Me will
live even if he dies, 26 and everyone who lives and
believes in Me [A]will never die. Do you believe this?"
27 She *said to Him, "Yes, Lord; I have believed that

11:3 [A]Luke 7:13; John 11:2, 21, 32; 13:13f [B]John 11:5, 11, 36 11:4 [A]John 9:3; 10:38; 11:40 11:5 [A]John 11:1 11:7 [A]John 10:40 11:8 [A]Matt 23:7 [B]John 8:59; 10:31 11:9 [A]Luke 13:33; John 9:4; 12:35 11:11 [A]John 11:3 [B]Matt 27:52; Mark 5:39; John 11:13; Acts 7:60 11:12 [a]Lit *be saved* 11:13 [a]Lit *the slumber of sleep* [A]Matt 9:24; Luke 8:52 11:16 [a]I.e. the Twin [A]Matt 10:3; Mark 3:18; Luke 6:15; John 14:5; 20:26-28; Acts 1:13 [B]John 20:24; 21:2 11:17 [A]John 11:39 11:18 [a]Lit *15 stadia* (9,090 ft) [A]John 11:1 11:19 [A]John 1:19; 11:8 [B]John 11:1 [C]1 Sam 31:13; 1 Chr 10:12; Job 2:11; John 11:31 11:20 [a]Lit *was sitting* [A]Luke 10:38-42 11:21 [A]John 11:2 [B]John 11:32, 37 11:22 [A]John 9:31; 11:41f 11:24 [A]Dan 12:2; John 5:28f; Acts 24:15 11:25 [A]John 1:4; 5:26; 6:39f; Rev 1:18 11:26 [A]John 6:47, 50, 51; 8:51

presented (water into wine [2:1–11]; healing of the nobleman's son [4:46–54]; restoring the impotent man [5:1–15]; multiplying the loaves and fishes [6:1–14], walking on the water [6:15–21]; and curing the man born blind [9:1–12]). Lazarus' resurrection is more potent than all those and even more monumental than the raising of the widow's son in Nain (Lk 7:11–16) or Jairus' daughter (Lk 8:40–56) because those two resurrections occurred immediately after death. Lazarus was raised after 4 days of being in the grave with the process of decomposition already having started (v. 39). **Bethany.** This Bethany is different from the other "Bethany beyond the Jordan" in 1:28 (*see note there*). It lies on the E side of the Mt. of Olives about two mi. from Jerusalem (v. 18) along the road leading toward Jericho. **Mary . . . Martha.** This is the first mention of this family in John. John related the story of Mary's anointing of Jesus in 12:1–8, but this reference may indicate that the original readers were already familiar with the event. Cf. Lk 10:38–42.

11:3 sent *word* to Him. Since Jesus was in the Transjordan and Lazarus was near Jerusalem, the message to Jesus would most likely have taken one whole day to reach Him. Surely by omniscience, Jesus already knew of Lazarus' condition (see v. 6; 1:47). He may have died before the messenger reached Jesus, since he was dead 4 days (v. 17) when Jesus arrived, after a two day delay (v. 6) and a one day journey. **he whom You love.** This phrase is a touching hint at the close friendship that Jesus had with Lazarus. Cf. 13:1.

11:4 the Son of God may be glorified. This phrase reveals the real purpose behind Lazarus' sickness, i.e., not death, but that the Son of God might be glorified through his resurrection (cf. v. 4; *see note on 9:3*).

11:6 He . . . stayed two days *longer*. The decision to delay coming did not bring about Lazarus' death, since Jesus already supernaturally knew his plight. Most likely by the time the messenger arrived to inform Jesus, Lazarus was already dead. The delay was because He loved the family (v. 5) and that love would be clear as He greatly strengthened their faith by raising Lazarus from the dead. The delay also ensured that Lazarus had been dead long enough that no one could misinterpret the miracle as a fraud or mere resuscitation.

11:7, 8 The disciples realized that the animosity toward Jesus was so great that His return could result in His death because of the murderous Jews (cf. 8:59; 10:31).

11:9, 10 During the light of the sun, most people did their work safely. When darkness came, they stopped. The proverbial saying, however, had a deeper meaning. As long as the Son performed His Father's will (i.e., during the daylight period of His ministry when He is able to work), He was safe. The time would soon come (nighttime) when, by God's design, His earthly work would end and He would "stumble" in death. Jesus was stressing that as long as He was on earth doing God's will, even at this late time in His ministry, He would safely complete God's purposes.

11:11–13 fallen asleep. A euphemistic term used in the NT to refer to death, particularly with reference to believers who will be physically raised to eternal life (cf. 1Co 11:30; 15:51; 1Th 4:13).

11:14, 15 The resurrection of Lazarus was designed to strengthen His disciples' faith in Him as the Messiah and Son of God in the face of the strong Jewish rejection of Him.

11:16 Thomas' words reflect loyal devotion and, at the same time, pessimism over the fact that they would probably all die. His fears were not unrealistic in the face of bitter hostility toward Jesus, and had not the Lord protected them in the garden (18:1–11), they may also have been arrested and executed. Cf. 20:24–29.

11:17 in the tomb. The term "tomb" means a stone sepulcher. In first-century Israel such a grave was common. Either a cave or rock area would be hewn out, the floor inside leveled and graded to make a shallow descent. Shelves were cut out or constructed inside the area in order to bury additional family members. A rock was rolled in front to prevent wild animals or grave robbers from entering (see also v. 38). The evangelist made special mention of the fourth day (*see note on v. 3*) in order to stress the magnitude of the miracle, for the Jews did not embalm, and by then the body would have been in a state of rapid decomposition.

11:18, 19 The implication of these verses is that the family was rather prominent. The mention of the Jews also heightens the reader's awareness of the great risk that Jesus took in coming so close to Jerusalem, which was seething with the leaders' hatred for Him.

11:21 if You had been here. Cf. v. 32. Not a rebuke of Jesus, but a testimony of her trust in His healing power.

11:22 whatever You ask of God. Based on her statement in v. 39, Martha was not saying she believed Jesus could raise Lazarus from the dead, but that she knew He had a special relationship to God so that His prayers could bring some good from this sad event.

11:25, 26 This is the fifth in a series of 7 great "I am" statements of Jesus (see 6:35; 8:12; 10:7, 9; 10:11, 14). With this statement, Jesus moved Martha from an abstract belief in the resurrection that will take place "on the last day" (cf. 5:28, 29) to a personalized trust in Him who alone can raise the dead. No resurrection or eternal life exists outside of the Son of God. Time ("on the last day") is no barrier to the One who has the power of resurrection and life (1:4), for He can give life at any time.

11:27 She said to Him. Martha's confes-

You are [a,A]the Christ, the Son of God, *even* [b,B]He who
comes into the world."
28 When she had said this, she [A]went away and
called Mary her sister, saying secretly, "[B]The Teacher
is here and is calling for you." 29 And when she heard
it, she *got up quickly and was coming to Him.
30 Now Jesus had not yet come into the village,
but [A]was still in the place where Martha met Him.
31 [A]Then the Jews who were with her in the house,
and [B]consoling her, when they saw that Mary got
up quickly and went out, they followed her, supposing that she was going to the tomb to weep there.
32 Therefore, when Mary came where Jesus was, she
saw Him, and fell at His feet, saying to Him, "[A]Lord,
[B]if You had been here, my brother would not have
died." 33 When Jesus therefore saw her weeping,
and [A]the Jews who came with her *also* weeping,
He [B]was deeply moved in spirit and [a,C]was troubled,
34 and said, "Where have you laid him?" They *said
to Him, "Lord, come and see." 35 Jesus [A]wept. 36 So
[A]the Jews were saying, "See how He [B]loved him!"
37 But some of them said, "Could not this man, who
[A]opened the eyes of the blind man, [a]have kept this
man also from dying?"
38 So Jesus, again being deeply moved within,
*came to the tomb. Now it was a [A]cave, and a stone
was lying against it. 39 Jesus *said, "Remove the
stone." Martha, the sister of the deceased, *said to
Him, "Lord, by this time [a]there will be a stench, for
he has been *dead* [A]four days." 40 Jesus *said to her,
"[A]Did I not say to you that if you believe, you will
see the glory of God?" 41 So they removed the [A]stone.
Then Jesus [B]raised His eyes, and said, "[C]Father, I
thank You that You have heard Me. 42 I knew that
You always hear Me; but [A]because of the [a]people
standing around I said it, so that they may believe
that [B]You sent Me." 43 When He had said these things,
He cried out with a loud voice, "Lazarus, come forth."
44 The man who had died came forth, [A]bound hand
and foot with wrappings, and [B]his face was wrapped
around with a cloth. Jesus *said to them, "Unbind
him, and let him go."
45 [A]Therefore many of the Jews [B]who came to
Mary, and [C]saw what He had done, believed in Him.
46 But some of them went to the [A]Pharisees and told
them the things which Jesus had done.

CONSPIRACY TO KILL JESUS

47 Therefore [A]the chief priests and the Pharisees
[B]convened a [C]council, and were saying, "What are
we doing? For this man is performing many [a,D]signs.
48 If we let Him *go on* like this, all men will believe
in Him, and the Romans will come and take away
both our [A]place and our nation." 49 But one of them,
[A]Caiaphas, [B]who was high priest that year, said to
them, "You know nothing at all, 50 nor do you take
into account that [A]it is expedient for you that one
man die for the people, and that the whole nation

11:27 [a]I.e. the Messiah [b]The Coming One was the Messianic title [A]Matt 16:16; Luke 2:11 [B]John 6:14 11:28 [A]John 11:30 [B]Matt 26:18; Mark 14:14; Luke 22:11; John 13:13 11:30 [A]John 11:20 11:31 [A]John 11:19, 33 [B]John 11:19 11:32 [A]John 11:2 [B]John 11:21 11:33 [a]Lit *troubled Himself* [A]John 11:19 [B]John 11:38 [C]John 12:27; 13:21 11:35 [A]Luke 19:41; John 11:33 11:36 [A]John 11:19 [B]John 11:3 11:37 [a]Lit *have caused that this man also not die* [A]John 9:7 11:38 [A]Matt 27:60; Mark 15:46; Luke 24:2; John 20:1 11:39 [a]Lit *he stinks* [A]John 11:17 11:40 [A]John 11:4, 23ff 11:41 [A]Matt 27:60; Mark 15:46; Luke 24:2; John 20:1 [B]John 17:1; Acts 7:55 [C]Matt 11:25 11:42 [a]Lit *crowd* [A]John 12:30; 17:21 [B]John 3:17 11:44 [A]John 19:40 [B]John 20:7 11:45 [A]John 7:31 [B]John 11:19; 12:17f [C]John 2:23 11:46 [A]John 7:32, 45; 11:57 11:47 [a]Or *attesting miracles* [A]John 7:32, 45; 11:57 [B]Matt 26:3 [C]Matt 5:22 [D]John 2:11 11:48 [A]Matt 24:15 11:49 [A]Matt 26:3 [B]John 11:51; 18:13 11:50 [A]John 18:14

sion is representative of the very reason John wrote this inspired gospel (cf. 20:30, 31). See Peter's confession in Mt 16:16.

11:32 *See note on v. 21.*

11:33 saw ... the Jews ... weeping. According to Jewish oral tradition, the funeral custom indicated that even a poor family must hire at least two flute players and a professional wailing woman to mourn the dead. Because the family may have been well-to-do, a rather large group appears present. **He was deeply moved in spirit and was troubled.** The phrase here does not mean merely that Jesus was deeply touched or moved with sympathy at the sight. The Gr. term "deeply moved" always suggests anger, outrage, or emotional indignation (see v. 38; cf. Mt 9:30; Mk 1:43; 14:5). Most likely Jesus was angered at the emotional grief of the people because it implicitly revealed unbelief in the resurrection and the temporary nature of death. The group was acting like pagans who had no hope (1Th 4:13). While grief is understandable, the group was acting in despair, thus indicating a tacit denial of the resurrection and the Scripture that promised it. Jesus may also have been angered because He was indignant at the pain and sorrow in death that sin brought into the human condition.

11:35 Jesus wept. The Gr. word here has the connotation of silently bursting into tears in contrast to the loud lament of the group (see v. 33). His tears here were not generated out of mourning, since He was to raise Lazarus, but out of grief for a fallen world entangled in sin-caused sorrow and death. He was "a man of sorrows and acquainted with grief" (Is 53:3).

11:39 stench. Although Jews used aromatic spices, their custom was not to embalm the body, but to use the spices to counteract the repulsive odors from decomposition. They would wrap the body in linen cloth, adding spice in the layers and folds. The Jews did not wrap the body tightly like Egyptian mummies, but rather loosely with the head wrapped separately. This is indicated by the fact that Lazarus could move out of the tomb before he was unwrapped (v. 44; cf. 20:7).

11:41, 42 Jesus' prayer was not really a petition, but thanksgiving to the Father. The reason for the miracle was to authenticate His claims to be the Messiah and Son of God.

11:43 This was a preview of the power to be fully displayed in the final resurrection when all the dead hear the voice of the Son of God and live (5:25, 28, 29).

11:45, 46 Jesus' teaching and actions often divided the Jews (e.g., 6:14, 15; 7:10–13, 45–52). While some believed (cf. v. 40), others, apparently with malicious intent, informed the Pharisees of Jesus' action.

11:47 convened a council. Alerted by the Pharisees, a Sanhedrin committee consisting of chief priests (former High Priests and members of High Priestly families) and Pharisees called the Sanhedrin to session. The Pharisees could not by themselves take any judicial action against Jesus. Though subject to Roman control, the Sanhedrin was the highest judicial body in Israel and exercised judicial, legislative, and executive powers at that time. In Jesus' day, the 70 members of the Sanhedrin were dominated by the chief priests, and virtually all the priests were Sadducees. The Pharisees constituted an influential minority. While the Pharisees and Sadducees were often in conflict, their mutual hatred of Jesus united them into action.

11:48 the Romans will come. The Jews were not willing to believe in Jesus as the Son of God even though Lazarus had been raised. They feared that escalating messianic expectations could start a movement against Roman oppression and occupation that would cause the Romans to come and take away all their rights and freedoms.

11:49 Caiaphas. Caiaphas became High Priest ca. A.D. 18, being appointed by the Roman prefect, Valerius Gratus. His father-in-law was Annas, who had previously functioned in that same position from ca. A.D. 7–14 and who exercised great influence over the office even after his tenure (see 18:12–14). Caiaphas remained in office until A.D. 36 when, along with Pontius Pilate, he was removed by the Romans. He took a leading part in the trial and condemnation of Jesus. In his court or palace, the chief priests (Sadducees) and Pharisees assembled "and plotted together to seize Jesus by stealth and kill Him" (see Mt 26:3, 4).

11:50 one man die for the people. He only meant that Jesus should be executed in order to spare their own positions and nation from Roman reprisals, but Caiaphas unwittingly used sacrificial, substitutionary language and

not perish." 51 Now he did not say this [a]on his own
initiative, but [A]being high priest that year, he prophesied that Jesus was going to die for the nation,
52 and not for the nation only, but in order that He
might also [A]gather together into one the children of
God who are scattered abroad. 53 So from that day
on they [A]planned together to kill Him.

54 Therefore Jesus [A]no longer continued to walk
publicly among the Jews, but went away from there
to the country near the wilderness, into a city called
[B]Ephraim; and there He stayed with the disciples.

55 Now [A]the Passover of the Jews was near, and
many went up to Jerusalem out of the country before the Passover [B]to purify themselves. 56 So they
[A]were seeking for Jesus, and were saying to one
another as they stood in the temple, "What do you
think; that He will not come to the feast at all?"
57 Now [A]the chief priests and the Pharisees had given
orders that if anyone knew where He was, he was
to report it, so that they might seize Him.

MARY ANOINTS JESUS

12 [A]Jesus, therefore, six days before [B]the Passover, came to [C]Bethany where Lazarus was,
whom Jesus had raised from the dead. 2 So they
made Him a supper there, and [A]Martha was serving;
but Lazarus was one of those reclining *at the table* with Him. 3 [A]Mary then took a [a]pound of very
costly [B]perfume of pure nard, and anointed the feet
of Jesus and wiped His feet with her hair; and the
house was filled with the fragrance of the perfume.
4 But [A]Judas Iscariot, one of His disciples, who was
intending to [a]betray Him, *said, 5 "Why was this perfume not sold for [a]three hundred denarii and given
to poor *people?*" 6 Now he said this, not because he
was concerned about the poor, but because he was
a thief, and as he [A]had the money box, he used to
pilfer [B]what was put into it. 7 Therefore Jesus said,
"Let her alone, so that she may keep [a]it for [A]the day
of My burial. 8 [A]For you always have the poor with
you, but you do not always have Me."

9 The [A]large crowd of the Jews then learned that
He was there; and they came, not for Jesus' sake
only, but that they might also see Lazarus, [B]whom
He raised from the dead. 10 But the chief priests
planned to put Lazarus to death also; 11 because
[A]on account of him [B]many of the Jews were going
away and were believing in Jesus.

JESUS ENTERS JERUSALEM

12 On the next day [A]the large crowd who had
come to [B]the feast, when they heard that Jesus was

11:51 [a]Lit *from himself* [A]John 18:13 11:52 [A]John 10:16 11:53 [A]Matt 26:4 11:54 [A]John 7:1 [B]2 Chr 13:19 mg 11:55 [A]Matt 26:1f; Mark 14:1; Luke 22:1; John 2:13; 12:1; 13:1 [B]Num 9:10; 2 Chr 30:17f; John 18:28 11:56 [A]John 7:11 11:57 [A]John 11:47 12:1 [A]John 12:1-8: *Matt 26:6-13; Mark 14:3-9; Luke 7:37-39* [B]John 11:55; 12:20 [C]Matt 21:17; John 11:43f 12:2 [A]Luke 10:38 12:3 [a]I.e. a Roman pound, equaling 12 oz [A]Luke 7:37f; John 11:2 [B]Mark 14:3 12:4 [a]Or *hand Him over* [A]John 6:71 12:5 [a]Equivalent to 11 months' wages 12:6 [A]John 13:29 [B]Luke 8:3 12:7 [a]I.e. the custom of preparing the body for burial [A]John 19:40 12:8 [A]Deut 15:11; Matt 26:11; Mark 14:7 12:9 [A]Mark 12:37; John 12:12 mg [B]John 11:43f; 12:1, 17f 12:11 [A]John 11:45f; 12:18 [B]John 7:31; 11:42 12:12 [A]John 12:12-15: *Matt 21:4-9; Mark 11:7-10; Luke 19:35-38* [B]John 12:1

prophesied the death of Christ for sinners. Cf. 2Co 5:21; 1Pe 2:24.

11:51 he prophesied. Caiaphas did not realize the implications of what he spoke. While he uttered blasphemy against Christ, God parodied his statement into truth (cf. Ps 76:10). The responsibility for the wicked meaning of his words belonged to Caiaphas, but God's providence directed the choice of words so as to express the heart of God's glorious plan of salvation (Ac 4:27, 28). He actually was used by God as a prophet because he was the High Priest and originally the High Priest was the means of God's will being revealed (2Sa 15:27).

11:52 gather together into one the children of God. In context, this had reference to believing Jews of the dispersion who would be gathered together in the Promised Land to share the kingdom of God (Is 43:5; Eze 34:12). In a wider sense, this also anticipated the Gentile mission (see 12:32). As a result of Christ's sacrificial death and resurrection, both Jew and Gentile have been made into one group, the church (Eph 2:11–18).

11:53 from that day on. The phrase indicates that their course of action toward Jesus was then fixed. It remained only to accomplish it. Notice that Jesus was not arrested to be tried. He had already been judged guilty of blasphemy. The trial was a mere formality for a sentence already passed (Mk 14:1, 2).

11:54 Ephraim. This probably refers to the OT city of Ephron (see 2Ch 13:19). Its modern village name is Et-Taiyibeh, and it is located 4 mi. NE of Bethel and about 12 mi. from Jerusalem. The location was far enough away for temporary safety until the time of Passover (v. 55).

11:55 Passover. This is the third Passover mentioned in John (see 2:13; 6:4) and the last in Jesus' earthly ministry at which His sacrificial death occurred. For the chronology of the Passover Week, see Introduction to Luke: Outline.

11:56 they were seeking for Jesus. The Jews who filled Jerusalem for Passover were wondering if Jesus would show Himself at this time and were actively seeking to find Him. The plot of the chief priests and Pharisees (see v. 47; 7:12) was known widely enough to pique their curiosity as to whether Jesus would dare show Himself in Jerusalem.

11:57 if anyone knew. The plotters ensured that the whole city was filled with potential informants.

12:1–50 This chapter focuses on the reactions of love and hate, belief and rejection toward Christ, leading to the cross.

12:1 six days before the Passover. This most likely was the previous Saturday with Passover coming 6 days later on Thursday evening through sunset Friday. See Introduction: Interpretive Challenges.

12:3 a pound of very costly perfume of pure nard. The term used for "pound" actually indicates a weight around three-fourths of a pound (approximately 12 ounces). "Nard" was an oil extracted from the root of a plant grown in India. **anointed the feet of Jesus.** Since those who were eating reclined at the table, their feet extended away from it, making it possible for Mary to anoint the feet of Jesus. The act symbolized Mary's humble devotion and love for Him.

12:5 three hundred denarii. Since one denarius was a day's wage given to common laborers, 300 was equivalent to a year's wages (no money was earned on the Sabbath or other holy days).

12:6 a thief. Judas' altruism was really a front for his own personal avarice. Because he was the apostolic band's treasurer, he was able to secretly pilfer the group treasury for his own desires.

12:7 keep it for the day of My burial. Mary performed this act to signal her devotion but, as in the case of Caiaphas (11:49–52), her act revealed more than she realized at the time. During the first century, lavish sums were spent on funerals, which included costly perfumes to cover the smell of decay (*see note on 11:39*).

12:8 This does not mean that alms should not be distributed to the poor (Dt 15:11) but was a reminder that, while the poor would remain, Jesus would not always be with them. See Mt 26:11; Mk 14:7.

12:11 going away . . . believing. This phrase signaled both a conscious, deliberate move away from the religion of the authorities and a move toward genuine faith in Jesus as Messiah and Son of God.

12:12–19 This section marks Jesus' triumphal entry into Jerusalem. It is one of the few incidents in Jesus' life reported in all 4 Gospels (Mt 21:1–11; Mk 11:1–11; Lk 19:29–38). By this action, He presented Himself officially to the nation as the Messiah and Son of God. The Sanhedrin and other Jewish leaders wanted Him dead but did not want Him killed during the Passover time because they feared stirring up the multitudes with whom He was popular (Mt 26:5; Mk 14:2; Lk 22:2). Jesus entered the city, however, on His own time and forced the whole issue in order that it might happen exactly on the Passover day when the lambs were being sacrificed. As the Scripture says, "Christ, our Passover, also has been sacrificed" (1Co 5:7). In God's perfect timing (see 7:30; 8:20), at the precise time foreordained from eternity, He presented Himself to die (v. 23; 10:17, 18; 17:1; 19:10, 11; cf. Ac 2:23; 4:27, 28; Gal 4:4).

12:12 the next day. The day after the

coming to Jerusalem, 13 took the branches of the
palm trees and went out to meet Him, and *began*
to shout, "[A]Hosanna! Blessed is He who comes in
the name of the Lord, even the [B]King of Israel."
14 Jesus, finding a young donkey, sat on it; as it is
written, 15 "[A]Fear not, daughter of Zion; behold,
your King is coming, seated on a donkey's colt."
16 [A]These things His disciples did not understand at
the first; but when Jesus [B]was glorified, then they
remembered that these things were written of Him,
and that they had done these things to Him. 17 So
[A]the [a]people, who were with Him when He called
Lazarus out of the tomb and raised him from the
dead, continued to testify *about Him.* 18 [A]For this
reason also the [a]people went and met Him, [B]because
they heard that He had performed this [b]sign. 19 So
the Pharisees said to one another, "You see that
you are not doing any good; look, the world has
gone after Him."

GREEKS SEEK JESUS

20 Now there were some [A]Greeks among those
who were going up to worship at [B]the feast; 21 these
then came to [A]Philip, who was from [B]Bethsaida of
Galilee, and *began to* ask him, saying, "Sir, we wish
to see Jesus." 22 Philip *came and *told [A]Andrew; Andrew and Philip *came and *told Jesus. 23 And Jesus
*answered them, saying, "[A]The hour has come for
the Son of Man to [B]be glorified. 24 Truly, truly, I say
to you, [A]unless a grain of wheat falls into the earth
and dies, it remains alone; but if it dies, it bears
much fruit. 25 [A]He who loves his [a]life loses it, and
he who [B]hates his [a]life in this world will keep it to
life eternal. 26 If anyone [a]serves Me, he must follow
Me; and [A]where I am, there My servant will be also;
if anyone [a]serves Me, the Father will [B]honor him.

JESUS FORETELLS HIS DEATH

27 "[A]Now My soul has become troubled; and what
shall I say, '[B]Father, save Me from [C]this hour'? But
for this purpose I came to this hour. 28 [A]Father, glorify Your name." Then a [B]voice came out of heaven:
"I have both glorified it, and will glorify it again."
29 So the crowd *of people* who stood by and heard
it were saying that it had thundered; others were
saying, "[A]An angel has spoken to Him." 30 Jesus
answered and said, "[A]This voice has not come for
My sake, but for your sakes. 31 [A]Now judgment is
upon this world; now [B]the ruler of this world will
be cast out. 32 And I, if I [A]am lifted up from the
earth, will [B]draw all men to Myself." 33 But He was
saying this [A]to indicate the kind of death by which
He was to die. 34 The crowd then answered Him, "We
have heard out of [A]the Law that [a,B]the Christ is to
remain forever; and how can You say, 'The [C]Son of
Man must be [D]lifted up'? Who is this [C]Son of Man?"

12:13 [A]Ps 118:26 [B]John 1:49 12:15 [A]Zech 9:9 12:16 [A]Mark 9:32; John 2:22; 14:26 [B]John 7:39; 12:23 12:17 [a]Lit *crowd* [A]John 11:42 12:18 [a]Lit *crowd* [b]Or *attesting miracle* [A]Luke 19:37; John 12:12 [B]John 12:11 12:20 [A]John 7:35 [B]John 12:1 12:21 [A]John 1:44 [B]Matt 11:21 12:22 [A]John 1:44 12:23 [A]Matt 26:45; Mark 14:35, 41; John 13:1; 17:1 [B]John 7:39; 12:16; 13:32 12:24 [A]Rom 14:9; 1 Cor 15:36 12:25 [a]Lit *soul* [A]Matt 10:39; 16:25; Mark 8:35; Luke 9:24; 17:33 [B]Luke 14:26 12:26 [a]Or *is serving* [A]John 14:3; 17:24; 2 Cor 5:8; Phil 1:23; 1 Thess 4:17 [B]1 Sam 2:30; Ps 91:15; Luke 12:37 12:27 [A]Matt 26:38; Mark 14:34; John 11:33 [B]Matt 11:25 [C]John 12:23 12:28 [A]Matt 11:25 [B]Matt 3:17; 17:5; Mark 1:11; 9:7; Luke 3:22; 9:35 12:29 [A]Acts 23:9 12:30 [A]John 11:42 12:31 [A]John 3:19; 9:39; 16:11 [B]John 14:30; 16:11; 2 Cor 4:4; Eph 2:2; 6:12; 1 John 4:4; 5:19 12:32 [A]John 3:14; 8:28; 12:34 [B]John 6:44 12:33 [A]John 18:32; 21:19 12:34 [a]I.e. the Messiah [A]John 10:34 [B]Ps 110:4; Is 9:7; Ezek 37:25; Dan 7:14 [C]Matt 8:20 [D]John 3:14; 8:28; 12:32

crowds came to visit Him and Lazarus in Bethany (cf. 12:9). Jesus arrived in Bethany on Saturday (see note on 12:1). Then on Sunday a great number of Jews visited Him, angering the Jewish leaders (12:9–11). It would not have been until the following day (Monday) that Jesus prepared to enter Jerusalem through the East Gate of the city.

12:13 took the branches of the palm trees. The supply of date palms was plentiful; they still grow in Jerusalem today. From about two centuries earlier, the waving of palm branches had become a national, if not nationalistic, symbol, which signaled the fervent hope that a messianic liberator was arriving on the scene (6:14, 15). **Hosanna!** The term "hosanna" is a transliteration of a Heb. word that means "give salvation now." It was a term of acclamation or praise occurring in Ps 118:25 which was familiar to every Jew, since that psalm was part of the Hallel (Pss 113–118) sung each morning by the temple choir during the Feast of Tabernacles (7:37) and associated with the Feast of Dedication (10:22) and especially the Passover. After shouting out the "Hosanna," the crowds shouted Ps 118:26; significantly, the original context of Ps 118 may well have been the pronouncement of blessing upon a Davidic king. Jewish commentaries have understood the verse to bear messianic implications. "HE WHO COMES IN THE NAME OF THE LORD" refers to Messiah, especially in context with the phrase, "the King of Israel," though that messianic title is not from Ps 118.

12:14, 15 The Synoptic Gospels give more information here regarding Jesus' selection of a young donkey (see Mt 21:1–9; Mk 11:1–10; Lk 19:29–38). They convey the fact that Jesus deliberately planned to present Himself to the nation in this manner as a conscious fulfillment of the messianic prophecy of Zec 9:9 (quoted here). The words, "FEAR NOT," are not found in the Zechariah passage but were added from Is 40:9. Only after His ascension did the disciples grasp the meaning of the triumphal entry (cf. 14:26).

12:19 the world has gone after Him. "The world" means the people in general, as opposed to everyone in particular. Clearly, most people in the world did not even know of Jesus at that time, and many in Israel did not believe in Him. Often, "world" is used in this general sense (v. 47; 1:29; 3:17; 4:42; 14:22; 17:9, 21).

12:20, 21 Most likely Gentile proselytes to Judaism who had come up for the Passover and who, in their desire to see Jesus, stood in direct antithesis to the attitude of the national leaders who desired to kill Him. At the very moment when the Jewish authorities plotted virulently to kill Him, Gentiles began to desire His attention.

12:23 hour. Refers to the time of Jesus' death, resurrection, and exaltation (v. 27; 13:1; 17:1). Up to this point, Jesus' hour had always been future (2:4; 4:21, 23; 7:30; 8:20). **Son of Man.** *See note on 1:51.*

12:24 As the sown kernel dies to bring forth a rich harvest, so also the death of the Son of God will result in the salvation of many.

12:25, 26 Not only is the principle of death applicable to Jesus (see v. 24), but it is also applicable to His followers. They, too, as His disciples may have to lose their life in service and witness for Him (see Mt 10:37–39; 16:24, 25).

12:27 My soul has become troubled. The term used here is strong and signifies horror, anxiety, and agitation. Jesus' contemplation of taking on the wrath of God for the sins of the world caused revulsion in the sinless Savior (cf. 2Co 5:21).

12:28 glorify Your name. This request embodied the principle that Jesus lived by and would die by. See 7:18; 8:29, 50. **I have . . . and will glorify.** The Father answered the Son in an audible voice. This is only one of 3 instances during Jesus' ministry when this took place (cf. Mt 3:17—His baptism; 17:5—His transfiguration).

12:31 the ruler of this world. A reference to Satan (see 14:30; 16:11; cf. Mt 4:8, 9; Lk 4:6, 7; 2Co 4:4; Eph 2:2; 6:12). Although the cross might have appeared to signal Satan's victory over God, in reality it marked Satan's defeat (cf. Ro 16:20; Heb 2:14).

12:32 lifted up from the earth. This refers to His crucifixion (v. 33; 18:32). *See note on 3:14.*

12:34 remain forever. The term "Law" was used broadly enough to include not only the 5 books of Moses but also the whole of the OT (see Ro 10:4). Perhaps they had in mind Is 9:7 which promised that Messiah's kingdom would last forever, or Eze 37:25 where God promised that the final David would be Israel's prince forever (see also Ps 89:35–37).

35 So Jesus said to them, "[A]For a little while longer
[B]the Light is among you. [C]Walk while you have the
Light, so that darkness will not overtake you; he
who [D]walks in the darkness does not know where
he goes. 36 While you have the Light, [A]believe in
the Light, so that you may become [B]sons of Light."
These things Jesus spoke, and He went away
and [a,C]hid Himself from them. 37 But though He had
performed so many [a]signs before them, *yet* they
were not believing in Him. 38 *This was* to fulfill the
word of Isaiah the prophet which he spoke: "[A]LORD,
WHO HAS BELIEVED OUR REPORT? AND TO WHOM HAS
THE ARM OF THE LORD BEEN REVEALED?" 39 For this
reason they could not believe, for Isaiah said again,
40 "[A]HE HAS BLINDED THEIR EYES AND HE [B]HARDENED
THEIR HEART, SO THAT THEY WOULD NOT SEE WITH
THEIR EYES AND PERCEIVE WITH THEIR HEART, AND
[a]BE CONVERTED AND I HEAL THEM." 41 These things
Isaiah said because [A]he saw His glory, and [B]he
spoke of Him. 42 Nevertheless [A]many even of [B]the
rulers believed in Him, but [C]because of the Pharisees they were not confessing *Him,* for fear that
they would be [a,D]put out of the synagogue; 43 [A]for
they loved the [a]approval of men rather than the
[a]approval of God.

44 And Jesus cried out and said, "[A]He who believes in Me, does not believe in Me but in Him who
sent Me. 45 [A]He who sees Me sees the One who sent
Me. 46 [A]I have come *as* Light into the world, so that
everyone who believes in Me will not remain in
darkness. 47 If anyone hears My sayings and does
not keep them, I do not judge him; for [A]I did not
come to judge the world, but to save the world.
48 [A]He who rejects Me and does not receive My sayings, has one who judges him; [B]the word I spoke is
what will judge him at [C]the last day. 49 [A]For I did not
speak [a]on My own initiative, but the Father Himself
who sent Me [B]has given Me a commandment *as to*
what to say and what to speak. 50 I know that [A]His
commandment is eternal life; therefore the things
I speak, I speak [B]just as the Father has told Me."

THE LORD'S SUPPER

13 Now before the Feast of [A]the Passover, Jesus
knowing that [B]His hour had come that He
would depart out of this world [C]to the Father,
having loved His own who were in the world,
He loved them [a]to the end. 2 During supper, [A]the
devil having already put into the heart of [B]Judas
Iscariot, *the son* of Simon, to betray Him, 3 *Jesus,*
[A]knowing that the Father had given all things into
His hands, and that [B]He had come forth from God
and was going back to God, 4 *got up from supper,
and *laid aside His garments; and taking a towel,
He [A]girded Himself.

JESUS WASHES THE DISCIPLES' FEET

5 Then He *poured water into the basin, and began to [A]wash the disciples' feet and to wipe them
with the towel with which He was girded. 6 So He

12:35 [A]John 7:33; 9:4 [B]John 12:46; 1 John 2:10 [C]Gal 6:10; Eph 5:8 [D]1 John 1:6; 2:11 12:36 [a]Lit *was hidden* [A]John 12:46 [B]Luke 16:8; John 8:12 [C]John 8:59 12:37 [a]Or *attesting signs* 12:38 [A]Is 53:1; Rom 10:16 12:40 [a]Lit *be turned;* i.e. turn about [A]Is 6:10; Matt 13:14f [B]Mark 6:52 12:41 [A]Is 6:1ff [B]Luke 24:27 12:42 [a]I.e. excommunicated [A]John 7:48; 12:11 [B]Luke 23:13 [C]John 7:13 [D]John 9:22 12:43 [a]Or *glory* [A]John 5:41, 44 12:44 [A]Matt 10:40; John 5:24 12:45 [A]John 14:9 12:46 [A]John 1:4; 3:19; 8:12; 9:5; 12:35f 12:47 [A]John 3:17; 8:15f 12:48 [A]Luke 10:16 [B]Deut 18:18f; John 5:45ff; 8:47 [C]Matt 10:15; John 6:39; Acts 17:31; 1 Pet 1:5; 2 Pet 3:3, 7; Heb 10:25 12:49 [a]Lit *of Myself* [A]John 3:11; 7:16; 8:26, 28, 38; 14:10, 24 [B]John 14:31; 17:8 12:50 [A]John 6:68 [B]John 5:19; 8:28 13:1 [a]Or *to the uttermost;* or *eternally* [A]John 2:13; 11:55 [B]John 12:23 [C]John 13:3; 16:28 13:2 [A]John 6:70; 13:27 [B]John 6:71 13:3 [A]John 3:35 [B]John 8:42 13:4 [A]Luke 12:37; 17:8 13:5 [A]Gen 18:4; 19:2; 43:24; Judg 19:21; Luke 7:44; 1 Tim 5:10

12:35, 36 Jesus said to them. A final invitation from Jesus was recorded by John to focus on his theme of believing in the Messiah and Son of God (see 20:30, 31).

12:37–40 In these verses, John gave the scriptural explanation for such large-scale, catastrophic unbelief on the part of the Jewish nation. The explanation was that the unbelief was not only foreseen in Scripture but necessitated by it. In v. 38, John quotes Is 53:1 and in v. 40 he quotes Is 6:10 (see Ro 10:16), both of which stress the sovereign plan of God in His judicial hardening of Israel (cf. Paul's argument in Ro 9–11). Although God predestined such judgment, it was not apart from human responsibility and culpability (see 8:24).

12:41 Isaiah . . . saw His glory, and . . . spoke of Him. This is a reference to Isaiah 6:1 (*see notes there*). John unambiguously ties Jesus to God or Yahweh of the OT (*see note on 8:58*). Therefore, since v. 41 refers to Jesus, it makes Him the author of the judicial hardening of Israel. That fits His role as Judge (see 5:22, 23, 27, 30; 9:39).

12:42, 43 The indictment of vv. 37–41 is followed by the exceptions of vv. 42, 43 (see 1:10, 11 vs. 1:12, 13). While the people seemed to trust Jesus with much more candor and fervency, the leaders of Israel who believed in Him demonstrated inadequate, irresolute, even spurious faith (*see note on 2:23–25*). The faith of the latter was so weak that they refused to take any position that would threaten their position in the synagogue. This is one of the saddest statements about spiritual leadership, for they preferred the praises of men above the praises of God in their refusal to publicly acknowledge Jesus as Messiah and Son of God.

13:1–17:16 In these remaining chapters before His crucifixion, the record looks at Jesus' devoting Himself to His own disciples. While chaps. 1–12 center on the rejection of Jesus by the nation (cf. 1:11), chaps. 13–17 center on those who did receive Him (see 1:12). Beginning in chap. 13, Jesus moved completely away from public ministry to private ministry with those who had received Him. Chapters 13–17 were spoken by Jesus as a farewell on the night of His betrayal and arrest to communicate His coming legacy to His followers (chaps. 13–16) and pray for them (chap. 17). The cross was only one day away.

13:1 to the end. Meaning "to perfection" with perfect love. God loves the world (3:16), and sinners (3:16; Mt 5:44, 45; Tit 3:4) with compassion and common grace, but loves His own with perfect, saving, eternal love.

13:2 supper. Passover on Thursday night after sunset. See Introduction: Interpretive Challenges. **the devil . . . the heart of Judas.** This does not exonerate Judas, because his wicked heart desired exactly what the devil desired, the death of Jesus. The devil and Judas were in accord.

13:3 going back to God. Jesus faced the betrayal, agony, and death because He knew He would be exalted to the Father afterward, where He would receive the glory and fellowship He had eternally enjoyed within the Trinity (see 17:4, 5). This was the "joy set before Him" that enabled Him to "endure the cross" (Heb 12:2).

13:4, 5 The dusty and dirty conditions of the region necessitated the need for footwashing. Although the disciples most likely would have been happy to wash Jesus' feet, they could not conceive of washing one another's feet. This was because in the society of the time footwashing was reserved for the lowliest of menial servants. Peers did not wash one another's feet, except very rarely and as a mark of great love. Luke points out (22:24) that they were arguing about who was the greatest of them, so that none was willing to stoop to wash feet. When Jesus moved to wash their feet, they were shocked. His actions serve also as symbolic of spiritual cleansing (vv. 6–9) and a model of Christian humility (vv. 12–17). Through this action Jesus taught the lesson of selfless service that was supremely exemplified by His death on the cross.

13:6–10 These proceedings embarrassed all of the disciples. While others remained silent, Peter, perhaps on behalf of others (see Mt 16:13–23), spoke up in indignation that Jesus would stoop so low as to wash his feet. He failed to see beyond the humble service

*came to Simon Peter. He *said to Him, "Lord, do
You wash my feet?" 7 Jesus answered and said to
him, "What I do you do not realize now, but you
will understand [A]hereafter." 8 Peter *said to Him,
"Never shall You wash my feet!" Jesus answered
him, "[A]If I do not wash you, [B]you have no part with
Me." 9 Simon Peter *said to Him, "Lord, *then wash*
not only my feet, but also my hands and my head."
10 Jesus *said to him, "He who has bathed needs
only to wash his feet, but is completely clean; and
[A]you are clean, but not all *of you.*" 11 For [A]He knew
the one who was betraying Him; for this reason He
said, "Not all of you are clean."

12 So when He had washed their feet, and [A]taken
His garments and reclined *at the table* again, He
said to them, "Do you know what I have done to
you? 13 You call Me [A]Teacher and [B]Lord; and [a]you
are right, for *so* I am. 14 If I then, [A]the Lord and the
Teacher, washed your feet, you also ought to wash
one another's feet. 15 For I gave you [A]an example
that you also should do as I did to you. 16 Truly,
truly, I say to you, [A]a slave is not greater than his
master, nor *is* [B]one who is sent greater than the one
who sent him. 17 If you know these things, you are
[A]blessed if you do them. 18 [A]I do not speak of all of
you. I know the ones I have [B]chosen; but *it is* [C]that
the Scripture may be fulfilled, '[D]HE WHO EATS MY
BREAD HAS LIFTED UP HIS HEEL AGAINST ME.' 19 From
now on [A]I am telling you before *it* comes to pass,
so that when it does occur, you may believe that [B]I
am *He.* 20 Truly, truly, I say to you, [A]he who receives
whomever I send receives Me; and he who receives
Me receives Him who sent Me."

JESUS PREDICTS HIS BETRAYAL

21 When Jesus had said this, He [A]became troubled
in spirit, and testified and said, "Truly, truly, I say
to you, that [B]one of you will [a]betray Me." 22 The disciples *began* looking at one another, [A]at a loss *to
know* of which one He was speaking. 23 There was
reclining on [A]Jesus' bosom one of His disciples,
[B]whom Jesus loved. 24 So Simon Peter *gestured to
him, and *said to him, "Tell *us* who it is of whom
He is speaking." 25 He, [A]leaning back thus on Jesus'
bosom, *said to Him, "Lord, who is it?" 26 Jesus then
*answered, "That is the one for whom I shall dip the
morsel and give it to him." So when He had dipped
the morsel, He *took and *gave it to Judas, [A]*the son*
of Simon Iscariot. 27 After the morsel, [A]Satan then
[B]entered into him. Therefore Jesus *said to him,
"What you do, do quickly." 28 Now no one of those
reclining *at the table* knew for what purpose He
had said this to him. 29 For some were supposing,
because Judas [A]had the money box, that Jesus was
saying to him, "Buy the things we have need of [B]for
the feast"; or else, that he should [C]give something
to the poor. 30 So after receiving the morsel he went
out immediately; and [A]it was night.

31 Therefore when he had gone out, Jesus *said,
"Now [a]is [A]the Son of Man [B]glorified, and [C]God [a]is
glorified in Him; 32 [a]if God is glorified in Him, [A]God
will also glorify Him in Himself, and will glorify
Him immediately. 33 [A]Little children, I am with you
[B]a little while longer. [C]You will seek Me; and as I
said to the Jews, now I also say to you, 'Where I am
going, you cannot come.' 34 A [A]new commandment
I give to you, [B]that you love one another, [C]even as I

13:7 [A]John 13:12ff 13:8 [A]Ps 51:2, 7; Ezek 36:25; Acts 22:16; 1 Cor 6:11; Heb 10:22 [B]Deut 12:12; 2 Sam 20:1; 1 Kin 12:16 13:10 [A]John 15:3; Eph 5:26 13:11 [A]John 6:64; 13:2 13:12 [A]John 13:4 13:13 [a]Lit *you say well* [A]John 11:28 [B]John 11:2; 1 Cor 12:3; Phil 2:11 13:14 [A]John 11:2; 1 Cor 12:3; Phil 2:11 13:15 [A]1 Pet 5:3 13:16 [A]Matt 10:24; Luke 6:40; John 15:20 [B]2 Cor 8:23; Phil 2:25 13:17 [A]Matt 7:24ff; Luke 11:28; James 1:25 13:18 [A]John 13:10f [B]John 6:70; 15:16, 19 [C]John 15:25; 17:12; 18:32; 19:24, 36 [D]Ps 41:9; Matt 26:21ff; Mark 14:18f; Luke 22:21ff; John 13:21, 22, 26 13:19 [A]John 14:29; 16:4 [B]John 8:24 13:20 [A]Matt 10:40; Mark 9:37; Luke 9:48; 10:16; Gal 4:14 13:21 [a]Or *hand Me over* [A]John 11:33 [B]Matt 26:21f; Mark 14:18ff; Luke 22:21ff; John 13:18, 22, 26 13:22 [A]Matt 26:21ff; Mark 14:18ff; Luke 22:21ff; John 13:18, 21, 26 13:23 [A]John 1:18 [B]John 19:26; 20:2; 21:7, 20 13:25 [A]John 21:20 13:26 [A]John 6:71 13:27 [A]Matt 4:10 [B]Luke 22:3; John 13:2 13:29 [A]John 12:6 [B]John 13:1 [C]John 12:5 13:30 [A]Luke 22:53 13:31 [a]Or *was* [A]Matt 8:20 [B]John 7:39 [C]John 14:13; 17:4; 1 Pet 4:11 13:32 [a]Most early mss do not contain this phrase [A]John 17:1 13:33 [A]1 John 2:1 [B]John 7:33 [C]John 7:34 13:34 [A]John 15:12, 17; 1 John 2:7f; 3:11, 23; 2 John 5 [B]Lev 19:18; Matt 5:44; Gal 5:14; 1 Thess 4:9; Heb 13:1; 1 Pet 1:22; 1 John 4:7 [C]Eph 5:2; 1 John 4:10f

itself to the symbolism of spiritual cleansing involved (v. 7; cf. 1Jn 1:7–9). Jesus' response made the real point of His actions clear: unless the Lamb of God cleanses a person's sin (i.e., as portrayed in the symbolism of washing), one can have no part with Him.

13:10 needs only to wash his feet. The cleansing that Christ does at salvation never needs to be repeated—atonement is complete at that point. But all who have been cleansed by God's gracious justification need constant washing in the experiential sense as they battle sin in the flesh. Believers are justified and granted imputed righteousness (Php 3:8, 9), but still need sanctification and personal righteousness (Php 3:12–14).

13:11, 12 Not all of you are clean. This verse refers to Judas (6:70), who was soon to lead the mob to capture Jesus (18:3).

13:15 an example. The word used here suggests both "example" and "pattern" (Heb 4:11; 8:5; 9:25; Jas 5:10; 2Pe 2:6). Jesus' purpose in this action was to establish the model of loving humility.

13:17 you are blessed if you do them. Joy is always tied to obedience to God's revealed Word (see 15:14).

13:18 the ones I have chosen. A reference to the 12 disciples whom the Lord had selected (see 15:16), whom the Lord knew perfectly, including Judas, who was chosen that the prophecy of Ps 41:9 would be fulfilled.

13:21 troubled. For the meaning of this word, *see note on 12:27.*

13:23 one of His disciples, whom Jesus loved. This is the first reference to John the apostle, the author of the gospel (see Introduction: Author and Date). He specifically mentioned himself at the cross (19:26, 27), at the empty tomb (20:2–9), by the Sea of Tiberias (21:1, 20–23), and in the next to last verse where he is referenced as the author of the gospel (21:24).

13:26 He ... gave it to Judas. The host at a feast (whose role was filled by Jesus) would dip into a common bowl and pull out a particularly tasty bit and pass it to a guest as a special mark of honor or friendship. Because Jesus passed it so easily to Judas, it has been suggested that he was seated near the Lord in a place of honor. Jesus was demonstrating a final gesture of His love for Judas even though he would betray Him.

13:27 Satan then entered into him. Judas was personally possessed by Satan himself in his betrayal of Jesus. *See note on v. 2.*

13:30 it was night. Although this was a historical reminiscence of John, the phrase may also be imbued with profound theological implications. It was the hour for Judas to be handed over completely to the power of darkness (Satan; cf. Lk 22:53).

13:31–33 glorified. With Judas gone, the final events were set in motion. Rather than looking at the agony of the cross, Jesus looked past the cross, anticipating the glory that He would have with the Father when it was over (see 17:4, 5; Heb 12:2).

13:33 as I said to the Jews. That statement is recorded in 8:21.

13:34, 35 Having announced His departure and having insisted that His disciples could not come with Him, Jesus began to lay out what He expected of them after His leaving. Love is to serve as the distinguishing characteristic of discipleship (v. 35; cf. 1Jn 2:7–11; 3:10–12; 4:7–10, 20, 21).

13:34 A new commandment ... as I have loved you. The commandment to love was not new. Deuteronomy 6:5 commanded love for God, and Lv 19:18 commanded loving one's neighbor as oneself (cf. Mt 22:34–40; Ro 13:8–10; Gal 5:14; Jas 2:8). However, Jesus' command regarding love presented a distinctly new standard for two reasons: 1) it

have loved you, that you also love one another. 35 [A]By
this all men will know that you are My disciples, if
you have love for one another."
36 Simon Peter *said to Him, "Lord, where are You
going?" Jesus answered, "[A]Where I go, you cannot
follow Me now; but [B]you will follow later." 37 Peter
*said to Him, "Lord, why can I not follow You right
now? [A]I will lay down my life for You." 38 Jesus *answered, "Will you lay down your life for Me? Truly,
truly, I say to you, [A]a rooster will not crow until you
deny Me three times.

JESUS COMFORTS HIS DISCIPLES

14 "[A]Do not let your heart be troubled; [a]believe in
God, believe also in Me. 2 In My Father's house
are many dwelling places; if it were not so, I would
have told you; for [A]I go to prepare a place for you. 3 If
I go and prepare a place for you, [A]I will come again
and receive you to Myself, that [B]where I am, *there*
you may be also. 4 And you know the way where I
am going." 5 [A]Thomas *said to Him, "Lord, we do not
know where You are going, how do we know the way?"
6 Jesus *said to him, "I am [A]the way, and [B]the truth, and
[C]the life; no one comes to the Father but through Me.

ONENESS WITH THE FATHER

7 [A]If you had known Me, you would have known
My Father also; from now on you [B]know Him, and
have [C]seen Him."
8 [A]Philip *said to Him, "Lord, show us the Father, and it is enough for us." 9 Jesus *said to him,
"Have I been so long with you, and *yet* you have
not come to know Me, Philip? [A]He who has seen
Me has seen the Father; how *can* you say, 'Show us
the Father'? 10 Do you not believe that [A]I am in the
Father, and the Father is in Me? [B]The words that I
say to you I do not speak on My own initiative, but
the Father abiding in Me does His works. 11 Believe
Me that [A]I am in the Father and the Father is in
Me; otherwise [B]believe because of the works themselves. 12 Truly, truly, I say to you, he who believes
in Me, the works that I do, he will do also; and
[A]greater *works* than these he will do; because [B]I
go to the Father. 13 [A]Whatever you ask in My name,
that will I do, so that [B]the Father may be glorified
in the Son. 14 If you ask Me anything [A]in My name,
I will do *it*.
15 "[A]If you love Me, you will keep My commandments.

13:35 [A]1 John 3:14; 4:20 13:36 [A]John 13:33; 14:2; 16:5 [B]John 21:18f; 2 Pet 1:14 13:37 [A]John 13:37, 38: *Matt 26:33-35; Mark 14:29-31; Luke 22:33-34* 13:38 [A]Mark 14:30; John 18:27 14:1 [a]Or *you believe in God* [A]John 14:27; 16:22, 24 14:2 [A]John 13:33, 36 14:3 [A]John 14:18, 28 [B]John 12:26 14:5 [A]John 11:16 14:6 [A]John 10:9; Rom 5:2; Eph 2:18; Heb 10:20 [B]John 1:14 [C]John 1:4; 11:25; 1 John 5:20 14:7 [A]John 8:19 [B]1 John 2:13 [C]John 6:46 14:8 [A]John 1:43 14:9 [A]John 1:14; 12:45; Col 1:15; Heb 1:3 14:10 [A]John 10:38; 14:11, 20 [B]John 5:19; 14:24 14:11 [A]John 10:38; 14:10, 20 [B]John 5:36 14:12 [A]John 4:37f; 5:20 [B]John 7:33; 14:28 14:13 [A]Matt 7:7 [B]John 13:31 14:14 [A]John 15:16; 16:23f 14:15 [A]John 14:21, 23; 15:10; 1 John 5:3; 2 John 6

was sacrificial love modeled after His love ("as I have loved you"; cf. 15:13), and 2) it is produced through the New Covenant by the transforming power of the Holy Spirit (cf. Jer 31:29–34; Eze 36:24–26; Gal 5:22).

13:36 you cannot follow. His work was nearly finished, but theirs was just beginning (Mt 28:16–20; Mk 16:15; Lk 24:47). Particularly, Peter had a work to do (*see notes on 21:15–19*). Only Jesus, as the sinless sacrifice for the trespasses of the world, could go to the cross and die (1Pe 2:22–24). Also, only He could be glorified in the presence of the Father with the glory that He possessed before His incarnation (see 12:41; 17:1–5).

13:38 See 18:25–27; cf. Mt 26:71–75; Mk 14:69–72; Lk 22:54–62.

14:1–31 This whole chapter centers in the promise that Christ is the One who gives the believer comfort, not only in His future return but also in the present with the ministry of the Holy Spirit (v. 26). The scene continues to be the upper room where the disciples had gathered with Jesus before He was arrested. Judas had been dismissed (13:30), and Jesus had begun His valedictory address to the remaining 11. The world of the disciples was about to be shattered; they would be bewildered, confused, and ridden with anxiety because of the events that would soon transpire. Anticipating their devastation, Jesus spoke to comfort their hearts.

14:1 Instead of the disciples lending support to Jesus in the hours before His cross, He had to support them spiritually as well as emotionally. This reveals His heart of serving love (cf. Mt 20:26–28). **troubled.** Faith in Him can stop the heart from being agitated. *See note on 12:27.*

14:2 dwelling places. Lit. rooms, or even apartments (in modern terms). All are in the large "Father's house."

14:2, 3 I go to prepare. His departure would be for their advantage since He was going away to prepare a heavenly home for them and will return to take them so that they may be with Him. This is one of the passages that refers to the rapture of the saints at the end of the age when Christ returns. The features in this description do not describe Christ coming to earth with His saints to establish His kingdom (Rev 19:11–15), but taking believers from earth to live in heaven. Since no judgment on the unsaved is described here, this is not the event of His return in glory and power to destroy the wicked (cf. Mt 13:36–43, 47–50). Rather, this describes His coming to gather His own who are alive and raise the bodies of those who have died to take them all to heaven. This rapture event is also described in 1Co 15:51–54; 1Th 4:13–18. After being raptured, the church will celebrate the marriage supper (Rev 19:7–10), be rewarded (1Co 3:10–15; 4:5; 2Co 5:9, 10), and later return to earth with Christ when He comes again to set up His kingdom (Rev 19:11–20:6).

14:6 This is the sixth "I am" statement of Jesus in John (see 6:35; 8:12; 10:7, 9; 10:11, 14; 11:25; 15:1, 5). In response to Thomas' query (v. 4), Jesus declared that He is the way to God because He is the truth of God (1:14) and the life of God (1:4; 3:15; 11:25). In this verse, the exclusiveness of Jesus as the only approach to the Father is emphatic. Only one way, not many ways, exist to God, i.e., Jesus Christ (10:7–9; cf. Mt 7:13, 14; Lk 13:24; Ac 4:12).

14:7–11 from now on you know Him. They know God because they had come to know Christ in His ministry and soon in His death and resurrection. To know Him is to know God. This constant emphasis on Jesus as God incarnate is unmistakably clear in this gospel (v. 11; 1:1–3, 14, 17, 18; 5:10–23, 26; 8:58; 9:35; 10:30, 38; 12:41; 17:1–5; 20:28).

14:12 greater *works* than these he will do. Jesus did not mean greater works in power, but in extent. They would become witnesses to all the world through the power of the indwelling and infilling of the Holy Spirit (Ac 1:8) and would bring many to salvation because of the Comforter dwelling in them. The focus is on spiritual rather than physical miracles. The book of Acts constitutes the beginning historical record of the impact that the Spirit-empowered disciples had on the world (cf. Ac 17:6). **because I go to the Father.** The only way Jesus' disciples would be able to be used to do those greater works was through the power of the Holy Spirit and He could not be sent as the Comforter until Jesus returned to the Father (v. 26; 7:39).

14:13, 14 In their hour of loss at the departure of Jesus, He comforted them with the means that would provide them with the necessary resources to accomplish their task without His immediate presence which they had come to depend upon. To ask in Jesus' "name" does not mean to tack such an expression on the end of a prayer as a mere formula. It means: 1) the believer's prayer should be for His purposes and kingdom and not selfish reasons; 2) the believer's prayer should be on the basis of His merits and not any personal merit or worthiness; and 3) the believer's prayer should be in pursuit of His glory alone. *See note on 16:26–28;* on the disciples' prayer, *see notes on Mt 6:9, 10.*

14:15–31 In these verses, Jesus promises believers comfort from 5 supernatural blessings that the world does not enjoy: 1) a supernatural Helper (vv. 15–17); 2) a supernatural life (vv. 18, 19); 3) a supernatural union (vv. 20–25), 4) a supernatural teacher (v. 26); and 5) a supernatural peace (vv. 27–31). The key to all of this is v. 15 which relates that these supernatural promises are for those who love Jesus Christ, whose love is evidenced by obedience.

14:15 If you love Me ... keep My commandments. Cf. vv. 21–24. Love for Christ

ROLE OF THE SPIRIT

16 I will ask the Father, and He will give you another [a,A]Helper, that He may be with you forever;
17 *that is* [A]the Spirit of truth, [B]whom the world cannot receive, because it does not see Him or know
Him, *but* you know Him because He abides with
you and will be in you.
18 "I will not leave you as orphans; [A]I will come
to you. 19 [a,A]After a little while [B]the world will no
longer see Me, but you *will* see Me; [C]because I live,
you will live also. 20 [A]In that day you will know that
[B]I am in My Father, and you in Me, and I in you.
21 [A]He who has My commandments and keeps them
is the one who loves Me; and [B]he who loves Me will
be loved by My Father, and I will love him and will
[C]disclose Myself to him." 22 [A]Judas (not Iscariot)
*said to Him, "Lord, what then has happened [B]that
You are going to disclose Yourself to us and not to
the world?" 23 Jesus answered and said to him, "[A]If
anyone loves Me, he will [B]keep My word; and [C]My
Father will love him, and We [D]will come to him and
make Our abode with him. 24 He who does not love
Me [A]does not keep My words; and [B]the word which
you hear is not Mine, but the Father's who sent Me.
25 "These things I have spoken to you while abiding with you. 26 But the [A]Helper, the Holy Spirit,
[B]whom the Father will send in My name, [C]He will
teach you all things, and [D]bring to your remembrance all that I said to you. 27 [A]Peace I leave with
you; My peace I give to you; not as the world gives
do I give to you. [B]Do not let your heart be troubled,
nor let it be fearful. 28 [A]You heard that I said to you,
'I go away, and [B]I will come to you.' If you loved
Me, you would have rejoiced because [C]I go to the
Father, for [D]the Father is greater than I. 29 Now
[A]I have told you before it happens, so that when
it happens, you may believe. 30 I will not speak
much more with you, for [A]the ruler of the world
is coming, and he has nothing in Me; 31 but so that
the world may know that I love the Father, [a]I do
exactly as [A]the Father commanded Me. Get up, [B]let
us go from here.

14:16 [a]Gr *Paracletos*, one called alongside to help; or *Comforter, Advocate, Intercessor* [A]John 7:39; 14:26; 15:26; 16:7; Rom 8:26; 1 John 2:1
14:17 [A]John 15:26; 16:13; 1 John 4:6; 5:7 [B]1 Cor 2:14 14:18 [A]John 14:3, 28 14:19 [a]Lit *Yet a little and the world* [A]John 7:33 [B]John 16:16, 22 [C]John 6:57
14:20 [A]John 16:23, 26 [B]John 10:38; 14:11 14:21 [A]John 14:15, 23; 15:10; 1 John 5:3; 2 John 6 [B]John 14:23; 16:27 [C]Ex 33:18f; Prov 8:17
14:22 [A]Luke 6:16; Acts 1:13 [B]Acts 10:40, 41 14:23 [A]John 14:15, 21; 15:10; 1 John 5:3; 2 John 6 [B]John 8:51; 1 John 2:5 [C]John 14:21
[D]2 Cor 6:16; Eph 3:17; 1 John 2:24; Rev 3:20; 21:3 14:24 [A]John 14:23 [B]John 7:16; 14:10 14:26 [A]John 14:16 [B]Luke 24:49;
John 1:33; 15:26; 16:7; Acts 2:33 [C]John 16:13f; 1 John 2:20, 27 [D]John 2:22 14:27 [A]John 16:33; 20:19; Phil 4:7; Col 3:15
[B]John 14:1 14:28 [A]John 14:2-4 [B]John 14:3, 18 [C]John 14:12 [D]John 10:29; Phil 2:6 14:29 [A]John 13:19
14:30 [A]John 12:31 14:31 [a]Lit *and as the Father...so I do* [A]John 10:18; 12:49 [B]John 13:1; 18:1

is inseparable from obedience (see Lk 6:46; 1Jn 5:2, 3). "My commandments" are not only Jesus' ethical commandments in context (vv. 23, 24), but the entire revelation from the Father (see 3:31, 32; 12:47–49; 17:6).

14:16 ask the Father. The priestly and intercessory work of Christ began with the request that the Father send the Holy Spirit to indwell in the people of faith (7:39; 15:26; 16:7; *see note on 20:22*; cf. Ac 1:8; 2:4, 33). **another.** The Gr. word specifically means another of the same kind, i.e., someone like Jesus Himself who will take His place and do His work. The Spirit of Christ is the Third Person of the Trinity, having the same essence of deity as Jesus and as perfectly one with Him as He is with the Father. **Helper.** The Gr. term here lit. means "one called alongside to help" and has the idea of someone who encourages and exhorts (*see note on 16:7*). "Be with you" has to do with His permanent residence in believers (Ro 8:9; 1Co 6:19, 20; 12:13).

14:17 Spirit of truth. He is the Spirit of truth in that He is the source of truth and communicates the truth to His own (v. 26; 16:12–15). Apart from Him, people cannot know God's truth (1Co 2:12–16; 1Jn 2:20, 27). **abides with you and will be in you.** This indicates some distinction between the ministry of the Holy Spirit to believers before and after Pentecost. While clearly the Holy Spirit has been with all who have ever believed throughout redemptive history as the source of truth, faith, and life, Jesus is saying something new is coming in His ministry. John 7:37–39 indicates this unique ministry would be like "rivers of living water." Acts 19:1–7 introduces some Old Covenant believers who had not received the Holy Spirit in this unique fullness and intimacy. Cf. Ac 1:8; 2:1–4; 1Co 12:11–13.

14:18 orphans. In this veiled reference to His death, Jesus promised not to leave them alone (Ro 8:9).

14:18, 19 I will come to you ... you *will* see Me. First, He was referring to His resurrection, after which they would see Him (20:19–29). There is no record that any unbelievers saw Him after He rose (see 1Co 15:1–9). In another sense, this has reference to the mystery of the Trinity. Through the coming and indwelling of the Holy Spirit at Pentecost, Jesus would be back with His children (16:16; cf. Mt 28:20; Ro 8:9; 1Jn 4:13).

14:19 you will live also. Because of His resurrection and by the indwelling life of the Spirit of Christ, believers possess eternal life (see Ro 6:1–11; Col 3:1–4).

14:20 In that day. This refers to His resurrection when He returns to them alive.

14:21–24 Once again, Jesus emphasized the need for the habitual practice of obedience to His commands as evidence of the believer's love for Him and the Father (*see note on v. 15*). This is consistent with the teaching of Jas 2:14–26 that true saving faith is manifest by works produced by God in the transforming, regenerating power of the Spirit. Those works are expressions of the love which the Spirit pours into the believer's heart (Ro 5:5; Gal 5:22).

14:26 will teach you all things. The Holy Spirit energized the hearts and minds of the apostles in their ministry, helping them to produce the NT Scripture. The disciples had failed to understand many things about Jesus and what He taught; but because of this supernatural work, they came to an inerrant and accurate understanding of the Lord and His work, and recorded it in the gospels and the rest of the NT Scriptures (2Ti 3:16; 2Pe 1:20, 21). *See note on 16:7.*

14:27 Peace I leave ... not as the world gives. The word "peace" reflects the Heb. "Shalom," which became a greeting to His disciples after the resurrection (20:19–26). At the individual level this peace, unknown to the unsaved, secures composure in difficult trouble (cf. v. 1), dissolves fear (Php 4:7), and rules in the hearts of God's people to maintain harmony (Col 3:15). The greatest reality of this peace will be in the messianic kingdom (Nu 6:26; Ps 29:11; Is 9:6, 7; 52:7; 54:13; 57:19; Eze 37:26; Hag 2:9; cf. Ac 10:36; Ro 1:7; 5:1; 14:17).

14:28 greater than I. Jesus was not admitting inferiority to the Father (after claiming equality repeatedly, *see note on vv. 7–11*), but was saying that if the disciples loved Him, they would not be reluctant to let Him go to the Father because He was returning to the realm where He belonged and to the full glory He gave up (17:5). He was going back to share equal glory with the Father which would be greater than what He had experienced in His incarnation. He will in no way be inferior in that glory, because His humiliation was over.

14:30 the ruler of the world. Judas was only a tool of the "prince" who rules the system of darkness—Satan (6:70; 13:21, 27). **nothing in Me.** The Heb. idiom means that Satan had nothing on Jesus, could make no claim on Him, nor charge Him with any sin. Therefore, Satan could not hold Him in death. Christ would triumph and destroy Satan (Heb 2:14). His death was no sign that Satan won, but that God's will was being done. (v. 31).

JESUS IS THE VINE—FOLLOWERS ARE BRANCHES

15 "[A]I am the true vine, and My Father is the
[B]vinedresser. 2 Every branch in Me that does
not bear fruit, He takes away; and every *branch* that
bears fruit, He [a]prunes it so that it may bear more
fruit. 3 [A]You are already [a]clean because of the word
which I have spoken to you. 4 [A]Abide in Me, and I in
you. As the branch cannot bear fruit [a]of itself unless
it abides in the vine, so neither *can* you unless you
abide in Me. 5 I am the vine, you are the branches;
he who abides in Me and I in him, he [A]bears much
fruit, for apart from Me you can do nothing. 6 If anyone does not abide in Me, he is [A]thrown away as a
branch and dries up; and they gather them, and cast
them into the fire and they are burned. 7 If you abide
in Me, and My words abide in you, [A]ask whatever
you wish, and it will be done for you. 8 My [A]Father
is glorified by this, that you bear much fruit, and *so*
[a,B]prove to be My disciples. 9 Just as [A]the Father has
loved Me, I have also loved you; abide in My love.
10 [A]If you keep My commandments, you will abide
in My love; just as [B]I have kept My Father's commandments and abide in His love. 11 [A]These things
I have spoken to you so that My joy may be in you,
and *that* your [B]joy may be made full.

DISCIPLES' RELATION TO EACH OTHER

12 "This is [A]My commandment, that you love one
another, just as I have loved you. 13 [A]Greater love has
no one than this, that one [B]lay down his life for his
friends. 14 You are My [A]friends if [B]you do what I command you. 15 No longer do I call you slaves, for the
slave does not know what his master is doing; but
I have called you friends, for [A]all things that I have
heard from My Father I have made known to you.
16 [A]You did not choose Me but I chose you, and appointed you that you would go and [B]bear fruit, and
that your fruit would remain, so that [C]whatever you
ask of the Father in My name He may give to you.
17 This [A]I command you, that you love one another.

DISCIPLES' RELATION TO THE WORLD

18 "[A]If the world hates you, [a]you know that it has
hated Me before *it hated* you. 19 If you were of the
world, the world would love its own; but because
you are not of the world, but [A]I chose you out of
the world, [B]because of this the world hates you.

15:1 [A]Ps 80:8ff; Is 5:1ff; Ezek 19:10ff; Matt 21:33ff [B]Matt 15:13; Rom 11:17; 1 Cor 3:9 15:2 [a]Lit *cleans;* used to describe pruning 15:3 [a]I.e. pruned like a branch [A]John 13:10; 17:17; Eph 5:26 15:4 [a]Lit *from* [A]John 6:56; 15:4-7; 1 John 2:6 15:5 [A]John 15:16 15:6 [A]John 15:2 15:7 [A]Matt 7:7; John 15:16 15:8 [a]Or *become My disciples* [A]Matt 5:16 [B]John 8:31 15:9 [A]John 3:35; 17:23, 24, 26 15:10 [A]John 14:15 [B]John 8:29 15:11 [A]John 17:13 [B]John 3:29 15:12 [A]John 13:34; 15:17; 1 John 3:23; 2 John 5 15:13 [A]Rom 5:7f [B]John 10:11 15:14 [A]Luke 12:4 [B]Matt 12:50 15:15 [A]John 8:26; 16:12 15:16 [A]John 6:70; 13:18; 15:19 [B]John 15:5 [C]John 14:13; 15:7; 16:23 15:17 [A]John 15:12 15:18 [a]Or (imperative) *know that* [A]John 7:7; 1 John 3:13 15:19 [A]John 15:16 [B]Matt 10:22; 24:9; John 17:14

15:1–17 Through this extended metaphor of the vine and branches, Jesus set forth the basis of Christian living. Jesus used the imagery of agricultural life at the time; i.e., vines and vine crops (see also Mt 20:1–16; 21:23–41; Mk 12:1–9; Lk 13:6–9; 20:9–16). In the OT, the vine is used commonly as a symbol for Israel, (Ps 80:9–16; Is 5:1–7; 27:2–6; Jer 2:21; 12:10; Eze 15:1–8; 17:1–21; 19:10–14; Hos 10:1, 2). He specifically identified Himself as the "true vine" and the Father as the "vinedresser" or caretaker of the vine. The vine has two types of branches: 1) branches that bear fruit (vv. 2, 8), and 2) branches that do not (vv. 2, 6). The branches that bear fruit are genuine believers. Though in immediate context the focus is upon the 11 faithful disciples, the imagery also encompasses all believers down through the ages. The branches that do not bear fruit are those who profess to believe, but their lack of fruit indicates genuine salvation has never taken place and they have no life from the vine. Especially in the immediate context, Judas was in view, but the imagery extends from him to all those who make a profession of faith in Christ but do not actually possess salvation. The image of non-fruit-bearing branches being burned pictures eschatological judgment and eternal rejection (see Eze 15:6–8).

15:1 **I am the true vine.** This is the last of 7 claims to deity in the form of "I am" statements by Jesus in the Gospel of John (see 6:35; 8:12; 10:7, 9; 10:11, 14; 11:25; 14:6).

15:2 **He takes away.** The picture is of the vinedresser (i.e., the Father) getting rid of dead wood so that the living, fruit-bearing branches may be sharply distinguished. This is a picture of apostate Christians who never genuinely believed and will be taken away in judgment (v. 6; Mt 7:16; Eph 2:10); the transforming life of Christ has never pulsated within them (8:31, 32; cf. Mt 13:18–23; 24:12; Heb 3:14–19; 6:4–8; 10:27–31; 1Jn 2:19; 2Jn 9). **He prunes.** God removes all things in the believer's life that would hinder fruit-bearing, i.e., He chastises to cut away sin and hindrances that would drain spiritual life just as the farmer removes anything on the branches that keep them from bearing maximum fruit (Heb 12:3–11).

15:4–6 **Abide in Me.** The word "abide" means to remain or stay around. The "remaining" is evidence that salvation has already taken place (1Jn 2:19) and not vice versa. The fruit or evidence of salvation is continuance in service to Him and in His teaching (8:31; Col 1:23; 1Jn 2:24). The abiding believer is the only legitimate believer. Abiding and believing actually are addressing the same issue of genuine salvation (Heb 3:6–19). For a discussion of the perseverance of the saints, *see note on Mt 24:13.*

15:6 The imagery here is one of destruction (cf. Mt 3:10–12; 5:22; 13:40–42, 50; 25:41; Mk 9:43–49; Lk 3:17; 2Th 1:7–9; Rev 20:10–15). It pictures the judgment awaiting all those who were never saved.

15:7–10 True believers obey the Lord's commands, submitting to His Word (14:21, 23). Because of their commitment to God's Word, they are devoted to His will, thus their prayers are fruitful (14:13, 14), which puts God's glory on display as He answers.

15:9, 10 **abide in My love.** Cf. Jude 21. This is not emotional or mystical, but defined in v. 10 as obedience. Jesus set the model by His perfect obedience to the Father, which we are to use as the pattern for our obedience to Him.

15:11 **your joy may be made full.** Just as Jesus maintained that His obedience to the Father was the basis of His joy, so also the believers who are obedient to His commandments will experience the same joy (17:13; cf. 16:24).

15:12 Cf. 13:34, 35. *See note on 1Jn 2:7–11.*

15:13 This is a reference to the supreme evidence and expression of Jesus' love (v. 12), His sacrificial death upon the cross. Christians are called to exemplify the same kind of sacrificial giving toward one another, even if such sacrifice involves the laying down of one's own life in imitation of Christ's example (cf. 1Jn 3:16).

15:14, 15 **friends.** Just as Abraham was called the "friend of God" (2Ch 20:7; Jas 2:23) because he enjoyed extraordinary access to the mind of God through God's revelation to him which he believed, so also those who follow Christ are privileged with extraordinary revelation through the Messiah and Son of God and, believing, become "friends" of God also. It was for His "friends" that the Lord laid down His life (v. 13; 10:11, 15, 17).

15:16 **I chose you.** Cf. v. 19. In case any pretense might exist among the disciples in terms of spiritual pride because of the privileges they enjoyed, Jesus made it clear that such privilege rested not in their own merit, but on His sovereign choice of them. God chose Israel (Is 45:4; Am 3:2), but not for any merit (Dt 7:7; 9:4–6). God elected angels to be forever holy (1Ti 5:21). He elected believers to salvation apart from any merit (Mt 24:24, 31; *see notes on Ro 8:29–33; Eph 1:3–6; Col 3:12; Tit 1:1; 1Pe 1:2*). **bear fruit.** One purpose of God's sovereign election is that the disciples who have been blessed with such revelation and understanding should produce spiritual fruit. The NT describes fruit as godly attitudes (Gal 5:22, 23), righteous behavior (Php 1:11), praise (Heb 13:15), and especially leading others to faith in Jesus as Messiah and Son of God (Ro 1:13–16).

15:18, 19 Since Satan is the one who dominates the evil world system in rebellion against God (14:30), the result is that the world hates not only Jesus, but those who follow Him (2Ti 3:12). Hatred toward Jesus means also hatred toward the Father who sent Him (v. 23).

20 Remember the word that I said to you, '[A]A slave is
not greater than his master.' If they persecuted Me,
[B]they will also persecute you; if they [C]kept My word,
they will keep yours also. 21 But all these things they
will do to you [A]for My name's sake, [B]because they
do not know the One who sent Me. 22 [A]If I had not
come and spoken to them, they would not have [a]sin,
but now they have no excuse for their sin. 23 He who
hates Me hates My Father also. 24 [A]If I had not done
among them [B]the works which no one else did, they
would not have [a]sin; but now they have both seen
and hated Me and My Father as well. 25 But *they have
done this* to fulfill the word that is written in their
[A]Law, '[B]THEY HATED ME WITHOUT A CAUSE.'
26 "When the [a,A]Helper comes, [B]whom I will send
to you from the Father, *that is* [C]the Spirit of truth
who proceeds from the Father, [D]He will testify about
Me, 27 [a]and [A]you *will* testify also, because you have
been with Me [B]from the beginning.

JESUS' WARNING

16 "[A]These things I have spoken to you so that
you may be kept from [B]stumbling. 2 [a]They will
[A]make you outcasts from the synagogue, but [B]an
hour is coming for everyone [C]who kills you to think
that he is offering service to God. 3 These things they
will do [A]because they have not known the Father
or Me. 4 But these things I have spoken to you, [A]so
that when their hour comes, you [a]may remember
that I told you of them. These things I did not say
to you [B]at the beginning, because I was with you.

THE HOLY SPIRIT PROMISED

5 "But now [A]I am going to Him who sent Me; and
none of you asks Me, '[B]Where are You going?' 6 But
because I have said these things to you, [A]sorrow
has filled your heart. 7 But I tell you the truth, it is
to your advantage that I go away; for if I do not go
away, the [a,A]Helper will not come to you; but if I go, [B]I
will send Him to you. 8 And He, when He comes, will
convict the world concerning sin and righteousness
and judgment; 9 concerning sin, [A]because they do
not believe in Me; 10 and concerning [A]righteousness,
because [B]I go to the Father and you no longer see
Me; 11 [A]and concerning judgment, because the ruler
of this world has been judged.

15:20 [A]Matt 10:24; John 13:16 [B]1 Cor 4:12; 2 Cor 4:9; 2 Tim 3:12 [C]John 8:51 15:21 [A]Matt 10:22; 24:9; Mark 13:13; Luke 21:12, 17; Acts 4:17; 5:41; 9:14; 26:9; 1 Pet 4:14; Rev 2:3 [B]John 8:19, 55; 16:3; 17:25; Acts 3:17; 1 John 3:1 15:22 [a]I.e. guilt [A]John 9:41; 15:24 15:24 [a]I.e. guilt [A]John 9:41; 15:21 [B]John 5:36; 10:37 15:25 [A]John 10:34 [B]Ps 35:19; 69:4 15:26 [a]Gr *Paracletos*, one called alongside to help; or *Comforter, Advocate, Intercessor* [A]John 14:16 [B]John 14:26 [C]John 14:17 [D]1 John 5:7 15:27 [a]Or (imperative) *and bear witness* [A]Luke 24:48; John 19:35; 21:24; 1 John 1:2; 4:14 [B]Luke 1:2 16:1 [A]John 15:18-27 [B]Matt 11:6 16:2 [a]Or *They will have you excommunicated* [A]John 9:22 [B]John 4:21; 16:25 [C]Is 66:5; Acts 26:9-11; Rev 6:9 16:3 [A]John 8:19, 55; 15:21; 17:25; Acts 3:17; 1 John 3:1 16:4 [a]Or *will remember them, that I told you* [A]John 13:19 [B]Luke 1:2 16:5 [A]John 7:33; 16:10, 17, 28 [B]John 13:36; 14:5 16:6 [A]John 14:1; 16:22 16:7 [a]Gr *Paracletos*, one called alongside to help; or *Comforter, Advocate, Intercessor* [A]John 14:16 [B]John 14:26 16:9 [A]John 15:22, 24 16:10 [A]Acts 3:14; 7:52; 17:31; 1 Pet 3:18 [B]John 16:5 16:11 [A]John 12:31

15:20 slave . . . master. That axiom, spoken also in 13:16, reflects the obvious truth that led Jesus to inform His disciples. They could expect to be treated as He was treated because those who hated Him don't know God (v. 21) and would hate them also; and conversely, those who listened with faith to Him would hear them also.

15:22–24 they would not have sin. Jesus did not mean that if He had not come, they would have been sinless. But His coming incited the severest and most deadly sin, that of rejecting and rebelling against God and His truth. It was the decisive sin of rejection, the deliberate and fatal choice of darkness over light and death over life of which He spoke. He had done so many miracles and spoken innumerable words to prove He was Messiah and Son of God, but they were belligerent in their love of sin and rejection of the Savior. See Heb 4:2–5; 6:4–6; 10:29–31.

15:25 Jesus quotes Pss 35:19; 69:4. The logic here is that if David, a mere man, could have been hated in such a terrible manner by the enemies of God, how much more would the wicked hate David's perfect, divine Son who was the promised king who would confront sin and reign forever over His kingdom of righteousness (see 2 Sam 7:16).

15:26, 27 When the Helper comes. Again, Jesus promised to send the Holy Spirit (7:39; 14:16, 17, 26; 16:7, 13, 14). This time He emphasized the Spirit's help for witnessing—proclaiming the gospel. *See note on 16:7.*

16:1–15 Jesus continued the thoughts of 15:18–25 regarding the world's hatred of His disciples and its opposition to the testimony of the Holy Spirit regarding Him as Messiah and Son of God. In this section, He specified in greater detail how the Spirit confronts the world, i.e., not only does He testify about Jesus, but He convicts men of sin. Through conviction of sin and testimony of the gospel, the Spirit turns the hostile hearts of men away from rebellion against God into belief regarding Jesus as Savior and Lord. This section may be divided into 4 parts: 1) the killing of the disciples by the world (vv. 1–4); 2) the comforting of the disciples by the Lord (vv. 5–7); 3) the conviction of men by the Holy Spirit (vv. 8–12); and 4) the guidance of the believer into all truth by the Holy Spirit (vv. 13–15).

16:1 These things. This is what He had just said in 15:18–25. **stumbling.** The connotation of this word has the idea of setting a trap. The hatred of the world was such that it would seek to trap and destroy the disciples in an effort to prevent their witness to Jesus as Messiah and Son of God. Jesus did not want them to be caught unaware (v. 4).

16:2 he is offering service to God. Paul, before he was saved, personified this attitude as he persecuted the church thinking that he was doing service for God (Ac 22:4, 5; 26:9–11; Gal 1:13–17; Php 3:6; 1Ti 1:12–17). After Paul's conversion, the persecutor became the persecuted because of the hatred of the world (2Co 11:22–27; cf. Stephen in Ac 7:54–8:3).

16:4 I was with you. Jesus didn't need to warn them because He was there to protect them.

16:5 none of you asks. Earlier they had done so (13:36; 14:5), but they were then so absorbed in their own sorrow and confusion that they lost interest in where He was going. They were apparently consumed with what would happen to them (v. 6).

16:7 the Helper will not come. Again, the promise of the Holy Spirit being sent is given to comfort the disciples. *See note on 15:26, 27.* The first emphasis was on His life-giving power (7:37–39). The next featured His indwelling presence (14:16, 17). The next marked His teaching ministry (14:26). His ministry of empowering for witness is marked in 15:26.

16:8 when He comes. The coming of the Holy Spirit at Pentecost was approximately 40 or more days away at this point (see Ac 2:1–13). **convict.** This word has two meanings: 1) the judicial act of conviction with a view toward sentencing (i.e., a courtroom term—conviction of sin) or 2) the act of convincing. Here the second idea is best, since the purpose of the Holy Spirit is not condemnation but conviction of the need for the Savior. The Son does the judgment, with the Father (5:22, 27, 30). In v. 14, it is said that He will reveal the glories of Christ to His people. He will also inspire the writing of the NT, guiding the apostles to write it (v. 13), and He will reveal "what is to come," through the NT prophecies (v. 13).

16:9 sin. The singular indicates that a specific sin is in view; i.e., that of not believing in Jesus as Messiah and Son of God. This is the only sin, ultimately, that damns people to hell (*see note on 8:24*). Though all men are depraved, cursed by their violation of God's law and sinful by nature, what ultimately damns them to hell is their unwillingness to believe in the Lord Jesus Christ as Savior (cf. 8:24).

16:10 righteousness. The Holy Spirit's purpose here is to shatter the pretensions of self-righteousness (hypocrisy), exposing the darkness of the heart (3:19–21; 7:7; 15:22, 24). While Jesus was on the earth, He performed this task especially toward the shallowness and emptiness of Judaism that had degenerated into legalistic modes without life-giving reality (e.g., 2:13–22; 5:10–16; 7:24; Is 64:5, 6). With Jesus gone to the Father, the Holy Spirit continues His convicting role.

16:11 judgment. The judgment here in context is that of the world under Satan's

12 "I have many more things to say to you, but
you cannot bear *them* now. 13 But when He, [A]the
Spirit of truth, comes, He will [B]guide you into all the
truth; for He will not speak on His own initiative,
but whatever He hears, He will speak; and He will
disclose to you what is to come. 14 He will [A]glorify
Me, for He will take of Mine and will disclose *it*
to you. 15 [A]All things that the Father has are Mine;
therefore I said that He takes of Mine and will disclose *it* to you.

JESUS' DEATH AND RESURRECTION FORETOLD

16 "[A]A little while, and [B]you will no longer see
Me; and again a little while, and [C]you will see Me."
17 *Some* of His disciples then said to one another,
"What is this thing He is telling us, '[A]A little while,
and you will not see Me; and again a little while, and
you will see Me'; and, 'because [B]I go to the Father'?"
18 So they were saying, "What is this that He says,
'A little while'? We do not know what He is talking
about." 19 [A]Jesus knew that they wished to question
Him, and He said to them, "Are you deliberating together about this, that I said, 'A little while, and you
will not see Me, and again a little while, and you will
see Me'? 20 Truly, truly, I say to you, that [A]you will
weep and lament, but the world will rejoice; you
will grieve, but [B]your grief will be turned into joy.
21 [A]Whenever a woman is in labor she has [a]pain, because her hour has come; but when she gives birth
to the child, she no longer remembers the anguish
because of the joy that a [b]child has been born into
the world. 22 Therefore [A]you too have grief now; but
[B]I will see you again, and your heart will rejoice, and
no one *will* take your joy away from you.

PRAYER PROMISES

23 [A]In that day [B]you will not question Me about
anything. Truly, truly, I say to you, [C]if you ask the
Father for anything in My name, He will give it to
you. 24 [A]Until now you have asked for nothing in
My name; ask and you will receive, so that your
[B]joy may be made full.
25 "These things I have spoken to you in [a][A]figu-
rative language; [B]an hour is coming when I will no
longer speak to you in [a]figurative language, but will
tell you plainly of the Father. 26 [A]In that day [B]you
will ask in My name, and I do not say to you that I
will request of the Father on your behalf; 27 for [A]the
Father Himself loves you, because you have loved
Me and [B]have believed that [C]I came forth from the
Father. 28 [A]I came forth from the Father and have
come into the world; I am leaving the world again
and [B]going to the Father."
29 His disciples *said, "Lo, now You are speaking
plainly and are not [a]using [A]a figure of speech. 30 Now
we know that You know all things, and have no need
for anyone to question You; by this we [A]believe that
You [B]came from God." 31 Jesus answered them, "Do
you now believe? 32 Behold, [A]an hour is coming, and
has *already* come, for [B]you to be scattered, each to
[C]his own *home,* and to leave Me alone; and *yet* [D]I am

16:13 [A]John 14:17 [B]John 14:26 16:14 [A]John 7:39 16:15 [A]John 17:10 16:16 [A]John 7:33 [B]John 14:18-24; 16:16-24 [C]John 16:22 16:17 [A]John 16:16 [B]John 16:5 16:19 [A]Mark 9:32; John 6:61 16:20 [A]Mark 16:10; Luke 23:27 [B]John 20:20 16:21 [a]Lit *grief* [b]Lit *human being* [A]Is 13:8; 21:3; 26:17; 66:7; Hos 13:13; Mic 4:9; 1 Thess 5:3 16:22 [A]John 16:6 [B]John 16:16 16:23 [A]John 14:20; 16:26 [B]John 16:19, 30 [C]John 15:16 16:24 [A]John 14:14 [B]John 3:29; 15:11 16:25 [a]Lit *proverbs;* or *figures of speech* [A]Matt 13:34; John 10:6; 16:29 [B]John 16:2 16:26 [A]John 14:20; 16:23 [B]John 16:19, 30 16:27 [A]John 14:21, 23 [B]John 2:11; 16:30 [C]John 8:42 16:28 [A]John 8:42; 16:30 [B]John 13:1, 3; 16:5, 10, 17 16:29 [a]Lit *saying a proverb* [A]Matt 13:34; John 10:6; 16:25 16:30 [A]John 2:11; 16:27 [B]John 8:42; 16:28 16:32 [A]John 4:23; 16:2, 25 [B]Zech 13:7; Matt 26:31 [C]John 19:27 [D]John 8:29

control. Its judgments are blind, faulty, and evil as evidenced in their verdict on Christ. The world can't make righteous judgments (7:24), but the Spirit of Christ does (8:16). All Satan's adjudications are lies (8:44–47), so the Spirit convicts men of their false judgment of Christ. Satan, the ruler of the world (14:30; Eph 2:1–3) who, as the god of this world, has perverted the world's judgment and turned people from believing in Jesus as the Messiah and Son of God (2Co 4:4), was defeated at the cross. While Christ's death looked like Satan's greatest victory, it actually was Satan's destruction (cf. Col 2:15; Heb 2:14, 15; Rev 20:10). The Spirit will lead sinners to true judgment.

16:13 all the truth. This verse, like 14:26, points to the supernatural revelation of all truth by which God has revealed Himself in Christ (vv. 14, 15), particularly. This is the subject of the inspired NT writings. *See note on v. 7.*

16:14 He will glorify Me. This is really the same as v. 13, in that all NT truth revealed by God centers in Christ (Heb 1:1, 2). Christ was the theme of the OT, as the NT claims (1:45; 5:37; Lk 24:27, 44; Ac 10:43; 18:28; Ro 1:1, 2; 1Co 15:3; 1Pe 1:10, 11; Rev 19:10).

16:16–19 Jesus was referring to His ascension ("you will no longer see Me") and the coming of the Holy Spirit ("you will see Me"), emphatically claiming that the Spirit and He are one (Ro 8:9; Php 1:19; 1Pe 1:11; Rev 19:10). Christ dwells in believers through the Holy Spirit—in that sense they see Him. *See notes on 14:16–18.*

16:20 grief will be turned into joy. The very event that made the hateful realm of mankind ("world") rejoice and cause grief to Jesus' disciples will be the same event that will lead to the world's sorrow and the believer's joy. The disciples would soon realize the marvelous nature of God's gift of salvation and the Spirit through what He accomplished, and the blessing of answered prayer (v. 24). Acts records the coming of the Holy Spirit and the power and joy (Ac 2:4–47; 13:52) of the early church.

16:22 I will see you. After the resurrection, Jesus did see His disciples (20:19–29; 21:1–23; cf. 1Co 15:1–8). Beyond that brief time of personal fellowship (Ac 1:1–3), He would be with them permanently in His Spirit (*see notes on vv. 16–19; 14:16–19*).

16:23 In that day. This is a reference to Pentecost when the Holy Spirit came (Ac 2:1–13) and sorrow turned to joy. This is a reference also to the "last days" which were inaugurated after His resurrection and the Spirit's coming (Ac 2:17; 2Ti 3:1; Heb 1:2; Jas 5:3; 2Pe 3:3; 1Jn 2:18). **not question Me.** After His departure and sending of the Spirit, believers will no longer ask Him since He is not present. Instead, they will ask the Father in His name (*see notes on vv. 26–28; 14:13, 14*).

16:24 joy may be made full. In this case, the believer's joy will be related to answered prayer and a full supply of heavenly blessing for everything consistent with the purpose of the Lord in one's life. *See note on 15:11.*

16:25 in figurative language. The word means "veiled, pointed statement" that is pregnant with meaning, i.e., something that is obscure. What seemed hard to understand for the disciples during the life of Jesus would become clear after His death, resurrection, and the coming of the Holy Spirit (see vv. 13, 14; 14:26; 15:26, 27). They would actually understand the ministry of Christ better than they had while they were with Him, as the Spirit inspired them to write the Gospels and Epistles and ministered in and through them.

16:26–28 I do not say. Christ was clarifying what He meant by praying in His name. He did not mean asking Him to ask the Father, as if the Father was indifferent to believers, but not to His Son. On the contrary, the Father loves Christ's own. In fact, the Father sent the Son to redeem them and then return. Asking in Jesus' name means simply asking on the basis of His merit, His righteousness, and for whatever would honor and glorify Him so as to build His kingdom.

not alone, because the Father is with Me. 33 These
things I have spoken to you, so that [A]in Me you may
have peace. [B]In the world you have tribulation, but
[C]take courage; [D]I have overcome the world."

THE HIGH PRIESTLY PRAYER

17 Jesus spoke these things; and [A]lifting up His
eyes to heaven, He said, "Father, the hour has
come; [B]glorify Your Son, that the Son may glorify
You, 2 even as [A]You gave Him authority over all
flesh, that [B]to [a]all whom You have given Him, [C]He
may give eternal life. 3 This is eternal life, that they
may know You, [A]the only true God, and Jesus Christ
whom [B]You have sent. 4 [A]I glorified You on the earth,
[a,B]having accomplished the work which You have
given Me to do. 5 Now, Father, [A]glorify Me together
with Yourself, with the glory which I had [B]with You
before the world was.
6 "[A]I have manifested Your name to the men
whom [B]You gave Me out of the world; they were
[C]Yours and You gave them to Me, and they have
[D]kept Your word. 7 Now they have come to know
that everything You have given Me is from You;
8 for [A]the words which You gave Me [B]I have given
to them; and they received *them* and truly understood that [C]I came forth from You, and they believed
that [D]You sent Me. 9 [A]I ask on their behalf; [B]I do
not ask on behalf of the world, but of those whom
[C]You have given Me; for [D]they are Yours; 10 and [A]all
things that are Mine are Yours, and Yours are Mine;
and I have been glorified in them. 11 I am no longer
in the world; and *yet* [A]they themselves are in the
world, and [B]I come to You. [C]Holy Father, keep them
in Your name, *the name* [D]which You have given Me,
that [E]they may be one even as We *are*. 12 While I was
with them, I was keeping them in Your name [A]which
You have given Me; and I guarded them and [B]not
one of them perished but [C]the [a]son of perdition, so
that the [D]Scripture would be fulfilled.

THE DISCIPLES IN THE WORLD

13 But now [A]I come to You; and [B]these things I
speak in the world so that they may have My [C]joy
made full in themselves. 14 I have given them Your
word; and [A]the world has hated them, because [B]they
are not of the world, even as I am not of the world.
15 I do not ask You to take them out of the world, but
to keep them [a]from [b,A]the evil *one*. 16 [A]They are not

16:33 [A]John 14:27 [B]John 15:18ff [C]Matt 9:2 [D]Rom 8:37; 2 Cor 2:14; 4:7ff; 6:4ff; Rev 3:21; 12:11 17:1 [A]John 11:41 [B]John 7:39; 13:31f 17:2 [a]Lit *everything that You have given Him, to them He may* [A]John 3:35 [B]John 10:28 [C]John 6:37, 39; 17:6, 9, 24 17:3 [A]John 5:44 [B]John 3:17; 17:8, 21, 23, 25 17:4 [a]Or *by accomplishing* [A]John 13:31 [B]Luke 22:37; John 4:34 17:5 [A]John 17:1 [B]John 1:1; 8:58; 17:24; Phil 2:6 17:6 [A]John 17:26 [B]John 6:37, 39; 17:2, 9, 24 [C]John 17:9 [D]John 8:51 17:8 [A]John 6:68; 12:49 [B]John 15:15; 17:14, 26 [C]John 8:42; 16:27, 30 [D]John 3:17; 17:18, 21, 23, 25 17:9 [A]Luke 22:32; John 14:16 [B]Luke 23:34; John 17:20f [C]John 6:37, 39; 17:2, 6, 24 [D]John 17:6 17:10 [A]John 16:15 17:11 [A]John 13:1 [B]John 7:33; 17:13 [C]John 17:25 [D]John 17:6; Phil 2:9; Rev 19:12 [E]John 17:21f; Rom 12:5; Gal 3:28 17:12 [a]Heb idiom for one destined to perish [A]John 17:6; Phil 2:9; Rev 19:12 [B]John 6:39; 18:9 [C]John 6:70 [D]Ps 41:9; John 13:18 17:13 [A]John 7:33; 17:11 [B]John 15:11 [C]John 3:29 17:14 [A]John 15:19 [B]John 8:23; 17:16 17:15 [a]Or *out of* the power of [b]Or *evil* [A]Matt 5:37 17:16 [A]John 17:14

16:33 in Me you may have peace. *See note on 14:27.* **tribulation.** This word often refers to eschatological woes (Mk 13:9; Ro 2:9) and to persecution of believers because of their testimony for Christ (cf. 15:18–16:4; Ac 11:19; Eph 3:13). **overcome.** The fundamental ground for endurance in persecution is the victory of Jesus over the world (12:31; 1Co 15:57). Through His impending death, He rendered the world's opposition null and void. While the world continues to attack His people, such attacks fall harmlessly, for Christ's victory has already accomplished a smashing defeat of the whole evil rebellious system. *See notes on Ro 8:35–39.*

17:1–26 Although Mt 6:9–13 and Lk 11:2–4 have become known popularly as the "Lord's Prayer," that prayer was actually a prayer taught to the disciples by Jesus as a pattern for their prayers. The prayer recorded here is truly the Lord's Prayer, exhibiting the face-to-face communion the Son had with the Father. Very little is recorded of the content of Jesus' frequent prayers to the Father (Mt 14:23; Lk 5:16), so this prayer reveals some of the precious content of the Son's communion and intercession with Him. This chapter is a transitional chapter, marking the end of Jesus' earthly ministry and the beginning of His intercessory ministry for believers (Heb 7:25). In many respects, the prayer is a summary of John's entire gospel. Its principal themes include: 1) Jesus' obedience to His Father; 2) the glorification of His Father through His death and exaltation; 3) the revelation of God in Jesus Christ; 4) the choosing of the disciples out of the world; 5) their mission to the world; 6) their unity modeled on the unity of the Father and Son; and 7) the believer's final destiny in the presence of the Father and Son. The chapter divides into three parts: 1) Jesus' prayer for Himself (vv. 1–5); 2) Jesus' prayer for the apostles (vv. 6–19); and 3) Jesus' prayer for all NT believers who will form the church (vv. 20–26).

17:1 the hour has come. The time of His death. *See note on 12:23.* **glorify Your Son.** The very event that would glorify the Son was His death. By it, He has received the adoration, worship, and love of millions whose sins He bore. He accepted this path to glory, knowing that by it He would be exalted to the Father. The goal is that the Father may be glorified for His redemptive plan in the Son. So He sought by His own glory the glory of His Father (13:31, 32).

17:2 authority over all flesh. Cf. 5:27; *see note on Mt 28:18.* **to all whom You have given Him.** A reference to God's choosing of those who will come to Christ (*see notes on 6:37, 44*). The biblical doctrine of election or predestination is presented throughout the NT (15:16, 19; Ac 13:48; Ro 8:29–33; Eph 1:3–6; 2Th 2:13; Tit 1:1; 1Pe 1:2).

17:3 eternal life. *See notes on 3:15, 16; 5:24;* cf. 1Jn 5:20.

17:5 glorify Me together with Yourself. Having completed His work (v. 4), Jesus looked past the cross and asked to be returned to the glory that He shared with the Father before the world began (*see notes on 1:1; 8:58; 12:41*). The actual completion of bearing judgment wrath for sinners was declared by Christ in the cry, "It is finished" (19:30).

17:6–10 they were Yours. This phrase sums up all of Jesus' ministry, including the cross that was just hours away. Again, the Son emphasized that those who believed in Him were given by the Father (*see note on v. 2*). "They were Yours" (cf. v. 9) is a potent assertion that before conversion, they belonged to God (cf. 6:37). That is true because of God's election. They were chosen before the foundation of the world (Eph 1:4), when their names were written in the Lamb's book of life (Rev 17:8). Cf. Ac 18:10, where God says He has many people in Corinth who belong to Him but are not yet saved. *See notes on 10:1–5, 16.*

17:8 they believed. The Son of God affirmed the genuine saving faith of His disciples.

17:11 I am no longer in the world. So sure was His death and departure back to the Father that Jesus treated His departure as an already accomplished fact. He prayed here for His disciples because they would have to face the world's temptation and hatred without His immediate presence and protection (15:18–16:4). Based on the eternal nature of immutable God ("name"), He prayed for the eternal security of those who believed. He prayed that as the Trinity experiences eternal unity, so may believers. See Ro 8:31–39.

17:12 I was keeping them in Your name. Jesus protected them and kept them safe from the world as He said in 6:37–40, 44. One illustration of that can be seen in 18:1–11. Believers are secure forever because they are held by Christ and by God. *See note on 10:28, 29.* **son of perdition.** This identifies Judas by pointing to his destiny, i.e., eternal damnation (Mt 7:13; Ac 8:20; Ro 9:22; Php 1:28; 3:19; 1Ti 6:9; Heb 10:39; 2Pe 2:1; 3:7; Rev 17:8, 11). The defection of Judas was not a failure on Jesus' part, but was foreseen and foreordained in Scripture (Pss 41:9; 109:8; cf. 13:18).

17:15 keep them from the evil *one*. The reference here refers to protection from Satan and all the wicked forces following him (Mt 6:13; 1Jn 2:13, 14; 3:12; 5:18, 19). Though Jesus' sacrifice on the cross was the defeat of Satan, he is still loose and orchestrating his evil system against believers. He seeks to

of the world, even as I am not of the world. 17 [A]Sanc-
tify them in the truth; Your word is truth. 18 As [A]You
sent Me into the world, [B]I also have sent them into
the world. 19 For their sakes I [A]sanctify Myself, that
they themselves also may be [B]sanctified [C]in truth.
20 "I do not ask on behalf of these alone, but for
those also who believe in Me through their word;
21 that they may all be one; [A]even as You, Father,
are in Me and I in You, that they also may be in Us,
[B]so that the world may [a]believe that [C]You sent Me.

THEIR FUTURE GLORY

22 The [A]glory which You have given Me I have
given to them, that they may be one, just as We are
one; 23 [A]I in them and You in Me, that they may be
perfected [a]in unity, so that the world may [b]know that
[B]You sent Me, and [C]loved them, even as You have
loved Me. 24 Father, I desire that [A]they also, whom
You have given Me, [B]be with Me where I am, so that
they may see My [C]glory which You have given Me, for
You loved Me before [D]the foundation of the world.
25 "O [A]righteous Father, [a]although [B]the world has
not known You, yet I have known You; and these
have known that [C]You sent Me; 26 and [A]I have made
Your name known to them, and will make it known,
so that [B]the love with which You loved Me may be
in them, and I in them."

JUDAS BETRAYS JESUS

18 When Jesus had spoken these words, [A]He went
forth with His disciples over [B]the [a]ravine of
the Kidron, where there was [C]a garden, in which He
entered [b]with His disciples. 2 Now Judas also, who
was [a]betraying Him, knew the place, for Jesus had
[A]often met there with His disciples. 3 [A]Judas then,
having received [B]the *Roman* [a]cohort and [C]officers
from the chief priests and the Pharisees, *came
there with lanterns and [D]torches and weapons. 4 So
Jesus, [A]knowing all the things that were coming
upon Him, went forth and *said to them, "[B]Whom
do you seek?" 5 They answered Him, "Jesus the Nazarene." He *said to them, "I am *He*." And Judas also,
who was betraying Him, was standing with them.
6 So when He said to them, "I am *He*," they drew
back and fell to the ground. 7 Therefore He again
asked them, "[A]Whom do you seek?" And they said,
"Jesus the Nazarene." 8 Jesus answered, "I told you
that I am *He;* so if you seek Me, let these go their

17:17 [A]John 15:3 17:18 [A]John 3:17; 17:3, 8, 21, 23, 25 [B]Matt 10:5; John 4:38; 20:21 17:19 [A]John 15:13 [B]John 15:3 [C]2 Cor 7:14; Col 1:6; 1 John 3:18 17:21 [a]Gr tense indicates *continually believe* [A]John 10:38; 17:11, 23 [B]John 17:8 [C]John 3:17; 17:3, 8, 18, 23, 25 17:22 [A]John 1:14; 17:24 17:23 [a]Lit *into one* [b]Gr tense indicates *continually know* [A]John 10:38; 17:11, 21 [B]John 3:17; 17:3, 8, 18, 21, 25 [C]John 16:27 17:24 [A]John 17:2 [B]John 12:26 [C]John 1:14; 17:22 [D]Matt 25:34; John 17:5 17:25 [a]Lit *even the world* [A]John 17:11; 1 John 1:9 [B]John 7:29; 15:21 [C]John 3:17; 17:3, 8, 18, 21, 23 17:26 [A]John 17:6 [B]John 15:9 18:1 [a]Lit *winter-torrent* [b]Lit *and* [A]Matt 26:30, 36; Mark 14:26, 32; Luke 22:39 [B]2 Sam 15:23; 1 Kin 2:37; 15:13; 2 Kin 23:4, 6, 12; 2 Chr 15:16; 29:16; 30:14; Jer 31:40 [C]Matt 26:36; Mark 14:32; John 18:26 18:2 [a]Or *handing Him over* [A]Luke 21:37; 22:39 18:3 [a]Normally 600 men; *a battalion* [A]John 18:3-11: *Matt 26:47-56; Mark 14:43-50; Luke 22:47-53* [B]John 18:12; Acts 10:1 [C]John 7:32; 18:12, 18 [D]Matt 25:1 18:4 [A]John 6:64; 13:1, 11 [B]John 18:7 18:7 [A]John 18:4

destroy believers (1Pe 5:8), as with Job and Peter (Lk 22:31, 32), and in general (Eph 6:12), but God is their strong protector (12:31; 16:11; cf. Ps 27:1–3; 2Co 4:4; Jude 24, 25).

17:17 Sanctify. This verb also occurs in John's gospel at v. 19; 10:36. The idea of sanctification is the setting apart of something for a particular use. Accordingly, believers are set apart for God and His purposes alone so that the believer does only what God wants and hates all that God hates (Lv 11:44, 45; 1 Peter 1:16). Sanctification is accomplished by means of the truth, which is the revelation that the Son gave regarding all that the Father commanded Him to communicate and is now contained in the Scriptures left by the apostles. Cf. Eph 5:26; 2Th 2:13; Jas 1:21; 1Pe 1:22, 23.

17:19 I sanctify Myself. Meaning only that He was totally set apart for the Father's will (cf. 4:34; 5:19; 6:38; 7:16; 9:4). He did that in order that believers might be set apart to God by the truth He brought.

17:21 they may all be one. The basis of this unity centers in adherence to the revelation the Father mediated to His first disciples through His Son. Believers are also to be united in the common belief of the truth that was received in the Word of God (Php 2:2). This is not still a wish, but it became a reality when the Spirit came (cf. Ac 2:4; 1Co 12:13). It is not experiential unity, but the unity of common eternal life shared by all who believe the truth, and it results in the one body of Christ all sharing His life. *See notes on Eph 4:4–6.*

17:22 The glory which You have given Me. This refers to the believer's participation in all of the attributes and essence of God through the indwelling presence of the Holy Spirit (v. 10; cf. Col 1:27; 2Pe 1:4), as v. 23 makes clear ("I in them").

17:23 perfected in unity. The idea here is that they may be brought together in the same spiritual life around the truth that saves. That prayer was answered by the reality of 1Co 12:12, 13; Eph 2:14–22.

17:24 be with Me. This will be in heaven, where one can see the full glory that is His (cf. v. 5). Someday believers will not only see His glory, but share it (Php 3:20, 21; 1Jn 3:2). Until then, we participate in it spiritually (2Co 3:18).

17:25, 26 This summarizes the prayer of this chapter and promises the continuing indwelling Christ and His love. Cf. Ro 5:5.

18:1–40 The events of Jesus' arrest and trial receive emphasis in this chapter. Since John's purpose was to present Jesus as the Messiah and Son of God, he produced evidence to substantiate this purpose throughout his account of Jesus' passion. Through all of the debasing, shameful acts that were directed toward Jesus, John skillfully shows that these events, rather than detracting from His person and mission, actually constitute decisive evidence confirming who He was and the reason for which He came (1:29; cf. 2Co 5:21).

18:1 He went forth. Jesus' supreme courage is seen in His determination to go to the cross, where His purity and sinlessness would be violated as He bore the wrath of God for the sins of the world (3:16; *see note on 12:27*). The time of "the power of darkness" had come (Lk 22:53; *see notes on 1:5; 9:4; 13:30*). **ravine of the Kidron.** The Kidron valley was between the temple mount on the E of Jerusalem and the Mt. of Olives further to the E. **a garden.** On the slopes of the Mt. of Olives, named for ever-present olive groves, were many gardens. Matthew 26:36 and Mark 14:32 call this particular garden "Gethsemane," which means "oil press." **entered.** The wording here suggests a walled enclosure around the garden.

18:3 the *Roman* cohort and officers from the chief priests and the Pharisees. A full auxiliary Roman cohort had the potential strength of 1,000 men (i.e., 760 foot soldiers and 240 cavalry led by a *chiliarch* or "leader of a thousand"). Usually, however, in practice a cohort normally numbered 600 men, but could sometimes refer to as little as 200 (i.e., a "maniple"). Roman auxiliary troops were usually stationed at Caesarea, but during feast days they were garrisoned in the Antonia Fortress, on the NW perimeter of the temple complex (in order to ensure against mob violence or rebellion because of the large population that filled Jerusalem). The second group designated as "officers" refers to temple police who were the primary arresting officers since Jesus' destination after the arrest was to be brought before the High Priest (vv. 12–14). They came ready for resistance from Jesus and His followers ("weapons").

18:4 knowing all ... things. John, in a matter-of-fact way, states that Jesus was omniscient, thus God.

18:4–8 Whom do you seek? By twice asking that question (vv. 4, 7), to which they replied, "Jesus the Nazarene" (vv. 5, 7), Jesus was forcing them to acknowledge that they had no authority to take His disciples. In fact, He demanded that they let the disciples go (v. 8). The force of His demand was established by the power of His words. When He spoke, "I am *He*" (v. 6), a designation He had used before to declare Himself God (8:28, 58; cf. 6:35; 8:12; 10:7, 9, 11, 14; 11:25; 14:6; 15:1, 5), they were jolted backward and to the ground (v. 6). This power display and the authoritative demand not to take the disciples were of immense significance, as the next verse indicates.

way," 9 to fulfill the word which He spoke, "[A]Of those whom You have given Me I lost not one." 10 Simon Peter then, [A]having a sword, drew it and struck the high priest's slave, and cut off his right ear; and the slave's name was Malchus. 11 So Jesus said to Peter, "Put the sword into the sheath; [A]the cup which the Father has given Me, shall I not drink it?"

JESUS BEFORE THE PRIESTS

12 [A]So [B]the *Roman* [a]cohort and the [b]commander and the [B]officers of the Jews, arrested Jesus and bound Him, 13 and led Him to [A]Annas first; for he was father-in-law of [B]Caiaphas, who was high priest that year. 14 Now Caiaphas was the one who had advised the Jews that [A]it was expedient for one man to die on behalf of the people.

15 [A]Simon Peter was following Jesus, and *so was* another disciple. Now that disciple was known to the high priest, and entered with Jesus into [B]the court of the high priest, 16 [A]but Peter was standing at the door outside. So the other disciple, who was known to the high priest, went out and spoke to the doorkeeper, and brought Peter in. 17 [A]Then the slave-girl who kept the door *said to Peter, "[B]You are not also *one* of this man's disciples, are you?" He *said, "I am not." 18 Now the slaves and the [A]officers were standing *there,* having made [B]a charcoal fire, for it was cold and they were [C]warming themselves; and Peter was also with them, standing and warming himself.

19 [A]The high priest then questioned Jesus about His disciples, and about His teaching. 20 Jesus answered him, "I [A]have spoken openly to the world; I always [B]taught in [a]synagogues and [C]in the temple, where all the Jews come together; and I spoke nothing in secret. 21 Why do you question Me? Question those who have heard what I spoke to them; they know what I said." 22 When He had said this, one of the [A]officers standing nearby [B]struck Jesus, saying, "Is that the way You answer the high priest?" 23 [A]Jesus answered him, "If I have spoken wrongly, testify of the wrong; but if rightly, why do you strike Me?" 24 [A]So Annas sent Him bound to [A]Caiaphas the high priest.

PETER'S DENIAL OF JESUS

25 [A]Now [B]Simon Peter was standing and warming himself. So they said to him, "[C]You are not also *one* of His disciples, are you?" He denied *it,* and said, "I am not." 26 One of the slaves of the high priest, being a relative of the one [A]whose ear Peter cut off, *said, "Did I not see you in [B]the garden with Him?" 27 Peter then denied *it* again, and immediately [A]a rooster crowed.

JESUS BEFORE PILATE

28 [A]Then they *led Jesus from [B]Caiaphas into [C]the [a]Praetorium, and it was early; and they themselves did not enter into [C]the [a]Praetorium so that [D]they would not be defiled, but might eat the Passover.

18:9 [A]John 17:12 18:10 [A]Matt 26:51; Mark 14:47 18:11 [A]Matt 20:22; 26:39; Mark 14:36; Luke 22:42 18:12 [a]Or *battalion* [b]I.e. chiliarch, in command of a thousand troops [A]John 18:12f: *Matt 26:57ff* [B]John 18:3 18:13 [A]Luke 3:2; John 18:24 [B]Matt 26:3; John 11:49, 51 18:14 [A]John 11:50 18:15 [A]Matt 26:58; Mark 14:54; Luke 22:54 [B]Matt 26:3; John 18:24, 28 18:16 [A]John 18:16-18: *Matt 26:69f; Mark 14:66-68; Luke 22:55-57* 18:17 [A]Acts 12:13 [B]John 18:25 18:18 [A]John 18:3 [B]John 21:9 [C]Mark 14:54, 67 18:19 [A]John 18:19-24: *Matt 26:59-68; Mark 14:55-65; Luke 22:63-71* 18:20 [a]Lit *a synagogue* [A]John 7:26; 8:26 [B]Matt 4:23; John 6:59 [C]Matt 26:55 18:22 [A]John 18:3 [B]John 19:3 18:23 [A]Matt 5:39; Acts 23:2-5 18:24 [A]John 18:13 18:25 [A]John 18:25-27: *Matt 26:71-75; Mark 14:69-72; Luke 22:58-62* [B]John 18:18 [C]John 18:17 18:26 [A]John 18:10 [B]John 18:1 18:27 [A]John 13:38 18:28 [a]I.e. governor's official residence [A]Matt 27:2; Mark 15:1; Luke 23:1 [B]John 18:13 [C]Matt 27:27; John 18:33; 19:9 [D]John 11:55; Acts 11:3

18:9 I lost not one. Jesus was saying that He protected the disciples from being arrested, so He would not lose any of them, thus fulfilling the promises He made earlier (6:39, 40, 44; 10:28; 17:12). He knew that being arrested and perhaps imprisoned or executed was more than they could bear, and it could shatter their faith. So He made sure it did not happen. All believers are weak and vulnerable if not protected by the Lord. But He will never let them be tempted beyond what they can bear (1Co 10:13), as evidenced here. Believers are eternally secure, not in their own strength, but by the gracious and constant protection of the Savior (cf. Ro 8:35–39).

18:10 Simon Peter. He surely aimed for Malchus' head, ready to start the battle in defense of his Lord, but his was an ignorant love and courage. Christ healed Malchus' ear (Lk 22:51).

18:11 cup ... given Me ... not drink it? Peter's impetuous bravery in v. 10 was not only misguided, but exhibited failure to understand the centrality of the death that Jesus came to die. The "cup" in the OT is associated with suffering and especially judgment, i.e., the cup of God's wrath (Ps 75:8; Is 51:17, 22; Jer 25:15; Eze 23:31–34; *see notes on Mt 26:39; Mk 14:36; Lk 22:42*; cf. Rev 14:10; 16:19).

18:13 Annas first. Annas held the High Priesthood office from A.D. 6–15 when Valerius Gratus, Pilate's predecessor, removed him from office. In spite of this, Annas continued to wield influence over the office, most likely because he was still regarded as the true High Priest and also because no fewer than 5 of his sons, and his son-in-law Caiaphas, held the office at one time or another. Two trials occurred: one Jewish and one Roman. The Jewish phase began with the informal examination by Annas (vv. 12–14, 19–23), probably giving time for the members of the Sanhedrin to hurriedly gather together. A session before the Sanhedrin was next (Mt 26:57–68) at which consensus was reached to send Jesus to Pilate (Mt 27:1, 2). The Roman phase began with a first examination before Pilate (vv. 28–38a; Mt 27:11–14), and then Herod Antipas ("that fox"—Lk 13:32) interrogated Him (Lk 23:6–12). Lastly, Jesus appeared again before Pilate (vv. 38b–19:16; Mt 27:15–31).

18:13, 14 Caiaphas. *See notes on 11:49.* The examination under Caiaphas was not reported by John (see Mt 26:57–68).

18:15 another disciple ... that disciple. Traditionally, this person has been identified with the "disciple whom Jesus loved" (13:23, 24), i.e., John the apostle who authored this gospel, but he never mentioned his own name (see Introduction: Author and Date).

18:16–18 Peter. Here is the record of the first of Peter's predicted 3 denials (*see note on 18:25–27*).

18:16 known to the high priest. Apparently, John was more than just an acquaintance, because the term for "known" can mean a friend (Lk 2:44). The fact that he mentioned Nicodemus (3:1) and Joseph (19:38) may indicate his knowledge of other prominent Jews.

18:19 At the core of their concern was Jesus' claim that He was the Son of God (19:7). In a formal Jewish hearing, to question the defendant may have been illegal because a case had to rest on the weight of the testimony of witnesses (*see note on 1:7*). If this was an informal interrogation before the High Priest emeritus and not before the Sanhedrin, Annas may have thought that he was not bound by such rules. Jesus, however, knew the law and demanded that witnesses be called (vv. 20, 21). An official knew Jesus was rebuking Annas and retaliated (v. 22).

18:23 In essence, Jesus was asking for a fair trial, while His opponents, who had already decided on the sentence (see 11:47–57), had no intention of providing one.

18:24 Annas recognized that he was not getting anywhere with Jesus and sent Him to Caiaphas because, if Jesus was to be brought before Pilate for execution, the legal accusation must be brought by the current reigning High Priest (i.e., Caiaphas) in his capacity as chairman of the Sanhedrin (*see also note on v. 13*).

18:25–27 Simon Peter. Here was the final fulfillment of Jesus' prediction that Peter would deny Him 3 times (cf. Mt 26:34).

18:28–19:16 This section deals with Jesus' trial before Pilate. Although Pilate appears in every scene here, Jesus Himself and the nature of His kingdom occupy center stage.

18:28 Praetorium. The headquarters of the commanding officer of the Roman military camp or the headquarters of the Roman military governor (i.e., Pilate). Pilate's normal

29 [A]Therefore Pilate went out to them and *said,
"What accusation do you bring against this Man?"
30 They answered and said to him, "If this Man were
not an evildoer, we would not have delivered Him to
you." 31 So Pilate said to them, "Take Him yourselves,
and judge Him according to your law." The Jews
said to him, "We are not permitted to put anyone
to death," 32 to fulfill [A]the word of Jesus which He
spoke, signifying by what kind of death He was
about to die.
33 Therefore Pilate [A]entered again into the Praetorium, and summoned Jesus and said to Him, "[B]Are
You the King of the Jews?" 34 Jesus answered, "Are
you saying this [a]on your own initiative, or did others
tell you about Me?" 35 Pilate answered, "I am not a
Jew, am I? Your own nation and the chief priests
delivered You to me; what have You done?" 36 Jesus
answered, "[A]My kingdom [a]is not of this world. If
My kingdom were of this world, then My servants
would be fighting so that I would not be handed
over to the Jews; but as it is, My kingdom is not [b]of
this realm." 37 Therefore Pilate said to Him, "So You
are a king?" Jesus answered, "[A]You say *correctly*
that I am a king. For this I have been born, and for
this I have come into the world, [B]to testify to the
truth. [C]Everyone who is of the truth hears My voice."
38 Pilate *said to Him, "What is truth?"
And when he had said this, he [A]went out again to
the Jews and *said to them, "[B]I find no guilt in Him.
39 [A]But you have a custom that I release someone [a]for
you at the Passover; do you wish then that I release
[a]for you the King of the Jews?" 40 So they cried out
again, saying, "[A]Not this Man, but Barabbas." Now
Barabbas was a robber.

THE CROWN OF THORNS

19 Pilate then took Jesus and [a,A]scourged Him.
2 [A]And the soldiers twisted together a crown
of thorns and put it on His head, and put a purple
robe on Him; 3 and they *began* to come up to Him
and say, "[A]Hail, King of the Jews!" and to [B]give Him
slaps *in the face*. 4 Pilate [A]came out again and *said to
them, "Behold, I am bringing Him out to you so that
you may know that [B]I find no guilt in Him." 5 Jesus
then came out, [A]wearing the crown of thorns and the
purple robe. *Pilate* *said to them, "Behold, the Man!"

18:29 [A]John 18:29-38: *Matt 27:11-14; Mark 15:2-5; Luke 23:2, 3* 18:32 [A]Matt 20:19; 26:2; Mark 10:33f; Luke 18:32f; John 3:14; 8:28; 12:32f 18:33 [A]John 18:28, 29; 19:9 [B]Luke 23:3; John 19:12 18:34 [a]Lit *from yourself* 18:36 [a]Or *is not derived from* [b]Lit *from here* [A]Matt 26:53; Luke 17:21; John 6:15 18:37 [A]Matt 27:11; Mark 15:2; Luke 22:70; 23:3 [B]John 1:14; 3:32; 8:14 [C]John 8:47; 1 John 4:6 18:38 [A]John 18:33; 19:4 [B]Luke 23:4; John 19:4, 6 18:39 [a]Or *to you* [A]John 18:39-19:16: *Matt 27:15-26; Mark 15:6-15; Luke 23:18-25* 18:40 [A]Acts 3:14 19:1 [a]Or *had Him scourged* [A]Matt 27:26 19:2 [A]Matt 27:27-30: *Mark 15:16-19* 19:3 [A]Matt 27:29; Mark 15:18 [B]John 18:22 19:4 [A]John 18:33, 38 [B]Luke 23:4; John 18:38; 19:6 19:5 [A]John 19:2

headquarters was in Caesarea, in the palace that Herod the Great had built for himself. However, Pilate and his predecessors made it a point to be in Jerusalem during the feasts in order to quell any riots. Jerusalem became his *praetorium* or headquarters. **early.** The word is ambiguous. Most likely, it refers to around 6:00 a.m. since many Roman officials began their day very early and finished by 10:00 or 11:00 a.m. **not be defiled.** Jewish oral law gives evidence that a Jew who entered the dwelling places of Gentiles became ceremonially unclean. Their remaining outside in the colonnade avoided that pollution. John loads this statement with great irony by noting the chief priests' scrupulousness in the matter of ceremonial cleansing, when all the time they were incurring incomparably greater moral defilement by their proceedings against Jesus.

18:29 What accusation . . . ? This question formally opened the Roman civil phase of proceedings against Jesus (in contrast to the religious phase before the Jews in v. 24). The fact that Roman troops were used at the arrest (*see note on v. 3*) proves that the Jewish authorities communicated something about this case to Pilate in advance. Although they most likely had expected Pilate to confirm their judgment against Jesus and order His death sentence, Pilate ordered instead a fresh hearing in his presence.

18:31 We are not permitted. When Rome took over Judea and began direct rule through a prefect in A.D. 6, capital jurisdiction (i.e., the right to execute) was taken away from the Jews and given to the Roman governor. Capital punishment was the most jealously guarded of all the attributes in Roman provincial administration.

18:32 to fulfill the word of Jesus. Jesus had said that He would die by being "lifted up" (3:14; 8:28; 12:32, 33). If the Jews had executed Him it would have been by throwing Him down and stoning Him. But God providentially controlled all the political procedures to assure that when sentence was finally passed, He would be crucified by the Romans and not stoned by the Jews, as was Stephen (Ac 7:59). The Jews may have preferred this form of execution based on Dt 21:23.

18:34 others. Again (cf. vv. 20, 21), Jesus demanded witnesses.

18:36 My kingdom is not of this realm. By this phrase, Jesus meant that His kingdom is not connected to earthly political and national entities, nor does it have its origin in the evil world system that is in rebellion against God. If His kingdom was of this world, He would have fought. The kingships of this world preserve themselves by fighting with force. Messiah's kingdom does not originate in the efforts of man, but with the Son of Man forcefully and decisively conquering sin in the lives of His people and someday conquering the evil world system at His second coming when He establishes the earthly form of His kingdom. His kingdom was no threat to the national identity of Israel or the political and military identity of Rome. It exists in the spiritual dimension until the end of the age (Rev 11:15).

18:38 What is truth? In response to Jesus' mention of "truth" in v. 37, Pilate responded rhetorically with cynicism, convinced that no answer existed to the question. The retort proved that he was not among those whom the Father had given to the Son ("Everyone who is of the truth hears My voice"—v. 37; *see notes on 10:1–5*). **no guilt.** Cf. 19:4. John made it clear that Jesus was not guilty of any sin or crime, thus exhibiting the severe injustice and guilt of both the Jews and Romans who executed Him.

18:40 Now Barabbas was a robber. The word "robber" means "one who seizes plunder" and may depict not only a robber but a terrorist or guerrilla fighter who participated in bloody insurrection (see Mk 15:7).

19:1 scourged. Pilate appears to have flogged Jesus as a strategy to set Him free (see vv. 4–6). He was hoping that the Jews would be appeased by this action and that sympathy for Jesus' suffering would result in their desire that He be released (see Lk 23:13–16). Scourging was a horribly cruel act in which the victim was stripped, tied to a post and beaten by several torturers, i.e., soldiers who alternated when exhausted. For victims who were not Roman citizens, the preferred instrument was a short wooden handle to which several leather thongs were attached. Each leather thong had pieces of bones or metal on the end. The beatings were so savage that sometimes victims died. The body could be torn or lacerated to such an extent that muscles, veins or bones were exposed. Such flogging often preceded execution in order to weaken and dehumanize the victim (Is 53:5). Apparently, however, Pilate intended this to create sympathy for Jesus.

19:2 crown of thorns. This "crown" was made from the long spikes (up to 12 inches) of a date palm formed into an imitation of the radiating crowns which oriental kings wore. The long thorns would have cut deeply into Jesus' head, adding to the pain and bleeding. **purple robe.** The color represented royalty. The robe probably was a military cloak flung around Jesus' shoulders, intended to mock His claim to be King of the Jews.

19:4 I find no guilt in Him. *See note on 18:38.*

19:5 "Behold, the Man!" Pilate dramatically presented Jesus after His torturous treatment by the soldiers. Jesus would have been swollen, bruised, and bleeding. Pilate displayed Jesus as a beaten and pathetic figure hoping to gain the people's choice of Jesus for release. Pilate's phrase is filled with sarcasm since he was attempting to impress upon the Jewish authorities that Jesus was not the dangerous man that they had made Him out to be.

6 So when the chief priests and the [A]officers saw Him,
they cried out saying, "Crucify, crucify!" Pilate *said
to them, "Take Him yourselves and crucify Him, for
[B]I find no guilt in Him." 7 The Jews answered him,
"[A]We have a law, and by that law He ought to die
because He [B]made Himself out *to be* the Son of God."
8 Therefore when Pilate heard this statement, he
was *even* more afraid; 9 and he [A]entered into the
[a]Praetorium again and *said to Jesus, "Where are
You from?" But [B]Jesus gave him no answer. 10 So Pilate *said to Him, "You do not speak to me? Do You
not know that I have authority to release You, and
I have authority to crucify You?" 11 Jesus answered,
"[A]You would have no authority [a]over Me, unless it
had been given you from above; for this reason [B]he
who delivered Me to you has *the* greater sin." 12 As
a result of this Pilate [a]made efforts to release Him,
but the Jews cried out saying, "[A]If you release this
Man, you are no friend of Caesar; everyone who
makes himself out *to be* a king [b]opposes Caesar."
13 Therefore when Pilate heard these words, he
brought Jesus out, and [A]sat down on the judgment
seat at a place called [a]The Pavement, but [B]in [b]Hebrew,
Gabbatha. 14 Now it was [A]the day of preparation for
the Passover; it was about the [a,B]sixth hour. And he
*said to the Jews, "Behold, [C]your King!" 15 So they cried
out, "[A]Away with *Him,* away with *Him,* crucify Him!"
Pilate *said to them, "Shall I crucify your King?" The
chief priests answered, "We have no king but Caesar."

THE CRUCIFIXION

16 So he then [A]handed Him over to them to be
crucified.
17 [A]They took Jesus, therefore, and He went out,
[a,B]bearing His own cross, to the place called [C]the Place of
a Skull, which is called [D]in [b]Hebrew, Golgotha. 18 There
they crucified Him, and with Him [A]two other men, one
on either side, and Jesus in between. 19 Pilate also wrote
an inscription and put it on the cross. It was written,

"[A]JESUS THE NAZARENE, [B]THE KING
OF THE JEWS."

20 Therefore many of the Jews read this inscription, for the place where Jesus was crucified was
near the city; and it was written [A]in [a]Hebrew, Latin

19:6 [A]Matt 26:58; John 18:3 [B]Luke 23:4; John 18:38; 19:4 19:7 [A]Lev 24:16; Matt 26:63-66 [B]John 5:18; 10:33 19:9 [a]I.e. governor's official residence [A]John 18:33 [B]Matt 26:63; 27:12, 14; John 18:34-37 19:11 [a]Lit *against* [A]Rom 13:1 [B]John 18:13f, 28ff; Acts 3:13 19:12 [a]Lit *was seeking to* [b]Or *speaks against* [A]Luke 23:2; John 18:33ff 19:13 [a]Gr *The Lithostrotos* [b]I.e. Jewish Aramaic [A]Matt 27:19 [B]John 5:2; 19:17, 20 19:14 [a]Perhaps 6 a.m. [A]Matt 27:62; John 19:31, 42 [B]Matt 27:45; Mark 15:25 [C]John 19:19, 21 19:15 [A]Luke 23:18 19:16 [A]Matt 27:26; Mark 15:15; Luke 23:25 19:17 [a]Lit *bearing the cross for Himself* [b]I.e. Jewish Aramaic [A]John 19:17-24: *Matt 27:33-44; Mark 15:22-32; Luke 23:33-43* [B]Matt 27:32; Mark 15:21; Luke 14:27; 23:26 [C]Luke 23:33 [D]John 19:13 19:18 [A]Luke 23:32 19:19 [A]Matt 27:37; Mark 15:26; Luke 23:38 [B]John 19:14, 21 19:20 [a]I.e. Jewish Aramaic [A]John 19:13

19:6 Take Him yourselves and crucify Him. The pronouns "yourselves" and "Him" have an emphatic force indicating Pilate's disgust and indignation at the Jews for their callousness toward Jesus.

19:7 We have a law. This probably refers to Lv 24:16: "the one who blasphemes the name of the LORD shall surely be put to death." The charge of blasphemy (5:18; 8:58, 59; 10:33, 36) was central in Jesus' trial before Caiaphas (see Mt 26:57–68).

19:8 more afraid. Many Roman officials were deeply superstitious. While Jews interpreted Jesus' claims as messianic, to the Greco-Roman person, the title "Son of God" would place Jesus in the category of "divine men" who were gifted with supernatural powers. Pilate was afraid because he had just whipped and tortured someone who, in his mind, could bring down a curse or vengeance upon him.

19:9 Where are You from? Pilate was concerned about Jesus' origins. His superstitious mind was wondering just what kind of person he was dealing with.

19:11 Jesus' statement here indicates that even the worst evil cannot escape the sovereignty of God. Pilate had no real control (vv. 10, 11), yet still stood as a responsible moral agent for his actions. When confronted with opposition and evil, Jesus often found solace in the sovereignty of His Father (e.g., 6:43, 44, 65; 10:18, 28, 29). **he who delivered Me to you has *the* greater sin.** This could refer either to Judas or Caiaphas. Since Caiaphas took such an active part in the plot against Jesus (11:49–53) and presided over the Sanhedrin, the reference may center on him (18:30, 35). The critical point is not the identity of the person, but guilt because of the deliberate, high-handed, and coldly calculated act of handing Jesus over to Pilate, after having seen and heard the overwhelming evidence that He was Messiah and Son of God. Pilate had not been exposed to that. *See notes on 9:41; 15:22–24; Heb 10:26–31.*

19:12 no friend of Caesar. This statement by the Jews was loaded with irony, for the Jews' hatred of Rome certainly indicated they too were no friends of Caesar. But they knew Pilate feared Tiberius Caesar (the Roman emperor at the time of Jesus' crucifixion) since he had a highly suspicious personality and exacted ruthless punishment. Pilate had already created upheaval in Jerusalem by several foolish acts that had infuriated the Jews, and so was under the scrutiny of Rome to see if his ineptness continued. The Jews were intimidating him by threatening another upheaval that could spell the end of his power in Jerusalem, if he did not execute Jesus.

19:13 the judgment seat. Pilate capitulated under pressure (v. 12) and prepared to render judgment on the original charge of sedition against Rome. This "judgment seat" was the place Pilate sat to render the official verdict. The seat was placed on an area paved with stones known as "The Pavement." The irony is that Pilate rendered judgment on the One whom the Father Himself entrusted with all judgment (5:22) and who would render a just condemnation of Pilate.

19:14 day of preparation for the Passover. Since this refers to the day before the Passover when preparation for the Passover was done, John presents Jesus as being sent to execution about the time Passover lambs were being slaughtered. For the chronology of the week, see Introduction: Interpretive Challenges. **about the sixth hour.** John is here reckoning time by the Roman method of the day beginning at midnight. *See note on Mk 15:25.* **Behold, your King!** That was Pilate's mockery—that such a brutalized and helpless man was a fitting king for them. This mockery continued in the placard on the cross (vv. 19–22).

19:17 bearing His own cross. This refers to the cross-member, the horizontal bar. The condemned man carried it on his shoulders to the place of execution. Jesus carried His cross as far as the city gate, but due to the effects of the previous brutal beating, someone else had to eventually carry it for Him, i.e., Simon of Cyrene (Mt 27:32; Mk 15:21; Lk 23:26). **Golgotha.** This term is an Eng. transliteration of the Gr. which, in turn, is a translation of the Aram. word meaning "skull." The place probably derived its name from its appearance. The precise location of the site today is uncertain.

19:18 crucified Him. Jesus was made to lie on the ground while His arms were stretched out and nailed to the horizontal beam that He carried. The beam was then hoisted up, along with the victim, and fastened to the vertical beam. His feet were nailed to the vertical beam to which sometimes was attached a piece of wood that served as a kind of seat that partially supported the weight of the body. The latter, however, was designed to prolong and increase the agony, not relieve it. Having been stripped naked and beaten, Jesus could hang in the hot sun for hours if not days. To breathe, it was necessary to push with the legs and pull with the arms, creating excruciating pain. Terrible muscle spasms wracked the entire body; but since collapse meant asphyxiation, the struggle for life continued (*see note on Mt 27:31*). **two other men.** Matthew (27:38) and Luke (23:33) use the same word for these two as John used for Barabbas, i.e., guerrilla fighters. *See note on 18:40.*

19:19–22 wrote an inscription. The custom in such executions was to place a placard or tablet around the neck of the victim as he made his way to execution. The tablet would then be nailed to the victim's cross (see Mt 27:37; Mk 15:26; Lk 23:38). Pilate used this opportunity for mocking revenge on the

and in Greek. 21 So the chief priests of the Jews were
saying to Pilate, "Do not write, '[A]The King of the
Jews'; but that He said, 'I am [A]King of the Jews.' "
22 Pilate answered, "[A]What I have written I have
written."
23 Then [A]the soldiers, when they had crucified
Jesus, took His outer garments and made [B]four
parts, a part to every soldier and *also* the [a]tunic;
now the tunic was seamless, woven [b]in one piece.
24 So they said to one another, "[A]Let us not tear it, but
cast lots for it, *to decide* whose it shall be"; [B]*this was*
to fulfill the Scripture: "THEY [C]DIVIDED MY OUTER
GARMENTS AMONG THEM, AND FOR MY CLOTHING
THEY CAST [a]LOTS." 25 Therefore the soldiers did these
things.
[A]But standing by the cross of Jesus were [B]His
mother, and His mother's sister, Mary the *wife* of
Clopas, and [C]Mary Magdalene. 26 When Jesus then
saw His mother, and [A]the disciple whom He loved
standing nearby, He *said to His mother, "[B]Woman,
behold, your son!" 27 Then He *said to the disciple,
"Behold, your mother!" From that hour the disciple
took her into [A]his own *household.*
28 After this, Jesus, [A]knowing that all things had
already been accomplished, [B]to fulfill the Scripture,
*said, "[C]I am thirsty." 29 A jar full of sour wine was
standing there; so [A]they put a sponge full of the
sour wine upon *a branch of* hyssop and brought
it up to His mouth. 30 Therefore when Jesus had
received the sour wine, He said, "[A]It is finished!"
And He bowed His head and [B]gave up His spirit.

CARE OF THE BODY OF JESUS

31 Then the Jews, because it was [A]the day of preparation, so that [B]the bodies would not remain on
the cross on the Sabbath ([a]for that Sabbath was a
[C]high day), asked Pilate that their legs might be
broken, and *that* they might be taken away. 32 So the
soldiers came, and broke the legs of the first man
and of the other who was [A]crucified with Him; 33 but
coming to Jesus, when they saw that He was already
dead, they did not break His legs. 34 But one of the
soldiers pierced His side with a spear, and immediately [A]blood and water came out. 35 And he who
has seen has [A]testified, and his testimony is true;
and he knows that he is telling the truth, so that you
also may believe. 36 For these things came to pass
[A]to fulfill the Scripture, "[B]NOT A BONE OF HIM SHALL
BE [a]BROKEN." 37 And again another Scripture says,
"[A]THEY SHALL LOOK ON HIM WHOM THEY PIERCED."

19:21 [A]John 19:14, 19 19:22 [A]Gen 43:14; Esth 4:16 19:23 [a]Gr *khiton,* the garment worn next to the skin [b]Lit *from the upper part through the whole* [A]Matt 27:35; Mark 15:24; Luke 23:34 [B]Acts 12:4 19:24 [a]Lit *a lot* [A]Ex 28:32; Matt 27:35; Mark 15:24; Luke 23:34 [B]John 19:28, 36f [C]Ps 22:18 19:25 [A]Matt 27:55f; Mark 15:40f; Luke 23:49 [B]Matt 12:46 [C]Luke 8:2; John 20:1, 18 19:26 [A]John 13:23 [B]John 2:4 19:27 [A]Luke 18:28; John 1:11; 16:32; Acts 21:6 19:28 [A]John 13:1; 17:4 [B]John 19:24, 36f [C]Ps 69:21 19:29 [A]John 19:29, 30: *Matt 27:48, 50; Mark 15:36f; Luke 23:36* 19:30 [A]John 17:4 [B]Matt 27:50; Mark 15:37; Luke 23:46 19:31 [a]Lit *for the day of that Sabbath was great* [A]John 19:14, 42 [B]Deut 21:23; Josh 8:29; 10:26f [C]Ex 12:16 19:32 [A]John 19:18 19:34 [A]1 John 5:6, 8 19:35 [A]John 15:27; 21:24 19:36 [a]Or *crushed* or *shattered* [A]John 19:24, 28 [B]Ex 12:46; Num 9:12; Ps 34:20 19:37 [A]Zech 12:10; Rev 1:7

Jews who had so intimidated him into this execution (*see note on v. 12*).

19:23 His outer garments ... and *also* the tunic. By custom, the clothes of the condemned person were the property of the executioners. The division of the garments suggests that the execution squad was made up of 4 soldiers (cf. Ac 12:4). The tunic was worn next to the skin. The plural "garments" probably refers to other clothes, including an outer garment, belt, sandals, and head covering.

19:24 John cites Ps 22:18. In the psalm, David, beset by physical distress and mockery by his opponents, used the symbolism of the common practice in an execution scene in which the executioner divided the victim's clothes to portray the depth of his trouble. It is notable that David precisely described a form of execution that he had never seen. The passage was typologically prophetic of Jesus, David's heir to the messianic throne (see Mt 27:46; Mk 15:34).

19:25 Although the exact number of women mentioned here is questioned, John probably refers to 4 women rather than 3, i.e., two by name and two without naming them: 1) "His mother" (Mary); 2) "His mother's sister" (probably Salome [Mk 15:40] the sister of Mary and mother of James and John, the sons of Zebedee [Mt 27:56, 57; Mk 15:40]); 3) "Mary the *wife* of Cleopas" (the mother of James the younger and Joses—Mt 27:56); and 4) Mary Magdalene ("Magdalene" signifies "Magdala" a village on the W shore of Galilee, 2 or 3 mi. N of Tiberias). Mary Magdalene figures prominently in the resurrection account (see 20:1–18; cf. Lk 8:2, 3 where Jesus healed her from demon possession).

19:26 the disciple whom He loved. This is a reference to John (*see note on 13:23*; cf. Introduction: Author and Date). Jesus, as first-born and breadwinner of the family before He started His ministry, did not give the responsibility to His brothers because they were not sympathetic to His ministry nor did they believe in Him (7:3–5) and they likely were not present at the time (i.e., their home was in Capernaum—see 2:12).

19:29 The drink here is not to be confused with the wine "mixed with gall" offered to Him on the way to the cross (Mt 27:34) intended to help deaden pain. The purpose of this drink (cf. Mk 15:36) was to prolong life and increase the torture and pain. It was a cheap, sour wine used by soldiers. The use of this word recalls Ps 69:21 where the same noun occurs in the LXX. Hyssop is a little plant that is ideal for sprinkling (see Ex 12:22).

19:30 It is finished! The verb here carries the idea of fulfilling one's task and, in religious contexts, has the idea of fulfilling one's religious obligations (see 17:4). The entire work of redemption had been brought to completion. The single Gr. word here (translated "it is finished") has been found in the papyri being placed on receipts for taxes meaning "paid in full" (see Col 3:13, 14). **He ... gave up His spirit.** The sentence signaled that Jesus "handed over" His spirit as an act of His will. No one took His life from Him, for He voluntarily and willingly gave it up (see 10:17, 18).

19:31 day of preparation. This refers to Friday, the day before or the "preparation" day for the Sabbath. See Introduction: Interpretive Challenges. **would not remain on the cross on the Sabbath.** The normal Roman practice was to leave crucified men and women on the cross until they died (and this could take days) and then leave their rotting bodies hanging there to be devoured by vultures. The Mosaic law insisted that anyone being impaled (usually after execution) should not remain there overnight (Dt 21:22, 23). Such a person was under God's curse, and to leave him exposed would be to desecrate the land in their minds. **their legs might be broken.** In order to hasten death for certain reasons, soldiers would smash the legs of the victim with an iron mallet. Not only did this action induce shock and additional loss of blood, but it prevented the victim from pushing with his legs to keep breathing (*see note on v. 18.*), and thus the victim died due to asphyxiation.

19:34 The soldier's stabbing of Jesus' side caused significant penetration because of the sudden flow of blood and water. Either the spear pierced Jesus' heart, or the chest cavity was pierced at the bottom. In either event, John mentioned the outflow of "blood and water" to emphasize that Jesus was unquestionably dead.

19:35 he who has seen. This has reference to John the apostle who was an eyewitness of these events (v. 26; 13:23; 20:2; 21:7, 20; cf. 1Jn 1:1–4).

19:36, 37 John quoted from either Ex 12:46 or Nu 9:12, both of which specify that no bone of the Passover lamb may be broken. Since the NT portrays Jesus as the Passover Lamb that takes away the sins of the world (1:29; cf. 1Co 5:7; 1Pe 1:19), these verses have special typologically prophetic significance for Him. The quote in v. 37 comes from Zec 12:10, which indicates God Himself was pierced when His representative, the Shepherd (Zec 13:7; cf. Zec 11:4, 8, 9, 15–17) was pierced. The anguish and contrition of the Jews in the Zechariah passage, because of their wounding of God's Shepherd, is typologically prophetic of the time of the coming of the Son of God, Messiah,

38 [A]After these things Joseph of Arimathea, being
a disciple of Jesus, but a [B]secret *one* for [C]fear of the
Jews, asked Pilate that he might take away the body
of Jesus; and Pilate granted permission. So he came
and took away His body. 39 [A]Nicodemus, who had first
come to Him by night, also came, [B]bringing a [a]mix-
ture of [C]myrrh and aloes, about a [D]hundred [b]pounds
weight. 40 So they took the body of Jesus and [A]bound
it in [B]linen wrappings with the spices, as is the burial
custom of the Jews. 41 Now in the place where He was
crucified there was a garden, and in the garden a [A]new
tomb [B]in which no one had yet been laid. 42 Therefore
because of the Jewish day of [A]preparation, since the
tomb was [B]nearby, they laid Jesus there.

THE EMPTY TOMB

20 [A]Now on the first *day* of the week [B]Mary Magdalene *came early to the tomb, while it *was
still dark, and *saw [C]the stone *already* taken away
from the tomb. 2 So she *ran and *came to Simon
Peter and to the other [A]disciple whom Jesus loved,
and *said to them, "[B]They have taken away the Lord
out of the tomb, and we do not know where they
have laid Him." 3 [A]So Peter and the other disciple
went forth, and they were going to the tomb. 4 The
two were running together; and the other disciple
ran ahead faster than Peter and came to the tomb
first; 5 and [A]stooping and looking in, he *saw the
[B]linen wrappings lying *there;* but he did not go in.
6 And so Simon Peter also *came, following him, and
entered the tomb; and he *saw the linen wrappings
lying *there,* 7 and [A]the face-cloth which had been on
His head, not lying with the [B]linen wrappings, but
rolled up in a place by itself. 8 So the other disciple
who [A]had first come to the tomb then also entered,
and he saw and believed. 9 For as yet [A]they did not
understand the Scripture, [B]that He must rise again
from the dead. 10 So the disciples went away again
[A]to their own homes.

11 [A]But Mary was standing outside the tomb
weeping; and so, as she wept, she [B]stooped and
looked into the tomb; 12 and she *saw [A]two angels
in white sitting, one at the head and one at the
feet, where the body of Jesus had been lying. 13 And
they *said to her, "[A]Woman, why are you weeping?"
She *said to them, "Because [B]they have taken away

19:38 [A]John 19:38-42: *Matt 27:57-61; Mark 15:42-47; Luke 23:50-56* [B]Mark 15:43 [C]John 7:13 19:39 [a]Two early mss read *package of* [b]Lit *100 litras* (12 oz each) [A]John 3:1 [B]Mark 16:1 [C]Ps 45:8; Prov 7:17; Song 4:14; Matt 2:11 [D]John 12:3 19:40 [A]Matt 26:12; Mark 14:8; John 11:44 [B]Luke 24:12; John 20:5, 7 19:41 [A]Matt 27:60 [B]Luke 23:53 19:42 [A]John 19:14, 31 [B]John 19:20, 41 20:1 [A]John 20:1-8: *Matt 28:1-8; Mark 16:1-8; Luke 24:1-10* [B]John 19:25; 20:18 [C]Matt 27:60, 66; 28:2; Mark 15:46; 16:3f; Luke 24:2; John 11:38 20:2 [A]John 13:23 [B]John 20:13 20:3 [A]John 20:3-10: *Luke 24:12* 20:5 [A]John 20:11 [B]John 19:40 20:7 [A]John 11:44 [B]John 19:40 20:8 [A]John 20:4 20:9 [A]Matt 22:29; John 2:22 [B]Luke 24:26ff, 46 20:10 [A]Luke 24:12 20:11 [A]Mark 16:5 [B]John 20:5 20:12 [A]Matt 28:2f; Mark 16:5; Luke 24:4 20:13 [A]John 20:15 [B]John 20:2

when at His return, Israel shall mourn for the rejection and killing of their King (cf. Rev 1:7).

19:38 Joseph of Arimathea. This man appears in all 4 Gospels, only in connection with Jesus' burial. The Synoptics relate that he was a member of the Sanhedrin (Mk 15:43), he was rich (Mt 27:57), and he was looking for the kingdom of God (Lk 23:51). John treated the idea of secret disciples negatively (see 12:42, 43), but since Joseph publicly risked his reputation and even his life in asking for the body of Jesus, John pictured him in a more positive light.

19:39 Nicodemus. *See notes on 3:1–10.* **about a hundred pounds.** An inaccurate understanding of the term used in the original, this mixture of spices weighed closer to 65 pounds. Myrrh was a very fragrant gummy resin, which the Jews turned into a powdered form and mixed with aloes, a powder from the aromatic sandalwood. The Jews did not embalm but did this procedure to stifle the smell of putrefaction (*see note on 11:39*).

19:40 linen wrappings . . . spices. The spices most likely were laid on the entire length of the strips of linen which were then wound around Jesus' body. More spices were laid under the body and perhaps packed around it. The sticky resin would help the cloth adhere.

19:41, 42 garden . . . new tomb. Only John relates that the tomb was near the place where Jesus was crucified. Since the Sabbath, when all work had to cease, was nearly upon them (6:00 p.m., sunset), the nearness of the tomb was helpful. John does not mention that Joseph of Arimathea rolled a stone across the tomb's mouth or that Mary Madgdalene and Mary the mother of Joses saw where He was laid (Mt 27:58–61). For the time of the Lord's death and burial, *see note on Mt 27:45.*

20:1–31 This chapter records the appearances of Jesus to His own followers: 1) the appearance to Mary Magdalene (vv. 1–18); 2) the appearance to the 10 disciples (vv. 19–23); and 3) the appearance to Thomas (vv. 24–29). Jesus did not appear to unbelievers (see 14:19; 16:16, 22) because the evidence of His resurrection would not have convinced them, as the miracles had not (Lk 16:31). The god of this world had blinded them and prevented their belief (2Co 4:4). Jesus, therefore, appears exclusively to His own in order to confirm their faith in the living Christ. Such appearances were so profound that they transformed the disciples from cowardly men hiding in fear to bold witnesses for Jesus (e.g., Peter; see 18:27; cf. Ac 2:14–39). Once again John's purpose in recording these resurrection appearances was to demonstrate that Jesus' physical and bodily resurrection was the crowning proof that He truly is the Messiah and Son of God who laid down His life for His own (10:17, 18; 15:13; cf. Ro 1:4).

20:1 first *day* of the week. A reference to Sunday. From then on, believers set aside Sunday to meet and remember the marvelous resurrection of the Lord (see Ac 20:7; 1Co 16:2). It became known as the Lord's Day (Rev 1:10). *See notes on Lk 24:4, 34.* **Mary Magdalene came early to the tomb, while it was still dark.** Perhaps the reason why Jesus first appeared to Mary Magdalene was to demonstrate grace by His personal, loving faithfulness to someone who formerly had a sordid past; but clearly also because she loved Him so dearly and deeply that she appeared before anyone else at the tomb. Her purpose in coming was to finish the preparation of Jesus' body for burial by bringing more spices to anoint the corpse (Lk 24:1).

20:2 other disciple whom Jesus loved. This is the author John. **They have taken.** Though Jesus had predicted His resurrection numerous times, it was more than she could believe at that point. It would take His showing Himself alive to them by many "convincing proofs" (Ac 1:3) for them to believe.

20:5–7 saw the linen wrappings lying *there.* A contrast existed between the resurrection of Lazarus (11:44) and that of Jesus. While Lazarus came forth from the grave wearing his graveclothes, Jesus' body, though physical and material, was glorified and was now able to pass through the graveclothes much in the same way that He later appeared in the locked room (see vv. 19, 20; cf. Php 3:21). **linen wrappings . . . face-cloth.** The state of those items indicates no struggle, no hurried unwrapping of the body by grave robbers, who wouldn't unwrap the body anyway, since transporting it elsewhere would be easier and more pleasant if it was left in its wrapped and spiced condition. All appearances indicated that no one had taken the body, but that it had moved through the cloth and left it behind in the tomb.

20:8 the other disciple. John saw the graveclothes and was convinced by them that He had risen.

20:9 did not understand the Scripture. Neither Peter nor John understood that Scripture said Jesus would rise (Ps 16:10). This is evident by the reports of Luke (24:25–27, 32, 44–47). Jesus had foretold His resurrection (2:19; Mt 16:21; Mk 8:31; 9:31; Lk 9:22), but they would not accept it (Mt 16:22; Lk 9:44, 45). By the time John wrote this gospel, the church had developed an understanding of the OT prediction of Messiah's resurrection (cf. "as yet").

20:11–13 weeping. Mary's sense of grief and loss may have driven her back to the tomb. She apparently had not crossed paths with Peter or John and thus did not know of Jesus' resurrection (see v. 9).

20:12 two angels. Luke (24:4) describes both. Matthew (28:2, 3) and Mark (16:5) report only one. John's reason for the mention of angels is to demonstrate that no grave robbers took the body. This was an operation of the power of God.

my Lord, and I do not know where they have laid
Him." 14 When she had said this, she turned around
and *[A]saw Jesus standing *there,* and [B]did not know
that it was Jesus. 15 Jesus *said to her, "[A]Woman,
why are you weeping? Whom are you seeking?"
Supposing Him to be the gardener, she *said to
Him, "Sir, if you have carried Him away, tell me
where you have laid Him, and I will take Him away."
16 Jesus *said to her, "Mary!" She turned and *said
to Him [A]in [a]Hebrew, "[B]Rabboni!" (which means,
Teacher). 17 Jesus *said to her, "Stop clinging to
Me, for I have not yet ascended to the Father; but
go to [A]My brethren and say to them, 'I [B]ascend to
My Father and your Father, and My God and your
God.'" 18 [A]Mary Magdalene *came, [B]announcing to
the disciples, "I have seen the Lord," and *that* He
had said these things to her.

JESUS AMONG HIS DISCIPLES

19 So when it was evening on that day, the first
day of the week, and when the doors were shut
where the disciples were, for [A]fear of the Jews, Jesus
came and stood in their midst and *said to them,
"[a,B]Peace *be* with you." 20 And when He had said this,
[A]He showed them both His hands and His side. The
disciples then [B]rejoiced when they saw the Lord.
21 So Jesus said to them again, "[A]Peace *be* with you;
[B]as the Father has sent Me, I also send you." 22 And
when He had said this, He breathed on them and
*said to them, "Receive the Holy Spirit. 23 [A]If you
forgive the sins of any, *their sins* [a]have been forgiven them; if you retain the *sins* of any, they have
been retained."
24 But [A]Thomas, one of [B]the twelve, called [a,A]Did-
ymus, was not with them when Jesus came. 25 So
the other disciples were saying to him, "We have
seen the Lord!" But he said to them, "Unless I see
in [A]His hands the imprint of the nails, and put my
finger into the place of the nails, and put my hand
into His side, [B]I will not believe."
26 [a]After eight days His disciples were again inside, and Thomas with them. Jesus *came, the doors
having been [b]shut, and stood in their midst and said,
"[A]Peace *be* with you." 27 Then He *said to Thomas,
"[A]Reach here with your finger, and see My hands;
and reach here your hand and put it into My side;
and do not be unbelieving, but believing." 28 Thomas
answered and said to Him, "My Lord and my God!"
29 Jesus *said to him, "Because you have seen Me,
have you believed? [A]Blessed *are* they who did not
see, and *yet* believed."

WHY THIS GOSPEL WAS WRITTEN

30 [A]Therefore many other [a,B]signs Jesus also performed in the presence of the disciples, which are
not written in this book; 31 but these have been written [A]so that you may believe that Jesus is [a]the Christ,
[B]the Son of God; and that [C]believing you may have
life in His name.

20:14 [A]Matt 28:9; Mark 16:9 [B]John 21:4 20:15 [A]John 20:13 20:16 [a]I.e. Jewish Aramaic [A]John 5:2 [B]Matt 23:7; Mark 10:51 20:17 [A]Matt 28:10 [B]Mark 12:26; 16:19; John 7:33 20:18 [A]John 20:1 [B]Mark 16:10; Luke 24:10, 23 20:19 [a]Lit *Peace to you* [A]John 7:13 [B]Luke 24:36; John 14:27; 20:21, 26 20:20 [A]Luke 24:39, 40; John 19:34 [B]John 16:20, 22 20:21 [A]Luke 24:36; John 14:27; 20:19, 26 [B]John 17:18 20:23 [a]I.e. have previously been forgiven [A]Matt 16:19; 18:18 20:24 [a]I.e. the Twin [A]John 11:16 [B]John 6:67 20:25 [A]John 20:20 [B]Mark 16:11 20:26 [a]Or *A week later* [b]Or *locked* [A]Luke 24:36; John 14:27; 20:19, 21 20:27 [A]Luke 24:40; John 20:25 20:29 [A]1 Pet 1:8 20:30 [a]Or *attesting miracles* [A]John 21:25 [B]John 2:11 20:31 [a]I.e. the Messiah [A]John 19:35 [B]Matt 4:3 [C]John 3:15

20:14 did not know that it was Jesus. The reason for Mary's failure to recognize Jesus is uncertain. She may not have recognized Him because her tears blurred her eyes (v. 11). Possibly also, the vivid memories of Jesus' bruised and broken body were still etched in her mind, and Jesus' resurrection appearance was so dramatically different that she failed to recognize Him. Perhaps, however, like the disciples on the road to Emmaus, she was supernaturally prevented from recognizing Him until He chose for her to do so (see Lk 24:16).

20:16 Mary! Whatever the reason for her failure to recognize Jesus, the moment He spoke the single word, "Mary," she immediately recognized Him. This is reminiscent of Jesus' words "My sheep hear My voice, and I know them, and they follow Me" (10:27; cf. 10:3, 4).

20:17 Stop clinging to Me, for I have not yet ascended. Mary was expressing a desire to hold on to His physical presence for fear that she would once again lose Him. Jesus' reference to His ascension signifies that He would only be temporarily with them, and though she desperately wanted Him to stay, He could not. Jesus was with them only for 40 more days, and then He ascended (Ac 1:3–11). After He went to the Father, He sent the Holy Spirit ("The Helper") so that they would not feel abandoned (*see note on 14:18, 19*). **My brethren.** Disciples have been called "slaves" or "friends" (15:15), but not "brothers," until here. Because of Jesus' work on the cross in place of the sinner, this new relationship to Christ was made possible (Ro 8:14–17; Gal 3:26, 27; Eph 1:5; Heb 2:10–13).

20:19 on that day. *See note on v. 1.* **the doors were shut.** The Gr. word indicates the doors were locked for fear of the Jews. Since the authorities had executed their leader, they reasonably expected that Jesus' fate could be their own. **Peace *be* with you.** *See notes on 14:27; 16:33.* Jesus' greeting complements His "It is finished," for His work on the cross accomplished peace between God and His people (Ro 5:1; Eph 2:14–17).

20:20 Jesus proved that He who appeared to them was the same One who was crucified (cf. Lk 24:39).

20:21 This commission builds on 17:18. See Mt 28:19, 20.

20:22 Since the disciples did not actually receive the Holy Spirit until the day of Pentecost, some 40 days in the future (Ac 1:8; 2:1–3), this statement must be understood as a pledge on Christ's part that the Holy Spirit would be coming.

20:23 *See notes on Mt 16:19; 18:18.* This verse does not give authority to Christians to forgive sins. Jesus was saying that the believer can boldly declare the certainty of a sinner's forgiveness by the Father because of the work of His Son if that sinner has repented and believed the gospel. The believer with certainty can also tell those who do not respond to the message of God's forgiveness through faith in Christ that their sins, as a result, are not forgiven.

20:24–26 Thomas has already been portrayed as loyal but pessimistic. Jesus did not rebuke Thomas for his failure, but instead compassionately offered him proof of His resurrection. Jesus lovingly met him at the point of his weakness. Thomas' actions indicated that Jesus had to convince the disciples rather forcefully of His resurrection, i.e., they were not gullible people predisposed to believing in resurrection. The point is they would not have fabricated it or hallucinated it, since they were so reluctant to believe even with the evidence they could see.

20:28 My Lord and my God! With these words, Thomas declared his firm belief in the resurrection and, therefore, the deity of Jesus the Messiah and Son of God (Tit 2:13). This is the greatest confession a person can make. Thomas' confession functions as the fitting capstone of John's purpose in writing (see vv. 30, 31).

20:29 Jesus foresaw the time when such tangible evidence as Thomas received would not be available. When Jesus ascended permanently to the Father, all those who believe would do so without the benefit of seeing the resurrected Lord. Jesus pronounced a special blessing on those who believe without having Thomas' privilege (1Pe 1:8, 9).

20:30, 31 These verses constitute the goal and purpose for which John wrote the gospel (see Introduction: Background and Setting).

JESUS APPEARS AT THE SEA OF GALILEE

21 After these things Jesus [a,A]manifested Himself
[B]again to the disciples at the [C]Sea of Tiberias,
and He manifested *Himself* in this way. 2 Simon Peter, and [A]Thomas called [a]Didymus, and [B]Nathanael
of [C]Cana in Galilee, and [D]the *sons* of Zebedee, and
two others of His disciples were together. 3 Simon
Peter *said to them, "I am going fishing." They *said
to him, "We will also come with you." They went out
and got into the boat; and [A]that night they caught
nothing.
4 But when the day was now breaking, Jesus stood
on the beach; yet the disciples did not [A]know that it
was Jesus. 5 So Jesus *said to them, "Children, [A]you
do not have [a]any fish, do you?" They answered Him,
"No." 6 And He said to them, "[A]Cast the net on the
right-hand side of the boat and you will find *a catch.*"
So they cast, and then they were not able to haul it
in because of the great number of fish. 7 [A]Therefore
that disciple whom Jesus loved *said to Peter, "It is
the Lord." So when Simon Peter heard that it was
the Lord, he put his outer garment on (for he was
stripped *for work*), and threw himself into the sea.
8 But the other disciples came in the little boat, for
they were not far from the land, but about [a]one
hundred yards away, dragging the net *full* of fish.
9 So when they got out on the land, they *saw
a charcoal [A]fire *already* laid and [B]fish placed on
it, and bread. 10 Jesus *said to them, "Bring some
of the [A]fish which you have now caught." 11 Simon
Peter went up and drew the net to land, full of large
fish, a hundred and fifty-three; and although there
were so many, the net was not torn.

JESUS PROVIDES

12 Jesus *said to them, "Come *and* have [A]break-
fast." None of the disciples ventured to question
Him, "Who are You?" knowing that it was the Lord.
13 Jesus *came and *took [A]the bread and *gave *it* to
them, and the [B]fish likewise. 14 This is now the [A]third
time that Jesus [a]was manifested to the disciples,
after He was raised from the dead.

THE LOVE MOTIVATION

15 So when they had [A]finished breakfast, Jesus
*said to Simon Peter, "Simon, *son* of John, do you
[a,B]love Me more than these?" He *said to Him, "Yes,
Lord; You know that I [b]love You." He *said to him,
"Tend [C]My lambs." 16 He *said to him again a second time, "Simon, *son* of John, do you [a]love Me?"
He *said to Him, "Yes, Lord; You know that I [b]love
You." He *said to him, "[A]Shepherd My sheep." 17 He
*said to him the third time, "Simon, *son* of John, do
you [a]love Me?" Peter was grieved because He said to
him [A]the third time, "Do you [a]love Me?" And he said
to Him, "Lord, [B]You know all things; You know that
I [a]love You." Jesus *said to him, "[C]Tend My sheep.

21:1 [a]Or *made Himself visible* [A]Mark 16:12; John 21:14 [B]John 20:19, 26 [C]John 6:1 21:2 [a]I.e. the Twin [A]John 11:16 [B]John 1:45ff [C]John 2:1 [D]Matt 4:21; Mark 1:19; Luke 5:10 21:3 [A]Luke 5:5 21:4 [A]Luke 24:16; John 20:14 21:5 [a]Lit *something eaten with bread* [A]Luke 24:41 21:6 [A]Luke 5:4ff 21:7 [A]John 13:23; 21:20 21:8 [a]Lit *200 cubits* 21:9 [A]John 18:18 [B]John 6:9, 11; 21:10, 13 21:10 [A]John 6:9, 11; 21:9, 13 21:12 [A]John 21:15 21:13 [A]John 21:9 [B]John 6:9, 11; 21:9, 10 21:14 [a]Or *made Himself visible* [A]John 20:19, 26 21:15 [a]Gr *agapao* [b]Gr *phileo* [A]John 21:12 [B]Matt 26:33; Mark 14:29; John 13:37 [C]Luke 12:32 21:16 [a]Gr *agapao* [b]Gr *phileo* [A]Matt 2:6; Acts 20:28; 1 Pet 5:2; Rev 7:17 21:17 [a]Gr *phileo* [A]John 13:38 [B]John 16:30 [C]John 21:15, 16

21:1–25 The epilogue or appendix of John's gospel. While 20:30, 31 constitutes the conclusion of the body of the fourth gospel, the information here at the end of his work provides a balance to his prologue in 1:1–18. The epilogue essentially ties up 5 loose ends that were unanswered in chap. 20. 1) Will Jesus no longer directly provide for His own (cf. 20:17)? This question is answered in vv. 1–14. 2) What happened to Peter? Peter had denied Christ 3 times and fled. The last time Peter was seen was in 20:6–8 where both he and John saw the empty tomb, but only John believed (20:8). This question is answered in vv. 15–17. 3) What about the future of the disciples now that they are without their Master? This question is answered in vv. 18, 19. 4) Was John going to die? Jesus answers this question in vv. 20–23. 5) Why weren't other things that Jesus did recorded by John? John gives the answer to that in vv. 24, 25.

21:1 Sea of Tiberias. An alternate name for the Sea of Galilee, found only in John (see 6:1).

21:2 Simon Peter. In all lists of the apostles, he is named first, indicating his general leadership of the group (e.g., Mt 10:2).

21:3 I am going fishing. The most reasonable explanation for Peter and the others to go to Galilee in order to fish was that they went in obedience to the Lord's command to meet Him in Galilee (Mt 28:16). Peter and the others occupied themselves with fishing, which was their former livelihood, while they awaited Jesus' appearance.

21:4 This could be another instance in which the Lord kept His disciples from recognizing Him (20:14, 15; cf. Lk 24:16).

21:7 that disciple whom Jesus loved. John immediately recognized that the stranger was the risen Lord, for only He had such supernatural knowledge and power (v. 6). Peter impulsively jumped in and headed to see the Lord.

21:9 fish ... and bread. Apparently, the Lord created this breakfast as He had created food for the multitudes (6:1–13).

21:11 a hundred and fifty-three. John's recording of the precise number reinforces the fact that he was an eyewitness author of the events he recorded (1Jn 1:1–4). Jesus' action here in providing the fish also indicated that He would still provide for His disciples' needs (see Php 4:19; Mt 6:25–33).

21:14 the third time. The reference to the "third time" refers only to the appearances reported in John's gospel, i.e., the first being in 20:19–23 and the second in 20:26–29.

21:15–17 The meaning of this section hinges upon the usage of two synonyms for love. In terms of interpretation, when two synonyms are placed in close proximity in context, a difference in meaning, however slight, is emphasized. When Jesus asked Peter if he loved Him, He used a word for love that signified total commitment. Peter responded with a word for love that signified his love for Jesus, but not necessarily his total commitment. This was not because he was reluctant to express that greater love, but because he had been disobedient and denied the Lord in the past. He was, perhaps, now reluctant to make a claim of supreme devotion when, in the past, his life did not support such a claim. Jesus pressed home to Peter the need for unswerving devotion by repeatedly asking Peter if he loved Him supremely. The essential message here is that Jesus demands total commitment from His followers. Their love for Him must place Him above their love for all else. Jesus confronted Peter with love because He wanted Peter to lead the apostles (Mt 16:18), but in order for Peter to be an effective shepherd, his overwhelming drive must exemplify supreme love for his Lord.

21:15, 16 more than these? This probably refers to the fish (v. 11), representing Peter's profession as a fisherman, for he had gone back to it while waiting for Jesus (see v. 3). Jesus wanted Peter to love Him so supremely as to forsake all that he was familiar with and be exclusively devoted to being a fisher of men (Mt 4:19). The phrase may refer to the other disciples, since Peter had claimed he would be more devoted than all the others (Mt 26:33). **Tend My lambs.** The word "tend" conveys the idea of being devoted to the Lord's service as an undershepherd who cares for His flock (see 1Pe 5:1–4). The word has the idea of constantly feeding and nourishing the sheep. This served as a reminder that the primary duty of the messenger of Jesus Christ is to teach the Word of God (2Ti 4:2). Acts 1–12 records Peter's obedience to this commission.

21:17 Peter was grieved. The third time Jesus asked Peter, He used Peter's word for love that signified something less than total devotion, questioning even that level of love Peter thought he was safe in claiming (*see note on vv. 15–17*). The lessons driven home

OUR TIMES ARE IN HIS HAND

18 Truly, truly, I say to you, when you were younger, you used to gird yourself and walk wherever
you wished; but when you grow old, you will stretch
out your hands and someone else will gird you, and
bring you where you do not wish to *go.*" 19 Now
this He said, [A]signifying by [B]what kind of death he
would glorify God. And when He had spoken this,
He *said to him, "[C]Follow Me!"
20 Peter, turning around, *saw the [A]disciple whom
Jesus loved following *them;* the one who also had
[B]leaned back on His bosom at the supper and said,
"Lord, who is the one who betrays You?" 21 So Peter
seeing him *said to Jesus, "Lord, and what about
this man?" 22 Jesus *said to him, "If I want him to
remain [A]until I come, what *is that* to you? You [B]fol-
low Me!" 23 Therefore this saying went out among
[A]the brethren that that disciple would not die; yet
Jesus did not say to him that he would not die, but
only, "If I want him to remain [B]until I come, what
is that to you?"
24 This is the disciple who [A]is testifying to these
things and wrote these things, and we know that
his testimony is true.
25 And there are also [A]many other things which
Jesus did, which if they *were written in detail, I
suppose that even the world itself *would not contain the books that *would be written.

21:19 [A]John 12:33; 18:32 [B]2 Pet 1:14 [C]Matt 8:22; 16:24; John 21:22 21:20 [A]John 21:7 [B]John 13:25 21:22 [A]Matt 16:27f; 1 Cor 4:5; 11:26; James 5:7; Rev 2:25 [B]Matt 8:22; 16:24; John 21:19 21:23 [A]Acts 1:15 [B]Matt 16:27f; 1 Cor 4:5; 11:26; James 5:7; Rev 2:25 21:24 [A]John 15:27 21:25 [A]John 20:30

to Peter grieved his heart, so that he sought for a proper understanding of his heart, not by what he said or had done, but based on the Lord's omniscience (cf. 2:24, 25).

21:18, 19 A prophecy of Peter's martyrdom. Jesus' call of devotion to Him would also mean that Peter's devotion would entail his own death (Mt 10:37–39). Whenever any Christian follows Christ, he must be prepared to suffer and die (Mt 16:24–26). Peter lived 3 decades serving the Lord and anticipating the death that was before him (2Pe 1:12–15), but he wrote that such suffering and death for the Lord brings praise to God (1Pe 4:14–16). Church tradition records that Peter suffered martyrdom under Nero (ca. A.D. 67–68), being crucified upside down, because he refused to be crucified like his Lord.

21:20–22 Jesus' prophecy regarding Peter's martyrdom prompted Peter to ask what would happen to John ("the disciple whom Jesus loved"—see 13:23). He may have asked this because of his deep concern for John's future, since he was an intimate friend. Jesus' reply, "You follow Me," signified that his primary concern must not be John, but his continued devotion to the Lord and His service, i.e., Christ's service must be his all-consuming passion and nothing must detract from it.

21:22, 23 until I come. Jesus' hypothetical statement for emphasis was that, if John lived until His second coming, it was none of Peter's concern. He needed to live his own life in faithfulness, not compare it with any other.

21:24 the disciple who is testifying. John is a personal witness of the truth of the events that he recorded. The "we" most likely is an editorial device referring only to John (see 1:14; 1Jn 1:1–4; 3Jn 12), or it may include the collective witness of his apostolic colleagues.

21:25 John explained that he had been selective rather than exhaustive in his testimony. Although selective, the truth revealed in John's gospel is sufficient to bring anyone to faith in the Messiah and Son of God (14:26; 16:13).

THE ACTS OF THE APOSTLES

TITLE

As the second book Luke addressed to Theophilus (see Lk 1:3), Acts may originally have had no title. The Greek manuscripts title it "Acts," and many add "of the Apostles." The Greek word translated "Acts" (*praxeis*) was often used to describe the achievements of great men. Acts does feature the notable figures in the early years of the church, especially Peter (chaps. 1–12) and Paul (chaps. 13–28). But the book could more properly be called "The Acts of the Holy Spirit through the Apostles," since His sovereign, superintending work was far more significant than that of any man. It was the Spirit's directing, controlling, and empowering ministry that strengthened the church and caused it to grow in numbers, spiritual power, and influence.

AUTHOR AND DATE

Since Luke's gospel was the first book addressed to Theophilus (Lk 1:3), it is logical to conclude that Luke is also the author of Acts, although he is not named in either book. The writings of the early church fathers such as Irenaeus, Clement of Alexandria, Tertullian, Origen, Eusebius, and Jerome affirm Luke's authorship, and so does the Muratorian Canon (ca. A.D. 170). Because he is a relatively obscure figure, mentioned only 3 times in the NT (Col 4:14; 2Ti 4:11, Phm 24), it is unlikely that anyone would have forged a work to make it appear to be Luke's. A forger surely would have attributed his work to a more prominent person.

Luke was Paul's close friend, traveling companion, and personal physician (Col 4:14). He was a careful researcher (Lk 1:1–4) and an accurate historian, displaying an intimate knowledge of Roman laws and customs, as well as the geography of Israel, Asia Minor, and Italy. In writing Acts, Luke drew on written sources (15:23–29; 23:26–30), and also no doubt interviewed key figures, such as Peter, John, and others in the Jerusalem church. Paul's two-year imprisonment at Caesarea (24:27) gave Luke ample opportunity to interview Philip and his daughters (who were considered important sources of information on the early days of the church). Finally, Luke's frequent use of the first person plural pronouns "we" and "us" (16:10–17; 20:5–21:18; 27:1–28:16) reveals that he was an eyewitness to many of the events recorded in Acts.

Some believe Luke wrote Acts after the fall of Jerusalem (A.D. 70; his death was probably in the mid-eighties). It is more likely, however, that he wrote much earlier, before the end of Paul's first Roman imprisonment (ca. A.D. 60–62). That date is the most natural explanation for the abrupt ending of Acts—which leaves Paul awaiting trial before Caesar. Surely Luke, who devoted more than half of Acts to Paul's ministry, would have given the outcome of that trial, and described Paul's subsequent ministry, second imprisonment (cf. 2Ti 4:11), and death, if those events had happened before he wrote Acts. Luke's silence about such notable events as the martyrdom of James, head of the Jerusalem church (A.D. 62 according to the Jewish historian Josephus), the persecution under Nero (A.D. 64), and the fall of Jerusalem (A.D. 70) also suggests he wrote Acts before those events transpired.

BACKGROUND AND SETTING

As Luke makes clear in the prologue to his gospel, he wrote to give Theophilus (and the others who would read his work) an "account of the things" (Lk 1:1) which Jesus had accomplished during His earthly ministry. Accordingly, Luke's gospel records those momentous events "in consecutive order" (Lk 1:3). Acts continues that record, noting what Jesus accomplished through the early church. Beginning with Jesus' ascension, through the birth of the church on the Day of Pentecost, to Paul's preaching at Rome, Acts chronicles the spread of the gospel and the growth of the church (cf. 1:15; 2:41, 47; 4:4; 5:14; 6:7; 9:31; 12:24; 13:49; 16:5; 19:20). It also records the mounting opposition to the gospel (cf. 2:13; 4:1–22; 5:17–42; 6:9–8:4; 12:1–5; 13:6–12, 45–50; 14:2–6, 19, 20; 16:19–24; 17:5–9; 19:23–41; 21:27–36; 23:12–21; 28:24).

Theophilus, whose name means "lover of God," is unknown to history apart from his mention in Luke and Acts. Whether he was a believer whom Luke was instructing, or a pagan whom Luke sought to convert is not known. Luke's address of him as "most excellent Theophilus" (Lk 1:3) suggests he was a Roman official of some importance (cf. Ac 24:3; 26:25).

HISTORICAL AND THEOLOGICAL THEMES

As the first work of church history ever penned, Acts records the initial response to the Great Commission (Mt 28:19, 20). It provides information on the first 3 decades of the church's existence—material found nowhere else in the NT. Though not primarily a doctrinal work, Acts nonetheless emphasizes that Jesus of Nazareth was Israel's long-awaited Messiah, shows that the gospel is offered to all men (not merely the Jewish people), and stresses the work of the Holy Spirit (mentioned more than 50 times). Acts also makes frequent use of the OT: e.g., 2:17–21 (Joel 2:28–32); 2:25–28 (Ps 16:8–11); 2:35 (Ps 110:1); 4:11 (Ps 118:22); 4:25, 26 (Ps 2:1, 2); 7:49, 50 (Is 66:1, 2); 8:32, 33 (Is 53:7, 8); 28:26, 27 (Is 6:9, 10).

Acts abounds with transitions: from the ministry of Jesus to that of the apostles; from the Old Covenant to the New Covenant; from Israel as God's witness nation to the church (composed of both Jews and Gentiles) as God's witness people. The book of Hebrews sets forth the theology of the transition from the Old Covenant to the New; Acts depicts the New Covenant's practical outworking in the life of the church.

INTERPRETIVE CHALLENGES

Because Acts is primarily a historical narrative, not a theological treatise like Romans or Hebrews, it contains relatively few interpretive challenges. Those that exist mainly concern the book's transitional nature (see Historical and Theological Themes) and involve the role of signs and wonders. Those issues are addressed in the notes to the relevant passages (e.g., 2:1–47; 15:1–29).

OUTLINE

I. Prologue (1:1–8)

II. The Witness to Jerusalem (1:9–8:3)
- A. The Anticipation of the Church (1:9–26)
- B. The Founding of the Church (2:1–47)
- C. The Growth of the Church (3:1–8:3)
  1. Apostles: Preaching, healing, and enduring persecution (3:1–5:42)
  2. Deacons: Praying, teaching, and enduring persecution (6:1–8:3)

III. The Witness to Judea and Samaria (8:4–12:25)
- A. The Gospel to the Samaritans (8:4–25)
- B. The Conversion of a Gentile (8:26–40)
- C. The Conversion of Saul (9:1–31)
- D. The Gospel to Judea (9:32–43)
- E. The Gospel to the Gentiles (10:1–11:30)
- F. The Persecution by Herod (12:1–25)

IV. The Witness to the Ends of the Earth (13:1–28:31)
- A. Paul's First Missionary Journey (13:1–14:28)
- B. The Jerusalem Council (15:1–35)
- C. Paul's Second Missionary Journey (15:36–18:22)
- D. Paul's Third Missionary Journey (18:23–21:16)
- E. Paul's Jerusalem and Caesarean Trials (21:17–26:32)
- F. Paul's Journey to Rome (27:1–28:31)

INTRODUCTION

1 The first account I [a]composed, [A]Theophilus,
about all that Jesus [B]began to do and teach,
2 until the day when He [A]was taken up *to heaven,*
after He [B]had [a]by the Holy Spirit given orders to
[C]the apostles whom He had [D]chosen. 3 To [a]these [A]He
also presented Himself alive after His suffering,
by many convincing proofs, appearing to them
over *a period of* forty days and speaking of [B]the
things concerning the kingdom of God. 4 [a]Gathering
them together, He commanded them [A]not to leave
Jerusalem, but to wait for [b,B]what the Father had
promised, "Which," *He said,* "you heard of from
Me; 5 for [A]John baptized with water, but you will
be baptized [a]with the Holy Spirit [b,B]not many days
from now."
6 So when they had come together, they were
asking Him, saying, "Lord, [A]is it at this time You
are restoring the kingdom to Israel?" 7 He said to
them, "It is not for you to know times or epochs
which [A]the Father has fixed by His own authority;
8 but you will receive power [A]when the Holy Spirit
has come upon you; and you shall be [B]My witnesses
both in Jerusalem, and in all Judea and [C]Samaria,
and even to [D]the remotest part of the earth."

THE ASCENSION

9 And after He had said these things, [A]He was lifted
up while they were looking on, and a cloud received
Him out of their sight. 10 And as they were gazing intently into [a]the sky while He was going, behold, [A]two
men in white clothing stood beside them. 11 They also
said, "[A]Men of Galilee, why do you stand looking into
[a]the sky? This Jesus, who [B]has been taken up from
you into heaven, will [C]come in just the same way as
you have watched Him go into heaven."

THE UPPER ROOM

12 Then they [A]returned to Jerusalem from the
[a,B]mount called [b]Olivet, which is near Jerusalem,
a [c]Sabbath day's journey away. 13 When they had
entered *the city,* they went up to [A]the upper room
where they were staying; [B]that is, Peter and John
and [a]James and Andrew, Philip and Thomas, Bartholomew and Matthew, [a]James *the son* of Alphaeus,
and Simon the Zealot, and [C]Judas *the* [b]*son* of [a]James.

1:1 [a]Lit *made* [A]Luke 1:3 [B]Luke 3:23 1:2 [a]Or *through* [A]Mark 16:19; Acts 1:9, 11, 22 [B]Matt 28:19f; Mark 16:15; John 20:21f; Acts 10:42 [C]Mark 6:30 [D]John 13:18; Acts 10:41 1:3 [a]Lit *whom* [A]Matt 28:17; Mark 16:12, 14; Luke 24:34, 36; John 20:19, 26; 21:1, 14; 1 Cor 15:5-7 [B]Acts 8:12; 19:8; 28:23, 31 1:4 [a]Or *eating with;* or *lodging with* [b]Lit *the promise of the Father* [A]Luke 24:49 [B]John 14:16, 26; 15:26; Acts 2:33 1:5 [a]Or *in* [b]Lit *not* long *after these many days* [A]Matt 3:11; Mark 1:8; Luke 3:16; John 1:33; Acts 11:16 [B]Acts 2:1-4 1:6 [A]Matt 17:11; Mark 9:12; Luke 17:20; 19:11 1:7 [A]Matt 24:36; Mark 13:32 1:8 [A]Acts 2:1-4 [B]Luke 24:48; John 15:27 [C]Acts 8:1, 5, 14 [D]Matt 28:19; Mark 16:15; Rom 10:18; Col 1:23 1:9 [A]Luke 24:50, 51; Acts 1:2 1:10 [a]Or *heaven* [A]Luke 24:4; John 20:12 1:11 [a]Or *heaven* [A]Acts 2:7; 13:31 [B]Mark 16:19; Acts 1:9, 22 [C]Matt 16:27f; Acts 3:21 1:12 [a]Or *hill* [b]Or *Olive Grove* [c]I.e. 2K cubits, or approx 3/5 mile [A]Luke 24:52 [B]Matt 21:1 1:13 [a]Or *Jacob* [b]Or *brother* [A]Mark 14:15; Luke 22:12; Acts 9:37, 39; 20:8 [B]Acts 1:13: *Matt 10:2-4; Mark 3:16-19; Luke 6:14-16* [C]John 14:22

1:1 first account. The Gospel of Luke (Lk 1:1–4; see Introduction: Background and Setting). That account chronicled the life and teaching of Jesus, through His death, resurrection, and ascension (Lk 24:51). **Theophilus.** The original recipient of this book. *See note on Lk 1:3.* **all that Jesus began to do and teach.** Jesus taught the disciples by word and deed the truth necessary to carry on His work. On the cross, He finished the work of redemption, but He had only started the proclamation of its glories.

1:2 taken up. Christ's ascension to the Father (cf. Lk 24:51). Luke uses this term 3 other times (vv. 9, 11, 22) to describe the end of the Lord's earthly ministry (cf. Jn 6:62; 13:1, 3; 16:28; 17:13; 20:17). **by the Holy Spirit given orders.** The Spirit was the source and power of Jesus' earthly ministry (cf. Mt 4:1; 12:18; Mk 1:12; Lk 3:22; 4:1, 14, 18) and of the apostles' service (cf. Lk 24:49; Jn 14:16, 17; 16:7). "Orders" or commandments are authoritative NT truths, revealed to the apostles (cf. Jn 14:26; 16:13–15). **He had chosen.** The Lord sovereignly chose the apostles for salvation and service (cf. Jn 6:70; 15:16).

1:3 presented Himself … by many convincing proofs. Cf. Jn 20:30; 1Co 15:5–8. To give the apostles confidence to present His message, Jesus entered a locked room (Jn 20:19), showed His crucifixion wounds (Lk 24:39), and ate and drank with the disciples (Lk 24:41–43). **forty days.** The time period between Jesus' resurrection and ascension during which He appeared at intervals to the apostles and others (1Co 15:5–8) and provided convincing evidence of His resurrection. **kingdom of God.** Cf. 8:12; 14:22; 19:8; 20:25; 28:23, 31. Here this expression refers to the sphere of salvation, the gracious domain of divine rule over believers' hearts (*see notes on 1Co 6:9; Eph 5:5;* cf. 17:7; Col 1:13, 14; Rev 11:15; 12:10). This was the dominant theme during Christ's earthly ministry (cf. Mt 4:23; 9:35; Mk 1:15; Lk 4:43; 9:2; Jn 3:3–21).

1:4 Gathering them together. An alternative reading, "eating with them," is preferred (cf. 10:41; Lk 24:42, 43). The fact that Jesus ate provides additional proof of His bodily resurrection. **wait for what the Father had promised.** Jesus repeatedly promised that God would send them His Spirit (Lk 11:13; 24:49; Jn 7:39; 14:16, 26; 15:26; 16:7; *see note on Jn 20:22*).

1:5 John baptized with water. *See note on 2:38.* **baptized with the Holy Spirit.** The apostles had to wait until the Day of Pentecost, but since then all believers are baptized with the Holy Spirit at salvation (*see note on 1Co 12:13;* cf. Ro 8:9; 1Co 6:19, 20; Tit 3:5, 6). **not many days from now.** God's promise was fulfilled just 10 days later.

1:6 restoring the kingdom to Israel. The apostles still believed the earthly form of the kingdom of Messiah would soon be reestablished (cf. Lk 19:11; 24:21). They also knew that Eze 36 and Joel 2 connected the coming of the kingdom with the outpouring of the Spirit whom Jesus had promised.

1:7 This verse shows that the apostles' expectation of a literal, earthly kingdom mirrored what Christ taught and what the OT predicted. Otherwise, He would have corrected them about such a crucial aspect of His teaching. **times or epochs.** These two words refer to features, eras, and events that will be part of His earthly kingdom reign, which will begin at the second coming (Mt 25:21–34). The exact time of His return, however, remains unrevealed (Mk 13:32; cf. Dt 29:29).

1:8 The apostles' mission of spreading the gospel was the major reason the Holy Spirit empowered them. This event dramatically altered world history, and the gospel message eventually reached all parts of the earth (Mt 28:19, 20). **receive power.** The apostles had already experienced the Holy Spirit's saving, guiding, teaching, and miracle-working power. Soon they would receive His indwelling presence and a new dimension of power for witness (*see notes on 2:4; 1Co 6:19, 20; Eph 3:16, 20*). **witnesses.** People who tell the truth about Jesus Christ (cf. Jn 14:26; 1Pe 3:15). The Gr. word means "one who dies for his faith" because that was commonly the price of witnessing. **Judea.** The region in which Jerusalem was located. **Samaria.** The region immediately to the N of Judea (*see note on 8:5*).

1:9 lifted up. *See note on v. 2.* God the Father took Jesus, in His resurrection body, from this world to His rightful place at the Father's right hand (Lk 24:51; cf. 2:33; Jn 17:1–6). **a cloud.** A visible reminder that God's glory was present as the apostles watched the ascension. For some of them, this was not the first time they had witnessed divine glory (Mk 9:26); neither will it be the last time clouds accompany Jesus (Mk 13:26; 14:62; *see note on Rev 1:7*).

1:10 two men in white clothing. Two angels in the form of men (cf. Ge 18:2; Jos 5:13–15; Mk 16:5).

1:11 Men of Galilee. All the apostles were from Galilee except for Judas, who had killed himself by this time (cf. v. 18). **just the same way.** Christ one day will return to earth (to the Mt. of Olives), in the same way He ascended (with clouds), to set up His kingdom (cf. Da 7:13; Zec 14:4; Mt 24:30; 26:64; Rev 1:7; 14:14).

1:12 mount called Olivet. Located across the Kidron Valley, E of Jerusalem, this large hill rising about 200 ft. higher in elevation than the city was the site from which Jesus ascended into heaven (Lk 24:50, 51). **Sabbath day's journey.** One-half of a mi. (about 2,000 cubits), the farthest distance a faithful Jew could travel on the Sabbath to accommodate the prohibition of Ex 16:29. This measurement was derived from tradition based on Israel's encampments in the wilderness. The tents farthest out on the camp's perimeter were 2,000 cubits from the center tabernacle—the longest distance anyone had to walk to reach the tabernacle on the Sabbath (Jos 3:4; cf. Nu 35:5).

1:13 upper room. Where the Last Supper

14 These all with one mind [A]were continually devoting
themselves to prayer, along with [B]*the* women, and
Mary the [C]mother of Jesus, and with His [C]brothers.
15 [a]At this time Peter stood up in the midst of
[A]the brethren (a gathering of about one hundred
and twenty [b]persons was there together), and said,
16 "Brethren, [A]the Scripture had to be fulfilled, which
the Holy Spirit foretold by the mouth of David concerning Judas, [B]who became a guide to those who
arrested Jesus. 17 For he was [A]counted among us and
received his share in [B]this ministry." 18 (Now this man
[A]acquired a field with [B]the price of his wickedness, and
falling headlong, he burst open in the middle and all
his intestines gushed out. 19 And it became known to
all who were living in Jerusalem; so that in [A]their own
language that field was called Hakeldama, that is, Field
of Blood.) 20 "For it is written in the book of Psalms,

'[A]LET HIS HOMESTEAD BE MADE DESOLATE,
AND LET NO ONE DWELL IN IT';

and,

'[B]LET ANOTHER MAN TAKE HIS [a]OFFICE.'

1:14 [A]Acts 2:42; 6:4; Rom 12:12; Eph 6:18; Col 4:2 [B]Luke 8:2f [C]Matt 12:46 1:15 [a]Lit *In these days* [b]Lit *names* [A]John 21:23; Acts 6:3; 9:30; 10:23; 11:1, 12, 26, 29; 12:17; 14:2; 15:1, 3, 22, 23, 32f, 40; 16:2, 40; 17:6, 10, 14; 18:18, 27; 21:7, 17; 22:5; 28:14f; Rom 1:13 1:16 [A]John 13:18; 17:12; Acts 1:20 [B]Matt 26:47; Mark 14:43; Luke 22:47; John 18:3 1:17 [A]John 6:70f [B]Acts 1:25; 20:24; 21:19 1:18 [A]Matt 27:3-10 [B]Matt 26:14f 1:19 [A]Matt 27:8; Acts 21:40 1:20 [a]Lit *position as overseer* [A]Ps 69:25 [B]Ps 109:8

may have been celebrated (Mk 14:15) and where Jesus had appeared to the apostles after His resurrection. **Bartholomew.** This disciple is also called Nathanael (Jn 1:45–49; 21:2). **James *the son of* Alphaeus.** *See note on Mt 10:2.* The same person as James the younger, also called "the Less" to distinguish him from James, the brother of John (Mk 15:40). **Zealot.** *See note on Mt 10:4.* **Judas *the son of* James.** The preferred rendering is "the brother of." *See note on Mt 10:3.* He was also known as Thaddaeus (Mk 3:18).

1:14 continually devoting themselves to prayer. The pattern of praying in the name of Jesus started at this time (cf. Jn 14:13, 14). **with *the* women.** Doubtless they included Mary Magdalene, Mary the wife of Clopas, the sisters Mary and Martha, and Salome. Some of the apostles' wives also may have been present (cf. 1Co 9:5). **Mary the mother of Jesus.** *See notes on Lk 1:27, 28.* Mary's name does not appear again in the NT. **brothers.** Jesus' half-brothers, named in Mk 6:3 as James, Joses, Judas, and Simon. James was the leader of the Jerusalem church (12:17; 15:13–22) and author of the epistle that bears his name. Judas (Jude) wrote the epistle of Jude. At this time they were new believers in Jesus as God, Savior, and Lord, whereas only 8 months earlier John had mentioned their unbelief (Jn 7:5).

1:15 At this time. Some unspecified time during the believers' 10 days of prayer and fellowship between the ascension and Pentecost. **Peter.** *See note on Mt 10:2.* The acknowledged leader of the apostles took charge.

1:16 Brethren. The 120 believers who were gathered (v. 15). **the Scripture had to be fulfilled.** The two OT passages Peter quotes in v. 20 are Pss 69:25; 109:8. When God gives prophecies, they will come to pass (cf. Ps 115:3; Is 46:10; 55:11). **the Holy Spirit … by the mouth of David.** Scripture contains no clearer description of divine inspiration. God spoke through David's mouth, actually referring to his writing (*see note on 2Pe 1:21*).

1:17 received his share in this ministry. Judas Iscariot was a member of the 12, but was never truly saved which is why he was called "the son of perdition" (Jn 17:12). See Mt 26:24; Jn 6:64, 70, 71; cf. 2:23; Lk 22:22.

1:18 this man acquired a field. Because the field was bought with the money the Jewish leaders paid Judas to betray Jesus, which he returned to them (Mt 27:3–10), Luke refers to Judas as if he was the buyer (cf. Zec 11:12, 13). **price of his wickedness.** The 30 pieces of silver paid to Judas. **falling headlong.** Apparently, the tree on which Judas chose to hang himself (Mt 27:5) overlooked a cliff. Likely, the rope or branch broke (or the knot slipped), and his body was shattered on the rocks below.

1:19 Hakeldama … Field of Blood. This is the Aram. name of the field bought by the Jewish leaders. Traditionally, the field is located S of Jerusalem in the Valley of Hinnom, where that valley crosses the Kidron Valley. The soil there was good for making pottery, thus Matthew identifies it as "the Potter's Field" (Mt 27:7, 10; *see notes on v. 18*).

1:20 it is written. *See note on v. 16.* Peter

MINISTRIES OF THE HOLY SPIRIT

Ministry	Reference(s)
Baptismal Medium	1Co 12:13
Calls to Ministry	Ac 13:2–4
Channel of Divine Revelation	2Sa 23:2; Ne 9:30; Zec 7:12; Jn 14:17
Empowers	Ex 31:2, 3; Jdg 13:25; Ac 1:8
Fills	Lk 4:1; Ac 2:4; Eph 5:18
Guarantees	2Co 1:22; 5:5; Eph 1:14
Guards	2Ti 1:14
Helps	Jn 14:16, 26; 15:26; 16:7
Illuminates	1Co 2:10–13
Indwells	Ro 8:9–11; 1Co 3:16; 6:19
Intercedes	Ro 8:26, 27
Produces Fruit	Gal 5:22, 23
Provides Spiritual Character	Gal 5:16, 18, 25
Regenerates	Jn 3:5, 6, 8
Restrains/Convicts of Sin	Ge 6:3; Jn 16:8–10; Ac 7:51
Sanctifies	Ro 15:16; 1Co 6:11; 2Th 2:13
Seals	2Co 1:22; Eph 1:14; 4:30
Selects Overseers	Ac 20:28
Source of Fellowship	2Co 13:14; Php 2:1
Source of Liberty	2Co 3:17, 18
Source of Power	Eph 3:16
Source of Unity	Eph 4:3, 4
Source of Spiritual Gifts	1Co 12:4–11
Teaches	Jn 14:26; Ac 15:28; 1Jn 2:20, 27

21 Therefore it is necessary that of the men who have
accompanied us all the time that [A]the Lord Jesus
went in and out [a]among us— 22 [A]beginning [a]with
the baptism of John until the day that He [B]was taken
up from us—one of these *must* become a [C]witness
with us of His resurrection." 23 So they put forward
two men, Joseph called Barsabbas (who was also
called Justus), and [A]Matthias. 24 And they [A]prayed
and said, "You, Lord, [B]who know the hearts of all
men, show which one of these two You have chosen
25 to [a]occupy [A]this ministry and [B]apostleship from
which Judas turned aside to go to his own place."
26 And they [a,A]drew lots for them, and the lot fell [b]to
[B]Matthias; and he was [c]added to [C]the eleven apostles.

THE DAY OF PENTECOST

2 When [A]the day of Pentecost [a]had come, they were
all together in one place. 2 And suddenly there
came from heaven a noise like a violent rushing
wind, and it filled [A]the whole house where they were
sitting. 3 And there appeared to them tongues as of
fire [a]distributing themselves, and [b]they [c]rested on
each one of them. 4 And they were all [A]filled with the
Holy Spirit and began to [B]speak with other [a]tongues,
as the Spirit was giving them [b]utterance.
5 Now there were Jews living in Jerusalem, [A]de-
vout men from every nation under heaven. 6 And
when [A]this sound occurred, the crowd came together, and were bewildered because each one of
them was hearing them speak in his own [a]language.
7 [A]They were amazed and astonished, saying, "[a]Why,
are not all these who are speaking [B]Galileans? 8 And
how is it that we each hear *them* in our own [a]lan-
guage [b]to which we were born? 9 Parthians and
Medes and Elamites, and residents of Mesopotamia, Judea and [A]Cappadocia, [B]Pontus and [a,C]Asia,
10 [A]Phrygia and [B]Pamphylia, Egypt and the districts
of Libya around [C]Cyrene, and [a,D]visitors from Rome,
both Jews and [b,E]proselytes, 11 Cretans and Arabs—
we hear them in our *own* tongues speaking of the

1:21 [a]Lit *to us* [A]Luke 24:3 1:22 [a]Lit *from* [A]Matt 3:16; Mark 1:1-4, 9; Luke 3:21 [B]Mark 16:19; Acts 1:2 [C]Acts 1:8; 2:32 1:23 [A]Acts 1:26 1:24 [A]Acts 6:6; 13:3; 14:23 [B]1 Sam 16:7; Jer 17:10; Acts 15:8; Rom 8:27 1:25 [a]Lit *take the place of* [A]Acts 1:17 [B]Rom 1:5; 1 Cor 9:2; Gal 2:8 1:26 [a]Lit *gave* [b]Or *upon* [c]Lit *voted together with* [A]Lev 16:8; Josh 14:2; 1 Sam 14:41f; Neh 10:34; 11:1; Prov 16:33 [B]Acts 1:23 [C]Acts 2:14 2:1 [a]Lit *was being fulfilled* [A]Lev 23:15f; Acts 20:16; 1 Cor 16:8 2:2 [A]Acts 4:31 2:3 [a]Or *being distributed* [b]Lit *it* [c]Or *sat* 2:4 [a]Or *languages* [b]Or *ability to speak out* [A]Matt 10:20; Acts 1:5, 8; 4:8, 31; 6:3, 5; 7:55; 8:17; 9:17; 11:15; 13:9, 52 [B]Mark 16:17; 1 Cor 12:10f; 14:21 2:5 [A]Luke 2:25; Acts 8:2 2:6 [a]Or *dialect* [A]Acts 2:2 2:7 [a]Lit *Behold* [A]Acts 2:12 [B]Matt 26:73; Acts 1:11 2:8 [a]Or *dialect* [b]Lit *in* 2:9 [a]I.e. west coast province of Asia Minor [A]1 Pet 1:1 [B]Acts 18:2; 1 Pet 1:1 [C]Acts 6:9; 16:6; 19:10; 20:4; 21:27; 24:18; 27:2; Rom 16:5; 1 Cor 16:19; 2 Cor 1:8; 2 Tim 1:15; Rev 1:4 2:10 [a]Lit *the sojourning Romans* [b]I.e. Gentile converts to Judaism [A]Acts 16:6; 18:23 [B]Acts 13:13; 14:24; 15:38; 27:5 [C]Matt 27:32 [D]Acts 17:21 [E]Matt 23:15

used the most compelling proof, Scripture, to reassure the believers that Judas' defection and the choice of his replacement were both in God's purpose (cf. Ps 55:12–15).

1:21 went in and out among us. The first requirement for Judas' successor was that he had participated in Jesus' earthly ministry.

1:22 baptism of John. Jesus' baptism by John the Baptist (Mt 3:13–17; Mk 1:9–11; Lk 3:21–23). a witness with us of His resurrection. A second requirement for Judas' successor was that he had to have seen the resurrected Christ. The resurrection was central to apostolic preaching (cf. 2:24, 32; 3:15; 5:30; 10:40; 13:30–37).

1:23 Barsabbas ... Justus. Barsabbas means "son of the Sabbath." Justus ("the righteous") was Joseph's Lat. name. Many Jews in the Roman Empire had equivalent Gentile names. Matthias. The name means "gift of God." The ancient historian Eusebius claims Matthias was among the 70 of Luke 10:1.

1:24 You have chosen. Judas' successor was sovereignly determined (*see notes on v. 20*).

1:25 his own place. Judas chose his own fate of hell by rejecting Christ. It is not unfair to say that Judas and all others who go to hell belong there (cf. Jn 6:70).

1:26 drew lots. A common OT method of determining God's will (cf. Lv 16:8–10; Jos 7:14; Pr 18:18; *see note on Pr 16:33*). This is the last biblical mention of lots—the coming of the Spirit made them unnecessary.

2:1 day of Pentecost. "Pentecost" means "fiftieth" and refers to the Feast of Weeks (Ex 34:22, 23) or Harvest (Lv 23:16), which was celebrated 50 days after Passover in May/June (Lv 23:15–22). It was one of 3 annual feasts for which the nation was to come to Jerusalem (*see note on Ex 23:14–19*). At Pentecost, an offering of firstfruits was made (Lv 23:20). The Holy Spirit came on this day as the firstfruits of the believer's inheritance (cf. 2Co 5:5; Eph 1:11, 14). Those gathered into the church then were also the firstfruits of the full harvest of all believers to come after. in one place. The upper room mentioned in 1:13.

2:2 a noise like a violent rushing wind. Luke's simile described God's action of sending the Holy Spirit. Wind is frequently used in Scripture as a picture of the Spirit (cf. Eze 37:9, 10; Jn 3:8).

2:3 The disciples could not comprehend the significance of the Spirit's arrival without the Lord sovereignly illustrating what was occurring with a visible phenomenon. tongues as of fire. Just as the sound, like wind, was symbolic, these were not literal flames of fire but supernatural indicators, like fire, that God had sent the Holy Spirit upon each believer. In Scripture, fire often denoted the divine presence (cf. Ex 3:2–6). God's use of a fire-like appearance here parallels what He did with the dove when Jesus was baptized (Mt 3:11; Lk 3:16).

2:4 all. The apostles and the 120. Cf. Joel 2:28–32. filled with the Holy Spirit. In contrast to the baptism with the Spirit, which is the one-time act by which God places believers into His body (*see notes on 1Co 12:13*), the filling is a repeated reality of Spirit-controlled behavior that God commands believers to maintain (*see notes on Eph 5:18*). Peter and many others in Ac 2 were filled with the Spirit again (e.g., 4:8, 31; 6:5; 7:55) and so spoke boldly the Word of God. The fullness of the Spirit affects all areas of life, not just speaking boldly (cf. Eph 5:19–33). with other tongues. Known languages (*see notes on v. 6; 1Co 14:1–25*), not ecstatic utterances. These languages given by the Spirit were a sign of judgment to unbelieving Israel (*see notes on 1Co 14:21, 22*). They also showed that from then on God's people would come from all nations, and marked the transition from Israel to the church. Tongues speaking occurs only twice more in Acts (10:46; 19:6).

2:5 Jews ... devout men. Hebrew males who made the pilgrimage to Jerusalem. They were expected to celebrate Pentecost (*see note on v. 1*) in Jerusalem, as part of observing the Jewish religious calendar. *See note on Ex 23:14–19*.

2:6 this sound. The noise like gusty wind (v. 2), not the sound of the various languages. speak in his own language. As the believers were speaking, each pilgrim in the crowd recognized the language or dialect from his own country.

2:7 Galileans. Inhabitants of the mostly rural area of northern Israel around the Sea of Galilee. Galilean Jews spoke with a distinct regional accent and were considered to be unsophisticated and uneducated by the southern Judean Jews. When Galileans were seen to be speaking so many different languages, the Judean Jews were astonished.

2:9–11 The listing of specific countries and ethnic groups proves again that these utterances were known human languages.

2:9 Parthians. They lived in what is modern Iran. Medes. In Daniel's time, they ruled with the Persians, but had settled in Parthia. Elamites. They were from the southwestern part of the Parthian Empire. Mesopotamia. This means "between the rivers" (the Tigris and Euphrates). Many Jews still lived there, descendants of those who were in captivity and who never returned to the land of Israel (cf. 2Ch 36:22, 23). Judea. All the region once controlled by David and Solomon, including Syria.

2:9, 10 Cappadocia, Pontus and Asia, Phrygia and Pamphylia. All were districts in Asia Minor, in what is now Turkey.

2:10 Egypt. Many Jews lived there, especially in the city of Alexandria. The nation then covered the same general area as modern Egypt. Libya around Cyrene. These districts were W of Egypt, along the North African coast. Rome. The capital of the Empire had a sizeable Jewish population, dating from the second century B.C. proselytes. Gentile converts to Judaism. Jews in Rome were especially active in seeking such converts.

2:11 Cretans. Residents of the island of Crete, off the southern coast of Greece. Arabs. Jews who lived S of Damascus, among the Nabatean Arabs (cf. Gal 1:17). we hear them ...

mighty deeds of God." 12 And [A]they all continued
in amazement and great perplexity, saying to one
another, "What does this mean?" 13 But others were
mocking and saying, "[A]They are full of [a]sweet wine."

PETER'S SERMON

14 But Peter, [a]taking his stand with [A]the eleven,
raised his voice and declared to them: "Men of Judea and all you who live in Jerusalem, let this be
known to you and give heed to my words. 15 For
these men are not drunk, as you suppose, [A]for it is
only the [a]third hour of the day; 16 but this is what
was spoken of through the prophet Joel:

17 '[A]And it shall be in the last
days,' God says,
'That I will pour forth of My
Spirit on all [a]mankind;
And your sons and your
daughters shall prophesy,
And your young men shall see visions,
And your old men shall
dream dreams;
18 Even on My bondslaves,
both men and women,
I will in those days pour
forth of My Spirit
And they shall prophesy.
19 'And I will grant wonders
in the sky above
And signs on the earth below,
Blood, and fire, and vapor of smoke.
20 'The sun will be turned
into darkness
And the moon into blood,
Before the great and glorious
day of the Lord shall come.
21 'And it shall be that [A]everyone
who calls on the name of
the Lord will be saved.'

22 "Men of Israel, listen to these words: [A]Jesus
the Nazarene, [B]a man [a]attested to you by God with
[b]miracles and [C]wonders and [c]signs which God performed through Him in your midst, just as you
yourselves know— 23 this *Man,* delivered over by
the [A]predetermined plan and foreknowledge of God,
[B]you nailed to a cross by the hands of [a]godless men
and put *Him* to death. 24 [a]But [A]God raised Him up
again, putting an end to the [b]agony of death, since
it [B]was impossible for Him to be held [c]in its power.
25 For David says of Him,

'[A]I saw the Lord always in my presence;
For He is at my right hand, so
that I will not be shaken.

2:12 [A]Acts 2:7 2:13 [a]I.e. new wine [A]1 Cor 14:23 2:14 [a]Or *being put forward* as spokesman [A]Acts 1:26 2:15 [a]I.e. 9 a.m. [A]1 Thess 5:7 2:17 [a]Lit *flesh* [A]Joel 2:28-32 2:21 [A]Rom 10:13 2:22 [a]Or *exhibited or accredited* [b]Or *works of power* [c]Or *attesting miracles* [A]Acts 3:6; 4:10; 10:38 [B]John 3:2 [C]John 4:48; Acts 2:19, 43 2:23 [a]Lit *men without the Law;* i.e. pagan [A]Luke 22:22; Acts 3:18; 4:28; 1 Pet 1:20 [B]Matt 27:35; Mark 15:24; Luke 23:33; 24:20; John 19:18; Acts 3:13 2:24 [a]Lit *Whom God raised up* [b]Lit *birth pains* [c]Lit *by it* [A]Matt 28:5, 6; Mark 16:6; Luke 24:5, 6; Acts 2:32; 3:15, 26; 4:10; 5:30; 10:40; 13:30, 33, 34, 37; 17:31; Rom 4:24; 6:4; 8:11; 10:9; 1 Cor 6:14; 15:15; 2 Cor 4:14; Gal 1:1; Eph 1:20; Col 2:12; 1 Thess 1:10; Heb 13:20; 1 Pet 1:21 [B]John 20:9 2:25 [A]Ps 16:8-11

speaking. *See note on v. 6.* **mighty deeds of God.** The Christians were quoting from the OT what God had done for His people (cf. Ex 15:11; Pss 40:5; 77:11; 96:3; 107:21). Such praises were often heard in Jerusalem during festival times.

2:13 sweet wine. A drink that could have made one drunk.

2:14–40 After the Holy Spirit's arrival, the first major event of church history was Peter's sermon, which led to 3,000 conversions and established the church (vv. 41–47).

2:14 with the eleven. This number of the apostles included the newly appointed Matthias, who replaced Judas Iscariot (*see notes on 1:23, 24*).

2:15 the third hour. Calculated in Jewish fashion from sunrise, this was 9:00 a.m.

2:16–21 See Introduction to Joel: Interpretive Challenges; *see notes on Joel 2:28–32.* Joel's prophecy will not be completely fulfilled until the millennial kingdom. But Peter, by using it, shows that Pentecost was a pre-fulfillment, a taste of what will happen in the millennial kingdom when the Spirit is poured out on all flesh (cf. 10:45).

2:17 last days. This phrase refers to the present era of redemptive history from the first coming of Christ (Heb 1:2; 1Pe 1:20; 1Jn 2:18) to His return. **My Spirit.** *See notes on 1:2, 5, 8.* **all mankind.** This indicates all people will receive the Holy Spirit, because everyone who enters the millennial kingdom will be redeemed (cf. Mt 24:29–25:46; Rev 20:4–6). **visions ... dreams.** Dreams (Ge 20:3; Da 7:1) and visions (Ge 15:1; Rev 9:17) were some of God's most memorable means of revelation since they were pictorial in nature. While they were not limited to believers (e.g., Abimelech, Ge 20:3 and Pharaoh, Ge 41:1–8), they were primarily reserved for prophets and apostles (cf. Nu 12:6). While frequent in the OT, they were rare in the NT. In Acts, most of God's visions were associated with either Peter (chaps. 10, 11) or Paul (chaps. 9, 18; cf. 2Co 12:1). Most frequently they were used to reveal apocalyptic imagery (cf. Eze, Da, Zec, Rev). They were not considered normal in biblical times, nor should they be so now. The time will come, however, when God will use visions and dreams during the Tribulation period as predicted by Joel 2:28–32.

2:18 prophesy. The proclamation of God's truth will be pervasive in the millennial kingdom.

2:19 wonders ... signs. Cf. 4:30; 5:12; 14:3; 15:12. "Wonders" is the amazement people experience when witnessing supernatural works (miracles). "Signs" point to the power of God behind miracles—marvels have no value unless they point to God and His truth. Such works were often done by the Holy Spirit through the apostles (5:12–16) and their associates (6:8) to authenticate them as the messengers of God's truth. Cf. 2Co 12:12; Heb 2:3, 4. **blood ... fire ... vapor of smoke.** These phenomena are all connected with events surrounding Christ's second coming and signal the establishment of the earthly kingdom: blood (Rev 6:8; 8:7, 8; 9:15; 14:20; 16:3); fire (Rev 8:5, 7, 8, 10); and smoke (Rev 9:2, 3, 17, 18; 18:9, 18).

2:20 sun ... darkness ... moon into blood. Cf. Mt 24:29, 30; *see note on Rev 6:12.* **day of the LORD.** See Introduction to Joel: Interpretive Challenges; *see note on 1Th 5:2.* This Day of the Lord will come with the return of Jesus Christ (cf. 2Th 2:2; Rev 19:11–15).

2:21 everyone who calls. Up to that hour of judgment and wrath, any who turn to Christ as Lord and Savior will be saved (*see notes on Ro 10:10–13*).

2:22–36 Here is the main body of Peter's sermon, in which he presented and defended Jesus Christ as Israel's Messiah.

2:22 Jesus the Nazarene. The humble name that often identified the Lord during His earthly ministry (Mt 21:11; Mk 10:47; Lk 24:19; Jn 18:5). **attested ... with miracles and wonders and signs.** By a variety of supernatural means and works, God validated Jesus as the Messiah (cf. Mt 11:1–6; Lk 7:20–23; Jn 3:2; 5:17–20; 8:28; Php 2:9; *see notes on 1:3; 2:19*).

2:23 by the predetermined plan and foreknowledge of God. From eternity past (2Ti 1:9; Rev 13:8) God predetermined that Jesus would die an atoning death as part of His preordained plan (4:27, 28; 13:27–29). **hands of godless men.** An indictment against "men of Israel" (v. 22), those unbelieving Jews who instigated Jesus' death, which was carried out by the Romans. That the crucifixion was predetermined by God does not absolve the guilt of those who caused it.

2:24 impossible. Because of His divine power (Jn 11:25; Heb 2:14) and God's promise and purpose (Lk 24:46; Jn 2:18–22; 1Co 15:16–26), death could not keep Jesus in the grave.

2:25–28 David says. The Lord was speaking of His resurrection prophetically through David (*see note on Ps 16:10*).

26 'Therefore my heart was glad
and my tongue exulted;
Moreover my flesh also
will live in hope;
27 Because You will not abandon
my soul to [A]Hades,
[B]Nor [a]allow Your [b]Holy One
to [C]undergo decay.
28 'You have made known to
me the ways of life;
You will make me full of gladness
with Your presence.'

29 "[a]Brethren, I may confidently say to you regarding the [A]patriarch David that he both [B]died and [C]was
buried, and [D]his tomb is [b]with us to this day. 30 And
so, because he was [A]a prophet and knew that [B]God
had sworn to him with an oath to seat *one* [a]of
his descendants on his throne, 31 he looked ahead
and spoke of the resurrection of [a]the Christ, that [A]He
was neither abandoned to Hades, nor did His
flesh [b]suffer decay. 32 This Jesus [A]God raised up
again, to which we are all [B]witnesses. 33 Therefore
having been exalted [a,A]to the right hand of God, and
[B]having received from the Father [C]the promise of
the Holy Spirit, He has [D]poured forth this which
you both see and hear. 34 For it was not David who
ascended into [a]heaven, but he himself says:

'[A]The Lord said to my Lord,
"Sit at My right hand,
35 Until I make Your enemies a
footstool for Your feet." '

36 Therefore let all the [A]house of Israel know for
certain that God has made Him both [B]Lord and
[a]Christ—this Jesus [C]whom you crucified."

THE INGATHERING

37 Now when they heard *this,* they were [a]pierced to
the heart, and said to Peter and the rest of the apostles,
"[b]Brethren, [c,A]what shall we do?" 38 Peter *said* to them,
"[A]Repent, and each of you be [B]baptized in the name
of Jesus Christ for the forgiveness of your sins; and
you will receive the gift of the Holy Spirit. 39 For [A]the
promise is for you and your children and for all who
are [B]far off, as many as the Lord our God will call to
Himself." 40 And with many other words he solemnly
[A]testified and kept on exhorting them, saying, "[a]Be
saved from this [B]perverse generation!" 41 So then, those
who had received his word were baptized; and that
day there were added about three thousand [a,A]souls.

2:27 [a]Lit *give* [b]Or *devout* or *pious* [c]Lit *see corruption* [A]Matt 11:23; Acts 2:31 [B]Acts 13:35 2:29 [a]Lit *Men brothers* [b]Lit *among* [A]Acts 7:8f; Heb 7:4 [B]Acts 13:36 [C]1 Kin 2:10 [D]Neh 3:16 2:30 [a]Lit *of the fruit of his loins* [A]Matt 22:43 [B]Ps 132:11; 2 Sam 7:12f; Ps 89:3f 2:31 [a]I.e. the Messiah [b]Lit *see corruption* [A]Matt 11:23; Acts 2:27 2:32 [A]Acts 2:24; 3:15, 26; 4:10; 5:30; 10:40; 13:30, 33, 34, 37; 17:31; Rom 4:24; 6:4; 8:11; 10:9; 1 Cor 6:14; 15:15; 2 Cor 4:14; Gal 1:1; Eph 1:20; Col 2:12; 1 Thess 1:10; Heb 13:20; 1 Pet 1:21 [B]Acts 1:8 2:33 [a]Or *by* [A]Mark 16:19; Acts 5:31 [B]Acts 1:4 [C]John 7:39; Gal 3:14 [D]Acts 2:17; 10:45 2:34 [a]Lit *the heavens* [A]Ps 110:1; Matt 22:44f 2:36 [a]I.e. Messiah [A]Ezek 36:22, 32, 37; 45:6 [B]Acts 2:23 [C]Luke 2:11 2:37 [a]Or *wounded in conscience* [b]Lit *Men brothers* [c]Or *what are we to do* [A]Luke 3:10, 12, 14 2:38 [A]Mark 1:15; Luke 24:47; Acts 3:19; 5:31; 20:21 [B]Mark 16:16; Acts 8:12, 16; 22:16 2:39 [A]Is 44:3; 54:13; 57:19; Joel 2:32; Rom 9:4; Eph 2:12 [B]Eph 2:13, 17 2:40 [a]Or *Escape* [A]Luke 16:28 [B]Deut 32:5; Matt 17:17; Phil 2:15 2:41 [a]I.e. persons [A]Acts 3:23; 7:14; 27:37; Rom 13:1; 1 Pet 3:20; Rev 16:3

2:27 Hades. Cf. v. 31; *see note on Lk 16:23.* The NT equivalent of the OT grave or "Sheol." Though sometimes it identifies hell (Mt 11:23), here it refers to the general place of the dead.

2:29 his tomb is with us. A reminder to the Jews that David's body had never been raised, so he could not be the fulfillment of the prophecy of Ps 16.

2:30–32 Peter exposits the meaning of Ps 16 as referring not to David, but to Jesus Christ. He would be raised to reign (v. 30; cf. Pss 2:1–9; 89:3).

2:30 because he was a prophet. Peter quoted Ps 132:11. As God's spokesman, David knew that God would keep His oath (2Sa 7:11–16) and Christ would come.

2:31 Peter quoted Ps 16:10.

2:32 God raised up. Cf. v. 24; 10:40; 17:31; 1Co 6:14; Eph 1:20. That He did so attests to His approval of Christ's work on the cross. **we are all witnesses.** The early preachers preached the resurrection (3:15, 26; 4:10; 5:30; 10:40; 13:30, 33, 34, 37; 17:31).

2:33 After Jesus was risen and ascended, God's promise to send the Holy Spirit was fulfilled (cf. Jn 7:39; Gal 3:14) and manifest that day. **exalted to the right hand of God.** *See note on 7:55.*

2:34 The **LORD** said to my **LORD.** Peter quoted another psalm (Ps 110:1) concerning the exaltation of Messiah by ascension to the right hand of God, and reminds the reader that it was not fulfilled by David (as bodily resurrection had not yet been; *see note on v. 29*), but by Jesus Christ (v. 36). Peter had been an eyewitness to that ascension (1:9–11).

2:36 Peter summarizes his sermon with a powerful statement of certainty: the OT prophecies of resurrection and exaltation provide evidence that overwhelmingly points to the crucified Jesus as the Messiah. **both Lord and Christ.** Jesus is God as well as anointed Messiah (cf. Ro 1:4; 10:9; 1Co 12:3; Php 2:9, 11).

2:37 pierced to the heart. The Gr. word for "pierced" means "stab," and thus denotes something sudden and unexpected. In grief, remorse, and intense spiritual conviction, Peter's listeners were stunned by his indictment that they had killed their Messiah.

2:38 Repent. This refers to a change of mind and purpose that turns an individual from sin to God (1Th 1:9). Such change involves more than fearing the consequences of God's judgment. Genuine repentance knows that the evil of sin must be forsaken and the person and work of Christ totally and singularly embraced. Peter exhorted his hearers to repent, otherwise they would not experience true conversion (*see note on Mt 3:2;* cf. 3:19; 5:31; 8:22; 11:18; 17:30; 20:21; 26:20; Mt 4:17). **be baptized.** This Gr. word lit. means "be dipped or immersed" in water. Peter was obeying Christ's command from Mt 28:19 and urging the people who repented and turned to the Lord Christ for salvation to identify, through the waters of baptism, with His death, burial, and resurrection (cf. 19:5; Ro 6:3, 4; 1Co 12:13; Gal 3:27; *see notes on Mt 3:2*). This is the first time the apostles publicly enjoined people to obey that ceremony. Prior to this, many Jews had experienced the baptism of John the Baptist (*see notes on Mt 3:1–3*), and were also familiar with the baptism of Gentile converts to Judaism (proselytes). **in the name of Jesus Christ.** For the new believer, it was a crucial but costly identification to accept. **for the forgiveness of your sins.** This might better be translated "because of the forgiveness of sins." Baptism does not produce forgiveness and cleansing from sin. *See notes on 1Pe 3:20, 21.* The reality of forgiveness precedes the rite of baptism (v. 41). Genuine repentance brings from God the forgiveness of sins (cf. Eph 1:7), and because of that the new believer was to be baptized. Baptism, however, was to be the ever-present act of obedience, so that it became synonymous with salvation. Thus to say one was baptized for forgiveness was the same as saying one was saved. *See note on "one baptism" in Eph 4:5.* Every believer enjoys the complete forgiveness of sins (Mt 26:28; Lk 24:47; Eph 1:7; Col 2:13; 1Jn 2:12). **the gift of the Holy Spirit.** *See notes on 1:5, 8.*

2:39 the promise. *See note on 1:4.* **all who are far off.** Gentiles, who would also share in the blessings of salvation (cf. Eph 2:11–13). **as many as the Lord our God will call.** Salvation is ultimately from the Lord. *See note on Ro 3:24.*

2:41 those who had received his word were baptized. *See note on v. 38.* **three thousand.** Luke's use of a specific number suggests records were kept of conversions and baptisms (*see note on v. 38*). Archeological work on the S side of the temple mount has uncovered numerous Jewish *mikvahs,* large baptistry-like facilities where Jewish worshipers would immerse themselves in ritual purification before entering the temple. More than enough existed to facilitate the large number of baptisms in a short amount of time.

42They were [A]continually devoting themselves to the
apostles' teaching and to fellowship, to [B]the breaking
of bread and [a,A]to prayer.
43[a]Everyone kept feeling a sense of awe; and
many [A]wonders and [b]signs were taking place
through the apostles. 44And all those who had believed [a]were together and [A]had all things in common; 45and they [A]*began* selling their property and
possessions and were sharing them with all, as
anyone might have need. 46[A]Day by day continuing with one mind in the temple, and [B]breaking
bread [a]from house to house, they were taking their
[b]meals together with gladness and [c]sincerity of
heart, 47praising God and [A]having favor with all the
people. And the Lord [B]was adding [a]to their number
day by day [C]those who were being saved.

HEALING THE LAME BEGGAR

3 Now [A]Peter and John were going up to the
temple at the [a]ninth *hour,* [B]the hour of prayer.
2And [A]a man who had been lame from his mother's
womb was being carried along, whom they [B]used
to set down every day at the gate of the temple
which is called Beautiful, [C]in order to beg [a]alms
of those who were entering the temple. 3When he
saw [A]Peter and John about to go into the temple,
he *began* asking to receive alms. 4But Peter, along
with John, [A]fixed his gaze on him and said, "Look
at us!" 5And he *began* to give them his attention,
expecting to receive something from them. 6But
Peter said, "I do not possess silver and gold, but
what I do have I give to you: [A]In the name of Jesus
Christ the Nazarene—walk!" 7And seizing him by
the right hand, he raised him up; and immediately
his feet and his ankles were strengthened. 8[a,A]With
a leap he stood upright and *began* to walk; and he
entered the temple with them, walking and leaping
and praising God. 9And [A]all the people saw him
walking and praising God; 10and they were taking
note of him as being the one who used to [A]sit at the
Beautiful Gate of the temple to *beg* alms, and they
were filled with wonder and amazement at what
had happened to him.

PETER'S SECOND SERMON

11While he was clinging to [A]Peter and John, all
the people ran together to them at the so-called
[a,B]portico of Solomon, full of amazement. 12But when
Peter saw *this,* he replied to the people, "Men of
Israel, why are you amazed at this, or why do you
gaze at us, as if by our own power or piety we had
made him walk? 13[A]The God of Abraham, Isaac and
Jacob, [B]the God of our fathers, has glorified His
[a,C]servant Jesus, *the one* whom [D]you delivered and
disowned in the presence of [E]Pilate, when he had
[F]decided to release Him. 14But you disowned [A]the
Holy and Righteous One and [B]asked for a murderer
to be granted to you, 15but put to death the [a,A]Prince
of life, *the one* whom [B]God raised from the dead, *a
fact* to which we are [C]witnesses. 16And on the basis

2:42 [a]Lit *the prayers* [A]Acts 1:14 [B]Luke 24:30; Acts 2:46; 20:7; 1 Cor 10:16 2:43 [a]Lit *fear was occurring to every soul* [b]Or *attesting miracles* [A]Acts 2:22 2:44 [a]One early ms does not contain *were* and *and* [A]Acts 4:32, 37; 5:2 2:45 [A]Matt 19:21; Acts 4:34 2:46 [a]Or *in the various private homes* [b]Lit *food* [c]Or *simplicity* [A]Acts 5:42 [B]Luke 24:30; Acts 2:42; 20:7; 1 Cor 10:16 2:47 [a]Lit *together* [A]Acts 5:13 [B]Acts 2:41; 4:4; 5:14; 6:1, 7; 9:31, 35, 42; 11:21, 24; 14:1, 21; 16:5; 17:12 [C]1 Cor 1:18 3:1 [a]I.e. 3 p.m. [A]Luke 22:8; Acts 3:3, 4, 11 [B]Ps 55:17; Matt 27:45; Acts 10:30 3:2 [a]Or *a gift of charity* [A]Acts 14:8 [B]Luke 16:20 [C]John 9:8; Acts 3:10 3:3 [A]Luke 22:8; Acts 3:1, 4, 11 3:4 [A]Acts 10:4 3:6 [A]Acts 2:22; 3:16; 4:10 3:8 [a]Lit *Leaping up* [A]Acts 14:10 3:9 [A]Acts 4:16, 21 3:10 [A]John 9:8; Acts 3:2 3:11 [a]Or *colonnade* [A]Luke 22:8; Acts 3:3, 4 [B]John 10:23; Acts 5:12 3:13 [a]Or *Son* [A]Matt 22:32 [B]Ex 3:13, 15; Acts 5:30; 7:32; 22:14 [C]Acts 3:26; 4:27, 30 [D]Matt 20:19; John 19:11; Acts 2:23 [E]Matt 27:2 [F]Luke 23:4 3:14 [A]Mark 1:24; Acts 4:27; 7:52; 2 Cor 5:21 [B]Matt 27:20; Mark 15:11; Luke 23:18, 25 3:15 [a]Or *Author* [A]Acts 5:31; Heb 2:10; 12:2 [B]Acts 2:24 [C]Luke 24:48

2:42 apostles' teaching. The foundational content for the believer's spiritual growth and maturity was the Scripture, God's revealed truth, which the apostles received (*see notes on Jn 14:26; 15:26, 27; 16:13*) and taught faithfully. *See notes on 2Pe 1:19–21; 3:1, 2, 16.* **fellowship.** Lit. "partnership," or "sharing." Because Christians become partners with Jesus Christ and all other believers (1Jn 1:3), it is their spiritual duty to stimulate one another to righteousness and obedience (cf. Ro 12:10; 13:8; 15:5; Gal 5:13; Eph 4:2, 25; 5:21; Col 3:9; 1Th 4:9; Heb 3:13; 10:24, 25; 1Pe 4:9, 10). **breaking of bread.** A reference to the Lord's Table, or Communion, which is mandatory for all Christians to observe (cf. 1Co 11:24–29). **prayer.** Of individual believers and the church corporately (see 1:14, 24; 4:24–31; cf. Jn 14:13, 14).

2:43 wonders and signs. *See note on v. 19.* In the NT, the ability to perform miracles was limited to the apostles and their close colleagues (e.g., Philip in 8:13; cf. 2Co 12:12; Heb 2:3, 4). These produced awe and respect for divine power.

2:44 all things in common. See 4:32. This phrase conveys not that the early Christians lived in a commune or pooled and redistributed everything equally, but that they held their own possessions lightly, ready to use them at any moment for someone else, as needs arose.

2:45 selling ... their possessions. This indicates that they had not pooled their resources (*see note on v. 44*) but sold their own possessions to provide money for those of the church in need (cf. v. 46; 4:34–37; 2Co 8:13, 14).

2:46 Day by day ... in the temple. Believers went to the temple to praise God (v. 47), observe the daily hours of prayer (cf. 3:1), and witness to the gospel (v. 47; 5:42). **breaking bread from house to house.** This has reference to the daily means that believers shared with one another. **gladness and sincerity of heart.** The Jerusalem church was joyful because its single focus was on Jesus Christ. *See notes on 2Co 11:3; Php 3:13, 14.*

2:47 the Lord was adding. Cf. v. 39; 5:14. *See note on Mt 16:18.* Salvation is God's sovereign work.

3:1 the ninth *hour,* the hour of prayer. 3:00 p.m. The Jews had 3 daily times of prayer (Ps 55:17); the other two were 9:00 a.m. (third hour) and 12:00 noon (sixth hour).

3:2 gate of the temple ... called Beautiful. A large and ornate gate inside the temple mount on the eastern side, separating the Court of the Gentiles from the Court of the Women. **alms.** A charitable donation of money.

3:3 into the temple. Beggars considered the temple the best site to operate because the daily throngs came to impress God with their pious good works, including offerings at the temple treasury.

3:10 Beautiful Gate. *See note on v. 2.*

3:11 portico of Solomon. A portico surrounding the temple's Court of the Gentiles. This was also where Jesus had taught about the Good Shepherd (Jn 10:23). Cf. Is 35:6.

3:13 The God of Abraham, Isaac and Jacob. A description of God familiar to Peter's Jewish audience (cf. Ex 3:6, 15; 1Ki 18:36; 1Ch 29:18; 2Ch 30:6; Mt 22:32). He used this formula, which stressed God's covenant faithfulness, to demonstrate that he declared the same God and Messiah whom the prophets had proclaimed. **His servant Jesus.** Peter depicted Jesus as God's personal representative. This is an unusual NT title for Jesus, used only 4 other places (v. 26; 4:27, 30; Mt 12:18), but a more familiar OT name for Messiah (Is 42:1–4, 19; 49:5–7; *see notes on 52:13–53:12*; cf. Mt 20:28; Jn 6:38; 8:28; 13:1–7). **Pilate ... decided to release *Him*.** Pontius Pilate, the Roman governor at Jesus' trial, came from a national tradition that strongly supported justice (cf. 16:37, 38; 22:25–29; 25:16). He knew Jesus' crucifixion would be unjust and therefore declared Him innocent 6 times (Lk 23:4, 14, 15, 22; Jn 18:38; 19:4, 6) and repeatedly sought to release Him (Lk 23:13–22; *see notes on Jn 19:12, 13*).

3:14 the Holy and Righteous One. Cf. Ps 16:10; Lk 4:34; Jn 6:69. **murderer.** Barabbas (Mt 27:16–21; Mk 15:11; Lk 23:18; Jn 18:40).

3:15 put to death ... God raised ... we are witnesses. Peter's confident and forceful declaration (cf. 1Co 15:3–7) was a clear defense of and provided further evidence for Christ's resurrection. Peter's claim was undeniable; the Jews never showed any evidence, such as Jesus' corpse, to disprove it. **Prince of life.** The

of faith [A]in His name, *it is* [a]the name of Jesus which
has strengthened this man whom you see and know;
and the faith which *comes* through Him has given
him this perfect health in the presence of you all.
17 "And now, brethren, I know that you acted [A]in
ignorance, just as your [B]rulers did also. 18 But the
things which [A]God announced beforehand by the
mouth of all the prophets, [B]that His [a]Christ would
suffer, He has thus fulfilled. 19 Therefore [A]repent
and return, so that your sins may be wiped away, in
order that [B]times of refreshing may come from the
presence of the Lord; 20 and that He may send Jesus,
the [a]Christ appointed for you, 21 [A]whom heaven
must receive until *the* [a]period of [B]restoration of
all things about which [C]God spoke by the mouth of
His holy prophets from ancient time. 22 Moses said,
'[A]THE LORD GOD WILL RAISE UP FOR YOU A PROPHET
[a]LIKE ME FROM YOUR BRETHREN; TO HIM YOU SHALL
GIVE HEED to everything He says to you. 23 [A]And
it will be that every [B]soul that does not heed that
prophet [C]shall be utterly destroyed from among the
people.' 24 And likewise, [A]all the prophets who have
spoken, from Samuel and *his* successors onward,
also announced these days. 25 It is you who are [A]the
sons of the prophets and of the [B]covenant which
God [a]made with your fathers, saying to Abraham,
'[C]AND IN YOUR SEED ALL THE FAMILIES OF THE EARTH
SHALL BE BLESSED.' 26 For you [A]first, God [B]raised up
His [a]Servant and sent Him to bless you by turning
every one *of you* from your wicked ways."

PETER AND JOHN ARRESTED

4 As they were speaking to the people, the priests
and [A]the captain of the temple *guard* and [B]the
Sadducees [C]came up to them, 2 being greatly disturbed because they were teaching the people and
proclaiming [a,A]in Jesus the resurrection from the
dead. 3 And they laid hands on them and [A]put them

3:16 [a]Lit *His name* [A]Acts 3:6 3:17 [A]Luke 23:34; John 15:21; Acts 13:27; 26:9; Eph 4:18 [B]Luke 23:13 3:18 [a]Or *Anointed One;* i.e. Messiah [A]Acts 2:23 [B]Luke 24:27; Acts 17:3; 26:23 3:19 [A]Acts 2:38; 26:20 [B]2 Thess 1:7; Heb 4:1ff 3:20 [a]Or *Anointed One;* i.e. Messiah 3:21 [a]Lit *periods, times* [A]Acts 1:11 [B]Matt 17:11; Rom 8:21 [C]Luke 1:70 3:22 [a]Or *as* He raised up *me* [A]Deut 18:15, 18; Acts 7:37 3:23 [A]Deut 18:19 [B]Acts 2:41 [C]Lev 23:29 3:24 [A]Luke 24:27; Acts 17:3; 26:23 3:25 [a]Lit *covenanted* [A]Acts 2:39 [B]Rom 9:4f [C]Gen 22:18 3:26 [a]Or *Son* [A]Matt 15:24; John 4:22; Acts 13:46; Rom 1:16; 2:9f [B]Acts 2:24 4:1 [A]Luke 22:4 [B]Matt 3:7 [C]Luke 20:1; Acts 6:12 4:2 [a]Or *in the case of* [A]Acts 3:15; 17:18 4:3 [A]Acts 5:18

Gr. word for "prince" means originator, pioneer, or beginner of something. It describes Jesus as the Divine Originator of life (cf. Ps 36:9; Heb 2:10; 12:2; 1Jn 5:11, 20).

3:18 announced beforehand by the mouth of all the prophets. Cf. Ge 3:15; Ps 22; Is 53; Zec 12:10.

3:19 repent and return. *See notes on 2:38; Mt 3:2.* "Return" is a frequent NT word that relates to sinners turning to God (9:35; 14:15; 26:18, 20; Lk 1:16, 17; 2Co 3:16; 1Pe 2:25). **your sins . . . wiped away.** Cf. Ps 51:9; Is 43:25; 44:22. "Wiped away" compares forgiveness to the complete wiping away of ink from the surface of a document (Col 2:14).

3:19–21 times of refreshing . . . period of restoration of all things. "Times" or "period" means epoch, era, or season. Two descriptions are given to the coming era of the millennial kingdom. This is clear because they bracket the reference to Jesus Christ being sent from God to bring those times. Peter points to Christ's earthly reign (*see notes on 1:7*; cf. Ro 11:26). The period will be marked by all kinds of blessings and renewal (cf. Is 11:6–10; 35:1–10; Eze 34:26; 44:3; Joel 2:26; Mt 19:28; Rev 19:1–10).

3:22 Quoted from Dt 18:15. Moses was revered by the Jews as their first and greatest prophet, and the Jews viewed the prophet "like him" to refer to the Messiah.

3:23 Quoted from Dt 18:19; cf. Lv 23:29. Peter's audience was in the precarious position of losing covenant blessings by rejecting the Messiah.

3:24 prophets . . . from Samuel. Samuel was called a prophet in the OT (1Sa 3:20). Although he did not directly prophesy about Christ, he did anoint David as king and speak of his kingdom (1Sa 13:14; 15:28; 16:13; 28:17), and the promises David received were and will be fulfilled in Christ (cf. 2Sa 7:10–16).

3:25 in your seed. Quoted from Ge 22:18; 26:4. Jesus Christ was the ultimate fulfillment of the Abrahamic Covenant and its blessings (Gal 3:16), which are still available to the Jews.

3:26 God raised up. *See note on 2:32.* **His Servant.** *See note on v. 13.*

4:1 priests. The office of priest in the OT began with Aaron and his sons (Lv 8). They became the human intermediaries between holy God and sinful humanity. They were characterized by 3 qualities: 1) they were chosen and set apart for priestly service by God; 2) they were to be holy in character; and 3) they were the only ones allowed to come near to God on behalf of the people with the High Priest being the chief go-between on the Day of Atonement (Lv 16). Cf. Nu 16:5. **the captain of the temple *guard*.** Chief of the temple police force (composed of Levites) and second-ranking official to the High Priest. The Romans had delegated the temple-policing responsibility to the Jews. **Sadducees.** *See notes on 23:8; Mt 3:7.*

4:2 proclaiming in Jesus the resurrection. This part of the apostles' message was the most objectionable to the Jewish leaders. They had executed Christ as a blasphemer, and now Peter and John were proclaiming His resurrection.

4:3 already evening. The Jews detained Peter and John overnight in jail because Jewish law did not permit trials at night. It had been too late to convene the Sanhedrin (*see*

MAJOR SERMONS IN ACTS

Sermon	Theme	Reference
Peter to crowds at Pentecost	Peter's explanation of the meaning of Pentecost	Ac 2:14–40
Peter to crowds at the temple	The Jewish people should repent for crucifying the Messiah	Ac 3:12–26
Peter to the Sanhedrin	Testimony that a helpless man was healed by the power of Jesus	Ac 4:5–12
Stephen to the Sanhedrin	Stephen's rehearsal of Jewish history, accusing the Jews of killing the Messiah	Ac 7:2–53
Peter to Gentiles	Gentiles can be saved in the same manner as Jews	Ac 10:28–47
Peter to church at Jerusalem	Peter's testimony of his experiences at Joppa and a defense of his ministry to the Gentiles	Ac 11:4–18
Paul to synagogue at Antioch	Jesus was the Messiah in fulfillment of Old Testament prophecies	Ac 13:16–41
Peter to Jerusalem Council	Salvation by grace available to all	Ac 15:7–11
James to Jerusalem Council	Gentile converts do not require circumcision	Ac 15:13–21
Paul to Ephesian elders	Remain faithful in spite of false teachers and persecution	Ac 20:17–35
Paul to crowd at Jerusalem	Paul's statement of his conversion and his mission to the Gentiles	Ac 22:1–21
Paul to Sanhedrin	Paul's defense, declaring himself a Pharisee and a Roman citizen	Ac 23:1–6
Paul to King Agrippa	Paul's statement of his conversion and his zeal for the gospel	Ac 26:2–23
Paul to Jewish leaders at Rome	Paul's statement about his Jewish heritage	Ac 28:17–20

in jail until the next day, for it was already evening.
4 But many of those who had heard the [a]message
believed; and [A]the number of the men came to be
about five thousand.
5 On the next day, their [A]rulers and elders and
scribes were gathered together in Jerusalem;
6 and [A]Annas the high priest *was there,* and [B]Caia-
phas and John and Alexander, and all who were of
high-priestly descent. 7 When they had placed them
in the center, they *began to* inquire, "By what power,
or in what name, have you done this?" 8 Then Peter,
[a,A]filled with the Holy Spirit, said to them, "[b,B]Rulers
and elders of the people, 9 if we are [a]on trial today for
[A]a benefit done to a sick man, [b]as to how this man
has been made well, 10 let it be known to all of you
and to all the people of Israel, that [a,A]by the name
of Jesus Christ the Nazarene, whom you crucified,
whom [B]God raised from the dead—[a]by [b]this *name*
this man stands here before you in good health.
11 [a,A]He is the [B]STONE WHICH WAS [C]REJECTED by you,
THE BUILDERS, *but* WHICH BECAME THE CHIEF CORNER
stone. 12 And there is salvation in [A]no one else; for
there is no other name under heaven that has been
given among men by which we must be saved."

THREAT AND RELEASE

13 Now as they observed the [A]confidence of [B]Peter
and John and understood that they were uneducated and untrained men, they were amazed, and
[C]*began* to recognize them [a]as having been with
Jesus. 14 And seeing the man who had been healed
standing with them, they had nothing to say in reply. 15 But when they had ordered them to leave the
[a,A]Council, they *began* to confer with one another,
16 saying, "[A]What shall we do with these men? For
the fact that a [B]noteworthy [a]miracle has taken place
through them is apparent to all who live in Jerusalem, and we cannot deny it. 17 But so that it will
not spread any further among the people, let us
warn them to speak no longer to any man [A]in this
name." 18 And when they had summoned them, they
[A]commanded them not to speak or teach at all [a]in
the name of Jesus. 19 But [A]Peter and John answered
and said to them, "[B]Whether it is right in the sight
of God to give heed to you rather than to God, you
be the judge; 20 for [A]we cannot stop speaking about
what we have seen and heard." 21 When they had
threatened them further, they let them go (finding
no basis on which to punish them) [A]on account of
the people, because they were all [B]glorifying God for
what had happened; 22 for the man was more than
forty years old on whom this [a]miracle of healing
had been performed.
23 When they had been released, they went to their
own *companions* and reported all that the chief
priests and the elders had said to them. 24 And when
they heard *this,* they lifted their voices to God with
one accord and said, "O [a]Lord, it is You who [A]MADE
THE HEAVEN AND THE EARTH AND THE SEA, AND ALL
THAT IS IN THEM, 25 who [A]by the Holy Spirit, *through*
the mouth of our father David Your servant, said,

'[B]WHY DID THE [a]GENTILES RAGE,
AND THE PEOPLES DEVISE FUTILE THINGS?
26 '[A]THE KINGS OF THE EARTH
[a]TOOK THEIR STAND,
AND THE RULERS WERE
GATHERED TOGETHER
AGAINST THE LORD AND
AGAINST HIS [b,B]CHRIST.'

4:4 [a]Lit *word* [A]Acts 2:41 4:5 [A]Luke 23:13; Acts 4:8 4:6 [A]Luke 3:2 [B]Matt 26:3 4:8 [a]Or *having just been filled* [b]Lit *Rulers of the people and elders* [A]Acts 2:4; 13:9 [B]Luke 23:13; Acts 4:5 4:9 [a]Lit *answering* [b]Or *by whom* [A]Acts 3:7f 4:10 [a]Or *in* [b]Or *Him* [A]Acts 2:22; 3:6 [B]Acts 2:24 4:11 [a]Lit *This One* [A]Matt 21:42 [B]Ps 118:22 [C]Mark 9:12 4:12 [A]Matt 1:21; Acts 10:43; 1 Tim 2:5 4:13 [a]Lit *that they had been* [A]Acts 4:31 [B]Luke 22:8; Acts 4:19 [C]John 7:15 4:15 [a]Or *Sanhedrin* [A]Matt 5:22 4:16 [a]Or *sign* [A]John 11:47 [B]Acts 3:7-10 4:17 [A]John 15:21 4:18 [a]Or *on the basis of* [A]Acts 5:28f 4:19 [A]Acts 4:13 [B]Acts 5:28f 4:20 [A]1 Cor 9:16 4:21 [A]Acts 5:26 [B]Matt 9:8 4:22 [a]Or *sign* 4:24 [a]Or *Master* [A]Ex 20:11; Neh 9:6; Ps 146:6 4:25 [a]Or *nations* [A]Acts 1:16 [B]Ps 2:1 4:26 [a]Or *approached* [b]Or *Anointed One;* i.e. Messiah [A]Ps 2:2 [B]Dan 9:24f; Luke 4:18; Acts 10:38; Heb 1:9

note on v. 15) that afternoon, so the apostles would face a hearing the next day before that council.

4:4 five thousand. The cumulative total of men in the Jerusalem church by this time, not the number of those converted after Peter's latest message.

4:5 rulers and elders and scribes. These positions made up the Jewish ruling body, the Sanhedrin (*see note on v. 15*).

4:6 Annas ... Caiaphas. *See note on Jn 18:13.* Even though Annas (A.D. 6–15) had been replaced and Caiaphas was now High Priest (A.D. 18–36), he retained his title and wielded great influence. **John ... Alexander.** Their identities are uncertain. "John" could be an alternate reading for "Jonathan," who was one of Annas' sons and replaced Caiaphas as High Priest in A.D. 36.

4:8–12 Peter put the Sanhedrin on trial by preaching the gospel to those same men who condemned Jesus Christ and made themselves enemies of God.

4:8 filled with the Holy Spirit. *See note on 2:4.* Because Peter was under the control of the Spirit, he was able to face persecution and preach the gospel with power (cf. Lk 12:11, 12). **Rulers ... elders.** *See note on v. 5.*

4:11 rejected ... the chief corner *stone.* Quoted from Ps 118:22 (*see note*); cf. Eph 2:19–22; 1Pe 2:4–8.

4:12 no other name. This refers to the exclusivism of salvation by faith in Jesus Christ. There are only two religious paths: the broad way of works salvation leading to eternal death, and the narrow way of faith in Jesus, leading to eternal life (Mt 7:13, 14; cf. Jn 10:7, 8; 14:6). Sadly, the Sanhedrin and its followers were on the first path.

4:13 uneducated and untrained men. Peter and John were not educated in the rabbinical schools and had no formal training in OT theology.

4:15–17 It would be risky to punish the two apostles when they had broken no laws and had performed a miracle that captured the entire city's attention. But the Sanhedrin believed it had to stop the preaching of the incriminating truth that its members had executed the Messiah.

4:15 Council. The Sanhedrin, the Jews' national ruling body and supreme court. It had 71 members, including the High Priest (*see note on v. 5*).

4:19 to give heed to you rather than to God. Christians should obey governmental authority (Ro 13:1–7; 1Pe 2:13–17), but when government decrees are clearly contrary to God's Word, God must be obeyed (cf. Ex 1:15–17; Da 6:4–10).

4:23 chief priests. A small group within the Sanhedrin (*see note on v. 15*), composed of former High Priests and members of influential priestly families (*see note on Mt 2:4*). **elders.** *See note on v. 5.*

4:24–30 Peter and John's experience did not frighten or discourage the other disciples, but exhilarated them. They took confidence in God's sovereign control of all events, even their sufferings. Furthermore, they were comforted that the opposition whom they were facing was foreseen in the OT (vv. 25, 26).

4:24 Lord. The Gr. word is an uncommon NT title for God that means "absolute master" (Lk 2:29; 2Ti 2:21; 2Pe 2:1; Jude 4; Rev 6:10), which represented the disciples' recognition of God's sovereignty.

4:25 *through* the mouth of our father David. *See note on 1:16.* In the events of recent days, the disciples saw a fulfillment of Ps 2:1, 2 which they quoted.

27 For truly in this city there were gathered together against Your holy [a,A]servant Jesus, whom
You anointed, both [B]Herod and [C]Pontius Pilate, along
with [D]the [b]Gentiles and the peoples of Israel, 28 to do
whatever Your hand and [A]Your purpose predestined
to occur. 29 And [a]now, Lord, take note of their threats,
and grant that Your bond-servants may [A]speak Your
word with all [B]confidence, 30 while You extend Your
hand to heal, and [a,A]signs and wonders take place
through the name of Your holy [b,B]servant Jesus."
31 And when they had prayed, the [A]place where they
had gathered together was shaken, and they were
all [B]filled with the Holy Spirit and *began* to [C]speak
the word of God with [D]boldness.

SHARING AMONG BELIEVERS

32 And the [a]congregation of those who believed
were of one heart and soul; and not one *of them*
[b]claimed that anything belonging to him was his
own, but [A]all things were common property to them.
33 And [A]with great power the apostles were giving
[B]testimony to the resurrection of the Lord Jesus, and
abundant grace was upon them all. 34 For there was
not a needy person among them, for all who were
owners of land or houses [A]would sell them and
bring the [a]proceeds of the sales 35 and [A]lay them at
the apostles' feet, and they would be [B]distributed
to each as any had need.
36 Now Joseph, a Levite of [A]Cyprian birth, who
was also called [B]Barnabas by the apostles (which
translated means Son of [a,C]Encouragement), 37 and
who owned a tract of land, sold it and brought the
money and [A]laid it at the apostles' feet.

FATE OF ANANIAS AND SAPPHIRA

5 But a man named Ananias, with his wife Sapphira, sold a piece of property, 2 and [A]kept back
some of the price for himself, with his wife's [a]full
knowledge, and bringing a portion of it, he [B]laid it at
the apostles' feet. 3 But Peter said, "Ananias, why has
[A]Satan filled your heart to lie [B]to the Holy Spirit and
to [C]keep back *some* of the price of the land? 4 While it
remained *unsold,* did it not remain your own? And
after it was sold, was it not [a]under your control? Why
is it that you have [b]conceived this deed in your heart?
You have not lied to men but [A]to God." 5 And as he
heard these words, Ananias [A]fell down and breathed
his last; and [B]great fear came over all who heard of
it. 6 The young men got up and [A]covered him up, and
after carrying him out, they buried him.
7 Now there elapsed an interval of about three
hours, and his wife came in, not knowing what had
happened. 8 And Peter responded to her, "Tell me
whether you sold the land [a,A]for such and such a
price?" And she said, "Yes, [a]that was the price." 9 Then
Peter *said* to her, "Why is it that you have agreed
together to [A]put [B]the Spirit of the Lord to the test? Behold, the feet of those who have buried your husband
are at the door, and they will carry you out *as well.*"
10 And immediately she [A]fell at his feet and breathed
her last, and the young men came in and found her
dead, and they carried her out and buried her beside
her husband. 11 And [A]great fear came over the whole
church, and over all who heard of these things.
12 [a]At the hands of the apostles many [A]signs and
wonders were taking place among the people; and
they were all with one accord in [B]Solomon's portico.

4:27 [a]Or *Son* [b]Or *nations* [A]Acts 3:13; 4:30 [B]Matt 14:1; Luke 23:7-11 [C]Matt 27:2; Mark 15:1; Luke 23:1, 12; John 18:28, 29 [D]Matt 20:19 4:28 [A]Acts 2:23 4:29 [a]Or *as for the present situation* [A]Phil 1:14 [B]Acts 4:13, 31; 14:3 4:30 [a]Or *attesting miracles* [b]Or *Son* [A]John 4:48 [B]Acts 3:13; 4:27 4:31 [A]Acts 2:1 [B]Acts 2:4 [C]Phil 1:14 [D]Acts 4:13; 14:3 4:32 [a]Or *multitude* [b]Lit *was saying* [A]Acts 2:44 4:33 [A]Acts 1:8 [B]Luke 24:48 4:34 [a]Lit *the prices of the things being sold* [A]Matt 19:21; Acts 2:45 4:35 [A]Acts 4:37; 5:2 [B]Acts 2:45; 6:1 4:36 [a]Or *Exhortation* or *Consolation* [A]Acts 11:19f; 13:4; 15:39; 21:3, 16; 27:4 [B]Acts 9:27; 11:22, 30; 12:25; 13:1, 2, 7; 1 Cor 9:6; Gal 2:1, 9, 13; Col 4:10 [C]Acts 2:40; 11:23; 13:15; 1 Cor 14:3; 1 Thess 2:3 4:37 [A]Acts 4:35; 5:2 5:2 [a]Or *collusion* [A]Acts 5:3 [B]Acts 4:35, 37 5:3 [A]Matt 4:10; Luke 22:3; John 13:2, 27 [B]Acts 5:4, 9 [C]Acts 5:2 5:4 [a]Or *in your authority* [b]Lit *placed* [A]Acts 5:3, 9 5:5 [A]Ezek 11:13; Acts 5:10 [B]Acts 2:43; 5:11 5:6 [A]John 19:40 5:8 [a]Lit *for so much* [A]Acts 5:2 5:9 [A]Acts 15:10 [B]Acts 5:3, 4 5:10 [A]Ezek 11:13; Acts 5:5 5:11 [A]Acts 2:43; 5:5 5:12 [a]Lit *Through* [A]John 4:48 [B]John 10:23; Acts 3:11

4:28 Your hand and Your purpose. God has written all of history according to His eternal plan. The crucifixion of Jesus was no exception (*see note on 2:23*; cf. Ro 8:29, 30; 1Co 2:7; Eph 1:5–11).

4:30 signs and wonders. *See note on 2:19.* **holy servant.** *See note on 3:13.*

4:31 was shaken. As on Pentecost, a physical phenomenon indicated the presence of the Holy Spirit (*see notes on 2:2, 3*). **filled with the Holy Spirit.** *See notes on v. 8; 2:4.*

4:32–35 all things were common property. *See notes on 2:44–46.* Believers understood that all they had belonged to God, and therefore when a brother or sister had a need, those who could meet it were obligated to do so (cf. Jas 2:15, 16; 1Jn 3:17). The method was to give the money to the apostles who would distribute it (vv. 35, 37).

4:33 giving testimony to the resurrection. *See note on 1:22.* **abundant grace.** This means "favor" and carries a twofold meaning here: 1) favor from the people outside the church. Because of the believers' love and unity, the common people were impressed (cf. 2:47); and 2) favor from God who was granting blessing.

4:36 Joseph, a Levite … called Barnabas. Luke introduces Barnabas as a role model from among those who donated property proceeds. Barnabas was a member of the priestly tribe of the Levites and a native of the island of Cyprus. He becomes an associate of Paul and a prominent figure later in the book (cf. 9:26, 27; 11:22–24, 30; chaps. 13–15). **Cyprian.** Barnabas was from Cyprus, the third largest island in the Mediterranean after Sicily and Sardinia, located some 60 mi. W off the Syrian coast (*see note on 13:4*).

4:37 owned … land, sold it. The OT prohibited Levites from owning property in Israel (Nu 18:20, 24; Dt 10:9), but that law was apparently no longer in force. It is also possible that the land was in Cyprus.

5:1 Ananias … Sapphira. These are two classic examples of hypocrisy among Christians who faked their spirituality to impress others (cf. Mt 6:1–6, 16–18; 15:7; 23:13–36). They were in the "congregation of those who believed" (4:32) and were involved with the Holy Spirit (v. 3), but remained hypocrites.

5:2 kept back *some* of the price. This was not a sin in and of itself. However, they had promised, perhaps publicly, that they were giving the full amount received to the Lord. Their outward sin was lying about how much they were giving to the church, but the deeper, more devastating sin was their spiritual hypocrisy based on selfishness.

5:3 Satan filled your heart. Ananias and Sapphira were satanically inspired in contrast to Barnabas' Spirit-filled gesture (4:37).

5:3, 4 lie to the Holy Spirit. Ananias must have promised the Lord he would give the whole amount. He lied to the ever-present Holy Spirit in him (1Co 6:19, 20) and in the church (Eph 2:21, 22).

5:5 great fear. See v. 11. They were afraid about the seriousness of hypocrisy and sin in the church. The people learned that death can be the consequence of sin (see 1Co 11:30–32; 1Jn 5:16). That fear extended beyond those present to all who heard about the divine judgment (v. 11). Cf. 1Pe 3:10; 4:17.

5:6–10 The Jews did not embalm, but customarily buried the dead the same day, especially someone who died by divine judgment (see Dt 21:22, 23).

5:9 put the Spirit of the Lord to the test? Sapphira had gone too far in presuming upon God's forbearance. The folly of such blatant human presumption had to be shown as a sin, hence the ultimate divine chastening that followed.

5:11 church. This is the first use of "church" in Acts, although it is the most common word used to describe the assembly of those who had believed (cf. 4:32).

5:12 signs and wonders. *See note on 2:19.* **Solomon's portico.** *See note on 3:11.*

13 But none of the rest dared to associate with them;
however, [A]the people held them in high esteem.
14 And all the more [A]believers in the Lord, multitudes
of men and women, were constantly [B]added to *their*
number, 15 to such an extent that they even carried
the sick out into the streets and laid them on cots
and pallets, so that when Peter came by [A]at least his
shadow might fall on any one of them. 16 Also the
[a]people from the cities in the vicinity of Jerusalem
were coming together, bringing people who were
sick [b]or afflicted with unclean spirits, and they were
all being healed.

IMPRISONMENT AND RELEASE

17 But the high priest rose up, along with all his
associates (that is [A]the sect of [B]the Sadducees), and
they were filled with jealousy. 18 They laid hands on
the apostles and [A]put them in a public jail. 19 But
during the night [A]an angel of the Lord opened the
gates of the prison, and taking them out he said,
20 "Go, stand and [a]speak to the people in the temple
[b,A]the whole message of this Life." 21 Upon hearing
this, they entered into the temple [A]about daybreak
and *began* to teach.

Now when [B]the high priest and his associates
came, they called [C]the [a]Council together, even all
the Senate of the sons of Israel, and sent *orders* to
the prison house for them to be brought. 22 But [A]the
officers who came did not find them in the prison;
and they returned and reported back, 23 saying,
"We found the prison house locked quite securely
and the guards standing at the doors; but when we
had opened up, we found no one inside." 24 Now
when [A]the captain of the temple *guard* and the
chief priests heard these words, they were greatly
perplexed about them as to what [a]would come of
this. 25 But someone came and reported to them,
"The men whom you put in prison are standing in
the temple and teaching the people!" 26 Then [A]the
captain went along with [B]the officers and *proceeded*
to bring them *back* without violence (for [C]they were
afraid of the people, that they might be stoned).

27 When they had brought them, they stood them
[a]before [A]the Council. The high priest questioned
them, 28 saying, "We gave you [A]strict orders not to
continue teaching in this name, and [a]yet, you have
filled Jerusalem with your teaching and [B]intend to
bring this man's blood upon us." 29 But Peter and
the apostles answered, "[A]We must obey God rather
than men. 30 [A]The God of our fathers [B]raised up Jesus,
[a]whom you had [C]put to death by hanging Him on
a [b]cross. 31 [A]He is the one whom God exalted [a]to His
right hand as a [b,B]Prince and a [C]Savior, to grant [D]re-
pentance to Israel, and forgiveness of sins. 32 And we
are [A]witnesses [a]of these things; and [B]*so is* the Holy
Spirit, whom God has given to those who obey Him."

GAMALIEL'S COUNSEL

33 But when they heard this, they were [A]cut [a]to the
quick and intended to kill them. 34 But a Pharisee
named [A]Gamaliel, a [B]teacher of the Law, respected
by all the people, stood up in [C]the Council and gave
orders to put the men outside for a short time. 35 And
he said to them, "Men of Israel, take care what you
propose to do with these men. 36 For some time ago
Theudas rose up, [A]claiming to be somebody, and a
group of about four hundred men joined up with
him. [a]But he was killed, and all who [b]followed him
were dispersed and came to nothing. 37 After this
man, Judas of Galilee rose up in the days of [A]the
census and drew away *some* people after him; he
too perished, and all those who [a]followed him were

5:13 [A]Acts 2:47; 4:21 5:14 [A]2 Cor 6:15 [B]Acts 2:47; 11:24 5:15 [A]Acts 19:12 5:16 [a]Lit *multitude* [b]Lit *and* 5:17 [A]Acts 15:5 [B]Matt 3:7; Acts 4:1 5:18 [A]Acts 4:3 5:19 [A]Matt 1:20, 24; 2:13, 19; 28:2; Luke 1:11; 2:9; Acts 8:26; 10:3; 12:7, 23; 27:23 5:20 [a]Or *continue to speak* [b]Lit *all the words* [A]John 6:63, 68 5:21 [a]Or *Sanhedrin* [A]John 8:2 [B]Acts 4:6 [C]Matt 5:22; Acts 5:27, 34, 41 5:22 [A]Matt 26:58; Acts 5:26 5:24 [a]Lit *this would become* [A]Acts 4:1; 5:26 5:26 [A]Acts 5:24 [B]Acts 5:22 [C]Acts 4:21; 5:13 5:27 [a]Lit *in* [A]Matt 5:22; Acts 5:21, 34, 41 5:28 [a]Lit *behold* [A]Acts 4:18 [B]Matt 23:35; 27:25; Acts 2:23, 36; 3:14f; 7:52 5:29 [A]Acts 4:19 5:30 [a]Or *on whom you had laid violent hands* [b]Lit *wood* [A]Acts 3:13 [B]Acts 2:24 [C]Acts 10:39; 13:29; Gal 3:13; 1 Pet 2:24 5:31 [a]Or *by* [b]Or *Leader* [A]Acts 2:33 [B]Acts 3:15 [C]Luke 2:11 [D]Luke 24:47; Acts 2:38 5:32 [a]One early ms adds *in Him* [A]Luke 24:48 [B]John 15:26; Acts 15:28; Rom 8:16; Heb 2:4 5:33 [a]Or *in their hearts* [A]Acts 2:37; 7:54 5:34 [A]Acts 22:3 [B]Luke 2:46; 5:17 [C]Acts 5:21 5:36 [a]Lit *Who was killed* [b]Lit *were obeying* [A]Acts 8:9; Gal 2:6; 6:3 5:37 [a]Lit *were obeying* [A]Luke 2:2

5:13 none ... dared to associate with them. *See note on v. 5.* These unbelievers had respect for the followers of Jesus, but feared the deadly potential of joining the church.

5:14 believers ... men and women. While the unbelievers stayed away due to fear of the consequence of sin, there were multitudes who heard the gospel witness, gladly believed, and joined the church.

5:15 Peter ... his shadow. The people truly believed he had divine healing power and that it might even extend to them through his shadow (cf. 3:1–10). But Scripture does not say Peter's shadow ever healed anyone; in fact, the healing power of God through him seemed to go far beyond his shadow (v. 16, "people ... all being healed"). This outpouring of healing was an answer to the prayer in 4:29, 30.

5:16 unclean spirits. Cf. Mt 10:1; 12:43–45; Mk 1:23–27; 5:1–13; 6:7; 9:25; Lk 4:36; 8:29; 9:42. They are demons, fallen angels (Rev 12:3) who are so designated because of their vile wickedness. They frequently live inside unbelievers, particularly those who vent their wicked nature.

5:17 high priest. *See note on 4:6.* Here the title could refer to Annas (cf. 4:6) or Caiaphas. **Sadducees.** *See notes on 23:8; Mt 3:7.*

5:19 an angel of the Lord. This person should not be confused with "the angel of the LORD" in the OT (*see note on Ex 3:2*).

5:20 the whole message of this Life. The gospel (cf. Php 2:16; 1Jn 1:1–4). Jesus Christ came into this world to provide abundant and eternal life to spiritually dead people (cf. Jn 1:4; 11:25; 1Jn 5:20).

5:28 teaching. The gospel of Jesus Christ (*see notes on 2:14–40; 4:12, 13*). **this man's blood upon us.** The Sanhedrin had apparently forgotten the brash statement its supporters had made before Pilate that the responsibility for Jesus' death should be on them and their children (Mt 27:25).

5:29 obey God rather than men. *See note on 4:19.*

5:30 hanging Him on a cross. Cf. Dt 21:23; Gal 3:13.

5:31 God exalted to His right hand. *See notes on 1:9; Mk 16:19; Php 2:9–11.* **Prince.** *See note on 3:15.* **repentance to Israel.** Salvation for the Jews. Salvation demands repentance (cf. 2:38; 3:19; 17:30; 20:21; 26:20). For the nature of repentance, *see notes on 2Co 7:9–12.*

5:32 *so is* the Holy Spirit. Every believer receives the Spirit the moment one is saved by obeying the gospel (*see note on 2:4*; cf. Ro 8:9; 1Co 6:19, 20).

5:34 Gamaliel. Like his grandfather, the prominent rabbi Hillel, Gamaliel, the most noted rabbi of his time, led the liberal faction of the Pharisees. His most famous student was the apostle Paul (22:3).

5:36 Theudas. An otherwise unknown individual who led a revolt in Judea in the early years of the first century, not to be confused with a later Theudas cited in Josephus as a revolutionary.

5:37 Judas of Galilee rose up. The founder of the Zealots who led another revolt in Israel early in the first century. Zealots, a party of Jews who were fanatical nationalists, believed that radical action was required to overthrow the Roman power in Israel. They even sought to take up arms against Rome. **days of the census.** One ordered by Quirinius, governor of Syria, in 6–7 B.C. (cf. Lk 2:2).

scattered. 38 So in the present case, I say to you,
stay away from these men and let them alone, for
if this plan or [a]action [A]is of men, it will be overthrown; 39 but if it is of God, you will not be able
to overthrow them; or else you may even be found
[A]fighting against God.”
40 They [a]took his advice; and after calling the
apostles in, they [A]flogged them and ordered them
not to [b]speak in the name of Jesus, and *then* released them. 41 So they went on their way from the
presence of the [a,A]Council, [B]rejoicing that they had
been considered worthy to suffer shame [C]for *His*
name. 42 [A]And every day, in the temple and [a]from
house to house, they [b]kept right on teaching and
[c,B]preaching Jesus *as* the [d]Christ.

CHOOSING OF THE SEVEN

6 Now [a]at this time while the [A]disciples were
[B]increasing *in number,* a complaint arose on
the part of the [b,C]Hellenistic *Jews* against the *na-*
tive [D]Hebrews, because their [E]widows were being
overlooked in [F]the daily serving *of food.* 2 So the
twelve summoned the [a]congregation of the disciples
and said, “It is not desirable for us to neglect the
word of God in order to serve tables. 3 Therefore,
[A]brethren, select from among you seven men of
good reputation, [B]full of the Spirit and of wisdom,
whom we may put in charge of this task. 4 But we
will [A]devote ourselves to prayer and to the [a]ministry
of the word.” 5 The statement found approval with
the whole [a]congregation; and they chose [A]Stephen, a
man [B]full of faith and of the Holy Spirit, and [C]Philip,
Prochorus, Nicanor, Timon, Parmenas and [b]Nico-
las, a [c,D]proselyte from [E]Antioch. 6 And these they
brought before the apostles; and after [A]praying,
they [B]laid their hands on them.
7 [A]The word of God kept on spreading; and [B]the
number of the disciples continued to increase
greatly in Jerusalem, and a great many of the priests
were becoming obedient to [C]the faith.
8 And Stephen, full of grace and power, was performing great [A]wonders and [a]signs among the
people. 9 But some men from what was called the
Synagogue of the Freedmen, *including* both [A]Cyre-
nians and [B]Alexandrians, and some from [C]Cilicia and
[a,D]Asia, rose up and argued with Stephen. 10 But they
were unable to cope with the wisdom and the Spirit
with which he was speaking. 11 Then they secretly
induced men to say, “We have heard him speak blasphemous words against Moses and *against* God.”

5:38 [a]Or *work* [A]Mark 11:30 5:39 [A]Prov 21:30; Acts 11:17 5:40 [a]Lit *were persuaded by him* [b]Lit *be speaking* [A]Matt 10:17 5:41 [a]Or *Sanhedrin* [A]Acts 5:21 [B]1 Pet 4:14, 16 [C]John 15:21 5:42 [a]Or *in the various private homes* [b]Lit *were not ceasing to* [c]Lit *telling the good news of* [d]I.e. Messiah [A]Acts 2:46 [B]Acts 8:35; 11:20; 17:18; Gal 1:16 6:1 [a]Lit *in these days* [b]Jews who adopted the Gr language and much of Gr culture through acculturation [A]Acts 11:26 [B]Acts 2:47; 6:7 [C]Acts 9:29; 11:20 [D]2 Cor 11:22; Phil 3:5 [E]Acts 9:39, 41; 1 Tim 5:3 [F]Acts 4:35; 11:29 6:2 [a]Lit *multitude* 6:3 [A]John 21:23; Acts 1:15 [B]Acts 2:4 6:4 [a]Or *service* [A]Acts 1:14 6:5 [a]Lit *multitude* [b]Gr *Nikolaos* [c]I.e. a Gentile convert to Judaism [A]Acts 6:8ff; 11:19; 22:20 [B]Acts 6:3; 11:24 [C]Acts 8:5ff; 21:8 [D]Matt 23:15 [E]Acts 11:19 6:6 [A]Acts 1:24 [B]Num 8:10; 27:18; Deut 34:9; Mark 5:23; Acts 8:17ff; 9:17; 13:3; 19:6; 1 Tim 4:14; 2 Tim 1:6; Heb 6:2 6:7 [A]Acts 12:24; 19:20 [B]Acts 6:1 [C]Acts 13:8; 14:22; Gal 1:23; 6:10; Jude 3, 20 6:8 [a]Or *attesting miracles* [A]John 4:48 6:9 [a]I.e. west coast province of Asia Minor [A]Matt 27:32; Acts 2:10 [B]Acts 18:24 [C]Acts 15:23, 41; 21:39; 22:3; 23:34; 27:5; Gal 1:21 [D]Acts 16:6; 19:10; 21:27; 24:18

5:38, 39 Members of the Sanhedrin heeded Gamaliel’s words concerning the apostles. But, based on his knowledge of Scripture, Gamaliel should have been more decisive and less pragmatic about accepting Jesus as the risen Messiah.

5:40 **flogged them.** The apostles were unjustly flogged, probably with 39 lashes, the standard number given to avoid exceeding the OT legal limit of 40 (cf. Dt 25:3).

6:1 **increasing *in number*.** *See note on 4:4.* The figure could have reached over 20,000 men and women. **Hellenistic *Jews* ... Hebrews.** “Hellenistic Jews” were Jews from the Diaspora; “Hebrews” were the native Jewish population of Israel. The Hellenists’ absorption of aspects of Gr. culture made them suspect to the Jews of Israel. **widows were being overlooked.** The Hellenists believed their widows were not receiving an adequate share of the food the church provided for their care (cf. 1Ti 5:3–16).

6:2 **serve tables.** The word translated “tables” can refer to tables used in monetary matters (cf. Mt 21:12; Mk 11:15; Jn 2:15), as well as those used for serving meals. To be involved either in financial matters or in serving meals would take the 12 away from their first priority (*see note on v. 4*).

6:3 **seven men.** These were not deacons in terms of the later church office (1Ti 3:8–13), although they performed some of the same duties. Stephen and Philip (the only ones of the 7 mentioned elsewhere in Scripture) clearly were evangelists, not deacons. Acts later mentions elders (14:23; 20:17), but not deacons. It seems, therefore, that a permanent order of deacons was not established at that time. **full of the Spirit.** Cf. v. 5; *see notes on 2:4.*

6:4 Prayer and the ministry of the Word (cf. v. 2) define the highest priorities of church leaders.

6:5 The 7 men chosen by the church all had Gr. names, implying they were all Hellenists. The church, in a display of love and unity, may have chosen them to rectify the apparent imbalance involving the Hellenistic widows. **they chose Stephen ... Nicolas.** For Stephen’s ministry, see 6:9–7:60. His martyrdom became the catalyst for the spread of the gospel beyond Palestine (8:1–4; 11:19). Philip also played a key role in the spread of the gospel (cf. 8:4–24, 26–40). Nothing certain is known of the other 5. According to some early traditions, Prochorus became the apostle John’s amanuensis (scribe) when he wrote his Gospel and Nicolas was a Gentile convert to Judaism from Antioch.

6:6 **after praying, they laid their hands on them.** This expression was used of Jesus when He healed (Mk 6:5; Lk 4:40; 13:13; cf. 28:8) and sometimes indicated being taken prisoner (5:18; Mk 14:46). In the OT, offerers of sacrifices laid their hands on the animal as an expression of identification (Lv 8:14, 18, 22; Heb 6:2). But in the symbolic sense, it signified the affirmation, support, and identification with someone and his ministry. See 1Ti 4:14; 5:22; 2Ti 1:6; cf. Nu 27:23.

6:7 One of Luke’s periodic statements summarizing the growth of the church and the spread of the gospel (cf. 2:41, 47; 4:4; 5:14; 9:31; 12:24; 13:49; 16:5; 19:20). **great many of the priests.** The conversion of large numbers of priests may account for the vicious opposition that arose against Stephen. **were ... obedient to the faith.** *See note on Ro 1:5.*

6:8 **wonders and signs.** *See note on 2:19.*

6:9 It seems that this verse describes 3 synagogues: the Synagogue of the Freedmen, a second composed of Cyrenians and Alexandrians, and a third composed of those from Cilicia and Asia. Cultural and linguistic differences among the 3 groups make it unlikely they all attended the same synagogue. **Synagogue.** These were meeting places which began in the intertestamental period where the dispersed Jews (usually Hellenists), who did not have temple access, could meet in their community to worship and read the OT. *See note on Mk 1:21.* **Freedmen.** Descendants of Jewish slaves captured by Pompeii (63 B.C.) and taken to Rome. They were later freed and formed a Jewish community there. **Cyrenians.** Men from Cyrene, a city in North Africa. Simon, the man conscripted to carry Jesus’ cross, was a native of Cyrene (Lk 23:26). **Alexandrians.** Alexandria, another major North African city, was located near the mouth of the Nile River. The powerful preacher Apollos was from Alexandria (*see note on 18:24*). **Cilicia and Asia.** Roman provinces in Asia Minor (modern Turkey). Since Paul’s hometown (Tarsus) was located in Cilicia, he probably attended this synagogue. **argued with Stephen.** The word translated “argued” signifies a formal debate. They no doubt focused on such themes as the death and resurrection of Jesus, and the OT evidence that He was the Messiah.

6:11 **blasphemous words against Moses and ... God.** Unable to prevail over Stephen in open debate, his enemies resorted to deceit and conspiracy. As with Jesus (Mt 26:59–61), they secretly recruited false witnesses to spread lies about Stephen. The charges were serious, since blasphemy was punishable by death (Lv 24:16).

12 And they stirred up the people, the elders and the
scribes, and they [A]came up to him and dragged him
away and brought him [a]before [B]the [b]Council. 13 They
put forward [A]false witnesses who said, "This man
incessantly speaks against this [B]holy place and the
Law; 14 for we have heard him say that [A]this Nazarene, Jesus, will destroy this place and alter [B]the
customs which Moses handed down to us." 15 And
fixing their gaze on him, all who were sitting in
the [a,A]Council saw his face like the face of an angel.

STEPHEN'S DEFENSE

7 The high priest said, "Are these things so?"
2 And he said, "Hear me, [A]brethren and fathers!
[B]The God of glory [C]appeared to our father Abraham
when he was in Mesopotamia, before he lived in
[a]Haran, 3 and said to him, '[A]LEAVE YOUR COUNTRY AND
YOUR RELATIVES, AND COME INTO THE LAND THAT I
WILL SHOW YOU.' 4 [A]Then he left the land of the Chaldeans and settled in [a]Haran. [B]From there, after his father
died, *God* had him move to this country in which you
are now living. 5 But He gave him no inheritance in
it, not even a foot of ground, and *yet,* even when he
had no child, [A]He promised that HE WOULD GIVE IT
TO HIM AS A POSSESSION, AND TO HIS DESCENDANTS
AFTER HIM. 6 But [A]God spoke to this effect, that his DE-
SCENDANTS WOULD BE ALIENS IN A FOREIGN LAND, AND
THAT THEY WOULD [a]BE ENSLAVED AND MISTREATED
FOR FOUR HUNDRED YEARS. 7 'AND WHATEVER NATION
TO WHICH THEY WILL BE IN BONDAGE I MYSELF WILL
JUDGE,' said God, 'AND [A]AFTER THAT THEY WILL COME
OUT AND [a]SERVE ME IN THIS PLACE.' 8 And He [A]gave
him [a]the covenant of circumcision; and so [B]*Abraham*
became the father of Isaac, and circumcised him on
the eighth day; and [C]Isaac *became the father of* Jacob,
and [D]Jacob *of* the twelve [E]patriarchs.
9 "The patriarchs [A]became jealous of Joseph and
sold him into Egypt. *Yet* God was with him, 10 and
rescued him from all his afflictions, and [A]granted
him favor and wisdom in the sight of Pharaoh, king
of Egypt, and he made him governor over Egypt
and all his household.
11 "Now [A]a famine came over all Egypt and Canaan,
and great affliction *with it,* and our fathers [a]could
find no food. 12 But [A]when Jacob heard that there was
grain in Egypt, he sent our fathers *there* the first time.
13 On the second *visit* [A]Joseph [a]made himself known
to his brothers, and [B]Joseph's family was disclosed
to Pharaoh. 14 Then [A]Joseph sent *word* and invited
Jacob his father and all his relatives to come to him,
[B]seventy-five [a,C]persons *in all.* 15 And [A]Jacob went down
to Egypt and *there* he and our fathers died. 16 *From
there* they were removed to [a,A]Shechem and laid in
the tomb which Abraham had purchased for a sum
of money from the sons of [b]Hamor in [a]Shechem.
17 "But as the [A]time of the promise was approaching which God had assured to Abraham, [B]the people
increased and multiplied in Egypt, 18 until [A]THERE
AROSE ANOTHER KING OVER EGYPT WHO KNEW NOTH-
ING ABOUT JOSEPH. 19 It was he who took [A]shrewd
advantage of our race and mistreated our fathers
so that they would [a,B]expose their infants and they
would not survive. 20 It was at this time that [A]Moses
was born; and he was lovely [a]in the sight of God,

6:12 [a]Lit *into* [b]Or *Sanhedrin* [A]Luke 20:1; Acts 4:1 [B]Matt 5:22 6:13 [A]Matt 26:59-61; Acts 7:58 [B]Matt 24:15; Acts 21:28; 25:8 6:14 [A]Matt 26:61 [B]Acts 15:1; 21:21; 26:3; 28:17 6:15 [a]Or *Sanhedrin* [A]Matt 5:22 7:2 [a]Gr *Charran* [A]Acts 22:1 [B]Ps 29:3; 1 Cor 2:8 [C]Gen 11:31; 15:7 7:3 [A]Gen 12:1 7:4 [a]Gr *Charran* [A]Gen 11:31; 15:7 [B]Gen 12:4, 5 7:5 [A]Gen 12:7; 13:15; 15:18; 17:8 7:6 [a]Lit *enslave them and mistreat them* [A]Gen 15:13f 7:7 [a]Or *worship* [A]Ex 3:12 7:8 [a]Or *a* [A]Gen 17:10ff [B]Gen 21:2-4 [C]Gen 25:26 [D]Gen 29:31ff; 30:5ff; 35:23ff [E]Acts 2:29 7:9 [A]Gen 37:11, 28; 39:2, 21f; 45:4 7:10 [A]Gen 39:21; 41:40-46; Ps 105:21 7:11 [a]Lit *were not finding* [A]Gen 41:54f; 42:5 7:12 [A]Gen 42:2 7:13 [a]Or *was made known* [A]Gen 45:1-4 [B]Gen 45:16 7:14 [a]Lit *souls* [A]Gen 45:9, 10, 17, 18 [B]Gen 46:26f; Ex 1:5; Deut 10:22 [C]Acts 2:41 7:15 [A]Gen 46:1-7; 49:33; Ex 1:6 7:16 [a]Gr *Sychem* [b]Gr *Emmor* [A]Gen 23:16; 33:19; 50:13; Josh 24:32 7:17 [A]Gen 15:13 [B]Ex 1:7f 7:18 [A]Ex 1:8 7:19 [a]Or *put out to die* [A]Ex 1:10f, 16ff [B]Ex 1:22 7:20 [a]Lit *to God* [A]Ex 2:2; Heb 11:23

6:14 Jesus, will destroy this place. Another lie, since Jesus' words (Jn 2:19) referred to His own body (Jn 2:21).

6:15 face of an angel. Pure, calm, unruffled composure, reflecting the presence of God (cf. Ex 34:29–35).

7:1 high priest. *See notes on 4:6.* Probably Caiaphas (*see note on Jn 18:13, 14*), who remained in office until A.D. 36. **Are these things so?** In modern legal terminology, "How do you plead?"

7:2–53 Stephen's response does not seem to answer the High Priest's question. Instead, he gave a masterful, detailed defense of the Christian faith from the OT and concluded by condemning the Jewish leaders for rejecting Jesus.

7:2 The God of glory. A title used only here and in Ps 29:3. God's glory is the sum of His attributes (*see notes on Ex 33:18, 19*). **Abraham … Mesopotamia, before he lived in Haran.** Genesis 12:1–4 refers to the repeat of this call after Abraham had settled in Haran (ca. 500 mi. NW of Ur). Evidently, God had originally called Abraham while he was living in Ur (cf. Ge 15:7; Ne 9:7), then repeated that call at Haran (*see notes on Ge 11:31–12:1-3*).

7:3 Quoted from Ge 12:1.

7:4 land of the Chaldeans. Where Abraham's original home city of Ur was located (Ge 11:28, 31; 15:7; Ne 9:7). **after his father died.** At first glance, Ge 11:26, 32 and 12:4 seem to indicate that Terah lived for 60 years after Abraham's departure from Haran. Terah was 70 when his first son was born (Ge 11:26); Abraham was 75 when he left Haran (Ge 12:4; Terah would have been 145); and Terah lived to be 205 (Ge 11:32). The best solution to this apparent difficulty is that Abraham was not Terah's firstborn son, but was mentioned first (Ge 11:26) because he was most prominent. Abraham, then, would have been born when Terah was 130.

7:5 Quoted from Ge 17:8; 48:4.

7:6 four hundred years. This is taken directly from Ge 15:13, 14 where God Himself rounded off the exact length of Israel's sojourn in Egypt (430 years, Ex 12:40).

7:7 Quoted from Ex 3:12.

7:8 covenant of circumcision. Circumcision was the sign of the Abrahamic Covenant (*see notes on Ge 17:11*). **twelve patriarchs.** The 12 sons of Jacob, who became the heads of the 12 tribes of Israel (Ge 35:22–26).

7:13 second *visit*. Joseph revealed himself to his brothers on their second trip to Egypt to buy grain (Ge 43:1–3; 45:1–3).

7:14 Jacob … and all his relatives … seventy-five persons. Genesis 46:26, 27; Ex 1:5; Dt 10:22 give the figure as 70. However the LXX (the Gr. translation of the OT, which as a Hellenist Stephen would have used) in Ge 46:27 reads "seventy-five." The additional 5 people were Joseph's descendants born in Egypt. *See notes on Ge 46:26, 27.*

7:16 they were … laid in the tomb. "They" refers to Joseph (Jos 24:32) and his brothers, but not Jacob, who was buried in Abraham's tomb at Machpelah (Ge 50:13). **the tomb which Abraham had purchased … of Hamor in Shechem.** Joshua 24:32 states that Jacob bought this tomb, although Abraham had earlier built an altar at Shechem (Ge 12:6, 7), and probably purchased the land on which he built it. Abraham did not settle there, however, and the land apparently reverted to the people of Hamor. Jacob then repurchased it from Shechem (Ge 33:18–20), much like Isaac repurchased the well at Beersheba (Ge 26:28–31) that Abraham had originally bought (Ge 21:27–30). It is clear that Joseph was buried at Shechem as he requested (Ge 50:25; Ex 13:19; Jos 24:32). The OT does not record where Joseph's brothers were buried, but Stephen reveals it was in Shechem.

7:18 king … knew nothing about Joseph. *See note on Ex 1:8.*

7:19 expose their infants. Only the male babies (Ex 1:15–22).

7:20, 21 Moses … set outside. In God's providence, however, he was rescued by Pharaoh's daughter. *See notes on Ex 2:5–10.*

and he was nurtured three months in his father's
home. 21 And after he had been set outside, [A]Phar-
aoh's daughter [a]took him away and nurtured him
as her own son. 22 Moses was educated in all [A]the
learning of the Egyptians, and he was a man of
power in words and deeds. 23 But when he was approaching the age of forty, [A]it entered his [a]mind to
visit his brethren, the sons of Israel. 24 And when
he saw one *of them* being treated unjustly, he defended him and took vengeance for the oppressed
by striking down the Egyptian. 25 And he supposed
that his brethren understood that God was granting
them [a]deliverance [b]through him, but they did not
understand. 26 [A]On the following day he appeared
to them as they were fighting together, and he tried
to reconcile them in peace, saying, 'Men, you are
brethren, why do you injure one another?' 27 But
the one who was injuring his neighbor pushed him
away, saying, '[A]WHO MADE YOU A RULER AND JUDGE
OVER US? 28 [A]YOU DO NOT MEAN TO KILL ME AS YOU
KILLED THE EGYPTIAN YESTERDAY, DO YOU?' 29 At
this remark, [A]MOSES FLED AND BECAME AN ALIEN
IN THE LAND OF [a]MIDIAN, where he [B]became the
father of two sons.
30 "After forty years had passed, [A]AN ANGEL AP-
PEARED TO HIM IN THE WILDERNESS OF MOUNT Sinai,
IN THE FLAME OF A BURNING THORN BUSH. 31 When
Moses saw it, he marveled at the sight; and as he
approached to look *more* closely, there came the
voice of the Lord: 32 '[A]I AM THE GOD OF YOUR FA-
THERS, THE GOD OF ABRAHAM AND ISAAC AND JA-
COB.' Moses shook with fear and would not venture
to look. 33 [A]BUT THE LORD SAID TO HIM, '[B]TAKE OFF
THE SANDALS FROM YOUR FEET, FOR THE PLACE ON
WHICH YOU ARE STANDING IS HOLY GROUND. 34 [A]I HAVE
CERTAINLY SEEN THE OPPRESSION OF MY PEOPLE IN
EGYPT AND HAVE HEARD THEIR GROANS, AND I HAVE
COME DOWN TO RESCUE THEM; [a,B]COME NOW, AND I
WILL SEND YOU TO EGYPT.'
35 "This Moses whom they [A]disowned, saying,
'WHO MADE YOU A RULER AND A JUDGE?' is the one
whom God [a]sent *to be* both a ruler and a deliverer
with the [b]help of the angel who appeared to him in
the thorn bush. 36 [A]This man led them out, performing [B]wonders and [a]signs in the land of Egypt and in
the Red Sea and in the [C]wilderness for forty years.
37 This is the Moses who said to the sons of Israel,
'[A]GOD WILL RAISE UP FOR YOU A PROPHET [a]LIKE ME
FROM YOUR BRETHREN.' 38 This is the one who was in
[A]the [a]congregation in the wilderness together with
[B]the angel who was speaking to him on Mount Sinai,
and *who was* with our fathers; and he received [C]liv-
ing [D]oracles to pass on to you. 39 Our fathers were
unwilling to be obedient to him, but [A]repudiated him
and in their hearts turned back to Egypt, 40 [A]SAYING
TO AARON, 'MAKE FOR US GODS WHO WILL GO BEFORE
US; FOR THIS MOSES WHO LED US OUT OF THE LAND
OF EGYPT—WE DO NOT KNOW WHAT HAPPENED TO
HIM.' 41 [a]At that time [A]they made a [b]calf and brought
a sacrifice to the idol, and were rejoicing in [B]the
works of their hands. 42 But God [A]turned away and
delivered them up to [a]serve the [b]host of heaven; as
it is written in the book of the prophets, '[B]IT WAS NOT
TO ME THAT YOU OFFERED VICTIMS AND SACRIFICES
[C]FORTY YEARS IN THE WILDERNESS, WAS IT, O HOUSE
OF ISRAEL? 43 [A]YOU ALSO TOOK ALONG THE TABERNA-
CLE OF MOLOCH AND THE STAR OF THE GOD [a]ROMPHA,
THE IMAGES WHICH YOU MADE TO WORSHIP. I ALSO
WILL REMOVE YOU BEYOND BABYLON.'
44 "Our fathers had [A]the tabernacle of testimony
in the wilderness, just as He who spoke to Moses
directed *him* to make it [B]according to the pattern

7:21 [a]Or *adopted him* [A]Ex 2:5f, 10 7:22 [A]1 Kin 4:30; Is 19:11 7:23 [a]Lit *heart* [A]Ex 2:11f; Heb 11:24-26 7:25 [a]Or *salvation* [b]Lit *through his hand* 7:26 [A]Ex 2:13f 7:27 [A]Ex 2:14; Acts 7:35 7:28 [A]Ex 2:14 7:29 [a]Gr *Madiam* [A]Ex 2:15, 22 [B]Ex 18:3, 4 7:30 [A]Ex 3:1f; Is 63:9 7:32 [A]Ex 3:6; Matt 22:32 7:33 [A]Ex 3:5 [B]Josh 5:15 7:34 [a]Lit *and now come!* [A]Ex 3:7f [B]Ex 3:10 7:35 [a]Lit *has sent* [b]Lit *hand* [A]Ex 2:14; Acts 7:27 7:36 [a]Or *attesting miracles* [A]Ex 12:41; 33:1; Heb 8:9 [B]Ex 7:3; 14:21; John 4:48 [C]Ex 16:35; Num 14:33; Ps 95:8-10; Acts 7:42; 13:18; Heb 3:8f 7:37 [a]Or *as* He raised up *me* [A]Deut 18:15, 18; Acts 3:22 7:38 [a]Gr *ekklesia* [A]Ex 19:17 [B]Acts 7:53 [C]Deut 32:47; Heb 4:12 [D]Rom 3:2; Heb 5:12; 1 Pet 4:11 7:39 [A]Num 14:3f 7:40 [A]Ex 32:1, 23 7:41 [a]Lit *in those days* [b]Or *young bull* [A]Ex 32:4, 6 [B]Rev 9:20 7:42 [a]Or *worship* [b]I.e. heavenly bodies [A]Josh 24:20; Is 63:10; Jer 19:13; Ezek 20:39 [B]Amos 5:25 [C]Acts 7:36 7:43 [a]Other mss spell it: *Romphan,* or *Rempham,* or *Raiphan,* or *Rephan* [A]Amos 5:26, 27 7:44 [A]Ex 25:8, 9; 38:21 [B]Ex 25:40

7:23 approaching the age of forty. Moses' life may be divided into three 40-year periods. The first 40 years encompassed his birth and life in Pharaoh's court; the second his exile in Midian (vv. 29, 30); and the third revolved around the events of the Exodus and the years of Israel's wilderness wandering (v. 36).

7:27, 28 Cf. v. 35. Quoted from Ex 2:14.

7:29 fled ... Midian. Because he feared Pharaoh would learn of his killing of the Egyptian (v. 28) and view him as the leader of a Jewish rebellion. **two sons.** Gershom (Ex 2:22), and Eliezer (Ex 18:4).

7:30 angel. *See note on Ex 3:2.* Mount **Sinai.** *See notes on Ex 19:3–10.*

7:32 Quoted from Ex 3:6, 15.

7:33 Quoted from Ex 3:5.

7:34 Quoted from Ex 3:7, 8.

7:35 This Moses ... sent *to be* both a ruler and a deliverer. Thus began Israel's long history of rejecting her God-sent deliverers (cf. Mt 21:33–46; 23:37). Who made you. Quoted from Ex 2:14. **angel.** The Angel of the Lord (v. 30). *See note on Ex 3:2.*

7:36 wonders and signs. The 10 plagues in Egypt, and the miracles during the wilderness wandering (e.g., the parting of the Red Sea, Ex 14:1–31; the miraculous provision of water at Rephidim, Ex 17:1–7; and the destruction of Korah, Dathan, and Abiram, Nu 16:1–40). *See note on 2:19.*

7:37 prophet like me. Quoted from Dt 18:15, this refers to the Messiah (cf. Jn 1:21, 25; 6:14; 7:40).

7:38 the congregation in the wilderness. Israel (cf. Ex 12:3, 6, 19, 47; 16:1, 2, 9, 10; 17:1; 35:1; Lv 4:13; 16:5; Nu 1:2; 8:9; 13:26; 14:2; Jos 18:1). **the angel ... on Mount Sinai.** Most likely this is the Angel of the Lord (vv. 30, 35) who was assisted by a multitude of angels (cf. Dt 33:3; Gal 3:19; Heb 2:2). *See note on v. 53.* **living oracles.** The law given to Moses by God through the Angel of the Lord and a whole host of angels (cf. Heb 4:12; 1Pe 1:23).

7:39 unwilling to be obedient. Israel rejected Moses' leadership and longed to return to slavery in Egypt (cf. Nu 11:5).

7:40 Make for us gods. A man-made representation of a false god (Ex 32:1–5) which was forbidden (Ex 20:4). Quoted from Ex 32:1, 23.

7:41 a calf. *See note on Ex 32:4.*

7:42 God ... delivered them up. Quoted from Am 5:25–27. Judicially abandoning the people to their sin and idolatry (cf. Hos 4:17; *see notes on Ro 1:24, 26, 28*). **the host of heaven.** Israel's idolatrous worship of the sun, moon, and stars began in the wilderness and lasted through the Babylonian captivity (cf. Dt 4:19; 17:3; 2Ki 17:16; 21:3–5; 23:4; 2Ch 33:3, 5; Jer 8:2; 19:13; Zep 1:5).

7:43 Babylon. Amos wrote Damascus (Am 5:27), while Stephen said Babylon. Amos was prophesying the captivity of the northern kingdom in Assyria, a deportation beyond Damascus. Later the southern kingdom was taken captive to Babylon. Stephen, inspired to do so, extended the prophecy to embrace the judgment on the whole nation, summarizing their idolatrous history and its results.

7:44–50 To counter the false charge that he blasphemed the temple (6:13, 14), Stephen recounted its history to show his respect for it.

7:44 tabernacle of testimony. The predecessor of the temple (Ex 25:8, 9, 40).

which he had seen. 45 And having received it in their turn, our fathers [A]brought it in with [a]Joshua upon dispossessing the [b]nations whom God drove out before our fathers, until the time of David. 46 [A]*David* found favor in God's sight, and [B]asked that he might find a dwelling place for the [a]God of Jacob. 47 But it was [A]Solomon who built a house for Him. 48 However, [A]the Most High does not dwell in *houses* made by *human* hands; as the prophet says:

49 '[A]HEAVEN IS MY THRONE,
AND EARTH IS THE FOOTSTOOL OF MY FEET;
WHAT KIND OF HOUSE WILL YOU
BUILD FOR ME?' says the Lord,
'OR WHAT PLACE IS THERE FOR MY REPOSE?
50 '[A]WAS IT NOT MY HAND WHICH
MADE ALL THESE THINGS?'

51 "You men who are [A]stiff-necked and uncircumcised in heart and ears are always resisting the Holy Spirit; you are doing just as your fathers did. 52 [A]Which one of the prophets did your fathers not persecute? They killed those who had previously announced the coming of [B]the Righteous One, whose betrayers and murderers [C]you have now become; 53 you who received the law as [A]ordained by angels, and *yet* did not keep it."

STEPHEN PUT TO DEATH

54 Now when they heard this, they were [A]cut to the quick, and they *began* gnashing their teeth at him. 55 But being [A]full of the Holy Spirit, he [B]gazed intently into heaven and saw the glory of God, and Jesus standing [C]at the right hand of God; 56 and he said, "Behold, I see the [A]heavens opened up and [B]the Son of Man standing at the right hand of God." 57 But they cried out with a loud voice, and covered their ears and rushed at him with one impulse. 58 When they had [A]driven him out of the city, they *began* stoning *him;* and [B]the witnesses [C]laid aside their robes at the feet of [D]a young man named Saul. 59 They went on stoning Stephen as he [A]called on *the Lord* and said, "Lord Jesus, receive my spirit!" 60 Then [A]falling on his knees, he cried out with a loud voice, "Lord, [B]do not hold this sin against them!" Having said this, he [a,C]fell asleep.

SAUL PERSECUTES THE CHURCH

8 [A]Saul was in hearty agreement with putting him to death.

And on that day a great persecution [a]began against [B]the church in Jerusalem, and they were all [C]scattered throughout the regions of Judea and [D]Samaria, except the apostles. 2 *Some* devout men buried Stephen, and made loud lamentation over him. 3 But [A]Saul *began* ravaging the church, entering house after house, and [B]dragging off men and women, he would put them in prison.

PHILIP IN SAMARIA

4 Therefore, those [A]who had been scattered went about [a,B]preaching the word. 5 [A]Philip went down to the city of Samaria and *began* proclaiming [a]Christ

7:45 [a]Gr *Jesus* [b]Or *Gentiles* [A]Deut 32:49; Josh 3:14ff; 18:1; 23:9; 24:18; Ps 44:2f 7:46 [a]The earliest mss read *house* instead of *God;* the Septuagint reads *God* [A]2 Sam 7:8ff; Ps 132:1-5; Acts 13:22 [B]2 Sam 7:1-16; 1 Chr 17:1-14 7:47 [A]1 Kin 6:1-38; 8:20; 2 Chr 3:1-17 7:48 [A]Luke 1:32 7:49 [A]Is 66:1; Matt 5:34f 7:50 [A]Is 66:2 7:51 [A]Ex 32:9; 33:3, 5; Lev 26:41; Num 27:14; Is 63:10; Jer 6:10; 9:26 7:52 [A]2 Chr 36:15f; Matt 5:12; 23:31, 37 [B]Acts 3:14; 22:14; 1 John 2:1 [C]Acts 3:14; 5:28 7:53 [A]Deut 33:2; Acts 7:38; Gal 3:19; Heb 2:2 7:54 [A]Acts 5:33 7:55 [A]Acts 2:4 [B]John 11:41 [C]Mark 16:19 7:56 [A]John 1:51 [B]Matt 8:20 7:58 [A]Lev 24:14, 16; Luke 4:29 [B]Deut 13:9f; 17:7; Acts 6:13 [C]Acts 22:20 [D]Acts 8:1; 22:20; 26:10 7:59 [A]Acts 9:14, 21; 22:16; Rom 10:12-14; 1 Cor 1:2; 2 Tim 2:22 7:60 [a]I.e. died [A]Luke 22:41 [B]Matt 5:44; Luke 23:34 [C]Dan 12:2; Matt 27:52; John 11:11f; Acts 13:36; 1 Cor 15:6, 18, 20; 1 Thess 4:13ff; 2 Pet 3:4 8:1 [a]Lit *occurred* [A]Acts 7:58; 22:20; 26:10 [B]Acts 9:31 [C]Acts 8:4; 11:19 [D]Acts 1:8; 8:5, 14; 9:31 8:3 [A]Acts 9:1, 13, 21; 22:4, 19; 26:10f; 1 Cor 15:9; Gal 1:13; Phil 3:6; 1 Tim 1:13 [B]James 2:6 8:4 [a]Or *bringing the good news of* [A]Acts 8:1 [B]Acts 8:12; 15:35 8:5 [a]I.e. the Messiah [A]Acts 6:5; 8:26, 30

7:48 Most High. A common OT title for God (cf. Ge 14:18–20, 22; Nu 24:16; Dt 32:8; 2Sa 22:14; Pss 7:17; 9:2; 18:13; 21:7; 73:11; 87:5; 91:1; 107:11; Is 14:14; La 3:35, 38; Da 4:17, 24, 25, 32, 34; 7:25).

7:49, 50 Quoted from Is 66:1, 2. Stephen's point is that God is greater than the temple, and thus the Jewish leaders were guilty of blaspheming by confining God to it.

7:51–53 The climax of Stephen's sermon indicted the Jewish leaders for rejecting God in the same way that their ancestors had rejected Him in the OT.

7:51 stiff-necked. Obstinate, like their fathers (Ex 32:9; 33:5). **uncircumcised in heart and ears.** Thus as unclean before God as the uncircumcised Gentiles (*see notes on Dt 10:16; Jer 4:4; Ro 2:28, 29*). **resisting the Holy Spirit.** By rejecting the Spirit's messengers and their message. Cf. Jesus' sermon in Mt 23:13–39.

7:52 the Righteous One. *See note on 3:14.*

7:53 law as ordained by angels. See Dt 33:2; Gal 3:19; Heb 2:2. Scripture does not delineate their precise role in the giving of the law, but clearly states the fact of their presence.

7:54 gnashing their teeth. In anger and frustration (cf. Pss 35:16; 37:12; Mt 8:11, 12; 13:41, 42, 50; 22:13; 24:51; 25:30; Lk 13:28).

7:55 full of the Holy Spirit. *See note on 2:4.* **the glory of God.** Isaiah (Is 6:1–3), Ezekiel (Eze 1:26–28), Paul (2Co 12:2–4), and John (Rev 1:10) also received visions of God's glory in heaven. **at the right hand of God.** Jesus is frequently so depicted (2:34; cf. Mt 22:44; 26:64; Lk 22:69; Eph 1:20; Col 3:1; Heb 1:3; 8:1; 10:11, 12; 12:2).

7:56 Son of Man. *See note on Da 7:13, 14.*

7:58 laid aside their robes ... Saul. Paul's first appearance in Scripture. That he was near enough to the action to be holding the clothes of Stephen's killers reflects his deep involvement in the sordid affair (*see note on 8:1*).

7:59 stoning. This was the punishment prescribed in the law for blasphemy (Lv 24:16); however, this was not a formal execution but an act of mob violence.

7:60 do not hold this sin against them! As had Jesus before him (Lk 23:34), Stephen prayed for God to forgive his killers. **he fell asleep.** A common NT euphemism for the death of believers (cf. Jn 11:11–14; 1Co 11:30; 15:20, 51; 1Th 4:14; 5:10).

8:1 in ... agreement. Paul's murderous hatred of all believers was manifested here in his attitude toward Stephen (1Ti 1:13–15). **scattered.** Led by a Jew named Saul of Tarsus, the persecution scattered the Jerusalem fellowship and led to the first missionary outreach of the church. Not all members of the Jerusalem church were forced to flee; the Hellenists, because Stephen was likely one, bore the brunt of the persecution (cf. 11:19, 20). **except the apostles.** They remained because of their devotion to Christ, to care for those at Jerusalem, and to continue evangelizing the region (cf. 9:26, 27).

8:2 devout men. Probably pious Jews (cf. 2:5; Lk 2:25) who publicly protested Stephen's death.

8:3 ravaging the church. "Ravaging" was used in extrabiblical writings to refer to the destruction of a city or mangling by a wild animal.

8:4 went about. This Gr. word is used frequently in Acts for missionary efforts (v. 40; 9:32; 13:6; 14:24; 15:3, 41; 16:6; 18:23; 19:1, 21; 20:2).

8:5 Philip. Cf. 6:5. The first missionary named in Scripture and the first to be given the title "evangelist" (21:8). **the city of Samaria.** The ancient capital of the northern kingdom of Israel, which eventually fell to the Assyrians (722 B.C.) after over 200 years of idolatry and rebellion against God. After resettling many of the people in other lands, the Assyrians located Gentiles from other areas into the region, resulting in a mix of Jews and Gentiles who became known as Samaritans (*see notes on Jn 4:4, 20*).

to them. 6 The crowds with one accord were giving
attention to what was said by Philip, as they heard
and saw the [a]signs which he was performing. 7 For
in the case of many who had [A]unclean spirits, they
were coming out *of them* shouting with a loud voice;
and many who had been [B]paralyzed and lame were
healed. 8 So there was [A]much rejoicing in that city.
9 Now there was a man named Simon, who formerly was practicing [A]magic in the city and astonishing the people of Samaria, [B]claiming to be someone great; 10 and they all, from smallest to greatest,
were giving attention to him, saying, "[A]This man is
what is called the Great Power of God." 11 And they
were giving him attention because he had for a long
time astonished them with his [A]magic arts. 12 But
when they believed Philip [A]preaching the good
news about the kingdom of God and the name of
Jesus Christ, they were being [B]baptized, men and
women alike. 13 Even Simon himself believed; and
after being baptized, he continued on with Philip,
and as he observed [A]signs and [B]great miracles taking place, he was constantly amazed.
14 Now when [A]the apostles in Jerusalem heard
that Samaria had received the word of God, they
sent them [B]Peter and John, 15 who came down and
prayed for them [A]that they might receive the Holy
Spirit. 16 For He had [A]not yet fallen upon any of them;
they had simply been [B]baptized [a]in the name of
the Lord Jesus. 17 Then they [A]*began* laying their
hands on them, and they were [B]receiving the Holy
Spirit. 18 Now when Simon saw that the Spirit was
bestowed through the laying on of the apostles'
hands, he offered them money, 19 saying, "Give this
authority to me as well, so that everyone on whom
I lay my hands may receive the Holy Spirit." 20 But
Peter said to him, "May your silver perish with you,
because you thought you could [A]obtain the gift of
God with money! 21 You have [A]no part or portion
in this [a]matter, for your heart is not [B]right before
God. 22 Therefore repent of this wickedness of yours,
and pray the Lord that, [A]if possible, the intention of
your heart may be forgiven you. 23 For I see that you
are in the gall of bitterness and in [A]the [a]bondage of
iniquity." 24 But Simon answered and said, "[A]Pray
to the Lord for me yourselves, so that nothing of
what you have said may come upon me."

AN ETHIOPIAN RECEIVES CHRIST

25 So, when they had solemnly [A]testified and spoken [B]the word of the Lord, they started back to Jerusalem, and were [C]preaching the gospel to many
villages of the [D]Samaritans.
26 But [A]an angel of the Lord spoke to [B]Philip saying, "Get up and go south to the road that descends
from Jerusalem to [C]Gaza." ([a]This is a desert *road*.)
27 So he got up and went; and [A]there was an Ethiopian eunuch, a court official of Candace, queen of
the Ethiopians, who was in charge of all her treasure; and he [B]had come to Jerusalem to worship,
28 and he was returning and sitting in his [a]chariot,
and was reading the prophet Isaiah. 29 Then [A]the
Spirit said to Philip, "Go up and join this [a]chariot."
30 Philip ran up and heard him reading Isaiah the
prophet, and said, "Do you understand what you
are reading?" 31 And he said, "Well, how could I,
unless someone guides me?" And he invited Philip

8:6 [a]Or *attesting miracles* 8:7 [A]Mark 16:17 [B]Matt 4:24 8:8 [A]John 4:40-42; Acts 8:39 8:9 [A]Acts 8:11; 13:6 [B]Acts 5:36 8:10 [A]Acts 14:11; 28:6 8:11 [A]Acts 8:9; 13:6 8:12 [A]Acts 1:3; 8:4 [B]Acts 2:38 8:13 [A]Acts 8:6 [B]Acts 19:11 8:14 [A]Acts 8:1 [B]Luke 22:8 8:15 [A]Acts 2:38; 19:2 8:16 [a]Lit *into* [A]Matt 28:19; Acts 19:2 [B]Acts 2:38; 10:48 8:17 [A]Mark 5:23; Acts 6:6 [B]Acts 2:4 8:20 [A]2 Kin 5:16; Is 55:1; Dan 5:17; Matt 10:8; Acts 2:38 8:21 [a]Or *teaching;* lit *word* [A]Deut 10:9; 12:12; Eph 5:5 [B]Ps 78:37 8:22 [A]Is 55:7 8:23 [a]Lit *bond* [A]Is 58:6 8:24 [A]Gen 20:7; Ex 8:8; Num 21:7; James 5:16 8:25 [A]Luke 16:28 [B]Acts 13:12 [C]Acts 8:40 [D]Matt 10:5 8:26 [a]Or *This city is deserted* [A]Acts 5:19; 8:29 [B]Acts 8:5 [C]Gen 10:19 8:27 [A]Ps 68:31; 87:4; Is 56:3ff [B]1 Kin 8:41f; John 12:20 8:28 [a]Or *carriage* 8:29 [a]Or *carriage* [A]Acts 8:39; 10:19; 11:12; 13:2; 16:6, 7; 20:23; 21:11; 28:25; Heb 3:7

8:7 unclean spirits. *See note on 5:16.*

8:9 magic. This word originally referred to the practices of the Medo-Persians: a mixture of science and superstition, including astrology, divination, and the occult (*see notes on Dt 18:9–12; Rev 9:21*).

8:10, 11 the Great Power of God. Simon claimed to be united to God. The early church Fathers claimed he was one of the founders of gnosticism, which asserted there were a series of divine emanations reaching up to God. They were called "Powers," and the people believed he was at the top of the ladder.

8:13 Simon … believed. His belief was motivated by purely selfish reasons and could never be considered genuine. Cf. Jn 2:23, 24. He saw it as an external act useful to gain the power he believed Philip possessed. By following Philip, he also was able to maintain contact with his former audience.

8:15 receive the Holy Spirit. *See note on 2:4.*

8:16 not yet fallen upon any of them. This verse does not support the false notion that Christians receive the Holy Spirit subsequent to salvation. This was a transitional period in which confirmation by the apostles was necessary to verify the inclusion of a new group of people into the church. Because of the animosity that existed between Jews and Samaritans, it was essential for the Samaritans to receive the Spirit, in the presence of the leaders of the Jerusalem church, for the purpose of maintaining a unified church. The delay also revealed the Samaritans' need to come under apostolic authority. The same transitional event occurred when the Gentiles were added to the church (10:44–46; cf. 15:6–12; 19:6).

8:17 laying their hands on them. This signified apostolic affirmation and solidarity. *See note on 6:6.* **receiving the Holy Spirit.** That this actually occurred likely demonstrated that believers also spoke in tongues here, just as those who received the Spirit did on the Day of Pentecost (*see note on 2:4*), as the Gentiles did when they received the Spirit (10:46), and as those followers of John did (19:6). As Samaritans, Gentiles, and believers from the Old Covenant were added to the church, the unity of the church was established. No longer could one nation (Israel) be God's witness people, but the church was made up of Jews, Gentiles, half-breed Samaritans, and OT saints who became NT believers (19:1–7). To demonstrate the unity, it was imperative that there be some replication in each instance of what had occurred at Pentecost with the believing Jews, such as the presence of the apostles and the coming of the Spirit manifestly indicated through speaking in the languages of Pentecost (2:5–12).

8:22–24 Although Simon was certainly fearful, he was unwilling to repent and seek forgiveness, wanting only to escape the consequences of his sin.

8:26 Gaza. One of 5 chief cities of the Philistines. The original city was destroyed in the first century B.C., and a new city was built near the coast.

8:27 Ethiopian. In those days, Ethiopia was a large kingdom located S of Egypt. **eunuch.** This can refer to one who had been emasculated or generally, to a government official. It is likely he was both since Luke refers to him as a eunuch and as one who held a position of authority in the queen's court—that of treasurer, much like a minister of finance or secretary of the treasury. As a physical eunuch, he would have been denied access to the temple (Dt 23:1) and the opportunity to become a full proselyte to Judaism. **Candace.** Probably not a name, but an official title (like Pharaoh or Caesar) given to the queen mothers in that land.

8:28 reading … Isaiah. He knew the importance of seeking God through the Scripture (Lk 24:25–27; Jn 5:39, 46; Ro 10:12–15).

to come up and sit with him. 32 Now the passage of
Scripture which he was reading was this:

"[A]He was led as a sheep to slaughter;
And as a lamb before its
shearer is silent,
So He does not open His mouth.
33 "[A]In humiliation His judgment
was taken away;
Who will [a]relate His [b]generation?
For His life is removed from the earth."

34 The eunuch answered Philip and said, "Please *tell*
me, of whom does the prophet say this? Of himself or
of someone else?" 35 Then Philip [A]opened his mouth,
and [B]beginning from this Scripture he [C]preached
Jesus to him. 36 As they went along the road they
came to some water; and the eunuch *said, "Look!
Water! [A]What prevents me from being baptized?"
37 [[a]And Philip said, "If you believe with all your
heart, you may." And he answered and said, "I believe
that Jesus Christ is the Son of God."] 38 And he ordered the [a]chariot to stop; and they both went down
into the water, Philip as well as the eunuch, and he
baptized him. 39 When they came up out of the water,
[A]the Spirit of the Lord snatched Philip away; and the
eunuch no longer saw him, [a]but went on his way
rejoicing. 40 But Philip [a]found himself at [b,A]Azotus,
and as he passed through he [B]kept preaching the
gospel to all the cities until he came to [C]Caesarea.

THE CONVERSION OF SAUL

9 [A]Now [a]Saul, still [B]breathing [b]threats and murder against the disciples of the Lord, went to
the high priest, 2 and asked for [A]letters from him to
[B]the synagogues at [C]Damascus, so that if he found
any belonging to [D]the Way, both men and women,
he might bring them bound to Jerusalem. 3 As he
was traveling, it happened that he was approaching Damascus, and [A]suddenly a light from heaven
flashed around him; 4 and [A]he fell to the ground
and heard a voice saying to him, "Saul, Saul, why
are you persecuting Me?" 5 And he said, "Who are
You, Lord?" And He *said,* "I am Jesus whom you
are persecuting, 6 but get up and enter the city,
and [A]it will be told you what you must do." 7 The
men who traveled with him [A]stood speechless,
[B]hearing the [a]voice but seeing no one. 8 Saul got
up from the ground, and [A]though his eyes were
open, he [a]could see nothing; and leading him by
the hand, they brought him into [B]Damascus. 9 And
he was three days without sight, and neither ate
nor drank.
10 Now there was a disciple at [A]Damascus named
[B]Ananias; and the Lord said to him in [C]a vision,
"Ananias." And he said, "Here I am, Lord." 11 And
the Lord *said* to him, "Get up and go to the street
called Straight, and inquire at the house of Judas for
a man from [A]Tarsus named Saul, for he is praying,
12 and he has seen [a]in a vision a man named Ananias come in and [A]lay his hands on him, so that he
might regain his sight." 13 But Ananias answered,
"Lord, I have heard from many about this man,
[A]how much harm he did to [B]Your [a]saints at Jerusalem; 14 and here he [A]has authority from the chief
priests to bind all who [B]call on Your name." 15 But
the Lord said to him, "Go, for [A]he is a chosen [a]instru-
ment of Mine, to bear My name before [B]the Gentiles
and [C]kings and the sons of Israel; 16 for [A]I will show
him how much he must suffer for My name's sake."

8:32 [A]Is 53:7 8:33 [a]Or *describe* [b]Or *family* or *origin* [A]Is 53:8 8:35 [A]Matt 5:2 [B]Luke 24:27; Acts 17:2; 18:28; 28:23 [C]Acts 5:42 8:36 [A]Acts 10:47 8:37 [a]Early mss do not contain this v 8:38 [a]Or *carriage* 8:39 [a]Lit *for he was going* [A]1 Kin 18:12; 2 Kin 2:16; Ezek 3:12, 14; 8:3; 11:1, 24; 43:5; 2 Cor 12:2 8:40 [a]Or *was found* [b]OT: Ashdod [A]Josh 11:22; 1 Sam 5:1 [B]Acts 8:25 [C]Acts 9:30; 10:1, 24; 11:11; 12:19; 18:22; 21:8, 16; 23:23, 33; 25:1, 4, 6, 13 9:1 [a]Later called Paul [b]Lit *threat* [A]Acts 9:1-22; 22:3-16; 26:9-18 [B]Acts 8:3; 9:13-21 9:2 [A]Acts 9:14, 21; 22:5; 26:10 [B]Matt 10:17 [C]Gen 14:15; 2 Cor 11:32; Gal 1:17 [D]John 14:6; Acts 18:25f; 19:9, 23; 22:4; 24:14, 22 9:3 [A]1 Cor 15:8 9:4 [A]Acts 22:7; 26:14 9:6 [A]Acts 9:16 9:7 [a]Or *sound* [A]Acts 26:14 [B]John 12:29f; Acts 22:9 9:8 [a]Lit *was seeing* [A]Acts 9:18; 22:11 [B]Gen 14:15; 2 Cor 11:32; Gal 1:17 9:10 [A]Gen 14:15; 2 Cor 11:32; Gal 1:17 [B]Acts 22:12 [C]Acts 10:3, 17, 19; 11:5; 12:9; 16:9f; 18:9 9:11 [A]Acts 9:30; 11:25; 21:39; 22:3 9:12 [a]A few early mss do not contain *in a vision* [A]Mark 5:23; Acts 6:6; 9:17 9:13 [a]Or *holy ones* [A]Acts 8:3 [B]Acts 9:32, 41; 26:10; Rom 1:7; 15:25, 26, 31; 16:2, 15; 1 Cor 1:2 9:14 [A]Acts 9:2, 21 [B]Acts 7:59 9:15 [a]Or *vessel* [A]Acts 13:2; Rom 1:1; 9:23; Gal 1:15; Eph 3:7 [B]Acts 22:21; 26:17; Rom 1:5; 11:13; 15:16; Gal 1:16; 2:7ff; Eph 3:1, 8; 1 Tim 2:7; 2 Tim 4:17 [C]Acts 25:22f; 26:1, 32; 2 Tim 4:17 9:16 [A]Acts 20:23; 21:4, 11, 13; 2 Cor 6:4f; 11:23-27; 1 Thess 3:3

8:32, 33 passage … he was reading. Isaiah 53:7, 8.

8:34 of whom does the prophet say this? His confusion was understandable. Even the Jewish religious experts were divided on the meaning of this passage. Some believed the slaughtered sheep represented Israel, others thought Isaiah was referring to himself, and others thought the Messiah was Isaiah's subject.

8:37 This verse is not found in the oldest and most reliable manuscripts.

8:39 snatched Philip away. Elijah (1Ki 18:12; 2Ki 2:16) and Ezekiel (Eze 3:12, 14; 8:3) were also snatched away in a miraculous fashion. This was a powerful confirmation to the caravan that Philip was God's representative.

8:40 Azotus. The first-century name for the ancient Philistine city of Ashdod, located 20 mi. N of Gaza. **Caesarea.** Where Philip and his family probably lived (21:9; *see note on 9:30*).

9:1 Saul. See Introduction to Romans: Author and Date. The apostle Paul was originally named Saul, after the first king of Israel. He was born a Jew, studied in Jerusalem under Gamaliel (22:3), and became a Pharisee (23:6). He was also a Roman citizen, a right he inherited from his father (22:28). Verses 1–19 record the external facts of his conversion (see also 22:1–22; 26:9–20). Philippians 3:1–14 records the internal spiritual conversion (*see notes there*). **threats and murder.** See 1Ti 1:12, 13; 1Co 15:9.

9:2 Damascus. An ancient city, the capital of Syria, located 60 mi. inland from the Mediterranean and ca. 160 mi. NE of Jerusalem. Apparently, it had a large population of Jews, including Hellenist believers who fled Jerusalem to avoid persecution (8:2). **belonging to the Way.** This description of Christianity, derived from Jesus' description of Himself (Jn 14:6), appears several times in Acts (19:9, 23; 22:4; 24:14, 22). This is an appropriate title because Christianity is the way of God (18:26), the way into the Holy Place (Heb 10:19, 20), and the way of truth (Jn 14:6; 2Pe 2:2).

9:3–6 This was the first of 6 visions to be seen by Paul in Acts (cf. 16:9, 10; 18:9, 10; 22:17, 18; 23:11; 27:23, 24).

9:3 a light from heaven. The appearance of Jesus Christ in glory (cf. 22:6; 26:13), visible only to Saul (26:9).

9:4 why are you persecuting Me? An inseparable union exists between Christ and His followers. Saul's persecution represented a direct attack on Christ. Cf. Mt 18:5, 6.

9:10 Ananias. One of the leaders of the Damascus church, and therefore, one of Saul's targets (cf. 22:12).

9:11 street called Straight. This street, which runs through Damascus from the E gate to the W, still exists and is called Darb el-Mustaqim. **Tarsus.** The birthplace of Paul and a key city in the Roman province of Cilicia, located on the banks of the Cydnus River near the border of Asia Minor and Syria. It served as both a commercial and educational center. The wharves on the Cydnus were crowded with commerce, while its university ranked with those of Athens and Alexandria as the finest in the Roman world.

9:15 chosen instrument. Lit. "a vessel of election." There was perfect continuity between Paul's salvation and his service; God chose him to convey His grace to all people

17 So Ananias departed and entered the house, and
after [A]laying his hands on him said, "[B]Brother Saul,
the Lord Jesus, who appeared to you on the road by
which you were coming, has sent me so that you
may regain your sight and be [C]filled with the Holy
Spirit." 18 And immediately there fell from his eyes
something like scales, and he regained his sight,
and he got up and was baptized; 19 and he took food
and was strengthened.

SAUL BEGINS TO PREACH CHRIST

Now [A]for several days he was with [B]the disciples who were at Damascus, 20 and immediately
he *began* to proclaim Jesus [A]in the synagogues,
[a]saying, "He is [B]the Son of God." 21 All those hearing him continued to be amazed, and were saying,
"Is this not he who in Jerusalem [A]destroyed those
who [B]called on this name, and *who* had come here
for the purpose of bringing them bound before the
chief priests?" 22 But Saul kept increasing in strength
and confounding the Jews who lived at Damascus
by proving that this *Jesus* is the [a]Christ.
23 When [A]many days had elapsed, [B]the Jews plotted together to do away with him, 24 but [A]their plot
became known to Saul. [B]They were also watching
the gates day and night so that they might put him
to death; 25 but his disciples took him by night and
let him down through *an opening in* the wall, low-
ering him in a large basket.
26 [A]When he came to Jerusalem, he was trying
to associate with the disciples; [a]but they were all
afraid of him, not believing that he was a disciple.
27 But [A]Barnabas took hold of him and brought him
to the apostles and described to them how he had
[B]seen the Lord on the road, and that He had talked
to him, and how [C]at Damascus he had [D]spoken out
boldly in the name of Jesus. 28 And he was with
them, [a]moving about freely in Jerusalem, [A]speaking
out boldly in the name of the Lord. 29 And he was
talking and arguing with the [a,A]Hellenistic *Jews;* but
they were attempting to put him to death. 30 But
when [A]the brethren learned *of it,* they brought him
down to [B]Caesarea and [C]sent him away to [D]Tarsus.
31 So [A]the church throughout all Judea and Galilee
and Samaria [a]enjoyed peace, being built up; and
going on in the fear of the Lord and in the comfort
of the Holy Spirit, it continued to increase.

PETER'S MINISTRY

32 Now as Peter was traveling through all *those
regions,* he came down also to [A]the [a]saints who
lived at [b,B]Lydda. 33 There he found a man named
Aeneas, who had been bedridden eight years, for he
was paralyzed. 34 Peter said to him, "Aeneas, Jesus
Christ heals you; get up and make your bed." Immediately he got up. 35 And all who lived at [a,A]Lydda
and [B]Sharon saw him, and they [C]turned to the Lord.
36 Now in [A]Joppa there was a disciple named Tabitha (which translated *in Greek* is called [a]Dorcas);
this woman was abounding with deeds of kindness
and charity which she continually did. 37 And it
happened [a]at that time that she fell sick and died;
and when they had washed her body, they laid it
in an [A]upper room. 38 Since Lydda was near [A]Joppa,
[B]the disciples, having heard that Peter was there,
sent two men to him, imploring him, "Do not delay
in coming to us." 39 So Peter arose and went with
them. When he arrived, they brought him into the
[A]upper room; and all the [B]widows stood beside him,
weeping and showing all the [a]tunics and garments

9:17 [A]Mark 5:23; Acts 6:6; 9:12 [B]Acts 22:13 [C]Acts 2:4 9:19 [A]Acts 26:20 [B]Acts 9:26, 38; 11:26 9:20 [a]Lit *that* [A]Acts 13:5, 14; 14:1; 16:13; 17:2, 10; 18:4, 19; 19:8 [B]Matt 4:3; Acts 9:22; 13:33 9:21 [A]Acts 8:3; 9:13; Gal 1:13, 23 [B]Acts 9:14 9:22 [a]I.e. Messiah 9:23 [A]Gal 1:17, 18 [B]1 Thess 2:16 9:24 [A]Acts 20:3, 19; 23:12, 30; 25:3 [B]2 Cor 11:32f 9:26 [a]Lit *and* [A]Acts 22:17-20; 26:20 9:27 [A]Acts 4:36 [B]Acts 9:3-6 [C]Acts 9:20, 22 [D]Acts 4:13, 29; 9:29 9:28 [a]Lit *going in and going out* [A]Acts 4:13, 29; 9:29 9:29 [a]Jews who adopted the Gr language and much of Gr culture through acculturation [A]Acts 6:1 9:30 [A]Acts 1:15 [B]Acts 8:40 [C]Gal 1:21 [D]Acts 9:11 9:31 [a]Lit *was having* [A]Acts 5:11; 8:1; 16:5 9:32 [a]Or *holy ones* [b]OT: Lod [A]Acts 9:13 [B]1 Chr 8:12; Ezra 2:33; Neh 7:37; 11:35 9:35 [a]OT: Lod [A]1 Chr 8:12; Ezra 2:33; Neh 7:37; 11:35 [B]1 Chr 5:16; 27:29; Is 33:9; 35:2; 65:10 [C]Acts 2:47; 9:42; 11:21 9:36 [a]I.e. Gazelle [A]Josh 19:46; 2 Chr 2:16; Ezra 3:7; Jon 1:3; Acts 9:38, 42f; 10:5, 8, 23, 32; 11:5, 13 9:37 [a]Lit *in those days* [A]Acts 1:13; 9:39 9:38 [A]Josh 19:46; 2 Chr 2:16; Ezra 3:7; Jon 1:3; Acts 9:36, 42f; 10:5, 8, 23, 32; 11:5, 13 [B]Acts 11:26 9:39 [a]Or *inner garments* [A]Acts 1:13; 9:37 [B]Acts 6:1

(Gal 1:1; cf. 1Ti 2:7; 2Ti 1:11). Paul used this same word 4 times (Ro 9:21, 23; 2Co 4:7; 2Ti 2:21). **before the Gentiles and kings and the sons of Israel.** Paul began his ministry preaching to Jews (13:14; 14:1; 17:1, 10; 18:4; 19:8), but his primary calling was to Gentiles (Ro 11:13; 15:16). God also called him to minister to kings such as Agrippa (25:23–26:32) and likely Caesar (cf. 25:10–12; 2Ti 4:16, 17).

9:17 laying his hands on him. *See note on 6:6.* **be filled with the Holy Spirit.** *See note on 2:4.* The Spirit had already been active in Paul's life: convicting him of sin (Jn 16:9), convincing him of the Lordship of Christ (1Co 12:3), transforming him (Tit 3:5), and indwelling him permanently (1Co 12:13). He was then filled with the Spirit and empowered for service (cf. 2:4, 14; 4:8, 31; 6:5, 8; *see also note on Eph 5:18*). Saul received the Spirit without any apostles present because he was a Jew (the inclusion of Jews in the church had already been established at Pentecost) and because he was an apostle in his own right because Christ personally chose him and commissioned him for service (Ro 1:1).

9:20 He is the Son of God. The content of Paul's message was that Jesus Christ is God (*see notes on Heb 1:4, 5*).

9:23 When many days had elapsed. A period of 3 years, in which he ministered in Nabatean Arabia, an area encompassing Damascus S to the Sinai peninsula (*see notes on Gal 1:17, 18*).

9:24 gates. Damascus was a walled city, thus the gates were the only conventional means of escape.

9:25 let him down ... in a large basket. "Basket" was a large woven hamper suitable for hay, straw, or bales of wool.

9:27 Barnabas. *See note on 4:36.*

9:29 Hellenistic *Jews*. The same group Stephen debated (*see note on 6:1*).

9:30 Caesarea. Cf. 8:40. An important port city on the Mediterranean located 30 mi. N of Joppa. As the capital of the Roman province of Judea and the home of the Roman procurator, it served as the headquarters of a large Roman garrison. **sent him away to Tarsus.** Paul disappeared from prominent ministry for several years, although he possibly founded some churches around Syria and Cilicia (15:23; Gal 1:21).

9:31 the church ... enjoyed peace, being built up. Paul's conversion and political changes contributed to the rest. A stricter Roman governor and the expansion of Herod Agrippa's authority restricted the persecution.

9:32 Lydda. Lod in the OT. Located about 10 mi. SE of Joppa, it was a hub servicing roads from Egypt to Syria and from Joppa to Jerusalem.

9:33 Aeneas. Apparently an unbeliever (cf. v. 36), whose paralysis was incurable by the limited medical knowledge of that day.

9:35 Sharon. The plain surrounding Lydda and Joppa and extending N to Caesarea.

9:36 Joppa. A seacoast town today known as Jaffa, S of Tel Aviv. **Tabitha.** She was more commonly known by her Gr. name, "Dorcas." Both names mean "gazelle."

9:37 upper room. This arrangement was similar to that of the upstairs room in 1:13; 2:1. While it was customary to bury a body immediately, the believers in Joppa had another plan.

9:38 near Joppa. 10 mi. SE.

9:39 tunics and garments. Close-fitting undergarments and long outer robes.

that Dorcas used to make while she was with them.
40 But Peter [A]sent them all out and [B]knelt down and
prayed, and turning to the body, he said, "[C]Tabitha,
arise." And she opened her eyes, and when she saw
Peter, she sat up. 41 And he gave her his hand and
raised her up; and calling [A]the [a]saints and [B]wid-
ows, he presented her alive. 42 It became known
all over [A]Joppa, and [B]many believed in the Lord.
43 And Peter stayed many days in [A]Joppa with [B]a
tanner *named* Simon.

CORNELIUS'S VISION

10 Now *there was* a man at [A]Caesarea named
Cornelius, a centurion of what was [B]called the
Italian [a]cohort, 2 a devout man and [A]one who feared
God with all his household, and [B]gave many [a]alms
to the *Jewish* people and prayed to God continually.
3 About [A]the [a]ninth hour of the day he clearly saw
[B]in a vision [C]an angel of God who had *just* come in
and said to him, "Cornelius!" 4 And [A]fixing his gaze
on him and being much alarmed, he said, "What
is it, Lord?" And he said to him, "Your prayers and
[a]alms [B]have ascended [C]as a memorial before God.
5 Now dispatch *some* men to [A]Joppa and send for a
man *named* Simon, who is also called Peter; 6 he is
staying with a tanner *named* [A]Simon, whose house
is by the sea." 7 When the angel who was speaking
to him had left, he summoned two of his [a]servants
and a devout soldier of those who were his personal
attendants, 8 and after he had explained everything
to them, he sent them to [A]Joppa.
9 On the next day, as they were on their way and
approaching the city, [A]Peter went up on [B]the housetop about [C]the [a]sixth hour to pray. 10 But he became
hungry and was desiring to eat; but while they were
making preparations, he [A]fell into a trance; 11 and
he *saw [A]the [a]sky opened up, and an [b]object like a
great sheet coming down, lowered by four corners
to the ground, 12 and there were in it all *kinds of*
four-footed animals and [a]crawling creatures of the
earth and birds of the [b]air. 13 A voice came to him,
"Get up, Peter, [a]kill and eat!" 14 But Peter said, "By
no means, [A]Lord, for [B]I have never eaten anything
[a]unholy and unclean." 15 Again a voice *came* to him
a second time, "[A]What God has cleansed, no *longer*
consider [a]unholy." 16 This happened three times, and
immediately the [a]object was taken up into the [b]sky.
17 Now while Peter was greatly perplexed in [a]mind
as to what [A]the vision which he had seen might
be, behold, [B]the men who had been sent by Cornelius, having asked directions for Simon's house,
appeared at the gate; 18 and calling out, they were
asking whether Simon, who was also called Peter,
was staying there. 19 While Peter was reflecting on
[A]the vision, [B]the Spirit said to him, "Behold, [a]three
men are looking for you. 20 But get up, go down-
stairs and [A]accompany them [a]without misgivings,
for I have sent them Myself." 21 Peter went down to
the men and said, "Behold, I am the one you are
looking for; what is the reason for which you have
come?" 22 They said, "Cornelius, a centurion, a righteous and [A]God-fearing man well spoken of by the
entire nation of the Jews, [B]was *divinely* directed by
a [C]holy angel to send for you *to come* to his house
and hear [a,D]a message from you." 23 So he invited
them in and gave them lodging.

PETER AT CAESAREA

And on the next day he got up and went away
with them, and [A]some of [B]the brethren from
[C]Joppa accompanied him. 24 On the following day
he entered [A]Caesarea. Now Cornelius was waiting for them and had called together his relatives
and close friends. 25 When Peter entered, Cornelius met him, and fell at his feet and [a,A]worshiped
him. 26 But Peter raised him up, saying, "[A]Stand
up; I too am *just* a man." 27 As he talked with him,
he entered and *found [A]many people assembled.

9:40 [A]Matt 9:25 [B]Luke 22:41; Acts 7:60 [C]Mark 5:41 9:41 [a]Or *holy ones* [A]Acts 9:13, 32 [B]Acts 6:1 9:42 [A]Josh 19:46; 2 Chr 2:16; Jon 1:3; Acts 9:38, 42f; 10:5, 8, 23, 32; 11:5, 13 [B]Acts 9:35 9:43 [A]Josh 19:46; 2 Chr 2:16; Ezra 3:7; Jon 1:3; Acts 9:38, 42f; 10:5, 8, 23, 32; 11:13, 15 [B]Acts 10:6 10:1 [a]Or *battalion* [A]Acts 8:40; 10:24 [B]Matt 27:27; Mark 15:16; John 18:3, 12; Acts 21:31; 27:1 10:2 [a]Or *gifts of charity* [A]Acts 10:22, 35; 13:16, 26 [B]Luke 7:4f 10:3 [a]I.e. 3 p.m. [A]Acts 3:1 [B]Acts 9:10; 10:17, 19 [C]Acts 5:19 10:4 [a]Or *deeds of charity* [A]Acts 3:4 [B]Rev 8:4 [C]Matt 26:13; Phil 4:18; Heb 6:10 10:5 [A]Acts 9:36 10:6 [A]Acts 9:43 10:7 [a]Or *household slaves* 10:8 [A]Acts 9:36 10:9 [a]I.e. noon [A]Acts 10:9-32; 11:5-14 [B]Jer 19:13; 32:29; Zeph 1:5; Matt 24:17 [C]Ps 55:17; Acts 10:3 10:10 [A]Acts 11:5; 22:17 10:11 [a]Or *heaven* [b]Or *vessel* [A]John 1:51 10:12 [a]Or *reptiles* [b]Or *heaven* 10:13 [a]Or *sacrifice* 10:14 [a]Or *profane;* lit *common* [A]Matt 8:2ff; John 4:11ff; Acts 9:5; 22:8 [B]Lev 11:20-25; Deut 14:4-20; Ezek 4:14; Dan 1:8; Acts 10:28 10:15 [a]Lit *make common* [A]Matt 15:11; Mark 7:19; Rom 14:14; 1 Cor 10:25ff; 1 Tim 4:4f; Titus 1:15 10:16 [a]Or *vessel* [b]Or *heaven* 10:17 [a]Lit *himself* [A]Acts 10:3 [B]Acts 10:8 10:19 [a]One early ms reads *two* [A]Acts 10:3 [B]Acts 8:29 10:20 [a]Lit *doubting nothing* [A]Acts 15:7-9 10:22 [a]Lit *words* [A]Acts 10:2 [B]Matt 2:12 [C]Mark 8:38; Luke 9:26; Rev 14:10 [D]Acts 11:14 10:23 [A]Acts 10:45; 11:12 [B]Acts 1:15 [C]Acts 9:36 10:24 [A]Acts 8:40; 10:1 10:25 [a]Or *prostrated himself in reverence* [A]Matt 8:2 10:26 [A]Acts 14:15; Rev 19:10; 22:8f 10:27 [A]Acts 10:24

9:43 a tanner *named* Simon. Cf. 10:5, 6. Peter breaks down a cultural barrier by staying with a tanner, an occupation despised by Jewish society because the tanner dealt with the skins of dead animals. The local synagogue probably shunned Simon.

10:1 a centurion. One of 60 officers in a Roman legion, each of whom commanded 100 men (*see note on Mt 8:5*). **Italian cohort.** Ten cohorts of 600 men each made up a legion.

10:2 feared God. A technical term used by Jews to refer to Gentiles who had abandoned their pagan religion in favor of worshiping Jehovah God. Such a person, while following the ethics of the OT, had not become a full proselyte to Judaism through circumcision. Cornelius was to receive the saving knowledge of God in Christ (*see note on Ro 1:20*).

10:3 About the ninth hour. 3:00 p.m. (*see note on 3:1*).

10:4 memorial. A remembrance. Cornelius's prayers, devotion, faith, and goodness were like a fragrant offering rising up to God.

10:7 devout soldier. *See note on vv. 1, 2.*

10:9 housetop ... to pray. All kinds of worship occurred on the flat roofs of Jewish homes (2Ki 23:12; Jer 19:13; 32:29). **sixth hour.** 12:00 noon.

10:12 all *kinds of* four-footed animals. Both clean and unclean animals. To keep the Israelites separate from their idolatrous neighbors, God set specific dietary restrictions regarding the consumption of such animals (cf. Lv 11:25, 26).

10:13 kill and eat! With the coming of the New Covenant and the calling of the church, God ended the dietary restrictions (cf. Mk 7:19).

10:14 unholy and unclean. Impure or defiled.

10:15 God has cleansed. More than just abolishing the OT dietary restrictions, God made unity possible in the church of both Jews, symbolized by the clean animals, and Gentiles, symbolized by the unclean animals, through the comprehensive sacrificial death of Christ (*see note on Eph 2:14*).

10:22 directed by a holy angel. Cf. vv. 3–6.

10:23 invited them in. Self-respecting Jews did not invite any Gentiles into their home, especially soldiers of the hated Roman army. **some ... brethren.** Six Jewish believers (11:12), identified as "the circumcised believers" in v. 45.

10:26 I too am *just* a man. Cf. 14:11–15;

[28]And he said to them, "You yourselves know how
[A]unlawful it is for a man who is a Jew to associate
with a foreigner or to visit him; and *yet* [B]God has
shown me that I should not call any man [a]unholy or
unclean. [29]That is why I came without even raising
any objection when I was sent for. So I ask for what
reason you have sent for me."
[30]Cornelius said, "[A]Four days ago to this hour, I was
praying in my house during [B]the [a]ninth hour; and
behold, [C]a man stood before me in shining garments,
[31]and he *said, 'Cornelius, your prayer has been heard
and your [a]alms have been remembered before God.
[32]Therefore send to [A]Joppa and invite Simon, who is
also called Peter, to come to you; he is staying at the
house of Simon *the* tanner by the sea.' [33]So I sent for
you immediately, and you have [a]been kind enough to
come. Now then, we are all here present before God to
hear all that you have been commanded by the Lord."

GENTILES HEAR GOOD NEWS

[34][A]Opening his mouth, Peter said:
"I most certainly understand *now* that [B]God is not
one to show partiality, [35]but [A]in every nation the man
who [a,B]fears Him and [b]does what is right is welcome
to Him. [36]The word which He sent to the sons of Israel, [A]preaching [a,B]peace through Jesus Christ (He is
[C]Lord of all)— [37]you yourselves know the thing which
took place throughout all Judea, starting from Galilee, after the baptism which John proclaimed. [38][a]*You
know of* [A]Jesus of Nazareth, how God [B]anointed Him
with the Holy Spirit and with power, [b,C]and *how* He
went about doing good and healing all who were
oppressed by the devil, for [D]God was with Him. [39]We
are [A]witnesses of all the things He did both in the
[a]land of the Jews and in Jerusalem. They also [B]put
Him to death by hanging Him on a [b]cross. [40][A]God
raised Him up on the third day and granted that He
become visible, [41][A]not to all the people, but to [B]wit-
nesses who were chosen beforehand by God, *that is,*
to us [C]who ate and drank with Him after He arose
from the dead. [42]And He [A]ordered us to [a]preach to
the people, and solemnly to [B]testify that this is the
One who has been [C]appointed by God as [D]Judge of
the living and the dead. [43]Of Him [A]all the prophets
bear witness that through [B]His name everyone who
believes in Him receives forgiveness of sins."
[44]While Peter was still speaking these words,
[A]the Holy Spirit fell upon all those who were listening to the [a]message. [45][A]All the [a]circumcised believers who came with Peter were amazed, because
the gift of the Holy Spirit had been [B]poured out on
the Gentiles also. [46]For they were hearing them

10:28 [a]Or *profane;* lit *common* [A]John 4:9; 18:28; Acts 11:3 [B]Acts 10:14f, 35; 15:9 10:30 [a]I.e. 3 to 4 p.m. [A]Acts 10:9, 22f [B]Acts 3:1; 10:3 [C]Acts 10:3-6, 30-32 10:31 [a]Or *deeds of charity* 10:32 [A]John 4:9; 18:28; Acts 11:3 10:33 [a]Lit *done well in coming* 10:34 [A]Matt 5:2 [B]Deut 10:17; 2 Chr 19:7; Rom 2:11; Gal 2:6; Eph 6:9; Col 3:25; 1 Pet 1:17 10:35 [a]Or *reverences* [b]Lit *works righteousness* [A]Acts 10:28 [B]Acts 10:2 10:36 [a]Or *the gospel of peace* [A]Acts 13:32 [B]Luke 1:79; 2:14; Rom 5:1; Eph 2:17 [C]Matt 28:18; Acts 2:36; Rom 10:12 10:38 [a]Or *How God anointed Jesus of Nazareth* [b]Lit *who went* [A]Acts 2:22 [B]Acts 4:26 [C]Matt 4:23 [D]John 3:2 10:39 [a]Or *countryside* [b]Lit *wood* [A]Luke 24:48; Acts 10:41 [B]Acts 5:30 10:40 [A]Acts 2:24 10:41 [A]John 14:19, 22; 15:27 [B]Luke 24:48; Acts 10:39 [C]Luke 24:43; Acts 1:4 mg 10:42 [a]Or *proclaim* [A]Acts 1:2 [B]Luke 16:28 [C]Luke 22:22 [D]John 5:22, 27; Acts 17:31; 2 Tim 4:1; 1 Pet 4:5 10:43 [A]Acts 3:18 [B]Luke 24:47; Acts 2:38; 4:12 10:44 [a]Lit *word* [A]Acts 11:15; 15:8 10:45 [a]Lit *believers from among the circumcision;* i.e. Jewish Christians [A]Acts 10:23 [B]Acts 2:33, 38

Rev 22:8, 9. Only the triune God deserves our worship.

10:28 unlawful. Lit. "breaking a taboo." Peter followed the Jewish standards and traditions his whole life. His comments reveal his acceptance of a new standard in which Jews no longer were to consider Gentiles profane.

10:34 God is not one to show partiality. Taught in both the OT (Dt 10:17; 2Ch 19:7; Job 34:19) and NT (Ro 2:11; 3:29, 30; Jas 2:1). The reality of this truth was taking on new dimensions for Peter.

10:35 welcome. This Gr. word means "marked by a favorable manifestation of the divine pleasure."

10:36 preaching peace. Christ, by paying the price of sin through His sacrificial death, established peace between man and God (*see note on Ro 5:1–11*).

10:37 the baptism which John proclaimed. Cf. 1:22; 13:24; 18:25; 19:34; *see notes on Mt 3:2–12.*

10:38 Jesus … how God anointed Him. Cf. 4:27. The beginning of Jesus' earthly ministry (cf. Mt 3:13–17; Lk 3:21, 22).

10:41 to witnesses … chosen. Jesus became visible after His resurrection only to believers (cf. 1Co 15:5–8).

10:43 believes in Him. The means of salvation—faith in Christ alone (*see note on Ro 1:16*; cf. Jn 3:14–17; 6:69; Ro 10:11; Gal 3:22; Eph 2:8, 9).

10:44 the Holy Spirit fell. *See notes on 2:4; 8:17.*

10:45 the circumcised believers. Cf. 11:2. Jewish Christians (*see note on v. 23*).

10:46 tongues. *See notes on 2:4; 8:17.*

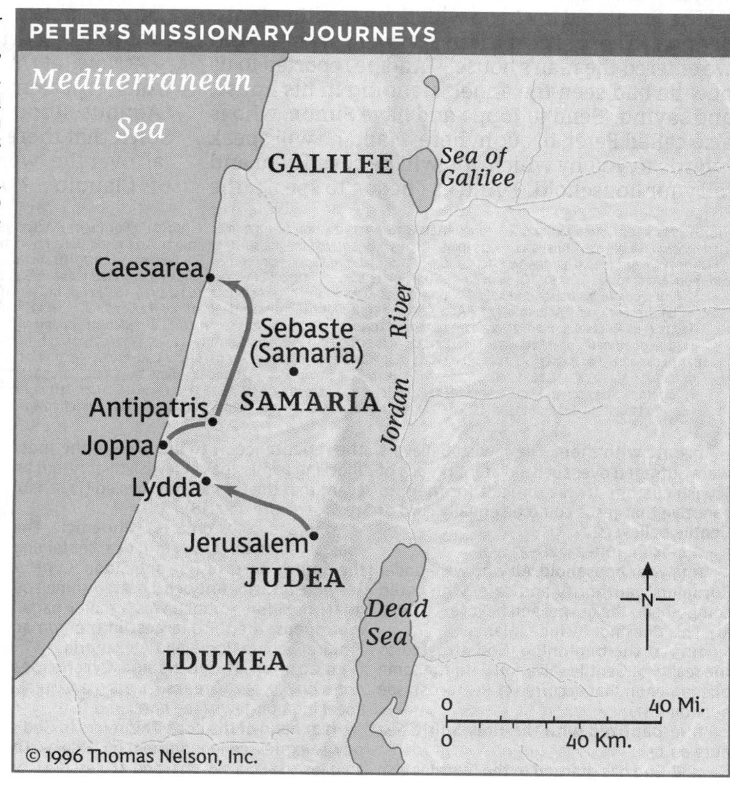

[A]speaking with tongues and exalting God. Then Peter answered, 47 "[A]Surely no one can refuse the water
for these to be baptized who [B]have received the Holy
Spirit just as we *did,* can he?" 48 And he [A]ordered
them to be baptized [B]in the name of Jesus Christ.
Then they asked him to stay on for a few days.

PETER REPORTS AT JERUSALEM

11 Now the apostles and [A]the brethren who were
throughout Judea heard that the Gentiles also
had received the word of God. 2 And when Peter
came up to Jerusalem, [a,A]those who were circumcised took issue with him, 3 saying, "[A]You [a]went to
uncircumcised men and ate with them." 4 But Peter
began *speaking* [a]and *proceeded* to explain to them
[A]in orderly sequence, saying, 5 "[A]I was in the city
of Joppa praying; and in a trance I saw [B]a vision,
an [a]object coming down like a great sheet lowered
by four corners from [b]the sky; and it came right
down to me, 6 and when I had fixed my gaze on it
and was observing it [a]I saw the four-footed animals
of the earth and the wild beasts and the [b]crawling
creatures and the birds of the [c]air. 7 I also heard a
voice saying to me, 'Get up, Peter; [a]kill and eat.' 8 But
I said, 'By no means, Lord, for nothing [a]unholy or
unclean has ever entered my mouth.' 9 But a voice
from heaven answered a second time, '[A]What God
has cleansed, no longer [a]consider unholy.' 10 This
happened three times, and everything was drawn
back up into [a]the sky. 11 And behold, at that moment
three men appeared at the house in which we were
staying, having been sent to me from [A]Caesarea.
12 [A]The Spirit told me to go with them [a,B]without misgivings. [C]These six brethren also went with me and
we entered the man's house. 13 And he reported to us
how he had seen the angel [a]standing in his house,
and saying, 'Send to Joppa and have Simon, who is
also called Peter, brought here; 14 and he will speak
[A]words to you by which you will be saved, you and
[B]all your household.' 15 And as I began to speak, [A]the
Holy Spirit fell upon them just [B]as *He did* upon us
at the beginning. 16 And I remembered the word of
the Lord, how He used to say, '[A]John baptized with
water, but you will be baptized [a]with the Holy Spirit.'
17 Therefore if [A]God gave to them the same gift as
He gave to us also after believing in the Lord Jesus
Christ, [B]who was I that I could [a]stand in God's way?"
18 When they heard this, they [a]quieted down and
[A]glorified God, saying, "Well then, God has granted
to the Gentiles also the [B]repentance *that leads* to life."

THE CHURCH AT ANTIOCH

19 [A]So then those who were scattered because of
the [a]persecution that occurred in connection with
Stephen made their way [b]to [B]Phoenicia and [C]Cyprus
and [D]Antioch, speaking the word to no one except
to Jews alone. 20 But there were some of them, men
of [A]Cyprus and [B]Cyrene, who came to [C]Antioch and
began speaking to the [a,D]Greeks also, [b,E]preaching the
Lord Jesus. 21 And [A]the hand of the Lord was with
them, and [B]a large number who believed turned to
the Lord. 22 The [a]news about them [b]reached the ears
of the church at Jerusalem, and they sent [A]Barnabas
off [c]to [B]Antioch. 23 Then when he arrived and [a]wit-
nessed [A]the grace of God, he rejoiced and *began* to
encourage them all with [b]resolute heart to remain
true to the Lord; 24 for he was a good man, and [A]full
of the Holy Spirit and of faith. And [B]considerable
[a]numbers were [b]brought to the Lord. 25 And he left
for [A]Tarsus to look for Saul; 26 and when he had
found him, he brought him to [A]Antioch. And for an
entire year they [a]met with the church and taught
considerable [b]numbers; and [B]the disciples were
first called [C]Christians in [A]Antioch.
27 Now [a]at this time [A]some prophets came down
from Jerusalem to [B]Antioch. 28 One of them named
[A]Agabus stood up and *began* to indicate [a]by the
Spirit that there would certainly be a great famine
[B]all over the [b]world. [c]And this took place in the *reign*
of [C]Claudius. 29 And in the proportion that any of

10:46 [A]Mark 16:17; Acts 2:4; 19:6 10:47 [A]Acts 8:36 [B]Acts 2:4; 10:44f; 11:17; 15:8 10:48 [A]1 Cor 1:14-17 [B]Acts 2:38; 8:16; 19:5 11:1 [A]Acts 1:15 11:2 [a]Lit *those of the circumcision;* i.e. Jewish Christians [A]Acts 10:45 11:3 [a]Or *entered the house of* [A]Matt 9:11; Acts 10:28; Gal 2:12 11:4 [a]Lit *and was explaining* [A]Luke 1:3 11:5 [a]Or *vessel* [b]Or *heaven* [A]Acts 10:9-32; 11:5-14 [B]Acts 9:10 11:6 [a]Lit *and I saw* [b]Or *reptiles* [c]Or *heaven* 11:7 [a]Or *sacrifice* 11:8 [a]Or *profane;* lit *common* 11:9 [a]Lit *make common* [A]Acts 10:15 11:10 [a]Or *heaven* 11:11 [A]Acts 8:40 11:12 [a]Or *without making any distinction* [A]Acts 8:29 [B]Acts 15:9; Rom 3:22 [C]Acts 10:23 11:13 [a]Or *after he had stood in his house and said* 11:14 [A]Acts 10:22 [B]John 4:53; Acts 10:2; 16:15, 31-34; 18:8; 1 Cor 1:16 11:15 [A]Acts 10:44 [B]Acts 2:4 11:16 [a]Or *in* [A]Acts 1:5 11:17 [a]Lit *prevent God* [A]Acts 10:45, 47 [B]Acts 5:39 11:18 [a]Lit *became silent* [A]Matt 9:8 [B]2 Cor 7:10 11:19 [a]Lit *tribulation* [b]Lit *as far as* [A]Acts 8:1, 4 [B]Acts 15:3; 21:2 [C]Acts 4:36 [D]Acts 6:5; 11:20, 22, 27; 13:1; 14:26; 15:22f, 30, 35; 18:22; Gal 2:11 11:20 [a]Lit *Hellenists;* people who lived by Greek customs and culture [b]Or *bringing the good news of* [A]Acts 4:36 [B]Matt 27:32; Acts 2:10; 6:9; 13:1 [C]Acts 6:5; 11:19, 22, 27; 13:1; 14:26; 15:22f, 30, 35; 18:22; Gal 2:11 [D]John 7:35; Acts 6:1 [E]Acts 5:42 11:21 [A]Luke 1:66 [B]Acts 2:47 11:22 [a]Lit *word* [b]Lit *was heard in* [c]Lit *as far as* [A]Acts 4:36 [B]Acts 6:5; 11:19, 20, 27; 13:1; 18:22; Gal 2:11 11:23 [a]Lit *saw* [b]Lit *purpose of heart* [A]Acts 13:43; 14:26; 15:40; 20:24, 32 11:24 [a]Lit *crowd was* [b]Lit *added* [A]Acts 2:4 [B]Acts 2:47; 5:14; 11:21 11:25 [A]Acts 9:11 11:26 [a]Or *were gathered together* [b]Lit *crowd* [A]Acts 6:5; 11:20, 22, 27 [B]John 2:2; Acts 1:15 [C]Acts 26:28; 1 Pet 4:16 11:27 [a]Lit *in these days* [A]Luke 11:49; Acts 2:17; 13:1; 1 Cor 12:10, 28f [B]Acts 6:5; 11:20, 22, 26; 13:1; 14:26; 15:22f, 30, 35; 18:22; Gal 2:11 11:28 [a]Or *through* [b]Lit *inhabited earth* [c]Lit *which* [A]Acts 21:10 [B]Matt 24:14 [C]Acts 18:2

11:3 ate with them. The Jewish believers were outraged over such a blatant breach of Jewish custom. It was difficult for them to conceive that Jesus could be equally Lord of Gentile believers.

11:4–14 Cf. 10:1–23, 28–33.

11:14 your household. All who were under Cornelius's authority and care, who could comprehend the gospel and believe (cf. 16:15, 31). This does not include infants.

11:15 at the beginning. God attested to the reality of Gentile salvation with the same phenomenon that occurred at Pentecost (*see note on 8:17*).

11:16 baptized with the Holy Spirit. *See note on 1:5.*

11:18 God has granted to the Gentiles also the repentance ... to life. One of the most shocking admissions in Jewish history, but an event that the OT had prophesied (Is 42:1, 6; 49:6; *see note on 2:38*).

11:19 *See notes on 8:1–3.* **Phoenicia.** The coastal region directly N of Judea, containing the trading ports of Tyre and Sidon. **Cyprus.** *See note on 4:36.* **Antioch.** Located some 200 mi. N of Sidon, Antioch was a major pagan metropolis, the third largest in the Roman Empire, behind Rome and Alexandria.

11:20 men of Cyprus and Cyrene. *See notes on 6:9; 13:4.* **Greeks.** Cf. 6:1; 9:29. Greek-speaking non-Jews (*see note on 6:1*).

11:21 hand of the Lord. This refers to God's power expressed in judgment (cf. Ex 9:33; Dt 2:15; Jos 4:24; 1Sa 5:6; 7:13) and in blessing (Ezr 7:9; 8:18; Ne 2:8, 18). Here, it refers to blessing.

11:22 Barnabas. *See note on 4:36.* Since he was a Cypriot Jew, he came from a similar background to the founders of the Antioch church.

11:25 Tarsus. *See note on 9:11.* **to look for Saul.** This was to be no easy task. Several years had elapsed since Saul fled Jerusalem (9:30). Apparently, he had been disinherited and forced to leave his home due to his new allegiance to Christianity (Php 3:8).

11:26 Christians. A term of derision meaning "of the party of Christ." Cf. 26:28; 1Pe 4:16.

11:27 prophets. Preachers of the NT (cf. 1Co 14:32; Eph 2:20; *see notes on 13:1; 21:9; Eph 4:11*).

11:28 Agabus. One of the Jerusalem prophets who years later played an important part in Paul's ministry (21:10, 11). **a great famine.** Several

[A]the disciples had means, each of them determined
to send *a contribution* for the [a]relief of [B]the brethren
living in Judea. 30 [A]And this they did, sending it [a]in
charge of [B]Barnabas and Saul to the [C]elders.

PETER'S ARREST AND DELIVERANCE

12 Now about that time [a]Herod the king laid
hands on some who belonged to the church
in order to mistreat them. 2 And he [A]had James the
brother of John [B]put to death with a sword. 3 When
he saw that it [A]pleased the Jews, he proceeded to
arrest Peter also. Now [a]it was during [B]the days of
Unleavened Bread. 4 When he had seized him, he put
him in prison, delivering him to four [a,A]squads of
soldiers to guard him, intending after [B]the Passover
to bring him out before the people. 5 So Peter was
kept in the prison, but prayer for him was being
made fervently by the church to God.
6 On [a]the very night when Herod was about to
bring him forward, Peter was sleeping between
two soldiers, [A]bound with two chains, and guards
in front of the door were watching over the prison.
7 And behold, [A]an angel of the Lord suddenly [B]ap-
peared and a light shone in the cell; and he struck
Peter's side and woke him up, saying, "Get up
quickly." And [C]his chains fell off his hands. 8 And
the angel said to him, "Gird yourself and [a]put on
your sandals." And he did so. And he *said to him,
"Wrap your cloak around you and follow me." 9 And
he went out and continued to follow, and he did not
know that what was being done by the angel was
real, but thought he was seeing [A]a vision. 10 When
they had passed the first and second guard, they
came to the iron gate that leads into the city, which
[A]opened for them by itself; and they went out and
went along one street, and immediately the angel
departed from him. 11 When Peter [A]came [a]to himself,
he said, "Now I know for sure that [B]the Lord has sent
forth His angel and rescued me from the hand of
Herod and from all [b]that the Jewish people were
expecting." 12 And when he realized *this,* he went to
the house of Mary, the mother of [A]John who was also
called Mark, where many were gathered together
and [B]were praying. 13 When he knocked at the door
of the gate, [A]a servant-girl named Rhoda came to
answer. 14 When she recognized Peter's voice, [A]be-
cause of her joy she did not open the gate, but ran
in and announced that Peter was standing in front
of the gate. 15 They said to her, "You are out of your
mind!" But she kept insisting that it was so. They
kept saying, "It is [A]his angel." 16 But Peter continued knocking; and when they had opened *the door,*
they saw him and were amazed. 17 But [A]motioning
to them with his hand to be silent, he described to
them how the Lord had led him out of the prison.
And he said, "Report these things to [a,B]James and [C]the
brethren." Then he left and went to another place.
18 Now when day came, there was no small disturbance among the soldiers *as to* [a]what could have
become of Peter. 19 When Herod had searched for
him and had not found him, he examined the guards
and ordered that they [A]be led away *to execution.*
Then he went down from Judea to [B]Caesarea and
was spending time there.

DEATH OF HEROD

20 Now he was very angry with the people of [A]Tyre
and Sidon; and with one accord they came to him,
and having won over Blastus the king's chamberlain,
they were asking for peace, because [B]their country

11:29 [a]Lit *service* [A]John 2:2; Acts 1:15; 6:1f; 9:19, 25, 26, 38; 11:26; 13:52; 14:20, 22, 28 [B]Acts 11:1 11:30 [a]Lit *by the hand of* [A]Acts 12:25 [B]Acts 4:36 [C]Acts 14:23; 15:2, 4, 6, 22f; 16:4; 20:17; 21:18; 1 Tim 5:17, 19; Titus 1:5; James 5:14; 1 Pet 5:1; 2 John 1; 3 John 1 12:1 [a]I.e. Herod Agrippa I 12:2 [A]Matt 4:21; 20:23 [B]Mark 10:39 12:3 [a]Lit *they were the days* [A]Acts 24:27; 25:9 [B]Ex 12:15; 23:15; Acts 20:6 12:4 [a]Lit *quaternions;* a quaternion was composed of four soldiers [A]John 19:23 [B]Ex 12:1-27; Mark 14:1; Acts 12:3 12:6 [a]Lit *that night* [A]Acts 21:33 12:7 [A]Acts 5:19 [B]Luke 2:9; 24:4 [C]Acts 16:26 12:8 [a]Lit *bind* 12:9 [A]Acts 9:10 12:10 [A]Acts 5:19; 16:26 12:11 [a]Lit *in himself* [b]Lit *the expectation of the people of the Jews* [A]Luke 15:17 [B]Dan 3:28; 6:22 12:12 [A]Acts 12:25; 13:5, 13; 15:37, 39; Col 4:10; 2 Tim 4:11; Philem 24; 1 Pet 5:13 [B]Acts 12:5 12:13 [A]John 18:16f 12:14 [A]Luke 24:41 12:15 [A]Matt 18:10 12:17 [a]Or *Jacob* [A]Acts 13:16; 19:33; 21:40 [B]Mark 6:3; Acts 15:13; 21:18; 1 Cor 15:7; Gal 1:19; 2:9, 12 [C]Acts 1:15 12:18 [a]Lit *what therefore had become* 12:19 [A]Acts 16:27; 27:42 [B]Acts 8:40 12:20 [A]Matt 11:21 [B]1 Kin 5:11; Ezra 3:7; Ezek 27:17

ancient writers (Tacitus [*Annals* XI.43], Josephus [*Antiquities* XX.ii.5], and Suetonius [*Claudius* 18]) affirm the occurrence of great famines in Israel ca. A.D. 45–46. **all over the world.** The famine reached beyond the region of Israel. **Claudius.** Emperor of Rome (A.D. 41–54).

11:30 elders. This is the first mention of the men who were pastor-overseers of the churches (15:4, 6, 22, 23; 16:4; 21:18); i.e., a plurality of godly men responsible to lead the church (*see notes on 1Ti 3:1–7; Tit 1:5–9*). They soon began to occupy the leading role in the churches, transitioning from the apostles and prophets, who were foundational (cf. Eph 2:20; 4:11).

12:1 Herod the king. Herod Agrippa I reigned from A.D. 37–44 and was the grandson of Herod the Great. He ran up numerous debts in Rome and fled to Israel. Imprisoned by Emperor Tiberius after some careless comments, he eventually was released following Tiberius' death, and was made ruler of northern Israel, to which Judea and Samaria were added in A.D. 41. As a hedge against his shaky relationship with Rome, he curried favor with the Jews by persecuting Christians.

12:2 James. The first of the apostles to be martyred (*see note on Mt 10:2*). **with a sword.** The manner of his execution indicates James was accused of leading people to follow false gods (cf. Dt 13:12–15).

12:3 during the days of Unleavened Bread. The weekly feast following Passover (*see notes on Ex 23:14–19; Mt 26:17*).

12:4 four squads. Each squad contained four soldiers and rotated the watch on Peter. At all times two guards were chained to him in his cell, while the other two stood guard outside the cell door (v. 6).

12:12 Mary. Mark is called the cousin of Barnabas in Col 4:10, so she was his aunt. **John … Mark.** Cousin of Barnabas (Col 4:10), acquaintance of Peter in his youth (1Pe 5:13), he accompanied Barnabas and Paul to Antioch (v. 25) and later to Cyprus (13:4, 5). He deserted them at Perga (13:13) and Paul refused to take him on his second missionary journey because of that desertion (15:36–41). He accompanied Barnabas to Cyprus (15:39). He disappeared until he was seen with Paul at Rome as an accepted companion and coworker (Col 4:10; Phm 24). During Paul's second imprisonment at Rome, Paul sought John Mark's presence as useful to him (2Ti 4:11). He wrote the second gospel that bears his name, being enriched in his task by the aid of Peter (1Pe 5:13).

12:15, 16 his angel. According to Jewish superstition, each person had his own guardian angel who could assume that person's form.

12:17 James. The Lord's brother, now head of the Jerusalem church (see Introduction to James; *see note on 15:13*). **he left.** Except for a brief appearance in chap. 15, Peter fades from the scene as the rest of Acts revolves around Paul and his ministry.

12:19 Herod. *See note on v. 1.* **led away to execution.** According to Justinian's *Code* (ix. 4:4), a guard who allowed a prisoner to escape would suffer the same fatal penalty that awaited the prisoner. **Caesarea.** *See note on 9:30.*

12:20 Tyre and Sidon. Two port cities N of Caesarea, in a region called Phoenicia. Mutual interdependence existed between these cities and Galilee, although Tyre and Sidon were more dependent on Galilee (*see note on Mk 3:8*). **Blastus.** The king's "chamberlain," or treasurer, acted as an intermediary between Herod and the representatives of Tyre and Sidon.

was fed by the king's country. 21 On an appointed day
Herod, having put on his royal apparel, took his seat
on the [a]rostrum and *began* delivering an address to
them. 22 The people kept crying out, "The voice of a
god and not of a man!" 23 And immediately [A]an angel
of the Lord struck him because he did not give God
the glory, and he was eaten by worms and [a]died.

24 But [A]the word of the Lord continued to grow
and to be multiplied.

25 And [A]Barnabas and [A]Saul returned [a]from Jerusalem [B]when they had fulfilled their [b]mission, taking
along with *them* [C]John, who was also called Mark.

FIRST MISSIONARY JOURNEY

13 Now there were at [A]Antioch, in the [B]church
that was *there*, [C]prophets and [D]teachers: [E]Bar-
nabas, and Simeon who was called Niger, and Lucius
of [F]Cyrene, and Manaen who had been brought up
with [G]Herod the tetrarch, and Saul. 2 While they were
ministering to the Lord and fasting, [A]the Holy Spirit
said, "Set apart for Me [B]Barnabas and Saul for [C]the
work to which I have called them." 3 Then, when
they had fasted and [A]prayed and [B]laid their hands
on them, [C]they sent them away.

4 So, being [A]sent out by the Holy Spirit, they went
down to Seleucia and from there they sailed to [B]Cy-
prus. 5 When they reached Salamis, they *began* to
proclaim the word of God in [A]the synagogues of
the Jews; and they also had [B]John as their helper.
6 When they had gone through the whole island as
far as Paphos, they found a [A]magician, a Jewish [B]false
prophet whose name was Bar-Jesus, 7 who was with
the [A]proconsul, Sergius Paulus, a man of intelligence.
This man summoned Barnabas and Saul and sought
to hear the word of God. 8 But Elymas the [A]magician
(for so his name is translated) was opposing them,
seeking to turn the [B]proconsul away from [C]the faith.
9 But Saul, who was also *known as* Paul, [a,A]filled with
the Holy Spirit, fixed his gaze on him, 10 and said,
"You who are full of all deceit and fraud, you [A]son
of the devil, you enemy of all righteousness, will
you not cease to make crooked [B]the straight ways
of the Lord? 11 Now, behold, [A]the hand of the Lord is
upon you, and you will be blind and not see the sun
for a time." And immediately a mist and a darkness
fell upon him, and he went about seeking those who
would lead him by the hand. 12 Then the [A]proconsul
believed when he saw what had happened, being
amazed at [B]the teaching of the Lord.

13 Now Paul and his companions put out to sea from
[A]Paphos and came to [B]Perga in [C]Pamphylia; but [D]John
left them and returned to Jerusalem. 14 But going on
from Perga, they arrived at [A]Pisidian [B]Antioch, and
on [C]the Sabbath day they went into [D]the synagogue

12:21 [a]Or *judgment seat* 12:23 [a]Lit *breathed his last breath* [A]2 Sam 24:16; 2 Kin 19:35; Acts 5:19 12:24 [A]Acts 6:7; 19:20 12:25 [a]Two early mss read *to Jerusalem* [b]Lit *ministry* [A]Acts 4:36; 13:1ff [B]Acts 11:30 [C]Acts 12:12 13:1 [A]Acts 11:19 [B]Acts 11:26 [C]Acts 11:27; 15:32; 19:6; 21:9; 1 Cor 11:4f; 13:2, 8f; 14:29, 32, 37 [D]Rom 12:6f; 1 Cor 12:28f; Eph 4:11; James 3:1 [E]Acts 4:36 [F]Matt 27:32; Acts 11:20 [G]Matt 14:1 13:2 [A]Acts 8:29; 13:4 [B]Acts 4:36 [C]Acts 9:15 13:3 [A]Acts 1:24 [B]Acts 6:6 [C]Acts 13:4; 14:26 13:4 [A]Acts 13:2f [B]Acts 4:36 13:5 [A]Acts 9:20; 13:14 [B]Acts 12:12 13:6 [A]Acts 8:9 [B]Matt 7:15 13:7 [A]Acts 13:8, 12; 18:12; 19:38 13:8 [A]Acts 8:9 [B]Acts 13:7, 12; 18:12; 19:38 [C]Acts 6:7 13:9 [a]Or *having* just *been filled* [A]Acts 2:4; 4:8 13:10 [A]Matt 13:38; John 8:44 [B]Hos 14:9; 2 Pet 2:15 13:11 [A]Ex 9:3; 1 Sam 5:6f; Job 19:21; Ps 32:4; Heb 10:31 13:12 [A]Acts 13:7, 8; 18:12; 19:38 [B]Acts 8:25; 13:49; 15:35f; 19:10, 20 13:13 [A]Acts 13:6 [B]Acts 14:25 [C]Acts 2:10; 14:24; 15:38; 27:5 [D]Acts 12:12 13:14 [A]Acts 14:24 [B]Acts 14:19, 21; 2 Tim 3:11 [C]Acts 13:42, 44; 16:13; 17:2; 18:4 [D]Acts 9:20; 13:5

12:21 On an appointed day. A feast in honor of Herod's patron, the Roman emperor Claudius. **put on his royal apparel.** According to Josephus, he wore a garment made of silver.

12:23 did not give God the glory. The crime for which Herod was executed by God (A.D. 44), who will eventually condemn and execute all who are guilty of this crime (Ro 1:18–23). **eaten by worms.** According to Josephus, Herod endured terrible pain for 5 days before he died.

12:25 had fulfilled their mission. After Herod's death, they delivered the famine relief to the Jerusalem church (11:30). **John ... Mark.** *See note on v. 12.*

13:1 Chapter 13 marks a turning point in Acts. The first 12 chapters focus on Peter; the remaining chapters revolve around Paul. With Peter, the emphasis is the Jewish church in Jerusalem and Judea; with Paul, the focus is the spread of the Gentile church throughout the Roman world, which began at the church in Antioch. **prophets.** These had a significant role in the apostolic church (*see notes on 1Co 12:28; Eph 2:20*). They were preachers of God's Word and were responsible in the early years of the church to instruct local congregations. On some occasions, they received new revelation that was of a practical nature (cf. 11:28; 21:10), a function that ended with the cessation of the temporary sign gifts. Their office was also replaced by pastor-teachers and evangelists (*see note on Eph 4:11*). **Barnabas.** *See note on 4:36.* **Simeon ... called Niger.** "Niger" means "black." He may have been a dark-skinned man, an African, or both. No direct evidence exists to equate him with Simon of Cyrene (Mk 15:21). **Lucius of Cyrene.** Not the Lucius of Ro 16:21, or Luke, the physician and author of Acts. **who had been brought up with.** Can be translated "foster-brother." Manean was reared in Herod the Great's household. **Herod the tetrarch.** Herod Antipas, the Herod of the Gospels (*see note on Mt 14:1*).

13:2 ministering. This is from a Gr. word which in Scripture describes priestly service. Serving in leadership in the church is an act of worship to God, and consists of offering spiritual sacrifices to Him, including prayer, oversight of the flock, plus preaching and teaching the Word. **fasting.** This is often connected with vigilant, passionate prayer (cf. Ne 1:4; Ps 35:13; Da 9:3; Mt 17:21; Lk 2:37), and includes either a loss of desire for food or the purposeful setting aside of eating to concentrate on spiritual issues (*see note on Mt 6:16, 17*).

13:3 laid their hands on them. *See note on 6:6.*

13:4 Seleucia. This city served as the port for Antioch, some 16 mi. away at the mouth of the Orontes River. **Cyprus.** *See note on 4:36.* Saul and Barnabas chose to begin their missionary outreach there because it was Barnabas' home, which was only a two-day journey from Antioch, and had a large Jewish population.

13:5 reached Salamis. The chief port and commercial center of Cyprus. **synagogues.** *See note on 6:9.* Paul established the custom of preaching to the Jews first whenever he entered a new city (cf. v. 14, 42; 14:1; 17:1, 10, 17; 18:4, 19, 26; 19:8) because he had an open door, as a Jew, to speak and introduce the gospel. Also, if he preached to Gentiles first, the Jews would never have listened to him. **John as their helper.** *See note on 12:12.*

13:6 Paphos. The capital of Cyprus and thus the seat of the Roman government. It also was a great center for the worship of Aphrodite (Venus), and thus a hotbed for all kinds of immorality. **a magician ... Jewish.** "Magician" originally carried no evil connotation, but later was used to describe all kinds of practitioners and dabblers in the occult. This particular magician put his knowledge to evil use (*see note on 8:9*).

13:7 the proconsul. A Roman official who served as provincial governor (cf. 18:12).

13:8 Elymas. The Gr. name of Bar-Jesus, a transliteration of the Arab. word for magician.

13:9 Saul ... *known as* Paul. Paul's Hebrew and Roman names.

13:13 came to Perga in Pamphylia. Perga was a major city in the Roman province of Pamphylia, in Asia Minor—some 200 mi. N across the Mediterranean from Cyprus. **John left them.** Whatever reason John Mark gave for leaving, Paul didn't accept it (15:38). While his desertion did not hamper the mission, it did later create dissension between Paul and Barnabas (15:36–40). This was finally resolved (cf. Col 4:10; 2Ti 4:11). *See note on 12:12.*

13:14 Pisidian Antioch. Not to be confused with Antioch in Syria, the location of the first Gentile church. This Antioch was located in the mountains of Asia Minor (modern Turkey).

and sat down. 15 After [A]the reading of the Law and [B]the Prophets [C]the synagogue officials sent to them, saying, "Brethren, if you have any word of exhortation for the people, say it." 16 Paul stood up, and [A]motioning with his hand said,

"Men of Israel, and [B]you who fear God, listen: 17 The God of this people Israel [A]chose our fathers and [a,B]made the people great during their stay in the land of Egypt, and with an uplifted arm [C]He led them out from it. 18 For [A]a period of about forty years [B]He put up with them in the wilderness. 19 [A]When He had destroyed [B]seven nations in the land of Canaan, He [C]distributed their land as an inheritance—*all of which took* [D]about four hundred and fifty years. 20 After these things He [A]gave *them* judges until [B]Samuel the prophet. 21 Then they [A]asked for a king, and God gave them [B]Saul the son of Kish, a man of the tribe of Benjamin, for forty years. 22 After He had [A]removed him, He raised up David to be their king, concerning whom He also testified and said, '[B]I HAVE FOUND DAVID the son of Jesse, A MAN AFTER MY HEART, who will do all My [a]will.' 23 [A]From the descendants of this man, [B]according to promise, God has brought to Israel [C]a Savior, Jesus, 24 after [A]John had proclaimed before [a]His coming a [B]baptism of repentance to all the people of Israel. 25 And while John [A]was completing his course, [B]he kept saying, 'What do you suppose that I am? I am not *He*. But behold, one is coming after me the sandals of whose feet I am not worthy to untie.'

26 "Brethren, sons of Abraham's family, and those among you who fear God, to us the message of [A]this salvation has been sent. 27 For those who live in Jerusalem, and their [A]rulers, [B]recognizing neither Him nor the [a]utterances of [C]the prophets which are [D]read every Sabbath, fulfilled *these* by condemning *Him*. 28 And though they found no ground for *putting Him to death*, they [A]asked Pilate that He be [a]executed. 29 When they had [A]carried out all that was written concerning Him, [B]they took Him down from [C]the [a]cross and [D]laid Him in a tomb. 30 But God [A]raised Him from the dead; 31 and for many days [A]He appeared to those who came up with Him from Galilee to Jerusalem, the very ones who are now [B]His witnesses to the people. 32 And we [A]preach to you the good news of [B]the promise made to the fathers, 33 that God has fulfilled this *promise* [a]to our children in that He [A]raised up Jesus, as it is also written in the second Psalm, '[B]YOU ARE MY SON; TODAY I HAVE BEGOTTEN YOU.' 34 *As for the fact* that He [A]raised Him up from the dead, no longer to return to decay, He has spoken in this way: '[B]I WILL GIVE YOU THE HOLY *and* [a]SURE *blessings* OF DAVID.' 35 Therefore He also says in another *Psalm*, '[A]YOU WILL NOT [a]ALLOW YOUR [b]HOLY ONE TO [c]UNDERGO DECAY.' 36 For [A]David, after he had [a]served [B]the purpose of God in his own generation, [C]fell asleep, and was laid among his fathers and [b]underwent decay; 37 but He whom God [A]raised did not [a]undergo decay. 38 Therefore let it be known to you, brethren, that [A]through [a]Him forgiveness of sins is proclaimed to you, 39 and [a]through Him [A]everyone who believes is [b]freed [c]from all things, from which you could not be [b]freed [c]through the Law of Moses. 40 Therefore take heed, so that the thing spoken of [A]in the Prophets may not come upon *you*:

41 '[A]BEHOLD, YOU SCOFFERS, AND
MARVEL, AND [a]PERISH;
FOR I AM ACCOMPLISHING A
WORK IN YOUR DAYS,
A WORK WHICH YOU WILL NEVER
BELIEVE, THOUGH SOMEONE
SHOULD DESCRIBE IT TO YOU.' "

42 As [a]Paul and Barnabas were going out, the people kept begging that these [b]things might be

13:15 [A]Acts 15:21; 2 Cor 3:14f [B]Acts 13:27 [C]Mark 5:22 13:16 [A]Acts 12:17 [B]Acts 10:2; 13:26 13:17 [a]Or *exalted* [A]Ex 6:1, 6; 13:14, 16; Deut 7:6-8; Acts 7:17ff [B]Ex 1:7 [C]Ex 12:51 13:18 [A]Num 14:34; Acts 7:36 [B]Deut 1:31 13:19 [A]Acts 7:45 [B]Deut 7:1 [C]Josh 14:1; 19:51; Ps 78:55 [D]Judg 11:26; 1 Kin 6:1 13:20 [A]Judg 2:16 [B]1 Sam 3:20; Acts 3:24 13:21 [A]1 Sam 8:5 [B]1 Sam 9:1f; 10:1, 21 13:22 [a]Lit *wishes* [A]1 Sam 15:23, 26, 28; 16:1, 13 [B]1 Sam 13:14; Ps 89:20; Acts 7:46 13:23 [A]Matt 1:1 [B]Acts 13:32f [C]Luke 2:11; John 4:42 13:24 [a]Lit *the face of His entering* [A]Mark 1:1-4; Acts 1:22; 19:4 [B]Luke 3:3 13:25 [A]Acts 20:24 [B]Matt 3:11; Mark 1:7; Luke 3:16; John 1:20, 27 13:26 [A]John 6:68; Acts 4:12; 5:20; 13:46; 28:28 13:27 [a]Lit *voices* [A]Luke 23:13 [B]Acts 3:17 [C]Luke 24:27 [D]Acts 13:15 13:28 [a]Lit *destroyed* [A]Matt 27:22, 23; Mark 15:13, 14; Luke 23:21-23; John 19:15; Acts 3:14 13:29 [a]Lit *wood* [A]Acts 26:22 [B]Luke 23:53 [C]Acts 5:30 [D]Matt 27:57-61; Mark 15:42-47; Luke 23:50-56; John 19:38-42 13:30 [A]Acts 2:24; 13:33, 34, 37 13:31 [A]Acts 1:3 [B]Luke 24:48 13:32 [A]Acts 5:42; 14:15 [B]Acts 13:23; 26:6; Rom 1:2; 4:13; 9:4 13:33 [a]Late mss read *to us their children* [A]Acts 2:24; 13:30, 34, 37 [B]Ps 2:7 13:34 [a]Lit *trustworthy* [A]Acts 2:24; 13:30, 33, 37 [B]Is 55:3 13:35 [a]Lit *give* [b]Or *Devout* or *Pious* [c]Lit *see corruption* [A]Ps 16:10; Acts 2:27 13:36 [a]Or *served his own generation by the purpose of God* [b]Lit *saw corruption* [A]Acts 2:29 [B]Acts 13:22; 20:27 [C]1 Kin 2:10; Acts 8:1 13:37 [a]Lit *see corruption* [A]Acts 2:24; 13:30, 33, 34 13:38 [a]Lit *this One* [A]Luke 24:47; Acts 2:38 13:39 [a]Lit *in* or *by* [b]Lit *justified* [c]Lit *by* [A]Acts 10:43; Rom 3:28; 10:4 13:40 [A]Luke 24:44; John 6:45; Acts 7:42 13:41 [a]Lit *disappear* [A]Hab 1:5 13:42 [a]Lit *they* [b]Lit *words*

13:15 reading of the Law and the Prophets. The reading of the Scriptures. This occupied the third part in the liturgy of the synagogue, after the recitation of the *shema* (Dt 6:4) and further prayers, but before the teaching, which was usually based on what had been read from the Scriptures. **synagogue officials.** Those who had general oversight of the synagogue (*see note on 6:9*), including designating who would read from the Scriptures.

13:16 who fear God. *See note on 10:2.*

13:19 seven nations. *See note on Dt 7:1.*

13:20 See Introduction to Judges.

13:21 Saul. *See note on 1Sa 9:2.*

13:22 a man after My heart. *See note on 1Sa 13:14.* Some would question the reality of this designation for David since he proved to be such a sinner at times (cf. 1Sa 11:1–4; 12:9; 21:10–22:1). No man after God's own heart is perfect; yet he will recognize sin and repent of it, as did David (cf. Pss 32, 38, 51). Paul quoted from 1Sa 13:14 and Ps 89:20.

13:23 according to promise. OT prophecy points to Messiah as a descendant of David (cf. 2Sa 7:12–16; Ps 132:11; Is 11:10; Jer 23:5). Jesus is the fulfillment of the OT prophecies of the coming Messiah (Mt 1:1, 20, 21; Ro 1:3; 2Ti 2:8).

13:24 baptism of repentance. Cf. 1:22; 10:37.

13:26 who fear God. *See note on 10:2.*

13:27 rulers. The supposed experts in the OT, including the scribes, Pharisees, Sadducees, and priests.

13:28 Pilate. *See notes on 3:13; Mt 27:2.*

13:29, 30 cross ... tomb ... God raised. The OT predicted the crucifixion of Christ on a cross (Ps 22; Dt 21), at the time when this particular form of execution was not used. His burial in a "tomb" was also prophesied (Is 53:9), yet victims of crucifixions were commonly tossed into mass graves. The climax of Paul's message was the resurrection of Christ, the ultimate proof that Jesus is the Messiah, and the fulfillment of 3 specific prophecies (*see notes on vv. 33–35*).

13:31 witnesses. More than 500 (cf. 1Co 15:5–8).

13:33 Quoted from Ps 2:7.

13:34 Quoted from Is 55:3.

13:35 Quoted from Ps 16:10; *see note on 2:27.*

13:39 you could not be freed through the Law of Moses. Keeping the law of Moses did not free anyone from their sins (cf. Ro 3:28; 1Co 1:30; Gal 2:16; 3:11; Php 3:9). But the atoning death of Jesus completely satisfied the demands of God's law, making forgiveness of all sins available to all who believe (Gal 3:16; Col 2:13, 14). Only the forgiveness Christ offers can free people from their sins (Ro 3:20, 22).

13:41 Quoted from Hab 1:5.

spoken to them the next [A]Sabbath. 43 Now when *the meeting of* the synagogue had broken up, many of the Jews and of the [A]God-fearing [a,B]proselytes followed Paul and Barnabas, who, speaking to them, were urging them to continue in [C]the grace of God.

PAUL TURNS TO THE GENTILES

44 The next [A]Sabbath nearly the whole city assembled to hear the word of [a]the Lord. 45 But when [A]the Jews saw the crowds, they were filled with jealousy and *began* contradicting the things spoken by Paul, and were [a]blaspheming. 46 Paul and Barnabas spoke out boldly and said, "It was necessary that the word of God be spoken to you [A]first; since you repudiate it and judge yourselves unworthy of eternal life, behold, [B]we are turning to the Gentiles. 47 For so the Lord has commanded us,

'[A]I HAVE PLACED YOU AS A [B]LIGHT
FOR THE GENTILES,
THAT YOU MAY [a]BRING SALVATION
TO THE END OF THE EARTH.' "

48 When the Gentiles heard this, they *began* rejoicing and glorifying [A]the word of [a]the Lord; and as many as [B]had been appointed to eternal life believed. 49 And [A]the word of the Lord was being spread through the whole region. 50 But [A]the Jews incited the [a,B]devout women [C]of prominence and the leading men of the city, and instigated a persecution against Paul and Barnabas, and drove them out of their [b]district. 51 But [A]they shook off the dust of their feet *in protest* against them and went to [B]Iconium. 52 And the disciples were continually [A]filled with joy and with the Holy Spirit.

ACCEPTANCE AND OPPOSITION

14 In [A]Iconium [B]they entered the synagogue of the Jews together, and spoke in such a manner [C]that a large number of people believed, both of Jews and of [D]Greeks. 2 But [A]the Jews who [a,B]disbelieved stirred up the [b]minds of the Gentiles and embittered them against [C]the brethren. 3 Therefore they spent a long time *there* [A]speaking boldly *with reliance* upon the Lord, who was testifying to the word of His grace, granting that [a,B]signs and wonders be done by their hands. 4 [A]But the [a]people of the city were divided; and some [b]sided with [B]the Jews, and some with [C]the apostles. 5 And when an attempt was made by both the Gentiles and [A]the Jews with their rulers, to mistreat and to [B]stone them, 6 they became aware of it and fled to the cities of [A]Lycaonia, [B]Lystra and [C]Derbe, and the surrounding region; 7 and there they continued to [A]preach the gospel.

8 At [A]Lystra [B]a man was sitting who had no strength in his feet, lame from his mother's womb, who had never walked. 9 This man was listening to Paul as he spoke, who, [A]when he had fixed his gaze on him and had seen that he had [B]faith to be [a]made well, 10 said with a loud voice, "Stand upright on your feet." [A]And he leaped up and *began* to walk. 11 When the crowds saw what Paul had done, they raised their voice, saying in the [A]Lycaonian language, "[B]The gods have become like men and have come down to

13:42 [A]Acts 13:14 13:43 [a]I.e. Gentile converts to Judaism [A]Acts 13:50; 16:14; 17:4, 17; 18:7 [B]Matt 23:15 [C]Acts 11:23 13:44 [a]One early ms reads *God* [A]Acts 13:14 13:45 [a]Or *slandering* him [A]Acts 13:50; 14:2, 4, 5, 19; 1 Thess 2:16 13:46 [A]Acts 3:26; 9:20; 13:5, 14 [B]Acts 18:6; 19:9; 22:21; 26:20; 28:28 13:47 [a]Lit *be for salvation* [A]Is 42:6; 49:6 [B]Luke 2:32 13:48 [a]Two early mss read *God* [A]Acts 13:12 [B]Rom 8:28ff; Eph 1:4f, 11 13:49 [A]Acts 13:12 13:50 [a]Or *worshiping* [b]Lit *boundaries* [A]Acts 13:45; 14:2, 4, 5, 19; 1 Thess 2:14ff [B]Acts 13:43; 16:14; 17:4, 17; 18:7 [C]Mark 15:43 13:51 [A]Matt 10:14; Mark 6:11; Luke 9:5; 10:11; Acts 18:6 [B]Acts 14:1, 19, 21; 16:2; 2 Tim 3:11 13:52 [A]Acts 2:4 14:1 [A]Acts 13:51; 14:19, 21; 16:2; 2 Tim 3:11 [B]Acts 13:5 [C]Acts 2:47 [D]John 7:35; Acts 18:4 14:2 [a]Or *disobeyed* [b]Lit *souls* [A]Acts 13:45, 50; 14:4, 5, 19; 1 Thess 2:14ff [B]John 3:36 [C]Acts 1:15 14:3 [a]Or *attesting miracles* [A]Acts 4:29f; 20:32; Heb 2:4 [B]John 4:48 14:4 [a]Lit *multitude* [b]Lit *were* [A]Acts 17:4f; 19:9; 28:24 [B]Acts 13:45, 50; 14:2, 5, 19; 1 Thess 2:14ff [C]Acts 14:14 14:5 [A]Acts 13:45, 50; 14:2, 4, 19; 1 Thess 2:14ff [B]Acts 14:19 14:6 [A]Acts 14:11 [B]Acts 14:8, 21; 16:1f; 2 Tim 3:11 [C]Acts 14:20; 16:1; 20:4 14:7 [A]Acts 14:15, 21; 16:10 14:8 [A]Acts 14:6, 21; 16:1f; 2 Tim 3:11 [B]Acts 3:2 14:9 [a]Lit *saved* [A]Acts 3:4; 10:4 [B]Matt 9:28 14:10 [A]Acts 3:8 14:11 [A]Acts 14:6 [B]Acts 8:10; 28:6

13:43 God-fearing proselytes. Full converts to Judaism who had been circumcised. **continue in the grace of God.** Those who are truly saved persevere and validate the reality of their salvation by continuing in the grace of God (cf. Jn 8:31; 15:1–6; Col 1:21–23; 1Jn 2:19). With such encouragement, Paul and Barnabas hoped to prevent those who were intellectually convinced of the truths of the gospel, yet had stopped short of saving faith, from reverting to legalism rather than embracing Christ completely.

13:46 to you first. God offered the plan of salvation to the Jews first (Mt 10:5, 6; 15:24; Lk 24:47; Ro 1:16). Although the thrust of Paul's ministry was to Gentiles, he had a desire to see Jews saved (Ro 9:1–5; 10:1), preaching to them first in many cities (*see note on v. 5*). **we are turning to the Gentiles.** Because the Jews rejected the gospel. But God never planned *salvation as an exclusive possession of the* Jews (Is 42:1, 6; 49:6).

13:47 Quoted from Is 49:6.

13:48 appointed to eternal life. One of Scripture's clearest statements on the sovereignty of God in salvation. God chooses man for salvation, not the opposite (Jn 6:65; Eph 1:4; Col 3:12; 2Th 2:13). Faith itself is a gift from God (Eph 2:8, 9).

13:51 shook off the dust of their feet. The Jews' antagonism toward Gentiles extended to their unwillingness to even bring Gentile dust into Israel. The symbolism of Paul and Barnabas' act is clear that they considered the Jews at Antioch no better than heathen. There could have been no stronger condemnation.

13:52 filled … with the Holy Spirit. *See notes on 2:4; Eph 5:18.*

14:1 Iconium. A cultural melting pot of native Phrygians, Greeks, Jews, and Roman colonists, located 80 mi. SE of Pisidian Antioch.

14:3 granting that signs and wonders. *See notes on 2:19.* Acts of such divine power confirmed that Paul and Barnabas spoke for God.

14:4 apostles. *See notes on Ro 1:1; Eph 4:11.* Barnabas was not an apostle in the same sense as Paul and the 12 since he was not an eyewitness of the resurrected Christ nor had he been called by Him. It is best to translate "apostles" here as "messengers" (cf. 2Co 8:23; Php 2:25). The verb means "to send." The 12 and Paul were "apostles of Christ," (2Co 11:13; 1Th 2:6), while Barnabas and others were "messengers of the churches" (2Co 8:23).

14:5 stone them. This proves that their Jewish opponents were the instigators, since stoning was a Jewish form of execution, usually for blasphemy.

14:6 cities of Lycaonia, Lystra and Derbe. Lycaonia was a district in the Roman province of Galatia. Lystra was about 18 mi. from Iconium, and was the home of Lois, Eunice, and Timothy (16:1; 2Ti 1:5). Luke mentions no synagogue in connection with Lystra, and since Paul began his ministry there by preaching to a crowd, it likely had a small Jewish population. Derbe was about 40 mi. SE of Lystra.

14:11–13 The strange reaction by the people of Lystra to the healing had its roots in local folklore. According to tradition, the gods Zeus and Hermes visited Lystra incognito, asking for food and lodging. All turned them away except for a peasant named Philemon and his wife, Baucis. The gods took vengeance by drowning everyone in a flood. But they turned the lowly cottage of Philemon and Baucis into a temple, where they were to serve as priest and priestess. Not wanting to repeat their ancestors' mistake, the people of Lystra believed Barnabas to be Zeus and Paul to be Hermes.

14:11 Lycaonian language. Paul and Barnabas were unable to understand the intentions of the people.

us." [12] And they *began* calling Barnabas, [a]Zeus, and Paul, [b]Hermes, because he was [c]the chief speaker. [13] The priest of Zeus, whose *temple* was [a]just outside the city, brought oxen and garlands to the gates, and [A]wanted to offer sacrifice with the crowds. [14] But when [A]the apostles Barnabas and Paul heard of it, they [B]tore their [a]robes and rushed out into the crowd, crying out [15] and saying, "Men, why are you doing these things? We are also [A]men of the same nature as you, and [B]preach the gospel to you that you should turn from these [a,C]vain things to a [D]living God, [E]WHO MADE THE HEAVEN AND THE EARTH AND THE SEA AND ALL THAT IS IN THEM. [16] [a]In the generations gone by He [A]permitted all the [b]nations to [B]go their own ways; [17] and yet [A]He did not leave Himself without witness, in that He did good and [B]gave you rains from heaven and fruitful seasons, [a]satisfying your hearts with food and gladness." [18] *Even* saying these things, with difficulty they restrained the crowds from offering sacrifice to them.

[19] But [A]Jews came from [B]Antioch and [C]Iconium, and having won over the crowds, they [D]stoned Paul and dragged him out of the city, supposing him to be dead. [20] But while [A]the disciples stood around him, he got up and entered the city. The next day he went away with Barnabas to [B]Derbe. [21] After they had [A]preached the gospel to that city and had [B]made many disciples, they returned to [C]Lystra and to [D]Iconium and to [E]Antioch, [22] strengthening the souls of [A]the disciples, encouraging them to continue in [B]the faith, and *saying,* "[C]Through many tribulations we must enter the kingdom of God." [23] When [A]they had appointed [B]elders for them in every church, having [C]prayed with fasting, they [D]commended them to the Lord in whom they had believed.

[24] They passed through [A]Pisidia and came into [B]Pamphylia. [25] When they had spoken the word in [A]Perga, they went down to Attalia. [26] From there they sailed to [A]Antioch, from [B]which they had been [C]commended to the grace of God for the work that they had [a]accomplished. [27] When they had arrived and gathered the church together, they *began* to [A]report all things that God had done with them and [a]how He had opened a [B]door of faith to the Gentiles. [28] And they spent [a]a long time with [A]the disciples.

THE COUNCIL AT JERUSALEM

15 [A]Some men came down from Judea and *began* teaching [B]the brethren, "Unless you are [C]circumcised according to [D]the custom of Moses, you cannot be saved." [2] And when Paul and Barnabas had [a]great dissension and [A]debate with them, [B]*the brethren* determined that Paul and Barnabas and some others of them should go up to Jerusalem to the [C]apostles and elders concerning this issue. [3] Therefore, being [A]sent on their way by the church, they were passing through both [B]Phoenicia and Samaria, [C]describing in detail the conversion of the Gentiles, and were bringing great joy to all [D]the brethren. [4] When they arrived at Jerusalem, they were received by the church and [A]the apostles and the elders, and they [B]reported all that God had done with them. [5] But some of [A]the sect of the [B]Pharisees who had believed stood up, saying, "It is necessary to [C]circumcise them and to direct them to observe the Law of Moses."

14:12 [a]Lat *Jupiter*, the chief pagan god [b]Lat *Mercury,* considered the messenger or spokesman for the pagan gods of Greece and Rome [c]Lit *the leader of the speaking* 14:13 [a]Lit *in front of* [A]Dan 2:46 14:14 [a]Or *outer garments* [A]Acts 14:4 [B]Num 14:6; Matt 26:65; Mark 14:63 14:15 [a]I.e. idols [A]Acts 10:26; James 5:17 [B]Acts 13:32; 14:7, 21 [C]Deut 32:21; 1 Sam 12:21; Jer 8:19; 14:22; 1 Cor 8:4 [D]Matt 16:16 [E]Ex 20:11; Ps 146:6; Acts 4:24; 17:24; Rev 14:7 14:16 [a]Lit *Who in the generations gone by permitted* [b]Or *Gentiles* [A]Acts 17:30 [B]Ps 81:12; Mic 4:5 14:17 [a]Lit *filling* [A]Acts 17:26f; Rom 1:19f [B]Deut 11:14; Job 5:10; Ps 65:10f; Ezek 34:26f; Joel 2:23 14:19 [A]Acts 13:45, 50; 14:2, 4, 5; 1 Thess 2:14ff [B]Acts 13:14; 14:21, 26 [C]Acts 13:51; 14:1, 21 [D]Acts 14:5; 2 Cor 11:25; 2 Tim 3:11 14:20 [A]Acts 11:26; 14:22, 28 [B]Acts 14:6 14:21 [A]Acts 14:7 [B]Acts 2:47 [C]Acts 14:6 [D]Acts 13:51; 14:1, 19 [E]Acts 13:14; 14:19, 26 14:22 [A]Acts 11:26; 14:28 [B]Acts 6:7 [C]Mark 10:30; John 15:18, 20; 16:33; Acts 9:16; 1 Thess 3:3; 2 Tim 3:12; 1 Pet 2:21; Rev 1:9 14:23 [A]2 Cor 8:19; Titus 1:5 [B]Acts 11:30 [C]Acts 1:24; 13:3 [D]Acts 20:32 14:24 [A]Acts 13:14 [B]Acts 13:13 14:25 [A]Acts 13:13 14:26 [a]Lit *fulfilled* [A]Acts 11:19 [B]Acts 13:3 [C]Acts 11:23; 15:40 14:27 [a]Lit *that* [A]Acts 15:3, 4, 12; 21:19 [B]1 Cor 16:9; 2 Cor 2:12; Col 4:3; Rev 3:8 14:28 [a]Lit *not a little* [A]Acts 11:26; 14:22 15:1 [A]Acts 15:24 [B]Acts 1:15; 15:3, 22, 32 [C]Lev 12:3; Acts 15:5; 1 Cor 7:18; Gal 2:11, 14; 5:2f [D]Acts 6:14 15:2 [a]Lit *not a little* [A]Acts 15:7 [B]Gal 2:2 [C]Acts 11:30; 15:4, 6, 22, 23; 16:4 15:3 [A]Acts 20:38; 21:5; Rom 15:24; 1 Cor 16:6, 11; 2 Cor 1:16; Titus 3:13; 3 John 6 [B]Acts 11:19 [C]Acts 14:27; 15:4, 12 [D]Acts 1:15; 15:22, 32 15:4 [A]Acts 11:30; 15:6, 22, 23; 16:4 [B]Acts 14:27; 15:12 15:5 [A]Acts 5:17; 24:5, 14; 26:5; 28:22 [B]Matt 3:7; Acts 26:5 [C]1 Cor 7:18; Gal 2:11, 14; 5:2f

14:13 priest of Zeus. It was his job to lead the people in worship of the two men they believed to be gods.

14:14 tore their robes. A Jewish expression of horror and revulsion at blasphemy (*see note on Mt 26:65*).

14:15–17 *See note on 17:23, 24.* Because the crowd at Lystra was pagan and had no knowledge of the OT, Paul adjusted his message to fit the audience. Instead of proclaiming the God of Abraham, Isaac, and Jacob, he appealed to the universal and rational knowledge of the One who created the world (cf. 17:22–26; Jon 1:9).

14:15 vain things. An appropriate description of idolatry and all false religions.

14:16 permitted all the nations. The path that they all have walked is described in Ro 1:18–32.

14:17 did not leave Himself without witness. God's providence and His creative power testify to man's reason of His existence (Ro 1:18–20), as does man's own conscience, which contains His moral law (Ro 2:13–15).

14:19 they stoned Paul ... supposing him to be dead. Paul did not die from the stoning as some claim, who link it to his third-heaven experience in 2Co 12. "Supposing" usually means "to suppose something that is not true." The main NT use of this word argues that the crowd's supposition was incorrect and that Paul was not dead. Another argument in favor of this position is that if Paul was resurrected, why didn't Luke mention it? Also, the dates of Paul's third-heaven experience and the time of the stoning do not reconcile.

14:20 Derbe. *See note on v. 6.*

14:22 kingdom of God. *See note on 1:3.*

14:23 appointed elders. *See note on 11:30.*

14:24 Pisidia. A mountainous and rugged region that offered no opportunities for evangelism. **Pamphylia.** *See note on 13:13.*

14:25 Perga. *See note on 13:13.*

14:26 From there. Thus ended Paul's first missionary journey. **Antioch.** *See note on 11:19.*

14:28 a long time. About one year.

15:1–30 Throughout its history, the church's leaders have met to settle doctrinal issues. Historians point to 7 ecumenical councils in the church's early history, especially the Councils of Nicea (A.D. 325) and Chalcedon (A.D. 451). Yet the most important council was the first one—the Jerusalem Council—because it established the answer to the most vital doctrinal question of all: "What must a person do to be saved?" The apostles and elders defied efforts to impose legalism and ritualism as necessary prerequisites for salvation. They forever affirmed that salvation is totally by grace through faith in Christ alone.

15:1 Some men. Judaizers—false teachers who were self-appointed guardians of legalism, teaching a doctrine of salvation by works. **from Judea.** *See note on 1:8.* **Unless you are circumcised ... you cannot be saved.** Cf. v. 24. The heresy propagated by the Judaizers. *See notes on Ge 17:9–14.*

15:2 up to Jerusalem. *See note on 18:22.* **elders.** Leaders of the Jerusalem church (*see note on 11:30*).

15:4 Paul and Barnabas and others went into great detail to report the many works God was accomplishing through their efforts. No doubt they provided sufficient evidence to verify the genuineness of the Gentiles' salvation (cf. 10:44–48; 11:17, 18).

6[A]The apostles and the elders came together to [a]look
into this [b]matter. 7After there had been much [A]debate,
Peter stood up and said to them, "Brethren, you know
that [a]in the early days [B]God made a choice among you,
that by my mouth the Gentiles would hear the word
of [C]the gospel and believe. 8And God, [A]who knows the
heart, testified to them [B]giving them the Holy Spirit,
just as He also did to us; 9and [A]He made no distinction
between us and them, [B]cleansing their hearts by faith.
10Now therefore why do you [A]put God to the test by
placing upon the neck of the disciples a yoke which
[B]neither our fathers nor we have been able to bear?
11But we believe that we are saved through [A]the grace
of the Lord Jesus, in the same way as they also are."
12All the people kept silent, and they were listening to Barnabas and Paul as they were [A]relating
what [B]signs and wonders God had done through
them among the Gentiles.

JAMES'S JUDGMENT

13After they had stopped speaking, [a,A]James answered, saying, "Brethren, listen to me. 14[A]Simeon
has related how God first concerned Himself about
taking from among the Gentiles a people for His
name. 15With this the words of [A]the Prophets agree,
just as it is written,

16 '[A]After these things [B]I will return,
And I will rebuild the [a]tabernacle
of David which has fallen,
And I will rebuild its ruins,
And I will restore it,
17 [A]So that the rest of [a]mankind
may seek the Lord,
And all the Gentiles [b,B]who
are called by My name,'
18 [A]Says the Lord, who [a,B]makes these
things known from long ago.

19Therefore it is [A]my judgment that we do not trouble those who are turning to God from among the
Gentiles, 20but that we write to them that they abstain from [a,A]things contaminated by idols and from
[B]fornication and from [C]what is strangled and from
blood. 21For [A]Moses from ancient generations has in
every city those who preach him, since [a]he is read
in the synagogues every Sabbath."
22Then it seemed good to [A]the apostles and the
elders, with the whole church, to choose men from
among them to send to [B]Antioch with Paul and
Barnabas—Judas called Barsabbas, and [C]Silas, leading men among [D]the brethren, 23and they [a]sent this
letter by them,

"[A]The apostles and the brethren who are
elders, to [B]the brethren in [C]Antioch and
[D]Syria and [E]Cilicia who are from the Gentiles,
[F]greetings. 24Since we have heard that
[A]some [a]of our number to whom we gave no
instruction have [B]disturbed you with *their*

15:6 [a]Lit *see about* [b]Lit *word* [A]Acts 11:30; 15:4, 22, 23; 16:4 15:7 [a]Lit *from days of old* [A]Acts 15:2 [B]Acts 10:19f [C]Acts 20:24 15:8 [A]Acts 1:24 [B]Acts 2:4; 10:44, 47 15:9 [A]Acts 10:28, 34; 11:12 [B]Acts 10:43 15:10 [A]Acts 5:9 [B]Matt 23:4; Gal 5:1 15:11 [A]Rom 3:24; 5:15; 2 Cor 13:14; Eph 2:5-8 15:12 [A]Acts 14:27; 15:3, 4 [B]John 4:48 15:13 [a]Or *Jacob* [A]Acts 12:17 15:14 [A]Acts 15:7; 2 Pet 1:1 15:15 [A]Acts 13:40 15:16 [a]Or *tent* [A]Amos 9:11 [B]Jer 12:15 15:17 [a]Gr *anthropoi* [b]Lit *upon whom My name is called* [A]Amos 9:12 [B]Deut 28:10; Is 63:19; Jer 14:9; Dan 9:19; James 2:7 15:18 [a]Or *does these things* which were *known* [A]Amos 9:12 [B]Is 45:21 15:19 [A]Acts 15:28; 21:25 15:20 [a]Lit *the pollutions of* [A]Ex 34:15-17; Dan 1:8; Acts 15:29; 1 Cor 8:7, 13; 10:7f, 14-28; Rev 2:14, 20 [B]Lev 18:6-23 [C]Gen 9:4; Lev 3:17; 7:26; 17:10, 14; 19:26; Deut 12:16, 23; 15:23; 1 Sam 14:33 15:21 [a]I.e. the books of Moses, Gen through Deut [A]Acts 13:15; 2 Cor 3:14f 15:22 [A]Acts 15:2 [B]Acts 11:20 [C]Acts 15:27, 32, 40; 16:19, 25, 29; 17:4, 10, 14f; 18:5; 2 Cor 1:19; 1 Thess 1:1; 2 Thess 1:1; 1 Pet 5:12 [D]Acts 15:1 15:23 [a]Lit *wrote by their hand* [A]Acts 15:2 [B]Acts 15:1 [C]Acts 11:20 [D]Matt 4:24; Acts 15:41; Gal 1:21 [E]Acts 6:9 [F]Acts 23:26; James 1:1; 2 John 10f 15:24 [a]Lit *from us* [A]Acts 15:1 [B]Gal 1:7; 5:10

15:7 Peter stood up. Peter gave the first of 3 speeches at the Council that amount to one of the strongest defenses of salvation by grace through faith alone contained in Scripture. Peter began his defense by reviewing how God saved Gentiles in the early days of the church without a requirement of circumcision, law keeping, or ritual—referring to the salvation of Cornelius and his household (10:44–48; 11:17, 18). If God did not require any additional qualifications for salvation, neither should the legalists. **by my mouth.** See 10:1–48.

15:8 giving them the Holy Spirit. The Judaizers could have argued that Cornelius and the others could not have been saved because they did not meet the legalistic requirements. To thwart that potential argument, Peter reiterates that God gave them the Holy Spirit, thus proving the genuineness of their salvation (*see note on 2:4*).

15:10 a yoke. A description of the law and the legalism of the scribes and Pharisees (Mt 23:4; cf. Lk 11:46). The legalists expected the Gentiles to carry a load they themselves were unwilling to bear.

15:11 through the grace of the Lord Jesus. A resounding affirmation of salvation by grace through faith alone (*see notes on Ro 3:24, 25*).

15:12 Barnabas and Paul. They delivered the second speech in which they recounted the work of God on their just completed first missionary journey among Gentiles. **signs and wonders.** *See note on 2:19.*

15:13 James answered. He delivers the third speech in defense of salvation by faith alone by relating how God's future plans for Gentile salvation agree with His current work.

15:14 people for His name. *See notes on chaps. 10, 11.* Cf. Mal 2:2, 5; 3Jn 7.

15:15–17 James quotes Amos' prophecy (9:11, 12) of the millennial kingdom to prove that Gentile salvation was not contrary to God's plan for Israel. In fact, in the kingdom God's messengers will announce salvation to the Gentiles (Zec 8:20–23).

15:17 Gentiles ... called by My name. James' point is that Amos makes no mention of Gentiles becoming Jewish proselytes. If Gentiles can be saved without becoming Jews in the kingdom, there is no need for Gentiles to become proselytes in the present age.

15:19 we do not trouble. The Gr. word for "trouble" means "to throw something in the path of someone to annoy them." The decision of the Jerusalem Council, after considering all the evidence, was that keeping the law and observing rituals were not requirements for salvation. The Judaizers were to cease troubling and annoying the Gentiles.

15:20 James and the other leaders did not want the Gentiles to revel in their freedom in Christ, which could cause the Jewish believers to follow that same liberty and violate their consciences. So James proposed that the Gentiles abstain from 4 pagan, idolatrous practices that were violations of the law of Moses so as not to offend Jews. **things contaminated by idols.** Food offered to pagan gods and then sold in temple butcher shops. Because idolatry was so repulsive to Jews and forbidden by God (cf. Ex 20:3; 34:17; Dt 5:7), they would avoid anything to do with idols, including meat offered to idols (cf. 1Co 8:1–13). **fornication.** Sexual sins in general, but particularly the orgies associated with the worship of pagan gods. The Gentiles were to avoid being offensive to Jewish sensibilities in their marriages and any relationship with the opposite sex. **what is strangled and from blood.** Dietary restrictions (Ge 9:4; Lv 3:17; 7:26; 17:12–14; 19:26; Dt 12:16, 23; 15:23; 1Sa 14:34; Eze 33:25).

15:22 Judas. Nothing more is known about him except that he was a prophet (v. 32). **Silas.** *See note on v. 40.* Also known as Silvanus, he accompanied Paul on his second missionary journey (v. 40; 16:19, 25, 29; 17:4, 10, 14, 15; 18:5) and later was Peter's amanuensis (scribe) for his first epistle (1Pe 5:12).

15:23 in Antioch and Syria and Cilicia. Antioch was the capital of Syria and Cilicia, which was administered as a single Roman district. The churches in Cilicia were probably founded by Paul when he went there after fleeing Jerusalem (9:30).

15:24 disturbed ... unsettling. "Disturbed"

words, unsettling your souls, 25 [A]it seemed good to us, having [a]become of one mind, to select men to send to you with our beloved Barnabas and Paul, 26 men who have [a,A]risked their lives for the name of our Lord Jesus Christ. 27 Therefore we have sent [A]Judas and [B]Silas, who themselves will also report the same things by word *of mouth.* 28 For [A]it seemed good to [B]the Holy Spirit and to [C]us to lay upon you no greater burden than these essentials: 29 that you abstain from [A]things sacrificed to idols and from [A]blood and from [A]things strangled and from [A]fornication; [a]if you keep yourselves free from such things, you will do well. Farewell."

30 So when they were sent away, [A]they went down to Antioch; and having gathered the [a]congregation together, they delivered the letter. 31 When they had read it, they rejoiced because of its [a]encouragement. 32 [A]Judas and [B]Silas, also being [C]prophets themselves, [a]encouraged and strengthened [D]the brethren with a lengthy message. 33 After they had spent time *there,* they were sent away from the brethren [A]in peace to those who had [B]sent them out. 34 [[a]But it seemed good to Silas to remain there.] 35 But [A]Paul and Barnabas stayed in Antioch, teaching and [B]preaching with many others also, [C]the word of the Lord.

SECOND MISSIONARY JOURNEY

36 After some days Paul said to Barnabas, "Let us return and visit the brethren in [A]every city in which we proclaimed [B]the word of the Lord, *and see* how they are." 37 Barnabas wanted to take [A]John, called Mark, along with them also. 38 But Paul kept insisting that they should not take him along who had [A]deserted them [a]in Pamphylia and had not gone with them to the work. 39 And there occurred such a sharp disagreement that they separated from one another, and Barnabas took [A]Mark with him and sailed away to [B]Cyprus. 40 But Paul chose [A]Silas and left, being [B]committed by the brethren to the grace of the Lord. 41 And he was traveling through [A]Syria and [B]Cilicia, strengthening the churches.

THE MACEDONIAN VISION

16 Paul came also to [A]Derbe and to [A]Lystra. And a disciple was there, named [B]Timothy, the son of a [C]Jewish woman who was a believer, but his father was a Greek, 2 and he was well spoken of by [A]the brethren who were in [B]Lystra and [C]Iconium. 3 Paul wanted this man to [a]go with him; and he [A]took him and circumcised him because of the Jews who were in those parts, for they all knew that his father was a Greek. 4 Now while they were passing through the cities, they were delivering [A]the decrees which had been decided upon by [B]the apostles and [C]elders who were in Jerusalem, for them to observe. 5 So [A]the churches were being strengthened [a]in the faith, and were [B]increasing in number daily.

6 They passed through the [a,A]Phrygian and [B]Galatian region, having been forbidden by the Holy Spirit to speak the word in [b,C]Asia; 7 and after they came to [A]Mysia, they were trying to go into [B]Bithynia, and the [C]Spirit of Jesus did not permit them; 8 and passing by [A]Mysia, they came down to [B]Troas.

15:25 [a]Or *met together* [A]Acts 15:28 15:26 [a]Lit *given over* [A]Acts 9:23ff; 14:19 15:27 [A]Acts 15:22, 32 [B]Acts 15:22 15:28 [A]Acts 15:25 [B]Acts 5:32; 15:8 [C]Acts 15:19, 25 15:29 [a]Lit *from which keeping yourselves free* [A]Acts 15:20 15:30 [a]Or *multitude* [A]Acts 15:22f 15:31 [a]Or *exhortation* 15:32 [a]Or *exhorted* [A]Acts 15:22, 27 [B]Acts 15:22 [C]Acts 13:1 [D]Acts 15:1 15:33 [A]Mark 5:34; Acts 16:36; 1 Cor 16:11; Heb 11:31 [B]Acts 15:22 15:34 [a]Early mss do not contain this v 15:35 [A]Acts 12:25 [B]Acts 8:4 [C]Acts 13:12 15:36 [A]Acts 13:4, 13, 14, 51; 14:6, 24f [B]Acts 13:12 15:37 [A]Acts 12:12 15:38 [a]Lit *from* [A]Acts 13:13 15:39 [A]Acts 12:12; 15:37; Col 4:10 [B]Acts 4:36 15:40 [A]Acts 15:22 [B]Acts 11:23; 14:26 15:41 [A]Matt 4:24; Acts 15:23 [B]Acts 6:9 16:1 [A]Acts 14:6 [B]Acts 17:14f; 18:5; 19:22; 20:4; Rom 16:21; 1 Cor 4:17; 16:10; 2 Cor 1:1, 19; Phil 1:1; 2:19; Col 1:1; 1 Thess 1:1; 3:2, 6; 2 Thess 1:1; 1 Tim 1:2, 18; 6:20; 2 Tim 1:2; Philem 1; Heb 13:23 [C]2 Tim 1:5; 3:15 16:2 [A]Acts 16:40 [B]Acts 14:6 [C]Acts 13:51 16:3 [a]Lit *go out* [A]Gal 2:3 16:4 [A]Acts 15:28f [B]Acts 15:2 [C]Acts 11:30 16:5 [a]Or *in faith* [A]Acts 9:31 [B]Acts 2:47 16:6 [a]Or *Phrygia and the Galatian region* [b]I.e. west coast province of Asia Minor [A]Acts 2:10; 18:23 [B]Acts 18:23; 1 Cor 16:1; Gal 1:2; 3:1; 2 Tim 4:10; 1 Pet 1:1 [C]Acts 2:9 16:7 [A]Acts 16:8 [B]1 Pet 1:1 [C]Luke 24:49; Acts 8:29; Rom 8:9; Gal 4:6; Phil 1:19; 1 Pet 1:11 16:8 [A]Acts 16:7 [B]Acts 16:11; 20:5f; 2 Cor 2:12; 2 Tim 4:13

is a different Gr. word from the one in v. 19, meaning "to deeply upset," "to deeply trouble," "to perplex," or "to create fear." The Gr. word for "unsettling" was used in extrabiblical writings to speak of someone going bankrupt. Together these words aptly describe the chaos caused by the Judaizers.

15:26 risked their lives. On the first missionary journey they faced persecution (13:50) and Paul was nearly killed (14:19, 20).

15:29 *See notes on v. 20.*

15:34 This verse is not in the best manuscripts.

15:36 ***see* how they are.** In addition to proclaiming the gospel, Paul also recognized his responsibility to mature the new believers in their faith (Mt 28:19, 20; Eph 4:12, 13; Php 1:8; Col 1:28; 1Th 2:17). So he planned his second missionary journey to retrace his first one.

15:37, 38 John, called Mark. *See notes on 12:12; 13:13.*

15:39 disagreement ... separated. This was not an amicable parting—they were in sharp disagreement regarding John Mark. The weight of the evidence favors Paul's decision, especially since he was an apostle of Jesus Christ. That alone should have caused Barnabas to submit to his authority. But they eventually did reconcile (1Co 9:6). **Cyprus.** *See note on 13:4.*

15:40 Silas. He was perfectly suited to be Paul's companion, since he was a prophet and could proclaim and teach the Word. Being a Jew gave him access to the synagogues (*see note on 6:9*). Because he was a Roman citizen (16:37), he enjoyed the same benefits and protection as Paul. His status as a respected leader in the Jerusalem fellowship helped to reinforce Paul's teaching that Gentile salvation was by grace alone through faith alone (*see note on v. 22*).

15:41 Syria and Cilicia. Paul visited congregations he had most likely founded before his connection with the Antioch church (Gal 1:21). The circumcision question had been raised there also.

16:1 to Derbe and to Lystra. *See note on 14:6.* **a disciple ... Timothy.** A young man (late teens or early 20s) of high regard, a "true child in the faith" (1Ti 1:2; cf. 2Ti 1:2), who eventually became Paul's right-hand man (1Co 4:17; 1Th 3:2; Php 2:19; see Introduction to 1 Timothy). In essence, he became John Mark's replacement. After being commissioned by the elders of the local church (1Ti 4:14; 2Ti 1:6), he joined Paul and Silas. **his father was a Greek.** The grammar likely suggests his father was dead. By being both Jew and Gentile, Timothy had access to both cultures—an indispensable asset for missionary service.

16:3 circumcised him. This was done to aid his acceptance by the Jews and provide full access to the synagogues (*see note on 6:9*) he would be visiting with Paul and Silas. If Timothy had not been circumcised, the Jews could have assumed he had renounced his Jewish heritage and had chosen to live as a Gentile.

16:4 the decrees. The determinations of the Jerusalem Council (*see notes on 15:23–29*).

16:6 Holy Spirit ... Asia. Paul was not allowed to fulfill his intention to minister in Asia Minor (modern Turkey) and to such cities as Ephesus, Smyrna, Philadelphia, Laodicea, Colosse, Sardis, Pergamos, and Thyatira.

16:7 Bithynia. A separate Roman province NE of Mysia. **the Spirit of Jesus did not permit them.** Once the Holy Spirit had providentially stopped their travel N, they had nowhere else to go but Troas, a seaport on the Aegean Sea.

16:8 Mysia ... Troas. The NW part of the province of Asia Minor.

9 [A]A vision appeared to Paul in the night: a man of
[B]Macedonia was standing and appealing to him,
and saying, "Come over to Macedonia and help us."
10 When he had seen [A]the vision, immediately [B]we
sought to [a]go into Macedonia, concluding that God
had called us to [C]preach the gospel to them.
11 So putting out to sea from [A]Troas, we ran [B]a
straight course to Samothrace, and on the day following to Neapolis; 12 and from there to [A]Philippi,
which is a leading city of the district of [B]Macedonia,
[C]a *Roman* colony; and we were staying in this city
for some days. 13 And on [A]the Sabbath day we went
outside the gate to a riverside, where we were supposing that there would be a place of prayer; and
we sat down and began speaking to the women
who had assembled.

FIRST CONVERT IN EUROPE

14 A woman named Lydia, from the city of [A]Thya-
tira, a seller of purple fabrics, [B]a worshiper of God,
was listening; [a]and the Lord [C]opened her heart to
respond to the things spoken by Paul. 15 And when
she and [A]her household had been baptized, she
urged us, saying, "If you have judged me to be faithful to the Lord, come into my house and stay." And
she prevailed upon us.
16 It happened that as we were going to [A]the place
of prayer, a slave-girl having [B]a spirit of divination
met us, who was bringing her masters much
profit by fortune-telling. 17 Following after Paul
and us, she kept crying out, saying, "These men
are bond-servants of [A]the Most High God, who are
proclaiming to you [a]the way of salvation." 18 She
continued doing this for many days. But Paul was
greatly annoyed, and turned and said to the spirit,
"I command you [A]in the name of Jesus Christ to
come out of her!" And it came out at that very
[a]moment.
19 But when her masters saw that their hope of
[A]profit was [a]gone, they seized [B]Paul and Silas and
[C]dragged them into the market place before the
authorities, 20 and when they had brought them
to the chief magistrates, they said, "These men are
throwing our city into confusion, being Jews, 21 and
[A]are proclaiming customs which it is not lawful for
us to accept or to observe, being [B]Romans."

PAUL AND SILAS IMPRISONED

22 The crowd rose up together against them, and
the chief magistrates tore their [a]robes off them and
proceeded to order [b]*them* to be [A]beaten with rods.
23 When they had struck them with many blows, they
threw them into prison, commanding [A]the jailer to
guard them securely; 24 [a]and he, having received
such a command, threw them into the inner prison
and fastened their feet in [A]the [b]stocks.

16:9 [A]Acts 9:10 [B]Acts 16:10, 12; 18:5; 19:21f, 29; 20:1, 3; 27:2; Rom 15:26 16:10 [a]Lit *go out* [A]Acts 9:10 [B][we] Acts 16:10-17; 20:5-15; 21:1-18; 27:1-28:16 [C]Acts 14:7 16:11 [A]Acts 16:8; 20:5f; 2 Cor 2:12; 2 Tim 4:13 [B]Acts 21:1 16:12 [A]Acts 20:6; Phil 1:1; 1 Thess 2:2 [B]Acts 16:9, 10; 18:5; 19:21f, 29; 20:1, 3; 27:2; Rom 15:26 [C]Acts 16:21 16:13 [A]Acts 13:14 16:14 [a]Lit *whose heart the Lord opened* [A]Rev 1:11; 2:18, 24 [B]Acts 13:43; 18:7 [C]Luke 24:45 16:15 [A]Acts 11:14 16:16 [A]Acts 16:13 [B]Lev 19:31; 20:6, 27; Deut 18:11; 1 Sam 28:3, 7; 2 Kin 21:6; 1 Chr 10:13; Is 8:19 16:17 [a]Lit *a way* [A]Mark 5:7 16:18 [a]Lit *hour* [A]Mark 16:17 16:19 [a]Lit *gone out* [A]Acts 16:16; 19:25f [B]Acts 15:22, 40; 16:25, 29 [C]Acts 8:3; 17:6f; 21:30; James 2:6 16:21 [A]Esth 3:8 [B]Acts 16:12 16:22 [a]Or *outer garments* [b]Lit *to beat with rods* [A]2 Cor 11:25; 1 Thess 2:2 16:23 [A]Acts 16:27, 36 16:24 [a]Lit *who* [b]Lit *wood* [A]Job 13:27; 33:11; Jer 20:2f; 29:26

16:9, 10 This was the second of 6 visions received by the apostle (cf. 9:3–6; 18:9, 10; 22:17, 18; 23:11; 27:23, 24).

16:9 Macedonia. The region located across the Aegean Sea on the mainland of Greece. The cities of Philippi and Thessalonica were located there. Most significantly, going there was to take the gospel from Asia into Europe.

16:10 we. A change from the third person pronoun to the first person indicates that Luke joined up with Paul, Silas, and Timothy (see Introduction: Author and Date).

16:11 Samothrace. An island in the Aegean Sea about halfway between Asia Minor and the Greek mainland. They stayed there overnight to avoid the hazards associated with sailing in the dark. **Neapolis.** The port city for Philippi.

16:12 Philippi. See Introduction to Philippians. Located 10 mi. inland from Neapolis, Philippi was named for Philip II of Macedon (the father of Alexander the Great). **a *Roman* colony.** Philippi became a Roman colony in 31 B.C., so it carried the right of freedom (it was self-governing and independent of the provincial government), the right of exemption from tax, and the right of holding land in full ownership.

16:13 to a riverside. Evidently, the Jewish community did not have the minimum of 10 Jewish men who were heads of households required to form a synagogue. In such cases, a place of prayer under the open sky and near a river or sea was adopted as a meeting place. Most likely this spot was located where the road leading out of the city crossed the Gangites River. **women who had assembled.** In further evidence of the small number of Jewish men, it was women who met to pray, worship, and recite from the OT Scriptures.

16:14 Lydia, from the city of Thyatira. Her home city was located in the Roman province of Lydia, thus the name "Lydia" was probably associated with her place of origin. **seller of purple fabrics.** Because purple dye was extremely expensive, purple garments were usually worn by royalty and the wealthy. As a result, Lydia's business turned a nice profit, which enabled her to have a house large enough to accommodate the missionary team (v. 15) and the new church at Philippi (v. 40). **a worshiper of God.** Like Cornelius, she believed in the God of Israel but had not become a full proselyte (cf. 10:2). **the Lord opened her heart.** This is another proof of the sovereignty of God in salvation (*see note on 13:48*).

16:15 household. *See note on 11:14.* Cf. v. 31.

16:16 a spirit of divination. Lit. "a python spirit." That expression comes from Gr. mythology; Python was a snake that guarded the oracle at Delphi. Essentially, this girl was a medium in contact with demons who could supposedly predict the future. *See note on Dt 18:9–12.*

16:17 the Most High God. El Elyon, the Absolutely Sovereign God, is an OT title (used about 50 times) for the God of Israel (see Ge 14:18–22; Ps 78:35; Da 5:18).

16:18 I command you in the name of Jesus Christ. The demon left the girl in obedience to Paul's command and his apostolic authority. The ability to cast out demons was a special ability of Christ's apostles (Mk 3:15; 2Co 12:12).

16:20 throwing our city into confusion, being Jews. Anti-Semitism was alive even then. The Emperor Claudius issued an order around that time expelling the Jews from Rome (18:2). This may explain why they apprehended only Paul and Silas, since Luke was a Gentile and Timothy half-Gentile.

16:21 proclaiming customs … not lawful for us … Romans. It was technically true that Roman citizens were not to engage in any foreign religion that had not been sanctioned by the state. But it was a false charge that they were creating chaos.

16:22 magistrates. Every Roman colony had two of these men serving as judges. In this case, they did not uphold Roman justice: they did not investigate the charges, conduct a proper hearing, or give Paul and Silas the chance to defend themselves. **beaten.** This was an illegal punishment since they had not been convicted of any crime. The officers (v. 35) under the command of the magistrates administered the beating with rods tied together in a bundle. Paul received the same punishment on two other occasions (2Co 11:25).

16:24 inner prison … in the stocks. The most secure part of the prison. The jailer took further precautions by putting their feet "in the stocks." This particular security measure was designed to produce painful cramping so the prisoner's legs were spread as far apart as possible.

25 But about midnight [A]Paul and Silas were praying and [B]singing hymns of praise to God, and the
prisoners were listening to them; 26 and suddenly
[A]there came a great earthquake, so that the foundations of the prison house were shaken; and immediately [B]all the doors were opened and everyone's
[C]chains were unfastened. 27 When [A]the jailer awoke
and saw the prison doors opened, he drew his sword
and was about [B]to kill himself, supposing that the
prisoners had escaped. 28 But Paul cried out with a
loud voice, saying, "Do not harm yourself, for we are
all here!" 29 And he called for lights and rushed in,
and trembling with fear he fell down before [A]Paul
and Silas, 30 and after he brought them out, he said,
"Sirs, [A]what must I do to be saved?"

THE JAILER CONVERTED

31 They said, "[A]Believe in the Lord Jesus, and you
will be saved, you and [B]your household." 32 And they
spoke the word of [a]the Lord to him together with all
who were in his house. 33 And he took them [A]that
very hour of the night and washed their wounds,
and immediately he was baptized, he and all his
household. 34 And he brought them into his house
and set [a]food before them, and rejoiced [b]greatly,
having believed in God with [A]his whole household.
35 Now when day came, the chief magistrates sent
their policemen, saying, "Release those men." 36 And
[A]the jailer reported these words to Paul, *saying,* "The
chief magistrates have sent to release you. Therefore
come out now and go [B]in peace." 37 But Paul said
to them, "They have beaten us in public without
trial, [A]men who are Romans, and have thrown us
into prison; and now are they sending us away secretly? No indeed! But let them come themselves
and bring us out." 38 The policemen reported these
words to the chief magistrates. [A]They were afraid
when they heard that they were Romans, 39 and
they came and appealed to them, and when they
had brought them out, they kept begging them [A]to
leave the city. 40 They went out of the prison and
entered *the house of* [A]Lydia, and when they saw [B]the
brethren, they [a]encouraged them and departed.

PAUL AT THESSALONICA

17 Now when they had traveled through Amphipolis and Apollonia, they came to [A]Thessalonica,
where there was a synagogue of the Jews. 2 And
[A]according to Paul's custom, he went to them, and
for three [B]Sabbaths reasoned with them from [C]the
Scriptures, 3 [a]explaining and [b]giving evidence that the
[c]Christ [A]had to suffer and [B]rise again from the dead,
and *saying,* "[C]This Jesus whom I am proclaiming to
you is the [c]Christ." 4 [A]And some of them were persuaded and joined [B]Paul and Silas, [a]along with a large
number of the [C]God-fearing [D]Greeks and [b]a number
of the [E]leading women. 5 But [A]the Jews, becoming
jealous and taking along some wicked men from the
market place, formed a mob and set the city in an
uproar; and attacking the house of [B]Jason, they were
seeking to bring them out to the people. 6 When they
did not find them, they *began* [A]dragging Jason and
some brethren before the city authorities, shouting,
"These men who have upset [a,B]the world have come

16:25 [A]Acts 16:19 [B]Eph 5:19 16:26 [A]Acts 4:31 [B]Acts 12:10 [C]Acts 12:7 16:27 [A]Acts 16:23, 36 [B]Acts 12:19 16:29 [A]Acts 16:19 16:30 [A]Acts 2:37; 22:10 16:31 [A]Mark 16:16 [B]Acts 11:14; 16:15 16:32 [a]Two early mss read *God* 16:33 [A]Acts 16:25 16:34 [a]Lit *a table* [b]Or *greatly with his whole household, having believed in God* [A]Acts 11:14; 16:15 16:36 [A]Acts 16:27 [B]Acts 15:33 16:37 [A]Acts 22:25-29 16:38 [A]Acts 22:29 16:39 [A]Matt 8:34 16:40 [a]Or *exhorted* [A]Acts 16:14 [B]Acts 1:15; 16:2 17:1 [A]Acts 17:11, 13; 20:4; 27:2; Phil 4:16; 1 Thess 1:1; 2 Thess 1:1; 2 Tim 4:10 17:2 [A]Acts 9:20; 17:10, 17 [B]Acts 13:14 [C]Acts 8:35 17:3 [a]Lit *opening* [b]Lit *placing before* [c]I.e. Messiah [A]Acts 3:18 [B]John 20:9 [C]Acts 9:22; 18:5, 28 17:4 [a]Lit *and a large* [b]Lit *not a few* [A]Acts 14:4 [B]Acts 15:22, 40; 17:10, 14f [C]Acts 13:43; 17:17 [D]John 7:35 [E]Acts 13:50 17:5 [A]Acts 17:13; 1 Thess 2:14ff [B]Acts 17:6, 7, 9; Rom 16:21 17:6 [a]Lit *the inhabited earth* [A]Acts 16:19f [B]Matt 24:14; Acts 17:31

16:27 prison doors opened … about to kill himself. Instead of waiting to face humiliation and a painful execution. A Roman soldier who let a prisoner escape paid for his negligence with his life (12:19; 27:42).

16:31 Believe in the Lord Jesus. One must believe He is who He claimed to be (Jn 20:31) and believe in what He did (1Co 15:3, 4; *see note on Ro 1:16*). **you and your household.** All of his family, servants, and guests who could comprehend the gospel and believe heard the gospel and believed (*see note on 11:14*). This does not include infants. Cf. v. 15.

16:37 Romans. To inflict corporal punishment on a Roman citizen was a serious crime, and made more so since Paul and Silas did not receive a trial. As a result, the magistrates faced the possibility of being removed from office, and having Philippi's privileges as a Roman colony revoked (*see note on v. 12*).

17:1 Amphipolis and Apollonia … Thessalonica. SW from Philippi along the Egnatian Way. "Amphipolis" was about 30 mi. from Philippi, and "Apollonia" another 30 mi. beyond. The narrative indicates that the travelers stopped only for the night in those cities. Forty mi. beyond "Apollonia" was "Thessalonica," the capital city of Macedonia with a population of 200,000. It was a major port city and an important commercial center. **synagogue.** *See note on 13:5.* Luke refers to a synagogue only in Thessalonica, which may explain why Paul and his companions did not stay in the other two cities.

17:2 according to Paul's custom. Paul began his ministry in each town with the Jews (*see note on 13:5*). **three Sabbaths.** The length of his initial public ministry. The actual amount of time spent in Thessalonica would have been longer, extending perhaps to 4–6 months.

17:5 the house of Jason. The mob assumed Paul, Silas, and Timothy were staying there. Nothing is known of Jason except that he was probably Jewish, since Jason was a name adopted by many of the dispersed Jews.

HYMNS AND SONGS OF THE NEW TESTAMENT

Personality	Description	Biblical Reference
Jesus and Disciples	A song in the Upper Room as they celebrated the Passover together just before the arrest of Jesus	Matthew 26:30
Mary	The Song of Mary, upon learning that she as a virgin would give birth to the Messiah	Luke 1:46–55
Zacharias	A song of joy at the circumcision of his son, who would serve as the Messiah's forerunner	Luke 1:68–79
Paul and Silas	A song of praise to God at midnight from their prison cell in Philippi	Acts 16:25
All believers	The spiritual songs of thanksgiving and joy, which God wants all believers to sing	Colossians 3:16
144,000 believers	A new song of the redeemed in heaven, sung to glorify God	Revelation 14:1–3

here also; 7 [a]and Jason [A]has welcomed them, and
they all act [B]contrary to the decrees of Caesar, saying
that there is another king, Jesus." 8 They stirred up
the crowd and the city authorities who heard these
things. 9 And when they had received a [a]pledge from
[A]Jason and the others, they released them.

PAUL AT BEREA

10 [A]The brethren immediately sent [B]Paul and Silas away by night to [C]Berea, [a]and when they arrived, they went into [D]the synagogue of the Jews.
11 Now these were more noble-minded than those
in [A]Thessalonica, [a]for they received the word with
[b]great eagerness, examining the Scriptures daily
to see whether these things were so. 12 Therefore
[A]many of them believed, [a]along with a number of
[B]prominent Greek [C]women and men. 13 But when
the Jews of [A]Thessalonica found out that the word
of God had been proclaimed by Paul in [B]Berea also,
they came there as well, agitating and stirring up
the crowds. 14 Then immediately [A]the brethren sent
Paul out to go as far as the sea; and [B]Silas and [C]Tim-
othy remained there. 15 Now [A]those who escorted
Paul brought him as far as [B]Athens; and receiving
a command for [C]Silas and Timothy to [D]come to him
as soon as possible, they left.

PAUL AT ATHENS

16 Now while Paul was waiting for them at [A]Ath-
ens, his spirit was being provoked within him as
he was observing the city full of idols. 17 So he was
reasoning [A]in the synagogue with the Jews and
[B]the God-fearing *Gentiles,* and in the market place
every day with those who happened to be present.
18 And also some of the Epicurean and Stoic philosophers were [a]conversing with him. Some were
saying, "What would [A]this [b]idle babbler wish to say?"
Others, "He seems to be a proclaimer of strange
deities,"—because he was preaching [B]Jesus and the
resurrection. 19 And they [A]took him and brought him
[a]to the [b,B]Areopagus, saying, "May we know what
[C]this new teaching is [c]which you are proclaiming?
20 For you are bringing some strange things to our
ears; so we want to know what these things mean."
21 (Now all the Athenians and the strangers [A]visiting
there used to spend their time in nothing other than
telling or hearing something new.)

SERMON ON MARS HILL

22 So Paul stood in the midst of the [a]Areopagus
and said, "Men of [A]Athens, I observe that you are
very [B]religious in all respects. 23 For while I was
passing through and examining the [A]objects of
your worship, I also found an altar with this inscription,

'TO AN UNKNOWN GOD.'

Therefore what [B]you worship in ignorance, this I
proclaim to you. 24 [A]The God who made the world
and all things in it, since He is [B]Lord of heaven and
earth, does not [C]dwell in temples made with hands;
25 nor is He served by human hands, [A]as though
He needed anything, since He Himself gives to all
people life and breath and all things; 26 and [A]He
made from one *man* every nation of mankind to
live on all the face of the earth, having [B]determined
their appointed times and the boundaries of their

17:7 [a]Lit *whom Jason has welcomed* [A]Luke 10:38; James 2:25 [B]Luke 23:2 17:9 [a]Or *bond* [A]Acts 17:5 17:10 [a]Lit *who when...arrived went* [A]Acts 1:15; 17:6, 14f [B]Acts 17:4 [C]Acts 17:13; 20:4 [D]Acts 17:1f 17:11 [a]Lit *who received* [b]Lit *all* [A]Acts 17:1 17:12 [a]Lit *and not a few* [A]Acts 2:47 [B]Mark 15:43 [C]Acts 13:50 17:13 [A]Acts 17:1 [B]Acts 17:10; 20:4 17:14 [A]Acts 1:15; 17:6, 10 [B]Acts 15:22; 17:4, 10 [C]Acts 16:1 17:15 [A]Acts 15:3 [B]Acts 17:16, 21f; 18:1; 1 Thess 3:1 [C]Acts 17:14 [D]Acts 18:5 17:16 [A]Acts 17:15, 21f; 18:1; 1 Thess 3:1 17:17 [A]Acts 9:20; 17:2 [B]Acts 17:4 17:18 [a]Or *disputing* [b]I.e. one who makes his living by picking up scraps [A]1 Cor 1:20; 4:10 [B]Acts 4:2; 17:31f 17:19 [a]Or *before* [b]Or *Hill of Ares,* god of war [c]Lit *which is being spoken by you* [A]Acts 23:19 [B]Acts 17:22 [C]Mark 1:27 17:21 [A]Acts 2:10 17:22 [a]Or *the Council of the Areopagus* [A]Acts 17:15 [B]Acts 25:19 17:23 [A]2 Thess 2:4 [B]John 4:22 17:24 [A]Is 42:5; Acts 14:15 [B]Deut 10:14; Ps 115:16; Matt 11:25 [C]1 Kin 8:27; Acts 7:48 17:25 [A]Job 22:2; Ps 50:10-12 17:26 [A]Mal 2:10 [B]Deut 32:8; Job 12:23

17:7 contrary to the decrees of Caesar. One of the most serious crimes in the Roman Empire was to acknowledge allegiance to any king but Caesar (cf. Jn 19:15).

17:9 received a pledge. A bond, which would be forfeited by Jason should Paul and his companions cause more trouble. As a result, they had no choice but to leave Thessalonica.

17:10 Berea. An important town that was not on a main route. **synagogue.** *See note on 13:5.*

17:15 Athens. The cultural center of Greece. At its zenith, Athens was home to the most renowned philosophers in history, including Socrates, Plato, and Aristotle, who was arguably the most influential philosopher of all. Two other significant philosophers taught there: Epicurus, founder of Epicureanism, and Zeno, founder of Stoicism—two of the dominant philosophies in that day (*see note on v. 18*).

17:16 city full of idols. Athens was also the religious center of Greece—virtually every deity known to man could be worshiped there. Paul viewed Athens as a city of lost humanity, all doomed to a Christless eternity because of rampant pagan idolatry.

17:17 synagogue. *See note on 13:5.*

17:18 Epicurean and Stoic philosophers. Epicurean philosophy taught that the chief end of man was the avoidance of pain. Epicureans were materialists—they did not deny the existence of God, but they believed He did not become involved with the affairs of men. When a person died, they believed his body and soul disintegrated. Stoic philosophy taught self-mastery—that the goal in life was to reach a place of indifference to pleasure or pain. **babbler.** Lit. "seed picker." Some of the philosophers viewed Paul as an amateur philosopher—one who had no ideas of his own but only picked among prevailing philosophies and constructed one with no depth.

17:19 the Areopagus. A court named for the hill on which it once met. Paul was not being formally tried; only being asked to defend his teaching.

17:22 religious. Lit. "in fear of Gods."

17:23, 24 TO AN UNKNOWN GOD. The Athenians were supernaturalists—they believed in supernatural powers that intervened in the course of natural laws. They at least acknowledged the existence of someone beyond their ability to understand who had made all things. Paul thus had the opportunity to introduce them to the Creator-God who could be known (Dt 4:35; 1Ki 8:43; 1Ch 28:9; Ps 9:10; Jer 9:24; 24:7; 31:34; Jn 17:3). When evangelizing pagans, Paul started from creation, the general revelation of God (cf. 14:15–17). When evangelizing Jews, he started from the OT (vv. 10–13).

17:24 God who made the world. This teaching flatly contradicted both the Epicureans, who believed matter was eternal and therefore had no creator, and the Stoics, who as pantheists believed God was part of everything and could not have created Himself. Paul's teaching finds its support throughout Scripture (Ge 1:1; Ps 146:5, 6; Is 40:28; 45:18; Jer 10:12; 32:17; Jon 1:9; Zec 12:1; Eph 3:9; Col 1:16; Rev 4:11; 10:6).

17:26 one *man*. All men are equal in God's sight since all came from one man, Adam. This teaching was a blow to the national pride of the Greeks, who believed all non-Greeks were barbarians (*see note on Ro 1:14*). **determined *their* appointed times.** God sovereignly controls the rise and fall of nations and empires (cf. Da 2:36–45; Lk 21:24). **the boundaries of their habitation.** God is responsible for establishing nations as to their racial identity and their specific geographical locations (Dt 32:8) and determining the extent of their conquests (cf. Is 10:12–15).

habitation, 27 that they would seek God, if perhaps
they might grope for Him and find Him, [A]though
He is not far from each one of us; 28 for [A]in Him
we live and move and [a]exist, as even some of your
own poets have said, 'For we also are His children.'
29 Being then the children of God, we [A]ought not to
think that the Divine Nature is like gold or silver
or stone, an image formed by the art and thought
of man. 30 Therefore having [A]overlooked [B]the times
of ignorance, God is [C]now declaring to men that
all *people* everywhere should repent, 31 because
He has fixed [A]a day in which [B]He will judge [a,C]the
world in righteousness [b]through a Man whom He
has [D]appointed, having furnished proof to all men
[c]by [E]raising Him from the dead."

32 Now when they heard of [A]the resurrection of
the dead, some *began* to sneer, but others said, "We
shall hear you [a]again concerning this." 33 So Paul
went out of their midst. 34 But some men joined
him and believed, among whom also were Dionysius the [A]Areopagite and a woman named Damaris
and others with them.

PAUL AT CORINTH

18 After these things he left [A]Athens and went to
[B]Corinth. 2 And he found a Jew named [A]Aquila,
a native of [B]Pontus, having recently come from [C]It-
aly with his wife [A]Priscilla, because [D]Claudius had
commanded all the Jews to leave Rome. He came
to them, 3 and because he was of the same trade, he
stayed with them and [A]they were working, for by
trade they were tent-makers. 4 And he was reasoning [A]in the synagogue every [B]Sabbath and trying
to persuade [C]Jews and Greeks.

5 But when [A]Silas and Timothy [B]came down from
[C]Macedonia, Paul *began* devoting himself completely
to the word, solemnly [D]testifying to the Jews that
[E]Jesus was the [a]Christ. 6 But when they resisted and
blasphemed, he [A]shook out his garments and said
to them, "Your [B]blood *be* on your own heads! I am
clean. From now on I will go [C]to the Gentiles." 7 Then
he left there and went to the house of a man named
[a]Titius Justus, [A]a worshiper of God, whose house
was next to the synagogue. 8 [A]Crispus, [B]the leader
of the synagogue, believed in the Lord [C]with all his
household, and many of the [D]Corinthians when they
heard were believing and being baptized. 9 And the
Lord said to Paul in the night by [A]a vision, "Do not
be afraid *any longer*, but go on speaking and do
not be silent; 10 for I am with you, and no man will
attack you in order to harm you, for I have many
people in this city." 11 And he settled *there* a year and
six months, teaching the word of God among them.

12 But while Gallio was [A]proconsul of [B]Achaia,
[C]the Jews with one accord rose up against Paul
and brought him before [D]the judgment seat,

17:27 [A]Deut 4:7; Jer 23:23f; Acts 14:17 17:28 [a]Lit *are* [A]Job 12:10; Dan 5:23 17:29 [A]Is 40:18ff; Rom 1:23 17:30 [A]Acts 14:16; Rom 3:25 [B]Acts 17:23 [C]Luke 24:47; Acts 26:20; Titus 2:11f 17:31 [a]Lit *the inhabited earth* [b]Lit *by* or *in* [c]Or *when He raised* [A]Matt 10:15 [B]Ps 9:8; 96:13; 98:9; John 5:22, 27; Acts 10:42 [C]Matt 24:14; Acts 17:6 [D]Luke 22:22 [E]Acts 2:24 17:32 [a]Lit *also again* [A]Acts 17:18, 31 17:34 [A]Acts 17:19, 22 18:1 [A]Acts 17:15 [B]Acts 18:8; 19:1; 1 Cor 1:2; 2 Cor 1:1, 23; 6:11; 2 Tim 4:20 18:2 [A]Acts 18:18, 26; Rom 16:3; 1 Cor 16:19; 2 Tim 4:19 [B]Acts 2:9 [C]Acts 27:1, 6; Heb 13:24 [D]Acts 11:28 18:3 [A]Acts 20:34; 1 Cor 4:12; 9:14f; 2 Cor 11:7; 12:13; 1 Thess 2:9; 4:11; 2 Thess 3:8 18:4 [A]Acts 9:20; 18:19 [B]Acts 13:14 [C]Acts 14:1 18:5 [a]I.e. Messiah [A]Acts 15:22; 16:1; 17:14 [B]Acts 17:15 [C]Acts 16:9 [D]Luke 16:28; Acts 20:21 [E]Acts 17:3; 18:28 18:6 [A]Neh 5:13; Acts 13:51 [B]2 Sam 1:16; 1 Kin 2:33; Ezek 18:13; 33:4, 6, 8; Matt 27:25; Acts 20:26 [C]Acts 13:46 18:7 [a]One early ms reads *Titus;* two other early mss omit the name [A]Acts 13:43; 16:14 18:8 [A]1 Cor 1:14 [B]Mark 5:22 [C]Acts 11:14 [D]Acts 18:1; 19:1; 1 Cor 1:2; 2 Cor 1:1, 23; 6:11; 2 Tim 4:20 18:9 [A]Acts 9:10 18:12 [A]Acts 13:7 [B]Acts 18:27; 19:21; Rom 15:26; 1 Cor 16:15; 2 Cor 1:1; 9:2; 11:10; 1 Thess 1:7f [C]1 Thess 2:14ff [D]Matt 27:19

17:27 seek God. The Lord's objective for man in revealing Himself as the creator, ruler, and controller of the world. Men have no excuse for not knowing about God because He has revealed Himself in man's conscience and in the physical world (*see notes on Ro 1:19, 20; 2:15*).

17:28 in Him we live and move and exist. A quote from the Cretan poet Epimenides.

17:29 the children of God. A quote from Aratus, who came from Paul's home region of Cilicia. **not ... like gold or silver.** If man is the offspring of God, as the Greek poet suggested, it is foolish to think that God could be nothing more than a man-made idol. Such reasoning points out the absurdity of idolatry (cf. Is 44:9–20).

17:30 overlooked the times of ignorance. *See note on Ro 3:25.*

17:31 Man whom He has appointed. Jesus Christ (Jn 5:22–27).

17:32 resurrection of the dead. Gr. philosophy did not believe in bodily resurrection.

17:34 the Areopagite. A member of the Areopagus court (*see note on v. 19*).

18:1 Corinth. See Introduction to 1 Corinthians. The leading political and commercial center in Greece. It was located at a strategic point on the isthmus of Corinth, which connected the Peloponnesian peninsula with the rest of Greece. Virtually all traffic between northern and southern Greece had to pass through the city. Because Corinth was a trade center and host to all sorts of travelers, it had an unsettled population that was extremely debauched. It also housed the temple of Aphrodite, the goddess of love. One thousand temple priestesses, who were ritual prostitutes, came each evening into the city to practice their trade.

18:2 Aquila ... Priscilla. This husband and wife team were to become Paul's close friends who even risked their lives for him (Ro 16:3, 4). Priscilla is listed first 4 times in Scripture (NU), which could imply she had a higher social rank than Aquila or that she was the more prominent of the two in the church. They probably were Christians when Paul met them, having come from Rome where a church already existed (Ro 1:7, 8). **Claudius.** *See note on 11:28.* **commanded all the Jews to leave Rome.** The decree that forced Priscilla and Aquila to leave Rome ca. A.D. 49 (*see note on 16:20*).

18:3 tent-makers. This could also refer to leatherworkers.

18:4 synagogue. *See note on 13:5.* **Greeks.** Gentile God-fearers in the synagogue (*see note on 10:2*).

18:5 Silas and Timothy came down from Macedonia. As Paul desired, Silas and Timothy joined him in Athens (17:15). From there he sent Timothy back to Thessalonica (1Th 3:1–6). Paul evidently sent Silas somewhere in Macedonia, possibly Philippi (cf. 2Co 11:9; Php 4:15), since he returned to Corinth from that province.

18:6 Your blood *be* on your own heads! Paul held his opponents completely responsible for blaspheming Christ and rejecting his message (cf. Jos 2:19; 2Sa 1:16; 1Ki 2:37; Eze 18:13; 33:4; Mt 27:25).

18:7 house of ... Justus. A Gentile who showed interest in the God of Israel and was associated with the synagogue next door. His name indicates he was a Roman, and since Romans usually had 3 names, his may have been Gaius Titius Justus, meaning he was the same Gaius mentioned in Ro 16:23 and 1Co 1:14. **a worshiper of God.** *See note on 16:14.*

18:8 Crispus, the leader of the synagogue. The conversion of this respected leader must have sent shock waves throughout the Jewish community (*see note on 6:9*). **all his household.** *See note on 11:14.*

18:9, 10 This was the third of 6 visions given to Paul (cf. 9:3–6; 16:9, 10; 22:17, 18; 23:11; 27:23, 24).

18:10 I have many people in this city. God had appointed a number of people in Corinth for salvation, who had not yet heard the gospel (cf. 13:48; Ro 10:13–15). The effect of Paul's preaching would be to bring the elect to faith (Tit 1:1).

18:11 a year and six months. Paul's longest stay in any city, except Ephesus (20:31) and Rome (28:30).

18:12 while Gallio was proconsul of Achaia. From July, A.D. 51 to June, A.D. 52. **judgment seat.** A large, raised stone platform in the marketplace, situated in front of the residence of the proconsul, where he would try public cases.

13 saying, "This man persuades men to worship God
contrary to [A]the law." 14 But when Paul was about to
[A]open his mouth, Gallio said to the Jews, "If it were
a matter of wrong or of vicious crime, O Jews, it
would be reasonable for me to put up with you;
15 but if there are [A]questions about words and names
and your own law, look after it yourselves; I am
unwilling to be a judge of these matters." 16 And he
drove them away from [A]the judgment seat. 17 And
they all took hold of [A]Sosthenes, [B]the leader of the
synagogue, and *began* beating him in front of [C]the
judgment seat. But Gallio was not concerned about
any of these things.
18 Paul, having remained many days longer,
[A]took leave of [B]the brethren and put out to sea for
[C]Syria, and with him were [D]Priscilla and [D]Aquila.
In [E]Cenchrea [a]he [F]had his hair cut, for he was
keeping a vow. 19 They came to [A]Ephesus, and
he left them there. Now he himself entered [B]the
synagogue and reasoned with the Jews. 20 When
they asked him to stay for a longer time, he did
not consent, 21 but [A]taking leave of them and saying, "I will return to you again [B]if God wills," he
set sail from [C]Ephesus.
22 When he had landed at [A]Caesarea, he went up
and greeted the church, and went down to [B]Antioch.

THIRD MISSIONARY JOURNEY

23 And having spent some time *there,* he left and
passed successively through the [A]Galatian region
and Phrygia, strengthening all the disciples.
24 Now a Jew named [A]Apollos, an [B]Alexandrian
by birth, [a]an eloquent man, came to [C]Ephesus; and
he was mighty in the Scriptures. 25 This man had
been instructed in [A]the way of the Lord; and being
fervent in spirit, he was speaking and teaching
accurately the things concerning Jesus, being acquainted only with [B]the baptism of John; 26 and [a]he
began to speak out boldly in the synagogue. But
when [A]Priscilla and Aquila heard him, they took him
aside and explained to him [B]the way of God more
accurately. 27 And when he wanted to go across to
[A]Achaia, [B]the brethren encouraged him and wrote
to [C]the disciples to welcome him; and when he had
arrived, he greatly [a]helped those who had believed
through grace, 28 for he powerfully refuted the Jews
in public, demonstrating [A]by the Scriptures that
[B]Jesus was the [a]Christ.

18:13 [A]John 19:7; Acts 18:15 18:14 [A]Matt 5:2 18:15 [A]Acts 23:29; 25:19 18:16 [A]Matt 27:19 18:17 [A]1 Cor 1:1 [B]Acts 18:8 [C]Matt 27:19 18:18 [a]Lit *having his hair cut* [A]Mark 6:46 [B]Acts 1:15; 18:27 [C]Matt 4:24 [D]Acts 18:2, 26 [E]Rom 16:1 [F]Num 6:2, 5, 9, 18; Acts 21:24 18:19 [A]Acts 18:21, 24; 19:1, 17, 26, 28, 34f; 20:16f; 21:29; 1 Cor 15:32; 16:8; Eph 1:1; 1 Tim 1:3; 2 Tim 1:18; 4:12; Rev 1:11; 2:1 [B]Acts 18:4 18:21 [A]Mark 6:46 [B]Rom 1:10; 15:32; 1 Cor 4:19; 16:7; Heb 6:3; James 4:15; 1 Pet 3:17 [C]Acts 18:19, 24; 19:1, 17, 26, 28, 34f; 20:16f; 21:29; 1 Cor 15:32; 16:8; Eph 1:1; 1 Tim 1:3; 2 Tim 1:18; 4:12; Rev 1:11; 2:1 18:22 [A]Acts 8:40 [B]Acts 11:19 18:23 [A]Acts 16:6 18:24 [a]Or *a learned man* [A]Acts 19:1; 1 Cor 1:12; 3:5, 6, 22; 4:6; 16:12; Titus 3:13 [B]Acts 6:9 [C]Acts 18:19 18:25 [A]Acts 9:2; 18:26 [B]Luke 7:29; Acts 19:3 18:26 [a]Lit *this man* [A]Acts 18:2, 18 [B]Acts 18:25 18:27 [a]Or *helped greatly through grace those who had believed* [A]Acts 18:12; 19:1 [B]Acts 18:18 [C]Acts 11:26 18:28 [a]I.e. Messiah [A]Acts 8:35 [B]Acts 18:5

18:13 contrary to the law. While Judaism was not an official religion, it was officially tolerated in the Roman world, and Christianity was viewed as a sect of Judaism. The Jews in Corinth claimed that Paul's teaching was external to Judaism, and therefore should be banned. Had Gallio ruled in the Jews' favor, Christianity could have been outlawed throughout the Empire.

18:14–16 Gallio was no fool and saw through the Jews' plan. He refused to get caught up in what he viewed as an internal squabble within Judaism. In essence, he rendered what would be called a summary judgment—he officially ruled that no crime had been committed, that the dispute was over semantics, and threw the case out.

18:17 Sosthenes ... *began* beating him. The Greeks had reasons for being hostile to Sosthenes; they were venting general hostility toward Jews on him, or they may have been angry with his unsuccessful attempt, as leader of the Jews, at prosecuting the case against Paul. Since he was the ruler of the synagogue, he would have presented the case to Gallio. Later, he converted to Christ (1Co 1:1).

18:18 Priscilla and Aquila. *See note on v. 2.* That they could accompany Paul means there was sufficient leadership in Corinth, with men such as Gaius, Sosthenes, Stephanas, and Crispus. **Cenchrea.** The eastern port of Corinth. **he had his hair cut, for he was keeping a vow.** To show God his gratitude for helping him through a difficult time in Corinth, he took a Nazirite vow—a special pledge of separation and devotion to God (cf. Nu 6:2–5, 13–21). The vow generally lasted a specific period of time, although Samson (Jdg 13:5), Samuel (1Sa 1:11), and John the Baptist (Lk 1:15) were Nazirites for life. In Paul's day, if someone made the vow while away from Jerusalem, at the termination of his vow he would shave his head, as Paul did, and afterwards present the shorn hair at the temple within 30 days.

18:19 Ephesus. The most important city in Asia Minor (see Introduction to Ephesians). **left them there.** Priscilla and Aquila remained in Ephesus to establish their business. Apparently, they lived in Ephesus for several years—a church met in their home (1Co 16:19)—before they returned to Rome (16:3–5). **synagogue.** *See note on 13:5.*

18:22 went up ... went down to Antioch. Although Luke does not mention it in detail, his description of the geography indicates Paul went to Jerusalem to greet the church. Because Jerusalem was elevated over the surrounding region, travelers had to go "up" to get there and "down" to any other place. Paul also had to return to Jerusalem so he could fulfill his vow. This ended the second missionary journey.

18:23 some time *there*. Possibly from the summer of A.D. 52 to the spring of A.D. 53. **Galatian region and Phrygia.** *See note on 16:6.* Paul's return to those regions marked the beginning of his third missionary journey.

18:24 Apollos. An OT saint and follower of John the Baptist (v. 25). After further instruction by Aquila and Priscilla (v. 26), he became a powerful Christian preacher. His ministry profoundly influenced the Corinthians (cf. 1Co 1:12). **Alexandrian by birth.** Alexandria was an important city in Egypt located near the mouth of the Nile. In the first century, it had a large Jewish population. Thus Apollos, though born outside of Israel, was reared in a Jewish cultural setting. **mighty in the Scriptures.** Used only here, this phrase refers to Apollos' knowledge of the OT Scriptures. That knowledge, combined with his eloquence, allowed him to crush his Jewish opponents in debate (v. 28).

18:25 the way of the Lord. This did not include the Christian faith (cf. v. 26). The OT uses the phrase to describe the spiritual and moral standards God required His people to observe (Ge 18:19; Jdg 2:22; 1Sa 12:23; 2Sa 22:22; 2Ki 21:22; 2Ch 17:6; Pss 18:21; 25:8, 9; 138:5; Pr 10:29; Jer 5:4, 5; Eze 18:25, 29; 33:17, 20; Hos 14:9). **baptism of John.** Despite his knowledge of the OT, Apollos did not fully understand Christian truth. John's baptism was to prepare Israel for the Messiah's arrival (cf. Lk 1:16, 17; *see notes on 2:38; Mt 3:6*). Apollos accepted that message, even acknowledging that Jesus of Nazareth was Israel's Messiah. He did not, however, understand such basic Christian truths as the significance of Christ's death and resurrection, the ministry of the Holy Spirit, and the church as God's new witness people. He was a redeemed OT believer (v. 24).

18:26 the way of God more accurately. Aquila and Priscilla completed Apollos' training in divine truth by instructing him in the fullness of the Christian faith.

18:27 Achaia. *See note on v. 12.* Apollos planned to cross from Asia Minor (modern Turkey) to Corinth on the Greek mainland (19:1). **the brethren ... wrote.** Such letters of commendation were common in the early church (cf. Rom 16:1, 2; 1Co 16:10; 2Co 3:1, 2; Col 4:10). The Ephesian Christians wrote to inform their Corinthian brethren that Apollos was now a fully informed Christian.

18:28 the Christ. The Messiah of Israel.

PAUL AT EPHESUS

19 It happened that while [A]Apollos was at [B]Cor-
inth, Paul passed through the [C]upper country
and came to [D]Ephesus, and found some disciples.
2 He said to them, "[A]Did you receive the Holy Spirit
when you believed?" And they *said* to him, "No, [B]we
have not even heard whether [a]there is a Holy Spirit."
3 And he said, "Into what then were you baptized?"
And they said, "[A]Into John's baptism." 4 Paul said,
"[A]John baptized with the baptism of repentance,
telling the people [B]to believe in Him who was coming after him, that is, in Jesus." 5 When they heard
this, they were [A]baptized [a]in the name of the Lord
Jesus. 6 And when Paul had [A]laid his hands upon
them, the Holy Spirit came on them, and they *began*
[B]speaking with tongues and [C]prophesying. 7 There
were in all about twelve men.
8 And he entered [A]the synagogue and continued
speaking out boldly for three months, reasoning and
persuading *them* [B]about the kingdom of God. 9 But
when [A]some were becoming hardened and disobedient, speaking evil of [B]the Way before the [a]people, he
withdrew from them and took away [C]the disciples,
reasoning daily in the school of Tyrannus. 10 This took
place for [A]two years, so that all who lived in [a,B]Asia
heard [C]the word of the Lord, both Jews and Greeks.

MIRACLES AT EPHESUS

11 God was performing [A]extraordinary [a]miracles
by the hands of Paul, 12 [A]so that handkerchiefs or
aprons were even carried from his body to the
sick, and the diseases left them and [B]the evil spirits went out. 13 But also some of the Jewish [A]exor-
cists, who went from place to place, attempted to
name over those who had the evil spirits the name
of the Lord Jesus, saying, "I adjure you by Jesus
whom Paul preaches." 14 Seven sons of one Sceva,
a Jewish chief priest, were doing this. 15 And the
evil spirit answered and said to them, "I recognize Jesus, and I know about Paul, but who are
you?" 16 And the man, in whom was the evil spirit,
leaped on them and subdued all of them and overpowered them, so that they fled out of that house
naked and wounded. 17 This became known to all,
both Jews and Greeks, who lived in [A]Ephesus;
and fear fell upon them all and the name of the
Lord Jesus was being magnified. 18 Many also of
those who had believed kept coming, confessing
and disclosing their practices. 19 And many of
those who practiced magic brought their books
together and *began* burning them in the sight of
everyone; and they counted up the price of them
and found it [a]fifty thousand [A]pieces of silver. 20 So

19:1 [A]Acts 18:24; 1 Cor 1:12; 3:5, 6, 22; 4:6; 16:12; Titus 3:13 [B]Acts 18:1 [C]Acts 18:23 [D]Acts 18:21, 24; 19:17, 26, 28, 34f; 20:16f; 21:29; 1 Cor 15:32; 16:8; Eph 1:1; 1 Tim 1:3; 2 Tim 1:18; 4:12; Rev 1:11; 2:1 19:2 [a]Or *the Holy Spirit has been* given [A]Acts 8:15f; 11:16f [B]John 7:39 19:3 [A]Luke 7:29; Acts 18:25 19:4 [A]Matt 3:11; Mark 1:4, 7, 8; Luke 3:16; John 1:26, 27; Acts 13:24 [B]John 1:7 19:5 [a]Lit *into* [A]Acts 8:12, 16; 10:48 19:6 [A]Acts 6:6; 8:17 [B]Mark 16:17; Acts 2:4; 10:46 [C]Acts 13:1 19:8 [A]Acts 9:20; 18:26 [B]Acts 1:3 19:9 [a]Lit *multitude* [A]Acts 14:4 [B]Acts 9:2; 19:23 [C]Acts 11:26; 19:30 19:10 [a]I.e. west coast province of Asia Minor [A]Acts 19:8; 20:31 [B]Acts 16:6; 19:22, 26, 27 [C]Acts 13:12; 19:20 19:11 [a]Or *works of power* [A]Acts 8:13 19:12 [A]Acts 5:15 [B]Mark 16:17 19:13 [A]Matt 12:27; Luke 11:19 19:17 [A]Acts 18:19 19:19 [a]Probably fifty thousand Greek drachmas; a drachma approximated a day's wage [A]Luke 15:8

19:1 the upper country. The area of Asia Minor N of Ephesus, where Luke left Paul before the interlude describing Apollos' ministry (18:23). By going through that area, Paul took the direct route to Ephesus, not the more common trade route. **Ephesus.** See Introduction to Ephesians. **some disciples.** They were of John the Baptist (v. 3); hence OT seekers. That they did not yet fully understand the Christian faith is evident from their reply to Paul's question (v. 2). The word "disciple" means "learner," or "follower," and does not always refer to Christians (cf. Mt 9:14; 11:2; Mk 2:18; Lk 5:33; 7:18, 19; 11:1; Jn 1:35; 6:66). Followers of John the Baptist, like this group, existed into the second century.

19:2 Did you receive the Holy Spirit when you believed? The question reflects Paul's uncertainty about their spiritual status. Since all Christians receive the Holy Spirit at the moment of salvation (*see notes on Ro 8:9; 1Co 12:13*), their answer revealed they were not yet fully Christians. They had not yet received Christian baptism (having been baptized only "into John's baptism") which further evidenced that they were not Christians (*see note on 2:38*).

19:4 baptism of repentance ... believe in ... Jesus. These disciples did not realize Jesus of Nazareth was the One to whom John's baptism pointed. Paul gave them instruction not on how to receive the Spirit, but about Jesus Christ.

19:5 baptized in the name of the Lord Jesus. They believed Paul's presentation of the gospel and came to saving faith in the Lord Jesus Christ (cf. 2:41). Although required of all Christians, baptism does not save (*see note on 2:38*).

19:6 Paul ... laid his hands upon them. This signified their inclusion into the church (*see note on 8:17*). Apostles were also present when the church was born (chap. 2), and when the Samaritans (chap. 8) and Gentiles (chap. 10) were included. In each case, God's purpose was to emphasize the unity of the church. **speaking with tongues and prophesying.** This served as proof that they were part of the church (*see note on 8:17*). They also needed tangible evidence that the Holy Spirit now indwelt them, since they had not heard that He had come (v. 2).

19:8 synagogue. *See note on 13:5.* **three months.** Paul's longest stay in any synagogue, with the possible exception of the one at Corinth. **kingdom of God.** *See note on 1:3.*

19:9 hardened. The Gr. word always refers to defiance against God (Ro 9:18; Heb 3:8, 13, 15; 4:7). Truth rejected leads to a hardened heart, causing the life-giving message of salvation to become "an aroma from death to death" (2Co 2:16). **the Way.** *See note on 9:2.* **the school of Tyrannus.** Tyrannus was either the owner of the lecture hall, or a philosopher who taught there. If the latter, his name, which means "our tyrant," may have been a nickname given him by his students. Paul used the hall during the afternoon break (from about 11:00 a.m. to 4:00 p.m.), when it would otherwise be unoccupied.

19:10 two years. The length of time Paul taught in the school of Tyrannus, not the total length of his ministry at Ephesus (cf. 20:31). **all ... in Asia heard.** Though Paul probably never left Ephesus, his converts (cf. 2Ti 2:2) spread the gospel throughout the province of Asia Minor (modern Turkey). This two-year period saw the founding of the churches at Colosse and Hierapolis, and possibly some of the 7 churches mentioned in Rev 2, 3, beyond the one at Ephesus.

19:11 extraordinary miracles. These confirmed that Paul was God's messenger, since there was no completed NT to use to determine the truth of his message (cf. 2Co 12:12; Heb 2:3, 4).

19:12 handkerchiefs ... aprons. The headbands and outer clothing Paul wore while making tents. The belief that mystical power could be so transmitted was widespread in the ancient world, e.g., believing that Peter's shadow could heal (cf. 5:15; Mt 9:21).

19:13 Jewish exorcists. Simon Magus (8:9–25) and Bar-Jesus (13:6–12) were other possible examples of such charlatans (cf. Mt 12:27). In contrast to the absolute authority exercised by Jesus and the apostles over demons, those exorcists sought to expel the demons by attempting to call on a more potent spirit being—in this case the Lord Jesus.

19:14 Sceva, a Jewish chief priest. Since there is no record of a Jewish High Priest by that name, he probably assumed that title falsely to impress people.

19:15 recognize Jesus, and I know about Paul. Recognizing that the exorcists had no authority over him (unlike Jesus and Paul), the demon rejected their attempt to expel him from his victim. This confirms that the power to cast out demons belonged to Jesus and the apostles and no one else. Even the demons give testimony to that.

19:16 Cf. Mk 5:1–4.

19:19 books. Of secret magical spells. Burning them proved the genuineness of the magicians' repentance (*see note on 2:38*); having destroyed these books, they could not easily resume their practices. **fifty thousand pieces of silver.** Fifty thousand days' wages for a common laborer—an astonishing sum

[a,A]the word of the Lord [B]was growing mightily and
prevailing.
21 Now after these things were finished, Paul purposed in the [a]Spirit to [A]go to Jerusalem [B]after he had
passed through [C]Macedonia and [D]Achaia, saying,
"After I have been there, [E]I must also see Rome."
22 And having sent into [A]Macedonia two of [B]those
who ministered to him, [C]Timothy and [D]Erastus, he
himself stayed in [a,E]Asia for a while.
23 About that time there occurred no small disturbance concerning [A]the Way. 24 For a man named
Demetrius, a silversmith, who made silver shrines
of [a]Artemis, [A]was bringing no little [b]business to
the craftsmen; 25 these he gathered together with
the workmen of similar *trades,* and said, "Men, you
know that our prosperity [a]depends upon this business. 26 You see and hear that not only in [A]Ephesus,
but in almost all of [a,B]Asia, this Paul has persuaded
and turned away a considerable number of people,
saying that [b,C]gods made with hands are no gods *at*
all. 27 Not only is there danger that this trade of ours
fall into disrepute, but also that the temple of the
great goddess [a]Artemis be regarded as worthless
and that she whom all of [b,A]Asia and [B]the [c]world worship will even be dethroned from her magnificence."
28 When they heard *this* and were filled with rage,
they *began* crying out, saying, "Great is [a]Artemis
of the [A]Ephesians!" 29 The city was filled with the
confusion, and they rushed [a]with one accord into
the theater, dragging along [A]Gaius and [B]Aristarchus,
Paul's traveling [C]companions from [D]Macedonia.
30 And when Paul wanted to go into the [a]assembly,
[A]the disciples would not let him. 31 Also some of
the [a]Asiarchs who were friends of his sent to him
and repeatedly urged him not to [b]venture into the
theater. 32 [A]So then, some were shouting one thing
and some another, for the [a]assembly was in confusion and the majority did not know [b]for what reason they had come together. 33 Some of the crowd
[a]concluded *it was* Alexander, since the Jews had
put him forward; and having [A]motioned with his
hand, Alexander was intending to make a defense
to the [b]assembly. 34 But when they recognized that
he was a Jew, a *single* outcry arose from them all as
they shouted for about two hours, "Great is [a]Arte-
mis of the Ephesians!" 35 After quieting the crowd,
the town clerk *said, "Men of [A]Ephesus, what man
is there after all who does not know that the city of
the Ephesians is guardian of the temple of the great
[a]Artemis and of the *image* which fell down from
[b]heaven? 36 So, since these are undeniable facts, you
ought to keep calm and to do nothing rash. 37 For
you have brought these men *here* who are neither
[A]robbers of temples nor blasphemers of our goddess. 38 So then, if Demetrius and the craftsmen
who are with him have a complaint against any

19:20 [a]Or *according to the power of the Lord the word was growing* [A]Acts 19:10 [B]Acts 6:7; 12:24 19:21 [a]Or *spirit* [A]Acts 20:16, 22; 21:15; Rom 15:25; 2 Cor 1:16 [B]Acts 20:1; 1 Cor 16:5 [C]Acts 16:9; 19:22, 29; Rom 15:26; 1 Thess 1:7f [D]Acts 18:12 [E]Acts 23:11; Rom 15:24, 28 19:22 [a]I.e. west coast province of Asia Minor [A]Acts 16:9; 19:21, 29 [B]Acts 13:5; 19:29; 20:34; 2 Cor 8:19 [C]Acts 16:1 [D]Rom 16:23; 2 Tim 4:20 [E]Acts 19:10 19:23 [A]Acts 19:9 19:24 [a]Lat *Diana* [b]Or *profit* [A]Acts 16:16, 19f 19:25 [a]Lit *is from* 19:26 [a]V 22, note 1 [b]Lit *those* [A]Acts 18:19 [B]Acts 19:10 [C]Deut 4:28; Ps 115:4; Is 44:10-20; Jer 10:3ff; Acts 17:29; 1 Cor 8:4; 10:19; Rev 9:20 19:27 [a]Lat *Diana* [b]V 22, note 1 [c]Lit *the inhabited earth* [A]Acts 19:10 [B]Matt 24:14 19:28 [a]Lat *Diana* [A]Acts 18:19 19:29 [a]Or *together* [A]Acts 20:4 [B]Acts 20:4; 27:2; Col 4:10; Philem 24 [C]Acts 13:5; 19:22; 20:34; 2 Cor 8:19 [D]Acts 16:9; 19:22 19:30 [a]Lit *people* [A]Acts 19:9 19:31 [a]I.e. political or religious officials of the province of Asia [b]Lit *give himself* 19:32 [a]Gr *ekklesia* [b]Or *on whose account* [A]Acts 21:34 19:33 [a]Or *advised* *Alexander* [b]Lit *people* [A]Acts 12:17 19:34 [a]Lat *Diana* 19:35 [a]Lat *Diana* [b]Lit *Zeus;* Lat *Jupiter* [A]Acts 18:19 19:37 [A]Rom 2:22

of money given to indicate how widespread the practice of magic was in Ephesus.

19:21 **purposed in the Spirit.** Probably his own spirit, not the Holy Spirit (see the NAS footnote). **Macedonia and Achaia.** *See notes on 16:9; 18:12.* Located on the Greek mainland, these provinces were in the opposite direction from Jerusalem. Paul, however, took this roundabout route to collect an offering for the needy in the Jerusalem church (Ro 15:25–27; 1Co 16:1–4; 2Co 8, 9). **I must also see Rome.** Paul had not visited the Imperial capital, but because of the strategic importance of the church there, he could stay away no longer. In addition, Paul intended to use Rome as a jumping-off point for ministry in the strategic region of Spain (Ro 15:22–24). This simple declaration marked a turning point in Acts; from this point on, Rome became Paul's goal. He would ultimately arrive there as a Roman prisoner (28:16).

19:22 **Timothy and Erastus.** For Timothy, *see note on 16:1.* Nothing more is known of Erastus. Though the name appears two other times in Scripture (Ro 16:23; 2Ti 4:20), he cannot with certainty be identified with either one. Paul sent these two ahead of him to assist in his collection of the offering.

19:23 **the Way.** *See note on 9:2.*

19:24 **Demetrius, a silversmith.** Probably not the individual commended by John (3Jn 12), since the name was a common one. **silver shrines.** These were of the goddess Diana (Artemis). These shrines were used as household idols, and in the worship at the temple of Diana. **Artemis.** She was also known as "Diana." Worship of her, centered at the great temple of Diana at Ephesus (one of the Seven Wonders of the Ancient World), was widespread throughout the Roman Empire. It is likely that the riot described in this passage took place during the annual spring festival held in her honor at Ephesus. **bringing no little business.** This statement suggests Demetrius may have been the head of the silversmiths' guild—which would explain his taking the lead in opposing the Christian preachers.

19:27 Demetrius cleverly played upon his hearers' fears of financial ruin, religious zeal, and concern for their city's prestige. The Christian preachers, he argued, threatened the continued prosperity of Ephesus. His audience's violent reaction shows they took the threat seriously (v. 28).

19:29 **Gaius and Aristarchus.** These men are described as Macedonians, though 20:4 lists Gaius' hometown as Derbe, a city in Galatia. Possibly the Gaius of 20:4 was a different person.

19:31 **Asiarchs.** These members of the aristocracy were dedicated to promoting Roman interests. Though only one Asiarch ruled at a time, they bore the title for life. That such powerful, influential men were Paul's friends shows that they did not regard him or his message as criminal. Hence, there was no legitimate cause for the riot.

19:32 **assembly.** The frenzied mob gathered in the theater. Though Paul courageously sought to address them, the Asiarchs (along with the Ephesian Christians, v. 30) begged him to stay away (v. 31). They feared both for the apostle's safety, and that his presence would exacerbate the already explosive situation.

19:33 **Alexander.** Probably not the false teacher later active at Ephesus (1Ti 1:20), or the individual who opposed Paul at Rome (2Ti 4:14), since the name was common. He was either a Christian Jew or a spokesman for Ephesus' Jewish community. Either way, the Jews' motive for putting him forward was the same—to disassociate themselves from the Christians and avoid a massacre of the Jews. **make a defense.** Either of the Christians, or the Jews, depending on which group he represented.

19:34 **a Jew.** Whatever the Jews intended by putting Alexander forward backfired; the crowd shouted him down, and in a mindless display of religious frenzy, they chanted the name of their goddess for two hours.

19:35 **town clerk.** In modern terms, he was Ephesus' mayor. He was the liaison between the town council and the Roman authorities—who would hold him personally responsible for the riot. ***image* which fell down from heaven.** This probably refers to a meteorite, since meteorites were incorporated with the worship of Diana.

19:38–40 The town clerk (v. 35) correctly blamed the crowd for the riot, noting that they should have followed proper judicial procedure and gone to the courts and proconsuls

man, the courts are in session and [a,A]proconsuls
are *available;* let them bring charges against one
another. 39 But if you want anything beyond this,
it shall be settled in the [a]lawful [b]assembly. 40 For
indeed we are in danger of being accused of a riot
in connection with today's events, since there is no
real cause *for it,* and in this connection we will be
unable to account for this disorderly gathering."
41 After saying this he dismissed the [a]assembly.

PAUL IN MACEDONIA AND GREECE

20 After the uproar had ceased, Paul sent for [A]the
disciples, and when he had exhorted them and
taken his leave of them, he left [B]to go to [C]Macedonia.
2 When he had gone through those districts and had
given them much exhortation, he came to Greece.
3 And *there* he spent three months, and when [A]a plot
was formed against him by the Jews as he was about
to set sail for [B]Syria, he decided to return through
[C]Macedonia. 4 And [a]he was accompanied by Sopater
of [A]Berea, *the son* of Pyrrhus, and by [B]Aristarchus and
Secundus of the [C]Thessalonians, and [B]Gaius of [D]Derbe,
and [E]Timothy, and [F]Tychicus and [G]Trophimus of [b,H]Asia.
5 But these had gone on ahead and were waiting for [A]us
at [B]Troas. 6 [A]We sailed from [B]Philippi after [C]the days of
Unleavened Bread, and came to them at [D]Troas within
five days; and there we stayed seven days.
7 On [A]the first day of the week, when [B]we were
gathered together to [C]break bread, Paul *began* talking to them, intending to leave the next day, and
he prolonged his [a]message until midnight. 8 There
were many [A]lamps in the [B]upper room where we
were gathered together. 9 And there was a young
man named [a]Eutychus sitting [b]on the window sill,
sinking into a deep sleep; and as Paul kept on talking, he was overcome by sleep and fell down from
the third floor and was picked up dead. 10 But Paul
went down and [A]fell upon him, and after embracing
him, he [B]said, "[a]Do not be troubled, for his life is in
him." 11 When he had gone *back* up and had [A]broken
the bread and [a]eaten, he talked with them a long
while until daybreak, and then left. 12 They took
away the boy alive, and were [a]greatly comforted.

TROAS TO MILETUS

13 But [A]we, going ahead to the ship, set sail for
Assos, intending from there to take Paul on board;
for so he had arranged it, intending himself to go
[a]by land. 14 And when he met us at Assos, we took
him on board and came to Mitylene. 15 Sailing from
there, we arrived the following day opposite Chios;
and the next day we crossed over to Samos; and the
day following we came to [A]Miletus. 16 For Paul had
decided to sail past [A]Ephesus so that he would not

19:38 [a]Or *provincial governors* [A]Acts 13:7 19:39 [a]Or *regular* [b]Gr *ekklesia* 19:41 [a]Gr *ekklesia* 20:1 [A]Acts 11:26 [B]Acts 19:21 [C]Acts 16:9; 20:3 20:3 [A]Acts 9:23f; 20:19 [B]Matt 4:24 [C]Acts 16:9; 20:1 20:4 [a]Lit *there accompanied him* [b]I.e. west coast province of Asia Minor [A]Acts 17:10 [B]Acts 19:29 [C]Acts 17:1 [D]Acts 14:6 [E]Acts 16:1 [F]Eph 6:21; Col 4:7; 2 Tim 4:12; Titus 3:12 [G]Acts 21:29; 2 Tim 4:20 [H]Acts 16:6; 20:16, 18 20:5 [A]Acts 16:10; 20:5-15 [B]Acts 16:8 20:6 [A]Acts 16:10; 20:5-15 [B]Acts 16:12 [C]Acts 12:3 [D]Acts 16:8 20:7 [a]Lit *word, speech* [A]1 Cor 16:2; Rev 1:10 [B]Acts 16:10; 20:5-15 [C]Acts 2:42; 20:11 20:8 [A]Matt 25:1 [B]Acts 1:13 20:9 [a]*Eutychus* means *Good fortune*, i.e. 'Lucky' [b]Or *at the window* 20:10 [a]Or *Stop being troubled* [A]1 Kin 17:21; 2 Kin 4:34 [B]Matt 9:23f; Mark 5:39 20:11 [a]Lit *tasted* [A]Acts 2:42; 20:7 20:12 [a]Lit *not moderately* 20:13 [a]Or *on foot* [A]Acts 16:10; 20:5-15 20:15 [A]Acts 20:17; 2 Tim 4:20 20:16 [A]Acts 18:19

if they had any complaints, so as not to incur serious consequences from Rome.

20:1 left. Paul departed on his trip to Jerusalem via Greece (*see note on 19:21*). **Macedonia.** *See note on 16:9.*

20:2 he had gone through those districts. Macedonia and Achaia (*see note on 19:21*).

20:3 three months. Most or all of it were likely spent in Corinth. **a plot … against him by the Jews.** See 9:20, 23; 13:45; 14:2, 19; 17:5–9, 13; 18:6, 12, 13; 19:9; 21:27–36; 23:12–15. Tragically, most of the opposition to Paul's ministry stemmed from his fellow countrymen (cf. 2Co 11:26). The Jewish community of Corinth hated Paul because of its humiliating debacle before Gallio (18:12–17), and the stunning conversions of two of its most prominent leaders, Crispus (18:8) and Sosthenes (18:17; 1Co 1:1). Luke does not record the details of the Jews' plot, but it undoubtedly involved murdering Paul during the voyage to Syria. The apostle would have been an easy target on a small ship packed with Jewish pilgrims. Because of that danger, Paul canceled his plans to sail from Greece to Syria. Instead, he decided to go N into Macedonia, cross the Aegean Sea to Asia Minor, and catch another ship from there. That delay cost Paul his opportunity to reach Jerusalem in time for Passover; but he hurried to be there in time for Pentecost (v. 16).

20:4 Sopater of Berea … Trophimus of Asia. Paul's traveling companions came from the various provinces in which he had ministered. These men were likely the official representatives of their churches, chosen to accompany Paul as he took the offering to Jerusalem (*see note on 19:21*; cf. 1Co 16:3, 4).

20:5 for us. The first person plural pronoun reveals that Luke rejoined Paul in Philippi (v. 6). Being a Gentile, he was able to remain there to minister after Paul and Silas were forced to leave (16:20, 39, 40). This verse begins the second of the three "we passages" in which Luke accompanied Paul on his travels (see Introduction: Author and Date). **Troas.** *See note on 16:7, 8.*

20:6 from Philippi. Paul, along with Luke, and possibly Titus, crossed the Aegean Sea from Philippi to Troas. That crossing, due to unfavorable winds, took 5 days; Paul's earlier crossing from Troas to Neapolis (Philippi's port) had taken only two days (16:11). In Troas, they were reunited with the rest of their party. **days of Unleavened Bread.** I.e., Passover (Ex 12:17).

20:7 first day of the week. Sunday, the day the church gathered for worship, because it was the day of Christ's resurrection. Cf. Mt 28:1; Mk 16:2, 9; Lk 24:1; Jn 20:1, 19; 1Co 16:2. The writings of the early church Fathers confirm that the church continued to meet on Sunday after the close of the NT period. Scripture does not require Christians to observe the Saturday Sabbath: 1) the Sabbath was the sign of the Mosaic Covenant (Ex 31:16, 17; Ne 9:14; Eze 20:12), whereas Christians are under the New Covenant (2Co 3; Heb 8); 2) there is no NT command to keep the Sabbath; 3) the first command to keep the Sabbath was not until the time of Moses (Ex 20:8); 4) the Jerusalem Council (chap. 15) did not order Gentile believers to keep the Sabbath; 5) Paul never cautioned Christians about breaking the Sabbath; and 6) the NT explicitly teaches that Sabbath keeping was not a requirement (*see notes on Ro 14:5; Gal 4:10, 11; Col 2:16, 17*). **to break bread.** The common meal associated with the communion service (1Co 11:20–22).

20:8 lamps. The fumes given off by these oil-burning lamps help explain why Eutychus fell asleep (v. 9). **upper room.** *See note on 1:13.* The early church met in homes (Ro 16:5; 1Co 16:19; Col 4:15; Phm 2); the first church buildings date from the third century.

20:9 young man. The Gr. word suggests he was between 7 and 14 years old. His youth, the fumes from the lamps, and the lateness of the hour (v. 7) gradually overcame his resistance. He dozed off, fell out of the open window, and was killed.

20:10 his life is in him. This does not mean that he had not died, but that his life had been restored. As a physician, Luke knew whether someone had died, as he plainly states (v. 9) was the case with Eutychus.

20:13 Assos. Located 20 mi. S of Troas, across the neck of a small peninsula. **by land.** Because the ship had to sail around the peninsula, Paul could have arrived in Assos not long after it did. Paul presumably chose to walk to Assos so he could continue to teach the believers from Troas who accompanied him.

20:14 Mitylene. Chief city of the island of Lesbos, S of Assos.

20:15 Chios. An island off the coast of Asia Minor, S of Lesbos. Chios was the birthplace of the Greek poet Homer. **Samos.** An island off the coast near Ephesus. The famed mathematician Pythagoras was born on Samos. **Miletus.** A city in Asia Minor, about 30 mi. S of Ephesus.

20:16 decided to sail past Ephesus. Still trying to reach Jerusalem before Pentecost (50 days after Passover), Paul decided to

have to spend time in [a,B]Asia; for he was hurrying [C]to
be in Jerusalem, if possible, [D]on the day of Pentecost.

FAREWELL TO EPHESUS

17 From Miletus he sent to [A]Ephesus and called
to him [B]the elders of the church. 18 And when they
had come to him, he said to them,
"You yourselves know, [A]from the first day that I
set foot in [a]Asia, how I was with you the whole time,
19 serving the Lord with all humility and with tears
and with trials which came upon me [a]through [A]the
plots of the Jews; 20 how I [A]did not shrink from declaring to you anything that was profitable, and teaching
you publicly and [a]from house to house, 21 solemnly
[A]testifying to both Jews and Greeks of [B]repentance
toward God and [C]faith in our Lord Jesus Christ. 22 And
now, behold, bound by the [a]Spirit, [A]I am on my way to
Jerusalem, not knowing what will happen to me there,
23 except that [A]the Holy Spirit solemnly [B]testifies to me
in every city, saying that [C]bonds and afflictions await
me. 24 But [A]I do not consider my life of any account as
dear to myself, so that I may [B]finish my course and
[C]the ministry which I received from the Lord Jesus,
to [D]testify solemnly of the gospel of [E]the grace of God.
25 "And now, behold, I know that all of you,
among whom I went about [A]preaching the
kingdom, will no longer see my face. 26 Therefore, I [a]testify to you this day that [A]I am [b]innocent
of the blood of all men. 27 For I [A]did not shrink
from declaring to you the whole [B]purpose of God.
28 Be on guard for yourselves and for all [A]the flock,
among which the Holy Spirit has made you [a]over-
seers, to shepherd [B]the church of God which [C]He
[b]purchased [c]with His own blood. 29 I know that
after my departure [A]savage wolves will come in
among you, not sparing [B]the flock; 30 and from
among your own selves men will arise, speaking
perverse things, to draw away [A]the disciples after
them. 31 Therefore be on the alert, remembering
that night and day for a period of [A]three years I
did not cease to admonish each one [B]with tears.
32 And now I [A]commend you to God and to [B]the
word of His grace, which is able to [C]build *you* up
and to give *you* [D]the inheritance among all those
who are sanctified. 33 [A]I have coveted no one's silver or gold or clothes. 34 You yourselves know that
[A]these hands ministered to my *own* needs and to
the [B]men who were with me. 35 In everything I
showed you that by working hard in this manner
you must help the weak and remember the words
of the Lord Jesus, that He Himself said, 'It is more
blessed to give than to receive.' "

20:16 [a]I.e. west coast province of Asia Minor [B]Acts 16:6; 20:4, 18 [C]Acts 19:21; 20:6, 22; 1 Cor 16:8 [D]Acts 2:1 20:17 [A]Acts 18:19 [B]Acts 11:30 20:18 [a]V 16, note 1 [A]Acts 18:19; 19:1, 10; 20:4, 16 20:19 [a]Lit *by* [A]Acts 20:3 20:20 [a]Or *in the various private homes* [A]Acts 20:27 20:21 [A]Luke 16:28; Acts 18:5; 20:23, 24 [B]Acts 2:38; 11:18; 26:20 [C]Acts 24:24; 26:18; Eph 1:15; Col 2:5; Philem 5 20:22 [a]Or *in spirit* [A]Acts 17:16; 20:16 20:23 [A]Acts 8:29 [B]Luke 16:28; Acts 18:5; 20:21, 24 [C]Acts 9:16; 21:33 20:24 [A]Acts 21:13 [B]Acts 13:25; 2 Tim 4:7 [C]Acts 1:17 [D]Luke 16:28; Acts 18:5; 20:21 [E]Acts 11:23; 20:32 20:25 [A]Matt 4:23; Acts 28:31 20:26 [a]Or *call you to witness* [b]Lit *pure from* [A]Acts 18:6 20:27 [A]Acts 20:20 [B]Acts 13:36 20:28 [a]Or *bishops* [b]Lit *acquired* [c]Lit *through* [A]Luke 12:32; John 21:15-17; Acts 20:29; 1 Pet 5:2f [B]Matt 16:18; Rom 16:16; 1 Cor 10:32 [C]Eph 1:7, 14; Titus 2:14; 1 Pet 1:19; 2:9; Rev 5:9 20:29 [A]Ezek 22:27; Matt 7:15 [B]Luke 12:32; John 21:15-17; Acts 20:28; 1 Pet 5:2f 20:30 [A]Acts 11:26 20:31 [A]Acts 19:8, 10; 24:17 [B]Acts 20:19 20:32 [A]Acts 14:23 [B]Acts 14:3; 20:24 [C]Acts 9:31 [D]Acts 26:18; Eph 1:14; 5:5; Col 1:12; 3:24; Heb 9:15; 1 Pet 1:4 20:33 [A]1 Cor 9:4-18; 2 Cor 11:7-12; 12:14-18; 1 Thess 2:5f 20:34 [A]Acts 18:3 [B]Acts 19:22

have the elders (i.e., pastors, overseers) of the Ephesian church meet him in Miletus.

20:19 with tears. Paul wept because of: 1) those who did not know Christ (cf. Ro 9:2, 3); 2) struggling, immature believers (2Co 2:4); and 3) the threat of false teachers (v. 29, 30). **plots of the Jews.** See 2Co 11:24, 26. Ironically, it was the plot of the Jews at Corinth that allowed the Ephesian elders this opportunity to spend time with Paul (*see note on v. 3*).

20:20 publicly and from house to house. Paul taught in the synagogue (19:8; *see note on 6:9*) and the school of Tyrannus (19:10). He reinforced that public teaching with practical instruction of individuals and households.

20:21 repentance. An essential element of the gospel (*see notes on 2:38*; cf. 26:20; Mt 4:17; Lk 3:8; 5:32; 24:47).

20:22 bound by the Spirit. Paul's deep sense of duty toward the Master who had redeemed him and called him to service drove him onward despite the threat of danger and hardship (v. 23).

20:23 Holy Spirit … testifies. Paul knew he faced persecution in Jerusalem (cf. Ro 15:31), though he would not know the details until he heard Agabus' prophecy (21:10, 11).

20:24 the ministry … received from the Lord Jesus. Cf. 2Ti 4:7. **gospel of the grace of God.** An apt description, since salvation is solely by God's grace (Eph 2:8, 9; Tit 2:11).

20:25 all of you … will no longer see my face. Aware that he faced severe opposition in Jerusalem, Paul did not anticipate ever returning to Asia Minor. Though he may have done so after his release from his first Roman imprisonment, he could not at this time have foreseen that possibility. **the kingdom.** *See note on 1:3.*

20:26 innocent of the blood. Cf. Eze 33:7–9; Jas 3:1.

20:27 whole purpose of God. The entire plan and purpose of God for man's salvation in all its fullness: divine truths of creation, election, redemption, justification, adoption, conversion, sanctification, holy living, and glorification. Paul strongly condemned those who adulterate the truth of Scripture (2Co 2:17; 2Ti 4:3, 4; cf. Rev 22:18, 19).

20:28–30 A timely warning, proven true by later events at Ephesus (1Ti 1:3–7, 19, 20; 6:20, 21; Rev 2:2). False teachers were already plaguing the churches of Galatia (Gal 1:6) and the Corinthian church (2Co 11:4).

20:28 Be on guard for yourselves. Paul repeated this call to self-examination to Timothy when his young son in the faith served as pastor of the Ephesian congregation (1Ti 4:16; 2Ti 2:20, 21). **overseers.** These are the same as elders and pastors (*see note on 1Ti 3:1*). The word stresses the leaders' responsibility to watch over and protect their congregations—an appropriate usage in the context of a warning against false teachers. Church rule, which minimizes the biblical authority of elders in favor of a cultural, democratic process, is foreign to the NT (cf. 1Th 5:12, 13; Heb 13:17). **with His own blood.** *See note on 1Pe 1:18.* Paul believed so strongly in the unity of God the Father and the Lord Jesus Christ that he could speak of Christ's death as shedding the blood of God—who has no body (Jn 4:24; cf. Lk 24:39) and hence no blood.

20:29 savage wolves. Borrowed from Jesus (Mt 7:15; 10:16), this metaphor stresses the extreme danger false teachers pose to the church.

20:30 from among your own selves. Even more deadly than attacks from outside the church are the defections of those (especially leaders) within the church (1Ti 1:20; 2Ti 1:15; 2:17; cf. Jude 3, 4, 10–13). **perverse things.** The Gr. word means "distorted," or "twisted." False teachers twist God's Word for their own evil ends (13:10; 2Pe 3:16).

20:31 three years. The total length of Paul's Ephesian ministry, including the two years he taught in the school of Tyrannus (19:10).

20:32 word of His grace. The Scriptures, the record of God's gracious dealings with mankind. **build *you* up.** The Bible is the source of spiritual growth (1Th 2:13; 2Ti 3:16, 17; 1Pe 2:2) for all Christians. And since the church is "the pillar and support of the truth" (1Ti 3:15), its leaders must be familiar with that truth. **inheritance.** *See note on 1Pe 1:4.*

20:33 coveted. Love of money is a hallmark of false teachers (cf. Is 56:11; Jer 6:13; 8:10; Mic 3:11; Tit 1:11; 2Pe 2:3), but did not characterize Paul's ministry. *See notes on 1Ti 6:3, 5.*

20:34 these hands ministered to my *own* needs. Paul had the right to earn his living from the gospel (1Co 9:3–14) and sometimes accepted support (2Co 11:8, 9; Php 4:10–19). Yet, he often worked to support himself so he could "offer the gospel without charge" (1Co 9:18).

20:35 help the weak. Cf. 1Co 4:12; 1Th 2:9; 2Th 3:8, 9. **the words of the Lord Jesus.** This is the only direct quote from Jesus' earthly ministry recorded outside the Gospels. The Bible does not record all the words or deeds of Jesus (Jn 21:25).

36 When he had said these things, he [A]knelt down
and prayed with them all. 37 And [a]they *began* to
weep aloud and [b,A]embraced Paul, and repeatedly
kissed him, 38 [a]grieving especially over [A]the word
which he had spoken, that they would not see his
face again. And they were [B]accompanying him to
the ship.

PAUL SAILS FROM MILETUS

21 When [A]we had parted from them and had set
sail, we ran [B]a straight course to Cos and the
next day to Rhodes and from there to Patara; 2 and
having found a ship crossing over to [A]Phoenicia, we
went aboard and set sail. 3 When we came in sight
of [A]Cyprus, leaving it on the left, we kept sailing to
[B]Syria and landed at [C]Tyre; for there the ship was
to unload its cargo. 4 After looking up [A]the disciples,
we stayed there seven days; and they kept telling
Paul [a,B]through the Spirit not to set foot in Jerusalem. 5 When [a]our days there were ended, we left and
started on our journey, while they all, with wives
and children, [A]escorted us until *we were* out of the
city. After [B]kneeling down on the beach and praying,
we said farewell to one another. 6 Then we went on
board the ship, and they returned [A]home again.

7 When we had finished the voyage from [A]Tyre,
we arrived at Ptolemais, and after greeting [B]the
brethren, we stayed with them for a day. 8 On the
next day we left and came to [A]Caesarea, and entering the house of [B]Philip the [C]evangelist, who was
[B]one of the seven, we stayed with him. 9 Now this
man had four virgin daughters who were [A]proph-
etesses. 10 As we were staying there for some days,
a prophet named [A]Agabus came down from Judea.
11 And coming to us, he [A]took Paul's belt and bound
his own feet and hands, and said, "This [B]is what the
Holy Spirit says: 'In this way the Jews at Jerusalem
will [C]bind the man who owns this belt and [D]deliver
him into the hands of the Gentiles.'" 12 When we had
heard this, we as well as the local residents *began*
begging him [A]not to go up to Jerusalem. 13 Then
Paul answered, "What are you doing, weeping and
breaking my heart? For [A]I am ready not only to be
bound, but even to die at Jerusalem for [B]the name
of the Lord Jesus." 14 And since he would not be
persuaded, we fell silent, remarking, "[A]The will of
the Lord be done!"

PAUL AT JERUSALEM

15 After these days we got ready and [A]started on
our way up to Jerusalem. 16 *Some* of [A]the disciples
from [B]Caesarea also came with us, taking us to Mnason of [C]Cyprus, a [D]disciple of long standing with
whom we were to lodge.

20:36 [A]Acts 9:40; 21:5; Luke 22:41 20:37 [a]Lit *a considerable weeping of all occurred* [b]Lit *threw themselves on Paul's neck* [A]Luke 15:20 20:38 [a]Lit *suffering pain* [A]Acts 20:25 [B]Acts 15:3 21:1 [A][we] Acts 16:10; 21:1-18 [B]Acts 16:11 21:2 [A]Acts 11:19; 21:3 21:3 [A]Acts 4:36; 21:16 [B]Matt 4:24 [C]Acts 12:20; 21:7 21:4 [a]I.e. because of impressions made by the Spirit [A]Acts 11:26; 21:16 [B]Acts 20:23; 21:11 21:5 [a]Lit *we had completed the days* [A]Acts 15:3 [B]Luke 22:41; Acts 9:40; 20:36 21:6 [A]John 19:27 21:7 [A]Acts 12:20; 21:3 [B]Acts 1:15; 21:17 21:8 [A]Acts 8:40; 21:16 [B]Acts 6:5; 8:5 [C]Eph 4:11; 2 Tim 4:5 21:9 [A]Luke 2:36; Acts 13:1; 1 Cor 11:5 21:10 [A]Acts 11:28 21:11 [A]1 Kin 22:11; Is 20:2; Jer 13:1-11; 19:1, 11; John 18 [B]Acts 8:29 [C]Acts 9:16; 21:33 [D]Matt 20:19 21:12 [A]Acts 21:15 21:13 [A]Acts 20:24 [B]Acts 5:41; 9:16 21:14 [A]Luke 22:42 21:15 [A]Acts 21:12 21:16 [A]Acts 21:4 [B]Acts 8:40 [C]Acts 4:36; 21:3 [D]Acts 15:7

20:37 embraced Paul. A common biblical way of expressing extreme emotion and affection (cf. Ge 33:4; 45:14; 46:29).

21:1 parted. Lit. means "to tear away." It reiterates the difficulty of Paul's leaving the Ephesian elders (20:37, 38). **straight course to Cos.** The chief city of the island of Cos. **Rhodes.** An island SE of Cos; also the name of its capital city. Its harbor was home to the great statue known as the Colossus of Rhodes, one of the 7 Wonders of the Ancient World. **Patara.** A busy port city in the extreme southern portion of Asia Minor. Paul and the others had now rounded the southwestern corner of Asia Minor. Each of the ports they stopped in represented one day's sailing; the ship did not sail at night.

21:2 found a ship ... to Phoenicia. Realizing he would never reach Jerusalem in time for Pentecost if he continued to hug the coast, Paul decided to risk sailing directly across the Mediterranean Sea to Tyre (v. 3). The ship they embarked on would have been considerably larger than the small coastal vessels on which they had been sailing. The ship that later took Paul on his ill-fated voyage to Rome held 276 people (27:37); this one was probably of comparable size.

21:3 Cyprus. *See note on 11:19.* **Tyre.** *See note on 12:20*; cf. Jos 19:29; Mt 11:21. The voyage across the Mediterranean from Patara to Tyre normally took 5 days.

21:4 disciples. The church in Tyre had been founded by some of those who fled Jerusalem after Stephen's martyrdom (11:19)—a persecution Paul himself had spearheaded. **telling Paul ... not to set foot in Jerusalem.** This was not a command from the Spirit for Paul not to go to Jerusalem. Rather, the Spirit had revealed to the believers at Tyre that Paul would face suffering in Jerusalem. Understandably, they tried (as his friends shortly would, v. 12) to dissuade him from going there. Paul's mission to Jerusalem had been given him by the Lord Jesus (20:24); the Spirit would never command him to abandon it.

21:7 Ptolemais. Old Testament Acco (Jdg 1:31), located 25 mi. S of Tyre.

21:8 Caesarea. *See note on 8:40.* **Philip the evangelist.** *See note on 6:5.* No one else in Scripture is called an evangelist, though Paul commanded Timothy to do the work of an evangelist (2Ti 4:5). Once enemies, Philip and Paul were now fellow preachers of God's gospel of grace. **the seven.** *See note on 6:3.*

21:9 virgin daughters. That they were virgins may indicate that they had been called by God for special ministry (cf. 1Co 7:34). The early church regarded these women as important sources of information in the early years of the church (see Introduction: Author and Date). **prophetesses.** Luke does not reveal the nature of their prophecy. They may have had an ongoing prophetic ministry, or prophesied only once. Since women are not to be preachers or teachers in the church (1Co 14:34–36; 1Ti 2:11, 12), they probably ministered to individuals. For an explanation of NT prophets *see notes on 11:27; 1Co 12:28; Eph 4:11.*

21:10 prophet named Agabus. *See note on 11:28.* **down from Judea.** Although it was located in Judea, the Jews considered Caesarea, seat of the Roman government, to be a foreign city (*see note on 18:22*).

21:11 belt. Old Testament prophets sometimes acted out their prophecies (cf. 1Ki 11:29–39; Is 20:2–6; Jer 13:1–11; Eze 4, 5). Agabus' action foreshadowed Paul's arrest and imprisonment by the Romans. **hands of the Gentiles.** Though falsely accused by the Jews (vv. 27, 28), Paul was arrested and imprisoned by the Romans (vv. 31–33).

21:12 we as well as the local residents. Both Paul's friends (Luke and the others traveling with him) and the Caesarean Christians.

21:13 for the name. Baptism (*see note on 2:38*; cf. 8:16; 10:48; 19:5), healing (3:6, 16; 4:10), signs and wonders (4:30), and preaching (4:18; 5:40; 8:12), were all done in the name of the Lord Jesus. His name represents all that He is.

21:14 will of the Lord be done! A confident expression of trust that God's will is best (cf. 1Sa 3:18; Mt 6:10; Lk 22:42; Jas 4:13–15).

21:15 up to Jerusalem. Jerusalem was SE of Caesarea, located on a plateau so travelers were always said to go up to it (cf. 11:2; 15:2; 18:22; Mk 10:32; Lk 2:22; Jn 2:13; Gal 1:17, 18).

21:16 Mnason. His Gr. name may mean he was a Hellenistic Jew. If so, Paul and his Gentile companions may have chosen to stay with him because of his acquaintance with Gr. culture. That would have made him more comfortable in housing a party of Gentiles than the Palestinian Jews would have been. **disciple of long standing.** Possibly one of those saved on the Day of Pentecost. If so, Mnason could have been another source of historical information for Luke.

17 After we arrived in Jerusalem, [A]the brethren
received us gladly. 18 And the following day Paul
went in with us to [a,A]James, and all [B]the elders were
present. 19 After he had greeted them, he [A]*began* to
relate one by one the things which God had done
among the Gentiles through his [B]ministry. 20 And
when they heard it they *began* [A]glorifying God;
and they said to him, "You see, brother, how many
[a]thousands there are among the Jews of those who
have believed, and they are all [B]zealous for the Law;
21 and they have been told about you, that you are
[A]teaching all the Jews who are among the Gentiles
to forsake Moses, telling them [B]not to circumcise
their children nor to [a]walk according to [C]the customs. 22 What, then, is *to be done?* They will certainly
hear that you have come. 23 Therefore do this that
we tell you. We have four men who [a,A]are under a
vow; 24 take them and [A]purify yourself along with
them, and [a]pay their expenses so that they may
[B]shave their [b]heads; and all will know that there is
nothing to the things which they have been told
about you, but that you yourself also walk orderly,
keeping the Law. 25 But concerning the Gentiles
who have believed, we wrote, [A]having decided that
they should abstain from [a]meat sacrificed to idols
and from blood and from what is strangled and
from fornication." 26 Then Paul [a]took the men, and
the next day, [A]purifying himself along with them,
[B]went into the temple giving notice of the completion of the days of purification, until the sacrifice
was offered for each one of them.

PAUL SEIZED IN THE TEMPLE

27 When [A]the seven days were almost over, [B]the
Jews from [a,C]Asia, upon seeing him in the temple,
began to stir up all the crowd and laid hands on
him, 28 crying out, "Men of Israel, come to our aid!
[A]This is the man who preaches to all men everywhere against our people and the Law and this
place; and besides he has even brought Greeks
into the temple and has [B]defiled this holy place."
29 For they had previously seen [A]Trophimus the
[B]Ephesian in the city with him, and they supposed
that Paul had brought him into the temple. 30 Then
all the city was provoked, and [a]the people rushed
together, and taking hold of Paul they [A]dragged
him out of the temple, and immediately the doors
were shut. 31 While they were seeking to kill him,
a report came up to the [a]commander of the [A]*Ro-*
man [b]cohort that all Jerusalem was in confusion.

21:17 [A]Acts 1:15; 21:7 21:18 [a]Or *Jacob* [A]Acts 12:17 [B]Acts 11:30 21:19 [A]Acts 14:27 [B]Acts 1:17 21:20 [a]Lit *ten thousands* [A]Matt 9:8 [B]Acts 15:1; 22:3; Rom 10:2; Gal 1:14 21:21 [a]I.e. observe or live by [A]Acts 21:28 [B]Acts 15:19ff; 1 Cor 7:18f [C]Acts 6:14 21:23 [a]Lit *have a vow on them* [A]Num 6:13-21; Acts 18:18 21:24 [a]Lit *spend on them* [b]Lit *head* [A]John 11:55; Acts 21:26; 24:18 [B]Acts 18:18 21:25 [a]Lit *the thing* [A]Acts 15:19f, 29 21:26 [a]Or *took the men the next day, and purifying himself* [A]John 11:55; Acts 21:24; 24:18 [B]Num 6:13; Acts 24:18 21:27 [a]I.e. west coast province of Asia Minor [A]Num 6:9, 13-20 [B]Acts 20:19; 24:18 [C]Acts 16:6 21:28 [A]Acts 6:13 [B]Matt 24:15; Acts 6:13f; 24:6 21:29 [A]Acts 20:4 [B]Acts 18:19 21:30 [a]Lit *a running together of the people occurred* [A]2 Kin 11:15; Acts 16:19; 26:21 21:31 [a]I.e. chiliarch, in command of one thousand troops [b]Or *battalion* [A]Acts 10:1

21:17 arrived in Jerusalem. Presumably in time to celebrate Pentecost, as Paul had planned (20:16). **the brethren received us gladly.** This was because of the much-needed offering they brought. Also, and more importantly, the Jerusalem believers rejoiced because the Gentile converts with Paul provided visible evidence of God's work of salvation in the Roman world. This initial, unofficial reception may have taken place at Mnason's house.

21:18 James. The brother of Jesus and head of the Jerusalem church (*see note on 12:17*), not James, the brother of John, who had been executed by Herod (12:2). **all the elders.** The mention of elders indicates that the apostles, often away on evangelistic work, had turned over rule of the Jerusalem church to them. Some have speculated that there were 70 elders, paralleling the Sanhedrin. Given the large size of the Jerusalem church, there probably were at least that many. God had decreed that after the apostles were gone, the church was to be ruled by elders (cf. 14:23; 20:17; 1Ti 5:17; Tit 1:5; Jas 5:14; 1Pe 5:1, 5).

21:19 *began* to relate one by one. Paul's official report of his missionary work did not involve meaningless generalities; he related specific incidents from his journeys (cf. 11:4). As always (cf. 14:27; 15:4, 12), Paul gave all credit and glory for his accomplishments to God.

21:20 zealous for the Law. Some Jewish believers continued to observe the ceremonial aspects of the Mosaic law. Unlike the Judaizers (*see note on 15:1*), they did not view the law as a means of salvation.

21:21 to forsake Moses. The Judaizers were spreading false reports that Paul was teaching Jewish believers to forsake their heritage. That Paul had not abandoned Jewish customs is evident from his circumcision of Timothy (16:1–3) and his own taking of a Nazirite vow (18:18).

21:23 under a vow. A Nazirite vow, symbolizing total devotion to God (*see notes on 18:18; Nu 6:1–21*).

21:24 purify yourself. Having just returned from an extended stay in Gentile lands, Paul was considered ceremonially unclean. He therefore needed to undergo ritual purification before participating (as their sponsor) in the ceremony marking the end of the 4 men's vows. **pay their expenses.** For the temple ceremony in which the 4 would shave their heads, and the sacrifices associated with the Nazirite vow. Paying those expenses for another was considered an act of piety, and by so doing, Paul would give further proof that he had not forsaken his Jewish heritage. **shave their heads.** A practice commonly associated with a Nazirite vow (Nu 6:18).

21:25 *See notes on 15:19, 20.* James made it clear that what he was asking Paul to do by no means changed the decision of the Jerusalem Council regarding Gentiles. Since Paul was Jewish, that decision did not apply to him.

21:26 purifying himself. *See note on v. 24.*

21:27 seven days. The length of the purification process (*see note on v. 24*). Paul had to appear at the temple on the third and seventh days. The incident that follows took place on the seventh day, when the process was almost completed. **Jews from Asia.** Probably from Ephesus, since they recognized Trophimus as a Gentile (v. 29). They were in Jerusalem celebrating the Feast of Pentecost.

21:28 our people and the Law and this place. Paul's enemies leveled 3 false charges against him. They claimed that he taught Jews to forsake their heritage—the same lie told by the Judaizers (*see note on v. 21*). The second charge, that Paul opposed the law, was a very dangerous one, albeit false, in this setting. Originally, Pentecost was a celebration of the firstfruits of the harvest. But by this time, it had become a celebration of Moses' receiving the law on Mt. Sinai. Thus, the Jewish people were especially zealous for the law during this feast. The third charge, of blaspheming or defiling the temple, had helped bring about the deaths of Jesus (Mk 14:57, 58) and Stephen (6:13). All 3 charges were, of course, totally false. **brought Greeks into the temple.** The Asian Jews accused Paul of having brought Trophimus past the Court of the Gentiles into the part of the temple where Gentiles were forbidden. Such a charge was absurd, for it would have entailed Paul's risking his friend's life (the Romans had granted the Jews permission to execute any Gentile who so defiled the temple).

21:30 doors were shut. This was done by the temple guards, since Paul's death on the temple grounds would defile the temple (cf. 2Ki 11:15). They made no effort, however, to rescue the apostle from the crowd, which was intent on beating him to death.

21:31 commander. The tribune (Claudias Lysias, 23:26) commanding the Roman cohort based in Jerusalem. He was the highest-ranking Roman official stationed in Jerusalem (the governor's official residence was in Caesarea, *see note on 8:40*). ***Roman* cohort.** The 1,000 man Roman occupation force. Their headquarters was Fort Antonia, located on a precipice overlooking the temple complex. From that vantage point, Roman sentries spotted the riot and informed their commander.

32 At once he [A]took along *some* soldiers and centurions and ran down to them; and when they saw
the [a]commander and the soldiers, they stopped
beating Paul. 33 Then the [a]commander came up
and took hold of him, and ordered him to be
[A]bound with [B]two chains; and he *began* asking
who he was and what he had done. 34 But among
the crowd [A]some were shouting one thing *and*
some another, and when he could not find out the
[a]facts because of the uproar, he ordered him to be
brought into [B]the barracks. 35 When he got to [A]the
stairs, he was carried by the soldiers because of
the violence of the [a]mob; 36 for the multitude of
the people kept following them, shouting, "[A]Away
with him!"
37 As Paul was about to be brought into [A]the barracks, he said to the [a]commander, "May I say something to you?" And he *said, "Do you know Greek?
38 Then you are not [A]the Egyptian who some [a]time
ago stirred up a revolt and led the four thousand
men of the Assassins out [B]into the wilderness?"
39 But Paul said, "[A]I am a Jew of Tarsus in [B]Cilicia,
a citizen of no insignificant city; and I beg you,
allow me to speak to the people." 40 When he had
given him permission, Paul, standing on [A]the stairs,
[B]motioned to the people with his hand; and when
there [a]was a great hush, he spoke to them in the
[b,C]Hebrew dialect, saying,

PAUL'S DEFENSE BEFORE THE JEWS

22 "[A]Brethren and fathers, hear my defense
which I now *offer* to you."
2 And when they heard that he was addressing
them in the [a,A]Hebrew dialect, they became even
more quiet; and he *said,
3 "[A]I am [B]a Jew, born in [C]Tarsus of [D]Cilicia, but
brought up in this city, educated [a]under [E]Gamaliel,
[b,F]strictly according to the law of our fathers, being
zealous for God just as [G]you all are today. 4 [A]I persecuted this [B]Way to the death, binding and putting
both men and women into prisons, 5 as also [A]the
high priest and all [B]the Council of the elders [a]can
testify. From them I also [C]received letters to [D]the
brethren, and started off for [C]Damascus in order
to bring even those who were there to Jerusalem
[b]as prisoners to be punished.
6 "[A]But it happened that as I was on my way, approaching Damascus about noontime, a very bright
light suddenly flashed from heaven all around me,
7 and I fell to the ground and heard a voice saying
to me, 'Saul, Saul, why are you persecuting Me?'
8 And I answered, 'Who are You, Lord?' And He said
to me, 'I am [A]Jesus the Nazarene, whom you are
persecuting.' 9 And those who were with me [A]saw
the light, to be sure, but [B]did not [a]understand the
voice of the One who was speaking to me. 10 And I
said, '[A]What shall I do, Lord?' And the Lord said to
me, 'Get up and go on into Damascus, and there you
will be told of all that has been appointed for you
to do.' 11 But since I [A]could not see because of the
[a]brightness of that light, I was led by the hand by
those who were with me and came into Damascus.
12 "A certain [A]Ananias, a man who was devout
by the standard of the Law, *and* [B]well spoken of

21:32 [a]V 31, note 1 [A]Acts 23:27 21:33 [a]V 31, note 1 [A]Acts 20:23; 21:11; 22:29; 26:29; 28:20; Eph 6:20; 2 Tim 1:16; 2:9 [B]Acts 12:6 21:34 [a]Lit *certainty* [A]Acts 19:32 [B]Acts 21:37; 22:24; 23:10, 16, 32 21:35 [a]Lit *crowd* [A]Acts 21:40 21:36 [A]Luke 23:18; John 19:15; Acts 22:22 21:37 [a]V 31, note 1 [A]Acts 21:34; 22:24; 23:10, 16, 32 21:38 [a]Lit *days* [A]Acts 5:36 [B]Matt 24:26 21:39 [A]Acts 9:11; 22:3 [B]Acts 6:9 21:40 [a]Lit *occurred* [b]I.e. Jewish Aramaic [A]Acts 21:35 [B]Acts 12:17 [C]John 5:2; Acts 1:19; 22:2; 26:14 22:1 [A]Acts 7:2 22:2 [a]I.e. Jewish Aramaic [A]Acts 21:40 22:3 [a]Lit *at the feet of* [b]Lit *according to the strictness of the ancestral law* [A]Acts 9:1-22; 22:3-16; 26:9-18 [B]Acts 21:39 [C]Acts 9:11 [D]Acts 6:9 [E]Acts 5:34 [F]Acts 23:6; 26:5; Phil 3:6 [G]Acts 21:20 22:4 [A]Acts 8:3; 22:19f; 26:9-11 [B]Acts 9:2 22:5 [a]Lit *testifies for me* [b]Lit *having been bound* [A]Acts 9:1 [B]Luke 22:66; Acts 5:21; 1 Tim 4:14 [C]Acts 9:2 [D]Acts 2:29; 3:17; 13:26; 23:1; 28:17, 21; Rom 9:3 22:6 [A]Acts 22:6-11: *Acts 9:3-8; 26:12-18* 22:8 [A]Acts 26:9 22:9 [a]Or *hear* (with comprehension) [A]Acts 26:13 [B]Acts 9:7 22:10 [A]Acts 16:30 22:11 [a]Lit *glory* [A]Acts 9:8 22:12 [A]Acts 9:10 [B]Acts 6:3; 10:22

21:32 soldiers and centurions. The use of the plural "centurions" suggests Lysias took at least 200 soldiers with him, since each centurion commanded 100 men.

21:33 two chains. Assuming Paul to be guilty of something (since the Jews were so enraged at him), Lysias arrested him. The tribune thought he knew who Paul was (v. 38).

21:34 barracks. In Fort Antonia, overlooking the temple grounds.

21:36 Away with him! Or, "Kill him" (cf. 22:22; Lk 23:18; Jn 19:15).

21:37 Do you know Greek? Paul's use of the language of educated people startled Lysias, who assumed his prisoner was an uncultured criminal.

21:38 the Egyptian … stirred up a revolt. Lysias' question revealed who he (wrongly) assumed Paul was. The Egyptian was a false prophet who, several years earlier, had promised to drive out the Romans. Before he could do so, however, his forces were attacked and routed by Roman troops led by governor Felix. Though several hundred of his followers were killed or captured, he managed to escape. Lysias assumed he had returned and been captured by the crowd. **Assassins.** Called "sicarii," they were a terrorist group whose Jewish nationalism led them to murder Romans and Jews perceived as sympathetic to Rome. Since they often used the cover of a crowd to stab their victims, Lysias assumed the mob had caught one of their leaders in the act.

21:39 Tarsus. *See note on 9:11.* Tarsus was an important cultural city, with a university rivaling those at Athens and Alexandria.

22:1–22 Paul's first of 6 defenses (cf. 22:30–23:10; 24:10–21; 25:1–12; 26:1–29; 28:17–29).

22:2 Hebrew dialect. Aramaic, the language commonly spoken in Israel (cf. 2Ki 18:26; Is 36:11). *See note on 21:37.*

22:3 I am a Jew. A response to the false charges raised by the Asian Jews (*see note on 21:21*). **born in Tarsus.** *See note on 21:39.* **Cilicia.** *See note on 6:9.* Tarsus was the chief city of Cilicia. **brought up in this city.** Paul was born among the Hellenistic Jews of the Diaspora, but had been brought up in Jerusalem. **Gamaliel.** *See note on 5:34.* That Paul had studied under the most celebrated rabbi of that day was further evidence that the charges against him were absurd. **law of our fathers.** As a student of Gamaliel, Paul received extensive training both in the OT law and in the rabbinic traditions. Also, though he did not mention it to the crowd, he also had been a Pharisee. In light of all that, the charge that Paul opposed the law (*see note on 21:21*) was ridiculous.

22:4 I persecuted this Way. *See note on 9:2.* As the leading persecutor of the Christian church after Stephen's martyrdom (cf. Gal 1:13), Paul's zeal for his Jewish heritage far outstripped that of his hearers.

22:5 Council of the elders. The Sanhedrin (*see notes on 4:15; Mt 26:59*).

22:6–16 The second of 3 NT accounts of Paul's conversion (cf. 9:1–19; 26:12–18).

22:6 about noontime. Paul's reference to the time of day emphasizes how bright the light from heaven really was. It outshone the sun at its peak.

22:7, 8 Cf. 9:4, 5.

22:9 did not understand the voice. This is no contradiction with 9:7. Since Jesus spoke only to Paul, only he understood the Lord's words. His companions heard the sound, but could not make out the words (cf. Jn 12:29).

22:11 brightness of that light. Paul's companions saw the light, but only he saw the Lord Jesus Christ (v. 14; 9:7, 17, 27; 26:16; 1Co 9:1; 15:8).

22:12 Ananias. *See note on 9:10.* His testimony as a respected member of Damascus' Jewish community would carry weight with Paul's hostile audience.

by all the Jews who lived there, 13 came to me, and
standing near said to me, '[A]Brother Saul, receive
your sight!' And [a,B]at that very time I looked up at
him. 14 And he said, '[A]The God of our fathers has
[B]appointed you to know His will and to [C]see the
[D]Righteous One and to hear an [a]utterance from His
mouth. 15 For you will be [A]a witness for Him to all
men of [B]what you have seen and heard. 16 Now why
do you delay? [A]Get up and be baptized, and [B]wash
away your sins, [C]calling on His name.'
17 "It happened when I [A]returned to Jerusalem and
was praying in the temple, that I [B]fell into a trance,
18 and I saw Him saying to me, '[A]Make haste, and
get out of Jerusalem quickly, because they will not
accept your testimony about Me.' 19 And I said, 'Lord,
they themselves understand that in one synagogue
after another [A]I used to imprison and [B]beat those
who believed in You. 20 And [A]when the blood of Your
witness Stephen was being shed, I also was standing by approving, and watching out for the coats of
those who were slaying him.' 21 And He said to me,
'Go! For I will send you far away [A]to the Gentiles.' "
22 They listened to him up to this statement, and
then they raised their voices and said, "[A]Away with
such a fellow from the earth, for [B]he should not be
allowed to live!" 23 And as they were crying out and
[A]throwing off their cloaks and [B]tossing dust into the
air, 24 the [a]commander ordered him to be brought into
[A]the barracks, stating that he should be [B]examined by
scourging so that he might find out the reason why
they were shouting against him that way. 25 But when
they stretched him out [a]with thongs, Paul said to the
centurion who was standing by, "Is it [b]lawful for you to
scourge [A]a man who is a Roman and uncondemned?"
26 When the centurion heard *this,* he went to the [a]com-
mander and told him, saying, "What are you about
to do? For this man is a Roman." 27 The [a]commander
came and said to him, "Tell me, are you a Roman?"
And he said, "Yes." 28 The [a]commander answered, "I
acquired this citizenship with a large sum of money."
And Paul said, "But I was actually born *a citizen.*"
29 Therefore those who were about to [A]examine him
immediately [a]let go of him; and the [b]commander also
[B]was afraid when he found out that he was a Roman,
and because he had [c,C]put him in chains.
30 But on the next day, [A]wishing to know for certain why he had been accused by the Jews, he [B]re-
leased him and ordered the chief priests and all
[C]the [a]Council to assemble, and brought Paul down
and set him before them.

PAUL BEFORE THE COUNCIL

23 Paul, looking intently at [A]the [a]Council, said,
"[B]Brethren, [C]I have [b]lived my life with a perfectly good conscience before God up to this day." 2 The
high priest [A]Ananias commanded those standing beside him [B]to strike him on the mouth. 3 Then Paul said
to him, "God is going to strike you, [A]you whitewashed
wall! Do you [B]sit to try me according to the Law,
and in violation of the Law order me to be struck?"

22:13 [a]Or *instantly;* lit *at the very hour* [A]Acts 9:17 [B]Acts 9:18 22:14 [a]Or *message;* lit *voice* [A]Acts 3:13 [B]Acts 9:15; 26:16 [C]Acts 9:17; 26:16; 1 Cor 9:1; 15:8 [D]Acts 7:52 22:15 [A]Acts 23:11; 26:16 [B]Acts 22:14 22:16 [A]Acts 9:18 [B]Acts 2:38; 1 Cor 6:11; Eph 5:26; Heb 10:22 [C]Acts 7:59 22:17 [A]Acts 9:26; 26:20 [B]Acts 10:10 22:18 [A]Acts 9:29 22:19 [A]Acts 8:3; 22:4 [B]Matt 10:17; Acts 26:11 22:20 [A]Acts 7:58f; 8:1; 26:10 22:21 [A]Acts 9:15 22:22 [A]Acts 21:36; 1 Thess 2:16 [B]Acts 25:24 22:23 [A]Acts 7:58 [B]2 Sam 16:13 22:24 [a]I.e. chiliarch, in command of one thousand troops [A]Acts 21:34 [B]Acts 22:29 22:25 [a]Or *for the whip* [b]Interrogation by torture was a procedure used with slaves [A]Acts 16:37 22:26 [a]V 24, note 1 22:27 [a]V 24, note 1 22:28 [a]V 24, note 1 22:29 [a]Lit *withdrew from* [b]V 24, note 1 [c]Lit *bound him* [A]Acts 22:24 [B]Acts 16:38 [C]Acts 21:33 22:30 [a]Or *Sanhedrin* [A]Acts 23:28 [B]Acts 21:33 [C]Matt 5:22 23:1 [a]Or *Sanhedrin* [b]Or *conducted myself as a citizen* [A]Acts 22:30; 23:6, 15, 20, 28 [B]Acts 22:5 [C]Acts 24:16; 2 Cor 1:12; 2 Tim 1:3 23:2 [A]Acts 24:1 [B]John 18:22 23:3 [A]Matt 23:27 [B]Lev 19:15; Deut 25:2; John 7:51

22:14 the Righteous One. A title given to the Messiah (cf. 3:14; 7:52; Is 53:11).

22:15 a witness. Paul never wavered in his claim to have seen the risen, glorified Christ on the Damascus road (*see note on v. 11*).

22:16 wash away your sins. Grammatically the phrase, "calling on His name," precedes "Get up and be baptized." Salvation comes from calling on the name of the Lord (Ro 10:9, 10, 13), not from being baptized (*see note on 2:38*).

22:17 when I returned to Jerusalem. After a brief ministry in Damascus (9:20–25) and 3 years in Nabatean Arabia (Gal 1:17, 18). **a trance.** Paul was carried beyond his senses into the supernatural realm to receive revelation from Jesus Christ. The experience was unique to the apostles, since only Peter (10:10; 11:5) and John (Rev 1:10) had similar revelations. This was the fourth of 6 visions received by Paul in Acts (cf. 9:3–6; 16:9, 10; 18:9, 10; 23:11; 27:23, 24).

22:20 Your witness Stephen. *See notes on 6:5; 7:54–60.* **approving.** See 8:1.

22:21–23 Paul's insistence that the Lord had sent *him to minister to the despised Gentiles* was too much for the crowd. They viewed the teaching that Gentiles could be saved without first becoming Jewish proselytes (thus granting them equal status with the Jewish people before God) as intolerable blasphemy.

22:23 throwing off their cloaks. They did this in preparation to stone Paul, in horror at his "blasphemy" (*see note on 14:14*) or in uncontrollable rage—or, most likely, for all 3 reasons. Their passions inflamed by racial pride, the members of the crowd lost any semblance of self-control. **tossing dust.** A sign of intense emotion (cf. 2Sa 16:13; Job 2:12; Rev 18:19).

22:24 the commander ordered him to be brought into the barracks. Lysias realized he would have to interrogate Paul privately. He ordered his soldiers to bring the prisoner into Fort Antonia, away from the angry mob. **that he should be examined by scourging.** A brutal Roman interrogation method. Prisoners frequently died after being flogged with the Roman *flagellum* (metal-tipped leather thongs attached to a wooden handle).

22:25 stretched him out with thongs. This was done in preparation for his examination by scourging. Stretching Paul taut would magnify the effects of the *flagellum* on his body. **centurion.** *See notes on 10:1; Mt 8:5.* There would have been 10 centurions in the 1,000-man Roman garrison in Jerusalem. **who is a Roman.** Roman citizens were exempted (by the Valerian and Porcian laws) from such brutal methods of interrogation. Paul now exerted his rights as a Roman citizen. His claim would not have been questioned, because the penalty for falsely claiming Roman citizenship was death.

22:26 What are you about to do? For this man is a Roman. The centurion informed his commander of Paul's citizenship, cautioning him against an act that could have ended Lysias' military career—or even cost him his life.

22:28 with a large sum. Roman citizenship was officially not for sale, but could sometimes be obtained by bribing corrupt officials.

22:30–23:10 Paul's second of 6 defenses (cf. vv. 1–21; 24:10–21; 25:1–12; 26:1–29; 28:17–29).

22:30 chief priests and all the Council. He convened an unofficial meeting of the Sanhedrin (*see notes on 4:15, 23*).

23:1 the Council. The Sanhedrin (*see notes on 4:15; Mt 26:59*). **good conscience.** *See note on 2Co 1:12;* cf. 24:16; 2Ti 1:3.

23:2 high priest Ananias. Not the Annas of the Gospels (*see note on Lk 3:2*), this man was one of Israel's cruelest and most corrupt High Priests (*see note on 4:6*). His pro-Roman policies alienated him from the Jewish people, who murdered him at the outset of the revolt against Rome (A.D. 66). **commanded . . . to strike him.** An illegal act in keeping with Ananias' brutal character. The verb translated "strike" is used of the mob's beating of Paul (21:32) and the Roman soldiers' beating of Jesus (Mt 27:30). It was no mere slap on the face, but a vicious blow.

23:3 whitewashed wall! Cf. Eze 13:10–16; Mt 23:27. **in violation of the Law.** Outraged by the High Priest's flagrant violation of Jewish law, Paul flared up in anger. When Jesus was similarly struck in violation of the law, He reacted by calmly asking the reason for the

4 But the bystanders said, "Do you revile God's high
priest?" 5 And Paul said, "I was not aware, brethren,
that he was high priest; for it is written, '[A]YOU SHALL
NOT SPEAK EVIL OF A RULER OF YOUR PEOPLE.' "
6 But perceiving that one group were [A]Sadducees
and the other Pharisees, Paul *began* crying out in
[B]the [a]Council, "[C]Brethren, [D]I am a Pharisee, a son of
Pharisees; I am on trial for [E]the hope and resurrection of the dead!" 7 As he said this, there occurred a
dissension between the Pharisees and Sadducees,
and the assembly was divided. 8 For [A]the Sadducees
say that there is no resurrection, nor an angel, nor
a spirit, but the Pharisees acknowledge them all.
9 And there occurred a great uproar; and some of
[A]the scribes of the Pharisaic party stood up and
began to argue heatedly, saying, "[B]We find nothing
wrong with this man; [C]suppose a spirit or an angel
has spoken to him?" 10 And as a great dissension
was developing, the [a]commander was afraid Paul
would be torn to pieces by them and ordered the
troops to go down and take him away from them
by force, and bring him into [A]the barracks.
11 But on [A]the night *immediately* following, the
Lord stood at his side and said, "[B]Take courage;
for [C]as you have [D]solemnly witnessed to My cause
at Jerusalem, so you must witness at Rome also."

A CONSPIRACY TO KILL PAUL

12 When it was day, [A]the Jews formed a [a]conspir-
acy and [B]bound themselves under an oath, saying
that they would neither eat nor drink until they
had killed Paul. 13 There were more than forty who
formed this plot. 14 They came to the chief priests
and the elders and said, "We have [A]bound ourselves
under a solemn oath to taste nothing until we have
killed Paul. 15 Now therefore, you [a]and [A]the [b]Council
notify the [c]commander to bring him down to you,
as though you were going to determine his case
by a more thorough investigation; and we for our
part are ready to slay him before he comes near
the place."
16 But the son of Paul's sister heard of their ambush, [a]and he came and entered [A]the barracks and
told Paul. 17 Paul called one of the centurions to him
and said, "Lead this young man to the [a]commander,
for he has something to report to him." 18 So he took
him and led him to the [a]commander and *said, "Paul
[A]the prisoner called me to him and asked me to lead
this young man to you since he has something to
tell you." 19 The [a]commander took him by the hand
and stepping aside, *began* to inquire of him privately, "What is it that you have to report to me?"
20 And he said, "[A]The Jews have agreed to ask you
to bring Paul down tomorrow to [B]the [a]Council, as
though they were going to inquire somewhat more
thoroughly about him. 21 So do not [a]listen to them,
for more than forty of them are [A]lying in wait for
him who have [B]bound themselves under a curse
not to eat or drink until they slay him; and now
they are ready and waiting for the promise from

23:5 [A]Ex 22:28 23:6 [a]Or *Sanhedrin* [A]Matt 3:7; 22:23 [B]Acts 22:30; 23:1, 15, 20, 28 [C]Acts 22:5 [D]Acts 26:5; Phil 3:5 [E]Acts 24:15, 21; 26:8 23:8 [A]Matt 22:23; Mark 12:18; Luke 20:27 23:9 [A]Mark 2:16; Luke 5:30 [B]Acts 23:29 [C]John 12:29; Acts 22:6ff 23:10 [a]I.e. chiliarch, in command of one thousand troops [A]Acts 21:34; 23:16, 32 23:11 [A]Acts 18:9 [B]Matt 9:2 [C]Acts 19:21 [D]Luke 16:28; Acts 28:23 23:12 [a]Or *mob* [A]Acts 9:23; 23:30; 1 Thess 2:16 [B]Acts 23:14, 21 23:14 [A]Acts 23:12, 21 23:15 [a]Lit *with* [b]Or *Sanhedrin* [c]V 10, note 1 [A]Acts 22:30; 23:1, 6, 20, 28 23:16 [a]Or *having been present* with them, *and he entered* [A]Acts 21:34; 23:10, 32 23:17 [a]V 10, note 1 23:18 [a]V 10, note 1 [A]Eph 3:1 23:19 [a]V 10, note 1 23:20 [a]Or *Sanhedrin* [A]Acts 23:14f [B]Acts 22:30; 23:1, 6, 15, 28 23:21 [a]Lit *be persuaded by them* [A]Acts 23:12, 14 [B]Luke 11:54

blow (Jn 18:23). Paul's reaction was wrong, as he would shortly admit (v. 5). Although an evil man, Ananias still held a God-ordained office, and was to be granted the respect that position demanded.

23:4 revile. Those standing near Paul were appalled by his harsh rebuke of the High Priest. "Revile" is the same word used in Jn 9:28 to describe the Jewish leaders' insulting remarks to the blind man whom Jesus had healed. Peter used it to speak of the abuse Jesus endured (1Pe 2:23).

23:5 I was not aware. Some believe this to be another manifestation of Paul's eye problems (cf. Gal 4:15); or that Paul was so angry that he forgot to whom he was speaking; or that he was being sarcastic, since Ananias was not acting like a High Priest should. The simplest explanation is to take Paul's words at face value. He had been gone from Jerusalem for many years and would not likely have recognized Ananias by sight. That this was an informal gathering of the Sanhedrin (*see note on 22:30*) would have meant the High Priest would not have been wearing his official garments. **it is written.** Quoted from Ex 22:28.

23:6 Ananias' haughty attitude and illegal act convinced Paul he would not receive a fair hearing before the Sanhedrin. Accordingly, he decided on a bold step. As a Pharisee, and possibly a former member of the Sanhedrin (*see note on 26:10*), Paul was well aware of the tensions between the Sanhedrin's two factions. He appealed to the Pharisees for support, reminding them that he himself was a Pharisee, and appealing to the major theological difference between them and the Sadducees (*see note on v. 7*). Paul thus created a split between the Sanhedrin's factions. **Sadducees ... Pharisees.** *See note on Mt 3:7.* **Council.** *See note on 4:15.*

23:7 a dissension. There were major social, political, and theological differences between the Sadducees and Pharisees. By raising the issue of the resurrection, Paul appealed to the Pharisees for support on perhaps the most important theological difference (*see note on v. 8*). Since the resurrection of Jesus Christ is also the central theme of Christianity, this was no cynical ploy on Paul's part to divide the Sanhedrin over a trivial point of theology.

23:8 Sadducees ... Pharisees. The Sadducees accepted only the Pentateuch as divinely inspired Scripture. Since they claimed (wrongly, cf. Mt 22:23–33) that the Pentateuch did not teach that there would be a resurrection, they rejected it. The Pharisees, however, believed in the resurrection and afterlife. Their beliefs were thus closer to Christianity than those of the Sadducees. Significantly, the Scripture records the conversion of Pharisees (15:5; Jn 3:1), but not of Sadducees.

23:9 scribes of the Pharisaic party. So intense was their theological disagreement with the Sadducees that they were willing to defend Paul—even though he was a leader of the hated sect of the Christians (cf. 24:5).

23:11 the Lord stood at his side. The fifth of 6 visions Paul received in Acts (cf. 9:3–6; 16:9, 10; 18:9, 10; 22:17, 18; 27:23, 24), all coming at crucial points in his ministry. **you must witness at Rome.** Jesus encouraged Paul by telling him that his desire (Ro 1:9–11; 15:23) to visit Rome would be granted.

23:12 bound themselves under an oath. Lit. they "anathematized" themselves (cf. Gal 1:8, 9), thus invoking divine judgment if they failed (cf. 1Sa 14:44; 2Sa 3:35; 19:13; 1Ki 2:23; 2Ki 6:31).

23:14 chief priests and the elders. *See notes on 4:23;* cf. Mt 16:21. Being Sadducees, they would be more inclined to help the conspirators. Significantly excluded are the scribes who, being mostly Pharisees, had already shown their willingness to defend Paul (v. 9).

23:16 son of Paul's sister. The only clear reference in Scripture to Paul's family (for other possible references see Ro 16:7, 11, 21). Why he was in Jerusalem, away from the family home in Tarsus, is not known. Nor is it evident why he would want to warn his uncle, since Paul's family possibly disinherited him when he became a Christian (Php 3:8). **entered the barracks and told Paul.** Since Paul was not under arrest, but merely in protective custody, he was able to receive visitors.

23:17 centurions. *See note on 22:25.*

you." 22 So the [a]commander let the young man go,
instructing him, "Tell no one that you have notified
me of these things."

PAUL MOVED TO CAESAREA

23 And he called to him two of the centurions and
said, "Get two hundred soldiers ready by [a]the third
hour of the night to proceed to [A]Caesarea, [b]with
seventy horsemen and two hundred [c]spearmen."
24 *They were* also to provide mounts to put Paul on
and bring him safely to [A]Felix the governor. 25 And
he wrote a letter having this form:

26 "Claudius Lysias, to the [A]most excellent
governor Felix, [B]greetings.

27 "When this man was arrested by the Jews
and was about to be slain by them, [A]I came
up to them with the troops and rescued him,
[B]having learned that he was a Roman. 28 And
[A]wanting to ascertain the charge for which
they were accusing him, I [B]brought him down
to their [a,C]Council; 29 and I found him to be
accused over [A]questions about their Law, but
[a]under [B]no accusation deserving death or
[b]imprisonment.

30 "When I was [A]informed that there would
be [B]a plot against the man, I sent him to you at
once, also instructing [C]his accusers to [a]bring
charges against him before you."

31 So the soldiers, in accordance with their orders,
took Paul and brought him by night to Antipatris.
32 But the next day, leaving [A]the horsemen to go on
with him, they returned to [B]the barracks. 33 When
these had come to [A]Caesarea and delivered the letter
to [B]the governor, they also presented Paul to him.
34 When he had read it, he asked from what [A]prov-
ince he was, and when he learned that [B]he was from
Cilicia, 35 he said, "I will give you a hearing after
your [A]accusers arrive also," giving orders for him
to be [B]kept in Herod's [a]Praetorium.

PAUL BEFORE FELIX

24 After [A]five days the high priest [B]Ananias came
down with some elders, [a]with an [b]attorney
named Tertullus, and they [c]brought charges to [C]the
governor against Paul. 2 After *Paul* had been summoned, Tertullus began to accuse him, saying *to
the governor,*

"Since we have through you attained much
peace, and since by your providence reforms are
being carried out for this nation, 3 we acknowledge
this in every way and everywhere, [A]most excellent
Felix, with all thankfulness. 4 But, that I may not
weary you any further, I beg you [a]to grant us, by
your kindness, a brief hearing. 5 For we have found
this man a real pest and a fellow who stirs up dissension among all the Jews throughout [a]the world,
and a ringleader of the [A]sect of the Nazarenes.

23:22 [a]V 10, note 1 23:23 [a]I.e. 9 p.m. [b]Lit *and* [c]Or *slingers* or *bowmen* [A]Acts 8:40; 23:33 23:24 [A]Acts 23:26, 33; 24:1, 3, 10; 25:14 23:26 [A]Luke 1:3; Acts 24:3; 26:25 [B]Acts 15:23 23:27 [A]Acts 21:32f [B]Acts 22:25-29 23:28 [a]Or *Sanhedrin* [A]Acts 22:30 [B]Acts 23:10 [C]Acts 23:1 23:29 [a]Lit *having* [b]Lit *bonds* [A]Acts 18:15; 25:19 [B]Acts 23:9; 25:25; 26:31; 28:18 23:30 [a]Lit *speak against him* [A]Acts 23:20f [B]Acts 9:24; 23:12 [C]Acts 23:35; 24:19; 25:16 23:32 [A]Acts 23:23 [B]Acts 23:10 23:33 [A]Acts 8:40; 23:23 [B]Acts 23:24, 26; 24:1, 3, 10; 25:14 23:34 [A]Acts 25:1 [B]Acts 6:9; 21:39 23:35 [a]I.e. governor's official residence [A]Acts 23:30; 24:19; 25:16 [B]Acts 24:27 24:1 [a]Lit *and* [b]Lit *orator* [c]Or *presented their evidence* or *case* [A]Acts 24:11 [B]Acts 23:2 [C]Acts 23:24 24:3 [A]Acts 23:26; 26:25 24:4 [a]Lit *to hear...briefly* 24:5 [a]Lit *the inhabited earth* [A]Acts 15:5; 24:14

23:23, 24 To foil the conspirators' plot, avoid a potentially explosive confrontation with the Jews, and save Paul's life, Lysias realized he had to get the apostle out of Jerusalem and to his superior, Governor Felix in Caesarea.

23:23 soldiers ... horsemen ... spearmen. The "soldiers" were legionnaires, the elite soldiers of the Roman army; the "horsemen" were from the garrison's cavalry detachment; and the "spearmen," or javelin throwers, were soldiers less heavily armed than the legionnaires. Lysias sent almost half of his 1,000-man garrison, showing how seriously he viewed the plot against Paul. **third hour of the night.** 9:00 p.m.

23:26 governor Felix. *See note on 24:2.*

23:27 having learned that he was a Roman. Actually, Lysias did not find this out until after he arrested Paul (22:25, 26). Lysias sought to portray himself in the best possible light before the governor. For that reason, he also neglected to mention his order to have Paul scourged (22:24), and his mistaken assumption that he was the notorious Egyptian assassin (21:38).

23:29 questions about their Law. Lysias' failure to mention any crimes against Roman law was tantamount to declaring Paul innocent.

23:30 to bring charges against him before you. The plot against Paul's life rendered any further hearings at Jerusalem unsafe, thus requiring Lysias to burden Felix with the case.

23:31 Antipatris. A Roman military post about 40 mi. from Jerusalem. Travelers from Jerusalem to Caesarea often rested there. To get there from Jerusalem in one night (v. 32) would have been an exhausting forced march for the foot soldiers.

23:32 horsemen. Since there was much less danger of ambush in the largely Gentile region of Samaria, the foot soldiers were no longer needed.

23:33 Caesarea. *See note on 9:30.*

23:34 from what province he was. Felix needed to determine whether he had jurisdiction to hear Paul's case. **from Cilicia.** Judea and Cilicia were at that time both under the legate of Syria, so Felix had the authority to hear his case.

23:35 Herod's Praetorium. Felix's official residence in Caesarea.

24:1 After five days. A very short period of time for the Jewish leaders to put their case together, hire an attorney, and make the trip to Caesarea. Perhaps they feared Felix would dismiss the case against Paul if they did not pursue it rapidly. **the high priest Ananias.** *See note on 23:2.* **elders.** Important leaders of the Sanhedrin (*see note on 4:5*). **Tertullus.** Possibly a Roman, but more likely a Hellenistic Jew (cf. v. 6).

24:3 Felix. Governor of Judea from A.D. 52 to 59. Felix was a former slave whose brother (a favorite of Emperor Claudius) had obtained for him the position as governor. He was not highly regarded by the influential Romans of his day and accomplished little during his term as governor. He defeated the Egyptian and his followers (*see note on 21:38*), but his brutality angered the Jews and led to his ouster as governor by Emperor Nero two years after Paul's hearing (v. 27).

24:5–7 Having dispensed with the obligatory flattery of Felix, Tertullus set forth the specific charges against Paul. They included sedition (a violation of Roman law), sectarianism (a violation of Jewish law), and sacrilege (a violation of God's law).

24:5 a real pest. This statement, while reflecting the Sanhedrin's hatred of the apostle and Christianity, was not a specific charge of wrongdoing. **stirs up dissension.** The first and (in a Roman court) most serious charge leveled against Paul: sedition (rebellion). The Romans did not tolerate those who incited rebellion (as the Jews present would learn a few years later in A.D. 66). Had the Jewish leaders been able to substantiate this charge, Paul would have faced severe punishment, possibly even execution. Tertullus carefully avoided naming any specific incidents, since Felix could then have transferred Paul's case to the governor in whose jurisdiction the incident took place. The Jews wanted Paul tried before a governor over whom they had some influence. **ringleader ... sect of the Nazarenes.** The second charge brought against Paul was sectarianism (heresy). Tertullus' contemptuous reference to Christianity as "the sect of the Nazarenes" (cf. 6:14; Jn 1:46; 7:41, 52) was intended to portray Paul as the leader of a messianic sect posing a danger to Rome.

6 And he even tried to [A]desecrate the temple; and
[a]then we arrested him. [[b]We wanted to judge him according to our own Law. 7 But Lysias the commander
came along, and with much violence took him out
of our hands, 8 ordering his accusers to come before
you.] By examining him yourself concerning all
these matters you will be able to ascertain the things
of which we accuse him." 9 [A]The Jews also joined
in the attack, asserting that these things were so.
10 When [A]the governor had nodded for him to
speak, Paul responded:

"Knowing that for many years you have been
a judge to this nation, I cheerfully make my defense, 11 since you can take note of the fact that no
more than [A]twelve days ago I went up to Jerusalem
to worship. 12 [A]Neither in the temple, nor in the
synagogues, nor in the city *itself* did they find me
carrying on a discussion with anyone or [B]causing
[a]a riot. 13 [A]Nor can they prove to you *the charges* of
which they now accuse me. 14 But this I admit to
you, that according to [A]the Way which they call a
[B]sect I do serve [a,C]the God of our fathers, [D]believing
everything that is in accordance with the Law and
that is written in the Prophets; 15 having a hope in
God, which [A]these men cherish themselves, that
there shall certainly be a resurrection of both the
righteous and the wicked. 16 In view of this, [A]I also
[a]do my best to maintain always a blameless conscience *both* before God and before men. 17 Now
[A]after several years I [B]came to bring [a]alms to my
nation and to present offerings; 18 in which they
found me *occupied* in the temple, having been [A]pu-
rified, without *any* [B]crowd or uproar. But *there were*
some [C]Jews from [a]Asia— 19 who ought to have been
present before you and to [A]make accusation, if they
should have anything against me. 20 Or else let these
men themselves tell what misdeed they found when
I stood before [A]the [a]Council, 21 other than for this
one statement which [A]I shouted out while standing
among them, 'For the resurrection of the dead I am
on trial before you today.' "

22 But Felix, [a]having a more exact knowledge
about [A]the Way, put them off, saying, "When Lysias
the [b]commander comes down, I will decide your
case." 23 Then he gave orders to the centurion for
him to be [A]kept in custody and *yet* [B]have *some* freedom, and not to prevent any of [C]his friends from
ministering to him.

24 But some days later Felix arrived with Drusilla,
his [a]wife who was a Jewess, and sent for Paul and
heard him *speak* about [A]faith in Christ Jesus. 25 But
as he was discussing [A]righteousness, [B]self-control
and [C]the judgment to come, Felix became frightened
and said, "Go away for the present, and when I find

24:6 [a]Lit *also* [b]The early mss do not contain the remainder of v 6, v 7, nor the first part of v 8 [A]Acts 21:28 24:9 [A]1 Thess 2:16 24:10 [A]Acts 23:24 24:11 [A]Acts 21:18, 27; 24:1 24:12 [a]Lit *an attack of a mob* [A]Acts 25:8 [B]Acts 24:18 24:13 [A]Acts 25:7 24:14 [a]Lit *the ancestral God* [A]Acts 9:2; 24:22 [B]Acts 15:5; 24:5 [C]Acts 3:13 [D]Acts 25:8; 26:4ff, 22f; 28:23 24:15 [A]Dan 12:2; John 5:28f; 11:24; Acts 23:6 24:16 [a]Lit *practice myself* [A]Acts 23:1 24:17 [a]Or *gifts to charity* [A]Acts 20:31 [B]Acts 11:29f; Rom 15:25-28; 1 Cor 16:1-4; 2 Cor 8:1-4; 9:1, 2, 12; Gal 2:10 24:18 [a]I.e. west coast province of Asia Minor [A]Acts 21:26 [B]Acts 24:12 [C]Acts 21:27 24:19 [A]Acts 23:30 24:20 [a]Or *Sanhedrin* [A]Matt 5:22 24:21 [A]Acts 23:6; 24:15 24:22 [a]Lit *knowing more accurately* [b]I.e. chiliarch, in command of one thousand troops [A]Acts 24:14 24:23 [A]Acts 23:35 [B]Acts 28:16 [C]Acts 23:16; 27:3 24:24 [a]Lit *own wife* [A]Acts 20:21 24:25 [A]Titus 2:12 [B]Gal 5:23; Titus 1:8; 2 Pet 1:6 [C]Acts 10:42

24:6–8a **he even ... before you.** Many ancient manuscripts omit this passage, raising the question of whom Tertullus was urging Felix to examine. If the passage is omitted, Tertullus would be asking Felix to examine Paul; but the apostle would merely have denied Tertullus' false accusations. If the passage is genuine, Tertullus would be falsely accusing Lysias of overstepping his authority by meddling in a proper Jewish legal proceeding. He would then be claiming that an examination of Lysias would confirm the Jewish leaders' false interpretation of the events. That would help explain Felix's decision to adjourn the hearing until he sent for Lysias (v. 22).

24:6 **tried to desecrate the temple.** The third accusation leveled against Paul was sacrilege, blasphemy against God. The Jewish leaders, through their spokesman, repeated the false charges of the Asian Jews (21:28). Trying to whitewash the angry crowd's savage beating of Paul, they claimed (falsely) to have arrested him.

24:7, 8a Another falsehood, intended to shift the blame for the incident. Actually, it was the Jewish mob that was guilty of violence; Lysias put a stop to the riot and rescued Paul.

24:10–21 Paul's third of 6 defenses (cf. 22:1–21; 22:30–23:10; 25:1–12; 26:1–29; 28:17–19).

24:10 **many years .... judge.** Both as governor, and before that during his service under the governor of Samaria. Unlike Tertullus, Paul was not flattering Felix, but reminding him of his acquaintance with Jewish laws, customs, and beliefs. Felix was thus bound to give a just verdict.

24:11 **twelve days.** Five of which had been spent at Caesarea waiting for his accusers to arrive (v. 1). Several of the remaining 7 had been taken up with his purification rites (*see notes on 21:24, 27*). Paul's point was that, even if he had wanted to, he had not had the time to incite a revolt.

24:14 **the Way.** *See note on 9:2.* **the Law and ... in the Prophets.** The "Law and the Prophets" refers to the OT (see Mt 7:12). The Sadducees rejected much of the OT (*see note on 23:8*), while both they and the Pharisees rejected the OT's witness to Jesus Christ (cf. Lk 24:27, 44; Jn 1:45; 5:39, 46). In contrast, Paul viewed the entire OT as the inspired Word of God, and believed everything it taught.

24:15 **hope in God.** The great hope of the Jewish people was the resurrection (Job 19:25–27; Da 12:2). It was Paul, not the skeptical Sadducees, who stood in the mainstream of traditional Jewish theology.

24:16 **blameless conscience.** *See note on 23:1.*

24:17 **alms ... offerings.** The only reference in Acts to the delivery of the offering Paul had been collecting for the poor saints in Jerusalem (*see note on 19:21*). Far from seeking to stir up strife, Paul had gone to Jerusalem on a humanitarian mission.

24:18 **purified.** *See note on 21:24.* **Jews from Asia.** *See note on 21:27.*

24:21 **For the resurrection of the dead.** Belief in the resurrection was not a crime under either Jewish or Roman law. Nor was Paul responsible for the longstanding feud between the Sadducees and Pharisees that erupted into open dissension when he made his statement.

24:22 **having a more exact knowledge about the Way.** Probably from his wife Drusilla, who was Jewish (v. 24). **put them off.** The witnesses to Paul's alleged crime (the Jews from Asia) had failed to show up for the hearing. Nor could the Jewish leaders prove him guilty of a crime. The only verdict Felix could render consistent with Roman law was not guilty, which would infuriate the Jews, and possibly lead to further trouble. Since as governor, Felix's primary responsibility was to maintain order, he decided the best decision was no decision, and adjourned the proceedings on the pretext of needing further information from Lysias. **commander comes down.** Lysias' written report had already stated that the dispute involved questions of Jewish law (23:29), and that Paul was not guilty of any crime (23:29). It is difficult to see what more he could have added, and there is no evidence that Felix ever summoned him.

24:24 **Drusilla.** The youngest daughter of Agrippa I (*see note on 12:1*), and Felix's third wife. Felix, struck by her beauty, had lured her away from her husband. At the time of Paul's hearing, she was not yet 20 years old.

24:25 **righteousness, self-control and the judgment.** God demands "righteousness" of all people, because of His holy nature (Mt 5:48; 1Pe 1:15, 16). For men and women to conform to that absolute standard requires "self-control." The result of failing to exhibit self-control and to conform oneself to God's righteous standard is (apart from salvation) "judgment." **Felix became frightened.** Living with a woman he had lured away from her husband, Felix obviously lacked "righteousness" and "self-control." The

time I will summon you.” 26 At the same time too, he was hoping that [A]money would be given him by Paul; therefore he also used to send for him quite often and converse with him. 27 But after two years had passed, Felix [a]was succeeded by Porcius [A]Festus, and [B]wishing to do the Jews a favor, Felix left Paul [C]imprisoned.

PAUL BEFORE FESTUS

25 Festus then, having arrived in [A]the province, three days later went up to Jerusalem from [B]Caesarea. 2 And the chief priests and the leading men of the Jews [A]brought charges against Paul, and they were urging him, 3 requesting a [a]concession against [b]Paul, that he might [c]have him brought to Jerusalem (*at the same time,* [A]setting an ambush to kill him on the way). 4 Festus then [A]answered that Paul [B]was being kept in custody at [C]Caesarea and that he himself was about to leave shortly. 5 “Therefore,” he *said, “let the influential men among you [a]go there with me, and if there is anything wrong [b]about the man, let them [c]prosecute him.”

6 After he had spent not more than eight or ten days among them, he went down to [A]Caesarea, and on the next day he took his seat on [B]the tribunal and ordered Paul to be brought. 7 After Paul arrived, the Jews who had come down from Jerusalem stood around him, bringing [A]many and serious charges against him [B]which they could not prove, 8 while Paul said in his own defense, “[A]I have committed no offense either against the Law of the Jews or against the temple or against Caesar.” 9 But Festus, [A]wishing to do the Jews a favor, answered Paul and said, “[B]Are you willing to go up to Jerusalem and [a]stand trial before me on these *charges?*” 10 But Paul said, “I am standing before Caesar’s [A]tribunal, where I ought to be tried. I have done no wrong to *the* Jews, as you also very well know. 11 If, then, I am a wrongdoer and have committed anything worthy of death, I do not refuse to die; but if none of those things is *true* of which these men accuse me, no one can hand me over to them. I [A]appeal to Caesar.” 12 Then when Festus had conferred with [a]his council, he answered, “You have appealed to Caesar, to Caesar you shall go.”

13 Now when several days had elapsed, King Agrippa and Bernice arrived at [A]Caesarea [a]and paid their respects to Festus. 14 While they were spending many days there, Festus laid Paul’s case before the king, saying, “There is a man who was [A]left as a prisoner by Felix; 15 and when I was at Jerusalem, the chief priests and the elders of the Jews [A]brought charges against him, asking for a sentence of condemnation against him. 16 I [A]answered them that it is not the custom of the Romans to hand over any man before [B]the accused meets his accusers face to face and has an opportunity to make his defense against the charges. 17 So after they had assembled here, I did not delay, but on the next day took my seat on [A]the tribunal and ordered the man to be brought before me. 18 When the accusers stood up, they *began* bringing charges against him not of such crimes as I was expecting, 19 but they *simply* had some [A]points of disagreement with him about their own [a,B]religion and about a dead man, Jesus, whom Paul asserted to be alive. 20 [A]Being at a loss how to investigate [a]such matters, I asked whether he was willing to go to Jerusalem and there stand

24:26 [A]Acts 24:17 24:27 [a]Lit *received a successor, Porcius Festus* [A]Acts 25:1, 4, 9, 12; 26:24f, 32 [B]Acts 12:3; 25:9 [C]Acts 23:35; 25:14 25:1 [A]Acts 23:34 [B]Acts 8:40; 25:4, 6, 13 25:2 [A]Acts 24:1; 25:15 25:3 [a]Or *favor* [b]Lit *him* [c]Lit *send for him to Jerusalem* [A]Acts 9:24 25:4 [A]Acts 25:16 [B]Acts 24:23 [C]Acts 8:40; 25:1, 6, 13 25:5 [a]Lit *go down* [b]Lit *in* [c]Or *accuse* 25:6 [A]Acts 8:40; 25:1, 4, 13 [B]Matt 27:19; Acts 25:10, 17 25:7 [A]Acts 24:5f [B]Acts 24:13 25:8 [A]Acts 6:13; 24:12; 28:17 25:9 [a]Lit *be judged* [A]Acts 12:3; 24:27 [B]Acts 25:20 25:10 [A]Matt 27:19; Acts 25:6, 17 25:11 [A]Acts 25:21, 25; 26:32; 28:19 25:12 [a]A different group from that mentioned in Acts 4:15 and 24:20 25:13 [a]Lit *greeting Festus* [A]Acts 8:40; 25:1, 4, 6 25:14 [A]Acts 24:27 25:15 [A]Acts 24:1; 25:2 25:16 [A]Acts 25:4f [B]Acts 23:30 25:17 [A]Matt 27:19; Acts 25:6, 10 25:19 [a]Or *superstition* [A]Acts 18:15; 23:29 [B]Acts 17:22 25:20 [a]Lit *these* [A]Acts 25:9

realization that he faced “judgment” alarmed him, and he hastily dismissed Paul. **when I find time.** The moment of conviction passed, and Felix foolishly passed up his opportunity to repent (cf. 2Co 6:2).

24:26 money would be given him by Paul. Roman law prohibited the taking of bribes, which was nonetheless commonplace.

24:27 Felix was succeeded by Porcius Festus. *See note on v. 3.* Festus was a member of the Roman nobility, unlike the former slave, Felix. Little is known of his brief tenure as governor (he died two years after assuming office), but the Jewish historian Josephus described him as better than either his predecessor or his successor. **do the Jews a favor.** He did this since Jewish complaints to Rome about his brutality eventually led to his ouster from office. He had brutally suppressed a riot in Caesarea and infuriated the Jews who managed to complain to Rome and have him replaced. Emperor Nero recalled him to Rome, where he would have faced severe punishment if his influential brother, Pallas, had not interceded for him.

25:1–12 Paul’s fourth of 6 defenses (cf. 22:1–21; 22:30–23:10; 24:10–21; 26:1–29; 28:17–29).

25:1 three days later . . . to Jerusalem from Caesarea. To acquaint himself with the situation in his new province.

25:3 ambush. A second ambush plot. This time, however, the members of the Sanhedrin were not accomplices (cf. 23:14, 15), but the plotters.

25:4 Festus. *See note on 24:27.* **Caesarea.** *See note on 8:40.* As the headquarters of Roman government in Judea, Caesarea was the proper place for Paul, a Roman citizen, to be tried.

25:6 took his seat on the tribunal. This signified that this hearing was an official Roman trial (see vv. 10, 17; 18:12; Mt 27:19; Jn 19:13).

25:9 wishing to do the Jews a favor. Cf. 24:27.

25:10 Caesar’s tribunal. Festus’ compromise gave the Jewish leaders all that they hoped for; they intended to murder Paul before he got to Jerusalem. The apostle therefore rejected Festus’ attempt at compromise and reminded the governor that he was standing at Caesar’s judgment seat where, as a Roman citizen, he had every right to be judged.

25:11 I appeal to Caesar. He declared his right as a Roman citizen to have a trial in Rome.

25:12 his council. Festus’ advisers. **to Caesar you shall go.** By granting the appeal, the governor removed himself from the case and transferred it to the emperor.

25:13 King Agrippa. Herod Agrippa II, son of the Herod who killed James and imprisoned Peter (*see note on 12:1*). He was the last of the Herods, who play a prominent role in NT history. His great-uncle, Herod Antipas, was the Herod of the Gospels (Mk 6:14–29; Lk 3:1; 13:31–33; 23:7–12), while his great-grandfather, Herod the Great, ruled at the time Jesus was born (Mt 2:1–19; Lk 1:5). Though not the ruler of Judea, Agrippa was well versed in Jewish affairs (cf. 26:3). **Bernice.** Not Agrippa’s wife, but his consort and sister. (Their sister, Drusilla, was married to the former governor, Felix). Their incestuous relationship was the talk of Rome, where Agrippa grew up. Bernice for a while became the mistress of Emperor Vespasian, then of his son, Titus, but always returned to her brother.

25:19 religion. Such charges did not belong in a Roman court (cf. 18:12–16).

25:20 at a loss how to investigate such matters. Festus, a pagan Roman and new in Judea, could not be expected to understand the theological differences between Christians and Jews.

trial on these matters. 21 But when Paul [A]appealed
to be held in custody for [a]the Emperor's decision, I
ordered him to be kept in custody until I send him
to Caesar." 22 Then [A]Agrippa *said* to Festus, "I also
would like to hear the man myself." "Tomorrow,"
he *said, "you shall hear him."

PAUL BEFORE AGRIPPA

23 So, on the next day when [A]Agrippa came [a]to-
gether with [A]Bernice amid great pomp, and entered
the auditorium [b]accompanied by the [c]commanders
and the prominent men of the city, at the command
of Festus, Paul was brought in. 24 Festus *said, "King
Agrippa, and all you gentlemen here present with
us, you see this man about whom [A]all the people
of the Jews appealed to me, both at Jerusalem and
here, loudly declaring that [B]he ought not to live
any longer. 25 But I found that he had committed
[A]nothing worthy of death; and since he himself
[B]appealed to [a]the Emperor, I decided to send him.
26 [a]Yet I have nothing definite about him to write
to my lord. Therefore I have brought him before
you *all* and especially before you, King Agrippa, so
that after the investigation has taken place, I may
have something to write. 27 For it seems absurd to
me in sending a prisoner, not to indicate also the
charges against him."

PAUL'S DEFENSE BEFORE AGRIPPA

26 [A]Agrippa said to Paul, "You are permitted
to speak for yourself." Then Paul stretched
out his hand and *proceeded* to make his defense:
2 "In regard to all the things of which I am accused by the Jews, I consider myself fortunate, King
Agrippa, that I am about to make my defense before
you today; 3 [a]especially because you are an expert
in all [A]customs and [b]questions among *the* Jews;
therefore I beg you to listen to me patiently.
4 "So then, all Jews know [A]my manner of life from
my youth up, which from the beginning was spent
among my *own* nation and at Jerusalem; 5 since they
have known about me for a long time, if they are
willing to testify, that I lived *as* a [A]Pharisee [B]accord-
ing to the strictest [C]sect of our religion. 6 And now
I am [a]standing trial [A]for the hope of [B]the promise
made by God to our fathers; 7 *the promise* [A]to which
our twelve tribes hope to attain, as they earnestly
serve *God* night and day. And for this [B]hope, O King,
I am being [C]accused by Jews. 8 Why is it considered
incredible among you *people* [A]if God does raise
the dead?
9 "So then, [A]I thought to myself that I had to do
many things hostile to [B]the name of Jesus of Nazareth. 10 And this is [a]just what I [A]did in Jerusalem;
not only did I lock up many of the [b]saints in prisons,
having [B]received authority from the chief priests,
but also when they were being put to death I [C]cast
my vote against them. 11 And [A]as I punished them
often in all the synagogues, I tried to force them to
blaspheme; and being [B]furiously enraged at them, I
kept pursuing them [C]even to [a]foreign cities.
12 "[a]While so engaged [A]as I was journeying to Damascus with the authority and commission of the
chief priests, 13 at midday, O King, I saw on the way
a light from heaven, [a]brighter than the sun, shining
all around me and those who were journeying with
me. 14 And when we had [A]all fallen to the ground,
I heard a voice saying to me in the [a,B]Hebrew dialect, 'Saul, Saul, why are you persecuting Me? [b]It
is hard for you to kick against the goads.' 15 And
I said, 'Who are You, Lord?' And the Lord said, 'I
am Jesus whom you are persecuting. 16 But get up
and [A]stand on your feet; for this purpose I have
appeared to you, to [B]appoint you a [C]minister and
[D]a witness not only to the things which you have
[a]seen, but also to the things in which I will appear

25:21 [a]Lit *the Augustus's* (in this case Nero) [A]Acts 25:11f 25:22 [A]Acts 9:15 25:23 [a]Lit *and Bernice* [b]Lit *and with* [c]I.e. chiliarchs, in command of one thousand troops [A]Acts 25:13; 26:30 25:24 [A]Acts 25:2, 7 [B]Acts 22:22 25:25 [a]V 21, note 1 [A]Luke 23:4; Acts 23:29 [B]Acts 25:11f 25:26 [a]Lit *About whom I have nothing definite* 26:1 [A]Acts 9:15 26:3 [a]Or *because you are especially expert* [b]Or *controversial issues* [A]Acts 6:14; 25:19; 26:7 26:4 [A]Gal 1:13f; Phil 3:5 26:5 [A]Acts 23:6; Phil 3:5 [B]Acts 22:3 [C]Acts 15:5 26:6 [a]Lit *being tried* [A]Acts 24:15; 28:20 [B]Acts 13:32 26:7 [A]James 1:1 [B]Acts 24:15; 28:20 [C]Acts 26:2 26:8 [A]Acts 23:6 26:9 [A]John 16:2; 1 Tim 1:13 [B]John 15:21 26:10 [a]Lit *also* [b]Or *holy ones* [A]Acts 8:3; 9:13 [B]Acts 9:1f [C]Acts 22:20 26:11 [a]Or *outlying* [A]Matt 10:17; Acts 22:19 [B]Acts 9:1 [C]Acts 22:5 26:12 [a]Lit *In which things* [A]Acts 26:12-18: *9:3-8; 22:6-11* 26:13 [a]Lit *above the brightness of* 26:14 [a]I.e. Jewish Aramaic [b]An idiom referring to an animal's futile resistance to being prodded with goads [A]Acts 9:7 [B]Acts 21:40 26:16 [a]Two early mss read *seen Me* [A]Ezek 2:1; Dan 10:11 [B]Acts 22:14 [C]Luke 1:2 [D]Acts 22:15

25:21 Caesar. The "Caesar" ruling at this time was the infamous Nero.

25:22 I also would like to hear. The Gr. verb tense implies Herod had been wanting to hear Paul for a long time. As an expert on Jewish affairs (cf. 26:3), he relished hearing Christianity's leading spokesman in person.

25:23 Agrippa ... Bernice. The two are inseparable in Luke's account (cf. v. 13; 26:30); she is a constant reminder of Agrippa's scandalous private life (*see note on v. 13*). commanders. The 5 tribunes commanding the 5 cohorts stationed in Caesarea (*see note on 10:1*). prominent men. The civic leaders of the city.

25:26 I have nothing definite. Since Festus did not understand the nature of the charges against Paul, he did not know what to write in his official report to Nero. For a provincial governor to send a prisoner to the emperor with no clear charges against him was foolish, if not dangerous. especially before you, King Agrippa. Festus hoped Herod's expertise in Jewish affairs (26:3) would enable him to make sense of the charges against Paul.

26:1–29 Paul's fifth of 6 defenses (cf. 22:1–21; 22:30–23:10; 24:10–21; 25:1–12; 28:17–19).

26:1 permitted to speak. Since no one was there to accuse Paul, Herod permitted him to speak in his defense. stretched out his hand. A common gesture at the beginning of a speech (cf. 12:17; 13:16; 19:33).

26:3 expert in all customs and questions among *the* Jews. *See note on 25:26.* Paul's main purpose was not to defend himself but to convert Agrippa and the others (vv. 28, 29).

26:5 lived *as* a Pharisee. *See note on Mt 3:7*; cf. Php 3:5.

26:6 the hope of the promise. The coming of the Messiah and His kingdom (cf. 1:6; 3:22–24; 13:23–33; Ge 3:15; Is 7:14; 9:6; Da 7:14; Mic 5:2; Tit 2:13; 1Pe 1:11, 12).

26:7 twelve tribes. A common NT designation for Israel (cf. Mt 19:28; Jas 1:1; Rev 21:12). The 10 northern tribes were not lost. Representatives from each intermingled with the two southern tribes before and after the Exile—a process that had begun during the reigns of Hezekiah (2Ch 30:1–11) and Josiah (2Ch 34:1–9).

26:8 Paul found it inconceivable that he should be condemned for believing in the resurrection—the great hope of the Jewish people (*see note on 24:15*).

26:10 saints. Christian believers (1Co 1:2). I cast my vote. Lit. "I threw my pebble"—a reference to the ancient custom of recording votes by means of colored pebbles. This verse may also indicate that Paul had once been a member of the Sanhedrin.

26:11 tried to force them to blaspheme. To renounce their faith in Jesus Christ.

26:12–14 The third NT account of Paul's conversion (*see notes on 9:1–17; 22:6–23*).

26:16 things in which I will appear to you. See 18:9, 10; 22:17–21; 23:11; 2Co 12:1–7; Gal 1:11, 12.

to you; 17 [A]rescuing you [B]from the *Jewish* people
and from the Gentiles, to whom I am sending you,
18 to [A]open their eyes so that they may turn from
[B]darkness to light and from the dominion of [C]Satan
to God, that they may receive [D]forgiveness of sins
and an [E]inheritance among those who have been
sanctified by [F]faith in Me.'

19 "So, King Agrippa, I did not prove disobedient
to the heavenly vision, 20 but *kept* declaring both
[A]to those of Damascus first, and *also* [B]at Jerusalem
and *then* throughout all the region of Judea, and
even [C]to the Gentiles, that they should [D]repent
and turn to God, performing deeds [E]appropri-
ate to repentance. 21 For this reason *some* Jews
[A]seized me in the temple and tried [B]to put me
to death. 22 So, having obtained help from God,
I stand to this day [A]testifying both to small and
great, stating nothing but what [B]the Prophets and
Moses said was going to take place; 23 [a,A]that [b]the
Christ was [c]to suffer, *and* [a]that [B]by reason of *His*
resurrection from the dead He would be the first
to proclaim [C]light both to the *Jewish* people and
to the Gentiles."

24 While *Paul* was saying this in his defense, Festus *said in a loud voice, "Paul, you are out of your
mind! [a]*Your* great [A]learning is [b]driving you mad."
25 But Paul *said, "I am not out of my mind, [A]most
excellent Festus, but I utter words [a]of sober truth.
26 For the king [a,A]knows about these matters, and
I speak to him also with confidence, since I am
persuaded that none of these things escape his notice; for this has not been done in a [b]corner. 27 King
Agrippa, do you believe the Prophets? I know that
you [a]do." 28 Agrippa *replied* to Paul, "[a]In a short
time you [b]will persuade me to [c]become a [A]Chris-
tian." 29 And Paul *said,* "[a]I would wish to God, that
whether [b]in a short or long time, not only you, but
also all who hear me this day, might become such
as I am, except for these [A]chains."

30 [A]The king stood up and the governor and Bernice, and those who were sitting with them, 31 and
when they had gone aside, they *began* talking to one
another, saying, "[A]This man is not doing anything
worthy of death or [a]imprisonment." 32 And Agrippa
said to Festus, "This man might have been [A]set free
if he had not [B]appealed to Caesar."

PAUL IS SENT TO ROME

27 When it was decided that [A]we [B]would sail
for [C]Italy, they proceeded to deliver Paul and
some other prisoners to a centurion of the Augustan [a,D]cohort named Julius. 2 And embarking in an
Adramyttian ship, which was about to sail to the
regions along the coast of [a,A]Asia, we put out to sea
accompanied by [B]Aristarchus, a [C]Macedonian of
[D]Thessalonica. 3 The next day we put in at [A]Sidon;
and Julius [B]treated Paul with consideration and
[C]allowed him to go to his friends and receive care.

26:17 [A]Jer 1:8, 19 [B]1 Chr 16:35; Acts 9:15 26:18 [A]Is 35:5; 42:7, 16; Eph 5:8; Col 1:13; 1 Pet 2:9 [B]John 1:5; Eph 5:8; Col 1:12f; 1 Thess 5:5; 1 Pet 2:9 [C]Matt 4:10 [D]Luke 24:47; Acts 2:38 [E]Acts 20:32 [F]Acts 20:21 26:20 [A]Acts 9:19ff [B]Acts 9:26-29; 22:17-20 [C]Acts 9:15; 13:46 [D]Acts 3:19 [E]Matt 3:8; Luke 3:8 26:21 [A]Acts 21:27, 30 [B]Acts 21:31 26:22 [A]Luke 16:28 [B]Acts 10:43; 24:14 26:23 [a]Lit *whether* [b]I.e. the Messiah [c]Lit *subject to suffering* [A]Matt 26:24; Acts 3:18 [B]1 Cor 15:20, 23; Col 1:18; Rev 1:5 [C]Is 42:6; 49:6; Luke 2:32; 2 Cor 4:4 26:24 [a]Lit *The many letters* [b]Lit *turning you to madness* [A]John 7:15; 2 Tim 3:15 26:25 [a]Lit *of truth and rationality* [A]Acts 23:26; 24:3 26:26 [a]Or *understands* [b]I.e. a hidden or secret place [A]Acts 26:3 26:27 [a]Lit *believe* 26:28 [a]Or *With a little* [b]Or *are trying to convince* [c]Lit *make* [A]Acts 11:26 26:29 [a]Or *I would pray to* [b]Or *with a little or with much* [A]Acts 21:33 26:30 [A]Acts 25:23 26:31 [a]Lit *bonds* [A]Acts 23:29 26:32 [A]Acts 28:18 [B]Acts 25:11 27:1 [a]Or *battalion* [A][we] Acts 16:10; 27:1-28 [B]Acts 25:12, 25 [C]Acts 18:2; 27:6 [D]Acts 10:1 27:2 [a]I.e. west coast province of Asia Minor [A]Acts 2:9 [B]Acts 19:29 [C]Acts 16:9 [D]Acts 17:1 27:3 [A]Matt 11:21 [B]Acts 27:43 [C]Acts 24:23

26:17 **Gentiles, to whom I am sending you.** Paul's commissioning as the apostle to the Gentiles (Ro 11:13; 1Ti 2:7).

26:18 **to open their eyes.** Unbelievers are blinded to spiritual truth by Satan (2Co 4:4; 6:14; cf. Mt 15:14). **from darkness to light.** Since unbelievers are in the darkness of their spiritual blindness, the Bible often uses light to picture salvation (v. 23; 13:47; Mt 4:16; Jn 1:4, 5, 7–9; 3:19–21; 8:12; 9:5; 12:36; 2Co 4:4; 6:14; Eph 5:8, 14; Col 1:12, 13; 1Th 5:5; 1Pe 2:9; 1Jn 1:7; 2:8–10). **forgiveness of sins.** This is the most significant result of salvation (*see note on 2:38*; cf. 3:19; 5:31; 10:43; 13:38; Mt 1:21; 26:28; Lk 1:77; 24:47; 1Co 15:3; Gal 1:4; Col 1:14; Heb 8:12; 9:28; 10:12; 1Pe 2:24; 3:18; 1Jn 2:1, 2; 3:5; 4:10; Rev 1:5). **an inheritance.** The blessings believers will enjoy throughout eternity in heaven (cf. 20:32; Eph 1:11, 14, 18; Col 1:12; 3:24; Heb 9:15). **sanctified by faith.** The Bible plainly and repeatedly teaches that salvation comes solely through faith apart from human works (13:39; 15:9; 16:31; Jn 3:14–17; 6:69; Ro 3:21–28; 4:5; 5:1; 9:30; 10:9–11; Gal 2:16; 3:11, 24; Eph 2:8, 9; Php 3:9).

26:20 **deeds appropriate to repentance.** Genuine repentance is inseparably linked to a changed lifestyle (*see notes on 2:38; Mt 3:8; Jas 2:18*).

26:21 **Jews … tried to put me to death.** See 21:27–32. The true reason in contrast to the lies of the Jewish leaders (24:6).

26:22 **the Prophets and Moses.** *See note on 24:14.* The term "Moses" is used interchangeably with "law," since he was the author of the Pentateuch, the 5 books of law.

26:23 **Christ was to suffer … resurrection from the dead.** Messiah's suffering (Ps 22; Is 53) and resurrection (Ps 16:10; cf. 13:30–37), the central themes of Paul's preaching, are clearly taught in the OT.

26:24 **you are out of your mind!** Festus was astonished that a learned scholar like Paul could actually believe that the dead would live again—something no intelligent Roman would accept. Unable to contain himself, he interrupted the proceedings, shouting that Paul's tremendous learning had driven him insane (cf. Mk 3:21; Jn 8:48, 52; 10:20).

26:26 **none of these things escape his notice.** The death of Jesus and the Christians' claim that He rose from the dead were common knowledge in Israel.

26:27 **do you believe the Prophets?** Paul's shrewd question put Herod in a dilemma. If he affirmed his belief in the prophets, he would also have to admit that what they taught about Jesus' death and resurrection was true—an admission that would make him appear foolish before his Roman friends. Yet to deny the prophets would outrage his Jewish subjects.

26:28 **In a short time you will persuade me.** Agrippa was saying, "Do you think you can convince me to become a Christian in such a short time?" Recognizing his dilemma, Agrippa parried Paul's question with one of his own.

26:30–32 The hearing over, Agrippa and Festus met privately to discuss Paul's case. Both agreed that he was innocent of any crime and could be set free, had he not appealed to Caesar.

27:1 **we.** The use of the pronoun "we" marks the return of Paul's close friend Luke, who has been absent since 21:18. He had likely been living near Caesarea so he could care for Paul during his imprisonment. Now he rejoined the apostle for the journey to Rome. **centurion of the Augustan cohort.** A cohort (regiment) of that name was stationed in Judea during the reign of Agrippa II (*see note on 25:13*). Julius may have been on detached duty, performing such tasks as escorting important prisoners.

27:2 **Adramyttian ship.** Adramyttium was a city on the NW coast of Asia Minor (modern Turkey) near Troas, where the centurion planned to find a ship sailing to Italy. **we put out to sea.** From Caesarea the ship sailed 70 mi. N to Sidon. **accompanied by Aristarchus.** He had been seized by the crowd during the riot at Ephesus (19:29), while accompanying Paul to Jerusalem with the offering (20:4). Aristarchus would be with Paul during the apostle's first Roman imprisonment (Col 4:10).

27:3 **put in at Sidon.** *See note on 12:20.* The Christians there ministered to Paul—possibly by providing him with provisions for his trip.

4 From there we put out to sea and sailed under the
shelter of [A]Cyprus because [B]the winds were contrary.
5 When we had sailed through the sea along the
coast of [A]Cilicia and [B]Pamphylia, we landed at Myra
in Lycia. 6 There the centurion found an [A]Alexan-
drian ship sailing for [B]Italy, and he put us aboard it.
7 When we had sailed slowly for a good many days,
and with difficulty had arrived off Cnidus, [A]since
the wind did not permit us *to go* farther, we sailed
under the shelter of [B]Crete, off Salmone; 8 and with
difficulty [A]sailing past it we came to a place called
Fair Havens, near which was the city of Lasea.

9 When considerable time had passed and the
voyage was now dangerous, since even [A]the [a]fast
was already over, Paul *began* to admonish them,
10 and said to them, "Men, I perceive that the voyage will certainly be with [A]damage and great loss,
not only of the cargo and the ship, but also of our
lives." 11 But the centurion was more persuaded by
the [A]pilot and the [a]captain of the ship than by what
was being said by Paul. 12 Because the harbor was
not suitable for wintering, the majority reached
a decision to put out to sea from there, if somehow they could reach Phoenix, a harbor of [A]Crete,
facing southwest and northwest, and spend the
winter *there*.

13 [a]When a moderate south wind came up, supposing that they had attained their purpose, they
weighed anchor and *began* [A]sailing along [B]Crete,
close *inshore*.

SHIPWRECK

14 But before very long there [A]rushed down from
[a]the land a violent wind, called [b]Euraquilo; 15 and
when the ship was caught *in it* and could not face
the wind, we gave way *to it* and let ourselves be
driven along. 16 Running under the shelter of a small
island called Clauda, we were scarcely able to get the
ship's [a]boat under control. 17 After they had hoisted
it up, they used [a]supporting cables in undergirding
the ship; and fearing that they might [A]run aground
on *the shallows* of Syrtis, they let down the [b]sea
anchor and in this way let themselves be driven
along. 18 The next day as we were being violently
storm-tossed, [a]they began to [A]jettison the cargo;
19 and on the third day they threw the ship's tackle
overboard with their own hands. 20 Since neither
sun nor stars appeared for many days, and no small
storm was assailing *us*, from then on all hope of our
being saved was gradually abandoned.

21 [a]When they had gone a long time without food,
then Paul stood up in their midst and said, "[A]Men,
you ought to have [b]followed my advice and not to
have set sail from [B]Crete and [c]incurred this [A]damage
and loss. 22 *Yet* now I urge you to [A]keep up your courage, for there will be no loss of life among you, but
only of the ship. 23 For this very night [A]an angel of the
God to whom I belong and [B]whom I serve [C]stood before me, 24 saying, 'Do not be afraid, Paul; [A]you must
stand before Caesar; and behold, God has granted
you [B]all those who are sailing with you.' 25 Therefore,
[A]keep up your courage, men, for I believe God that
[a]it will turn out exactly as I have been told. 26 But we
must [A]run aground on a certain [B]island."

27 But when the fourteenth night came, as
we were being driven about in the Adriatic
Sea, about midnight the sailors *began* to surmise that [a]they were approaching some land.

27:4 [A]Acts 4:36 [B]Acts 27:7 27:5 [A]Acts 6:9 [B]Acts 13:13 27:6 [A]Acts 28:11 [B]Acts 18:2; 27:1 27:7 [A]Acts 27:4 [B]Acts 2:11; 27:12f, 21; Titus 1:5, 12 27:8 [A]Acts 27:13 27:9 [a]I.e. Day of Atonement in September or October, which was a dangerous time of year for navigation [A]Lev 16:29-31; 23:27-29; Num 29:7 27:10 [A]Acts 27:21 27:11 [a]Or *owner* [A]Rev 18:17 27:12 [A]Acts 2:11; 27:13, 21; Titus 1:5, 12 27:13 [a]Lit *a south wind having gently blown* [A]Acts 27:8 [B]Acts 2:11; 27:12f, 21; Titus 1:5, 12 27:14 [a]Lit *it* [b]I.e. a northeaster [A]Mark 4:37 27:16 [a]Or *skiff:* a small boat in tow or carried on board for emergency use, transportation to and from shore, etc. 27:17 [a]Lit *helps* [b]Or *gear* [A]Acts 27:26, 29 27:18 [a]Lit *they were doing a throwing out* [A]Jon 1:5; Acts 27:38 27:21 [a]Lit *there being much abstinence from food* [b]Lit *obeyed me* [c]Lit *gained* [A]Acts 27:10 [B]Acts 27:7 27:22 [A]Acts 27:25, 36 27:23 [A]Acts 5:19 [B]Rom 1:9 [C]Acts 18:9; 23:11; 2 Tim 4:17 27:24 [A]Acts 23:11 [B]Acts 27:31, 42, 44 27:25 [a]Lit *it will be* [A]Acts 27:22, 36 27:26 [A]Acts 27:17, 29 [B]Acts 28:1 27:27 [a]Lit *some land was approaching them*

27:4 **sailed under the shelter of Cyprus.** They kept to the lee side of the island (passing between it and the mainland), seeking shelter from the strong winds.

27:5 **coast of Cilicia and Pamphylia.** *See notes on 2:9, 10; 6:9.* **Myra ... Lycia.** One of the main ports of the imperial grain fleet, whose ships brought Egyptian grain to Italy.

27:6 **Alexandrian ship.** Part of the imperial grain fleet.

27:7 **Cnidus.** Located on a peninsula in extreme SW Asia Minor, this port also served ships of the imperial grain fleet. Having reached Cnidus, the ship could not sail farther W due to the strong headwinds. It was forced to turn S and head for the island of Crete. **the shelter of Crete.** This large island off the SW coast of Asia Minor provided some relief from the strong NW winds buffeting the ship. **Salmone.** A promontory on Crete's NE coast.

27:8 **Fair Havens ... Lasea.** The ship fought its way around the SE corner of Crete, finally reaching the shelter of the bay known as Fair Havens.

27:9 **the fast was already over.** *See note on Zec 7:3*; cf. Lv 23:26–32. Travel in the open sea was dangerous from mid-Sept. to mid-Nov., after which it ceased altogether until Feb. Since the fast (the Day of Atonement) of late Sept. or early Oct. was past, further travel was already extremely hazardous.

27:10 **voyage ... with damage.** Because of the lateness of the season, and the difficulties they had already experienced, Paul wisely counseled them to spend the winter at Fair Havens.

27:11 **centurion.** *See note on 10:1.* Because the ship was part of the imperial grain fleet (*see note on v. 5*) Julius, not the helmsman nor the ship's owner, was the ranking official on board. **pilot.** The ship's captain.

27:12 **not suitable for wintering.** The professional sailors deemed Fair Havens an unsuitable location to wait out the winter (*see note on v. 9*). **Phoenix.** Located 40 mi. from Fair Havens with a harbor that provided better shelter from the winter storms.

27:14 **Euraquilo.** From the Gr. word *euros* ("east wind") and the Lat. word *aquilo* ("north wind"). This is a strong, dangerous windstorm greatly feared by those who sailed the Mediterranean.

27:16 **Clauda.** An island 23 mi. SW of Crete. ***ship's* boat.** Taking advantage of Clauda's shelter, the sailors began to rig the ship for the storm by hauling the ship's dinghy on board.

27:17 **used supporting cables in undergirding the ship.** A procedure known as frapping. The cables, wrapped around the hull and winched tight, helped the ship endure the battering of the wind and waves. **Syrtis.** A region of sandbars and shoals off the coast of Africa, much feared as a graveyard of ships. **let down the sea anchor.** The sailors probably also took down the sails, since putting out an anchor with the sails up would be self-defeating.

27:18 **jettison the cargo.** Throwing all unnecessary gear and cargo overboard would lighten the ship, enabling it to ride more easily over the waves.

27:23, 24 The last of 6 visions Paul received as recorded by Luke (cf. 9:3–6; 16:9, 10; 18:9, 10; 22:17, 18; 23:11).

27:24 **stand before Caesar.** The angel reaffirmed the promise Jesus Himself had earlier made to Paul (23:11).

27:27 **fourteenth night.** Since they sailed from Fair Havens (v. 13). **Adriatic Sea.** The central Mediterranean Sea, not the present Adriatic Sea located between Italy and Croatia. The modern Adriatic was known in Paul's day as the Gulf of Adria. ***began* to surmise.** The sailors probably heard the sound of waves breaking on a shore.

28 They took soundings and found *it to be* twenty
fathoms; and a little farther on they took another
sounding and found *it to be* fifteen fathoms. 29 Fearing that we might [A]run aground somewhere on the
[a]rocks, they cast four anchors from the stern and
[b]wished for daybreak. 30 But as the sailors were
trying to escape from the ship and had let down
[A]the *ship's* boat into the sea, on the pretense of intending to lay out anchors from the bow, 31 Paul said
to the centurion and to the soldiers, "Unless these
men remain in the ship, you yourselves cannot be
saved." 32 Then the soldiers cut away the [A]ropes of
the *ship's* boat and let it fall away.
33 Until the day was about to dawn, Paul was encouraging them all to take some food, saying, "Today
is the fourteenth day that you have been constantly
watching and going without eating, having taken
nothing. 34 Therefore I encourage you to take some
food, for this is for your preservation, for [A]not a hair
from the head of any of you will perish." 35 Having
said this, he took bread and [A]gave thanks to God in
the presence of all, and he broke it and began to eat.
36 All [A]of them [a]were encouraged and they themselves also took food. 37 All of us in the ship were
two hundred and seventy-six [a,A]persons. 38 When
they had eaten enough, they *began* to lighten the
ship by [A]throwing out the wheat into the sea.
39 When day came, [A]they [a]could not recognize the
land; but they did observe a bay with a beach, and
they resolved to drive the ship onto it if they could.
40 And casting off [A]the anchors, they left them in
the sea while at the same time they were loosening
the ropes of the rudders; and hoisting the foresail
to the wind, they were heading for the beach. 41 But
striking a [a]reef where two seas met, they ran the vessel aground; and the prow stuck fast and remained
immovable, but the stern *began* to be broken up by
the force *of the waves*. 42 The soldiers' plan was to
[A]kill the prisoners, so that none *of them* would swim
away and escape; 43 but the centurion, [A]wanting to
bring Paul safely through, kept them from their
intention, and commanded that those who could
swim should [a]jump overboard first and get to land,
44 and the rest *should follow*, some on planks, and
others on various things from the ship. And so it
happened that [A]they all were brought safely to land.

SAFE AT MALTA

28 When [A]they had been brought safely through,
[B]then we found out that [C]the island was
called [a]Malta. 2 [A]The [a]natives showed us extraordinary kindness; for because of the rain that had
set in and because of the cold, they kindled a fire
and [B]received us all. 3 But when Paul had gathered
a bundle of sticks and laid them on the fire, a viper
came out [a]because of the heat and fastened itself
on his hand. 4 When [A]the [a]natives saw the creature
hanging from his hand, they *began* saying to one
another, "[B]Undoubtedly this man is a murderer, and
though he has been saved from the sea, [b]justice has
not allowed him to live." 5 However [A]he shook the
creature off into the fire and suffered no harm. 6 But
they were expecting that he was about to swell up or
suddenly fall down dead. But after they had waited
a long time and had seen nothing unusual happen
to him, they changed their minds and [A]*began* to
say that he was a god.
7 Now in the neighborhood of that place were lands
belonging to the leading man of the island, named
Publius, who welcomed us and entertained us courteously three days. 8 And it happened that the father
of Publius was lying *in bed* afflicted with *recurrent*
fever and dysentery; and Paul went in *to see* him and
after he had [A]prayed, he [B]laid his hands on him and
healed him. 9 After this had happened, the rest of the
people on the island who had diseases were coming
to him and getting cured. 10 They also honored us
with many [a]marks of respect; and when we were
setting sail, they [b]supplied *us* with [c]all we needed.

PAUL ARRIVES AT ROME

11 At the end of three months we set sail on [A]an
Alexandrian ship which had wintered at the island,
and which had [a]the Twin Brothers for its figurehead.

27:29 [a]Lit *rough places* [b]Lit *they were praying for it to become day* [A]Acts 27:17, 26 27:30 [A]Acts 27:16 27:32 [A]John 2:15 27:34 [A]Matt 10:30 27:35 [A]Matt 14:19 27:36 [a]Lit *became cheerful* [A]Acts 27:22, 25 27:37 [a]Lit *souls* [A]Acts 2:41 27:38 [A]Jon 1:5; Acts 27:18 27:39 [a]Lit *were not recognizing* [A]Acts 28:1 27:40 [A]Acts 27:29 27:41 [a]Lit *place* 27:42 [A]Acts 12:19 27:43 [a]Lit *throw themselves* [A]Acts 27:3 27:44 [A]Acts 27:22, 31 28:1 [a]Or *Melita* [A][they] Acts 16:10; 27:1 [B]Acts 27:39 [C]Acts 27:26 28:2 [a]Lit *barbarians* [A]Acts 28:4; Rom 1:14; 1 Cor 14:11; Col 3:11 [B]Rom 14:1 28:3 [a]Or *from the heat* 28:4 [a]Lit *barbarians* [b]Or *Justice*, i.e. the personification of a goddess [A]Acts 28:2 [B]Luke 13:2, 4 28:5 [A]Mark 16:18 28:6 [A]Acts 14:11 28:8 [A]Acts 9:40; James 5:14f [B]Matt 9:18; Mark 5:23; 6:5 28:10 [a]Lit *honors* [b]Or *put on board* [c]Lit *the things pertaining to the needs* 28:11 [a]Gr *Dioscuri;* i.e. Castor and Pollux, twin sons of Zeus [A]Acts 27:6

27:28 took soundings. With a weight attached to a length of rope they measured the depth of the sea. **twenty fathoms . . . fifteen fathoms.** 120 feet . . . 90 feet. The decreasing depth of the water confirmed the ship was approaching land.

27:29 cast four anchors from the stern. An attempt to hold the ship in place and keep the bow pointed toward the shore.

27:30 *ship's* boat. The same dinghy hauled aboard earlier (v. 16). **lay out anchors from the bow.** This would have been for additional stability (cf. v. 29).

27:33 going without eating. Because of seasickness and the difficulty of preparing and preserving food, the passengers and crew had eaten little or nothing in the two weeks since they left Fair Havens.

27:34 not a hair . . . will perish. A common Jewish saying (1Sa 14:45; 2Sa 14:11; 1Ki 1:52; Lk 21:18) denoting absolute protection.

27:37 two hundred and seventy-six persons. As an ocean-going vessel, this ship was considerably larger than the smaller vessel Paul sailed in from Caesarea to Lycia.

27:38 lighten the ship. *See note on v. 18.*

27:41 a reef where two seas met. A sandbar or reef short of the shore.

27:42 The soldiers' plan was to kill the prisoners. Knowing they could face punishment or death if their prisoners escaped (cf. 12:19; 16:27).

28:1 Malta. An island, 17 mi. long and 9 mi. wide, about 60 mi. S of Sicily. None of the sailors had previously been to the bay (known today as St. Paul's Bay) where they were shipwrecked.

28:3 a viper. A venomous snake. Cf. Mk 16:18.

28:6 *began* to say that he was a god. See 14:11, 12.

28:7 leading man. The Gr. phrase indicates Publius was the Roman governor of Malta.

28:8 afflicted with . . . fever and dysentery. The gastric fever (caused by a microbe found in goat's milk) that was common on Malta. Dysentery, often the result of poor sanitation, was widespread in the ancient world.

28:11 At the end of three months. Since sea travel was dangerous during this period (*see note on 27:9*). **Alexandrian ship.** Probably another in the imperial grain fleet (*see notes on 27:5, 6*). **Twin Brothers.** Castor and Pollux, Zeus' sons according to Gr. mythology, were believed to protect sailors.

12 After we put in at Syracuse, we stayed there for
three days. 13 From there we sailed around and arrived at Rhegium, and a day later a south wind
sprang up, and on the second day we came to Puteoli. 14 [a]There we found *some* [A]brethren, and were
invited to stay with them for seven days; and thus
we came to Rome. 15 And the [A]brethren, when they
heard about us, came from there as far as the [a]Mar-
ket of Appius and [b]Three Inns to meet us; and when
Paul saw them, he thanked God and took courage.
16 When we entered Rome, Paul was [A]allowed to
stay by himself, with the soldier who was guarding him.
17 After three days [a]Paul called together those who
were [A]the leading men of the Jews, and when they
came together, he *began* saying to them, "[B]Brethren,
[C]though I had done nothing against our people or
[D]the customs of our [b]fathers, yet I was delivered as
a prisoner from Jerusalem into the hands of the
Romans. 18 And when they had [A]examined me, they
[B]were willing to release me because there was [C]no
ground [a]for putting me to death. 19 But when the
Jews [a]objected, I was forced to [A]appeal to Caesar,
not that I had any accusation against my nation.
20 For this reason, therefore, I [a]requested to see you
and to speak with you, for I am wearing [A]this chain
for [B]the sake of the hope of Israel." 21 They said to
him, "We have neither received letters from Judea
concerning you, nor have any of [A]the brethren come
here and reported or spoken anything bad about
you. 22 But we desire to hear from you what [a]your
views are; for concerning this [A]sect, it is known to
us that [B]it is spoken against everywhere."
23 When they had set a day for Paul, they came to
him at [A]his lodging in large numbers; and he was
explaining to them by solemnly [B]testifying about
the kingdom of God and trying to persuade them
concerning Jesus, [C]from both the Law of Moses and
from the Prophets, from morning until evening.
24 [A]Some were being persuaded by the things spoken, but others would not believe. 25 And when they
did not agree with one another, they *began* leaving
after Paul had spoken one *parting* word, "The Holy
Spirit rightly spoke through Isaiah the prophet to
your fathers, 26 saying,

'[A]GO TO THIS PEOPLE AND SAY,
"[a,B]YOU WILL KEEP ON HEARING, [b]BUT
WILL NOT UNDERSTAND;
AND [C]YOU WILL KEEP ON SEEING,
BUT WILL NOT PERCEIVE;
27 [A]FOR THE HEART OF THIS PEOPLE
HAS BECOME DULL,
AND WITH THEIR EARS THEY
SCARCELY HEAR,
AND THEY HAVE CLOSED THEIR EYES;
OTHERWISE THEY MIGHT SEE
WITH THEIR EYES,
AND HEAR WITH THEIR EARS,
AND UNDERSTAND WITH THEIR
HEART AND RETURN,
AND I WOULD HEAL THEM."'

28 Therefore let it be known to you that [A]this salvation
of God has been sent [B]to the Gentiles; they will also
listen." 29 [[a]When he had spoken these words, the Jews
departed, having a great dispute among themselves.]
30 And he stayed two full years [a]in his own rented
quarters and was welcoming all who came to him,
31 [a,A]preaching the kingdom of God and teaching
concerning the Lord Jesus Christ [B]with all openness,
unhindered.

28:14 [a]Lit *Where* [A]John 21:23; Acts 1:15; 6:3; 9:30; 28:15; Rom 1:13; 28:15 [a]Lat *Appii Forum*, a station about 43 miles from Rome [b]Lat *Tres Tabernae*, a station about 33 miles from Rome [A]Acts 1:15; 10:23; 11:1, 12, 29; 12:17 28:16 [A]Acts 24:23 28:17 [a]Lit *he* [b]Or *forefathers* [A]Acts 13:50; 25:2 [B]Acts 22:5 [C]Acts 25:8 [D]Acts 6:14 28:18 [a]Lit *of death in me* [A]Acts 22:24 [B]Acts 26:32 [C]Acts 23:29; 25:25; 26:31 28:19 [a]Lit *spoke against* [A]Acts 25:11, 21, 25; 26:32 28:20 [a]Or *invited you to see me and speak with me* [A]Acts 21:33 [B]Acts 26:6f 28:21 [A]Acts 3:17; 22:5; 28:14; Rom 9:3 28:22 [a]Lit *you think* [A]Acts 24:14 [B]1 Pet 2:12; 3:16; 4:14, 16 28:23 [A]Philem 22 [B]Luke 16:28; Acts 1:3; 23:11 [C]Acts 8:35 28:24 [A]Acts 14:4 28:26 [a]Lit *with a hearing* [b]Lit *and* [c]Lit *seeing you will see* [A]Is 6:9 [B]Matt 13:14f 28:27 [A]Is 6:10 28:28 [A]Ps 98:3; Luke 2:30; Acts 13:26 [B]Acts 9:15; 13:46 28:29 [a]Early mss do not contain this v 28:30 [a]Or *at his own expense* 28:31 [a]Or *proclaiming* [A]Matt 4:23; Acts 20:25; 28:23 [B]2 Tim 2:9

28:12 Syracuse. An important city on the island of Sicily. Tradition holds that Paul established a church during the ship's 3-day stopover there.

28:13 Rhegium. A harbor on the southern tip of the Italian mainland. There the ship waited one day for a favorable wind to permit it to sail through the Straits of Messina (separating Sicily from the Italian mainland). Puteoli. Modern Pozzuoli, located on the Bay of Naples near Pompeii. Rome's main port and the most important one in Italy, Puteoli was also the main port for the Egyptian grain fleet (*see note on 27:5*).

28:14 Rome. Almost as a footnote, Luke mentions the party's arrival in the Imperial capital—Paul's longtime goal (*see note on 19:21*).

28:15 Market of Appius. A market town 43 mi. S of Rome on the Appian Way. Three Inns. A rest stop on the Appian Way, about 30 mi. S of Rome.

28:16 stay by himself ... guarding. Possibly through Julius' intervention, Paul was allowed to live under guard in his own rented quarters (cf. v. 30).

28:17–29 Paul's sixth and final defense recorded in Acts (cf. 22:1–21; 22:30–23:10; 24:10–21; 25:1–12; 26:1–29).

28:17 leading men of the Jews. The most prominent men from Rome's synagogues (*see note on 6:9*). the customs of our fathers. Paul began by denying that he was guilty of any infraction against the Jewish people or their traditions (cf. 22:3; 24:14; 26:4, 5).

28:19 appeal to Caesar. *See note on 25:11.*

28:20 the hope of Israel. *See notes on 24:15; 26:6.*

28:23 kingdom of God. *See note on 1:3.* persuade them ... Law of Moses ... Prophets. Paul's method of Jewish evangelism throughout Acts was to prove from the OT that Jesus was the Messiah (cf. 13:16–41).

28:26, 27 Quoted from Is 6:9, 10 (*see note there*).

28:28 salvation of God has been sent to the Gentiles. See 11:18; 13:46, 47; 14:27; 15:14–17; 18:6.

28:29 Many ancient manuscripts omit this verse.

28:30, 31 The best explanation for this rather abrupt ending to the book is that Luke wrote Acts before Paul's release from his first Roman imprisonment (see Introduction: Author and Date).

28:31 with all openness, unhindered. Helped by his loyal fellow workers (cf. Col 4:10; Phm 24), Paul evangelized Rome (cf. Php 1:13; 4:22).

THE EPISTLE OF PAUL TO THE ROMANS

TITLE

This epistle's name comes from its original recipients: the members of the church in Rome, the capital of the Roman Empire (1:7).

AUTHOR AND DATE

No one disputes that the apostle Paul wrote Romans. Like his namesake, Israel's first king (Saul was Paul's Hebrew name; Paul his Greek name), Paul was from the tribe of Benjamin (Php 3:5). He was also a Roman citizen (Ac 16:37; 22:25). Paul was born about the time of Christ's birth in Tarsus (Ac 9:11), an important city (Ac 21:39) in the Roman province of Cilicia, located in Asia Minor (modern Turkey). He spent much of his early life in Jerusalem as a student of the celebrated rabbi Gamaliel (Ac 22:3). Like his father before him, Paul was a Pharisee (Ac 23:6), a member of the strictest Jewish sect (cf. Php 3:5).

Miraculously converted while on his way to Damascus (ca. A.D. 33–34) to arrest Christians in that city, Paul immediately began proclaiming the gospel message (Ac 9:20). After narrowly escaping from Damascus with his life (Ac 9:23–25; 2Co 11:32, 33), Paul spent 3 years in Nabatean Arabia, south and east of the Dead Sea (Gal 1:17, 18). During that time, he received much of his doctrine as direct revelation from the Lord (Gal 1:11, 12).

More than any other individual, Paul was responsible for the spread of Christianity throughout the Roman Empire. He made 3 missionary journeys through much of the Mediterranean world, tirelessly preaching the gospel he had once sought to destroy (Ac 26:9). After he returned to Jerusalem bearing an offering for the needy in the church there, he was falsely accused by some Jews (Ac 21:27–29), savagely beaten by an angry mob (Ac 21:30, 31), and arrested by the Romans. Though two Roman governors, Felix and Festus, as well as Herod Agrippa, did not find him guilty of any crime, pressure from the Jewish leaders kept Paul in Roman custody. After two years, the apostle exercised his right as a Roman citizen and appealed his case to Caesar. After a harrowing trip (Ac 27, 28), including a violent, two-week storm at sea that culminated in a shipwreck, Paul reached Rome. Eventually released for a brief period of ministry, he was arrested again and suffered martyrdom at Rome in ca. A.D. 65–67 (cf. 2Ti 4:6).

Though physically unimpressive (cf. 2Co 10:10; Gal 4:14), Paul possessed an inner strength granted him through the Holy Spirit's power (Php 4:13). The grace of God proved sufficient to provide for his every need (2Co 12:9, 10), enabling this noble servant of Christ to successfully finish his spiritual race (2Ti 4:7).

Paul wrote Romans from Corinth, as the references to Phoebe (Ro 16:1, Cenchrea was Corinth's port), Gaius (Ro 16:23), and Erastus (Ro 16:23)—all of whom were associated with Corinth—indicate. The apostle wrote the letter toward the close of his third missionary journey (most likely in A.D. 56), as he prepared to leave for Israel with an offering for the poor believers in the Jerusalem church (Ro 15:25). Phoebe was given the great responsibility of delivering this letter to the Roman believers (16:1, 2).

BACKGROUND AND SETTING

Rome was the capital and most important city of the Roman Empire. It was founded in 753 B.C., but is not mentioned in Scripture until NT times. Rome is located along the banks of the Tiber River, about 15 miles from the Mediterranean Sea. Until an artificial harbor was built at nearby Ostia, Rome's main harbor was Puteoli, some 150 miles away (*see note on Ac 28:13*). In Paul's day, the city had a population of over one million people, many of whom were slaves. Rome boasted magnificent buildings, such as the Emperor's palace, the Circus Maximus, and the Forum, but its beauty was marred by the slums in which so many lived. According to tradition, Paul was martyred outside Rome on the Ostian Way during Nero's reign (A.D. 54–68).

Some of those converted on the Day of Pentecost probably founded the church at Rome (cf. Ac 2:10). Paul had long sought to visit the Roman church, but had been prevented from doing so (1:13). In God's providence, Paul's inability to visit Rome gave the world this inspired masterpiece of gospel doctrine.

Paul's primary purpose in writing Romans was to teach the great truths of the gospel of grace to believers who had never received apostolic instruction. The letter also introduced him to a church where he was personally unknown, but hoped to visit soon for several important reasons: to edify the believers (1:11); to preach the gospel (1:15); and to get to know the Roman Christians, so they could encourage him (1:12; 15:32), better pray for him (15:30), and help him with his planned ministry in Spain (15:28).

FIRST CENTURY ROME

Unlike some of Paul's other epistles (e.g., 1, 2Co, Gal), his purpose for writing was not to correct aberrant theology or rebuke ungodly living. The Roman church was doctrinally sound, but, like all churches, it was in need of the rich doctrinal and practical instruction this letter provides.

FIRST-CENTURY ROME

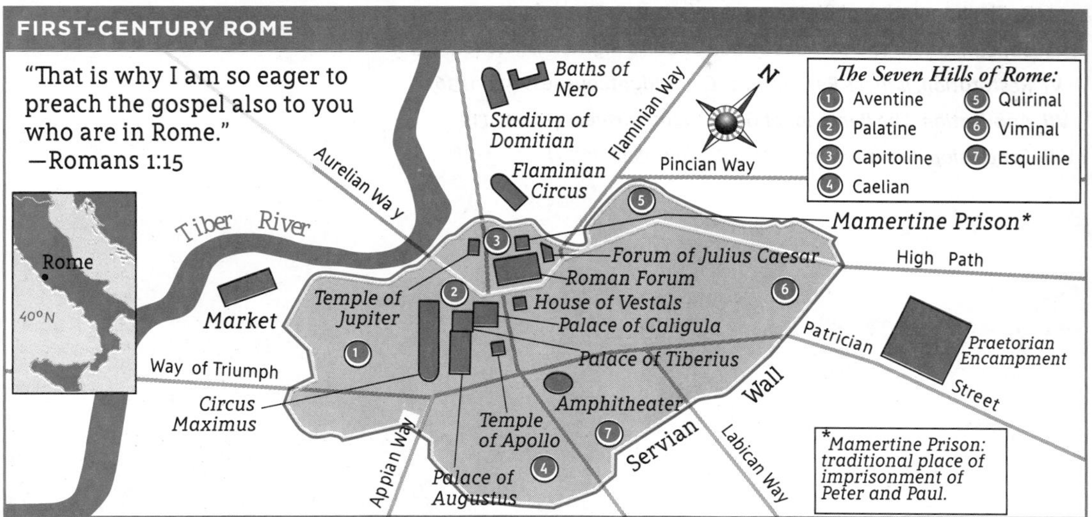

HISTORICAL AND THEOLOGICAL THEMES

Since Romans is primarily a work of doctrine, it contains little historical material. Paul does use such familiar OT figures as Abraham (chap. 4), David (4:6–8), Adam (5:12–21), Sarah (9:9), Rebekah (9:10), Jacob and Esau (9:10–13), and Pharaoh (9:17) as illustrations. He also recounts some of Israel's history (chaps. 9–11). Chapter 16 provides insightful glimpses into the nature and character of the first-century church and its members.

The overarching theme of Romans is the righteousness that comes from God: the glorious truth that God justifies guilty, condemned sinners by grace alone through faith in Christ alone. Chapters 1–11 present the theological truths of that doctrine, while chaps. 12–16 detail its practical outworking in the lives of individual believers and the life of the whole church. Some specific theological topics include principles of spiritual leadership (1:8–15); God's wrath against sinful mankind (1:18–32); principles of divine judgment (2:1–16); the universality of sin (3:9–20); an exposition and defense of justification by faith alone (3:21–4:25); the security of salvation (5:1–11); the transference of Adam's sin (5:12–21); sanctification (chaps. 6–8); sovereign election (chap. 9); God's plan for Israel (chap. 11); spiritual gifts and practical godliness (chap. 12); the believer's responsibility to human government (chap. 13); and principles of Christian liberty (14:1–15:12).

INTERPRETIVE CHALLENGES

As the preeminent doctrinal work in the NT, Romans naturally contains a number of difficult passages. Paul's discussion of the perpetuation of Adam's sin (5:12–21) is one of the deepest, most profound theological passages in all of Scripture. The nature of mankind's union with Adam, and how his sin was transferred to the human race has always been the subject of intense debate. Bible students also disagree on whether 7:7–25 describes Paul's experience as a believer or unbeliever, or is a literary device not intended to be autobiographical at all. The closely related doctrines of election (8:28–30) and the sovereignty of God (9:6–29) have confused many believers. Others question whether chaps. 9–11 teach that God has a future plan for the nation of Israel. Some have ignored Paul's teaching on the believer's obedience to human government (13:1–7) in the name of Christian activism, while others have used it to defend slavish obedience to totalitarian regimes.

All of these and more interpretive challenges are addressed in the notes to the respective passages.

OUTLINE

I. Greetings and Introduction (1:1–15)

II. Theme (1:16, 17)

III. Condemnation: The Need of God's Righteousness (1:18–3:20)
   A. Unrighteous Gentiles (1:18–32)
   B. Unrighteous Jews (2:1–3:8)
   C. Unrighteous Mankind (3:9–20)

IV. Justification: The Provision of God's Righteousness (3:21–5:21)
   A. The Source of Righteousness (3:21–31)
   B. The Example of Righteousness (4:1–25)
   C. The Blessings of Righteousness (5:1–11)
   D. The Imputation of Righteousness (5:12–21)

V. Sanctification: The Demonstration of God's Righteousness (6:1–8:39)

VI. Restoration: Israel's Reception of God's Righteousness (9:1–11:36)

VII. Application: The Behavior of God's Righteousness (12:1–15:13)

VIII. Conclusion, Greetings, and Benediction (15:14–16:27)

THE GOSPEL EXALTED

1 Paul, a bond-servant of Christ Jesus, [a,A]called *as* an
apostle, [B]set apart for [C]the gospel of God, 2 which
He [A]promised beforehand through His [B]prophets in
the holy Scriptures, 3 concerning His Son, who was
born [A]of a [a]descendant of David [B]according to the
flesh, 4 who was declared [A]the Son of God with power
[a]by the resurrection from the dead, according to the
[b]Spirit of holiness, Jesus Christ our Lord, 5 through
whom we have received grace and [A]apostleship [a]to
bring about *the* [B]obedience of faith among [C]all the
Gentiles for His name's sake, 6 among whom you
also are the [A]called of Jesus Christ;
7 to all who are [A]beloved of God in Rome, called
as [a,B]saints: [C]Grace to you and peace from God our
Father and the Lord Jesus Christ.
8 First, [A]I thank my God through Jesus Christ [a]for
you all, because [B]your faith is being proclaimed
throughout the whole world. 9 For [A]God, whom I
[B]serve in my spirit in the *preaching of the* gospel
of His Son, is my witness *as to* how unceasingly
[C]I make mention of you, 10 always in my prayers

1:1 [a]Lit *a called apostle* [A]1 Cor 1:1; 9:1; 2 Cor 1:1 [B]Acts 9:15; 13:2; Gal 1:15 [C]Mark 1:14; Rom 15:16 1:2 [A]Titus 1:2 [B]Luke 1:70; Rom 3:21; 16:26 1:3 [a]Lit *seed* [A]Matt 1:1 [B]John 1:14; Rom 4:1; 9:3, 5; 1 Cor 10:18 1:4 [a]Or *as a result of* [b]Or *spirit* [A]Matt 4:3 1:5 [a]Lit *for obedience* [A]Acts 1:25; Gal 1:16 [B]Acts 6:7; Rom 16:26 [C]Acts 9:15 1:6 [A]Jude 1; Rev 17:14 1:7 [a]Or *holy ones* [A]Rom 5:5ff; 8:39 [B]Acts 9:13; Rom 8:28ff; 1 Cor 1:2, 24 [C]Num 6:25f; 1 Cor 1:3; 2 Cor 1:2; Gal 1:3; Eph 1:2; Phil 1:2; Col 1:2; 1 Thess 1:1; 2 Thess 1:2 1:8 [a]Or *concerning you all, that...* [A]1 Cor 1:4; Eph 1:15f; Phil 1:3f; Col 1:3f; 1 Thess 1:2; 2:13 [B]Acts 28:22; Rom 16:19 1:9 [A]Rom 9:1 [B]Acts 24:14; 2 Tim 1:3 [C]Eph 1:16; Phil 1:3f

1:1 Paul. See Introduction: Author and Date. **bond-servant.** *Doulos,* the common NT word for servant. Although in Gr. culture it most often referred to the involuntary, permanent service of a slave, Paul elevates this word by using it in its Heb. sense to describe a servant who willingly commits himself to serve a master he loves and respects (Ex 21:5, 6; Gal 1:10; Titus 1:1; cf. Ge 26:24; Nu 12:7; 2Sa 7:5; Is 53:11). **apostle.** The Gr. word means "one who is sent." In the NT, it primarily refers to the 12 men Christ chose to accompany Him (Mk 3:13–19) and Matthias, whom the other apostles chose to replace Judas (Ac 1:15–26). Christ gave them power to confirm their apostleship with miracles (Mt 10:1; 2Co 12:12), and authority to speak as His proxies—every NT book was written either by an apostle or under his auspices (cf. Jn 14:26). Their teaching is the foundation of the church (Eph 2:20). Christ Himself selected Paul for this position (Ac 9:15; 22:14; 26:16; cf. Gal 1:1) and trained him to fulfill this ministry (Gal 1:12, 16). **gospel of God.** Used in its verb and noun forms some 60 times in this epistle, the Gr. word for this phrase means "good news" (see Mk 1:1). Rome incorporated it into its emperor worship. The town herald used this word to begin important favorable announcements about the emperor—such as the birth of a son. But Paul's good news is not from the emperor but "of God"; it originated with Him. Its message that God will forgive sins, deliver from sin's power, and give eternal hope (1:16; cf. 1Co 15:1–4) comes not only as a gracious offer, but also as a command to be obeyed (10:16). Paul was consumed with this message (1Co 9:23).

1:2 which He promised beforehand. Paul's Jewish antagonists accused him of preaching a revolutionary new message unrelated to Judaism (Ac 21:28). But the OT is replete with prophecies concerning Christ and the gospel (1Pe 1:10–12; cf. Mt 5:17; Heb 1:1). **His prophets.** All the writers of the OT. The "Law and the Prophets" constitute all the OT (Ac 24:14). But the law—or the Pentateuch—was written by Moses, whom Scripture also calls a prophet (Dt 18:15). **holy Scriptures.** While the rabbinical writings popular in the first century—and often studied more diligently than Scripture itself—may not have taught the gospel of God, the divinely inspired OT certainly did (cf. Lk 24:25, 27, 32; Jn 5:39; Ac 3:18; 7:52; 10:43; 13:32; 26:22, 23; *see note on Ge 3:15*). The prophets spoke clearly of a New Covenant (Jer 31:31–34; Eze 36:25–27; cf. Heb 8:6–13) and of the Messiah whose sacrifice would make it possible (Is 9:6, 7; 53:1–12).

1:3 born. Jesus was conceived in a virgin's womb by the Holy Spirit (Lk 1:35; cf. Is 7:14), and was delivered normally. This word emphasizes that He is an actual historical figure. Many well-known ancient writers, including the Roman historian Tacitus (*Annals* 15.44), the familiar Jewish historian Josephus (*Antiquities,* 2.18.3), and Pliny the Younger (*Letters* 10.96,97) verify Jesus' historicity. **descendant of David.** The OT had prophesied that Messiah would be in the lineage of David (2Sa 7:12, 13; Ps 89:3, 4, 19, 24; Is 11:1–5; Jer 23:5, 6). Both Mary, Jesus' mother (Lk 3:23, 31), and Joseph, His legal father (Mt 1:6, 16; Lk 1:27), were descendants of David. John makes believing that Christ has come in the flesh a crucial test of orthodoxy (1Jn 4:2, 3). Because He is fully human—as well as fully God—He can serve as man's substitute (Jn 1:29; 2Co 5:21) and as a sympathetic High Priest (Heb 4:15, 16).

1:4 declared. The Gr. word, from which the English word "horizon" comes, means "to distinguish." Just as the horizon serves as a clear demarcation line, dividing earth and sky, the resurrection of Jesus Christ clearly divides Him from the rest of humanity, providing irrefutable evidence that He is the Son of God (*see note on 10:9*). **Son of God.** This title, used nearly 30 times in the Gospels, identifies Jesus Christ as the same in essence as God. *See notes on Jn 1:34, 49; 11:27; 19:7* (cf. Heb 1:5; 2Sa 7:14). The resurrection clearly declared that Jesus was deity, the expression of God Himself in human form. While He was eternally the Son in anticipation of His incarnation, it was when He entered the world in incarnation that He was declared to all the world as the Son of God and took on the role of submission to the Father (*see notes on Ps 2:7; Heb 1:5, 6*). **resurrection from the dead.** His victory over death was the supreme demonstration and most conclusive evidence that He is God the Son (*see note on 10:9*; cf. Ac 13:29–33; 1Co 15:14–17). **Spirit of holiness.** In His incarnation, Christ voluntarily submitted Himself to do the will of the Father only through the direction, agency, and power of the Holy Spirit (Mt 3:16; Lk 4:1; Jn 3:34; *see note on Ac 1:2*).

1:5 grace. The unmerited favor which God shows guilty sinners. This is the book's first reference to the most crucial part of the gospel message: salvation is a gift from God wholly separate from any human effort or achievement (3:24, 27; 4:1–5; 5:20, 21; *see note on Eph 2:8*). **apostleship.** Although the term "apostle" refers to the 12 in a unique way (*see note on 1:1*), in a broader and less official sense it can describe anyone whom God has sent with the message of salvation (cf. Ac 14:14; Ro 16:7; Heb 3:1). **obedience of faith.** True saving faith always produces obedience and submission to the Lordship of Jesus Christ (16:19, 26; cf. 10:9, 10; cf. Mt 7:13, 14, 22–27; Jas 2:17–20).

1:6 called. *See note on 1:7.* Always in the NT Epistles the "call" of God refers to God's effectual call of elect sinners to salvation (cf. 8:28–30), rather than the general call to all people to believe (cf. Mt 20:16).

1:7 beloved of God ... called *as* saints. The Gr. text records these as 3 separate privileges: 1) God has set His love on His own (5:5; 8:35; Eph 1:6; 2:4, 5; 1Jn 3:1); 2) He has extended to them not only the general, external invitation to believe the gospel (Is 45:22; 55:6; Eze 33:11; Mt 11:28; Jn 7:37; Rev 22:17), but His effectual calling—or His drawing to Himself all those He has chosen for salvation (8:30; 2Th 2:13, 14; 2Ti 1:9; *see note on Jn 6:44*); and 3) God has set believers apart from sin unto Himself, so that they are holy ones (1Co 3:16, 17; 1Pe 2:5, 9). **Rome.** See Introduction: Background and Setting. **Grace ... peace.** Paul's standard greeting (1Co 1:3; 2Co 1:2; Gal 1:3; Eph 1:2; Php 1:2; Col 1:2; 1Th 1:1; 2Th 1:2; 1Ti 1:2; 2Ti 1:2; Titus 1:4; Phm 3).

1:8 I thank my God. In every letter Paul wrote, he expressed his gratitude for those who would receive it (e.g., 1Co 1:4), except in his letter to the Galatians, whose defection from the true gospel caused him to dispense with any opening commendations (Gal 1:6–12). **your faith.** The genuineness of their salvation. The testimony of the church in Rome was so strong that in A.D. 49 the emperor Claudius expelled all the Jews because of the influence of "Chrestus," which was undoubtedly a reference to Christ (cf. Ac 18:2). **throughout the whole world.** As the center of the Roman Empire and the inhabited world, whatever happened in Rome became known universally.

1:9 serve in my spirit. In the NT, this Gr. word for "serve" always refers to religious service, and is sometimes translated "worship." Paul had seen the shallow, hypocritical religion of the Pharisees and the superstitious hedonism of pagan idolatry. His spiritual service (*see note on 12:1*), however, did not result from abject fear or legal obligation, but was genuine and sincere (cf. Php 3:3; 2Ti 1:3; 2:22).

1:10 in my prayers. Paul frequently recorded the content of his requests (Eph 3:14–19; Php 1:9–11; Col 1:9–11; 2Th 1:11, 12) and urged his readers to join him in prayer (15:30–32; 1Th 5:17; Eph 6:18). **will of God.** God's sovereign orchestration of Paul's circumstances (cf. Mt 6:10; Ac 21:11–14; Jas 4:13, 14).

making request, if perhaps now at last by [A]the will
of God I may succeed in coming to you. 11 For [A]I
long to see you so that I may impart some spiritual
gift to you, that you may be [a]established; 12 that
is, that I may be encouraged together with you
while among you, each of us by the other's faith,
both yours and mine. 13 [A]I do not want you to be
unaware, [B]brethren, that often I [C]have planned to
come to you (and have been prevented so far) so
that I may obtain some [D]fruit among you also, even
as among the rest of the Gentiles. 14 [A]I am [a]under
obligation both to Greeks and to [B]barbarians, both
to the wise and to the foolish. 15 So, for my part, I
am eager to [A]preach the gospel to you also who
are in Rome.

16 For I am not [A]ashamed of the gospel, for [B]it is
the power of God for salvation to everyone who believes, to the [C]Jew first and also to [D]the Greek. 17 For
in it [A]*the* righteousness of God is revealed [a]from
faith to faith; as it is written, "[b,B]BUT THE RIGHTEOUS
man SHALL LIVE BY FAITH."

UNBELIEF AND ITS CONSEQUENCES

18 For [A]the wrath of God is revealed from heaven
against all ungodliness and unrighteousness of
men who [B]suppress the truth [a]in unrighteousness,

1:10 [A]Acts 18:21; Rom 15:32 1:11 [a]Or *strengthened* [A]Acts 19:21; Rom 15:23 1:13 [A]Rom 11:25; 1 Cor 10:1; 12:1; 2 Cor 1:8; 1 Thess 4:13 [B]Acts 1:15; Rom 7:1; 1 Cor 1:10; 14:20, 26; Gal 3:15 [C]Acts 19:21; Rom 15:22f [D]John 4:36; 15:16; Phil 1:22; Col 1:6 1:14 [a]Lit *debtor* [A]1 Cor 9:16 [B]Acts 28:2 1:15 [A]Rom 15:20 1:16 [A]Mark 8:38; 2 Tim 1:8, 12, 16 [B]1 Cor 1:18, 24 [C]Acts 3:26; Rom 2:9 [D]John 7:35 1:17 [a]Or *by* [b]Or *But he who is righteous by faith shall live* [A]Rom 3:21; 9:30; Phil 3:9 [B]Hab 2:4; Gal 3:11; Heb 10:38 1:18 [a]Or *by* [A]Rom 5:9; Eph 5:6; Col 3:6 [B]2 Thess 2:6f

1:11 spiritual gift. The Gr. word translated "gift" is *charisma,* which means a "gift of grace"—a spiritual enablement whose source is the Spirit of God. Romans uses this same term to describe: 1) Christ Himself (5:15, 16); 2) general blessings from God (11:29; cf. 1Ti 6:17); and 3) specific spiritual gifts given to members of the body to minister to the whole (12:6–8; cf. 1Co 12:1–31; 1Pe 4:10, 11). Paul probably intends to encompass all 3.

1:12 each . . . by the other's faith. A glimpse of Paul's genuine humility (cf. 1Pe 5:3, 4).

1:13 fruit. Scripture catalogs 3 kinds of spiritual fruit: 1) spiritual attitudes that characterize a Spirit-led believer (Gal 5:22, 23); 2) righteous actions (6:22; Php 4:16, 17; Heb 13:15); and 3) new converts (16:5). In this context, Paul is probably referring to the third one—a desire that was eventually realized during his imprisonment in Rome (Php 4:22). **among the rest of the Gentiles.** This implies the church in Rome consisted primarily of non-Jews.

1:14 under obligation. Paul had an obligation to God (cf. 1Co 9:16–17) to fulfill His divine mandate to minister to Gentiles (1:5; Ac 9:15). **Greeks.** People of many different nationalities who had embraced the Gr. language, culture, and education. They were the sophisticated elite of Paul's day. Because of their deep interest in Greek philosophy, they were considered "wise." Because of this prevalence of Greek culture, Paul sometimes used this word to describe all Gentiles (cf. 3:9). **barbarians.** A derisive term coined by the Greeks for all who had not been trained in Gr. language and culture. When someone spoke in another language, it sounded to the Greeks like "bar-bar-bar," or unintelligible chatter. Although in the narrowest sense "barbarian" referred to the uncultured, uneducated masses, it was often used to describe all non-Greeks—the unwise of the world. Paul's point is that God is no respecter of persons—the gospel must reach both the world's elite and its outcasts (cf. Jn 4:4–42; Jas 2:1–9).

1:15 gospel. *See note on 1:1.*

1:16, 17 These two verses crystallize the thesis of the entire book—the gospel of Jesus Christ—which Paul will unfold and explain in the following chapters.

1:16 I am not ashamed. He had been imprisoned in Philippi (Ac 16:23, 24), chased out of Thessalonica (Ac 17:10), smuggled out of Berea (Ac 17:14), laughed at in Athens (Ac 17:32), regarded as a fool in Corinth (1Co 1:18, 23), and stoned in Galatia (Ac 14:19), but Paul remained eager to preach the gospel in Rome—the seat of contemporary political power and pagan religion. Neither ridicule, criticism, nor physical persecution could curb his boldness. *See notes on 2Co 4:5–18; 11:23–28; 12:9, 10.* **power.** The Eng. word "dynamite" comes from this Gr. word. Although the message may sound foolish to some (1Co 1:18), the gospel is effective because it carries with it the omnipotence of God (cf. Ex 15:6; Dt 32:39; Job 9:4; Pss 33:8, 9; 89:13; 106:8, 9; Is 26:4; 43:13; Jer 10:12; 27:5; Mt 28:18; Ro 9:21). Only God's power is able to overcome man's sinful nature and give him new life (5:6; 8:3; Jn 1:12; 1Co 1:18, 23–25; 2:1–4; 4:20; 1Pe 1:23). **salvation.** Used 5 times in Romans (the verb form occurs 8 times), this key word basically means "deliverance" or "rescue." The power of the gospel delivers people from lostness (Mt 18:11), from the wrath of God (Ro 5:9), from willful spiritual ignorance (Hos 4:6; 2Th 1:8), from evil self-indulgence (Lk 14:26), and from the darkness of false religion (Col 1:13; 1Pe 2:9). It rescues them from the ultimate penalty of their sin, i.e., eternal separation from God and eternal punishment (*see note on Rev 20:6*). **believes.** To trust, rely on, or have faith in. When used of salvation, this word usually occurs in the present tense, which stresses that faith is not simply a onetime event, but an ongoing condition. True saving faith is supernatural, a gracious gift of God that He produces in the heart (*see note on Eph 2:8*) and is the only means by which a person can appropriate true righteousness (cf. 3:22, 25; 4:5, 13, 20; 5:1; *see notes on 4:1–25*). Saving faith consists of 3 elements: 1) mental: the mind understands the gospel and the truth about Christ (10:14–17); 2) emotional: one embraces the truthfulness of those facts with sorrow over sin and joy over God's mercy and grace (6:17; 15:13); and 3) volitional: the sinner submits his will to Christ and trusts in Him alone as the only hope of salvation (*see note on 10:9*). Genuine faith will always produce authentic obedience (*see note on 4:3;* cf. Jn 8:31; 14:21–24). **Jew first.** God chose Israel to be His witness nation (Ex 19:6) and gave her distinct privileges (3:2; 9:4, 5). Christ's ministry was first to Israel (Mt 15:24), and it was through Israel that salvation was to come to the world (Jn 4:22; Acts 13:46). **Greek.** *See note on 1:14.*

1:17 righteousness of God. Better translated "righteousness from God." A major theme of the book, appearing over 30 times in one form or another, righteousness is the state or condition of perfectly conforming to God's perfect law and holy character. Other terms from the same Gr. root also occur some 30 times and are usually translated "justified," "justification" or similarly. Only God is inherently righteous (Dt 32:4; Pss 11:7; 116:5; Jn 17:25; 1Jn 2:1; Rev 16:5), and man falls woefully short of the divine standard of moral perfection (3:10, 23; Job 9:2; Mt 5:48). But the gospel reveals that on the basis of faith—and faith alone—God will impute His righteousness to ungodly sinners (*see notes on 3:21–24; 4:5; 2Co 5:21; Php 3:8, 9*). **from faith to faith.** This may be a parallel expression to "everyone who believes" (1:16), as if Paul were singling out the faith of each individual believer—from one person's faith to another's faith to another's and so on. Or perhaps Paul's point is that the righteousness from God is completely on the basis of faith from beginning to end. **as it is written.** *See note on Hab 2:4.* **But the righteous *man* shall live by faith.** Paul intends to prove that it has always been God's way to justify sinners by grace on the basis of faith alone. God established Abraham as a pattern of faith (4:22–25; Gal 3:6, 7) and thus calls him the father of all who believe (4:11, 16). Elsewhere, Paul uses this same phrase to argue that no one has ever been declared righteous before God except by faith alone (Gal 3:11) and that true faith will demonstrate itself in action (Php 2:12, 13). This expression emphasizes that true faith is not a single event, but a way of life—it endures. That endurance is called the perseverance of the saints (cf. Col 1:22, 23; Heb 3:12–14). One central theme of the story of Job is that no matter what Satan does, saving faith cannot be destroyed. *See notes on 8:31–39.*

1:18–3:20 After introducing the righteousness which comes from God (1:17), a theme he develops at length (3:21–5:21), Paul presents the overwhelming evidence of man's sinfulness, underscoring how desperately he needs this righteousness that only God can provide. He presents God's case against the irreligious, immoral pagan (1:18–32; the Gentiles) and the religious, outwardly moral person (2:1–3:8; the Jews); and concludes by showing that all men alike deserve God's judgment (3:9–20).

1:18 wrath of God. This is not an impulsive outburst of anger aimed capriciously at people whom God does not like. It is the settled, determined response of a righteous God against sin (cf. Pss 2:5, 12; 45:7; 75:8; 76:6, 7; 78:49–51; 90:7–9; Is 51:17; Jer 25:15, 16; Jn 3:36; Ro 9:22; Eph 5:6; Col 3:5, 6). **is revealed.** More accurately, "is constantly revealed." The word

19 because [A]that which is known about God is evident [a]within them; for God made it evident to them.
20 For [A]since the creation of the world His invisible
attributes, His eternal power and divine nature,
have been clearly seen, [B]being understood through
what has been made, so that they are without excuse. 21 For even though they knew God, they did
not [a]honor Him as God or give thanks, but they
became [A]futile in their speculations, and their foolish heart was darkened. 22 [A]Professing to be wise,
they became fools, 23 and [A]exchanged the glory of
the incorruptible God for an image in the form of
corruptible man and of birds and four-footed animals and [a]crawling creatures.
24 Therefore [A]God gave them over in the lusts of
their hearts to impurity, so that their bodies would
be [B]dishonored among them. 25 For they exchanged
the truth of God for [a]a [A]lie, and worshiped and
served the creature rather than the Creator, [B]who
is blessed [b]forever. Amen.
26 For this reason [A]God gave them over to [B]de-
grading passions; for their women exchanged the
natural function for that which is [a]unnatural, 27 and
in the same way also the men abandoned the natural function of the woman and burned in their desire
toward one another, [A]men with men committing
[a]indecent acts and receiving in [b]their own persons
the due penalty of their error.
28 And just as they did not see fit [a]to acknowledge
God any longer, [A]God gave them over to a depraved
mind, to do those things which are not proper,
29 being filled with all unrighteousness, wickedness, greed, evil; full of envy, murder, strife, deceit,
malice; *they are* [A]gossips, 30 slanderers, [a,A]haters of

1:19 [a]Or *among* [A]Acts 14:17; 17:24ff 1:20 [A]Mark 10:6 [B]Job 12:7-9; Ps 19:1-6; Jer 5:21f 1:21 [a]Lit *glorify* [A]2 Kin 17:15; Jer 2:5; Eph 4:17f 1:22 [A]Jer 10:14; 1 Cor 1:20 1:23 [a]Or *reptiles* [A]Deut 4:16-18; Ps 106:20; Jer 2:11; Acts 17:29 1:24 [A]Rom 1:26, 28; Eph 4:19 [B]Eph 2:3 1:25 [a]Lit *the lie* [b]Lit *unto the ages* [A]Is 44:20; Jer 10:14; 13:25; 16:19 [B]Rom 9:5; 2 Cor 11:31 1:26 [a]Lit *against nature* [A]Rom 1:24 [B]1 Thess 4:5 1:27 [a]Lit *the shameless deed* [b]Lit *themselves* [A]Lev 18:22; 20:13; 1 Cor 6:9 1:28 [a]Lit *to have God in knowledge* [A]Rom 1:24 1:29 [A]2 Cor 12:20 1:30 [a]Or *hateful to God* [A]Ps 5:5

essentially means "to uncover, make visible, or make known." God reveals His wrath in two ways: 1) indirectly, through the natural consequences of violating His universal moral law, and 2) directly through His personal intervention (the OT record—from the sentence passed on Adam and Eve to the worldwide flood, from the fire and brimstone that leveled Sodom to the Babylonian captivity—clearly displays this kind of intervention). The most graphic revelation of God's holy wrath and hatred against sin was when He poured out divine judgment on His Son on the cross. God has various kinds of wrath: 1) eternal wrath, which is hell; 2) eschatological wrath, which is the final day of the Lord; 3) cataclysmic wrath like the Flood and the destruction of Sodom and Gomorrah; 4) consequential wrath, which is the principle of sowing and reaping; and 5) the wrath of abandonment, which is removing restraint and letting people go to their sins (for examples of this wrath, see Ps 81:11, 12; Pr 1:23–31; *see note on Hos 4:17*). Here, it is that fifth form, God's abandoning the wicked continually through history to pursue their sin and its consequences (vv. 24–32). **ungodliness.** This indicates a lack of reverence for, devotion to, and worship of the true God—a defective relationship with Him (cf. Jude 14, 15). **unrighteousness.** This refers to the result of ungodliness: a lack of conformity in thought, word, and deed to the character and law of God (*see note on 1:17*). **suppress the truth.** Although the evidence from conscience (1:19; 2:14), creation (1:20), and God's Word is irrefutable, men choose to resist and oppose God's truth by holding fast to their sin (cf. Ps 14:1; Jn 3:19, 20).

1:19 is evident within them. God has sovereignly planted evidence of His existence in the very nature of man by reason and moral law (1:20, 21, 28, 32; 2:15).

1:20 invisible attributes. This refers specifically to the two mentioned in this verse. **His eternal power.** The Creator, who made all that we see around us and constantly sustains it, must be a being of awesome power. **divine nature.** That is, His faithfulness (Ge 8:21, 22), kindness, and graciousness (Ac 14:17). **through what has been made.** The creation delivers a clear, unmistakable message about God's person (cf. Pss 19:1–8; 94:9; Ac 14:15–17; 17:23–28). **they are without excuse.** God holds all men responsible for their refusal to acknowledge what He has shown them of Himself in His creation. Even those who have never had an opportunity to hear the gospel have received a clear witness about the existence and character of God—and have suppressed it. If a person will respond to the revelation he has, even if it is solely natural revelation, God will provide some means for that person to hear the gospel (cf. Ac 8:26–39; 10:1–48; 17:27).

1:21 knew God. Man is conscious of God's existence, power, and divine nature through general revelation (vv. 19, 20). **they did not honor Him.** Man's chief end is to glorify God (Lv 10:3; 1Ch 16:24–29; Ps 148; Ro 15:5, 6), and Scripture constantly demands it (Ps 29:1, 2; 1Co 10:31; Rev 4:11). To glorify Him is to honor Him, to acknowledge His attributes, and to praise Him for His perfections (cf. Ex 34:5–7). It is to recognize His glory and extol Him for it. Failing to give Him glory is man's greatest affront to his Creator (Ac 12:22, 23). **or give thanks.** They refused to acknowledge that every good thing they enjoyed came from God (Mt 5:45; Ac 14:15–17; 1Ti 6:17; Jas 1:17). **futile.** Man's search for meaning and purpose will produce only vain, meaningless conclusions. **heart was darkened.** When man rejects the truth, the darkness of spiritual falsehood replaces it (cf. Jn 3:19, 20).

1:22 Professing to be wise, they became fools. Man rationalizes his sin and proves his utter foolishness by devising and believing his own philosophies about God, the universe, and himself (cf. Pss 14:1; 53:1).

1:23 exchanged the glory . . . for an image. They substitute the worship of idols for the worship of the true God. Historians report that many ancient cultures did not originally have idols. For example, Persia (Herodotus; *The Histories,* 1:31), Rome (Varro in Augustine; *The City of God,* 4:31), even Greece and Egypt (Lucian; *The Syrian Goddess,* 34) had no idolatry at their founding. The fourth-century A.D. historian Eusebius reported that the oldest civilizations had no idols. The earliest biblical record of idolatry was among Abram's family in Ur (Jos 24:2). The first commandment forbids it (Ex 20:3–5), and the prophets continually ridiculed those who foolishly practiced it (Is 44:9–17; cf. 2Ki 17:13–16). Although the false gods which men worship do not exist, demons often impersonate them (1Co 10:20).

1:24–32 This section describes the downward spiral of the wrath of abandonment (*see note on v. 18*) in the life of man when God abandons him. Paul shows the essence (vv. 24, 25), the expression (vv. 26, 27), and the extent (vv. 28–32) of man's sinfulness.

1:24 God gave them over. This is a judicial term in Gr., used for handing over a prisoner to his sentence. When men consistently abandon God, He will abandon them (cf. Jdg 10:13; 2Ch 15:2; 24:20; Ps 81:11, 12; Hos 4:17; Mt 15:14; Ac 7:38–42; 14:16). He accomplishes this 1) indirectly and immediately, by removing His restraint and allowing their sin to run its inevitable course, and 2) directly and eventually, by specific acts of divine judgment and punishment. **impurity.** A general term often used of decaying matter, like the contents of a grave. It speaks here of sexual immorality (2Co 12:21; cf. Gal 5:19–23; Eph 5:3; 1Th 4:7), which begins in the heart and moves to the shame of the body.

1:25 a lie. A denial of God's existence and His right to be obeyed and glorified (vv. 19–21; Is 44:20; Jer 13:25; cf. Jn 8:44).

1:26 God gave them over. *See notes on vv. 18, 24.* **degrading passions.** Identified in vv. 26, 27 as homosexuality, a sin roundly condemned in Scripture (Ge 19; Lv 18:22; 1Co 6:9–11; cf. Gal 5:19–21; Eph 5:3–5; 1Ti 1:9, 10; Jude 7). **women.** Rather than the normal Gr. term for women, this is a general word for female. Paul mentions women first to show the extent of debauchery under the wrath of abandonment, because in most cultures women are the last to be affected by moral collapse.

1:27 receiving in their own persons the due penalty. Here the law of sowing and reaping (Gal 6:7, 8) takes effect, as Paul refers to the self-destructive nature of this sin, of which AIDS is one frightening evidence.

1:28 God gave them over. *See notes on vv. 18, 24.* **depraved.** This translates a Gr. word that means "not passing the test." It was often used to describe useless, worthless metals, discarded because they contained too much impurity. God has tested man's minds and found them worthless and useless (cf. Jer 6:30).

God, insolent, arrogant, boastful, inventors of evil,
[B]disobedient to parents, 31without understanding,
untrustworthy, [A]unloving, unmerciful; 32and although they know the ordinance of God, that those
who practice such things are worthy of [A]death, they
not only do the same, but also [B]give hearty approval
to those who practice them.

THE IMPARTIALITY OF GOD

2 Therefore you have [A]no excuse, [a,B]everyone of
you who passes judgment, for in that which
[C]you judge another, you condemn yourself; for you
who judge practice the same things. 2And we know
that the judgment of God [a]rightly falls upon those
who practice such things. 3But do you suppose
this, [A]O man, [a]when you pass judgment on those
who practice such things and do the same *yourself,*
that you will escape the judgment of God? 4Or do
you think lightly of [A]the riches of His [B]kindness
and [C]tolerance and [D]patience, not knowing that
the kindness of God leads you to repentance? 5But
[a]because of your stubbornness and unrepentant
heart [A]you are storing up wrath for yourself [B]in the
day of wrath and revelation of the righteous judgment of God, 6[A]who WILL RENDER TO EACH PERSON
ACCORDING TO HIS DEEDS: 7to those who by [A]perse-
verance in doing good seek for [B]glory and honor
and [C]immortality, [D]eternal life; 8but to those who
are [A]selfishly ambitious and [B]do not obey the truth,
but obey unrighteousness, wrath and indignation.
9*There will be* [A]tribulation and distress [a]for every
soul of man who does evil, of the Jew [B]first and also
of the Greek, 10but [A]glory and honor and peace to
everyone who does good, to the Jew [B]first and also
to the Greek. 11For [A]there is no partiality with God.
12For all who have sinned [a,A]without the Law will
also perish [a]without the Law, and all who have sinned
[b]under the Law will be judged [c]by the Law; 13for *it is*
[A]not the hearers [a]of the Law *who* are [b]just before God,
but the doers [a]of the Law will be justified. 14For when
Gentiles who do not have [a]the Law do [b,A]instinctively
the things of the Law, these, not having [a]the Law, are

1:30 [B]2 Tim 3:2 1:31 [A]2 Tim 3:3 1:32 [A]Rom 6:21 [B]Luke 11:48; Acts 8:1; 22:20 2:1 [a]Lit *O man, everyone who* [A]Rom 1:20 [B]Luke 12:14; Rom 2:3; 9:20 [C]2 Sam 12:5-7; Matt 7:1; Luke 6:37; Rom 14:22 2:2 [a]Lit *is according to truth against* 2:3 [a]Lit *who passes judgment* [A]Luke 12:14; Rom 2:1; 9:20 2:4 [A]Rom 9:23; 11:33; 2 Cor 8:2; Eph 1:7, 18; 2:7; Phil 4:19; Col 1:27; 2:2; Titus 3:6 [B]Rom 11:22 [C]Rom 3:25 [D]Ex 34:6; Rom 9:22; 1 Tim 1:16; 1 Pet 3:20; 2 Pet 3:9, 15 2:5 [a]Or *in accordance with* [A]Deut 32:34f; Prov 1:18 [B]Ps 110:5; 2 Cor 5:10; 2 Thess 1:5; Jude 6 2:6 [A]Ps 62:12; Prov 24:12; Matt 16:27 2:7 [A]Luke 8:15; Heb 10:36 [B]Rom 2:10; Heb 2:7; 1 Pet 1:7 [C]1 Cor 15:42, 50, 53f; Eph 6:24; 2 Tim 1:10 [D]Matt 25:46 2:8 [A]2 Cor 12:20; Gal 5:20; Phil 1:17; 2:3; James 3:14, 16 [B]2 Thess 2:12 2:9 [a]Lit *upon* [A]Rom 8:35 [B]Acts 3:26; Rom 1:16; 1 Pet 4:17 2:10 [A]Rom 2:7; Heb 2:7; 1 Pet 1:7 [B]Rom 2:9 2:11 [A]Deut 10:17; Acts 10:34 2:12 [a]Or *without law* [b]Or *under law* [c]Or *by law* [A]Acts 2:23; 1 Cor 9:21 2:13 [a]Or *of law* [b]Or *righteous* [A]Matt 7:21, 24ff; John 13:17; James 1:22f, 25 2:14 [a]Or *law* [b]Lit *by nature* [A]Acts 10:35; Rom 1:19; 2:15

1:32 know. Not ignorance, but blatant rebellion (*see note on 2:15*).

2:1–16 Having demonstrated the sinfulness of the immoral pagan (1:18–32), Paul presents his case against the religious moralist—Jew or Gentile—by cataloging 6 principles that govern God's judgment: 1) knowledge (v. 1); 2) truth (vv. 2, 3); 3) guilt (vv. 4, 5); 4) deeds (vv. 6–10); 5) impartiality (vv. 11–15); and 6) motive (v. 16).

2:1 no excuse . . . you who passes judgment. Both Jews (Paul's primary audience here; cf. v. 17) and moral Gentiles who think they are exempt from God's judgment because they have not indulged in the immoral excesses described in chap. 1 are tragically mistaken. They have more knowledge than the immoral pagan (3:2; 9:4) and thus a greater accountability (cf. Heb 10:26–29; Jas 3:1). **condemn yourself.** If someone has sufficient knowledge to judge others, he condemns himself, because he shows he has the knowledge to evaluate his own condition. **practice the same things.** In their condemnation of others they have excused and overlooked their own sins. Self-righteousness exists because of two deadly errors: 1) minimizing God's moral standard usually by emphasizing externals; and 2) underestimating the depth of one's own sinfulness (cf. Mt 5:20–22, 27, 28; 7:1–3; 15:1–3; Lk 18:21).

2:2 rightly falls. Whatever God does is by nature right (cf. 3:4; 9:14; Pss 9:4, 8; 96:13; 145:17; Is 45:19).

2:3 *See note on v. 1.*

2:4 think lightly. Lit. "to think down on," thus to underestimate someone's or something's value, and even to treat with contempt. **kindness.** This refers to "common grace," the benefits God bestows on all men (cf. Mt 5:45; Ac 14:15–17). **tolerance.** This word, which means "to hold back," was sometimes used of a truce between warring parties. Rather than destroying every person the moment he or she sins, God graciously holds back His judgment (cf. 3:25). He saves sinners in a physical and temporal way from what they deserve (*see note on 1Ti 4:10*), to show them His saving character, that they might come to Him and receive salvation that is spiritual and eternal. **patience.** This word indicates the duration for which God demonstrates His kindness and tolerance—for long periods of time (cf. 2Pe 2:5). Together these 3 words speak of God's common grace—the way He demonstrates His grace to all mankind (cf. Job 12:10; Pss 119:68; 145:9). **repentance.** The act of turning from sin to Christ for forgiveness and salvation. *See notes on 2Co 7:9–11.*

2:5 stubbornness. The Eng. word "sclerosis" (as in arteriosclerosis, a hardening of the arteries) comes from this Gr. word. But here the danger is not physical, but spiritual hardness (Eze 36:26; Mt 19:8; Mk 3:5; 6:52; 8:17; Jn 12:40; Heb 3:8, 15; 4:7). **unrepentant heart.** A refusal to repent (cf. v. 4) and accept God's pardon of sin through Jesus Christ. **storing up wrath.** To reject God's offer of forgiveness and cling to one's sin is to accumulate more of God's wrath and earn a severer judgment (*see notes on Heb 10:26–30; Rev 20:12*). **day of wrath and . . . judgment.** Refers to the final judgment of wicked men that comes at the Great White Throne at the end of the Millennium (*see notes on Rev 20:11–15*).

2:6–10 *See notes on vv. 1–16.* Although Scripture everywhere teaches that salvation is not on the basis of works (*see notes on 4:1–4; Eph 2:8*), it consistently teaches that God's judgment is always on the basis of a person's deeds (Is 3:10, 11; Jer 17:10; Jn 5:28, 29; 1Co 3:8; 2Co 5:10; Gal 6:7–9; cf. Ro 14:12). Paul describes the deeds of two distinct groups: the redeemed (vv. 7, 10) and the unredeemed (vv. 8, 9). The deeds of the redeemed are not the basis of their salvation but the evidence of it. They are not perfect and are prone to sin, but there is undeniable evidence of righteousness in their lives (*see notes on Jas 2:14–20*).

2:7 eternal life. Not simply in duration, because even unbelievers will live forever (2Th 1:9; Rev 14:9–11), but also in quality (*see note on Jn 17:3*). Eternal life is a kind of life, the holy life of the eternal God given to believers.

2:8 selfishly ambitious. This word may have originally been used to describe a hireling or mercenary; someone who does what he does for money regardless of how his actions affect others. **wrath.** *See note on 1:18.*

2:9 the Jew first. Just as the Jews were given the first opportunity to hear and respond to the gospel (1:16), they will be first to receive God's judgment if they refuse (cf. Am 3:2). Israel will receive severer punishment because she was given greater light and blessing (see 9:3, 4).

2:11 partiality. Lit. "to receive a face," that is, to give consideration to someone simply because of his position, wealth, influence, popularity, or appearance. Because it is God's nature to be just, it is impossible for Him to be anything but impartial (Ac 10:34; Gal 2:6; Eph 6:7, 8; Col 3:25; 1Pe 1:17).

2:12 sinned without the Law. The Gentiles who never had the opportunity to know God's moral law (Ex 20:1ff.) will be judged on their disobedience in relationship to their limited knowledge (*see notes on 1:19, 20*). **judged by the Law.** The Jews and many Gentiles who had access to God's moral law will be accountable for their greater knowledge (cf. Mt 11:20–23; Heb 6:4–6; 10:26–31).

2:13 will be justified. *See note on 3:24;* cf. Jas 2:20–26.

2:14 do instinctively the things of the Law. Without knowing the written law of God, people in pagan society generally value and attempt to practice its most basic tenets. This is normal for cultures instinctively (*see note on v. 15*) to value justice, honesty, compassion, and goodness toward others, reflecting the divine law written in the heart. **law**

a law to themselves, 15 in that they show [A]the work of the Law written in their hearts, their conscience bearing witness and their thoughts alternately accusing or else defending them, 16 on the day when, [A]according to my gospel, [B]God will judge the secrets of men through Christ Jesus.

THE JEW IS CONDEMNED BY THE LAW

17 But if you bear the name "Jew" and [A]rely [a]upon the Law and boast in God, 18 and know *His* will and [a,A]approve the things that are essential, being instructed out of the Law, 19 and are confident that you yourself are a guide to the blind, a light to those who are in darkness, 20 a [a]corrector of the foolish, a teacher of [b]the immature, having in the Law [A]the embodiment of knowledge and of the truth, 21 you, therefore, [A]who teach another, do you not teach yourself? You who [a]preach that one shall not steal, do you steal? 22 You who say that one should not commit adultery, do you commit adultery? You who abhor idols, do you [A]rob temples? 23 You who [A]boast [a]in the Law, through your breaking the Law, do you dishonor God? 24 For "[A]THE NAME OF GOD IS BLASPHEMED AMONG THE GENTILES [B]BECAUSE OF YOU," just as it is written.

25 For indeed circumcision is of value if you [A]practice [a]the Law; but if you are a transgressor [b]of the Law, [B]your circumcision has become uncircumcision. 26 [A]So if [B]the [a]uncircumcised man [C]keeps the requirements of the Law, will not his uncircumcision be regarded as circumcision? 27 And [A]he who is physically uncircumcised, if he keeps the Law, will he not [B]judge you who [a]though having the letter *of the Law* and circumcision are a transgressor [b]of the Law? 28 For [A]he is not a Jew who is one outwardly, nor is circumcision that which is outward in the flesh. 29 But [A]he is a Jew who is one inwardly; and [B]circumcision is that which is of the heart, by the [C]Spirit, not by the letter; [D]and his praise is not from men, but from God.

ALL THE WORLD GUILTY

3 Then what [a]advantage has the Jew? Or what is the benefit of circumcision? 2 Great in every respect. First of all, that [A]they were entrusted with the [B]oracles of God. 3 What then? If [A]some [a]did not believe, their [b]unbelief will not nullify the faithfulness

2:15 [A]Rom 2:14, 27 2:16 [A]Rom 16:25; 1 Cor 15:1; Gal 1:11; 1 Tim 1:11; 2 Tim 2:8 [B]Acts 10:42; 17:31; Rom 3:6; 14:10 2:17 [a]Or *upon law* [A]Mic 3:11; John 5:45; Rom 2:23; 9:4 2:18 [a]Or *distinguish between the things which differ* [A]Phil 1:10 2:20 [a]Or *instructor* [b]Lit *infants* [A]Rom 3:31; 2 Tim 1:13 2:21 [a]Or *proclaim* [A]Matt 23:3ff 2:22 [A]Acts 19:37 2:23 [a]Or *in law* [A]Mic 3:11; John 5:45; Rom 2:17; 9:4 2:24 [A]Is 52:5; Ezek 36:20ff [B]2 Pet 2:2 2:25 [a]Or *law* [b]Or *of law* [A]Rom 2:13f, 27 [B]Jer 4:4; 9:25f 2:26 [a]Lit *uncircumcision* [A]1 Cor 7:19 [B]Rom 3:30; Eph 2:11 [C]Rom 2:25, 27; 8:4 2:27 [a]Lit *through the letter* [b]Or *of law* [A]Rom 3:30; Eph 2:11 [B]Matt 12:41 2:28 [A]John 8:39; Rom 2:17; 9:6; Gal 6:15 2:29 [A]Phil 3:3; Col 2:11 [B]Deut 30:6 [C]Rom 2:27; 7:6; 2 Cor 3:6 [D]John 5:44; 12:43; 1 Cor 4:5; 2 Cor 10:18 3:1 [a]Lit *is the advantage of the Jew* 3:2 [A]Deut 4:8; Ps 147:19; Rom 9:4 [B]Acts 7:38 3:3 [a]Or *were unfaithful* [b]Or *unfaithfulness* [A]Rom 10:16; Heb 4:2

to themselves. Their practice of some good deeds and their aversion to some evil ones demonstrate an innate knowledge of God's law—a knowledge that will actually witness against them on the day of judgment.

2:15 work of the Law. Probably best understood as "the same works the Mosaic law prescribes." **conscience.** Lit. "with knowledge." That instinctive sense of right and wrong that produces guilt when violated. In addition to an innate awareness of God's law, men have a warning system that activates when they choose to ignore or disobey that law. Paul urges believers not to violate their own consciences or cause others to (13:5; 1Co 8:7, 12; 10:25, 29; 2Co 5:11; cf. 9:1; Ac 23:1; 24:16), because repeatedly ignoring the conscience's warnings desensitizes it and eventually silences it (1Ti 4:2). See 2Co 1:12; 4:2.

2:16 the day. *See note on 2:5.* **my gospel.** Not his own personal message, but the divinely revealed message of Jesus Christ (*see note on 1:1*), which is "good news" in light of the bad news of judgment. **secrets.** This primarily refers to the motives that lie behind men's actions (1Ch 28:9; Ps 139:1–3; Jer 17:10; Mt 6:4, 6, 18; cf. Lk 8:17; Heb 4:12). **through Christ Jesus.** *See note on Jn 5:23.*

2:17–29 Having shown that outwardly moral people—Jew and Gentiles alike—will stand condemned by God's judgment, Paul turns his argument exclusively to the Jews, God's covenant people. Neither their heritage (v. 17a), their knowledge (vv. 17b–24), nor their ceremonies, specifically circumcision (vv. 25–29), will protect them from God's righteous judgment.

2:17 Jew. Previously called Hebrews and Israelites, by the first-century "Jew" had become the most common name for the descendants of Abraham through Isaac. "Jew" comes from "Judah" (meaning "praise"), one of the 12 tribes and the designation for the southern half of Solomon's kingdom after his death. From the time of the Babylonian captivity, the whole race bore this title. Their great heritage, however (cf. Ge 12:3), became a source of pride and complacency (cf. Jon 4:2; Mic 3:11, 12; Mt 3:7–9; Jn 8:31–34, 40–59), which led to judgment instead of "praise."

2:19, 20 the blind … immature. Because they possessed the law, the Jews were confident that they were spiritually superior teachers: guides to blind pagans (cf. Mt 23:24–28), light (cf. Is 42:6), wise in God's ways, and able to teach the immature (probably a reference to Gentile proselytes to Judaism).

2:21–23 A series of questions designed to contrast most Jews' practice with what they knew and taught (cf. Ps 50:16–20; Mt 23:3, 4; Jas 3:1).

2:22 do you rob temples? May refer to fraudulently skimming funds from money given to the temple or withholding part of their temple tax or offerings (cf. Mal 3:8–10). More likely, however, it refers to the common practice—in direct violation of God's command (Dt 7:25)—of looting pagan temples and selling the idols and vessels for personal profit (cf. Ac 19:37) under the pretext of religion.

2:24 it is written. Quoted from Is 52:5.

2:25 circumcision. *See note on Ge 17:11.* **of value.** As an act of obedience and a reminder of their covenant relationship to God (*see notes on Ge 17:9–14*). **uncircumcision.** A Jew who continually transgressed God's law had no more of a saving relationship to God than an uncircumcised Gentile. The outward symbol was nothing without the inner reality.

2:26 regarded as circumcision. God will regard the believing Gentile as favorably as a circumcised, believing Jew.

2:27 A Gentile's humble obedience to the law should serve as a stern rebuke to a Jew who, in spite of his great advantages, lives in disobedience.

2:28 outwardly. This refers to physical descendants of Abraham who have been properly circumcised (cf. 9:6; Mt 3:9).

2:29 he is a Jew. A true child of God; the true spiritual descendant of Abraham. (See 4:16; cf. Gal 3:29). **circumcision is … of the heart.** The outward rite is of value only when it reflects the inner reality of a heart separated from sin unto God. Cf. Dt 10:16; 30:6. **Spirit … letter.** Salvation results from the work of God's Spirit in the heart, not mere external efforts to conform to His law.

3:2 oracles. This Gr. word is *logion,* a diminutive form of the common NT word *logos,* which is normally translated "word." These are important sayings or messages, especially supernatural ones. Here Paul uses the word to encompass the entire OT—the Jews received the very words of the true God (Dt 4:1, 2; 6:1, 2; cf. Mk 12:24; Lk 16:29; Jn 5:39). The Jews had a great advantage in having the OT, because it contained the truth about salvation (2Ti 3:15) and about the gospel in its basic form (Gal 3:8). When Paul said "preach the word" (2Ti 4:2), he meant the "utterances (or oracles) of God" (1Pe 4:11) recorded in Scripture.

3:3, 4 Paul anticipated that Jewish readers would disagree with his statements that God has not guaranteed to fulfill His promises to every physical descendant of Abraham. They would argue that such teaching nullifies all the promises God made to the Jews in the OT. But his answer reflects both the explicit and implicit teaching of the OT; before any Jew, regardless of the purity of his lineage, can inherit the promises, he must come to repentance and faith (cf. 9:6, 7; Is 55:6, 7).

3:3 the faithfulness of God. God will fulfill all the promises He made to the nation, even if individual Jews are not able to receive them because of their unbelief.

of God, will it? 4 [A]May it never be! Rather, let God be
found true, though every man *be found* [B]a liar, as
it is written,

"[C]THAT YOU MAY BE JUSTIFIED
IN YOUR WORDS,
AND PREVAIL WHEN YOU [a]ARE JUDGED."

5 But if our unrighteousness [a,A]demonstrates the
righteousness of God, [B]what shall we say? The God
who inflicts wrath is not unrighteous, is He? ([C]I am
speaking in human terms.) 6 [A]May it never be! For
otherwise, how will [B]God judge the world? 7 But if
through my lie [A]the truth of God abounded to His
glory, [B]why am I also still being judged as a sinner?
8 And why not *say* (as we are slanderously reported
and as some claim that we say), "[A]Let us do evil
that good may come"? [a]Their condemnation is just.
9 What then? [a,A]Are we better than they? Not at
all; for we have already charged that both [B]Jews
and [C]Greeks are [D]all under sin; 10 as it is written,

"[A]THERE IS NONE RIGHTEOUS,
NOT EVEN ONE;
11 THERE IS NONE WHO UNDERSTANDS,
THERE IS NONE WHO SEEKS FOR GOD;
12 ALL HAVE TURNED ASIDE, TOGETHER
THEY HAVE BECOME USELESS;
THERE IS NONE WHO DOES GOOD,
THERE IS NOT EVEN ONE."
13 "[A]THEIR THROAT IS AN OPEN GRAVE,
WITH THEIR TONGUES THEY
KEEP DECEIVING,"
"[B]THE POISON OF ASPS IS
UNDER THEIR LIPS";
14 "[A]WHOSE MOUTH IS FULL OF CURSING
AND BITTERNESS";
15 "[A]THEIR FEET ARE SWIFT TO SHED BLOOD,
16 DESTRUCTION AND MISERY
ARE IN THEIR PATHS,
17 AND THE PATH OF PEACE THEY
HAVE NOT KNOWN."
18 "[A]THERE IS NO FEAR OF GOD
BEFORE THEIR EYES."

19 Now we know that whatever the [A]Law says, it
speaks to [B]those who are [a]under the Law, so that
every mouth may be closed and [C]all the world may
become accountable to God; 20 because [A]by the
works [a]of the Law no flesh will be justified in His
sight; for [b,B]through the Law *comes* the knowledge
of sin.

3:4 [a]Lit *in Your judging* [A]Luke 20:16; Rom 3:6, 31 [B]Ps 116:11; Rom 3:7 [C]Ps 51:4 3:5 [a]Or *commends* [A]Rom 5:8; 2 Cor 6:4; 7:11 [B]Rom 4:1; 7:7; 8:31; 9:14, 30 [C]Rom 6:19; 1 Cor 9:8; 15:32; Gal 3:15 3:6 [A]Luke 20:16; Rom 3:4, 31 [B]Rom 2:16 3:7 [A]Rom 3:4 [B]Rom 9:19 3:8 [a]Lit *Whose* [A]Rom 6:1 3:9 [a]Or *Are we worse* [A]Rom 3:1 [B]Rom 2:1-29 [C]Rom 1:18-32 [D]Rom 3:19, 23; 11:32; Gal 3:22 3:10 [A]Ps 14:1-3; 53:1-3 3:13 [A]Ps 5:9 [B]Ps 140:3 3:14 [A]Ps 10:7 3:15 [A]Is 59:7f 3:18 [A]Ps 36:1 3:19 [a]Lit *in* [A]John 10:34 [B]Rom 2:12 [C]Rom 3:9 3:20 [a]Or *of law* [b]Or *through law* [A]Ps 143:2; Acts 13:39; Gal 2:16 [B]Rom 4:15; 5:13, 20; 7:7

3:4 every man .... liar. If all mankind were to agree that God had been unfaithful to His promises, it would only prove that all are liars and God is true. Cf. Titus 1:1. **it is written.** This is quoted from Ps 51:4.

3:5–8 Paul anticipates and answers the objection that his teaching actually impugned the very holiness and purity of God's character (*see note on 3:3, 4*).

3:5 demonstrates the righteousness of God. *See note on 1:17.* By contrast, like a jeweler who displays a diamond on black velvet to make the stone appear even more beautiful. **I am speaking in human terms.** He is simply paraphrasing the weak, unbiblical logic of his opponents—the product of their natural, unregenerate minds.

3:6 judge. A major theme of Scripture (Ge 18:25; Pss 50:6; 58:11; 94:2), here it probably refers to the great future day of judgment (*see note on 2:5*). Paul's point is that if God condoned sin, He would have no equitable, righteous basis for judgment.

3:8 slanderously reported. Tragically, the apostle's gospel message of salvation by grace through faith alone had been perverted by his opponents who argued it provided not only a license to sin, but outright encouragement to do so (5:20; 6:1, 2).

3:9–20 Paul concludes his indictment of mankind with this summary: Jew and Gentile alike stand guilty before God (*see note on 1:18–3:20*).

3:9 Are we better ... ? "We" probably refers to the Christians in Rome who will receive this letter. Christians do not have an intrinsically superior nature to all those Paul has shown to stand under God's condemnation. **Greeks.** *See note on 1:14.* **under sin.** Completely enslaved and dominated by sin.

3:10–18 Paul strings together a series of OT quotations that indict the character (vv. 10–12), conversation (vv. 13, 14), and conduct (vv. 15–18) of all men. Seven times he uses words such as "none" and "all" to show the universality of human sin and rebellion.

3:10–12 This is quoted from Pss 14:1–3; 53:1–3.

3:10 as it is written. The common introduction to OT quotations (cf. 1:17; 2:24; 3:4; Mt 4:4, 6, 7, 10). The tense of the Gr. verb stresses continuity and permanence, and implies its divine authority. none righteous. Man is universally evil (cf. Ps 14:1; *see notes on 1:17*).

3:11 none who understands. Man is unable to comprehend the truth of God or grasp His standard of righteousness (see Pss 14:2; 53:3; cf. 1Co 2:14). Sadly, his spiritual ignorance does not result from a lack of opportunity (1:19, 20; 2:15), but is an expression of his depravity and rebellion (Eph 4:18). **none who seeks.** See Ps 14:2. This verse clearly implies that the world's false religions are fallen man's attempts to escape the true God—not to seek Him. Man's natural tendency is to seek his own interests (cf. Php 2:21), but his only hope is for God to seek him (Jn 6:37, 44). It is only as a result of God's work in the heart that anyone seeks Him (Ps 16:8; Mt 6:33).

3:12 turned aside. See Ps 14:3. This word basically means "to lean in the wrong direction." It was used to describe a soldier's running the wrong way, or deserting. All men are inclined to leave God's way and pursue their own (cf. Is 53:6). **none who does good.** *See note on v. 10.*

3:13 open grave. See Ps 5:9. Graves were sealed not only to show respect for the deceased, but to hide the sight and stench of the body's decay. As an unsealed grave allows those who pass to see and smell what is inside, the unregenerate person's open throat—that is, the foul words that come from it—reveal the decay of his heart (cf. Pr 10:31, 32; 15:2, 28; Jer 17:9; Mt 12:34, 35; 15:18; Jas 3:1–12). asps. See Ps 140:3; cf. Mt 3:7; 12:34.

3:14 cursing. This is quoted from Ps 10:7. It refers to wanting the worst for someone and publicly expressing that desire in caustic, derisive language. **bitterness.** The open, public expression of emotional hostility against one's enemy (cf. Ps 64:3, 4).

3:15–17 This is quoted from Is 59:7, 8.

3:16 Destruction and misery. Man damages and destroys everything he touches, leaving a trail of pain and suffering in his wake.

3:17 path of peace. Not the lack of an inner sense of peace, but man's tendency toward strife and conflict, whether between individuals or nations (cf. Jer 6:14).

3:18 no fear of GOD. See Ps 36:1. Man's true spiritual condition is nowhere more clearly seen than in the absence of a proper submission to and reverence for God. Biblical fear for God consists of: 1) awe of His greatness and glory, and 2) dread of the results of violating that holy nature (*see note on Pr 1:7*; cf. Pr 9:10; 16:6; Ac 5:1–11; 1Co 11:30).

3:19 those ... under the Law. Every unredeemed human being. Jews received the written law through Moses (3:2), and Gentiles have the works of the law written on their hearts (2:15), so that both groups are accountable to God. **every mouth ... closed ... accountable.** There is no defense against the guilty verdict God pronounces on the entire human race.

3:20 works of the Law. Doing perfectly what God's moral law requires is impossible, so that every person is cursed by that inability (*see notes on Gal 3:10, 13*). **justified.** *See note on v. 24.* **through the Law *comes* the knowledge of sin.** The law makes sin known, but can't save. *See note on 7:7.*

JUSTIFICATION BY FAITH

21 But now apart [a]from the Law [A]*the* righteousness of God has been manifested, being [B]witnessed
by the Law and the Prophets, 22 even *the* [A]righ-
teousness of God through [B]faith [C]in Jesus Christ
for [D]all those [a]who believe; for [E]there is no distinction; 23 for all [a,A]have sinned and fall short of
the glory of God, 24 being justified as a gift [A]by
His grace through [B]the redemption which is in
Christ Jesus; 25 whom God displayed publicly as
[A]a [a]propitiation [b,B]in His blood through faith. *This
was* to demonstrate His righteousness, [c]because in
the [C]forbearance of God He [D]passed over the sins
previously committed; 26 for the demonstration, *I
say,* of His righteousness at the present time, so
that He would be just and the justifier of the one
who [a]has faith in Jesus.

27 Where then is [A]boasting? It is excluded. By
[B]what kind of law? Of works? No, but by a law of
faith. 28 [a]For [A]we maintain that a man is justified
by faith apart from works [b]of the Law. 29 Or [A]is God
the God of Jews only? Is He not *the God* of Gentiles
also? Yes, of Gentiles also, 30 since indeed [A]God [B]who
will justify the [a]circumcised [b]by faith and the [c]un-
circumcised through faith [C]is one.

31 Do we then nullify [a]the Law through faith? [A]May
it never be! On the contrary, we [B]establish the Law.

JUSTIFICATION BY FAITH EVIDENCED IN OLD TESTAMENT

4 What then shall we say that Abraham, [a]our
forefather [A]according to the flesh, has found?
2 For if Abraham was justified [a]by works, he has
something to boast about, but [A]not [b]before God.

3:21 [a]Or *from law* [A]Rom 1:17; 9:30 [B]Acts 10:43; Rom 1:2 3:22 [a]Or *who believe. For there is no distinction, since they all have sinned...and are being justified* [A]Rom 1:17; 9:30 [B]Rom 4:5 [C]Acts 3:16; Gal 2:16, 20; 3:22; Eph 3:12 [D]Rom 4:11, 16; 10:4 [E]Rom 10:12; Gal 3:28; Col 3:11 3:23 [a]Or *sinned* [A]Rom 3:9 3:24 [A]Rom 4:4f, 16; Eph 2:8 [B]1 Cor 1:30; Eph 1:7; Col 1:14; Heb 9:15 3:25 [a]Or *a propitiatory sacrifice* [b]Or *by* [c]Lit *because of the passing over of the sins previously committed in the forbearance of God* [A]1 John 2:2; 4:10 [B]1 Cor 5:7; Heb 9:14, 28; 1 Pet 1:19; Rev 1:5 [C]Rom 2:4 [D]Acts 14:16; 17:30 3:26 [a]Lit *is of the faith of Jesus* 3:27 [A]Rom 2:17, 23; 4:2; 1 Cor 1:29ff [B]Rom 9:31 3:28 [a]One early ms reads *Therefore* [b]Or *of law* [A]Acts 13:39; Rom 3:20, 21; Eph 2:9; James 2:20, 24, 26 3:29 [A]Acts 10:34f; Rom 9:24; 10:12; 15:9; Gal 3:28 3:30 [a]Lit *circumcision* [b]Lit *out of* [c]Lit *uncircumcision* [A]Rom 10:12; Gal 3:20 [B]Rom 3:22; 4:11f, 16; Gal 3:8 [C]Deut 6:4 3:31 [a]Or *law* [A]Luke 20:16; Rom 3:4 [B]Matt 5:17; Rom 3:4, 6; 8:4 4:1 [a]Or *our forefather, has found according to the flesh* [A]Rom 1:3 4:2 [a]Lit *out of* [b]Lit *toward* [A]1 Cor 1:31

3:21–5:21 Having conclusively proved the universal sinfulness of man and his need for righteousness (1:18–3:20), Paul develops the theme he introduced in 1:17, i.e., God has graciously provided a righteousness that comes from Him on the basis of faith alone (3:21–5:21).

3:21 **But now.** Not a reference to time, but a change in the flow of the apostle's argument. Having shown the impossibility of gaining righteousness by human effort, he turns to explain the righteousness that God Himself has provided. **apart from the Law.** Entirely apart from obedience to any law (4:15; Gal 2:16; 3:10, 11; 5:1, 2, 6; Eph 2:8, 9; cf. Php 3:9; 2Ti 1:9; Titus 3:5). **righteousness.** *See note on 1:17.* This righteousness is unique: 1) God is its source (Is 45:8); 2) it fulfills both the penalty and precept of God's law. Christ's death as a substitute pays the penalty exacted on those who failed to keep God's law, and His perfect obedience to every requirement of God's law fulfills God's demand for comprehensive righteousness (2Co 5:21; 1Pe 2:24; cf. Heb 9:28); and 3) because God's righteousness is eternal (Ps 119:142; Is 51:8; Da 9:24), the one who receives it from Him enjoys it forever. **witnessed by the Law and the Prophets.** *See note on 1:2.*

3:22 **through faith ... all ... who believe.** *See note on 1:16.*

3:22, 23 **there is no distinction ... glory of God.** A parenthetical comment explaining that God can bestow His righteousness on all who believe, Jew or Gentile, because all people—without distinction—fail miserably to live up to the divine standard.

3:23 **all have sinned.** Paul has already made this case (1:18–3:20).

3:24 **justified.** This verb, and related words from the same Gr. root (e.g., justification), occur some 30 times in Romans and are concentrated in 2:13–5:1. This legal or forensic term comes from the Gr. word for "righteous" and means "to declare righteous." This verdict includes: pardon from the guilt and penalty of sin, and the imputation of Christ's righteousness to the believer's account, which provides for the positive righteousness man needs to be accepted by God. God declares a sinner righteous solely on the basis of the merits of Christ's righteousness. God imputed a believer's sin to Christ's account in His sacrificial death (Is 53:4, 5; 1Pe 2:24), and He imputes Christ's perfect obedience to God's law to Christians (cf. 5:19; 1Co 1:30; *see notes on 2Co 5:21; Php 3:9*). The sinner receives this gift of God's grace by faith alone (3:22, 25; *see notes on 4:1–25*). Sanctification, the work of God by which He makes righteous those whom He has already justified, is distinct from justification but, without exception, always follows it (8:30). **a gift by His grace.** Justification is a gracious gift God extends to the repentant, believing sinner, wholly apart from human merit or work (*see note on 1:5*). **redemption.** The imagery behind this Gr. word comes from the ancient slave market. It meant paying the necessary ransom to obtain the prisoner or slave's release. The only adequate payment to redeem sinners from sin's slavery and its deserved punishment was "in Christ Jesus" (1Ti 2:6; 1Pe 1:18, 19), and was paid to God to satisfy His justice.

3:25 **whom God displayed.** This great sacrifice was not accomplished in secret, but God publicly displayed His Son on Calvary for all to see. **propitiation.** Crucial to the significance of Christ's sacrifice, this word carries the idea of appeasement or satisfaction—in this case Christ's violent death satisfied the offended holiness and wrath of God against those for whom Christ died (Is 53:11; Col 2:11–14). The Heb. equivalent of this word was used to describe the mercy seat—the cover to the ark of the covenant—where the High Priest sprinkled the blood of the slaughtered animal on the Day of Atonement to make atonement for the sins of the people. In pagan religions, it is the worshiper, not the god, who is responsible to appease the wrath of the offended deity. But in reality, man is incapable of satisfying God's justice apart from Christ, except by spending eternity in hell. Cf. 1Jn 2:2. **through faith.** *See note on 1:16.* **forbearance.** *See note on 2:4.* **passed over the sins.** This means neither indifference nor remission. God's justice demands that every sin and sinner be punished. God would have been just, when Adam and Eve sinned, to destroy them, and with them, the entire human race. But in His goodness and forbearance (see 2:4), He withheld His judgment for a certain period of time (cf. Ps 78:38, 39; Ac 17:30, 31; 2Pe 3:9).

3:26 **demonstration ... of His righteousness.** Through the incarnation, sinless life, and substitutionary death of Christ. **just and the justifier.** The wisdom of God's plan allowed Him to punish Jesus in the place of sinners and thereby justify those who are guilty without compromising His justice.

3:27 **Where then is boasting?** Cf. 4:1, 2; 1Co 1:26–29.

3:28 **justified by faith.** *See note on v. 24.* Paul's clear meaning is that a person is justified on the basis of faith alone (cf. 4:3–5; *see note on Jas 2:21*). **works of the Law.** *See note on v. 20.*

3:29 ***God* of Gentiles.** There is only one true God (cf. 1Co 8:5, 6).

3:31 Knowing he would be accused of antinomianism (being against the law) for arguing that a man was justified apart from keeping the law, Paul introduced here the defense he later developed in chaps. 6, 7. **through faith ... we establish the Law.** Salvation by grace through faith does not denigrate the law, but underscores its true importance: 1) by providing a payment for the penalty of death, which the law required for failing to keep it; 2) by fulfilling the law's original purpose, which is to serve as a tutor to show mankind's utter inability to obey God's righteous demands and to drive people to Christ (Gal 3:24); and 3) by giving believers the capacity to obey it (8:3, 4).

4:1 **Abraham, our forefather.** Paul uses the model of Abraham to prove justification by faith alone because the Jews held him up as the supreme example of a righteous man (Jn 8:39), and because it clearly showed that Judaism with its works-righteousness had deviated from the faith of the Jews' patriarchal ancestors. In a spiritual sense, Abraham was the forerunner of the primarily Gentile church in Rome as well (*see notes on 1:13; 4:11, 16;* cf. Gal 3:6, 7).

4:2 **justified by works.** Declared righteous on the basis of human effort (*see note on 3:24*). **boast.** If Abraham's own works had

3 For what does the Scripture say? "[A]ABRAHAM BE-
LIEVED GOD, AND IT WAS CREDITED TO HIM AS RIGH-
TEOUSNESS." 4 Now to the one who [A]works, his wage
is not credited as a favor, but as what is due. 5 But
to the one who does not work, but [A]believes in Him
who justifies the ungodly, his faith is credited as
righteousness, 6 just as David also speaks of the
blessing on the man to whom God credits righteousness apart from works:

7 "[A]BLESSED ARE THOSE WHOSE LAWLESS
DEEDS HAVE BEEN FORGIVEN,
AND WHOSE SINS HAVE BEEN COVERED.
8 "[A]BLESSED IS THE MAN WHOSE SIN THE LORD
WILL NOT [B]TAKE INTO ACCOUNT."

9 Is this blessing then on [a,A]the circumcised, or on
[b]the uncircumcised also? For [B]we say, "[C]FAITH WAS
CREDITED TO ABRAHAM AS RIGHTEOUSNESS." 10 How
then was it credited? While he was [a]circumcised,
or [b]uncircumcised? Not while [a]circumcised, but
while [b]uncircumcised; 11 and he [A]received the sign
of circumcision, [B]a seal of the righteousness of the
faith which [a]he had while uncircumcised, so that
he might be [C]the father of [D]all who believe without
being circumcised, that righteousness might be
credited to them, 12 and the father of circumcision
to those who not only are of the circumcision, but
who also follow in the steps of the faith of our father Abraham which [a]he had while uncircumcised.
13 For [A]the promise to Abraham or to his [a]descen-
dants [B]that he would be heir of the world was not
[b]through the Law, but through the righteousness of
faith. 14 For [A]if those who are [a]of the Law are heirs,
faith is made void and the promise is nullified; 15 for
[A]the Law brings about wrath, but [B]where there is
no law, there also is no violation.
16 For this reason *it is* [a]by faith, in order that *it may*
be in accordance with [A]grace, so that the promise
will be guaranteed to [B]all the [b]descendants, not only
to [c]those who are of the Law, but also to [c,C]those who
are of the faith of Abraham, who is [D]the father of us
all, 17 (as it is written, "[A]A FATHER OF MANY NATIONS
HAVE I MADE YOU") in the presence of Him whom
he believed, *even* God, [B]who gives life to the dead
and [a,C]calls into being [D]that which does not exist.

4:3 [A]Gen 15:6; Rom 4:9, 22; Gal 3:6; James 2:23 4:4 [A]Rom 11:6 4:5 [A]John 6:29; Rom 3:22 4:7 [A]Ps 32:1 4:8 [A]Ps 32:2 [B]2 Cor 5:19 4:9 [a]Lit *circumcision* [b]Lit *uncircumcision* [A]Rom 3:30 [B]Rom 4:3 [C]Gen 15:6 4:10 [a]Lit *in circumcision* [b]Lit *in uncircumcision* 4:11 [a]Lit *was in uncircumcision* [A]Gen 17:10f [B]John 3:33 [C]Luke 19:9; Rom 4:16f [D]Rom 3:22; 4:16 4:12 [a]Lit *was in uncircumcision* 4:13 [a]Lit *seed* [b]Or *through law* [A]Rom 9:8; Gal 3:16, 29 [B]Gen 17:4-6; 22:17f 4:14 [a]Or *of law* [A]Gal 3:18 4:15 [A]Rom 7:7, 10-25; 1 Cor 15:56; Gal 3:10 [B]Rom 3:20 4:16 [a]Or *out of* [b]Lit *seed* [c]Lit *that which is* [A]Rom 3:24 [B]Rom 4:11; 9:8; 15:8 [C]Gal 3:7 [D]Luke 19:9; Rom 4:11 4:17 [a]Lit *calls the things which do not exist as existing* [A]Gen 17:5 [B]John 5:21 [C]Is 48:13; 51:2 [D]1 Cor 1:28

been the basis of his justification, he would have had every right to boast in God's presence. That makes the hypothetical premise of v. 2 unthinkable (Eph 2:8, 9; 1Co 1:29).

4:3 A quotation of Ge 15:6, one of the clearest statements in all Scripture about justification (*see note on 3:24*). **believed.** Abraham was a man of faith (*see note on 1:16*; cf. 4:18–21; Gal 3:6, 7, 9; Heb 11:8–10). But faith is not a meritorious work. It is never the ground of justification—it is simply the channel through which it is received, and it, too, is a gift. *See note on Eph 2:8.* **credited.** Cf. vv. 5, 6, 8, 9, 10, 11, 22, 23, 24. Used in both financial and legal settings, this Gr. word, which occurs 9 times in chap. 4 alone, means to take something that belongs to someone and credit it to another's account. It is a one-sided transaction—Abraham did nothing to accumulate it; God simply credited it to him. God took His own righteousness and credited it to Abraham as if it were actually his. This God did because Abraham believed in Him (*see note on Ge 15:6*). **righteousness.** *See notes on 1:17; 3:21.*

4:4, 5 Broadening his argument from Abraham to all men, the apostle here makes it clear that the forensic act of declaring a person righteous is completely apart from any kind of human work. If salvation were on the basis of one's own effort, God would owe salvation as a debt—but salvation is always a sovereignly given gift of God's grace (3:24; Eph 2:8, 9) to those who believe (cf. 1:16). Since faith is contrasted with work, faith must mean the end of any attempt to earn God's favor through personal merit.

4:5 justifies the ungodly. Only those who relinquish all claims to goodness and acknowledge they are ungodly are candidates for justification (cf. Lk 5:32). **credited.** *See note on v. 3.*

4:6–8 Paul turns for support of his argument to Ps 32:1, 2, a penitential psalm written by David after his adultery with Bathsheba and his murder of her husband (2Sa 11). In spite of the enormity of his sin and the utter absence of personal merit, David knew the blessing of imputed righteousness.

4:9–12 Paul anticipated what his Jewish readers would be thinking: if Abraham was justified by his faith alone, why did God command him and his descendants to be circumcised? His response not only answers those concerned with circumcision, but the millions who still cling to some other kind of religious ceremony or activity as their basis for righteousness. *See notes on Ge 15:6.*

4:9 circumcised. This refers to Jews (*see notes on Ge 17:11–14*; cf. Ac 15:19–29; Ro 2:25–29; 4:11; Gal 5:1–4; 6:12; Php 3:2–5). **uncircumcised.** All Gentiles (*see notes on 2:25–29*).

4:10 Not while … but while uncircumcised. The chronology of Genesis proves Paul's case. Abraham was 86 when Ishmael was born (Ge 16:16), and Abraham was 99 when he was circumcised. But God declared him righteous before Ishmael had even been conceived (Ge 15:6; 16:2–4)—at least 14 years before Abraham's circumcision.

4:11, 12 the father of all who believe. Racially, Abraham is the father of all Jews (circumcised); spiritually, he is the father of both believing Jews (v. 12) and believing Gentiles (uncircumcised; v. 11). Cf. 4:16; Gal 3:29.

4:11 sign. This indicates man's need for spiritual cleansing (cf. 2:28, 29; Jer 4:3, 4; 9:24–26) and of the covenant relationship between God and His people (*see note on Ge 17:11*). **seal.** An outward demonstration of the righteousness God had credited to him by faith.

4:13–15 Just as Abraham was not justified by the rite of circumcision (vv. 9–12), neither was he justified by keeping the Mosaic law (vv. 13–15).

4:13 promise … heir of the world. This refers to Christ and is the essence of the covenant God made with Abraham and his descendants (*see notes on Ge 12:3*; cf. Ge 15:5; 18:18; 22:18). The final provision of that covenant was that through Abraham's descendants all the world would be blessed (Ge 12:3). Paul argues that "his descendants" refers specifically to Christ and that this promise really constituted the gospel (Gal 3:8, 16; cf. Jn 8:56). All believers, by being in Christ, become heirs of the promise (Gal 3:29; cf. 1Co 3:21–23). **not through the Law.** That is, not as a result of Abraham's keeping the law. **righteousness of faith.** Righteousness received from God by faith (*see note on 1:17*).

4:14 those who are of the Law. If only those who perfectly keep the law—an impossibility—receive the promise, faith has no value. **promise is nullified.** Making a promise contingent on an impossible condition nullifies the promise (*see note on v. 13*).

4:15 Law brings about wrath. By exposing man's sinfulness (cf. 7:7–11; Gal 3:19, 24).

4:16 by faith. Justification is through faith alone (*see notes on 1:16, 17 and 3:24*). **in accordance with grace.** But the power of justification is God's great grace (*see note on 1:5*), not man's faith. **promise.** *See note on v. 13.* **those who are of the Law.** Believing Jews. **those who are of the faith of Abraham.** Believing Gentiles. **father of us all.** *See note on v. 11.*

4:17 as it is written. Quoted from Ge 17:5. **gives life to the dead.** Abraham had experienced this firsthand (Heb 11:11, 12; cf. Ro 4:19). **calls into being that which does not exist.** This is another reference to the forensic nature of justification. God can declare believing sinners to be righteous even though they are not, by imputing His righteousness to them, just as God made or declared Jesus "sin" and punished Him, though He was not a sinner. Those whom He justifies, He will conform to the image of His Son (8:29, 30).

18 In hope against hope he believed, so that he
might become [A]a father of many nations according
to that which had been spoken, "[B]SO SHALL YOUR
[a]DESCENDANTS BE." 19 Without becoming weak in
faith he contemplated his own body, now [A]as good
as dead since [B]he was about a hundred years old,
and [C]the deadness of Sarah's womb; 20 yet, with
respect to the promise of God, he did not waver in
unbelief but grew strong in faith, [A]giving glory to
God, 21 and [A]being fully assured that [B]what God had
promised, He was able also to perform. 22 Therefore [A]IT WAS ALSO CREDITED TO HIM AS RIGHTEOUS-
NESS. 23 Now [A]not for his sake only was it written
that it was credited to him, 24 but for our sake
also, to whom it will be credited, as those [A]who
believe in Him who [B]raised Jesus our Lord from
the dead, 25 *He* who was [A]delivered over because
of our transgressions, and was [B]raised because of
our justification.

RESULTS OF JUSTIFICATION

5 [A]Therefore, having been justified by faith, [a,B]we
have peace with God through our Lord Jesus
Christ, 2 through whom also we have [A]obtained
our introduction by faith into this grace [B]in which
we stand; and [a]we exult in hope of the glory of
God. 3 [A]And not only this, but [a]we also [B]exult in our
tribulations, knowing that tribulation brings about
[C]perseverance; 4 and [A]perseverance, [B]proven character; and proven character, hope; 5 and hope [A]does
not disappoint, because the love of God has been
[B]poured out within our hearts through the Holy
Spirit who was given to us.
6 For while we were still [A]helpless, [B]at the right
time [C]Christ died for the ungodly. 7 For one will
hardly die for a righteous man; [a]though perhaps
for the good man someone would dare even to die.
8 But God [A]demonstrates [B]His own love toward us,
in that while we were yet sinners, [C]Christ died for

4:18 [a]Lit *seed* [A]Rom 4:17 [B]Gen 15:5 4:19 [A]Heb 11:12 [B]Gen 17:17 [C]Gen 18:11 4:20 [A]Matt 9:8 4:21 [A]Rom 14:5 [B]Gen 18:14; Heb 11:19 4:22 [A]Gen 15:6; Rom 4:3 4:23 [A]Rom 15:4; 1 Cor 9:9f; 10:11; 2 Tim 3:16f 4:24 [A]Rom 10:9; 1 Pet 1:21 [B]Acts 2:24 4:25 [A]Is 53:4, 5; Rom 5:6, 8; 8:32; Gal 2:20; Eph 5:2 [B]Rom 5:18; 1 Cor 15:17; 2 Cor 5:15 5:1 [a]Two early mss read *let us have* [A]Rom 3:28 [B]Rom 5:11 5:2 [a]Or *let us exult* [A]Eph 2:18; 3:12; Heb 10:19f; 1 Pet 3:18 [B]1 Cor 15:1 5:3 [a]Or *let us also exult* [A]Rom 5:11; 8:23; 9:10; 2 Cor 8:19 [B]Matt 5:12; James 1:2f [C]Luke 21:19 5:4 [A]Luke 21:19 [B]Phil 2:22; James 1:12 5:5 [A]Ps 119:116; Rom 9:33; Heb 6:18f [B]Acts 2:33; 10:45; Gal 4:6; Titus 3:6 5:6 [A]Rom 5:8, 10 [B]Gal 4:4 [C]Rom 4:25; 5:8; 8:32; Gal 2:20; Eph 5:2 5:7 [a]Lit *for* 5:8 [A]Rom 3:5 [B]John 3:16; 15:13; Rom 8:39 [C]Rom 4:25; 5:6; 8:32; Gal 2:20; Eph 5:2

4:18–25 Having shown that justification is through faith not works (vv. 1–8), and that it is by grace, not the keeping of law (vv. 9–17), Paul now concludes by showing that it results from divine power, not human effort (vv. 18–25).

4:18 **hope against hope.** From the human perspective, it seemed impossible (cf. v. 19). Cf. Ge 17:5. **which had been spoken.** Quoted from Ge 15:5.

4:19 **weak in faith.** When doubt erodes one's confidence in God's Word. **the deadness of Sarah's womb.** She was only 10 years younger than Abraham (Ge 17:17), 90 years old (well past childbearing age), when they received the promise of Isaac.

4:20 **the promise.** Of the birth of a son (Ge 15:4; 17:16; 18:10). **giving glory to God.** Believing God affirms His existence and character and thus gives Him glory (cf. Heb 11:6; 1Jn 5:10).

4:22 **Therefore.** Because of his genuine faith (see Ge 15:6).

4:23 **not for his sake only.** All Scripture has universal application (cf. 15:4; 2Ti 3:16, 17), and Abraham's experience is no exception. If Abraham was justified by faith, then all others are justified on the same basis.

4:25 A paraphrase of the LXX (Gr. translation of the OT) rendering of Is 53:12. Perhaps these words were adapted to and quoted from an early Christian confession or hymn. **delivered over.** I.e., crucified. **because of our justification.** The resurrection provided proof that God had accepted the sacrifice of His Son and would be able to be just and yet justify the ungodly.

5:1–11 Paul completed his case that God justifies sinners on the basis of faith alone, and he turned his pen to counter the notion that although believers receive salvation by faith, they will preserve it by good works. He argues that they are bound eternally to Jesus Christ, preserved by His power and not by human effort (cf. Is 11:5; Ps 36:5; La 3:23; Eph 1:18–20; 2Ti 2:13; Heb 10:23). For the Christian, the evidences of that eternal tie are: 1) his peace with God (v. 1); 2) his standing in grace (v. 2a); 3) his hope of glory (vv. 2b–5a); 4) his receiving of divine love (vv. 5b–8); 5) his certain escape of divine wrath (vv. 9, 10); and 6) his joy in the Lord (v. 11).

5:1 **having been justified.** The Gr. construction—and its Eng. translation—underscores that justification is a onetime legal declaration with continuing results (*see note on 3:24*), not an ongoing process. **peace with God.** Not a subjective, internal sense of calm and serenity, but an external, objective reality. God has declared Himself to be at war with every human being because of man's sinful rebellion against Him and His laws (v. 10; cf. 1:18; 8:7; Ex 22:24; Dt 32:21, 22; Ps 7:11; Jn 3:36; Eph 5:6). But the first great result of justification is that the sinner's war with God is ended forever (Col 1:21, 22). Scripture refers to the end of this conflict as a person's being reconciled to God (vv. 10, 11; 2Co 5:18–20).

5:2 **obtained our introduction.** This refers to the believer's access to God through Jesus Christ. What was unthinkable to the OT Jew (cf. Ex 19:9, 20, 21; 28:35) is now available to all who come (Jer 32:38, 40; Heb 4:16; 10:19–22; cf. Mt 27:51). **stand.** This refers to the permanent, secure position believers enjoy in God's grace (cf. v. 10; 8:31–34; Jn 6:37; Php 1:6; 2Ti 1:12; Jude 24). **hope of the glory of God.** Unlike the Eng. word "hope," the NT word contains no uncertainty; it speaks of something that is certain, but not yet realized. The believer's ultimate destiny is to share in the very glory of God (8:29, 30; Jn 17:22; 2Co 3:18; Php 3:20, 21; 1Jn 3:1, 2), and that hope will be realized because Christ Himself secures it (1Ti 1:1). Without the clear and certain promises of the Word of God, the believer would have no basis for hope (15:4; Ps 119:81,114; Eph 2:12; cf. Jer 14:8).

5:3 **tribulations.** A word used for pressure, like that of a press squeezing the fluid from olives or grapes. Here they are not the normal pressures of living (cf. 8:35), but the inevitable troubles that come to followers of Christ because of their relationship with Him (Mt 5:10–12; Jn 15:20; 2Co 4:17; 1Th 3:3; 2Ti 3:12; 1Pe 4:19). Such difficulties produce rich spiritual benefits (vv. 3, 4). **perseverance.** Sometimes translated "patience," this word refers to endurance, the ability to remain under tremendous weight and pressure without succumbing (15:5; Col 1:22, 23; 2Th 1:4; Rev 14:12).

5:4 **proven character.** The Gr. word simply means "proof." It was used of testing metals to determine their purity. Here the proof is Christian character (cf. Jas 1:12). Christians can glory in tribulations because of what those troubles produce.

5:5 **love of God … poured out.** God's love for us (cf. v. 8) has been lavishly poured out to the point of overflowing within our hearts. Paul moves from the objective aspects of our security in Christ to the internal, more subjective. God has implanted within our hearts evidence that we belong to Him in that we love the One who first loved us (1Co 16:22; cf. Gal 5:22; Eph 3:14–19; 1Jn 4:7–10). **Spirit who was given.** A marvelous testimony to God's love for us (8:9, 14, 16, 17; Jn 7:38, 39; 1Co 6:19, 20; 12:13; Eph 1:18).

5:6 **helpless.** Unregenerate sinners are spiritually dead and incapable of doing anything to help themselves (Jn 6:44; Eph 2:1). **at the right time.** At the moment God had chosen (cf. Gal 4:4). **Christ died for the ungodly.** God's love for His own is unwavering because it is not based on how lovable we are, but on the constancy of His own character; God's supreme act of love came when we were at our most undesirable (cf. Mt 5:46).

5:7 **righteous man … good man.** As uncommon as such a sacrifice is, Paul's point is that we were neither of these persons—yet Christ sacrificed Himself for us.

us. 9 Much more then, having now been justified
[a,A]by His blood, we shall be saved [B]from the wrath
of God through Him. 10 For if while we were [A]ene-
mies we were reconciled to God through the death
of His Son, much more, having been reconciled, we
shall be saved [a,B]by His life. 11 [A]And not only this,
[a]but we also exult in God through our Lord Jesus
Christ, through whom we have now received [B]the
reconciliation.
12 Therefore, just as through [A]one man sin entered
into the world, and [B]death through sin, and [C]so
death spread to all men, because all sinned— 13 for
[a]until the Law sin was in the world, but [A]sin is not
imputed when there is no law. 14 Nevertheless death
reigned from Adam until Moses, even over those
who had not sinned [A]in the likeness of the offense
of Adam, who is a [a,B]type of Him who was to come.
15 But [a]the free gift is not like the transgression.
For if by the transgression of [A]the one [B]the many
died, much more did the grace of God and the gift
by [C]the grace of the one Man, Jesus Christ, abound
to the many. 16 The gift is not like *that which came*
through the one who sinned; for on the one hand
[A]the judgment *arose* from one *transgression* [a]re-
sulting in condemnation, but on the other hand the
free gift *arose* from many transgressions [b]resulting
in justification. 17 For if by the transgression of the
one, death reigned [A]through the one, much more
those who receive the abundance of grace and of
the gift of righteousness will [B]reign in life through
the One, Jesus Christ.
18 So then as through [A]one transgression [a]there resulted condemnation to all men, even so through one
[B]act of righteousness [b]there resulted [C]justification

5:9 [a]Or *in* [A]Rom 3:25 [B]Rom 1:18; 1 Thess 1:10 5:10 [a]Or *in* [A]Rom 11:28; 2 Cor 5:18f; Eph 2:3; Col 1:21f [B]Rom 8:34; Heb 7:25; 1 John 2:1 5:11 [a]Lit *but also exulting* [A]Rom 5:3; 8:23; 9:10; 2 Cor 8:19 [B]Rom 5:10; 11:15; 2 Cor 5:18f 5:12 [A]Gen 2:17; 3:6, 19; Rom 5:15-17; 1 Cor 15:21f [B]Rom 6:23; 1 Cor 15:56; James 1:15 [C]Rom 5:14, 19, 21; 1 Cor 15:22 5:13 [a]Or *until law* [A]Rom 4:15 5:14 [a]Or *foreshadowing* [A]Hos 6:7 [B]1 Cor 15:45 5:15 [a]Lit *not as the transgression, so also is the free gift* [A]Rom 5:12, 18, 19 [B]Rom 5:19 [C]Acts 15:11 5:16 [a]Lit *to condemnation* [b]Lit *to an act of righteousness* [A]1 Cor 11:32 5:17 [A]Gen 2:17; 3:6, 19; Rom 5:12, 15, 16; 1 Cor 15:21f [B]2 Tim 2:12; Rev 22:5 5:18 [a]Lit *to condemnation* [b]Lit *to justification* [A]Rom 5:12, 15 [B]Rom 3:25 [C]Rom 4:25

5:9 Much more. What Paul is about to say is even more amazing and wonderful. **justified.** *See note on 3:24.* **by His blood.** Through His violent, substitutionary death. References to the blood of the Savior include the reality that He bled in His death (a necessity to fulfill the OT imagery of sacrifice), but are not limited to the fluid itself. NT writers also use the term "blood" as a graphic way to describe violent death (see Mt 23:30, 35; 27:4–8, 24, 25; Jn 6:53–56; Ac 5:28; 20:26). References to the Savior's blood are not simply pointing to the fluid, but at His death and entire atoning work (cf. 3:25; Eph 1:7; 2:13; Col 1:14, 20; Heb 9:12; 10:19; 13:12; 1Pe 1:2, 19; 1Jn 1:7; Rev 1:5). **wrath.** *See note on 1:18.* Christ bore the full fury of God's wrath in the believing sinner's place, and there is none left for him (see 8:1; 1Th 1:10; 5:9).

5:10 saved by His life. When we were God's enemies, Christ was able by His death to reconcile us to God. Certainly now that we are God's children, the Savior can keep us by His living power.

5:11 reconciliation. This is between God and sinners. *See notes on 2Co 5:18–20.*

5:12–21 In one of the most enigmatic passages in the entire book, Paul sets out to show how one man's death can provide salvation for many. To prove his point, he uses Adam to establish the principle that one man's actions can—and did—inexorably affect many other people.

5:12 just as … sin entered. Not a particular sin, but the inherent propensity to sin entered the human realm; men became sinners by nature. Adam passed to all his descendants the inherent sinful nature he possessed because of his first disobedience. That nature is present from the moment of conception (Ps 51:5), making it impossible for man to live in a way that pleases God. Satan, the father of sin (1Jn 3:8), first brought temptation to Adam and Eve (Ge 3:1–7). **through one man.** God appointed Adam to be the representative of the entire human race that descended from him. When Adam sinned, all mankind sinned—that is, God imputed the guilt of his sin to all those yet in his loins (v. 18; cf. Heb 7:7–10). And since his sin transformed his inner nature and brought spiritual death and depravity, that sinful nature would be passed on to his posterity as well (Ps 51:5). **death.** Adam was not originally subject to death, but through his sin it became a grim certainty for him and his posterity. Death has three distinct manifestations: 1) spiritual death or separation from God (cf. Eph 2:1–2; 4:18); 2) physical death (Heb 9:27); and 3) eternal death (also called the second death), which includes not only eternal separation from God, but also eternal torment in the lake of fire (Rev 20:11–15). **because all sinned.** Because all humanity existed in the loins of Adam, and have through procreation inherited his fallenness and depravity, it can be said that all sinned in him. Some object to the concept of imputed guilt. But if God's imputation of the guilt of Adam's sin to us were not true, it would be impossible to argue that God can impute to us the righteousness of Christ (cf. 5:15–19; 1Co 15:22).

5:13 sin is not imputed. *See note on 2Co 5:19.* Though all men were regarded as sinners (v. 12), because there was no explicit list of commands, there was no strict accounting of their specific points of violation. **when there is no law.** The period from Adam to Moses, when God had not yet given the Mosaic law.

5:14 Nevertheless death reigned. But even without the law, death was universal. All men from Adam to Moses were subject to death, not because of their sinful acts against the Mosaic law (which they did not yet have), but because of their own inherited sinful nature. **not sinned … likeness … of Adam.** Those who had no specific revelation as did Adam (Ge 2:16, 17) or those who had the Mosaic law (cf. v. 13), but nevertheless sinned against the holiness of God, i.e., those who "sinned without the Law" (2:12). **a type of Him … to come.** Both Adam and Christ were similar in that their acts affected many others. This phrase serves as transition from the apostle's discussion of the transference of Adam's sin to the crediting of Christ's righteousness.

5:15–21 In this passage Paul explores the contrasts between the condemning act of Adam and the redemptive act of Christ. They were different in their effectiveness (v. 15), their extent (v. 16), their efficacy (v. 17), their essence (vv. 18, 19), and their energy (vv. 20, 21).

5:15 many died. Paul uses the word "many" with two distinct meanings in v. 15, just as he will with the word "all" in v. 18. He has already established that all men, without exception, bear the guilt of sin and are therefore subject to death (*see notes on v. 12*). So the "many" who die must refer to all Adam's descendants. **much more.** Christ's one act of redemption was immeasurably greater than Adam's one act of condemnation.

5:16 The gift. Salvation by grace. **the judgment *arose* from one *transgression*.** *See notes on v. 12.* **condemnation.** The divine guilty verdict; the opposite of justification. **many transgressions.** Adam brought upon all men the condemnation for only one offense—his willful act of disobedience. Christ, however, delivers the elect from the condemnation of many offenses. **justification.** *See note on 3:24.*

5:17 death reigned. Adam's sin brought universal death—exactly opposite the result he expected and Satan had promised: "You will be like God" (Ge 3:5). Christ's sacrifice brought salvation to those who believe. **gift of righteousness.** *See notes on 1:17 and 3:24*; see also 2Co 5:21; Php 3:8, 9. **will reign in life.** Unlike Adam's act, Christ's act has—and will—accomplish exactly what He intended (cf. Php 1:6), i.e., spiritual life (cf. Eph 2:5).

5:18, 19 Summaries of the analogy of Adam and Christ.

5:18 condemnation. *See note on v. 16.* **one act of righteousness.** Not a reference to a single event, but generally to Christ's obedience (cf. v. 19; Lk 2:49; Jn 4:34; 5:30; 6:38), culminating in the greatest demonstration of that obedience, death on a cross (Php 2:8). **justification … to all men.** This cannot mean that all men will be saved; salvation is only for those who exercise faith in Jesus Christ (cf. 1:16, 17; 3:22, 28; 4:5, 13). Rather, like the word "many" in v. 15, Paul is using "all" with two different meanings for the sake of parallelism, a common practice in the Heb. OT.

of life to all men. 19 For as through the one man's
disobedience [A]the many [B]were made sinners, even
so through [C]the obedience of the One [A]the many
will be made righteous. 20 [a],[A]The Law came in so
that the transgression would increase; but where
sin increased, [B]grace abounded all the more, 21 so
that, as [A]sin reigned in death, even so [B]grace would
reign through righteousness to eternal life through
Jesus Christ our Lord.

BELIEVERS ARE DEAD TO SIN, ALIVE TO GOD

6 [A]What shall we say then? Are we to [B]continue in
sin so that grace may increase? 2 [A]May it never
be! How shall we who [B]died to sin still live in it?
3 Or do you not know that all of us who have been
[A]baptized into [B]Christ Jesus have been baptized into
His death? 4 Therefore we have been [A]buried with
Him through baptism into death, so that as Christ
was [B]raised from the dead through the [C]glory of the
Father, so we too might walk in [D]newness of life.
5 For [A]if we have become [a]united with *Him* in the
likeness of His death, certainly we shall also be [b]*in
the likeness* of His resurrection, 6 knowing this, that
our [A]old [a]self was [B]crucified with *Him,* in order that
our [C]body of sin might be [b]done away with, so that
we would no longer be slaves to sin; 7 for [A]he who
has died is [a]freed from sin.
8 Now [A]if we have died with Christ, we believe that
we shall also live with Him, 9 knowing that Christ,
having been [A]raised from the dead, [a]is never to die
again; [B]death no longer is master over Him. 10 For
the death that He died, He died to sin once for all;
but the life that He lives, He lives to God. 11 Even so
consider yourselves to be [A]dead to sin, but alive to
God in Christ Jesus.

5:19 [A]Rom 5:15, 18 [B]Rom 5:12; 11:32 [C]Phil 2:8 5:20 [a]Or *law* [A]Rom 3:20; 7:7f; Gal 3:19 [B]Rom 6:1; 1 Tim 1:14 5:21 [A]Rom 5:12, 14 [B]John 1:17; Rom 6:23 6:1 [A]Rom 3:5 [B]Rom 3:8; 6:15 6:2 [A]Luke 20:16; Rom 6:15 [B]Rom 6:11; 7:4, 6; Gal 2:19; Col 2:20; 3:3; 1 Pet 2:24 6:3 [A]Matt 28:19 [B]Acts 2:38; 8:16; 19:5; Gal 3:27 6:4 [A]Col 2:12 [B]Acts 2:24; Rom 6:9 [C]John 11:40; 2 Cor 13:4 [D]Rom 7:6; 2 Cor 5:17; Gal 6:15; Eph 4:23f; Col 3:10 6:5 [a]Or *united with the likeness* [b]Or *with* [A]2 Cor 4:10; Phil 3:10f; Col 2:12; 3:1 6:6 [a]Gr *anthropos* [b]Or *made powerless* [A]Eph 4:22; Col 3:9 [B]Gal 2:20; 5:24; 6:14 [C]Rom 7:24 6:7 [a]Or *acquitted* [A]1 Pet 4:1 6:8 [A]Rom 6:4; 2 Cor 4:10; 2 Tim 2:11 6:9 [a]Lit *no longer dies* [A]Acts 2:24; Rom 6:4 [B]Rev 1:18 6:11 [A]Rom 6:2; 7:4, 6; Gal 2:19; Col 2:20; 3:3; 1 Pet 2:24

5:19 made righteous. This expression probably refers to one's legal status before God and not an actual change in character, since Paul is contrasting justification and condemnation throughout this passage, and he has not yet introduced the doctrine of sanctification (chaps. 6–8) which deals with the actual transformation of the sinner as a result of redemption.

5:20 The Law came in. Cf. Gal 3:19. Although the Mosaic law is not flawed (7:12), its presence caused man's sin to increase (cf. 7:8–11). Thus it made men more aware of their own sinfulness and inability to keep God's perfect standard (7:7; Gal 3:21, 22), and it served as a tutor to drive them to Christ (Gal 3:24).

5:21 This is the final summary of the analogy of Adam and Christ.

6:1–8:39 Paul moves from demonstrating the doctrine of justification, which is God's declaring the believing sinner righteous (3:20–5:21), to demonstrating the practical ramifications of salvation on those who have been justified. He specifically discusses the doctrine of sanctification, which is God's producing actual righteousness in the believer (6:1–8:39).

6:1–10 He begins his lesson on sanctification by arguing that in spite of their past, all whom God has justified will experience personal holiness (cf. 1Co 6:9–11a; 1Ti 1:12, 13).

6:1 Are we to continue in sin . . . ? Because of his past Pharisaic experience, Paul was able to anticipate the major objections of his critics. He had already alluded to this criticism, that by preaching a justification based solely on the free grace of God, he was encouraging people to sin (cf. 3:5, 6, 8).

6:2 May it never be! Used 14 times in Paul's epistles (10 in Romans: 3:4, 6, 31; 6:2, 15; 7:7, 13; 9:14; 11:1, 11), this expression is the strongest Gr. idiom for repudiating a statement, and it contains a sense of outrage that anyone would ever think the statement was true. **we . . . died to sin.** Not a reference to the believer's ongoing daily struggle with sin, but to a onetime event completed in the past. Because we are "in Christ" (6:11; 8:1), and He died in our place (5:6–8), we are counted dead with Him. This is the fundamental premise of chap. 6, and Paul spends the remainder of the chapter explaining and supporting it.

6:3 baptized into Christ Jesus. This does not refer to water baptism. Paul is actually using the word "baptized" in a metaphorical sense, as we might in saying someone was immersed in his work, or underwent his baptism of fire when experiencing some trouble. All Christians have, by placing saving faith in Him, been spiritually immersed into the person of Christ, that is, united and identified with Him (cf. 1Co 6:17; 10:2; Gal 3:27; 1Pe 3:21; 1Jn 1:3; *see note on Ac 2:38*). Certainly water baptism pictures this reality, which is the purpose—to show the transformation of the justified. **into His death.** This means that immersion or identification is specifically with Christ's death and resurrection, as the apostle will explain (see 6:4–7).

6:4 buried with Him. Since we are united by faith with Him, as baptism symbolizes, His death and burial become ours. **newness of life.** This is true if, in Christ, we died and were buried with Him, we have also been united with Him in His resurrection. There is a new quality and character to our lives, a new principle of life. This speaks of the believer's regeneration (cf. Eze 36:26; 2Co 5:17; Gal 6:15; Eph 4:24). Whereas sin describes the old life, righteousness describes the new.

6:6 our old self. A believer's unregenerate self. The Gr. word for "old" does not refer to something old in years but to something that is worn out and useless. Our old self died with Christ, and the life we now enjoy is a new divinely given life that is the life of Christ Himself (cf. Gal 2:20). We have been removed from the unregenerate self's presence and control, so we should not follow the remaining memories of its old sinful ways as if we were still under its evil influence (*see notes on Eph 4:20–24; Gal 5:24; Col 3:9, 10*). **body of sin.** Essentially synonymous with "our old self." Paul uses the terms "body" and "flesh" to refer to sinful propensities that are intertwined with physical weaknesses and pleasures (e.g., 8:10, 11, 13, 23). Although the old self is dead, sin retains a foothold in our temporal flesh or our unredeemed humanness, with its corrupted desires (7:14–24). The believer does not have two competing natures, the old and the new; but one new nature that is still incarcerated in unredeemed flesh (*see note on v. 12*). But the term "flesh" is not equivalent to the physical body, which can be an instrument of holiness (v. 19; 12:1; 1Co 6:20). **done away with.** Rendered powerless or inoperative.

6:7 has died. Through his union with Christ (*see note on v. 3*). **freed from sin.** No longer under its domination and control.

6:8 we shall also live with Him. The context suggests that Paul means not only that believers will live in the presence of Christ for eternity, but also that all who have died with Christ, which is true of all believers, will live a life here that is fully consistent with His holiness.

6:9 master. Control or domination. Cf. vv. 11, 12.

6:10 He died to sin. Christ died to sin in two senses: 1) in regard to sin's penalty—He met its legal demands upon the sinner; and 2) in regard to sin's power—forever breaking its power over those who belong to Him. And His death will never need repeating (Heb 7:26, 27; 9:12, 28; 10:10; cf. 1Pe 3:18). Paul's point is that believers have died to sin in the same way. **He lives to God.** For God's glory.

6:11–14 Paul addresses the logical conclusion of his readers: if the old self is dead, why is there continually a struggle with sin, and how can the new self become dominant (see also 7:1–25)? His exhortation is contained in 2 key words: "consider" (vv. 11b, 12) and "present" (vv. 13, 14).

6:11 Even so. This implies the importance of his readers' knowing what he just explained. Without that foundation, what he is about to teach will not make sense. Scripture always identifies knowledge as the foundation for one's practice (cf. Col 3:10). **consider.** This word was often used metaphorically to refer to having an absolute, unreserved confidence in what one's mind knows to be true—the kind of heartfelt confidence that

12 Therefore do not let sin [A]reign in your mortal
body so that you obey its lusts, 13 and do not go
on [A]presenting [a]the members of your body to sin
as [b]instruments of unrighteousness; but [B]present
yourselves to God as those alive from the dead, and
your members *as* [b]instruments of righteousness to
God. 14 For [A]sin shall not [B]be master over you, for
[C]you are not under law but [D]under grace.
15 What then? [A]Shall we sin because we are not
under law but under grace? [B]May it never be! 16 Do
you not [A]know that when you present yourselves to
someone *as* [B]slaves for obedience, you are slaves of
the one whom you obey, either of [C]sin [a]resulting in
death, or of obedience [b]resulting in righteousness?
17 But [A]thanks be to God that [a]though you were slaves
of sin, you became obedient from the heart to that
[B]form of teaching to which you were committed,
18 and having been [A]freed from sin, you became
slaves of righteousness. 19 [A]I am speaking in human
terms because of the weakness of your flesh. For
just [B]as you presented your members as slaves to
impurity and to lawlessness, [a]resulting in *further*
lawlessness, so now present your members as slaves
to righteousness, [b]resulting in sanctification.
20 For [A]when you were slaves of sin, you were
free in regard to righteousness. 21 Therefore what
[a,A]benefit were you then [b]deriving [c]from the things
of which you are now ashamed? For the outcome
of those things is [B]death. 22 But now having been
[A]freed from sin and [B]enslaved to God, you [a]derive
your [b,C]benefit, [c]resulting in sanctification, and [D]the
outcome, eternal life. 23 For the wages of [A]sin is
death, but the free gift of God is [B]eternal life in Christ
Jesus our Lord.

BELIEVERS UNITED TO CHRIST

7 Or do you not know, [A]brethren (for I am speaking to those who know the law), that the law
has jurisdiction over a person as long as he lives?
2 For [A]the married woman is bound by law to her
[a]husband while he is living; but if her husband
dies, she is released from the law [b]concerning the

6:12 [A]Rom 6:14 6:13 [a]Lit *your members to sin* [b]Or *weapons* [A]Rom 6:16, 19; 7:5; Col 3:5 [B]Rom 12:1; 2 Cor 5:14f; 1 Pet 2:24 6:14 [A]Rom 8:2, 12 [B]Rom 6:12 [C]Rom 5:18; 7:4, 6; Gal 4:21 [D]Rom 5:17, 21 6:15 [A]Rom 6:1 [B]Luke 20:16; Rom 6:2 6:16 [a]Lit *to death* [b]Lit *to righteousness* [A]Rom 11:2; 1 Cor 3:16; 5:6; 6:2, 3, 9, 15, 16, 19; 9:13, 24 [B]John 8:34; 2 Pet 2:19 [C]Rom 6:21, 23 6:17 [a]Lit *you were slaves…but you became* [A]Rom 1:8; 2 Cor 2:14 [B]2 Tim 1:13 6:18 [A]John 8:32; Rom 6:22; 8:2 6:19 [a]Lit *to lawlessness* [b]Lit *to sanctification* [A]Rom 3:5 [B]Rom 6:13 6:20 [A]Matt 6:24; Rom 6:16 6:21 [a]Lit *fruit* [b]Lit *having* [c]Lit *in* [A]Jer 12:13; Ezek 16:63; Rom 7:5 [B]Rom 1:32; 5:12; 6:16, 23; 8:6, 13; Gal 6:8 6:22 [a]Lit *have* [b]Lit *fruit* [c]Lit *to sanctification* [A]John 8:32; Rom 6:18; 8:2 [B]1 Cor 7:22; 1 Pet 2:16 [C]Rom 7:4 [D]1 Pet 1:9 6:23 [A]Rom 1:32; 5:12; 6:16, 21; 8:6, 13; Gal 6:8 [B]Matt 25:46; Rom 5:21; 8:38, 39 7:1 [A]Rom 1:13 7:2 [a]Lit *living husband* [b]Lit *of* [A]1 Cor 7:39

affects his actions and decisions. Paul is not referring to mind games in which we trick ourselves into thinking a certain way. Rather, he is urging us to embrace by faith what God has revealed to be true. **dead to sin.** See vv. 2–7. **in Christ.** Paul's favorite expression of our union with Christ. This is its first occurrence in Romans (cf. Eph 1:3–14).

6:12 mortal body. The only remaining repository where sin finds the believer vulnerable. The brain and its thinking processes are part of the body and thus tempt our souls with its sinful lusts (*see note on v. 6*; cf. 8:22, 23; 1Co 15:53; 1Pe 2:9–11).

6:13 presenting. Refers to a decision of the will. Before sin can have power over a believer, it must first pass through his will (cf. Php 2:12, 13). **members.** The parts of the physical body, the headquarters from which sin operates in the believer (7:18, 22–25; cf. 12:1; 1Co 9:27). **instruments of unrighteousness.** Tools for accomplishing that which violates God's holy will and law.

6:14 sin shall not be master over you. Sin must be able to exercise control in our bodies, or Paul's admonition becomes unnecessary (v. 13). But sin does not have to reign there; so the apostle expresses his confidence that those who are Christ's will not allow it to. **not under law but under grace.** This does not mean God has abrogated His moral law (3:31; cf. Mt 5:17–19). The law is good, holy, and righteous (7:12; cf. 1Ti 1:8), but it cannot be kept, so it curses. Since it cannot assist anyone to keep God's moral standard (cf. 7:7–11), it can only show the standard and thus rebuke and condemn those who fail to keep it. But the believer is no longer under the law as a condition of acceptance with God—an impossible condition to meet and one designed only to show man his sinfulness (*see notes on 3:19, 20*; cf. Gal 3:10–13)—but under grace, which enables him to truly fulfill the law's righteous requirements (7:6; 8:3, 4). Chapter 7 is Paul's complete commentary on this crucial expression.

6:15–23 This section continues Paul's discussion of sanctification by reminding his readers of their past slavery to sin and their new slavery to righteousness. He wants them to live in submission to their new master, Jesus Christ, and not to be entangled again with the sins that characterized their old life, sins which no longer have any claim over them.

6:15 Shall we sin … ? Cf. 3:5, 6, 8; 6:1. **not under law but under grace.** *See note on v. 14.*

6:17 form of teaching … committed. In the Gk. "form" is a word for a mold such as a craftsman would use to cast molten metal. Paul's point is that God pours His new children into the mold of divine truth (12:2; cf. Titus 2:1). New believers have an innate and compelling desire to know and obey God's Word (1Pe 2:2).

6:18 having been freed. *See note on v. 2.* **slaves of righteousness.** See v. 16.

6:19 human terms … weakness of your flesh. Paul's use of the master/slave analogy was an accommodation to their humanness and their difficulty in grasping divine truth. **your members.** *See note on v. 13.* ***further* lawlessness.** Like a vicious animal, sin's appetite only grows when it is fed (Ge 4:7).

6:22 freed from sin. *See note on v. 2.* **having become slaves of God.** Paul describes a *doulos*/ slave salvation relationship to one's *kurios*/ Lord who redeemed him. The *doulos* word group (used over 160 times in the NT) should always be translated with the sense of "slave" and never "servant" or "bond servant," which would be foreign to the first-century intent of *doulos*, which conveyed at least five comprehensive ideas: 1) absolute obedience (Mt 8:5–9; Lk 7:2–10); 2) compulsory obedience (Lk 6:46); 3) consistent obedience (Jn 13:16); 4) exclusive obedience (Mt 6:24); and 5) loyal obedience (Mt 10:24; Jn 15:20). *Doulos* is always employed in the context of being owned by, belonging to, and being wholly subordinate to one's master. Christ is the supreme example of both slave (Php 2:7) and Lord (Php 2:11). The lordship of Christ in authentic salvation (both inauguration and continuation) comes across clearly in texts such as Ro 10:9 (see note) and Col 2:6. The Savior possesses sovereign authority over those whom He has saved; the redeemed by virtue of their salvation are obliged to obey as those who have been bought with a price and therefore are not their own (Ac 20:28; 1Co 16:19, 20; 1Pe 1:17–19). **sanctification.** The benefit of being slaves to God is sanctification, the outcome of which is eternal life.

6:23 This verse describes two inexorable absolutes: 1) spiritual death is the paycheck for every man's slavery to sin; and 2) eternal life is a free gift God gives undeserving sinners who believe in His Son (cf. Eph 2:8, 9).

7:1–8:4 Knowing that his readers—especially Jewish ones—would have many questions about how the law relates to their faith in Christ, Paul sets out to explain that relationship (he refers to the law 27 times in this passage). In a detailed explanation of what it means not to be under law, but under grace (6:14, 15), Paul teaches that: 1) the law can no longer condemn a believer (7:1–6); 2) it convicts unbelievers (and believers) of sin (7:7–13); 3) it cannot deliver a believer from sin (7:14–25); and 4) believers who walk in the power of the Spirit can fulfill the law (8:1–4).

7:1 know the law. Lit. "those who know law." Although Paul intends to include God's written law, he is not referring to any specific law code, but to a principle that is true of all law—Greek, Roman, Jewish, or biblical. **jurisdiction.** No matter how serious a criminal's offenses may be, he is no longer subject to prosecution and punishment after he dies.

7:2, 3 These two verses are not a complex allegory, but a simple analogy, using marriage law to illustrate the point Paul just made about law's jurisdiction (v. 1). This passage is

husband. 3 So then, if while her husband is living
she is joined to another man, she shall be called an
adulteress; but if her husband dies, she is free from
the law, so that she is not an adulteress though she
is joined to another man.
4 Therefore, my brethren, you also were [A]made to
die [B]to the Law [C]through the body of Christ, so that
you might be joined to another, to Him who was
raised from the dead, in order that we might bear
fruit for God. 5 For while we were [A]in the flesh, the
sinful passions, which were [B]*aroused* by the Law,
were at work [C]in [a]the members of our body to bear
fruit for death. 6 But now we have been [A]released
from the Law, having [B]died to that by which we
were bound, so that we serve in [C]newness of [D]the
[a]Spirit and not in oldness of the letter.
7 [A]What shall we say then? Is the Law sin? [B]May
it never be! On the contrary, [C]I would not have
come to know sin except [a]through the Law; for I
would not have known about [b]coveting if the Law
had not said, "[D]YOU SHALL NOT [b]COVET." 8 But sin,
[A]taking opportunity [B]through the commandment,
produced in me [a]coveting of every kind; for [C]apart
[b]from the Law sin *is* dead. 9 I was once alive apart
[a]from the Law; but when the commandment came,
sin became alive and I died; 10 and this commandment, which was [a,A]to result in life, proved [b]to result
in death for me; 11 for sin, [A]taking an opportunity
[B]through the commandment, [C]deceived me and
through it killed me. 12 [A]So then, the Law is holy,
and the commandment is holy and righteous and
good.
13 Therefore did that which is good become *a*
cause of death for me? [A]May it never be! Rather it
was sin, in order that it might be shown to be sin
by effecting my death through that which is good,
so that through the commandment sin would become utterly sinful.

7:4 [A]Rom 6:2; 7:6 [B]Rom 8:2; Gal 2:19; 5:18 [C]Col 1:22 7:5 [a]Lit *our members to bear* [A]Rom 8:8f; 2 Cor 10:3 [B]Rom 7:7f [C]Rom 6:13, 21, 23 7:6 [a]Or *spirit* [A]Rom 7:2 [B]Rom 6:2 [C]Rom 6:4 [D]Rom 2:29 7:7 [a]Or *through law* [b]Or *lust* [A]Rom 3:5 [B]Luke 20:16 [C]Rom 3:20; 4:15; 5:20 [D]Ex 20:17; Deut 5:21 7:8 [a]Or *lust* [b]Or *from law* [A]Rom 7:11 [B]Rom 3:20; 7:11 [C]1 Cor 15:56 7:9 [a]Or *from law* 7:10 [a]Lit *to life* [b]Lit *to death* [A]Lev 18:5; Luke 10:28; Rom 10:5; Gal 3:12 7:11 [A]Rom 7:8 [B]Rom 3:20; 7:8 [C]Gen 3:13 7:12 [A]Rom 7:16; 1 Tim 1:8 7:13 [A]Luke 20:16

not teaching that only the death of a spouse frees a Christian to remarry; it is not teaching about divorce and remarriage at all. Both Christ and Paul have fully addressed those issues elsewhere (cf. Mt 5:31, 32; 19:3–12; 1Co 7:10–15).

7:3 The law that governs a married woman's actions no longer has any jurisdiction over her once her husband dies. Widows are free to marry again, and Paul even encourages younger ones to remarry as long as their potential mate is a believer (1Co 7:39; 1Ti 5:14). Even the legitimately divorced can marry again (*see notes on 1Co 7:8, 9*).

7:4 Therefore. The logical conclusion or application of Paul's brief argument (vv. 1–3) follows. **made to die.** The Gr. construction of this verb emphasizes two important points: 1) this death happened at a point in time, with results that are complete and final; and 2) someone else—in this case God Himself—initiated this death (lit. "you also were made to die"). In response to faith in His Son, God makes the believing sinner forever dead to the condemnation and penalty of the law (cf. 8:1). **through the body of Christ.** Because, as the substitute for sinners, He suffered the penalty of death that the law demanded. **be joined to another.** Just as the widow in Paul's analogy (vv. 2, 3) was freed to remarry, the believer has been freed from his hostile relationship to a law that condemned him, and can, therefore, be remarried—this time to Christ (cf. 2Co 11:2; Eph 5:24–27). **fruit.** A transformed life that manifests new attitudes (Gal 5:22, 23) and actions (Jn 15:1, 2; Php 1:11; cf. 2Co 5:21; Gal 2:19, 20; Eph 2:10; *see note on 1:13*).

7:5 flesh. Scripture uses this term in a nonmoral sense to describe man's physical being (Jn 1:14), and in a morally evil sense to describe man's unredeemed humanness (*see notes on 6:6; Ro 8; Gal 5; Eph 2*), i.e., that remnant of the old self which will remain with each believer until each receives his or her glorified body (8:23). "In the flesh" here describes a person who is able to operate only in the sphere of fallen mankind—an unredeemed, unregenerate person (8:9). Although the believer can manifest some of the deeds of the flesh, he can never again be "in the flesh." **sinful passions.** The overwhelming impulses to think and do evil, which characterize those who are "in the flesh" (Eph 2:3). ***aroused* by the Law.** The unbeliever's rebellious nature is awakened when restrictions are placed on him and make him want to do the very things the law forbids (*see note on v. 8*; cf. 1:32). **members.** *See note on 6:13.* **fruit for death.** The sinful passions at work in unbelievers produce a harvest of eternal death (*see note on 5:12*; cf. Gal 6:7, 8).

7:6 released from the Law. Not freedom to do what God's law forbids (6:1, 15; 8:4; cf. 3:31), but freedom from the spiritual liabilities and penalties of God's law (*see note on v. 4*; cf. Gal 3:13). Because we died in Christ when He died (*see note on 6:2*), the law with its condemnation and penalties no longer has jurisdiction over us (vv. 1–3). **serve.** This is the verb form of the word for "bond-servant" (*see note on 1:1*), but here it is parallel to being slaves of righteousness (cf. 6:18, 19, 22), emphasizing that this service is not voluntary. Not only is the believer able to do what is right, he will do what is right. **newness of the Spirit.** A new state of mind which the Spirit produces, characterized by a new desire and ability to keep the law of God (*see note on 8:4*). **oldness of the letter.** The external, written law code that produced only hostility and condemnation.

7:7 Is the Law sin? Paul wanted to make certain his readers did not conclude (from vv. 4–6) that the law itself was evil (cf. v. 12). **I would not have come to know sin.** The law reveals the divine standard, and as believers compare themselves against that standard, they can accurately identify sin, which is the failure to meet the standard. Paul uses the personal pronoun "I" throughout the rest of the chapter, using his own experience as an example of what is true of unredeemed mankind (vv. 7–12) and true of Christians (vv. 13–25). covet. Quoted from Ex 20:17; Dt 5:21.

7:8 opportunity through the commandment. The word "opportunity" describes a starting point or base of operations for an expedition. Sin uses the specific requirements of the law as a base of operation from which to launch its evil work. Confronted by God's law, the sinner's rebellious nature finds the forbidden thing more attractive, not because it is inherently attractive, but because it furnishes an opportunity to assert one's self-will. **sin *is* dead.** Not lifeless or nonexistent (*see notes on 5:12, 13*), but dormant. When the law comes, sin becomes fully active and overwhelms the sinner.

7:9 from the Law. Not ignorance of or lack of concern for the law (cf. Php 3:6), but a purely external, imperfect conception of it. **when the commandment came.** When he began to understand the true requirements of God's moral law at some point prior to his conversion. **sin became alive.** He realized his true condition as a desperately wicked sinner (cf. 1Ti 1:15). **I died.** He realized his deadness, spiritually; that all his religious credentials and accomplishments were rubbish (Php 3:7, 8).

7:10 was to result in life. Theoretically, perfect obedience to the law could bring eternal life, and with it happiness and holiness. But no one except Christ has—or could—ever fully obey it (2Co 5:21; *see note on 10:5*).

7:11 sin ... deceived me. By leading him to expect life from his keeping of the law, when what he found was death (v. 10); and by convincing him that he is acceptable to God because of his own merit and good works.

7:12 The fact that the law reveals, arouses, and condemns sin, bringing death to the sinner, does not mean that the law is evil (cf. v. 7). Rather the law is a perfect reflection of God's holy character (cf. vv. 14, 16, 22; Ps 19:7–11) and the standard for believers to please Him.

7:13 did that which is good become ... death. Sin is the cause of spiritual death, not the good law. **sin would become ... sinful.** An awareness of the true nature of sin and its deadly character, which brings the sinner to see his need of salvation—the very purpose God intended the law to serve (Gal 3:19–22).

THE CONFLICT OF TWO NATURES

14 For we know that the Law is [A]spiritual, but I am
[A]of flesh, [B]sold [a,C]into bondage to sin. 15 For what I
am doing, [A]I do not understand; for I am not practicing [B]what I *would* like to *do,* but I am doing the
very thing I hate. 16 But if I do the very thing I do
not want *to do,* I agree with [A]the Law, *confessing*
that the Law is good. 17 So now, [A]no longer am I
the one doing it, but sin which dwells in me. 18 For
I know that nothing good dwells in me, that is,
in my [A]flesh; for the willing is present in me, but
the doing of the good *is* not. 19 For [A]the good that I
want, I do not do, but I practice the very evil that
I do not want. 20 But if I am doing the very thing I
do not want, [A]I am no longer the one doing it, but
sin which dwells in me.
21 I find then [A]the [a]principle that evil is present
in me, the one who wants to do good. 22 For I joyfully concur with the law of God [a]in [A]the inner man,
23 but I see [A]a different law in [a]the members of my
body, waging war against the [B]law of my mind and
making me a prisoner [b]of [C]the law of sin which is
in my members. 24 Wretched man that I am! Who
will set me free from [a,A]the body of this [B]death?
25 [A]Thanks be to God through Jesus Christ our Lord!
So then, on the one hand I myself with my mind
am serving the law of God, but on the other, with
my flesh [B]the law of sin.

7:14 [a]Lit *under sin* [A]1 Cor 3:1 [B]1 Kin 21:20, 25; 2 Kin 17:17; Rom 6:6; Gal 4:3 [C]Rom 3:9 7:15 [A]John 15:15 [B]Rom 7:19; Gal 5:17 7:16 [A]Rom 7:12; 1 Tim 1:8 7:17 [A]Rom 7:20 7:18 [A]John 3:6; Rom 7:25; 8:3 7:19 [A]Rom 7:15 7:20 [A]Rom 7:17 7:21 [a]Lit *law* [A]Rom 7:23, 25; 8:2 7:22 [a]Or *concerning* [A]2 Cor 4:16; Eph 3:16; 1 Pet 3:4 7:23 [a]Lit *my members* [b]Lit *in* [A]Rom 6:19; Gal 5:17; James 4:1; 1 Pet 2:11 [B]Rom 7:25 [C]Rom 7:21, 25; 8:2 7:24 [a]Or *this body of death* [A]Rom 6:6; Col 2:11 [B]Rom 8:2 7:25 [A]1 Cor 15:57 [B]Rom 7:21, 23; 8:2

7:14–25 Some interpret this chronicle of Paul's inner conflict as describing his life before Christ. They point out that Paul describes the person as "sold ... to sin" (v. 14); as having "nothing good" in him (v. 18); and as a "wretched man" trapped in a "body of death" (v. 24). Those descriptions seem to contradict the way Paul describes the believer in chap. 6 (cf. vv. 2, 6, 7, 11, 17, 18, 22). However, it is correct to understand Paul here to be speaking about a believer. This person desires to obey God's law and hates his sin (vv. 15, 19, 21); he is humble, recognizing that nothing good dwells in his humanness (v. 18); he sees sin in himself, but not as all that is there (vv. 17, 20–22); and he serves Jesus Christ with his mind (v. 25). Paul has already established that none of those attitudes ever describe the unsaved (cf. 1:18–21, 32; 3:10–20). Paul's use of present tense verbs in vv. 14–25 strongly supports the idea that he is describing his life currently as a Christian. For those reasons, it seems certain that chap. 7 describes a believer. However, of those who agree that this is a believer, there is still disagreement. Some see a carnal, fleshly Christian; others a legalistic Christian, frustrated by his feeble attempts in his own power to please God by keeping the Mosaic law. But the personal pronoun "I" refers to the apostle Paul, a standard of spiritual health and maturity. So, in vv. 14–25 Paul must be describing all Christians—even the most spiritual and mature—who, when they honestly evaluate themselves against the righteous standard of God's law, realize how far short they fall. He does so in a series of 4 laments (vv. 14–17, 18–20, 21–23, 24, 25).

7:14 **the Law is spiritual.** I.e., it reflects God's holy character. **flesh.** This means earthbound, mortal, and still incarcerated in unredeemed humanness. Paul does not say he is still "in the flesh" (*see note on 7:5*), but the flesh is in him. **sold ... to sin.** Sin no longer controls the whole man (as with an unbeliever; cf. 6:6), but it does hold captive the believer's members, or his fleshly body (v. 23; cf. v. 18). Sin contaminates him and frustrates his inner desire to obey the will of God.

7:15 **understand.** This refers to knowledge that goes beyond the factual and includes the idea of an intimate relationship (cf. Gal 4:9). By extension, this word was sometimes used to express approving or accepting (cf. 1Co 8:3). That is its sense here, i.e., Paul found himself doing things he did not approve of.

7:16 **I agree with the Law, *confessing* that the Law is good.** Paul's new nature defends the divine standard—the perfectly righteous law is not responsible for his sin (v. 12). His new self longs to honor the law and keep it perfectly (v. 22).

7:17 **no longer am I the one doing it.** The Gr. adverb for "no longer" signifies a complete and permanent change. Paul's new inner self (*see note on 6:6*), the new "I," no longer approved of the sin that was still residing in his flesh, as his old self did (cf. v. 22; Gal 2:20), but rather, strongly disapproved. Many have misconstrued Paul's comments as abdicating personal responsibility for his sin by embracing a form of Greek dualism (which would later spawn gnosticism; see Introduction to 1 John). Dualism taught that the body is evil and the spirit is good, so its adherents sinned with impunity by claiming they were not responsible; their sin was entirely the product of their physical bodies, while their spirits remained untouched and unsullied. But the apostle has already acknowledged personal guilt for his sin (v. 14; cf. 1Jn 1:10). **sin which dwells in me.** His sin does not flow out of his new redeemed innermost self ("I"), but from his unredeemed humanness, his flesh "in me" (Gal 5:17).

7:18 **nothing good dwells in me.** The flesh serves as a base camp from which sin operates in the Christian's life. It is not sinful inherently (*see note 6:6*), but because of its fallenness, it is still subject to sin and is thoroughly contaminated. **my flesh.** The part of the believer's present being that remains unredeemed (*see notes on 6:6, 12; 7:5*).

7:20 **no longer the one doing it, but sin.** *See note on v. 17.*

7:21 **principle.** A reference to an inviolable spiritual principle.

7:22 **I joyfully concur with the law of God.** The believer's justified, new inner self no longer sides with sin, but joyfully agrees with the law of God against sin (Pss 1:2; 119:14, 47, 77,105,140; cf. 2Co 4:16; Eph 3:16).

7:23 **a different law.** A corresponding spiritual principle to the one in v. 21. But this principle, which Paul identifies as "the law of sin," operates in the members of his body—that is, his unredeemed and still sinful humanness (*see note on 6:6*)—waging war against his desire to obey God's law. **law of my mind.** Equivalent to the new inner self (2Co 5:17; *see notes on 6:6*), which longs to obey the law of God (*see notes on vv. 21, 22*). Paul is not saying his mind is spiritual and his body is inherently evil (*see note on v. 17*).

7:24 **Wretched man.** In frustration and grief, Paul laments his sin (cf. Pss 38:14; 130:1–5). A believer perceives his own sinfulness in direct proportion to how clearly he sees the holiness of God and perfection of His law. **set me free.** This word means "to rescue from danger" and was used of a soldier pulling his wounded comrade from the battlefield. Paul longed to be rescued from his sinful flesh (cf. 8:23). **body of ... death.** The believer's unredeemed humanness, which has its base of operation in the body (*see notes on 6:6, 12; 7:5*). Tradition says that an ancient tribe near Tarsus tied the corpse of a murder victim to its murderer, allowing its spreading decay to slowly infect and execute the murderer—perhaps that is the image Paul has in mind.

7:25 The first half of this verse answers the question Paul just raised (v. 24)—he is certain that Christ will eventually rescue him when He returns (cf. 8:18, 23; 1Co 15:52, 53, 56, 57; 2Co 5:4). The second half summarizes the two sides of the struggle Paul has described (vv. 14–24). **I myself.** Paul's new redeemed self (*see note on 6:6*). **with my mind.** *See note on v. 23.* **my flesh.** *See notes on 6:6, 12; 7:5.* **law of sin.** *See note on v. 23.*

DELIVERANCE FROM BONDAGE

8 Therefore there is now no [A]condemnation for
those who are [B]in [C]Christ Jesus. 2 For [A]the law
of the Spirit of life [a]in [B]Christ Jesus [C]has set you
free from the law of sin and of death. 3 For [A]what
the Law could not do, [a,B]weak as it was through the
flesh, God *did:* sending His own Son in [C]the likeness
of [b]sinful flesh and *as an offering* for sin, He condemned sin in the flesh, 4 so that the [A]requirement
of the Law might be fulfilled in us, who [B]do not walk
according to the flesh but according to the Spirit.
5 For those who are according to the flesh set their
minds on [A]the things of the flesh, but those who
are according to the Spirit, [B]the things of the Spirit.
6 [A]For the mind set on the flesh is [B]death, but the
mind set on the Spirit is life and peace, 7 because
the mind set on the flesh is [A]hostile toward God; for
it does not subject itself to the law of God, for it is
not even able *to do so,* 8 and those who are [A]in the
flesh cannot please God.
9 However, you are not [A]in the flesh but in the
Spirit, if indeed the Spirit of God [B]dwells in you. But
[C]if anyone does not have the Spirit of Christ, he does
not belong to Him. 10 [A]If Christ is in you, though the
body is dead because of sin, yet the spirit is [a]alive
because of righteousness. 11 But if the Spirit of Him
who [A]raised Jesus from the dead dwells in you, [B]He
who raised [C]Christ Jesus from the dead will also
give life to your mortal bodies [a]through His Spirit
who dwells in you.
12 So then, brethren, we are under obligation, not
to the flesh, to live according to the flesh— 13 for [A]if
you are living according to the flesh, you [a]must die;
but if by the Spirit you are [B]putting to death the deeds

8:1 [A]Rom 5:16; 8:34 [B]Rom 8:9f [C]Rom 8:2, 11, 39; 16:3 8:2 [a]Or *has set you free in Christ Jesus* [A]1 Cor 15:45 [B]Rom 8:1, 11, 39; 16:3 [C]John 8:32, 36; Rom 6:14, 18; 7:4 8:3 [a]Lit *in which it was weak* [b]Lit *flesh of sin* [A]Acts 13:39; Heb 10:1ff [B]Rom 7:18f; Heb 7:18 [C]Phil 2:7; Heb 2:14, 17; 4:15 8:4 [A]Luke 1:6; Rom 2:26 [B]Gal 5:16, 25 8:5 [A]Gal 5:19-21 [B]Gal 5:22-25 8:6 [A]Gal 6:8 [B]Rom 6:21; 8:13 8:7 [A]James 4:4 8:8 [A]Rom 7:5 8:9 [A]Rom 7:5 [B]John 14:23; Rom 8:11; 1 Cor 3:16; 6:19; 2 Cor 6:16; Gal 4:6; Phil 1:19; 2 Tim 1:14; 1 John 4:13 [C]John 14:17 8:10 [a]Lit *life* [A]John 17:23; Gal 2:20; Eph 3:17; Col 1:27 8:11 [a]One early ms reads *because of* [A]Acts 2:24; Rom 6:4 [B]John 5:21 [C]Rom 8:1, 2, 39; 16:3 8:13 [a]Or *are going to* [A]Rom 8:6 [B]Col 3:5

8:1 **Therefore.** The result or consequence of the truth just taught. Normally, it marks the conclusion of the verses immediately preceding it. But here it introduces the staggering results of Paul's teaching in the first 7 chapters: that justification is by faith alone on the basis of God's overwhelming grace. **no condemnation.** Occurring only 3 times in the NT, all in Romans (cf. 5:16, 18), "condemnation" is used exclusively in judicial settings as the opposite of justification. It refers to a verdict of guilty and the penalty that verdict demands. No sin a believer can commit—past, present, or future—can be held against him, since the penalty was paid by Christ and righteousness was imputed to the believer. And no sin will ever reverse this divine legal decision (*see note on v. 33*). **those ... in Christ Jesus.** I.e., every true Christian; to be in Christ means to be united with Him (*see notes on 6:2, 11*; cf. 6:1–11; 1Co 12:13, 27; 15:22).

8:2–30 The Spirit, who was mentioned only once in chaps. 1–7 (cf. 1:4), is referred to nearly 20 times in chap. 8. He frees us from sin and death (vv. 2, 3); enables us to fulfill God's law (v. 4); changes our nature and grants us strength for victory over our unredeemed flesh (vv. 5–13); confirms our adoption as God's children (vv. 14–16); and guarantees our ultimate glory (vv. 17–30).

8:2 The word "for" introduces the reason there is no condemnation for the believer; the Spirit has replaced the law that produced only sin and death (7:5, 13) with a new, simple law that produces life: the law of faith (3:27), or the message of the gospel. **the law of the Spirit of life.** Synonymous with the gospel, the law of faith. **the law of sin and of death.** The law of God. Although it is good, holy, and righteous (7:12), because of the weakness of the flesh (*see notes on 7:7–11; 8:3*), it can produce only sin and death (7:5, 13).

8:3 **what the Law could not do.** Deliver sinners from its penalty (Ac 13:38, 39; Gal 3:10) or make them righteous (Gal 3:21). **weak ... the flesh.** Because of the sinful corruption of unregenerate men, the law was powerless to produce righteousness (Gal 3:21). **His own Son.** *See notes on Ps 2:7; Gal 4:4; Php 2:6, 7; Heb 1:1–5.* **in the likeness of sinful flesh.** Although in His incarnation Christ became fully man (*see note on 1:3*), He took only the outward appearance of sinful flesh, because He was completely without sin (Heb 4:15). **condemned sin in the flesh.** God's condemnation against sin was fully poured out on the sinless flesh of Christ (Is 53:4–8; cf. Php 2:7).

8:4 **requirement of the Law.** The thoughts, words, and deeds which the moral law of God demands. The ceremonial aspect of the Mosaic law has been set aside (Col 2:14–17), and the basic responsibility for the civil aspect, which shows the application of the moral law in a community, has been transferred to human government (13:1–7). The moral law finds its basis in the character of God and is presented in outline form in the Ten Commandments; its most condensed form is in Jesus' commands to love God and to love one's neighbor as one's self. It has never been abrogated, but finds its authority in the New Covenant. Every unbeliever is still under its requirement of perfection and its condemnation, until he comes to Christ (Gal 3:23–25), and every believer still finds in it the standard for behavior. **fulfilled.** Although the believer is no longer in bondage to the moral law's condemnation and penalty (7:6), the law still reflects the moral character of God and His will for His creatures. But what the external, written code was unable to accomplish, the Spirit is able to do by writing the law on our hearts (Jer 31:33, 34) and giving us the power to obey it. **not walk according to the flesh but ... the Spirit.** Not an admonition, but a statement of fact that applies to all believers. "Walk" refers to a lifestyle, the habits of living and thinking that characterize a person's life (cf. Lk 1:6; Eph 4:17; 1Jn 1:7). Since every true Christian is indwelt by the Spirit (v. 9), every Christian will manifest the fruit He produces in his life (Gal 5:22, 23).

8:5 **those who are according to the flesh.** All unbelievers (*see note on v. 4*). **set their minds.** This Gr. verb refers to a basic orientation of the mind—a mindset that includes one's affections, mental processes, and will (cf. Php 2:2, 5; 3:15, 19; Col 3:2). Paul's point is that unbelievers' basic disposition is to satisfy the cravings of their unredeemed flesh (Php 3:19; 2Pe 2:10). **those who are according to the Spirit.** All believers (*see note on v. 4*).

8:6 **mind set on the flesh.** This is a simple spiritual equation: The person with the mind set on the flesh is spiritually dead (cf. 1Co 2:14; Eph 2:1). **mind set on the Spirit.** This describes every Christian. The person with his mind set on the things of the Spirit is very much spiritually alive and at peace with God (*see note on 5:1*; cf. Eph 2:5).

8:7 **hostile toward God.** The unbeliever's problem is much deeper than acts of disobedience, which are merely outward manifestations of inner fleshly compulsions. His basic inclinations and orientation toward gratifying himself—however outwardly religious or moral he may appear—are directly hostile to God. Even the good deeds unbelievers perform are not truly a fulfillment of God's law, because they are produced by the flesh, for selfish reasons, and from a heart that is in rebellion (*see note on 5:1*).

8:8 **in the flesh.** *See note on 7:5.*

8:9 **dwells.** Refers to being in one's own home. The Spirit of God makes His home in every person who trusts in Jesus Christ. Cf. 1Co 6:19, 20; 12:13. When there is no evidence of His presence by the fruit He produces (Gal 5:22, 23), a person has no legitimate claim to Christ as Savior and Lord.

8:10 **the body is dead because of sin.** The body is unredeemed and dead in sin (*see notes on 6:6, 12; 7:5*; cf. 8:11, 23). **the spirit is alive because of righteousness.** It is best to translate the word "spirit" as the person's spirit, not the Holy Spirit. Paul is saying that if God's Spirit indwells you (v. 9), the human spirit is alive (cf. Eph 2:5) and can manifest true righteousness (cf. v. 4).

8:11 **your mortal bodies.** *See note on 6:12;* cf. 8:23.

8:12 **the flesh.** Our unredeemed humanness—that complex of sinful passions that sin generates through its one remaining domain, our bodies (*see notes on 6:6, 12; 7:5*).

8:13 **putting to death the deeds of the body.** Paul's first instruction concerning what his readers must do in the struggle with sin destroys several false views of how believers are made holy: 1) that in a crisis moment we

of the body, you will live. 14 For all who are [A]being led
by the Spirit of God, these are [B]sons of God. 15 For you
[A]have not received a spirit of slavery [a]leading to fear
again, but you [B]have received [b]a spirit of adoption
as sons by which we cry out, "[C]Abba! Father!" 16 The
Spirit Himself [A]testifies with our spirit that we are
[B]children of God, 17 and if children, [A]heirs also, heirs of
God and fellow heirs with Christ, [B]if indeed we suffer
with *Him* so that we may also be glorified with *Him*.
18 For I consider that the sufferings of this present
time [A]are not worthy to be compared with the [B]glory
that is to be revealed to us. 19 For the [A]anxious longing of the creation waits eagerly for [B]the revealing of
the [C]sons of God. 20 For the creation [A]was subjected
to [B]futility, not willingly, but [C]because of Him who
subjected it, [a]in hope 21 that [A]the creation itself also
will be set free from its slavery to corruption into
the freedom of the glory of the children of God.
22 For we know that the whole creation [A]groans
and suffers the pains of childbirth together until
now. 23 [A]And not only this, but also we ourselves,
having [B]the first fruits of the Spirit, even we ourselves [C]groan within ourselves, [D]waiting eagerly for
our adoption as sons, [E]the redemption of our body.
24 For [A]in hope we have been saved, but [B]hope that is
seen is not hope; for who hopes for what he *already*
sees? 25 But [A]if we hope for what we do not see, with
perseverance we wait eagerly for it.

OUR VICTORY IN CHRIST

26 In the same way the Spirit also helps our weakness; for [A]we do not know how to pray as we should,
but [B]the Spirit Himself intercedes for *us* with groanings too deep for words; 27 and [A]He who searches
the hearts knows what [B]the mind of the Spirit is,
because He [C]intercedes for the [a]saints according
to *the will of* God.
28 And we know that [a]God causes [A]all things to
work together for good to those who love God, to
those who are [B]called according to *His* purpose.

8:14 [A]Gal 5:18 [B]Hos 1:10; Matt 5:9; John 1:12; Rom 8:16, 19; 9:8, 26; 2 Cor 6:18; Gal 3:26; 1 John 3:1; Rev 21:7 8:15 [a]Lit *for fear again* [b]Or *the Spirit* [A]2 Tim 1:7; Heb 2:15 [B]Rom 8:23; Gal 4:5f [C]Mark 14:36; Gal 4:6 8:16 [A]Acts 5:32 [B]Hos 1:10; Matt 5:9; John 1:12; Rom 8:14, 19; 9:8, 26; 2 Cor 6:18; Gal 3:26; 1 John 3:1; Rev 21:7 8:17 [A]Acts 20:32; Gal 3:29; 4:7; Eph 3:6; Titus 3:7; Heb 1:14; Rev 21:7 [B]2 Cor 1:5, 7; Phil 3:10; Col 1:24; 2 Tim 2:12; 1 Pet 4:13 8:18 [A]2 Cor 4:17; 1 Pet 4:13 [B]Col 3:4; Titus 2:13; 1 Pet 1:5; 5:1 8:19 [A]Phil 1:20 [B]Rom 8:18; 1 Cor 1:7f; Col 3:4; 1 Pet 1:7, 13; 1 John 3:2 [C]Hos 1:10; Matt 5:9; John 1:12; Rom 8:14, 16; 9:8, 26; 2 Cor 6:18; Gal 3:26; 1 John 3:1; Rev 21:7 8:20 [a]Or *in hope; because the creation* [A]Gen 3:17-19 [B]Ps 39:5f; Eccl 1:2 [C]Gen 3:17; 5:29 8:21 [A]Acts 3:21; 2 Pet 3:13; Rev 21:1 8:22 [A]Jer 12:4, 11 8:23 [A]Rom 5:3 [B]Rom 8:16; 2 Cor 1:22 [C]2 Cor 5:2, 4 [D]Rom 8:15, 19, 25; Gal 5:5 [E]Rom 7:24 8:24 [A]Rom 8:20; 1 Thess 5:8; Titus 3:7 [B]Rom 4:18; 2 Cor 5:7; Heb 11:1 8:25 [A]1 Thess 1:3 8:26 [A]Matt 20:22; 2 Cor 12:8 [B]John 14:16; Rom 8:15f; Eph 6:18 8:27 [a]Or *holy ones* [A]Ps 139:1f; Luke 16:15; Acts 1:24; Rev 2:23 [B]Rom 8:6 [C]Rom 8:34 8:28 [a]One early ms reads *all things work together for good* [A]Rom 8:32 [B]Rom 8:30; 9:24; 11:29; 1 Cor 1:9; Gal 1:6, 15; 5:8; Eph 1:11; 3:11; 2 Thess 2:14; Heb 9:15; 1 Pet 2:9; 3:9

are immediately made perfect; 2) that we must "let God" take over while we remain idle; and 3) that some turning-point decision will propel us to a higher level of holiness. Rather, the apostle says the Spirit provides us with the energy and power to continually and gradually be killing our sins, a process never completed in this life. The means the Spirit uses to accomplish this process is our faithful obedience to the simple commands of Scripture (*see notes on Eph 5:18; Col 3:16*; cf. 13:14; Pss 1:2; 119:11; Lk 22:40; Jn 17:17; 1Co 6:18; 9:25–27; 1Pe 2:11).

8:14 led by the Spirit. Believers are not led through subjective, mental impressions or promptings to provide direction in making life's decisions—something Scripture nowhere teaches. Instead, God's Spirit objectively leads His children sometimes through the orchestration of circumstances (Ac 16:7) but primarily through: 1) illumination, divinely clarifying Scripture to make it understandable to our sinful, finite minds (Lk 24:44, 45; 1Co 2:14–16; Eph 1:17–19; cf. Eph 3:16–19; Col 1:9); and 2) sanctification, divinely enabling us to obey Scripture (Gal 5:16, 17; 5:25). **sons of God.** When a person experiences the Spirit's leading in those ways, he gains assurance that God has adopted him into His family (*see notes on 8:15–17; 1Jn 3:2*; for other tests of true faith see Introduction to 1 John: Historical and Theological Themes).

8:15 spirit of slavery ... to fear. Because of their life of sin, unregenerate people are slaves to their fear of death (Heb 2:14, 15), and to their fear of final punishment (1Jn 4:18). **spirit of adoption.** Not primarily a reference to the transaction by which God adopts us (*see notes on Eph 1:5; Gal 4:5, 6*), but to a Spirit-produced awareness of the rich reality that God has made us His children, and, therefore, that we can come before Him without fear or hesitation as our beloved Father. It includes the confidence that we are truly sons of God. **Abba!** An informal, Aram. term for Father that conveys a sense of intimacy. Like the Eng. terms "Daddy" or "Papa," it connotes tenderness, dependence, and a relationship free of fear or anxiety (cf. Mk 14:36).

8:16 testifies with our spirit. In Roman culture, for an adoption to be legally binding, 7 reputable witnesses had to be present, attesting to its validity. God's Holy Spirit confirms the validity of our adoption, not by some inner, mystical voice, but by the fruit He produces in us (Gal 5:22, 23) and the power He provides for spiritual service (Ac 1:8).

8:17 heirs. Every believer has been made an heir of God, our Father (Mt 25:34; Gal 3:29; Eph 1:11; Col 1:12; 3:24; Heb 6:12; 9:15; 1Pe 1:4). We will inherit eternal salvation (Titus 3:7), God Himself (La 3:24; cf. Ps 73:25; Rev 21:3), glory (5:2), and everything in the universe (Heb 1:2). Unlike the Jewish practice of the primacy of the firstborn son, under Roman law the inheritance was divided equally between the children, where the law more carefully protected possessions that had been inherited. **fellow heirs.** God has appointed His Son to be heir of all things (Heb 1:2). Every adopted child will receive by divine grace the full inheritance Christ receives by divine right (cf. Mt 25:21; Jn 17:22; 2Co 8:9). **if ... we suffer with *Him*.** Proof of the believer's ultimate glory is that he suffers—whether it comes as mockery, ridicule, or physical persecution—because of his Lord (Mt 5:10–12; Jn 15:18–21; 2Co 4:17; 2Ti 3:12).

8:18 glory ... revealed to us. This looks forward to the resurrection of the body (v. 23) and the subsequent complete Christlikeness which is the believer's eternal glory. See Php 3:20, 21; Col 3:4; 1Jn 3:2.

8:19 the creation. This includes everything in the physical universe except human beings, whom he contrasts with this term (vv. 22, 23). All creation is personified to be, as it were, longing for transformation from the curse and its effects. **the revealing.** Lit. "an uncovering," or "an unveiling." When Christ returns, God's children will share His glory. *See note on v. 18.*

8:20 futility. This refers to the inability to achieve a goal or purpose. Because of man's sin, God cursed the physical universe (Ge 3:17–19), and now, no part of creation entirely fulfills God's original purpose.

8:21 set free. Cf. 2Pe 3:10; Rev 21:4, 5.

8:23 first fruits of the Spirit. Just as the first pieces of produce to appear on a tree provide hope of a future harvest, the fruit which the Spirit produces in us now (Gal 5:22, 23) provides hope that we will one day be like Christ. **groan.** With grief over our remaining sinfulness (7:24; cf. Ps 38:4, 9, 10). **adoption.** The process that began with God's choice (Eph 1:5) and included our actually becoming His children at salvation (Gal 4:5–7) will culminate with our glorification—the full realization of our inheritance (see vv. 29, 30). **redemption of our body.** Not the physical body only, but all of man's remaining fallenness (*see notes on 6:6, 12; 7:5*; cf. 1Co 15:35–44; Php 3:20, 21; 2Pe 1:3, 4; 1Jn 3:2).

8:24 hope. *See note on 5:2.*

8:26 In the same way. As the creation (v. 22) and believers (v. 23) both groan for ultimate restoration, the Spirit does as well. **groanings too deep for words.** Divine articulations within the Trinity that cannot be expressed in words, but carry profound appeals for the welfare of every believer (cf. 1Co 2:11). This work of the Holy Spirit parallels the high priestly work of intercession by the Lord Jesus on behalf of believers (see Heb 2:17, 18; 4:14–16; 7:24–26).

8:27 the mind of the Spirit. No words are necessary because the Father understands and agrees with what the Spirit thinks. *See note on Jude 20.*

8:28 good. In His providence, God orchestrates every event in life—even suffering, temptation, and sin—to accomplish both our temporal and eternal benefit (cf. Dt 8:15, 16).

29 For those whom He [A]foreknew, He also [B]predes-
tined *to become* [C]conformed to the image of His Son,
so that He would be the [D]firstborn among many
brethren; 30 and these whom He [A]predestined, He
also [B]called; and these whom He called, He also [C]justi-
fied; and these whom He justified, He also [D]glorified.
31 [A]What then shall we say to these things? [B]If
God *is* for us, who *is* against us? 32 He who [A]did not
spare His own Son, but [B]delivered Him over for us
all, how will He not also with Him freely give us all
things? 33 Who will bring a charge against [A]God's
elect? [B]God is the one who justifies; 34 who is the one
who [A]condemns? Christ Jesus is He who [B]died, yes,
rather who was [a,C]raised, who is [D]at the right hand of
God, who also [E]intercedes for us. 35 Who will separate
us from [A]the love of [a]Christ? Will [B]tribulation, or
distress, or [C]persecution, or [C]famine, or [C]nakedness,
or [C]peril, or sword? 36 Just as it is written,

"[A]FOR YOUR SAKE WE ARE BEING PUT
TO DEATH ALL DAY LONG;
WE WERE CONSIDERED AS SHEEP
TO BE SLAUGHTERED."

37 But in all these things we overwhelmingly [A]con-
quer through [B]Him who loved us. 38 For I am convinced that neither [A]death, nor life, nor [B]angels, nor
principalities, nor [A]things present, nor things to
come, nor powers, 39 nor height, nor depth, nor any
other created thing, will be able to separate us from
[A]the love of God, which is [B]in Christ Jesus our Lord.

SOLICITUDE FOR ISRAEL

9 [A]I am telling the truth in Christ, I am not lying,
my conscience testifies with me in the Holy Spirit,
2 that I have great sorrow and unceasing grief in my
heart. 3 For [A]I could [a]wish that I myself were [B]accursed,
separated from Christ for the sake of my brethren,
my kinsmen [C]according to the flesh, 4 who are [A]Isra-
elites, to whom belongs [B]the adoption as sons, and
[C]the glory and [D]the covenants and [E]the giving of
the Law and [F]the *temple* service and [G]the promises,

8:29 [A]Rom 11:2; 1 Cor 8:3; 2 Tim 1:9; 1 Pet 1:2, 20 [B]Rom 9:23; 1 Cor 2:7; Eph 1:5, 11 [C]1 Cor 15:49; Phil 3:21 [D]Col 1:18; Heb 1:6 8:30 [A]Rom 9:23; 11:29; 1 Cor 2:7; Eph 1:5, 11 [B]Rom 8:28; 9:24; 1 Cor 1:9; Gal 1:6, 15; 5:8; Eph 1:11; 3:11; 2 Thess 2:14; Heb 9:15; 1 Pet 2:9; 3:9 [C]1 Cor 6:11 [D]John 17:22; Rom 8:21; 9:23 8:31 [A]Rom 3:5; 4:1 [B]Ps 118:6; Matt 1:23 8:32 [A]John 3:16; Rom 5:8 [B]Rom 4:25 8:33 [A]Luke 18:7 [B]Is 50:8f 8:34 [a]One early ms reads *raised from the dead* [A]Rom 8:1 [B]Rom 5:6f [C]Acts 2:24 [D]Mark 16:19 [E]Rom 8:27; Heb 7:25 8:35 [a]Two early mss read *God* [A]Rom 8:37f [B]Rom 2:9; 2 Cor 4:8 [C]1 Cor 4:11; 2 Cor 11:26f 8:36 [A]Ps 44:22; Acts 20:24; 1 Cor 4:9; 15:30f; 2 Cor 1:9; 4:10f; 6:9; 11:23 8:37 [A]John 16:33; 1 Cor 15:57 [B]Gal 2:20; Eph 5:2; Rev 1:5 8:38 [A]1 Cor 3:22 [B]1 Cor 15:24; Eph 1:21; 1 Pet 3:22 8:39 [A]Rom 5:8 [B]Rom 8:1 9:1 [A]2 Cor 11:10; Gal 1:20; 1 Tim 2:7 9:3 [a]Lit *pray* [A]Ex 32:32 [B]1 Cor 12:3; 16:22; Gal 1:8f [C]Rom 1:3; 11:14; Eph 6:5 9:4 [A]Deut 7:6; 14:1f; Rom 9:6 [B]Ex 4:22; Rom 8:15 [C]Ex 40:34; 1 Kin 8:11; Ezek 1:28; Heb 9:5 [D]Gen 17:2; Deut 29:14; Luke 1:72; Acts 3:25; Eph 2:12 [E]Deut 4:13f; Ps 147:19 [F]Heb 9:1, 6 [G]Acts 2:39; 13:32; Eph 2:12

called. Cf. v. 30; *see note on 1:7.* As always, in the NT Epistles, this call is God's effectual calling of His elect that brings them to salvation.

8:29 foreknew. Not a reference simply to God's omniscience—that in eternity past He knew who would come to Christ. Rather, it speaks of a predetermined choice to set His love on us and establish an intimate relationship—or His election (cf. Ac 2:23 rule of Gr. grammar, called the Granville Sharp rule, equates [pre]determination and "foreknowledge"; *see notes on 1Pe 1:1, 2,* and cf. with 1:20—the term must be interpreted the same in both verses). *See notes on election in 9:11–23.* **predestined.** Lit. "to mark out, appoint, or determine beforehand." Those God chooses, He destines for His chosen end—that is, likeness to His Son (*see notes on Eph 1:4, 5, 11*). **conformed to the image of His Son.** The goal of God's predestined purpose for His own is that they would be made like Jesus Christ. This is the "prize of the upward call" (Php 3:14; cf. Eph 4:13; Col 1:28; Php 3:20, 21; 1Jn 3:2). **firstborn.** The preeminent one, the only one who is the rightful heir (cf. Ps 89:27; Col 1:15–18; Rev 1:5). Jesus Christ is the most notable one among those who have become "brethren" by being made like Him.

8:30 predestined. *See note on v. 29.* **called.** *See note on 1:7.* **justified.** *See note on 3:24.* **glorified.** Paul uses the past tense for a future event to stress its certainty (cf. vv. 18, 21; 2Ti 2:10).

8:31–39 Paul closes his teaching about the believer's security in Christ with a crescendo of questions and answers for the concerns his readers might still have. The result is an almost poetic expression of praise for God's grace in bringing salvation to completion for all who are chosen and believe—a hymn of security.

8:31 If God *is* for us. The Gr. construction is better translated, "Since God is for us."

8:32 Paul's point is: Would God do less for His children than He did for His enemies? **freely give.** This word means "to bestow out of grace." Paul often uses it to denote forgiveness (2Co 2:7, 10; 12:13; Col 2:13; 3:13) and may intend that here. **all things.** Referring either to every sin the believer commits (if "freely give" is translated "forgiveness") or to whatever is necessary to complete the purpose He had in choosing us (vv. 29, 30; cf. Php 1:6).

8:33, 34 The setting of these verses is the divine courtroom.

8:33 God's elect. *See notes on vv. 29, 30.* **God is the one who justifies.** *See note on 3:24.* Who can successfully accuse someone whom God has declared righteous?

8:34 condemns. To declare guilty and sentence to punishment. There are 4 reasons the believer can never be found guilty: 1) Christ's death; 2) His resurrection; 3) His exalted position; and 4) His continual intercession for them. **intercedes.** Cf. Is 53:12; Heb 7:25.

8:35–39 This list of experiences and persons that can't separate the believer from God's love in Christ was not just theory to Paul. It was rather personal testimony from one who had personally survived assaults from these entities and emerged triumphant.

8:35 the love of Christ. Not our love for Christ, but His love for us (Jn 13:1), specifically here as He demonstrated it in salvation (1Jn 4:9, 10). **tribulation.** *See note on 5:3.* Here the word probably refers to the kind of adversity common to all men. **distress.** This refers to being strictly confined in a narrow, difficult place or being helplessly hemmed in by one's circumstances. **persecution.** Suffering inflicted on us by men because of our relationship with Christ (Mt 5:10–12).

8:36 This is a quotation from the LXX (the ancient Gr. translation of the Heb. OT) of Ps 44:22.

8:37 overwhelmingly conquer. A compound Gr. word, which means to over-conquer, to conquer completely, without any real threat to personal life or health.

8:38 principalities. Fallen angels or demons (cf. Eph 6:12; Col 2:15; Jude 6). **powers.** The plural form of this common word for "power" is used to refer to either miracles or to persons in positions of authority.

8:39 nor height, nor depth. Common astronomical terms used to refer to the high and low points of a star's path; nothing in life's path, from beginning to end, can separate us from Christ's love. Possibly, Paul may intend to describe all of space from top to bottom. **nor any other created thing.** In case anything or anyone might be left out, this covers everything but the Creator Himself. **the love of God.** Cf. 5:5–11.

9:1 conscience. *See note on 2:15.* **in the Holy Spirit.** Only when the Spirit controls the conscience can it be trusted—but it remains imperfect, and its warnings must always be evaluated against the Word of God (cf. 1Co 4:3–5).

9:3 accursed. The Gr. word is *anathema,* which means "to devote to destruction in eternal hell" (cf. 1Co 12:3; 16:22; Gal 1:8, 9). Although Paul understood the exchange he was suggesting was impossible (8:38, 39; Jn 10:28), it was still the sincere expression of his deep love for his fellow Jews (cf. Ex 32:32).

9:4 Israelites. The descendants of Abraham through Jacob, whose name God changed to Israel (Ge 32:28). **adoption.** Not in the sense of providing salvation to every person born a Jew (*see notes on 8:15–23*; cf. 9:6), but sovereignly selecting an entire nation to receive His special calling, covenant, and blessing and to serve as His witness nation (Ex 4:22; 19:6; Hos 11:1; cf. Is 46:3, 4). **glory.** The glory cloud (Shekinah) that pictured God's presence in the OT (Ex 16:10; 24:16, 17; 29:42, 43; Lv 9:23). His glory was supremely present in the Holy of Holies in both the tabernacle and the temple, which served as the throne room of Yahweh, Israel's King (Ex 25:22; 40:34; 1Ki 8:11). **covenants.** *See note on Ge 9:16.* A covenant is a legally binding promise, agreement, or contract. Three times in the NT the word "covenants" is used in

5 whose are [A]the fathers, and [B]from whom is [a]the
Christ according to the flesh, [C]who is over all, [D]God
[E]blessed [b]forever. Amen.
6 But *it is* not as though [A]the word of God has failed.
[B]For they are not all Israel who are *descended* from
Israel; 7 nor are they all children [A]because they are
Abraham's [a]descendants, but: "[b,B]THROUGH ISAAC
YOUR [a]DESCENDANTS WILL BE NAMED." 8 That is, it is not
the children of the flesh who are [A]children of God, but
the [B]children of the promise are regarded as [a]descen-
dants. 9 For this is the word of promise: "[A]AT THIS TIME
I WILL COME, AND SARAH SHALL HAVE A SON." 10 [A]And
not only this, but there was [B]Rebekah also, when she
had conceived *twins* by one man, our father Isaac;
11 for though *the twins* were not yet born and had not
done anything good or bad, so that [A]God's purpose
according to *His* choice would [a]stand, not [b]because
of works but [b]because of Him who calls, 12 it was said
to her, "[A]THE OLDER WILL SERVE THE YOUNGER." 13 Just
as it is written, "[A]JACOB I LOVED, BUT ESAU I HATED."
14 [A]What shall we say then? [B]There is no injustice
with God, is there? [C]May it never be! 15 For He says
to Moses, "[A]I WILL HAVE MERCY ON WHOM I HAVE
MERCY, AND I WILL HAVE COMPASSION ON WHOM I
HAVE COMPASSION." 16 So then it *does* not *depend*
on the man who wills or the man who [A]runs, but
on [B]God who has mercy. 17 For the Scripture says
to Pharaoh, "[A]FOR THIS VERY PURPOSE I RAISED YOU
UP, TO DEMONSTRATE MY POWER IN YOU, AND THAT
MY NAME MIGHT BE PROCLAIMED [a]THROUGHOUT THE
WHOLE EARTH." 18 So then He has mercy on whom He
desires, and He [A]hardens whom He desires.
19 [A]You will say to me then, "[B]Why does He still
find fault? For [C]who resists His will?" 20 On the

9:5 [a]I.e. the Messiah [b]Lit *unto the ages* [A]Acts 3:13; Rom 11:28 [B]Matt 1:1-16; Rom 1:3 [C]Col 1:16-19 [D]John 1:1 [E]Rom 1:25 9:6 [A]Num 23:19 [B]John 1:47; Rom 2:28f; Gal 6:16 9:7 [a]Lit *seed* [b]Lit *in* [A]John 8:33, 39; Gal 4:23 [B]Gen 21:12; Heb 11:18 9:8 [a]Lit *seed* [A]Rom 8:14 [B]Rom 4:13, 16; Gal 3:29; 4:28; Heb 11:11 9:9 [A]Gen 18:10 9:10 [A]Rom 5:3 [B]Gen 25:21 9:11 [a]Lit *remain* [b]Lit *from* [A]Rom 4:17; 8:28 9:12 [A]Gen 25:23 9:13 [A]Mal 1:2f 9:14 [A]Rom 3:5 [B]2 Chr 19:7; Rom 2:11 [C]Luke 20:16 9:15 [A]Ex 33:19 9:16 [A]Gal 2:2 [B]Eph 2:8 9:17 [a]Lit *in* [A]Ex 9:16 9:18 [A]Ex 4:21; 7:3; 9:12; 10:20, 27; 11:10; 14:4, 17; Deut 2:30; Josh 11:20; John 12:40; Rom 11:7, 25 9:19 [A]Rom 11:19; 1 Cor 15:35; James 2:18 [B]Rom 3:7 [C]2 Chr 20:6; Job 9:12; Dan 4:35

the plural (Gal 4:24; Eph 2:12). All but one of God's covenants with man are eternal and unilateral—that is, God promised to accomplish something based on His own character and not on the response or actions of the promised beneficiary. The 6 biblical covenants include: 1) the covenant with Noah (Ge 9:8–17); 2) the covenant with Abraham (Ge 12:1–3; *see note on 4:13*); 3) the covenant of law given through Moses at Sinai (Ex 19–31; cf. Dt 29, 30); 4) the priestly covenant (Nu 25:10–13); 5) the covenant of an eternal kingdom through David's greatest Son (2Sa 7:8–16); and 6) the New Covenant (Jer 31:31–34; Eze 37:26; cf. Heb 8:6–13). All but the Mosaic Covenant are eternal and unilateral. It is neither, since Israel's sin abrogated it and it has been replaced by the New Covenant (cf. Heb 8:7–13). ***temple* service.** This refers to the entire sacrificial and ceremonial system that God revealed through Moses (cf. Ex 29:43–46). **promises.** Probably this refers to the promised Messiah, who would come out of Israel, bringing eternal life and an eternal kingdom (cf. Ac 2:39; 13:32–34; 26:6; Gal 3:16, 21).

9:5 fathers. The patriarchs Abraham, Isaac, and Jacob, through whom the promises of the Messiah were fulfilled. **Christ . . . God blessed forever.** This is not intended primarily as a benediction, but as an affirmation of the sovereignty and deity of Christ.

9:6 word of God. This refers specifically to the privileges and promises God had revealed to Israel (v. 4; cf. Is 55:11; Jer 32:42). **not all Israel who are *descended* from Israel.** Not all the physical descendants of Abraham are true heirs of the promise (*see notes on 2:28, 29*).

9:7 To illustrate the truth of v. 6, Paul reminds his readers that even the racial and national promises made to Abraham were not made to every physical descendant of his, but only to those who came through Isaac. Cf. Ge 21:12. **children.** Only Isaac's descendants could truly be called the children of Abraham, the inheritors of those racial and national promises (Ge 17:19–21).

9:8 children of the flesh. Abraham's other children by Hagar and Keturah were not chosen to receive the national promises made to him. **children of God.** Paul's point is that just as not all of Abraham's descendants belonged to the physical people of God—or national Israel—not all of those who are true children of Abraham through Isaac are the true spiritual people of God and enjoy the promises made to Abraham's spiritual children (4:6, 11; cf. 11:3, 4).

9:9 Quoted from Ge 18:10.

9:11 *the twins.* The twins Jacob and Esau. **done anything good or bad.** God's choice of Jacob, instead of Esau, to continue the physical line was not based on his personal merit or demerit. **God's purpose according to *His* choice.** Rather, God's choice of Jacob resides solely in His own sovereign plan, a perfect example of election unto salvation. God has chosen some Jews—and some Gentiles—but not all, for salvation. **not because of works but because of Him who calls.** The fact that God made His choice of Jacob before the boys were born and apart from personal merit demonstrates that election unto spiritual life is unrelated to any human effort, and is based only on the prerogative of God who makes His selection (*see note on 8:29*; cf. 1Co 1:9).

9:12 Quoted from Ge 25:23.

9:13 Jacob I loved, but Esau I hated. Quoted from Mal 1:2, 3. Actual emotional hatred for Esau and his offspring is not the point here. Malachi, who wrote this declaration more than 1,500 years after their death, was looking back at these two men—and by extension the nations (Israel and Edom) that came from their loins. God chose one for divine blessing and protection, and the other He left to divine judgment.

9:14 There is no injustice with God. Paul once again anticipates his readers' objection to Paul's theology: if God were to choose some people for salvation and pass over others apart from their merits or actions, that would make God arbitrary and unfair (cf. Ge 18:25; Pss 7:9; 48:10; 71:19; 119:137, 142; Jer 9:23, 24).

9:15 Quoted from Ex 33:19. In response to the accusation that such a teaching about God's sovereign election is inconsistent with His fairness, Paul cites this text from the OT that clearly indicates that God is absolutely sovereign and does elect who will be saved without violating His other attributes. He determines who receives mercy.

9:16 it. God's gracious choice of certain people unto eternal life (*see note on 8:29*). **who wills.** Salvation is not initiated by human choice—even faith is a gift of God (*see note on 1:16*; cf. Jn 6:37; Eph 2:8, 9). **who runs.** Salvation is not merited by human effort (*see notes on v. 11*).

9:17 Quoted from Ex 9:16. This again (as v. 15) is an OT quote to prove that God does sovereignly choose who will serve His purposes and how. raised you up. Refers to bringing forward or lifting up and was often used to describe the rise of leaders and countries to positions of prominence (cf. Hab 1:6; Zec 11:16). Undoubtedly, Pharaoh thought his position and actions were of his own free choice to accomplish his own purposes, but in reality he was there to serve God's purpose. My name. The sum of the character of God (cf. Ex 34:5–7).

9:18 The mighty act of God in freeing Israel from the hand of Pharaoh demonstrated two corollary truths. Both Moses and Pharaoh were wicked sinners, even murderers, and were equally worthy of God's wrath and eternal punishment. But Moses received mercy, while Pharaoh received God's judgment, because that was God's sovereign will (cf. 11:7; Jos 11:18–20; 1Th 5:9; 2Pe 2:12). **hardens.** The Gr. word literally means to make something hard, but is often used figuratively to refer to making stubborn or obstinate. Ten times Exodus refers to God's hardening Pharaoh's heart (e.g., 4:21; 7:3, 13), and other times to Pharaoh's hardening his own heart (e.g., 8:32; 9:34). This does not mean that God actively created unbelief or some other evil in Pharaoh's heart (cf. Jas 1:13), but rather that He withdrew all the divine influences that ordinarily acted as a restraint to sin and allowed Pharaoh's wicked heart to pursue its sin unabated (cf. 1:24, 26, 28).

9:19 Why does He still find fault? The objection is: how can God blame anyone for sin and unbelief when He has sovereignly determined that person's destiny?

9:20 who are you, O man, who answers back to God? The nature of Paul's reply makes it clear that he is not addressing those with honest questions about this difficult doctrine, but those who seek to use it to excuse their own sin and unbelief.

9:20, 21 Using the familiar OT analogy of

contrary, who are you, [A]O man, who [B]answers
back to God? [C]The thing molded will not say to the
molder, "Why did you make me like this," will it?
21 Or does not the potter have a right over the clay,
to make from the same lump one vessel [a]for honorable use and another [b]for common use? 22 [a]What
if God, although willing to demonstrate His wrath
and to make His power known, endured with much
[A]patience vessels of wrath [B]prepared for destruction? 23 And *He did so* to make known [A]the riches
of His glory upon [B]vessels of mercy, which He [C]pre-
pared beforehand for glory, 24 *even* us, whom He
also [A]called, [B]not from among Jews only, but also
from among Gentiles. 25 As He says also in Hosea,

"[A]I WILL CALL THOSE WHO WERE NOT
MY PEOPLE, 'MY PEOPLE,'
AND HER WHO WAS NOT
BELOVED, 'BELOVED.'"
26 "[A]AND IT SHALL BE THAT IN THE PLACE
WHERE IT WAS SAID TO THEM,
'YOU ARE NOT MY PEOPLE,'
THERE THEY SHALL BE CALLED
SONS OF [B]THE LIVING GOD."

27 Isaiah cries out concerning Israel, "[A]THOUGH
THE NUMBER OF THE SONS OF ISRAEL BE [B]LIKE THE
SAND OF THE SEA, IT IS [C]THE REMNANT THAT WILL BE
SAVED; 28 [A]FOR THE LORD WILL EXECUTE HIS WORD
ON THE EARTH, [a]THOROUGHLY AND [b]QUICKLY." 29 And
just as Isaiah foretold,

"[A]UNLESS [B]THE LORD OF [a]SABAOTH
HAD LEFT TO US A [b]POSTERITY,
[C]WE WOULD HAVE BECOME LIKE SODOM, AND
WOULD HAVE [c]RESEMBLED GOMORRAH."

30 [A]What shall we say then? That Gentiles, who did
not pursue righteousness, attained righteousness,
even [B]the righteousness which is [a]by faith; 31 but Israel, [A]pursuing a law of righteousness, did not [B]arrive
at *that* law. 32 Why? Because *they did* not *pursue it* [a]by
faith, but as though *it were* [a]by works. They stumbled over [A]the stumbling stone, 33 just as it is written,

"[A]BEHOLD, I LAY IN ZION [B]A STONE OF
STUMBLING AND A ROCK OF OFFENSE,
[C]AND HE WHO BELIEVES IN HIM
[D]WILL NOT BE [a]DISAPPOINTED."

THE WORD OF FAITH BRINGS SALVATION

10 Brethren, my heart's desire and my prayer
to God for them is for *their* salvation. 2 For I
testify about them that they have [A]a zeal for God, but
not in accordance with knowledge. 3 For not knowing about [A]God's righteousness and [B]seeking to establish their own, they did not subject themselves to

9:20 [A]Rom 2:1 [B]Job 33:13 [C]Is 29:16; 45:9; 64:8; Jer 18:6; Rom 9:22f; 2 Tim 2:20 9:21 [a]Lit *for honor* [b]Lit *for dishonor* 9:22 [a]Lit *But* [A]Rom 2:4 [B]Prov 16:4; 1 Pet 2:8 9:23 [A]Rom 2:4; Eph 3:16 [B]Acts 9:15 [C]Rom 8:29f 9:24 [A]Rom 8:28 [B]Rom 3:29 9:25 [A]Hos 2:23; 1 Pet 2:10 9:26 [A]Hos 1:10 [B]Matt 16:16 9:27 [A]Is 10:22 [B]Gen 22:17; Hos 1:10 [C]Rom 11:5 9:28 [a]Lit *finishing it* [b]Lit *cutting it short* [A]Is 10:23 9:29 [a]I.e. Hosts [b]Lit *seed* [c]Lit *been made like* [A]Is 1:9 [B]James 5:4 [C]Deut 29:23; Is 13:19; Jer 49:18; 50:40; Amos 4:11 9:30 [a]Lit *out of* [A]Rom 9:14 [B]Rom 1:17; 3:21f; 10:6; Gal 2:16; 3:24; Phil 3:9; Heb 11:7 9:31 [A]Is 51:1; Rom 9:30; 10:2f, 20; 11:7 [B]Gal 5:4 9:32 [a]Lit *out of* [A]Is 8:14; 1 Pet 2:6, 8 9:33 [a]Lit *put to shame* [A]Is 28:16 [B]Is 8:14 [C]Rom 10:11 [D]Rom 5:5 10:2 [A]Acts 21:20 10:3 [A]Rom 1:17 [B]Is 51:1; Rom 10:2f, 20; 11:7

the potter (cf. Is 64:6–8; Jer 18:3–16), Paul argues that it is as irrational, and far more arrogant, for men to question God's choice of certain sinners for salvation, as for a piece of pottery to question the purposes of the potter.

9:22, 23 These verses are not intended to identify the origin of evil or explain fully why God has allowed it, but they do provide 3 reasons He has permitted its presence and contamination: 1) to demonstrate His wrath; 2) to make His power known; and 3) to put the riches of His glorious mercy on display. No one is treated unfairly: some receive the justice they earn and deserve (6:23), others graciously receive mercy.

9:22 **What if.** This introduces a statement of fact in the form of a rhetorical question. **willing.** The Gr. word speaks of divine intention, not passive resignation. **endured.** God could justly destroy sinners the first time they sin. But He patiently endures their rebellion rather than giving them what every sin immediately deserves: eternal punishment. *See note on 2:4.* **vessels of wrath.** Continuing the analogy of a potter, Paul refers to those whom God has not chosen for salvation, but rather allowed to incur the just penalty for their sin—God's wrath (*see note on 1:18*). **prepared for destruction.** By their own rejection of Him. God does not make men sinful, but He leaves them in the sin they have chosen (*see note on v. 18*).

9:23 **glory.** The greatness of His character, seen especially in the grace, mercy, compassion, and forgiveness He grants sinners in Christ. **vessels of mercy.** Those He has chosen for salvation. **He prepared beforehand.** Refers to divine election (*see note on v. 29*).

9:25–33 Paul finishes his argument that Israel's unbelief is not inconsistent with God's plan of redemption by using the OT to show that her unbelief reflects exactly what the prophets recorded (vv. 25–29), and that it is consistent with God's prerequisite of faith (vv. 30–33).

9:25, 26 Paul quotes Hos 1:9, 10; 2:23. Hosea spoke of the ultimate restoration of Israel to God, but Paul's emphasis is that restoration necessarily implies her present alienation from God. Therefore, Israel's unbelief is consistent with the OT revelation.

9:27, 28 See Is 10:22, 23. Isaiah prophesied that the southern kingdom of Judah would be conquered and scattered—temporarily rejected by God—because of her unbelief. Paul's point is that the scattering Isaiah described was only a preview of Israel's rejection of the Messiah and her subsequent destruction and scattering.

9:29 See Is 1:9. Again, only a remnant of Israel will survive God's wrath, solely because of His mercy. **LORD OF** Sabaoth. Cf. Jas 5:4. This OT title for God is translated "Lord of hosts" and refers to His all-encompassing sovereignty.

9:30–32 Paul concludes the lesson on God's divine choice by reminding his readers that although God chooses some to receive His mercy, those who receive His judgment do so not because of something God has done to them, but because of their own unwillingness to believe the gospel (cf. 2Th 2:10). Sinners are condemned for their personal sins, the supreme one being rejection of God and Christ (cf. 2:2–6, 9, 12; Jn 8:21–24; 16:8–11).

9:30 **righteousness ... by faith.** Righteousness which comes from God on the basis of faith (*see note on 1:17*).

9:31 **law of righteousness.** Righteousness earned by keeping the law (cf. 3:20; *see note on 8:3*).

9:32 **not ... by faith.** *See notes on 3:21–24.* **works.** By doing everything the law prescribed (cf. Gal 2:16; 3:2, 5, 10).

9:33 See Is 8:14 and 28:16. Long before His coming, the OT prophets had predicted that Israel would reject her Messiah, illustrating again that her unbelief is perfectly consistent with the Scripture.

10:1 **prayer to God for them.** Paul's calling as an apostle to the Gentiles (11:13; Ac 9:15) did not diminish his continual entreaties to God (cf. 1Ti 2:1–3) for Israel to be saved (cf. 1:16; Jn 4:22; Ac 1:8), or his own evangelistic efforts toward Jews.

10:2 **zeal for God.** Demonstrated by legalistic conformity to the law and fierce opposition to Judaism's opponents (Ac 22:3; 26:4, 5; Gal 1:13, 14; Php 3:5, 6).

10:3 **not knowing about God's righteousness.** Ignorant both of God's inherent righteousness revealed in the law and the rest of the OT (which should have shown the Jews their own unrighteousness) and of the righteousness which comes from Him on the basis of faith (*see note on 1:17*). **seeking ... their**

the righteousness of God. 4 For [A]Christ is the [a]end of
the law for righteousness to [B]everyone who believes.
5 For Moses writes that the man who practices the
righteousness which is [a]based on law [A]shall live [b]by
that righteousness. 6 But [A]the righteousness [a]based
on faith speaks as follows: "[B]DO NOT SAY IN YOUR
HEART, 'WHO WILL ASCEND INTO HEAVEN?' (that is,
to bring Christ down), 7 or 'WHO WILL DESCEND INTO
THE [A]ABYSS?' (that is, to [B]bring Christ up from the
dead)." 8 But what does it say? "[A]THE WORD IS NEAR
YOU, IN YOUR MOUTH AND IN YOUR HEART"—that is,
the word of faith which we are preaching, 9 [a]that
[A]if you confess with your mouth Jesus *as* Lord, and
[B]believe in your heart that [C]God raised Him from
the dead, you will be saved; 10 for with the heart a
person believes, [a]resulting in righteousness, and
with the mouth he confesses, [b]resulting in salvation. 11 For the Scripture says, "[A]WHOEVER BELIEVES
IN HIM WILL NOT BE [a]DISAPPOINTED." 12 For [A]there
is no distinction between Jew and Greek; for the
same *Lord* is [B]Lord of [C]all, abounding in riches for
all who call on Him; 13 for "[A]WHOEVER WILL CALL ON
THE NAME OF THE LORD WILL BE SAVED."
14 How then will they call on Him in whom they
have not believed? How will they believe in Him
[A]whom they have not heard? And how will they
hear without [B]a preacher? 15 How will they preach
unless they are sent? Just as it is written, "[A]HOW
BEAUTIFUL ARE THE FEET OF THOSE WHO [a,B]BRING
GOOD NEWS OF GOOD THINGS!"
16 However, they [A]did not all heed the [a]good news;
for Isaiah says, "[B]LORD, WHO HAS BELIEVED OUR RE-
PORT?" 17 So faith *comes* from [A]hearing, and hearing
by [B]the word [a]of Christ.
18 But I say, surely they have never heard, have
they? Indeed they have;

"[A]THEIR VOICE HAS GONE OUT
INTO ALL THE EARTH,
AND THEIR WORDS TO THE
ENDS OF THE [a]WORLD."

19 But I say, surely Israel did not know, did they?
First Moses says,

"[A]I WILL [B]MAKE YOU JEALOUS BY THAT
WHICH IS NOT A NATION,
BY A NATION WITHOUT UNDERSTANDING
WILL I ANGER YOU."

20 And Isaiah is very bold and says,

"[A]I WAS FOUND BY THOSE WHO
DID NOT SEEK ME,
I BECAME MANIFEST TO THOSE
WHO DID NOT ASK FOR ME."

10:4 [a]Or *goal* [A]Rom 7:1-4; Gal 3:24; 4:5 [B]Rom 3:22 10:5 [a]Lit *out of, from* [b]Lit *by it* [A]Lev 18:5; Neh 9:29; Ezek 20:11, 13, 21; Rom 7:10 10:6 [a]Lit *out of, from* [A]Rom 9:30 [B]Deut 30:12 10:7 [A]Luke 8:31 [B]Heb 13:20 10:8 [A]Deut 30:14 10:9 [a]Or *because* [A]Matt 10:32; Luke 12:8; Rom 14:9; 1 Cor 12:3; Phil 2:11 [B]Acts 16:31; Rom 4:24 [C]Acts 2:24 10:10 [a]Lit *to righteousness* [b]Lit *to salvation* 10:11 [a]Lit *put to shame* [A]Is 28:16; Rom 9:33 10:12 [A]Rom 3:22, 29 [B]Acts 10:36 [C]Rom 3:29 10:13 [A]Joel 2:32; Acts 2:21 10:14 [A]Eph 2:17; 4:21 [B]Acts 8:31; Titus 1:3 10:15 [a]Or *preach the gospel* [A]Is 52:7 [B]Rom 1:15; 15:20 10:16 [a]Or *gospel* [A]Rom 3:3 [B]Is 53:1; John 12:38 10:17 [a]Or *concerning Christ* [A]Gal 3:2, 5 [B]Col 3:16 10:18 [a]Or *inhabited earth* [A]Ps 19:4; Rom 1:8; Col 1:6, 23; 1 Thess 1:8 10:19 [A]Deut 32:21 [B]Rom 11:11, 14 10:20 [A]Is 65:1; Rom 9:30

own. Based on their conformity to God's law and often to the less demanding standards of their own traditions (Mk 7:1–13).

10:4 Christ is the end of the law. Although the Gr. word translated "end" can mean either "fulfillment" or "termination," this is not a reference to Christ's having perfectly fulfilled the law through His teaching (Mt 5:17, 18) or through His sinless life (2Co 5:21). Instead, as the second half of the verse shows, Paul means that belief in Christ as Lord and Savior ends the sinner's futile quest for righteousness through his imperfect attempts to save himself by efforts to obey the law (cf. 3:20–22; Is 64:6; Col 2:13, 14).

10:5 the man who practices … righteousness … shall live by that righteousness. Quoted from Lv 18:5. To hope for a righteousness based on obedience to the law requires perfect conformity in every detail (Gal 3:10; Jas 2:10; cf. Dt 27:26)—an utter impossibility. **the righteousness which is based on law.** A righteous standing before God on the basis of obedience to the law.

10:6, 7 Paul speaks of the righteousness based on faith as if it were a person and puts in its mouth a quotation from Dt 30:12, 13. His point is that the righteousness of faith does not require some impossible odyssey through the universe to find Christ.

10:8 The word is near you. Quoted from Dt 30:14. The journey of vv. 6, 7 is unnecessary because God has clearly revealed the way of salvation: it is by faith. **word of faith.** The message of faith is the way to God.

10:9 confess … Jesus *as* Lord. Not a simple acknowledgment that He is God and the Lord of the universe, since even demons acknowledge that to be true (Jas 2:19). This is the deep personal conviction, without reservation, that Jesus is that person's own master or sovereign. This phrase includes repenting from sin, trusting in Jesus for salvation, and submitting to Him as Lord. This is the volitional element of faith (*see note on 1:16*). **believe in your heart.** *See note on 1:16.* **God raised Him from the dead.** Christ's resurrection was the supreme validation of His ministry (cf. Jn 2:18–21). Belief in it is necessary for salvation because it proved that Christ is who He claimed to be and that the Father had accepted His sacrifice in the place of sinners (4:24; cf. Ac 13:32, 33; 1Pe 1:3, 4). Without the resurrection, there is no salvation (1Co 15:14–17). *See note on 1:4.* **will be saved.** *See note on 1:16.*

10:10 confesses. This Gr. word basically means to say the same thing, or to be in agreement with someone. The person who confesses Jesus as Lord (v. 9) agrees with the Father's declaration that Jesus is Savior and Lord.

10:11 Quoted from Is 28:16 and 49:23. This quotation not only demonstrates that salvation by grace through faith alone has always been God's salvation plan, but that no one—including Gentiles—was ever to be excluded (1:16; 3:21, 22; 2Pe 3:9; see also Jon 3:5).

10:12 there is no distinction. Cf. 3:22, 23; Gal 3:28, 29; Eph 2:11–13; 3:4–6.

10:13 Paul quoted Joel (2:32) to further emphasize that salvation is available for people of all nations and races. call on the name. This familiar OT expression (e.g., Pss 79:5, 6; 105:1; 116:4, 5) does not refer to some desperate cry to just any deity, but to the one true God as He has revealed Himself—a revelation which now includes recognition of Jesus as Lord (v. 9) and of the One who raised up Jesus from the dead (v. 9).

10:14, 15 Paul's main point in this series of rhetorical questions is that a clear presentation of the gospel message must precede true saving faith. True faith always has content—the revealed Word of God. Salvation comes to those who hear and believe the facts of the gospel.

10:15 beautiful are the feet of those who bring good news. Quoted from Is 52:7. It is the message of good news which those feet carry that is so welcome.

10:16 heed the good news. The good news is not only a gracious offer, but a command to believe and repent (1:4–6; 2:8; 6:17; Ac 6:7; 2Th 1:7, 8; Heb 5:9). believed our report. Quoted from Is 53:1. The report Isaiah described was of the substitutionary death of Christ (53:5)—the good news of the gospel.

10:17 faith *comes* from hearing. *See note on vv. 14, 15.* **the word of Christ.** This means "the message about Christ"—the gospel (cf. Mt 28:19, 20; Ac 20:21).

10:18 Paul cited this quotation from the LXX (the Gr. translation of the Heb. OT) version of Ps 19:4 to show that even David understood that God's revelation of Himself has reached the entire earth (cf. 1:18–20; Jer 29:13; Mt 24:14; Jn 1:9; Col 1:5, 6).

10:19–21 Israel was ignorant of the salvation truth contained in her own Scriptures, including that the gospel would reach the Gentiles, as promised in Dt 32:21; Is 65:1, 2.

10:19 that which is not a nation. The Gentiles, who are not a part of Israel, God's special, chosen nation.

10:20, 21 Quoted from Is 65:1, 2.

21 But as for Israel He says, "[A]ALL THE DAY LONG I
HAVE STRETCHED OUT MY HANDS TO A DISOBEDIENT
AND OBSTINATE PEOPLE."

ISRAEL IS NOT CAST AWAY

11 I say then, God has not [A]rejected His people, has
He? [B]May it never be! For [C]I too am an Israelite,
[a]a descendant of Abraham, of the tribe of Benjamin.
2 God [A]has not rejected His people whom He [B]fore-
knew. [C]Or do you not know what the Scripture says
in *the passage about* Elijah, how he pleads with God
against Israel? 3 "Lord, [A]THEY HAVE KILLED YOUR
PROPHETS, THEY HAVE TORN DOWN YOUR ALTARS, AND
I ALONE AM LEFT, AND THEY ARE SEEKING MY LIFE."
4 But what [a]is the divine response to him? "[A]I HAVE
KEPT for Myself SEVEN THOUSAND MEN WHO HAVE
NOT BOWED THE KNEE TO BAAL." 5 In the same way
then, there has also come to be at the present time
[A]a remnant according to *God's* [a]gracious choice.
6 But [A]if it is by grace, it is no longer [a]on the basis
of works, otherwise grace is no longer grace.

7 What then? What [A]Israel is seeking, it has not
obtained, but [a]those who were chosen obtained it,
and the rest were [B]hardened; 8 just as it is written,

"[A]GOD GAVE THEM A SPIRIT OF STUPOR,
EYES TO SEE NOT AND EARS TO HEAR NOT,
DOWN TO THIS VERY DAY."

9 And David says,

"[A]LET THEIR TABLE BECOME A
SNARE AND A TRAP,
AND A STUMBLING BLOCK AND
A RETRIBUTION TO THEM.
10 "[A]LET THEIR EYES BE DARKENED
TO SEE NOT,
AND BEND THEIR BACKS FOREVER."

11 [A]I say then, they did not stumble so as to fall, did
they? [B]May it never be! But by their transgression
[C]salvation *has come* to the Gentiles, to [D]make them
jealous. 12 Now if their transgression is riches for
the world and their failure is riches for the Gentiles,
how much more will their [a,A]fulfillment be! 13 But I
am speaking to you who are Gentiles. Inasmuch
then as [A]I am an apostle of Gentiles, I magnify my
ministry, 14 if somehow I might [A]move to jealousy
[B]my [a]fellow countrymen and [C]save some of them.
15 For if their rejection is the [A]reconciliation of the
world, what will *their* acceptance be but [B]life from
the dead? 16 If the [A]first piece *of dough* is holy, the
lump is also; and if the root is holy, the branches
are too.

17 But if some of the [A]branches were broken off, and
[B]you, being a wild olive, were grafted in among them
and became partaker with them of the [a]rich root of the

10:21 [A]Is 65:2 11:1 [a]Lit *of the seed of Abraham* [A]1 Sam 12:22; Jer 31:37; 33:24-26 [B]Luke 20:16 [C]2 Cor 11:22; Phil 3:5 11:2 [A]Ps 94:14 [B]Rom 8:29 [C]Rom 6:16 11:3 [A]1 Kin 19:10, 14 11:4 [a]Lit *says* [A]1 Kin 19:18 11:5 [a]Lit *choice of grace* [A]2 Kin 19:4; Rom 9:27 11:6 [a]Lit *out of* [A]Rom 4:4 11:7 [a]Lit *the election* [A]Rom 9:31 [B]Mark 6:52; Rom 9:18; 11:25; 2 Cor 3:14 11:8 [A]Deut 29:4; Is 29:10; Matt 13:13f 11:9 [A]Ps 69:22 11:10 [A]Ps 69:23 11:11 [A]Rom 11:1 [B]Luke 20:16 [C]Acts 28:28 [D]Rom 11:14 11:12 [a]Or *fullness* [A]Rom 11:25 11:13 [A]Acts 9:15 11:14 [a]Lit *flesh* [A]Rom 11:11 [B]Gen 29:14; 2 Sam 19:12f; Rom 9:3 [C]1 Cor 1:21; 7:16; 9:22; 1 Tim 1:15; 2:4; 2 Tim 1:9; Titus 3:5 11:15 [A]Rom 5:11 [B]Luke 15:24, 32 11:16 [A]Num 15:18ff; Neh 10:37; Ezek 44:30 11:17 [a]Lit *root of the fatness* [A]Jer 11:16; John 15:2 [B]Eph 2:11ff

10:21 **disobedient.** Lit. "to contradict," or "to speak against." As throughout her history, Israel once again had contradicted the Word of God—this time it was the truth of the gospel (cf. Mt 21:33–41; Lk 14:21–24).

11:1–36 In this section Paul answers the question that logically arises from 10:19–21: "Is God's setting aside of Israel for rejecting Christ permanent?" At stake is whether God can be trusted to keep His unconditional promises to that nation (cf. Jer 33:19–26).

11:1 **rejected.** To thrust away from oneself. The form of the question in the Gr. text expects a negative answer. Despite Israel's disobedience (9:1–13; 10:14–21), God has not rejected His people (cf. 1Sa 12:22; 1Ki 6:13; Pss 89:31–37; 94:14; Is 49:15; 54:1–10; Jer 33:19–26). **May it never be!** The strongest form of negation in Gr. (*see note on 6:2*).

11:2 **whom He foreknew.** *See note on 8:29.* Israel's disobedience does not nullify God's predetermined love relationship with her. **Elijah.** *See note on 1Ki 17:1.*

11:3 Quoted from 1Ki 19:10.

11:4 Quoted from 1Ki 19:18. Baal. *See note on 1Ki 16:31, 32;* cf. Nu 22:41.

11:5 **a remnant.** Although the nation had rejected Jesus, thousands of individual Jews had come to faith in Him (cf. Ac 2:41; 4:4; 6:1). ***God's* gracious choice.** God did not choose this remnant because of its foreseen faith, good works, spiritual worthiness, or racial descent, but solely because of His grace (cf. Dt 7:7, 8; Eph 2:8, 9; 2Ti 1:9).

11:6 **by grace ... no longer ... of works.** Human effort and God's grace are mutually exclusive ways to salvation (cf. 3:21–31; 4:1–11; 9:11; Gal 2:16, 21; 3:11, 12, 18; Titus 3:5).

11:7 **Israel is seeking.** In spite of their intense religious zeal, the Jews of Paul's day had failed to obtain God's righteousness (9:31, 32; 10:2, 3). **those ... chosen.** Those whom God graciously had chosen in turn sought and found His righteousness (*see notes on 9:30; 10:4*). **were hardened.** By a judicial act of God (cf. Ex 4:21; 7:3; 9:12; 10:20, 27; 11:10; 14:4, 8, 17; Dt 2:30; Jn 12:40), in response to their stubbornness or rebellion (cf. Ex 8:15, 32; 9:34; 10:1; 2Ch 36:13; Ps 95:8; Pr 28:14; Mt 19:8; Mk 3:5; Eph 4:18; Heb 3:8, 15; 4:7).

11:8–10 These OT quotes both illustrate God's judicial hardening of unbelieving Israel, and show that what Paul is teaching is not in violation of or inconsistent with the OT.

11:8 **it is written.** *See note on 3:10.* The first line was quoted from Is 29:10, and the last lines are adapted from Dt 29:4.

11:9 Adapted from Ps 69:22, 23. A person's "table" was thought to be a place of safety, but the table of the ungodly is a trap. Many people trust in the very things that damn them.

11:11 **stumble ... fall.** The form of Paul's question (*see note on v. 1*) and his strong response confirm that Israel's blindness, hardening, and apostasy are not irreversible. **their transgression.** Israel's rejection of Jesus Christ. **salvation ... to the Gentiles.** Something the OT had long prophesied (cf. Ge 12:3; Is 49:6; Mt 8:11, 12; 21:43; 22:1–14; Ac 13:46, 47; 28:25–28). **to make them jealous.** God intends to use His offer of salvation to the despised Gentiles (*see note on Ac 22:21–23*) to draw the nation back to Him (vv. 25–27).

11:12 **riches for the world.** The rich truths of salvation (Ge 12:3; Is 49:6; cf. 2Co 8:9). **their failure.** To acknowledge Jesus of Nazareth as their Messiah and be God's witness nation resulted in the Gentile church being given that privilege. **their fulfillment.** Their future spiritual renewal (Rev 7:4, 9; cf. Zec 8:23; 12:10; 13:1; 14:9, 11, 16). Israel's "transgression" and "failure" are temporary (vv. 25–27).

11:13 **apostle of Gentiles.** See Ac 18:6; 22:21; 26:17, 18; Eph 3:8; 1Ti 2:7.

11:14 **move to jealousy.** *See note on v. 11.* **my fellow countrymen.** His fellow Israelites (*see note on 9:3*).

11:15 **their rejection ... reconciliation of the world ... acceptance.** *See notes on v. 12.* **life from the dead.** Not bodily resurrection, but the passing from spiritual death to spiritual life (Jn 5:24). This phrase also describes the future spiritual rebirth of Israel (cf. vv. 25–27; Zec 12:10; 13:1).

11:16 **first piece.** The first portion of the harvest, which was to be given to the Lord (Ex 23:19; 34:26; Lv 2:12; 23:10; Nu 15:19–21; 18:12, 13; Dt 18:4). ***dough* is holy, the lump is also.** Because the firstfruit offering represented the entire portion, the entire piece of dough could be said to be holy, set apart to God (cf. Ex 31:15; Lv 27:14, 30, 32; Jos 6:19). **root.** The patriarchs Abraham, Isaac, and Jacob. *See note on 4:13.* **branches.** The patriarchs' descendants: the nation of Israel.

11:17–24 In this section, Paul sternly warns the Gentiles against pride and arrogance (cf. vv. 18, 20) because of Israel's rejection and their being grafted in.

11:17 **branches were broken off.** See Jer 5:10; 11:16, 17; Mt 21:43. Some, but not all,

olive tree, 18 do not be arrogant toward the branches;
but if you are arrogant, *remember that* [A]it is not you
who supports the root, but the root *supports* you.
19 [A]You will say then, "Branches were broken off
so that I might be grafted in." 20 Quite right, they
were broken off for their unbelief, but you [A]stand
by your faith. [B]Do not be conceited, but fear; 21 for
if God did not spare the natural branches, He will
not spare you, either. 22 Behold then the kindness
and severity of God; to those who fell, severity, but
to you, God's [A]kindness, [B]if you continue in His kindness; otherwise you also [C]will be cut off. 23 And they
also, [A]if they do not continue in their unbelief, will
be grafted in, for God is able to graft them in again.
24 For if you were cut off from what is by nature a
wild olive tree, and were grafted contrary to nature
into a cultivated olive tree, how much more will
these who are the natural *branches* be grafted into
their own olive tree?

25 For [A]I do not want you, brethren, to be uninformed of this [B]mystery—so that you will not
be [C]wise in your own estimation—that a partial
[D]hardening has happened to Israel until the [E]full-
ness of the Gentiles has come in; 26 and so all Israel
will be saved; just as it is written,

> "[A]The Deliverer will
> come from Zion,
> He will remove ungodliness
> from Jacob."
> 27 "[A]This is [a]My covenant with them,
> [B]When I take away their sins."

28 [a]From the standpoint of the gospel they are [A]en-
emies for your sake, but [b]from the standpoint of
God's choice they are beloved for [B]the sake of the
fathers; 29 for the gifts and the [A]calling of God [B]are
irrevocable. 30 For just as you once were disobedient
to God, but now have been shown mercy because
of their disobedience, 31 so these also now have
been disobedient, that because of the mercy shown
to you they also may now be shown mercy. 32 For
[A]God has shut up all in disobedience so that He may
show mercy to all.

11:18 [A]John 4:22 11:19 [A]Rom 9:19 11:20 [A]Rom 5:2; 1 Cor 10:12; 2 Cor 1:24 [B]Rom 12:16; 1 Tim 6:17; 1 Pet 1:17 11:22 [A]Rom 2:4 [B]1 Cor 15:2; Heb 3:6, 14 [C]John 15:2 11:23 [A]2 Cor 3:16 11:25 [A]Rom 1:13 [B]Matt 13:11; Rom 16:25; 1 Cor 2:7-10; Eph 3:3-5, 9 [C]Rom 12:16 [D]Rom 11:7 [E]Luke 21:24; John 10:16; Rom 11:12 11:26 [A]Is 59:20 11:27 [a]Lit *the covenant from Me* [A]Is 59:21; Jer 31:33, 34; Heb 8:10 [B]Is 27:9; Heb 8:12 11:28 [a]Lit *According to the gospel* [b]Lit *according to the election* [A]Rom 5:10 [B]Deut 7:8; 10:15; Rom 9:5 11:29 [A]Rom 8:28; 1 Cor 1:26; Eph 1:18; 4:1, 4; Phil 3:14; 2 Thess 1:11; 2 Tim 1:9; Heb 3:1; 2 Pet 1:10 [B]Heb 7:21 11:32 [A]Rom 3:9; Gal 3:22f

of the branches of Israel (*see note on v. 16*) were removed; God always preserved a believing remnant (cf. vv. 3, 4). **a wild olive … grafted in.** Olives were an important crop in the ancient world. Although trees often lived for hundreds of years, individual branches eventually stopped producing olives. When that happened, branches from younger trees were grafted in to restore productivity. Paul's point is that the old, unproductive branches (Israel) were broken off and branches from a wild olive tree (Gentiles) were grafted in. **rich root.** Once grafted in, Gentiles partake of the richness of God's covenant blessings as the spiritual heirs of Abraham (*see notes on 4:11, 12; Gal 3:29*). **the olive tree.** The place of divine blessing; God's covenant of salvation made with Abraham (Ge 12:1–3; 15:1–21; 17:1–27).

11:18 do not be arrogant. There is no place in the church for spiritual pride, still less for anti-Semitism—we are the spiritual offspring of Abraham (4:11, 16; Gal 3:29). **branches.** The unbelieving Jews who had been broken off. **the root *supports* you.** Gentiles are not the source of blessing, but have been grafted into the covenant of salvation that God made with Abraham (cf. Gal 3:6–9, 13, 14).

11:19 Branches. *See note on v. 17.* **grafted in.** *See note on v. 17.*

11:20 unbelief … faith. Branches were broken off and others grafted in based solely on the issue of faith, not race, ethnicity, social, or intellectual background, or external morality. Salvation is ever and always by faith alone (cf. 1:16, 17; Eph 2:8, 9). **fear.** See 1Co 10:12; 2Co 13:5. God will judge the apostate church (cf. Rev 2:15, 16; 3:16) just as surely as He judged apostate Israel.

11:21 If Israel (the "natural branches") was not spared despite being God's covenant nation, why should Gentiles, strangers to God's covenants (Eph 2:11, 12; *see note on 9:4*), expect to be spared if they sin against the truth of the gospel?

11:22 Behold then the kindness and severity. All of God's attributes work in harmony; there is no conflict between His goodness and love, and His justice and wrath. Those who accept His gracious offer of salvation experience His goodness (2:4); those who reject it experience His severity (2:5). **those who fell.** The unbelieving Jews described in vv. 12–21. "Fell" translates a Gr. word meaning "to fall so as to be completely ruined." Those who reject God's offer of salvation bring upon themselves utter spiritual ruin. **if you continue.** Genuine saving faith always perseveres (cf. Jn 8:31; 15:5, 6; Col 1:22, 23; Heb 3:12–14; 4:11; 1Jn 2:19). **cut off.** God will deal swiftly and severely with those who reject Him.

11:23, 24 In the future, Israel will repent of unbelief and embrace the Messiah (Zec 12:10). In the terms of Paul's analogy, God will at that time gladly graft the (believing) Jewish people back into the olive tree of His covenant blessings because it was theirs originally (9:4)—unlike the wild branches (the Gentiles, cf. Eph 2:11, 12).

11:25 mystery. This word is used to refer to NT truth previously not revealed (*see notes on 1Co 2:7; Eph 3:2–6*). This mystery has two components: 1) Israel has experienced a partial spiritual hardening, and 2) that hardening will last only for a divinely specified period of time. *See note on 16:25.* **wise in your own estimation.** Another warning to the Gentiles against spiritual pride and arrogance (*see notes on vv. 17–24*). **partial hardening.** The nation's "hardening," or blindness, does not extend to every individual Jew. Through all of history God has always preserved a believing remnant (*see notes on vv. 5, 17*). **until the fullness of the Gentiles has come in.** "Until" refers to a specific point in time; "fullness" refers to completion; "has come in" translates a Gr. verb often used to speak of coming to salvation (cf. Mt 5:20; Mk 9:43, 45, 47; Jn 3:5; Ac 14:22). Israel's spiritual hardening (which began with rejecting Jesus as Messiah) will last until the complete number of elect Gentiles has come to salvation.

11:26, 27a Quoted from Is 59:20, 21.

11:26 all Israel. All the elect Jewish people alive at the end of the Tribulation, not the believing remnant of Jews within the church during this church age (*see notes on vv. 5, 17*). Since the remnant has already embraced the truth of the gospel (*see note on v. 25*), it could not be in view here, since it no longer needs the salvation this verse promises. The Deliverer will come from Zion. See Pss 14:7; 53:6; Is 46:13. The Lord Jesus Christ's millennial rule will be associated with Mt. Zion (*see notes on Ps 110:2; Heb 12:22*). Zion. *See note on 9:33.*

11:27 covenant. The New Covenant (Is 59:21; Jer 31:31–34). When I take away their sins. Quoted from Is 27:9. A necessary prerequisite for Israel's salvation (cf. Eze 36:25–29; Heb 8:12).

11:28 gospel … enemies. Israel's temporary situation during her time of spiritual hardening (*see note on v. 25*). **from … *God's* choice.** From the perspective of God's eternal choice, Israel will always be His covenant people (*see note on v. 1*). **the sake of the fathers.** The patriarchs (Abraham, Isaac, and Jacob), recipients of the Abrahamic Covenant (Ex 2:24; Lv 26:42; 2Ki 13:23).

11:29 the gifts … are irrevocable. *See note on v. 1.* God's sovereign election of Israel, like that of individual believers, is unconditional and unchangeable, because it is rooted in His immutable nature and expressed in the unilateral, eternal Abrahamic Covenant (*see note on 9:4*).

11:30, 31 God will extend His grace to unbelieving Israel, just as He did to unbelieving Gentiles (cf. Ro 5:8). Salvation, whether of Jews or Gentiles, flows from God's mercy (cf. 1Ti 1:12–14).

11:32 Though not the author of sin (Ps 5:4; Hab 1:13; Jas 1:13), God allowed man to pursue his sinful inclinations so that He could receive glory by demonstrating His grace and mercy to disobedient sinners (cf. Eph 2:2; 5:6).

33 Oh, the depth of [A]the riches [a]both of the [B]wis-
dom and knowledge of God! [C]How unsearchable are
His judgments and unfathomable His ways! 34 For
[A]WHO HAS KNOWN THE MIND OF THE LORD, OR WHO
BECAME HIS COUNSELOR? 35 Or [A]WHO HAS FIRST GIVEN
TO HIM [a]THAT IT MIGHT BE PAID BACK TO HIM AGAIN?
36 For [A]from Him and through Him and to Him are
all things. [B]To Him *be* the glory [a]forever. Amen.

DEDICATED SERVICE

12 Therefore [A]I urge you, brethren, by the mercies
of God, to [B]present your bodies a living and holy
sacrifice, [a]acceptable to God, *which is* your [b]spiritual
service of worship. 2 And do not [A]be conformed to
[B]this [a]world, but be transformed by the [C]renewing of
your mind, so that you may [b,D]prove what the will of
God is, that which is good and [c]acceptable and perfect.
3 For through [A]the grace given to me I say to everyone among you [B]not to think more highly of
himself than he ought to think; but to think so as
to have sound judgment, as God has allotted to
[C]each a measure of faith. 4 For [A]just as we have many
members in one body and all the members do not
have the same function, 5 so we, [A]who are many,
are [B]one body in Christ, and individually members
one of another. 6 Since we have gifts that [A]differ
according to the grace given to us, *each of us is to*
exercise them accordingly: if [B]prophecy, [a]according

11:33 [a]Or *and the wisdom* [A]Rom 2:4; Eph 3:8 [B]Eph 3:10; Col 2:3 [C]Job 5:9; 11:7; 15:8 11:34 [A]Is 40:13f; 1 Cor 2:16 11:35 [a]Lit *and it will be paid back* [A]Job 35:7; 41:11 11:36 [a]Lit *to the ages* [A]1 Cor 8:6; 11:12; Col 1:16; Heb 2:10 [B]Rom 16:27; Eph 3:21; Phil 4:20; 1 Tim 1:17; 2 Tim 4:18; 1 Pet 4:11; 5:11; 2 Pet 3:18; Jude 25; Rev 1:6; 5:13; 7:12 12:1 [a]Or *well-pleasing* [b]Or *rational* [A]1 Cor 1:10; 2 Cor 10:1-4; Eph 4:1; 1 Pet 2:11 [B]Rom 6:13, 16, 19; 1 Cor 6:20; Heb 13:15; 1 Pet 2:5 12:2 [a]Or *age* [b]Or *approve* [c]Or *well-pleasing* [A]1 Pet 1:14 [B]Matt 13:22; Gal 1:4; 1 John 2:15 [C]Eph 4:23; Titus 3:5 [D]Eph 5:10, 17; Col 1:9 12:3 [A]Rom 1:5; 15:15; 1 Cor 3:10; 15:10; Gal 2:9; Eph 3:7f [B]Rom 11:20; 12:16 [C]1 Cor 7:17; 2 Cor 10:13; Eph 4:7; 1 Pet 4:11 12:4 [A]1 Cor 12:12-14; Eph 4:4, 16 12:5 [A]1 Cor 10:17, 33 [B]1 Cor 12:20, 27; Eph 4:12, 25 12:6 [a]Or *in agreement with the faith* [A]Rom 12:3; 1 Cor 7:7; 12:4; 1 Pet 4:10 [B]Acts 13:1; 1 Cor 12:10

11:33–36 The majesty, grandeur, and wisdom of God's plan revealed in vv. 1–32 caused Paul to burst out in praise. This doxology is a fitting response not only to God's future plans for Israel (chaps. 9–11), but to Paul's entire discussion of justification by faith (chaps. 1–11).

11:33 **wisdom.** See Ps 104:24; Da 2:20; Eph 3:10; Rev 7:12. **knowledge.** God's omniscience (cf. 1Sa 2:3; 1Ki 8:39; Pss 44:21; 147:5). **judgments.** God's purposes or decrees, which are beyond human understanding (cf. Ps 36:6). **ways.** The methods God chooses to accomplish His purposes (cf. Job 5:9; 9:10; 26:14).

11:34 Quoted from Is 40:13.

11:35 Quoted from Job 41:11.

11:36 See 1Co 8:6; 15:28; Eph 1:23; 4:6; Heb 2:10. God is the source, the sustainer, and the rightful end of everything that exists.

12:1–16:27 In these final 5 chapters, Paul explains in great detail how believers are to practically live out the rich theological truths of chaps. 1–11. God has graciously given believers so much, that Paul exhorts them to respond in grateful obedience.

12:1 **Therefore.** This refers to the last refrain of his doxology of praise in 11:36. Since all things are for His glory, we must respond by offering ourselves for that purpose. **urge.** This Gr. word comes from a root which means "to call alongside to help." Jesus used a related word, often translated "comforter," in reference to the Holy Spirit (Jn 14:16, 26; 15:26; 16:7). This family of words later came to connote exhorting, encouraging, or counseling. Paul was speaking as a counselor to his readers, but his counsel carried the full weight of his apostleship. **mercies of God.** The gracious, extravagant, divine graces Paul expounded in the first 11 chapters, including God's love (1:7; cf. 5:5; 8:35, 39), grace (1:6, 7; 3:24; 5:2, 20, 21; 6:15), righteousness (1:17; 3:21, 22; 4:5, 6, 22–24; 5:17, 19), and the gift of faith (1:5, 17; 3:22, 26; 4:5, 13; 5:1; 10:17; 12:3). **present your bodies a living … sacrifice.** Under the Old Covenant, God accepted the sacrifices of dead animals. But because of Christ's ultimate sacrifice, the OT sacrifices are no longer of any effect (Heb 9:11, 12). For those in Christ, the only acceptable worship is to offer themselves completely to the Lord. Under God's control, the believer's yet-unredeemed body (*see note on 6:6, 12; 7:5*; cf. 8:11, 23) can and must be yielded to Him as an instrument of righteousness (6:12, 13; cf. 8:11–13). **spiritual service.** In light of all the spiritual riches believers enjoy solely as the fruit of God's mercies (Ro 11:33, 36), it logically follows that they owe God their highest form of service. Understood here is the idea of priestly, spiritual service, which was such an integral part of OT worship.

12:2 **do not be conformed.** "Conformed" refers to assuming an outward expression that does not reflect what is really inside, a kind of masquerade or act. The word's form implies that Paul's readers were already allowing this to happen and must stop. **this world.** Better translated "age," which refers to the system of beliefs, values—or the spirit of the age—at any time current in the world. This sum of contemporary thinking and values forms the moral atmosphere of our world and is always dominated by Satan (cf. 2Co 4:4). **transformed.** The Gr. word, from which the Eng. word "metamorphosis" comes, connotes a change in outward appearance. Matthew uses the same word to describe the Transfiguration (Mt 17:2). Just as Christ briefly and in a limited way displayed outwardly His inner, divine nature and glory at the Transfiguration, Christians should outwardly manifest their inner, redeemed natures, not once, however, but daily (cf. 2Co 3:18; Eph 5:18). **renewing of your mind.** That kind of transformation can occur only as the Holy Spirit changes our thinking through consistent study and meditation of Scripture (Ps 119:11; cf. Col 1:28; 3:10, 16; Php 4:8). The renewed mind is one saturated with and controlled by the Word of God. **good … acceptable … perfect.** Holy living of which God approves. These words borrow from OT sacrificial language and describe a life that is morally and spiritually spotless, just as the sacrificial animals were to be (cf. Lv 22:19–25).

12:3 **grace.** The divine, undeserved favor that called Paul to be an apostle and gave him spiritual authority (Ro 1:1–5; cf. 1Co 3:10; Gal 2:9) and also produced sincere humility (1Ti 1:12–14). **sound judgment.** The exercise of sound judgment, which will lead believers to recognize that in themselves they are nothing (cf. 1Pe 5:5), and will yield the fruit of humility (cf. 3Jn 9). **measure of faith.** The correct proportion of the spiritual gift—or supernatural endowment and ability—the Holy Spirit gives each believer (*see note on 1Pe 4:10*) so he may fulfill his role in the body of Christ (1Co 12:7, 11). "Faith" is not saving faith, but rather faithful stewardship, the kind and quantity required to use one's own particular gift (cf. 1Co 12:7, 11). Every believer receives the exact gift and resources he needs to fulfill his role in the body of Christ.

12:4–8 One of two NT passages (cf. 1Co 12:12–14) listing the general categories of spiritual gifts. The emphasis in each list is not on believers' identifying their gift perfectly, but on faithfully using the unique enablement God has given each. The fact that the two lists differ clearly implies the gifts are like a palette of basic colors, from which God selects to blend a unique hue for each disciple's life (*see notes on vv. 6–8; 1Co 12:12–14*).

12:4 **many members … one body.** Just as in the natural body, God has sovereignly given the body of Christ a unified diversity (*see note on 1Co 12:14–20*).

12:5 **in Christ.** *See notes on 8:1; Eph 1:3–14.*

12:6 **gifts.** *See note on 12:3.* **according to the grace given.** Undeserved and unmerited (*see note on v. 3*). The gift itself (1Co 12:4), the specific way in which it is used (1Co 12:5), and the spiritual results (1Co 12:6) are all sovereignly chosen by the Spirit completely apart from personal merit (1Co 12:11). **prophecy.** *See note on 1Co 12:10.* This Gr. word means "speaking forth" and does not necessarily include prediction of the future or any other mystical or supernatural aspects. Although some prophets in Acts did make predictions of future events (Ac 11:27, 28; 21:10, 11), others made no predictions but spoke the truth of God to encourage and strengthen their hearers (Ac 15:32; cf. vv. 22–31). The evidence does suggest, however, that in the first century, before the NT was complete and the sign gifts had ceased (*see note on 1Co 13:8–10*), this word may have had both nonrevelatory and revelatory facets. In its nonrevelatory sense, the word "prophecy" simply identifies the skill of public proclamation of the Word of God (*see notes on 1Co 14:3, 24, 25; 1Pe 4:11*). **the proportion of his faith.** Lit. "the faith," or the full revealed message or body of Christian faith (Jude 3; cf. 2Ti 4:2). The preacher must be careful to preach the same message the apostles delivered. Or, it could also refer to the believer's personal understanding and insight regarding the gospel (*see note on v. 3*).

to the proportion of his faith; 7 if [a,A]service, in his
serving; or he who [B]teaches, in his teaching; 8 or
he who [A]exhorts, in his exhortation; he who gives,
with [a,B]liberality; [C]he who [b]leads, with diligence; he
who shows mercy, with [D]cheerfulness.
9 *Let* [A]love *be* without hypocrisy. [B]Abhor what is evil;
cling to what is good. 10 *Be* [A]devoted to one another
in brotherly love; [a]give preference to one another [B]in
honor; 11 not lagging behind in diligence, [A]fervent in
spirit, [B]serving the Lord; 12 [A]rejoicing in hope, [B]perse-
vering in tribulation, [C]devoted to prayer, 13 [A]contribut-
ing to the needs of the [a]saints, [b,B]practicing hospitality.
14 [A]Bless those who persecute [a]you; bless and do
not curse. 15 [A]Rejoice with those who rejoice, and weep
with those who weep. 16 [A]Be of the same mind toward one another; [B]do not be haughty in mind, but
[a]associate with the lowly. [C]Do not be wise in your own
estimation. 17 [A]Never pay back evil for evil to anyone.
[a,B]Respect what is right in the sight of all men. 18 If possible, [A]so far as it depends on you, [B]be at peace with
all men. 19 [A]Never take your own revenge, beloved,
but [a]leave room for the wrath *of God,* for it is written,
"[B]VENGEANCE IS MINE, I WILL REPAY," says the Lord.
20 "[A]BUT IF YOUR ENEMY IS HUNGRY, FEED HIM, AND IF
HE IS THIRSTY, GIVE HIM A DRINK; FOR IN SO DOING YOU
WILL HEAP BURNING COALS ON HIS HEAD." 21 Do not
be overcome by evil, but overcome evil with good.

BE SUBJECT TO GOVERNMENT

13 Every [a,A]person is to be in [B]subjection to the
governing authorities. For [C]there is no authority except [b]from God, and those which exist

12:7 [a]Or *office of service* [A]Acts 6:1; 1 Cor 12:5, 28 [B]Acts 13:1; 1 Cor 12:28; 14:26 12:8 [a]Or *simplicity* [b]Or *gives aid* [A]Acts 4:36; 11:23; 13:15 [B]2 Cor 8:2; 9:11, 13 [C]1 Cor 12:28; 1 Tim 5:17 [D]2 Cor 9:7 12:9 [A]2 Cor 6:6; 1 Tim 1:5 [B]1 Thess 5:21f 12:10 [a]Or *outdo one another in showing honor* [A]John 13:34; 1 Thess 4:9; Heb 13:1; 2 Pet 1:7 [B]Rom 13:7; Phil 2:3; 1 Pet 2:17 12:11 [A]Acts 18:25 [B]Acts 20:19 12:12 [A]Rom 5:2 [B]Heb 10:32, 36 [C]Acts 1:14 12:13 [a]Or *holy ones* [b]Lit *pursuing* [A]Rom 15:25; 1 Cor 16:15; 2 Cor 9:1; Heb 6:10 [B]Matt 25:35; 1 Tim 3:2 12:14 [a]Two early mss do not contain *you* [A]Matt 5:44; Luke 6:28; 1 Cor 4:12 12:15 [A]Job 30:25; Heb 13:3 12:16 [a]Or *accommodate yourself to lowly things* [A]Rom 15:5; 2 Cor 13:11; Phil 2:2; 4:2; 1 Pet 3:8 [B]Rom 11:20; 12:3 [C]Prov 3:7; Rom 11:25 12:17 [a]Lit *Take thought for* [A]Prov 20:22; 24:29; Rom 12:19 [B]2 Cor 8:21 12:18 [A]Rom 1:15 [B]Mark 9:50; Rom 14:19 12:19 [a]Lit *give a place* [A]Prov 20:22; 24:29; Rom 12:17 [B]Deut 32:35; Ps 94:1; 1 Thess 4:6; Heb 10:30 12:20 [A]2 Kin 6:22; Prov 25:21f; Matt 5:44; Luke 6:27 13:1 [a]Or *soul* [b]Lit *by* [A]Acts 2:41 [B]Titus 3:1; 1 Pet 2:13f [C]Dan 2:21; 4:17; John 19:11

12:7 service. From the same Gr. word as "deacon," "deaconess" come from, it refers to those who serve. This gift, similar to the gift of helps (1Co 12:28), has broad application to include every kind of practical help (cf. Ac 20:35; 1Co 12:28). **teaching.** The ability to interpret, clarify, systematize, and explain God's truth clearly (cf. Ac 18:24, 25; 2Ti 2:2). Pastors must have the gift of teaching (1Ti 3:2; Titus 1:9; cf. 1Ti 4:16), but many mature, qualified laymen also have this gift. This differs from preaching (prophecy), not in content, but in the unique skill for public proclamation (*see note on v. 6*).

12:8 exhortation. The gift which enables a believer to effectively call others to obey and follow God's truth (*see note on v. 1*). It may be used negatively to admonish and correct regarding sin (2Ti 4:2), or positively, to encourage, comfort, and strengthen struggling believers (cf. 2Co 1:3–5; Heb 10:24, 25). **gives.** This denotes the sacrificial sharing and giving of one's resources and self to meet the needs of others (cf. 2Co 8:3–5, 9, 11; Eph 4:28). **liberality.** Simplicity, single-mindedness, and openhearted generosity. The believer who gives with a proper attitude does not do so for thanks and personal recognition, but to glorify God (cf. Mt 6:2; Ac 2:44, 45; 4:37–5:11; 2Co 8:2–5). **leads.** Lit. "standing before." Paul calls this gift "administrations" (1Co 12:28), a word that means "to guide" and is used of the person who steers a ship (Ac 27:11; Rev 18:17). In the NT, this word is used to describe only leadership in the home (1Ti 3:4, 5, 12) and the church (1Co 12:28; 1Ti 5:17; cf. Ac 27:11; Rev 18:17). Again, the church's leaders must exercise this gift, but it is certainly not limited to them. **shows mercy.** One who actively shows sympathy and sensitivity to those in suffering and sorrow, and who has both the willingness and the resources to help lessen their afflictions. Frequently, this gift accompanies the gift of exhortation. **cheerfulness.** This attitude is crucial to ensure that the gift of mercy becomes a genuine help, not a discouraging commiseration with those who are suffering (cf. Pr 14:21, 31; Lk 4:18, 19).

12:9–21 This passage provides a comprehensive and mandatory list of traits that characterize the Spirit-filled life (cf. Jn 15:8; Eph 2:10). Paul presents these characteristics under 4 categories: 1) personal duties (v. 9); 2) family duties (vv. 10–13); 3) duties to others (vv. 14–16); and 4) duties to those who consider us enemies (vv. 17–21).

12:9 love. The supreme NT virtue, which centers completely on the needs and welfare of the one loved and does whatever necessary to meet those needs (cf. Mt 22:37–39; Gal 5:22; 1Pe 4:8; 1Jn 4:16; *see notes on 1Co 13*). **hypocrisy.** *See note on Mt 6:2.* Christian love is to be shown purely and sincerely, without self-centeredness or guile.

12:10 devoted ... in brotherly love. To be devoted to other Christians with a family sort of love, not based on personal attraction or desirability (cf. 1Th 4:9). This quality is the primary way the world can recognize us as followers of Christ (Jn 13:35; cf. 1Jn 3:10, 17–19). **give preference ... in honor.** To show genuine appreciation and admiration for fellow believers by putting them first (Php 2:3).

12:11 Whatever is worth doing in the Christian life is valuable enough to be done with enthusiasm and care (Jn 9:4; Gal 6:10; Heb 6:10, 11; cf. Ecc 9:10; 2Th 3:13). Sloth and indifference not only prevent good, but allow evil to prosper (Pr 18:9; Eph 5:15, 16). **fervent in spirit.** Lit. "to boil in spirit." This phrase suggests having plenty of heat to produce adequate, productive energy, but not so much heat that one goes out of control (cf. Ac 18:25; 1Co 9:26; Gal 6:9).

12:12 rejoicing in hope. Of Christ's return and our ultimate redemption (*see notes on 5:2; 8:19*; cf. Mt 25:21; 1Co 15:58; 2Ti 4:8). **persevering in tribulation.** *See note on 5:3.* **devoted to prayer.** Cf. Ac 2:42; 1Th 5:17; 1Ti 2:8.

12:13 contributing. From a Gr. word that means commonality, partnership, or mutual sharing, which is often translated "fellowship," and "communion" (Ac 2:42, 44; cf. 4:32; 1Ti 6:17, 18). **practicing hospitality.** Lit. "pursuing the love of strangers" (Heb 13:2)—not merely entertaining one's friends. In NT times, travel was dangerous and inns were evil, scarce, and expensive. So the early believers often opened their homes to travelers, especially to fellow believers (2Ti 1:16–18; 3Jn 5–8; cf. Lk 14:12–14; 1Pe 4:9). Church leaders should be role models of this virtue (Titus 1:8).

12:14 Bless those who persecute you. Treat enemies as if they were your friends (Lk 6:27–33; cf. Mt 5:44; Lk 23:34; Ac 7:60; 1Pe 2:21–23).

12:15 Rejoice ... weep. To be glad in the blessings, honor, and welfare of others—no matter what one's own situation (cf. 1Co 12:26; 2Co 2:3), and to be sensitive or compassionate to the hardships and sorrows of others (Col 3:12; Jas 5:11; cf. Lk 19:41–44; Jn 11:35).

12:16 same mind toward one another. To be impartial (*see notes on 2:11; Jas 2:1–4, 9*; cf. Ac 10:34; 1Ti 5:21; 1Pe 1:17). **not be haughty in mind.** To be haughty with self-seeking pride (cf. Php 2:3). **wise in your own estimation.** Christians are not to have conceit or feelings of superiority toward fellow believers (cf. 1:22).

12:17 Never pay back evil for evil. The OT law of "eye for eye, tooth for tooth" was never intended to be applied by individuals in the OT or NT; but it was a standard for the collective society to use to enforce good conduct among people (1Th 5:15; *see note on Ex 21:23, 24*; cf. Lv 24:20; Dt 19:21; 1Pe 3:8, 9). **Respect what is right.** Christians are to respect what is intrinsically proper and honest and have the right behavior when they are around others, especially unbelievers.

12:18 If possible. Although we should do everything possible to be at peace with others, it will not always come, because it also depends on others' attitudes and responses.

12:19 wrath. Of God (*see note on 1:18*). Vengeance. Divine retribution as quoted from Dt 32:35.

12:20 heap burning coals on his head. Refers to an ancient Egyptian custom in which a person who wanted to show public contrition carried a pan of burning coals on his head. The coals represented the burning pain of his shame and guilt. When believers lovingly help their enemies, it should bring shame to such people for their hate and animosity (cf. Pr 25:21, 22).

13:1 be in subjection. This Gr. word was used of a soldier's absolute obedience to his superior officer. Scripture makes one exception to this command: when obedience to civil authority would require disobedience to God's Word (Ex 1:17; Da 3:16–18; 6:7, 10; *see note on Ac 4:19*). **governing authorities.** Every position of

are established by God. 2 Therefore [a]whoever resists authority has opposed the ordinance of God;
and they who have opposed will receive condemnation upon themselves. 3 For [A]rulers are not a
cause of fear for [a]good behavior, but for evil. Do
you want to have no fear of authority? Do what
is good and you will have praise from the same;
4 for it is a minister of God to you for good. But if
you do what is evil, be afraid; for it does not bear
the sword for nothing; for it is a minister of God,
an [A]avenger who brings wrath on the one who
practices evil. 5 Therefore it is necessary to be in
subjection, not only because of wrath, but also
[A]for conscience' sake. 6 For because of this you also
pay taxes, for *rulers* are servants of God, devoting
themselves to this very thing. 7 [A]Render to all what
is due them: [B]tax to whom tax *is due;* [C]custom to
whom custom; fear to whom fear; honor to whom
honor.

8 Owe nothing to anyone except to love one another; for [A]he who loves [a]his neighbor has fulfilled
the law. 9 For this, "[A]YOU SHALL NOT COMMIT ADUL-
TERY, YOU SHALL NOT MURDER, YOU SHALL NOT STEAL,
YOU SHALL NOT COVET," and if there is any other
commandment, it is summed up in this saying,
"[B]YOU SHALL LOVE YOUR NEIGHBOR AS YOURSELF."
10 Love [a]does no wrong to a neighbor; therefore
[A]love is the fulfillment of *the* law.
11 *Do* this, knowing the time, that it is [A]already the
hour for you to [B]awaken from sleep; for now [a]salva-
tion is nearer to us than when we believed. 12 [A]The
night is almost gone, and [B]the day is near. Therefore
let us lay aside [C]the deeds of darkness and put on
[D]the armor of light. 13 Let us [a,A]behave properly as
in the day, [B]not in carousing and drunkenness, not
in sexual promiscuity and sensuality, not in strife
and jealousy. 14 But [A]put on the Lord Jesus Christ, and
make no provision for the flesh [B]in regard to *its* lusts.

13:2 [a]Lit *he who* 13:3 [a]Lit *good work* [A]1 Pet 2:14 13:4 [A]1 Thess 4:6 13:5 [A]Eccl 8; 1 Pet 2:13, 19 13:7 [A]Matt 22:21; Mark 12:17; Luke 20:25 [B]Luke 20:22; 23:2 [C]Matt 17:25 13:8 [a]Lit *the other* [A]Matt 7:12; 22:39f; John 13:34; Rom 13:10; Gal 5:14; James 2:8 13:9 [A]Ex 20:13ff; Deut 5:17ff [B]Lev 19:18; Matt 19:19 13:10 [a]Lit *works no evil* [A]Matt 7:12; 22:39f; John 13:34; Rom 13:8; Gal 5:14; James 2:8 13:11 [a]Or *our salvation is nearer than when* [A]1 Cor 7:29f; 10:11; James 5:8; 1 Pet 4:7; 2 Pet 3:9, 11; 1 John 2:18; Rev 1:3; 22:10 [B]Mark 13:37; 1 Cor 15:34; Eph 5:14; 1 Thess 5:6 13:12 [A]1 Cor 7:29f; 10:11; James 5:8; 1 Pet 4:7; 2 Pet 3:9, 11; 1 John 2:18; Rev 1:3; 22:10 [B]Heb 10:25; 1 John 2:8; Rev 1:3; 22:10 [C]Eph 5:11 [D]2 Cor 6:7; 10:4; Eph 6:11, 13; 1 Thess 5:8 13:13 [a]Lit *walk* [A]1 Thess 4:12 [B]Luke 21:34; Gal 5:21; Eph 5:18; 1 Pet 4:3 13:14 [A]Job 29:14; Gal 3:27; Eph 4:24; Col 3:10, 12 [B]Gal 5:16; 1 Pet 2:11

civil authority without regard to competency, morality, reasonableness, or any other caveat (1Th 4:11, 12; 1Ti 2:1, 2; Titus 3:1, 2). **there is no authority except from God.** Since He alone is the sovereign ruler of the universe (Pss 62:11; 103:19; 1Ti 6:15), He has instituted 4 authorities on earth: 1) the government over all citizens; 2) the church over all believers; 3) the parents over all children; and 4) the masters over all employees. **established.** Human government's authority derives from and is defined by God. He instituted human government to reward good and to restrain sin in an evil, fallen world.

13:2 **opposed the ordinance of God.** Since all government is God-ordained, disobedience is rebellion against God. **condemnation.** Not God's judgment, but punishment from the government for breaking the law (*see note on v. 4*).

13:3 **not a cause of fear for good behavior, but for evil.** Even the most wicked, godless governments act as a deterrent to crime. **Do what is good … have praise.** Peaceful, law-abiding citizens need not fear the authorities. Few governments will harm those who obey their laws. In fact, governments usually commend such people.

13:4 **minister of God … for good.** By helping restrain evil and protecting life and property. Paul took advantage of his government's role in promoting what is good when he exercised his rights as a Roman citizen to obtain justice (Ac 16:37; 22:25, 29; 25:11). **bear the sword.** This symbolizes the government's right to inflict punishment on wrongdoers—especially capital punishment (Ge 9:6; cf. Mt 26:52; Ac 25:11). **brings wrath.** Not God's wrath, but the punishment inflicted by the civil authorities.

13:5 **be in subjection.** *See note on v. 1.* **for conscience' sake.** Out of a sense of obligation to God and to keep a clear conscience before Him (*see note on 2Co 1:12*), not merely to avoid punishment from the civil authorities.

13:6 **because of this.** Because God ordained human government and demands submission to it (vv. 1–5). **taxes.** The Gr. word referred specifically to taxes paid by individuals, particularly those living in a conquered nation to their foreign rulers—which makes the tax even more onerous. That tax was usually a combined income and property tax. In this context, however, Paul uses the term in the broadest possible sense to speak of all kinds of taxes. Jesus explicitly taught that taxes are to be paid—even to the pagan Roman government (Mt 22:17–21). He also set an example by willingly paying the temple tax (Mt 17:24–27).

13:7 **Render to all what is due.** "Render" translates a Gr. word signifying the payment of something owed—not a voluntary contribution—and is reinforced by the word "due." The apostle reiterates that paying taxes is mandatory (*see note on v. 6*). **custom.** Tolls or taxes on goods. **fear … honor.** God demands that we show sincere respect and an attitude of genuine high esteem for all public officials.

13:8 **Owe nothing to anyone.** Not a prohibition against borrowing money, which Scripture permits and regulates (cf. Ex 22:25; Lv 25:35–37; Dt 15:7–9; Ne 5:7; Pss 15:5; 37:21, 26; Eze 22:12; Mt 5:42; Lk 6:34). Paul's point is that all our financial obligations must be paid when they are due. *See notes on Dt 23:19, 20; 24:10–13.* **love one another.** Believers are commanded to love not only other Christians (Jn 13:34, 35; 1Co 14:1; Php 1:9; Col 3:14; 1Th 4:9; 1Ti 2:15; Heb 6:10; 1Pe 1:22; 4:8; 1Jn 2:10; 3:23; 4:7, 21), but also non-Christians (Mt 5:44; Lk 6:27, 35; cf. Lk 6:28, 34; Ro 12:14, 20; Gal 6:10; 1Th 5:15). **fulfilled *the* law.** *See note on 13:10.*

13:9 To demonstrate that love fulfills the law, Paul cites 4 of the Ten Commandments dealing with human relations and ties them in with an overarching OT command. He quotes Ex 20:13–15, 17 (cf. Dt 5:17–19, 21). **summed up … love your neighbor as yourself.** This command, quoting Lv 19:18, encompasses all of God's laws concerning human relationships (Mt 22:39); if we truly love our neighbor (anyone with whom we have contact, cf. Lk 10:25–37), we will only do what is in his or her best interest (13:10).

13:10 **love is the fulfillment of *the* law.** If we treat others with the same care that we have for ourselves, we will not violate any of God's laws regarding interpersonal relationships (Mt 7:12; Jas 2:8).

13:11 **time.** The Gr. word views time not in terms of chronology, but as a period, era, or age (cf. 3:26; Mt 16:3; Mk 1:15; Lk 21:8; Ac 1:7; 3:19; Rev 1:3). **sleep.** Spiritual apathy and lethargy, i.e. unresponsiveness to the things of God. **salvation.** Not our justification, but the final feature of our redemption, glorification (*see note on 8:23*). **is nearer.** We will be glorified when Jesus returns (*see note on 8:23*), which draws closer with each passing day. The Bible frequently uses the return of Jesus Christ to motivate believers to holy living (2Co 5:10; Titus 2:11–13; Heb 10:24, 25; Jas 5:7, 8; 1Pe 4:7–11; 2Pe 3:11–14).

13:12 **night.** Of man's depravity and Satan's dominion (cf. 1Th 5:4, 5). **day.** Of Christ's return and reign (cf. 1Th 5:2–4). **lay aside.** In light of Christ's imminent return, Paul exhorts believers to repent of and forsake their sins (2Pe 3:14; 1Jn 2:28; cf. Eph 4:22; Col 3:8–10; Heb 12:1, 14; Jas 1:21; 1Pe 2:1; 4:1–3). **the armor of light.** The protection that practical righteousness provides (cf. Eph 6:11–17).

13:13 **Let us behave properly.** By living a life pleasing to God, manifesting in our outward behavior the inner reality of a redeemed life (cf. 6:4; 8:4; Lk 1:6; Gal 5:16, 25; Eph 2:10; 4:1, 17; 5:2, 8, 15; Php 1:27; 3:16, 17; Col 1:10; 2:6; 1Th 2:12; 4:1, 12; 1Pe 2:12; 1Jn 2:6; 2Jn 4, 6). **carousing.** Wild parties, sexual orgies, brawls, riots (cf. Gal 5:21; 1Pe 4:3). **sexual promiscuity and sensuality.** Sexual immorality (cf. 1Co 6:18; Eph 5:3; Col 3:5; 1Th 4:3; 2Ti 2:22). **strife and jealousy.** Closely associated iniquities (cf. 1Co 3:3; 2Co 12:20; Gal 5:20; Php 1:15; 1Ti 6:4), since the former is often the result of the latter.

13:14 **But put on the Lord Jesus Christ.** This phrase summarizes sanctification, the continuing spiritual process in which those who have been saved by faith are transformed into His image and likeness (cf. 2Co 3:18;

PRINCIPLES OF CONSCIENCE

14 Now [A]accept the one who is [B]weak in faith, *but*
not for *the purpose of* passing judgment on
his opinions. 2 [A]One person has faith that he may
eat all things, but he who is [B]weak eats vegetables
only. 3 The one who eats is not to [A]regard with contempt the one who does not eat, and the one who
does not eat is not to [B]judge the one who eats, for
God has [C]accepted him. 4 [A]Who are you to judge the
[a]servant of another? To his own [b]master he stands
or falls; and he will stand, for the Lord is able to
make him stand.
5 [A]One person [a]regards one day above another,
another regards every day *alike*. Each person must
be [B]fully convinced in his own mind. 6 He who observes the day, observes it for the Lord, and he who
eats, [a]does so for the Lord, for he [A]gives thanks
to God; and he who eats not, for the Lord he does
not eat, and gives thanks to God. 7 For not one of
us [A]lives for himself, and not one dies for himself;
8 for if we live, we live for the Lord, or if we die, we
die for the Lord; therefore [A]whether we live or die,
we are the Lord's. 9 For to this end [A]Christ died and
lived again, that He might be [B]Lord both of the dead
and of the living.
10 But you, why do you judge your brother? Or
you again, why do you [A]regard your brother with
contempt? For [B]we will all stand before the judgment seat of God. 11 For it is written,

> "[A]As I live, says the Lord, [B]every
> knee shall bow to Me,
> And every tongue shall
> [a]give praise to God."

12 So then [A]each one of us will give an account of
himself to God.
13 Therefore let us not [A]judge one another anymore, but rather determine this—[B]not to put an
obstacle or a stumbling block in a brother's way.

14:1 [A]Acts 28:2; Rom 11:15; 14:3; 15:7 [B]Rom 14:2; 15:1; 1 Cor 8:9ff; 9:22 14:2 [A]Rom 14:14 [B]Rom 14:1; 15:1; 1 Cor 8:9ff; 9:22 14:3 [A]Luke 18:9; Rom 14:10 [B]Rom 14:10, 13; Col 2:16 [C]Acts 28:2; Rom 11:15; 14:1; 15:7 14:4 [a]Or *house-servant* [b]Lit *lord* [A]Rom 9:20; James 4:12 14:5 [a]Lit *judges* [A]Gal 4:10 [B]Luke 1:1; Rom 4:21; 14:23 14:6 [a]Lit *eats* [A]Matt 14:19; 15:36; 1 Cor 10:30; 1 Tim 4:3f 14:7 [A]Rom 8:38f; 2 Cor 5:15; Gal 2:20; Phil 1:20f 14:8 [A]Luke 20:38; Phil 1:20; 1 Thess 5:10; Rev 14:13 14:9 [A]Rev 1:18; 2:8 [B]Matt 28:18; John 12:24; Phil 2:11; 1 Thess 5:10 14:10 [A]Luke 18:9; Rom 14:3 [B]Rom 2:16; 2 Cor 5:10 14:11 [a]Or *confess* [A]Is 45:23 [B]Phil 2:10f 14:12 [A]Matt 12:36; 16:27; 1 Pet 4:5 14:13 [A]Matt 7:1; Rom 14:3 [B]1 Cor 8:13

Gal 4:19; Php 3:13, 14; Col 2:7; 1Jn 3:2, 3). The image Paul uses to describe that process is taking off and putting on clothing, which is symbolic of thoughts and behavior. *See notes on Eph 4:20–24.* **no provision.** This word has the basic meaning of planning ahead or forethought. Most sinful behavior results from wrong ideas and lustful desires we allow to linger in our minds (cf. Jas 1:14, 15). **the flesh.** *See note on 7:5.* **its lusts.** See Gal 5:17; Eph 2:3.

14:1–12 The diversity of the church displays Christ's power to bring together dissimilar people in genuine unity. Yet Satan often works on man's unredeemed flesh to create division and threaten that unity. The threat to unity Paul addresses in this passage arises when mature (strong) believers—both Jews and Gentiles—conflict with immature (weak) believers. The strong Jewish believers understood their freedom in Christ and realized the ceremonial requirements of the Mosaic law were no longer binding. The mature Gentiles understood that idols are not gods and, therefore, that they could eat meat that had been offered to them. But in both cases the weaker brothers' consciences were troubled, and they were even tempted to violate their consciences (a bad thing to train oneself to do). Knowing that the mature Jews and Gentiles would be able to understand these struggles, Paul addresses most of his comments to them.

14:1 accept. The Gr. word refers to personal and willing acceptance of another. **weak in faith.** This characterizes those believers who are unable to let go of the religious ceremonies and rituals of their past. The weak Jewish believer had difficulty abandoning the rites and prohibitions of the Old Covenant; he felt compelled to adhere to dietary laws, observe the Sabbath, and offer sacrifices in the temple. The weak Gentile believer had been steeped in pagan idolatry and its rituals; he felt that any contact with anything remotely related to his past, including eating meat that had been offered to a pagan deity and then sold in the marketplace, tainted him with sin. Both had very sensitive consciences in these areas, and were not yet mature enough to be free of those convictions. Cf. 1Co 8:1–13. **passing judgment on his opinions.** The mature believer should not sit in judgment on the sincere but underdeveloped thoughts that govern the weak believer's conduct.

14:2 One … has faith. The strong believer, whose mature faith allows him to exercise his freedom in Christ by eating the inexpensive meat sold at the pagan meat markets—inexpensive because a worshiper had first offered it as a sacrifice to a pagan deity (*see notes on 1Co 8:1–13*). **vegetables *only*.** The strict diet weak Jewish and Gentile believers ate to avoid eating meat that was unclean or may have been sacrificed to idols.

14:3 regard with contempt … judge. To "regard with contempt" is to consider someone as worthless. "Judge" is equally strong and means "to condemn." Paul uses them synonymously: the strong hold the weak in contempt as legalistic and self-righteous; the weak judge the strong to be irresponsible at best and perhaps depraved.

14:4 To his own master he stands or falls. How Christ evaluates each believer is what matters, and His judgment does not take into account religious tradition or personal preference (cf. 8:33, 34; 1Co 4:3–5).

14:5 regards one day. Though it was no longer required by God, the weak Jewish believer felt compelled to observe the Sabbath and other special days associated with Judaism (cf. Gal 4:9, 10; *see notes on Col 2:16, 17*). On the other hand, the weak Gentile wanted to separate himself from the special days of festivities associated with his former paganism because of its immorality and idolatry. **regards every day *alike*.** The mature believers were unaffected by those concerns. **Each … must be fully convinced.** Each Christian must follow the dictates of his own conscience in matters not specifically commanded or prohibited in Scripture. Since conscience is a God-given mechanism to warn, and responds to the highest standard of moral law in the mind (2:14, 15), it is not sensible to train yourself to ignore it. Rather, respond to its compunctions, and as you mature, by learning more, your mind will not alert it to those things which are not essential.

14:6 The strong believer eats whatever he pleases and thanks the Lord. The weak brother eats according to his ceremonial diet and thanks the Lord that he made a sacrifice on His behalf. In either case, the believer thanks the Lord, so the motive is the same. **for the Lord.** Whether weak or strong, the motive behind a believer's decisions about issues of conscience must be to please the Lord.

14:7 lives for himself … dies for himself. The focus of Christian living is never oneself—everything we do should be to please our sovereign Lord (cf. 1Co 6:20; 10:31).

14:9 Lord both of the dead and of the living. Christ died not only to free us from sin, but to enslave us to Himself (6:22); to establish Himself as Sovereign over the saints in His presence and those still on earth (cf. Php 2:11; 1Ti 6:15; Rev 17:14; 19:16).

14:10 judge … with contempt. *See note on v. 3.* **your brother.** A fellow believer in Christ. **the judgment seat of God.** *See notes on 1Co 3:13–15.* Every believer will give an account of himself, and the Lord will judge the decisions he made—including those concerning issues of conscience. That verdict is the only one that matters (*see notes on 1Co 4:1–5; 2Co 5:9, 10*).

14:11 it is written. Paul quotes Is 45:23; 49:18 (cf. Php 2:10, 11).

14:13 judge. *See note on v. 3.* **but rather determine.** The same Gr. word translated "judge" (14:3, 10, 13) is here translated "determine." In vv. 3, 10, 13a, the meaning is negative: to condemn. In v. 13b, the meaning is positive: to determine or make a careful decision. The point of Paul's play on words is that instead of passing judgment on their brothers, they should use their best judgment to help fellow believers. **stumbling block.** Anything a believer does—even though Scripture may permit it—that causes another to fall into sin (1Co 8:9).

14 I know and am convinced [a]in the Lord Jesus that [A]nothing is unclean in itself; but to him who [B]thinks anything to be unclean, to him it is unclean. 15 For if because of food your brother is hurt, you are no longer [A]walking according to love. [B]Do not destroy with your food him for whom Christ died. 16 Therefore [A]do not let what is for you a good thing be [a]spoken of as evil; 17 for the kingdom of God [A]is not eating and drinking, but righteousness and [B]peace and [B]joy in the Holy Spirit. 18 For he who in this *way* [A]serves Christ is [B]acceptable to God and approved by men. 19 So then [a]we [A]pursue the things which make for peace and the [B]building up of one another. 20 [A]Do not tear down the work of God for the sake of food. [B]All things indeed are clean, but [C]they are evil for the man who eats [a]and gives offense. 21 [A]It is good not to eat meat or to drink wine, or *to do anything* by which your brother stumbles. 22 The faith which you have, have [a]as your own conviction before God. Happy is he who [A]does not condemn himself in what he approves. 23 But [A]he who doubts is condemned if he eats, because *his eating is* not from faith; and whatever is not from faith is sin.

SELF-DENIAL ON BEHALF OF OTHERS

15 Now we who are strong ought to bear the weaknesses of [A]those without strength and not *just* please ourselves. 2 Each of us is to [A]please his neighbor [a]for his good, to his [B]edification. 3 For even [A]Christ did not please Himself; but as it is written, "[B]THE REPROACHES OF THOSE WHO REPROACHED YOU FELL ON ME." 4 For [A]whatever was written in earlier times was written for our instruction, so that through perseverance and the encouragement of the Scriptures we might have hope. 5 Now may the [A]God [a]who gives perseverance and encouragement grant you [B]to be of the same mind with one another according to Christ Jesus,

14:14 [a]Lit *through* [A]Acts 10:15; Rom 14:2, 20 [B]1 Cor 8:7 14:15 [A]Eph 5:2 [B]Rom 14:20; 1 Cor 8:11 14:16 [a]Lit *blasphemed* [A]1 Cor 10:30; Titus 2:5 14:17 [A]1 Cor 8:8 [B]Rom 15:13; Gal 5:22 14:18 [A]Rom 16:18 [B]2 Cor 8:21; Phil 4:8; 1 Pet 2:12 14:19 [a]Later mss read *let us pursue* [A]Ps 34:14; Rom 12:18; 1 Cor 7:15; 2 Tim 2:22; Heb 12:14 [B]Rom 15:2; 1 Cor 10:23; 14:3f, 26; 2 Cor 12:19; Eph 4:12, 29 14:20 [a]Lit *with offense* [A]Rom 14:15 [B]Acts 10:15; Rom 14:2, 14 [C]1 Cor 8:9-12 14:21 [A]1 Cor 8:13 14:22 [a]Lit *according to yourself* [A]1 John 3:21 14:23 [A]Rom 14:5 15:1 [A]Rom 14:1; Gal 6:2; 1 Thess 5:14 15:2 [a]Lit *for what is good to edification* [A]1 Cor 9:22; 10:24, 33; 2 Cor 13:9 [B]Rom 14:19; 1 Cor 10:23; 14:3f, 26; 2 Cor 12:19; Eph 4:12, 29 15:3 [A]2 Cor 8:9 [B]Ps 69:9 15:4 [A]Rom 4:23f; 2 Tim 3:16 15:5 [a]Lit *of perseverance* [A]2 Cor 1:3 [B]Rom 12:16

14:14 I know and am convinced in the Lord Jesus. This truth was not the product of Paul's own thinking or the teaching of others, but of divine revelation (cf. Gal 1:12). *See note on 1Co 7:12.* **nothing is unclean in itself.** *See note on Ac 10:15;* cf. Mk 7:15; 1Ti 4:3–5; Titus 1:15). **unclean.** The Gr. word originally meant "common" but came to mean "impure" or "evil" (*see note on Ac 10:14*). **to him who thinks … to him it is unclean.** If a believer is convinced a certain behavior is sin—even if his assessment is wrong—he should never do it. If he does, he will violate his conscience, experience guilt (cf. 1Co 8:4–7; *see note on 2:15*), and perhaps be driven back into deeper legalism instead of moving toward freedom (*see note on v. 5*).

14:15 hurt. The Gr. word refers to causing pain or distress. A weak believer may be hurt when he sees a brother do something he believes is sinful. But still worse, the strong believer may cause his weaker brother to violate his own conscience (cf. 1Co 8:8–13). **love.** *See notes on 1Co 13:1–13.* Love will ensure that the strong Christian is sensitive and understanding of his brother's weaknesses (1Co 8:8–13). **destroy.** This refers to complete devastation. In the NT, it is often used to indicate eternal damnation (Mt 10:28; Lk 13:3; Jn 3:16; Ro 2:12). In this context, however, it refers to a serious devastation of one's spiritual growth (cf. Mt 18:3, 6, 14). **him for whom Christ died.** Any Christian (cf. 1Co 8:11).

14:16 good thing. The rightful exercise of one's Christian liberty (cf. 1Co 10:23–32). **spoken of as evil.** To blaspheme. When unbelievers see a strong Christian abusing his freedom in Christ and harming a weaker brother, they will conclude that Christianity is filled with unloving people, which reflects badly on God's reputation (cf. 2:24).

14:17 kingdom of God. The sphere of salvation where God rules in the hearts of those He has saved (*see notes on Ac 1:3; 1Co 6:9*). **eating and drinking.** Non-essentials and external observances. **righteousness.** Holy, obedient living (cf. Eph 6:14; Php 1:11). **peace.** The loving tranquillity, produced by the Spirit, that should characterize believers' relationships with God and one another (Gal 5:22). **joy in the Holy Spirit.** Another part of the Spirit's fruit, this describes an abiding attitude of praise and thanksgiving regardless of circumstances, which flows from one's confidence in God's sovereignty (Gal 5:22; 1Th 1:6).

14:18 approved by men. This refers to approving something after a careful examination, like a jeweler inspecting a stone to determine its quality and value. Christians are under the microscope of a skeptical world that is assessing how they live with and treat one another (cf. Jn 13:35; Php 2:15).

14:20 work of God. A fellow Christian who has been redeemed by the efforts of the Father, Son, and Holy Spirit, not his own (cf. v. 15; Eph 2:10). **All things … clean.** The discretionary liberties which God has given to believers and are good in themselves (cf. vv. 14, 16). **who eats and gives offense.** One who uses those God-given liberties carelessly and selfishly, offending his weaker brother.

14:21 stumbles. *See note on v. 13.*

14:22, 23 The strongest Christian can bring harm to himself in the area of Christian liberty by denouncing or belittling the freedom God has given him (Gal 5:1), or by carelessly flaunting his liberty without regard for how that might affect others (cf. 1Co 10:23–32).

14:22 have as your own conviction before God. Paul urges the strong believer to understand his liberty, enjoy it, and keep it between God and himself. **what he approves.** The strong believer maintains a healthy conscience because he does not give a weak believer a cause to stumble.

14:23 who doubts is condemned. When the weak brother violates his conscience, he sins. **whatever is not from faith.** The thoughts and actions that our conscience condemns.

15:1 we who are strong. *See notes on 14:1–13.* **to bear.** The word means "to pick up and carry a weight." It is used of carrying a pitcher of water (Mk 14:13), of carrying a man (Ac 21:35), and figuratively of bearing an obligation (Ac 15:10). The strong are not to simply tolerate the weaknesses of their weaker brothers; they are to help the weak shoulder their burdens by showing loving and practical consideration for them (Gal 6:2; cf. 1Co 9:19–22; Php 2:2–4). **weaknesses.** *See note on 14:1.*

15:2 edification. To build up and strengthen. This is essentially the same appeal Paul made earlier (14:19), only with the additional qualification of self-sacrifice (1Co 10:23, 24; cf. Php 2:2–5).

15:3 Christ did not please Himself. His ultimate purpose was to please God and accomplish His will (Jn 4:34; 5:30; 6:38; 8:25, 27–29; Php 2:6–8). **it is written.** Quoted from Ps 69:9. The reproaches … fell on Me. "Reproaches" refers to slander, false accusations, and insults. Men hate God, and they manifested that same hate toward the One He sent to reveal Himself (cf. Jn 1:10, 11, 18).

15:4 whatever was written in earlier times. The divinely revealed OT. **written for our instruction.** Although Christians live under the New Covenant and are not under the authority of the Old Covenant, God's moral law has not changed, and all Scripture is of spiritual benefit (1Co 10:6, 10, 11; 2Pe 1:20, 21). Paul's description of the benefits of Scripture certainly includes the NT, but speaks primarily about "the sacred writings"—or the OT (2Ti 3:15–17). **perseverance.** *See note on 5:3.* **encouragement.** The Word of God not only informs believers how to endure, but it also encourages them in the process. **hope.** *See note on 5:2.* Without the clear and certain promises of the Word of God, the believer has no basis for hope (cf. Ps 119:81,114; Eph 2:12; Jer 14:8).

15:5 to be of the same mind with one another. Paul urges the strong and the weak (*see notes on 14:1–13*), despite their differing views on these nonessential issues, to pursue loving, spiritual harmony in regard to matters on which the Bible is silent.

6 so that with one accord you may with one [a]voice
glorify [A]the God and Father of our Lord Jesus Christ.
7 Therefore, [A]accept one another, just as Christ
also accepted [a]us to the glory of God. 8 For I say that
Christ has become a servant to [A]the circumcision on
behalf of the truth of God to confirm [B]the promises
given to the fathers, 9 and for [A]the Gentiles to [B]glorify
God for His mercy; as it is written,

> "[C]THEREFORE I WILL [a]GIVE PRAISE TO
> YOU AMONG THE GENTILES,
> AND I WILL SING TO YOUR NAME."

10 Again he says,

> "[A]REJOICE, O GENTILES, WITH HIS PEOPLE."

11 And again,

> "[A]PRAISE THE LORD ALL YOU GENTILES,
> AND LET ALL THE PEOPLES PRAISE HIM."

12 Again Isaiah says,

> "[A]THERE SHALL COME [B]THE ROOT OF JESSE,
> AND HE WHO ARISES TO RULE
> OVER THE GENTILES,
> [C]IN HIM SHALL THE GENTILES HOPE."

13 Now may the God of hope fill you with all [A]joy
and peace in believing, so that you will abound in
hope [B]by the power of the Holy Spirit.
14 And concerning you, my brethren, I myself also
am convinced that you yourselves are full of [A]good-
ness, filled with [B]all knowledge and able also to admonish one another. 15 But I have written very boldly
to you on some points so as to remind you again,
because of [A]the grace that was given me [a]from God,
16 to be [A]a minister of Christ Jesus to the Gentiles,
ministering as a priest the [B]gospel of God, so that
my [C]offering of the Gentiles may become acceptable,
sanctified by the Holy Spirit. 17 Therefore in Christ
Jesus I have found [A]reason for boasting in [B]things
pertaining to God. 18 For I will not presume to speak
of anything [a]except what [A]Christ has accomplished
through me, [b]resulting in the obedience of the Gentiles by word and deed, 19 in the power of [a,A]signs and
wonders, [B]in the power of the Spirit; so that [C]from
Jerusalem and round about as [D]far as Illyricum I
have [b]fully preached the gospel of Christ. 20 And thus
I aspired to [A]preach the gospel, not where Christ
was *already* named, [B]so that I would not build on
another man's foundation; 21 but as it is written,

> "[A]THEY WHO HAD NO NEWS OF HIM SHALL SEE,
> AND THEY WHO HAVE NOT HEARD
> SHALL UNDERSTAND."

15:6 [a]Lit *mouth* [A]Rev 1:6 15:7 [a]One early ms reads *you* [A]Rom 14:1 15:8 [A]Matt 15:24; Acts 3:26 [B]Rom 4:16; 2 Cor 1:20 15:9 [a]Or *confess* [A]Rom 3:29; 11:30f [B]Matt 9:8 [C]2 Sam 22:50; Ps 18:49 15:10 [A]Deut 32:43 15:11 [A]Ps 117:1 15:12 [A]Is 11:10 [B]Rev 5:5; 22:16 [C]Matt 12:21 15:13 [A]Rom 14:17 [B]Rom 15:19; 1 Cor 2:4; 1 Thess 1:5 15:14 [A]Eph 5:9; 2 Thess 1:11 [B]1 Cor 1:5; 8:1, 7, 10; 12:8; 13:2 15:15 [a]One early ms reads *by God* [A]Rom 12:3 15:16 [A]Acts 9:15; Rom 11:13 [B]Rom 1:1; 15:19, 20 [C]Rom 12:1; Eph 5:2; Phil 2:17 15:17 [A]Phil 3:3 [B]Heb 2:17; 5:1 15:18 [a]Lit *which Christ has not accomplished* [b]Lit *to the obedience* [A]Acts 15:12; 21:19; Rom 1:5; 2 Cor 3:5 15:19 [a]Or *attesting miracles* [b]Lit *fulfilled* [A]John 4:48 [B]Rom 15:13; 1 Cor 2:4; 1 Thess 1:5 [C]Acts 22:17-21 [D]Acts 20:1f 15:20 [A]Rom 1:15; 10:15; 15:16 [B]1 Cor 3:10; 2 Cor 10:15f 15:21 [A]Is 52:15

15:6 with one accord . . . one voice. Our unity should be both real ("one accord") and apparent ("one voice"). But the consummate purpose of unity is not to please other believers but to glorify God. **God and Father.** This expression emphasizes the deity of Christ. Jesus is not an adopted son of God; He is of the same essential being and nature as God. This is such an important connection that it appears frequently in the NT (2Co 1:3; 11:31; Eph 1:3; Col 1:3; 1Pe 1:3).

15:7 accept. *See note on 14:1.* **as Christ . . . accepted us.** If the perfect, sinless Son of God was willing to bring sinners into God's family, how much more should forgiven believers be willing to warmly embrace and accept each other in spite of their disagreements over issues of conscience (Mt 10:24; 11:29; Eph 4:32–5:2).

15:8 a servant to the circumcision. Jesus was born a Jew (*see note on Mt 1:1*), and as a child, He was circumcised and identified physically with the sign of the covenant (*see notes on 4:11; Ge 17:11–14*). **promises *given* to the fathers.** The covenant with Abraham that God reiterated to both Isaac and Jacob (*see note on 4:13*).

15:9–12 To show that God's plan has always been to bring Jew and Gentile alike into His kingdom and to soften the prejudice of Christian Jews against their Gentile brothers, Paul quotes from the Law, the Prophets, and twice from the Psalms—all the recognized divisions of the OT—proving God's plan from their own Scriptures.

15:9 for the Gentiles to glorify God for His mercy. Because He extended His grace and mercy to a people outside the covenant (*see notes on 10:11–21; 11:11–18*). **it is written.** Quoted from 2Sa 22:50; Ps 18:49. The psalmist sings praise to God among the nations, which alludes to Gentile salvation.

15:10 Quoted from Dt 32:43.

15:11 Quoted from Ps 117:1.

15:12 Quoted from Is 11:10. **root of Jesse.** A way of referring to Jesus as the descendant of David, and thus of David's father Jesse (*see note on Rev 5:5*).

15:13 God of hope. God is the source of eternal hope, life, and salvation, and He is the object of hope for every believer (*see note on 5:2*). **by the power of the Holy Spirit.** The believer's hope comes through the Scripture (cf. 15:4; Eph 1:13, 14), which was written and is applied to every believing heart by the Holy Spirit.

15:14–22 Not wanting to jeopardize his relationship with the believers in Rome by seeming to be insensitive, presumptuous, or unloving, Paul sets out to explain how he could write such a forthright letter to a church he did not found and had never visited.

15:14 goodness. High moral character. The believers in Rome hated evil and loved righteousness, attitudes their lives clearly displayed. **knowledge.** Refers to deep, intimate knowledge indicating that the Roman believers were doctrinally sound (Col 2:2, 3), illustrating the fact that truth and virtue are inseparable (cf. 1Ti 1:19). **admonish.** To encourage, warn, or advise—a comprehensive term for preaching (1Co 14:3) and personal counseling (*see note on 12:1*). Every believer is responsible to encourage and strengthen other believers with God's Word and is divinely equipped to do so (2Ti 3:16).

15:15 as to remind you. In spite of their spiritual strength, these Christians needed to be reminded of truths they already knew but could easily neglect or even forget (cf. 1Ti 4:6; 2Ti 2:8–14; Titus 3:1).

15:16 minister. "Minister" was a general Gr. term used of public officials. But in the NT it is used most often of those who serve God in some form of public worship (e.g., Php 2:17; Heb 1:7, 14; 8:1, 2, 6), including that of a priest (Lk 1:23). **to the Gentiles.** Although Paul's practice was always to present the gospel to the Jews first in every city he visited (*see note on Ac 13:5*), his primary apostolic calling was to the Gentiles (11:13; Ac 9:15). ***my* offering.** Having referred to himself as a minister, a word with priestly overtones, Paul explains that his priestly ministry is to present to God an offering of a multitude of Gentile converts.

15:17 boasting. Paul never boasted in his accomplishments as an apostle, but only in what Christ had accomplished through him (1Co 1:27–29, 31; 2Co 10:13–17; 12:5, 9; Gal 6:14; 1Ti 1:12–16).

15:19 signs and wonders. *See notes on Ac 2:19; 2Co 12:12.* God used them to authenticate true preaching and teaching. **Illyricum.** The region that roughly corresponds to former Yugoslavia and current northern Albania. In Paul's day, this area was more commonly known as Dalmatia (2Ti 4:10). Jerusalem to Illyricum covered some 1400 miles.

15:20 gospel. *See note on 1:1.* **another man's foundation.** Paul's goal was to reach those who had never heard the gospel—the primary function of a NT evangelist (Eph 4:11). But for pastor-teachers, building on the foundation laid by such an evangelist is the crucial part of their ministry (cf. 1Co 3:6).

15:21 it is written. Quoted from Is 52:15;

22 For this reason [A]I have often been prevented
from coming to you; 23 but now, with no further
place for me in these regions, and since I [A]have had
for many years a longing to come to you 24 whenever
I [A]go to Spain—for I hope to see you in passing, and
to be [B]helped on my way there by you, when I have
first [C]enjoyed your company [a]for a while— 25 but
now, [A]I am going to Jerusalem [B]serving the [a]saints.
26 For [A]Macedonia and [B]Achaia have been pleased to
make a contribution for the poor among the [a]saints
in Jerusalem. 27 Yes, they were pleased *to do so,* and
they are indebted to them. For [A]if the Gentiles have
shared in their spiritual things, they are indebted to
minister to them also in material things. 28 Therefore, when I have finished this, and [A]have [a]put my
seal on this fruit of theirs, I will [B]go on by way of
you to Spain. 29 I know that when [A]I come to you, I
will come in the fullness of the blessing of Christ.
30 Now I urge you, brethren, by our Lord Jesus
Christ and by [A]the love of the Spirit, to [B]strive together
with me in your prayers to God for me, 31 that I may be
[A]rescued from those who are disobedient in Judea, and
that my [B]service for Jerusalem may prove acceptable
to the [a,C]saints; 32 so that [A]I may come to you in joy by
[B]the will of God and find *refreshing* rest in your company. 33 Now [A]the God of peace be with you all. Amen.

GREETINGS AND LOVE EXPRESSED

16 I [A]commend to you our sister Phoebe, who is a
[a]servant of the church which is at [B]Cenchrea;
2 that you [A]receive her in the Lord in a manner worthy of the [a,B]saints, and that you help her in whatever
matter she may have need of you; for she herself has
also been a helper of many, [b]and of myself as well.
3 Greet [A]Prisca and Aquila, my fellow workers
[B]in [C]Christ Jesus, 4 who for my life risked their own
necks, to whom not only do I give thanks, but also
all the churches of the Gentiles; 5 also *greet* [A]the
church that is in their house. Greet Epaenetus, my
beloved, who is the [B]first convert to Christ from
[a,C]Asia. 6 Greet Mary, who has worked hard for you.
7 Greet Andronicus and [a]Junias, my [A]kinsmen and
my [B]fellow prisoners, who are outstanding among
the apostles, who also [b]were [C]in Christ before me.

15:22 [A]Rom 1:13; 1 Thess 2:18 15:23 [A]Acts 19:21; Rom 1:10f; 15:29, 32 15:24 [a]Lit *in part* [A]Rom 15:28 [B]Acts 15:3 [C]Rom 1:12 15:25 [a]Or *holy ones* [A]Acts 19:21 [B]Acts 24:17 15:26 [a]V 25, note 1 [A]Acts 16:9; 1 Cor 16:5; 2 Cor 1:16; 2:13; 7:5; 8:1; 9:2, 4; 11:9; Phil 4:15; 1 Thess 1:7f; 4:10; 1 Tim 1:3 [B]Acts 18:12; 19:21 15:27 [A]1 Cor 9:11 15:28 [a]Lit *sealed to them this fruit* [A]John 3:33 [B]Rom 15:24 15:29 [A]Acts 19:21; Rom 1:10f; 15:23, 32 15:30 [A]Gal 5:22; Col 1:8 [B]2 Cor 1:11; Col 4:12 15:31 [a]V 25, note 1 [A]2 Cor 1:10; 2 Thess 3:2; 2 Tim 3:11; 4:17 [B]Rom 15:25f; 2 Cor 8:4; 9:1 [C]Acts 9:13, 15 15:32 [A]Rom 15:23 [B]Acts 18:21; Rom 1:10 15:33 [A]Rom 16:20; 2 Cor 13:11; Phil 4:9; 1 Thess 5:23; 2 Thess 3:16; Heb 13:20 16:1 [a]Or *deaconess* [A]2 Cor 3:1 [B]Acts 18:18 16:2 [a]Or *holy ones* [b]Lit *and of me, myself* [A]Phil 2:29 [B]Acts 9:13, 15 16:3 [A]Acts 18:2 [B]Rom 8:11ff; 16:7, 9, 10; 2 Cor 5:17; 12:2; Gal 1:22 [C]Rom 8:1 16:5 [a]I.e. west coast province of Asia Minor [A]1 Cor 16:19; Col 4:15; Philem 2 [B]1 Cor 16:15 [C]Acts 16:6 16:7 [a]Or *Junia* (fem) [b]Lit *have become* [A]Rom 9:3; 16:11, 21 [B]Col 4:10; Philem 23 [C]Rom 8:11ff; 16:3, 9, 10; 2 Cor 5:17; 12:2; Gal 1:22

see note on 3:10. The OT quotation refers primarily to Christ's second coming, but in its broader application it refers to the process of evangelism that began in Paul's day and continues throughout church history until Christ returns.

15:22 prevented from coming. The form of this Gr. verb indicates an ongoing problem, and that something external created the hindrance. Paul was providentially being prevented by God from going to Rome (cf. Ac 16:7).

15:23, 24 Careful and sensible planning does not demonstrate a lack of trust in God's providence. But plans must always be subject to the Lord's control and alteration—just as Paul's were (cf. Pr 16:9).

15:23 no further place. Paul believed he had covered the region with the gospel sufficiently and could move on to other areas. **a longing to come to you.** *See notes on 1:10–13.*

15:24 Spain. The city and region referred to in the OT as Tarshish (1Ki 10:22; Jon 1:3), located on the far western end of the European continent. It had become a major center of commerce and culture, made accessible by the vast network of Roman roads. Its most famous ancient son was Seneca, the philosopher and statesman who tutored Nero and served as prime minister of the Empire. **helped on my way there by you.** Paul hoped the church at Rome would supply him with an escort and supplies to make the journey to Spain.

15:25 serving. *See note on Ac 6:2.*

15:26 Macedonia and Achaia. *See notes on Ac 16:9; 1Th 1:7.* Paul ministered in these regions during his first and second missionary journeys. **contribution.** The Gr. word carries the basic idea of sharing and is usually translated "fellowship" or "communion." The context indicates that here it is the sharing of a financial gift to help support the poor in Jerusalem (1Co 16:1; 2Co 8:2–4; Gal 2:9, 10).

15:27 their spiritual things. The "things" were gospel truths first preached to the Gentile believers by the Jewish apostles, prophets, teachers, and evangelists.

15:28 this fruit. The financial gift for the Jerusalem church; the fruit of their genuine love and gratitude. **Spain.** *See note on 15:24.*

15:30 the love of the Spirit. This phrase occurs only here in Scripture and refers to Paul's love for the Holy Spirit, not the Spirit's love for him (cf. Ps 143:10).

15:30, 31 prayers ... that I may be rescued. Many Jews in Judea rejected the gospel and were prepared to attack Paul when he returned. Aware of the trouble that awaited him (Ac 20:22–24), he wanted the Roman Christians to pray for his deliverance only so he could complete the ministry the Lord had given him. Their prayers were answered in that he met with success in Jerusalem (Ac 21:17, 19, 20) and was delivered from death, but not imprisonment (Ac 21:10, 11; 23:11).

15:31 may prove acceptable. Paul wanted the Jewish Christians in Jerusalem to receive the financial gift from the Gentiles with loving gratitude, recognizing it as a gesture of brotherly love and kindness.

15:32 the will of God. *See note on 1:10.* **find *refreshing* rest in your company.** Paul eventually found the joy and rest he was looking for (Ac 28:15).

15:33 the God of peace. Just as He is the God of hope (*see note on v. 13*), God is also the source of true peace (cf. Eph 2:11–14; Php 4:7).

16:1–27 This chapter, which has almost no explicit teaching and contains several lists of mostly unknown people, is the most extensive and intimate expression of Paul's love and affection for other believers and coworkers found anywhere in his NT letters. It also provides insights into the lives of ordinary first-century Christians and gives an inside look at the nature and character of the early church.

16:1 Phoebe. Means "bright and radiant," which aptly fits Paul's brief description of her personality and Christian character. **servant.** The term from which we get "deacon" and "deaconess" (*see notes on 1Ti 3:10, 11, 12*). In the early church, women servants cared for sick believers, the poor, strangers, and those in prison. They instructed the women and children (cf. Titus 2:3–5). Whether Phoebe had an official title or not, she had the great responsibility of delivering this letter to the Roman church. When they had served faithfully and become widowed and destitute, such women were to be cared for by the church (*see notes on 1Ti 5:3–16*). **Cenchrea.** A neighboring port city of Corinth, where Paul wrote Romans. The church in Cenchrea was probably planted by the Corinthian church.

16:3 Prisca and Aquila. *See notes on Ac 18:1–3.*

16:4 for my life risked their own necks. Probably at Corinth or Ephesus, but the details are not known.

16:5 Epaenetus. Probably saved through Paul's preaching and lovingly discipled by the apostle. **first convert.** *See note on 1:13.* He was the first convert in Asia Minor (modern Turkey).

16:6 Mary, who has worked hard for you. "Worked hard" connotes hard labor to the point of exhaustion. The context suggests she might have ministered in the church at Rome since its founding and been mentioned to Paul by others (possibly Prisca and Aquila). But nothing more is known of her.

16:7 Andronicus and Junias. Perhaps

8 Greet Ampliatus, my beloved in the Lord. 9 Greet
Urbanus, our fellow worker [A]in Christ, and Stachys
my beloved. 10 Greet Apelles, the approved [A]in Christ.
Greet those who are of the *household* of Aristobulus.
11 Greet Herodion, my [A]kinsman. Greet those of the
household of Narcissus, who are in the Lord. 12 Greet
Tryphaena and Tryphosa, workers in the Lord. Greet
Persis the beloved, who has worked hard in the
Lord. 13 Greet [A]Rufus, a choice man in the Lord, also
his mother and mine. 14 Greet Asyncritus, Phlegon,
Hermes, Patrobas, Hermas and the brethren with
them. 15 Greet Philologus and Julia, Nereus and his
sister, and Olympas, and all [A]the [a]saints who are
with them. 16 [A]Greet one another with a holy kiss.
All the churches of Christ greet you.
17 Now I urge you, brethren, keep your eye on
those who cause dissensions and [a]hindrances [A]con-
trary to the teaching which you learned, and [B]turn
away from them. 18 For such men are [A]slaves, not
of our Lord Christ but of [B]their own [a]appetites;
and by their [C]smooth and flattering speech they
deceive the hearts of the unsuspecting. 19 For the
report of your obedience [A]has reached to all; therefore I am rejoicing over you, but [B]I want you to
be wise in what is good and innocent in what is
evil. 20 [A]The God of peace will soon crush [B]Satan
under your feet.
[C]The grace of our Lord Jesus be with you.
21 [A]Timothy my fellow worker greets you, and *so
do* [B]Lucius and [C]Jason and [D]Sosipater, my [E]kinsmen.
22 I, Tertius, who [A]write this letter, greet you in
the Lord.
23 [A]Gaius, host to me and to the whole church,
greets you. [B]Erastus, the city treasurer greets you,
and Quartus, the brother. 24 [[a]The grace of our Lord
Jesus Christ be with you all. Amen.]
25 [A]Now to Him who is able to establish you [B]ac-
cording to my gospel and the preaching of Jesus
Christ, according to the revelation of [C]the mystery
which has been kept secret for [D]long ages past,

16:9 [A]Rom 8:11ff; 16:3, 7, 10; 2 Cor 5:17; 12:2; Gal 1:22 16:10 [A]Rom 8:11ff; 16:3, 7, 9; 2 Cor 5:17; 12:2; Gal 1:22 16:11 [A]Rom 9:3; 16:7, 21 16:13 [A]Mark 15:21 16:15 [a]V 2, note 1 [A]Rom 16:2, 14 16:16 [A]1 Cor 16:20; 2 Cor 13:12; 1 Thess 5:26; 1 Pet 5:14 16:17 [a]Lit *occasions of stumbling* [A]1 Tim 1:3; 6:3 [B]Matt 7:15; Gal 1:8f; 2 Thess 3:6, 14; Titus 3:10; 2 John 10 16:18 [a]Lit *belly* [A]Rom 14:18 [B]Phil 3:19 [C]Col 2:4; 2 Pet 2:3 16:19 [A]Rom 1:8 [B]Jer 4:22; Matt 10:16; 1 Cor 14:20 16:20 [A]Rom 15:33 [B]Matt 4:10 [C]1 Cor 16:23; 2 Cor 13:14; Gal 6:18; Phil 4:23; 1 Thess 5:28; 2 Thess 3:18; Rev 22:21 16:21 [A]Acts 16:1 [B][Acts 13:1] [C][Acts 17:5] [D][Acts 20:4] [E]Rom 9:3; 16:7, 11 16:22 [A]1 Cor 16:21; Gal 6:11; Col 4:18; 2 Thess 3:17; Philem 19 16:23 [A][Acts 19:29; 20:4]; 1 Cor 1:14 [B]Acts 19:22; 2 Tim 4:20 16:24 [a]Early mss do not contain this v 16:25 [A]Eph 3:20; Jude 24 [B]Rom 2:16 [C]Matt 13:35; Rom 11:25; 1 Cor 2:1, 7; 4:1; Eph 1:9; 3:3, 9; 6:19; Col 1:26f; 2:2; 4:3; 1 Tim 3:16 [D]2 Tim 1:9; Titus 1:2

a married couple, since "Junias" can be a woman's name. **fellow prisoners.** Probably a reference to their actually sharing the same cell or adjacent cells at some point. **outstanding among the apostles.** Their ministry with Paul, and perhaps with Peter and some of the other apostles in Jerusalem before Paul was converted, was well known and appreciated by the apostles.

16:8 Ampliatus. A common name among the emperor's household slaves at that time; he may have been one of those in "Caesar's household" (Php 4:22).

16:9 Stachys. An uncommon Gr. name meaning "ear of corn." He was obviously close to Paul, but the details are unknown.

16:10 Aristobulus. Since Paul does not greet him personally, he was probably not a believer, although some relatives and household servants apparently were. One noted biblical scholar believes that he was the brother of Herod Agrippa I and the grandson of Herod the Great.

16:11 Herodion. Related to the Herod family, and so perhaps associated with the household of Aristobulus. **my kinsman.** He may have been one of Paul's Jewish relatives. **Narcissus.** *See note on 16:10.* Some scholars believe that this was the Emperor Claudius' secretary. If so, two households within the palace had Christians in them (cf. Php 4:22).

16:12 Tryphaena and Tryphosa. Possibly twin sisters, whose names mean "delicate" and "dainty." **Persis.** Named after her native Persia; since her work is spoken of in the past tense, she was probably older than the other two women in this verse.

16:13 Rufus. Biblical scholars generally agree that he was one of the sons of Simon of Cyrene, the man enlisted to carry Jesus' cross (cf. Mk 15:21) and was likely saved through that contact with Christ. Mark wrote his gospel in Rome, possibly after the letter to Rome was written, and circulated. Paul would not have mentioned Rufus if that name were not well known to the church in Rome. **choice man in the Lord.** Elected to salvation. This indicates he was widely known as an extraordinary believer because of his great love and service. **his mother and mine.** Rufus was not Paul's natural brother. Rather, Rufus' mother, the wife of Simon of Cyrene, at some time had cared for Paul during his ministry travels.

16:14, 15 "Brethren" in this context, probably refers to both men and women, which indicates that these names represent the outstanding leaders of two of the assemblies in Rome.

16:16 holy kiss. Kissing of friends on the forehead, cheek, or beard was common in the OT. The Jews in the NT church carried on the practice, and it became especially precious to new believers, who were often outcasts from their own families because of their faith, because of the spiritual kinship it signified.

16:17–20 Paul considered it necessary to insert into his greetings of love this caution against harmful teachings and practices that undermine the truth of Christianity and are its greatest threat. Genuine love will be ready to forgive evil, but it will not condone or ignore it. Those such as Paul, who truly love other believers who are dear to them, will warn them about sin and harm (cf. 1Co 13:6).

16:17 dissensions and hindrances. Doctrinal falsehood and unrighteous practices (cf. Mt 24:24; Ac 20:27–32; Gal 1:6–8; Eph 4:14).

16:18 appetites. Driven by self-interest and self-gratification, often seen in their pretentious, extravagant, and immoral lifestyles (cf. Php 3:18, 19; 2Ti 3:7, 8; 2Pe 1:20–2:3, 10–19; Jude 12, 13). **unsuspecting.** The naive person (cf. 2Co 11:13–15).

16:19 reached. *See note on 1:8.*

16:20 God of peace. See 15:33; Heb 13:20. **will … crush Satan.** *See note on Ge 3:15.* **soon.** "Speedily, quickly" (Ac 12:7; 22:18; cf. Rev 22:7, 12, 20). **grace of our Lord Jesus.** *See note on 1:7.*

16:21 Lucius. Either 1) a native of Cyrene, one of the prophets and teachers in Antioch who participated in Paul and Barnabas' commissioning (Ac 13:1–3) or 2) another form of "Luke," the author of the Gospel of Luke and the book of Acts. **Jason.** One of the first converts in Thessalonica, who evidently let Paul stay in his home for a short time before Paul and Silas were sent to Berea (*see notes on Ac 17:5–10*). **Sosipater.** A longer form of "Sopater" (Ac 20:4–6), a Berean (cf. Ac 17:10–12) who joined other believers in meeting Paul at Troas after the apostle left Ephesus. **my kinsmen.** *See note on v. 11.*

16:22 Tertius. Paul's secretary, who wrote this letter as Paul dictated it, inserts a personal greeting.

16:23 Gaius. One of Paul's converts at Corinth (cf. 1Co 1:14). His full name was most likely "Gaius Titius Justus" (Ac 18:7). **the whole church.** The congregation that met in Gaius' house. **Erastus.** A common name in NT times, but probably not the same man referred to in Ac 19:22 or 2Ti 4:20. **treasurer.** In Corinth. This was a prominent position with political clout. **Quartus.** May have been a physical brother of Erastus, but more likely just the final brother in Christ listed here.

16:24 This verse is not found in the earliest Gr. manuscripts of Romans, which is understandable in view of the longer, more explicit benediction that follows.

16:25–27 The letter concludes with a beautiful doxology that praises God for His work through Jesus Christ and thereby summarizes the major themes in Romans (*see notes on 11:33–36*; cf. Mt 6:13; Lk 19:37, 38; Eph 3:20, 21; Heb 13:20, 21; Rev 5:9, 10).

16:25 my gospel. *See notes on 1:1; 2:16*; cf. Gal 1:11; 2:2. **preaching of Jesus Christ.** Synonymous with the gospel, it was Paul's

26 but now is manifested, and by [A]the Scriptures of the prophets, according to the commandment of the eternal God, has been made known to all the nations, *leading* to [B]obedience of faith; 27 to the only wise God, through Jesus Christ, [A]be the glory forever. Amen.

16:26 [A]Rom 1:2 [B]Rom 1:5 16:27 [A]Rom 11:36

supreme life commitment (*see notes on 10:14, 15, 17*; cf. 1Co 1:23, 24; 2Co 4:5, 6). **the mystery.** *See note on 11:25.* In the NT, this word does not have its modern connotation. Instead, it refers to something hidden in former times but now made known (1Co 4:1; Eph 5:32; 6:19; Col 1:25, 26; 2Th 2:7, 8; 1Ti 3:9, 16). The NT's most common mystery is that God would provide salvation for Gentiles as well as Jews (Eph 3:3–9).

16:26 Scriptures of the prophets ... made known. God had told Israel that He would not only call her to righteousness, but appoint her as a light (of the gospel) to the nations (*see notes on Is 42:6; 49:6; 1Pe 1:10, 11*; cf. Ge 12:3; Ex 19:6; Is 49:22; 53:11; 60:3–5; Jer 31:31, 33).

16:27 to ... God ... be the glory. It was through the Father that the gospel was ultimately revealed, therefore He deserves all the credit, praise, and worship.

THE FIRST EPISTLE OF PAUL TO THE CORINTHIANS

TITLE

The letter is named for the city of Corinth, where the church to whom it was written was located. With the exception of personal epistles addressed to Timothy, Titus, and Philemon, all Paul's letters bear the name of the city where the church addressed existed.

AUTHOR AND DATE

As indicated in the first verse, the epistle was written by the apostle Paul, whose authorship cannot be seriously questioned. Pauline authorship has been universally accepted by the church since the first century, when 1 Corinthians was penned. Internally, the apostle claimed to have written the epistle (1:1, 13; 3:4–6; 4:15; 16:21). Externally, this correspondence has been acknowledged as genuine since A.D. 95 by Clement of Rome, who was writing to the Corinthian church. Other early Christian leaders who authenticated Paul as author include Ignatius (ca. A.D. 110), Polycarp (ca. A.D. 135), and Tertullian (ca. A.D. 200).

This epistle was most likely written in the first half of A.D. 55 from Ephesus (16:8, 9, 19) while Paul was on his third missionary journey. The apostle intended to remain on at Ephesus to complete his 3-year stay (Ac 20:31) until Pentecost (May/June) A.D. 55 (16:8). Then he hoped to winter (A.D. 55–56) at Corinth (16:6; Ac 20:2). His departure for Corinth was anticipated even as he wrote (4:19; 11:34; 16:8).

BACKGROUND AND SETTING

The city of Corinth was located in southern Greece, in what was the Roman province of Achaia, ca. 45 mi. W from Athens. This lower part, the Peloponnesus, is connected to the rest of Greece by a 4-mile-wide isthmus, which is bounded on the E by the Saronic Gulf and on the W by the Gulf of Corinth. Corinth is near the middle of the isthmus and is prominently situated on a high plateau. For many centuries, all N-S land traffic in that area had to pass through or near this ancient city. Since travel by sea around the Peloponnesus involved a 250-mile voyage that was dangerous and obviously time consuming, most captains carried their ships on skids or rollers across the isthmus directly past Corinth. Corinth understandably prospered as a major trade city, not only for most of Greece but for much of the Mediterranean area, including North Africa, Italy, and Asia Minor. A canal across the isthmus was begun by the emperor Nero during the first century A.D., but was not completed until near the end of the nineteenth century.

The Isthmian games, one of the two most famous athletic events of that day (the other being the Olympian games), were hosted by Corinth, causing more people-traffic. Even by the pagan standards of its own culture, Corinth became so morally corrupt that its very name became synonymous with debauchery and moral depravity. To "corinthianize" came to represent gross immorality and drunken debauchery. In 6:9, 10, Paul lists some of the specific sins for which the city was noted and which formerly had characterized many believers in the church there. Tragically, some of the worst sins were still found among some church members. One of those sins, incest, was condemned even by most pagan Gentiles (5:1).

Like most ancient Greek cities, Corinth had an acropolis (lit. "a high city"), which rose 2,000 feet and was used both for defense and for worship. The most prominent edifice on the acropolis was a temple to Aphrodite, the Greek goddess of love. Some 1,000 priestesses, who were "religious" prostitutes, lived and worked there and came down into the city in the evening to offer their services to male citizens and foreign visitors.

The church in Corinth was founded by Paul on his second missionary journey (Ac 18:1ff.). As usual, his ministry began in the synagogue, where he was assisted by two Jewish believers, Priscilla and Aquila, with whom he lived for a while and who were fellow tradesmen. Soon after, Silas and Timothy joined them and Paul began preaching even more intensely in the synagogue. When most of the Jews resisted the gospel, he left the synagogue, but not before Crispus, the leader of the synagogue, his family, and many other Corinthians were converted (Ac 18:5–8).

After ministering in Corinth for over a year and a half (Ac 18:11), Paul was brought before a Roman tribunal by some of the Jewish leaders. Because the charges were strictly religious and not civil, the proconsul, Gallio, dismissed the case. Shortly thereafter, Paul took Priscilla and Aquila with him to Ephesus. From there he returned to Israel (vv. 18–22).

Unable to fully break with the culture from which it came, the church at Corinth was exceptionally factional, showing its carnality and immaturity. After the gifted Apollos had ministered in the church for some time, a group of his admirers established a clique and had little to do with the rest of the church. Another group developed that was loyal to Paul, another claimed special allegiance to Peter (Cephas), and still another to Christ alone (see 1:10–13; 3:1–9).

The most serious problem of the Corinthian church was worldliness, an unwillingness to divorce the culture around them. Most of the believers could not consistently separate themselves from their old, selfish, immoral, and pagan ways. It became necessary for Paul to write to correct this, as well as to command the faithful Christians not only to break fellowship with the disobedient and unrepentant members, but to put those members out of the church (5:9–13).

Before he wrote this inspired letter, Paul had written the church other correspondence (see 5:9), which was also corrective in nature. Because a copy of that letter has never been discovered, it has been referred to as "the lost epistle." There was another noncanonical letter after 1 Corinthians, usually called "the severe letter" (2Co 2:4).

HISTORICAL AND THEOLOGICAL THEMES

Although the major thrust of this epistle is corrective of behavior rather than of doctrine, Paul gives seminal teaching on many doctrines that directly relate to the matters of sin and righteousness. In one way or another, wrong living always stems from wrong belief. Sexual sins for example, including divorce, are inevitably related to disobeying God's plan for marriage and the family (7:1–40). Proper worship is determined by such things as recognition of God's holy character (3:17), the spiritual identity of the church (12:12–27), and pure partaking of the Lord's Supper (11:17–34). It is not possible for the church to be edified faithfully and effectively unless believers understand and exercise their spiritual gifts (12:1–14:40). The importance of the doctrine of the resurrection, of course, cannot be overestimated because if there is no resurrection of the dead, then Christ is not risen. And if Christ is not risen, then preaching is empty and so is faith (15:13, 14).

In addition to those themes, Paul deals briefly with God's judgment of believers, the right understanding of which will produce right motives for godly living (see 3:13–15). The right understanding of idols and of false gods, in general, was to help the immature Corinthians think maturely about such things as eating meat that had been sacrificed to idols (8:1–11:1). The right understanding and expression of genuine, godly love was mandatory to right use of the gifts and even to right knowledge about all the things of God (13:1–13).

So Paul deals with the cross, divine wisdom and human wisdom, the work of the Spirit in illumination, carnality, eternal rewards, the transformation of salvation, sanctification, the nature of Christ, union with Him, the divine role for women, marriage and divorce, Spirit baptism, indwelling and gifting, the unity of the church in one body, the theology of love, and the doctrine of resurrection. All these establish foundational truth for godly behavior.

INTERPRETIVE CHALLENGES

By far the most controversial issue for interpretation is that of the sign gifts discussed in chaps. 12–14, particularly the gifts of miracles and tongues-speaking. Many believe that all the gifts are permanent, so that the gift of speaking in tongues will cease (13:8) only at the time the gifts of prophecy and of knowledge cease, namely, when that which is perfect has come (v. 10). Those who maintain that tongues and miracles are still valid spiritual gifts in the church today believe they should be exercised with the same power they were in NT times by the apostles. Others believe the miraculous sign gifts have ceased. This controversy will be resolved in the appropriate notes on chaps. 12–14.

The issue of divorce is a troubling one for many. Chapter 7 addresses the subject, but calls for careful interpretation to yield consistent biblical doctrine on the matter.

Advocates of universalism, the idea that all men will eventually be saved, use 15:22 in support of that view, claiming that, just as every human being died spiritually because of Adam's sin, they will all be saved through Christ's righteousness. The note on that verse will confront the challenge of such universalists.

From that same chapter, the obscure phrase "baptized for the dead" (v. 29) is used to defend the notion that a dead person can be saved by being baptized vicariously through a living Christian. There have been over 40 suggested explanations for this baptism. As the notes will point out, regardless of how that particular verse is interpreted, the falsehood of dead people having the opportunity to be saved is proven by many other texts that are indisputably clear.

A much less serious issue concerns the meaning of 6:4, which pertains to Christians taking other Christians to court before unbelievers. The resolution of that problem lies primarily in being obedient to a verse which is unambiguous.

OUTLINE

I. Introduction: The Calling and Benefits of Sainthood (1:1–9)

II. Disunity in the Church (1:10–4:21)
- A. The Need for Unity (1:10–3:23)
- B. The Need for Servanthood (4:1–21)

III. Immorality in the Church (5:1–6:20)

IV. Marriage in the Church (7:1–40)

V. Liberty in the Church (8:1–11:1)

VI. Worship in the Church (11:2–14:40)

A. Roles of Men and Women in the Church (11:2–16)
B. The Lord's Supper (11:17–34)
C. Spiritual Gifts (12:1–14:40)

VII. The Hope of the Church: Resurrection (15:1–58)

VIII. A Charge to the Church (16:1–24)

A. Stewardship (16:1–4)
B. Personal Plans and Greetings (16:5–24)

APPEAL TO UNITY

1 Paul, [A]called *as* an apostle of Jesus Christ [a]by [B]the
will of God, and [C]Sosthenes our [D]brother,
2 To [A]the church of God which is at [B]Corinth, to
those who have been sanctified in Christ Jesus,
[a]saints [C]by calling, with all who in every place [D]call
on the name of our Lord Jesus Christ, their *Lord*
and ours:
3 [A]Grace to you and peace from God our Father
and the Lord Jesus Christ.
4 [A]I thank [a]my God always concerning you for the
grace of God which was given you in Christ Jesus,
5 that in everything you were [A]enriched in Him, in all
[B]speech and [B]all knowledge, 6 even as [A]the testimony
concerning Christ was confirmed [a]in you, 7 so that
you are not lacking in any gift, [A]awaiting eagerly
the revelation of our Lord Jesus Christ, 8 [A]who will
also confirm you to the end, blameless in [B]the day
of our Lord Jesus Christ. 9 [A]God is faithful, through
whom you were [B]called into [C]fellowship with His
Son, Jesus Christ our Lord.
10 Now [A]I exhort you, [B]brethren, by the name of
our Lord Jesus Christ, that you all [a]agree and that
there be no [b,C]divisions among you, but that you
be [c]made complete in [D]the same mind and in the
same judgment. 11 For I have been informed concerning you, my brethren, by Chloe's *people,* that
there are quarrels among you. 12 Now I mean this,
that [A]each one of you is saying, "I am of Paul," and
"I of [B]Apollos," and "I of [C]Cephas," and "I of Christ."
13 [a]Has Christ been divided? Paul was not crucified
for you, was he? Or were you [A]baptized [b]in the name
of Paul? 14 [a]I thank God that I [A]baptized none of you
except [A]Crispus and [B]Gaius, 15 so that no one would
say you were baptized [a]in my name. 16 Now I did
baptize also the [A]household of Stephanas; beyond
that, I do not know whether I baptized any other.
17 [A]For Christ did not send me to baptize, but to

1:1 [a]Lit *through* [A]Rom 1:1 [B]Rom 1:10; 2 Tim 1:1 [C]Acts 18:17 [D]Acts 1:15 1:2 [a]Or *holy ones* [A]1 Cor 10:32 [B]Acts 18:1 [C]Rom 1:7; 8:28 [D]Acts 7:59 1:3 [A]Rom 1:7 1:4 [a]Two early mss do not contain *my* [A]Rom 1:8 1:5 [A]2 Cor 9:11 [B]Rom 15:14; 2 Cor 8:7 1:6 [a]Or *among* [A]2 Thess 1:10; 1 Tim 2:6; 2 Tim 1:8; Rev 1:2 1:7 [A]Luke 17:30; Rom 8:19, 23; Phil 3:20; 2 Pet 3:12 1:8 [A]Rom 8:19; Phil 1:6; Col 2:7; 1 Thess 3:13; 5:23 [B]Luke 17:24, 30; 1 Cor 5:5; 2 Cor 1:14; Phil 1:6, 10; 2:16; 1 Thess 5:2; 2 Thess 2:2 1:9 [A]Deut 7:9; Is 49:7; 1 Cor 10:13; 2 Cor 1:18; 1 Thess 5:24; 2 Thess 3:3 [B]Rom 8:28 [C]1 John 1:3 1:10 [a]Lit *speak the same thing* [b]Lit *schisms* [c]Or *united* [A]Rom 12:1 [B]Rom 1:13 [C]1 Cor 11:18 [D]Rom 12:16; Phil 1:27 1:12 [A]Matt 23:8-10; 1 Cor 3:4 [B]Acts 18:24; 1 Cor 3:22 [C]John 1:42; 1 Cor 3:22; 9:5; 15:5 1:13 [a]Or *Christ has been divided!* or *Christ is divided!* [b]Lit *into* [A]Matt 28:19; Acts 2:38 1:14 [a]Two early mss read *I give thanks that* [A]Acts 18:8 [B]Rom 16:23 1:15 [a]Lit *into* 1:16 [A]1 Cor 16:15, 17 1:17 [A]John 4:2; Acts 10:48

1:1 apostle. Lit. "a sent one." Paul establishes his authority as an emissary of the Lord Jesus by God's appointment (9:1; 15:8; cf. Ac 9:3–6, 17; 22:11–15), made especially necessary because so much of the message of this epistle is corrective (2:1–7). *See notes on Ro 1:1; Eph 4:11.* Since he was delegated by God to speak and write, resisting him was resisting God. **Sosthenes.** Probably Paul's secretary, a former leader of the Corinthian synagogue who had become a brother in Christ. On one occasion, he was beaten for bringing Paul before the civil court at Corinth (Ac 18:12–17).

1:2 saints. Not referring to a specially pious or revered person canonized by an ecclesiastical body, but a reference to everyone who by salvation has been sanctified, that is, set apart from sin in Christ Jesus (cf. Gal 1:6; Eph 4:1, 4; Col 3:15–17; 1Ti 6:12; Heb 10:10, 14; 1Pe 2:9, 21; 3:9; 2Pe 1:3; Jude 1).

1:3 Grace to you and peace. A greeting Paul used in all his letters. The basic meaning of "grace" is favor; "peace" is a result of God's saving grace (Jn 14:27; Php 4:7).

1:4 grace of God ... given. This looks at the past, i.e., their salvation, when God justified them by undeserved and unrepayable love and mercy, forgiving their sin through the work of His Son.

1:5 in everything ... enriched in Him. In the present, the believer has everything the Lord has to give and therefore everything he needs (see 3:21; Eph 1:3; Col 2:10; 2Pe 1:3). The two particular blessings spoken of here are related to presenting the truth of God's Word. **speech.** In regard to speaking for God (cf. Ac 4:29, 31; Eph 6:19; 2Ti 2:15; 1Pe 3:15), believers are able to speak when God wants them to because of His enablement. Prayer reaches out for that ability (cf. Ac 4:29, 31; Eph 6:19), and diligence in study of God's Word aids it (2Ti 2:15; 1Pe 3:15). **all knowledge.** God provides believers with all the knowledge they need in order to speak effectively for Him (cf. 2:9; Mt 11:15; 2Co 4:6; Col 1:9, 10).

1:6 testimony concerning Christ was confirmed in you. This is a reference to the moment of salvation when the gospel was heard and believed and settled in the heart. At that moment, the enabling of v. 4 took place, because one became a recipient of the grace of God.

1:7 not lacking in any gift. "Gift" in Gr. is specifically "a gift of grace." While the blessings of speech and knowledge were primarily for evangelizing the lost, the spiritual gifts (chaps. 12–14) edify the church. Because these gifts are given to each believer (12:11, 12) without regard for maturity or spirituality, the Corinthians, though sinful, had them in full. **the revelation.** Paul looks to the blessing of future grace. At the Lord's second coming, His full glory, honor, and majesty will be revealed in blazing splendor (Rev 4:11; 5:12; 17:14), at which time all true believers will be fixed solidly forever as holy and without sin in full resurrected glory and purity to live in heaven with God forever. See Eph 5:25–27; 2Co 11:2.

1:8 the day of our Lord Jesus Christ. Cf. 5:5; 2Co 1:14. This refers to the coming of the Lord for His church, the Rapture (Jn 14:1–3; 1Th 4:13–18; Rev 3:10). This is to be distinguished from the day of the Lord (1Th 5:2, 4; 2Th 2:2), a term referring to judgment on the ungodly (see Introduction to Joel: Historical and Theological Themes).

1:9 God is faithful. Because of God's sovereign and unchangeable promise, believers are assured of this grace—past, present, and future—and will remain saved, assured of future glory at Christ's appearing (Eph 5:26, 27). **through whom you were called.** This call, as always in the epistles of the NT, refers to an effectual call that saves (*see note on Ro 8:30*). God who calls to salvation and heaven will be faithful to give the grace needed to fulfill that call. **fellowship with His Son.** *See notes on 1Jn 1:3–7.*

1:10 all agree. Paul is emphasizing the unity of doctrine in the local assembly of believers, not the spiritual unity of His universal church. Doctrinal unity, clearly and completely based on Scripture, must be the foundation of all church life (cf. Jn 17:11, 21–23; Ac 2:46, 47). Both weak commitment to doctrine and commitment to disunity of doctrine will severely weaken a church and destroy the true unity. In its place, there can be only shallow sentimentalism or superficial harmony. **made complete.** The basic idea is that of putting back together something that was broken or separated so it is no longer divided. The term is used in both the NT and in classical Gr. to speak of mending such things as nets, broken bones or utensils, torn garments, and dislocated joints. Cf. Ro 16:17; Php 1:27. **same mind ... same judgment.** Cf. Php 3:15, 16. The demand is for unity internally in their individual minds and externally in decisions made among themselves—unified in truth by beliefs, convictions, standards, and in behavior by applied principles of living (Ac 4:32; Eph 4:3). The only source of such unity is God's Word which establishes the standard of truth on which true unity rests.

1:11–13 Cf. 3:4–8.

1:11 Chloe's *people*. Probably a prominent person in the Corinthian church who had written or come to visit Paul in Ephesus to tell him of the factions in the church. It is not known whether Chloe was a man or a woman.

1:12 Apollos. *See notes on 16:12; Ac 18:24–28.* **Cephas.** The apostle Peter.

1:13 Has Christ been divided? No human leader, not even an apostle, should be given the loyalty that belongs only to the Lord. Such elevation of leaders leads only to contention, disputes, and a divided church. Christ is not divided and neither is His body, the church. Paul depreciates his worth in comparison to the Lord Jesus. For passages on unity, see 12:12, 13; Ro 12:5; Eph 4:4–6.

1:14 Crispus. The leader of the synagogue in Corinth who was converted under Paul's preaching (Ac 18:8). His conversion led to that of many others. **Gaius.** Since Romans was written from Corinth, this man was probably the host referred to in Ro 16:23.

1:16 Stephanas. Nothing is known of this family.

1:17 This verse does not mean that people should not be baptized (cf. Ac 2:38), but that God did not send Paul to start a private cult

preach the gospel, [B]not in [a]cleverness of speech,
so that the cross of Christ would not be made void.

THE WISDOM OF GOD

18 For the word of the cross is [A]foolishness to
[B]those who [a]are perishing, but to us who [b]are being
saved it is [C]the power of God. 19 For it is written,

> "[A]I WILL DESTROY THE WISDOM OF THE WISE,
> AND THE CLEVERNESS OF THE
> CLEVER I WILL SET ASIDE."

20 [A]Where is the wise man? Where is the scribe?
Where is the debater of [B]this age? Has not God [C]made
foolish the wisdom of [D]the world? 21 For since in
the wisdom of God [A]the world through its wisdom
did not *come to* know God, [B]God was well-pleased
through the [C]foolishness of the [a]message preached
to [D]save those who believe. 22 For indeed [A]Jews ask
for [a]signs and Greeks search for wisdom; 23 but we
preach [a,A]Christ crucified, [B]to Jews a stumbling block
and to Gentiles [C]foolishness, 24 but to those who
are [A]the called, both Jews and Greeks, Christ [B]the
power of God and [C]the wisdom of God. 25 Because
the [A]foolishness of God is wiser than men, and [B]the
weakness of God is stronger than men.
26 For [a]consider your [A]calling, brethren, that there
were [B]not many wise according to [b]the flesh, not
many mighty, not many noble; 27 but [A]God has chosen the foolish things of [B]the world to shame the
wise, and God has chosen the weak things of [B]the
world to shame the things which are strong, 28 and
the base things of [A]the world and the despised God
has chosen, [B]the things that are not, so that He may
[C]nullify the things that are, 29 so that [A]no [a]man may
boast before God. 30 But [a]by His doing you are in
[A]Christ Jesus, who became to us [B]wisdom from God,
[b]and [C]righteousness and [D]sanctification, and [E]re-
demption, 31 so that, just as it is written, "[A]LET HIM
WHO BOASTS, BOAST IN THE LORD."

PAUL'S RELIANCE UPON THE SPIRIT

2 And when I came to you, brethren, I [A]did not
come with superiority of speech or of wisdom,
proclaiming to you [B]the [a]testimony of God. 2 For I
determined to know nothing among you except
[A]Jesus Christ, and Him crucified. 3 I was with you
in [A]weakness and in [B]fear and in much trembling,

1:17 [a]Lit *wisdom* [B]1 Cor 2:1, 4, 13; 2 Cor 10:10; 11:6 1:18 [a]Or *perish* [b]Or *are saved* [A]1 Cor 1:21, 23, 25; 2:14; 4:10 [B]Acts 2:47; 2 Cor 2:15; 4:3; 2 Thess 2:10 [C]Rom 1:16; 1 Cor 1:24 1:19 [A]Is 29:14 1:20 [A]Job 12:17; Is 19:11f; 33:18 [B]Matt 13:22; 1 Cor 2:6, 8; 3:18, 19 [C]Rom 1:20ff [D]John 12:31; 1 Cor 1:27f; 6:2; 11:32; James 4:4 1:21 [a]Lit *preaching* [A]John 12:31; 1 Cor 1:27f; 6:2; 11:32; James 4:4 [B]Luke 12:32; Gal 1:15; Col 1:19 [C]1 Cor 1:18, 23, 25; 2:14; 4:10 [D]Rom 11:14; James 5:20 1:22 [a]Or *attesting miracles* [A]Matt 12:38 1:23 [a]I.e. Messiah [A]1 Cor 2:2; Gal 3:1; 5:11 [B]Luke 2:34; 1 Pet 2:8 [C]1 Cor 1:18, 21, 25; 2:14; 4:10 1:24 [A]Rom 8:28 [B]Rom 1:16; 1 Cor 1:18 [C]Luke 11:49; 1 Cor 1:30 1:25 [A]1 Cor 1:18, 21, 23; 2:14; 4:10 [B]2 Cor 13:4 1:26 [a]Lit *see* [b]I.e. human standards [A]Rom 11:29 [B]Matt 11:25; 1 Cor 1:20; 2:8 1:27 [A]James 2:5 [B]1 Cor 1:20 1:28 [A]1 Cor 1:20 [B]Rom 4:17 [C]Job 34:19; 1 Cor 2:6; 2 Thess 2:8; Heb 2:14 1:29 [a]Lit *flesh* [A]Eph 2:9 1:30 [a]Lit *of Him* [b]Or *both* [A]Rom 8:1; 1 Cor 4:15 [B]1 Cor 1:24 [C]Jer 23:5f; 33:16; 2 Cor 5:21; Phil 3:9 [D]1 Cor 1:2; 6:11; 1 Thess 5:23 [E]Rom 3:24; Eph 1:7, 14; Col 1:14 1:31 [A]Jer 9:23f; 2 Cor 10:17 2:1 [a]One early ms reads *mystery* [A]1 Cor 1:17; 2:4, 13 [B]1 Cor 2:7 2:2 [A]1 Cor 1:23; Gal 6:14 2:3 [A]1 Cor 4:10; 2 Cor 11:30; 12:5, 9f; 13:9 [B]Is 19:16; 2 Cor 7:15; Eph 6:5

of people personally baptized by him. See Ac 26:16–18. He was called to preach the gospel and bring people to oneness in Christ, not baptize a faction around himself.

1:18 word of the cross. God's total revelation, i.e., the gospel in all its fullness, which centers in the incarnation and crucifixion of Christ (2:2); the entire divine plan and provision for the redemption of sinners, which is the theme of all Scripture, is in view. **foolishness.** Translates the word from which "moron" is derived. **perishing … being saved.** Every person is either in the process of salvation (though not completed until the redemption of the body; see Ro 8:23; 13:11) or the process of destruction. One's response to the cross of Christ determines which. To the Christ-rejectors who are in the process of being destroyed (cf. Eph 2:1, 2) the gospel is nonsense. To those who are believers it is powerful wisdom.

1:19 it is written. Quoted from Is 29:14 (*see note there*) to emphasize that man's wisdom will be destroyed. Isaiah's prophecy will have its ultimate fulfillment in the last days when Christ sets up His kingdom (cf. Rev 17:14) and all of human wisdom dies.

1:20 Where is the wise man? Paul paraphrased Is 19:12, where the prophet was referring to the wise men of Egypt who promised, but never produced wisdom. Human wisdom always proves to be unreliable and impermanent (*cf. v. 17; Pr 14:12; Is 29:14; Jer 8:9;* Ro 1:18–23). **scribe.** Probably Paul has in mind the Assyrians, who sent scribes along with their soldiers to record the booty taken in battle. God saw to it they had nothing to record (Is 33:18). **debater.** This was a Gr. word with no OT counterpart, identifying those who were adept at arguing philosophy.

1:21 in the wisdom of God. God wisely established that men could not come to know Him by human wisdom. That would exalt man, so God designed to save helpless sinners through the preaching of a message that was so simple the "worldly wise" deemed it nonsense. Cf. Rom 1:18–23. **who believe.** From the human side, salvation requires and comes only through faith. Cf. Jn 1:12; Ro 10:8–17.

1:22 signs. Unbelieving Jews still wanted supernatural signs (Mt 12:38–44), yet they refused to accept the most glorious of all the supernatural sign-works of God, namely providing salvation through a virgin-born, crucified, and risen Messiah. In fact, the sign was a stumbling block to them (cf. Ro 9:31–33). **wisdom.** Gentiles wanted proof by means of human reason, through ideas they could set forth, discuss, and debate. Like the Athenian philosophers, they were not sincere, with no interest in divine truth, but merely wanting to argue intellectual novelty (Ac 17:21).

1:23 Christ crucified. The only true sign and the only true wisdom. This alone was the message Paul would preach (2:2) because it alone had the power to save all who believed.

1:24, 25 called. *See note on v. 9.* To all the "called," the message of the cross, which seems so pointless and irrelevant to man's proud, natural mind, actually exhibits God's greatest power and greatest wisdom.

1:26–28 God disdained human wisdom, not only by disallowing it as a means to knowing Him, but also by choosing to save the lowly. He does not call to salvation many whom the world would call wise, mighty, and noble (cf. Mt 11:25; 18:3, 4). God's wisdom is revealed to the foolish, weak, and common, i.e., those considered nothing by the elite, who trust in Jesus Christ as Savior and Lord. God clearly received all the credit and the glory for causing such lowly ones to know Him and the eternal truths of His heavenly kingdom. No saved sinner can boast that he has achieved salvation by his intellect (v. 29).

1:30, 31 The redeemed not only are given salvation by God's wisdom rather than by their own, but are also graciously given ("by His doing") a measure of His divine wisdom, as well as imputed righteousness (Ro 4:5; 2Co 5:21), sanctification from sin (Eph 2:10), and redemption by God (Eph 1:14; 1Pe 1:18, 19) in order that, above all else, the Lord will be glorified (cf. Gal 6:4).

1:31 Quoted from Jer 9:24.

2:1 superiority of speech or of wisdom. *See notes on 1:20–22.*

2:2 crucified. Though Paul expounded the whole counsel of God to the church (Ac 20:27) and taught the Corinthians the Word of God (Ac 18:11), the focus of his preaching and teaching to unbelievers was Jesus Christ, who paid the penalty for sin on the cross (Ac 20:20; 2Co 4:2; 2Ti 4:1, 2). Until someone understands and believes the gospel, there is nothing more to say to them. The preaching of the cross (1:18) was so dominant in the early church that believers were accused of worshiping a dead man.

2:3 weakness … fear … trembling. Paul came to Corinth after being beaten and imprisoned in Philippi, run out of Thessalonica and Berea, and scoffed at in Athens (Ac 16:22–24; 17:10, 13, 14, 32), so he may have been physically weak. But in that weakness, he was most powerful (see vv. 4, 5; 2Co 12:9, 10) There were no theatrics or techniques to manipulate people's response. His fear and shaking were because of the seriousness of his mission.

4 and my [a]message and my preaching were [A]not in persuasive words of wisdom, but in demonstration of [B]the Spirit and of power, 5 so that your faith would not [a]rest on the wisdom of men, but on [A]the power of God.

6 Yet we do speak wisdom among those who are [A]mature; a wisdom, however, not of [B]this age nor of the rulers of [B]this age, who are [C]passing away; 7 but we speak God's wisdom in a [A]mystery, the hidden *wisdom* which God [B]predestined before the [C]ages to our glory; 8 *the wisdom* [A]which none of the rulers of [B]this age has understood; for if they had understood it they would not have crucified [C]the Lord of glory; 9 but just as it is written,

> "[A]Things which eye has not seen
> And ear has not heard,
> And *which* have not entered
> the heart of man,
> All that God has prepared for
> those who love Him."

10 [a,A]For to us God revealed *them* [B]through the Spirit; for the Spirit searches all things, even the [C]depths of God. 11 For who among men knows the *thoughts* of a man except the [A]spirit of the man which is in him? Even so the *thoughts* of God no one knows except the Spirit of God. 12 Now we [A]have received, not the spirit of [B]the world, but the Spirit who is from God, so that we may know the things freely given to us by God, 13 which things we also speak, [A]not in words taught by human wisdom, but in those taught by the Spirit, [a]combining spiritual *thoughts* with spiritual *words*.

14 But [a]a [A]natural man [B]does not accept the things of the Spirit of God, for they are [C]foolishness to him; and he cannot understand them, because they are spiritually [b]appraised. 15 But he who is [A]spiritual appraises all things, yet he himself is appraised by no one. 16 For [A]who has known the mind of the Lord, that he will instruct Him? But [B]we have the mind of Christ.

FOUNDATIONS FOR LIVING

3 And I, brethren, could not speak to you as to [A]spiritual men, but as to [B]men of flesh, as to [C]infants in Christ. 2 I gave you [A]milk to drink, not solid food; for you [B]were not yet able *to receive it*. Indeed, even now you are not yet able, 3 for you are still fleshly. For since there is [A]jealousy and strife among you, are you not fleshly, and are you not walking [a,B]like mere men? 4 For when [A]one says, "I am of Paul," and another, "I am of Apollos," are you not *mere* [B]men?

2:4 [a]Lit *word* [A]1 Cor 1:17; 2:1, 13 [B]Rom 15:19; 1 Cor 4:20 2:5 [a]Lit *be* [A]2 Cor 4:7; 6:7; 12:9 2:6 [A]Eph 4:13; Phil 3:15; Heb 5:14; 6:1 [B]Matt 13:22; 1 Cor 1:20 [C]1 Cor 1:28 2:7 [A]Rom 11:25; 16:25f; 1 Cor 2:1 [B]Rom 8:29f [C]Heb 1:2; 11:3 2:8 [A]1 Cor 1:26; 2:6 [B]Matt 13:22; 1 Cor 1:20 [C]Acts 7:2; James 2:1 2:9 [A]Is 64:4; 65:17 2:10 [a]One early ms reads *But* [A]Matt 11:25; 13:11; 16:17; Gal 1:12; Eph 3:3, 5 [B]John 14:26 [C]Rom 11:33ff 2:11 [A]Prov 20:27 2:12 [A]Rom 8:15 [B]1 Cor 1:27 2:13 [a]Or *interpreting spiritual* things *for spiritual* men [A]1 Cor 1:17; 2:1, 4 2:14 [a]Or *an unspiritual* [b]Or *examined* [A]1 Cor 15:44, 46; James 3:15; Jude 19 mg [B]John 14:17 [C]1 Cor 1:18 2:15 [A]1 Cor 3:1; 14:37; Gal 6:1 2:16 [A]Is 40:13; Rom 11:34 [B]John 15:15 3:1 [A]1 Cor 2:15; 14:37; Gal 6:1 [B]Rom 7:14; 1 Cor 2:14 [C]1 Cor 2:6; Eph 4:14; Heb 5:13 3:2 [A]Heb 5:12f; 1 Pet 2:2 [B]John 16:12 3:3 [a]Lit *according to man* [A]Rom 13:13; 1 Cor 1:10f; 11:18 [B]1 Cor 3:4 3:4 [A]1 Cor 1:12 [B]1 Cor 3:3

2:6 mature. Paul uses this word to refer to genuine believers who have been saved by Christ, as in Heb 6:1; 10:14. **rulers.** Those in authority. *See notes on 1:19, 20.* **this age.** All periods of human history until the Lord returns.

2:7 mystery. This term does not refer to something puzzling, but to truth known to God before time, which He has kept secret until the appropriate time for Him to reveal it. *See notes on Mt 13:11; Eph 3:4, 5.* **to our glory.** The truth God established before time and revealed in the NT wisdom of the gospel is the truth that God will save and glorify sinners. *See notes on Eph 3:8–12.*

2:8 if they had understood. The crucifixion is proof that the rulers/Jewish religious leaders lacked wisdom. Cf. 1Ti 1:12, 13.

2:9 These words from Is 64:4, often incorrectly thought to refer to the wonders of heaven, refer rather to the wisdom God has prepared for believers. God's truth is not discoverable by eye or ear (objective, empirical evidence), nor is it discovered by the mind (subjective, rational conclusions).

2:10–16 The wisdom that saves, which man's wisdom can't know, is revealed to us by God. He makes it known by revelation, inspiration, and illumination. Revelation (vv. 10, 11) and inspiration (vv. 12, 13) were given to those who wrote the Bible; illumination (vv. 14–16) is given to all believers who seek to know and understand that divinely written truth. In each case, the Holy Spirit is the divine agent doing the work (cf. 2Pe 1:21).

2:10 to us. As with the "we's" in vv. 6, 7 and vv. 12, 13, Paul is, first of all, speaking of himself (as in Jn 14:26; 15:26, 27; *see notes there*), and, in a sense, of believers who have been given the Word as recorded by the apostles and their associates who wrote the NT. **God revealed *them*.** By the Holy Spirit, God disclosed His saving truth (cf. Mt 11:25; 13:10–13). The Spirit alone was qualified because He knows all that God knows, Himself being God.

2:12 we have received ... given to us. The "we" and "us" refer to the apostles and other writers of the Word of God. The means was inspiration (*see notes on 2Ti 3:16; 2Pe 1:20, 21*), by which God freely gave the gift of His Word. It was this process of inspiration that turned the spiritual thoughts into spiritual words (v. 13) to give life (cf. Mt 4:4).

2:14 natural man. This refers to the unconverted, who lack supernatural life and wisdom. **spiritually appraised.** Through illumination of the Word, the Holy Spirit provides His saints the capacity to discern divine truth (see Ps 119:18), which the spiritually dead are unable to comprehend (cf. Jn 5:37–39; *see notes on 1Jn 2:20, 27*). The doctrine of illumination does not mean we know everything (cf. Dt 29:29), that we do not need teachers (cf. Eph 4:11, 12), or that understanding does not require hard work (cf. 2Ti 2:15).

2:15 appraised by no one. Obviously, unbelievers are able to recognize Christians' faults and shortcomings; but they are not able to evaluate their true nature as spiritual people who have been transformed into children of God (cf. 1Jn 3:2).

2:16 the mind of the **LORD.** Quoted from Is 40:13. The same word can be translated "understanding." Believers are allowed, by the Word and the Spirit, to know the thoughts of their Lord. Cf. Lk 24:45.

3:1 The cause of problems in the church was more than external, worldly influence. It was also internal carnality. The pressures of the world were combined with the weakness of the flesh. **flesh.** Although Corinthian believers were no longer "natural," they were not "spiritual" (fully controlled by the Holy Spirit). In fact, they were controlled by the fallen flesh. Though all believers have the Holy Spirit (cf. Ro 8:9) they still battle the fallen "flesh" (*see notes on Ro 7:14–25; 8:23*). **infants in Christ.** The carnality of those believers was indicative of their immaturity. They had no excuse for not being mature, since Paul implied that he should have been able to write to them as mature, in light of all he had taught them (v. 2). *See notes on Heb 5:12–14; 1Pe 2:1, 2.*

3:2 milk. Not a reference to certain doctrines, but to the more easily digestible truths of doctrine that were given to new believers. **solid food.** The deeper features of the doctrines of Scripture. The difference is not in kind of truth, but degree of depth. Spiritual immaturity makes one unable to receive the richest truths.

3:3 jealousy and strife. The fallen flesh, or carnality, produces the attitude of jealousy, a severe form of selfishness, which produces the action of strife and the subsequent divisions. **mere men.** Apart from the will of the Spirit, hence carnal, not spiritual.

3:4 Paul ... Apollos. Factionalism was the divisive product of carnality. Cf. 1:11–13.

5 What then is Apollos? And what is Paul? [A]Ser-
vants through whom you believed, even [B]as the
Lord gave *opportunity* to each one. 6 [A]I planted,
[B]Apollos watered, but [C]God was causing the
growth. 7 So then neither the one who plants nor
the one who waters is anything, but God who
causes the growth. 8 Now he who plants and he
who waters are one; but each will [A]receive his
own [a]reward according to his own labor. 9 For we
are God's [A]fellow workers; you are God's [a,B]field,
God's [C]building.

10 According to [A]the grace of God which was given
to me, like a wise master builder [B]I laid a foundation,
and [C]another is building on it. But each man must
be careful how he builds on it. 11 For no man can
lay a [A]foundation other than the one which is laid,
which is Jesus Christ. 12 Now if any man builds on
the foundation with gold, silver, [a]precious stones,
wood, hay, straw, 13 [A]each man's work will become
evident; for [B]the day will show it because it is *to be*
revealed with fire, and the fire itself will test [a]the
quality of each man's work. 14 If any man's work
which he has built on it remains, he will [A]receive a
reward. 15 If any man's work is burned up, he will
suffer loss; but he himself will be saved, yet [A]so as
through fire.

16 [A]Do you not know that [B]you are a [a]temple of
God and *that* the Spirit of God dwells in you? 17 If
any man destroys the [a]temple of God, God will destroy him, for the [a]temple of God is holy, and [b]that
is what you are.

18 [A]Let no man deceive himself. [B]If any man
among you thinks that he is wise in [C]this age, he
must become foolish, so that he may become wise.
19 For [A]the wisdom of this world is foolishness before
God. For it is written, "*He is* [B]THE ONE WHO CATCHES
THE WISE IN THEIR CRAFTINESS"; 20 and again, "[A]THE
LORD KNOWS THE REASONINGS of the wise, THAT THEY
ARE USELESS." 21 So then [A]let no one boast in men.
For [B]all things belong to you, 22 [A]whether Paul or
Apollos or Cephas or the world or [B]life or death or
things present or things to come; all things belong
to you, 23 and [A]you belong to Christ; and [B]Christ
belongs to God.

SERVANTS OF CHRIST

4 Let a man regard us in this manner, as [A]ser-
vants of Christ and [B]stewards of [C]the mysteries

3:5 [A]Rom 15:16; 2 Cor 3:3, 6; 4:1; 5:18; 6:4; Eph 3:7; Col 1:25; 1 Tim 1:12 [B]Rom 12:6; 1 Cor 3:10 3:6 [A]1 Cor 4:15; 9:1; 15:1; 2 Cor 10:14f [B]Acts 18:24-27; 1 Cor 1:12 [C]1 Cor 15:10 3:8 [a]Or *wages* [A]1 Cor 3:14; 4:5; 9:17; Gal 6:4 3:9 [a]Or *cultivated land* [A]Mark 16:20; 2 Cor 6:1 [B]Is 61:3; Matt 15:13 [C]1 Cor 3:16; Eph 2:20-22; Col 2:7; 1 Pet 2:5 3:10 [A]Rom 12:3; 1 Cor 15:10 [B]Rom 15:20; 1 Cor 3:11f [C]1 Thess 3:2 3:11 [A]Is 28:16; Eph 2:20; 1 Pet 2:4ff 3:12 [a]Or *costly* 3:13 [a]Lit *of what sort each man's work is* [A]1 Cor 4:5 [B]Matt 10:15; 1 Cor 1:8; 2 Thess 1:7-10; 2 Tim 1:12, 18; 4:8 3:14 [A]1 Cor 3:8; 4:5; 9:17; Gal 6:4 3:15 [A]Job 23:10; Ps 66:10, 12; Jude 23 3:16 [a]Or *sanctuary* [A]Rom 6:16 [B]Rom 8:9; 1 Cor 6:19; 2 Cor 6:16; Eph 2:21f 3:17 [a]Or *sanctuary* [b]Lit *who you are* 3:18 [A]Is 5:21 [B]1 Cor 8:2; Gal 6:3 [C]1 Cor 1:20 3:19 [A]1 Cor 1:20 [B]Job 5:13 3:20 [A]Ps 94:11 3:21 [A]1 Cor 4:6 [B]Rom 8:32 3:22 [A]1 Cor 1:12; 3:5, 6 [B]Rom 8:38 3:23 [A]1 Cor 15:23; 2 Cor 10:7; Gal 3:29 [B]1 Cor 11:3; 15:28 4:1 [A]Luke 1:2 [B]1 Cor 9:17; Titus 1:7; 1 Pet 4:10 [C]Rom 11:25; 16:25

3:5–7 What then is Apollos … Paul? A humble, but accurate assessment of the roles that ministers play. **the Lord gave … God who causes the growth.** It is the Lord alone who can give the faith to the spiritually ignorant and dead. Salvation is God's work of grace to whom He chooses to give it (*see notes on Ro 9:15–19; Eph 2:8, 9*).

3:8 are one. All the human instruments God uses to produce salvation life are equally considered and rewarded for their willingness to be used by God. But all the glory goes to Him, who alone saves. Because of that, the silly favoritism of v. 4; 1:12 is condemned. *See notes on Mt 20:1–16.*

3:9 we. Paul, Apollos, Peter, and all ministers are equal workers in the field, but the spiritual life from that field is entirely by God's grace and power. **God's building.** Paul shifts the imagery from agricultural to construction (vv. 10–17).

3:10 master builder … foundation. The Gr. word is the root for architect, but contained the idea of builder as well as designer. Paul's specialty was designing and building spiritual foundations (cf. Ro 15:20). He was used by God to establish the groundwork for churches in Asia Minor, Macedonia, and Greece. Others (e.g., Timothy, Apollos) built the churches up from his foundations. That God used him in that way was all of grace (cf. v. 7; 15:20; Ro 15:18; Eph 3:7, 8; Col 1:29). **each man.** This primarily refers to evangelists and pastor-teachers.

3:11 no … foundation other than. Paul did not design the foundation, he only laid it down by preaching Christ. Cf. 1Pe 2:6–8.

3:12 if any man builds. This is, first of all, in reference to the evangelists and pastors (v. 9), and then to all believers who are called to build the church through faithful ministry. **gold, silver, precious stones.** His quality materials represent dedicated, spiritual service to build the church. **wood, hay, straw.** Inferior materials implying shallow activity with no eternal value. They do not necessarily refer to activities that are evil (*see note on v. 13*).

3:13 the day. Refers to the time of the Judgment Seat of Christ (*see notes on 2Co 5:10*). **revealed with fire.** The fire of God's discerning judgment (cf. Job 23:10; Zec 13:9; 1Pe 1:17, 18; Rev 3:18). Second Corinthians 5:10 indicates that the wood, hay, and straw are "worthless" things that don't stand the test of judgment fire (*see note there*; cf. Col 2:18).

3:14 remains. All that which has been accomplished in His power and for His glory will survive (cf. Mt 25:21, 23; 2Co 5:9; Php 3:13, 14; 1Th 2:19, 20; 2Ti 4:7, 8; Jas 1:12; 1Pe 5:4; Rev 22:12). **reward.** Cf. Rev 22:12. This is not a judgment for sin. Christ has paid that price (Ro 8:1), so that no believer will ever be judged for sin. This is only to determine eternal reward (cf. 4:5, "each man's praise").

3:15 be saved. No matter how much is worthless, no believer will forfeit salvation.

3:16, 17 Here is a severe warning to any who would try to interfere with or destroy the building of the church on the foundation of Christ. *See notes on Mt 18:6, 7.*

3:18, 19a deceive himself. *See notes on 1:18–25.* Those who defile the church and think they can succeed in destroying it by their human wisdom would be far better to reject that wisdom and accept the foolishness of Christ's cross.

3:19b, 20 With quotations from Job 5:13 and Ps 94:11, Paul reinforces his point from 1:18–25 by reminding them that human wisdom which cannot save, also cannot either build a church or prevent its growth.

3:21 boast in men. Cf. v. 4; 1:12. Paul, Apollos, and all others receive no credit for the building of the church. **all things belong to you.** All believers share equally in God's most important and valuable provisions and glories; human boasting, therefore, is ludicrous as well as sinful.

3:22 the world. Although the universe is now in Satan's grip, it is still the God-given and God-made possession of Christians (2Co 4:15; 1Jn 5:19). In the millennial kingdom and throughout eternity, however, believers will possess both the recreated and eternal earth in an infinitely more complete and rich way (Mt 5:5; Rev 21). **life.** Spiritual, eternal life (cf. Jn 14:23; cf. 2Pe 1:3, 4). **death.** Spiritual and eternal death (15:54–57; Php 1:21–24). **things present.** Everything the believer has or experiences in this life (cf. Ro 8:37–39). **things to come.** All the blessings of heaven. Cf. 1Pe 1:3, 4. **all things belong to you.** In Christ, all good and holy things are for believers' blessing and for God's glory. Cf. Eph 1:3; 2Pe 1:3.

3:23 Christ … God. Knowing that believers belong to Christ and therefore to one another is the greatest incentive for unity in the church (6:17; Jn 9:9, 10, 21–23; Php 2:1–4).

4:1 regard us. Paul wanted everyone to view him and his fellow ministers only as the humble messengers God ordained them to be (cf. 3:9, 22). **servants.** Paul expresses his humility by using a word lit. meaning "under rowers," referring to the lowest, most menial, and most despised galley slaves, who rowed on the bottom tier of a ship (9:16; see Lk 1:2; Ac 20:19). **stewards.** Paul defines his responsibilities as an apostle by using a word originally referring to a person entrusted with and responsible for his master's entire household: e.g., buildings, fields, finances, food,

of God. 2 In this case, moreover, it is required [a]of stewards that one be found trustworthy. 3 But to me it is a very small thing that I may be examined by you, or by *any* human [a]court; in fact, I do not even examine myself. 4 For I [A]am conscious of nothing against myself, yet I am not by this [B]acquitted; but the one who examines me is the Lord. 5 Therefore [A]do not go on [a]passing judgment before [b]the time, *but wait* [B]until the Lord comes who will both [C]bring to light the things hidden in the darkness and disclose the motives of *men's* hearts; and then each man's [D]praise will come to him from God.

6 Now these things, brethren, I have figuratively applied to myself and Apollos for your sakes, so that in us you may learn not to exceed [A]what is written, so that no one of you will [B]become [a]arrogant [C]in behalf of one against the other. 7 For who regards you as superior? [A]What do you have that you did not receive? And if you did receive it, why do you boast as if you had not received it?

8 You are [A]already filled, you have already become rich, you have become kings without us; and indeed, *I* wish that you had become kings so that we also might reign with you. 9 For, I think, God has exhibited us apostles last of all, as men [A]condemned to death; because we [B]have become a spectacle to the world, [a]both to angels and to men. 10 We are [A]fools for Christ's sake, but [B]you are prudent in Christ; [C]we are weak, but you are strong; you are distinguished, but we are without honor. 11 To this present hour we are both [A]hungry and thirsty, and are poorly clothed, and are roughly treated, and are homeless; 12 and we toil, [A]working with our own hands; when we are [B]reviled, we bless; when we are [C]persecuted, we endure; 13 when we are slandered, we try to [a]conciliate; we have [A]become as the scum of the world, the dregs of all things, *even* until now.

14 I do not write these things to [A]shame you, but to admonish you as my beloved [B]children. 15 For if you were to have countless [A]tutors in Christ, yet *you would* not *have* many fathers, for in [B]Christ Jesus I [C]became your father through the [D]gospel. 16 Therefore I exhort you, be [A]imitators of me. 17 For this reason I [A]have sent to you [B]Timothy, who is my [C]beloved and faithful child in the Lord, and he will remind you of my ways which are in Christ, [D]just as I teach

4:2 [a]Lit *in* 4:3 [a]Lit *day* 4:4 [A]Acts 23:1; 2 Cor 1:12 [B]Ps 143:2; Rom 2:13 4:5 [a]Lit *judging anything* [b]I.e. the appointed time of judgment [A]Matt 7:1; Rom 2:1 [B]John 21:22; Rom 2:16 [C]1 Cor 3:13 [D]Rom 2:29; 1 Cor 3:8; 2 Cor 10:18 4:6 [a]Lit *puffed up* [A]1 Cor 1:19, 31; 3:19f [B]1 Cor 4:18f; 8:1; 13:4 [C]1 Cor 1:12; 3:4 4:7 [A]John 3:27; Rom 12:3, 6; 1 Pet 4:10 4:8 [A]Rev 3:17f 4:9 [a]Or *and to angels and to men* [A]Rom 8:36; 1 Cor 15:31; 2 Cor 11:23 [B]Heb 10:33 4:10 [A]Acts 17:18; 26:24; 1 Cor 1:18 [B]1 Cor 1:19f; 3:18; 2 Cor 11:19 [C]1 Cor 2:3; 2 Cor 13:9 4:11 [A]Rom 8:35; 2 Cor 11:23-27 4:12 [A]Acts 18:3 [B]1 Pet 3:9 [C]John 15:20; Rom 8:35 4:13 [a]Or *console* [A]Lam 3:45 4:14 [A]1 Cor 6:5; 15:34 [B]2 Cor 6:13; 12:14; 1 Thess 2:11; 1 John 2:1; 3 John 4 4:15 [A]Gal 3:24f [B]1 Cor 1:30 [C]Num 11:12; 1 Cor 3:8; Gal 4:19; Philem 10 [D]1 Cor 9:12, 14, 18, 23; 15:1 4:16 [A]1 Cor 11:1; Phil 3:17; 4:9; 1 Thess 1:6; 2 Thess 3:9 4:17 [A]1 Cor 16:10 [B]Acts 16:1 [C]1 Cor 4:14; 1 Tim 1:2, 18; 2 Tim 1:2 [D]1 Cor 7:17; 14:33; 16:1; Titus 1:5

other servants, and sometimes even children of the owner. Cf. 1Pe 4:10. **mysteries of God.** "Mysteries" is used in the NT to refer to divine revelation previously hidden. *See notes on 2:7; Mt 13:11; Eph 3:4, 5.* Here the word is used in its broadest sense as God's full revealed truth in the NT (Ac 20:20, 21, 27; 2Ti 2:15; 3:16). It was all that truth which Paul had to oversee and dispense as God's servant and steward.

4:2 trustworthy. The most essential quality of a servant or steward is obedient loyalty to his master (v. 17; 7:25; cf. Mt 24:45–51; Col 1:7; 4:7).

4:3 human court. Paul is not being arrogant or saying that he is above fellow ministers, other Christians, or even certain unbelievers. He is saying that a human verdict on his life is not the one that matters, even if it was his own.

4:4 nothing against myself. Paul was not aware of any unconfessed or habitual sin in his own life, but his limited understanding assumed that his was not the final verdict (*see note on 2Co 1:12*). **not by this acquitted.** Paul's own sincere evaluation of his life did not acquit him of all failures to be faithful. **the Lord.** He is the ultimate and only qualified Judge of any man's obedience and faithfulness (2Ti 2:15). *See notes on 2Co 5:9, 10.*

4:5 things hidden in the darkness ... motives of *men's* hearts. These refer to the inner motives, thoughts, and attitudes which only God can know. Since final rewards will be based, not just on outward service, but on inward devotion (cf. 10:31), only God can give the praise each deserves. *See notes on 3:12–14.*

4:6 these things. Paul is referring to the analogies he used to depict those who minister for the Lord, including himself and Apollos: farmers (3:6–9), builders (3:10–15), and servant-stewards (vv. 1–5). **your sakes.** Paul's humility, expressed in light of God's judgment on the greatest apostles and preachers, was useful to teach believers not to exalt any of them (cf. Ge 18:27; 32:10; Ex 3:11; Jdg 6:15; Mt 3:14; Lk 5:8; Jn 1:26, 27; Ac 20:19; 2Co 3:5; Eph 3:8). **what is written.** God's faithful servants are to be treated with respect only within the bounds of what is scriptural (1Th 5:12; 1Ti 5:17; Heb 13:7, 17). **arrogant.** Pride and arrogance were great problems in the Corinthian church (see vv. 18, 19; 5:2; 8:1; 13:4; 2Co 12:20).

4:7 boast. Pride is deception, since everything a person possesses is from God's providential hand (cf. 1Ch 29:11–16; Job 1:21; Jas 1:17).

4:8 filled ... rich ... reign. In a severe rebuke, Paul heaps on false praise, sarcastically suggesting that those Corinthians who were self-satisfied had already achieved spiritual greatness. They were similar to the Laodiceans (see Rev 3:17). Cf. Php 3:12; 2Ti 4:8; Jas 1:12; 1Pe 5:4. **reign.** Yet, Paul genuinely wished it really were the coronation time of the Millennium, so that they all might share in the glory of the Lord.

4:9 last. The imagery is of condemned prisoners brought into a Roman arena to fight and die; the last ones brought out for slaughter were the grand finale. In His sovereign wisdom and for His ultimate glory, God chose to display the apostles figuratively before men and angels during the present age as just such worthless and condemned spectacles (cf. Mt 19:28). Like doomed gladiators, they were ridiculed, spit on, imprisoned, and beaten; yet, God glorified His name through them as He used them to build His kingdom.

4:10 fools ... prudent. Again using sarcasm, this time on himself as if mimicking the attitude of the proud Corinthians toward him, Paul rebukes them (cf. Ac 17:18).

4:11–13 The apostles and early preachers lived at the lowest levels of society. While the Corinthian believers thought they were kings (v. 8), the apostle knew he was a suffering slave (cf. 2Co 1:8, 9; 4:8–12; 6:4–10; 11:23–28).

4:12 our own hands. The apostles did manual labor which Greeks, including some in the church at Corinth, considered beneath their dignity and suitable only for slaves. But Paul was not resentful about any necessary labor needed to support gospel preaching (cf. Ac 18:3; 20:34; 2Co 11:23–28; 1Th 2:9; 2Th 3:8; 2Ti 3:12).

4:13 scum ... dregs. The filth scraped from a dirty dish or garbage pot, figuratively used of the lowest, most degraded criminals who were often sacrificed in pagan ceremonies. Not in God's sight, but in the world's, Paul and his fellow preachers were so designated. What a rebuke of the proud, fleshly Corinthians who saw themselves at the top, while the humble apostle considered himself at the bottom.

4:14 admonish. Lit. "put in mind," with the purpose of admonishing and reproving, presupposing that something is wrong and should be corrected (cf. Mt 18:15–20; Ac 20:31; 1Th 2:7–12; 5:14). **beloved children.** Despite their fleshly, even sometimes hateful, immaturity, Paul always looked on the Corinthian believers with affection (cf. 2Co 12:14, 15; Gal 4:19; Php 1:23–27; 3Jn 4).

4:15 countless tutors. This refers to an unlimited number of moral guardians used with children. Only Paul was their spiritual father; hence, no one cared like him.

4:16 be imitators of me. See 11:1. A bold, but justified exhortation. Spiritual leaders must set an example of Christlikeness to follow (cf. 1Ti 4:12; Heb 13:7).

4:17 Timothy. He had been so faithfully discipled by Paul that he could be sent in the great apostle's place with confidence that he would perfectly represent him. Cf. 2Ti 2:2; 3:10–14. **I teach.** Referring to doctrine, not advice. By his own instruction and example, Timothy would reinforce the eternal truths Paul had taught him.

everywhere in every church. 18 Now some have become [a][A]arrogant, as though I were not [B]coming to
you. 19 But I [A]will come to you soon, [B]if the Lord wills,
and I shall find out, not the [a]words of those who are
[C]arrogant but their power. 20 For the kingdom of God
does [A]not consist in [a]words but in power. 21 What do
you desire? [A]Shall I come to you with a rod, or with
love and a spirit of gentleness?

IMMORALITY REBUKED

5 It is actually reported that there is immorality among you, and immorality of such a kind
as does not exist even among the Gentiles, that
someone has [A]his father's wife. 2 [a]You [A]have become
[b]arrogant and [a]have not [B]mourned instead, so that
the one who had done this deed would be [C]removed
from your midst.

3 For I, on my part, though [A]absent in body but
present in spirit, have already judged him who has
so committed this, as though I were present. 4 [A]In
the name of our Lord Jesus, when you are assembled, and [a]I with you in spirit, [B]with the power of
our Lord Jesus, 5 *I have decided* to [A]deliver such
a one to [B]Satan for the destruction of his flesh,
so that his spirit may be saved in [C]the day of the
Lord [a]Jesus.

6 [A]Your boasting is not good. [B]Do you not know
that [C]a little leaven leavens the whole lump *of*
dough? 7 Clean out the old leaven so that you may
be a new lump, just as you are *in fact* unleavened.
For Christ our [A]Passover also has been sacrificed.
8 Therefore let us celebrate the feast, [A]not with old
leaven, nor with the leaven of malice and wickedness, but with the unleavened bread of sincerity
and truth.

9 I wrote you in my letter [A]not to associate with
immoral people; 10 I *did* not at all *mean* with the
immoral people of this world, or with the covetous
and swindlers, or with [A]idolaters, for then you would
have to go out of the world. 11 But [a]actually, I wrote
to you not to associate [b]with any so-called [A]brother
if he is an immoral person, or covetous, or [B]an idolater, or a reviler, or a drunkard, or a swindler—not
even to eat with such a one. 12 For what have I to do
with judging [A]outsiders? [B]Do you not judge those
who are within *the church?* 13 But those who are
outside, God [a]judges. [A]REMOVE THE WICKED MAN
FROM AMONG YOURSELVES.

4:18 [a]Lit *puffed up* [A]1 Cor 4:6 [B]1 Cor 4:21 4:19 [a]Lit *word* [A]Acts 19:21; 20:2; 1 Cor 11:34; 16:5f; 16:7-9; 2 Cor 1:15f [B]Acts 18:21 [C]1 Cor 4:6 4:20 [a]Lit *word* [A]1 Cor 2:4 4:21 [A]2 Cor 1:23; 2:1, 3; 12:20; 13:2, 10 5:1 [A]Lev 18:8; Deut 22:30; 27:20 5:2 [a]Or *have you...?* [b]Lit *puffed up* [A]1 Cor 4:6 [B]2 Cor 7:7-10 [C]1 Cor 5:13 5:3 [A]Col 2:5; 1 Thess 2:17 5:4 [a]Lit *my spirit, with the power* [A]2 Thess 3:6 [B]John 20:23; 2 Cor 2:10; 13:3, 10 5:5 [a]Two early mss do not contain *Jesus* [A]Prov 23:14; Luke 22:31; 1 Tim 1:20 [B]Matt 4:10 [C]1 Cor 1:8 5:6 [A]1 Cor 5:2; James 4:16 [B]Rom 6:16 [C]Hos 7:4; Matt 16:6, 12; Gal 5:9 5:7 [A]Mark 14:12; 1 Pet 1:19 5:8 [A]Ex 12:19; 13:7; Deut 16:3 5:9 [A]2 Cor 6:14; Eph 5:11; 2 Thess 3:6 5:10 [A]1 Cor 10:27 5:11 [a]Lit *now* [b]Lit *together if any man called a brother is* [A]Acts 1:15; 2 Thess 3:6 [B]1 Cor 10:7, 14, 20f 5:12 [A]Mark 4:11 [B]1 Cor 5:3-5; 6:1-4 5:13 [a]Or *will judge* [A]Deut 13:5; 17:7, 12; 21:21; 22:21; 1 Cor 5:2

4:18, 19 arrogant. They were full of pride, thinking they would never have to face Paul again. But, if God allowed, he was planning to see them soon. He would not let their proud sinning go unchallenged, for their own sake as well as the gospel's (cf. Heb 12:6). The reality of how much real spiritual power they had would become clear in that confrontation.

4:20 words ... power. Spiritual character is measured not by the impressiveness of words, but in the power of the life (cf. Mt 7:21–23).

4:21 rod. Spiritual leaders need to use the rod of correction if people persist in sin. The pattern for that correction is illustrated and explained in 5:1–13; cf. Mt 18:15–18.

5:1 immorality. This sin was so vile that even the church's pagan neighbors were doubtless scandalized by it. The Corinthians had rationalized or minimized this sin which was common knowledge, even though Paul had written them before about it (v. 9). The Gr. for "immorality" is the root of the Eng. word "pornography." **his father's wife.** The man's stepmother, with whom having sexual relations bore the same sinful stigma as if between him and his natural mother. Incest was punishable by death in the OT (Lv 18:7, 8, 29; cf. Dt 22:30) and was both uncommon ("does not exist") and illegal under Roman law.

5:2 arrogant. So prideful and fleshly as to excuse even that extreme wickedness. **removed.** Excommunicated as in v. 7 (see Mt 18:15–17; Eph 5:3, 11; 2Th 3:6).

5:3 already judged. Paul had passed judgment on the sinner, and the church also needed to.

5:4 name of our Lord. Consistent with His holy person and will. **assembled.** This action is to be done when the church meets publicly (*see notes on Mt 18:15–18*). **power.** Authority is in view. Action against unrepentant sinning in the church carries the weight of the Lord's authority.

5:5 deliver ... to Satan. "Deliver" is a strong term, used of judicial sentencing. This is equal to excommunicating the professed believer. It amounts to putting that person out of the blessing of Christian worship and fellowship by thrusting him into Satan's realm, the world system. *See note on 1Ti 1:20.* **the destruction of his flesh.** This refers to divine chastening for sin that can result in illness and even death. *See notes on 11:29–32*; cf. Ac 5:1–11. **spirit ... saved.** The unrepentant person may suffer greatly under God's judgment, but will not be an evil influence in the church; and he will more likely be saved under that judgment than if tolerated and accepted in the church. **day of the Lord Jesus.** This is the time when the Lord returns with His rewards for His people. *See note on 1:8.*

5:6 boasting. It was not good because their proud sense of satisfaction blinded them to their duty in regard to blatant sin that devastated the church. **leaven.** *See note on Mk 8:15.* In Scripture, it is used to represent influence, in most cases evil influence, although in Mt 13:33 it refers to the good influence of the kingdom of heaven (cf. Ex 13:3, 7). **whole lump.** When tolerated, sin will permeate and corrupt the whole local church.

5:7 Christ our Passover. Just as unleavened bread symbolized being freed from Egypt by the Passover (Ex 12:15–17), so the church is to be unleavened, since it has been separated from the dominion of sin and death by the perfect Passover Lamb, the Lord Jesus Christ. The church is, therefore, to remove everything sinful in order to be separate from the old life, including the influence of sinful church members.

5:8 celebrate the feast. In contrast to the OT Passover feast celebrated annually, believers constantly celebrate the "feast" of the new Passover—Jesus Christ. As the Jews who celebrate Passover do so with unleavened bread, so believers celebrate their continual Passover with unleavened lives.

5:9 my letter. A previous letter that Paul had written the church at Corinth instructed them to disassociate with the immoral (cf. v. 11; 2Th 3:6–15).

5:10 people of this world. Evidently, the church had misinterpreted the advice in that letter and had stopped having contact with the unsaved in the world, while continuing to tolerate the sin of those in the church, which was even more dangerous to the fellowship. See Jn 17:15, 18. God intends us to be in the world as witnesses (cf. Mt 5:13–16; Ac 1:8; Php 2:15).

5:11 any so-called brother. Paul clarifies his intention in the earlier letter. He expected them to disassociate with all who said they were brothers, but had a consistent pattern of sin. **not even to eat.** The meal was a sign of acceptance and fellowship in those days. See 2Th 3:6, 14.

5:12, 13 outsiders. Paul never intended himself or the church to be judges of unbelievers outside the church, but to judge those inside (cf. 1Pe 4:17). Those on the outside are for God to judge and believers to evangelize. Those who sin on the inside, the church is to put out. Verse 13 is quoted from Dt 17:7.

LAWSUITS DISCOURAGED

6 Does any one of you, when he has a [a]case against
his neighbor, dare to go to law before the unrighteous and [A]not before the [b]saints? 2 Or [A]do you
not know that [B]the [a]saints will judge [C]the world? If
the world is judged by you, are you not competent
to [b]*constitute* the smallest law courts? 3 [A]Do you not
know that we will judge angels? How much more
matters of this life? 4 So if you have law courts dealing with matters of this life, [a]do you appoint them as
judges who are of no account in the church? 5 [A]I say
this to your shame. *Is it* so, *that* there is not among
you one wise man who will be able to decide between his [B]brethren, 6 but brother goes to law with
brother, and that before [A]unbelievers?
7 Actually, then, it is already a defeat for you, that
you have lawsuits with one another. [A]Why not rather
be wronged? Why not rather be defrauded? 8 On the
contrary, you yourselves wrong and defraud. *You
do* this even to *your* [A]brethren.
9 Or [A]do you not know that the unrighteous will
not [B]inherit the kingdom of God? [C]Do not be deceived; [D]neither fornicators, nor idolaters, nor adulterers, nor [a]effeminate, nor homosexuals, 10 nor
thieves, nor *the* covetous, nor drunkards, nor revilers, nor swindlers, will [A]inherit the kingdom
of God. 11 [A]Such were some of you; but you were
[B]washed, but you were [C]sanctified, but you were
[D]justified in the name of the Lord Jesus Christ and
in the Spirit of our God.

THE BODY IS THE LORD'S

12 [A]All things are lawful for me, but not all things
are profitable. All things are lawful for me, but I

6:1 [a]Lit *matter* [b]Or *holy ones* [A]Matt 18:17 6:2 [a]V 1, note 2 [b]Or try *the trivial cases?* [A]Rom 6:16 [B]Dan 7:18, 22, 27; Matt 19:28 [C]1 Cor 1:20 6:3 [A]Rom 6:16 6:4 [a]Or *appoint them…church* 6:5 [A]1 Cor 4:14; 15:34 [B]Acts 1:15; 9:13; 1 Cor 6:1 6:6 [A]2 Cor 6:14f; 1 Tim 5:8 6:7 [A]Matt 5:39f 6:8 [A]1 Thess 4:6 6:9 [a]I.e. effeminate by perversion [A]Rom 6:16 [B]Acts 20:32; 1 Cor 15:50; Gal 5:21; Eph 5:5 [C]Luke 21:8; 1 Cor 15:33; Gal 6:7; James 1:16; 1 John 3:7 [D]Rom 13:13; 1 Cor 5:11; Gal 5:19-21; Eph 5:5; 1 Tim 1:10; Rev 21:8; 22:15 6:10 [A]Acts 20:32; 1 Cor 15:50; Gal 5:21; Eph 5:5 6:11 [A]1 Cor 12:2; Eph 2:2f; Col 3:5-7; Titus 3:3-7 [B]Acts 22:16; Eph 5:26 [C]1 Cor 1:2, 30 [D]Rom 8:30 6:12 [A]1 Cor 10:23

6:1 a case against his neighbor. The phrase in Gr. was commonly used of a lawsuit ("go to law"). **dare.** Suing another believer in a secular law court is a daring act of disobedience because of its implications related to all sin—the displeasure of God. **unrighteous.** This does not refer to their moral character, but to their unsaved spiritual condition. **before the saints.** Believers are to settle all issues between themselves within the church.

6:2 judge the world. Because Christians will assist Christ to judge the world in the millennial kingdom (Rev 2:26, 27; 3:21; cf. Da 7:22), they are more than qualified with the truth, the Spirit, the gifts, and the resources they presently have in Him to settle small matters that come up among themselves in this present life.

6:3 judge angels. The Gr. word can mean "rule or govern." Since the Lord Himself will judge fallen angels (2Pe 2:4; Jude 6), it is likely this means we will have some rule in eternity over holy angels. Since angels are "ministering spirits" to serve the saints (Heb 1:14), it seems reasonable that they will serve us in glory.

6:4 This is a difficult verse to translate, as suggested by the widely varying Eng. renderings. But the basic meaning is clear: when Christians have earthly quarrels and disputes among themselves, it is inconceivable that they would turn to those least qualified (unbelievers) to resolve the matter. The most legally untrained believers, who know the Word of God and are obedient to the Spirit, are far more competent to settle disagreements between believers than the most experienced unbeliever, void of God's truth and Spirit.

6:5, 6 shame. Such conduct as suing a fellow believer is not only a sinful shame (v. 5), but a complete failure to act obediently and righteously. Christians who take fellow Christians to court suffer moral defeat and spiritual loss even before the case is heard, and they become subject to divine chastening (cf. Heb 12:3ff.).

6:7 Why not rather be wronged? The implied answer is because of the shameful sin (v. 5) and the moral defeat (v. 8) that result from selfishness, a willingness to discredit God, His wisdom, power, and sovereign purpose, and to harm the church and the testimony of Christ's gospel. **defrauded.** Christians have no right to insist on legal recourse in a public court. It is far better to trust God's sovereign purposes in trouble and lose financially than to be disobedient and suffer spiritually (*see notes on Mt 5:39; 18:21–34*).

6:8 you yourselves wrong and defraud. He is referring to those who sue their brothers in Christ being as guilty of the same misconduct they are suing to rectify.

6:9, 10 This catalog of sins, though not exhaustive, represents the major types of moral sin that characterize the unsaved.

6:9 not inherit the kingdom. The kingdom is the spiritual sphere of salvation where God rules as king over all who belong to Him by faith (*see notes on Mt 5:3, 10*). All believers are in that spiritual kingdom, yet are waiting to enter into the full inheritance of it in the age to come. People who are characterized by these iniquities are not saved (v. 10). *See notes on 1Jn 3:9, 10.* While believers can and do commit these sins, they do not characterize them as an unbroken life pattern. When they do, it demonstrates that the person is not in God's kingdom. True believers who do sin resent that sin and seek to gain the victory over it (cf. Ro 7:14–25). **fornicators.** All who indulge in sexual immorality, but particularly unmarried persons. **idolaters.** Those who worship any false god or follow any false religious system. **adulterers.** Married persons who indulge in sexual acts outside their marriage. **effeminate … homosexuals.** These terms refer to those who exchange and corrupt normal male-female sexual roles and relations. Transvestism, sex changes, and other gender perversions are included (cf. Ge 1:27; Dt 22:5). Those whom some translations refer to as "sodomites," and Paul as "effeminate," are so-called because the sin of male-male sex dominated the city of Sodom (Ge 18:20; 19:4, 5). This sinful perversion is condemned always, in any form, by Scripture (cf. Lv 18:22; 20:13; Ro 1:26, 27; 1Ti 1:10).

6:10 thieves … covetous. Both are guilty of the same basic sin of greed. Those who are covetous desire what belongs to others; thieves actually take it. **revilers.** People who try to destroy others with words. **swindlers.** Extortioners and embezzlers who steal indirectly, taking unfair advantage of others for their own financial gain.

6:11 some of you. Though not all Christians have been guilty of all those particular sins, every Christian is equally an ex-sinner, since Christ came to save sinners (cf. Mt 9:13; Ro 5:20). Some who used to have those patterns of sinful life were falling into those old sins again, and needed reminding that if they went all the way back to live as they used to, they were not going to inherit eternal salvation, because it would indicate that they never were saved (cf. 2Co 5:17). **washed.** Refers to new life, through spiritual cleansing and regeneration (cf. Jn 3:3–8; 2Co 5:17; Eph 2:10; Titus 3:5). **sanctified.** This results in new behavior, which a transformed life always produces. Sin's total domination is broken and replaced by a new pattern of obedience and holiness. Though not perfection, this is a new direction (see Ro 6:17, 18, 22). **justified.** This refers to a new standing before God, in which the Christian is clothed in Christ's righteousness. In His death, the believer's sins were put to His account and He suffered for them, so that His righteousness might be put to an account, so that we might be blessed for it (Ro 3:26; 4:22–25; 2Co 5:21; Php 3:8, 9; 1Pe 3:18). **in the Spirit.** The Holy Spirit is the agent of salvation's transformation (cf. Jn 3:3–5).

6:12–20 As one who is washed, sanctified, and justified eternally by God's grace, the believer is set free (cf. Ro 8:21, 33; Gal 5:1, 13). The Corinthians had done with that freedom just what Paul had warned the Galatians not to do: "Do not turn your freedom into an opportunity for the flesh" (Gal 5:13). So in this section, Paul exposed the error in the Corinthian Christians' rationalization that they were free to sin, because it was covered by God's grace.

6:12 All things are lawful … but not … profitable. That may have been a Corinthian slogan. It was true that no matter what sins a believer commits, God forgives (Eph 1:7), but not everything they did was profitable or beneficial. The price of abusing freedom and grace was very high. Sin always produces loss. **not be mastered.** Cf. Ro 6:14. Sin has power, and no sin is more enslaving than sexual sin. While it can never be the unbroken pattern of

will not be mastered by anything. 13 [A]Food is for the [a]stomach and the [a]stomach is for food, but God will [B]do away with both [b]of them. Yet the body is not for immorality, but [C]for the Lord, and [D]the Lord is for the body. 14 Now God has not only [A]raised the Lord, but [B]will also raise us up through His power. 15 [A]Do you not know that [B]your bodies are members of Christ? Shall I then take away the members of Christ and make them members of a prostitute? [C]May it never be! 16 Or [A]do you not know that the one who joins himself to a prostitute is one body *with her?* For He says, "[B]THE TWO SHALL BECOME ONE FLESH." 17 But the one who joins himself to the Lord is [A]one spirit *with Him.* 18 [A]Flee immorality. Every *other* sin that a man commits is outside the body, but the [a]immoral man sins against his own body. 19 Or [A]do you not know that [B]your body is a [a]temple of the Holy Spirit who is in you, whom you have from [b]God, and that [C]you are not your own? 20 For [A]you have been bought with a price: therefore glorify God in [B]your body.

TEACHING ON MARRIAGE

7 Now concerning the things about which you wrote, it is [A]good for a man not to touch a woman. 2 But because of immoralities, each man is to have his own wife, and each woman is to have her own husband. 3 The husband must [a]fulfill his duty to his wife, and likewise also the wife to her husband. 4 The wife does not have authority over her own body, but the husband *does;* and likewise also the husband does not have authority over his own body, but the wife *does.* 5 [A]Stop depriving one another, except by agreement for a time, so that you may devote yourselves to prayer, and [a]come together again so that [B]Satan will not tempt you because of your lack of self-control. 6 But this I say by way of concession, [A]not of command.

6:13 [a]Lit *belly* [b]Lit *it and them* [A]Matt 15:17 [B]Col 2:22 [C]1 Cor 6:15, 19 [D]Gal 5:24; Eph 5:23 6:14 [A]Acts 2:24 [B]John 6:39f; 1 Cor 15:23 6:15 [A]1 Cor 6:3 [B]Rom 12:5; 1 Cor 6:13; 12:27; Eph 5:30 [C]Luke 20:16 6:16 [A]1 Cor 6:3 [B]Gen 2:24; Matt 19:5; Mark 10:8; Eph 5:31 6:17 [A]John 17:21-23; Rom 8:9-11; 1 Cor 6:15; Gal 2:20 6:18 [a]Or *one who practices immorality* [A]1 Cor 6:9; 2 Cor 12:21; Eph 5:3; Col 3:5; Heb 13:4 6:19 [a]Or *sanctuary* [b]Or *God? And you...own* [A]1 Cor 6:3 [B]John 2:21; 1 Cor 3:16; 2 Cor 6:16 [C]Rom 14:7f 6:20 [A]Acts 20:28; 1 Cor 7:23; 1 Pet 1:18f; 2 Pet 2:1; Rev 5:9 [B]Rom 12:1; Phil 1:20 7:1 [A]1 Cor 7:8, 26 7:3 [a]Lit *render* 7:5 [a]Lit *be* [A]Ex 19:15; 1 Sam 21:5 [B]Matt 4:10 7:6 [A]2 Cor 8:8

a true believer's life, it can be the recurring habit that saps joy, peace, usefulness and brings divine chastening and even church discipline (cf. 5:1ff.). *See notes on 1Th 4:3–5.* Sexual sin controls, so the believer must never allow sin to have that control, but must master it in the Lord's strength (*see note on 9:27*). Paul categorically rejects the ungodly notion that freedom in Christ gives license to sin (cf. Ro 7:6; 8:13, 21).

6:13 Food ... stomach. Perhaps this was a popular proverb to celebrate the idea that sex is purely biological, like eating. The influence of philosophical dualism may have contributed to this idea since it made only the body evil; therefore, what one did physically was not preventable and thus inconsequential. Because the relationship between these two is purely biological and temporal, the Corinthians, like many of their pagan friends, probably used that analogy to justify sexual immorality. **the body ... the Lord.** Paul rejects the convenient justifying analogy. Bodies and food are temporal relations that will perish.

6:14 Cf. Ac 2:32; Eph 1:19. Bodies of believers and the Lord have an eternal relationship that will never perish. He is referring to the believer's body to be changed, raised, glorified, and made heavenly. See 15:35–54; cf. Php 3:20, 21.

6:15 members. The believer's body is not only for the Lord here and now (v. 14) but is of the Lord, a part of His body, the church (Eph 1:22, 23). The Christian's body is a spiritual temple in which the Spirit of Christ lives (12:3; Jn 7:38, 39; 20:22; Ac 1:8; Ro 8:9; 2Co 6:16); therefore, when a believer commits a sexual sin, it involves Christ with a harlot. All sexual sin is harlotry. **May it never be!** These words translate the strongest Gr. negative—"this should never be so."

6:16 one flesh. Paul supports his point in the previous verse by appealing to the truth of Ge 2:24 that defines the sexual union between a man and a woman as "one flesh." When a person is joined to a harlot, it is a one flesh experience; therefore, Christ spiritually is joined to that harlot.

6:17 one spirit *with Him.* Further strengthening the point, Paul affirms that all sex outside of marriage is sin; but illicit relationships by believers are especially reprehensible because they profane Jesus Christ with whom believers are one (Jn 14:18–23; 15:4, 7; 17:20–23; Ro 12:5). This argument should make such sin unthinkable.

6:18 Every *other* sin ... is outside. There is a sense in which sexual sin destroys a person like no other, because it is so intimate and entangling, corrupting on the deepest human level. But Paul is probably alluding to venereal disease, prevalent and devastating in his day and today. No sin has greater potential to destroy the body, something a believer should avoid because of the reality given in vv. 19, 20.

6:19 not your own. A Christian's body belongs to the Lord (v. 13), is a member of Christ (v. 15), and is the Holy Spirit's temple. *See notes on Ro 12:1, 2.* Every act of fornication, adultery, or any other sin is committed by the believer in the sanctuary, the Holy of Holies, where God dwells. In the OT, the High Priest only went in there once a year, and only after extensive cleansing, lest he be killed (Lv 16).

6:20 a price. The precious blood of Christ (*see notes on 1Pe 1:18*). **glorify God.** The Christian's supreme purpose (10:31).

7:1–11:34 This section comprises Paul's answers to practical questions about which the Corinthians had written him (7:1) in a letter probably delivered by Stephanas, Fortunatus, and Achaicus (16:17). The first of those questions had to do with marriage, an area of trouble due to the moral corruption of the culture which tolerated fornication, adultery, homosexuality, polygamy, and concubinage.

7:1–7 Some had the notion that because of all the sexual sin and marital confusion, it would be better to be single, even more spiritual to be celibate. This could lead some falsely pious people to advocate divorce in order to be single. These verses elevate singleness, as long as it is celibate, but they in no way teach that marriage is either wrong or inferior.

7:1 touch a woman. This is a Jewish euphemism for sexual intercourse (see, e.g., Ge 20:6; Ru 2:9; Pr 6:29). Paul is saying that it is good not to have sex, that is, to be single and celibate. It is not, however, the only good or even better than marriage (cf. Ge 1:28; 2:18).

7:2 immoralities. There is a great danger of sexual sin when single (cf. Mt 19:12). Marriage is God's only provision for sexual fulfillment. Marriage should not be reduced simply to that, however. Paul has a much higher view and articulates it in Eph 5:22, 23. He is, here, stressing the issue of sexual sin for people who are single.

7:3 fulfill his duty. Married believers are not to sexually deprive their spouses. While celibacy is right for the single, it is wrong for the married. The practice of deprivation may have been most common when a believer had an unsaved spouse (for more on unsaved spouses, *see notes on vv. 10–17*).

7:4 authority. By the marriage covenant, each partner is given the right over the spouse's body for the satisfaction of the other.

7:5 depriving. This command may indicate that this kind of deprivation was going on among believers, perhaps reacting to the gross sexual sins of their past and wanting to leave all that behind. Husbands and wives may abstain temporarily from sexual activity, but only when they mutually agree to do so for intercession, as a part of their fasting. **come together again.** Sexual intercourse is to be soon renewed after the spiritual interruption. **so that Satan will not tempt.** Cf. 1Th 3:5. After the agreed-upon "time" of abstinence, sexual desires intensify and a spouse becomes more vulnerable to sinful desire. *See notes on Mt 4:1–11; 2Co 2:11.*

7:6 concession. A better translation of the Gr. would be "awareness" or "to have a mutual opinion." Paul was very aware of the God-ordained advantages of both singleness and marriage, and was not commanding marriage because of the temptation of singleness. Spirituality is not connected at all to marital status, though marriage is God's good gift (see 1Pe 3:7, "the grace of life").

7 [a]Yet I wish that all men were [A]even as I myself am.
However, [B]each man has his own gift from God, one
in this manner, and another in that.
8 But I say to the unmarried and to widows that
it is [A]good for them if they remain [B]even as I. 9 But
if they do not have self-control, [A]let them marry;
for it is better to marry than to burn *with passion.*
10 But to the married I give instructions, [A]not I,
but the Lord, that the wife should not [a]leave her
husband 11 (but if she does leave, she must remain
unmarried, or else be reconciled to her husband),
and that the husband should not [a]divorce his wife.
12 But to the rest [A]I say, not the Lord, that if any
brother has a wife who is an unbeliever, and she
consents to live with him, he must not [a]divorce her.
13 And a woman who has an unbelieving husband,
and he consents to live with her, she must not [a]send
her husband away. 14 For the unbelieving husband
is sanctified through his wife, and the unbelieving
wife is sanctified through [a]her believing husband;
for otherwise your children are unclean, but now
they are [A]holy. 15 Yet if the unbelieving one leaves,
let him leave; the brother or the sister is not under bondage in such *cases,* but God has called
[a]us [b,A]to peace. 16 For how do you know, O wife,
whether you will [A]save your husband? Or how
do you know, O husband, whether you will save
your wife?
17 Only, [A]as the Lord has assigned to each one, as
God has called each, in this manner let him walk.
And [B]so I direct in [C]all the churches. 18 Was any man
called *when he was already* circumcised? He is not
to become uncircumcised. Has anyone been called
in uncircumcision? [A]He is not to be circumcised.
19 [A]Circumcision is nothing, and uncircumcision
is nothing, but *what matters is* [B]the keeping of the
commandments of God. 20 [A]Each man must remain
in that [a]condition in which he was called.

7:7 [a]One early ms reads *For* [A]1 Cor 7:8; 9:5 [B]Matt 19:11f; Rom 12:6; 1 Cor 12:4, 11 7:8 [A]1 Cor 7:1, 26 [B]1 Cor 7:7; 9:5 7:9 [A]1 Tim 5:14 7:10 [a]Lit *depart from* [A]Mal 2:16; Matt 5:32; 19:3-9; Mark 10:2-12; Luke 16:18; 1 Cor 7:6 7:11 [a]Or *leave his wife* 7:12 [a]Or *leave her* [A]1 Cor 7:6; 2 Cor 11:17 7:13 [a]Or *leave her husband* 7:14 [a]Lit *the brother* [A]Ezra 9:2; Mal 2:15 7:15 [a]One early ms reads *you* [b]Lit *in* [A]Rom 14:19 7:16 [A]Rom 11:14; 1 Pet 3:1 7:17 [A]Rom 12:3 [B]1 Cor 4:17 [C]1 Cor 11:16; 14:33; 2 Cor 8:18; 11:28; Gal 1:22; 1 Thess 2:14; 2 Thess 1:4 7:18 [A]Acts 15:1ff 7:19 [A]Rom 2:27, 29; Gal 3:28; 5:6; 6:15; Col 3:11 [B]Rom 2:25 7:20 [a]Lit *calling* [A]1 Cor 7:24

7:7 even as I myself am. As a single person, Paul recognized the special freedom and independence he had to serve Christ (*see notes on vv. 32–34*). But he did not expect all believers to be single, nor all who were single to stay that way, nor all who were married to act celibate as if they were single. **gift from God.** Both singleness and marriage are God's gracious gifts.

7:8 unmarried ... widows. "Unmarried" is a term used 4 times in the NT, and only in 1 Corinthians (cf. vv. 11, 32, 34). This verse makes it clear that the unmarried and widows are distinct. Verse 11 identifies the divorced as the "unmarried" to be distinguished from "widows" (vv. 39, 40; single by death) and virgins (vv. 25, 28; never married). Each use of "unmarried," then, refers to those formerly married, presently single, but not widowed. They are the divorced. It is likely these people who were formerly married wanted to know if they, as Christians, could or should remarry. **even as I.** Paul was possibly a widower, and could here affirm his former marriage by identifying with the unmarried and widows. His first suggestion is that they stay single because of its freedoms in serving the Lord (vv. 25–27, 32–34). *See notes on Anna in Lk 2:36, 37.*

7:9 let them marry. The Gr. tense indicates a command, since a person can't live a happy life and serve the Lord effectively if dominated by unfulfilled sexual passion—especially in that Corinthian society.

7:10 not I, but the Lord. What Paul writes to these believers was already made clear by Jesus during His earthly ministry (Mt 5:31, 32; 19:5–8; cf. Ge 2:24; Mal 2:16). **leave.** This word is used as a synonym for divorce, as indicated by the parallel use of the word "divorce," in v. 11.

7:11 remain unmarried. If a Christian divorces another Christian except for adultery (*see notes on Mt 5:31, 32; 19:8, 9*), neither partner is free to marry another person. They should reconcile, or at least remain unmarried.

7:12 to the rest. Those not covered by the instruction of vv. 10, 11. **I say.** Not a denial of inspiration or an indication that Paul is giving human opinion, but simply a way of saying that Jesus had not spoken on this, and God had not previously given revelation on the matter, as Paul was then writing. Apparently, some Christians felt they should divorce their unsaved spouses, to live celibately or marry a believer.

7:12, 13 Some believers must have felt that being married to an unbeliever was somehow defiling. However, just the opposite is true (v. 14).

7:14 sanctified. This does not refer to salvation; otherwise, the spouse would not be spoken of as unbelieving. The sanctification is matrimonial and familial, not personal or spiritual, and means that the unsaved partner is set apart for temporal blessing because the other belongs to God. One Christian in a marriage brings grace that spills over on the spouse—even possibly leading them to salvation. **children ... are holy.** The Christian need not separate from an unbeliever because of fear that the unbelieving spouse may defile the children. God promises the opposite. They would be unclean if both parents were unsaved, but the presence of one believing parent exposes the children to blessing and brings them protection. The presence of even one Christian parent will protect children from undue spiritual harm, and they will receive many blessings, and often that includes salvation.

7:15 let him leave. A term referring to divorce (cf. vv. 10, 11). When an unbelieving spouse cannot tolerate the partner's faith and wants a divorce, it is best to let that happen in order to preserve peace in the family (cf. Ro 12:18). The bond of marriage is broken only by death (Ro 7:2), adultery (Mt 19:9), or an unbeliever's leaving. **not under bondage.** When the bond is broken in any of those ways, a Christian is free to marry another believer. Throughout Scripture, whenever legitimate divorce occurs, remarriage is assumed. When divorce is permitted, so is remarriage. By implication, the permission for a widow to remarry (vv. 39, 40; Ro 7:3), because the "bond" is broken, extends to this case where there is no more "bondage."

7:16 Some may have been reluctant to let go of their unsaved spouse, who wanted out and was creating discord in the home—thinking they could evangelize the spouse by hanging on for the purpose of seeing that one converted. Paul says there are no such assurances, and it is better to divorce and be at peace (v. 15), if the unsaved partner wants to end the marriage that way.

7:17–24 Discontent was prevalent among these new believers in the Corinthian church. As noted up to this point (vv. 1–16), some wanted to change their marital status, some were slaves who wanted to be free, and some used their freedom in Christ to rationalize sinning. In a general response to that, this passage plainly repeats the basic principle that Christians should willingly accept the marital condition and social situations into which God has placed them and be content to serve Him there until He leads them elsewhere.

7:17 For the first of 3 times (vv. 20, 24), Paul states the principle of contentment which is required of all Christians.

7:18 called. As always in the Epistles, this term refers to God's effectual call that saves (*see note on Ro 8:30*). **circumcised ... uncircumcised.** With Judaizers demanding all Gentile believers in Christ to be circumcised (Gal 5:1–6), and with some Christian Jews wanting to disassociate with Judaism and thus having a surgery to become uncircumcised (as addressed in rabbinic literature), Paul needed to clarify the issue by saying that neither was necessary. Figuratively, the idea is that when a Jew became a Christian, he was not to give up his racial and cultural identity in order to appear like a Gentile. Likewise, a Gentile was not to become culturally like a Jew (v. 19). Culture, social order, and external ceremony have no bearing on spiritual life. What matters is faith and obedience.

21 Were you called while a slave? [a]Do not worry about it; but if you are able also to become free, rather [b]do that. 22 For he who was called in the Lord while a slave, is [A]the Lord's freedman; likewise he who was called while free, is [B]Christ's slave. 23 [A]You were bought with a price; do not become slaves of men. 24 Brethren, [A]each one is to remain with God in that *condition* in which he was called.

25 Now concerning virgins I have [A]no command of the Lord, but I give an opinion as one who [a,B]by the mercy of the Lord is trustworthy. 26 I think then that this is good in view of the [a]present [A]distress, that [B]it is good for a man [b]to remain as he is. 27 Are you bound to a wife? Do not seek to be released. Are you released from a wife? Do not seek a wife. 28 But if you marry, you have not sinned; and if a virgin marries, she has not sinned. Yet such will have [a]trouble in this life, and I am trying to spare you. 29 But this I say, brethren, [A]the time has been shortened, so that from now on those who have wives should be as though they had none; 30 and those who weep, as though they did not weep; and those who rejoice, as though they did not rejoice; and those who buy, as though they did not possess; 31 and those who use the world, as though they did not [A]make full use of it; for [B]the form of this world is passing away.

32 But I want you to be free from concern. One who is [A]unmarried is concerned about the things of the Lord, how he may please the Lord; 33 but one who is married is concerned about the things of the world, how he may please his wife, 34 and *his interests* are divided. The woman who is unmarried, and the virgin, is concerned about the things of the Lord, that she may be holy both in body and spirit; but one who is married is concerned about the things of the world, how she may please her husband. 35 This I say for your own benefit; not to put a restraint upon you, but [a]to promote what is appropriate and *to secure* undistracted devotion to the Lord.

36 But if any man thinks that he is acting unbecomingly toward his virgin *daughter,* if she is past her youth, and if it must be so, let him do what he wishes, he does not sin; let [a]her marry. 37 But he who stands firm in his heart, [a]being under no constraint, but has authority [b]over his own will, and has decided this in his own heart, to keep his own virgin

7:21 [a]Lit *Let it not be a care to you* [b]Lit *use* 7:22 [A]John 8:32, 36; Philem 16 [B]Eph 6:6; Col 3:24; 1 Pet 2:16 7:23 [A]1 Cor 6:20 7:24 [A]1 Cor 7:20 7:25 [a]Lit *has had mercy shown on him by the Lord to be trustworthy* [A]1 Cor 7:6 [B]2 Cor 4:1; 1 Tim 1:13, 16 7:26 [a]Or *impending* [b]Lit *so to be* [A]Luke 21:23; 2 Thess 2:2 [B]1 Cor 7:1, 8 7:28 [a]Lit *tribulation in the flesh* 7:29 [A]Rom 13:11f; 1 Cor 7:31 7:31 [A]1 Cor 9:18 [B]1 Cor 7:29; 1 John 2:17 7:32 [A]1 Tim 5:5 7:35 [a]Lit *for what is seemly* 7:36 [a]Lit *them* 7:37 [a]Lit *having no necessity* [b]Lit *pertaining to*

7:21 while a slave. Paul is not approving all slavery, but is teaching that a person who is a slave is still able to obey and honor Christ (Eph 6:5–8; Col 3:23; 1Ti 6:1, 2). **Do not worry about it.** In modern society, this seems an insensitive command to those who wrongly assume that freedom is some God-given right, rather than a preferable option.

7:22 the Lord's freedman. In the ways that truly count, no man is freer than a Christian. No bondage is as terrible as that of sin, from which Christ frees the believer. **Christ's slave.** Those who are not slaves, but free in the social sense, are in the spiritual sense made slaves of Christ in salvation (Ro 6:22).

7:23 price. The blood of Christ (6:20; 1Pe 1:19). **slaves of men.** This refers to sinful slavery, i.e., becoming slaves to the ways of men, the ways of the world, and of the flesh. This is the slavery about which to be concerned.

7:25–40 Having already established that both marriage and singleness are good and right before the Lord (vv. 1–9), and for the person who has the gift of singleness (v. 7), that state has many practical advantages, Paul continued to answer the questions about which the Corinthians had written him (*see note on v. 1*). Paul gives 6 reasons for never marrying, in relationship to the downside of marriage, but remaining single (virgins): 1) pressure from the system (vv. 25–27); 2) problems of the flesh (v. 28); 3) passing of the world (vv. 29–31); 4) preoccupations of marriage (vv. 32–35); 5) promises from fathers (vv. 36–38); and 6) permanency of marriage (vv. 39, 40).

7:25 I have no command. *See note on v. 12.* The conviction given here is not a command, but is thoroughly dependable and sound advice to remain a virgin, which is counsel included by the inspiration of the Spirit from a trustworthy man.

7:26 present distress. An unspecified, current calamity. Perhaps Paul anticipated the imminent Roman persecutions which began within 10 years after this epistle was written. **remain as he is.** Persecution is difficult enough for a single person to endure, but problems and pain are multiplied for those who are married, especially if they have children.

7:27 The benefits of singleness notwithstanding, married people must remain married. **released.** Divorce is in view.

7:28 marry, you have not sinned. Marriage is a fully legitimate and godly option for both the divorced (on biblical grounds; *see note on v. 15*) and virgins. **trouble in this life.** "Trouble" means lit. "pressed together, or under pressure." Marriage can involve conflicts, demands, difficulties, and adjustments that singleness does not, because it presses two fallen people into intimate life that leads to inevitable "trouble." The troubles of singleness may be exceeded by the conflicts of marriage.

7:29 time has been shortened. Human life is brief (cf. Jas 4:14; 1Pe 1:24). **as though they had none.** This does not teach that marriage is no longer binding or treated with seriousness (cf. Eph 5:22–33; Col 3:18, 19), nor should there be any physical deprivation (vv. 3–5); but Paul is teaching that marriage should not at all reduce one's devotion to the Lord and service to Him (cf. Col 3:2). He means to keep the eternal priority (see v. 31).

7:30 The mature Christian does not get so swept up in the emotion of this life, so as to lose motivation, hope, and purpose.

7:31 use … make full use. This refers to the normal commercial materialism and pleasures that govern in the world. Believers are not to be swept up in earthly enterprises so that heavenly matters become secondary. **form.** This refers to a manner of life, a fashion, or way of doing things.

7:32, 33 free from concern. A single person is free from concern about the earthly needs of a spouse and therefore potentially better able to set himself apart exclusively for the Lord's work.

7:33 things of the world. These are earthly matters connected to the passing system (v. 31).

7:33, 34 how he may please his wife … husband. Here is a basic and expected principle for a good marriage—each seeking to please the other.

7:34 The first part of this verse is preferably rendered in some manuscripts as "and his interests are divided. And the woman who is unmarried and the virgin …." This is important because it distinguishes clearly between the "unmarried" and "virgins," who, therefore, can't be the same. "Virgins" are single people never married, while "unmarried" must be single by divorce. Widows is the term for those made single by death (*see note on v. 8*).

7:35 Marriage does not prevent great devotion to the Lord, but it brings more potential matters to interfere with it. Singleness has fewer hindrances, though not guaranteed greater spiritual virtue. **undistracted devotion.** *See notes on vv. 26, 29, 33.*

7:36 his virgin. That is, a man's daughter. Apparently in Corinth some of the fathers intending devotion to the Lord, had dedicated their young daughters to the Lord as permanent virgins. **past her youth.** Fully matured as a woman capable of child-bearing. **it must be.** When daughters became of marriageable age and insisted on being married, their fathers were free to break the vow and let them marry.

7:37 no constraint. This means the father who has kept his daughter a virgin and is not under constraint by the daughter to change his mind, does well to fulfill his desire for her to be singularly devoted to the Lord (v. 34). As with those who remain single (v. 28), the choice was not between right and wrong.

daughter, he will do well. 38 So then both he who
gives his own virgin *daughter* in marriage does
well, and he who does not give her in marriage
will do better.
39 [A]A wife is bound as long as her husband lives;
but if her husband [a]is dead, she is free to be married
to whom she wishes, only [B]in the Lord. 40 But [A]in my
opinion she is happier if she remains as she is; and
I think that I also have the Spirit of God.

TAKE CARE WITH YOUR LIBERTY

8 Now concerning [A]things sacrificed to idols, we
know that we all have [B]knowledge. Knowledge
[a,C]makes arrogant, but love [D]edifies. 2 [A]If anyone
supposes that he knows anything, he has not yet
[B]known as he ought to know; 3 but if anyone loves
God, he [A]is known by Him.
4 Therefore concerning the eating of [A]things
sacrificed to idols, we know that [a]there is [B]no such
thing as an idol in the world, and that [C]there is
no God but one. 5 For even if [A]there are so-called
gods whether in heaven or on earth, as indeed
there are many gods and many lords, 6 yet for us
[A]there is *but* one God, [B]the Father, [C]from whom are
all things and we *exist* for Him; and [D]one Lord,
Jesus Christ, [E]by whom are all things, and we *exist*
through Him.
7 However not all men [A]have this knowledge; but
[B]some, being accustomed to the idol until now, eat
food as if it were sacrificed to an idol; and their
conscience being weak is defiled. 8 But [A]food will
not [a]commend us to God; we are neither [b]the worse
if we do not eat, nor [c]the better if we do eat. 9 But
[A]take care that this [a]liberty of yours does not somehow become a stumbling block to the [B]weak. 10 For
if someone sees you, who have [A]knowledge, dining
in an idol's temple, will not his conscience, if he is
weak, be strengthened to eat [B]things sacrificed to
idols? 11 For through [A]your knowledge he who is
weak [B]is ruined, the brother for whose sake Christ
died. 12 [A]And so, by sinning against the brethren
and wounding their conscience when it is weak, you
sin [B]against Christ. 13 Therefore, [A]if food causes my
brother to stumble, I will never eat meat again, so
that I will not cause my brother to stumble.

PAUL'S USE OF LIBERTY

9 Am I not [A]free? Am I not an [B]apostle? Have I not
[C]seen Jesus our Lord? Are you not [D]my work in
the Lord? 2 If to others I am not an apostle, at least
I am to you; for you are the [A]seal of my [B]apostleship
in the Lord.
3 My defense to those who examine me is
this: 4 [a,A]Do we not have a right to eat and drink?

7:39 [a]Lit *falls asleep* [A]Rom 7:2 [B]2 Cor 6:14 7:40 [A]1 Cor 7:6, 25 8:1 [a]Lit *puffs up* [A]Acts 15:20; 1 Cor 8:4, 7, 10 [B]Rom 15:14; 1 Cor 8:7, 10; 10:15 [C]1 Cor 4:6 [D]Rom 14:19 8:2 [A]1 Cor 3:18 [B]1 Cor 13:8-12; 1 Tim 6:4 8:3 [A]Ps 1:6; Jer 1:5; Amos 3:2; Rom 8:29; 11:2; Gal 4:9 8:4 [a]Lit *nothing is an idol in the world;* i.e. an idol has no real existence [A]Acts 15:20; 1 Cor 8:1, 7, 10 [B]Acts 14:15; 1 Cor 10:19; Gal 4:8 [C]Deut 4:35, 39; 6:4; 1 Cor 8:6 8:5 [A]2 Thess 2:4 8:6 [A]Deut 4:35, 39; 6:4; Is 46:9; Jer 10:6, 7; 1 Cor 8:4 [B]Mal 2:10; Eph 4:6 [C]Rom 11:36 [D]John 13:13; 1 Cor 1:2; Eph 4:5; 1 Tim 2:5 [E]John 1:3; Col 1:16 8:7 [A]1 Cor 8:4ff [B]Rom 14:14, 22f 8:8 [a]Or *present* [b]Lit *lacking* [c]Lit *abounding* [A]Rom 14:17 8:9 [a]Lit *right* [A]Rom 14:13, 21; 1 Cor 10:28; Gal 5:13 [B]Rom 14:1; 1 Cor 8:10f 8:10 [A]1 Cor 8:4ff [B]Acts 15:20; 1 Cor 8:1, 4, 7 8:11 [A]1 Cor 8:4ff [B]Rom 14:15, 20 8:12 [A]Matt 18:6; Rom 14:20 [B]Matt 25:45 8:13 [A]Rom 14:21; 1 Cor 10:32; 2 Cor 6:3; 11:29 9:1 [A]1 Cor 9:19; 10:29 [B]Acts 14:14; Rom 1:1; 2 Cor 12:12; 1 Thess 2:6; 1 Tim 2:7; 2 Tim 1:11 [C]Acts 9:3, 17; 18:9; 22:14, 18; 23:11; 1 Cor 15:8 [D]1 Cor 3:6; 4:15 9:2 [A]John 3:33; 2 Cor 3:2f [B]Acts 1:25 9:4 [a]Lit *It is not that we have no right to eat and drink, is it?* [A]1 Cor 9:14; 1 Thess 2:6, 9; 2 Thess 3:8f

7:39 bound. God's law designed marriage for life (cf. Ge 2:24; Mal 2:16; Ro 7:1–3). It is so permanent that the disciples thought it may be better not to marry (*see note on Mt 19:10*). **only in the Lord.** That is, free to marry a believer only. This is true for all believers who marry or remarry (see 2Co 6:14–16).

7:40 I also have the Spirit. Perhaps with a touch of sarcasm, Paul affirmed that this sound advice was given by the Holy Spirit.

8:1–11:1 Paul addresses liberty in the church (*see notes on Ro 14*).

8:1 things sacrificed to idols. The Greeks and Romans were polytheistic (worshiping many gods) and polydemonistic (believing in many evil spirits). They believed that evil spirits would try to invade human beings by attaching themselves to food before it was eaten, and that the spirits could be removed only by the food's being sacrificed to a god. The sacrifice was meant not only to gain favor with the god, but also to cleanse the meat from demonic contamination. Such decontaminated meat was offered to the gods as a sacrifice. That which was not burned on the altar was served at wicked pagan feasts. What was left was sold in the market. After conversion, believers resented eating such food bought out of idol markets, because it reminded sensitive Gentile believers of their previous pagan lives and the demonic worship. **we all have knowledge.** Paul and mature believers knew better than to be bothered by such food offered once to idols and then sold in the marketplace. They knew the deities did not exist and that evil spirits did not contaminate the food. *See note on 1Ti 4:3.* **love edifies.** Knowledge mingled with love prevents a believer from exercising freedoms that offend weaker believers and, rather, builds the others up in truth and wisdom (cf. 13:1–4).

8:2, 3 Love is the proof of knowing God. Cf. 1Jn 4:19–5:1.

8:4 Paul states his agreement with the well-taught believers who knew idols were nothing, so food offered to idols was not defiled.

8:5 so-called gods. Some were outright fakes and some were manifestations of demons, but none were truly gods (Ps 115:4–7; Ac 19:26).

8:6 one God, the Father . . . one Lord, Jesus Christ. A powerful and clear affirmation of the essential equality of God the Father and God the Son (cf. Eph 4:4–6).

8:7 conscience . . . is defiled. The consciences of some newer converts were still accusing them strongly with regard to allowing them to eat idol food without feeling spiritually corrupted and guilty. They still imagined that idols were real and evil. A defiled conscience is one that has been violated, bringing fear, shame, and guilt. *See notes on Ro 14:20–23.*

8:8 commend us to God. The idea is of bringing us nearer to God or making us approved by Him. Food is spiritually neutral.

8:9–11 stumbling block. Some believers would be caused to fall back into old sins by getting involved with foods offered to idols.

8:11 ruined. *See note on Mt 18:14.* **for whose sake Christ died.** Christ died for all who believe, actually bearing the penalty for their sin and fully satisfying the wrath of God.

8:12 you sin against Christ. A strong warning that causing a brother or sister in Christ to stumble is more than simply an offense against that person; it is a serious offense against the Lord Himself (*see notes on Mt 18:6–14*).

8:13 *See notes on Ro 14:14, 15, 17, 20.*

9:1, 2 In chap. 8, Paul set out the limits of Christian liberty. In this chapter he sets forth how he followed them in his own life. In vv. 1–18, he discusses his right to be financially supported by those to whom he ministers. In vv. 19–27, he explains how he would give up all rights to win people to Christ. All of these questions are rhetorical, the "yes" answer to each being assumed.

9:2 seal of my apostleship. The existence of the church in Corinth was evidence of Paul's apostolic authenticity.

9:3 examine. Using this Gr. legal term for a preliminary investigation required before a decision was reached in a case, Paul sets out to defend his rights.

9:4 right to eat and drink. Cf. 1Ti 5:17, 18. He was entitled to be married (v. 5) and to receive financial support from those to whom he ministered.

5[a,A]Do we not have a right to take along a [b]believ-
ing wife, even as the rest of the apostles and the
[B]brothers of the Lord and [C]Cephas? 6Or do only
[a,A]Barnabas and I not have a right to refrain from
working? 7Who at any time serves [A]as a soldier at
his own expense? Who [B]plants a vineyard and does
not eat the fruit of it? Or who tends a flock and does
not [a]use the milk of the flock?
8I am not speaking these things [A]according to
[a]human judgment, am I? Or does not the Law also
say these things? 9For it is written in the Law of
Moses, "[A]YOU SHALL NOT MUZZLE THE OX WHILE HE
IS THRESHING." God is not concerned about [B]oxen, is
He? 10Or is He speaking altogether for our sake? Yes,
[A]for our sake it was written, because [B]the plowman
ought to plow in hope, and the thresher *to thresh* in
hope of sharing *the crops.* 11[A]If we sowed spiritual
things in you, is it too much if we reap material
things from you? 12If others share the right over
you, do we not more? Nevertheless, we [A]did not
use this right, but we endure all things [B]so that we
will cause no hindrance to the [C]gospel of Christ.
13[A]Do you not know that those who [B]perform sacred services eat the *food* of the temple, *and* those
who attend regularly to the altar have their share
[a]from the altar? 14So also [A]the Lord directed those
who proclaim the [B]gospel to [C]get their living from
the gospel.
15But I have [A]used none of these things. And I
am not writing these things so that it will be done
so in my case; for it would be better for me to die
than have any man make [B]my boast an empty one.
16For if I preach the gospel, I have nothing to boast
of, for [A]I am under compulsion; for woe is me if I
do not preach [B]the gospel. 17For if I do this voluntarily, I have a [A]reward; but if against my will, I
have a [B]stewardship entrusted to me. 18What then
is my [A]reward? That, when I preach the gospel, I
may offer the gospel [B]without charge, so as [C]not to
make full use of my right in the gospel.
19For though I am [A]free from all *men,* I have made
myself [B]a slave to all, so that I may [C]win more. 20[A]To
the Jews I became as a Jew, so that I might win Jews;
to those who are under [a]the Law, as under [a]the Law
though [B]not being myself under [a]the Law, so that I
might win those who are under [a]the Law; 21to those
who are [A]without law, [B]as without law, though not
being without the law of God but [C]under the law of
Christ, so that I might win those who are without
law. 22To the [A]weak I became weak, that I might win
the weak; I have become [B]all things to all men, [C]so
that I may by all means save some. 23I do all things
for the sake of the gospel, so that I may become a
fellow partaker of it.
24[A]Do you not know that those who run in a
race all run, but *only* one receives [B]the prize? [C]Run

9:5 [a]Lit *It is not that we have no right to take along…Cephas, is it?* [b]Lit *sister, as wife* [A]1 Cor 7:7f [B]Matt 12:46 [C]Matt 8:14; John 1:42 9:6 [a]Lit *I and Barnabas* [A]Acts 4:36 9:7 [a]Lit *eat of* [A]2 Cor 10:4; 1 Tim 1:18; 2 Tim 2:3f [B]Deut 20:6; Prov 27:18; 1 Cor 3:6, 8 9:8 [a]Lit *man* [A]Rom 3:5 9:9 [A]Deut 25:4; 1 Tim 5:18 [B]Deut 22:1-4; Prov 12:10 9:10 [A]Rom 4:23f [B]2 Tim 2:6 9:11 [A]Rom 15:27; 1 Cor 9:14 9:12 [A]Acts 18:3; 20:33; 1 Cor 9:15, 18 [B]2 Cor 6:3; 11:12 [C]1 Cor 4:15; 9:14, 16, 18, 23; 2 Cor 2:12 9:13 [a]Lit *with* [A]Rom 6:16 [B]Lev 6:16, 26; 7:6, 31ff; Num 5:9f; 18:8-20, 31; Deut 18:1 9:14 [A]Matt 10:10; Luke 10:7; 1 Tim 5:18 [B]1 Cor 4:15; 9:12, 16, 18, 23; 2 Cor 2:12 [C]Luke 10:8; 1 Cor 9:4 9:15 [A]Acts 18:3; 20:33; 1 Cor 9:12, 18 [B]2 Cor 11:10 9:16 [A]Acts 9:15; Rom 1:14 [B]1 Cor 4:15; 9:12, 14, 18, 23; 2 Cor 2:12 9:17 [A]John 4:36; 1 Cor 3:8; 9:18 [B]1 Cor 4:1; Gal 2:7; Eph 3:2; Phil 1:16; Col 1:25 9:18 [A]John 4:36; 1 Cor 3:8; 9:17 [B]Acts 18:3; 2 Cor 11:7; 12:13 [C]1 Cor 7:31; 9:12 9:19 [A]1 Cor 9:1 [B]2 Cor 4:5; Gal 5:13 [C]Matt 18:15; 1 Pet 3:1 9:20 [a]Or *law* [A]Acts 16:3; 21:23-26; Rom 11:14 [B]Gal 2:19 9:21 [A]Rom 2:12, 14 [B]Gal 2:3; 3:2 [C]1 Cor 7:22; Gal 6:2 9:22 [A]Rom 14:1; 15:1; 2 Cor 11:29 [B]1 Cor 10:33 [C]Rom 11:14 9:24 [A]1 Cor 9:13 [B]Phil 3:14; Col 2:18 [C]Gal 2:2; 2 Tim 4:7; Heb 12:1

9:5 Cephas. Peter, who was married (cf. Mk 1:29–31).

9:6 working. With sarcasm, Paul, a tentmaker (Ac 18:3), let the Corinthians know that he and Barnabas had as much right as others to receive full financial support from their work. Except for help from a few churches (e.g., Php 4:15, 16), they paid their own expenses not because of obligation or necessity, but voluntarily.

9:7 Who plants a vineyard. Cf. 2Ti 2:6.

9:9 Law. The Scripture, as quoted from Dt 25:4.

9:10 for our sake. As in agriculture, men should earn their living from their labor.

9:11 material things. Financial support. *See note on 1Ti 5:17.* Cf. 2Co 8:1–5.

9:12 others share the right. Apparently, the church had financially supported other ministers. **endure.** False teachers sought money. Paul wanted to be certain he was not classed with them, so he endured not accepting support, so as not to offend. Cf. Ac 20:34; 2Th 3:8.

9:13 share from the altar. OT priests were supported by the tithes of crops and animals, as well as of financial gifts (Nu 18:8–24; cf. Ge 14:18–21).

9:14 get their living from the gospel. This refers to earning a living by preaching the good news.

9:15 none of these things. The 6 reasons given in vv. 1–14 that indicate his right to financial support. **I am not writing.** He was not underhandedly hoping that, despite his protest, the Corinthians would feel obligated to pay him (2Co 11:8, 9; cf. 1Th 2:9; 2Th 3:8; 1Pe 5:2). **better … to die.** He preferred death to having anyone think he ministered with a financial motive. See Ac 20:33–35; 1Pe 5:2. **make my boast … empty.** The term "boast" refers to that in which one glories or to the basis of one's glorying, and carries the idea of rejoicing. It is a statement of sincere joy, not pride (cf. 1:31; Ro 15:17). Paul was genuinely overjoyed for the privilege of serving the Lord and did not want material support to rob him of it in any way.

9:16 nothing to boast of. That is to say, his boast (cf. v. 15) was not personal. He was not proud as if it were his gospel; nor was he proud about the way he preached it, as if it were his ability. **under compulsion.** Paul did not preach from personal pride, but from divine compulsion. He had no other choice, because God had sovereignly set him apart for service (see Ac 9:3–6, 15; 26:13–19; Gal 1:15; Col 1:25; cf. Jer 1:5; 20:9; Lk 1:13–17). **woe.** God's severest chastening is reserved for unfaithful ministers (Heb 13:17; Jas 3:1).

9:17 against my will. This does not indicate that Paul was unwilling to obey but that his will had no part in the call itself. Since it was God's sovereign choice and call, he received not a "reward," but a "stewardship" (a valuable responsibility or duty to be carefully managed).

9:18 my reward. Not money, but the privilege of preaching the gospel without support, was Paul's reward, so that he set aside his liberty ("right").

9:19 a slave. By choice, he set aside his right to be supported, and thus "enslaved" himself to self-support, in order to remove a potential offense and win more people to Jesus Christ (cf. Pr 11:30).

9:20 became as a Jew. Within the limits of God's Word and his Christian conscience, Paul would be as culturally and socially Jewish as necessary when witnessing to Jews (cf. Ro 9:3; 10:1; 11:14). He was not bound to ceremonies and traditions of Judaism. All legal restraints had been removed, but there was the constraint of love (cf. Ro 9:3; 10:1; 11:14). For examples of this identification with customs of the Jews, *see notes on Ac 16:3; 18:18; 21:20–26.*

9:21 those … without law. Gentiles. Paul was not suggesting the violating of God's moral law, but, as he explained, not being lawless toward God, but abiding by the law of Jesus Christ (cf. Jas 1:25; 2:8, 12).

9:22 weak. He stooped to make the gospel clear at the lower level of comprehension, which Paul no doubt had done often while dealing with the Corinthians themselves (cf. 2:1–5). **all things … all means.** Within the bounds of God's Word, he would not offend the Jew, Gentile, or those weak in understanding. Not changing Scripture or compromising the truth, he would condescend in ways that could lead to salvation.

9:24–27 Liberty cannot be limited without self-control, since the flesh resists limits on its freedom. Here, Paul speaks of his personal self-control.

9:24 race. The Greeks enjoyed two great

in such a way that you may win. 25 Everyone who
[A]competes in the games exercises self-control in
all things. They then *do it* to receive a perishable
[B]wreath, but we an imperishable. 26 Therefore I [A]run
in such a way, as not without aim; I box in such a
way, as not [B]beating the air; 27 but I [a]discipline [A]my
body and make it my slave, so that, after I have
preached to others, I myself will not be disqualified.

AVOID ISRAEL'S MISTAKES

10 For [A]I do not want you to be unaware, brethren, that our fathers were all [B]under the cloud
and all [C]passed through the sea; 2 and all were [A]bap-
tized into Moses in the cloud and in the sea; 3 and
all [A]ate the same spiritual food; 4 and all [A]drank the
same spiritual drink, for they were drinking from
a spiritual rock which followed them; and the rock
was [a]Christ. 5 Nevertheless, with most of them God
was not well-pleased; for [A]they were laid low in the
wilderness.
6 Now these things happened as [A]examples for
us, so that we would not crave evil things as [B]they
also craved. 7 Do not be [A]idolaters, as some of them
were; as it is written, "[B]THE PEOPLE SAT DOWN TO EAT
AND DRINK, AND STOOD UP TO [C]PLAY." 8 Nor let us act
immorally, as [A]some of them [a]did, and [B]twenty-three
thousand fell in one day. 9 Nor let us try the Lord,
as [A]some of them [a]did, and were destroyed by the
serpents. 10 Nor [A]grumble, as some of them [a]did,
and [B]were destroyed by the [C]destroyer. 11 Now these
things happened to them as an [A]example, and [B]they
were written for our instruction, upon whom [C]the
ends of the ages have come. 12 Therefore let him
who [A]thinks he stands take heed that he does not
fall. 13 No temptation has overtaken you but such as
is common to man; and [A]God is faithful, who will
not allow you to be [B]tempted beyond what you are
able, but with the temptation will provide the way
of escape also, so that you will be able to endure it.
14 Therefore, my [A]beloved, flee from [B]idolatry.
15 I speak as to wise men; you judge what I say.
16 Is not the [A]cup of blessing which we bless a
sharing in the blood of Christ? Is not the [a,B]bread
which we break a sharing in the body of Christ?

9:25 [A]Eph 6:12; 1 Tim 6:12; 2 Tim 2:5; 4:7 [B]2 Tim 4:8; James 1:12; 1 Pet 5:4; Rev 2:10; 3:11 9:26 [A]Gal 2:2; 2 Tim 4:7; Heb 12:1 [B]1 Cor 14:9 9:27 [a]Lit *bruise* [A]Rom 8:13 10:1 [A]Rom 1:13 [B]Ex 13:21; Ps 105:39 [C]Ex 14:22, 29; Neh 9:11; Ps 66:6 10:2 [A]Rom 6:3; 1 Cor 1:13; Gal 3:27 10:3 [A]Ex 16:4, 35; Deut 8:3; Neh 9:15, 20; Ps 78:24f; John 6:31 10:4 [a]I.e. the Messiah [A]Ex 17:6; Num 20:11; Ps 78:15 10:5 [A]Num 14:29ff, 37; 26:65; Heb 3:17; Jude 5 10:6 [A]1 Cor 10:11 [B]Num 11:4, 34; Ps 106:14 10:7 [A]Ex 32:4; 1 Cor 5:11; 10:14 [B]Ex 32:6 [C]Ex 32:19 10:8 [a]Lit *acted immorally* [A]Num 25:1ff [B]Num 25:9 10:9 [a]Lit *made trial* [A]Num 21:5f 10:10 [a]Lit *grumbled* [A]Num 16:41; 17:5, 10 [B]Num 16:49 [C]Ex 12:23; 2 Sam 24:16; 1 Chr 21:15; Heb 11:28 10:11 [A]1 Cor 10:6 [B]Rom 4:23 [C]Rom 13:11 10:12 [A]Rom 11:20; 2 Pet 3:17 10:13 [A]1 Cor 1:9 [B]2 Pet 2:9 10:14 [A]Heb 6:9 [B]1 Cor 10:7, 19f; 1 John 5:21 10:16 [a]Lit *loaf* [A]Matt 26:27f; Mark 14:23f; Luke 22:20; 1 Cor 11:25 [B]Matt 26:26; Luke 22:19; Acts 2:42; 1 Cor 11:23f

athletic events, the Olympic games and the Isthmian games, and because the Isthmian events were held in Corinth, believers there were quite familiar with this analogy of running to win.

9:25 self-control. Self-control is crucial to victory. **wreath.** A wreath of greenery given to the winner of the race. Cf. 2Ti 4:8; 1Pe 5:4.

9:26 not without aim. Four times he has mentioned his goal of winning people to salvation (vv. 19, 22). **beating the air.** Paul changes the metaphor to boxing to illustrate the point that he was no shadow boxer, just waving his arms without effect (cf. 1Ti 1:18).

9:27 discipline. From a term lit. meaning "to hit under the eye." He knocked out the bodily impulses to keep them from preventing him from his mission of winning souls to Christ. **disqualified.** Another metaphor from the athletic games. A contestant who failed to meet basic training requirements could not participate at all, much less have an opportunity to win. Paul may be especially referring to such fleshly sins that disqualify a man from preaching and leading the church, particularly being blameless and above reproach in the sexual area, since such sin is a disqualification (*see notes on Ps 101:6; 1Ti 3:2; Titus 1:6*).

10:1–13 Ancient Israel's 40-year journey between Egypt and Canaan (Ex 13:21; 14:16; 16:15; 17:6) is a sobering illustration of the misuse of freedom and the dangers of overconfidence. The Israelites misused their newfound freedom, fell into idolatry, immorality, and rebelliousness, disqualifying themselves from receiving the Lord's blessing.

10:1 unaware. This transition leads from the lack of self-discipline and subsequent disqualification spoken of in 9:27 to an illustration of it in ancient Israel. **our fathers.** Paul is referring to ancient Israel, of whom he was a descendant. In particular, he asked his readers to remember what had happened to Israel in the wilderness, because of freedom without self-control. **under the cloud.** Guided by God's presence as a cloud by day and column of fire at night (see Ex 13:21). **through the sea.** The Red Sea, which opened for Israel to pass through and closed to drown the Egyptian army (see Ex 14:26–31).

10:2 baptized. Israel was immersed, not in the sea, but "into Moses," indicating their oneness, or solidarity, with him as their leader.

10:3, 4 spiritual food ... drink. Actual food provided by the spiritual power of God. See Ex 16:15; 17:6.

10:4 a spiritual rock. The Jews had a legend that the actual rock Moses struck followed them throughout their wilderness wanderings, providing water for them. Paul says they have a Rock providing all they need, but it is Christ. Rock (*petra*) refers to a massive cliff, not simply a large stone or boulder, signifying the preincarnate Messiah (Christ), who protected and sustained His people. Cf. Mt 16:18.

10:5 not well-pleased. This is an understatement. Because of Israel's extreme disobedience, God allowed only two of the men over 19 who had originally left Egypt (Joshua and Caleb) to enter the Promised Land; all the others died in the wilderness, including Moses and Aaron who were disqualified from entering the Land (Nu 20:8–12, 24).

10:6 examples for us. They died in the wilderness because of their failure of self-discipline and consequent indulgence of every desire (*see note on 9:27*). Four major sins characterized them: idolatry (v. 7); sexual immorality (v. 8); testing God (v. 9); and complaining (v. 10).

10:7 idolaters. The Israelites were barely out of Egypt when they fell into idol worship. Exodus 32 records the story (v. 6 is quoted here). Some 3,000 were executed for instigating an immoral orgy at Sinai (Ex 32:28). See Ex 20:3; Eze 14:3; 1Jn 5:21; Rev 22:9. **play.** A euphemism for the gross sexual relations which followed the excessive feasting.

10:8 twenty-three thousand. Having just quoted from Ex 32 in v. 7, this very likely also refers to the incident in Ex 32, not to the incident at Shittim in Nu 25 (contra. marginal ref.). Apparently 3,000 were killed by the Levites (Ex 32:28) and 20,000 died in the plague (Ex 32:35).

10:9 try the Lord. Numbers 21 records this story of the people questioning the goodness and plan of the One carrying them through the wilderness, the Protector and Provider, the spiritual Rock, Christ pre-incarnate (*see note on v. 4*). **serpents.** See Nu 21:6; cf. 11:30.

10:10 destroyer. This incident is recorded in Nu 16:3–41. The same angel had slain the firstborn of the Egyptians (Ex 12:23), the 70,000 men because of David's census (2Sa 24:15, 16), and the entire Assyrian army that was besieging Jerusalem (2Ch 32:21).

10:11 the ends of the ages. The time of Messiah; the last days of redemptive history before the messianic kingdom. See Heb 9:26; 1Jn 2:18.

10:12 Cf. Pr 16:18. The Bible is filled with examples of overconfidence (see Est 3–5; Is 37:36–38; Lk 22:33, 34, 54–62; Rev 3:1–3, 17).

10:13 temptation. *See notes on Jas 1:13–15*; cf. Mt 6:13. **common to man.** One Gr. word meaning "that which is human."

10:16 cup of blessing. The proper name given to the third cup during the Passover Feast. At the last Passover with the disciples, Jesus used the third cup as the symbol of His blood shed for sin. That cup became the one used to institute the Lord's Supper. He set the cup apart as a token of salvation blessing before passing it to the 12 (*see notes on Lk 22:17, 20*). **a sharing.** This word means "to have in common, to participate and have partnership with." The same Gr. word is used in 1:9; 2Co 8:4; Php 2:1; 3:10. Commemorating the Lord's

17 Since there is one [a]bread, we [A]who are many are one body; for we all partake of the one [a]bread. 18 Look at [a]the nation [A]Israel; are not those who [B]eat the sacrifices sharers in the altar? 19 What do I mean then? That a thing sacrificed to idols is anything, or [A]that an idol is anything? 20 *No,* but *I say* that the things which the Gentiles sacrifice, they [A]sacrifice to demons and not to God; and I do not want you to become sharers in demons. 21 [A]You cannot drink the cup of the Lord and the cup of demons; you cannot partake of the table of the Lord and [B]the table of demons. 22 Or do we [A]provoke the Lord to jealousy? We are not [B]stronger than He, are we?

23 [A]All things are lawful, but not all things are profitable. All things are lawful, but not all things [B]edify. 24 Let no one [A]seek his own *good,* but that of his [a]neighbor. 25 [A]Eat anything that is sold in the meat market without asking questions for conscience' sake; 26 [A]FOR THE EARTH IS THE LORD'S, AND [a]ALL IT CONTAINS. 27 If [A]one of the unbelievers invites you and you want to go, [B]eat anything that is set before you without asking questions for conscience' sake. 28 But [A]if anyone says to you, "This is meat sacrificed to idols," do not eat *it,* for the sake of the one who informed *you,* and for conscience' sake; 29 I mean not your own conscience, but the other *man's;* for [A]why is my freedom judged by another's conscience? 30 If I partake with thankfulness, [A]why am I slandered concerning that for which I [B]give thanks?

31 Whether, then, you eat or drink or [A]whatever you do, do all to the glory of God. 32 [A]Give no offense either to Jews or to Greeks or to [B]the church of God; 33 just as I also [A]please all men in all things, [B]not seeking my own profit but the *profit* of the many, [C]so that they may be saved.

CHRISTIAN ORDER

11 [A]Be imitators of me, just as I also am of Christ. 2 Now [A]I praise you because you [B]remember me in everything and [C]hold firmly to the traditions, just as I delivered them to you. 3 But I want you to understand that [a]Christ is the [A]head of every man, and [B]the man is the head of a woman, and God is the [C]head of [a]Christ. 4 Every man who has *something* on his head while praying or [A]prophesying

10:17 [a]Lit *loaf* [A]Rom 12:5; 1 Cor 12:12f, 27; Eph 4:4, 16; Col 3:15 10:18 [a]Lit *Israel according to the flesh* [A]Rom 1:3 [B]Lev 7:6, 14f; Deut 12:17f 10:19 [A]1 Cor 8:4 10:20 [A]Deut 32:17; Ps 106:37; Gal 4:8; Rev 9:20 10:21 [A]2 Cor 6:16 [B]Is 65:11 10:22 [A]Deut 32:21 [B]Eccl 6:10; Is 45:9 10:23 [A]1 Cor 6:12 [B]Rom 14:19 10:24 [a]Lit *the other* [A]Rom 15:2; 1 Cor 10:33; 13:5; 2 Cor 12:14; Phil 2:21 10:25 [A]Acts 10:15; 1 Cor 8:7 10:26 [a]Lit *its fullness* [A]Ps 24:1; 50:12; 1 Tim 4:4 10:27 [A]1 Cor 5:10 [B]Luke 10:8 10:28 [A]1 Cor 8:7, 10-12 10:29 [A]Rom 14:16; 1 Cor 9:19 10:30 [A]1 Cor 9:1 [B]Rom 14:6 10:31 [A]Col 3:17; 1 Pet 4:11 10:32 [A]Acts 24:16; 1 Cor 8:13 [B]Acts 20:28; 1 Cor 1:2; 7:17; 11:22; 15:9; 2 Cor 1:1; Gal 1:13; Phil 3:6; 1 Tim 3:5, 15 10:33 [A]Rom 15:2; 1 Cor 9:22; Gal 1:10 [B]Rom 15:2; 1 Cor 13:5; 2 Cor 12:14; Phil 2:21 [C]Rom 11:14; 1 Thess 2:16 11:1 [A]1 Cor 4:16; Phil 3:17 11:2 [A]1 Cor 11:17, 22 [B]1 Cor 4:17; 15:2; 1 Thess 1:6; 3:6 [C]2 Thess 2:15; 3:6 11:3 [a]I.e. the Messiah [A]Eph 1:22; 4:15; 5:23; Col 1:18; 2:19 [B]Gen 3:16; Eph 5:23 [C]1 Cor 3:23 11:4 [A]Acts 13:1; 1 Thess 5:20

Supper was a regular and cherished practice in the early church, by which believers remembered their Savior's death and celebrated their common salvation and eternal life which reflected their perfect spiritual oneness. **the blood of Christ.** A vivid phrase used to represent Christ's sacrificial death and full atoning work. *See note on Ro 5:9.* See Ac 20:28; Ro 3:25; Eph 1:7; 2:13; Col 1:20; 1Pe 1:19; 1Jn 1:7; Rev 1:5; 5:9. **the bread.** This symbolized our Lord's body as the cup symbolized His blood. Both point to His death as a sacrifice for the salvation of men.

10:17 is one bread. This refers to the bread of communion as the symbol of Christ's body given for all who believe. Since we all partake of that body, we are one. *See note on 6:17.*

10:18 Look at . . . Israel. In the OT sacrifices, the offering was on behalf of all who ate (see Lv 7:15–18). By such action, the people were identifying with the offering and affirming their devotion to God to whom it was offered. Paul was, by this, implying how any sacrifice made to an idol (see vv. 7, 14) was identifying with and participating with that idol. It is completely inconsistent for believers to participate in any such worship (v. 21).

10:19, 20 Idols and the things sacrificed to them have no spiritual nature or power in themselves (cf. 8:4, 8), but they do represent the demonic. If pagan worshipers believe an idol was a god, demons act out the part of the imagined god (cf. 2Th 2:9–11). There is not a true god in the idol, but there is a satanic spiritual force (cf. Dt 32:17; Ps 106:37).

10:22 jealousy. God tolerates no competition and will not allow idolatry to go unpunished. (Dt 32:21; Jer 25:6, 9; Rev 21:8; cf. 11:30).

10:23–30 Paul gives 4 principles for Christian liberty: 1) edification over gratification (v. 23); 2) others over self (v. 24); 3) liberty over legalism (vv. 25–27); and 4) condescension over condemnation (vv. 28–30).

10:23 *See note on 6:12.* **edify.** To build up in Christian doctrine (cf. 8:1; 14:3, 4, 26; Ac 20:32; 2Co 12:19; Eph 4:12; 2Ti 3:16, 17).

10:24 *See notes on Php 2:3.*

10:25, 26 Quoting Ps 24:1, Paul declares that believers, though not participating in idol ceremonies (*see notes on vv. 18–20*), should not hesitate to buy meat once used in such ceremonies and eat it without guilt (*see note on 1Ti 4:4, 5*).

10:27 eat anything. So as not to offend the unbeliever.

10:28, 29 Even if you are the guest of an unbeliever and don't want to offend him, it is better to offend the unbeliever and not eat for the sake of the weaker Christian who would be offended to eat, since love to other believers is the strongest witness we have (Jn 13:34, 35).

10:29 my freedom judged by another's conscience. Offending a weaker brother with one's freedom will cause the offended person to condemn us.

10:30 We can't truly offer thanks to God for some food by which we cause another believer to stumble.

10:31 glory. Christian liberty, as well as the most common behavior, is to be conducted to the honor of God. Cf. Eze 36:23.

10:32 Those 3 groups cover all humanity. We are to be careful to offend none.

10:33 please all men. *See notes on 9:19–22.*

11:1 Be imitators of me. *See notes on 4:16; Eph 5:1; Php 3:17; 4:9.*

11:2 traditions. In the strict sense used here, a synonym for God's Word (cf. 2Th 2:15). The NT sometimes uses the word in a negative way, referring to man-made ideas or practices, especially those that conflict with Scripture (cf. Mt 15:2–6; Gal 1:14; Col 2:8).

11:3–15 There is no distinction between men and women as far as personal worth, intellect, or spirituality are concerned (cf. Gal 3:28). That women function uniquely in God's order, however, submitting to men's authority, Paul affirms by several points: 1) the pattern in the Godhead (v. 3); 2) the divine design of male and female (v. 7); 3) the order of creation (v. 8); 4) the purpose of woman in regard to man (v. 9); 5) the concern of the angels (v. 10); and 6) the characteristics of natural physiology (vv. 13–15).

11:3 Christ. Christ is the head of the church as its Savior and Lord (cf. Eph 1:22, 23; 4:15; Col 1:18). He is also the Lord over every unbeliever (cf. Mt 28:18; Heb 2:8). Someday all will acknowledge His authority (cf. Php 2:10, 11). **man.** Men have authority over women in the basic order of creation (cf. vv. 8, 9; cf. Is 3:12; Eph 5:22–33). *See notes on 1Ti 2:11–15.* **God.** Christ has never been in any way inferior in essence to the Father (Jn 10:30; 17:21–24), but in His incarnation He willingly submitted Himself to the Father's will in humble obedience (3:23; 15:24–28; cf. Jn 4:34; 5:30; 6:38).

11:4 ***something* on his head . . . disgraces.** Lit. "having down from head" is probably a reference to men wearing a head covering, which seems to have been a local custom. Jews began wearing head coverings during the fourth century A.D., although some may already have been wearing them in NT times. Apparently, Corinthian men were doing the same, and Paul informs them that it is a disgrace. Paul is not stating a universal law from God, but acknowledging a local custom, which did reflect divine principle. In that society, a man's uncovered head was a sign of his authority over women, who were to have their heads covered. For a man to cover his head was to suggest a reversal of proper roles.

disgraces his head. 5 But every [A]woman who has her head uncovered while praying or prophesying disgraces her head, for she is one and the same as the woman [a]whose head is [B]shaved. 6 For if a woman does not cover [a]her head, let her also [b]have her hair cut off; but if it is disgraceful for a woman to [b]have her hair cut off or [a]her head shaved, let her cover [a]her head. 7 For a man ought not to have his head covered, since he is the [A]image and glory of God; but the woman is the glory of man. 8 For [A]man [a]does not originate from woman, but woman from man; 9 for indeed man was not created for the woman's sake, but [A]woman for the man's sake. 10 Therefore the woman ought to have *a symbol of* authority on her head, because of the angels. 11 However, in the Lord, neither is woman [a]independent of man, nor is man [a]independent of woman. 12 For as the woman [a]originates from the man, so also the man *has his birth* through the woman; and [A]all things [b]originate [B]from God. 13 [A]Judge [a]for yourselves: is it proper for a woman to pray to God *with her head* uncovered? 14 Does not even nature itself teach you that if a man has long hair, it is a dishonor to him, 15 but if a woman has long hair, it is a glory to her? For her hair is given to her for a covering. 16 But if one is inclined to be contentious, [A]we have no [a]other practice, nor have [B]the churches of God.

17 But in giving this instruction, [A]I do not praise you, because you come together not for the better but for the worse. 18 For, in the first place, when you come together [a]as a church, I hear that [b,A]divisions exist among you; and in part I believe it. 19 For there [A]must also be factions among you, [B]so that those who are approved may become [a]evident among you. 20 Therefore when you meet together, it is not to eat the Lord's Supper, 21 for in your eating each one takes his own supper first; and one is hungry and [A]another is drunk. 22 What! Do you not have houses in which to eat and drink? Or do you despise the [A]church of God and [B]shame those who have nothing? What shall I say to you? Shall [C]I praise you? In this I will not praise you.

THE LORD'S SUPPER

23 For [A]I received from the Lord that which I also delivered to you, that [B]the Lord Jesus in the night in which He was betrayed took bread; 24 and when He had given thanks, He broke it and said, "This is My body, which is for you; do this in remembrance of

11:5 [a]Lit *who is shaved* [A]Luke 2:36; Acts 21:9; 1 Cor 14:34 [B]Deut 21:12 11:6 [a]Lit *herself* [b]Lit *shear herself* 11:7 [A]Gen 1:26; 5:1; 9:6; James 3:9 11:8 [a]Lit *is not from* [A]Gen 2:21-23; 1 Tim 2:13 11:9 [A]Gen 2:18 11:11 [a]Lit *without* 11:12 [a]Lit *is* [b]Lit *are* [A]2 Cor 5:18 [B]Rom 11:36 11:13 [a]Lit *in* [A]Luke 12:57 11:16 [a]Lit *such* [A]1 Cor 4:5; 9:1-3, 6 [B]1 Cor 7:17 11:17 [A]1 Cor 11:2, 22 11:18 [a]Lit *in church* [b]Lit *schisms* [A]1 Cor 1:10; 3:3 11:19 [a]Or *manifest* [A]Matt 18:7; Luke 17:1; 1 Tim 4:1; 2 Pet 2:1 [B]Deut 13:3; 1 John 2:19 11:21 [A]Jude 12 11:22 [A]1 Cor 10:32 [B]James 2:6 [C]1 Cor 11:2, 17 11:23 [A]1 Cor 15:3; Gal 1:12; Col 3:24 [B]1 Cor 11:23-25: *Matt 26:26-28; Mark 14:22-24; Luke 22:17-20;* 1 Cor 10:16

11:5 woman . . . while praying or prophesying. Paul makes clear directives that women are not to lead or speak in the services of the church (cf. 14:34; 1Ti 2:12), but they may pray and proclaim the truth to unbelievers, as well as teaching children and other women (cf. 1Ti 5:16; Titus 2:3, 4). *See note on Ac 21:9.* Wherever and whenever women do pray and proclaim the Word appropriately, they must do so maintaining a proper distinction from men. **uncovered.** In the culture of Corinth, a woman's covered head while ministering or worshiping was a symbol to signify a subordinate relationship to her husband. The apostle is not laying down an absolute law for women to wear veils or coverings in all churches for all time, but is declaring that the symbols of the divinely established male and female roles are to be genuinely honored in every culture. As in the case of meat offered to idols (chaps. 8, 9), there is nothing spiritual about wearing or not wearing a covering. But manifesting rebellion against God's order was wrong. **disgraces her head.** "Head" may refer to her own self being disgraced by refusing to conform to recognized symbols of submission, or to her husband, who is disgraced by her behavior.

11:6 disgraceful . . . hair cut off. In that day only a prostitute or a feminist would shave her head. If a Christian woman rejected the covering that symbolized her submission in that culture, she might as well have shaved her head—the shame was similar.

11:7 image and glory of God. Though men and women were both created in God's image (Ge 1:27), it is man who bears the glory of God uniquely by his role. Like God, he is given a sphere of sovereignty as the earthly sovereign over God's created order. *See notes on Ge 3:16, 17.*

11:7, 8 woman is the glory of man. As man carries authority delegated to him by God, so woman carries authority delegated to her by God through her husband. Man came from God; woman came from man (cf. Ge 2:9–23; 1Ti 2:11–13).

11:9 See Ge 2:18–23.

11:10 angels. Women are to be submissive by wearing the symbol of authority so as not to offend these most holy and submissive creatures who watch the church (cf. Mt 18:10; Eph 3:9, 10), who were present (Job 38:4, 7) at creation, when God designed the order of authority for men and women.

11:11, 12 All believers, male and female, are equal in the Lord and complementary in the Lord's work. Their roles are different in function and relationships, not in spirituality or importance (cf. Gal 3:28). *See note on 1Ti 2:15.*

11:13 is it proper. Aside from apostolic command, Paul asked, in effect, "Isn't it self-evident that women should not be uncovered?"

11:14, 15 nature. The term can convey the idea of basic human awareness, i.e., the innate sense of what is normal and right. The male hormone, testosterone, speeds up the loss of hair in men. Estrogen causes women's hair to grow longer and for a longer time. Women are rarely bald, no matter how old. This physiology is reflected in most cultures in the custom of longer hair on women. God has given her hair as a covering to show tenderness, softness, and beauty.

11:16 no other practice. Neither the Lord, the apostles, nor the churches would allow female rebellion. Women were to maintain their distinctively feminine hairdos; and when custom dictated, they should wear a covering.

11:17–34 The early church love feasts (cf. Jude 12) usually closed with observance of the Lord's Supper. The worldly, fleshly church at Corinth had turned those sacred meals into gluttonous, drunken revelries (v. 17; cf. 2Pe 2:13). Beyond that, wealthy believers brought ample food and drink for themselves but refused to share, letting their poorer brethren go away hungry (v. 21).

11:17 worse. A comparative Gr. word which refers to moral evil.

11:18 divisions. The church was torn by dissension (see 1:10–17; 3:1–3).

11:19 approved . . . evident. Factions revealed who passed the test of spiritual genuineness and purity (cf. 1Th 2:4).

11:20 it is not to eat the Lord's Supper. The love feast and communion celebration had become so perverted that it was a sinful, selfish mockery. They could not legitimately say it was devoted to the Lord, since it was not honoring to Him.

11:21, 22 If they intended to selfishly indulge themselves, they might as well have stayed at home.

11:23–26 While the information was not new to the Corinthians, because Paul had previously "delivered" it, it is an important reminder. This description of Christ's final supper with His disciples is one of the most beautiful in all of Scripture, yet it was given in the midst of a strong rebuke of carnal selfishness. If this letter was written before any of the Gospels (see Mt 26:26–30; Mk 14:22–26; Lk 22:17–20; Jn 13:2), as most conservative scholars believe, then Paul's instruction was the first biblical record of the institution of the Lord's Supper—given directly from the Lord and not through his reading of any other apostles (cf. Gal 1:10–12).

Me." 25 In the same way *He took* [A]the cup also after
supper, saying, "This cup is the [B]new covenant in
My blood; do this, as often as you drink *it,* in remembrance of Me." 26 For as often as you eat this
bread and drink the cup, you proclaim the Lord's
death [A]until He comes.
27 Therefore whoever eats the bread or drinks the
cup of the Lord in an unworthy manner, shall be
[A]guilty of the body and the blood of the Lord. 28 But
a man must [A]examine himself, and in so doing he
is to eat of the bread and drink of the cup. 29 For he
who eats and drinks, eats and drinks judgment to
himself if he does not judge the body rightly. 30 For
this reason many among you are weak and sick,
and a number [a,A]sleep. 31 But if we judged ourselves
rightly, we would not be judged. 32 But when we
are judged, we are [A]disciplined by the Lord so that
we will not be condemned along with [B]the world.
33 So then, my brethren, when you come together
to eat, wait for one another. 34 If anyone is [A]hungry,
let him eat [B]at home, so that you will not come together for judgment. The remaining matters I will
[C]arrange [D]when I come.

THE USE OF SPIRITUAL GIFTS

12 Now concerning [A]spiritual *gifts,* brethren, [B]I
do not want you to be unaware. 2 [A]You know
that when you were pagans, *you were* [B]led astray to
the [C]mute idols, however you were led. 3 Therefore
I make known to you that no one speaking [a,A]by the
Spirit of God says, "Jesus is [b,B]accursed"; and no one
can say, "Jesus is [C]Lord," except [a,A]by the Holy Spirit.
4 Now there are [A]varieties of gifts, but the same
Spirit. 5 And there are varieties of ministries, and
the same Lord. 6 There are varieties of effects, but
the same [A]God who works all things in all *persons.*

11:25 [A]1 Cor 10:16 [B]Ex 24:6-8; Luke 22:20; 2 Cor 3:6 11:26 [A]John 21:22; 1 Cor 4:5 11:27 [A]Heb 10:29 11:28 [A]Matt 26:22; 2 Cor 13:5; Gal 6:4 11:30 [a]I.e. are dead [A]Acts 7:60 11:32 [A]2 Sam 7:14; Ps 94:12; Heb 12:7-10; Rev 3:19 [B]1 Cor 1:20 11:34 [A]1 Cor 11:21 [B]1 Cor 11:22 [C]1 Cor 4:17; 7:17; 16:1 [D]1 Cor 4:19 12:1 [A]1 Cor 12:4; 14:1 [B]Rom 1:13 12:2 [A]1 Cor 6:11; Eph 2:11f; 1 Pet 4:3 [B]1 Thess 1:9 [C]Ps 115:5; Is 46:7; Jer 10:5; Hab 2:18f 12:3 [a]Or *in* [b]Gr *anathema* [A]Matt 22:43; 1 John 4:2f; Rev 1:10 [B]Rom 9:3 [C]John 13:13; Rom 10:9 12:4 [A]Rom 12:6f; 1 Cor 12:11; Eph 4:4ff, 11; Heb 2:4 12:6 [A]1 Cor 15:28; Eph 1:23; 4:6

11:25 new covenant in My blood. The Old Covenant was practiced repeatedly by the blood of animals offered by men; but the New Covenant has been ratified once and for all by the death of Christ (cf. Heb 9:28). **in remembrance of Me.** Jesus transformed the third cup of the Passover into the cup of remembrance of His offering (*see note on 10:16*).

11:26 The gospel is presented through the service of communion as the elements are explained. They point to His physical incarnation, sacrificial death, resurrection, and coming kingdom.

11:27 in an unworthy manner. I.e., ritualistically, indifferently, with an unrepentant heart, a spirit of bitterness, or any other ungodly attitude. **guilty.** To come to the Lord's Table clinging to one's sin does not only dishonor the ceremony, but it also dishonors His body and blood, treating lightly the gracious sacrifice of Christ for us. It is necessary to set all sin before the Lord (v. 28), then partake, so as not to mock the sacrifice for sin, by holding on to it.

11:29 judgment. I.e., chastisement. **not judge the body rightly.** When believers do not properly judge the holiness of the celebration of communion, they treat with indifference the Lord Himself—His life, suffering, and death (cf. Ac 7:52; Heb 6:6; 10:29).

11:30 sleep. I.e., are dead. *See note on 15:18.* The offense was so serious that God put the worst offenders to death, an extreme but effective form of church purification (cf. Lk 13:1–5; Ac 5:1–11; 1Jn 5:16).

11:32 Believers are kept from being consigned to hell, not only by divine decree, but by divine intervention. The Lord chastens to drive His people back to righteous behavior and even sends death to some in the church (v. 30) to remove them before they could fall away (cf. Jude 24).

11:34 There is no point in gathering together to sin and be chastened.

12:1–14:40 This section focuses on spiritual gifts in the church, dealing with a vital, but controversial, subject. The false religion situation in Corinth caused counterfeit spiritual manifestations that had to be confronted. The church was being informed on this subject by Paul and its behavior would be regulated by the truth and the Spirit.

12:1 spiritual *gifts.* The NASB translators italicized "*gifts*" to indicate that the word is not in the original but is implied by the context (cf. vv. 4, 9, 28, 30, 31; 14:1). The Gr. lit. means "pertaining to the Spirit," referring to that which has spiritual qualities or characteristics or is under some form of spiritual control. Spiritual gifts are divine enablements for ministry that the Holy Spirit gives in some measure to all believers and that are to be completely under His control and used for the building of the church to Christ's glory (*see notes on Ro 12:4–8*). These had to be distinguished from the mystical experiences called "ecstasy" (supernatural, sensuous communion with a deity) and "enthusiasm" (divination, dreams, revelations, visions) that were found in the pagan religions of Corinth.

12:2 pagans. That is, Gentiles (1Th 4:5; 1Pe 2:12). **led astray.** Incredibly, some church members were mimicking certain dramatic and bizarre practices of the mystery religions in which they had been formerly involved. The practice of ecstasy, considered to be the highest expression of religious experience, involved supposed supernatural interaction with a deity, induced through frenzied hypnotic chants and ceremonies. The practice frequently included drunkenness (cf. Eph 5:18) and sexual orgies, to which the devotees willfully yielded themselves to be led into gross sin.

12:3 accursed. This is the most severe kind of condemnation. Some of the Corinthians were fleshly and given over to ecstasies that were controlled by demons. In that condition, they actually claimed to be prophesying or teaching in the Spirit while demonically blaspheming the name of the Lord whom they were supposed to be worshiping. They had been judging the use of gifts on the basis of experience and not content. Satan always assaults the person of Christ. It is possible that the curser of Christ was a Gentile claiming to be a Christian, but holding to a philosophy that all matter was evil, including the human Jesus (i.e., pre-gnosticism). They might have said that the Christ spirit left the human Jesus before His death, and therefore Jesus died a cursed death as a mere man. **Jesus is Lord.** Cf. Ac 2:36; Ro 10:9, 10; Eph 1:20, 21; Php 2:9–11. The validity of any speaking exercise is determined by the truthfulness of it. If the speaker affirms the lordship of Jesus, it is the truth from the Holy Spirit. What a person believes and says about Jesus Christ is the test of whether he speaks from the Holy Spirit. He always leads people to Christ's lordship (cf. 2:8–14; Jn 15:26; 1Jn 5:6–8).

12:4 gifts. These categories of giftedness are not natural talents, skills, or abilities, such as are possessed by believers and unbelievers alike. They are sovereignly and supernaturally bestowed by the Holy Spirit on all believers (vv. 7, 11), enabling them to spiritually edify each other effectively and thus honor the Lord. The varieties of gifts fall into two general types, speaking and serving (see vv. 8–10; cf. Ro 12:6–8; 1Pe 4:10, 11). The speaking, or verbal, gifts (prophecy, knowledge, wisdom, teaching, and exhortation) and the serving, nonverbal gifts (leadership, helps, giving, mercy, faith, and discernment) are all permanent gifts that will operate throughout the church age. Their purpose is to edify the church and glorify God. The list here and in Ro 12:3–8 is best seen as representative of categories of giftedness which the Holy Spirit draws from to give each believer whatever kind or combination of kinds He chooses (v. 11). Some believers may be gifted categorically similar to others but are personally unique as the Spirit suits each grace gift to the individual. Miracles, healing, tongues, and the interpretation of tongues were temporary sign gifts limited to the apostolic age and have, therefore, ceased. Their purpose was to authenticate the apostles and their message as the true Word of God, until God's written Word was completed and became self-authenticating. *See notes on vv. 9, 10.*

12:5, 6 varieties of ministries … varieties of effects. The Lord gives believers unique ministry arenas in which to fulfill their giftedness, and provides varieties of power to energize and accomplish them (cf. Ro 12:6).

7 But to each one is given the manifestation of the
Spirit [A]for the common good. 8 For to one is given
the word of [A]wisdom through the Spirit, and to
another the word of [B]knowledge according to the
same Spirit; 9 to another [A]faith [a]by the same Spirit,
and to another [B]gifts of [b]healing [a]by the one Spirit,
10 and to another the [a]effecting of [b,A]miracles, and to
another [B]prophecy, and to another the [c,C]distinguish-
ing of spirits, to another *various* [D]kinds of tongues,
and to another the [E]interpretation of tongues. 11 But
one and the same Spirit works all these things, [A]dis-
tributing to each one individually just as He wills.
12 For even [A]as the body is one and *yet* has many
members, and all the members of the body, though
they are many, are one body, [B]so also is Christ. 13 For
[a,A]by one Spirit we were all baptized into one body,
whether [B]Jews or Greeks, whether slaves or free, and
we were all made to [C]drink of one Spirit.

12:7 [A]1 Cor 12:12-30; 14:26; Eph 4:12 12:8 [A]1 Cor 2:6; 2 Cor 1:12 [B]Rom 15:14; 1 Cor 2:11, 16; 2 Cor 2:14; 4:6; 8:7; 11:6 12:9 [a]Or *in* [b]Lit *healings* [A]1 Cor 13:2; 2 Cor 4:13 [B]1 Cor 12:28, 30 12:10 [a]Lit *effects* [b]Or *works of power* [c]Lit *distinguishings* [A]1 Cor 12:28f; Gal 3:5 [B]1 Cor 11:4; 13:2, 8 [C]1 Cor 14:29; 1 John 4:1 [D]Mark 16:17; 1 Cor 12:28, 30; 13:1; 14:2ff [E]1 Cor 12:30; 14:26 12:11 [A]1 Cor 12:4 12:12 [A]Rom 12:4f; 1 Cor 10:17 [B]1 Cor 12:27 12:13 [a]Or *in* [A]Eph 2:18 [B]Rom 3:22; Gal 3:28; Eph 2:13-18; Col 3:11 [C]John 7:37-39

12:7 manifestation of the Spirit. No matter what the gift, ministry, or effect, all spiritual gifts are from the Holy Spirit. They make Him known, understood, and evident in the church and in the world, by spiritually profiting all who receive their ministry.

12:8 the word of wisdom. "Word" indicates a speaking gift (*see note on v. 4*; cf. 1Pe 4:11). In the NT, "wisdom" is most often used of the ability to understand God's Word and His will, and to skillfully apply that understanding to life (cf. Mt 11:19; 13:54; Mk 6:2; Lk 7:35; Ac 6:10; Jas 1:5; 3:13, 17; 2Pe 3:15). **the word of knowledge.** This gift may have been revelatory in the first century, but it is today the ability to understand and speak God's truth, with insight into the mysteries of His Word, that cannot be known apart from God's revelation (Ro 16:25; Eph 3:3; Col 1:26; 2:2; 4:3; cf. 13:2). Knowledge majors on grasping the meaning of the truth; wisdom emphasizes the practical conviction and conduct that applies it.

12:9 faith. Distinct from saving faith or persevering faith, both of which all believers possess, this gift is exercised in persistent prayer and endurance in intercession, along with a strong trust in God in the midst of difficult circumstances (cf. Mt 17:20). **healing.** A temporary sign gift used by Christ (Mt 8:16, 17), the apostles (Mt 10:1), the seventy (Lk 10:1), and a few associates of the apostles, such as Philip (Ac 8:5–7). This ability was identified as a gift belonging to the apostles (cf. 2Co 12:12). Although Christians today do not have the gifts of healings, God certainly still hears and answers the faithful prayers of His children (see Jas 5:13–16). Some people feel that healing should be common and expected in every era, but this is not the case. Physical healings are very rare throughout the OT record. Only a few are recorded. There was never a time before the coming of Christ when healings were common. Only in His lifetime and that of His apostles was there a veritable explosion of healing. This was due to the unique need to accredit the Messiah and to authenticate the first miracles of the gospel. Jesus and His apostles temporarily banished disease from Israel, but that was the most monumental era of redemptive history and called for such authentication. To normalize healing would be to normalize the arrival of the Savior. This gift belonged to the sign gifts for that era only. The gifts of healings were never used solely for bringing people physical health. Paul was sick but never healed himself or asked another human to heal him. His friend Epaphroditus was near death (Php 2:27), and Paul did not heal him. God intervened. When Timothy was sick, Paul did not heal him, but told him to take some wine (1Ti 5:23). Paul left Trophimus "sick at Miletus" (2Ti 4:20). Healings were not the everyday norm in Paul's ministry, but did occur when he entered a new region, e.g., Malta, where the gospel and its preacher needed authentication (see Ac 28:8, 9). That healing was the first mention of healing since the lame man was healed in Lystra (Ac 14:9) in connection with the arrival of Paul and the gospel there. Prior to that, the nearest healing was by Peter in Ac 9:34, and the resurrection of Tabitha in 9:41, so that people would believe the gospel Peter preached (9:42).

12:10 miracles. This temporary sign gift was for the working of divine acts contrary to nature, so that there was no explanation for the action except that it was by the power of God. This, too, was to authenticate Christ and the apostolic preachers of the gospel. John 2:11 notes that Jesus did His first miracle at Cana to "manifest His glory," not enhance the party (cf. John's purpose for recording the miracles of Jesus in this Gospel, 20:30, 31). Ac 2:22 affirms that Jesus did miracles to "attest" that God was working through Him, so that people would believe in Him as Lord and Savior. Jesus performed miracles and healed only for the 3 years of His ministry, not at all in the 30 years before. His miracles began when His ministry began. Though Jesus did miracles related to nature (made wine, created food, walked on water with Peter, ascended), no apostle ever is reported to have done a miracle in the natural realm. What miracle did the apostles do? The answer is in the word "miracles," meaning "power," and is frequently connected to casting out demons (Lk 4:36; 6:18; 9:42). It is precisely that power that the Lord gave the disciples (Lk 9:1; 10:17–19; cf. Ac 6:8; 8:7; 13:6–12). *See notes on Ac 19:14–16.* **prophecy.** The meaning is simply that of "speaking forth," or "proclaiming publicly" to which the connotation of prediction was added sometime in the Middle Ages. Since the completion of Scripture, prophecy has not been a means of new revelation, but is limited to proclaiming what has already been revealed in the written Word. Even the biblical prophets were preachers, proclaimers of God's truth both by revelation and reiteration. Old Testament prophets like Isaiah, Jeremiah, and Ezekiel spent lifetimes proclaiming God's Word. Only a comparatively small amount of what they preached is recorded in the Bible as God's direct revelation. They must have continually repeated and reemphasized those truths, as preachers today repeat, explain, and reemphasize the Word of God in Scripture. The best definition for this gift is given in 14:3. The importance of this gift is given in 14:1, 39. Its supremacy to other gifts, especially tongues, is the theme of chap. 14. *See notes on 1Th 5:20; Rev 19:10.* **distinguishing of spirits.** Satan is the great deceiver (Jn 8:44), and his demons counterfeit God's message and work. Christians with the gift of discernment have the God-given ability to recognize lying spirits and to identify deceptive and erroneous doctrine (cf. Ac 17:11; 1Jn 4:1). Paul illustrated the use of this gift in Ac 16:16–18, as Peter had exercised it in Ac 5:3. When it was not being exercised in the Corinthian church, grave distortion of the truth occurred (see v. 3; 14:29). Though its operation has changed since apostolic times, because of the completion of Scripture, it is still essential to have people in the church who are discerning. They are the guardians, the watchmen who protect the church from demonic lies, false doctrines, perverted cults, and fleshly elements. As it requires diligent study of the Word to exercise gifts of knowledge, wisdom, preaching, and teaching, so it does with discernment. *See notes on 1Th 5:20–22.* **tongues ... interpretation.** These temporary sign gifts, using the normal words for speaking a foreign language and translating it, like the others (miracles, healings) were for the authentication of the truth and those who preached it. This true gift was clearly identified in Ac 2:5–12 as languages, which validated the gospel as divine. They were, however, because of their counterfeit in the culture, disproportionately exalted and seriously abused in Corinth. Here, Paul identified them, but throughout chap. 14 he discussed them in detail. *See notes on 14:1–39.*

12:11 one and the same Spirit. While stressing the diversity of gifts (vv. 4–11), Paul also stressed the singular source in the Spirit (cf. vv. 4, 5, 6, 8, 9). This is the fifth mention, in this chapter, of the source of gifts being the Holy Spirit. It emphasizes that gifts are not something to seek, but to be received from the Spirit "as He wills." It is He alone who "works" or energizes (v. 6) all gifts as He chooses.

12:12 body ... members. Paul used the human body as an analogy (cf. 10:17) for the unity of the church in Christ. From this point on to v. 27, he used "body" 18 times (cf. Ro 12:5; Eph 1:23; 2:16; 4:4, 12, 16; Col 1:18).

12:13 baptized. The church, the spiritual body of Christ, is formed as believers are immersed by Christ with the Holy Spirit. Christ is the baptizer (*see note on Mt 3:11*) who immerses each believer with the Spirit into unity with all other believers. Paul is not writing of water baptism. That outward sign depicts the believer's union with Christ in His death and resurrection (*see notes on*

14 For [A]the body is not one member, but many.
15 If the foot says, "Because I am not a hand, I am
not *a part* of the body," it is not for this reason
[a]any the less *a part* of the body. 16 And if the ear
says, "Because I am not an eye, I am not *a part* of
the body," it is not for this reason [a]any the less *a*
part of the body. 17 If the whole body were an eye,
where would the hearing be? If the whole were
hearing, where would the sense of smell be? 18 But
now God has [A]placed the members, each one of
them, in the body, [B]just as He desired. 19 If they
were all one member, where would the body be?
20 But now [A]there are many members, but one
body. 21 And the eye cannot say to the hand, "I
have no need of you"; or again the head to the feet,
"I have no need of you." 22 On the contrary, [a]it is
much truer that the members of the body which
seem to be weaker are necessary; 23 and those
members of the body which we [a]deem less honorable, [b]on these we bestow more abundant honor,
and our less presentable members become much
more presentable, 24 whereas our more presentable members have no need *of it.* But God has *so*
composed the body, giving more abundant honor
to that *member* which lacked, 25 so that there may
be no [a]division in the body, but *that* the members
may have the same care for one another. 26 And if
one member suffers, all the members suffer with
it; if *one* member is [a]honored, all the members
rejoice with it.
27 Now you are [A]Christ's body, and [B]individually
members of it. 28 And God has [a,A]appointed in [B]the
church, first [C]apostles, second [D]prophets, third
[E]teachers, then [b,F]miracles, then [G]gifts of healings,
helps, [H]administrations, *various* [I]kinds of tongues.
29 All are not apostles, are they? All are not prophets,
are they? All are not teachers, are they? All are not
workers of [a]miracles, are they? 30 All do not have
gifts of healings, do they? All do not speak with
tongues, do they? All do not [A]interpret, do they?
31 But [A]earnestly desire the greater gifts.

And I show you a still more excellent way.

12:14 [A]1 Cor 12:20 12:15 [a]Lit *not* a part 12:16 [a]Lit *not* a part 12:18 [A]1 Cor 12:28 [B]Rom 12:6; 1 Cor 12:11 12:20 [A]1 Cor 12:12, 14 12:22 [a]Lit *to a much greater degree the members* 12:23 [a]Or *think to be* [b]Or *these we clothe with* 12:25 [a]Lit *schism* 12:26 [a]Lit *glorified* 12:27 [A]1 Cor 1:2; 12:12; Eph 1:23; 4:12; Col 1:18, 24; 2:19 [B]Rom 12:5; Eph 5:30 12:28 [a]Lit *set some in* [b]Or *works of power* [A]1 Cor 12:18 [B]1 Cor 10:32 [C]Eph 4:11 [D]Acts 13:1; Eph 2:20; 3:5 [E]Acts 13:1 [F]1 Cor 12:10, 29 [G]1 Cor 12:9, 30 [H]Rom 12:8 [I]1 Cor 12:10 12:29 [a]Or *works of power* 12:30 [A]1 Cor 12:10 12:31 [A]1 Cor 14:1, 39

Ro 6:3, 4). Similarly, all believers are also immersed into the body of Christ by means of the Holy Spirit. Paul's point is to emphasize the unity of believers. There cannot be any believer who has not been Spirit-baptized, nor can there be more than one Spirit baptism, or the whole point of unity in the body of Christ is convoluted. Believers have all been Spirit-baptized and thus are all in one body. *See notes on Eph 4:4–6.* This is not an experience to seek, but a reality to acknowledge. *See also notes on Ac 8:17; 10:44, 45; 11:15, 16.* **drink of one Spirit.** At salvation, all believers not only become full members of Christ's body, the church, but the Holy Spirit is placed within each of them (Ro 8:9; cf. 6:19; Col 2:10; 2Pe 1:3, 4). There is no need (or divine provision) for any such thing as a second blessing, a triumphalistic experience of a deeper life, or a formula for instantly increased spirituality (cf. Jn 3:34). Christ's salvation provision is perfect, and He calls only for obedience and trust in what has already been given (Heb 10:14).

12:14–20 By his illustration of how every part of a human body is essential to the function of that body, Paul showed that unity is an indispensable need of the church; but divinely provided diversity within that unity is also necessary. His words additionally implied that some selfish members were discontent with their gifts, wanting the gifts they had not been given (v. 11). With that attitude, they in effect questioned God's wisdom and implied He had made a mistake in assignments (cf. v. 3; Ro 9:20, 21). In seeking showy abilities and power, they also became vulnerable to carnal, demonically counterfeited gifts.

12:18 Here again, *as in v. 11,* Paul dealt with the foolish and carnal Corinthians who were discontent with what had been given them sovereignly for the edification of the church and the glory of its Lord. *See note on v. 31.*

12:21 no need. While some in Corinth were bemoaning the fact that they did not have the showy gifts (*see note on vv. 14–20*), those who did were belittling those with the more quiet and less prominent gifts. The "eye" and the "head," which are highly visible and the focus of all who engage each other, represent the people with public gifts. They so overestimated their own importance that they disdained those whom they perceived as less gifted and less significant. They were apparently indifferent ("I have no need") and self-sufficient.

12:22–24 Paul's answer to the pride of the more visibly gifted was to engage his analogy again and remind them that the more fragile and less lovely, in fact, ugly parts of the body which are not publicly "presentable" (v. 24) are given the greater respect for their necessity. He spoke of the internal organs.

12:25 God has designed visible, public gifts to have a crucial place, but equally designed and more vital to life are the hidden gifts, thus maintaining the perspective of unity—all are essential to the working of the body of Christ.

12:26, 27 This is a call to mutual love and concern in the fellowship of believers (cf. Php 2:1–4) which maintains the unity that honors the Lord. There is one body in which all function, yet never do they lose their personal identity and the essential necessity of ministry as God has designed them to do it.

12:28–30 God has appointed. Again emphasizing the sovereignty of God (cf. vv. 7, 11, 18), Paul illustrates the individuality and unity of the body by a repeat of the representative categories of ministries, callings, and giftedness.

12:28 apostles ... prophets. *See notes on Eph 4:11.* Their purpose was: 1) to lay the foundation of the church (Eph 2:20); 2) to receive and declare the revelation of God's Word (Ac 11:28; 21:10, 11; Eph 3:5); and 3) to give confirmation of that Word through signs, wonders, and miracles (2Co 12:12; cf. Ac 8:6, 7; Heb 2:3, 4). "Apostles" refers, primarily, to those 12 chosen by our Lord plus Paul and Matthias (Ac 1:26). *See note on Ro 1:1.* In a secondary sense, others served as messengers of the church: Barnabas (Ac 14:14), Silas and Timothy (1Th 2:6), and others (Ro 16:7; 2Co 8:23; Php 2:25). Apostles of Christ were the source of the church's doctrine (Ac 2:42); apostles of the church (2Co 8:23) were its early leaders. "Prophets" were especially gifted men in the local churches, who preached God's Word (Ac 11:21–28; 13:1). Any message preached by a prophet had to be judged by the word of the apostles (*see note on 14:36, 37*). **teachers.** Could be the same as pastor-teachers (*see note on Eph 4:11*), but probably should be broadened to include all who are gifted for teaching in the church, whether they have the office of pastor or not. **miracles ... healings ... tongues.** *See notes on vv. 9, 10.* **helps, administrations.** These less public gifts are mingled with the more public manifestations of the Spirit to show their vital necessity (v. 22). "Helps" is an ability for service; in fact, the gift of ministry ("service") in Ro 12:7 is in the same category. "Administrations" is leadership. The word comes from the Gr., meaning "to pilot a ship" (Ac 27:11) and speaks of one who can lead ministries of the church efficiently and effectively.

12:29, 30 Each of these rhetorical queries expects a "no" answer. The body of Christ is diverse, and God sovereignly designs it that way.

12:31 earnestly desire. In context, this could not mean that believers should desire the more prominent gifts, when the whole chapter has just been confronting the fact that they have sinfully been doing just that. Desiring a gift for selfish reasons is wrong, since they are sovereignly given by God as He wills (vv. 7, 11, 18, 28). Therefore, this must be rendered not as an imperative (command), but, as the verb form allows, as an indicative (statement of fact), "You are desiring the showy gifts, wrongly." The real imperative is to stop doing that and learn the "more excellent way," the way of love, which Paul will explain in chap. 13.

THE EXCELLENCE OF LOVE

13 If I speak with the [A]tongues of men and of
[B]angels, but do not have love, I have become
a noisy gong or a [C]clanging cymbal. 2 If I have *the*
gift of [A]prophecy, and know all [B]mysteries and all
[C]knowledge; and if I have [D]all faith, so as to [E]remove
mountains, but do not have love, I am nothing. 3 And
if I [A]give all my possessions to feed *the poor,* and
if I [B]surrender my body [a]to be burned, but do not
have love, it profits me nothing.
4 Love [A]is patient, love is kind *and* [B]is not jealous;
love does not brag *and* is not [C]arrogant, 5 does not
act unbecomingly; it [A]does not seek its own, is not
provoked, [B]does not take into account a wrong *suf-*
fered, 6 [A]does not rejoice in unrighteousness, but
[B]rejoices with the truth; 7 [a,A]bears all things, believes
all things, hopes all things, endures all things.
8 Love never fails; but if *there are gifts of* [a,A]proph-
ecy, they will be done away; if *there are* [B]tongues,
they will cease; if *there is* knowledge, it will be done
away. 9 For we [A]know in part and we prophesy in
part; 10 but when the perfect comes, the partial will
be done away. 11 When I was a child, I used to speak
like a child, think like a child, reason like a child;
when I [a]became a man, I did away with childish
things. 12 For now we [A]see in a mirror [a]dimly, but
then [B]face to face; now I know in part, but then I
will know fully just as I also [C]have been fully known.
13 But now faith, hope, love, abide these three; but
the [a]greatest of these is [A]love.

13:1 [A]1 Cor 12:10 [B]2 Cor 12:4; Rev 14:2 [C]Ps 150:5 13:2 [A]Matt 7:22; Acts 13:1; 1 Cor 11:4; 13:8; 14:1, 39 [B]1 Cor 14:2; 15:51 [C]Rom 15:14 [D]1 Cor 12:9 [E]Matt 17:20; 21:21; Mark 11:23 13:3 [a]Early mss read *that I may boast* [A]Matt 6:2 [B]Dan 3:28 13:4 [A]Prov 10:12; 17:9; 1 Thess 5:14; 1 Pet 4:8 [B]Acts 7:9 [C]1 Cor 4:6 13:5 [A]1 Cor 10:24; Phil 2:21 [B]2 Cor 5:19 13:6 [A]2 Thess 2:12 [B]2 John 4; 3 John 3f 13:7 [a]Or *covers* [A]1 Cor 9:12 13:8 [a]Lit *prophecies* [A]1 Cor 13:2 [B]1 Cor 13:1 13:9 [A]1 Cor 8:2; 13:12 13:11 [a]Lit *have become... have done away with* 13:12 [a]Lit *in a riddle* [A]2 Cor 5:7; Phil 3:12; James 1:23 [B]Gen 32:30; Num 12:8; 1 John 3:2 [C]1 Cor 8:3 13:13 [a]Lit *greater* [A]Gal 5:6

13:1–13 Spiritual gifts were present in Corinth (1:7); right doctrine was even in place (11:2); but love was absent. This led to the quarrels and exhibitions of selfishness and pride that plagued the church—notably in the area of spiritual gifts (*see notes on 12:14–31*). Instead of selfishly and jealously desiring showy gifts which they don't have, believers should pursue the greatest thing of all—love for one another. This chapter is considered by many the greatest literary passage ever penned by Paul. It is central to his earnestly dealing with spiritual gifts (chaps. 12–14), because after discussing the endowment of gifts (chap. 12) and before presenting the function of gifts (chap. 14), he addresses the attitude necessary in all ministry in the church (chap. 13).

13:1 **tongues of men.** Cf. 12:10, 28; 14:4–33. That this gift was actual languages is established in Ac 2:1–13 (*see notes there*), affirmed in this text by Paul's calling it "of men"—clearly a reference to human language. This was the gift which the Corinthians prized so highly, abused so greatly, and counterfeited so disastrously. God gave the ability to speak in a language not known to the speaker, as a sign with limited function (*see notes on 14:1–33*). **tongues ... of angels.** The apostle was writing in general hypothetical terms. There is no biblical teaching of any special angelic language that people could learn to speak. **love.** Self-giving love that is more concerned with giving than receiving (Jn 3:16; cf. 14:1; Mt 5:44, 45; Jn 13:1, 34, 35; 15:9; Ro 5:10; Eph 2:4–7; Php 2:2; Col 3:14; Heb 10:24). The word was not admired and thus seldom used in ancient Gr. literature, but it is common in the NT. Without love, no matter how linguistically gifted one is to speak his own language, other languages, or even (hypothetically) the speech of angels, his speech is noise only. In NT times, rites honoring the pagan deities Cybele, Bacchus, and Dionysius included ecstatic noises accompanied by gongs, cymbals, and trumpets. Unless the speech of the Corinthians was done in love, it was no better than the gibberish of pagan ritual.

13:2 ***the gift of* prophecy.** *See notes on 12:10.* In 14:1–5, Paul speaks of this gift as the most essential one because it brings God's truth to people. Even this gift must be ministered in love (cf. Eph 4:15). **know all mysteries and all knowledge.** This encompasses gifts of wisdom, knowledge, and discernment (*see notes on 12:8, 10*), which are to be exercised in love (see Php 1:9). **all faith.** *See note on Mt 17:20.* This refers to the gift of faith (enduring, believing prayer; *see note on 12:9*), which is useless without selfless love for the church.

13:3 **burned.** The practice of burning Christians at the stake did not begin until some years later, but it was clearly understood to be an extremely horrible death. Neither volunteering for giving up all your possessions or being burned would produce any spiritual benefit if not done out of love for the body of Christ.

13:4–7 In the previous comments (vv. 1–3), the focus is on the emptiness produced when love is absent from ministry. In these verses, the fullness of love is described, in each case by what love does. Love is action, not abstraction. Positively, love is patient with people and gracious to them with generosity. Negatively, love never envies, or brags, or is arrogant, since that is the opposite of selfless service to others. Never rude or overbearing, love never wants its own way, is not irritated or angered in personal offense, and finds no pleasure in someone else's sin, even the sin of an enemy. On the positive side again, love is devoted to truth in everything. With regard to "all things" within God's righteous and gracious will, love protects, believes, hopes, and endures what others reject.

13:8–10 **never fails.** This refers to love's lastingness or permanence as a divine quality. Love outlasts all failures (cf. 1Pe 4:8; 1Jn 4:16). Paul strengthens his point on the permanence of love by comparing it to the spiritual gifts which the Corinthians so highly prized: prophecy, knowledge, and tongues, all of which will have an end. There may be a distinction made on how prophecy and knowledge come to an end, and how the gift of tongues does. This is indicated by the Gr. verb forms used. In the case of prophecy and knowledge, they are both said to "be done away" (in both cases the verb indicates that something will put an end to those two functions). Verses 9, 10 indicate that what will abolish knowledge and prophecy is that which is "perfect." When that occurs, those gifts will be rendered inoperative. The "perfect" is not the completion of Scripture, since there is still the operation of those two gifts and will be in the future kingdom (cf. Joel 2:28; Ac 2:17; Rev 11:3). The Scriptures do not allow us to see "face to face" or have perfect knowledge as God does (v. 12). The "perfect" is not the rapture of the church or the second coming of Christ, since the kingdom to follow these events will have an abundance of preachers and teachers (cf. Is 29:18; 32:3, 4; Joel 2:28; Rev 11:3). The perfect must be the eternal state, when we in glory see God face to face (Rev 22:4) and have full knowledge in the eternal new heavens and new earth. Just as a child grows to full understanding, believers will come to perfect knowledge, and no such gifts will be necessary.

On the other hand, Paul uses a different word for the end of the gift of tongues, or languages, thus indicating it will "cease" by itself, as it did at the end of the apostolic age. It will not end by the coming of the "perfect," for it will already have ceased. The uniqueness of the gift of tongues and its interpretations was, as all sign gifts, to authenticate the message and messengers of the gospel before the NT was completed (Heb 2:3, 4). "Tongues" was also limited by being a judicial sign from the God of Israel's judgment (*see note on 14:21*; cf. Is 28:11, 12). "Tongues" were also not a sign to believers, but unbelievers (*see note on 14:22*), specifically those unbelieving Jews. Tongues also ceased because there was no need to verify the true messages from God once the Scripture was given. It became the standard by which all are to be deemed true. "Tongues" was a means of edification in a way far inferior to preaching and teaching (*see notes on 14:5, 12, 27, 28*). In fact, chap. 14 was designed to show the Corinthians, so preoccupied with tongues, that it was an inferior means of communication (vv. 1–12), an inferior means of praise (vv. 13–19), and an inferior means of evangelism (vv. 20–25). Prophecy was and is, far superior (vv. 1, 3–6, 24, 29, 31, 39). That tongues have ceased should be clear from their absence from any other books in the NT, except Acts. Tongues ceased to be an issue of record or practice in the early church, as the Scripture was being written. That tongues has ceased should be clear also from its absence through church history since the first century, appearing only sporadically and then only in questionable groups. A more detailed discussion is given in the notes on chap. 14.

13:13 **love.** The objects of faith and hope will be fulfilled and perfectly realized in heaven, but love, the God-like virtue, is everlasting (cf. 1Jn 4:8). Heaven will be the place for the expression of nothing but perfect love toward God and one another.

PROPHECY A SUPERIOR GIFT

14 [A]Pursue love, yet [B]desire earnestly [C]spiritual
gifts, but especially that you may [D]prophesy.
2 For one who [A]speaks in a tongue does not speak
to men but to God; for no one [a]understands, but
[b]in *his* spirit he speaks [B]mysteries. 3 But one who
prophesies speaks to men for [A]edification and [B]ex-
hortation and consolation. 4 One who [A]speaks in a
tongue [B]edifies himself; but one who [C]prophesies
[B]edifies the church. 5 Now I wish that you all [A]spoke
in tongues, but [B]*even* more that you would prophesy; and greater is one who prophesies than one
who [A]speaks in tongues, unless he interprets, so
that the church may receive [C]edifying.

6 But now, brethren, if I come to you speaking in
tongues, what will I profit you unless I speak to you
either by way of [A]revelation or of [B]knowledge or of
[C]prophecy or of [D]teaching? 7 Yet *even* lifeless things,
either flute or harp, in producing a sound, if they do
not produce a distinction in the tones, how will it be
known what is played on the flute or on the harp? 8 For
if [A]the [a]bugle produces an indistinct sound, who will
prepare himself for battle? 9 So also you, unless you
utter by the tongue speech that is clear, how will it
be known what is spoken? For you will be [A]speaking
into the air. 10 There are, perhaps, a great many kinds
of [a]languages in the world, and no *kind* is without
meaning. 11 If then I do not know the meaning of the
language, I will be to the one who speaks a [a,A]barbar-
ian, and the one who speaks will be a [a]barbarian [b]to
me. 12 So also you, since you are zealous of [a]spiritual
gifts, seek to abound for the [A]edification of the church.

14:1 [A]1 Cor 16:14 [B]1 Cor 12:31; 14:39 [C]1 Cor 12:1 [D]1 Cor 13:2 14:2 [a]Lit *hears* [b]Or *by the Spirit* [A]Mark 16:17; 1 Cor 12:10, 28, 30; 13:1; 14:18ff [B]1 Cor 13:2 14:3 [A]Rom 14:19; 1 Cor 14:5, 12, 17, 26 [B]Acts 4:36 14:4 [A]Mark 16:17; 1 Cor 12:10, 28, 30; 13:1; 14:18ff, 26f [B]Rom 14:19; 1 Cor 14:5, 12, 17, 26 [C]1 Cor 13:2 14:5 [A]Mark 16:17; 1 Cor 12:10, 28, 30; 13:1; 14:18ff, 26f [B]Num 11:29 [C]Rom 14:19; 1 Cor 14:4, 12, 17, 26 14:6 [A]1 Cor 14:26; Eph 1:17 [B]1 Cor 12:8 [C]1 Cor 13:2 [D]Acts 2:42; Rom 6:17; 1 Cor 14:26 14:8 [a]Lit *trumpet* [A]Num 10:9; Jer 4:19; Ezek 33:3-6; Joel 2:1 14:9 [A]1 Cor 9:26 14:10 [a]Lit *voices* 14:11 [a]Or *foreigner* [b]Or *in my estimation* [A]Acts 28:2 14:12 [a]Lit *spirits* [A]Rom 14:19; 1 Cor 14:4, 5, 17, 26

14:1 Pursue love. A command for every believer. Because lovelessness was a root spiritual problem in the Corinthian church, the godly love just described should have been sought after by them with particular determination and diligence. **desire ... spiritual *gifts*.** Love does not preclude the use of these enablements. Since Paul has addressed not desiring showy gifts (12:31) and not elevating one over the other (12:14–25), some might think it best to set them all aside for unity's sake. Spiritual gifts, on the other hand, are sovereignly bestowed by God on each believer and necessary for the building of the church (12:1–10). Desire for them, in this context, is in reference to their use collectively and faithfully in His service—not a personal yearning to have an admired gift that one did not possess. As a congregation, the Corinthians should be wanting the full expression of all the gifts to be exercised. "You" is plural, emphasizing the corporate desire of the church. **especially ... prophesy.** This spiritual gift was desirable in the life of the church to serve in a way that tongues cannot, namely, by edifying the entire church (v. 5).

14:2–39 Although it is not indicated consistently in some translations, the distinction between the singular *tongue* and the plural *tongues* is foundational to the proper interpretation of this chapter. Paul seems to use the singular to distinguish the counterfeit gift of pagan gibberish and the plural to indicate the genuine gift of a foreign language (*see note on v. 2*). It was perhaps in recognition of that, that the King James Version (KJV) translators added consistently the word "unknown" before every singular form (see vv. 2, 4, 13, 14, 19, 27). The implications of that distinction will be noted as appropriate. Against the backdrop of carnality and counterfeit ecstatic speech learned from the experience of the pagans, Paul covers 3 basic issues with regard to speaking in languages by the gift of the Holy Spirit: 1) its position, inferior to prophecy (vv. 1–19); 2) its purpose, a sign to unbelievers not believers (vv. 20–25); and 3) its procedure, systematic, limited, and orderly (vv. 26–40).

14:2 one who speaks in a tongue. This is singular (*see previous note*; cf. vv. 4, 13, 14, 19, 27), indicating that it refers to the false gibberish of the counterfeit pagan ecstatic speech. The singular is used because gibberish can't be plural; there are not various kinds of non-language. There are, however, various languages; hence when speaking of the true gift of language, Paul uses the plural to make the distinction (vv. 6, 18, 22, 23, 29). The only exception is in vv. 13, 27, 28 (*see note there*), where it refers to a single person speaking a single genuine language. **does not speak to men but to God.** This is better translated "to a god." The Gr. text has no definite article (see similar translation in Ac 17:23, "an unknown god"). Their gibberish was worship of pagan deities. The Bible records no incident of any believer ever speaking to God in any other than normal human language. **no one understands ... in *his* spirit he speaks mysteries.** The fleshly, or carnal, Corinthians using the counterfeit ecstatic speech of paganism were not interested in being understood, but in making a dramatic display. The spirit by which they spoke was not the Holy Spirit, but their own human spirit or some demon; and the mysteries they declared were the type associated with the pagan mystery religions, which was espoused to be the depths that only the initiated few were privileged to know and understand. Those mysteries were totally unlike the ones mentioned in Scripture (e.g., Mt 13:11; Eph 3:9), which are divine revelations of truths previously hidden (*see notes on 12:7; Eph 3:4–6*).

14:3 prophesies. In dramatic contrast to the bedlam of counterfeit tongues was the gift of genuine prophecy or preaching of the truth (*see note on 12:10*). It produced the building up in truth, the encouragement to obedience, and the comfort in trouble that God desired for His church. Spiritual gifts are always for the benefit of others, never self.

14:4 a tongue. Again (as in v. 2), Paul uses the singular to refer to the pagan counterfeit gibberish and sarcastically (cf. v. 16; 4:8–10 for other sarcasm) marks its selfishness as some kind of self-edification. This illicit building up of self comes from pride-induced emotion which only produces more pride. **edifies the church.** *See note on 12:7.*

14:5 all spoke in tongues ... that you would prophesy. Here the plural, "tongues," appears as Paul was referring to the real gift of tongues, or languages (*see note on v. 2*). Obviously, this was not Paul's true desire, even for the true gift, since the very idea was impossible and contrary to God's sovereign distribution of gifts (12:11, 30). He was simply suggesting hypothetically that, if they insisted on clamoring after gifts they did not possess, they at least should seek the one that was more enduring and more valuable for the church. The only purpose tongues renders to the church is when it is interpreted (the normal Gr. word for translation). Wherever God gave the gift of tongues, He also gave the gift for translation, so that the sign would also be edifying. Never was the gift to be used without such translation (v. 28), so that the church would always be edified.

14:6 if I come to you ... what will I profit ... ? Even an apostle who spoke in tongues did not spiritually benefit a congregation unless, through interpretation, his utterance was clarified so that the revelation and knowledge could be understandably preached and taught. Any private use of this gift is excluded for several reasons: 1) it is a sign to unbelievers (v. 22); 2) it must have a translator to have any meaning, even to the speaker (v. 2); and 3) it must edify the church (v. 6).

14:7–9 Here, Paul illustrates his previous point about the uselessness of even the true gift apart from translation for the church to understand. If even inanimate musical instruments are expected to make sensible sounds, how much more should human speech make sense, especially when it deals with the things of God? *See note on v. 23.*

14:10, 11 Paul simply points up the obvious: the purpose of *every* language is to communicate, not to impress and certainly not to confuse, as the Corinthians had been doing with their counterfeits. That was clearly the point in the first instance of tongues: each heard the apostles speak in his own language (Ac 2:6, cf. v. 8). This section makes an undeniable case for the fact that the true gift of tongues was never some unintelligible gibberish, but was human language that was to be translated (v. 13).

14:12 Again Paul returned to the issue of edification, central to all gifts (12:7).

13 Therefore let one who speaks in a tongue pray
that he may interpret. 14 For if I pray in a tongue,
my spirit prays, but my mind is unfruitful. 15 [A]What
is *the outcome* then? I will pray with the spirit and
I will pray with the mind also; I will [B]sing with the
spirit and I will sing with the mind also. 16 Otherwise if you bless [a]in the spirit *only,* how will the one
who fills the place of the [b]ungifted say [A]the "Amen"
at your [B]giving of thanks, since he does not know
what you are saying? 17 For you are giving thanks
well enough, but the other person is not [A]edified.
18 I thank God, I speak in tongues more than you
all; 19 however, in the church I desire to speak five
words with my mind so that I may instruct others
also, rather than ten thousand words in a tongue.

INSTRUCTION FOR THE CHURCH

20 [A]Brethren, [B]do not be children in your thinking; yet in evil [C]be infants, but in your thinking be
mature. 21 In [A]the Law it is written, "[B]BY MEN OF
STRANGE TONGUES AND BY THE LIPS OF STRANGERS
I WILL SPEAK TO THIS PEOPLE, AND EVEN SO THEY
WILL NOT LISTEN TO ME," says the Lord. 22 So then
tongues are for a sign, not to those who believe but
to unbelievers; but [A]prophecy *is for a sign,* not to
unbelievers but to those who believe. 23 Therefore if
the whole church assembles together and all speak
in tongues, and [a]ungifted men or unbelievers enter, will they not say that [A]you are mad? 24 But if all
[A]prophesy, and an unbeliever or an [a]ungifted man
enters, he is [B]convicted by all, he is called to account
by all; 25 [A]the secrets of his heart are disclosed; and
so he will [B]fall on his face and worship God, [C]declar-
ing that God is certainly among you.

26 [A]What is *the outcome* then, [B]brethren? When
you assemble, [C]each one has a [D]psalm, has a [E]teach-
ing, has a [E]revelation, has a [F]tongue, has an [G]inter-
pretation. Let [H]all things be done for edification.

14:15 [A]Acts 21:22; 1 Cor 14:26 [B]Eph 5:19; Col 3:16 14:16 [a]Or *with the* [b]I.e. unversed in spiritual gifts [A]Deut 27:15-26; 1 Chr 16:36; Neh 5:13; 8:6; Ps 106:48; Jer 11:5; 28:6; Rev 5:14; 7:12 [B]Matt 15:36 14:17 [A]Rom 14:19; 1 Cor 14:4, 5, 12, 26 14:20 [A]Rom 1:13 [B]Eph 4:14; Heb 5:12f [C]Ps 131:2; Matt 18:3; Rom 16:19; 1 Pet 2:2 14:21 [A]John 10:34; 1 Cor 14:34 [B]Is 28:11f 14:22 [A]1 Cor 14:1 14:23 [a]V 16, note 2 [A]Acts 2:13 14:24 [a]V 16, note 2 [A]1 Cor 14:1 [B]John 16:8 14:25 [A]John 4:19 [B]Luke 17:16 [C]Is 45:14; Dan 2:47; Zech 8:23; Acts 4:13 14:26 [A]1 Cor 14:15 [B]Rom 1:13 [C]1 Cor 12:8-10 [D]Eph 5:19 [E]1 Cor 14:6 [F]1 Cor 14:2 [G]1 Cor 12:10; 14:5, 13, 27f [H]Rom 14:19

14:14–17 Paul continued to speak sarcastically (cf. v. 16; 4:8–10) about counterfeit tongues, so he used the singular "tongue" (*see note on vv. 2–39*), which refers to the fake gift. He was speaking hypothetically to illustrate the foolishness and pointlessness of speaking in ecstatic gibberish. The speaker could not understand, and what virtue is there in praying to God or praising God without understanding? No one can "Amen" such nonsense.

14:16 **ungifted.** From the Gr. word meaning ignorant or unlearned.

14:18 **I speak in tongues more than you all.** Paul emphasized that by writing all of this, he was not condemning genuine tongues (plural); nor, as some may have thought to accuse him, was he envious of a gift he did not possess. At that point, he stopped speaking hypothetically about counterfeit tongue-speaking. He actually had more occasions to use the true gift than all of them (though we have no record of a specific instance). He knew the true gift and had used it properly. It is interesting, however, that the NT makes no mention of Paul's actually exercising that gift. Nor does Paul in his own writings make mention of a *specific* use of it by *any* Christian.

14:19 **instruct others.** This is the general principle that summarizes what he has been saying, i.e., teaching others is the important matter and that requires understanding.

14:20–25 This very important passage deals with the primary purpose of the gift of languages. Paul has clearly indicated that such speaking was not something for all believers to do, since it was dispensed sovereignly like all other gifts (12:11); nor was it connected to the baptism with the Holy Spirit which all believers receive (12:13); nor was it some superior sign of spirituality, but rather an inferior gift (v. 5). Because of all that, and the corruption of the real gift by the Corinthians, the apostle gives the principles for its proper and limited operation as a sign.

14:20 **in evil be infants, but in your thinking be mature.** Most of the Corinthian believers were the opposite of what Paul here admonished. They were extremely experienced in evil, but greatly lacking in wisdom. Yet mature understanding was especially essential for proper comprehension and use of the gift of tongues, because the conspicuous and fascinating nature of that gift made it so attractive to the flesh. He was asking his readers to put aside emotion and experience, along with the desires of the flesh and pride, to think carefully about the purpose of tongues.

14:21 **it is written.** In a freely rendered quotation from Is 28:11, 12, Paul explains that centuries earlier the Lord had predicted that one day He would use men of other tongues, that is, foreigners speaking unknown languages, as a sign to *unbelieving Israel,* who "WILL NOT LISTEN TO ME." These "STRANGE TONGUES" are what they knew as the gift of languages, given solely as a sign to unbelieving Israel. That sign was 3-fold: cursing, blessing, and authority. To emphasize the cursing, Paul quoted Isaiah's words of warning to Judah of the judgment from Assyria (*see note on Is 28:11, 12*). The leaders thought his words were too simple and rejected him. The time would come, the prophet said, when they would hear Assyrian, a language they could not understand, indicating judgment. Jeremiah spoke similarly of the Babylonians who were also to come and destroy Judah (cf. Jer 5:15). When the apostles spoke at Pentecost in all those foreign languages (Ac 2:3–12), the Jews should have known that the judgment prophesied and historically fulfilled first by the Assyrians and then by the Babylonian captivity was about to fall on them again for their rejection of Christ, including the destruction of Jerusalem (A.D. 70) as it had happened in 586 B.C. under Babylonian power.

14:22 **So then tongues are for a sign, not to those who believe but to unbelievers.** Explaining further, Paul says explicitly that all tongues are for the sake of unbelievers. In other words, that gift has no purpose in the church when everyone present is a believer. And once the sign served its purpose to pronounce judgment or cursing on Israel, and the judgment fell, the purpose ceased along with the sign gift. The blessing of that sign was that God would build a new nation of Jews and Gentiles to be His people (Gal 3:28), to make Israel jealous and someday repent (see Ro 11:11, 12, 25–27). The sign was thus repeated when Gentiles were included in the church (Ac 10:44–46). The sign also gave authority to those who preached both the judgment and blessing (2Co 12:12), including Paul (v. 18). **but prophecy *is* ... to those who believe.** In the completely opposite way, the gift of prophesying benefits only believers, who are able, by their new natures and the indwelling Holy Spirit, to understand spiritual truth (cf. 2:14; 1Jn 2:20, 27).

14:23 **Therefore if ... all speak in tongues.** As Paul explains in more detail later (vv. 27, 28), even for unbelievers, even when the gift of tongues was exercised in its proper time in history, when it was dominant and uncontrolled in the church, bedlam ensued and the gospel was disgraced and discredited. **you are mad.** The Gr. word means to be in an uncontrolled frenzy. When the real gift was used in Ac 2, there was no madness, and everyone understood in his own language (v. 11). In Corinth, there was charismatic chaos.

14:24, 25 **But if all prophesy.** This means to publicly proclaim the Word of God (*see note on 12:10*). "All" does not mean all at once (see v. 31), but rather means that hypothetically if the cacophony of all the Corinthians could be replaced by all of them preaching the Word, the effect on unbelievers would be amazingly powerful, the gospel would be honored, and souls would be converted to worshiping God.

14:26–40 In this last section on the topic of tongues, the stress is on how they were to be systematically limited for use in the church in an orderly way. For the sake of hypothetical discussion, it is noteworthy that even if one granted that the gift was still in use today, the modern movement would be totally discredited as illegitimate by its failure to follow the clear, controlling commands in these verses.

14:26 **each one has.** It seems that chaos and lack of order was rampant in that assembly (v. 33). It is interesting that no elders or pastors are mentioned, and the prophets were not even exercising control (see vv. 29, 32, 37). Everyone was participating with whatever expression they desired whenever they

27 If anyone speaks in a [A]tongue, *it should be* by two or at the most three, and *each* in turn, and one must [B]interpret; 28 but if there is no interpreter, he must keep silent in the church; and let him speak to himself and to God. 29 Let two or three [A]prophets speak, and let the others [B]pass judgment. 30 But if a revelation is made to another who is seated, the first one must keep silent. 31 For you can all prophesy one by one, so that all may learn and all may be exhorted; 32 and the spirits of prophets are subject to prophets; 33 for God is not *a God* of [A]confusion but of [a]peace, as in [B]all the churches of the [C]saints.

34 The women are to [A]keep silent in the churches; for they are not permitted to speak, but [B]are to subject themselves, just as [C]the Law also says. 35 If they desire to learn anything, let them ask their own husbands at home; for it is [a]improper for a woman to speak in church. 36 [a]Was it from you that the word of God *first* went forth? Or has it come to you only?

37 [A]If anyone thinks he is a prophet or [B]spiritual, let him recognize that the things which I write to you [C]are the Lord's commandment. 38 But if anyone does not recognize *this,* he [a]is not recognized.

39 Therefore, my brethren, [A]desire earnestly to [B]prophesy, and do not forbid to speak in tongues. 40 But [A]all things must be done properly and in an orderly manner.

THE FACT OF CHRIST'S RESURRECTION

15 Now [A]I make known to you, brethren, the [B]gospel which I preached to you, which also you received, [C]in which also you stand, 2 by which also you are saved, [A]if you hold fast [a]the word which I preached to you, [B]unless you believed in vain.

3 For [A]I delivered to you [a]as of first importance what I also received, that Christ died [B]for our sins [C]according to the Scriptures, 4 and that He was buried, and that He was [A]raised on the third day [B]according to the Scriptures, 5 and that [A]He appeared to [B]Cephas, then [C]to the twelve. 6 After that He appeared to more than five hundred brethren at one

14:27 [A]1 Cor 14:2 [B]1 Cor 12:10; 14:5, 13, 26ff 14:29 [A]1 Cor 13:2; 14:32, 37 [B]1 Cor 12:10 14:33 [a]Or *peace. As in all...saints, let* [A]1 Cor 14:40 [B]1 Cor 4:17; 7:17 [C]Acts 9:13 14:34 [A]1 Cor 11:5, 13 [B]1 Tim 2:11f; 1 Pet 3:1 [C]1 Cor 14:21 14:35 [a]Or *disgraceful* 14:36 [a]Lit *Or was* 14:37 [A]2 Cor 10:7 [B]1 Cor 2:15 [C]1 John 4:6 14:38 [a]Two early mss read *is not to be recognized* 14:39 [A]1 Cor 12:31 [B]1 Cor 13:2; 14:1 14:40 [A]1 Cor 14:33 15:1 [A]Rom 2:16; Gal 1:11 [B]Rom 2:16; 1 Cor 3:6; 4:15 [C]Rom 5:2; 11:20; 2 Cor 1:24 15:2 [a]Lit *to what word I* [A]Rom 11:22 [B]Gal 3:4 15:3 [a]Lit *among the first* [A]1 Cor 11:23 [B]John 1:29; Gal 1:4; Heb 5:1, 3; 1 Pet 2:24 [C]Is 53:5-12; Matt 26:24; Luke 24:25-27; Acts 8:32f; 17:2f; 26:22 15:4 [A]Matt 16:21; John 2:20ff; Acts 2:24 [B]Ps 16:8ff; Acts 2:31; 26:22f 15:5 [A]Luke 24:34 [B]1 Cor 1:12 [C]Mark 16:14; Luke 24:36; John 20:19

desired. **a psalm.** The reading or singing of an OT psalm. **a teaching.** This probably refers to a doctrine or subject of special interest (v. 33). **a revelation.** Some supposed word from God, whether spurious or genuine. **a tongue.** In the singular, this refers to the counterfeit. *See note on vv. 2–39.* **an interpretation.** This refers to that of a tongue's message. **for edification.** This was Paul's way of calling a halt to the chaos. Edification is the goal (cf. vv. 3–5, 12, 17, 26, 31) and the Corinthian chaos could not realize it (cf. 1Th 5:11; Ro 15:2, 3).

14:27, 28 These verses provide regulations for the exercise of the gift: 1) only two or three persons in a service; 2) only speaking in turn, one at a time; and 3) only with an interpreter. Without those conditions, one was to meditate and pray silently.

14:29–31 Since Paul's pastoral epistles (1, 2Ti; Titus) do not mention prophets, it seems evident that this unique office had ceased to function in the church even before the end of the apostolic age. When Paul wrote the Corinthians, however, prophets were still central to the work of that church (cf. Ac 13:1). Here he gave 4 regulations for their preaching: 1) only two or three were to speak; 2) the other prophets were to judge what was said; 3) if while one was speaking, God gave a revelation, the speaker was to defer to the one hearing from God; and 4) each prophet was to speak in turn. *See notes on Eph 2:20; 4:11.*

14:32 Not only were the prophets to judge others with discernment, but they were also to have control over themselves. God does not desire out-of-spirit or out-of-mind experiences. Those who received and proclaimed the truth were to have clear minds. There was nothing bizarre, ecstatic, trance-like, or wild about receiving and preaching God's Word, as with demonic experiences.

14:33 confusion. Here is the key to the whole chapter. The church at worship before God should reflect His character and nature because He is a God of peace and harmony, order and clarity, not strife and confusion (cf. Ro 15:33; 2Th 3:16; Heb 13:20). **as in all the churches.** This phrase does not belong in v. 33, but at the beginning of v. 34, as a logical introduction to a universal principle for churches.

14:34, 35 women are to keep silent in the churches. The principle of women not speaking in church services is universal; this applies to all the churches, not just locally, geographically, or culturally. The context in this verse concerns prophecy, but includes the general theme of the chapter, i.e., tongues. Rather than leading, they are to be submissive as God's Word makes clear (*see notes on 11:3–15; Ge 3:16; 1Ti 2:11–15*). It is not coincidental that many modern churches that have tongues-speaking and claim gifts of healings and miracles also permit women to lead worship, preach, and teach. Women may be gifted teachers, but they are not permitted by God "to speak" in churches. In fact, for them to do so is "improper," meaning "disgraceful." Apparently, certain women were out of order in disruptively asking questions publicly in the chaotic services.

14:36, 37 Paul knew that the Corinthians would react to all these firm regulations that would end the free-for-all in their services. The prophets, tongues-speakers, and women may all have been resistant to words, so he anticipated that resistance by sarcastically challenging those who put themselves above his word, and thus, above Scripture by either ignoring it or interpreting it to fit their predisposed ideas. If anyone was genuinely a prophet or had the true spiritual gift of tongues, he or she would submit to the principles God had revealed through the apostle.

14:36 Was it from you ... word ... went forth ... to you only? *See notes on 1Th 2:13; 2Ti 3:15–17; 2Pe 1:19–21.*

14:38 not recognized. Anyone who does not recognize the authority of Paul's teaching should himself not be recognized as a legitimate servant gifted by God.

14:39 do not forbid ... tongues. Legitimate languages were limited in purpose and in duration, but as long as it was still active in the early church, it was not to be hindered. But prophecy was the most desirable gift to be exercised because of its ability to edify, exhort, and comfort with the truth (v. 3).

14:40 *See notes on v. 33.*

15:1–58 This chapter is the most extensive treatment of resurrection in the Bible. Both the resurrection of Jesus Christ as recorded in the gospels and the resurrection of believers as promised in the gospels are here explained.

15:1–11 To begin his teachings about the resurrection of believers, Paul reviewed the evidences for Jesus' resurrection: 1) the church (vv. 1, 2); 2) the Scriptures (vv. 3, 4); 3) the eyewitnesses (vv. 5–7); 4) the apostle himself (vv. 8–10); and 5) the common message (v. 11).

15:1, 2 preached ... received ... stand. This was not a new message. They had heard of the resurrection, believed in it, and had been saved by it.

15:2 unless you believed in vain. By this qualifying statement, Paul recognized and called to their attention that some may have had a shallow, nonsaving faith (see Mt 7:13, 14, 22–27; 13:24–30, 34–43, 47–50; 25:1–30). Some believed only as the demons believed (Jas 2:19), i.e., they were convinced the gospel was true, but had no love for God, Christ, and righteousness. True believers "hold fast" to the gospel (cf. Jn 8:31; 2Co 13:5; 1Jn 2:24; 2Jn 9).

15:3, 4 according to the Scriptures. The OT spoke of the suffering and resurrection of Christ (see Lk 24:25–27; Ac 2:25–31; 26:22, 23). Jesus, Peter, and Paul quoted or referred to such OT passages regarding the work of Christ as Pss 16:8–11; 22; Is 53.

15:5–7 The testimony of eyewitnesses, recorded in the NT, was added to support the reality of the resurrection. These included: 1) John and Peter together (Jn 20:19, 20), but probably also separately before (Lk 24:34); 2) the 12 (Jn 20:19, 20; Lk 24:36; Ac 1:22); 3) the 500, only referred to here (*see note on 2Pe*

time, most of whom remain until now, but some
[A]have fallen asleep; 7 then He appeared to [a,A]James,
then to [B]all the apostles; 8 and last of all, as [a]to one
untimely born, [A]He appeared to me also. 9 For I am
[A]the least of the apostles, [a]and not fit to be called an
apostle, because I [B]persecuted the church of God.
10 But by [A]the grace of God I am what I am, and His
grace toward me did not prove vain; but I [B]labored
even more than all of them, yet [C]not I, but the grace
of God with me. 11 Whether then *it was* I or they, so
we preach and so you believed.
12 Now if Christ is preached, that He has been
raised from the dead, how do some among you say
that there [A]is no resurrection of the dead? 13 But if
there is no resurrection of the dead, not even Christ
has been raised; 14 and [A]if Christ has not been raised,
then our preaching is vain, your faith also is vain.
15 Moreover we are even found *to be* false witnesses
of God, because we testified [a]against God that He
[A]raised [b]Christ, whom He did not raise, if in fact
the dead are not raised. 16 For if the dead are not
raised, not even Christ has been raised; 17 and if
Christ has not been raised, your faith is worthless;
[A]you are still in your sins. 18 Then those also who
[A]have fallen asleep in Christ have perished. 19 If we
have hoped in Christ in this life only, we are [A]of all
men most to be pitied.

THE ORDER OF RESURRECTION

20 But now Christ [A]has been raised from the
dead, the [B]first fruits of those who [C]are asleep. 21 For
since [A]by a man *came* death, by a man also *came*
the resurrection of the dead. 22 For [A]as in Adam
all die, so also in [a]Christ all will be made alive.

15:6 [A]Acts 7:60; 1 Cor 15:18, 20 15:7 [a]Or *Jacob* [A]Acts 12:17 [B]Luke 24:33, 36f; Acts 1:3f 15:8 [a]Lit *to an untimely birth* [A]Acts 9:3-8; 22:6-11; 26:12-18; 1 Cor 9:1 15:9 [a]Lit *who am* [A]2 Cor 12:11; Eph 3:8; 1 Tim 1:15 [B]Acts 8:3 15:10 [A]Rom 12:3 [B]2 Cor 11:23; Col 1:29; 1 Tim 4:10 [C]1 Cor 3:6; 2 Cor 3:5; Phil 2:13 15:12 [A]Acts 17:32; 23:8; 2 Tim 2:18 15:14 [A]1 Thess 4:14 15:15 [a]Or *concerning* [b]I.e. the Messiah [A]Acts 2:24 15:17 [A]Rom 4:25 15:18 [A]1 Cor 15:6; 1 Thess 4:16; Rev 14:13 15:19 [A]1 Cor 4:9; 2 Tim 3:12 15:20 [A]Acts 2:24; 1 Pet 1:3 [B]Acts 26:23; 1 Cor 15:23; Rev 1:5 [C]1 Cor 15:6; 1 Thess 4:16; Rev 14:13 15:21 [A]Rom 5:12 15:22 [a]I.e. the Messiah [A]Rom 5:14-18

3:15, 16), had all seen the risen Christ (cf. Mt 28:9; Mk 16:9, 12, 14; Lk 24:31–39; Jn 21:1–23); 4) James, either one of the two so-named apostles (son of Zebedee or son of Alphaeus; cf. Mk 3:17, 18) or even James the half-brother of the Lord, the author of the epistle by that name and the key leader in the Jerusalem church (Ac 15:13–21); and 5) the apostles (Jn 20:19–29). Such unspecified appearances occurred over a 40-day period (Ac 1:3) to all the apostles.

15:8 one untimely born. Paul was saved too late to be one of the 12 apostles. Christ had ascended before he was converted. But through a miraculous appearance (Ac 9:1–8; cf. 18:9, 10; 23:11; 2Co 12:1–7), Christ revealed Himself to Paul and, according to divine purpose, Paul was made an apostle. *See note on 1:1.* He was "last of all" the apostles, and felt himself to be the "least" (vv. 9, 10; 1Ti 1:12–17).

15:10 labored even more than all of them. In terms of years and extent of ministry, he exceeded all those named (vv. 5–7). John outlived him but did not have the extensive ministry of Paul.

15:12 some among you say. The Corinthian Christians believed in Christ's resurrection, or else they could not have been Christians (cf. Jn 6:44; 11:25; Ac 4:12; 2Co 4:14; 1Th 4:16). But some had particular difficulty accepting and understanding the resurrection of believers. Some of this confusion was a result of their experiences with pagan philosophies and religions. A basic tenet of much of ancient Gr. philosophy was dualism, which taught that everything physical was intrinsically evil; so the idea of a resurrected body was repulsive and disgusting (Ac 17:32). In addition, perhaps some Jews in the Corinthian church formerly may have been influenced by the Sadducees, who did not believe in the resurrection even though it is taught in the OT (Job 19:26; Pss 16:8–11; 17:15; Da 12:2). On the other hand, NT teaching in the words of our Lord Himself was extensive on the resurrection (Jn 5:28, 29; 6:44; 11:25; 14:19) and it was the theme of the apostolic preaching (Ac 4:1, 2). In spite of that clarity, the church at Corinth was in doubt about the resurrection.

15:13–19 In these verses, Paul gives 6 disastrous consequences if there were no resurrection: 1) preaching Christ would be senseless (v. 14); 2) faith in Christ would be useless (v. 14); 3) all the witnesses and preachers of the resurrection would be liars (v. 15); 4) no one would be redeemed from sin (v. 17); 5) all former believers would have perished (v. 18); and 6) Christians would be the most pitiable people on earth (v. 19).

15:13, 16 The two resurrections, Christ's and believers', stand or fall together; if there is no resurrection, then Christ is dead. Cf. Rev 1:17, 18.

15:17 still in your sins. *See notes on Ac 5:30, 31; Ro 4:25.*

15:18 fallen asleep. A common euphemism for death (cf. vv. 6, 20; 11:30; Mt 27:52; Ac 7:60; 2Pe 3:4). This is not soul sleep, in which the body dies and the soul, or spirit, supposedly rests in unconsciousness.

15:19 most to be pitied. This is because of the sacrifices made in this life in light of the hope of life to come. If there is no life to come, we would be better "to eat, drink and be merry" before we die.

15:20 first fruits. This speaks of the first installment of harvest to eternal life, in which Christ's resurrection will precipitate and guarantee that all of the saints who have died will be resurrected also. See Jn 14:19. **those . . . asleep.** *See note on v. 18.*

15:21, 22 man . . . man. Adam, who through his sin brought death on the whole human race, was human. So was Christ, who by His resurrection brought life to the race. *See notes on Ro 5:12–19.*

15:22 all . . . all. The two "alls" are alike only in the sense that they both apply to descendants. The second "all" applies only to believers (see Gal 3:26, 29; 4:7; Eph 3:6; cf. Ac 20:32; Titus 3:7) and does not imply universalism (the salvation of everyone without faith). Countless other passages clearly teach

THE APPEARANCES OF THE RISEN CHRIST

Central to Christian faith is the bodily resurrection of Jesus. By recording the resurrection appearances, the New Testament leaves no doubt about this event.

> In or around Jerusalem:
•• To Mary Magdalene (Mk 16:9; Jn 20:11–18)
•• To other women (Mt 28:8–10)
•• To Peter (Lk 24:34)
•• To ten disciples (Lk 24:36–43; Jn 20:19–25)
•• To the Eleven, including Thomas (Mk 16:14; Jn 20:26–29)
•• At the Ascension (Mk 16:19, 20; Lk 24:50–53; Ac 1:4–12)
> To the disciples on the Emmaus road (Mk 16:12, 13; Lk 24:13–35)
> In Galilee (Mt 28:16–20; Jn 21:1–24)
> To 500 people (1Co 15:6)
> To James and the apostles (1Co 15:7)
> To Paul on the road to Damascus (Ac 9:1–6; 22:1–10; 26:12–18; 1Co 15:8)

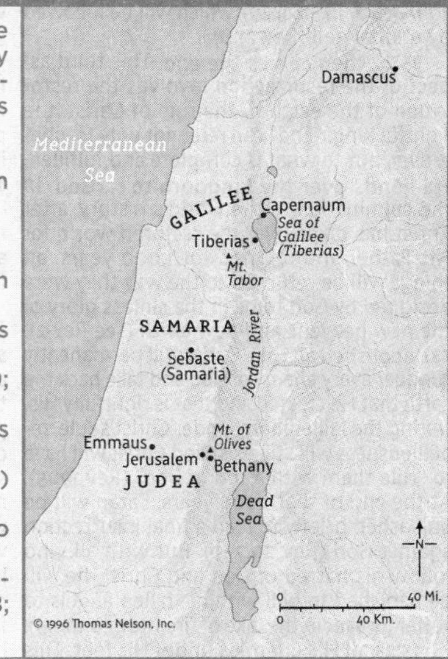

23 But each in his own order: Christ [A]the first fruits,
after that [B]those who are Christ's at [C]His coming,
24 then *comes* the end, when He hands over [A]the
kingdom to the [B]God and Father, when He has abolished [C]all rule and all authority and power. 25 For
He must reign [A]until He has put all His enemies
under His feet. 26 The last enemy that will be [A]abol-
ished is death. 27 For [A]HE HAS PUT ALL THINGS IN
SUBJECTION UNDER HIS FEET. But when He says,
"[B]All things are put in subjection," it is evident that
He is excepted who put all things in subjection
to Him. 28 When [A]all things are subjected to Him,
then the Son Himself also will be subjected to the
One who subjected all things to Him, so that [B]God
may be all in all.

29 Otherwise, what will those do who are baptized
for the dead? If the dead are not raised at all, why
then are they baptized for them? 30 Why are we
also [A]in danger every hour? 31 I affirm, brethren,
by the boasting in you which I have in Christ Jesus
our Lord, [A]I die daily. 32 If [a]from human motives I
[A]fought with wild beasts at [B]Ephesus, what does it
profit me? If the dead are not raised, [C]LET US EAT
AND DRINK, FOR TOMORROW WE DIE. 33 [A]Do not be
deceived: "Bad company corrupts good morals."
34 [A]Become sober-minded [a]as you ought, and stop
sinning; for some have [B]no knowledge of God. [C]I
speak *this* to your shame.

35 But [A]someone will say, "How are [B]the dead
raised? And with what kind of body do they come?"
36 [A]You fool! That which you [B]sow does not come to
life unless it dies; 37 and that which you sow, you do
not sow the body which is to be, but a bare grain,
perhaps of wheat or of [a]something else. 38 But God

15:23 [A]Acts 26:23; 1 Cor 15:20; Rev 1:5 [B]1 Cor 6:14; 15:52; 1 Thess 4:16 [C]1 Thess 2:19 15:24 [A]Dan 2:44; 7:14, 27; 2 Pet 1:11 [B]Eph 5:20 [C]Rom 8:38 15:25 [A]Ps 110:1; Matt 22:44 15:26 [A]2 Tim 1:10; Rev 20:14; 21:4 15:27 [A]Ps 8:6 [B]Matt 11:27; 28:18; Eph 1:22; Heb 2:8 15:28 [A]Phil 3:21 [B]1 Cor 3:23; 12:6 15:30 [A]2 Cor 11:26 15:31 [A]Rom 8:36 15:32 [a]Lit *according to man* [A]2 Cor 1:8 [B]Acts 18:19; 1 Cor 16:8 [C]Is 22:13; 56:12; Luke 12:19 15:33 [A]1 Cor 6:9 15:34 [a]Lit *righteously* [A]Rom 13:11 [B]Matt 22:29; Acts 26:8 [C]1 Cor 6:5 15:35 [A]Rom 9:19 [B]Ezek 37:3 15:36 [A]Luke 11:40 [B]John 12:24 15:37 [a]Lit *some of the rest*

the eternal punishment of the unbelieving (e.g., Mt 5:29; 10:28; 25:41, 46; Lk 16:23; 2Th 1:9; Rev 20:15).

15:23 in his own order. Christ was first, as the firstfruits of the resurrection harvest (vv. 20–23a). Because of His resurrection, "those who are Christ's" will be raised and enter the eternal heavenly state in 3 stages at Christ's coming (cf. Mt 24:36, 42, 44, 50; 25:13): 1) those who have come to saving faith from Pentecost to the Rapture will be joined by living saints at the Rapture to meet the Lord in the air and ascend to heaven (1Th 4:16, 17); 2) those who come to faith during the Tribulation, with the OT saints as well, will be raised up to reign with Him during the Millennium (Rev 20:4; cf. Da 12:2; cf. Is 26:19, 20); and 3) those who die during the millennial kingdom may well be instantly transformed at death into their eternal bodies and spirits. The only people left to be raised will be the ungodly, and that will occur at the end of the Millennium at the Great White Throne Judgment of God (*see notes on Rev 20:11–15*; cf. Jn 5:28, 29), which will be followed by eternal hell (Rev 21:8).

15:24 then *comes* the end. This third aspect of the resurrection involves the restoration of the earth to the rule of Christ, the rightful King. "End" can refer not only to what is over, but to what is complete and fulfilled. **He hands over the kingdom to … God.** In the culmination of the world's history, after Christ has taken over the restored world for His Father and reigned for 1,000 years, all things will be returned to the way they were designed by God to be in the sinless glory of the new heavens and new earth (see Rev 21, 22). **abolished all rule.** Christ will permanently conquer every enemy of God and take back the earth that He created and that is rightfully His. During the Millennium, under Christ's rule, rebelliousness will still exist and Christ will have to "rule them with a rod of iron" (Rev 19:15). At the end of that 1,000 years, Satan will be unleashed briefly to lead a final insurrection against God (Rev 20:7–9). But with all who follow his hatred of God and Christ, he will be banished to hell with his fallen angels to suffer forever in the lake of fire (Rev 20:10–15).

15:25 all His enemies under His feet. This figure comes from the common practice of kings always sitting enthroned above their subjects, so that when the subjects bowed or kneeled, they were lower than the sovereign's feet. With enemies, the monarch might put his foot on the neck of a conquered ruler, symbolizing that enemy's total subjugation. In the millennial kingdom, Christ's foes will be in subjection to Him.

15:26, 27 last enemy … death. Christ has broken the power of Satan, who held the power of death (Heb 2:14), at the cross. But Satan will not be permanently divested of his weapon of death until the end of the Millennium (*see notes on Rev 20:1–10*). At that point, having fulfilled completely the prophecy of Ps 8:6 (v. 27a), Christ then will deliver the kingdom to His Father, and the eternal glory of Rev 21, 22 will begin.

15:27 it is evident. Lest anyone misunderstand what should be "evident," Paul does not mean by the phrase "PUT ALL THINGS IN SUBJECTION UNDER HIS FEET" that God the Father is so included. It is actually the Father who gave Christ His authority (Mt 28:18; Jn 5:26, 27) and whom the Son perfectly serves.

15:28 all in all. Christ will continue to rule because His reign is eternal (Rev 11:15), but He will reign in His former, full, and glorious place within the Trinity, subject to God (v. 28) in the way eternally designed for Him in full Trinitarian glory.

15:29–34 Paul points out that the resurrection gives men compelling incentives for salvation (v. 19), for service (vv. 30–32), and for sanctification (vv. 33, 34).

15:29 This difficult verse has numerous possible interpretations. Other Scripture passages, however, clarify certain things which it does *not* mean. It does not teach, for example, that a dead person can be saved by another person's being baptized on his behalf, because baptism never has a part in a person's salvation (Eph 2:8; cf. Ro 3:28; 4:3; 6:3, 4). A reasonable view seems to be that "those … who are baptized" refers to living believers who give outward testimony to their faith in baptism by water because they were first drawn to Christ by the exemplary lives, faithful influence, and witness of believers who had subsequently died. Paul's point is that if there is no resurrection and no life after death, then why are people coming to Christ to follow the hope of those who have died?

15:30, 31 I die daily. Paul continually risked his life in self-sacrificing ministry. Why would he risk death daily, even hourly, if there were no life after death, no reward, and no eternal joy for all his pain? Cf. 1Pe 1:3, 4.

15:32 beasts at Ephesus. Perhaps literal wild animals, or, metaphorically, the fierce crowd of Ephesians incited against him by Demetrius (Ac 19:23–34). In either case, these were life-threatening dangers (cf. 2Co 11:23–28). eat … drink … die. A direct quote from Is 22:13 reflecting the hopelessness of the backslidden Israelites. Cf. Heb 11:33, 34, 38 for a litany of sufferers who were willing to die because they looked forward to resurrection (v. 35).

15:33, 34 Bad company. The Gr. term behind this word can also refer to a spoken message. By word or example, bad, or evil, friends are a corrupting influence. Hope in the resurrection is sanctifying; it leads to godly living, not corruption. Some in the church did not know God and were a corrupting influence, but not for those who hoped for life in God's presence (see 1Jn 3:2, 3).

15:35 They had the truth but shamefully did not believe and follow it (cf. 2Co 13:5); thus, these questions did not reflect a genuine interest in the resurrection but were mocking taunts, by those who denied the resurrection, perhaps under the influence of gnostic-oriented philosophy. But supposing it were true, they queried as to how it could ever happen. Cf. Ac 26:8.

15:36–49 To the questions posed in v. 35, Paul here gives 4 responses: 1) an illustration from nature (vv. 36–38); 2) a description of resurrection bodies (vv. 39–42a); 3) contrasts of earthly and resurrection bodies (vv. 42b–44); and 4) a reminder of the prototype resurrection of Jesus Christ (vv. 45–49).

15:36–38 When a seed is planted in the ground it dies; decomposing, it ceases to exist in its seed form, but life comes from inside that dead seed (see Jn 12:24). Just as God gives a new body to that plant that rises from the dead seed, so He can give a resurrection body to a man who dies.

gives it a body just as He wished, and [A]to each of the
seeds a body of its own. 39 All flesh is not the same
flesh, but there is one *flesh* of men, and another flesh
of beasts, and another flesh of birds, and another of
fish. 40 There are also heavenly bodies and earthly
bodies, but the glory of the heavenly is one, and the
glory of the earthly is another. 41 There is one glory of
the sun, and another glory of the moon, and another
glory of the stars; for star differs from star in glory.
42 [A]So also is the resurrection of the dead. It is
sown [a,B]a perishable *body,* it is raised [b,C]an imperishable *body;* 43 it is sown in dishonor, it is raised in
[A]glory; it is sown in weakness, it is raised in power;
44 it is sown a [A]natural body, it is raised a [B]spiritual
body. If there is a natural body, there is also a spiritual *body.* 45 So also it is written, "The first [A]MAN,
Adam, BECAME A LIVING SOUL." The [B]last Adam *became* a [C]life-giving spirit. 46 However, the spiritual
is not first, but the natural; then the spiritual. 47 The
first man is [A]from the earth, [a,B]earthy; the second
man is from heaven. 48 As is the earthy, so also are
those who are earthy; and as is the heavenly, [A]so
also are those who are heavenly. 49 Just as we have
[A]borne the image of the earthy, [a]we [B]will also bear
the image of the heavenly.

THE MYSTERY OF RESURRECTION

50 Now I say this, brethren, that [A]flesh and blood
cannot [B]inherit the kingdom of God; nor does [a]the
perishable inherit [b,C]the imperishable. 51 Behold, I tell
you a [A]mystery; we will not all sleep, but we will all
be [B]changed, 52 in a moment, in the twinkling of an
eye, at the last trumpet; for [A]the trumpet will sound,
and [B]the dead will be raised [a]imperishable, and [C]we
will be changed. 53 For this [a]perishable must put on
[b,A]the imperishable, and this [B]mortal must put on
immortality. 54 But when this [a]perishable will have
put on [b]the imperishable, and this mortal will have
put on immortality, then will come about the saying
that is written, "[A]DEATH IS SWALLOWED UP in victory.
55 [A]O DEATH, WHERE IS YOUR VICTORY? O DEATH, WHERE
IS YOUR STING?" 56 The sting of [A]death is sin, and [B]the
power of sin is the law; 57 but [A]thanks be to God, who
gives us the [B]victory through our Lord Jesus Christ.
58 [A]Therefore, my beloved brethren, be steadfast, immovable, always abounding in [B]the work
of the Lord, knowing that your toil is not *in* vain
in the Lord.

INSTRUCTIONS AND GREETINGS

16 Now concerning [A]the collection for [B]the saints,
as [C]I directed the churches of [D]Galatia, so do
you also. 2 On [A]the first day of every week each one
of you is to [a]put aside and save, as he may prosper, so
that [B]no collections be made when I come. 3 When I
arrive, [A]whomever you may approve, I will send them
with letters to carry your gift to Jerusalem; 4 and if
it is fitting for me to go also, they will go with me.
5 But I [A]will come to you after I go through [B]Mac-
edonia, for I [C]am going through Macedonia; 6 and

15:38 [A]Gen 1:11 15:42 [a]Lit *in corruption* [b]Lit *in incorruption* [A]Dan 12:3; Matt 13:43 [B]Rom 8:21; 1 Cor 15:50; Gal 6:8 [C]Rom 2:7 15:43 [A]Phil 3:21; Col 3:4 15:44 [A]1 Cor 2:14 [B]1 Cor 15:50 15:45 [A]Gen 2:7 [B]Rom 5:14 [C]John 5:21; 6:57f; Rom 8:2 15:47 [a]Lit *made of dust* [A]John 3:31 [B]Gen 2:7; 3:19 15:48 [A]Phil 3:20f 15:49 [a]Two early mss read *let us also* [A]Gen 5:3 [B]Rom 8:29 15:50 [a]Lit *corruption* [b]Lit *incorruption* [A]Matt 16:17; John 3:5f [B]1 Cor 6:9 [C]Rom 2:7 15:51 [A]1 Cor 13:2 [B]2 Cor 5:2, 4 15:52 [a]Lit *incorruptible* [A]Matt 24:31 [B]John 5:28 [C]1 Thess 4:15, 17 15:53 [a]Lit *corruptible* [b]Lit *incorruption* [A]Rom 2:7 [B]2 Cor 5:4 15:54 [a]V 53, note 1 [b]V 53, note 2 [A]Is 25:8 15:55 [A]Hos 13:14 15:56 [A]Rom 5:12 [B]Rom 3:20; 4:15; 7:8 15:57 [A]Rom 7:25; 2 Cor 2:14 [B]Rom 8:37; Heb 2:14f; 1 John 5:4; Rev 21:4 15:58 [A]2 Pet 3:14 [B]1 Cor 16:10 16:1 [A]Acts 24:17; Rom 15:25f [B]Acts 9:13 [C]1 Cor 4:17 [D]Acts 16:6 16:2 [a]Lit *put by himself* [A]Acts 20:7 [B]2 Cor 9:4f 16:3 [A]2 Cor 3:1; 8:18f 16:5 [A]1 Cor 4:19 [B]Rom 15:26 [C]Acts 19:21

15:39–42a As there are vastly different bodies and forms in God's created universe which are suited for all kinds of existence, so God can design a body perfect for resurrection life.

15:42b–44 Focusing directly on the resurrection body, Paul gives 4 sets of contrasts to show how the new body will differ from the present one (cf. v. 54; Php 3:20, 21): 1) no more sickness and death ("perishable *body*"); 2) no more shame because of sin ("dishonor"); 3) no more frailty in temptation ("weakness"); and 4) no more limits to the time/space sphere ("natural").

15:45–49 Here Paul answers the question (v. 35) more specifically by showing that the resurrection body of Jesus Christ is the prototype. He begins with a quotation from Ge 2:7 with the addition of two words, "first" and "Adam." Adam was created with a natural body, not perfect, but good in every way (Ge 1:31). The "last Adam" is Jesus Christ (Ro 5:19, 21). He is saying that through the first Adam we received our natural bodies, but through the last Adam we will receive our spiritual bodies in resurrection. Adam's body was the prototype of the natural, Christ's body of the resurrection. We will bear the image of His body fit for heaven (Ac 1:11; Php 3:20, 21; 1Jn 3:1–3) as we have borne the image of Adam's on earth.

15:50 People cannot live in God's eternal heavenly glory the way they are. *See notes on Ro 8:23.* We have to be changed (v. 51).

15:51 mystery. This term refers to truth hidden in the past and revealed in the NT. *See notes on 2:7 and Eph 3:4, 5.* In this case, the rapture of the church was never revealed in the OT. It was first mentioned in Jn 14:1–3, when it is specifically explained and is detailed in 1Th 4:13–18 (*see notes there*). sleep. *See note on v. 18.*

15:52 twinkling of an eye. This was Paul's way of showing how brief the "moment" will be. The Gr. word for "twinkling" refers to any rapid movement. Since the eye can move more rapidly than any other part of our visible bodies, it seems to well illustrate the sudden transformation of raptured believers. trumpet will sound. To herald the end of the church era, when all believers will be removed from the earth at the Rapture (1Th 4:16). dead ... raised. According to 1Th 4:16, they are first and the living saints follow (1Th 4:17).

15:54–57 Paul enhanced his joy at the reality of resurrection by quoting from Is 25:8 and Hos 13:14. The latter quote taunts death as if it were a bee whose sting was removed. That sting was the sin that was exposed by the law of God (*see notes on Ro 3:23; 4:15; 6:23; Gal 3:10–13*), but conquered by Christ in His death (*see notes on Ro 5:17; 2Co 5:21*).

15:58 The hope of resurrection makes all the efforts and sacrifices in the Lord's work worth it. No work done in His name is wasted in light of eternal glory and reward.

16:1 collection. An offering for destitute believers in the overpopulated, famine stricken city of Jerusalem (v. 3; see Ac 11:28). Paul had previously solicited funds from the churches of Galatia, Macedonia, and Achaia (Ro 15:26; cf. Lk 10:25–37; 2Co 8:1–5; 9:12–15; Gal 6:10; 1Jn 3:17).

16:2 first day of every week. This evidences that the early church met on Sunday (Ac 20:7). The point is that giving must occur regularly, not just when one feels generous, particularly led to do so, or instructed to do so for some special purpose (cf. Lk 6:38; cf. 2Co 9:6, 7). as he may prosper. No required amount or percentage for giving to the Lord's work is specified in the NT. All giving to the Lord is to be free-will giving and completely discretionary (see Lk 6:38; 2Co 9:6–8). This is not to be confused with the OT required giving of 3 tithes (see Lv 27:30; Nu 18:21–26; Dt 14:28, 29; Mal 3:8–10) which totaled about 23 percent annually to fund the national government of Israel, take care of public festivals, and provide welfare. Modern parallels to the OT tithe are found in the taxation system of countries (Ro 13:6). OT giving to God was not regulated as to amount (see Ex 25:1, 2; 35:21; 36:6; Pr 3:9, 10; 11:24).

16:3, 4 This matter of getting the money to Jerusalem was important enough for Paul to go, if necessary.

16:5 At the end of a 3-year stay in Ephesus, Paul wrote his letter and probably gave it to Timothy to deliver (v. 10). Paul originally

perhaps I will stay with you, or even spend the winter,
so that you may [A]send me on my way wherever I may
go. 7 For I do not wish to see you now [A]*just* in passing;
for I hope to remain with you for some time, [B]if the
Lord permits. 8 But I will remain in [A]Ephesus until
[B]Pentecost; 9 for a [A]wide door [a]for effective *service*
has opened to me, and [B]there are many adversaries.
10 Now if [A]Timothy comes, see that he is with
you without [a]cause to be afraid, for he is doing [B]the
Lord's work, as I also am. 11 [A]So let no one despise
him. But [B]send him on his way [C]in peace, so that he
may come to me; for I expect him with the brethren.
12 But concerning [A]Apollos our brother, I encouraged him greatly to come to you with the brethren;
and it was not at all *his* desire to come now, but he
will come when he has opportunity.
13 [A]Be on the alert, [B]stand firm in the faith, [C]act
like men, [D]be strong. 14 Let all that you do be done
[A]in love.

15 Now I urge you, brethren (you know the [A]house-
hold of Stephanas, that [a]they were the [B]first fruits
of [C]Achaia, and that they have devoted themselves
for [D]ministry to [E]the saints), 16 that [A]you also be in
subjection to such men and to everyone who helps
in the work and labors. 17 I rejoice over the [a,A]coming
of Stephanas and Fortunatus and Achaicus, because
they have [b]supplied [B]what was lacking on your part.
18 For they [A]have refreshed my spirit and yours.
Therefore [B]acknowledge such men.
19 The churches of [A]Asia greet you. [B]Aquila and
Prisca greet you heartily in the Lord, with [C]the
church that is in their house. 20 All the brethren
greet you. [A]Greet one another with a holy kiss.
21 The greeting is in [A]my own hand—[a]Paul. 22 If
anyone does not love the Lord, he is to be [a,A]ac-
cursed. [b,B]Maranatha. 23 [A]The grace of the Lord Jesus
be with you. 24 My love be with you all in Christ
Jesus. Amen.

16:6 [A]Acts 15:3; 1 Cor 16:11 16:7 [A]2 Cor 1:15f [B]Acts 18:21 16:8 [A]Acts 18:19 [B]Acts 2:1 16:9 [a]Lit *and* [A]Acts 14:27 [B]Acts 19:9 16:10 [a]Lit *fear; for* [A]Acts 16:1; 1 Cor 4:17; 2 Cor 1:1 [B]1 Cor 15:58 16:11 [A]1 Tim 4:12; Titus 2:15 [B]Acts 15:3; 1 Cor 16:6 [C]Acts 15:33 16:12 [A]Acts 18:24; 1 Cor 1:12; 3:5f 16:13 [A]Matt 24:42 [B]1 Cor 15:1; Gal 5:1; Phil 1:27; 4:1; 1 Thess 3:8; 2 Thess 2:15 [C]1 Sam 4:9; 2 Sam 10:12 [D]Ps 31:24; Eph 3:16; 6:10; Col 1:11 16:14 [A]1 Cor 14:1 16:15 [a]Lit *it was* [A]1 Cor 1:16 [B]Rom 16:5 [C]Acts 18:12 [D]Rom 15:31 [E]1 Cor 16:1 16:16 [A]1 Thess 5:12; Heb 13:17 16:17 [a]Or *presence* [b]Or *made up for your absence* [A]2 Cor 7:6f [B]2 Cor 11:9; Phil 2:30 16:18 [A]2 Cor 7:13; Philem 7, 20 [B]Phil 2:29; 1 Thess 5:12 16:19 [A]Acts 16:6 [B]Acts 18:2 [C]Rom 16:5 16:20 [A]Rom 16:16 16:21 [a]Lit *Paul's* [A]Rom 16:22; Gal 6:11; Col 4:18; 2 Thess 3:17; Philem 19 16:22 [a]Gr *anathema* [b]I.e. O [our] Lord come! [A]Rom 9:3 [B]Phil 4:5; Rev 22:20 16:23 [A]Rom 16:20

planned to follow Timothy a short while after (4:19), visiting Corinth on the way to and from Macedonia (2Co 1:15, 16). He had to change his plan and visit only after a longer stay in Ephesus (v. 8), then on to Corinth after Macedonia, to stay for a while (vv. 6, 7).

16:9 many adversaries. Perhaps no NT church had such fierce opposition as the one in Ephesus (see 2Co 1:8–10 where he described his experience in Ephesus; cf. Ac 19:1–21). In spite of that opposition, the door for the gospel was open wide (cf. 2Co 2:12, 13 where Paul also had an open door, but no heart to remain and preach), and Paul stayed. At the end of the experience of opposition described in 2Co 1:8–10, he wrote 1 Corinthians.

16:10 Timothy. Paul had sent him with Erastus to Macedonia (Ac 19:22), and then he was to travel to Corinth, perhaps to carry this epistle (4:17). **without cause to be afraid.** I.e., of intimidation or frustration by believers in Corinth.

16:12 Apollos. *See note on Ac 18:24.* Paul felt Apollos should accompany the other brothers, Timothy and Erastus, to Corinth. Apollos refused, staying in Ephesus longer. Paul respected his convictions.

16:13, 14 Paul gives 5 final commands. The Corinthians are to be alert, firm, mature, strong, and loving.

16:13 the faith. The Christian faith, i.e., sound doctrine, as in Php 1:27; 1Ti 6:21; Jude 3.

16:15 first fruits. The members of the household of Stephanas were among the first converts in Corinth, which is located in Achaia, the southern province of Greece. Stephanas was one of the Corinthian believers Paul baptized personally (1:16), and was visiting with Paul in Ephesus at the time this epistle was written. With Fortunatus and Achaicus (v. 17), he probably delivered the earlier letter from Corinth mentioned in 7:1 (*see note there*).

16:17, 18 Paul was glad about the arrival of his 3 friends in Ephesus who went there to be with him (cf. Pr 25:25). The Corinthians were to give those men respect for their service to the Lord (cf. 1Th 5:12, 13).

16:19 Aquila and Prisca. *See note on Ac 18:2.* They had become good friends with Paul, since he stayed in their house during his first ministry in Corinth (Ac 18:1–3). He may have stayed with them the entire year and a half (cf. Ac 18:18, 19, 24–26). **in their house.** The early church used homes of believers for worship and many other activities (see, e.g., Ac 2:46; 5:42; 10:23, 27–48; 20:7, 8; 28:23).

16:20 kiss. A pure expression of Christian love between men with men and women with women, with no sexual overtones (cf. Ro 16:16; 2Co 13:12; 1Th 5:26; 1Pe 5:14).

16:21 my own hand. Paul dictated the main part of the letter to a scribe (Ro 16:22), but finished and signed it himself.

16:22 accursed. I.e., devoted to destruction. **Maranatha.** In this context, Paul perhaps appeals for the Lord to take away the nominal, false Christians who threatened the spiritual well-being of the church. This was also an expression of eagerness for the Lord's return (cf. Rev 22:20). The Aram. words may be translated, "O Lord, come!" (see marginal note).

THE SECOND EPISTLE
OF PAUL TO THE

CORINTHIANS

TITLE

This is the second NT epistle the apostle Paul wrote to the Christians in the city of Corinth (see Introduction to 1 Corinthians).

AUTHOR AND DATE

That the Apostle Paul wrote 2 Corinthians is uncontested; the lack of any motive for a forger to write this highly personal, biographical epistle has led even the most critical scholars to affirm Paul as its author.

Several considerations establish a feasible date for the writing of this letter. Extrabiblical sources indicate that July, A.D. 51 is the most likely date for the beginning of Gallio's proconsulship (cf. Ac 18:12). Paul's trial before him at Corinth (Ac 18:12–17) probably took place shortly after Gallio assumed office. Leaving Corinth (probably in A.D. 52), Paul sailed for Syria (Ac 18:18), thus concluding his second missionary journey. Returning to Ephesus on his third missionary journey (probably in A.D. 52), Paul ministered there for about 2 1/2 years (Ac 19:8, 10). The apostle wrote 1 Corinthians from Ephesus toward the close of that period (1Co 16:8), most likely in A.D. 55. Since Paul planned to stay in Ephesus until the following spring (cf. the reference to Pentecost in 1Co 16:8), and 2 Corinthians was written after he left Ephesus (see Background and Setting), the most likely date for 2 Corinthians is late A.D. 55 or very early A.D. 56.

BACKGROUND AND SETTING

Paul's association with the important commercial city of Corinth (see Introduction to 1 Corinthians: Title) began on his second missionary journey (Ac 18:1–18), when he spent 18 months (Ac 18:11) ministering there. After leaving Corinth, Paul heard of immorality in the Corinthian church and wrote a letter (since lost) to confront that sin, referred to in 1Co 5:9. During his ministry in Ephesus, he received further reports of trouble in the Corinthian church in the form of divisions among them (1Co 1:11). In addition, the Corinthians wrote Paul a letter (1Co 7:1) asking for clarification of some issues. Paul responded by writing the letter known as 1 Corinthians. Planning to remain at Ephesus a little longer (1Co 16:8, 9), Paul sent Timothy to Corinth (1Co 4:17; 16:10, 11). Disturbing news reached the apostle (possibly from Timothy) of further difficulties at Corinth, including the arrival of self-styled false apostles (11:13; *see note on 11:4*).

To create the platform to teach their false gospel, they began by assaulting the character of Paul. They had to convince the people to turn from Paul to them if they were to succeed in preaching demon doctrine. Temporarily abandoning the work at Ephesus, Paul went immediately to Corinth. The visit (known as the "painful visit," 2:1) was not a successful one from Paul's perspective; someone in the Corinthian church (possibly one of the false apostles) even openly insulted him (2:5–8, 10; 7:12). Saddened by the Corinthians' lack of loyalty to defend him, seeking to spare them further reproof (cf. 1:23), and perhaps hoping time would bring them to their senses, Paul returned to Ephesus. From Ephesus, Paul wrote what is known as the "severe letter" (2:4) and sent it with Titus to Corinth (7:5–16). Leaving Ephesus after the riot sparked by Demetrius (Ac 19:23–20:1), Paul went to Troas to meet Titus (2:12, 13). But Paul was so anxious for news of how the Corinthians had responded to the "severe letter" that he could not minister there, though the Lord had opened the door (2:12; cf. 7:5). So he left for Macedonia to look for Titus (2:13). To Paul's immense relief and joy, Titus met him with the news that the majority of the Corinthians had repented of their rebellion against Paul (7:7). Wise enough to know that some rebellious attitudes still smoldered under the surface, and could erupt again, Paul wrote (possibly from Philippi, cf. 11:9 with Php 4:15; also, some early manuscripts list Philippi as the place of writing) the Corinthians the letter called 2 Corinthians. In this letter, though the apostle expressed his relief and joy at their repentance (7:8–16), his main concern was to defend his apostleship (chaps. 1–7), exhort the Corinthians to resume preparations for the collection for the poor at Jerusalem (chaps. 8, 9), and confront the false apostles head on (chaps. 10–13). He then went to Corinth, as he had written (12:14; 13:1, 2). The Corinthians' participation in the Jerusalem offering (Ro 15:26) implies that Paul's third visit to that church was successful.

HISTORICAL AND THEOLOGICAL THEMES

Second Corinthians complements the historical record of Paul's dealings with the Corinthian church recorded in Acts and 1 Corinthians. It also contains important biographical data on Paul throughout.

Although an intensely personal letter, written by the apostle in the heat of battle against those attacking his credibility, 2 Corinthians contains several important theological themes. It portrays God the Father as a merciful comforter (1:3; 7:6), the Creator (4:6), the One who raised Jesus from the dead (4:14; cf. 13:4), and who will raise believers as well (1:9). Jesus Christ is the One who suffered (1:5), who fulfilled God's promises (1:20), who was the proclaimed Lord (4:5), who manifested God's glory (4:6), and the One who in His incarnation became poor for believers (8:9; cf. Php 2:5–8). The letter portrays the Holy Spirit as God (3:17, 18) and the guarantee of believers' salvation (1:22; 5:5). Satan is identified as the "god of this world" (4:4; cf. 1Jn 5:19), a deceiver (11:14), and the leader of human and angelic deceivers (11:15). The end times include both the believer's glorification (4:16–5:8) and his judgment (5:10). The glorious truth of God's sovereignty in salvation is the theme of 5:14–21, while 7:9, 10 sets forth man's response to God's offer of salvation—genuine repentance. Second Corinthians also presents the clearest, most concise summary of the substitutionary atonement of Christ to be found anywhere in Scripture (5:21; cf. Is 53) and defines the mission of the church to proclaim reconciliation (5:18–20). Finally, the nature of the New Covenant receives its fullest exposition outside the book of Hebrews (3:6–16).

INTERPRETIVE CHALLENGES

The main challenge confronting the interpreter is the relationship of chaps. 10–13 to chaps. 1–9 (*see note on 10:1–13:14*). The identity of Paul's opponents at Corinth has produced various interpretations, as has the identity of the brother who accompanied Titus to Corinth (8:18, 22). Whether the offender mentioned

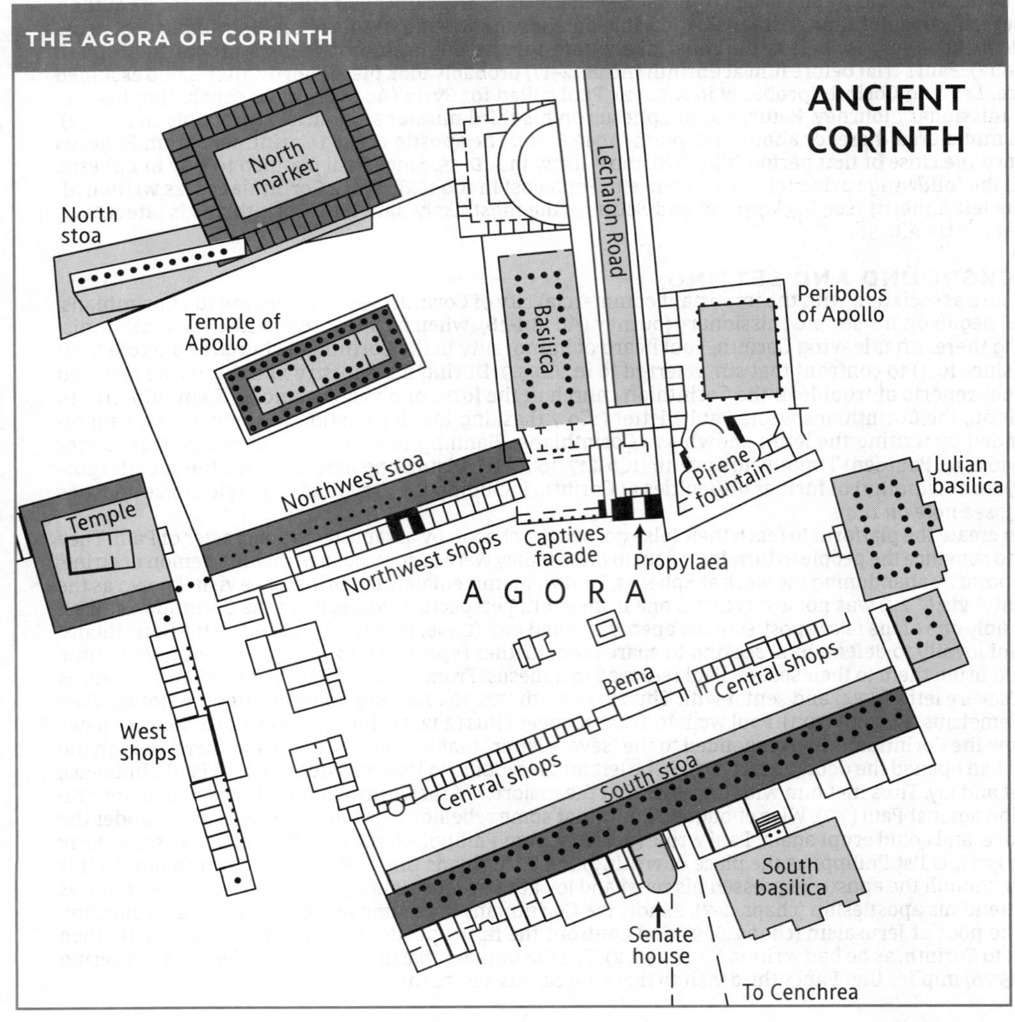

in 2:5–8 is the incestuous man of 1Co 5 is also uncertain. It is difficult to explain Paul's vision (12:1–5) and to identify specifically his "thorn in the flesh," the "messenger of Satan [sent] to torment [him]" (12:7). These and other interpretive problems will be dealt with in the notes on the appropriate passages.

OUTLINE

I. Paul's Greeting (1:1–11)

II. Paul's Ministry (1:12–7:16)

- A. Paul's Plans (1:12–2:4)
- B. The Offender's Punishment (2:5–11)
- C. Titus' Absence (2:12, 13)
- D. The Ministry's Nature (2:14–6:10)
    1. The triumph of the ministry (2:14–17)
    2. The commendation of the ministry (3:1–6)
    3. The basis of the ministry (3:7–18)
    4. The theme of the ministry (4:1–7)
    5. The trials of the ministry (4:8–18)
    6. The motivation of the ministry (5:1–10)
    7. The message of the ministry (5:11–21)
    8. The conduct of the ministry (6:1–10)
- E. The Corinthians Exhorted (6:11–7:16)
    1. To open their hearts to Paul (6:11–13)
    2. To separate themselves from unbelievers (6:14–7:1)
    3. To be assured of Paul's love (7:2–16)

III. Paul's Collection (8:1–9:15)

- A. The Patterns of Giving (8:1–9)
    1. The Macedonians (8:1–7)
    2. Jesus Christ (8:8, 9)
- B. The Purpose of Giving (8:10–15)
- C. The Procedures of Giving (8:16–9:5)
- D. The Promise of Giving (9:6–15)

IV. Paul's Apostleship (10:1–12:13)

- A. Apostolic Authority (10:1–18)
- B. Apostolic Conduct (11:1–15)
- C. Apostolic Suffering (11:16–33)
- D. Apostolic Credentials (12:1–13)

V. Paul's Visit (12:14–13:14)

- A. Paul's Unselfishness (12:14–18)
- B. Paul's Warnings (12:19–13:10)
- C. Paul's Benediction (13:11–14)

INTRODUCTION

1 Paul, [A]an apostle of [B]Christ Jesus [C]by the will of
God, and [D]Timothy *our* brother,
To [E]the church of God which is at [F]Corinth with
all the [a]saints who are throughout [G]Achaia:
2 [A]Grace to you and peace from God our Father
and the Lord Jesus Christ.
3 [A]Blessed *be* the God and Father of our Lord Jesus
Christ, the Father of mercies and [B]God of all comfort, 4 who [A]comforts us in all our affliction so that
we will be able to comfort those who are in [a]any
affliction with the comfort with which we ourselves
are comforted by God. 5 For just [A]as the sufferings of
Christ are [a]ours in abundance, so also our comfort is
abundant through Christ. 6 But if we are afflicted, it
is [A]for your comfort and salvation; or if we are comforted, it is for your comfort, which is effective in
the patient enduring of the same sufferings which
we also suffer; 7 and our hope for you is firmly
grounded, knowing that [A]as you are sharers of our
sufferings, so also you are *sharers* of our comfort.
8 For [A]we do not want you to be unaware, brethren, of our [B]affliction which came *to us* in [a,C]Asia,
that we were burdened excessively, beyond our
strength, so that we despaired even of life; 9 [a]indeed,
we had the sentence of death within ourselves so
that we would not trust in ourselves, but in God who
raises the dead; 10 who [A]delivered us from so great a
peril of death, and will deliver *us*, [a]He [B]on whom we
have set our hope. And He will yet deliver us, 11 you
also joining in [A]helping us through your prayers,
so that thanks may be given by [B]many persons on
our behalf for the favor bestowed on us through
the prayers of many.

1:1 [a]Or *holy ones* [A]Rom 1:1; Gal 1:1; Eph 1:1; Col 1:1; 2 Tim 1:1; Titus 1:1 [B]Gal 3:26 [C]1 Cor 1:1 [D]Acts 16:1; 1 Cor 16:10; 2 Cor 1:19 [E]1 Cor 10:32 [F]Acts 18:1 [G]Acts 18:12 1:2 [A]Rom 1:7 1:3 [A]Eph 1:3; 1 Pet 1:3 [B]Rom 15:5 1:4 [a]Lit *every* [A]Is 51:12; 66:13; 2 Cor 7:6, 7, 13 1:5 [a]Lit *to us* [A]2 Cor 4:10; Phil 3:10; Col 1:24 1:6 [A]2 Cor 4:15; 12:15; Eph 3:1, 13; 2 Tim 2:10 1:7 [A]Rom 8:17 1:8 [a]I.e. west coast province of Asia Minor [A]Rom 1:13 [B]Acts 19:23; 1 Cor 15:32 [C]Acts 16:6 1:9 [a]Lit *but we ourselves* 1:10 [a]One early ms reads *on whom we have set our hope that He will also* [A]Rom 15:31 [B]1 Tim 4:10 1:11 [A]Rom 15:30; Phil 1:19; Philem 22 [B]2 Cor 4:15; 9:11f

1:1 apostle. This refers to Paul's official position as a messenger sent by Christ (*see note on Ro 1:1*; Introduction to 1 Corinthians: Author and Date). **by the will of God.** Paul's mission was not a self-appointed one, or based on his own achievements. Rather, his credentials were by divine appointment, and his letter reflected not his own message, but the words of Christ (see Introduction to Romans: Author and Date; cf. Ac 26:15–18). **Timothy *our* brother.** Paul's cherished son in the faith and a dominant person in Paul's life and ministry (see Introduction to 1 Timothy: Background and Setting; *see note on 1Ti 1:2*). Paul first met Timothy in Derbe and Lystra on his first missionary journey (Ac 16:1–4). Timothy was with him during the founding of the church in Corinth (Ac 18:1–5), which, along with Paul's mention of Timothy in 1 Corinthians (4:17; 16:10, 11), indicated the Corinthians knew Timothy. Perhaps Paul mentioned him here to remind them Timothy was indeed a brother and to smooth over any hard feelings left from his recent visit (*see notes on 1Co 16:10*).

1:2 Grace … peace. Part of Paul's normal salutation in his letters (*see note on Ro 1:7*). "Grace" is God's unmerited favor, and "peace" one of its benefits.

1:3 God and Father of our Lord Jesus Christ. Paul praised the true God who revealed Himself in His Son, who is of the same essence with the Father (*see notes on Jn 1:14, 18; 17:3–5*; cf. Jn 5:17; 14:9–11; Eph 1:3; Heb 1:2, 3; 2Jn 3). He is the anointed one (Christ) and sovereign (Lord) Redeemer (Jesus). Although the Son enjoyed this lofty position, He was willing to become a servant and submit Himself in His incarnation (*see notes on Php 2:5–8*). This great benediction comprehends the entire Gospel. **Father of mercies.** Paul borrowed from Jewish liturgical language and a synagogue prayer that called for God to treat the sinful individual with kindness, love, and tenderness (*see note on Ro 12:1*; cf. 2Sa 24:14; Ps 103:13, 14; Mic 7:18–20). **God of all comfort.** An OT description of God (cf. Is 40:1; 51:3, 12; 66:13), who is the ultimate source of every true act of comfort. The Gr. word for "comfort" is related to the familiar word *paraclete*, "one who comes alongside to help," another name for the Holy Spirit (*see notes on Jn 14:26; Php 2:1*). "Comfort" often connotes softness and ease, but that is not its meaning here. Paul was saying that God came to him in the middle of his sufferings and troubles to strengthen him and give him courage and boldness (cf. vv. 4–10).

1:4 affliction. This term refers to crushing pressure, because in Paul's life and ministry there was always something attempting to weaken him, restrict or confine his ministry, or even crush out his life. But no matter what confronted him, Paul knew God would sustain and strengthen him (*see notes on 12:9, 10; Ro 8:31–38*; cf. Php 1:6). **that we will be able to comfort.** Comfort from God is not an end in itself. Its purpose is that believers also might be comforters. Having humiliated and convicted the Corinthians, God used Paul to return to them with a strengthening message after he himself had received divine strengthening (6:1–13; 12:6–11; cf. Lk 22:31, 32).

1:5 sufferings of Christ … in abundance. God's comfort to believers extends to the boundaries of their suffering for Christ. The more they endure righteous suffering, the greater will be their comfort and reward (cf. 1Pe 4:12–14). Paul knew firsthand that these many sufferings would seem never-ending (4:7–11; 6:5–10; 11:23–27; cf. Gal 6:17; Php 3:10; Col 1:24), and all genuine believers should expect the same (cf. Mt 10:18–24).

1:6 Paul was referring to the body of Christ's partnership of suffering, which mutually builds godly patience and endurance (1Co 12:26). All believers need to realize this process, avoid any sense of self-pity when suffering for Him, and share in one anothers' lives the encouragement of divine comfort they receive from their experiences. **salvation.** This refers to the Corinthians' ongoing perseverance to final, completed salvation when they will be glorified (*see note on Ro 13:11*). Paul's willingness, by God's grace and the Spirit's power, to suffer and be comforted and then comfort and strengthen the Corinthians enabled them to persevere.

1:7 sharers of our sufferings. Some in the church at Corinth, perhaps the majority, were suffering for righteousness, as Paul was. Although that church had caused him much pain and concern, Paul saw its members as partners to be helped, because of their faithfulness in mutual suffering.

1:8 our. An editorial plural, which Paul used throughout the letter. It usually was a humble reference to Paul himself, but in this instance it could include others as well. **affliction which came *to us* in Asia.** This was a recent occurrence (following the writing of 1 Corinthians) that happened in or around the city of Ephesus. The details of this situation are not known. **despaired even of life.** Paul faced something that was beyond human survival and was extremely discouraging because he believed it threatened to end his ministry prematurely. The Gr. word for "despaired" lit. means "no passage," the total absence of an exit (cf. 2Ti 4:6). The Corinthians were aware of what had happened to Paul, but they did not realize the utter severity of it, or what God was doing through those circumstances.

1:9 the sentence of death. The word for "sentence" is a technical term that indicated the passing of an official resolution, in this case the death sentence. Paul was so absolutely sure he was going to die for the gospel that he had pronounced the sentence upon himself. **not trust in ourselves, but in God.** God's ultimate purpose for Paul's horrible extremity. The Lord took him to the point at which he could not fall back on any intellectual, physical, or emotional human resource (cf. 12:9, 10). **who raises the dead.** A Jewish descriptive term for God used in synagogue worship language (*see note on v. 3*). Paul understood that trust in God's power to raise the dead was the only hope of rescue from his extreme circumstances.

1:10 He will yet deliver us. *See notes on 2Ti 4:16, 17; 2Pe 2:9.*

1:11 helping us through your prayers. Intercessory prayer is crucial to the expression of God's power and sovereign purpose. In this regard, Paul wanted the faithful Corinthians to know he needed their prayers then and in the future (cf. Eph 6:18; Jas 5:16). **thanks may be given.** Prayer's duty is not to change God's plans, but to glorify Him and give thanks for them. Paul was confident that God's sovereign purpose would be accomplished, balanced by the prayerful participation of believers. **the favor.** Probably better translated "gift," or "blessing," as in God's undeserved favor or the divine answer

PAUL'S INTEGRITY

12 For our [a]proud confidence is this: the testimony
of [A]our conscience, that in holiness and [B]godly sincerity, [C]not in fleshly wisdom but in the grace of God, we
have conducted ourselves in the world, and especially
toward you. 13 For we write nothing else to you than
what you read and understand, and I hope you will
understand [A]until the end; 14 just as you also partially
did understand us, that we are your reason to be proud
as you also are ours, in [A]the day of our Lord Jesus.
15 In this confidence I intended at first to [A]come to
you, so that you might [a]twice receive a [b,B]blessing;
16 [a]that is, to [A]pass [b]your way into [B]Macedonia, and
again from Macedonia to come to you, and by you
to be [C]helped on my journey to Judea. 17 Therefore, I
was not vacillating when I intended to do this, was
I? Or what I purpose, do I purpose [A]according to
the flesh, so that with me there will be yes, yes and
no, no *at the same time?* 18 But as [A]God is faithful,
[B]our word to you is not yes and no. 19 For [A]the Son
of God, Christ Jesus, who was preached among you
by us—by me and [B]Silvanus and [C]Timothy—was not
yes and no, but is yes [D]in Him. 20 For [A]as many as are
the promises of God, [B]in Him they are yes; therefore
also through Him is [C]our Amen to the glory of God
through us. 21 Now He who [A]establishes us with you
in Christ and [B]anointed us is God, 22 who also [A]sealed
us and [B]gave *us* the Spirit in our hearts as a [a]pledge.
23 But [A]I call God as witness [a]to my soul, that [B]to
spare you I did not come again to [C]Corinth. 24 Not that
we [A]lord it over your faith, but are workers with you
for your joy; for in your faith you are [B]standing firm.

1:12 [a]Lit *boasting* [A]Acts 23:1; 1 Thess 2:10; Heb 13:18 [B]2 Cor 2:17 [C]1 Cor 1:17; James 3:15 1:13 [A]1 Cor 1:8 1:14 [A]1 Cor 1:8 1:15 [a]Lit *have a second grace* [b]One early ms reads *joy* [A]1 Cor 4:19 [B]Rom 1:11; 15:29 1:16 [a]Lit *and* [b]Lit *through you into* [A]Acts 19:21; 1 Cor 16:5-7 [B]Acts 19:21; Rom 15:26 [C]Acts 15:3; 1 Cor 16:6, 11 1:17 [A]2 Cor 10:2f; 11:18 1:18 [A]1 Cor 1:9 [B]2 Cor 2:17 1:19 [A]Matt 4:3; 16:16; 26:63 [B]Acts 15:22; 1 Thess 1:1; 2 Thess 1:1; 1 Pet 5:12 [C]Acts 18:5; 2 Cor 1:1 [D]Heb 13:8 1:20 [A]Rom 15:8 [B]Heb 13:8 [C]1 Cor 14:16; Rev 3:14 1:21 [A]1 Cor 1:8 [B]1 John 2:20, 27 1:22 [a]Or *down payment* [A]John 3:33 [B]Rom 8:16; 2 Cor 5:5; Eph 1:14 1:23 [a]Lit *upon* [A]Rom 1:9; Gal 1:20 [B]1 Cor 4:21; 2 Cor 2:1, 3 [C]2 Cor 1:1 1:24 [A]2 Cor 4:5; 11:20; 1 Pet 5:3 [B]Rom 11:20; 1 Cor 15:1

to prayer Paul would receive in being delivered from death.

1:12 Paul faced his critics' many accusations against his character and integrity (they had accused him of being proud, self-serving, untrustworthy and inconsistent, mentally unbalanced, incompetent, unsophisticated, and an incompetent preacher) by appealing to the highest human court, his conscience. **proud confidence.** Paul often used this word. Used negatively, it refers to unwarranted bragging about one's own merits and achievements; but Paul used it positively to denote legitimate confidence in what God had done in his life (cf. Jer 9:23, 24; Ro 15:18; 1Co 1:31; 15:9, 10; 1Ti 1:12–17). **conscience.** The soul's warning system, which allows human beings to contemplate their motives and actions and make moral evaluations of what is right and wrong (*see note on Ro 2:14, 15*). In order to work as God designed it, the conscience must be informed to the highest moral and spiritual level and best standard, which means submitting it to the Holy Spirit through God's Word (cf. Ro 12:1, 2; 1Ti 1:19; 2Ti 2:15; Heb 9:14; 10:22). Paul's fully enlightened conscience exonerated him completely (cf. Ac 23:1; 24:16; 1Ti 1:5; 3:9; 2Ti 1:3). But ultimately, only God can accurately judge a man's motives (1Co 4:1–5). **fleshly wisdom.** Wisdom that is based on worldly, human insight (*see note on Jas 3:15*).

1:13 This broadly answers the accusation that Paul had engaged in deceptive personal relationships (cf. 7:2; 11:9). His continuing flow of information to the Corinthians was always clear, straightforward and understandable, consistent, and genuine. Paul wanted them to know that he was not holding anything back, nor did he have any secret agenda (10:11). He simply wanted them to understand all that he had written and spoken to them.

1:14 partially. As the Corinthians read and heard Paul's unfolding instruction to them, they continued to understand more. **we are your reason to be proud.** *See note on v. 12.* **the day of our Lord Jesus.** When He returns (*see notes on Php 1:6; 2Ti 1:12; 4:8*). Paul eagerly longed for the Lord's coming when they would rejoice over one another in glory (cf. 1Th 2:19, 20).

1:15 twice receive a blessing. Paul's original plan was to visit the Corinthians twice so that they might receive a double blessing. His travel plans were not the result of selfishness, but of the genuine relationship he enjoyed with the Corinthians and their mutual loyalty and godly pride in one another.

1:16 again … come. Paul had planned to leave Ephesus, stop at Corinth on the way to Macedonia, and return to Corinth again after his ministry in Macedonia (cf. 1Co 16:5–7). For some reason, Paul's plans changed and he was unable to stop in Corinth the first time. The false apostles who had invaded the church seized upon that honest change of schedule as evidence of his untrustworthiness and tried to use it to discredit him.

1:17 Paul is probably quoting some actual accusations of dishonesty brought by his opponents. **Therefore … not vacillating … was I?** The Gr. words that introduce this question call for an indignant, negative answer. Paul declared that he was in no way operating as a vacillating, fickle, unstable person who could not be trusted. **according to the flesh.** Purely from a human viewpoint, apart from the leading of the Holy Spirit, this is someone who is unregenerate (*see notes on Gal 5:19–21*). He affirmed that his "yes" and "no" words to them really meant what they said.

1:18 as God is faithful. Paul may have been making an oath and calling God to give testimony (cf. 11:10, 31; Ro 1:9; Gal 1:20; Php 1:8; 1Th 2:5, 10). Whatever the case, he refers to God's trustworthiness and the fact that he represented such a God as an honest spokesman. **not yes and no.** He was not saying "yes" and meaning "no." There was no duplicity with Paul (nor with Timothy and Silas). He said what he meant and did what he said, unless there was compelling reason to change his plans.

1:19 The firmness of Paul's statement, and his use of Jesus' full title, indicates that the person and work of Christ were under attack from the false teachers at Corinth. The proof of his truthfulness with them was the truthful gospel which he faithfully preached. **Silvanus.** The Lat. name for Silas, Paul's companion on his second missionary journey (Ac 16–18) and fellow preacher at Corinth (*see note on Ac 15:22*). **Timothy.** *See note on v. 1.*

1:20 in Him they are yes. All God's OT and NT promises of peace, joy, love, goodness, forgiveness, salvation, sanctification, fellowship, hope, glorification, and heaven are made possible and fulfilled in Jesus Christ (cf. Lk 24:44). **Amen.** The Heb. word of affirmation (cf. Mt 5:18; Jn 3:3; Ro 1:25). Paul reminded them that they had said a collective "yes" to the truth of his preaching and teaching.

1:21 He who establishes us. Christ's saving work of grace stabilizes believers and places them on a firm foundation in Him (cf. Ro 16:25; 1Co 15:58; 1Pe 5:10).

1:21, 22 Christ … God … Spirit. A clear reference to the 3 members of the Trinity. The authenticity of Paul's spiritual life and that of every genuine believer is verified by these 4 divine works ("establishes us," "anointed us," "sealed us," "gave *us* the Spirit") accomplished in their lives. For the critics to attack Paul's authenticity was equal to tearing down God's work as well as the church's unity.

1:21 anointed. This word is borrowed from a commissioning service that would symbolically set apart kings, prophets, priests, and special servants. The Holy Spirit sets apart believers and empowers them for the service of gospel proclamation and ministry (cf. Ac 1:8; 1Jn 2:20, 27).

1:22 sealed us. Refers to the ancient practice of placing soft wax on a document and imprinting the wax with a stamp that indicated authorship or ownership, authenticity, and protection. The Holy Spirit attaches all these meanings to His act of spiritually sealing believers (*see notes on Eph 1:13*; cf. Hag 2:23; Eph 4:30). **pledge.** A guarantee or down payment. The Spirit is the down payment on the believer's eternal inheritance (*see note on Eph 1:13, 14*; cf. 2Pe 1:4, 11).

1:23 God as witness. *See note on v. 18.* **to spare you.** Paul finally explained why he said he was coming, but did not. He did not come earlier because he wanted them to have time to repent of and correct their sinful behavior (see Introduction to 1 Corinthians: Background and Setting; *see note on 1Co 4:21*). He waited instead for a report from Titus before taking further action (see chap. 7), hoping he would not have to come again, as he had earlier, to face their rebellion.

1:24 Not that we lord it over your faith. Paul did not want to dominate and control the

REAFFIRM YOUR LOVE

2 But I determined this [a]for my own sake, that I
[A]would not come to you in sorrow again. 2 For
if I [A]cause you sorrow, who then makes me glad but
the one whom I made sorrowful? 3 This is the very
thing I [A]wrote you, so that [B]when I came, I would
not have sorrow from those who ought to make
me rejoice; having [C]confidence in you all that my
joy would be *the joy* of you all. 4 For out of much
affliction and anguish of heart I [A]wrote to you with
many tears; not so that you would be made sorrowful, but that you might know the love which I have
especially for you.

5 But [A]if any has caused sorrow, he has caused
sorrow not to me, but in some degree—[a]in order not
to say too much—to all of you. 6 Sufficient for such a
one is [A]this punishment which *was inflicted* by the
majority, 7 so that on the contrary you should rather
[A]forgive and comfort *him,* otherwise such a one
might be overwhelmed by excessive sorrow. 8 Wherefore I urge you to reaffirm *your* love for him. 9 For
to this end also [A]I wrote, so that I might [a,B]put you
to the test, whether you are [C]obedient in all things.
10 But one whom you forgive anything, I *forgive* also;
for indeed what I have forgiven, if I have forgiven
anything, *I did it* for your sakes [A]in the presence of
Christ, 11 so that no advantage would be taken of us
by [A]Satan, for [B]we are not ignorant of his schemes.

12 Now when I came to [A]Troas for the [B]gospel
of Christ and when a [C]door was opened for me in
the Lord, 13 I [A]had no rest for my spirit, not finding
[B]Titus my brother; but [C]taking my leave of them, I
went on to [D]Macedonia.

14 [A]But thanks be to God, who always [B]leads us
in triumph in Christ, and manifests through us the
[C]sweet aroma of the [D]knowledge of Him in every

2:1 [a]Or *as far as I am concerned* [A]1 Cor 4:21; 2 Cor 12:21 2:2 [A]2 Cor 7:8 2:3 [A]2 Cor 2:9; 7:8, 12 [B]1 Cor 4:21; 2 Cor 12:21 [C]Gal 5:10; 2 Thess 3:4; Philem 21 2:4 [A]2 Cor 2:9; 7:8, 12 2:5 [a]Lit *so that I not be burdensome* [A]1 Cor 5:1f 2:6 [A]1 Cor 5:4f; 2 Cor 7:11 2:7 [A]Gal 6:1; Eph 4:32 2:9 [a]Lit *know the proof of you* [A]2 Cor 2:3f [B]2 Cor 8:2; Phil 2:22 [C]2 Cor 7:15; 10:6 2:10 [A]1 Cor 5:4; 2 Cor 4:6 2:11 [A]Matt 4:10 [B]Luke 22:31; 2 Cor 4:4; 1 Pet 5:8 2:12 [A]Acts 16:8 [B]Rom 1:1; 2 Cor 4:3, 4; 8:18; 9:13; 10:14; 11:4, 7; 1 Thess 3:2 [C]Acts 14:27 2:13 [A]2 Cor 7:5 [B]2 Cor 7:6, 13f; 8:6, 16, 23; 12:18; Gal 2:1, 3; 2 Tim 4:10; Titus 1:4 [C]Mark 6:46 [D]Rom 15:26 2:14 [A]Rom 1:8; 6:17; 1 Cor 15:57; 2 Cor 8:16; 9:15 [B]Col 2:15 [C]Song 1:3; Ezek 20:41; Eph 5:2; Phil 4:18 [D]1 Cor 12:8

Corinthians when he ministered and worked among them (*see notes on 1Pe 5:2, 3*).

2:1 come to you in sorrow again. Paul, who had already had a painful confrontation at Corinth (see Introduction: Background and Setting), was not eager to have another one (*see note on 1:23*).

2:2 Although Paul was sensitive to the Corinthians' pain and sadness from the past confrontation, because of his commitment to purity he would confront them again if necessary. "The one whom I made sorrowful" refers to one convicted by his sin. In particular, there was apparently on Paul's last visit a man in the church who confronted him with the accusations taken from the false teachers. The church had not dealt with that man in Paul's defense, and Paul was deeply grieved over that lack of loyalty. The only thing that would bring Paul joy would be repentance from such a one and any who agreed with him, and Paul had been waiting for it.

2:3 the very thing I wrote. Paul's reason for writing was that those in sin would repent—then there could be mutual joy when the apostle came.

2:4 Paul again wanted them to know that his motive in dealing with them in the severe letter (see Introduction: Background and Setting) and 1 Corinthians (see Introduction to 1 Corinthians: Background and Setting) was not harsh but loving.

2:5–11 This passage is one of the best texts in all of Scripture on the godly motivation and rationale for forgiveness.

2:5 if any has caused sorrow. The Gr. construction of this clause assumes the condition to be true—Paul is acknowledging the reality of the offense and its ongoing effect, not on him, but on the church. With this deflection of any personal vengeance, he sought to soften the charge against the penitent offender and allow the church to deal with the man and those who were with him objectively, apart from Paul's personal anguish or offense.

2:6 Sufficient. The process of discipline and punishment was enough; now it was time to show mercy because the man had repented (cf. Mt 18:18, 23–35; Gal 6:1, 2; Eph 4:32; Col 3:13; Heb 12:11). **punishment ... *inflicted* by the majority.** This indicates that the church in Corinth had followed the biblical process in disciplining the sinning man (cf. Mt 18:15–20; 1Co 5:4–13; 2Th 3:6, 14). The Gr. word for "punishment," used frequently in secular writings but only here in the NT, denoted an official legal penalty or commercial sanction that was enacted against an individual or group (city, nation).

2:7 you should rather forgive. It was time to grant forgiveness so the man's joy would be restored (cf. Ps 51:12, 14; Is 42:2, 3). Paul knew there was—and is—no place in the church for man-made limits on God's grace, mercy, and forgiveness toward repentant sinners. Such restrictions could only rob the fellowship of the joy of unity (cf. Mt 18:34, 35; Mk 11:25, 26).

2:10 in the presence of Christ. Paul was constantly aware that his entire life was lived in the sight of God, who knew everything he thought, did, and said (cf. v. 17; 4:2; 2Ti 4:1).

2:11 schemes. The devil wants to produce sin and animosity that will destroy church unity. He uses every possible approach to accomplish this—from legalism to libertinism, intolerance to excessive tolerance (cf. 11:13, 14; Eph 4:14; 6:11, 12; 1Pe 5:8). Paul used a different Greek word (but with similar meaning) translated "schemes" in Eph 6:11. It, along with the words for "take advantage" and "ignorant," strongly implies that Satan targets the believer's mind, but God has provided protection by unmasking Satan's schemes in Scripture, along with providing the counteracting truth.

2:12 when I came to Troas. "Troas" was a seaport city N of Ephesus in the western Asia Minor province of Mysia (cf. Ac 16:7). The riots in Ephesus probably caused Paul to leave for Troas, but his main reason for going was to meet Titus, returning from Corinth after delivering "the severe letter" (v. 4), and to hear how the Corinthians had responded to that letter (see Introduction: Background and Setting). **a door was opened for me.** God sovereignly provided a great evangelistic opportunity for Paul, which may have led to the planting of the church in Troas (cf. Ac 20:5–12). Because of the success of his preaching, Paul was assured that this opportunity was from God (cf. 1Co 16:8, 9).

2:13 I had no rest for my spirit. Paul's concern for the problems in the Corinthian church and how its members were responding to both those problems and his instructions caused Paul debilitating restlessness and anxiety (cf. 7:5, 6). These concerns became so heavy and distracting that he was unable to give full attention to his ministry. **Titus.** One of Paul's most important Gentile converts and closest associates in ministry (*see notes on v. 12; Gal 2:1;* see Introduction to Titus: Background and Setting). **taking my leave of them.** Because of his troubled heart and mind and his anxiety to see Titus, Paul turned his back on the open door in Troas. **Macedonia.** A province that bordered the NW shore of the Aegean Sea, N of Achaia (see Introduction to 1 Thessalonians: Background and Setting; *see note on Ac 16:9*). Paul headed there in hopes of intersecting with Titus, whom he knew would have to pass through there on his journey back from Corinth.

2:14 But thanks be to God. Paul made an abrupt transition from his narrative and looked above and beyond his troubles to praise and thank God. By turning from the difficulties of ministry and focusing on the privileges of his position in Christ, Paul regained his joyful perspective. He picked the narrative back up in 7:5. **leads us in triumph in Christ.** Paul drew from the imagery of the official and exalted Roman ceremony called the Triumph, in which a victorious general was honored with a festive, ceremonial parade through the streets of Rome. First, Paul gave thanks for being led by a sovereign God at all times (cf. 1Ti 1:17); and second, for the promised victory in Jesus Christ (cf. Mt 16:18; Ro 8:37; Rev 6:2). **manifests ... the sweet aroma of the knowledge of Him.** Paul was also grateful for the privilege of being used as an influence for Christ (cf. Ro 10:14, 15) wherever he went. The imagery comes from the strong, sweet smell of incense from censers in the Triumph parade, which, along with the fragrance of crushed flowers strewn under horses' hooves, produced a powerful aroma that filled the city. By analogy, every believer is transformed and called by the Lord to be an influence for His gospel throughout the world.

place. 15 For we are a [A]fragrance of Christ to God
among [B]those who are being saved and among
those who are perishing; 16 [A]to the one an aroma
from death to death, to the other an aroma from
life to life. And who is [B]adequate for these things?
17 For we are not like many, [a,A]peddling the word of
God, but [B]as from sincerity, but as from God, we
speak in Christ [C]in the sight of God.

MINISTERS OF A NEW COVENANT

3 Are we beginning to [A]commend ourselves
again? Or do we need, as some, [B]letters of commendation to you or from you? 2 [A]You are our letter,
written in our hearts, known and read by all men;
3 being manifested that you are a letter of Christ,
[a,A]cared for by us, written not with ink but with the
Spirit of [B]the living God, not on [C]tablets of stone but
on [D]tablets of [b,E]human hearts.
4 Such [A]confidence we have through Christ toward
God. 5 Not that we are adequate in ourselves to consider anything as *coming* from ourselves, but [A]our
adequacy is from God, 6 who also made us adequate *as*
[A]servants of a [B]new covenant, not of [C]the letter but of
the Spirit; for the letter kills, but [D]the Spirit gives life.
7 But if the [A]ministry of death, [B]in letters engraved
on stones, came [a]with glory, [C]so that the sons of
Israel could not look intently at the face of Moses
because of the glory of his face, fading *as* it was,

2:15 [A]Song 1:3; Ezek 20:41; Eph 5:2; Phil 4:18 [B]1 Cor 1:18 2:16 [A]Luke 2:34; John 9:39; 1 Pet 2:7f [B]2 Cor 3:5f 2:17 [a]Or *corrupting* [A]2 Cor 4:2; Gal 1:6-9 [B]1 Cor 5:8; 2 Cor 1:12; 1 Thess 2:4; 1 Pet 4:11 [C]2 Cor 12:19 3:1 [A]2 Cor 5:12; 10:12, 18; 12:11 [B]Acts 18:27; 1 Cor 16:3 3:2 [A]1 Cor 9:2 3:3 [a]Lit *served* [b]Lit *hearts of flesh* [A]2 Cor 3:6 [B]Matt 16:16 [C]Ex 24:12; 31:18; 32:15f; 2 Cor 3:7 [D]Prov 3:3; 7:3; Jer 17:1 [E]Jer 31:33; Ezek 11:19; 36:26 3:4 [A]Eph 3:12 3:5 [A]1 Cor 15:10 3:6 [A]1 Cor 3:5 [B]Jer 31:31; Luke 22:20 [C]Rom 2:29 [D]John 6:63; Rom 7:6 3:7 [a]Or *in glory* [A]Rom 4:15; 5:20; 7:5f; 2 Cor 3:9; Gal 3:10, 21f [B]Ex 24:12; 31:18; 32:15f; 2 Cor 3:3 [C]Ex 34:29-35; 2 Cor 3:13

2:15 **a fragrance of Christ to God.** Paul was further thankful for the privilege of pleasing God. Continuing his analogy, Paul pictured God as the emperor at the end of the Triumph who also smells the pervasive fragrance and is pleased with the victorious efforts it represents. Wherever God's servant is faithful and is an influence for the gospel, God is pleased (cf. 5:9; Mt 25:21).

2:16 **an aroma from death … life.** Paul used the style of Heb. superlatives to emphasize the twofold effect of gospel preaching. To some, the message brings eternal life and ultimate glorification. To others, it is a stumbling stone of offense that brings eternal death (cf. 1Pe 2:6–8). **adequate for these things.** No one in his own strength is adequate or competent to serve God in the ways and with the power that Paul has been describing (cf. 3:5; 1Co 15:10; Gal 2:20; Eph 1:19; 3:20; Php 2:13; Col 1:29).

2:17 **not like many.** Or, "not as the majority." This specifically refers to the false teachers in Corinth and to the many other teachers and philosophers of that day who operated by human wisdom (cf. 1Co 1:19, 20). **peddling.** From a Gr. verb that means "to corrupt," this word came to refer to corrupt hucksters, or con men who by their cleverness and deception were able to sell as genuine an inferior product that was only a cheap imitation. The false teachers in the church were coming with clever, deceptive rhetoric to offer a degraded, adulterated message that mixed paganism and Jewish tradition. They were dishonest men seeking personal profit and prestige at the expense of gospel truth and people's souls. **in the sight of God.** *See note on v. 10.*

3:1–6 The false teachers in Corinth constantly attacked Paul's competency as a minister of the gospel; these verses form his defense.

3:1 Because Paul did not want to allow the false teachers to accuse him of being proud, he began his defense by posing two questions rather than making any overt claims. **Are we beginning to commend ourselves again?** The Gr. word for "commend" means "to introduce." Thus Paul was asking the Corinthians if he needed to reintroduce himself, as if they had never met, and prove himself once more. The form of the question demanded a negative answer. **letters of commendation.** The false teachers also accused Paul of not possessing the appropriate documents to prove his legitimacy. Such letters were often used to introduce and authenticate someone to the first-century churches (cf. 1Co 16:3, 10, 11). The false teachers undoubtedly arrived in Corinth with such letters, which they may have forged (cf. Ac 15:1, 5) or obtained under false pretenses from prominent members of the Jerusalem church. Paul's point was that he did not need secondhand testimony when the Corinthians had firsthand proof of his sincere and godly character, as well as the truth of his message that regenerated them.

3:2 **written in our hearts.** An affirmation of Paul's affection for the believers in Corinth—he held them close to his heart (cf. 12:15). **known and read by all men.** The transformed lives of the Corinthians were Paul's most eloquent testimonial, better than any secondhand letter. Their changed lives were like an open letter that could be seen and read by all men as a testimony to Paul's faithfulness and the truth of his message.

3:3 **letter of Christ.** The false teachers did not have a letter of commendation signed by Christ, but Paul had the Corinthian believers' changed lives as proof that Christ had transformed them. **written not with ink.** Paul's letter was no human document written with ink that can fade. It was a living one. **Spirit of the living God.** Paul's letter was alive, written by Christ's divine, supernatural power through the transforming work of the Holy Spirit (cf. 1Co 2:4, 5; 1Th 1:5). **tablets of stone.** A reference to the Ten Commandments (*see notes on Ex 24:12; 25:16*). **tablets of human hearts.** More than just writing His law on stone, God was writing His law on the hearts of those people He transformed (cf. Jer 31:33; 32:38, 39; Eze 11:19; 36:26, 27). The false teachers claimed external adherence to the Mosaic law as the basis of salvation, but the transformed lives of the Corinthians proved that salvation was an internal change wrought by God in the heart.

3:4 **Such confidence.** The Gr. word for "confidence" can mean "to win." Paul was confident in his ministry, and that confidence resulted in his ability to stay the course and continue moving toward the goal (cf. Ac 4:13, 29).

3:5 **adequate.** *See note on 2:16.* **to consider anything.** Paul disdained his own ability to reason, judge, or assess truth. Left to his own abilities, he was useless. He was dependent on divine revelation and the Holy Spirit's power. **our adequacy is from God.** Only God can make a person adequate to do His work, and Paul realized that truth (*see note on 2:16*; cf. 9:8, 10; 2Th 2:13).

3:6 **new covenant.** The covenant that provides forgiveness of sins through the death of Christ (*see notes on Jer 31:31–34; Mt 26:28; Heb 8:7–12*). **the letter.** A shallow, external conformity to the law that missed its most basic requirement of absolutely holy and perfect love for God and man (Mt 22:34–40) and distorted its true intention, which was to make a person recognize his sinfulness (cf. Ro 2:27–29). **the Spirit.** The Holy Spirit. **the letter kills, but the Spirit gives life.** The letter kills in two ways: 1) it results in a living death. Before Paul was converted, he thought he was saved by keeping the law, but all it did was kill his peace, joy, and hope; and 2) it results in spiritual death. His inability to truly keep the law sentenced him to an eternal death (*see notes on Ro 7:9–11*; cf. Ro 5:12; Gal 3:10). Only Jesus Christ through the agency of the Holy Spirit can produce eternal life in one who believes.

3:7–18 A true minister of God preaches the New Covenant; thus Paul featured the glory of the New Covenant in these verses.

3:7 **the ministry of death.** The law is a killer (v. 6) in the sense that it brings knowledge of sin. It acts as a ministry of death because no one can satisfy the demands of the law on his own and is therefore condemned (cf. Gal 3:22; *see notes on Ro 7:1–13; 8:4; Gal 3:10–13; 3:19–4:5*). **came with glory.** When God gave Moses the law, His glory appeared on the mountain (Ex 19:10–25; 20:18–26). Paul was not depreciating the law; he was acknowledging that it was glorious because it reflected God's nature, will, and character (*see notes on Ex 33:18–34:7*). **could not look intently at the face of Moses.** The Israelites could not look intently or stare at Moses' face for too long because the reflective glory of God was too bright for them. It was similar to staring into the sun (*see notes on Ex 34:29–35*). **the glory of his face.** When God manifested Himself, He did so by reducing His attributes to visible light. That's how God manifested Himself to Moses (Ex 34:29), whose face in turn reflected the glory of God to the people (cf. the Transfiguration of Jesus in Mt 17:1–8; 2Pe 1:16–18; and His second coming in Mt 24:29, 30; 25:31).

8 how will the ministry of the Spirit fail to be even more with glory? 9 For if [A]the ministry of condemnation has glory, much more does the [B]ministry of righteousness abound in glory. 10 For indeed what had glory, in this case has no glory because of the glory that surpasses *it.* 11 For if that which fades away *was* [a]with glory, much more that which remains *is* in glory.

12 [A]Therefore having such a hope, [B]we use great boldness in *our* speech, 13 and *are* not like Moses, [A]*who* used to put a veil over his face so that the sons of Israel would not look intently at the end of what was fading away. 14 But their minds were [A]hardened; for until this very day at the [B]reading of [C]the old covenant the same veil [a]remains unlifted, because it is removed in Christ. 15 But to this day whenever Moses is read, a veil lies over their heart; 16 [A]but whenever a person turns to the Lord, the veil is taken away. 17 Now the Lord is the Spirit, and where [A]the Spirit of the Lord is, [B]*there* is liberty. 18 But we all, with unveiled face, [A]beholding as in a mirror the [B]glory of the Lord, are being [C]transformed into the same image from glory to glory, just as from [D]the Lord, the Spirit.

PAUL'S APOSTOLIC MINISTRY

4 Therefore, since we have this [A]ministry, as we [B]received mercy, we [C]do not lose heart, 2 but we have renounced the [A]things hidden because of shame, not walking in craftiness or [B]adulterating the word of God, but by the manifestation of truth [C]commending ourselves to every man's conscience in the sight of God. 3 And even if our [A]gospel is [B]veiled, it is veiled [a]to [C]those who are perishing, 4 in whose case [A]the god of [B]this [a]world has [C]blinded the minds of the unbelieving [b]so that they might not see the [D]light of the gospel of the [E]glory of Christ, who is the [F]image of God.

3:9 [A]Deut 27:26; 2 Cor 3:7; Heb 12:18-21 [B]Rom 1:17; 3:21f 3:11 [a]Lit *through* 3:12 [A]2 Cor 7:4 [B]Acts 4:13, 29; 2 Cor 7:4; Eph 6:19; 1 Thess 2:2 3:13 [A]Ex 34:33-35; 2 Cor 3:7 3:14 [a]*Or remains, it not being revealed that it is done away in Christ* [A]Rom 11:7; 2 Cor 4:4 [B]Acts 13:15 [C]2 Cor 3:6 3:16 [A]Ex 34:34; Rom 11:23 3:17 [A]Is 61:1f; Gal 4:6 [B]John 8:32; Gal 5:1, 13 3:18 [A]1 Cor 13:12 [B]John 17:22, 24; 2 Cor 4:4, 6 [C]Rom 8:29 [D]2 Cor 3:17 4:1 [A]1 Cor 3:5 [B]1 Cor 7:25 [C]Luke 18:1; 2 Cor 4:16; Gal 6:9; Eph 3:13; 2 Thess 3:13 4:2 [A]Rom 6:21; 1 Cor 4:5 [B]2 Cor 2:17 [C]2 Cor 5:11f 4:3 [a]Lit *in* [A]2 Cor 2:12 [B]1 Cor 2:6ff; 2 Cor 3:14 [C]1 Cor 1:18; 2 Cor 2:15 4:4 [a]Lit *age* [b]*Or that the light...image of God, would not dawn* upon them [A]John 12:31 [B]Matt 13:22 [C]2 Cor 3:14 [D]Acts 26:18; 2 Cor 4:6 [E]2 Cor 3:18; 4:6 [F]John 1:18; Phil 2:6; Col 1:15; Heb 1:3

3:8, 9 ministry of the Spirit ... righteousness abound in glory. The "ministry of the Spirit" is Paul's descriptive term for the New Covenant (*see notes on Jer 31:31–34; Mt 26:28; 1Co 11:25; Heb 8:8, 13; 9:15; 12:24*). Paul is arguing that if such glory attended the giving of the law under the ministry that brought death, how much more glorious will be the ministry of the Spirit in the New Covenant which brings righteousness. The law pointed to the superior New Covenant and thus a glory that must also be superior.

3:9 ministry of condemnation. Another name for the ministry of death (*see note on v. 7*). **ministry of righteousness.** The New Covenant. The emphasis here is on the righteousness it provides (cf. Ro 3:21, 22; Php 3:9).

3:11 that which fades away. The law had a fading glory (cf. v. 7). It was not the final solution or the last word on the plight of sinners. **that which remains.** The New Covenant is what remains because it is the consummation of God's plan of salvation. It has permanent glory.

3:12 such a hope. The belief that all the promises of the New Covenant will occur. It is hope in total and complete forgiveness of sins for those who believe the gospel (cf. Ro 8:24, 25; Gal 5:5; Eph 1:18; 1Pe 1:3, 13, 21). **boldness in *our* speech.** The Gr. word for "boldness" means "courageously." Because of his confidence, Paul preached the New Covenant fearlessly, without any hesitation or timidity.

3:13 Moses ... put a veil over his face. This physical action pictured the fact that Moses did not have the confidence or boldness of Paul because the Old Covenant was veiled. It was shadowy. It was made up of types, pictures, symbols, and mystery. Moses communicated the glory of the Old Covenant with a certain obscurity (cf. 1Pe 1:10, 11).

3:14, 15 the same veil remains .... veil lies over their heart. The "veil" here represents unbelief. Those Israelites did not grasp the glory of the Old Covenant because of their unbelief. As a result, the meaning of the Old Covenant was obscure to them (cf. Heb 3:8, 15; 4:7). Paul's point was that just as the Old Covenant was obscure to the people of Moses' day, it was still obscure to those who trusted in it as a means of salvation in Paul's day. The veil of ignorance obscures the meaning of the Old Covenant to the hardened heart (cf. Jn 5:38).

3:14 the same veil ... is removed in Christ. Without Christ the OT is unintelligible. But when a person comes to Christ, the veil is lifted and his spiritual perception is no longer impaired (Is 25:6–8). With the veil removed, believers are able to see the glory of God revealed in Christ (Jn 1:14). They understand that the law was never given to save them, but to lead them to the One who would.

3:17 the Lord is the Spirit. Yahweh of the OT is the same Lord who is saving people in the New Covenant through the agency of the Holy Spirit. The same God is the minister of both the Old and New Covenants. ***there* is liberty.** Freedom from sin and the futile attempt to keep the demands of the law as a means of earning righteousness (cf. Jn 8:32–36; Ro 3:19, 20). The believer is no longer in bondage to the law's condemnation and Satan's dominion.

3:18 we all. Not just Moses, or prophets, apostles, and preachers, but all believers. **with unveiled face.** Believers in the New Covenant have nothing obstructing their vision of Christ and His glory as revealed in the Scripture. **beholding as in a mirror.** Paul's emphasis here is not so much on the reflective capabilities of the mirror as it is on the intimacy of it. A person can bring a mirror right up to his face and get an unobstructed view. Mirrors in Paul's day were polished metal (*see note on Jas 1:23*), and thus offered a far from perfect reflection. Though the vision is unobstructed and intimate, believers do not see a perfect representation of God's glory now, but will one day (cf. 1Co 13:12). **being transformed.** A continual, progressive transformation (*see note on Ro 12:2*). **into the same image.** As they gaze at the glory of the Lord, believers are continually being transformed into Christlikeness. The ultimate goal of the believer is to be like Christ (cf. Ro 8:29; Php 3:12–14; 1Jn 3:2), and by continually focusing on Him the Spirit transforms the believer more and more into His image. **from glory to glory.** From one level of glory to another level of glory—from one level of manifesting Christ to another. This verse describes progressive sanctification. The more believers grow in their knowledge of Christ, the more He is revealed in their lives (cf. Php 3:12–14).

4:1 this ministry. The New Covenant gospel of Jesus Christ. **lose heart.** A strong Gr. term which refers to abandoning oneself to cowardly surrender. That was not how Paul responded to the continual attacks he faced. The task of ministering the New Covenant was too noble to lose heart over (cf. Gal 6:9; Eph 3:13). Since God had called him to proclaim it, Paul could not abandon his calling. Instead, he trusted God to strengthen him (cf. Ac 20:24; 1Co 9:16, 17; Col 1:23, 25).

4:2 we have renounced the things hidden because of shame. "Renounced" means "to turn away from" or "to repent," and "shame" means "ugly" or "disgraceful." The phrase "things hidden" refers to secret immoralities, hypocrisies, and the sins hidden deep in the darkness of one's life. At salvation every believer repents and turns away from such sin and devotes his life to the pursuit of godliness. This appears to be a reply by Paul to a direct and slanderous accusation against him, that he was a hypocrite, whose mask of piety hid a corrupt and shameful life. **adulterating.** This Gr. word means "to tamper with," and was used in nonbiblical sources to speak of the dishonest business practice of diluting wine with water. The false teachers accused Paul of being a deceiver ("craftiness") who was twisting and perverting the teaching of Jesus and the OT Scripture.

4:3 if our gospel is veiled ... to those who are perishing. The false teachers accused Paul of preaching an antiquated message. So Paul showed that the problem was not with the message or the messenger, but with the hearers headed for hell (cf. 1Co 2:14). The preacher cannot persuade people to believe; only God can do that.

4:4 the god of this world. Satan (cf. Mt 4:8; Jn 12:31; 14:30; 16:11; Eph 2:2; 2Ti 2:26; 1Jn

5 For we [A]do not preach ourselves but Christ Jesus
as Lord, and ourselves as your bond-servants [a]for
Jesus' sake. 6 For God, who said, "[A]Light shall shine
out of darkness," is the One who has [B]shone in our
hearts to give the [C]Light of the knowledge of the
glory of God in the face of Christ.
7 But we have this treasure in [A]earthen vessels, so
that the surpassing greatness of [B]the power will be of
God and not from ourselves; 8 *we are* [A]afflicted in every
way, but not [B]crushed; [C]perplexed, but not despairing;
9 [A]persecuted, but not [B]forsaken; [C]struck down, but not
destroyed; 10 [A]always carrying about in the body the
dying of Jesus, so that [B]the life of Jesus also may be
manifested in our body. 11 For we who live are constantly being delivered over to death for Jesus' sake,
so that the life of Jesus also may be manifested in our
mortal flesh. 12 So death works in us, but life in you.
13 But having the same [A]spirit of faith, according
to what is written, "[B]I BELIEVED, THEREFORE I SPOKE,"
we also believe, therefore we also speak, 14 knowing
that He who [A]raised the Lord Jesus [B]will raise us also
with Jesus and will [C]present us with you. 15 For all
things *are* [A]for your sakes, so that the grace which
is [a,B]spreading to more and more people may cause
the giving of thanks to abound to the glory of God.
16 Therefore we [A]do not lose heart, but though
our outer man is decaying, yet our [B]inner man is
[C]being renewed day by day. 17 For momentary, [A]light
affliction is producing for us an eternal weight of
glory far beyond all comparison, 18 while we [A]look
not at the things which are seen, but at the things
which are not seen; for the things which are seen
are temporal, but the things which are not seen
are eternal.

4:5 [a]Two early mss read *through Jesus* [A]1 Cor 4:15f; 1 Thess 2:6f 4:6 [A]Gen 1:3 [B]2 Pet 1:19 [C]Acts 26:18; 2 Cor 4:4 4:7 [A]Job 4:19; 10:9; 33:6; Lam 4:2; 2 Cor 5:1; 2 Tim 2:20 [B]Judg 7:2; 1 Cor 2:5 4:8 [A]2 Cor 1:8; 7:5 [B]2 Cor 6:12 [C]Gal 4:20 4:9 [A]John 15:20; Rom 8:35f [B]Ps 129:2; Heb 13:5 [C]Ps 37:24; Prov 24:16; Mic 7:8 4:10 [A]Rom 6:5; 8:36; Gal 6:17 [B]Rom 6:8 4:13 [A]1 Cor 12:9 [B]Ps 116:10 4:14 [A]Acts 2:24 [B]1 Thess 4:14 [C]Luke 21:36; Eph 5:27; Col 1:22; Jude 24 4:15 [a]Lit *being multiplied through the many* [A]Rom 8:28; 2 Cor 1:6 [B]1 Cor 9:19; 2 Cor 1:11 4:16 [A]2 Cor 4:1 [B]Rom 7:22 [C]Is 40:29, 31; Col 3:10 4:17 [A]Rom 8:18 4:18 [A]Rom 8:24; 2 Cor 5:7; Heb 11:1, 13

5:19). **this world.** The current world mindset expressed by the ideals, opinions, goals, hopes, and views of the majority of people. It encompasses the world's philosophies, education, and commerce. *See notes on 10:5.* **has blinded.** Satan blinds men to God's truth through the world system he has created. Without a godly influence, man left to himself will follow that system, which panders to the depravity of unbelievers and deepens their moral darkness (cf. Mt 13:19). Ultimately, it is God who allows such blindness (Jn 12:40). **image of God.** Jesus Christ is the exact representation of God Himself (*see notes on Col 1:15; 2:9; Heb 1:3*).

4:5 we do not preach ourselves. The false teachers accused Paul of preaching for his own benefit, yet they were the ones guilty of doing so. In contrast, Paul was always humble (12:5, 9; cf. 1Co 2:3); he never promoted himself, but always preached Christ Jesus as Lord (1Co 2:2).

4:6 God, who said, "Light shall shine out of darkness." A direct reference to God as Creator, who commanded physical light into existence (Ge 1:3). **the Light of the knowledge of the glory of God.** The same God who created physical light in the universe is the same God who must create supernatural light in the soul and usher believers from the kingdom of darkness to His kingdom of light (Col 1:13). The light is expressed as "the knowledge of the glory of God." That means to know that Christ is God incarnate. To be saved, one must understand that the glory of God shone in Jesus Christ. That is the theme of John's gospel (*see note on Jn 1:4, 5*).

4:7 this treasure. *See note on v. 1.* **earthen vessels.** The Gr. word means "baked clay," and refers to clay pots. They were cheap, breakable, and replaceable, but they served necessary household functions. Sometimes they were used as a vault to store valuables, such as money, jewelry, or important documents. But they were most often used for holding garbage and human waste. The latter is the use Paul had in mind, and it was how Paul viewed himself—as lowly, common, expendable, and replaceable (cf. 1Co 1:20–27; 2Ti 2:20, 21). **surpassing greatness of the power will be of God and not from ourselves.** By using frail and expendable people, God makes it clear that salvation is the result of His power and not any power His messengers could generate (cf. 2:16). The great power of God overcomes and transcends the clay pot. The messenger's weakness is not fatal to what he does; it is essential (cf. 12:9, 10).

4:8, 9 Here Paul gave 4 contrasting metaphors to show that his weakness did not cripple him, but actually strengthened him (cf. 6:4–10; 12:7–10).

4:10 always carrying about in the body the dying of Jesus. "Always" indicates that the suffering Paul experienced was endless. And the suffering was a result of attacks against Jesus, not Paul and other believers. Those who hated Jesus took out their vengeance on those who represented Him (cf. Jn 15:18–21; Gal 6:17; Col 1:24). **that the life of Jesus also may be manifested in our body.** Through Paul's weakness, Christ was put on display (cf. Gal 2:20). His suffering, the false apostles said, was evidence that God was not with him and he was a fraud. On the contrary, Paul affirmed that his suffering was the badge of his loyalty to Christ and the source of his power (12:9, 10).

4:11 delivered over to death. Refers to the transferring of a prisoner to the executioner. It was used to refer to Christ's being delivered to those who crucified Him (Mt 27:2). In this case, it refers to the potential physical death constantly faced by those who represented Christ. **our mortal flesh.** Another term for Paul's humanness—his physical body (cf. v. 10; 5:3).

4:12 Paul faced death every day, yet he was willing to pay that price if it meant salvation for those to whom he preached (cf. Php 2:17; Col 1:24; 2Ti 2:10).

4:13 Paul remained true to his convictions, no matter the cost. He was not a pragmatist who would alter his message to suit his listeners. He was convinced of the power of God to act through the message he preached. **spirit of faith.** The attitude of faith, not the Holy Spirit. Paul had the same conviction about the power of the message as did the psalmist (*see following note*). **I believed, therefore I spoke.** A quotation from the LXX (the Gr. translation of the OT) version of Ps 116:10. In the midst of his troubles, the psalmist confidently asked God to deliver him out of his troubles. He could confidently do so because he believed God would answer his prayer.

4:15 to the glory of God. The ultimate goal of all that the believer does (*see note on 1Co 10:31*).

4:16 we do not lose heart. *See note on v. 1.* **our outer man is decaying.** The physical body is in the process of decay and will eventually die. On the surface Paul was referring to the normal aging process, but with the added emphasis that his lifestyle sped up that process. While not an old man, Paul wore himself out in ministry, both in the effort and pace he maintained, plus the number of beatings and attacks he absorbed from his enemies (cf. 6:4–10; 11:23–27). **inner man.** The soul of every believer i.e., the new creation—the eternal part of the believer (cf. Eph 4:24; Col 3:10). **being renewed.** The growth and maturing process of the believer is constantly occurring. While the physical body is decaying, the inner self of the believer continues to grow and mature into Christlikeness (cf. Eph 3:16–20).

4:17 momentary, light affliction. The Gr. word for "light" means "a weightless trifle" and "affliction" refers to intense pressure. From a human perspective, Paul's own testimony lists a seemingly unbearable litany of sufferings and persecutions he endured throughout his life (11:23–33), yet he viewed them as weightless and lasting for only a brief moment. **eternal weight of glory.** The Gr. word for "weight" refers to a heavy mass. For Paul, the future glory he would experience with the Lord far outweighed any suffering he experienced in this world (cf. Ro 8:17, 18; 1Pe 1:6, 7). Paul understood that the greater the suffering, the greater would be his eternal glory (cf. 1Pe 4:13).

4:18 things which are seen ... not seen. Endurance is based on a person's ability to look beyond the physical to the spiritual; beyond the present to the future, and beyond the visible to the invisible. Believers must look past what is temporary—what is perishing (i.e., the things of the world). **things ... not seen are eternal.** Pursuing God, Christ, the Holy Spirit, and the souls of men should consume the believer.

THE TEMPORAL AND ETERNAL

5 For we know that if [a]the [A]earthly [B]tent which is our
house is torn down, we have a building from God,
a house [C]not made with hands, eternal in the heavens.
2 For indeed in this *house* we [A]groan, longing to be
[B]clothed with our dwelling from heaven, 3 inasmuch
as we, having put it on, will not be found naked. 4 For
indeed while we are in this tent, we [A]groan, being burdened, because we do not want to be unclothed but to
be [B]clothed, so that what is [C]mortal will be swallowed
up by life. 5 Now He who prepared us for this very
purpose is God, who [A]gave to us the Spirit as a [a]pledge.
6 Therefore, being always of good courage, and
knowing that [A]while we are at home in the body we
are absent from the Lord— 7 for [A]we walk by faith,
not by [a]sight— 8 we are of good courage, I say, and
[A]prefer rather to be absent from the body and [B]to
be at home with the Lord. 9 Therefore we also have
as our ambition, whether at home or absent, to be
[A]pleasing to Him. 10 For we must all appear before
[A]the judgment seat of Christ, so that each one may
be recompensed for [a]his deeds in the body, according to what he has done, whether good or bad.
11 Therefore, knowing the [A]fear of the Lord, we
persuade men, but we are made manifest to God;
and I hope that we are [B]made manifest also in your
consciences. 12 We are not [A]again commending ourselves to you but *are* giving you an [B]occasion to be

5:1 [a]Lit *our earthly house of the tent* [A]Job 4:19; 1 Cor 15:47; 2 Cor 4:7 [B]2 Pet 1:13f [C]Mark 14:58; Acts 7:48; Heb 9:11, 24 5:2 [A]Rom 8:23; 2 Cor 5:4 [B]1 Cor 15:53f; 2 Cor 5:4 5:4 [A]2 Cor 5:2 [B]1 Cor 15:53f; 2 Cor 5:2 [C]1 Cor 15:54 5:5 [a]Or *down payment* [A]Rom 8:23; 2 Cor 1:22 5:6 [A]Heb 11:13f 5:7 [a]Or *appearance* [A]1 Cor 13:12; 2 Cor 4:18 5:8 [A]Phil 1:23 [B]John 12:26; Phil 1:23 5:9 [A]Rom 14:18; Col 1:10; 1 Thess 4:1 5:10 [a]Lit *the things through the body* [A]Matt 16:27; Acts 10:42; Rom 2:16; 14:10, 12; Eph 6:8 5:11 [A]Heb 10:31; 12:29; Jude 23 [B]2 Cor 4:2 5:12 [A]2 Cor 3:1 [B]2 Cor 1:14; Phil 1:26

5:1 earthly tent … house. Paul's metaphor for the physical body (cf. 2Pe 1:13, 14). The imagery was quite natural for that time because many people were nomadic tent dwellers, and Paul as a tentmaker (Ac 18:3) knew much about tents' characteristics. Also, the Jewish tabernacle had symbolized God's presence among the people as they left Egypt and became a nation. Paul's point is that like a temporary tent, man's earthly existence is fragile, insecure, and lowly (cf. 1Pe 2:11). **a building from God.** Paul's metaphor for the believer's resurrected, glorified body (cf. 1Co 15:35–50). "Building" implies solidity, security, certainty, and permanence, as opposed to the frail, temporary, uncertain nature of a tent. Just as the Israelites replaced the tabernacle with the temple, so believers ought to long to exchange their earthly bodies for glorified ones (*see notes on 4:16; Ro 8:19–23; 1Co 15:35–50; Php 3:20, 21*). **a house … in the heavens.** A heavenly, eternal body. Paul wanted a new body that would forever perfectly express his transformed nature. **not made with hands.** A glorified body, by definition, is not of this earthly creation (*see notes on Mk 14:58; Heb 9:11*; cf. Jn 2:19; Col 2:11).

5:2 we groan. Paul had a passionate longing to be free from his earthly body and all the accompanying sins, frustrations, and weaknesses that were so relentless (*see notes on Ro 7:24; 8:23*). **clothed with our dwelling from heaven.** The perfections of immortality (*see notes on v. 1*).

5:3 we … will not be found naked. Paul clarified the fact that the believer's hope for the next life is not a disembodied spiritual life, but a real, eternal, resurrection body. Unlike the pagans who viewed matter as evil and spirit as good, Paul knew that Christian death would not mean being released into a nebulous, spiritual infinity. Rather, it would mean the receiving of a glorified, spiritual, immortal, perfect, qualitatively different but nonetheless real body, just as Jesus received (*see notes on 1Co 15:35–44; Php 3:20, 21*; cf. 1Jn 3:2).

5:4 unclothed … clothed. *See notes on vv. 2, 3.* Paul reiterated that he could hardly wait to get his glorified body (cf. Php 1:21–23). **mortal will be swallowed up by life.** Paul wanted the fullness of all that God had planned for him in eternal life, when all that is earthly and human will cease to be.

5:5 for this very purpose. Paul emphatically states that the believer's heavenly existence will come to pass according to God's sovereign purpose (*see notes on Ro 8:28–30*; cf. Jn 6:37–40, 44). **God … gave to us the Spirit.** *See notes on 1:22; Ro 5:5; Eph 1:13*; cf. Php 1:6. **pledge.** *See notes on 1:22; Eph 1:13.*

5:6 at home in the body … absent from the Lord. While a believer is alive on earth, he is away from the fullness of God's presence. However, Paul was not saying he had absolutely no contact, because there is prayer, the indwelling Spirit, and fellowship through the Word. Paul was simply expressing a heavenly homesickness, a strong yearning to be at home with his Lord (cf. Ps 73:25; 1Th 4:17; Rev 21:3, 23; 22:3).

5:7 The Christian can hope for a heaven he has not seen. He does so by believing what Scripture says about it and living by that belief (*see note on Heb 11:1*; cf. Jn 20:29).

5:8 absent from the body … at home with the Lord. Because heaven is a better place than earth, Paul would rather have been there, with God. This sentiment simply states Paul's feelings and longings of v. 6 from a reverse perspective (*see notes on Php 1:21, 23*).

5:9 we also have as our ambition. Paul was speaking of his ambition in life, but not the kind of proud, selfish desire that "ambition" expresses in English. "Ambition" is from the Gr. word that means "to love what is honorable." Paul demonstrated that it is right and noble for the believer to strive for excellence, spiritual goals, and all that is honorable before God (cf. Ro 15:20; 1Ti 3:1). **whether at home or absent.** *See notes on vv. 6, 8.* Paul's ambition was not altered by his state of being—whether he should be in heaven or on earth—he cared how he lived for the Lord (*see notes on Ro 14:6; Php 1:20*; cf. 1Co 9:27). **pleasing to Him.** This was Paul's highest goal (cf. 1Co 4:1–5), and should be so for every believer (cf. Ro 12:2; Eph 5:10; Col 1:9; 1Th 4:1). The term translated "pleasing" is the same one used in Titus 2:9 to describe slaves who were passionate to please their masters.

5:10 This describes the believer's deepest motivation and highest aim in pleasing God—the realization that every Christian is inevitably and ultimately accountable to Him. **the judgment seat of Christ.** "Judgment seat" metaphorically refers to the place where the Lord will sit to evaluate believers' lives for the purpose of giving them eternal rewards. It is translated from the Gr. word *bēma,* which was an elevated platform where victorious athletes (e.g., during the Olympics) went to receive their crowns. The term is also used in the NT to refer to the place of judging, as when Jesus stood before Pontius Pilate (Mt 27:19; Jn 19:13), but here the reference is definitely from the athletic analogy. Corinth had such a platform where both athletic rewards and legal justice were dispensed (Ac 18:12–16), so the Corinthians understood Paul's reference. **deeds in the body.** Actions which happened during the believer's time of earthly ministry. This does not include sins, since their judgment took place at the cross (Eph 1:7). Paul was referring to all those activities believers do during their lifetimes, which relate to their eternal reward and praise from God. What Christians do in their temporal bodies will, in His eyes, have an impact for eternity (*see notes on 1Co 4:3–5*; cf. Ro 12:1, 2; Rev 22:12). **whether good or bad.** These Gr. terms do not refer to moral good and moral evil. Matters of sin have been completely dealt with by the death of the Savior. Rather, Paul was comparing worthwhile, eternally valuable activities with useless ones. His point was not that believers should not enjoy certain wholesome, earthly things, but that they should glorify God in them and spend most of their energy and time with what has eternal value (*see notes on 1Co 3:8–14*).

5:11 the fear of the Lord. This is not referring to being afraid, but to Paul's worshipful reverence for God as his essential motivation to live in such a way as to honor his Lord and maximize his reward for his Lord's glory (cf. 7:1; Pr 9:10; Ac 9:31). **we persuade men.** The Gr. word for "persuade" means to seek someone's favor, as in getting the other person to see you in a certain favorable or desired way (cf. Gal 1:10). This term can mean gospel preaching (Ac 18:4; 28:23), but here Paul was persuading others not about salvation, but about his own integrity. The Corinthians' eternal reward would be affected if they defected to the false teachers and left the divine teaching of Paul. **made manifest.** Paul's true spiritual condition of sincerity and integrity was manifest to God (*see notes on 1:12*; cf. Ac 23:1; 24:16), and he also wanted the Corinthians to believe the truth about him.

5:12 take pride in appearance. Those who have no integrity, such as Paul's opponents at Corinth, have to take pride in externals, which can be any false doctrine accompanied by showy hypocrisy (cf. Mt 5:20; 6:1; Mk 7:6, 7).

proud of us, so that you will have *an answer* for those
who take pride in appearance and not in heart. 13 For
if we [a]are [A]beside ourselves, it is for God; if we are
of sound mind, it is for you. 14 For the love of Christ
[A]controls us, having concluded this, that [B]one died
for all, therefore all died; 15 and He died for all, so that
they who live might no longer [A]live for themselves,
but for Him who died and rose again on their behalf.
16 Therefore from now on we recognize no one
[a,A]according to the flesh; even though we have
known Christ [a]according to the flesh, yet now we
know *Him in this way* no longer. 17 Therefore if
anyone is [A]in Christ, [a]*he is* [B]a new creature; [C]the
old things passed away; behold, new things have
come. 18 Now [A]all *these* things are from God, [B]who
reconciled us to Himself through Christ and gave us
the [C]ministry of reconciliation, 19 namely, that [A]God
was in Christ reconciling the world to Himself, [B]not
counting their trespasses against them, and [a]He
has [b]committed to us the word of reconciliation.
20 Therefore, we are [A]ambassadors for Christ, [B]as
though God were making an appeal through us; we
beg you on behalf of Christ, be [C]reconciled to God.
21 He made Him who [A]knew no sin *to be* [B]sin on our
behalf, so that we might become the [C]righteousness
of God in Him.

5:13 [a]Lit *were* [A]Mark 3:21; 2 Cor 11:1, 16ff; 12:11 5:14 [A]Acts 18:5 [B]Rom 5:15; 6:6f; Gal 2:20; Col 3:3 5:15 [A]Rom 14:7-9 5:16 [a]I.e. by what he is in the flesh [A]John 8:15; 2 Cor 11:18; Phil 3:4 5:17 [a]Or there is *a new creation* [A]Rom 16:7 [B]John 3:3; Rom 6:4; Gal 6:15 [C]Is 43:18f; 65:17; Eph 4:24; Rev 21:4f 5:18 [A]1 Cor 11:12 [B]Rom 5:10; Col 1:20 [C]1 Cor 3:5 5:19 [a]Lit *having* [b]Lit *placed in us* [A]Col 2:9 [B]Rom 4:8; 1 Cor 13:5 5:20 [A]Mal 2:7; Eph 6:20 [B]2 Cor 6:1 [C]Rom 5:10; Col 1:20 5:21 [A]Acts 3:14; Heb 4:15; 7:26; 1 Pet 2:22; 1 John 3:5 [B]Rom 3:25; 4:25; 8:3; Gal 3:13 [C]Rom 1:17; 3:21f; 1 Cor 1:30

5:13 beside ourselves. This Gr. phrase usually means to be insane, or out of one's mind, but here Paul used the expression to describe himself as one dogmatically devoted to truth. In this way, he answered those critics who claimed he was nothing more than an insane fanatic (cf. Jn 8:48; Ac 26:22–24). **of sound mind.** The original word meant to be moderate, sober minded, and in complete control. Paul also behaved this way among the Corinthians as he defended his integrity and communicated truth to them.

5:14 the love of Christ. Christ's love for Paul and all believers at the cross (cf. Ro 5:6–8). Christ's loving, substitutionary death motivated Paul's service for Him (cf. Gal 2:20; Eph 3:19). **controls.** This refers to pressure that causes action. Paul emphasized the strength of his desire to offer his life to the Lord. **one died for all.** This expresses the truth of Christ's substitutionary death. The preposition "for" indicates He died "in behalf of," or "in the place of" all (cf. Is 53:4–12; Gal 3:13; Heb 9:11–14). This truth is at the heart of the doctrine of salvation. God's wrath against sin required death; Jesus took that wrath and died in the sinner's place. Thus He took away God's wrath and satisfied God's justice as a perfect sacrifice (*see notes on v. 21; Ro 5:6–11, 18, 19; 1Ti 2:5, 6*; cf. Eph 5:2; 1Th 5:10; Titus 2:14; 1Pe 2:24). **therefore all died.** Everyone who died in Christ receives the benefits of His substitutionary death (*see notes on Ro 3:24–26; 6:8*). With this short phrase, Paul defined the extent of the atonement and limited its application. This statement logically completes the meaning of the preceding phrase, in effect saying, "Christ died for all who died in Him," or "One died for all, therefore all died" (*see notes on vv. 19–21*; cf. Jn 10:11–16; Ac 20:28). Paul was overwhelmed with gratitude that Christ loved him and was so gracious as to make him a part of the "all" who died in Him.

5:15 As he defended his integrity to the Corinthians, Paul wanted them to know that his old, self-centered life was finished and that he had an all-out desire to live righteously. For all genuine believers, their death in Christ is not only a death to sin, but a resurrection to a new life of righteousness (*see notes on Ro 6:3, 4, 8, 10*; cf. Gal 2:19, 20; Col 3:3).

5:16 Since Paul's conversion, his priority was to meet people's spiritual needs (cf. Ac 17:16; Ro 1:13–16; 9:1–3; 10:1). **according to the flesh.** Paul no longer evaluated people according to external, human, worldly standards (cf. 10:3). **we know *Him in this way* no longer.** Paul, as a Christian, also no longer had merely a fallible, human assessment of Jesus Christ (cf. Ac 9:1–6; 26:9–23).

5:17 in Christ. These two words comprise a brief but most profound statement of the inexhaustible significance of the believer's redemption, which includes the following: 1) the believer's security in Christ, who bore in His body God's judgment against sin; 2) the believer's acceptance in Him with whom God alone is well pleased; 3) the believer's future assurance in Him who is the resurrection to eternal life and the sole guarantor of the believer's inheritance in heaven; and 4) the believer's participation in the divine nature of Christ, the everlasting Word (cf. 2Pe 1:4). **new creature.** This describes something that is created at a qualitatively new level of excellence. It refers to regeneration or the new birth (cf. Jn 3:3; Eph 2:1–3; Titus 3:5; 1Pe 1:23; 1Jn 2:29; 3:9; 5:4). This expression encompasses the Christian's forgiveness of sins paid for in Christ's substitutionary death (cf. Gal 6:15; Eph 4:24). **old things passed away.** After a person is regenerate, old value systems, priorities, beliefs, loves, and plans are gone. Evil and sin are still present, but the believer sees them in a new perspective (*see note on v. 16*), and they no longer control him. **new things have come.** The Gr. grammar indicates that this newness is a continuing condition of fact. The believer's new spiritual perception of everything is a constant reality for him, and he now lives for eternity, not temporal things. James identifies this transformation as the faith that produces works (*see notes on Eph 2:10; Jas 2:14–25*).

5:18 all *these* things are from God. All the aspects related to someone's conversion and newly transformed life in Christ are accomplished by a sovereign God. Sinners on their own cannot decide to participate in these new realities (*see note on Ro 5:10*; cf. 1Co 8:6; 11:12; Eph 2:1). **ministry of reconciliation.** This speaks to the reality that God wills sinful men to be reconciled to Himself (cf. Ro 5:10; Eph 4:17–24). God has called believers to proclaim the gospel of reconciliation to others (cf. 1Co 1:17). The concept of service, such as waiting on tables, derives from the Gr. word for "ministry." Lit. God wants Christians to accept the privilege of serving unbelievers by proclaiming a desire to be reconciled.

5:19 God was in Christ. God by His own will and design used His Son, the only acceptable and perfect sacrifice, as the means to reconcile sinners to Himself (*see notes on v. 18; Ac 2:23; Col 1:19, 20*; cf. Jn 14:6; Ac 4:12; 1Ti 2:5, 6). **reconciling the world.** God initiates the change in the sinner's status in that He brings him from a position of alienation to a state of forgiveness and right relationship with Himself. This again is the essence of the gospel. The word "world" should not be interpreted in any universalistic sense, which would say that everyone will be saved, or even potentially reconciled. "World" refers rather to the entire sphere of mankind or humanity (cf. Titus 2:11; 3:4), the category of beings to whom God offers reconciliation—people from every ethnic group, without distinction. The intrinsic merit of Christ's reconciling death is infinite, and the offer is unlimited. However, actual atonement was made only for those who believe (cf. Jn 10:11, 15; 17:9; Ac 13:48; 20:28; Ro 8:32, 33; Eph 5:25). The rest of humanity will pay the price personally for their own sin in eternal hell. **counting.** This may also be translated "reckoning." This is the heart of the doctrine of justification whereby God declares the repentant sinner righteous and does not count his sins against him because He covers him with the righteousness of Christ the moment he places wholehearted faith in Christ and His sacrificial death (*see notes on Ro 3:24–4:5*; cf. Ps 32:2; Ro 4:8). **word of reconciliation.** *See note on v. 18.* Here Paul presents another aspect to the meaning of the gospel. He used the Gr. word for "word" (cf. Ac 13:26), which indicated a true and trustworthy message, as opposed to a false or unsure one. In a world filled with false messages, believers have the solid, truthful message of the gospel.

5:20 ambassadors. A term that is related to the more familiar Gr. word often translated "elder." It described an older, more experienced man who served as a representative of a king from one country to another. Paul thus described his role—and the role of all believers—as a messenger representing the King of heaven with the gospel, who pleads with the people of the world to be reconciled to God, who is their rightful King (cf. Ro 10:13–18). **as though God were making an appeal.** As believers present the gospel, God speaks (lit. "calls," or "begs") through them and urges unbelieving sinners to come in an attitude of faith and accept the gospel, which means to repent of their sins and believe on Jesus (cf. Ac 16:31; Jas 4:8).

5:21 Here Paul summarized the heart of the gospel, resolving the mystery and paradox of vv. 18–20, and explaining how sinners can be reconciled to God through Jesus Christ. These

THEIR MINISTRY COMMENDED

6 And [A]working together *with Him,* [B]we also urge
you not to receive [C]the grace of God in vain—
2 for He says,

"[A]AT THE ACCEPTABLE TIME I
LISTENED TO YOU,
AND ON THE DAY OF SALVATION
I HELPED YOU."

Behold, now is "THE ACCEPTABLE TIME," behold, now
is "THE DAY OF SALVATION"— 3 [A]giving no cause for
offense in anything, so that the ministry will not
be discredited, 4 but in everything [A]commending
ourselves as [a,B]servants of God, [C]in much endurance,
in afflictions, in hardships, in distresses, 5 in [A]beat-
ings, in imprisonments, in [B]tumults, in labors, in
sleeplessness, in [C]hunger, 6 in purity, in [A]knowledge,
in [B]patience, in kindness, in the [C]Holy Spirit, in [D]gen-
uine love, 7 in [A]the word of truth, in [B]the power of
God; by [C]the weapons of righteousness for the right
hand and the left, 8 by glory and [A]dishonor, by [B]evil
report and good report; *regarded* as [C]deceivers
and yet [D]true; 9 as unknown [a]yet well-known, as
[A]dying [a]yet behold, [B]we live; as [b]punished [a]yet not
put to death, 10 as [A]sorrowful yet always [A]rejoicing,
as [B]poor yet making many rich, as [C]having nothing
[a]yet possessing [D]all things.
11 [A]Our mouth [a]has spoken freely to you, O Corinthians, our [B]heart is opened wide. 12 You are not
restrained [a]by us, but [A]you are restrained in your
own [b]affections. 13 Now in a like [A]exchange—I speak
as to [B]children—open wide *to us* also.
14 [A]Do not be [a]bound together with [B]unbeliev-
ers; for what [C]partnership have righteousness and
lawlessness, or what fellowship has light with

6:1 [A]1 Cor 3:9 [B]2 Cor 5:20 [C]Acts 11:23 6:2 [A]Is 49:8 6:3 [A]1 Cor 8:9, 13; 9:12 6:4 [a]Or *ministers* [A]Rom 3:5 [B]1 Cor 3:5; 2 Tim 2:24f [C]Acts 9:16; 2 Cor 4:8-11; 6:4ff; 11:23-27; 12:10 6:5 [A]Acts 16:23 [B]Acts 19:23ff [C]1 Cor 4:11 6:6 [A]1 Cor 12:8; 2 Cor 11:6 [B]2 Cor 1:23; 2:10; 13:10 [C]1 Cor 2:4; 1 Thess 1:5 [D]Rom 12:9 6:7 [A]2 Cor 2:17; 4:2 [B]1 Cor 2:5 [C]Rom 13:12; 2 Cor 10:4; Eph 6:11ff 6:8 [A]1 Cor 4:10 [B]Rom 3:8; 1 Cor 4:13; 2 Cor 12:16 [C]Matt 27:63 [D]2 Cor 1:18; 4:2; 1 Thess 2:3f 6:9 [a]Lit *and* [b]Or *disciplined* [A]Rom 8:36 [B]2 Cor 1:8, 10; 4:11 6:10 [a]Lit *and* [A]John 16:22; 2 Cor 7:4; Phil 2:17; 4:4; Col 1:24; 1 Thess 1:6 [B]1 Cor 1:5; 2 Cor 8:9 [C]Acts 3:6 [D]Rom 8:32; 1 Cor 3:21 6:11 [a]Lit *is open to you* [A]Ezek 33:22; Eph 6:19 [B]Is 60:5; 2 Cor 7:3 6:12 [a]Or *in us* [b]Lit *inward parts* [A]2 Cor 7:2 6:13 [A]Gal 4:12 [B]1 Cor 4:14 6:14 [a]Lit *unequally yoked* [A]Deut 22:10; 1 Cor 5:9f [B]1 Cor 6:6 [C]Eph 5:7, 11; 1 John 1:6

15 Gr. words express the doctrines of imputation and substitution like no other single verse. **who knew no sin.** Jesus Christ, the sinless Son of God (*see notes on Gal 4:4, 5*; cf. Lk 23:4, 14, 22, 47; Jn 8:46; Heb 4:15; 7:26; 1Pe 1:19; 2:22–24; 3:18; Rev 5:2–10). **sin on our behalf.** God the Father, using the principle of imputation (*see note on v. 19*), treated Christ as if He were a sinner though He was not, and had Him die as a substitute to pay the penalty for the sins of those who believe in Him (cf. Is 53:4–6; Gal 3:10–13; 1Pe 2:24). On the cross, He did not become a sinner (as some suggest), but remained as holy as ever. He was treated as if He were guilty of all the sins ever committed by all who would ever believe, though He committed none. The wrath of God was exhausted on Him and the just requirement of God's law met for those for whom He died. **the righteousness of God.** Another reference to justification and imputation. The righteousness that is credited to the believer's account is the righteousness of Jesus Christ, God's Son (*see notes on Ro 1:17; 3:21–24; Php 3:9*). As Christ was not a sinner, but was treated as if He were, so believers who have not yet been made righteous (until glorification) are treated as if they were righteous. He bore their sins so that they could bear His righteousness. God treated Him as if He committed believers' sins, and treats believers as if they did only the righteous deeds of the sinless Son of God.

6:1 to receive the grace of God in vain. Most of the Corinthians were saved but hindered by legalistic teaching regarding sanctification (*see notes on 11:3; Gal 6:1*). Some were not truly saved but deceived by a gospel of works (cf. 13:5; Gal 5:4), which was being taught by the false teachers. In either case, Paul's proclamation of the gospel of grace would not have been having its desired effect, and he would have had cause for serious concern that his many months of ministry at Corinth were for nothing. Both cases also prevented the people from effectively assuming any "ministry of reconciliation" (5:18).

6:2 Paul emphasized his point by quoting Is 49:8. He was passionately concerned that the Corinthians adhere to the truth because it was God's time to save, and they were messengers for helping to spread that message. **now is "the day of salvation."** Paul applied Isaiah's words to the present situation. There is a time in God's economy when He listens to sinners and responds to those who are repentant—and it was and is that time (cf. Pr 1:20–23; Is 55:6; Heb 3:7, 8; 4:7). However, there will also be an end to that time (cf. Ge 6:3; Pr 1:24–33; Jn 9:4), which is why Paul's exhortation was so passionate.

6:3–10 Like Paul, any believer who engages in a faithful ministry of reconciliation should expect to be rejected and accepted, to be hated and loved, to encounter joy and hardship. This is what Jesus had already taught His disciples (cf. Mt 5:10–16; Lk 12:2–12).

6:3 giving no cause for offense in anything. The faithful ambassador of Christ does nothing to discredit his ministry, but everything he can to protect its integrity, the gospel's integrity, and God's integrity (cf. Ro 2:24; 1Co 9:27; Titus 2:1–10).

6:4 commending ourselves as servants of God. "Commending" means "introducing," with the connotation of proving oneself (*see note on 3:1*). The most convincing proof is the patient endurance of character reflected in Paul's hardships (v. 5) and the nature of his ministry (vv. 6, 7).

6:5 Here Paul commended himself to them by mentioning his faithfulness in enduring persecution and citing his diligence in ministry labors, to the point of anguished deprivations when necessary (*see note on 4:17*).

6:6 Paul commended himself positively by listing the important elements of the righteousness God had granted to him. **in the Holy Spirit.** Paul lived and walked by the power of the Spirit (*see note on Gal 5:16*). It was the central reason that all the other positive elements of his endurance were a reality.

6:7 in the word of truth. The Scriptures, the revealed Word of God (cf. Col 1:5; Jas 1:18). During his entire ministry, Paul never operated beyond the boundaries of the direction and guidance of divine revelation. **in the power of God.** Paul did not rely on his own strength when he ministered (*see notes on 1Co 1:18; 2:1–3*; cf. Ro 1:16). **by the weapons of righteousness.** Paul did not fight Satan's kingdom with human resources, but with spiritual virtue (*see notes on 10:3–5; Eph 6:10–18*). **the right hand . . . the left.** Paul had both offensive tools, such as the sword of the Spirit, and defensive tools, such as the shield of faith and the helmet of salvation, at his disposal (*see notes on Eph 6:16, 17*).

6:8–10 The mark of a ministry that has genuine character is paradoxical, and here Paul gave a series of paradoxes regarding his service for Christ.

6:8 as deceivers. Paul's opponents at Corinth had accused him of being an impostor and a false apostle (cf. Jn 7:12).

6:9 as unknown. This is a twofold reference to: 1) the fact that Christians did not know him before he began persecuting them (cf. Ac 8:1; 1Ti 1:12, 13); and 2) his rejection by the community of leading Jews and Pharisees following his conversion. He had become unknown to his former world, and well-known and well-loved by the Christian community.

6:10 making many rich. The spiritual wealth Paul possessed and imparted did much to make his hearers spiritually wealthy (cf. Ac 3:6).

6:11–13 Paul proved his genuine love for the Corinthians by defining love's character. This passage confirms the reality of his profession of love for them (cf. 2:4; 3:2; 12:15, 19).

6:11 our heart is opened wide. Lit. "our heart is enlarged" (cf. 1Ki 4:29). The evidence of Paul's genuine love for the Corinthians was that no matter how some of them had mistreated him, he still loved them and had room for them in his heart (cf. Php 1:7).

6:14 not be bound together. Lit. "unequally yoked," an illustration taken from OT prohibitions to Israel regarding the work-related joining together of two different kinds of livestock (*see note on Dt 22:10*). By this analogy, Paul taught that it is not right to join together in common spiritual enterprise with those who are not of the same nature (unbelievers). It is impossible under such an arrangement for things to be done to God's glory. **with**

darkness? 15 Or what [A]harmony has Christ with [a]Be-
lial, or [b]what has a [B]believer in common with an
[C]unbeliever? 16 Or [A]what agreement has the temple
of God with idols? For we are [B]the temple of [C]the
living God; just as God said,

"[D]I WILL [E]DWELL IN THEM AND
[F]WALK AMONG THEM;
AND I WILL BE THEIR GOD, AND
THEY SHALL BE MY PEOPLE.
17 "[A]Therefore, [B]COME OUT
FROM THEIR MIDST AND BE
SEPARATE," says the Lord.
"AND DO NOT TOUCH WHAT
IS UNCLEAN;
And I will welcome you.
18 "[A]And I will be a father to you,
And you shall be [B]sons and
daughters to Me,"
Says the Lord Almighty.

PAUL REVEALS HIS HEART

7 Therefore, having these promises, [A]beloved, [B]let
us cleanse ourselves from all defilement of flesh
and spirit, perfecting holiness in the fear of God.
2 [A]Make room for us *in your hearts;* we wronged no
one, we corrupted no one, we took advantage of no
one. 3 I do not speak to condemn you, for I have said
[A]before that you are [B]in our hearts to die together and
to live together. 4 Great is my [A]confidence [a]in you; great
is my [B]boasting on your behalf. I am filled with [C]com-
fort; I am overflowing with [D]joy in all our affliction.
5 For even when we came into [A]Macedonia our
flesh had no rest, but we were [B]afflicted on every
side: [C]conflicts without, fears within. 6 But [A]God, who
comforts the [a]depressed, [B]comforted us by the coming of [C]Titus; 7 and not only by his coming, but also
by the comfort with which he was comforted in you,
as he reported to us your longing, your mourning,
your zeal for me; so that I rejoiced even more. 8 For
though I [A]caused you sorrow by my letter, I do not

6:15 [a]Gr *Beliar* [b]Lit *what part has a believer with an unbeliever* [A]1 Cor 10:21 [B]Acts 5:14; 1 Pet 1:21 [C]1 Cor 6:6 6:16 [A]1 Cor 10:21 [B]1 Cor 3:16; 6:19 [C]Matt 16:16 [D]Ex 29:45; Lev 26:12; Jer 31:1; Ezek 37:27 [E]Ex 25:8; John 14:23 [F]Rev 2:1 6:17 [A]Is 52:11 [B]Rev 18:4 6:18 [A]2 Sam 7:14; 1 Chr 17:13; Is 43:6; Hos 1:10 [B]Rom 8:14 7:1 [A]Heb 6:9 [B]1 Pet 1:15f 7:2 [A]2 Cor 6:12f; 12:15 7:3 [A]2 Cor 6:11f [B]Phil 1:7 7:4 [a]Lit *toward* [A]2 Cor 3:12 [B]2 Cor 7:14; 8:24; 9:2f; 10:8; Phil 1:26; 2 Thess 1:4 [C]2 Cor 1:4 [D]2 Cor 6:10 7:5 [A]Rom 15:26; 2 Cor 2:13 [B]2 Cor 4:8 [C]Deut 32:25 7:6 [a]Or *humble* [A]2 Cor 1:3f [B]2 Cor 7:13 [C]2 Cor 2:13; 7:13f 7:8 [A]2 Cor 2:2

unbelievers. Christians are not to be bound together with non-Christians in any spiritual enterprise or relationship that would be detrimental to the Christian's testimony within the body of Christ (*see notes on 1Co 5:9–13;* cf. 1Co 6:15–18; 10:7–21; Jas 4:4; 1Jn 2:15). This was especially important for the Corinthians because of the threats from the false teachers and the surrounding pagan idolatry. But this command does not mean believers should end all associations with unbelievers; that would defy the purpose for which God saved believers and left them on earth (cf. Mt 28:19, 20; 1Co 9:19–23). The implausibility of such religious alliances is made clear in vv. 14b–17.

6:15 Belial. An ancient name for Satan, the utterly worthless one (*see note on Dt 13:13*). This contrasts sharply with Jesus Christ, the worthy One with whom believers are to be in fellowship.

6:16 agreement … temple of God with idols? The temple of God (true Christianity) and idols (idolatrous, demonic false religions) are utterly incompatible (cf. 1Sa 4–6; 2Ki 21:1–15; Eze 8). **we are the temple of the living God.** Believers individually are spiritual houses (cf. 5:1) in which the Spirit of Christ dwells (*see notes on 1Co 3:16, 17; 6:19, 20; Eph 2:22*). **as God said.** Paul supported his statement by referring to a blend of OT texts (Lv 26:11, 12; Jer 24:7; 31:33; Eze 37:26, 27; Hos 2:2, 3).

6:17 Paul drew from Is 52:11 and elaborated on the command to be spiritually separated. It is not only irrational and sacrilegious but disobedient to be bound together with unbelievers. When believers are saved, they are to disengage themselves from all forms of false religion and make a clean break from all sinful habits and old idolatrous patterns (*see notes on Eph 5:6–12; 2Ti 2:20–23;* cf. Rev 18:4). **be separate.** This is a command for believers to be as Christ was (Heb 7:26).

6:18 As a result of separating themselves from false doctrine and practice, believers will know the full richness of what it means to be children of God (*see notes on Ro 8:14–17;* cf. 2Sa 7:14; Eze 20:34).

7:1 these promises. The OT promises Paul quoted in 6:16–18. Scripture often encourages believers to action based on God's promises (cf. Ro 12:1; 2Pe 1:3). **let us cleanse ourselves.** The form of this Gr. verb indicates that this is something each Christian must do in his own life. **defilement.** This Gr. word, which appears only here in the NT, was used in the Greek OT to refer to religious defilement, or unholy alliances with idols, idol feasts, temple prostitutes, sacrifices, and festivals of worship. **flesh and spirit.** False religion panders to the human appetites, represented by both "flesh and spirit." While some believers for a time might avoid succumbing to fleshly sins associated with false religion, the Christian who exposes his mind to false teaching cannot avoid contamination by the devilish ideologies and blasphemies that assault the purity of divine truth and blaspheme God's name. *See note on 6:17.* **perfecting holiness.** The Gr. word for "perfecting" means "to finish" or "to complete" (cf. 8:6). "Holiness" refers to separation from all that would defile both the body and the mind. Complete or perfect holiness was embodied only in Christ, thus believers are to pursue Him (cf. 3:18; Lv 20:26; Mt 5:48; Ro 8:29; Php 3:12–14; 1Jn 3:2, 3).

7:2 we wronged no one. The Gr. word for "wronged" means "to treat someone unjustly," "to injure someone," or "to cause someone to fall into sin." Paul could never be accused of injuring or leading any Corinthian into sin (*see notes on Mt 18:5–14*). **we corrupted no one.** "Corrupted" could refer to corruption by doctrine or money, but probably refers to corrupting one's morals (cf. 1Co 15:33). Paul could never be accused of encouraging any immoral conduct.

7:3 Paul had a forgiving heart. Rather than only condemning the Corinthians for believing the false teachers and rejecting him, Paul reminded them of his love for them and his readiness to forgive them.

7:4 Great is my confidence. "Confidence" can be translated "boldness." Paul was confident of God's ongoing work in their lives (cf. Php 1:6)—another proof of Paul's love for the Corinthian believers.

7:5–16 These verses catalog the restoration of Paul's joy over the repentance of the Corinthian believers.

7:5 Here, Paul continued the narrative he left off in 2:13. When he arrived in Macedonia after leaving Troas, he had no rest from external "conflicts." The Gr. word is used of quarrels and disputes, and probably refers to the ongoing persecution Paul faced. He was also burdened by internal "fears"—the concern he had for the church and the anti-Paul faction prevalent there. **Macedonia.** *See note on 2:13.*

7:6 the depressed. This refers not to the spiritually humble, but to those who are humiliated. Such people are lowly in the economic, social, or emotional sense (cf. Ro 12:16).

7:6, 7 comforted us by the coming of Titus … as he reported to us. The Gr. word for "coming" refers to the actual presence of Titus with Paul. But comforting Paul beyond just the arrival of Titus, which was a blessing, was the encouraging report he gave regarding the repentance of the Corinthians and their positive response to Paul's letter carried by Titus.

7:7 Paul was encouraged by the manner in which the Corinthians comforted Titus, since he brought them such a confrontational letter (see Introduction: Background and Setting). Paul was also encouraged by their response to himself, which was manifested in 3 ways: 1) "longing"—they were eager to see Paul again and resume their relationship with him; 2) "mourning"—they were sorrowful over their sin and the breach it created between themselves and Paul; and 3) "zeal"—they loved Paul to such a degree that they were willing to defend him against those who sought to harm him, specifically the false teachers.

7:8 I caused you sorrow. *See note on 2:1.* **my letter.** The severe letter that confronted the mutiny in the church at Corinth (*see note on 2:3;* see Introduction: Background and Setting).

7:8, 9 I do not regret it …. did regret it …. I now rejoice. Paul did not regret sending the letter, even though it caused them sorrow,

regret it; though I did regret it—*for* I see that that
letter caused you sorrow, though only for a while—
9 I now rejoice, not that you were made sorrowful,
but that you were made sorrowful to *the point of*
repentance; for you were made sorrowful according to *the will of* God, so that you might not suffer
loss in anything [a]through us. 10 For the sorrow
that is according to *the will of* God produces a
[A]repentance [a]without regret, *leading* to salvation,
but the sorrow of the world produces death. 11 For
behold what earnestness this very thing, this [a]godly
sorrow, has produced in you: what vindication
of yourselves, what indignation, what fear, what
[A]longing, what zeal, what [B]avenging of wrong! In
everything you [C]demonstrated yourselves to be
innocent in the matter. 12 So although [A]I wrote to
you, *it was* not for the sake of [B]the offender nor
for the sake of the one offended, but that your earnestness on our behalf might be made known to
you in the sight of God. 13 For this reason we have
been [A]comforted.

And besides our comfort, we rejoiced even much
more for the joy of [B]Titus, because his [C]spirit has
been refreshed by you all. 14 For if in anything I have
[A]boasted to him about you, I was not put to shame;
but as we spoke all things to you in truth, so also
our boasting before [B]Titus proved to be *the* truth.
15 His [a]affection abounds all the more toward you,
as he remembers the [A]obedience of you all, how you
received him with [B]fear and trembling. 16 I rejoice
that in everything [A]I have confidence in you.

GREAT GENEROSITY

8 Now, brethren, we *wish to* make known to you
the grace of God which has been [A]given in the
churches of [B]Macedonia, 2 that in a great ordeal of
affliction their abundance of joy and their deep
poverty overflowed in the [A]wealth of their liberality. 3 For I testify that [A]according to their ability,
and beyond their ability, *they gave* of their own
accord, 4 begging us with much urging for the [A]fa-
vor [a]of participation in the [b,B]support of the [C]saints,

7:9 [a]Lit *from* 7:10 [a]Or leading *to a salvation without regret* [A]Acts 11:18 7:11 [a]Lit *sorrow according to God* [A]2 Cor 7:7 [B]2 Cor 2:6 [C]Rom 3:5 7:12 [A]2 Cor 2:3, 9; 7:8 [B]1 Cor 5:1f 7:13 [A]2 Cor 7:6 [B]2 Cor 2:13; 7:6, 14 [C]1 Cor 16:18 7:14 [A]2 Cor 7:4; 8:24; 9:2f; 10:8; Phil 1:26; 2 Thess 1:4 [B]2 Cor 2:13; 7:6, 13 7:15 [a]Lit *inward parts* [A]2 Cor 2:9 [B]1 Cor 2:3; Phil 2:12 7:16 [A]2 Cor 2:3 8:1 [A]2 Cor 8:5 [B]Acts 16:9 8:2 [A]Rom 2:4 8:3 [A]1 Cor 16:2; 2 Cor 8:11 8:4 [a]Lit *and* [b]Lit *service to the saints* [C]Or *holy ones* [A]Acts 24:17; Rom 15:25f [B]Rom 15:31; 2 Cor 8:19f; 9:1, 12f

because he knew that sorrow over their sin would affect in them repentance leading to obedience. Yet Paul did regret having sent it for a brief time while awaiting Titus' return, fearing that his letter was too harsh, and that he might have driven them further away from him. In the end, however, he rejoiced because the letter accomplished what he had hoped.

7:9 sorrowful to *the point of* repentance. The letter produced a sorrow in the Corinthian believers that led them to repent of their sins. "Repentance" refers to the desire to turn from sin and restore one's relationship to God (*see notes on Mt 3:2, 8*).

7:10 sorrow … produces a repentance … *leading* to salvation. "Sorrow" here refers to sorrow that is according to the will of God and produced by the Holy Spirit (*see note on 2Ti 2:25*). True repentance cannot occur apart from such a genuine sorrow over one's sin. The word "*leading*" is supplied by the translators; Paul was saying that repentance belongs to the realm or sphere of salvation. Repentance is at the very heart of and proves one's salvation: unbelievers repent of their sin initially when they are saved, and then as believers, repent of their sins continually to keep the joy and blessing of their relationship to God (*see notes on 1Jn 1:7–9*). **sorrow of the world produces death.** Human sorrow is unsanctified remorse and has no redemptive capability. It is nothing more than the wounded pride of getting caught in a sin and having one's lusts go unfulfilled. That kind of sorrow leads only to guilt, shame, despair, depression, self-pity, and hopelessness. People can die from such sorrow (cf. Mt 27:3).

7:11 This verse provides a look at how genuine repentance will manifest itself in one's attitudes. **earnestness.** It is the initial reaction of true repentance to eagerly and aggressively pursue righteousness. This is an attitude that ends indifference to sin and complacency about evil and deception. **what vindication of yourselves.** A desire to clear one's name of the stigma that accompanies sin. The repentant sinner restores the trust and confidence of others by making his genuine repentance known. **indignation.** Often associated with righteous indignation and holy anger. Repentance leads to anger over one's sin and displeasure at the shame it has brought on the Lord's name and His people. **fear.** This is reverence toward God, who is the One most offended by sin. Repentance leads to a healthy fear of the One who chastens and judges sin. **longing.** This could be translated "yearning," and refers to the desire of the repentant sinner to restore the relationship with the one who was sinned against. **zeal.** This refers to loving someone or something so much that one hates anyone or anything that harms the object of this love (*see note on v. 7*). **avenging of wrong.** This refers to the desire to see justice done. The repentant sinner no longer tries to protect himself; he wants to see the sin avenged no matter what it might cost him. **to be innocent in the matter.** The essence of repentance is an aggressive pursuit of holiness, which was characteristic of the Corinthians. The Gr. word for "innocent" means "pure" or "holy." They demonstrated the integrity of their repentance by their purity.

7:12 the offender. The leader of the mutiny in the Corinthian church (*see note on 12:7*).

7:15 fear and trembling. Reverence toward God and a healthy fear of judgment (*see note on 1Co 2:3*).

8:1–9:15 While this section specifically deals with Paul's instruction to the Corinthians about a particular collection for the saints in Jerusalem, it also provides the richest, most detailed model of Christian giving in the NT.

8:1 grace of God. The generosity of the churches of Macedonia was motivated by God's grace. Paul did not merely commend those churches for a noble human work, but instead gave the credit to God for what He did through them. **churches of Macedonia.** Macedonia was the northern Roman province of Greece. Paul's reference was to the churches at Philippi, Thessalonica, and Berea (cf. Ac 17:11). This was basically an impoverished province that had been ravaged by many wars and even then was being plundered by Roman authority and commerce.

8:2 abundance of joy. "Abundance" means "surplus." In spite of their difficult circumstances, the churches' joy rose above their pain because of their devotion to the Lord and the causes of His kingdom. **deep poverty.** "Deep" means "according to the depth," or "extremely deep." "Poverty" refers to the most severe type of economic deprivation, the kind that caused a person to become a beggar. **wealth of their liberality.** The Gr. word for "liberality" can be translated "generosity" or "sincerity." It is the opposite of duplicity or being double-minded. The Macedonian believers were rich in their single-minded, selfless generosity to God and to others.

8:3 Paul highlighted 3 elements of the Macedonians' giving which summed up the concept of freewill giving: 1) "according to their ability." Giving is proportionate—God sets no fixed amount or percentage and expects His people to give based on what they have (Lk 6:38; 1Co 16:2); 2) "beyond their ability." Giving is sacrificial. God's people are to give according to what they have, yet it must be in proportions that are sacrificial (cf. Mt 6:25–34; Mk 12:41–44; Php 4:19); and 3) "their own accord"—lit. "one who chooses his own course of action." Giving is voluntary—God's people are not to give out of compulsion, manipulation, or intimidation. Freewill giving has always been God's plan (cf. 9:6; Ge 4:2–4; 8:20; Ex 25:1, 2; 35:4, 5, 21, 22; 36:5–7; Nu 18:12; Dt 16:10, 17; 1Ch 29:9; Pr 3:9, 10; 11:24; Lk 19:1–8). Freewill giving is not to be confused with tithing, which related to the national taxation system of Israel (*see note on Lv 27:30–32*) and is paralleled in the NT and the present by paying taxes (*see notes on Mt 22:21; Ro 13:6, 7*).

8:4 favor of participation. The Macedonian Christians implored Paul for the special grace of being able to have fellowship and be partners in supporting the poor saints in Jerusalem. They viewed giving as a privilege, not an obligation (cf. 9:7).

5 and *this,* not as we had [a]expected, but they first
[A]gave themselves to the Lord and to us by [B]the will
of God. 6 So we [A]urged [B]Titus that as he had previously [C]made a beginning, so he would also complete
in you [D]this gracious work as well.
7 But just as you [A]abound [B]in everything, in faith
and utterance and knowledge and in all earnestness and in the [a]love we inspired in you, *see* that
you [A]abound in this gracious work also. 8 I [A]am
not speaking *this* as a command, but as proving
through the earnestness of others the sincerity
of your love also. 9 For you know [A]the grace of our
Lord Jesus Christ, that [B]though He was rich, yet for
your sake He became poor, so that you through His
poverty might become rich. 10 I [A]give *my* opinion in
this matter, for this is to your advantage, who were
the first to begin [B]a year ago not only to do *this,*
but also to desire *to do it.* 11 But now finish [a]doing
it also, so that just as *there was* the [A]readiness to
desire it, so *there may be* also the completion of it
by your ability. 12 For if the readiness is present, it
is acceptable [A]according to what *a person* has, not
according to what he does not have. 13 For *this* is
not for the ease of others *and* for your affliction,
but by way of equality— 14 at this present time your
abundance *being a supply* for [A]their need, so that
their abundance also may become *a supply* for [A]your
need, that there may be equality; 15 as it is written,
"[A]HE WHO *gathered* MUCH DID NOT HAVE TOO MUCH,
AND HE WHO *gathered* LITTLE HAD NO LACK."
16 But [A]thanks be to God who [B]puts the same earnestness on your behalf in the heart of [C]Titus. 17 For
he not only accepted our [A]appeal, but being himself
very earnest, he has gone to you of his own accord.
18 We have sent along with him [A]the brother whose
fame in *the things of* the [B]gospel *has spread* through
[C]all the churches; 19 [A]and not only *this,* but he has
also been [B]appointed by the churches to travel with
us in [C]this gracious work, which is being administered by us for the glory of the Lord Himself, and *to
show* our [D]readiness, 20 [a]taking precaution so that
no one will discredit us in our administration of
this generous gift; 21 for we [A]have regard for what
is honorable, not only in [B]the sight of the Lord,
but also in the sight of men. 22 We have sent with
them our brother, whom we have often tested and
found diligent in many things, but now even more
diligent because of *his* great confidence in you.

8:5 [a]Lit *hoped* [A]2 Cor 8:1 [B]1 Cor 1:1 8:6 [A]2 Cor 8:17; 12:18 [B]2 Cor 2:13; 8:16, 23 [C]2 Cor 8:10 [D]Acts 24:17; Rom 15:25f 8:7 [a]Lit *love from us in you;* one early ms reads *your love for us* [A]2 Cor 9:8 [B]Rom 15:14; 1 Cor 1:5; 12:8 8:8 [A]1 Cor 7:6 8:9 [A]2 Cor 13:14 [B]Matt 20:28; 2 Cor 6:10; Phil 2:6f 8:10 [A]1 Cor 7:25, 40 [B]1 Cor 16:2f; 2 Cor 9:2 8:11 [a]Lit *the doing* [A]2 Cor 8:12, 19; 9:2 8:12 [A]Mark 12:43f; Luke 21:3, 4; 2 Cor 9:7 8:14 [A]Acts 4:34; 2 Cor 9:12 8:15 [A]Ex 16:18 8:16 [A]2 Cor 2:14 [B]Rev 17:17 [C]2 Cor 2:13; 8:6, 23 8:17 [A]2 Cor 8:6; 12:18 8:18 [A]1 Cor 16:3; 2 Cor 12:18 [B]2 Cor 2:12 [C]1 Cor 4:17; 7:17 8:19 [A]Rom 5:3 [B]Acts 14:23; 1 Cor 16:3f [C]2 Cor 8:4, 6 [D]2 Cor 8:11, 12; 9:2 8:20 [a]Lit *avoiding this* 8:21 [A]Rom 12:17 [B]Prov 3:4; Rom 14:18

8:5 not as we had expected. The response of the Macedonian churches was far more than Paul had expected. **first.** Refers not to time but priority. Of first priority to the Macedonians was to present themselves as sacrifices to God (cf. Ro 12:1, 2; 1Pe 2:5). Generous giving follows personal dedication.

8:6 we urged Titus. Titus initially encouraged the Corinthians to begin the collection at least one year earlier. When he returned to Corinth with the severe letter (see Introduction: Background and Setting), Paul encouraged him to help the believers finish the collection of the money for the support of the poor saints in Jerusalem.

8:7 you abound in everything. The giving of the Corinthians was to be in harmony with other Christian virtues that Paul already recognized in them: "faith"—sanctifying trust in the Lord; "utterance"—sound doctrine; "knowledge"—the application of doctrine; "earnestness"—eagerness and spiritual passion; and "love"—the love of choice, inspired by their leaders.

8:8 not . . . as a command. Freewill giving is never according to obligation or command (*see note on v. 3*).

8:9 though He was rich. A reference to the eternality and pre-existence of Christ. As the second person of the Trinity, Christ is as rich as God is rich. He owns everything and possesses all power, authority, sovereignty, glory, honor, and majesty (cf. Is 9:6; Mic 5:2; Jn 1:1; 8:58; 10:30; 17:5; Col 1:15–18; 2:9; Heb 1:3). **He became poor.** A reference to Christ's incarnation (cf. Jn 1:14; Ro 1:3; 8:3; Gal 4:4; Col 1:20; 1Ti 3:16; Heb 2:7). He laid aside the independent exercise of all His divine prerogatives, left His place with God, took on human form, and died on a cross like a common criminal (Php 2:5–8). **that you . . . might become rich.** Believers become spiritually rich through the sacrifice and impoverishment of Christ (Php 2:5–8). They become rich in salvation, forgiveness, joy, peace, glory, honor, and majesty (cf. 1Co 1:4, 5; 3:22; Eph 1:3; 1Pe 1:3, 4). They become joint heirs with Christ (Ro 8:17).

8:10 opinion. Paul was not commanding the Corinthians to give any specific amount. It was his opinion, however, that it was to their advantage to give generously so they might receive abundantly more from God in either material blessings, spiritual blessings, or eternal reward (cf. 9:6; Lk 6:38).

8:11 finish doing it. The Corinthians needed to finish what they had started by completing the collection (cf. Lk 9:62; 1Co 16:2). They needed this reminder since they likely stopped the process due to the influence of the false teachers, who probably accused Paul of being a huckster who would keep the money for himself (cf. 2:17).

8:12 readiness. Paul spoke of a readiness and eagerness to give. God is most concerned with the heart attitude of the giver, not the amount he gives (cf. 9:7; Mk 12:41–44). **according to what *a person* has.** Whatever a person has is the resource out of which he should give (*see note on v. 3*). That is why there are no set amounts or percentages for giving anywhere stated in the NT. The implication is that if one has much, he can give much; if he has little, he can give only little (cf. 9:6). **not according to what he does not have.** Believers do not need to go into debt to give, nor lower themselves to a poverty level. God never asks believers to impoverish themselves. The Macedonians received a special blessing of grace from God to give the way they did.

8:14 equality. This Gr. word gives us the Eng. word "isostasy," which refers to a condition of equilibrium. Thus the term could also be translated "balance" or "equilibrium." The idea is that in the body of Christ some believers who have more than they need should help those who have far less than they need (cf. 1Ti 6:17, 18). This is not, however, a scheme of Paul's to redistribute wealth within the church, but rather to meet basic needs.

8:15 as it is written. Quoted from Ex 16:18. The collecting of the manna by the Israelites in the wilderness was an appropriate illustration of sharing of resources. Some were able to gather more than others, and apparently shared it so that no one lacked what they needed.

8:16 Titus. *See note on v. 6.*

8:18 the brother. This man is unnamed because he was so well-known, prominent, and unimpeachable. He was a distinguished preacher, and he was able to add credibility to the enterprise of taking the collection to Jerusalem.

8:19 appointed by the churches. To protect Paul and Titus from false accusations regarding the mishandling of the money, the churches picked the unbiased brother (v. 18) as their representative to lend accountability to the enterprise. **for the glory of the Lord Himself.** Paul wanted careful scrutiny as protection against bringing dishonor to Christ for any misappropriation of the money. He wanted to avoid any offenses worthy of justifiable criticisms or accusations.

8:21 regard for what is honorable. A better rendering is "take into consideration what is honorable." Paul cared greatly about what people thought of his actions, especially considering how large the gift was.

8:22 our brother. A third member of the delegation sent to deliver the gift, also unnamed.

23 As for [A]Titus, *he is* my [B]partner and fellow worker
[a]among you; as for our [C]brethren, *they are* [b,D]mes-
sengers of the churches, [E]a glory to Christ. 24 Therefore [a]openly before the churches, [b]show them the
proof of your love and of our [A]reason for boasting
about you.

GOD GIVES MOST

9 For [A]it is superfluous for me to write to you
about this [B]ministry to the [a]saints; 2 for I know
your readiness, of which I [A]boast about you to the
[B]Macedonians, *namely,* that [C]Achaia has been prepared since [D]last year, and your zeal has stirred
up most of them. 3 But I have sent the brethren,
in order that our [A]boasting about you may not be
made empty in this case, so that, [B]as I was saying,
you may be prepared; 4 otherwise if any [A]Mace-
donians come with me and find you unprepared,
we—not to speak of you—will be put to shame by
this confidence. 5 So I thought it necessary to urge
the [A]brethren that they would go on ahead to you
and arrange beforehand your previously promised [a,B]bountiful gift, so that the same would be
ready as a [a,C]bountiful gift and not [b,D]affected by
covetousness.

6 Now this *I say,* [A]he who sows sparingly will also
reap sparingly, and he who sows [a]bountifully will also
reap [a]bountifully. 7 Each one *must do* just as he has
purposed in his heart, not [A]grudgingly or under compulsion, for [B]God loves a cheerful giver. 8 And [A]God is
able to make all grace abound to you, so that always
having all sufficiency in everything, you may have
an abundance for every good deed; 9 as it is written,

"[A]He scattered abroad, he
gave to the poor,
His righteousness [a]endures forever."

10 Now He who supplies [A]seed to the sower and
bread for food will supply and multiply your seed
for sowing and [B]increase the harvest of your righteousness; 11 you will be [A]enriched in everything
for all liberality, which through us is producing
[B]thanksgiving to God. 12 For the ministry of this
service is not only fully supplying [A]the needs of
the [a]saints, but is also overflowing [B]through many

8:23 [a]Lit *for you* [b]Lit *apostles* [A]2 Cor 8:6 [B]Philem 17 [C]2 Cor 8:18, 22 [D]John 13:16; Phil 2:25 [E]1 Cor 11:7 8:24 [a]Lit *in the face of the churches* [b]Or *show the proof…for boasting to them about you* [A]2 Cor 7:4 9:1 [a]Or *holy ones* [A]1 Thess 4:9 [B]2 Cor 8:4 9:2 [A]2 Cor 7:4 [B]Rom 15:26 [C]Acts 18:12 [D]2 Cor 8:10 9:3 [A]2 Cor 7:4 [B]1 Cor 16:2 9:4 [A]Rom 15:26 9:5 [a]Lit *blessing* [b]Lit *as covetousness* [A]2 Cor 9:3 [B]Gen 33:11; Judg 1:15; 2 Cor 9:6 [C]Phil 4:17 [D]2 Cor 12:17f 9:6 [a]Lit *with blessings* [A]Prov 11:24f; 22:9; Gal 6:7, 9 9:7 [A]Deut 15:10; 1 Chr 29:17; Rom 12:8; 2 Cor 8:12 [B]Ex 25:2 9:8 [A]Eph 3:20 9:9 [a]Lit *abides* [A]Ps 112:9 9:10 [A]Is 55:10 [B]Hos 10:12 9:11 [A]1 Cor 1:5 [B]2 Cor 1:11 9:12 [a]Or *holy ones* [A]2 Cor 8:14 [B]2 Cor 1:11

8:23 partner and fellow worker. Titus was Paul's "partner"—his close companion—and fellow laborer among the Corinthians. They already knew of his outstanding character. **messengers of the churches.** The two men who went with Titus were apostles in the sense of being commissioned and sent by the churches. They were not apostles of Christ (11:13; 1Th 2:6), because they were not eyewitnesses of the resurrected Lord or commissioned directly by Him (*see note on Ro 1:1*). **glory to Christ.** The greatest of all commendations is to be characterized as bringing glory to Christ. Such was the case of the two messengers.

9:1 ministry to the saints. The offering they were collecting for the believers in Jerusalem (*see note on 8:4*).

9:2 Paul was simply calling the Corinthians back to their original eagerness and readiness to participate in the offering project. The confusion and lies spread by the false teachers (i.e., Paul was a deceiver ministering only for the money) had sidetracked the believers on this issue. **the Macedonians.** Believers in the churches in the province of Macedonia, which was the northern part of Greece (*see notes on 8:1–5; Ac 16:9;* see Introduction to 1 Thessalonians: Background and Setting). **Achaia.** A province in southern Greece, where Corinth was located (see Introduction to 1 Corinthians: Background and Setting).

9:5 your … bountiful gift. On first hearing of the need, the Corinthians had undoubtedly promised Paul that they would raise a large amount. **covetousness.** This denotes a grasping to get more and keep it at the expense of others. This attitude emphasizes selfishness and pride, which can have a very detrimental effect on giving, and is natural for unbelievers but should not be for professed believers (cf. Ps 10:3; Ecc 5:10; Mic 2:2; Mk 7:22; Ro 1:29; 1Co 5:11; 6:9, 10; Eph 5:3–5; 1Ti 6:10; 2Pe 2:14).

9:6 The simple, self-evident agrarian principle—which Paul applied to Christian giving—that the harvest is directly proportionate to the amount of seed sown (cf. Pr 11:24, 25; 19:17; Lk 6:38; Gal 6:7). **bountifully.** This is derived from the Gr. word which gives us the word "eulogy" ("blessing"). When a generous believer gives by faith and trust in God, with a desire to produce the greatest possible blessing, that person will receive that kind of a harvest of blessing (cf. Pr 3:9, 10; 28:27; Mal 3:10). God gives a return on the amount one invests with Him. Invest a little, receive a little, and vice versa (cf. Lk 6:38).

9:7 as he has purposed. The term translated "purposed" occurs only here in the NT and indicates a premeditated, predetermined plan of action that is done from the heart voluntarily, but not impulsively. This is an age-old biblical principle of giving (*see note on 8:3;* cf. Ex 25:2). **grudgingly.** Lit. "with grief," "sorrow," or "sadness," which indicates an attitude of depression, regret, and reluctance that accompanies something done strictly out of a sense of duty and obligation, but not joy. **under compulsion.** This refers to external pressure and coercion, quite possibly accompanied by legalism. Believers are not to give based on the demands of others, or according to any arbitrary standards or set amounts. **God loves a cheerful giver.** God has a unique, special love for those who are happily committed to generous giving. The Gr. word for "cheerful" is the word from which we get "hilarious," which suggests that God loves a heart that is enthusiastically thrilled with the pleasure of giving.

9:8 all grace abound to you. God possesses an infinite amount of grace, and He gives it lavishly, without holding back (cf. 1Ch 29:14). Here "grace" does not refer to spiritual graces, but to money and material needs. When the believer generously—and wisely—gives of his material resources, God graciously replenishes them so he always has plenty and will not be in need (cf. 2Ch 31:10). **all sufficiency.** In secular Greek philosophy, this was the proud contentment of self-sufficiency that supposedly led to true happiness. Paul sanctifies the secular term and says that God, not man, will supply everything needed for real happiness and contentment (cf. Php 4:19). **abundance for every good deed.** God gives back lavishly to generous, cheerful givers, not so they may satisfy selfish, nonessential desires, but so they may meet the variety of needs others have (cf. Dt 15:10, 11).

9:9 Paul marshals OT support (Ps 112:9) for what he has been saying about the divine principles of giving. God replenishes and rewards the righteous giver both in time and eternity.

9:10 Paul drew on Is 55:10 for additional OT support. The same God who is faithful to supply all His creatures' physical needs, and is kind to all people, is uniquely gracious to His children. He always fulfills His promise to replenish their generosity. **harvest of your righteousness.** God's temporal and eternal blessings to the cheerful giver (cf. Hos 10:12).

9:12 ministry of this service. The Gr. word translated "ministry" is a priestly word from which we get "liturgy." Paul viewed the entire collection project as a spiritual, worshipful enterprise that was primarily being offered to God to glorify Him. **supplying the needs of the saints.** The Gr. word for "supplying" is a doubly intense term that could be rendered "really, fully supplying." This indicates the Jerusalem church had an extremely great need. Many of its members had gone to Jerusalem as pilgrims to celebrate the feast of Pentecost (*see notes on Ac 2:1, 5–11*), had been converted through

thanksgivings to God. 13 Because of the proof given
by this [A]ministry, they will [B]glorify God for *your*
obedience to your [C]confession of the [D]gospel of
Christ and for the liberality of your [a]contribution
to them and to all, 14 while they also, by prayer on
your behalf, yearn for you because of the surpassing grace of God in you. 15 [A]Thanks be to God for His
indescribable [B]gift!

PAUL DESCRIBES HIMSELF

10 Now [A]I, Paul, myself [B]urge you by the [C]meek-
ness and gentleness of Christ—I who [D]am
[a]meek when face to face with you, but bold toward
you when absent! 2 I ask that [A]when I am present
I *need* not be bold with the confidence with which
I propose to be courageous against [B]some, who
regard us as if we walked [C]according to the flesh.
3 For though we walk in the flesh, we do not war
[A]according to the flesh, 4 for the [A]weapons of our
warfare are not of the flesh, but [a]divinely powerful
[B]for the destruction of fortresses. 5 *We are* destroying speculations and every [A]lofty thing raised up
against the knowledge of God, and *we are* taking
every thought captive to the [B]obedience of Christ,
6 and we are ready to punish all disobedience, whenever [A]your obedience is complete.

9:13 [a]Or *sharing with them* [A]Rom 15:31; 2 Cor 8:4 [B]Matt 9:8 [C]1 Tim 6:12f; Heb 3:1; 4:14; 10:23 [D]2 Cor 2:12 9:15 [A]2 Cor 2:14 [B]Rom 5:15f 10:1 [a]Lit *lowly* [A]Gal 5:2; Eph 3:1; Col 1:23 [B]Rom 12:1 [C]Matt 11:29; 1 Cor 4:21; Phil 4:5 [D]1 Cor 2:3f; 2 Cor 10:10 10:2 [A]1 Cor 4:21; 2 Cor 13:2, 10 [B]1 Cor 4:18f [C]Rom 8:4; 2 Cor 1:17 10:3 [A]Rom 8:4; 2 Cor 1:17 10:4 [a]Or *mighty before God* [A]1 Cor 9:7; 2 Cor 6:7; 1 Tim 1:18 [B]Jer 1:10; 2 Cor 10:8; 13:10 10:5 [A]Is 2:11f [B]2 Cor 9:13 10:6 [A]2 Cor 2:9

Peter's message, and had then remained in the city without adequate financial support. Many residents of Jerusalem had undoubtedly lost their jobs in the waves of persecution that came after the martyrdom of Stephen (Ac 8:1). However, the Corinthians were wealthy enough (they had not yet suffered persecution and deprivation like the Macedonians; 8:1–4) to help meet the huge need with a generous monetary gift (*see note on 9:5*).

9:13 proof given by this ministry. The collection also provided an important opportunity for the Corinthians to test the genuineness of their faith (cf. Jas 1:22; 1Jn 2:3, 4). The Jewish believers, who already doubted the validity of Gentile salvation, were especially skeptical of the Corinthians since their church had so many problems. The Corinthians' involvement in the collection would help to put those doubts to rest. **obedience to your confession.** Obedient submission to God's Word is always evidence of a true confession of Christ as Lord and Savior (Eph 2:10; Jas 2:14–20; cf. Ro 10:9, 10). If the Corinthians had a proper response to and participation in Paul's collection ministry, the Jewish believers would know the Gentile conversions had been real.

9:14 This verse illustrates the truth that mutual prayer is at the heart of authentic Christian unity. When the Jerusalem believers recognized God was at work in the Corinthian church as a result of its outreach through the collection (*see notes on v. 13*), they would have become friends in Christ and prayed for the Corinthians, thanking God for their loving generosity. **the surpassing grace of God.** The Spirit of God was at work in the Corinthians in a special way (*see note on v. 13*).

9:15 Paul summarized his discourse by comparing the believer's act of giving with what God did in giving Jesus Christ (cf. Ro 8:32), "His indescribable gift." God buried His Son and reaped a vast harvest of those who put their faith in the resurrected Christ (cf. Jn 12:24). That makes it possible for believers to joyfully, sacrificially, and abundantly sow and reap. As they give in this manner, they show forth Christ's likeness (cf. Jn 12:25, 26; Eph 5:1, 2).

10:1–13:14 The abrupt change in tone from chaps. 1–9 has prompted various explanations of the relationship between chaps. 10–13 and 1–9. Some argue that chaps. 10–13 were originally part of the "severe letter" (2:4), and hence belong chronologically before chaps. 1–9. Chapters 10–13 cannot, however, have been written before chaps. 1–9, since they refer to Titus' visit as a past event (12:18; cf. 8:6). Further, the offender whose defiance of Paul prompted the "severe letter" (2:5–8) is nowhere mentioned in chaps. 10–13. Others agree that chaps. 10–13 belong after chaps. 1–9, but believe they form a separate letter. They assume that Paul, after sending chaps. 1–9 to the Corinthians, received reports of new trouble at Corinth and wrote chaps. 10–13 in response. A variation of this view is that Paul paused in his writing of 2 Corinthians after chaps. 1–9, then heard bad news from Corinth before he resumed writing chaps. 10–13. This view preserves the unity of 2 Corinthians; however, Paul does not mention anywhere in chaps. 10–13 that he received any fresh news from Corinth. The best interpretation views 2 Corinthians as a unified letter, with chaps. 1–9 addressed to the repentant majority (cf. 2:6) and chaps. 10–13 to the minority still influenced by the false teachers. The support for this view is that: 1) there is no historical evidence (from Gr. manuscripts, the writings of the church Fathers, or early translations) that chaps. 10–13 ever circulated as a separate letter; all Gr. manuscripts have them following chaps. 1–9; 2) the differences in tone between chaps. 10–13 and 1–9 have been exaggerated (cf. 11:11; 12:14 with 6:11; 7:2); and 3) chaps. 10–13 form the logical conclusion to chaps. 1–9, as Paul prepared the Corinthians for his promised visit (1:15, 16; 2:1–3).

10:1 meekness. The humble and gentle attitude that expresses itself in patient endurance of unfair treatment. A meek person is not bitter or angry, and he does not seek revenge when wronged. *See note on Mt 5:5.* **gentleness.** This is similar in meaning to meekness. When applied to someone in a position of authority it refers to leniency. Gentle people refuse to retaliate, even when it is in their power to do so (Php 4:5). **meek ... bold toward you.** Paul sarcastically repeated another feature of the Corinthians' accusation against him; sadly, they had mistaken his gentleness and meekness toward them for weakness. Further, they accused him of cowardice, of being bold only when writing to them from a safe distance (cf. v. 10).

10:2 Paul was quite capable of bold, fearless confrontation (cf. Gal 2:11). But seeking to spare the Corinthians (cf. 1:23), the apostle begged the rebellious minority not to force him to display his boldness by confronting them—something he would do, he warned, if necessary.

10:3 walk in the flesh. Paul's opponents at Corinth had wrongly accused him of walking in the flesh in a moral sense (cf. Ro 8:4). Playing off that, Paul affirmed that he did walk in the flesh in a physical sense; though possessing the power and authority of an apostle of Jesus Christ, he was a real human being (cf. 4:7, 16; 5:1). **war according to the flesh.** Although a man, Paul did not fight the spiritual battle for men's souls using human ingenuity, worldly wisdom, or clever methodologies (cf. 1Co 1:17–25; 2:1–4). Such impotent weapons are powerless to free souls from the forces of darkness and bring them to maturity in Christ. They cannot successfully oppose satanic assaults on the gospel, such as those made by the false apostles at Corinth.

10:4 our warfare. The motif of the Christian life as warfare is a common one in the NT (cf. 6:7; Eph 6:10–18; 1Ti 1:18; 2Ti 2:3, 4; 4:7). **of the flesh.** Human. *See note on v. 3.* **fortresses.** The metaphor would have been readily understandable to the Corinthians since Corinth, like most ancient cities, had a fortress (on top of a hill S of the city) in which its residents could take refuge. The formidable spiritual strongholds manned by the forces of hell can be demolished only by spiritual weapons wielded by godly believers—singularly the "sword of the Spirit" (Eph 6:17), since only the truth of God's Word can defeat satanic falsehoods. This is the true spiritual warfare. Believers are not instructed in the NT to assault demons or Satan (*see note on Jude 9*), but to assault error with the truth. That is our battle (cf. Jn 17:17; Heb 4:12).

10:5 speculations. Thoughts, ideas, reasonings, philosophies, and false religions are the ideological forts in which men barricade themselves against God and the gospel (cf. 1Co 3:20). **every thought captive.** Emphasizes the total destruction of the fortresses of human and satanic wisdom and the rescuing of those inside from the damning lies that had enslaved them.

10:6 Paul would not stand idly by while enemies of the faith assaulted a church under his care. He was ready to purge them out (as he did at Ephesus; 1Ti 1:19, 20) as soon as the Corinthian church was complete in its obedience. When that happened, the lines would be clearly drawn between the repentant, obedient majority and the recalcitrant, disobedient minority.

7 [a,A]You are looking at [b]things as they are outwardly.
[B]If anyone is confident in himself that he is Christ's,
let him consider this again within himself, that just
as he is Christ's, [C]so also are we. 8 For even if [A]I boast
somewhat [a]further about our [B]authority, which the
Lord gave for building you up and not for destroying
you, I will not be put to shame, 9 [a]for I do not wish
to seem as if I would terrify you by my letters. 10 For
they say, "His letters are weighty and strong, but his
[a]personal presence is [A]unimpressive and [B]his speech
contemptible." 11 Let such a person consider this, that
what we are in word by letters when absent, such
persons *we are* also in deed when present.
12 For we are not bold to class or compare ourselves with [a]some of those who [A]commend themselves; but when they measure themselves by themselves and compare themselves with themselves,
they are without understanding. 13 But we will not
boast [A]beyond *our* measure, but [a,B]within the measure of the sphere which God apportioned to us as
a measure, to reach even as far as you. 14 For we are
not overextending ourselves, as if we did not reach
to you, for [A]we were the first to come even as far
as you in the [B]gospel of Christ; 15 not boasting [A]be-
yond *our* measure, *that is,* in [B]other men's labors,
but with the hope that as [C]your faith grows, we will
be, [a]within our sphere, [D]enlarged even more by you,
16 so as to [A]preach the gospel even to [B]the regions
beyond you, *and* not to boast [a,C]in what has been
accomplished in the sphere of another. 17 But [A]HE
WHO BOASTS IS TO BOAST IN THE LORD. 18 For it is not
he who [A]commends himself that is approved, but
he [B]whom the Lord commends.

PAUL DEFENDS HIS APOSTLESHIP

11 I wish that you would [A]bear with me in a little [B]foolishness; but [a]indeed you are bearing
with me. 2 For I am jealous for you with a godly
jealousy; for I [A]betrothed you to one husband, so
that to Christ I might [B]present you *as* a pure virgin.

10:7 [a]Or *Look at…* or *Do you look at…?* [b]Lit *what is before your face* [A]John 7:24; 2 Cor 5:12 [B]1 Cor 1:12; 14:37 [C]1 Cor 9:1; 2 Cor 11:23; Gal 1:12 10:8 [a]Or *more abundantly* [A]2 Cor 7:4 [B]2 Cor 13:10 10:9 [a]Lit *so that I may not seem* 10:10 [a]Lit *bodily presence is weak* [A]1 Cor 2:3; 2 Cor 12:7; Gal 4:13f [B]1 Cor 1:17; 2 Cor 11:6 10:12 [a]Or *any* [A]2 Cor 3:1; 10:18 10:13 [a]Lit *according to the measure* [A]2 Cor 10:15 [B]Rom 12:3; 2 Cor 10:15f 10:14 [A]1 Cor 3:6 [B]2 Cor 2:12 10:15 [a]Lit *according to our sphere* [A]2 Cor 10:13 [B]Rom 15:20 [C]2 Thess 1:3 [D]Acts 5:13 10:16 [a]Lit *to the things prepared in the* [A]2 Cor 11:7 [B]Acts 19:21 [C]Rom 15:20 10:17 [A]Jer 9:24; 1 Cor 1:31 10:18 [A]2 Cor 10:12 [B]Rom 2:29; 1 Cor 4:5 11:1 [a]Or *do indeed bear with me* [A]Matt 17:17; 2 Cor 11:4, 16, 19f [B]2 Cor 5:13; 11:17, 21 11:2 [A]Hos 2:19f; Eph 5:26f [B]2 Cor 4:14

10:7 looking at things … outwardly. The Gr. verb "looking" is better translated as an imperative, or command: "Look at what is obvious, face the facts, consider the evidence." In light of what they knew about him (cf. 1Co 9:1, 2), how could some of the Corinthians possibly believe that Paul was a false apostle and the false teachers were true apostles? Unlike Paul, the false apostles had founded no churches, and had suffered no persecution for the cause of Christ. Paul could call on his companions and even Ananias as witnesses to the reality of his Damascus Road experience; there were no witnesses to verify the false apostles' alleged encounters with the risen, glorified Christ. **If anyone is confident … that he is Christ's.** The false apostles' claim to belong to Christ can be understood in 4 ways: 1) that they were Christians; 2) that they had known Jesus during His earthly life; 3) that they had an apostolic commission from Him; or 4) that they had an elevated, secret knowledge of Him. Their claim that some or all of those things were true about themselves implies that they denied all of them to be true of Paul. **as he is Christ's, so also are we.** For the sake of argument, Paul did not at this point deny the false apostles' claims (as he did later in 11:13–15). He merely pointed out that he, too, can and does claim to belong to Christ. To decide between the conflicting personal claims, the Corinthians needed only to consider the objective evidence, as he commanded them to do earlier in this verse.

10:8 The debate with the false apostles had forced Paul to emphasize his authority more than he cared to; Paul's claims for his authority normally were restrained by his humility. But no matter how much he said about his authority, Paul would never be ashamed. Since he had the authority of which he spoke, he would never be proved guilty of making an empty boast. The Lord gave Paul his authority to edify and strengthen the church; that he had done so at Corinth proves the genuineness of his claim to apostolic calling. Far from edifying the Corinthian church, the false apostles had brought confusion, divisiveness, and turmoil to it. That showed that their authority did not come from the Lord, who seeks only to build His church (cf. Mt 16:18), not tear it down.

10:9 terrify you by my letters. The false apostles had accused Paul of being an abusive leader, of trying to intimidate the Corinthians in his letters (such as the "severe letter," see Introduction: Background and Setting). Paul's goal, however, was not to terrify the Corinthians, but to bring them to repentance (cf. 7:9, 10), because he loved them (cf. 7:2, 3; 11:11; 12:15).

10:10 In their continuing attempt to discredit Paul, the false apostles claimed that in contrast to his bold, forceful letters, in person he lacked the presence, charisma, and personality of a truly great leader. They no doubt supported their point by portraying Paul's departure after his "painful" visit (2:1; cf. Introduction: Background and Setting) as a retreat of abject failure. And in a culture that highly valued skillful rhetoric and eloquent oration, Paul's "contemptible" speech was also taken as evidence that he was a weak, ineffective person.

10:11 Paul denied the false charges against him and affirmed his integrity. What he was in his letters he was to be when present with them.

10:12 class or compare ourselves. It is a mark of Paul's humility that he refused to compare himself with others, or engage in self-promotion. His only personal concern was what the Lord thought of him (cf. 1Co 4:4), though he needed to defend his apostleship so the Corinthians would not, in turning from him, turn from the truth to lies. **comparing themselves with themselves.** Paul pointed out the folly of the false apostles' boasting. They invented false standards that they could meet, then proclaimed themselves superior for meeting them.

10:13 not boast beyond *our* measure. In contrast to the proud, arrogant, boastful false apostles, Paul refused to say anything about himself or his ministry that was not true and God-given. **the measure of the sphere which God apportioned to us.** Paul was content to stay within the bounds of the ministry God had given him—that of being the apostle to the Gentiles (Ro 1:5; 11:13; 1Ti 2:7; 2Ti 1:11). Thus, contrary to the claims of the false apostles, Paul's sphere of ministry included Corinth. The apostle again demonstrated his humility by refusing to boast of his own accomplishments, preferring to speak only of what Christ had done through him (Ro 15:18; Col 1:29).

10:15 within our sphere, enlarged … by you. When the crisis in Corinth had been resolved and the Corinthians' faith strengthened, Paul would, with their help, expand his ministry into new areas.

10:16 regions beyond you. Areas such as Rome (Ac 19:21) and Spain (Ro 15:24, 28).

10:17 The thought of self-glory was repugnant to Paul; he boasted only in the Lord (cf. Jer 9:23, 24; 1Co 1:31; *see note on v. 13*).

10:18 whom the Lord commends. *See note on v. 12.* Self-commendation is both meaningless and foolish; the only true, meaningful commendation comes from God.

11:1 a little foolishness. Having just pointed out the folly of self-commendation (10:18), Paul certainly did not want to engage in it. But the Corinthians' acceptance of the false apostles' claims forced Paul to set forth his own apostolic credentials (cf. 12:11); that was the only way he could get them to see the truth (*see note on 10:7*). Unlike the false apostles, however, Paul's boasting was in the Lord (10:17) and motivated by concern for the Corinthians' well-being under the threat of false teaching (cf. v. 2; 12:19).

11:2 I am jealous for you. The reason for Paul's "foolishness" (*see note on v. 1*) was his deep concern for the Corinthians—concern to the point of jealousy, not for his own reputation, but zeal for their spiritual purity (*see note on v. 3*). **godly jealousy.** Jealousy inspired by zeal for God's causes, and thus similar to God's own jealousy for His holy name and His people's loyalty (cf. Ex 20:5; 34:14; Dt 4:24; 5:9;

3 But I am afraid that, as the [A]serpent deceived Eve
by his craftiness, your minds will be led astray from
the simplicity and purity *of devotion* to Christ. 4 For
if [a]one comes and preaches [A]another Jesus whom
we have not preached, or you receive a [B]different
spirit which you have not received, or a [C]differ-
ent gospel which you have not accepted, you [D]bear
this [E]beautifully. 5 For I consider myself [A]not in the
least inferior to the [a]most eminent apostles. 6 But
even if I am [A]unskilled in speech, yet I am not *so* in
[B]knowledge; in fact, in every way we have [C]made
this evident to you in all things.
7 Or [A]did I commit a sin in humbling myself so
that you might be exalted, because I preached the
[B]gospel of God to you [C]without charge? 8 I robbed
other churches by [A]taking wages *from them* to serve
you; 9 and when I was present with you and was in
need, I was [A]not a burden to anyone; for when [B]the
brethren came from [C]Macedonia they fully supplied
my need, and in everything I kept myself from [A]be-
ing a burden to you, [a]and will continue to do so.
10 [A]As the truth of Christ is in me, [B]this boasting of
mine will not be stopped in the regions of [C]Achaia.
11 Why? [A]Because I do not love you? [B]God knows *I do!*
12 But what I am doing I will continue to do, [A]so
that I may cut off opportunity from those who
desire an opportunity to be [a]regarded just as we
are in the matter about which they are boasting.
13 For such men are [A]false apostles, [B]deceitful workers, disguising themselves as apostles of Christ.

11:3 [A]Gen 3:4, 13; John 8:44; 1 Thess 3:5; 1 Tim 2:14; Rev 12:9, 15 11:4 [a]Lit *the one who comes preaches* [A]1 Cor 3:11 [B]Rom 8:15 [C]Gal 1:6 [D]2 Cor 11:1 [E]Mark 7:9 11:5 [a]Or *super-apostles* [A]2 Cor 12:11; Gal 2:6 11:6 [A]1 Cor 1:17 [B]1 Cor 12:8; Eph 3:4 [C]2 Cor 4:2 11:7 [A]2 Cor 12:13 [B]Rom 1:1; 2 Cor 2:12 [C]Acts 18:3; 1 Cor 9:18 11:8 [A]1 Cor 4:12; 9:6; Phil 4:15, 18 11:9 [a]Lit *and I will keep* [A]2 Cor 12:13f, 16 [B]Acts 18:5 [C]Rom 15:26; Phil 4:15-18 11:10 [A]Rom 1:9; 9:1; 2 Cor 1:23; Gal 2:20 [B]1 Cor 9:15 [C]Acts 18:12 11:11 [A]2 Cor 12:15 [B]Rom 1:9; 2 Cor 2:17; 11:31; 12:2f 11:12 [a]Lit *found* [A]1 Cor 9:12 11:13 [A]Acts 20:30; Gal 1:7; 2:4; Phil 1:15; Titus 1:10f; 2 Pet 2:1; Rev 2:2 [B]Phil 3:2

6:15; 32:16, 21; Jos 24:19; Ps 78:58; Eze 39:25; Na 1:2). **I betrothed you to one husband.** As their spiritual father (12:14; 1Co 4:15; cf. 9:1, 2), Paul portrayed the Corinthians like a daughter, whom he betrothed to Jesus Christ (at their conversion). The OT pictures Israel as the wife of the Lord (cf. Is 54:5; Jer 3:14; Hos 2:19, 20), while the NT pictures the church as the bride of Christ (Eph 5:22–32; Rev 19:7). **pure virgin.** Having betrothed or pledged the Corinthians to Christ, Paul wanted them to be pure until the marriage day finally arrived (cf. Rev 19:7). It was that passionate concern which provoked Paul's jealousy (*see note on v. 1*) and prompted him to set forth his apostolic credentials.

11:3 Paul compared the danger facing the Corinthian church to Eve's deception by Satan. He feared the Corinthians, like Eve, would fall prey to satanic lies and have their minds corrupted. The tragic result would be the abandonment of their simple devotion to Christ in favor of the sophisticated error of the false apostles. Paul's allusion to Ge 3 implies that the false apostles were Satan's emissaries—a truth that he later made explicit (vv. 13–15).

11:4 if one comes. The false apostles came into the Corinthian church from the outside—just as Satan did into the Garden. Likely they were Palestinian Jews (cf. v. 22; Ac 6:1) who allegedly sought to bring the Corinthians under the sway of the Jerusalem church. They were in a sense Judaizers, seeking to impose Jewish customs on the Corinthians. Unlike the Judaizers who plagued the Galatian churches (cf. Gal 5:2), however, the false apostles at Corinth apparently did not insist that the Corinthians be circumcised. Nor did they practice a rigid legalism; in fact, they apparently encouraged licentiousness (cf. 12:21). Their fascination with rhetoric and oratory (cf. 10:10) suggests they had been influenced by Greek culture and philosophy. They claimed (falsely, cf. Ac 15:24) to represent the Jerusalem church, even possessing letters of commendation (*see note on 3:1*). Claiming to be the most eminent of apostles (v. 5), they scorned Paul's apostolic claims. Though their teaching may have differed from the Galatian Judaizers, it was just as deadly. **another Jesus .... different spirit .... different gospel.** Despite their vicious attacks on him, Paul's quarrel with the false apostles was not personal, but doctrinal. He could tolerate those hostile to him, as long as they preached the gospel of Jesus Christ (cf. Php 1:15–18). Those who adulterated the true gospel, however, received Paul's strongest condemnation (cf. Gal 1:6–9). Though the precise details of what the false apostles taught are unknown and don't matter, they preached "another Jesus" and "a different spirit," which added up to "a different gospel." **you bear *this* beautifully.** Paul's fear that the Corinthians would embrace the damning lies of the false apostles prompted his jealous concern for them (*see notes on vv. 2, 3*).

11:5 the most eminent apostles. Possibly a reference to the 12 apostles, in which case Paul was asserting that, contrary to the claims of the false apostles (who said they were sent from the Jerusalem church; *see note on v. 4*), he was in no way inferior to the 12 (cf. 1Co 15:7–9). More likely, Paul was making a sarcastic reference to the false apostles, based on their exalted view of themselves. It is unlikely that he would refer to the 12 in the context of false teaching (cf. vv. 1–4), nor does the comparison that follows seem to be between Paul and the 12 (Paul certainly would not have had to defend his speaking skills against those of the 12; cf. Ac 4:13).

11:6 unskilled in speech. Paul acknowledged his lack of training in the rhetorical skills so prized in Greek culture (*see note on 10:10*; cf. Ac 18:24); he was a preacher of the gospel, not a professional orator. **I am not so in knowledge.** Whatever deficiencies Paul may have had as an orator, he had none in terms of knowledge. Paul did not refer here to his rabbinic training under Gamaliel (Ac 22:3), but to his knowledge of the gospel (cf. 1Co 2:6–11; Eph 3:1–5), which he had received directly from God (Gal 1:12).

11:7 without charge. Greek culture measured the importance of a teacher by the fee he could command. The false apostles therefore accused Paul of being a counterfeit, since he refused to charge for his services (cf. 1Co 9:1–15). They convinced the Corinthians to be offended by Paul's refusal to accept support from them, offering that as evidence that he did not love them (cf. v. 11). Paul's resort to manual labor to support himself (Ac 18:1–3) also embarrassed the Corinthians, who felt such work to be beneath the dignity of an apostle. With biting irony Paul asked his accusers how foregoing his right to support could possibly be a sin. In fact, by refusing support he had humbled himself so they could be exalted; that is, lifted out of their sin and idolatry.

11:8 I robbed other churches. "Robbed" is a very strong word, used in extrabiblical Gr. to refer to pillaging. Paul, of course, did not take money from churches without their consent; his point is that the churches who supported him while he ministered in Corinth received no direct benefit from the support they gave him. Why Paul refused to accept the support he was entitled to from the Corinthians (1Co 9:15) is not clear; perhaps some of them were suspicious of his motives in promoting the offering for the Jerusalem church (cf. 12:16–18).

11:9 brethren came from Macedonia. Silas and Timothy (Ac 18:5), bringing money from Philippi (Php 4:15) and, possibly, Thessalonica (cf. 1Th 3:6). The Macedonians' generous financial support allowed Paul to devote himself full time to preaching the gospel.

11:10 this boasting. About his ministering without charge (*see note on v. 7*; cf. 1Co 9:15, 18). **the regions of Achaia.** The Roman province of which Corinth was the capital and leading city (*see note on 9:2*). The false apostles apparently were affecting more than just the city of Corinth.

11:12 continue to do. That Paul refused to accept financial support from the Corinthians was a source of embarrassment to the false apostles, who eagerly sought money for their services. Paul intended to keep his ministry free of charge and thereby undermine the false apostles' claims that they operated on the same basis as he did.

11:13–15 No longer speaking with veiled irony or defending himself, Paul bluntly and directly exposed the false apostles for what they were—emissaries of Satan. Not only was their claim to apostleship false, so also was their doctrine (*see note on v. 4*). As satanic purveyors of false teaching, they were under the curse of Gal 1:8, 9. Paul's forceful language may seem harsh, but it expressed the godly jealousy he felt for the Corinthians (*see note on v. 2*). Paul was unwilling to sacrifice truth for the sake of unity. Cf. 1Ti 4:12; 2Pe 2:1–17; Jude 8–13.

11:13 false apostles. *See note on v. 4.*

14 No wonder, for even [A]Satan disguises himself as an
[B]angel of light. 15 Therefore it is not surprising if his
servants also disguise themselves as servants of righteousness, [A]whose end will be according to their deeds.
16 [A]Again I say, let no one think me foolish; but
if *you do,* receive me even as foolish, so that I also
may boast a little. 17 What I am saying, I am not
saying [a,A]as the Lord would, but as [B]in foolishness,
in this confidence of boasting. 18 Since [A]many boast
[B]according to the flesh, I will boast also. 19 For you,
[A]being *so* wise, tolerate the foolish gladly. 20 For you
tolerate it if anyone [A]enslaves you, anyone [B]devours
you, anyone [C]takes advantage of you, anyone [D]exalts
himself, anyone [E]hits you in the face. 21 To *my* [A]shame
I *must* say that we have been [B]weak *by comparison.*
But in whatever respect anyone *else* [C]is bold—I
[D]speak in foolishness—I am just as bold myself.
22 Are they [A]Hebrews? [B]So am I. Are they [C]Israelites?
[C]So am I. Are they [a,D]descendants of Abraham? [E]So
am I. 23 Are they [A]servants of Christ?—I speak as if
insane—I more so; in [a,B]far more labors, in [a,C]far more
imprisonments, [b,D]beaten times without number,
often in [E]danger of death. 24 Five times I received
from the Jews [A]thirty-nine *lashes.* 25 Three times I
was [A]beaten with rods, once I was [B]stoned, three
times I was shipwrecked, a night and a day I have
spent in the deep. 26 *I have been* on frequent journeys, in dangers from rivers, dangers from robbers,
dangers from *my* [A]countrymen, dangers from the
[B]Gentiles, dangers in the [C]city, dangers in the wilderness, dangers on the sea, dangers among [D]false
brethren; 27 *I have been* in [A]labor and hardship,
[a]through many sleepless nights, in [B]hunger and
thirst, often [C]without food, in cold and [b,D]exposure.
28 Apart from *such* [a]external things, there is the daily
pressure on me *of* concern for [A]all the churches.

11:14 [A]Matt 4:10; Eph 6:12; Col 1:13 [B]Col 1:12 11:15 [A]Rom 2:6; 3:8 11:16 [A]2 Cor 11:1 11:17 [a]Lit *in accordance with the Lord* [A]1 Cor 7:12, 25 [B]2 Cor 11:21 11:18 [A]Phil 3:3f [B]2 Cor 5:16 11:19 [A]1 Cor 4:10 11:20 [A]2 Cor 1:24; Gal 2:4; 4:3, 9; 5:1 [B]Mark 12:40 [C]2 Cor 11:3; 12:16 [D]2 Cor 10:5 [E]1 Cor 4:11 11:21 [A]2 Cor 6:8 [B]2 Cor 10:10 [C]2 Cor 10:2 [D]2 Cor 11:17 11:22 [a]Lit *seed* [A]Acts 6:1 [B]Phil 3:5 [C]Rom 9:4 [D]Gal 3:16 [E]Rom 11:1 11:23 [a]Lit *more abundant* [b]Lit *exceedingly in stripes* [A]1 Cor 3:5; 2 Cor 3:6; 10:7 [B]1 Cor 15:10 [C]2 Cor 6:5 [D]Acts 16:23; 2 Cor 6:5 [E]Rom 8:36 11:24 [A]Deut 25:3 11:25 [A]Acts 16:22 [B]Acts 14:19 11:26 [A]Acts 9:23; 13:45, 50; 14:5; 17:5, 13; 18:12; 20:3, 19; 21:27; 23:10, 12; 25:3; 1 Thess 2:15 [B]Acts 14:5, 19; 19:23ff; 27:42 [C]Acts 21:31 [D]Gal 2:4 11:27 [a]Lit *often in wakefulness* [b]Lit *nakedness;* i.e. lack of clothing [A]1 Thess 2:9; 2 Thess 3:8 [B]1 Cor 4:11; Phil 4:12 [C]2 Cor 6:5 [D]1 Cor 4:11 11:28 [a]Or *the things unmentioned* [A]1 Cor 7:17

11:14, 15 Since the Prince of Darkness (cf. Lk 22:53; Ac 26:18; Eph 6:12; Col 1:13) masquerades as an angel of light—that is, deceptively, disguised as a messenger of truth—it is not surprising that his emissaries do as well. Satan deceived Eve (*see notes on v. 3; Gen 3:1-7*) and holds unbelievers captive (4:4; cf. Eph 2:1–3); his emissaries were attempting to deceive and enslave the Corinthians. The terrifying "end" these self-styled "servants of righteousness" will face is God's judgment—the fate of all false teachers (Ro 3:8; 1Co 3:17; Php 3:19; 2Th 2:8; 2Pe 2:1, 3, 17; Jude 4, 13).

11:16–33 After digressing to discuss the issue of financial support (vv. 7–12) and to expose the false teachers as emissaries of Satan (vv. 13–15), Paul returned to the "foolish" boasting the Corinthians had forced him into (vv. 1–6; *see note on v. 1*).

11:16 let no one think me foolish. *See note on v. 1.* Since some of the Corinthians (following the false apostles' lead) were comparing Paul unfavorably to the false apostles, he decided to answer fools according to their folly (Pr 26:5). Paul's concern was not personal preservation; rather, the apostle knew that by rejecting him in favor of the false apostles, the Corinthians would be rejecting the true gospel for a false one. So by establishing himself and his ministry as genuine, Paul was defending the true gospel of Jesus Christ.

11:17, 18 Paul acknowledged that boasting was not commended by the Lord (cf. 10:1), but the desperate situation in Corinth (where the false apostles made their "boast according to the flesh") forced him to boast, not for self-glorification (Gal 6:14), but to counter the false doctrine threatening the Corinthian church (*see note on v. 16*).

11:19–21 These verses contain some of the most scathing sarcasm Paul ever penned, demonstrating the seriousness of the situation at Corinth and revealing the jealous concern of a godly pastor (*see note on v. 2*). Paul did not view his disagreement with the false apostles as a mere academic debate; the souls of the Corinthians and the purity of the gospel were at stake.

11:19 The Corinthians, wrote Paul sarcastically, should have no trouble bearing with a "fool" like him, since they themselves were so wise (cf. 1Co 4:10)!

11:20 enslaves you. The Gr. verb translated by this phrase appears elsewhere in the NT only in Gal 2:4, where it speaks of the Galatians' enslavement by the Judaizers. The false apostles had robbed the Corinthians of their freedom in Christ (cf. Gal 5:1). **devours you.** Or "preys upon you." This probably refers to the false teachers' demands for financial support (the same verb appears in Lk 20:47 where Jesus denounces the Pharisees for devouring widows' houses). **takes advantage of you.** This is translated "I took you in by deceit" in 12:16. The false apostles were attempting to catch the Corinthians like fish in a net (cf. Lk 5:5, 6). **exalts himself.** This refers to one who is presumptuous, puts on airs, acts arrogantly, or lords it over people (cf. 1Pe 5:3). **hits you in the face.** The false apostles may have physically abused the Corinthians, but the phrase is more likely used in a metaphorical sense (cf. 1Co 9:27) to speak of the false teachers' humiliation of the Corinthians. To strike someone on the face was a sign of disrespect and contempt (cf. 1Ki 22:24; Lk 22:64; Ac 23:2).

11:21 weak *by comparison.* Paul's sarcasm reached its peak as he noted that he was too weak to abuse the Corinthians as the false apostles had done (v. 20).

11:22–33 The third and most comprehensive list recorded in this letter of Paul's sufferings for the cause of Christ (cf. 4:8–12; 6:4–10).

11:22 Are they Hebrews ... Israelites ... descendants of Abraham? To each of these questions Paul replied simply and powerfully, "so am I" (cf. Php 3:5).

11:23 Are they servants of Christ? Paul had already emphatically denied that they were (v. 13); however, some of the Corinthians still believed they were. Paul accepted that belief for the sake of argument, then went on to show that his ministry was in every way superior to the false apostles' so-called "ministry." **I speak as if insane.** *See note on v. 1.* Once again Paul expressed his extreme distaste for the boasting the Corinthians had forced him into. **in far more labors ... in danger of death.** A general summation of Paul's sufferings for the gospel; the next few verses give specific examples, many of which are not found in Acts. Paul was often in danger of death (Ac 9:23, 29; 14:5, 19, 20; 17:5; 21:30–32).

11:24 thirty-nine *lashes.* Deuteronomy 25:1–3 set 40 as the maximum number that could legally be administered; in Paul's day the Jews reduced that number by one to avoid accidentally going over the maximum. Jesus warned that His followers would receive such beatings (Mt 10:17).

11:25 beaten with rods. Refers to Roman beatings with flexible sticks tied together (cf. Ac 16:22, 23). **once I was stoned.** At Lystra (Ac 14:19, 20). **three times I was shipwrecked.** Not including the shipwreck on his journey as a prisoner to Rome (Ac 27), which had not yet taken place. Paul had been on several sea voyages up to this time (cf. Ac 9:30; 11:25, 26; 13:4, 13; 14:25, 26; 16:11; 17:14, 15; 18:18, 21), giving ample opportunity for the 3 shipwrecks to have occurred. **a night and a day I have spent in the deep.** At least one of the shipwrecks was so severe that Paul spent an entire day floating on the wreckage, waiting to be rescued.

11:26, 27 in dangers. Those connected with his frequent travels. "Rivers" and "robbers" posed a serious danger to travelers in the ancient world. Paul's journey from Perga to Pisidian Antioch (Ac 13:14), for example, required him to travel through the robber-infested Taurus Mountains, and to cross two dangerous, flood-prone rivers. Paul was frequently in danger from his own "countrymen" (Ac 9:23, 29; 13:45; 14:2, 19; 17:5; 18:6, 12–16; 20:3, 19; 21:27–32) and, less often, from "Gentiles" (Ac 16:16–40; 19:23–20:1).

11:26 false brethren. Those who appeared to be Christians, but were not, such as the false apostles (v. 13) and the Judaizers (Gal 2:4).

11:28, 29 Far worse than the occasional physical suffering Paul endured was the constant, daily burden of concern for the churches that he felt. Those who were "weak" (cf. Ro 14; 1Co 8) in faith, or were "led into sin" caused him intense emotional pain. Cf. 1Th 5:14.

29 Who is [A]weak without my being weak? Who is
[a]led into sin [b]without my intense concern?
30 If I have to boast, I will boast of what pertains to
my [A]weakness. 31 The God and Father of the Lord Jesus,
[A]He who is blessed forever, [B]knows that I am not lying.
32 In [A]Damascus the ethnarch under Aretas the king
was [B]guarding the city of the Damascenes in order to
seize me, 33 and I was let down in a basket [A]through a
window [a]in the wall, and *so* escaped his hands.

PAUL'S VISION

12 [A]Boasting is necessary, though it is not profitable; but I will go on to visions and [B]rev-
elations [a]of the Lord. 2 I know a man [A]in Christ
who fourteen years ago—whether in the body I do
not know, or out of the body I do not know, [B]God
knows—such a man was [C]caught up to the [D]third
heaven. 3 And I know how such a man—whether in
the body or apart from the body I do not know, [A]God
knows— 4 was [A]caught up into [B]Paradise and heard
inexpressible words, which a man is not permitted
to speak. 5 [A]On behalf of such a man I will boast; but
on my own behalf I will not boast, except in regard
to *my* [B]weaknesses. 6 For if I do wish to boast I will
not be [A]foolish, [B]for I will be speaking the truth;
but I refrain *from this,* so that no one will credit
me with more than he sees *in* me or hears from me.

A THORN IN THE FLESH

7 Because of the surpassing greatness of the [A]rev-
elations, for this reason, to keep me from exalting
myself, there was given me a [B]thorn in the flesh, a
[C]messenger of Satan to [a]torment me—to keep me from
exalting myself! 8 Concerning this I implored the Lord
[A]three times that it might leave me. 9 And He has said
to me, "My grace is sufficient for you, for [A]power
is perfected in weakness." Most gladly, therefore, I
will rather [B]boast [a]about my weaknesses, so that the
power of Christ may dwell in me. 10 Therefore [A]I am
well content with weaknesses, with [a]insults, with
[B]distresses, with [C]persecutions, with [B]difficulties, [D]for
Christ's sake; for [E]when I am weak, then I am strong.

11:29 [a]Lit *made to stumble* [b]Lit *and I do not burn* [A]1 Cor 8:9, 13; 9:22 11:30 [A]1 Cor 2:3 11:31 [A]Rom 1:25 [B]2 Cor 11:11 11:32 [A]Acts 9:2 [B]Acts 9:24 11:33 [a]Lit *through* [A]Acts 9:25 12:1 [a]Or *from* [A]2 Cor 11:16, 18, 30; 12:5, 9 [B]1 Cor 14:6; 2 Cor 12:7; Gal 1:12; 2:2; Eph 3:3 12:2 [A]Rom 16:7 [B]2 Cor 11:11 [C]Ezek 8:3; Acts 8:39; 2 Cor 12:4; 1 Thess 4:17; Rev 12:5 [D]Deut 10:14; Ps 148:4; Eph 4:10; Heb 4:14 12:3 [A]2 Cor 11:11 12:4 [A]Ezek 8:3; Acts 8:39; 2 Cor 12:2; 1 Thess 4:17; Rev 12:5 [B]Luke 23:43 12:5 [A]2 Cor 12:1 [B]1 Cor 2:3; 2 Cor 12:9f 12:6 [A]2 Cor 5:13; 11:16f; 12:11 [B]2 Cor 7:14 12:7 [a]Lit *beat* [A]2 Cor 12:1 [B]Num 33:55; Ezek 28:24; Hos 2:6 [C]Job 2:6; Matt 4:10; 1 Cor 5:5 12:8 [A]Matt 26:44 12:9 [a]Lit *in* [A]1 Cor 2:5; Eph 3:16; Phil 4:13 [B]1 Cor 2:3; 2 Cor 12:5 12:10 [a]Or *mistreatment* [A]Rom 5:3; 8:35 [B]2 Cor 6:4 [C]2 Thess 1:4; 2 Tim 3:11 [D]2 Cor 5:15, 20 [E]2 Cor 13:4

11:30 I will boast … my weakness. To do so magnified God's power at work in him (cf. 4:7; Col 1:29; 2Ti 2:20, 21).

11:31 Realizing how incredible the list of his sufferings must have seemed, Paul called on God to witness that he was telling the truth (cf. v. 10; 1:23; Ro 1:9; 9:1; Gal 1:20; 1Th 2:5, 10; 1Ti 2:7)—that these things really happened.

11:32, 33 Paul related his humiliating escape from Damascus (cf. Ac 9:23–25) as the crowning example of the weakness and infirmity in which he boasted (v. 30). The Acts narrative names the hostile Jews as those who sought Paul's life, whereas Paul here mentioned the governor under the Nabatean Arab king Aretas (9 B.C.–A.D. 40) as the one who sought him. Evidently, the Jews stirred up the secular authorities against him, as they were later to do repeatedly in Acts (cf. Ac 13:50; 14:2; 17:13).

12:1–7 Paul continued, reluctantly, with his boasting (*see note on 11:1*). Though it was "not profitable," since it could tempt his own flesh to be proud, the Corinthians' fascination with the alleged visions and revelations of the false apostles left him little choice (v. 11).

12:1 visions and revelations. Six of Paul's visions are recorded in Acts (9:12; 16:9, 10; 18:9; 22:17, 18; 23:11; 27:23, 24), and his letters speak of revelations he had received (cf. Gal 1:12; 2:2; Eph 3:3).

12:2–4 Since it took place 14 years before the writing of 2 Corinthians, the specific vision Paul relates cannot be identified with any incident recorded in Acts. It probably took place between his return to Tarsus from Jerusalem (Ac 9:30) and the start of his missionary journeys (Ac 13:1–3). **caught up to the third heaven … caught up into Paradise.** Paul was not describing two separate visions; "the third heaven" and "Paradise" are the same place (cf. Rev 2:7, which says the tree of life is in Paradise, with Rev 22:14, which says it is in heaven). The first heaven is the earth's atmosphere (Ge 8:2; Dt 11:11; 1Ki 8:35); the second is interplanetary and interstellar space (Ge 15:5; Ps 8:3; Is 13:10); and the third is the abode of God (1Ki 8:30; 2Ch 30:27; Ps 123:1).

12:2 a man in Christ. Though Paul's reluctance to boast caused him to refer to himself in the third person, the context makes it obvious that he was speaking about himself; relating the experience of another man would hardly have enhanced Paul's apostolic credentials. Also, Paul's thorn in the flesh afflicted him, not someone else (v. 7).

12:2, 3 whether in … or … apart from the body. Paul was so overwhelmed by his heavenly vision that he did not know the precise details. However, whether he was caught up bodily into heaven (like Enoch, Ge 5:24 and Elijah, 2Ki 2:11), or his spirit was temporarily separated from his body, was not important.

12:4 inexpressible words … not permitted to speak. Because the words were for him alone, Paul was forbidden to repeat them, even if he could have expressed them coherently.

12:5 of such a man I will boast. *See note on v. 2.*

12:6 If Paul wished to boast about his unique experience (vv. 1–4) he would not be a fool, because it really happened. He refrained from boasting about it, however, because he wanted the Corinthians to judge him based on their observations of his ministry, not on his visions.

12:7 the revelations. *See note on v. 1.* **a thorn in the flesh, a messenger of Satan.** This was sent to him by God, to keep him humble. As with Job, Satan was the immediate cause, but God was the ultimate cause. Paul's use of the word "messenger" (Gr., *angelos,* or angel) from Satan suggests the "thorn in the flesh" (lit. "a stake for the flesh") was a demonized person, not a physical illness. Of the 175 uses of the Gr. word, *angelos,* in the NT, most are in reference to angels. This angel was from Satan, a demon afflicting Paul. Possibly, the best explanation for this demon was that he was indwelling the ring leader of the Corinthian conspiracy, the leader of the false apostles. Through them he was tearing up Paul's beloved church and thus driving a painful stake through Paul. Further support for this view comes from the context of chaps. 10–13, which is one of fighting adversaries (the false prophets). The verb translated "torment" always refers to ill treatment from other people (Mt 26:67; Mk 14:65; 1Co 4:11; 1Pe 2:20). Finally, the OT describes Israel's personal opponents as thorns (Nu 33:55; Jos 23:13; Jdg 2:3; Eze 28:24). **to keep me from exalting myself.** The assault was painful, but purposeful. God was allowing Satan to bring this severe trouble in the church for the purpose of humbling Paul who, having had so many revelations, including a trip to heaven and back, would have been proud. The demonized false apostle attacking his work in Corinth was the stake being driven through his otherwise proud flesh.

12:8 I implored … three times. Paul, longing for relief from this painful hindrance to his ministry, went to his Lord, begging Him (the use of the definite article with "Lord" shows Paul's prayer was directed to Jesus) to remove it. The demons are only subject to His authority. The 3-fold repetition of Paul's request parallels that of Jesus in Gethsemane (Mk 14:32–41). Both Paul and Jesus had their requests denied, but were granted grace to endure their ordeals.

12:9 My grace is sufficient for you. The present tense of the verb translated "is sufficient" reveals the constant availability of divine grace. God would not remove the thorn, as Paul had requested, but would continually supply him with grace to endure it (cf. 1Co 15:10; Php 4:13; Col 1:29). **power is perfected in weakness.** Cf. 4:7–11. The weaker the human instrument, the more clearly God's grace shines forth.

12:9, 10 Paul took no pleasure in the pain itself, but rejoiced in the power of Christ that it revealed through him.

11 I have become [A]foolish; you yourselves compelled me. Actually I should have been commended by you, for [B]in no respect was I inferior to the [a]most eminent apostles, even though [C]I am a nobody. 12 The [a,A]signs [b]of a true apostle were performed among you with all perseverance, by [a]signs and wonders and [c]miracles. 13 For in what respect were you treated as inferior to the rest of the churches, except that [A]I myself did not become a burden to you? Forgive me [B]this wrong!

14 Here [A]for this third time I am ready to come to you, and I [B]will not be a burden to you; for I [C]do not seek what is yours, but [D]you; for [E]children are not responsible to save up for *their* parents, but [F]parents for *their* children. 15 I will [A]most gladly spend and be expended for your souls. If [B]I love you more, am I to be loved less? 16 But be that as it may, I [A]did not burden you myself; nevertheless, crafty fellow that I am, I [B]took you in by deceit. 17 [A]*Certainly* I have not taken advantage of you through any of those whom I have sent to you, have I? 18 I [A]urged [B]Titus *to go,* and I sent [C]the brother with him. Titus did not take any advantage of you, did he? Did we not [a]conduct ourselves [b]in the same [D]spirit *and walk* [E]in the same steps?

19 All this time [a]you have been thinking that we are defending ourselves to you. *Actually,* [A]it is in the sight of God that we have been speaking in Christ; and [B]all for your upbuilding, [C]beloved. 20 For I am afraid that perhaps [A]when I come I may find you to be not what I wish and may be found by you to be not what you wish; that perhaps *there will be* [B]strife, jealousy, [C]angry tempers, [D]disputes, [E]slanders, [F]gossip, [G]arrogance, [H]disturbances; 21 I am afraid that when I come again my God may humiliate me before you, and I may mourn over many of those who have [A]sinned in the past and not repented of the [B]impurity, [a]immorality and sensuality which they have practiced.

EXAMINE YOURSELVES

13 [A]This is the third time I am coming to you. [B]EVERY [a]FACT [b]IS TO BE CONFIRMED BY THE [c]TESTIMONY OF TWO OR THREE WITNESSES. 2 I have previously said when present the second time, and though now absent I say in advance to those who have [A]sinned in the past and to all the rest *as well,* that [B]if I come again I will not [C]spare *anyone,* 3 since you are [A]seeking for proof of the [B]Christ who speaks in me, and who is not weak toward you, but [C]mighty in you. 4 For indeed He was [A]crucified because of weakness, yet He lives [B]because of the power of God. For we also are [C]weak [a]in Him, yet [D]we will live with Him because of the power of God *directed* toward you.

12:11 [a]Or *super-apostles* [A]2 Cor 5:13; 11:16f; 12:6 [B]1 Cor 15:10; 2 Cor 11:5 [C]1 Cor 3:7; 13:2; 15:9 12:12 [a]Or *attesting miracles* [b]Lit *of the apostle* [c]Or *works of power* [A]John 4:48; Rom 15:19; 1 Cor 9:1 12:13 [A]1 Cor 9:12, 18; 2 Cor 11:9; 12:14 [B]2 Cor 11:7 12:14 [A]2 Cor 1:15; 13:1, 2 [B]1 Cor 9:12, 18; 2 Cor 11:9; 12:13 [C]1 Cor 10:24, 33 [D]1 Cor 9:19 [E]1 Cor 4:14f; Gal 4:19 [F]Prov 19:14; Ezek 34:2 12:15 [A]Rom 9:3; 2 Cor 1:6; Phil 2:17; Col 1:24; 1 Thess 2:8; 2 Tim 2:10 [B]2 Cor 11:11 12:16 [A]2 Cor 11:9 [B]2 Cor 11:20 12:17 [A]2 Cor 9:5 12:18 [a]Lit *walk* [b]Or *by the same Spirit* [A]2 Cor 8:6 [B]2 Cor 2:13 [C]2 Cor 8:18 [D]1 Cor 4:21 [E]Rom 4:12 12:19 [a]Or *have you been thinking...?* [A]Rom 9:1; 2 Cor 2:17 [B]Rom 14:19; 2 Cor 10:8; 1 Thess 5:11 [C]Heb 6:9 12:20 [A]1 Cor 4:21; 2 Cor 2:1-4 [B]1 Cor 1:11; 3:3 [C]Gal 5:20 [D]Rom 2:8; 1 Cor 11:19 [E]Rom 1:30; James 4:11; 1 Pet 2:1 [F]Rom 1:29 [G]1 Cor 4:6, 18; 5:2 [H]1 Cor 14:33 12:21 [a]I.e. sexual immorality [A]2 Cor 13:2 [B]1 Cor 6:9, 18; Gal 5:19; Col 3:5 13:1 [a]Lit *word* [b]Lit *shall be* [c]Lit *mouth* [A]2 Cor 12:14 [B]Deut 17:6; 19:15; Matt 18:16 13:2 [A]2 Cor 12:21 [B]1 Cor 4:21; 2 Cor 13:10 [C]2 Cor 1:23; 10:11 13:3 [A]2 Cor 10:1, 10 [B]Matt 10:20; 1 Cor 5:4; 7:40 [C]2 Cor 9:8; 10:4 13:4 [a]One early ms reads *with Him* [A]Phil 2:7f; 1 Pet 3:18 [B]Rom 1:4; 6:4; 1 Cor 6:14 [C]1 Cor 2:3; 2 Cor 13:9 [D]Rom 6:8

12:11 become foolish. *See notes on 11:1, 16;* cf. 11:17, 21, 23. **you ... compelled me.** *See note on 11:1.* **the most eminent apostles.** *See note on 11:5.*

12:12 The signs of a true apostle. Including, but not limited to, "signs and wonders and miracles" (the miracle of the Corinthians' salvation was also a mark of Paul's apostleship, 1Co 9:2). The purpose of miraculous signs was to authenticate the apostles as God's messengers (cf. Ac 2:22, 43; 4:30; 5:12; 14:3; Ro 15:18, 19; Heb 2:3, 4).

12:13 Paul had not slighted the Corinthians except by refusing to be a burden (*see note on 11:7*). With a touch of irony, he begged their forgiveness for that "wrong."

12:14 for this third time. The first was the visit recorded in Ac 18; the second was the "painful visit" (2:1; see Introduction: Background and Setting). **not be a burden.** On his upcoming visit, Paul wished to continue his practice of refusing to accept support from the Corinthians. **I do not seek what is yours, but you.** Paul sought the Corinthians (cf. 6:11–13; 7:2, 3), not their money. **children ... parents ... parents ... children.** To reinforce his point, Paul cited the axiomatic truth that parents are financially responsible for their children, not children (when they are young, cf. 1Ti 5:4) for their parents.

12:15 Far from seeking to take from the Corinthians, Paul sought to give. The verb translated "spend" refers to spending money, and probably describes Paul's willingness to work to support himself while in Corinth (Ac 18:3). "Be expended" describes Paul's willingness to give of himself—even to the point of sacrificing his life.

12:16–18 Although it was obvious to all that Paul had not personally taken advantage of the Corinthians, his opponents circulated an even more vicious rumor—that he was using craftiness and cunning to deceive the Corinthians (cf. 4:2). Specifically, the false apostles accused Paul of sending his assistants to collect the Jerusalem offering from the Corinthians while intending to keep some of it for himself. Thus, according to his opponents, Paul was both a deceitful hypocrite (because he really did take money from the Corinthians after all, despite his words in vv. 14, 15) and a thief. This charge was all the more painful to Paul because it impugned the character of his friends. Outraged that the Corinthians could believe such ridiculous lies, Paul pointed out that his associates did not take advantage of the Corinthians during their earlier visits regarding the collection (8:6, 16–22). The simple truth was that neither Paul nor his representatives had in any way defrauded the Corinthians.

12:19 Lest the Corinthians view themselves as judges before whom Paul was on trial, the apostle quickly set them straight: only God was his judge (cf. 5:10; 1Co 4:3–5). Paul sought to edify the Corinthians, not exonerate himself.

12:21 When he visited them, Paul did not want to find the Corinthians in the same sorry spiritual condition as on his last visit (the "painful visit," 2:1; see Introduction: Background and Setting). If he found that they were not what he wished (i.e., still practicing the sins he listed), they would find him not as they wished—he would have had to discipline them (cf. 13:2). To find the Corinthians still living in unrepentant sin would both humiliate and sadden Paul. This warning (and the one in 13:2) was designed to prevent that from happening.

13:1 the third time. *See note on 12:14.* **two or three witnesses.** Not a reference to Paul's 3 visits to Corinth, since he could be only one witness no matter how many visits he made. Paul informed the Corinthians that he would deal biblically (cf. Dt 19:15; Mt 18:16; Jn 8:17; Heb 10:28) with any sin he found in Corinth.

13:2 I will not spare. *See note on 12:21.*

13:3 proof of the Christ who speaks in me. Those Corinthians still seeking proof that Paul was a genuine apostle would have it when he arrived. They may have gotten more than they bargained for, however, for Paul was going to use his apostolic authority and power to deal with any sin and rebellion he found there (v. 2; *see note on 12:21*). **who is not weak.** Christ's power was to be revealed through Paul against the sinning Corinthians (cf. 1Co 11:30–32). By rebelling against Christ's chosen apostle (1:1), they were rebelling against Him.

13:4 Paul was to come to Corinth armed with the irresistible power of the risen, glorified Christ (cf. Php 3:10).

5 [A]Test yourselves *to see* if you are in the faith;
[B]examine yourselves! Or do you not recognize this
about yourselves, that Jesus Christ is in you—unless
indeed you [a,C]fail the test? 6 But I trust that you will
realize that we ourselves [a]do not fail the test. 7 Now
we pray to God that you do no wrong; not that we
ourselves may appear approved, but that you may
do what is right, even though we may [a]appear unapproved. 8 For we can do nothing against the truth,
but *only* for the truth. 9 For we rejoice when we
ourselves are [A]weak but you are strong; this we
also pray for, [a]that you be [B]made complete. 10 For
this reason I am writing these things while absent,
so that when present [A]I *need* not use [B]severity, in
accordance with the [C]authority which the Lord gave
me for building up and not for tearing down.

11 [A]Finally, brethren, [a]rejoice, [b,B]be made complete,
be comforted, [C]be like-minded, [D]live in peace; and
[E]the God of love and peace will be with you. 12 [A]Greet
one another with a holy kiss. 13 [A]All the [a]saints greet
you.

14 [A]The grace of the Lord Jesus Christ, and the
[B]love of God, and the [C]fellowship of the Holy Spirit,
be with you all.

13:5 [a]Lit *are unapproved* [A]John 6:6 [B]1 Cor 11:28 [C]1 Cor 9:27 13:6 [a]Lit *are not unapproved* 13:7 [a]Lit *be as* 13:9 [a]Lit *your completion* [A]2 Cor 12:10; 13:4 [B]1 Cor 1:10; 2 Cor 13:11; Eph 4:12; 1 Thess 3:10 13:10 [A]2 Cor 2:3 [B]Titus 1:13 [C]1 Cor 5:4; 2 Cor 10:8 13:11 [a]Or *farewell* [b]Or *put yourselves in order* [A]1 Thess 4:1; 2 Thess 3:1 [B]1 Cor 1:10; 2 Cor 13:9; Eph 4:12; 1 Thess 3:10 [C]Rom 12:16 [D]Mark 9:50 [E]Rom 15:33; Eph 6:23 13:12 [A]Rom 16:16 13:13 [a]Or *holy ones* [A]Phil 4:22 13:14 [A]Rom 16:20; 2 Cor 8:9 [B]Rom 5:5; Jude 21 [C]Phil 2:1

13:5, 6 The Gr. grammar places great emphasis on the pronouns "yourselves" and "you." Paul turned the tables on his accusers; instead of presuming to evaluate his apostleship, they needed to test the genuineness of their faith (cf. Jas 2:14–26). He pointed out the incongruity of the Corinthians' believing (as they did) that their faith was genuine and his apostleship false. Paul was their spiritual father (1Co 4:15); if his apostleship was counterfeit, so was their faith. The genuineness of their salvation was proof of the genuineness of his apostleship.

13:5 **fail the test.** Lit. "not approved." Here it referred to the absence of genuine saving faith.

13:7 **do what is right.** Paul's deepest longing was for his spiritual children to lead godly lives (cf. 7:1)—even if they persisted in doubting him. Paul was even willing to appear "unapproved," as long as the Corinthians turned from their sin (cf. Ro 9:3).

13:8, 9 Lest anyone think his reference to being unapproved (v. 7) was an admission of wrongdoing on his part, Paul hastened to add that he had not violated "the truth" of the gospel. The apostle may also have meant that he needed to take no action against the Corinthians if he found them living according to "the truth." In that case, he would rejoice in his "weakness" (that is, his lack of opportunity to exercise his apostolic power), because that would mean that the Corinthians were spiritually "strong."

13:10 A one-sentence summary of Paul's purpose in writing this letter.

13:11 Paul's concluding exhortations expressed the attitudes he prayed (v. 9) would characterize the Corinthians. **the God of love and peace will be with you.** An encouragement to the Corinthians to carry out the exhortations in the first part of the verse. Only here in the NT is God called "the God of love" (cf. 1Jn 4:8).

13:12 **a holy kiss.** A sign of greeting in biblical times (Mt 26:49; Lk 7:45), much like the modern handshake. For Christians, it further expressed brotherly love and unity (Ro 16:16; 1Co 16:20; 1Th 5:26; 1Pe 5:14).

13:13 **All the saints.** Those in Macedonia (possibly Philippi; see Introduction: Background and Setting), from where Paul wrote 2 Corinthians. While encouraging unity within the Corinthian church, Paul did not want the Corinthians to lose sight of their unity with other churches.

13:14 The Trinitarian benediction reminded the Corinthians of the blessings they had received: "grace" from the Lord Jesus Christ (cf. 8:9), "love" from God the Father (cf. v. 11), and "fellowship" with God and one another through the Holy Spirit (cf. 1:22; 5:5). Jesus was mentioned before the Father because His sacrificial death is the ultimate expression of God's love.

THE EPISTLE OF
PAUL TO THE

GALATIANS

TITLE

Galatians derives its title (*pros Galatas*) from the region in Asia Minor (modern Turkey) where the churches addressed were located. It is the only one of Paul's epistles specifically addressed to churches in more than one city (1:2; cf. 3:1; 1Co 16:1).

AUTHOR AND DATE

There is no reason to question the internal claims that the apostle Paul wrote Galatians (1:1; 5:2). Paul was born in Tarsus, a city in the province of Cilicia, not far from Galatia. Under the famous rabbi, Gamaliel, Paul received a thorough training in the OT Scriptures and in the rabbinic traditions at Jerusalem (Ac 22:3). A member of the ultraorthodox sect of the Pharisees (Ac 23:6), he was one of first-century Judaism's rising stars (1:14; cf. Php 3:5, 6).

The course of Paul's life took a sudden and startling turn when, on his way to Damascus from Jerusalem to persecute Christians, he was confronted by the risen, glorified Christ (*see notes on Ac 9*). That dramatic encounter turned Paul from Christianity's chief persecutor to its greatest missionary. His 3 missionary journeys and trip to Rome turned Christianity from a faith that included only a small group of Palestinian Jewish believers into an Empire-wide phenomenon. Galatians is one of 13 inspired letters he addressed to Gentile congregations or his fellow workers. For further biographical information on Paul, see Introduction to Romans: Author and Date.

In chap. 2, Paul described his visit to the Jerusalem Council of Ac 15 (*see note on 2:1*), so he must have written Galatians after that event. Since most scholars date the Jerusalem Council about A.D. 49, the most likely date for Galatians is shortly thereafter.

BACKGROUND AND SETTING

In Paul's day, the word *Galatia* had two distinct meanings. In a strict ethnic sense, Galatia was the region of central Asia Minor inhabited by the Galatians. They were a Celtic people who had migrated to that region from Gaul (modern France) in the third century B.C. The Romans conquered the Galatians in 189 B.C. but allowed them to have some measure of independence until 25 B.C. when Galatia became a Roman province, incorporating some regions not inhabited by ethnic Galatians (e.g., parts of Lycaonia, Phrygia, and Pisidia). In a political sense, *Galatia* came to describe the entire Roman province, not merely the region inhabited by the ethnic Galatians.

Paul founded churches in the southern Galatian cities of Antioch, Iconium, Lystra, and Derbe (Ac 13:14–14:23). These cities, although within the Roman province of Galatia, were not in the ethnic Galatian region. There is no record of Paul's founding churches in that northern, less populated region.

Those two uses of the word *Galatia* make it more difficult to determine who the original recipients of the epistle were. Some interpret *Galatia* in its strict racial sense and argue that Paul addressed this epistle to churches in the northern Galatian region, inhabited by the ethnic descendants of the Gauls. Although the apostle apparently crossed the border into the fringes of ethnic Galatia on at least two occasions (Ac 16:6; 18:23), Acts does not record that he founded any churches or engaged in any evangelistic ministry there.

Because neither Acts nor Galatians mentions any cities or people from northern (ethnic) Galatia, it is reasonable to believe that Paul addressed this epistle to churches located in the southern part of the Roman province, but outside of the ethnic Galatian region. Acts records the apostle's founding of such churches at Pisidian Antioch (13:14–50), Iconium (13:51–14:7; cf. 16:2), Lystra (14:8–19; cf. 16:2), and Derbe (14:20, 21; cf. 16:1). In addition, the churches Paul addressed had apparently been established before the Jerusalem Council (2:5), and the churches of southern Galatia fit that criterion, having been founded during Paul's first missionary journey before the Council met. Paul did not visit northern (ethnic) Galatia until after the Jerusalem Council (Ac 16:6).

Paul wrote Galatians to counter Judaizing false teachers who were undermining the central NT doctrine of justification by faith (*see note on Ro 3:31*). Ignoring the express decree of the Jerusalem Council (Ac 15:23–29), they spread their dangerous teaching that Gentiles must first become Jewish proselytes and submit to all the Mosaic law before they could become Christians (see 1:7; 4:17, 21; 5:2–12; 6:12, 13). Shocked by the Galatians' openness to that damning heresy (cf. 1:6), Paul wrote this letter to defend justification by faith, and warn these churches of the dire consequences of abandoning that essential doctrine. Galatians is the only epistle Paul wrote that does not contain a commendation for its readers—that obvious omission reflects how urgently he felt about confronting the defection and defending the essential doctrine of justification.

HISTORICAL AND THEOLOGICAL THEMES

Galatians provides valuable historical information about Paul's background (chaps. 1, 2), including his 3-year stay in Nabatean Arabia (1:17, 18), which Acts does not mention; his 15-day visit with Peter after his stay in Arabia (1:18, 19); his trip to the Jerusalem Council (2:1–10); and his confrontation of Peter (2:11–21).

As already noted, the central theme of Galatians (like that of Romans) is justification by faith. Paul defends that doctrine (which is the heart of the gospel) both in its theological (chaps. 3, 4) and practical (chaps. 5, 6) ramifications. He also defends his position as an apostle (chaps. 1, 2) since, as in Corinth, false teachers had attempted to gain a hearing for their heretical teaching by undermining Paul's credibility. The main theological themes of Galatians are strikingly similar to those of Romans, e.g., the inability of the law to justify (2:16; cf. Ro 3:20); the believer's deadness to the law (2:19; cf. Ro 7:4); the believer's crucifixion with Christ (2:20; cf. Ro 6:6); Abraham's justification by faith (3:6; cf. Ro 4:3); that believers are Abraham's spiritual children (3:7; cf. Ro 4:10, 11) and therefore blessed (3:9; cf. Ro 4:23, 24); that the law brings not salvation but God's wrath (3:10; cf. Ro 4:15); that the just shall live by faith (3:11; cf. Ro 1:17); the universality of sin (3:22; cf. Ro 11:32); that believers are spiritually baptized into Christ (3:27; cf. Ro 6:3); believers' adoption as God's spiritual children (4:5–7; cf. Ro 8:14–17); that love fulfills the law (5:14; cf. Ro 13:8–10); the importance of walking in the Spirit (5:16; cf. Ro 8:4); the warfare of the flesh against the Spirit (5:17; cf. Ro 7:23, 25); and the importance of believers bearing one anothers' burdens (6:2; cf. Ro 15:1).

INTERPRETIVE CHALLENGES

First, Paul described a visit to Jerusalem and a subsequent meeting with Peter, James, and John (2:1–10). There is a question to be resolved in that text, as to whether that was his visit to the Jerusalem Council (Ac 15), or his earlier visit bringing famine relief to the Jerusalem church (Ac 11:27–30). Second, those who teach baptismal regeneration (the false doctrine that baptism is necessary for salvation) support their view from 3:27. Third, others have used this epistle to support their attacks on the biblical roles of men and women, claiming that the spiritual equality taught in 3:28 is incompatible with the traditional concept of authority and submission. Fourth, those who reject the doctrine of eternal security argue that the phrase "you have fallen from grace" (5:4) describes believers who lost their salvation. Fifth, there is disagreement whether Paul's statement "see with what large letters I am writing to you with my own hand" refers to the entire letter, or merely the concluding verses. Finally, many claim that Paul erased the line between Israel and the church when he identified the church as the "Israel of God" (6:16). Those challenges will be addressed in the notes to the appropriate passages.

OUTLINE

I. Personal: The Preacher of Justification (1:1–2:21)
- A. Apostolic Chastening (1:1–9)
- B. Apostolic Credentials (1:10–2:10)
- C. Apostolic Confidence (2:11–21)

II. Doctrinal: The Principles of Justification (3:1–4:31)
- A. The Experience of the Galatians (3:1–5)
- B. The Blessing of Abraham (3:6–9)
- C. The Curse of the Law (3:10–14)
- D. The Promise of the Covenant (3:15–18)
- E. The Purpose of the Law (3:19–29)
- F. The Sonship of Believers (4:1–7)
- G. The Futility of Ritualism (4:8–20)
- H. The Illustration from Scripture (4:21–31)

III. Practical: The Privileges of Justification (5:1–6:18)
- A. Freedom from Ritual (5:1–6)
- B. Freedom from Legalists (5:7–12)
- C. Freedom in the Spirit (5:13–26)
- D. Freedom from Spiritual Bondage (6:1–10)
- E. Conclusion (6:11–18)

INTRODUCTION

1 Paul, [A]an apostle ([B]not *sent* from men nor through
the agency of man, but [C]through Jesus Christ and
God the Father, who [D]raised Him from the dead),
2 and all [A]the brethren who are with me,
To [B]the churches of Galatia:
3 [A]Grace to you and peace from [a]God our Father
and the Lord Jesus Christ, 4 who [A]gave Himself for
our sins so that He might rescue us from [B]this present evil [a]age, according to the will of [C]our God and
Father, 5 [A]to whom *be* the glory forevermore. Amen.

PERVERSION OF THE GOSPEL

6 I am amazed that you are so quickly deserting
[A]Him who called you [a]by the grace of Christ, for a
[B]different gospel; 7 which is *really* not another; only
there are some who are [A]disturbing you and want to
distort the gospel of Christ. 8 But even if we, or [A]an
angel from heaven, should preach to you a gospel
[a]contrary to what we have preached to you, he is
to be [b,B]accursed! 9 As we [A]have said before, so I say
again now, [B]if any man is preaching to you a gospel
[a]contrary to what you received, he is to be [b,C]accursed!
10 For am I now [A]seeking the favor of men, or of
God? Or am I striving to please men? If I were still
trying to please men, I would not be a [B]bond-ser-
vant of Christ.

PAUL DEFENDS HIS MINISTRY

11 For [A]I would have you know, brethren, that the
gospel which was preached by me is [B]not according
to man. 12 For [A]I neither received it from man, nor
was I taught it, but *I received it* through a [B]revela-
tion of Jesus Christ.

1:1 [A]2 Cor 1:1 [B]Gal 1:11f [C]Acts 9:15; Gal 1:15f [D]Acts 2:24 1:2 [A]Phil 4:21 [B]Acts 16:6; 1 Cor 16:1 1:3 [a]Two early mss read *God the Father, and our Lord Jesus Christ* [A]Rom 1:7 1:4 [a]Or *world* [A]Gal 2:20 [B]Matt 13:22; Rom 12:2; 2 Cor 4:4 [C]Phil 4:20 1:5 [A]Rom 11:36 1:6 [a]Lit *in* [A]Rom 8:28; Gal 1:15; 5:8 [B]2 Cor 11:4; Gal 1:7, 11; 2:2, 7; 5:14; 1 Tim 1:3 1:7 [A]Acts 15:24; Gal 5:10 1:8 [a]Or *other than, more than* [b]Gr *anathema* [A]2 Cor 11:14 [B]Rom 9:3 1:9 [a]Or *other than, more than* [b]Gr *anathema* [A]Acts 18:23 [B]Rom 16:17 [C]Rom 9:3 1:10 [A]1 Cor 10:33; 1 Thess 2:4 [B]Rom 1:1; Phil 1:1 1:11 [A]Rom 2:16; 1 Cor 15:1 [B]1 Cor 3:4; 9:8 1:12 [A]1 Cor 11:23; Gal 1:1 [B]1 Cor 2:10; 2 Cor 12:1; Gal 1:16; 2:2

1:1 Paul. See Introduction to Romans: Author and Date; *see note on Ac 9:1.* **apostle.** In general terms, it means "one who is sent with a commission." The apostles of Jesus Christ—the 12 and Paul—were special ambassadors or messengers chosen and trained by Christ to lay the foundation of the early church and be the channels of God's completed revelation (*see note on Ro 1:1;* cf. Ac 1:2; 2:42; Eph 2:20). **not *sent* from men ... but through Jesus Christ.** To defend his apostleship against the false teachers' attack, Paul emphasized that Christ Himself appointed him as an apostle before he met the other apostles (cf. vv. 17, 18; Ac 9:3–9). **raised Him from the dead.** *See notes on Ro 1:4.* Paul included this important fact to show that the risen and ascended Christ Himself appointed him (*see notes on Ac 9:1–3, 15*), thus Paul was a qualified witness of His resurrection (cf. Ac 1:22).

1:2 churches of Galatia. The churches Paul founded at Antioch of Pisidia, Iconium, Lystra, and Derbe during his first missionary journey (Ac 13:14–14:23; see Introduction: Background and Setting).

1:3–5 Paul's deep concern over the churches' defection from the gospel is evident from his greeting, which lacks his customary commendations and courtesies, and is instead brief and impersonal.

1:3 Grace to you and peace. *See note on Ro 1:1.* Even Paul's typical greeting attacked the Judaizers' legalistic system. If salvation is by works as they claimed, it is not of "grace" and cannot result in "peace," since no one can be sure he has enough good works to be eternally secure.

1:4 for our sins. No one can avoid sin by human effort or law-keeping (Ro 3:20); therefore it must be forgiven, which Christ accomplished through His atoning death on the cross (3:13; *see notes on 2Co 5:19–21; 1Pe 2:24*). **present evil age.** The Gr. word for "age" does not refer to a period of time, but an order or system, and in particular to the current world system ruled by Satan (*see notes on Ro 12:2; 1Jn 2:15, 16; 5:19*). **the will of our God.** The sacrifice of Christ for salvation was the will of God designed and fulfilled for His glory. Cf. Mt 26:42; Jn 6:38–40; Ac 2:22, 23; Ro 8:3, 31, 32; Eph 1:7, 11; Heb 10:4–10.

1:6 so quickly. This Gr. word can mean either "easily" or "quickly" and sometimes both. No doubt both senses characterized the Galatians' response to the false teachers' heretical doctrines. **deserting.** The Gr. word was used of military desertion, which was punishable by death. The form of this Gr. verb indicates that the Galatian believers were voluntarily deserting grace to pursue the legalism taught by the false teachers (*see notes on 5:4*). **called you.** This could be translated "who called you once and for all" (cf. 2Th 2:13, 14; 2Ti 1:8, 9; 1Pe 1:15), and refers to God's effectual call to salvation (*see note on Ro 1:7*). **grace of Christ.** God's free and sovereign act of mercy in granting salvation through the death and resurrection of Christ, totally apart from any human work or merit (*see note on Ro 3:24*). **different gospel.** Cf. 2Co 11:4. The Judaizers' perversion of the true gospel. They added the requirements, ceremonies, and standards of the Old Covenant as necessary prerequisites to salvation. *See notes on 3:3; 4:9; 5:7; Php 3:2.*

1:7 disturbing. The Gr. word means "to shake back and forth," meaning "to agitate or stir up." Here, it refers to the deep emotional disturbance the Galatian believers experienced. **distort.** To turn something into its opposite. By adding law to the gospel of Christ, the false teachers were effectively destroying grace, turning the message of God's undeserved favor toward sinners into a message of earned and merited favor. **the gospel of Christ.** The good news of salvation by grace alone through faith alone in Christ alone (*see notes on Ro 1:1; 1Co 15:1–4*).

1:8, 9 Throughout history God has devoted certain objects, individuals, and groups of people to destruction (Jos 6:17, 18; 7:1, 25, 26). The NT offers many examples of one such group: false teachers (Mt 24:24; Jn 8:44; 1Ti 1:20; Titus 1:16). Here the Judaizers are identified as members of this infamous company.

1:8 we, or an angel from heaven. Paul's point is hypothetical, calling on the most unlikely examples for false teaching—himself and holy angels. The Galatians should receive no messenger, regardless of how impeccable his credentials, if his doctrine of salvation differs in the slightest degree from God's truth revealed through Christ and the apostles. **accursed.** The translation of the familiar Gr. word *anathema,* which refers to devoting someone to destruction in eternal hell (cf. Ro 9:3; 1Co 12:3; 16:22).

1:9 As we have said before. This refers to what Paul taught during an earlier visit to these churches, not to a previous comment in this epistle. **any man.** Paul turns from the hypothetical case of v. 8 (the apostle or heavenly angels preaching a false gospel) to the real situation faced by the Galatians. The Judaizers were doing just that, and were to be devoted to destruction because of their damning heresy.

1:10–12 Because the false teachers sought to undermine Paul's spiritual credentials, he set out to defend his apostleship, explaining once again (cf. v. 1) that he was appointed by God and not by men.

1:10 still trying to please men. Paul's previous motivation when he used to persecute Christians on behalf of his fellow Jews. **a bond-servant of Christ.** *See note on Ro 1:1.* Paul had become a willing slave of Christ, which cost him a great deal of suffering from others (6:17). Such personal sacrifice is exactly opposite the goal of pleasing men (6:12).

1:11 would have you know. The strong Gr. verb Paul used here often introduced an important and emphatic statement (1Co 12:3; 2Co 8:1). **the gospel ... not according to man.** The gospel Paul preached was not human in origin, or it would have been like all other human religion, permeated with works righteousness born of man's pride and Satan's deception (Ro 1:16).

1:12 neither received it from man, nor was I taught it. In contrast to the Judaizers, who received their religious instruction from rabbinic tradition. Most Jews did not study the actual Scriptures; instead, they used human interpretations of Scripture as their religious authority and guide. Many of their traditions not only were not taught in Scripture but also contradicted it (Mk 7:13). **through a revelation.** This refers to the unveiling of something previously kept secret—in this case, Jesus Christ. While he knew about Christ, Paul subsequently met Him personally on the road to Damascus and received the truth of the gospel from Him (Ac 9:1–16).

13 For you have heard of [A]my former manner
of life in Judaism, how I [B]used to persecute [C]the
church of God beyond measure and [D]tried to destroy it; 14 and I [A]was advancing in Judaism beyond
many of my contemporaries among my [a]coun-
trymen, being more extremely zealous for my
[B]ancestral traditions. 15 But when God, who had
set me apart *even* from my mother's womb and
[A]called me through His grace, was pleased 16 to
reveal His Son in me so that I might [A]preach Him
among the Gentiles, [B]I did not immediately consult with [a,C]flesh and blood, 17 [A]nor did I go up to
Jerusalem to those who were apostles before me;
but I went away to Arabia, and returned once more
to [B]Damascus.
18 Then [A]three years later I went up [B]to Jerusalem
to [a]become acquainted with [C]Cephas, and stayed
with him fifteen days. 19 But I did not see any other
of the apostles except [a,A]James, the Lord's brother.
20 (Now in what I am writing to you, [a]I assure you
[A]before God that I am not lying.) 21 Then [A]I went
into the regions of [B]Syria and [C]Cilicia. 22 I was *still*
unknown by [a]sight to [A]the churches of Judea which
were [B]in Christ; 23 but only, they kept hearing, "He
who once persecuted us is now preaching [A]the faith
which he once [B]tried to destroy." 24 And they [A]were
glorifying God [a]because of me.

THE COUNCIL AT JERUSALEM

2 Then after an interval of fourteen years I [A]went
up again to Jerusalem with [B]Barnabas, taking
[C]Titus along also. 2 [a]It was because of a [A]revelation
that I went up; and I submitted to them the [B]gos-
pel which I preach among the Gentiles, but *I did*
so in private to those who were of reputation, for
fear that I might be [C]running, or had run, in vain.

1:13 [A]Acts 26:4f [B]Acts 8:3; 22:4, 5 [C]1 Cor 10:32 [D]Acts 9:21 1:14 [a]Lit *race* [A]Acts 22:3 [B]Jer 9:14; Matt 15:2; Mark 7:3; Col 2:8 1:15 [A]Is 49:1, 5; Jer 1:5; Acts 9:15; Rom 1:1; Gal 1:6 1:16 [a]I.e. human beings [A]Acts 9:15; Gal 2:9 [B]Acts 9:20 [C]Matt 16:17 1:17 [A]Acts 9:19-22 [B]Acts 9:2 1:18 [a]Or *visit Cephas* [A]Acts 9:22f [B]Acts 9:26 [C]John 1:42; Gal 2:9, 11, 14 1:19 [a]Or *Jacob* [A]Matt 12:46; Acts 12:17 1:20 [a]Lit *behold before God* [A]Rom 9:1; 2 Cor 1:23; 11:31 1:21 [A]Acts 9:30 [B]Acts 15:23, 41 [C]Acts 6:9 1:22 [a]Lit *face* [A]1 Cor 7:17; 1 Thess 2:14 [B]Rom 16:7 1:23 [A]Acts 6:7; Gal 6:10 [B]Acts 9:21 1:24 [a]Lit *in me* [A]Matt 9:8 2:1 [A]Acts 15:2 [B]Acts 4:36; Gal 2:9, 13 [C]2 Cor 2:13; Gal 2:3 2:2 [a]Lit *according to revelation I went up* [A]Acts 15:2; Gal 1:12 [B]Gal 1:6 [C]Rom 9:16; 1 Cor 9:24ff; Gal 5:7; Phil 2:16; 2 Tim 4:7; Heb 12:1

1:13–2:21 Paul offers a brief biographical sketch of important events in his life to further defend his apostleship and prove the authenticity of the gospel of grace he proclaimed.

1:13 Judaism. The Jewish religious system of works righteousness, based not primarily on the OT text, but on rabbinic interpretations and traditions. In fact, Paul will argue that a proper understanding of the OT can lead only to Christ and His gospel of grace through faith (3:6–29). **persecute.** The tense of this Gr. verb emphasizes Paul's persistent and continual effort to hurt and ultimately exterminate Christians. *See notes on Ac 8:1–3; 9:1; 1Ti 1:12–14.*

1:14 advancing ... beyond. The Gr. word for "advancing" means "to chop ahead," much like one would blaze a trail through a forest. Paul blazed his path in Judaism (cf. Php 3:5, 6), and because he saw Jewish Christians as obstacles to its advancement, he worked to cut them down. **extremely zealous.** Paul demonstrated this by the extent to which he pursued and persecuted Christians (cf. Ac 8:1–3; 26:11). **ancestral traditions.** The oral teachings about OT law commonly known as the "Halakah." This collection of interpretations of the law eventually carried the same authority as, or even greater than, the law (Torah) itself. Its regulations were so hopelessly complex and burdensome that even the most astute rabbinical scholars could not master it by either interpretation or conduct.

1:15 set me apart *even* from my mother's womb. Paul is not talking about being born, separated physically from his mother, but being separated or set apart to God for service from the time of his birth. The phrase refers to God's election of Paul without regard for his personal merit or effort (cf. Is 49:1; Jer 1:5; Lk 1:13–17; Ro 9:10–23). **called me through His grace.** This refers to God's effectual call (*see note on Ro 1:7*). On the Damascus Road God actually brought Saul, whom He had already chosen, to salvation.

1:16 reveal His Son in me. Not only was Christ revealed *to* Paul on the Damascus Road, but *in* him as God gave him the life, light, and faith to believe in Him. **preach Him among the Gentiles.** Paul's specific call to proclaim the gospel to non-Jews (*see notes on Ac 9:15; 26:12–18*; cf. Ro 1:13–16; 11:13; 15:18). **consult with flesh and blood.** Paul did not look to Ananias or other Christians at Damascus for clarification of or addition to the revelation he received from Christ (Ac 9:19, 20).

1:17 Jerusalem ... Arabia ... Damascus. Rather than immediately travel to Jerusalem to be instructed by the apostles, Paul instead went to Nabatean Arabia, a wilderness desert that stretched E of Damascus down to the Sinai peninsula. After being prepared for ministry by the Lord, he returned to minister in nearby Damascus.

1:18 three years. The approximate time from Paul's conversion to his first journey to Jerusalem. During those years he made a visit to Damascus and resided in Arabia, under the instruction of the Lord. This Jerusalem visit is discussed in Ac 9:26–30 (*see note on Ac 9:23*). **up to Jerusalem.** Travelers in Israel always speak of going up to Jerusalem because of its higher elevation (*see note on Ac 18:22*). **Cephas.** *See notes on Mt 10:2;* see Introduction to 1 Peter: Author and Date. The apostle Peter, who was the personal companion of the Lord and the most powerful spokesman in the early years of the Jerusalem church (Ac 1–12).

1:19 James, the Lord's brother. Cf. 2:9, 12; *see note on Ac 15:13;* see Introduction to James: Author and Date.

1:20 The directness of this statement indicates that Paul had been accused by the Jewish legalists of being a liar, who was shameless or deluded.

1:21 Syria and Cilicia. *See note on Ac 15:23;* cf. Ac 9:30. This area included his hometown of Tarsus. He was preaching in that region for several years. When word of revival in that area reached Jerusalem, they sent Barnabas (see Ac 11:20–26). Paul stayed on in that region as a pastor in the church at Antioch. With Barnabas, they went from there on the first missionary journey (Ac 13:1–3), and afterward returned to Antioch (Ac 14:26), from where they were sent to the Jerusalem Council (Ac 14:26–15:4).

1:22 Judea. *See note on Ac 1:8.*

1:23 Over the 14 years before the Jerusalem Council (*see note on 2:1*), Paul had come only twice to Jerusalem (Ac 9:26–30; 11:30) so the Christians there only knew him by reputation.

1:24 they were glorifying God because of me. Proof that the gospel Paul preached was the same one the other apostles had taught the Judean believers.

2:1–10 By recounting the details of his most significant trip to Jerusalem after his conversion, Paul offered convincing proof that the message he proclaimed was identical to that of the other 12 apostles.

2:1 fourteen years ... again to Jerusalem. This was the period from the time of his first visit to Jerusalem (1:18) to the one Paul refers to here, which probably was for the Jerusalem Council (Ac 15:1–22) called to resolve the issue of Gentile salvation. Linguistically, the word "again" need not refer to the next visit; it can just as easily mean "once again" without respect to how many visits took place in between. And in fact, Paul did visit Jerusalem during that 14-year period to deliver famine relief to the church there (Ac 11:27–30; 12:24, 25), but he does not refer to that visit here since it had no bearing on his apostolic authority. **Barnabas.** *See note on Ac 4:36.* Paul's first ally who vouched for him before the apostles at Jerusalem (Ac 9:27) and became his traveling companion on his first missionary journey (Ac 13:2, 3). **Titus.** A spiritual child of Paul and a coworker (Titus 1:4, 5). As an uncircumcised Gentile, Titus was fitting proof of the effectiveness of Paul's ministry. See Introduction to Titus: Author and Date.

2:2 because of a revelation. This revelation from God was the voice of the Holy Spirit (*see notes on Ac 13:2–4*). He refers to the divine commissioning of his visit in order to refute any suggestion by the Judaizers that they had sent Paul to Jerusalem to have the apostles correct his doctrine. **gospel.** *See note on 1:7.* **those who were of reputation.** The 3 main leaders of the Jerusalem church: Peter, James (the Lord's brother, 1:19), and John (cf. v. 9). This phrase was typically used of authorities and implied a position of honor. Paul refers to them in a similar way two other times (vv. 6, 9), suggesting a hint of sarcasm directed toward the Judaizers, who claimed they had apostolic approval for their doctrine

3 But not even [A]Titus, who was with me, though he
was a Greek, was [B]compelled to be circumcised.
4 But *it was* because of the [A]false brethren secretly
brought in, who [B]had sneaked in to spy out our
[C]liberty which we have in Christ Jesus, in order to
[D]bring us into bondage. 5 But we did not yield in
subjection to them for even an hour, so that [A]the
truth of the gospel would remain with you. 6 But
from those who [a]were of high [A]reputation (what
they were makes no difference to me; [B]God [b]shows
no partiality)—well, those who were of reputation
contributed nothing to me. 7 But on the contrary,
seeing that I had been [A]entrusted with the [B]gospel
[a]to the uncircumcised, just as [C]Peter *had been* [b]to
the circumcised 8 (for He who effectually worked
for Peter in *his* [A]apostleship [a]to the circumcised
effectually worked for me also to the Gentiles), 9 and
recognizing [A]the grace that had been given to me,
[a,B]James and [C]Cephas and John, who were [D]reputed
to be [E]pillars, gave to me and [F]Barnabas the [G]right
[b]hand of fellowship, so that we *might* [H]*go* to the
Gentiles and they to the circumcised. 10 *They* only
asked us to remember the poor—[A]the very thing I
also was eager to do.

PETER (CEPHAS) OPPOSED BY PAUL

11 But when [A]Cephas came to [B]Antioch, I opposed
him to his face, because he [a]stood condemned. 12 For
prior to the coming of certain men from [a,A]James,
he used to [B]eat with the Gentiles; but when they
came, he *began* to withdraw and hold himself aloof,
[C]fearing [b]the party of the circumcision. 13 The rest
of the Jews joined him in hypocrisy, with the result that even [A]Barnabas was carried away by their

2:3 [A]2 Cor 2:13; Gal 2:1 [B]Acts 16:3; 1 Cor 9:21 2:4 [A]Acts 15:1, 24; 2 Cor 11:13, 26; Gal 1:7 [B]2 Pet 2:1; Jude 4 [C]Gal 5:1, 13; James 1:25 [D]Rom 8:15; 2 Cor 11:20 2:5 [A]Gal 1:6; 2:14; Col 1:5 2:6 [a]Lit *seemed to be something* [b]Lit *does not receive a face* [A]2 Cor 11:5; 12:11; Gal 2:9; 6:3 [B]Acts 10:34 2:7 [a]Lit *of the uncircumcision* [b]Lit *of the circumcision* [A]1 Cor 9:17; 1 Thess 2:4; 1 Tim 1:11 [B]Acts 9:15; Gal 1:16 [C]Gal 1:18; 2:9, 11, 14 2:8 [a]Lit *of the circumcision* [A]Acts 1:25 2:9 [a]Or *Jacob* [b]Lit *hands* [A]Rom 12:3 [B]Acts 12:17; Gal 2:12 [C]Luke 22:8; Gal 1:18; 2:7, 11, 14 [D]2 Cor 11:5; 12:11; Gal 2:2, 6; 6:3 [E]1 Tim 3:15; Rev 3:12 [F]Acts 4:36; Gal 2:1, 13 [G]2 Kin 10:15 [H]Gal 1:16 2:10 [A]Acts 24:17 2:11 [a]Or *was to be condemned;* lit *was one who was condemned,* or, *was self-condemned* [A]Gal 1:18; 2:7, 9, 14 [B]Acts 11:19; 15:1 2:12 [a]Or *Jacob* [b]Or converts *from the circumcised;* lit *those from the circumcision* [A]Acts 12:17; Gal 2:9 [B]Acts 11:3 [C]Acts 11:2 2:13 [A]Acts 4:36; Gal 2:1, 9

and Paul did not. They had likely made a habit of exalting these 3 leaders at the expense of Paul. **might be running … in vain.** Paul hoped the Jerusalem leaders would support his ministry to the Gentiles and not soften their opposition to legalism. He did not want to see his ministry efforts wasted because of conflict with the other apostles.

2:3 Greek. *See note on Ro 1:14.* **compelled to be circumcised.** At the core of the Judaizers' works system was the Mosaic prescription of circumcision (*see notes on Ge 17:9–14; Ro 4:9–12*). They were teaching that there could be no salvation without circumcision (Ac 15:1, 5, 24). Paul and the apostles denied that, and it was settled at the Jerusalem Council (Ac 15:1–22). *See notes on 5:2–12; 6:15; Ro 4:10–12;* cf. 1Co 7:19. As a true believer, Titus was living proof that circumcision and the Mosaic regulations were not prerequisites or necessary components of salvation. The apostles' refusal to require Titus' circumcision verified the church's rejection of the Judaizers' doctrine (cf. Timothy, Ac 16:1–3).

2:4 false brethren. The Judaizers, who pretended to be true Christians. Yet, their doctrine, because it claimed allegiance to Christ, was opposed to traditional Judaism, and because it demanded circumcision and obedience to the Mosaic law as prerequisites for salvation, was opposed to Christianity. **to spy out.** This Gr. word pictures spies or traitors entering by stealth into an enemy's camp. The Judaizers were Satan's undercover agents sent into the midst of the church to sabotage the true gospel. **liberty.** Christians are free from the law as a means of salvation, from its external ceremonial regulations as a way of living, and from its curse for disobedience to the law—a curse that Christ bore for all believers (3:13). This freedom is not, however, a license to sin (5:13; Ro 6:18; 1Pe 2:16). **bondage.** Conveys the idea of absolute slavery to an impossible system of works righteousness.

2:5 we did not yield. Paul and Titus (v. 3) never budged from their position of salvation by grace alone through faith alone. **truth of the gospel.** The true gospel as opposed to the different (1:6–8) and false one propagated by the Judaizers (*see note on Ro 1:1*).

2:6 those who were of high reputation. Another reference to Peter, James, and John (*see note on v. 2*). **partiality.** The unique privileges of the 12 did not make their apostleship more legitimate or authoritative than Paul's—Christ commissioned them all (cf. Ro 2:11). Paul never saw himself as apostolically inferior (see 2Co 12:11, 12).

2:7 The Judaizers claimed Paul was preaching a deviant gospel, but the apostles confirmed that he proclaimed the true gospel. It was the same gospel Peter proclaimed, but to a different audience. **to the uncircumcised.** Paul preached the gospel primarily to the Gentiles (also to Jews in Gentile lands, as his pattern was to go to the synagogue first; cf. Ac 13:5). **Peter *had been* to the circumcised.** Peter's ministry was primarily to the Jews.

2:8 He who effectively worked for Peter … for me. The Holy Spirit, who has but one gospel, empowered both Peter and Paul in their ministries.

2:9 grace … given to me. The only conclusion these leaders could make was that God's grace was responsible for the powerful preaching of the gospel and the building of the church through Paul's efforts. **James and Cephas and John.** This James was Jesus' half-brother (1:19), who had risen to a prominent role in the Jerusalem church (see Introduction to James). Cephas (Peter) and John (the brother of James the apostle, martyred in Ac 12:2), were two of Christ's closest companions and became the main apostles in the Jerusalem church (see Ac 2–12). **pillars.** Emphasizing the role of James, Peter, and John in establishing and supporting the church. **Barnabas.** *See notes on v. 1; Ac 4:36.* **the right hand of fellowship.** In the Near East, this represented a solemn vow of friendship and a mark of partnership. This act signified the apostles' recognition of Paul as a teacher of the true gospel and a partner in ministry. **we *might go* to the Gentiles.** Further confirmation of Paul's divine call to ministry and a blow to the Judaizers, since the apostles directed him to continue in his already flourishing ministry to the Gentiles. **circumcised.** *See note on v. 7.*

2:10 remember the poor. A practical reminder for Paul and the growing ranks of Gentile Christians. The number of Christians in Jerusalem grew rapidly at first (cf. Ac 2:41–45; 6:1), and many who were visiting the city for the feast of Pentecost (Ac 2:1, 5) remained and never returned to their homes. While the believers initially shared their resources (Ac 2:45; 4:32–37), many had little money. For years the Jerusalem church was economically pressed. *See note on Ac 11:28.*

2:11–13 A brief account of the darkest of days in the history of the gospel. By withdrawing from the Gentile believers to fellowship with the Judaizers who held a position he knew was wrong, Peter had in appearance supported their doctrine and nullified Paul's divine teaching, especially the doctrine of salvation by grace alone through faith alone. *See notes on 2Co 6:14–18; 2Jn 10, 11.*

2:11 Antioch. *See note on Ac 11:19.* The location of the first Gentile church. **stood condemned.** Peter was guilty of sin by aligning himself with men he knew to be in error and because of the harm and confusion he caused his Gentile brethren.

2:12 certain men from James. Peter, knowing the decision the Jerusalem Council had made (Ac 15:7–29), had been in Antioch for some time, eating with Gentiles. When Judaizers came, pretending to be sent by James, they lied, giving false claims of support from the apostles. Peter had already given up all Mosaic ceremony (Ac 10:9–22) and James had at times held only to some of it (Ac 21:18–26). **withdraw.** The Gr. term refers to strategic military withdrawal. The verb's form may imply that Peter's withdrawal was gradual and deceptive. To eat with the Judaizers and decline invitations to eat with the Gentiles, which he had previously done, meant that Peter was affirming the very dietary restrictions he knew God had abolished (Ac 10:15) and thus striking a blow at the gospel of grace. **fearing the party of the circumcision.** The true motivation behind Peter's defection. He was afraid of losing popularity with the legalistic, Judaizing segment of people in the church, even though they were self-righteous hypocrites promoting a heretical doctrine.

2:13 The rest of the Jews. The Jewish be-

hypocrisy. 14 But when I saw that they [A]were not
[a]straightforward about [B]the truth of the gospel, I
said to [C]Cephas in the presence of all, "If you, being a
Jew, [D]live like the Gentiles and not like the Jews, how
is it that you compel the Gentiles to live like Jews?[b]
15 "We *are* [A]Jews by nature and not [B]sinners from
among the Gentiles; 16 nevertheless knowing that
[A]a man is not justified by the works of [a]the Law but
through faith in Christ Jesus, even we have believed
in Christ Jesus, so that we may be justified by [B]faith
in Christ and not by the works of [a]the Law; since
[C]by the works of [a]the Law no [b]flesh will be justified.
17 But if, while seeking to be justified in Christ, we
ourselves have also been found [A]sinners, is Christ
then a minister of sin? [B]May it never be! 18 For if I
rebuild what I have *once* destroyed, I [A]prove myself to be a transgressor. 19 For through [a]the Law I
[A]died to [a]the Law, so that I might live to God. 20 I
have been [A]crucified with Christ; and it is no longer I who live, but [B]Christ lives in me; and [a]the *life*
which I now live in the flesh I live by faith in [C]the
Son of God, who [D]loved me and [E]gave Himself up
for me. 21 I do not nullify the grace of God, for [A]if
righteousness *comes* through [a]the Law, then Christ
died needlessly."

FAITH BRINGS RIGHTEOUSNESS

3 [a]You foolish [A]Galatians, who has bewitched
you, before whose eyes Jesus Christ [B]was publicly portrayed *as* crucified? 2 This is the only thing
I want to find out from you: did you receive the
Spirit by the works of [a]the Law, or by [b,A]hearing with
faith? 3 Are you so foolish? Having begun [a]by the
Spirit, are you now [b]being perfected by the flesh?

2:14 [a]Or *progressing toward;* lit *walking straightly* [b]Some close the direct quotation here, others extend it through v 21 [A]Heb 12:13 [B]Gal 1:6; 2:5; Col 1:5 [C]Gal 1:18; 2:7, 9, 11 [D]Acts 10:28; Gal 2:12 2:15 [A]Phil 3:4f [B]1 Sam 15:18; Luke 24:7 2:16 [a]Or *law* [b]Or *mortal man* [A]Acts 13:39; Gal 3:11 [B]Rom 3:22; 9:30 [C]Ps 143:2; Rom 3:20 2:17 [A]Gal 2:15 [B]Luke 20:16; Gal 3:21 2:18 [A]Rom 3:5 2:19 [a]Or *law* [A]Rom 6:2; 7:4; 1 Cor 9:20 2:20 [a]Or *insofar as I* [A]Rom 6:6; Gal 5:24; 6:14 [B]Rom 8:10 [C]Matt 4:3 [D]Rom 8:37 [E]Gal 1:4 2:21 [a]Or *law* [A]Gal 3:21 3:1 [a]Lit *O* [A]Gal 1:2 [B]1 Cor 1:23; Gal 5:11 3:2 [a]Or *law* [b]Lit *the hearing of faith* [A]Rom 10:17 3:3 [a]Or *with* [b]Or *ending with*

lievers in Antioch. **hypocrisy.** The Gr. word "hypocrite" refers to an actor who wore a mask to depict a mood or certain character. In the spiritual sense, it refers to someone who masks his true character by pretending to be something he is not (cf. Mt 6:1–6). They were committed to the gospel of grace, but pretended to accept Jewish legalism.

2:14 straightforward. Lit. to walk "straight" or "uprightly." By withdrawing from the Gentile Christians, Peter and the other Jewish believers were not walking in line with God's Word. **truth of the gospel.** *See note on v. 5.* **live like the Gentiles.** Before his gradual withdrawal, Peter regularly had fellowship and ate with the Gentiles, thus modeling the ideal of Christian love and liberty between Jew and Gentile. **compel the Gentiles to live like Jews.** By his Judaizing mandate, he was declaring theirs was the right way.

2:15, 16 Paul's rebuke of Peter serves as one of the most dynamic statements in the NT on the absolute and unwavering necessity of the doctrine of justification by grace through faith (*see note on Ro 3:24*). Peter's apparent repentance acknowledged Paul's apostolic authority and his own submission to the truth (cf. 2Pe 3:15, 16).

2:15 sinners from among the Gentiles. This is used in the legal sense since Gentiles were sinners by nature because they had no revealed divine written law to guide them toward salvation or living righteously.

2:16 works ... faith. Three times in this verse Paul declares that salvation is only through faith in Christ and not by law. The first is general, "a *man* is not justified"; the second is personal, "*we* may be justified"; and the third is universal, "no *flesh* will be justified." **justified.** This basic forensic Gr. word describes a judge declaring an accused person not guilty and therefore innocent before the law. Throughout Scripture it refers to God's declaring a sinner not guilty and fully righteous before Him by imputing to him the divine righteousness of Christ and imputing the man's sin to his sinless Savior for punishment, (*see notes on Ro 3:24; Php 3:8, 9*). **works of the Law.** Keeping the law is a totally unacceptable means of salvation because the root of sinfulness is in the fallenness of man's heart, not his actions. The law served as a mirror to reveal sin, not a cure for it (*see notes on 3:22–24; Ro 7:7–13; 1Ti 1:8–11*).

2:17 we ... have also been found sinners. If the Judaizers' doctrine was correct, then Paul, Peter, Barnabas, and the other Jewish believers fell back into the category of sinners because they had been eating and fellowshiping with Gentiles, who according to the Judaizers were unclean. **minister of sin.** If the Judaizers were right, then Christ was wrong and had been teaching people to sin because He taught that food could not contaminate a person (Mk 7:19; cf. Ac 10:13–15). He also declared that all who belong to Him are one with Him and therefore one another (Jn 17:21–23). Paul's airtight logic condemned Peter, because by his actions he had in effect made it appear as if Christ was lying. This thought is utterly objectionable and causes Paul to use the strongest Gr. negative ("certainly not"; cf. 3:21; Ro 6:1, 2; 7:13).

2:18 what I have *once* destroyed. The false system of salvation through legalism (*see note on 1:13*), done away with by the preaching of salvation by grace alone through faith alone.

2:19 died to the Law. When a person is convicted of a capital crime and executed, the law has no further claim on him. So it is with the Christian who has died in Christ (who paid the penalty for his sins in full) and rises to new life in Him—justice has been satisfied and he is forever free from any further penalty. *See notes on Ro 7:1–6.*

2:20 I have been crucified with Christ. *See notes on Ro 6:2–6.* When a person trusts in Christ for salvation, he spiritually participates with the Lord in His crucifixion and His victory over sin and death. **no longer I who live, but Christ lives in me.** The believer's old self is dead (*see note on Eph 4:22*), having been crucified with Christ (Ro 6:3, 5). The believer's new self has the privilege of the indwelling Christ empowering him and living through him (*see notes on Ro 8:9, 10*). **gave Himself up for me.** The manifestation of Christ's love for the believer through His sacrificial death on the cross (Jn 10:17, 18; Ro 5:6–8; Eph 5:25–30).

2:21 Paul concluded that Peter, by taking his stand with the Judaizers and thus against Christ, was in effect denying the need for God's grace and thereby nullifying the benefit of Christ's death. **righteousness.** *See note on Ro 1:17.* **Christ died needlessly.** Those who insist they can earn salvation by their own efforts undermine the foundation of Christianity and render unnecessary the death of Christ.

3:1 foolish. This refers not to lack of intelligence, but to lack of obedience (cf. Lk 24:25; 1Ti 6:9; Titus 3:3). Paul expressed his shock, surprise, and outrage at the Galatians' defection. **who.** The Judaizers, the Jewish false teachers who were plaguing the Galatian churches (see Introduction: Background and Setting). **bewitched.** Charmed or misled by flattery and false promises. The term suggests an appeal to the emotions by the Judaizers. **publicly portrayed.** The Gr. word describes the posting of official notices in public places. Paul's preaching had publicly displayed the true gospel of Jesus Christ before the Galatians. **crucified.** The crucifixion of Christ was a onetime historical fact with continuing results into eternity. Christ's sacrificial death provides eternal payment for believers' sins (cf. Heb 7:25), and does not need to be supplemented by any human works.

3:2 did you receive the Spirit ... ? The answer to Paul's rhetorical question is obvious. The Galatians had received the Spirit when they were saved (Ro 8:9; 1Co 12:13; 1Jn 3:24; 4:13), not through keeping the law, but through saving faith granted when hearing the gospel (cf. Ro 10:17). The hearing *of* faith is actually hearing *with* faith. Paul appealed to the Galatians' own salvation to refute the Judaizers' false teaching that keeping the law is necessary for salvation.

3:3 Are you so foolish? Incredulous at how easily the Galatians had been duped, Paul asked a second rhetorical question, again rebuking them for their foolishness. **begun by the Spirit ... by the flesh.** The notion that sinful, weak (Mt 26:41; Ro 6:19), fallen human nature could improve on the saving work of the Holy Spirit was ludicrous to Paul.

4 Did you [a]suffer so many things in vain—[A]if indeed
it was in vain? 5 So then, does He who [A]provides
you with the Spirit and [B]works [a]miracles among
you, do it by the works of [b]the Law, or by [c,C]hearing
with faith?
6 [a]Even so [A]Abraham [B]BELIEVED GOD, AND IT WAS
RECKONED TO HIM AS RIGHTEOUSNESS. 7 Therefore,
[a]be sure that [A]it is those who are of faith who are
[B]sons of Abraham. 8 The Scripture, foreseeing that
God [a]would justify the [b]Gentiles by faith, preached
the gospel beforehand to Abraham, *saying,* "[A]ALL
THE NATIONS WILL BE BLESSED IN YOU." 9 So then
[A]those who are of faith are blessed with [a]Abraham,
the believer.
10 For as many as are of the works of [a]the Law are
under a curse; for it is written, "[A]CURSED IS EVERY-
ONE WHO DOES NOT ABIDE BY ALL THINGS WRITTEN
IN THE BOOK OF THE LAW, TO PERFORM THEM." 11 Now
that [A]no one is justified [a]by [b]the Law before God is
evident; for, "[c,B]THE RIGHTEOUS MAN SHALL LIVE BY
FAITH." 12 [a]However, the Law is not [b]of faith; on the
contrary, "[A]HE WHO PRACTICES THEM SHALL LIVE
[c]BY THEM." 13 Christ [A]redeemed us from the curse
of the Law, having become a curse for us—for it is
written, "[B]CURSED IS EVERYONE WHO HANGS ON [C]A
[a]TREE"— 14 in order that [A]in Christ Jesus the blessing of Abraham might [a]come to the Gentiles, so
that we [B]would receive [C]the promise of the Spirit
through faith.

INTENT OF THE LAW

15 [A]Brethren, [B]I speak [a]in terms of human relations: [c]even though it is *only* a man's [b]covenant,
yet when it has been ratified, no one sets it aside

3:4 [a]Or *experience* [A]1 Cor 15:2 3:5 [a]Or *works of power* [b]Or *law* [c]Lit *the hearing of faith* [A]2 Cor 9:10; Phil 1:19 [B]1 Cor 12:10 [C]Rom 10:17 3:6 [a]Lit *Just as* [A]Rom 4:3 [B]Gen 15:6 3:7 [a]Lit *know* [A]Rom 4:16; Gal 3:9 [B]Luke 19:9; Gal 6:16 3:8 [a]Lit *justifies* [b]Lit *nations* [A]Gen 12:3 3:9 [a]Lit *the believing Abraham* [A]Gal 3:7 3:10 [a]Or *law* [A]Deut 27:26 3:11 [a]Or *in* [b]Or *law* [c]Or *But he who is righteous by faith shall live* [A]Gal 2:16 [B]Hab 2:4; Rom 1:17; Heb 10:38 3:12 [a]Or *And* [b]Or *based on* [c]Or *in* [A]Lev 18:5; Rom 10:5 3:13 [a]Or *cross;* lit *wood* [A]Gal 4:5 [B]Deut 21:23 [C]Acts 5:30 3:14 [a]Or *occur* [A]Rom 4:9, 16; Gal 3:28 [B]Gal 3:2 [C]Acts 2:33; Eph 1:13 3:15 [a]Lit *according to man* [b]Or *will or testament* [A]Acts 1:15; Rom 1:13; Gal 6:18 [B]Rom 3:5 [C]Heb 6:16

3:4 suffer. The Gr. word has the basic meaning of "experience," and does not necessarily imply pain or hardship. Paul used it to describe the Galatians' personal experience of salvation in Jesus Christ. **many things.** This refers to all the blessings of salvation from God, Christ, and the Holy Spirit (cf. Eph 1:3). **if indeed it was in vain?** See Lk 8:13; Ac 8:13, 21; 1Co 15:2; 2Co 6:1; 13:5, 6.

3:5 hearing with faith. *See note on v. 2.*

3:6 As he does in Romans (*see note on Ro 4:3*), Paul, quoting Ge 15:6, uses Abraham as proof that there has never been any other way of salvation than by grace through faith. Even the OT teaches justification by faith.

3:7 sons of Abraham. Believing Jews and Gentiles are the true spiritual children of Abraham because they follow his example of faith (cf. v. 29; Ro 4:11, 16).

3:8 Scripture, foreseeing. Personifying the Scriptures was a common Jewish figure of speech (cf. 4:30; Jn 7:38, 42; 19:37; Ro 9:17; 10:11; 11:2; 1Ti 5:18). Because Scripture is God's Word, when it speaks, God speaks. **preached the gospel ... to Abraham.** The "good news" to Abraham was the news of salvation for all the nations (quoted from Ge 12:3; 18:18). See Ge 22:18; Jn 8:56; Ac 26:22, 23. Salvation has always, in every age, been by faith.

3:9 those who are of faith ... with Abraham. Whether Jew or Gentile. The OT predicted that Gentiles would receive the blessings of justification by faith, as did Abraham. Those blessings are poured out on all because of Christ (cf. Jn 1:16; Ro 8:32; Eph 1:3; 2:6, 7; Col 2:10; 1Pe 3:9; 2Pe 1:3, 4).

3:10 as many as are of the works of the Law. Those attempting to earn salvation by keeping the law. **under a curse.** Quoted from Dt 27:26 to show that failure to perfectly keep the law brings divine judgment and condemnation. One violation of the law deserves the curse of God. Cf. Dt 27, 28. **all things.** See Jas 2:10. No one can keep all the commands of the law—not even strict Pharisees like Saul of Tarsus (Ro 7:7–12).

3:11 no one is justified by the Law. Cf. Ro 3:20. **justified.** Made righteous before God. *See note on Ro 3:24.* The righteous man shall live by faith. *See note on Ro 1:17.* Paul's earlier OT quote (v. 10; cf. Dt 27:26) showed that justification does not come from keeping the law; this quote from Hab 2:4 shows that justification is by faith alone (cf. Heb 10:38).

3:12 the Law is not of faith. Justification by faith and justification by keeping the law are mutually exclusive, as Paul's OT quote from Lv 18:5 proves.

3:13 Christ redeemed us from the curse of the Law. The Gr. word translated "redeemed" was often used to speak of buying a slave's or debtor's freedom. Christ's death, because it was a death of substitution for sin, satisfied God's justice and exhausted His wrath toward His elect, so that Christ actually purchased believers from slavery to sin and from the sentence of eternal death (4:5; Titus 2:14; 1Pe 1:18; cf. Ro 3:24; 1Co 1:30; Eph 1:7; Col 1:14; Heb 9:12). **having become a curse for us.** By bearing God's wrath for believers' sins on the cross (*see note on 2Co 5:21*; cf. Heb 9:28; 1Pe 2:24; 3:18), Christ took upon Himself the curse pronounced on those who violated the law (*see note on v. 10*). **it is written.** The common NT way (61 times) of introducing OT quotes, (*see note on Ro 3:10*). Dt 21:23 is quoted.

3:14 the blessing of Abraham. Faith in God's promise of salvation. *See note on v. 9.* **promise of the Spirit.** From God the Father. Cf. Is 32:15; 44:3; 59:19–21; Eze 36:26, 27; 37:14; 39:29; Joel 2:28, 29; Lk 11:13; 24:49; Jn 7:37–39; 14:16, 26.

3:15–22 Paul anticipated and refuted a possible objection to his use of Abraham to prove the doctrine of justification by faith, that the giving of the law at Sinai after Abraham brought about a change and a better method of salvation. The apostle dismissed that argument by showing the superiority of the Abrahamic Covenant (vv. 15–18), and the inferiority of the law (vv. 19–22).

3:15 Brethren. This term of endearment reveals Paul's compassionate love for the Galatians—which they may have begun to question in light of his stern rebuke (vv. 1, 3). **man's covenant.** Even human covenants, once confirmed, are considered irrevocable and unchangeable, how much more a covenant made by an unchanging God (Mal 3:6; Jas 1:17).

LAW AND GRACE

The Function		The Effect	
Of Law	**Of Grace**	**Of Law**	**Of Grace**
Based on works (3:10)	Based on faith (3:11, 12)	Works put us under a curse (3:10)	Justifies us by faith (3:3, 24)
Our guardian (3:23; 4:2)	Centered in Christ (3:24)	Keeps us for faith (3:23)	Christ lives in us (2:20)
Our tutor (3:24)	Our certificate of freedom (4:30, 31)	Brings us to Christ (3:24)	Adopts us as sons and heirs (4:7)

The law functions to 1) declare our guilt, 2) drive us to Christ, and 3) direct us in a life of obedience. However, the law is powerless to save.

or adds [c]conditions to it. 16 Now the promises were
spoken [A]to Abraham and to his seed. He does not
say, "And to seeds," as *referring* to many, but *rather*
to one, "[B]And to your seed," that is, Christ. 17 What I
am saying is this: the Law, which came [A]four hundred and thirty years later, does not invalidate a
covenant previously ratified by God, so as to nullify
the promise. 18 For [A]if the inheritance is [a]based on
law, it is no longer [a]based on a promise; but [B]God
has granted it to Abraham by means of a promise.
19 [A]Why the Law then? It was added [a]because of
transgressions, having been [B]ordained through
angels [C]by the [b]agency of a mediator, until [D]the
seed would come to whom the promise had been
made. 20 Now [A]a mediator is not [a]for one *party*
only; whereas God is *only* one. 21 Is the Law then
contrary to the promises of God? [A]May it never
be! For [B]if a law had been given which was able
to impart life, then righteousness [a]would indeed
have been [b]based on law. 22 But the Scripture has
[A]shut up [a]everyone under sin, so that the promise
by faith in Jesus Christ might be given to those
who believe.
23 But before faith came, we were kept in custody
under the law, [A]being shut up to the faith which was
later to be revealed. 24 Therefore the Law has become
our [A]tutor *to lead us* to Christ, so that [B]we may be
justified by faith. 25 But now that faith has come, we
are no longer under a [a,A]tutor. 26 For you are all [A]sons
of God through faith in [B]Christ Jesus. 27 For all of you
who were [A]baptized into Christ have [B]clothed yourselves with Christ. 28 [A]There is neither Jew nor Greek,
there is neither slave nor free man, there is [a]neither
male nor female; for [B]you are all one in [C]Christ Jesus.

3:15 [c]Or *a codicil* 3:16 [A]Luke 1:55; Rom 4:13, 16; 9:4 [B]Acts 3:25 3:17 [A]Gen 15:13f; Ex 12:40; Acts 7:6 3:18 [a]Lit *out of, from* [A]Rom 4:14 [B]Heb 6:14 3:19 [a]Or *for the sake of defining* [b]Lit *hand* [A]Rom 5:20 [B]Acts 7:53 [C]Ex 20:19; Deut 5:5 [D]Gal 3:16 3:20 [a]Lit *of one* [A]1 Tim 2:5; Heb 8:6; 9:15; 12:24 3:21 [a]Or *would indeed be* [b]Lit *out of, from* [A]Luke 20:16; Gal 2:17 [B]Gal 2:21 3:22 [a]Lit *things* [A]Rom 11:32 3:23 [A]Rom 11:32 3:24 [A]1 Cor 4:15 [B]Gal 2:16 3:25 [a]Lit *child-conductor* [A]1 Cor 4:15 3:26 [A]Rom 8:14; Gal 4:5 [B]Rom 8:1; Gal 3:28; 4:14; 5:6, 24; Eph 1:1; Phil 1:1; Col 1:4; 1 Tim 1:12; 2 Tim 1:1; Titus 1:4 3:27 [A]Matt 28:19; Rom 6:3; 1 Cor 10:2 [B]Rom 13:14 3:28 [a]Lit *not male and female* [A]Rom 3:22; 1 Cor 12:13; Col 3:11 [B]John 17:11; Eph 2:15 [C]Rom 8:1; Gal 3:26; 4:14; 5:6, 24; Eph 1:1; Phil 1:1; Col 1:4; 1 Tim 1:12; 2 Tim 1:1; Titus 1:4

3:16 **promises.** Those associated with the Abrahamic Covenant (Ge 12:3, 7; 13:15, 16; 15:5, 18; 17:8; 22:16–18; 26:3, 4; 28:13, 14). Because they were made both to Abraham and his descendants, they did not become void when Abraham died, or when the law came. **seed.** Cf. v. 19. The quote is from Ge 12:7. The singular form of the Heb. word, like its Eng. and Gr. counterparts, can be used in a collective sense. Paul's point is that in some OT passages (e.g., Ge 3:15; 22:18), "seed" refers to the greatest of Abraham's descendants, Jesus Christ.

3:17 **four hundred and thirty years.** From Israel's sojourn in Egypt (cf. Ex 12:40) to the giving of the law at Sinai (ca. 1445 B.C.). The law actually came 645 years after the initial promise to Abraham (ca. 2090 B.C.; cf. Ge 12:4; 21:5; 25:26; 47:9), but the promise was repeated to Isaac (Ge 26:24) and later to Jacob (ca. 1928 B.C.; Ge 28:15). The last known reaffirmation of the Abrahamic Covenant to Jacob occurred in Ge 46:2–4 (ca. 1875 B.C.) just before he went to Egypt—430 years before the Mosaic law was given. **a covenant.** The Abrahamic Covenant (*see note on v. 16*). For a discussion of the biblical covenants, *see notes on Ge 9:16; 12:1–3; Ro 9:4.* **previously ratified by God.** *See note on v. 15.* Once God ratified the covenant officially (*see notes on Ge 15:9–21*), it had lasting authority so that nothing and no one could annul it. The Abrahamic Covenant was unilateral (God made the promise to Himself), eternal (it provided for everlasting blessing), irrevocable (it will never cease), unconditional (in that it depended on God, not man), but its complete fulfillment awaits the salvation of Israel and the millennial kingdom of Jesus Christ.

3:18 Paul again emphasized that there is no middle ground between law (works) and promise (grace); the two principles are mutually exclusive ways of salvation (cf. Rom 4:14). An "inheritance" by definition is something granted, not worked for, as proven in the case of Abraham.

3:19–22 Having shown the superiority of the promise to Abraham (vv. 15–18), Paul described the inferiority of the law, and its purpose.

3:19 **was added because of transgressions.** Paul's persuasive argument that the promise is superior to the law raises an obvious question: what was the purpose of the law? Paul's answer is that the law reveals man's utter sinfulness, inability to save himself, and desperate need of a Savior—it was never intended to be the way of salvation (cf. Ro 7:1–13). **through angels.** The Bible teaches that angels were involved in the giving of the law (cf. Ac 7:53; Heb 2:2), but does not explain the precise role they played. **seed.** *See note on v. 16.*

3:20 **mediator.** Paul's point is apparently that a "mediator" is required when more than one party is involved, but God alone ratified the covenant with Abraham (*see notes on Ge 15:7–21*).

3:21 Paul uses the strongest Gr. negative (*see note on 2:17*) to disdain the idea that the law and the promise are at opposite purposes. Since God gave them both and does not work against Himself, law and promise work in harmony; the law reveals man's sinfulness and need for the salvation freely offered in the promise. If the law could have provided righteousness and eternal life, there would be no gracious promise.

3:22 **shut up everyone under sin.** The Gr. verb translated "shut up" means "to enclose on all sides." Paul portrays all mankind as hopelessly trapped in sin, like a school of fish caught in a net. That all people are sinners is the express teaching of Scripture (*see note on Ro 3:19*; cf. 1Ki 8:46; Ps 143:2; Pr 20:9; Ecc 7:20; Is 53:6; Ro 3:9–19, 23; 11:32).

3:23 **before faith came.** From the viewpoints of both the history of redemption and through all times in the area of individual salvation (cf. vv. 19, 24, 25; 4:1–4), only saving faith unlocks the door of the prison where the law keeps men bound. **kept in custody under the law.** Paul personifies the law as a jailer of guilty, condemned sinners, on death row awaiting God's judgment (Ro 6:23). **the faith . . . later to be revealed.** Again Paul was looking at the coming of Christ, historically and at each believer's salvation, individually. Faith in Christ alone releases people from bondage to law, whether the Mosaic law, or the law written on the hearts of Gentiles (Ro 2:14–16).

3:24 **tutor.** The Gr. word denotes a slave whose duty it was to take care of a child until adulthood. The "tutor" escorted the children to and from school and watched over their behavior at home. Tutors were often strict disciplinarians, causing those under their care to yearn for the day when they would be free from their tutor's custody. The law was our tutor which, by showing us our sins, was escorting us to Christ.

3:25, 26 Believers, through faith in Jesus Christ, have come of age as God's children. Thus, they are not under the tutelage of the law (Ro 6:14), although they are still obligated to obey God's holy and unchanging righteous standards which are now given authority in the New Covenant (6:2; Ro 8:4; 1Co 9:21).

3:26 **sons of God.** While God is the Father of all people in a general sense because He created them (Ac 17:24–28), only those who have put their faith in Jesus Christ are God's true spiritual children. Unbelievers are the children of Satan (Mt 13:38; Jn 8:38, 41, 44; Ac 13:10; 1Jn 3:10; cf. Eph 2:3; 1Jn 5:19).

3:27 **baptized into Christ.** This is not water baptism, which cannot save (*see notes on Ac 2:38; 22:16*). Paul used the word "baptized" in a metaphorical manner to speak of being "immersed," or "placed into" Christ (cf. 2:20) by the spiritual miracle of union with Him in His death and resurrection. *See notes on Ro 6:3, 4;* cf. 1Co 6:17. **clothed yourselves with Christ.** The result of the believer's spiritual union with Christ. Paul was emphasizing the fact that we have been united with Christ through salvation. Positionally before God, we have put on Christ, His death, resurrection, and righteousness (*see notes on Php 3:8–10*). Practically, we need to clothe ourselves with Christ before men, in our conduct (Ro 13:14).

3:28 **you are all one in Christ Jesus.** All those who are one with Jesus Christ are one with one another. This verse does not deny that God has designed racial, social, and sexual distinctions among Christians, but it affirms that those do not imply spiritual inequality before God. Nor is this spiritual equality incompatible with the God-ordained roles of headship and submission in the church, society, and at home. Jesus Christ, though fully equal with the Father, assumed a submissive role during His incarnation (Php 2:5–8).

29 And if [A]you [a]belong to Christ, then you are Abraham's [b]descendants, heirs according to [B]promise.

SONSHIP IN CHRIST

4 Now I say, as long as the heir is a [a]child, he
does not differ at all from a slave although he
is [b]owner of everything, 2 but he is under guardians and [a]managers until the date set by the father.
3 So also we, while we were children, were held
[A]in bondage under the [a,B]elemental things of the
world. 4 But when [A]the fullness of the time came,
God sent forth His Son, [B]born of a woman, born
[C]under [a]the Law, 5 so that He might redeem those
who were under [a]the Law, that we might receive
the adoption as [A]sons. 6 Because you are sons, [A]God
has sent forth the Spirit of His Son into our hearts,
crying, "[B]Abba! Father!" 7 Therefore you are no longer a slave, but a son; and [A]if a son, then an heir
[a]through God.
8 However at that time, [A]when you did not know
God, you were [B]slaves to [C]those which by nature are
no gods. 9 But now that you have come to know God,
or rather to be [A]known by God, [B]how is it that you
turn back again to the weak and worthless [a,C]ele-
mental things, to which you desire to be enslaved
all over again? 10 You [A]observe days and months and
seasons and years. 11 I fear for you, that perhaps I
have labored [a]over you in vain.
12 I beg of you, [A]brethren, [B]become as I *am,* for
I also *have become* as you *are.* You have done me

3:29 [a]Lit *are Christ's* [b]Lit *seed* [A]Rom 4:13; 1 Cor 3:23 [B]Rom 9:8; Gal 3:18; 4:28 4:1 [a]Or *minor* [b]Lit *lord* 4:2 [a]Or *stewards* 4:3 [a]Or *rudimentary teachings* or *principles* [A]Gal 2:4; 4:8f, 24f [B]Gal 4:9; Col 2:8, 20; Heb 5:12 4:4 [a]Or *law* [A]Mark 1:15 [B]John 1:14; Rom 1:3; 8:3; Phil 2:7 [C]Luke 2:21f, 27 4:5 [a]Or *law* [A]Rom 8:14; Gal 3:26 4:6 [A]Acts 16:7; Rom 5:5; 8:9, 16; 2 Cor 3:17 [B]Mark 14:36; Rom 8:15 4:7 [a]I.e. through the gracious act of [A]Rom 8:17 4:8 [A]1 Cor 1:21; Eph 2:12; 1 Thess 4:5; 2 Thess 1:8 [B]Gal 4:3 [C]2 Chr 13:9; Is 37:19; Jer 2:11; 1 Cor 8:4f; 10:20 4:9 [a]Or *rudimentary teachings* or *principles* [A]1 Cor 8:3 [B]Col 2:20 [C]Gal 4:3 4:10 [A]Rom 14:5; Col 2:16 4:11 [a]Or *for* 4:12 [A]Gal 6:18 [B]2 Cor 6:11, 13

3:29 Abraham's descendants. *See note on v. 7.* Not all physical children of Abraham are the "Israel of God" (cf. 6:16), that is, true spiritual children of Abraham (Ro 9:6–8). Gentile believers who are not physical children of Abraham are, however, his spiritual children in the sense that they followed the pattern of his faith (*see note on Ro 4:11, 12*). **heirs according to promise.** All believers are heirs of the spiritual blessing that accompanied the Abrahamic Covenant—justification by faith (Ge 15:6; cf. Ro 4:3–11).

4:1–7 Paul expands on the analogy of a child's coming of age (3:24–26), contrasting believers' lives before salvation (as children and servants), with their lives after salvation (as adults and sons). Both Paul's Jewish and Gentile readers readily understood this imagery, since the Jews, Greeks, and Romans all had a ceremony to mark a child's coming of age.

4:1 child. The Gr. word refers to a child too young to talk; a minor, spiritually and intellectually immature and not ready for the privileges and responsibilities of adulthood.

4:2 guardians and managers. "Guardians" were slaves entrusted with the care of underage boys, while "managers" managed their property for them until they came of age. Along with the tutor (3:24), they had almost complete charge of the child—so that, for all practical purposes, a child under their care did not differ from a slave.

4:3 while we were children ... in bondage. Before our "coming of age" when we came to saving faith in Jesus Christ. **the elemental things of the world.** "Elemental" is from a Gr. word meaning "row," or "rank," and was used to speak of basic, foundational things like the letters of the alphabet. In light of its use in v. 9, it is best to see it here as a reference to the basic elements and rituals of human religion (*see note on Col 2:8*). Paul describes both Jewish and Gentile religions as elemental because they are merely human, never rising to the level of the divine. Both Jewish religion and Gentile religion centered on man-made systems of works. They were filled with laws and ceremonies to be performed so as to achieve divine acceptance. All such rudimentary elements are immature, like behaviors of children under bondage to a guardian.

4:4 the fullness of the time. In God's timetable, when the exact religious, cultural, and political conditions demanded by His perfect plan were in place, Jesus came into the world. **God sent forth His Son.** As a father set the time for the ceremony of his son becoming of age and being released from the guardians, managers, and tutors, so God sent His Son at the precise moment to bring all who believe out from under bondage to the law—a truth Jesus repeatedly affirmed (Jn 5:30, 36, 37; 6:39, 44, 57; 8:16, 18, 42; 12:49; 17:21, 25; 20:21). That the Father sent Jesus into the world teaches His preexistence as the eternal second member of the Trinity. *See notes on Php 2:6, 7; Heb 1:3–5*; cf. Ro 8:3, 4. **born of a woman.** This emphasizes Jesus' full humanity, not merely His virgin birth (Is 7:14; Mt 1:20–25). Jesus had to be fully God for His sacrifice to be of the infinite worth needed to atone for sin. But, He also had to be fully man so He could take upon Himself the penalty of sin as the substitute for man. See Lk 1:32, 35; Jn 1:1, 14, 18. **under the Law.** Like all men, Jesus was obligated to obey God's law. Unlike anyone else, however, He perfectly obeyed that law (Jn 8:46; 2Co 5:21; Heb 4:15; 7:26; 1Pe 2:22; 1Jn 3:5). His sinlessness made Him the unblemished sacrifice for sins, who perfectly obeyed God in everything. That perfect righteousness is what is imputed to those who believe in Him.

4:5 redeem. *See note on 3:13.* **those ... under the Law.** Guilty sinners who are under the law's demands and its curses (*see notes on 3:10, 13*) and in need of a Savior (*see note on 3:23*). **the adoption as sons.** "Adoption" is the act of bringing someone who is the offspring of another into one's own family. Since unregenerate people are by nature children of the devil (*see note on 3:26*), the only way they can become God's children is by spiritual adoption (Ro 8:15, 23; Eph 1:5).

4:6 Spirit of His Son. It is the Holy Spirit's work to confirm to believers their adoption as God's children (*see note on Ro 8:15*). Assurance of salvation is a gracious work of the Holy Spirit and does not come from any human source. **Abba!** An Aram. term of endearment, used by young children to speak to their fathers; the equivalent of the word "Daddy" (*see note on Ro 8:15*).

4:8–11 While salvation is the free gift of God (Ro 5:15, 16, 18; 6:23; Eph 2:8), it brings with it serious responsibility (cf. Lk 12:48). God requires believers to live a holy life because they are children of a holy God and desire to love and worship Him (Mt 5:48; 1Pe 1:15–18). That obligation was to the unchanging moral and spiritual principles that forever reflect the nature of God; however, it did not include the rituals and ceremonies unique to Israel under Mosaic law as the Judaizers falsely claimed.

4:8 when you did not know God. Before coming to saving faith in Christ, no unsaved person knows God. *See notes on Eph 4:17–19; 2Co 4:3–6.* **by nature are no gods.** The Greco-Roman pantheon of non-existent deities the Galatians had imagined they worshiped before their conversion (cf. Ro 1:23; 1Co 8:4; 10:19, 20; 12:2; 1Th 1:9).

4:9 known by God. We can know God only because He first knew us, just as we choose Him only because He first chose us (Jn 6:44; 15:16), and we love Him only because He first loved us (1Jn 4:19). **turn back again.** *See notes on 3:1–3.* **weak ... elemental things ... enslaved ... again.** *See note on v. 3.*

4:10 days ... years. The rituals, ceremonies, and festivals of the Jewish religious calendar which God had given, but were never required for the church. Paul warns the Galatians, as he did the Colossians (*see notes on Ro 14:1–6; Col 2:16, 17*), against legalistically observing them as if they were required by God or could earn favor with Him.

4:11 labored ... in vain. Paul feared that his effort in establishing and building the Galatian churches might prove to be futile if they fell back into legalism (cf. 3:4; 1Th 3:5).

4:12–20 Having sternly rebuked the Galatians, Paul changes his approach and makes an appeal based on his strong affection for them.

4:12 become as I *am,* for I also *have become* as you *are.* Paul had been a proud, self-righteous Pharisee, trusting in his own righteousness to save him (cf. Php 3:4–6). But when he came to Christ, he abandoned all efforts to save himself, trusting wholly in God's grace (Php 3:7–9). He urged the Galatians to follow his example and avoid the legalism of the Judaizers. **You have done me no wrong.** Though the Jews persecuted him when he first went to Galatia, the Galatian believers had not harmed Paul, but had enthusiastically received him when he preached the gospel to them (cf. Ac 13:42–50; 14:19). How, he asked, could they reject him now?

no wrong; 13but you know that it was because of a
[a]bodily illness that I preached the gospel to you the
[b]first time; 14and that which was a [a]trial to you in
my [b]bodily condition you did not despise or [c]loathe,
but [A]you received me as an angel of God, as [B]Christ
Jesus *Himself.* 15Where then is [a]that sense of blessing
you had? For I bear you witness that, if possible, you
would have plucked out your eyes and given them to
me. 16So have I become your enemy [A]by [a]telling you
the truth? 17They eagerly seek you, not commendably,
but they wish to shut you out so that you will seek
them. 18But it is good always to be eagerly sought
in a commendable [a]manner, and [A]not only when I
am present with you. 19[A]My children, with whom [B]I
am again in labor until [C]Christ is formed in you—
20but I could wish to be present with you now and
to change my tone, for [A]I am perplexed about you.

BOND AND FREE

21Tell me, you who want to be under law, do
you not [A]listen to the law? 22For it is written that
Abraham had two sons, [A]one by the bondwoman
and [B]one by the free woman. 23But [A]the son by the
bondwoman [a]was born according to the flesh, and
[B]the son by the free woman through the promise.
24[a,A]This is allegorically speaking, for these *women*
are two covenants: one *proceeding* from [B]Mount
Sinai bearing children [b]who are to be [c]slaves; [c]she
is Hagar. 25Now this Hagar is Mount Sinai in Arabia and corresponds to the present Jerusalem,
for she is in slavery with her children. 26But [A]the
Jerusalem above is free; [a]she is our mother. 27For
it is written,

> "[A]REJOICE, BARREN WOMAN
> WHO DOES NOT BEAR;
> BREAK FORTH AND SHOUT, YOU
> WHO ARE NOT IN LABOR;
> FOR MORE NUMEROUS ARE THE
> CHILDREN OF THE DESOLATE
> THAN OF THE ONE WHO
> HAS A HUSBAND."

4:13 [a]Lit *weakness of the flesh* [b]Or *former* 4:14 [a]Or *temptation* [b]Lit *flesh* [c]Lit *spit out at* [A]Matt 10:40; 1 Thess 2:13 [B]Gal 3:26 4:15 [a]Lit *the congratulation of yourselves* 4:16 [a]Or *dealing truthfully with you* [A]Amos 5:10 4:18 [a]Or *thing* [A]Gal 4:13f 4:19 [A]1 John 2:1 [B]1 Cor 4:15 [C]Eph 4:13 4:20 [A]2 Cor 4:8 4:21 [A]Luke 16:29 4:22 [A]Gen 16:15 [B]Gen 21:2 4:23 [a]Lit *has been born* [A]Rom 9:7; Gal 4:29 [B]Gen 17:16ff; 18:10ff; 21:1; Gal 4:28; Heb 11:11 4:24 [a]Lit *Which* [b]Lit *into slavery* [c]Lit *which* [A]1 Cor 10:11 [B]Deut 33:2 [C]Gal 4:3 4:26 [a]Lit *which* [A]Heb 12:22; Rev 3:12; 21:2, 10 4:27 [A]Is 54:1

4:13 bodily illness. Some think the illness Paul refers to was malaria, possibly contracted in the coastal lowlands of Pamphylia. That could explain why Paul and Barnabas apparently did not preach at Perga, a city in Pamphylia (cf. Ac 13:13, 14). The cooler and healthier weather in Galatia and especially at Pisidian Antioch (3,600 ft. above sea level), where Paul went when he left Perga, would have brought some relief to the fever caused by malaria. Although malaria is a serious, debilitating disease, its attacks are not continuous; Paul could have ministered between bouts with fever.

4:14 you received me. The Galatians welcomed Paul in spite of his illness, which in no way was a barrier to his credibility or acceptance. **as Christ Jesus.** *See notes on Mt 18:5–10.*

4:15 blessing you had. "Blessing" can also be translated "happiness," or "satisfaction." Paul points out that the Galatians had been happy and content with his gospel preaching (cf. Ac 13:48) and wonders why they had turned against him. **plucked out your eyes.** This may be a figure of speech (cf. Mt 5:29; 18:9), or an indication that Paul's bodily illness (*see note on v. 13*) had somehow affected his eyes (cf. 6:11). In either case, it reflects the great love the Galatians had initially expressed for the apostle.

4:16 your enemy. The Galatians had become so confused that, in spite of their previous affection for Paul, some had come to regard him as their enemy. The apostle reminds them that he had not harmed them, but merely told them the truth—a truth that had once brought them great joy (*see note on v. 15*).

4:17 They. The Judaizers (see Introduction: Background and Setting). **eagerly.** With a serious concern, or warm interest (the same word is used in 1:14 to describe Paul's former zeal for Judaism). The Judaizers appeared to have a genuine interest in the Galatians, but their true motive was to exclude the Galatians from God's gracious salvation and win recognition for themselves.

4:18 not only when I am present. Paul encouraged the Galatians to have the same zeal for the true gospel of grace that they had had when he was with them.

4:19 My children. Paul's only use of this affectionate phrase, which John uses frequently ("My little children," 1Jn 2:1, 18, 28; 3:7, 18; 4:4; 5:21). **until Christ is formed in you.** In contrast to the evil motives of the Judaizers (*see note on 3:1*), Paul sought to bring the Galatians to Christlikeness. This is the goal of salvation (*see notes on Ro 8:29*).

4:20 am perplexed. The verb means "to be at wits end."

4:21–5:1 Paul, continuing to contrast grace and law, faith and works, employs an OT story as an analogy or illustration of what he has been teaching.

4:21 under law. *See note on 3:10.*

4:22 two sons. Ishmael, son of Sarah's Egyptian maid Hagar (Ge 16:1–16), and Isaac, Sarah's son (Gen 21:1–7).

4:23 according to the flesh. Ishmael's birth was motivated by Abraham and Sarah's lack of faith in God's promise and fulfilled by sinful human means. **through the promise.** God miraculously enabled Abraham and Sarah to have Isaac when Sarah was well past childbearing age and had been barren her entire life.

4:24 allegorically speaking. The Gr. word was used of a story that conveyed a meaning beyond the literal sense of the words. In this passage, Paul uses historical people and places from the OT to illustrate spiritual truth. This is actually not an allegory, nor are there any allegories in Scripture. An allegory is a fictional story where real truth is the secret, mysterious, hidden meaning. The story of Abraham, Sarah, Hagar, Ishmael, and Isaac is actual history and has no secret or hidden meaning. Paul uses it only as an illustration to support his contrast between law and grace. **two covenants.** Paul uses the two mothers, their two sons, and two locations as a further illustration of two covenants. Hagar, Ishmael, and Mt. Sinai (earthly Jerusalem) represent the covenant of law; Sarah, Isaac, and the heavenly Jerusalem the covenant of promise. However, Paul cannot be contrasting these two covenants as different ways of salvation, one way for OT saints, another for NT saints—a premise he has already denied (2:16; 3:10–14, 21, 22). The purpose of the Mosaic Covenant was only to show all who were under its demands and condemnation their desperate need for salvation by grace alone (3:24)—it was never intended to portray the way of salvation. Paul's point is that those, like the Judaizers, who attempt to earn righteousness by keeping the law receive only bondage and condemnation (3:10, 23). While those who partake of salvation by grace—the only way of salvation since Adam's sin—are freed from the law's bondage and condemnation. **Mount Sinai.** An appropriate symbol for the old covenant, since it was at Mt. Sinai that Moses received the law (Ex 19). **Hagar.** Since she was Sarah's slave (Ge 16:1), Hagar is a fitting illustration of those under bondage to the law (cf. vv. 5, 21; 3:23). She was actually associated with Mt. Sinai through her son Ishmael, whose descendants settled in that region.

4:25 corresponds to . . . Jerusalem. The law was given at Sinai and received its highest expression in the temple worship at Jerusalem. The Jewish people were still in bondage to the law.

4:26 Jerusalem above is free. Heaven (Heb 12:18, 22). Those who are citizens of heaven (Php 3:20) are free from the Mosaic law, works, bondage, and trying endlessly and futilely to please God by the flesh. **our mother.** Believers are children of the heavenly Jerusalem, the "mother-city" of heaven. In contrast to the slavery of Hagar's children, believers in Christ are free (5:1; Is 61:1; Lk 4:18; Jn 8:36; Ro 6:18, 22; 8:2; 2Co 3:17).

4:27 Paul applies the passage from Is 54:1 to the Jerusalem above.

28 And you brethren, [A]like Isaac, are [B]children of
promise. 29 But as at that time [A]he who was born
according to the flesh [B]persecuted him *who was*
born according to the Spirit, [C]so it is now also. 30 But
what does the Scripture say?

"[A]CAST OUT THE BONDWOMAN AND HER SON,
FOR [B]THE SON OF THE BONDWOMAN
SHALL NOT BE AN HEIR WITH THE
SON OF THE FREE WOMAN."

31 So then, brethren, we are not children of a bondwoman, [a]but of the free woman.

WALK BY THE SPIRIT

5 [a,A]It was for freedom that Christ set us free;
therefore [B]keep standing firm and do not be
subject again to a [C]yoke of slavery.
2 Behold I, [A]Paul, say to you that if you receive
[B]circumcision, Christ will be of no benefit to you.
3 And I [A]testify again to every man who receives
[B]circumcision, that he is under obligation to [C]keep
the whole Law. 4 You have been severed from Christ,
you who [a]are seeking to be justified by law; you have
[A]fallen from grace. 5 For we [a]through the Spirit, [b]by
faith, are [A]waiting for the hope of righteousness.
6 For in [A]Christ Jesus [B]neither circumcision nor uncircumcision means anything, but [C]faith working
through love.
7 You were [A]running well; who hindered you from
obeying the truth? 8 This persuasion *did* not *come*
from [A]Him who calls you. 9 [A]A little leaven leavens
the whole lump *of dough*. 10 [A]I have confidence [a]in
you in the Lord that you [B]will adopt no other view;
but the one who is [C]disturbing you will bear his
judgment, whoever he is. 11 But I, brethren, if I still
preach circumcision, why am I still [A]persecuted?
Then [B]the stumbling block of the cross has been
abolished. 12 I wish that [A]those who are troubling
you would even [a,B]mutilate themselves.

4:28 [A]Gal 4:23 [B]Rom 9:7ff; Gal 3:29 4:29 [A]Gal 4:23 [B]Gen 21:9 [C]Gal 5:11 4:30 [A]Gen 21:10, 12 [B]John 8:35 4:31 [a]V 5:1, note 1 5:1 [a]Some authorities prefer to join with 4:31 and render *but with the freedom of the free woman Christ set us free* [A]John 8:32, 36; Rom 8:15; 2 Cor 3:17; Gal 2:4; 5:13 [B]1 Cor 16:13 [C]Acts 15:10; Gal 2:4 5:2 [A]2 Cor 10:1 [B]Acts 15:1; Gal 5:3, 6, 11 5:3 [A]Luke 16:28 [B]Acts 15:1; Gal 5:2, 6, 11 [C]Rom 2:25 5:4 [a]Or *would be* [A]Heb 12:15; 2 Pet 3:17 5:5 [a]Lit *by* [b]Lit *out of* [A]Rom 8:23; 1 Cor 1:7 5:6 [A]Gal 3:26 [B]1 Cor 7:19; Gal 6:15 [C]Col 1:4f; 1 Thess 1:3; James 2:18, 20, 22 5:7 [A]Gal 2:2 5:8 [A]Rom 8:28; Gal 1:6 5:9 [A]1 Cor 5:6 5:10 [a]Lit *toward* [A]2 Cor 2:3 [B]Gal 5:7; Phil 3:15 [C]Gal 1:7; 5:12 5:11 [A]Gal 4:29; 6:12 [B]Rom 9:33; 1 Cor 1:23 5:12 [a]Or *cut themselves off* [A]Gal 2:4; 5:10 [B]Deut 23:1

4:28 children of promise. Just as Isaac inherited the promises made to Abraham (Ge 26:1–3), so also are believers the recipients of God's redemptive promises (1Co 3:21–23; Eph 1:3), because they are spiritual heirs of Abraham (*see note on 3:29*).

4:29 he who was born according to the flesh. Ishmael. *See note on v. 23.* **persecuted him *who was born* according to the Spirit.** Isaac, whom Ishmael mocked at the feast celebrating Isaac's weaning (see Ge 21:8, 9). **so it is now also.** Ishmael's descendants (Arabs) have always persecuted Isaac's (Jews). So unbelievers have always persecuted believers (cf. Mt 5:11; 10:22–25; Mk 10:30; Jn 15:19, 20; 16:2, 33; 17:14; Ac 14:22; 2Ti 3:12; Heb 11:32–37; 1Pe 2:20, 21; 3:14; 4:12–14).

4:30 Cast out the bondwoman. Quoted from Ge 21:10 to illustrate that those who are attempting to be justified on the basis of keeping the law will be cast out of God's presence forever (Mt 8:12; 22:12, 13; 25:30; Lk 13:28; 2Th 1:9).

4:31 we are not children of a bondwoman. *See notes on 4:24, 26.*

5:1 free. Deliverance from the curse that the law pronounces on the sinner who has been striving unsuccessfully to achieve his own righteousness (3:13, 22–26; 4:1–7), but who has now embraced Christ and the salvation granted to him by grace (*see notes on 2:4; 4:26*; cf. Ro 7:3; 8:2). **keep standing firm.** Stay where you are, Paul asserts, because of the benefit of being free from law and the flesh as a way of salvation and the fullness of blessing by grace. **subject again.** Better translated "to be burdened by" or "to be oppressed by" because of its connection with a yoke. **yoke of slavery.** "Yoke" refers to the apparatus used to control a domesticated animal. The Jews thought of the "yoke of the law" as a good thing, the essence of true religion. Paul argued that for those who pursued it as a way of salvation, the law was a yoke of slavery. *See note on Mt 11:28–30.*

5:2 circumcision. *See notes on 2:3.* Paul had no objection to circumcision itself (cf. Ac 16:1–3; Php 3:5). But he objected to the notion that it had some spiritual benefit or merit with God and was a prerequisite or necessary component of salvation. Circumcision had meaning in Israel when it was a physical symbol of a cleansed heart (cf. Dt 30:6; Jer 4:4; 9:24–26) and served as a reminder of God's covenant of salvation promise (Ge 17:9, 10). **Christ will be of no benefit to you.** The atoning sacrifice of Christ cannot benefit anyone who trusts in law and ceremony for salvation.

5:3 under obligation to keep the whole Law. God's standard is perfect righteousness, thus a failure to keep only one part of the law falls short of the standard (*see note on 3:10*).

5:4 severed from Christ ... fallen from grace. The Gr. word for "severed" means "to be separated," or "to be estranged." The word for "fallen" means "to lose one's grasp on something." Paul's clear meaning is that any attempt to be justified by the law is to reject salvation by grace alone through faith alone. Those once exposed to the gracious truth of the gospel, who then turn their backs on Christ (Heb 6:4–6) and seek to be justified by the law are separated from Christ and lose all prospects of God's gracious salvation. Their desertion of Christ and the gospel only proves that their faith was never genuine (cf. Lk 8:13, 14; 1Jn 2:19). **justified.** *See notes on 2:16; Ro 3:24.*

5:5 by faith ... the hope of righteousness. Christians already possess the imputed righteousness of Christ, but they still await the completed and perfected righteousness that is yet to come at glorification (Ro 8:18, 21).

5:6 neither circumcision nor uncircumcision means anything. Cf. 6:15. Nothing done or not done in the flesh, even religious ceremony, makes any difference in one's relationship to God. What is external is immaterial and worthless, unless it reflects genuine internal righteousness (cf. Ro 2:25–29). **faith working through love.** Saving faith proves its genuine character by works of love. The person who lives by faith is internally motivated by love for God and Christ (cf. Mt 22:37–40), which supernaturally issues forth in reverent worship, genuine obedience, and self-sacrificing love for others.

5:7 You were running well. Cf. 3:3. Paul compares the Galatians' life of faith with a race, a figure he used frequently (2:2; Ro 9:16; 1Co 9:24). They had a good beginning—they had received the gospel message by faith and had begun to live their Christian lives by faith as well. **obeying the truth.** *See note on 1 Peter 1:22.* A reference to believers' true way of living, including both their response to the true gospel in salvation (cf. Ac 6:7; Ro 2:8; 6:17; 2Th 1:8), and their consequent response to obey the Word of God in sanctification. Paul wrote more about salvation and sanctification being a matter of obedience in Ro 1:5; 6:16, 17; 16:26. The legalistic influence of the Judaizers prevented the unsaved from responding in faith to the gospel of grace and true believers from living by faith.

5:8 This persuasion. Salvation by works. God does not promote legalism. Any doctrine that claims His gracious work is insufficient to save is false (*see notes on 1:6, 7*).

5:9 leaven. A common axiomatic saying (cf. 1Co 5:6) regarding the influence of yeast in dough. Leaven is often used in Scripture to denote sin (Mt 16:6, 12) because of its permeating power.

5:10 confidence in you. Paul expresses encouraging assurance that the Lord will be faithful to keep His own from falling into gross heresy. See Jn 6:39, 40; 10:28, 29; Ro 8:31–39; Php 1:6, 7. They will persevere and be preserved (Jude 24). **judgment.** All false teachers will incur strict and devastating eternal condemnation. *See notes on 2Pe 2:2, 3, 9.*

5:11 still preach circumcision. Apparently, the Judaizers had falsely claimed that Paul agreed with their teaching. But he makes the point that if he was preaching circumcision as necessary for salvation, why were the Judaizers persecuting him instead of supporting him? **stumbling block of the cross.** The Gr. word for "stumbling block" can mean "trap," "snare," or "offense." Any offer of salvation that strips man of the opportunity to earn it by his own merit breeds opposition (cf. Ro 9:33).

5:12 mutilate themselves. The Gr. word was often used of castration, such as in the

[13] For you were called to [A]freedom, brethren; [B]only
do not *turn* your freedom into an opportunity for the
flesh, but through love [C]serve one another. [14] For [A]the
whole Law is fulfilled in one word, in the *statement*,
"[B]YOU SHALL LOVE YOUR NEIGHBOR AS YOURSELF."
[15] But if you [A]bite and devour one another, take care
that you are not consumed by one another.
[16] But I say, [A]walk by the Spirit, and you will not
carry out [B]the desire of the flesh. [17] For [A]the flesh
[a]sets its desire against the Spirit, and the Spirit
against the flesh; for these are in opposition to
one another, [B]so that you may not do the things
that you [b]please. [18] But if you are [A]led by the Spirit,
[B]you are not under the Law. [19] Now the deeds of the
flesh are evident, which are: [a,A]immorality, impurity,
sensuality, [20] idolatry, [A]sorcery, enmities, [B]strife,
jealousy, outbursts of anger, [C]disputes, dissensions,
[a,D]factions, [21] envying, [A]drunkenness, carousing, and
things like these, of which I forewarn you, just as
I have forewarned you, that those who practice
such things will not [B]inherit the kingdom of God.
[22] But [A]the fruit of the Spirit is [B]love, joy, peace, patience, kindness, goodness, faithfulness, [23] gentleness, [A]self-control; against such things [B]there is no

5:13 [A]Gal 5:1 [B]1 Cor 8:9; 1 Pet 2:16 [C]1 Cor 9:19; Eph 5:21 5:14 [A]Matt 7:12; 22:40; Rom 13:8, 10; Gal 6:2 [B]Lev 19:18; Matt 19:19; John 13:34 5:15 [A]Gal 5:20; Phil 3:2 5:16 [A]Rom 8:4; 13:14; Gal 5:24f [B]Rom 13:14; Eph 2:3 5:17 [a]Lit *lusts against* [b]Lit *wish* [A]Rom 7:18, 23; 8:5ff [B]Rom 7:15ff 5:18 [A]Rom 8:14 [B]Rom 6:14; 7:4; 1 Tim 1:9 5:19 [a]I.e. sexual immorality [A]1 Cor 6:9, 18; 2 Cor 12:21 5:20 [a]Or *heresies* [A]Rev 21:8 [B]2 Cor 12:20 [C]Rom 2:8; James 3:14ff [D]1 Cor 11:19 5:21 [A]Rom 13:13 [B]1 Cor 6:9 5:22 [A]Matt 7:16ff; Eph 5:9 [B]Rom 5:1-5; 1 Cor 13:4; Col 3:12-15 5:23 [A]Acts 24:25 [B]Gal 5:18

cult of Cybele, whose priests were self-made eunuchs. Paul's ironic point is that since the Judaizers were so insistent on circumcision as a means of pleasing God, they should go to the extreme of religious devotion and mutilate themselves.

5:13 freedom. *See note on 2:4.* **opportunity for the flesh.** The Gr. word for "opportunity" was often used to refer to a central base of military operations (cf. Ro 7:8). In the context, "flesh" refers to the sinful inclinations of fallen man (*see note on Ro 7:5*). The freedom Christians have is not a base from which they can sin freely and without consequence. **serve one another.** Christian freedom is not for selfish fulfillment, but for serving others. Cf. Ro 14:1–15.

5:14 the whole Law. The ethics of the former OT law are the same as those of the NT gospel as indicated in the quote from Lv 19:18 (*see notes on Ro 7:12; 8:4*; cf. Jas 2:8–10). When a Christian genuinely loves others, he fulfills all the moral requirements of the former Mosaic law concerning them (Mt 22:36–40; cf. Dt 6:5; Ro 13:8–10). This is the ruling principle of Christian freedom (vv. 6, 13).

5:15 bite and devour one another. The imagery is of wild animals savagely attacking and killing one another—a graphic picture of what happens in the spiritual realm when believers do not love and serve each other.

5:16 walk by the Spirit. All believers have the presence of the indwelling Holy Spirit (cf. Ro 8:9; 1Co 6:19, 20) as the personal power for living to please God. The form of the Gr. verb translated "walk" indicates continuous action, or a habitual lifestyle. Walking also implies progress; as a believer submits to the Spirit's control—that is, responds in obedience to the simple commands of Scripture—he grows in his spiritual life (*see notes on Ro 8:13; Eph 5:18; Col 3:16*). **the flesh.** This is not simply the physical body, but includes the mind, will, and emotions which are all subject to sin. It refers in general to our unredeemed humanness. *See notes on Ro 7:5; 8:23*; cf. v. 13.

5:17 opposition to one another. The flesh opposes the work of the Spirit and leads the believer toward sinful behavior he would not otherwise be compelled to do (*see notes on Ro 7:14–25*).

5:18 led by the Spirit ... not under the Law. Take your choice; these are mutually exclusive. Either you live by the power of the Holy Spirit which results in righteous behavior and spiritual attitudes (vv. 22–26) or by the law which can only produce unrighteous behavior and attitudes (vv. 19–21). Cf. 1Co 15:56.

5:19–21 These sins characterize all unredeemed mankind living under the impotent commands of the law which produces only iniquity, though not every person manifests all these sins nor exhibits them to the same degree. Paul's list, which is not exhaustive, encompasses 3 areas of human life: sex, religion, and human relationships. For other such lists, see Ro 1:24–32; 1Co 6:9, 10.

5:19 evident. The flesh manifests itself in obvious and certain ways. **immorality.** The Gr. word is *porneia*, from which the Eng. word "pornography" comes. It refers to all illicit sexual activity, including (but not limited to) adultery, premarital sex, homosexuality, bestiality, incest, and prostitution. **sensuality.** The word originally referred to any excessive behavior or lack of restraint, but eventually became associated with sexual excess and indulgence.

5:20 sorcery. The Gr. word *pharmakeia*, from which the Eng. word "pharmacy" comes, originally referred to medicines in general, but eventually only to mood- and mind-altering drugs, as well as the occult, witchcraft, and magic. Many pagan religious practices required the use of these drugs to aid in the communication with deities. **strife ... factions.** Many of these sins manifested in the area of human relationships have to do with some form of anger: "Hatred" results in "strife." "Jealousy" (hateful resentment) results in "outbursts of anger" (sudden, unrestrained expressions of hostility). The next 4 represent animosity between individuals and groups.

5:21 drunkenness, carousing. Probably a specific reference to the orgies that characterized pagan, idolatrous worship. Generally, it refers to all rowdy, boisterous, and crude behavior. **practice.** Here is the key word in Paul's warning. The sense of this Gr. verb describes continual, habitual action. Although believers undoubtedly can commit these sins, those people whose basic character is summed up in the uninterrupted and unrepentant practice of them cannot belong to God (*see notes on 1Co 6:11; 1Jn 3:4–10*). **will not inherit the kingdom of God.** *See note on Mt 5:3.* The unregenerate are barred from entering the spiritual kingdom of redeemed people over whom Christ now rules, and they will be excluded from His millennial kingdom and the eternal state of blessing that follows it. *See note on Eph 5:5.*

5:22 fruit of the Spirit. Godly attitudes that characterize the lives of only those who belong to God by faith in Christ and possess the Spirit of God. The Spirit produces fruit which consists of 9 characteristics or attitudes that are inextricably linked with each and are commanded of believers throughout the NT. **love.** One of several Gr. words for love, *agape*, is the love of choice, referring not to an emotional affection, physical attraction, or a familial bond, but to respect, devotion, and affection that leads to willing, self-sacrificial service (Jn 15:13; Ro 5:8; 1Jn 3:16, 17). **joy.** A happiness based on unchanging divine promises and eternal spiritual realities. It is the sense of well-being experienced by one who knows all is well between himself and the Lord (1Pe 1:8). Joy is not the result of favorable circumstances, and even occurs when those circumstances are the most painful and severe (Jn 16:20–22). Joy is a gift from God, and as such, believers are not to manufacture it but to delight in the blessing they already possess (Ro 14:17; Php 4:4). **peace.** The inner calm that results from confidence in one's saving relationship with Christ. The verb form denotes binding together and is reflected in the expression "having it all together." Like joy, peace is not related to one's circumstances (Jn 14:27; Ro 8:28; Php 4:6, 7, 9). **patience.** The ability to endure injuries inflicted by others and the willingness to accept irritating or painful situations (Eph 4:2; Col 3:12; 1Ti 1:15, 16). **kindness.** Tender concern for others, reflected in a desire to treat others gently, just as the Lord treats all believers (Mt 11:28, 29; 19:13, 14; 2Ti 2:24). **goodness.** Moral and spiritual excellence manifested in active kindness (Ro 5:7). Believers are commanded to exemplify goodness (6:10; 2Th 1:11). **faithfulness.** Loyalty and trustworthiness (La 3:22; Php 2:7–9; 1Th 5:24; Rev 2:10).

5:23 gentleness. Better translated "meekness." It is a humble and gentle attitude that is patiently submissive in every offense, while having no desire for revenge or retribution. In the NT, it is used to describe 3 attitudes: submission to the will of God (Col 3:12), teachability (Jas 1:21), and consideration of others (Eph 4:2). **self-control.** This refers to restraining passions and appetites (1Co 9:25; 2Pe 1:5, 6). **no law.** When a Christian walks by the Spirit and manifests His fruit, he needs no external law to produce the attitudes and behavior that please God (cf. Ro 8:4).

law. 24 [a]Now those who [a]belong to [A]Christ Jesus have
[B]crucified the flesh with its passions and [C]desires.
25 If we live by the Spirit, let us also [a]walk [A]by the
Spirit. 26 Let us not become [A]boastful, challenging
one another, envying one another.

BEAR ONE ANOTHER'S BURDENS

6 [A]Brethren, even if [a]anyone is caught in any trespass, you who are [B]spiritual, [C]restore such a one
[D]in a spirit of gentleness; *each one* looking to yourself,
so that you too will not be tempted. 2 [A]Bear one another's burdens, and thereby fulfill [B]the law of Christ. 3 For
[A]if anyone thinks he is something when he is nothing,
he deceives himself. 4 But each one must [A]examine his
own work, and then he will have *reason for* [B]boasting
in regard to himself alone, and not in regard to another. 5 For [A]each one will bear his own load.
6 [A]The one who is taught [B]the word is to share all
good things with the one who teaches *him*. 7 [A]Do
not be deceived, [B]God is not mocked; for [C]whatever
a man sows, this he will also reap. 8 [A]For the one
who sows to his own flesh will from the flesh reap
[B]corruption, but [C]the one who sows to the Spirit
will from the Spirit reap eternal life. 9 [A]Let us not
lose heart in doing good, for in due time we will
reap if we [B]do not grow weary. 10 So then, [a,A]while
we have opportunity, let us do good to all people,
and especially to those who are of the [B]household
of [C]the faith.
11 See with what large letters I [a]am writing to you
[A]with my own hand. 12 Those who desire [A]to make a
good showing in the flesh try to [B]compel you to be
circumcised, simply so that they [C]will not be persecuted [a]for the cross of Christ. 13 For those who [a]are
circumcised do not even [A]keep [b]the Law themselves,
but they desire to have you circumcised so that they
may [B]boast in your flesh. 14 But [A]may it never be that
I would boast, [B]except in the cross of our Lord Jesus

5:24 [a]Lit *are of Christ Jesus* [A]Gal 3:26 [B]Rom 6:6; Gal 2:20; 6:14 [C]Gal 5:16f 5:25 [a]Or *follow the Spirit* [A]Gal 5:16 5:26 [A]Phil 2:3 6:1 [a]Gr *anthropos* [A]Gal 6:18; 1 Thess 4:1 [B]1 Cor 2:15 [C]2 Cor 2:7; 2 Thess 3:15; Heb 12:13; James 5:19f [D]1 Cor 4:21 6:2 [A]Rom 15:1 [B]Rom 8:2; 1 Cor 9:21; James 1:25; 2:12; 2 Pet 3:2 6:3 [A]Acts 5:36; 1 Cor 3:18; 2 Cor 12:11 6:4 [A]1 Cor 11:28 [B]Phil 1:26 6:5 [A]Prov 9:12; Rom 14:12; 1 Cor 3:8 6:6 [A]1 Cor 9:11, 14 [B]2 Tim 4:2 6:7 [A]1 Cor 6:9 [B]Job 13:9 [C]2 Cor 9:6 6:8 [A]Job 4:8; Hos 8:7; Rom 6:21 [B]1 Cor 15:42 [C]Rom 8:11; James 3:18 6:9 [A]1 Cor 15:58; 2 Cor 4:1 [B]Matt 10:22; Heb 12:3, 5; James 5:7f 6:10 [a]Or *as* [A]Prov 3:27; John 12:35 [B]Eph 2:19; Heb 3:6; 1 Pet 2:5; 4:17 [C]Acts 6:7; Gal 1:23 6:11 [a]Or *have written* [A]1 Cor 16:21 6:12 [a]Or *because of* [A]Matt 23:27f [B]Acts 15:1 [C]Gal 5:11 6:13 [a]Two early mss read *have been* [b]Or *law* [A]Rom 2:25 [B]Phil 3:3 6:14 [A]Luke 20:16; Gal 2:17; 3:21 [B]1 Cor 2:2

5:24 have crucified the flesh. One of 4 uses of "crucified" that does not refer to Christ's crucifixion (cf. 2:20; 6:14; Ro 6:6). Here Paul states that the flesh has been executed, yet the spiritual battle still rages in the believer (*see notes on Ro 7:14–25*). Paul's use looks back to the cross of Christ, where the death of the flesh and its power to reign over believers was actually accomplished (Ro 6:1–11). Christians must wait until their glorification before they are finally rid of their unredeemed humanness (Ro 8:23), yet by walking in the Spirit they can please God in this world.

5:25 walk by the Spirit. *See note on v. 16.*

6:1 caught. This word may imply the person was actually seen committing the sin or that he was caught or snared by the sin itself. **you … spiritual.** Those believers who are walking in the Spirit (*see note on 5:16*), filled with the Spirit (*see notes on Eph 5:18–20; Col 3:16*), and evidencing the fruit of the Spirit (*see notes on 5:22, 23*). **restore.** Sometimes used metaphorically of settling disputes or arguments, it lit. means "to mend" or "repair," and was used of setting a broken bone or repairing a dislocated limb (Heb 12:12, 13; *see notes on Ro 15:1; 1Th 5:14, 15*). The basic process of restoration is outlined in Mt 18:15–20 (*see notes there*). **spirit of gentleness.** *See note on 5:23* (cf. 2Co 2:7; 2Th 3:15). **looking.** Also "observing." The Gr. form strongly emphasizes a continual, diligent attentiveness.

6:2 Bear one another's burdens. "Burdens" are extra heavy loads, which here represent difficulties or problems people have trouble dealing with. "Bear" connotes carrying something with endurance. **the law of Christ.** The law of love which fulfills the entire law (*see notes on 5:14; Jn 13:34; Ro 13:8, 10*).

6:4 examine. Lit. "to approve something after testing it." Believers first must be sure their lives are right with God before giving spiritual help to others (cf. Mt 7:3–5). ***reason for* boasting.** If a believer rejoices or boasts, it should be only boasting in the Lord for what God has done in him (cf. 2Co 10:12–18), not for what he supposedly has accomplished compared to other believers (*see note on 1Co 1:30, 31*).

6:5 bear his own load. This is not a contradiction to v. 2. "Load" has no connotation of difficulty; it refers to life's routine obligations and each believer's ministry calling (cf. Mt 11:30; 1Co 3:12–15; 2Co 5:10). God requires faithfulness in meeting those responsibilities.

6:6 all good things. Although this expression could refer to material compensation, the context suggests that Paul is referring to the spiritually and morally excellent things learned from the Word, in which they fellowship together. Paul uses this same term to describe the gospel (Ro 10:15; cf. Heb 9:11).

6:7 whatever a man sows … reap. This agricultural principle, applied metaphorically to the moral and spiritual realm, is universally true (cf. Job 4:8; Pr 1:31–33; Hos 8:7; 10:12). This law is a form of God's wrath. *See note on Ro 1:18.*

6:8 sows to his own flesh. *See notes on 5:16–19; Ro 7:18; 8:23.* Here it means pandering to the flesh's evil desires. **corruption.** From the Gr. word for degeneration, as in decaying food. Sin always corrupts and, when left unchecked, always makes a person progressively worse in character (cf. Ro 6:23). **sows to the Spirit.** To walk by the Holy Spirit (*see notes on 5:16–18; Eph 5:18*; cf. Jn 8:31; 15:7; Ro 12:1, 2; Col 2:6; 3:2). **eternal life.** This expression describes not only a life that endures forever but, primarily, the highest quality of living that one can experience (cf. Ps 51:12; Jn 10:10; Eph 1:3, 18).

6:10 opportunity. This Gr. word refers to a distinct, fixed time period, rather than occasional moments. Paul's point is that the believer's entire life provides the unique privilege by which he can serve others in Christ's name. **especially … the household of the faith.** Our love for fellow Christians is the primary test of our love for God (*see notes on Jn 13:34, 35; Ro 12:10–13; 1Jn 4:21*).

6:11–17 This closing section of the letter is Paul's final rhetorical attack against the Judaizers' doctrine (*see notes on 1:7–9*) and motives. It is also a positive statement of his own godly motives in preaching the true gospel.

6:11 with what large letters. This can be interpreted in two ways: 1) Paul's poor eyesight forced him to use large letters (cf. 4:13, 15); or 2) instead of the normal cursive style of writing used by professional scribes, he used the large block letters (frequently employed in public notices) to emphasize the letter's content rather than its form. It was a visible picture that contrasted his concern with the content of the gospel for the Judaizers' only concern: appearances. The expression served as a transition to his concluding remarks. **I am writing … my own hand.** As a good translation of the Gr. verb, this indicates that Paul wrote the entire letter by his own hand, not merely penning a brief statement at the end of dictation to a secretary as he did other times (cf. 1Co 16:21; Col 4:18; 2Th 3:17). Paul wrote this letter himself to make sure the Galatians knew he—not some forger—was writing it, and to personalize the document, given the importance and severity of its contents.

6:12 good showing. The Judaizers were motivated by religious pride and wanted to impress others with their external piety (cf. Mt 6:1–7). **compel you to be circumcised.** *See notes on 2:3; 5:2–6.* **will not be persecuted.** The Judaizers were more concerned about their personal safety than correct doctrine. By adhering more to the Mosaic law than to the gospel of Jesus, they hoped to avoid social and financial ostracism from other Jews and maintain their protected status as Jews within the Roman Empire.

6:13 circumcised. Specifically, in this case, the Judaizers (*see notes on 2:7, 8*; cf. Ac 10:45; 11:2). **boast in your flesh.** They zealously worked to win Gentile converts to the law so they could brag about their effective proselytizing (cf. Mt 23:15).

6:14 boast, except in the cross. The Gr word for "boast" is a basic expression of praise, unlike the Eng. word, which necessar-

Christ, [C]through [a]which the world has been crucified
to me, and [D]I to the world.
15 For [A]neither is circumcision anything, nor uncircumcision, but a [B]new [a]creation.
16 And those who will [a]walk by this rule, peace and mercy *be* upon them, and upon the [A]Israel of God.
17 From now on let no one cause trouble for me, for I bear on my body the [A]brand-marks of Jesus.
18 [A]The grace of our Lord Jesus Christ be [B]with your spirit, [C]brethren. Amen.

6:14 [a]Or *whom* [C]Gal 2:20; Col 2:20 [D]Rom 6:2, 6; Gal 2:19f; 5:24 6:15 [a]Or *creature* [A]Rom 2:26, 28; 1 Cor 7:19; Gal 5:6 [B]2 Cor 5:17; Eph 2:10, 15; 4:24; Col 3:10 6:16 [a]Or *follow this rule* [A]Rom 9:6; Gal 3:7, 29; Phil 3:3 6:17 [A]Is 44:5; Ezek 9:4; 2 Cor 4:10; 11:23; Rev 13:16 6:18 [A]Rom 16:20 [B]2 Tim 4:22 [C]Acts 1:15; Rom 1:13; Gal 3:15; 4:12, 28, 31

ily includes the aspect of pride. Paul glories and rejoices in the sacrifice of Jesus Christ (cf. Ro 8:1–3; 1Co 2:2; 1Pe 2:24). **the world.** The evil, Satanic system (*see notes on 1Jn 2:15, 16; 5:19*). **crucified to me, and I to the world.** The world is spiritually dead to believers, and they are dead to the world (*see notes on 2:20; Ro 6:2–10; 1Jn 5:4, 5*; cf. Php 3:20, 21).

6:15 circumcision … nor uncircumcision. *See notes on 5:6.* **a new creation.** The new birth (*see notes on Jn 3:3; 2Co 5:17*).

6:16 peace and mercy. The results of salvation: "Peace" is the believer's new relationship to God (Ro 5:1; 8:6; Col 3:15), and "mercy" is the forgiveness of all his sins and the setting aside of God's judgment (Ps 25:6; Da 9:18; Mt 5:7; Lk 1:50; Ro 12:1; Eph 2:4; Titus 3:5). **Israel of God.** All Jewish believers in Christ, i.e., those who are both physical and spiritual descendants of Abraham (*see notes on 3:7, 18; Ro 2:28, 29; 9:6, 7*).

6:17 brand-marks. The physical results of persecution (scars, wounds, etc.) that identified Paul as one who had suffered for the Lord (cf. Ac 14:19; 16:22; 2Co 11:25; *see notes on 2Co 1:5; 4:10; Col 1:24*).

6:18 Even Paul's final benediction implicitly extols the superiority of the gospel of grace over any man-made system of works righteousness.

THE EPISTLE OF PAUL TO THE EPHESIANS

TITLE

The letter is addressed to the church in the city of Ephesus, capital of the Roman province of Asia (Asia Minor, modern Turkey). Because the name Ephesus is not mentioned in every early manuscript, some scholars believe the letter was an encyclical, intended to be circulated and read among all the churches in Asia Minor and was simply sent first to believers in Ephesus.

AUTHOR AND DATE

There is no indication that the authorship of Paul should be in question. He is indicated as author in the opening salutation (1:1; 3:1). The letter was written from prison in Rome (Ac 28:16–31) sometime between A.D. 60–62 and is, therefore, often referred to as a prison epistle (along with Philippians, Colossians, and Philemon). It may have been composed almost contemporaneously with Colossians and initially sent with that epistle and Philemon by Tychicus (Eph 6:21, 22; Col 4:7, 8). See Introduction to Philippians: Author and Date for a discussion of the city from which Paul wrote.

BACKGROUND AND SETTING

It is likely that the gospel was first brought to Ephesus by Priscilla and Aquila, an exceptionally gifted couple (see Ac 18:26) who were left there by Paul on his second missionary journey (Ac 18:18, 19). Located at the mouth of the Cayster River, on the east side of the Aegean Sea, the city of Ephesus was perhaps best known for its magnificent temple of Artemis, or Diana, one of the 7 wonders of the ancient world. It was also an important political, educational, and commercial center, ranking with Alexandria in Egypt, and Antioch of Pisidia, in southern Asia Minor.

The fledgling church begun by Priscilla and Aquila was later firmly established by Paul on his third missionary journey (Ac 19) and was pastored by him for some 3 years. After Paul left, Timothy pastored the congregation for perhaps a year and a half, primarily to counter the false teaching of a few influential men (such as Hymenaeus and Alexander), who were probably elders in the congregation there (1Ti 1:3, 20). Because of those men, the church at Ephesus was plagued by "myths and endless genealogies" (1Ti 1:4) and by such ascetic and unscriptural ideas as the forbidding of marriage and abstaining from certain foods (1Ti 4:3). Although those false teachers did not rightly understand Scripture, they propounded their ungodly interpretations with confidence (1Ti 1:7), which produced in the church harmful "speculation rather than ... the administration of God which is by faith" (1Ti 1:4). Thirty years or so later, Christ gave to the apostle John a letter for this church indicating its people had left their first love for Him (Rev 2:1–7).

HISTORICAL AND THEOLOGICAL THEMES

The first 3 chapters are theological, emphasizing NT doctrine, whereas the last 3 chapters are practical and focus on Christian behavior. Perhaps, above all, this is a letter of encouragement and admonition, written to remind believers of their immeasurable blessings in Jesus Christ; and not only to be thankful for those blessings, but also to live in a manner worthy of them. Despite, and partly even because of, a Christian's great blessings in Jesus Christ, he is sure to be tempted by Satan to self-satisfaction and complacency. It was for that reason that, in the last chapter, Paul reminds believers of the full and sufficient spiritual armor supplied to them through God's Word and by His Spirit (6:10–17) and of their need for vigilant and persistent prayer (6:18).

A key theme of the letter is the mystery (meaning a heretofore unrevealed truth) of the church, which is "that the Gentiles are fellow heirs and fellow members of the body, and fellow partakers of the promise in Christ Jesus through the gospel" (3:6), a truth completely hidden from the OT saints (cf. 3:5, 9). All believers in Jesus Christ, the Messiah, are equal before the Lord as His children and as citizens of His eternal kingdom, a marvelous truth that only believers of this present age possess. Paul also speaks of the mystery of the church as the bride of Christ (5:32; cf. Rev 21:9).

A major truth emphasized is that of the church as Christ's present spiritual, earthly body, also a distinct and formerly unrevealed truth about God's people. This metaphor depicts the church, not as an organization, but as a living organism composed of mutually related and interdependent parts. Christ is Head of the body and the Holy Spirit is its lifeblood, as it were. The body functions through the faithful use of its members' various spiritual gifts, sovereignly and uniquely bestowed by the Holy Spirit on each believer.

Other major themes include the riches and fullness of blessing to believers. Paul writes of "the riches of His [God's] grace" (1:7), "the unfathomable riches of Christ" (3:8), and "the riches of His glory" (3:16). Paul admonishes believers to "be filled up to all the fullness of God" (3:19), to "attain to the unity of the faith and of the knowledge of the Son of God, to a mature man, to the measure of the stature which belongs to the fullness of Christ" (4:13), and to "be filled with the Spirit" (5:18). Their riches in Christ are based on His grace (1:2, 6, 7; 2:7), His peace (1:2), His will (1:5), His pleasure and purpose (1:9), His glory (1:12, 14), His calling and inheritance (1:18), His power and strength (1:19; 6:10), His love (2:4), His workmanship (2:10), His Holy Spirit (3:16), His offering and sacrifice (5:2), and His armor (6:11, 13). The word "riches" is used 5 times in this letter; "grace" is used 12 times; "glory" 9 times; "fullness" or "filled" 6 times; and the key phrase "in Christ" (or "in Him") some 11 times.

INTERPRETIVE CHALLENGES

The general theology of Ephesians is direct, unambiguous, and presents no ideas or interpretations whose meanings are seriously contended. There are, however, some texts that require careful thought to rightly interpret, namely: 1) 2:8, in which one must decide if the salvation or the faith is the gift; 2) 4:5, in which the type of baptism must be discerned; and 3) 4:8, in its relationship to Ps 68:18.

OUTLINE

I. Salutation (1:1, 2)

II. God's Purpose for the Church (1:3–3:13)
- A. Predestination in Christ (1:3–6a)
- B. Redemption in Christ (1:6b–10)
- C. Inheritance in Christ (1:11–14)
- D. Resources in Christ (1:15–23)
- E. New Life in Christ (2:1–10)
- F. Unity in Christ (2:11–3:13)

III. God's Fullness for the Church (3:14–21)

IV. God's Plan for Faithful Living in the Church (4:1–6)

V. God's Son Endows and Builds the Church (4:7–16)

VI. God's Pattern and Principles for Members of the Church (4:17–32)

VII. God's Standards for Faithfulness in the Church (5:1–21)
- A. Walking in Love (5:1–7)
- B. Living in Light (5:8–14)
- C. Walking in Wisdom and Sobriety (5:15–18a)
- D. Filled with God's Spirit (5:18b–21)

VIII. God's Standards for Authority and Submission in the Church (5:22–6:9)
- A. Husbands and Wives (5:22–33)
- B. Parents and Children (6:1–4)
- C. Employers and Employees (6:5–9)

IX. God's Provision for His Children's Spiritual Battles (6:10–17)
- A. The Believer's Warfare (6:10–13)
- B. The Believer's Armor (6:14–17)

X. God's Appeal for Prayer in the Church (6:18–20)

XI. Benediction (6:21–24)

THE BLESSINGS OF REDEMPTION

1 Paul, [A]an apostle of [B]Christ Jesus [a,C]by the will
of God,
To the [b,D]saints who are [c]at [E]Ephesus and [F]*who are*
faithful in [B]Christ Jesus: 2 [A]Grace to you and peace
from God our Father and the Lord Jesus Christ.
3 [A]Blessed *be* the God and Father of our Lord
Jesus Christ, who has blessed us with every
spiritual blessing in [B]the heavenly *places* in
Christ, 4 just as [A]He chose us in Him before [B]the
foundation of the world, that we would be [C]holy
and blameless before [a]Him. [D]In love 5 [a]He [A]predes-
tined us to [B]adoption as sons through Jesus Christ
to Himself, [C]according to the [b]kind intention of
His will, 6 [A]to the praise of the glory of His grace,
which He freely bestowed on us in [B]the Beloved.

1:1 [a]Lit *through* [b]Or *holy ones* [c]Three early mss do not contain *at Ephesus* [A]2 Cor 1:1 [B]Rom 8:1 [C]1 Cor 1:1 [D]Acts 9:13 [E]Acts 18:19 [F]Col 1:2 1:2 [A]Rom 1:7 1:3 [A]2 Cor 1:3 [B]Eph 1:20; 2:6; 3:10; 6:12 1:4 [a]Or *Him, in love* [A]Eph 2:10; 2 Thess 2:13f [B]Matt 25:34 [C]Eph 5:27; Col 1:22 [D]Eph 4:2, 15, 16; 5:2 1:5 [a]Lit *having predestined* [b]Lit *good pleasure* [A]Acts 13:48; Rom 8:29f [B]Rom 8:14ff [C]Phil 2:13; Col 1:19 1:6 [A]Eph 1:12, 14 [B]Matt 3:17

1:1 apostle. The word means "messenger" and served as an official title for Paul and the 12 disciples (including Matthias, Ac 1:26), who were eyewitnesses of the resurrected Jesus and were chosen by God to lay the foundation for the church by preaching, teaching, and writing Scripture, accompanied by miracles (cf. 2Co 12:12). *See note on 4:11.* **saints . . . faithful.** Designates those whom God has set apart from sin to Himself, made holy through their faith in Jesus Christ.

1:2 Grace to you and peace. A common greeting in the early church which Paul used in all his letters. **God our Father and the Lord Jesus Christ.** From them came the authority with which Paul spoke (v. 1) as well as the blessings of grace and peace to all believers. The conjunction "and" indicates equivalence; that is, the Lord Jesus Christ is equally divine with the Father.

1:3–14 This passage describes God's master plan for salvation in terms of the past (election, vv. 3–6a), the present (redemption, vv. 6b–11), and the future (inheritance, vv. 12–14). It can also be viewed as emphasizing the Father (vv. 3–6), the Son (vv. 7–12), and the Spirit (vv. 13–16).

1:3 Blessed. Derived from the same Gr. word as "eulogy," which means to praise or commend. This is the supreme duty of all creatures (*see notes on Ro 1:18–21*; cf. Rev 5:13). **God . . . who has blessed us with every spiritual blessing.** In His providential grace, God has already given believers total blessing (Ro 8:28; Col 2:10; Jas 1:17; 2Pe 1:3). "Spiritual" does not refer to immaterial blessings as opposed to material ones, but rather to the work of God, who is the divine and spiritual source of all blessings. **in the heavenly *places*.** Lit. "in the heavenlies." This refers to the realm of God's complete, heavenly domain, from which all His blessings come (cf. v. 20; 2:6; 3:10; 6:12). **in Christ.** God's superabundant blessings belong only to believers who are His children, by faith in Christ, so that what He has is theirs—including His righteousness, resources, privilege, position, and power (cf. Ro 8:16, 17).

1:4 He chose us. The doctrine of election is emphasized throughout Scripture (cf. Dt 7:6; Is 45:4; Jn 6:44; Ac 13:48; Ro 8:29; 9:11; 1Th 1:3, 4; 2Th 2:13; 2Ti 2:10; *see note on 1Pe 1:2*). The form of the Gr. verb behind "chose" indicates that God not only chose *by* Himself but *for* Himself to the praise of His own glory (vv. 6, 12, 14). God's election or predestination does not operate apart from or nullify man's responsibility to believe in Jesus as Lord and Savior (cf. Mt 3:1, 2; 4:17; Jn 5:40). **before the foundation of the world.** Through God's sovereign will before the creation of the world and, therefore, obviously independent of human influence and apart from any human merit, those who are saved have become eternally united with Christ Jesus. Cf. 1Pe 1:20; Rev 13:8; 17:8. **holy and blameless before Him.** This describes both a purpose and a result of God's choosing those who are to be saved. Unrighteous persons are declared righteous, unworthy sinners are declared worthy of salvation, all because they are chosen "in Him" (Christ). This refers to Christ's imputed righteousness granted to us (*see notes on 2Co 5:21; Php 3:9*), a perfect righteousness which places believers in a holy and blameless position before God (5:27; Col 2:10), though daily living inevitably falls far short of His holy standard. **In love.** This phrase belongs at the start of v. 5, since it introduces the divine motive for God's elective purpose. Cf. 2:4, 5; Dt 7:8.

1:5 He predestined us to adoption as sons. Human parents can bestow their love, resources, and inheritance on an adopted child, but not their own distinct characteristics. But God miraculously gives His own nature to those whom He has elected and who have trusted in Christ. He makes them His children in the image of His divine Son, giving them not just Christ's riches and blessings but also His very nature (cf. Jn 15:15; Ro 8:15).

1:6 to the praise of the glory of His grace. The ultimate purpose of election to salvation is the glory of God (cf. vv. 12, 14; Php 2:13; 2Th 1:11, 12). **which He . . . bestowed . . . in the Beloved.** "Which" refers to the divine grace (undeserved love and favor) that has made it possible for sinners to be accepted by God through the substitutionary death and imputed righteousness provided by Jesus Christ ("the Beloved," cf. Mt 3:17; Col 1:13). Because believers are accepted in Him, then they, like Him, are beloved of God.

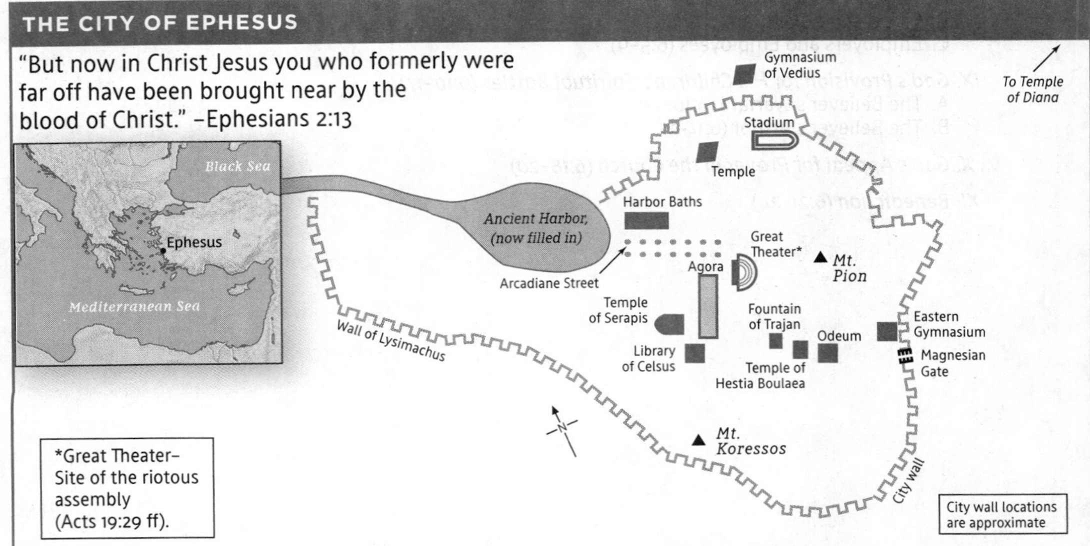

7 [A]In [a]Him we have [B]redemption [C]through His blood,
the [D]forgiveness of our trespasses, according to [E]the
riches of His grace 8 which He [a]lavished on [b]us. In
all wisdom and insight 9 He [a,A]made known to us
the mystery of His will, [B]according to His [b]kind intention which He [C]purposed in Him 10 with a view
to an administration [a]suitable to [A]the fullness of
the times, *that is,* [B]the summing up of all things
in Christ, things [b]in the heavens and things on the
earth. In Him 11 [a]also we [b,A]have obtained an inheritance, having been [B]predestined [C]according to His
purpose who works all things [D]after the counsel of
His will, 12 to the end that we who were the first to
hope in [a]Christ would be [A]to the praise of His glory.
13 In [a]Him, you also, after listening to [A]the message
of truth, the gospel of your salvation—having also
[b]believed, you were [B]sealed in [a]Him with [C]the Holy
Spirit of promise, 14 who is [a,A]given as a pledge of
[B]our inheritance, with a view to the [C]redemption of
[D]*God's own* possession, [E]to the praise of His glory.
15 For this reason I too, [A]having heard of the faith
in the Lord Jesus which *exists* among you and [a]your
love for [B]all the [b]saints, 16 [A]do not cease giving thanks
for you, [B]while making mention *of you* in my prayers;
17 that the [A]God of our Lord Jesus Christ, [B]the Father
of glory, may give to you a spirit of [C]wisdom and of
[D]revelation in the [a]knowledge of Him. 18 *I pray that*
[A]the eyes of your heart [a]may be enlightened, so that
you will know what is the [B]hope of His [C]calling, what
are [D]the riches of the glory of [E]His inheritance in
[F]the [b]saints, 19 and what is the surpassing greatness
of His power toward us who believe. [A]*These are* in
accordance with the working of the [B]strength of His
might 20 which He brought about in Christ, when He

1:7 [a]Lit *whom* [A]Col 1:14 [B]Rom 3:24; 1 Cor 1:30; Eph 1:14 [C]Acts 20:28; Rom 3:25 [D]Acts 2:38 [E]Rom 2:4; Eph 1:18; 2:7; 3:8, 16 1:8 [a]Lit *made abundant toward* [b]Or *us, in all wisdom and insight* 1:9 [a]Lit *making known* [b]Lit *good pleasure* [A]Rom 11:25; Eph 3:3 [B]1 Cor 1:21; Gal 1:15 [C]Rom 8:28; Eph 1:11 1:10 [a]Lit *of* [b]Lit *upon* [A]Mark 1:15 [B]Eph 3:15; Phil 2:9f; Col 1:16, 20 1:11 [a]Lit *in whom also* [b]Or *were made a heritage* [A]Deut 4:20; Eph 1:14; Titus 2:14 [B]Eph 1:5 [C]Rom 8:28f; Eph 3:11 [D]Rom 9:11; Heb 6:17 1:12 [a]I.e. the Messiah [A]Eph 1:6, 14 1:13 [a]Lit *whom* [b]Or *believed in Him, you were sealed* [A]Eph 4:21; Col 1:5 [B]Eph 4:30 [C]Acts 2:33 1:14 [a]Or *a down payment* [A]2 Cor 1:22 [B]Acts 20:32 [C]Eph 1:7 [D]Eph 1:11 [E]Eph 1:6, 12 1:15 [a]Three early mss do not contain *your love* [b]V 1, note 2 [A]Col 1:4; Philem 5 [B]Eph 1:1; 3:18 1:16 [A]Rom 1:8f; Col 1:9 [B]Rom 1:9 1:17 [a]Or *true knowledge* [A]John 20:17; Rom 15:6 [B]Acts 7:2; 1 Cor 2:8 [C]Col 1:9 [D]1 Cor 14:6 1:18 [a]Lit *being* [b]Or *holy ones* [A]Acts 26:18; 2 Cor 4:6; Heb 6:4 [B]Eph 4:4 [C]Rom 11:29 [D]Eph 1:7 [E]Eph 1:11 [F]Col 1:12 1:19 [A]Eph 3:7; Col 1:29 [B]Eph 6:10

1:7a redemption through His blood. The term used here relates to paying the required ransom to God for the release of a person from bondage. Christ's sacrifice on the cross paid that price for every elect person enslaved by sin, buying them out of the slave market of iniquity (*see notes on 2Co 5:18, 19*). The price of redemption was death (cf. Lv 17:11; Ro 3:24, 25; Heb 9:22; 1Pe 1:18, 19; Rev 5:8–10).

1:7b, 8 the forgiveness of our trespasses . . . In all wisdom and insight. Redemption brings in the limitless grace of God (Ro 5:20) and forgiveness of sin (cf. Mt 26:28; Ac 13:38, 39; Eph 4:32; Col 2:13; 1Jn 1:9). It brings divinely bestowed spiritual understanding. Cf. 1Co 2:6, 7, 12, 16.

1:10 the summing up of all things. At the end of this world's history, God will gather believers together in the millennial kingdom, called here "an administration suitable to the fullness of the times," meaning the completion of history (Rev 20:1–6). After that, God will gather everything to Himself in eternity future, and the new heaven and new earth will be created (Rev 21:1ff.). The new universe will be totally unified under Christ (cf. 1Co 15:27, 28; Php 2:10, 11).

1:11 we have obtained an inheritance. Christ is the source of the believer's divine inheritance, which is so certain that it is spoken of as if it has already been received. Cf. 1Co 3:22, 23; 2Pe 1:3, 4. **having been predestined.** Before the earth was formed, God sovereignly determined that every elect sinner—however vile, useless, and deserving of death—by trusting in Christ would be made righteous. *See note on v. 4.* **who works all things.** The word translated "works" is the same one from which "energy," "energetic," and "energize" are derived. When God created the world, He gave it sufficient energy to begin immediately to operate as He had planned. It was not simply ready to function, but was created functioning. As God works out His plan according to "the counsel of His will," He energizes every believer with the power necessary for his spiritual completion (cf. Phil 1:6; 2:13).

1:12 to the praise of His glory. God's glory is the supreme purpose of redemption (cf. vv. 6, 14).

1:13 after listening to the . . . truth . . . also believed. The God-revealed gospel of Jesus Christ must be heard (Ro 10:17) and believed (Jn 1:12) to bring salvation.

1:13, 14 sealed . . . with the Holy Spirit. God's own Spirit comes to indwell the believer and secures and preserves his eternal salvation. The sealing of which Paul speaks refers to an official mark of identification placed on a letter, contract, or other document. That document was thereby officially under the authority of the person whose stamp was on the seal. Four primary truths are signified by the seal: 1) security (cf. Da 6:17; Mt 27:62–66); 2) authenticity (cf. 1Ki 21:6–16); 3) ownership (cf. Jer 32:10); and 4) authority (cf. Est 8:8–12). The Holy Spirit is given by God as His pledge of the believer's future inheritance in glory (cf. 2Co 1:21).

1:15 your love for all the saints. Love for other believers evidences saving faith (cf. Jn 13:34, 35; 1Jn 4:16–18; 4:20; 5:1) and is a cause of thanksgiving (v. 16).

1:17 the God of our Lord Jesus Christ. This is a designation of God that links Father and Son in essential nature as deity (cf. v. 3a; Ro 1:1–4; 1Co 1:3; Phil 2:9–11; 1Pe 1:3; 2Jn 3).

1:17, 18 a spirit of wisdom . . . hope. Paul was praying that believers will have the disposition of godly knowledge and insight of which the sanctified mind is capable (v. 8), so as to grasp the greatness of the hope (Ro 8:29; 1Jn 3:2) and the inheritance that is theirs in Christ (vv. 3–14).

1:18 the eyes of your heart may be enlightened. A spiritually enlightened mind is the only means of truly understanding and appreciating the hope and inheritance in Christ and of living obediently for Him.

1:19, 20 surpassing greatness of His power. God's great power, that very power which raised Jesus from the dead and lifted Him by ascension back to glory to take His seat at God's right hand, is given to every believer at the time of salvation and is always available (cf. Ac 1:8; Col 1:29). Paul therefore did not pray that God's power be given to believers, but that they be aware of the power they already possessed in Christ and use it (cf. 3:20).

EPHESIANS AND COLOSSIANS COMPARED

Though written near the same time and reflecting similar themes, the Books of Ephesians and Colossians have their own distinctive emphases. One could say that Ephesians is the epistle portraying the "Church of Christ," while the focus of Colossians is the "Christ of the Church."

Ephesians	Colossians
Jesus Christ; Lord of the church	Jesus Christ: Lord of the cosmos
Emphasis on the church as the body of Christ, with Christ as the Head of the church	Emphasis on Christ as the Head of the cosmos and the church
Less personal and probably a circular epistle	More personal and local church oriented
Addresses the errors of false teaching less directly	Speaks to the errors of particular false doctrines
Common themes treated extensively	Common themes treated briefly

[A]raised Him from the dead and [B]seated Him at His
right hand in [C]the heavenly *places,* 21 far above [A]all
rule and authority and power and dominion, and
every [B]name that is named, not only in [C]this age but
also in the one to come. 22 And He [A]put all things in
subjection under His feet, and gave Him as [B]head
over all things to the church, 23 which is His [A]body,
the [B]fullness of Him who [C]fills [D]all in all.

MADE ALIVE IN CHRIST

2 And you [a]were [A]dead [b]in your trespasses and
sins, 2 in which you [A]formerly walked according to the [a]course of [B]this world, according to [C]the
prince of the power of the air, of the spirit that is
now working in [D]the sons of disobedience. 3 Among
them we too all [A]formerly lived in [B]the lusts of our
flesh, [a]indulging the desires of the flesh and of the
[b]mind, and were [C]by nature [D]children of wrath, [E]even
as the rest. 4 But God, being [A]rich in mercy, because
of [B]His great love with which He loved us, 5 even
when we were [A]dead [a]in our transgressions, made us
alive together [b]with Christ ([B]by grace you have been
saved), 6 and [A]raised us up with Him, and [B]seated us
with Him in [C]the heavenly *places* in [D]Christ Jesus,
7 so that in the ages to come He might show the surpassing [A]riches of His grace in [B]kindness toward us
in Christ Jesus. 8 For [A]by grace you have been saved
[B]through faith; and [a]that not of yourselves, *it is* [C]the
gift of God; 9 [A]not as a result of works, so that [B]no one
may boast. 10 For we are His workmanship, [A]created
in [B]Christ Jesus for [C]good works, which God [D]pre-
pared beforehand so that we would [E]walk in them.
11 Therefore remember that [A]formerly [B]you, the
Gentiles in the flesh, who are called "[C]Uncircum-
cision" by the so-called "[C]Circumcision," *which
is* performed in the flesh by human hands—
12 *remember* that you were at that time separate
from Christ, [a,A]excluded from the commonwealth of
Israel, and strangers to [B]the covenants of promise,
having [C]no hope and [D]without God in the world.

1:20 [A]Acts 2:24 [B]Mark 16:19 [C]Eph 1:3 1:21 [A]Matt 28:18; Col 1:16 [B]Phil 2:9; Rev 19:12 [C]Matt 12:32 1:22 [A]Ps 8:6; 1 Cor 15:27 [B]1 Cor 11:3; Eph 4:15; Col 1:18 1:23 [A]1 Cor 12:27; Eph 4:12; Col 1:18, 24 [B]John 1:16; Eph 3:19 [C]Eph 4:10 [D]Col 3:11 2:1 [a]Lit *being* [b]Or *by reason of* [A]Eph 2:5; Col 2:13 2:2 [a]Lit *age* [A]1 Cor 6:11; Eph 2:3 [B]Eph 1:21 [C]John 12:31; Eph 6:12 [D]Eph 5:6 2:3 [a]Lit *doing* [b]Lit *thoughts* [A]Eph 2:2 [B]Gal 5:16f [C]Rom 2:14; Gal 2:15 [D]Rom 5:9; Col 1:21; 2 Pet 2:14 [E]Rom 5:12 2:4 [A]Eph 1:7 [B]John 3:16 2:5 [a]Or *by reason of* [b]Two early mss read *in Christ* [A]Eph 2:1 [B]Acts 15:11 2:6 [A]Col 2:12 [B]Eph 1:20 [C]Eph 1:3 [D]Eph 1:1; 2:10, 13 2:7 [A]Rom 2:4; Eph 1:7 [B]Titus 3:4 2:8 [a]I.e. that salvation [A]Acts 15:11; Eph 2:5 [B]1 Pet 1:5 [C]John 4:10 2:9 [A]Rom 3:28; 2 Tim 1:9 [B]1 Cor 1:29 2:10 [A]Eph 2:15; 4:24; Col 3:10 [B]Eph 1:1; 2:6, 13 [C]Titus 2:14 [D]Eph 1:4 [E]Eph 4:1 2:11 [A]Eph 2:2 [B]1 Cor 12:2; Eph 5:8 [C]Rom 2:28f; Col 2:11 2:12 [a]Or *alienated* [A]Rom 9:4; Col 1:21 [B]Gal 3:17; Heb 8:6 [C]1 Thess 4:13 [D]Gal 4:8; 1 Thess 4:5

1:21 Paul wanted believers to comprehend the greatness of God compared to other heavenly beings. "Rule and authority and power and dominion" were traditional Jewish terms to designate angelic beings having a high rank among God's hosts. God is above them all (cf. Rev 20:10–15).

1:22 feet … head. This is a quote from Ps 8:6 indicating that God has exalted Christ over everything (cf. Heb 2:8), including His church (cf. Col 1:18). Christ is clearly the authoritative Head (not "source") because all things have been placed under His feet. *See notes on 4:15; 5:23.*

1:23 His body. A metaphor for God's redeemed people, used exclusively in the NT of the church (cf. 4:12–16; 1Co 12:12–27).

2:1 dead in your trespasses and sins. A sobering reminder of the total sinfulness and lostness from which believers have been redeemed. "In" indicates the realm or sphere in which unregenerate sinners exist. They are not dead because of sinful acts that have been committed, but because of their sinful nature (cf. Mt 12:35; 15:18, 19).

2:2 course of this world. *See note on Jn 1:9.* This refers to the world order, i.e., humanity's values and standards apart from God and Christ. In 2Co 10:4, 5, Paul refers to these ideologies that are like fortresses in which people are imprisoned, need to be set free, and brought captive to Christ and obedience to the truth (*see notes there*). **the prince of the power of the air.** Satan. Cf. Jn 12:31; 14:30; 16:11; 2Co 4:4.

2:4 mercy … love. Salvation is for God's glory by putting on display His boundless mercy and love for those who are spiritually dead because of their sinfulness.

2:5 when we were dead … made us alive. Far more than anything else, a spiritually dead person needs to be made alive by God. Salvation brings spiritual life to the dead. The power that raises believers out of death and makes them alive (cf. Ro 6:1–7) is the same power that energizes every aspect of Christian living (cf. Ro 6:11–13).

2:6 raised us up … seated us with Him. The tense of "raised" and "seated" indicates that these are immediate and direct results of salvation. Not only is the believer dead to sin and alive to righteousness through Christ's resurrection, but he also enjoys his Lord's exaltation and shares in His preeminent glory. **in the heavenly *places*.** The supernatural realm where God reigns. In 3:10 and 6:12, however, it also refers to the supernatural sphere where Satan temporarily rules. This spiritual realm is where believers' blessings are (cf. 1:3), their inheritance is (1Pe 1:4), their affections should be (Col 3:3), and where they enjoy fellowship with the Lord. It is the realm from which all divine revelation has come and where all praise and petitions go.

2:7 riches of His grace. Salvation, of course, is very much for the believer's blessing, but it is even more for the purpose of eternally glorifying God for bestowing on believers His endless and limitless grace and kindness. The whole of heaven glorifies Him for what He has done in saving sinners (cf. 3:10; Rev 7:10–12).

2:8 faith; and that not of yourselves. "That" refers to the entire previous statement of salvation, not only the grace but the faith. Although men are required to believe for salvation, even that faith is part of the gift of God which saves and cannot be exercised by one's own power. God's grace is preeminent in every aspect of salvation (cf. Ro 3:20; Gal 2:16).

2:10 created in … for good works. Good works cannot produce salvation but are subsequent and resultant God-empowered fruits and evidences of it (cf. Jn 15:8; Php 2:12, 13; 2Ti 3:17; Titus 2:14; Jas 2:16–26). **which God prepared beforehand.** Like his salvation, a believer's sanctification and good works were ordained before time began (*see notes on Ro 8:29, 30*).

2:11, 12 Gentiles (the "Uncircumcision") experienced two types of alienation. The first was social, resulting from the animosity that had existed between Jews and Gentiles for thousands of years. Jews considered Gentiles to be outcasts, objects of derision, and reproach. The second and more significant type of alienation was spiritual, because Gentiles as a people were cut off from God in 5 different ways: 1) they were "separate from Christ," the Messiah, having no Savior and Deliverer and without divine purpose or destiny. 2) They were "excluded from the commonwealth of Israel." God's chosen people, the Jews, were a nation whose supreme King and Lord was God Himself, and from whose unique blessing and protection they benefitted. 3) Gentiles were "strangers to the covenants of promise," not able to partake of God's divine covenants in

SALVATION

Justification (past tense)	Sanctification (present tense)	Glorification (future tense)
Saved *immediately* from sin's penalty	Saved *progressively* from sin's power	Saved *ultimately* from sin's presence

"For by grace you have been saved through faith; and that not of yourselves, it is the gift of God." Eph. 2:8

13 But now in [A]Christ Jesus you who [B]formerly were
[C]far off [a]have [C]been brought near [b,D]by the blood of
Christ. 14 For He Himself is [A]our peace, [B]who made
both *groups into* one and broke down the [a]barrier of
the dividing wall, 15 [a]by [A]abolishing in His flesh the
enmity, *which is* [B]the Law of commandments *contained* in ordinances, so that in Himself He might
[b,C]make the two into [D]one new man, *thus* establishing
[E]peace, 16 and might [A]reconcile them both in [B]one
body to God through the cross, [a]by it having [C]put to
death the enmity. 17 AND [A]HE CAME AND PREACHED
[B]PEACE TO YOU WHO WERE [C]FAR AWAY, AND PEACE
TO THOSE WHO WERE [C]NEAR; 18 for through Him we
both have [A]our access in [B]one Spirit to [C]the Father.
19 So then you are no longer [A]strangers and aliens,
but you are [B]fellow citizens with the [a]saints, and are
of [C]God's household, 20 having been [A]built on [B]the
foundation of [C]the apostles and prophets, [D]Christ
Jesus Himself being the [E]corner *stone*, 21 [A]in whom
the whole building, being fitted together, is growing into [B]a holy [a]temple in the Lord, 22 in whom
you also are being [A]built together into a [B]dwelling
of God in the Spirit.

PAUL'S STEWARDSHIP

3 For this reason I, Paul, [A]the prisoner of [B]Christ
Jesus [C]for the sake of you [D]Gentiles— 2 if indeed you
have heard of the [A]stewardship of God's grace which
was given to me for you; 3 [A]that [B]by revelation there
was [C]made known to me [D]the mystery, [E]as I wrote
before in brief. 4 [a]By referring to this, when you read
you can understand [A]my insight [b]into the [B]mystery

2:13 [a]Lit *became;* or *were made* [b]Or *in* [A]Eph 1:1; 2:6 [B]Eph 2:2 [C]Is 57:19; Acts 2:39; Eph 2:17 [D]Rom 3:25; Col 1:20 2:14 [a]Lit *the dividing wall of the barrier* [A]Is 9:6; Eph 2:15; Col 3:15 [B]1 Cor 12:13; Gal 3:28; Col 3:11 2:15 [a]Or *the enmity, by abolishing in His flesh the Law* [b]Lit *create* [A]Eph 2:16; Col 1:21f [B]Col 2:14, 20 [C]Gal 3:28; Eph 2:10; Col 3:10, 11 [D]Gal 3:28; Col 3:10f [E]Is 9:6; Eph 2:14; Col 3:15 2:16 [a]Or *in Himself* [A]2 Cor 5:18; Col 1:20, 22 [B]1 Cor 10:17; Eph 4:4 [C]Eph 2:15 2:17 [A]Is 57:19; Rom 10:14 [B]Acts 10:36; Eph 2:14 [C]Eph 2:13 2:18 [A]Rom 5:2; Eph 3:12 [B]1 Cor 12:13; Eph 4:4 [C]Col 1:12 2:19 [a]Or *holy ones* [A]Eph 2:12; Heb 11:13; 1 Pet 2:11 [B]Phil 3:20; Heb 12:22f [C]Gal 6:10 2:20 [A]1 Cor 3:9 [B]Matt 16:18; 1 Cor 3:10; Rev 21:14 [C]1 Cor 12:28; Eph 3:5 [D]1 Cor 3:11 [E]Ps 118:22; Luke 20:17 2:21 [a]Or *sanctuary* [A]Eph 4:15f; Col 2:19 [B]1 Cor 3:16f 2:22 [A]1 Cor 3:9, 16; 2 Cor 6:16 [B]Eph 3:17 3:1 [A]Acts 23:18; Eph 4:1; 2 Tim 1:8; Philem 1, 9, 23 [B]Gal 5:24 [C]2 Cor 1:6; Eph 3:13 [D]Eph 3:8 3:2 [A]Eph 1:10; 3:9; Col 1:25; 1 Tim 1:4 3:3 [A]Acts 22:17, 21; 26:16ff [B]Gal 1:12 [C]Eph 1:9; 3:4, 6, 9 [D]Rom 11:25; 16:25; Eph 3:4, 9; 6:19; Col 1:26f; 4:3 [E]Eph 1:9f; Heb 13:22; 1 Pet 5:12 3:4 [a]Lit *To which, when you read* [b]Lit *in* [A]2 Cor 11:6 [B]Rom 11:25; 16:25; Eph 3:3, 9; 6:19; Col 1:26f; 4:3

which He promised to give His people a land, a priesthood, a people, a nation, a kingdom, and a King—and to those who believe in Him, eternal life and heaven. 4) They had "no hope" because they had been given no divine promise. 5) They were "without God in the world." While Gentiles had many gods, they did not recognize the true God because they did not want Him (*see notes on Ro 1:18–26*).

2:13 far off. A common term in rabbinical writings used to describe Gentiles, those who were apart from the true God (cf. Is 57:19; Ac 2:39). **brought near.** Every person who trusts in Christ alone for salvation, Jew or Gentile, is brought into spiritual union and intimacy with God. This is the reconciliation of 2Co 5:18–21. The atoning work accomplished by Christ's death on the cross washes away the penalty of sin and ultimately even its presence.

2:14 He Himself. This emphatically indicates that Jesus alone is the believer's source of peace (cf. Is 9:6). **the barrier of the dividing wall.** This alludes to a wall in the temple that partitioned off the Court of the Gentiles from the areas accessible only to Jews. Paul referred to that wall as symbolic of the social, religious, and spiritual separation that kept Jews and Gentiles apart.

2:15 abolishing in His flesh the enmity. Through His death, Christ abolished OT ceremonial laws, feasts, and sacrifices which uniquely separated Jews from Gentiles. God's moral law (as summarized in the Ten Commandments and written on the hearts of all men, Ro 2:15) was not abolished but subsumed in the New Covenant, however, because it reflects His own holy nature (Mt 5:17–19). *See notes on Mt 22:37–40; Ro 13:8–10.* **one new man.** Christ does not exclude anyone who comes to Him, and those who are His are not spiritually distinct from one another. "New" translates a Gr. word that refers to something completely unlike what it was before. It refers to being different in kind and quality. Spiritually, a new person in Christ is no longer Jew or Gentile, only Christian (cf. Ro 10:12, 13; Gal 3:28).

2:16 reconcile them both … to God. As Jews and Gentiles are brought to God through Christ Jesus, they are brought together with one another. This was accomplished by the cross where Jesus became a curse (Gal 3:10–13), taking God's wrath so that divine justice was satisfied and reconciliation with God became a reality (*see notes on 2Co 5:19–21*). For more on reconciliation, see Ro 5:8–10; Col 1:19–23.

2:17 preached peace. The Gr. word for "preached" lit. means "to bring or announce good news," and in the NT is almost always used of proclaiming the good news that sinners can be reconciled to God by the salvation which is through Jesus Christ. In this context, Christ, the One who "Himself is our peace" (v. 14), also announced the good news of peace. **far away, and … near.** That is to Gentiles and Jews alike.

2:18 access in one Spirit to the Father. No sinner has any right or worthiness in himself for access to God, but believers have been granted that right through faith in Christ's sacrificial death (cf. 3:12; Ro 5:2). The resources of the Trinity belong to believers the moment they receive Christ, and the Holy Spirit presents them before the heavenly throne of God the Father, where they are welcome to come with boldness at any time. *See notes on Ro 8:15–17; Gal 4:6, 7; Heb 4:16.*

2:19 fellow citizens with the saints. God's kingdom is made up of the people from all time who have trusted in Him. There are no strangers, foreigners, or second-class citizens there (cf. Php 3:20). **of God's household.** Redeemed sinners not only become heavenly citizens but also members of God's own family. The Father bestows on believers the same infinite love He gives His Son. *See note on 1:5*; cf. Heb 3:6.

2:20 the foundation of the apostles and prophets. For discussion of these gifted men, *see note on 4:11.* As important as they were, it was not them personally, but the divine revelation they taught, as they authoritatively spoke the word of God to the church before the completion of the NT, that provided the foundation (cf. Ro 15:20). **corner *stone*.** Cf. Ps 118:22; Is 28:16; Mt 21:42; Ac 4:11; 1Pe 2:6, 7. This stone set the foundation and squared the building.

2:21 a holy temple in the Lord. Every new believer is a new stone in Christ's temple, the church, Christ's body of believers (*see note on 1Pe 2:5*). Christ's building of His church will not be complete until every person who will believe in Him has done so (2Pe 3:9).

2:22 a dwelling of God in the Spirit. The term for "dwelling" connotes a permanent home. God the Holy Spirit takes up permanent residence in His earthly sanctuary, the church, the vast spiritual body of all the redeemed (cf. 1Co 6:19, 20; 2Co 6:16).

3:1 For this reason. This refers back to the truths about the unity of believers that Paul has just discussed and introduces the motive for his prayer which begins in v. 14. **the prisoner of Christ Jesus.** Although Paul had been a prisoner for about two years in Caesarea and two years in Rome, he did not consider himself to be a prisoner of any government or person. Rather, he knew he was under Christ's control, and every aspect of his life was in the Lord's hands. He suffered imprisonment for preaching to Gentiles. See 2Co 4:8–15.

3:2–13 In this parenthetical passage, Paul interrupted the thought begun in v. 1 to reemphasize and to expand upon the truths he had just written. He was compelled to affirm his authority for teaching the oneness of Jew and Gentile in Christ (vv. 2–7), a new and far-reaching truth that most of the Ephesians doubtless found difficult to comprehend or accept.

3:2 stewardship … given to me. "Stewardship" means an administration, or management. Paul did not choose the stewardship of his apostleship or ministry. God had sovereignly commissioned him with the calling, spiritual gifts, opportunities, knowledge, and authority to minister as the apostle to the Gentiles (see Ac 9:1–19; 1Ti 1:12, 13; cf. Ro 15:15, 16; 1Co 4:1; 9:16, 17; Gal 2:9).

3:4 the mystery of Christ. *See notes on 1:10–12; 2:11, 12; Mt 13:11; 1Co 2:7; Col 1:26, 27.* There were many truths hidden and later revealed in the NT that are called mysteries. Here is one: Jew and Gentile brought together in one body in the Messiah. For others, *see notes on 1Co 15:51; Col 1:27; 1Ti 3:16.* Paul not

of Christ, 5 which in other generations was not made
known to the sons of men, as it has now been revealed
to His holy [A]apostles and prophets [a]in the Spirit; 6 *to
be specific,* that the Gentiles are [A]fellow heirs and
[B]fellow members of the body, and [C]fellow partakers
of the promise in [D]Christ Jesus through the gospel,
7 [A]of which I was made a [B]minister, according to the
gift of [C]God's grace which was given to me [D]according
to the working of His power. 8 To me, [A]the very least
of all [a]saints, this grace was given, to [B]preach to the
Gentiles the unfathomable [C]riches of Christ, 9 and to
[a]bring to light what is the administration of the [A]mys-
tery which for ages has been [B]hidden in God [C]who
created all things; 10 so that the manifold [A]wisdom of
God might now be [B]made known through the church
to the [C]rulers and the authorities in [D]the heavenly
places. 11 *This was* in [A]accordance with the [a]eternal
purpose which He [b]carried out in [B]Christ Jesus our
Lord, 12 in whom we have boldness and [a,A]confident
[B]access through faith [b]in Him. 13 Therefore I ask [a]you
not [A]to lose heart at my tribulations [B]on your behalf,
[b]for they are your glory.

14 For this reason I [A]bow my knees before the
Father, 15 from whom [a]every family in heaven and
on earth derives its name, 16 that He would grant
you, according to [A]the riches of His glory, to be
[B]strengthened with power through His Spirit in
[C]the inner man, 17 so that [A]Christ may dwell in your
hearts through faith; *and* that you, being [B]rooted
and [C]grounded in love, 18 may be able to comprehend with [A]all the [a]saints what is [B]the breadth and
length and height and depth, 19 and to know [A]the
love of Christ which [B]surpasses knowledge, that you
may be [C]filled up to all the [D]fullness of God.

3:5 [a]Or *by* [A]1 Cor 12:28; Eph 2:20 3:6 [A]Gal 3:29 [B]Eph 2:16 [C]Eph 5:7 [D]Gal 5:24 3:7 [A]Col 1:23, 25 [B]1 Cor 3:5 [C]Acts 9:15; Rom 12:3; Eph 3:2 [D]Eph 1:19; 3:20 3:8 [a]Or *holy ones* [A]1 Cor 15:9 [B]Acts 9:15; Eph 3:1f [C]Rom 2:4; Eph 1:7; 3:16 3:9 [a]Two early mss read *make all know* [A]Rom 11:25; 16:25; Eph 3:3, 4; 6:19; Col 1:26f; 4:3 [B]Col 3:3 [C]Rev 4:11 3:10 [A]Rom 11:33; 1 Cor 2:7 [B]Eph 1:23; 1 Pet 1:12 [C]Eph 1:21; 6:12; Col 2:10, 15 [D]Eph 1:3 3:11 [a]Lit *purpose of the ages* [b]Or *formed* [A]Eph 1:11 [B]Gal 5:24; Eph 3:1 3:12 [a]Lit *access in confidence* [b]Lit *of Him* [A]2 Cor 3:4; Heb 4:16; 10:19, 35; 1 John 2:28; 3:21 [B]Eph 2:18 3:13 [a]Or *that I may not lose* [b]Lit *which are* [A]2 Cor 4:1 [B]Eph 3:1 3:14 [A]Phil 2:10 3:15 [a]Or *the whole* 3:16 [A]Eph 1:18; 3:8 [B]1 Cor 16:13; Phil 4:13; Col 1:11 [C]Rom 7:22 3:17 [A]John 14:23; Rom 8:9f; 2 Cor 13:5; Eph 2:22 [B]1 Cor 3:6; Col 2:7 [C]Col 1:23 3:18 [a]V 8, note 1 [A]Eph 1:15 [B]Job 11:8f 3:19 [A]Rom 8:35, 39 [B]Phil 4:7 [C]Col 2:10 [D]Eph 1:23

only wrote of the mystery that, in Christ, Jew and Gentile become one in God's sight and in His kingdom and family, but also explained and clarified that truth. He realized that spiritual knowledge must precede practical application. What is not properly understood cannot be properly applied.

3:5 in other generations was not made known. Though God had promised universal blessing through Abraham (Ge 12:3), the full meaning of that promise became clear when Paul wrote Gal 3:28. Isaiah 49:6 predicted salvation to all races, but it was Paul who wrote of the fulfillment of that pledge (Ac 13:46, 47). Paul disclosed a truth that not even the greatest prophets understood—that within the church, composed of all the saved since Pentecost in one united body, there would be no racial, social, or spiritual distinctions.

3:6 Gentiles are fellow heirs. A summary of 2:11–22. *See notes on 1Co 12:12, 13; Gal 3:29.*

3:7 made a minister. No man can make himself a minister (lit. servant) of God, because the calling, message, work, and empowering of genuine ministry to and for God are His prerogative alone to give. See Ac 26:16; 1Co 15:10; Col 1:23, 25, 29.

3:8 the very least of all saints. In light of God's perfect righteousness, Paul's assessment of himself was not false humility but simple honesty. He knew his unworthiness. See 1Ti 1:12, 13 (cf. Jdg 6:15, 16; Is 6:1–9). **the unfathomable riches of Christ.** All God's truths, all His blessings, all that He is and has (cf. 1:3; Col 2:3; 2Pe 1:3).

3:9 administration ... mystery. *See notes on vv. 4, 5.*

3:10 rulers ... authorities. Angels, both holy and unholy (1:21; 6:12; *see note on Col 1:16*). God, through the church manifests His glory to all the angels. The holy angels rejoice (see Lk 15:10; cf. 1Pe 1:12) because they are involved with the church (see 1Co 11:10; Heb 1:14). Although they have no desire or capacity to praise God, even fallen angels see the glory of God in the salvation and preservation of the church. **in the heavenly *places*.** As in 1:3; 6:12, this refers to the entire realm of spiritual beings.

3:11 the eternal purpose. The supreme purpose of the church is to glorify God, which includes the displaying of His wisdom (v. 10) before the angels, who then honor Him with even greater praise.

3:12 confident access. Every person who comes to Christ in faith can come before God at any time, not in self-confidence but in Christ-confidence. *See notes on Heb 4:15, 16.*

3:13 tribulations ... your glory. Through trouble and suffering, God produces glory. *See note on Ro 8:18.*

3:14 For this reason. Paul repeated what he wrote in v. 1 (*see note there*) as he began his prayer. Because of their new identity in Christ, stated in chap. 2, believers are spiritually alive (v. 5), they are unified into God's household (v. 19), and, as the church, they are the dwelling place of God, built on the words and work of the apostles and prophets (vv. 20–22). **I bow my knees.** Not an instruction for physical posture during prayer, but suggesting an attitude of submission, reverence, and intense passion (cf. Ezr 9:5, 6; Ps 95:1–6; Da 6:10; Ac 20:36).

3:15 every family in heaven and on earth. Paul was not teaching the universal fatherhood of God and the universal brotherhood of man (cf. Jn 8:39–42; 1Jn 3:10), but was simply referring to believers from every era of history, those who are dead (in heaven) and those who are alive (on earth).

3:16 that He would grant you. Paul's prayers are almost always for the spiritual welfare of others (cf. Php 1:4; Col 1:9–11; 1Th 1:2). **according to the riches of His glory.** They are limitless and available to every believer. **strengthened ... His Spirit in the inner man.** Spiritual power is a mark of every Christian who submits to God's Word and Spirit. It is not reserved for some special class of Christian, but for all those who discipline their minds and spirits to study the Word, understand it, and live by it. Although the outer, physical person becomes weaker with age (cf. 2Co 4:16), the inner, spiritual person should grow stronger through the Holy Spirit, who will energize, revitalize, and empower the obedient, committed Christian (cf. Ac 1:8; Ro 8:5–9, 13; Gal 5:16).

3:17 that Christ may dwell in your hearts. Every believer is indwelt by Christ at the moment of salvation (Ro 8:9; 1Co 12:13), but He is "at home," finding comfort and satisfaction, only where hearts are cleansed of sin and filled with His Spirit (cf. Jn 14:23). **through faith.** This speaks of Christians' continuing trust in Christ to exercise His lordship over them. **rooted and grounded in love.** I.e., established on the strong foundation of self-giving, serving love for God and for His people (cf. Mt 22:37–39; 1Jn 4:9–12, 19–21).

3:18 able to comprehend. A believer cannot understand the fullness of God's love apart from genuine, Spirit-empowered love in his own life. **with all the saints.** Love is both granted to (Ro 5:5; 1Th 4:9) and commanded of (Jn 13:34, 35) every Christian, not just those who have a naturally pleasant temperament or have great spiritual maturity. **breadth ... length ... height ... depth.** Not 4 different features of love, but an effort to suggest its vastness and completeness.

3:19 to know the love of Christ. Not the love believers have for Christ, but the love of and from Christ that He places in their hearts before they can truly and fully love Him or anyone else (Ro 5:5). **which surpasses knowledge.** Knowledge of Christ's love is far beyond the capability of human reason and experience. It is only known by those who are God's children (cf. Php 4:7). **filled up to all the fullness of God.** To be so strong spiritually, so compelled by divine love, that one is totally dominated by the Lord with nothing left of self. Human comprehension of the fullness of God is impossible, because even the most spiritual and wise believer cannot completely grasp the full extent of God's attributes and characteristics—His power, majesty, wisdom, love, mercy, patience, kindness, and everything He is and does. But believers can experience the greatness of God in their lives as a result of total devotion to Him. Note the fullness of God, here; the fullness of Christ in 4:13; and the fullness of the Spirit in 5:18. Paul prayed for believers to become as Godlike as possible (Mt 5:48; 1Pe 1:15, 16).

20 [A]Now to Him who is [B]able to do far more abundantly beyond all that we ask or think, [C]according
to the power that works within us, 21 [A]to Him *be*
the glory in the church and in Christ Jesus to all
generations [a]forever and ever. Amen.

UNITY OF THE SPIRIT

4 Therefore I, [A]the prisoner of the Lord, [B]implore
you to [C]walk in a manner worthy of the [D]call-
ing with which you have been [E]called, 2 with all
[A]humility and gentleness, with patience, showing
tolerance for one another [B]in love, 3 being diligent
to preserve the unity of the Spirit in the [A]bond of
peace. 4 *There is* [A]one body and one Spirit, just as
also you were called in one [B]hope of your calling;
5 [A]one Lord, one faith, one baptism, 6 one God and
Father of all [A]who is over all and through all and
in all.
7 But [A]to each one of us [B]grace was given [C]ac-
cording to the measure of Christ's gift. 8 Therefore
[a]it says,

"[A]WHEN HE ASCENDED ON HIGH,
HE [B]LED CAPTIVE A HOST
OF CAPTIVES,
AND HE GAVE GIFTS TO MEN."

9 (Now this *expression,* "He [A]ascended," what [a]does
it mean except that He also [b]had descended into
[B]the lower parts of the earth? 10 He who descended
is Himself also He who ascended [A]far above all
the heavens, so that He might [B]fill all things.)

3:20 [A]Rom 16:25 [B]2 Cor 9:8 [C]Eph 3:7 3:21 [a]Lit *of the age of the ages* [A]Rom 11:36 4:1 [A]Eph 3:1 [B]Rom 12:1 [C]Eph 2:10; Col 1:10; 2:6; 1 Thess 2:12 [D]Rom 11:29 [E]Rom 8:28f 4:2 [A]Col 3:12f [B]Eph 1:4 4:3 [A]Col 3:14f 4:4 [A]1 Cor 12:4ff; Eph 2:16, 18 [B]Eph 1:18 4:5 [A]1 Cor 8:6 4:6 [A]Rom 11:36 4:7 [A]1 Cor 12:7, 11 [B]Eph 3:2 [C]Rom 12:3 4:8 [a]Or *He* [A]Ps 68:18 [B]Col 2:15 4:9 [a]Lit *is it except* [b]One early ms reads *had first descended* [A]John 3:13 [B]Is 44:23 4:10 [A]Eph 1:20f; Heb 4:14; 7:26 [B]Eph 1:23

3:20 When the conditions of vv. 16–19 are met, God's power working in and through believers is unlimited and far beyond their comprehension.

3:21 to Him *be* the glory. Only when His children meet this level of faithfulness will Christ be fully glorified with the honor He deserves from His church.

4:1 Therefore. This word marks the transition from doctrine to duty, principle to practice, position to behavior. This is typical of Paul (see Ro 12:1; Gal 5:1; Php 2:1; Col 3:5; 1Th 4:1). **the prisoner of the Lord.** By mentioning his imprisonment again (see 3:1), Paul gently reminded Ephesian believers that the faithful Christian walk can be costly and that he had paid a considerable personal price because of his obedience to the Lord. **walk … worthy.** "Walk" is frequently used in the N.T. to refer to daily conduct. It sets the theme for the final 3 chapters. "Worthy" has the idea of living to match one's position in Christ. The apostle urged his readers to be everything the Lord desires and empowers them to be. **calling.** This refers to God's sovereign call to salvation, as always in the Epistles. *See note on Ro 1:7.* The effectual call that saves is mentioned in 1:18; Ro 11:29; 1Co 1:26; Php 3:14; 2Th 1:11; 2Ti 1:9; Heb 3:1.

4:2 humility. "Humility" is a term not found in the Lat. or Gr. vocabularies of Paul's day. The Gr. word apparently was coined by Christians, perhaps even by Paul himself, to describe a quality for which no other word was available. Humility, the most foundational Christian virtue (Jas 4:6), is the quality of character commanded in the first beatitude (Mt 5:3), and describes the noble grace of Christ (Php 2:7, 8). **gentleness.** "Meekness," an inevitable product of humility, refers to that which is mild-spirited and self-controlled (cf. Mt 5:5; 11:29; Gal 5:23; Col 3:12). **patience.** The Gr. word lit. means long-tempered, and refers to a resolved patience that is an outgrowth of humility and gentleness (cf. 1Th 5:14; Jas 5:10). **showing tolerance for one another in love.** Humility, gentleness, and patience are reflected in a forbearing love for others that is continuous and unconditional (cf. 1Pe 4:8).

4:3 unity of the Spirit. The Spirit-bestowed oneness of all true believers (see 1Co 6:17; 12:11–13; Php 1:27; 2:2) has created the bond of peace, the spiritual cord that surrounds and binds God's holy people together. This bond is love (Col 3:14).

4:4–6 In this passage, Paul lists the particular areas of oneness, or unity: body, Spirit, hope, Lord, faith, baptism, and God and Father. He focuses on the Trinity—the Spirit in v. 4, the Son in v. 5, and the Father in v. 6. His point is not to distinguish between the Persons of the Godhead, but to emphasize that, although they have unique roles, they are completely unified in every aspect of the divine nature and plan.

4:4 one body. The church, the body of Christ, is composed of every believer since Pentecost without distinction, by the work of the "one Spirit" (see 1Co 12:11–13). **one hope.** This is the pledge and promise of eternal inheritance given each believer (1:11–14) and sealed to each believer by the one Spirit (v. 13).

4:5 one Lord. See Ac 4:12; Ro 10:12; Gal 1:8. **one faith.** The body of doctrine revealed in the NT (cf. Jude 3). **one baptism.** This probably refers to the water baptism following salvation, a believer's public confession of faith in Jesus Christ. Spiritual baptism, by which all believers are placed into the body of Christ (1Co 12:11–13) is implied in v. 4.

4:6 one God. This is the basic doctrine of God taught in Scripture (see Dt 4:35; 6:4; 32:39; Is 45:14; 46:9; 1Co 8:4–6).

4:7 But to each one. This could be translated "in spite of that," or "on the other hand," contrasting what has just been said with what is about to be said, moving from the subject of the unity of believers ("all," v. 6) to that of the uniqueness of believers ("each one"). **grace.** Grace is a single-word definition of the gospel, the good news of God's offering salvation to sinful and unworthy mankind. God is the God of grace because He is a God who freely gives; His giving has nothing to do with anything we have done, but is unmerited, unearned, and undeserved. *See notes on 2:7–10.* **the measure of Christ's gift.** Each believer has a unique spiritual gift that God individually portions out according to His sovereign will and design. The Gr. term for "gift" focuses not on the Spirit as the source like the term used in 1Co 12:1, nor on the grace that prompted it in Ro 12:6, but on the freeness of the gift. For discussions of the gifts, *see notes on Ro 12:6–8; 1Co 12:4–10; 1Pe 4:10.*

4:8 When He ascended on high. Paul used an interpretive rendering of Ps 68:18 as a parenthetical analogy to show how Christ received the right to bestow the spiritual gifts (v. 7). Psalm 68 is a victory hymn composed by David to celebrate God's conquest of the Jebusite city of Jerusalem and the triumphant ascent of God up to Mt. Zion (cf. 2Sa 6, 7; 1Ch 13). After such a triumph, the king would bring home the spoils and the prisoners. Here Paul depicts Christ returning from His battle on earth back into the glory of the heavenly city with the trophies of His great victory at Calvary (*see notes on 2Co 2:14–16*). led captive a host of captives. Through His crucifixion and resurrection, Christ conquered Satan and death, and in triumph returned to God those who were once sinners and prisoners of Satan (cf. Col 2:15). gave gifts to men. He distributes the spoils throughout His kingdom. After His ascension came all the spiritual gifts empowered by the Spirit, who was then sent (see Jn 7:39; 14:12; Ac 2:33).

4:9 ascended. Jesus' ascension from earth to heaven (Ac 1:9–11), where He forever reigns with His Father. **descended.** This refers to Christ's incarnation, when He came down from heaven as a man into the earth of suffering and death. **the lower parts of the earth.** These are in contrast to the highest heavens to which He afterward ascended (cf. Ps 139:8, 15; Is 44:23). The phrase here does not point to a specific place, but to the great depth, as it were, of the incarnation, including Christ's descent, between His crucifixion and resurrection beyond the earth, the grave, and death, into the very pit of the demons, "the spirits in prison" (*see notes on Col 2:14, 15; 1Pe 3:18, 19*).

4:10 that He might fill all things. After the Lord ascended, having fulfilled all prophecies and all His divinely ordained redemptive tasks, He gained the right to rule the church and to give gifts, as He was then filling the entire universe with His divine presence, power, sovereignty, and blessing (cf. Php 2:9–11).

11And He [A]gave [B]some *as* apostles, and some *as*
prophets, and some *as* [C]evangelists, and some *as*
pastors and [D]teachers, 12[A]for the equipping of the
[a]saints for the work of service, to the building up of
[B]the body of Christ; 13until we all attain to [A]the unity
of the faith, and of the [a,B]knowledge of the Son of
God, to a [C]mature man, to the measure of the stature [b]which belongs to the [D]fullness of Christ. 14[a]As
a result, we are [A]no longer to be children, [B]tossed
here and there by waves and carried about by every
wind of doctrine, by the trickery of men, by [C]craft-
iness [b]in [D]deceitful scheming; 15but [a]speaking the
truth [A]in love, [b]we are to [B]grow up in all *aspects* into
Him who is the [C]head, *even* Christ, 16from whom
[A]the whole body, being fitted and held together [a]by
what every joint supplies, according to the [b]proper
working of each individual part, causes the growth
of the body for the building up of itself [B]in love.

THE CHRISTIAN'S WALK

17[A]So this I say, and affirm together with the Lord,
[B]that you walk no longer just as the Gentiles also
walk, in the [C]futility of their mind, 18being [A]dark-
ened in their understanding, [a,B]excluded from the
life of God because of the [C]ignorance that is in them,
because of the [D]hardness of their heart; 19and they,
having [A]become callous, [B]have given themselves
over to [C]sensuality [a]for the practice of every kind of

4:11 [A]Eph 4:8 [B]Acts 13:1; 1 Cor 12:28 [C]Acts 21:8 [D]Acts 13:1 4:12 [a]Or *holy ones* [A]2 Cor 13:9 [B]1 Cor 12:27; Eph 1:23 4:13 [a]Or *true knowledge* [b]Lit *of the fullness* [A]Eph 4:3, 5 [B]John 6:69; Eph 1:17; Phil 3:10 [C]1 Cor 14:20; Col 1:28; Heb 5:14 [D]John 1:16; Eph 1:23 4:14 [a]Lit *So that we will no longer be* [b]Lit *with regard to the scheming of deceit* [A]1 Cor 14:20 [B]James 1:6; Jude 12 [C]1 Cor 3:19; 2 Cor 4:2; 11:3 [D]Eph 6:11 4:15 [a]Or *holding to or being truthful in* [b]Or *let us grow up* [A]Eph 1:4 [B]Eph 2:21 [C]Eph 1:22 4:16 [a]Lit *through every joint of the supply* [b]Lit *working in measure* [A]Rom 12:4f; Col 2:19 [B]Eph 1:4 4:17 [A]Col 2:4 [B]Eph 2:2; 4:22 [C]Rom 1:21; Col 2:18; 1 Pet 1:18; 2 Pet 2:18 4:18 [a]Or *alienated* [A]Rom 1:21 [B]Eph 2:1, 12 [C]Acts 3:17; 17:30; 1 Cor 2:8; Heb 5:2; 9:7; 1 Pet 1:14 [D]Mark 3:5; Rom 11:7, 25; 2 Cor 3:14 4:19 [a]Or *greedy for the practice of every kind of impurity* [A]1 Tim 4:2 [B]Rom 1:24 [C]Col 3:5

4:11 He gave some. As evidenced by His perfect fulfillment of His Father's will, Christ possessed the authority and sovereignty to assign the spiritual gifts (vv. 7, 8) to those He has called into service in His church. He gave not only gifts, but gifted men. **apostles.** *See note on 2:20.* A term used particularly of the 12 disciples who had seen the risen Christ (Ac 1:22), including Matthias, who replaced Judas. Later, Paul was uniquely set apart as the apostle to the Gentiles (Gal 1:15–17) and was numbered with the other apostles. He, too, miraculously encountered Jesus at his conversion on the Damascus Road (Ac 9:1–9; Gal 1:15–17). Those apostles were chosen directly by Christ, so as to be called "apostles of Jesus Christ" (Gal 1:1; 1Pe 1:1). They were given 3 basic responsibilities: 1) to lay the foundation of the church (2:20); 2) to receive, declare, and write God's Word (3:5; Ac 11:28; 21:10, 11); and 3) to give confirmation of that Word through signs, wonders, and miracles (2Co 12:12; cf. Ac 8:6, 7; Heb 2:3, 4). The term "apostle" is used in more general ways of other men in the early church, such as Barnabas (Ac 14:4), Silas, Timothy (1Th 2:6), and others (Ro 16:7; Php 2:25). They are called "messengers (or apostles) of the churches" (2Co 8:23), rather than "apostles of Jesus Christ" like the 13. They were not self-perpetuating, nor was any apostle who died replaced. **prophets.** *See note on 2:20.* Not ordinary believers who had the gift of prophecy but specially commissioned men in the early church. The office of prophet seems to have been exclusively for work within a local congregation. They were not "sent ones" as were the apostles (see Ac 13:1–4), but, as with the apostles, their office ceased with the completion of the NT. They sometimes spoke practical direct revelation for the church from God (Ac 11:21–28) or expounded revelation already given (implied in Ac 13:1). They were not used for the reception of Scripture. Their messages were to be judged by other prophets for validity (1Co 14:32) and had to conform to the teaching of the apostles (v. 37). Those two offices were replaced by the evangelists and teaching pastors. **evangelists.** Men who proclaim the good news of salvation in Jesus Christ to unbelievers. Cf. the use of this term in Ac 21:8; 2Ti 4:5. The related verb translated "to preach the gospel" is used 54 times and the related noun translated "gospel" is used 76 times in the NT. **pastors and teachers.** This phrase is best understood in context as a single office of leadership in the church. The Gr. word translated "and" can mean "in particular" (see 1Ti 5:17). The normal meaning of pastor is "shepherd," so the two functions together define the teaching shepherd. He is identified as one who is under the "great Shepherd" Jesus (Heb 13:20, 21; 1Pe 2:25). One who holds this office is also called an "elder" (*see notes on Titus 1:5–9*) and "bishop," or "overseer" (*see notes on 1Ti 3:1–7*). Ac 20:28 and 1Pe 5:1, 2 bring all 3 terms together.

4:12 equipping. This refers to restoring something to its original condition, or its being made fit or complete. In this context, it refers to leading Christians from sin to obedience. Scripture is the key to this process (*see notes on 2Ti 3:16, 17*; cf. Jn 15:3). **saints.** All who believe in Jesus Christ. *See note on 1:1.* **the work of service.** The spiritual service required of every Christian, not just of church leaders (cf. 1Co 15:58). **the building up of the body of Christ.** The spiritual edification, nurturing, and development of the church (cf. Ac 20:32).

4:13 unity of the faith. Faith here refers to the body of revealed truth that constitutes Christian teaching, particularly featuring the complete content of the gospel. Oneness and harmony among believers are possible only when they are built on the foundation of sound doctrine. **the knowledge of the Son of God.** This does not refer to salvation knowledge, but to the deep knowledge of Christ that a believer comes to have through prayer, faithful study of His Word, and obedience to His commands (cf. Php 3:8–10, 12; Col 1:9, 10; 2:2; *see note on 1Jn 2:12–14*). **the fullness of Christ.** God wants every believer to manifest the qualities of His Son, who is Himself the standard for their spiritual maturity and perfection. *See notes on Ro 8:29; 2Co 3:18; Col 1:28, 29.*

4:14 carried about by every wind of doctrine. Spiritually immature believers who are not grounded in the knowledge of Christ through God's Word are inclined to uncritically accept every sort of beguiling doctrinal error and fallacious interpretation of Scripture promulgated by deceitful, false teachers in the church. They must learn discernment (1Th 5:21, 22). See 3:1; 4:20. The NT is replete with warnings of such danger (Ac 20:30, 31; Ro 16:17, 18; Gal 1:6, 7; 1Ti 4:1–7; 2Ti 2:15–18; 2Pe 2:1–3).

4:15 speaking the truth in love. Evangelism is most effective when the truth is proclaimed in love. This can be accomplished only by the spiritually mature believer who is thoroughly equipped in sound doctrine. Without maturity, the truth can be cold and love little more than sentimentality. **grow up ... into Him.** Christians are to be completely yielded and obedient to the Lord's will, subject to His controlling power and Christlike in all areas of their lives (cf. Gal 2:20; Php 1:21). **the head.** Given the picture of the church as a body whose head is Christ, "head" is used in the sense of authoritative leader, not "source," which would have required a different anatomical picture. See 1:22; 5:23.

4:16 from whom. This refers to the Lord. Power for producing mature, equipped believers comes not from the effort of those believers alone, but from their Head, the Lord Jesus Christ (cf. Col 2:19). **proper working of each ... part.** Godly, biblical church growth results from every member of the body fully using his spiritual gift, in submission to the Holy Spirit and in cooperation with other believers (cf. Col 2:19).

4:17–19 In these verses, Paul gives 4 characteristics of the ungodly lifestyles which believers are to forsake.

4:17 walk no longer. "Walk" expresses daily conduct and refers back to what Paul has said about the believer's high calling in Christ Jesus (v. 1). Because Christians are part of the body of Christ, have been spiritually gifted by the Holy Spirit, and are edified through other believers, they should not continue to live like the rest of the ungodly (1Jn 2:6). **Gentiles.** All ungodly, unregenerate pagans (cf. 1Th 4:5 which defines them). **the futility of their mind.** First, unbelievers are intellectually unproductive. As far as spiritual and moral issues are concerned, their rational processes are distorted and inadequate, inevitably failing to produce godly understanding or moral living. Their life is empty, vain, and without meaning (cf. Ro 1:21–28; 1Co 2:14; Col 2:18).

4:18 excluded from the life of God. Second, unbelievers are spiritually separated from God, thus ignorant of God's truth (1Co 2:14), and their willing spiritual darkness and moral blindness is the result (cf. Ro 1:21–24; 2Ti 3:7). They are blind, or "hard" like a rock.

4:19 having become callous. Third,

impurity with greediness. 20 But you did not [A]learn
[a]Christ in this way, 21 if indeed you [A]have heard Him
and have [B]been taught in Him, just as truth is in
Jesus, 22 that, in reference to your former manner
of life, you [A]lay aside the [B]old [a]self, which is being
corrupted in accordance with the [C]lusts of deceit,
23 and that you be [A]renewed in the spirit of your
mind, 24 and [A]put on the [B]new [a]self, which [b,C]in *the
likeness of* God has been created in righteousness
and holiness of the truth.

25 Therefore, [A]laying aside falsehood, [B]SPEAK
TRUTH EACH ONE *of you* WITH HIS NEIGHBOR, for
we are [C]members of one another. 26 [A]BE ANGRY,
AND *yet* DO NOT SIN; do not let the sun go down
on your anger, 27 and do not [A]give the devil [a]an
opportunity. 28 He who steals must steal no longer; but rather [A]he must labor, [B]performing with
his own hands what is good, [C]so that he will have
something to share with [a]one who has need. 29 Let
no [a,A]unwholesome word proceed from your
mouth, but only such *a word* as is good for [B]ed-
ification [b]according to the need *of the moment,*
so that it will give grace to those who hear. 30 [A]Do
not grieve the Holy Spirit of God, [a]by whom you
were [B]sealed for the day of redemption. 31 [A]Let all
bitterness and wrath and anger and clamor and
slander be [B]put away from you, along with all
[C]malice. 32 [A]Be kind to one another, tender-hearted,
forgiving each other, [B]just as God in Christ also
has forgiven [a]you.

4:20 [a]I.e. the Messiah [A]Matt 11:29 4:21 [A]Rom 10:14; Eph 1:13; 2:17; Col 1:5 [B]Col 2:7 4:22 [a]Lit *man* [A]Eph 4:25, 31; Col 3:8; Heb 12:1; James 1:21; 1 Pet 2:1 [B]Rom 6:6 [C]2 Cor 11:3; Heb 3:13 4:23 [A]Rom 12:2 4:24 [a]Lit *man* [b]Lit *according to God* [A]Rom 13:14 [B]Rom 6:4; 7:6; 12:2; 2 Cor 5:17; Col 3:10 [C]Eph 2:10 4:25 [A]Eph 4:22, 31; Col 3:8; Heb 12:1; James 1:21; 1 Pet 2:1 [B]Zech 8:16; Eph 4:15; Col 3:9 [C]Rom 12:5 4:26 [A]Ps 4:4 4:27 [a]Lit *a place* [A]Rom 12:19; James 4:7 4:28 [a]Lit *the one* [A]Acts 20:35; 1 Cor 4:12; Gal 6:10 [B]1 Thess 4:11; 2 Thess 3:8, 11f; Titus 3:8, 14 [C]Luke 3:11; 1 Thess 4:12 4:29 [a]Lit *rotten* [b]Lit *of the need* [A]Matt 12:34; Eph 5:4; Col 3:8 [B]Eccl 10:12; Rom 14:19; Col 4:6 4:30 [a]Lit *in* [A]Is 63:10; 1 Thess 5:19 [B]John 3:33; Eph 1:13 4:31 [A]Rom 3:14; Col 3:8, 19 [B]Eph 4:22 [C]1 Pet 2:1 4:32 [a]Two early mss read *us* [A]1 Cor 13:4; Col 3:12f; 1 Pet 3:8 [B]Matt 6:14f; 2 Cor 2:10

unbelievers are morally insensitive. As they continue to sin and turn away from God, they become still more apathetic about moral and spiritual things (cf. Ro 1:32). **sensuality ... impurity.** Fourth, unbelievers are behaviorally depraved (cf. Ro 1:28). As they willingly keep succumbing to sensuality and licentiousness, they increasingly lose moral restraint, especially in the area of sexual sins. Impurity is inseparable from greediness, which is a form of idolatry (5:5; Col 3:5). That some souls may not reach the extremes of vv. 17–19 is due only to God's common grace and the restraining influence of the Holy Spirit.

4:20, 21 learn ... heard ... taught. Three figurative descriptions of salvation, the new birth.

4:21 as truth is in Jesus. The truth about salvation leads to the fullness of truth about God, man, creation, history, life, purpose, relationships, heaven, hell, judgment, and everything else that is truly important. John summed this up in 1Jn 5:20.

4:22 lay aside. To strip away, as in taking off old, filthy clothes. This describes repentance from sin and submission to God at the point of salvation. *See notes on Col 3:3–9* (cf. Is 55:6, 7; Mt 19:16–22; Ac 2:38–40; 20:21; 1Th 1:9). **the old self.** The worn out, useless, and unconverted sinful nature corrupted by deceit. Salvation is a spiritual union with Jesus Christ that is described as the death plus burial of the old self and the resurrection of the new self walking in newness of life. This transformation is Paul's theme in Ro 6:2–8 (*see notes there*).

4:23 be renewed in the spirit of your mind. Salvation involves the mind (*see notes on Ro 12:2; 2Co 10:5*), which is the center of thought, understanding, and belief, as well as of motive and action (cf. Col 3:1, 2, 10). When a person becomes a Christian, God gives him a completely new spiritual and moral capability that a mind apart from Christ could never achieve (cf. 1Co 2:9–16).

4:24 put on the new self. The renewal of the mind in salvation brings not simply a renovation of character, but transformation of the old to the new self (cf. 2Co 5:17). **in *the likeness of* God has been created.** In Christ, the old self no longer exists as it had in the past; the new self is created in the very likeness of God (cf. Gal 2:20). **in righteousness and holiness.** Righteousness relates to the Christian's moral responsibility to his fellow men reflecting the second table of the law (Ex 20:12–17), while holiness refers to his responsibilities to God, reflecting the first table (Ex 20:3–11). There is still sin in the believer's unredeemed human flesh (*see notes on Ro 7:17, 18, 20, 23, 25; 8:23*).

4:25 laying aside falsehood. More than simply telling direct falsehoods, lying also includes exaggeration and adding fabrications to something that is true. Cheating, making foolish promises, betraying a confidence, and making false excuses are all forms of lying, with which Christians should have no part (cf. Jn 8:44; 1Co 6:9; Rev 21:8). speak truth ... with his neighbor. Quoted from Zec 8:16. God's work in the world is based on truth, and neither the church nor individual believers can be fit instruments for the Lord to use if they are not truthful.

4:26 Be angry, and ... do not sin Quoted from Ps 4:4. By NT standards, anger can be either good or bad, depending on motive and purpose. Paul may have been sanctioning righteous indignation, anger at evil. This type of anger hates injustice, immorality, ungodliness, and every other sin. When such anger is unselfish and based on love for God and others, it not only is permissible but commanded. Jesus expressed this righteous anger (see Mt 21:12; Mk 3:5; Jn 2:15). **sun go down.** Even righteous anger can turn to bitterness, so it should be set aside by the end of each day. If anger is prolonged, it may become hostile and violate the instruction of Ro 12:17–21.

4:28 steal no longer. Stealing in any form is a sin and has no part in the life of a Christian. Rather, let him work, producing what is beneficial (cf. Ex 20:15). The alternative to stealing is to provide for oneself, one's family, and others what is God-honoring through honest, honorable means (cf. 2Th 3:10, 11; 1Ti 5:8). **share with one who has need.** A Christian not only should harm no one but should continually endeavor to help those who are in need. See Lk 14:13, 14; Ac 20:33–35.

4:29 unwholesome word. The word for "unwholesome" refers to that which is foul or rotten, such as spoiled fruit or putrid meat. Foul language of any sort should never pass a Christian's lips, because it is totally out of character with his new life in Christ (see Col 3:8; Jas 3:6–8; cf. Ps 141:3). **good for edification.** The Christian's speech should be instructive, encouraging, uplifting, (even when it must be corrective), and suited for the moment (cf. Pr 15:23; 25:11; 24:26). **grace to those who hear.** Cf. Col 4:6. Because believers have been saved by grace and kept by grace, they should live and speak with grace. Our Lord set the standard (Lk 4:22).

4:30 Do not grieve the Holy Spirit of God. God is grieved when His children refuse to change the old ways of sin for those righteous ways of the new life. It should be noted that such responses by the Holy Spirit indicate He is a person. His personhood is also indicated by personal pronouns (Jn 14:17; 16:13), His personal care of believers (Jn 14:16, 26; 15:26), His intellect (1Co 2:11), feelings (Ro 8:27), will (1Co 12:11), speaking (Ac 13:2), convicting (Jn 16:8–11), interceding (Ro 8:26), guiding (Jn 16:13), glorifying Christ (Jn 16:14), and serving God (Ac 16:6, 7). **sealed for the day of redemption.** The Holy Spirit is the guarantor of eternal redemption in Christ for those who believe in Him (*see note on 1:13, 14*).

4:31, 32 These verses summarize the changes in the life of a believer mentioned in vv. 17–30. "Bitterness" reflects a smoldering resentment. "Wrath" has to do with rage, the passion of a moment. "Anger" is a more internal, deep hostility. "Clamor" is the outcry of strife out of control. "Slander" is evil speaking. "Malice" is the general Gr. term for evil, the root of all vices.

4:32 just as God in Christ also has forgiven you. Those who have been forgiven so much by God should, of all people, forgive the relatively small offenses against them by others. The most graphic illustration of this truth is the parable of Mt 18:21–35.

BE IMITATORS OF GOD

5 [A]Therefore be imitators of God, as beloved
children; 2 and [A]walk in love, just as Christ also
[B]loved [a]you and [C]gave Himself up for us, an [D]offer-
ing and a sacrifice to God [b]as a [E]fragrant aroma.
3 But [A]immorality [a]or any impurity or greed must
not even be named among you, as is proper among
[b]saints; 4 and *there must be no* [A]filthiness and silly
talk, or coarse jesting, which [B]are not fitting, but
rather [C]giving of thanks. 5 For this you know with
certainty, that [A]no [a]immoral or impure person or
covetous man, who is an idolater, has an inheritance
in the kingdom [B]of Christ and God.
6 [A]Let no one deceive you with empty words, for
because of these things [B]the wrath of God comes
upon [C]the sons of disobedience. 7 Therefore do not
be [A]partakers with them; 8 for [A]you were formerly
[B]darkness, but now you are Light in the Lord; walk
as [C]children of Light 9 (for [A]the fruit of the Light
consists in all [B]goodness and righteousness and
truth), 10 [a,A]trying to learn what is pleasing to the
Lord. 11 [A]Do not participate in the unfruitful [B]deeds
of [C]darkness, but instead even [a,D]expose them; 12 for
it is disgraceful even to speak of the things which
are done by them in secret. 13 But all things become
visible [A]when they are [a]exposed by the light, for
everything that becomes visible is light. 14 For this
reason [a]it says,

> "[A]Awake, sleeper,
> And arise from [B]the dead,
> And Christ [C]will shine on you."

5:1 [A]Matt 5:48; Luke 6:36; Eph 4:32 5:2 [a]One early ms reads *us* [b]Lit *for an odor of fragrance* [A]Rom 14:15; Col 3:14 [B]John 13:34; Rom 8:37 [C]John 6:51; Rom 4:25; Gal 2:20; Eph 5:25 [D]Heb 7:27; 9:14; 10:10, 12 [E]Ex 29:18, 25; 2 Cor 2:14 5:3 [a]Lit *and all* [b]Or *holy ones* [A]Col 3:5 5:4 [A]Matt 12:34; Eph 4:29; Col 3:8 [B]Rom 1:28 [C]Eph 5:20 5:5 [a]I.e. one who commits sexual immorality [A]1 Cor 6:9; Col 3:5 [B]Col 1:13 5:6 [A]Col 2:8 [B]Rom 1:18; Col 3:6 [C]Eph 2:2 5:7 [A]Eph 3:6 5:8 [A]Eph 2:2 [B]Acts 26:18; Col 1:12f [C]John 12:36; Rom 13:12 5:9 [A]Gal 5:22 [B]Rom 15:14 5:10 [a]Lit *proving what* [A]Rom 12:2 5:11 [a]Or *reprove* [A]1 Cor 5:9; 2 Cor 6:14 [B]Rom 13:12 [C]Acts 26:18; Col 1:12f [D]1 Tim 5:20 5:13 [a]Or *reproved* [A]John 3:20f 5:14 [a]Or *He* [A]Is 26:19; 51:17; 52:1; 60:1; Rom 13:11 [B]Eph 2:1 [C]Luke 1:78f

5:1 be imitators of God. The Christian has no greater calling or purpose than that of imitating his Lord (*see notes on 3:16, 19*). That is the very purpose of sanctification, growing in likeness to the Lord while serving Him on earth (cf. Mt 5:48). The Christian life is designed to reproduce godliness as modeled by the Savior and Lord, Jesus Christ, in whose image believers have been recreated through the new birth (cf. Ro 8:29; 2Co 3:18; 1Pe 1:14–16). As God's dear children, believers are to become more and more like their heavenly Father (Mt 5:48; 1Pe 1:15, 16).

5:2 Christ also loved you and gave Himself up for us. The Lord is the supreme example in His self-sacrificing love for lost sinners (4:32; Ro 5:8–10). He took human sin upon Himself and gave up His very life that men might be redeemed from their sin, receive a new and holy nature, and inherit eternal life (*see note on 2Co 5:21*). They are henceforth to be imitators of His great love in the newness and power of the Holy Spirit, who enables them to demonstrate divine love. **a fragrant aroma.** Christ's offering of Himself for fallen man pleased and glorified His heavenly Father, because it demonstrated in the most complete and perfect way God's sovereign, perfect, unconditional, and divine kind of love. Leviticus describes 5 offerings commanded by God for Israel. The first 3 were: 1) the burnt offering (Lv 1:1–17), depicting Christ's perfection; 2) the grain offering (Lv 2:1–16), depicting Christ's total devotion to God in giving His life to please the Father; and 3) the peace offering (Lv 3:1–17), depicting His peacemaking between God and man. All 3 of these were a "soothing aroma to the LORD" (Lv 1:9, 13, 17; 2:2, 9, 12; 3:5, 16). The other two offerings, the sin offering (Lv 4:1–5:13) and the guilt, or trespass, offering (Lv 5:14–6:7), were repulsive to God because, though they depicted Christ, they depicted Him as bearing sin (cf. Mt 27:46). In the end, when redemption was accomplished, the whole work pleased God completely.

5:3 immorality ... greed. In absolute contrast to God's holiness and love, such sins as these exist (also in v. 5), by which Satan seeks to destroy God's divine work in His children and turn them as far away as possible from His image and will. As do many other Scriptures, this verse shows the close connection between sexual sin and other forms of impurity and greed. An immoral person is inevitably greedy. Such sins are so godless that the world should never have reason even to suspect their presence in Christians.

5:4 not fitting. These 3 inappropriate sins of the tongue include any speech that is obscene and degrading or foolish and dirty, as well as suggestive and immoral. All such are destructive of holy living and godly testimony and should be confessed, forsaken, and replaced by open expressions of thankfulness to God (cf. Col 3:8).

5:5 For this you know. Paul had taught this truth many times when he pastored the church at Ephesus, and it should have been clear in their minds. God never tolerates sin, which has no place at all in His kingdom, nor will any person whose life pattern is one of habitual immorality, impurity, and greed (see v. 3) be in His kingdom, because no such person is saved (*see notes on 1Co 6:9, 10; Gal 5:17–21; 1Jn 3:9, 10*). **the kingdom of Christ and God.** A reference to the sphere of salvation where Christ rules the redeemed. *See note on Ac 1:3.*

5:6 deceive you. No Christian will be sinless in this present life, but it is dangerously deceptive for Christians to offer assurance of salvation to a professing believer whose life is characterized by persistent sin and who shows no shame for that sin or hunger for the holy and pure things of God. They are headed for wrath (2:2), and believers must not partner in any of their wickedness (v. 7).

5:8 darkness ... Light. "Darkness" describes the character of the life of the unconverted as void of truth and virtue in intellectual and moral matters (cf. 1Jn 1:5–7). The realm of darkness is presided over by the "power of darkness" (Lk 22:53; Col 1:13), who rules those headed for "outer darkness" (Mt 8:12; 2Pe 2:17). Tragically, sinners love the darkness (Jn 3:19–21). It is that very darkness from which salvation in Christ delivers sinners (*see notes on Jn 8:12; Col 1:13; 1Pe 2:9*; cf. Ps 27:1).

5:9 fruit of the Light. This speaks of that which is produced by walking in the light (cf. 1Jn 1:5–7), namely moral excellence of heart, righteous behavior, and truthfulness (honesty or integrity). *See notes on Gal 5:22, 23.*

5:10 trying to learn what is pleasing to the Lord. "Trying to learn" carries the idea of testing or proving to learn by clear and convincing evidence what is truly honoring to God. The point is that, as believers walk in the light of the truth, the knowledge of the Lord's will becomes clear. See Ro 12:1, 2 where Paul says the same thing, stating that it is only after presenting ourselves as living sacrifices to God that we can know His acceptable will. This relates to assurance of salvation also (see 1Pe 1:5–11).

5:11 Do not participate in ... darkness. Paul's instruction is plain and direct: Christians are to faithfully live in righteousness and purity and have nothing at all to do with the evil ways and works of Satan and the world. The two ways of living are unalterably opposed to each other and mutually exclusive. Cf. 1Co 5:9–11; 2Co 6:14–18; 2Th 3:6, 14. **instead ... expose them.** The Christian's responsibility does not stop with his own rejection of evil. He is also responsible for exposing and opposing darkness wherever it is found, especially when it is found in the church. *See notes on Mt 18:15–17; Gal 6:1, 2.*

5:12 disgraceful even to speak. Some sins are so despicable that they should be sealed off from direct contact and not even mentioned, much less discussed, except in order to contradict and oppose them. Merely talking about them can be morally and spiritually corruptive. Positive proclamation of the pure truth in the light of the Word exposes all evil (cf. Pr 6:23; 2Ti 3:16).

5:13 everything that becomes visible is light. This phrase should probably be part of v. 14, and is better translated "for it is light that makes everything visible." The pure and illuminating light of God's Word exposes all the secrets of sin.

5:14 Using this quotation from Is 60:1, Paul extended an invitation for salvation to the unsaved, in order that they may be transformed from children of darkness into children of God's holy light (cf. Pr 4:18). These words may have been part of an early church Easter hymn used as an invitation to unbelievers. They express a capsule view of the gospel. Cf. the invitations in Is 55:1–3, 6, 7 and in Jas 4:6–10.

15 Therefore [a]be careful how you [A]walk, not [B]as
unwise men but as wise, 16 [a,A]making the most of
your time, because [B]the days are evil. 17 So then do
not be foolish, but [A]understand what the will of the
Lord is. 18 And [A]do not get drunk with wine, [a]for
that is [B]dissipation, but be [C]filled with the Spirit,
19 [A]speaking to [a]one another in [B]psalms and [C]hymns
and spiritual [D]songs, [E]singing and making melody
with your heart to the Lord; 20 [A]always giving thanks
for all things in the name of our Lord Jesus Christ
to [a,B]God, even the Father; 21 [a,A]and be subject to one
another in the [b,B]fear of Christ.

MARRIAGE LIKE CHRIST AND THE CHURCH

22 [A]Wives, [B]*be subject* to your own husbands, [C]as
to the Lord. 23 For [A]the husband is the head of the
wife, as Christ also is the [B]head of the church, He
Himself [C]*being* the Savior of the body. 24 But as the
church is subject to Christ, so also the wives *ought
to be* to their husbands in everything.
25 [A]Husbands, love your wives, just as Christ also
loved the church and [B]gave Himself up for her, 26 [A]so
that He might sanctify her, having [B]cleansed her
by the [C]washing of water with [D]the word, 27 that

5:15 [a]Lit *look carefully* [A]Eph 5:2 [B]Col 4:5 5:16 [a]Lit *redeeming the time* [A]Col 4:5 [B]Gal 1:4; Eph 6:13 5:17 [A]Rom 12:2; Col 1:9; 1 Thess 4:3 5:18 [a]Lit *in which is* [A]Prov 20:1; 23:31f; Rom 13:13; 1 Cor 5:11; 1 Thess 5:7 [B]Titus 1:6; 1 Pet 4:4 [C]Luke 1:15 5:19 [a]Or *yourselves* [A]Col 3:16 [B]1 Cor 14:26 [C]Acts 16:25 [D]Rev 5:9 [E]1 Cor 14:15 5:20 [a]Lit *the God and Father* [A]Rom 1:8; Eph 5:4; Col 3:17 [B]1 Cor 15:24 5:21 [a]Lit *being subject* [b]Or *reverence* [A]Gal 5:13; Phil 2:3; 1 Pet 5:5 [B]2 Cor 5:11 5:22 [A]Eph 5:22-6:9: *Col 3:18-4:1* [B]1 Cor 14:34f; Titus 2:5; 1 Pet 3:1 [C]Eph 6:5 5:23 [A]1 Cor 11:3 [B]Eph 1:22 [C]1 Cor 6:13 5:25 [A]Eph 5:28, 33; Col 3:19; 1 Pet 3:7 [B]Eph 5:2 5:26 [A]Titus 2:14; Heb 10:10, 14, 29; 13:12 [B]2 Pet 1:9 [C]Acts 22:16; 1 Cor 6:11; Titus 3:5 [D]John 15:3; 17:17; Rom 10:8f; Eph 6:17

5:15 be careful how you walk, not as unwise men but as wise. To live morally is to live wisely. Biblically, an "unwise man" is not so named because of intellectual limits, but because of unbelief and the consequent abominable deeds (Ps 14:1; Ro 1:22). He lives apart from God and against God's law (Pr 1:7, 22; 14:9), and can't comprehend the truth (1Co 2:14) or his true condition (Ro 1:21, 22). Certainly, believers are to avoid behaving like fools (see Lk 24:25; Gal 3:1–3).

5:16 making the most of your time. The Gr. word for "time" denotes a fixed, measured, allocated season. We are to make the most of our time on this evil earth in fulfilling God's purposes, lining up every opportunity for useful worship and service. *See note on 1Pe 1:17.* Be aware of the brevity of life (Pss 39:4, 5; 89:46, 47; Jas 4:14, 17).

5:17 do not be foolish, but understand what the will of the Lord is. Knowing and understanding God's will through His Word is spiritual wisdom. For example, God's will revealed to us is that people should be saved (1Ti 2:3, 4), Spirit-filled (v. 18), sanctified (1Th 4:3), submissive (1Pe 2:13–15), suffering (1Pe 2:20), and thankful (1Th 5:18). Jesus is the supreme example for all (see Jn 4:34; 5:19, 30; 1Pe 4:1, 2).

5:18 And do not get drunk with wine. Although Scripture consistently condemns all drunkenness (*see notes on Pr 23:29–35; 31:4, 5; Is 5:11, 12; 28:7, 8*; cf. 1Co 5:11; 1Pe 4:3), the context suggests that Paul is speaking here especially about the drunken orgies commonly associated with many pagan worship ceremonies of that day. They were supposed to induce some ecstatic communion with the deities. Paul refers to such as the "cup of demons" (*see note on 1Co 10:19, 20*). **but be filled with the Spirit.** *See notes on Ac 2:4; 4:8, 31; 6:3.* True communion with God is not induced by drunkenness, but by the Holy Spirit. Paul is not speaking of the Holy Spirit's indwelling (Ro 8:9) or the baptism by Christ with the Holy Spirit (1Co 12:13), because every Christian is indwelt and baptized by the Spirit at the time of salvation. He is rather giving a command for believers to live continually under the influence of the Spirit by letting the Word control them (*see note on Col 3:16*), pursuing pure lives, confessing all known sin, dying to self, surrendering to God's will, and depending on His power in all things. Being filled with the Spirit is living in the conscious presence of the Lord Jesus Christ, letting His mind, through the Word, dominate everything that is thought and done. Being filled with the Spirit is the same as walking in the Spirit (*see notes on Gal 5:16–23*). Christ exemplified this way of life (Lk 4:1).

5:19–21 These verses summarize the immediate personal consequences of obeying the command to be filled with the Spirit, namely singing, giving thanks, and humbly submitting to others. The rest of the epistle features instruction based on obedience to this command.

5:19 speaking to one another. This is to be public (Heb 2:12). Cf. Pss 33:1; 40:3; 96:1, 2; 149:1; Ac 16:25; Rev 14:3. **psalms.** Old Testament psalms put to music, primarily, but the term was used also of vocal music in general. The early church sang the Psalms. **hymns.** Perhaps songs of praise distinguished from the Psalms which exalted God, in that they focused on the Lord Jesus Christ. **spiritual songs.** Probably songs of personal testimony expressing truths of the grace of salvation in Christ. **making melody.** Lit. means to pluck a stringed instrument, so it could refer primarily to instrumental music, while including vocal also. **with your heart to the Lord.** Not just public, but private. The Lord Himself is both the source and the object of the believer's song-filled heart. That such music pleases God can be seen in the account of the temple dedication, when the singing so honored the Lord that His glory came down (2Ch 5:12, 14).

5:20 always giving thanks for all things. *See note on 1Th 5:18*; cf. 2Co 4:15; 9:12, 15; Php 4:6; Col 2:7; Heb 13:15. Believers' thankfulness is for who God is and for what He has done through His Son, their Savior and Lord.

5:21 be subject to one another. Paul here made a transition and introduced his teaching about specific relationships of authority and submission among Christians (5:22–6:9) by declaring unequivocally that every Spirit-filled Christian is to be a humble, submissive Christian. This is foundational to all the relationships in this section. No believer is inherently superior to any other believer. In their standing before God, they are equal in every way (Gal 3:28). **in the fear of Christ.** The believer's continual reverence for God is the basis for his submission to other believers. Cf. Pr 9:10.

5:22 Wives, *be subject* to your own husbands. Having established the foundational principle of submission (v. 21), Paul applied it first to the wife. The command is unqualified, applying to every Christian wife, no matter what her own abilities, education, knowledge of Scripture, spiritual maturity, or any other qualifications might be in relation to those of her husband. The submission is not the husband's to command, but for the wife to willingly and lovingly offer. "Your own husbands" limits her submission to the one man God has placed over her, and also gives a balancing emphasis that he is hers as a personal intimate possession (SS 2:16; 6:3; 7:10). She submits to the man she possesses as her own. **as to the Lord.** Because the obedient, spiritual wife's supreme submission is to the Lord, her attitude is that she lovingly submits as an act of obedience to the Lord who has given this command as His will for her, regardless of her husband's personal worthiness or spiritual condition. Cf. vv. 5–9.

5:23 husband is the head … Christ … is the head. The Spirit-filled wife recognizes that her husband's role in giving leadership is not only God-ordained, but is a reflection of Christ's own loving, authoritative headship of the church. *See notes on 1Co 11:3*; cf. 1:22, 23; 4:15; Col 1:18; Titus 2:4, 5. **Savior.** As the Lord delivered His church from the dangers of sin, death, and hell, so the husband provides for, protects, preserves, and loves his wife, leading her to blessing as she submits. Cf. Titus 1:4; 2:13; 3:6.

5:25 love your wives. Though the husband's authority has been established (vv. 22–24), the emphasis moves to the supreme responsibility of husbands in regard to their wives, which is to love them with the same unreserved, selfless, and sacrificial love that Christ has for His church. Christ gave everything He had, including His own life, for the sake of His church, and that is the standard of sacrifice for a husband's love of his wife. Cf. Col 3:19.

5:26, 27 sanctify … cleansed … holy … blameless. This speaks of the love of Christ for His church. Saving grace makes believers holy by the agency of the Word of God (Titus 2:1–9; 3:5) so that they may be a pure bride. For husbands to love their wives as Christ does His church demands a purifying love. Since divine love seeks to completely cleanse those who are loved from every form of sin and evil, a Christian husband should not be able to bear the thought of anything sinful in the life of his wife that displeases God. His greatest desire for her should be that she become perfectly conformed to Christ, so he leads her to purity. *See note on 2Co 11:2.*

He might [A]present to Himself the church [a]in all
her glory, having no spot or wrinkle or any such
thing; but that she would be [B]holy and blameless.
28 So husbands ought also to [A]love their own wives
as their own bodies. He who loves his own wife
loves himself; 29 for no one ever hated his own flesh,
but nourishes and cherishes it, just as Christ also
does the church, 30 because we are [A]members of
His [B]body. 31 [A]FOR THIS REASON A MAN SHALL LEAVE
HIS FATHER AND MOTHER AND SHALL BE JOINED TO
HIS WIFE, AND THE TWO SHALL BECOME ONE FLESH.
32 This mystery is great; but I am speaking with
reference to Christ and the church. 33 Nevertheless,
each individual among you also is to [A]love his own
wife even as himself, and the wife must *see to it* that
she [a,B]respects her husband.

FAMILY RELATIONSHIPS

6 [A]Children, obey your parents in the Lord, for this
is right. 2 [A]HONOR YOUR FATHER AND MOTHER
(which is the first commandment with a promise),
3 SO THAT IT MAY BE WELL WITH YOU, AND THAT YOU
MAY LIVE LONG ON THE EARTH.
4 [A]Fathers, do not provoke your children to anger,
but [B]bring them up in the discipline and instruction
of the Lord.
5 [A]Slaves, be obedient to those who are your
[a]masters according to the flesh, with [B]fear and
trembling, in the sincerity of your heart, [C]as to
Christ; 6 [A]not [a]by way of eyeservice, as [B]men-pleas-
ers, but as [C]slaves of Christ, [D]doing the will of God
from the [b]heart. 7 With good will [a]render service,
[A]as to the Lord, and not to men, 8 [A]knowing that
[B]whatever good thing each one does, this he will
receive back from the Lord, [C]whether slave or
free.
9 And masters, do the same things to them, and
[A]give up threatening, knowing that [B]both their Master and yours is in heaven, and there is [C]no partiality
with Him.

5:27 [a]Lit *glorious* [A]2 Cor 4:14; 11:2; Col 1:22 [B]Eph 1:4 5:28 [A]Eph 5:25, 33; 1 Pet 3:7 5:30 [A]1 Cor 6:15; 12:27 [B]Eph 1:23 5:31 [A]Gen 2:24; Matt 19:5; Mark 10:7f 5:33 [a]Lit *fear* [A]Eph 5:25, 28; 1 Pet 3:7 [B]1 Pet 3:2, 5f 6:1 [A]Prov 6:20; 23:22; Col 3:20 6:2 [A]Ex 20:12; Deut 5:16 6:4 [A]Col 3:21 [B]Gen 18:19; Deut 6:7; 11:19; Ps 78:4; Prov 22:6; 2 Tim 3:15 6:5 [a]I.e. earthly masters, with fear [A]Col 3:22; 1 Tim 6:1; Titus 2:9 [B]1 Cor 2:3 [C]Eph 5:22 6:6 [a]Lit *according to* [b]Lit *soul* [A]Col 3:22 [B]Gal 1:10 [C]1 Cor 7:22 [D]Mark 3:35 6:7 [a]Lit *rendering* [A]Col 3:23 6:8 [A]Col 3:24 [B]Matt 16:27; 2 Cor 5:10; Col 3:24f [C]1 Cor 12:13; Col 3:11 6:9 [A]Lev 25:43 [B]Job 31:13ff; John 13:13; Col 4:1 [C]Deut 10:17; Acts 10:34; Col 3:25

5:28 as their own bodies. Here is one of the most poignant and compelling descriptions of the oneness that should characterize Christian marriage. A Christian husband is to care for his wife with the same devotion that he naturally manifests as he cares for himself (v. 29)—even more so, since his self-sacrificing love causes him to put her first (cf. Php 2:1–4). **loves his own wife loves himself.** In the end, a husband who loves his wife in these ways brings great blessing to himself from her and from the Lord.

5:29 nourishes and cherishes. These express the twin responsibilities of providing for her needs so as to help her grow mature in Christ and to provide warm and tender affection to give her comfort and security.

5:30 members of His body. The Lord provides for His church because it is so intimately and inseparably connected to Him. If He did not care for His church, He would be diminishing His own glory which the church brings to Him by praise and obedience. So, in marriage, the husband's life is so intimately joined to the wife's that they are one. When he cares for her, he cares for himself (v. 29).

5:31 Quoted from Ge 2:24 (*see note there*). Paul reinforces the divine plan for marriage which God instituted at creation, emphasizing its permanence and unity. The union of marriage is intimate and unbreakable. "Joined" is a word used to express having been glued or cemented together, emphasizing the permanence of the union (*see notes on Mal 2:16; Mt 19:5–9*).

5:32 mystery is great. In the NT, "mystery" identifies some reality hidden in the past and revealed in the NT age to be written in Scripture. Marriage is a sacred reflection of the magnificent and beautiful mystery of union between the Messiah and His church, completely unknown until the NT. *See notes on 3:4, 5; Mt 13:11; 1Co 2:7.*

5:33 each individual among you. The intimacy and sacredness of the love relationship between believing marriage partners are to be a visual expression of the love between Christ and His church.

6:1 obey ... in the Lord. See Col 3:20. The child in the home is to be willingly under the authority of parents with obedient submission to them as the agents of the Lord placed over him, obeying parents as if obeying the Lord Himself. The reasoning here is simply that such is the way God has designed and required it ("right"). Cf. Hos 14:9.

6:2, 3 Honor. While v. 1 speaks of action, this term speaks of attitude, as Paul deals with the motive behind the action. When God gave His law in the Ten Commandments, the first law governing human relationships was this one (Ex 20:12; Dt 5:16). It is the only command of the 10 that relates to the family because that principle alone secures the family's fulfillment. Cf. Ex 21:15, 17; Lv 20:9; Mt 15:3–6. Proverbs affirms this principle (see 1:8; 3:1; 4:1–4; 7:1–3; 10:1; 17:21; 19:13, 26; 28:24).

6:2 the first commandment with a promise. Although submission to parents should first of all be for the Lord's sake, He has graciously added the promise of special blessing for those who obey this command. *See note on Ex 20:12*, the verse from which Paul quotes (cf. Dt 5:16).

6:4 Fathers. The word technically refers to male parents, but was also used of parents in general. Since Paul had been speaking of both parents (vv. 1–3), he probably had both in mind here. The same word is used in Heb 11:23 for Moses' parents. **do not provoke.** In the pagan world of Paul's day, and even in many Jewish households, most fathers ruled their families with rigid and domineering authority. The desires and welfare of wives and children were seldom considered. The apostle makes clear that a Christian father's authority over his children does not allow for unreasonable demands and strictures that might drive his children to anger, despair, and resentment. **discipline and instruction of the Lord.** This calls for systematic discipline and instruction, which brings children to respect the commands of the Lord as the foundation of all of life, godliness, and blessing. Cf. Pr 13:24; Heb 12:5–11.

6:5 Slaves, be obedient. *See note on Col 3:22–4:1.* Slaves in both Greek and Roman culture had no rights legally and were treated as commodities. There was much abuse and seldom good treatment of slaves. The Bible does not speak against slavery itself, but against its abuses (cf. Ex 21:16, 26, 27; Lv 25:10; Dt 23:15, 16). Paul's admonition applies equally well to all employees. The term "obedient" refers to continuous, uninterrupted submission to one's earthly master or employer, the only exception being in regard to a command that involves clear disobedience of God's Word as illustrated in Ac 4:19, 20. *See notes on 1Ti 6:1, 2; Titus 2:9, 10; 1Pe 2:18–20.* **according to the flesh.** Human masters, that is. **with fear and trembling.** This is not fright, but respect for their authority. Even if an employer does not deserve respect in his own right (see 1Pe 2:18), it should nevertheless be given to him with genuine sincerity as if one was serving Christ Himself. To serve one's employer well is to serve Christ well. Cf. Col 3:23, 24.

6:6 eyeservice. Working well only when being watched by the boss. **men-pleasers.** Working only to promote one's welfare, rather than to honor the employer and the Lord, whose servants we really are.

6:7, 8 Cf. Col 3:23. God's credits and rewards will be appropriate to the attitude and action of our work. No good thing done for His glory will go unrewarded.

6:9 And masters, do the same things to them. There should be mutual honor and respect from Christian employers to their employees, based on their common allegiance to the Lord. **give up threatening.** The Spirit-filled boss uses his authority and power with justice and grace—never putting people under threats, never abusive or inconsiderate. He realizes that he has a heavenly Master who is impartial (cf. Ac 10:34; Ro 2:11; Jas 2:9).

THE ARMOR OF GOD

10 Finally, [A]be strong in the Lord and in [B]the
strength of His might. 11 [A]Put on the full armor of
God, so that you will be able to stand firm against
the [B]schemes of the devil. 12 For our [A]struggle is not
against [a,B]flesh and blood, but [C]against the rulers,
against the powers, against the [D]world forces of this
[E]darkness, against the [F]spiritual *forces* of wickedness in [G]the heavenly *places*. 13 Therefore, take up
[A]the full armor of God, so that you will be able to
[B]resist in [C]the evil day, and having done everything,
to stand firm. 14 Stand firm therefore, [A]HAVING GIRD-
ED YOUR LOINS WITH TRUTH, and HAVING [B]PUT ON THE
BREASTPLATE OF RIGHTEOUSNESS, 15 and having [A]shod
YOUR FEET WITH THE PREPARATION OF THE GOSPEL
OF PEACE; 16 [a]in addition to all, taking up the [A]shield
of faith with which you will be able to extinguish
all the [B]flaming arrows of [C]the evil *one*. 17 And take
[A]THE HELMET OF SALVATION, and the [B]sword of the
Spirit, which is [C]the word of God.

6:10 [A]1 Cor 16:13; 2 Tim 2:1 [B]Eph 1:19 6:11 [A]Rom 13:12; Eph 6:13 [B]Eph 4:14 6:12 [a]Lit *blood and flesh* [A]1 Cor 9:25 [B]Matt 16:17 [C]Eph 1:21; 2:2; 3:10 [D]John 12:31 [E]Acts 26:18; Col 1:13 [F]Eph 3:10 [G]Eph 1:3 6:13 [A]Eph 6:11 [B]James 4:7 [C]Eph 5:16 6:14 [A]Is 11:5; Luke 12:35; 1 Pet 1:13 [B]Is 59:17; Rom 13:12; Eph 6:13; 1 Thess 5:8 6:15 [A]Is 52:7; Rom 10:15 6:16 [a]Lit *in all* [A]1 Thess 5:8 [B]Ps 7:13; 120:4 [C]Matt 5:37 6:17 [A]Is 59:17 [B]Is 49:2; Hos 6:5; Heb 4:12 [C]Eph 5:26; Heb 6:5

6:10–17 The true believer described in chaps. 1–3, who lives the Spirit-controlled life of 4:1–6:9, can be sure to be in a spiritual war, as described here. Paul closes this letter with both warning about that war and instructions on how to win it. The Lord provides His saints with sufficient armor to combat and thwart the adversary. In vv. 10–13, the apostle briefly sets forth the basic truths regarding the believer's necessary spiritual preparation as well as truths regarding his enemy, his battle, and his victory. In vv. 14–17, he specifies the 6 most necessary pieces of spiritual armor with which God equips His children to resist and overcome Satan's assaults.

6:10 **be strong in the Lord and in the strength of His might.** Cf. Php 4:13; 2Ti 2:1. Ultimately, Satan's power over Christians is already broken, and the great war is won through Christ's crucifixion and resurrection, which forever conquered the power of sin and death (Ro 5:18–21; 1Co 15:56, 57; Heb 2:14). However, in life on earth, battles of temptation go on regularly. The Lord's power, the strength of His Spirit, and the force of biblical truth are required for victory (*see notes on 2Co 10:3–5*).

6:11 **Put on the full armor of God.** "Put on" conveys the idea of permanence, indicating that armor should be the Christian's sustained, life-long attire. Paul uses the common armor worn by Roman soldiers as the analogy for the believer's spiritual defense and affirms its necessity if one is to hold his position while under attack. **schemes.** This Gr. word carries the idea of cleverness, crafty methods, cunning, and deception. Satan's schemes are propagated through the evil world system over which he rules, and are carried out by his demon hosts. "Schemes" is all-inclusive, encompassing every sin, immoral practice, false theology, false religion, and worldly enticement. *See note on 2Co 2:11.* **the devil.** Scripture refers to him as "the anointed cherub" (Eze 28:14), "the ruler of the demons" (Lk 11:15), "the god of this world" (2Co 4:4), and "the prince of the power of the air" (Eph 2:2). Scripture depicts him opposing God's work (Zec 3:1), perverting God's Word (Mt 4:6), hindering God's servant (1Th 2:18), hindering the gospel (2Co 4:4), snaring the righteous (1Ti 3:7), and holding the world in his power (1Jn 5:19).

6:12 **struggle.** A term used of hand-to-hand combat, rendered as "wrestle" by some translations. Struggling or wrestling features trickery and deception, like Satan and his hosts when they attack. Coping with deceptive temptation requires truth and righteousness. The 4 designations describe the different strata and rankings of those demons and the evil supernatural empire in which they operate. Satan's forces of darkness are highly structured for the most destructive purposes. Cf. Col 2:15; 1Pe 3:22. **not against flesh and blood.** See 2Co 10:3–5. **spiritual *forces* of wickedness.** This possibly refers to the most depraved abominations, including such things as extreme sexual perversions, occultism, and Satan worship. *See note on Col 1:16.* **in the heavenly *places*.** As in 1:3; 3:10, this refers to the entire realm of spiritual beings.

6:13 **Therefore, take up the full armor of God.** Paul again emphasized the necessity of the Christian's appropriating God's full spiritual armor by obedience in taking it up, or putting it on (v. 11). The first 3 pieces of armor (girdle, breastplate, and shoes/boots, vv. 14, 15) were worn continually on the battlefield; the last 3 (shield, helmet, and sword, vv. 16, 17) were kept ready for use when actual fighting began. **the evil day.** Since the fall of man, every day has been evil, a condition that will persist until the Lord returns and establishes His own righteous kingdom on earth. **having done everything, to stand firm.** Standing firm against the enemy without wavering or falling is the goal. *See notes on Jas 4:17; 1Pe 5:8, 9.*

6:14 **Stand firm therefore.** For the third time (see vv. 11, 13), the apostle calls Christians to take a firm position in the spiritual battle against Satan and his minions. Whether confronting Satan's efforts to distrust God, forsaking obedience, producing doctrinal confusion and falsehood, hindering service to God, bringing division, serving God in the flesh, living hypocritically, being worldly, or in any other way rejecting biblical obedience, this armor is our defense. **girded … with truth.** The soldier wore a tunic of loose-fitting cloth. Since ancient combat was largely hand-to-hand, a loose tunic was a potential hindrance and danger. A belt was necessary to cinch up the loosely hanging material. Cf. Ex 12:11; Lk 12:35; 1Pe 1:13. Girding up was a matter of pulling in the loose ends as preparation for battle. The belt that pulls all the spiritual loose ends in is "truth," or better, "truthfulness." The idea is of sincere commitment to fight and win without hypocrisy—self-discipline in devotion to victory. Everything that hinders is tucked away. Cf. 2Ti 2:4; Heb 12:1. **the breastplate of righteousness.** The breastplate was usually a tough, sleeveless piece of leather or heavy material with animal horn or hoof pieces sewn on, covering the soldier's full torso, protecting his heart and other vital organs. Because righteousness, or holiness, is such a distinctive characteristic of God Himself, it is not hard to understand why that is the Christian's chief protection against Satan and his schemes. As believers faithfully live in obedience to and communion with Jesus Christ, His own righteousness produces in them the practical, daily righteousness that becomes their spiritual breastplate. Lack of holiness, on the other hand, leaves them vulnerable to the great enemy of their souls (cf. Is 59:17; 2Co 7:1; 1Th 5:8).

6:15 **shod … with … the gospel of peace.** Roman soldiers wore boots with nails in them to grip the ground in combat. The gospel of peace pertains to the good news that, through Christ, believers are at peace with God and He is on their side (Ro 5:6–10). It is that confidence of divine support which allows the believer to stand firm, knowing that since he is at peace with God, God is his strength (see Ro 8:31, 37–39).

6:16 **the shield of faith.** This Gr. word usually refers to the large shield (2.5 x 4.5 ft.) that protected the entire body. The faith to which Paul refers is not the body of Christian doctrine (as the term is used in 4:13), but basic trust in God. The believer's continual trust in God's word and promise is "in addition to all" necessary to protect him from temptations to every sort of sin. All sin comes when the victim falls to Satan's lies and promises of pleasure, rejecting the better choice of obedience and blessing. **flaming arrows.** Temptations are likened to the flaming arrows shot by the enemy and quenched by the oil-treated leather shield (cf. Ps 18:30; Pr 30:5, 6; 1Jn 5:4).

6:17 **the helmet of salvation.** The helmet protected the head, always a major target in battle. Paul is speaking to those who are already saved, and is therefore not speaking here about attaining salvation. Rather, Satan seeks to destroy a believer's assurance of salvation with his weapons of doubt and discouragement. This is clear from Paul's reference to the helmet as "the hope of salvation" (Is 59:17; *see note on 1Th 5:8*). But although a Christian's feelings about his salvation may be seriously damaged by Satan-inspired doubt, his salvation itself is eternally protected and he need not fear its loss. Satan wants to curse the believer with doubts, but the Christian can be strong in God's promises of eternal salvation in Scripture (see Jn 6:37–39; 10:28, 29; Ro 5:10; 8:31–39; Php 1:6; 1Pe 1:3–5). Security is a fact; assurance is a feeling that comes to the obedient Christian (1Pe 1:3–10). **the sword of the Spirit.** As the sword was the soldier's only weapon, so God's Word is the only needed weapon, infinitely more powerful than any of Satan's. The Gr. term refers to a small weapon (6–18 in. long). It was used

18[a]With all [A]prayer and petition [b,B]pray at all times
[C]in the Spirit, and with this in view, [c,D]be on the alert
with all [E]perseverance and [F]petition for all the saints,
19and [A]*pray* on my behalf, that utterance may be given
to me [B]in the opening of my mouth, to make known
with [C]boldness [D]the mystery of the gospel, 20for which
I am an [A]ambassador [B]in [a]chains; that [b]in *proclaiming*
it I may speak [C]boldly, [D]as I ought to speak.
21[A]But that you also may know about my circumstances, [a]how I am doing, [B]Tychicus, [C]the beloved
brother and faithful minister in the Lord, will make
everything known to you. 22[a,A]I have sent him to
you for this very purpose, so that you may know
[b]about us, and that he may [B]comfort your hearts.
23[A]Peace be to the brethren, and [B]love with faith,
from God the Father and the Lord Jesus Christ.
24Grace be with all those who love our Lord Jesus
Christ [a]with incorruptible *love*.

6:18 [a]Lit *Through* [b]Lit *praying* [c]Lit *being* [A]Phil 4:6 [B]Luke 18:1; Col 1:3; 4:2; 1 Thess 5:17 [C]Rom 8:26f [D]Mark 13:33 [E]Acts 1:14 [F]1 Tim 2:1 6:19 [A]Col 4:3; 1 Thess 5:25 [B]2 Cor 6:11 [C]2 Cor 3:12 [D]Eph 3:3 6:20 [a]Lit *a chain* [b]Two early mss read *I may speak it boldly* [A]2 Cor 5:20; Philem 9 mg [B]Acts 21:33; 28:20; Eph 3:1; Phil 1:7; Col 4:3 [C]2 Cor 3:12 [D]Col 4:4 6:21 [a]Lit *what* [A]Eph 6:21, 22: *Col 4:7-9* [B]Acts 20:4; 2 Tim 4:12 [C]Col 4:7 6:22 [a]Lit *Whom I have sent to you* [b]Lit *the things about us* [A]Col 4:8 [B]Col 2:2; 4:8 6:23 [A]Rom 15:33; Gal 6:16; 2 Thess 3:16; 1 Pet 5:14 [B]Gal 5:6; 1 Thess 5:8 6:24 [a]Lit *in incorruption*

both defensively to fend off Satan's attacks, and offensively to help destroy the enemy's strategies. It is the truth of Scripture. *See notes on 2Co 10:3–5; Heb 4:12.*

6:18 This verse introduces the general character of a believer's prayer life: 1) "all prayer and petition" focuses on the variety; 2) "at all times" focuses on the frequency (cf. Ro 12:12; Php 4:6; 1Th 5:17); 3) "in the Spirit" focuses on submission, as we line up with the will of God (cf. Ro 8:26, 27); 4) "be on the alert" focuses on the manner (cf. Mt 26:41; Mk 13:33); 5) "all perseverance" focuses on the persistence (cf. Lk 11:9; 18:7, 8); and 6) "all the saints" focuses on the objects (cf. 1Sa 12:23).

6:19, 20 Paul does not ask for prayer for his personal well-being or physical comfort in the imprisonment from which he wrote, but for boldness and faithfulness to continue proclaiming the gospel to the unsaved no matter what the cost. **mystery.** *See note on 3:4.* **ambassador.** *See notes on 2Co 5:18–20.*

6:21, 22 Tychicus. A convert from Asia Minor (modern Turkey) who was with the apostle during his first imprisonment in Rome, from where this epistle was written (see 3:1). He accompanied Paul in taking an offering to the church in Jerusalem (Ac 20:4–6) and was sent by him on several missions (2Ti 4:12; Titus 3:12).

6:23, 24 This beautiful benediction sums up the major themes of this very personal letter, reminding readers of the peace (v. 15; 1:2; 2:14, 15, 17; 4:3), love (1:15; 4:2, 15, 16; 5:25, 28, 33), and faith (v. 16; 1:15; 2:8; 3:12, 17; 4:5, 13) from God and Jesus Christ.

THE EPISTLE OF
PAUL TO THE

PHILIPPIANS

TITLE

Philippians derives its name from the Greek city where the church to which it was addressed was located. Philippi was the first town in Macedonia where Paul established a church.

AUTHOR AND DATE

The unanimous testimony of the early church was that the apostle Paul wrote Philippians. Nothing in the letter would have motivated a forger to write it.

The question of when Philippians was written cannot be separated from that of where it was written. The traditional view is that Philippians, along with the other Prison Epistles (Ephesians, Colossians, Philemon), was written during Paul's first imprisonment at Rome (ca. A.D. 60–62). The most natural understanding of the references to the "praetorian guard" (1:13) and the "saints ... of Caesar's household" (4:22) is that Paul wrote from Rome, where the emperor lived. The similarities between the details of Paul's imprisonment given in Acts and in the Prison Epistles also argue that those epistles were written from Rome (e.g., Paul was guarded by soldiers, Ac 28:16; cf. 1:13, 14; was permitted to receive visitors, Ac 28:30; cf. 4:18; and had the opportunity to preach the gospel, Ac 28:31; cf. 1:12–14; Eph 6:18–20; Col 4:2–4).

Some have held that Paul wrote the Prison Epistles during his two-year imprisonment at Caesarea (Ac 24:27). But Paul's opportunities to receive visitors and proclaim the gospel were severely limited during that imprisonment (cf. Ac 23:35). The Prison Epistles express Paul's hope for a favorable verdict (1:25; 2:24; cf. Phm 22). In Caesarea, however, Paul's only hope for release was either to bribe Felix (Ac 24:26), or agree to stand trial at Jerusalem under Festus (Ac 25:9). In the Prison Epistles, Paul expected the decision in his case to be final (1:20–23; 2:17, 23). That could not have been true at Caesarea, since Paul could and did appeal his case to the emperor.

Another alternative has been that Paul wrote the Prison Epistles from Ephesus. But at Ephesus, like Caesarea, no final decision could be made in his case because of his right to appeal to the emperor. Also, Luke was with Paul when he wrote Colossians (Col 4:14), but he apparently was not with the apostle at Ephesus. Acts 19, which records Paul's stay in Ephesus, is not in one of the "we sections" of Acts (see Introduction to Acts: Author and Date). The most telling argument against Ephesus as the point of origin for the Prison Epistles, however, is that there is no evidence that Paul was ever imprisoned at Ephesus.

In light of the serious difficulties faced by both the Caesarean and Ephesian views, there is no reason to reject the traditional view that Paul wrote the Prison Epistles—including Philippians—from Rome.

Paul's belief that his case would soon be decided (2:23, 24) points to Philippians being written toward the close of the apostle's two-year Roman imprisonment (ca. A.D. 61).

BACKGROUND AND SETTING

Originally known as Krenides ("The Little Fountains") because of the numerous nearby springs, Philippi ("city of Philip") received its name from Philip II of Macedon (the father of Alexander the Great). Attracted by the nearby gold mines, Philip conquered the region in the fourth century B.C. In the second century B.C., Philippi became part of the Roman province of Macedonia.

The city existed in relative obscurity for the next two centuries until one of the most famous events in Roman history brought it recognition and expansion. In 42 B.C., the forces of Antony and Octavian defeated those of Brutus and Cassius at the Battle of Philippi, thus ending the Roman Republic and ushering in the Empire. After the battle, Philippi became a Roman colony (cf. Ac 16:12), and many veterans of the Roman army settled there. As a colony, Philippi had autonomy from the provincial government and the same rights granted to cities in Italy, including the use of Roman law, exemption from some taxes, and Roman citizenship for its residents (Ac 16:21). Being a colony was also the source of much civic pride for the Philippians, who used Latin as their official language, adopted Roman customs, and modeled their city government after that of Italian cities. Acts and Philippians both reflect Philippi's status as a Roman colony.

Paul's description of Christians as citizens of heaven (3:20) was appropriate, since the Philippians prided themselves on being citizens of Rome (cf. Ac 16:21). The Philippians may well have known some of the members of the palace guard (1:13) and Caesar's household (4:22).

The church at Philippi, the first one founded by Paul in Europe, dates from the apostle's second missionary journey (Ac 16:12–40). Philippi evidently had a very small Jewish population. Because there were not enough men to form a synagogue (the requirement was for 10 Jewish men who were heads of a household), some devout women met outside the city at a place of prayer (Ac 16:13) alongside the Gangites River. Paul preached the gospel to them and Lydia, a wealthy merchant dealing in expensive purple dyed goods (Ac 16:14), became a believer (16:14, 15). It is likely that the Philippian church initially met in her spacious home.

Satanic opposition to the new church immediately arose in the person of a demon-possessed, fortune-telling slave girl (Ac 16:16, 17). Not wanting even agreeable testimony from such an evil source, Paul cast the demon out of her (Ac 16:18). The apostle's act enraged the girl's masters, who could no longer sell her services as a fortune-teller (Ac 16:19). They hauled Paul and Silas before the city's magistrates (Ac 16:20) and inflamed the civic pride of the Philippians by claiming the two preachers were a threat to Roman customs (Ac 16:20, 21). As a result, Paul and Silas were beaten and imprisoned (Ac 16:22–24).

The two preachers were miraculously released from prison that night by an earthquake, which unnerved the jailer and opened his heart and that of his household to the gospel (Ac 16:25–34). The next day the magistrates, panicking when they learned they had illegally beaten and imprisoned two Roman citizens, begged Paul and Silas to leave Philippi.

Paul apparently visited Philippi twice during his third missionary journey, once at the beginning (cf. 2Co 8:1–5), and again near the end (Ac 20:6). About 4 or 5 years after his last visit to Philippi, while a prisoner at Rome, Paul received a delegation from the Philippian church. The Philippians had generously supported Paul in the past (4:15, 16), and had also contributed abundantly for the needy at Jerusalem (2Co 8:1–4). Now, hearing of Paul's imprisonment, they sent another contribution to him (4:10), and along with it Epaphroditus to minister to Paul's needs. Unfortunately, Epaphroditus suffered a near-fatal illness (2:26, 27), either while en route to Rome, or after he arrived. Accordingly, Paul decided to send Epaphroditus back to Philippi (2:25, 26) and wrote the letter to the Philippians to send back with him.

Paul had several purposes in composing this epistle. First, he wanted to express in writing his thanks for the Philippians' gift (4:10–18). Second, he wanted the Philippians to know why he decided to return Epaphroditus to them, so they would not think his service to Paul had been unsatisfactory (2:25, 26). Third, he wanted to inform them about his circumstances at Rome (1:12–26). Fourth, he wrote to exhort them to unity (2:1, 2; 4:2). Finally, he wrote to warn them against false teachers (3:1–4:1).

HISTORICAL AND THEOLOGICAL THEMES

Since it is primarily a practical letter, Philippians contains little historical material (there are no OT quotes), apart from the momentous treatment of Paul's spiritual autobiography (3:4–7). There is, likewise, little direct theological instruction, also with one momentous exception. The magnificent passage describing Christ's humiliation and exaltation (2:5–11) contains some of the most profound and crucial teaching on the Lord Jesus Christ in all the Bible. The major theme of pursuing Christlikeness, as the most defining element of spiritual growth and the one passion of Paul in his own life, is presented in 3:12–14. In spite of Paul's imprisonment, the dominant tone of the letter is joyful (1:4, 18, 25, 26; 2:2, 16–18, 28; 3:1, 3; 4:1, 4, 10).

INTERPRETIVE CHALLENGES

The major difficulty connected with Philippians is determining where it was written (see Author and Date). The text itself presents only one significant interpretive challenge: the identity of the "enemies of the cross" (*see notes on 3:18, 19*).

OUTLINE

I. Paul's Greeting (1:1–11)

II. Paul's Circumstances (1:12–26)

III. Paul's Exhortations (1:27–2:18)
- A. To Stand Firm Amid Persecution (1:27–30)
- B. To Be United by Humility (2:1–4)
- C. To Remember the Example of Christ (2:5–11)
- D. To Be Light in a Dark World (2:12–18)

IV. Paul's Companions (2:19–30)
- A. Timothy (2:19–24)
- B. Epaphroditus (2:25–30)

V. Paul's Warnings (3:1–4:1)
- A. Against Legalism (3:1–16)
- B. Against Lawlessness (3:17–4:1)

VI. Paul's Admonition (4:2–9)

VII. Paul's Thankfulness (4:10–20)

VIII. Paul's Farewell (4:21–23)

THANKSGIVING

1 [A]Paul and [B]Timothy, [C]bond-servants of [D]Christ
Jesus,
To [E]all the [a,F]saints in Christ Jesus who are in
[G]Philippi, [b]including the [H]overseers and [I]deacons:
2 [A]Grace to you and peace from God our Father and
the Lord Jesus Christ.
3 [A]I thank my God in all my remembrance of
you, 4 always offering prayer with joy in [A]my every
prayer for you all, 5 in view of your [a,A]participation
in the [B]gospel [C]from the first day until now. 6 *For I
am* confident of this very thing, that He who began
a good work in you will perfect it until [A]the day of
Christ Jesus. 7 [a]For [A]it is only right for me to feel
this way about you all, because I [B]have you in my
heart, since both in my [b,C]imprisonment and in the
[D]defense and confirmation of the [E]gospel, you all
are partakers of grace with me. 8 For [A]God is my
witness, how I long for you all with the [a]affection of
[B]Christ Jesus. 9 And this I pray, that [A]your love may
abound still more and more in [B]real knowledge
and all discernment, 10 so that you may [a,A]approve
the things that are excellent, in order to be sincere
and blameless [b]until [B]the day of Christ; 11 having
been filled with the [A]fruit of righteousness which
comes through Jesus Christ, to the glory and
praise of God.

THE GOSPEL IS PREACHED

12 Now I want you to know, brethren, that my circumstances [A]have turned out for the greater progress of the [B]gospel, 13 so that my [a,A]imprisonment in
the cause of Christ has become well known throughout the whole [b]praetorian guard and to [B]everyone

1:1 [a]Or *holy ones* [b]Lit *with* [A]2 Cor 1:1 [B]Acts 16:1 [C]Rom 1:1; Gal 1:10 [D]Gal 3:26 [E]2 Cor 1:1; Col 1:2 [F]Acts 9:13 [G]Acts 16:12 [H]Acts 20:28; 1 Tim 3:1f; Titus 1:7 [I]1 Tim 3:8ff
1:2 [A]Rom 1:7 1:3 [A]Rom 1:8 1:4 [A]Rom 1:9 1:5 [a]Or *sharing in the preaching of the gospel* [A]Acts 2:42; Phil 4:15 [B]Phil 1:7; 2:22; 4:3, 15 [C]Acts 16:12-40; Phil 2:12; 4:15
1:6 [A]1 Cor 1:8; Phil 1:10; 2:16 1:7 [a]Lit *Just as it is right* [b]Lit *bonds* [A]2 Pet 1:13 [B]2 Cor 7:3 [C]Acts 21:33; Eph 6:20; Phil 1:13f, 17 [D]Phil 1:16 [E]Phil 1:5, 12, 16, 27; 2:22; 4:3, 15
1:8 [a]Lit *inward parts* [A]Rom 1:9 [B]Gal 3:26 1:9 [A]1 Thess 3:12 [B]Col 1:9 1:10 [a]Or *discover; or distinguish between the things which differ* [b]Or *for* [A]Rom 2:18 [B]1 Cor 1:8; Phil 1:6; 2:16 1:11 [A]James 3:18 1:12 [A]Luke 21:13 [B]Phil 1:5, 7, 16, 27; 2:22; 4:3, 15 1:13 [a]Lit *bonds* [b]Or *governor's palace* [A]Phil 1:7; 2 Tim 2:9 [B]Acts 28:30

1:1, 2 First century letters normally began by identifying the sender and the recipient with a basic greeting. One notable variation here is that Paul includes Timothy's name because Timothy was an important gospel coworker in and around Philippi and a trusted, corroborating witness to the truths Paul expounded.

1:1 **Paul.** See Introduction to Romans: Author and Date; *see note on Ac 9:1.* Paul wrote this letter from a Roman prison (see Introduction: Author and Date). **Timothy.** Timothy, Paul's beloved son in the faith (see Introduction to 1 Timothy: Author and Date; Ac 16:1–3), was not the coauthor of the letter, but possibly the one to whom Paul dictated it. Regardless, Paul had good reason for including Timothy's name (*see note on vv. 1, 2*). **bond-servants.** This denotes a willing slave who was happily and loyally linked to his master (*see note on Ro 1:1*; cf. Jas 1:1; 2Pe 1:1; Jude 1). **saints.** *See note on 1Co 1:2.* These were believers in the church at Philippi, including those who led the assembly. **in Christ Jesus.** This describes the Philippian believers' union with Christ in His death and resurrection (*see notes on Ro 6:2–9; Gal 2:20*), which was the reason they could be called "saints." **Philippi.** See Introduction: Background and Setting. **overseers.** *See note on 1Ti 3:1.* This is a term used to emphasize the leadership responsibilities of those who are elders, who are also called pastors and bishops. All 3 terms are used in the NT to describe the same men. **deacons.** Lit. "those who serve"; *see note on 1Ti 3:8.*

1:2 **Grace … peace.** Paul's standard greeting (*see note on Ro 1:7*) reminded the believers of their relationship to God.

1:3 **I thank my God.** Paul's letters usually included such commendation (*see note on Gal 1:3–5*).

1:4 **offering prayer with joy.** The Gr. word for "prayer" denotes a petition for, or a request made on behalf of, someone else. It was a delight for Paul to intercede for fellow believers.

1:5 **participation.** This can also be translated "fellowship" or "partnership." Cf. 2Co 8:4. **from the first day.** These believers eagerly assisted Paul in evangelizing Philippi from the beginning of the church there (Ac 16:12–40).

1:6 **He … will perfect it.** The Gr. verb translated "began" is used only here and in Gal 3:3—both times in reference to salvation itself. When God begins a work of salvation in a person, He finishes and perfects that work. Thus the verb "will perfect" points to the eternal security of the Christian (*see notes on Jn 6:40, 44; Ro 5:10; 8:29–39; Eph 1:13, 14; Heb 7:25; 12:2*). **day of Christ Jesus.** This phrase is not to be confused with the "Day of the Lord" (see Introduction to Joel: Historical and Theological Themes), which describes final divine judgment and wrath (cf. Is 13:9; Joel 1:15; 2:11; 1Th 5:2; 2Pe 3:10). "Day of Christ Jesus" is also called the "day of Christ" (v. 10; 2:16) and the "day of our Lord Jesus Christ" (1Co 1:8), which looks to the final salvation, reward, and glorification of believers. Cf. 1Co 3:10–15; 4:5; 2Co 5:9, 10.

1:7 **heart.** A common biblical word used to describe the center of thought and feeling (cf. Pr 4:23). **defense and confirmation.** Two judicial terms referring either to the first phase of Paul's trial in Rome in which he defended his gospel ministry or in a general sense to his continual defense of the faith, which was the heart of his ministry. **partakers of grace with me.** *See notes on v. 5.* During his imprisonment, the Philippians sent Paul money and Epaphroditus' services to support the apostle, thus sharing in God's gracious blessing on his ministry (cf. 2:30).

1:8 **affection.** The word lit. refers to the internal organs, which are the part of the body that reacts to intense emotion. It became the strongest Gr. word to express compassionate love—a love that involves one's entire being.

1:9 **in … knowledge.** This is from the Gr. word that describes genuine, full, or advanced knowledge. Biblical love is not an empty sentimentalism but is anchored deeply in the truth of Scripture and regulated by it (cf. Eph 5:2, 3; 1Pe 1:22). **discernment.** The Eng. word "aesthetic" comes from this Gr. word, which speaks of moral perception, insight, and the practical application of knowledge. Love is not blind, but perceptive, and it carefully scrutinizes to distinguish between right and wrong. *See note on 1Th 5:21, 22.*

1:10 **approve the … excellent.** "Approve" in classical Gr. described the assaying of metals or the testing of money for authenticity (cf. Lk 12:56; 14:19). "Excellent" means "to differ." Believers need the ability to distinguish those things that are truly important so they can establish the right priorities. **sincere and blameless.** "Sincere" means "genuine," and may have originally meant "tested by sunlight." In the ancient world, dishonest pottery dealers filled cracks in their inferior products with wax before glazing and painting them, making worthless pots difficult to distinguish from expensive ones. The only way to avoid being defrauded was to hold the pot to the sun, making the wax-filled cracks obvious. Dealers marked their fine pottery that could withstand "sun testing" as *sine cera*—"without wax." "Blameless" can be translated "without offense," referring to relational integrity. Christians are to live lives of true integrity that do not cause others to sin (*see notes on Ro 12:9; 1Co 10:31, 32; 2Co 1:12*; cf. Ro 14; 1Co 8). **the day of Christ.** *See note on v. 6.*

1:11 **fruit of righteousness.** This is better translated "the fruit righteousness produces" (*see note on Ro 1:13*; cf. Pr 11:30; Am 6:12; Jas 3:17, 18). **which *comes* through Jesus Christ.** See Jn 15:1–5; Eph 2:10. This speaks of the salvation transformation provided by our Lord and His ongoing work of power through His Spirit in us. **to the glory and praise of God.** See Jn 15:8; Eph 1:12–14; 3:20, 21. The ultimate end of all Paul's prayers was that God be glorified.

1:12 **my circumstances.** The events in Paul's life, namely, his journey to Rome and imprisonment there (see Introduction: Background and Setting; Ac 21–28). **for the greater progress.** This refers to the forward movement of something—often of armies—in spite of obstacles, dangers, and distractions. Paul's imprisonment proved to be no hindrance to spreading the message of salvation (cf. Ac 28:30, 31). Actually, it created new opportunities (*see note on 4:22*).

1:13 **imprisonment … *cause of* Christ … well known.** People around him recognized that Paul was no criminal, but had become a prisoner because of preaching Jesus Christ and the gospel (cf. Eph 6:20). **whole praetorian guard.** The Gr. word "praetorian"

else, [14] and that most of the [a]brethren, trusting in
the Lord because of my [b,A]imprisonment, have [B]far
more courage to speak the word of God without
fear. [15] [A]Some, to be sure, are preaching Christ even
[a]from envy and strife, but some also [a]from good
will; [16] the latter *do it* out of love, knowing that I
am appointed for the defense of the [A]gospel; [17] the
former proclaim Christ [A]out of selfish ambition
[a]rather than from pure motives, thinking to cause
me distress in my [b,B]imprisonment. [18] What then?
Only that in every way, whether in pretense or in
truth, Christ is proclaimed; and in this I rejoice.
Yes, and I will rejoice, [19] for I know that this will
turn out for my [a]deliverance [A]through your [b]prayers
and the provision of [B]the Spirit of Jesus Christ, [20] according to my [A]earnest expectation and [B]hope, that
I will not be put to shame in anything, but *that* with
[C]all boldness, Christ will even now, as always, be
[D]exalted in my body, [E]whether by life or by death.

TO LIVE IS CHRIST

[21] For to me, [A]to live is Christ and to die is gain.
[22] [a]But if *I am* to live *on* in the flesh, this *will mean*
[A]fruitful labor for me; and I do not know [b]which to
choose. [23] But I am hard-pressed from both *directions,*
having the [A]desire to depart and [B]be with Christ, for
that is very much better; [24] yet to remain on in the
flesh is more necessary for your sake. [25] [A]Convinced
of this, I know that I will remain and continue with
you all for your progress and joy [a]in the faith, [26] so
that your [A]proud confidence in me may abound in
Christ Jesus through my coming to you again.
[27] Only conduct yourselves in a manner [A]worthy
of the [B]gospel of Christ, so that whether I come and
see you or remain absent, I will hear of you that you
are [C]standing firm in [D]one spirit, with one [a]mind
[E]striving together for the faith of the gospel; [28] in no
way alarmed by *your* opponents—which is a [A]sign of
destruction for them, but of salvation for you, and

1:14 [a]Or *brethren in the Lord, trusting because of my bonds* [b]Lit *bonds* [A]Phil 1:7; 2 Tim 2:9 [B]Acts 4:31; 2 Cor 3:12; 7:4; Phil 1:20 1:15 [a]Lit *because of* [A]2 Cor 11:13 1:16 [A]Phil 1:5, 7, 12, 27; 2:22; 4:3, 15 1:17 [a]Lit *not sincerely* [b]Lit *bonds* [A]Rom 2:8; Phil 2:3 [B]Phil 1:7; 2 Tim 2:9 1:19 [a]Or *salvation* [b]Lit *supplication* [A]2 Cor 1:11 [B]Acts 16:7 1:20 [A]Rom 8:19 [B]Rom 5:5; 1 Pet 4:16 [C]Acts 4:31; 2 Cor 3:12; 7:4; Phil 1:14 [D]1 Cor 6:20 [E]Rom 14:8 1:21 [A]Gal 2:20 1:22 [a]Or *But if to live in the flesh, this will be fruitful labor for me, then I* [b]Lit *what I shall choose* [A]Rom 1:13 1:23 [A]2 Cor 5:8; 2 Tim 4:6 [B]John 12:26 1:25 [a]Lit *of* [A]Phil 2:24 1:26 [A]2 Cor 5:12; 7:4; Phil 2:16 1:27 [a]Lit *soul* [A]Eph 4:1 [B]Phil 1:5 [C]1 Cor 16:13; Phil 4:1 [D]Acts 4:32 [E]Jude 3 1:28 [A]2 Thess 1:5

can denote either a special building (e.g., a commander's headquarters, the emperor's palace) or the group of men in the Imperial guard. Because Paul was in a private house in Rome, "praetorian guard" probably refers to the members of the Imperial guard who guarded Paul day and night. Cf. Ac 28:16. **everyone else.** Others in the city of Rome who met and heard Paul (cf. Ac 28:23, 24, 30, 31).

1:14 most of the brethren. With the exception of those detractors identified in vv. 15, 16, who were attacking Paul. **far more courage to speak.** Paul's example of powerful witness to the gospel as a prisoner demonstrated God's faithfulness to His persecuted children and that their imprisonment would not halt the progress of the gospel. This encouraged others to be bold and not fear imprisonment.

1:15 from envy and strife. The attitude of Paul's detractors, who really did preach the gospel but were jealous of his apostolic power and authority, his success, and immense giftedness. "Strife" connotes contention, rivalry, and conflict, which resulted when Paul's critics began discrediting him. **from good will.** "Good will" speaks of satisfaction and contentment, the attitude that Paul's supporters had for him personally and for his ministry.

1:16 the latter *do it* out of love. Paul's supporters were motivated by genuine affection for him and confidence in his virtue (cf. 1Co 13:1, 2). **appointed.** The Gr. word describes a soldier's being placed on duty. Paul was in prison because he was destined to be there by God's will, so as to be in a strategic position to proclaim the gospel. **defense of the gospel.** *See note on v. 7.*

1:17 selfish ambition. This describes those who were interested only in self-advancement, or who ruthlessly sought to get ahead at any cost. Paul's detractors used his incarceration as an opportunity to promote their own prestige by accusing Paul of being so sinful the Lord had chastened him by imprisonment. **rather than ... pure motives.** *See note on v. 10.*

1:18 I rejoice ... will rejoice. Paul's joy was not tied to his circumstances or his critics (cf. Ps 4:7, 8; Ro 12:12; 2Co 6:10). He was glad when the gospel was proclaimed with authority, no matter who received credit. He endured the unjust accusations without bitterness at his accusers. Rather, he rejoiced that they preached Christ, even in a pretense of godliness.

1:19 my deliverance. "Deliverance" is from the basic Gr. term for salvation. But it can also be rendered "well-being" or "escape," which presents 4 possible interpretations: 1) it refers to Paul's ultimate salvation; 2) it alludes to his deliverance from threatened execution; 3) he would finally be vindicated by the emperor's ruling; or 4) Paul is talking about his eventual release from prison. Whatever Paul's precise meaning, he was certain he would be freed from his temporary distress (Job 13:16; cf. Job 19:26; Pss 22:4, 5, 8; 31:1; 33:18, 19; 34:7; 41:1). **Spirit of Jesus Christ.** The Holy Spirit (Ro 8:9; Gal 4:6). Paul had supreme confidence in the Spirit (cf. Zec 4:6; Jn 14:16; Ro 8:26; Eph 3:20).

1:20 earnest expectation. This Gr. word indicates keen anticipation of the future, as when someone stretches his neck to see what lies ahead. Paul was very confident and excited about Christ's promise (see Mt 10:32). **not be put to shame.** See Is 49:23; Ro 9:33; cf. Pss 25:2, 3; 40:15, 16; 119:80; Is 1:27–29; 45:14–17; Jer 12:13; Zep 3:11.

1:21 to me, to live is Christ. For Paul, life is summed up in Jesus Christ; Christ was his reason for being. *See notes on 3:12–14.* **to die is gain.** Death would relieve him of earthly burdens and let him focus totally on glorifying God (*see notes on vv. 23, 24;* cf. Ac 21:13).

1:22 the flesh. Cf. v. 24. Here this word refers not to one's fallen humanness (as in Ro 7:5, 18; 8:1), but simply to physical life (as in 2Co 10:3; Gal 2:20). **fruitful labor.** *See notes on Ro 1:13.* Paul knew that the only reason to remain in this world was to bring souls to Christ and build up believers to do the same. *See note on 2Co 4:15.*

1:23 hard-pressed. The Gr. word pictures a traveler on a narrow path, a rock wall on either side allowing him to go only straight ahead. **depart and be with Christ.** Paul knew if he died he would have complete, conscious, intimate, unhindered fellowship with his Lord (*see notes on 2Co 5:1, 8; 2Ti 4:6–8*). **very much better.** The highest superlative.

1:24 more necessary for your sake. Paul yielded his personal desire to be with his Lord for the necessity of the building of the church (see 2:3, 4).

1:25 Convinced .... will remain. Paul's conviction—not a supernatural revelation—that their need would determine that he stay on earth longer. **progress ... in the faith.** "Progress" pictures trail blazing so that an army can advance (*see note on v. 12*). Paul wanted to cut a new path for the Philippians to follow to victory; the increasing of their faith would result in the increasing of their joy.

1:26 confidence ... abound in Christ Jesus. The Gr. word order is "that your confidence of joy may be more abundant in Jesus Christ for me." The point is, as Paul lived on fruitfully, their joy and confidence would overflow because of Christ's working in him, not because of anything he himself did by his own ability.

1:27 worthy of the gospel. Believers are to have integrity, i.e., to live consistent with what they believe, teach, and preach. Cf. Eph 4:1; Col 1:10; 1Th 2:11, 12; 4:1; Titus 2:10; 2Pe 3:11, 14. **one spirit ... one mind.** This introduces Paul's theme of unity that continues through 2:4. His call for genuine unity of heart and mind is based on 1) the necessity of oneness to win the spiritual battle for the faith (vv. 28–30); 2) the love of others in the fellowship (2:1, 2); 3) genuine humility and self-sacrifice (2:3, 4); and 4) the example of Jesus Christ who proved that sacrifice produces eternal glory (2:5–11). **striving together.** Lit. "to struggle along with someone." Paul changed the metaphor from that of a soldier standing at his post ("standing firm") to one of a team struggling for victory against a common foe. **the faith of the gospel.** The Christian faith as revealed by God and recorded in the Scripture (Jude 3; cf. Ro 1:1; Gal 1:7).

1:28 sign of destruction. When believers willingly suffer without being "alarmed," it is a sign that God's enemies will be destroyed and eternally lost (*see notes on 2Th 1:4–8*).

that *too,* from God. 29 For to you [A]it has been granted
for Christ's sake, not only to believe in Him, but also
to [B]suffer for His sake, 30 experiencing the same [A]con-
flict which [B]you saw in me, and now hear *to be* in me.

BE LIKE CHRIST

2 Therefore if there is any encouragement in
Christ, if there is any consolation of love, if there
is any [A]fellowship of the Spirit, if any [a,B]affection and
compassion, 2 [A]make my joy complete [a]by [B]being of
the same mind, maintaining the same love, united
in spirit, intent on one purpose. 3 Do nothing [a]from
[b,A]selfishness or [B]empty conceit, but with humility of
mind [C]regard one another as more important than
yourselves; 4 [A]do not *merely* look out for your own
personal interests, but also for the interests of others. 5 [A]Have this attitude [a]in yourselves which was
also in [B]Christ Jesus, 6 who, although He [A]existed in
the [B]form of God, [C]did not regard equality with God
a thing to be [a]grasped, 7 but [a,A]emptied Himself, taking the form of a [B]bond-servant, *and* [C]being made
in the likeness of men. 8 Being found in appearance
as a man, [A]He humbled Himself by becoming [B]obe-
dient to the point of death, even [C]death [a]on a cross.
9 [A]For this reason also, God [B]highly exalted Him,
and bestowed on Him [C]the name which is above

1:29 [A]Matt 5:11, 12 [B]Acts 14:22 1:30 [A]Col 1:29; 2:1; 1 Thess 2:2; 1 Tim 6:12; 2 Tim 4:7; Heb 10:32; 12:1 [B]Acts 16:19-40; Phil 1:13 2:1 [a]Lit *inward parts* [A]2 Cor 13:14 [B]Col 3:12 2:2 [a]Lit *that you be* [A]John 3:29 [B]Rom 12:16; Phil 4:2 2:3 [a]Lit *according to* [b]Or *contentiousness* [A]Rom 2:8; Phil 1:17 [B]Gal 5:26 [C]Rom 12:10; Eph 5:21 2:4 [A]Rom 15:1f 2:5 [a]Or *among* [A]Matt 11:29; Rom 15:3 [B]Phil 1:1 2:6 [a]I.e. utilized or asserted [A]John 1:1 [B]2 Cor 4:4 [C]John 5:18; 10:33; 14:28 2:7 [a]I.e. laid aside His privileges [A]2 Cor 8:9 [B]Matt 20:28 [C]John 1:14; Rom 8:3; Gal 4:4; Heb 2:17 2:8 [a]Lit *of* [A]2 Cor 8:9 [B]Matt 26:39; John 10:18; Rom 5:19; Heb 5:8 [C]Heb 12:2 2:9 [A]Heb 1:9 [B]Matt 28:18; Acts 2:33; Heb 2:9 [C]Eph 1:21

1:29 granted … to suffer. *See notes on 3:10; 1Pe 2:19–21*; cf. Mt 5:10–12; Ac 5:41. The Gr. verb translated "granted" is from the noun for grace. Believers' suffering is a gift of grace which brings power (2Co 7:9, 10; 1Pe 5:10) and eternal reward (1Pe 4:13).

1:30 same conflict. The same kind of suffering Paul had experienced (vv. 12–14; Ac 16:22–24). **you saw.** This refers to what the Philippians witnessed when Paul and Silas were imprisoned at Philippi (Ac 16:19–40).

2:1 encouragement in Christ. "Encouragement" is from the Gr. word that means "to come alongside and help, counsel, exhort" (*see notes on Jn 14:26; Ro 12:1*), which our beloved Lord does for His own. **consolation of love.** The Gr. word translated "consolation" portrays the Lord coming close and whispering words of gentle cheer or tender counsel in a believer's ear. **fellowship of the Spirit.** "Fellowship" refers to the partnership, of common eternal life, provided by the indwelling Holy Spirit (1Co 3:16; 12:13; 2Co 13:14; 1Jn 1:4–6). **affection and compassion.** God has extended His deep affection (*see note on 1:8*) and compassion to every believer (cf. Ro 12:1; 2Co 1:3; Col 3:12), and that reality should result in unity.

2:2 make my joy complete. Paul's joy was tied to concern for the unity of believers (cf. Heb 13:17). **same mind.** Cf. 3:15, 16; 4:2; 1Pe 3:8. The Gr. word means "think the same way." This exhortation is not optional or obscure, but is repeated throughout the NT (cf. Ro 15:5; 1Co 1:10; 2Co 13:11–13). **same love.** Believers are to love others in the body of Christ equally—not because they are all equally attractive, but by showing the same kind of sacrificial, loving service to all that was shown to them by Christ (Jn 15:13; Ro 12:10; 1Jn 3:17; cf. Jn 3:16). **united in spirit.** This is perhaps a term specially coined by Paul. It lit. means "one-souled" and describes people who are knit together in harmony, having the same desires, passions, and ambitions.

2:3 selfishness. This Gr. word, which is sometimes rendered "strife" because it refers to factionalism, rivalry, and partisanship (*see note on Gal 5:20*), speaks of the pride that prompts people to push for their own way. **empty conceit.** Lit. "empty glory." This word refers to the pursuit of personal glory, which is the motivation for selfish ambition. **humility of mind.** This translates a Gr. word that Paul and other NT writers apparently coined. It was a term of derision, with the idea of being low, shabby, and humble (cf. 1Co 15:9; 1Ti 1:15). **regard one another as more important than yourselves.** The basic definition of true humility (cf. Ro 12:10; Gal 5:13; Eph 5:21; 1Pe 5:5).

2:5 Christ is the ultimate example of selfless humility (cf. Mt 11:29; Jn 13:12–17).

2:6–11 This is the classic Christological passage in the NT, dealing with the incarnation. It was probably sung as a hymn in the early church (*see note on Col 3:16*).

2:6 He existed in the form of God. Paul affirms that Jesus eternally has been God. The usual Gr. word for "existed" or "being" is not used here. Instead, Paul chose another term that stresses the essence of a person's nature—his continuous state or condition. Paul also could have chosen one of two Gr. words for "form," but he chose the one that specifically denotes the essential, unchanging character of something—what it is in and of itself. The fundamental doctrine of Christ's deity has always encompassed these crucial characteristics (cf. Jn 1:1, 3, 4, 14; 8:58; Col 1:15–17; Heb 1:3). **equality with God.** The Gr. word for "equality" defines things that are exactly the same in size, quantity, quality, character, and number. In every sense, Jesus is equal to God and constantly claimed to be so during His earthly ministry (cf. Jn 5:18; 10:33, 38; 14:9; 20:28; Heb 1:1–3). **grasped.** The Gr. word originally meant "a thing seized by robbery." It eventually came to mean anything clutched, embraced, or prized, and thus is sometimes translated "held onto." Though Christ had all the rights, privileges, and honors of deity—which He was worthy of and could never be disqualified from—His attitude was not to cling to those things or His position but to be willing to give them up for a season. *See notes on Jn 17:1–5.*

2:7 emptied Himself. From this Gr. word comes the theological word "kenosis"; i.e., the doctrine of Christ's self-emptying in His incarnation. This was a self-renunciation, not an emptying Himself of deity nor an exchange of deity for humanity (*see notes on v. 6*). Jesus did, however, renounce or set aside His privileges in several areas: 1) heavenly glory—while on earth He gave up the glory of a face-to-face relationship with God and the continuous outward display and personal enjoyment of that glory (cf. Jn 17:5); 2) independent authority—during His incarnation Christ completely submitted Himself to the will of His Father (*see note on v. 8*; cf. Mt 26:39; Jn 5:30; Heb 5:8); 3) divine prerogatives—He set aside the voluntary display of His divine attributes and submitted Himself to the Spirit's direction (cf. Mt 24:36; Jn 1:45–49); 4) eternal riches—while on earth Christ was poor and owned very little (cf. 2Co 8:9); and 5) a favorable relationship with God—He felt the Father's wrath for human sin while on the cross (cf. Mt 27:46; *see note on 2Co 5:21*). **form of a bond-servant.** Again, Paul uses the Gr. word "form," which indicates exact essence (*see note on v. 6*). As a true servant (*see note on 1:1*), Jesus submissively did the will of His Father (cf. Is 52:13, 14). **the likeness of men.** Christ became more than God in a human body, but He took on all the essential attributes of humanity (Lk 2:52; Gal 4:4; Col 1:22), even to the extent that He identified with basic human needs and weaknesses (cf. Heb 2:14, 17; 4:15). He became the God-Man: fully God and fully man.

2:8 in appearance as a man. This is not simply a repetition of the last phrase in v. 7, but a shift from the heavenly focus to an earthly one. Christ's humanity is described from the viewpoint of those who saw Him. Paul is implying that although He outwardly looked like a man, there was much more to Him (His deity) than many people recognized naturally (cf. Jn 6:42; 8:48). **He humbled Himself.** After the humbling of incarnation, Jesus further humbled Himself in that He did not demand normal human rights, but subjected Himself to persecution and suffering at the hands of unbelievers (cf. Is 53:7; Mt 26:62–64; Mk 14:60, 61; 1Pe 2:23). **obedient … death.** Beyond even persecution, Jesus went to the lowest point or furthest extent in His humiliation in dying as a criminal, following God's plan for Him (cf. Mt 26:39; Ac 2:23). **a cross.** *See notes on Mt 27:29–50.* Even further humiliation was His because Jesus' death was not by ordinary means, but was accomplished by crucifixion—the cruelest, most excruciating, most degrading form of death ever devised. The Jews hated this manner of execution (Dt 21:23; *see note on Gal 3:13*).

2:9 For this reason also, God. Christ's humiliation (vv. 5–8) and exaltation by God (vv. 9–11) are causally and inseparably linked. **highly exalted Him.** Christ's exaltation was fourfold. The early sermons of the apostles affirm His resurrection and coronation (His position at the right hand of God), and allude to His intercession for believers (Ac 2:32, 33; 5:30, 31; cf. Eph 1:20, 21; Heb 4:15; 7:25, 26).

every name, 10 so that at the name of Jesus [A]EVERY
KNEE WILL BOW, of [B]those who are in heaven and on
earth and under the earth, 11 and that every tongue
will confess that Jesus Christ is [A]Lord, to the glory
of God the Father.
12 So then, my beloved, [A]just as you have always
obeyed, not as in my presence only, but now much
more in my absence, work out your [B]salvation with
[C]fear and trembling; 13 for it is [A]God who is at work in
you, both to will and to work [B]for *His* good pleasure.
14 Do all things without [A]grumbling or disputing;
15 so that you will [a]prove yourselves to be [A]blameless
and innocent, [B]children of God above reproach in
the midst of a [C]crooked and perverse generation,
among whom you [b,D]appear as [c]lights in the world,
16 holding [a]fast the word of life, so that in [A]the day
of Christ I will have reason to glory because I did
not [B]run in vain nor [C]toil in vain. 17 But even if I am
being [A]poured out as a drink offering upon [B]the sacrifice and service of your faith, I rejoice and share
my joy with you all. 18 You too, *I urge you*, rejoice in
the same way and share your joy with me.

TIMOTHY AND EPAPHRODITUS

19 But I hope [a]in the Lord Jesus to [A]send [B]Timothy
to you shortly, so that I also may be encouraged when

2:10 [A]Is 45:23; Rom 14:11 [B]Eph 1:10 2:11 [A]John 13:13; Rom 10:9; 14:9 2:12 [A]Phil 1:5, 6; 4:15 [B]Heb 5:9 [C]2 Cor 7:15 2:13 [A]Rom 12:3; 1 Cor 12:6; 15:10; Heb 13:21 [B]Eph 1:5 2:14 [A]1 Cor 10:10; 1 Pet 4:9 2:15 [a]Or *become* [b]Or *shine* [c]Or *luminaries, stars* [A]Luke 1:6; Phil 3:6 [B]Matt 5:45; Eph 5:1 [C]Deut 32:5; Acts 2:40 [D]Matt 5:14-16 2:16 [a]Or *forth* [A]Phil 1:6 [B]Gal 2:2 [C]Is 49:4; Gal 4:11; 1 Thess 3:5 2:17 [A]2 Cor 12:15; 2 Tim 4:6 [B]Num 28:6, 7; Rom 15:16 2:19 [a]Or *trusting in* [A]Phil 2:23 [B]Phil 1:1

Hebrews 4:14 refers to the final element, His ascension. The exaltation did not concern Christ's nature or eternal place within the Trinity, but His new identity as the God-Man (cf. Jn 5:22; Ro 1:4; 14:9; 1Co 15:24, 25). In addition to receiving back His glory (Jn 17:5), Christ's new status as the God-Man meant God gave Him privileges He did not have prior to the incarnation. If He had not lived among men, He could not have identified with them as the interceding High Priest. Had He not died on the cross, He could not have been elevated from that lowest degree back to heaven as the substitute for sin. **name ... above every name.** Christ's new name which further describes His essential nature and places Him above and beyond all comparison is "Lord." This name is the NT synonym for OT descriptions of God as sovereign ruler. Both before (Is 45:21–23; Mk 15:2; Lk 2:11; Jn 13:13; 18:37; 20:28) and after (Ac 2:36; 10:36; Ro 14:9–11; 1Co 8:6; 15:57; Rev 17:14; 19:16) the exaltation, Scripture affirms that this was Jesus' rightful title as the God-Man.

2:10, 11 bow ... **confess.** The entire intelligent universe is called to worship Jesus Christ as Lord (cf. Ps 2). This mandate includes the angels in heaven (Rev 4:2–9), the spirits of the redeemed (Rev 4:10, 11), obedient believers on earth (Ro 10:9), the disobedient rebels on earth (2Th 1:7–9), and demons and lost humanity in hell (1Pe 3:18–22). The Gr. word for "confess" means "to acknowledge," "affirm," or "agree," which is what everyone will eventually do in response to Christ's lordship, willingly and blessedly or unwillingly and painfully.

2:10 at the name of Jesus. "Jesus" was the name bestowed at His birth (Mt 1:21), not His new name. The name for Jesus given in the fullest sense after His exaltation was "Lord" (*see note on v. 11*).

2:11 Lord. *See note on v. 9.* "Lord" primarily refers to the right to rule, and in the NT it denotes mastery over or ownership of people and property. When applied to Jesus, it certainly implies His deity, but it mainly refers to sovereign authority. **glory of God the Father.** The purpose of Christ's exaltation (cf. Mt 17:5; Jn 5:23; 13:31, 32; 1Co 15:28).

2:12 obeyed. Their faithful response to the divine commands Paul had taught them (cf. Ro 1:5; 15:18; 2Co 10:5, 6). **work out your salvation.** The Gr. verb rendered "work out" means "to continually work to bring something to fulfillment or completion." It cannot refer to salvation by works (cf. Ro 3:21–24; Eph 2:8, 9), but it does refer to the believer's responsibility for active pursuit of obedience in the process of sanctification (*see notes on 3:13, 14; Ro 6:19*; cf. 1Co 9:24–27; 15:58; 2Co 7:1; Gal 6:7–9; Eph 4:1; Col 3:1–17; Heb 6:10, 11; 12:1, 2; 2Pe 1:5–11). **fear and trembling.** The attitude with which Christians are to pursue their sanctification. It involves a healthy fear of offending God and a righteous awe and respect for Him (cf. Pr 1:7; 9:10; Is 66:1, 2).

2:13 God who is at work in you. Although the believer is responsible to work (v. 12), the Lord actually produces the good works and spiritual fruit in the lives of believers (Jn 15:5; 1Co 12:6). This is accomplished because He works through us by His indwelling Spirit (Ac 1:8; 1Co 3:16, 17; 6:19, 20; cf. Gal 3:3). **to will and to work.** God energizes both the believer's desires and his actions. The Gr. word for "will" indicates that He is not focusing on mere desires or whimsical emotions, but on the studied intent to fulfill a planned purpose. God's power makes His church willing to live godly lives (cf. Ps 110:3). **good pleasure.** God wants Christians to do what satisfies Him. Cf. Eph 1:5, 9; 2Th 1:11.

2:14 without grumbling or disputing. The Gr. word for "grumbling" is a term that actually sounds like what it means. Its pronunciation is much like muttering or grumbling in a low tone of voice. It is an emotional rejection of God's providence, will, and circumstances for one's life. The word for "disputing" is more intellectual and here means "questionings," or "criticisms" directed negatively toward God.

2:15 that you will prove yourselves. This introduces the reasons believers should have the right attitude in pursuing godliness. "Prove yourselves" indicates a process—they are to be growing toward something they do not yet fully possess as children of God (cf. Eph 5:1; Titus 2:1). **blameless and innocent.** "Blameless" describes a life that cannot be criticized because of sin or evil. "Innocent" describes a life that is pure, unmixed, and unadulterated with sin, much like high-quality metal without any alloy (cf. Mt 10:16; Ro 16:19; 2Co 11:3; Eph 5:27). **above reproach.** In the Gr. OT, this word is used several times of the kind of sacrifice to be brought to God, i.e., spotless and without blemish (cf. Nu 6:14; 19:2; 2Pe 3:14). **crooked and perverse generation.** See Dt 32:5. "Crooked" is the word from which the Eng. "scoliosis" (curvature of the spinal column) comes. It describes something that is deviated from the standard, which is true of all who stray from God's path (cf. Pr 2:15; Is 53:6). "Perverse" intensifies this meaning by referring to a person who has strayed so far off the path that his deviation is severely twisted and distorted (cf. Lk 9:41). Paul applies this condition to the sinful world system. **appear as lights.** A metaphorical reference to spiritual character. "Appear" can be more precisely rendered "you have to shine," which means believers must show their character in the midst of a dark culture, as the sun, moon, and stars shine in an otherwise dark sky (*see notes on Mt 5:16; 2Co 4:6; Eph 5:8*).

2:16 holding fast. A slightly different translation—"holding forth"—more accurately reflects the verb in the original text. Here it refers to believers' holding out or offering something for others to take. **the word of life.** The gospel which, when believed, produces spiritual and eternal life (cf. Eph 2:1). **day of Christ.** *See note on 1:6.* **I will ... glory.** *See notes on v. 2; 4:1; 1Th 2:19.* **run ... nor toil in vain.** *See note on Gal 2:2.* Paul wanted to look back on his ministry and see that all his efforts were worthwhile (cf. 1Co 9:27; 1Th 5:12; 2Ti 4:7; Heb 13:17; 3Jn 4).

2:17, 18 rejoice ... share my joy ... your joy. An attitude of mutual joy ought to accompany any sacrificial Christian service (*see notes on 1:4, 18, 26*; cf. 2Co 7:4; Col 1:24; 1Th 3:9).

2:17 being poured out. From the Gr. that means "to be offered as a libation or drink offering." Some connect this with Paul's future martyrdom, but the verb is in the present tense, which means he is referring to his sacrificial ministry among the Philippians. **drink offering.** This refers to the topping off of an ancient animal sacrifice. The offerer poured wine either in front of or on top of the burning animal, and the wine would be vaporized. That steam symbolized the rising of the offering to the deity for whom the sacrifice was made (cf. Ex 29:38–41; 2Ki 16:13; Jer 7:18; Hos 9:4). Paul viewed his entire life as a drink offering, and here it was poured on the Philippians' sacrificial service. **service of your faith.** "Service" comes from a word that refers to sacred, priestly service (cf. Ro 12:1; 1Co 9:13) and was so used in the Gr. OT. Paul sees the Philippians as priests who were offering their lives sacrificially and faithfully in service to God (cf. 1Pe 2:9).

2:19–23 Paul tells the Philippians of his plans to send Timothy to Philippi to set him forth as a model spiritual servant.

2:19 Timothy. *See note on 1:1.*

I learn of your condition. 20 For I have no one *else*
[A]of kindred spirit who will genuinely be concerned
for your welfare. 21 For they all [A]seek after their own
interests, not those of Christ Jesus. 22 But you know
[A]of his proven worth, that [B]he served with me in the
furtherance of the gospel [C]like a child *serving* his father. 23 [A]Therefore I hope to send him immediately, as
soon as I see how things *go* with me; 24 and [A]I trust
in the Lord that I myself also will be coming shortly.
25 But I thought it necessary to send to you [A]Epaph-
roditus, my brother and [B]fellow worker and [C]fellow
soldier, who is also your [a,D]messenger and [A]minister
to my need; 26 because he was longing [a]for you all and
was distressed because you had heard that he was
sick. 27 For indeed he was sick to the point of death,
but God had mercy on him, and not on him only but
also on me, so that I would not have sorrow upon
sorrow. 28 Therefore I have sent him all the more eagerly so that when you see him again you may rejoice
and I may be less concerned *about you.* 29 [A]Receive
him then in the Lord with all joy, and [B]hold men like
him in high regard; 30 because he came close to death
[a,A]for the work of Christ, risking his life to [B]complete
[b]what was deficient in your service to me.

THE GOAL OF LIFE

3 Finally, my brethren, [A]rejoice in the Lord. To
write the same things *again* is no trouble to
me, and it is a safeguard for you.
2 Beware of the [A]dogs, beware of the [B]evil workers,
beware of the [a]false circumcision; 3 for [A]we are the *true*
[a]circumcision, who [B]worship in the Spirit of God and
[C]glory in [D]Christ Jesus and put no confidence in the
flesh, 4 although [A]I myself might have confidence even
in the flesh. If anyone else has a mind to put confidence in the flesh, I far more: 5 [A]circumcised the eighth
day, of the [B]nation of Israel, of the [C]tribe of Benjamin,
a [B]Hebrew of Hebrews; as to the Law, [D]a Pharisee;

2:20 [A]1 Cor 16:10; 2 Tim 3:10 2:21 [A]1 Cor 10:24; 13:5; Phil 2:4 2:22 [A]Rom 5:4; Acts 16:2 [B]Acts 16:3; 1 Cor 16:10; 2 Tim 3:10 [C]1 Cor 4:17 2:23 [A]Phil 2:19 2:24 [A]Phil 1:25 2:25 [a]Lit *apostle* [A]Phil 4:18 [B]Rom 16:3, 9, 21; Phil 4:3; Philem 1, 24 [C]Philem 2 [D]John 13:16; 2 Cor 8:23 2:26 [a]One early ms reads *to see you all* 2:29 [A]Rom 16:2 [B]1 Cor 16:18 2:30 [a]Lit *because of* [b]Lit *your deficiency of service* [A]Acts 20:24 [B]1 Cor 16:17; Phil 4:10 3:1 [A]Phil 2:18; 4:4 3:2 [a]Lit *mutilation;* Gr *katatome* [A]Ps 22:16, 20; Gal 5:15; Rev 22:15 [B]2 Cor 11:13 3:3 [a]Gr *peritome* [A]Rom 2:29; 9:6; Gal 6:15 [B]Gal 5:25 [C]Rom 15:17; Gal 6:14 [D]Rom 8:39; Phil 1:1; 3:12 3:4 [A]2 Cor 5:16; 11:18 3:5 [A]Luke 1:59 [B]Rom 11:1; 2 Cor 11:22 [C]Rom 11:1 [D]Acts 22:3; 23:6; 26:5

2:20, 21 I have no one *else* of kindred spirit. *See notes on v. 2.* Lit. "one souled." Timothy was one in thought, feeling, and spirit with Paul in love for the church. He was unique in being Paul's protege (*see note on 1Co 4:17;* cf. 1Ti 1:2; 2Ti 1:2). Paul had no other like Timothy because, sadly, "all" the others were devoted to their own purposes rather than Christ's. *See notes on 2Ti 1:15.*

2:23, 24 Paul was eventually released from prison (cf. Ac 28:30), after which he may have visited the church at Philippi.

2:24 in the Lord. Paul knew his plans were subject to God's sovereignty (cf. Jas 4:13–17).

2:25–30 This passage is a compelling look at love and unity among believers. All the parties show selfless affection for one another.

2:25 Epaphroditus. Paul wanted to send Timothy (v. 23) and come himself (v. 24), but found it necessary to send this man, a native Philippian of whom, outside this passage, little is known. His name was a common Gr. one, taken from a familiar word that originally meant "favorite of Aphrodite" (Gr. goddess of love). Later, the name came to mean "lovely" or "loving." He was sent to Paul with gifts (4:18) and was to remain and serve Paul as he could (v. 30). **messenger.** This comes from the same word that yields the Eng. "apostle." He was not an apostle of Christ (*see note on Ro 1:1*), but an apostle ("sent one") in the broader sense (*see note on Ro 1:5*) that he was an apostle of the church in Philippi, sent to Paul with their monetary love gift (*see note on 1:7;* cf. 2Co 8:23). Paul's sending him back to the church with this letter needed an explanation, lest they think Epaphroditus had not served Paul well.

2:26 distressed. The Gr. term describes the confused, chaotic, heavy state of restlessness that results from a time of turmoil or great trauma. Epaphroditus was more concerned about the Philippians' worry for him than he was about his own difficult situation.

2:27 sick to the point of death. Perhaps by the time he arrived in Rome, he had become seriously ill, but now was recovered enough to go back home to labor with the church, who needed him more than Paul did.

2:28 concerned. Paul had a great burden for all the people in the churches (cf. 2Co 11:2), and he was concerned here because the Philippians were so distressed about Epaphroditus (*see note on 1:8*).

2:29 high regard. Men like him are worthy of honor. *See notes on 1Th 5:12, 13.*

2:30 close to death. This refers to the same thing mentioned as sickness in vv. 26, 27.

3:1 Finally. Paul has reached a transition point—not a conclusion, since 44 verses remain. Cf. 4:8. **rejoice in the Lord.** Cf. 4:4. Paul's familiar theme throughout the epistle (see Introduction: Historical and Theological Themes), which has already been heard in chaps. 1, 2. This, however, is the first time he adds "in the Lord," which signifies the sphere in which the believers' joy exists—a sphere unrelated to the circumstances of life, but related to an unassailable, unchanging relationship to the sovereign Lord. **the same things.** What he is about to teach them in the verses that follow, he had previously given them instruction in, regarding their opponents (cf. 1:27–30). **a safeguard.** A safeguard to protect the Philippians from succumbing to the false teachers.

3:2 dogs. During the first century, dogs roamed the streets and were essentially wild scavengers. Because dogs were such filthy animals, the Jews loved to refer to Gentiles as dogs. Yet here Paul refers to Jews, specifically the Judaizers, as dogs to describe their sinful, vicious, and uncontrolled character. For more on those who taught that circumcision was necessary for salvation, see Introduction to Galatians: Background and Setting; *see notes on Ac 15:1; Gal 2:3.* **evil workers.** The Judaizers prided themselves on being workers of righteousness. Yet Paul described their works as evil, since any attempt to please God by one's own efforts and draw attention away from Christ's accomplished redemption is the worst kind of wickedness. **false circumcision.** In contrast to the Gr. word for "circumcision," which means "to cut around," this term means "to cut down (off)" or "to mutilate." Like the prophets of Baal (1Ki 18:28) and pagans who mutilated their bodies in their frenzied rituals, which were forbidden in the OT (Lv 19:28; 21:5; Dt 14:1; Is 15:2; Hos 7:14), the Judaizers' circumcision was, ironically, no spiritual symbol; it was merely physical mutilation (*see note on Gal 5:12*).

3:3 we are the *true* circumcision. The true people of God do not possess merely a symbol of the need for a clean heart (*see note on Ge 17:11*), they actually have been cleansed of sin by God (*see notes on Ro 2:25–29*). **worship in the Spirit of God.** The first characteristic Paul uses to define a true believer. The Gr. word for "worship" means to render respectful spiritual service, while "Spirit" should have a small "s," to indicate the inner person. *See notes on Jn 4:23, 24.* **glory in Christ Jesus.** The Gr. word for "glory" means "to boast with exultant joy." The true Christian gives all the credit for all that he is to Christ (cf. Ro 15:17; 1Co 1:31; 2Co 10:17; *see note on v. 1*). **no confidence in the flesh.** By "flesh" Paul is referring to man's unredeemed humanness, his own ability and achievements apart from God (*see note on Ro 7:5*). The Jews placed their confidence in being circumcised, being descendants of Abraham, and performing the external ceremonies and duties of the Mosaic law—things that could not save them (*see notes on Ro 3:20; Gal 5:1–12*). The true believer views his flesh as sinful, without any capacity to merit salvation or please God.

3:4–7 To counteract the Judaizers' claim that certain ceremonies and rituals of Judaism were necessary for salvation, Paul described his own lofty attainments as a Jew, which were greater than those his opponents could claim, but were of no benefit for salvation.

3:5 the eighth day. Paul was circumcised on the prescribed day (Ge 17:12; 21:4; Lv 12:3). **of Israel.** All true Jews were direct descendants of Abraham, Isaac, and Jacob (Israel). Paul's Jewish heritage was pure. **of the tribe of Benjamin.** Benjamin was the second son of Rachel (Ge 35:18), and one of the elite tribes of Israel who, along with Judah, remained loyal to the Davidic dynasty and formed the southern kingdom (1Ki 12:21). **Hebrew of Hebrews.** Paul was born to Hebrew parents and

6 as to zeal, [A]a persecutor of the church; as to the [B]righ-
teousness which is in the Law, found [C]blameless.
7 But [A]whatever things were gain to me, those
things I have counted as loss for the sake of Christ.
8 More than that, I count all things to be loss [a]in
view of the surpassing value of [b,A]knowing [B]Christ
Jesus my Lord, [a]for whom I have suffered the loss
of all things, and count them but rubbish so that
I may gain Christ, 9 and may be found in Him, not
having [A]a righteousness of my own derived from
the Law, but that which is through faith in Christ,
[B]the righteousness which *comes* from God on the
basis of faith, 10 that I may [A]know Him and [B]the
power of His resurrection and [a,C]the fellowship of
His sufferings, being [D]conformed to His death; 11 [a]in
order that I may [A]attain to the resurrection from
the dead.
12 Not that I have already [A]obtained *it* or have
already [B]become perfect, but I press on [a]so that
I may [C]lay hold of that [b]for which also I [D]was laid
hold of by [E]Christ Jesus. 13 Brethren, I do not regard
myself as having laid hold of *it* yet; but one thing
I do: [A]forgetting what *lies* behind and reaching
forward to what *lies* ahead, 14 I [A]press on toward
the goal for the prize of the [B]upward call of God
in [C]Christ Jesus. 15 Let us therefore, as many as are
[a,A]perfect, have this attitude; and if in anything you
have a [B]different attitude, [C]God will reveal that also
to you; 16 however, let us keep [a,A]living by that same
standard to which we have attained.

3:6 [A]Acts 8:3; 22:4, 5; 26:9-11 [B]Phil 3:9 [C]Phil 2:15 3:7 [A]Luke 14:33 3:8 [a]Lit *because of* [b]Lit *the knowledge of* [A]Jer 9:23f; John 17:3; Eph 4:13; Phil 3:10; 2 Pet 1:3 [B]Rom 8:39; Phil 1:1; 3:12 3:9 [A]Rom 10:5; Phil 3:6 [B]Rom 9:30; 1 Cor 1:30 3:10 [a]Or *participation in* [A]Jer 9:23f; John 17:3; Eph 4:13; Phil 3:8; 2 Pet 1:3 [B]Rom 6:5 [C]Rom 8:17 [D]Rom 6:5; 8:36; Gal 6:17 3:11 [a]Lit *if somehow* [A]Acts 26:7; 1 Cor 15:23; Rev 20:5f 3:12 [a]Lit *if I may even* [b]Or *because also* [A]1 Cor 9:24f; 1 Tim 6:12, 19 [B]1 Cor 13:10 [C]1 Tim 6:12, 19 [D]Acts 9:5f [E]Rom 8:39; Phil 1:1; 3:3, 8 3:13 [A]Luke 9:62 3:14 [A]1 Cor 9:24; Heb 6:1 [B]Rom 8:28; 11:29; 2 Tim 1:9 [C]Phil 3:3 3:15 [a]Or *mature* [A]Matt 5:48; 1 Cor 2:6 [B]Gal 5:10 [C]John 6:45; Eph 1:17; 1 Thess 4:9 3:16 [a]Lit *following in line* [A]Gal 6:16

maintained the Hebrew tradition and language, even while living in a pagan city (cf. Ac 21:40; 26:4, 5). **a Pharisee.** The legalistic fundamentalists of Judaism, whose zeal to apply the OT Scriptures directly to life led to a complex system of tradition and works righteousness (*see note on Mt 3:7*). Paul may have come from a line of Pharisees (cf. Ac 22:3; 23:6; 26:5).

3:6 zeal, a persecutor of the church. To the Jew, "zeal" was the highest single virtue of religion. It combines love and hate; because Paul loved Judaism, he hated whatever might threaten it (*see notes on Ac 8:3; 9:1*). **the righteousness which is in the Law.** The standard of righteous living advocated by God's law. Paul outwardly kept this, so that no one could accuse him of violation. Obviously his heart was sinful and self-righteous. He was not an OT believer, but a proud and lost legalist.

3:7 whatever things were gain .... have counted as loss. The Gr. word for "gain" is an accounting term that means "profit." The Gr. word for "loss" also is an accounting term, used to describe a business loss. Paul used the language of business to describe the spiritual transaction that occurred when Christ redeemed him. All his Jewish religious credentials that he thought were in his profit column were actually worthless and damning (cf. Lk 18:9–14). Thus, he put them in his loss column when he saw the glories of Christ (cf. Mt 13:44, 45; 16:25, 26).

3:8–11 Paul described the benefits that accrued to his profit column when he came to Christ.

3:8 knowing Christ Jesus. To "know" Christ is not simply to have intellectual knowledge about Him; Paul used the Gr. verb that means to know "experientially" or "personally" (cf. Jn 10:27; 17:3; 2Co 4:6; 1Jn 5:20). It is equivalent to shared life with Christ (*see note on Gal 2:20*). It also corresponds to a Heb. word used of God's knowledge of His people (Am 3:2) and their knowledge of Him in love and obedience (Jer 31:34; Hos 6:3; 8:2). **rubbish.** The Gr. word refers to garbage or waste, and can even be translated "dung" or "manure."

3:9 be found in Him. Paul was "in Christ" (*see note on 1:1*). His union with Christ was possible only because God imputed Christ's righteousness to him so that it was reckoned by God as his own (*see notes on Ro 1:17; 3:24*). **not having a righteousness of my own derived from *the* Law.** This is the proud self-righteousness of external morality, religious ritual and ceremony, and good works. It is the righteousness produced by the flesh, which cannot save from sin (Ro 3:19, 20; Gal 3:6–25). **faith in Christ.** Faith is the confident, continuous confession of total dependence on and trust in Jesus Christ for the necessary requirement to enter God's kingdom (*see note on Ro 1:16*). And that requirement is the righteousness of Christ, which God imputes to every believer (*see note on Ro 3:24*).

3:10 I may know Him. *See note on v. 8.* Paul's emphasis here is on gaining a deeper knowledge and intimacy with Christ. **the power of His resurrection.** Christ's resurrection most graphically demonstrated the extent of His power. By raising Himself from the dead, Christ displayed His power over both the physical and spiritual worlds. **fellowship of His sufferings.** This refers to a partnership—a deep communion of suffering that every believer shares with Christ, who is able to comfort suffering Christians because He has already experienced the same suffering, and infinitely more (Heb 2:18; 4:15; 12:2–4; cf. 2Co 5:21; 1Pe 2:21–24). **conformed to His death.** As Christ died for the purpose of redeeming sinners, so Paul had that same purpose in a lesser sense; he lived and would willingly die to reach sinners with the gospel. His life and death, though not redemptive, were for the same purpose as his Lord's.

3:11 in order that. Reflecting his humility, he didn't care how God brought it to pass, but longed for death and for the fulfillment of his salvation in his resurrection body (cf. Ro 8:23). **the resurrection from the dead.** Lit. "the resurrection out from the corpses." This is a reference to the resurrection which accompanies the rapture of the church (1Th 4:13–17; cf. 1Co 15:42–44).

3:12–14 Paul uses the analogy of a runner to describe the Christian's spiritual growth. The believer has not reached his goal of Christlikeness (cf. vv. 20, 21), but like the runner in a race, he must continue to pursue it. That this is the goal for every believer is also clear from Ro 8:29; 2Th 2:13, 14; 1Jn 3:2 (*see notes there*).

3:12 Not that I have already obtained. The race toward Christlikeness begins with a sense of honesty and dissatisfaction. **press on.** The Gr. word was used of a sprinter, and refers to aggressive, energetic action. Paul pursued sanctification with all his might, straining every spiritual muscle to win the prize (1Co 9:24–27; 1Ti 6:12; Heb 12:1). **lay hold ... laid hold.** "Lay hold" means "to make one's own possession." Christ chose Paul for the ultimate purpose of conforming Paul to His glorious image (Ro 8:29), and that is the very goal Paul pursued to attain.

3:13 one thing *I do*. Paul had reduced the whole of sanctification to the simple and clear goal of doing "one thing"—pursuing Christlikeness (*see notes on 2Co 11:1–3*). **forgetting what *lies* behind.** The believer must refuse to rely on past virtuous deeds and achievements in ministry or to dwell on sins and failures. To be distracted by the past debilitates one's efforts in the present.

3:14 the goal. Christlikeness here and now (*see note on v. 12*). **the prize.** Christlikeness in heaven (cf. vv. 20, 21; 1Jn 3:1, 2). **the upward call of God.** The time when God calls each believer up to heaven and into His presence will be the moment of receiving the prize which has been an unattainable goal in earthly life.

3:15 as many as are perfect. Since the spiritual perfection of Christlikeness is possible only when the believer receives the upward call, Paul is referring here to mature spirituality. He could be referring to the mature believers who were like-minded with him in this pursuit or he may also have used "mature" here to refer sarcastically to the Judaizers, who thought they had reached perfection. **have this attitude.** Believers are to have the attitude of pursuing the prize of Christlikeness. **have a different attitude.** Those who continue to dwell on the past and make no progress toward the goal. **God will reveal.** The Gr. word for "reveal" means "to uncover" or "unveil." Paul left in God's hands those who were not pursuing spiritual perfection. He knew God would reveal the truth to them eventually, even if it meant chastening (Heb 12:5–11).

3:16 keep living ... same *standard* ... we have attained. The Gr. word for "living" refers to walking in line. Paul's directive for the Philippian believers was to stay in line spiritually and keep progressing in sanctification by the

17 Brethren, [A]join in following my example, and
observe those who walk according to the [B]pattern
you have in us. 18 For [A]many walk, of whom I often told you, and now tell you even [B]weeping, *that
they are* enemies of [C]the cross of Christ, 19 whose
end is destruction, whose god is *their* [a,A]appetite,
and *whose* [B]glory is in their shame, who [C]set their
minds on earthly things. 20 For [A]our [a]citizenship is
in heaven, from which also we eagerly [B]wait for a
Savior, the Lord Jesus Christ; 21 who will [A]transform
[a]the body of our humble state into [B]conformity
with [b]the [C]body of His glory, [D]by the exertion of
the power that He has even to [E]subject all things
to Himself.

THINK OF EXCELLENCE

4 Therefore, my beloved brethren [a]whom I [A]long
to see, my joy and crown, in this way [B]stand firm
in the Lord, my beloved.
2 I urge Euodia and I urge Syntyche to [a,A]live in
harmony in the Lord. 3 Indeed, true companion, I
ask you also to help these women who have shared
my struggle in *the cause of* the gospel, together with
Clement also and the rest of my [A]fellow workers,
whose [B]names are in the book of life.
4 [A]Rejoice in the Lord always; again I will say, rejoice! 5 Let your gentle *spirit* be known to all men.
[A]The Lord is [a]near. 6 [A]Be anxious for nothing, but
in everything by [B]prayer and supplication with

3:17 [A]1 Cor 4:16; 11:1; Phil 4:9 [B]1 Pet 5:3 3:18 [A]2 Cor 11:13 [B]Acts 20:31 [C]Gal 6:14 3:19 [a]Lit *belly* [A]Rom 16:18; Titus 1:12 [B]Rom 6:21; Jude 13 [C]Rom 8:5f; Col 3:2 3:20 [a]Lit *commonwealth* [A]Eph 2:19; Phil 1:27; Col 3:1; Heb 12:22 [B]1 Cor 1:7 3:21 [a]Or *our lowly body* [b]Or *His glorious body* [A]1 Cor 15:43-53 [B]Rom 8:29; Col 3:4 [C]1 Cor 15:43, 49 [D]Eph 1:19 [E]1 Cor 15:28 4:1 [a]Lit *and longed for* [A]Phil 1:8 [B]1 Cor 16:13; Phil 1:27 4:2 [a]Or *be of the same mind* [A]Phil 2:2 4:3 [A]Phil 2:25 [B]Luke 10:20 4:4 [A]Phil 3:1 4:5 [a]Or *at hand* [A]1 Cor 16:22 mg; Heb 10:37; James 5:8f 4:6 [A]Matt 6:25 [B]Eph 6:18; 1 Tim 2:1; 5:5

same principles that had brought them to this point in their spiritual growth (cf. 1Th 3:10; 1Pe 2:2).

3:17 my example. Lit. "be imitators of me." Since all believers are imperfect, they need examples of less imperfect people who know how to deal with imperfection and who can model the process of pursuing the goal of Christlikeness. Paul was that model (1Co 11:1; 1Th 1:6). **observe those who walk.** The Philippian believers were to focus on other godly examples, such as Timothy and Epaphroditus (2:19, 20), and see how they conducted themselves in service to Christ.

3:18 often told you. Apparently, Paul had warned the Philippians on numerous occasions about the dangers of false teachers, just as he did the Ephesians (Ac 20:28–30). **weeping.** Paul had a similar response as he warned the Ephesian elders about the dangers of false teachers (Ac 20:31). **enemies of the cross.** Implied in Paul's language is that these men did not claim to oppose Christ, His work on the cross, or salvation by grace alone through faith alone, but they did not pursue Christlikeness in manifest godliness. Apparently, they were posing as friends of Christ, and possibly had even reached positions of leadership in the church.

3:19 These enemies of the cross could have been either Jews (the Judaizers; v. 2) or Gentile libertines—precursors of gnosticism, who maintained a dualistic philosophy that tended toward antinomianism, which is a discarding of any moral law. **end is destruction.** The Gr. word for "end" refers to one's ultimate destiny. The Judaizers were headed for eternal damnation because they depended on their works to save them. The Gentile libertines were headed for the same destiny because they trusted in their human wisdom and denied the transforming power of the gospel. **god ... appetite.** This may refer to the Judaizers' fleshly accomplishments, which were mainly religious works. It could also refer to their observance of the dietary laws they believed were necessary for salvation. If the Gentile libertines are in view, it could easily refer to their sensual desires and fleshly appetites. As always, false teachers are evident by their wickedness. *See notes on 2Pe 2:10–19; Jude 8–13.* **glory ... shame.** The Judaizers boasted of their self-effort; but even the best of their accomplishments were no better than filthy rags or dung (vv. 7, 8; Is 64:6). The Gentile libertines boasted about their sin and abused Christian liberty to defend their behavior (1Co 6:12). **earthly things.** The Judaizers were preoccupied with ceremonies, feasts, sacrifices, and other kinds of physical observances. The Gentile libertines simply loved the world itself and all the things in it (cf. Jas 4:4; 1Jn 2:15).

3:20 our citizenship. The Gr. term refers to a colony of foreigners. In one secular source, it was used to describe a capital city that kept the names of its citizens on a register. **in heaven.** The place where God dwells and where Christ is present. It is the believers' home (Jn 14:2, 3), where their names are registered (Lk 10:20) and their inheritance awaits (1Pe 1:4). Other believers are there (Heb 12:23). We belong to the kingdom under the rule of our heavenly King, and obey heaven's laws. Cf. 1Pe 2:11. **eagerly wait.** The Gr. verb is found in most passages dealing with the second coming and expresses the idea of waiting patiently, but with great expectation (Ro 8:23; 2Pe 3:11, 12).

3:21 transform the body of our humble state. The Gr. word for "transform" gives us the word "schematic," which is an internal design of something. Those who are already dead in Christ, but alive with Him in spirit in heaven (1:23; 2Co 5:8; Heb 12:23), will receive new bodies at the resurrection and rapture of the church, when those alive on earth will have their bodies transformed (*see notes on Ro 8:18–23; 1Co 15:51–57; 1Th 4:16*). **conformity with the body of His glory.** The believer's new body will be like Christ's after His resurrection, and will be redesigned and adapted for heaven (1Co 15:42, 43; 1Jn 3:2). **subject.** The Gr. word refers to arranging things in order of rank or managing something. Christ has the power both to providentially create natural laws and miraculously overrule them (1Co 15:23–27).

4:1 beloved ... long *to see.* Paul reveals his deep affection for the Philippian believers. The Gr. term for "long to see" refers to the deep pain of separation from loved ones. **my joy and crown.** Paul did not derive his joy from circumstances, but from his fellow believers in Philippi (cf. 1Th 2:19, 20; 3:9). The Gr. term for "crown" refers to the laurel wreath received by an athlete for winning a contest (1Co 9:25) or by a person honored by his peers at a banquet as a symbol of success or a fruitful life. The Philippian believers were proof that Paul's efforts were successful (cf. 1Co 9:2). **stand firm.** This Gr. word was often used to describe a soldier standing at his post; here it is a military command (cf. 1:27) which is the dominant expression of vv. 1–9.

4:2 I urge. The Gr. term means "to implore," or "to appeal." **Euodia ... Syntyche.** These two women were prominent church members (v. 3), who may have been among the women meeting for prayer when Paul first preached the gospel in Philippi (Ac 16:13). Apparently, they were leading two opposing factions in the church, most likely over a personal conflict. **live in harmony.** Spiritual stability depends on the mutual love, harmony, and peace between believers. Apparently the disunity in the Philippian church was about to destroy the integrity of its testimony.

4:3 companion. The Gr. word pictures two oxen in a yoke, pulling the same load. A companion is a partner or an equal in a specific endeavor—in this case a spiritual one. It is possible that this individual is unnamed, but it is best to take the Gr. word translated "companion" as a proper name ("Syzygos"). He was likely one of the church elders (1:1). **with Clement.** Nothing is known of him. **book of life.** In eternity past, God registered all the names of His elect in that book which identifies those inheritors of eternal life (*see note on Rev 3:5*; cf. Da 12:1; Mal 3:16, 17; Lk 10:20; Rev 17:8; 20:12).

4:4 Rejoice in the Lord. *See note on 3:1.*

4:5 gentle *spirit.* This refers to contentment with and generosity toward others. It can also refer to mercy or leniency toward the faults and failures of others. It can even refer to patience in someone who submits to injustice or mistreatment without retaliating. Graciousness with humility encompasses all the above. **near.** Can refer to nearness in space or time. The context suggests nearness in space: the Lord encompasses all believers with His presence (Ps 119:151).

4:6 Be anxious for nothing. *See notes on Mt 6:26–33.* Fret and worry indicate a lack of trust in God's wisdom, sovereignty, or power. Delighting in the Lord and meditating on His Word are a great antidote to anxiety (Ps 1:2). **in everything.** All difficulties are within God's purposes. **prayer and supplication with thanksgiving ... requests.** Gratitude to God accompanies all true prayer.

thanksgiving let your requests be made known to
God. 7 And [A]the peace of God, which surpasses all
[a]comprehension, will [B]guard your hearts and your
[C]minds in [D]Christ Jesus.
8 Finally, brethren, [A]whatever is true, whatever
is honorable, whatever is right, whatever is pure,
whatever is [a]lovely, whatever is of good repute,
if there is any excellence and if anything worthy
of praise, [b]dwell on these things. 9 The things you
have learned and received and heard and seen [A]in
me, practice these things, and [B]the God of peace
will be with you.

GOD'S PROVISIONS

10 But I rejoiced in the Lord greatly, that now at
last [A]you have revived your concern for me; indeed,
you were concerned *before,* but you lacked opportunity. 11 Not that I speak [a]from want, for I have
learned to be [b,A]content in whatever circumstances I
am. 12 I know how to get along with humble means,
and I also know how to live in prosperity; in any
and every circumstance I have learned the secret
of being filled and going [A]hungry, both of having
abundance and [B]suffering need. 13 I can do all things
[a]through Him who [A]strengthens me. 14 Nevertheless, you have done well to [A]share *with me* in my
affliction.
15 You yourselves also know, Philippians, that at
the [a,A]first preaching of the gospel, after I left [B]Mac-
edonia, no church [C]shared with me in the matter
of giving and receiving but you alone; 16 for even
in [A]Thessalonica you sent *a gift* more than once
for my needs. 17 [A]Not that I seek the gift itself, but I
seek for the [a]profit which increases to your account.
18 But I have received everything in full and have an
abundance; I am [a]amply supplied, having received
from [A]Epaphroditus [b]what you have sent, [c,B]a fragrant aroma, an acceptable sacrifice, well-pleasing
to God. 19 And [A]my God will supply [a]all your needs
according to His [B]riches in glory in Christ Jesus.

4:7 [a]Lit *mind* [A]Is 26:3; John 14:27; Phil 4:9; Col 3:15 [B]1 Pet 1:5 [C]2 Cor 10:5 [D]Phil 1:1; 4:19, 21 4:8 [a]Or *lovable and gracious* [b]Lit *ponder these things* [A]Rom 14:18; 1 Pet 2:12 4:9 [A]Phil 3:17 [B]Rom 15:33 4:10 [A]2 Cor 11:9; Phil 2:30 4:11 [a]Lit *according to* [b]Or *self-sufficient* [A]2 Cor 9:8; 1 Tim 6:6, 8; Heb 13:5 4:12 [A]1 Cor 4:11 [B]2 Cor 11:9 4:13 [a]Lit *in* [A]2 Cor 12:9; Eph 3:16; Col 1:11 4:14 [A]Heb 10:33; Rev 1:9 4:15 [a]Lit *beginning of* [A]Phil 1:5 [B]Rom 15:26 [C]2 Cor 11:9 4:16 [A]Acts 17:1; 1 Thess 2:9 4:17 [a]Lit *fruit* [A]1 Cor 9:11f; 2 Cor 9:5 4:18 [a]Lit *made full* [b]Lit *the things from you* [c]Lit *an odor of fragrance* [A]Phil 2:25 [B]Ex 29:18; 2 Cor 2:14; Eph 5:2 4:19 [a]Or *every need of yours* [A]2 Cor 9:8 [B]Rom 2:4

4:7 peace of God. *See note on v. 9.* Inner calm or tranquillity is promised to the believer who has a thankful attitude based on unwavering confidence that God is able and willing to do what is best for His children (cf. Ro 8:28). **surpasses all comprehension.** This refers to the divine origin of peace. It transcends human intellect, analysis, and insight (Is 26:3; Jn 16:33). **guard.** A military term meaning "to keep watch over." God's peace guards believers from anxiety, doubt, fear, and distress. **hearts ... minds.** Paul was not making a distinction between the two—he was giving a comprehensive statement referring to the whole inner person. Because of the believer's union with Christ, He guards his inner being with His peace.

4:8 true. What is true is found in God (2Ti 2:25), in Christ (Eph 4:20, 21), in the Holy Spirit (Jn 16:13), and in God's Word (Jn 17:17). **honorable.** The Gr. term means "worthy of respect." Believers are to meditate on whatever is worthy of awe and adoration, i.e., the sacred as opposed to the profane. **right.** The believer is to think in harmony with God's divine standard of holiness. **pure.** That which is morally clean and undefiled. **lovely.** The Gr. term means "pleasing" or "amiable." By implication, believers are to focus on whatever is kind or gracious. **of good repute.** That which is highly regarded or thought well of. It refers to what is generally considered reputable in the world, such as kindness, courtesy, and respect for others.

4:9 in me. The Philippians were to follow the truth of God proclaimed, along with the example of that truth lived by Paul before them (*see note on Heb 13:7*). **the God of peace.** *See note on Ro 15:33;* cf. 1Co 14:33. God is peace (Ro 16:20; Eph 2:14), makes peace with sinners through Christ (2Co 5:18–20), and gives perfect peace in trouble (v. 7).

4:10–19 Paul expressed his gratitude to the Philippians for their kind expressions of love and the generous gift they sent him and thus provides a powerful example of how a Christian can be content regardless of his circumstances.

4:10 at last ... you lacked opportunity. About ten years had passed since the Philippians first gave a gift to Paul to help meet his needs when he was first in Thessalonica (vv. 15, 16). Paul was aware of their desire to continue to help, but he realized, within God's providence, that they had not had the "opportunity" (season) to help.

4:11 content. The Gr. term means "to be self-sufficient" or "to be satisfied." It is the same word translated "sufficiency" in 2Co 9:8. It indicates independence from any need for help (cf. Lk 3:14; 1Th 4:12; 1Ti 6:6, 8; Heb 13:5). **whatever circumstances I am.** Paul defined the circumstances in the following verse.

4:12 humble means ... prosperity. Paul knew how to get along with humble means (food, clothing, daily necessities) and how to live in prosperity. **being filled and going hungry.** The Gr. word translated "being filled" was used of feeding and fattening animals. Paul knew how to be content when he had plenty to eat and when he was deprived of enough to eat.

4:13 I can do all things. Paul uses a Gr. verb that means "to be strong" or "to have strength" (cf. Ac 19:16, 20; Jas 5:16). He had strength to withstand "all things" (vv. 11, 12), including both difficulty and prosperity in the material world. **through Him who strengthens me.** The Gr. word for strengthen means "to put power in." Because believers are in Christ (Gal 2:20), He infuses them with His strength to sustain them until they receive some provision (Eph 3:16–20; 2Co 12:10).

4:14 Paul adds a word of clarification here so the Philippians would not think he was being ungrateful for their most recent gift, because of what he just wrote (vv. 11–13). **share.** To join in a partnership with someone.

4:15 at the first preaching of the gospel. When Paul first preached the gospel in Philippi (Ac 16:13). **after I left.** When Paul first left Philippi approximately 10 years before (Ac 16:40). **Macedonia.** In addition to Philippi, Paul also ministered in two other towns in Macedonia: Thessalonica and Berea (Ac 17:1–14). **matter of giving and receiving.** Paul used 3 business terms. "Matter of" could be translated "account." "Giving and receiving" refer to expenditures and receipts. Paul was a faithful steward of God's resources and kept careful records of what he received and spent. **but you alone.** Only the Philippians sent Paul provisions to meet his needs.

4:16 even in Thessalonica. *See note on Ac 17:1;* see also Introduction to 1 Thessalonians. Paul preached there for a few months, during his second missionary journey.

4:17 increases to your account. The Philippians were in effect storing up for themselves treasure in heaven (Mt 6:20). The gifts they gave to Paul were accruing eternal dividends to their spiritual account (Pr 11:24, 25; 19:17; Lk 6:38; 2Co 9:6).

4:18 Epaphroditus. *See note on 2:25.* **a fragrant aroma, an acceptable sacrifice, well-pleasing to God.** In the OT sacrificial system, every sacrifice was to provide a fragrant aroma and be acceptable to God. Only if it was offered with the correct attitude would it be pleasing to Him (Ge 8:20, 21; Ex 29:18; Lv 1:9, 13, 17). The Philippians' gift was a spiritual sacrifice (cf. Ro 12:1; 1Pe 2:5) that pleased God.

4:19 all your needs. Paul addressed all the Philippians' material needs, which had probably been depleted to some extent because of their gracious gift (Pr 3:9). **according to His riches.** God would give increase to the Philippians in proportion to His infinite resources, not just a small amount out of His riches.

20 Now to [A]our God and Father [B]*be* the glory [a]forever
and ever. Amen.
21 Greet every [a]saint in Christ Jesus. [A]The brethren who are with me greet you. 22 [A]All the [a,B]saints
greet you, especially those of Caesar's household.
23 [A]The grace of the Lord Jesus Christ [B]be with
your spirit.

4:20 [a]Lit *to the ages of the ages* [A]Gal 1:4 [B]Rom 11:36 4:21 [a]Or *holy one* [A]Gal 1:2
4:22 [a]V 21, note 1 [A]2 Cor 13:13 [B]Acts 9:13 4:23 [A]Rom 16:20 [B]2 Tim 4:22

4:20 This doxology is Paul's praise in direct response to the great truth that God supplies all the needs of the saints. In a more general sense, this is praise in response to the character of God and His faithfulness.

4:21 every saint. *See note on 1:1.* Instead of using the collective "all," Paul used the individualistic "every" to declare that each saint was worthy of his concern. **brethren who are with me.** They certainly included Timothy and Epaphroditus (2:19, 25). Others who were preaching the gospel in Rome were present (1:14). It is possible that Tychicus, Aristarchus, Onesimus, and Jesus Justus were also there (Col 4:7, 9–11).

4:22 Caesar's household. A significant number of people, not limited to Caesar's family, which would include courtiers, princes, judges, cooks, food-tasters, musicians, custodians, builders, stablemen, soldiers, accountants. Within that large group, Paul had in mind those who, through the proclamation of the gospel by members of the church at Rome, had been saved prior to his coming. Newly added to their number were those led to Christ by Paul himself, including those soldiers who were chained to him while he was a prisoner (1:13).

4:23 The common conclusion to Paul's epistles (*see note on Ro 16:24*).

THE EPISTLE OF PAUL TO THE COLOSSIANS

TITLE

Colossians is named for the city of Colosse, where the church it was addressed to was located. It was also to be read in the neighboring church at Laodicea (4:16).

AUTHOR AND DATE

Paul is identified as author at the beginning (1:1; cf. v. 23; 4:18), as customarily in his epistles. The testimony of the early church, including such key figures as Irenaeus, Clement of Alexandria, Tertullian, Origen, and Eusebius, confirms that the opening claim is genuine. Additional evidence for Paul's authorship comes from the book's close parallels with Philemon, which is universally accepted as having been written by Paul. Both were written (ca. A.D. 60–62) while Paul was a prisoner in Rome (4:3, 10, 18; Phm 9, 10, 13, 23); plus the names of the same people (e.g., Timothy, Aristarchus, Archippus, Mark, Epaphras, Luke, Onesimus, and Demas) appear in both epistles, showing that both were written by the same author at about the same time. For biographical information on Paul see Introduction to Romans: Author and Date.

BACKGROUND AND SETTING

Colosse was a city in Phrygia, in the Roman province of Asia (part of modern Turkey), about 100 mi. E of Ephesus in the region of the 7 churches of Rev 1–3. The city lay alongside the Lycus River, not far from where it flowed into the Maender River. The Lycus Valley narrowed at Colosse to a width of about two mi., and Mt. Cadmus rose 8,000 feet above the city.

Colosse was a thriving city in the fifth century B.C. when the Persian king Xerxes (Ahasuerus, cf. Est 1:1) marched through the region. Black wool and dyes (made from the nearby chalk deposits) were important products. In addition, the city was situated at the junction of the main north-south and east-west trade routes. By Paul's day, however, the main road had been rerouted through nearby Laodicea, thus bypassing Colosse and leading to its decline and the rise of the neighboring cities of Laodicea and Hierapolis.

Although Colosse's population was mainly Gentile, there was a large Jewish settlement dating from the days of Antiochus the Great (223–187 B.C.). Colosse's mixed population of Jews and Gentiles manifested itself both in the composition of the church and in the heresy that plagued it, which contained elements of both Jewish legalism and pagan mysticism.

The church at Colosse began during Paul's 3-year ministry at Ephesus (Ac 19). Its founder was not Paul, who had never been there (2:1); but Epaphras (1:5–7), who apparently was saved during a visit to Ephesus, then likely started the church in Colosse when he returned home. Several years after the Colossian church was founded, a dangerous heresy arose to threaten it—one not identified with any particular historical system. It contained elements of what later became known as gnosticism: that God is good, but matter is evil, that Jesus Christ was merely one of a series of emanations descending from God and being less than God (a belief that led them to deny His true humanity), and that a secret, higher knowledge above Scripture was necessary for enlightenment and salvation. The Colossian heresy also embraced aspects of Jewish legalism, e.g., the necessity of circumcision for salvation, observance of the ceremonial rituals of the OT law (dietary laws, festivals, Sabbaths), and rigid asceticism. It also called for the worship of angels and mystical experience. Epaphras was so concerned about this heresy that he made the long journey from Colosse to Rome (4:12, 13), where Paul was a prisoner.

This letter was written from prison in Rome (Ac 28:16–31) sometime between A.D. 60–62 and is, therefore, referred to as a Prison Epistle (along with Ephesians, Philippians, and Philemon). It may have been composed almost contemporaneously with Ephesians and initially sent with that epistle and Philemon by Tychicus (Eph 6:21, 22; Col 4:7, 8). See Introduction to Philippians: Author and Date for a discussion of the city from which Paul wrote. He wrote this letter to warn the Colossians against the heresy they faced, and sent the letter to them with Tychicus, who was accompanying the runaway slave Onesimus back to his master, Philemon, a member of the Colossian church (4:7–9; see Introduction to Philemon: Background and Setting). Epaphras remained behind in Rome (cf. Phm 23), perhaps to receive further instruction from Paul.

HISTORICAL AND THEOLOGICAL THEMES

Colossians contains teaching on several key areas of theology, including the deity of Christ (1:15–20; 2:2–10), reconciliation (1:20–23), redemption (1:13, 14; 2:13, 14; 3:9–11), election (3:12), forgiveness (3:13), and the nature of the church (1:18, 24, 25; 2:19; 3:11, 15). Also, as noted above, it refutes the heretical teaching that threatened the Colossian church (chap. 2).

INTERPRETIVE CHALLENGES

Those cults that deny Christ's deity have seized upon the description of Him as "the firstborn of all creation" (1:15) as proof that He was a created being. Paul's statement that believers will be "holy and blameless and beyond reproach" if they "continue in the faith" (1:22, 23) has led some to teach that believers can lose their salvation. Some have argued for the existence of purgatory based on Paul's statement, "I do my share ... in filling up what is lacking in Christ's afflictions" (1:24), while others see support for baptismal regeneration (2:12). The identity of the "letter ... from Laodicea" (4:16) has also prompted much discussion. These issues will be treated in the notes.

OUTLINE

I. Personal Matters (1:1–14)
- A. Paul's Greeting (1:1, 2)
- B. Paul's Thankfulness (1:3–8)
- C. Paul's Prayer (1:9–14)

II. Doctrinal Instruction (1:15–2:23)
- A. About Christ's Deity (1:15–23)
- B. About Paul's Ministry (1:24–2:7)
- C. About False Philosophy (2:8–23)

III. Practical Exhortations (3:1–4:18)
- A. Christian Conduct (3:1–17)
- B. Christian Households (3:18–4:1)
- C. Christian Speech (4:2–6)
- D. Christian Friends (4:7–18)

THANKFULNESS FOR SPIRITUAL ATTAINMENTS

1 [A]Paul, [B]an apostle of Jesus Christ [a,C]by the will of
God, and [D]Timothy [b]our brother,
2 To the [a,A]saints and faithful brethren in Christ
who are at Colossae: [B]Grace to you and peace from
God our Father.
3 [A]We give thanks to God, [B]the Father of our Lord
Jesus Christ, praying always for you, 4 [A]since we heard
of your faith in Christ Jesus and the [B]love which you
have [a]for [C]all the [b]saints; 5 because of the [A]hope [B]laid
up for you in [a]heaven, of which you previously [C]heard
in the word of truth, [b]the gospel 6 which has come to
you, just as [a,A]in all the world also it is constantly bearing [B]fruit and [b]increasing, even as *it has been doing*
in you also since the day you [C]heard *of it* and [c]under-
stood the grace of God in truth; 7 just as you learned
it from [A]Epaphras, our [B]beloved fellow bond-servant,
who is a faithful servant of Christ on our behalf,
8 and he also informed us of your [A]love in the Spirit.

1:1 [a]Lit *through* [b]Lit *the* [A]Phil 1:1 [B]2 Cor 1:1 [C]1 Cor 1:1 [D]2 Cor 1:1; 1 Thess 3:2 1:2 [a]Or *holy ones* [A]Acts 9:13 [B]Rom 1:7 1:3 [A]Rom 1:8 [B]Rom 15:6; 2 Cor 1:3 1:4 [a]Or *toward* [b]Or *holy ones* [A]Eph 1:15; Philem 5 [B]Gal 5:6 [C]Eph 6:18 1:5 [a]Lit *the heavens* [b]Or *of the gospel* [A]Acts 23:6 [B]2 Tim 4:8 [C]Eph 1:13 1:6 [a]Or *it is in the world* [b]Or *spreading abroad* [c]Or *came really to know* [A]Rom 10:18 [B]Rom 1:13 [C]Eph 4:21 1:7 [A]Col 4:12 [B]Col 4:7 1:8 [A]Rom 15:30

1:1 Paul. For details on the Apostle Paul, see Introduction to Romans: Author and Date; *see note on Ac 9:1.* **Timothy.** Paul's colaborer and true child in the faith (see Introduction to 1 Timothy: Background and Setting; *see note on Ac 16:1*) was able to be with him because, although Paul was a prisoner, he had personal living quarters (Ac 28:16–31).

1:2 saints. Those who have been separated from sin and set apart to God—the believers in Colosse (*see note on 1Co 1:2*). **faithful.** A word used in the NT exclusively for believers. Cf. v. 4. **Colossae.** One of 3 cities in the Lycus River valley in the region of Phrygia, in the Roman province of Asia (part of modern Turkey), about 100 mi. E of Ephesus (see Introduction: Background and Setting). **Grace . . . and peace.** Paul's greeting in all 13 of his epistles (*see note on Ro 1:7*).

1:3 God, the Father of our Lord Jesus Christ. This designation was often used to show that Jesus was one in nature with God, as any true son is with his father. It was an affirmation of Christ's deity (cf. Ro 15:6; 2Co 1:3; 11:13; Eph 1:3; 3:14; 1Pe 1:3).

1:4 faith in Christ Jesus. For discussion of saving faith *see notes on Ro 1:16; 10:4–17; Jas 2:14–26.* **love . . . for all the saints.** Cf. v. 8. One of the visible fruits of true saving faith is love for fellow believers (Jn 13:34, 35; Gal 5:22; 1Jn 2:10; 3:14–16).

1:5 the hope laid up for you. The believer's hope is inseparable from his faith. *See notes on Ro 5:2; 1Pe 1:3–5.* **the gospel.** *See note on Ro 1:1.* The Gr. word lit. means "good news," and was used in classical Greek to express the good news of victory in a battle. The gospel is the good news of Christ's victory over Satan, sin, and death.

1:6 in all the world. Cf. v. 23, "all creation under heaven." The gospel was never intended for an exclusive group of people; it is good news for the whole world (Mt 24:14; 28:19, 20; Mk 16:15; Ro 1:8, 14, 16; 1Th 1:8). It transcends all ethnic, geographic, cultural, and political boundaries. **fruit.** Refers to the saving effect of gospel preaching and to the growth of the church. *See notes on Ro 1:13; Php 1:22;* cf. Mt 13:3–8, 31, 32.

1:7 Epaphras. The likely founder of the church at Colossae (see Introduction: Background and Setting).

THE GLORIES OF CHRIST

"Not that we are adequate in ourselves to consider anything as coming from ourselves, but our adequacy is from God . . ." (2Co 3:5)

One of the great tenets of Scripture is the claim that Jesus Christ is completely sufficient for all matters of life and godliness (2Pe 1:3, 4)! He is sufficient for creation (Col 1:16, 17), salvation (Heb 10:10–12), sanctification (Eph 5:26, 27), and glorification (Ro 8:30). So pure is He that there is no blemish, stain, spot of sin, defilement, lying, deception, corruption, error, or imperfection (1Pe 1:18–20).

So complete is He that there is no other God besides Him (Is 45:5); He is the only begotten Son (Jn 1:14, 18); all the treasures of wisdom and knowledge are in Him (Col 2:3); the fullness of Deity dwells bodily in Him (Col 2:9); He is heir of all things (Heb 1:2); He created all things and all things were made by Him, through Him, and for Him (Col 1:16); He upholds all things by the word of His power (Col 1:17; Heb 1:3); He is the firstborn of all creation (Col 1:15); He is the exact representation of God (Heb 1:3).

He is the only Mediator between God and man; He is the Sun that enlightens; the Physician who heals; the Wall of Fire that defends; the Friend that comforts; the Pearl that enriches; the Ark that supports; and the Rock to sustain under the heaviest of pressures; He is seated at the right hand of the throne of the Majesty on high (Heb 1:3; 8:1); He is better than the angels (Heb 1:4–14); better than Moses; better than Aaron; better than Joshua; better than Melchizedek; better than all the prophets; greater than Satan (Lk 4:1–12); and stronger than death (1Co 15:55).

He has no beginning and no end (Rev 1:17, 18); He is the spotless Lamb of God; He is our Peace (Eph 2:14); He is our Hope (1Ti 1:1); He is our Life (Col 3:4); He is the living and true Way (Jn 14:6); He is the Strength of Israel (1Sa 15:29); He is the Root and Descendant of David, the Bright Morning Star (Rev 22:16); He is Faithful and True (Rev 19:11); He is the Author and Perfecter of our faith (Heb 12:1, 2); He is the Author of our Salvation (Heb 2:10); He is the Champion; He is the Chosen One (Is 42:1); He is the Apostle and High Priest of our confession (Heb 3:1); He is the Righteous Servant (Is 53:11).

He is the Lord of Hosts, the Redeemer—the Holy One of Israel, the God of the whole earth (Is 54:5); He is the Man of Sorrows (Is 53:3); He is the Light; He is the Son of Man (Mt 20:28); He is the Vine; He is the Bread of Life; He is the Door; He is Lord (Php 2:10–13); He is Prophet, Priest and King (Heb 1:1–3); He is our Sabbath rest (Heb 4:9); He is our Righteousness (Jer 23:6); He is the Wonderful Counselor, the Mighty God, the Everlasting Father, the Prince of Peace (Is 9:6); He is the Chief Shepherd (1Pe 5:4); He is Lord God of hosts; He is Lord of the nations; He is the Lion of Judah; the Living Word; the Rock of Salvation; the Eternal Spirit; He is the Ancient of Days; Creator and Comforter; Messiah; and He is the great I AM (Jn 8:58)!

9 For this reason also, [A]since the day we heard *of*
it, [B]we have not ceased to pray for you and to ask
that you may be filled with the [a,C]knowledge of His
will in all spiritual [D]wisdom and understanding,
10 so that you will [A]walk in a manner worthy of the
Lord, [a,B]to please *Him* in all respects, [C]bearing fruit in
every good work and [b]increasing in the [c]knowledge
of God; 11 [A]strengthened with all power, according to
[a]His glorious might, [b]for the attaining of all steadfastness and [c]patience; [B]joyously 12 giving thanks to
[A]the Father, who has qualified us [a]to share in [B]the
inheritance of the [b]saints in [C]Light.

THE INCOMPARABLE CHRIST

13 [a]For He rescued us from the [b,A]domain of darkness, and transferred us to the kingdom of [c,B]His
beloved Son, 14 [A]in whom we have redemption, the
forgiveness of sins.
15 [a]He is the [A]image of the [B]invisible God, the [C]first-
born of all creation. 16 For [a,A]by Him all things were
created, [A]*both* in the heavens and on earth, visible
and invisible, whether [B]thrones or dominions or
rulers or authorities—[C]all things have been created through Him and for Him. 17 He [a,A]is before
all things, and in Him all things [b]hold together.

1:9 [a]Or *real knowledge* [A]Col 1:4 [B]Eph 1:16 [C]Phil 1:9 [D]Eph 1:17 1:10 [a]Lit *unto all pleasing* [b]Or *growing by the knowledge* [c]Or *real knowledge* [A]Eph 4:1 [B]Eph 5:10 [C]Rom 1:13 1:11 [a]Lit *the might of His glory* [b]Lit *unto all* [c]Or *patience with joy* [A]1 Cor 16:13 [B]Eph 4:2 1:12 [a]Lit *unto the portion of* [b]Or *holy ones* [A]Eph 2:18 [B]Acts 20:32 [C]Acts 26:18 1:13 [a]Lit *Who rescued* [b]Lit *authority* [c]Lit *the Son of His love* [A]Eph 6:12 [B]Eph 1:6 1:14 [A]Rom 3:24 1:15 [a]Lit *Who is* [A]2 Cor 4:4 [B]John 1:1 [C]Rom 8:29 1:16 [a]Or *in* [A]Eph 1:10 [B]Eph 1:20f; Col 2:15 [C]John 1:3; Rom 11:36; 1 Cor 8:6 1:17 [a]Or *has existed prior to* [b]Or *endure* [A]John 1:1; 8:58

1:9 the knowledge of His will. The Gr. word for "knowledge" is the usual one, with an added preposition that intensifies its meaning. This is not an inner impression or feeling, but a deep and thorough knowledge of the will of God that is finally and completely revealed in the Word of God (3:16; Eph 5:17; 1Th 4:3; 5:18; 1Ti 2:4; 1Pe 2:13, 15; 4:19). **spiritual wisdom and understanding.** "Spiritual" modifies both "wisdom" (the ability to accumulate and organize principles from Scripture) and "understanding" (the application of those principles to daily living).

1:10 walk . . . worthy. This is a key NT concept which calls the believer to live in a way that is consistent with his identification with the Lord who saved him. *See notes on Eph 4:1; Php 1:27.* **bearing fruit in every good work.** *See notes on Ro 1:13; Php 4:17.* Spiritual fruit is the by-product of a righteous life. The Bible identifies spiritual fruit as leading people to Christ (1Co 16:15), praising God (Heb 13:15), giving money (Ro 15:26–28), living a godly life (Heb 12:11), and displaying holy attitudes (Gal 5:22, 23). **increasing in the knowledge of God.** Spiritual growth cannot occur apart from this knowledge (1Pe 2:2; 2Pe 3:18). The evidences of spiritual growth include a deeper love for God's Word (Ps 119:97), a more perfect obedience (1Jn 2:3–5), a strong doctrinal foundation (1Jn 2:12–14), an expanding faith (2Th 1:3; cf. 2Co 10:5), and a greater love for others (Php 1:9).

1:11 strengthened with all power. *See notes on Eph 3:16–20.* **steadfastness and patience.** These terms are closely related and refer to the attitude one has during trials. "Patience" looks more at enduring difficult circumstances while "steadfastness" looks at enduring difficult people.

1:12 qualified us. The Gr. word for "qualified" means "to make sufficient," "to empower," or "to authorize." God qualifies us only through the finished work of the Savior. Apart from God's grace through Jesus Christ, all people would be qualified only to receive His wrath. **inheritance.** Lit. "for the portion of the lot." Each believer will receive his own individual portion of the total divine inheritance (*see note on Ro 8:17*), an allusion to the partitioning of Israel's inheritance in Canaan (cf. Nu 26:52–56; 33:51–54; Jos 14:1, 2). *See notes on 1Pe 1:3–5.* **in Light.** Scripture represents "light" intellectually as divine truth (Ps 119:130) and morally as divine purity (Eph 5:8–14; 1Jn 1:5). The saints' inheritance exists in the spiritual realm of truth and purity where God Himself dwells (1Ti 6:16). Light, then, is a synonym for God's kingdom. Cf. Jn 8:12; 2Co 4:6; Rev 21:23; 22:5.

1:13 rescued us. The Gr. term means "to draw to oneself" or "to deliver," and refers to the believer's spiritual liberation by God from Satan's kingdom, which, in contrast to the realm of light with truth and purity, is the realm of darkness (cf. Lk 22:53) with only deception and wickedness (1Jn 2:9, 11). *See note on Ac 26:18.* **kingdom.** In its basic sense, a group of people ruled by a king. More than just the future, earthly millennial kingdom, this everlasting kingdom (2Pe 1:11) speaks of the realm of salvation in which all believers live in current and eternal spiritual relationship with God under the care and authority of Jesus Christ (*see note on Mt 3:2*). **His beloved Son.** Cf. Mt 3:17; 12:18; 17:5; Mk 1:11; 9:7; Lk 3:22; 9:35; Eph 1:6; 2Pe 1:17; *see notes on Jn 17:23–26.* The Father gave this kingdom to the Son He loves, as an expression of eternal love. That means that every person the Father calls and justifies is a love gift from Him to the Son. *See notes on Jn 6:37, 44.*

1:14 redemption. The Gr. word means "to deliver by payment of a ransom," and was used of freeing slaves from bondage. Here it refers to Christ freeing believing sinners from slavery to sin (cf. Eph 1:7; 1Co 1:30; *see note on Ro 3:24*). Some later manuscripts follow "redemption" with "through His blood." Cf. v. 20, a reference not limited to the fluid as if the blood had saving properties in its chemistry, but an expression pointing to the totality of Christ's atoning work as a sacrifice for sin. This is a frequently used metonym in the NT (see Eph 1:7; 2:13; Heb 9:14; 1Pe 1:19). The word "cross" (as in v. 20) is used similarly to refer to the whole atoning work (see 1Co 1:18; Gal 6:12, 14; Eph 2:16). *See note on Ro 5:9.* **the forgiveness of sins.** The Gr. word is a composite of two words that mean "to pardon" or "grant remission of a penalty." Cf. Ps 103:12; Mic 7:19; Eph 1:7; *see notes on 2Co 5:19–21.*

1:15–20 One component in the heresy threatening the Colossian church was the denial of the deity of Christ. Paul combats that damning element of heresy with an emphatic defense of Christ's deity.

1:15 image of the invisible God. *See note on Heb 1:3.* The Gr. word for "image" is *eikōn*, from which the Eng. word "icon" derives. It means, "copy" or "likeness." Jesus Christ is the perfect image—the exact likeness—of God and is in the very form of God (Php 2:6; cf. Jn 1:14; 14:9), and has been so from all eternity. By describing Jesus in this manner, Paul emphasizes that He is both the representation and manifestation of God. Thus, He is fully God in every way (cf. 2:9; Jn 8:58; 10:30–33; Heb 1:8). **the firstborn of all creation.** Cf. v. 18. The Gr. word for "firstborn" can refer to one who was born first chronologically, but most often refers to preeminence in position, or rank (*see note on Heb 1:6*; cf. Ro 8:29). In both Greek and Jewish culture, the firstborn was the ranking son who had received the right of inheritance from his father, whether he was born first or not. It is used of Israel who, not being the first nation, was however the preeminent nation (cf. Ex 4:22; Jer 31:9). Firstborn in this context clearly means highest in rank, not first created (cf. Ps 89:27; Rev 1:5) for several reasons: 1) Christ cannot be both "first begotten" and "only begotten" (cf. Jn 1:14, 18; 3:16, 18; 1Jn 4:9); 2) when the "firstborn" is one of a class, the class is in the plural form (cf. v. 18; Ro 8:29), but "creation," the class here, is in a singular form; 3) if Paul was teaching that Christ was a created being, he was agreeing with the heresy he was writing to refute; and 4) it is impossible for Christ to be both created, and the Creator of everything (v. 16). Thus Jesus is the firstborn in the sense that He has the preeminence (v. 18) and possesses the right of inheritance over "all creation" (cf. Heb 1:2; Rev 5:1–7, 13). He existed before the creation and is exalted in rank above it. *See notes on Ps 2:7; Ro 8:29.*

1:16 thrones or dominions or rulers or authorities. Cf. 2:15; Ro 8:38; Eph 1:21; 3:10; 6:12; 1Pe 3:22; Jude 6. These are various categories of angels whom Christ created and rules over. There is no comment regarding whether they are holy or fallen, since He is Lord of both groups. The false teachers had incorporated into their heresy the worship of angels (*see note on 2:18*), including the lie that Jesus was one of them, merely a spirit created by God and inferior to Him. Paul rejected that and made it clear that angels, whatever their rank, whether holy or fallen, are mere creatures, and their Creator is none other than the preeminent One, the Lord and Savior, Jesus Christ. The purpose of his catalog of angelic ranks is to show the immeasurable superiority of Christ over any being the false teachers might suggest. **all things have been created through Him and for Him.** Cf. Ro 11:33–36. *See notes on Jn 1:3; Heb 1:2.* As God, Jesus created the material and spiritual universe for His pleasure and glory.

1:17 He is before all things. When the universe had its beginning, Christ already existed, thus by definition He must be eternal (Mic 5:2; Jn 1:1, 2; 8:58; 1Jn 1:1; Rev 22:13).

18 He is also [A]head of [B]the body, the church; and
He is [C]the beginning, [D]the firstborn from the dead,
so that He Himself will come to have first place in
everything. 19 For [a]it was [A]the *Father's* good pleasure for all [B]the [b]fullness to dwell in Him, 20 and
through Him to [A]reconcile all things to Himself,
having made [B]peace through [C]the blood of His cross;
through Him, *I say,* [D]whether things on earth or
things in [a]heaven.

21 And although you were [A]formerly alienated and
hostile in mind, *engaged* in evil deeds, 22 yet He has now
[A]reconciled you in His fleshly [B]body through death, in
order to [C]present you before Him [D]holy and blameless
and beyond reproach— 23 if indeed you continue in
[a]the faith firmly [A]established and steadfast, and not
moved away from the [B]hope of the gospel that you have
heard, which was proclaimed [C]in all creation under
heaven, [D]and of which I, Paul, [b]was made a [c,E]minister.

1:18 [A]Eph 1:22 [B]Eph 1:23; Col 1:24; 2:19 [C]Rev 3:14 [D]Acts 26:23 1:19 [a]*Or all the fullness was pleased to dwell* [b]I.e. fullness of deity [A]Eph 1:5 [B]John 1:16 1:20 [a]*Lit the heavens* [A]2 Cor 5:18; Eph 2:16 [B]Rom 5:1; Eph 2:14 [C]Eph 2:13 [D]Col 1:16 1:21 [A]Rom 5:10; Eph 2:3, 12 1:22 [A]2 Cor 5:18; Eph 2:16 [B]Rom 7:4 [C]Eph 5:27; Col 1:28 [D]Eph 1:4 1:23 [a]*Or in faith* [b]*Lit became* [c]*Or servant* [A]Eph 3:17; Col 2:7 [B]Col 1:5 [C]Mark 16:15; Acts 2:5; Col 1:6 [D]Eph 3:7; Col 1:25 [E]1 Cor 3:5

hold together. Christ sustains the universe, maintaining the power and balance necessary to life's existence and continuity (cf. Heb 1:3).

1:18 head of the body. Cf. 2:19. Paul uses the human body as a metaphor for the church, of which Christ serves as the "head." Just as a body is controlled from the brain, so Christ controls every part of the church and gives it life and direction. Cf. Eph 4:15; 5:23. For a detailed discussion of the church as a body, *see notes on 1Co 12:4–27*. **the beginning**. This refers to both source and preeminence. The church had its origins in the Lord Jesus (Eph 1:4), and He gave life to the church through His sacrificial death and resurrection to become its Sovereign. **the firstborn from the dead**. *See note on v. 15*. Jesus was the first chronologically to be resurrected, never to die again. Of all who have been or ever will be raised from the dead, and that includes all men (Jn 5:28, 29), Christ is supreme (*see notes on v. 15; Php 2:8–11*).

1:19 all the fullness. A term likely used by those in the Colossian heresy to refer to divine powers and attributes they believed were divided among various emanations (see Introduction: Background and Setting). Paul countered that by asserting that the fullness of deity—all the divine powers and attributes—was not spread out among created beings, but completely dwelt in Christ alone (cf. 2:9).

1:20 reconcile all things to Himself. The Gr. word for "reconcile" means "to change" or "exchange." Its NT usage refers to a change in the sinner's relationship to God. *See notes on Ro 5:10; 2Co 5:18–21*. Man is reconciled to God when God restores man to a right relationship with Him through Jesus Christ. An intensified form for "reconcile" is used in this verse to refer to the total and complete reconciliation of believers and ultimately "all things" in the created universe (cf. Ro 8:21; 2Pe 3:10–13; Rev 21:1). This text does not teach that, as a result, all will believe; rather it teaches that all will ultimately submit (cf. Php 2:9–11). **having made peace**. *See note on Ro 5:1*. God and those He saved are no longer at enmity with one another. **the blood of His cross**. *See note on v. 14*.

1:21 alienated . . . hostile. The Gr. term for "alienated" means "estranged," "cut off," or "separated." Before they were reconciled, all people were completely estranged from God (cf. Eph 2:12, 13). The Gr. word for "hostile" can also be translated "hateful." Unbelievers hate God and resent His holy standard because they love "evil deeds" (cf. Jn 3:19, 20; 15:18, 24, 25). Actually, there is alienation from both sides, since God hates "all who do iniquity" (Ps 5:5).

1:22 reconciled . . . through death. Christ's substitutionary death on the cross that paid the full penalty for the sin of all who believe made reconciliation possible and actual. *See notes on 2Co 5:18–21*; cf. Ro 3:25; 5:9, 10; 8:3. **reconciled**. *See note on v. 20*. **present you holy**. "Holy" refers to the believer's positional relationship to God—he is separated from sin and set apart to God by imputed righteousness. This is justification (*see notes on Ro 3:24–26; Php 3:8, 9*). As a result of the believer's union with Christ in His death and resurrection, God considers Christians as holy as His Son (Eph 1:4; 2Co 5:21). Christians are also "blameless" (without blemish) and "beyond reproach" (no one can bring a charge against them; Ro 8:33; cf. Php 2:15). We are to be presented to Christ, when we meet Him, as a chaste bride (Eph 5:25–27; 2Co 11:2).

1:23 continue in the faith. Cf. Ac 11:23; 14:22. Those who have been reconciled will persevere in faith and obedience because, in addition to being declared righteous, they are actually made new creatures (2Co 5:17) with a new disposition that loves God, hates sin, desires obedience, and is energized by

TITLES OF CHRIST

Name or Title	Significance	Biblical Reference
Adam, Last Adam	First of the new race of the redeemed	1Co 15:45
Alpha and Omega	The beginning and ending of all things	Rev 21:6
Bread of Life	The one essential food	Jn 6:35
Corner Stone	A sure foundation for life	Eph 2:20
Chief Shepherd	Protector, sustainer, and guide	1Pe 5:4
Firstborn from the Dead	Leads us into resurrection and eternal life	Col 1:18
Good Shepherd	Provider and caretaker	Jn 10:11
Great Shepherd of the Sheep	Trustworthy guide and protector	Heb 13:20
High Priest	A perfect sacrifice for our sins	Heb 3:1
Holy One of God	Sinless in His nature	Mk 1:24
Immanuel (God With Us)	Stands with us in all life's circumstances	Mt 1:23
King of Kings, Lord of Lords	The Almighty, before whom every knee will bow	Rev 19:16
Lamb of God	Gave His life as a sacrifice on our behalf	Jn 1:29
Light of the World	Brings hope in the midst of darkness	Jn 9:5
Lord of Glory	The power and presence of the living God	1Co 2:8
Mediator between God and Men	Brings us into God's presence redeemed and forgiven	1Ti 2:5
Only Begotten of the Father	The unique, one-of-a-kind Son of God	Jn 1:14
Prophet	Faithful proclaimer of the truths of God	Ac 3:22
Savior	Delivers from sin and death	Lk 1:47
Seed of Abraham	Mediator of God's covenant	Gal 3:16
Son of Man	Identifies with us in our humanity	Mt 18:11
The Word	Present with God at the creation	Jn 1:1

24 [A]Now I rejoice in my sufferings for your sake,
and in my flesh [B]I [a]do my share on behalf of [C]His
body, which is the church, in filling up what is lacking [b]in Christ's afflictions. 25 [A]Of *this church* I [a]was
made a minister according to the [B]stewardship from
God bestowed on me for your benefit, so that I might
[b]fully carry out the *preaching of* the word of God,
26 *that is,* [A]the mystery which has been hidden from
the *past* ages and generations, but has now been
manifested to His [a]saints, 27 to whom [A]God willed
to make known what is [B]the riches of the glory of
this mystery among the Gentiles, which is [C]Christ
in you, the [D]hope of glory. 28 We proclaim Him, [A]ad-
monishing every man and teaching every man
[a]with all [B]wisdom, so that we may [C]present every
man [b,D]complete in Christ. 29 For this purpose also
I [A]labor, [B]striving [C]according to His [a]power, which
[b]mightily works within me.

YOU ARE BUILT UP IN CHRIST

2 For I want you to know how great a [A]struggle
I have on your behalf and for those who are
at [B]Laodicea, and for all those who have not [a]per-
sonally seen my face, 2 that their [A]hearts may be
encouraged, having been [B]knit together in love,
and *attaining* to all [C]the wealth [a]that comes from
the full assurance of understanding, *resulting* in a
[D]true knowledge of [E]God's mystery, *that is,* Christ
Himself, 3 in whom are hidden all [A]the treasures of
wisdom and knowledge. 4 [A]I say this so that no one
will delude you with [B]persuasive argument. 5 For
even though I am [A]absent in body, nevertheless I
am with you in spirit, rejoicing [a]to see [b]your [B]good
discipline and the [C]stability of your faith in Christ.
6 Therefore as you have received [A]Christ Jesus the
Lord, *so* [a,B]walk in Him, 7 having been firmly [A]rooted
and now being [B]built up in Him and [C]established

1:24 [a]Or *representatively...fill up* [b]Lit *of* [A]Rom 8:17; 2 Cor 1:5; 12:15; Phil 2:17 [B]2 Tim 1:8; 2:10 [C]Col 1:18 1:25 [a]Lit *became* [b]Lit *make full the word of God* [A]Col 1:23 [B]Eph 3:2 1:26 [a]Or *holy ones* [A]Rom 16:25f; Eph 3:3f; Col 2:2; 4:3 1:27 [A]Matt 13:11 [B]Eph 1:7, 18; 3:16 [C]Rom 8:10 [D]1 Tim 1:1 1:28 [a]Lit *in* [b]Or *perfect* [A]Acts 20:31; Col 3:16 [B]1 Cor 2:6f; Col 2:3 [C]Col 1:22 [D]Matt 5:48; Eph 4:13 1:29 [a]Lit *working* [b]Lit *in power* [A]1 Cor 15:10 [B]Col 2:1; 4:12 [C]Eph 1:19; Col 2:12 2:1 [a]Lit *in the flesh* [A]Col 1:29; 4:12 [B]Col 4:13, 15f; Rev 1:11 2:2 [a]Lit *of the full assurance* [A]1 Cor 14:31; Eph 6:22; Col 4:8 [B]Col 2:19 [C]Eph 1:7, 18; 3:16 [D]Matt 13:11 [E]Rom 16:25f; Eph 3:3f; Col 1:26; 4:3 2:3 [A]Is 11:2; Rom 11:33 2:4 [A]Eph 4:17 [B]Rom 16:18 2:5 [a]Lit *and seeing* [b]Or *your good order* [A]1 Cor 5:3 [B]1 Cor 14:40 [C]1 Pet 5:9 2:6 [a]Or *lead your life* [A]Gal 3:26 [B]Col 1:10 2:7 [A]Eph 3:17 [B]1 Cor 3:9; Eph 2:20 [C]1 Cor 1:8

the indwelling Holy Spirit (cf. Jn 8:30–32; 1Jn 2:19). Rather than defect from the gospel they heard, true believers will remain solid on Christ who is the only foundation (1Co 3:11), and faithful by the enabling grace of God (Php 1:6; 2:11–13). For discussion on perseverance of the saints, *see note on Mt 24:13.* **proclaimed in all creation.** Cf. Mk 16:15. The gospel has no racial boundaries. Having reached Rome, where Paul was when he wrote Colossians, it had reached the center of the known world.

1:24 my sufferings. Paul's present imprisonment (Ac 28:16, 30; see Introduction to Ephesians: Background and Setting). **on behalf of His body.** Paul's motivation for enduring suffering was to benefit and build Christ's church. Cf. Php 1:13, 29, 30; *see notes on 2Co 4:8–15; 6:4–10; 11:23–29; 12:9, 10.* **filling up what is lacking.** Paul was experiencing the persecution intended for Christ. In spite of His death on the cross, Christ's enemies had not gotten their fill of inflicting injury on Him. So they turned their hatred on those who preached the gospel (cf. Jn 15:18, 24; 16:1–3). It was in that sense that Paul filled up what was lacking in Christ's afflictions (*see notes on 2Co 1:5; Gal 6:17*).

1:25 stewardship. Cf. 1Co 4:1, 2; 9:17. A steward was a slave who managed his master's household, supervising the other servants, dispensing resources, and handling business and financial affairs. Paul viewed his ministry as a stewardship from the Lord. The church is God's household (1Ti 3:16), and Paul was given the task of caring for, feeding, and leading the churches, for which he was accountable to God (cf. Heb 13:17). All believers are responsible for managing the abilities and resources God gives them (*see note on 1Pe 4:10*). **carry out ... the word of God.** This refers to Paul's single-minded devotion to completely fulfill the ministry God gave him to preach the whole counsel of God to those to whom God sent him (Ac 20:27; 2Ti 4:7).

1:26 mystery. Cf. 2:2; 4:3. *See notes on Mt 13:11; 1Co 2:7; Eph 3:4, 5.* This refers to truth, hidden until now, but revealed for the first time to the saints in the NT. Such truth includes the mystery of the incarnate God (2:2, 3, 9), Israel's unbelief (Ro 11:25), lawlessness (2Th 2:7), the unity of Jew and Gentile made one in the church (Eph 3:3–6), and the rapture of the church (1Co 15:51). In this passage, the mystery is specifically identified in v. 27.

1:27 Gentiles ... Christ in you. The OT predicted the coming of the Messiah and that the Gentiles would partake of salvation (cf. Is 42:6; 45:21, 22; 49:6; 52:10; 60:1–3; Pss 22:27; 65:5; 98:2, 3), but it did not reveal that the Messiah would actually live in each member of His redeemed church, made up mostly of Gentiles. That believers, both Jew and Gentile, now possess the surpassing riches of the indwelling Christ is the glorious revealed mystery (Jn 14:23; Ro 8:9, 10; Gal 2:20; Eph 1:7, 17, 18; 3:8–10, 16–19). **the hope of glory.** The indwelling Spirit of Christ is the guarantee to each believer of future glory (Ro 8:11; Eph 1:13, 14; 1Pe 1:3, 4).

1:28 complete. To be perfect or mature—to be like Christ. *See notes on Ro 8:29; Php 3:12–14, 19, 20; 1Jn 2:6; 3:2.* This spiritual maturity is defined in 2:2.

1:29 I labor, striving according to His power. Here is the balance of Christian living. Paul gave the effort to serve and honor God with all his might. "Labor" refers to working to the point of exhaustion. The Gr. word for "striving" gives us the Eng. word "agonize" and refers to the effort required to compete in an athletic event. At the same time, he knew the effective "striving" or work, with spiritual and eternal results, was being done by God through him (*see notes on Php 2:11–13;* cf. 1Co 15:10, 58).

2:1 great ... struggle. The word means "striving" and comes from the same root as in 1:29. Both the Colossians and Laodiceans were among those for whom Paul struggled so hard in order to bring them to maturity. **Laodicea.** The chief city of Phrygia in the Roman province of Asia, located just S of Hierapolis in the Lycus River valley (see Introduction: Background and Setting; *see note on Rev 3:14;* cf. 4:13).

2:2 full assurance of understanding. "Understanding" of the fullness of the gospel, along with inner encouragement and shared love, mark mature believers who, thereby, enjoy the "assurance" of salvation (*see notes on 2Pe 1:5–8*). **mystery ... Christ *Himself.*** *See note on 1:26.* The mystery Paul referred to here is that the Messiah Christ is God incarnate Himself (cf. 1Ti 3:16).

2:3 all the treasures. Cf. vv. 9, 10; 1:19. The false teachers threatening the Colossians claimed to possess a secret wisdom and transcendent knowledge available only to the spiritual elite. In sharp contrast, Paul declared that all the richness of truth necessary for salvation, sanctification, and glorification is found in Jesus Christ, who Himself is God revealed. Cf. Jn 1:14; Ro 11:33–36; 1Co 1:24, 30; 2:6–8; Eph 1:8, 9; 3:8, 9.

2:4 so that no one will delude you. Paul did not want the Colossians to be deceived by the persuasive rhetoric of the false teachers which assaulted the person of Christ. That is why throughout chaps. 1, 2 he stressed Christ's deity, and His sufficiency both to save believers and bring them to spiritual maturity.

2:5 absent in body ... with you in spirit. Because he was a prisoner, Paul was unable to be present with the Colossians. That did not mean, however, that his love and concern for them was any less (cf. 1Co 5:3, 4; 1Th 2:17). Their "good discipline" and "stability" of faith (both military terms depicting a solid rank of soldiers drawn up for battle) brought great joy to the apostle's heart.

2:6 walk in Him. "Walk" is the familiar NT term denoting the believer's daily conduct (1:10; 4:5; Ro 6:4; 8:1, 4; 13:13; 1Co 7:17; 2Co 5:7; 10:3; 12:18; Gal 5:16, 25; 6:16; Eph 2:10; 4:1, 17; 5:2, 8, 15; Php 3:16–18; 1Th 2:12; 4:1, 12; 2Th 3:11; 1Jn 1:6, 7; 2:6; 2Jn 6; 3Jn 3, 4). To walk in Christ is to live a life patterned after His.

2:7 your faith. The sense here is objective, referring to the truth of Christian doctrine. Spiritual maturity develops upward from the foundation of biblical truth as taught and recorded by the apostles. Cf. 3:16. This rooting, building, and establishing is in sound doctrine (cf. 1Ti 4:6; 2Ti 3:16, 17; Titus 2:1).

[a]in your faith, just as you [D]were instructed, *and*
overflowing [b]with gratitude.
8 [A]See to it that no one takes you captive through
[B]philosophy and empty deception, according to the
tradition of men, according to the [C]elementary principles of the world, [a]rather than according to Christ.
9 For in Him all the [A]fullness of Deity dwells in bodily
form, 10 and in Him you have been [A]made [a]complete,
and [B]He is the head [b]over all [C]rule and authority;
11 and in Him [A]you were also circumcised with a circumcision made without hands, in the removal of
[B]the body of the flesh by the circumcision of Christ;
12 having been [A]buried with Him in baptism, in which
you were also [B]raised up with Him through faith in
the working of God, who [C]raised Him from the dead.
13 When you were [A]dead [a]in your transgressions and
the uncircumcision of your flesh, He [B]made you alive
together with Him, having forgiven us all our transgressions, 14 having canceled out [A]the certificate of
debt consisting of decrees against us, which was hostile to us; and [B]He has taken it out of the way, having
nailed it to the cross. 15 When He had [a,A]disarmed the
[B]rulers and authorities, He [A]made a public display of
them, having [C]triumphed over them through [b]Him.
16 Therefore no one is to [a,A]act as your judge in regard to [B]food or [B]drink or in respect to a [C]festival or a
[D]new moon or a [E]Sabbath [b]day— 17 things which are [A]a
mere shadow of what is to come; but the [a]substance
[b]belongs to Christ. 18 Let no one keep [a,A]defrauding
you of your prize by [B]delighting in [b]self-abasement
and the worship of the angels, [c]taking his stand on
visions he has seen, [d,C]inflated without cause by his

2:7 [a]Or *by* [b]One early ms reads *in it with* [D]Eph 4:21 2:8 [a]Lit *and not* [A]1 Cor 8:9; 10:12; Gal 5:15; Heb 3:12 [B]Eph 5:6; Col 2:23; 1 Tim 6:20 [C]Gal 4:3; Col 2:20 2:9 [A]2 Cor 5:19; Col 1:19 2:10 [a]Lit *full* [b]Lit *of* [A]Eph 3:19 [B]Eph 1:21f [C]1 Cor 15:24; Eph 3:10; Col 2:15 2:11 [A]Rom 2:29; Eph 2:11 [B]Rom 6:6; 7:24; Gal 5:24; Col 3:5 2:12 [A]Rom 6:4f [B]Rom 6:5; Eph 2:6; Col 2:13; 3:1 [C]Acts 2:24 2:13 [a]Or *by reason of* [A]Eph 2:1 [B]Eph 2:5; Col 2:12 2:14 [A]Eph 2:15; Col 2:20 [B]1 Pet 2:24 2:15 [a]Or *divested Himself of* [b]Or *it;* i.e. the cross [A]Eph 4:8 [B]John 12:31; 1 Cor 15:24; Eph 3:10; Col 2:10 [C]2 Cor 2:14 2:16 [a]Lit *judge you* [b]Or *days* [A]Rom 14:3 [B]Mark 7:19; Rom 14:17; Heb 9:10 [C]Lev 23:2; Rom 14:5 [D]1 Chr 23:31; 2 Chr 31:3; Neh 10:33 [E]Mark 2:27f; Gal 4:10 2:17 [a]Lit *body* [b]Lit *of Christ* [A]Heb 8:5; 10:1 2:18 [a]Or *deciding against you* [b]Or *humility* [c]Or *going into detail about* [d]Or *conceited* [A]1 Cor 9:24; Phil 3:14 [B]Col 2:23 [C]1 Cor 4:6

2:8 takes you captive. Here is the term for robbery. False teachers who are successful in getting people to believe lies then rob them of truth, salvation, and blessing. **philosophy and empty deception.** "Philosophy" (lit. "love of wisdom") appears only here in the NT. The word referred to more than merely the academic discipline, but described any theory about God, the world, or the meaning of life. Those embracing the Colossian heresy used it to describe the supposed higher knowledge they claimed to have attained. Paul, however, equates the false teachers' philosophy with "empty" or worthless "deception." Cf. 1Ti 6:20; *see note on 2Co 10:5.* **the elementary principles of the world.** *See note on v. 20; Gal 4:3.* Far from being advanced, profound knowledge, the false teachers' beliefs were simplistic and immature like all the rest of the speculations, ideologies, philosophies, and psychologies the fallen satanic and human system invents.

2:9 the fullness of Deity. Christ possesses the fullness of the divine nature and attributes (*see notes on 1:19; Jn 1:14–16*). **bodily.** In Greek philosophical thought, matter was evil; spirit was good. Thus, it was unthinkable that God would ever take on a human body. Paul refutes that false teaching by stressing the reality of Christ's incarnation. Jesus was not only fully God, but fully human as well. *See notes on Php 2:5–11.*

2:10 in Him . . . made complete. *See notes on vv. 3, 4*; cf. Jn 1:16; Eph 1:3. Believers are complete in Christ, both positionally by the imputed perfect righteousness of Christ (*see note on 1:22*), and the complete sufficiency of all heavenly resources for spiritual maturity (*see notes on 2Pe 1:3, 4*). **the head over all rule and authority.** Jesus Christ is the creator and ruler of the universe and all its spiritual beings (*see note on 1:16*), not a lesser being emanating from God as the Colossian errorists maintained (see Introduction: Background and Setting).

2:11, 12 circumcision made without hands. *See note on Ge 17:11.* Circumcision symbolized man's need for cleansing of the heart (cf. Dt 10:16; 30:6; Jer 4:4; 9:26; Ac 7:51; Ro 2:29) and was the outward sign of that cleansing of sin that comes by faith in God (Ro 4:11; Php 3:3). At salvation, believers undergo a spiritual "circumcision" by putting off the sins of the flesh (cf. Ro 6:6; 2Co 5:17; Php 3:3; Titus 3:5). This is the new birth, the new creation in conversion. The outward affirmation of the already accomplished inner transformation is now the believer's baptism by water (Ac 2:38).

2:13 dead in your transgressions. *See notes on Eph 2:1, 5.* So bound in the sphere of sin, the world (Eph 2:12), the flesh (Ro 8:8), and the devil (1Jn 5:19) as to be unable to respond to spiritual stimuli; totally devoid of spiritual life. Paul further defines this condition of the unsaved in 1Co 2:14; Eph 4:17–19; Titus 3:3. **He made you alive together with Him.** *See notes on Eph 2:1, 5.* Only through union with Jesus Christ (vv. 10–12) can those hopelessly dead in their sins receive eternal life (cf. Eph 2:5). Note that God takes the initiative and exerts the life-giving power to awaken and unite sinners with His Son; the spiritually dead have no ability to make themselves alive (cf. Ro 4:17; 2Co 1:9). **forgiven us all our transgressions.** Cf. 1:14. God's free (Ro 3:24) and complete (Ro 5:20; Eph 1:7) forgiveness of guilty sinners who put their faith in Jesus Christ is the most important reality in Scripture (cf. Pss 32:1; 130:3, 4; Is 1:18; 55:7; Mic 7:18; Mt 26:28; Ac 10:43; 13:38, 39; Titus 3:4–7; Heb 8:12).

2:14 canceled out the certificate of debt. This refers to the handwritten certificate of debt by which a debtor acknowledged his indebtedness. All people (Ro 3:23) owe God an unpayable debt for violating His law (Gal 3:10; Jas 2:10; cf. Mt 18:23–27), and are thus under sentence of death (Ro 6:23). Paul graphically compares God's forgiveness of believers' sins to wiping ink off a parchment. Through Christ's sacrificial death on the cross, God has totally erased our certificate of indebtedness and made our forgiveness complete. **nailed it to the cross.** This is another metaphor for forgiveness. The list of the crimes of a crucified criminal was nailed to the cross with that criminal to declare the violations he was being punished for (as in the case of Jesus, as noted in Mt 27:37). Believers' sins were all put to Christ's account, nailed to His cross as He paid the penalty in their place for them all, thus satisfying the just wrath of God against crimes requiring punishment in full.

2:15 had disarmed. In yet another element of the cross work, Paul tells that the cross spelled the ultimate doom of Satan and his evil host of fallen angels (cf. Ge 3:15; Jn 12:31; 16:11; Heb 2:14). **rulers and authorities.** *See note on 1:16.* While His body was dead, His living, divine spirit actually went to the abode of demons and announced His triumph over sin, Satan, death, and hell. *See notes on 1Pe 3:18, 19.* **made a public display . . . triumphed over them.** The picture is that of a victorious Roman general parading his defeated enemies through the streets of Rome (*see notes on 2Co 2:14–16*). Christ won the victory over the demon forces on the cross, where their efforts to halt God's redemptive plan were ultimately defeated. For more on that triumphant imagery, *see notes on 2Co 2:14–16.*

2:16, 17 Paul warns the Colossians against trading their freedom in Christ for a set of useless, man-made, legalistic rules (cf. Gal 5:1). Legalism is powerless to save or to restrain sin.

2:16 food or drink. The false teachers sought to impose some sort of dietary regulations, probably based on those of the Mosaic law (cf. Lv 11). Since they were under the New Covenant, the Colossians (like all Christians) were not obligated to observe the OT dietary restrictions (cf. Mk 7:14–19; Ac 10:9–15; Ro 14:17; 1Co 8:8; 1Ti 4:1–5; Heb 9:9, 10). **festival.** The annual religious celebrations of the Jewish calendar (e.g., Passover, Pentecost, or Tabernacles (Booths); cf. Lv 23). **new moon.** The monthly sacrifice offered on the first day of each month (Nu 10:10; 28:11–14; Ps 81:3). **Sabbath day.** The weekly celebration of the seventh day, which pictured God's rest from creation. The NT clearly teaches that Christians are not required to keep it (*see notes on Ac 20:7; Ro 14:5, 6*).

2:17 shadow . . . substance. The ceremonial aspects of the OT law (dietary regulations, festivals, sacrifices) were mere shadows pointing to Christ. Since Christ, the reality has come, the shadows have no value. Cf. Heb 8:5; 10:1.

2:18 defrauding you. Paul warns the Colossians not to allow the false teachers to cheat or defraud them of their temporal blessings or eternal reward (cf. 2Jn 8) by luring them into irrational mysticism. **self-abasement.** Since the false teachers took great delight in it, their "self-abasement" was actually pride, which God hates (Pr 6:16, 17). **worship of the**

[D]fleshly mind, 19 and not holding fast to [A]the head,
from whom [B]the entire body, being supplied and
held together by the joints and [a]ligaments, grows
with a growth [b]which is from God.
20 [A]If you have died with Christ [a]to the [B]elementary
principles of the world, [C]why, as if you were living in
the world, do you submit yourself to [D]decrees, such as,
21 "Do not handle, do not taste, do not touch!" 22 (which
all *refer* [A]*to* things destined to perish [a]with use)—in
accordance with the [B]commandments and teachings
of men? 23 These are matters which have, to be sure,
the [a]appearance of wisdom in [b,A]self-made religion
and self-abasement and [B]severe treatment of the
body, *but are* of no value against [C]fleshly indulgence.

PUT ON THE NEW SELF

3 Therefore if you have been [A]raised up with Christ,
keep seeking the things above, where Christ is,
[B]seated at the right hand of God. 2 [a,A]Set your mind on
the things above, not on the things that are on earth.
3 For you have [A]died and your life is hidden with Christ
in God. 4 When Christ, [A]who is our life, is revealed,
[B]then you also will be revealed with Him in glory.
5 [A]Therefore [a]consider [B]the members of your
earthly body as dead to [b,C]immorality, impurity,
passion, evil desire, and greed, which [c]amounts to
idolatry. 6 For it is because of these things that [A]the
wrath of God will come [a]upon the sons of disobedience, 7 and [A]in them you also once walked, when
you were living [a]in them. 8 But now you also, [A]put
them all aside: [B]anger, wrath, malice, slander, *and*
[C]abusive speech from your mouth. 9 [a,A]Do not lie
to one another, since you [B]laid aside the old [b]self
with its *evil* practices, 10 and have [A]put on the new
self who is being [a,B]renewed to a true knowledge
[C]according to the image of the One who [D]created

2:18 [D]Rom 8:7 2:19 [a]Lit *bonds* [b]Lit *of God* [A]Eph 1:22 [B]Eph 1:23; 4:16 2:20 [a]Lit *from* [A]Rom 6:2 [B]Col 2:8 [C]Gal 4:9 [D]Col 2:14, 16 2:22 [a]Or *by being consumed* [A]1 Cor 6:13 [B]Is 29:13; Matt 15:9; Titus 1:14 2:23 [a]Lit *report;* Gr *logos* [b]Or *would-be religion* [A]Col 2:18 [B]1 Tim 4:3 [C]Rom 13:14; 1 Tim 4:8 3:1 [A]Col 2:12 [B]Ps 110:1; Mark 16:19 3:2 [a]Or *Be intent on* [A]Matt 16:23; Phil 3:19, 20 3:3 [A]Rom 6:2; 2 Cor 5:14; Col 2:20 3:4 [A]John 11:25; Gal 2:20 [B]1 Cor 1:7; Phil 3:21; 1 Pet 1:13; 1 John 2:28; 3:2 3:5 [a]Lit *put to death the members which are upon the earth* [b]Lit *fornication* [c]Lit *is* [A]Rom 8:13 [B]Col 2:11 [C]Mark 7:21f; 1 Cor 6:9f, 18; 2 Cor 12:21; Gal 5:19f; Eph 4:19; 5:3, 5 3:6 [a]Two early mss do not contain *upon the sons of disobedience* [A]Rom 1:18; Eph 5:6 3:7 [a]Or *among these* [A]Eph 2:2 3:8 [A]Eph 4:22 [B]Eph 4:31 [C]Eph 4:29 3:9 [a]Or *Stop lying* [b]Gr *anthropos* [A]Eph 4:25 [B]Eph 4:22 3:10 [a]Lit *renovated* [A]Eph 4:24 [B]Rom 12:2; 2 Cor 4:16; Eph 4:23 [C]Gen 1:26; Rom 8:29 [D]Eph 2:10

angels. The beginning of a heresy that was to plague the region around Colossae for several centuries and far beyond—a practice the Bible clearly prohibits (Mt 4:10; Rev 19:10; 22:8, 9). ***visions*** **he has seen.** Like virtually all cults and false religions, the Colossian false teachers based their teaching on visions and revelations they had supposedly received. Their claims were false, since Jesus Christ is God's final and complete (*see notes on vv. 3, 4*) revelation to mankind (Heb 1:1, 2). **fleshly mind.** *See note on Ro 8:6.* This describes the unregenerate and is further defined in Eph 4:17–19.

2:19 Cf. 1:18; *see note on Eph 4:15, 16.* There is no spiritual growth for the body (the church) apart from union with the Head, Christ (cf. Jn 15:4, 5; 2Pe 1:3).

2:20 died with Christ. Refers to the believer's union with Christ in His death and resurrection (*see notes on Ro 6:1–11*) by which he has been transformed to new life from all worldly folly. **elementary principles.** *See note on v. 8.* These are the same as "the commandments and teachings of men" (v. 22).

2:21–23 These verses point out the futility of asceticism, which is the attempt to achieve holiness by rigorous self-neglect (v. 23), self-denial (v. 21), and even self-infliction. Since it focuses on temporal "things destined to perish with use," asceticism is powerless to restrain sin or bring one to God. While reasonable care and discipline of one's body is of temporal value (1Ti 4:8), it has no eternal value, and the extremes of asceticism serve only to gratify the flesh. All too often, ascetics seek only to put on a public show of their supposed holiness (Mt 6:16–18).

3:1 if. Better translated "since." **you have been raised.** This verb actually means "to be co-resurrected." Because of their union with Christ, believers spiritually entered His death and resurrection at the moment of their conversion (*see notes on Ro 6:3, 4; Gal 2:20*) and have been and are now alive in Him so as to understand spiritual truths, realities, blessings, and the will of God. Those glorious benedictions (cf. Eph 1:3) are the privileges and riches of the heavenly kingdom, all of which are at our disposal. Paul called them "things above." To understand what these are, *see note on 2:3.* **seated at the right hand of God.** The position of honor and majesty (cf. Ps 110:1; Lk 22:69; Ac 2:33; 5:31; 7:56; Eph 1:20; Heb 1:3; 8:1; 1Pe 3:22) that Christ enjoys as the exalted Son of God (*see note on Php 2:9*). That exaltation makes Him the fountain of blessing for His people (Jn 14:13, 14; cf. 2Co 1:20).

3:2 Set your mind. This can also be translated "think," or "have this inner disposition." As a compass points N, the believer's entire disposition should point itself toward the things of heaven. Heavenly thoughts can only come by understanding heavenly realities from Scripture (cf. Ro 8:5; 12:2; Php 1:23; 4:8; 1Jn 2:15–17; *see note on Mt 6:33*).

3:3 you have died. *See notes on Ro 6:1–11; 2Co 5:17; Gal 6:14.* The verb's tense indicates that a death occurred in the past, in this case at the death of Jesus Christ, where believers were united with Him, their penalty of sin was paid, and they arose with Him in new life. **hidden with Christ in God.** This rich expression has a threefold meaning: 1) believers have a common spiritual life with the Father and Son (1Co 6:17; 2Pe 1:4); 2) the world cannot understand the full import of the believer's new life (1Co 2:14; 1Jn 3:2); and 3) believers are eternally secure, protected from all spiritual enemies, and with access to all God's blessings (Jn 10:28; Ro 8:31–39; Heb 7:25; 1Pe 1:4).

3:4 When Christ ... is revealed. At His second coming (cf. Rev 19:11–13, 15, 16).

3:5 consider ... as dead. *See note on Ro 8:13;* cf. Zec 4:6; Eph 5:18; 6:17; 1Jn 2:14. This refers to a conscious effort to slay the remaining sin in our flesh. **immorality.** This refers to any form of sexual sin (*see note on Gal 5:19;* cf. 1Th 4:3). **impurity.** This term goes beyond sexual acts of sin to encompass evil thoughts and intentions as well (*see note on Gal 5:19;* cf. Mt 5:28; Mk 7:21, 22; 1Th 4:7). **passion, evil desire.** Similar terms that refer to sexual lust. "Passion" is the physical side of that vice, and "evil desire" is the mental side (*see notes on Ro 1:26; 1Th 4:3;* cf. Jas 1:15). **greed.** Lit. this term means "to have more." It is the insatiable desire to gain more, especially of things that are forbidden (cf. Ex 20:17; Dt 5:21; Jas 4:2). **which amounts to idolatry.** When people engage in either greed or the sexual sins Paul has cataloged, they follow their desires rather than God's, in essence worshiping themselves—which is idolatry (Nu 25:1–3; Eph 5:3–5).

3:6 wrath of God. His constant, invariable reaction against sin (*see notes on Jn 3:36; Ro 1:18; Rev 11:18*). **sons of disobedience.** *See note on Eph 2:2.* This expression designates unbelievers as bearing the very nature and character of the disobedient, rebellious sinfulness they love.

3:7 in them you also once walked. Before their conversion (cf. Eph 2:1–5; Titus 3:3, 4).

3:8 put ... aside. A Gr. word used for taking off clothes (cf. Ac 7:58; Ro 13:12–14; 1Pe 2:1). Like one who removes his dirty clothes at day's end, believers must discard the filthy garments of their old, sinful lives. **anger.** A deep, smoldering bitterness; the settled heart attitude of an angry person (cf. Eph 4:31; Jas 1:19, 20). **wrath.** Unlike God's settled and righteous wrath (*see note on Ro 1:18*), this is a sudden outburst of sinful anger, usually the eruption that flows out of "anger" (*see note on Gal 5:20;* cf. Lk 4:28; Ac 19:28; Eph 4:31). **malice.** From the Gr. term that denotes general moral evil. Here it probably refers to the damage caused by evil speech (cf. 1Pe 2:1). **slander.** The normal translation when this word refers to God is "blasphemy." But here, since it refers to people, it is better translated "slander." To slander people, however, is to blaspheme God (Jas 3:9; cf. Mt 5:22; Jas 3:10).

3:9, 10 laid aside ... put on. *See notes on v. 8; Eph 4:24, 25.* These words are the basis for the command of v. 8. Because the old man died in Christ, and the new man lives in Christ—because that is the fact of new creation or regeneration (2Co 5:17)—believers must put off remaining sinful deeds and be continually renewed into the Christlikeness to which they are called.

3:9 old self. The old, unregenerate self, originating in Adam (*see notes on Ro 5:12–14; 6:6;* cf. Eph 4:22).

3:10 new self. The new, regenerate self, which replaces the old self; this is the essence

him— 11 *a renewal* in which [A]there is no *distinction*
between Greek and Jew, [B]circumcised and uncircumcised, [a,C]barbarian, Scythian, [D]slave and freeman,
but [E]Christ is all, and in all.
12 So, as those who have been [A]chosen of God, holy
and beloved, [B]put on a [C]heart of compassion, kindness, [D]humility, gentleness and [a,E]patience; 13 [A]bear-
ing with one another, and [B]forgiving each other,
whoever has a complaint against anyone; [B]just as
the Lord forgave you, so also should you. 14 Beyond
all these things *put on* love, which is [a,A]the perfect
bond of [B]unity. 15 Let [A]the peace of Christ [a]rule in
your hearts, to which [b]indeed you were called in [B]one
body; and [c]be thankful. 16 Let [A]the word of [a]Christ
richly dwell within you, [b]with all wisdom [B]teaching
and admonishing [c]one another [C]with psalms *and*
hymns *and* spiritual songs, [D]singing [d]with thankfulness in your hearts to God. 17 [A]Whatever you do in
word or deed, *do* all in the name of the Lord Jesus,
[B]giving thanks through Him to God the Father.

FAMILY RELATIONS

18 [A]Wives, [B]be subject to your husbands, as is fitting in the Lord. 19 [A]Husbands, love your wives and
do not be embittered against them. 20 [A]Children, be
obedient to your parents in all things, for this is
well-pleasing [a]to the Lord. 21 [A]Fathers, do not exasperate your children, so that they will not lose heart.
22 [A]Slaves, in all things obey those who are your
masters [a]on earth, [B]not with [b]external service, as
those who *merely* please men, but with sincerity
of heart, fearing the Lord. 23 Whatever you do, do

3:11 [a]I.e. those who were not Greeks, either by birth or by culture [A]Rom 10:12; 1 Cor 12:13; Gal 3:28 [B]1 Cor 7:19; Gal 5:6 [C]Acts 28:2 [D]Eph 6:8 [E]Eph 1:23 3:12 [a]I.e. forbearance toward others [A]Luke 18:7 [B]Eph 4:24 [C]Luke 1:78; Gal 5:22f; Phil 2:1 [D]Eph 4:2; Phil 2:3 [E]1 Cor 13:4; 2 Cor 6:6 3:13 [A]Eph 4:2 [B]Rom 15:7; Eph 4:32 3:14 [a]Lit *the uniting bond of perfection* [A]Eph 4:3 [B]John 17:23; Heb 6:1 3:15 [a]Or *act as arbiter* [b]Lit *also* [c]Or *show yourselves thankful* [A]John 14:27 [B]Eph 2:16 3:16 [a]One early ms reads *the Lord* [b]Or *in* [c]Or *one another, singing with psalms...* [d]Or *by*; lit *in His grace* [A]Rom 10:17; Eph 5:26; 1 Thess 1:8 [B]Col 1:28 [C]Eph 5:19 [D]1 Cor 14:15 3:17 [A]1 Cor 10:31 [B]Eph 5:20; Col 3:15 3:18 [A]Col 3:18-4:1: *Eph 5:22-6:9* [B]Eph 5:22 3:19 [A]Eph 5:25; 1 Pet 3:7 3:20 [a]Lit *in* [A]Eph 6:1 3:21 [A]Eph 6:4 3:22 [a]Lit *according to the flesh* [b]Lit *eyeservice* [A]Eph 6:5 [B]Eph 6:6

of what believers are in Christ (cf. Eph 4:17; 5:1, 8, 15). The reason believers still sin is their unredeemed flesh (*see notes on Ro 6:6, 12; 7:5*). **renewed.** *See note on 2Co 4:16*; cf. Ro 12:2; 2Co 3:18. This Gr. verb contains a sense of contrast with the former reality. It describes a new quality of life that never before existed (cf. Ro 12:2; Eph 4:22). Just like a baby is born complete but immature, the new self is complete, but has the capacity to grow. **knowledge.** *See note on 1:9.* A deep, thorough knowledge, without which there can be no spiritual growth or renewal (2Ti 3:16, 17; 1Pe 2:2). **image of the One who created him.** It is God's plan that believers become progressively more like Jesus Christ, the one who made them (cf. Ro 8:29; 1Co 15:49; 1Jn 3:2). *See notes on Php 3:12–14, 19, 20.*

3:11 Even as individual believers must discard old, sinful habits, the body of Christ must realize its unity and destroy the old barriers that separated people (cf. Gal 3:28; Eph 2:15). **Greek.** A Gentile, or non-Jew (*see note on Ro 1:14*). **Jew.** A descendant of Abraham through Isaac (*see note on Ro 2:17*). **barbarian.** *See note on Ro 1:14.* **Scythian.** An ancient nomadic and warlike people that invaded the Fertile Crescent in the seventh century B.C. Noted for their savagery, they were the most hated and feared of all the so-called barbarians. **slave and freeman.** A social barrier had always existed between slaves and freemen; Aristotle had referred to slaves as "a living tool." But faith in Christ removed the separation (1Co 12:13; Gal 3:28; cf. Phm 6). **Christ is all, and in all.** Because Jesus Christ is the Savior of all believers, He is equally the all-sufficient Lord of them all.

3:12 So. In view of what God has done through Jesus Christ for the believer, Paul described the behavior and attitude God expects in response (vv. 12–17). **chosen of God.** This designates true Christians as those who have been chosen by God. No one is converted solely by his own choice, but only in response to God's effectual, free, uninfluenced, and sovereign grace (*see notes on Jn 15:16; Ro 8:29; 9:14–23; Eph 1:4; 2Th 2:13, 14; 2Ti 1:8, 9; 1Pe 1:1, 2*; cf. Ac 13:46–48; Ro 11:4, 5). **beloved.** Election means believers are the objects of God's incomprehensible special love (cf. Jn 13:1; Eph 1:4, 5). **put on.** *See note on vv. 9, 10.* **heart of compassion.** It is a Hebraism that connotes the internal organs of the human body as used figuratively to describe the seat of the emotions (cf. Mt 9:36; Lk 6:36; Jas 5:11). **kindness.** Refers to a goodness toward others that pervades the entire person, mellowing all harsh aspects (cf. Mt 11:29, 30; Lk 10:25–37). **humility.** *See notes on Ro 12:3, 10; Php 2:3*; cf. Mt 18:4; Jn 13:14–16; Jas 4:6, 10. This is the perfect antidote to the self-love that poisons human relationships. **gentleness.** *See notes on Mt 5:5, Gal 5:23.* Sometimes translated "meekness," it is the willingness to suffer injury or insult rather than to inflict such hurts. **patience.** *See note on 1:11*; cf. Ro 2:4. It is also translated "longsuffering," the opposite of quick anger, resentment, or revenge and thus epitomizes Jesus Christ (1Ti 1:16; cf. 2Pe 3:15). It endures injustice and troublesome circumstances with hope for coming relief.

3:13 as the Lord forgave you. *See notes on Mt 18:23–34; Eph 4:32.* Because Christ as the model of forgiveness has forgiven all our sins totally (1:14; 2:13, 14), believers must be willing to forgive others.

3:14 perfect bond of unity. *See notes on Eph 4:3; Php 1:27; 2:2.* Supernatural love poured into the hearts of believers is the adhesive of the church. Cf. Ro 5:5; 1Th 4:9.

3:15 the peace of Christ. The Gr. word "peace" here refers to both the call of God to salvation and consequent peace with Him (*see note on Ro 5:1*), and the attitude of rest or security (Php 4:7) believers have because of that eternal peace.

3:16 word of Christ. This is Scripture, the Holy Spirit inspired Scripture, the word of revelation He brought into the world. **richly dwell within you.** *See notes on Eph 5:18.* "Richly" may be more fully rendered "abundantly or extravagantly rich," and "dwell" means "to live in" or "to be at home." Scripture should permeate every aspect of the believer's life and control every thought, word, and deed (cf. Ps 119:11; Mt 13:9; Php 2:16; 2Ti 2:15). This concept is parallel to being filled with the Spirit in Eph 5:18 since the results of each are the same. In Eph 5:18, the power and motivation for all the effects is the filling of the Holy Spirit; here it is the word richly dwelling. Those two realities are really one. The Holy Spirit fills the life controlled by His Word. This emphasizes that the filling of the Spirit is not some ecstatic or emotional experience, but a steady controlling of the life by obedience to the truth of God's Word. **psalms *and* hymns *and* spiritual songs.** *See note on Eph 5:19.*

3:17 *do* all in the name of the Lord Jesus. This simply means to act consistently with who He is and what He wants (*see note on 1Co 10:31*).

3:18–4:1 Paul discusses the new self's relationships to others. This passage is also a brief parallel to Eph 5:19–6:9 (*see notes there*).

3:18 be subject. *See notes on Eph 5:22, 23.* The Gr. verb denotes willingly putting oneself under someone or something (cf. Lk 2:51; 10:17, 20; Ro 8:7; 13:1, 5; 1Co 15:27, 28; Eph 1:22).

3:19 love. *See notes on Eph 5:25–29.* This is a call for the highest form of love which is rendered selflessly (cf. Ge 24:67; Eph 5:22–28; 1Pe 3:7). **be embittered.** The form of this Gr. verb is better translated "stop being bitter," or "do not have the habit of being bitter." Husbands must not be harsh or angrily resentful toward their wives.

3:20 in all things. *See notes on Eph 6:1–3.* The only limit on a child's obedience is when parents demand something contrary to God's Word. For example, some children will act contrary to their parents' wishes even in coming to Christ (cf. Lk 12:51–53; 14:26).

3:21 exasperate. *See notes on Eph 6:4.* Also translated "provoke," this word has the connotation of not stirring up or irritating.

3:22–4:1 *See notes on Eph 6:5–9;* see Introduction to Philemon: Historical and Theological Themes. Paul upholds the duties of slave and master, of which the modern parallel is the duties of employee and employer. Scripture never advocates slavery, but recognizes it as an element of ancient society that could have been more beneficial if slaves and masters had treated one another properly. Here, Paul followed Christ's example and used slavery as a motif for spiritual instruction, likening the believer to one who is a slave and servant to Jesus Christ and seeing service to an earthly master as a way to serve the Lord.

3:22 Slaves. *See note on Ro 1:1.* **external service.** *See notes on Eph 6:6.* This refers to working only when the master is watching, rather than recognizing the Lord is always watching, and how our work concerns Him (vv. 23, 24). Cf. 1Ti 6:1, 2; Titus 2:9, 10; 1Pe 2:18–21.

your work [a]heartily, [A]as for the Lord [b]rather than
for men, 24 [A]knowing that from the Lord you will
receive the reward [a]of [B]the inheritance. It is the
Lord Christ whom you [C]serve. 25 For [A]he who does
wrong will receive the consequences of the wrong
which he has done, and [a,B]that without partiality.

FELLOW WORKERS

4 Masters, grant to your slaves justice and fairness,
[A]knowing that you too have a Master in heaven.
2 [A]Devote yourselves to prayer, keeping alert in it
with *an attitude of* thanksgiving; 3 praying at the same
time [A]for us as well, that God will open up to us a [B]door
for [C]the word, so that we may speak forth [D]the mystery of Christ, for which I have also [E]been imprisoned;
4 that I may make it clear [A]in the way I ought to speak.
5 [a,A]Conduct yourselves with wisdom toward
[B]outsiders, [b,C]making the most of the opportunity.
6 [A]Let your speech always be [a]with grace, *as though*
seasoned with [B]salt, so that you will know how you
should [C]respond to each person.
7 [A]As to all my affairs, [B]Tychicus, *our* [C]beloved
brother and faithful servant and fellow bond-servant in the Lord, will bring you information. 8 [A]*For*
I have sent him to you for this very purpose, that
you may know about our circumstances and that
he may [B]encourage your hearts; 9 [a]and with him
[A]Onesimus, *our* faithful and [B]beloved brother, [C]who
is one of your *number*. They will inform you about
the whole situation here.
10 [A]Aristarchus, my [B]fellow prisoner, sends you his
greetings; and *also* [C]Barnabas's cousin Mark (about
whom you received [a]instructions; [D]if he comes to
you, welcome him); 11 and *also* Jesus who is called
Justus; these are the only [A]fellow workers for the
kingdom of God [B]who are from the circumcision,
and they have proved to be an encouragement to
me. 12 [A]Epaphras, [B]who is one of your number, a
bondslave of Jesus Christ, sends you his greetings,
always [C]laboring earnestly for you in his prayers,
that you may [a]stand [b,D]perfect and [c]fully assured in all
the will of God. 13 For I testify for him that he has [a]a
deep concern for you and for those who are in [A]Laod-
icea and Hierapolis. 14 [A]Luke, the beloved physician,
sends you his greetings, and *also* [B]Demas. 15 Greet
the brethren who are in [A]Laodicea and also [a]Nym-
pha and [B]the church that is in [b]her house. 16 [A]When
[a]this letter is read among you, have it also read in
the church of the Laodiceans; and you, for your part
[A]read [a]my letter *that is coming* from [B]Laodicea. 17 Say
to [A]Archippus, "Take heed to the [B]ministry which you
have received in the Lord, that you may [a]fulfill it."
18 [a]I, Paul, [A]write this greeting with my own hand.
[B]Remember my [b,C]imprisonment. [D]Grace be with you.

3:23 [a]Lit *from the soul* [b]Lit *and not* [A]Eph 6:7 3:24 [a]I.e. consisting of [A]Eph 6:8 [B]Acts 20:32; 1 Pet 1:4 [C]1 Cor 7:22 3:25 [a]Lit *there is no partiality* [A]Eph 6:8 [B]Deut 10:17; Acts 10:34; Eph 6:9 4:1 [A]Eph 6:9 4:2 [A]Acts 1:14; Eph 6:18 4:3 [A]Eph 6:19 [B]Acts 14:27 [C]2 Tim 4:2 [D]Eph 3:3, 4; 6:19 [E]Eph 6:20 4:4 [A]Eph 6:20 4:5 [a]Lit *Walk* [b]Lit *redeeming the time* [A]Eph 5:15 [B]Mark 4:11 [C]Eph 5:16 4:6 [a]Or *gracious* [A]Eph 4:29 [B]Mark 9:50 [C]1 Pet 3:15 4:7 [A]Col 4:7-9: *Eph 6:21, 22* [B]Acts 20:4; 2 Tim 4:12 [C]Eph 6:21; Col 1:7 4:8 [A]Eph 6:22 [B]Col 2:2 4:9 [a]Lit *along with Onesimus* [A]Philem 10 [B]Col 1:7 [C]Col 4:12 4:10 [a]Or *orders* [A]Acts 19:29; 27:2; Philem 24 [B]Rom 16:7 [C]Acts 4:36; 12:12, 25; 15:37, 39 [D]2 Tim 4:11 4:11 [A]Rom 16:3 [B]Acts 11:2 4:12 [a]Or *stand firm* [b]Or *complete* or *mature* [c]Or *made complete* [A]Col 1:7; Philem 23 [B]Col 4:9 [C]Rom 15:30 [D]Col 1:28 4:13 [a]Or *much toil* or *great pain* [A]Col 2:1; 4:15f 4:14 [A]2 Tim 4:11; Philem 24 [B]2 Tim 4:10; Philem 24 4:15 [a]Or *Nymphas* (masc) [b]One early ms reads *their* [A]Col 2:1; 4:13, 16 [B]Rom 16:5 4:16 [a]Lit *the* [A]1 Thess 5:27; 2 Thess 3:14 [B]Col 2:1; 4:13, 15 4:17 [a]Or *continually fulfill* [A]Philem 2 [B]2 Tim 4:5 4:18 [a]Lit *The greeting by my hand of Paul* [b]Lit *bonds* [A]1 Cor 16:21 [B]Heb 13:3 [C]Phil 1:7; Col 4:3 [D]1 Tim 6:21; 2 Tim 4:22; Titus 3:15; Heb 13:25

3:24, 25 reward of the inheritance. *See note on Eph 6:7, 8.* The Lord ensures the believer that he will receive a just, eternal compensation for his efforts (cf. Rev 20:12, 13), even if his earthly boss or master does not compensate fairly (v. 25). God deals with obedience and disobedience impartially (cf. Ac 10:34; Gal 6:7). Christians are not to presume on their faith in order to justify disobedience to an authority or employer (cf. Phm 18).

4:1 Masters. *See note on Eph 6:9.*

4:2 Devote yourselves. The Gr. word for "devote" means "to be courageously persistent" or "to hold fast and not let go" and refers here to persistent prayer (Ac 1:14; Ro 12:12; Eph 6:18; 1Th 5:17; cf. Lk 11:5–10; 18:1–8). **keeping alert.** In its most general sense this means to stay awake while praying. But Paul has in mind the broader implication of staying alert for specific needs about which to pray, rather than being vague and unfocused. Cf. Mt 26:41; Mk 14:38; Lk 21:36.

4:3 a door. An opportunity (1Co 16:8, 9; 2Co 2:12). **the mystery of Christ.** *See notes on 1:26, 27; 2:2, 3.*

4:5 outsiders. This refers to unbelievers. *See notes on Eph 5:15, 16.* Believers are called to so live that they establish the credibility of the Christian faith and that they make the most of every evangelistic opportunity.

4:6 with grace. To speak what is spiritual, wholesome, fitting, kind, sensitive, purposeful, complimentary, gentle, truthful, loving, and thoughtful (*see notes on Eph 4:29–31*). **seasoned with salt.** Just as salt not only flavors, but prevents corruption, the Christian's speech should act not only as a blessing to others, but as a purifying influence within the decaying society of the world.

4:7 Tychicus. The name means "fortuitous" or "fortunate." He was one of the Gentile converts Paul took to Jerusalem as a representative of the Gentile churches (Ac 20:4). He was a reliable companion of Paul and a capable leader, since he was considered as a replacement for Titus and Timothy on separate occasions (2Ti 4:12; Titus 3:12). He had the responsibility to deliver Paul's letters to the Colossians, the Ephesians (Eph 6:21), and Philemon (v. 9).

4:9 Onesimus. The runaway slave whose return to his master was the basis for Paul's letter to Philemon (see Introduction to Philemon: Background and Setting).

4:10 Aristarchus. The Gr. name of a Jewish (cf. v. 11) native of Thessalonica (Ac 20:4; 27:2). He was one of Paul's companions who was seized by a rioting mob in Ephesus (Ac 19:29) and also accompanied Paul on his trip to Jerusalem and his voyage to Rome (Ac 27:2). **Mark.** *See notes on Ac 13:5, 13;* see Introduction to Mark: Author and Date. After having fallen out of favor with Paul for some time, Mark is seen here as one of Paul's key helpers (cf. 2Ti 4:11).

4:11 Jesus who is called Justus. Possibly one of the Roman Jews who believed Paul's message (Ac 28:24). **kingdom of God.** *See note on 1:13.*

4:12 Epaphras. See Introduction: Background and Setting. **perfect and fully assured.** His goal for the Colossian believers was the same as Paul's (cf. 1:28–2:2).

4:13 Laodicea. *See note on 2:1.* **Hierapolis.** A city in Phrygia 20 mi. W of Colosse and 6 mi. N of Laodicea (see Introduction: Background and Setting).

4:14 Luke. Paul's personal physician and close friend who traveled frequently with him on his missionary journeys and wrote the Gospel of Luke and Acts (see Introductions to the Gospel of Luke and Acts: Author and Date). **Demas.** A man who demonstrated substantial commitment to the Lord's work before the attraction of the world led him to abandon Paul and the ministry (2Ti 4:9, 10; Phm 24).

4:15 Nympha and the church. A church met in her house, probably in Laodicea.

4:16 When this letter is read among you. This letter was to be publicly read in the churches in Colossae and in Laodicea. **letter . . . from Laodicea.** A separate letter from Paul, usually identified as the epistle to the Ephesians. The oldest manuscripts of Ephesians do not contain the words "in Ephesus," indicating that in all likelihood it was a circular letter intended for several churches in the region. Tychicus may have delivered Ephesians to the church at Laodicea first.

4:17 Archippus. Most likely the son of Philemon (Phm 2). Paul's message to him to fulfill his ministry is similar to the exhortation to Timothy (2Ti 4:5).

4:18 with my own hand. Paul usually dictated his letters to an amanuensis (recording secretary), but would often add his own greeting in his own writing at the end of his letters (cf. 1Co 16:21; Gal 6:11; 2Th 3:17; Phm 19). **Remember my imprisonment.** *See note on Php 1:16;* see Introduction to Ephesians: Background and Setting. Cf. Heb 13:3.

THE FIRST EPISTLE OF PAUL TO THE

THESSALONIANS

TITLE

In the Greek NT, 1 Thessalonians is listed literally as "To *the* Thessalonians." This represents the apostle Paul's first canonical correspondence to the church in the city of Thessalonica (cf. 1:1).

AUTHOR AND DATE

The apostle Paul identified himself twice as the author of this letter (1:1; 2:18). Silvanus (Silas) and Timothy (3:2, 6), Paul's traveling companions on the second missionary journey when the church was founded (Ac 17:1–9), were also mentioned in Paul's greeting (1:1). Though Paul was the single inspired author, most of the first person plural pronouns (we, us, our) refer to all 3. However, during Timothy's visit back to Thessalonica, they refer only to Paul and Silvanus (3:1, 2, 6). Paul commonly used such editorial plurals because the letters came with the full support of his companions.

Paul's authorship has not been questioned until recently by radical critics. Their attempts to undermine Pauline authorship have failed in light of the combined weight of evidence favoring Paul such as: 1) the direct assertions of Paul's authorship (1:1; 2:18); 2) the letter's perfect correlation with Paul's travels in Ac 16–18; 3) the multitude of intimate details regarding Paul; and 4) the confirmation by multiple, early historical verifications starting with Marcion's canon in A.D. 140.

The first of Paul's two letters written from Corinth to the church at Thessalonica is dated ca. A.D. 51. This date has been archeologically verified by an inscription in the temple of Apollos at Delphi (near Corinth) which dates Gallio's service as proconsul in Achaia to A.D. 51–52 (Ac 18:12–17). Since Paul's letter to the churches of Galatia was probably written ca. A.D. 49–50, this was his second piece of canonical correspondence.

BACKGROUND AND SETTING

Thessalonica (modern Salonica) lies near the ancient site of Therma on the Thermaic Gulf at the northern reaches of the Aegean Sea. This city became the capital of Macedonia (ca. 168 B.C.) and enjoyed the status of a "free city" which was ruled by its own citizenry (Ac 17:6) under the Roman Empire. Because it was located on the main east-west highway, Via Egnatia, Thessalonica served as the hub of political and commercial activity in Macedonia, and became known as "the mother of all Macedonia." The population in Paul's day reached 200,000 people.

Paul had originally traveled 100 mi. from Philippi via Amphipolis and Apollonia to Thessalonica on his second missionary journey (A.D. 50; Ac 16:1–18:22). As his custom was upon arrival, he sought out the synagogue in which to teach the local Jews the gospel (Ac 17:1, 2). On that occasion, he dialogued with them from the OT concerning Christ's death and resurrection in order to prove that Jesus of Nazareth was truly the promised Messiah (Ac 17:2, 3). Some Jews believed and soon after, Hellenistic proselytes and some wealthy women of the community also were converted (Ac 17:4). Mentioned among these new believers were Jason (Ac 17:5), Gaius (Ac 19:29), Aristarchus (Ac 20:4), and Segundus (Ac 20:4).

Because of their effective ministry, the Jews had Paul's team evicted from the city (Ac 17:5–9), so they went south to evangelize Berea (Ac 17:10). There Paul had a similar experience to Thessalonica with conversions followed by hostility, so the believers sent Paul away. He headed for Athens, while Silvanus and Timothy remained in Berea (Ac 17:11–14). They rejoined Paul in Athens (cf. Ac 17:15, 16 with 3:1), from which Timothy was later dispatched back to Thessalonica (3:2). Apparently, Silas afterwards traveled from Athens to Philippi while Paul journeyed on alone to Corinth (Ac 18:1). It was after Timothy and Silvanus rejoined Paul in Corinth (Ac 18:5) that he wrote 1 Thessalonians in response to Timothy's good report of the church.

Paul undoubtedly had multiple reasons for writing, all coming out of his supreme concern for the flock from which he had been separated. Some of Paul's purposes clearly included: 1) encouraging the church (1:2–10); 2) answering false allegations (2:1–12); 3) comforting the persecuted flock (2:13–16); 4) expressing his joy in their faith (2:17–3:13); 5) reminding them of the importance of moral purity (4:1–8); 6) condemning the sluggard lifestyle (4:9–12); 7) correcting a wrong understanding of prophetic events (4:13–5:11); 8) defusing tensions within the flock (5:12–15); and 9) exhorting the flock in the basics of Christian living (5:16–22).

HISTORICAL AND THEOLOGICAL THEMES

Both letters to Thessalonica have been referred to as "the eschatological epistles." However, in light of their more extensive focus upon the church, they would better be categorized as the Church Epistles. Five major themes are woven together in 1 Thessalonians: 1) an apologetic theme with the historical correlation between Acts and 1 Thessalonians; 2) an ecclesiastical theme with the portrayal of a healthy, growing church; 3) a pastoral theme with the example of shepherding activities and attitudes; 4) an eschatological theme with the focus on future events as the church's hope; and 5) a missionary theme with the emphasis on gospel proclamation and church planting.

INTERPRETIVE CHALLENGES

Primarily, the challenges for understanding this epistle involve the sections that are eschatological in nature: 1) the coming wrath (1:10; 5:9); 2) Christ's return (2:19; 3:13; 4:15; 5:23); 3) the rapture of the church (4:13–18); and 4) the meaning and time of the Day of the Lord (5:1–11).

OUTLINE

I. Paul's Greeting (1:1)

II. Paul's Personal Thoughts (1:2–3:13)
- A. Thanksgiving for the Church (1:2–10)
- B. Reminders for the Church (2:1–16)
- C. Concerns for the Church (2:17–3:13)

III. Paul's Practical Instructions (4:1–5:22)
- A. On Moral Purity (4:1–8)
- B. On Disciplined Living (4:9–12)
- C. On Death and the Rapture (4:13–18)
- D. On Holy Living and the Day of the Lord (5:1–11)
- E. On Church Relationships (5:12–15)
- F. On the Basics of Christian Living (5:16–22)

IV. Paul's Benediction (5:23, 24)

V. Paul's Final Remarks (5:25–28)

THANKSGIVING FOR THESE BELIEVERS

1 [A]Paul and [B]Silvanus and [C]Timothy,
To the [D]church of the Thessalonians in God the
Father and the Lord Jesus Christ: [E]Grace to you and
peace.
2 [A]We give thanks to God always for all of you, [B]mak-
ing mention of *you* in our prayers; 3 constantly bearing in mind your [A]work of faith and labor of [B]love and
[a,C]steadfastness of hope [b]in our Lord Jesus Christ in the
presence of [D]our God and Father, 4 knowing, [A]brethren
beloved by God, [B]*His* choice of you; 5 for our [A]gospel
did not come to you in word only, but also [B]in power
and in the Holy Spirit and with [C]full conviction; just as
you know [D]what kind of men we [a]proved to be among
you for your sake. 6 You also became [A]imitators of us
and of the Lord, [B]having received [C]the word in much
tribulation with the [D]joy of the Holy Spirit, 7 so that
you became an example to all the believers in [A]Mace-
donia and in [B]Achaia. 8 For [A]the word of the Lord has
[B]sounded forth from you, not only in [C]Macedonia and
[D]Achaia, but also [E]in every place your faith toward
God has gone forth, so that we have no need to say
anything. 9 For they themselves report about us what
kind of a [a,A]reception we had [b]with you, and how you
[B]turned to God [c]from [C]idols to serve [d,D]a living and true
God, 10 and to [A]wait for His Son from [a]heaven, whom
He [B]raised from the dead, *that is* Jesus, who [C]rescues
us from [D]the wrath to come.

PAUL'S MINISTRY

2 For you yourselves know, brethren, that our [a,A]com-
ing to you [B]was not in vain, 2 but after we had
already suffered and been [A]mistreated in [B]Philippi, as
you know, we had the boldness in our God [C]to speak
to you the [D]gospel of God amid much [a,E]opposition.

1:1 [A]2 Thess 1:1 [B]2 Cor 1:19 [C]Acts 16:1 [D]Acts 17:1 [E]Rom 1:7 1:2 [A]Rom 1:8; 2 Thess 1:3 [B]Rom 1:9 1:3 [a]Or *perseverance* [b]Lit *of* [A]John 6:29 [B]1 Cor 13:13 [C]Rom 8:25; 15:4 [D]Gal 1:4 1:4 [A]Rom 1:7; 2 Thess 2:13 [B]2 Pet 1:10 1:5 [a]Or *became* [A]1 Cor 9:14 [B]Rom 15:19 [C]Luke 1:1; Col 2:2 [D]1 Thess 2:10 1:6 [A]1 Cor 4:16; 11:1f [B]Acts 17:5-10 [C]2 Tim 4:2 [D]Acts 13:52; 2 Cor 6:10; Gal 5:22 1:7 [A]Rom 15:26 [B]Acts 18:12 1:8 [A]Col 3:16; 2 Thess 3:1 [B]Rom 10:18 [C]Rom 15:26 [D]Acts 18:12 [E]Rom 1:8; 16:19; 2 Cor 2:14 1:9 [a]Lit *entrance* [b]Lit *to* [c]Or *the idols* [d]Or *the* [A]1 Thess 2:1 [B]Acts 14:15 [C]1 Cor 12:2 [D]Matt 16:16 1:10 [a]Lit *the heavens* [A]Matt 16:27f; 1 Cor 1:7 [B]Acts 2:24 [C]Rom 5:9 [D]Matt 3:7; 1 Thess 2:16; 5:9 2:1 [a]Lit *entrance* [A]1 Thess 1:9 [B]2 Thess 1:10 2:2 [a]Or *struggle, conflict* [A]Acts 14:5; 16:19-24; Phil 1:30 [B]Acts 16:22-24 [C]Acts 17:1-9 [D]Rom 1:1 [E]Phil 1:30

1:1 Paul. Biographical details for the former Saul of Tarsus (Ac 9:11) can be found in Ac 9:1–30; 11:19–28:31; *see note on Ro 1:1.* For autobiographical material, see 2Co 11:16–12:10; Gal 1:11–2:21; Php 3:4–6; and 1Ti 1:12–17. **Silvanus.** A companion of Paul on the second missionary journey (Ac 15–18), later a writer for Peter (1Pe 5:12), also called Silas. **Timothy.** Paul's most notable disciple (Php 2:17–23) who traveled on the second and third missionary journeys and stayed near Paul during his first Roman imprisonment (Php 1:1; Col 1:1; Phm 1). Later he served in Ephesus (1Ti 1:3) and spent some time in prison (Heb 13:23). Paul's first letter to Timothy, while he was ministering in the church at Ephesus, instructed him regarding life in the church (cf. 1Ti 3:15). In his second letter, Paul called Timothy to be strong (2Ti 2:1) and faithfully preach as he faced death and was about to turn his ministry over to Timothy (2Ti 4:1–8). **God the Father and the Lord Jesus Christ.** Since Paul's initial converts were Jewish, he made it unmistakably clear that this "church" was not a Jewish assembly, but rather one which gathered in the name of Jesus, the Son of God (Ac 17:2, 3), who is both Lord God and Messiah. This emphasis on the equality between God and the Lord Jesus is a part of the introduction in all Paul's epistles (cf. 1Jn 2:23).

1:2 our prayers. Paul and his companions prayed frequently for the entire flock, and 3 of those prayers are offered in this letter (1:2, 3; 3:11–13; 5:23, 24).

1:3 work of faith. The 3-fold combination of faith, hope, and love is a Pauline favorite (5:8; 1Co 13:13; Col 1:4, 5). Paul refers here to the fulfillment of ministry duties which resulted from these three spiritual attitudes (cf. vv. 9, 10).

1:4 *His* choice of you. The church is commonly called "the elect" (cf. Ro 8:33; Col 3:12; 2Ti 2:10; Titus 1:1). In salvation, the initiating will is God's, not man's (cf. Jn 1:13; Ac 13:46–48; Ro 9:15, 16; 1Co 1:30; Col 1:13; 2Th 2:13; 1Pe 1:1, 2; *see notes on Eph 1:4, 5*). Man's will participates in response to God's promptings as Paul makes clear when he says the Thessalonians received the Word (v. 6) and they turned to God from idols (v. 9). These two responses describe faith and repentance, which God repeatedly calls sinners to do throughout Scripture (e.g., Ac 20:21).

1:5 our gospel. Paul called his message "our gospel," because it was for him and all sinners to believe and especially for him to preach. He knew it did not originate with him, but was divinely authored; thus he also called it "the gospel of God" (2:2, 9; Ro 1:1). Because the person who made forgiveness possible is the Lord Jesus, he also referred to it as "the gospel of Christ" (3:2). **word only.** It had to come in word (cf. Ro 10:13–17), and not word only, but in Holy Spirit power (cf. 2Co 2:4, 5) and in confidence (cf. Is 55:11). **what kind of men.** The quality of the message was confirmed by the character of the lives of the preachers. Paul's exemplary life served as an open book for all men to read, establishing the credibility of the power and grace of God essential to making the message of redemption believable to sinners (*see note on 2Co 1:12*).

1:6 imitators. The Thessalonians had become third-generation mimics of Christ. Christ is the first; Paul is the second; and the Thessalonians are the third (1Co 4:16; 11:1). **joy of the Holy Spirit.** Cf. Ro 14:17. Joy in the midst of suffering evidenced the reality of their salvation, which included the indwelling Holy Spirit (1Co 3:16; 6:19).

1:7 example. The Gr. word was used to describe a seal that marked wax or a stamp that minted coins. Paul commended the Thessalonians for being model believers leaving their mark on others. **in Macedonia and in Achaia.** The two Roman provinces which comprised Greece, Macedonia being to the N and Achaia to the S.

1:8 sounded forth. The idea is to reverberate. Wherever the Thessalonians went, the gospel given by the word of the Lord was heard. It resulted in a local outreach to Thessalonica, a national outreach to Macedonia and Achaia, and an international outreach to regions beyond. **we have no need to say anything.** Though it may appear that this church developed such a testimony in only 3 Sabbaths of preaching (cf. Ac 17:2) spanning as little as 15 days, it is better to understand that Paul preached 3 Sabbaths in the synagogue before he had to relocate elsewhere in the city. In all likelihood, Paul spent months not weeks, which accounts for: 1) the two collections he received from Philippi (Php 4:16); 2) the time he worked night and day (2:9; 2Th 3:8); and 3) the depth of pastoral care evidenced in the letter (2:7, 8, 11).

1:9 turned. This word describes what the Bible elsewhere calls repentance (Mt 3:1, 2; 4:17; Ac 2:38; 3:19; 5:31; 20:21). Salvation involves a person's turning from sin and trusting in false gods to Christ. *See notes on 2Co 7:8–11.* **to serve a living and true God.** Those converted to Christ abandoned the worship of dead idols to become willing slaves to the living God.

1:10 to wait. This is a recurring theme in the Thessalonian letters (3:13; 4:15–17; 5:8, 23; 2Th 3:6–13; cf. Ac 1:11; 2Ti 4:8; Titus 2:11–13). These passages indicate the imminency of the deliverance; it was something Paul felt could happen in their lifetime. **rescues us from the wrath to come.** This can mean to evacuate out of a current distress (Ro 7:24; Col 1:13) or to exempt from entering into a distress (Jn 12:27; 2Co 1:10). The wrath can refer either to God's temporal wrath to come on the earth (Rev 6:16, 17; 19:15) or to God's eternal wrath (Jn 3:36; Ro 5:9, 10). First Thessalonians 5:9 develops the same idea (*see note there*). The emphasis in both passages on Christ's work of salvation from sin favors this being understood as the deliverance from the eternal wrath of God in hell because of salvation.

2:1 not in vain. Paul's ministry among the Thessalonians was so fruitful that not only were people saved and a vibrant, reproducing church planted, but the church also grew and flourished even after Paul left (cf. 1:5–8).

2:2 mistreated in Philippi. Paul and Silas had been brutalized in Philippi before coming to Thessalonica (cf. Ac 16:19–24, 37). They suffered physically when beaten (Ac 16:22, 23) and incarcerated (Ac 16:24). They were arrogantly mistreated with false accusations (Ac 16:20, 21) and illegally punished in spite

3 For our [A]exhortation does not *come* from [B]error or
[C]impurity or [a]by way of [D]deceit; 4 [A]but just as we have
been approved by God to be [B]entrusted with the gospel, so we speak, [C]not as pleasing men, but God who
[a,D]examines our hearts. 5 For we never came [a]with
flattering speech, as you know, nor with [A]a pretext for
greed—[B]God is witness— 6 nor did we [A]seek glory from
men, either from you or from others, even though
as [B]apostles of Christ [a]we might have [b]asserted our
authority. 7 But we [a]proved to be [b,A]gentle [c]among
you, [B]as a nursing *mother* [d]tenderly cares for her
own children. 8 Having so fond an affection for you,
we were well-pleased to [A]impart to you not only the
[B]gospel of God but also our own [a]lives, because you
had become [b]very dear to us.
9 For you recall, brethren, our [A]labor and hardship, *how* [B]working night and day so as not to be
a [C]burden to any of you, we proclaimed to you the
[D]gospel of God. 10 You are witnesses, and *so is* [A]God,
[B]how devoutly and uprightly and blamelessly we
[a]behaved toward you [b]believers; 11 just as you know
how we *were* [A]exhorting and encouraging and [a,B]im-
ploring each one of you as [C]a father *would* his own
children, 12 so that you would [A]walk in a manner
worthy of the God who [B]calls you into His own kingdom and [C]glory.
13 For this reason we also constantly [A]thank God
that when you received the [B]word of God which
you heard from us, you accepted *it* [C]not *as* the word
of men, but *for* what it really is, the word of God,
[D]which also performs its work in you who believe.
14 For you, brethren, became [A]imitators of [B]the
churches of God in Christ Jesus that are [C]in Judea,
for [D]you also endured the same sufferings at the
hands of your own countrymen, [E]even as they *did*
from the Jews, 15 [A]who both killed the Lord Jesus
and [B]the prophets, and [a]drove us out. [b]They are not
pleasing to God, [b]but hostile to all men, 16 [A]hindering
us from speaking to the Gentiles [B]so that they may
be saved; with the result that they always [C]fill up the
measure of their sins. But [D]wrath has come upon
them [a]to the utmost.

2:3 [a]Lit *in deceit* [A]Acts 13:15 [B]2 Thess 2:11 [C]1 Thess 4:7 [D]2 Cor 4:2 2:4 [a]Or *approves* [A]2 Cor 2:17 [B]Gal 2:7 [C]Gal 1:10 [D]Rom 8:27 2:5 [a]Lit *in a word of flattery* [A]Acts 20:33; 2 Pet 2:3 [B]Rom 1:9; 1 Thess 2:10 2:6 [a]Lit *being able to* [b]Or *be burdensome* [A]John 5:41, 44; 2 Cor 4:5 [B]1 Cor 9:1f 2:7 [a]Or *became gentle* [b]Three early mss read *babes* [c]Lit *in the midst of you* [d]Or *cherishes* [A]2 Tim 2:24 [B]Gal 4:19; 1 Thess 2:11 2:8 [a]Or *souls* [b]Lit *beloved* [A]2 Cor 12:15; 1 John 3:16 [B]Rom 1:1 2:9 [A]Phil 4:16; 2 Thess 3:8 [B]Acts 18:3 [C]1 Cor 9:4f; 2 Cor 11:9 [D]Rom 1:1 2:10 [a]Lit *became* [b]Or who *believe* [A]1 Thess 2:5 [B]2 Cor 1:12; 1 Thess 1:5 2:11 [a]Or *testifying to* [A]1 Thess 5:14 [B]Luke 16:28; 1 Thess 4:6 [C]1 Cor 4:14; 1 Thess 2:7 2:12 [A]Eph 4:1 [B]Rom 8:28; 1 Thess 5:24; 2 Thess 2:14 [C]2 Cor 4:6; 1 Pet 5:10 2:13 [A]Rom 1:8; 1 Thess 1:2 [B]Rom 10:17; Heb 4:2 [C]Matt 10:20; Gal 4:14 [D]Heb 4:12 2:14 [A]1 Thess 1:6 [B]1 Cor 7:17; 10:32 [C]Gal 1:22 [D]Acts 17:5; 1 Thess 3:4; 2 Thess 1:4f [E]Heb 10:33f 2:15 [a]Or *persecuted us* [b]Lit *and* [A]Luke 24:20; Acts 2:23 [B]Matt 5:12; Acts 7:52 2:16 [a]Or *forever* or *altogether;* lit *to the end* [A]Acts 9:23; 13:45, 50; 14:2, 5, 19; 17:5, 13; 18:12; 21:21f, 27; 25:2, 7 [B]1 Cor 10:33 [C]Gen 15:16; Dan 8:23; Matt 23:32 [D]1 Thess 1:10

of their Roman citizenship (Ac 16:37). **much opposition.** Like their treatment in Philippi, Paul's team was falsely accused of civil treason in Thessalonica (Ac 17:7) and suffered physical intimidation (Ac 17:5, 6).

2:3 error or impurity ... deceit. Paul used 3 distinctly different words to affirm the truthfulness of his ministry, each expressing a contrast with what was characteristic of false teachers. He first asserted that "his message" was true and not erroneously false. His "manner of life" was pure, not sexually wicked. His "method of ministry" was authentic, not deceptive (*see notes on 2Co 4:2*).

2:4 approved by God. It could be that some false teachers came into the church to discredit Paul's ministry. This would account for his emphasis in vv. 1–12 on his divine appointment, approval, integrity, and devotion to them. Cf. Ac 9:15; 16:9, 10.

2:5, 6 flattering speech. Paul used 3 disclaimers to affirm the purity of his motives for ministry: 1) he denied being a smooth-talking preacher who tried to make favorable impressions in order to gain influence for selfish advantage; 2) he did not pretend to be poor and work night and day (cf. v. 9) as a pretense to get rich in the ministry at their expense; and 3) he didn't use his honored position as an apostle to seek personal glory, only God's glory (cf. 1Co 10:31).

2:6 apostles of Christ. This plural is designed to include Paul with the 12 for the sake of emphasizing his unique authority. Silvanus and Timothy were "apostles (messengers) of the church" (cf. Ro 16:7; Php 2:25).

2:7, 8 gentle ... as a nursing *mother*. Paul may have had in mind Moses' portrayal of himself as a nursing mother to Israel (cf. Nu 11:12). He used the same tender picture with the Corinthians (cf. 2Co 12:14, 15) and the Galatians (cf. Gal 4:19). Paul's affection for the Thessalonians was like that felt by a mother willing to sacrifice her life for her child as was Christ who was willing to give up His own life for those who would be born again into the family of God (cf. Mt 20:28).

2:9 working night and day. Paul explained this in 2Th 3:7–9. He did not ask for any money from the Thessalonians but rather lived on what he earned and what the Philippians sent (Php 4:16), so that his motives could not be questioned, unlike the false teachers who always sought money (cf. 1Pe 5:2). **the gospel of God.** Cf. Ro 1:1. The good news from God which Paul preached included these truths: 1) the authority and truthfulness of Scripture (v. 13); 2) the deity of Christ (Ro 10:9); 3) the sinfulness of mankind (Ro 3:23); 4) Christ's death and resurrection (1Co 15:4, 5); and 5) salvation by God's grace through man's faith (Eph 2:8, 9). Paul's summary of the gospel is in 1Co 15:1–5.

2:10 You are witnesses. Under OT law it took two or more witnesses to verify truth (Nu 35:30; Dt 17:6; 19:15; 2Co 13:1). Here Paul called on both the Thessalonians and God as witnesses to affirm his holy conduct in the ministry. Cf. 2Co 1:12.

2:11 exhorting ... encouraging ... imploring. Paul used these 3 words to describe his fatherly relationship with the Thessalonians since they were his children in the faith. They emphasized the personal touch of a loving father (cf. 1Co 4:14, 15).

2:12 His own kingdom and glory. This speaks of the sphere of eternal salvation (cf. Col 1:13, 14) culminating in the splendor of heaven.

2:13 the word of God. Paul's message from God is equated with the OT (Mk 7:13). It was the message taught by the apostles (Ac 4:31; 6:2). Peter preached it to the Gentiles (Ac 11:1). It was the word Paul preached on his first missionary journey (Ac 13:5, 7, 44, 48, 49), his second (Ac 16:32; 17:13; 18:11), and his third (Ac 19:10). Cf. Col 1:25. **performs its work.** The work of God's Word includes: saving (Ro 10:17; 1Pe 1:23); teaching and training (2Ti 3:16, 17); guiding (Ps 119:105); counseling (Ps 119:24); reviving (Ps 119:154); restoring (Ps 19:7); warning and rewarding (Ps 19:11); nourishing (1Pe 2:2); judging (Heb 4:12); sanctifying (Jn 17:17); freeing (Jn 8:31, 32); enriching (Col 3:16); protecting (Ps 119:11); strengthening (Ps 119:28); making wise (Ps 119:97–100); rejoicing the heart (Ps 19:8); and prospering (Jos 1:8, 9). All this is summarized in Ps 19:7–9 (*see notes there*).

2:14 imitators. Not only were the Thessalonians imitators of Paul and the Lord (cf. 1:6), but also of the churches in Judea in the sense that they both were persecuted for Christ's sake (cf. Ac 4:1–4; 5:26; 8:1). They drank Christ's cup of suffering (Mt 26:39) and walked in the way of the OT prophets (Mt 21:33–46; Lk 13:34).

2:15 who ... killed the Lord Jesus. There is no question that the Jews were responsible for the death of their Messiah, though the Romans carried out the execution. It was the Jews who brought the case against Him and demanded His death (cf. Lk 23:1–24, 34–38), just as they had killed the prophets (cf. Ac 7:51, 52).

2:15, 16 hostile to all men. Just as it is God's will that all men be saved (1Ti 2:4; 2Pe 3:9), so it was the will of the Jews that no one find salvation in Christ (v. 16). Paul at one time had embraced this blasphemy of trying to prevent gospel preaching (cf. 1Ti 1:12–17).

2:16 wrath has come upon them. God's wrath (cf. 1:10; 5:9) on the Jews who "fill up the measure of their sins" (cf. Mt 23:32; Ro 2:5), thus filling up the cup of wrath, can be understood: 1) historically of the Babylonian exile (Eze 8–11); 2) prophetically of Jerusalem's destruction in A.D. 70; 3) eschatologically of Christ's second coming in judgment (Rev 19); or 4) soteriologically in the sense that God's promised eternal wrath for unbelievers is so certain that it is spoken of as having come already as does the apostle John (cf. Jn 3:18, 36). This context relates to the fourth option.

17 But we, brethren, having been taken away from
you for a [a]short while—[A]in [b]person, not in [c]spirit—
were all the more eager with great desire [B]to see
your face. 18 [a]For [A]we wanted to come to you—I, Paul,
[b,B]more than once—and *yet* [C]Satan [D]hindered us.
19 For who is our hope or [A]joy or crown of exultation?
Is it not even you, in the presence of our Lord Jesus
at His [a,B]coming? 20 For you are [A]our glory and joy.

ENCOURAGEMENT OF TIMOTHY'S VISIT

3 Therefore [A]when we could endure *it* no longer,
we thought it best to be left behind at [B]Athens
alone, 2 and we sent [A]Timothy, our brother and God's
fellow worker in the gospel of Christ, to strengthen
and encourage you as to your faith, 3 so that no
one would be [a]disturbed by these afflictions; for
you yourselves know that [A]we have been destined
for this. 4 For indeed when we were with you, we
kept telling you in advance that we were going to
suffer affliction; [a,A]and so it came to pass, [b]as you
know. 5 For this reason, [A]when I could endure *it* no
longer, I also [B]sent to [a]find out about your faith, for
fear that [C]the tempter might have tempted you, and
[D]our labor would be in vain.
6 But now that [A]Timothy has come to us from
you, and has brought us good news of [B]your faith
and love, and that you always [C]think kindly of us,
longing to see us just as we also long to see you,
7 for this reason, brethren, in all our distress and
affliction we were comforted about you through
your faith; 8 for now we *really* live, if you [A]stand
firm in the Lord. 9 For [A]what thanks can we render
to God for you in return for all the joy with which
we rejoice before our God on your account, 10 as we
[A]night and day keep praying most earnestly that
we may [B]see your face, and may [C]complete what is
lacking in your faith?
11 [A]Now may [B]our God and Father [C]Himself and
Jesus our Lord [D]direct our way to you; 12 and may
the Lord cause you to increase and [A]abound in love
for one another, and for all people, just as we also

2:17 [a]Lit *occasion of an hour* [b]Lit *face* [c]Lit *heart* [A]1 Cor 5:3 [B]1 Thess 3:10 2:18 [a]Or *Because* [b]Lit *both once and twice* [A]Rom 15:22 [B]Phil 4:16 [C]Matt 4:10 [D]Rom 1:13; 15:22 2:19 [a]Or *presence* [A]Phil 4:1 [B]Matt 16:27; Mark 8:38; John 21:22; 1 Thess 3:13; 4:15; 5:23 2:20 [A]2 Cor 1:14 3:1 [A]1 Thess 3:5 [B]Acts 17:15f 3:2 [A]2 Cor 1:1; Col 1:1 3:3 [a]Or *deceived* [A]Acts 9:16; 14:22 3:4 [a]Lit *just as* [b]Lit *and* [A]1 Thess 2:14 3:5 [a]Or *to know, to ascertain* [A]Phil 2:19; 1 Thess 3:1 [B]1 Thess 3:2 [C]Matt 4:3 [D]2 Cor 6:1; Phil 2:16 3:6 [A]Acts 18:5 [B]1 Thess 1:3 [C]1 Cor 11:2 3:8 [A]1 Cor 16:13 3:9 [A]1 Thess 1:2 3:10 [A]2 Tim 1:3 [B]1 Thess 2:17 [C]2 Cor 13:9 3:11 [A]2 Thess 2:16 [B]Gal 1:4; 1 Thess 3:13 [C]1 Thess 4:16; 5:23; 2 Thess 2:16; 3:16; Rev 21:3 [D]2 Thess 3:5 3:12 [A]Phil 1:9; 1 Thess 4:1, 10; 2 Thess 1:3

2:17 having been taken away. Paul had been forcedly separated from his spiritual children (cf. Ac 17:5–9). His motherly (v. 7) and fatherly instincts (v. 11) had been dealt a severe blow. Lit. the Thessalonians had been orphaned by Paul's forced departure.

2:18 Satan hindered us. Satan, which means "adversary," continually attempted to tear down the church that Christ promised to build (cf. Mt 16:18). He was said to be present at the churches of Jerusalem (Ac 5:1–10), Smyrna (Rev 2:9, 10), Pergamum (Rev 2:13), Thyatira (Rev 2:24), Philadelphia (Rev 3:9), Ephesus (1Ti 3:6, 7), and Corinth (2Co 2:1–11). He thwarted Paul in the sense that a military foe would hinder the advance of his enemy. This could very possibly refer to the pledge that Jason made (Ac 17:9), if that pledge was a promise that Paul would not return to Thessalonica.

2:19 crown of exultation. The Bible speaks of eternal life like a wreath awarded for an athletic victory. It is spoken of in terms of: 1) the imperishable wreath that celebrates salvation's victory over corruption (1Co 9:25); 2) the righteous wreath that celebrates salvation's victory over unrighteousness (2Ti 4:8); 3) the unfading wreath of glory that celebrates salvation's victory over defilement (1Pe 5:4); 4) the wreath of life that celebrates salvation's victory over death (Jas 1:12, Rev 2:10); and here 5) the wreath of exultation which celebrates salvation's victory over Satan and mankind's persecution of believers. **at His coming.** "Coming," or *parousia,* lit. means "to be present." It can be understood as: 1) actual presence (Php 2:2); 2) moment of arrival (1Co 16:17); or 3) expected coming (2Co 7:6). In regard to Christ and the future, it can refer to: 1) Christ's coming at the Rapture (4:15), or 2) Christ's second coming prior to His 1,000-year millennial reign (Mt 24:37; Rev 19:11–20:6). Paul referred directly to Christ's coming 4 times in 1Th (see also 3:13; 4:15; 5:23) and once indirectly (1:10). Context indicates Paul most likely refers here to Christ's coming for the rapture of the church.

3:1 endure *it* no longer. The agony of separation between spiritual parent Paul and his children in Thessalonica became unbearably painful (cf. v. 5). **at Athens alone.** Paul and Silas stayed behind while Timothy returned (v. 2). This would not be the last time that Timothy went to a church in Paul's place (cf. 1Co 4:17; 16:10; Php 2:19–24; 1Ti 1:3).

3:2 strengthen ... encourage ... your faith. This was a common ministry concern and practice of Paul (cf. Ac 14:22; 15:32; 18:23). Paul's concern did not focus on health, wealth, self-esteem, or ease of life, but rather the spiritual quality of life. Their faith was of supreme importance in Paul's mind as evidenced by 5 mentions in vv. 1–10 (see also vv. 5, 6, 7, 10). Faith includes the foundation of the body of doctrine (cf. Jude 3) and their believing response to God in living out that truth (cf. Heb 11:6).

3:3 destined. God had promised Paul future sufferings when He commended him to ministry through Ananias (Ac 9:16). Paul reminded the Thessalonians of this divine appointment so that they would not think that: 1) God's plan was not working out as evidenced by Paul's troubles, or 2) Paul's afflictions demonstrated God's displeasure with him. To think that way would upset the church's confidence in Paul and fulfill Satan's deceptive purposes (v. 5). Cf. 2Co 4:8–15; 6:1–10; 11:23–27; 12:7–10.

3:4 suffer affliction. Paul had told them to expect him to suffer as he had already suffered before his Thessalonian experience (2:14–16; Ac 13, 14). During (Ac 17:1–9) and following (Ac 17:10–18:11) his time at Thessalonica, Paul also knew tribulation.

3:5 the tempter. Satan had already been characterized as a hinderer (2:18) and now as a tempter in the sense of trying/testing for the purpose of causing failure (cf. Mt 4:3; 1Co 7:5; Jas 1:12–18). Paul was not ignorant of Satan's schemes (2Co 2:11; 11:23) nor vulnerable to his methods (Eph 6:11), so Paul took action to counterattack Satan's expected maneuver and to assure that all his efforts were not useless (cf. 2:1).

3:6 your faith and love. Timothy returned to report the Thessalonians' trust in God, their response to one another, and to Paul's ministry. This news convinced Paul that Satan's plans to disrupt God's work had not been successful and settled Paul's anxiety (v. 7).

3:8 stand firm. Pictured here is an army that refuses to retreat even though it is being assaulted by the enemy. This is a frequent Pauline injunction (1Co 16:13; Gal 5:1; Eph 6:11, 13, 14; Php 1:27; 4:1; 2Th 2:15).

3:9 joy. Paul, like John (3Jn 4), found the highest sense of ministry joy in knowing that his children in the faith were growing and walking in the truth. It led him to the worship of God in thanksgiving and rejoicing.

3:10 praying. As to frequency, Paul prayed night and day just as he worked night and day (2:9). As to fervency, Paul prayed superabundantly (cf. Eph 3:20). **lacking.** Paul was not criticizing the church, but rather acknowledging that they had not yet reached their full potential, for which he prayed and labored (v. 10). The themes of chaps. 4, 5 deal with areas of this lack.

3:11 direct our way. Paul knew that Satan had hindered his return (2:18). Even though Timothy had visited and returned with a good report, Paul still felt the urgency to see his spiritual children again. Paul followed the biblical admonition of the Psalms (Ps 37:1–5) and Proverbs (Pr 3:5, 6) to entrust difficult situations to God.

3:12 love for one another. With over 30 positive and negative "one anothers" in the NT, love appears by far most frequently (cf. 4:9; Ro 12:10; 13:8; 2Th 1:3; 1Pe 1:22; 1Jn 3:11, 23; 4:7, 11; 2Jn 5). It is the overarching term that includes all of the other "one anothers."

do for you; 13 so that He may [A]establish your hearts
[B]without blame in holiness before [C]our God and
Father at the [a,D]coming of our Lord Jesus [E]with all
His [b]saints.

SANCTIFICATION AND LOVE

4 [A]Finally then, [B]brethren, we request and exhort
you in the Lord Jesus, that as you received from
us *instruction* as to how you ought to [a,C]walk and
[D]please God (just as you actually do [a]walk), that
you [E]excel still more. 2 For you know what commandments we gave you [a]by *the authority of* the
Lord Jesus. 3 For this is the will of God, your sanctification; *that is,* that you [A]abstain from [a]sexual
immorality; 4 that [A]each of you know how to [a]pos-
sess his own [b,B]vessel in sanctification and [C]honor,
5 not in [a,A]lustful passion, like the Gentiles who [B]do
not know God; 6 *and* that no man transgress and
[A]defraud his brother [B]in the matter because [C]the
Lord is *the* avenger in all these things, just as we
also [D]told you before and solemnly warned *you.*
7 For [A]God has not called us for [B]the purpose of impurity, but [a]in sanctification. 8 So, he who rejects
this is not rejecting man but the God who [A]gives
His Holy Spirit to you.
9 Now as to the [A]love of the brethren, you [B]have no
need for *anyone* to write to you, for you yourselves
are [C]taught by God to love one another; 10 for indeed
[A]you do practice it toward all the brethren who are
in all Macedonia. But we urge you, brethren, to [B]ex-
cel still more, 11 and to make it your ambition [A]to
lead a quiet life and [B]attend to your own business
and [C]work with your hands, just as we commanded
you, 12 so that you will [a,A]behave properly toward
[B]outsiders and [b,C]not be in any need.

THOSE WHO DIED IN CHRIST

13 But [A]we do not want you to be uninformed,
brethren, about those who [B]are asleep, so that you
will not grieve as do [C]the rest who have [D]no hope.

3:13 [a]*Or presence* [b]*Or holy ones* [A]1 Cor 1:8; 1 Thess 3:2 [B]Luke 1:6 [C]Gal 1:4; 1 Thess 3:11 [D]1 Thess 2:19 [E]Matt 25:31; Mark 8:38; 1 Thess 4:17; 2 Thess 1:7 4:1 [a]*Or conduct yourselves* [A]2 Cor 13:11; 2 Thess 3:1 [B]Gal 6:1; 1 Thess 5:12; 2 Thess 1:3; 2:1; 3:1, 13 [C]Eph 4:1 [D]2 Cor 5:9 [E]Phil 1:9; 1 Thess 3:12; 4:10; 2 Thess 1:3 4:2 [a]Lit *through the Lord* 4:3 [a]*Or fornication* [A]1 Cor 6:18 4:4 [a]*Or acquire* [b]I.e. body; or wife [A]1 Cor 7:2, 9 [B]2 Cor 4:7; 1 Pet 3:7 [C]Rom 1:24 4:5 [a]Lit *passion of lust* [A]Rom 1:26 [B]Gal 4:8 4:6 [A]1 Cor 6:8 [B]2 Cor 7:11 [C]Rom 12:19; 13:4; Heb 13:4 [D]Luke 16:28; 1 Thess 2:11; Heb 2:6 4:7 [a]I.e. in the state or sphere of [A]1 Pet 1:15 [B]1 Thess 2:3 4:8 [A]Rom 5:5; 2 Cor 1:22; Gal 4:6; 1 John 3:24 4:9 [A]John 13:34; Rom 12:10 [B]2 Cor 9:1; 1 Thess 5:1 [C]Jer 31:33f; John 6:45; 1 John 2:27 4:10 [A]1 Thess 1:7 [B]1 Thess 3:12 4:11 [A]2 Thess 3:12 [B]1 Pet 4:15 [C]Acts 18:3; Eph 4:28; 2 Thess 3:10-12 4:12 [a]Lit *walk* [b]Lit *have need of nothing* [A]Rom 13:13; Col 4:5 [B]Mark 4:11 [C]Eph 4:28 4:13 [A]Rom 1:13 [B]Acts 7:60 [C]Eph 2:3; 1 Thess 5:6 [D]Eph 2:12

Its focus is on believers in the church. **for all.** In light of the fact that God loved the world and sent His Son to die for human sin (Jn 3:16), believers who were loved when they were unlovely (Ro 5:8) are to love unbelievers (*see notes on Mt 5:43, 44*). Other NT commands concerning all men include pursuing peace (Ro 12:18), doing good (Gal 6:10), being patient (Php 4:5), praying (1Ti 2:1), showing consideration (Titus 3:2), and honoring (1Pe 2:17).

3:13 without blame in holiness. Paul prayed that there would be no grounds of accusation because of unholiness. Cf. 1Co 1:8; 2Co 11:2; Eph 5:25–27; 1Pe 4:16, 17; Jude 24. **His saints.** Since this exact term is not used elsewhere in the NT of angels (*see note on Jude 14*), but is commonly used for believers, it is best to understand the coming of the Lord to rapture all His church (*see notes on 4:13–18*) and take them to heaven to enjoy His presence (*see notes on Jn 14:1–3*).

4:1 in the Lord Jesus. To give added weight to his words, Paul appealed here to the fact that he wrote with the authority of Christ Himself (see vv. 2, 15; 5:27; 2Th 3:6, 12). **please God.** Cf. 2:4, 15; 2Co 5:9; Eph 5:10, 17; Col 1:10; Heb 11:6; 13:15, 16; 1Jn 3:22. This is done by obedience to the Word of God (cf. v. 3).

4:3 the will of God. All of God's Word contains God's will—both affirmations and prohibitions. Specifically, God's will includes salvation (1Ti 2:4), self-sacrifice (Ro 12:1, 2), Spirit filling (Eph 5:18), submission (1Pe 2:13–15), suffering (1Pe 3:17), satisfaction (5:18), settledness (Heb 10:36), and particularly here—sanctification, which literally refers to a state of being set apart from sin to holiness. In this context, it means being set apart from sexual impurity in particular, holding oneself away from immorality by following the instruction in vv. 4–8.

4:4 possess his own vessel. Two interpretations of "vessel" are usually offered. The term can mean: 1) the wife (cf. Ru 4:10 LXX; 1Pe 3:7) which one acquires, or 2) the body (2Co 4:7; 2Ti 2:21) which one possesses. The latter is most likely since: 1) the reference in 1Pe 3:7 is used only in a comparative sense ("someone weaker") referring to general humanity, not femaleness; 2) being married does not guarantee sexual purity; 3) Paul would be contradicting what he taught in 1Co 7 about the superlative state of singleness (cf. 7:8, 9); and 4) if taken in the sense of marrying a wife, Paul would be talking to men only and ignoring how women were to stay pure. Therefore, "possess his own body" is the preferred translation/interpretation. Cf. note on 1Co 9:27.

4:5 the Gentiles. Used here in a spiritual sense referring to non-Christians, and indicated by the defining statement, "who do not know God." *See notes on Eph 4:17, 18.*

4:6 defraud his brother. The context, which remains unchanged throughout vv. 1–8, demands that this refer to all the destructive social and spiritual implications of illegitimate sexual activity. *See notes on Mt 18:6–10.* **avenger.** This means it is God who ultimately works out just recompense for such sins (cf. Col 3:4–7; Heb 13:4).

4:7 called us. Whenever the epistles refer to the "call" of God, it is always a reference to His effectual, saving call, never to a general plea. It is linked to justification (cf. Ro 8:30).

4:8 gives His Holy Spirit to you. God's Spirit is a free gift to all who believe in the Lord Jesus Christ for salvation. Cf. Ac 2:38; Ro 8:9; 1Co 3:16; 12:13; 2Co 6:16.

4:9, 10 taught by God to love. Through God's Word (Ps 119:97–102) and by God Himself, they were loving believers (cf. Ro 5:5; 1Jn 2:7–11; 3:14; 4:7, 8, 12).

4:11 a quiet life. This refers to one who does not present social problems (*see note on 1Ti 2:2*) or generate conflict among those people in his life, but whose soul rests easy even in the midst of difficulty (cf. 1Pe 3:4). Paul later deals with those who did not "attend to their own business" at Thessalonica (cf. 2Th 3:6–15). **work with your hands.** Greek culture looked down on manual labor, but Paul exalts it (*see note on Eph 4:28*).

4:12 outsiders. Non-Christians are in view here (cf. 1Co 5:2; Col 4:5; 1Ti 3:7).

4:13–18 Even though Paul's ministry in Thessalonica was brief, it is clear the people had come to believe in and hope for the reality of their Savior's return (cf. 1:3, 9, 10; 2:19; 5:1, 2; 2Th 2:1, 5). They were living in expectation of that coming, eagerly awaiting Christ. Verse 13 (cf. 2Th 2:1–3) indicates they were even agitated about some things that were happening to them that might affect their participation in it. They knew Christ's return was the climactic event in redemptive history and didn't want to miss it. The major question they had was "What happens to the Christians who die before He comes? Do they miss His return?" Clearly, they had an imminent view of Christ's return, and Paul had left the impression it could happen in their lifetime. Their confusion came as they were being persecuted, an experience they thought they were to be delivered from by the Lord's return (cf. 3:3, 4).

4:13 those who are asleep. Sleep is the familiar NT euphemism for death which describes the appearance of the deceased (*see note on 1Co 11:30*). It describes the dead body, not the soul (cf. 2Co 5:1–9; Php 1:23). Sleep is used of Jarius' daughter (Mt 9:24) whom Jesus raised from the dead and Stephen who was stoned to death (Ac 7:60; cf. Jn 11:11; 1Co 7:39; 15:6, 18, 51; 2Pe 3:4). Those who sleep are identified in v. 16 as "the dead in Christ." The people, in ignorance, had come to the conclusion that those who die miss the Lord's return, and they were grieved over their absence at such a glorious event. Thus the departure of a loved one brought great anguish to the soul. But there is no reason for Christians to sorrow when a brother dies as if some great loss to that person has come.

14 For if we believe that Jesus died and rose again,
[A]even so God will bring with Him [B]those who have
fallen asleep [a]in Jesus. 15 For this we say to you [A]by
the word of the Lord, that [B]we who are alive [a]and remain until [C]the coming of the Lord, will not precede
[D]those who have fallen asleep. 16 For the Lord [A]Him-
self [B]will descend from heaven with a [a,C]shout, with
the voice of [D]*the* archangel and with the [E]trumpet
of God, and [F]the dead in Christ will rise first. 17 Then
[A]we who are alive [a]and remain will be [B]caught up
together with them [C]in the clouds to meet the Lord
in the air, and so we shall always [D]be with the Lord.
18 Therefore comfort one another with these words.

THE DAY OF THE LORD

5 Now as to the [A]times and the epochs, brethren,
you [B]have no need of anything to be written to
you. 2 For you yourselves know full well that [A]the day
of the Lord [a]will come [B]just like a thief in the night.
3 While they are saying, "[A]Peace and safety!" then
[a,B]destruction [b]will come upon them suddenly like
[C]labor pains upon a woman with child, and they will

4:14 [a]Lit *through* [A]Rom 14:9; 2 Cor 4:14 [B]1 Cor 15:18; 1 Thess 4:13 4:15 [a]Lit *who* [A]1 Kin 13:17f; 20:35; 2 Cor 12:1; Gal 1:12 [B]1 Cor 15:52; 1 Thess 5:10 [C]1 Thess 2:19 [D]1 Cor 15:18; 1 Thess 4:13 4:16 [a]Or *cry of command* [A]1 Thess 3:11 [B]1 Thess 1:10; 2 Thess 1:7 [C]Joel 2:11 [D]Jude 9 [E]Matt 24:31 [F]1 Cor 15:23; 2 Thess 2:1; Rev 14:13 4:17 [a]Lit *who* [A]1 Cor 15:52; 1 Thess 5:10 [B]2 Cor 12:2 [C]Dan 7:13; Acts 1:9; Rev 11:12 [D]John 12:26 5:1 [A]Acts 1:7 [B]1 Thess 4:9 5:2 [a]Lit *is coming* [A]1 Cor 1:8 [B]Luke 21:34; 1 Thess 5:4; 2 Pet 3:10; Rev 3:3; 16:15 5:3 [a]Or *sudden destruction* [b]Lit *comes upon* [A]Jer 6:14; 8:11; Ezek 13:10 [B]2 Thess 1:9 [C]John 16:21

4:14 God will bring with Him. As Jesus died and rose, so also will those who die believing in Him rise again so they can be taken to heaven with the Lord (*see notes on Jn 14:1–3; 1Co 15:51–58*). These texts describe the rapture of the church, which takes place when Jesus comes to collect His redeemed and take them back to heaven. Those who have died before that time (called "those who have fallen asleep") will be gathered and taken back to heaven with the Lord.

4:15 the word of the Lord. Was Paul referring to some saying of Jesus found in the Gospels? No. There are none exact or even close. The only explicit reference to the Rapture in the Gospels is Jn 14:1–3. Some suggest that Jesus had said the words while on earth, their substance being recorded later in such places as Mt 24:30, 31 and Jn 6:39, 40; 11:25, 26. Similarities between this passage in 1Th and the gospel accounts include a trumpet (Mt 24:31), a resurrection (Jn 1:26), and a gathering of the elect (Mt 24:31). Yet dissimilarities between it and the canonical sayings of Christ far outweigh the resemblances. Some of the differences between Mt 24:30, 31 and vv. 15–17 are as follows: 1) in Mt the Son of Man is coming on the clouds (but see Mk 13:26; Lk 21:27), in 1Th ascending believers are in them; 2) in the former the angels gather, in the latter Christ does personally; 3) in the former nothing is said about resurrection, while in the latter this is the main theme; and 4) Matthew records nothing about the order of ascent, which is the principal lesson in Thessalonians. On the other hand, did he mean a statement of Jesus that was spoken but not recorded in the gospels (Ac 20:35)? No. There is reason to conclude this since Paul affirmed that he taught the Rapture as a heretofore hidden truth (1Co 15:51), i.e., "mystery." Apparently, the Thessalonians were informed fully about the day of the Lord judgment (cf. 5:1, 2), but not the preceding event—the rapture of the church. Until Paul revealed it as the revelation from God to him, it had been a secret, with the only prior mention being Jesus' teaching in Jn 14:1–3. This was new revelation of what had previously been an unrevealed mystery. **we who are alive and remain.** This refers to Christians alive at the time of the Rapture, those who live on this earth to see the coming of the Lord for His own. Since Paul didn't know God's timing, he lived and spoke as if it could happen in his lifetime. As with all early Christians, he believed the event was near (cf. Ro 13:11; 1Co 6:14; 10:11; 16:22; Php 3:20, 21; 1Ti 6:14; Titus 2:13). Those alive at the Rapture will follow those dead who rise first (v. 16).

4:16 the Lord Himself will descend. This fulfills the pledge of Jn 14:1–3 (cf. Ac 1:11). Until then, He remains in heaven (cf. 1:10; Heb 1:1–3). **archangel.** Very little is known about the organization or rank of angels (cf. Col 1:17). While only Michael is named as an archangel (Jude 9), there seems to be more than one in the archangelic ranks (Da 10:13). Perhaps it is Michael, the archangel, whose voice is heard as he is identified with Israel's resurrection in Da 12:1–3. At that moment (cf. 1Co 15:52, "twinkling of an eye"), the dead rise first. They will not miss the Rapture, but be the first participants. **trumpet of God.** Cf. 1Co 15:52. This trumpet is not the judgment trumpets of Rev 8–11, but is illustrated by the trumpet of Ex 19:16–19, which called the people out of the camp to meet God. It will be a trumpet of deliverance (cf. Zep 1:16; Zec 9:14).

4:17 caught up. After the dead come forth, their spirits, already with the Lord (2Co 5:8; Php 1:23), are now being joined to resurrected new bodies (*see notes on 1Co 15:35–50*); the living Christians will be raptured, lit. snatched away (cf. Jn 10:28; Ac 8:39). This passage, along with Jn 14:1–3 and 1Co 15:51, 52, forms the biblical basis for "the Rapture" of the church. The time of the Rapture cannot be conclusively determined from this passage alone. However, when other texts such as Rev 3:10 and Jn 14:3 are consulted and compared to the texts about Christ's coming in judgment (Mt 13:34–50; 24:29–44; Rev 19:11–21) at the end of a 7-year tribulation, it has to be noted that there is a clear difference between the character of the "Rapture" in that there is no mention of any judgment, while the other texts feature judgment. So then, it is best to understand that the Rapture occurs at a time different from the coming of Christ in judgment. Thus, the Rapture has been described as pretribulational (before the wrath of God unfolded in the judgments of Rev 6–19). This event includes complete transformation (cf. 1Co 15:51, 52; Phil 3:20, 21) and union with the Lord Jesus Christ that never ends.

4:18 comfort one another. The primary purpose of this passage is not to teach a scheme of prophecy, but rather to provide encouragement to those Christians whose loved ones have died. The comfort here is based on the following: 1) the dead will be resurrected and will participate in the Lord's coming for His own; 2) when Christ comes the living will be reunited forever with their loved ones; and 3) they all will be with the Lord eternally (v. 17).

5:1 Now. Paul used familiar Gr. words here to indicate a change of topics within the same general subject of prophecy (cf. 4:9, 13; 1Co 7:1, 25; 8:1; 12:1; 16:1). The expression here points to the idea that within the broader context of the end time coming of the Lord Jesus, the subject is changing from a discussion of the blessings of the rapture of believers to the judgment of unbelievers. **times and the epochs.** These two terms mean the measurement of time and the character of the times respectively (cf. Da 2:21; Ac 1:7). Many of them expected the Lord to come in their lifetime and were confused and grieved when their fellow believers died before His coming (*see notes on 4:13–18*). They were concerned about the delay. Apparently, the Thessalonians knew all that God intended believers to know about coming judgment, and Paul had taught them what they hadn't known about the Rapture (4:13–18), so Paul exhorted them to live godly lives in light of coming judgment on the world, rather than to be distracted by probing into issues of prophetic timing. They could not know the timing of God's final judgment, but they knew well that it was coming unexpectedly (v. 2).

5:2 day of the Lord. There are 19 indisputable uses of "the Day of the Lord" in the OT and 4 in the NT (cf. Ac 2:20; 2Th 2:2; 2Pe 3:10). The OT prophets used "Day of the Lord" to describe near historical judgments (see Is 13:6–22; Eze 30:2–19; Joel 1:15; Am 5:18–20; Zep 1:14–18) or far eschatological divine judgments (see Joel 2:30–32; 3:14; Zec 14:1; Mal 4:1, 5). It is also referred to as the "day of doom" and the "day of vengeance." The NT calls it a day of "wrath," day of "visitation," and the "great day of God Almighty" (Rev 16:14). These are terrifying judgments from God (cf. Joel 2:30, 31; 2Th 1:7–10) for the overwhelming sinfulness of the world. The future "Day of the Lord," which unleashes God's wrath, falls into two parts: 1) the end of the 7-year tribulation period (cf. Rev 19:11–21), and 2) the end of the Millennium. These two are actually 1,000 years apart, and Peter refers to the end of the 1,000-year period in connection with the final "Day of the Lord" (cf. 2Pe 3:10; Rev 20:7–15). Here, Paul refers to that aspect of the "Day of the Lord," which concludes the tribulation period. **a thief in the night.** This phrase is never used to refer to the rapture of the church. It is used of Christ's coming in judgment on the day of the Lord at the end of the 7-year tribulation which is distinct from the rapture of the church (*see note on 4:15*) and it is used of the judgment that concludes the Millennium (2Pe 3:10). As a thief comes unexpectedly and without warning, so will the day of the Lord come in both its final phases.

5:3 "Peace and safety!" Just as false

not escape. 4 But you, brethren, are not in [A]darkness, that the day would overtake you [a,B]like a thief; 5 for you are all [A]sons of light and sons of day. We are not of night nor of [B]darkness; 6 so then let us not [A]sleep as [a,B]others do, but let us be alert and [b,C]sober. 7 For those who sleep do their sleeping at night, and those who get drunk get [A]drunk at night. 8 But since [A]we are of *the* day, let us [B]be [a]sober, having put on the [C]breastplate of [D]faith and love, and as a [E]helmet, the [F]hope of salvation. 9 For God has not destined us for [A]wrath, but for [B]obtaining salvation through our Lord Jesus Christ, 10 [A]who died for us, so that whether we are awake or asleep, we will live together with Him. 11 Therefore [a]encourage one another and [A]build up one another, just as you also are doing.

CHRISTIAN CONDUCT

12 But we request of you, brethren, that you [a,A]appreciate those [B]who diligently labor among you, and [C]have charge over you in the Lord and give you [b]instruction, 13 and that you esteem them very highly in love because of their work. [A]Live in peace with one another. 14 We urge you, brethren, admonish [A]the [a]unruly, encourage [B]the fainthearted, help [C]the weak, be [D]patient with everyone. 15 See that [A]no one repays another with evil for evil, but always [B]seek after that which is good for one another and for all people. 16 [A]Rejoice always; 17 [A]pray without ceasing; 18 in everything [A]give thanks; for this is God's will for you in Christ Jesus. 19 [A]Do not quench the Spirit; 20 do not despise [A]prophetic [a]utterances.

5:4 [a]One early ms reads *like thieves* [A]Acts 26:18; 1 John 2:8 [B]Luke 21:34; 1 Thess 5:2; 2 Pet 3:10; Rev 3:3; 16:15 5:5 [A]Luke 16:8 [B]Acts 26:18; 1 John 2:8 5:6 [a]Lit *the remaining ones* [b]Or *self-controlled* [A]Rom 13:11; 1 Thess 5:10 [B]Eph 2:3; 1 Thess 4:13 [C]1 Pet 1:13 5:7 [A]Acts 2:15; 2 Pet 2:13 5:8 [a]Or *self-controlled* [A]1 Thess 5:5 [B]1 Pet 1:13 [C]Is 59:17; Eph 6:14 [D]Eph 6:23 [E]Eph 6:17 [F]Rom 8:24 5:9 [A]1 Thess 1:10 [B]2 Thess 2:13f 5:10 [A]Rom 14:9 5:11 [a]Or *comfort* [A]Eph 4:29 5:12 [a]Lit *know* [b]Or *admonition* [A]1 Cor 16:18; 1 Tim 5:17 [B]Rom 16:6, 12; 1 Cor 15:10; 16:16 [C]Heb 13:17 5:13 [A]Mark 9:50 5:14 [a]Or *undisciplined* [A]2 Thess 3:6, 7, 11 [B]Is 35:4 [C]Rom 14:1f; 1 Cor 8:7ff; Rom 15:1 [D]1 Cor 13:4 5:15 [A]Matt 5:44; Rom 12:17; 1 Pet 3:9 [B]Rom 12:9; Gal 6:10; 1 Thess 5:21 5:16 [A]Phil 4:4 5:17 [A]Eph 6:18 5:18 [A]Eph 5:20 5:19 [A]Eph 4:30 5:20 [a]Or *gifts* [A]Acts 13:1; 1 Cor 14:31

prophets of old fraudulently forecast a bright future, in spite of the imminence of God's judgment (Jer 6:14; 8:11; 14:13, 14; La 2:14; Eze 13:10, 16; Mic 3:5), so they will again in future days just before the final day of the Lord destruction. **labor pains.** The Lord used this same illustration in the Olivet Discourse (*see note on Mt 24:8*). It portrays the inevitability, suddenness, inescapable nature, and painfulness of the day of the Lord.

5:4 But you, brethren. Paul dramatically shifts from the third person plural pronoun (3 times in v. 3) to the second person plural. Because the church is raptured before the judgment of the Day of the Lord, believers will not be present on earth to experience its terrors and destruction (v. 3). **not in darkness.** Believers have no part in the Day of the Lord, because they have been delivered from the domain of darkness and transferred to the kingdom of light (Col 1:13). Jesus taught that to believe in Him would remove a person from spiritual darkness (Jn 8:12; 12:46). The contrast between believers and the lost is emphatic, and Paul draws it out all the way through v. 7. Believers will not experience the wrath of God because they are different in nature. Unbelievers are in darkness (cf. v. 2, "in the night"), engulfed in mental, moral, and spiritual darkness because of sin and unbelief (cf. Jn 1:5; 3:19; 8:12; 2Co 4:6; Eph 4:17, 18; 5:8, 11). All these people are children of Satan (cf. Jn 8:44) who is called "the power of darkness" (Lk 22:53). The day of the Lord will overtake them suddenly and with deadly results.

5:5 sons of light. This is a Heb. expression that characterizes believers as children of God, their heavenly Father, who is light and in whom is no darkness at all (1Jn 1:5–7). Cf. Lk 16:8; Jn 8:12; 12:36. Believers live in a completely different sphere of life than those who will be in the day of the Lord.

5:6 let us not sleep. Because believers have been delivered from the domain of darkness, they are taken out of the night of sin and ignorance and put into the light of God. Because Christians are in the light, they should not sleep in spiritual indifference and comfort, but be alert to the spiritual issues around them. They are not to live like the sleeping, darkened people who will be jolted out of their coma by the day of the Lord (v. 7), but to live alert, balanced, godly lives under control of the truth.

5:8 breastplate. Paul pictured the Christian life in military terms as being a life of soberness (alertness) and proper equipping. The "breastplate" covers the vital organs of the body. "Faith" is an essential protection against temptations, because it is trust in God's promise, plan, and truth. It is unwavering belief in God's Word that protects us from temptation's arrows. Looking at it negatively, it is unbelief that characterizes all sin. When believers sin, they have believed Satan's lie. Love for God is essential, as perfect love for Him yields perfect obedience to Him. Elsewhere the warrior's breastplate has been used to represent righteousness (Is 59:17; Eph 6:14). Faith elsewhere is represented by a soldier's shield (Eph 6:16). The "helmet" is always associated with salvation in its future aspects (cf. Is 59:17; Eph 6:17). Our future salvation is guaranteed nothing can take it away (Ro 13:11). Paul again combined faith, love, and hope (cf. 1:3). *See notes on Eph 6:10–17.*

5:9 wrath. This is the same wrath referred to in 1:10 (*see notes there*). In this context (note especially the contrast), it appears obvious that this wrath refers to God's eternal wrath, not His temporal wrath during the tribulation period (cf. Ro 5:9).

5:10 awake or asleep. This analogy goes back to 4:13–15 and refers to being physically alive or dead with the promise that, in either case, we will one day live together (cf. 4:17; Jn 14:1–3) forever with the Savior who died as the substitute for our sins. Cf. Ro 4:9; Gal 1:4; 2Co 5:15, 21.

5:12 appreciate. This means that the people are to know their pastors well enough to have an intimate appreciation for them and to respect them because of their value. The work of pastors is summarized in a 3-fold description which includes: 1) laboring, working to the point of exhaustion; 2) overseeing, lit. standing before the flock to lead them in the way of righteousness; and 3) instructing in the truths of God's Word. Cf. Heb 13:7, 17.

5:13 esteem. In addition to knowing pastors (*see notes on v. 12*), congregations are to think rightly and lovingly of their pastors, not because of their charm or personality, but because of the fact that they work for the Chief Shepherd as His special servants (cf. 1Pe 5:2–4). They are also to submit to their leadership so that "peace" prevails in the church.

5:14, 15 We urge you. Paul has discussed how the pastors are to serve the people and how the people are to respond to the pastors (vv. 12, 13). In these verses, he presents how the people are to treat one another in the fellowship of the church. The "unruly," those out of line, must be warned and taught to get back in line. The "fainthearted," those in fear and doubt, must be encouraged and made bold. The "weak," those without spiritual and moral strength, must be held up firmly. Patience, forgiveness, and acts of goodness must prevail among all the people.

5:16–22 Paul gave a summary of the Christian's virtues. These verses provide the foundational principles for a sound spiritual life in brief, staccato statements that, in spite of their brevity, give believers the priorities for successful Christian living.

5:16 Rejoice. Joy is appropriate at all times. Cf. Php 2:17, 18; 3:1; 4:4.

5:17 pray. This does not mean pray repetitiously or continuously without a break (cf. Mt 6:7, 8), but rather pray persistently (cf. Lk 11:1–13; 18:1–8) and regularly (cf. Eph 6:18; Php 4:6; Col 4:2, 12).

5:18 give thanks. Thanklessness is a trait of unbelievers (cf. Ro 1:21; 2Ti 3:1–5). "This is God's will" includes vv. 16, 17.

5:19 quench. The fire of God's Spirit is not to be doused with sin. Believers are also instructed to not grieve the Holy Spirit (Eph 4:30), but to be controlled by the Holy Spirit (Eph 5:18) and to walk by the Holy Spirit (Gal 5:16).

5:20 prophetic utterances. This phrase can refer to a spoken revelation from God (cf. Ac 11:27, 28; 1Ti 1:18; 4:14), but most often refers to the written word of Scripture (cf. Mt 13:14; 2Pe 1:19–21; Rev 1:3; 22:7, 10, 18, 19). These "prophetic utterances" are authoritative messages from God through a well-recognized spokesman for God that, because of their divine origin, are not to be treated lightly. When God's Word is preached or read, it is to be received with great seriousness.

21 But [A]examine everything *carefully;* [B]hold fast
to that which is good; 22 abstain from every [a]form
of evil.
23 Now [A]may the God of peace [B]Himself sanctify
you entirely; and may your [C]spirit and soul and
body be preserved complete, [D]without blame at
[E]the coming of our Lord Jesus Christ. 24 [A]Faithful
is He who [B]calls you, and He also will bring it to
pass.
25 Brethren, [A]pray for us[a].
26 [A]Greet all the brethren with a holy kiss. 27 I
adjure you by the Lord to [A]have this letter read to
all the [B]brethren.
28 [A]The grace of our Lord Jesus Christ be with you.

5:21 [A]1 Cor 14:29; 1 John 4:1 [B]Rom 12:9; Gal 6:10; 1 Thess 5:15 5:22 [a]Or *appearance* 5:23 [A]Rom 15:33 [B]1 Thess 3:11 [C]Luke 1:46f; Heb 4:12 [D]James 1:4; 2 Pet 3:14 [E]1 Thess 2:19 5:24 [A]1 Cor 1:9; 2 Thess 3:3 [B]1 Thess 2:12 5:25 [a]Two early mss add *also* [A]Eph 6:19; 2 Thess 3:1; Heb 13:18 5:26 [A]Rom 16:16 5:27 [A]Col 4:16 [B]Acts 1:15 5:28 [A]Rom 16:20; 2 Thess 3:18

5:21, 22 examine everything. This call for careful testing and discernment is in response to the command of v. 20. One is never to downgrade the proclamation of God's Word, but to examine the preached word carefully (cf. Ac 17:10, 11). What is found to be "good" is to be wholeheartedly embraced. What is "evil" or unbiblical is to be shunned.

5:23 God ... sanctify you. Having concluded all the exhortations beginning in 4:1, and especially from vv. 16–22, Paul's ending benediction acknowledged the source for obeying and fulfilling them all. It is not within human power to be sanctified in all these ways (cf. Zec 4:6; 1Co 2:4, 5; Eph 3:20, 21; Col 1:29). Only God (cf. Ro 15:33; 16:20; Php 4:9; Heb 13:20 for references to God as "peace") "Himself" can separate us from sin to holiness "entirely." **spirit and soul and body.** This comprehensive reference makes the term "complete" more emphatic. By using spirit and soul, Paul was not indicating that the immaterial part of man could be divided into two substances (cf. Heb 4:12). The two words are used interchangeably throughout Scripture (cf. Heb 6:19; 10:39; 1Pe 2:11; 2Pe 2:8). There can be no division of these realities, but rather they are used as other texts use multiple terms for emphasis (cf. Dt 6:5; Mt 22:37; Mk 12:30; Lk 10:27). Nor was Paul a believer in a 3-part human composition (cf. Ro 8:10; 1Co 2:11; 5:3–5; 7:34; 2Co 7:1; Gal 6:18; Col 2:5; 2Ti 4:22), but rather two parts: material and immaterial. **at the coming.** This fourth mention of Christ's *parousia* refers to the rapture of the church as it has previously at 2:19; 3:13; 4:15.

5:24 calls you. This, as every time the divine call is mentioned in the NT, refers to God's effectual call of His chosen ones to salvation (cf. 2:12; 4:7; Ro 1:6, 7; 8:28; 1Co 1:9; Eph 4:1, 4; 2Ti 1:9; 1Pe 2:9; 5:10; 2Pe 1:10). The God who calls will also bring those whom He calls to glory and none will be lost (cf. Jn 6:37–44; 10:28, 29; Ro 8:28–39; Php 1:6; Jude 24).

5:26 holy kiss. This gesture of affection is commanded 5 times in the NT (Ro 16:16; 1Co 16:20; 2Co 13:12; 1Pe 5:14) and refers to the cultural hug and kiss greeting of the first century which for Christians was to be done righteously in recognition that believers are brothers and sisters in the family of God.

5:27 Public reading was the foundation of spiritual accountability (cf. Col 4:16; 2Th 3:14).

5:28 Cf. Ro 16:20, 24; 2Th 3:18.

THE SECOND EPISTLE
OF PAUL TO THE

THESSALONIANS

TITLE

In the Greek NT, 2 Thessalonians is listed as "To *the* Thessalonians." This represents the apostle Paul's second canonical correspondence to the fellowship of believers in the city of Thessalonica (cf. 1:1).

AUTHOR AND DATE

Paul, as in 1 Thessalonians, identified himself twice as the author of this letter (1:1; 3:17). Silvanus (Silas) and Timothy, Paul's co-laborers in founding the church, were present with him when he wrote. Evidence, both within this letter and with regard to vocabulary, style, and doctrinal content, strongly supports Paul as the only possible author. The time of this writing was surely a few months after the first epistle, while Paul was still in Corinth with Silas and Timothy (1:1; Ac 18:5) in late A.D. 51 or early A.D. 52 (see Introduction to 1 Thessalonians: Author and Date).

BACKGROUND AND SETTING

For the history of Thessalonica, see Introduction to 1 Thessalonians: Background and Setting. Some have suggested that Paul penned this letter from Ephesus (Ac 18:18–21), but his 18-month stay in Corinth provided ample time for both of the Thessalonian epistles to be authored (Ac 18:11).

Apparently, Paul had stayed apprised of the happenings in Thessalonica through correspondence and/or couriers. Perhaps the bearer of the first letter brought Paul back an update on the condition of the church, which had matured and expanded (1:3); but pressure and persecution had also increased. The seeds of false doctrine concerning the Lord had been sown, and the people's behavior was disorderly. So Paul wrote to his beloved flock who were: 1) discouraged by persecution and needed incentive to persevere; 2) deceived by false teachers who confused them about the Lord's return; and 3) disobedient to divine commands, particularly by refusing to work. Paul wrote to address those 3 issues by offering: 1) comfort for the persecuted believers (1:3–12); 2) correction for the falsely taught and frightened believers (2:1–15); and 3) confrontation for the disobedient and undisciplined believers (3:6–15).

HISTORICAL AND THEOLOGICAL THEMES

Although chaps. 1, 2 contain much prophetic material because the main issue was a serious misunderstanding generated by false teachers about the coming Day of the Lord (Paul reveals that the Day had not come and would not until certain other events occur), it is still best to call this "a pastoral letter." The emphasis is on how to maintain a healthy church with an effective testimony in proper response to sound eschatology and obedience to the truth.

Eschatology dominates the theological issues. One of the clearest statements on personal eschatology for unbelievers is found in 1:9. Church discipline is the major focus of 3:6–15, which needs to be considered along with Mt 18:15–20; 1Co 5:1–13; Gal 6:1–5, and 1Ti 5:19, 20 for understanding the complete Biblical teaching on this theme.

INTERPRETIVE CHALLENGES

Eternal reward and retribution are discussed in 1:5–12 in such general terms that it is difficult precisely to identify some of the details with regard to exact timing. Matters concerning the Day of the Lord (2:2), the restrainer (2:6, 7), and the lawless one (2:3, 4, 8–10) provide challenging prophetic material to interpret.

OUTLINE

I. Paul's Greeting (1:1, 2)

II. Paul's Comfort for Affliction (1:3–12)
- A. By Way of Encouragement (1:3, 4)
- B. By Way of Exhortation (1:5–12)

III. Paul's Correction for Prophetic Error (2:1–17)
- A. Prophetic Crisis (2:1, 2)
- B. Apostolic Correction (2:3–12)
- C. Pastoral Comfort (2:13–17)

IV. Paul's Concern for the Church (3:1–15)
- A. Regarding Prayer (3:1–5)
- B. Regarding Undisciplined Living (3:6–15)

V. Paul's Benediction (3:16–18)

THANKSGIVING FOR FAITH AND PERSEVERANCE

1 [A]Paul and [B]Silvanus and [C]Timothy,
To the [D]church of the Thessalonians in God our
Father and the Lord Jesus Christ: 2 [A]Grace to you and
peace from God the Father and the Lord Jesus Christ.
3 We ought always [A]to give thanks to God for you,
[B]brethren, as is *only* fitting, because your faith is
greatly enlarged, and the [C]love of each one of you
toward one another grows *ever* greater; 4 therefore,
we ourselves [A]speak proudly of you among [B]the
churches of God for your [a]perseverance and faith
[B]in the midst of all your persecutions and afflictions
which you endure. 5 *This is* a [A]plain indication of
God's righteous judgment so that you will be [B]consid-
ered worthy of the kingdom of God, for which indeed
you are suffering. 6 [a]For after all [A]it is *only* just [b]for
God to repay with affliction those who afflict you,
7 and *to give* relief to you who are afflicted [a]and to us
as well [b,A]when the Lord Jesus will be revealed [B]from
heaven [c]with [C]His mighty angels [D]in flaming fire,
8 dealing out retribution to those who [A]do not know
God and to those who [B]do not obey the gospel of our
Lord Jesus. 9 These will pay the penalty of [A]eternal
destruction, [B]away from the presence of the Lord
and from the glory of His power, 10 when He comes
to be [A]glorified [a]in His [b]saints on that [B]day, and to be
marveled at among all who have believed—for our
[C]testimony to you was believed. 11 To this end also we
[A]pray for you always, that our God will [a,B]count you
worthy of your [C]calling, and fulfill every desire for
[D]goodness and the [E]work of faith with power, 12 so
that the [A]name of our Lord Jesus will be glorified
in you, and you in Him, according to the grace of
our God and *the* Lord Jesus Christ.

MAN OF LAWLESSNESS

2 Now we request you, [A]brethren, with regard to
the [a,B]coming of our Lord Jesus Christ and our
[C]gathering together to Him, 2 that you not be quickly

1:1 [A]1 Thess 1:1 [B]2 Cor 1:19 [C]Acts 16:1 [D]Acts 17:1; 1 Thess 1:1 1:2 [A]Rom 1:7 1:3 [A]Rom 1:8; Eph 5:20; 1 Thess 1:2; 2 Thess 2:13 [B]1 Thess 4:1; 2 Thess 2:1 [C]1 Thess 3:12 1:4 [a]Or *steadfastness* [A]2 Cor 7:4; 1 Thess 2:19 [B]1 Cor 7:17; 1 Thess 2:14 1:5 [A]Phil 1:28 [B]Luke 20:35; 2 Thess 1:11 1:6 [a]Lit *If indeed* [b]Or *in the sight of* [A]Ex 23:22; Col 3:25; Heb 6:10 1:7 [a]Lit *along with us* [b]Lit *at the revelation of the Lord Jesus* [c]Lit *the angels of His power* [A]Luke 17:30 [B]1 Thess 4:16 [C]Jude 14 [D]Ex 3:2; 19:18; Is 66:15; Ezek 1:13; Dan 7:9; Matt 25:41; 1 Cor 3:13; Heb 10:27; 12:29; 2 Pet 3:7; Jude 7; Rev 14:10 1:8 [A]Gal 4:8 [B]Rom 2:8 1:9 [A]Phil 3:19; 1 Thess 5:3 [B]Is 2:10, 19, 21; 2 Thess 2:8 1:10 [a]Or *in the persons of* [b]Or *holy ones* [A]Is 49:3; John 17:10; 1 Thess 2:12 [B]Is 2:11ff; 1 Cor 3:13 [C]1 Cor 1:6; 1 Thess 2:1 1:11 [a]Or *make* [A]Col 1:9 [B]2 Thess 1:5 [C]Rom 11:29 [D]Rom 15:14 [E]1 Thess 1:3 1:12 [A]Is 24:15; 66:5; Mal 1:11; Phil 2:9ff 2:1 [a]Or *presence* [A]2 Thess 1:3 [B]1 Thess 2:19 [C]Mark 13:27; 1 Thess 4:15-17

1:1, 2 *See note on 1Th 1:1.*

1:3 ought always to give thanks. There is a spiritual obligation to thank God in prayer when He accomplishes great things in the lives of His saints. That was the case with the obedient Thessalonians, who had demonstrated growth in faith and love since the first letter. This was in direct answer to Paul's prayers (cf. 1Th 1:3; 3:12).

1:4 perseverance and faith. Nowhere was their growth in faith and love (v. 3) more evident than in the way they patiently and faithfully endured hostilities and suffering from the enemies of Christ. Although there was no need to speak, since the Thessalonians' lives spoke clearly enough (1Th 1:8), Paul's joy before the Lord over their perseverance bubbled up.

1:5 suffering. Having a right attitude toward suffering is essential, and that required attitude is concern for the kingdom of God. They were not self-centered, but concentrated on God's kingdom. Their focus was not on personal comfort, fulfillment, and happiness, but on the glory of God and the fulfillment of His purposes. They were not moaning about the injustice of their persecutions. Rather, they were patiently enduring the sufferings they did not deserve (v. 4). This very attitude was positive proof that God's wise process of purging, purifying, and perfecting through suffering was working to make His beloved people worthy of the kingdom (cf. 2:12) by being perfected (cf. Jas 1:2–4; 1Pe 5:10). For believers, afflictions are to be expected (cf. 1Th 3:3) as they live and develop Christian character in a satanic world. Suffering is not to be thought of as evidence that God has forsaken them, but evidence that He is with them, perfecting them (cf. Mt 5:10; Rom 8:18; 2Co 12:10). So the Thessalonians demonstrated that their salvation, determined by faith alone in the Lord Jesus Christ, was genuine because they, like Christ, were willing to suffer on account of God and His kingdom. They suffered unjustly as objects of man's wrath against Christ and His kingdom (Ac 5:41; Php 3:10; Col 1:24). "Kingdom of God" is used here in its spiritual sense of salvation (*see note on Mt 3:2*).

1:6 God to repay. Just as the righteous judgment of God works to perfect believers (v. 5), so it works to "repay" the wicked (cf. v. 8). Vindication and retribution are to be exercised by God, not man, in matters of spiritual persecution (cf. Dt 32:35; Pr 25:21, 22; Ro 12:19–21; 1Th 5:15; Rev 19:2). When God repays and how God repays are to be determined by Him.

1:7 relief . . . to us as well. Paul was a fellow-sufferer for the just cause of Christ. He, like the Thessalonians, hoped for that ultimate rest and reward for their suffering for the kingdom that was to come when Christ returned to judge the ungodly. The Lord Jesus promised this twofold coming for rest and retribution (cf. Mt 13:40–43; 24:39–41; 25:31–33; Lk 21:27, 28, 34–36; Jn 5:24–29). **when the Lord Jesus will be revealed.** This undoubtedly refers to Christ being unveiled in His coming as Judge. The first aspect of this revealing occurs at the end of the 7-year tribulation period (cf. Mt 13:24–30, 36–43; 24:29–51; 25:31–46; Rev 19:11–15). The final and universal revelation of Christ as Judge occurs at the Great White Throne judgment following Christ's millennial reign on the earth (Rev 20:11–15). Angels always accompany Christ in His coming for judgment (cf. Mt 13:41, 49; 24:30, 31; 25:31; Rev 14:14, 15). **in flaming fire.** Fire is a symbol of judgment (cf. Ex 3:2; 19:16–20; Dt 5:4; Ps 104:4; Is 66:15, 16; Mt 3:11, 12; Rev 19:12).

1:8 dealing out retribution. Lit. these words mean "to give full punishment" (cf. Dt 32:35; Is 59:17; 66:15; Eze 25:14; Ro 12:19). **do not know God.** Cf. 1Th 4:5. This speaks to the lack of a personal relationship with God through Jesus Christ (cf. Jn 17:3; Gal 4:8; Eph 2:12; 4:17, 18; Titus 1:16). Retribution is not dealt out because of persecuting Christians, but rather because they did not obey God's command to believe (cf. Ac 17:30, 31; Ro 1:5; 10:16; 15:18; 16:19) and call upon the name of the Lord to be saved from their sin (Ro 10:9–13; 1Co 16:22; Heb 10:26–31). Salvation is never obtained by works, but always by placing one's faith alone in the Lord Jesus Christ (Eph 2:8–10).

1:9 eternal destruction. *See note on Mt 25:46.* Paul explained the duration and extent of what is elsewhere in Scripture called "hell." First, it is forever, thus it is not a reversible experience. Second, destruction means ruin and does not involve annihilation, but rather a new state of conscious being which is significantly worse than the first (cf. Rev 20:14, 15). This is described as the absence of God's presence and glory (cf. Mt 8:12; 22:13; 25:30; Lk 16:24–26).

1:10 when He comes. When the day of the Lord arrives bringing retribution and ruin for unbelievers. As Christ's great glory is displayed, the result will be rest and relief for believers and the privilege of sharing His glory (cf. Php 3:21; 1Jn 3:2). This is the glorious manifestation of believers of which Paul spoke (Ro 8:18, 19). At the time, all believers will adore and worship Him, including those in the Thessalonian church who believed Paul's testimony of the gospel.

1:11 we pray . . . always. Paul's prayer life is exemplified 4 times in this letter (cf. v. 12; 2:16, 17; 3:1–5, 16). Here he prayed as he did in v. 5, that they might behave in ways consistent with their identity as Christians (cf. 1Th 2:19; Eph 4:1; Col 1:10), living up to their calling to salvation (cf. Rom 8:30; 11:29; Gal 4:13–15; 1Co 1:26; Col 1:3–5; 1Th 2:12) with lives marked by goodness and powerful works of faith.

1:12 so that. The worthy walk of v. 11 allows God to be glorified in us, the light of all purposes (cf. 2:14; 1Co 10:31; 1Pe 4:11).

2:1 coming of our Lord Jesus Christ. This is the fifth mention of Christ's coming in the Thessalonian letters (cf. 1Th 2:19; 3:13; 4:15; 5:23; *see note at 1Th 2:19*). The aspect of His particular coming in view here is identified by the next phrase "our gathering together," which conveys the idea of all believers meeting together with the Lord Jesus, obviously referring to the rapture of the church described in 1Th 4:13–18 and Jn 14:1–3. Cf. Heb 10:25 for the only other use of this phrase in the NT. This was the event the Thessalonians were anticipating (cf. 1Th 1:10; 3:13; 5:9).

2:2 quickly shaken. This term has been used of an earthquake (Ac 16:26) and a ship

shaken from your [a]composure or be disturbed either
by a [A]spirit or a [b,B]message or a [C]letter as if from us,
to the effect that [D]the day of the Lord [E]has come.
3 [A]Let no one in any way deceive you, for *it will not*
come unless the [a,B]apostasy comes first, and the [C]man
of lawlessness is revealed, the [D]son of destruction,
4 who opposes and exalts himself above [a,A]every
so-called god or object of worship, so that he takes
his seat in the temple of God, [B]displaying himself
as being God. 5 Do you not remember that [A]while I
was still with you, I was telling you these things?
6 And you know [A]what restrains him now, so that in
his time he will be revealed. 7 For [A]the mystery of
lawlessness is already at work; only [B]he who now
restrains *will do so* until he is taken out of the way.
8 Then that lawless one [A]will be revealed whom the
Lord will slay [B]with the breath of His mouth and
bring to an end by the [C]appearance of His [a]coming;

2:2 [a]Lit *mind* [b]Lit *word* [A]1 Cor 14:32; 1 John 4:1 [B]1 Thess 5:2; 2 Thess 2:15 [C]2 Thess 3:17 [D]1 Cor 1:8 [E]1 Cor 7:26 2:3 [a]Or *falling away* from the faith [A]Eph 5:6 [B]1 Tim 4:1 [C]Dan 7:25; 8:25; 11:36; 2 Thess 2:8; Rev 13:5ff [D]John 17:12 2:4 [a]Or *everyone who is called God* [A]1 Cor 8:5 [B]Is 14:14; Ezek 28:2 2:5 [A]1 Thess 3:4 2:6 [A]2 Thess 2:7 2:7 [A]Rev 17:5, 7 [B]2 Thess 2:6 2:8 [a]Or *presence* [A]Dan 7:25; 8:25; 11:36; 2 Thess 2:3; Rev 13:5ff [B]Is 11:4; Rev 2:16; 19:15 [C]1 Tim 6:14; 2 Tim 1:10; 4:1, 8; Titus 2:13

at anchor slipping its mooring in the midst of a heavy wind. Along with the word "disturbed," it describes the state of agitation and alarm that had gripped the church. They were greatly distressed because they had expected the Rapture, the gathering together to the Lord, to take place before the day of the Lord. They had expected to be taken to glory and heavenly rest, not left to persecution and divine wrath. Paul must have taught them that they would miss the day of the Lord (1Th 5:2–5; cf. Rev 3:10), but they had become confused by the persecution they were experiencing, thinking they may have been in the day of the Lord. This error had been reinforced by some messages to them claiming that they were indeed in the day of the Lord. Paul noted the source of these as "spirit," "message," and "letter." A "spirit" would most likely refer to a false prophet claiming divine revelation as in 1Jn 4:1–3. A "message" would refer to a sermon or speech given, while a "letter" indicated a written report. The powerful but harmful effect of this false information was gained by claiming it was from the apostle Paul ("as if from us"). Whoever was telling them they were in the day of the Lord claimed that it came from Paul who heard it, preached it, and wrote it. Thus their lie was given supposed apostolic sanction. The result was shock, fear, and alarm. Obviously, they had expected the Rapture before the day of the Lord. For if they had expected it after, they would have rejoiced because Christ's coming was to be soon. Apostolic authenticity in this letter which corrects the error was important and accounts for Paul's care to close the letter in his distinctive handwriting (3:17; cf. Gal 6:11). **the day of the Lord.** *See note on 1Th 5:2* for discussion of this "day." The idea that the day of the Lord had already come conflicted with what Paul had previously taught them about the Rapture. This error, which so upset the Thessalonians, is what Paul corrected in vv. 3–12, where he showed that the day hadn't come and couldn't until certain realities were in place, most especially "the man of lawlessness" (v. 3).

2:3, 4 the apostasy. The day of the Lord cannot occur until a deliberate abandonment of a formerly professed position, allegiance, or commitment occurs (the term was used to refer to military, political, or religious rebellion). Some have suggested, on questionable linguistic evidence, that this refers to "departure" in the sense of the Rapture. Context, however, points to a religious defection, which is further described in v. 4. The language indicates a specific event, not general apostasy which exists now and always will. Rather, Paul has in mind *the* apostasy. This is an event which is clearly and specifically identifiable and unique, the consummate act of rebellion, an event of final magnitude. The key to identifying the event is to identify the main person, which Paul does, calling him the "man of lawlessness." Some texts have "man of sin," but there is no real difference in meaning since sin equals lawlessness (1Jn 3:4). This is the one who is called "the prince who is to come" (Da 9:26) and "the little horn" (Da 7:8), whom John calls "the beast" (Rev 13:2–10, 18) and most know as the Antichrist. The context and language clearly identify a real person in future times who actually does the things prophesied of him in Scripture. He is also called "the son of perdition" or destruction, a term used of Judas Iscariot (Jn 17:12). This "apostasy" is the abomination of desolation that takes place at the midpoint of the Tribulation, spoken of in Da 9:27; 11:31 and Mt 24:15 (*see notes there*). This man is not Satan, although Satan is the force behind him (v. 9), and he has motives like the desires of the devil (cf. Is 14:13, 14). Paul is referring to the very act of ultimate apostasy which reveals the final Antichrist and sets the course for the events that usher in the day of the Lord. Apparently, he will be seen as supportive of religion so that God and Christ will not appear as his enemies until the apostasy. He exalts himself and opposes God by moving into the temple, the place for worship of God, declaring himself to be God and demanding the worship of the world. In this act of Satanic self-deification, he commits the great apostasy in defiance of God. For the first 3 1/2 years of the Tribulation, he maintains relations with Israel, but halts those (cf. Da 9:27); and for the last 3 1/2 years, there is great tribulation under his reign (cf. Da 7:25; 11:36–39; Mt 24:15–21; Rev 13:1–8) culminating with the day of the Lord.

2:5 I was telling you. The imperfect tense is used indicating repeated action in past time. Apparently, Paul on numerous occasions had taught them the details of God's future plans. Here, he reminded them of the issues which proved the false teachers wrong about the day of the Lord. Paul had before told them that the revealing of the Antichrist preceded the day of the Lord; since he has not yet been revealed they could not possibly be in that Day.

2:6 restrains. While the Thessalonians already had been taught and thus knew what was restraining the coming of the Antichrist, Paul does not say specifically in this letter; thus many suggestions have been made to identify the restraining force of vv. 6, 7. These include: 1) human government; 2) preaching of the gospel; 3) the binding of Satan; 4) the providence of God; 5) the Jewish state; 6) the church; 7) the Holy Spirit; and 8) Michael. Whatever now restrains the Antichrist of vv. 3, 4, 8–10 from being revealed in the fullness of his apostasy and evil must be more than human or even angelic power. The power that holds back Satan from bringing the final apostasy and unveiling of his Satan-possessed false Christ must be divinely supernatural. It must be God's power in operation that holds back Satan, so that the man of sin, the son of destruction, won't be able to come until God permits it by removing the restraining power. The reason for the restraint was so that Antichrist would be revealed at God's appointed time and no sooner, just as was Christ (cf. Gal 4:4), because God controls Satan.

2:7 the mystery of lawlessness. This is the spirit of lawlessness already prevalent in society (cf. 1Jn 3:4; 5:17), but still a mystery in that it is not fully revealed as it will be in the one who so blatantly opposes God that he blasphemously assumes the place of God on earth, which God has reserved for Jesus Christ. The spirit of such a man is already in operation (cf. 1Jn 2:18; 4:3), but the man who fully embodies that spirit has not come. For more on mystery, *see notes on Mt 13:11; 1Co 2:7; Eph 3:4, 5.* **taken out of the way.** This refers not to spatial removal (therefore it could not be the rapture of the church) but rather "a stepping aside." The idea is "out of the way," not gone (cf. Col 2:14 where our sins are taken out of the way as a barrier to God); *see note on vv. 3, 4.* This restraint will be in place until the Antichrist is revealed, at the midpoint of the Tribulation, leaving him 42 months to reign (Da 7:25; Rev 13:5).

2:8 Then that lawless one will be revealed. At the divinely decreed moment in the middle of the Tribulation when God removes the divine restraint, Satan, who has been promoting the spirit of lawlessness (v. 7), is finally allowed to fulfill his desire to imitate God by indwelling a man who will perform his will as Jesus did God's. This also fits God's plan for the consummation of evil and the judgment of the day of the Lord. **the Lord will slay.** Death occurs at God's hand (cf. Dan 7:26; Rev 17:11), and this man and his partner, the false prophet, will be cast alive into the lake of fire which burns with brimstone, where he will be eternally separated from God. (Rev 19:20; 20:10). **His coming.** The aspect of His coming in view here is not the rapture of the church, but the Lord's coming in judgment on that day when He conquers the forces of Satan and sets up His millennial kingdom (Rev 19:11–21).

9 *that is,* the one whose [a]coming is in accord with
the activity of [A]Satan, with all power and [b,B]signs and
false wonders, 10 and with [a]all the deception of wickedness for [A]those who perish, because they did not
receive the love of [B]the truth so as to be saved. 11 For
this reason [A]God [a]will send upon them [b]a [B]deluding
influence so that they will believe [c]what is false, 12 in
order that they all may be [a]judged who [A]did not believe the truth, but [b,B]took pleasure in wickedness.
13 [A]But we should always give thanks to God for
you, [B]brethren beloved by the Lord, because [C]God
has chosen you [a]from the beginning [D]for salvation
[b,E]through sanctification [c]by the Spirit and faith in
the truth. 14 It was for this He [A]called you through
[B]our gospel, [a]that you may gain the glory of our
Lord Jesus Christ. 15 So then, brethren, [A]stand firm
and [B]hold to the traditions which you were taught,
whether [C]by word *of mouth* or [C]by letter [a]from us.
16 [A]Now may our Lord Jesus Christ [A]Himself and
God our Father, who has [B]loved us and given us eternal comfort and [C]good hope by grace, 17 [A]comfort and
[B]strengthen your hearts in every good work and word.

EXHORTATION

3 [A]Finally, brethren, [B]pray for us that [C]the word of
the Lord will [a]spread rapidly and be glorified,
just as *it did* also with you; 2 and that we will be
[A]rescued from [a]perverse and evil men; for not all
have [b]faith. 3 But [A]the Lord is faithful, [a]and He will
strengthen and protect you [b]from [B]the evil *one.* 4 We
have [A]confidence in the Lord concerning you, that
you [B]are doing and will *continue to* do what we
command. 5 May the Lord [A]direct your hearts into
the love of God and into the steadfastness of Christ.
6 Now we command you, brethren, [A]in the name
of our Lord Jesus Christ, that you [a,B]keep away from
every brother who [b]leads an [c,C]unruly life and not
according to [D]the tradition which [d]you received
from us. 7 For you yourselves know how you ought
to [a,A]follow our example, because we did not act
in an undisciplined manner among you, 8 nor did
we [A]eat [a]anyone's bread [b]without paying for it, but
with [B]labor and hardship we *kept* [C]working night
and day so that we would not be a burden to any of
you; 9 not because we do not have [A]the right *to this,*
but in order to offer ourselves [B]as a model for you,
so that you would [a]follow our example. 10 For even
[A]when we were with you, we used to give you this
order: [B]if anyone is not willing to work, then he is
not to eat, either. 11 For we hear that some among
you are [A]leading an undisciplined life, doing no
work at all, but acting like [B]busybodies. 12 Now such
persons we command and [A]exhort in the Lord Jesus
Christ to [B]work in quiet fashion and eat their own

2:9 [a]Or *presence* [b]Or *attesting miracles* [A]Matt 4:10 [B]Matt 24:24; John 4:48 2:10 [a]Or *every deception* [A]1 Cor 1:18 [B]2 Thess 2:12, 13 2:11 [a]Lit *is sending* [b]Lit *an activity of error* [c]Or *the lie* [A]1 Kin 22:22; Rom 1:28 [B]1 Thess 2:3; 2 Tim 4:4 2:12 [a]Or *condemned* [b]Or *approved* [A]Rom 2:8 [B]Rom 1:32; 1 Cor 13:6 2:13 [a]One early ms reads *first fruits* [b]Lit *in* [c]Lit *of* [A]2 Thess 1:3 [B]1 Thess 1:4 [C]Eph 1:4ff [D]1 Cor 1:21; 1 Thess 2:12; 5:9; 1 Pet 1:5 [E]1 Thess 4:7; 1 Pet 1:2 2:14 [a]Lit *to the gaining of* [A]1 Thess 2:12 [B]1 Thess 1:5 2:15 [a]Lit *of* [A]1 Cor 16:13 [B]1 Cor 11:2; 2 Thess 3:6 [C]2 Thess 2:2 2:16 [A]1 Thess 3:11 [B]John 3:16 [C]Titus 3:7; 1 Pet 1:3 2:17 [A]1 Thess 3:2, 13 [B]2 Thess 3:3 3:1 [a]Lit *run* [A]1 Thess 4:1 [B]1 Thess 5:25 [C]1 Thess 1:8 3:2 [a]Lit *improper* [b]Or *the faith* [A]Rom 15:31 3:3 [a]Lit *who will* [b]Or *from evil* [A]1 Cor 1:9; 1 Thess 5:24 [B]Matt 5:37 3:4 [A]2 Cor 2:3 [B]1 Thess 4:10 3:5 [A]1 Thess 3:11 3:6 [a]Or *avoid* [b]Lit *walks disorderly* [c]Or *undisciplined* [d]One early ms reads *they* [A]1 Cor 5:4 [B]Rom 16:17; 1 Cor 5:11; 2 Thess 3:14 [C]1 Thess 5:14; 2 Thess 3:7, 11 [D]1 Cor 11:2; 2 Thess 2:15 3:7 [a]Lit *imitate us* [A]1 Thess 1:6; 2 Thess 3:9 3:8 [a]Lit *from anyone* [b]Lit *freely* [A]1 Cor 9:4 [B]1 Thess 2:9 [C]Acts 18:3; Eph 4:28 3:9 [a]Lit *imitate us* [A]1 Cor 9:4ff [B]2 Thess 3:7 3:10 [A]1 Thess 3:4 [B]1 Thess 4:11 3:11 [A]2 Thess 3:6 [B]1 Tim 5:13; 1 Pet 4:15 3:12 [A]1 Thess 4:1 [B]1 Thess 4:11

2:9, 10 the one. This "lawless one" will do mighty acts pointing to himself as supernaturally empowered. His whole operation will be deceptive, luring the world to worship him and be damned. The career of the coming lawless one is more fully described in Rev 13:1–18 (*see notes there*).

2:10 those who perish. His influence is limited to deceiving the unsaved, who will believe his lies (cf. Mt 24:24; Jn 8:41–44). They perish in the deception because of Satan-imposed blindness to the truth of the saving gospel. Cf. Jn 3:19, 20; 2Co 4:4.

2:11 a deluding influence. People who prefer to love sin and lies rather than gospel truth will receive severe, divine recompense, as do all sinners. God Himself will send judgment that ensures their fate in the form of a "deluding influence" so that they continue to believe what is false. They accept evil as good and a lie as the truth. Thus does God use Satan and Antichrist as His instruments of judgment (cf. 1Ki 22:19–23).

2:12 judged. As God has always judged willful rejection by giving men over to impurity and degrading passions (Ro 1:24–28), so in the last days God will sovereignly seal the fate of those who persist in following Satan and his counterfeit Christ. As in all ages, those who habitually reject the truth are judged by being left to the consequences of their sin.

2:13, 14 salvation … sanctification. Just as there were specific elements in the character of the Antichrist (vv. 10–12), so there are characteristics of the saved. In these two verses, Paul swept through the features of salvation, noting that believers are "beloved by the Lord," chosen for salvation from eternity past (cf. Rev 13:8; 17:8), set apart from sin by the Spirit, and called to eternal glory, i.e., the sharing of the very "glory of our Lord Jesus Christ." Paul's main point in this section was to remind the Thessalonians that there was no need to be agitated or troubled (v. 2) thinking they had missed the rapture and thus were in the Day of the Lord judgment. They were destined for glory, not judgment and would not be included with those deceived and judged in that Day.

2:15 stand firm … hold. This direct exhortation called for appropriate response to the great truths Paul had just written. In place of agitation should come strength and a firm stand. In place of false teaching should come faithful adherence to the truth.

2:16, 17 Now may. This is one of many benedictions Paul has given in his letters. In it, he invoked God's power based on His love and grace, as the true source of encouragement and strength (cf. 3:5, 16).

3:1 pray for us. Paul frequently enlisted prayer support from the churches for his ministry (cf. Ro 15:30–32; Eph 6:18, 19; Col 4:2, 3; 1Th 5:25; Phm 22). In particular, he asked them to pray that the Word of God would continue to spread rapidly as it had been already (cf. Ac 6:7; 12:24; 13:44–49), and be received with the honor it deserved.

3:2 perverse and evil men. These were Paul's enemies at Corinth, where he ministered when he wrote (cf. Ac 18:9–17), who were perverse and aggressively unrighteous in their opposition of him and the gospel.

3:3 the Lord is faithful. Cf. La 3:23. God is faithful in regard to creation (Ps 119:90), His promises (Dt 7:9; 2Co 1:18; Heb 10:23), salvation (1Th 5:24), temptation (1Co 10:13), suffering (1Pe 4:19), and here faithful to strengthen and protect from Satan (cf. Jn 17:15; Eph 6:16; 1Th 3:5).

3:5 Another of Paul's benedictions (cf. v. 16; 2:16, 17), so common in his letters.

3:6 we command you. Paul's directions were not mere suggestions, but rather they carried the weight and authority of a judge's court order which the apostle delivered and enforced (cf. vv. 4, 6, 10, 12). Here, he required separation so that obedient Christians were not to fellowship with habitually disobedient believers. This is further explained at v. 14. **the tradition.** There were false traditions (Mk 7:2–13; Col 2:8) and true (cf. 2:15). Paul's traditions were the inspired teachings he had given.

3:7 follow our example. Paul called for them to imitate him (cf. v. 9; 1Th 1:6) because he imitated Christ's example (cf. 1Co 4:16; 11:1; Eph 5:1).

3:8–10 working. The specific issue related to working diligently to earn one's living. Though Paul had the "right" as an apostle to receive support, he chose rather to earn his own living to set an example (cf. 1Co 9:3–14; Gal 6:4; 1Ti 5:17, 18).

3:11, 12 we hear. Word had come that, in spite of Paul teaching them to work and writing to them about it (1Th 4:11), some were still

bread. 13 But as for you, [A]brethren, [B]do not grow weary of doing good.

14 If anyone does not obey our [a]instruction [b,A]in this letter, take special note of that person [c,B]and do not associate with him, so that he will be [C]put to shame. 15 *Yet* [A]do not regard him as an enemy, but [a,B]admonish him as a [C]brother.

16 Now [A]may the Lord of peace [B]Himself continually grant you peace in every [a]circumstance. [C]The Lord be with you all!

17 [a]I, Paul, write this greeting [A]with my own hand, and this is a distinguishing mark in every letter; this is the way I write. 18 [A]The grace of our Lord Jesus Christ be with you all.

3:13 [A]1 Thess 4:1 [B]2 Cor 4:1; Gal 6:9 3:14 [a]Lit *word* [b]Lit *through* [c]Lit *not to associate* [A]Col 4:16 [B]2 Thess 3:6 [C]1 Cor 4:14
3:15 [a]Or *keep admonishing* [A]Gal 6:1 [B]1 Thess 5:14 [C]2 Thess 3:6, 13 3:16 [a]Lit *way* [A]Rom 15:33 [B]1 Thess 3:11 [C]Ruth 2:4
3:17 [a]Lit *The greeting by my hand of Paul* [A]1 Cor 16:21 3:18 [A]Rom 16:20; 1 Thess 5:28

not willing to work (cf. 1Ti 5:13). These were commanded to settle down and begin an ordered life of work.

3:13 do not grow weary. The hard working believers were tired of having to support the lazy, and were ready to stop all help to those in need, giving up all charity. Paul reminded them that the truly needy still required help and that the Thessalonians must not be negligent toward them.

3:14 do not associate with him. This means to "mix it up" in the sense of social interaction. Blatantly disobedient Christians were to be disfellowshipped (v. 6) to produce shame and, hopefully, repentance if they refused to obey the Word of God. See Mt 18:15–17; 1Co 5:9–13; Gal 6:1 for additional details on how to deal with those engaged in unrepentant and repeated sin.

3:15 enemy . . . brother. The purpose of this disfellowship discipline is not final rejection. While an unrepentant pattern of sin is to be dealt with decisively, it is to be continually kept in mind that the one with whom one deals is a brother in the Lord, so all further warnings to him about his sin are done with a brotherly attitude. For instruction on the manner of church discipline, *see notes on Mt 18:15–20.*

3:16 the Lord of peace. Paul knew this characteristic of God would be most meaningful to reflect upon in light of the intense spiritual battle that raged all around the Thessalonians (cf. 1:2; 1Th 1:1; 5:23). Cf. Paul's other benedictions to this church in v. 5; 2:16, 17; 1Th 3:11–13; 5:23.

3:17 a distinguishing mark. Paul often wrote through a secretary (cf. Ro 16:22). When that was the case, as most likely with this letter, Paul added an identifying signature (cf. 1Co 16:21; Col 4:18) so that readers could be sure he was truly the author (*see note on 2:2*).

3:18 Cf. 1Th 5:28.

THE FIRST EPISTLE OF PAUL TO

TIMOTHY

TITLE

This is the first of two inspired letters Paul wrote to his beloved son in the faith. Timothy received his name, which means "one who honors God," from his mother (Eunice) and grandmother (Lois), devout Jews who became believers in the Lord Jesus Christ (2Ti 1:5) and taught Timothy the OT Scriptures from his childhood (2Ti 3:15). His father was a Greek (Ac 16:1) who may have died before Timothy met Paul.

Timothy was from Lystra (Ac 16:1–3), a city in the Roman province of Galatia (part of modern Turkey). Paul led Timothy to Christ (1:2, 18; 1Co 4:17; 2Ti 1:2), undoubtedly during his ministry in Lystra on his first missionary journey (Ac 14:6–23). When he revisited Lystra on his second missionary journey, Paul chose Timothy to accompany him (Ac 16:1–3). Although Timothy was very young (probably in his late teens or early twenties, since about 15 years later Paul referred to him as a young man, 4:12), he had a reputation for godliness (Ac 16:2). Timothy was to be Paul's disciple, friend, and co-laborer for the rest of the apostle's life, ministering with him in Berea (Ac 17:14), Athens (Ac 17:15), Corinth (Ac 18:5; 2Co 1:19), and accompanying him on his trip to Jerusalem (Ac 20:4). He was with Paul in his first Roman imprisonment and went to Philippi (Php 2:19–23) after Paul's release. In addition, Paul frequently mentions Timothy in his epistles (Ro 16:21; 2Co 1:1; Php 1:1; Col 1:1; 1Th 1:1; 2Th 1:1; Phm 1). Paul often sent Timothy to churches as his representative (1Co 4:17; 16:10; Php 2:19; 1Th 3:2), and 1 Timothy finds him on another assignment, serving as pastor of the church at Ephesus (1:3). According to Heb 13:23, Timothy was imprisoned somewhere and released.

AUTHOR AND DATE

Many modernist critics delight in attacking the plain statements of Scripture and, for no good reason, deny that Paul wrote the Pastoral Epistles (1, 2 Timothy, Titus). Ignoring the testimony of the letters themselves (1:1; 2Ti 1:1; Titus 1:1) and that of the early church (which is as strong for the Pastoral Epistles as for any of Paul's epistles, except Romans and 1 Corinthians), these critics maintain that a devout follower of Paul wrote the Pastoral Epistles in the second century. As proof, they offer 5 lines of supposed evidence: 1) the historical references in the Pastoral Epistles cannot be harmonized with the chronology of Paul's life given in Acts; 2) the false teaching described in the Pastoral Epistles is the fully developed gnosticism of the second century; 3) the church organizational structure in the Pastoral Epistles is that of the second century, and is too well developed for Paul's day; 4) the Pastoral Epistles do not contain the great themes of Paul's theology; 5) the Greek vocabulary of the Pastoral Epistles contains many words not found in Paul's other letters, nor in the rest of the NT.

While it is unnecessary to dignify such unwarranted attacks by unbelievers with an answer, occasionally such an answer does enlighten. Thus, in reply to the critics' arguments, it can be pointed out that: 1) this contention of historical incompatibility is valid only if Paul was never released from his Roman imprisonment mentioned in Acts. But he was released, since Acts does not record Paul's execution, and Paul himself expected to be released (Php 1:19, 25, 26; 2:24; Phm 22). The historical events in the Pastoral Epistles do not fit into the chronology of Acts because they happened after the close of the Acts narrative, which ends with Paul's first imprisonment in Rome. 2) While there are similarities between the heresy of the Pastoral Epistles and second-century gnosticism (see Introduction to Colossians: Background and Setting), there are also important differences. Unlike second-century gnosticism, the false teachers of the Pastoral Epistles were still within the church (cf. 1:3–7), and their teaching was based on Judaistic legalism (1:7; Titus 1:10, 14; 3:9). 3) The church organizational structure mentioned in the Pastoral Epistles is, in fact, consistent with that established by Paul (Ac 14:23; Php 1:1). 4) The Pastoral Epistles do mention the central themes of Paul's theology, including the inspiration of Scripture (2Ti 3:15–17); election (2Ti 1:9; Titus 1:1, 2); salvation (Titus 3:5–7); the deity of Christ (Titus 2:13); His mediatorial work (2:5), and substitutionary atonement (2:6). 5) The different subject matter in the Pastoral Epistles required a different vocabulary from that in Paul's other epistles. Certainly a pastor today would use a different vocabulary in a personal letter to a fellow pastor than he would in a work of systematic theology.

The idea that a "pious forger" wrote the Pastoral Epistles faces several further difficulties: 1) The early church did not approve of such practices and surely would have exposed this as a ruse, if there had actually been one (cf. 2Th 2:1, 2; 3:17). 2) Why forge 3 letters that include similar material and no deviant doctrine? 3) If a counterfeit, why not invent an itinerary for Paul that would have harmonized with Acts? 4) Would a later, devoted follower of Paul have put the words of 1:13, 15 into his master's mouth? 5) Why would he include warnings against deceivers (2Ti 3:13; Titus 1:10), if he himself were one?

The evidence seems clear that Paul wrote 1 Timothy and Titus shortly after his release from his first Roman imprisonment (ca. A.D. 62–64), and 2 Timothy from prison during his second Roman imprisonment (ca. A.D. 66–67), shortly before his death.

BACKGROUND AND SETTING

After being released from his first Roman imprisonment (cf. Ac 28:30), Paul revisited several of the cities in which he had ministered, including Ephesus. Leaving Timothy behind there to deal with problems that had arisen in the Ephesian church, such as false doctrine (1:3–7; 4:1–3; 6:3–5), disorder in worship (2:1–15), the need for qualified leaders (3:1–14), and materialism (6:6–19), Paul went on to Macedonia, from where he wrote Timothy this letter to help him carry out his task in the church (cf. 3:14, 15).

HISTORICAL AND THEOLOGICAL THEMES

First Timothy is a practical letter containing pastoral instruction from Paul to Timothy (cf. 3:14, 15). Since Timothy was well versed in Paul's theology, the apostle had no need to give him extensive doctrinal instruction. This epistle does, however, express many important theological truths, such as the proper function of the law (1:5–11); salvation (1:14–16; 2:4–6); the attributes of God (1:17); the Fall (2:13, 14); the person of Christ (3:16; 6:15, 16); election (6:12); and the second coming of Christ (6:14, 15).

INTERPRETIVE CHALLENGES

There is disagreement over the identity of the false teachers (1:3) and the genealogies (1:4) involved in their teaching. What it means to be "handed over to Satan" (1:20) has also been a source of debate. The letter contains key passages in the debate over the extent of the atonement (2:4–6; 4:10). Paul's teaching on the role of women (2:9–15) has generated much discussion, particularly his declaration that they are not to assume leadership roles in the church (2:11, 12). How women can be saved by bearing children (2:15) has also confused many. Whether the fact that an elder must be "the husband of one wife" excludes divorced or unmarried men has been disputed, as well as whether Paul refers to deacons' wives or deaconesses (3:11). Those who believe Christians can lose their salvation cite 4:1 as support for their view. There is a question about the identity of the widows in 5:3–16—are they needy women ministered to by the church, or an order of older women ministering to the church? Does "double honor" accorded to elders who rule well (5:17, 18) refer to respect or money? These will all be dealt with in their respective notes.

OUTLINE

I. Greeting (1:1, 2)

II. Instructions Concerning False Doctrine (1:3–20)
- A. The False Doctrine at Ephesus (1:3–11)
- B. The True Doctrine of Paul (1:12–17)
- C. The Exhortation to Timothy (1:18–20)

III. Instructions Concerning the Church (2:1–3:16)
- A. The Importance of Prayer (2:1–8)
- B. The Role of Women (2:9–15)
- C. The Qualifications for Leaders (3:1–13)
- D. The Reason for Paul's Letter (3:14–16)

IV. Instructions Concerning False Teachers (4:1–16)
- A. The Description of False Teachers (4:1–5)
- B. The Description of True Teachers (4:6–16)

V. Instructions Concerning Pastoral Responsibilities (5:1–6:2)
- A. The Responsibility to Sinning Members (5:1, 2)
- B. The Responsibility to Widows (5:3–16)
- C. The Responsibility to Elders (5:17–25)
- D. The Responsibility to Slaves (6:1, 2)

VI. Instructions Concerning the Man of God (6:3–21)
- A. The Peril of False Teaching (6:3–5)
- B. The Peril of Loving Money (6:6–10)
- C. The Proper Character and Motivation of a Man of God (6:11–16)
- D. The Proper Handling of Treasure (6:17–19)
- E. The Proper Handling of Truth (6:20, 21)

MISLEADINGS IN DOCTRINE AND LIVING

1 Paul, [A]an apostle of [B]Christ Jesus [C]according to
the commandment of [C]God our Savior, and of
[B]Christ Jesus, *who is* our [D]hope,
2 To [A]Timothy, [A]*my* true child in *the* faith: [B]Grace,
mercy *and* peace from God the Father and [C]Christ
Jesus our Lord.
3 As I urged you [a]upon my departure for [A]Macedo-
nia, [b]remain on at [B]Ephesus so that you may instruct
certain men not to [C]teach strange doctrines, 4 nor to
[a]pay attention to [A]myths and endless [B]genealogies,
which give rise to mere [C]speculation rather than
[D]*furthering* [b]the administration of God which is by
faith. 5 But the goal of our [a,A]instruction is love [B]from
a pure heart and a [C]good conscience and a sincere
[D]faith. 6 For some men, straying from these things,
have turned aside to [A]fruitless discussion, 7 [A]wanting
to be [B]teachers of the Law, even though they do not
understand either what they are saying or the matters about which they make confident assertions.
8 But we know that [A]the Law is good, if one uses
it lawfully, 9 realizing the fact that [A]law is not made
for a righteous person, but for those who are lawless
and [B]rebellious, for the [C]ungodly and sinners, for the
unholy and [D]profane, for those who kill their fathers

1:1 [A]2 Cor 1:1 [B]1 Tim 1:12 [C]Titus 1:3 [D]Col 1:27 1:2 [A]2 Tim 1:2 [B]Rom 1:7; 2 Tim 1:2; Titus 1:4 [C]1 Tim 1:12 1:3 [a]Lit *while going to* [b]Lit *to remain* [A]Rom 15:26 [B]Acts 18:19 [C]Rom 16:17; 2 Cor 11:4; Gal 1:6f; 1 Tim 6:3 1:4 [a]Or *occupy themselves with* [b]Lit *God's provision* [A]1 Tim 4:7; 2 Tim 4:4; Titus 1:14; 2 Pet 1:16 [B]Titus 3:9 [C]2 Tim 2:23 [D]Eph 3:2 1:5 [a]Lit *commandment* [A]1 Tim 1:18 [B]2 Tim 2:22 [C]1 Tim 1:19; 3:9; 2 Tim 1:3; 1 Pet 3:16, 21 [D]2 Tim 1:5 1:6 [A]Titus 1:10 1:7 [A]James 3:1 [B]Luke 2:46 1:8 [A]Rom 7:12, 16 1:9 [A]Gal 5:23 [B]Titus 1:6, 10 [C]1 Pet 4:18; Jude 15 [D]1 Tim 4:7; 6:20; Heb 12:16

1:1 apostle of Christ Jesus. *See notes on 2Co 12:11, 12*; cf. Ac 1:2; 2:42; Ro 1:1; Eph 2:20. **God our Savior.** A title unique to the Pastoral Epistles (1, 2Ti, Titus) that has its roots in the OT (Pss 18:46; 25:5; 27:9; Mic 7:7; Hab 3:18). God is by nature a saving God and the source of our salvation, which He planned from eternity past (*see note on 4:10*; cf. 2Th 2:13). **Christ Jesus ... our hope.** Christians have hope for the future because Christ purchased salvation for them on the cross in the past (Ro 5:1, 2), sanctifies them through His Spirit in the present (Gal 5:16–25), and will lead them to glory in the future (Col 1:27; 1Jn 3:2, 3).

1:2 Timothy. See Introduction: Title. **true child in *the* faith.** Only Timothy (2Ti 1:2; 2:1) and Titus (1:4) received this special expression of Paul's favor. "Child" emphasizes Paul's role as spiritual father to Timothy. "True" speaks of the genuineness of Timothy's faith (cf. 2Ti 1:5). Timothy was Paul's most cherished pupil, and protégé (1Co 4:17; Php 2:19–22). **Grace, mercy *and* peace.** Paul's familiar greeting that appears in all his epistles (*see note on Ro 1:7*), but with the addition here of "mercy" (cf. 2Ti 1:2). Mercy frees believers from the misery that accompanies the consequences of sin.

1:3–11 In his opening charge to halt the spread of false teaching in the church at Ephesus, Paul characterizes the false teachers and their doctrine.

1:3 my departure for Macedonia, remain on at Ephesus. Before Paul left Ephesus, he likely began the confrontation with the expulsion of Hymenaeus and Alexander (v. 20), then assigned Timothy to stay on and complete what he had begun. **instruct.** This refers to a military command—it demands that a subordinate obey an order from a superior (cf. 2Ti 4:1). **certain men.** The false teachers were few in number, yet had a wide influence. Several reasons point toward these men being elders in the church at Ephesus and in the churches in the surrounding region: 1) they presumed to be teachers (v. 7), a role reserved for elders (3:2; 5:17). 2) Paul himself had to excommunicate Hymenaeus and Alexander, which implies they occupied the highest pastoral positions. 3) Paul detailed the qualifications of an overseer (3:1–7), implying that unqualified men, who needed to be replaced by qualified ones, were occupying those roles. 4) Paul stressed that sinning overseers were to be publicly disciplined (5:19–22). **not to teach strange doctrines.** A compound word made up of two Gr. words that mean "of a different kind" and "to teach." The false teachers were teaching doctrine different from apostolic doctrine (cf. 6:3, 4; Ac 2:42; Gal 1:6, 7). This had to do with the gospel of salvation. Apparently they were teaching another gospel (*see notes on Gal 1:6–9*) and not the "glorious gospel of the blessed God" (v. 11).

1:4 myths and endless genealogies. Legends and fanciful stories manufactured from elements of Judaism (v. 7; cf. Titus 1:14), which probably dealt with allegorical or fictitious interpretations of OT genealogical lists. In reality, they were "doctrines of demons" (4:1), posing as God's truth (cf. 4:7).

1:5 our instruction. *See note on v. 3*, where the verb form "instruct" is used. The purpose of the instruction in vv. 3, 4 is the spiritual virtue defined in v. 5. Timothy was to deliver this charge to the church. The goal of preaching the truth and warning of error is to call men to true salvation in Christ, which produces a love for God from a purified heart (2Ti 2:22; 1Pe 1:22), a cleansed conscience (Heb 9:22; 10:14), and genuine faith (Heb 10:22). **love.** This is the love of choice and the will, characterized by self-denial and self-sacrifice for the benefit of others, and it is the mark of a true Christian (Jn 13:35; Ro 13:10; 1Jn 4:7, 8; *see notes on 1Co 13:1–7*). In contrast, false doctrine produces only conflict and "speculation" (v. 4; 6:3–5). **good conscience.** Cf. v. 19; 3:9; 4:2; *see note on 2Co 1:12*. The Gr. word for "good" refers to that which is perfect and produces pleasure and satisfaction. God created man with a "conscience" as his self-judging faculty. Because God has written His law on man's heart (*see note on Ro 2:15*), man knows the basic standard of right and wrong. When he violates that standard, his conscience produces guilt, which acts as the mind's security system that produces fear, guilt, shame, and doubt as warnings of threats to the soul's well-being (cf. Jn 8:9; 1Co 8:7, 10, 12; Titus 1:15; Heb 10:22). On the other hand, when a believer does God's will, he enjoys the affirmation, assurance, peace, and joy of a good conscience (cf. Ac 23:1; 24:16; 2Ti 1:3; Heb 13:18; 1Pe 3:16, 21).

1:6 fruitless discussion. Cf. Titus 1:10. Refers to speech that is aimless and has no logical end. It is essentially irrelevant and will not accomplish anything spiritual or edifying to believers. False doctrine leads nowhere, but to the deadening end of human speculation and demonic deception (cf. 6:3–5).

1:7 wanting to be teachers. The false teachers wanted the kind of prestige enjoyed by Jewish rabbis; but they were not concerned at all about truly learning the law and teaching it to others (cf. 6:4; Mt 23:5–7). Instead, they imposed on believers in Ephesus a legalistic heresy that offered salvation by works.

1:7, 8 the Law. The Mosaic law is in view here, not just law in general. These were Jewish would-be teachers who wanted to impose circumcision and the keeping of Mosaic ceremonies on the church as necessary for salvation. They plagued the early church (*see notes on Gal 3–5; Php 3:1–8*).

1:8 the Law is good. The Gr. word for "good" can be translated "useful." The law is good or useful because it reflects God's holy will and righteous standard (Ps 19:7; Ro 7:12), which accomplishes its purpose in showing sinners their sin (Ro 3:19) and their need for a Savior (Gal 3:24). The law forces people to recognize that they are guilty of disobeying God's commands, and it thereby condemns every person and sentences them to hell (*see notes on Ro 3:19, 20*).

1:9, 10 kill their fathers ... perjurers. These sins are violations of the second half of the Ten Commandments—those dealing with relationships among people. These specific sins undoubtedly characterized the false teachers, since they are characteristic behaviors related to false doctrine (v. 10). Killing of "fathers" and "mothers" is a violation of the fifth commandment (Ex 20:12; cf. 21:15–17), which forbids everything from dishonor to murder. Murder is in violation of the sixth commandment (Ex 20:13). "Immoral men" and "homosexuals" violate the seventh commandment (Ex 20:14), which prohibits sexual activity outside the marriage bed. Because the theft of children was commonplace in Paul's day, he mentions "kidnappers" in connection with the eighth commandment (Ex 20:15), which prohibits stealing. Finally, "liars" and "perjurers" are violators of the ninth commandment (Ex 20:16).

1:9 not made for a righteous person. Those who think they are righteous will never be saved (Lk 5:32) because they do not understand the true purpose of the law. The false teachers, with their works system of personally achieved self-righteousness (in their own minds), had shown clearly that they misunderstood the law completely. It was not a means to self-righteousness, but a means to self-condemnation, sin, conviction, repentance, and pleading to God for mercy (v. 15).

or mothers, for murderers 10 [a]and [b,A]immoral men
[a]and [B]homosexuals [a]and [C]kidnappers [a]and [D]liars [a]and
[E]perjurers, and whatever else is contrary to [F]sound
teaching, 11 according to [A]the glorious gospel of [B]the
blessed God, with which I have been [C]entrusted.
12 I thank [A]Christ Jesus our Lord, who has
[B]strengthened me, because He considered me
faithful, [C]putting me into service, 13 even though
I was formerly a blasphemer and a [A]persecutor
and a violent aggressor. Yet I was [B]shown mercy
because [C]I acted ignorantly in unbelief; 14 and the
[A]grace of our Lord was more than abundant, with
the [B]faith and love which are *found* in Christ Jesus.
15 [A]It is a trustworthy statement, deserving full acceptance, that [B]Christ Jesus came into the world to
[C]save sinners, among whom [D]I am foremost *of all.*
16 Yet for this reason I [A]found mercy, so that in me
as the foremost, Jesus Christ might [B]demonstrate
His perfect patience as an example for those [a]who
would believe in Him for eternal life. 17 Now to the
[A]King [a]eternal, [B]immortal, [C]invisible, the [D]only God,
[E]*be* honor and glory [b]forever and ever. Amen.
18 This [A]command I entrust to you, Timothy, [B]*my*
[a]son, in accordance with the [C]prophecies previously
made concerning you, that by them you [D]fight the
good fight, 19 keeping [A]faith and a good conscience,
which some have rejected and suffered shipwreck in
regard to [a,B]their faith. 20 [a]Among these are [A]Hyme-
naeus and [B]Alexander, whom I have [C]handed over to
Satan, so that they will be [D]taught not to blaspheme.

1:10 [a]Lit *for* [b]Or *fornicators* [A]1 Cor 6:9 [B]Lev 18:22 [C]Ex 21:16; Rev 18:13 [D]Rev 21:8, 27; 22:15 [E]Matt 5:33 [F]1 Tim 4:6; 6:3; 2 Tim 4:3; Titus 1:9, 13; 2:1, 2 1:11 [A]2 Cor 4:4 [B]1 Tim 6:15 [C]Gal 2:7 1:12 [A]Gal 3:26 [B]Acts 9:22; Phil 4:13; 2 Tim 4:17 [C]Acts 9:15 1:13 [A]Acts 8:3 [B]1 Cor 7:25 [C]Acts 26:9 1:14 [A]Rom 5:20; 1 Cor 3:10; 2 Cor 4:15; Gal 1:13-16 [B]1 Thess 1:3; 1 Tim 2:15; 4:12; 6:11; 2 Tim 1:13; 2:22; Titus 2:2 1:15 [A]1 Tim 3:1; 4:9; 2 Tim 2:11; Titus 3:8 [B]Mark 2:17; Luke 15:2ff; 19:10 [C]Rom 11:14 [D]1 Cor 15:9; Eph 3:8 1:16 [a]Or *destined to* [A]1 Cor 7:25; 1 Tim 1:13 [B]Eph 2:7 1:17 [a]Lit *of the ages* [b]Lit *to the ages of the ages* [A]Rev 15:3 [B]1 Tim 6:16 [C]Col 1:15 [D]John 5:44; 1 Tim 6:15; Jude 25 [E]Rom 2:7, 10; 11:36; Heb 2:7 1:18 [a]Or *child* [A]1 Tim 1:5 [B]1 Tim 1:2 [C]1 Tim 4:14 [D]2 Cor 10:4; 1 Tim 6:12; 2 Tim 2:3f; 4:7 1:19 [a]Lit *the* [A]1 Tim 1:5 [B]1 Tim 6:12, 21; 2 Tim 2:18 1:20 [a]Lit *Of* [A]2 Tim 2:17 [B]2 Tim 4:14 [C]1 Cor 5:5 [D]1 Cor 11:32; Heb 12:5ff

See notes on Lk 18:9–14; Ro 5:20; Gal 3:10–13, 19. **lawless … profane.** These first 6 characteristics, expressed in 3 couplets, delineate sins from the first half of the Ten Commandments, which deal with a person's relationship to God. "Lawless" describes those who have no commitment to any law or standard, which makes such people "rebellious." Those who are "ungodly" have no regard for anything sacred, which means they are "sinners" because they disregard God's law. "Unholy" people are indifferent to what is right, which leads them to be the "profane," who step on or trample what is sacred (cf. Heb 10:29).

1:10 sound teaching. A familiar emphasis in the Pastoral Epistles (cf. 2Ti 4:3; Titus 1:9; 2:1). "Sound" refers to that which is healthy and wholesome. It is the kind of teaching that produces spiritual life and growth, which implies that false doctrine produces spiritual disease and debilitation.

1:11 the glorious gospel. The gospel reveals God's glory; that is, the perfections of His person or His attributes, including His holiness (hatred of sin) and justice (demand of punishment for violations of His law) and grace (forgiveness of sin). Those particular attributes are key to any effective gospel presentation. **entrusted.** This Gr. word refers to committing something of value to another. God entrusted Paul with the communication and guardianship of His revealed truth. Cf. 2:7; 6:20, 21; Ro 15:15, 16; 1Co 4:1, 2; 9:17; 2Co 5:18–20; Gal 2:7; Col 1:25; 1Th 2:4.

1:12–17 Paul's testimony of his own salvation in these verses provides a contrast between his proper understanding of the law and the misconceptions of the false teachers, and between the glory of the true gospel and the emptiness of false doctrine.

1:12 considered me faithful. God's sovereign purpose for Paul and for all believers works through personal faith. Until Paul was turned by the Holy Spirit from self-righteous works (see Php 3:4–7) to faith alone in Christ, he could not be used by God. He was in the same condition as the useless false teachers (vv. 6, 7).

1:13 a blasphemer and a persecutor and a violent aggressor. This verse indicates that experience of Paul when he saw himself, in the light of God's law, for who he really was (*see notes on Ro 7:7–12*). A "blasphemer" speaks evil of and slanders God. Paul violated the first half of the Ten Commandments through his overt attacks against Christ (cf. Ac 9:4, 5; 22:7, 8; 26:9, 14, 15). As a "persecutor" and a "violent aggressor," Paul violated the second half through his attacks on believers. Cf. note on v. 20. **I acted ignorantly in unbelief.** Paul was neither a Jewish apostate nor a Pharisee who clearly understood Jesus' teaching and still rejected Him. He was a zealous, fastidious Jew trying to earn his salvation, thus lost and damned (*see notes on Php 3:4–7*). His plea of ignorance was not a claim to innocence nor an excuse denying his guilt. It was simply a statement indicating that he did not understand the truth of Christ's gospel and was honestly trying to protect his religion. His willing repentance when confronted by Christ (cf. Ro 7:9; Php 3:8, 9) is evidence that he had not understood the ramifications of his actions—he truly thought he was doing God a service (Ac 26:9).

1:14 grace. God's loving forgiveness, by which He grants salvation apart from any merit on the part of those He saves (*see notes on Ro 3:24; Gal 1:6*). **faith and love.** Attitudes frequently linked with salvation in the NT (cf. Eph 1:15; 3:17; Col 1:4, 23). They are gifts of God's grace in Christ.

1:15 It is a trustworthy statement. A phrase unique to the Pastoral Epistles (cf. 3:1; 4:9; 2Ti 2:11; Titus 3:8), which announces a statement summarizing key doctrines. The phrase "deserving full acceptance" gives the statement added emphasis. Apparently, these sayings were well known in the churches, as concise expressions of cardinal gospel truth. **to save sinners.** This faithful saying was based on the statements of Jesus recorded in Mt 9:13; Lk 19:10. **I am foremost *of all*.** Lit. "first," in rank. Few could be considered a worse sinner than someone who blasphemed God and persecuted His church (*see note on Eph 3:8*). Paul's attitude toward himself dramatically changed (cf. Php 3:7–9; *see notes on Rom 7:7–12*).

1:16 for this reason. Paul was saved so that God could display to all His gracious and merciful patience with the most wretched sinners. **an example.** Paul was living proof that God could save any sinner, no matter how great a one he might be. The account of Paul's conversion has been instrumental in the salvation of many. Paul's testimony is repeated 6 other times in the NT (Ac 9, 22, 26; Gal 1, 2; Php 3:1–14).

1:17 God receives all the praise for sovereignly saving Paul. This is one of the many doxologies Paul wrote (cf. Ro 11:33–36).

1:18 Timothy. See Introduction: Title. **prophecies previously made concerning you.** The Gr. word for "previously made" lit. means "leading the way to," implying that a series of prophecies had been given about Timothy in connection with his receiving his spiritual gift (*see note on 4:14*). These prophecies specifically and supernaturally called Timothy into God's service. **fight the good fight.** Paul urged Timothy to fight the battle against the enemies of Christ and the gospel. Cf. 2Co 10:3–5; 2Ti 2:3, 4; 4:7.

1:19 faith … faith. The first is subjective and means continuing to believe the truth. The second is objective, referring to the content of the Christian gospel. **a good conscience.** *See note on v. 5.* **shipwreck.** A good conscience serves as the rudder that steers the believer through the rocks and reefs of sin and error. The false teachers ignored their consciences and the truth, and as a result, suffered shipwreck of the Christian faith (the true doctrine of the gospel), which implies severe spiritual catastrophe. This does not imply loss of salvation of a true believer (*see notes on Ro 8:31–39*), but likely indicates the tragic loss that comes to the apostate. They had been in the church, heard the gospel, and rejected it in favor of the false doctrine defined in vv. 3–7. Apostasy is a turning away from the gospel, having once known it. *See notes on Heb 2:3, 4; 3:12–19; 6:1–8; 10:26–31.*

1:20 Hymenaeus and Alexander. Hymenaeus is mentioned in 2Ti 2:17 in connection with Philetus, another false teacher. Alexander may be the opponent of the faith referred to in 2Ti 4:14, 15. Nothing else is known about these two men (*see note on v. 3*). **I have handed over to Satan.** Paul put both men out of the church, thus ending their influence and removing them from the protection and insulation of God's people. They were no longer in the environment of God's blessing but under Satan's control. In some instances God has turned believers over to Satan for

A CALL TO PRAYER

2 First of all, then, I urge that [A]entreaties *and*
prayers, petitions *and* thanksgivings, be made
on behalf of all men, 2 [A]for kings and all who are in
[a]authority, so that we may lead a tranquil and quiet
life in all godliness and [b]dignity. 3 This is good and
acceptable in the sight of [A]God our Savior, 4 [A]who
desires all men to be [B]saved and to [C]come to the
[a]knowledge of the truth. 5 For there is [A]one God, *and*
[B]one mediator also between God and men, *the* [C]man
Christ Jesus, 6 who [A]gave Himself as a ransom for
all, the [B]testimony [a]*given* at [b,C]the proper time. 7 [A]For
this I was appointed a [a]preacher and [B]an apostle ([C]I
am telling the truth, I am not lying) as a teacher of
[D]the Gentiles in faith and truth.
8 Therefore [A]I want the men [B]in every place to
pray, [C]lifting up [D]holy hands, without wrath and
dissension.

2:1 [A]Eph 6:18 2:2 [a]Or *a high position* [b]Or *seriousness* [A]Ezra 6:10; Rom 13:1 2:3 [A]Luke 1:47; 1 Tim 1:1; 4:10 2:4 [a]Or *recognition* [A]Ezek 18:23, 32; John 3:17; 1 Tim 4:10; Titus 2:11; 2 Pet 3:9 [B]Rom 11:14 [C]2 Tim 2:25; 3:7; Titus 1:1; Heb 10:26 2:5 [A]Rom 3:30; 10:12; 1 Cor 8:4 [B]1 Cor 8:6; Gal 3:20 [C]Matt 1:1; Rom 1:3 2:6 [a]Or *to be given* [b]Lit *its own times* [A]Matt 20:28; Gal 1:4 [B]1 Cor 1:6 [C]Mark 1:15; Gal 4:4; 1 Tim 6:15; Titus 1:3 2:7 [a]Or *herald* [A]Eph 3:8; 1 Tim 1:11; 2 Tim 1:11 [B]1 Cor 9:1 [C]Rom 9:1 [D]Acts 9:15 2:8 [A]Phil 1:12; 1 Tim 5:14; Titus 3:8 [B]John 4:21; 1 Cor 1:2; 2 Cor 2:14; 1 Thess 1:8 [C]Ps 63:4; Luke 24:50 [D]Ps 24:4; James 4:8

positive purposes, such as revealing the genuineness of saving faith, keeping them humble and dependent on Him, enabling them to strengthen others, or offering God praise (cf. Job. 1:1–22; Mt 4:1–11; Lk 22:31–33; 2Co 12:1–10; Rev 7:9–15). God hands some people over to Satan for judgment, such as King Saul (1Sa 16:12–16; 28:4–20), Judas (Jn 13:27), and the sinning member in the Corinthian church (*see notes on 1Co 5:1–5*). **will be taught not to blaspheme.** *See note on v. 13.* Paul learned not to blaspheme when confronted by the true understanding of the law and the gospel. That was what those men needed. God, the inspired text seems to indicate, would teach them and show them grace as He had Paul. But that evangelistic work could not go on at the expense of the purity of the church.

2:1–8 The Ephesian church had evidently stopped praying for the lost, since Paul urged Timothy to make it a priority again. The Judaistic false teachers in Ephesus, by a perverted gospel and the teaching that salvation was only for Jews and Gentile proselytes to Judaism, would have certainly restricted evangelistic praying. Religious exclusivism (salvation only for the elite) would preclude the need for prayer for the lost.

2:1 entreaties. The Gr. word is from a root that means "to lack," "to be deprived," or "to be without." Thus this kind of prayer occurs because of a need. The lost have a great need for salvation, and believers should always be asking God to meet that need. **petitions.** This word comes from a root meaning "to fall in with someone," or "to draw near so as to speak intimately." The verb from which this word derives is used of Christ's and the Spirit's intercession for believers (Ro 8:26; Heb 7:25). Paul's desire is for the Ephesian Christians to have compassion for the lost, to understand the depths of their pain and misery, and to come intimately to God pleading for their salvation. *See notes on Titus 3:3, 4.* **all men.** The lost in general, not the elect only. God's decree of election is secret—believers have no way of knowing who is elect until they respond. The scope of God's evangelistic efforts is broader than election (Mt 22:14; Jn 17:21, 23; *see note on v. 4*).

2:2 kings and all who are in authority. Because so many powerful and influential political rulers are hostile to God, they are often the targets of bitterness and animosity. But Paul urges believers to pray that these leaders might repent of their sins and embrace the gospel, which meant that the Ephesians were even to pray for the salvation of the Roman emperor, Nero, a cruel and vicious blasphemer and persecutor of the faith. **a tranquil and quiet life.** "Quiet" refers to the absence of external disturbances; "tranquil" refers to the absence of internal ones. While it remains uncompromising in its commitment to the truth, the church is not to agitate or disrupt the national life. When it manifests love and goodness to all and prays passionately for the lost, including rulers, the church may experience a certain amount of religious freedom. Persecution should only be the result of righteous living, not civil disobedience (*see notes on Titus 3:1–4; 1Pe 2:13–23*). **godliness and dignity.** "Godliness" is a key word in this letter (3:16; 4:7, 8; 6:3, 5, 6, 11; cf. 2Ti 3:5; Titus 1:1), indicating that there needed to be a call back to holy living, which had been negatively affected by the false doctrine. Godliness refers to having the proper attitude and conduct before God in everything; "dignity" can be translated "moral earnestness," and refers to holy behavior before men.

2:3 God our Savior. *See note on 1:1.*

2:4 desires all men to be saved. The Gr. word for "desires" is not that which normally expresses God's will of decree (His eternal purpose), but God's will of desire. There is a distinction between God's desire and His eternal saving purpose, which must transcend His desires. God does not want men to sin. He hates sin with all His being (Pss 5:4; 45:7); thus, He hates its consequences—eternal wickedness in hell. God does not want people to remain wicked forever in eternal remorse and hatred of Himself. Yet, God, for His own glory, and to manifest that glory in wrath, chose to endure "vessels ... prepared for destruction" for the supreme fulfillment of His will (Ro 9:22). In His eternal purpose, He chose only the elect out of the world (Jn 17:6) and passed over the rest, leaving them to the consequences of their sin, unbelief, and rejection of Christ (cf. Ro 1:18–32). Ultimately, God's choices are determined by His sovereign, eternal purpose, not His desires. *See note on 2Pe 3:9.* **the knowledge of the truth.** Meaning "to be saved." *See note on 2Ti 3:7.*

2:5 there is one God. There is no other way of salvation (Ac 4:12); hence, there is the need to pray for the lost to come to know the one true God (cf. Dt 4:35, 39; 6:4; Is 43:10; 44:6; 45:5, 6, 21, 22; 46:9; 1Co 8:4, 6). **mediator.** This refers to someone who intervenes between two parties to resolve a conflict or ratify a covenant. Jesus Christ is the only "mediator" who can restore peace between God and sinners (Heb 8:6; 9:15; 12:24). ***the* man Christ Jesus.** The absence of the article before "man" in the Gr. suggests the translation, "Christ Jesus, Himself a man." Only the perfect God-Man could bring God and man together. Cf. Job 9:32, 33.

2:6 a ransom. This describes the result of Christ's substitutionary death for believers, which He did voluntarily (Jn 10:17, 18) and reminds one of Christ's own statement in Mt 20:28, "a ransom for many." The "all" is qualified by the "many." Not all will be ransomed (though His death would be sufficient), but only the many who believe by the work of the Holy Spirit and for whom the actual atonement was made. *See note on 2Pe 3:9.* Christ did not pay a ransom only; He became the object of God's just wrath in the believer's place—He died his death and bore his sin (cf. 2Co 5:21; 1Pe 2:24). **for all.** This should be taken in two senses: 1) there are temporal benefits of the atonement that accrue to all people universally (*see note on 4:10*), and 2) Christ's death was sufficient to cover the sins of all people. Yet the substitutionary aspect of His death is applied to the elect alone (*see above and notes on 2Co 5:14–21*). Christ's death is therefore unlimited in its sufficiency, but limited in its application. Because Christ's expiation of sin is indivisible, inexhaustible, and sufficient to cover the guilt of all the sins that will ever be committed, God can clearly offer it to all. Yet only the elect will respond and be saved, according to His eternal purpose (cf. Jn 17:12). **at the proper time.** At the appropriate time in God's redemptive plan (*see note on Gal 4:4*).

2:7 For this. Paul's divine commission was based on the truths delineated in vv. 3–6. **preacher.** The Gr. word derives from the verb that means "to herald," "to proclaim," or "to speak publicly." Paul was a public herald proclaiming the gospel of Christ. **apostle.** *See note on 1:1.* **I am telling the truth ... not lying.** Paul's emphatic outburst of his apostolic authority and integrity is to emphasize that he was a teacher of the Gentiles. **teacher of the Gentiles.** The distinctive feature of Paul's apostolic appointment, which demonstrates the universal scope of the gospel. Paul's need to make this distinction suggests he was dealing with some form of Jewish exclusivism that had crippled the Ephesians' interest in praying for Gentiles to be saved.

2:8 men. The Gr. word for "men" as opposed to women. God intends for men to be the leaders when the church meets for corporate worship. When prayer for the lost is offered during those times, the men are to lead it. **every place.** Paul's reference to the official assembly of the church (cf. 1Co 1:2; 2Co 2:14; 1Th 1:8). **lifting up holy hands.** Paul is not emphasizing a specific posture necessary for prayer, but a prerequisite for effective prayer (cf. Ps 66:18). Though this posture is described in the OT (1Ki 8:22; Pss 28:2; 63:4; 134:2), so are many others. The Gr. word for "holy" means "unpolluted" or "unstained by evil." "Hands" symbolize the activities of life; thus "holy hands" represent a holy life. This basis of effective prayer is a righteous life (Jas 5:16). **without wrath and**

WOMEN INSTRUCTED

9 Likewise, *I want* [A]women to adorn themselves
with proper clothing, [a]modestly and discreetly, not
with braided hair and gold or pearls or costly garments, 10 but rather by means of good works, as is
proper for women making a claim to godliness. 11 [A]A
woman must quietly receive instruction with entire submissiveness. 12 [A]But I do not allow a woman
to teach or exercise authority over a man, but to
remain quiet. 13 [A]For it was Adam who was first
[a]created, *and* then Eve. 14 And *it was* not Adam *who*
was deceived, but [A]the woman being deceived, [a]fell
into transgression. 15 But *women* will be [a]preserved
through the bearing of children if they continue
in [A]faith and love and sanctity with [b]self-restraint.

OVERSEERS AND DEACONS

3 [A]It is a trustworthy statement: if any man aspires
to the [B]office of [a]overseer, it is a fine work he
desires *to do.* 2 [a,A]An overseer, then, must be above
reproach, [B]the husband of one wife, [C]temperate,
prudent, respectable, [D]hospitable, [E]able to teach,

2:9 [a]Lit *with modesty* [A]1 Pet 3:3 2:11 [A]1 Cor 14:34; Titus 2:5 2:12 [A]1 Cor 14:34; Titus 2:5 2:13 [a]Or *formed* [A]Gen 2:7, 22; 3:16; 1 Cor 11:8ff 2:14 [a]Lit *has come* [A]Gen 3:6, 13; 2 Cor 11:3 2:15 [a]Lit *saved* [b]Or *discretion* [A]1 Tim 1:14 3:1 [a]Or *bishop* [A]1 Tim 1:15 [B]Acts 20:28; Phil 1:1 3:2 [a]Lit *The* [A]1 Tim 3:2-4; Titus 1:6-8 [B]Luke 2:36f; 1 Tim 5:9; Titus 1:6 [C]1 Tim 3:8, 11; Titus 2:2 [D]Rom 12:13; Titus 1:8; Heb 13:2; 1 Pet 4:9 [E]2 Tim 2:24

dissension. "Wrath" and righteousness are mutually exclusive (Jas 1:20; cf. Lk 9:52–56). "Dissension" refers to a hesitant reluctance to be committed to prayer.

2:9–15 Women in the church were living impure and self-centered lives (cf. 5:6, 11–15; 2Ti 3:6), and that practice carried over into the worship service, where they became distractions. Because of the centrality of worship in the life of the church, Paul calls on Timothy to confront the problem.

2:9 adorn ... proper clothing. The Gr. word for "adorn" means "to arrange," "to put in order," or "to make ready." A woman is to arrange herself appropriately for the worship service, which includes wearing decent clothing which reflects a properly adorned chaste heart. **modestly and discreetly.** "Modestly" refers to modesty mixed with humility, which carries the underlying idea of shame. It can also refer to a rejection of anything dishonorable to God, or refer to grief over sin. "Discreetly" basically refers to self-control over sexual passions. Godly women hate sin and control their passions so as not to lead another into sin. *See notes on 1Pe 3:3, 4.* **braided hair and gold or pearls or costly garments.** Specific practices that were causing distraction and discord in the church. Women in the first century often wove "gold or pearls" or other jewelry into their hair styles ("braided hair") to call attention to themselves and their wealth or beauty. The same was true of those women who wore "costly garments." By doing so they would draw attention to themselves and away from the Lord, likely causing the poorer women to be envious. Paul's point was to forbid the preoccupation of certain women with flaunting their wealth and distracting people from worshiping the Lord.

2:10 Those women who have publicly committed themselves to pursuing godliness should support that claim not only in their demeanor, wardrobe, and appearance, but by being clothed with righteous behavior.

2:11 A woman must ... receive instruction. Women are not to be the public teachers when the church assembles, but neither are they to be shut out of the learning process. The form of the Gr. verb translated "receive instruction" is an imperative: Paul is commanding that women be taught in the church. That was a novel concept, since neither first-century Judaism nor Greek culture held women in high esteem. Some of the women in Ephesus probably overreacted to the cultural denigration they had typically suffered and took advantage of their opportunity in the church by seeking a dominant role in leadership. **quietly ... submissiveness.** "Quietly" and "submissiveness" ("to line up under") were to characterize the role of a woman as a learner in the context of the church assembly. Paul explains his meaning in v. 12: women are to be silent by not teaching, and they are to demonstrate submission by not usurping the authority of the pastors or elders.

2:12 I do not allow. The Gr. word for "allow" is used in the NT to refer to allowing someone to do what he desires. Paul may have been addressing a real situation in which several women in Ephesus desired to be public preachers. **to teach.** Paul used a verbal form of this Gr. word that indicates a condition or process and is better translated "to be a teacher." This was an important, official function in the church (*see Ac 13:1; 1Co 12:28; Eph 4:11*). Thus Paul is forbidding women from filling the office and role of the pastor or teacher. He is not prohibiting them from teaching in other appropriate conditions and circumstances (cf. Ac 18:26; Titus 2:3, 4). **exercise authority over.** Paul forbids women from exercising any type of authority over men in the church assembly, since the elders are those who rule (5:17). They are all to be men (as is clear from the requirements in 3:2, 5). **remain quiet.** *See note on v. 11.*

2:13, 14 A woman's subordinate role did not result after the Fall as a cultural, chauvinistic corruption of God's perfect design; rather, God established her role as part of His original creation (v. 13). God made woman after man to be his suitable helper (*see note on Ge 2:18*; cf. 1Co 11:8, 9). The Fall actually corroborates God's divine plan of creation (*see notes on Ge 3:1–7*). By nature Eve was not suited to assume the position of ultimate responsibility. By leaving Adam's protection and usurping his headship, she was vulnerable and fell, thus confirming how important it was for her to stay under the protection and leadership of her husband (*see notes on 5:11, 12; 2Ti 3:6, 7*). Adam then violated his leadership role, followed Eve in her sin, and plunged the human race into sinfulness—all connected with violating God's planned roles for the sexes. Ultimately, the responsibility for the Fall still rests with Adam, since he chose to disobey God apart from being deceived (Ro 5:12–21; 1Co 15:21, 22).

2:15 *women.* That Paul does not have Eve in mind here is clear because the verb translated "will be preserved" is future, and he also uses the plural pronoun "they." He is talking about women after Eve. **will be preserved.** The Gr. word can also mean "to rescue," "to preserve safe and unharmed," "to heal," or "to deliver from." It appears several times in the NT without reference to spiritual salvation (cf. Mt 8:25; 9:21, 22; 24:22; 27:40, 42, 49; 2Ti 4:18). Paul is not advocating that women are eternally saved from sin through childbearing or that they maintain their salvation by having babies, both of which would be clear contradictions of the NT teaching of salvation by grace alone through faith alone (Ro 3:19, 20) sustained forever (Ro 8:31–39). Paul is teaching that even though a woman bears the stigma of being the initial instrument who led the race into sin, it is women through childbearing who may be preserved or freed from that stigma by raising a generation of godly children (cf. 5:10). **through the bearing of children.** Because mothers have a unique bond and intimacy with their children, and spend far more time with them than do fathers, they have far greater influence in their lives and thus a unique responsibility and opportunity for rearing godly children. While a woman may have led the human race into sin, women have the privilege of leading many out of sin to godliness. Paul is speaking in general terms; God does not want all women to be married (1Co 7:25–40), let alone bear children. **if they continue in faith and love and sanctity with self-restraint.** The godly appearance, demeanor, and behavior commanded of believing women in the church (vv. 9–12) is motivated by the promise of deliverance from any inferior status and the joy of raising godly children.

3:1–13 Paul's purpose in writing this letter was to instruct Timothy regarding the church (vv. 14, 15). Of primary importance to any church is that its leaders be qualified to teach and set the example for the rest. These verses delineate those qualifications for pastors and deacons (*see also notes on Titus 1:5–9*).

3:1 It is a trustworthy statement: *See note on 1:15.* **aspires ... desires.** Two different Gr. words are used. The first means "to reach out after." It describes external action, not internal motive. The second means "a strong passion," and refers to an inward desire. Taken together, these two words aptly describe the type of man who belongs in the ministry—one who outwardly pursues it because he is driven by a strong internal desire. **overseer.** The word identifies the men who are responsible to lead the church (cf. 5:17; 1Th 5:12; Heb 13:7). In the NT the words "elder," "overseer," and "pastor" are used interchangeably to describe the same men (Ac 20:17, 28; Titus 1:5–9; 1Pe 5:1, 2). Pastors are responsible to lead (5:17), preach and teach (5:17), help the spiritually weak (1Th 5:12–14), care for the church (1Pe 5:1, 2), and ordain other leaders (4:14).

3:2 must. The use of this Gr. particle stresses emphatically that living a blameless life is absolutely necessary for church leaders. **above reproach.** Lit. "not able to be held" in a criminal

3 [A]not addicted to wine [a]or pugnacious, but gentle,
peaceable, [B]free from the love of money. 4 *He must*
be one who [A]manages his own household well, keeping his children under control with all dignity 5 (but
if a man does not know how to manage his own
household, how will he take care of [A]the church of
God?), 6 *and* not a new convert, so that he will not
become [A]conceited and fall into the [B]condemnation
[a]incurred by the devil. 7 And he must [A]have a good
reputation with [B]those outside *the church,* so that he
will not fall into reproach and [C]the snare of the devil.
8 [A]Deacons likewise *must be* men of dignity, not
[a]double-tongued, [b,B]or addicted to much wine [b,C]or
fond of sordid gain, 9 [A]*but* holding to the mystery of
the faith with a clear conscience. 10 [A]These men must
also first be tested; then let them serve as deacons if
they are beyond reproach. 11 [a]Women *must* likewise
be dignified, [A]not malicious gossips, but [B]temperate,

3:3 [a]Lit *not* [A]Titus 1:7 [B]1 Tim 3:8; 6:10; Titus 1:7; Heb 13:5 3:4 [A]1 Tim 3:12 3:5 [A]1 Cor 10:32; 1 Tim 3:15 3:6 [a]Lit *of the devil* [A]1 Tim 6:4; 2 Tim 3:4 [B]1 Tim 3:7 3:7 [A]2 Cor 8:21 [B]Mark 4:11 [C]1 Tim 6:9; 2 Tim 2:26 3:8 [a]Or *given to double-talk* [b]Lit *not* [A]Phil 1:1; 1 Tim 3:12 [B]1 Tim 5:23; Titus 2:3 [C]1 Tim 3:3; Titus 1:7; 1 Pet 5:2 3:9 [A]1 Tim 1:5, 19 3:10 [A]1 Tim 5:22 3:11 [a]I.e. either deacons' wives or deaconesses [A]2 Tim 3:3; Titus 2:3 [B]1 Tim 3:2

sense; there is no valid accusation of wrongdoing that can be made against him. No overt, flagrant sin can mar the life of one who must be an example for his people to follow (cf. v. 10; 4:16; 5:7; Ps 101:6; Php 3:17; 2Th 3:9; Heb 13:7; 1Pe 5:3). This is the overarching requirement for elders; the rest of the qualifications elaborate on what it means to be blameless. Titus 1:6, 7 uses another Gr. word to mean the same thing. **the husband of one wife.** Lit. in Gr. a "one-woman man." This says nothing about marriage or divorce (for comments on that, *see note on v. 4*). The issue is not the elder's marital status, but his moral and sexual purity. This qualification heads the list, because it is in this area that leaders are most prone to fail. Various interpretations of this qualification have been offered. Some see it as a prohibition against polygamy—an unnecessary injunction since polygamy was not common in Roman society and clearly forbidden by Scripture (Gen 2:24), the teaching of Jesus (Mt 19:5, 6; Mk 10:6–9), and Paul (Eph 5:31). A polygamist could not even have been a church member, let alone a church leader. Others see this requirement as barring those who remarried after the death of their wives. But, as already noted, the issue is sexual purity, not marital status. Further, the Bible encourages remarriage after widowhood (5:14; 1Co 7:39). Some believe that Paul here excludes divorced men from church leadership. That again ignores the fact that this qualification does not deal with marital status. Nor does the Bible prohibit all remarriage after divorce (*see notes on Mt 5:31, 32; 19:9; 1Co 7:15*). Finally, some think that this requirement excludes single men from church leadership. But if that were Paul's intent, he would have disqualified himself (1Co 7:8). A "one-woman man" is one totally devoted to his wife, maintaining singular devotion, affection, and sexual purity in both thought and deed. To violate this is to forfeit blamelessness and no longer be "above reproach" (Titus 1:6, 7). Cf. Pr 6:32, 33. **temperate.** The Gr. word lit. means "wineless," but is here used metaphorically to mean "alert," "watchful," "vigilant," or "clear-headed." Elders must be able to think clearly. **prudent.** A "prudent" man is disciplined, knows how to properly order his priorities, and is serious about spiritual matters. **respectable.** The Gr. word means "orderly." Elders must not lead chaotic lives; if they cannot order their own lives, how can they bring order to the church? **hospitable.** From a compound Gr. word meaning "love of strangers" (*see notes on Ro 12:13; Heb 13:2*; cf. 1Pe 4:9). As with all spiritual virtues, elders must set the example; their lives and homes are to be open so all can see their spiritual character. **able to teach.** Used only here and in 2Ti 2:24. The only qualification relating to an elder's giftedness and spiritual ability, and the only one that distinguishes elders from deacons. The preaching and teaching of God's Word is the overseer/pastor/elder's primary duty (4:6, 11, 13; 5:17; 2Ti 2:15, 24; Titus 2:1).

3:3 not addicted to wine. More than a mere prohibition against drunkenness (*see note on Eph 5:18*). An elder must not have a reputation as a drinker; his judgment must never be clouded by alcohol (cf. Pr 31:4, 5; 1Co 6:12). His lifestyle must be radically different from the world and lead others to holiness, not sin (Ro 14:21). *See note on 5:23.* **not ... pugnacious.** Lit. "not a giver of blows." Elders must react to difficult situations calmly and gently (2Ti 2:24, 25), and under no circumstances with physical violence. **gentle.** Considerate, genial, gracious, quick to pardon failure, and one who does not hold a grudge. **peaceable.** "Peaceful," "reluctant to fight"; one who does not promote disunity or disharmony. **free from the love of money.** Elders must be motivated by love for God and His people, not money (cf. Titus 1:7; 1Pe 5:2). A leader who is in the ministry for money reveals a heart set on the world, not the things of God (Mt 6:24; 1Jn 2:15). Covetousness characterizes false teachers (Titus 1:11; 2Pe 2:1–3, 14; Jude 11), but not Paul's ministry (Ac 20:33; 1Co 9:1–16; 2Co 11:9; 1Th 2:5).

3:4 who manages his own household well. The elder's homelife, like his personal life, must be exemplary. He must be one who "manages" (presides over, has authority over) "his own household" (everything connected with his home, not merely his wife and children) "well" (intrinsically good; excellently). Issues of divorce should be related to this matter. A divorced man gives no evidence of a well-managed home, but rather that divorce shows weakness in his spiritual leadership. If there has been a biblically permitted divorce, it must have been so far in the past as to have been overcome by a long pattern of solid family leadership and the rearing of godly children (v. 4; Titus 1:6). **under control.** A military term referring to soldiers ranked under one in authority. An elder's children must be believers (*see note on "believe" in Titus 1:6*), well-behaved, and respectful.

3:5 take care of the church of God? An elder must first prove in the intimacy and exposure of his own home his ability to lead others to salvation and sanctification. There he proves God has gifted him uniquely to spiritually set the example of virtue, to serve others, resolve conflicts, build unity, and maintain love. If he cannot do those essential things there, why would anyone assume he would be able to do them in the church?

3:6 not a new convert ... not become conceited. Putting a new convert into a leadership role would tempt him to pride. Elders, therefore, are to be drawn from the spiritually mature men of the congregation (*see notes on 5:22*). **fall into the condemnation incurred by the devil.** Satan's condemnation was due to pride over his position. It resulted in his fall from honor and authority (Is 14:12–14; Eze 28:11–19; cf. Pr 16:18). The same kind of fall and judgment could easily happen to a new and weak believer put in a position of spiritual leadership.

3:7 good reputation ... outside. A leader in the church must have an unimpeachable reputation in the unbelieving community, even though people there may disagree with his moral and theological stands. How can he make a spiritual impact on those who do not respect him? Cf. Mt 5:48; Php 2:15.

3:8 Deacons. From a word group meaning "to serve." Originally referring to menial tasks such as waiting on tables (*see notes on Ac 6:1–4*), "deacon" came to denote any service in the church. Deacons serve under the leadership of elders, helping them exercise oversight in the practical matters of church life. Scripture defines no official or specific responsibilities for deacons; they are to do whatever the elders assign them or whatever spiritual ministry is necessary. **men of dignity.** Serious in mind and character; not silly or flippant about important matters. **not double-tongued.** Deacons must not say one thing to some people and something else to others; their speech must not be hypocritical, but honest and consistent. **not ... addicted to much wine.** Not preoccupied with drink (*see note on v. 3*). **not ... fond of sordid gain.** Like elders (*see note on v. 3*), deacons must not abuse their office to make money. Such a qualification was especially important in the early church, where deacons routinely handled money, distributing it to those in need.

3:9 the mystery. *See notes on Mt 13:11; 1Co 2:7; Eph 3:4, 5.* Appearing frequently in Paul's writings (cf. Ro 11:25; 16:25; Eph 1:9; 3:9; 6:19; Col 2:2), the word "mystery" describes truth previously hidden, but now revealed, including Christ's incarnation (v. 16), Christ's indwelling of believers (Col 1:26, 27), the unity of Jews and Gentiles in the church (Eph 3:4–6), the gospel (Col 4:3), lawlessness (2Th 2:7), and the rapture of the church (1Co 15:51, 52). **a clear conscience.** *See note on 1:5.*

3:10 first be tested. The present tense of this verb indicates an ongoing evaluation of deacons' character and service by the church. **beyond reproach.** *See note on v. 2.*

3:11 Women. Paul likely here refers not to deacons' wives, but to the women who serve as deacons. The use of the word "likewise" (cf. v. 8) suggests a third group in addition to elders and deacons. Also, since Paul gave no requirements for elders' wives, there is no reason to assume these would be qualifications for deacons' wives. **dignified.** *See note on v. 8.* **not malicious gossips.** "Malicious

faithful in all things. 12 [A]Deacons must be [B]husbands
of *only* one wife, *and* [a,C]good managers of *their* children and their own households. 13 For those who
have served well as deacons [A]obtain for themselves
a [a]high standing and great confidence in the faith
that is in Christ Jesus.

14 I am writing these things to you, hoping to
come to you before long; 15 but [a]in case I am delayed,
I write so that you will know how [b]one ought to conduct himself in [A]the household of God, which is the
[B]church of [C]the living God, the [D]pillar and support
of the truth. 16 By common confession, great is [A]the
mystery of godliness:

> He who was [B]revealed in the flesh,
> Was [a,C]vindicated [b]in the Spirit,
> [D]Seen by angels,
> [E]Proclaimed among the nations,
> [F]Believed on in the world,
> [G]Taken up in glory.

APOSTASY

4 But [A]the Spirit explicitly says that [B]in later
times some will [a]fall away from the faith, paying attention to [C]deceitful spirits and [D]doctrines
of demons, 2 by means of the hypocrisy of liars
[A]seared in their own conscience as with a branding iron, 3 *men* who [A]forbid marriage *and advocate*
[B]abstaining from foods which [C]God has created to
be [D]gratefully shared in by those who believe and
know the truth. 4 For [A]everything created by God is
good, and nothing is to be rejected if it is [B]received

3:12 [a]Lit *managing well* [A]Phil 1:1; 1 Tim 3:8 [B]1 Tim 3:2 [C]1 Tim 3:4 3:13 [a]Lit *good* [A]Matt 25:21 3:15 [a]Lit *if I delay* [b]Or *you ought to conduct yourself* [A]1 Cor 3:16; 2 Cor 6:16; Eph 2:21f; 1 Pet 2:5; 4:17 [B]1 Tim 3:5 [C]Matt 16:16; 1 Tim 4:10 [D]Gal 2:9; 2 Tim 2:19 3:16 [a]Or *justified* [b]Or *by* [A]Rom 16:25 [B]John 1:14; 1 Pet 1:20; 1 John 3:5, 8 [C]Rom 3:4 [D]Luke 2:13; 24:4; 1 Pet 1:12 [E]Rom 16:26; 2 Cor 1:19; Col 1:23 [F]2 Thess 1:10 [G]Mark 16:19; Acts 1:9 4:1 [a]I.e. apostacize [A]John 16:13; Acts 20:23; 21:11; 1 Cor 2:10f [B]2 Thess 2:3ff; 2 Tim 3:1; 2 Pet 3:3; Jude 18 [C]1 John 4:6 [D]James 3:15 4:2 [A]Eph 4:19 4:3 [A]Heb 13:4 [B]Col 2:16, 23 [C]Gen 1:29; 9:3 [D]Rom 14:6; 1 Cor 10:30f; 1 Tim 4:4 4:4 [A]1 Cor 10:26 [B]Rom 14:6; 1 Cor 10:30f; 1 Tim 4:3

gossips" is the plural form of *diabolos*—a title frequently given to Satan (Mt 4:5, 8, 11; 13:39; Lk 4:3, 5, 6, 13; 8:12; 1Pe 5:8; 1Jn 3:8; Rev 2:10; 12:9, 12; 20:2, 10). The women who serve must not be slanderous and malicious in their speech. **temperate.** *See note on v. 2.* **faithful in all things.** Women servants in the church, like their male counterparts (*see note on v. 2*), must be absolutely trustworthy in all aspects of their lives and ministries.

3:12 husbands of *only* one wife. *See note on v. 2.* **good managers of *their* children … households.** *See note on v. 4.*

3:14–16 These verses mark a transition point between the positive instruction of the first 3 chapters and the warnings of the last 3. They reveal the heart of the church's mission (v. 15) and message (v. 16).

3:14, 15 hoping to come to you before long. The Gr. grammar suggests Paul's meaning is "These things I write, although I had hoped to come to you sooner." Delayed in Macedonia (see Introduction: Background and Setting), Paul sent Timothy this letter.

3:15 how one ought to conduct himself. The second half of this verse expresses the theme of this epistle—setting things right in the church. **household of God.** Believers are members of God's household (Gal 6:10; Eph 2:19; Heb 3:6; 1Pe 4:17) and must act accordingly. This is not a reference to any building, but to the people who make up the true church. **church of the living God.** The church is God's possession (Ac 20:28; Eph 1:14; Titus 2:14; 1Pe 2:9). The title "the living God" has a rich OT heritage (Dt 5:26; Jos 3:10; 1Sa 17:26, 36; 2Ki 19:4, 16; Pss 42:2; 84:2; Is 37:4, 17; Jer 10:10; 23:26; Da 6:20, 26; Hos 1:10). **pillar and support.** Paul's imagery may have referred to the magnificent temple of Diana (Artemis) in Ephesus, which was supported by 127 gold-plated marble pillars. The word translated "support" appears only here in the NT and *denotes the foundation on* which a building rests. The church upholds the truth of God's revealed Word. **the truth.** The content of the Christian faith recorded in Scripture and summed up in v. 16.

3:16 This verse contains part of an early church hymn, as its uniformity, rhythm, and parallelism indicate. Its 6 lines form a concise summary of the truth of the gospel. **mystery of godliness.** "Mystery" is that term used by Paul to indicate truth hidden in the OT age and revealed in the NT (*see note on v. 9*). "Godliness" refers to the truths of salvation and righteousness in Christ, which produce holiness in believers; namely, the manifestation of true and perfect righteousness in Jesus Christ. **He who was revealed.** This reference is clearly to Christ, who manifested the invisible God to mankind (Jn 1:1–4; 14:9; Col 1:15; Heb 1:3; 2Pe 1:16–18). **in the flesh.** Not sinful, fallen human nature here (cf. Ro 7:18, 25; 8:8; Gal 5:16, 17), but merely humanness (cf. Jn 1:14; Ro 1:3; 8:3; 9:5; 1Pe 3:18; 1Jn 4:2, 3; 2Jn 7). **vindicated in the Spirit.** "Vindicated" means "righteous," so that "spirit" may be written with lower case "s" indicating a declaration of Christ's sinless spiritual righteousness (Jn 8:46; 2Co 5:21; Heb 4:15; 5:9; 7:26; 1Pe 2:21, 22; 1Jn 2:1), or it could refer to His vindication by the Holy Spirit (Ro 1:4). **Seen by angels.** Both by fallen (*see notes on Col 2:15; 1Pe 3:18–20*) and elect (Mt 28:2; Lk 24:4–7; Ac 1:10, 11; Heb 1:6–9) angels. **Proclaimed among the nations.** Or, Gentiles. See Mt 24:14; 26:13; 28:19, 20; Mk 13:10; Ac 1:8. **Taken up in glory.** See Ac 1:9, 10; Php 2:8–11; Heb 1:3. Christ's ascension and exaltation showed that the Father was pleased with Him and accepted His work fully.

4:1–5 After already noting the presence of false teachers at Ephesus (1:3–7, 18–20), and countering some of their erroneous teaching with the positive instruction of chaps. 2, 3, Paul deals directly with the false teachers themselves in this passage, focusing on their origin and content.

4:1 the Spirit explicitly says. Paul repeats to Timothy the warning he had given many years earlier to the Ephesian elders (Ac 20:29, 30). The Holy Spirit through the Scriptures has repeatedly warned of the danger of apostasy (cf. Mt 24:4–12; Ac 20:29, 30; 2Th 2:3–12; Heb 3:12; 5:11–6:8; 10:26–31; 2Pe 3:3; 1Jn 2:18; Jude 18). **in later times.** The period from the first coming of Christ until His return (Ac 2:16, 17; Heb 1:1, 2; 9:26; 1Pe 1:20; 1Jn 2:18). Apostasy will exist throughout that period, reaching a climax shortly before Christ returns (cf. Mt 24:12). **fall away from the faith.** Those who fall prey to the false teachers will abandon the Christian faith. The Gr. word for "fall away" is the source of the Eng. word "apostatize," and refers to someone moving away from an original position. These are professing or nominal Christians who associate with those who truly believe the gospel, but defect after believing lies and deception, thus revealing their true nature as unconverted. *See notes on 1Jn 2:19; Jude 24.* **deceitful spirits.** Those demonic spirits, either directly or through false teachers, who have wandered away from the truth and lead others to do the same. The most defining word to describe the entire operation of Satan and his demons is "deception" (cf. Jn 8:44; 1Jn 4:1–6). **doctrines of demons.** Not teaching about demons, but false teaching that originates from them. To sit under such teaching is to hear lies from the demonic realm (Eph 6:12; Jas 3:15; 2Jn 7–11). The influence of demons will reach its peak during the Tribulation (2Th 2:9; Rev 9:2–11; 16:14; 20:2, 3, 8, 10). Satan and demons constantly work the deceptions that corrupt and pervert God's Word.

4:2 hypocrisy of liars. Lit. "hypocritical lie-speakers." These are the human false teachers who propagate demon doctrine (cf. 1Jn 4:1). **seared.** A medical term referring to cauterization. False teachers can teach their hypocritical lies because their consciences have been desensitized (cf. Eph 4:19), as if all the nerves that make them feel had been destroyed and turned into scar tissue by the burning of demonic deception. **conscience.** *See note on 1:5.*

4:3 forbid marriage … abstaining from foods. A sample of the false teaching at Ephesus. Typically, it contained elements of truth, since Scripture commends both singleness (1Co 7:25–35) and fasting (Mt 6:16, 17; 9:14, 15). The deception came in making such human works a prerequisite for salvation—a distinguishing mark of all false religion. This ascetic teaching was probably influenced both by the Jewish sect known as the Essenes, and contemporary Greek thought (which viewed matter as evil and spirit as good). Paul addressed this asceticism in Col 2:21–23 (*see notes there*). Neither celibacy nor any form of diet saves or sanctifies.

4:4 everything created by God is good. The false teachers' asceticism contradicted Scripture, which teaches that since God created both marriage and food (Ge 1:28–31; 2:18–24;

with gratitude; 5 for it is sanctified by means of [A]the
word of God and prayer.

A GOOD MINISTER'S DISCIPLINE

6 In pointing out these things to [A]the brethren,
you will be a good [B]servant of Christ Jesus, *constantly* nourished on the words of the faith and of
the [a,C]sound doctrine which you [D]have been following. 7 But [a]have nothing to do with [A]worldly [B]fables
fit only for old women. On the other hand, discipline
yourself for the purpose of [C]godliness; 8 for [A]bodily
discipline is only of little profit, but [B]godliness is
profitable for all things, since it [C]holds promise for
the [D]present life and *also* for the *life* to come. 9 [A]It is
a trustworthy statement deserving full acceptance.
10 For it is for this we labor and strive, because we
have fixed [A]our hope on [B]the living God, who is [C]the
Savior of all men, especially of believers.
11 [a,A]Prescribe and teach these things. 12 [A]Let no
one look down on your youthfulness, but *rather*
in speech, conduct, [B]love, faith *and* purity, show
yourself [C]an example [a]of those who believe. 13 [A]Un-
til I come, give attention to the *public* [B]reading *of
Scripture,* to exhortation and teaching. 14 Do not
neglect the spiritual gift within you, which was bestowed on you through [A]prophetic utterance with
[B]the laying on of hands by the [a,C]presbytery. 15 Take
pains with these things; be *absorbed* in them, so

4:5 [A]Gen 1:25, 31; Heb 11:3 4:6 [a]Lit *good* [A]Acts 1:15 [B]2 Cor 11:23 [C]1 Tim 1:10 [D]Luke 1:3; Phil 2:20, 22; 2 Tim 3:10 4:7 [a]Or *reject* [A]1 Tim 1:9 [B]1 Tim 1:4 [C]1 Tim 4:8; 6:3, 5f; 2 Tim 3:5 4:8 [A]Col 2:23 [B]1 Tim 4:7; 6:3, 5f; 2 Tim 3:5 [C]Ps 37:9, 11; Prov 19:23; 22:4; Matt 6:33 [D]Matt 6:33; 12:32; Mark 10:30 4:9 [A]1 Tim 1:15 4:10 [A]2 Cor 1:10; 1 Tim 6:17 [B]1 Tim 3:15 [C]John 4:42; 1 Tim 2:4 4:11 [a]Or *Keep commanding and teaching* [A]1 Tim 5:7; 6:2 4:12 [a]Or *to* [A]1 Cor 16:11; Titus 2:15 [B]Titus 2:7; 1 Pet 5:3 [C]1 Tim 1:14 4:13 [A]1 Tim 3:14 [B]2 Tim 3:15ff 4:14 [a]Or *board of elders* [A]1 Tim 1:18 [B]Acts 6:6; 1 Tim 5:22; 2 Tim 1:6 [C]Acts 11:30

9:3), they are intrinsically good (Ge 1:31) and to be enjoyed with gratitude by believers. Obviously, food and marriage are essential for life and procreation.

4:5 sanctified. Set apart or dedicated to God for holy use. The means for so doing are thankful prayer and an understanding that the Word of God has set aside the temporary Mosaic dietary restrictions (Mk 7:19; Ac 10:9–15; Ro 14:1–12; Col 2:16, 17). Contrast the unbeliever whose inner corruption and evil motives corrupt every good thing (Titus 1:15).

4:6 nourished ... words of the faith ... sound doctrine. Continual feeding on the truths of Scripture is essential to the spiritual health of all Christians (2Ti 3:16, 17), but especially of spiritual leaders like Timothy. Only by reading the Word, studying it, meditating on it, and mastering its contents can a pastor fulfill his mandate (2Ti 2:15). Timothy had been doing so since childhood (2Ti 3:15), and Paul urged him to continue (cf. v. 16; 2Ti 3:14). "Words of the faith" is a general reference to Scripture, God's revealed truth. "Sound doctrine" indicates the theology Scripture teaches.

4:7 have nothing to do with worldly fables. In addition to being committed to God's Word (*see note on v. 6*), believers must avoid all false teaching. Paul denounced such error as "worldly" (the opposite of what is holy) "fables" (*muthos,* from which the Eng. word "myths" derives), fit only for "old women" (a common epithet denoting something fit only for the uneducated and philosophically unsophisticated). *See notes on 2Ti 2:14–18.* **discipline ... godliness.** "Godliness" (a proper attitude and response toward God; *see note on 2:2*) is the prerequisite from which all effective ministry flows. "Discipline" is an athletic term denoting the rigorous, self-sacrificing training an athlete undergoes. Spiritual self-discipline is the path to godly living (cf. 1Co 9:24–27).

4:8 little profit. Bodily exercise is limited both in extent and duration; it affects only the physical body during this earthly life. **profitable for all things.** In time and eternity.

4:9 trustworthy statement. *See note on 1:15.*

4:10 hope. Believers are saved in hope and live and serve in light of that hope of eternal life (Titus 1:2; 3:7; *see note on Ro 5:2*). Working to the point of exhaustion and suffering rejection and persecution are acceptable because believers understand they are doing God's work—which is the work of salvation. That makes it worth all of the sacrifices (Php 1:12–18, 27–30; 2:17; Col 1:24, 25; 2Ti 1:6–12; 2:3, 4, 9, 10; 4:5–8). **the Savior of all men, especially of believers.** Paul is obviously not teaching universalism, that all people will be saved in the spiritual and eternal sense, since the rest of Scripture clearly teaches that God will not save everyone. Most will reject Him and spend eternity in hell (Mt 25:41, 46; Rev 20:11–15). Yet, the Gr. word translated "especially" must mean that all people enjoy God's salvation in some way like those who believe enjoy His salvation. The simple explanation is that God is the Savior of all people, only in a temporal sense, while of believers in an eternal sense. Paul's point is that while God graciously delivers believers from sin's condemnation and penalty because He was their substitute (2Co 5:21), all people experience some earthly benefits from the goodness of God. Those benefits are: 1) common grace—a term that describes God's goodness shown to all mankind universally (Ps 145:9) in restraining sin (Ro 2:15) and judgment (Ro 2:3–6), maintaining order in society through government (Ro 13:1–5), enabling man to appreciate beauty and goodness (Ps 50:2), and showering him with temporal blessings (Mt 5:45; Ac 14:15–17; 17:25); 2) compassion—the broken-hearted love of pity God shows to undeserving, unregenerate sinners (Ex 34:6, 7; Ps 86:5; Da 9:9; Mt 23:37; Lk 19:41–44; cf. Is 16:11–13; Jer 48:35–37); 3) admonition to repent—God constantly warns sinners of their fate, demonstrating the heart of a compassionate Creator who has no pleasure in the death of the wicked (Eze 18:30–32; 33:11); 4) the gospel invitation—salvation in Christ is indiscriminately offered to all (Mt 11:28, 29; 22:2–14; Jn 6:35–40; Rev 22:17; cf. Jn 5:39, 40). God is, by nature, a saving God. That is, He finds no pleasure in the death of sinners. His saving character is revealed even in how He deals with those who will never believe, but only in those 4 temporal ways. *See notes on 2:6.*

4:12 Let no one look down on your youthfulness. Greek culture placed great value on age and experience. Since Timothy was in his thirties, still young by the standards of that culture, he would have to earn respect by being a godly example. Because he had been with Paul since a young teenager, Timothy had much experience to mature him, so that looking down on him because he was under 40 was inexcusable. **show yourself an example.** Paul lists 5 areas (the better Gr. manuscripts omit "in spirit") in which Timothy was to be an example to the church: "speech" (cf. Mt 12:34–37; Eph 4:25, 29, 31); "conduct" (righteous living; cf. Titus 2:10; 1Pe 1:15; 2:12; 3:16); "love" (self-sacrificial service for others; cf. Jn 15:13); "faith" (not belief, but faithfulness or commitment; cf. 1Co 4:2); "purity" (especially sexual purity; cf. 3:2). Timothy's exemplary life in those areas would offset the disadvantage of his youth.

4:13 Until I come. *See note on 3:14.* **give attention to ... teaching.** These things were to be Timothy's constant practice; his way of life. "Reading" refers to the custom of public reading of Scripture in the church's worship service, followed by the exposition of the passage that had been read (cf. Ne 8:1–8; Lk 4:16–27). "Exhortation" challenges those who hear the Word to apply it in their daily lives. It may involve rebuke, warning, encouragement, or comfort. "Teaching" refers to systematic instruction from the Word of God (cf. 3:2; Titus 1:9).

4:14 the spiritual gift. That grace given to Timothy and to all believers at salvation which consisted of a God-designed, Spirit-empowered spiritual ability for the use of ministry (*see notes on Ro 12:4–8; 1Co 12:4–12; 1Pe 4:10, 11*). Timothy's gift (cf. 2Ti 1:6) was leadership with special emphasis on preaching (2Ti 4:2), and teaching (vv. 6, 11, 13; 6:2). **through prophetic utterance.** Timothy's gift was identified by a revelation from God (*see note on 1:18*) and apostolic confirmation (2Ti 1:6), probably when he joined Paul on the apostle's second missionary journey (Ac 16:1–3). **laying on of hands by the presbytery.** *See note on 5:22.* This public affirmation of Timothy's call to the ministry likely took place at the same time as the prophecy (cf. 2Ti 1:6). His call to the ministry was thus confirmed subjectively (by means of his spiritual gift), objectively (through the prophecy made about him), and collectively (by the affirmation of apostles and the church, represented by the elders).

4:15 progress. The word was used in military terms of an advancing force and in general terms of advancement in learning, understanding, or knowledge. Paul exhorted Timothy to let his progress toward Christlikeness be evident to all.

that your progress will be evident to all. 16 [A]Pay
close attention to yourself and to your teaching;
persevere in these things, for as you do this you
will [a,B]ensure salvation both for yourself and for
those who hear you.

HONOR WIDOWS

5 [A]Do not sharply rebuke an [B]older man, but *rather*
appeal to *him* as a father, *to* [C]the younger men
as brothers, 2 the older women as mothers, *and* the
younger women as sisters, in all purity.
3 Honor widows who are [A]widows indeed; 4 but
if any widow has children or grandchildren, [A]they
must first learn to practice piety in regard to their
own family and to [a]make some return to their
parents; for this is [B]acceptable in the sight of God.
5 Now she who is a [A]widow indeed and who has
been left alone, [B]has fixed her hope on God and
continues in [C]entreaties and prayers night and
day. 6 But she who [A]gives herself to wanton pleasure is [B]dead even while she lives. 7 [a,A]Prescribe
these things as well, so that they may be above
reproach. 8 But if anyone does not provide for his
own, and especially for those of his household,
he has [A]denied the faith and is worse than an
unbeliever.
9 A widow is to be [A]put on the list only if she
is not less than sixty years old, *having been* [B]the
wife of one man, 10 having a reputation for [A]good
works; *and* if she has brought up children, if she
has [B]shown hospitality to strangers, if she [C]has
washed the [a]saints' feet, if she has [D]assisted those
in distress, *and* if she has devoted herself to every
good work. 11 But refuse *to put* younger widows
on the list, for when they feel [A]sensual desires in
disregard of Christ, they want to get married, 12 *thus*
incurring condemnation, because they have set
aside their previous [a]pledge. 13 At the same time they

4:16 [a]Lit *save both yourself and those* [A]Acts 20:28 [B]1 Cor 1:21 5:1 [A]Lev 19:32 [B]Titus 2:2 [C]Titus 2:6 5:3 [A]Acts 6:1; 9:39, 41; 1 Tim 5:5, 16 5:4 [a]Lit *give back recompenses* [A]Eph 6:2 [B]1 Tim 2:3 5:5 [A]Acts 6:1; 9:39, 41; 1 Tim 5:3, 16 [B]1 Cor 7:34; 1 Pet 3:5 [C]Luke 2:37; 1 Tim 2:1; 2 Tim 1:3 5:6 [A]James 5:5 [B]Luke 15:24; 2 Tim 3:6; Rev 3:1 5:7 [a]Or *Keep commanding* [A]1 Tim 4:11 5:8 [A]2 Tim 2:12; Titus 1:16; 2 Pet 2:1; Jude 4 5:9 [A]1 Tim 5:16 [B]1 Tim 3:2 5:10 [a]Or *holy ones* [A]Acts 9:36; 1 Tim 6:18; Titus 2:7; 3:8; 1 Pet 2:12 [B]1 Tim 3:2 [C]Luke 7:44; John 13:14 [D]1 Tim 5:16 5:11 [A]Rev 18:7 5:12 [a]Lit *faith*

4:16 to yourself and to your teaching. The priorities of a godly leader are summed up in his personal holiness and public teaching. All of Paul's exhortations in vv. 6–16 fit into one or the other of those two categories. **you will ensure salvation ... for yourself.** Perseverance in believing the truth always accompanies genuine conversion (*see note on Mt 24:13*; cf. Jn 8:31; Ro 2:7; Php 2:12, 13; Col 1:23). **those who hear you.** By careful attention to his own godly life and faithful preaching of the Word, Timothy would continue to be the human instrument God used to bring the gospel and to save some who heard him. Though salvation is God's work, it is His pleasure to do it through human instruments.

5:1 rebuke. Some translations add "sharply" to the word "rebuke," which fills out the intensity of the Gr. term. An older sinning believer is to be shown respect by not being addressed with harsh words (cf. 2Ti 2:24, 25). **an older man.** In this context, the Gr. is indicating older men generally, not the office of elder. The younger Timothy was to confront sinning older men with deference and honor, which is clearly inferred from OT principles (cf. Lv 19:32; Job 32:4, 6; Pr 4:1–4; 16:31; 20:29). **appeal.** This Gr. word, which is related to a title for the Holy Spirit (*paraclētos;* cf. Jn 14:16, 26; 15:26; 16:7), refers to coming alongside someone to help. It may best be translated strengthen. We are to strengthen our fellow believers (cf. Gal 6:1, 2) in the same way the Scripture (Ro 15:4) and the Holy Spirit do.

5:3–16 This section supports the mandate of Scripture that women who have lost the support of their husbands are to be cared for (cf. Ex 22:22–24; Dt 27:19; Is 1:17). God's continual compassion for widows only reinforces this command (cf. Pss 68:5; 146:9; Mk 12:41–44; Lk 7:11–17).

5:3 Honor. "To show respect or care," "to support," or "to treat graciously." Although it includes meeting all kinds of needs, Paul had in mind here not only this broad definition, but primarily financial support (cf. Ex 20:12; Mt 15:1–6; 27:9). **widows indeed.** Not all widows are truly alone and without resources. Financial support from the church is mandatory only for widows who have no means to provide for their daily needs.

5:4 widow has children or grandchildren. Families, not the church, have the first responsibility for their own widows. **return to their parents.** Children and grandchildren are indebted to those who brought them into the world, reared them, and loved them. Fulfilling this responsibility is a mark of godly obedience (cf. Ex 20:12).

5:5 left alone. *See note on v. 3.* The form of this Gr. word denotes a permanent condition of being forsaken and left without resources. She is "really" a widow, since there is no family to support her. **fixed her hope on God.** A continual state or settled attitude of hope in God (cf. 1Ki 17:8–16; Jer 49:11). Since she has no one else, she pleads with God as her only hope.

5:6 dead even while she lives. A widow who lives a worldly, immoral, ungodly life may be alive physically, but her lifestyle proves she is unregenerate and spiritually dead (cf. Eph 2:1).

5:7 above reproach. *See notes on 3:2; Php 2:15.* "Above reproach" means "blameless," so that no one can fault their conduct.

5:8 if. Better translated "since." Paul negatively restated the positive principle of v. 4, using the Gr. construction that implies the condition is true, suggesting that there were numerous violations of that principle at Ephesus. Any believer who fails to obey this command is guilty of: 1) denying the principle of compassionate Christian love (cf. Jn 13:35; Ro 5:5; 1Th 4:9); and 2) being "worse than an unbeliever." Most pagans naturally fulfill this duty, so believers who have God's command and power to carry it out and do not, behave worse than pagans. Cf. 1Co 5:1, 2.

5:9 put on the list. This was not a list of those widows eligible for specially recognized church support (all widows in the church who had no other means of support were; v. 3), but rather those eligible for specially recognized church ministry (cf. Titus 2:3–5). **not less than sixty.** In NT culture, 60 was considered retirement age. By that age, older women would have completed their child rearing and would have the time, maturity, and character to devote their lives in service to God and the church. They also would not be likely to remarry and become preoccupied with that commitment. **the wife of one man.** Lit. "one-man woman" (cf. 3:2, 12). It does not exclude women who have been married more than once (cf. v. 14; 1Co 7:39), but it refers to a woman totally devoted and faithful to her husband, a wife who had displayed purity of thought and action in her marriage.

5:10 has brought up children. This views the godly widow as a Christian mother who has nourished or reared children that have followed the Lord (*see note on 2:15*). **washed the saints' feet.** The menial duty of slaves. It is used literally and metaphorically of widows who have humble servants' hearts (*see notes on Jn 13:4–17*). **every good work.** Cf. Dorcas in Ac 9:36–39.

5:11 feel sensual desires. This is an expression that includes all that is involved in the marriage relationship, including sexual passion. Paul saw the danger that younger widows might want to escape from their vows to remain single (*see note on v. 12*) and be devoted only to God's service (cf. Nu 30:9); he knew the negative impact such feelings could have on young widows' personal lives and ministry within the church. Such women were also marked out by false teachers as easy prey (2Ti 3:6, 7), causing them to leave the truth (v. 15).

5:12 set aside their previous pledge. This refers to a specific covenant young widows made when asking to be included on the widows' list. Likely, they promised to devote the rest of their lives in service to the church and the Lord. Though well-meaning at the time of their need and bereavement, they were surely to desire marriage again (see v. 11), and thus renege on their original pledge.

5:13 gossips. Such people speak nonsense, talk idly, make empty charges, or even accuse others with malicious words. This idleness and talk also made them suitable targets for the false teachers (1:6). **busybodies.** Lit. "one who moves around." The implication is that such people pry into things that do not concern them; they do not mind their own business.

also learn *to be* idle, as they go around from house
to house; and not merely idle, but also [A]gossips
and [B]busybodies, talking about [C]things not proper
to mention. 14Therefore, I want younger *widows*
to get [A]married, bear children, [B]keep house, *and*
[C]give the enemy no occasion for reproach; 15for
some [A]have already turned aside to follow [B]Satan.
16If any woman who is a believer [A]has *dependent*
widows, she must [B]assist them and the church must
not be burdened, so that it may assist those who
are [C]widows indeed.

CONCERNING ELDERS

17[A]The elders who [B]rule well are to be considered
worthy of double honor, especially those who [C]work
hard [a]at preaching and teaching. 18For the Scripture
says, "[A]YOU SHALL NOT MUZZLE THE OX WHILE HE
IS THRESHING," and "[B]The laborer is worthy of his
wages." 19Do not receive an accusation against an
[A]elder except on the basis of [B]two or three witnesses.
20Those who continue in sin, [A]rebuke in the presence of all, [B]so that the rest also will be fearful *of*
sinning. 21[A]I solemnly charge you in the presence of

5:13 [A]3 John 10 [B]2 Thess 3:11 [C]Titus 1:11 5:14 [A]1 Cor 7:9; 1 Tim 4:3 [B]Titus 2:5 [C]1 Tim 6:1 5:15 [A]1 Tim 1:20 [B]Matt 4:10 5:16 [A]1 Tim 5:4 [B]1 Tim 5:10 [C]1 Tim 5:3 5:17 [a]Lit *in word* [A]Acts 11:30; 1 Tim 4:14; 5:19 [B]Rom 12:8 [C]1 Thess 5:12 5:18 [A]Deut 25:4; 1 Cor 9:9 [B]Lev 19:13; Deut 24:15; Matt 10:10; Luke 10:7; 1 Cor 9:14 5:19 [A]Acts 11:30; 1 Tim 4:14; 5:17 [B]Deut 17:6; 19:15; Matt 18:16 5:20 [A]Gal 2:14; Eph 5:11; 2 Tim 4:2 [B]2 Cor 7:11 5:21 [A]Luke 9:26; 1 Tim 6:13; 2 Tim 2:14; 4:1

5:14 bear children. The younger widows were still of childbearing age. Although they had lost their first husbands, there was still the potential privilege and blessing of remarrying and having children (*see notes on 2:15*; cf. Ps 127:3, 5). **keep house.** The Gr. term denotes all the aspects of household administration, not merely the rearing of children. The home is the domain where a married woman fulfills herself in God's design. *See notes on Titus 2:4, 5.*

5:15 Some of the young widows had given up their commitment to serve Christ (*see notes on vv. 11, 12*), perhaps either by following false teachers and spreading their false doctrine or by marrying unbelievers and bringing disgrace upon the church. **Satan.** The devil, the believer's adversary (*see notes on Job 1:6–12; 2:1–7; Is 14:12–15; Eze 28:12–15; Rev 12:9*).

5:16 woman. Paul restates the message of vv. 4–8 with the addition that as the situation warrants, Christian women are included in this responsibility for support of widows.

5:17–25 The source of much of the Ephesian church's difficulties was the inadequacy of the pastors. So Paul explains to Timothy how to restore proper pastoral oversight. He sets forth the church's obligations in regard to honoring, protecting, rebuking, and selecting elders.

5:17 elders. This identifies the "overseer" (3:1) or bishop, who is also called pastor (Eph 4:11). *See notes on 3:1–7; Titus 1:6–9.* **rule well.** Elders are spiritual rulers in the church. Cf. 1Th 5:12, 13; Heb 13:7, 17. **double honor.** Elders who serve with greater commitment, excellence, and effort should have greater acknowledgment from their congregations. This expression does not mean such men should receive exactly twice as much remuneration as others, but because they have earned such respect they should be paid more generously. **especially.** Means "chiefly" or "particularly." Implicit is the idea that some elders will work harder than others and be more prominent in ministry. **work hard.** Lit. "work to the point of fatigue or exhaustion." The Gr. word stresses the effort behind the work more than the amount of work. **preaching and teaching.** *See note on 4:13.* The first emphasizes proclamation, along with exhortation and admonition, and calls for a heart response to the Lord. The second is an essential fortification against heresy and puts more stress on instruction.

5:18 For the Scripture says. A typical formula for introducing biblical references, in this instance both an OT (Dt 25:4) and NT (Lk 10:7) one. It is also very significant that this is a case of one NT writer (Paul) affirming the inspiration of another by referring to Luke's writing as "Scripture" (cf. 2Pe 3:15, 16), which shows the high view that the early church took of NT Scripture.

5:19 two or three witnesses. Serious accusations against elders must be investigated and confirmed by the same process as established in Mt 18:15–20 (*see notes there*). This process for the whole church also applies to elders. This demand does not place elders beyond accusation, but protects them from frivolous, evil accusers, by demanding the same process of confirmation of sin as for all in the church.

5:20 Those who continue in sin. Elders who continue in any kind of sin after the confrontation of 2 or 3 witnesses, especially any that violates the qualifications to serve (3:2–7). **in the presence of all.** The other elders and the congregation. The third step of confrontation, established in Mt 18:17, is to tell the church, so that they can all confront the person and call him to repentance.

5:21 charge . . . God . . . Christ Jesus. Cf. 6:13; *see note on 2Ti 4:1.* ***His chosen angels.*** The unfallen angels, as opposed to Satan and his demons. This indicates that God's sovereign purpose to choose those beings who would be part of His eternal kingdom included angels whom He chose to eternal glory. Christians are also called "elect" (Ro 8:33). **without bias . . . partiality.** All discipline of elders is to be done fairly, without prejudgment or personal preference, according to the standards of Scripture.

NAMES OF SATAN

1. Accuser	Opposes believers before God	Rev 12:10
2. Adversary	Against God	1Pe 5:8
3. Beelzebul	Lord of the fly	Mt 12:24
4. Belial	Worthless	2Co 6:15
5. Devil	Slanderer	Mt 4:1
6. Dragon	Destructive	Rev 12:3, 7, 9
7. Enemy	Opponent	Mt 13:28
8. Evil one	Intrinsically evil	Jn 17:15
9. God of this world	Influences thinking of world	2Co 4:4
10. Liar	Perverts the truth	Jn 8:44
11. Murderer	Leads people to eternal death	Jn 8:44
12. Prince of the power of the air	Control of unbelievers	Eph 2:2
13. Roaring lion	One who destroys	1Pe 5:8
14. Ruler of demons	Leader of fallen angels	Mk 3:22
15. Ruler of this world	Rules in world system	Jn 12:31
16. Satan	Adversary	1Ti 5:15
17. Serpent of old	Deceiver in garden	Rev 12:9; 20:2
18. Tempter	Solicits people to sin	1Th 3:5

God and of Christ Jesus and of *His* chosen angels, to
maintain these *principles* without bias, doing nothing in a *spirit of* partiality. 22 [A]Do not lay hands upon
anyone *too* hastily and [a]thereby share [B]*responsibility*
for the sins of others; keep yourself [b]free from sin.
23 No longer drink water *exclusively*, but [A]use a
little wine for the sake of your stomach and your
frequent ailments.
24 The sins of some men are quite evident, going before them to judgment; for others, their *sins*
[A]follow after. 25 Likewise also, deeds that are good
are quite evident, and [A]those which are otherwise
cannot be concealed.

INSTRUCTIONS TO THOSE WHO MINISTER

6 [A]All who are under the yoke as slaves are to regard their own masters as worthy of all honor
so [B]that the name of God and *our* doctrine will not
be [a]spoken against. 2 Those who have believers as
their masters must not be disrespectful to them
because they are [A]brethren, but must serve them
all the more, because those who [a]partake of the benefit are believers and beloved. [B]Teach and [b]preach
these *principles*.
3 If anyone [A]advocates a different doctrine and
does not [a]agree with [B]sound words, those of our Lord
Jesus Christ, and with the doctrine [C]conforming to
godliness, 4 he is [A]conceited *and* understands nothing; but he [a]has a morbid interest in [B]controversial
questions and [C]disputes about words, out of which
arise envy, strife, abusive language, evil suspicions,
5 and constant friction between [A]men of depraved
mind and deprived of the truth, who [B]suppose that
[a]godliness is a means of gain. 6 [A]But godliness *ac-*
tually is a means of [B]great gain when accompanied
by [C]contentment. 7 For [A]we have brought nothing
into the world, so we cannot take anything out of it

5:22 [a]Lit *do not share* [b]Lit *pure* [A]1 Tim 3:10; 4:14 [B]Eph 5:11; 1 Tim 3:2-7 5:23 [A]1 Tim 3:8 5:24 [A]Rev 14:13 5:25 [A]Prov 10:9 6:1 [a]Or *blasphemed* [A]Eph 6:5; Titus 2:9; 1 Pet 2:18 [B]Titus 2:5 6:2 [a]Or *devote themselves to kindness* [b]Lit *exhort, urge* [A]Acts 1:15; Gal 3:28; Philem 16 [B]1 Tim 4:11 6:3 [a]Lit *come to;* or *come with* [A]1 Tim 1:3 [B]1 Tim 1:10 [C]Titus 1:1 6:4 [a]Lit *is sick about* [A]1 Tim 3:6 [B]1 Tim 1:4 [C]Acts 18:15; 2 Tim 2:14 6:5 [a]Or *religion* [A]2 Tim 3:8; Titus 1:15 [B]Titus 1:11; 2 Pet 2:3 6:6 [A]Luke 12:15-21; 1 Tim 6:6-10 [B]1 Tim 4:8 [C]Phil 4:11; Heb 13:5 6:7 [A]Job 1:21; Eccl 5:15

5:22 Do not lay hands upon … hastily. The ceremony that affirmed a man's suitability for and acceptance into public ministry as an elder/pastor/overseer. This came from the OT practice of laying hands on a sacrificial animal to identify with it (Ex 29:10, 15, 19; Lv 4:15; cf. Nu 8:10; 27:18–23; Dt 34:9; Mt 19:15; Ac 8:17, 18; 9:17; Heb 6:2). "Hastily" refers to proceeding with this ceremony without a thorough investigation and preparation period to be certain of the man's qualifications (as in 3:1–7). **not … share *responsibility* … sins of others.** This refers to the sin of hasty ordination, which makes those responsible culpable for the man's sin of serving as an unqualified elder and, thus, misleading people. **keep yourself free from sin.** Paul wanted Timothy, by not participating in the recognition of unqualified elders, to remain untainted by others' sins. The church desperately needed qualified spiritual leaders, but the selection had to be carefully executed.

5:23 No longer drink water *exclusively*. "Water" in the ancient world was often polluted and carried many diseases. Therefore, Paul urged Timothy not to risk illness, not even for the sake of a commitment to abstinence from wine. Apparently, Timothy avoided wine, so as not to place himself in harm's way (*see note on 3:3*). **use a little wine … ailments.** Paul wanted Timothy to use wine which, because of fermentation, acted as a disinfectant to protect his health problems due to the harmful effects of impure water. With this advice, however, Paul was not advocating that Timothy lower the high standard of behavior for leaders (cf. Nu 6:1–4; Pr 31:4, 5).

5:24 sins … are quite evident. The sins of some people are manifest for all to see, thus disqualifying them out of hand for service as elders. **going before them to judgment.** The known sins of the unqualified announce those men's guilt and unfitness before all. "Judgment" refers to the church's process for determining men's suitability to serve as elders. **follow after.** The sins of other candidates for elder will come to light in time, perhaps even during the scrutiny of the evaluation process.

5:25 The same is true of good works. Some are evident; others come to light later. Time and truth go hand in hand. The whole emphasis in this instruction regarding choosing elders, according to the qualifications of 3:1–7, is to be patient, fair, impartial, and pure (vv. 21–25). Such an approach will yield the right choices.

6:1, 2 The Ephesian believers may have been struggling to maintain a biblical work ethic in the world of slavery, so these verses form Paul's instruction on that subject. Essentially, first-century slaves resembled the indentured servants of the American colonial period. In many cases, slaves were better off than day-laborers, since much of their food, clothing, and shelter was provided. The system of slavery served as the economic structure in the Roman world, and the master-slave relationship closely parallels the twentieth-century employer-employee relationship. For more on slaves, see Introduction to Philemon: Background and Setting.

6:1 under the yoke. A colloquial expression describing submissive service under another's authority, not necessarily describing an abusive relationship (cf. Mt 11:28–30). **slaves.** They are people who are in submission to another. It carries no negative connotation and is often positive when used in connection with the Lord serving the Father (Php 2:7), and believers serving God (1Pe 2:16), the Lord (Ro 1:1; Gal 1:10; 2Ti 2:24; Jas 1:1), non-Christians (1Co 9:19), and other believers (Gal 5:13). **masters.** The Gr. word for "master," while giving us the Eng. word "despot," does not carry a negative connotation. Instead, it refers to one with absolute and unrestricted authority. **all honor.** This translates into diligent and faithful labor for one's employer. *See notes on Eph 6:5–9; Col 3:22–25.* ***our* doctrine.** The revelation of God summed up in the gospel. How believers act while under the authority of another affects how people view the message of salvation Christians proclaim (*see notes on Titus 2:5–14*). Displaying a proper attitude of submission and respect, and performing quality work, help make the gospel message believable (Mt 5:48).

6:2 believers as their masters. The tendency might be to assume one's equality in Christ with a Christian master, and disdain the authority related to work roles. On the contrary, working for a Christian should produce more loyal and diligent service out of love for the brethren. **preach.** Lit. "to call to one's side." The particular emphasis here is on a strong urging, directing, and insisting on following the principles for correct behavior in the workplace.

6:3 Paul identifies 3 characteristics of false teachers: 1) they "advocate a different doctrine"—a different teaching that contradicts God's revelation in Scripture (*see notes on Gal 1:6–9*); 2) they do "not agree with sound words"—they do not accept sound, healthy teaching, specifically the teaching contained in Scripture (2Pe 3:16); and 3) they reject "doctrine conforming to godliness"—teaching not based on Scripture will always result in an unholy life. Instead of godliness, false teachers will be marked by sin (*see notes on 2Pe 2:10–22*; cf. Jude 4, 8–16).

6:4 questions and disputes about words. "Questions" refers to idle speculation; "disputes about words" lit. means "word battles." Because proud, ignorant false teachers do not understand divine truth (2Co 2:14), they obsess over terminology and attack the reliability and authority of Scripture. Every kind of strife is mentioned to indicate that false teachers produce nothing of benefit out of their fleshly, corrupt, and empty minds (v. 5).

6:5 deprived of the truth. False teachers are in a state of apostasy; that is, although they once knew and seemed to embrace the truth, they turned to openly reject it. The Gr. word for "deprived" means "to steal" or "to rob," and its form here indicates that someone or something was pulled away from contact with the truth (it does not mean they were ever saved; *see note on 1:19*; cf. 2Ti 2:18; 3:8; Heb 6:4–6; 2Pe 2:1, 4–9). **a means of gain.** Almost always behind all the efforts of the hypocritical, lying (4:2) false teachers is the driving motivation of monetary gain (cf. Ac 8:18–23; 2Pe 2:15).

6:6 contentment. This Gr. word means "self-sufficiency," and was used by Sto

either. 8 If we [A]have food and covering, with these
we shall be content. 9 [A]But those who want to get
rich fall into temptation and [B]a snare and many
foolish and harmful desires which plunge men into
ruin and destruction. 10 For [A]the love of money is a
root of all [a]sorts of evil, and some by longing for it
have [B]wandered away from the faith and pierced
themselves with many griefs.
11 But [A]flee from these things, you [B]man of God,
and pursue righteousness, godliness, [C]faith, [D]love,
[a]perseverance *and* gentleness. 12 [A]Fight the good
fight of [B]faith; [C]take hold of the eternal life [D]to which
you were called, and you made the good [E]confes-
sion in the presence of [F]many witnesses. 13 [A]I charge
you in the presence of God, who [a]gives life to all
things, and of [B]Christ Jesus, who testified the [C]good
confession [D]before Pontius Pilate, 14 that you keep
the commandment without stain or reproach until
the [A]appearing of our Lord Jesus Christ, 15 which
He will [a]bring about at [A]the proper time—He who
is [B]the blessed and [C]only Sovereign, [D]the King of
[b]kings and [E]Lord of [c]lords, 16 [A]who alone possesses
immortality and [B]dwells in unapproachable light,
[C]whom no man has seen or can see. [A]To Him *be*
honor and eternal dominion! Amen.
17 Instruct those who are rich in [A]this present
world [B]not to be conceited or to [C]fix their hope
on the uncertainty of riches, but on God, [D]who
richly supplies us with all things to enjoy. 18 *Instruct them* to do good, to be rich in [A]good [a]works,
[B]to be generous and ready to share, 19 [A]storing up
for themselves the treasure of a good foundation

6:8 [A]Prov 30:8 6:9 [A]Prov 15:27; 23:4; 28:20; Luke 12:21; 1 Tim 6:17 [B]1 Tim 3:7 6:10 [a]Lit *the evils* [A]Col 3:5; 1 Tim 3:3; 6:9 [B]James 5:19 6:11 [a]Or *steadfastness* [A]2 Tim 2:22 [B]2 Tim 3:17 [C]1 Tim 1:14 [D]2 Tim 3:10 6:12 [A]1 Cor 9:25f; Phil 1:30; 1 Tim 1:18 [B]1 Tim 1:19 [C]Phil 3:12; 1 Tim 6:19 [D]Col 3:15 [E]2 Cor 9:13; 1 Tim 6:13 [F]1 Tim 4:14; 2 Tim 2:2 6:13 [a]Or *preserves alive* [A]1 Tim 5:21 [B]Gal 3:26; 1 Tim 1:12, 15; 2:5 [C]2 Cor 9:13; 1 Tim 6:12 [D]Matt 27:2; John 18:37 6:14 [A]2 Thess 2:8 6:15 [a]Lit *show* [b]Lit *those who reign as kings* [c]Lit *those who rule as lords* [A]1 Tim 2:6 [B]1 Tim 1:11 [C]1 Tim 1:17 [D]Deut 10:17; Rev 17:14; 19:16 [E]Ps 136:3 6:16 [A]1 Tim 1:17 [B]Ps 104:2; James 1:17; 1 John 1:5 [C]John 1:18 6:17 [A]Matt 12:32; 2 Tim 4:10; Titus 2:12 [B]Ps 62:10; Luke 12:20; Rom 11:20; 1 Tim 6:9 [C]1 Tim 4:10 [D]Acts 14:17 6:18 [a]Or *deeds* [A]1 Tim 5:10 [B]Rom 12:8; Eph 4:28 6:19 [A]Matt 6:20

philosophers to describe a person who was unflappable and unmoved by external circumstances. Christians are to be satisfied and sufficient, and not to seek for more than what God has already given them. He is the source of true contentment (2Co 3:5; 9:8; Php 4:11–13, 19).

6:8 have food and covering … be content. The basic necessities of life are what ought to make Christians content. Paul does not condemn having possessions, as long as God graciously provides them (v. 17). He does, however, condemn a self-indulgent desire for money, which results from discontentment. *See note on Mt 6:33.*

6:9 those who want to get rich fall into temptation. Greedy people are compulsive—they are continually trapped in sins by their consuming desire to acquire more. **ruin and destruction.** Such greed may lead these people to suffer the tragic end of destruction and hell. These terms refer to the eternal punishment of the wicked.

6:10 love of money. Lit. "affection for silver." In the context, this sin applies to false teachers specifically, but the principle is true universally. Money itself is not evil since it is a gift from God (Dt 8:18); Paul condemns only the love of it (cf. Mt 6:24), which is so characteristic of false teachers (*see notes on 1Pe 5:2; 2Pe 2:1–3, 15*). **wandered away from the faith.** From the body of Christian truth. Gold has replaced God for these apostates, who have turned away from pursuing the things of God in favor of money.

6:11 these things. Love of money and all that goes with it (vv. 6–10), along with the other proud obsessions of false teachers (vv. 3–5). **you man of God.** Cf. 2Ti 3:17. This is a term used in the NT only for Timothy; as a technical term it is used about 70 times in the OT, always to refer to a man who officially spoke for God (*see note on Dt 33:1*). This, along with 1:2; 2:1, indicates that the letter is primarily directed to Timothy, exhorting him to be faithful and strong in light of persecution and difficulty—and particularly with Paul's death near (see Introduction to 2 Timothy: Background and Setting). The man of God is known by what he: 1) flees from (v. 11); 2) follows after (v. 11); 3) fights for (v. 12); and 4) is faithful to (vv. 13, 14). The key to his success in all these endeavors is the perfection produced in him by the Scripture (2Ti 3:16, 17). **righteousness, godliness.** "Righteousness" means to do what is right, in relation to both God and man, and it emphasizes outward behavior. "Godliness" (*see note on 2:2*) refers to one's reverence for God and could be translated "God-likeness."

6:12 Fight the good fight of faith. The Gr. word for "fight" gives us the Eng. word "agonize," and was used in both military and athletic endeavors to describe the concentration, discipline, and extreme effort needed to win. The "good fight of faith" is the spiritual conflict with Satan's kingdom of darkness in which all men of God are necessarily involved. *See notes on 2Co 10:3–5; 2Ti 4:2.* **take hold of the eternal life.** Paul is here admonishing Timothy to "get a grip" on the reality of the matters associated with eternal life, so that he would live and minister with a heavenly and eternal perspective (cf. Php 3:20; Col 3:2). **to which you were called.** Refers to God's effectual, sovereign call of Timothy to salvation (*see note on Ro 1:7*). **good confession.** Timothy's public confession of faith in the Lord Jesus Christ, which likely occurred at his baptism and again when he was ordained to the ministry (4:14; 2Ti 1:6).

6:13 charge … God … Christ Jesus. Cf. 5:21; *see note on 2Ti 4:1.* **the good confession before Pontius Pilate.** Knowing that such a confession would cost Him His life, Jesus nevertheless confessed that He was truly the King and Messiah (Jn 18:33–37). He rarely evaded danger (cf. Jn 7:1); He boldly and trustfully committed Himself to God who raises the dead (cf. Col 2:12).

6:14 the commandment. The entire revealed Word of God, which Paul charged Timothy to preach (2Ti 4:2). Paul also repeatedly encouraged Timothy to guard it (v. 20; 1:18, 19; 4:6, 16; 2Ti 1:13, 14; 2:15–18). **appearing.** When the Lord returns to earth in glory (cf. 2Ti 4:1, 8; Titus 2:13) to judge and to establish His kingdom (Mt 24:27, 29, 30; 25:31). Because Christ's return is imminent, that ought to be motivation enough for the man of God to remain faithful to his calling until he dies or the Lord returns (cf. Ac 1:8–11; 1Co 4:5; Rev 22:12).

6:15 at the proper time. The time, known only to Him, that God established in eternity past for Christ to return (Mk 13:32; Ac 1:7). **Sovereign.** This word comes from a Gr. word group that basically means "power." God is absolutely sovereign and omnipotently rules everything everywhere. **King of kings and Lord of lords.** A title used of Christ (Rev 17:14; 19:16) is here used of God the Father. Paul probably used this title for God to confront the cult of emperor worship, intending to communicate that only God is sovereign and worthy of worship.

6:16 whom no man has seen or can see. God in spirit is invisible (cf. 1:17; Job 23:8, 9; Jn 1:18; 5:37; Col 1:15) and, therefore, unapproachable in the sense that sinful man has never seen nor can he ever see His full glory (cf. Ex 33:20; Is 6:1–5).

6:17–19 Paul counsels Timothy what to teach those who are rich in material possessions, those who have more than the mere essentials of food, clothing, and shelter. Paul does not condemn such people, nor command them to get rid of their wealth. He does call them to be good stewards of their God-given resources (cf. Dt 8:18; 1Sa 2:7; 1Ch 29:12).

6:17 conceited. "To have an exalted opinion of oneself." Those who have an abundance are constantly tempted to look down on others and act superior. Riches and pride often go together, and the wealthier a person is, the more he is tempted to be proud (Pr 18:23; 28:11; Jas 2:1–4). **uncertainty of riches … richly supplies us.** Those who have much tend to trust in their wealth (cf. Pr 23:4, 5). But God provides far more security than any earthly investment can ever give (Ecc 5:18–20; Mt 6:19–21).

6:18 ready to share. The Gr. word means "liberal," or "bountiful." Those believers who have money must use it in meeting the needs of others, unselfishly and generously (*see notes on Ac 4:32–37; 2Co 8:1–4*).

6:19 storing up …. good foundation. "Storing up" can be translated "amassing a treasure," while "foundation" can refer to a fund. The idea is that the rich in this world should not be concerned with receiving a

for the future, so that they may [B]take hold of that
which is life indeed.
20 O [A]Timothy, guard [B]what has been entrusted
to you, avoiding [C]worldly *and* empty chatter *and*
the opposing arguments of what is falsely called
"knowledge"— 21 which some have professed and
thus [A]gone astray [a]from [B]the faith.
[C]Grace be with you.

6:19 [B]1 Tim 6:12 6:20 [A]1 Tim 1:2 [B]2 Tim 1:12, 14 [C]1 Tim 1:9; 2 Tim 2:16
6:21 [a]Lit *concerning* [A]2 Tim 2:18 [B]1 Tim 1:19 [C]Col 4:18

return on their earthly investment. Those who make eternal investments will be content to receive their dividends in heaven. *See notes on Lk 16:1–13.* **take hold of … life indeed.** *See note on v. 12.*

6:20, 21 The church's main responsibility is to guard and proclaim the truths of Scripture, so Paul here instructs Timothy on how to guard and protect the Word of God.

6:20 what has been entrusted to you. This translates one Gr. word, which means "deposit." The deposit Timothy was to guard is the truth—the divine revelation that God committed to his care. Every Christian, especially if he is in ministry, has that sacred trust to guard the revelation of God (cf. 1Co 4:1; 1Th 2:3, 4). **what is falsely called "knowledge."** False doctrine—anything claiming to be the truth that is in fact a lie. False teachers typically claim to have the superior knowledge (as in gnosticism). They claim to know the transcendent secrets, but actually are ignorant and infantile in their understanding (*see notes on Col 2:8*).

6:21 Grace be with you. Paul's closing salutation is plural, i.e., "you all"—it goes beyond Timothy to the entire congregation at Ephesus. All believers require the grace of God to preserve the truth and pass it on to the next generation.

THE SECOND EPISTLE OF PAUL TO

TIMOTHY

TITLE

This epistle is the second of two inspired letters Paul the apostle wrote to his son in the faith, Timothy (1:2; 2:1). For biographical information on Timothy, see Introduction to 1 Timothy: Title. It is titled, as are the other personal letters of Paul to individuals (1 Timothy, Titus, and Philemon), with the name of the addressee (1:2).

AUTHOR AND DATE

The issue of Paul's authorship of the Pastoral Epistles is discussed in the Introduction to 1 Timothy: Author and Date. Paul wrote 2 Timothy, the last of his inspired letters, shortly before his martyrdom (ca. A.D. 67).

BACKGROUND AND SETTING

Paul was released from his first Roman imprisonment for a short period of ministry during which he wrote 1 Timothy and Titus. Second Timothy, however, finds Paul once again in a Roman prison (1:16; 2:9), apparently rearrested as part of Nero's persecution of Christians. Unlike Paul's confident hope of release during his first imprisonment (Php 1:19, 25, 26; 2:24; Phm 22), this time he had no such hopes (4:6–8). In his first imprisonment in Rome (ca. A.D. 60–62), before Nero had begun the persecution of Christians (A.D. 64), he was only under house arrest and had opportunity for much interaction with people and ministry (Ac 28:16–31). At this time, 5 or 6 years later (ca. A.D. 66–67), however, he was in a cold cell (4:13), in chains (2:9), and with no hope of deliverance (4:6). Abandoned by virtually all of those close to him for fear of persecution (cf. 1:15; 4:9–12, 16) and facing imminent execution, Paul wrote to Timothy, urging him to hasten to Rome for one last visit with the apostle (4:9, 21). Whether Timothy made it to Rome before Paul's execution is not known. According to tradition, Paul was not released from this second Roman imprisonment, but suffered the martyrdom he had foreseen (4:6).

In this letter, Paul, aware the end was near, passed the nonapostolic mantle of ministry to Timothy (cf. 2:2) and exhorted him to continue faithful in his duties (1:6), hold on to sound doctrine (1:13, 14), avoid error (2:15–18), accept persecution for the gospel (2:3, 4; 3:10–12), put his confidence in the Scripture, and preach it relentlessly (3:15–4:5).

HISTORICAL AND THEOLOGICAL THEMES

It seems that Paul may have had reason to fear that Timothy was in danger of weakening spiritually. This would have been a grave concern for Paul since Timothy needed to carry on Paul's work (cf. 2:2). While there are no historical indications elsewhere in the NT as to why Paul was so concerned, there is evidence in the epistle itself from what he wrote. This concern is evident, for example, in Paul's exhortation to "kindle afresh" his gift (1:6), to replace fear with power, love, and a sound mind (1:7), to not be ashamed of Paul and the Lord, but willingly suffer for the gospel (1:8), and to hold on to the truth (1:13, 14). Summing up the potential problem of Timothy, who might be weakening under the pressure of the church and the persecution of the world, Paul calls him to 1) generally "be strong" (2:1), the key exhortation of the first part of the letter, and to 2) continue to "preach the word" (4:2), the main admonition of the last part. These final words to Timothy include few commendations but many admonitions, including about 25 imperatives.

Since Timothy was well versed in Paul's theology, the apostle did not instruct him further doctrinally. He did, however, allude to several important doctrines, including salvation by God's sovereign grace (1:9, 10; 2:10), the person of Christ (2:8; 4:1, 8), and perseverance (2:11–13); plus Paul wrote the crucial text of the NT on the inspiration of Scripture (3:16, 17).

INTERPRETIVE CHALLENGES

There are no major challenges in this letter involving theological issues. There is limited data regarding several individuals named in the epistle; e.g., Phygellus and Hermogenes (1:15), Onesiphorus (1:16; cf. 4:19), Hymenaeus and Philetus (2:17, 18), Jannes and Jambres (3:8), and Alexander (4:14).

OUTLINE

I. Greeting and Thanksgiving (1:1–5)

II. The Perseverance of a Man of God (1:6–18)
- A. The Exhortation (1:6–11)
- B. The Examples (1:12–18)
  1. Paul (1:12–14)
  2. Onesiphorus (1:15–18)

III. The Patterns of a Man of God (2:1–26)
- A. Paul (2:1, 2)
- B. A Soldier (2:3, 4)
- C. An Athlete (2:5)
- D. A Farmer (2:6, 7)
- E. Jesus (2:8–13)
- F. A Worker (2:14–19)
- G. A Vessel (2:20–23)
- H. A Servant (2:24–26)

IV. The Perils of a Man of God (3:1–17)
- A. Facing Apostasy (3:1–9)
- B. Defeating Apostasy (3:10–17)

V. The Preaching of the Man of God (4:1–5)
- A. The Charge to Preach (4:1, 2)
- B. The Need for Preaching (4:3–5)

VI. Concluding Remarks (4:6–18)
- A. Paul's Triumph (4:6–8)
- B. Paul's Needs (4:9–18)

VII. Paul's Farewells (4:19–22)

TIMOTHY CHARGED TO GUARD HIS TRUST

1 Paul, [A]an apostle of [B]Christ Jesus [a,C]by the will of
God, according to the promise of [D]life in Christ
Jesus,
2 To [A]Timothy, my beloved [a,B]son: [C]Grace, mercy *and*
peace from God the Father and Christ Jesus our Lord.
3 [A]I thank God, whom I [B]serve with a [C]clear conscience [a]the way my forefathers did, [D]as I constantly
remember you in my [b]prayers night and day, 4 [A]long-
ing to see you, [B]even as I recall your tears, so that
I may be filled with joy. 5 [a]For I am mindful of the
[A]sincere faith within you, which first dwelt in your
grandmother Lois and [B]your mother Eunice, and I
am sure that *it is* in you as well. 6 For this reason I
remind you to kindle afresh [A]the gift of God which
is in you through [A]the laying on of my hands. 7 For
God has not given us a [A]spirit of [a]timidity, but of
power and love and [b]discipline.
8 Therefore [A]do not be ashamed of the [B]testimony
of our Lord or of me [C]His prisoner, but join with
me in [D]suffering for the [E]gospel according to the
power of God, 9 who has [A]saved us and [B]called us
with a holy [C]calling, [D]not according to our works,
but according to His own [B]purpose and grace which
was granted us in [E]Christ Jesus from [F]all eternity,

1:1 [a]Lit *through* [A]2 Cor 1:1 [B]Gal 3:26 [C]1 Cor 1:1 [D]1 Tim 6:19 1:2 [a]Or *child* [A]Acts 16:1; 1 Tim 1:2 [B]1 Tim 1:2; 2 Tim 2:1; Titus 1:4 [C]Rom 1:7 1:3 [a]Lit *from my forefathers* [b]Or *petitions* [A]Rom 1:8 [B]Acts 24:14 [C]Acts 23:1; 24:16; 1 Tim 1:5 [D]Rom 1:9 1:4 [A]2 Tim 4:9, 21 [B]Acts 20:37 1:5 [a]Lit *Receiving remembrance of* [A]1 Tim 1:5 [B]Acts 16:1; 2 Tim 3:15 1:6 [A]1 Tim 4:14 1:7 [a]Or *cowardice* [b]Or *sound judgment* [A]John 14:27; Rom 8:15 1:8 [A]Mark 8:38; Rom 1:16; 2 Tim 1:12, 16 [B]1 Cor 1:6 [C]Eph 3:1; 2 Tim 1:16 [D]2 Tim 2:3, 9; 4:5 [E]2 Tim 1:10; 2:8 1:9 [A]Rom 11:14 [B]Rom 8:28ff [C]Rom 11:29 [D]Eph 2:9 [E]2 Tim 1:1 [F]Rom 16:25; Eph 1:4; Titus 1:2

1:1, 2 Paul reminded Timothy that, despite their intimate spiritual relationship, the apostle wrote to him with spiritual authority given him by God. This established the necessity that not only Timothy, but also all others comply with the inspired mandates of the epistle.

1:1 apostle of Christ Jesus by the will of God. *See note on 1Ti 1:1.* His call was according to God's sovereign plan and purpose (cf. 1Co 1:1; 2Co 1:1; Eph 1:1; Col 1:1). **promise of life in Christ Jesus.** The gospel promises that those who are spiritually dead but by faith embrace the gospel's message will be united to Christ and find eternal life in Him (Jn 3:16; 10:10; 14:6; Col 3:4).

1:2 Timothy, my beloved son. *See note on 1Ti 1:2.* **Grace … our Lord.** *See note on 1Ti 1:2.* More than a standard greeting by Paul, this expressed his genuine desire for God's best in Timothy's life.

1:3 I thank God … in my prayers. *See notes on Php 1:3, 4.* **clear conscience.** *See note on 1Ti 1:5.*

1:4 longing to see you. Because of Paul's affection for Timothy and the urgency of the hour in Paul's life, as he faced death, Paul had an intense yearning to see Timothy again (cf. 4:9, 13, 21). **recall your tears.** Paul perhaps remembered this occurring at their latest parting, which occurred after a short visit to Ephesus, following the writing of 1 Timothy, and prior to Paul's arrest at Troas (*see note on 4:13*) and his second imprisonment in Rome. Years before, Paul had a similar parting with the elders at Ephesus (Ac 20:36–38).

1:5 Lois … Eunice. Mention of their names suggests that Paul knew them personally, perhaps because he (with Barnabas) led them to faith in Christ during his first missionary journey (cf. Ac 13:13–14:21). The women were true OT Jewish believers, who understood the Scripture well enough to prepare themselves and Timothy (3:15) to immediately accept Jesus as Messiah when they first heard the gospel from Paul.

1:6 kindle afresh the gift of God. This seems to indicate Paul was unsatisfied with Timothy's level of current faithfulness. "Kindle afresh" means lit. "to keep the fire alive," and "gift" refers to the believer's spiritual gift (*see notes on Ro 12:4–8; 1Co 12:7–11;* regarding Timothy's spiritual gift, *see notes on 4:2–6; 1Ti 4:14*). Paul reminds Timothy that as a steward of his God-given gift for preaching, teaching, and evangelizing, he could not let it fall into disuse (cf. 4:2–5). **laying on of my hands.** *See notes on 1Ti 4:14; 5:22;* cf. 6:12. Paul might have done this at the time of Timothy's conversion, in which case it would have corresponded to when Timothy received his spiritual gift. The expression may also refer to an extraordinary spiritual endowment, which was received or enhanced at some point after his conversion.

1:7 a spirit of timidity. The Gr. word, which can also be translated "fear," denotes a cowardly, shameful fear caused by a weak, selfish character. The threat of Roman persecution, which was escalating under Nero, the hostility of those in the Ephesian church who resented Timothy's leadership, and the assaults of false teachers with their sophisticated systems of deceptions may have been overwhelming Timothy. But if he was fearful, it didn't come from God. **power.** Positively, God has already given believers all the spiritual resources they need for every trial and threat (cf. Mt 10:19, 20). Divine power—effective, productive spiritual energy—belongs to believers (Eph 1:18–20; 3:20; cf. Zec 4:6). **love.** *See note on 1Ti 1:5.* This kind of love centers on pleasing God and seeking others' welfare before one's own (cf. Ro 14:8; Gal 5:22, 25; Eph 3:19; 1Pe 1:22; 1Jn 4:18). **discipline.** Refers to a self-controlled and properly prioritized mind. This is the opposite of fear and cowardice that cause disorder and confusion. Focusing on the sovereign nature and perfect purposes of our eternal God allows believers to control their lives with godly wisdom and confidence in every situation (cf. Ro 12:3; 1Ti 3:2; Titus 1:8; 2:2).

1:8 the testimony of our Lord. The gospel message concerning Jesus Christ. Paul did not want Timothy to be "ashamed" to name the name of Christ because he was afraid of the potential persecution (cf. vv. 12, 16). **me His prisoner.** See Introduction: Author and Date; *see notes on Eph 3:1; Php 1:12–14.* Being linked to Paul, who was a prisoner because of his preaching of the gospel, could have put Timothy's life and freedom in jeopardy (cf. Heb 13:23).

1:9 with a holy calling. As always in the NT Epistles, this calling is not a general invitation to sinners to believe the gospel and be saved (as in Mt 20:16), but refers to God's effectual call of the elect to salvation (*see note on Ro 1:7*). This calling results in holiness, imputed (justification) and imparted (sanctification), and finally completed (glorification). **not … works, but … grace.** This truth is the foundation of the gospel. Salvation is by grace through faith, apart from works (*see notes on Ro 3:20–25; Gal 3:10, 11; Eph 2:8, 9; Php 3:8, 9*). Grace is also the basis for God's sustaining work in believers (cf. Php 1:6; Jude 24, 25). **according to His own purpose.** God's sovereign plan of election (*see notes on 2:10; Jn 6:37–40, 44; Ac 13:48; Ro 8:29; 9:6–23; Eph 1:4; 3:11; 2Th 2:13; Titus 1:1, 2; 1Pe 1:2*). **in Christ Jesus.** His sacrifice made God's salvation plan possible, because He became the substitute sacrifice for the sins of God's people (*see notes on 2Co 5:21*). **from all eternity.** The same Gr. phrase appears in Titus 1:2. The destiny of God's chosen was determined and sealed from eternity past (Jn 17:24; cf. Eph 1:4, 5; Php 1:29; 1Pe 1:2).

A COMPARISON OF PAUL'S TWO ROMAN IMPRISONMENTS

First Imprisonment	Second Imprisonment
Acts 28—Wrote the Prison Epistles	2 Timothy
Accused by Jews of heresy and sedition	Persecuted by Rome and arrested as a criminal against the Empire
Local sporadic persecutions (A.D. 60–63)	Neronian persecution (A.D. 64–68)
Decent living conditions in a rented house (Acts 28:30, 31)	Poor conditions, in a cold, dark dungeon
Many friends visited him	Virtually alone (only Luke with him)
Many opportunities for Christian witness were available	Opportunities for witness were restricted
Was optimistic for release and freedom (Php 1:24–26)	Anticipated his execution (2Ti 4:6)

10 but [A]now has been revealed by the [B]appearing of
our Savior [C]Christ Jesus, who [D]abolished death and
brought life and immortality to light through the
gospel, 11 [A]for which I was appointed a preacher and
an apostle and a teacher. 12 For this reason I also suffer these things, but [A]I am not ashamed; for I know
[B]whom I have believed and I am convinced that He
is able to [C]guard what I have entrusted to Him [a]until
[D]that day. 13 [a,A]Retain the [B]standard of [C]sound words
[D]which you have heard from me, in the [E]faith and
love which are in [F]Christ Jesus. 14 Guard, through
the Holy Spirit who [A]dwells in us, the [a,B]treasure
which has been entrusted to *you*.
15 You are aware of the fact that all who are in
[a,A]Asia [B]turned away from me, among whom are
Phygelus and Hermogenes. 16 The Lord grant mercy
to [A]the house of Onesiphorus, for he often refreshed
me and [B]was not ashamed of my [a,C]chains; 17 but
when he was in Rome, he eagerly searched for me
and found me— 18 the Lord grant to him to find
mercy from the Lord on [A]that day—and you know
very well what services he rendered at [B]Ephesus.

BE STRONG

2 You therefore, my [a,A]son, [B]be strong in the grace
that is in [C]Christ Jesus. 2 The things [A]which you
have heard from me in the presence of [B]many witnesses, [C]entrust these to [D]faithful men who will be
[E]able to teach others also. 3 [A]Suffer hardship with
me, as a good [B]soldier of [C]Christ Jesus. 4 No soldier
in active service [A]entangles himself in the affairs
of everyday life, so that he may please the one who
enlisted him as a soldier. 5 Also if anyone [A]competes
as an athlete, he [a]does not win the prize unless he
competes according to the rules. 6 [A]The hard-working farmer ought to be the first to receive his share
of the crops. 7 Consider what I say, for the Lord will
give you understanding in everything.

1:10 [A]Rom 16:26 [B]2 Thess 2:8; 2 Tim 4:1, 8; Titus 2:11 [C]2 Tim 1:1 [D]1 Cor 15:26; Heb 2:14f 1:11 [A]1 Tim 2:7 1:12 [a]Or *for* [A]2 Tim 1:8, 16 [B]Titus 3:8 [C]1 Tim 6:20; 2 Tim 1:14 [D]1 Cor 1:8; 3:13; 2 Tim 1:18; 4:8 1:13 [a]Or *Hold the example* [A]2 Tim 3:14; Titus 1:9 [B]Rom 2:20; 6:17 [C]1 Tim 1:10 [D]2 Tim 2:2 [E]1 Tim 1:14 [F]2 Tim 1:1 1:14 [a]Lit *good deposit* [A]Rom 8:9 [B]1 Tim 6:20; 2 Tim 1:12 1:15 [a]I.e. the province of Asia [A]Acts 2:9 [B]2 Tim 4:10, 11, 16 1:16 [a]Lit *chain* [A]2 Tim 4:19 [B]2 Tim 1:8 [C]Eph 6:20 1:18 [A]1 Cor 1:8; 3:13; 2 Tim 1:12; 4:8 [B]Acts 18:19; 1 Tim 1:3 2:1 [a]Or *child* [A]2 Tim 1:2 [B]Eph 6:10 [C]2 Tim 1:1 2:2 [A]2 Tim 1:13 [B]1 Tim 6:12 [C]1 Tim 1:18 [D]1 Tim 1:12 [E]2 Cor 2:14ff; 3:5 2:3 [A]2 Tim 1:8 [B]1 Cor 9:7; 1 Tim 1:18 [C]2 Tim 1:1 2:4 [A]2 Pet 2:20 2:5 [a]Lit *is not crowned* [A]1 Cor 9:25 2:6 [A]1 Cor 9:10

1:10 appearing. "Epiphany" is the Eng. equivalent of this Gr. word, most often used of Christ's second coming (4:18; 1Ti 6:14; Titus 2:13), but here of His first coming. **abolished death ... immortality to light.** "Abolished" means "rendered inoperative." Physical death still exists, but it is no longer a threat or an enemy for Christians (1Co 15:54, 55; Heb 2:14). It was not until the incarnation and the gospel that God chose to fully make known the truth of immortality and eternal life, a reality only partially understood by OT believers (cf. Job 19:26).

1:11 preacher ... teacher. *See notes on 1Ti 2:7.*

1:12 I also suffer. Cf. v. 8; *see notes on 2Co 4:8–18; 6:4–10; 11:23–28; Gal 6:17; Php 3:10.* **I am not ashamed.** *See notes on v. 8; Ro 1:16; 1Pe 4:16.* Paul had no fear of persecution and death from preaching the gospel in a hostile setting, because he was so confident God had sealed his future glory and blessing. **know whom I have believed.** "Know" describes the certainty of Paul's intimate, saving knowledge—the object of which was God Himself. The form of the Gr. verb translated "I have believed" refers to something that began in the past and has continuing results (*see note on Ro 1:16*). This knowing is equal to "the knowledge of the truth" (3:7; 1Ti 2:4). **He is able to guard.** *See notes on Jude 24, 25.* **what I have entrusted.** Paul's life in time and eternity had been given to his Lord. He lived with unwavering confidence and boldness because of the revealed truth about God's power and faithfulness, and his own experience of an unbreakable relationship to the Lord (Ro 8:31–39). **that day.** Cf. v. 18; 4:8; *see notes on Php 1:6.* Also called "day of Christ" (*see notes on Php 1:10*), when believers will stand before the judgment seat and be rewarded (*see notes on 1Co 3:13; 2Co 5:10; 1Pe 1:5*).

1:13 sound words. Cf. 1Ti 4:6; 6:3. The Scripture and the doctrine it teaches (*see notes on 3:15–17*). **from me.** Paul had been the source of this divine revelation (cf. 2:2; 3:10, 14; Php 4:9; *see notes on Eph 3:1–5*). **faith and love ... in Christ Jesus.** "Faith" is confidence that God's Word is true, and "love" is kindness and compassion in teaching that truth (cf. Eph 4:15).

1:14 the treasure ... entrusted to *you*. The treasure of the good news of salvation revealed in the Scripture (*see note on 1Ti 6:20*).

1:15 Asia. A Roman province that is part of modern Turkey; this is not a reference to the entire region of Asia Minor. **Phygelus and Hermogenes.** Nothing else is known about these two men, who apparently had shown promise as leaders, had been close to Paul, and were well known among the Asian churches, but deserted Paul under the pressure of persecution.

1:16 Onesiphorus. One of Paul's loyal coworkers who had not deserted Paul, but befriended him in prison and was not ashamed or afraid to visit the apostle there regularly and minister to his needs. Since Paul asks Timothy to greet those in his house (4:19), the family obviously lived in or near Ephesus.

1:17 when he was in Rome. For notes on Rome, see Introduction to Romans: Background and Setting. Onesiphorus was perhaps on a business trip, and the text implies that his search involved time, effort, and possibly even danger.

1:18 that day. *See note on v. 12.* **Ephesus.** See Introduction to Ephesians: Background and Setting. Onesiphorus' faithfulness began here many years earlier, when Paul ministered on his third or fourth missionary journey.

2:1 my son. Paul had led Timothy to Christ during his first missionary journey (cf. 1Co 4:17; 1Ti 1:2, 18). **be strong.** Here is the main admonition in the first part of the letter. Paul is calling for Timothy to overcome his apparent drift toward weakness and renew his commitment to his ministry (see Introduction: Historical and Theological Themes).

2:2 heard from me. *See notes on 1:13;* cf. 3:14. During Timothy's many years of close association with Paul (see Introduction to 1 Timothy: Author and Date), he had heard divine truth which God had revealed through the apostle. **presence of many witnesses.** Such as Silas, Barnabas, and Luke, and many others in the churches who could attest to the divine authenticity of Paul's teaching—a needed reminder to Timothy in light of the many defections at Ephesus (cf. 1:15). **faithful men who will be able to teach others.** Timothy was to take the divine revelation he had learned from Paul and teach it to other faithful men—men with proven spiritual character and giftedness, who would in turn pass on those truths to another generation. From Paul to Timothy to faithful men to others encompasses 4 generations of godly leaders. That process of spiritual reproduction, which began in the early church, is to continue until the Lord returns.

2:3 a good soldier. The metaphor of the Christian life as warfare (against the evil world system, the believer's sinful human nature, and Satan) is a familiar one in the NT (cf. 2Co 10:3–5; Eph 6:10–20; 1Th 4:8; 1Ti 1:18; 4:7; 6:12). Here Paul is dealing with the conflict against the hostile world and the persecution (cf. v. 9; 1:8; 3:11, 12; 4:7).

2:4 entangles himself. Just as a soldier called to duty is completely severed from the normal affairs of civilian life, so also must the good soldier of Jesus Christ refuse to allow the things of the world to distract him (cf. Jas 4:4; 1Jn 2:15–17).

2:5 competes as an athlete. The Gr. verb (*athleō*) expresses the effort and determination needed to compete successfully in an athletic event (cf. 1Co 9:24). This is a useful picture of spiritual effort and untiring pursuit of the victory to those familiar with events such as the Olympic Games and the Isthmian Games (held in Corinth). **prize ... rules.** All an athlete's hard work and discipline will be wasted if he or she fails to compete according to the rules. This is a call to obey the Word of God in the pursuit of spiritual victory.

2:6 The hard-working farmer. "Hard-working" is from a Gr. verb meaning "to labor to the point of exhaustion." Ancient farmers worked long hours of backbreaking labor under all kinds of conditions, with the hope that their physical effort would be rewarded by a good harvest. Paul is urging Timothy not to be lazy or indolent, but to labor intensely (cf. Col 1:28, 29) with a view to the harvest. Cf. 1Co 3:5–8.

2:7 Consider. The Gr. word denotes clear perception, full understanding, and careful consideration. The form of the verb suggests

8 Remember Jesus Christ, [A]risen from the dead,
[B]descendant of David, [C]according to my gospel,
9 [a]for which I [A]suffer hardship even to [B]imprison-
ment as a [C]criminal; but [D]the word of God [E]is not
imprisoned. 10 For this reason [A]I endure all things
for [B]the sake of those who are chosen, [C]so that they
also may obtain the [D]salvation which is in [E]Christ
Jesus *and* with *it* [F]eternal glory. 11 [A]It is a trustworthy statement:

For [B]if we died with Him, we
will also live with Him;
12 If we endure, [A]we will also
reign with Him;
If we [a,B]deny Him, He also will deny us;
13 If we are faithless, [A]He
remains faithful, for [B]He
cannot deny Himself.

AN UNASHAMED WORKMAN

14 Remind *them* of these things, and solemnly
[A]charge *them* in the presence of God not to [B]wrangle
about words, which is useless *and leads* to the ruin
of the hearers. 15 Be diligent to [A]present yourself approved to God as a workman who does not need to be
ashamed, accurately handling [B]the word of truth. 16 But
[A]avoid [B]worldly *and* empty chatter, for [a]it will lead to
further ungodliness, 17 and their [a]talk will spread like
[b]gangrene. Among them are [A]Hymenaeus and Philetus,
18 *men* who have gone astray from the truth saying
that [A]the resurrection has already taken place, and
they upset [B]the faith of some. 19 Nevertheless, the [A]firm
foundation of God stands, having this [B]seal, "[C]The Lord
knows those who are His," and, "[D]Everyone who names
the name of the Lord is to abstain from wickedness."
20 Now in a large house there are not only gold
and silver vessels, but also vessels of wood and

2:8 [A]Acts 2:24 [B]Matt 1:1 [C]Rom 2:16 2:9 [a]Lit *in which* [A]2 Tim 1:8; 2:3 [B]Phil 1:7 [C]Luke 23:32 [D]1 Thess 1:8 [E]Acts 28:31; 2 Tim 4:17 2:10 [A]Col 1:24 [B]Luke 18:7; Titus 1:1 [C]2 Cor 1:6; 1 Thess 5:9 [D]1 Cor 1:21 [E]2 Tim 1:1; 2:1, 3 [F]2 Cor 4:17; 1 Pet 5:10 2:11 [A]1 Tim 1:15 [B]Rom 6:8; 1 Thess 5:10 2:12 [a]Lit *will deny* [A]Matt 19:28; Luke 22:29; Rom 5:17; 8:17 [B]Matt 10:33; Luke 12:9; 1 Tim 5:8 2:13 [A]Rom 3:3; 1 Cor 1:9 [B]Num 23:19; Titus 1:2 2:14 [A]1 Tim 5:21; 2 Tim 4:1 [B]1 Tim 6:4; 2 Tim 2:23; Titus 3:9 2:15 [A]Rom 6:13; James 1:12 [B]Eph 1:13; James 1:18 2:16 [a]Lit *they will make further progress in ungodliness* [A]Titus 3:9 [B]1 Tim 1:9; 6:20 2:17 [a]Lit *word* [b]Or *cancer* [A]1 Tim 1:20 2:18 [A]1 Cor 15:12 [B]1 Tim 1:19; Titus 1:11 2:19 [A]Is 28:16f; 1 Tim 3:15 [B]John 3:33 [C]John 10:14; 1 Cor 8:3 [D]Luke 13:27; 1 Cor 1:2

a strong admonition by Paul, not mere advice, to give deep thought to what he was writing.

2:8 Remember Jesus Christ. The supreme model of a faithful teacher (v. 2), soldier (vv. 3, 4), athlete (v. 5), and farmer (v. 6). Timothy was to follow His example in teaching, suffering, pursuing the prize, and planting the seeds of truth for a spiritual harvest. **risen from the dead.** The resurrection of Christ is the central truth of the Christian faith (1Co 15:3, 4, 17, 19). By it, God affirmed the perfect redemptive work of Jesus Christ (*see note on Ro 1:4*). **descendant of David.** *See notes on Ro 1:3; Rev 22:16.* As David's descendant, Jesus is the rightful heir to his throne (Lk 1:32, 33). The Lord's humanity is stressed.

2:9 I suffer ... but the word ... is not imprisoned. Paul contrasts his imprisonment for the sake of the gospel to the unfettered power of the Word of God.

2:10 for the sake of those who are chosen. Those of the elect, having been chosen for salvation from before the world began (*see note on 1:9*), who had not yet come to faith in Jesus Christ (*see notes on Ac 18:10; Titus 1:1*). **the salvation which is in Christ Jesus.** There is salvation in no one else (Ac 4:12; cf. Ro 8:29; Eph 1:4, 5). The gospel must be proclaimed (Mt 28:19; Ac 1:8) because the elect are not saved apart from faith in Christ (Ro 10:14). **eternal glory.** The ultimate outcome of salvation (*see notes on Ro 5:2; 8:17*).

2:11 trustworthy statement. The saying is in vv. 11–13. *See note on 1Ti 1:15.* **died with Him ... live with Him.** This refers to believers' spiritual participation in Christ's death and resurrection (Ro 6:4–8), including also the possibility of suffering martyrdom for the sake of Christ, as the context would indicate.

2:12 endure. Believers who persevere give evidence of the genuineness of their faith (*see note on Mt 24:13*; cf. Mt 10:22; Jn 8:31; Ro 2:7; Col 1:23). **reign with Him.** In His future eternal kingdom (Rev 1:6; 5:10; 20:4, 6). **If we deny Him, He also will deny us.** Speaks of a final, permanent denial, such as that of an apostate (*see note on 1Ti 1:19*), not the temporary failure of a true believer like Peter (Mt 26:69–75). Those who so deny Christ give evidence that they never truly belonged to Him (1Jn 2:19) and face the fearful reality of one day being denied by Him (Mt 10:33).

2:13 faithless. This refers to a lack of saving faith, not to weak or struggling faith. Unbelievers will ultimately deny Christ because their faith was not genuine (cf. Jas 2:14–26). **He remains faithful, for He cannot deny Himself.** As faithful as Jesus is to save those who believe in Him (Jn 3:16), He is equally faithful to judge those who do not (Jn 3:18). To act any other way would be inconsistent with His holy, unchangeable nature. Cf. Heb 10:23.

2:14 wrangle about words. Arguing with false teachers, i.e., deceivers who use human reason to subvert God's Word, is not only foolish (Pr 14:7) and futile (Mt 7:6), but dangerous (vv. 16, 17; cf. v. 23). This is the first of 3 warnings to avoid useless arguments. *See notes on vv. 16, 23; 1Ti 4:6, 7; 6:3–5; 2Pe 2:1–3.* **ruin.** The Gr. word means "overturned," or "overthrown." It appears only one other time in the NT (2Pe 2:6), where it describes the destruction of Sodom and Gomorrah. Because it replaces the truth with lies, false teaching brings spiritual catastrophe to those who heed it. The ruin can be eternal.

2:15 Be diligent. This word denotes zealous persistence in accomplishing a goal. Timothy, like all who preach or teach the Word, was to give his maximum effort to impart God's Word completely, accurately, and clearly to his hearers. This is crucial to counter the disastrous effects of false teaching (vv. 14, 16, 17). **accurately handling.** Lit. "cutting it straight"—a reference to the exactness demanded by such trades as carpentry, masonry, and Paul's trade of leather working and tentmaking. Precision and accuracy are required in biblical interpretation, beyond all other enterprises, because the interpreter is handling God's Word. Anything less is shameful. **the word of truth.** All of Scripture in general (Jn 17:17), and the gospel message in particular (Eph 1:13; Col 1:5).

2:16 avoid worldly *and* empty chatter. *See notes on v. 14; 1Ti 6:20*; cf. Titus 3:9. Such destructive heresy leads only to "further ungodliness." Heresy can't save or sanctify. This is Paul's second such warning. Cf. vv. 14, 23.

2:17 gangrene. The word refers to a disease which spreads rapidly in a deadly manner. The metaphor emphasizes the insidious danger of false teaching. It attacks and consumes one's life. **Hymenaeus.** *See note on 1Ti 1:20.* **Philetus.** Alexander's replacement (1Ti 1:20) as Hymenaeus' accomplice.

2:18 the resurrection has already taken place. Like the false teachers who troubled the Corinthians (1Co 15:12), Hymenaeus and Philetus denied the reality of believers' bodily resurrection. They probably taught that believers' spiritual identification with Christ's death and resurrection (Ro 6:4, 5, 8) was the only resurrection they would experience and that had already happened. Such heretical teaching reflects the contemporary Greek philosophical view that matter was evil and spirit was good. **upset the faith.** This speaks of those whose faith was not genuine (cf. Mt 24:24). Genuine saving faith cannot be finally and completely overthrown (*see note on v. 12*). False, nonsaving faith is common (cf. 4:10). *See notes on Mt 7:21–28; 13:19–22; Jn 2:23, 24; 6:64–66; 8:31; 1Jn 2:19.*

2:19 the firm foundation of God. This is likely a reference to the church (cf. 1Ti 3:15), which cannot be overcome by the forces of hell (Mt 16:18) and is made up of those who belong to Him. **seal.** A symbol of ownership and authenticity. Paul gives two characteristics of those with the divine seal of authenticity. **The Lord knows those who are His.** This is likely a reference to Nu 16:5. He "knows," not in the sense of awareness, but as a husband knows his wife in the sense of intimate relationship (*see notes on Jn 10:26–29; Gal 4:9*). God has known His own ever since He chose them before time began. *See note on 1:9.* **Everyone ... abstain from wickedness.** This statement is likely adapted from Nu 16:26, and reflects a second mark of God's ownership of believers, which is their pursuit of holiness (cf. 1Co 6:19, 20; 1Pe 1:15, 16).

2:20 vessels. The Gr. word is very general and was used to describe various tools, utensils, and furniture found in the home. In this "large house" analogy, Paul contrasts two kinds of utensils or serving dishes. **some to honor.** In a wealthy home, the ones made of precious "gold and silver" were used for honorable purposes

of earthenware, and [A]some to honor and some to
dishonor. 21 Therefore, if anyone cleanses himself
from [A]these *things,* he will be a vessel for honor,
sanctified, useful to the Master, [B]prepared for every
good work. 22 Now [A]flee from youthful lusts and
pursue righteousness, [B]faith, love *and* peace, with
those who [C]call on the Lord [D]from a pure heart.
23 But refuse foolish and ignorant [A]speculations,
knowing that they [B]produce [a]quarrels. 24 [A]The Lord's
bond-servant must not be quarrelsome, but be kind
to all, [B]able to teach, patient when wronged, 25 [A]with
gentleness correcting those who are in opposition,
[B]if perhaps God may grant them repentance leading to [C]the knowledge of the truth, 26 and they may
come to their senses *and escape* from [A]the snare
of the devil, having been [B]held captive [a]by him to
do his will.

"DIFFICULT TIMES WILL COME"

3 But realize this, that [A]in the last days difficult
times will come. 2 For men will be [A]lovers of self,
[B]lovers of money, [C]boastful, [C]arrogant, [D]revilers,
[C]disobedient to parents, [E]ungrateful, [F]unholy, 3 [A]un-
loving, irreconcilable, [B]malicious gossips, without
self-control, brutal, [a,C]haters of good, 4 [A]treacherous,
[B]reckless, [C]conceited, [D]lovers of pleasure rather than
lovers of God, 5 holding to a form of [a,A]godliness,
although they have [B]denied its power; [C]Avoid such
men as these. 6 For among them are those who [a,A]en-
ter into households and captivate [b,B]weak women
weighed down with sins, led on by [C]various impulses, 7 always learning and never able to [A]come
to the [a]knowledge of the truth. 8 Just as [A]Jannes and
Jambres [B]opposed Moses, so these *men* also oppose
the truth, [C]men of depraved mind, rejected in regard to the faith. 9 But they will not make further
progress; for their [A]folly will be obvious to all, just
[B]as [a]Jannes's and Jambres's folly was also.
10 Now you [A]followed my teaching, conduct, purpose, faith, patience, [B]love, [a]perseverance, 11 [A]perse-
cutions, *and* [B]sufferings, such as happened to me
at [C]Antioch, at [D]Iconium *and* at [E]Lystra; what [F]per-
secutions I endured, and out of them all [G]the Lord
rescued me! 12 Indeed, all who desire to live godly in

2:20 [A]Rom 9:21 2:21 [A]1 Tim 6:11; 2 Tim 2:16-18 [B]2 Cor 9:8; Eph 2:10; 2 Tim 3:17 2:22 [A]1 Tim 6:11 [B]1 Tim 1:14 [C]Acts 7:59 [D]1 Tim 1:5 2:23 [a]Lit *fightings* [A]1 Tim 6:4; 2 Tim 2:14; Titus 3:9 [B]Titus 3:9; James 4:1 2:24 [A]1 Tim 3:3; Titus 1:7 [B]1 Tim 3:2 2:25 [A]Gal 6:1; Titus 3:2; 1 Pet 3:15 [B]Acts 8:22 [C]1 Tim 2:4 2:26 [a]Or *by him, to do His will* [A]1 Tim 3:7 [B]Luke 5:10 3:1 [A]1 Tim 4:1 3:2 [A]Phil 2:21 [B]Luke 16:14; 1 Tim 3:3; 6:10 [C]Rom 1:30 [D]2 Pet 2:10-12 [E]Luke 6:35 [F]1 Tim 1:9 3:3 [a]Lit *not loving good* [A]Rom 1:31 [B]1 Tim 3:11 [C]Titus 1:8 3:4 [A]Acts 7:52 [B]Acts 19:36 [C]1 Tim 3:6 [D]Phil 3:19 3:5 [a]Or *religion* [A]1 Tim 4:7 [B]1 Tim 5:8 [C]Matt 7:15; 2 Thess 3:6 3:6 [a]Or *creep into* [b]Or *idle* [A]Jude 4 [B]1 Tim 5:6; Titus 3:3 [C]Titus 3:3 3:7 [a]Or *recognition* [A]2 Tim 2:25 3:8 [A]Ex 7:11 [B]Acts 13:8 [C]1 Tim 6:5 3:9 [a]Lit *that of those* [A]Luke 6:11 [B]Ex 7:11, 12; 8:18; 9:11 3:10 [a]Or *steadfastness* [A]Phil 2:20, 22; 1 Tim 4:6 [B]1 Tim 6:11 3:11 [A]2 Cor 12:10 [B]2 Cor 1:5, 7 [C]Acts 13:14, 45, 50 [D]Acts 14:1-7, 19 [E]Acts 14:8-20 [F]2 Cor 11:23-27 [G]Rom 15:31

such as serving food to the family and guests. **some to dishonor.** Those made of "wood and of earthenware" were not for any honorable use, but rather those uses which were repulsive—disposing of garbage and the filthy waste of the household. *See notes on 2Co 4:7.*

2:21 anyone. Whoever wants to be useful to the Lord for noble purposes. Even a common wood bucket or clay pot becomes useful when purged and made holy. **cleanses himself.** *See note on v. 19.* The Gr. word means "to thoroughly clean out," or "to completely purge." For any wastebucket in the house to be used for a noble purpose, it would have had to be vigorously scoured, cleansed, and purged of all vestiges of its former filth. **these *things*.** The vessels of dishonor (v. 20). Associating with anyone who teaches error and lives in sin is corrupting (Pr 1:10–19; 13:20; 1Co 5:6, 11; 15:33; Titus 1:16)—all the more so when they are leaders in the church. This is clearly a call to separate from all who claim to serve God, but do so as filthy implements useful only for the most dishonorable duties.

2:22 youthful lusts. Not merely illicit sexual desires, but also such lusts as pride, desire for wealth and power, jealousy, self-assertiveness, and an argumentative spirit.

2:23 speculations . . . quarrels. Paul's third warning to avoid useless arguments with false teachers (*see notes on vv. 14, 16*).

2:24 able to teach. This is one word in Gr. meaning "skilled in teaching." *See note on 1Ti 3:2.*

2:25 those who are in opposition. Primarily unbelievers (captive to Satan, v. 26), but also could include believers deceived by the "foolish and ignorant" (v. 23) speculations of the false teachers; and, possibly, the false teachers themselves. **God may grant them repentance.** Cf. Ac 11:18; see 2Co 7:9, 10. All true repentance is produced by God's sovereign grace (Eph 2:7), and without such grace human effort to change is futile (cf. Jer 13:23). **knowledge of the truth.** *See note on 3:7.* When God, by grace, grants saving faith, it includes the granting of repentance from sin. Neither is a human work.

2:26 the snare of the devil. Deception is Satan's trap. He is an inveterate, scheming, clever, and subtle purveyor of lies. *See notes on Ge 3:4–6; Jn 8:44; 2Co 11:13–15; Rev 12:9.*

3:1 the last days. This phrase refers to this age, the time since the first coming of the Lord Jesus. *See note on 1Ti 4:1.* **difficult times.** "Difficult" is used to describe the savage nature of two demon-possessed men (Mt 8:28). The word for "times" had to do with epochs, rather than clock or calendar time. Such savage, dangerous eras or epochs will increase in frequency and severity as the return of Christ approaches (v. 13). The church age is fraught with these dangerous movements accumulating strength as the end nears. Cf. Mt 7:15; 24:11, 12, 24; 2Pe 2:1, 2.

3:2–4 This list of attributes characterizing the leaders of the dangerous seasons is a description of unbelievers similar to the Lord's in Mk 7:21, 22.

3:5 holding to a form of godliness . . . denied its power. "Form" refers to outward shape or appearance. Like the unbelieving scribes and Pharisees, false teachers and their followers are concerned with mere external appearances (cf. Mt 23:25; Titus 1:16). Their outward form of Christianity and virtue makes them all the more dangerous.

3:6 weak women. Weak in virtue and the knowledge of the truth, and weighed down with emotional and spiritual guilt over their sins, these women were easy prey for the deceitful false teachers. *See notes on 1Ti 2:13, 14; 5:11, 12.*

3:7 the knowledge of the truth. First Timothy 2:4 uses this same phrase, equating it with being saved. Here Paul identified those women (v. 6) and men who were often jumping from one false teacher or cult to another without ever coming to an understanding of God's saving truth in Jesus Christ. The present age, since the coming of Jesus Christ, has been loaded with perilous false teaching that can't save, but does damn (cf. vv. 14, 16, 17; 1Ti 4:1).

3:8 Jannes and Jambres. Although their names are not mentioned in the OT, they were likely two of the Egyptian magicians that opposed Moses (Ex 7:11, 22; 8:7, 18, 19; 9:11). According to Jewish tradition, they pretended to become Jewish proselytes, instigated the worship of the golden calf, and were killed with the rest of the idolaters (Ex 32). Paul's choice of them as examples may indicate the false teachers at Ephesus were practicing deceiving signs and wonders. **the truth.** *See note on v. 7.* **rejected.** The same word is translated "depraved" in Ro 1:28 (*see note there*) and comes from a Gr. word meaning "useless" in the sense of being tested (like metal) and shown to be worthless.

3:9 folly . . . obvious. Sooner or later, it will be clear that these false teachers are lost fools, as it became clear in the case of Jannes and Jambres.

3:11 persecutions. From a Gr. verb that lit. means "to put to flight." Paul had been forced to flee from Damascus (Ac 9:23–25), Pisidian Antioch (Ac 13:50), Iconium (Ac 14:6), Thessalonica (Ac 17:10), and Berea (Ac 17:14). **Antioch . . . Iconium . . . Lystra.** As a native of Lystra (Ac 16:1), Timothy vividly recalled the persecution Paul faced in those 3 cities. **the Lord rescued me!** Cf. 4:17, 18; Pss 34:4, 6, 19; 37:40; 91:2–6, 14; Is 41:10; 43:2; Da 3:17; Ac 26:16, 17; 2Co 1:10. The Lord's repeated deliverance of Paul should have encouraged Timothy in the face of persecution by those at Ephesus who opposed the gospel.

3:12 all who desire to live godly in Christ Jesus will be persecuted. Faithful believers

Christ Jesus [A]will be persecuted. **13** But evil men and
impostors [A]will proceed *from bad* to worse, [B]deceiv-
ing and being deceived. **14** You, however, [A]continue
in the things you have learned and become convinced of, knowing from whom you have learned
them, **15** and that [A]from childhood you have known
[B]the sacred writings which are able to [C]give you the
wisdom that leads to [D]salvation through faith which
is in [E]Christ Jesus. **16** [A]All Scripture is [a]inspired by
God and profitable for teaching, for reproof, for
correction, for [b]training in righteousness; **17** so that
[A]the man of God may be adequate, [B]equipped for
every good work.

"PREACH THE WORD"

4 [A]I solemnly charge *you* in the presence of God
and of Christ Jesus, who is to [B]judge the living
and the dead, and by His [C]appearing and His kingdom: **2** preach [A]the word; be ready in season *and*
out of season; [B]reprove, rebuke, exhort, with [a]great
[C]patience and instruction. **3** For [A]the time will come
when they will not endure [B]sound doctrine; but

3:12 [A]John 15:20; Acts 14:22; 2 Cor 4:9f 3:13 [A]2 Tim 2:16 [B]Titus 3:3 3:14 [A]2 Tim 1:13; Titus 1:9 3:15 [A]2 Tim 1:5 [B]John 5:47; Rom 2:27 [C]Ps 119:98f [D]1 Cor 1:21 [E]2 Tim 1:1 3:16 [a]Lit *God-breathed* [b]Lit *training which is in* [A]Rom 4:23f; 15:4; 2 Pet 1:20f 3:17 [A]1 Tim 6:11 [B]2 Tim 2:21; Heb 13:21 4:1 [A]1 Tim 5:21; 2 Tim 2:14 [B]Acts 10:42 [C]2 Thess 2:8; 2 Tim 1:10; 4:8 4:2 [a]Lit *all* [A]Gal 6:6; Col 4:3; 1 Thess 1:6 [B]1 Tim 5:20; Titus 1:13; 2:15 [C]2 Tim 3:10 4:3 [A]2 Tim 3:1 [B]1 Tim 1:10; 2 Tim 1:13

must expect persecution and suffering at the hands of the Christ-rejecting world (cf. Jn 15:18–21; Ac 14:22).

3:13 All the dangerous movements of the false teachers (cf. vv. 1–9) will become increasingly more successful until Christ comes. Cf. 2Th 2:11.

3:14 from whom you have learned. *See note on 1:13.* To further encourage Timothy to stand firm, Paul reminds him of his godly heritage. The plural form of the pronoun "whom" suggests Timothy was indebted not just to Paul, but to others as well (1:5).

3:15 from childhood. Lit. "from infancy." Two people whom Timothy was especially indebted to were his mother and grandmother (*see note on 1:5*), who faithfully taught him the truths of OT Scripture from his earliest childhood, so that he was ready to receive the gospel when Paul preached it. **you have known the sacred writings.** A common designation of the OT by Greek-speaking Jews. **wisdom that leads to salvation.** The OT Scriptures pointed to Christ (Jn 5:37–39) and revealed the need for faith in God's promises (Ge 15:6; cf. Ro 4:1–3). Thus, they were able to lead people to acknowledge their sin and need for justification in Christ (Gal 3:24). Salvation is brought by the Holy Spirit using the Word. *See notes on Ro 10:14–17; Eph 5:26, 27; 1Pe 1:23–25.* **faith which is in Christ Jesus.** Though not understanding all the details involved (cf. 1Pe 1:10–12), OT believers, including Abraham (Jn 8:56) and Moses (Heb 11:26) looked forward to the coming of the Messiah (Is 7:14; 9:6) and His atonement for sin (Is 53:5, 6). So did Timothy, who responded when he heard the gospel.

3:16 All Scripture. Grammatically similar Gr. constructions (Ro 7:12; 2Co 10:10; 1Ti 1:15; 2:3; 4:4) argue persuasively that the translation "all Scripture is inspired ...." is accurate. Both OT and NT Scripture are included (*see notes on 2Pe 3:15, 16,* which identify NT writings as Scripture). **inspired by God.** Lit. "breathed out by God," or "God-breathed." Sometimes God told the Bible writers the exact words to say (e.g., Jer 1:9), but more often He used their minds, vocabularies, and experiences to produce His own perfect infallible, inerrant Word (*see notes on 1Th 2:13; Heb 1:1; 2Pe 1:20, 21*). It is important to note that inspiration applies only to the original autographs of Scripture, not the Bible writers; there are no inspired Scripture writers, only inspired Scripture. So identified is God with His Word that when Scripture speaks, God speaks (cf. Ro 9:17; Gal 3:8). Scripture is called "the oracles of God" (Ro 3:2), and cannot be altered (Jn 10:35; Mt 5:17, 18; Lk 16:17; Rev 22:18, 19). **teaching.** The divine instruction or doctrinal content of both the OT and the NT (cf. 2:15; Ac 20:18, 20, 21, 27; 1Co 2:14–16; Col 3:16; 1Jn 2:20, 24, 27). The Scripture provides the comprehensive and complete body of divine truth necessary for life and godliness. Cf. Ps 119:97–105. **reproof.** Rebuke for wrong behavior or wrong belief. The Scripture exposes sin (Heb 4:12, 13) that can then be dealt with through confession and repentance. **correction.** The restoration of something to its proper condition. The word appears only here in the NT, but was used in extrabiblical Gr. of righting a fallen object, or helping back to their feet those who had stumbled. Scripture not only rebukes wrong behavior, but also points the way back to godly living. Cf. Ps 119:9–11; Jn 15:1, 2. **training in righteousness.** Scripture provides positive training (originally used in reference to training a child) in godly behavior, not merely rebuke and correction of wrong behavior (Ac 20:32; 1Ti 4:6; 1Pe 2:1, 2).

3:17 man of God. A technical term for an official preacher of divine truth. *See note on 1Ti 6:11.* **adequate.** Capable of doing everything one is called to do (cf. Col 2:10). **equipped for every good work.** Enabled to meet all the demands of godly ministry and righteous living. The Word not only accomplishes this in the life of the man of God but in all who follow him (Eph 4:11–13).

4:1 I solemnly charge *you*. Or better "command." The Gr. has the idea of issuing a forceful order or directive (cf. 2:14; 1Ti 1:18; 5:21). **in the presence of God and of Christ Jesus.** The Gr. construction also allows the translation "in the presence of God, even Christ Jesus," which is probably the best rendering since He is about to be introduced as the judge (cf. Jn 5:22). Everyone who ministers the Word of God is under the omniscient scrutiny of Christ (*see notes on 2Co 2:17; Heb 13:17*). **Christ Jesus, who is to judge.** The grammatical construction suggests imminency—that Christ is about to judge. Paul is emphasizing the unique accountability that all believers, and especially ministers of the Word of God, have to Christ as Judge. Service to Christ is rendered both under His watchful eye and with the knowledge that as Judge He will one day appraise the works of every believer (*see notes on 1Co 3:12–15; 4:1–5; 2Co 5:10*). That is not a judgment of condemnation, but one of evaluation. With regard to salvation, believers have been judged already and declared righteous—they are no longer subject to the condemnation of sin (Ro 8:1–4). **the living and the dead.** Christ will ultimately judge all men in 3 distinct settings: 1) the judgment of believers after the Rapture (1Co 3:12–15; 2Co 5:10); 2) the sheep and goats judgment of the nations, in which believers will be separated from unbelievers (Mt 25:31–33, for entrance into the millennial kingdom); and 3) the Great White Throne judgment of unbelievers only (Rev 20:11–15). Here, the apostle is referring to judgment in a general sense, encompassing all those elements. **His appearing.** The Gr. word translated "appearing" lit. means "a shining forth" and was used by the ancient Greeks of the supposed appearance to men of a pagan god. Here, Paul is referring generally to Christ's second coming, when He will judge "the living and the dead" (*see previous note*) and establish His millennial and eternal kingdom (*see note on 1Ti 6:14*).

4:2 the word. The entire written Word of God, His complete revealed truth as contained in the Bible (cf. 3:15, 16; Ac 20:27). **be ready.** The Gr. word has a broad range of meanings, including suddenness (Lk 2:9; Ac 12:7) or forcefulness (Lk 20:1; Ac 4:1; 6:12; 23:27). Here the form of the verb suggests the complementary ideas of urgency, preparedness, and readiness. It was used of a soldier prepared to go into battle or a guard who was continually alert for any surprise attack—attitudes which are imperative for a faithful preacher (Jer 20:9; Ac 21:11–13; Eph 5:15, 16; 1Pe 3:15). **in season *and* out of season.** The faithful preacher must proclaim the Word when it is popular and/or convenient, and when it is not; when it seems suitable to do so, and when it seems not. The dictates of popular culture, tradition, reputation, acceptance, or esteem in the community (or in the church) must never alter the true preacher's commitment to proclaim God's Word. **reprove, rebuke.** The negative side of preaching the Word (the "reproof" and "correction"; cf. 3:16). The Gr. word for "reprove" refers to correcting behavior or false doctrine by using careful biblical argument to help a person understand the error of his actions. The Gr. word for "rebuke" deals more with correcting the person's motives by convicting him of his sin and leading him to repentance. **exhort ... instruction.** The positive side of preaching (the "teaching" and "training"; cf. 3:16).

4:3 not endure. This refers to holding up under adversity, and can be translated "tolerate." Paul here warns Timothy that, in the dangerous seasons of this age, many people

wanting to have their ears tickled, they will accumulate for themselves teachers in accordance to
their own desires, 4 and [A]will turn away their ears
from the truth and [B]will turn aside to myths. 5 But
you, [A]be sober in all things, [B]endure hardship, do
the work of an [C]evangelist, fulfill your [D]ministry.
6 For I am already being [A]poured out as a drink
offering, and the time of [B]my departure has come.
7 [A]I have fought the good fight, I have finished [B]the
course, I have kept [C]the faith; 8 in the future there [A]is
laid up for me [B]the crown of righteousness, which
the Lord, the righteous Judge, will award to me on
[C]that day; and not only to me, but also to [D]all who
have loved His [E]appearing.

PERSONAL CONCERNS

9 [A]Make every effort to come to me soon; 10 for [A]De-
mas, having loved [B]this present [a]world, has deserted
me and gone to [C]Thessalonica; Crescens *has gone* to
[b,D]Galatia, [E]Titus to Dalmatia. 11 [A]Only [B]Luke is with
me. Pick up [C]Mark and bring him with you, [D]for he is
useful to me for service. 12 But [A]Tychicus I have sent
to [B]Ephesus. 13 When you come bring the cloak which
I left at [A]Troas with Carpus, and the books, especially

4:4 [A]2 Thess 2:11; Titus 1:14 [B]1 Tim 1:4 **4:5** [A]1 Pet 1:13 [B]2 Tim 1:8 [C]Acts 21:8 [D]Eph 4:12; Col 4:17 **4:6** [A]Phil 2:17 [B]Phil 1:23; 2 Pet 1:14 **4:7** [A]1 Cor 9:25f; Phil 1:30; 1 Tim 1:18; 6:12 [B]Acts 20:24; 1 Cor 9:24 [C]2 Tim 3:10 **4:8** [A]Col 1:5; 1 Pet 1:4 [B]1 Cor 9:25; 2 Tim 2:5; James 1:12 [C]2 Tim 1:12 [D]Phil 3:11 [E]2 Tim 4:1 **4:9** [A]2 Tim 1:4; 4:21; Titus 3:12 **4:10** [a]Or *age* [b]One early ms reads *Gaul* [A]Col 4:14 [B]1 Tim 6:17 [C]Acts 17:1 [D]Acts 16:6 [E]2 Cor 2:13; 8:23; Gal 2:3; Titus 1:4 **4:11** [A]2 Tim 1:15 [B]Col 4:14; Philem 24 [C]Acts 12:12, 25; 15:37-39; Col 4:10 [D]2 Tim 2:21 **4:12** [A]Acts 20:4; Eph 6:21, 22; Col 4:7f [B]Acts 18:19 **4:13** [A]Acts 16:8

would become intolerant of the confrontive, demanding preaching of God's Word (1:13, 14; 1Ti 1:9, 10; 6:3–5). **sound doctrine.** *See notes on 1:13; 1Ti 4:6; Titus 2:1.* **their ears tickled ... their own desires.** Professing Christians, nominal believers in the church follow their own desires and flock to preachers who offer them God's blessings apart from His forgiveness, and His salvation apart from their repentance. They want to be entertained by teachings that will produce pleasant sensations and leave them with good feelings about themselves. Their goal is that men preach "in accordance to their own desires." Under those conditions, people will dictate what men preach, rather than God dictating it by His Word.

4:4 myths. This refers to false idealogies, viewpoints, and philosophies in various forms that oppose sound doctrine (*see notes on 2Co 10:3–5; 1Ti 1:4; 4:7*; cf. Titus 1:14; 2Pe 1:16).

4:5 an evangelist. Used only two other times in the NT (*see notes on Ac 21:8; Eph 4:11*), this word always refers to a specific office of ministry for the purpose of preaching the gospel to non-Christians. Based on Eph 4:11, it is very basic to assume that all churches would have both pastor-teachers and evangelists. But the related verb "to preach the gospel" and the related noun "gospel" are used throughout the NT not only in relation to evangelists, but also to the call for every Christian, especially preachers and teachers, to proclaim the gospel. Paul did not call Timothy to the office of an evangelist, but to "do the work" of one.

4:6–8 As Paul neared the end of his life, he was able to look back without regret or remorse. In these verses, he examines his life from 3 perspectives: the present reality of the end of his life, for which he was ready (v. 6); the past, when he had been faithful (v. 7); and the future, as he anticipated his heavenly reward (v. 8).

4:6 already. Meaning his death was imminent. **a drink offering.** In the OT sacrificial system, this was the final offering that followed the burnt and grain offerings prescribed for the people of Israel (Nu 15:1–16). Paul saw his coming death as his final offering to God in a life that had already been full of sacrifices to Him (*see note on Php 2:17*). **my departure.** Paul's death. The Gr. word essentially refers to the loosening of something, such as the mooring ropes of a ship or the ropes of a tent; thus it eventually acquired the secondary meaning of "departure."

4:7 The form of the 3 Gr. verbs "have fought, have finished, have kept," indicates completed action with continuing results. Paul saw his life as complete—he had been able to accomplish through the Lord's power all that God called him to do. He was a soldier (2:3, 4; 2Co 10:3; 1Ti 6:12; Phm 2), an athlete (1Co 9:24–27; Eph 6:12), and a guardian (1:13, 14; 1Ti 6:20, 21). **the faith.** The truths and standards of the revealed Word of God.

4:8 the crown of righteousness. The Gr. word for "crown" lit. means "surrounding," and it was used of the plaited wreaths or garlands placed on the heads of dignitaries and victorious military officers or athletes. Linguistically, "of righteousness" can mean either that righteousness is the source of the crown, or that righteousness is the nature of the crown. Like the "crown of life" (Jas 1:12), the "crown of exultation" (1Th 2:19), the "imperishable crown" (1Co 9:25), and the "crown of glory" (1Pe 5:4), in which life, rejoicing, imperishability, and glory describe the nature of the crown, the context here seems to indicate the crown represents eternal righteousness. Believers receive the imputed righteousness of Christ (justification) at salvation (Ro 4:6, 11). The Holy Spirit works practical righteousness (sanctification) in the believer throughout his lifetime of struggle with sin (Ro 6:13, 19; 8:4; Eph 5:9; 1Pe 2:24). But only when the struggle is complete will the Christian receive Christ's righteousness perfected in him (glorification) when he enters heaven (*see note on Gal 5:5*). **the righteous Judge.** *See note on v. 1.* **that day.** *See note on 1:12.* **His appearing.** *See notes on v. 1; 1Ti 6:14.*

4:9–22 In these closing verses, Paul brings Timothy up to date on the spiritual condition, activities, and whereabouts of certain men and women who either helped or harmed his ministry.

4:9 Make every effort to come to me soon. Paul longed to see his beloved coworker, but it was imperative that Timothy make haste because Paul knew his days were numbered (v. 6).

4:10 Demas. He had been one of Paul's closest associates along with Luke and Epaphras (*see notes on Col 4:14; Phm 24*). **loved this present world.** *See notes on Jas 4:4; 1Jn 2:15–17.* **deserted.** This Gr. word means "to utterly abandon," with the idea of leaving someone in a dire situation. Demas was a fair-weather disciple who had never counted the cost of genuine commitment to Christ. His kind are described by our Lord in Mt 13:20, 21; cf. Jn 8:31; 1Jn 2:1. **Thessalonica.** Demas may have considered this city a safe haven (see Introduction to 1 Thessalonians: Background and Setting). **Crescens.** In contrast to Demas, Crescens must have been faithful and dependable, since Paul sent him to Galatia, a Roman province in central Asia Minor, where Paul ministered on each of his 3 missionary journeys. **Titus.** Paul's closest friend and coworker next to Timothy (Titus 1:5; see Introduction to Titus: Title). **Dalmatia.** Also known as Illyricum (Ro 15:19), a Roman province on the E coast of the Adriatic Sea, just N of Macedonia.

4:11 Luke. The author of the Gospel of Luke and Acts, and Paul's devoted friend and personal physician, who could not carry the burden of ministry in Rome by himself (see Introductions to Luke and Acts: Author and Date). **Pick up Mark and bring him with you.** Evidently, Mark lived somewhere along the route Timothy would take from Ephesus to Rome. The one who was the author of the Gospel of Mark (sometimes called John), cousin of Barnabas (Col 4:10), and devoted fellow worker (Phm 24), had once left Paul and Barnabas in shame (*see notes on Ac 13:13; 15:36–39*), but had become by this time a valued servant (see Introduction to Mark: Author and Date).

4:12 Tychicus. Paul had either sent him to Ephesus earlier, or he was sending him there to deliver this second letter to Timothy, just as Tychicus had previously delivered Paul's letters to the churches at Ephesus (Eph 6:21), Colosse (Col 4:7), and possibly to Titus (Titus 3:12; *see note on Col 4:7*). **Ephesus.** See Introduction to Ephesians: Background and Setting; *see note on Rev 2:1.*

4:13 cloak. A large, heavy wool garment that doubled as a coat and blanket in cold weather, which Paul would soon face (v. 21). **Troas.** A seaport of Phrygia, in Asia Minor. **Carpus.** An otherwise unknown acquaintance of Paul whose name means "fruit." **the books, especially the parchments.** "Books" refers to papyrus scrolls, possibly OT books. "Parchments" were vellum sheets made of treated animal hides, thus they were extremely expensive. They may have been copies of letters he had written or blank sheets for writing other letters. That Paul did not have these already in his possession leads to the possible conclusion that he was arrested in Troas and had no opportunity to retrieve them.

the parchments. 14 [A]Alexander the coppersmith did
me much harm; [B]the Lord will repay him according
to his deeds. 15 Be on guard against him yourself, for
he vigorously opposed our [a]teaching.
16 At my first defense no one supported me, but all
deserted me; [A]may it not be counted against them.
17 But the Lord stood with me and [A]strengthened
me, so that through me [B]the proclamation might [a]be
[C]fully accomplished, and that all [D]the Gentiles might
hear; and I was [E]rescued out of [F]the lion's mouth.
18 The Lord will rescue me from every evil deed, and
will [a,A]bring me safely to His [B]heavenly kingdom; [C]to
[b]Him *be* the glory forever and ever. Amen.
19 Greet Prisca and [A]Aquila, and [B]the household of
Onesiphorus. 20 [A]Erastus remained at [B]Corinth, but
[C]Trophimus I left sick at [D]Miletus. 21 [A]Make every effort to come before [B]winter. Eubulus greets you, also
Pudens and Linus and Claudia and all the brethren.
22 [A]The Lord be with your spirit. [B]Grace be with
you.

4:14 [A]Acts 19:33; 1 Tim 1:20 [B]Ps 62:12; Rom 2:6; 12:19 4:15 [a]Lit *words* 4:16 [A]Acts 7:60; 1 Cor 13:5 4:17 [a]Or *be fulfilled* [A]1 Tim 1:12; 2 Tim 2:1 [B]Titus 1:3 [C]2 Tim 4:5 [D]Acts 9:15; Phil 1:12ff [E]Rom 15:31; 2 Tim 3:11 [F]1 Sam 17:37; Ps 22:21 4:18 [a]Or *save me for* [b]Lit *Whom* [A]1 Cor 1:21 [B]1 Cor 15:50; 2 Tim 4:1; Heb 11:16; 12:22 [C]Rom 11:36; 2 Pet 3:18 4:19 [A]Acts 18:2 [B]2 Tim 1:16 4:20 [A]Acts 19:22; Rom 16:23 [B]Acts 18:1 [C]Acts 20:4; 21:29 [D]Acts 20:15 4:21 [A]2 Tim 4:9 [B]Titus 3:12 4:22 [A]Gal 6:18; Phil 4:23; Philem 25 [B]Col 4:18

4:14 **Alexander the coppersmith.** Probably not the same man whom Paul delivered to Satan along with Hymenaeus (1Ti 1:20), since Paul singles him out as the one who was a "coppersmith." This Alexander, however, may have been an idol maker (cf. Ac 19:24). **did me much harm.** Alexander opposed Paul's teaching and likely spread his own false doctrine. He may have been instrumental in Paul's arrest and may even have borne false witness against him. Cf. Ac 19:23ff. **the Lord will repay him.** Paul left vengeance in God's hands (Dt 32:35; Ro 12:19).

4:16 **first defense.** The Gr. word for "defense" gives us the Eng. words "apology" and "apologetics." It referred to a verbal defense used in a court of law. In the Roman legal system, an accused person received two hearings: the *prima actio,* much like a contemporary arraignment, established the charge and determined if there was a need for a trial. The *secunda actio* then established the accused's guilt or innocence. The defense Paul referred to was the *prima actio.* **may it not be counted against them.** Like Stephen (Ac 7:60) and the Lord Himself (Lk 23:34).

4:17 **But the Lord stood with me.** The Lord fulfills His promise never to "leave or forsake" His children (Dt 31:6, 8; Jos 1:5; Heb 13:5). **proclamation ... accomplished.** As he had done in the past (Ac 26:2–29), Paul was able to proclaim the gospel before a Roman tribunal. **all the Gentiles might hear.** By proclaiming the gospel to such a cosmopolitan, pagan audience, Paul could say that he had reached all the Gentiles with the gospel. This was a fulfillment of his commission (Ac 9:15, 16; 26:15–18). **the lion's mouth.** Cf. Da 6:26, 27. A common figure for mortal danger (Pss 22:21; 35:17) and a common occurrence for Paul (cf. Ac 14:19; 2Co 4:8–12; 6:4–10; 11:23–27). Peter pictured Satan as a lion in 1Pe 5:8.

4:18 **will rescue me from every evil deed.** On the basis of the Lord's present work—strengthening Paul and standing with him (v. 17)—Paul had hope for the Lord's future work. He knew God would deliver him from all temptations and plots against him (2Co 1:8–10). **bring me safely to His heavenly kingdom.** Paul knew the completion of his own salvation was nearer than when he first believed (cf. Ro 13:11; 2Co 5:8; Php 1:21).

4:19 **Prisca and Aquila.** Paul first met these two faithful friends in Corinth after they fled Italy (*see note on Ac 18:2*). They ministered for some time in Ephesus (Ac 18:18, 19), later returned to Rome for a period of time (Ro 16:3), and had returned to Ephesus. **the household of Onesiphorus.** *See note on 1:16.*

4:20 **Erastus.** Probably the city treasurer of Corinth, who sent greetings through Paul to the church at Rome (*see note on Ro 16:23*). **Corinth.** The leading city in Greece (*see note on Ac 18:1*; see Introduction to 1 Corinthians: Title). **Trophimus.** A native of Asia, specifically Ephesus, who had accompanied Paul from Greece to Troas (*see note on Ac 20:4*). **Miletus.** A city and seaport in the province of Lycia, located 30 mi. S of Ephesus.

4:21 **before winter.** In view of the coming season and the cold Roman jail cell, Paul needed the cloak for warmth. He would also have less opportunity to use the books and parchments as the duration of light grew shorter in winter. **Eubulus ... Pudens ... Linus ... Claudia.** The first 3 names are Latin, which could indicate they were from Italy and had been members in the church at Rome. "Claudia" was a believer and close friend of whom nothing else is known.

4:22 **Grace be with you.** This is the same benediction as in Paul's previous letter to Timothy (*see note on 1Ti 6:21*). The "you" is plural, which means it extended to the entire Ephesian congregation.

THE EPISTLE OF
PAUL TO

TITUS

TITLE

This epistle is named for its recipient, Titus, who is mentioned by name 13 times in the NT (1:4; Gal 2:1, 3; 2Ti 4:10; for the 9 times in 2 Corinthians, see Background and Setting). The title in the Greek NT literally reads "To Titus." Along with 1, 2 Timothy, these letters to Paul's sons in the faith are traditionally called "The Pastoral Epistles."

AUTHOR AND DATE

Authorship by the apostle Paul (1:1) is essentially uncontested (see Introduction to 1 Timothy). Titus was written between A.D. 62–64, while Paul ministered to Macedonian churches between his first and second Roman imprisonments, from either Corinth or Nicopolis (cf. 3:12). Most likely, Titus served with Paul on both the second and third missionary journeys. Titus, like Timothy (2Ti 1:2), had become a beloved disciple (1:4) and fellow worker in the gospel (2Co 8:23). Paul's last mention of Titus (2Ti 4:10) reports that he had gone for ministry in Dalmatia—modern Yugoslavia. The letter probably was delivered by Zenas and Apollos (3:13).

BACKGROUND AND SETTING

Although Luke did not mention Titus by name in the book of Acts, it seems probable that Titus, a Gentile (Gal 2:3), met and may have been led to faith in Christ by Paul (1:4) before or during the apostle's first missionary journey. Later, Titus ministered for a period of time with Paul on the Island of Crete and was left behind to continue and strengthen the work (1:5). After Artemas or Tychicus (3:12) arrived to direct the ministry there, Paul wanted Titus to join him in the city of Nicopolis, in the province of Achaia in Greece, and stay through the winter (3:12).

Because of his involvement with the church at Corinth during Paul's third missionary journey, Titus is mentioned 9 times in 2 Corinthians (2:13; 7:6, 13, 14; 8:6, 16, 23; 12:18), where Paul refers to him as "my brother" (2:13) and "my partner and fellow worker" (8:23). The young elder was already familiar with Judaizers, false teachers in the church, who among other things insisted that all Christians, Gentile as well as Jew, were bound by the Mosaic law. Titus had accompanied Paul and Barnabas years earlier to the Council of Jerusalem where that heresy was the subject (Ac 15; Gal 2:1–5).

Crete, one of the largest islands in the Mediterranean Sea, measuring 160 mi. long by 35 mi. at its widest, lying S of the Aegean Sea, had been briefly visited by Paul on his voyage to Rome (Ac 27:7–9, 12, 13, 21). He returned there for ministry and later left Titus to continue the work, much as he left Timothy at Ephesus (1Ti 1:3), while he went on to Macedonia. He most likely wrote to Titus in response to a letter from Titus or a report from Crete.

HISTORICAL AND THEOLOGICAL THEMES

Like Paul's two letters to Timothy, the apostle gives personal encouragement and counsel to a young pastor who, though well-trained and faithful, faced continuing opposition from ungodly men within the churches where he ministered. Titus was to pass on that encouragement and counsel to the leaders he was to appoint in the Cretan churches (1:5).

In contrast to several of Paul's other letters, such as those to the churches in Rome and Galatia, the book of Titus does not focus on explaining or defending doctrine. Paul had full confidence in Titus' theological understanding and convictions, evidenced by the fact that he entrusted him with such a demanding ministry. Except for the warning about false teachers and Judaizers, the letter gives no theological correction, strongly suggesting that Paul also had confidence in the doctrinal grounding of most church members there, despite the fact that the majority of them were new believers. Doctrines that this epistle affirms include: 1) God's sovereign election of believers (1:1, 2); 2) His saving grace (2:11; 3:5); 3) Christ's deity and second coming (2:13); 4) Christ's substitutionary atonement (2:14); and 5) the regeneration and renewing of believers by the Holy Spirit (3:5).

God and Christ are regularly referred to as Savior (1:3, 4; 2:10, 13; 3:4, 6), and the saving plan is so emphasized in 2:11–14 that it indicates the major thrust of the epistle is that of equipping the churches of

Crete for effective evangelism. This preparation required godly leaders who not only would shepherd believers under their care (1:5–9), but also would equip those Christians for evangelizing their pagan neighbors, who had been characterized by one of their own famous natives as liars, evil beasts, and lazy gluttons (1:12). In order to gain a hearing for the gospel among such people, the believers' primary preparation for evangelization was to live among themselves with the unarguable testimony of righteous, loving, selfless, and godly lives (2:2–14) in marked contrast to the debauched lives of the false teachers (1:10–16). How they behaved with reference to governmental authorities and unbelievers was also crucial to their testimony (3:1–8).

Several major themes repeat themselves throughout Titus. They include: work(s) (1:16; 2:7, 14; 3:1, 5, 8, 14); soundness in faith and doctrine (1:4, 9, 13; 2:1, 2, 7, 8, 10; 3:15); and salvation (1:3, 4; 2:10, 13; 3:4, 6).

INTERPRETIVE CHALLENGES

The letter to Titus presents itself in a straightforward manner which should be taken at face value. The few interpretive challenges include: What is the "blessed hope" of 2:13?

OUTLINE

I. Salutation (1:1–4)

II. Essentials for Effective Evangelism (1:5–3:11)

- A. Among Leaders (1:5–16)
  1. Recognition of elders (1:5–9)
  2. Rebuke of false teachers (1:10–16)
- B. In the Church (2:1–15)
  1. Holy living (2:1–10)
  2. Sound doctrine (2:11–15)
- C. In the World (3:1–11)
  1. Holy living (3:1–4)
  2. Sound doctrine (3:5–11)

III. Conclusion (3:12–14)

IV. Benediction (3:15)

SALUTATION

1 Paul, [A]a bond-servant of God and an [B]apostle of
Jesus Christ, [a]for the faith of those [C]chosen of God
and [D]the knowledge of the truth which is [E]according
to godliness, 2 in [A]the hope of eternal life, which
God, [B]who cannot lie, [C]promised [a,D]long ages ago,
3 but [A]at the proper time manifested, *even* His word,
in [B]the proclamation [C]with which I was entrusted
[D]according to the commandment of [E]God our Savior,
4 To [A]Titus, [B]my true child [a]in a [C]common faith:
[D]Grace and peace from God the Father and [E]Christ
Jesus our Savior.

QUALIFICATIONS OF ELDERS

5 For this reason I left you in [A]Crete, that you would
set in order what remains and [B]appoint [C]elders in
every city as I directed you, 6 *namely,* [A]if any man is
above reproach, the [B]husband of one wife, having children who believe, not accused of [C]dissipation or [D]re-
bellion. 7 For the [a,A]overseer must be above reproach
as [B]God's steward, not [C]self-willed, not quick-tempered, not [D]addicted to wine, not pugnacious, [E]not
fond of sordid gain, 8 but [A]hospitable, [B]loving what is
good, sensible, just, devout, self-controlled, 9 [A]holding
fast the faithful word which is in accordance with
the teaching, so that he will be able both to exhort in
[B]sound doctrine and to refute those who contradict.
10 [A]For there are many [B]rebellious men, [C]empty
talkers and deceivers, especially [D]those of the circumcision, 11 who must be silenced because they
are upsetting [A]whole families, teaching [B]things
they should not *teach* [C]for the sake of sordid gain.

1:1 [a]Or *according to* [A]Rom 1:1; James 1:1; Rev 1:1 [B]2 Cor 1:1 [C]Luke 18:7 [D]1 Tim 2:4 [E]1 Tim 6:3 1:2 [a]Lit *before times eternal* [A]2 Tim 1:1; Titus 3:7 [B]2 Tim 2:13; Heb 6:18 [C]Rom 1:2 [D]2 Tim 1:9 1:3 [A]1 Tim 2:6 [B]Rom 16:25; 2 Tim 4:17 [C]1 Tim 1:11 [D]1 Tim 1:1 [E]Luke 1:47; 1 Tim 1:1; Titus 2:10; 3:4 1:4 [a]Lit *according to* [A]2 Cor 2:13; 8:23; Gal 2:3; 2 Tim 4:10 [B]2 Tim 1:2 [C]2 Pet 1:1 [D]Rom 1:7 [E]1 Tim 1:12; 2 Tim 1:1 1:5 [A]Acts 27:7; Titus 1:12 [B]Acts 14:23 [C]Acts 11:30 1:6 [A]1 Tim 3:2-4; Titus 1:6-8 [B]1 Tim 3:2 [C]Eph 5:18 [D]Titus 1:10 1:7 [a]Or *bishop* [A]1 Tim 3:2 [B]1 Cor 4:1 [C]2 Pet 2:10 [D]1 Tim 3:3 [E]1 Tim 3:3, 8 1:8 [A]1 Tim 3:2 [B]2 Tim 3:3 1:9 [A]2 Thess 2:15; 1 Tim 1:19; 2 Tim 1:13 [B]1 Tim 1:10; Titus 2:1 1:10 [A]2 Cor 11:13 [B]Titus 1:6 [C]1 Tim 1:6 [D]Acts 11:2 1:11 [A]1 Tim 5:4; 2 Tim 3:6 [B]1 Tim 5:13 [C]1 Tim 6:5

1:1–3 This salutation emphasizes the nature of Paul's service as an apostle of Jesus Christ. He proclaimed: 1) salvation: God's purpose to save the elect by the gospel; 2) sanctification: God's purpose to build up the saved by the Word of God; and 3) glorification: God's purpose to bring believers to eternal glory.

1:1 Paul. See Introduction: Title; Author and Date; Background and Setting. **bond-servant.** Paul pictures himself as the most menial slave of NT times (*see notes on 2:9; 1Co 4:1, 2*), indicating his complete and willing servitude to the Lord, by whom all believers have been "bought with a price" (1Co 6:20; cf. 1Pe 1:18, 19). This is the only time Paul referred to himself as a "bond-servant of God" (cf. Ro 1:1; Gal 1:10; Php 1:1). He was placing himself alongside OT men of God (cf. Rev 15:3). **apostle.** Cf. Ro 1:1; 1Co 1:1; 2Co 1:1; Eph 1:1. The word has the basic meaning of messenger or lit. "sent one" and, though often used of royal emissaries who ministered with the extended authority of their sovereign, Paul's exalted position as "an apostle" also was an extension of his bondservice to "God," which came with great authority, responsibility, and sacrifice. *See note on Ac 20:24.* **those chosen of God.** *See notes on Eph 1:4, 5.* Those who have been graciously chosen for salvation "before the foundation of the world" (Eph 1:4), but who must exercise personal faith prompted and empowered by the Holy Spirit. God's choice of believers always precedes and enables their choice of Him (cf. Jn 15:16; Ac 13:46–48; Ro 9:15–21; 2Th 2:13; 2Ti 1:8, 9; 2:10; 1Pe 1:1, 2). **the truth.** Paul had in mind gospel truth, the saving message of the death and resurrection of Jesus Christ (1Ti 2:3, 4; 2Ti 2:25). It is that saving truth that leads to "godliness" or sanctification (see 2:11, 12).

1:2 hope. This is divinely promised and divinely guaranteed to all believers, providing endurance and patience (cf. Jn 6:37–40; Ro 8:18–23; 1Co 15:51–58; Eph 1:13, 14; Php 3:8–11, 20, 21; 1Th 4:13–18; 1Jn 3:2, 3). *See notes on 1Pe 1:3–9.* **cannot lie.** Cf. 1Sa 15:29; Heb 6:18. Because God Himself is truth and the source of truth, it is impossible for Him to say anything untruthful (Jn 14:6, 17; 15:26; cf. Nu 23:19; Ps 146:6). **long ages ago.** God's plan of salvation for sinful mankind was determined and decreed before man was even created. The promise was made to God the Son (*see notes on Jn 6:37–44; Eph 1:4, 5; 2Ti 1:9*).

1:3 His word . . . proclamation. God's Word is the sole source of content for all faithful preaching and teaching. Cf. 1Co 1:18–21; 9:16, 17; Gal 1:15, 16; Col 1:25. **God our Savior.** Cf. 2:10; 3:4. The plan of salvation originated in eternity past with God.

1:4 true child. A spiritual son, a genuine believer in Christ, like Timothy (1Ti 1:2). **common faith.** This may refer to saving faith or to the content of the Christian faith, e.g., "The faith which was once for all handed down to the saints" (Jude 3). **our Savior.** Christ is called Savior each time He is mentioned after v. 1 (cf. 2:13; 3:6).

1:5–9 God's standards for all believers are high; His requirement for church leaders is to set that standard and model it. Such leaders are not qualified on the basis of natural ability, intelligence, or education, but on the basis of moral and spiritual character and the ability to teach with skill as the Spirit sovereignly has equipped them.

1:5 Crete. See Introduction: Background and Setting. **set in order.** Titus was to correct wrong doctrine and practices in the Cretan churches, a task that Paul had been unable to complete. This ministry is mentioned nowhere else. **elders.** Cf. similar qualifications in 1Ti 3:1–7. Mature spiritual leaders of the church, also known as bishops or overseers (v. 7; cf. 1Ti 3:2) and pastors (lit. shepherds; see Eph 4:11), were to care for each city's congregation. See also Ac 20:17, 28; 1Pe 5:1, 2. This ministry of appointing leaders is consistently Pauline (cf. Ac 14:23). **directed you.** A reminder of past apostolic instructions.

1:6 above reproach. This word does not refer to sinless perfection, but to a personal life that is beyond legitimate accusation and public scandal. It is a general and primary requirement of spiritual leaders that is repeated (v. 7) and explained in the next verses (cf. 1Ti 3:2, 10). **husband of one wife.** Lit. "a one-woman man," i.e., a husband who is consistently, both inwardly and outwardly, devoted and faithful to his wife (cf. 1Ti 3:2). An otherwise qualified single man is not necessarily disqualified. This is not speaking of divorce, but of internal and external purity in the sexual area. See Pr 6:32, 33. This necessity was motivation for Paul's commitment to control his body (1Co 9:27). **children who believe.** This refers to children who have saving faith in Christ and reflect it in their conduct. Since 1Ti 3:4 requires children to be in submission, it may be directed at young children in the home, while this text looks at those who are older. **dissipation or rebellion.** "Dissipation" connotes debauchery, suggesting, again, that the reference is to grown children. "Rebellion" carries the idea of rebelliousness to the gospel. Here the elder shows his ability to lead his family to salvation and sanctification (see 1Ti 3:4, 5), an essential prerequisite for leading the church.

1:7 overseer. This is not a hierarchical title, but a word meaning "elder" or "bishop." Cf. Ac 20:28; Heb 13:17; 1Pe 5:2. **steward.** The term refers to one who manages someone else's properties for the well-being of those his master cares for. In this context, one who manages spiritual truths, lives on God's behalf, and is wholly accountable to Him. The church is God's (Ac 20:28; 1Ti 3:15; 1Pe 5:2–4), and elders or overseers are accountable to Him for the way they lead it (Heb 13:17). **wine.** Applies to drinking any alcoholic beverage in any way that dulls the mind or subdues inhibitions (cf. Pr 23:29–35; 31:4–7). By application, it also indicts any other substance, e.g., drugs, which would cloud the mind. **sordid gain.** Even in the early church, some men became pastors in order to gain wealth (see v. 11; 1Pe 5:2; cf. 2Pe 2:1–3).

1:8 hospitable. The word actually means "a lover of strangers." **sensible.** Serious, with the right priorities.

1:9 faithful word. Sound biblical doctrine not only should be taught but also adhered to with deep conviction. Cf. 1Ti 4:6; 5:17; 2Ti 2:15; 3:16, 17; 4:2–4. **exhort . . . refute.** The faithful teaching and defending of Scripture which encourages godliness and confronts sin and error (those who contradict). *See notes on vv. 10–16; 3:10, 11; Ac 20:29, 30.*

1:10–16 The false teachers in the Cretan churches were much like those with whom Timothy had to deal in Ephesus (see 1Ti 1:3–7; cf. Ro 16:17, 18; 2Pe 2:1–3).

1:10 rebellious men. Because those men were so numerous, Titus' job was especially difficult, which made the appointment of additional godly elders (v. 5) all the more crucial. Some of the false teachers may have opposed even Paul's apostolic authority during his brief ministry on Crete. **deceivers.** Cf. Jer 14:14; 23:2, 21, 32. **the circumcision.** Cf. Ac 10:45; 11:2. These were Jews who taught that salvation required the physical cutting of circumcision (*see notes on Ge 17:9–14*) and adherence to Mosaic ceremonies. *See notes on Ac 15:1–12; Gal 3:1–12; Eph 2:11, 12; Col 2:11, 12.*

1:11 whole families. Cf. 2Ti 3:6. **sordid gain.**

12 One of themselves, a prophet of their own, said,
"[A]Cretans are always liars, evil beasts, lazy gluttons."
13 This testimony is true. For this reason [A]reprove
them [B]severely so that they may be [C]sound in the
faith, 14 not paying attention to Jewish [A]myths and
[B]commandments of men who [C]turn away from the
truth. 15 [A]To the pure, all things are pure; but [B]to
those who are defiled and unbelieving, nothing
is pure, but both their [C]mind and their conscience
are defiled. 16 [A]They profess to know God, but by
their deeds they [B]deny *Him,* being [C]detestable and
[D]disobedient and [E]worthless [F]for any good deed.

DUTIES OF THE OLDER AND YOUNGER

2 But as for you, speak the things which are fitting for [A]sound doctrine. 2 [A]Older men are to be
[B]temperate, dignified, sensible, [C]sound [D]in faith, in
love, in [a]perseverance.
3 Older women likewise are to be reverent in their
behavior, [A]not malicious gossips nor [B]enslaved to
much wine, teaching what is good, 4 so that they may
[a]encourage the young women to love their husbands,
to love their children, 5 *to be* sensible, pure, [A]workers
at home, kind, being [B]subject to their own husbands,
[C]so that the word of God will not be dishonored.
6 Likewise urge [A]the young men to be [a]sensible;
7 in all things show yourself to be [A]an example of
good deeds, *with* [a]purity in doctrine, dignified,
8 sound *in* speech which is beyond reproach, so
[A]that the opponent will be put to shame, having
nothing bad to say about us.
9 *Urge* [A]bondslaves to be subject to their own
masters in everything, to be well-pleasing, not [a]ar-
gumentative, 10 not pilfering, but showing all good
faith so that they will adorn the doctrine of [A]God
our Savior in every respect.

1:12 [A]Acts 2:11; 27:7 1:13 [A]1 Tim 5:20; 2 Tim 4:2; Titus 2:15 [B]2 Cor 13:10 [C]Titus 2:2 1:14 [A]1 Tim 1:4 [B]Col 2:22 [C]2 Tim 4:4 1:15 [A]Luke 11:41; Rom 14:20 [B]Rom 14:14, 23 [C]1 Tim 6:5 1:16 [A]1 John 2:4 [B]1 Tim 5:8 [C]Rev 21:8 [D]Titus 3:3 [E]2 Tim 3:8 [F]2 Tim 3:17; Titus 3:1 2:1 [A]Titus 1:9 2:2 [a]Or *steadfastness* [A]Philem 9 [B]1 Tim 3:2 [C]Titus 1:13 [D]1 Tim 1:2, 14 2:3 [A]1 Tim 3:11 [B]1 Tim 3:8 2:4 [a]Or *train* 2:5 [A]1 Tim 5:14 [B]Eph 5:22 [C]1 Tim 6:1 2:6 [a]Or *sensible in all things; show* [A]1 Tim 5:1 2:7 [a]Or *soundness;* lit *uncorruptness* [A]1 Tim 4:12 2:8 [A]2 Thess 3:14; 1 Pet 2:12 2:9 [a]Lit *contradicting* [A]Eph 6:5; 1 Tim 6:1 2:10 [A]Titus 1:3

False teachers are always in it for the money (1Ti 6:5; 1Pe 5:2).

1:12 a prophet. Epimenides, the highly esteemed sixth century B.C. Greek poet and native of Crete, had characterized his own people as the dregs of Greek culture. Elsewhere, Paul also quoted pagan sayings (cf. Ac 17:28; 1Co 15:33). This quote is directed at the false teachers' character.

1:13 sound in the faith. True and pure doctrine was to be required of all who spoke to the church. Any who fell short of that were to be rebuked.

1:14 myths and commandments of men. Paul reemphasized (see v. 10, "those of the circumcision") that most of the false teachers were Jewish. They taught the same kind of externalism and unscriptural laws and traditions that both Isaiah and Jesus railed against (Is 29:13; Mt 15:1–9; Mk 7:5–13).

1:15, 16 False teachers are corrupt on the inside ("mind" and "conscience") and the outside ("deeds" and "disobedient"). Cf. Mt 7:15, 16.

1:15 defiled. The outwardly despicable things that those men practiced (vv. 10–12) were simply reflections of their inner corruption. See Mt 15:15–20. **mind ... conscience.** If the mind is defiled, it cannot accurately inform the conscience, so conscience cannot warn the person. When conscience is accurately and fully infused with God's truth, it functions as the warning system God designed. *See notes on 2Co 1:12; 4:2; 1Ti 1:19, 20.*

1:16 profess ... deny. Some of the false teachers in the church were not believers at all. Eventually, even the seemingly noble "deeds" of unbelievers will betray them. **worthless.** They can do nothing that pleases God. *See note on 1Co 9:27;* cf. 2Ti 3:8.

2:1–10 Sound doctrine for older men (v. 2), older women (v. 3), younger women (vv. 4, 5), young men (vv. 6–8), and bondslaves (vv. 9, 10) reflects the duty of everyone in the church.

2:1 sound. Meaning healthy—Paul uses this word 9 times in the Pastoral Epistles (5 times in Titus), always in the sense that the truth produces spiritual well-being. The "things" Paul mentions in vv. 2–10 pertain to truths, attitudes, and actions that correspond to and are based on biblical truth. In order not only to please God, but also to have an effective witness to unbelievers, God's people must know the truth that leads to spiritual health.

2:2 Older men. Paul used this term for himself (Phm 9) when he was over 60. It refers to those of advanced age, using a different term from the one translated "elders" in 1:5. **dignified.** This requirement is not limited to reverence for God, which is assumed, but also refers to being honorable. They are to be sensible and spiritually healthy.

2:3 Older women. Those who no longer had child-rearing responsibilities, typically around age 60 (cf. 1Ti 5:3–10). **reverent.** Or "dignified." *See note on v. 2.* Cf. 1Ti 2:9–11, 15. **not malicious gossips.** A term used 34 times in the NT to describe Satan, the arch-slanderer. **what is good.** Those things that please God (cf. 1:16), particularly the lessons in vv. 4, 5.

2:4 encourage the young women. Their own examples of godliness (v. 3) give older women the right and the credibility to instruct younger women in the church. The obvious implication is that older women must exemplify the virtues (vv. 4, 5) that they "encourage." **love their husbands.** Like the other virtues mentioned here, this one is unconditional. It is based on God's will, not on a husband's worthiness. The Gr. word *phileō* emphasizes affection. *See notes on Eph 5:22, 23.*

2:5 workers at home. Cf. 1Ti 5:14. Keeping a godly home with excellence for one's husband and children is the Christian woman's nonnegotiable responsibility. **subject to.** The ideas of radical feminism were an integral part of ancient Babylonian and Assyrian mythology as well as of Greek gnosticism, which flourished throughout the Roman Empire during NT times and posed a constant danger to the early church. Modern feminism is neither new nor progressive; it is age-old and regressive. *See notes on Eph 5:22.* **not be dishonored.** This is the purpose of godly conduct—to eliminate any reproach on Scripture. For a person to be convinced God can save from sin, one needs to see someone who lives a holy life. When Christians claim to believe God's Word but do not obey it, the Word is dishonored. Many have mocked God and His truth because of the sinful behavior of those who claim to be Christians. Cf. Mt 5:16; 1Pe 2:9.

2:6 young men. Males, 12 and older.

2:6, 7 sensible. See v. 2.

2:7 in all things. This rightly goes at the end of v. 6, qualifying young men and emphasizing the comprehensiveness of this admonition. **example.** Titus had a special obligation to exemplify the moral and spiritual qualities about which he was to admonish others. Cf. 1Co 4:16; 11:1; Php 3:17; 2Th 3:8, 9; 1Ti 4:12; Heb 13:7.

2:8 sound *in* speech. Daily conversation. Cf. Eph 4:31; Col 3:16, 17; 4:6. **nothing bad to say.** Again, as in v. 5, the purpose of godly living is to silence the opponents of Christianity and the gospel (*see notes on 1Pe 2:11, 12*), and make the power of Christ believable.

2:9 bondslaves. The term applies generally to all employees, but direct reference is to slaves—men, women, and children who, in the Roman Empire and in much of the ancient world, were owned by their masters. They had few, if any, civil rights and often were accorded little more dignity or care than domestic animals. The NT nowhere condones or condemns the practice of slavery, but it everywhere teaches that freedom from the bondage of sin is infinitely more important than freedom from any human bondage a person may have to endure (see Ro 6:22). **subject to ... masters ... well-pleasing.** Paul clearly teaches that, even in the most servile of circumstances, believers are "to be subject" and seek to please those for whom they work, whether their "masters" are believers or unbelievers, fair or unfair, kind or cruel. How much more obligated are believers to respect and obey employers for whom they work voluntarily! As with wives' obedience to their husbands (v. 5), the only exception would involve a believer's being required to disobey God's Word. Cf. Eph 6:5–9; Col 3:22–4:1; 1Ti 6:1, 2.

2:10 not pilfering. A term used to refer to embezzlement. **all good faith.** Loyalty. **adorn the doctrine.** Again (cf. v. 5), Paul stresses that the supreme purpose of a virtuous life is to make attractive the teaching that God saves sinners.

11For the grace of God has [A]appeared, [a,B]bringing
salvation to all men, 12[a]instructing us to deny ungodliness and [A]worldly desires and [B]to live sensibly,
righteously and godly [C]in the present age, 13looking
for the blessed hope and the [A]appearing of the glory
of [a,B]our great God and Savior, Christ Jesus, 14who
[A]gave Himself for us [B]to redeem us from every lawless deed, and to [C]purify for Himself a [D]people for
His own possession, [E]zealous for good deeds.
15These things speak and [A]exhort and [A]reprove
with all [a]authority. [B]Let no one disregard you.

GODLY LIVING

3 [A]Remind them [B]to be subject to rulers, to authorities, to be obedient, to be [C]ready for every good
deed, 2to malign no one, [A]to be peaceable, [A]gentle,
[B]showing every consideration for all men. 3[A]For
we also once were foolish ourselves, [B]disobedient,
[C]deceived, [D]enslaved to [E]various lusts and pleasures,
spending our life in [F]malice and [F]envy, hateful, hating one another. 4But when the [A]kindness of [B]God
our Savior and *His* love for mankind [C]appeared,
5[A]He saved us, [B]not on the basis of deeds which
we have done in righteousness, but [C]according to
His mercy, by the [D]washing of regeneration and
[E]renewing by the Holy Spirit, 6[A]whom He poured
out upon us [B]richly through Jesus Christ our Savior,
7so that being justified by His grace we would be
made [A]heirs [a]according to *the* hope of eternal life.
8[A]This is a trustworthy statement; and concerning
these things I [B]want you to speak confidently, so
that those who have [C]believed God will be careful to
[D]engage in good deeds. These things are good and
profitable for men. 9But [A]avoid [B]foolish controversies and [C]genealogies and strife and [D]disputes about
the Law, for they are [E]unprofitable and worthless.

2:11 [a]*Or to all men, bringing* [A]2 Tim 1:10; Titus 3:4 [B]1 Tim 2:4 2:12 [a]*Or disciplining* [A]1 Tim 6:9; Titus 3:3 [B]2 Tim 3:12 [C]1 Tim 6:17 2:13 [a]*Or the great God and our Savior* [A]2 Thess 2:8 [B]1 Tim 1:1; 2 Tim 1:2; Titus 1:4; 2 Pet 1:1 2:14 [A]1 Tim 2:6 [B]Ps 130:8; 1 Pet 1:18f [C]Ezek 37:23; Heb 1:3; 9:14; 1 John 1:7 [D]Ex 19:5; Deut 4:20; 7:6; 14:2; Eph 1:11; 1 Pet 2:9 [E]Eph 2:10; Titus 3:8; 1 Pet 3:13 2:15 [a]*Lit command* [A]1 Tim 4:13; 5:20; 2 Tim 4:2 [B]1 Tim 4:12 3:1 [A]2 Tim 2:14 [B]Rom 13:1 [C]2 Tim 2:21 3:2 [A]1 Tim 3:3; 1 Pet 2:18 [B]2 Tim 2:25 3:3 [A]Rom 11:30; Col 3:7 [B]Titus 1:16 [C]2 Tim 3:13 [D]Rom 6:6, 12 [E]2 Tim 3:6; Titus 2:12 [F]Rom 1:29 3:4 [A]Rom 2:4; Eph 2:7; 1 Pet 2:3 [B]Titus 2:10 [C]Titus 2:11 3:5 [A]Rom 11:14; 2 Tim 1:9 [B]Eph 2:9 [C]Eph 2:4; 1 Pet 1:3 [D]John 3:5; Eph 5:26; 1 Pet 3:21 [E]Rom 12:2 3:6 [A]Rom 5:5 [B]Rom 2:4; 1 Tim 6:17 3:7 [a]*Or of eternal life according to hope* [A]Matt 25:34; Mark 10:17; Rom 8:17, 24; Titus 1:2 3:8 [A]1 Tim 1:15 [B]1 Tim 2:8 [C]2 Tim 1:12 [D]Titus 2:7, 14; 3:14 3:9 [A]2 Tim 2:16 [B]1 Tim 1:4; 2 Tim 2:23 [C]1 Tim 1:4 [D]James 4:1 [E]2 Tim 2:14

2:11–13 This is the heart of the letter, emphasizing that God's sovereign purpose in calling out elders (1:5) and in commanding His people to live righteously (vv. 1–10) is to provide the witness that brings God's plan and purpose of salvation to fulfillment. Paul condensed the saving plan of God into 3 realities: 1) salvation from the penalty (v. 11); 2) the power (v. 12); and 3) the presence (v. 13) of sin.

2:11 grace of God. Not simply the divine attribute of grace, but Jesus Christ Himself, grace incarnate, God's supremely gracious gift to fallen mankind. Cf. Jn 1:14. **all men.** This does not teach universal salvation. "Mankind" (3:4) refers to humanity in general, as a category, not to every individual. *See notes on 2Co 5:19; 2Pe 3:9.* Jesus Christ made a sufficient sacrifice to cover every sin of every one who believes (Jn 3:16–18; 1Ti 2:5, 6; 4:10; 1Jn 2:2). Paul makes clear in the opening words of this letter to Titus that salvation becomes effective only through "the faith of those chosen of God" (1:1). *See note on 3:2.* Out of all humanity, only those who believe will be saved (Jn 1:12; 3:16; 5:24, 38, 40; 6:40; 10:9; Ro 10:9–17).

2:12 deny ... live. Salvation is transforming (2Co 5:17; Eph 2:8–10), and transformation (new birth) produces a new life in which the power of sin has been broken (*see notes on Ro 6:4–14; Php 3:8, 9; Col 3:9, 10*).

2:13 blessed hope. A general reference to the second coming of Jesus Christ, including the resurrection (cf. Ro 8:22, 23; 1Co 15:51–58; Php 3:20, 21; 1Th 4:13–18; 1Jn 3:2, 3) and the reign of the saints with Christ in glory (2Ti 2:10). **appearing of the glory.** Cf. 2Ti 1:10. This will be our salvation from the presence of sin. **God and Savior.** A clear reference to the deity of Jesus. Cf. 2Pe 1:1.

2:14 redeem ... purify. Another expression (cf. v. 12) summarizes the dual effect of salvation (regeneration and sanctification). To "redeem" is to release someone held captive, on the payment of a ransom. The price was Christ's blood paid to satisfy God's justice. *See notes on Ac 20:28; Gal 1:4; 2:20; 1Pe 1:18*; cf. Mk 10:45. **a people for His own possession.** People who are special by virtue of God's decree and confirmed by the grace of salvation which they have embraced (*see notes on 1:1–4*). Cf. 1Co 6:19, 20; 1Pe 2:9. **zealous.** Cf. 3:8. Good works are the product, not the means, of salvation. Cf. Eph 2:10.

2:15 speak ... exhort ... reprove. These 3 verbs identify the need for proclamation, application, and correction by the Word. **authority.** "Authority" to command people in the spiritual realm comes only from God's Word. Cf. Mt 7:28, 29. **Let no one disregard you.** See 3:9–11. Rebellion against the truth has to be dealt with. Cf. Mt 18:15–20; 1Co 5:9–13; 2Th 3:14, 15.

3:1–11 In his closing remarks, Paul admonished Titus to remind believers under his care of their attitudes toward: 1) the unsaved rulers (v. 1) and people in general (v. 2); 2) their previous state as unbelievers lost in sin (v. 3); 3) of their gracious salvation through Jesus Christ (vv. 4–7); 4) of their righteous testimony to the unsaved world (v. 8); 5) and of their responsibility to oppose false teachers and factious members within the church (vv. 9–11). All of these matters are essential to effective evangelism.

3:1 subject. Submission to the authority of Scripture demands submission to human authorities as part of a Christian's testimony (*see notes on Ro 13:1–7; 1Pe 2:12–17*).

3:2 all men. Christians are to exemplify these godly virtues in their dealings with everyone. The admonition applies especially to dealings with unbelievers. The use of this phrase here to refer to mankind in general (particularly those who cross our paths), rather than every person who lives, supports the fact that it has the same meaning in 2:11.

3:3 ourselves. It is not that every believer has committed every sin listed here, but rather that before salvation every life is characterized by such sins. That sobering truth should make believers humble in dealing with the unsaved, even those who are grossly immoral and ungodly. If it weren't for God's grace to His own, they would all be wicked. *See note on 1Pe 3:15*; cf. 2Ti 2:25. For other lists of sins, see Ro 1:18–32; 1Co 6:9, 10; Gal 5:19–21; Eph 4:17–19.

3:4 kindness ... appeared. As in 2:11, Paul is speaking of Jesus Christ, who was kindness and love incarnate, appearing in human form. Cf. Eph 2:4–6.

3:5 not on the basis of deeds. Salvation has never been by deeds, or works (see Eph 2:8, 9; cf. Ro 3:19–28). **according to His mercy.** Cf. Eph 2:4; 1Ti 1:13; 1Pe 1:3; 2:10. **washing of regeneration.** *See notes on Eze 36:25–31; Eph 5:26, 27; Jas 1:18; 1Pe 1:23.* Salvation brings divine cleansing from sin and the gift of a new, Spirit-generated, Spirit-empowered, and Spirit-protected life as God's own children and heirs (v. 7). This is the new birth (cf. Jn 3:5; 1Jn 2:29; 3:9; 4:7; 5:1). **renewing by the Holy Spirit.** Cf. Ro 8:2. He is the agent of the "washing of regeneration."

3:6 richly. When believers are saved, Christ's Spirit blesses them beyond measure (cf. Ac 2:38, 39; 1Co 12:7, 11, 13; Eph 3:20; 5:18).

3:7 justified. The central truth of salvation is justification by faith alone. When a sinner repents and places his faith in Jesus Christ, God declares him just, imputes the righteousness of Christ to him, and gives him eternal life by virtue of the substitutionary death of Christ as the penalty for that sinner's iniquity. *See notes on Ro 3:21–5:21; Gal 3:6–22; Php 3:8, 9.* **heirs.** As adopted children of God through faith in Jesus Christ, believers become "heirs of God and fellow heirs with Christ" (Ro 8:17; cf. 1Pe 1:3, 4).

3:8 trustworthy statement. A common expression in the early church, used 5 times in the Pastoral Epistles (cf. 1Ti 1:15; 3:1; 4:9; 2Ti 2:11). **profitable for men.** That is, for the sake of evangelism. Again "men" (cf. v. 2; 2:11) is general, referring to those who respond by the holy witness to the gospel.

3:9 foolish controversies. Paul again warns against becoming embroiled in senseless discussions with the many false teachers on Crete (see 1:10, 14–16), especially the Judaizers who contended that a Christian must

10 [A]Reject a [B]factious man [C]after a first and second
warning, 11 knowing that such a man is [A]perverted
and is sinning, being self-condemned.

PERSONAL CONCERNS

12 When I send Artemas or [A]Tychicus to you,
[B]make every effort to come to me at Nicopolis,
for I have decided to [C]spend the winter there.
13 Diligently help Zenas the [A]lawyer and [B]Apollos
on their way so that nothing is lacking for them.
14 [A]Our people must also learn to [B]engage in good
[a]deeds to meet [C]pressing needs, so that they will
not be [D]unfruitful.
15 [A]All who are with me greet you. Greet those
who love us [B]in *the* faith.
[C]Grace be with you all.

3:10 [A]2 John 10 [B]Rom 16:17 [C]Matt 18:15f 3:11 [A]Titus 1:14 3:12 [A]Acts 20:4; Eph 6:21f; Col 4:7f; 2 Tim 4:12 [B]2 Tim 4:9 [C]2 Tim 4:21 3:13 [A]Matt 22:35 [B]Acts 18:24; 1 Cor 16:12 3:14 [a]Or *occupations* [A]Titus 2:8 [B]Titus 3:8 [C]Rom 12:13; Phil 4:16 [D]Matt 7:19; Phil 1:11; Col 1:10 3:15 [A]Acts 20:34 [B]1 Tim 1:2 [C]Col 4:18

be obedient to "the (Mosaic) Law," a view that assaulted the doctrine of justification by grace through faith alone and, contrary to holy living, which was good and profitable, was "unprofitable and worthless." Proclaiming the truth, not arguing error, is the biblical way to evangelize.

3:10 Reject. Anyone in the church who is unsubmissive, self-willed, and divisive should be expelled. Two warnings are to be given, following the basic pattern for church discipline set forth by Christ (*see notes on Mt 18:15–17*; cf. Ro 16:17, 18; 2Th 3:14, 15).

3:11 self-condemned. By his own ungodly behavior, a factious believer brings judgment on himself.

3:12–14 Paul gives Titus special instructions.

3:12 Artemas. Nothing is known of this man beyond Paul's obvious confidence in him. **Tychicus.** This "beloved brother and faithful servant" (Col 4:7) accompanied Paul from Corinth to Asia Minor (Ac 20:4), carried the apostle's letter to the Colossian church (Col 4:7), and possibly his letter to Ephesus (see Eph 6:21). **Nicopolis.** The name means "city of victory," and this was but one of perhaps 9 different cities so named because of decisive military battles that were won in or near them. This particular Nicopolis was probably in southern Greece, on the W coast of Achaia, which was a good place "to spend the winter."

3:13 Zenas. Nothing is known of this believer whose expertise was either in biblical law or Roman law. **Apollos.** Originally from Alexandria, he was an outstanding teacher of Scripture who was converted to Christ after being acquainted only with the teaching of John the Baptist (Ac 18:24–28). Some of his followers apparently formed a faction in the church at Corinth (1Co 1:11, 12; 3:4).

3:14 good deeds. Again the emphasis is on good deeds as the platform for witnessing effectively (cf. v. 8; 1:13–16; 2:5, 8, 10, 12, 14).

3:15 All who are with me. Cf. 1Co 16:20; 2Co 13:12; Php 4:22; cf. also Ro 16:21–23; Col 4:10–14, where those with Paul are mentioned by name.

THE EPISTLE OF PAUL TO

PHILEMON

TITLE

Philemon, the recipient of this letter, was a prominent member of the church at Colosse (vv. 1, 2; cf. Col 4:9), which met in his house (v. 2). The letter was for him, his family, and the church.

AUTHOR AND DATE

The book claims that the apostle Paul was its writer (vv. 1, 9, 19), a claim that few in the history of the church have disputed, especially since there is nothing in Philemon that a forger would have been motivated to write. It is one of the Prison Epistles, along with Ephesians, Philippians, and Colossians. Its close connection with Colossians, which Paul wrote at the same time (ca. A.D. 60–62; cf. vv. 1, 16), brought early and unquestioned vindication of Paul's authorship by the early church fathers (e.g., Jerome, Chrysostom, and Theodore of Mopsuestia). The earliest of NT canons, the Muratorian (ca. A.D. 170), includes Philemon. For biographical information on Paul, see Introduction to Romans: Author and Date; for the date and place of Philemon's writing, see Introductions to Ephesians and Philippians: Author and Date.

BACKGROUND AND SETTING

Philemon had been saved under Paul's ministry, probably at Ephesus (v. 19), several years earlier. Wealthy enough to have a large house (cf. v. 2), Philemon also owned at least one slave, a man named Onesimus (lit. "useful"; a common name for slaves). Onesimus was not a believer at the time he stole some money (v. 18) from Philemon and ran away. Like countless thousands of other runaway slaves, Onesimus fled to Rome, seeking to lose himself in the Imperial capital's teeming and nondescript slave population. Through circumstances not recorded in Scripture, Onesimus met Paul in Rome and became a Christian.

The apostle quickly grew to love the runaway slave (vv. 12, 16) and longed to keep Onesimus in Rome (v. 13), where he was providing valuable service to Paul in his imprisonment (v. 11). But by stealing and running away from Philemon, Onesimus had both broken Roman law and defrauded his master. Paul knew those issues had to be dealt with, and decided to send Onesimus back to Colosse. It was too hazardous for him to make the trip alone (because of the danger of slave-catchers), so Paul sent him back with Tychicus, who was returning to Colosse with the epistle to the Colossians (Col 4:7–9). Along with Onesimus, Paul sent Philemon this beautiful personal letter, urging him to forgive Onesimus and welcome him back to service as a brother in Christ (vv. 15–17).

HISTORICAL AND THEOLOGICAL THEMES

Philemon provides valuable historical insights into the early church's relationship to the institution of slavery. Slavery was widespread in the Roman Empire (according to some estimates, slaves constituted one-third, perhaps more, of the population) and an accepted part of life. In Paul's day, slavery had virtually eclipsed free labor. Slaves could be doctors, musicians, teachers, artists, librarians, or accountants; in short, almost all jobs could be and were filled by slaves.

Slaves were not legally considered persons, but were the tools of their masters. As such, they could be bought, sold, inherited, exchanged, or seized to pay their master's debt. Their masters had virtually unlimited power to punish them, and sometimes did so severely for the slightest infractions. By the time of the NT, however, slavery was beginning to change. Realizing that contented slaves were more productive, masters tended to treat them more leniently. It was not uncommon for a master to teach a slave his own trade, and some masters and slaves became close friends. While still not recognizing them as persons under the law, the Roman Senate in A.D. 20 granted slaves accused of crimes the right to a trial. It also became more common for slaves to be granted (or to purchase) their freedom. Some slaves enjoyed very favorable and profitable service under their masters and were better off than many freemen because they were assured of care and provision. Many freemen struggled in poverty.

The NT nowhere directly attacks slavery; had it done so, the resulting slave insurrections would have been brutally suppressed and the message of the gospel hopelessly confused with that of social reform. Instead, Christianity undermined the evils of slavery by changing the hearts of slaves and masters. By stressing the spiritual equality of master and slave (v. 16; Gal 3:28; Eph 6:9; Col 4:1; 1Ti 6:1, 2), the Bible did away with slavery's abuses. The rich theological theme that alone dominates the letter is forgiveness, a featured theme throughout NT Scripture (cf. Mt 6:12–15; 18:21–35; Eph 4:32; Col 3:13). Paul's instruction here provides the biblical definition of forgiveness, without ever using the word.

INTERPRETIVE CHALLENGES

There are no significant interpretive challenges in this personal letter from Paul to his friend Philemon.

OUTLINE

I. Greeting (1–3)

II. The Character of One Who Forgives (4–7)

III. The Actions of One Who Forgives (8–18)

IV. The Motives of One Who Forgives (19–25)

SALUTATION

[1] [A]Paul, [B]a prisoner of [C]Christ Jesus, and [D]Timothy
[a]our brother,
To Philemon our beloved *brother* and [E]fellow
worker, [2] and to Apphia [a,A]our sister, and to [B]Ar-
chippus our [C]fellow soldier, and to [D]the church in
your house: [3] [A]Grace to you and peace from God our
Father and the Lord Jesus Christ.

PHILEMON'S LOVE AND FAITH

[4] [A]I thank my God always, making mention of
you in my prayers, [5] because I [A]hear of your love
and of the faith which you have toward the Lord
Jesus and toward all the [a]saints; [6] *and I pray* that
the fellowship of your faith may become effective
[a]through the [A]knowledge of every good thing which
is in you [b]for Christ's sake. [7] For I have come to have
much [A]joy and comfort in your love, because the
[a]hearts of the [b]saints have been [B]refreshed through
you, brother.

[8] Therefore, [A]though I have [a]enough confidence
in Christ to order you *to do* what is [B]proper, [9] yet
for love's sake I rather [A]appeal *to you*—since I am
such a person as Paul, [a]the [B]aged, and now also [C]a
prisoner of [D]Christ Jesus—

PLEA FOR ONESIMUS, A FREE MAN

[10] I [A]appeal to you for my [B]child [a,C]Onesimus,
whom I have begotten in my [b]imprisonment, [11] who
formerly was useless to you, but now is useful both
to you and to me. [12] I have sent him back to you in
person, that is, *sending* my very heart, [13] whom I
wished to keep with me, so that on your behalf he
might minister to me in my [a,A]imprisonment for
the gospel; [14] but without your consent I did not
want to do anything, so that your goodness would
[A]not be, in effect, by compulsion but of your own
free will. [15] For perhaps [A]he was for this reason separated *from you* for a while, that you would have
him back forever, [16] [A]no longer as a slave, but more

1:1 [a]Lit *the* [A]Phil 1:1 [B]Eph 3:1 [C]Gal 3:26 [D]2 Cor 1:1; Col 1:1 [E]Phil 2:25; Philem 24 1:2 [a]Lit *the* [A]Rom 16:1 [B]Col 4:17 [C]Phil 2:25; 2 Tim 2:3 [D]Rom 16:5 1:3 [A]Rom 1:7 1:4 [A]Rom 1:8f 1:5 [a]Or *holy ones* [A]Eph 1:15; Col 1:4; 1 Thess 3:6 1:6 [a]Or *in* [b]Lit *toward Christ* [A]Phil 1:9; Col 1:9; 3:10 1:7 [a]Lit *inward parts* [b]Or *holy ones* [A]2 Cor 7:4, 13 [B]1 Cor 16:18; Philem 20 1:8 [a]Lit *much* [A]2 Cor 3:12; 1 Thess 2:6 [B]Eph 5:4 1:9 [a]Or *an ambassador* [A]Rom 12:1 [B]Titus 2:2 [C]Philem 1 [D]Gal 3:26; 1 Tim 1:12; Philem 23 1:10 [a]I.e. useful [b]Lit *bonds* [A]Rom 12:1 [B]1 Cor 4:14f [C]Col 4:9 1:13 [a]Lit *bonds* [A]Phil 1:7; Philem 10 1:14 [A]2 Cor 9:7; 1 Pet 5:2 1:15 [A]Gen 45:5, 8 1:16 [A]1 Cor 7:22

1, 2 Following first-century custom, the salutation contains the names of the letter's author and its recipient. This is a very personal letter and Philemon was one of only 3 individuals (Timothy and Titus are the others) to receive a divinely inspired letter from Paul.

1 prisoner of Christ Jesus. At the time of writing, Paul was a prisoner in Rome (see Introductions to Ephesians and Philippians: Author and Date). Paul was imprisoned for the sake of and by the sovereign will of Christ (cf. Eph 3:1; 4:1; 6:19, 20; Php 1:13; Col 4:3). By beginning with his imprisonment and not his apostolic authority, Paul made this letter a gentle and singular appeal to a friend. A reminder of Paul's severe hardships was bound to influence Philemon's willingness to do the comparatively easy task Paul was about to request. **Timothy.** See Introduction to 1 Timothy: Background and Setting; *see notes on Ac 16:1–3; Php 1:1; 1Ti 1:2.* He was not the coauthor of this letter, but probably had met Philemon at Ephesus and was with Paul when the apostle wrote the letter. Paul mentions Timothy here and in the other epistles (e.g., 2Co 1:1; Php 1:1; Col 1:1; 1Th 1:1; 2Th 1:1) because he wanted him recognized as a leader and the non-apostolic heir apparent to Paul. **Philemon.** A wealthy member of the Colossian church which met in his house (see Introduction: Background and Setting). Church buildings were unknown until the third century.

2 Apphia … Archippus. Philemon's wife and son, respectively. **in your house.** First-century churches met in homes, and Paul wanted this personal letter read in the church that met at Philemon's. This reading would hold Philemon accountable, as well as instruct the church on the matter of forgiveness.

3 Grace to you. The standard greeting that appears in all 13 of Paul's NT letters. It highlighted salvation's means (grace) and its results (peace) and linked the Father and Son, thus affirming the deity of Christ.

5 In the Gr. text, this verse is arranged in what is called a chiastic construction. "Love" relates to the final phrase "toward all the saints." This love of will, choice, self-sacrifice, and humility (Gal 5:22) was a manifestation of Philemon's genuine faith "toward the Lord Jesus" (cf. Ro 5:5; Gal 5:6; 1Jn 3:14).

6 fellowship. The Gr. word here means much more than simply enjoying one another's company. It refers to a mutual sharing of all life, which believers do because of their common life in Christ and mutual partnership or "belonging to one another" in the "faith." **effective.** Lit. "powerful." Paul wanted Philemon's actions to send a powerful message to the church about the importance of forgiveness. **knowledge.** The deep, rich, full, experiential knowledge of the truth (*see notes on Col 1:9; 3:10*).

7 hearts. This Gr. word denotes the seat of human feelings (*see note on Col 3:12* where the same Gr. word is translated "compassion"). **refreshed.** This comes from the Gr. military term that describes an army at rest from a march.

8 confidence … to order. Because of his apostolic authority (*see notes on Ro 1:1; 1Th 2:6*), Paul could have ordered Philemon to accept Onesimus.

9 I rather appeal. In this situation, however, Paul did not rely on his authority but called for a response based on the bond of love between himself and Philemon (v. 7; cf. 2Co 10:1). **the aged.** More than a reference to his chronological age (which at the time of this letter was about 60), this description includes the toll that all the years of persecution, illnesses, imprisonments, difficult journeys, and constant concern for the churches had taken on Paul (*see notes on 2Co 11:23–30*), making him feel and appear even older than he actually was. **prisoner.** *See note on v. 1.*

10 my child Onesimus. See Introduction: Background and Setting. To Paul, he was a son in the faith (*see note on 1Ti 1:2*). **begotten in my imprisonment.** While in prison at Rome, Paul had led him to faith in Christ.

11 useless … useful. This play on words carries the same root meaning as the Gr. word from which the name Onesimus comes. Paul was basically saying, "Useful formerly was useless, but now is useful"—Paul's point is that Onesimus had been radically transformed by God's grace.

14 own free will. Paul wanted Onesimus to minister alongside him, but only if Philemon openly and gladly agreed to release him.

15 perhaps. Paul was suggesting that God providentially ordered the overturning of the evil of Onesimus' running away to produce eventual good (cf. Ge 50:20; Ro 8:28).

16 more than a slave, a beloved brother. Paul did not call for Onesimus' freedom (cf. 1Co 7:20–22), but that Philemon would receive his slave now as a fellow-believer in Christ (cf. Eph 6:9; Col 4:1; 1Ti 6:2). Christianity never

CHARACTERISTICS OF CHRISTIAN LOVE	
Grateful for the best in others	v. 4
Seeks the welfare of others	v. 10
Deals honestly with others	v. 12
Bears the burdens of others	v. 18
Believes the best of others	v. 21

than a slave, [B]a beloved brother, especially to me,
but how much more to you, both [C]in the flesh and
in the Lord.
17 If then you regard me a [A]partner, accept him
as *you would* me. 18 But if he has wronged you in
any way or owes you anything, charge that to my
account; 19 [A]I, Paul, am writing this with my own
hand, I will repay it ([B]not to [a]mention to you that
you owe to me even your own self as well). 20 Yes,
brother, let me benefit from you in the Lord; [A]refresh my heart in Christ.

21 [A]Having confidence in your obedience, I write
to you, since I know that you will do even more
than what I say.
22 At the same time also prepare me a [A]lodging,
for [B]I hope that through [C]your prayers [D]I will be
given to you.
23 [A]Epaphras, my [B]fellow prisoner in Christ Jesus,
greets you, 24 *as do* [A]Mark, [B]Aristarchus, [C]Demas,
[C]Luke, my [D]fellow workers.
25 [A]The grace of the Lord Jesus Christ be [B]with
your spirit.[a]

1:16 [B]Matt 23:8; 1 Tim 6:2 [C]Eph 6:5; Col 3:22 1:17 [A]2 Cor 8:23 1:19 [a]Lit *say* [A]1 Cor 16:21; 2 Cor 10:1; Gal 5:2 [B]2 Cor 9:4 1:20 [A]Philem 7 1:21 [A]2 Cor 2:3 1:22 [A]Acts 28:23 [B]Phil 1:25; 2:24 [C]2 Cor 1:11 [D]Acts 27:24; Heb 13:19 1:23 [A]Col 1:7; 4:12 [B]Rom 16:7; Philem 1 1:24 [A]Acts 12:12, 25; 15:37-39; Col 4:10 [B]Acts 19:29; 27:2; Col 4:10 [C]Col 4:14; 2 Tim 4:10f [D]Philem 1 1:25 [a]One early ms adds *Amen* [A]Gal 6:18 [B]2 Tim 4:22

sought to abolish slavery, but rather to make the relationships within it just and kind. **in the flesh.** In this physical life (*see note on Php 1:22*), as they worked together. **in the Lord.** The master and slave were to enjoy spiritual oneness and fellowship as they worshiped and ministered together.

17–19 Paul offered to pay whatever restitution was necessary for Onesimus to be reconciled to Philemon, following the example of Jesus in reconciling sinners to God.

19 with my own hand. *See notes on Gal 6:11; Col 4:18*; cf. 2Th 3:17. **even your own self.** Philemon owed Paul something far greater than the material debt Paul was offering to repay, since Paul had led him to saving faith, a debt Philemon could never repay.

20 let me benefit from you. *See note on Php 2:2*. By forgiving Onesimus, Philemon would keep the unity in the church at Colosse and bring joy to the chained apostle (cf. v. 7).

21 even more than what I say. The more than forgiveness that Paul was urging upon Philemon was either: 1) to welcome Onesimus back enthusiastically, not grudgingly (cf. Lk 15:22–24); 2) to permit Onesimus, in addition to his menial tasks, to minister spiritually with Philemon; or 3) to forgive any others who might have wronged Philemon. Whichever Paul intended, he was not subtly urging Philemon to grant Onesimus freedom (*see note on v. 16*).

22 a lodging. A place where Paul could stay when he visited Colosse. **I will be given to you.** Paul expected to be released from prison in the near future (cf. Php 2:23, 24), after which he could be with Philemon and the other Colossians again.

23 Epaphras. *See note on Col 4:12.*

24 Mark, Aristarchus. *See note on Col 4:10*. The story of the once severed but now mended relationship between Paul and Mark (Ac 15:38–40; 2Ti 4:11) would have been well known to the believers in Colosse (Col 4:10). Listing Mark's name here would serve to remind Philemon that Paul himself had worked through the issues of forgiveness, and that the instructions he was passing on to his friend were ones the apostle himself had already implemented in his relationship with John Mark. **Demas, Luke.** *See note on Col 4:14.*

THE EPISTLE TO THE HEBREWS

TITLE

When the various NT books were formally brought together into one collection shortly after A.D. 100, the titles were added for convenience. This epistle's title bears the traditional Greek title, "To the Hebrews," which was attested by at least the second century A.D. Within the epistle itself, however, there is no identification of the recipients as either Hebrews (Jews) or Gentiles. Since the epistle is filled with references to Hebrew history and religion and does not address any particular Gentile or pagan practice, the traditional title has been maintained.

AUTHOR AND DATE

The author of Hebrews is unknown. Paul, Barnabas, Silas, Apollos, Luke, Philip, Priscilla, Aquila, and Clement of Rome have been suggested by different scholars, but the epistle's vocabulary, style, and various literary characteristics do not clearly support any particular claim. It is significant that the writer includes himself among those people who had received confirmation of Christ's message from others (2:3). That would seem to rule out someone like Paul who claimed that he had received such confirmation directly from God and not from men (Gal 1:12). Whoever the author was, he preferred citing OT references from the Greek OT (LXX) rather than from the Hebrew text. Even the early church expressed various opinions on authorship, and current scholarship admits the puzzle still has no solution. Therefore, it seems best to accept the epistle's anonymity. Ultimately, of course, the author was the Holy Spirit (2Pe 1:21).

The use of the present tense in 5:1–4; 7:21, 23, 27, 28; 8:3–5, 13; 9:6–9, 13, 25; 10:1, 3, 4, 8, 11; and 13:10, 11 would suggest that the Levitical priesthood and sacrificial system were still in operation when the epistle was composed. Since the temple was destroyed by General (later Emperor) Titus Vespasian in A.D. 70, the epistle must have been written prior to that date. In addition, it may be noted that Timothy had just been released from prison (13:23) and that persecution was becoming severe (10:32–39; 12:4; 13:3). These details suggest a date for the epistle around A.D. 67–69.

BACKGROUND AND SETTING

Emphases on the Levitical priesthood and on sacrifices, as well as the absence of any reference to the Gentiles, support the conclusion that a community of Hebrews was the recipient of the epistle. Although these Hebrews were primarily converts to Christ, there were probably a number of unbelievers in their midst, who were attracted by the message of salvation, but who had not yet made a full commitment of faith in Christ (see Interpretive Challenges). One thing is clear from the contents of the epistle: the community of Hebrews was facing the possibility of intensified persecution (10:32–39; 12:4). As they confronted this possibility, the Hebrews were tempted to cast aside any identification with Christ. They may have considered demoting Christ from God's Son to a mere angel. Such a precedent had already been set in the Qumran community of messianic Jews living near the Dead Sea. They had dropped out of society, established a religious commune, and included the worship of angels in their brand of reformed Judaism. The Qumran community had even gone so far as to claim that the angel Michael was higher in status than the coming Messiah. These kinds of doctrinal aberrations could explain the emphasis in Hebrews chapter one on the superiority of Christ over the angels.

Possible locations for the recipients of the epistle include Israel, Egypt, Italy, Asia Minor, and Greece. The community that was the primary recipient may have circulated the epistle among those of Hebrew background in neighboring areas and churches. Those believers probably had not seen Christ personally. Apparently, they had been evangelized by "those who heard" Christ and whose ministries had been authenticated "by signs and wonders and by various miracles" (2:3, 4). Thus the recipients could have been in a church outside Judea and Galilee or in a church in those areas, but established among people in the generation following those who had been eyewitnesses of Christ. The congregation was not new or untaught ("by this time you ought to be teachers"), yet some of them still needed "milk and not solid food" (5:12).

"Those from Italy" (13:24) is an ambiguous reference since it could mean either those who had left Italy and were living elsewhere, or those who were still in Italy and being singled out as native residents of that country. Greece or Asia Minor must also be considered because of the apparently early establishment of the church there, and because of the consistent use of the LXX.

The generation of Hebrews receiving this epistle had practiced the Levitical sacrifices at the temple in Jerusalem. Jews living in exile had substituted the synagogue for the temple but still felt a deep attraction to the temple worship. Some had the means to make regular pilgrimages to the temple in Jerusalem. The writer of this epistle emphasized the superiority of Christianity over Judaism and the superiority of Christ's once-for-all sacrifice over the repeated and imperfect Levitical sacrifices observed in the temple.

HISTORICAL AND THEOLOGICAL THEMES

Since the book of Hebrews is grounded in the work of the Levitical priesthood, an understanding of the book of Leviticus is essential for properly interpreting Hebrews. Israel's sin had continually interrupted God's fellowship with His chosen and covenant people, Israel. Therefore, He graciously and sovereignly established a system of sacrifices that symbolically represented the inner repentance of sinners and His divine forgiveness. However, the need for sacrifices never ended because the people and priests continued to sin. The need of all mankind was for a perfect priest and a perfect sacrifice that would once and for all actually remove sin. God's provision for that perfect priest and sacrifice in Christ is the central message of Hebrews.

The epistle to the Hebrews is a study in contrast, between the imperfect and incomplete provisions of the Old Covenant, given under Moses, and the infinitely better provisions of the New Covenant offered by the perfect High Priest, God's only Son and the Messiah, Jesus Christ. Included in the "better" provisions are: a better hope, testament, promise, sacrifice, substance, country, and resurrection. Those who belong to the New Covenant dwell in a completely new and heavenly atmosphere, they worship a heavenly Savior, have a heavenly calling, receive a heavenly gift, are citizens of a heavenly country, look forward to a heavenly Jerusalem, and have their very names written in heaven.

One of the key theological themes in Hebrews is that all believers now have direct access to God under the New Covenant and, therefore, may approach the throne of God boldly (4:16; 10:22). One's hope is in the very presence of God, into which he follows the Savior (6:19, 20; 10:19, 20). The primary teaching symbolized by the tabernacle service was that believers under the covenant of law did not have direct access to the presence of God (9:8), but were shut out of the Holy of Holies. The book of Hebrews may briefly be summarized in this way: believers in Jesus Christ, as God's perfect sacrifice for sin, have the perfect High Priest through whose ministry everything is new and better than under the covenant of law.

This epistle is more than a doctrinal treatise, however. It is intensely practical in its application to everyday living (see chap. 13). The writer himself even refers to his letter as a "word of exhortation" (13:22; cf. Ac 13:15). Exhortations designed to stir the readers into action are found throughout the text. Those exhortations are given in the form of 6 warnings:

- Warning against drifting from "what we have heard" (2:1–4)
- Warning against disbelieving the "voice" of God (3:7–14)
- Warning against degenerating from "the elementary teaching about the Christ" (5:11–6:20)
- Warning against despising "the knowledge of the truth" (10:26–39)
- Warning against devaluing "the grace of God" (12:15–17)
- Warning against departing from Him "who is speaking" (12:25–29)

Another significant aspect of this epistle is its clear exposition of selected OT passages. The writer was clearly a skilled expositor of the Word of God. His example is instructive for preachers and teachers:

1:1–2:4	Exposition of verses from Pss; 2Sa 7; Dt 32
2:5–18	Exposition of Ps 8:4–6
3:1–4:13	Exposition of Ps 95:7–11
4:14–7:28	Exposition of Ps 110:4
8:1–10:18	Exposition of Jer 31:31–34
10:32–12:3	Exposition of Hab 2:3, 4
12:4–13	Exposition of Pr 3:11, 12
12:18–29	Exposition of Ex 19; 20

INTERPRETIVE CHALLENGES

A proper interpretation of this epistle requires the recognition that it addresses 3 distinct groups of Jews: 1) believers; 2) unbelievers who were intellectually convinced of the gospel; and 3) unbelievers who were attracted by the gospel and the person of Christ but who had reached no final conviction about Him. Failure to acknowledge these groups leads to interpretations inconsistent with the rest of Scripture.

The primary group addressed were Hebrew Christians who suffered rejection and persecution by fellow Jews (10:32–34), although none as yet had been martyred (12:4). The letter was written to give them encouragement and confidence in Christ, their Messiah and High Priest. They were an immature group of believers who were tempted to hold on to the symbolic and spiritually powerless rituals and traditions of Judaism.

The second group addressed were Jewish unbelievers who were convinced of the basic truths of the gospel but who had not placed their faith in Jesus Christ as their own Savior and Lord. They were intellectually persuaded but spiritually uncommitted. These unbelievers are addressed in such passages as 2:1–3; 6:4–6; 10:26–29; and 12:15–17.

The third group addressed were Jewish unbelievers who were not convinced of the gospel's truth but had had some exposure to it. Chapter 9 is largely devoted to them (see especially vv. 11, 14, 15, 27, 28).

By far, the most serious interpretive challenge is found in 6:4–6. The phrase "once been enlightened" is often taken to refer to Christians, and the accompanying warning taken to indicate the danger of losing their salvation if they "have fallen away" and "again crucify to themselves the Son of God." But there is no mention of their being saved, and they are not described with any terms that apply only to believers (such as holy, born again, righteous, or saints). This problem arises from inaccurately identifying the spiritual condition of the ones being addressed. In this case, they were unbelievers who had been exposed to God's redemptive truth, and perhaps made a profession of faith, but had not exercised genuine saving faith. In 10:26, the reference once again is to apostate Christians, not to genuine believers who are often incorrectly thought to lose their salvation because of their sins.

OUTLINE

I. The Superiority of Jesus Christ's Position (1:1–4:13)

A. A Better Name (1:1–3)
B. Better Than the Angels (1:4–2:18)
  1. A greater messenger (1:4–14)
  2. A greater message (2:1–18)
    a. A greater salvation (2:1–4)
    b. A greater savior (2:5–18)
C. Better Than Moses (3:1–19)
D. A Better Rest (4:1–13)

II. The Superiority of Jesus Christ's Priesthood (4:14–7:28)

A. Christ as High Priest (4:14–5:10)
B. Exhortation to Full Commitment to Christ (5:11–6:20)
C. Christ's Priesthood like Melchizedek's (7:1–28)

III. The Superiority of Jesus Christ's Priestly Ministry (8:1–10:18)

A. Through a Better Covenant (8:1–13)
B. In a Better Sanctuary (9:1–12)
C. By a Better Sacrifice (9:13–10:18)

IV. The Superiority of the Believer's Privileges (10:19–12:29)

A. Saving Faith (10:19–25)
B. False Faith (10:26–39)
C. Genuine Faith (11:1–3)
D. Heroes of the Faith (11:4–40)
E. Persevering Faith (12:1–29)

V. The Superiority of Christian Behavior (13:1–21)

A. In Relation to Others (13:1–3)
B. In Relation to Ourselves (13:4–9)
C. In Relation to God (13:10–21)
Postscript (13:22–25)

GOD'S FINAL WORD IN HIS SON

1 God, after He [A]spoke long ago to the fathers in [B]the
prophets in many portions and [C]in many ways,
2 [a,A]in these last days [B]has spoken to us [b]in [C]His Son,
whom He appointed [D]heir of all things, [E]through
whom also He made the [c,F]world. 3 [a]And He is the radiance of His glory and the exact [A]representation of His
nature, and [b,B]upholds all things by the word of His
power. When He had made [C]purification of sins, He
[D]sat down at the right hand of the [E]Majesty on high,
4 having become as much better than the angels, as
He has inherited a more excellent [A]name than they.
5 For to which of the angels did He ever say,

"[A]YOU ARE MY SON,
TODAY I HAVE BEGOTTEN YOU"?

And again,

"[B]I WILL BE A FATHER TO HIM
AND HE SHALL BE A SON TO ME"?

6 And [a]when He again [A]brings the firstborn into
[b,B]the world, He says,

"[C]AND LET ALL THE ANGELS OF
GOD WORSHIP HIM."

1:1 [A]John 9:29; 16:13; Heb 2:2f; 3:5; 4:8; 5:5; 11:18; 12:25 [B]Acts 2:30; 3:21 [C]Num 12:6, 8; Joel 2:28 1:2 [a]Or *at the end of these days* [b]Lit *in Son;* or in the person of a Son [c]Lit *ages* [A]Matt 13:39; 1 Pet 1:20 [B]John 9:29 [C]John 5:26, 27; Heb 3:6; 5:8; 7:28 [D]Ps 2:8; Matt 28:18; Mark 12:7; Rom 8:17; Heb 2:8 [E]John 1:3; 1 Cor 8:6; Col 1:16 [F]1 Cor 2:7; Heb 11:3 1:3 [a]Lit *Who being* [b]Lit *upholding* [A]2 Cor 4:4 [B]Col 1:17 [C]Titus 2:14; Heb 9:14 [D]Mark 16:19; Heb 8:1; 10:12; 12:2 [E]2 Pet 1:17 1:4 [A]Eph 1:21 1:5 [A]Ps 2:7; Acts 13:33; Heb 5:5 [B]2 Sam 7:14 1:6 [a]Or *again when He brings* [b]Lit *the inhabited earth* [A]Heb 10:5 [B]Matt 24:14 [C]Ps 97:7

1:1 many portions. Over the course of possibly 1,800 years (from Job, ca. 2200 B.C. [?] to Nehemiah, ca. 400 B.C.) the OT was written in 39 different books reflecting different historical times, locations, cultures, and situations. **many ways.** These included visions, symbols, and parables, written in both poetry and prose. Though the literary form and style varied, it was always God's revelation of what He wanted His people to know. The progressive revelation of the OT described God's program of redemption (1Pe 1:10–12) and His will for His people (Ro 15:4; 2Ti 3:16, 17).

1:2 last days. Jews understood the "last days" to mean the time when Messiah (Christ) would come (cf. Nu 24:14; Jer 33:14–16; Mic 5:1, 2; Zec 9:9, 16). The fulfillment of the messianic prophecies commenced with the advent of the Messiah. Since He came, it has been the "last days" (cf. 1Co 10:11; Jas 5:3; 1Pe 1:20; 4:7; 1Jn 2:18). In the past God gave revelation through His prophets, but in these times, beginning with the Messiah's advent, God spoke the message of redemption through the Son. **heir.** Everything that exists will ultimately come under the control of the Son of God, the Messiah (cf. Pss 2:8, 9; 89:27; Ro 11:36; Col 1:16). This "inheritance" is the full extension of the authority which the Father has given to the Son (cf. Da 7:13, 14; Mt 28:18), as the "firstborn" (*see note on v. 6*). **world.** The word can also be translated "ages." It refers to time, space, energy, and matter—the entire universe and everything that makes it function (cf. Jn 1:3).

1:3 radiance. The term is used only here in the NT. It expresses the concept of sending forth light or shining (cf. Jn 8:12; 2Co 4:4, 6). The meaning of "reflection" is not appropriate here. The Son is not just reflecting God's glory; He is God and radiates His own essential glory. **exact representation of His nature.** The term translated "exact representation" is used only here in the NT. In extrabiblical literature, it was employed for an engraving on wood, an etching in metal, a brand on animal hide, an impression in clay, and a stamped image on coins. The Son is the perfect imprint, the exact representation of the nature and essence of God in time and space (cf. Jn 14:9; Col 1:15; 2:9). **upholds.** The universe and everything in it is constantly sustained by the Son's powerfully effective word (Col 1:17). The term also conveys the concept of movement or progress—the Son of God directs all things toward the consummation of all things according to God's sovereign purpose. He who spoke all things into existence also sustains His creation and consummates His purpose by His word. **purification of sins.** By the substitutionary sacrifice of Himself on the cross (cf. Titus 2:14; Rev 1:5). **sat down at the right hand.** The right hand is the place of power, authority, and honor (cf. v. 13; Ro 8:34; 1Pe 3:22). It is also the position of subordination, implying that the Son is under the authority of the Father (cf. 1Co 15:27, 28). The seat that Christ has taken is the throne of God (8:1; 10:12; 12:2) where He rules as sovereign Lord. This depicts a victorious Savior, not a defeated martyr. While the primary thrust of this phrase is the enthronement of Christ, His sitting might also imply the completion of His atoning work.

1:4 having become. The Gr. verb used here refers to a change of state, not a change of existence. The Son in His divine essence has eternally existed, but for a while He was made lower than the angels (2:9) and afterward was exalted to an infinitely higher position by virtue of what He had accomplished in His redemptive work (*see notes on Php 2:9–11*). **angels.** Spirit beings created by God to minister to Him and do His bidding. The Jews held angels in very high regard as the highest beings next to God. The sect of Judaism which had established a community at Qumran taught that the archangel Michael's authority rivaled or surpassed that of the Messiah. The writer of Hebrews clearly disclaims any such concept. The Son of God is superior to the angels. **more excellent name.** That name is Lord (*see notes on Php 2:9–11*). No angel is Sovereign Lord (vv. 6, 13, 14).

1:5 Quoting from Ps 2:7 and 2Sa 7:14, the writer presents the unique relationship which the Son has with the Father. No angel ever experienced such a relationship. **Son.** A reference to the essential nature of Christ, the Second Person of the Godhead, in relation to the First Person—the Son shares the same substance of deity with the Father from eternity past (*see note on 2Ti 1:9*). Cf. vv. 2, 8; 3:6; 4:14; 5:5, 8; 6:6; 7:3, 28; 10:29; 11:17 and many other references in the NT. His sonship was also expressed in the OT (cf. Ps 2:12; Pr 30:4). The word "TODAY" indicates that God's Son was born in a point of time. He was always God, but He demonstrated His role as Son in space and time at His incarnation and was affirmed as such by His resurrection (Ro 1:4).

1:6 again. This adverb can be taken with "brings" as a reference to the second coming of Christ or with "says" to indicate yet another quotation from the OT ("and again, when He brings the firstborn into the world, He says"; cf. v. 5; 2:13). **firstborn.** *See notes on Ro 8:29; Col 1:15*, where it refers to prominence of position or title, not to the order of time. Christ was not the first to be born on the earth, but He holds the highest position of sovereignty. As "firstborn" He is also set apart to the service of God and, being preeminent, is entitled

CHRIST'S SUPERIORITY

Jesus Is Greater Than the Prophets 1:1–3 Seven affirmations	Jesus Is Greater Than the Angels 1:4–14 Seven quotations
Heir of all things (v. 2)	Psalm 2:7 (v. 5)
Creator (v. 2)	2 Samuel 7:14 (v. 5)
Manifestation of God's Being (v. 3)	Deuteronomy 32:43 or Psalm 97:7 (v. 6)
Perfect representation of God (v.3)	Psalm 104:4 (v. 7)
Sustainer of all things (v. 3)	Psalm 45:6, 7 (vv. 8, 9)
Savior (v. 3)	Psalm 102:25–27 (vv. 10–12)
Exalted Lord (v. 3)	Psalm 110:1 (v. 13)

7 And of the angels He says,

"[A]WHO MAKES HIS ANGELS WINDS,
AND HIS MINISTERS A FLAME OF FIRE."

8 But of the Son *He says,*

"[A]YOUR THRONE, O GOD, IS
FOREVER AND EVER,
AND THE RIGHTEOUS SCEPTER IS THE
SCEPTER OF [a]HIS KINGDOM.
9 "[A]YOU HAVE LOVED RIGHTEOUSNESS
AND HATED LAWLESSNESS;
[B]THEREFORE GOD, YOUR GOD,
HAS [C]ANOINTED YOU
WITH THE OIL OF GLADNESS ABOVE
YOUR COMPANIONS."

10 And,

"[A]YOU, LORD, IN THE BEGINNING LAID
THE FOUNDATION OF THE EARTH,
AND THE HEAVENS ARE THE
WORKS OF YOUR HANDS;
11 [A]THEY WILL PERISH, BUT YOU REMAIN;
[B]AND THEY ALL WILL BECOME
OLD LIKE A GARMENT,
12 [A]AND LIKE A MANTLE YOU
WILL ROLL THEM UP;
LIKE A GARMENT THEY WILL
ALSO BE CHANGED.
BUT YOU ARE [B]THE SAME,
AND YOUR YEARS WILL NOT
COME TO AN END."

13 But to which of the angels has He ever said,

"[A]SIT AT MY RIGHT HAND,
[B]UNTIL I MAKE YOUR ENEMIES
A FOOTSTOOL FOR YOUR FEET"?

14 Are they not all [A]ministering spirits, sent out to render service for the sake of those who will [B]inherit [C]salvation?

GIVE HEED

2 For this reason we must pay much closer attention to [a]what we have heard, so that [A]we
do not drift away *from it.* 2 For if the word [A]spoken
through [B]angels proved [a]unalterable, and [C]every
transgression and disobedience received a just
[b,D]penalty, 3 [A]how will we escape if we neglect so
great a [B]salvation? [a]After it was at the first [C]spoken
through the Lord, it was [D]confirmed to us by those

1:7 [A]Ps 104:4 1:8 [a]Late mss read *Your* [A]Ps 45:6 1:9 [A]Ps 45:7 [B]John 10:17; Phil 2:9; Heb 2:9 [C]Is 61:1, 3 1:10 [A]Ps 102:25 1:11 [A]Ps 102:26 [B]Is 51:6; Heb 8:13 1:12 [A]Ps 102:26, 27 [B]Heb 13:8 1:13 [A]Ps 110:1; Matt 22:44; Heb 1:3 [B]Josh 10:24; Heb 10:13 1:14 [A]Ps 103:20f; Dan 7:10 [B]Matt 25:34; Mark 10:17; Titus 3:7; Heb 6:12 [C]Rom 11:14; 1 Cor 1:21; Heb 2:3; 5:9; 9:28 2:1 [a]Lit *the things that have been heard* [A]Prov 3:21 2:2 [a]Or *steadfast* [b]Or *recompense* [A]Heb 1:1 [B]Acts 7:53 [C]Heb 10:28 [D]Heb 10:35; 11:26 2:3 [a]Lit *Which was* [A]Heb 10:29; 12:25 [B]Rom 11:14; 1 Cor 1:21; Heb 1:14; 5:9; 9:28 [C]Heb 1:1 [D]Mark 16:20; Luke 1:2; 1 John 1:1

to the inheritance (cf. v. 2; Ge 43:33; Ex 13:2; 22:29; Dt 21:17; Ps 89:27). let all the angels. Quoted from the LXX translation of Dt 32:43 (cf. Ps 97:7). Since the angels are commanded to worship the Messiah, the Messiah must be superior to them. Five of the 7 OT passages quoted in this first chapter of Hebrews are in contexts related to the Davidic Covenant, which emphasizes the concepts of sonship, kingship, and kingdom. Although Dt 32:43 is not in a Davidic Covenant context, it has an affinity to the teaching of Ps 89:6 (a psalm of the Davidic Covenant), which declares that the heavenly beings themselves must recognize the lordship of God. Reference is made to "the firstborn" in the introduction to the Deuteronomy quote. In addition, "firstborn" is mentioned in Ps 89:27.

1:7 of the angels. The writer continues biblical proofs that the angels are subservient to the Son of God by citing Ps 104:4. This is the only one of the 7 OT quotations in chap. 1 which has no connection at all to the Davidic Covenant. The quote merely defines the primary nature and purpose of angels.

1:8, 9 *He says.* Quoting from Ps 45:6, 7, the writer argues for the deity and the lordship of the Son over creation (cf. v. 3). The text is all the more significant since the declaration of the Son's deity is presented as the words of the Father Himself (cf. Is 9:6; Jer 23:5, 6; Jn 5:18; Titus 2:13; 1Jn 5:20). It is clear that the writer of Hebrews had the 3 messianic offices in mind: Prophet (v. 1), Priest (v. 3), and King (vv. 3, 8). Induction into those 3 offices required anointing (v. 9). The title Messiah (Christ) means "anointed one" (cf. Is 61:1–3; Lk 4:16–21).

1:9 companions. The term is used only in Hebrews (3:1, 14; 6:4; 12:8) and in Lk 5:7, where it is rendered as "partners.". In this occurrence, it might refer to angels or to other men who were similarly anointed for their offices: the OT prophets, priests, and kings. If the "OIL OF GLADNESS" here is the same as "oil of gladness" referred to in Is 61:3, the reference would clearly be to those who had mourned in Zion but who would one day be clothed with praise and called "oaks of righteousness"—references to men, not angels. No matter how noble such men were, Christ is superior.

1:10–12 Quoted from Ps 102:25–27. The Son who created the universe (Jn 1:1–3) one day will destroy the heavens and earth that He created (*see notes on 2Pe 3:10–12*), but He remains unchanged. Immutability is yet another characteristic of the divine essence. Once again the OT testifies of the Son's deity.

1:13, 14 The writer reemphasizes the lordship of the Son by quoting Ps 110:1. While Christ's destiny is to reign (cf. v. 3; Mt 22:44; Ac 2:35), the angels' destiny is to serve the recipients of salvation (*see note on 1Co 6:3*). This is the seventh and final quotation from the OT to bolster the argument that as Son and Lord the Messiah is superior to the angels.

1:13 Your enemies a footstool. This quote from Ps 110:1 is repeated in the NT at 10:13; Mt 22:44; Mk 12:36; Lk 20:43; Ac 2:35, and expresses the sovereignty of Christ over all (cf. Php 2:10).

1:14 *See note on Mt 18:10.*

2:1–4 In order to drive home the importance of the superiority of the Son of God over angels, the writer urges the readers to respond. "We" includes all those who are Hebrews. Some had given intellectual assent to the doctrine of Messiah's superiority to the angels, but had not yet committed themselves to Him as God and Lord. He deserves their worship as much as He deserves the worship of the angels.

2:1 closer attention . . . drift away. Both phrases have nautical connotations. The first refers to mooring a ship, tying it up at the dock. The second was often used of a ship that had been allowed to drift past the harbor. The warning is to secure oneself to the truth of the gospel, being careful not to pass by the only harbor of salvation. The closest attention must be paid to these very serious matters of the Christian faith. The readers in their tendency to apathy are in danger of making shipwreck of their lives (cf. 6:19; *see note on 1Ti 1:19*).

2:2 if. The Gr. term assumes a fulfilled condition and here carries the idea: "In view of the fact that . . . ." **angels.** Angels were instrumental in bringing God's law to His people at Mt. Sinai (cf. Dt 33:1, 2; Ps 68:17; Ac 7:38, 53; Gal 3:19). **transgression and disobedience.** The former means to step across the line, in an overt sin of commission. The latter carries the idea of shutting one's ears to God's commands, thereby committing a sin of omission. Both are willful, serious, and require just judgment.

2:3 how will we escape. If disobedience to the older covenant of law brought swift judgment, how much more severe will be the judgment of disobedience to the New Covenant gospel of salvation, which was mediated by the Son who is superior to the angels (cf. Mt 10:14, 15; 11:20–24)? The messenger and message of the New Covenant are greater than the messengers and message of the older covenant. The greater the privilege, the greater the

who heard, 4 God also testifying with them, both
by [A]signs and wonders and by [B]various [a]miracles
and by [b,C]gifts of the Holy Spirit [D]according to His
own will.

EARTH SUBJECT TO MAN

5 For He did not subject to angels [a,A]the world to
come, concerning which we are speaking. 6 But one
has testified [A]somewhere, saying,

> "[B]What is man, that You
> remember him?
> Or the son of man, that You
> are concerned about him?
> 7 "[A]You have made him [a]for
> a little while lower
> than the angels;
> You have crowned him with
> glory and honor,
> [b]And have appointed him over
> the works of Your hands;
> 8 [A]You have put all things in
> subjection under his feet."

For in subjecting all things to him, He left nothing
that is not subject to him. But now [B]we do not yet
see all things subjected to him.

JESUS BRIEFLY HUMBLED

9 But we do see Him who was [A]made [a]for a little
while lower than the angels, *namely,* Jesus, [B]because
of the suffering of death [C]crowned with glory and
honor, so that [D]by the grace of God He might [E]taste
death [F]for everyone.
10 For [A]it was fitting for Him, [B]for whom are all
things, and through whom are all things, in bringing many sons to glory, to [C]perfect the [a,D]author of
their salvation through sufferings. 11 For both He
who [A]sanctifies and those who [B]are [a]sanctified are
all [C]from one *Father;* for which reason He is not
ashamed to call them [D]brethren, 12 saying,

> "[A]I will proclaim Your name
> to My brethren,
> In the midst of the congregation
> I will sing Your praise."

13 And again,

> "[A]I will put My trust in Him."

And again,

> "[B]Behold, I and the children
> whom God has given Me."

2:4 [a]Or *works of power* [b]Lit *distributions* [A]John 4:48 [B]Mark 6:14 [C]1 Cor 12:4, 11; Eph 4:7 [D]Eph 1:5 2:5 [a]Lit *the inhabited earth* [A]Matt 24:14; Heb 6:5 2:6 [A]Heb 4:4 [B]Ps 8:4 2:7 [a]Or *...him a little lower than...* [b]Two early mss do not contain *And...hands* [A]Ps 8:5, 6 2:8 [A]Ps 8:6; 1 Cor 15:27 [B]1 Cor 15:25 2:9 [a]Or *a little lower* [A]Heb 2:7 [B]Acts 2:33; 3:13; 1 Pet 1:21 [C]Phil 2:9; Heb 1:9 [D]John 3:16 [E]Matt 16:28; John 8:52 [F]Heb 7:25 2:10 [a]Or *leader* [A]Luke 24:26 [B]Rom 11:36 [C]Heb 5:9; 7:28 [D]Acts 3:15; 5:31 2:11 [a]Or *being sanctified* [A]Heb 13:12 [B]Heb 10:10 [C]Acts 17:28 [D]Matt 25:40; Mark 3:34f; John 20:17 2:12 [A]Ps 22:22 2:13 [A]Is 8:17 [B]Is 8:18

punishment for disobedience or neglect (10:29; cf. Lk 12:47). **by those who heard.** This phrase reveals the succession of evangelism. That generation of Hebrews would not have heard if the previous generation of witnesses had not passed the message along (cf. 1Ti 2:5–7).

2:4 signs ... wonders ... miracles ... gifts. The supernatural powers demonstrated by Jesus and by His apostles were the Father's divine confirmation of the gospel of Jesus Christ, His Son (cf. Jn 10:38; Ac 2:22; Ro 15:19; 1Co 14:22; *see note on 2Co 12:12*). This authentication of the message was the purpose of such miraculous deeds. **the Holy Spirit.** The epistle's first reference to the Holy Spirit refers in passing to His ministry of confirming the message of salvation by means of miraculous gifts. Mentioned elsewhere in the epistle are the Holy Spirit's involvement in the revelation of Scripture (3:7; 10:15), in teaching (9:8), in pre-salvation operations (6:4, perhaps His convicting work; 10:29, common grace), and in ministry to Christ (9:14).

2:5 world. The term refers to the inhabited earth. The reference is to the great millennial kingdom (cf. Zec 14:9; Rev 20:1–5). Angels will not reign over the messianic kingdom.

2:6–8 Quoted from Ps 8:4–6 (cf. 1Co 15:27, 28; Eph 1:22).

2:6 somewhere. This is not an indication that the writer was ignorant of the source of the quotation that follows. The location of the quotation is not as significant as its divine authorship. Perhaps it is significant that the author of Hebrews is not identified either. The writer may have desired that his readers understand that the Holy Spirit is the real author of all Scripture (cf. 2Ti 3:16; 2Pe 1:21). **man ... son of man.** Both refer to mankind, not to Christ. The passage asks why God would ever bother with man. As the following verses demonstrate (vv. 9, 10), the incarnation of Christ is the greatest proof of God's love and regard for mankind. Christ was not sent in the form of an angel. He was sent in the form of a man.

2:7 angels. Angels were given supernatural powers by the Creator. They have continual access to the throne of God (cf. Job 1:6; 2:1; Rev 5:11) and are not subject to death.

2:8 subjection. In spite of the superiority of angels to mankind, God had originally placed the administration of the earth into the hands of mankind (Ge 1:26–28). Due to the Fall (Ge 3), however, mankind has been incapable of fulfilling that divinely ordained position.

2:9 glory and honor. Because Jesus became "obedient to the point of death ... God highly exalted Him" (Php 2:8, 9). By His redemptive work, Christ has fulfilled all that is required as the supreme representative of mankind. By His incarnation, substitutionary sacrifice, and victory over sin and death (cf. Ro 6:23; 1Jn 4:10), He has fulfilled man's original purpose. As the Second Adam (1Co 15:47), He was for a short time lower than the angels. Now He has glory and honor, and all things (including angels) are subject to Him. **taste death for everyone.** Everyone who believes, that is. The death of Christ can only be applied in its efficacy to those who come to God repentantly in faith, asking for saving grace and forgiveness of sins. *See notes on 2Co 5:21; 1Ti 2:6; 4:10; Titus 2:11.*

2:10 fitting. What God did through the humiliation of Jesus Christ was perfectly consistent with His sovereign righteousness and holiness. Without Christ's humiliation and suffering, there could be no redemption. Without redemption, there could be no glorification (cf. Ro 8:18, 29, 30). **perfect.** In His divine nature, Christ was already perfect. However, His human nature was perfected through obedience, including suffering in order that He might be an understanding High Priest, an example for believers (cf. 5:8, 9; 7:25–28; Php 2:8; 1Pe 2:21), and establish the perfect righteousness (Mt 3:15) to be imputed to believers (2Co 5:21; Php 3:8, 19). **author.** The term is also used in 12:2 and Ac 5:31. It could be translated "pioneer," "leader," "captain," or "originator." Christ is the source (cf. 5:9, which has the meaning of cause), the initiator, and the leader in regard to salvation. He has led the way into heaven as our forerunner (6:20).

2:11 sanctifies. Sanctification sets a person apart for service through purification from sin and conformity to the holiness of God (cf. 10:10).

2:12 My brethren. Quoted from Ps 22:22. Jesus had taught that those who do the will of the Father in obedience to His Word are His brothers and mother (Mt 12:50; Lk 8:21). He never directly referred to His disciples by the title of "brethren" or "brothers" until after His resurrection (Mt 28:10; Jn 20:17). Not until He had paid the price for their salvation did they truly become His spiritual brothers and sisters. The use of the term demonstrates His full identification with mankind in order to provide complete redemption (Php 2:7–9).

2:13 The citation of Is 8:17, 18 (cf. 2Sa 22:3) emphasizes the point made in vv. 9–11: that Christ had fully identified Himself with mankind by taking a human nature. He demonstrated the reality of His human nature by His reliance upon God during His earthly sojourn.

14 Therefore, since the children share in [a,A]flesh
and blood, [B]He Himself likewise also partook of the
same, that [C]through death He might render powerless [D]him who had the power of death, that is, the
devil, 15 and might free those who through [A]fear of
death were subject to slavery all their lives. 16 For
assuredly He does not [a]give help to angels, but He
gives help to the [b]descendant of Abraham. 17 Therefore, He [a]had [A]to be made like His brethren in all
things, so that He might [B]become a merciful and
faithful [C]high priest in [D]things pertaining to God, to
[E]make propitiation for the sins of the people. 18 For
since He Himself was [A]tempted in that which He
has suffered, He is able to come to the aid of those
who are tempted.

JESUS OUR HIGH PRIEST

3 Therefore, [A]holy brethren, partakers of a [B]heav-
enly calling, consider Jesus, [C]the Apostle and
[D]High Priest of our [E]confession; 2 [a]He was faithful
to Him who appointed Him, as [A]Moses also was
in all His house. 3 [A]For He has been counted worthy of more glory than Moses, by just so much as
the builder of the house has more honor than the
house. 4 For every house is built by someone, but the
builder of all things is God. 5 Now [A]Moses was faithful in all His house as [B]a servant, [C]for a testimony of
those things [D]which were to be spoken later; 6 but
Christ *was faithful* as [A]a Son over His house—[B]whose
house we are, [C]if we hold fast our [D]confidence and
the boast of our [E]hope firm until the end.

2:14 [a]Lit *blood and flesh* [A]Matt 16:17 [B]John 1:14 [C]1 Cor 15:54-57; 2 Tim 1:10 [D]John 12:31; 1 John 3:8 2:15 [A]Rom 8:15 2:16 [a]Lit *take hold of angels, but He takes hold of* [b]Lit *seed* 2:17 [a]Lit *was obligated to be* [A]Phil 2:7; Heb 2:14 [B]Heb 4:15f; 5:2 [C]Heb 3:1; 4:14f; 5:5, 10; 6:20; 7:26, 28; 8:1, 3; 9:11; 10:21 [D]Rom 15:17; Heb 5:1 [E]Dan 9:24; 1 John 2:2; 4:10 2:18 [A]Heb 4:15 3:1 [A]Acts 1:15; Heb 2:11; 3:12; 10:19; 13:22 [B]Phil 3:14 [C]John 17:3 [D]Heb 2:17; 4:14f; 5:5, 10; 6:20; 7:26, 28; 8:1, 3; 9:11; 10:21 [E]2 Cor 9:13; Heb 4:14; 10:23 3:2 [a]Lit *Being faithful* [A]Ex 40:16; Num 12:7; Heb 3:5 3:3 [A]2 Cor 3:7-11 3:5 [A]Ex 40:16; Num 12:7; Heb 3:2 [B]Ex 14:31; Num 12:7 [C]Deut 18:18f [D]Heb 1:1 3:6 [A]Heb 1:2 [B]1 Cor 3:16; 1 Tim 3:15 [C]Rom 11:22; Heb 3:14; 4:14 [D]Eph 3:12; Heb 4:16; 10:19, 35 [E]Heb 6:11; 7:19; 10:23; 11:1; 1 Pet 1:3

2:14 share … partook. The Gr. word for "partook" means fellowship, communion, or partnership. "Share" means to take hold of something that is not related to one's own kind. The Son of God was not by nature "flesh and blood," but took upon Himself that nature for the sake of providing redemption for mankind. **death … power of death.** This is the ultimate purpose of the incarnation: Jesus came to earth to die. By dying, He was able to conquer death in His resurrection (Jn 14:19). By conquering death, He rendered Satan powerless against all who are saved. Satan's using the power of death is subject to God's will (cf. Job 2:6).

2:15 fear of death. For the believer, "death is swallowed up in victory" (1Co 15:54). Therefore, the fear of death and its spiritual bondage have been brought to an end through the work of Christ.

2:16 give help. The literal meaning is to "take hold of." The sense of "giving help" is from the picture of a taking hold of someone in order to push or pull them to safety, to rescue them. However, there was no thought in Judaism that the Messiah's entrance into the world would be to give help to the angels. The contrast, using this translation, is weak in comparison with all that has been previously said about Christ's superiority to the angels. The context presents the identification of Christ with mankind in His incarnation—He took upon Himself a human nature (vv. 9–14, 17). When the writer wished to express the concept of giving help, he chose a different Gr. word in v. 18 (also, 4:16). Therefore, the translation, "take on *the nature of,*" is to be preferred. **descendant of Abraham.** Christ is that promised descendant (*see notes on Gal 3:16*). Since the readers are Hebrews, they would certainly identify themselves with this description. The Messiah had been born in the line of Abraham in fulfillment of the OT prophecies (Mt 1:1). One of the chief purposes for the incarnation was the salvation of Israel (Mt 1:21). Yet another purpose was the fulfillment of the Abrahamic Covenant in regard to the promised descendant. Of all peoples, the Hebrews should be first to recognize the significance and importance of the incarnation.

2:17 propitiation. The word means "to conciliate" or "satisfy." *See note on Ro 3:25.* Christ's work of propitiation is related to His high priestly ministry. By His partaking of a human nature, Christ demonstrated His mercy to mankind and His faithfulness to God by satisfying God's requirement for sin and thus obtaining for His people full forgiveness. Cf. 1Jn 2:2; 4:10.

2:18 tempted. The genuineness of Christ's humanity is demonstrated by the fact that He was subject to temptation. By experiencing temptation, Jesus became fully capable of understanding and sympathizing with His human brethren (cf. 4:15). He felt the full force of temptation. Though we often yield to temptation before we feel its full force, Jesus resisted temptation even when the greatest enticement for yielding had become evident (cf. Lk 4:1–13). **able to come to the aid … tempted.** *See notes on 4:15, 16; 1Co 10:13.*

3:1–6 This section presents the superiority of Jesus over the highly revered Moses. The Lord had spoken with Moses "face to face, just as a man speaks to his friend" (Ex 33:11) and had given the law to him (Ne 9:13, 14). The commandments and rituals of the law were the Jews' supreme priorities, and to them Moses and the law were synonymous. Both the OT and the NT refer to the commands of God as the "law of Moses" (Jos 8:31; 1Ki 2:3; Lk 2:22; Ac 13:39). Yet, as great as Moses was, Jesus was infinitely greater.

3:1 holy brethren. The phrase occurs only here and in 1Th 5:27, where some manuscripts omit "holy." The writer addresses believers who have a "heavenly calling" (cf. Php 3:14). They are elsewhere described as desiring a "heavenly country" (11:16) and as coming to "the heavenly Jerusalem" (12:22). They are "holy" in the sense that they are set apart unto God and identified with the heavenly realm—citizens of heaven more than citizens of earth. **calling.** The reference, as always in the NT epistles, is to the effective summons to salvation in Christ (cf. Ro 8:30; 1Co 7:21). **consider.** The writer asks for the readers' complete attention and diligent observation of the superiority of Jesus Christ. **Apostle and High Priest.** An apostle is a "sent one" who has the rights, power, and authority of the one who sends him. Jesus was sent to earth by the Father (cf. Jn 3:17, 34; 5:36–38; 8:42). The topic of the High Priesthood of Christ, which was begun in 2:17, 18 and is mentioned again here, will be taken up again in greater detail in 4:14–10:18. Meanwhile, the writer presents the supremacy of Christ to Moses (vv. 1–6), to Joshua (4:8), and to all other national heroes and OT preachers whom Jews held in high esteem. Jesus Himself spoke of His superiority to Moses in the same context in which He spoke of His being sent by the Father (Jn 5:36–38, 45–47; cf. Lk 16:29–31). Moses had been sent by God to deliver His people from historical Egypt and its bondage (Ex 3:10). Jesus was sent by God to deliver His people from spiritual Egypt and its bondage (2:15). **of our confession.** Christ is the center of our confession of faith in the gospel, both in creed and public testimony. The term is used again in 4:14 and 10:23 (cf. 2Co 9:13; 1Ti 6:12). In all 3 uses in Hebrews there is a sense of urgency. Surely, the readers would not give up Christ, whom they had professed, and reject what He had done for them, if they could understand the superiority of His person and work.

3:2 house. The term refers to a family of people rather than a building or dwelling (cf. v. 6; 1Ti 3:15). Those who were stewards of a household must above all be faithful (1Co 4:2). Both Moses (Nu 12:7) and Christ (2:17) faithfully fulfilled their individual, divine appointments to care for the people of God.

3:3, 4 builder of the house. Moses was only a part of God's household of faith, whereas Jesus was the creator of that household (cf. 2Sa 7:13; Zec 6:12, 13; Eph 2:19–22; 1Pe 2:4, 5) and, therefore, is greater than Moses and equal to God.

3:5, 6 servant … Son. The term for "servant" implies a position of dignity and freedom, not slavery (cf. Ex 14:31; Jos 1:2). However, even as the highest-ranking servant, Moses could never hold the position of Son, which is Christ's alone (cf. Jn 8:35).

3:5 spoken later. Moses was faithful primarily as a testimony to that which was to come in Christ (cf. 11:24–27; *see note on Jn 5:46*).

3:6 whose house we are. *See notes on v. 2; Eph 2:22; 1Ti 3:15; 1Pe 2:5; 4:17.* **if we hold fast.** Cf. v. 14. This is not speaking of how to be saved or remain saved (cf. 1Co 15:2). It means rather that perseverance in faithfulness is proof of real faith. The person who returns to the rituals of the Levitical system to contribute to his own salvation proves he was never truly part of God's household (*see note on 1Jn 2:19*), whereas the one who abides in Christ gives evidence of his genuine membership in that household (cf. Mt 10:22; Lk 8:15; Jn 8:31; 15:4–6). The promise of God will fulfill this holding fast (1Th 5:24; Jude 24, 25). *See note*

7 Therefore, just as [A]the Holy Spirit says,

"[B]TODAY IF YOU HEAR HIS VOICE,
8 [A]DO NOT HARDEN YOUR HEARTS AS
[a]WHEN THEY PROVOKED ME,
AS IN THE DAY OF TRIAL IN
THE WILDERNESS,
9 [A]WHERE YOUR FATHERS TRIED
Me BY TESTING *Me*,
AND SAW MY WORKS FOR [B]FORTY YEARS.
10 "[A]THEREFORE I WAS ANGRY WITH
THIS GENERATION,
AND SAID, 'THEY ALWAYS GO
ASTRAY IN THEIR HEART,
AND THEY DID NOT KNOW MY WAYS';
11 [A]AS I SWORE IN MY WRATH,
'THEY SHALL NOT ENTER MY REST.' "

THE PERIL OF UNBELIEF

12 [A]Take care, brethren, that there not be in any
one of you an evil, unbelieving heart [a]that falls
away from [B]the living God. 13 But [A]encourage one
another day after day, as long as it is *still* called
"Today," so that none of you will be hardened by
the [B]deceitfulness of sin. 14 For we have become
partakers of Christ, [A]if we hold fast the beginning of
our [B]assurance firm until the end, 15 while it is said,

"[A]TODAY IF YOU HEAR HIS VOICE,
DO NOT HARDEN YOUR HEARTS, AS
[a]WHEN THEY PROVOKED ME."

16 For who [A]provoked *Him* when they had heard?
Indeed, [B]did not all those who came out of Egypt *led*
by Moses? 17 And with whom was He angry for forty
years? Was it not with those who sinned, [A]whose
bodies fell in the wilderness? 18 And to whom did
He swear [A]that they would not enter His rest, but
to those who were [B]disobedient? 19 *So* we see that
they were not able to enter because of [A]unbelief.

THE BELIEVER'S REST

4 Therefore, let us fear if, while a promise remains of entering His rest, any one of you may
seem to have [A]come short of it. 2 For indeed we have
had good news preached to us, just as they also;
but [A]the word [a]they heard did not profit them, because [b]it was not united by faith in those who heard.

3:7 [A]Acts 28:25; Heb 9:8; 10:15 [B]Ps 95:7; Heb 3:15; 4:7 3:8 [a]Lit *in the provocation* [A]Ps 95:8 3:9 [A]Ps 95:9-11 [B]Acts 7:36 3:10 [A]Ps 95:10 3:11 [A]Ps 95:11; Heb 4:3, 5 3:12 [a]Lit *in falling* [A]Col 2:8; Heb 12:25 [B]Matt 16:16; Heb 9:14; 10:31; 12:22 3:13 [A]Heb 10:24f [B]Eph 4:22 3:14 [A]Heb 3:6 [B]Heb 11:1 3:15 [a]Lit *in the rebellion* [A]Ps 95:7f; Heb 3:7; 4:7 3:16 [A]Jer 32:29; 44:3, 8 [B]Num 14:2, 11, 30; Deut 1:35, 36, 38 3:17 [A]Num 14:29; 1 Cor 10:5 3:18 [A]Num 14:23; Deut 1:34f; Heb 4:2 [B]Rom 11:30-32; Heb 4:6, 11 3:19 [A]John 3:18, 36; Rom 11:23; Heb 3:12 4:1 [A]2 Cor 6:1; Gal 5:4; Heb 12:15 4:2 [a]Lit *of hearing* [b]Two early mss read *they were...faith with those who heard* [A]Rom 10:17; Gal 3:2; 1 Thess 2:13

on Mt 24:13. **hope.** See the writer's further description of this hope in 6:18, 19. This hope rests in Christ Himself, whose redemptive work has accomplished our salvation (Ro 5:1, 2; *see note on 1Pe 1:3*).

3:7–11 The writer cites Ps 95:7–11 as the words of its ultimate author, the Holy Spirit (cf. 4:7; 9:8; 10:15). This passage describes the Israelites' wilderness wanderings after their delivery from Egypt. Despite God's miraculous works and His gracious, providential faithfulness to them, the people still failed to commit themselves to Him in faith (cf. Ex 17; Nu 14:22, 23; Ps 78:40–53). The writer of Hebrews presents a 3-point exposition of the OT passage: 1) beware of unbelief (vv. 12–19); 2) be afraid of falling short (4:1–10); and 3) be diligent to enter (4:11–13). The themes of the exposition include urgency, obedience (including faith), perseverance, and rest.

3:7 **Today.** The reference is to the present moment while the words of God are fresh in the mind. There is a sense of urgency to immediately give heed to the voice of God. This urgency is emphasized by repeating the reference to "today" from Ps 95:7 three more times (vv. 13, 15; 4:7) and is the theme of the writer's exposition (cf. 2Co 6:2).

3:11 **My rest.** The earthly rest which God promised to give was life in the land of Canaan which Israel would receive as their inheritance (Dt 12:9, 10; Jos 21:44; 1Ki 8:56). Because of rebellion against God, an entire generation of the children of Israel was prohibited from entering into that rest in the Promised Land (cf. Dt 28:65; La 1:3). The application of this picture is to an individual's spiritual rest in the Lord, which has precedent in the OT (cf. Ps 116:7; Is 28:12). At salvation, every believer enters the true rest, the realm of spiritual promise, never again laboring to achieve through personal effort a righteousness that pleases God. The Lord wanted both kinds of rest for the generation that was delivered from Egypt.

3:12 **brethren.** This admonition is addressed to those having the same potential characteristics as the generation which perished in the wilderness without ever seeing the Land of Promise. They were unbelieving Jewish brethren who were in the company of the "holy brethren" (v. 1). They were admonished to believe and be saved before it was too late. See Introduction: Interpretive Challenges. **an evil, unbelieving heart.** All men are born with such a heart (Jer 17:9). In the case of these Hebrews, that evil manifested itself in disbelief of the gospel which moved them in the opposite way from God.

3:13 **encourage one another day after day.** Both individual accountability and corporate responsibility are intended in this admonition. As long as the distressing days were upon them and they were tempted to return to the ineffective Levitical system, they were to encourage one another to identify completely with Jesus Christ. **hardened.** Repeated rejection of the gospel concerning Jesus results in a progressive hardening of the heart and will ultimately result in outright antagonism to the gospel. Cf. 6:4–6; 10:26–29; Ac 19:9. **deceitfulness.** Sin lies and deceives, using every trickery and stratagem possible (cf. Ro 7:11; 2Th 2:10; Jas 1:14–16). The Hebrews deceived themselves with the reasoning that their rejection of Jesus Christ was being faithful to the older system. Their willingness to hang on to the Levitical system was really a rejection of the living Word (4:12) of the "living God" (v. 12), who through Christ had opened up a "new and living way" (10:20). Choosing the path of unbelief always leads only to death (v. 17; 10:26–29; cf. 2:14, 15; Jude 5).

3:14 The exhortation is similar to that in v. 6. It repeats the theme of perseverance.

3:15–19 The quotation from Ps 95:7, 8 is repeated (cf. v. 7). The first quotation was followed with exposition emphasizing "today" and the urgency that word conveys. This second quotation is followed with exposition emphasizing rebellion (vv. 15, 16) and presenting the theme of obedience by means of its antithesis, disobedience. Four different terms are employed to drive the point of rebellion home: "provoked" (v. 16), "sinned" (v. 17), "disobedient" (v. 18), and "unbelief" (v. 19). This initial third (*see notes on vv. 7–11*) of the writer's exposition of Ps 95:7–11 is summed up by the obvious conclusion that the Israelites who died in the wilderness were victims of their own unbelief (v. 19).

4:1–10 The second section of the writer's exposition of Ps 95:7–11 goes beyond the description of unbelief and its dire consequences (3:12–19) to define the nature of the "rest" which the disobedient had forfeited. The first section had dealt primarily with Ps 95:7, 8; the second section deals primarily with Ps 95:11.

4:1 **promise.** This is the first use of this important word in Hebrews. The content of this promise is defined as "entering His rest." **His rest.** *See note on 3:11.* This is the rest which God gives; therefore it is called "My rest" (Ps 95:11) and "His rest." For believers, God's rest includes His peace, confidence of salvation, reliance on His strength, and assurance of a future heavenly home (cf. Mt 11:29). **come short.** The entire phrase could be translated "lest you think you have come too late to enter into the rest of God" (cf. 12:15). With reverential fear all are to examine their own spiritual condition (cf. 1Co 10:12; 2Co 13:5) and to actively press for commitment on the part of others (cf. Jude 23).

4:2 **faith.** Mere knowledge of God's message is not sufficient. It must be appropriated by saving faith. Later in the epistle a much longer exposition will take up this topic of

3 For we who have believed enter that rest, just as
He has said,

"[A]As I swore in My wrath,
They shall not enter My rest,"

although His works were finished [B]from the foundation of the world. 4 For He has said [A]somewhere
concerning the seventh *day:* "[B]And God [C]rested
on the seventh day from all His works"; 5 and
again in this *passage,* "[A]They shall not enter
My rest." 6 Therefore, since it remains for some to
enter it, and those who formerly had good news
preached to them failed to enter because of [A]dis-
obedience, 7 He again fixes a certain day, "Today,"
saying [a]through David after so long a time just [A]as
has been said before,

"[B]Today if you hear His voice,
Do not harden your hearts."

8 For [A]if [a]Joshua had given them rest, He would
not have spoken of another day after that. 9 So
there remains a Sabbath rest for the people of
God. 10 For the one who has entered His rest has
himself also [A]rested from his works, as [B]God did
from His. 11 Therefore let us be diligent to enter
that rest, so that no one will fall, through *following*
the same [A]example of [B]disobedience. 12 For [A]the
word of God is [B]living and [C]active and sharper
than any two-edged [D]sword, and piercing as far
as the division of [E]soul and [E]spirit, of both joints
and marrow, and [F]able to judge the thoughts and
intentions of the heart. 13 And [A]there is no creature
hidden from His sight, but all things are [B]open
and laid bare to the eyes of Him with whom we
have to do.

14 Therefore, since we have a great [A]high priest
who has [B]passed through the heavens, Jesus [C]the Son
of God, let us hold fast our [D]confession. 15 For we do
not have [A]a high priest who cannot sympathize with

4:3 [A]Ps 95:11; Heb 3:11 [B]Matt 25:34 4:4 [A]Heb 2:6 [B]Gen 2:2 [C]Ex 20:11; 31:17 4:5 [A]Ps 95:11; Heb 3:11 4:6 [A]Heb 3:18; 4:11 4:7 [a]Or *in* [A]Heb 3:7f [B]Ps 95:7f 4:8 [a]Gr *Jesus* [A]Josh 22:4 4:10 [A]Rev 14:13 [B]Gen 2:2; Heb 4:4 4:11 [A]2 Pet 2:6 [B]Heb 3:18; 4:6 4:12 [A]Jer 23:29; Eph 5:26; Heb 6:5; 1 Pet 1:23 [B]Acts 7:38 [C]1 Thess 2:13 [D]Eph 6:17 [E]1 Thess 5:23 [F]John 12:48; 1 Cor 14:24f 4:13 [A]2 Chr 16:9; Ps 33:13-15 [B]Job 26:6 4:14 [A]Heb 2:17 [B]Eph 4:10; Heb 6:20; 8:1; 9:24 [C]Matt 4:3; Heb 1:2; 6:6; 7:3; 10:29 [D]Heb 3:1 4:15 [A]Heb 2:17

faith (10:19–12:29). The writer's point of comparison is that, like the Jews who left Egypt (3:16–19), his generation had also received God's message through the preaching of the gospel—they had been evangelized.

4:3 we … enter. Those who exercise faith in the message of God will enter into their spiritual rest. This is the corollary of Ps 95:11 which states the opposite side: that the unbeliever will not enter into the rest which God provides. **finished from the foundation of the world.** The spiritual rest which God gives is not something incomplete or unfinished. It is a rest which is based upon a finished work which God purposed in eternity past, just like the rest which God took after He finished creation (v. 4).

4:4, 5 By way of explanation for the statement in v. 3, the writer cites the illustration of the seventh day of creation and quotes Ge 2:2. Then he repeats the last part of Ps 95:11.

4:6, 7 The opportunity to enter God's rest remains open (cf. "a promise remains" in v. 1). It is not yet too late. God had offered the rest to His people in Moses' time and continued to offer it in David's time. He is still patiently inviting His people to enter His rest (cf. Ro 10:21). Quoting Ps 95:7, 8 once again (see 3:7, 15), the author urges an immediate, positive response. The themes of urgency and obedience are thus combined in a clear invitation to the readers.

4:8–10 God's true rest did not come through Joshua or Moses, but through Jesus Christ, who is greater than either one. Joshua led the nation of Israel into the land of their promised rest (*see note on 3:11*; Jos 21:43–45). However, that was merely the earthly rest which was only the shadow of what was involved in the heavenly rest. The very fact that, according to Ps 95, God was still offering His rest in the time of David (long after Israel had been in the Land) meant that the rest being offered was spiritual—superior to that which Joshua obtained. Israel's earthly rest was filled with the attacks of enemies and the daily cycle of work. The heavenly rest is characterized by the fullness of heavenly promise (Eph 1:3) and the absence of any labor to obtain it.

4:9 rest. A different Gr. word for "rest" meaning "Sabbath rest" is introduced here, and this is its only appearance in the NT. The writer chose the word to draw the readers' attention back to the "seventh *day*" mentioned in v. 4 and to set up the explanation in v. 10 ("rested from his works, as God did from His").

4:11–13 The concluding third part of the exposition of Ps 95:7–11 emphasizes the accountability which comes to those who have heard the Word of God. Scripture records the examples of those in the wilderness with Moses, those who entered Canaan with Joshua, and those who received the same opportunity in David's day. It is the Word which must be believed and obeyed and the Word which will judge the disobedient (cf. 1Co 10:5–13).

4:12 two-edged sword. While the Word of God is comforting and nourishing to those who believe, it is a tool of judgment and execution for those who have not committed themselves to Jesus Christ. Some of the Hebrews were merely going through the motions of belonging to Christ. Intellectually, they were at least partly persuaded, but inside they were not committed to Him. God's Word would expose their shallow beliefs and even their false intentions (cf. 1Sa 16:7; 1Pe 4:5). **division of soul and spirit.** These terms do not describe two separate entities (any more than "thoughts and intentions" do) but are used as one might say "heart and soul" to express fullness (cf. Lk 10:27; Ac 4:32; *see note on 1Th 5:23*). Elsewhere these two terms are used interchangeably to describe man's immaterial self, his eternal inner person.

4:13 open … to the eyes of Him. "Open" is a specialized term used just this one time in the NT. It originally meant to expose the neck either in preparation for sacrifice or for beheading. Perhaps the use of "sword" in the previous verse triggered the term. Each individual is judged not only by the Word of God (cf. Jn 12:48), but by God Himself. We are accountable to the living, written Word (cf. Jn 6:63, 68; Ac 7:38) and to the living God who is its author.

4:14–7:28 Next, the writer expounds on Ps 110:4, quoted in 5:6. Not only is Christ as Apostle superior to Moses and to Joshua, but as High Priest, He is superior to Aaron (4:14–5:10; cf. 3:1). In the midst of his exposition, the writer gives an exhortation related to the spiritual condition of his readers (5:11–6:20). At the conclusion of the exhortation, he then returns to the subject of Christ's priesthood (7:1–28).

4:14 passed through the heavens. Just as the High Priest under the Old Covenant passed through 3 areas (the outer court, the Holy Place, and the Holy of Holies) to make the atoning sacrifice, Jesus passed through 3 heavens (the atmospheric heaven, the stellar heaven, and God's abode; cf. 2Co 12:2–4) after making the perfect, final sacrifice. Once a year on the Day of Atonement the High Priest of Israel would enter the Holy of Holies to make atonement for the sins of the people (Lv 16). That tabernacle was only a limited copy of the heavenly reality (cf. 8:1–5). When Jesus entered into the heavenly Holy of Holies, having accomplished redemption, the earthly facsimile was replaced by the reality of heaven itself. Freed from that which is earthly, the Christian faith is characterized by the heavenly (3:1; Eph 1:3; 2:6; Php 3:20; Col 1:5; 1Pe 1:4). **Jesus the Son of God.** The use of both the title of humanity (Jesus) and of deity (Son of God) is significant. One of the few cases of such a juxtaposition is in 1Jn 1:7, where His sacrifice for sins is emphasized (cf. 1Th 1:10; 1Jn 4:15; 5:5). **hold fast our confession.** *See notes on 3:1, 6; 10:23.*

4:15 tempted in all things. *See notes on 2:17, 18.* The writer here adds to his statements in 2:18 that Jesus was sinless. He was able to be tempted (Mt 4:1–11), but not able to sin (*see notes on 7:26*).

our weaknesses, but One who has been [B]tempted in
all things as *we are, yet* [C]without sin. 16 Therefore
let us [A]draw near with [B]confidence to the throne of
grace, so that we may receive mercy and find grace
to help in time of need.

THE PERFECT HIGH PRIEST

5 For every high priest [A]taken from among men
is appointed on behalf of men in [B]things pertaining to God, in order to [C]offer both gifts and
sacrifices [D]for sins; 2 [a,A]he can deal gently with the
[B]ignorant and [C]misguided, since he himself also
is [b,D]beset with weakness; 3 and because of it he is
obligated to offer *sacrifices* [A]for sins, [B]as for the
people, so also for himself. 4 And [A]no one takes the
honor to himself, but *receives it* when he is called
by God, even [B]as Aaron was.
5 So also Christ [A]did not glorify Himself so as to
become a [B]high priest, but He who [C]said to Him,

"[D]YOU ARE MY SON,
TODAY I HAVE BEGOTTEN YOU";

6 just as He says also in another *passage,*

"[A]YOU ARE A PRIEST FOREVER
ACCORDING TO [B]THE ORDER OF MELCHIZEDEK."

7 [a]In the days of His flesh, [b,A]He offered up both
prayers and supplications with [B]loud crying and
tears to the One [C]able to save Him [c]from death, and
He [d]was heard because of His [D]piety. 8 Although He
was [A]a Son, He learned [B]obedience from the things
which He suffered. 9 And having been made [A]perfect,
He became to all those who obey Him the source of
eternal salvation, 10 being designated by God as [A]a
high priest according to [B]the order of Melchizedek.
11 Concerning [a]him we have much to say, and
it is hard to explain, since you have become dull

4:15 [B]Heb 2:18 [C]2 Cor 5:21; Heb 7:26 4:16 [A]Heb 7:19 [B]Heb 3:6 5:1 [A]Ex 28:1 [B]Heb 2:17 [C]Heb 7:27; 8:3f; 9:9; 10:11 [D]1 Cor 15:3; Heb 7:27; 10:12 5:2 [a]Lit *being able to* [b]Or *subject to weakness* [A]Heb 2:18; 4:15 [B]Eph 4:18; Heb 9:7 mg [C]James 5:19; 1 Pet 2:25 [D]Heb 7:28 5:3 [A]1 Cor 15:3; Heb 7:27; 10:12 [B]Lev 9:7; 16:6; Heb 7:27; 9:7 5:4 [A]Num 16:40; 18:7; 2 Chr 26:18 [B]Ex 28:1; 1 Chr 23:13 5:5 [A]John 8:54 [B]Heb 2:17; 5:10 [C]Heb 1:1, 5 [D]Ps 2:7 5:6 [A]Ps 110:4; Heb 7:17 [B]Heb 5:10; 6:20; 7:11, 17 5:7 [a]I.e. during Christ's earthly life [b]Lit *who having offered up* [c]Or *out of* [d]Lit *having been heard* [A]Matt 26:39, 42, 44; Mark 14:36, 39; Luke 22:41, 44 [B]Matt 27:46, 50; Mark 15:34, 37; Luke 23:46 [C]Mark 14:36 [D]Heb 11:7; 12:28 5:8 [A]Heb 1:2 [B]Phil 2:8 5:9 [A]Heb 2:10 5:10 [A]Heb 2:17; 5:5 [B]Heb 5:6 5:11 [a]Lit *whom or which*

4:16 draw near with confidence to the throne of grace. Most ancient rulers were unapproachable by anyone but their highest advisers (cf. Est 4:11). In contrast, the Holy Spirit calls for all to come confidently before God's throne to receive mercy and grace through Jesus Christ (cf. 7:25; 10:22; Mt 27:51; see Introduction: Historical and Theological Themes). The ark of the covenant was viewed as the place on earth where God sat enthroned between the cherubim (cf. 2Ki 19:15; Jer 3:16, 17). Oriental thrones included a footstool—yet another metaphor for the ark (cf. Ps 132:7). It was at the throne of God that Christ made atonement for sins, and it is there that grace is dispensed to believers for all the issues of life (cf. 2Co 4:15; 9:8; 12:9; Eph 1:7; 2:7). "Grace to you" became a standard greeting among believers who celebrated this provision (Ro 1:7; 16:20, 24; 1Co 1:3; 16:23; 2Co 1:2; 13:14; Gal 1:3; 6:18; Eph 1:2; 6:24; Php 1:2; 4:18; Col 1:2; 4:18; 1Th 1:1; 5:28; 2Th 1:2; 3:18; 1Ti 1:2; 6:21; 2Ti 1:2; 4:22; Titus 1:4; 3:15; Phm 3, 25). **to help in time of need.** *See notes on 2:16, 18.*

5:1–4 No angel with supernatural power could serve as High Priest. Only men with the weaknesses of humanity could serve as High Priest (v. 2; 7:28). The position of High Priest in the Levitical system was by appointment only. No man could legitimately appoint himself High Priest. The use of the present tense in these verses would seem to indicate that the Levitical system was still being practiced at the time of this epistle (see Introduction: Author and Date).

5:1 gifts and sacrifices. The first term might refer especially to the grain offerings under the Old Covenant, which were for thanksgiving or dedication. That would leave the second term to refer to blood offerings for the expiation of sins (see Lv 1–5). However, "gifts" is used in 8:4 to refer to all of the various sacrifices (cf. 8:3). The 3 occurrences of the phrase in the NT (cf. 8:3; 9:9) employ a Gr. construction which expresses a closer relationship between the two terms than is normally indicated by the word "and." This could indicate that no distinction should be made between the terms, and that "for sins" should be taken with both.

5:2 deal gently. This verb occurs only here in the NT. It carries the idea of maintaining a controlled but gentle attitude in the treatment of those who are spiritually ignorant and wayward. Impatience, loathing, and indignation have no part in priestly ministry. Such moderation and gentleness come from realizing one's own human frailty. The priest would be reminded of his own sinful humanity every time he offered sacrifices for his own sins (v. 3).

5:4 called by God. A High Priest was selected and called by God into service (cf. Ex 28; Nu 16:1–40; 1Sa 16:1–3).

5:5, 6 With the quotations of Pss 2:7 and 110:4, the writer demonstrates that Christ's incarnation (*see notes on 1:5*) and His priesthood were both by divine appointment (cf. Jn 8:54). Jesus' humanity does not in any way diminish His eternal deity, nor does it alter the essential equality within the Trinity (cf. Jn 10:30; 14:9–11). It is noteworthy that Ps 2 recognizes the Son as both King and Messiah. Christ is the King-Priest.

5:6 Quoted from Ps 110:4, from which this whole section is expounded (*see note on 4:14–7:28*). Melchizedek. As king of Salem and priest of the Most High God in the time of Abraham, he was also a king-priest (Ge 14:18–20). The Melchizedekian priesthood is discussed in detail in chap. 7.

5:7, 8 Having established the first requirement that a High Priest be appointed (vv. 1, 4, 5, 6), the writer focused on the requirement of being humanly sympathetic (vv. 2, 3).

5:7 He. The subsequent context makes it clear that this refers back to Christ, the main subject in v. 5. In Gethsemane, Jesus agonized and wept, but committed Himself to do the Father's will in accepting the cup of suffering which would bring His death (Mt 26:38–46; Lk 22:44, 45). Anticipating bearing the burden of judgment for sin, Jesus felt its fullest pain and grief (cf. Is 52:14; 53:3–5, 10). Though He bore the penalty in silence and did not seek to deliver Himself from it (Is 53:7), He did cry out from the agony of the fury of God's wrath poured on His perfectly holy and obedient person (Mt 27:46; cf. 2Co 5:21). Jesus asked to be saved from remaining in death, i.e., to be resurrected (cf. Ps 16:9, 10).

5:8 learned obedience. Christ did not need to suffer in order to conquer or correct any disobedience. In His deity (as the Son of God), He understood obedience completely. As the incarnate Lord, He humbled Himself to learn (cf. Lk 2:52). He learned obedience for the same reasons He bore temptation: to confirm His humanity and experience its sufferings to the fullest (*see notes on 2:10*; cf. Lk 2:52; Php 2:8). Christ's obedience was also necessary so that He could fulfill all righteousness (Mt 3:15) and thus prove to be the perfect sacrifice to take the place of sinners (1Pe 3:18). He was the perfectly righteous One, whose righteousness would be imputed to sinners (cf. Ro 3:24–26).

5:9 perfect ... source of eternal salvation. *See notes on 2:10.* Because of the perfect righteousness of Jesus Christ and His perfect sacrifice for sin, He became the cause of salvation. **obey Him.** True salvation evidences itself in obedience to Christ, from the initial obedience to the gospel command to repent and believe (cf. Ac 5:32; Ro 1:5; 2Th 1:8; 1Pe 1:2, 22; 4:17) to a life pattern of obedience to the Word (cf. Ro 6:16).

5:10 Referring to Ps 110:4 a second time (cf. v. 6), the writer mentions again the call of God to the priesthood (v. 4).

5:11 Concerning him. An alternate translation would be "of which" (meaning the relationship of Christ's High Priesthood to that of Melchizedek). Logically and stylistically, v. 11 appears to introduce the entire section from 5:11–6:12. The same Gr. verb "become" forms brackets around the section: "become dull" (v. 11) and "be sluggish" (6:12). **dull.** The Hebrews' spiritual lethargy and slow response to gospel teaching prevented additional teaching at this time. This is a reminder that failure to appropriate the truth of the gospel produces stagnation in spiritual advancement and the inability to understand or assimilate addi-

of hearing. 12 For though [a]by this time you ought
to be teachers, you have need again for someone
to teach you [A]the [b,B]elementary principles of the
[C]oracles of God, and you have come to need [D]milk
and not solid food. 13 For everyone who partakes
only of milk is not accustomed to the word of
righteousness, for he is an [A]infant. 14 But solid
food is for [A]the mature, who because of practice
have their senses [B]trained to [C]discern good and
evil.

THE PERIL OF FALLING AWAY

6 Therefore [A]leaving [B]the [a]elementary teaching
about the [b]Christ, let us press on to [c,C]maturity, not
laying again a foundation of repentance from [D]dead
works and of faith toward God, 2 of [A]instruction about
washings and [B]laying on of hands, and the [C]resurrec-
tion of the dead and [C]eternal judgment. 3 And this we
will do, [A]if God permits. 4 For in the case of those who
have once been [A]enlightened and have tasted of [B]the
heavenly gift and have been made [C]partakers of the

5:12 [a]Lit *because of the time* [b]Lit *elements of the beginning* [A]Gal 4:3 [B]Heb 6:1 [C]Acts 7:38 [D]1 Cor 3:2; 1 Pet 2:2 5:13 [A]1 Cor 3:1; 14:20; 1 Pet 2:2 5:14 [A]1 Cor 2:6; Eph 4:13; Heb 6:1 [B]1 Tim 4:7 [C]Rom 14:1ff 6:1 [a]Lit *word of the beginning* [b]I.e. Messiah [c]Or *perfection* [A]Phil 3:13f [B]Heb 5:12 [C]Heb 5:14 [D]Heb 9:14 6:2 [A]John 3:25; Acts 19:3f [B]Acts 6:6 [C]Acts 17:31f 6:3 [A]Acts 18:21 6:4 [A]2 Cor 4:4, 6; Heb 10:32 [B]John 4:10; Eph 2:8 [C]Gal 3:2; Heb 2:4

tional teaching (cf. Jn 16:12). Such a situation exists also among the Gentiles who have received revelatory truth (natural or general revelation) from God in the creation (Ro 1:18–20). Rejection of that revelation results in a process of hardening (Ro 1:21–32). The Hebrews had not only received the same general revelation, they had also received special revelation consisting of the OT Scriptures (Ro 9:4), the Messiah Himself (Ro 9:5), and the teaching of the apostles (2:3, 4). Until the Hebrews obeyed the revelation they had received and obtained eternal salvation (v. 8), additional teaching about the Messiah's Melchizedekian priesthood would be of no profit to them.

5:12 teachers. Every believer is to be a teacher (Col 3:16; 1Pe 3:15; cf. Dt 6:7; 2Ti 3:15). If these Hebrews had really obeyed the gospel of Christ, they would have been passing that message on to others. The Jews were instructed in the law and prided themselves because they taught the law, but they had not really understood or appropriated its truths to themselves (*see notes on Ro 2:17–23*). **oracles.** These are contained in the OT Scripture, which had laid the foundation for the gospel and had been committed into the care of the Hebrews (Ro 3:1, 2). The ABC's of the law tutored the Hebrews in order to lead them to faith in the Messiah (Gal 3:23, 24). They had also heard the NT gospel (2:2–4; 1Pe 4:11).

5:12, 13 milk. Knowledge without obedience does not advance a person. In fact, by rejecting saving faith, the Hebrews were regressing in their understanding concerning the Messiah. They had long enough been exposed to the gospel to be teaching it to others, but were babies, too infantile and unskilled to comprehend, let alone teach, the truth of God.

5:13 word of righteousness. This is the message about the righteousness of Christ which we have by faith (Ro 3:21, 22; 1Co 1:30; 2Co 5:21; Php 3:9; Titus 3:5). The phrase is equivalent to the gospel of salvation by faith rather than works.

5:14 mature. The same Gr. root is also translated "maturity" in 6:1 and is elsewhere translated "perfect" (7:11, 19, 28; 9:9; 10:1, 14; 11:40; 12:23). It is used in Hebrews, including this text, as a synonym for salvation. In that sense, it refers to the completion which comes when one becomes a believer in Christ, rather than referring to a Christian who has become mature. Jesus invited unbelieving Jews to the salvation perfection which came only through following Him in faith (Mt 19:21). Paul wrote that those who had come to Christ by faith were thereby mature and able to receive the wisdom of God (1Co 2:6). Paul also declared that the apostles warned and taught everyone "that we may present every man complete in Christ Jesus" (Col 1:28). **trained.** The deeper, more "solid" truths about the priesthood of the Lord Jesus could only be given to those who knew Him as Savior. Athletic training and competition form the metaphor implied by this particular word (cf. 1Ti 4:7, 8). The person who has come to Christ for spiritual completion is then trained by the Word to discern truth from error and holy behavior from unholy (cf. 2Ti 3:16, 17).

6:1 leaving. This "leaving" does not mean to despise or abandon the basic doctrines. They are the place to start, not stop. They are the gate of entrance on the road to salvation in Christ. **elementary teaching about the Christ.** As "the oracles of God" in 5:12 refers to the OT, so does this phrase. The writer is referring to basic OT teaching that prepared the way for Messiah—the beginning teaching about Christ. This OT "teaching" includes the 6 features listed in vv. 1, 2. **press on to maturity.** Salvation by faith in Messiah Jesus. *See note on 5:14.* The verb is passive, so as to indicate "let us be carried to salvation." That is not a matter of learners being carried by teachers, but both being carried forward by God. The writer warns his Jewish readers that there is no value in stopping with the OT basics and repeating ("laying again") what was only intended to be foundational. **repentance from dead works.** This OT form of repentance is the turning away from evil deeds that bring death (cf. Eze 18:4; Ro 6:23) and turning to God. Too often the Jew only turned to God in a superficial fashion—fulfilling the letter of the law as evidence of his repentance. The inner man was still dead (Mt 23:25–28; Ro 2:28, 29). Such repentance was not the kind which brought salvation (v. 6; 12:17; cf. Ac 11:18; 2Co 7:10). Under the New Covenant, however, "repentance ... toward God" is coupled with "faith in our Lord Jesus Christ" (Ac 20:21). Christ's atoning sacrifice saves from "dead works" (9:14; cf. Jn 14:6). **faith toward God.** Faith directed only toward the Father is unacceptable without faith in His Son, Jesus Christ (Ac 4:12; cf. Jas 2:14–20).

6:2 washings. In the OT Levitical system, there were many ceremonial cleansings, which were outward signs of heart cleansing (cf. Ex 30:18–21; Lv 16:4, 24, 26, 28; Mk 7:4, 8). The New Covenant called for an inner washing (Titus 3:5) that regenerated the soul. **laying on of hands.** Under the Old Covenant, the person who brought a sacrifice placed his hands on it to symbolize his identification with it as a substitute sacrifice for sin (Lv 1:4; 3:8, 13; 16:21). There could also be a reference here to solemn priestly blessings (cf. Mt 19:13). **resurrection ... and eternal judgment.** The Pharisees believed in the resurrection from the dead (Ac 23:8) but were still spiritually dead (Mt 23:27). They also believed in the judgment of God and were headed for it. It is significant that all of the doctrines listed in vv. 1, 2 can be associated with the Pharisees, who were attracted to and sometimes associated with Jesus (Lk 7:36–50; 13:31; 14:1; Jn 3:1). Paul was a Pharisee before his conversion (Php 3:5). The Pharisees were products of the pursuit of righteousness by works of the law rather than by faith (Ro 9:30–32; 10:1–3). A portion of the Hebrews to whom this epistle was written may have been Pharisees.

6:3 we will do. The writer is likely both giving his own testimony about going on from OT teaching to embrace the New Covenant in Jesus Christ and also identifying himself with the readers. Salvation always requires God's enablement (cf. Jn 6:44).

6:4–6 See Introduction: Interpretive Challenges. Five advantages possessed by the Jews are yet insufficient for their salvation.

6:4 enlightened. They had received instruction in biblical truth which was accompanied by intellectual perception. Understanding the gospel is not the equivalent of regeneration (cf. 10:26, 32). In Jn 1:9 it is clear that enlightening is not the equivalent of salvation. Cf. 10:29. **tasted of the heavenly gift.** Tasting in the figurative sense in the NT refers to consciously experiencing something (cf. 2:9). The experience might be momentary or continuing. Christ's "tasting" of death (2:9) was obviously momentary and not continuing or permanent. All men experience the goodness of God, but that does not mean they are all saved (cf. Mt 5:45; Ac 17:25). Many Jews, during the Lord's earthly ministry, experienced the blessings from heaven He brought—in healings and deliverance from demons, as well as eating the food He created miraculously (Jn 6). Whether the gift refers to Christ (cf. Jn 6:51; 2Co 9:15) or to the Holy Spirit (cf. Ac 2:38; 1Pe 1:12), experiencing either one was not the equivalent of salvation (cf. Jn 16:8; Ac 7:51). **partakers of the Holy Spirit.** *See notes on 2:4.* Even though the concept of partaking is used in 3:1; 3:14; and 12:8 of a relationship which believers have, the context must be the final determining factor. This context in vv. 4–6 seems to preclude a reference to true believers. It could be a reference to their participation, as noted above, in the miraculous ministry of Jesus who was empowered by the Spirit (*see notes on Mt 12:18–32*; cf. Lk 4:14, 18) or in the convicting ministry of the Holy Spirit (Jn 16:8) which obviously can be resisted without experiencing salvation (cf. Ac 7:51).

Holy Spirit, 5 and [A]have tasted the good [B]word of God
and the powers of [C]the age to come, 6 and *then* have
fallen away, it is [A]impossible to renew them again to
repentance, [a,B]since they again crucify to themselves
the Son of God and put Him to open shame. 7 For
ground that drinks the rain which often [a]falls on it
and brings forth vegetation useful to those [A]for whose
sake it is also tilled, receives a blessing from God;
8 but if it yields thorns and thistles, it is worthless and
[A]close [a]to being cursed, and [b]it ends up being burned.

BETTER THINGS FOR YOU

9 But, [A]beloved, we are convinced of better things
concerning you, and things that [a]accompany salvation, though we are speaking in this way. 10 For
[A]God is not unjust so as to forget [B]your work and
the love which you have shown toward His name,
in having [C]ministered and in still ministering to the
[a]saints. 11 And we desire that each one of you show
the same diligence [a]so as to realize the [A]full assurance of [B]hope until the end, 12 so that you will not
be sluggish, but [A]imitators of those who through
[B]faith and patience [C]inherit the promises.
13 For [A]when God made the promise to Abraham,
since He could swear by no one greater, He [B]swore
by Himself, 14 saying, "[A]I WILL SURELY BLESS YOU
AND I WILL SURELY MULTIPLY YOU." 15 And so, [A]having
patiently waited, he obtained the promise. 16 [A]For
men swear by [a]one greater *than themselves,* and
with them [B]an oath *given* as confirmation is an end
of every dispute. 17 [a]In the same way God, desiring
even more to show to [A]the heirs of the promise [B]the
unchangeableness of His purpose, [b]interposed with
an oath, 18 so that by two unchangeable things in
which [A]it is impossible for God to lie, we who have
[a]taken refuge would have strong encouragement to

6:5 [A]1 Pet 2:3 [B]Eph 6:17 [C]Heb 2:5 6:6 [a]Or *while* [A]Matt 19:26; Heb 10:26f; 2 Pet 2:21; 1 John 5:16 [B]Heb 10:29 6:7 [a]Lit *comes* [A]2 Tim 2:6 6:8 [a]Lit *near to a curse* [b]Lit *whose end is for burning* [A]Gen 3:17f; Deut 29:22ff 6:9 [a]Or *belong to* [A]1 Cor 10:14; 2 Cor 7:1; 12:19; 1 Pet 2:11; 2 Pet 3:1; 1 John 2:7; Jude 3 6:10 [a]Or *holy ones* [A]Prov 19:17; Matt 10:42; 25:40; Acts 10:4 [B]1 Thess 1:3 [C]Rom 15:25; Heb 10:32-34 6:11 [a]Lit *to the full* [A]Heb 10:22 [B]Heb 3:6 6:12 [A]Heb 13:7 [B]2 Thess 1:4; James 1:3; Rev 13:10 [C]Heb 1:14 6:13 [A]Gal 3:15, 18 [B]Gen 22:16; Luke 1:73 6:14 [A]Gen 22:17 6:15 [A]Gen 12:4; 21:5 6:16 [a]Or *Him who is greater* [A]Gal 3:15 [B]Ex 22:11 6:17 [a]Lit *In which* [b]Or *guaranteed* [A]Heb 11:9 [B]Ps 110:4; Prov 19:21; Heb 6:18 6:18 [a]Lit *in which* [A]Num 23:19; Titus 1:2

6:5 tasted. *See note on v. 4.* This has an amazing correspondence to what was described in 2:1–4 (*see notes there*). Like Simon Magus (Ac 8:9–24), these Hebrews had not yet been regenerated in spite of all they had heard and seen (cf. Mt 13:3–9; Jn 6:60–66). They were repeating the sins of those who died in the wilderness after seeing the miracles performed through Moses and Aaron and hearing the voice of God at Sinai.

6:6 fallen away. This Gr. term occurs only here in the NT. In the LXX, it was used to translate terms for severe unfaithfulness and apostasy (cf. Eze 14:13; 18:24; 20:27). It is equivalent to the apostasy in 3:12. The seriousness of this unfaithfulness is seen in the severe description of rejection within this verse: they re-crucify Christ and treat Him contemptuously (see also the strong descriptions in 10:29). Those who sinned against Christ in such a way had no hope of restoration or forgiveness (cf. 2:2, 3; 10:26, 27; 12:25). The reason is that they had rejected Him with full knowledge and conscious experience (as described in the features of vv. 5, 6). With full revelation they rejected the truth, concluding the opposite of the truth about Christ, and thus had no hope of being saved. They can never have more knowledge than they had when they rejected it. They have concluded that Jesus should have been crucified, and they stand with His enemies. There is no possibility of these verses referring to losing salvation. Many Scripture passages make unmistakably clear that salvation is eternal (cf. Jn 10:27–29; Ro 8:35, 38, 39; Php 1:6; 1Pe 1:4, 5). Those who want to make this verse mean that believers can lose salvation will have to admit that it would then also say that one could never get it back again. See Introduction: Interpretive Challenges.

6:7, 8 Here are illustrations showing that those who hear the gospel message and respond in faith are blessed; those who hear and reject it are cursed (cf. Mt 13:18–23).

6:8 worthless. See the use of the term in Ro 1:28 ("depraved"); 2Co 13:5 ("fail the test"); and 2Ti 3:8 ("rejected").

6:9 beloved. This term shows a change of audience and a change from a message of warning to a message of encouragement. That the address is to believers is further confirmed by the expression of confidence that "better things" could be said of them (as compared to those who were being warned in the preceding verses). The "things that accompany salvation" are their works which verify their salvation (v. 10; cf. Eph 2:10; Jas 2:18, 26). The very statement implies that the things described in 5:11–6:5 do not accompany salvation but are indicative of unbelief and apostasy. **though we are speaking in this way.** Though it had been necessary to speak about judgment in the preceding verses, the writer assures the "beloved," those who are believers, that he is confident of their salvation.

6:10 work and ... love. See 1Th 1:3, 4. **toward His name.** Throughout this epistle "name" has the Hebraic sense of the authority, character, and attributes of the Son of God (1:4) or of God the Father (2:12; 13:15; cf. Jn 14:13, 14). **saints.** All true Christians are saints, or "holy ones" (cf. 13:24; Ac 9:13; Ro 1:7; *see note on 1Co 1:2*).

6:11 you. The author is speaking again to unbelievers but appears to intentionally distance this particular group from the would-be apostates of vv. 4–6, who are in danger of being impossible to restore. **diligence.** This term can carry the idea of eagerness or haste. It is a plea for unbelieving Jews to come to Christ immediately. If these uncommitted Jews followed the example of the active faith of the saints (vv. 9, 10, 12), they would obtain the salvation which gives "full assurance of hope until the end" (cf. 10:22; Col 2:2). Salvation should not be postponed.

6:12 sluggish. *See note on 5:11,* where the same Gr. word is translated "dull." **imitators.** This concept is repeated in 13:7 and is inherent in the many illustrations of faith given in chap. 11. **inherit the promises.** The inheritance and the promises of salvation are a theme of this epistle (cf. vv. 13, 15, 17; 1:14; 4:1, 3; 9:15; 10:36; 11:7, 8, 9, 11, 13, 17, 33, 39).

6:13–20 The persecution and trials which the believing Hebrews faced required patient perseverance. That persevering faith would enable them to inherit the promises of God, which at the time of suffering seemed so distant. Regardless of their circumstances, they were to remember that God is faithful (cf. v. 10) and that in Him their hope was secure (cf. v. 11).

6:13 Abraham. To encourage the Hebrews to rely upon faith as opposed to holding on to the Levitical system of worship, the writer cited the example of Abraham, who, as the great model of faith (cf. Ro 4), should be imitated (v. 12). **swore by Himself.** As recorded in Ge 22:15–19, God promised unilaterally to fulfill the Abrahamic Covenant.

6:14 Quoted from Ge 22:17, this summarizes the essence of God's promise. The fact that God had said it assured its fulfillment. It is significant that the quote in Genesis is in the context of Abraham's sacrifice of Isaac, who was the immediate fulfillment of God's promise to Abraham. Ultimate fulfillment would also take place through Isaac and his descendants.

6:15 patiently waited. Abraham was an example of the patience mentioned in v. 12. He received the promise in the beginning of its fulfillment by the birth of Isaac (*see note on v. 14*), but he did not live to see all the promises fulfilled (11:13).

6:16–18 God's Word does not need any confirmation from someone else. It is reliable because God Himself is faithful. People confirm their promises by appealing to someone greater (especially to God) as witness. Since no one is greater than God, He can only provide an oath from Himself. By doing so He is willingly (v. 17) accommodating Himself to human beings who desire the confirmation because of the characteristic unreliability of human promises.

6:18 two unchangeable things. These are God's promise and His oath. The Gr. term behind "unchangeable" was used of a legal will, which was unchangeable by anyone but the maker of the will. **taken refuge.** In the LXX, the Gr. word is used for the cities of refuge God provided for those who sought protection from avengers for an accidental killing (Nu 35:9–34; Dt 19:1–13; Jos 20:1–9; cf. Ac 14:5, 6). **hope.** *See note on 3:6.* Hope is one of the themes of Hebrews. It is also the product of

take hold of [B]the hope set before us. 19 [a]This [A]hope
we have as an anchor of the soul, a *hope* both sure
and steadfast and one which [B]enters [b]within the veil,
20 [A]where Jesus has entered as a forerunner for us,
having become a [B]high priest forever according to
the order of Melchizedek.

MELCHIZEDEK'S PRIESTHOOD LIKE CHRIST'S

7 For this [A]Melchizedek, king of Salem, priest of
the [B]Most High God, who met Abraham as he
was returning from the slaughter of the kings and
blessed him, 2 to whom also Abraham apportioned
a tenth part of all *the spoils,* was first of all, by the
translation *of his name,* king of righteousness, and
then also king of Salem, which is king of peace.
3 Without father, without mother, [A]without genealogy, having neither beginning of days nor end
of life, but made like [B]the Son of God, he remains a
priest perpetually.
4 Now observe how great this man was to whom
Abraham, the [A]patriarch, [B]gave a tenth of the choicest spoils. 5 And those indeed of [A]the sons of Levi
who receive the priest's office have commandment
[a]in the Law to collect [b]a tenth from the people,
that is, from their brethren, although these [c]are
descended from Abraham. 6 But the one [A]whose
genealogy is not traced from them [B]collected [a]a
tenth from Abraham and [b,B]blessed the one who [C]had
the promises. 7 But without any dispute the lesser
is blessed by the greater. 8 In this case mortal men
receive tithes, but in that case one *receives them,*
[A]of whom it is witnessed that he lives on. 9 And, so
to speak, through Abraham even Levi, who received
tithes, paid tithes, 10 for he was still in the loins of
his father when Melchizedek met him.
11 [A]Now if perfection was through the Levitical
priesthood (for on the basis of it [B]the people received the Law), what further need *was there* for
another priest to arise [C]according to the order of
Melchizedek, and not be designated according to
the order of Aaron? 12 For when the priesthood is
changed, of necessity there takes place a change of
law also. 13 For [A]the one concerning whom [B]these
things are spoken belongs to another tribe, from
which no one has officiated at the altar. 14 For it is
evident that our Lord [a]was [A]descended from Judah,
a tribe with reference to which Moses spoke nothing concerning priests. 15 And this is clearer still,
if another priest arises according to the likeness
of Melchizedek, 16 who has become *such* not on
the basis of a law of [a,A]physical requirement, but

6:18 [B]Heb 3:6; 7:19 **6:19** [a]Lit *Which* hope *we have* [b]Or *inside* [A]Ps 39:7; 62:5; Acts 23:6; Rom 4:18; 5:4, 5; 1 Cor 13:13; Col 1:27; 1 Pet 1:3 [B]Lev 16:2, 15; Heb 9:3, 7 **6:20** [A]John 14:2; Heb 4:14 [B]Ps 110:4; Heb 2:17; 5:6 **7:1** [A]Gen 14:18-20; Heb 7:6 [B]Mark 5:7 **7:3** [A]Heb 7:6 [B]Matt 4:3; Heb 7:1, 28 **7:4** [A]Acts 2:29; 7:8f [B]Gen 14:20 **7:5** [a]Lit *according to* [b]Or *tithes* [c]Lit *have come out of the loins of* [A]Num 18:21, 26; 2 Chr 31:4f **7:6** [a]Or *tithes* [b]Lit *has blessed* [A]Heb 7:3 [B]Heb 7:1f [C]Rom 4:13 **7:8** [A]Heb 5:6; 6:20 **7:11** [A]Heb 7:18f; 8:7 [B]Heb 9:6; 10:1 [C]Heb 5:6; 7:17 **7:13** [A]Heb 7:14 [B]Heb 7:11 **7:14** [a]Lit *has arisen from* [A]Num 24:17; Is 11:1; Mic 5:2; Matt 2:6; Rev 5:5 **7:16** [a]Lit *fleshly commandment;* i.e. to be a descendant of Levi [A]Heb 9:10

OT studies (Ro 15:4). Hope for the fulfillment of God's salvation promises is the "anchor of the soul" (v. 19) keeping the believer secure during the times of trouble and turmoil.

6:19, 20 Our hope is embodied in Christ Himself who has entered into God's presence in the heavenly Holy of Holies on our behalf (*see note on 4:14*). By this line of reasoning, the writer returned to the topic which he left in 5:10, the Melchizedekian priesthood.

7:1–28 Using the two OT references to Melchizedek (Ge 14:18–20; Ps 110:4), chap. 7 explains the superiority of Christ's priesthood to that of this unique High Priest, who was a type of Christ in certain respects (*see note on 5:6*). Chapter 7 is the focal point of the epistle to the Hebrews because of its detailed comparison of the priesthood of Christ and the Levitical High Priesthood.

7:1, 2 A summary of the account of Melchizedek in Ge 14:18–20 (*see notes there*).

7:3 The Levitical priesthood was hereditary, but Melchizedek's was not. His parentage and origin are unknown because they were irrelevant to his priesthood. Contrary to some interpretations, Melchizedek did have a father and a mother. The ancient Syriac Peshitta gives a more accurate translation of what was intended by the Gr. phrase: "whose father and mother are not written in genealogies." No record existed of Melchizedek's birth or death. This is quite a contrast to the details of Aaron's death (Nu 20:22–29). **like.** Lit. "made to be like"; this word is used nowhere else in the NT. The implication is that the resemblance to Christ rests upon the way Melchizedek's history is reported in the OT, not upon Melchizedek himself. Melchizedek was not the preincarnate Christ, as some maintain, but was similar to Christ in that his priesthood was universal (v. 1), royal (v. 1, 2; cf. Zec 6:13), righteous (v. 2; cf. Ps 72:2; Jer 23:5; 1Co 1:30), peaceful (v. 2; cf. Ps 72:7; Is 9:6; Ro 5:1), and unending (v. 3; cf. vv. 24, 25).

7:4–28 This section presents the superiority of the Melchizedekian priesthood to the Levitical. The major arguments for superiority are related to the receiving of tithes (vv. 2–10), the giving of blessing (vv. 1, 6, 7), the replacement of the Levitical priesthood (vv. 11–19), and the perpetuity of the Melchizedekian priesthood (vv. 3, 8, 16, 17, 20–28).

7:4 In antiquity, it was common for people to give a tithe to a god or his representative. Abraham, the father of the Hebrew faith, gave a tithe to Melchizedek. That proves that Melchizedek was superior to Abraham. The lesser person tithes to the greater (v. 7).

7:5 By the authority invested in them after the establishment of the Mosaic law, the Levitical priests collected tithes from their fellow Israelites (*see note on Nu 18:21–24*). The submission of the Israelites was not to honor the priests but to honor the law of God.

7:6, 7 Melchizedek not only received a tithe from Abraham, he also blessed him. This proves again Melchizedek's superiority.

7:8 this case . . . that case. This refers to the Levitical law whose system was still active at the time ("this case") and to the earlier historical incident recorded in Ge 14 ("that case"). The Levitical priesthood changed as each priest died until it passed away altogether, whereas Melchizedek's priesthood is perpetual since the record about his priesthood does not record his death (cf. v. 3).

7:9, 10 In an argument based upon seminal headship, the writer observes that it is possible to speak of Levi paying tithes to Melchizedek. It is the same kind of argument Paul employed to demonstrate that when Adam sinned we all sinned (*see notes on Ro 5:12–14*).

7:11–28 In this section the argument is extended a step further. Since the Melchizedekian priesthood is superior to the Levitical priesthood (vv. 1–10), Christ's priesthood is also superior to the Levitical priesthood, since Christ's priesthood is Melchizedekian rather than Levitical.

7:11 perfection. *See note on 5:14.* Throughout Hebrews, the term refers to complete reconciliation with God and unhindered access to God—salvation. The Levitical system and its priesthood could not save anyone from their sins. *See notes on 10:1–4.*

7:12–14 Since Christ is the Christian's High Priest and He was of the tribe of Judah, not Levi (cf. Mt 2:1, 6; Rev 5:5), His priesthood is clearly beyond the law, which was the authority for the Levitical priesthood (cf. v. 11). This is proof that the Mosaic law had been abrogated. The Levitical system was replaced by a new Priest, offering a new sacrifice, under a New Covenant. He abrogated the law by fulfilling it (cf. Mt 5:17) and providing the perfection which the law could never accomplish (cf. Mt 5:20).

7:13, 15 another. In both cases, the term is "another of a different kind" (*heteros*) emphasizing the contrast with the Levitical priesthood.

7:16 law of physical requirement. The law dealt only with the temporal existence of Israel. The forgiveness which could be obtained even on the Day of Atonement was temporary. Those who ministered as priests under the law were mortals receiving their

according to the power of [B]an indestructible life.
17 For it is attested *of Him,*

> "[A]You are a priest forever
> According to the order
> of Melchizedek."

18 For, on the one hand, there is a setting aside of a
former commandment [A]because of its weakness and
uselessness 19 (for [A]the Law made nothing perfect),
and on the other hand there is a bringing in of a
better [B]hope, through which we [C]draw near to God.
20 And inasmuch as *it was* not without an oath 21 (for
they indeed became priests without an oath, but
He with an oath through the One who said to Him,

> "[A]The Lord has sworn
> And [B]will not change His mind,
> 'You are a priest [C]forever' ");

22 so much the more also Jesus has become the
[A]guarantee of [B]a better covenant.
23 [a]The *former* priests, on the one hand, existed
in greater numbers because they were prevented
by death from continuing, 24 but Jesus, on the other
hand, because He continues [A]forever, holds His
priesthood permanently. 25 Therefore He is able
also to [A]save [a]forever those who [B]draw near to God
through Him, since He always lives to [C]make intercession for them.
26 For it was fitting for us to have such a [A]high
priest, [B]holy, [C]innocent, undefiled, separated from
sinners and [D]exalted above the heavens; 27 who does
not need daily, like those high priests, to [A]offer up
sacrifices, [B]first for His own sins and then for the
sins of the people, because this He did [C]once for
all when He [D]offered up Himself. 28 For the Law
appoints men as high priests [A]who are weak, but
the word of the oath, which came after the Law,
appoints [B]a Son, [C]made perfect forever.

A BETTER MINISTRY

8 Now the main point in what has been said *is this:*
we have such a [A]high priest, who has taken His
seat at [B]the right hand of the throne of the [B]Majesty
in the heavens, 2 a [A]minister [a]in the sanctuary and
[a]in the [B]true [b]tabernacle, which the Lord [C]pitched,
not man. 3 For every [A]high priest is appointed [B]to
offer both gifts and sacrifices; so it is necessary
that this *high priest* also have something to offer.

7:16 [B]Heb 9:14 7:17 [A]Ps 110:4; Heb 5:6; 6:20; 7:21 7:18 [A]Rom 8:3; Gal 3:21; Heb 7:11 7:19 [A]Acts 13:39; Rom 3:20; 7:7f; Gal 2:16; 3:21; Heb 9:9; 10:1 [B]Heb 3:6 [C]Lam 3:57; Heb 4:16; 7:25; 10:1, 22; James 4:8 7:21 [A]Ps 110:4; Heb 5:6; 7:17 [B]Num 23:19; 1 Sam 15:29; Rom 11:29 [C]Heb 7:23f, 28 7:22 [A]Ps 119:122; Is 38:14 [B]Heb 8:6 7:23 [a]Lit *The greater number have become priests…* 7:24 [A]Is 9:7; John 12:34; Rom 9:5; Heb 7:23f, 28 7:25 [a]Or *completely* [A]1 Cor 1:21 [B]Heb 7:19 [C]Rom 8:34; Heb 9:24 7:26 [A]Heb 2:17 [B]2 Cor 5:21; Heb 4:15 [C]1 Pet 2:22 [D]Heb 4:14 7:27 [A]Heb 5:1 [B]Lev 9:7; Heb 5:3 [C]Heb 9:12, 28; 10:10 [D]Eph 5:2; Heb 9:14, 28; 10:10, 12 7:28 [A]Heb 5:2 [B]Heb 1:2 [C]Heb 2:10 8:1 [A]Col 3:1; Heb 2:17; 3:1 [B]Ps 110:1; Heb 1:3 8:2 [a]Or *of* [b]Or *sacred tent* [A]Heb 10:11 [B]Heb 9:11, 24 [C]Ex 33:7 8:3 [A]Heb 2:17 [B]Rom 4:25; 5:6, 8; Gal 2:20; Eph 5:2; Heb 5:1; 8:4

office by heredity. The Levitical system was dominated by matters of physical existence and transitory ceremonialism. **power of an indestructible life.** Because He is the eternal Second Person of the Godhead, Christ's priesthood cannot end. He obtained His priesthood, not by virtue of the law, but by virtue of His deity.

7:17 Quoted from Ps 110:4 again (*see notes on 5:6, 10*).

7:18 setting aside. *See note on vv. 12–14.* The law was weak in that it could not save or bring about inward change in a person (cf. Ro 8:3; Gal 4:9).

7:19 the Law made nothing perfect. *See note on v. 11.* The law saved no one (cf. Ro 3:19, 20); rather it cursed everyone (cf. Gal 3:10–13). **a better hope.** *See notes on 3:6; 6:18.* **draw near to God.** See Introduction: Historical and Theological Themes; *see note on 4:16.* This is the key phrase in this passage. Drawing near to God is the essence of Christianity as compared with the Levitical system, which kept people outside His presence. As believer priests, we are all to draw near to God—that is a characteristic of priesthood (cf. Ex 19:22; *see notes on Mt 27:51*).

7:20, 21 oath. God's promises are unchangeable, sealed with an oath (cf. 6:17). The Melchizedekian priesthood of Christ is confirmed with God's oath in Ps 110:4. God's mind on this matter will not change (v. 21).

7:22 guarantee. This is the only use of the Gr. term in the NT and could also be translated "surety." Jesus Himself guarantees the success of His New Covenant of salvation. **a better covenant.** The New Covenant (8:8, 13; 9:15). *See notes on Jer 31:31–34; Mt 26:28.* The first mention of "covenant" in this epistle is coupled with one of the key themes of the book ("better," cf. v. 19; see Introduction: Historical and Theological Themes). This covenant will be more fully discussed in chap. 8.

7:23, 24 *See notes on vv. 3, 8, 16.*

7:23 greater numbers. It is claimed that there were 84 High Priests who served from Aaron until the destruction of the temple by the Romans in A.D. 70. The lesser priests' numbers were much larger.

7:25 forever. Virtually the same concept as was expressed in "perfection" (v. 11) and "make perfect" (v. 19). The Gr. term is used only here and in Lk 13:11 (the woman's body could not be straightened completely). **who draw near to God.** *See note on 4:16* (cf. Jn 6:37). **intercession.** The word means "to intercede on behalf of another." It was used to refer to bringing a petition to a king on behalf of someone. *See note on Ro 8:34.* Cf. the High Priestly intercessory prayer of Christ in Jn 17. Since rabbis assigned intercessory powers to angels, perhaps the people were treating angels as intercessors. The writer makes it clear that only Christ is the intercessor (cf. 1Ti 2:5).

7:26–28 Christ's divine and holy character is yet another proof of the superiority of His priesthood.

7:26 In His relationship to God, Christ is "holy" (piety without any pollution; Mt 3:17; 17:5; Mk 1:24; Lk 4:34; Ac 2:27; 13:35). In His relationship to man, He is "innocent" (without evil or malice; Jn 8:46). In relationship to Himself, He is "undefiled" (free from contamination; 1Pe 1:19) and "separated from sinners" (He had no sin nature which would be the source of any act of sin; cf. "without sin" in 4:15). *See notes on 2Co 5:21.* **exalted above the heavens.** *See notes on 3:1; 4:14.*

7:27 daily. Whenever the Levitical High Priest sinned, he was required to offer sacrifices for himself (Lv 4:3). Whenever the people sinned, he also had to offer a sacrifice for them (Lv 4:13). These occasions could be daily. Then, annually, on the Day of Atonement, he had to again offer sacrifices for himself and for the people (Lv 16:6, 11, 15). Christ had no sin and needed no sacrifice for Himself. And only one sacrifice (by Him) was needed—one time only, for all men, for all time. **once for all.** A key emphasis in Hebrews. The sacrificial work of Christ never needed to be repeated, unlike the OT priestly sacrifices. Cf. 9:12, 26, 28; 10:2, 10; 1Pe 3:18.

7:28 word of the oath. God confirmed Christ as High Priest. *See notes on vv. 20, 21; 6:16–18.* **made perfect forever.** *See note on 2:10.*

8:1–10:18 This entire section is an exposition of the New Covenant promised in Jer 31:31–34 and its contrast to the Old Covenant of Law.

8:1–5 A brief description of Jesus' priesthood in the heavenly sanctuary, which is better than Aaron's because He serves in a better sanctuary (vv. 1–5; cf. 9:1–12).

8:1 main point. Here the writer arrived at his central message. The fact is that "we have" (current possession) a superior High Priest, Jesus Christ, who is the fulfillment of all that was foreshadowed in the OT. **taken His seat.** *See notes on 1:3, 13.*

8:2 minister. This is the same word used of the angels in 1:7. In Jer 33:21 it was used of the priests. **sanctuary.** Cf. 9:3. The holiest place where God dwelt (cf. Ex 15:17; 25:8; 26:23, 24; 1Ch 22:17). **true tabernacle.** The definition is given in the phrase "which the Lord pitched, not man," as well as in 9:11, 24 (cf. v. 5). It refers to the heavenly dwelling place of God.

8:3 gifts and sacrifices. *See note on 5:1.*

4 Now if He were on earth, He would not be a priest at
all, since there are those who [A]offer the gifts according
to the Law; 5 who serve [A]a copy and [B]shadow of the
heavenly things, just as Moses [a]was [C]warned *by God*
when he was about to erect the [b]tabernacle; for, "[D]See,"
He says, "That you make all things according to the
pattern which was shown you on the mountain."
6 But now He has obtained a more excellent ministry,
by as much as He is also the [A]mediator of [B]a better
covenant, which has been enacted on better promises.

A NEW COVENANT

7 For [A]if that first *covenant* had been faultless,
there would have been no occasion sought for a
second. 8 For finding fault with them, He says,

"[A]Behold, days are coming, says the Lord,
[a]When I will effect [B]a new covenant
With the house of Israel and
with the house of Judah;
9 [A]Not like the covenant which I
made with their fathers
On the day when I took
them by the hand
To lead them out of the land of Egypt;
For they did not continue
in My covenant,
And I did not care for
them, says the Lord.
10 "[A]For this is the covenant that I will
make with the house of Israel
After those days, says the Lord:
[a]I will put My laws into their minds,
And I will write them
[B]on their hearts.
And I will be their God,
And they shall be My people.
11 "[A]And they shall not teach
everyone his fellow citizen,
And everyone his brother,
saying, 'Know the Lord,'
For [B]all will know Me,
From [a]the least to the
greatest of them.
12 "[A]For I will be merciful to
their iniquities,
[B]And I will remember their
sins no more."

13 [a]When He said, "[A]A new *covenant*," He has made
the first obsolete. [B]But whatever is becoming obsolete and growing old is [b]ready to disappear.

THE OLD AND THE NEW

9 Now even the first *covenant* had [A]regulations of
divine worship and [B]the earthly sanctuary. 2 For
there was [A]a [a]tabernacle prepared, the [b]outer one, in
which *were* [B]the lampstand and [C]the table and [D]the
[c]sacred bread; this is called the holy place. 3 Behind
[A]the second veil there was a [a]tabernacle which is
called the [B]Holy of Holies, 4 having a golden [a,A]altar
of incense and [B]the ark of the covenant covered on
all sides with gold, in which was [C]a golden jar holding the manna, and [D]Aaron's rod which budded, and
[E]the tables of the covenant; 5 and above it *were* the
[A]cherubim of glory [B]overshadowing the mercy seat;
but of these things we cannot now speak in detail.
6 Now when these things have been so prepared, the priests [A]are continually entering the
[a]outer [b]tabernacle performing the divine worship,

8:4 [A]Heb 5:1; 7:27; 8:3; 9:9; 10:11 8:5 [a]Lit *has been* [b]Or *sacred tent* [A]Heb 9:23 [B]Col 2:17; Heb 10:1 [C]Matt 2:12; Heb 11:7; 12:25 [D]Ex 25:40 8:6 [A]1 Tim 2:5 [B]Luke 22:20; Heb 7:22; 8:8; 9:15; 12:24 8:7 [A]Heb 7:11 8:8 [a]Lit *And* [A]Jer 31:31 [B]Luke 22:20; 2 Cor 3:6; Heb 7:22; 8:6, 13; 9:15; 12:24 8:9 [A]Ex 19:5; 24:6-8; Deut 5:2, 3; Jer 31:32 8:10 [a]Lit *Putting my laws into…* [A]Jer 31:33; Rom 11:27; Heb 10:16 [B]2 Cor 3:3 8:11 [a]Lit *small to great of them* [A]Jer 31:34 [B]Is 54:13; John 6:45; 1 John 2:27 8:12 [A]Is 43:25; Jer 31:34; 50:20; Mic 7:18, 19 [B]Heb 10:17 8:13 [a]Or *In His saying* [b]Or *near* [A]Luke 22:20; 2 Cor 3:6; Heb 7:22; 8:6, 8; 9:15; 12:24 [B]2 Cor 5:17; Heb 1:11 9:1 [A]Heb 9:10 [B]Ex 25:8; Heb 8:2; 9:11, 24 9:2 [a]Or *sacred tent* [b]Lit *first* [c]Lit *loaves of presentation* [A]Ex 25:8, 9; 26:1-30 [B]Ex 25:31-39 [C]Ex 25:23-29 [D]Ex 25:30; Lev 24:5ff; Matt 12:4 9:3 [a]Or *sacred tent* [A]Ex 26:31-33; 40:3 [B]Ex 26:33 9:4 [a]Or *censer* [A]Ex 30:1-5; 37:25f [B]Ex 25:10ff; 37:1ff [C]Ex 16:32f [D]Num 17:10 [E]Ex 25:16; 31:18; 32:15; Deut 9:9, 11, 15; 10:3-5 9:5 [A]Ex 25:18ff [B]Ex 25:17, 20; Lev 16:2; 1 Kin 8:7 9:6 [a]Lit *first* [b]Or *sacred tent* [A]Num 18:2-6; 28:3

8:4 **not be a priest.** Jesus was not qualified to be a Levitical priest because He was not of the tribe of Levi. *See note on 7:12–14.* Because of its use of the present tense, this verse indicates that the Levitical system was still in operation at the time of writing, indicating it was before the destruction of the temple in A.D. 70 (*see note on 5:1–4*).

8:5 The quote is from Ex 25:40. **copy and shadow.** This does not mean that there are actual buildings in heaven which were copied in the tabernacle, but rather that the heavenly realities were adequately symbolized and represented in the earthly tabernacle model.

8:6 **mediator.** Cf. 9:15. The word describes a go-between or an arbitrator, in this case between man and God. *See note on 1Ti 2:5* (cf. Gal 3:19, 20). **better covenant … better promises.** *See notes on 7:19, 22; Jn 1:17, 18.* This covenant is identified as the "new covenant" in vv. 8, 13; 9:15.

8:7 Cf. the same argument in 7:11. The older covenant, incomplete and imperfect, was only intended to be temporary.

8:8–12 Quoted from Jer 31:31–34 (*see notes there*).

8:9 **I did not care for them.** Jeremiah 31:32 says, "although I was a husband to them." The NT writer is quoting from the LXX, which uses a variant reading that does not essentially change the meaning.

8:10 **minds … hearts.** By its nature, the Covenant of Law was primarily external, but the New Covenant is internal (cf. Eze 36:26, 27).

8:12 The LXX represents a slight expansion of the last sentence of Jer 31:34.

8:13 **ready to disappear.** Soon after the book of Hebrews was written, the temple in Jerusalem was destroyed and its Levitical worship ended (*see note on 5:1–4*; see Introduction: Author and Date).

9:1–10 In these verses, the author gives a brief description of the tabernacle, to which some 50 chaps. in the OT are devoted, including the tabernacle service (cf. Ex 25–40). The section is marked off by its beginning with a reference to "regulations" (v. 1) and closing with a reference to "regulations" (v. 10).

9:2 **outer one … holy place.** This is the Holy Place, the first room of the tabernacle (Ex 26:33). For the items in the Holy Place, see Ex 25:23–40; 40:22–25; Lv 24:5–9.

9:3 **Holy of Holies.** This is the Most Holy Place where the ark of the covenant and the mercy seat dwelt—the place of atonement (Ex 26:33, 34).

9:4 **golden altar of incense.** *See note on Ex 30:1–10* (cf. Ex 40:5, 26, 27). Though it was outside the Most Holy Place (Ex 30:6), the writer of Hebrews pictures the golden altar inside the Most Holy Place because uppermost in his mind is its role in the liturgy of the Day of Atonement. On that day, the High Priest brought incense from that altar into the Most Holy Place (Lv 16:12, 13). The altar of golden incense marked the boundary of the Holy of Holies as well as the curtain. The High Priest went beyond the altar of incense only once a year. **the ark.** *See notes on Ex 25:11–18; 26:31–34.* **golden jar holding the manna.** *See note on Ex 16:32–36.* **Aaron's rod.** *See notes on Nu 17:2–10.* **tables of the covenant.** *See note on Ex 25:16* (cf. 1Ki 8:9).

9:5 **cherubim … mercy seat.** *See notes on Ex 25:17, 18.* **cannot now speak in detail.** The writer has no desire to obscure his main point with details (cf. 8:1).

7 but into [A]the second, only [B]the high priest *enters*
[C]once a year, [D]not without *taking* blood, which he
[E]offers for himself and for the [a,F]sins of the people
committed in ignorance. 8 [A]The Holy Spirit *is* signifying this, [B]that the way into the holy place has
not yet been disclosed while the [a]outer tabernacle
is still standing, 9 which *is* a symbol for the present time. Accordingly [A]both gifts and sacrifices
are offered which [B]cannot make the worshiper
perfect in conscience, 10 since they *relate* only to
[A]food and [B]drink and various [C]washings, [D]reg-
ulations for the [a]body imposed until [E]a time of
reformation.

11 But when Christ appeared *as* a [A]high priest of
the [B]good things [a]to come, *He entered* through [C]the
greater and more perfect [b]tabernacle, [D]not made with
hands, that is to say, [E]not of this creation; 12 and not
through [A]the blood of goats and calves, but [B]through
His own blood, He [C]entered the holy place [D]once for
all, [a]having obtained [E]eternal redemption. 13 For if [A]the
blood of goats and bulls and [B]the ashes of a heifer
sprinkling those who have been defiled sanctify for
the [a]cleansing of the flesh, 14 how much more will [A]the
blood of Christ, who through [a,B]the eternal Spirit [C]of-
fered Himself without blemish to God, [D]cleanse [b]your
conscience from [E]dead works to serve [F]the living God?

9:7 [a]Lit *ignorance of the people* [A]Heb 9:3 [B]Lev 16:12ff [C]Ex 30:10; Lev 16:34; Heb 10:3 [D]Lev 16:11, 14 [E]Heb 5:3 [F]Num 15:25; Heb 5:2 9:8 [a]Lit *first* [A]Heb 3:7 [B]John 14:6; Heb 10:20 9:9 [A]Heb 5:1 [B]Heb 7:19 9:10 [a]Lit *flesh* [A]Lev 11:2ff; Col 2:16 [B]Num 6:3 [C]Lev 11:25; Num 19:13; Mark 7:4 [D]Heb 7:16 [E]Heb 7:12 9:11 [a]Two early mss read *that have come* [b]Or *sacred tent* [A]Heb 2:17 [B]Heb 10:1 [C]Heb 8:2; 9:24 [D]Mark 14:58; 2 Cor 5:1 [E]2 Cor 4:18; Heb 12:27; 13:14 9:12 [a]Or *obtaining* [A]Lev 4:3; 16:6, 15; Heb 9:19 [B]Heb 9:14; 13:12 [C]Heb 9:24 [D]Heb 7:27 [E]Heb 5:9; 9:15 9:13 [a]Lit *purity* [A]Lev 16:15; Heb 9:19; 10:4 [B]Num 19:9, 17f 9:14 [a]Or His *eternal spirit* [b]One early ms reads *our* [A]Heb 9:12; 13:12 [B]1 Cor 15:45; 1 Pet 3:18 [C]Eph 5:2; Heb 7:27; 10:10, 12 [D]Acts 15:9; Titus 2:14; Heb 1:3; 10:2, 22 [E]Heb 6:1 [F]Matt 16:16; Heb 3:12

9:7 This was the Day of Atonement. *See notes on 4:14; 7:27; Lv 16:16, 20–22, 30.* **not without *taking* blood.** *See note on v. 22.* This is the first of many references to the blood of sacrifice. The term is especially central to 9:1–10:18 where it identifies the deaths of OT sacrifices and of Christ (cf. vv. 12–14). Note, however, that the shedding of blood in and of itself is an insufficient sacrifice. Christ had not only to shed His blood, but to die. Hebrews 10:10 indicates that He gave His body as the sacrificial offering. Without His death, His blood had no saving value. *See notes on v. 14, 18, 22; 10:10.*

9:8 The Levitical system did not provide any direct access into God's presence for His people. Rather, it kept them away. Nearness had to be provided by another way (v. 12). This is the primary lesson which the Holy Spirit taught concerning the tabernacle. It teaches how inaccessible God is apart from the death of Jesus Christ. See Introduction: Historical and Theological Themes. See the counterpart to this lesson in 10:20. **Holy Spirit.** *See note on 2:4.* By the Spirit-inspired instruction given for the Holiest of All, He was indicating that there was no way to God in the ceremonial system. Only Christ could open the way (cf. Jn 14:6).

9:9 symbol. The Gr. word is *parabolē*, from which the Eng. word parable is derived. The Levitical system was a parable, an object lesson, about what was to come in Christ. **for the present time.** "For" is ambiguous enough to allow for two different meanings and interpretations: 1) "during" the time of the OT, or 2) "until" and "pointing to" the current Christian era. The second interpretation is "according to which" (from an alternate Gr. reading) referring to the "parable" rather than to the time. It was an object lesson from the past pointing to the present time. This latter interpretation is preferable because of the explanation in v. 10. "The present time" is "the time of reformation." **gifts and sacrifices.** *See note on 5:1.* **perfect in conscience.** Again, this term refers to salvation. *See notes on 5:14; 7:11; 10:1* (cf. 7:25). The sacrifices of the OT did not remove the offerers' guilty conscience or provide them with full forgiveness for their sins (cf. 10:1–4). It was only symbolic of something else that would—namely Christ. The conscience is a divinely given warning device that reacts to sin and produces accusation and guilt (*see notes on Ro 2:14, 15*) that cannot be relieved apart from the work of Christ (cf. v. 14; 10:22). At the time of salvation, it is quieted from its convicting ravings, but it is not deactivated. Rather, it continues its work, warning the believer about sin. Believers should seek a clear conscience (*see notes on 2Co 1:12*).

9:10 food and drink. *See notes on Lv 11:1–47; Dt 14:3–21* (cf. Col 2:16). **washings.** *See note on 6:2.* **regulations for the body.** The Levitical ordinances regulated the visible actions without changing the inner man (cf. 10:4). **reformation.** The Gr. term means "restoring what is out of line." All things are set straight in Christ. The reformation is the New Covenant and its application. *See note on v. 9.*

9:11 the good things to come. The reference appears to be to the "eternal redemption" (v. 12). In 10:1, the "good things" refer back to the "salvation" of v. 28 (cf. Ro 10:15). Most Gr. editions of the NT accept the reading "that have come." In the context, both readings refer to the things of the New Covenant. It is just a matter of perspective: whether from the viewpoint of the Levitical system where the realities of redemption were "to come," or the viewpoint of those in the Christian era where the realities of redemption "have come" because Christ has completed His work. **not of this creation.** The phrase is the explanation of "not made with hands"—it is the creation of God alone. The sanctuary where Christ serves is heaven itself (cf. v. 24; 8:2).

9:12 goats and calves. Only one of each was sacrificed on the Day of Atonement (cf. Lv 16:5–10). The plural here represents the numbers sacrificed as the Day of Atonement was observed year after year. **through His own blood.** The same phrase is used in 13:12. Nothing is said which would indicate that Christ carried His actual physical blood with Him into the heavenly sanctuary. The Sacrificer was also the Sacrifice. **once for all.** *See note on 7:27.* **eternal redemption.** This word for redemption is found only here and in Lk 1:68; 2:38. Its original use was for the release of slaves by payment of a ransom.

9:13–22 Christ's death was necessary for the fulfillment of the older covenant and the establishment of the new.

9:13 ashes of a heifer. *See notes on Nu 19.* It is said that, in the history of Israel, only 6 red heifers were killed and their ashes used. One heifer's ashes would suffice for centuries since only a minute amount of the ash was required. **defiled.** The Gr. term is literally "common" or "profane." Not that it was ceremonially unclean, but that it was not sanctified or set apart unto God. The word was used in Jesus' discourse on what defiles a man (cf. Mt 15:11, 18, 20; Mk 7:15, 18, 20, 23), in the Jews' complaint that Paul had defiled the temple by bringing Gentiles into it (Ac 21:28), and in reference to the meats which Peter had been invited to eat (Ac 10:15; 11:9). According to the Mosaic regulation, the red heifer's ashes were to be placed "outside the camp" and used in a ceremony for symbolic purifying from sin (Nu 19:9; cf. 13:11–13).

9:14 how much more. Superior to the cleansing capability of the ashes of an animal is the cleansing power of the sacrifice of Christ. **the blood of Christ.** This is an expression that refers not simply to the fluid, but the whole atoning sacrificial work of Christ in His death. Blood is used as a substitute word for death (cf. Mt 23:30, 35; 27:6, 8, 24, 25; Jn 6:54–56; Ac 18:6; 20:26). *See notes on Mt 26:28; Ro 3:25; 5:9; Col 1:14.* **the eternal Spirit.** *See note on 2:4* (cf. Is 42:1; 61:1; Lk 4:1, 14). Some interpreters argue that the lack of the definite article in the Gr. makes this a reference to Christ's own "eternal spirit" (in the sense of an endless life, cf. 7:16). However, the references to the Holy Spirit in 2:4 and 6:4 are also without the definite article. The use of "eternal" as a qualifier serves to relate the Spirit to the "eternal redemption" (v. 12) and the "eternal inheritance" (v. 15) which Christ accomplished by His sacrificial death. **offered Himself.** *See notes on v. 7; Jn 10:17, 18.* The animals in the Levitical system were brought involuntarily and without understanding to their deaths. Christ came of His own volition with a full understanding of the necessity and consequences of His sacrifice. His sacrifice was not just His blood; it was His entire human nature (cf. 10:10). **without blemish.** In the LXX, the term is used for describing acceptable sacrifices including the red heifer (Nu 19:3; cf. Ex 29:1; Lv 1:3). A similar reference is found in 1Pe 1:19. **conscience.** *See note on v. 9.* **dead works.** *See note on 6:1.* The works are dead because the unregenerate are "dead in ... trespasses and sins" (Eph 2:1), their works are worthless and unproductive (Gal 2:16; 5:19–21), and they end in death (Ro 6:23). **to serve the living God.** Salvation is not an end in itself. The believer has been freed from sin to serve God, saved to serve (cf. Ro 6:16–18; 1Th 1:9). The contrast between dead works and the living God (cf. 3:12; 10:31; 12:22) is basic. Cf. Jas 2:14–26.

15 For this reason [A]He is the [B]mediator of a [C]new
covenant, so that, since a death has taken place for
the redemption of the transgressions that were
committed under the first covenant, those who
have been [D]called may [E]receive the promise of [F]the
eternal inheritance. 16 For where a [a]covenant is,
there must of necessity [b]be the death of the one
who made it. 17 For a [a]covenant is valid *only* when
[b]men are dead, [c]for it is never in force while the
one who made it lives. 18 Therefore even the first
covenant was not inaugurated without blood. 19 For
when every commandment had been [A]spoken by
Moses to all the people according to the Law, [B]he
took the [C]blood of the calves and the goats, with
[D]water and scarlet wool and hyssop, and sprinkled
both [E]the book itself and all the people, 20 saying,
"[A]THIS IS THE BLOOD OF THE COVENANT WHICH GOD
COMMANDED YOU." 21 And in the same way he [A]sprin-
kled both the [a]tabernacle and all the vessels of the
ministry with the blood. 22 And according to the
[a]Law, *one may* [A]almost *say,* all things are cleansed
with blood, and [B]without shedding of blood there
is no forgiveness.

23 Therefore it was necessary for the [A]copies of
the things in the heavens to be cleansed with these,
but [A]the heavenly things themselves with better
sacrifices than these. 24 For Christ [A]did not enter a
holy place made with hands, a *mere* copy of [B]the
true one, but into [C]heaven itself, now [D]to appear
in the presence of God for us; 25 nor was it that He
would offer Himself often, as [A]the high priest enters [B]the holy place [A]year by year with blood that is

9:15 [A]Rom 3:24 [B]1 Tim 2:5; Heb 8:6; 12:24 [C]Heb 8:8 [D]Matt 22:3ff; Rom 8:28f; Heb 3:1 [E]Heb 6:15; 10:36; 11:39 [F]Acts 20:32 9:16 [a]Or *testament* [b]Lit *be brought*
9:17 [a]Or *testament* [b]Lit *over the dead* [c]Two early mss read *for is it then...lives?* 9:19 [A]Heb 1:1 [B]Ex 24:6ff [C]Heb 9:12 [D]Lev 14:4, 7; Num 19:6, 18 [E]Ex 24:7
9:20 [A]Ex 24:8; Matt 26:28 9:21 [a]Or *sacred tent* [A]Ex 24:6; 40:9; Lev 8:15, 19; 16:14-16 9:22 [a]Or *Law, almost all things* [A]Lev 5:11f [B]Lev 17:11
9:23 [A]Heb 8:5 9:24 [A]Heb 4:14; 9:12 [B]Heb 8:2 [C]Heb 9:12 [D]Matt 18:10; Heb 7:25 9:25 [A]Heb 9:7 [B]Heb 9:2; 10:19

9:15 mediator. *See note on 8:6.* **death.** In the making of some biblical covenants, sacrifices were involved. When God made the covenant with Abraham, 5 different animals were sacrificed in the ceremony (Ge 15:9, 10). The Mosaic Covenant was affirmed by animal sacrifices (Ex 24:5–8). **redemption.** The term used here is found more frequently than the term used in v. 12 (cf. 11:35; Lk 21:28; Ro 3:24). Jesus' death retroactively redeemed all those who had believed in God under the Old Covenant (cf. Ro 3:24–26). This is in keeping with symbolism of the Day of Atonement. Annually, the High Priest would atone for or cover the sins that the people had committed in the preceding year (Lv 16:16, 21, 30). **first covenant.** *See note on Ge 9:16.* The actual first covenant historically was made with Noah (Ge 6:18; 9:9). Next came the covenant made with Abraham (Ge 15:18). By context, however, the older covenant under discussion in this epistle is that which is called the Mosaic Covenant or the Covenant of Law (Ex 19:1–20:21). "First" in this verse, therefore, means the former, older covenant with which the Levitical system is connected. **those who have been called.** Lit. "the ones having been called," looking back to those under the Old Covenant who were called to salvation by God on the basis of the sacrifice of Jesus Christ to come long after most of them had died. The reference, as always in the NT Epistles, is to the effectual calling related to salvation (cf. 3:1), which in this context refers to OT believers. **promise of the eternal inheritance.** That is, salvation in its fullness (*see notes on 3:11; 4:1, 9; 6:12; 1Pe 1:3–5*).

9:16, 17 A last will and testament illustrates the necessity of Christ's death. "Covenant" is the same Gr. word translated "testament," but the term takes on the more specialized meaning in this context. The benefits and provisions of a will are only promises until the one who wrote the will dies. Death activates the promises into realities.

9:18–20 The shedding of blood in the covenant ratification ceremony at Sinai (Ex 24:1–8) also illustrates the necessity of Christ's death (*see note on v. 15*).

9:18 blood. "Death" in vv. 15, 16 is replaced by "blood" (*see notes on vv. 7, 14*). The term is used to emphasize the violent aspect of His sacrificial death.

9:19 water and scarlet wool and hyssop. These items were used at the Passover in Egypt (Ex 12:22) for sprinkling of blood, and in the ritual cleansing for lepers (Lv 14:4), and in the red heifer ceremony (Nu 19:6). More of those are in view here. These elements were a part of the sprinkling of blood in the covenant ceremony described in Ex 24:1–8, though not mentioned there. The added details came either by direct revelation to the writer or had been preserved in other records or traditions known to the writer and his readers. **the book ... the people.** *See note on Ex 24:8.* The consecration of Aaron and his sons to the priesthood is the only other occasion in the OT when any persons were sprinkled with blood (Ex 29:21; Lv 8:30; cf. 1Pe 1:2). The detail about the book also being sprinkled with the blood is not recorded in the Exodus account.

9:20 This is the blood. Cf. Ex 24:8 with Mt 26:28. The same formula was utilized in the inaugural ceremonies for the Mosaic Covenant and for the New Covenant.

9:21 in the same way. The dedication of the tabernacle and its vessels was accompanied by a blood sprinkling ritual similar to that observed at the inauguration of the Mosaic Covenant (cf. Ex 29:10–15, 21, 36, 37).

9:22 almost ... all. There were a few exceptions. Water, incense, and fire were also used to purify (cf. Ex 19:10; Lv 15:5; Nu 16:46, 47; 31:21–24). Those who were too poor to bring even a small animal for sacrifice were allowed to bring fine flour instead (Lv 5:11). **blood ... forgiveness.** "It is the blood ... that makes atonement" (Lv 17:11). The phraseology is reminiscent of Christ's own words (Mt 26:28). "Shedding of blood" refers to death (*see notes on vv. 7, 14, 18*). "Forgiveness" is the emphatic last word in this section (vv. 18–22) of the Gr. NT, and it forms the transition to the next section (vv. 23–28).

9:23–28 Christ's High Priestly ministry is to be exercised in the perfect tabernacle of heaven. The real High Priest who offered the real sacrifice for sin serves in the real tabernacle. He is the complete fulfillment of the shadowy copies in the Levitical system.

9:23 copies. *See note on 8:5.* The earthly tabernacle and its vessels were only symbolic replicas of the true heavenly tabernacle (8:2), and were also made unclean by the transgressions of the people (Lv 16:16). **the heavenly things.** As the preceding context indicated, the inauguration of the Mosaic Covenant by sacrifices was necessary (vv. 18–21). That concept is here applied to the heavenly sanctuary—it is dedicated or inaugurated as the central sanctuary of the New Covenant by Christ's sacrifice. The better covenant required a better sacrifice. **better sacrifices.** Christ's superior sacrifice is a major theme in 9:13–10:18. The many sacrifices of the Levitical system were to be superseded by better sacrifices that would be represented in the one, all-inclusive, perfect sacrifice of Christ (cf. 10:12). *See note on 7:22.*

9:24 copy. The term is not the same as that used in v. 23 and 8:5. This is lit. "antitype." It is used only twice in the NT. The antitype either prefigures the type (as here), or is a later illustration of the type (as in 1Pe 3:21). In both cases, the antitype is not the real thing, but only a copy of it. The earthly "holy place" in the tabernacle was only a type of the heavenly abode of God. **now to appear.** On the Day of Atonement, the High Priest entered the Most Holy Place where God made an appearance (Lv 16:2). The High Priest, however, was hidden from the presence of God by the cloud of incense (Lv 16:12, 13). See also "has been manifested" (v. 26) and "will appear" (v. 28). Each verb is a different term in the Gr. The term for Christ's present appearance in heaven (v. 24) alludes to His official presentation to report to the Father on the fulfillment of His mission. The concept of making an appearance or being revealed is involved in the incarnational appearance in order to die once for sin (v. 26). At Christ's appearing at the Second Advent (v. 28), the term used stresses the visible nature of the appearance (cf. 2:8; 12:14). All 3 tenses of Christ's soteriological ministry are also covered: 1) His First Advent to save us from the penalty of sin; 2) His present intercessory ministry in heaven to save us from the power of sin; and 3) His Second Advent to deliver us from the presence of sin. **for us.** Christ is our representative and the provider of our spiritual benefits (cf. 2:9; 6:20; 7:25; Jn 14:12–14; Eph 1:3).

not his own. 26 Otherwise, He would have needed to suffer often since [A]the foundation of the world; but now [B]once at [C]the consummation of the ages He has been [D]manifested to put away sin [a],[E]by the sacrifice of Himself. 27 And inasmuch as [A]it is [a]appointed for men to die once and after this [B]*comes* judgment, 28 so Christ also, having been [A]offered once to [B]bear the sins of many, will appear [C]a second time for [D]salvation [E]without *reference to* sin, to those who [F]eagerly await Him.

ONE SACRIFICE OF CHRIST IS SUFFICIENT

10 For the Law, since it has *only* [A]a shadow of [B]the good things to come *and* not the very [a]form of things, [b]can [C]never, by the same sacrifices which they offer continually year by year, [D]make perfect those who draw near. 2 Otherwise, would they not have ceased to be offered, because the worshipers, having once been cleansed, would no longer have had [A]consciousness of sins? 3 But [A]in [a]those *sacrifices* there is a reminder of sins year by year. 4 For it is [A]impossible for the [B]blood of bulls and goats to take away sins. 5 Therefore, [A]when He comes into the world, He says,

"[B]SACRIFICE AND OFFERING YOU
HAVE NOT DESIRED,
BUT [C]A BODY YOU HAVE PREPARED FOR ME;
6 [A]IN WHOLE BURNT OFFERINGS AND
sacrifices FOR SIN YOU HAVE
TAKEN NO PLEASURE.
7 "[A]THEN I SAID, 'BEHOLD, I HAVE COME
(IN [B]THE SCROLL OF THE BOOK
IT IS WRITTEN OF ME)
TO DO YOUR WILL, O GOD.' "

8 After saying above, "[A]SACRIFICES AND OFFERINGS AND [B]WHOLE BURNT OFFERINGS AND *sacrifices* [C]FOR SIN YOU HAVE NOT DESIRED, NOR HAVE YOU TAKEN PLEASURE *in them*" (which are offered according to the Law), 9 then He [a]said, "[A]BEHOLD, I HAVE COME TO DO YOUR WILL." He takes away the first in order to establish the second. 10 By [a]this will we have been [A]sanctified through [B]the offering of [C]the body of Jesus Christ [D]once for all.

9:26 [a]Or *by His sacrifice* [A]Matt 25:34; Heb 4:3 [B]Heb 7:27; 9:12 [C]Matt 13:39; Heb 1:2 [D]1 John 3:5, 8 [E]Heb 9:12, 14 9:27 [a]Lit *laid up* [A]Gen 3:19 [B]2 Cor 5:10; 1 John 4:17 9:28 [A]Heb 7:27 [B]Is 53:12; 1 Pet 2:24 [C]Acts 1:11 [D]Heb 5:9 [E]Heb 4:15 [F]1 Cor 1:7; Titus 2:13 10:1 [a]Lit *image* [b]Two early mss read *they can* [A]Heb 8:5 [B]Heb 9:11 [C]Rom 8:3; Heb 9:9; 10:4, 11 [D]Heb 7:19 10:2 [A]1 Pet 2:19 10:3 [a]Lit *them there is* [A]Heb 9:7 10:4 [A]Heb 10:1, 11 [B]Heb 9:12f 10:5 [A]Heb 1:6 [B]Ps 40:6 [C]Heb 2:14; 5:7; 1 Pet 2:24 10:6 [A]Ps 40:6 10:7 [A]Ps 40:7, 8 [B]Ezra 6:2; Jer 36:2; Ezek 2:9; 3:1f 10:8 [A]Ps 40:6; Heb 10:5f [B]Mark 12:33 [C]Rom 8:3 10:9 [a]Lit *has said* [A]Ps 40:7, 8; Heb 10:7 10:10 [a]Lit *which* [A]John 17:19; Eph 5:26; Heb 2:11; 10:14, 29; 13:12 [B]John 6:51; Eph 5:2; Heb 7:27; 9:14, 28; 10:12 [C]Heb 2:14; 5:7; 1 Pet 2:24 [D]Heb 7:27

9:26 since the foundation of the world. This is a reference to creation (*see notes on 4:3*). **consummation of the ages.** All the eras and ages came together and were consummated in the coming of the Messiah. The eschatological era was inaugurated (*see note on 1:2*; cf. Gal 4:4).

9:27 to die once. This is a general rule for all mankind. There have been very rare exceptions (e.g., Lazarus died twice; cf. Jn 11:43, 44). Those, like Lazarus, who were raised from the dead by a miraculous act of our Lord were not resurrected to a glorified body and unending life. They only experienced resuscitation. Another exception will be those who don't die even once, but who will be "caught up … to meet the Lord in the air" (1Th 4:17; cf. Enoch, Ge 5:24; Elijah, 2Ki 2:11). **judgment.** A general term encompassing the judgment of all people, believers (*see note on 2Co 5:10*) and unbelievers (*see notes on Rev 20:11–15*).

9:28 to bear the sins of many. *See note on Is 53:12* (cf. 2Co 5:21; 1Pe 2:24). **second time.** On the Day of Atonement, the people eagerly waited for the High Priest to come back out of the Holy of Holies. When he appeared, they knew that the sacrifice on their behalf had been accepted by God. In the same way, when Christ appears at His second coming, it will be confirmation that the Father has been fully satisfied with the Son's sacrifice on behalf of believers. At that point salvation will be consummated (cf. 1Pe 1:3–5). **without *reference to* sin.** *See notes on 2:17, 18; 4:15.* This phrase testifies to the completed work of Christ in removing sins by His sacrifice at His first coming. No such burden will be upon Him in His second coming. **eagerly await.** *See note on Php 3:20.*

10:1–18 Christ's offering was a once-for-all sacrifice which is superior to all the sacrifices of the Levitical system.

10:1 shadow. *See note on 8:5.* The Gr. term translated "shadow" refers to a pale reflection, as contrasted with a sharp, distinct one. The term behind "very form," on the other hand, indicates an exact and distinct replica (cf. Col 2:17). **good things.** *See note on 9:11.* **perfect.** This term is used repeatedly in Hebrews to refer to salvation. *See notes on 5:14; 7:11; 9:9.* As much as those living under the law desired to approach God, the Levitical system provided no way to enter His holy presence (cf. Pss 15:1; 16:11; 24:3, 4).

10:2 consciousness of sins. This is the same word translated "conscience" in v. 22; 9:9; 13:18. *See note on 9:9.* If sin had really been overpowered by that system of sacrifices, the OT believers' consciences would have been cleansed from condemning guilt (cf. v. 22). There was not freedom of conscience under the Old Covenant.

10:3 reminder. The OT sacrifices not only could not remove sin, but their constant repetition was a constant reminder of that deficiency. The promise of the New Covenant was that the sin would be removed and even God would "remember" their sins "no more" (8:12, quoting Jer 31:34).

10:4 impossible. The Levitical system was not designed by God to remove or forgive sins. It was preparatory for the coming of the Messiah (Gal 3:24) in that it made the people expectant (cf. 1Pe 1:10). It revealed the seriousness of their sinful condition, in that even temporary covering required the death of an animal. It revealed the reality of God's holiness and righteousness by indicating that sin had to be covered. Finally, it revealed the necessity of full and complete forgiveness so that God could have desired fellowship with His people.

10:5–7 Quoted from Ps 40:6–8.

10:5, 6 You have not desired. God was not pleased with sacrifices given by a person who did not give them out of a sincere heart (cf. Ps 51:17; Is 1:11; Jer 6:20; Hos 6:6; Am 5:21–25). To sacrifice only as a ritual, without obedience, was a mockery and worse than no sacrifice at all (cf. Is 1:11–18).

10:5 a body You have prepared for Me. Psalm 40:6 reads, "My ears you have opened." This does not represent a significant alteration in the meaning of the psalm, as indicated by the fact that the writer quoted the LXX version of the Heb. idiom, which was an accurate representation for Greek readers. The Greek translators regarded the Heb. words as a figure of speech, in which a part of something signified the whole, i.e., the hollowing out of ears was part of the total work of fashioning a human body. And ears were selected as the part to emphasize because they were symbols of obedience as the organ of the reception of God's Word and will (cf. 1Sa 15:22). Christ needed a body in order to offer Himself as the final sacrifice (2:14).

10:7 To do Your will. Cf. Mt 26:39, 42.

10:8, 9 The writer quotes from Ps 40:6–8 again, but in a condensed form.

10:9 first … second. The old, repetitious sacrificial system was removed to make way for the new, once-for-all sacrifice of Christ, who had obediently done God's will (cf. 5:8; Php 2:8).

10:10 sanctified. "Sanctify" means to "make holy," to be set apart from sin for God (cf. 1Th 4:3). When Christ fulfilled the will of God, He provided for the believer a continuing, permanent condition of holiness (Eph 4:24; 1Th 3:13). This is the believer's positional sanctification as opposed to the progressive sanctification that results from daily walking by the will of God (*see notes on Ro 6:19; 12:1, 2; 2Co 7:1*). **body.** Refers to His atoning death, as the term "blood" has been used to do (9:7, 12, 14, 18, 22). Mention of the body of Christ in such a statement is unusual in the NT, but it is logically derived from the quotation from Ps 40:6.

11 Every priest stands daily ministering and [A]of-
fering time after time the same sacrifices, which
[B]can never take away sins; 12 but He, having offered
one sacrifice [A]for [a]sins [B]for all time, [C]SAT DOWN AT
THE RIGHT HAND OF GOD, 13 waiting from that time
onward [A]UNTIL HIS ENEMIES BE MADE A FOOTSTOOL
FOR HIS FEET. 14 For by one offering He has [A]per-
fected [B]for all time those who are [a]sanctified. 15 And
[A]the Holy Spirit also testifies to us; for after saying,

16 "[A]THIS IS THE COVENANT THAT I
WILL MAKE WITH THEM
AFTER THOSE DAYS, SAYS THE LORD:
I WILL PUT MY LAWS UPON THEIR HEART,
AND ON THEIR MIND I WILL WRITE THEM,"

He then says,

17 "[A]AND THEIR SINS AND THEIR LAWLESS DEEDS
I WILL REMEMBER NO MORE."

18 Now where there is forgiveness of these things,
there is no longer *any* offering for sin.

A NEW AND LIVING WAY

19 Therefore, brethren, since we [A]have confidence to [B]enter the holy place by the blood of Jesus,
20 by [A]a new and living way which He inaugurated
for us through [B]the veil, that is, His flesh, 21 and
since *we have* [A]a great priest [B]over the house of
God, 22 let us [A]draw near with a [a]sincere heart in
[B]full assurance of faith, having our hearts [C]sprin-
kled *clean* from an evil conscience and our bodies
[D]washed with pure water. 23 Let us hold fast the
[A]confession of our [B]hope without wavering, for
[C]He who promised is faithful; 24 and let us consider
how [A]to stimulate one another to love and [B]good
deeds, 25 not forsaking our own [A]assembling together, as is the habit of some, but [B]encouraging
one another; and all the more as you see [C]the day
drawing near.

10:11 [A]Heb 5:1 [B]Mic 6:6-8; Heb 10:1, 4 10:12 [a]Or *sins, forever sat down* [A]Heb 5:1 [B]Heb 10:14 [C]Ps 110:1; Heb 1:3 10:13 [A]Ps 110:1; Heb 1:13 10:14 [a]Or *being sanctified* [A]Heb 10:1 [B]Heb 10:12 10:15 [A]Heb 3:7 10:16 [A]Jer 31:33; Heb 8:10 10:17 [A]Jer 31:34; Heb 8:12 10:19 [A]Heb 3:6; 10:35 [B]Heb 9:25 10:20 [A]Heb 9:8 [B]Heb 6:19; 9:3 10:21 [A]Heb 2:17 [B]1 Tim 3:15; Heb 3:6 10:22 [a]Lit *true* [A]Heb 7:19; 10:1 [B]Heb 6:11 [C]Ezek 36:25; Heb 9:19; 12:24; 1 Pet 1:2 [D]Acts 22:16; 1 Cor 6:11; Eph 5:26; Titus 3:5; 1 Pet 3:21 10:23 [A]Heb 3:1 [B]Heb 3:6 [C]1 Cor 1:9; 10:13; Heb 11:11 10:24 [A]Heb 13:1 [B]Titus 3:8 10:25 [A]Acts 2:42 [B]Heb 3:13 [C]1 Cor 3:13

10:11, 12 The old and new are contrasted: thousands of priests versus one Priest; the old priests continually standing versus the sitting down of the new; repeated offerings versus a once-for-all offering; and the ineffective sacrifices that only covered sin versus the effective sacrifice that completely removes sin.

10:11 stands. *See note on 1:3.* In 2Ch 6:10, 12, Solomon sat on his throne as king, but stood at the altar when acting in a priestly role (cf. Dt 17:12; 18:7).

10:13 footstool. *See note on 1:13.* This is yet another reference to Ps 110:1. This prediction will be fulfilled when Christ returns and all creation acknowledges His lordship by bowing at His feet (Php 2:10).

10:14 perfected. *See note on v. 1.* This involves a perfect standing before God in the righteousness of Christ (*see notes on Ro 3:22; Php 3:8, 9*). **sanctified.** *See notes on v. 10.*

10:15–17 The writer confirms his interpretation of Ps 40:6–8 by repeating from Jer 31:31–34 what he had already quoted in 8:8–12.

10:19–25 For the second time (cf. 8:1–6 for the first), the writer gives a summary of the arguments for the superiority of Christ's priestly ministry.

10:19 brethren. *See note on 3:12.* As on the earlier occasion, the writer addresses his Jewish brethren with an invitation to leave behind the Levitical system and to appropriate the benefits of the New Covenant in Christ. **confidence.** An important emphasis in the epistle (*see note on 4:16*). Because of the high priestly ministry of Christ and His finished sacrifice, the Hebrews can enter boldly into the presence of God.

10:20 new. In Gr., this word originally meant "newly slain," but was understood as "recent" when the epistle was written. The way is new because the covenant is new. It is not a way provided by the Levitical system. **living way.** Though it is the path of eternal life, it was not opened by Christ's sinless life—it required His death. *See notes on 2:17, 18; 4:16.* The Hebrews were invited to embark on this way which is characterized by the eternal life of the Son of God who loved them and gave Himself for them (cf. Jn 14:6; Gal 2:20). The Christian faith was known as "the Way" among the Jews of Jerusalem (Ac 9:2) as well as among the Gentiles (Ac 19:23). Those receiving this epistle understood quite clearly that the writer was inviting them to become Christians—to join those who had been persecuted for their faith. True believers in their midst were even then suffering persecution, and those who had not committed themselves to the Way were asked to become targets of the same persecution. **veil ... flesh.** When Jesus' flesh was torn at His crucifixion, so was the temple veil that symbolically separated men from God's presence (Mt 27:51). When the High Priest on the Day of Atonement entered the Holy of Holies, the people waited outside for him to return. When Christ entered the heavenly temple He did not return. Instead, He opened the curtain and exposed the Holy of Holies so that we could follow Him. Here "flesh" is used as was "body" (v. 10) and "blood" (9:7, 12, 14, 18, 22) to refer to the sacrificial death of the Lord Jesus.

10:21 the house of God. *See note on 3:6.*

10:22 let us draw near. *See note on 7:19.* Based on what had been written, this was the heart of the invitation to those in the assembly who had not come to Christ. The same invitation is found in the first NT book to be written (Jas 4:8), where James reveals the corollary of drawing near to God: God will draw near to you. Asaph taught that it is a good thing to draw near to God (Ps 73:28). The full restoration of Israel to God's blessing is dependent upon them drawing near to Him (Jer 30:18–22). In other words, it is an eschatological invitation coming to them in "these last days" (1:2). This verse describes the prerequisites for entering the presence of God (cf. Ps 15): sincerity, security, salvation, and sanctification. **sincere heart.** The Gr. term behind "sincere" carries the ideas of being true, genuine, and without ulterior motive (cf. Jer 24:7; Mt 15:8). This one thing these particular Hebrews lacked: genuine commitment to Christ. **full assurance of faith.** *See note on 6:11.* Utter confidence in the promises of God is intended by the phrase. Such confidence will result in heartfelt assurance or security which will allow them to persevere through the coming trials. This is the first of a familiar triad: faith, hope (v. 23), and love (v. 24). **hearts sprinkled.** *See notes on 9:9, 14; 10:1–4; 1Pe 1:2.* **pure water.** The imagery in this verse is taken from the sacrificial ceremonies of the Old Covenant, where blood was sprinkled as a sign of cleansing, and the priests were continually washing themselves and the sacred vessels in basins of clear water. Being "washed with pure water" does not refer to Christian baptism, but to the Holy Spirit's purifying a person's life by means of the Word of God (cf. Eph 5:25, 26; Titus 3:5). This is purely a New Covenant picture (Jer 31:33; Eze 36:25, 26).

10:23 hold fast. Holding on, or the perseverance of the saints, is the human side of eternal security. It is not something done to maintain salvation, but is rather an evidence of salvation. *See note on 3:6.* **confession of our hope.** Affirmation of salvation. *See note on 3:1.* **without wavering.** The idea is not to follow any inclination that leads back to the Old Covenant. In other ancient literature, the same Gr. term is used of enduring torture. Persecution will come (2Ti 3:12), but God is faithful. Temptations will abound, but God is faithful to provide an escape (cf. 1Co 10:13). God's promises are reliable (1Co 10:13; 1Th 5:24; Jude 24, 25). With that confidence, the believer can persevere.

10:24 consider. The same verb is used about Jesus in 3:1. The invitation must be responded to individually, but the response also has a corporate side. They are members of a community of Hebrews whose initial attraction to Christ is in danger of eroding. They have been considering a return to the Levitical system of Judaism to avoid the persecution (cf. Jn 12:42, 43). Mutual encouragement to make full commitment is crucial. **stimulate.** The Eng. word "paroxysm" is derived from the Gr. term used here. The meaning in this context is that of stimulating or inciting someone to do something. **love and good deeds.** An example of such mutual effort in the midst of persecution was to be found at Corinth (cf. 2Co 8:1–7).

10:25 not forsaking our own assembling.

CHRIST OR JUDGMENT

26 For if we go on [A]sinning willfully after receiving [B]the knowledge of the truth, there no longer remains a sacrifice for sins, 27 but a terrifying expectation of [A]judgment and [B]THE FURY OF A FIRE WHICH WILL CONSUME THE ADVERSARIES. 28 [A]Anyone who has set aside the Law of Moses dies without mercy on *the testimony of* two or three witnesses. 29 [A]How much severer punishment do you think he will deserve [B]who has trampled under foot the Son of God, and has regarded as unclean [C]the blood of the covenant [D]by which he was sanctified, and has [E]insulted the Spirit of grace? 30 For we know Him who said, "[A]VENGEANCE IS MINE, I WILL REPAY." And again, "[B]THE LORD WILL JUDGE HIS PEOPLE." 31 It is a [A]terrifying thing to fall into the hands of the [B]living God.

32 But remember [A]the former days, [a]when, after being [B]enlightened, you endured a great [C]conflict of sufferings, 33 partly by being [A]made a public spectacle through reproaches and tribulations, and partly by becoming [B]sharers with those who were so treated. 34 For you [A]showed sympathy to the prisoners and accepted [B]joyfully the seizure of your property, knowing that you have for yourselves [C]a better possession and a lasting one. 35 Therefore, do not throw away your [A]confidence, which has a great [B]reward. 36 For you have need of [A]endurance, so that when you have [B]done the will of God, you may [C]receive [a]what was promised.

10:26 [A]Num 15:30; Heb 6:4-8; 2 Pet 2:20f [B]1 Tim 2:4 **10:27** [A]John 5:29; Heb 9:27 [B]Is 26:11; 2 Thess 1:7 **10:28** [A]Deut 17:2-6; 19:15; Matt 18:16; Heb 2:2 **10:29** [A]Heb 2:3 [B]Heb 6:6 [C]Ex 24:8; Matt 26:28; Heb 13:20 [D]Eph 5:26; Heb 9:13f; Rev 1:5 [E]1 Cor 6:11; Eph 4:30; Heb 6:4 **10:30** [A]Deut 32:35; Rom 12:19 [B]Deut 32:36 **10:31** [A]2 Cor 5:11 [B]Matt 16:16; Heb 3:12 **10:32** [a]Lit *in which* [A]Heb 5:12 [B]Heb 6:4 [C]Phil 1:30 **10:33** [A]1 Cor 4:9; Heb 12:4 [B]Phil 4:14; 1 Thess 2:14 **10:34** [A]Heb 13:3 [B]Matt 5:12 [C]Heb 9:15; 11:16; 13:14; 1 Pet 1:4f **10:35** [A]Heb 10:19 [B]Heb 2:2 **10:36** [a]Lit *the promise* [A]Luke 21:19; Heb 12:1 [B]Mark 3:35 [C]Heb 9:15

Collective and corporate worship is a vital part of spiritual life. The warning here is against apostasy in an eschatological context (cf. 2Th 2:1). The reference is to the approaching "day" (the second coming of Christ; cf. Ro 13:12; 1Co 3:13; 1Th 5:4). **encouraging.** Encouraging takes the form of comfort, warning, or strengthening. There is an eschatological urgency to the encouraging which requires an increased activity as the coming of Christ approaches (cf. 3:13; cf. 1Th 4:18).

10:26–39 *See notes on 6:1–8.* This warning passage deals with the sin of apostasy, an intentional falling away, or defection. Apostates are those who move toward Christ, hear and understand His gospel, and are on the verge of saving belief, but then rebel and turn away. This warning against apostasy is one of the most serious warnings in all of Scripture. Not all of the Hebrews would respond to the gentle invitation of vv. 19–25. Some were already beyond response.

10:26 we. The author is speaking rhetorically. In v. 39, he excludes himself and genuine believers from this category. **sinning willfully.** The Gr. term carries the idea of deliberate intention that is habitual. The sin is rejecting Christ deliberately. These are not isolated acts. According to the Mosaic legislation, such acts of deliberate, premeditated sin required exclusion from the congregation of Israel (cf. Nu 15:30, 31) and from its worship (cf. Ex 21:14). Such sins also excluded the individual from sanctuary in the cities of refuge (cf. Dt 19:11–13). **knowledge.** The Gr. term denotes specific knowledge, not general spiritual knowledge (cf. 6:4; cf. 1Ti 2:4). Though the knowledge was not defective or incomplete, the application of the knowledge was certainly flawed. Judas Iscariot is a good example of a disciple who had no lack of knowledge, but lacked faith and became the arch-apostate. **no longer.** *See note on 6:6.* The apostate is beyond salvation because he has rejected the only sacrifice that can cleanse him from sin and bring him into God's presence. To turn away from that sacrifice leaves him with no saving alternative. This is parallel to Mt 12:31 (*see note there*).

10:27 terrifying expectation. The judgment is certain to happen, so it engenders fear. **judgment and** the fury of a fire. The description is similar to that in Is 26:11 and Zep 1:18 (cf. 2Th 1:7–9). Ultimately, such judgment is that of eternity in the lake of fire (cf. Mt 13:38–42, 49, 50). **adversaries.** Actual opposition against God and toward the program of God in salvation (*see notes on Php 3:18, 19*).

10:28 Cf. Dt 17:2–7.

10:29 How much severer punishment. There will be degrees of punishment in hell. This is also clearly indicated in Mt 11:22–24 (*see notes there*). **trampled.** In the ancient Near East one of the gestures used to show contempt for someone was to "lift up the foot" against or toward them (cf. Ps 41:9). To walk on top of someone or something was a more extreme gesture showing utter contempt and scorn (cf. 2Ki 9:33; Is 14:19; Mic 7:10; Zec 10:5). Such contempt demonstrates a complete rejection of Christ as Savior and Lord. **regarded as unclean.** To reckon Christ's blood as something "unclean" is the same thing as saying that it is defiled (*see note on 9:13*) and implies that Christ was a sinner and a blemished sacrifice. Such thinking is truly blasphemous. **blood of the covenant.** *See notes on 9:14, 15.* Christ's death inaugurated or ratified the New Covenant. **sanctified.** This refers to Christ, in that He was set apart unto God (cf. Jn 17:19). It cannot refer to the apostate, because only true believers are sanctified. See Introduction: Interpretive Challenges. **insulted the Spirit of grace.** *See notes on 6:4 and 9:14.* The same title is utilized in Zec 12:10. Rejecting Christ insults the Spirit who worked through Him (Mt 12:31, 32) and who testifies of Him (Jn 15:26; 16:8–11).

10:30 Quoted from Dt 32:35, 36 (cf. Ps 135:4; Ro 12:19).

10:31 living God. *See note on 3:12.*

10:32–39 In this section, a word of encouragement is presented to counterbalance the preceding grave warning (vv. 19–31). The writer points out that the Hebrews' former experiences should stimulate them, the nearness of reward should strengthen them, and the fear of God's displeasure should prevent them from going back to Judaism.

10:32 remember. Carries the idea of carefully thinking back and reconstructing something in one's mind, not merely remembering (cf. Ac 5:41; 2Co 7:15). **enlightened.** *See note on 6:4* (cf. "knowledge of the truth" in v. 26). **a great conflict.** The word is only here in the NT. It is a picture of the struggling athlete engaged in a rigorous contest (cf. 2Ti 2:5). After being enlightened, they suffered (v. 33), became offended, and began to fall away (*see note on Mt 13:20*).

10:33 a public spectacle. The theater is alluded to with regard to the actors being placed on a stage where they can be observed by everyone. In the context of this verse, the idea is exposure to disgrace and ridicule (cf. 1Co 4:9). **sharers.** These unconverted Hebrews had been close to persecution when it happened to the believers they associated with. They perhaps had actually suffered for that identification, including the seizure of their property, but had not yet turned away because they were still interested in the prospects of heaven (v. 34). In the NT, there are examples of those who willingly exposed themselves to possible arrest and harassment because they sought to help those who were persecuted for their faith. Surprisingly, on one occasion, the Pharisees were among them. The Pharisees warned Jesus about Herod's pending attempt on Jesus' life (Lk 13:31). Among genuine believers who might be given as examples of helping the persecuted, there was Onesiphorus (2Ti 1:16–18).

10:34 the prisoners. This is one of the supposed indicators used for identifying the author of this epistle as the apostle Paul (cf. Eph 3:1; 2Ti 1:8). However, many other Christians were also imprisoned. **accepted joyfully.** Cf. Ac 5:41; 16:24, 25; Ro 5:3; Jas 1:2. **a better possession and a lasting one.** *See note on 9:15* (cf. Mt 6:19, 20; 1Pe 1:4).

10:35 throw away. Due to their current persecutions, they were tempted to run away from their outward identification with Christ and Christians and to apostatize (cf. v. 23; Dt 32:15, 18). **reward.** They are closer than ever to the eternal reward. It is no time to turn back.

10:36 done the will of God. To trust in Christ fully by living daily in the will of the Father. *See notes on Mt 7:21–28; Jas 1:22–25;* cf. Jn 6:29. **receive what was promised.** *See notes on 4:1; 6:12; 9:15.* If they would remain with the New Covenant and put their trust exclusively in Christ, they would obtain the promise of salvation for themselves.

37 [A]For yet in a very little while,
[B]He who is coming will come,
And will not delay.
38 [A]But My righteous one shall live by faith;
And if he shrinks back, My soul
has no pleasure in him.

39 But [a]we are not of those who shrink back to destruction, but of those who have faith to the [b]pre-
serving of the soul.

THE TRIUMPHS OF FAITH

11 Now faith is the [a,A]assurance of *things* [b,B]hoped
for, the [c]conviction of [C]things not seen. 2 For by
it the [A]men of old [a,B]gained approval.
3 By faith we understand that the [a,A]worlds
were prepared [B]by the word of God, so that what
is seen [C]was not made out of things which are
visible. 4 By faith [A]Abel offered to God a better
sacrifice than Cain, through which he [B]obtained
the testimony that he was righteous, God testifying [a]about his [C]gifts, and through [b]faith, though
[D]he is dead, he still speaks. 5 By faith [A]Enoch was
taken up so that he would not [B]see death; AND
HE WAS NOT FOUND BECAUSE GOD TOOK HIM UP;
for he obtained the witness that before his being taken up he was pleasing to God. 6 And without faith it is impossible to please *Him,* for he
who [A]comes to God must believe that He is and
that He is a rewarder of those who seek Him.

10:37 [A]Hab 2:3; Heb 10:25; Rev 22:20 [B]Matt 11:3 10:38 [A]Hab 2:4; Rom 1:17; Gal 3:11 10:39 [a]Lit *we are not of shrinking back...but of faith* [b]Or *possessing*
11:1 [a]Or *substance* [b]Or *expected* [c]Or *evidence* [A]Heb 3:14 [B]Heb 3:6 [C]Rom 8:24; 2 Cor 4:18; 5:7; Heb 11:7, 27 11:2 [a]Lit *obtained a* good *testimony* [A]Heb 1:1 [B]Heb 11:4, 39 11:3 [a]Lit *ages* [A]John 1:3; Heb 1:2 [B]Gen ch 1; Ps 33:6, 9; Heb 6:5; 2 Pet 3:5 [C]Rom 4:17 11:4 [a]I.e. by receiving his gifts [b]Lit *it* [A]Gen 4:4; Matt 23:35; 1 John 3:12 [B]Heb 11:2 [C]Heb 5:1 [D]Gen 4:8-10; Heb 12:24 11:5 [A]Gen 5:21-24 [B]Luke 2:26; John 8:51; Heb 2:9 11:6 [A]Heb 7:19

10:37, 38 The loose reference to Hab 2:3, 4 (cf. Ro 1:17; Gal 3:11) is introduced by a phrase taken from Is 26:20. This is the second reference to the Isaiah passage (cf. v. 27) which is part of a song of salvation. The passage in Is 26 (or, its greater context, Is 24–27) is perhaps uppermost in the writer's mind. The Habakkuk reference is altered considerably so that it is more of an interpretive paraphrase drawing on other OT concepts and contexts. Habakkuk 2:4, 5 is descriptive of the proud who do not live by faith. It is the proud who are self-sufficient and who fail to realize the necessity of patient endurance and trust in God. The proud Jew will be rejected if he does not exercise faith. He will be judged along with the nations.

10:38 My righteous one shall live by faith. *See note on Ro 1:17.* The opposite of apostasy is faith. This is a preview of the subsequent chapter. It is faith which pleases God. The individual who draws back from the knowledge of the gospel and faith will prove his apostasy.

10:39 **shrink back to destruction.** The writer expresses confidence that believing readers ("we") will not be counted among "those" who fall away to destruction. Apostates will draw back from Christ, but there are some who are near to believing who can be pulled "out of the fire" (cf. Jude 23). "Destruction," also translated "perdition," is commonly used in the NT of the everlasting punishment or judgment of unbelievers (cf. Mt 7:13; Ro 9:22; Php 1:28; 3:19; 1Ti 6:9). Judas is called the "son of perdition" (a Semitism meaning "perdition bound"; Jn 17:12). The man of lawlessness is referred to as the "son of destruction," i.e., destruction bound (2Th 2:3). **preserving of the soul.** Preservation from eschatological destruction is the concept of "preserving" in this context. In the context of Is 26:20, 21 (v. 19) the eschatological preservation includes resurrection from the dead. The writer connects faith and resurrection in the example of Abraham (11:19).

11:1–40 The 11th chapter is a moving account of faithful OT saints and given such titles as, "The Saints' Hall of Fame," "The Honor Roll of OT Saints," and "Heroes of Faith." They all attest to the value of living by faith. They compose the "cloud of witnesses" (12:1) who give powerful testimony to the Hebrews that they should come to faith in God's truth in Christ.

11:1 This verse is written in a style of Heb. poetry (used often in the Psalms), in which two parallel and nearly identical phrases are used to state the same thing. Cf. 1Pe 1:7—God tests our faith in the crucible. **assurance.** This is from the same Gr. word translated "exact representation" in 1:3 and "assurance" in 3:14. The faith described here involves the most solid possible conviction, the God-given present assurance of a future reality. **conviction of things not seen.** True faith is not based on empirical evidence, but on divine assurance, and is a gift of God (Eph 2:8).

11:2 **men of old.** In this context, the term refers to all saints, both men and women, under the older covenant, a select few of whom are described in vv. 4–40. **gained approval.** Lit. "were testified to" or "had witness given about them" (cf. vv. 4, 39). God bears witness on the behalf of these saints that they lived by faith and divine approval is granted to them.

11:3 **By faith.** Each example of faith in vv. 3–31 is formally introduced with this specific phrase. True saving faith works in obedience to God (*see notes on Jas 2:14–25*). **we.** This refers to the writer and all other true believers, present and past. **worlds.** The physical universe itself, as well as its operation and administration. **were prepared.** The concept involved in this verb (used also in 13:21) is that of equipping so that something might be made ready to fulfill its purpose. **word of God.** God's divine utterance (see, e.g., Ge 1:3, 6, 9, 11, 14). **not made.** God created the universe out of something which cannot be seen. There is the possibility that the invisible something was God's own energy or power. For more on creation, *see notes on Ge 1:1–31.*

11:4–40 Adam and Eve are passed over in this portion regarding creation because they had seen God, fellowshipped with Him, and talked with Him. Their children were the first to exercise faith in the unseen God.

11:4 **Abel.** See Ge 4:1–15. **better.** The precise reason for the superiority of Abel's sacrifice is not specifically revealed by the writer of Hebrews, but implied in 12:24 (*see notes there*). Here his concern is with Abel's faith. Both brothers knew what God required. Abel obeyed and Cain did not. Abel acted in faith, Cain in unbelief (*see notes on Ge 4:4, 5*). Through faith, Abel left testimony to all succeeding generations that a person comes to God by faith to receive righteousness. **righteous.** Because of his faith, evidenced in obedience to God's requirement for sacrifice, Abel was accounted as righteous by God (cf. Ro 4:4–8). Christ Himself referred to the righteousness of Abel (Mt 23:35). Cain's sacrifice was evidence that he was just going through the motions of ritual in a disobedient manner, not evidencing authentic faith. Without faith no one can receive imputed righteousness (cf. Ge 15:6). **testifying about his gifts.** Abel's offering proved something about his faith that was not demonstrated by Cain's offering.

11:5 The quote is from Ge 5:24. **Enoch.** *See note on Ge 5:24.* The LXX translated the Heb. idiom "Enoch walked with God" with "he pleased God." The writer combines both in the reference. Enoch was miraculously taken to heaven without dying (cf. 1Th 4:17).

11:6 **impossible to please.** Enoch pleased God because he had faith. Without such faith it is not possible for anyone to "walk with God" or "please *Him*" (cf. 10:38). **He is.** The emphasis here is on "He," the true God. Genuine faith does not simply believe that *a* divine

FAITH'S FEATURES IN HEBREWS 11	
Is certain of God's promises	v. 1
Is confident of God's power	v. 1
Perceives the divine design	v. 3
Acts on God's promises	vv. 8–22
Esteems Christ above all	v. 26
Overcomes tremendous trials	vv. 29–38

7 By faith [A]Noah, being [B]warned *by God* about [C]things not yet seen, [a,D]in reverence [E]prepared an ark for the salvation of his household, by which he condemned the world, and became an heir of [F]the righteousness which is according to faith.

8 By faith [A]Abraham, when he was called, obeyed [a]by going out to a place which he was to [B]receive for an inheritance; and he went out, not knowing where he was going. 9 By faith he lived as an alien in [A]the land of promise, as in a foreign *land,* [B]dwelling in tents with Isaac and Jacob, [C]fellow heirs of the same promise; 10 for he was looking for [A]the city which has [B]foundations, [C]whose architect and builder is God. 11 By faith even [A]Sarah herself received [a]ability to conceive, even beyond the proper time of life, since she considered Him [B]faithful who had promised. 12 Therefore there was born even of one man, and [A]him as good as dead [a]at that, *as many descendants* [B]AS THE STARS OF HEAVEN IN NUMBER, AND INNUMERABLE AS THE SAND WHICH IS BY THE SEASHORE.

13 [A]All these died in faith, [B]without receiving the promises, but [C]having seen them and having welcomed them from a distance, and [D]having confessed that they were strangers and exiles on the earth. 14 For those who say such things make it clear that they are seeking a country of their own. 15 And indeed if they had been [a]thinking of that *country* from which they went out, [A]they would have had opportunity to return. 16 But as it is, they desire a better *country,* that is, a [A]heavenly one. Therefore [B]God is not [a]ashamed to be [C]called their God; for [D]He has prepared a city for them.

17 By faith [A]Abraham, when he was tested, offered up Isaac, and he who had [B]received the promises was offering up his only begotten *son;* 18 *it was he* to whom it was said, "[A]IN ISAAC YOUR [a]DESCENDANTS SHALL BE CALLED." 19 [a]He considered that [A]God is able to raise *people* even from the dead, from which he also received him back [b]as a [B]type. 20 By faith [A]Isaac blessed Jacob and Esau, even regarding things to come. 21 By faith [A]Jacob, as he was dying, blessed each of the sons of Joseph, and [B]worshiped, *leaning* on the top of his staff. 22 By faith [A]Joseph, when he was dying, made mention of the exodus of the sons of Israel, and gave orders concerning his bones.

11:7 [a]Lit *having become reverent* [A]Gen 6:13-22 [B]Heb 8:5 [C]Heb 11:1 [D]Heb 5:7 [E]1 Pet 3:20 [F]Gen 6:9; Ezek 14:14, 20; Rom 4:13; 9:30 11:8 [a]Lit *to go out* [A]Gen 12:1-4; Acts 7:2-4 [B]Gen 12:7 11:9 [A]Acts 7:5 [B]Gen 12:8; 13:3, 18; 18:1, 9 [C]Heb 6:17 11:10 [A]Heb 12:22; 13:14 [B]Rev 21:14ff [C]Heb 11:16 11:11 [a]Lit *power for the laying down of seed* [A]Gen 17:19; 18:11-14; 21:2 [B]Heb 10:23 11:12 [a]Lit *in these things* [A]Rom 4:19 [B]Gen 15:5; 22:17; 32:12 11:13 [A]Matt 13:17 [B]Heb 11:39 [C]John 8:56; Heb 11:27 [D]Gen 23:4; 47:9; 1 Chr 29:15; Ps 39:12; Eph 2:19; 1 Pet 1:1; 2:11 11:15 [a]Or *remembering* [A]Gen 24:6-8 11:16 [a]Lit *ashamed of them, to be* [A]2 Tim 4:18 [B]Mark 8:38; Heb 2:11 [C]Gen 26:24; 28:13; Ex 3:6, 15; 4:5 [D]Heb 11:10; Rev 21:2 11:17 [A]Gen 22:1-10; James 2:21 [B]Heb 11:13 11:18 [a]Lit *seed* [A]Gen 21:12; Rom 9:7 11:19 [a]Lit *Considering* [b]Or *figuratively speaking;* lit *in a parable* [A]Rom 4:21 [B]Heb 9:9 11:20 [A]Gen 27:27-29, 39f 11:21 [A]Gen 48:1, 5, 16, 20 [B]Gen 47:31; 1 Kin 1:47 11:22 [A]Gen 50:24f; Ex 13:19

being exists, but that the God of Scripture is the *only* real and true God who exists. Not believing that God exists is equivalent to calling Him a liar (cf. 1Jn 5:10). **rewarder.** A person must believe not only that the true God exists, but also that He will reward men's faith in Him with forgiveness and righteousness, because He has promised to do so (cf. 10:35; Ge 15:1; Dt 4:29; 1Ch 28:9; Ps 58:11; Is 40:10).

11:7 Noah. See Ge 5:28–9:29; Eze 14:14. **things not yet seen.** *See notes on vv. 1, 6.* The world had not seen anything resembling the great Flood (not even rain; *see notes on Ge 7:11*), yet Noah spent 120 years (Ge 6:3) fulfilling God's command to build the massive ark (Ge 6:13–22). **reverence.** Noah treated God's message with great respect and awe (cf. 5:7). His faith was expressed in obedience (cf. Ge 6:22; 7:5). **condemned.** Noah warned the people of his time about God's impending judgment (cf. 1Pe 3:20), and is called "a preacher of righteousness" (2Pe 2:5). **heir of the righteousness.** *See notes on 6:12; 9:15.* He who was a preacher of righteousness (2Pe 2:5) also became an heir of righteousness. He believed the message he preached. Like Enoch before him (*see notes on v. 5*), Noah walked with God in faith and obedience (Ge 6:9).

11:8–19 Abraham. See Ge 11:27–25:11.

11:8 a place ... inheritance. The land of Canaan, far from his original home in Ur of the Chaldees (Ge 11:31). He went by faith.

11:9 promise. Neither Abraham, Isaac, nor Jacob were able to settle permanently in or possess the land God promised to them (v. 10). Abraham first went there in faith, and they all lived there in faith, believing in a promise of possession that would not be fulfilled for many generations beyond their lifetimes (Ge 12:7).

11:10 city. Abraham's ultimate and permanent Promised Land was heaven which, through faith, he knew he would ultimately inherit. This city is mentioned again in v. 16; 12:22; 13:14.

11:11, 12 Sarah. See Ge 11:27–23:2; 1Pe 3:5, 6.

11:11 beyond the proper time. At 90 (Ge 17:17), she was long past child-bearing age and had never been able to conceive. God enabled her, however, because of her faith in His promise (Ge 21:1–3).

11:12 as good as dead. At 99, Abraham was well beyond the age to father children apart from divine intervention (Ge 17:1, 15–17; 21:1–5). stars ... sand. This is hyperbole to stress the vastness of the population that would come from Abraham's loins. See Ge 15:4, 5; 22:17.

11:13 All these. The reference is to the patriarchs only (Abraham, Isaac, and Jacob). This interpretation is supported by the fact that the promises began with Abraham (cf. Ac 7:17; Ro 4:13; Gal 3:14–18) and were passed on to Isaac (Ge 26:2–5, 24) and Jacob (Ge 28:10–15). In addition, only those individuals fit the description in v. 15 and Enoch did not die. *See note on 6:15.* These people of faith didn't know when they would inherit the promise. They had a life in the land, but did not possess it.

11:13–16 strangers and exiles. See Ge 23:4. Their faith was patient and endured great hardships because they believed God had something better. They had no desire to go back to Ur, but did long for heaven (Job 19:25, 26; Ps 27:4).

11:16 their God. God referred to Himself as "the God of Abraham, the God of Isaac, and the God of Jacob" (Ex 3:6; cf. Ge 28:13; Mt 22:32). This is a significant covenant formula whereby an individual or a people identified with God and He with them (cf. Lv 26:12). **a city.** *See note on 12:22.*

11:17–19 See Ge 22:1–18. Abraham again proved his faith by his willingness to give back to God his son of promise, Isaac, whom he had miraculously received because of his faith. It would take an even greater miracle for them to replace Isaac by natural means. He trusted God for a resurrection. Cf. Ro 4:16–21.

11:17, 18 only begotten. Isaac was not the only son of Abraham—there was also Ishmael through Hagar (Ge 16:1–16). The term refers to someone who is unique, one of a kind (cf. Jn 1:14). Isaac was the only son born according to God's promise and was the only heir of that promise. The quotation from Ge 21:12 proves this latter point.

11:19 even from the dead. Believing that God's promise regarding Isaac was unconditional, Abraham came to the conclusion that God would fulfill that promise even if it required raising Isaac from the dead (cf. Ge 22:5). **type.** The word is the same as in 9:9, which is the basis for the Eng. word "parable." Abraham received Isaac back from the dead, as it were, even though Isaac had not been slain.

11:20 Isaac. See Ge 27:1–28:5.

11:21 Jacob. See Ge 47:28–49:33. **each of the sons.** Both of Joseph's sons, Ephraim and Manasseh, received a blessing from Jacob. Consequently, two tribes descended from Joseph, whereas only one tribe descended from each of his brothers (see Ge 47:31; 48:1, 5, 16). **top of his staff.** According to Ge 47:31, Jacob leaned upon his "bed." The two words (staff, bed) in Heb. have exactly the same consonants. Old Testament Heb. mss. were copied without vowels. Later Heb. mss., between the sixth and ninth centuries A.D., took the word as "bed." The LXX, in the third century B.C., rendered it "staff," which seems more likely although both could be factual.

11:22 Joseph. See Ge 37:1–50:26. Joseph spent all of his adult life in Egypt and, even though he was a fourth-generation heir of the promise given to Abraham, he never returned to Canaan while he was alive. Yet, facing death, he still had faith that God would fulfill His promise and demonstrated that

23 By faith [A]Moses, when he was born, was hidden
for three months by his parents, because they saw
he was a beautiful child; and they were not afraid
of the [B]king's edict. 24 By faith Moses, [A]when he had
grown up, refused to be called the son of Pharaoh's
daughter, 25 choosing rather to [A]endure ill-treatment
with the people of God than to enjoy the passing
pleasures of sin, 26 [A]considering the reproach of
[a]Christ greater riches than the treasures of Egypt;
for he was looking to the [B]reward. 27 By faith he [A]left
Egypt, not [B]fearing the wrath of the king; for he endured, as [C]seeing Him who is unseen. 28 By faith he
[a,A]kept the Passover and the sprinkling of the blood,
so that [B]he who destroyed the firstborn would not
touch them. 29 By faith they [A]passed through the
Red Sea as though *they were passing* through dry
land; and the Egyptians, when they attempted it,
were [a]drowned.
30 By faith [A]the walls of Jericho fell down [B]after
they had been encircled for seven days. 31 By faith
[A]Rahab the harlot did not perish along with those
who were disobedient, after she had welcomed the
spies [a]in peace.
32 And what more shall I say? For time will fail
me if I tell of [A]Gideon, [B]Barak, [C]Samson, [D]Jephthah,
of [E]David and [F]Samuel and the prophets, 33 who
by faith [A]conquered kingdoms, [B]performed *acts
of* righteousness, [C]obtained promises, [D]shut the
mouths of lions, 34 [A]quenched the power of fire,
[B]escaped the edge of the sword, from weakness
were made strong, [C]became mighty in war, [C]put foreign armies to flight. 35 [A]Women received *back* their
dead by resurrection; and others were tortured, not
accepting their [a]release, so that they might obtain
a better resurrection; 36 and others [a]experienced
mockings and scourgings, yes, also [A]chains and imprisonment. 37 They were [A]stoned, they were [B]sawn
in two, [a]they were tempted, they were [C]put to death
with the sword; they went about [D]in sheepskins,
in goatskins, being destitute, afflicted, [E]ill-treated

11:23 [A]Ex 2:2 [B]Ex 1:16, 22 11:24 [A]Ex 2:10, 11ff 11:25 [A]Heb 11:37 11:26 [a]I.e. the Messiah [A]Luke 14:33; Phil 3:7f [B]Heb 2:2 11:27 [A]Ex 2:15; 12:50f; 13:17f [B]Ex 2:14; 10:28f [C]Col 1:15; Heb 11:1, 13 11:28 [a]Lit *has kept* [A]Ex 12:21ff [B]Ex 12:23, 29f; 1 Cor 10:10 11:29 [a]Lit *swallowed up* [A]Ex 14:22-29 11:30 [A]Josh 6:20 [B]Josh 6:15f 11:31 [a]Lit *with* [A]Josh 2:9ff; 6:23; James 2:25 11:32 [A]Judg ch 6-8 [B]Judg ch 4, 5 [C]Judg ch 13-16 [D]Judg ch 11, 12 [E]1 Sam 16:1, 13 [F]1 Sam 1:20 11:33 [A]Judg ch 4, 7, 11, 14; 2 Sam 5:17-20; 8:1f; 10:12 [B]1 Sam 12:4; 2 Sam 8:15 [C]2 Sam 7:11f [D]Judg 14:6; 1 Sam 17:34ff; Dan 6:22 11:34 [A]Dan 3:23ff [B]Ex 18:4; 1 Sam 18:11; 19:10; 1 Kin ch 19; 2 Kin ch 6; Ps 144:10 [C]Judg 7:21; 15:8, 15f; 1 Sam 17:51f; 2 Sam 8:1-6; 10:15ff 11:35 [a]Lit *redemption* [A]1 Kin 17:23; 2 Kin 4:36f 11:36 [a]Lit *received the trial of* [A]Gen 39:20; 1 Kin 22:27; 2 Chr 18:26; Jer 20:2; 37:15 11:37 [a]One early ms does not contain *they were tempted* [A]1 Kin 21:13; 2 Chr 24:21 [B]2 Sam 12:31; 1 Chr 20:3 [C]1 Kin 19:10; Jer 26:23 [D]1 Kin 19:13, 19; 2 Kin 2:8, 13f; Zech 13:4 [E]Heb 11:25; 13:3

confidence by making his brothers promise to take his bones back to Canaan for burial (Ge 50:24, 25; cf. Ex 13:19; Jos 24:32).

11:23–29 Moses. See Ex 1–15; Ac 7:17–36.

11:23 beautiful child. Meaning "favored," in this case divinely favored (Ac 7:20; cf. Ex 2:2). The faith described here is actually that exercised by Moses' parents, although it is unclear how much Moses' parents understood about God's plan for their child.

11:24 Moses refused the fame he could have in Egypt if he would have capitalized on his position as the adopted son of Pharaoh's daughter (cf. Ex 2:10).

11:25 with the people of God. Moses would have sinned had he refused to take on the responsibility God gave him regarding Israel, and he had a clear and certain conviction that "God was granting them deliverance through him" (Ac 7:25). Moses repudiated the pleasures of Egypt.

11:26 reproach of Christ. Moses suffered reproach for the sake of Christ in the sense that he identified with Messiah's people in their suffering (v. 25). In addition, Moses identified himself with the Messiah because of his own role as leader and prophet (cf. 12:2; Dt 18:15; Pss 69:9; 89:51). Moses knew of the sufferings and glory of the Messiah (cf. Jn 5:46; Ac 26:22, 23; 1Pe 1:10–12). Anyone who suffers because of genuine faith in God and for the redemptive gospel suffers for the sake of Christ (cf. 13:12, 13; 1Pe 4:14).

11:27 left Egypt. Moses left Egypt for the first time when he fled for his life after killing the Egyptian slave master (Ex 2:14, 15). That time he did fear Pharaoh's wrath. On the second occasion, he turned his back on Egypt and all that it represented. This leaving was not for fear of Pharaoh, so it is the one in view here. **seeing Him.** Moses' faith was such that he responded to God's commands as though God were standing visibly before him. This was the basis for his loyalty to God, and it should be a believer's example for loyalty (cf. 2Co 4:16–18).

11:28 Passover. See Ex 12.

11:29 Red Sea. See Ex 14, 15. When they first reached the shores of the Red Sea, the people feared for their lives (Ex 14:11, 21). But upon hearing Moses' pronouncement of God's protection (Ex 14:13, 14), they went forward in faith.

11:30 Jericho. See Jos 6. The people did nothing militarily to cause the fall of Jericho; they simply followed God's instructions in faith. Cf. 2Co 10:4.

11:31 Rahab. See Jos 2:1–24; 6:22–25; Mt 1:5; Jas 2:25.

11:32 All of the men listed in this verse held a position of power or authority, but none of them is praised for his personal status or abilities. Instead, they are recognized for what each one had accomplished by faith in God. They are not listed chronologically, but are listed in pairs with the more important member mentioned first (cf. 1Sa 12:11). See Jdg 6–9 (Gideon); 4, 5 (Barak); 13–16 (Samson); 11, 12 (Jephthah). **David.** David is the only king mentioned in this verse. All the others are judges or prophets. David could also be considered a prophet (see 4:7; 2Sa 23:1–3; Mk 12:36). Cf. 1Sa 13:14; 16:1, 12; Ac 13:22. **Samuel and the prophets.** Samuel was the last of the judges and the first of the prophets (cf. 1Sa 7:15; Ac 3:24; 13:20). He anointed David as king (1Sa 16:13) and was known as a man of intercessory prayer (1Sa 12:19, 23; Jer 15:1).

11:33–38 The many accomplishments and sufferings described in these verses apply generally to those faithful saints. Some experienced great success, whereas others suffered great affliction. The point is that they all courageously and uncompromisingly followed God, regardless of the earthly outcome. They placed their trust in Him and in His promises (cf. 6:12; 2Ti 3:12).

11:33 conquered kingdoms. Joshua, the judges, David, and others. **performed *acts of* righteousness.** Righteous kings like David, Solomon, Asa, Jehoshaphat, Joash, Hezekiah, and Josiah. **obtained promises.** Abraham, Moses, David, and Solomon. **shut the mouths of lions.** Samson (Jdg 14:5, 6), David (1Sa 17:34, 35), Daniel (Da 6:22).

11:34 quenched the power of fire. Shadrach, Meshach, and Abednego (Da 3:19–30). **escaped the edge of the sword.** David (1Sa 18:4, 11; 19:9, 10), Elijah (1Ki 19:1–3, 10), and Elisha (2Ki 6:15–19). **weakness.** Ehud (Jdg 3:12–30), Jael (Jdg 4:17–24), Gideon (Jdg 6:15, 16; 7:1–25), Samson (Jdg 16:21–30), and Hezekiah (Is 38:1–6). Cf. 1Co 1:27; 2Co 12:10.

11:35 Women received *back* their dead. The widow of Zarephath (1Ki 17:22) and the woman of Shunem (2Ki 4:34). **tortured.** The word indicates that they were beaten to death while strapped to some sort of rack (cf. 2 Macc. 6, 7 about Eleazar and the mother with 7 sons who were martyrs). **better resurrection.** *See note on 9:27.* The deliverance from certain death or near death would be like returning from the dead, but would not be the promised resurrection. This was especially true of those who had died and were raised. The first time they were raised from the dead was merely resuscitation, not the true and glorious final resurrection (Da 12:2; cf. Mt 5:10; Jas 1:12).

11:36 others. Joseph (Ge 39:20), Micaiah (1Ki 22:27), Elisha (2Ki 2:23), Hanani (2Ch 16:10), Jeremiah (Jer 20:1–6; 37:15), and others (2Ch 36:16).

11:37 stoned. The prophet Zechariah (son of Jehoiada) was killed in this fashion (*see notes on 2Ch 24:20–22; Mt 23:35*). **sawn in two.** According to tradition, this was the method Manasseh employed to execute Isaiah. **put to death with the sword.** Uriah the prophet died in this fashion (Jer 26:23; cf. 1Ki 19:10). However, the expression here may refer to the mass execution of God's people; several such incidents occurred during the time of the Maccabees in the 400 years between the OT and NT (see Introduction to the Intertestamental Period). **went about.** Many of God's people suffered from poverty and persecution (cf. Ps 107:4–9).

38 (*men* of whom the world was not worthy), [A]wan-
dering in deserts and mountains and caves and
holes [a]in the ground.
39 And all these, having [a,A]gained approval
through their faith, [B]did not receive [b]what was
promised, 40 because God had [a]provided [A]something
better for us, so that [B]apart from us they would not
be made perfect.

JESUS, THE EXAMPLE

12 Therefore, since we have so great a cloud of
witnesses surrounding us, let us also [A]lay
aside every encumbrance and the sin which so easily entangles us, and let us [B]run with [C]endurance the
race that is set before us, 2 [a]fixing our eyes on Jesus,
the [b,A]author and perfecter of faith, who for the joy
set before Him [B]endured the cross, [C]despising the
shame, and has [D]sat down at the right hand of the
throne of God.
3 For [A]consider Him who has endured such hostility by sinners against Himself, so that you will
not grow weary [a,B]and lose heart.

A FATHER'S DISCIPLINE

4 [A]You have not yet resisted [a,B]to the point of shedding blood in your striving against sin; 5 and you
have forgotten the exhortation which is addressed
to you as sons,

"[A]MY SON, DO NOT REGARD LIGHTLY
THE DISCIPLINE OF THE LORD,
NOR [B]FAINT WHEN YOU ARE
REPROVED BY HIM;
6 [A]FOR THOSE [B]WHOM THE LORD
LOVES HE DISCIPLINES,
AND HE SCOURGES EVERY SON
WHOM HE RECEIVES."

7 It is for discipline that you endure; [A]God deals with
you as with sons; for what son is there whom *his*
father does not discipline? 8 But if you are without
discipline, [A]of which all have become partakers, then
you are illegitimate children and not sons. 9 Furthermore, we had [a]earthly fathers to discipline us,
and we [A]respected them; shall we not much rather
be subject to [B]the Father of [b]spirits, and [C]live? 10 For
they disciplined us for a short time as seemed best
to them, but He *disciplines us* for *our* good, [A]so that
we may share His holiness. 11 All discipline [A]for the
moment seems not to be joyful, but sorrowful; yet
to those who have been trained by it, afterwards it
yields the [B]peaceful fruit of righteousness.

11:38 [a]Lit *of* [A]1 Kin 18:4, 13; 19:9 11:39 [a]Lit *obtained a testimony* [b]Lit *the promise* [A]Heb 11:2 [B]Heb 10:36; 11:13 11:40 [a]Or *foreseen* [A]Heb 11:16 [B]Rev 6:11 12:1 [A]Rom 13:12; Eph 4:22 [B]1 Cor 9:24; Gal 2:2 [C]Heb 10:36 12:2 [a]Lit *looking to* [b]Or *leader* [A]Heb 2:10 [B]Phil 2:8f; Heb 2:9 [C]1 Cor 1:18, 23; Heb 13:13 [D]Heb 1:3 12:3 [a]Lit *fainting in your souls* [A]Rev 2:3 [B]Gal 6:9; Heb 12:5 12:4 [a]Lit *as far as blood* [A]Heb 10:32ff; 13:13 [B]Phil 2:8 12:5 [A]Job 5:17; Prov 3:11 [B]Heb 12:3 12:6 [A]Prov 3:12 [B]Ps 119:75; Rev 3:19 12:7 [A]Deut 8:5; 2 Sam 7:14; Prov 13:24; 19:18; 23:13f 12:8 [A]1 Pet 5:9 12:9 [a]Lit *fathers of our flesh* [b]Or *our spirits* [A]Luke 18:2 [B]Num 16:22; 27:16; Rev 22:6 [C]Is 38:16 12:10 [A]2 Pet 1:4 12:11 [A]1 Pet 1:6 [B]Is 32:17; 2 Tim 4:8; James 3:17f

11:38 See 1Ki 18:4, 13; 19:9.

11:39, 40 something better. They had faith in the ultimate fulfillment of the eternal promises in the covenant (v. 13). See Introduction: Historical and Theological Themes.

11:40 apart from us. The faith of OT saints looked forward to the promised salvation, whereas the faith of those after Christ looks back to the fulfillment of the promise. Both groups are characterized by genuine faith and are saved by Christ's atoning work on the cross (cf. Eph 2:8, 9).

12:1 Therefore. This is a very crucial transition word offering an emphatic conclusion (cf. 1Th 4:8) to the section which began in 10:19. **witnesses.** The deceased people of chap. 11 give witness to the value and blessing of living by faith. Motivation for running "the race" is not in the possibility of receiving praise from observing heavenly saints. Rather, the runner is inspired by the godly examples those saints set during their lives. The great crowd is not comprised of spectators but rather is comprised of ones whose past life of faith encourages others to live that way (cf. 11:2, 4, 5, 33, 39). **let us.** The reference is to those Hebrews who had made a profession of Christ, but had not gone all the way to full faith. They had not yet begun the race, which starts with salvation. The writer has invited them to accept salvation in Christ and join the race. **every encumbrance.** Different from the "sin" mentioned next, this refers to the main encumbrance weighing down the Hebrews, which was the Levitical system with its stifling legalism. The athlete would strip away every piece of unnecessary clothing before competing in the race. The outward things emphasized by the Levitical system not only impede, they "entangle." **sin.** In this context, this focuses first on the particular sin of unbelief—refusing to turn away from the Levitical sacrifices to the perfect sacrifice, Jesus Christ (cf. Jn 16:8–11), as well as other sins cherished by the unbeliever. **endurance.** Endurance is the steady determination to keep going, regardless of the temptation to slow down or give up (cf. 1Co 9:24, 25). **race.** The athletic metaphor presents the faith-filled life as a demanding, grueling effort. The Eng. word "agony" is derived from the Gr. word used here. *See note on Mt 7:14.*

12:2 fixing our eyes on. They were to look to Jesus as the object of faith and salvation (cf. 11:26, 27; Ac 7:55, 56; Php 3:8). **author.** *See note on 2:10.* The term means originator or preeminent example. **perfecter.** *See note on 5:14.* The term expresses the idea of carrying through to perfect completion (cf. Jn 19:30). **the joy.** Jesus persevered so that He might receive the joy of accomplishment of the Father's will and exaltation (cf. 1:9; Ps 16:9–11; Lk 10:21–24). **right hand.** *See note on 1:3.*

12:3 consider Him. Jesus is the supreme example of willingness to suffer in obedience to God. He faced "hostility" (the same word as "opposed" in Lk 2:34) and endured even the cruel cross. The same opposition is faced by all who follow Him (Ac 28:22; Gal 6:17; Col 1:24; 2Ti 3:12). **weary and lose heart.** Believers' pressures, exhaustion, and persecutions (cf. Gal 6:9) are as nothing compared to Christ's.

12:4 shedding blood. None of the Hebrews had experienced such intense exhaustion or persecution that it brought them to death or martyrdom. Since Stephen (Ac 7:60), James (Ac 12:1), and others (cf. Ac 9:1; 22:4; 26:10) had faced martyrdom in Jerusalem, it would appear to rule out that city as the residence of this epistle's recipients (see Introduction: Author and Date).

12:5, 6 Here the writer recalls and expounds Pr 3:11, 12. Trials and sufferings in the Christian's life come from God, who uses them to educate and discipline believers by such experiences. Such dealings are evidence of God's love for His own children (cf. 2Co 12:7–10).

12:6 scourges. This refers to flogging with a whip, a severe and painful form of beating that was a common Jewish practice (cf. Mt 10:17; 23:34).

12:7, 8 sons. Because all are imperfect and need discipline and training, all true children of God are chastened at one time or another, in one way or another.

12:8 illegitimate. The word is found only here in the NT, but is used elsewhere in Gr. literature of those born to slaves or concubines. There could be in this an implied reference to Hagar and Ishmael (Ge 16), Abraham's concubine and illegitimate son.

12:9 be subject. Respect for God equals submission to His will and law, and those who willingly receive the Lord's chastening will have a richer, more abundant life (cf. Ps 119:165). **Father of spirits.** Probably best translated as "Father of our spirits," it is in contrast to "human fathers" (lit. "fathers of our flesh").

12:10 ***our* good.** Imperfect human fathers discipline imperfectly; but God is perfect and therefore His discipline is perfect and always for the spiritual good of His children.

12:11 trained. The same word was used in 5:14 (*see note there*; cf. 1Ti 4:7). **fruit of righteousness.** This is the same phrase as in Jas 3:18.

12 Therefore, [a,A]strengthen the hands that are
weak and the knees that are feeble, 13 and [A]make
straight paths for your feet, so that *the limb* which
is lame may not be put out of joint, but rather [B]be
healed.

14 [A]Pursue peace with all men, and the [B]sancti-
fication without which no one will [C]see the Lord.
15 See to it that no one [A]comes short of the grace of
God; that no [B]root of bitterness springing up causes
trouble, and by it many be [C]defiled; 16 that *there be*
no [A]immoral or [B]godless person like Esau, [C]who sold
his own birthright for a *single* meal. 17 For you know
that even afterwards, [A]when he desired to inherit
the blessing, he was rejected, for he found no place
for repentance, though he sought for it with tears.

CONTRAST OF SINAI AND ZION

18 [A]For you have not come to [B]*a mountain* that can
be touched and to a blazing fire, and to darkness
and gloom and whirlwind, 19 and to the [A]blast of
a trumpet and the [B]sound of words which *sound
was such that* those who heard [C]begged that no
further word be spoken to them. 20 For they could
not bear the command, "[A]IF EVEN A BEAST TOUCHES
THE MOUNTAIN, IT WILL BE STONED." 21 And so terrible
was the sight, *that* Moses said, "[A]I AM FULL OF FEAR
and trembling." 22 But [A]you have come to Mount
Zion and to [B]the city of [C]the living God, [D]the heavenly Jerusalem, and to [E]myriads of [a]angels, 23 to the
general assembly and [A]church of the firstborn who
[B]are enrolled in heaven, and to God, [C]the Judge of
all, and to the [D]spirits of *the* righteous made perfect,
24 and to Jesus, the [A]mediator of a new covenant,
and to the [B]sprinkled blood, which speaks better
than [C]*the blood* of Abel.

THE UNSHAKEN KINGDOM

25 [A]See to it that you do not refuse Him who is
[B]speaking. For [C]if those did not escape when they
[D]refused him who [E]warned *them* on earth, [a]much
less *will* we *escape* who turn away from Him who
[E]*warns* from heaven. 26 And [A]His voice shook the
earth then, but now He has promised, saying, "[B]YET
ONCE MORE I WILL SHAKE NOT ONLY THE EARTH, BUT
ALSO THE HEAVEN." 27 This *expression,* "Yet once
more," denotes [A]the removing of those things
which can be shaken, as of created things, so that
those things which cannot be shaken may remain.

12:12 [a]Lit *make straight* [A]Is 35:3 12:13 [A]Prov 4:26; Gal 2:14 [B]Gal 6:1; James 5:16 12:14 [A]Rom 14:19 [B]Rom 6:22; Heb 12:10 [C]Matt 5:8; Heb 9:28 12:15 [A]2 Cor 6:1; Gal 5:4; Heb 4:1 [B]Deut 29:18 [C]Titus 1:15 12:16 [A]Heb 13:4 [B]1 Tim 1:9 [C]Gen 25:33f 12:17 [A]Gen 27:30-40 12:18 [A]2 Cor 3:7-13; Heb 12:18ff [B]Ex 19:12, 16ff; 20:18; Deut 4:11; 5:22 12:19 [A]Ex 19:16, 19; 20:18; Matt 24:31 [B]Ex 19:19; Deut 4:12 [C]Ex 20:19; Deut 5:25; 18:16 12:20 [A]Ex 19:12f 12:21 [A]Deut 9:19 12:22 [a]Or *angels in festive gathering, and to the church* [A]Rev 14:1 [B]Eph 2:19; Phil 3:20; Heb 11:10; Rev 21:2 [C]Heb 3:12 [D]Gal 4:26; Heb 11:16 [E]Rev 5:11 12:23 [A]Ex 4:22; Heb 2:12 [B]Luke 10:20 [C]Gen 18:25; Ps 50:6; 94:2 [D]Heb 11:40; Rev 6:9, 11 12:24 [A]1 Tim 2:5; Heb 8:6; 9:15 [B]Heb 9:19; 10:22; 1 Pet 1:2 [C]Gen 4:10; Heb 11:4 12:25 [a]Lit *much rather we* will not escape... [A]Heb 3:12 [B]Heb 1:1 [C]Heb 2:2f; 10:28f [D]Heb 12:19 [E]Ex 20:22; Heb 8:5; 11:7 12:26 [A]Ex 19:18; Judg 5:4f [B]Hag 2:6 12:27 [A]Is 34:4; 54:10; 65:17; Rom 8:19, 21; 1 Cor 7:31; Heb 1:10ff

12:12–17 This passage exhorts believers to act on the divine truths laid out in the previous passages. Truth that is known but not obeyed becomes a judgment rather than a benefit (cf. 13:22).

12:12, 13 The author returns to the race metaphor begun in vv. 1–3 (cf. Pr 4:25–27) and incorporates language taken from Is 35:3 to describe the disciplined individual's condition like a weary runner whose arms drop and knees wobble. When experiencing trials in his life, the believer must not allow the circumstances to get the best of him. Instead, he must endure and get his second wind so as to be renewed to continue the race.

12:14 **Pursue ... sanctification.** In this epistle, it is explained as 1) a drawing near to God with full faith and a cleansed conscience (10:14, 22), and 2) a genuine acceptance of Christ as the Savior and sacrifice for sin, bringing the sinner into fellowship with God. Unbelievers will not be drawn to accept Christ if believers' lives do not demonstrate the qualities God desires, including peace and holiness (cf. Jn 13:35; 1Ti 4:3; 1Pe 1:16).

12:15 **See to it.** Believers are to watch their own lives, so as to give a testimony of peace and holiness, as well as to look out for and help those in their midst who are in need of salvation. **comes short of the grace of God.** *See notes on 4:1; 6:6; 10:26.* This means to come too late and be left out. Here is another mention of the intellectually convinced Jews in that assembly, who knew the gospel and were enamored with Christ, but still stood on the edge of apostasy. **root of bitterness.** This is the attitude of apostates within the church who are corruptive influences. Cf. Dt 29:18.

12:16, 17 See Ge 25:29–34 and 27:1–39. Esau desired God's blessings, but he did not want God. He regretted what he had done, but he did not repent. Esau is an example of those who willfully sin against God and who are given no second chance because of their exposure to the truth and their advanced state of hardness (cf. 6:6; 10:26). Esau was an example of the "godless" person.

12:16 **immoral.** This refers to the sexually immoral in general. Apostasy is often closely linked with immorality (cf. 2Pe 2:10, 14, 18; Jude 8, 16, 18).

12:18–29 The writer proceeds to give an exposition based upon Israel's encounter with God at Mt. Sinai (see Ex 19, 20; Dt 4:10–24).

12:18 See Ex 19:12, 13; Dt 4:11; 5:22.

12:19 **blast of a trumpet.** See Ex 19:16, 19; Dt 4:12.

12:20 Quoted from Ex 19:12, 13 (cf. 20:19; Dt 5:23, 24).

12:21 Quoted from Dt 9:19.

12:22 **Mount Zion.** As opposed to Mt. Sinai, where God gave the Mosaic law which was foreboding and terrifying, Mt. Zion here is not the earthly one in Jerusalem, but God's heavenly abode, which is inviting and gracious. No one could please God on Sinai's terms, which was perfect fulfillment of the law (Gal 3:10–12). Zion, however, is accessible to all who come to God through Jesus Christ (cf. Ps 132:13, 14; Is 46:13; Zec 2:10; Gal 4:21–31). **Mount Zion ... city of the living God ... heavenly Jerusalem.** These are synonyms for heaven itself. For a description of the abode of God, the city of Jerusalem in heaven, *see notes on Rev 21:1–22:5.* **myriads.** The Gr. word is often translated 10,000. See Rev 5:11, 12.

12:23 **general assembly.** The term here means "a gathering for public festival." It does not likely describe a distinct group as if different from the church, but describes the attitude of the innumerable angels in heaven in a festal gathering around the throne of God. **church of the firstborn.** The firstborn is Jesus Christ (*see note on 1:6*). The "church" is comprised of believers who are fellow heirs with Christ, the preeminent One among many brethren (Ro 8:17, 29). **righteous made perfect.** *See notes on 5:14* (cf. 11:40). These are the OT saints in distinction from the "church of the firstborn," who are the NT believers.

12:24 **mediator.** *See note on 7:22* (cf. 8:6–10; 9:15). **better.** *See notes on 6:9; 9:23.* Abel's sacrifice was pleasing to God because it was offered in faith and obedience (cf. 11:4), but it had no atoning power. Jesus' blood alone was sufficient to cleanse sin (cf. 1Jn 1:7). The sacrifice of Christ brought redemption (9:12), forgiveness (9:26), and complete salvation (10:10, 14). **than *the blood* of Abel.** The blood of Abel's sacrifice only provided a temporary covering, but Christ's blood sacrifice declares eternal forgiveness (cf. Col 1:20).

12:25 **refused.** *See note on v. 19,* where the same word describes the conduct of the Israelites at Mt. Sinai. **much less.** The consequences for apostates are dire indeed. The judgment to be experienced and the expected terror is far in excess of that on Mt. Sinai.

12:26 Quoted from Hag 2:6.

12:26, 27 shake not only the earth. At Mt. Sinai, God shook the earth. From Zion, He will shake the heavens, the entire universe (cf. Is 13:13; 34:4; 65:17, 22; 2Pe 3:10–13; Rev 6:12–14; 20:11; 21:1).

12:27 Everything physical ("things ... shaken") will be destroyed; only eternal

28 Therefore, since we receive a [A]kingdom which
cannot be shaken, let us [a]show gratitude, by which
we may [B]offer to God an acceptable service with
reverence and awe; 29 for [A]our God is a consuming fire.

THE CHANGELESS CHRIST

13 Let [A]love of the brethren continue. 2 Do not
neglect to [A]show hospitality to strangers,
for by this some have [B]entertained angels without knowing it. 3 [A]Remember [B]the prisoners, as
though in prison with them, *and* those who are
ill-treated, since you yourselves also are in the
body. 4 [A]Marriage *is to be held* in honor among
all, and the *marriage* bed *is to be* undefiled; [B]for
fornicators and adulterers God will judge. 5 *Make
sure that* your character is [A]free from the love
of money, [B]being content with what you have;
for He Himself has said, "[C]I WILL NEVER DESERT
YOU, NOR WILL I EVER FORSAKE YOU," 6 so that we
confidently say,

"[A]THE LORD IS MY HELPER, I
WILL NOT BE AFRAID.
WHAT WILL MAN DO TO ME?"

7 Remember [A]those who led you, who spoke [B]the
word of God to you; and considering the [a]result of
their conduct, [C]imitate their faith. 8 [A]Jesus Christ *is*
the same yesterday and today and forever. 9 [A]Do not
be carried away by varied and strange teachings; for
it is good for the heart to [B]be strengthened by grace,
not by [C]foods, [D]through which those who [a]were so occupied were not benefited. 10 We have an altar [A]from
which those [B]who serve the [a]tabernacle have no right
to eat. 11 For [A]the bodies of those animals whose blood
is brought into the holy place by the high priest *as an
offering* for sin, are burned outside the camp. 12 Therefore Jesus also, [A]that He might sanctify the people
[B]through His own blood, suffered [C]outside the gate.
13 So, let us go out to Him outside the camp, [A]bearing
His reproach. 14 For here [A]we do not have a lasting
city, but we are seeking [B]*the city* which is to come.

12:28 [a]Lit *have* [A]Dan 2:44 [B]Heb 13:15, 21 12:29 [A]Deut 4:24; 9:3; Is 33:14; 2 Thess 1:7; Heb 10:27, 31 13:1 [A]Rom 12:10; 1 Thess 4:9; 1 Pet 1:22 13:2 [A]Matt 25:35; Rom 12:13; 1 Pet 4:9 [B]Gen 18:1ff; 19:1f 13:3 [A]Col 4:18 [B]Matt 25:36; Heb 10:34 13:4 [A]1 Cor 7:38; 1 Tim 4:3 [B]1 Cor 6:9; Gal 5:19, 21; 1 Thess 4:6 13:5 [A]Eph 5:3; Col 3:5; 1 Tim 3:3 [B]Phil 4:11 [C]Deut 31:6, 8; Josh 1:5 13:6 [A]Ps 118:6 13:7 [a]Or *end of their life* [A]Heb 13:17, 24 [B]Luke 5:1 [C]Heb 6:12 13:8 [A]2 Cor 1:19; Heb 1:12 13:9 [a]Lit *walked* [A]Eph 4:14; 5:6; Jude 12 [B]2 Cor 1:21; Col 2:7 [C]Col 2:16 [D]Heb 9:10 13:10 [a]Or *sacred tent* [A]1 Cor 10:18 [B]Heb 8:5 13:11 [A]Ex 29:14; Lev 4:12, 21; 9:11; 16:27; Num 19:3, 7 13:12 [A]Eph 5:26; Heb 2:11 [B]Heb 9:12 [C]John 19:17 13:13 [A]Luke 9:23; Heb 11:26; 12:2 13:14 [A]Heb 10:34; 12:27 [B]Eph 2:19; Heb 2:5; 11:10, 16; 12:22

things ("which cannot be shaken") will remain.

12:28 kingdom. God will create "a new heaven and a new earth … the holy city, new Jerusalem" (Rev 21:1, 2), which will be eternal and immovable. **let us show gratitude.** *See note on 4:16.* **with reverence and awe.** *See note on 11:7* (cf. 5:7). The second word has to do with the apprehension felt due to being in God's presence.

12:29 consuming fire. See Dt 4:24. God's law given at Sinai prescribed many severe punishments, but the punishment is far worse for those who reject His offer of salvation through His own Son, Jesus Christ (cf. Lk 3:16, 17). This verse is to be related to 10:29–31.

13:1 The last chapter of the epistle focuses on some of the essential practical ethics of Christian living. These ethics help portray the true gospel to the world, encourage others to believe in Christ, and bring glory to God. The first of these is love for fellow believers (cf. Jn 13:35). Although the primary reference would be to Christians, the writer must have had emotions similar to those of the apostle Paul when it came to considering his fellow Hebrews (see Ro 9:3, 4).

13:2 show hospitality. The second grace needing development was the extension of love to those who were strangers (cf. Ro 12:13; 1Ti 3:2). Hospitality in the ancient world often included putting up a guest overnight or longer. This is hardest to do when experiencing a time of persecution. The Hebrews would not know whether a guest would prove to be a spy or a fellow believer being pursued. **angels.** This is not given as the ultimate motivation for hospitality, but to reveal that one never knows how far-reaching an act of kindness might be (cf. Mt 25:40, 45). This is exactly what happened to Abraham and Sarah (Ge 18:1–3), Lot (Ge 19:1, 2), Gideon (Jdg 6:11–24), and Manoah (Jdg 13:6–20).

13:3 yourselves. Believers should be able to identify with the suffering of others because they also suffer physical ("in the body") pain and hardship.

13:4 in honor. God highly honors marriage, which He instituted at creation (Ge 2:24); but some people in the early church considered celibacy to be holier than marriage, an idea Paul strongly denounces in 1Ti 4:3 (*see notes on 1Co 7*). Sexual activity in a marriage is pure, but any sexual activity outside marriage brings one under divine judgment. **God will judge.** God prescribes serious consequences for sexual immorality (*see notes on Eph 5:3–6*).

13:5 love of money. Lusting after material riches is "a root of all sorts of evil, and some by longing for it have wandered away from the faith and pierced themselves with many griefs" (1Ti 6:10; cf. 1Ti 3:3). **I will never.** Quoted from Ge 28:15; Dt 31:6, 8; Jos 1:5; 1Ch 28:20. Believers can be content in every situation because of this promise. Several negatives are utilized in this statement to emphasize the impossibility of Christ deserting believers. It is like saying "there is absolutely no way whatsoever that I will ever, ever leave you."

13:6 confidently. This word has the idea of being bold and courageous. Cf. its use in Mt 9:2; 2Co 5:6, 8. Quoted from Ps 118:6.

13:7 In addition to the roll of the faithful in chap. 11, the writer reminds the Hebrews of their own faithful leaders within the church. In so doing, he outlines the duties of pastors: 1) rule; 2) speak the Word of God; and 3) establish the pattern of faith for the people to follow. Cf. Ac 20:28; 1Ti 3:1–7; Titus 1:5–9.

13:9 varied and strange teachings. These would include any teaching contrary to God's Word. The NT contains countless warnings against false teaching and false teachers (cf. Ac 20:29, 30; Ro 16:17; 2Co 10:4, 5; Gal 1:6–9; Eph 4:14; 2Ti 3:16). **strengthened by grace.** Those who are experiencing God's grace in Christ have hearts and minds that remain stable. **foods.** The Mosaic law had regulations for everything, including food (Lv 11). But for Christians, those laws have been abrogated (Ac 10:9–16; cf. 1Co 8:8; Ro 14:17; 1Ti 4:1–5).

13:10–13 *See notes on 11:26; 12:2.* The writer presents an analogy for the believers' identification with Christ in His rejection by Jews. The bodies of animals offered on the Day of Atonement were not eaten but burned "outside the camp" (Lv 4:21; 16:27). Jesus, who was the ultimate atoning sacrifice, was similarly crucified outside the gates of Jerusalem (Jn 19:17). Figuratively, believers must join Him outside the camp of the world, no longer being a part of its unholy systems and practices (cf. 2Ti 2:4). By extension, this would also depict the departure from the Levitical system. The uncommitted Hebrews needed to take the bold step of leaving that system and being outside the camp of Old Covenant Israel.

13:10 an altar. The altar, the offerer, and the sacrifice are all closely related. Association with an altar identifies the offerer with the sacrifice. With certain offerings, the individual further identified himself with the altar and sacrifice by eating some of the sacrifice. The apostle Paul referred to this relationship to an altar when giving instruction to the Corinthians regarding eating meat offered to idols (1Co 9:13) and regarding the observation of the Lord's Supper (1Co 10:18). Here, the altar is equivalent to the sacrifice of Christ, especially as seen in the comparison to the Day of Atonement.

GOD-PLEASING SACRIFICES

15 [A]Through Him then, let us continually offer up
a [B]sacrifice of praise to God, that is, [C]the fruit of lips
that [a]give thanks to His name. 16 And do not neglect
doing good and [A]sharing, for [B]with such sacrifices
God is pleased.
17 [A]Obey your leaders and submit *to them,* for
[B]they keep watch over your souls as those who will
give an account. [a]Let them do this with joy and not
[b]with grief, for this would be unprofitable for you.
18 [A]Pray for us, for we are sure that we have a
[B]good conscience, desiring to conduct ourselves
honorably in all things. 19 And I urge *you* all the
more to do this, [A]so that I may be restored to you
the sooner.

BENEDICTION

20 Now [A]the God of peace, who [B]brought up from
the dead the [C]great Shepherd of the sheep [a]through
[D]the blood of the [E]eternal covenant, *even* Jesus our
Lord, 21 [A]equip you in every good thing to do His
will, [B]working in us that [C]which is pleasing in His
sight, through Jesus Christ, [D]to whom *be* the glory
forever and ever. Amen.
22 But [A]I urge you, [B]brethren, [a]bear with [b]this
[B]word of exhortation, for [C]I have written to you
briefly. 23 [a]Take notice that [A]our brother Timothy
has been released, with whom, if he comes soon, I
will see you. 24 Greet [A]all of your leaders and all the
[a,B]saints. Those from [C]Italy greet you.
25 [A]Grace be with you all.

13:15 [a]Lit *confess* [A]1 Pet 2:5 [B]Lev 7:12 [C]Is 57:19; Hos 14:2 13:16 [A]Rom 12:13 [B]Phil 4:18 13:17 [a]Lit *in order that they may do this* [b]Lit *groaning* [A]1 Cor 16:16; Heb 13:7, 24 [B]Is 62:6; Ezek 3:17; Acts 20:28 13:18 [A]1 Thess 5:25 [B]Acts 24:16; 1 Tim 1:5 13:19 [A]Philem 22 13:20 [a]Lit *in* [A]Rom 15:33 [B]Acts 2:24; Rom 10:7 [C]Is 63:11; John 10:11; 1 Pet 2:25 [D]Zech 9:11; Heb 10:29 [E]Is 55:3; Jer 32:40; Ezek 37:26 13:21 [A]1 Pet 5:10 [B]Phil 2:13 [C]Heb 12:28; 1 John 3:22 [D]Rom 11:36 13:22 [a]Or *listen to* [b]Lit *the* [A]Acts 13:15; Heb 3:13; 10:25; 12:5; 13:19 [B]Heb 3:1 [C]1 Pet 5:12 13:23 [a]Lit *Know* [A]Acts 16:1; Col 1:1 13:24 [a]Or *holy ones* [A]1 Cor 16:16; Heb 13:7, 17 [B]Acts 9:13 [C]Acts 18:2 13:25 [A]Col 4:18

13:15 **praise … thanks.** As seen throughout the book of Hebrews, sacrifices were extremely important under the Old Covenant. Under the New Covenant, God desires the praise and thanksgiving of His people rather than offerings of animals or grain. Since NT believers are all priests (1Pe 2:5, 9), they have offerings of praise and thanks to God (cf. Ro 12:1). The "sacrifice of praise" or thanksgiving is also mentioned in Lv 7:12; Ps 54:6.

13:16 **doing good and sharing.** The sacrifices of praise coming from the lips of God's people please Him only when accompanied by loving action (cf. Is 58:6, 7; Jas 1:27; 1Jn 3:18).

13:17 **your leaders.** *See note on v. 7.* The pastors/elders of the church exercise the very authority of Christ when they preach, teach, and apply Scripture (*see notes on Ac 20:28; 1Th 5:12, 13*). They serve the church on behalf of Christ and must give Him an account of their faithfulness. *See notes on 1Co 4:1–5; 1Pe 5:1–4.* These may include both secular and spiritual leaders. Even those who do not acknowledge God are nevertheless ordained and used by Him (cf. Ro 13:1, 4). **joy.** The church is responsible to help its leaders do their work with satisfaction and delight. *See notes on 1Th 5:12, 13.*

13:19 **restored.** The author had been with these Hebrews and was anxious to once again be in their fellowship.

13:20, 21 This benediction is among the most beautiful in Scripture (cf. Nu 6:24–26; 2Co 13:14; Jude 24, 25). It is an example of how grace can be manifested in mutual blessing and prayer.

13:20 **God of peace.** Paul uses this title 6 times in his epistles (cf. 1Th 5:23). **great Shepherd of the sheep.** See Is 63:11. The figure of the Messiah as a Shepherd is found frequently in Scripture (cf. Ps 23; Is 40:11; Eze 34:23; Jn 10:11; 1Pe 2:25; 5:4). **through the blood of the eternal covenant.** This must refer, in the context of Hebrews, to the New Covenant that is eternal (in a future sense) compared to the Mosaic Covenant that was temporary and had been abrogated (*see notes on 8:6–13; 9:15*).

13:21 **equip you.** This is not the Gr. word for "perfect" or "perfection" used throughout Hebrews to indicate salvation (*see note on 5:14*) but is a word which is translated "prepared" in 10:5 and 11:3. It refers to believers being edified. The verb has the idea of equipping by means of adjusting, shaping, mending, restoring, or preparing (*see note on 11:3*; cf. 1Co 1:10; 2Co 13:11; 2Ti 3:17).

13:22 **bear with.** Readers are encouraged to receive this message with open minds and warm hearts, in contrast to those who "will not endure sound doctrine" (2Ti 4:3). **word of exhortation.** Cf. 3:13. This is the writer's own description of his epistle (see Introduction: Historical and Theological Themes).

13:23 **released.** The details of Timothy's imprisonment are unknown (cf. 2Ti 4:11, 21).

13:24 **Those from Italy.** The group to which the author wrote may have been in Italy, or the meaning might be that Italian Christians who were with him sent their greetings (see Introduction: Author and Date). The use of similar phrases elsewhere is ambiguous since some are clearly referring to people still in their location (Ac 10:23; 17:13) and those who were away from their homes (Ac 21:27).

THE
EPISTLE OF

JAMES

TITLE

James, like all of the general epistles except Hebrews, is named after its author (v. 1).

AUTHOR AND DATE

Of the 4 men named James in the NT, only two are candidates for authorship of this epistle. No one has seriously considered James the Less, the son of Alphaeus (Mt 10:3; Ac 1:13), or James the father of Judas, not Iscariot (Lk 6:16; Ac 1:13). Some have suggested James the son of Zebedee and brother of John (Mt 4:21), but he was martyred too early to have written it (Ac 12:2). That leaves only James, the oldest half-brother of Christ (Mk 6:3) and brother of Jude (Mt 13:55), who also wrote the epistle that bears his name (Jude 1). James had at first rejected Jesus as Messiah (Jn 7:5), but later believed (1Co 15:7). He became the key leader in the Jerusalem church (cf. Ac 12:17; 15:13; 21:18; Gal 2:12), being called one of the "pillars" of that church, along with Peter and John (Gal 2:9). Also known as James the Just because of his devotion to righteousness, he was martyred ca. A.D. 62, according to the first-century Jewish historian Josephus. Comparing James' vocabulary in the letter he wrote which is recorded in Ac 15 with that in the epistle of James further corroborates his authorship.

James		Acts 15
1:1	"greetings"	15:23
1:16, 19; 2:5	"beloved"	15:25
1:21; 5:20	"your souls"	15:24, 26
1:27	"visit"	15:14
2:10	"keep"	15:24
5:19, 20	"turn"	15:19

James wrote with the authority of one who had personally seen the resurrected Christ (1Co 15:7), who was recognized as an associate of the apostles (Gal 1:19), and who was the leader of the Jerusalem church.

James most likely wrote this epistle to believers scattered (1:1) as a result of the unrest recorded in Ac 12 (ca. A.D. 44). There is no mention of the Council of Jerusalem described in Ac 15 (ca. A.D. 49), which would be expected if that Council had already taken place. Therefore, James can be reliably dated ca. A.D. 44–49, making it the earliest written book of the NT canon.

BACKGROUND AND SETTING

The recipients of this book were Jewish believers who had been dispersed (1:1), possibly as a result of Stephen's martyrdom (Ac 7, A.D. 31–34), but more likely due to the persecution under Herod Agrippa I (Ac 12, ca. A.D. 44). The author refers to his audience as "brethren" 15 times (1:2, 16, 19; 2:1, 5, 14; 3:1, 10, 12; 4:11; 5:7, 9, 10, 12, 19), which was a common epithet among the first-century Jews. Not surprisingly, then, James is Jewish in its content. For example, the Gr. word translated "assembly" (2:2) is the word for "synagogue." Further, James contains more than 40 allusions to the OT (and more than 20 to the Sermon on the Mount, Mt 5–7).

HISTORICAL AND THEOLOGICAL THEMES

James, with its devotion to direct, pungent statements on wise living, is reminiscent of the book of Proverbs. It has a practical emphasis, stressing not theoretical knowledge, but godly behavior. James wrote with a passionate desire for his readers to be uncompromisingly obedient to the Word of God. He used at least 30 references to nature (e.g., "surf of the sea" [1:6]; "reptile" [3:7]; and "sky poured rain" [5:18]), as befits one who spent a great deal of time outdoors. He complements Paul's emphasis on justification by faith with his own emphasis on spiritual fruitfulness demonstrating true faith.

INTERPRETIVE CHALLENGES

At least two significant texts challenge the interpreter: 1) In 2:14–26, what is the relationship between faith and works? Does James' emphasis on works contradict Paul's focus on faith? 2) In 5:13–18, do the promises of healing refer to the spiritual or physical realm? These difficult texts are treated in the notes.

OUTLINE

There are a number of ways to outline the book to grasp the arrangement of its content. One way is to arrange it around a series of tests by which the genuineness of a person's faith may be measured.

OUTLINE

I. Introduction (1:1)

II. The Test of Perseverance in Suffering (1:2–12)

III. The Test of Blame in Temptation (1:13–18)

IV. The Test of Response to the Word (1:19–27)

V. The Test of Impartial Love (2:1–13)

VI. The Test of Righteous Works (2:14–26)

VII. The Test of the Tongue (3:1–12)

VIII. The Test of Humble Wisdom (3:13–18)

IX. The Test of Worldly Indulgence (4:1–12)

X. The Test of Dependence (4:13–17)

XI. The Test of Patient Endurance (5:1–11)

XII. The Test of Truthfulness (5:12)

XIII. The Test of Prayerfulness (5:13–18)

XIV. The Test of True Faith (5:19, 20)

TESTING YOUR FAITH

1 [a,A]James, a [B]bond-servant of God and [C]of the Lord
Jesus Christ,
To [D]the twelve tribes who are [b,E]dispersed abroad:
[F]Greetings.
2 [A]Consider it all joy, my brethren, when you encounter [B]various [a]trials, 3 knowing that [A]the testing
of your [B]faith produces [a,C]endurance. 4 And let [a,A]en-
durance have *its* perfect [b]result, so that you may be
[c,B]perfect and complete, lacking in nothing.
5 But if any of you [A]lacks wisdom, let him ask of
God, who gives to all generously and [a]without reproach, and [B]it will be given to him. 6 But he must
[A]ask in faith [B]without any doubting, for the one who
doubts is like the surf of the sea, [C]driven and tossed
by the wind. 7 For that man ought not to expect that
he will receive anything from the Lord, 8 *being* a
[a,A]double-minded man, [B]unstable in all his ways.
9 [A]But the [a]brother of humble circumstances is to
glory in his high position; 10 and the rich man *is to*
glory in his humiliation, because [A]like [a]flowering
grass he will pass away. 11 For the sun rises with
[a,A]a scorching wind and [B]withers the grass; and its
flower falls off and the beauty of its appearance is
destroyed; so too the rich man in the midst of his
pursuits will fade away.
12 [A]Blessed is a man who perseveres under trial;
for once he has [a]been approved, he will receive

1:1 [a]Or *Jacob* [b]Lit *in the Dispersion* [A]Acts 12:17 [B]Titus 1:1 [C]Rom 1:1 [D]Luke 22:30 [E]John 7:35 [F]Acts 15:23 1:2 [a]Or *temptations* [A]Matt 5:12; James 1:12; 5:11 [B]1 Pet 1:6 1:3 [a]Or *steadfastness* [A]1 Pet 1:7 [B]Heb 6:12 [C]Luke 21:19 1:4 [a]V 3, note 1 [b]Lit *work* [c]Or *mature* [A]Luke 21:19 [B]Matt 5:48; Col 4:12 1:5 [a]Lit *does not reproach* [A]1 Kin 3:9ff; James 3:17 [B]Matt 7:7 1:6 [A]Matt 21:21 [B]Mark 11:23; Acts 10:20 [C]Matt 14:28-31; Eph 4:14 1:8 [a]Or *doubting, hesitating* [A]James 4:8 [B]2 Pet 2:14 1:9 [a]I.e. church member [A]Luke 14:11 1:10 [a]Lit *the flower of the grass* [A]1 Cor 7:31; 1 Pet 1:24 1:11 [a]Lit *the* [A]Matt 20:12 [B]Ps 102:4, 11; Is 40:7f 1:12 [a]Or *passed the test* [A]Luke 6:22; James 5:11; 1 Pet 3:14; 4:14

1:1 James. The half-brother of the Lord Jesus (see Introduction: Author and Date; cf. Gal 1:19; 2:9). **bond-servant.** *See note on Ro 1:1.* **twelve tribes.** A common NT title for Jews (cf. Mt 19:28; Ac 26:7; Rev 7:4). When the kingdom split after Solomon's reign, 10 tribes constituted the northern kingdom, called Israel, and Benjamin and Judah combined to form the southern kingdom, called Judah. After the fall and deportation of the northern kingdom to Assyria (722 B.C.), some of the remnant of those in the 10 northern tribes filtered down into Judah and came to Jerusalem to worship (2Ch 29, 30, 34), thus preserving all 12 tribes in Judah's land. Although tribal identity could not be established with certainty after the southern kingdom was led captive by Babylon (586 B.C.), the prophets foresaw a time when God would reconstitute the whole nation and delineate each person's tribal membership once again (cf. Is 11:12, 13; Jer 3:18; 50:4; Eze 37; Rev 7:5–8). **dispersed abroad.** The Gr. word *diaspora,* which lit. means "through a sowing" (cf. Jn 7:35), became a technical term referring to Jews living outside the land of Israel (cf. 1Pe 1:1). Besides the expulsions from the land by the Assyrians (2Ki 17; 1Ch 5) and Babylonians (2Ki 24, 25; 2Ch 36), many Jews were taken to Rome as slaves when the Romans conquered them ca. 63 B.C. In addition, during the centuries leading up to Christ's first coming, thousands of Jews drifted out of Israel and settled throughout the Mediterranean world (*see notes on Ac 2:5–11*). But James' primary audience was those who were scattered because of persecution (see Introduction: Background and Setting).

1:2 Consider it all joy. The Gr. word for "consider" may also be translated "count" or "evaluate." The natural human response to trials is not to rejoice; therefore, the believer must make a conscious commitment to face them with joy (*see note on Php 3:1*). **brethren.** Believing Jews among those scattered (cf. 1Pe 1:1, 2; *see note on Ac 8:1*). **trials.** This Gr. word connotes trouble, or something that breaks the pattern of peace, comfort, joy, and happiness in someone's life. The verb form of this word means "to put someone or something to the test," with the purpose of discovering that person's nature or that thing's quality. God brings such tests to prove—and increase—the strength and quality of one's faith and to demonstrate its validity (vv. 2–12). Every trial becomes a test of faith designed to strengthen: if the believer fails the test by wrongly responding, that test then becomes a temptation, or a solicitation to evil (*see notes on vv. 13–15*).

1:3 testing. This means "proof," or "proving" (see Introduction: Outline). **endurance.** Through tests, a Christian will learn to withstand tenaciously the pressure of a trial until God removes it at His appointed time and even cherish the benefit. *See notes on 2Co 12:7–10.*

1:4 perfect. Not a reference to sinless perfection (cf. 3:2), but to spiritual maturity (cf. 1Jn 2:14). The testing of faith drives believers to deeper communion and greater trust in Christ—qualities that in turn produce a stable, godly, and righteous character (*see note on 1Pe 5:10*; cf. Gal 4:19). **complete.** From a compound Gr. word that lit. means "all the portions whole."

1:5 wisdom. James' Jewish audience recognized this as the understanding and practical skill that were necessary to live life to God's glory. It was not a wisdom of philosophical speculation, but the wisdom contained in the pure and peaceable absolutes of God's will revealed in His Word (cf. 3:13, 17) and lived out. Only such divine wisdom enables believers to be joyous and submissive in the trials of life. **ask of God.** This command is a necessary part of the believer's prayer life (cf. Job 28:12–23; Pr 3:5–7; 1Th 5:17). God intends that trials will drive believers to greater dependency on Him, by showing them their own inadequacy. As with all His riches (Eph 1:7; 2:7; 3:8; Php 4:19), God has wisdom in abundance (Ro 11:33) available for those who seek it. *See notes on Pr 2:1–8.*

1:6 ask in faith. Prayer must be offered with confident trust in a sovereign God (*see note on Heb 11:1*). **without any doubting.** This refers to having one's thinking divided within himself, not merely because of mental indecision but an inner moral conflict or distrust in God (*see note on v. 8*). **surf of the sea.** The person who doubts God's ability or willingness to provide this wisdom is like the billowing, restless sea, moving back and forth with its endless tides, never able to settle (cf. Jos 24:15; 1Ki 18:21; Rev 3:16).

1:8 double-minded man. A lit. translation of the Gr. expression that denotes having one's mind or soul divided between God and the world (*see note on 4:4*). This man is a hypocrite, who occasionally believes in God but fails to trust Him when trials come, and thus receives nothing. The use of this expression in 4:8 makes it clear that it refers to an unbeliever. **unstable.** *See notes on v. 6.*

1:9, 10 brother of humble circumstances ... the rich man. Trials make all believers equally dependent on God and bring them to the same level with one another by keeping them from becoming preoccupied with earthly things. Poor Christians and wealthy ones can rejoice that God is no respecter of persons and that they both have the privilege of being identified with Christ.

1:9 glory. This word refers to the boasting of a privilege or possession; it is the joy of legitimate pride. Although having nothing in this world, the poor believer can rejoice in his high spiritual standing before God by grace and the hope which that brings (cf. Ro 8:17, 18; 1Pe 1:4).

1:10 his humiliation. Refers to the rich believer's being brought low by trials. Such experiences help him rejoice and realize that genuine happiness and contentment depend on the true riches of God's grace, not earthly wealth.

1:11 grass ... flower. A picture of Palestine's flowers and flowering grasses, which colorfully flourish in Feb. and dry up by May. This is a clear allusion to Is 40:6–8, which speaks of the scorching sirocco wind that burns and destroys plants in its path. This picture from nature illustrates how divinely wrought death and judgment can quickly end the wealthy person's dependence on material possessions (*see note on v. 10*; cf. Pr 27:24).

1:12 Blessed. *See notes on Mt 5:3, 10.* Believers who successfully endure trials are truly happy (cf. 5:11). **perseveres.** *See note on v. 3.* In this context, it also describes the passive, painful survival of a trial and focuses on the victorious outcome. Such a person never relinquishes his saving faith in God; thus this concept is closely related to the doctrine of eternal security and perseverance of the believer (*see note on Mt 24:13*; cf. Jn 14:15, 23; 1Jn 2:5, 6, 15, 19; 4:19; 1Pe 1:6–8). **trial.** *See note on v. 2.* **approved.** Lit. "passed the test" (*see note on v. 2,* "trials"). The believer has successfully and victoriously gone through his trials, indicating he is genuine because his faith has endured like Job's. **crown of life.** Best translated "the crown which is life." "Crown" was the wreath put on the victor's head after

[B]the crown of life which *the Lord* [C]has promised
to those who [D]love Him. 13 Let no one say when
he is tempted, "[A]I am being tempted [a]by God"; for
God cannot be tempted [b]by evil, and He Himself
does not tempt anyone. 14 But each one is tempted
when he is carried away and enticed by his own
lust. 15 Then [A]when lust has conceived, it gives birth
to sin; and when [B]sin [a]is accomplished, it brings
forth death. 16 [A]Do not be [a]deceived, [B]my beloved
brethren. 17 Every good thing given and every perfect gift is [A]from above, coming down from [B]the
Father of lights, [C]with whom there is no variation
or [a]shifting shadow. 18 In the exercise of [A]His will
He [B]brought us forth by [C]the word of truth, so that
we would be [a]a kind of [D]first fruits [b]among His
creatures.

19 [a]*This* [A]you know, [B]my beloved brethren. But everyone must be quick to hear, [C]slow to speak *and* [D]slow
to anger; 20 for [A]the anger of man does not achieve
the righteousness of God. 21 Therefore, [A]putting aside
all filthiness and *all* [a]that remains of wickedness, in
[b]humility receive [B]the word implanted, which is able
to save your souls. 22 [A]But prove yourselves doers of
the word, and not merely hearers who delude themselves. 23 For if anyone is a hearer of the word and not
a doer, he is like a man who looks at his [a]natural face
[A]in a mirror; 24 for *once* he has looked at himself and
gone away, [a]he has immediately forgotten what kind
of person he was. 25 But one who looks intently at the
perfect law, [A]the *law* of liberty, and abides by it, not
having become a forgetful hearer but [a]an effectual
doer, this man will be [B]blessed in [b]what he does.

1:12 [B]1 Cor 9:25 [C]Ex 20:6; James 2:5 [D]1 Cor 2:9; 8:3 1:13 [a]Lit *from* [b]Lit *of evil things* [A]Gen 22:1 1:15 [a]Lit *is brought to completion* [A]Job 15:35; Ps 7:14; Is 59:4 [B]Rom 5:12; 6:23 1:16 [a]Or *misled* [A]1 Cor 6:9 [B]Acts 1:15; James 1:2, 19; 2:1, 5, 14; 3:1, 10; 4:11; 5:12, 19 1:17 [a]Lit *shadow of turning* [A]John 3:3; James 3:15, 17 [B]Ps 136:7; 1 John 1:5 [C]Mal 3:6 1:18 [a]Or *a certain first fruits* [b]Lit *of* [A]John 1:13 [B]James 1:15; 1 Pet 1:3, 23 [C]2 Cor 6:7; Eph 1:13; 2 Tim 2:15 [D]Jer 2:3; Rev 14:4 1:19 [a]Or *Know* this [A]1 John 2:21 [B]Acts 1:15; James 1:2, 16; 2:1, 5, 14; 3:1, 10; 4:11; 5:12, 19 [C]Prov 10:19; 17:27 [D]Prov 16:32; Eccl 7:9 1:20 [A]Matt 5:22; Eph 4:26 1:21 [a]Lit *abundance of malice* [b]Or *gentleness* [A]Eph 4:22; 1 Pet 2:1 [B]Eph 1:13; 1 Pet 1:22f 1:22 [A]Matt 7:24-27; Luke 6:46-49; Rom 2:13; James 1:22-25; 2:14-20 1:23 [a]Lit *the face of his birth; or nature* [A]1 Cor 13:12 1:24 [a]Lit *and he* 1:25 [a]Lit *a doer of a work* [b]Lit *his doing* [A]John 8:32; Rom 8:2; Gal 2:4; 6:2; James 2:12; 1 Pet 2:16 [B]John 13:17

ancient Greek athletic events. Here, it denotes the believer's ultimate reward, eternal life, which God has promised to him and will grant in full at death or at Christ's coming (*see notes on 2Ti 4:8; Rev 2:10*; cf. 1Pe 5:4).

1:13 The same Gr. word translated "trials" (vv. 2–12) is also translated "tempted" here. James' point is that every difficult circumstance that enters a believer's life can either strengthen him if he obeys God and remains confident in His care, or become a solicitation to evil if the believer chooses instead to doubt God and disobey His Word. **God cannot be tempted.** God by His holy nature has no capacity for evil, or vulnerability to it (Hab 1:13; cf. Lv 19:2; Is 6:3; 1Pe 1:16). **He Himself does not tempt anyone.** God purposes trials to occur and in them He allows temptation to happen, but He has promised not to allow more than believers can endure and never without a way to escape (1Co 10:13). They choose whether to take the escape God provides or to give in (*see note on v. 14*; cf. 2Sa 24:1; 1Ch 21:1).

1:14 **carried away.** This Gr. word was used to describe wild game being lured into traps. Just as animals can be drawn to their deaths by attractive baits, temptation promises people something good, which is actually harmful. **enticed.** A fishing term that means "to capture" or "to catch with bait" (cf. 2Pe 2:14, 18). It is a parallel to "carried away." **his own lust.** This refers to the strong desire of the human soul to enjoy or acquire something to fulfill the flesh. Man's fallen nature has the propensity to strongly desire whatever sin will satisfy it (*see notes on Ro 7:8–25*). "His own" describes the individual nature of lust—it is different for each person as a result of inherited tendencies, environment, upbringing, and personal choices. The Gr. grammar also indicates that this "lust" is the direct agent or cause of one's sinning. Cf. Mt 15:18–20.

1:15 Sin is not merely a spontaneous act, but the result of a process. The Gr. words for "has conceived" and "gives birth" liken the process to physical conception and birth. Thus James personifies temptation and shows that it can follow a similar sequence and produce sin with all its deadly results. While sin does not result in spiritual death for the believer, it can lead to physical death (1Co 11:30; 1Jn 5:16).

1:16 **Do not be deceived.** The Gr. expression refers to erring, going astray, or wandering. Christians are not to make the mistake of blaming God rather than themselves for their sin.

1:17 **Every good … perfect gift is from above.** Two different Gr. words for "gift" emphasize the perfection and inclusiveness of God's graciousness. The first denotes the act of giving, and the second is the object given. Everything related to divine giving is adequate, complete, and beneficial. **Father of lights.** An ancient Jewish expression for God as the Creator, with "lights" referring to the sun, moon, and stars (cf. Ge 1:14–19). **no variation or shifting shadow.** From man's perspective, the celestial bodies have different phases of movement and rotation, change from day to night, and vary in intensity and shadow. But God does not follow that pattern—He is changeless (cf. Mal 3:6; 1Jn 1:5).

1:18 **of His will.** This phrase translates a Gr. word that makes the point that regeneration is not just a wish, but an active expression of God's will, which He always has the power to accomplish. This phrase occurs at the beginning of the Gr. sentence, which means James intends to emphasize that the sovereign will of God is the source of this new life. **He brought us forth.** The divine act of regeneration, or the new birth (*see notes on Jn 3:3–8; 1Pe 1:23*; cf. Eze 36:25–27; Jn 1:12, 13; Eph 2:5, 6; 5:26). **word of truth.** Cf. Jn 17:17. Scripture, or the Word of God. He regenerates sinners through the power of that Word (cf. 2Co 6:7; Col 1:5; 1Th 2:13; Titus 3:5; 1Pe 1:23–25). **first fruits.** Originally an OT expression referring to the first and best harvest crops, which God expected as an offering (cf. Ex 23:19; Lv 23:9–14; Dt 26:1–19). Giving God that initial crop was an act of faith that He would fulfill His promise of a full harvest to come (Pr 3:9, 10). In the same way, Christians are the first evidence of God's new creation that is to come (cf. 2Pe 3:10–13) and enjoy presently in their new life a foretaste of future glory (*see notes on Ro 8:19–23*).

1:19 **quick to hear, slow to speak.** Believers are to respond positively to Scripture, and eagerly pursue every opportunity to know God's Word and will better (cf. Ps 119:11; 2Ti 2:15). But at the same time, they should be cautious about becoming a preacher or teacher too quickly (*see notes on 3:1, 2*; cf. Eze 3:17; 33:6, 7; 1Ti 3:6; 5:22).

1:20 **anger.** From the Gr. word that describes a deep, internal resentment and rejection, in this context, of God's Word (*see notes on 4:1–3*; cf. Gal 4:16).

1:21 **putting aside.** Lit. "having put off," as one would do with dirty clothes (*see notes on Ro 13:12–14; Eph 4:22; Col 3:8; Heb 12:1; 1Pe 2:1, 2*). The tense of this Gr. verb stresses the importance of putting off sin prior to receiving God's Word. **filthiness … wickedness.** The first term was used of moral vice as well as dirty garments. Sometimes it was even used of ear wax—here, of sin that would impede the believer's spiritual hearing. "Wickedness" refers to evil desire or intent. **word implanted.** *See note on v. 18.*

1:22 **prove yourselves doers.** The fact that James calls professing believers to be "doers," rather than simply *to do,* emphasizes that their entire personality should be characterized in that way. *See notes on Mt 7:21–28.* **delude.** Lit. "reason beside or alongside" (as in "beside oneself"). This word was used in mathematics to refer to a miscalculation. Professing Christians who are content with only hearing the Word have made a serious spiritual miscalculation.

1:23 **looks.** A forceful Gr. word meaning to observe carefully and cautiously, as opposed to taking a casual glance. **mirror.** First-century mirrors were not glass but metallic, made of bronze, silver—or for the wealthy—gold. The metals were beaten flat and polished to a high gloss, and the image they reflected was adequate but not perfect (cf. 1Co 13:12).

1:24 **forgotten what kind of person he was.** Unless professing Christians act promptly after they hear the Word, they will forget the changes and improvements that their reflection showed them they need to make.

1:25 **perfect law.** In both the OT and NT, God's revealed, inerrant, sufficient, and comprehensive Word is called "law" (cf. Ps 19:7). The presence of His grace does not mean there is no moral law or code of conduct for believers to obey. Believers are enabled by the

[26] If anyone thinks himself to be religious, and yet
does not [a,A]bridle his tongue but deceives his *own*
heart, this man's religion is worthless. [27] Pure and
undefiled religion [A]in the sight of *our* God and Father
is this: to [B]visit [C]orphans and widows in their distress, *and* to keep oneself unstained [a]by [D]the world.

THE SIN OF PARTIALITY

2 [A]My brethren, [B]do not hold your faith in our [C]glori-
ous Lord Jesus Christ with *an attitude of* [D]personal
favoritism. [2] For if a man comes into your [a]assembly
with a gold ring and dressed in [b,A]fine clothes, and
there also comes in a poor man in [B]dirty clothes, [3] and
you [a]pay special attention to the one who is wearing
the [A]fine clothes, and say, "You sit here in a good place,"
and you say to the poor man, "You stand over there,
or sit down by my footstool," [4] have you not made
distinctions among yourselves, and become judges
[A]with evil [a]motives? [5] Listen, [A]my beloved brethren: did
not [B]God choose the poor [a]of this world *to be* [C]rich in
faith and [D]heirs of the kingdom which He [E]promised
to those who love Him? [6] But you have dishonored
the poor man. Is it not the rich who oppress you and
[a]personally [A]drag you into [b]court? [7] [A]Do they not blaspheme the fair name [a]by which you have been called?
[8] If, however, you [A]are fulfilling the [a]royal law
according to the Scripture, "[B]YOU SHALL LOVE
YOUR NEIGHBOR AS YOURSELF," you are doing well.
[9] But if you [A]show partiality, you are committing
sin *and* are convicted by the [a]law as transgressors. [10] For whoever keeps the whole [a]law and yet
[A]stumbles in one *point,* he has become [B]guilty of all.

1:26 [a]Or *control* [A]Ps 39:1; 141:3; James 3:2-12 1:27 [a]Lit *from* [A]Rom 2:13; Gal 3:11 [B]Matt 25:36 [C]Deut 14:29; Job 31:16, 17, 21; Ps 146:9; Is 1:17, 23 [D]Matt 12:32; Eph 2:2; Titus 2:12; James 4:4; 2 Pet 1:4; 2:20; 1 John 2:15-17 2:1 [A]James 1:16 [B]Heb 12:2 [C]Acts 7:2; 1 Cor 2:8 [D]Acts 10:34; James 2:9 2:2 [a]Or *synagogue* [b]Or *bright* [A]Luke 23:11; James 2:3 [B]Zech 3:3f 2:3 [a]Lit *look at* [A]Luke 23:11 2:4 [a]Lit *reasonings* [A]Luke 18:6; John 7:24 2:5 [a]Lit *to the* [A]James 1:16 [B]Job 34:19; 1 Cor 1:27f [C]Luke 12:21; Rev 2:9 [D]Matt 5:3; 25:34 [E]James 1:12 2:6 [a]Lit *they themselves* [b]Lit *courts* [A]Acts 8:3; 16:19 2:7 [a]Lit *which has been called upon you* [A]Acts 11:26; 1 Pet 4:16 2:8 [a]Or *law of our King* [A]Matt 7:12 [B]Lev 19:18 2:9 [a]Or *Law* [A]Acts 10:34; James 2:1 2:10 [a]Or *Law* [A]James 3:2; 2 Pet 1:10; Jude 24 [B]Matt 5:19; Gal 5:3

Spirit to keep it (*see note on Ro 8:4*). **liberty.** Genuine freedom from sin. As the Holy Spirit applies the principles of Scripture to believers' hearts, they are freed from sin's bondage and enabled to obey God (Jn 8:34–36).

1:26 religious. This refers to ceremonial public worship (cf. Ac 26:5). James chose this term, instead of one referring to internal godliness, to emphasize the external trappings, rituals, routines, and forms that were not followed sincerely. **bridle his tongue.** "Bridle" means "control," or as another translation renders it, "keep a tight rein." Purity of heart is often revealed by controlled and proper speech (*see note on Mt 12:36*).

1:27 Pure and undefiled religion. James picks two synonymous adjectives to define the most spotless kind of religious faith—that which is measured by compassionate love (cf. Jn 13:35). **orphans and widows.** Those without parents or husbands were and are an especially needy segment of the church (*see notes on 1Ti 5:3*; cf. Ex 22:22; Dt 14:28, 29; Ps 68:5; Jer 7:6, 7; 22:16; Ac 6:1–6). Since they are usually unable to reciprocate in any way, caring for them clearly demonstrates true, sacrificial, Christian love. **world.** The evil world system (*see notes on 4:4; 1Jn 2:15*).

2:1 your faith. This refers not to the act of believing, but to the entire Christian faith (cf. Jude 3), which has as its central focus Jesus Christ. **our glorious Lord.** Christ is the One who reveals the glory of God (cf. Jn 1:14; 2Co 4:4–6; Heb 1:1–3). In His incarnation, He showed only impartiality (cf. Mt 22:16)—for example, consider the non-elite people included in His genealogy (*see notes on Mt 1:1–16*), His choice of the humble village of Nazareth as His residence for 30 years, and His willingness to minister in Galilee and Samaria, both regions held in contempt by Israel's leaders. **favoritism.** Originally, this word referred to raising someone's face or elevating the person, but it came to refer to exalting someone strictly on a superficial, external basis, such as appearance, race, wealth, rank, or social status (Lv 19:15; Job 34:19; cf. Dt 10:17; 15:7–10; 2Ch 19:7; Pr 24:23; 28:21; Mt 22:8–10; Ac 10:34, 35; Ro 2:11; Eph 6:9; Col 3:25; 4:1; 1Pe 1:17).

2:2 assembly. Lit. "a gathering together" or "synagogue." Since James was writing early in the church's history (see Introduction: Author and Date) to Jewish believers (1:1), he used both this general word and the normal Gr. word for "church" (5:14) to describe the church's corporate meetings during that period of transition. **gold ring.** While Jews commonly wore rings (cf. Lk 15:22), few could afford gold ones. However, there are some reports that in the ancient world the most ostentatious people wore rings on every finger but the middle one to show off their economic status (some ancient sources indicate that there were even ring rental businesses). **fine clothes.** This word refers to bright, shining garments and is used of the gorgeous garment Herod's soldiers put on Jesus to mock Him (Lk 23:11) and of the apparel of an angel (Ac 10:30). It can also refer to bright, flashy color and to brilliant, glittering, sparkling ornamentation. James is not condemning this unbeliever for his distracting dress, but the church's flattering reaction to it. **a poor man.** Although there were people of means in the early church (Mt 27:57–60; Jn 19:38, 39; Ac 4:36, 37; 8:27; 10:1, 2; 16:14; 17:4; 1Ti 6:17–19), it consisted mostly of common, poor people (cf. v. 5; Ac 2:45; 4:35–37; 6:1–6; 1Co 1:26; 2Co 8:2, 14). Throughout Scripture the poor are objects of God's special concern (1:27; Lv 25:25, 35–37, 39; Pss 41:1; 68:10; 72:4, 12; 113:7; Pr 17:5; 21:13; 28:27; 29:7; 31:9, 20; Is 3:14, 15; 10:1, 2; 25:4; Gal 2:10).

2:3 sit here in a good place. A more comfortable, prominent place of honor. The synagogues and assembly halls of the first century sometimes had benches around the outside wall and a couple of benches in front. Most of the congregation either sat cross-legged on the floor or stood. There were a limited number of good seats; they were the ones the Pharisees always wanted (Mk 12:38, 39).

2:4 made distinctions. *See note on v. 1.* The true nature of the sin in this passage, not the lavish apparel or rings of the rich man or that he was given a good seat. **judges with evil motives.** This is better translated "judges with vicious intentions." James feared that his readers would behave just like the sinful world by catering to the rich and prominent while shunning the poor and common.

2:5 did not God choose. *See note on Ro 8:29*; cf. 1Co 1:26–29. **the kingdom.** *See note on Mt 3:2.* Here James intends the kingdom in its present sense of the sphere of salvation—those over whom Christ rules—as well as its future millennial and eternal glory.

2:6 oppress. Lit. "to tyrannize." **drag you into court.** A reference to civil court.

2:7 blaspheme the fair name. Probably a reference to religious courts. Wealthy Jewish opponents of Christ were harassing these poor Christians. Cf. Jn 16:2–4.

2:8 royal law. This is better translated "sovereign law." The idea is that this law is supreme or binding. love your neighbor as yourself. This sovereign law (quoted from Lv 19:18), when combined with the command to love God (Dt 6:4, 5), summarizes all the Law and the Prophets (Mt 22:36–40; Ro 13:8–10). James is not advocating some kind of emotional affection for oneself—self-love is clearly a sin (2Ti 3:2). Rather, the command is to pursue meeting the physical health and spiritual well-being of one's neighbors (all within the sphere of our influence; Lk 10:30–37) with the same intensity and concern as one does naturally for one's self (cf. Php 2:3, 4).

2:9 if. Better translated as "since," the Gr. construction of this conditional statement indicates that this practice was in fact happening among James' readers. **show partiality.** *See note on v. 1.* The form of this Gr. verb indicates that their behavior was not an occasional slip but a continual practice. **convicted by the law.** Specifically by the commands in Dt 1:17 and 16:19. **transgressors.** This refers to one who goes beyond the law of God. Respect of persons makes one a violator of God's law.

2:10 whole law . . . one *point*. *See notes on Gal 3:10–13.* The law of God is not a series of detached injunctions, but a basic unity that requires perfect love of Him and our neighbors (Mt 22:36–40). Although all sins are not equally damaging or heinous, they all shatter that unity and render men transgressors, much like hitting a window with a hammer at only one point will shatter and destroy the whole window. **guilty of all.** Not in the sense of having violated every command, but in the sense of having violated the law's unity. One transgression makes fulfilling the law's most basic commands—to love God perfectly and to love one's neighbor as oneself—impossible.

11 For He who said, "[A]DO NOT COMMIT ADULTERY,"
also said, "[B]DO NOT COMMIT MURDER." Now if you
do not commit adultery, but do commit murder,
you have become a transgressor of the [a]law. 12 So
speak and so act as those who are to be judged by
[A]*the* law of liberty. 13 For [A]judgment *will be* merciless
to one who has shown no mercy; mercy [a]triumphs
over judgment.

FAITH AND WORKS

14 [A]What use is it, [B]my brethren, if someone says
he has faith but he has no works? Can [a]that faith
save him? 15 [A]If a brother or sister is without clothing and in need of daily food, 16 and one of you says
to them, "[A]Go in peace, [a]be warmed and be filled,"
and yet you do not give them what is necessary for
their body, what use is that? 17 Even so [A]faith, if it
has no works, is [a]dead, *being* by itself.
18 [A]But someone [a]may *well* say, "You have faith
and I have works; show me your [B]faith without the
works, and I will [C]show you my faith [D]by my works."
19 You believe that [a,A]God is one. [B]You do well; [C]the
demons also believe, and shudder. 20 But are you
willing to recognize, [A]you foolish fellow, that [B]faith
without works is useless? 21 [A]Was not Abraham our
father justified by works when he offered up Isaac
his son on the altar? 22 You see that [A]faith was working with his works, and [a]as a result of the [B]works,
faith was [b]perfected; 23 and the Scripture was fulfilled which says, "[A]AND ABRAHAM BELIEVED GOD,
AND IT WAS RECKONED TO HIM AS RIGHTEOUSNESS,"
and he was called [B]the friend of God. 24 You see
that a man is justified by works and not by faith
alone. 25 In the same way, was not [A]Rahab the harlot also justified by works [B]when she received the
messengers and sent them out by another way?

2:11 [a]Or *Law* [A]Ex 20:14; Deut 5:18 [B]Ex 20:13; Deut 5:17 2:12 [A]James 1:25 2:13 [a]Lit *boasts against* [A]Prov 21:13; Matt 5:7; 18:32-35; Luke 6:37f 2:14 [a]Lit *the* [A]James 1:22ff [B]James 1:16 2:15 [A]Matt 25:35f; Luke 3:11 2:16 [a]Or *warm yourselves and fill yourselves* [A]1 John 3:17f 2:17 [a]Or *dead by its own standards* [A]Gal 5:6; James 2:20, 26 2:18 [a]Lit *will* [A]Rom 9:19 [B]Rom 3:28; 4:6; Heb 11:33 [C]James 3:13 [D]Matt 7:16f; Gal 5:6 2:19 [a]One early ms reads *there is one God* [A]Deut 6:4; Mark 12:29 [B]James 2:8 [C]Matt 8:29; Mark 1:24; 5:7; Luke 4:34; Acts 19:15 2:20 [A]Rom 9:20; 1 Cor 15:36 [B]Gal 5:6; James 2:17, 26 2:21 [A]Gen 22:9, 10, 12, 16-18 2:22 [a]Or *by the deeds* [b]Or *completed* [A]John 6:29; Heb 11:17 [B]1 Thess 1:3 2:23 [A]Gen 15:6; Rom 4:3 [B]2 Chr 20:7; Is 41:8 2:25 [A]Heb 11:31 [B]Josh 2:4, 6, 15

2:11 These quotations are taken from Ex 20:13, 14 and Dt 5:17, 18.

2:12 judged. Cf. Ro 2:6–16. **law of liberty.** *See note on 1:25.*

2:13 A person who shows no mercy and compassion for people in need demonstrates that he has never responded to the great mercy of God, and as an unredeemed person will receive only strict, unrelieved judgment in eternal hell (cf. Mt 5:7). **mercy triumphs over judgment.** The person whose life is characterized by mercy is ready for the day of judgment, and will escape all the charges that strict justice might bring against him because by showing mercy to others he gives genuine evidence of having received God's mercy.

2:14–26 James continues his series of tests by which his readers can evaluate whether their faith is living or dead (see Introduction: Background and Setting). This passage contains the composite test—the one test that pulls the others together: the test of works, or righteous behavior that obeys God's Word and manifests a godly nature (cf. 1:22–25). James' point is not that a person is saved by works (he has already strongly and clearly asserted that salvation is a gracious gift from God; 1:17, 18; cf. Eph 2:8, 9), but that there is a kind of apparent faith that is dead and does not save (vv. 14, 17, 20, 24, 26; cf. Mt 3:7, 8; 5:16; 7:21; 13:18–23; Jn 8:30, 31; 15:6). It is possible James was writing to Jews (cf. 1:1) who had jettisoned the works righteousness of Judaism but, instead, had embraced the mistaken notion that since righteous works and obedience to God's will were not efficacious for salvation, they were not necessary at all. Thus, they reduced faith to a mere mental assent to the facts about Christ.

2:14 if someone says. This important phrase governs the interpretation of the entire passage. James does not say that this person actually has faith, but that he claims to have it. **faith.** This is best understood in a broad sense, speaking of any degree of acceptance of the truths of the gospel. **has no.** Again, the verb's form describes someone who continually lacks any external evidence of the faith he routinely claims. **works.** This refers to all righteous behavior that conforms to God's revealed Word, but specifically, in the context, to acts of compassion (v. 15). **Can that faith save him?** Better translated "Can that kind of faith save?" James is not disputing the importance of faith. Rather, he is opposing the notion that saving faith can be a mere intellectual exercise void of a commitment to active obedience (cf. Mt 7:16–18). The grammatical form of the question demands a negative answer. *See note on Ro 2:6–10.*

2:15, 16 James illustrates his point by comparing faith without works to words of compassion without acts of compassion (cf. Mt 25:31–46).

2:17 faith ... is dead ... by itself. Just as professed compassion without action is phony, the kind of faith that is without works is mere empty profession, not genuine saving faith.

2:18 someone. Interpreters disagree on whether 1) "someone" is James' humble way of referring to himself or whether it refers to one of James' antagonists who objected to his teaching; and 2) how much of the following passage should be attributed to this antagonist as opposed to James himself. Regardless, James' main point is the same: the only possible evidence of true faith is works (cf. 2Pe 1:3–11).

2:19 You believe that God is one. A clear reference to the passage most familiar to his Jewish readers: the *Shema* (Dt 6:4, 5), the most basic doctrine of the OT. **demons also believe.** Even fallen angels affirm the oneness of God and tremble at its implications. Demons are essentially orthodox in their doctrine (cf. Mt 8:29, 30; Mk 5:7; Lk 4:41; Ac 19:15). But orthodox doctrine by itself is no proof of saving faith. They know the truth about God, Christ, and the Spirit, but hate it and Them.

2:20 foolish. Lit. "empty, defective." The objector's claim of belief is fraudulent, and his faith is a sham. **faith without works is useless.** Lit. "the faith without the works." James is not contrasting two methods of salvation (faith versus works). Instead, he contrasts two kinds of faith: living faith that saves and dead faith that does not (cf. 1Jn 3:7–10).

2:21–26 James cites 3 illustrations of living faith: 1) Abraham (vv. 21–24); 2) Rahab (v. 25); and 3) the human body and spirit (v. 26).

2:21 justified by works. This does not contradict Paul's clear teaching that Abraham was justified before God by grace alone through faith alone (Ro 3:20; 4:1–25; Gal 3:6, 11). For several reasons, James cannot mean that Abraham was constituted righteous before God because of his own good works: 1) James already stressed that salvation is a gracious gift (1:17, 18); 2) in the middle of this disputed passage (v. 23), James quoted Ge 15:6, which forcefully claims that God credited righteousness to Abraham solely on the basis of his faith (*see notes on Ro 1:17; 3:24; 4:1–25*); and 3) the work that James said justified Abraham was his offering up of Isaac (Ge 22:9, 12), an event that occurred many years after he first exercised faith and was declared righteous before God (Ge 12:1–7; 15:6). Instead, Abraham's offering of Isaac demonstrated the genuineness of his faith and the reality of his justification before God. James is emphasizing the vindication before others of a person's claim to salvation. James' teaching perfectly complements Paul's writings; salvation is determined by faith alone (Eph 2:8, 9) and demonstrated by faithfulness to obey God's will alone (Eph 2:10).

2:22 was perfected. This refers to bringing something to its end, or to its fullness. Just as a fruit tree has not arrived at its goal until it bears fruit, faith has not reached its end until it demonstrates itself in a righteous life.

2:23 the Scripture ... says. Quoted from Ge 15:6; *see notes on Ro 4:1–5.* **friend of God.** Abraham is so called in 2Ch 20:7 and Is 41:8 because of his obedience (Jn 15:14, 15).

2:24 justified by works and not by faith alone. *See note on v. 21.*

2:25 Rahab the harlot. The OT records the content of her faith, which was the basis of her justification before God (*see note on Jos 2:11*). She demonstrated the reality of her saving faith when, at great personal risk, she protected the messengers of God (Jos 2:4, 15; 6:17; cf. Heb 11:31). James did not intend, however, for those words to be a commendation of her occupation or her lying. **justified by works.** *See note on v. 21.*

26 For just as the body without *the* spirit is dead, so
also [A]faith without works is dead.

THE TONGUE IS A FIRE

3 [A]Let not many *of you* become teachers, [B]my
brethren, knowing that as such we will incur a
[a]stricter judgment. 2 For we all [A]stumble in many
ways. [B]If anyone does not stumble in [a]what he says,
he is a [C]perfect man, able to [D]bridle the whole body
as well. 3 Now [A]if we put the bits into the horses'
mouths so that they will obey us, we direct their
entire body as well. 4 Look at the ships also, though
they are so great and are driven by strong winds,
are still directed by a very small rudder wherever
the inclination of the pilot desires. 5 So also the
tongue is a small part of the body, and *yet* it [A]boasts
of great things.

[B]See how great a forest is set aflame by such a
small fire! 6 And [A]the tongue is a fire, the *very* world
of iniquity; the tongue is set among our members
as that which [B]defiles the entire body, and sets on
fire the course of *our* [a]life, and is set on fire by [b,C]hell.
7 For every [a]species of beasts and birds, of reptiles
and creatures of the sea, is tamed and has been
tamed by the human [a]race. 8 But no one can tame
the tongue; *it is* a restless evil *and* full of [A]deadly
poison. 9 With it we bless [A]*our* Lord and Father, and
with it we curse men, [B]who have been made in the
likeness of God; 10 from the same mouth come *both*
blessing and cursing. My brethren, these things
ought not to be this way. 11 Does a fountain send
out from the same opening *both* [a]fresh and bitter *water?* 12 [A]Can a fig tree, my brethren, produce
olives, or a vine produce figs? Nor *can* salt water
produce [a]fresh.

WISDOM FROM ABOVE

13 Who among you is wise and understanding?
[A]Let him show by his [B]good behavior his deeds
in the gentleness of wisdom. 14 But if you have
bitter [A]jealousy and [a]selfish ambition in your
heart, do not be arrogant and *so* lie against [B]the
truth. 15 This wisdom is not that which comes
down [A]from above, but is [B]earthly, [a,C]natural, [D]de-
monic. 16 For where [A]jealousy and [a]selfish ambition exist, [b]there is disorder and every evil thing.

2:26 [A]Gal 5:6; James 2:17, 20 3:1 [a]Or *greater condemnation* [A]Matt 23:8; Rom 2:20f; 1 Tim 1:7 [B]James 1:16; 3:10 3:2 [a]Lit *word* [A]James 2:10 [B]Matt 12:34-37; James 3:2-12 [C]James 1:4 [D]James 1:26 3:3 [A]Ps 32:9 3:5 [A]Ps 12:3f; 73:8f [B]Prov 26:20f 3:6 [a]Or *existence, origin* [b]Gr *Gehenna* [A]Ps 120:2, 3; Prov 16:27 [B]Matt 12:36f; 15:11, 18f [C]Matt 5:22 3:7 [a]Lit *nature* 3:8 [A]Ps 140:3; Eccl 10:11; Rom 3:13 3:9 [A]James 1:27 [B]Gen 1:26; 1 Cor 11:7 3:11 [a]Lit *sweet* 3:12 [a]V 11, note 1 [A]Matt 7:16 3:13 [A]James 2:18 [B]1 Pet 2:12 3:14 [a]Or *strife* [A]Rom 2:8; 2 Cor 12:20; James 3:16 [B]1 Tim 2:4; James 1:18; 5:19 3:15 [a]Or *unspiritual* [A]James 1:17 [B]1 Cor 2:6; 3:19 [C]2 Cor 1:12; Jude 19 [D]2 Thess 2:9f; 1 Tim 4:1; Rev 2:24 3:16 [a]V 14, note 1 [b]I.e. in that place [A]Rom 2:8; 2 Cor 12:20; James 3:14

3:1–12 In this passage, James used the common Jewish literary device of attributing blame to a specific bodily member (cf. Ro 3:15; 2Pe 2:14). He personified the tongue as being representative of human depravity and wretchedness. In this way, he echoed the scriptural truth that the mouth is a focal point and vivid indicator of man's fallenness and sinful heart condition (cf. Is 6:5; Mt 15:11, 16–19; Mk 7:20–23; Ro 3:13, 14).

3:1 teachers. This word refers to a person who functions in an official teaching or preaching capacity (cf. Lk 4:16–27; Jn 3:10; Ac 13:14, 15; 1Co 12:28; Eph 4:11). **stricter judgment.** The word translated "judgment" usually expresses a negative verdict in the NT, and here refers to a future judgment: 1) for the unbelieving false teacher, at the second coming (Jude 14, 15); and 2) for the believer, when he is rewarded before Christ (1Co 4:3–5). This is not meant to discourage true teachers, but to warn the prospective teacher of the role's seriousness (cf. Eze 3:17, 18; 33:7–9; Ac 20:26, 27; Heb 13:17).

3:2 Scripture contains much about all the evil which the tongue can cause (cf. Pss 5:9; 34:13; 39:1; 52:4; Pr 6:17; 17:20; 26:28; 28:23; Is 59:3; Ro 3:13). The tongue has immense power to speak sinfully, erroneously, and inappropriately—human speech is a graphic representation of human depravity (*see notes on vv. 1–12*). **stumble.** This refers to sinning, or offending God's Person. The form of the Gr. verb emphasizes that everyone continually fails to do what is right. **perfect man.** "Perfect" may refer to true perfection, in which case James is saying that, hypothetically, if a human being were able to perfectly control his tongue, he would be a perfect man. But, of course, no one is actually immune from sinning with his tongue. More likely, "perfect" is describing those who are spiritually mature and thus able to control their tongues.

3:3–5 James provided several analogies that show how the tongue, even though small, has the power to control one's whole person and influence everything in his life.

3:6 tongue is a fire. Like fire, the tongue's sinful words can spread destruction rapidly, or as its accompanying smoke, those words can permeate and ruin everything around it. **defiles.** This means "to pollute or contaminate" (cf. Mk 7:20; Jude 23). **the course of *our* life.** Better translated "the circle of life," this underscores that the tongue's evil can extend beyond the individual to affect everything in his sphere of influence. **hell.** *See note on Mt 25:46.* A translation of the Gr. word *gehenna* (or valley of Hinnom). In Christ's time this valley that lay SW of Jerusalem's walls served as the city dump and was known for its constantly burning fire. Jesus used that place to symbolize the eternal place of punishment and torment (cf. Mk 9:43, 45). To James "hell" conjures up not just the place but the satanic host that will some day inherit it—they use the tongue as a tool for evil.

3:8 no one can tame the tongue. Only God, by His power, can do this (cf. Ac 2:1–11).

3:9 bless … curse. It was traditional for Jews to add "blessed be He" to a mention of God's name (cf. Ps 68:19, 35). However, the tongue also wishes evil on people made in God's image. This points out the hypocritical inconsistency of the tongue's activities. **made in the likeness of God.** Man was made in God's image (*see notes on Ge 1:26*).

3:11, 12 Three illustrations from nature demonstrate the sinfulness of cursing. The genuine believer will not contradict his profession of faith by the regular use of unwholesome words.

3:13–18 In v. 13, James makes a transition from discussing teachers and the tongue to dealing with wisdom's impact on everyone's life. He supports the truth of OT wisdom literature (Job to Song of Solomon), that wisdom is divided into two realms—man's and God's.

3:13 wise and understanding. "Wise" is the common Gr. word for speculative knowledge and philosophy, but the Hebrews infused it with the much richer meaning of skillfully applying knowledge to the matter of practical living. The word for "understanding" is used only here in the NT and means a specialist or professional who could skillfully apply his expertise to practical situations. James is asking who is truly skilled in the art of living. **gentleness.** This is the opposite of arrogance and self-promotion (*see note on Mt 5:5*; cf. 1:21; Nu 12:3; Gal 5:23). The Greeks described it as power under control. **wisdom.** The kind that comes only from God (*see note on 1:5*; cf. Job 9:4; 28; Pss 104:24; 111:10; Pr 1:7; 2:1–7; 3:19, 20; 9:10; Jer 10:7, 12; Da 1:17; 2:20–23; Ro 11:33; 1Co 1:30; Eph 3:10; Col 2:3).

3:14 bitter jealousy. The Gr. term for "bitter" was used of undrinkable water. When combined with "jealousy" it defines a harsh, resentful attitude toward others. **selfish ambition.** Sometimes translated "strife," it refers to self-seeking that engenders antagonism and factionalism. The Gr. word came to describe anyone who entered politics for selfish reasons and sought to achieve his agenda at any cost (i.e., even if that meant trampling on others).

3:15 from above. *See notes on v. 13.* Self-centered wisdom that is consumed with personal ambition is not from God. **earthly, natural, demonic.** A description of man's wisdom as: 1) limited to earth; 2) characterized by humanness, frailty, an unsanctified heart, and an unredeemed spirit; and 3) generated by Satan's forces (cf. 1Co 2:14; 2Co 11:14, 15).

3:16 disorder. This is the confusion that results from the instability and chaos of human wisdom (*see notes on 1:6, 8*; cf. v. 8). **every evil thing.** Lit. "every worthless (or vile) work." This denotes things that are not so much intrinsically evil as they are simply good for nothing.

17 But the wisdom [A]from above is first [B]pure, then
[C]peaceable, [D]gentle, [a]reasonable, [E]full of mercy and
good fruits, [F]unwavering, without [G]hypocrisy. 18 And
the [a,A]seed whose fruit is righteousness is sown in
peace [b]by those who make peace.

THINGS TO AVOID

4 [a]What is the source of quarrels and [A]conflicts
among you? [b]Is not the source your pleasures
that wage [B]war in your members? 2 You lust and
do not have; *so* you [A]commit murder. You are envious and cannot obtain; *so* you fight and quarrel.
You do not have because you do not ask. 3 You ask
and [A]do not receive, because you ask [a]with wrong
motives, so that you may spend *it* [b]on your pleasures. 4 You [A]adulteresses, do you not know that
friendship with [B]the world is [C]hostility toward
God? [D]Therefore whoever wishes to be a friend
of the world makes himself an enemy of God. 5 Or
do you think that the Scripture [A]speaks to no purpose: "[a]He [b]jealously desires [B]the Spirit which He
has made to dwell in us"? 6 But [A]He gives a greater
grace. Therefore *it* says, "[B]GOD IS OPPOSED TO THE
PROUD, BUT GIVES GRACE TO THE HUMBLE." 7 [A]Sub-
mit therefore to God. [B]Resist the devil and he will
flee from you. 8 [A]Draw near to God and He will
draw near to you. [B]Cleanse your hands, you sinners; and [C]purify your hearts, you [D]double-minded.

3:17 [a]Or *willing to yield* [A]James 1:17 [B]2 Cor 7:11; James 4:8 [C]Matt 5:9; Heb 12:11 [D]Titus 3:2 [E]Luke 6:36; James 2:13 [F]James 2:4 [G]Rom 12:9; 2 Cor 6:6 3:18 [a]Lit *fruit of righteousness* [b]Or *for* [A]Prov 11:18; Is 32:17; Hos 10:12; Amos 6:12; Gal 6:8; Phil 1:11 4:1 [a]Lit *From where wars and from where fightings* [b]Lit Are they *not from here,* from your [A]Titus 3:9 [B]Rom 7:23 4:2 [A]James 5:6; 1 John 3:15 4:3 [a]Lit *wickedly* [b]Lit *in* [A]1 John 3:22; 5:14 4:4 [A]Jer 2:2; Ezek 16:32 [B]James 1:27 [C]Rom 8:7; 1 John 2:15 [D]Matt 6:24; John 15:19 4:5 [a]Or *The spirit which He has made to dwell in us lusts with envy* [b]Lit *desires to jealousy* [A]Num 23:19 [B]1 Cor 6:19; 2 Cor 6:16 4:6 [A]Is 54:7f; Matt 13:12 [B]Ps 138:6; Prov 3:34; Matt 23:12; 1 Pet 5:5 4:7 [A]1 Pet 5:6 [B]Eph 4:27; 6:11f; 1 Pet 5:8f 4:8 [A]2 Chr 15:2; Zech 1:3; Mal 3:7; Heb 7:19 [B]Job 17:9; Is 1:16; 1 Tim 2:8 [C]Jer 4:14; James 3:17; 1 Pet 1:22; 1 John 3:3 [D]James 1:8

3:17 wisdom from above. *See note on v. 13.* **pure.** This refers to spiritual integrity and moral sincerity. Every genuine Christian has this kind of heart motivation (cf. Pss 24:3, 4; 51:7; Mt 5:8; Ro 7:22, 23; Heb 12:14). **peaceable.** Means "peace loving" or "peace promoting" (cf. Mt 5:9). **gentle.** This word is difficult to translate, but most nearly means a character trait of sweet reasonableness. Such a person will submit to all kinds of mistreatment and difficulty with an attitude of kind, courteous, patient humility, without any thought of hatred or revenge (cf. Mt 5:10, 11). **reasonable.** The original term described someone who was teachable, compliant, easily persuaded, and who willingly submitted to military discipline or moral and legal standards. For believers, it defines obedience to God's standards (cf. Mt 5:3–5). **full of mercy.** The gift of showing concern for those who suffer pain and hardship, and the ability to forgive quickly (cf. Mt 5:7; Ro 12:8). **without hypocrisy.** The Gr. word occurs only here in the NT and denotes a consistent, unwavering person who is undivided in his commitment and conviction and does not make unfair distinctions (*see notes on 2:1–13*).

3:18 fruit is righteousness. Good works that result from salvation (cf. v. 17; Mt 5:6; *see notes on 2:14–20; Gal 5:22, 23; Php 1:11*). **those who make peace.** *See note on v. 17.* Righteousness flourishes in a climate of spiritual peace.

4:1 quarrels and conflicts among you. These are between people in the church, not internal conflict in individual people. "Quarrels" speaks of the conflict in general; "conflicts" of its specific manifestations. Discord in the church is not by God's design (Jn 13:34, 35; 17:21; 2Co 12:20; Php 1:27), but results from the mix of tares (false believers) and wheat (truly redeemed people) that make up the church. **pleasures.** The Gr. word (from which the Eng. word "hedonism" derives) always has a negative connotation in the NT. The passionate desires for worldly pleasures that mark unbelievers (1:14; Eph 2:3; 2Ti 3:4; Jude 18) are the internal source of the external conflict in the church. Cf. 1:14, 15. **your members.** Not church members, but bodily members (*see note on Ro 6:13*). James, like Paul, uses "members" to speak of sinful, fallen human nature (cf. Ro 6:19; 7:5, 23). Unbelievers (who are in view here) fight (unsuccessfully) against the evil desires they cannot control.

4:2 murder. The ultimate result of thwarted desires. James had in mind actual murder, and the gamut of sins (hate, anger, bitterness) leading up to it. The picture is of unbelievers so driven by their uncontrollable evil desires that they will fight to the death to fulfill them. **you do not ask.** True joy, peace, happiness, meaning, hope, and fulfillment in life come only from God. Unbelievers, however, are unwilling to ask for them on His terms—they refuse to submit to God or acknowledge their dependence on Him.

4:3 wrong motives. This refers to acting in an evil manner, motivated by personal gratification and selfish desire. Unbelievers seek things for their own pleasures, not the honor and glory of God.

4:4 adulteresses. A metaphorical description of spiritual unfaithfulness (cf. Mt 12:39; 16:4; Mk 8:38). It would have been especially familiar to James' Jewish readers, since the OT often describes unfaithful Israel as a spiritual harlot (cf. 2Ch 21:11, 13; Jer 2:20; 3:1, 6, 8, 9; Eze 16:26–29; Hos 1:2; 4:15; 9:1). James has in view professing Christians, outwardly associated with the church, but holding a deep affection for the evil world system. **friendship.** Appearing only here in the NT, the Gr. word describes love in the sense of a strong emotional attachment. Those with a deep and intimate longing for the things of the world give evidence that they are not redeemed (1Jn 2:15–17). **world.** *See note on 1:27.* **hostility toward God.** The necessary corollary to friendship with the world. The sobering truth that unbelievers are God's enemies is taught throughout Scripture (cf. Dt 32:41–43; Pss 21:8; 68:21; 72:9; 110:1, 2; Is 42:13; Na 1:2, 8; Lk 19:27; Ro 5:10; 8:5–7; 1Co 15:25).

4:5 Scripture speaks. The quote that follows is not found as such in the OT; it is a composite of general OT teaching. **jealously desires the Spirit.** This difficult phrase is best understood by seeing the "Spirit" as a reference not to the Holy Spirit, but to the human spirit, and translating the phrase "jealously desires" in the negative sense of "lusts to envy." James' point is that an unbelieving person's spirit (inner person) is bent on evil (cf. Ge 6:5; 8:21; Pr 21:10; Ecc 9:3; Jer 17:9; Mk 7:21–23). Those who think otherwise defy the biblical diagnosis of fallen human nature; and those who live in worldly lusts give evidence that their faith is not genuine (cf. Ro 8:5–11; 1Co 2:14).

4:6 greater grace. The only ray of hope in man's spiritual darkness is the sovereign grace of God, which alone can rescue man from his propensity to lust for evil things. That God gives "greater grace" shows that His grace is greater than the power of sin, the flesh, the world, and Satan (cf. Ro 5:20). The OT quote (from Pr 3:34; cf. 1Pe 5:5) reveals who obtains God's grace—the humble, not the proud enemies of God. The word "HUMBLE" does not define a special class of Christians, but encompasses all believers (cf. Is 57:15; 66:2; Mt 18:3, 4).

4:7–10 In a series of 10 commands (10 imperative verbs in the Gr. text), James reveals how to receive saving grace. These verses delineate man's response to God's gracious offer of salvation, and disclose what it means to be humble.

4:7 Submit. Lit. "to line up under." The word was used of soldiers under the authority of their commander. In the NT, it describes Jesus' submission to His parents' authority (Lk 2:51), submission to human government (Ro 13:1), the church's submission to Christ (Eph 5:24), and servants' submission to their masters (Titus 2:9; 1Pe 2:18). James used the word to describe a willing, conscious submission to God's authority as sovereign ruler of the universe. A truly humble person will give his allegiance to God, obey His commands, and follow His leadership (cf. Mt 10:38). **Resist the devil and he will flee from you.** The flip side of the first command. "Resist" literally means "take your stand against." All people are either under the lordship of Christ or the lordship of Satan (Jn 8:44; Eph 2:2; 1Jn 3:8; 5:19); there is no middle ground. Those who transfer their allegiance from Satan to God will find that Satan "will flee from" them; he is a defeated foe.

4:8 Draw near. Pursue an intimate love relationship with God (cf. Php 3:10). The concept of drawing near to God was associated originally with the Levitical priests (Ex 19:22; Lv 10:3; Eze 44:13), but eventually came to describe anyone's approach to God (Ps 73:28; Is 29:13; Heb 4:16; 7:19; 10:22). Salvation involves more than submitting to God and resisting the devil; the redeemed heart longs for communion with God (Pss 27:8; 42:1, 2; 63:1, 2; 84:2;

9 [A]Be miserable and mourn and weep; let your laughter be turned into mourning and your joy to gloom.
10 [A]Humble yourselves in the presence of the Lord,
and He will exalt you.
11 [A]Do not speak against one another, [B]brethren.
He who speaks against a brother or [C]judges his
brother, speaks against [D]the law and judges the law;
but if you judge the law, you are not [E]a doer of the
law but a judge *of it.* 12 There is *only* one [A]Lawgiver
and Judge, the One who is [B]able to save and to destroy; but [C]who are you who judge your neighbor?
13 [A]Come now, you who say, "[B]Today or tomorrow
we will go to such and such a city, and spend a year
there and engage in business and make a profit."
14 [a]Yet you do not know [b]what your life will be like
tomorrow. [A]You are *just* a vapor that appears for a
little while and then vanishes away. 15 [a]Instead, *you
ought* to say, "[A]If the Lord wills, we will live and
also do this or that." 16 But as it is, you boast in your
[a]arrogance; [A]all such boasting is evil. 17 Therefore,
[A]to one who knows *the* [a]right thing to do and does
not do it, to him it is sin.

MISUSE OF RICHES

5 [A]Come now, [B]you rich, [C]weep and howl for your
miseries which are coming upon you. 2 [A]Your
riches have rotted and your garments have become moth-eaten. 3 Your gold and your silver have
rusted; and their rust will be a witness against you
and will consume your flesh like fire. It is [A]in the
last days that you have stored up your treasure!
4 Behold, [A]the pay of the laborers who mowed your
fields, *and* which has been withheld by you, cries
out *against you;* and [B]the outcry of those who did
the harvesting has reached the ears of [C]the Lord
of [a]Sabaoth. 5 You have [A]lived luxuriously on the
earth and led a life of wanton pleasure; you have
[a]fattened your hearts in [B]a day of slaughter. 6 You
have condemned and [a,A]put to death [B]the righteous
man; he does not resist you.

4:9 [A]Neh 8:9; Prov 14:13; Luke 6:25 4:10 [A]Job 5:11; Ezek 21:26; Luke 1:52; James 4:6 4:11 [A]2 Cor 12:20; James 5:9; 1 Pet 2:1 [B]James 1:16; 5:7, 9, 10 [C]Matt 7:1; Rom 14:4 [D]James 2:8 [E]James 1:22 4:12 [A]Is 33:22; James 5:9 [B]Matt 10:28 [C]Rom 14:4 4:13 [A]James 5:1 [B]Prov 27:1; Luke 12:18-20 4:14 [a]Lit *Who do not* [b]Or *what will happen tomorrow. What kind of life is yours?* [A]Job 7:7; Ps 39:5; 102:3; 144:4 4:15 [a]Lit *Instead of your saying* [A]Acts 18:21 4:16 [a]Or *pretensions* [A]1 Cor 5:6 4:17 [a]Or *good* [A]Luke 12:47; John 9:41; 2 Pet 2:21 5:1 [A]James 4:13 [B]Luke 6:24; 1 Tim 6:9 [C]Is 13:6; 15:3; Ezek 30:2 5:2 [A]Job 13:28; Is 50:9; Matt 6:19f 5:3 [A]James 5:7, 8 5:4 [a]I.e. Hosts [A]Lev 19:13; Job 24:10f; Jer 22:13; Mal 3:5 [B]Ex 2:23; Deut 24:15; Job 31:38f [C]Rom 9:29; Is 5:9 5:5 [a]Lit *nourished* [A]Ezek 16:49; Luke 16:19; 1 Tim 5:6; 2 Pet 2:13 [B]Jer 12:3; 25:34 5:6 [a]Or *murdered* [A]James 4:2 [B]Heb 10:38; 1 Pet 4:18

143:6; Mt 22:37). **Cleanse your hands.** The OT priests had to ceremonially wash their hands before approaching God (Ex 30:19–21), and sinners (a term used only for unbelievers; *see note on 5:20*) who would approach Him must recognize and confess their sin. **purify your hearts.** Cleansing the hands symbolizes external behavior; this phrase refers to the inner thoughts, motives, and desires of the heart (Ps 24:3, 4; Jer 4:4; Eze 18:31; 36:25, 26; 1Ti 1:5; 2Ti 2:22; 1Pe 1:22). **double-minded.** *See note on 1:8.*

4:9 Be miserable. Be afflicted and wretched. This is the state of those truly broken over their sin. **mourn.** *See note on Mt 5:4.* God will not turn away a heart broken and contrite over sin (Ps 51:17; 2Co 7:10). Mourning is the inner response to such brokenness. **weep.** The outward manifestation of inner sorrow over sin (cf. Mk 14:72). **laughter.** Used only here in the NT, the word signifies the flippant laughter of those foolishly indulging in worldly pleasures. The picture is of people who give no thought to God, life, death, sin, judgment, or holiness. James calls on such people to mourn over their sin (cf. Lk 18:13, 14).

4:10 See Ps 75:6; Mt 23:12. This final command sums up the preceding 9 (*see notes on vv. 7–10*) commands, which mark the truly humble person. "Humble" comes from a word meaning "to make oneself low." Those conscious of being in the presence of the majestic, infinitely holy God are humble (cf. Is 6:5).

4:11 Do not speak against. This means to slander or defame. James does not forbid confronting those in sin, which is elsewhere commanded in Scripture (Mt 18:15–17; Ac 20:31; 1Co 4:14; Col 1:28; Titus 1:13; 2:15; 3:10). Rather, he condemns careless, derogatory, critical, slanderous accusations against others (cf. Ex 23:1; Pss 50:20; 101:5; 140:11; Pr 10:18; 11:9; 16:28; 17:9; 26:20; Ro 1:29; 2Co 12:20; Eph 4:31; 1Ti 3:11; 2Ti 3:3; Titus 2:3; 3:2). **speaks against a brother ... speaks against the law.** Those who speak evil of other believers set themselves up as judges and condemn them (cf. 2:4). They thereby defame and disregard God's law, which expressly forbids such slanderous condemnation. **judges the law.** By refusing to submit to the law, slanderers place themselves above it as its judges.

4:12 one Lawgiver. God, who gave the law (cf. Is 33:22). He alone has the authority to save those who repent from its penalty, and destroy those who refuse to repent.

4:13 James does not condemn wise business planning, but rather planning that leaves out God. The people so depicted are practical atheists, living their lives and making their plans as if God did not exist. Such conduct is inconsistent with genuine saving faith, which submits to God (*see note on v. 7*).

4:14 not know what your life will be like tomorrow. See Pr 27:1. James exposes the presumptuous folly of the practical atheists he condemned in v. 13—those who do not know what the future holds for them (cf. Lk 12:16–21). God alone knows the future (cf. Is 46:9, 10). **vapor.** This refers either to a puff of smoke or one's breath that appears for a moment in cold air. It stresses the transitory nature of life (cf. 1:10; Job 7:6, 7; 9:25, 26; 14:1, 2; Pss 39:5, 11; 62:9; 89:47; 90:5, 6, 10).

4:15 If the Lord wills. The true Christian submits his plans to the lordship of Christ (*see note on v. 7*; cf. Pr 19:21; Ac 18:21; 21:14; Ro 1:10; 15:32; 1Co 4:19; 16:7).

4:16 boasting. Arrogant bragging about their anticipated business accomplishments (*see note on v. 13*).

4:17 sin. The implication is that they also did what they shouldn't do. Sins of omission lead directly to sins of commission.

5:1 rich. Those with more than they need to live. James condemns them not for being wealthy, but for misusing their resources. Unlike the believing rich in Timothy's congregation (1Ti 6:17–19), these are the wicked wealthy who profess Christian faith and have associated themselves with the church, but whose real god is money. For prostituting the goodness and generosity of God, they can anticipate only divine punishment (v. 5).

5:2, 3 rotted ... moth-eaten ... rusted. James points out the folly of hoarding food, expensive clothing, or money—all of which is subject to decay, theft, fire, or other forms of loss.

5:3 last days. The period between Christ's first and second comings (*see note on 1Ti 4:1*). James rebukes the rich for living as if Jesus were never coming back.

5:4 pay ... withheld by you. The rich had gained some of their wealth by oppressing and defrauding their day laborers—a practice strictly forbidden in the OT (cf. Lv 19:13; Dt 24:14, 15). **the Lord of Sabaoth.** An untranslated Gr. word meaning "hosts." The One who hears the cries of the defrauded laborers, James warns, is the Lord of hosts (a name for God used frequently in the OT), the commander of the armies of heaven (angels). The Bible teaches that angels will be involved in the judgment of unbelievers (Mt 13:39–41, 49; 16:27; 25:31; 2Th 1:7, 8).

5:5 lived luxuriously ... wanton pleasure. "Lived luxuriously" leads to vice when a person becomes consumed with the pursuit of pleasure, since a life without self-denial soon becomes out of control in every area. After robbing their workers to accumulate their wealth, the rich indulged themselves in an extravagant lifestyle. **a day of slaughter.** Like fattened cattle ready to be slaughtered, the rich that James condemns had indulged themselves to the limit. This is a vivid depiction of divine judgment, in keeping with the metaphor likening the overindulgent rich to fattened cattle.

5:6 condemned ... put to death. This describes the next step in the sinful progression of the rich. Hoarding led to fraud, which led to self-indulgence. Finally, that overindulgence has consumed the rich to the point that they will do anything to sustain their lifestyle. "Condemned" comes from a word meaning "to sentence." The implication is that the rich were using the courts to commit judicial murder (cf. 2:6).

EXHORTATION

7 Therefore be patient, [A]brethren, [B]until the coming of the Lord. [C]The farmer waits for the precious
produce of the soil, being patient about it, until
[a]it gets [D]the early and late rains. 8 [A]You too be patient; [B]strengthen your hearts, for [C]the coming
of the Lord is [D]near. 9 [A]Do not [a]complain, [B]breth-
ren, against one another, so that you yourselves
may not be judged; behold, [C]the Judge is standing
[b,D]right at the [c]door. 10 As an example, [A]brethren,
of suffering and patience, take [B]the prophets who
spoke in the name of the Lord. 11 We count those
[A]blessed who endured. You have heard of [B]the [a]en-
durance of Job and have seen [C]the [b]outcome of the
Lord's dealings, that [D]the Lord is full of compassion
and *is* merciful.
12 But above all, [A]my brethren, [B]do not swear, either by heaven or by earth or with any other oath;
but [a]your yes is to be yes, and your no, no, so that
you may not fall under judgment.
13 Is anyone among you [A]suffering? [B]*Then* he must
pray. Is anyone cheerful? He is to [C]sing praises. 14 Is
anyone among you sick? *Then* he must call for [A]the
elders of the church and they are to pray over him,
[a,B]anointing him with oil in the name of the Lord;
15 and the [A]prayer [a]offered in faith will [b,B]restore the
one who is sick, and the Lord will [C]raise him up, and
if he has committed sins, [c]they will be forgiven him.
16 Therefore, [A]confess your sins to one another, and
pray for one another so that you may be [B]healed.
[C]The effective [a]prayer of a righteous man can accomplish much. 17 Elijah was [A]a man with a nature
like ours, and [B]he prayed [a]earnestly that it would not
rain, and it did not rain on the earth for [C]three years
and six months. 18 Then he [A]prayed again, and [B]the
[a]sky [b]poured rain and the earth produced its fruit.
19 My brethren, [A]if any among you strays from [B]the
truth and one turns him back, 20 let him know that [a]he
who turns a sinner from the error of his way will [A]save
his soul from death and will [B]cover a multitude of sins.

5:7 [a]Or *he* [A]James 4:11; 5:9, 10 [B]John 21:22; 1 Thess 2:19 [C]Gal 6:9 [D]Deut 11:14; Jer 5:24; Joel 2:23 5:8 [A]Luke 21:19 [B]1 Thess 3:13 [C]John 21:22; 1 Thess 2:19 [D]Rom 13:11, 12; 1 Pet 4:7 5:9 [a]Lit *groan* [b]Lit *before* [c]Lit *doors* [A]James 4:11 [B]James 5:7, 10 [C]1 Cor 4:5; James 4:12; 1 Pet 4:5 [D]Matt 24:33; Mark 13:29 5:10 [A]James 4:11; 5:7, 9 [B]Matt 5:12 5:11 [a]Or *steadfastness* [b]Lit *end of the Lord* [A]Matt 5:10; 1 Pet 3:14 [B]Job 1:21f; 2:10 [C]Job 42:10, 12 [D]Ex 34:6; Ps 103:8 5:12 [a]Lit *yours is to be yes, yes, and no, no* [A]James 1:16 [B]Matt 5:34-37 5:13 [A]James 5:10 [B]Ps 50:15 [C]1 Cor 14:15; Col 3:16 5:14 [a]Lit *having anointed* [A]Acts 11:30 [B]Mark 6:13; 16:18 5:15 [a]Lit *of* [b]Or *save* [c]Lit *it* [A]James 1:6 [B]1 Cor 1:21; James 5:20 [C]John 6:39; 2 Cor 4:14 5:16 [a]Lit *supplication* [A]Matt 3:6; Mark 1:5; Acts 19:18 [B]Heb 12:13; 1 Pet 2:24 [C]Gen 18:23-32; John 9:31 5:17 [a]Lit *with prayer* [A]Acts 14:15 [B]1 Kin 17:1; 18:1 [C]Luke 4:25 5:18 [a]Lit *heaven* [b]Lit *gave* [A]1 Kin 18:42 [B]1 Kin 18:45 5:19 [A]Matt 18:15; Gal 6:1 [B]James 3:14 5:20 [a]Lit *he who has turned* [A]Rom 11:14; 1 Cor 1:21; James 1:21 [B]Prov 10:12; 1 Pet 4:8

5:7 **patient.** The word emphasizes patience with people (cf. 1Th 5:14), not trials or circumstances (as in 1:3). Specifically, James has in mind patience with the oppressive rich. **the coming.** The second coming of Christ (*see note on Mt 24:3*). Realizing the glory that awaits them at Christ's return should motivate believers to patiently endure mistreatment (Ro 8:18). **the early and late rains.** The "early" rain falls in Israel during October and November and softens the ground for planting. The "late" rain falls in March and April, immediately before the spring harvest. Just as the farmer waits patiently from the early rain to the latter for his crop to ripen, so must Christians patiently wait for the Lord's return (cf. Gal 6:9; 2Ti 4:8; Titus 2:13).

5:8 **strengthen your hearts.** A call for resolute, firm courage and commitment. James exhorts those about to collapse under the weight of persecution to shore up their hearts with the hope of the second coming. **near.** The imminency of Christ's return is a frequent theme in the NT (cf. Ro 13:12; Heb 10:25; 1Pe 4:7; 1Jn 2:18).

5:9 **Do not complain … the Judge is standing right at the door.** James pictured Christ as a judge about to open the doors to the courtroom and convene His court. Knowing that the strain of persecution could lead to grumbling, James cautioned his readers against that sin (Php 2:14), lest they forfeit their full reward (2Jn 8).

5:11 **the endurance of Job.** Job is the classic example of a man who patiently endured suffering and was blessed by God for his persevering faith. James reassured his readers that God had a purpose for their suffering, just as He did for Job's. Cf. Job 42. **full of compassion and *is* merciful.** Remembering the Lord's character is a great comfort in suffering. The Scriptures repeatedly affirm His compassion and mercy (Ex 34:6; Nu 14:18; 1Ch 21:13; 2Ch 30:9; Pss 25:6; 78:38; 86:5, 15; 103:8, 13; 116:5; 136:1; 145:8; La 3:22; Joel 2:13; Jon 4:2; Mic 7:18; Lk 6:36).

5:12 **above all.** Or "especially." As he has done repeatedly in his epistle, James stressed that a person's speech provides the most revealing glimpse of his spiritual condition (cf. 1:26; 2:12; 3:2–11; 4:11). **do not swear … any other oath.** As Jesus did before him (Mt 5:33–36; 23:16–22), James condemned the contemporary Jewish practice of swearing false, evasive, deceptive oaths by everything other than the name of the Lord (which alone was considered binding). **yes is to be yes.** Again echoing Jesus (Mt 5:37), James called for straightforward, honest, plain speech. To speak otherwise is to invite God's judgment.

5:13 **suffering.** The antidote to the suffering caused by evil treatment or persecution is seeking God's comfort through prayer (cf. Pss 27:13, 14; 55:22; Jon 2:7; Php 4:6; 1Pe 5:7). **He is to sing praises.** The natural response of a joyful heart is to sing praise to God.

5:14, 15 **sick.** James directs those who are "sick," meaning weakened by their suffering to call for the elders of the church for strength, support, and prayer.

5:14 **anointing him with oil.** Lit. "rubbing him with oil": 1) possibly this is a reference to ceremonial anointing (*see notes on Lv 14:18; Mk 6:13*); 2) on the other hand, James may have had in mind medical treatment of believers physically bruised and battered by persecution. Perhaps it is better to understand the anointing in a metaphorical sense of the elders' encouraging, comforting, and strengthening the believer.

5:15 **prayer offered in faith.** The prayer offered on their behalf by the elders. **restore the … sick.** Deliver them from their suffering because they have been weakened by their infirmity, not from their sin, which was confessed. **committed sins … be forgiven.** Not by the elders, since God alone can forgive sins (Is 43:25; Da 9:9; Mk 2:7). That those who are suffering called for the elders implies they had a contrite, repentant heart, and that part of their time with the overseers would involve confessing their sins to God.

5:16 **confess your sins.** Mutual honesty, openness, and sharing of needs will enable believers to uphold each other in the spiritual struggle. **effective prayer … can accomplish much.** The energetic, passionate prayers of godly people have the power to accomplish much. Cf. Nu 11:2.

5:17, 18 **Elijah … prayed … he prayed again.** Elijah provides one of the most notable illustrations of the power of prayer in the OT. His prayers (not mentioned in the OT account) both initiated and ended a 3-year, 6-month drought (cf. Lk 4:25).

5:19 **if any among you.** This introduces a third category of people in the church (cf. vv. 13, 14)—those professing believers who have strayed from the truth. **strays from the truth.** Apostatizes from the faith they once professed (cf. Heb 5:12–6:9; 10:29; 1Jn 2:19). Such people are in grave danger (v. 20), and the church must call them back to the true faith.

5:20 **sinner.** Cf. 4:8. A word used to describe the unregenerate (cf. Pr 11:31; 13:6, 22; Mt 9:13; Lk 7:37, 39; 15:7, 10; 18:13; Ro 5:8; 1Ti 1:9, 15; 1Pe 4:18). James has in mind here those with dead faith (cf. 2:14–26), not sinning, true believers. **the error of his way.** Those who go astray doctrinally (v. 19) will also manifest an errant lifestyle, one not lived according to biblical principles. **save his soul from death.** A person who wanders from the truth puts his soul in jeopardy. The "death" in view is not physical death, but eternal death—eternal separation from God and eternal punishment in hell (cf. Is 66:24; Da 12:2; Mt 13:40, 42, 50; 25:41, 46; Mk 9:43–49; 2Th 1:8, 9; Ro 6:23; Rev 20:11–15; 21:8). Knowing how high the stakes are should motivate Christians to aggressively pursue such people. **cover a multitude of sins.** See Ps 5:10. Since even one sin is enough to condemn a person to hell, James' use of the word "multitude" emphasizes the hopeless condition of lost, unregenerate sinners. The good news of the gospel is that God's forgiving grace (which is greater than any sin; Ro 5:20) is available to those who turn from their sins and exercise faith in the Lord Jesus Christ (Eph 2:8, 9).

THE FIRST
EPISTLE OF

PETER

TITLE

The letter has always been identified (as are most general epistles, like James, John, and Jude) with the name of the author, Peter, and with the notation that it was his first inspired letter.

AUTHOR AND DATE

The opening verse of the epistle claims it was written by Peter, who was clearly the leader among Christ's apostles. The Gospel writers emphasize this fact by placing his name at the head of each list of apostles (Mt 10; Mk 3; Lk 6; Ac 1), and including more information about him in the 4 Gospels than any person other than Christ. Originally known as Simon (Gr.) or Simeon (Heb.), cf. Mk 1:16; Jn 1:40, 41, Peter was the son of Jonas (Mt 16:17) who was also known as John (Jn 1:42), and a member of a family of fishermen who lived in Bethsaida and later in Capernaum. Andrew, Peter's brother, brought him to Christ (Jn 1:40–42). He was married, and his wife apparently accompanied him in his ministry (Mk 1:29–31; 1Co 9:5).

Peter was called to follow Christ in His early ministry (Mk 1:16, 17), and was later appointed to apostleship (Mt 10:2; Mk 3:14–16). Christ renamed him Peter (Gr.), or Cephas (Aram.), both words meaning "stone" or "rock" (Jn 1:42). The Lord clearly singled out Peter for special lessons throughout the Gospels (e.g., Mt 10; 16:13–21; 17:1–9; 24:1–7; 26:31–33; Jn 6:6; 21:3–7, 15–17). He was the spokesman for the 12, articulating their thoughts and questions as well as his own. His triumphs and weaknesses are chronicled in the Gospels and Ac 1–12.

After the resurrection and ascension, Peter initiated the plan for choosing a replacement for Judas (Ac 1:15). After the coming of the Holy Spirit (Ac 2:1–4), he was empowered to become the leading gospel preacher from the Day of Pentecost on (Ac 2–12). He also performed notable miracles in the early days of the church (Ac 3–9), and opened the door of the gospel to the Samaritans (Ac 8) and to the Gentiles (Ac 10). According to tradition, Peter had to watch as his wife was crucified, but encouraged her with the words, "Remember the Lord." When it came time for him to be crucified, he reportedly pled that he was not worthy to be crucified like his Lord, but rather should be crucified upside down (ca. A.D. 67–68), which tradition says he was.

Because of his unique prominence, there was no shortage in the early church of documents falsely claiming to be written by Peter. That the apostle Peter is the author of 1 Peter, however, is certain. The material in this letter bears definite resemblance to his messages in the book of Acts. The letter teaches, for example, that Christ is the Stone rejected by the builder (2:7, 8; Ac 4:10, 11), and that Christ is no respecter of persons (1:17; Ac 10:34). Peter teaches his readers to "clothe yourselves with humility" (5:5), an echo of the Lord's girding Himself with a towel and washing the disciples' feet (Jn 13:3–5). There are other statements in the letter similar to Christ's sayings (4:14; 5:7, 8). Moreover, the author claims to have been a witness of the sufferings of Christ (5:1; cf. 3:18; 4:1). In addition to these internal evidences, it is noteworthy that the early Christians universally recognized this letter as the work of Peter.

The only significant doubt to be raised about Peter's authorship arises from the rather classical style of Greek employed in the letter. Some have argued that Peter, being an "uneducated" fisherman (Ac 4:13), could not have written in sophisticated Greek, especially in light of the less classical style of Greek employed in the writing of 2 Peter. However, this argument is not without a good answer. In the first place, that Peter was "uneducated" does not mean that he was illiterate, but only that he was without formal, rabbinical training in the Scriptures. Moreover, though Aramaic may have been Peter's primary language, Greek would have been a widely spoken second language in this region. It is also apparent that at least some of the authors of the NT, though not highly educated, could read the Greek of the OT Septuagint (see James' use of the LXX in Ac 15:14–18).

Beyond these evidences of Peter's ability in Greek, Peter also explained (5:12) that he wrote this letter "through Silvanus," also known as Silas. Silvanus was likely the messenger designated to take this letter to its intended readers. But more is implied by this statement in that Peter is acknowledging that Silvanus served as his secretary, or amanuensis. Dictation was common in the ancient Roman world (cf. Paul and Tertius; Ro 16:22), and secretaries often could aid with syntax and grammar. So, Peter, under the superintendence of the Spirit of God, dictated the letter to Silvanus, while Silvanus, who also was a prophet (Ac 15:32), may have aided in some of the composition of the more classical Greek.

First Peter was most likely written just before or shortly after July, A.D. 64 when the city of Rome burned, thus a writing date of ca. A.D. 64–65.

BACKGROUND AND SETTING

When the city of Rome burned, the Romans believed that their emperor, Nero, had set the city on fire, probably because of his incredible lust to build. In order to build more, he had to destroy what already existed.

The Romans were totally devastated. Their culture, in a sense, went down with the city. All the religious elements of their life were destroyed—their great temples, shrines, and even their household idols were burned up. This had great religious implications because it made them believe that their deities had been unable to deal with this conflagration and were also victims of it. The people were homeless and hopeless. Many had been killed. Their bitter resentment was severe, so Nero realized that he had to redirect the hostility.

The emperor's chosen scapegoat was the Christians, who were already hated because they were associated with Jews, and because they were seen as being hostile to the Roman culture. Nero spread the word quickly that the Christians had set the fires. As a result, a vicious persecution against Christians began, and soon spread throughout the Roman Empire, touching places N of the Taurus mountains, like Pontus, Galatia, Cappadocia, Asia, and Bithynia (1:1), and impacting the Christians, whom Peter calls "aliens." These "aliens," who were probably Gentiles, for the most part (1:14, 18; 2:9, 10; 4:3), possibly led to Christ by Paul and his associates, and established on Paul's teachings, needed spiritual strengthening because of their sufferings. Thus the Apostle Peter, under the inspiration of the Holy Spirit, wrote this epistle to strengthen them.

Peter wrote that he was in "Babylon" when he penned the letter (5:13). Three locations have been suggested for this "Babylon." First, a Roman outpost in northern Egypt was named Babylon; but that place was too obscure, and there are no reasons to think that Peter was ever there. Second, ancient Babylon in Mesopotamia is a possibility; but it would be quite unlikely that Peter, Mark, and Silvanus were all at this rather small, distant place at the same time. Third, "Babylon" is an alias for Rome; perhaps even a code word for Rome. In times of persecution, writers exercised unusual care not to endanger Christians by identifying them. Peter, according to some traditions, followed James and Paul and died as a martyr near Rome about two years after he wrote this letter, thus he had written this epistle near the end of his life, probably while staying in the imperial city. He did not want the letter to be found and the church to be persecuted, so he may have hidden its location under the code word, "Babylon," which aptly fit because of the city's idolatry (cf. Rev 17, 18).

HISTORICAL AND THEOLOGICAL THEMES

Since the believers addressed were suffering escalating persecution (1:6; 2:12, 19–21; 3:9, 13–18; 4:1, 12–16, 19), the purpose of this letter was to teach them how to live victoriously in the midst of that hostility: 1) without losing hope; 2) without becoming bitter; 3) while trusting in their Lord; and 4) while looking for His second coming. Peter wished to impress on his readers that by living an obedient, victorious life under duress, a Christian can actually evangelize his hostile world (cf. 1:14; 2:1, 12, 15; 3:1–6, 13–17; 4:2; 5:8, 9).

Believers are constantly exposed to a world system energized by Satan and his demons. Their effort is to discredit the church and to destroy its credibility and integrity. One way these spirits work is by finding Christians whose lives are not consistent with the Word of God, and then parading them before the unbelievers to show what a sham the church is. Christians, however, must stand against the enemy and silence the critics by the power of holy lives.

In this epistle, Peter is rather effusive in reciting two categories of truth. The first category is positive and includes a long list of blessings bestowed on Christians. As he speaks about the identity of Christians and what it means to know Christ, Peter mentions one privilege and blessing after another. Interwoven into this list of privileges is the catalog of suffering. Christians, though most greatly privileged, should also know that the world will treat them unjustly. Their citizenship is in heaven, and they are strangers in a hostile, Satan-energized world. Thus the Christian life can be summed up as a call to victory and glory through the path of suffering. So, the basic question that Peter answers in this epistle is: how are Christians to deal with animosity? The answer features practical truths and focuses on Jesus Christ as the model of one who maintained a triumphant attitude in the midst of hostility.

First Peter also answers other important practical questions about Christian living such as: Do Christians need a priesthood to intercede with God for them (2:5–9)? What should be the Christian's attitude to secular government and civil disobedience (2:13–17)? What should a Christian employee's attitude be toward a hostile employer (2:18)? How should a Christian lady conduct herself (3:3, 4)? How can a believing wife win her unsaved husband to Christ (3:1, 2)?

INTERPRETIVE CHALLENGES

First Peter 3:18–22 stands as one of the most difficult NT texts to translate and then interpret. For example, does "Spirit" in 3:18 refer to the Holy Spirit, or to Christ's Spirit? Did Christ preach through Noah before the Flood, or did He preach Himself after the crucifixion (3:19)? Was the audience to this preaching composed of the humans in Noah's day, or demons in the abyss (3:19)? Does 3:20, 21 teach baptismal regeneration (salvation), or salvation by faith alone in Christ? Answers to these questions will be found in the notes.

OUTLINE

I. Salutation (1:1, 2)

II. Remember Our Great Salvation (1:3–2:10)

A. The Certainty of Our Future Inheritance (1:3–12)
   1. Preserved by the power of God (1:3–5)
   2. Proven by the trials of persecution (1:6–9)
   3. Predicted by the prophets of God (1:10–12)

B. The Consequences of Our Future Inheritance (1:13–2:10)
   1. Perseverance of hope (1:13–16)
   2. Persistence of wonder (1:17–21)
   3. Power of love (1:22–2:3)
   4. Praises of Christ (2:4–10)

III. Remember Our Example Before Men (2:11–4:6)

A. Honorable Living Before Unbelievers (2:11–3:7)
   1. Submission to the government (2:11–17)
   2. Submission to masters (2:18–25)
   3. Submission in the family (3:1–7)

B. Honorable Living Before Believers (3:8–12)

C. Honorable Living in the Midst of Suffering (3:13–4:6)
   1. The principle of suffering for righteousness (3:13–17)
   2. The paragon of suffering for righteousness (3:18–22)
   3. The purpose of suffering for righteousness (4:1–6)

IV. Remember Our Lord Will Return (4:7–5:11)

A. The Responsibilities of Christian Living (4:7–11)

B. The Rewards of Christian Suffering (4:12–19)

C. The Requirements for Christian Leadership (5:1–4)

D. The Realization of Christian Victory (5:5–11)
   1. Conclusion (5:12–14)

A LIVING HOPE, AND A SURE SALVATION

1 [A]Peter, an apostle of Jesus Christ,
To those who reside as [B]aliens, [C]scattered
throughout [D]Pontus, [E]Galatia, [D]Cappadocia, [D]Asia,
and [F]Bithynia, [G]who are chosen 2 according to the
[A]foreknowledge of God the Father, [B]by the sanctifying work of the Spirit, [a]to [C]obey Jesus Christ and
be [D]sprinkled with His blood: [E]May grace and peace
[b]be yours in the fullest measure.
3 [A]Blessed be the God and Father of our Lord Jesus
Christ, who [B]according to His great mercy [C]has
caused us to be born again to [D]a living hope through
the [E]resurrection of Jesus Christ from the dead,
4 to *obtain* an [A]inheritance *which is* imperishable
and undefiled and [B]will not fade away, [C]reserved in
heaven for you, 5 who are [A]protected by the power of
God [B]through faith for [C]a salvation ready [D]to be revealed in the last time. 6 [A]In this you greatly rejoice,
even though now [B]for a little while, [C]if necessary,

1:1 [A]2 Pet 1:1 [B]1 Pet 2:11 [C]James 1:1 [D]Acts 2:9 [E]Acts 16:6 [F]Acts 16:7 [G]Matt 24:22; Luke 18:7 1:2 [a]Lit *unto obedience and sprinkling* [b]Lit *be multiplied for you* [A]Rom 8:29; 1 Pet 1:20 [B]2 Thess 2:13 [C]1 Pet 1:14, 22 [D]Heb 10:22; 12:24 [E]2 Pet 1:2 1:3 [A]2 Cor 1:3 [B]Gal 6:16; Titus 3:5 [C]James 1:18; 1 Pet 1:23 [D]1 Pet 1:13, 21; 3:5, 15; 1 John 3:3 [E]1 Cor 15:20; 1 Pet 3:21 1:4 [A]Acts 20:32; Rom 8:17; Col 3:24 [B]1 Pet 5:4 [C]2 Tim 4:8 1:5 [A]John 10:28; Phil 4:7 [B]Eph 2:8 [C]1 Cor 1:21; 2 Thess 2:13 [D]1 Pet 4:13; 5:1 1:6 [A]Rom 5:2 [B]1 Pet 5:10 [C]1 Pet 3:17

1:1 Peter. See Introduction: Author and Date. **apostle of Jesus Christ.** Peter was one of a unique group of men who were personally called (Mt 10:1–4) and commissioned (Jn 20:19–23) by Christ, and who ministered with Christ after His resurrection. *See note on 5:1.* The church was built upon the foundation of their teaching (*see notes on Ac 2:42; Eph 2:20*). **aliens.** These were strangers dispossessed in a land not their own—temporary residents or foreigners. Like all believers, they were residents of an eternal city (Php 3:20; Heb 13:13, 14). **scattered.** With the Gr. definite article, "scattered," or "dispersion," is sometimes a technical term for the scattering of the Jews from Israel throughout the world (Jn 7:35; Jas 1:1). But here, without the article, "scattered" is used in a nontechnical sense referring to spiritual pilgrims, aliens to the earth, whether Jews or Gentiles (cf. v. 17; 2:11), i.e., the church. **Pontus . . . Bithynia.** Peter's letter is addressed to churches in provinces located in modern-day Turkey, which were part of the Roman Empire. **chosen.** From the Gr. word which connotes the "called out ones." The word means "to pick out" or "to select." In the OT, it was used of Israel (Dt 7:6), indicating that God sovereignly chose Israel from among all the nations of the world to believe in and belong to Him (cf. Dt 14:2; Pss 105:43; 135:4). Here the word is used as a term for Christians, those chosen by God for salvation (cf. Ro 8:33; Col 3:12; 2Ti 2:10). The word is also used for those who receive Christ during the tribulation time (Mt 24:22, 24), and holy, unfallen angels (1Ti 5:21). To be reminded that they were elected by God was a great comfort to those persecuted Christians (*see notes on Eph 1:3–14*).

1:2 foreknowledge. The same Gr. word is translated "foreknown" in v. 20. In both verses, the word does not refer to awareness of what is going to happen, but it clearly means a predetermined relationship in the knowledge of the Lord. God brought the salvation relationship into existence by decreeing it into existence ahead of time. Christians are foreknown for salvation in the same way Christ was foreordained before the foundation of the world to be a sacrifice for sins (cf. Ac 2:23). "Foreknowledge" means that God planned before, not that He observed before (cf. Ex 33:17; Jer 1:5; Am 3:2; Mt 7:23). Thus, God pre-thought and pre-determined or predestined each Christian's salvation (*see notes on Ro 8:29; Eph 1:4*). **sanctifying work of the Spirit.** To sanctify means "to consecrate," "to set apart." The objective of election is salvation, which comes to the elect through the sanctifying work of the Spirit. The Holy Spirit thus makes God's chosen holy, by savingly setting them apart from sin and unbelief unto faith and righteousness (cf. 1Th 1:4; 2Th 2:13). Sanctification thus begins with justification (declaring the sinner just before God by graciously imputing Christ's righteousness to him, cf. Php 3:9), and continues as a process of purification that goes on until glorification, when the Christian sees Jesus face-to-face. **to obey.** Believers are set apart from sin to God in order that they might obey Jesus Christ. True salvation produces obedience to Christ (cf. Eph 2:10; 1Th 1:4–10). **sprinkled with His blood.** This phrase is based on Moses' sprinkling sacrificial blood on the people of Israel as a symbol sealing their covenant as they promised to obey God's Word (*see notes on Ex 24:4–8*). Likewise, in the New Covenant, faith in the shedding of Christ's blood on the cross not only activates God's promise to give the believer perfect atonement for sin, but also brings the believer into the covenant by one's promise of obedience to the Lord and His Word.

1:3 Father of our Lord Jesus Christ. Though God was known as Creator and Redeemer in the OT, He was rarely called Father. Christ, however, always addressed God as His Father in the Gospels (as Jn 5:17), except in the separation on the cross (Mt 27:46). In so doing, Christ was claiming to be of the same nature, being, or essence as the Father (cf. Mt 11:27; Jn 10:29–39; 14:6–11; 2Co 1:3; Eph 1:3, 17; 2Jn 3). Also, by speaking of "our" Lord, Peter personalized the Christian's intimate relationship with the God of the universe through His Son (cf. 1Co 6:17), an important truth for suffering Christians to remember. **great mercy.** The reason God provided a glorious salvation for mankind is that He is merciful. Sinners need God's mercy because they are in a pitiful, desperate, wretched condition as sinners (cf. Eph 2:4; Titus 3:5; see also Ex 34:6; Ps 108:4; Is 27:4; La 3:22; Mic 7:18). **has caused us to be born again.** God gave the new birth as part of His provision in salvation. When a sinner comes to Christ and puts his faith in Him, he is born anew into God's family and receives a new nature (*see notes on v. 23; Jn 1:13; 3:1–21*). **a living hope.** The living hope is eternal life. "Hope" means confident optimism, and: 1) comes from God (Ps 43:5); 2) is a gift of grace (2Th 2:16); 3) is defined by Scripture (Ro 15:4); 4) is a reasonable reality (1Pe 3:15); 5) is secured by the resurrection of Jesus Christ (Jn 11:25, 26; 14:19; 1Co 15:17); 6) is confirmed in the Christian by the Holy Spirit (Ro 15:13); 7) defends the Christian against Satan's attacks (1Th 5:8); 8) is confirmed through trials (Ro 5:3, 4); 9) produces joy (Ps 146:5); and 10) is fulfilled in Christ's return (Titus 2:13).

1:4 inheritance. Peter showed those persecuted Christians how to look past their troubles to their eternal inheritance. Life, righteousness, joy, peace, perfection, God's presence, Christ's glorious companionship, rewards, and all else God has planned is the Christian's heavenly inheritance (v. 5; cf. Mt 25:34; Ac 26:18; Eph 1:11; Col 1:12; Heb 9:15; also Pss 16:5; 23; 26; 72; La 3:24). According to Eph 1:14, the indwelling Holy Spirit is the resident guarantee of that inheritance. **imperishable.** The inheritance is not subject to passing away, nor liable to decay. The word was used in secular Greek of something that was unravaged by an invading army (cf. Mt 6:19–21). **undefiled.** This word means unpolluted, unstained with evil. The undefiled inheritance of the Christian is in marked contrast to an earthly inheritance, all of which is corrupted and defiled. **will not fade away.** "Fading" was often used of flowers that wither and decay. Though earthly inheritances eventually fade away, the eternal inheritance of a Christian has no decaying elements.

1:5 protected by the power of God. Supreme power, omniscience, omnipotence, and sovereignty not only keep the inheritance (v. 4), but also keep the believer secure. No one can steal the Christian's treasure, and no one can disqualify him from receiving it. *See notes on Ro 8:31–39.* **through faith.** The Christian's response to God's election and the Spirit's conviction is faith, but even faith is empowered by God (*see note on Eph 2:8*). Moreover, the Christian's continued faith in God is the evidence of God's keeping power. At the time of salvation, God energizes faith, and continues to preserve it. Saving faith is permanent; it never dies. *See notes on Mt 24:13; Heb 3:14.*

1:6 greatly rejoice. That is, to be exceedingly glad, exuberantly jubilant. This kind of joy is not based on changing, temporal circumstances, but is used of joy that comes from the unchanging, eternal relationship with God. Peter relates this joy to 1) the assurance of one's protected eternal inheritance (vv. 4, 5; cf. Jn 16:16–33) and 2) the assurance from one's proven faith (v. 7). **various trials.** Peter teaches several important principles about trouble in this verse: 1) trouble does not last ("little while"); 2) trouble serves a purpose ("if necessary"); 3) trouble brings turmoil ("distressed"); 4) trouble comes in various forms ("trials"); and 5) trouble should not diminish the Christian's joy ("greatly rejoice").

you have been distressed by [D]various [a]trials, 7 so
that the [a,A]proof of your faith, *being* more precious
than gold which [b]is perishable, [B]even though tested
by fire, [C]may be found to result in praise and glory
and honor at [D]the revelation of Jesus Christ; 8 and
[A]though you have not seen Him, you [B]love Him, and
though you do not see Him now, but believe in Him,
you greatly rejoice with joy inexpressible and [a]full
of glory, 9 obtaining as [A]the outcome of your faith
the salvation of [a]your souls.

10 [A]As to this salvation, the prophets who [B]prophe-
sied of the [C]grace that *would come* to you made careful searches and inquiries, 11 [a]seeking to know what
person or time [A]the Spirit of Christ within them was
indicating as He [B]predicted the sufferings of Christ
and the glories [b]to follow. 12 It was revealed to them
that they were not serving themselves, but you, in
these things which now have been announced to
you through those who [A]preached the gospel to you
by [B]the Holy Spirit sent from heaven—things into
which [C]angels long to [a]look.

13 Therefore, [a,A]prepare your minds for action, [b,B]keep
sober *in spirit,* fix your [C]hope completely on the [D]grace
[c]to be brought to you at [E]the revelation of Jesus Christ.
14 As [a,A]obedient children, do not [b,B]be conformed to
the former lusts *which were yours* in your [C]ignorance,
15 but [a,A]like the Holy One who called you, [b,B]be holy
yourselves also [C]in all *your* behavior; 16 because it is
written, "[A]YOU SHALL BE HOLY, FOR I AM HOLY."

17 If you [A]address as Father the One who [B]impar-
tially [C]judges according to each one's work, conduct
yourselves [D]in fear during the time of your [E]stay *on
earth;* 18 knowing that you were not [a,A]redeemed
with perishable things like silver or gold from your
[B]futile way of life inherited from your forefathers,
19 but with precious [A]blood, as of a [B]lamb unblemished and spotless, *the blood* of Christ. 20 For He was
[A]foreknown before [B]the foundation of the world, but
has [C]appeared [a]in these last times [D]for the sake of
you 21 who through Him are [A]believers in God, who
raised Him from the dead and [B]gave Him glory, so
that your faith and [C]hope are in God.

1:6 [a]Or *temptations* [D]James 1:2; 1 Pet 4:12 1:7 [a]Or *genuineness* [b]Lit *perishes* [A]James 1:3 [B]1 Cor 3:13 [C]Rom 2:7 [D]Luke 17:30; 1 Pet 1:13; 4:13 1:8 [a]Lit *glorified* [A]John 20:29 [B]Eph 3:19 1:9 [a]One early ms does not contain *your* [A]Rom 6:22 1:10 [A]Matt 13:17; Luke 10:24 [B]Matt 26:24 [C]1 Pet 1:13 1:11 [a]Or *inquiring* [b]Lit *after these* [A]2 Pet 1:21 [B]Matt 26:24 1:12 [a]Or *gain a clear glimpse* [A]1 Pet 1:25; 4:6 [B]Acts 2:2-4 [C]1 Tim 3:16 1:13 [a]Lit *gird the loins of your mind* [b]Lit *be sober* [c]Or *which is announced* [A]Eph 6:14 [B]1 Thess 5:6, 8; 2 Tim 4:5; 1 Pet 4:7; 5:8 [C]1 Pet 1:3 [D]1 Pet 1:10 [E]1 Pet 1:7 1:14 [a]Lit *children of obedience* [b]Or *conform yourselves* [A]1 Pet 1:2 [B]Rom 12:2; 1 Pet 4:2f [C]Eph 4:18 1:15 [a]Lit *according to* [b]Or *become* [A]1 Thess 4:7; 1 John 3:3 [B]2 Cor 7:1 [C]James 3:13 1:16 [A]Lev 11:44f; 19:2; 20:7 1:17 [A]Ps 89:26; Jer 3:19; Matt 6:9 [B]Acts 10:34 [C]Matt 16:27 [D]2 Cor 7:1; Heb 12:28; 1 Pet 3:15 [E]1 Pet 2:11 1:18 [a]Or *ransomed* [A]Is 52:3; 1 Cor 6:20; Titus 2:14; Heb 9:12 [B]Eph 4:17 1:19 [A]Acts 20:28; 1 Pet 1:2 [B]John 1:29 1:20 [a]Lit *at the end of the times* [A]Acts 2:23; Eph 1:4; 1 Pet 1:2; Rev 13:8 [B]Matt 25:34 [C]Heb 9:26 [D]Heb 2:14 1:21 [A]Rom 4:24; 10:9 [B]John 17:5, 24; 1 Tim 3:16; Heb 2:9 [C]1 Pet 1:3

1:7 proof of your faith. God's purpose in allowing trouble is to test the reality of one's faith. But the benefit of such a testing, or "fire," is immediately for the Christian, not God. When a believer comes through a trial still trusting the Lord, he is assured that his faith is genuine (cf. Ge 22:1–12; Job 1:20–22). **revelation of Jesus Christ.** The revelation or unveiling of Christ refers to His second coming, particularly focusing on the time when He comes to call and reward His redeemed people (cf. v. 13; 4:13; 1Co 1:7), i.e., the Rapture (1Th 4:13–18).

1:8 have not seen. This is in the sense of His appearing (v. 7). Cf. 2Co 5:7. At that time, the fiery trials that believers have endured will benefit God by bringing Him "praise and glory and honor" eternally.

1:9 obtaining ... salvation. "Obtaining" could lit. be translated "presently receiving for yourselves." In one sense, Christians now possess the result of their faith, a constant deliverance from the power of sin. In another sense, we are waiting to receive the full salvation of eternal glory in the redemption of our bodies (Ro 8:23).

1:10 this salvation. In this section, Peter looks at the greatness of salvation from the viewpoint of the divine agents who made it possible: 1) OT prophets (vv. 10, 11); 2) the Holy Spirit (vv. 11, 12); 3) the NT apostles (v. 12); and 4) the angels (v. 12). **grace that *would come*.** God is by nature gracious and was so, even under the conditional Old Covenant (cf. Ex 33:19; Jon 4:2). But the prophets foretold an even greater exhibit of grace than what they had ever known (Is 45:20–25; 52:14, 15; 55:1–7; 61:1–3; cf. Ro 9:24–33; 10:11, 13, 20; 15:9–21). **careful searches and inquiries.** The OT prophets studied their own writings in order to know more about the promised salvation. Though they believed and were personally saved from their sin by that faith (through the sacrifice God would provide in Christ), they could not fully understand what was involved in the life and death of Jesus Christ (cf. Nu 24:17; Heb 11:13, 39, 40).

1:11 what person or time. "Who would be the person?" and "When would He come?" were the questions the OT prophets searched to know. **Spirit of Christ within them.** The Holy Spirit (see notes on Ac 16:7; Ro 8:9; Gal 4:6; Php 1:19) took up residence within the writers of the OT, enabling them to write about the glorious salvation to be consummated in the future (2Pe 1:19–21).

1:12 not serving themselves, but you. The OT prophets who wrote of the coming of salvation (vv. 10, 11) knew it was a future Savior who would come, and thus they were really writing for those who are on this side of the cross. **those who preached the gospel.** The NT apostles and preachers of the gospel had the privilege of proclaiming that the prophecies written by the OT prophets had come to pass (cf. 2Co 6:1, 2).

1:13 prepare your minds for action. Some translations render this, "Gird up the loins of your mind." The ancient practice of gathering up one's robes when needing to move in a hurry; here, it is metaphorically applied to one's thought process. The meaning is to pull in all the loose ends of one's thinking, by rejecting the hindrances of the world and focusing on the future grace of God (cf. Eph 6:14; Col 3:2). **keep sober.** Spiritual sober-mindedness includes the ideas of steadfastness, self-control, clarity of mind, and moral decisiveness. The sober Christian is correctly in charge of his priorities and not intoxicated with the various allurements of the world. **fix your hope completely.** In light of their great salvation, Christians, especially those undergoing suffering, should unreservedly live for the future, anticipating the consummation of their salvation at the second coming of Christ (see v. 7). Cf. Col 3:2–4. **grace to be brought to you.** Christ's future ministry of glorifying Christians and giving them eternal life in His presence will be the final culmination of the grace initiated at salvation (cf. Eph 2:7).

1:15 be holy yourselves. Holiness essentially defines the Christian's new nature and conduct in contrast with his pre-salvation lifestyle. The reason for practicing a holy manner of living is that Christians are associated with the holy God and must treat Him and His Word with respect and reverence. We therefore glorify Him best by being like Him (see vv. 16, 17; Mt 5:48; Eph 5:1; cf. Lv 11:44, 45; 18:30; 19:2; 20:7; 21:6–8).

1:17 if you address as Father. This is another way of saying, "if you are a Christian." The believer who knows God, and that He judges the works of all His children fairly, will respect God and His evaluation of his life, and long to honor his heavenly Father.

1:18 redeemed. *See note on 1Ti 2:6.* That is, to buy back someone from bondage by the payment of a price; to set free by paying a ransom. "Redemption" was a technical term for money paid to buy back a prisoner of war. Here it is used of the price paid to buy the freedom of one in the bondage of sin and under the curse of the law (i.e., eternal death, cf. Gal 3:13). The price paid to a holy God was the shed blood of His own Son (cf. Ex 12:1–13; 15:13; Ps 78:35; Ac 20:28; Ro 3:24; Gal 4:4, 5; Eph 1:7; Col 1:14; Titus 2:14; Heb 9:11–17).

1:20 foreknown. In eternity past, before Adam and Eve sinned, God planned the redemption of sinners through Jesus Christ (cf. Ac 2:23; 4:27, 28; 2Ti 1:9). *See note on v. 2.* **last times.** The "last times" are the times of the Messiah, from His first coming to His second coming (cf. Ac 2:17; 1Ti 4:1; 1Jn 2:18).

1:21 gave Him glory. God, through the ascension, returned Christ to the glory that He had with Him before the world began (cf. Lk 24:51–53; Jn 17:4, 5; Ac 1:9–11; Php 2:9–11; Heb 1:1–3; 2:9).

22 Since you have [A]in obedience to the truth
[B]purified your souls for a [a,C]sincere love of the
brethren, fervently love one another from [b]the
heart, 23 for you have been [A]born again [B]not of
seed which is perishable but imperishable, *that
is,* through the living and enduring [C]word of God.
24 For,

> "[A]ALL FLESH IS LIKE GRASS,
> AND ALL ITS GLORY LIKE THE
> FLOWER OF GRASS.
> THE GRASS WITHERS,
> AND THE FLOWER FALLS OFF,
> 25 [A]BUT THE WORD OF THE LORD
> ENDURES FOREVER."

And this is [B]the word which was [a]preached to you.

AS NEWBORN BABES

2 Therefore, [A]putting aside all [a]malice and all deceit and [b]hypocrisy and [b]envy and all [b,B]slander,
2 [A]like newborn babies, long for the [a,B]pure [b]milk of
the word, so that by it you may [C]grow [c]in respect
to salvation, 3 if you have [A]tasted [a,B]the kindness of
the Lord.

AS LIVING STONES

4 And coming to Him as to a living stone which
has been [A]rejected by men, but is [a]choice and precious in the sight of God, 5 [A]you also, as living stones,
[a]are being built up as a [B]spiritual house for a holy
[C]priesthood, to [D]offer up spiritual sacrifices acceptable to God through Jesus Christ. 6 For *this* is contained in [a]Scripture:

> "[A]BEHOLD, I LAY IN ZION A CHOICE STONE,
> A [B]PRECIOUS CORNER *stone,*
> AND HE WHO BELIEVES IN [b]HIM
> WILL NOT BE [C]DISAPPOINTED."

7 [A]This precious value, then, is for you who believe;
but for those who disbelieve,

> "[B]THE STONE WHICH THE
> BUILDERS [C]REJECTED,
> THIS BECAME THE VERY CORNER *stone,*"

8 and,

> "[A]A STONE OF STUMBLING AND
> A ROCK OF OFFENSE";

1:22 [a]Lit *unhypocritical* [b]Two early mss read *a clean heart* [A]1 Pet 1:2 [B]James 4:8 [C]John 13:34; Rom 12:10; Heb 13:1; 1 Pet 2:17; 3:8 1:23 [A]John 3:3; 1 Pet 1:3 [B]John 1:13 [C]Heb 4:12 1:24 [A]Is 40:6ff; James 1:10f 1:25 [a]Lit *preached as good news to you* [A]Is 40:8 [B]Heb 6:5 2:1 [a]Or *wickedness* [b]plural nouns [A]Eph 4:22, 25, 31; James 1:21 [B]James 4:11 2:2 [a]Or *unadulterated* [b]Or *spiritual* (Gr *logikos*) *milk* [c]Or *up to salvation* [A]Matt 18:3; 19:14; Mark 10:15; Luke 18:17; 1 Cor 14:20 [B]1 Cor 3:2 [C]Eph 4:15f 2:3 [a]Lit *that the Lord is kind* [A]Heb 6:5 [B]Ps 34:8; Titus 3:4 2:4 [a]Lit *chosen;* or *elect* [A]1 Pet 2:7 2:5 [a]Or *allow yourselves to be built up;* or *build yourselves up* [A]1 Cor 3:9 [B]Gal 6:10; 1 Tim 3:15 [C]Is 61:6; 66:21; 1 Pet 2:9; Rev 1:6 [D]Rom 15:16; Heb 13:15 2:6 [a]Or *a scripture* [b]Or *it* [c]Or *put to shame* [A]Is 28:16; Rom 9:32, 33; 10:11; 1 Pet 2:8 [B]Eph 2:20 2:7 [A]2 Cor 2:16; 1 Pet 2:7, 8 [B]Ps 118:22; Matt 21:42; Luke 2:34 [C]1 Pet 2:4 2:8 [A]Is 8:14

1:22 fervently love one another. The love indicated here by Peter is the love of choice, the kind of love that can respond to a command. "Fervently" means to stretch to the limits (cf. Lk 22:44; Ac 12:5; also Lk 10:27ff.). Only those whose "souls" have been "purified," i.e., saved, have the capacity to love like this. Such love exhibits itself by meeting others at the point of their need (cf. 2:17; 3:8; 4:8; also Jn 13:34; Ro 12:10; Php 2:1–8; Heb 13:1; 1Jn 3:11).

1:23 not of seed which is perishable but imperishable. The spiritual life implanted by the Holy Spirit to produce the new birth is unfailing and permanent. **through the ... word of God.** The Spirit uses the Word to produce life. It is the truth of the gospel that saves. *See note on Ro 10:17.*

1:24, 25 Peter enforces his point about the power of the Word to regenerate by quoting from Is 40:6–8 (*see note there*).

2:1 putting aside. The Christian's new life can't grow unless sins are renounced. When that purging takes place, then the Word does its work (v. 2). **malice.** The Gr. word for evil is used 11 times in the NT to indicate that wickedness which comes from within a person (cf. v. 16; Ro 1:29; Eph 4:31; Titus 3:3).

2:2 long for the pure milk of the word. Spiritual growth is always marked by a craving for and a delight in God's Word with the intensity with which a baby craves milk (cf. Job 23:12; Pss 1:1, 2; 19:7–11; 119:16, 24, 35, 47, 48, 72, 92, 97, 103, 111, 113, 127, 159, 167, 174; Jer 15:16). A Christian develops a desire for the truth of God's Word by: 1) remembering his life's source (1:25; cf. Is 55:10, 11; Jn 15:3; Heb 4:12); 2) eliminating sin from his life (v. 1); 3) admitting his need for God's truth (v. 2, "like newborn babies"; cf. Mt 4:4); 4) pursuing spiritual growth (v. 2, "by it you may grow"); and 5) surveying his blessings (v. 3, "kindness of the Lord").

2:3 tasted. At salvation, all believers experience how gracious the Lord is to those who trust Him. That should compel believers to seek more of that grace in pursuing His Word.

2:4 coming to Him. "Coming" in the Gr. here means to come with the idea of remaining. Here it means to remain in Christ's presence with intimate fellowship (cf. Jn 15:5–15). **a living stone.** Both a metaphor and a paradox, this phrase from the OT (see vv. 6–8) emphasizes that Christ, the "cornerstone" and "stone of stumbling," is alive from the dead and has a living relationship with saved humanity (v. 5; cf. 1Co 15:45; 1Jn 5:11, 12). **rejected ... choice.** See v. 7. The messianic credentials of Jesus were examined by the false religious leaders of Israel and contemptuously rejected (vv. 6–8; cf. Mt 12:22–24; Jn 1:10, 11). But Jesus Christ was God's precious and elect Son, ultimately authenticated through His resurrection from the dead (cf. Ps 2:10, 11; Mt 3:17; Ac 2:23, 24, 32; 4:11, 12; 5:30, 31; 10:39–41).

2:5 you also, as living stones. Christians are so closely identified and united with Christ that the very life that exists in Christ exists in them also (cf. Gal 2:20; Col 3:3, 4; 2Pe 1:4). **built up as a spiritual house.** Metaphorically, God is building a spiritual house, putting all believers in place, integrating each one with others, and each one with the life of Christ (cf. Eph 2:19; Heb 3:6). **a holy priesthood.** OT priests and NT believer-priests share a number of characteristics: 1) priesthood is an elect privilege (Ex 28:1; Jn 15:16); 2) priests are cleansed of sins (Lv 8:6–36; Titus 2:14); 3) priests are clothed for service (5:5; Ex 28:42; Lv 8:7ff.; Ps 132:9, 16); 4) priests are anointed for service (Lv 8:12, 30; 1Jn 2:20, 27); 5) priests are prepared for service (Lv 8:33; 9:4, 23; Gal 1:16; 1Ti 3:6); 6) priests are ordained to obedience (v. 4; Lv 10:1ff.); 7) priests are to honor the Word of God (v. 2; Mal 2:7); 8) priests are to walk with God (Mal 2:6; Gal 5:16, 25); 9) priests are to impact sinners (Mal 2:6; Gal 6:1); and 10) priests are messengers of God (Mal 2:7; Mt 28:19, 20). The main privilege of a priest, however, is access to God. **to offer up spiritual sacrifices.** Spiritual sacrifices mean God-honoring works done because of Christ under the direction of the Holy Spirit and the guidance of the Word of God. These would include: 1) offering the strength of one's body to God (Ro 12:1, 2); 2) praising God (Heb 13:15); 3) doing good (Heb 13:16); 4) sharing one's resources (Heb 13:16); 5) bringing people to Christ (Ro 15:16); 6) sacrificing one's desires for the good of others (Eph 5:2); and 7) praying (Rev 8:3).

2:6–8 Three OT passages employing the "stone" metaphor are used by Peter to show that Christ's position as chief cornerstone of the new spiritual house was foreordained by God. That same stone is also going to be the stumbling stone that brings down the unbelieving in judgment (cf. Mt 21:42, 44).

2:6 Zion. Quoted from Is 28:16. Figuratively, Zion, i.e., Jerusalem, is in the realm of the New Covenant, as Sinai is in the realm of the Old Covenant.

2:6, 7 corner ***stone.*** *See note on Eph 2:20;* cf. Ps 118:22.

2:8 A stone of stumbling and a rock of offense. Quoted from Is 8:14. To every human being, Christ is either the means of salvation if they believe, or the means of judgment if they reject the gospel. He is like a stone in the

[B]for they stumble because they are disobedient to the
word, [C]and to this *doom* they were also appointed.
9 But you are [A]A CHOSEN RACE, A royal [B]PRIEST-
HOOD, A [C]HOLY NATION, [D]A PEOPLE FOR *God's* OWN POS-
SESSION, so that you may proclaim the excellencies
of Him who has called you [E]out of darkness into His
marvelous light; 10 [A]for you once were NOT A PEOPLE,
but now you are THE PEOPLE OF GOD; you had NOT
RECEIVED MERCY, but now you have RECEIVED MERCY.
11 [A]Beloved, [B]I urge you as [C]aliens and strangers to abstain from [D]fleshly lusts which wage [E]war
against the soul. 12 [A]Keep your behavior excellent
among the Gentiles, so that in the thing in which
they [B]slander you as evildoers, they may [a]because
of your good deeds, as they observe *them,* [C]glorify
God [D]in the day of [b]visitation.

HONOR AUTHORITY

13 [A]Submit yourselves for the Lord's sake to every
human institution, whether to a king as the one in
authority, 14 or to governors as sent [a]by him [A]for the
punishment of evildoers and the [B]praise of those
who do right. 15 For [a,A]such is the will of God that
by doing right you may [B]silence the ignorance of
foolish men. 16 *Act* as [A]free men, and [a]do not use
your freedom as a covering for evil, but *use it* as
[B]bondslaves of God. 17 [A]Honor all people, [B]love the
brotherhood, [C]fear God, [D]honor the [a]king.

2:8 [B]1 Cor 1:23; Gal 5:11 [C]Rom 9:22 2:9 [A]Is 43:20f; Deut 10:15 [B]Is 61:6; 66:21; 1 Pet 2:5; Rev 1:6 [C]Ex 19:6; Deut 7:6 [D]Ex 19:5; Deut 4:20; 14:2; Titus 2:14 [E]Is 9:2; 42:16; Acts 26:18; 2 Cor 4:6 2:10 [A]Hos 1:10; 2:23; Rom 9:25; 10:19 2:11 [A]Heb 6:9; 1 Pet 4:12 [B]Rom 12:1 [C]Lev 25:23; Ps 39:12; Eph 2:19; Heb 11:13; 1 Pet 1:17 [D]Rom 13:14; Gal 5:16, 24 [E]James 4:1 2:12 [a]Or *as a result of* [b]I.e. Christ's coming again in judgment [A]2 Cor 8:21; Phil 2:15; Titus 2:8; 1 Pet 2:15; 3:16 [B]Acts 28:22 [C]Matt 5:16; 9:8; John 13:31; 1 Pet 4:11, 16 [D]Is 10:3; Luke 19:44 2:13 [A]Rom 13:1 2:14 [a]Lit *through* [A]Rom 13:4 [B]Rom 13:3 2:15 [a]Lit *so* [A]1 Pet 3:17 [B]1 Pet 2:12 2:16 [a]Lit *not having* [A]John 8:32; James 1:25 [B]Rom 6:22; 1 Cor 7:22 2:17 [a]Or *emperor* [A]Rom 12:10; 13:7 [B]1 Pet 1:22 [C]Prov 24:21 [D]Matt 22:21; 1 Pet 2:13

road that causes a traveler to fall. **disobedient to the word.** Unbelief is their disobedience, since the call of the gospel to repent and believe is a command from God. **they were also appointed.** These were not appointed by God to disobedience and unbelief. Rather, these were appointed to doom because of their disobedience and unbelief. Judgment on unbelief is as divinely appointed as salvation by faith. *See notes on Ro 9:22; 2Co 2:15, 16.*

2:9 a chosen race. Peter uses OT concepts to emphasize the privileges of NT Christians (cf. Dt 7:6–8). In strong contrast to the disobedient who are appointed by God to wrath (v. 8), Christians are chosen by God to salvation (cf. 1:2). **A royal** priesthood. The concept of a kingly priesthood is drawn from Ex 19:6. Israel temporarily forfeited this privilege because of its apostasy and because its wicked leaders executed the Messiah. At the present time, the church is a royal priesthood united with the royal priest, Jesus Christ. A royal priesthood is not only a priesthood that belongs to and serves the king, but is also a priesthood which exercises rule. This will ultimately be fulfilled in Christ's future kingdom (1Co 6:1–4; Rev 5:10; 20:6). a holy nation. Another allusion to Ex 19:6 (cf. Lv 19:2; 20:26; Dt 7:6; Is 62:12). Tragically, Israel temporarily forfeited the great privilege of being the unique people of God through unbelief. Until Israel's future acceptance of its Messiah, God has replaced the nation with the church. *See notes on Ro 11:1, 2, 25–29* for Israel's salvation. a people for ***God's*** own possession. This combines phraseology found in Ex 19:5; Is 43:21; Mal 3:17. Cf. Titus 2:14. **proclaim the excellencies.** "Proclaim," an unusual word found in no other place in the NT, means to tell forth, to tell something not otherwise known. "Excellencies" are praises, virtues, eminent qualities. **darkness ... light.** Cf. Ac 26:18; Eph 5:8; Col 1:13.

2:10 the people of **GOD.** The ideas of this verse come from Hos 1:6–10; 2:23. Cf. Ro 9:23–26 where the reference is explicitly to the calling of a people made up of Jews and Gentiles. **now you have** received mercy. God generally has temporal mercy and the compassion of common grace on His creation as a whole (Ps 145:9; La 3:22). Paul made reference to this when he said that God is the "Savior of all men" (*see note on 1Ti 4:10*). But God has eternal mercy on His elect church by forgiving their sins and eliminating their judgment (cf. Ro 9:15; Titus 3:5). In the OT, the prophet Hosea promised that Israel, though remaining outside of God's blessings for a long period of time, would eventually come under God's mercy. God's dealing with Israel was somewhat of a pattern for His dealings with the believers under the New Covenant, who previously were outside God's covenant, but have been brought under the mercy of God by faith in Christ (cf. Eph 2:4–13).

2:11 aliens and strangers. In this section, Peter called his readers to a righteous life in a hostile world. Christians are foreigners in a secular society because their citizenship is in heaven. There are 3 perspectives from which Christians can look at their obligations: 1) strangers (vv. 11, 12); 2) citizens (vv. 13–17); and 3) servants (vv. 18–20). In vv. 21–25, Peter shows how Christ set the example by living a perfect life in the midst of His hostile environment. **abstain from fleshly lusts.** Perhaps more lit. "hold yourself away from fleshly lusts." In order to have an impact on the world for God, Christians must be disciplined in an inward and private way by avoiding the desires of the fallen nature (cf. Gal 5:19–21, where "fleshly lusts" include much more than sexual temptations). **which wage war against the soul.** "War," i.e., to carry on a military campaign. Fleshly lusts are personified as if they were an army of rebels or guerrillas who incessantly search out and try to destroy the Christian's joy, peace and usefulness (cf. 4:2, 3).

2:12 behavior excellent. The Gr. word for "excellent" is rich in meaning and implies the purest, highest, noblest kind of goodness. It means "lovely," "winsome," "gracious," "noble," and "honorable." Having been disciplined in the inward and private side, the Christian must outwardly live among non-Christians in a way which reflects that inward discipline. **evildoers.** The early Christians were falsely accused of rebellion against the government with such false accusations as: terrorism (burning Rome; see Introduction: Background and Setting), atheism (no idols or emperor worship), cannibalism (rumors about the Lord's Supper), immorality (because of their love for one another), damaging trade and social progress, and leading slaves into insurrection. Cf. Ac 16:18–21; 19:19, 24–27. **day of visitation.** A common phrase in the OT (Is 10:3; Jer 27:22) warning of God's "visitation," His drawing near to people or nations in either judgment or blessing. In the NT, "visitation" speaks of redemption (Lk 1:68; 7:16; 19:44). Peter was teaching that when the grace of God visits the heart of an unbeliever, he will respond with saving faith and glorify God because he remembers the testimony of believers he had observed. Those who don't believe will experience the visitation of His wrath in the final judgment.

2:13 Submit yourselves. "Submit" is a military term meaning "to arrange in military fashion under the commander," "to put oneself in an attitude of submission." As citizens in the world and under civil law and authority, God's people are to live in a humble, submissive way in the midst of any hostile, godless, slandering society (cf. vv. 21–23; Pr 24:21; Jer 29:4–14; Mt 22:21; Ro 13:1ff., 1Ti 2:1; Heb 10:32–34). **for the Lord's sake.** Though the Christian's true citizenship is in heaven (Php 3:20) he still must live as an obedient citizen in this world so that God will be honored and glorified. Rebellious conduct by a Christian brings dishonor on Christ. *See notes on Ro 13:1–5; Titus 3:1, 2.*

2:14 governors. Christians are to live in obedience to every institution of civil and social order on earth. This includes obedience to the national government (v. 13, "king"), the state government, the police, and judges. Only when the government tries to force a Christian to do what is against the law of God explicitly stated in Scripture, should he refuse to submit (cf. Ac 4:18–20; 5:28, 29; Titus 1:6; 3:1, 2).

2:15 silence ... foolish men. Here is the purpose for our submission to authority, in order that we should avoid condemnation and win commendation that shuts the mouth of those obstinately set against the faith who are looking for reasons to criticize believers.

2:16 freedom as a covering for evil. Believers should enjoy their freedom in Christ, but ought not to put on a veil or mask of freedom to cover what really is wickedness. Christian freedom is never to be an excuse for self-indulgence or license. Cf. 1Co 7:22; 8:9–13; 2Th 3:7–9; *see notes on Ro 14:1–15:3.*

2:17 Honor. Highly esteem is the idea, and it refers not just to obedient duty but inner respect. **brotherhood.** The church. Cf. 1:22; 3:8; 4:8; 5:14.

18 [A]Servants, be submissive to your masters with
all respect, not only to those who are good and
[B]gentle, but also to those who are [a]unreasonable.
19 For this *finds* [a]favor, if for the sake of [A]conscience
toward God a person bears up under sorrows when
suffering unjustly. 20 For what credit is there if,
when you sin and are harshly treated, you endure
it with patience? But if [A]when you do what is right
and suffer *for it* you patiently endure it, this *finds*
[a]favor with God.

CHRIST IS OUR EXAMPLE

21 For [A]you have been called for this purpose,
[B]since Christ also suffered for you, leaving you [C]an
example for you to follow in His steps, 22 WHO [A]COM-
MITTED NO SIN, NOR WAS ANY DECEIT FOUND IN HIS
MOUTH; 23 [a]and while being [A]reviled, He did not revile in return; while suffering, He uttered no threats,
but kept entrusting *Himself* to Him who judges
righteously; 24 and He Himself [a,A]bore our sins in
His body on the [b,B]cross, so that we [C]might die to [c]sin
and live to righteousness; for [D]by His [d]wounds you
were [E]healed. 25 For you were [A]continually straying
like sheep, but now you have returned to the [B]Shep-
herd and [a]Guardian of your souls.

GODLY LIVING

3 [A]In the same way, you wives, [B]be submissive
to your own husbands so that even if any *of*
them are disobedient to the word, they may be [C]won
without a word by the behavior of their wives, 2 as
they observe your chaste and [a]respectful behavior.
3 [A]Your adornment must not be *merely* external—
braiding the hair, and wearing gold jewelry, or putting on dresses; 4 but *let it be* [A]the hidden person
of the heart, with the imperishable quality of a

2:18 [a]Or *perverse* [A]Eph 6:5 [B]James 3:17 2:19 [a]Or *grace* [A]Rom 13:5; 1 Pet 3:14, 16f 2:20 [a]V 19, note 1 [A]1 Pet 3:17 2:21 [A]Acts 14:22; 1 Pet 3:9 [B]1 Pet 3:18; 4:1, 13 [C]Matt 11:29; 16:24 2:22 [A]Is 53:9; 2 Cor 5:21 2:23 [a]Lit *who* [A]Is 53:7; Heb 12:3; 1 Pet 3:9 2:24 [a]Or *carried...up to the cross* [b]Lit *wood* [c]Lit *sins* [d]Lit *wound;* or *welt* [A]Is 53:4, 11; 1 Cor 15:3; Heb 9:28 [B]Acts 5:30 [C]Rom 6:2, 13 [D]Is 53:5 [E]Heb 12:13; James 5:16 2:25 [a]Or *Bishop, Overseer* [A]Is 53:6 [B]John 10:11; 1 Pet 5:4 3:1 [A]1 Pet 3:7 [B]Eph 5:22; Col 3:18 [C]1 Cor 9:19 3:2 [a]Lit *with respect* 3:3 [A]Is 3:18ff; 1 Tim 2:9 3:4 [A]Rom 7:22

2:18 Servants, be submissive. One's Christianity does not give the right to rebel against one's superior in the social structure (*see notes on 1Co 7:21–23; Eph 6:5; Col 3:22; Phm*; see also Ex 21:26, 27; Lv 25:39–43; Dt 23:15, 16), no matter how unfair or harsh he may be.

2:19, 20 favor with God. Favor with God is found when an employee, treated unjustly, accepts his poor treatment with faith in God's sovereign care, rather than responding in anger, hostility, discontent, pride, or rebellion (cf. Mt 5:11).

2:21 you have been called. The "call," as always in the NT epistles, is the efficacious call to salvation (v. 9; 5:10; Ro 8:30). Peter's point is that a person called to salvation will, sometimes at least, have to endure unfair treatment. Commendable behavior on the part of the believer in the midst of such trials results in the strengthening and perfecting of the Christian on earth (5:10; cf. Jas 1:2–4), and his increased eternal capacity to glorify God (cf. Mt 20:21–23; 2Co 4:17, 18; 2Ti 2:12). **for this purpose.** Patient endurance (v. 20). **leaving you an example.** The word "example" lit. means "writing under." It was writing put under a piece of paper on which to trace letters, thus a pattern. Christ is the pattern for Christians to follow in suffering with perfect patience. His death was efficacious, primarily, as an atonement for sin (2Co 5:21); but it was also exemplary, as a model of endurance in unjust suffering.

2:22 This is a quote from Is 53:9. He was the perfect example of patient endurance in unjust suffering because He was sinless, as the prophet said He would be. Cf. 1:19.

2:23 reviled. To "revile" is to pile up abusive and vile language against someone. Though verbally abused, Christ never retaliated with vicious words and threats (3:9; cf. Mt 26:57–65; 27:12–14; Lk 23:7–11). **entrusting *Himself*.** "To entrust" was "to hand over to someone to keep." Christ was "delivered" to Pilate (Jn 19:11); Pilate "handed Him over" to the Jews (Jn 19:16); Christ "handed over" Himself to God, suffering in surprising silence, because of His perfect confidence in the sovereignty and righteousness of His Father (cf. Is 53:7).

2:24 bore our sins. Christ suffered not simply as the Christian's pattern (vv. 21–23), but far more importantly as the Christian's substitute. To bear sins was to be punished for them (cf. Nu 14:33; Eze 18:20). Christ bore the punishment and the penalty for believers, thus satisfying a holy God (3:18; *see notes on 2Co 5:21; Gal 3:13*). This great doctrine of the substitutionary atonement is the heart of the gospel. Actual atonement, sufficient for the sins of the whole world, was made for all who would ever believe, namely, the elect (cf. Lv 16:17; 23:27–30; Jn 3:16; 2Co 5:19; 1Ti 2:6; 4:10; Titus 2:11; Heb 2:9; 1Jn 2:2; 4:9, 10). **we might die to sin.** This is true by the miracle of being in Christ. We died to sin in the sense that we paid its penalty, death, by being in Christ when He died as our substitute. *See notes on Ro 6:1–11.* **live to righteousness.** Not only have we been declared just, the penalty for our sins paid by His death, but we have risen to walk in new life, empowered by the Holy Spirit (*see notes on Ro 6:12–22*). **by His wounds you were healed.** From Is 53:5 (*see note*). Through the wounds of Christ at the cross, believers are healed spiritually from the deadly disease of sin. Physical healing comes at glorification only, when there is no more physical pain, illness, or death (Rev 21:4). *See notes on Is 53:4–6; Mt 8:17* for comments on healing in the atonement.

2:25 returned. Means "to turn toward," and refers to the repentant faith a person has at salvation. **Shepherd and Guardian.** Christ is not only the Christian's standard (vv. 21–23) and substitute (v. 24), but He is also the Christian's shepherd (5:4; cf. Is 53:6; Jn 10:11). In the OT, the title of "shepherd" for the Lord was often messianic (Eze 34:23, 24; 37:24; cf. Jn 10:1–18). Beyond that, "Shepherd and Guardian" were the most appropriate descriptions of Christ for Peter to use in order to comfort Christians who were being persecuted and slandered (v. 12). These two terms are also used for human spiritual leaders. "Shepherd" is the word for pastor, and "Guardian" is the word for bishop (cf. Eph 4:11; Titus 1:7), both referring to the same persons who lead the church (cf. Ac 20:28).

3:1 In the same way. In chap. 2, Peter taught that living successfully as a Christian in a hostile world would require relating properly in two places: the civil society (2:13–17), and the workplace (2:18–25). At the start of this chapter, he added two more places: the family (vv. 1–7) and the local church (vv. 8, 9). **be submissive.** Peter insisted that if Christians are to be a witness for their Lord, they must submit not only to the civil, but also to the social order which God has designed. **own husbands.** Women are not inferior to men in any way, any more than submissive Christians are inferior to pagan rulers or non-Christian bosses (cf. Gal 3:28). But wives have been given a role which puts them in submission to the headship which resides in their own husbands (*see notes on 1Co 11:1–9; Eph 5:22; Col 3:18; Titus 2:4, 5*). **any ... disobedient to the word.** Since obedience has been used in this letter to refer to believers and disobedience to nonbelievers (*see notes on 1:2; 2:8*), this is a non-Christian husband. In a culture in which women were viewed as lower than men, the potential for conflict and embarrassment in the marriage of a believer and unbeliever was significant, even as it is in contemporary society. Peter did not urge the Christian wife to leave her husband (cf. 1Co 7:13–16), to preach to her husband ("without a word"), or to demand her rights ("be submissive"). **won ... by the behavior of their wives.** The loving, gracious submission of a Christian woman to her unsaved husband is the strongest evangelistic tool she has. Added to submission is modesty, meekness, and respect for the husband (vv. 2–6).

3:2 chaste ... respectful. Purity of life with reverence for God is what the unsaved husband should observe consistently.

3:3 external. Peter was not here condemning all outward adornment. His condemnation is for incessant preoccupation with the outward to the disregard of one's character (v. 4; cf. 1Ti 2:9, 10). But every Christian woman is especially to concentrate on developing that chaste and reverent Christlike character.

3:4 gentle and quiet spirit. Here is beauty that never decays, as the outward body does. "Gentle" is actually "meek or humble" and "quiet" describes the character of her action and reaction to her husband and life in general. Such is precious not only to her husband, but also to God.

gentle and quiet spirit, which is precious in the
sight of God. 5 For in this way in former times the
holy women also, [A]who hoped in God, used to adorn
themselves, being submissive to their own husbands; 6 just as Sarah obeyed Abraham, [A]calling him
lord, and you have become her children if you do
what is right [a,B]without being frightened by any fear.
7 [A]You husbands in the same way, live with *your*
wives in an understanding way, as with [a,B]someone
weaker, since she is a woman; and show her honor
as a fellow heir of the grace of life, so that your
prayers will not be hindered.
8 [a]To sum up, [A]all of you be harmonious, sympathetic, [B]brotherly, [C]kindhearted, and [D]humble
in spirit; 9 [A]not returning evil for evil or [B]insult for
insult, but [a]giving a [C]blessing instead; for [D]you were
called for the very purpose that you might [E]inherit
a blessing. 10 For,

> "[A]The one who desires life, to
> love and see good days,
> Must keep his tongue from evil and
> his lips from speaking deceit.
> 11 "[A]He must turn away from
> evil and do good;
> He must seek peace and pursue it.
> 12 "[A]For the eyes of the Lord are
> toward the righteous,
> And His ears attend
> to their prayer,
> But the face of the Lord is
> against those who do evil."

13 [A]Who is [a]there to harm you if you prove zealous
for what is good? 14 But even if you should [A]suffer
for the sake of righteousness, [B]you [a]are blessed.
[C]And do not fear their [b]intimidation, and do
not be troubled, 15 but [a]sanctify [A]Christ as Lord
in your hearts, always *being* ready [B]to make a [b]de-
fense to everyone who asks you to give an account
for the [A]hope that is in you, yet [C]with gentleness
and [c,D]reverence; 16 [a]and keep a [A]good conscience
so that in the thing in which [B]you are slandered,
those who revile your good behavior in Christ will
be put to shame. 17 For [A]it is better, [B]if [a]God should
will it so, that you suffer for doing what is right
rather than for doing what is wrong. 18 For [A]Christ
also died for sins [B]once for all, *the* just for *the* unjust,
so that He might [C]bring us to God, having been put
to death [D]in the flesh, but made alive [E]in the [a]spirit;

3:5 [A]1 Tim 5:5; 1 Pet 1:3 3:6 [a]Lit *and are not* [A]Gen 18:12 [B]1 Pet 3:14 3:7 [a]Lit *a weaker vessel* [A]Eph 5:25; Col 3:19 [B]1 Thess 4:4 3:8 [a]Or *Finally* [A]Rom 12:16 [B]1 Pet 1:22 [C]Eph 4:32 [D]Eph 4:2; Phil 2:3; 1 Pet 5:5 3:9 [a]Lit *blessing instead* [A]Rom 12:17; 1 Thess 5:15 [B]1 Cor 4:12; 1 Pet 2:23 [C]Luke 6:28; Rom 12:14; 1 Cor 4:12 [D]1 Pet 2:21 [E]Gal 3:14; Heb 6:14; 12:17 3:10 [A]Ps 34:12, 13 3:11 [A]Ps 34:14 3:12 [A]Ps 34:15, 16 3:13 [a]Lit *the one who will harm you* [A]Prov 16:7 3:14 [a]Or *would be* [b]Lit *fear* [A]Matt 5:10; 1 Pet 2:19ff; 4:15f [B]James 5:11 [C]Is 8:12f; 1 Pet 3:6 3:15 [a]I.e. set apart [b]Or *argument;* or *explanation* [C]Or *fear* [A]1 Pet 1:3 [B]Col 4:6 [C]2 Tim 2:25 [D]1 Pet 1:17 3:16 [a]Lit *having a good* [A]1 Tim 1:5; Heb 13:18; 1 Pet 3:21 [B]1 Pet 2:12, 15 3:17 [a]Lit *the will of God* [A]1 Pet 2:20; 4:15f [B]Acts 18:21; 1 Pet 1:6; 2:15; 4:19 3:18 [a]Or *Spirit* [A]1 Pet 2:21 [B]Heb 9:26, 28; 10:10 [C]Rom 5:2; Eph 3:12 [D]Col 1:22; 1 Pet 4:1 [E]1 Pet 4:6

3:5 holy women. Certain OT saints (particularly Sarah, v. 6) are models of inner beauty, character, modesty, and submissiveness to their husbands (*see notes on Pr 31:10–31*).

3:6 frightened by any fear. There are potential fears for a Christian woman who sets out to be submissive to her unsaved husband, as to where such submission might lead. But Peter's instruction to the wife is that she should not be intimidated or fearful; as a principle, she is to submit to her husband. This precludes any coercion to sin, disobedience to God's Word, or imposition of physical harm (cf. Ac 4:18–20; 5:28, 29; Titus 1:6).

3:7 husbands in the same way. Submission is the responsibility of a Christian husband as well (cf. Eph 5:21). Though not submitting to his wife as a leader, a believing husband must submit to the loving duty of being sensitive to the needs, fears, and feelings of his wife. In other words, a Christian husband needs to subordinate his needs to hers, whether she is a Christian or not. Peter specifically notes consideration, chivalry, and companionship. **someone weaker.** While she is fully equal in Christ and not inferior spiritually because she is a woman (see Gal 3:28), she is physically weaker, and in need of protection, provision, and strength from her husband. **fellow heir of the grace of life.** Here the "grace of life" is not salvation, but marriage—the best relationship earthly life has to offer. The husband must cultivate companionship and fellowship with his wife, Christian or not (cf. Ecc 9:9). **prayers will not be hindered.** This refers specifically to the husband's prayer for the salvation of his wife (*see note on v. 1*). Such a prayer would be hindered if he were not respectful of her needs and fellowship.

3:8 be harmonious. From two Gr. words, meaning "to think the same," "to be like-minded." The idea is to maintain inward unity of heart. All Christians are to be examples and purveyors of peace and unity, not disruption and disharmony (Jn 13:35; 17; Ro 12:16; 15:5; 1Co 1:10; Php 2:1, 2). **brotherly.** A recurring theme in 1 Peter (see 1:22; 2:17; 4:8; 5:14).

3:9 giving a blessing instead. "Blessing" means "to speak well of," "to eulogize." The blessing that a Christian is to give to the reviler includes finding ways to serve him, praying for his salvation or spiritual progress, expressing thankfulness for him, speaking well of him, and desiring his well-being (2:23; cf. Lv 19:18; Pr 20:22; Lk 6:38). **you were called for the very purpose.** A person to whom God has given undeserved blessings instead of judgment should seek the blessing he will receive when giving a free gift of forgiveness to someone who has wronged him (cf. v. 21; Mt 18:21–35).

3:10 desires life, to love and see good days. Peter employed apt scriptural confirmation of his exhortation in v. 9, by quoting from Ps 34:12–16. The believer has been granted the legacy to enjoy his life (Jn 10:10). In this section, Peter gave straightforward advice on how to experience that rich joy and fullness of life, even in the midst of a hostile environment. The requirements of the fulfilled life include a humble, loving attitude toward everyone (v. 8), a nonvindictive response toward revilers (v. 9), pure and honest speech (v. 10), a disdain for sin and pursuit of peace (v. 11), and a right motive, i.e., to work the righteousness that pleases the omniscient Lord (v. 12; cf. Mt 5:38–48; Ro 12:14, 17; 1Co 4:12; 5:11; 1Th 5:15).

3:13 Who is there to harm you. It is unusual for people to mistreat those who are zealous for good. Even a hostile world is slow to hurt people who are benefactors of society, who are kind and caring (cf. 4:12), but it does happen (v. 14).

3:14 blessed. Here the idea is "privileged" or "honored" (cf. Mt 5:10). do not fear. The idea here is borrowed from Is 8:12, 13.

3:15 sanctify Christ as Lord in your hearts. The meaning is "set apart in your hearts Christ as Lord." The heart is the sanctuary in which He prefers to be worshiped. Live in submissive communion with the Lord Jesus, loving and obeying Him—and you have nothing to fear. **always *being* ready to make a defense.** The Eng. word "apologetics" comes from the Gr. word here translated "defense." Peter is using the word in an informal sense (cf. Php 1:16, 17) and is insisting that the believer must understand what he believes and why one is a Christian, and then be able to articulate one's beliefs humbly, thoughtfully, reasonably, and biblically. **the hope that is in you.** Salvation with its anticipation of eternal glory.

3:16 a good conscience. The conscience accuses (cf. Ro 2:14, 15) by notifying the person of sin by producing guilt, shame, doubt, fear, anxiety, or despair. A life free of ongoing and unconfessed sin, lived under the command of the Lord, will produce a "blameless conscience" (Ac 24:16; *see notes on 2Co 1:12; 4:2*). This will cause your false accusers to feel the "shame" of their own consciences (cf. 2:12, 15).

3:18 For Christ also died. Peter wished to encourage his readers in their suffering by again reminding them that even Christ suffered unjustly because it was God's will

19 in [a]which also He went and made proclamation
to the spirits *now* in prison, 20 who once were disobedient, when the [A]patience of God [B]kept waiting
in the days of Noah, during the construction of
[C]the ark, in which a few, that is, [D]eight [E]persons,
were brought safely through *the* [a]water. 21 [A]Cor-
responding to that, baptism now saves you—[B]not
the removal of dirt from the flesh, but an appeal
to God [a]for a [C]good conscience—through [D]the resurrection of Jesus Christ, 22 [A]who is at the right
hand of God, [B]having gone into heaven, [C]after
angels and authorities and powers had been subjected to Him.

KEEP FERVENT IN YOUR LOVE

4 Therefore, since [A]Christ has [a]suffered in the
flesh, [B]arm yourselves also with the same purpose, because [C]he who has [a]suffered in the flesh
has ceased from sin, 2 [A]so as to live [B]the rest of the
time in the flesh no longer for the lusts of men, but
for the [C]will of God. 3 For [A]the time already past is
sufficient *for you* to have carried out the desire of
the Gentiles, [a,B]having pursued a course of sensuality, lusts, drunkenness, carousing, drinking parties
and [b]abominable idolatries. 4 In *all* this, they are
surprised that you do not run with *them* into the
same excesses of [A]dissipation, and they [B]malign *you;*

3:19 [a]Or *whom* 3:20 [a]I.e. the great flood [A]Rom 2:4 [B]Gen 6:3, 5, 13f [C]Heb 11:7 [D]Gen 8:18; 2 Pet 2:5 [E]Acts 2:41; 1 Pet 1:9, 22; 2:25; 4:19 3:21 [a]Or *from* [A]Acts 16:33; Titus 3:5 [B]Heb 9:14; 10:22 [C]1 Tim 1:5; Heb 13:18; 1 Pet 3:16 [D]1 Pet 1:3 3:22 [A]Mark 16:19 [B]Heb 4:14; 6:20 [C]Rom 8:38f; Heb 1:6 4:1 [a]I.e. suffered death [A]1 Pet 2:21 [B]Eph 6:13 [C]Rom 6:7 4:2 [A]Rom 6:2; Col 3:3 [B]1 Pet 1:14 [C]Mark 3:35 4:3 [a]Lit *having gone in* [b]Lit *lawless* [A]1 Cor 12:2 [B]Rom 13:13; Eph 2:2; 4:17ff 4:4 [A]Eph 5:18 [B]1 Pet 3:16

(v. 17). Ultimately, however, Christ was marvelously triumphant to the point of being exalted to the right hand of God while all of those demon beings who were behind His suffering were made forever subject to Him (v. 22). God also caused Peter's suffering readers to triumph. **for sins once for all.** Under the Old Covenant, the Jewish people offered sacrifice after sacrifice, and then repeated it all the next year, especially at the Passover. But Christ's one sacrifice for sins was of such perpetual validity that it was sufficient for all and would never need to be repeated (*see notes on Heb 7:27; 9:26–28*). **the just for *the* unjust.** This is another statement of the sinlessness of Jesus (cf. Heb 7:26) and of His substitutionary and vicarious atonement. He, who personally never sinned and had no sin nature, took the place of sinners (cf. 2:24; 2Co 5:21). In so doing, Christ satisfied God's just penalty for sin required by the law and opened the way to God for all who repentantly believe (cf. Jn 14:6; Ac 4:12). **bring us to God.** In this life spiritually, and in the next life, wholly (cf. Mk 15:38). **put to death in the flesh.** A violent physical execution that terminated His earthly life (cf. Heb 5:7). **alive in the spirit.** This is not a reference to the Holy Spirit, but to Jesus' true inner life, His own spirit. Contrasted with His flesh (humanness) which was dead for 3 days, His spirit (deity) was alive, lit. "in spirit" (cf. Lk 23:46).

3:19 made proclamation. Between Christ's death and resurrection, His living spirit went to the demon spirits bound in the abyss and proclaimed that, in spite of His death, He had triumphed over them (*see notes on Col 2:14, 15*). **spirits *now* in prison.** This refers to fallen angels (demons), who were permanently bound because of heinous wickedness. The demons who are not so bound resist such a sentence (cf. Lk 8:31). In the end, they will all be sent to the eternal lake of fire (Mt 25:41; Rev 20:10).

3:20 disobedient ... in the days of Noah. Peter further explains that the abyss is inhabited by bound demons who have been there since the time of Noah, and who were sent there because they severely overstepped the bounds of God's tolerance with their wickedness. The demons of Noah's day were running riot through the earth, filling the world with their wicked, vile, anti-God activity, including sexual sin, so that even 120 years of Noah's preaching, while the ark was being built, could not convince any of the human race beyond the 8 people in Noah's family to believe in God (*see notes on 2Pe 2:4, 5; Jude 6, 7*; cf. Ge 6:1–8). Thus God bound these demons permanently in the abyss until their final sentencing. **safely through *the* water.** They had been rescued in spite of the water, not because of the water. Here, water was the agent of God's judgment, not the means of salvation (*see note on Ac 2:38*).

3:21 Corresponding to that ... now saves you. Peter is teaching that the fact that 8 people were in an ark and went through the whole judgment, and yet were unharmed, is analogous to the Christian's experience in salvation by being in Christ, the ark of one's salvation. **baptism ... through the resurrection of Jesus Christ.** Peter is not at all referring to water baptism here, but rather a figurative immersion into union with Christ as an ark of safety from the judgment of God. The resurrection of Christ demonstrates God's acceptance of Christ's substitutionary death for the sins of those who believe (Ac 2:30, 31; Ro 1:4). Judgment fell on Christ just as the judgment of the flood waters fell on the ark. The believer who is in Christ is thus in the ark of safety that will sail over the waters of judgment into eternal glory (cf. Ro 6:1–4). **not the removal of dirt from the flesh.** To be sure he is not misunderstood, Peter clearly says he is not speaking of water baptism. In Noah's flood, they were kept out of the water while those who went into the water were destroyed. Being in the ark and thus saved from God's judgment on the world prefigures being in Christ and thus saved from eternal damnation. **an appeal to God for a good conscience.** The word for "appeal" has the idea of a pledge, agreeing to certain conditions of a covenant (the New Covenant) with God. What saves a person plagued by sin and a guilty conscience is not some external rite, but the agreement with God to get in the ark of safety, the Lord Jesus, by faith in His death and resurrection (cf. Ro 10:9, 10; Heb 9:14; 10:22).

3:22 right hand of God. After Jesus accomplished His cross work and was raised from the dead, He was exalted to the place of prominence, honor, majesty, authority, and power (cf. Ro 8:34; Eph 1:20, 21; Php 2:9–11; Heb 1:3–9; 6:20; 8:1; 12:2). The point of application to Peter's readers is that suffering can be the context for one's greatest triumph, as seen in the example of the Lord Jesus.

4:1 Therefore. In light of the triumphant suffering and death of Christ, Peter's readers should also be willing to suffer in the flesh, knowing that it potentially produces the greatest triumph. **suffered in the flesh.** A reference to Christ's death on the cross (*see note on 3:18*). **the same purpose.** The Christian should be armed (terminology that realizes a battle) with the same thought that was manifest in the suffering of Christ, namely that one can be triumphant in suffering, even the suffering of death. In other words, the Christian should voluntarily accept the potential of death as a part of the Christian life (cf. Mt 10:38, 39; 2Co 4:8–11). Peter would have his opportunity to live this principle himself, when he faced martyrdom (see Jn 21:18, 19). **has ceased from sin.** The perfect tense of the verb emphasizes a permanent eternal condition free from sin. The worst that can happen to a believer suffering unjustly is death, and that is the best that can happen because death means the complete and final end of all sins. If the Christian is armed with the goal of being delivered from sin, and that goal is achieved through his death, the threat and experience of death are precious (cf. Ro 7:5, 18; 1Co 1:21; 15:42, 49). Moreover, the greatest weapon that the enemy has against the Christian, the threat of death, is not effective.

4:2 live ... no longer for the lusts of men. If the goal of the Christian's life is the freedom from sin which comes at death, then he should live the remainder of his life on earth pursuing the holy will of God rather than the ungodly lusts of the flesh.

4:3 sensuality ... abominable idolatries. "Sensuality" describes unbridled, unrestrained sin, an excessive indulgence in sensual pleasure. "Carousing" has the idea of an orgy. The Gr. word was used in extrabiblical literature to refer to a band of drunken, wildly acting people, swaggering and staggering through public streets, wreaking havoc. Thus the pleasures of the ungodly are described here from the perspective of God as despicable acts of wickedness. Though Peter's readers had indulged in such sins before salvation, they must never do so again. Sin in the believer is a burden which afflicts him rather than a pleasure which delights him.

4:4 they are surprised. The former friends are surprised, offended, and resentful because of the Christian's lack of interest in ungodly pleasures. **the same excesses of dissipation.** "Dissipation" refers to the state of evil in which a person thinks about nothing else. The picture here is of a large crowd running together in a mad, wild race—a melee pursuing sin.

5 but they will give account to Him who is ready to
judge [A]the living and the dead. 6 For [A]the gospel
has for this purpose been [a]preached even to those
who are dead, that though they are judged in the
flesh as men, they may live in the spirit according
to *the will of* God.
7 [A]The end of all things [a]is near; therefore, [B]be of
sound judgment and sober *spirit* for the purpose of
[b]prayer. 8 Above all, [A]keep fervent in your love for
one another, because [B]love covers a multitude of
sins. 9 [A]Be hospitable to one another without [B]com-
plaint. 10 [A]As each one has received a *special* gift,
employ it in serving one another as good [B]stewards
of the manifold grace of God. 11 [A]Whoever speaks, *is*
to do so [a]as one who is speaking the [B]utterances of
God; whoever serves *is to do so* as one who is serving [b,C]by the strength which God supplies; so that
[D]in all things God may be glorified through Jesus
Christ, [E]to whom belongs the glory and dominion
forever and ever. Amen.

SHARE THE SUFFERINGS OF CHRIST

12 [A]Beloved, do not be surprised at the [B]fiery ordeal among you, which comes upon you for your
testing, as though some strange thing were happening to you; 13 but to the degree that you [A]share the
sufferings of Christ, keep on rejoicing, so that also
at the [B]revelation of His glory [C]you may rejoice with

4:5 [A]Acts 10:42; Rom 14:9; 2 Tim 4:1 4:6 [a]I.e. preached in their lifetimes [A]1 Pet 3:18 4:7 [a]Lit *has come near* [b]Lit *prayers* [A]Rom 13:11; Heb 9:26; James 5:8; 1 John 2:18 [B]1 Pet 1:13 4:8 [A]1 Pet 1:22 [B]Prov 10:12; 1 Cor 13:4ff; James 5:20 4:9 [A]1 Tim 3:2; Heb 13:2 [B]Phil 2:14 4:10 [A]Rom 12:6f [B]1 Cor 4:1 4:11 [a]Lit *as utterances* [b]Lit *from* [A]1 Thess 2:4; Titus 2:1, 15; Heb 13:7 [B]Acts 7:38 [C]Eph 1:19; 6:10 [D]1 Cor 10:31; 1 Pet 2:12 [E]Rom 11:36; 1 Pet 5:11; Rev 1:6; 5:13 4:12 [A]1 Pet 2:11 [B]1 Pet 1:6f 4:13 [A]Rom 8:17; 2 Cor 1:5; 4:10; Phil 3:10 [B]2 Tim 2:12 [C]1 Pet 1:7; 5:1

4:5 give account. This verb means "to pay back." People who have "pursued a course of lewdness" (v. 3) and who "malign" believers (v. 4) are amassing a debt to God which they will spend all eternity paying back (cf. Mt 12:36; Ro 14:11, 12; Heb 4:13). **to judge the living and the dead.** All the unsaved, currently alive or dead, will be brought before the Judge, the Lord Jesus Christ at the Great White Throne Judgment (Rev 20:11–15; cf. Ro 3:19; 2Th 1:6–10).

4:6 to those who are dead. The preaching of the gospel not only offers a rich life (3:10), a ceasing from sin (v. 1), and a good conscience (3:21), but also an escape from final judgment. Peter had in mind believers who had heard and accepted the gospel of Christ when they were still alive, but who had died by the time Peter wrote this letter. Some of them, perhaps, had been martyred for their faith. Though these were dead physically, they were triumphantly alive in their spirits (cf. Heb 12:23). All their judgment had been fully accomplished while they were alive in this world ("in the flesh"), so they will live forever in God's presence.

4:7 The end of all things. The Gr. word for "end" is never used in the NT as a chronological end, as if something simply stops. Instead, the word means a consummation, a goal achieved, a result attained, or a realization. Having emphasized triumphant suffering through death, Peter here begins to emphasize triumphant suffering through the second coming of Christ (cf. 1:3; 2:12), which is the goal of all things. He is calling believers to live obediently and expectantly in the light of Christ's return. **is near.** The idea is that of a process consummated with a resulting nearness; that is, "imminent." Peter is reminding the readers of this letter that the return of Jesus Christ could be at any moment (cf. Ro 13:12; 1Th 1:10; Jas 5:7, 8; Rev 22:20). **be of sound judgment and sober *spirit*.** To be of "sound judgment and sober *spirit*" implies here not to be swept away by emotions or passions, thus maintaining a proper eternal perspective on life. The doctrine of the imminent return of Christ should not turn the Christian into a zealous fanatic who does nothing but wait for it to occur. Instead, it should lead the believer into a watchful pursuit of holiness. Moreover, a watchful attitude creates a pilgrim mentality (2:11). It reminds the Christian that he is a citizen of heaven only sojourning on earth. It should also remind him that he will face the record of his service to God and be rewarded for what stands the test at the judgment seat of Christ, which follows the return of Christ to rapture His church (see 1Co 3:10–15; 4:1–5; 2Co 5:9, 10). **purpose of prayer.** A mind victimized by emotion and passion, out of control, or knocked out of balance by worldly lusts and pursuits is a mind that cannot know the fullness of holy communion in prayer with God (cf. 3:7). A mind fixed on His return is purified (1Jn 3:3) and enjoys the fullness of fellowship with the Lord.

4:8 fervent in your love. "Fervent" means "to be stretched," "to be strained." It is used of a runner who is moving at maximum output with taut muscles straining and stretching to the limit (cf. 1:22). This kind of love requires the Christian to put another's spiritual good ahead of his own desires in spite of being treated unkindly, ungraciously, or even with hostility (cf. 1Co 13:4–7; Php 2:1–4). **love covers a multitude of sins.** Quoted from Pr 10:12. It is the nature of true spiritual love, whether from God to man or Christian to Christian, to cover sins (cf. Ro 5:8). This teaching does not preclude the discipline of a sinning, unrepentant church member (cf. Mt 18:15–18; 1Co 5). It means specifically that a Christian should overlook sins against him if possible, and always be ready to forgive insults and unkindnesses.

4:9 Be hospitable to one another. The Gr. word means "love of strangers." Love is intensely practical, not just emotional. In Peter's day, love included opening one's home and caring for other needy Christians, such as traveling preachers. It also included opening one's home for church services. Scripture also teaches that Christians should be hospitable to strangers (Ex 22:21; Dt 14:28, 29; Heb 13:1, 2).

4:10 received a *special* gift. A "*special*" or spiritual gift is a graciously given supernaturally designed ability granted to every believer by which the Holy Spirit ministers to the body of Christ. The Gr. word (*charisma*) emphasizes the freeness of the gift. A spiritual gift cannot be earned, pursued, or worked up. It is merely "received" through the grace of God (cf. 1Co 12:4, 7, 11, 18). The categories of spiritual gifts are given in Ro 12:3–8 and 1Co 12:4–10 (*see notes there*). Each believer has one specific gift, often a combination of the various categories of gifts blended together uniquely for each Christian. **employ it in serving one another.** Spiritual gifts were used, not for the exaltation of the person with the gift, but in loving concern for the benefit of others in the church (cf. 1Co 12:7; 13). **good stewards.** A steward is responsible for another's resources. A Christian does not own his gifts, but God has given him gifts to manage for the church and His glory. **manifold grace of God.** This emphasizes the vast designs of God for these gifts.

4:11 speaks ... serves. Peter is implying that there are two categories of gifts: speaking gifts and serving gifts. Such distinctions are clear in the lists in Ro 12 and 1Co 12. For a discussion of the gifts, *see notes on 1Co 12–14*. **utterances of God.** Elsewhere used of Scripture, the very words out of God's mouth (cf. Ro 3:2; Ac 7:38). **God may be glorified.** That is the goal of everything. Cf. Ro 11:33–36; Eph 3:21; 2Ti 4:18; 2Pe 3:18; Rev 1:6.

4:12 the fiery ordeal. Peter probably wrote this letter shortly before or after the burning of Rome (see Introduction: Background and Setting), and at the beginning of the horrors of a 200-year period of Christian persecution. Peter explains that 4 attitudes are necessary in order to be triumphant in persecution: 1) expect it (v. 12); 2) rejoice in it (vv. 13, 14); 3) evaluate its cause (vv. 15–18); and 4) entrust it to God (v. 19). **some strange thing were happening.** "Happening" means "to fall by chance." A Christian must not think that his persecution is something that happened accidentally. God allowed it and designed it for the believer's testing, purging, and cleansing.

4:13 to the degree ... sufferings. The Christian who is persecuted for his faith is a partner in the same kind of suffering Jesus endured—suffering for doing what is right (cf. Mt 5:10–12; Gal 6:17; Php 1:29; 3:10; Col 1:24). **at the revelation of His glory.** That is, at Christ's second coming (cf. Mt 24:30; 25:31; Lk 17:30). While Jesus is presently glorified in heaven, His glory is not yet fully revealed on earth. **rejoice with exultation.** That is, exult and rejoice with a rapturous joy (cf. Jas 1:2). A Christian who is persecuted for righteousness in this life will have overflowing joy in the future because of his reward (*see notes on Mt 20:20–23*). Such an awareness of future joy enables him also to "rejoice" (v. 13) at the present time (cf. Lk 6:22; *see note on Ro 8:17*).

exultation. [14] If you are reviled [a,A]for the name of
Christ, [B]you are blessed, [C]because the Spirit of glory
and of God rests on you. [15] Make sure that [A]none of
you suffers as a murderer, or thief, or evildoer, or a
[a,B]troublesome meddler; [16] but if *anyone suffers* as a
[A]Christian, he is not to be ashamed, but is to [B]glorify
God in this name. [17] For *it is* time for judgment [A]to
begin [a]with [B]the household of God; and if *it* [C]*begins*
with us first, what *will be* the outcome for those
[D]who do not obey the [E]gospel of God? [18] [A]AND IF IT
IS WITH DIFFICULTY THAT THE RIGHTEOUS IS SAVED,
[a]WHAT WILL BECOME OF THE [B]GODLESS MAN AND THE
SINNER? [19] Therefore, those also who suffer according to [A]the will of God shall entrust their souls to a
faithful Creator in doing what is right.

SERVE GOD WILLINGLY

5 [A]Therefore, I exhort the elders among you, as
your [B]fellow elder and [C]witness of the sufferings
of Christ, and a [D]partaker also of the glory that is to
be revealed, [2] shepherd [A]the flock of God among you,
exercising oversight [B]not under compulsion, but
voluntarily, according to *the will of* God; and [C]not for
sordid gain, but with eagerness; [3] nor yet as [A]lording
it over [a]those allotted to your charge, but [b]proving to
be [B]examples to the flock. [4] And when the Chief [A]Shep-
herd appears, you will receive the [B]unfading [a,C]crown
of glory. [5] [A]You younger men, likewise, [B]be subject to
your elders; and all of you, clothe yourselves with
[C]humility toward one another, for [D]GOD IS OPPOSED
TO THE PROUD, BUT GIVES GRACE TO THE HUMBLE.

4:14 [a]Lit *in* [A]John 15:21; Heb 11:26; 1 Pet 4:16 [B]Matt 5:11; Luke 6:22; Acts 5:41 [C]2 Cor 4:10f, 16 4:15 [a]Lit *one who oversees others' affairs* [A]1 Pet 2:19f; 3:17 [B]1 Thess 4:11; 2 Thess 3:11; 1 Tim 5:13 4:16 [A]Acts 5:41; 28:22; James 2:7 [B]1 Pet 4:11 4:17 [a]Lit *from* [A]Jer 25:29; Ezek 9:6; Amos 3:2 [B]1 Tim 3:15; Heb 3:6; 1 Pet 2:5 [C]Rom 2:9 [D]2 Thess 1:8 [E]Rom 1:1 4:18 [a]Lit *where will appear* [A]Prov 11:31; Luke 23:31 [B]1 Tim 1:9 4:19 [A]1 Pet 3:17 5:1 [A]Acts 11:30 [B]2 John 1; 3 John 1 [C]Luke 24:48; Heb 12:1 [D]1 Pet 1:5, 7; 4:13; Rev 1:9 5:2 [A]John 21:16; Acts 20:28 [B]Philem 14 [C]1 Tim 3:8 5:3 [a]Lit *the allotments* [b]Or *becoming* [A]Ezek 34:4; Matt 20:25f [B]John 13:15; Phil 3:17; 1 Thess 1:7; 2 Thess 3:9; 1 Tim 4:12; Titus 2:7 5:4 [a]Lit *wreath* [A]1 Pet 2:25 [B]1 Pet 1:4 [C]1 Cor 9:25 5:5 [A]Luke 22:26; 1 Tim 5:1 [B]Eph 5:21 [C]1 Pet 3:8 [D]Prov 3:34; James 4:6

4:14 **reviled for the name of Christ.** Insulted and treated unfairly for being a representative of all that Christ is, and for the public proclamation of the name of Christ (cf. Ac 4:12; 5:41; 9:15, 16; 15:26). **blessed.** Not a general, nondescript happiness so much as a specific benefit, in that suffering triumphantly for Christ shows God's approval. **Spirit of glory.** That is, the Spirit who has glory, or who is glorious. In the OT, the glory of God was represented by the Shekinah light, that luminous glow which signified the presence of God (see Ex 33:15–34:9). **rests on you.** When a believer suffers, God's presence specially rests and lifts him to strength and endurance beyond the physical dimension (cf. Ac 6:8–7:60; 2Co 12:7–10).

4:15 **troublesome meddler.** Someone who intrudes into matters that belong to someone else. Peter is dealing with matters that would lead to persecution, such as getting involved in revolutionary, disruptive activity, or interfering in the function and flow of government. It might also refer to being a troublesome meddler in the workplace. As a general rule, a Christian living in a non-Christian culture is to do his work faithfully, exalt Jesus Christ, and live a virtuous life, rather than try to overturn or disrupt his culture (2:13–16; cf. 1Th 4:11; 2Th 3:11; *see notes on 1Ti 2:1–3*).

4:16 **Christian.** In the earliest days of the church, "Christian" was a derisive term given to those followers of Christ (cf. Ac 11:26; 26:28). Eventually, followers of Christ came to love and adopt this name.

4:17 **judgment ... household of God.** Not condemnation, but the purging, chastening, and purifying of the church by the loving hand of God. It is far better and more important to kingdom work to endure suffering as the Lord purges and strengthens the church than to endure the eternal sufferings of the unbeliever in the lake of fire. And, if God so strongly and painfully judges His church which He loves, what will be His fury on the ungodly?

4:18 Quoted from the LXX of Pr 11:31, and reinforces the point that if the justified sinner is saved only with great difficulty, suffering, pain, and loss—what will be the end of the ungodly? Cf. 2Th 1:4–10.

4:19 **entrust their souls.** "Entrust" is a banking term meaning "to deposit for safe keeping." **faithful Creator.** Peter uses the word "Creator" to remind the readers of this letter that when they committed their lives to God, they were simply giving back to God what He had created. As Creator, God knows best the needs of His beloved creatures (2:23; cf. 2Ti 1:12).

5:1 **I exhort the elders.** Times of suffering and persecution in the church call for the noblest leadership. The "elder" is the same leader as the "shepherd" (v. 2), and "Guardian" (2:25), or "overseer" (*see note on Ac 20:28*). The word "elder" emphasizes their spiritual maturity. As in almost all other uses of the word (with the exception of Peter's reference to himself here and John's in 2Jn 1 and 3Jn 1), Peter wrote in the plural, indicating it was usual to have a plurality of godly leaders who oversaw and fed the flock. **fellow elder ... witness ... partaker also of the glory.** Peter loaded this exhortation to the elders with some rich motivation. First, there was motivation by identification with Peter, who refers to himself as a fellow-elder. As such, he could give relevant exhortation to the spiritual leaders. Second, there was motivation by authority. By noting that he had been an eyewitness of Christ's suffering, Peter was affirming his apostleship (cf. Lk 24:48; Ac 1:21, 22). Third, there was the motivation by anticipation. The fact that Christian leaders will one day receive from the hand of Christ a reward for their service should be a stimulant to faithful duty. The basis of this anticipation was Peter's experience in observing the transfiguration of Christ (cf. Mt 17:1–8; 2Pe 1:16). At that momentous event, he did partake of the Lord's glory.

5:2 **shepherd the flock of God.** After the motivation (v. 1) comes the exhortation (vv. 2–4). Since the primary objective of shepherding is feeding, that is, teaching, every elder must be able to teach (cf. Jn 21:15–17; *see notes on 1Ti 3:2; Titus 1:9*). Involved with the feeding of the flock is also protecting the flock (cf. Ac 20:28–30). In both duties, it must be remembered that the flock belongs to God, not to the pastor. God entrusts some of His flock to the pastor of a church to lead, care for, and feed (v. 3). **not under compulsion, but voluntarily.** Specifically, Peter may be warning the elders against a first danger—laziness. The divine calling (cf. 1Co 9:16), along with the urgency of the task (Ro 1:15), should prevent laziness and indifference. Cf. 2Co 9:7. **not for sordid gain.** False teachers are always motivated by a second danger, money, and use their power and position to rob people of their own wealth (*see notes on 2Pe 2:1–3*). Scripture is clear that churches should pay their shepherds well (1Co 9:7–14; 1Ti 5:17, 18); but a desire for undeserved money must never be a motive for ministers to serve (cf. 1Ti 3:3; 6:9–11; 2Ti 2:4; Titus 1:7; 2Pe 2:3; see also Jer 6:13; 8:10; Mic 3:11; Mal 1:10).

5:3 **nor yet as lording it over.** This is the third major temptation for a pastor: 1) laziness (v. 2); 2) dishonest finances (v. 2); and 3) demagoguery. In this context, "lording it over" means to dominate someone or some situation. It implies leadership by manipulation and intimidation. *See notes on Mt 20:25–28*. Rather, true spiritual leadership is by example (see 1Ti 4:12).

5:4 **Chief Shepherd appears.** The Chief Shepherd is Jesus Christ (cf. Is 40:11; Zec 13:7; Jn 10:2, 11, 12, 16; Heb 13:20, 21). When He appears at the second coming, He will evaluate the ministry of pastors at the judgment seat of Christ (cf. 1Co 3:9–15; 4:5; 2Co 5:9, 10). **unfading.** The Gr. word for "unfading" is the name of a flower, the amaranth. **crown of glory.** Lit. the crown which is eternal glory. In the NT world, crowns were given as marks of victorious achievements (cf. 1Co 9:24, 25). Believers are promised crowns of glory, life (Jas 1:12), righteousness (2Ti 4:8), and rejoicing (1Th 2:19), and all are imperishable (1Co 9:25). All the crowns describe certain characteristics of eternal life. *See note on 1Th 2:19)*.

5:5 **be subject to.** See 2:18–3:9. **elders.** The elders are the pastors, the spiritual leaders of the church (cf. v. 1; notes on 1Ti 3:1–7; Titus 1:5–9). The church members, especially the young people, are to give honor, deference, and respect to spiritual leadership. Submission is a fundamental attitude of spiritual maturity (cf. 1Co 16:15; 1Th 5:12–14; Titus 3:1, 2; Heb 13:7, 17). Lack of submission to the elders not only makes the ministry difficult, but also forfeits God's grace, as noted in the quote from Pr 3:34 (*see note on Jas 4:6*). **clothe yourselves with humility.** To "clothe yourselves" lit. means to tie something on oneself with a knot or a bow. This term was often used of a slave putting on an apron over his clothes

6 Therefore [A]humble yourselves under the mighty hand of God, that He may exalt you at the proper time, 7 casting all your [A]anxiety on Him, because He cares for you. 8 [A]Be of sober *spirit,* [B]be on the alert. Your adversary, [C]the devil, prowls around like a roaring [D]lion, seeking someone to devour. 9 [a,A]But resist him, [B]firm in *your* faith, knowing that [C]the same experiences of suffering are being accomplished by your [b]brethren who are in the world. 10 After you have suffered [A]for a little while, the [B]God of all grace, who [C]called you to His [D]eternal glory in Christ, will Himself [E]perfect, [F]confirm, strengthen *and* establish you. 11 [A]To Him *be* dominion forever and ever. Amen.

12 Through [A]Silvanus, our faithful brother [a](for so I regard *him*), [B]I have written to you briefly, exhorting and testifying that this is [C]the true grace of God. [D]Stand firm in it! 13 She who is in Babylon, chosen together with you, sends you greetings, and *so does* my son, [A]Mark. 14 [A]Greet one another with a kiss of love.

[B]Peace be to you all who are in Christ.

5:6 [A]Matt 23:12; Luke 14:11; 18:14; James 4:10 5:7 [A]Ps 55:22; Matt 6:25 5:8 [A]1 Pet 1:13 [B]Matt 24:42 [C]James 4:7 [D]2 Tim 4:17 5:9 [a]Lit *whom resist* [b]Lit *brotherhood* [A]James 4:7 [B]Col 2:5 [C]Acts 14:22 5:10 [A]1 Pet 1:6 [B]1 Pet 4:10 [C]1 Cor 1:9; 1 Thess 2:12 [D]2 Cor 4:17; 2 Tim 2:10 [E]1 Cor 1:10; Heb 13:21 [F]Rom 16:25; 2 Thess 2:17; 3:3 5:11 [A]Rom 11:36; 1 Pet 4:11 5:12 [a]Lit *(as I consider)* [A]2 Cor 1:19 [B]Heb 13:22 [C]Acts 11:23; 1 Pet 1:13; 4:10 [D]1 Cor 15:1 5:13 [A]Acts 12:12, 25; 15:37, 39; Col 4:10; Philem 24 5:14 [A]Rom 16:16 [B]Eph 6:23

in order to keep his clothes clean. "Humility" is lit. "lowly mindedness," an attitude that one is not too good to serve. Humility was not considered a virtue by the ancient world, any more than it is today (but cf. Jn 13:3–17; Php 2:3, 4; see also Pr 6:16, 17; 8:13; Is 57:15).

5:6 under the mighty hand of God. This is an OT symbol of the power of God working in the experience of men, always accomplishing His sovereign purpose (cf. Ex 3:19, 20; Job 30:20, 21; Eze 20:33, 37; Mic 6:8). The readers of Peter's letter were not to fight the sovereign hand of God, even when it brought them through testings. One of the evidences of lack of submission and humility is impatience with God in His work of humbling believers (*see notes on 2Co 12:7–10*). **exalt you at the proper time.** Cf. Lk 14:11. God will lift up the suffering, submissive believers in His wisely appointed time. *See notes on Job 42.*

5:7 casting all your anxiety on Him. This verse partly quotes and partly interprets Ps 55:22. "Casting" means "to throw something on something," as to throw a blanket on a donkey (Lk 19:35). Christians are to cast all of their discontent, discouragement, despair, and suffering on the Lord, and trust Him for knowing what He's doing with their lives (cf. 1Sa 1:10–18). Along with submission (v. 5) and humility (vv. 5, 6), trust in God is the third attitude necessary for victorious Christian living.

5:8 Be of sober *spirit*. *See notes on 1:13 and 4:7.* **be on the alert.** Strong confidence in God's sovereign care does not mean that the believer may live carelessly. The outside evil forces which come against the Christian demand that the Christian stay alert. **Your adversary.** Gr. for a legal opponent in a lawsuit. **the devil …. roaring lion.** The Gr. word for "devil" means "slanderer"; thus a malicious enemy who maligns believers. He and his forces are always active, looking for opportunities to overwhelm the believer with temptation, persecution, and discouragement (cf. Pss 22:13; 104:21; Eze 22:25). Satan sows discord, accuses God to men, men to God, and men to men. He will do what he can to drag the Christian out of fellowship with Christ and out of Christian service (cf. Job 1; Lk 22:3; Jn 13:27; 2Co 4:3, 4; Rev 12). And he constantly accuses believers before God's throne, attempting to convince God to abandon them (Job 1:6–12; Rev 12:10).

5:9 resist him, firm in *your* faith. Cf. Jas 4:7. "Resist" means "to stand up against." The way to resist the devil is not with special formulas, or words directed at him and his demons, but by remaining firm in the Christian faith. This means to continue to live in accord with the truth of God's Word (*see notes on 2Co 10:3–5*). As the believer knows sound doctrine and obeys God's truth, Satan is withstood (cf. Eph 6:17). **the same … suffering.** The whole brotherhood, the entire Christian community, is always going through similar trials brought on by the roaring lion who never stops trying to devour believers (cf. 1Co 10:13).

5:10 After you have suffered for a little while. Christians are to live with the understanding that God's purposes realized in the future require some pain in the present. While the believer is being personally attacked by the enemy, he is being personally perfected by the Lord, as the next phrase attests (cf. 1:6; also 2Co 1:3–7). **who called you.** As always in the NT Epistles, an effectual, saving call. *See notes on 1:5; 2:9, 21; 3:9.* **perfect, confirm, strengthen *and* establish.** These 4 words all speak of strength and resoluteness. God is working through the Christian's struggles to produce strength of character. In vv. 5–14, Peter elucidated briefly, but in wonderful richness, those attitudes which are necessary for the believer to grow in Christ to effective maturity. These include submission (v. 5), humility (vv. 5, 6), trust (v. 7), sober-mindedness (v. 8), vigilant defense (vv. 8, 9), hope (v. 10), worship (v. 11), faithfulness (v. 12), and affection (vv. 13, 14).

5:12 Silvanus. This is the Silas who traveled with Paul and is often mentioned in his epistles. He was a prophet (Ac 15:32) and a Roman citizen (Ac 16:37); he was apparently the one who wrote down Peter's words and later took this letter to its intended recipients (cf. Introduction: Author and Date).

5:13 She who is in Babylon. This refers to a church in Rome (cf. Rev 17, 18; Introduction: Background and Setting). **my son, Mark.** Mark, called John Mark, was the spiritual son of Peter. Tradition indicates that Peter helped him write the Gospel of Mark (cf. Ac 12:12). This is the same Mark who once failed Paul (Ac 13:13; 15:38, 39; Col 4:10), but later became useful again for ministry (2Ti 4:11).

THE SECOND EPISTLE OF PETER

TITLE

The clear claim to authorship in 1:1 by the apostle Peter gives the epistle its title. To distinguish it from Peter's first epistle, it was given the Greek title *"Petrou B,"* or 2 Peter.

AUTHOR AND DATE

The author of 2 Peter is the apostle Peter (see Introduction to 1 Peter). In 1:1, he makes that claim; in 3:1, he refers to his first letter; in 1:14, he refers to the Lord's prediction of his death (Jn 21:18, 19); and in 1:16–18, he claims to have been at the Transfiguration (Mt 17:1–4). However, critics have generated more controversy over 2 Peter's authorship and rightful place in the canon of Scripture than over any other NT book. The church fathers were slow in giving it their acceptance. No church father refers to 2 Peter by name until Origen near the beginning of the third century. The ancient church historian, Eusebius, only included 2 Peter in his list of disputed books, along with James, Jude, 2 John, and 3 John. Even the leading Reformers only hesitatingly accepted it.

The question about differences in Greek style between the two letters has been satisfactorily answered. Peter wrote that he used an amanuensis, Silvanus, in 1 Peter (cf. 1Pe 5:12). In 2 Peter, Peter either used a different amanuensis or wrote the letter by himself. The differences in vocabulary between the two letters can be explained by the differences in themes. First Peter was written to help suffering Christians. Second Peter was written to expose false teachers. On the other hand, there are remarkable similarities in the vocabulary of the two books. The salutation, "grace and peace be multiplied to you," is essentially the same in each book. The author uses such words as "precious," "virtue," "putting off," and "eyewitness," to name just a few examples, in both letters. Certain rather unusual words found in 2 Peter are also found in Peter's speeches in the Acts of the Apostles. These include "received" (1:1; Ac 1:17); "godliness" or "piety" (1:3, 6, 7; 3:11; Ac 3:12); and "price" or "wages" of wickedness or unrighteousness (2:13, 15; Ac 1:18). Both letters also refer to the same OT event (2:5; 1Pe 3:18–20). Some scholars have pointed out that there are as many similarities in vocabulary between 1 and 2 Peter as there are between 1 Timothy and Titus, two letters almost universally believed to have been written by Paul.

The differences in themes also explain certain emphases, such as why one letter teaches that the second coming is near, and one deals with its delay. First Peter, ministering especially to suffering Christians, focuses on the imminency of Christ as a means of encouraging the Christians. Second Peter, dealing with scoffers, emphasizes the reasons why that imminent return of Christ has not yet occurred. Other proposed differences invented by the critics, such as the contradiction between including the resurrection of Christ in one letter and the Transfiguration of Christ in the other, seem to be contrived.

Moreover, it is seemingly irrational that a false teacher would spuriously write a letter against false teachers. No unusual, new, or false doctrines appear in 2 Peter. So, if 2 Peter were a forgery, it would be a forgery written by a fool for no reason at all. This is too much to believe. The conclusion to the question of authorship is that, when the writer introduced the letter and referred to himself as Peter, he was writing the truth.

Nero died in A.D. 68, and tradition says Peter died in Nero's persecution. The epistle may have been written just before his death (1:14; ca. A.D. 67–68).

BACKGROUND AND SETTING

Since the time of the writing and sending of his first letter, Peter had become increasingly concerned about false teachers who were infiltrating the churches in Asia Minor. Though these false teachers had already caused trouble, Peter expected that their heretical doctrines and immoral lifestyles would result in more damage in the future. Thus Peter, in an almost last will and testament (1:13–15), wrote to warn the beloved believers in Christ about the doctrinal dangers they were facing.

Peter does not explicitly say where he was when he wrote this letter, as he does in 1 Peter (1Pe 5:13). But the consensus seems to be that Peter wrote this letter from prison in Rome, where he was facing imminent death. Shortly after this letter was written, Peter was martyred, according to reliable tradition, by being crucified upside down (*see note on Jn 21:18, 19*).

Peter says nothing in the salutation about the recipients of this letter. But according to 3:1, Peter was writing another epistle to the same people to whom he wrote 1 Peter. In his first letter, he spelled out that he was writing "to those who reside as aliens, scattered throughout Pontus, Galatia, Cappadocia, Asia, and Bithynia" (1Pe 1:1). These provinces were located in an area of Asia Minor, which is modern Turkey. The Christians to whom Peter wrote were mostly Gentiles (*see note on 1:1*).

HISTORICAL AND THEOLOGICAL THEMES

Second Peter was written for the purpose of exposing, thwarting, and defeating the invasion of false teachers into the church. Peter intended to instruct Christians in how to defend themselves against these false teachers and their deceptive lies. This book is the most graphic and penetrating exposé of false teachers in Scripture, comparable only to Jude.

The description of the false teachers is somewhat generic. Peter does not identify some specific false religion, cult, or system of teaching. In a general characterization of false teachers, he informs that they teach destructive heresies. They deny Christ and twist the Scriptures. They bring true faith into disrepute. And they mock the second coming of Christ. But Peter was just as concerned to show the immoral character of these teachers as he was to expose their teaching. Thus, he describes them in more detail than he describes their doctrines. Wickedness is not the product of sound doctrine, but of "destructive heresies" (2:1).

Other themes for this letter can be discerned in the midst of Peter's polemic against the false teachers. He wanted to motivate his readers to continue to develop their Christian character (1:5–11). In so doing, he explains wonderfully how a believer can have assurance of his salvation. Peter also wanted to persuade his readers of the divine character of the apostolic writings (1:12–21). Near the end of the letter, he presents reasons for the delay in Christ's second coming (3:1–13).

Another recurring theme is the importance of knowledge. The word "knowledge" appears in some form 16 times in these 3 short chapters. It is not too much to say that Peter's primary solution to false teaching is knowledge of true doctrine. Other distinctive features of 2 Peter include a precise statement on the divine origin of Scripture (1:20, 21); the future destruction of the world by fire (3:8–13); and the recognition of Paul's letters as inspired Scripture (3:15, 16).

INTERPRETIVE CHALLENGES

Perhaps the most important challenge in the epistle is to rightly interpret 1:19–21, because of its far-reaching implications with regard to the nature and authenticity of Scripture. That passage, along with 2Ti 3:15–17, is vital to a sound view of the Bible's inspiration. Peter's remark that the Lord "bought" false teachers (2:1) poses a challenge interpretively and theologically with regard to the nature of the atonement. The identity of the angels who sinned (2:4) also challenges the interpreter. Many who believe that the saved can be lost again use 2:18–22 for their argument. That passage, directed at false teachers, must be clarified so as not to contradict a similar statement to believers in 1:4. Further, whom does God not want to perish (3:9)? All of these matters will be treated in the notes.

OUTLINE

I. Salutation (1:1, 2)

II. Know Your Salvation (1:3–11)
- A. Sustained by God's Power (1:3, 4)
- B. Confirmed by Christian Graces (1:5–7)
- C. Honored by Abundant Reward (1:8–11)

III. Know Your Scriptures (1:12–21)
- A. Certified by Apostolic Witness (1:12–18)
- B. Inspired by the Holy Spirit (1:19–21)

IV. Know Your Adversaries (2:1–22)
- A. Deceptive in Their Infiltration (2:1–3)
- B. Doomed by Their Iniquity (2:4–10a)
- C. Disdainful in Their Impurity (2:10b–17)
- D. Devastating in Their Impact (2:18–22)

V. Know Your Prophecy (3:1–18)
- A. The Sureness of the Day of the Lord (3:1–10)
- B. The Sanctification of God's People (3:11–18)

GROWTH IN CHRISTIAN VIRTUE

1 [a]Simon Peter, a [A]bond-servant and [B]apostle of
Jesus Christ,
To those who have received [C]a faith of the same
[b]kind as ours, [c]by [D]the righteousness of [E]our God and
Savior, Jesus Christ: 2 [A]Grace and peace be multiplied
to you in [B]the knowledge of God and of Jesus our
Lord; 3 seeing that His [A]divine power has granted
to us everything pertaining to life and godliness,
through the true [B]knowledge of Him who [C]called us
[a]by His own glory and [b]excellence. 4 [a]For by these
He has granted to us His precious and magnificent [A]promises, so that by them you may become
[B]partakers of *the* divine nature, having [C]escaped
the [D]corruption that is in [E]the world by lust. 5 Now
for this very reason also, applying all diligence, in
your faith [A]supply [B]moral [a]excellence, and in *your*
moral excellence, [C]knowledge, 6 and in *your* knowledge, [A]self-control, and in *your* self-control, [B]per-
severance, and in *your* perseverance, [C]godliness,

1:1 [a]Two early mss read *Simeon* [b]Or *value* [c]Or *in* [A]Rom 1:1; Phil 1:1; James 1:1; Jude 1 [B]1 Pet 1:1 [C]Rom 1:12; 2 Cor 4:13; Titus 1:4 [D]Rom 3:21-26 [E]Titus 2:13 1:2 [A]Rom 1:7; 1 Pet 1:2 [B]John 17:3; Phil 3:8; 2 Pet 1:3, 8; 2:20; 3:18 1:3 [a]Or *to* [b]Or *virtue* [A]1 Pet 1:5 [B]John 17:3; Phil 3:8; 2 Pet 1:2, 8; 2:20; 3:18 [C]1 Thess 2:12; 2 Thess 2:14; 1 Pet 5:10 1:4 [a]Lit *Through which* (things) [A]2 Pet 3:9, 13 [B]Eph 4:13, 24; Heb 12:10; 1 John 3:2 [C]2 Pet 2:18, 20 [D]2 Pet 2:19 [E]James 1:27 1:5 [a]Or *virtue* [A]2 Pet 1:11 [B]2 Pet 1:3 [C]Col 2:3; 2 Pet 1:2 1:6 [A]Acts 24:25 [B]Luke 21:19 [C]2 Pet 1:3

1:1 Simon Peter. See Introduction. **a bond-servant and apostle.** Peter identifies himself with a balance of humility and dignity. As a servant, he was on equal basis with other Christians—an obedient slave of Christ. As an apostle, he was unique, divinely called, and commissioned as an eyewitness to the resurrection of Christ (*see notes on Ro 1:1*). **To those.** The recipients of this letter are the same as those who received Peter's first letter (cf. 3:1; 1Pe 1:1; see Introductions to 1, 2 Peter). **received.** An uncommon word often referring to obtaining something by lot (cf. Ac 1:17). It can mean "attaining by divine will." Here, Peter was emphasizing that salvation was not attained by personal effort, skill, or worthiness, but came purely from God's grace. **faith.** Peter is speaking of a subjective faith, i.e., the Christian's power to believe for his salvation. Faith is the capacity to believe (Eph 2:8, 9). Even though faith and belief express the human side of salvation, God still must grant that faith. God initiates faith when the Holy Spirit awakens the dead soul in response to hearing the Word of God (cf. Ac 11:21; Eph 2:8; Php 1:2). **of the same kind.** Generally the Gr. word which is translated "of the same kind" was used to designate equal in rank, position, honor, standing, price, or value. It was used in the ancient world with strangers and foreigners who were given equal citizenship in a city. Here, Peter was emphasizing that Christians have all received the same priceless saving faith. There are no first- and second-class Christians in spiritual, racial, or gender distinctions (cf. Gal 3:28). Since Peter was writing to mostly Gentiles, he may have been emphasizing that they have received the same faith as the Jews (cf. Ac 10:44–48; 11:17, 18). **by the righteousness.** Peter's point is that believers share the equal gift of salvation because God's righteousness is imputed to them. That righteousness recognizes no distinction between people except that the sins of some are more heinous than others. So, not only do they have faith because God gives it to them, they are saved only because God imputes righteousness to them (*see notes on Ro 3:26; 4:5; 2Co 5:21; Php 3:8, 9*). **our God and Savior, Jesus Christ.** The Gr. construction has only one article before this phrase, making the entire phrase refer to the same person. Thus, Peter is identifying Jesus Christ as both Savior and God (cf. Is 43:3, 11; 45:15, 21; 60:16; Ro 9:5; Col 2:9; Titus 2:13; Heb 1:8).

1:2 knowledge. This is a strengthened form of "knowledge" implying a larger, more thorough, and intimate knowledge. The Christian's precious faith is built on knowing the truth about God (cf. v. 3). Christianity is not a mystical religion, but is based in objective, historical, revealed, rational truth from God and intended to be understood and believed. The deeper and wider that knowledge of the Lord, the more "grace and peace" are multiplied.

1:3 His divine power. "His" refers to Jesus Christ. Christ's power is the source of the believer's sufficiency and perseverance (cf. Mt 24:30; Mk 5:30; Lk 4:14; 5:17; Ro 1:4; 2Co 12:9). **everything pertaining to life.** The genuine Christian is eternally secure in his salvation and will persevere and grow because he has received everything necessary to sustain eternal life through Christ's power. **godliness.** To be godly is to live reverently, loyally, and obediently toward God. Peter means that the genuine believer ought not to ask God for something more (as if something necessary to sustain his growth, strength, and perseverance was missing) to become godly, because he already has every spiritual resource to manifest, sustain, and perfect godly living. **knowledge of Him.** "Knowledge" is a key word in 2 Peter (vv. 2, 5, 6, 8; 2:20; 3:18). Throughout Scripture, it implies an intimate knowledge (Am 3:2). The knowledge of Christ emphasized here is not a superficial knowledge, or a mere surface awareness of the facts about Christ, but a genuine, personal sharing of life with Christ, based on repentance from sin and personal faith in Him (cf. Mt 7:21). **called us by His own glory and excellence.** This call, as always when mentioned in the NT Epistles, is the effectual call to salvation (cf. 1Pe 1:15; 2:21; 5:10; *see note on Ro 8:30*). This saving call is based on the sinner's understanding of Christ's revealed majesty and moral excellence evidencing that He is Lord and Savior. This implies that there must be a clear presentation of Christ's person and work as the God-Man in evangelism, which attracts men to salvation (cf. 1Co 2:1, 2). The cross and resurrection most clearly reveal His "glory and excellence."

1:4 precious and magnificent promises. That is, the promises of abundant and eternal life. **partakers of *the* divine nature.** This expression is not different from the concepts of being born again, born from above (cf. Jn 3:3; Jas 1:18; 1Pe 1:23), being in Christ (cf. Ro 8:1), or being the home of the Trinity (Jn 14:17–23). The precious promises of salvation result in becoming God's children in the present age (Jn 1:12; Ro 8:9; Gal 2:20; Col 1:27), and thereby sharing in God's nature by the possession of His eternal life. Christians do not become little gods, but they are "new creatures" (2Co 5:17) and have the Holy Spirit living in them (1Co 6:19, 20). Moreover, believers will partake of the divine nature in a greater way when they bear a glorified body like Jesus Christ (Php 3:20, 21; 1Jn 3:1–3). **escaped the corruption.** The word "corruption" has the idea of something decomposing or decaying. "Escaped" depicts a successful flight from danger. At the time of salvation, the believer escapes from the power which the rottenness in the world has over him through his fallen, sinful nature.

1:5 for this very reason. Because of all the God-given blessings in vv. 3, 4, the believer cannot be indifferent or self-satisfied. Such an abundance of divine grace calls for total dedication. **applying all diligence.** That is, making maximum effort. The Christian life is not lived to the honor of God without effort. Even though God has poured His divine power into the believer, the Christian himself is required to make every disciplined effort alongside of what God has done (cf. Php 2:12, 13; Col 1:28, 29). **in your faith supply.** "Supply" is to give lavishly and generously. In Greek culture, the word was used for a choirmaster who was responsible for supplying everything that was needed for his choir. The word never meant to equip sparingly, but to supply lavishly for a noble performance. God has given us faith and all the graces necessary for godliness (vv. 3, 4). We add to those by our diligent devotion to personal righteousness. **moral excellence.** First in Peter's list of virtues is a word that, in classical Gr., meant the God-given ability to perform heroic deeds. It also came to mean that quality of life which made someone stand out as excellent. It never meant cloistered excellence, or excellence of attitude, but excellence which is demonstrated in life. Peter is here writing of moral energy, the power that performs deeds of excellence. **knowledge.** This means understanding, correct insight, truth properly comprehended and applied. This virtue involves a diligent study and pursuit of truth in the Word of God.

1:6 self-control. Lit. "holding oneself in." In Peter's day, self-control was used of athletes who were to be self-restrained and self-disciplined. Thus, a Christian is to control the flesh, the passions, and the bodily desires, rather than allowing himself to be controlled by them (cf. 1Co 9:27; Gal 5:23). Moral excellence, guided by knowledge, disciplines desire and makes it the servant, not the master, of one's life. **perseverance.** That is, patience or endurance in doing what is right, never giving in to temptation or trial. Perseverance is that spiritual staying power that will die before it gives in. It is the virtue which can endure, not simply with resignation, but with a vibrant hope. **godliness.** *See note on v. 3.*

7 and in *your* godliness, [A]brotherly kindness, and in
your brotherly kindness, love. 8 For if these *qualities*
are yours and are increasing, they render you neither useless nor [A]unfruitful in the true [B]knowledge
of our Lord Jesus Christ. 9 For he who lacks these
qualities is [A]blind *or* short-sighted, having forgotten
his [B]purification from his former sins. 10 Therefore,
brethren, be all the more diligent to make certain
about His [A]calling and [B]choosing you; for as long
as you practice these things, you will never [C]stum-
ble; 11 for in this way the entrance into [A]the eternal
kingdom of our [B]Lord and Savior Jesus Christ will
be [C]abundantly [D]supplied to you.
12 Therefore, [A]I will always be ready to remind
you of these things, even though you *already* know
them, and have been established in [B]the truth which
is present with *you.* 13 I consider it [A]right, as long
as I am in [B]this *earthly* dwelling, to [C]stir you up by
way of reminder, 14 knowing that [A]the laying aside of
my *earthly* dwelling is imminent, [B]as also our Lord
Jesus Christ has made clear to me. 15 And I will also
be diligent that at any time after my [A]departure you
will be able to call these things to mind.

EYEWITNESSES

16 For we did not follow cleverly devised [A]tales
when we made known to you the [B]power and coming
of our Lord Jesus Christ, but we were [C]eyewitnesses of
His majesty. 17 For when He received honor and glory
from God the Father, such an [a,A]utterance as this was
[b]made to Him by the [B]Majestic Glory, "This is My beloved Son with whom I am well-pleased"— 18 and we
ourselves heard this [a]utterance made from heaven
when we were with Him on the [A]holy mountain.
19 [a]*So* we have [A]the prophetic word *made* more
[B]sure, to which you do well to pay attention as
to [C]a lamp shining in a dark place, until the [D]day
dawns and the [E]morning star arises [F]in your hearts.

1:7 [A]Rom 12:10; 1 Pet 1:22 1:8 [A]Col 1:10 [B]John 17:3; Phil 3:8; 2 Pet 1:2, 3; 2:20; 3:18 1:9 [A]1 John 2:11 [B]Eph 5:26; Titus 2:14 1:10 [A]Matt 22:14; Rom 11:29; 2 Pet 1:3 [B]1 Thess 1:4 [C]James 2:10; 2 Pet 3:17; Jude 24 1:11 [A]2 Tim 4:18 [B]2 Pet 2:20; 3:18 [C]Rom 2:4; 1 Tim 6:17 [D]2 Pet 1:5 1:12 [A]Phil 3:1; 1 John 2:21; Jude 5 [B]Col 1:5f; 2 John 2 1:13 [A]Phil 1:7 [B]2 Cor 5:1, 4; 2 Pet 1:14 [C]2 Pet 3:1 1:14 [A]2 Cor 5:1; 2 Tim 4:6 [B]John 13:36; 21:19 1:15 [A]Luke 9:31 1:16 [A]1 Tim 1:4; 2 Pet 2:3 [B]Mark 13:26; 14:62; 1 Thess 2:19 [C]Matt 17:1ff; Mark 9:2ff; Luke 9:28ff 1:17 [a]Lit *voice* [b]Lit *brought* [A]Matt 17:5; Mark 9:7; Luke 9:35 [B]Heb 1:3 1:18 [a]Lit *voice brought* [A]Ex 3:5; Josh 5:15 1:19 [a]Or *We have the* even *more sure prophetic word* [A]1 Pet 1:10f [B]Heb 2:2 [C]Ps 119:105 [D]Luke 1:78 [E]Rev 22:16 [F]2 Cor 4:6

1:7 brotherly kindness. I.e., brotherly affection, mutual sacrifice for one another (cf. 1Jn 4:20). **love.** See 1Co 13; 1Pe 4:8.

1:8 neither useless. To be useless is to be inactive, indolent, and empty (cf. Titus 1:12; Jas 2:20–22). With these virtues increasing in one's life (vv. 5–7), a Christian will not be useless or ineffective. **nor unfruitful.** I.e., unproductive (cf. Mt 13:22; Eph 5:11; 2Th 3:14; Jude 12). When these Christian qualities are not present in a believer's life (vv. 5–7), he will be indistinguishable from an evildoer or a superficial believer. But when these qualities are increasing in a Christian's life, there is the manifestation of the "divine nature" within the believer (*see note on v. 4*).

1:9 these *qualities*. The qualities mentioned in vv. 5–7 (see v. 10). **blind *or* short-sighted.** A professing Christian who is missing the virtues mentioned above is, therefore, unable to discern his true spiritual condition, and thus can have no assurance of his salvation. **forgotten.** The failure to diligently pursue spiritual virtues produces spiritual amnesia. Such a person, unable to discern his spiritual condition, will have no confidence about his profession of faith. He may be saved and possess all the blessings of vv. 3, 4, but without the excellencies of vv. 5–7, he will live in doubt and fear.

1:10 make certain about His calling and choosing you. This expresses the bull's-eye Peter has been shooting at in vv. 5–9. Though God is "certain" who His elect are and has given them an eternally secure salvation (*see notes on 1Pe 1:1–5*; cf. Ro 8:31–39), the Christian might not always have assurance of his salvation. Security is the Holy Spirit revealed fact that salvation is forever. Assurance is one's confidence that he possesses that eternal salvation. In other words, the believer who pursues the spiritual qualities mentioned above guarantees to himself by spiritual fruit that he was called (cf. v. 3; Ro 8:30; 1Pe 2:21) and chosen (cf. 1Pe 1:2) by God to salvation. **never stumble.** As the Christian pursues the qualities enumerated by Peter (vv. 5–7) and sees that his life is useful and fruitful (v. 8), he will not stumble into doubt, despair, fear, or questioning, but enjoy assurance that he is saved.

1:11 entrance into the eternal kingdom . . . abundantly supplied. Peter piles up the words to bring joy to the weary Christian's heart. An abundant entrance into eternal heaven is the hope and reality for a Christian who lives a faithful, fruitful life here on earth. Peter's point is that a Christian who pursues the listed virtues (vv. 5–7) will not only enjoy assurance in the present, but a full, rich reward in the future life (cf. 1Co 4:5; Rev 22:12)

1:12, 13 I will always be ready. Truth always needs repetition because believers forget so easily. Cf. 2Th 2:5; Jude 5.

1:13, 14 *earthly* dwelling. Death is described aptly as laying aside one's earthly dwelling (cf. 2Co 5:1). Peter was likely in his seventies as he wrote this letter (likely from a Roman prison) and anticipated dying soon. Nero's persecution had begun and he was martyred in it, soon after writing this epistle. Tradition says he was crucified upside down, refusing to be crucified like his Lord.

1:14 Christ has made clear to me. Christ had prophesied the death Peter would die almost 40 years earlier (*see note on Jn 21:18, 19*).

1:15 after my departure. Peter wanted to make certain that after he died, God's people would have a permanent reminder of the truth, thus he penned this inspired letter.

1:16 cleverly devised tales. The word for "tales" was used to refer to mythical stories about gods and miracles (cf. 1Ti 1:4; 4:7; 2Ti 4:4; Titus 1:14). Realizing that false leaders and their followers would try to discredit this letter, and that he was probably already being accused of concocting tales and myths in order to get people to follow him so he could amass wealth, power, and prestige as false teachers were motivated to do, Peter gave evidences in the following verses to prove that he wrote the truth of God as a genuinely inspired writer. **made known.** This word is a somewhat technical term for imparting a new revelation—something previously hidden, but now revealed. **the power and coming of our Lord Jesus Christ.** Since there is only one definite article with this phrase, the meaning is "the powerful coming," or "the coming in power." The false teachers who were opposing Peter had tried to debunk the doctrine of the second coming of Christ (see 3:3, 4) about which Peter had spoken and written (1Pe 1:3–7, 13; 4:13). **eyewitnesses of His majesty.** The "we" that begins this verse refers to the apostles. In one sense, all of the apostles had been eyewitnesses to Christ's majesty, especially His miracles, resurrection body, and ascension into heaven. Peter, however, is referring to a more specific event which he will describe in the next verse. The kingdom splendor of Christ revealed at this event was intended as a preview of His majesty to be manifested at His second coming (cf. Mt 16:28; *see notes on 17:1–6*). The Transfiguration was a glimpse of the glory to be unveiled at the final revelation, the apocalypse of Christ (Rev 1:1). It must be noted that Jesus' earthly ministry of healing, teaching, and gathering souls into His kingdom was a preview of the character of the earthly kingdom He will establish at His return.

1:17 Majestic Glory. A reference to the glory cloud on the Mt. of Transfiguration from which God spoke to the disciples (Mt 17:5). **This is My beloved Son.** This means "This One is in essence with Me." The Father is thus affirming the deity of Christ (cf. Mt 17:5; Lk 9:27–36).

1:18 when we were with Him. Peter implied that there was no reason to believe the false teachers who denied the majesty and second coming of Christ, since they were not on the Mt. of Transfiguration to see the preview of the kingdom and glory of Christ, as were he, James, and John.

1:19 the prophetic word. The "prophetic word" refers not just to the OT major and minor prophets, but to the entire OT. Of course, all of the OT was written by "prophets" in the truest sense, since they spoke and wrote God's Word, which was the task of a prophet, and they looked forward, in some sense, to the coming Messiah (cf. Lk 24:27). ***made* more sure.** This translation could indicate that the eyewitness account of Christ's majesty at the Transfiguration confirmed the Scriptures. However, the Gr. word order is crucial in that it does not

20 But [A]know this first of all, that [B]no prophecy of
Scripture is *a matter* of one's own interpretation, 21 for
[A]no prophecy was ever made by an act of human will,
but men [B]moved by the Holy Spirit spoke from God.

THE RISE OF FALSE PROPHETS

2 But [A]false prophets also arose among the people,
just as there will also be [B]false teachers [C]among
you, who will [D]secretly introduce [E]destructive
heresies, even [F]denying the [G]Master who [H]bought
them, bringing swift destruction upon themselves.
2 Many will follow their [A]sensuality, and because of
them [B]the way of the truth will be [C]maligned; 3 and
in *their* [A]greed they will [B]exploit you with [C]false
words; [D]their judgment from long ago is not idle,
and their destruction is not asleep.
4 For [A]if God did not spare angels when they
sinned, but cast them into hell and [B]committed them

1:20 [A]2 Pet 3:3 [B]Rom 12:6 1:21 [A]Jer 23:26; 2 Tim 3:16 [B]2 Sam 23:2; Luke 1:70; Acts 1:16; 3:18; 1 Pet 1:11 2:1 [A]Deut 13:1ff; Jer 6:13 [B]2 Cor 11:13 [C]Matt 7:15; 1 Tim 4:1 [D]Gal 2:4; Jude 4 [E]1 Cor 11:19; Gal 5:20 [F]Jude 4 [G]Rev 6:10 [H]1 Cor 6:20 2:2 [A]Gen 19:5ff; 2 Pet 2:7, 18; Jude 4 [B]Acts 16:17; 22:4; 24:14 [C]Rom 2:24 2:3 [A]1 Tim 6:5; 2 Pet 2:14; Jude 16 [B]2 Cor 2:17; 1 Thess 2:5 [C]Rom 16:18; 2 Pet 1:16 [D]Deut 32:35 2:4 [A]Jude 6 [B]Rev 20:1f

say that. It says, "And we have more sure the prophetic word." That original arrangement of the sentence supports the interpretation that Peter is ranking Scripture over experience. The prophetic word (Scripture) is more complete, more permanent, and more authoritative than the experience of anyone. More specifically, the Word of God is a more reliable verification of the teachings about the person, atonement, and second coming of Christ than even the genuine firsthand experiences of the apostles themselves. **you do well to pay attention.** Peter was warning believers that since they would be exposed to false teachers, they must pay careful attention to Scripture. **a lamp shining in a dark place.** The murky darkness of this fallen world keeps people from seeing the truth until the light shines. The light is the lamp of revelation, the Word of God (cf. Ps 119:105; Jn 17:17). **the day dawns and the morning star arises.** These simultaneous images mark the *parousia,* i.e., the appearing of Jesus Christ (cf. Lk 1:78; Rev 2:28; 22:16). **in your hearts.** The second coming will have not only an externally transforming impact on the universe (3:7–13), but also an internally transforming impact on those believers who are alive when Jesus returns, forever removing any of their remaining doubts. The perfect, but limited, revelation of the Scriptures will be replaced with the perfect and complete revelation of Jesus Christ at the second coming (cf. Jn 14:7–11; 21:25). Then the Scriptures will have been fulfilled; and believers, made like Christ (1Jn 3:1, 2), will have perfect knowledge and all prophecy will be abolished (*see note on 1Co 13:8–10*).

1:20 know this first. A call to recognize His truth as priority, namely that Scripture is not of human origin. **prophecy of Scripture.** I.e., all of Scripture. This refers primarily to all of the OT, and then by implication to all of the NT (*see notes on 3:15, 16*). **one's own interpretation.** The Gr. word for "interpretation" has the idea of a "loosing," as if to say no Scripture is the result of any human being privately "untying" and "loosing" the truth. Peter's point is not so much about how to interpret Scripture, but rather how Scripture originated, and what its source was. The false prophets untied and loosed their own ideas. But no part of God's revelation was unveiled or revealed from a human source or out of the prophet's unaided understanding (see v. 21).

1:21 by an act of human will. As Scripture is not of human origin, neither is it the result of human will. The emphasis in the phrase is that no part of Scripture was ever at any time produced because men wanted it so. The Bible is not the product of human effort. The prophets, in fact, sometimes wrote what they could not fully understand (1Pe 1:10, 11), but were nonetheless faithful to write what God revealed to them. **moved by the Holy Spirit.** Grammatically, this means that they were continually carried or borne along by the Spirit of God (cf. Lk 1:70; Ac 27:15, 17). The Holy Spirit thus is the divine author and originator, the producer of the Scriptures. In the OT alone, the human writers refer to their writings as the words of God over 3800 times (e.g., Jer 1:4; cf. 3:2; Ro 3:2; 1Co 2:10). Though the human writers of Scripture were active rather than passive in the process of writing Scripture, God the Holy Spirit superintended them so that, using their own individual personalities, thought processes, and vocabulary, they composed and recorded without error the exact words God wanted written. The original copies of Scripture are therefore inspired, i.e., God-breathed (cf. 2Ti 3:16) and inerrant, i.e., without error (Jn 10:34, 35; 17:17; Titus 1:2). Peter defined the process of inspiration which created an inerrant original text (cf. Pr 30:5; 1Co 14:36; 1Th 2:13).

2:1 false prophets. Peter described false teachers in detail in this chapter so that Christians would always recognize their characteristics and methods. The greatest sin of Christ-rejecters and the most damning work of Satan is misrepresentation of the truth and its consequent deception. Nothing is more wicked than for someone to claim to speak for God to the salvation of souls when in reality he speaks for Satan to the damnation of souls (cf. Dt 13:1–18; 18:20; Jer 23; Eze 13; Mt 7:15; 23:1–36; 24:4, 5; Ro 16:17; 2Co 11:13, 14; Gal 3:1, 2; 2Ti 4:3, 4). **among the people.** "The people" is used in the NT of Israel (cf. Ac 26:17, 23). Peter's point, though, is that Satan has always endeavored to infiltrate groups of believers with the deceptions of false teachers (cf. Jn 8:44). Since Eve, he has been in the deceit business (*see notes on 2Co 11:3, 4*). **secretly introduce destructive heresies.** The false teachers parade themselves as Christian pastors, teachers, and evangelists (cf. Jude 4). "Heresies" means self-designed religious lies which lead to division and faction (cf. 1Co 11:19; Gal 5:20). The Gr. word for "destructive" basically means damnation. This word is used 6 times in this letter and always speaks of final damnation (vv. 1–3; 3:7, 16). This is why it is so tragic when a church makes a virtue out of the toleration of unscriptural teachings and ideas in the name of love and unity (see 2Th 3:14; 1Ti 4:1–5; Titus 3:9–11). **denying the Master.** This phrase exposes the depth of the crime and guilt of the false teachers. This unusual Gr. word for "Master" or "Lord" appears 10 times in the NT and means one who has supreme authority, whether human authority or divine authority. Peter here warns that false prophets deny the sovereign lordship of Jesus Christ. Though their heresies may include the denial of the virgin birth, deity, bodily resurrection, and second coming of Christ, the false teachers' basic error is that they will not submit their lives to the rule of Christ. All false religions have an erroneous Christology. **who bought them.** The terms which Peter used here are more analogical than theological, speaking of a human master over a household. The master bought slaves, and the slaves owed the master allegiance as their sovereign. (For an OT parallel, see Dt 32:5, 6, where God is said to have bought Israel, though they rejected Him.) Doctrinally, this analogy can be viewed as responsibility for submission to God which the false teachers had refused. Beyond this, they are probably claiming that they were Christians, so that the Lord had bought them actually and personally. With some sarcasm, Peter mocks such a claim by writing of their coming damnation. Thus, the passage is describing the sinister character of the false teachers who claim Christ, but deny His lordship over their lives. **swift destruction.** This refers to either physical death or judgment at the return of Christ (Pr 29:1; 2Th 1:7–10).

2:2 Many will follow their sensuality. Many people will profess to be Christians but deny Christ's lordship over their lives, refusing to live as obedient servants to Christ and His Word, following instead the lusts of the flesh, the world, and the devil. Such nominal Christians tragically will be included in the Lord's condemnation of hypocrites at the judgment (Mt 7:21–23; cf. Jude 4, 7). Denying the lordship of Christ while claiming to be a believer destructively infects other people and discredits the gospel. **the way of the truth will be maligned.** The world mocks and scoffs at the gospel of Jesus Christ because of nominal Christians who do not follow the Lord they claim, and have been unmasked as hypocritical people.

2:3 in *their* greed. That is, uncontrolled greed. Peter observed that the underlying motive of the false teachers was not love of the truth, but love of money (see v. 14). They exploited people through their lies. **their judgment ... is not idle.** The principle that God is going to damn false teachers was set in place in eternity past, repeated throughout the OT, and is "not idle" in the sense that it has not worn out or become ineffective. It is still potent and will come to pass (see Jude 4). **their destruction is not asleep.** Peter is personifying destruction as if destruction were an executioner who is fully awake and alert, ready to act. Because God is by nature a God of truth, He will judge all liars and deceivers (cf. Pr 6:19; 19:5, 9; Is 9:15; 28:15, 22; Jer 9:3, 5; 14:14; 23:25, 26; Rev 21:8, 27).

2:4 if. This is better translated "since" because there is no doubt about the history of judgment which Peter is about to recount. Verses 4–10 are one long sentence with the conclusion to the "since" clause beginning in

to pits of darkness, reserved for judgment; 5 and did
not spare [A]the ancient world, but preserved [B]Noah, a
[a]preacher of righteousness, with seven others, when
He brought a [C]flood upon the world of the ungodly;
6 and *if* He [A]condemned the cities of Sodom and Gomorrah to destruction by reducing *them* to ashes,
having made them an [B]example to those who would
[C]live ungodly *lives* thereafter; 7 and *if* He [A]rescued
righteous Lot, oppressed by the [B]sensual conduct of
[C]unprincipled men 8 (for by what he saw and heard
that [A]righteous man, while living among them,
felt *his* righteous soul tormented day after day by
their lawless deeds), 9 [A]*then* the Lord knows how
to rescue the godly from [a]temptation, and to keep
the unrighteous under punishment for the [B]day of
judgment, 10 and especially those who [a,A]indulge the
flesh in *its* corrupt desires and [B]despise authority.
Daring, [C]self-willed, they do not tremble when they
[B]revile angelic [b]majesties, 11 [A]whereas angels who are
greater in might and power do not bring a reviling
judgment against them before the Lord. 12 But [A]these,
like unreasoning animals, [B]born as creatures of instinct to be captured and killed, reviling where they
have no knowledge, will in [a]the destruction of those
creatures also be destroyed, 13 suffering wrong as [A]the
wages of doing wrong. They count it a pleasure to
[B]revel in the [C]daytime. They are stains and blemishes,
[B]reveling in their [a]deceptions, as they [D]carouse with

2:5 [a]Or *herald* [A]Ezek 26:20; 2 Pet 3:6 [B]Gen 6:8, 9; 1 Pet 3:20 [C]2 Pet 3:6 2:6 [A]Gen 19:24; Jude 7 [B]Is 1:9; Matt 10:15; 11:23; Rom 9:29; Jude 7 [C]Jude 15 2:7 [A]Gen 19:16, 29 [B]Gen 19:5ff; 2 Pet 2:2, 18; Jude 4 [C]2 Pet 3:17 2:8 [A]Heb 11:4 2:9 [a]Lit *trial; or temptation* [A]1 Cor 10:13; Rev 3:10 [B]Matt 10:15; Jude 6 2:10 [a]Lit *go after* [b]Lit *glories* [A]2 Pet 3:3; Jude 16, 18 [B]Ex 22:28; Jude 8 [C]Titus 1:7 2:11 [A]Jude 9 2:12 [a]Lit *their destruction also* [A]Jude 10 [B]Jer 12:3; Col 2:22 2:13 [a]One early ms reads *love feasts* [A]2 Pet 2:15 [B]Rom 13:13 [C]1 Thess 5:7 [D]1 Cor 11:21; Jude 12

v. 9. Lest anyone think that God is too loving and merciful to judge the wicked false teachers and their deceived people, Peter gives 3 powerful illustrations of past divine judgment on the wicked. These illustrations set the precedents for the future and final judgment on liars and deceivers. Though God has no pleasure in the death of the wicked (Eze 33:11), He must judge wickedness because His holiness requires it (2Th 1:7–9). **angels when they sinned.** These angels, according to Jude 6, "did not keep their own domain," i.e., they entered men who promiscuously cohabited with women. Apparently, this is a reference to the fallen angels of Ge 6 (sons of God): 1) before the flood (v. 5; Ge 6:1–3) who left their normal state and lusted after women, and 2) before the destruction of Sodom and Gomorrah (v. 6; Ge 19). *See notes on Ge 6:1, 2; Jude 6.* **cast them into hell.** Peter borrows a word from Greek mythology for hell, *tartarus*. The Greeks taught that *tartarus* was a place lower than Hades reserved for the most wicked of human beings, gods, and demons. The Jews eventually came to use this term to describe the place where fallen angels were sent. It defined for them the lowest hell, the deepest pit, the most terrible place of torture and eternal suffering. Jesus, in spirit, entered that place when His body was in the grave, and proclaimed triumph over the demons during the time between His death and resurrection (*see notes on Col 2:14; 1Pe 3:18, 19*). **pits of darkness.** The demons feared going there and begged Jesus during His life on earth not to send them there (cf. Mt 8:29; Lk 8:31). Not all demons are bound. Many roam the heavens and earth (cf. Rev 12:7–9). Some are temporarily bound (*see notes on Rev 9:1–12*). These were, because of their sin in Ge 6, permanently bound in darkness. **reserved for judgment.** These permanently incarcerated demons are like prisoners who are incarcerated awaiting final sentencing. *Tartarus* is only temporary in the sense that in the day of judgment, the wicked angels confined there will be ultimately cast into the lake of fire (Rev 20:10).

2:5 did not spare the ancient world. The second illustration serving as precedent for God's future judgment on false teachers is the judgment on the ancient world through the world-wide flood (cf. Ge 6–8). The human race was reduced to 8 people by that judgment (cf. 1Pe 3:20). **a preacher of righteousness.** See Ge 6:9; 7:1. His life spoke of righteousness as he called people to repent and avoid the flood judgment.

2:6 Sodom and Gomorrah. The third precedent for a future divine judgment on the wicked is the total destruction of Sodom and Gomorrah and the other lesser surrounding cities (cf. Ge 13; 18:16–33; 19:1–38; Dt 29:23). This judgment destroyed every person in the area by incineration. *See notes on Jude 7.* **made them an example.** That is, a model, or a pattern. God sent an unmistakable message to all future generations that wickedness results in judgment.

2:7, 8 rescued righteous Lot. He was righteous, as all the saved are, by faith in the true God. Righteousness was imputed to him, by grace through faith, as it was to Abraham (Ge 15:6; Ro 4:3, 11, 22, 23). There was spiritual weakness in Lot (Ge 19:6), e.g., immorality (Ge 19:8) and drunkenness (Ge 19:33–35). His heart was in Sodom (Ge 19:16), yet he did hate the sins of his culture and strongly sought ways to protect God's angels from harm. He obeyed the Lord in not looking back at Sodom (Ge 19). In both of the illustrations where God rendered a wholesale judgment on all living people (once on the whole earth, and once in the whole region of the plain S of the Dead Sea), Peter pointed out that God's people were rescued (v. 5; cf. v. 9). The Gr. word for "oppressed" implies that Lot was troubled deeply and tortured (the meaning of "tormented") with the immoral, outrageous behavior of the people living in and around Sodom and Gomorrah. Tragically, it is ordinary for believers today no longer to be shocked by the rampant sin in their society.

2:9 to rescue the godly from temptation. The Gr. word for "temptation" can mean "an attack with intent to destroy" (cf. Mk 8:11; Lk 4:12; 22:28; Ac 20:29; Rev 3:10) and refers to severe divine judgment. The pattern of the plan of God is to rescue the godly before His judgment falls on the wicked. **to keep the unrighteous.** The wicked are kept like prisoners awaiting the sentencing that will send them to their eternal prison (cf. v. 4). The final judgment on the wicked is called the Great White Throne Judgment (Rev 20:11–15) where all the ungodly of all the ages will be raised, judged finally, and cast into the lake of fire.

2:10 indulge the flesh. Cf. Jude 6. Like the wicked of Noah's and Lot's time, the false teachers of Peter's era were slaves to the corrupt desires of the flesh. **despise authority.** "Authority" comes from the same Gr. word as "lord" (1:2). The false teachers identified with Christ outwardly, but they would not live under His lordship. The two major characteristics of false teachers are emphasized in this verse: 1) lust and 2) arrogance. **Daring, self-willed.** "Daring" is to be brazen, audacious, and defiant. "Self-willed" is to be obstinate, determined in one's own way. **revile angelic majesties.** Cf. Jude 8. To revile or speak evil is to ridicule and blaspheme. "Angelic majesties" were probably wicked angels. Wicked angels have a level of existence in the supernatural world that has a dignity and a transcendent quality about it that is beyond humanity (Eph 6:12). A certain honor belongs to those who transcend time. Consequently, there must be no flippancy regarding Satan and his angels. It may even be that these teachers tried to excuse their wicked lusts by pointing to the angels in Genesis 6 "who did not keep their own domain" (Jude 6). The blasphemy of even bad angels by the false teachers demonstrated their arrogance and antipathy toward any authority, be it good or bad.

2:11 angels who are greater in might and power. A reference to the holy angels, who are greater in power than human beings. **do not bring a reviling judgment.** Unlike false teachers who are defiant toward higher powers, the holy angels so revere their Lord that they will not speak insults against any authority. Even the archangel, Michael, recognizing the great presence and power of Satan, refused to speak evil of him (*see notes on Jude 8, 9*), but called on the Lord to do so (*see note on Zec 3:2*). No believer should be so boldly foolish as to mock or command the power of supernatural demons, especially Satan.

2:12 like unreasoning animals. Cf. Jude 10. The false teachers have no sensitivity to the power and presence of demons or holy angels, but like wild animals, insubordinate, insolent, and arrogant, they charge into the supernatural realm, cursing away at persons and matters they don't understand. **be destroyed.** Since they live like beasts who are "born … to be captured and killed," the false teachers will be killed like beasts. False teachers cannot get beyond their own instincts and thus will be destroyed by the folly of those passions.

2:13 the wages of doing wrong. Immorality and arrogant boldness will not pay in the end. It will rob and destroy. **revel in the daytime.** Sinning during the day without the cover of darkness was a sign of low-level wickedness in Roman society (cf. 1Th 5:7). But these

you, 14 having eyes full of adultery that never cease
from sin, [A]enticing [B]unstable souls, having a heart
trained in [C]greed, [D]accursed children; 15 forsaking
[A]the right way, they have gone astray, having followed [B]the way of Balaam, the *son* of Beor, who loved
[C]the wages of unrighteousness; 16 but he received a
rebuke for his own transgression, [A]*for* a mute donkey, speaking with a voice of a man, restrained the
madness of the prophet.
17 These are [A]springs without water and mists
driven by a storm, [B]for whom the [a]black darkness
has been reserved. 18 For speaking out [A]arrogant
words of [B]vanity they [C]entice by fleshly desires,
by [D]sensuality, those who barely [E]escape from the
ones who live in error, 19 promising them freedom
while they themselves are slaves of corruption; for
[A]by what a man is overcome, by this he is enslaved.
20 For if, after they have [A]escaped the defilements of
the world by [B]the knowledge of the [C]Lord and Savior Jesus Christ, they are again [D]entangled in them
and are overcome, [E]the last state has become worse
for them than the first. 21 [A]For it would be better for
them not to have known the way of righteousness,
than having known it, to turn away from [B]the holy
commandment [C]handed on to them. 22 [a]It has happened to them according to the true proverb, "[A]A
DOG RETURNS TO ITS OWN VOMIT," and, "A sow, after
washing, *returns* to wallowing in the mire."

PURPOSE OF THIS LETTER

3 This is now, [A]beloved, the second letter I am
writing to you in which I am [B]stirring up your

2:14 [A]2 Pet 2:18 [B]James 1:8; 2 Pet 3:16 [C]2 Pet 2:3 [D]Eph 2:3 2:15 [A]Acts 13:10 [B]Num 22:5, 7; Deut 23:4; Neh 13:2; Jude 11; Rev 2:14 [C]2 Pet 2:13 2:16 [A]Num 22:21, 23, 28, 30ff 2:17 [a]Lit *blackness of darkness* [A]Jude 12 [B]Jude 13 2:18 [A]Jude 16 [B]Eph 4:17 [C]2 Pet 2:14 [D]2 Pet 2:2 [E]2 Pet 1:4; 2:20 2:19 [A]John 8:34; Rom 6:16 2:20 [A]2 Pet 2:18 [B]2 Pet 1:2 [C]2 Pet 1:11; 3:18 [D]2 Tim 2:4 [E]Matt 12:45; Luke 11:26 2:21 [A]Ezek 18:24; Heb 6:4ff; 10:26f; James 4:17 [B]Gal 6:2; 1 Tim 6:14; 2 Pet 3:2 [C]Jude 3 2:22 [a]Lit *The thing of the true proverb has happened to them* [A]Prov 26:11 3:1 [A]1 Pet 2:11; 2 Pet 3:8, 14, 17 [B]2 Pet 1:13

false teachers are so consumed with lust and rebellion that they are pleased not to wait for the night. Their unbridled passions consume them. **stains and blemishes.** Cf. Jude 10. That is, dirt spots and scabs. They are opposite to the character of Christ (1Pe 1:19). The church should be like her Lord (Eph 5:27). **reveling . . . as they carouse with you.** The false teachers, feigning to be teachers of truth while sitting with Christians at church love-feasts, were behaving arrogantly and immorally even on such occasions intended for Christian fellowship. Though attempting to cover their corruption with religious talk, they were filthy defects on these church gatherings (cf. 2Jn 9–11; Jude 12).

2:14 eyes full of adultery. The false teachers had so totally lost moral control that they could not look at any woman without seeing her as a potential adulteress (cf. Mt 5:28). They were uncontrollably driven by lust, never resting from their sins. **enticing unstable souls.** The metaphor is from fishing and appears also in v. 18. To entice is to catch with bait. False teachers do not capture those strong in the Word, but prey on the weak, the unstable, and the young in the faith (see 3:16; cf. Eph 4:14; 1Jn 2:13). **heart trained in greed.** The word "trained" was often used for training in athletics. The false teachers have trained, prepared, and equipped their minds to concentrate on nothing but the forbidden things for which their passions lust. They are well schooled in the craft of self-fulfillment. **accursed children.** This is a Hebraism for the curse of sin being the dominant thing in their lives, thus saying that they are damned to hell for their blatant wickedness. Cf. Gal 3:10, 13; Eph 2:1–3; 1Pe 1:14.

2:15 forsaking the right way. The "right way" is an OT metaphor for obedience to God (cf. Ac 13:10). **Balaam.** Cf. Jude 11. Balaam served as an illustration and example of such false prophets. He was an OT compromising prophet for sale to whoever paid him, who preferred wealth and popularity over faithfulness and obedience to God (Nu 22–24). Through a talking donkey, God kept him from cursing Israel (v. 16; cf. Nu 22:21–35).

2:17 springs without water. In this verse, Peter uses two poetic figures ("springs" and "mists") which represent a precious commodity in the Middle East. A spring or well without water would be a major disappointment in a hot and dry land. Likewise, false teachers have a pretense of spiritual water to quench the thirsty soul, but they actually have nothing to give. **mists driven by a storm.** The coming of clouds or "mists" would seem to promise rain, but sometimes the storm would blow the clouds on by, leaving the land dry and hot. The false teachers might seem to promise spiritual refreshment, but were all show with no substance (cf. Jude 12). **black darkness.** That is, hell (cf. Mt 8:12; Jude 13).

2:18 arrogant *words* of vanity. Cf. Jude 16. That is, ostentatious verbosity. The false teachers deceive the weak with high-sounding words that masquerade as scholarship or profound spiritual insight, and even as direct revelation from God. They may contradict the plain historic teachings of Scripture which in some cases they are not able to explain properly because of their lack of adequate training and divine wisdom (cf. 1Co 2:14). In reality, they say nothing genuinely scholarly, or spiritual, or divine. **entice . . . by sensuality.** Nevertheless, in spite of all the empty talk, false teachers entice others to their philosophies by appealing to people on the baser level. Seduction, rather than the winsomeness of truth, is their ploy. They offer people a kind of religion that they can embrace and still hold on to their fleshly desires and sensuality. Peter may also be implying that false teachers particularly aim to seduce women through sensual methods. **barely escape . . . error.** The preferred translation is "barely escaping" or "trying to escape." This is a description not of saved people, but of people who are vulnerable because they have high levels of guilt and anxieties—people with broken marriages, people who are lonely and tired of the consequences of sin and are looking for a new start, even for religion or help from God. The false teachers exploit these kinds of people.

2:19 promising them freedom. False teachers promise those "trying to escape" the struggles of life the very freedom they seek. **slaves of corruption.** The false teachers can't deliver the freedom they promise, because they themselves are enslaved to the very corruption which people are trying to escape. **overcome . . . enslaved.** Whoever puts himself, in the name of freedom, into the hands of a false teacher, who is a prisoner himself, also becomes a prisoner. Bondage to corruption awaits all followers of false teachers.

2:20 escaped the defilements of the world. "Defilements" has the idea of putrid or poisonous vapors. Morally, the world gives off a deadly influence. Peter notes that at some point in time, these false teachers and their followers wanted to escape the moral contamination of the world system and sought religion, even Jesus Christ (on their terms, not His; *see notes on v. 1*). But these false teachers had never genuinely been converted to Christ. They heard the true gospel and moved toward it, but then rejected the Christ of that gospel. That is apostasy, like the people of Heb 10:26, 27. Their last end is far worse than the first (for examples of apostasy, see Lk 11:24–26; 12:47, 48; 1Co 10:1–12; Heb 3:12–18; 6:6; 10:26, 38ff.; 1Jn 2:19; Jude 4–6).

2:21 to turn away from the holy commandment. Lit., "to turn back." This verse describes the perversion and defection of the false teachers. They professed the Christian experience (the way of righteousness; cf. Mt 21:32), and even had access to the true teachings of Scripture. But by their lives they demonstrated that they ultimately had chosen to reject Christ (cf. Heb 10:26–31). Such false teachers as Peter was describing were not made outside Christianity. They are always bred in the church, half in and half out; but eventually they reject the truth and try to seduce others in their attempt to fulfill their self-gratification.

2:22 dog . . . sow. Two graphic analogies of an apostate. The first is from Proverbs 26:11; the second is Peter's own.

3:1 beloved. This attitude toward the readers of his letter reflects Peter's pastoral concern (cf. 1Pe 5:1–4). **the second letter.** That is, second to 1 Peter (see Introduction). **your sincere mind.** A good commendation which demonstrates that Peter believed that his readers were genuine Christians. "Sincere" means uncontaminated, unmixed by the seductive influences of the world, the flesh, and the devil. How different the true believers were from the corrupt apostate false teachers (2:10–22). Peter sought to impress on his readers the truth they already knew so that their sanctified reason and spiritual discernment would be able to detect and refute the purveyors of false doctrine.

sincere mind by way of reminder, 2 that you should
[A]remember the words spoken beforehand by [B]the
holy prophets and [C]the commandment of the Lord
and Savior *spoken* by your apostles.

THE COMING DAY OF THE LORD

3 [A]Know this first of all, that [B]in the last days
[C]mockers will come with *their* mocking, [D]following
after their own lusts, 4 and saying, "[A]Where is the
promise of His [B]coming? For *ever* since the fathers
[C]fell asleep, all continues just as it was [D]from the
beginning of creation." 5 For [a]when they maintain
this, it escapes their notice that [A]by the word of God
the heavens existed long ago and *the* earth was
[B]formed out of water and by water, 6 through which
[A]the world at that time was [B]destroyed, being flooded
with water. 7 But by His word [A]the present heavens
and earth are being reserved for [B]fire, kept for [C]the
day of judgment and destruction of ungodly men.
8 But do not let this one *fact* escape your notice,
[A]beloved, that with the Lord one day is like a thousand years, and [B]a thousand years like one day.

3:2 [A]Jude 17 [B]Luke 1:70; Acts 3:21; Eph 3:5 [C]Gal 6:2; 1 Tim 6:14; 2 Pet 2:21 3:3 [A]2 Pet 1:20 [B]1 Tim 4:1; Heb 1:2 [C]Jude 18 [D]2 Pet 2:10 3:4 [A]Is 5:19; Jer 17:15; Ezek 11:3; 12:22, 27; Mal 2:17; Matt 24:48 [B]1 Thess 2:19; 2 Pet 3:12 [C]Acts 7:60 [D]Mark 10:6 3:5 [a]*Or they are willfully ignorant of this fact, that* [A]Gen 1:6, 9; Heb 11:3 [B]Ps 24:2; 136:6 3:6 [A]2 Pet 2:5 [B]Gen 7:11, 12, 21f 3:7 [A]2 Pet 3:10, 12 [B]Is 66:15; Dan 7:9f; 2 Thess 1:7; Heb 12:29 [C]Matt 10:15; 1 Cor 3:13; Jude 7 3:8 [A]2 Pet 3:1 [B]Ps 90:4

3:2 holy prophets. The OT prophets are in view, who were holy in contrast to the unholy false teachers. God's Word was written by those prophets in the Scriptures (*see notes on 1:19–21*). In particular those prophets warned about coming judgment (e.g., Ps 50:1–4; Is 13:10–13; 24:19–23; Mic 1:4; Mal 4:1, 2), and even about the coming of the Lord (Zec 14:1–9). **the commandment of the Lord.** Peter is referring to the warnings which he and the other apostles had written regarding judgment (Jude 17). **your apostles.** The apostles (*see notes on Ro 1:1; Eph 4:11*) of Christ filled the 260 chapters of the NT with about 300 references to the second coming. NT revelation about the Christ coming to gather His own, warnings about eschatological judgments, information about the establishment of His kingdom, and teaching concerning God's bringing in eternal righteousness are the irrefutable proof for the second coming of Christ and the judgment of the wicked.

3:3 Know this first. "First" here means the preeminent matter, not the first in a list. Peter's priority in this section of his letter is to warn Christians about how the false teachers would try to deny this judgment and steal the hope of believers. **in the last days.** This phrase refers to that entire period of time from the arrival of the Messiah to His return (cf. Ac 2:17; Gal 4:4; 2Ti 3:1; Heb 1:2; Jas 5:3; 1Pe 1:20; 1Jn 2:18, 19; Jude 18). The entire age will be marked by saboteurs of the Christian truth and especially the hope of Christ's return. **mockers will come.** False teachers argue against the second coming of Christ or any teaching of Scripture through ridicule (cf. Is 5:19; Jude 18). **following after their own lusts.** Peter again speaks of the lifestyle of the false teachers, which was characterized by sexual lusts (cf. 2:2, 10, 13, 14, 18), pounding home his warning. False teachers who know not the truth and know not God have nothing to restrain their lusts. They particularly mock the second coming of Jesus Christ because they want to pursue impure sexual pleasure without consequence, or without having to face divine retribution. They want an eschatology that fits their conduct (cf. 1Jn 2:28, 29; 3:2, 3).

3:4 Where is the promise of His coming? The early church believed that Jesus was coming back imminently (cf. 1Co 15:51; 1Th 1:10; 2:19; 4:15–18; 5:1, 2). These scoffers employed an emotional argument against imminency rather than a biblical argument. Their argument played on ridicule and disappointment. **the fathers.** The OT patriarchs, Abraham, Isaac, and Jacob (cf. Ro 9:5; Heb 1:1). **all continues just as it was.** This argument against the second coming of Christ is based on the theory of uniformitarianism, which says that all natural phenomena have operated uniformly since the beginning of the earth. The false teachers were also implying that God is absent from earth affairs. In effect, they were teaching that, "There will not be a great cataclysmic judgmental event at the end of history, because that is not how the universe works. There never has been such a judgment, so why should we expect one in the future? Instead, everything in the universe is stable, closed, fixed, and governed by never varying patterns and principles of evolution. Nothing catastrophic has ever happened in the past, so nothing catastrophic ever will happen in the future. There will be no divine invasion, no supernatural judgment on mankind."

3:5 it escapes their notice. The false teachers, in their quest to avoid the doctrine of judgment, deliberately ignore the two major previous divine cataclysmic events—creation and the flood. **by the word of God *the* heavens existed long ago.** Creation was God's stepping into the emptiness and bringing the universe into existence, not by uniformitarianism, but by an instantaneous, explosive 6-day creation. Everything has not gone along in some consistent, unvarying evolutionary process. In six, 24-hour days the whole universe was created mature and complete (*see notes on Ge 1; 2*). **earth was formed out of water and by water.** The earth was formed between two realms of watery mass. During the early part of the creation week, God collected the upper waters into a canopy around the whole earth, and the lower waters into underground reservoirs, rivers, lakes, and seas. *See notes on Ge 1:2–10.*

3:6 through which. That is, by water. God, by creating water above and below, built into His creation the tool of its destruction. **the world at that time.** A reference to the pre-flood world order. This world included the physical arrangement with the canopy above, the waters in the underground reservoirs, rivers, lakes, and seas below, and the heavens in the middle. The pre-flood world, sheltered from the sun's destructive ultraviolet rays, and with a gentle climate without rain, storms, and winds, was characterized by long life of humans (Ge 5) and the ability of the earth (like a greenhouse) to produce extensively. **destroyed, being flooded with water.** The second great divine cataclysm that defeats the idea of uniformitarianism was the universal flood which drowned the whole earth and altered that originally created world order. According to Genesis 7:11ff., the flood occurred from two directions: first, the bursting open of the sources of water below as the earth cracked open and gas, dust, water, and air burst up; then came the breakup of the canopy when hit by all that upward flow, which sent the water from above crashing down on the earth. The deluge was so cataclysmic that the inhabitants of the earth were all destroyed, except 8 people and a representation of every kind of animal (*see notes on Ge 7:11–24*). Clearly, by those two great events, it is certain that the world is not in a uniformitarian process.

3:7 by His word. The present world system is reserved for future judgment, which will come by the Word of God just as creation and the flood came. God will speak it into existence as well, after the present order is again destroyed. **the present.** Humanity, since the flood, lives in the second world order. One of the obvious differences between the two world orders is that people live 70 years in the present world not 900 years, which was a common age of pre-flood human beings. And Peter was making the point that there is a third form of the heavens and earth yet to come following another cataclysm. **reserved for fire.** God put the rainbow in the sky to signify that He would never destroy the world again by water (Ge 9:13). In the future, God will destroy the heavens and the earth by fire (cf. Is 66:15; Da 7:9, 10; Mic 1:4; Mal 4:1; Mt 3:11, 12; 2Th 1:7, 8). In the present universe, the heavens are full of stars, comets, and asteroids. The core of the earth is also filled with a flaming, boiling, liquid lake of fire, the temperature of which is some 12,400 degrees Fahrenheit. The human race is separated from the fiery core of the earth by only a thin 10-mile crust. Far more than that, the whole of creation is a potential fire bomb due to its atomic structure. As man from atoms creates destructive bombs that burn a path of death, so God can disintegrate the whole universe in an explosion of atomic energy (*see notes on vv. 10–12*). **kept for the day of judgment ... of ungodly men.** The earth waits for the day of judgment and destruction of ungodly men. The godly will not be present on earth when God speaks into existence the judgment by fire (cf. 1Th 1:10; 5:9).

3:8 one day is like a thousand years. God understands time much differently from man. From man's viewpoint, Christ's coming seems like a long time away (cf. Ps 90:4). From God's viewpoint, it will not be long. Beyond that general reference, this may be a specific indication of the fact that there are actually 1,000 years between the first phase of the Day of the Lord at the end of the Tribulation (Rev 6:17), and the last phase 1,000 years later at

9 [A]The Lord is not slow about His promise, as some
count slowness, but [B]is patient toward you, [C]not
wishing for any to perish but for all to come to
repentance.

A NEW HEAVEN AND EARTH

10 But [A]the day of the Lord [B]will come like a
thief, in which [C]the heavens [D]will pass away with
a roar and the [E]elements will be destroyed with
intense heat, and [F]the earth and [a]its works will be
[b]burned up.
11 Since all these things are to be destroyed in this
way, what sort of people ought you to be in holy
conduct and godliness, 12 [A]looking for and hastening
the coming of the day of God, because of which [B]the
heavens will be destroyed by burning, and the [C]ele-
ments will melt with intense heat! 13 But according
to His [A]promise we are looking for [B]new heavens
and a new earth, [C]in which righteousness dwells.
14 [A]Therefore, [B]beloved, since you look for these
things, be diligent to be [C]found by Him in peace,
[D]spotless and blameless, 15 and regard the [A]patience
of our Lord *as* salvation; just as also [B]our beloved
brother Paul, [C]according to the wisdom given him,
wrote to you, 16 as also in all *his* letters, speaking in
them of [A]these things, [B]in which are some things
hard to understand, which the untaught and
[C]unstable distort, as *they do* also [D]the rest of the

3:9 [A]Hab 2:3; Rom 13:11; Heb 10:37 [B]Rom 2:4; Rev 2:21 [C]1 Tim 2:4; Rev 2:21 3:10 [a]Lit *the works in it* [b]Two early mss read *discovered* [A]1 Cor 1:8 [B]Matt 24:43; Luke 12:39; 1 Thess 5:2; Rev 3:3; 16:15 [C]Is 34:4; 2 Pet 3:7, 12 [D]Matt 24:35; Rev 21:1 [E]Is 24:19; Mic 1:4 [F]2 Pet 3:7 3:12 [A]1 Cor 1:7 [B]2 Pet 3:7, 10 [C]Is 24:19; 34:4; Mic 1:4 3:13 [A]Is 65:17; 66:22 [B]Rom 8:21; Rev 21:1 [C]Is 60:21; 65:25; Rev 21:27 3:14 [A]1 Cor 15:58; 2 Pet 1:10 [B]2 Pet 3:1 [C]1 Pet 1:7 [D]Phil 2:15; 1 Thess 5:23; 1 Tim 6:14; James 1:27 3:15 [A]2 Pet 3:9 [B]Acts 9:17; 15:25; 2 Pet 3:2 [C]1 Cor 3:10; Eph 3:3 3:16 [A]2 Pet 3:14 [B]Heb 5:11 [C]2 Pet 2:14 [D]2 Pet 3:2

the end of the millennial kingdom when the Lord creates the new heaven and new earth (*see notes on vv. 10, 13; Rev 20:1–21:1*).

3:9 not slow. That is, not loitering or late (cf. Gal 4; 4; Titus 2:13; Heb 6:18; 10:23, 37; Rev 19:11). **patient toward you.** "You" is the saved, the people of God. He waits for them to be saved. God has an immense capacity for patience before He breaks forth in judgment (cf. v. 15; Joel 2:13; Lk 15:20; Ro 9:22; 1Pe 3:15). God endures endless blasphemies against His name, along with rebellion, murders, and the ongoing breaking of His law, waiting patiently while He is calling and redeeming His own. It is not impotence or slackness that delays final judgment; it is patience. **not wishing for any to perish.** The "any" must refer to those whom the Lord has chosen and will call to complete the redeemed, i.e., the "you." Since the whole passage is about God's destroying the wicked, His patience is not so He can save all of them, but so that He can receive all His own. He can't be waiting for everyone to be saved, since the emphasis is that He will destroy the world and the ungodly. Those who do perish and go to hell go because they are depraved and worthy only of hell and have rejected the only remedy, Jesus Christ, not because they were created for hell and predetermined to go there. The path to damnation is the path of a nonrepentant heart; it is the path of one who rejects the person and provision of Jesus Christ and holds on to sin (cf. Is 55:1; Jer 13:17; Eze 18:32; Mt 11:28; 23:37; Lk 13:3; Jn 3:16; 8:21, 24; 1Ti 2:3, 4; Rev 22:17). **all to come to repentance.** "All" (cf. "you," "any") must refer to all who are God's people who will come to Christ to make up the full number of the people of God. The reason for the delay in Christ's coming and the attendant judgments is not because He is slow to keep His promise, or because He wants to judge more of the wicked, or because He is impotent in the face of wickedness. He delays His coming because He is patient and desires the time for His people to repent.

3:10 the day of the Lord. See *Introduction* to Joel: Historical and Theological Themes; *see note on 1Th 5:2*. The "Day of the Lord" is a technical term pointing to the special interventions of God in human history for judgment. It ultimately refers to the future time of judgment whereby God judges the wicked on earth and ends this world system in its present form. The OT prophets saw the final day of the Lord as unequaled darkness and damnation, a day when the Lord would act in a climactic way to vindicate His name, destroy His enemies, reveal His glory, establish His kingdom, and destroy the world (cf. Is 2:10–21; 13:6–22; Joel 1, 2; Am 5; Ob 15; Zec 14; Mal 4; 2Th 1:7; 2:2). It occurs at the time of the tribulation on earth (Rev 6:17), and again 1,000 years later at the end of the millennial kingdom before the creation of the new heavens and new earth (v. 13; Rev 20:1–21:1). **like a thief.** The day of the Lord will have a surprise arrival, sudden, unexpected, and disastrous to the unprepared (*see notes on 1Th 5:2*). **the heavens will pass away with a roar.** The "heavens" refer to the physical universe. The "roar" connotes a whistling or a crackling sound as of objects being consumed by flames. God will incinerate the universe, probably in an atomic reaction that disintegrates all matter as we know it (vv. 7, 11, 12, 13). **the elements will be destroyed with intense heat.** The "elements" are the atomic components into which matter is ultimately divisible, which make up the composition of all the created matter. Peter means that the atoms, neutrons, protons, and electrons are all going to disintegrate (v. 11). **the earth and its works.** The whole of the physical, natural earth in its present form, with its entire universe will be consumed. Cf. Is 24:19, 20; 34:4.

3:11 what sort of people ought you to be. This is an exclamation rather than a question. It means "How astoundingly excellent you ought to be!" This is a straightforward challenge for Christians to conform their lives to God's standards in light of the reality of coming judgment and eternity (cf. 1Co 4:15; 2Co 5:9). **holy conduct and godliness.** "Holy conduct" refers to the way a Christian should live life—separate from sin. "Godliness" refers to the spirit of reverence which should permeate a Christian's attitude—that which rules the heart.

3:12 looking for and hastening. One of the motives for holy conduct and godliness is expectation. "Hastening" means "eagerly desiring" that something will happen. Christians are not to fear the future day of God, but eagerly hope for it (cf. 1Co 1:7; 16:22; 1Jn 2:28; 3:3). **the day of God.** The "day of God" is not the same as the "Day of the Lord." The "day of God" refers to the eternal state, in preparation of which the heavens and the earth are burned up and the new creation is made. It is likely so named because of what Paul had in mind in 1Co 15:28, the eternal glory of the new creation, with God being all in all. When the day of God comes, man's "day" will be over. The corrupting of the universe by man and Satan will have been terminated and judged, finally and forever. **the heavens will be destroyed.** *See notes on vv. 7, 10, 11.* The new world in which righteousness dwells (v. 13) requires the Lord to first destroy the old, sin-cursed universe (cf. Ro 8:19–22).

3:13 new heavens and a new earth. The "promise" of a new universe is rooted in the OT (e.g., Ps 102:25; Is 65:17; 66:22). The word "new" means new in quality, i.e., different from before, not just new in chronology. **righteousness dwells.** The universe is new in quality because righteousness has settled in and taken up permanent and exclusive residence (cf. Is 60:19–22; Rev 21:1–7).

3:14 in peace. When Christ returns, each Christian should be found enjoying the peace of Christ which knows no worry or fear about the day of the Lord or the judgment of Christ (cf. Php 4:6, 7). To have this peace means that the Christian has a strong sense of assurance of his salvation and a life of obedience to Christ (cf. 1Jn 4:17). **spotless and blameless.** Christians should have a spotless character and a blameless reputation. These characteristics are in graphic contrast to the false teachers (cf. 2:13), but like Christ (1Pe 1:19).

3:15a the patience of our Lord *as* salvation. In addition to what he has already explained in v. 9 about the Lord's patience being the reason He delays judgment, here he adds that during the time of God's patience, Christians should engage in seeking the salvation of souls.

3:15b, 16 hard to understand. Since Paul had (by the time Peter wrote) written all his letters and died, the readers of 2 Peter would have already received letters about future events from Paul. Some of Paul's explanations were difficult (not impossible) to interpret. Nevertheless, Peter uses Paul as a support for his teaching.

3:16 untaught and unstable distort. In Peter's day (as today), there was a proliferation of foolish and hurtful perverting of apostolic teaching about the future (cf. vv. 3, 4; 2Th 2:1–5; 3:6–12). **the rest of the Scriptures.** This is one of the most clear-cut statements in the Bible to affirm that the writings of Paul are

Scriptures, to their own destruction. 17 You therefore, [A]beloved, knowing this beforehand, [B]be on
your guard so that you are not carried away by
[C]the error of [D]unprincipled men and [E]fall from your
own steadfastness, 18 but grow in the grace and
[A]knowledge of our [B]Lord and Savior Jesus Christ.
[C]To Him *be* the glory, both now and to the day of
eternity. Amen.

3:17 [A]2 Pet 3:1 [B]1 Cor 10:12 [C]2 Pet 2:18 [D]2 Pet 2:7 [E]Rev 2:5 3:18 [A]2 Pet 1:2 [B]2 Pet 1:11; 2:20 [C]Rom 11:36; 2 Tim 4:18; Rev 1:6

Scripture. Peter's testimony is that Paul wrote Scripture, but the false teachers distorted it. The NT apostles were aware that they spoke and wrote the Word of God (1Th 2:13) as surely as did the OT prophets. Peter realized that the NT writers brought the divine truth that completed the Bible (1Pe 1:10–12). **to their own destruction.** The fact that distorting Paul's writings leads to eternal damnation proves that Paul's writings were inspired of God.

3:17 knowing this beforehand. Since Christians now know that there will be false teachers who will appear, twisting and distorting the Scriptures, they should be all the more on their guard. **be on your guard ... not carried away ... and fall.** Any time a believer seriously listens to a false teacher, he runs the risk of being led astray (cf. 2Ti 2:14–18; Titus 1:10–16).

3:18 grow in the grace and knowledge. Peter ends this letter with a summary statement of the same instruction with which he began it (1:2–11). Pursuing Christian maturity and a deepening knowledge of the Lord Jesus Christ will lead to doctrinal stability and prevent a Christian from being led astray. **To Him *be* the glory.** Such a call for glory to Christ demonstrates again that Peter considered Jesus Christ to be deity, equal in honor with God the Father (cf. 1:1; Jn 5:23).

THE FIRST EPISTLE OF JOHN

TITLE

The epistle's title has always been "1 John." It is the first and largest in a series of 3 epistles that bear the apostle John's name. Since the letter identifies no specific church, location, or individual to whom it was sent, its classification is as a "general epistle." Although 1 John does not exhibit some of the general characteristics of an epistle common to that time (e.g., no introduction, greeting, or concluding salutation), its intimate tone and content indicate that the term "epistle" still applies to it.

AUTHOR AND DATE

The epistle does not identify the author, but the strong, consistent and earliest testimony of the church ascribes it to John the disciple and apostle (cf. Lk 6:13, 14). This anonymity strongly affirms the early church's identification of the epistle with John the apostle, for only someone of John's well-known and preeminent status as an apostle would be able to write with such unmistakable authority, expecting complete obedience from his readers, without clearly identifying himself (e.g., 4:6). He was well known to the readers so he didn't need to mention his name.

John and James, his older brother (Ac 12:2), were known as "the sons of Zebedee" (Mt 10:2–4), whom Jesus gave the name "Sons of Thunder" (Mk 3:17). John was one of the 3 most intimate associates of Jesus (along with Peter and James—cf. Mt 17:1; 26:37), being an eyewitness to and participant in Jesus' earthly ministry (1:1–4). In addition to the 3 epistles, John also authored the fourth gospel, in which he identified himself as the disciple "whom Jesus loved" and as the one who reclined on Jesus' breast at the Last Supper (Jn 13:23; 19:26; 20:2; 21:7, 20). He also wrote the book of Revelation (Rev 1:1).

Precise dating is difficult because no clear historical indications of date exist in 1 John. Most likely John composed this work in the latter part of the first century. Church tradition consistently identifies John in his advanced age as living and actively writing during this time at Ephesus in Asia Minor. The tone of the epistle supports this evidence since the writer gives the strong impression that he is much older than his readers (e.g., "my little children"—2:1, 18, 28). The epistle and John's gospel reflect similar vocabulary and manner of expression (see Historical and Theological Themes). Such similarity causes many to date the writing of John's epistles as occurring soon after he composed his gospel. Since many date the gospel during the latter part of the first century, they also prefer a similar date for the Epistles. Furthermore, the heresy John combats most likely reflects the beginnings of gnosticism (see Background and Setting) which was in its early stages during the latter third of the first century when John was actively writing. Since no mention is made of the persecution under Domitian, which began about A.D. 95, it may have been written before that began. In light of such factors, a reasonable date for 1 John is ca. A.D. 90–95. It was likely written from Ephesus to the churches of Asia Minor over which John exercised apostolic leadership.

BACKGROUND AND SETTING

Although he was greatly advanced in age when he penned this epistle, John was still actively ministering to churches. He was the sole remaining apostolic survivor who had intimate, eyewitness association with Jesus throughout His earthly ministry, death, resurrection, and ascension. The church Fathers (e.g., Justin Martyr, Irenaeus, Clement of Alexandria, Eusebius) indicate that after that time, John lived at Ephesus in Asia Minor, carrying out an extensive evangelistic program, overseeing many of the churches that had arisen, and conducting an extensive writing ministry (e.g., Epistles, The Gospel of John, and Revelation). One church Father (Papias) who had direct contact with John described him as a "living and abiding voice." As the last remaining apostle, John's testimony was highly authoritative among the churches. Many eagerly sought to hear the one who had firsthand experience with the Lord Jesus.

Ephesus (cf. Ac 19:10) lay within the intellectual center of Asia Minor. As predicted years before by the apostle Paul (Ac 20:28–31), false teachers arising from within the church's own ranks, saturated with the prevailing climate of philosophical trends, began infecting the church with false doctrine, perverting fundamental apostolic teaching. These false teachers advocated new ideas which eventually became known as "gnosticism" (from the Gr. word "knowledge"). After the Pauline battle for freedom from the law, Gnosticism was the most dangerous heresy that threatened the early church during the first 3 centuries. Most likely, John was combating the beginnings of this virulent heresy that threatened to destroy the fundamentals of the faith and the churches (see Interpretive Challenges).

Gnosticism, influenced by such philosophers as Plato, advocated a dualism asserting that matter was inherently evil and spirit was good. As a result of this presupposition, these false teachers, although attributing some form of deity to Christ, denied His true humanity to preserve Him from evil. It also claimed elevated knowledge, a higher truth known only to those in on the deep things. Only the initiated had the mystical knowledge of truth that was higher even than the Scripture.

Instead of divine revelation standing as judge over man's ideas, man's ideas judged God's revelation (2:15–17). The heresy featured two basic forms. First, some asserted that Jesus' physical body was not real but only "seemed" to be physical (known as "Docetism" from a Gr. word that means "to appear"). John forcefully affirmed the physical reality of Jesus by reminding his readers that he was an eyewitness to Him ("heard," "seen," "touched," "Jesus Christ has come in the flesh"—1:1–4; 4:2, 3). According to early tradition (Irenaeus), another form of this heresy which John may have attacked was led by a man named Cerinthus, who contended that the Christ's "spirit" descended on the human Jesus at his baptism but left him just before his crucifixion. John wrote that the Jesus who was baptized at the beginning of His ministry was the same person who was crucified on the cross (5:6).

Such heretical views destroy not only the true humanity of Jesus, but also the atonement, for Jesus must not only have been truly God, but also the truly human (and physically real) man who actually suffered and died upon the cross in order to be the acceptable substitutionary sacrifice for sin (cf. Heb 2:14–17). The biblical view of Jesus affirms His complete humanity as well as His full deity.

The gnostic idea that matter was evil and only spirit was good led to the idea that either the body should be treated harshly, a form of asceticism (e.g., Col 2:21–23), or sin committed in the body had no connection or effect on one's spirit. This led some, especially John's opponents, to conclude that sin committed in the physical body did not matter; absolute indulgence in immorality was permissible; one could deny sin even existed (1:8–10) and disregard God's law (3:4). John emphasized the need for obedience to God's laws, for he defined the true love of God as obedience to His commandments (5:3).

A lack of love for fellow believers characterizes false teachers, especially as they react against anyone rejecting their new way of thinking (3:10–18). They separated their deceived followers from the fellowship of those who remained faithful to apostolic teaching, leading John to reply that such separation outwardly manifested that those who followed false teachers lacked genuine salvation (2:19). Their departure left the other believers, who remained faithful to apostolic doctrine, shaken. Responding to this crisis, the aged apostle wrote to reassure those remaining faithful and to combat this grave threat to the church. Since the heresy was so acutely dangerous and the time period was so critical for the church in danger of being overwhelmed by false teaching, John gently, lovingly, but with unquestionable apostolic authority, sent this letter to churches in his sphere of influence to stem this spreading plague of false doctrine.

HISTORICAL AND THEOLOGICAL THEMES

In light of the circumstances of the epistle, the overall theme of 1 John is "a recall to the fundamentals of the faith" or "back to the basics of Christianity." The apostle deals with certainties, not opinions or conjecture. He expresses the absolute character of Christianity in very simple terms; terms that are clear and unmistakable, leaving no doubt as to the fundamental nature of those truths. A warm, conversational, and, above all, loving tone occurs, like a father having a tender, intimate conversation with his children.

First John also is pastoral, written from the heart of a pastor who has concern for his people. As a shepherd, John communicated to his flock some very basic, but vitally essential, principles reassuring them regarding the basics of the faith. He desired them to have joy regarding the certainty of their faith rather than being upset by the false teaching and current defections of some (1:4).

The book's viewpoint, however, is not only pastoral but also polemical; not only positive but also negative. John refutes the defectors with sound doctrine, exhibiting no tolerance for those who pervert divine truth. He labels those departing from the truth as "false prophets" (4:1), "those who are trying to deceive" (2:26; 3:7), and "antichrists" (2:18). He pointedly identifies the ultimate source of all such defection from sound doctrine as demonic (4:1–7).

The constant repetition of 3 subthemes reinforces the overall theme regarding faithfulness to the basics of Christianity: happiness (1:4), holiness (2:1), and security (5:13). By faithfulness to the basics, his readers will experience these 3 results continually in their lives. These 3 factors also reveal the key cycle of true spirituality in 1 John: a proper belief in Jesus produces obedience to His commands; obedience issues in love for God and fellow believers (e.g., 3:23, 24). When these 3 (sound faith, obedience, love) operate in concert together, they result in happiness, holiness, and assurance. They constitute the evidence, the litmus test, of a true Christian.

INTERPRETIVE CHALLENGES

Theologians debate the precise nature of the false teachers' beliefs in 1 John, because John does not directly specify their beliefs, but rather combats the heretics mainly through a positive restatement of the fundamentals of the faith. The main feature of the heresy, as noted above, seems to be a denial of the incarnation, i.e., Christ had not come in the flesh. This was most likely an incipient or beginning form of gnosticism, as was pointed out.

The interpreter is also challenged by the rigidity of John's theology. John presents the basics or fundamentals of the Christian life in absolute, not relative, terms. Unlike Paul, who presented exceptions, and dealt so often with believers' failures to meet the divine standard, John does not deal with the "what if I fail" issues. Only in 2:1, 2 does he give some relief from the absolutes. The rest of the book presents truths in black and white rather than shades of gray, often through a stark contrast, e.g., "light" vs. "darkness" (1:5, 7; 2:8–11); truth vs. lies (2:21, 22; 4:1); children of God vs. children of the devil (3:10). Those who claim to be Christians must absolutely display the characteristics of genuine Christians: sound doctrine, obedience, and love. Those who are truly born again have been given a new nature, which gives evidence of itself. Those who do not display characteristics of the new nature don't have it, so were never truly born again. The issues do not center (as much of Paul's writing does) in maintaining temporal or daily fellowship with God but the application of basic tests in one's life to confirm that salvation has truly occurred. Such absolute distinctions were also characteristic of John's gospel.

In a unique fashion, John challenges the interpreter by his repetition of similar themes over and over to emphasize the basic truths about genuine Christianity. Some have likened John's repetition to a spiral that moves outward, becoming larger and larger, each time spreading the same truth over a wider area and encompassing more territory. Others have seen the spiral as moving inward, penetrating deeper and deeper into the same themes while expanding on his thoughts. However one views the spiraling pattern, John uses repetition of basic truths as a means to accentuate their importance and to help his readers understand and remember them.

OUTLINE

I. The Fundamental Tests of Genuine Fellowship—SPIRAL I (1:1–2:17)
- A. The Fundamental Tests of Doctrine (1:1–2:2)
  1. A biblical view of Christ (1:1–4)
  2. A biblical view of sin (1:5–2:2)
- B. The Fundamental Tests of Morals (2:3–17)
  1. A biblical view of obedience (2:3–6)
  2. A biblical view of love (2:7–17)
     - a. The love that God requires (2:7–11)
     - b. The love that God hates (2:12–17)

II. The Fundamental Tests of Genuine Fellowship—SPIRAL II (2:18–3:24)
- A. Part 2 of the Doctrinal Test (2:18–27)
  1. Antichrists depart from Christian fellowship (2:18–21)
  2. Antichrists deny the Christian faith (2:22–25)
  3. Antichrists deceive the Christian faithful (2:26, 27)
- B. Part 2 of the Moral Test (2:28–3:24)
  1. The purifying hope of the Lord's return (2:28–3:3)
  2. The Christian's incompatibility with sin (3:4–24)
     - a. The requirement of righteousness (3:4–10)
     - b. The requirement of love (3:11–24)

III. The Fundamental Tests of Genuine Fellowship—SPIRAL III (4:1–21)
- A. Part 3 of the Doctrinal Test (4:1–6)
  1. The demonic source of false doctrine (4:1–3)
  2. The need for sound doctrine (4:4–6)
- B. Part 3 of the Moral Test (4:7–21)
  1. God's character of love (4:7–10)
  2. God's requirement of love (4:11–21)

IV. The Fundamental Tests of Genuine Fellowship—SPIRAL IV (5:1–21)
- A. The Victorious Life in Christ (5:1–5)
- B. The Witness of God for Christ (5:6–12)
- C. Christian Certainties Because of Christ (5:13–21)
  1. The certainty of eternal life (5:13)
  2. The certainty of answered prayer (5:14–17)
  3. The certainty of victory over sin and Satan (5:18–21)

INTRODUCTION, THE INCARNATE WORD

1 What was [A]from the beginning, what we have
[B]heard, what we have [C]seen with our eyes, what
we [D]have looked at and [E]touched with our hands,
concerning the [F]Word of Life— 2 and [A]the life was
manifested, and we have [B]seen and [C]testify and
proclaim to you [D]the eternal life, which was [E]with
the Father and was [A]manifested to us— 3 what we
have [A]seen and [B]heard we proclaim to you also, so
that you too may have fellowship with us; and indeed our [C]fellowship is with the Father, and with
His Son Jesus Christ. 4 [A]These things we write, so
that our [B]joy may be made complete.

GOD IS LIGHT

5 [A]This is the message we have heard from Him
and announce to you, that [B]God is Light, and in Him
there is no darkness at all. 6 [A]If we say that we have
fellowship with Him and *yet* walk in the darkness, we
[B]lie and [C]do not practice the truth; 7 but if we [A]walk
in the Light as [B]He Himself is in the Light, we have
fellowship with one another, and [C]the blood of Jesus
His Son cleanses us from all sin. 8 [A]If we say that we
have no sin, we are deceiving ourselves and the [B]truth
is not in us. 9 [A]If we confess our sins, He is faithful and
righteous to forgive us our sins and [B]to cleanse us from
all unrighteousness. 10 [A]If we say that we have not
sinned, we [B]make Him a liar and [C]His word is not in us.

1:1 [A]John 1:1f; 1 John 2:13, 14 [B]Acts 4:20; 1 John 1:3 [C]John 19:35; 2 Pet 1:16; 1 John 1:2 [D]John 1:14; 1 John 4:14 [E]Luke 24:39; John 20:27 [F]John 1:1, 4 1:2 [A]John 1:4; 1 John 3:5, 8; 5:20 [B]John 19:35; 1 John 1:1 [C]John 15:27; 1 John 4:14 [D]John 10:28; 17:3; 1 John 2:25; 5:11, 13, 20 [E]John 1:1 1:3 [A]John 19:35; 2 Pet 1:16; 1 John 1:1 [B]Acts 4:20; 1 John 1:1 [C]John 17:3, 21; 1 Cor 1:9 1:4 [A]1 John 2:1 [B]John 3:29 1:5 [A]John 1:19; 1 John 3:11 [B]1 Tim 6:16; James 1:17 1:6 [A]John 8:12; 1 John 2:11 [B]John 8:55; 1 John 2:4; 4:20 [C]John 3:21 1:7 [A]Is 2:5 [B]1 Tim 6:16 [C]Titus 2:14 1:8 [A]Job 15:14; Prov 20:9; Rom 3:10ff; James 3:2 [B]John 8:44; 1 John 2:4 1:9 [A]Ps 32:5; Prov 28:13 [B]Titus 2:14 1:10 [A]Job 15:14 [B]John 3:33; 1 John 5:10 [C]1 John 2:14

1:1–4 As an apostolic eyewitness to Jesus' ministry, including His death and resurrection, and as one of the 3 most intimate associates of the Lord (John, Peter, James), John affirms the physical reality of Jesus Christ's having come "in the flesh" (cf. 4:2, 3). In this way, John accentuated the gravity of the false teaching by immediately focusing on a strongly positive affirmation of the historic reality of Jesus' humanity and the certainty of the gospel. Although the false teachers claimed to believe in Christ, their denial of the true nature of Christ (i.e., His humanity) demonstrated their lack of genuine salvation (2:22, 23). The affirmation of a proper view of Christ constitutes the first test of genuine fellowship (v. 3; see 1:5–2:2 for test two).

1:1 What was. This phrase refers to the proclamation of the gospel that centers in Christ's person, words, and works as contained in apostolic testimony. **from the beginning.** Although John's gospel uses a similar phrase meaning eternity past (Jn 1:1, "in the beginning"), the phrase here, in the context of vv. 1–4, refers to the beginnings of gospel preaching when the readers first heard about Jesus (cf. 2:7, 24). The phrase also emphasizes the stability of the gospel message; its contents do not change but remain stable from the very beginning; it is not subject to change due to current worldly fads or philosophical thinking. **we have heard … we have seen … we have looked at … touched with our hands.** The words used here point to the vivid recollection of the person of Jesus that John still had even in his old age. For John, even 60 years later, those memories were permanently etched on his mind as if the events had just happened. He uses terms that strongly affirm the physical reality of Jesus, for a spirit cannot be heard, gazed at for long periods ("looked at") or touched as Jesus was by John during His earthly ministry and even after His resurrection. **the Word of Life.** This refers not only to Jesus Christ but the proclamation of His gospel.

1:2, 3 manifested … seen … testify … heard … proclaim. John dramatically reemphasizes through repetition of these terms in vv. 2, 3 (cf. v. 1) the authority of his own personal experience as an eyewitness of Jesus' life. Such repetition pointedly reminds his readers that John's personal testimony refutes the false teachers who boasted arrogantly and wrongly about the Christ they had never seen or known.

1:2 the eternal life … with the Father … manifested to us. With this phrase, John accentuates the eternality of Christ in His preincarnate glory (cf. 5:12; Jn 1:4; 5:26, 40; 11:25; 14:6).

1:3 fellowship with us. Fellowship does not mean social relations, but that his readers were to be partakers (or, partners) with John in possessing eternal life (cf. Php 1:5; 1Pe 5:1; 2Pe 1:4). John writes not only to affirm the physical reality of Jesus (vv. 1, 2) but also to produce salvation in the readers. That genuine Christians are never "out of fellowship" is clear, since this verse equates fellowship with salvation.

1:4 our joy may be made complete. A main goal for this epistle is to create joy in the readers. The proclamation of the reality of the gospel (vv. 1, 2) produces a fellowship in eternal life (v. 3) and l, in turn, fellowship in eternal life produces joy (v. 4).

1:5–2:2 To counter the false teachers who denied the existence or importance of sin, John affirms its reality. This affirmation of sin's reality constitutes the second test of true fellowship (cf. vv. 1–4 for test one and 2:3–6 for test three). Those who deny the reality of sin demonstrate their lack of genuine salvation. The "we" in vv. 6, 8, 10 is not a reference to genuine Christians, but a general reference to anyone claiming fellowship, but denying sin. The "we" and "ours" in vv. 7, 9 and 2:1, 2 is a specific reference to genuine Christians.

1:5 we have heard from Him. The message that John and the other apostles preached came from God not from men (cf. Gal 1:12). **God is Light.** In Scripture, light and darkness are very familiar symbols. Intellectually, "light" refers to biblical truth, while "darkness" refers to error or falsehood (cf. Ps 119:105; Pr 6:23; Jn 1:4; 8:12). Morally, "light" refers to holiness or purity, while "darkness" refers to sin or wrongdoing (Ro 13:11–14; 1Th 5:4–7). The heretics claimed to be the truly enlightened, walking in the real light, but John denied that because they do not recognize their sin. About that basic reality, they were unenlightened. **no darkness at all.** With this phrase, John forcefully affirms that God is absolutely perfect, and nothing exists in God's character that impinges upon His truth and holiness (cf. Jas 1:17).

1:6 In spite of their claims to enlightenment, and although the false teachers may have claimed fellowship with Christ, their walking in darkness refuted such claims and, consequently, demonstrated their lack of genuine salvation. The reference to "lie" in v. 6b refers to the claim of fellowship in v. 6a. **do not practice.** This points to their habitual failure regarding the practice of the truth.

1:7 A genuine Christian walks habitually in the light (truth and holiness), not in darkness (falsehood and sin). *See note on 3:9.* Their walk also results in cleansing from sin as the Lord continually forgives His own. Since those walking in the light share in the character of God, they will be habitually characterized by His holiness (3Jn 11), indicating their true fellowship with Him (Jas 1:27). A genuine Christian does not walk in darkness, but only in the light (2Co 6:14; Eph 5:8; Col 1:12, 13), and cleansing from sin continually occurs (cf. v. 9).

1:8 Not only did the false teachers walk in darkness (i.e., sin; v. 6), they went so far as to deny totally the existence of a sin nature in their lives. If someone never admits to being a sinner, salvation cannot result (see Mt 19:16–22 for the account of the young man who refused to recognize his sin). Not only did the false teachers make false claims to fellowship and disregard sin (v. 6), they are also characterized by deceit regarding sinlessness (Ecc 7:20; Ro 3:23).

1:9 Continual confession of sin is an indication of genuine salvation. While the false teachers would not admit their sin, the genuine Christian admitted and forsook it (Ps 32:3–5; Pr 28:13). The term "confess" means to say the same thing about sin as God does; to acknowledge His perspective about sin. While v. 7 is from God's perspective, v. 9 is from the Christian's perspective. Confession of sin characterizes genuine Christians, and God continually cleanses those who are confessing (cf. v. 7). Rather than focusing on confession for every single sin as necessary, John has especially in mind here a settled recognition and acknowledgment that one is a sinner in need of cleansing and forgiveness (Eph 4:32; Col 2:13).

1:10 make Him a liar. Since God has said that all people are sinners (cf. Ps 14:3; 51:5; Is 53:6; Jer 17:5, 6; Ro 3:10–19, 23; 6:23), to deny that fact is to blaspheme God with slander that defames His name.

CHRIST IS OUR ADVOCATE

2 [A]My little children, I am [B]writing these things to
you so that you may not sin. And if anyone sins,
[C]we have an [a,D]Advocate with the Father, Jesus Christ
the righteous; **2** and He Himself is [A]the [a]propitiation
for our sins; and not for ours only, but also [B]for *those*
of the whole world.
3 [A]By this we know that we have come to [B]know
Him, if we [C]keep His commandments. **4** The one who
says, "[A]I have come to [B]know Him," and does not
keep His commandments, is a [C]liar, and [D]the truth
is not in him; **5** but whoever [A]keeps His word, in him
the [B]love of God has truly been perfected. [C]By this
we know that we are in Him: **6** the one who says he
[A]abides in Him [B]ought himself to walk in the same
manner as He walked.
7 [A]Beloved, I am [B]not writing a new commandment
to you, but an old commandment which you have
had [C]from the beginning; the old commandment is
the word which you have heard. **8** [a]On the other hand,
I am writing [A]a new commandment to you, which
is true in Him and in you, because [B]the darkness is
passing away and [C]the true Light is already shining.
9 The one who says he is in the Light and *yet* [A]hates
his [B]brother is in the darkness until now. **10** [A]The one
who loves his brother abides in the Light and there
is no cause for stumbling in him. **11** But the one who
[A]hates his brother is in the darkness and [B]walks in
the darkness, and does not know where he is going
because the darkness has [C]blinded his eyes.
12 I am writing to you, [A]little children, because
[B]your sins have been forgiven you for His name's

2:1 [a]Gr *Paracletos,* one called alongside to help; or *Intercessor* [A]John 13:33; Gal 4:19; 1 John 2:12, 28; 3:7, 18; 4:4; 5:21 [B]1 John 1:4 [C]Rom 8:34; 1 Tim 2:5; Heb 7:25; 9:24 [D]John 14:16 2:2 [a]Or *satisfaction* [A]Rom 3:25; Heb 2:17; 1 John 4:10 [B]John 4:42; 11:51f; 1 John 4:14 2:3 [A]1 John 2:5; 3:24; 4:13; 5:2 [B]1 John 2:4; 3:6; 4:7f [C]John 14:15; 15:10; 1 John 3:22, 24; 5:3; Rev 12:17; 14:12 2:4 [A]Titus 1:10 [B]1 John 3:6; 4:7f [C]1 John 1:6 [D]1 John 1:8 2:5 [A]John 14:23 [B]1 John 4:12 [C]1 John 2:3; 3:24; 4:13; 5:2 2:6 [A]John 15:4 [B]John 13:15; 15:10; 1 Pet 2:21 2:7 [A]Heb 6:9; 1 John 3:2, 21; 4:1, 7, 11 [B]John 13:34; 1 John 3:11, 23; 4:21; 2 John 5 [C]1 John 2:24; 3:11; 2 John 5, 6 2:8 [a]Lit *Again* [A]John 13:34 [B]Rom 13:12; Eph 5:8; 1 Thess 5:4f [C]John 1:9 2:9 [A]1 John 2:11; 3:15; 4:20 [B]Acts 1:15; 1 John 3:10, 16; 4:20f 2:10 [A]John 11:9; 1 John 2:10, 11 2:11 [A]1 John 2:9; 3:15; 4:20 [B]John 12:35; 1 John 1:6 [C]2 Cor 4:4; 2 Pet 1:9 2:12 [A]1 John 2:1 [B]Acts 13:38; 1 Cor 6:11

2:1 so that you may not sin. Although a Christian must continually acknowledge and confess sin (1:9), he is not powerless against it. Fulfilling the duty of confession does not give license to sin. Sin can and should be conquered through the power of the Holy Spirit (see Ro 6:12–14; 8:12, 13; 1Co 15:34; Titus 2:11, 12; 1Pe 1:13–16). **Advocate.** John 16:7 translates this word as "Helper" (lit. "one called alongside"). Perhaps a modern concept of the term would be a defense attorney. Although Satan prosecutes believers night and day before the Father due to sin (Rev 12:10), Christ's High Priestly ministry guarantees not only sympathy but also acquittal (Heb 4:14–16).

2:2 propitiation. Cf. 4:10. The word means "appeasement" or "satisfaction." The sacrifice of Jesus on the cross satisfied the demands of God's holiness for the punishment of sin (cf. Ro 1:18; 2Co 5:21; Eph 2:3). So Jesus propitiated or satisfied God. *See notes on Heb 2:17; 9:15* for a clear illustration of propitiation. **for *those* *of* the whole world.** This is a generic term, referring not to every single individual, but to mankind in general. Christ actually paid the penalty only for those who would repent and believe. A number of Scriptures indicate that Christ died for the world (Jn 1:29; 3:16; 6:51; 1Ti 2:6; Heb 2:9). Most of the world will be eternally condemned to hell to pay for their own sins, so they could not have been paid for by Christ. The passages which speak of Christ's dying for the whole world must be understood to refer to mankind in general (as in Tit 2:11). "World" indicates the sphere, the beings toward whom God seeks reconciliation and has provided propitiation. God has mitigated His wrath on sinners temporarily, by letting them live and enjoy earthly life (*see note on 1Ti 4:10*). In that sense, Christ has provided a brief, temporal propitiation for the whole world. But He actually satisfied fully the wrath of God eternally only for the elect who believe. Christ's death in itself had unlimited and infinite value because He is Holy God. Thus His sacrifice was sufficient to pay the penalty for all the sins of all whom God brings to faith. But the actual satisfaction and atonement was made only for those who believe (cf. Jn 10:11, 15; 17:9, 20; Ac 20:28; Ro 8:32, 37; Eph 5:25). The pardon for sin is offered to the whole world, but received only by those who believe (cf. 4:9, 14; Jn 5:24). There is no other way to be reconciled to God.

2:3–6 Obedience to God's commands constitutes a third test of genuine fellowship. First John presents two external tests that demonstrate salvation: doctrinal and moral. The doctrinal test consists of confessing a proper view of Christ and of sin (see 1:1–4 and 1:5–2:2), while the moral test consists of obedience and love (see also vv. 7–11). While subjective assurance of salvation comes through the internal witness of the Holy Spirit (5:10; Ro 8:14–16; 2Co 1:12), the test of obedience constitutes objective assurance that one is genuinely saved. Obedience is the external, visible proof of salvation (*see notes on Jas 2:14–25; 2Pe 2:5–11*). The false teachers' failure to obey God's commands objectively demonstrated that they were not saved (Lk 6:46). Those who are truly enlightened and know God are obedient to His Word.

2:3, 4 know … keep. The repetition of these words emphasizes that those genuinely born again display the habit of obedience. Obedience results in assurance of salvation (cf. Eph 2:2; 1Pe 1:14). That these two words are among John's favorites is clear since he uses "know" approximately 40 times and "keep" approximately 10 times in this epistle.

2:6 abides. This word is one of John's favorite terms for salvation (*see notes on Jn 15:4–10*). **manner as He walked.** Jesus' life of obedience is the Christian's pattern. Those who claim to be Christians ought to live as He did (cf. Jn 6:38) since they possess His Spirit's presence and power.

2:7–17 Love of the brethren constitutes the fourth test of genuine fellowship. The primary focus of the moral test is obedience to the command of love because love is the fulfillment of the law (Mt 22:34–40; Ro 13:8–10; Jas 2:8) and is also Christ's new command (Jn 13:34; 15:12, 17). True enlightenment is to love. God's light is the light of love, so to walk in light is to walk in love.

2:7 new. Not referring to "new" in the sense of time, but something that is fresh in quality, kind or form; something that replaces something else that has been worn out. **new commandment … old commandment.** John makes a significant wordplay here. Though he doesn't state here what the command is, he does in 2Jn 5, 6. It is to love. Both of these phrases refer to the same commandment of love. The commandment of love was "new" because Jesus personified love in a fresh, new way, and it was shed abroad in believers' hearts (Ro 5:5) and energized by the Holy Spirit (Gal 5:22; 1Th 4:9). He raised love to a higher standard for the church and commanded His disciples to imitate His love ("as I have loved you"; cf. 3:16; Jn 13:34). The command was also "old" because the OT commanded love (Lv 19:18; Dt 6:5), and the readers of John's epistle had heard about Jesus' command to love when they first heard the gospel. **from the beginning.** This phrase refers not to the beginning of time, but the beginning of their Christian lives, as indicated by v. 24; 3:11; 2Jn 6. This was part of the ethical instruction they received from the day of their salvation and not some innovation invented by John, as the heretics may have said.

2:9 hates. The original language conveys the idea of someone who habitually hates or is marked by a lifestyle of hate. **in the darkness until now.** Those who profess to be Christians, yet are characterized by hate, demonstrate by such action that they have never been born again. The false teachers made claims to enlightenment, transcendent knowledge of God, and salvation, but their actions, especially the lack of love, proved all such claims false (see also v. 11).

2:12–14 Only two families exist from God's perspective: children of God and children of Satan (see Jn 8:39–44). John reminds his readers in these verses that as Christians they have been forgiven and come to know God as their heavenly Father. As a result, they are a part of God's family. They must not love Satan's family or give their allegiance to the world controlled by him (see v. 15). The word "little children" in v. 12 is general for offspring of any age, in contrast to a different Gr. word for "children" in v. 13, which refers to young children (*see note on vv. 13, 14*). **I am writing …. have written.** John repeats the message in these verses to emphasize the certainty of their belonging to God's family. "I am writing" is from John's perspective, while "I have written" anticipates his readers' perspective when they received the letter.

sake. 13 I am writing to you, fathers, because you
know Him [A]who has been from the beginning. I am
writing to you, young men, because [B]you have overcome [C]the evil one. I have written to you, children,
because [D]you know the Father. 14 I have written to
you, fathers, because you know Him [A]who has been
from the beginning. I have written to you, young
men, because you are [B]strong, and the [C]word of God
abides in you, and [D]you have overcome the evil one.

DO NOT LOVE THE WORLD

15 Do not love [A]the world nor the things in the world.
[B]If anyone loves the world, the love of the Father is
not in him. 16 For all that is in the world, [A]the lust of
the flesh and [B]the lust of the eyes and [C]the boastful
pride of life, is not from the Father, but is from the
world. 17 [A]The world is passing away, and *also* its lusts;
but the one who [B]does the will of God lives forever.
18 Children, [A]it is the last hour; and just as you
heard that [B]antichrist is coming, [C]even now many
antichrists have appeared; from this we know that
it is the last hour. 19 [A]They went out from us, but they
were not *really* of us; for if they had been of us, they
would have remained with us; but *they went out,*
[B]so that [a]it would be shown that they all are not of
us. 20 [a]But you have an [A]anointing from [B]the Holy
One, and [C]you all know. 21 I have not written to you
because you do not know the truth, but [A]because you
do know it, and [a]because no lie is [B]of the truth. 22 Who
is the liar but [A]the one who denies that Jesus is the
[a]Christ? This is [B]the antichrist, the one who denies
the Father and the Son. 23 [A]Whoever denies the Son

2:13 [A]1 John 1:1 [B]John 16:33; 1 John 2:14; 4:4; 5:4f; Rev 2:7 [C]Matt 5:37; 1 John 2:14; 3:12; 5:18f [D]John 14:7; 1 John 2:3 2:14 [A]1 John 1:1 [B]Eph 6:10 [C]John 5:38; 8:37; 1 John 1:10 [D]1 John 2:13 2:15 [A]Rom 12:2; James 1:27 [B]James 4:4 2:16 [A]Rom 13:14; Eph 2:3; 1 Pet 2:11 [B]Prov 27:20 [C]James 4:16 2:17 [A]1 Cor 7:31 [B]Mark 3:35 2:18 [A]Rom 13:11; 1 Tim 4:1; 1 Pet 4:7 [B]Matt 24:5, 24; 1 John 2:22; 4:3; 2 John 7 [C]Mark 13:22; 1 John 4:1, 3 2:19 [a]Lit *they would be revealed* [A]Acts 20:30 [B]1 Cor 11:19 2:20 [a]Lit *And* [A]2 Cor 1:21; 1 John 2:27 [B]Mark 1:24; Acts 10:38 [C]Prov 28:5; Matt 13:11; John 14:26; 1 Cor 2:15f; 1 John 2:27 2:21 [a]Or know *that* [A]James 1:19; 2 Pet 1:12; Jude 5 [B]John 8:44; 18:37; 1 John 3:19 2:22 [a]I.e. Messiah [A]1 John 4:3; 2 John 7 [B]Matt 24:5, 24; 1 John 2:18; 4:3; 2 John 7 2:23 [A]John 8:19; 16:3; 17:3; 1 John 4:15; 5:1; 2 John 9

2:13, 14 fathers … young men … children. These very clear distinctions identify 3 stages of spiritual growth in God's family. "Fathers," the most mature, have a deep knowledge of the Eternal God. The pinnacle of spiritual maturity is to know God in His fullness (cf. Php 3:10). "Young men" are those who, while not yet having the mature experience of knowing God in the Word and through life, do know sound doctrine. They are strong against sin and error because they have His Word in them. Thus they overcome the wiles of the devil, who makes havoc of children (cf. Eph 4:14). Since Satan's efforts are in falsehood and deception, they have overcome him. "Children" are those who have only the basic awareness of God and need to grow. All are in God's family and manifest Christ's character at different levels.

2:15 Do not love the world. Although John often repeats the importance of love and that God is love (4:7, 8), he also reveals that God hates a certain type of love: love of the world (Jn 15:18–20). In this text, John expresses a particular form of the fourth test (i.e., the test of love). Positively, the Christian loves God and fellow Christians. Negatively, an absence of love for the world must habitually characterize the love life of those to be considered genuinely born again. "Love" here signifies affection and devotion. God, not the world, must have the first place in the Christian's life (Mt 10:37–39; Php 3:20). **the world.** This is not a reference to the physical, material world, but the invisible spiritual system of evil dominated by Satan (*see notes on 2Co 10:3–5*) and all that it offers in opposition to God, His Word, and His people (cf. 5:19; Jn 12:31; 1Co 1:21; 2Co 4:4; Jas 4:4; 2Pe 1:4). **the love of the Father is not in him.** Either one is a genuine Christian marked by love and obedience to God, or one is a non-Christian in rebellion against God, i.e., in love with and enslaved by the satanically controlled world system (Eph 2:1–3; Col 1:13; Jas 4:4). No middle ground between these two alternatives exists for someone claiming to be born again. The false teachers had no such singular love, but were devoted to the world's philosophy and wisdom, thereby revealing their love for the world and their unsaved state (cf. Mt 6:24; Lk 16:13; 1Ti 6:20; 2Pe 2:12–22).

2:16 all that is in the world. Cf. Jas 4:4. While the world's philosophies and ideologies and much that it offers may appear attractive and appealing, that is deception. Its true and pervasive nature is evil, harmful, ruinous, and satanic. Its deadly theories are raised up against the knowledge of God and hold the souls of men captive (2Co 10:3–5). **lust.** John uses the term negatively here for a strong desire for evil things. **flesh.** The term refers to the sin nature of man; the rebellious self dominated by sin and in opposition to God (Ro 7:15–25; 8:2–8; Gal 5:19–21). Satan uses the evil world system to incite the flesh. **eyes.** Satan uses the eyes as a strategic avenue to incite wrong desires (Jos 7:20, 21; 2Sa 11:2; Mt 5:27–29). Satan's temptation of Eve involved being attracted to something beautiful in appearance, but the result was spiritual death (Ge 3:6 "a delight to the eyes"). **pride of life.** The phrase has the idea of arrogance over one's circumstances, which produced haughtiness or exaggeration, parading what one possessed to impress other people (Jas 4:16). **not from the Father.** The world is the enemy of the Christian because it is in rebellion and opposition against God and controlled by Satan (5:19; Eph 2:2; 2Co 4:4; 10:3–5). The 3 openings presented, if allowing access to sin, result in tragedy. Not only must the Christian reject the world for what it is but also for what it does.

2:17 The world is passing away. The Christian also must not love the satanic world system because of its temporary nature. It is in the continual process of disintegration, headed for destruction (Ro 8:18–22). **the one who does the will of God lives forever.** In contrast to the temporary world, God's will is permanent and unchangeable. Those who follow God's will abide as His people forever. While God offers eternal life to His children, the present age is doomed (cf. 1Co 7:31; 2Co 4:18).

2:18 antichrist. This is the first occurrence of the term "antichrist." Its usage is found only in John's epistles (4:3; 2Jn 7). Here it refers to the coming final world ruler energized by Satan who will seek to replace and oppose the true Christ (Da 8:9–11; 11:31–38; 12:11; Mt 24:15; 2Th 2:1–12; *see notes on Rev 13:1–5; 19:20*). **many antichrists have appeared.** While the term's first occurrence refers to a particular person prophesied in Scripture, this one is plural and refers to many individuals. John uses the plural to identify and characterize the false teachers who were troubling John's congregations because their false doctrine distorted the truth and opposed Christ (Mt 24:24; Mk 13:22; Ac 20:28–30). The term, therefore, refers to a principle of evil, incarnated in men, who are hostile and opposed to God (cf. 2Co 10:4, 5). John writes to expose the false teachers, the wolves in sheep's clothing, who purvey damning lies (cf. Eph 5:11). **the last hour.** The phrase refers to the "latter times" or "last days," i.e., the time period between the first and second comings of Christ (1Ti 4:1; Jas 5:3; 1Pe 4:7; 2Pe 3:3; Jude 18).

2:19 They went out from us … they were not *really* of us. The first characteristic mentioned of antichrists, i.e., false teachers and deceivers (vv. 22–26), is that they depart from the faithful (see vv. 22, 23 for the second characteristic and v. 26 for the third). They arise from within the church and depart from true fellowship and lead people out with them. The verse also places emphasis on the doctrine of the perseverance of the saints. Those genuinely born again endure in faith and fellowship and the truth (1Co 11:19; 2Ti 2:12). The ultimate test of true Christianity is endurance (Mk 13:13; Heb 3:14). The departure of people from the truth and the church is their unmasking.

2:20, 21 Two characteristics mark genuine Christians in contrast to the antichrists. First, the Holy Spirit ("the anointing," v. 27) guards them from error (cf. Ac 10:38; 2Co 1:21). Christ as the Holy One (Lk 4:34; Ac 3:14) imparts the Holy Spirit as their illuminating guardian from deception. Second, the Holy Spirit guides the believer into knowing "all things" (Jn 14:26; 16:13). True Christians have a built-in lie detector and persevere in the truth. Those who remain in heresy and apostasy manifest the fact that they were never genuinely born again (cf. v. 19).

2:22, 23 denies the Father and the Son. A second characteristic of antichrists is that they deny the faith (i.e., sound doctrine). Anyone denying the true nature of Christ as presented in the Scripture is an antichrist (cf. 4:3; 2Th 2:11). The denial of Christ also constitutes a denial of God Himself, who testified to His Son (5:9; Jn 5:32–38; 8:18).

does not have the Father; the one who confesses the
Son has the Father also. 24 As for you, let that abide
in you which you heard [A]from the beginning. If
what you heard from the beginning abides in you,
you also [B]will abide in the Son and in the Father.

THE PROMISE IS ETERNAL LIFE

25 [A]This is the promise which He Himself [a]made
to us: eternal life.

26 These things I have written to you concerning those who are trying to [A]deceive you. 27 As for
you, the [A]anointing which you received from Him
abides in you, and you have no need for anyone to
teach you; but as His anointing [B]teaches you about
all things, and is [C]true and is not a lie, and just as it
has taught you, [a]you abide in Him.

28 Now, [A]little children, abide in Him, so that when
He [B]appears, we may have [C]confidence and [D]not
[a]shrink away from Him in shame [b]at His [E]coming.
29 If you know that [A]He is righteous, you know that
everyone also who practices righteousness [B]is [a]born
of Him.

CHILDREN OF GOD LOVE ONE ANOTHER

3 See [a,A]how great a love the Father has bestowed
on us, that we would be called [B]children of God;
and *such* we are. For this reason the world does not
know us, because [C]it did not know Him. 2 [A]Beloved,
now we are [B]children of God, and [C]it has not appeared as yet what we will be. We know that when He
[D]appears, we will be [E]like Him, because we will [F]see

2:24 [A]1 John 2:7 [B]John 14:23; 1 John 1:3; 2 John 9 2:25 [a]Lit *promised us* [A]John 3:15; 6:40; 1 John 1:2 2:26 [A]1 John 3:7; 2 John 7 2:27 [a]Or *abide in Him;* Gr command [A]John 14:16; 1 John 2:20 [B]John 14:26; 1 Cor 2:12; 1 Thess 4:9 [C]John 14:17 2:28 [a]Lit *be put to shame from Him* [b]Or *in His presence* [A]1 John 2:1 [B]Luke 17:30; Col 3:4; 1 John 3:2 [C]Eph 3:12; 1 John 3:21; 4:17; 5:14 [D]Mark 8:38 [E]1 Thess 2:19 2:29 [a]Or *begotten* [A]John 7:18; 1 John 3:7 [B]John 1:13; 3:3; 1 John 3:9; 4:7; 5:1, 4, 18; 3 John 11 3:1 [a]Lit *what kind of love* [A]John 3:16; 1 John 4:10 [B]John 1:12; 11:52; Rom 8:16; 1 John 3:2, 10 [C]John 15:18, 21; 16:3 3:2 [A]1 John 2:7 [B]John 1:12; 11:52; Rom 8:16; 1 John 3:1, 10 [C]Rom 8:19, 23f [D]Luke 17:30; Col 3:4; 1 John 2:28 [E]Rom 8:29; 2 Pet 1:4 [F]John 17:24; 2 Cor 3:18

2:24, 25 heard from the beginning. The gospel that cannot change. Let it remain, do not follow false teachers (cf. 2Ti 3:1, 7, 13; 4:3). Christian truth is fixed and unalterable (Jude 3). If we stay faithful to the truth, we continue to experience intimate communion with God and Christ and persevere to the full eternal life (cf. 5:11, 12).

2:26 A third characteristic of antichrists is that they try to deceive the faithful (cf. also 1Ti 4:1).

2:27 anointing. *See note on vv. 20, 21.* John is not denying the importance of gifted teachers in the church (1Co 12:28; Eph 4:11) but indicates that neither those teachers nor those believers are dependent on human wisdom or the opinions of men for the truth. God's Holy Spirit guards and guides the true believer into the truth (see vv. 20, 21). If God is true (cf. 2Ch 15:3; Jer 10:10; Jn 17:3; 1Th 1:9) and Christ is the truth (cf. Jn 14:6), so is the Holy Spirit (cf. 5:6; Jn 15:26; 16:13). **abide in Him.** In response to such deceivers, the task of the genuine believer is to "walk in truth," i.e., persevere in faithfulness and sound doctrine (see vv. 20–21; 2Jn 4; 3Jn 4).

2:28–3:3 This section deals with the "purifying hope" of every Christian, i.e., the return of Christ. John uses this purifying hope to reiterate and elaborate on the moral test (love and obedience) of a true Christian. The hope of Christ's return has a sanctifying effect on moral behavior. In anticipation of Christ's return and reward (cf. 1Co 3:10–17; 4:1–5; 2Co 5:9, 10; Rev 22:12), a genuine Christian walks in holiness of life. Those who do not evidence such behavior manifest an unsaved life. In these 5 verses, John has given 5 features of the believer's hope.

2:28 abide in Him. John repeats his emphasis on abiding (v. 27) to introduce it as the first feature of the believer's hope in 2:28–3:3. Whenever John refers to abiding, he is referring to persevering in the faith of salvation, which is evidence of being a true believer (Jn 15:1–6). The hope of Christ's return produces the effect of continual abiding in every true believer as they long for the glorious future prepared for them. Paul called it "loving His appearing" (2Ti 4:8) and said those who do that are the ones who will be crowned with eternal righteousness in heaven. Abiding signifies a permanent remaining in Christ and guarantees the believer's hope. Those who truly abide continue in the faith and in fellowship with the saints (v. 19). In contrast to v. 27 ("you abide"), however, he commands (imperative) believers to abide. The command signals that abiding is not passive; continual, active abiding must be pursued by every genuine believer (Php 2:12). Salvation is eternal because of the Lord's side—He holds us (cf. Jn 6:37–44), and because of our side—we persevere in faith and obedience (cf. Jn 8:31, 32). It is not unlike salvation in which God sovereignly saves, but not apart from personal faith from the one He saves. Or in the case of sanctification, God conforms us to His Son, but not apart from obedience. The NT is rich with statements about God's work and the work of the believer. Paul said it well in Col 1:29. **when He appears.** This refers especially to the Rapture and gathering of the church (cf. Jn 14:1–6; 1Co 15:51–54; 1Th 4:13–18) and the Judgment Seat of Christ to follow (cf. 1Co 4:5; 2Co 5:9, 10). **confidence ... not shrink away from Him in shame.** The word "confidence" means "outspokenness" or "freedom of speech." Those who are saved will have confidence at Christ's coming because they will be blameless in holiness based on abiding in Christ (Eph 5:27; Col 1:22; 1Th 3:13; 5:23). In contrast, there will be many, like the soils in Matthew 13, who are temporary look-alike believers (see 13:20–22; cf. Jn 8:31), who did not believe, who did not persevere in abiding, and, consequently, face only shame at His appearance.

2:29 everyone ... who practices righteousness is born of Him. This is the second feature of the believer's hope in 2:28–3:3. The hope of Christ's return not only sustains faith (v. 28), but makes righteousness a habit. The term for "born" is the same verb used in Jn 3:7 where Jesus told Nicodemus that he must be "born" again. Those truly born again as God's children have their heavenly Father's righteous nature (1Pe 1:3, 13–16). As a result, they will display characteristics of God's righteousness. John looks from effect (righteous behavior) to cause (being truly born again) to affirm that righteous living is the proof of being born again (Jas 2:20, 26; 2Pe 3:11).

3:1 how great a love the Father has bestowed on us. This outburst of wonder introduces the third feature of the believer's hope in 2:28–3:3. The believer's hope is strengthened by the fact that God's love initiated his salvation (Eph 1:3–6). Christ's return will unite the believer with the heavenly Father who loves His child with an immeasurable love. John expresses utter astonishment at God's love for believers in making them His children (Ro 8:17). **the world does not know us.** The real aliens in the world are not extraterrestrials but Christians. Having been born again, given a new nature of heavenly origin, Christians display a nature and lifestyle like their Savior and heavenly Father; a nature totally foreign (other worldly) to the unsaved (1Co 2:15, 16; 1Pe 4:3, 4). No wonder Scripture describes Christians as "aliens," "exiles," and "strangers" (Heb 11:13; 1Pe 1:1; 2:11). The Lord Jesus was unearthly in origin, and so are those born again. Our true transformed lives have not yet been manifested (*see notes on Ro 8:18–24*).

3:2 now we are children of God. Everyone who exercises genuine saving faith becomes a child of God at the moment of belief (Jn 1:12; Ro 8:16; 2Pe 1:4), though the truly heavenly, divine life in that person (cf. Eph 4:24; Col 3:10) will not be revealed until Jesus appears (*see note on Ro 8:19*). In the meantime, the Holy Spirit is working into us the image of Christ (*see note on 2Co 3:18*). **we will be like Him.** This phrase introduces the fourth feature of the believer's hope in 2:28–3:3. When Christ returns He shall conform every believer to His image, i.e., His nature. A tension exists between the first part of the verse ("now we are children") and the latter part ("we will be like Him"). Such tension finds resolution in the solid hope that at Christ's return the believer will experience ultimate conformity to His likeness (*see notes on Ro 8:29; 1Co 15:42–49; Php 3:21*). The glorious nature of that conformity defies description, but as much as glorified humanity can be like incarnate deity, believers will be, without becoming deity.

Him just as He is. 3 And everyone who has this
[A]hope *fixed* on Him [B]purifies himself, just as He
is pure.
4 Everyone who practices sin also practices lawlessness; and [A]sin is lawlessness. 5 You know that He
[A]appeared in order to [B]take away sins; and [C]in Him
there is no sin. 6 No one who abides in Him [A]sins;
no one who sins has seen Him or [a,B]knows Him.
7 [A]Little children, make sure no one [B]deceives you;
[C]the one who practices righteousness is righteous,
just as He is righteous; 8 the one who practices sin
is [A]of the devil; for the devil [a]has sinned from the
beginning. [B]The Son of God [C]appeared for this purpose, [D]to destroy the works of the devil. 9 No one
who is [a,A]born of God [B]practices sin, because His
seed abides in him; and he cannot sin, because he
is [a]born of God. 10 By this the [A]children of God and
the [B]children of the devil are obvious: [a]anyone who
does not practice righteousness is not of God, nor
the one who [C]does not love his [D]brother.

3:3 [A]Rom 15:12; 1 Pet 1:3 [B]John 17:19; 2 Cor 7:1 3:4 [A]Rom 4:15; 1 John 5:17 3:5 [A]1 John 1:2; 3:8 [B]John 1:29; 1 Pet 1:18-20; 1 John 2:2 [C]2 Cor 5:21; 1 John 2:29 3:6 [a]Or *has known* [A]1 John 3:9 [B]1 John 2:3; 3 John 11 3:7 [A]1 John 2:1 [B]1 John 2:26 [C]1 John 2:29 3:8 [a]Lit *sins* [A]Matt 13:38; John 8:44; 1 John 3:10 [B]Matt 4:3 [C]1 John 3:5 [D]John 12:31; 16:11 3:9 [a]Or *begotten* [A]John 1:13; 3:3; 1 John 2:29; 4:7; 5:1, 4, 18; 3 John 11 [B]1 Pet 1:23; 1 John 3:6; 5:18 3:10 [a]Lit *everyone* [A]John 1:12; 11:52; Rom 8:16; 1 John 3:1, 2 [B]Matt 13:38; John 8:44; 1 John 3:8 [C]Rom 13:8ff; Col 3:14; 1 Tim 1:5; 1 John 4:8 [D]1 John 2:9

3:3 purifies himself, just as He is pure. This is the key verse to 2:28–3:3 and introduces the fifth feature of the believer's hope in this section. Living in the reality of Christ's return makes a difference in a Christian's behavior. Since Christians someday will be like Him, a desire should grow within the Christian to become like Him now. That was Paul's passion, expressed in Php 3:12–14 (*see notes there*). That calls for a purifying of sin, in which we play a part (*see notes on 2Co 7:1; 1Ti 5:22; 1Pe 1:22*).

3:4–24 The primary aim of this section is to combat false teachers who are corrupting the fundamentals of the faith. These verses further amplify, reiterate, and emphasize the moral test already presented by John (see 2:3–6, 7–11). Verses 4–10 convey that genuine believers practice righteousness, while vv. 11–24 relate that genuine believers practice love toward fellow believers. John was very concerned that Christians know how to tell the true from the false; the genuine from the artificial; true believers from false ones. He presents tests here and throughout this letter to help determine the validity of anybody's claim to be a Christian.

3:4–10 These verses deal with the Christian's incompatibility with sin. The false teachers that John combated, because of their gnostic-like concepts (see Introduction: Background and Setting), discounted the significance of sin and the need for obedience. Because of their philosophical dualism, they viewed matter as inherently bad, and as a result, any sins committed in the physical realm as inconsequential. In this section, John gives 4 reasons why true Christians cannot habitually practice sin (Jn 8:31, 34–36; Ro 6:11; 2Jn 9).

3:4 practices sin. The verb, "practices," in the Gr. conveys the idea of making sin a habitual practice. Although genuine Christians have a sin disposition (1:8), and do commit and need to confess sin (1:9; 2:1), that is not the unbroken pattern of their lives. A genuinely born again believer has a built-in check or guard against habitual sinning due to a new nature ("born of God"—v. 9; Ro 6:12). **sin is lawlessness.** The first reason why Christians cannot practice sin is because sin is incompatible with the law of God which they love (Ps 119:34, 77, 97; Ro 7:12, 22). The term "lawlessness" conveys more than transgressing God's law. It conveys the ultimate sense of rebellion, i.e., living as if there was no law or ignoring what laws exist (Jas 4:17).

3:5 He appeared in order to take away sins. A second reason why Christians cannot practice sin is because it is incompatible with the work of Christ. Christ died to sanctify (i.e., make holy) the believer (2Co 5:21; Eph 5:25–27). To sin is contrary to Christ's work of breaking the dominion of sin in the believer's life (Ro 6:1–15).

3:6 No one who abides … sins. Like the phrase "practices sin" of verse 4, the sense conveyed here is the idea of habitual, constant sinning. **No one who sins has seen Him or knows Him.** If no check against habitual sin exists in someone who professes to be a Christian, John's pronouncement is absolutely clear—salvation never took place.

3:7 make sure no one deceives you. The word "deceives" means "to lead astray." Since false teachers were attempting to pervert the fundamentals of the faith, the possibility existed that some Christians might be fooled into accepting what they were advocating. To prevent this deception from occurring, John repeatedly emphasized the basics of Christianity, e.g., the need for obedience, the need for love, and the need for a proper view of Christ (see Introduction: Historical and Theological Themes). **practices righteousness.** The genuine believer's habitual lifestyle of righteousness stands in sharp contrast to those false teachers who practiced sin (cf. vv. 4, 6). Since Christ died on the cross to transform sinners, those truly born again have replaced the habit of sin with the habit of righteous living (Ro 6:13, 14). **just as He is righteous.** Those who are truly born again reflect the divine nature of the Son. They behave like Him, manifesting the power of His life in them (Gal 2:20).

3:8 the one who practices sin. This phrase means "who habitually practice sin" (*see notes on vv. 4, 6*). **of the devil.** The phrase gives the source of the false teachers' actions. The term "devil" means "accuser" or "slanderer." Not only does Satan ("adversary") oppose God and His plan, but he is the originator and instigator of sin and rebellion against God and His law (v. 4; *see notes on Eph 6:10–17*). Therefore, all the unsaved are under the diabolic influence of Satan. Their sinful lifestyle reflects their satanic origin (*see note on Eph 2:1*). John contrasts the children of God with the children of Satan in terms of their actions. While those who are truly born again reflect the habit of righteousness, Satan's children practice sin. **from the beginning.** Since Satan was originally created as perfect and only later rebelled against God (Is 14:12–14; Eze 28:12–17), John probably means the moment of his rebellion against God, the beginning of his rebellious career. Since sin characterizes him completely, so everyone characterized by sin must derive from him (cf. Jn 8:44). **for this purpose, to destroy.** A third reason why Christians cannot practice sin is because Christ came to destroy the works of the arch-sinner, Satan. The devil is still operating, but he has been defeated, and in Christ we escape his tyranny. The day will come when all of Satan's activity will cease in the universe, and he will be sent to hell forever (Rev 20:10). **works of the devil.** This summarizes a variety of the devil's activities: sin, rebellion, temptation, ruling the world, persecution and accusation of saints, instigation of false teachers, power of death (e.g., Lk 8:12; Jn 8:44; Ac 5:3; 1Co 7:5; 2Co 4:4; Eph 6:11, 12; 1Th 2:18; Heb 2:14; Rev 12:10).

3:9 The fourth reason why Christians cannot practice sin is because it is incompatible with the ministry of the Holy Spirit, who has imparted a new nature to the believer (Jn 3:5–8). **born of God.** John wrote here of the new birth (Jn 3:7). When people become Christians, God makes them new creatures with new natures (2Co 5:17). Believers have God's characteristics because they have been born into God's family. This new nature exhibits the habitual character of righteousness produced by the Holy Spirit (Gal 5:22–24). John repeats this phrase twice for emphasis. **His seed.** The new birth involves the acquisition of a seed, which refers to the principle of life of God imparted to the believer at salvation's new birth. John uses this image of a planted seed to picture the divine element involved in being born again. *See notes on 1Pe 1:23–25.* **abides.** The word conveys the idea of the permanence of the new birth which cannot be reversed, for those who are truly born again are permanently transformed into a new creation (2Co 5:17; Gal 6:15; Eph 2:10). **he cannot sin.** This phrase once again conveys the idea of habitual sinning (see vv. 4, 6).

3:10 This summary verse is the key to vv. 4–10. Only two kinds of children exist in the world: children of God and children of Satan. No one can belong to both families simultaneously. Either one belongs to God's family and exhibits His righteous character, or one belongs to Satan's family and exhibits his sinful nature.

3:10b the one who does not love his brother. This phrase introduces the readers to the second aspect of the moral test, i.e., the test of love (as in 2:7–11). John develops this thought through vv. 11–24. The false teachers not only had an erroneous view of Christ's nature and displayed disobedience to God's commands, but they also displayed a distinct lack of love for true believers, who rejected their heretical teaching.

11 [A]For this is the message [B]which you have heard from the beginning, [C]that we should love one another; 12 not as [A]Cain, *who* was of [B]the evil one and slew his brother. And for what reason did he slay him? Because [C]his deeds were evil, and his brother's were righteous.

13 Do not be surprised, brethren, if [A]the world hates you. 14 We know that we have [A]passed out of death into life, [B]because we love the brethren. He who does not love abides in death. 15 Everyone who [A]hates his brother is a murderer; and you know that [B]no murderer has eternal life abiding in him. 16 We know love by this, that [A]He laid down His life for us; and [B]we ought to lay down our lives for the [C]brethren. 17 But [A]whoever has the world's goods, and sees his brother in need and [B]closes his [a]heart [b]against him, [C]how does the love of God abide in him? 18 [A]Little children, let us not love with word or with tongue, but in deed and [B]truth. 19 We will know by this that we are [A]of the truth, and will [a]assure our heart before Him 20 [a]in whatever our heart condemns us; for God is greater than our heart and knows all things. 21 [A]Beloved, if our heart does not condemn us, we have [B]confidence [a]before God; 22 and [A]whatever we ask we receive from Him, because we [B]keep His commandments and do [C]the things that are pleasing in His sight.

23 This is His commandment, that we [a,A]believe in [B]the name of His Son Jesus Christ, and love one another, just as [C]He [b]commanded us. 24 The one who [A]keeps His commandments [B]abides in Him, and He in him. [C]We know by this that [D]He abides in us, by the Spirit whom He has given us.

3:11 [A]1 John 1:5 [B]1 John 2:7 [C]John 13:4f; 15:12; 1 John 4:7, 11f, 21; 2 John 5 3:12 [A]Gen 4:8 [B]Matt 5:37; 1 John 2:13f [C]Ps 38:20; Prov 29:10; John 8:40, 41 3:13 [A]John 15:18; 17:14 3:14 [A]John 5:24 [B]John 13:35; 1 John 2:10 3:15 [A]Matt 5:21f; John 8:44 [B]Gal 5:20f; Rev 21:8 3:16 [A]John 10:11; 15:13 [B]Phil 2:17; 1 Thess 2:8 [C]1 John 2:9 3:17 [a]Lit *inward parts* [b]Lit *from* [A]James 2:15f [B]Deut 15:7 [C]1 John 4:20 3:18 [A]1 John 2:1; 3:7 [B]2 John 1; 3 John 1 3:19 [a]Lit *persuade* [A]1 John 2:21 3:20 [a]Or *that if our heart condemns us, that God...* 3:21 [a]Lit *toward* [A]1 John 3:2 [B]1 John 2:28; 5:14 3:22 [A]Job 22:26f; Matt 7:7; 21:22; John 9:31 [B]1 John 2:3 [C]John 8:29; Heb 13:21 3:23 [a]Or *believe the name* [b]Lit *gave us a commandment* [A]John 6:29 [B]John 1:12; 2:23; 3:18 [C]John 13:34; 15:12; 1 John 2:8 3:24 [A]1 John 2:3 [B]John 6:56; 10:38; 1 John 2:6, 24; 4:15 [C]John 14:17; Rom 8:9, 14, 16; 1 Thess 4:8; 1 John 4:13 [D]1 John 2:5

3:11–24 John elaborates on the love life of genuine believers. For those who are truly born again, love is an indispensable characteristic. The new nature or "seed" (v. 9) that God imparts not only exhibits holiness but also love as a habitual characteristic (Jn 13:35; Ro 5:5; 1Th 4:9). Those who practice love give proof of the new birth. Those who do not have never been born again.

3:11 from the beginning. Since the beginning of gospel proclamation, love has been a central theme of Christianity (*see notes on 1:1; 2:7*). John emphasizes what they heard "from the beginning" (1:1; 2:7, 24) to emphasize that the false teachers were preventing that which God, through the apostles, proclaimed. **we should love one another.** This phrase highlights the habit of love displayed by those possessing the new nature. Love is not merely an optional duty for someone claiming to be a Christian, but proof positive that one truly has been born again (Jn 15:12; 1Pe 1:22, 23).

3:12–24 As noted throughout this epistle, John often repeated the same truths, expanding on them to allow his readers to hear them in new and fresh ways. Each time he presents the same truths in "new" packages, which expand on a particular aspect of their significance or approach the subject from a slightly different angle. Verses 12–17 address the characteristic lack of love displayed by the children of the devil, while in vv. 18–24 he talks about the characteristics of love displayed by the children of God (*see note on v. 10*).

3:12 Cain. Scripture presents Cain outwardly as a God-worshiper who even offered sacrifice (Ge 4:3–5). Cain's murderous actions, however, revealed that inwardly he was a child of the Devil (cf. Jn 8:44). ***who* was of the evil one and slew his brother.** In vv. 12–17, John presents the first of three behaviors of the devil's children manifesting their lack of love—murder, the ultimate expression of hate. **his deeds were evil.** Cain's offering was not acceptable because he was sinful (cf. Ge 4:5). Jealousy was behind his hate and murder, as in the case of the religious leaders who had Christ executed.

3:13 the world hates you. History is filled with stories of the persecution of the saints by the world (Heb 11:36–40). This does not surprise believers because hateful Satan is their father (v. 10).

3:14 passed out of death into life, because we love. Becoming a Christian is a resurrection from death to life, and a turning of hate to love (cf. Gal 5:6, 22). A lack of love indicates that one is spiritually dead. Love is the sure test of whether someone has experienced the new birth or is still in the darkness of spiritual death (2:9, 11). **abides in death.** Someone who is characterized by hate has never experienced the new birth.

3:15 Everyone who hates his brother is a murderer. John presents the second of 3 characteristics of the devil's children with respect to their lack of love. Hatred is spiritually the same as murder in the eyes of God, i.e., the attitude is equal to the act. Hate is the seed that leads to murder, as seen in the example of the hatred of Cain for Abel that resulted in murder (*see notes on Mt 5:20–22*; cf. Gal 5:19–21; Rev 22:15).

3:16 We know love by this. With this phrase, John introduces the standard of love that is reflected in genuine Christianity. It becomes the measuring stick for every expression of love (see v. 18). John presents the third characteristic of Satan's children in terms of their lack of love. Satan's children are marked by indifference toward others' needs (see also vv. 12, 15). **He laid down His life for us.** This expression is unique to John (Jn 10:11, 15, 17, 18; 13:37, 38; 15:13) and speaks of divesting oneself of something. Christian love is self-sacrificing and giving. Christ's giving up His life for believers epitomized the true nature of Christian love (Jn 15:12, 13; Php 2:5–8; 1Pe 2:19–23). **we ought to lay down our lives for the brethren.** God calls Christians to that same standard of love for one another as He had for us (see v. 16a).

3:17 whoever has the world's goods ... and closes his heart. True love is not limited to supreme sacrifices (v. 16), but shows up in lesser ones. Genuine Christian love expresses itself in sacrificial giving to other Christians' needs (i.e., "his brother"). It is a practical love that finds motivation in helping others (1Ti 6:17–19; Heb 13:16; Jas 2:14–17). Where it does not exist, it is questionable that God's love is present. If that is so, it is also questionable whether the person is the Lord's child (v. 14).

3:18 with word or with tongue ... in deed and truth. Claiming to love is not enough. Love is not sentiment, but deeds.

3:19 We will know by this. A lifestyle of love in action is the demonstrable proof of salvation (see v. 16). **will assure our heart before Him.** John gives 3 benefits of love for the true Christian. The first benefit is assurance of salvation since love in action is the test of Christian profession (cf. 4:7; Jn 13:34, 35).

3:20 in whatever our heart condemns us ... God is greater. God knows those who are truly His (2Ti 2:19) and wants to assure His own of their salvation. Although Christians may have insecurities and doubts about salvation, God does not condemn them (Ro 8:1). Displaying love as a pattern of life is the proof that believers stand uncondemned before God.

3:21 confidence before God. Love banishes self-condemnation. When a Christian recognizes in his life the manifestation of love in deeds and actions, it results in confidence about his relationship with God.

3:22 The second benefit of love is answered prayer (see v. 19). Since love is the heart of obedience to the law (cf. Mt 22:37–40; Ro 13:8–10), its presence in a life evidences submission to God which He blesses by answered prayers.

3:23, 24 Cf. 4:13. These verses again repeat the 3 features of this epistle—believing, loving, and obeying—which are the major evidences of true salvation. The third benefit of love is the abiding presence and empowering of the Holy Spirit.

TESTING THE SPIRITS

4 [A]Beloved, do not believe every [B]spirit, but test the
spirits to see whether they are from God, because
[C]many false prophets have gone out into the world.
2 By this you know the Spirit of God: [A]every spirit that
[B]confesses that [C]Jesus Christ has come in the flesh is
from God; 3 and every spirit that [A]does not confess
Jesus is not from God; this is the *spirit* of the [B]anti-
christ, of which you have heard that it is coming, and
[C]now it is already in the world. 4 You are from God,
[A]little children, and [B]have overcome them; because
[C]greater is He who is in you than [D]he who is in the
world. 5 [A]They are from the world; therefore they speak
as from the world, and the world listens to them.
6 [A]We are from God; [B]he who knows God listens to us;
[C]he who is not from God does not listen to us. By this
we know [D]the spirit of truth and [E]the spirit of error.

GOD IS LOVE

7 [A]Beloved, let us [B]love one another, for love
is from God; and [C]everyone who loves is [a,D]born
of God and [E]knows God. 8 The one who does not
love does not know God, for [A]God is love. 9 By this
the love of God was manifested [a,A]in us, that [B]God
has sent His [b]only begotten Son into the world so
that we might live through Him. 10 In this is love,
[A]not that we loved God, but that [B]He loved us and
sent His Son *to be* [C]the propitiation for our sins.

4:1 [A]3 John 11 [B]Jer 29:8; 1 Cor 12:10; 1 Thess 5:20f; 2 Thess 2:2 [C]Jer 14:14; 2 Pet 2:1; 1 John 2:18 4:2 [A]1 Cor 12:3 [B]1 John 2:23 [C]John 1:14; 1 John 1:2 4:3 [A]1 John 2:22; 2 John 7 [B]1 John 2:18, 22 [C]2 Thess 2:3-7; 1 John 2:18 4:4 [A]1 John 2:1 [B]1 John 2:13 [C]Rom 8:31; 1 John 3:20 [D]John 12:31 4:5 [A]John 15:19; 17:14, 16 4:6 [A]John 8:23; 1 John 4:4 [B]John 8:47; 10:3ff; 18:37 [C]1 Cor 14:37 [D]John 14:17 [E]1 Tim 4:1 4:7 [a]Or *begotten* [A]1 John 2:7 [B]1 John 3:11 [C]1 John 5:1 [D]1 John 2:29 [E]1 Cor 8:3; 1 John 2:3 4:8 [A]1 John 4:7, 16 4:9 [a]Or *in our case* [b]Or *unique,* only one of His kind [A]John 9:3; 1 John 4:16 [B]John 3:16f; 1 John 4:10; 5:11 4:10 [A]Rom 5:8, 10; 1 John 4:19 [B]John 3:16f; 1 John 4:9; 5:11 [C]1 John 2:2

4:1–6 John turns from the importance of love to the importance of belief in God's truth. He focuses once again on the doctrinal test and emphasizes the need to obey sound teaching (Mt 24:11; 2Pe 2:2, 3; Jude 3). Scripture presents stern warnings against false doctrine. From his temptation of Eve on, Satan has sought to distort and deny God's Word (Ge 3:1–5). He is the ultimate demonic source behind all false teachers and false doctrine (2Co 11:13, 14). In this section, John gives two doctrinal tests to determine truth from error and false teachers from true teachers.

4:1 **do not believe every spirit.** The mention of the Holy Spirit in 3:24 prompts John to inform his readers that other spirits exist, i.e., demonic spirits, who produce false prophets and false teachers to propagate their false doctrine (*see notes on 1Ti 4:1, 2*). Christians are to have a healthy skepticism regarding any teaching, unlike some among John's congregations who were too open minded to anyone claiming a new teaching regarding the faith. Christians are to be like the Bereans who, as students of the Word, examined the Scriptures to determine truth and error (Ac 17:11, 12). **test.** The word "test" is a metallurgist's term used for assaying metals to determine their purity and value. Christians must test any teaching with a view to approving or disapproving it (*see notes on 1Th 5:20–22*), rigorously comparing any teaching to the Scripture. **the spirits ... many false prophets.** By juxtaposing "spirits" with "false prophets," John reminds his readers that behind human teachers who propagate false doctrine and error are demons inspired by Satan (*see notes on 1Th 5:20–22*; cf. Ac 20:28–30). Human false prophets and teachers are the physical expressions of demonic, spiritual sources (Mt 7:15; Mk 13:22).

4:2 **By this you know the Spirit of God.** John gives a measuring stick to determine whether the propagator of the message is a demon spirit or the Holy Spirit. **Jesus Christ has come in the flesh.** This is the first test of a true teacher: they acknowledge and proclaim that Jesus is God incarnate in human flesh. The Gr. construction does not mean that they confess Christ as having come to earth, but that they confess that He came in the flesh to the earth, i.e., His human body was physically real. Both the full humanity and full deity of Jesus must be equally maintained by the teacher who is to be considered genuinely of the Spirit. The Holy Spirit testifies to the true nature of the Son, while Satan and his forces distort and deny that true nature. John accentuates the crucial importance of sound doctrine expressed in God's Word as the only absolute and trustworthy standard (cf. Is 8:20).

4:3 **the *spirit* of the antichrist.** These false teachers who denied the true nature of the Son (see Introduction: Background and Setting) are to be identified among the antichrists in 2:18, 19 (2Jn 7). The same demonic deception that will work to produce the final world ruler (*see notes on Rev 13:1–8*) who rules as the false Christ is always actively seeking to distort Jesus Christ's true nature, perverting the gospel. The final Antichrist will not be something new, but will be the ultimate embodiment of all the antichrist spirits that have perverted truth and propagated satanic lies since the beginning. This is similar to 2Th 2:3–8, where the man of lawlessness (Antichrist) is still to be revealed, but the mystery of lawlessness is already at work.

4:4 **greater is He who is in you.** Believers need to be aware and alert to false teaching, but not afraid, since those who have experienced the new birth with its indwelling of the Holy Spirit have a built-in check against false teaching (cf. 2:20, 27). The Holy Spirit leads into sound doctrine for genuine Christians, evidencing that salvation has actually occurred (cf. Ro 8:17). True believers have nothing to fear, for even Satan's hosts with their perversions can't take them out of the Lord's hand. Here, as in 2:18–27, protection against error or victory over it are guaranteed by sound doctrine and the indwelling Holy Spirit who illumines the mind.

4:5, 6 **they speak *as* from the world ... he who knows God listens to us.** John gives the second test of a true teacher: they speak God's word, following apostolic doctrine.

4:6 **By this we know the spirit of truth and the spirit of error.** The OT and NT are the sole standards by which all teaching is to be tested. In contrast, demonically inspired teachers either reject the teaching of God's Word or add elements to it (2Co 4:2; Rev 22:18, 19).

4:7–21 True to his pattern to develop the same subjects, each time broadening, expanding, and enhancing their significance, John returns once again to the moral test of love. These verses constitute one long unit describing what perfect love is and that it is available to men. In John's third and last discussion of love in this letter (see also 2:7–11; 3:10–14), he gives 5 reasons why Christians love.

4:7, 8 **love is from God ... God is love.** John introduces the reader to the first of 5 reasons why Christians love: because God is the essence of love. The gnostics believed that God was immaterial spirit and light, but never defined the source of love as coming from His inmost being. As He is spirit (Jn 4:24), light (1:5), and a consuming fire (Heb 12:29), so He is love. Love is inherent in all He is and does. Even His judgment and wrath are perfectly harmonized with His love.

4:7 **let us love one another.** This phrase in v. 7 is the key to the entire section (see v. 21). The original conveys the idea of making sure that love is a habitual practice. He has already written that those who are truly born again do exhibit the characteristic habit of love (cf. 2:10, 11; 3:14). **everyone who loves is born of God.** Those who are born again receive God's nature (cf. 2Pe 1:4). Since God's nature exhibits love as a chief characteristic (see also v. 8), God's children will also reflect that love.

4:8 **The one who does not love does not know God.** Someone may profess to be a Christian, but only those who display love like their heavenly Father actually possess His divine nature and are truly born again.

4:9 John introduces the reader to the second of 5 reasons why Christians love: to follow the supreme example of God's sacrificial love in sending His Son for us. The judgment of sin on the cross was the supreme example of God's love, for He poured out His wrath on His beloved Son in place of sinners (Jn 3:14–16; Ro 5:8; 2Co 5:21; Eph 5:1, 2; *see note on Titus 3:4*). **only begotten.** Five of the NT's nine uses of this term are by John (Jn 1:14, 18; 3:16, 18). John always uses it of Christ to picture His unique relationship to the Father, His pre-existence, and His distinctness from creation. The term emphasizes the uniqueness of Christ, as the only one of His kind. It was He whom the Father sent into the world as the greatest gift ever given (Jn 17:3; 2Co 8:9) so that we might have life eternal (cf. Jn 3:14, 15; 12:24).

4:10 **propitiation for our sins.** For the word's meaning, *see note on 2:2*. Hebrews 9:5 translates a form of this word as "the mercy seat." Christ lit. became our mercy seat like the one in the Holy of Holies, where the High Priest splattered the blood of the sacrifice on

11 [A]Beloved, if God so loved us, [B]we also ought to
love one another. 12 [A]No one has seen God at any
time; if we love one another, God abides in us, and
His [B]love is perfected in us. 13 [A]By this we know
that we abide in Him and He in us, because He has
given us of His Spirit. 14 We have seen and [A]testify
that the Father has [B]sent the Son *to be* the Savior
of the world.
15 [A]Whoever confesses that [B]Jesus is the Son of
God, God [C]abides in him, and he in God. 16 [A]We have
come to know and have believed the love which
God has [a,B]for us. [C]God is love, and the one who
[D]abides in love abides in God, and God abides in
him. 17 By this, [A]love is perfected with us, so that
we may have [B]confidence in [C]the day of judgment;
because [D]as He is, so also are we in this world.
18 There is no fear in love; but [A]perfect love casts
out fear, because fear [a]involves punishment, and
the one who fears is not [B]perfected in love. 19 [A]We
love, because He first loved us. 20 [A]If someone says,
"I love God," and [B]hates his brother, he is a [C]liar;
for [D]the one who does not love his brother whom
he has seen, [E]cannot love God whom he has not
seen. 21 And [A]this commandment we have from
Him, that the one who loves God [B]should love his
brother also.

OVERCOMING THE WORLD

5 [A]Whoever believes that Jesus is the [a]Christ is
[b,B]born of God, and whoever loves the [C]Father
[C]loves the *child* [b]born of Him. 2 [A]By this we know
that [B]we love the children of God, when we love
God and [a]observe His commandments. 3 For [A]this
is the love of God, that we [B]keep His commandments; and [C]His commandments are not burdensome. 4 For whatever is [a,A]born of God [B]overcomes
the world; and this is the victory that has overcome
the world—our faith.
5 Who is the one who overcomes the world,
but he who [A]believes that Jesus is the Son of God?

4:11 [A]1 John 2:7 [B]1 John 4:7 4:12 [A]John 1:18; 1 Tim 6:16; 1 John 4:20 [B]1 John 2:5; 4:17f 4:13 [A]Rom 8:9; 1 John 3:24 4:14 [A]John 15:27; 1 John 1:2 [B]John 3:17; 4:42; 1 John 2:2 4:15 [A]1 John 2:23 [B]Rom 10:9; 1 John 3:23; 4:2; 5:1, 5 [C]1 John 2:24; 3:24 4:16 [a]Lit *in* [A]John 6:69 [B]John 9:3; 1 John 4:9 [C]1 John 4:7, 8 [D]1 John 4:12f 4:17 [A]1 John 2:5; 4:12 [B]1 John 2:28 [C]Matt 10:15 [D]John 17:22; 1 John 2:6; 3:1, 7, 16 4:18 [a]Lit *has* [A]Rom 8:15 [B]1 John 4:12 4:19 [A]1 John 4:10 4:20 [A]1 John 1:6, 8, 10; 2:4 [B]1 John 2:9, 11 [C]1 John 1:6 [D]1 John 3:17 [E]1 Pet 1:8; 1 John 4:12 4:21 [A]Lev 19:18; Matt 5:43f; 22:37ff; John 13:34 [B]1 John 3:11 5:1 [a]I.e. Messiah [b]Or *begotten* [C]Lit *one who begets* [A]1 John 2:22f; 4:2, 15 [B]John 1:3; 3:3; 1 John 2:29; 5:4, 18 [C]John 8:42 5:2 [a]Lit *do* [A]1 John 2:5 [B]1 John 3:14 5:3 [A]John 14:15; 2 John 6 [B]1 John 2:3 [C]Matt 11:30; 23:4 5:4 [a]Or *begotten* [A]John 1:13; 3:3; 1 John 2:29; 5:1, 18 [B]1 John 2:13; 4:4 5:5 [A]1 John 4:15; 5:1

the Day of Atonement (Lv 16:15). Christ did this when His blood, spilled on behalf of others, satisfied the demands of God's holy justice and wrath against sin.

4:11 God's sending His Son gives Christians not only salvation privilege, but obligation to follow this pattern of sacrificial love. Christian love must be self-sacrificing like God's love.

4:12 John introduces the reader to the third of 5 reasons why Christians love: because love is the heart of Christian witness. Nobody can see God loving since His love is invisible. Jesus no longer is in the world to manifest the love of God. The only demonstration of God's love in this age is the church. That testimony is critical (Jn 13:35; 2Co 5:18–20). John's argument in vv. 7–12 can be summed up as: love originated in God, was manifested in His Son, and demonstrated in His people.

4:13–16 John introduces the reader to the fourth of 5 reasons why Christians love: because love is the Christian's assurance (*see notes on 3:16–23*).

4:15 Whoever confesses. *See note on v. 2.* This refers to the doctrinal test (cf. vv. 1–6; 1:1–4; 2:23).

4:17–20 John introduces the reader to the fifth reason why Christians love: because love is the Christian's confidence in judgment (*see notes on 3:16–23*).

4:17 love is perfected with us. He is not suggesting sinless perfection, but rather mature love marked by confidence in the face of judgment. Confidence is a sign that love is mature. **as He is, so also are we.** Jesus was God's Son in whom He was well pleased on earth; we also are God's children (3:11) and the objects of His gracious goodness. If Jesus called God Father, so may we, since we are accepted in the Beloved (Eph 1:6). In v. 18, the same truth is stated negatively. The love that builds confidence also banishes fears. We love God and reverence Him, but we do not love God and come to Him in love, and at the same time, hide from Him in terror (cf. Ro 8:14, 15; 2Ti 1:7). Fear involves torment or punishment, a reality the sons of God will never experience, because they are forgiven.

4:21 This verse summarizes chap. 4. One cannot love God without first loving his fellow believer. A claim to love God is a delusion if not accompanied by unselfish love for other Christians.

5:1–5 John introduces the subject of the victorious life. While the Bible uses many terms to describe what Christians are (e.g., believers, friends, brothers, sheep, saints, soldiers, witnesses, etc.), John highlights one particular term in this chapter: the overcomer (*see note on v. 4* for the meaning of the term). Of the 24 times the word occurs in the NT, John uses it 21 times (cf. also Rev 2:7, 11, 17; 2:26; 3:5, 12, 21). Several different forms of this term appear in these verses to emphasize the victorious nature of the believer.

5:1 Whoever believes. Saving faith is the first characteristic of an overcomer. The term "believes" conveys the idea of continuing faith, making the point that the mark of genuine believers is that they continue in faith throughout their life. Saving belief is not simply intellectual acceptance, but whole-hearted dedication to Jesus Christ that is permanent. **Jesus is the Christ.** The object of the believer's faith is Jesus, particularly that He is the promised Messiah or "Anointed One" whom God sent to be the Savior from sin. Whoever places faith in Jesus Christ as the only Savior has been born again and, as a result, is an overcomer (v. 5). **born of God.** This is a reference to the new birth and is the same word that Jesus used in Jn 3:7. The tense of the Gr. verb indicates that ongoing faith is the result of the new birth and, therefore, the evidence of the new birth. The sons of God will manifest the reality that they have been born again by continuing to believe in God's Son, the Savior. The new birth brings us into a permanent faith relationship with God and Christ. **whoever loves the Father loves the *child* born of Him.** Love is the second characteristic of the overcomer. The overcomer not only believes in God, but loves both God and fellow believers. The moral test is again in view.

5:2, 3 observe ... keep His commandments. John repeats this phrase twice in these two verses. Obedience is the third characteristic of an overcomer. In these 5 verses, John weaves faith, love, and obedience all together inextricably. They exist mutually in a dynamic relationship, i.e., as the genuine proof of love is obedience, so the genuine proof of faith is love. The word "keep" conveys the idea of constant obedience (cf. Jn 8:31, 32; 14:15, 21; 15:10).

5:3 His commandments are not burdensome. For example, in contrast to the burdensome man-made religious traditions of the Jewish leaders (Mt 23:4), the yoke of Jesus is easy and the burden light (Mt 11:30).

5:4 overcomes. John clearly defines who these overcomers are: they are all who believe that Jesus is God's Son, and all that means. The overcomers are believers—all of them (cf. 2:13). The word for "overcomes" or "overcomer" comes from a Gr. word meaning "to conquer," "to have victory," "to have superiority" or "conquering power." The word reflects a genuine superiority that leads to overwhelming success. The victory is demonstrable; it involves overthrowing an enemy so that the victory is seen by all. Jesus also used this word to describe Himself (Jn 16:33). Because of believers' union with Christ, they too partake in His victory (Ro 8:37; 2Co 2:14). The word "overcomes" in the original language conveys the idea that the believer has continual victory over the world.

5:4, 5 the world. Satan's worldwide system of deception and wickedness. *See notes on 2:15.* Through Christ and His provision of salvation, the believer is a victor (v. 5) over the invisible system of demonic and human evil that Satan operates to capture men's souls for hell. John repeats the reference to overcoming the world 3 times—to press it home. **our faith ... he who believes.** Faith in Jesus Christ and dedication of one's life to Him make one an overcomer. John repeats the truth for emphasis.

6 This is the One who came [A]by water and blood,
Jesus Christ; not [a]with the water only, but [a]with
the water and [a]with the blood. It is [B]the Spirit who
testifies, because the Spirit is the truth. 7 For there
are [A]three that testify: 8 [a]the Spirit and the water
and the blood; and the three are [b]in agreement.
9 [A]If we receive the testimony of men, the testimony of God is greater; for the testimony of God
is this, that [B]He has testified concerning His Son.
10 The one who believes in the Son of God [A]has
the testimony in himself; the one who does not
believe God has [B]made Him a liar, because he has
not believed in the testimony that God has given
concerning His Son. 11 And the testimony is this,
that God has given us [A]eternal life, and [B]this life is
in His Son. 12 [A]He who has the Son has the life; he
who does not have the Son of God does not have
the life.

THIS IS WRITTEN THAT YOU MAY KNOW

13 [A]These things I have written to you who [B]be-
lieve in the name of the Son of God, so that you
may know that you have [C]eternal life. 14 This is [A]the
confidence which we have [a]before Him, that, [B]if we
ask anything according to His will, He hears us.
15 And if we know that He hears us *in* whatever we
ask, [A]we know that we have the requests which we
have asked from Him.

16 If anyone sees his brother [a]committing a sin not
leading to death, [A]he shall ask and [b]*God* will for him
give life to those who commit sin not *leading* to death.
[B]There is a sin *leading* to death; [C]I do not say that he
should make request for this. 17 [A]All unrighteousness
is sin, and [B]there is a sin not *leading* to death.

18 [A]We know that [B]no one who is [a]born of God
sins; but He who was [a]born of God [C]keeps him, and

5:6 [a]Lit *in* [A]John 19:34 [B]Matt 3:16f; John 15:26; 16:13-15 5:7 [A]Matt 18:16 5:8 [a]A few late mss add ...*in heaven, the Father, the Word, and the Holy Spirit, and these three are one. And there are three that testify on earth, the Spirit* [b]Lit *for the one thing* 5:9 [A]John 5:34, 37; 8:18 [B]Matt 3:17; John 5:32, 37 5:10 [A]Rom 8:16; Gal 4-6; Rev 12:17 [B]John 3:18, 33; 1 John 1:10 5:11 [A]John 3:36; 1 John 1:2; 2:25; 4:9; 5:13, 20 [B]John 1:4 5:12 [A]John 3:15f, 36 5:13 [A]John 20:31 [B]1 John 3:23 [C]1 John 1:2; 2:25; 4:9; 5:11, 20 5:14 [a]Lit *toward* [A]1 John 2:28; 3:21f [B]Matt 7:7; John 14:13; 1 John 3:22 5:15 [A]1 John 5:18-20 5:16 [a]Lit *sinning* [b]Or *God will give him life,* that is, *to those who...* [A]James 5:15 [B]Num 15:30; Heb 6:4-6; 10:26 [C]Jer 7:16; 14:11 5:17 [A]1 John 3:4 [B]1 John 2:1f; 5:16 5:18 [a]Or *begotten* [A]1 John 5:15, 19, 20 [B]1 John 3:9 [C]James 1:27; Jude 21

5:6–12 The terms "testify" and "testimony" are the themes of this section. The passage concerns the witness or testimony of God and the Spirit to the world regarding the great truth of the deity of Jesus Christ. The previous passage (5:1–5) described overcomers as those who believed in Jesus as Lord and Savior, and here John presents God's own testimony to confirm that Jesus is the Christ (Jn 5:31–37; 8:13–18). He gives two kinds of testimony: external (vv. 6–9) and internal (vv. 10–12).

5:6 water and blood. Water and the blood constitute external, objective witnesses to who Jesus Christ is. They refer to Jesus' baptism (water) and death (blood). John combats the dualism of false teachers who asserted that "Christ-spirit" departed from the man Jesus just prior to His death on the cross (see Introduction: Background and Setting). John writes to show that God has given testimony to the deity of Jesus through both His baptism and death. **testifies.** Both the verb "testifies" and the noun "testimony" come from the same Gr. word and are used a total of 9 times in this section. The basic meaning is "someone who has personal and immediate knowledge of something." **the Spirit is the truth.** John no longer stresses apostolic testimony (1:1–4; 4:14) but writes of the testimony of God that comes through the Holy Spirit. Since the Spirit of God cannot lie, His testimony is sure.

5:7 three that testify. The OT law required "the evidence of two witnesses or three witnesses" to establish the truth of a particular matter (Dt 17:6; 19:15; cf. Jn 8:17, 18; 1Ti 5:19).

5:8 the Spirit and the water and the blood. At the baptism of Jesus, the Father and the Spirit testified to the Son (see Mt 3:16, 17). The death of Jesus Christ also witnessed to who He was (Mt 27:54; Heb 9:14). The Holy Spirit testified throughout Jesus' life as to His identity (Mk 1:12; Lk 1:35; Ac 10:38).

5:10 has the testimony in himself. John writes of the internal subjective witness to the Son within the believer's heart (Ro 8:15, 16; Gal 4:6). **made Him a liar.** If someone refuses the testimony of God regarding His Son, such rejection is the ultimate form of blasphemy, for it is tantamount to calling God a liar (Titus 1:2; Heb 6:18).

5:11, 12 This summarizes the blessing of the believer's subjective witness—the very life that we possess in Christ expressed in the grace and power He provides all the time. It is the very experience of knowing Christ in one's life. Life is only in Him, so it is impossible to have it without Him.

5:13–21 John concludes his letter with a discussion regarding 5 Christian certainties that constitute a powerful climax to the entire epistle. He accentuates their certainty by using the word "know" 7 times in this section.

5:13 These things. This has reference to all that John has written in his letter. **that you may know that you have eternal life.** Assurance of eternal life constitutes the first Christian certainty. While John wrote his gospel to bring unbelievers to faith (Jn 20:31), he wrote the epistle to give believers confidence that they possessed eternal life. The false brethren's departure left John's congregations shaken (2:19). He assured those who remained that since they adhered to the fundamentals of the faith (a proper view of Christ, obedience, love), their salvation was sure. **eternal life.** This does not refer primarily to a period of time but a person (v. 20; Jn 17:3). Eternal life is a relationship with the person of Jesus Christ and possessing His nature (as in vv. 11, 12).

5:14–17 Answered prayer is the second Christian certainty.

5:14 confidence. For the meaning of the term, *see note on 3:21.* Christians can know with absolute confidence that God answers prayer when they approach the throne of grace (Heb 4:16). **according to His will.** This phrase constitutes a strategic key to answered prayer. To pray according to God's will is to pray in accord with what He would want, not what we would desire or insist that He do for us (Jn 14:13, 14). John already specified that answered prayer also depends on obedience to God's commandments and avoidance of sin (3:21; Ps 66:18; Jn 15:7; 1Pe 3:7). Since genuine believers know God's Word (i.e., His will) and practice those things that are pleasing to Him, they never insist on their own will, but supremely seek God's desires (Mt 26:39–42). **He hears us.** The word "hears" signifies that God always hears the prayers of His children (Ps 34:15–17), but not always in the manner they were presented.

5:16, 17 John illustrates praying according to God's will with the specific example of the "sin *leading* to death." Such a sin could be any premeditated and unconfessed sin that causes the Lord to determine to end a believer's life. It is not one particular sin like homosexuality or lying, but whatever sin is the final one in the tolerance of God. Failure to repent of and forsake sin may eventually lead to physical death as a judgment of God (Ac 5:1–11; 1Co 5:5; 11:30). No intercessory prayer will be effective for those who have committed such deliberate high-handed sin, i.e., God's discipline with physical death is inevitable in such cases as He seeks to preserve the purity of His church (*see notes on 1Co 5:5–7*). The contrast to the phrase "sin *leading* to death" with "sin not *leading* to death" signifies that the writer distinguishes between sins that may lead to physical death and those that do not. That is not to identify a certain kind of mortal or nonmortal sin, but to say not all sins are so judged by God.

5:18 Victory over sin and Satan is the third Christian certainty (3:9; Ro 6:15–22). **keeps him.** This refers to the fact that God protects the believer. **evil one.** This is a reference to Satan. **does not touch him.** John uses this word only here and in Jn 20:17. The word suggests "to lay hold of" or "to grasp" in order to harm. Because the believer belongs to God, Satan must operate within God's sovereignty and cannot function beyond what God allows, as in the example of Job (Job 2:5; Ro 16:20). While Satan may persecute, tempt, test, and accuse the believer, God protects His children and places definite limits on Satan's influence or power (2:13; Jn 10:28; 17:12–15).

[D]the evil one does not [E]touch him. 19 [A]We know that
[B]we are of God, and that [C]the whole world lies in *the*
power of the evil one. 20 And [A]we know that [B]the Son
of God has come, and has [C]given us understanding
so that we may know [D]Him who is true; and we [E]are
in Him who is true, in His Son Jesus Christ. [F]This is
the true God and [G]eternal life.
21 [A]Little children, guard yourselves from [B]idols.

5:18 [D]1 John 2:13 [E]John 14:30 5:19 [A]1 John 5:15, 18, 20 [B]1 John 4:6 [C]John 12:31; 17:15; Gal 1:4 5:20 [A]1 John 5:15, 18, 19 [B]John 8:42; 1 John 5:5 [C]Luke 24:45 [D]John 17:3; Rev 3:7 [E]John 1:18; 14:9; 1 John 2:23; Rev 3:7 [F]1 John 1:2 [G]1 John 5:11 5:21 [A]1 John 2:1 [B]1 Cor 10:7, 14; 1 Thess 1:9

5:19 we are of God. That Christians belong to God is the fourth Christian certainty. Only two types of people exist in the world according to John: children of God and children of Satan (*see note on 3:10*). One belongs either to God or to the evil world system that is Satan's domain. Because the whole world belongs to Satan, Christians should avoid its contamination.

5:20 true. The word means "genuine" as opposed to what is false (cf. v. 21). **God and eternal life.** That Jesus Christ is the true God is the fifth Christian certainty. This verse constitutes the summation of John's whole letter. The greatest certainty of all, the incarnation, guarantees the certainty of the rest. This is the doctrinal foundation, out of which comes love and obedience.

5:21 guard yourselves from idols. John contrasts the term "idols" with "the true God" of v. 20. He has reference here to the false teachers who withdrew from the brotherhood with which they had been formerly associated (2:19). Their false beliefs and practices are the idols from which the readers are commanded to protect themselves. The false teachers upheld the world's philosophy as superior to God's revelation as demonstrated in their perversion of basic Christian teaching (faith, love, and obedience). In closing, John once again highlights the importance of adherence to the fundamentals of the faith.

THE SECOND EPISTLE OF

JOHN

TITLE

The epistle's title is "2 John." It is the second in a series of 3 epistles that bear the apostle John's name. Second and Third John present the closest approximation in the NT to the conventional letter form of the contemporary Greco-Roman world, since they were addressed from an individual to individuals. Second and Third John are the shortest epistles in the NT, each containing less than 300 Greek words. Each letter could fit on a single papyrus sheet (cf. 3Jn 13).

AUTHOR AND DATE

The author is the apostle John. He describes himself in 2Jn 1 as "The Elder" which conveys the advanced age of the apostle, his authority, and status during the foundational period of Christianity when he was involved with Jesus' ministry. The precise date of the epistle cannot be determined. Since the wording, subject matter, and circumstances of 2 John closely approximate 1 John (v. 5 [cf. 1Jn 2:7; 3:11]; v. 6 [cf. 1Jn 5:3]; v. 7 [cf. 1Jn 2:18–26]; v. 9 [cf. 1Jn 2:23]; v. 12 [cf. 1Jn 1:4]), most likely John composed the letter at the same time or soon after 1 John, ca. A.D. 90–95, during his ministry at Ephesus in the latter part of his life.

BACKGROUND AND SETTING

Second John deals with the same problem as 1 John (see Introduction to 1 John: Background and Setting). False teachers influenced by the beginnings of gnostic thought were threatening the church (v. 7; cf. 1Jn 2:18, 19, 22, 23; 4:1–3). The strategic difference is that while 1 John has no specific individual or church specified to whom it was addressed, 2 John has a particular local group or house-church in mind (v. 1).

The focus of 2 John is that the false teachers were conducting an itinerant ministry among John's congregations, seeking to make converts, and taking advantage of Christian hospitality to advance their cause (vv. 10, 11; cf. Ro 12:13; Heb 13:2; 1Pe 4:9). The individual addressed in the greeting (v. 1) inadvertently or unwisely may have shown these false prophets hospitality, or John may have feared that the false teachers would attempt to take advantage of her kindness (vv. 10, 11). The apostle seriously warns his readers against showing hospitality to such deceivers (vv. 10, 11). Although his exhortation may appear on the surface to be harsh or unloving, the acutely dangerous nature of their teaching justified such actions, especially since it threatened to destroy the very foundations of the faith (v. 9).

HISTORICAL AND THEOLOGICAL THEMES

The overall theme of 2 John closely parallels 1 John's theme of a "recall to the fundamentals of the faith" or "back to the basics of Christianity" (vv. 4–6). For John, the basics of Christianity are summarized by adherence to the truth (v. 4), love (v. 5), and obedience (v. 6).

The apostle, however, conveys an additional but related theme in 2 John: "the biblical guidelines for hospitality." Not only are Christians to adhere to the fundamentals of the faith, but the gracious hospitality that is commanded of them (Ro 12:13) must be discriminating. The basis of hospitality must be common love of or interest in the truth, and Christians must share their love within the confines of that truth. They are not called to universal acceptance of anyone who claims to be a believer. Love must be discerning. Hospitality and kindness must be focused on those who are adhering to the fundamentals of the faith. Otherwise, Christians may actually aid those who are attempting to destroy those basic truths of the faith. Sound doctrine must serve as the test of fellowship and the basis of separation between those who profess to be Christians and those who actually are (vv. 10, 11; cf. Ro 16:17; Gal 1:8, 9; 2Th 3:6, 14; Titus 3:10).

INTERPRETIVE CHALLENGES

Second John stands in direct antithesis to the frequent cry for ecumenism and Christian unity among believers. Love and truth are inseparable in Christianity. Truth must always guide the exercise of love (cf. Eph 4:15). Love must stand the test of truth. The main lesson of this book is that truth determines the bounds of love, and as a consequence, of unity. Therefore, truth must exist before love can unite, for truth generates love (1Pe 1:22). When someone compromises the truth, true Christian love and unity are destroyed. Only a shallow sentimentalism exists where the truth is not the foundation of unity.

The reference to the "chosen lady and her children" (v. 1) should be understood in a normal, plain sense referring to a particular woman and her children, rather than interpreted in a nonliteral sense as a church and its membership. Similarly, the reference to "the children of your elect sister" (v. 13) should be understood as a reference to the nieces and/or nephews of the individual addressed in verse 1, rather than metaphorically to a sister church and its membership. In these verses, John conveys greetings to personal acquaintances that he has come to know through his ministry.

OUTLINE

I. The Basis of Christian Hospitality (1–3)

II. The Behavior of Christian Hospitality (4–6)

III. The Bounds of Christian Hospitality (7–11)

IV. The Blessings of Christian Hospitality (12, 13)

WALK ACCORDING TO HIS COMMANDMENTS

1 [A]The elder to the [B]chosen [C]lady and her children,
whom I [D]love in truth; and not only I, but also all
who [E]know the truth, 2 for [A]the sake of the truth
which abides [B]in us and will be [C]with us forever:
3 [A]Grace, mercy *and* peace will be with us, from
God the Father and from Jesus Christ, the Son of
the Father, in truth and love.
4 [A]I was very glad to find *some* of your children
walking in truth, just as we have received commandment *to do* from the Father. 5 Now I ask you, lady, [A]not
as though *I were* writing to you a new commandment, but the one which we have had [A]from the
beginning, that we [B]love one another. 6 And [A]this is
love, that we walk according to His commandments.
This is the commandment, [B]just as you have heard
[C]from the beginning, that you should walk in it.
7 For [A]many deceivers have [B]gone out into the
world, those who [C]do not acknowledge Jesus Christ
as coming in the flesh. This is [A]the deceiver and the
[D]antichrist. 8 [A]Watch yourselves, [B]that you do not
lose what we have accomplished, but that you may
receive a full reward. 9 [a]Anyone who [b]goes too far
and [A]does not abide in the teaching of Christ, does
not have God; the one who abides in the teaching, he
has both the Father and the Son. 10 If anyone comes
to you and does not bring this teaching, [A]do not
receive him into *your* house, and do not give him
a greeting; 11 for the one who gives him a greeting
[A]participates in his evil deeds.
12 [A]Though I have many things to write to you, I
do not want to *do so* with paper and ink; but I hope
to come to you and speak face to face, so that [a]your
[B]joy may be made full.
13 The children of your [A]chosen sister greet you.

1:1 [A]Acts 11:30; 1 Pet 5:1; 3 John 1 [B]Rom 16:13; 1 Pet 5:13; 2 John 13 [C]2 John 5 [D]1 John 3:18; 2 John 3; 3 John 1 [E]John 8:32; 1 Tim 2:4 1:2 [A]2 Pet 1:12 [B]1 John 1:8 [C]John 14:16 1:3 [A]Rom 1:7; 1 Tim 1:2 1:4 [A]3 John 3f 1:5 [A]1 John 2:7 [B]John 13:34, 35; 15:12, 17; 1 John 3:11; 4:7, 11 1:6 [A]1 John 2:5; 5:3 [B]1 John 2:24 [C]1 John 2:7 1:7 [A]1 John 2:26 [B]1 John 2:19; 4:1 [C]1 John 4:2f [D]1 John 2:18 1:8 [A]Mark 13:9 [B]1 Cor 3:8; Heb 10:35 1:9 [a]Lit *Everyone* [b]Lit *goes on ahead* [A]John 7:16; 8:31; 1 John 2:23 1:10 [A]1 Kin 13:16f; Rom 16:17; 2 Thess 3:6, 14; Titus 3:10 1:11 [A]Eph 5:11; 1 Tim 5:22; Jude 23 1:12 [a]One early ms reads *our* [A]3 John 13, 14 [B]John 3:29; 1 John 1:4 1:13 [A]2 John 1

1 The elder. John uses this title to emphasize his advanced age, his spiritual authority over the congregations in Asia Minor, and the strength of his own personal eyewitness testimony to the life of Jesus and all that He taught (vv. 4–6). **the chosen lady and her children.** Some think that this phrase refers metaphorically to a particular local church, while "her children" would refer to members of the congregation. The more natural understanding in context, however, is that it refers to a particular woman and her children (i.e., offspring) who were well known to John. **whom I love in truth.** The basis of Christian hospitality is the truth (vv. 1–3). John accentuates the need for truth by repeating the term "truth" 5 times in the opening 4 verses. Truth refers to the basics or fundamentals of the faith that John has discussed in 1 John (sound belief in Christ, obedience, love) as well as the truths expressed in 2 John (e.g., vv. 4–6). Truth is the necessary condition of unity and, as a result, the basis of hospitality.

2 truth ... abides in us ... will be with us forever. This is the cognitive truth of God's Word (cf. Col 3:16).

3 Grace, mercy *and* peace ... in truth and love. John's succession from grace to mercy and then peace marks the order from the first motion of God to the final satisfaction of man. The confines of these threefold blessings are within the sphere of truth and love.

4 children walking in truth, just as we have received commandment. The behavior of hospitality involves obedience to the truth (see vv. 5, 6). The word "walking" has reference to continual walking in the truth, i.e., making obedience to the truth a habit in one's life.

5 new commandment ... that we love one another. John ties the commandment of truth to the commandment of love (cf. 1Jn 2:7–11; 4:7–12). The word "love" has reference to practicing love as a habit in one's life. Both walking in the truth and in love is the behavior of hospitality.

6 this is love, that we walk according to His commandments. John defines love, not as a sentiment or an emotion, but as obedience to God's commands (*see notes on 1Jn 5:2, 3*). Those who are obedient to the truth as contained in God's commandments, the fundamentals of the faith (1Jn 2:3–11), are identified as walking in love. Cf. Jn 14:15, 21; 15:10.

7 many deceivers. Cf. Mk 13:22, 23; 1Ti 4:1–4; 2Pe 2:1ff.; 1Jn 4:1. In vv. 7–11, John gives limits for Christian hospitality. This is the centerpiece of John's thought in this epistle and expands the first two points. Since Satan comes as an angel of light (2Co 11:13–15), believers must be on guard against error by having an intimate acquaintance with the truth. **who do not acknowledge Jesus Christ *as* coming in the flesh.** The original language conveys the idea of a habitual denial of the undiminished deity and humanity of Christ. A biblical Christology maintains that Jesus Christ's nature was both fully God and fully man with all the implications for the fulfillment of redemptive purposes. The essence of the severest error in false religions, heresies, and cults is a denial of the true nature of Jesus Christ.

8 do not lose what we have accomplished. Although a reward is generally promised Christians for hospitality (e.g., Mt 10:41; 25:40; Mk 9:41), the idea here is of the fullness of a believer's reward for all the good he has done (see 1Co 3:10–17; 2Co 5:9, 10). A loss of that reward may occur to any believer who does not discriminate fellowship on the basis of adherence to the truth (Col 2:18, 19; 3:24, 25). This is a potent warning. All the eternal reward one earns by seeing Christ purely, eagerly, and effectively in the Spirit can be diminished by any aiding or abetting of false teaching.

9 does not abide in the teaching of Christ, does not have God. A failure to be faithful to the fundamental, sound doctrines of the faith (a proper view of the person and work of Christ, love, obedience) marks a person as having never been born again (1Jn 2:23; 3:6–10; 4:20, 21; 5:1–3). The word "abide" has the idea of constant adherence and warns that these fundamentals are not open to change or subject to the latest trends or philosophical fads.

10 do not receive him into *your* house ... not give him a greeting. John's prohibition is not a case of entertaining people who disagree on minor matters. These false teachers were carrying on a regular campaign to destroy the basic, fundamental truths of Christianity. Complete disassociation from such heretics is the only appropriate course of action for genuine believers. No benefit or aid of any type (not even a greeting) is permissible. Believers should aid only those who proclaim the truth (vv. 5–8).

11 participates in his evil deeds. Hospitality to such leaders aids the spread of their heresy and inevitably leaves the impression of sanctioning the teachings of these antichrists (cf. 1Jn 2:22). Supreme loyalty to God and His Word alone must characterize the actions of every true believer.

12 paper and ink. The word "paper" refers to a papyrus sheet. One papyrus sheet could contain the whole letter of 2 John. The term "ink" means "black" and refers to a mixture of water, charcoal, and gum resin that was used to write. **face to face.** John lit. wrote "mouth to mouth." Cf. Nu 12:8 where God spoke to Moses "mouth to mouth." **that your joy may be made full.** The blessing of hospitality is full joy (vv. 12, 13). John uses this same wording in 1Jn 1:4. When believers uphold the biblical standards for fellowship, the result is genuine joy among believers because the truths of the Word are maintained.

13 The children of your chosen sister. John refers to the nieces and/or nephews of the woman ("chosen lady") addressed in v. 1 who sent their greetings via John.

THE THIRD EPISTLE OF JOHN

TITLE

The epistle's title is "3 John." It is the third in a series of 3 epistles that bear the apostle John's name. Third John and Second John present the closest approximation in the New Testament to the conventional letter form of the contemporary Greco-Roman world, since they were addressed from an individual to individuals. Both 2 and 3 John are the shortest epistles in the NT, each containing less than 300 Greek words, so as to fit on a single papyrus sheet (cf. v. 13).

AUTHOR AND DATE

The author is the apostle John. He describes himself in v. 1 as "the elder," which conveys the advanced age of the apostle, his authority, and his eyewitness status, especially during the foundational period of Christianity when John was involved with Jesus' ministry (cf. 2Jn 1). The precise date of the epistle cannot be determined. Since the structure, style, and vocabulary closely approximate 2 John (v. 1 [cf. 2Jn 1]; v. 4 [cf. 2Jn 4]; v. 13 [cf. 2Jn 12]; v. 14 [cf. 2Jn 12]), most likely John composed the letter at the same time or soon after 2 John, ca. A.D. 90–95. As with 1 and 2 John, the apostle probably composed the letter during his ministry at Ephesus in the latter part of his life.

BACKGROUND AND SETTING

Third John is perhaps the most personal of John's 3 epistles. While 1 John appears to be a general letter addressed to congregations scattered throughout Asia Minor, and 2 John was sent to a lady and her family (2Jn 1), in 3 John the apostle clearly names the sole recipient as "the beloved Gaius" (v. 1). This makes the epistle one of a few letters in the NT addressed strictly to an individual (cf. Philemon). The name "Gaius" was very common in the first century (e.g., Ac 19:29; 20:4; Ro 16:23; 1Co 1:14), but nothing is known of this individual beyond John's salutation, from which it is inferred that he was a member of one of the churches under John's spiritual oversight.

As with 2 John, 3 John focuses on the basic issue of hospitality but from a different perspective. While 2 John warns against showing hospitality to false teachers (2Jn 7–11), 3 John condemns the lack of hospitality shown to faithful ministers of the Word (vv. 9, 10). Reports came back to the apostle that itinerant teachers known and approved by him (vv. 5–8) had traveled to a certain congregation where they were refused hospitality (e.g., lodging and provision) by an individual named Diotrephes who domineered the assembly (v. 10). Diotrephes went even further, for he also verbally slandered the apostle John with malicious accusations and excluded anyone from the assembly who dared challenge him (v. 10).

In contrast, Gaius, a beloved friend of the apostle and faithful adherent to the truth (vv. 1–4), extended the correct standard of Christian hospitality to itinerant ministers. John wrote to commend the type of hospitality exhibited by Gaius to worthy representatives of the gospel (vv. 6–8) and to condemn the high-handed actions of Diotrephes (v. 10). The apostle promised to correct the situation personally and sent this letter through an individual named Demetrius, whom he commended for his good testimony among the brethren (vv. 10–12).

HISTORICAL AND THEOLOGICAL THEMES

The theme of 3 John is the commendation of the proper standards of Christian hospitality and the condemnation for failure to follow those standards.

INTERPRETIVE CHALLENGES

Some think that Diotrephes may either have been a heretical teacher or at least favored the false teachers who were condemned by 2 John. However, the epistle gives no clear evidence to warrant such a conclusion, especially since one might expect that John would have mentioned Diotrephes' heretical views. The epistle indicates that his problems centered around arrogance and disobedience, which is a problem for the orthodox as well as the heretic.

OUTLINE

I. The Commendation Regarding Christian Hospitality (1–8)

II. The Condemnation Regarding Violating Christian Hospitality (9–11)

III. The Conclusion Regarding Christian Hospitality (12–14)

YOU WALK IN THE TRUTH

1 [A]The elder to the beloved [B]Gaius, whom I [C]love
in truth.
2 Beloved, I pray that in all respects you may
prosper and be in good health, just as your soul
prospers. 3 For I [A]was very glad when [B]brethren
came and testified to your truth, *that is,* how you
[A]are walking in truth. 4 I have no greater joy than
[a]this, to hear of [A]my children [B]walking in the truth.
5 Beloved, you are acting faithfully in whatever
you accomplish for the [A]brethren, and [a]especially
when they are [B]strangers; 6 and they have testified
to your love before the church. You will do well to
[A]send them on their way in a manner [B]worthy of
God. 7 For they went out for the sake of [A]the Name,
[B]accepting nothing from the Gentiles. 8 Therefore
we ought to [a]support such men, so that we may [b]be
fellow workers [c]with the truth.
9 I wrote something to the church; but Diotrephes,
who loves to [A]be first among them, does not accept
[a]what we say. 10 For this reason, [A]if I come, I will
call attention to his deeds which he does, unjustly
accusing us with wicked words; and not satisfied
with this, he himself does not [B]receive the [C]brethren,
either, and he forbids those who desire *to do so* and
[D]puts *them* out of the church.
11 Beloved, [A]do not imitate what is evil, but what
is good. [B]The one who does good is of God; [C]the one

1:1 [A]2 John 1 [B]Acts 19:29; 20:4; Rom 16:23; 1 Cor 1:14 [C]1 John 3:18; 2 John 1 1:3 [A]2 John 4 [B]Acts 1:15; Gal 6:10; 3 John 5, 10 1:4 [a]Lit *these things, that I hear* [A]1 Cor 4:14f; 2 Cor 6:13; Gal 4:19; 1 Thess 2:11; 1 Tim 1:2; 2 Tim 1:2; Philem 10; 1 John 2:1 [B]2 John 4 1:5 [a]Lit *this* [A]Acts 1:15; Gal 6:10; 3 John 3, 10 [B]Rom 12:13; Heb 13:2 1:6 [A]Acts 15:3; Titus 3:13 [B]Col 1:10; 1 Thess 2:12 1:7 [A]John 15:21; Acts 5:41; Phil 2:9 [B]Acts 20:33, 35 1:8 [a]Or *receive such men as guests* [b]Or *prove ourselves to be* [c]Or *for* 1:9 [a]Lit *us* [A]2 John 9 1:10 [A]2 John 12 [B]2 John 10; 3 John 5 [C]Acts 1:15; Gal 6:10; 3 John 3, 5 [D]John 9:34 1:11 [A]Ps 34:14; 37:27 [B]1 John 2:29; 3:10 [C]1 John 3:6

1 The elder. John uses the same term for himself as he did in 2Jn 1. The term probably has reference to his age, his apostolic eyewitness status of Jesus' life, and also that he had an official position of authority in the church. **the beloved.** The term "beloved" is only used of Christians in the NT (Col 3:12; Phm 1, 2; 2Pe 3:14; 1Jn 4:1). **Gaius.** Nothing is known of Gaius beyond the mention of his name in the salutation. The name was one of 18 common names from which Roman parents usually chose a name for one of their sons, making any specific identification doubtful. John, his fellow believers, and even strangers to whom Gaius extended hospitality held him in great esteem for his Christian walk and conduct (vv. 1–6). John conveyed his own appreciation for Gaius by calling him "beloved" 4 times in the letter (vv. 1, 2, 5, 11). He probably was a member of a church somewhere in Asia Minor that was under John's sphere of influence. The apostle planned to visit him sometime in the near future (v. 13). **whom I love in truth.** Because Christians have common knowledge of the truth, they have the common source of love (2Jn 1). While some have taken the phrase to mean simply "truly" (Mk 12:32), John's usage of this phrase elsewhere in these letters where truth takes on such a significant meaning suggests that the elder intended the kind of love that is consistent with the fundamental truths of the faith (cf. v. 4; 1Jn 2:21; 3:19).

2 I pray. John's prayer for Gaius is significant. Gaius' spiritual state was so excellent that John prayed that his physical health would match his spiritual vigor. To ask about one's health was standard custom in ancient letters, but John adapted this convention in a unique manner to highlight Gaius' vibrant spiritual state.

3 when brethren came and testified. The phrase indicates that Christians continually praised Gaius' exemplary obedience to the fundamentals of the faith. His spiritual reputation was well known. **you are walking in truth.** Gaius' walk matched his talk. His reputation for practicing what he preached was exemplary (2Jn 4). John's commendation of him is one of the greatest given in the NT, since the commendation centers not only in the fact that he knew the truth but that he faithfully practiced it. Gaius' actions were in stark contrast to Diotrephes' negative reputation (v. 10).

4 I have no greater joy. John's personal affection for Gaius radiated especially from his personal conduct (Lk 6:46). **my children.** The word "my" is emphatic in the original. John's heart delighted in the proper conduct of his spiritual children in the faith. Those who walk (conduct) in the truth (belief) have integrity; there is no dichotomy between professing and living. He had strong fatherly affection for them (cf. 1Co 4:14–16; 1Th 2:11; 3:1–10).

5 you are acting faithfully. Genuine faith always produces genuine good works (Jas 2:14–17). **brethren, and ... strangers.** Gaius practiced hospitality not only toward those whom he knew but also to those whom he did not know. The reference concerns especially itinerant gospel preachers that Gaius aided on their journeys.

6 they have testified to your love before the church. Gaius' reputation for hospitality and kindness (as well as obedience—v. 3) was also well known throughout the churches in the region. **You will do well.** John encouraged Gaius to keep practicing hospitality, especially because of the actions of Diotrephes who conducted a heavy-handed campaign against it (v. 10). **in a manner worthy of God.** Cf. Col 1:10; 1Th 2:12. The phrase has the connotation of treating people as God would treat them (see Mt 10:40), and becomes the key manner in which hospitality should be practiced (Mt 25:40–45).

7, 8 John gives several grounds for practicing hospitality in a "manner worthy of God" (v. 6). First, one must show hospitality to those who have pure motives. These itinerant missionaries went out "for the sake of the Name" (v. 7; cf. Ro 1:5). They must be doing their ministry for God's glory, not their own. Second, one must show hospitality to those who are not in ministry for money. Since the missionaries were "accepting nothing from the Gentiles" (v. 7), the church was their only means of support. They were free from avarice (2Co 2:17; 1Ti 5:17, 18). Third, those who show hospitality participate in the ministries of those to whom hospitality is shown (v. 8). Verse 8 gives the same reason to demonstrate hospitality to genuine teachers as does 2Jn 10 in forbidding hospitality toward false teachers, i.e., that those who extend hospitality share in the deeds (i.e., good or bad) of those receiving it.

9 I wrote ... to the church. John apparently had written a previous letter to the church, perhaps on the subject of hospitality, but it was lost. Perhaps Diotrephes never read it to the church because he rejected John's authority (cf. vv. 9, 10). **Diotrephes, who loves to be first.** In the second part of his epistle, John condemned the violation of hospitality toward faithful ministers of the Word. The word "first" conveys the idea of someone who is selfish, self-centered, and self-seeking. The language suggests a self-promoting demagogue, who served no one, but wanted all to serve only him. Diotrephes' actions directly contradict Jesus' and the NT's teaching on servant-leadership in the church (cf. Mt 20:20–28; Php 2:5–11; 1Ti 3:3; 1Pe 5:3). **does not accept what we say.** Diotrephes modeled the opposite of kindness and hospitality to God's servants, even denying John's apostolic authority over the local congregation, and as a result, denying the revelation of God that came through that authority. His pride endeavored to supplant the rule of Christ through John in the church. Diotrephes' character was the very opposite of the gentle and loving Gaius who readily showed hospitality.

10 if I come, I will call attention to his deeds. John's apostolic authority meant that Diotrephes had to answer for his behavior. The apostle did not overlook this usurping of Christ's place in the church. Verse 10 indicates that Diotrephes was guilty of 4 things: 1) "unjustly accusing us." The charges against John were completely unjustified; 2) "with wicked words." Not only were Diotrephes' charges false, they were evil; 3) "does not receive the brethren." He not only slandered John but also deliberately defied other believers; and 4) "puts *them* out of the church." The original language indicates that Diotrephes' habit was to excommunicate those who resisted his authority. **does not receive the brethren.** To accept John's authority (v. 9), as well as being hospitable to the traveling ministers, directly threatened the authority that Diotrephes coveted.

11 do not imitate what is evil, but what is good. The verse begins the introduction to the commendation of Demetrius in v. 12. Gaius was to imitate Demetrius as the correct role model for his actions. **The one who does good is of God; the one who does evil has not seen God.** John's statement indicates that Diotrephes' actions proved that he was never a Christian. This is a practical application of the moral test (*see notes on 1Jn 5:2, 3*).

who does evil has not seen God. 12 Demetrius [A]has
received a *good* testimony from everyone, and from
the truth itself; and we add our testimony, and [B]you
know that our testimony is true.
13 [A]I had many things to write to you, but I am
not willing to write *them* to you with pen and ink;
14 but I hope to see you shortly, and we will speak
face to face.
15 [A]Peace *be* to you. The friends greet you. Greet
the friends [B]by name.

1:12 [A]Acts 6:3; 1 Tim 3:7 [B]John 19:35; 21:24 1:13 [A]2 John 12 1:15 [A]John 20:19, 21, 26; Eph 6:23; 1 Pet 5:14 [B]John 10:3

12 Demetrius. As with Gaius, Demetrius was a very common name in the Roman world (Ac 19:24, 38). Nothing is known of him apart from this epistle. He may have delivered this letter, which also would serve to commend him to Gaius. **has received a *good* testimony from everyone.** Like Gaius, Demetrius' reputation was well known in the region. **from the truth itself.** Demetrius was an excellent role model preeminently because he practiced the truth of God's Word in his life.

13, 14 pen and ink … face to face. *See note on 2Jn 12.*

THE EPISTLE OF JUDE

TITLE

Jude, which is rendered "Judah" in Hebrew and "Judas" in Greek, was named after its author (v. 1), one of the 4 half-brothers of Christ (Mt 13:55; Mk 6:3). As the fourth shortest NT book (Philemon, 2 John, and 3 John are shorter), Jude is the last of 8 general epistles. Jude does not quote the OT directly, but there are at least 9 obvious allusions to it. Contextually, this "epistolary sermon" could be called "The Acts of the Apostates."

AUTHOR AND DATE

Although Jude (Judas) was a common name in Israel (at least 8 are named in the NT), the author of Jude generally has been accepted as Jude, Christ's half-brother. He is to be differentiated from the apostle Judas, the son of James (Lk 6:16; Ac 1:13). Several lines of thought lead to this conclusion: 1) Jude's appeal to being the "brother of James," the leader of the Jerusalem Council (Ac 15) and another half-brother of Jesus (v. 1; cf. Gal 1:19); 2) Jude's salutation being similar to James (cf. Jas 1:1); and 3) Jude's not identifying himself as an apostle (v. 1), but rather distinguishing between himself and the apostles (v. 17).

The doctrinal and moral apostasy discussed by Jude (vv. 4–18) closely parallels that of 2 Peter (2:1–3:4), and it is believed that Peter's writing predated Jude for several reasons: 1) 2 Peter anticipates the coming of false teachers (2Pe 2:1, 2; 3:3), while Jude deals with their arrival (vv. 4, 11, 12, 17, 18); and 2) Jude quotes directly from 2Pe 3:3 and acknowledges that it is from an apostle (vv. 17, 18). Since no mention of Jerusalem's destruction in A.D. 70 was made by Jude, though Jude most likely came after 2 Peter (ca. A.D. 68–70), it was almost certainly written before the destruction of Jerusalem. Although Jude did travel on missionary trips with other brothers and their wives (1Co 9:5), it is most likely that he wrote from Jerusalem. The exact audience of believers with whom Jude corresponded is unknown, but seems to be Jewish in light of Jude's illustrations. He undoubtedly wrote to a region recently plagued by false teachers.

Although Jude had earlier rejected Jesus as Messiah (Jn 7:1–9), he, along with other half-brothers of our Lord, was converted after Christ's resurrection (Ac 1:14). Because of his relation to Jesus, his eyewitness knowledge of the resurrected Christ, and the content of this epistle, it was acknowledged as inspired and was included in the Muratorian Canon (A.D. 170). The early questions about its canonicity also tend to support that it was written after 2 Peter. If Peter had quoted Jude, there would have been no question about canonicity, since Peter would thereby have given Jude apostolic affirmation. Clement of Rome (ca. A.D. 96) plus Clement of Alexandria (ca. A.D. 200) also alluded to the authenticity of Jude. Its diminutive size and Jude's quotations from uninspired writings account for any misplaced questions about its canonicity.

BACKGROUND AND SETTING

Jude lived at a time when Christianity was under severe political attack from Rome and aggressive spiritual infiltration from gnostic-like apostates and libertines who sowed abundant seed for a gigantic harvest of doctrinal error. It could be that this was the forerunner to full-blown gnosticism which the apostle John would confront over 25 years later in his epistles. Except for John, who lived at the close of the century, all of the other apostles had been martyred, and Christianity was thought to be extremely vulnerable. Thus, Jude called the church to fight, in the midst of intense spiritual warfare, for the truth.

HISTORICAL AND THEOLOGICAL THEMES

Jude is the only NT book devoted exclusively to confronting "apostasy," meaning defection from the true, biblical faith (vv. 3, 17). Apostates are described elsewhere in 2Th 2:10; Heb 10:29; 2Pe 2:1–22; 1Jn 2:18–23. He wrote to condemn the apostates and to urge believers to contend for the faith. He called for discernment on the part of the church and a rigorous defense of biblical truth. He followed the earlier examples of: 1) Christ (Mt 7:15ff.; 16:6–12; 24:11ff; Rev 2; 3); 2) Paul (Ac 20:29, 30; 1Ti 4:1; 2Ti 3:1–5; 4:3, 4); 3) Peter (2Pe 2:1, 2; 3:3, 4); and 4) John (1Jn 4:1–6; 2Jn 6–11).

Jude is replete with historical illustrations from the OT which include: 1) the Exodus (v. 5); 2) Satan's rebellion (v. 6); 3) Sodom and Gomorrah (v. 7); 4) Moses' death (v. 9); 5) Cain (v. 11); 6) Balaam (v. 11); 7) Korah (v. 11); 8) Enoch (vv. 14, 15); and 9) Adam (v. 14).

Jude also vividly described the apostates in terms of their character and unconscionable activities (vv. 4, 8, 10, 16, 18, 19). Additionally, he borrowed from nature to illustrate the futility of their teaching (vv. 12, 13). While Jude never commented on the specific content of their false teaching, it was enough to demonstrate that their degenerate personal lives and fruitless ministries betrayed their attempts to teach error as though it were truth. This emphasis on character repeats the constant theme regarding false teachers—their personal corruption. While their teaching is clever, subtle, deceptive, enticing, and delivered in myriads of forms, the common way to recognize them is to look behind their false spiritual fronts and see their wicked lives (2Pe 2:10, 12, 18, 19).

INTERPRETIVE CHALLENGES

Because there are no doctrinal issues discussed, the challenges of this letter have to do with interpretation in the normal process of discerning the meaning of the text. Jude does quote from noncanonical, pseudepigraphal (i.e., the actual author was not the one named in its title) sources such as *1 Enoch* (v. 14) and the *Assumption of Moses* (v. 9) to support his points. Was this acceptable? Since Jude was writing under the inspiration of the Holy Spirit (2Ti 3:16; 2Pe 1:20, 21) and included material that was accurate and true in its affirmations, he did no differently than Paul (cf. Ac 17:28; 1Co 15:33; Titus 1:12).

OUTLINE

I. Desires of Jude (1, 2)

II. Declaration of War Against Apostates (3, 4)

III. Damnable Outcome of Apostates (5–7)

IV. Denunciation of Apostates (8–16)

V. Defenses Against Apostates (17–23)

VI. Doxology of Jude (24, 25)

THE WARNINGS OF HISTORY TO THE UNGODLY

1 [a,A]Jude, a [B]bond-servant of Jesus Christ, and
brother of [b]James,
To [C]those who are the called, beloved in God the
Father, and [D]kept for Jesus Christ: 2 [A]May mercy and
peace and love [B]be multiplied to you.
3 [A]Beloved, while I was making every effort to
write you about our [B]common salvation, I felt the
necessity to write to you appealing that you [C]con-
tend earnestly for [D]the faith which was once for all
[E]handed down to [F]the [a]saints. 4 For certain persons
have [A]crept in unnoticed, those who were long beforehand [a,B]marked out for this condemnation, ungodly persons who turn [C]the grace of our God into
[D]licentiousness and [E]deny our only Master and Lord,
Jesus Christ.
5 Now I desire to [A]remind you, though [B]you
know all things once for all, that [a]the Lord, [C]after
saving a people out of the land of Egypt, [b]subse-
quently destroyed those who did not believe. 6 And
[A]angels who did not keep their own domain, but
abandoned their proper abode, He has [B]kept in
eternal bonds under darkness for the judgment

1:1 [a]Gr *Judas* [b]Or *Jacob* [A]Matt 13:55; Mark 6:3; [Luke 6:16; John 14:22; Acts 1:13] [B]Rom 1:1 [C]Rom 1:6f [D]John 17:11f; 1 Pet 1:5; Jude 21 1:2 [A]Gal 6:16; 1 Tim 1:2 [B]1 Pet 1:2; 2 Pet 1:2 1:3 [a]Or *holy ones* [A]Heb 6:9; Jude 1, 17, 20 [B]Titus 1:4 [C]1 Tim 6:12 [D]Acts 6:7; Jude 20 [E]2 Pet 2:21 [F]Acts 9:13 1:4 [a]Or *written about...long ago* [A]Gal 2:4; 2 Tim 3:6 [B]1 Pet 2:8 [C]Acts 11:23 [D]2 Pet 2:7 [E]2 Tim 2:12; Titus 1:16; 2 Pet 2:1; 1 John 2:22 1:5 [a]Two early mss read *Jesus* [b]Lit *the second time* [A]2 Pet 1:12f; 3:1f [B]1 John 2:20 [C]Ex 12:51; 1 Cor 10:5-10; Heb 3:16f 1:6 [A]2 Pet 2:4 [B]2 Pet 2:9

1 Jude. See Introduction: Author and Date. **bond-servant.** Before the crucifixion and resurrection, Jude had denied Jesus as Messiah (Mt 13:55; Mk 6:3; Jn 7:5), but afterward came to humbly acknowledge himself as His slave, having submitted to Christ's lordship. **brother of James.** James was the well-known leader of the Jerusalem church (Ac 12:17; 15:13; 21:18; Gal 2:9) and author of the epistle that carried his name. **called.** As always in the Epistles, this refers not to a general invitation to salvation, but to God's irresistible, elective call to salvation (cf. Ro 1:7; 1Co 1:23, 24; 1Th 5:24; 2Th 2:13, 14). This call yields: 1) fellowship with Christ (1Co 1:9); 2) peace (1Co 7:15); 3) freedom (Gal 5:13); 4) a worthy walk (Eph 4:1); 5) hope (Eph 4:4); 6) holiness (1Pe 1:15); 7) blessing (1Pe 3:9); and 8) eternal glory (1Pe 5:10). Cf. "grace of our God" (v. 4). **beloved.** Cf. Jn 13:1; 14:23; 16:27; 17:20, 23; Ro 5:8; 1Jn 3:1, which expand on the idea of unconditional, thus unending, love from God to the believer in Christ. It is because of that love that believers are set apart from sin to God by the transformation of conversion. **God the Father.** The plan of salvation and its fulfillment come from God, who is not only Father in the sense of creation and origin of all that exists, but is also "God our Savior" (v. 25; cf. 1Ti 2:4; Titus 1:3; 2:10; 3:4). *See note on 1Ti 4:10.* **kept.** *See note on v. 24.* God not only initiates salvation, but He also completes it through Christ, thus preserving or keeping the believer secure for eternal life (cf. Jn 6:37–44; 10:28–30; 17:11, 15; Ro 8:31–39; 2Ti 4:18; Heb 7:25; 9:24; 1Pe 1:3–5).

2 mercy and peace and love. "Mercy and peace" was a common Jewish greeting; "love" was added to make this distinctively Christian. Only here in the NT do these 3 qualities appear so closely together. Where law and works prevail, there is failure and death. Where grace prevails, there is mercy (Eph 2:4; Heb 4:16), peace (Ro 5:1), and love (Ro 5:5) in abundance.

3 Beloved. Cf. vv. 17, 20. **I felt the necessity.** Cf. 1Co 9:16. This verse implies that Jude had intended to write a letter on salvation as the common blessing enjoyed by all believers, perhaps to emphasize unity and fellowship among believers, and remind them that God is no respecter of persons. But he was compelled, instead, to write a call to battle for the truth in light of the arrival of apostate teachers. **contend earnestly.** While the salvation of those to whom he wrote was not in jeopardy, false teachers preaching and living out a counterfeit gospel were misleading those who needed to hear the true gospel. Jude wrote this urgent imperative for Christians to wage war against error in all forms and fight strenuously for the truth, like a soldier who has been entrusted with a sacred task of guarding a holy treasure (cf. 1Ti 6:12; 2Ti 4:7). **the faith.** This is the whole body of revealed salvation truth contained in the Scriptures (cf. Gal 1:23; Eph 4:5, 13; Php 1:27; 1Ti 4:1). Cf. v. 20. Here is a call to know sound doctrine (Eph 4:14; Col 3:16: 1Pe 2:2; 1Jn 2:12–14), to be discerning in sorting out truth from error (1Th 5:20–22), and to be willing to confront and attack error (*see notes on 2Co 10:3–5; Php 1:7, 27; 1Ti 1:18; 6:12; 2Ti 1:13; 4:7, 8; Titus 1:13*). **once for all handed down.** God's revelation was delivered once as a unit, at the completion of the Scripture, and is not to be edited by either deletion or addition (cf. Dt 4:2; 12:32; Pr 30:6; Rev 22:18, 19). Scripture is complete, sufficient, and finished; therefore it is fixed for all time. Nothing is to be added to the body of the inspired Word (*see notes on 2Ti 3:16, 17; 2Pe 1:19–21*) because nothing else is needed. It is the responsibility of believers now to study the Word (2Ti 2:15), preach the Word (2Ti 4:2), and fight for its preservation. **saints.** Believers are identified as holy, since they are set apart from sin to God. *See note on 1Co 1:2.*

4 certain persons have crept in unnoticed. These were infiltrating, false teachers pretending to be true, who on the surface looked like the real thing, but whose intentions were to lead God's people astray (cf. Mt 7:15; Ac 20:29; Gal 2:4, 5; 1Ti 4:1–3; 2Pe 2:1, 20; 1Jn 2:18–23). These apostates were Satan's counterfeits, most likely posing as itinerant teachers (cf. 2Co 11:13–15; 2Pe 2:1–3; 2Jn 7–11). Their stealth made them dangerous. They were characterized by 3 features: 1) they were ungodly; 2) they perverted grace; and 3) they denied Christ. **long beforehand marked out.** Apostasy and apostates in general were written about and condemned many centuries before, such as illustrated in vv. 5–7 and spoken of as Enoch did in vv. 14–16. Cf. Is 8:19–21; 47:9–15; Hos 9:9; Zep 3:1–8. Their doom was "prewritten" in Scripture as a warning to all who would come later. Jesus had warned about them in Mt 7:15–20 (cf. Ac 20:29). The most recent warning had been 2Pe 2:3, 17; 3:7. **this condemnation.** This refers to the judgment spoken of by others "long beforehand." Jude's present exposé of apostates placed them in the path of the very judgment of God, written of previously. **ungodly persons.** Lit. "impious" or "without worship." Their lack of reverence for God was demonstrated by the fact that they infiltrated the church of God to corrupt it and gain riches from its people. Cf. vv. 15, 16, 18, 19. **licentiousness.** Lit. "unrestrained vice" or "gross immorality," which describes the shameless lifestyle of one who irreverently flaunts God's grace by indulging in unchecked and open immorality (cf. Ro 6:15). **deny ... Master and Lord, Jesus Christ.** Two Gr. words for Jesus are used here. The apostates disowned Christ as sovereign Lord (*despotēs*) and disdained any recognition of Christ as honorable Lord (*kurios*) by their wicked behavior. The better NT mss. omit God in the text, placing the emphasis clearly on one person, the Lord Jesus Christ, and emphasizing that apostates deny Him. *See note on 2Pe 2:1.* Cf. Mt 10:33; 2Ti 2:12; Titus 1:16; 1Jn 2:22, 23. It is always true of apostates, false teachers, and false religions that they pervert what Scripture declares is true about the Lord Jesus Christ.

5–7 Jude provided 3 well known acts of apostasy from the OT as brief reminders (v. 5) to illustrate their damnable outcome as declared in v. 4.

5 saving ... destroyed. Cf. Heb 3:16–19. God miraculously delivered the nation of Israel out of Egyptian bondage (Ex 12:51; Dt 4:34) only to have them respond in unbelief, doubting, and defecting from faith in God that He could bring them into the Promised Land (Nu 13:25–14:4), even to the extent of worshiping an idol of their own making, as well as murmuring against God instead of adoring Him (Ex 16:7–12; 1Co 10:10, 11). That apostate generation died during 38 years of wilderness wanderings (Nu 14:22–30, 35)

6 angels who did not keep. This apostasy of fallen angels is described in Ge 6:1–3 as possessing men who then cohabited with women. *See note on 2Pe 2:4.* The transition to Sodom and Gomorrah in v. 7 points to the similitude of the sin of homosexuality and what these angels did in Ge 6. **judgment ... great day.** This refers to the final judgment when all demons and Satan are forever consigned to the "lake of fire" prepared for them (Mt 25:41; Rev 20:10) and all the ungodly (Rev 20:15).

of the great day, 7 just as [A]Sodom and Gomorrah
and the [B]cities around them, since they in the
same way as these indulged in gross immorality
and [C]went after [a]strange flesh, are exhibited as
an [b,D]example in undergoing the [E]punishment of
eternal fire.

8 Yet in the same way these men, also by dreaming, [A]defile the flesh, and reject authority, and revile
[a]angelic majesties. 9 But [A]Michael [B]the archangel,
when he disputed with the devil and argued about
[C]the body of Moses, did not dare pronounce against
him a railing judgment, but said, "[D]The Lord rebuke

1:7 [a]Lit *different* or *other flesh* [b]Or *example of eternal fire, in undergoing punishment* [A]Gen 19:24f; 2 Pet 2:6 [B]Deut 29:23; Hos 11:8 [C]2 Pet 2:2 [D]2 Pet 2:6 [E]Matt 25:41; 2 Thess 1:8f; 2 Pet 3:7 1:8 [a]Lit *glories* [A]2 Pet 2:10 1:9 [A]Dan 10:13, 21; 12:1; Rev 12:7 [B]1 Thess 4:16; 2 Pet 2:11 [C]Deut 34:6 [D]Zech 3:2

7 Sodom … Gomorrah. *See notes on 2Pe 2:6–10.* The destruction of these cities at the SE corner of the Dead Sea is used over 20 times in Scripture as an illustration of God's judgment during the days of Abraham and Lot (cf. Ge 18:22–19:29). This destruction was in view of their apostasy, since it occurred about 450 years after the Flood, when at least one of Noah's sons, Shem (Ge 11:10, 11) was still living. Since this was only 100 years after Noah's death (Ge 9:28), people would have known about the message of righteousness and judgment from God which Noah preached, and which they rejected. **same way as these.** This points back to v. 6. **gross immorality … strange flesh.** This refers to both the heterosexual (Ge 19:8) and homosexual lusts (Ge 19:4, 5) of the residents. Cf. Lv 18:22; 20:13; Ro 1:27; 1Co 6:9; 1Ti 1:10 for the absolute condemnation of homosexual activity. **eternal fire.** Sodom and Gomorrah illustrate God's fire of earthly judgment (cf. Rev 16:8, 9; 20:9) which was only a preview of the fire that can never be quenched in eternal hell (cf. Mt 3:12; 18:8; 25:41; Mk 9:43, 44, 46, 48; Lk 3:17; Rev 19:20; 20:14, 15; 21:8).

8 these men … by dreaming. *See notes on 2Pe 2:10–12.* This refers to a confused state of the soul or abnormal imagination, producing delusions and sensual confusion. These men's minds were numb to the truth of God's Word so that, being beguiled and deluded, they fantasized wicked perversions, being blind and deaf to reality and truth. Perhaps they falsely claimed these were dreams/visions from God. "These" occurs 5 more times (vv. 10, 12, 14, 16, 19) in reference to the apostates, who are characterized in 3 ways (v. 8). **defile the flesh.** Similar to the inhabitants of Sodom and Gomorrah (v. 7), apostates have few, if any, moral restraints and thus are frequently characterized by immoral lifestyles (v. 4). Cf. Titus 1:15; Heb 12:15; 2Pe 2:10–19; 3:3. **reject authority.** Like the sinning angels (v. 6), these pretenders rejected all authority, civil and spiritual, thus rejecting the Scriptures and denying Christ (v. 4). **revile angelic majesties.** Cf. v. 10. That the majesties (lit. "glories") are angels is supported by the illustration in v. 9.

9 Michael the archangel. The chief angel of God who especially watches over Israel (Da 10:13, 21; 12:1) and leads the holy angels (Rev 12:7). Nowhere else in Scripture is this struggle over the body of Moses mentioned. Michael had to fight with Satan to do God's bidding, as he did on another occasion in Da 10:13 (*see note there*). **the devil.** Another name for Satan which means "accuser" or "slanderer" (cf. Rev 12:9, 10). **body of Moses.** Moses died on Mt. Nebo in Moab without having entered the Promised Land and was secretly buried in a place not known to man (Dt 34:5, 6). It would likely be that this confrontation took place as Michael buried Moses to prevent Satan from using Moses' body for some diabolical purpose not stated. Perhaps Satan wanted to use it as an idol, an object of worship for Israel. God sent Michael, however, to be certain it was buried. This account was recorded in the pseudepigraphal *Assumption of Moses* (see Introduction: Interpretive Challenges). **railing judgment.** *See note on 2Pe 2:11.* Rather than

PROFILE OF AN APOSTATE
1. Ungodly (v. 4)
2. Morally perverted (v. 4)
3. Deny Christ (v. 4)
4. Defile the flesh (v. 8)
5. Rebellious (v. 8)
6. Revile holy angels (v. 8)
7. Dreamers (v. 10)
8. Ignorant (v. 8)
9. Self-destruction (v. 10)
10. Grumblers (v. 16)
11. Faultfinders (v. 16)
12. Self-seeking (v. 16)
13. Arrogant speakers (v. 16)
14. Flatterers (v. 16)
15. Mockers (v. 18)
16. Cause division (v. 19)
17. Worldly minded (v. 19)
18. Without the Spirit (v. 19)

you!" 10 But [A]these men revile the things which they
do not understand; and [B]the things which they know
by instinct, [A]like unreasoning animals, by these
things they are [a]destroyed. 11 Woe to them! For they
have gone [A]the way of Cain, and for pay [a]they have
rushed headlong into [B]the error of Balaam, and
[C]perished in the rebellion of Korah. 12 These are
the men who are [a]hidden reefs [A]in your love feasts
when they feast with you [B]without fear, caring for
themselves; [C]clouds without water, [D]carried along
by winds; autumn trees without fruit, [b]doubly dead,
[E]uprooted; 13 [A]wild waves of the sea, casting up [B]their
own [a]shame like foam; wandering stars, [C]for whom
the [b]black darkness has been reserved forever.
14 *It was* also about these men *that* [A]Enoch, *in* the
seventh *generation* from Adam, prophesied, saying,
"[B]Behold, the Lord came with [a]many thousands of
His holy ones, 15 [A]to execute judgment upon all,
and to convict all the ungodly of all their ungodly
deeds which they have done in an ungodly way,
and of all the harsh things which [B]ungodly sinners
have spoken against Him." 16 These are [A]grumblers,
finding fault, [B]following after their *own* lusts; [a]they
speak [C]arrogantly, flattering people [D]for the sake of
gaining an advantage.

KEEP YOURSELVES IN THE LOVE OF GOD

17 But you, [A]beloved, [B]ought to remember the words
that were spoken beforehand by [C]the apostles of our
Lord Jesus Christ, 18 that they were saying to you,
"[A]In the last time there will be mockers, [B]following

1:10 [a]Lit *corrupted* [A]2 Pet 2:12 [B]Phil 3:19 1:11 [a]Lit *they have poured themselves out* [A]Gen 4:3-8; Heb 11:4; 1 John 3:12 [B]Num 31:16; 2 Pet 2:15; Rev 2:14 [C]Num 16:1-3, 31-35 1:12 [a]Or *stains* [b]Lit *twice* [A]1 Cor 11:20ff; 2 Pet 2:13 and mg [B]Ezek 34:2, 8, 10 [C]Prov 25:14; 2 Pet 2:17 [D]Eph 4:14 [E]Matt 15:13 1:13 [a]Or *shameless deeds* [b]Lit *blackness of darkness; or netherworld gloom* [A]Is 57:20 [B]Phil 3:19 [C]2 Pet 2:17; Jude 6 1:14 [a]Lit *His holy ten thousands* [A]Gen 5:18, 21ff [B]Deut 33:2; Dan 7:10; Matt 16:27; Heb 12:22 1:15 [A]2 Pet 2:6ff [B]1 Tim 1:9 1:16 [a]Lit *their mouth speaks* [A]Num 16:11, 41; 1 Cor 10:10 [B]2 Pet 2:10; Jude 18 [C]2 Pet 2:18 [D]2 Pet 2:3 1:17 [A]Jude 3 [B]2 Pet 3:2 [C]Heb 2:3 1:18 [A]Acts 20:29; 1 Tim 4:1; 2 Tim 3:1f; 4:3; 2 Pet 3:3 [B]Jude 4, 16

personally cursing such a powerful angel as Satan, Michael deferred to the ultimate, sovereign power of God following the example of the Angel of the Lord in Zec 3:2. This is the supreme illustration of how Christians are to deal with Satan and demons. Believers are not to address them, but rather to seek the Lord's intervening power against them.

10 revile. Lit. "blaspheme." Cf. v. 8. Apostate teachers, in their brash, bold, egotistical infatuation with imagined power and authority, rail on that which they don't even understand. **things ... things.** *See note on 2Pe 2:12.* Apostates are intellectually arrogant and spiritually ignorant in that they don't know because they are blinded by Satan (2Co 4:4) and spiritual matters are beyond their unregenerate capacity to understand (1Co 2:14). In divine matters, they are no brighter than the dumbest beasts. **are destroyed.** This speaks of spiritual and moral self-destruction.

11 Woe. In declaring ultimate spiritual judgment on the apostates, Jude followed the example of the prophets (cf. Is 5:8–23) and of Christ (cf. Mt 23:13, 15, 16, 23, 25, 27, 29). The severest judgment of all (Heb 10:26), will come on apostates because they too followed the same path as Cain, Balaam, and Korah. **way of Cain.** Cain openly rebelled against God's revealed will regarding sacrifice (*see notes on Ge 4:1–15*; cf. Heb 11:4; 1Jn 3:12). **error of Balaam.** Cf. Nu 22–25; *see note on 2Pe 2:15.* For a large financial reward, Balaam devised a plan for Balak, king of Moab, to entice Israel into a compromising situation with idolatry and immorality which would bring God's own judgment on His people (cf. Nu 31:16; Rev 2:14). **rebellion of Korah.** *See notes on Nu 16:1–32.* Korah, plus 250 Jewish leaders, rejected the God-appointed leadership of Moses and Aaron in an attempt to impose his will upon God and the people. Apostates will unquestionably meet the same end as Korah—divine judgment.

12, 13 *See notes on 2Pe 2:13–17.*

12 hidden reefs ... love feasts. *See note on 2Pe 2:13.* These "hidden reefs" can be taken as "hidden rocks" or as "stains" (see marginal note). These apostates were dirt spots, filth on the garment of the church; or more likely, what God intended for the church as smooth sailing, they turned into a potential shipwreck through their presence. "Love feasts" were the regular gathering of the early church to partake of the bread and cup, plus share a common meal (cf. 1Co 11:20–30). **clouds without water.** *See note on 2Pe 2:17.* Apostates promise spiritual life but are empty clouds which bring the hope of rain, but actually deliver nothing but dryness and death (cf. Pr 25:14). They preach a false gospel that leads only to hell. **trees without fruit.** Apostates hold out the claim of providing a spiritual feast, but instead deliver famine (cf. Lk 13:6–9). Doubly dead trees will never yield fruit and, regardless of what they say, will always be barren because they are uprooted. Cf. Mt 7:17–20.

13 wild waves. Apostates promise powerful ministry, but are quickly exposed as wreakers of havoc and workers of worthless shame (cf. Is 57:20). **wandering stars.** This most likely refers to a meteor or shooting star which has an uncontrolled moment of brilliance and then fades away forever into nothing. Apostates promise enduring spiritual direction, but deliver a brief, aimless, and worthless flash.

14 Enoch. Following the genealogy of Ge 5:1–24; 1Ch 1:1–3, Enoch was the seventh in the line of Adam. Because Enoch "walked with God," he was taken directly to heaven without having to die (cf. Ge 5:24; Heb 11:5). **prophesied.** *See note on v. 4.* The source of this information was the Holy Spirit who inspired Jude. The fact that it was recorded in the nonbiblical and pseudepigraphal *Book of Enoch* had no effect on its accuracy. See Introduction: Interpretive Challenges. **Behold, the Lord ... holy ones.** Enoch, before the Flood, prophesied about Christ's second coming in judgment (cf. 1Th 3:13). "Holy ones" can refer to either angels or believers. Since both angels (Mt 24:31; 25:31; Mk 8:38; 2 Thess 1:7) and believers (Col 3:4; 1Th 3:13; Rev 19:14) will accompany Him, it may refer to both (cf. Zec 14:5), but the focus on judgment in v. 15 seems to favor angels, who are often seen in judgment action. While believers will have a role of judging during the Lord's earthly kingdom (*see note on 1Co 6:2*) and will return when Christ comes to judge (Rev 19:14), angels are the executioners of God at the second coming of Christ (see Mt 13:39–41, 49, 50; 24:29–31; 25:31; 2Th 1:7–10).

15 execute judgment. The sentence will be eternal hell (see Rev 20:11–15). Cf. Mt 5:22; 7:19; 8:12; 10:28; 13:40–42; 25:41, 46). **ungodly.** *See note on v. 4.* The 4-fold use of this word as a description of the apostates (cf. vv. 4, 18) identifies the core iniquity, which is failure to reverence God. See Peter's use of the term in 2Pe 2:5, 6; 3:7. It was for such that Christ died (Ro 5:6).

16 grumblers. *See note on v. 5.* The word, found only here in the NT, is used in the LXX to describe the murmurings of Israel against God (Ex 16:7–9; Nu 14:27, 29; 1Co 10:10). **finding fault.** They gave vent to dissatisfaction with God's will and way as was the case with Israel, Sodom, the fallen angels, Cain, Korah, and Balaam (cf. vv. 5–7, 11). **following ... own lusts.** *See notes on 2Pe 2:10, 18; 3:3.* This is a common phrase used to describe the unconverted (v. 18; 2Ti 4:3). Apostates are especially driven by a desire for sinful self-satisfaction. **speak arrogantly.** *See note on 2Pe 2:18.* They speak pompously and even magnificently, but with empty, lifeless words of no spiritual value. Their message has external attractiveness, but is void of the powerful substance of divine truth. **flattering people.** They tell people what they want to hear for their own profit (cf. 2Ti 4:3, 4), rather than proclaiming the truth of God's Word for the auditors' benefit. Cf. Pss 5:9; 12:2, 3; Pr 26:28; 29:5; Ro 3:13; 16:18.

17, 18 *See notes on 2Pe 3:1–3.*

17 words ... by the apostles. The apostles had warned the coming generation about apostates, so that they would be prepared and not be taken by surprise (cf. Ac 20:28–31; 1Ti 4:1, 2; 2Ti 3:1–5; 4:1–3; 2Pe 2:1–3:4; 1Jn 2:18; 2Jn 7–11). God's Word is designed to warn and protect (Ac 20:31; 1Co 4:14); as v. 18 indicates, there had been continually repeated warnings.

18 last time. Lit. at the chronological end of the current epoch or season (cf. 2Ti 3:1). This term refers to the time of Messiah from His first coming until His second (*see notes on 2Ti 3:1; 2Pe 3:3; 1Jn 2:18*). These characteristics will prevail until Christ returns. **mockers.** *See note on 2Pe 3:3.* These are the scoffers at God's future plans who pretend to know the truth but deny that judgment will ever come. **following ... ungodly lust.** *See note on v. 16.*

after their own ungodly lusts." 19 These are the ones
who cause divisions, [a,A]worldly-minded, [b]devoid of
the Spirit. 20 But you, [A]beloved, [B]building yourselves
up on your most holy [A]faith, [C]praying in the Holy
Spirit, 21 keep yourselves in the love of God, [A]waiting
anxiously for the mercy of our Lord Jesus Christ to
eternal life. 22 And have mercy on some, who are
doubting; 23 save others, [A]snatching them out of the
fire; and on some have mercy with fear, [B]hating even
the garment polluted by the flesh.
24 [A]Now to Him who is able to keep you from
stumbling, and to [B]make you stand in the presence
of His glory blameless with [C]great joy, 25 to the [A]only
[B]God our Savior, through Jesus Christ our Lord, [C]*be*
glory, majesty, dominion and authority, [D]before all
time and now and [a]forever. Amen.

1:19 [a]Or *merely natural* [b]Lit *not having* [A]1 Cor 2:14f; James 3:15 1:20 [A]Jude 3 [B]Col 2:7; 1 Thess 5:11 [C]Eph 6:18 1:21 [A]Titus 2:13; Heb 9:28; 2 Pet 3:12 1:23 [A]Amos 4:11; Zech 3:2; 1 Cor 3:15 [B]Zech 3:3f; Rev 3:4 1:24 [A]Rom 16:25 [B]2 Cor 4:14 [C]1 Pet 4:13 1:25 [a]Lit *to all the ages* [A]John 5:44; 1 Tim 1:17 [B]Luke 1:47 [C]Rom 11:36 [D]Heb 13:8

19 cause divisions. They fractured the church rather than united it (cf. Eph 4:4–6; Php 2:2). **worldly-minded.** Apostate teachers advertise themselves as having the highest spiritual knowledge, but are actually attracted to the most debased levels of life. They are "soulish" not "spiritual." Cf. Jas 3:15. **devoid of the Spirit.** To not have the Spirit is to not have spiritual life at all (*see notes on Ro 8:9; 1Co 6:19, 20*) or, in other words, to be an unbeliever.

20 building. True believers have a sure foundation (1Co 3:11) and cornerstone (Eph 2:20) in Jesus Christ. The truths of the Christian faith (cf. v. 3) have been provided in the teaching of the apostles and prophets (Eph 2:20), so that Christians can build themselves up by the Word of God (Ac 20:32). **praying in the Holy Spirit.** *See note on Eph 6:18.* This is not a call to some ecstatic form of prayer, but simply a call to pray consistently in the will and power of the Spirit, as one would pray in the name of Jesus Christ (cf. Ro 8:26, 27).

21 keep. Cf. Ac 13:43. This imperative establishes the believer's responsibility to be obedient and faithful by living out his salvation (cf. Php 2:12), while God works out His will (cf. Php 2:13). It means to remain in the place of obedience where God's love is poured out on His children, as opposed to being disobedient and incurring His chastening (cf. 1Co 11:27–31; Heb 12:5–11). This refers to the perseverance of the saints, the counterbalance to God's sovereign preservation of believers in Christ (cf. v. 1). This is accomplished by: 1) building one's self up in the Word of God (v. 20); 2) praying in the Holy Spirit (v. 20); and 3) looking for the finalization of eternal life (v. 21). For a related discussion of the perseverance of the saints, *see note on Mt 24:13*. **waiting.** An eager anticipation of Christ's second coming to provide eternal life in its ultimate, resurrection form (cf. Titus 2:13; 1Jn 3:1–3), which is the supreme expression of God's mercy on one to whom Christ's righteousness has undeservedly been imputed (cf. v. 2). Paul called this "loved His appearing" (2Ti 4:8) and John wrote that such a steady anticipation was purifying (1Jn 3:3).

22, 23 some. There are several textual variants here which could result in either two or three groups being indicated. They are: 1) sincere doubters who deserve compassion (v. 22); 2) those who are deeper in unbelief and urgently need to be pulled from the fire (v. 23); and 3) those declared disciples of apostasy who still deserve mercy, but are to be handled with much fear (v. 23), lest the would-be-rescuer also be spiritually sullied. Given the mss. evidence and Jude's pattern of writing in triads, 3 groups is the more likely scenario.

22 mercy. These victims of the apostate teachers need mercy and patience because they have not yet reached a firm conclusion about Christ and eternal life, and so remain doubters who could possibly be swayed to the truth.

23 save others. Others, who are committed to the errors taught by the apostates, need immediate and forthright attention before they are further entrenched on the road to the fire of hell (cf. v. 7) as a result of embracing deceptive lies. **with fear.** This third group also needs mercy, even though they are thoroughly polluted by apostate teaching. These people are to be given the true gospel, but with great fear, lest the deliverer be contaminated also. The defiled garment pictures the apostate's debauched life, which can spread its contagion to the well-meaning evangelist.

24, 25 Jude's lovely benediction/doxology stands as one of the most splendid in the NT (cf. Ro 11:33–36; 16:25–27; 2Co 13:14; Heb 13:20, 21). It returned to the theme of salvation which Jude had hoped to develop at the beginning (cf. v. 3) and bolstered the courage of believers to know that Christ would protect them from the present apostasy.

24 Him who is able. This speaks of omnipotent God. Cf. Ge 18:14; Dt 7:21; 1Sa 14:6; Mt 19:26. **keep you from stumbling.** *See notes on v. 1; 1Pe 1:3–5.* The power of Christ would sustain the sincere believer from falling to the temptation of apostasy (cf. Job 42:2; Pss 37:23, 24; 121:3; Jer 32:17; Mt 19:26; Lk 1:37; Jn 6:39, 40, 44; 10:27–30; Eph 3:20). **stand ... blameless.** Cf. 2Co 11:2; Eph 5:27. Christians possess Christ's imputed righteousness through justification by faith and have been made worthy of eternal life in heaven (*see notes on Ro 8:31–39*). **with great joy.** This refers primarily to the joy of the Savior (cf. Heb 12:2) but also includes the joy of believers (cf. 1Pe 1:8). Joy is the dominant expression of heaven (see Mt 25:23).

25 God our Savior. God is by nature a saving God, unlike the reluctant and indifferent false deities of human and demon invention (*see notes on 1Ti 2:2; 4:10; 2Ti 1:10; Titus 1:3; 2:10; 3:4; 2Pe 1:1*). **glory ... authority.** Both Jude on earth and the angels and saints in heaven (Rev 4:10, 11; 5:12–14) ascribed these kinds of qualities to our God and the Lord Jesus Christ.

THE REVELATION OF JESUS CHRIST

TITLE

Unlike most books of the Bible, Revelation contains its own title: "The Revelation of Jesus Christ" (1:1). "Revelation" (Gr., *apokalupsis*) means "an uncovering," "an unveiling," or "a disclosure." In the NT, this word describes the unveiling of spiritual truth (Ro 16:25; Gal 1:12; Eph 1:17; 3:3), the revealing of the sons of God (Ro 8:19), Christ's incarnation (Lk 2:32), and His glorious appearing at His second coming (2Th 1:7; 1Pe 1:7). In all its uses, "revelation" refers to something or someone, once hidden, becoming visible. What this book reveals or unveils is Jesus Christ in glory. Truths about Him and His final victory, that the rest of Scripture merely allude to, become clearly visible through revelation about Jesus Christ (see Historical and Theological Themes). This revelation was given to Him by God the Father, and it was communicated to the apostle John by an angel (1:1).

AUTHOR AND DATE

Four times the author identifies himself as John (1:1, 4, 9; 22:8). Early tradition unanimously identified him as John the apostle, author of the fourth gospel and three epistles. For example, important second century witnesses to the apostle John's authorship include Justin Martyr, Irenaeus, Clement of Alexandria, and Tertullian. Many of the book's original readers were still alive during the lifetimes of Justin Martyr and Irenaeus—both of whom held to apostolic authorship.

There are differences in style between Revelation and John's other writings, but they are insignificant and do not preclude one man from writing both. In fact, there are some striking parallels between Revelation and John's other works. Only John's gospel and Revelation refer to Jesus Christ as the Word (19:13; Jn 1:1). Revelation (1:7) and John's gospel (19:37) translate Zec 12:10 differently from the Septuagint, but in agreement with each other. Only Revelation and the Gospel of John describe Jesus as the Lamb (5:6, 8; Jn 1:29); both describe Jesus as a witness (cf. 1:5; Jn 5:31, 32).

Revelation was written in the last decade of the first century (ca. A.D. 94–96), near the end of Emperor Domitian's reign (A.D. 81–96). Although some date it during Nero's reign (A.D. 54–68), their arguments are unconvincing and conflict with the view of the early church. Writing in the second century, Irenaeus declared that Revelation had been written toward the end of Domitian's reign. Later writers, such as Clement of Alexandria, Origen, Victorinus (who wrote one of the earliest commentaries on Revelation), Eusebius, and Jerome affirm the Domitian date.

The spiritual decline of the 7 churches (chaps. 2, 3) also argues for the later date. Those churches were strong and spiritually healthy in the mid-60s, when Paul last ministered in Asia Minor. The brief time between Paul's ministry there and the end of Nero's reign was too short for such a decline to have occurred. The longer time gap also explains the rise of the heretical sect known as the Nicolaitans (2:6, 15), who are not mentioned in Paul's letters, not even to one or more of these same churches (Ephesians). Finally, dating Revelation during Nero's reign does not allow time for John's ministry in Asia Minor to reach the point at which the authorities would have felt the need to exile him.

BACKGROUND AND SETTING

Revelation begins with John, the last surviving apostle and an old man, in exile on the small, barren island of Patmos, located in the Aegean Sea southwest of Ephesus. The Roman authorities had banished him there because of his faithful preaching of the gospel (1:9). While on Patmos, John received a series of visions that laid out the future history of the world.

When he was arrested, John was in Ephesus, ministering to the church there and in the surrounding cities. Seeking to strengthen those congregations, he could no longer minister to them in person and, following the divine command (1:11), John addressed Revelation to them (1:4). The churches had begun to feel the effects of persecution; at least one man—probably a pastor—had already been martyred (2:13), and John himself had been exiled. But the storm of persecution was about to break in full fury upon the 7 churches so dear to the apostle's heart (2:10). To those churches, Revelation provided a message of hope: God is in sovereign control of all the events of human history, and though evil often seems pervasive and wicked men all powerful, their ultimate doom is certain. Christ will come in glory to judge and rule.

HISTORICAL AND THEOLOGICAL THEMES

Since it is primarily prophetic, Revelation contains little historical material, other than that in chaps. 1–3. The 7 churches to whom the letters were addressed were existing churches in Asia Minor (modern Turkey). Apparently, they were singled out because John had ministered in them.

Revelation is first and foremost a revelation about Jesus Christ (1:1). The book depicts Him as the risen, glorified Son of God ministering among the churches (1:10ff.); as "the faithful witness, the firstborn of the dead, and the ruler of the kings of the earth" (1:5); as "the Alpha and the Omega" (1:8); as the one "who is and who was and who is to come, the Almighty" (1:8); as a son of man (1:13); as the one who was dead, but now is alive forevermore (1:18); as the Son of God (2:18); as the one who is holy and true (3:7); as "the Amen, the faithful and true Witness, the Beginning of the creation of God" (3:14); as the Lion of the tribe of Judah (5:5); as the Lamb in heaven, with authority to open the title deed to the earth (6:1ff.); as the Lamb on the throne (7:17); as the Messiah who will reign forever (11:15); as the Word of God (19:13); as the majestic King of kings and Lord of lords, returning in glorious splendor to conquer His foes (19:11ff.); and as "the root and the descendant of David, the bright morning star" (22:16).

Many other rich theological themes find expression in Revelation. The church is warned about sin and exhorted to holiness. John's vivid pictures of worship in heaven both exhort and instruct believers. In few other books of the Bible is the ministry of angels so prominent. Revelation's primary theological contribution is to eschatology, i.e., the doctrine of last things. In it we learn about: the final political setup of the world; the last battle of human history; the career and ultimate defeat of Antichrist; Christ's 1,000-year earthly kingdom; the glories of heaven and the eternal state; and the final state of the wicked and the righteous. Finally, only Daniel rivals this book in declaring that God providentially rules over the kingdoms of men and will accomplish His sovereign purposes regardless of human or demonic opposition.

INTERPRETIVE CHALLENGES

No other NT book poses more serious and difficult interpretive challenges than Revelation. The book's vivid imagery and striking symbolism have produced 4 main interpretive approaches:

The *preterist* approach interprets Revelation as a description of first-century events in the Roman Empire (see Author and Date). This view conflicts with the book's own often repeated claim to be prophecy (1:3; 22:7, 10, 18, 19). It is impossible to see all the events in Revelation as already fulfilled. The second coming of Christ, for example, obviously did not take place in the first century.

The *historicist* approach views Revelation as a panoramic view of church history from apostolic times to the present—seeing in the symbolism such events as the barbarian invasions of Rome, the rise of the Roman Catholic Church (as well as various individual popes), the emergence of Islam, and the French Revolution. This interpretive method robs Revelation of any meaning for those to whom it was written. It also ignores the time limitations the book itself places on the unfolding events (cf. 11:2; 12:6, 14; 13:5). Historicism has produced many different—and often conflicting—interpretations of the actual historical events contained in Revelation.

The *idealist* approach interprets Revelation as a timeless depiction of the cosmic struggle between the forces of good and evil. In this view, the book contains neither historical allusions nor predictive prophecy. This view also ignores Revelation's prophetic character and, if carried to its logical conclusion, severs the book from any connection with actual historical events. Revelation then becomes merely a collection of stories designed to teach spiritual truth.

The *futurist* approach insists that the events of chaps. 6–22 are yet future, and that those chapters literally and symbolically depict actual people and events yet to appear on the world scene. It describes the events surrounding the second coming of Jesus Christ (chaps. 6–19), the Millennium and final judgment (chap. 20), and the eternal state (chaps. 21, 22). Only this view does justice to Revelation's claim to be prophecy and interprets the book by the same grammatical-historical method as chaps. 1–3 and the rest of Scripture.

OUTLINE

I. The Things which You Have Seen (1:1–20)

- A. The Prologue (1:1–8)
- B. The Vision of the Glorified Christ (1:9–18)
- C. The Apostle's Commission to Write (1:19, 20)

II. The Things which Are (2:1–3:22)

- A. The Letter to the Church at Ephesus (2:1–7)
- B. The Letter to the Church at Smyrna (2:8–11)
- C. The Letter to the Church at Pergamum (2:12–17)
- D. The Letter to the Church at Thyatira (2:18–29)
- E. The Letter to the Church at Sardis (3:1–6)
- F. The Letter to the Church at Philadelphia (3:7–13)
- G. The Letter to the Church at Laodicea (3:14–22)

III. The Things which Will Take Place after These Things (4:1–22:21)
   A. Worship in Heaven (4:1–5:14)
   B. The Great Tribulation (6:1–18:24)
   C. The Return of the King (19:1–21)
   D. The Millennium (20:1–10)
   E. The Great White Throne Judgment (20:11–15)
   F. The Eternal State (21:1–22:21)

THE REVELATION OF JESUS CHRIST

1 The Revelation of Jesus Christ, which [A]God gave
Him to [B]show to His bond-servants, [C]the things
which must soon take place; and He sent and
[a]communicated *it* [D]by His angel to His bond-servant [E]John, 2 who testified to [A]the word of God
and to [B]the testimony of Jesus Christ, *even* to all
that he saw. 3 [A]Blessed is he who reads and those
who hear the words of the prophecy, and [a]heed
the things which are written in it; [B]for the time
is near.

MESSAGE TO THE SEVEN CHURCHES

4 [A]John to [B]the seven churches that are in [C]Asia:
[D]Grace to you and peace, from [E]Him who is and
who was and who [a]is to come, and from [F]the seven
Spirits who are before His throne, 5 and from Jesus
Christ, [A]the faithful witness, the [B]firstborn of the
dead, and the [C]ruler of the kings of the earth. To
Him who [D]loves us and released us from our sins
[a]by His blood— 6 and He has made us *to be* a [A]king-
dom, [A]priests to [a,B]His God and Father—[C]to Him *be*
the glory and the dominion forever and ever. Amen.
7 [A]BEHOLD, HE IS COMING WITH THE CLOUDS, and [B]ev-
ery eye will see Him, even those who pierced Him;
and all the tribes of the earth will [C]mourn over Him.
So it is to be. Amen.
8 "I am [A]the Alpha and the Omega," says the [B]Lord
God, "[C]who is and who was and who [a]is to come,
the Almighty."

THE PATMOS VISION

9 [A]I, John, your [B]brother and [C]fellow partaker in
the tribulation and [D]kingdom and [a,E]perseverance
which are in Jesus, was on the island called Patmos
[F]because of the word of God and the testimony of
Jesus. 10 I was [a,A]in the Spirit on [B]the Lord's day, and
I heard behind me a loud voice [C]like *the sound* of a

1:1 [a]Or *signified* [A]John 17:8; Rev 5:7 [B]Rev 22:6 [C]Dan 2:28f; Rev 1:19 [D]Rev 17:1; 19:9f; 21:9; 22:16 [E]Rev 1:4, 9; 22:8 1:2 [A]Rev 1:9; 6:9; 12:17; 20:4 [B]1 Cor 1:6; Rev 12:17 1:3 [a]Or *keep* [A]Luke 11:28; Rev 22:7 [B]Rom 13:11; Rev 3:11; 22:7, 10, 12 1:4 [a]Or *is coming* [A]Rev 1:1, 9; 22:8 [B]Rev 1:11, 20 [C]Acts 2:9 [D]Rom 1:7 [E]Rev 1:8, 17; 4:8; 16:5 [F]Is 11:2; Rev 3:1; 4:5; 5:6; 8:2 1:5 [a]Or *in* [A]Rev 3:14; 19:11 [B]1 Cor 15:20; Col 1:18 [C]Rev 17:14; 19:16 [D]Rom 8:37 1:6 [a]Or *God and His Father* [A]Rev 5:10; 20:6 [B]Rom 15:6 [C]Rom 11:36 1:7 [A]Dan 7:13; 1 Thess 4:17 [B]Zech 12:10-14; John 19:37 [C]Luke 23:28 1:8 [a]Or *is coming* [A]Is 41:4; Rev 21:6; 22:13 [B]Rev 4:8; 11:17 [C]Rev 1:4 1:9 [a]Or *steadfastness* [A]Rev 1:1 [B]Acts 1:15 [C]Matt 20:23; Acts 14:22; 2 Cor 1:7; Phil 4:14 [D]2 Tim 2:12; Rev 1:6 [E]2 Thess 3:5; Rev 3:10 [F]Rev 1:2 1:10 [a]Or *in spirit* [A]Matt 22:43; Rev 4:2; 17:3; 21:10 [B]Acts 20:7 [C]Rev 4:1

1:1 The Revelation. The Gr. word from which the Eng. word "apocalypse" comes lit. means "to uncover, or to reveal." When it refers to a person, it means that person becomes clearly visible (see Introduction: Title; cf. Lk 2:30–32; Ro 8:19; 1Co 1:7; 1Pe 1:7). **Jesus Christ.** The gospels unveil Christ at His first coming in humiliation; Revelation reveals Him in His exaltation: 1) in blazing glory (vv. 7–20); 2) over His church, as its Lord (chaps. 2, 3); 3) in His second coming, as He takes back the earth from the usurper, Satan, and establishes His kingdom (chaps. 4–20); and 4) as He lights up the eternal state (chaps. 21, 22). The NT writers eagerly anticipate this unveiling (1Co 1:7; 2Th 1:7; 1Pe 1:7). **God gave Him.** As a reward for Christ's perfect submission and atonement, the Father now presented to Him the great record of His future glory (cf. Php 2:5–11). Readers eavesdrop on the gift of this book, from the Father to His Son. **soon.** This word (cf. 2:5, 16; 3:11; 11:14; 22:12; 2Ti 4:9) underscores the imminence of Christ's return.

1:3 Blessed. This is the only biblical book that comes with a blessing for the one who listens to it being read and explained and then responds in obedience. This is the first of 7 beatitudes in the book (v. 3; 14:13; 16:15; 19:9; 20:6; 22:7, 14). **time is near.** "Time" refers to epochs, eras, or seasons. The next great epoch of God's redemptive history is imminent. But although Christ's coming is the next event, it may be delayed so long that people begin to question whether He will ever come (cf. Mt 24:36–39; 2Pe 3:3, 4).

1:4 seven churches that are in Asia. Asia Minor, equivalent to modern Turkey, was composed of 7 postal districts. At the center of those districts were 7 key cities which served as central points for the dissemination of information. It is to the churches in those cities that John writes. **who is and who was and who is to come.** God's eternal presence is not limited by time. He has always been present and will come in the future. **the seven Spirits.** There are two possible meanings: 1) a reference to Isaiah's prophecy concerning the 7-fold ministry of the Holy Spirit (Is 11:2); or 2) more likely, it is a reference to the lampstand with 7 lamps (a menorah) in Zechariah—also a description of the Holy Spirit (*see notes on 4:5; 5:6; Zec 4:1–10*). In either case, 7 is the number of completeness, so John is identifying the fullness of the Holy Spirit.

1:5 firstborn. Of all who have been or will be raised from the dead, He is the preeminent one, the only one who is the rightful heir (cf. 3:14; Ps 89:27; Col 1:15).

1:6 a kingdom, priests. All who believe live in the sphere of God's rule, a kingdom entered by faith in Jesus Christ. And as priests, believers have the right to enter God's presence.

1:7 coming with the clouds. This echoes the promise of Daniel: The Son of Man will come with the clouds of heaven (Da 7:13)—not ordinary clouds but clouds of glory. In the OT, God often manifested Himself in an energized, blazing light, called the Shekinah or glory cloud. No one could see it fully and live (Ex 33:20), so it had to be veiled. But when Christ returns, the glory will be completely visible. Cf. Mt 24:29, 30; 25:31; *see notes on 6:12–17.* **those who pierced.** Not a reference to the 4 Roman soldiers usually involved in crucifixion, but to the Jews who were actually responsible for Christ's death (Ac 2:22, 23; 3:14, 15). Zechariah identified the ones who pierced Him as "the house of David" and "the inhabitants of Jerusalem," and prophesied that they will weep tears of genuine repentance because of what they did to their Messiah (Zec 12:10). **all the tribes … will mourn.** The mourning of the rest of the earth's inhabitants is not that which accompanies genuine repentance (cf. 9:21). It is the result of guilt for sin and fear of punishment (6:16; cf. Ge 3:8–10).

1:8 the Alpha and the Omega. These are the first and last letters of the Greek alphabet. An alphabet is an ingenious way to store and communicate knowledge. The 26 letters in the English alphabet, arranged in almost endless combinations, can hold and convey all knowledge. Christ is the supreme, sovereign alphabet; there is nothing outside His knowledge, so as there are no unknown factors that can sabotage His second coming. (cf. Col 2:3). **the Almighty.** "Almighty God" or "the Almighty" occurs 8 times in Revelation, underscoring that God's power is supreme over all the cataclysmic events it records (see also 4:8; 11:17; 15:3; 16:7, 14; 19:15; 21:22). He exercises sovereign control over every person, object, and event, and not one molecule in the universe is outside that dominion.

1:9–18 This vision of Christ is equaled in grandeur only by the vision of His final return as King of kings and Lord of lords (19:11–16).

1:9 tribulation and kingdom and perseverance. Four characteristics that John and his believing readers share: 1) persecution for their faith; 2) membership in the redeemed community over which Christ serves as Lord and King; 3) eager anticipation of the glory of His coming millennial reign on earth; and 4) endurance and perseverance in spite of difficult times. **island called Patmos.** Located in the Aegean Sea off the coast of Asia Minor (modern Turkey) and part of a group of about 50 islands, Patmos was a barren, rocky, crescent-shaped island in John's day that was about 10 mi. long and less than 6 mi. at its widest point. It served as a Roman penal colony. According to early Christian historian, Eusebius, the emperor Nerva (A.D. 96–98) released John from Patmos.

1:10 in the Spirit. This was not a dream. John was supernaturally transported out of the material world awake—not sleeping—to an experience beyond the normal senses. The Holy Spirit empowered his senses to perceive revelation from God (cf. Ac 10:11). **Lord's day.** This phrase appears in many early Christian writings and refers to Sunday, the day of the Lord's resurrection. Some have suggested this phrase refers to "the Day of the Lord," but the context doesn't support that interpretation. **loud voice.** Throughout Revelation, a loud sound or voice indicates the solemnity of what God is about to reveal.

trumpet, 11 saying, "[A]Write in a [a]book what you see,
and send *it* to the [B]seven churches: to [C]Ephesus and
to [D]Smyrna and to [E]Pergamum and to [F]Thyatira and
to [G]Sardis and to [H]Philadelphia and to [I]Laodicea."
12 Then I turned to see the voice that was speaking
with me. And having turned I saw [A]seven golden
lampstands; 13 and [A]in the middle of the lampstands
I saw one [B]like [a]a son of man, [C]clothed in a robe
reaching to the feet, and [D]girded across His chest
with a golden sash. 14 His head and His [A]hair were
white like white wool, like snow; and [B]His eyes were
like a flame of fire. 15 His [A]feet *were* like burnished
bronze, when it has been made to glow in a furnace,
and His [B]voice *was* like the sound of many waters.
16 In His right hand He held [A]seven stars, and out
of His mouth came a [B]sharp two-edged sword; and
His [C]face was like [D]the sun [a]shining in its strength.
17 When I saw Him, I [A]fell at His feet like a dead
man. And He [B]placed His right hand on me, saying, "[C]Do not be afraid; [D]I am the first and the
last, 18 and the [A]living One; and I [a,B]was dead, and
behold, I am alive forevermore, and I have [C]the
keys of death and of Hades. 19 Therefore [A]write
[B]the things which you have seen, and the things
which are, and the things which will take place
[C]after these things. 20 As for the [A]mystery of the
[B]seven stars which you saw in My right hand, and
the [C]seven golden lampstands: the [B]seven stars are
the angels of [D]the seven churches, and the seven
[E]lampstands are the seven churches.

1:11 [a]Or *scroll* [A]Rev 1:2, 19 [B]Rev 1:4, 20 [C]Rev 2:1 [D]Rev 2:8 [E]Rev 2:12 [F]Acts 16:14; Rev 2:18, 24 [G]Rev 3:1, 4 [H]Rev 3:7 [I]Col 2:1; Rev 3:14 1:12 [A]Ex 25:37; 37:23; Zech 4:2; Rev 1:20; 2:1 1:13 [a]Or *the Son of Man* [A]Rev 2:1 [B]Ezek 1:26; Dan 7:13; 10:16; Rev 14:14 [C]Dan 10:5 [D]Rev 15:6 1:14 [A]Dan 7:9 [B]Dan 7:9; 10:6; Rev 2:18; 19:12 1:15 [A]Ezek 1:7; Dan 10:6; Rev 2:18 [B]Ezek 1:24; 43:2; Rev 14:2; 19:6 1:16 [a]Lit *shines* [A]Rev 1:20; 2:1; 3:1 [B]Is 49:2; Heb 4:12; Rev 2:12, 16; 19:15 [C]Matt 17:2; Rev 10:1 [D]Judg 5:31 1:17 [A]Dan 8:17; 10:9, 10, 15 [B]Dan 8:18; 10:10, 12 [C]Matt 14:27; 17:7 [D]Is 41:4; 44:6; 48:12; Rev 2:8; 22:13 1:18 [a]Lit *became* [A]Luke 24:5; Rev 4:9f [B]Rom 6:9; Rev 2:8; 10:6; 15:7 [C]Job 38:17; Matt 11:23; 16:19; Rev 9:1; 20:1 1:19 [A]Rev 1:11 [B]Rev 1:12-16 [C]Rev 4:1 1:20 [A]Rom 11:25 [B]Rev 1:16; 2:1; 3:1 [C]Ex 25:37; 37:23; Zech 4:2; Rev 1:12; 2:1 [D]Rev 1:4, 11 [E]Matt 5:14f

1:11 book. The Gr. word refers to a scroll made of parchment formed from papyrus, a reed that grows plentifully along the Nile.

1:12 lampstands. These were portable gold lampstands that held small oil lamps. Each lampstand represented a church (v. 20), from which the light of life shone. Throughout Scripture, 7 is the number of completeness, so these 7 lampstands are representative of all the churches.

1:13 son of man. According to the Gospels, this is the title Christ used most often for Himself during His earthly ministry (81 times in the Gospels). Taken from the heavenly vision in Da 7:13, it is an implied claim to deity. **robe.** Most occurrences of this word in the Septuagint, the Gr. OT, refer to the garment of the High Priest. The golden sash across His chest completes the picture of Christ serving in His priestly role (cf. Lv 16:1–4; Heb 2:17).

1:14 like white wool. "White" does not refer to a flat white color but a blazing, glowing, white light (cf. Da 7:9). Like the glory cloud (or Shekinah), it is a picture of His holiness. **eyes ... flame of fire.** Like two lasers, the eyes of the exalted Lord look with penetrating gaze into the depths of His church (2:18; 19:12; Heb 4:13).

1:15 feet ... burnished bronze. The altar of burnt offering was covered with brass and its utensils were made of the same material (cf. Ex 38:1–7). Glowing hot, brass feet are a clear reference to divine judgment. Jesus Christ with feet of judgment is moving through His church to exercise His chastening authority upon sin. **voice ... sound of many waters.** No longer was His voice like the crystal clear note of a trumpet (v. 10), but John likened it to the crashing of the surf against the rocks of the island (cf. Eze 43:2). It was the voice of authority.

1:16 seven stars. These are the messengers who represent the 7 churches (*see note on v. 20*). Christ holds them in His hand, which means that He controls the church and its leaders. **a sharp two-edged sword.** A large, two-edged broad sword. It signifies judgment (cf. 2:16; 19:15) on those who attack His people and destroy His church.

1:17 fell at His feet. A common response to seeing the awesome glory of the Lord (Ge 17:3; Nu 16:22; Is 6:1–8; Eze 1:28; Ac 9:4). **first and the last.** Jesus Christ applies this OT name for Yahweh (22:13; Is 41:4; 44:6; 48:12) to Himself, clearly claiming to be God. Idols will come and go. He was before them, and He will remain after them.

1:18 keys of death and of Hades. *See note on Lk 16:23.* Death and Hades are essentially synonyms, but death is the condition and Hades, equivalent to the OT Sheol, the place of the dead (*see note on 20:13*). Christ decides who lives, who dies, and when.

1:19 This verse provides a simple outline for the entire book: "the things which you have seen" refers to the vision John has just seen (chap. 1); "the things which are" denotes the letters to the churches (chaps. 2, 3); and "the things which will take place after these things" refers to the revelation of future history (chaps. 4–22).

1:20 the angels. The word lit. means "messenger." Although it can mean angel—and does throughout the book—it cannot refer to angels here because angels are never leaders in the church. Most likely, these messengers are the 7 key elders representing each of those churches (*see note on v. 16*).

THE SEVEN CHURCHES OF THE APOCALYPSE

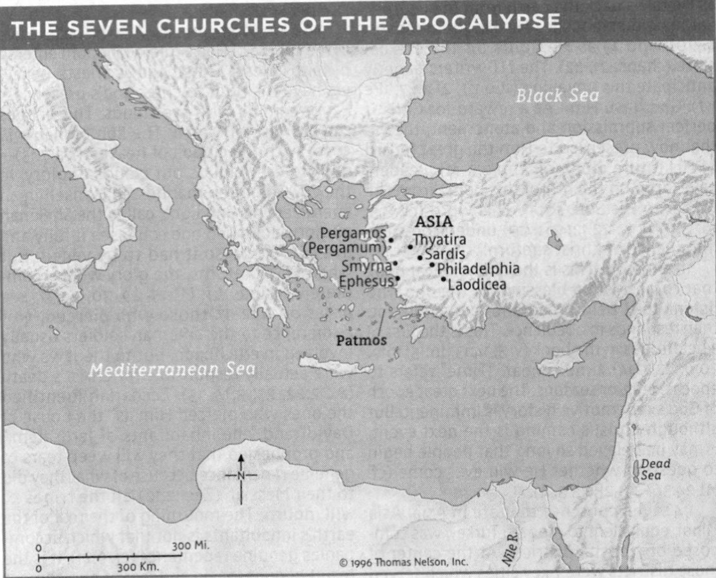

The churches of seven cities were recipients of an apocalyptic letter from the Lord Jesus through John. By commendation, rebuke, and warning, the people of God were exhorted to remain faithful in adversity. These churches held significant roles in the spread of Christianity in Asia Minor as a result of their location within a transportation network linking different parts of the region.

MESSAGE TO EPHESUS

2 "To the angel of the church in [A]Ephesus write:
The One who holds [B]the seven stars in His right
hand, the One who walks [a,C]among the seven golden
lampstands, says this:
2 'I know your deeds and your toil and [a]perse-
verance, and that you cannot tolerate evil men,
and you [B]put to the test those who call themselves
[C]apostles, and they are not, and you found them
to be false; 3 and you have [a]perseverance and have
endured [A]for My name's sake, and have not grown
weary. 4 But I have *this* against you, that you have
[A]left your first love. 5 Therefore remember from
where you have fallen, and [A]repent and [B]do the
[a]deeds you did at first; or else I am coming to you
and will remove your [C]lampstand out of its place—
unless you repent. 6 Yet this you do have, that you
hate the deeds of the [A]Nicolaitans, which I also hate.
7 [A]He who has an ear, let him hear what the Spirit
says to the churches. [B]To him who overcomes, I
will grant to eat of [C]the tree of life which is in the
[D]Paradise of God.'

MESSAGE TO SMYRNA

8 "And to the angel of the church in [A]Smyrna
write:
[B]The first and the last, who [a,C]was dead, and has
come to life, says this:
9 'I know your [A]tribulation and your [B]poverty (but
you are [B]rich), and the blasphemy by those who [C]say
they are Jews and are not, but are a synagogue of
[D]Satan. 10 Do not fear what you are about to suffer.
Behold, the devil is about to cast some of you into
prison, so that you will be [A]tested, and you will have
tribulation [B]for ten days. [a]Be [C]faithful until death,
and I will give you [D]the crown of life. 11 [A]He who
has an ear, let him hear what the Spirit says to the
churches. [B]He who overcomes will not be hurt by
the [C]second death.'

MESSAGE TO PERGAMUM

12 "And to the angel of the church in [A]Pergamum
write:
The One who has [B]the sharp two-edged sword
says this:

2:1 [a]Lit *in the middle of* [A]Rev 1:11 [B]Rev 1:16 [C]Rev 1:12f 2:2 [a]Or *steadfastness* [A]Rev 2:19; 3:1, 8, 15 [B]John 6:6; 1 John 4:1 [C]2 Cor 11:13 2:3 [a]V 2, note 1 [A]John 15:21 2:4 [A]Jer 2:2; Matt 24:12 2:5 [a]Lit *first deeds* [A]Rev 2:16, 22; 3:3, 19 [B]Heb 10:32; Rev 2:2 [C]Matt 5:14ff; Phil 2:15; Rev 1:20 2:6 [A]Rev 2:15 2:7 [A]Matt 11:15; Rev 2:11, 17; 3:6, 13, 22; 13:9 [B]Rev 2:11, 17, 26; 3:5, 12, 21; 21:7 [C]Gen 2:9; 3:22; Prov 3:18; 11:30; 13:12; 15:4; Rev 22:2, 14 [D]Ezek 28:13; 31:8f; Luke 23:43 2:8 [a]Lit *became* [A]Rev 1:11 [B]Is 44:6; 48:12; Rev 1:17; 22:13 [C]Rev 1:18 2:9 [A]Rev 1:9 [B]2 Cor 6:10; 8:9; James 2:5 [C]Rev 3:9 [D]Matt 4:10; Rev 2:13, 24 2:10 [a]Or *Prove yourself faithful* [A]Rev 3:10; 13:14ff [B]Dan 1:12, 14 [C]Rev 2:13; 12:11; 17:14 [D]1 Cor 9:25; Rev 3:11 2:11 [A]Matt 11:15; Rev 2:7, 17, 29; 3:6, 13, 22; 13:9 [B]Rev 2:7, 17, 26; 3:5, 12, 21; 21:7 [C]Rev 20:6, 14; 21:8 2:12 [A]Rev 1:11 [B]Rev 1:16; 2:16

2:1–3:22 Although these 7 churches were actual, historical churches in Asia Minor, they represent the types of churches that perennially exist throughout the church age. What Christ says to these churches is relevant in all times.

2:1 angel. The elder or pastor from the church (*see note on 1:20*). **Ephesus.** It was an inland city 3 mi. from the sea, but the broad mouth of the Cayster River allowed access and provided the greatest harbor in Asia Minor. Four great trade roads went through Ephesus; therefore, it became known as the gateway to Asia. It was the center of the worship of Artemis (Greek), or Diana (Roman), whose temple was one of the 7 Wonders of the Ancient World. Paul ministered there for 3 years (Ac 20:31), and later met with the Ephesian elders on his way to Jerusalem (Ac 20). Timothy, Tychicus, and the Apostle John all served this church. John was in Ephesus when he was arrested by Domitian and exiled 50 mi. SW to Patmos. **seven stars.** *See note on 1:16.* **seven golden lampstands.** *See note on 1:12.*

2:2 those who call themselves apostles. The Ephesian church exercised spiritual discernment. It knew how to evaluate men who claimed spiritual leadership by their doctrine and behavior (cf. 1Th 5:20, 21).

2:3 not grown weary. For over 40 years, since its founding, this church had remained faithful to the Word and the Lord. Through difficulty and persecution, the members had endured, always driven by the right motive, i.e., for Christ's name and reputation.

2:4 left your first love. To be a Christian is to love the Lord Jesus Christ (Jn 14:21, 23; 1Co 16:22). But the Ephesians' passion and fervor for Christ had become cold, mechanical orthodoxy. Their doctrinal and moral purity, their undiminished zeal for the truth, and their disciplined service were no substitute for the love for Christ they had forsaken.

2:5 remove your lampstand. God's judgment would bring an end to the Ephesian church.

2:6 the deeds of the Nicolaitans. A problem in Pergamum also (vv. 12–15), this heresy was similar to the teaching of Balaam (vv. 14, 15). Nicolas means "one who conquers the people." Irenaeus writes that Nicolas, who was made a deacon in Ac 6, was a false believer who later became apostate; but because of his credentials he was able to lead the church astray. And, like Balaam, he led the people into immorality and wickedness. The Nicolaitans, followers of Nicolas, were involved in immorality and assaulted the church with sensual temptations. Clement of Alexander says, "They abandoned themselves to pleasure like goats, leading a life of self-indulgence." Their teaching perverted grace and replaced liberty with license.

2:7 him who overcomes. According to John's own definition, to be an overcomer is to be a Christian (*see note on 1Jn 5:4*; cf. vv. 11, 17, 26; 3:5, 12, 21). **tree of life.** True believers enjoy the promise of heaven (*see notes on 22:2; Ge 2:9*).

2:8 angel. *See note on v. 1.* **Smyrna.** Smyrna means "myrrh," the substance used for perfume and often for anointing a dead body for aromatic purposes. Called the crown of Asia, this ancient city (modern Izmir, Turkey) was the most beautiful in Asia Minor and a center of science and medicine. Always on the winner's side in the Roman wars, Smyrna's intense loyalty to Rome resulted in a strong emperor-worship cult. Fifty years after John's death, Polycarp, the pastor of the church in Smyrna, was burned alive at the age of 86 for refusing to worship Caesar. A large Jewish community in the city also proved hostile to the early church. **The first and the last.** *See note on 1:17.*

2:9 who say they are Jews. Although they were Jews physically, they were not true Jews but spiritual pagans (cf. Ro 2:28). They allied with other pagans in putting Christians to death as they attempted to stamp out the Christian faith. **synagogue of Satan.** With the rejection of its Messiah, Judaism becomes as much a tool of Satan as emperor worship.

2:10 devil. The Gr. name for God's archenemy means "accuser." For discussion of Satan, *see notes on Eph 6:10–17.* **tribulation for ten days.** Their imprisonment will be brief. **crown of life.** It is the crown which is life, or the reward which is life, not an actual crown to adorn the head. "Crown" here does not refer to the kind royalty wear, but to the wreath awarded winning athletes.

2:11 who overcomes. This identifies every Christian (*see note on v. 7*). **the second death.** The first death is only physical; the second is spiritual and eternal (cf. 20:14).

2:12 angel. *See note on 1:20.* **Pergamum.** Pergamum lit. means "citadel" and is the word from which we get parchment—a writing material developed from animal skin, which apparently was first developed in that area. Pergamum (modern Bergama) was built on a 1,000-foot hill in a broad, fertile plain about 20 mi. inland from the Aegean Sea. It had served as the capital of the Roman province of Asia Minor for over 250 years. It was an important religious center for the pagan cults of Athena, Asklepios, Dionysius (or Bacchus, the god of drunkenness), and Zeus. It was the first city in Asia to build a temple to Caesar (29 B.C.) and became the capital of the cult of Caesar worship. **two-edged sword.** *See note on 1:16.*

13 'I know where you dwell, where [A]Satan's throne is; and you hold fast My name, and did not deny [B]My faith even in the days of Antipas, My [C]witness, My [D]faithful one, who was killed among you, [E]where Satan dwells. 14 But [A]I have a few things against you, because you have there some who hold the [B]teaching of Balaam, who kept teaching Balak to put a stumbling block before the sons of Israel, [C]to eat things sacrificed to idols and to commit *acts of* immorality. 15 So you also have some who in the same way hold the teaching of the [A]Nicolaitans. 16 Therefore [A]repent; or else [B]I am coming to you quickly, and I will make war against them with [C]the sword of My mouth. 17 [A]He who has an ear, let him hear what the Spirit says to the churches. [A]To him who overcomes, to him I will give *some* of the hidden [B]manna, and I will give him a white stone, and a [C]new name written on the stone [D]which no one knows but he who receives it.'

MESSAGE TO THYATIRA

18 "And to the angel of the church in [A]Thyatira write:

[B]The Son of God, [C]who has [a]eyes like a flame of fire, and His feet are like burnished bronze, says this:

19 '[A]I know your deeds, and your love and faith and service and [a]perseverance, and that your [b]deeds of late are greater than [c]at first. 20 But [A]I have *this* against you, that you tolerate the woman [B]Jezebel, who calls herself a prophetess, and she teaches and leads My bond-servants astray so that they [C]commit *acts of* immorality and eat things sacrificed to idols. 21 [A]I gave her time to repent, and she [B]does not want to repent of her immorality. 22 Behold, I will throw her [a]on a bed *of sickness,* and those who [A]commit adultery with her into great tribulation, unless they repent of [b]her deeds. 23 And I will kill her children with [a]pestilence, and all the churches will know that I am He who [A]searches the [b]minds and hearts; and [B]I will give to each one of you according to your deeds. 24 But I say to you, the rest who are in [A]Thyatira, who do not hold this teaching, who have not known the [B]deep things of Satan, as they call them—I [C]place no other burden on you. 25 Nevertheless [A]what you have, hold fast [B]until I come. 26 [A]He who overcomes, and he who keeps My deeds [B]until the end, [C]TO HIM I WILL GIVE AUTHORITY OVER THE [a]NATIONS; 27 AND HE SHALL [a,A]RULE THEM WITH A ROD OF IRON, [B]AS THE VESSELS OF THE POTTER ARE BROKEN TO PIECES, as I also have received *authority* from My Father; 28 and I will give him [A]the morning star. 29 [A]He who has an ear, let him hear what the Spirit says to the churches.'

2:13 [A]Matt 4:10; Rev 2:24 [B]1 Tim 5:8; Rev 14:12 [C]Acts 22:20; Rev 1:5; 11:3; 17:6 [D]Rev 2:10; 12:11; 17:14 [E]Rev 2:9 2:14 [A]Rev 2:20 [B]Num 31:16; 2 Pet 2:15 [C]Num 25:1f; Acts 15:29; 1 Cor 10:20; Rev 2:20 2:15 [A]Rev 2:6 2:16 [A]Rev 2:5 [B]Rev 22:7, 20 [C]2 Thess 2:8; Rev 1:16 2:17 [A]Rev 2:7 [B]Ex 16:33; John 6:49f [C]Is 56:5; 62:2; 65:15 [D]Rev 14:3; 19:12 2:18 [a]Lit *His eyes* [A]Rev 1:11; 2:24 [B]Matt 4:3 [C]Rev 1:14f 2:19 [a]Or *steadfastness* [b]Lit *last deeds* [c]Lit *the first* [A]Rev 2:2 2:20 [A]Rev 2:14 [B]1 Kin 16:31; 21:25; 2 Kin 9:7, 22, 30 [C]Acts 15:29; 1 Cor 10:20; Rev 2:14 2:21 [A]Rom 2:4; 2 Pet 3:9 [B]Rom 2:5; Rev 9:20f; 16:9, 11 2:22 [a]Lit *into* [b]One early ms reads *their* [A]Rev 17:2; 18:9 2:23 [a]Lit *death* [b]Lit *kidneys,* i.e. inner man [A]Ps 7:9; 26:2; 139:1; Jer 11:20; 17:10; Matt 16:27; Luke 16:15; Acts 1:24; Rom 8:27 [B]Ps 62:12 2:24 [A]Rev 2:18 [B]1 Cor 2:10 [C]Acts 15:28 2:25 [A]Rev 3:11 [B]John 21:22 2:26 [a]Or *Gentiles* [A]Rev 2:7 [B]Matt 10:22; Heb 3:6 [C]Ps 2:8; Rev 3:21; 20:4 2:27 [a]Lit *shepherd* [A]Ps 2:9; Rev 12:5; 19:15 [B]Is 30:14; Jer 19:11 2:28 [A]1 John 3:2; Rev 22:16 2:29 [A]Rev 2:7

2:13 where Satan's throne is. The headquarters of satanic opposition and a Gentile base for false religions. On the acropolis in Pergamum was a huge, throne-shaped altar to Zeus. In addition, Asklepios, the god of healing, was the god most associated with Pergamum. His snake-like form is still the medical symbol today. The famous medical school connected to his temple mingled medicine with superstition. One prescription called for the worshiper to sleep on the temple floor, allowing snakes to crawl over his body and infuse him with their healing power. **Antipas.** Probably the pastor of the church. **faithful one.** Tradition says Antipas was burned to death inside a brass bull. "Faithful one," or "martyr," a transliteration of the Gr. word, means "witness." Because so many of the witnesses faithful to Christ were put to death, the word "martyr" developed its current definition.

2:14 teaching of Balaam. Balaam tried unsuccessfully to prostitute his prophetic gift and curse Israel for money offered him by Balak, king of Moab. So he devised a plot to have Moabite women seduce Israelite men into intermarriage. The result was the blasphemous union of Israel with fornication and idolatrous feasts (for the story of Balaam, see Nu 22–25). **things sacrificed to idols.** See Ac 15:19–29.

2:15 So you also. The teaching of the Nicolaitans led to the same behavior as Balaam's schemes. **teaching of the Nicolaitans.** *See note on v. 6.*

2:16 sword of My mouth. *See note on 1:16.*

2:17 overcomes. *See note on v. 7.* **hidden manna.** Just as Israel received manna, God promises to give the true believer the spiritual bread the unbelieving world cannot see: Jesus Christ (cf. Jn 6:51). **white stone.** When an athlete won in the games, he was often given, as part of his prize, a white stone which was an admission pass to the winner's celebration afterwards. This may picture the moment when the overcomer will receive his ticket to the eternal victory celebration in heaven. **new name.** A personal message from Christ to the ones He loves, which serves as their admission pass into eternal glory. It is so personal that only the person who receives it will know what it is.

2:18 angel. *See note on 1:20.* **Thyatira.** Located halfway between Pergamum and Sardis, this city had been under Roman rule for nearly 3 centuries (ca. 190 B.C.). Since the city was situated in a long valley that swept 40 mi. to Pergamum, it had no natural defenses and had a long history of being destroyed and rebuilt. Originally populated by soldiers of Alexander the Great, it was little more than a military outpost to guard Pergamum. Lydia came from this city on business and was converted under Paul's ministry (Ac 16:14, 15). **eyes like a flame of fire.** *See note on 1:14.* **feet are like burnished bronze.** Cf. 19:15; *see note on 1:15.*

2:20 Jezebel. Probably a pseudonym for a woman who influenced the church in the way Jezebel influenced the OT Jews into idolatry and immorality (cf. 1Ki 21:25, 26). **immorality and eat things sacrificed to idols.** Cf. Ac 15:19–29; *see note on v. 14.*

2:22 bed *of sickness.* Lit. "bed." Having given this woman time to repent, God was to judge her upon a bed. Since she used a luxurious bed to commit her immorality, and the reclining couch at the idol feast to eat things offered to false gods, He was to give her a bed in hell where she would lie forever.

2:23 her children. The church was about 40 years old as John wrote, and her teaching had produced a second generation, advocating the same debauchery. **who searches the minds and hearts.** God has perfect, intimate knowledge of every human heart; no evil can be hidden from Him (Ps 7:9; Pr 24:12; Jer 11:20; 17:10; 20:12). **according to your deeds.** Always the basis for future judgment (20:12, 13; Mt 16:27; Ro 2:6). Deeds or works do not save (Eph 2:8, 9), but they do evidence salvation (Jas 2:14–26).

2:24 the deep things of Satan. This unbelievable libertinism and license was the fruit of pre-gnostic teaching that one was free to engage and explore the sphere of Satan and participate in evil with the body without harming the spirit (see Introduction to 1 John: Background and Setting).

2:26 overcomes. *See note on v. 7.*

2:27 rule them with a rod of iron. Lit. "shepherd them with an iron rod." During the millennial kingdom, Christ will enforce His will and protect His sheep with His iron scepter from any who would seek to harm them (cf. Ps 2:9).

2:28 the morning star. John later reveals Christ to be "the bright morning star" (22:16). Although the morning star has already dawned in our hearts (2Pe 1:19), someday we will have Him in His fullness.

MESSAGE TO SARDIS

3 "To the angel of the church in [A]Sardis write:
He who has [B]the seven Spirits of God and [C]the
seven stars, says this: '[D]I know your deeds, that you
have a name that you are alive, [a]but you are [E]dead.
2 Wake up, and strengthen the things that remain,
which were about to die; for I have not found your
deeds completed in the sight of My God. 3 So [A]remem-
ber [a]what you have received and heard; and keep *it,*
and [A]repent. Therefore if you do not wake up, [A]I will
come [B]like a thief, and you will not know at [C]what
hour I will come to you. 4 But you have a few [a,A]people
in [B]Sardis who have not [C]soiled their garments; and
they will walk with Me [D]in white, for they are worthy.
5 [A]He who overcomes will thus be clothed in [B]white
garments; and I will not [C]erase his name from the
book of life, and [D]I will confess his name before My
Father and before His angels. 6 [A]He who has an ear,
let him hear what the Spirit says to the churches.'

MESSAGE TO PHILADELPHIA

7 "And to the angel of the church in [A]Philadel-
phia write:
[B]He who is holy, [C]who is true, who has [D]the key
of David, who opens and no one will shut, and who
shuts and no one opens, says this:
8 '[A]I know your [a]deeds. Behold, I have put before
you [B]an open door which no one can shut, because
you have a little power, and have kept My word,
and [C]have not denied My name. 9 Behold, I [a]will
cause *those* of [A]the synagogue of Satan, who say
that they are Jews and are not, but lie—I will make
them [B]come and bow down [b]at your feet, and *make
them* know that [C]I have loved you. 10 Because you
have [A]kept the word of [B]My [a]perseverance, [C]I also
will keep you from the hour of [b,D]testing, that *hour*
which is about to come upon the whole [c,E]world, to
[d]test [F]those who dwell on the earth. 11 [A]I am coming
quickly; [B]hold fast what you have, so that no one
will take your [C]crown. 12 [A]He who overcomes, I will
make him a [B]pillar in the temple of My God, and he
will not go out from it anymore; and I will write
on him the [C]name of My God, and [D]the name of the
city of My God, [E]the new Jerusalem, which comes
down out of heaven from My God, and My [F]new
name. 13 [A]He who has an ear, let him hear what the
Spirit says to the churches.'

MESSAGE TO LAODICEA

14 "To the angel of the church in [A]Laodicea write:
[B]The Amen, [C]the faithful and true Witness, [D]the
[a]Beginning of the creation of God, says this:

3:1 [a]Lit *and* [A]Rev 1:11 [B]Rev 1:4 [C]Rev 1:16 [D]Rev 2:2; 3:8, 15 [E]1 Tim 5:6 3:3 [a]Lit *how* [A]Rev 2:5 [B]1 Thess 5:2; 2 Pet 3:10; Rev 16:15 [C]Matt 24:43; Luke 12:39f 3:4 [a]Lit *names* [A]Rev 11:13 [B]Rev 1:11 [C]Jude 23 [D]Eccl 9:8; Rev 3:5, 18; 4:4; 6:11; 7:9, 13f; 19:8, 14 3:5 [A]Rev 2:7 [B]Rev 3:4 [C]Ex 32:32f; Ps 69:28; Luke 10:20; Rev 13:8; 17:8; 20:12, 15; 21:27 [D]Matt 10:32; Luke 12:8 3:6 [A]Rev 2:7 3:7 [A]Rev 1:11 [B]Rev 6:10 [C]1 John 5:20; Rev 3:14; 19:11 [D]Job 12:14; Is 22:22; Matt 16:19; Rev 1:18 3:8 [a]Or *deeds (behold...shut), that you have* [A]Rev 3:1 [B]Acts 14:27 [C]Rev 2:13 3:9 [a]Lit *give* [b]Lit *before* [A]Rev 2:9 [B]Is 45:14; 49:23; 60:14 [C]Is 43:4; John 17:23 3:10 [a]Or *steadfastness* [b]Or *temptation* [c]Lit *inhabited earth* [d]Or *tempt* [A]John 17:6; Rev 3:8 [B]Rev 1:9 [C]2 Tim 2:12; 2 Pet 2:9 [D]Rev 2:10 [E]Matt 24:14; Rev 16:14 [F]Rev 6:10; 8:13; 11:10; 13:8, 14; 17:8 3:11 [A]Rev 1:3; 22:7, 12, 20 [B]Rev 2:25 [C]Rev 2:10 3:12 [A]Rev 3:5 [B]1 Kin 7:21; Jer 1:18; Gal 2:9 [C]Rev 14:1; 22:4 [D]Ezek 48:35; Rev 21:2 [E]Gal 4:26; Heb 13:14; Rev 21:2, 10 [F]Is 62:2; Rev 2:17 3:13 [A]Rev 3:6 3:14 [a]I.e. Origin or Source [A]Rev 1:11 [B]2 Cor 1:20 [C]Rev 1:5; 3:7 [D]Gen 49:3; Deut 21:17; Prov 8:22; John 1:3; Col 1:18; Rev 21:6; 22:13

3:1 angel. Messenger or pastor (*see note on 1:20*). **Sardis.** Situated on a natural acropolis rising 1,500 feet above the valley floor, the city (modern Sart) was nearly impregnable. Around 1200 B.C. it gained prominence as the capital of the Lydian kingdom. Its primary industry was harvesting wool, dying it, and making garments from it. The famous author, Aesop, came from Sardis, and tradition says that Melito, a member of the church in Sardis, wrote the first-ever commentary on certain passages in the book of Revelation. The church in Sardis was dead; that is, basically populated by unredeemed, unregenerate people. **seven Spirits.** *See note on 1:4.* **seven stars.** The pastors of these 7 churches (*see notes on 1:16, 20*).

3:3 come like a thief. Here the reference is not to Christ's second coming (cf. 16:15; 1Th 5:2; 2Pe 3:10), but to His sudden and unexpected coming to His unrepentant, dead church to inflict harm and destruction.

3:4 who have not soiled their garments. Soiled means "to smear," "to pollute," or "to stain," and garments refer to character. There were a few whose character was still godly (cf. Jude 23). **in white.** The white garments of all the redeemed (cf. 6:11; 7:9, 13; 19:8, 14) speak of holiness and purity. Such white robes are reserved for Christ (Mt 17:2; Mk 9:3), holy angels (Mt 28:3; Mk 16:5), and the glorified church (19:8, 14). In the ancient world, white robes were commonly worn at festivals and celebrations.

3:5 overcomes. All true Christians (*see note on 2:7*). **book of life.** A divine journal records the names of all those whom God has chosen to save and who, therefore, are to possess eternal life (13:8; 17:8; 20:12, 15; 21:27; cf. Da 12:1; Lk 10:20). Under no circumstances will He erase those names (*see note on Php 4:3*), as city officials often did of undesirable people on their rolls.

3:7 angel. *See note on 1:20.* **Philadelphia.** Located on a hillside about 30 mi. SE of Sardis, the city (modern Alashehir) was founded around 190 B.C. by Attalus II, king of Pergamum. His unusual devotion to his brother earned the city its name, "brotherly love." The city was an important commercial stop on a major trade route called the Imperial Post Road, a first-century mail route. Although Scripture does not mention this church elsewhere, it was probably the fruit of Paul's extended ministry in Ephesus (cf. Ac 19:10). **holy ... true.** A common description in this book (4:8; 6:10; 15:3; 16:7; 19:2, 11). Christ shares the holy, sinless, pure nature of His Father (Ps 16:10; Is 6:3; 40:25; 43:15; Hab 3:3; Mk 1:11, 24; Jn 6:69; Ac 3:14); that is, He is absolutely pure and separate from sin. "True" can refer both to one who speaks truth, and who is genuine or authentic as opposed to fake. **the key of David.** Christ has the sovereign authority to control entrance into the kingdom (Is 22:22; cf. Mt 16:19; Jn 14:6). In 1:18 He is pictured holding the keys to death and hell—here, the keys to salvation and blessing.

3:8 open door. This is either admission into the kingdom (see v. 7), or an opportunity for service (cf. 1Co 16:9; 2Co 2:12; Col 4:3).

3:9 synagogue of Satan. *See note on 2:9.* **who say that they are Jews.** *See note on 2:9.*

3:10 keep you from the hour of testing. Christ's description—an event still future that for a short time severely tests the whole world—must refer to the time of tribulation, the 7-year period before Christ's earthly kingdom is consummated, featuring the unleashing of divine wrath in judgments expressed as seals, trumpets, and bowls. This period is described in detail throughout chaps. 6–19. The latter half is called "the great tribulation" (7:14; Mt 24:21) and is identified as to time in 11:2, 3; 12:6, 14; 13:5. The verb "keep" is followed by a preposition whose normal meaning is "from" or "out of"—this phrase, "keep ... from" supports the pretribulational rapture of the church (*see notes on Jn 14:1–3; 1Co 15:51, 52; 1Th 4:13–17*). This period is the same as Daniel's 70th week (*see notes on Da 9:24–27*) and "the time of Jacob's distress" (*see notes on Jer 30:7*).

3:11 I am coming quickly. This isn't the threatening temporal judgment described in v. 3; 2:5, 16, nor the final judgment of chap. 19; it is a hopeful event. Christ will return to take His church out of the hour of trial (*see note on 2Th 2:1*).

3:12 He who overcomes. All Christians (*see note on 2:7*). **a pillar.** Believers will enjoy an unshakable, eternal, secure place in the presence of God. **temple.** *See note on 7:15.* **write ... name of My God.** In biblical times, one's name spoke of his character. Writing His name on us speaks of imprinting His character on us and identifying us as belonging to Him. **new Jerusalem.** The capital city of heaven (*see notes on 21:1–27*). The overcomer will enjoy eternal citizenship. **My new name.** At the moment we see Christ, whatever we may have called Him and understood by that name will pale in the reality of what we see. And He will give us a new, eternal name by which we will know Him.

3:14 angel. The pastor-messenger designated to deliver this letter (*see note on 1:20*). **Laodicea.** Located in the Lycus River Valley, the SW area of Phrygia, Laodicea became

15 '[A]I know your deeds, that you are neither cold
nor hot; [B]I wish that you were cold or hot. 16 So because you are lukewarm, and neither hot nor cold,
I will [a]spit you out of My mouth. 17 Because you say,
"[A]I am rich, and have become wealthy, and have
need of nothing," and you do not know that you
are wretched and miserable and poor and blind
and naked, 18 I advise you to [A]buy from Me [B]gold
refined by fire so that you may become rich, and
[C]white garments so that you may clothe yourself,
and *that* [D]the shame of your nakedness will not be
revealed; and eye salve to anoint your eyes so that
you may see. 19 [A]Those whom I love, I reprove and
discipline; therefore be zealous and [B]repent. 20 Behold, I stand [A]at the door and [B]knock; if anyone
hears My voice and opens the door, [C]I will come
in to him and will dine with him, and he with Me.
21 [A]He who overcomes, I will grant to him [B]to sit
down with Me on My throne, as [C]I also overcame
and sat down with My Father on His throne. 22 [A]He
who has an ear, let him hear what the Spirit says
to the churches.' "

SCENE IN HEAVEN

4 After [A]these things I looked, and behold, [B]a door
standing open in heaven, and the first voice
which I had heard, [C]like *the sound* of a trumpet
speaking with me, said, "[D]Come up here, and I will
[E]show you what must take place after these things."
2 Immediately I was [a,A]in the Spirit; and behold, [B]a
throne was standing in heaven, and [C]One sitting
on the throne. 3 And He who was sitting *was* like
a [A]jasper stone and a [B]sardius in appearance; and
there was a [a,C]rainbow around the throne, like an
[D]emerald in appearance. 4 [A]Around the throne *were*
[B]twenty-four thrones; and upon the thrones *I saw*
[C]twenty-four elders [D]sitting, clothed in [E]white garments, and [F]golden crowns on their heads.

THE THRONE AND WORSHIP OF THE CREATOR

5 Out from the throne come [A]flashes of lightning
and sounds and peals of thunder. And *there were*
[B]seven lamps of fire burning before the throne,
which are [C]the seven Spirits of God; 6 and before the

3:15 [A]Rev 3:1 [B]Rom 12:11 3:16 [a]Lit *vomit* 3:17 [A]Hos 12:8; Zech 11:5; Matt 5:3; 1 Cor 4:8 3:18 [A]Is 55:1; Matt 13:44 [B]1 Pet 1:7 [C]Rev 3:4 [D]Rev 16:15 3:19 [A]Prov 3:12; 1 Cor 11:32; Heb 12:6 [B]Rev 2:5 3:20 [A]Matt 24:33; James 5:9 [B]Luke 12:36; John 10:3 [C]John 14:23 3:21 [A]Rev 2:7 [B]Matt 19:28; 2 Tim 2:12; Rev 2:26; 20:4 [C]John 16:33; Rev 5:5; 6:2; 17:14 3:22 [A]Rev 2:7 4:1 [A]Rev 1:12ff, 19 [B]Ezek 1:1; Rev 19:11 [C]Rev 1:10 [D]Rev 11:12 [E]Rev 1:19; 22:6 4:2 [a]Or *in spirit* [A]Rev 1:10 [B]1 Kin 22:19; Is 6:1; Ezek 1:26; Dan 7:9; Rev 4:9f [C]Rev 4:9 4:3 [a]Or *halo* [A]Rev 21:11 [B]Rev 21:20 [C]Ezek 1:28; Rev 10:1 [D]Rev 21:19 4:4 [A]Rev 4:6; 5:11; 7:11 [B]Rev 11:16 [C]Rev 4:10; 5:6, 8, 14; 19:4 [D]Matt 19:28; Rev 20:4 [E]Rev 3:18 [F]Rev 4:10 4:5 [A]Ex 19:16; Rev 8:5; 11:19; 16:18 [B]Ex 25:37; Zech 4:2 [C]Rev 1:4

the wealthiest, most important commercial center in the region. It was primarily known for 3 industries: banking, wool, and medicine (notably its eye salve). An inadequate local water supply forced the city to build an underground aqueduct. All 3 industries, as well as the inadequate water supply, played a major part in this letter. The church began through the ministry of Epaphras, while Paul was ministering in Ephesus (cf. Col 1:7; Paul never personally visited Laodicea). **The Amen.** A common biblical expression signifying certainty and veracity (cf. Is 65:16, "the God of truth"). According to 2Co 1:20, all the promises of God are fulfilled in Christ; that is, all God's promises and unconditional covenants are guaranteed and affirmed by the person and work of Jesus Christ. **faithful and true Witness.** He is a completely trustworthy and perfectly accurate witness to the truth of God (Jn 14:6). **Beginning of the creation.** This corrects a heresy, apparently present in Laodicea as in Colossae, that Christ was a created being (cf. Col 1:15–20). Instead, He is the "Beginning" (lit. "beginner, originator, initiator") of creation (cf. Jn 1:3) and the "firstborn of creation"; that is, the most preeminent, supreme person ever born (Col 1:15). As a man, He had a beginning, but as God, He was the beginning. Sadly, this heresy concerning the person of Christ had produced an unregenerate church in Laodicea.

3:16 lukewarm. I.e., tepid. Nearby Hierapolis was famous for its hot springs, and Colossae for its cold, refreshing mountain stream. But Laodicea had dirty, tepid water that flowed for miles through an underground aqueduct. Visitors, unaccustomed to it, immediately spat it out. The church at Laodicea was neither cold, openly rejecting Christ, nor hot, filled with spiritual zeal. Instead, its members were lukewarm, hypocrites professing to know Christ, but not truly belonging to Him (cf. Mt 7:21ff.). **I will spit you out of My mouth.** Just like the dirty, tepid water of Laodicea, these self-deceived hypocrites sickened Christ.

3:18 gold ... white garments ... eye salve. *See note on v. 14.* He was offering them the spiritual counterparts to their 3 major industries. Each item was a way to refer to genuine salvation.

3:19 Those whom I love, I reprove and discipline. Both vv. 18, 20 indicate that Christ was speaking here to unbelievers. God certainly loves the unconverted (cf. Jn 3:16). And "reprove" and "discipline" often refer to God's convicting and punishing the unregenerate (Mt 18:17; 1Co 14:24; 2Ti 2:25).

3:20 I stand at the door and knock. Rather than allowing for the common interpretation of Christ's knocking on a person's heart, the context demands that Christ was seeking to enter this church that bore His name but lacked a single true believer. This poignant letter was His knocking. If one member would recognize his spiritual bankruptcy and respond in saving faith, He would enter the church.

3:21 overcomes. All true Christians (*see note on 2:7*). **sit down with Me on My throne.** A figurative expression meaning that we will share the privilege and authority that Christ enjoys as we reign with Him (1:6; Mt 19:28; Lk 22:29, 30).

4:1 Come up here. This is not a veiled reference to the rapture of the church, but a command for John to be temporarily transported to heaven "in the Spirit" (*see note on 1:10*) to receive revelation about future events. **what must take place after these things.** According to the outline given in 1:19, this begins the third and final section of the book, describing the events that will follow the church age.

4:2 I was in the Spirit. *See note on 1:10.* **throne.** Not so much a piece of furniture, but a symbol of sovereign rule and authority (7:15; 11:19; 16:17, 18; cf. Is 6:1). It is the focus of chap. 4, occurring 14 times, 11 times referring to God's throne.

4:3 jasper. John later describes this stone as "crystal-clear" (21:11), probably referring to a diamond, which refracts all the colors of the spectrum in wondrous brilliance. **sardius.** A fiery bright ruby stone named for the city near which it was found. **emerald.** A cool, emerald-green hue dominates the multicolored rainbow surrounding God's throne (cf. Eze 1:28). From the time of Noah, the rainbow became a sign of God's faithfulness to His Word, His promises, and His Noahic covenant (Ge 9:12–17).

4:4 twenty-four elders. Their joint rule with Christ, their white garments, and their golden crowns all seem to indicate that these 24 represent the redeemed (vv. 9–11; 5:5–14; 7:11–17; 11:16–18; 14:3; 19:4). The question is which redeemed? Not Israel, since the nation is not yet saved, glorified, and coronated. That is still to come at this point in the events of the end. Their resurrection and glory will come at the end of the 7-year tribulation time (cf. Da 12:1–3). Tribulation saints aren't yet saved (7:9, 10). Only one group will be complete and glorified at that point—the church. Here elders represent the church, which sings the song of redemption (5:8–10). They are the overcomers who have their crowns and live in the place prepared for them, where they have gone with Jesus (cf. Jn 14:1–4).

4:5 lightning ... thunder. Not the fury of nature, but the firestorm of righteous fury about to come from an awesome, powerful God upon a sinful world (8:5; 11:19; 16:18). **seven Spirits of God.** The Holy Spirit (*see note on 1:4*).

4:6 sea of glass. There is no sea in heaven (21:1), but the crystal pavement that serves as the floor of God's throne stretches out like a great, glistening sea (cf. Ex 24:10; Eze 1:22). **four living creatures.** Lit. "four living ones or beings." These are the cherubim (sing., cherub), those angels frequently referred to in the OT in connection with God's presence, power, and holiness. Although John's description is not identical to Ezekiel's, they are obviously both referring to the same supernatural and indescribable beings (Pss 80:1;

throne *there was something* like a [A]sea of glass, like
crystal; and in the [a]center and [B]around the throne,
[C]four living creatures [D]full of eyes in front and behind. 7 [A]The first creature *was* like a lion, and the
second creature like a calf, and the third creature
had a face like that of a man, and the fourth creature *was* like a flying eagle. 8 And the [A]four living
creatures, each one of them having [B]six wings, are
[C]full of eyes around and within; and [D]day and night
[a]they do not cease to say,

> "[E]HOLY, HOLY, HOLY *is* THE [F]LORD GOD, THE
> ALMIGHTY, [G]WHO WAS AND WHO IS AND
> WHO [b]IS TO COME."

9 And when the living creatures give glory and
honor and thanks to Him who [A]sits on the throne,
to [B]Him who lives forever and ever, 10 the [A]twen-
ty-four elders will [B]fall down before Him who [C]sits
on the throne, and will worship [D]Him who lives
forever and ever, and will cast their [E]crowns before
the throne, saying,

11 "[A]Worthy are You, our Lord and our God,
to receive glory and honor and power;
for You [B]created all things, and because
of Your will they [a]existed, and were
created."

THE BOOK WITH SEVEN SEALS

5 I saw [a]in the right hand of Him who [A]sat on the
throne a [b,B]book written inside and on the back,
[C]sealed up with seven seals. 2 And I saw a [A]strong
angel proclaiming with a loud voice, "Who is worthy to open the [a]book and to break its seals?" 3 And
no one [A]in heaven or on the earth or under the earth
was able to open the [a]book or to look into it. 4 Then
I *began* to weep greatly because no one was found
worthy to open the [a]book or to look into it; 5 and one
of the elders *said to me, "Stop weeping; behold, the
[A]Lion that is [B]from the tribe of Judah, the [C]Root of
David, has overcome so as to open the [a]book and its
seven seals."

6 And I saw [a]between the throne (with the four living
creatures) and [A]the elders a [B]Lamb standing, as if [C]slain,
having seven [D]horns and [E]seven eyes, which are [F]the
seven Spirits of God, sent out into all the earth. 7 And
He came and took [A]the book out of the right hand of
Him who [A]sat on the throne. 8 When He had taken the
[a]book, the [A]four living creatures and the [B]twenty-four
elders [C]fell down before the [D]Lamb, each one holding
a [E]harp and [F]golden bowls full of incense, which are
the [G]prayers of the [b]saints. 9 And they *sang a [A]new
song, saying,

> "[B]Worthy are You to take the [a]book and
> to break its seals; for You were [C]slain,

4:6 [a]Lit *middle of the throne and around* [A]Ezek 1:22; Rev 15:2; 21:18, 21 [B]Rev 4:4 [C]Ezek 1:5; Rev 4:8f; 5:6; 6:1, 6; 7:11; 14:3; 15:7; 19:4 [D]Ezek 1:18; 10:12 4:7 [A]Ezek 1:10; 10:14 4:8 [a]Lit *they have no rest, saying,* [b]Or *is coming* [A]Ezek 1:5; Rev 4:6, 9; 5:6; 6:1, 6; 7:11; 14:3; 15:7; 19:4 [B]Is 6:2 [C]Ezek 1:18; 10:12 [D]Rev 14:11 [E]Is 6:3 [F]Rev 1:8 [G]Rev 1:4 4:9 [A]Ps 47:8; Is 6:1; Rev 4:2 [B]Deut 32:40; Dan 4:34; 12:7; Rev 10:6; 15:7 4:10 [A]Rev 4:4 [B]Rev 5:8, 14; 7:11; 11:16; 19:4 [C]Ps 47:8; Is 6:1; Rev 4:2 [D]Deut 32:40; Dan 4:34; 12:7 [E]Rev 4:4; 10:6; 15:7 4:11 [a]Lit *were* [A]Rev 1:6; 5:12 [B]Acts 14:15; Rev 10:6; 14:7 5:1 [a]Lit *upon* [b]Or *scroll* [A]Rev 4:9; 5:7, 13 [B]Ezek 2:9, 10 [C]Is 29:11; Dan 12:4 5:2 [a]Or *scroll* [A]Rev 10:1; 18:21 5:3 [a]Or *scroll* [A]Phil 2:10; Rev 5:13 5:4 [a]Or *scroll* 5:5 [a]Or *scroll* [A]Gen 49:9 [B]Heb 7:14 [C]Is 11:1, 10; Rom 15:12; Rev 22:16 5:6 [a]Lit *in the middle of the throne and of the four living creatures, and in the middle of the elders* [A]Rev 4:4; 5:8, 14 [B]John 1:29; Rev 5:8, 12f; 13:8 [C]Rev 5:9, 12; 13:8 [D]Dan 8:3f [E]Zech 3:9; 4:10 [F]Rev 1:4 5:7 [A]Rev 5:1 5:8 [a]Or *scroll* [b]Or *holy ones* [A]Rev 4:6; 5:6, 11, 14 [B]Rev 4:4; 5:14 [C]Rev 4:10 [D]John 1:29; Rev 5:6, 12f; 13:8 [E]Rev 14:2; 15:2 [F]Rev 15:7 [G]Ps 141:2; Rev 8:3f 5:9 [a]Or *scroll* [A]Ps 33:3; 40:3; 98:1; 149:1; Is 42:10; Rev 14:3; 15:3 [B]Rev 4:11 [C]Rev 5:6, 12; 13:8

99:1; *see notes on Eze 1:4–25; 10:15*). **full of eyes.** Although not omniscient—an attribute reserved for God alone—these angels have a comprehensive knowledge and perception. Nothing escapes their scrutiny (cf. v. 8).

4:7 first ... like a lion. In what is obviously intended as symbolic language, John compares these 4 beings with 4 of God's earthly creations. Ezekiel indicates that every cherub has these 4 attributes. The likeness to a lion symbolizes strength and power. **second ... like a calf.** The image of a calf demonstrates that these beings render humble service to God. **third ... face like that of a man.** Their likeness to man shows they are rational beings. **fourth ... like a flying eagle.** The cherubim fulfill their service to God with the swiftness of eagles' wings.

4:8 full of eyes. *See note on v. 6.* **Holy, holy, holy.** Often God is extolled for His holiness in this 3-fold form, because it is the summation of all that He is—His most salient attribute (*see note on Is 6:3*). **who was and who is and who is to come.** *See note on 1:4.*

4:10 cast their crowns. Aware that God alone is responsible for the rewards they have received, they divest themselves of all honor and cast it at the feet of their King (*see note on 2:10*).

4:11 You created all things. It is the Creator God who set out to redeem His creation.

5:1 a book. *See note on 1:11.* **written inside and on the back.** This is typical of various kinds of contracts in the ancient world, including deeds, marriage contracts, rental and lease agreements, and wills. The inside of the scroll contained all the details of the contract, and the outside—or back—contained a summary of the document. In this case it almost certainly is a deed—the title deed to the earth (cf. Jer 32:7ff.) **sealed up with seven seals.** Romans sealed their wills 7 times—on the edge at each roll—to prevent unauthorized entry. Hebrew title deeds required a minimum of 3 witnesses and 3 separate seals, with more important transactions requiring more witnesses and seals.

5:2 strong angel. The identity of this angel is uncertain, but it may refer to the angel Gabriel, whose name means "strength of God" (Da 8:16).

5:3 in heaven or on the earth or under the earth. A common biblical expression denoting the entire universe and not intended to teach 3 precise divisions.

5:5 the Lion ... from the tribe of Judah. One of the earliest titles for the Messiah (*see notes on Ge 49:8–12*), it speaks of His fierceness and strength, which although glimpsed in His first coming, do not appear in their fullness until the moment anticipated here. **the Root of David.** Another clearly messianic title (*see notes on Is 11:1–10*), it anticipates His being a descendant of David, who with devastating force will compel the wicked of the earth to succumb to His authority.

5:6 Lamb. Hearing of a lion, John turns to see a lamb (lit. "a little, pet lamb"). God required the Jews to bring the Passover lamb into their houses for 4 days, essentially making it a pet, before it was to be violently slain (Ex 12:3, 6). This is the true Passover Lamb, God's Son (cf. Is 53:7; Jer 11:19; Jn 1:29). **as if slain.** The scars from its slaughter are still clearly visible, but it is standing—it is alive. **seven horns.** In Scripture, horns always symbolize power, because in the animal kingdom they are used to exert power and inflict wounds in combat. Seven horns signify complete or perfect power. Unlike other defenseless lambs, this One has complete, sovereign power. **seven eyes ... seven Spirits.** Cf. 4:5; *see note on 1:4.*

5:8 harp. These ancient stringed instruments not only accompanied the songs of God's people (1Ch 25:6; Ps 33:2), but also accompanied prophecy (cf. 1Sa 10:5). The 24 elders, representative of the redeemed church, played their harps in praise and in a symbolic indication that all the prophets had said was about to be fulfilled. **bowls full of incense.** These golden, wide-mouth saucers were common in the tabernacle and temple. Incense was a normal part of the OT ritual. Priests stood twice daily before the inner veil of the temple and burned incense so that the smoke would carry into the Holy of Holies and be swept into the nostrils of God. That symbolized the people's prayers rising to Him. **prayers of the saints.** Specifically, these prayers represent all that the redeemed have ever prayed concerning ultimate and final redemption.

5:9 new song. Cf. 15:3. The OT is filled with references to a new song that flows from a heart that has experienced God's redemption

and [D]purchased for God with Your blood
men from [E]every tribe and tongue and
people and nation. 10 You have made
them *to be* a [A]kingdom and [A]priests to
our God; and they will [B]reign upon the
earth."

ANGELS EXALT THE LAMB

11 Then I looked, and I heard the voice of many
angels [A]around the throne and the [B]living creatures and the [C]elders; and the number of them was
[D]myriads of myriads, and thousands of thousands,
12 saying with a loud voice,

"[A]Worthy is the [B]Lamb that was [B]slain to
receive power and riches and wisdom
and might and honor and glory and
blessing."

13 And [A]every created thing which is in heaven and
on the earth and under the earth and on the sea,
and all things in them, I heard saying,

"To Him who [B]sits on the throne, and to
the [C]Lamb, [D]*be* blessing and honor and
glory and dominion forever and ever."

14 And the [A]four living creatures kept saying,
"[B]Amen." And the [C]elders [D]fell down and worshiped.

THE FIRST SEAL—RIDER ON WHITE HORSE

6 Then I saw when the [A]Lamb broke one of the
[B]seven seals, and I heard one of the [C]four living creatures saying as with a [D]voice of thunder,
"Come[a]." 2 I looked, and behold, a [A]white horse, and
he who sat on it had a bow; and [B]a crown was given
to him, and he went out [C]conquering and to conquer.

THE SECOND SEAL—WAR

3 When He broke the second seal, I heard the [A]sec-
ond living creature saying, "Come[a]." 4 And another,
[A]a red horse, went out; and to him who sat on it, it
was granted to [B]take peace from the earth, and that
men would slay one another; and a great sword
was given to him.

THE THIRD SEAL—FAMINE

5 When He broke the third seal, I heard the [A]third
living creature saying, "Come[a]." I looked, and behold, a
[B]black horse; and he who sat on it had a [C]pair of scales
in his hand. 6 And I heard *something* like a voice in the
center of the [A]four living creatures saying, "A [a]quart of
wheat for a [b]denarius, and three [a]quarts of barley for
a [b]denarius; and [B]do not damage the oil and the wine."

THE FOURTH SEAL—DEATH

7 When the Lamb broke the fourth seal, I heard the
voice of the [A]fourth living creature saying, "Come[a]." 8 I
looked, and behold, an [a,A]ashen horse; and he who sat

5:9 [D]1 Cor 6:20; Rev 14:3f [E]Dan 3:4; 5:19; Rev 7:9; 10:11; 11:9; 13:7; 14:6; 17:15 5:10 [A]Rev 1:6 [B]Rev 3:21; 20:4 5:11 [A]Rev 4:4 [B]Rev 4:6; 5:6, 8, 14 [C]Rev 4:4; 5:6, 14 [D]Dan 7:10; Heb 12:22; Jude 14; Rev 9:16 5:12 [A]Rev 1:6; 4:11; 5:9 [B]John 1:29; Rev 5:6, 13; 13:8 5:13 [A]Phil 2:10; Rev 5:3 [B]Rev 5:1 [C]John 1:29; Rev 5:6, 12f; 13:8 [D]Rom 11:36; Rev 1:6 5:14 [A]Rev 4:6; 5:6, 8, 11 [B]1 Cor 14:16; Rev 7:12; 19:4 [C]Rev 4:4; 5:6, 8 [D]Rev 4:10 6:1 [a]One early ms reads *and see* [A]John 1:29; Rev 5:6, 12f; 13:8 [B]Rev 5:1 [C]Rev 4:6; 5:6, 8, 11, 14 [D]Rev 14:2; 19:6 6:2 [A]Zech 1:8; 6:3f; Rev 19:11 [B]Zech 6:11; Rev 9:7; 14:14; 19:12 [C]Rev 3:21 6:3 [a]One early ms reads *and see* [A]Rev 4:7 6:4 [A]Zech 1:8; 6:2 [B]Matt 10:34 6:5 [a]One early ms reads *and see* [A]Rev 4:7 [B]Zech 6:2, 6 [C]Ezek 4:16 6:6 [a]Gr *choenix;* i.e. a dry measure almost equal to a qt [b]The denarius was equivalent to a day's wages [A]Rev 4:6f [B]Rev 7:3; 9:4 6:7 [a]One early ms reads *and see* [A]Rev 4:7 6:8 [a]Or *sickly pale* [A]Zech 6:3

or deliverance (cf. 14:3; Pss 33:3; 96:1; 144:9). This new song anticipates the final, glorious redemption that God is about to begin. **purchased for God with Your blood.** The sacrificial death of Christ on behalf of sinners made Him worthy to take the scroll (cf. 1Co 6:20; 7:23; 2Co 5:21; Gal 3:13; 1Pe 1:18, 19; 2Pe 2:1).

5:10 a kingdom and priests. *See note on 1:6.* **reign upon the earth.** *See note on 20:2.*

5:11 myriads of myriads, and thousands of thousands. The number is to express an amount beyond calculation. The Gr. expression can also be translated "innumerable" or "many thousands" (Lk 12:1; Heb 12:22).

5:12 power . . . and blessing. This doxology records 7 qualities intrinsic to God and to the Lamb that demand our praise.

5:13 in heaven and on the earth and under the earth. *See note on v. 3.*

5:14 four living creatures. *See note on 4:6.* **elders.** *See note on 4:4.*

6:1–19:21 This lengthy section details the judgments and events of the time of tribulation (*see notes on 3:10*) from its beginning with the opening of the first seal (vv. 1, 2) through the 7 seal, trumpet, and bowl judgments to the return of Christ to destroy the ungodly (19:11–21).

6:1 the seven seals. In chap. 5, Christ was the only One found worthy to open the little scroll—the title deed to the universe. As He breaks the 7 seals that secure the scroll, each seal unleashes a new demonstration of God's judgment on the earth in the future tribulation period (*see notes on 5:1; Mt 24:3–9*). These seal judgments include all the judgments to the end. The seventh seal contains the 7 trumpets; the seventh trumpet contains the 7 bowls.

6:2 white horse. The animal represents an unparalleled time of world peace—a false peace that is to be short-lived (*see note on v. 4*). This peace will be ushered in by a series of false messiahs, culminating with the Antichrist (Mt 24:3–5). **he who sat on it.** The 4 horses and their riders do not represent specific individuals, but forces. Some, however, identify this rider with Antichrist. Although he will be the leading figure, John's point is that the entire world will follow him, being obsessed with pursuing this false peace. **bow.** The bow is a symbol of war, but the absence of arrows implies that this victory is a bloodless one—a peace won by covenant and agreement, not by war (cf. Da 9:24–27). **crown.** This word refers to the kind of laurel wreath awarded winning athletes. It "was given to him." Antichrist becomes king, elected by the world's inhabitants regardless of the cost, and will conquer the entire earth in a bloodless coup.

6:4 another, a red horse. Its blood-red appearance speaks of the holocaust of war (cf. Mt 24:7). God will grant this horse and its rider the power to create worldwide war. But as horrible as this judgment is, it will be only the "birth pangs," the beginning pains of God's wrath (Mt 24:8; Mk 13:7, 8; Lk 21:9). ***men* would slay one another.** Violent slaughter will become commonplace. **sword.** Not the long, broad sword, but the shorter, more easily maneuvered one that assassins often used and that soldiers carried into battle. It depicts assassination, revolt, massacre, and wholesale slaughter (cf. Da 8:24).

6:5 black horse. Black signifies famine (cf. La 5:8–10). Worldwide war will destroy the food supply which spawns global hunger. **pair of scales.** The common measuring device—two small trays hung from each end of a balance beam—indicates that the scarcity of food will lead to rationing and food lines.

6:6 quart of wheat. The approximate amount necessary to sustain one person for one day. **denarius.** One day's normal wage. One day's work will provide enough food for only one person. **three quarts of barley.** Usually fed to animals, this grain was low in nutrients and cheaper than wheat. A day's wage provides enough for only a small family's daily supply. **oil and the wine.** Although the point could be that these foods will not be affected by the famine, a more straightforward meaning is that bare staples—oil was used in the preparation of bread, and wine was considered necessary for cooking and purifying water—suddenly will become luxuries that have to be carefully protected.

6:8 ashen horse. "Ashen," the Gr. word from which the Eng. word "chlorophyll" comes, describes the pale, ashen-green, pallor characteristic of the decomposition of a corpse. God grants this horseman the

on it had the name [B]Death; and [B]Hades was following
with him. Authority was given to them over a fourth
of the earth, [C]to kill with sword and with famine and
with [b]pestilence and by the wild beasts of the earth.

THE FIFTH SEAL—MARTYRS

9 When the Lamb broke the fifth seal, I saw [A]un-
derneath the [B]altar the [C]souls of those who had been
slain [D]because of the word of God, and because of
the [E]testimony which they had maintained; 10 and
they cried out with a loud voice, saying, "[A]How long,
O [a,B]Lord, [C]holy and true, [b]will You refrain from [D]judg-
ing and avenging our blood on [E]those who dwell on
the earth?" 11 And [A]there was given to each of them a
white robe; and they were told that they should [B]rest
for a little while longer, [C]until *the number of* their fellow servants and their brethren who were to be killed
even as they had been, would be [D]completed also.

THE SIXTH SEAL—TERROR

12 I looked when He broke the sixth seal, and there
was a great [A]earthquake; and the [B]sun became black
as [C]sackcloth *made* of hair, and the whole moon became like blood; 13 and [A]the stars of the sky fell to the
earth, [B]as a fig tree casts its unripe figs when shaken
by a great wind. 14 [A]The sky was split apart like a scroll
when it is rolled up, and [B]every mountain and island
were moved out of their places. 15 Then [A]the kings
of the earth and the great men and the [a]command-
ers and the rich and the strong and every slave and
free man hid themselves in the caves and among
the rocks of the mountains; 16 and they *[A]said to the
mountains and to the rocks, "Fall on us and hide us
from the [a]presence of Him [B]who sits on the throne,
and from the [C]wrath of the Lamb; 17 for [A]the great day
of their wrath has come, and [B]who is able to stand?"

AN INTERLUDE

7 After this I saw [A]four angels standing at the
[B]four corners of the earth, holding back [C]the
four winds of the earth, [D]so that no wind would
blow on the earth or on the sea or on any tree. 2 And
I saw another angel ascending [A]from the rising of
the sun, having the [B]seal of [C]the living God; and he
cried out with a loud voice to the [D]four angels to
whom it was granted to harm the earth and the
sea, 3 saying, "[A]Do not harm the earth or the sea or
the trees until we have [B]sealed the bond-servants
of our God on their [C]foreheads."

THE 144,000

4 And I heard the [A]number of those who were
sealed, [B]one hundred and forty-four thousand sealed
from every tribe of the sons of Israel:

6:8 [b]Or *death* [B]Prov 5:5; Hos 13:14; Matt 11:23; Rev 1:18; 20:13f [C]Jer 14:12; 15:2f; 24:10; 29:17f; Ezek 5:12, 17; 14:21; 29:5 6:9 [A]Ex 29:12; Lev 4:7; John 16:2 [B]Rev 14:18; 16:7 [C]Rev 20:4 [D]Rev 1:2, 9 [E]Rev 12:17 6:10 [a]Or *Master* [b]Lit *do You not judge and avenge* [A]Zech 1:12 [B]Luke 2:29; 2 Pet 2:1 [C]Rev 3:7 [D]Deut 32:43; Ps 79:10; Luke 18:7; Rev 19:2 [E]Rev 3:10 6:11 [A]Rev 3:4, 5; 7:9 [B]2 Thess 1:7; Heb 4:10; Rev 14:13 [C]Heb 11:40 [D]Acts 20:24; 2 Tim 4:7 6:12 [A]Matt 24:7; Rev 8:5; 11:13; 16:18 [B]Is 13:10; Joel 2:10, 31; 3:15; Matt 24:29; Mark 13:24 [C]Is 50:3; Matt 11:21 6:13 [A]Matt 24:29; Mark 13:25; Rev 8:10; 9:1 [B]Is 34:4 6:14 [A]Is 34:4; 2 Pet 3:10; Rev 20:11; 21:1 [B]Is 54:10; Jer 4:24; Ezek 38:20; Nah 1:5; Rev 16:20 6:15 [a]I.e. chiliarchs, in command of one thousand troops [A]Is 2:10f, 19, 21; 24:21; Rev 19:18 6:16 [a]Lit *face* [A]Hos 10:8; Luke 23:30; Rev 9:6 [B]Rev 4:9; 5:1 [C]Mark 3:5 6:17 [A]Is 63:4; Jer 30:7; Joel 1:15; 2:1f, 11, 31; Zeph 1:14f; Rev 16:14 [B]Ps 76:7; Nah 1:6; Mal 3:2; Luke 21:36 7:1 [A]Rev 9:14 [B]Is 11:12; Ezek 7:2; Rev 20:8 [C]Jer 49:36; Dan 7:2; Zech 6:5; Matt 24:31 [D]Rev 7:3; 8:7; 9:4 7:2 [A]Is 41:2 [B]Rev 7:3; 9:4 [C]Matt 16:16 [D]Rev 9:14 7:3 [A]Rev 6:6 [B]John 3:33; Rev 7:3-8 [C]Ezek 9:4, 6; Rev 13:16; 14:1, 9; 20:4; 22:4 7:4 [A]Rev 9:16 [B]Rev 14:1, 3

authority to bring death to 25 percent of the world's population. **Hades.** *See note on Lk 16:23.* The place of the dead, which is identified as a common and fitting partner for death (20:13; *see note on 1:18*).

6:9 fifth seal. This seal describes the force of the saints' prayers for God's vengeance. Its events will begin in the first half and mark the midpoint and events following, in the 7-year period, which is called the Great Tribulation (2:22; 7:14; *see notes on Da 9:27; Mt 24:15; 2Th 2:3, 4*). The second 3 1/2 year period (11:2; 12:6; 13:5) features the day of the Lord, in which God unleashes His judgment and wrath on the earth in intensifying waves (*see note on 1Th 5:2*). **underneath the altar.** Probably a reference to the altar of incense, which pictured the saints' prayers ascending to God (5:8; cf. Ex 40:5). **the souls of those who had been slain.** Christians martyred for their faith (cf. 7:9, 13–15; 17:6; Mt 24:9–14; see also Mk 13:9–13; Lk 21:12–19).

6:11 white robe. *See note on 3:4.* **rest for a little while longer.** God will answer their prayer for vengeance, but in His time. **until *the number* ... would be completed.** God has predetermined the number of the righteous whose death He will allow before moving to destroy the rebels.

6:12 sixth seal. The force described in this seal is overpowering fear (cf. Lk 21:26). While the first 5 seals will result from human activity God used to accomplish His purposes, at this point He begins direct intervention (cf. Mt 24:29; Lk 21:25). The previous 5 seals will be precursors to the full fury of the day of the Lord which will begin with the sixth seal (v. 17). The events described in this seal unleash the seventh, which contains the trumpet judgments (chaps. 8, 9; 11:15ff.) and the bowl judgments (chap. 16). **great earthquake.** There have been many earthquakes prior to this (Mt 24:7), but this will be more than an earthquake. All the earth's faults will begin to fracture simultaneously, resulting in a cataclysmic, global earthquake. **moon became like blood.** Accompanying the earthquake will be numerous volcanic eruptions; and large amounts of ash and debris will be blown into the earth's atmosphere, blackening the sun and giving the moon a blood-red hue (cf. Zec 14:6, 7).

6:13 stars of the sky fell. The word "stars" can refer to any celestial body, large or small, and is not limited to normal English usage. The best explanation is a massive asteroid or meteor shower. **unripe figs.** Winter figs that grow without the protection of leaves and are easily blown from the tree.

6:14 sky was split apart like a scroll. The earth's atmosphere will be somehow dramatically affected and the sky as we know it disappears (cf. Is 34:4). **every mountain and island were moved.** Under the stress created by the global earthquake, great segments of the earth's plates will begin to slip and shift, realigning whole continents.

6:16 wrath of the Lamb. Earth's inhabitants will recognize for the first time the source of all their trouble (*see note on 9:6*). Incredibly, prior to this they will be living life as usual (Mt 24:37–39).

6:17 great day. The sixth seal will commence what the prophets call "the Day of the Lord." See Introduction to Joel: Historical and Theological Themes.

7:1–17 Chapter 7 forms a parenthesis between the sixth seal (6:12–17) and the seventh seal (8:1) and answers the question posed at the end of chap. 6. Two distinct groups will survive the divine fury: 1) 144,000 Jewish evangelists on earth (vv. 1–8) and 2) their converts in heaven (vv. 9–17).

7:1 four corners. The 4 quadrants of the compass; that is, the angels will take up key positions on earth. **four winds.** A figurative expression, indicating all the earth's winds—those from S, E, N, and W. The 4 angels will turn off, for a brief interlude, the essential engine of our earth's atmosphere.

7:2 seal of the living God. "Seal" often refers to a signet ring used to press its image into wax melted on a document. The resulting imprint implied authenticity and ownership and protected the contents (cf. 9:4; Eze 9:3, 4). In this case, the mark is the name of God (14:1).

7:4 One hundred and forty-four thousand. A missionary corps of redeemed Jews who are instrumental in the salvation of many Jews and Gentiles during the Tribulation (vv. 9–17). They will be the firstfruits of a new redeemed Israel (v. 4; Zec 12:10). Finally, Israel will be the witness nation she refused to be in the OT (*see notes on Ro 11:25–27*). **every tribe of the sons of Israel.** By sovereign election, God will seal 12,000 from each of the 12 tribes, promising His protection while they accomplish their mission.

5 from the tribe of Judah, twelve
thousand *were* sealed, from the tribe
of Reuben twelve thousand, from
the tribe of Gad twelve thousand,
6 from the tribe of Asher twelve
thousand, from the tribe of Naphtali
twelve thousand, from the tribe
of Manasseh twelve thousand,
7 from the tribe of Simeon twelve
thousand, from the tribe of Levi
twelve thousand, from the tribe
of Issachar twelve thousand,
8 from the tribe of Zebulun twelve
thousand, from the tribe of Joseph
twelve thousand, from the tribe of
Benjamin, twelve thousand *were* sealed.

A MULTITUDE FROM THE TRIBULATION

9 After these things I looked, and behold, a great
multitude which no one could count, from [A]every nation and *all* tribes and peoples and tongues, standing [B]before the throne and [C]before the Lamb, clothed
in [D]white robes, and [E]palm branches *were* in their
hands; 10 and they cry out with a loud voice, saying,
"[A]Salvation to our God [B]who sits on the throne,
and to the Lamb." 11 And all the angels were standing
[A]around the throne and *around* [A]the elders and the
[B]four living creatures; and they [C]fell on their faces
before the throne and worshiped God, 12 saying,
"[A]Amen, [B]blessing and glory and wisdom and
thanksgiving and honor and power and might, *be*
to our God forever and ever. [A]Amen."
13 Then one of the elders [A]answered, saying to me,
"These who are clothed in the [B]white robes, who are
they, and where have they come from?" 14 I [a]said to
him, "My lord, you know." And he said to me, "These are
the ones who come out of the [A]great tribulation, and
they have [B]washed their robes and made them [C]white
in the [D]blood of the Lamb. 15 For this reason, they are
[A]before the throne of God; and they [B]serve Him day
and night in His [a,C]temple; and [D]He who sits on the
throne will spread His [E]tabernacle over them. 16 [A]They
will hunger no longer, nor thirst anymore; nor will
the sun [a]beat down on them, nor any heat; 17 for the
Lamb in the center of the throne will be their [A]shep-
herd, and will guide them to springs of the [a,B]water
of life; and [C]God will wipe every tear from their eyes."

THE SEVENTH SEAL—THE TRUMPETS

8 When the Lamb broke the [A]seventh seal, there
was silence in heaven for about half an hour.
2 And I saw [A]the seven angels who stand before God,
and seven [B]trumpets were given to them.
3 [A]Another angel came and stood at the [B]altar, holding a [C]golden censer; and much [D]incense was given
to him, so that he might [a]add it to the [D]prayers of all
the [b]saints on the [E]golden altar which was before the
throne. 4 And [A]the smoke of the incense, [a]with the
prayers of the [b]saints, went up before God out of the
angel's hand. 5 Then the angel [a]took the censer and
[A]filled it with the fire of the altar, and [B]threw it to
the earth; and there followed [C]peals of thunder and
sounds and flashes of lightning and an [D]earthquake.
6 [A]And the seven angels who had the seven trumpets prepared themselves to sound them.
7 The first sounded, and there came [A]hail and
fire, mixed with blood, and they were thrown to
the earth; and [B]a third of the earth was burned up,
and [B]a third of the [C]trees were burned up, and all
the green [C]grass was burned up.

7:9 [A]Rev 5:9 [B]Rev 7:15 [C]Rev 22:3 [D]Rev 6:11; 7:14 [E]Lev 23:40 7:10 [A]Ps 3:8; Rev 12:10; 19:1 [B]Rev 22:3 7:11 [A]Rev 4:4 [B]Rev 4:6 [C]Rev 4:10 7:12 [A]Rev 5:14 [B]Rev 5:12 7:13 [A]Acts 3:12 [B]Rev 7:9 7:14 [a]Lit *have said* [A]Dan 12:1; Matt 24:21; Mark 13:19 [B]Zech 3:3-5; Rev 22:14 [C]Rev 6:11; 7:9 [D]Heb 9:14; 1 John 1:7 7:15 [a]Or *sanctuary* [A]Rev 7:9 [B]Rev 4:8f; 22:3 [C]Rev 11:19; 21:22 [D]Rev 4:9 [E]Lev 26:11; Ezek 37:27; John 1:14; Rev 21:3 7:16 [a]Lit *fall* [A]Ps 121:5f; Is 49:10 7:17 [a]Lit *waters* [A]Ps 23:1f; Matt 2:6; John 10:11 [B]John 4:14; Rev 21:6; 22:1 [C]Is 25:8; Matt 5:4; Rev 21:4 8:1 [A]Rev 5:1; 6:1, 3, 5, 7, 9, 12 8:2 [A]Rev 1:4; 8:6-13; 9:1, 13; 11:15 [B]1 Cor 15:52; 1 Thess 4:16 8:3 [a]Lit *give* [b]Or *holy ones* [A]Rev 7:2 [B]Amos 9:1; Rev 6:9 [C]Heb 9:4 [D]Ex 30:1; Rev 5:8 [E]Ex 30:3; Num 4:11; Rev 8:5; 9:13 8:4 [a]Or *for* [b]V 3, note 2 [A]Ps 141:2 8:5 [a]Lit *has taken* [A]Lev 16:12 [B]Ezek 10:2 [C]Ex 19:16; Rev 4:5; 11:19; 16:18 [D]Rev 6:12 8:6 [A]Rev 8:2 8:7 [A]Ex 9:23ff; Is 28:2; Ezek 38:22; Joel 2:30 [B]Zech 13:8, 9; Rev 8:7-12; 9:15, 18; 12:4 [C]Rev 9:4

7:9 a great multitude. While the tribulation period will be a time of judgment, it will also be a time of unprecedented redemption (cf. v. 14; 6:9–11; 20:4; Is 11:10; Mt 24:14). **every nation and *all* tribes and peoples and tongues.** All the earth's people groups. **white robes.** *See note on 3:4.* **palm branches.** In ancient times, they were associated with celebrations, including the Feast of Booths, or Tabernacles (Lv 23:40; Ne 8:17; Jn 12:13).

7:10 Salvation to our God. Salvation is the theme of their worship, and they recognize that it comes solely from Him.

7:11 elders. *See note on 4:4.* **four living creatures.** *See note on 4:6.*

7:12 blessing . . . and might. *See note on 5:12.*

7:13 white robes. *See note on 3:4.*

7:14 the great tribulation. *See notes on 3:10; 6:1, 9, 12.* These people didn't go with the raptured church, *since* they were not yet saved. During the 7-year period they will be saved, martyred, and enter heaven. Though it is a time of unparalleled judgment, it is also a time of unparalleled grace in salvation (cf. Mt 24:12–14). **washed their robes.** Cf. 19:8. Salvation's cleansing is in view (see Titus 2:11–14). **blood of the Lamb.** This refers to the atoning sacrifice of Christ (cf. 1:5; 5:9; Ro 3:24, 25; 5:9).

7:15 His temple. This refers to the heavenly throne of God (*see note on 11:19*). During the Millennium there will also be a temple on earth—a special holy place where God dwells in a partially restored, but still fallen, universe (see Eze 40–48). In the final, eternal state with its new heavens and earth, there is no temple; God Himself, who will fill all, will be its temple (21:22). **spread His tabernacle over them.** God's presence will become their canopy of shelter to protect them from all the terrors of a fallen world and the indescribable horrors they have experienced on the earth during the time of tribulation.

7:17 shepherd. In a beautiful mix of images, the Lamb has always been the Shepherd (Ps 23; Jn 10:14ff.; Heb 13:20).

8:1 the seventh seal. This seal includes not only an earthquake, but the 7 trumpet judgments (8:1–9:21; 11:15ff.) and the 7 bowl judgments (16:1–21), with the bowl judgments flowing out of the seventh trumpet and coming in rapid succession just before Christ's return (*see note on 6:1*). **silence in heaven.** The silence of awe and anticipation at the grim reality of the judgments God is about to unleash.

8:2 seven trumpets. In Revelation, trumpets primarily announce impending judgment. The trumpets are of greater intensity than the seals, but not as destructive as the final bowl judgments will be (cf. 16:1–21). They occur during the final 3 1/2 years, but the time of each is indefinite, except the effects of the fifth trumpet judgment, which will last 5 months (9:10). The first 4 announce the divine destruction of earth's ecology (vv. 6–12), while the final 3 involve demonic devastation of earth's inhabitants (9:1–21; 11:15ff.).

8:3 censer. A golden pan, suspended on a rope or chain, that was used to transport fiery coals from the brazen altar to the altar of incense, in order to ignite the incense, symbolizing the prayers of the people (5:8; Ex 27:3; cf. Lk 1:8, 9). This occurred twice daily at the time of the morning and evening sacrifices.

8:5 thunder . . . lightning. *See note on 4:5.* **an earthquake.** Surely of equal or greater intensity than the one described in the sixth seal (*see note on 6:12*).

8:7 hail and fire, mixed with blood. This may describe volcanic eruptions that could

8 The second angel sounded, and *something* like a
great [A]mountain burning with fire was thrown into
the sea; and [B]a third of the [C]sea became blood, 9 and [A]a
third of the creatures which were in the sea [a]and had
life, died; and a third of the [B]ships were destroyed.
10 The third angel sounded, and a great star [A]fell
from heaven, burning like a torch, and it fell on a
[B]third of the rivers and on the [C]springs of waters. 11 The
name of the star is called Wormwood; and a [A]third
of the waters became [B]wormwood, and many men
died from the waters, because they were made bitter.
12 The fourth angel sounded, and a [A]third of the
[B]sun and a third of the [B]moon and a [A]third of the
[B]stars were struck, so that a [A]third of them would be
darkened and the day would not shine for a [A]third
of it, and the night in the same way.
13 Then I looked, and I heard [a]an eagle flying in
[A]midheaven, saying with a loud voice, "[B]Woe, woe,
woe to [C]those who dwell on the earth, because of
the remaining blasts of the trumpet of the [D]three
angels who are about to sound!"

THE FIFTH TRUMPET—THE BOTTOMLESS PIT

9 Then the [A]fifth angel sounded, and I saw a [B]star
from heaven which had fallen to the earth; and
the [C]key of the [a,D]bottomless pit was given to him.
2 He opened the [a]bottomless pit, and [A]smoke went up
out of the pit, like the smoke of a great furnace; and
[B]the sun and the air were darkened by the smoke of
the pit. 3 Then out of the smoke came [A]locusts [a]upon
the earth, and power was given them, as the [B]scor-
pions of the earth have power. 4 They were told not
to [A]hurt the [B]grass of the earth, nor any green thing,
nor any tree, but only the men who do not have the
[C]seal of God on their foreheads. 5 And [a]they were not
permitted to kill [b]anyone, but to torment for [A]five
months; and their torment was like the torment of
a [B]scorpion when it [c]stings a man. 6 And in those
days [A]men will seek death and will not find it; they
will long to die, and death flees from them.
7 The [a,A]appearance of the locusts was like horses
prepared for battle; and on their heads appeared
to be crowns like gold, and their faces were like the
faces of men. 8 They had hair like the hair of women,
and their [A]teeth were like *the teeth* of lions. 9 They
had breastplates like breastplates of iron; and the
[A]sound of their wings was like the sound of chariots, of many horses rushing to battle. 10 They have
tails like [A]scorpions, and stings; and in their [B]tails
is their power to hurt men for [C]five months. 11 They
have as king over them, the angel of the [A]abyss; his
name in [B]Hebrew is [a,C]Abaddon, and in the Greek
he has the name [b]Apollyon.
12 [A]The first woe is past; behold, two woes are
still coming after these things.

8:8 [A]Jer 51:25 [B]Zech 13:8, 9; Rev 8:7-12; 9:15, 18; 12:4 [C]Ex 7:17ff; Rev 11:6; 16:3 8:9 [a]Lit *the ones having* [A]Zech 13:8, 9; Rev 8:7-12; 9:15, 18; 12:4 [B]Is 2:16 8:10 [A]Is 14:12; Rev 6:13; 9:1 [B]Zech 13:8, 9; Rev 8:7-12; 9:15, 18; 12:4 [C]Rev 14:7; 16:4 8:11 [A]Zech 13:8, 9; Rev 8:7-12; 9:15, 18; 12:4 [B]Jer 9:15; 23:15 8:12 [A]Zech 13:8, 9; Rev 8:7-12; 9:15, 18; 12:4 [B]Ex 10:21ff; Is 13:10; Ezek 32:7; Joel 2:10, 31; 3:15; Rev 6:12f 8:13 [a]Lit *one eagle* [A]Rev 14:6; 19:17 [B]Rev 9:12; 11:14; 12:12 [C]Rev 3:10 [D]Rev 8:2 9:1 [a]Lit *shaft of the abyss* [A]Rev 8:2 [B]Rev 8:10 [C]Rev 1:18 [D]Luke 8:31; Rev 9:2, 11 9:2 [a]V 1, note 1 [A]Gen 19:28; Ex 19:18 [B]Joel 2:2, 10 9:3 [a]Lit *into* [A]Ex 10:12-15; Rev 9:7 [B]2 Chr 10:11, 14; Ezek 2:6; Rev 9:5, 10 9:4 [A]Rev 6:6 [B]Rev 8:7 [C]Ezek 9:4; Rev 7:2, 3 9:5 [a]Lit *it was given to them* [b]Lit *them* [c]Lit *strikes* [A]Rev 9:10 [B]2 Chr 10:11, 14; Ezek 2:6; Rev 9:3, 10 9:6 [A]Job 3:21; 7:15; Jer 8:3; Rev 6:16 9:7 [a]Lit *likenesses* [A]Joel 2:4 9:8 [A]Joel 1:6 9:9 [A]Jer 47:3; Joel 2:5 9:10 [A]2 Chr 10:11, 14; Ezek 2:6; Rev 9:3, 5 [B]Rev 9:19 [C]Rev 9:5 9:11 [a]I.e. destruction [b]I.e. destroyer [A]Luke 8:31; Rev 9:1, 2 [B]John 5:2; Rev 16:16 [C]Job 26:6; 28:22; 31:12; Ps 88:11 mg; Prov 15:11 9:12 [A]Rev 8:13; 11:14

certainly result from the earthquake in v. 5. The steam and water thrown into the sky by such eruptions could easily condense into hail and fall to earth along with the fiery lava (cf. Ex 9:13–25). Dust and gases may so contaminate falling liquid water that it appears blood red. **a third of the trees were burned up.** The lava storm will create a blazing fire that devastates one-third of the earth's forests.

8:8 like a great mountain. Probably a huge meteor or asteroid surrounded by gases that will ignite as it enters earth's atmosphere. Its impact will create a tidal wave, destroying one-third of the world's ships. **sea became blood.** This may refer to an event known as red tides, caused by billions of dead micro-organisms poisoning the water—in this case the result of the meteor's collision. Or it may be actual blood, a clear act of eschatological judgment.

8:10 great star fell. Another celestial body, perhaps a comet in this case, since it leaves a fiery trail (*see notes on v. 8; 6:13*). It will disintegrate as it nears the earth, scattering over the globe.

8:11 Wormwood. A bitter, poisonous substance, derived from a root, that causes drunkenness and eventually death (Dt 29:18; Pr 5:4; Jer 9:15; La 3:15).

8:12 a third of the sun … struck. God will supernaturally reduce the intensity of the celestial bodies by one-third. The loss of solar heat will cause a radical drop in temperature, producing severe changes in meteorological, botanical, and biological cycles (Lk 21:25; cf. Ex 10:21–23). But this is temporary (cf. 16:8, 9).

8:13 Woe, woe, woe. One for each remaining trumpet blast. Although the first 4 trumpets are unimaginable, they will be nothing like the 3 to come (9:1–21; 11:15ff.).

9:1 a star from heaven which had fallen. Unlike the other stars that will have fallen (6:13; 8:8), this one will be an angelic being (cf. v. 2)—probably Satan himself (v. 4; 12:7; *see notes on Is 14:12–14; Lk 10:18*). **bottomless pit.** Lit. "pit of the abyss." Mentioned 7 times in Revelation, it always refers to the prison where some of the demonic hordes are incarcerated, the place of severest torment and isolation (vv. 1, 2, 11; 11:7; 17:8; 20:1, 3; *see notes on 2Pe 2:4; Jude 6, 7*).

9:3 locusts. A grasshopper-like insect that descends in swarms so thick they can obscure the sun and strip bare all vegetation. In the 1950s a locust swarm devoured every growing thing for several hundred thousand square miles in the Middle East. These are not normal locusts, however, but specially prepared ones that are merely the outward form of demons, who, like locusts, will bring swarming desolation (*see notes on Joel 2:2, 4*). "Like" appears several times in John's description; he finds it difficult to describe what he sees in a way the reader can understand. **scorpions.** An arachnid that inhabits warm, dry regions and has an erect tail tipped with a venomous stinger. A scorpion's victim often rolls on the ground in agony, foams at the mouth, and grinds his teeth in pain. The demons in locust form are able to inflict the physical—and perhaps, spiritual—pain like the scorpion (v. 5).

9:4 men who do not have the seal of God. Everyone on earth except the two groups mentioned in chap. 7—the 144,000 Jewish evangelists and their converts (*see note on 7:4*).

9:5 five months. The normal life cycle of locusts is 5 months, usually from May to Sep.

9:6 seek death and will not find it. The tormented will find no relief. Even their unimaginable attempts to end their misery in suicide will be unsuccessful.

9:7 faces of men. Probably a reference to these demonic creatures as rational, intelligent beings.

9:8 hair of women. Jeremiah 51:27 refers to locusts having bristles like hair. ***teeth* of lions.** They are fierce, powerful, and deadly (cf. Jer 51:27).

9:9 breastplates of iron. Breastplates were designed to protect the vital organs and sustain the life of the warrior. These creatures are invulnerable.

9:10 five months. *See note on v. 5.*

9:11 Abaddon … Apollyon. Although locusts normally have no king (Pr 30:27), these demonic creatures do. His name in both Heb. and Gr. means "destroyer." There is a hierarchy of power among the demons, just as among the holy angels. Apparently, "the angel of the abyss" is one of Satan's most trusted leaders or possibly Satan himself.

9:12 first woe. The first of the final 3 trumpets (*see note on 8:13*).

THE SIXTH TRUMPET—ARMY FROM THE EAST

13 Then the sixth angel sounded, and I heard [a]a
voice from the [b]four [A]horns of the [B]golden altar
which is before God, 14 one saying to the sixth angel
who had the trumpet, "Release the [A]four angels who
are bound at the [B]great river Euphrates." 15 And the
four angels, who had been prepared for the hour
and day and month and year, were [A]released, so that
they would kill a [B]third of [a]mankind. 16 The number
of the armies of the horsemen was [A]two hundred
million; [B]I heard the number of them. 17 And [a]this is
how I saw [A]in the vision the horses and those who
sat on them: *the riders* had breastplates *the color*
of fire and of hyacinth and of [b,B]brimstone; and
the heads of the horses are like the heads of lions;
and [C]out of their mouths proceed fire and smoke
and [b,B]brimstone. 18 A [A]third of [a]mankind was killed
by these three plagues, by the [B]fire and the smoke
and the [b]brimstone which proceeded out of their
mouths. 19 For the power of the horses is in their
mouths and in their tails; for their tails are like serpents and have heads, and with them they do harm.
20 The rest of [a]mankind, who were not killed by
these plagues, [A]did not repent of [B]the works of their
hands, so as not to [C]worship demons, and [D]the idols
of gold and of silver and of brass and of stone and of
wood, which can neither see nor hear nor walk; 21 and
they [A]did not repent of their murders nor of their
[B]sorceries nor of their [C]immorality nor of their thefts.

THE ANGEL AND THE LITTLE BOOK

10 I saw another [A]strong angel [B]coming down
out of heaven, clothed with a cloud; and the
[C]rainbow was upon his head, and [D]his face was like
the sun, and his [E]feet like pillars of fire; 2 and he had
in his hand a [A]little book which was open. He placed
[B]his right foot on the sea and his left on the land;
3 and he cried out with a loud voice, [A]as when a lion
roars; and when he had cried out, the [B]seven peals
of thunder [a]uttered their voices. 4 When the seven
peals of thunder had spoken, [A]I was about to write;
and I [B]heard a voice from heaven saying, "[C]Seal up
the things which the seven peals of thunder have
spoken and do not write them." 5 Then the angel
whom I saw standing on the sea and on the land
[A]lifted up his right hand to heaven, 6 [A]and swore
by [B]Him who lives forever and ever, [C]WHO CREATED
HEAVEN AND THE THINGS IN IT, AND THE EARTH AND
THE THINGS IN IT, AND THE SEA AND THE THINGS IN IT,
that [D]there will be delay no longer, 7 but in the days
of the voice of the [A]seventh angel, when he is about
to sound, then [B]the mystery of God is finished, as
He [a]preached to His servants the prophets.

9:13 [a]Lit *one voice* [b]Two early mss do not contain *four* [A]Ex 30:2f, 10 [B]Rev 8:3 9:14 [A]Rev 7:1 [B]Gen 15:18; Deut 1:7; Josh 1:4; Rev 16:12 9:15 [a]Gr *anthropoi* [A]Rev 20:7 [B]Rev 8:7; 9:18 9:16 [A]Rev 5:11 [B]Rev 7:4 9:17 [a]Lit *thus I saw* [b]I.e. burning sulphur [A]Dan 8:2; 9:21 [B]Rev 9:18; 14:10; 19:20; 20:10; 21:8 [C]Rev 11:5 9:18 [a]Gr *anthropoi* [b]I.e. burning sulphur [A]Rev 8:7; 9:15 [B]Rev 9:17 9:20 [a]Gr *anthropoi* [A]Rev 2:21 [B]Deut 4:28; Jer 1:16; Mic 5:13; Acts 7:41 [C]1 Cor 10:20 [D]Ps 115:4-7; 135:15-17; Dan 5:23 9:21 [A]Rev 9:20 [B]Is 47:9, 12; Rev 18:23 [C]Rev 17:2, 4, 5 10:1 [A]Rev 5:2 [B]Rev 18:1; 20:1 [C]Rev 4:3 [D]Matt 17:2; Rev 1:16 [E]Rev 1:15 10:2 [A]Rev 5:1; 10:8-10 [B]Rev 10:5, 8 10:3 [a]Or *spoke* [A]Is 31:4; Hos 11:10 [B]Ps 29:3-9; Rev 4:5 10:4 [A]Rev 1:11, 19 [B]Rev 10:8 [C]Dan 8:26; 12:4, 9; Rev 22:10 10:5 [A]Deut 32:40; Dan 12:7 10:6 [A]Gen 14:22; Ex 6:8; Num 14:30; Ezek 20:5 [B]Rev 4:9 [C]Ex 20:11; Rev 4:11 [D]Rev 6:11; 12:12; 16:17; 21:6 10:7 [a]Lit *preached the gospel* [A]Rev 11:15 [B]Amos 3:7; Rom 16:25

9:13 horns of the golden altar. God's design for the golden altar of incense included small protrusions (horns) on each corner (Ex 30:2; *see note on 6:9*). Normally a place of mercy, as God responds to His people's prayers, the altar will resound with a cry for vengeance.

9:14 four angels. Scripture never refers to holy angels as being bound. These are fallen angels—another segment of Satan's force whom God had bound but will free to accomplish His judgment through their horsemen (vv. 15–19). God's control extends even to the demonic forces—they are bound or freed at His command. **Euphrates.** One of the 4 rivers that flowed through the Garden of Eden (*see note on 16:12*; cf. Ge 2:14). Starting with Babel, this region has spawned many of the world's pagan religions.

9:15 the hour and day and month and year. God works according to His predetermined plan (cf. Mt 24:36; Ac 1:7).

9:16 the armies. Some see this as a reference to forces accompanying the kings of the east (16:12) and identify them with a human army coming from Asia. But that event occurs in connection with the seventh trumpet, not the sixth. The language is better understood as referring to a demon force that makes war with the earth's inhabitants and kills one-third of humanity (v. 15).

9:17 breastplates. *See note on v. 9.* **brimstone.** Brimstone is a yellowish, sulfuric rock that often attends fire and smoke in Revelation (14:10; 19:20; 20:10). Common in the Dead Sea region, when ignited such deposits melt and produce burning streams and suffocating gas.

9:19 tails are like serpents and have heads. John's language represents the demons' ability to vent their destructive power in both directions.

9:20, 21 God lists 5 sins that are representative of their defiance.

9:20 demons. Reminiscent of Paul's comments about idolatry (*see note on 1Co 10:19, 20*); demons impersonate the stone and wood idols men make.

9:21 they did not repent. Cf. 16:9, 11, 21. **sorceries.** This Gr. word is the root of the Eng. word "pharmacy." Drugs in the ancient world were used to dull the senses and induce a state suitable for religious experiences such as séances, witchcraft, incantations, and cavorting with mediums (21:8; 22:15). *See note on Eph 5:18.*

10:1–11:14 These verses serve as an interlude between the sixth trumpet and the seventh trumpet (11:15). The seals and the bowls also have a brief interlude between their sixth and seventh judgments (7:1–17; 16:15). God's intention is to encourage and comfort His people in the midst of the fury and to remind them that He is still sovereign, that He remembers His people, and that they will ultimately be victorious.

10:1 another strong angel. Many commentators understand this to be Jesus Christ. But the Gr. word translated "another" means one of the same kind, that is, a created being. This is not one of the 7 angels responsible for sounding the trumpets (8:2), but one of the highest ranking in heaven, filled with splendor, greatness, and strength (cf. 5:2; 8:3; 18:1). **rainbow.** *See note on 4:3.* Perhaps God included this to remind John, that even in judgment, He will always remember His Noahic Covenant and protect His own. **feet like pillars of fire.** This angel's feet and legs indicate the firm resolve with which he will execute the day of the Lord.

10:2 little book. The 7-sealed scroll that is the title deed to the earth (*see note on 5:1*) will be fully opened and all the final judgments made visible. **right foot on the sea and his left on the land.** Although Satan has temporarily usurped the sea and the earth, this symbolic act demonstrates that all creation belongs to the Lord and He rules it with sovereign authority.

10:3 seven peals of thunder. *See note on 4:5*; cf. 6:1; 8:5.

10:4 Seal up. John was told he must conceal the message of the 7 thunders until God's time (cf. 22:10; Da 8:26, 27; 12:9).

10:5 lifted up his right hand. This Gr. verb appears often in the technical sense of raising the hand to take an oath or a solemn vow (cf. Da 12:7; *see notes on Mt 5:33, 34*). The hand is raised toward heaven because that is where God dwells. The angel is taking an oath.

10:6 there will be delay no longer. This initiates the last plagues of the Day of the Lord (11:15), indicating that the time the disciples anticipated has come (Mt 24:3; Ac 1:6). The prayers of the saints will be answered (6:9–11; Mt 6:10).

10:7 the mystery. A Gr. term meaning "to shut" or "to close." In the NT, a "mystery" is a truth that God concealed but has revealed through Christ and His apostles (*see notes on Eph 3:4, 5*; cf. Ro 16:25). Here the mystery is the final consummation of all things as God destroys sinners and establishes His righteous

8 Then [A]the voice which I heard from heaven, *I heard* again speaking with me, and saying, "Go, take [B]the [a]book which is open in the hand of the angel who [B]stands on the sea and on the land."
9 So I went to the angel, telling him to give me the little book. And he *said to me, "[A]Take it and eat it; it will make your stomach bitter, but in your mouth it will be sweet as honey."
10 I took the little book out of the angel's hand and ate it, and in my mouth it was sweet as honey; and when I had eaten it, my stomach was made bitter.
11 And [A]they *said to me, "You must [B]prophesy again concerning [C]many peoples and nations and tongues and [D]kings."

THE TWO WITNESSES

11 Then there was given me a [a,A]measuring rod like a staff; [b]and [B]someone said, "Get up and measure the [c]temple of God and the altar, and those who worship in it.
2 [a]Leave out the [A]court which is outside the [b]temple and do not measure it, for [B]it has been given to the nations; and they will [B]tread under foot [C]the holy city for [D]forty-two months.
3 And I will grant *authority* to my two [A]witnesses, and they will prophesy for [B]twelve hundred and sixty days, clothed in [C]sackcloth."
4 These are the [A]two olive trees and the two lampstands that stand before the Lord of the earth.
5 And if anyone wants to harm them, [A]fire flows out of their mouth and devours their enemies; so if anyone wants to harm them, [B]he must be killed in this way.
6 These have the power to [A]shut up the sky, so that rain will not fall during [B]the days of their prophesying; and they have power over the waters to [C]turn them into blood, and [D]to strike the earth with every plague, as often as they desire.
7 When they have finished their testimony, [A]the beast that comes up out of the [B]abyss will [C]make war with them, and overcome them and kill them.
8 And their dead bodies *will lie* in the street of the [A]great city which [a]mystically is called [B]Sodom and [C]Egypt, where also their Lord was crucified.

10:8 [a]Or *scroll* [A]Rev 10:4 [B]Rev 10:2 10:9 [A]Jer 15:16; Ezek 2:8; 3:1-3 10:11 [A]Rev 11:1 [B]Ezek 37:4, 9 [C]Rev 5:9 [D]Rev 17:10, 12 11:1 [a]Lit *reed* [b]Lit *saying* [c]Or *sanctuary* [A]Ezek 40:3-42:20; Zech 2:1; Rev 21:15f [B]Rev 10:11 11:2 [a]Lit *Throw out* [b]Or *sanctuary* [A]Ezek 40:17, 20 [B]Luke 21:24 [C]Is 52:1; Matt 4:5; 27:53; Rev 21:2, 10; 22:19 [D]Dan 7:25; 12:7; Rev 12:6; 13:5 11:3 [A]Rev 1:5; 2:13 [B]Dan 7:25; 12:7; Rev 12:6; 13:5 [C]Gen 37:34; 2 Sam 3:31; 1 Kin 21:27; 2 Kin 19:1f; Neh 9:1; Esth 4:1; Ps 69:11; Joel 1:13; Jon 3:5f, 8 11:4 [A]Ps 52:8; Jer 11:16; Zech 4:3, 11, 14 11:5 [A]2 Kin 1:10-12; Jer 5:14; Rev 9:17f [B]Num 16:29, 35 11:6 [A]1 Kin 17:1; Luke 4:25 [B]Rev 11:3 [C]Ex 7:17ff; Rev 8:8 [D]1 Sam 4:8 11:7 [A]Rev 13:1ff; 17:8 [B]Rev 9:1 [C]Dan 7:21; Rev 13:7 11:8 [a]Lit *spiritually* [A]Rev 14:8; 16:19; 17:18; 18:2, 10, 16, 18, 19, 21 [B]Is 1:9, 10; 3:9; Jer 23:14; Ezek 16:46, 49 [C]Ezek 23:3, 8, 19, 27

kingdom on earth. **as He preached.** This mystery, though not fully revealed, was declared to God's prophets (cf. Am 3:7).

10:9 Take it and eat it. This act graphically illustrates taking in God's Word. John's physical reactions demonstrate what every believer's proper response to God's judgment should be (cf. Eze 3:1)—sweet anticipation of God's glory and our victory, and at the same time, the bitterness of seeing God's wrath poured out on those who reject His Son. **your stomach bitter.** As he truly digests what the seal, trumpet, and bowl judgments hold in store for the sinner, John becomes nauseated. **in your mouth it will be sweet as honey.** But still God's final victory and vindication are sweet realities to the believer.

10:11 prophesy again. A call for John to warn men about the bitter judgment in the seventh trumpet and the 7 bowls. **peoples and nations and tongues and kings.** *See note on 7:9.*

11:1 a measuring rod. This was a hollow, bamboo-like cane plant that grew in the Jordan Valley. Because of its light weight and rigidity, it was commonly used as a measuring rod (cf. Eze 40:3, 5). Measuring the temple signified God's ownership of it (cf. 21:15; Zec 2:1–5). **the temple of God.** Refers to the Holy of Holies and the Holy Place, not the entire temple complex (cf. v. 2). A rebuilt temple will exist during the time of the Tribulation (Da 9:27; 12:11; Mt 24:15; 2Th 2:4). **altar.** The reference to worshipers suggests this is the bronze altar in the courtyard, not the incense altar in the Holy Place, since only the priests were permitted inside the Holy Place (cf. Lk 1:8–10).

11:2 court which is outside. The court of the Gentiles, separated from the inner court in the Herodian temple by a low wall. Gentiles were forbidden to enter the inner court on penalty of death. That John is instructed not to measure the outer court symbolizes God's rejection of the unbelieving Gentiles who have oppressed His covenant people. **tread under foot the holy city.** Assyria, Babylon, Medo-Persia, Greece, and Rome all oppressed Jerusalem in ancient times (cf. 2Ki 25:8–10; Ps 79:1; Is 63:18; La 1:10). This verse refers to the future devastating destruction and oppression of Jerusalem by the forces of the Antichrist. **forty-two months.** This 3 1/2 year period covers the second half of the Tribulation and coincides with the visibly evil career of the Antichrist (v. 3; 12:6; 13:5). During this same time, the Jews will be sheltered by God in the wilderness (12:6, 14).

11:3 two witnesses. Individuals granted special power and authority by God to preach a message of judgment and salvation during the second half of the Tribulation. The OT required two or more witnesses to confirm testimony (cf. Dt 17:6; 19:15; Mt 18:16; Jn 8:17; Heb 10:28), and these two prophets will be the culmination of God's testimony to Israel: a message of judgment from God and of His gracious offer of the gospel to all who will repent and believe. **twelve hundred and sixty days.** Forty-two months or 3 1/2 years (cf. 12:6; 13:5; *see note on v. 2*). **sackcloth.** Coarse, rough cloth made from goat or camel hair. Wearing garments made from it expressed penitence, humility, and mourning (cf. Ge 37:34; 2Sa 3:31; 2Ki 6:30; 19:1; Est 4:1; Is 22:12; Jer 6:26; Mt 11:21). The witnesses are mourning because of the wretched wickedness of the world, God's judgment on it, and the desecration of the temple and the holy city by the Antichrist.

11:4 This imagery is drawn from Zec 3, 4 (*see notes there*). Zechariah's vision had both a near fulfillment (the rebuilding of the temple by Joshua and Zerubbabel) and a far future fulfillment (the two witnesses, whose ministry points toward Israel's final restoration in the Millennium). **two olive trees and the two lampstands.** Olive oil was commonly used in lamps; together the olive trees and lampstands symbolize the light of spiritual revival. The two witnesses' preaching will spark a revival, just as Joshua's and Zerubbabel's did in Israel after the Babylonian captivity.

11:5, 6 While it is impossible to be dogmatic about the identity of these two witnesses, several observations suggest they might be Moses and Elijah: 1) like Moses, they strike the earth with plagues, and like Elijah, they have the power to keep it from raining; 2) Jewish tradition expected both Moses (cf. Dt 18:15–18) and Elijah (cf. Mal 4:5, 6) to return in the future (cf. Jn 1:21); 3) both Moses and Elijah were present at the Transfiguration, the preview of Christ's second coming; 4) both Moses and Elijah used supernatural means to provoke repentance; 5) Elijah was taken up alive into heaven, and God buried Moses' body where it would never be found; and 6) the length of the drought the two witnesses bring (3 1/2 years; cf. v. 3) is the same as that brought by Elijah (Jas 5:17).

11:5 fire flows out . . . and devours. Probably this refers to literal fire. These two will be invincible during their ministry, protected by supernatural power. The false prophet will counterfeit this sign (13:3).

11:6 power to shut up the sky. Miracles have often authenticated God's messengers. Here, bringing a 3 1/2 year drought (as did Elijah before them) will add immeasurable torment to those experiencing the worldwide disasters of the Tribulation—and exacerbate their hatred of the two witnesses. **waters to turn them into blood.** The earth's water, already devastated by the effects of the second and third trumpets, will become undrinkable, adding immensely to the suffering caused by the drought.

11:7 the beast. The first of 36 references to this person in Revelation, who is none other than the Antichrist (see chap. 13). That he will ascend out of the bottomless pit indicates that his power is satanic. **kill them.** Their ministry completed, God will withdraw the two witnesses' supernatural protection. The beast will then be able to accomplish what many had died trying to do.

11:8 bodies *will lie* in the street. Refusing to bury one's enemies was a way to dishonor and show contempt for them (cf. Ac 14:19). The OT expressly forbids this practice (Dt 21:22, 23). **the great city.** Identifying Jerusalem as a city like Sodom and Egypt stresses the city's wickedness. Its Jewish population will apparently be the focus of the witnesses' ministry, leading to the conversions of v. 13.

9 Those from [A]the peoples and tribes and tongues and
nations *will* look at their dead [a]bodies for three and
a half days, and [b,B]will not permit their dead bodies
to be laid in a tomb. 10 And [A]those who dwell on the
earth *will* rejoice over them and celebrate; and they
will [B]send gifts to one another, because these two
prophets tormented [A]those who dwell on the earth.
11 But after the three and a half days, [A]the breath
of life from God came into them, and they stood on
their feet; and great fear fell upon those who were
watching them. 12 And they heard a loud voice from
heaven saying to them, "[A]Come up here." Then they
[B]went up into heaven in the cloud, and their enemies
watched them. 13 And in that hour there was a great
[A]earthquake, and a tenth of the city fell; [a]seven thousand people were killed in the earthquake, and the rest
were terrified and [B]gave glory to the [C]God of heaven.
14 The second [A]woe is past; behold, the third woe
is coming quickly.

THE SEVENTH TRUMPET—CHRIST'S REIGN FORESEEN

15 Then the [A]seventh angel sounded; and there
were [B]loud voices in heaven, saying,

"[C]The kingdom of the world has become *the kingdom* of our Lord and of [D]His [a]Christ; and [E]He will
reign forever and ever." 16 And the twenty-four elders, who [A]sit on their thrones before God, [B]fell on
their faces and worshiped God, 17 saying,
"We give You thanks, [A]O Lord God, the Almighty,
who are and who were, because You have taken
Your great power and have begun to [B]reign. 18 And
[A]the nations were enraged, and [B]Your wrath came,
and [C]the time *came* for the dead to be judged, and
the time to [a]reward Your [D]bond-servants the prophets and the [b]saints and those who fear Your name,
[E]the small and the great, and to destroy those who
destroy the earth."
19 And [A]the [a]temple of God which is in heaven was
opened; and [B]the ark of His covenant appeared in
His [a]temple, and there were flashes of [C]lightning
and sounds and peals of thunder and an earthquake
and a [D]great [b]hailstorm.

THE WOMAN, ISRAEL

12 A great [A]sign appeared [B]in heaven: [C]a woman
[D]clothed with the sun, and the moon under
her feet, and on her head a crown of twelve stars;

11:9 [a]Lit *body* [b]Lit *do not permit* [A]Rev 5:9; 10:11 [B]1 Kin 13:22; Ps 79:2f 11:10 [A]Rev 3:10 [B]Neh 8:10, 12; Esth 9:19, 22 11:11 [A]Ezek 37:5, 9, 10, 14 11:12 [A]Rev 4:1 [B]2 Kin 2:11; Acts 1:9 11:13 [a]Lit *names of people, seven thousand* [A]Rev 6:12; 8:5; 11:19; 16:18 [B]John 9:24; Rev 14:7; 16:9; 19:7 [C]Rev 16:11 11:14 [A]Rev 8:13; 9:12 11:15 [a]I.e. Messiah [A]Rev 8:2; 10:7 [B]Rev 16:17; 19:1 [C]Rev 12:10 [D]Ps 2:2; Acts 4:26 [E]Ex 15:18; Dan 2:44; 7:14, 27; Luke 1:33 11:16 [A]Matt 19:28; Rev 4:4 [B]Rev 4:10 11:17 [A]Rev 1:8 [B]Rev 19:6 11:18 [a]Lit *give the reward to* [b]Or *holy ones* [A]Ps 2:1 [B]Ps 2:5; 110:5 [C]Dan 7:10; Rev 20:12 [D]Rev 10:7; 16:6 [E]Ps 115:13; Rev 13:16; 19:5 11:19 [a]Or *sanctuary* [b]Lit *hail* [A]Rev 4:1; 15:5 [B]Heb 9:4 [C]Rev 4:5; 8:5; 16:18 [D]Rev 16:21 12:1 [A]Matt 24:30; Rev 12:3 [B]Rev 11:19 [C]Gal 4:26 [D]Ps 104:2; Song 6:10

11:9 three and a half days. The entire world will watch (undoubtedly on the latest form of visual media) and glorify the Antichrist as the bodies of the dead prophets who have been killed begin to decay.

11:10 rejoice ... celebrate ... send gifts. Wild with joy over the death of their tormentors, those who dwell on the earth (a phrase used 11 times in Revelation to speak of unbelievers) will celebrate the two witnesses' deaths as a holiday.

11:11 breath of life from God came into them. The festivities, however, are short-lived as God vindicates His faithful witnesses by resurrecting them.

11:12 went up into heaven in the cloud. Some may wonder why God will not allow them to preach, assuming their message would have more force following their resurrection. But that ignores Christ's clear statement to the contrary (Lk 16:31). **enemies watched them.** Those who hated and dishonored the two witnesses will watch their vindication.

11:13 earthquake. God punctuates the ascension of His prophets with a shattering earthquake. The destruction and loss of life may be primarily among the leaders of the Antichrist's forces. **the rest.** This refers to the Jews still living, who will not yet have come to faith in Christ. **gave glory to the God of heaven.** A genuine experience of the salvation of Jews (cf. Lk 17:18, 19), in contrast to those who blaspheme and refuse to glorify God (16:9). This makes a key fulfilment of Zechariah's prophecy (12:10; 13:1) and Paul's (Ro 11:25–27).

11:14 second woe. The sixth trumpet (*see note on 9:12*). The interlude between the sixth and seventh trumpets ends (*see note on 10:1*). Israel's repentance will shortly usher in the millennial kingdom (Ac 3:19–21; Ro 11:25, 26). But first will come the final, climactic judgments.

11:15 seventh angel sounded. The seventh trumpet includes the 7 bowl, final judgments depicted in chap. 16 and all the events leading up to the establishing of the millennial kingdom (chap. 20) and the coronation of Jesus as King (chap. 19). ***kingdom* of our Lord and of His Christ.** Despite its many political and cultural divisions, the Bible views the world spiritually as one kingdom, with one ruler—Satan (Jn 12:31; 14:30; 16:11; 2Co 4:4). Following Satan's lead, the human rulers of this world are generally hostile to Christ (Ps 2:2; Ac 4:26). The long rebellion of the world kingdom will end with the victorious return of the Lord Jesus Christ to defeat His enemies and establish His messianic kingdom (Is 2:2, 3; Da 2:44; 7:13, 14, 18, 22, 27; Lk 1:31–33). This kingdom also belongs to God the Father (*see notes on 1Co 15:24*).

11:16 twenty-four elders. *See note on 4:4.*

11:17 the Almighty, who are and who were. The coming of the kingdom is no longer future, it will be immediate.

11:18 nations were enraged. No longer terrified (cf. 6:15–17), they will be filled with defiant rage. Their hostility will shortly manifest itself in a foolish attempt to fight against Christ—a doomed, futile effort that is the apex of human rebellion against God (16:14; 19:17–21). **Your wrath.** Almighty God answers the feeble, impotent fury of the nations (cf. Ps 2:1–9). The 24 elders speak of God's future wrath (20:11–15) as if it were already present, signifying its certainty. That God will one day pour out His wrath on rebellious men is a major theme in Scripture (cf. Is 24:17–23; 26:20, 21; 30:27–33; Eze 38:16ff.; 2Th 1:5–10). **dead ... judged.** The final outpouring of God's wrath includes judging the dead (cf. Mt 25:31–46; Jn 5:25–29). The judgment has two parts: 1) God rewards OT saints (Da 12:1–3; cf. 22:12; 1Co 3:8; 4:5), the raptured church (1Co 15:51, 52; 1Th 4:13–18), and Tribulation saints (20:4); and 2) God condemns unbelievers to the lake of fire forever (20:15).

11:19 temple of God ... heaven. See 3:12; 7:15; 14:15, 17; 15:5–8; 16:1, 17. The heavenly Holy of Holies (*see notes on Ex 26:31–36*), where God dwells in transcendent glory, already is identified as His throne (chaps. 4, 5). Cf. Heb 9:24. John had seen the throne (4:5), the altar (6:9; 8:3–5), and here the Holy of Holies. **ark of His covenant.** This piece of furniture in the OT tabernacle and temple (*see notes on Ex 25:11–18*) symbolized God's presence, atonement, and covenant with His people. That earthly ark was only a picture of this heavenly one (see Heb 9:23; 10:20). It was there God provided mercy and atonement for sin. As the earthly Holy of Holies was open when the price of sin was paid (Mt 27:51; Heb 10:19, 20), so the Holy of Holies in heaven is opened to speak of God's saving New Covenant and redeeming purpose in the midst of judgment. **lightning ... thunder ... earthquake ... hailstorm.** What was anticipated in 4:5 and 8:5 will become a terrifying reality. These events occur as part of the seventh bowl (16:17–21) and are the climax of the seventh trumpet. Since heaven is the source of vengeance, judgment also comes out of God's Holy of Holies (14:15, 17; 15:5–8; 16:1, 7, 17). *See note on 6:1.*

12:1 sign. A symbol pointing to something else. This is the first of 7 signs in the last half of Revelation. Cf. v. 3; 13:13, 14; 15:1; 16:14; 19:20. **a woman.** Not an actual woman, but a symbolic representation of Israel, pictured in the OT as the wife of God (Is 54:5, 6; Jer 3:6–8; 31:32; Eze 16:32; Hos 2:16). Three other symbolic women appear in Revelation: 1) Jezebel, who represents paganism (2:20); 2) the scarlet woman (17:3–6), symbolizing

[2] and she was with child; and she *[A]cried out, being
in labor and in pain to give birth.

THE RED DRAGON, SATAN

[3] Then [A]another sign appeared in heaven: and
behold, a great red [B]dragon having [C]seven heads
and [D]ten horns, and on his heads *were* [E]seven diadems. [4] And his tail *swept away a [A]third of the stars
of heaven and [B]threw them to the earth. And the
[C]dragon stood before the woman who was about to
give birth, so that when she gave birth [D]he might
devour her child.

THE MALE CHILD, CHRIST

[5] And [A]she gave birth to a son, a male *child,* who
is to [a,B]rule all the [b]nations with a rod of iron; and
her child was [C]caught up to God and to His throne.
[6] Then the woman fled into the wilderness where
she *had a place prepared by God, so that there
[a]she would be nourished for [A]one thousand two
hundred and sixty days.

THE ANGEL, MICHAEL

[7] And there was war in heaven, [A]Michael and his
angels waging war with the [B]dragon. The dragon
and [C]his angels waged war, [8] and they were not
strong enough, and there was no longer a place
found for them in heaven. [9] And the great [A]dragon
was thrown down, the [B]serpent of old who is called
the devil and [C]Satan, who [D]deceives the whole
[a]world; he was [E]thrown down to the earth, and his
angels were thrown down with him. [10] Then I heard
[A]a loud voice in heaven, saying,
"Now the [B]salvation, and the power, and the [A]king-
dom of our God and the authority of His Christ
have come, for the [C]accuser of our brethren has
been thrown down, he who accuses them before
our God day and night. [11] And they [A]overcame him
because of [B]the blood of the Lamb and because of
[C]the word of their testimony, and they [D]did not love
their life even [a]when faced with death. [12] For this
reason, [A]rejoice, O heavens and [B]you who [a]dwell in
them. [C]Woe to the earth and the sea, because [D]the
devil has come down to you, having great wrath,
knowing that he has *only* [E]a short time."
[13] And when the [A]dragon saw that he was thrown
down to the earth, he persecuted [B]the woman who
gave birth to the male *child.* [14] But the [A]two wings
of the great eagle were given to the woman, so that
she could fly [B]into the wilderness to her place, where
she *was nourished for [C]a time and times and half a
time, from the [a]presence of the serpent. [15] And the

12:2 [A]Is 26:17; 66:6-9; Mic 4:9f 12:3 [A]Rev 12:1; 15:1 [B]Is 27:1; Rev 12:4, 7, 9, 13, 16f; 13:2, 4, 11; 16:13; 20:2 [C]Rev 13:1; 17:3, 7, 9ff [D]Dan 7:7, 20, 24; Rev 13:1; 17:12, 16 [E]Rev 13:1; 19:12 12:4 [A]Rev 8:7, 12 [B]Dan 8:10 [C]Is 27:1; Rev 12:3, 7, 9, 13, 16f; 13:2, 4, 11; 16:13; 20:2 [D]Matt 2:16 12:5 [a]Or *shepherd* [b]Or *Gentiles* [A]Is 66:7 [B]Ps 2:9; Rev 2:27 [C]2 Cor 12:2ff 12:6 [a]Lit *they would nourish her for* [A]Rev 11:3; 13:5 12:7 [A]Dan 10:13, 21; 12:1; Jude 9 [B]Rev 12:3 [C]Matt 25:41 12:9 [a]Lit *inhabited earth* [A]Rev 12:3 [B]Gen 3:1; 2 Cor 11:3; Rev 12:15; 20:2 [C]Matt 4:10; 25:41 [D]Rev 13:14; 20:3, 8, 10 [E]Luke 10:18; John 12:31 12:10 [A]Rev 11:15 [B]Rev 7:10 [C]Job 1:11; 2:5; Zech 3:1; Luke 22:31; 1 Pet 5:8 12:11 [a]Lit *to death* [A]John 16:33; 1 John 2:13; Rev 15:2 [B]Rev 7:14 [C]Rev 6:9 [D]Luke 14:26; Rev 2:10 12:12 [a]Or *tabernacle* [A]Ps 96:11; Is 44:23; Rev 18:20 [B]Rev 13:6 [C]Rev 8:13 [D]Rev 12:9 [E]Rev 10:6 12:13 [A]Rev 12:3 [B]Rev 12:5 12:14 [a]Lit *face* [A]Ex 19:4; Deut 32:11; Is 40:31 [B]Rev 12:6 [C]Dan 7:25; 12:7

the apostate church; and 3) the wife of the Lamb (19:7), symbolizing the true church. That this woman does not represent the church is clear from the context. **clothed with the sun … moon under her feet … twelve stars.** Cf. Ge 37:9–11. Being clothed with the sun speaks of the glory, dignity, and exalted status of Israel, the people of promise who will be saved and given a kingdom. The picture of the moon under her feet possibly describes God's covenant relationship with Israel, since new moons were associated with worship (1Ch 23:31; 2Ch 2:4; 8:13; Ezr 3:5; Ps 81:3). The 12 stars represent the 12 tribes of Israel.

12:2 cried out … in pain. Israel, often pictured as a mother giving birth (cf. Is 26:17, 18; 54:1; 66:7–12; Hos 13:13; Mic 4:10; 5:2, 3; Mt 24:8), had agonized and suffered for centuries, longing for the Messiah to come and destroy Satan, sin, and death, and usher in the kingdom.

12:3 great red dragon. The woman's mortal enemy is Satan, who appears as a dragon 13 times in this book (cf. v. 9; 20:2). Red speaks of bloodshed (cf. Jn 8:44). **seven heads … ten horns … seven diadems.** Figurative language depicting Satan's domination of 7 past worldly kingdoms and 10 future kingdoms (cf. Da 7:7, 20, 24). *See notes on 13:1; 17:9, 10.* Satan has and will rule the world until the seventh trumpet blows (11:15). He has inflicted relentless pain on Israel (Da 8:24), desiring to kill the woman before she could bring forth the child that would destroy him (*see notes on Est 3:6–15*).

12:4 a third of the stars of heaven. Satan's original rebellion (cf. Is 14:12ff.; Eze 28:11ff.) resulted in one-third of the angelic host joining his insurrection and becoming demons. **devour her child.** Unable to prevent the virgin birth of Christ, Satan tried to kill the child in a general massacre of male children commanded by Herod (Mt 2:13–18; cf. Lk 4:28, 29).

12:5 a male *child*. Jesus Christ in His incarnation was of Jewish descent (Mt 1:1; 2Ti 2:8). Despite Satan's efforts to destroy Israel and the messianic line, Jesus' birth took place as predicted by the prophets (cf. Is 7:14; 9:6; Mic 5:2). **rod of iron.** Describes Jesus' coronation as King over the nations of the world (cf. 11:15; 19:15; Ps 2:6–9). **her child was caught up to God.** Christ's ascension is in view (Ac 1:9; 2:33; Heb 1:1–3; 12:2).

12:6 wilderness. God will protect Israel from Satan by hiding her in the wilderness, perhaps in the region of Moab, Ammon, and Edom, east of Israel. Interestingly, those countries will be specifically spared from the Antichrist's attack against the Holy Land (cf. Da 11:41). **one thousand two hundred and sixty days.** At the midpoint of the Tribulation, the Antichrist breaks his covenant with Israel, puts a stop to temple worship, sets up the abomination of desolation (Da 9:27; Mt 24:15), and devastates Jerusalem (11:2). At that time, many Jews flee for their lives (Mt 24:16ff.). God will preserve them during the last 1,260 days (42 months; 3 1/2 years) constituting the Great Tribulation. *See notes on 3:10; 6:1, 9.*

12:7 war in heaven. The tumultuous events on earth during the Tribulation find their counterpart in heaven. A state of war has existed since the fall of Satan (cf. v. 4; cf. Da 10:13; Jude 9). Something will intensify that warfare—possibly the raptured saints passing through the realm of the prince of the power of the air (cf. Eph 2:2).

12:9 dragon was thrown down … to the earth. Satan and his demons were cast out of heaven at the time of their original rebellion, but still have access to it (cf. Job 1:6; 2:1). That access will then be denied, and they will be forever barred from heaven. **devil and Satan.** Cf. 20:2. "Devil" comes from a Gr. verb meaning "to slander" or "to falsely accuse." He is a malignant liar (Jn 8:44; 1Jn 3:8). His accusations against believers (v. 10) are unsuccessful because of Christ our Advocate (1Jn 2:1). Satan, meaning "adversary," or "enemy," appears especially in Job and the gospels. **deceives the whole world.** As he has throughout human history, Satan will deceive people during the Tribulation (cf. 13:14; 20:3; Jn 8:44). After his temporary release from the bottomless pit at the end of the Millennium, he will briefly resume his deceitful ways (20:8, 10).

12:10 accuser. *See note on v. 9.* Satan will no longer accuse believers before the throne of God because he will no longer have access to heaven.

12:11 blood of the Lamb. No accusation can stand against those whose sins have been forgiven because of Christ's sacrificial death (see Ro 8:33–39).

12:12 he has *only* a short time. Knowing that his time is limited, Satan will intensify his efforts against God and mankind, and specifically target Israel (v. 13, 17).

12:14 wings of the great eagle. Not actual birds' wings, but a graphic depiction of God's providential protection of Israel (cf. Ex 19:4). Wings often speak of protection (cf. Dt 32:9–12; Ps 91:4; Is 40:31). Eagles—probably vulture-like griffins—were the largest birds known in Palestine. **a time and times and half a time.** Three and one-half years; the second half of the Tribulation (cf. v. 6; 11:2, 3; 13:5).

[A]serpent [a]poured water like a river out of his mouth after the woman, so that he might cause her to be swept away with the flood. 16 [a]But the earth helped the woman, and the earth opened its mouth and drank up the river which the dragon [b]poured out of his mouth. 17 So the dragon was enraged with the woman, and went off to [A]make war with the rest of her [a,B]children, who [C]keep the commandments of God and [D]hold to the testimony of Jesus.

THE BEAST FROM THE SEA

13 And the dragon stood on the sand of the [a]seashore.

Then I saw a [A]beast coming up out of the sea, having [B]ten horns and [B]seven heads, and on his horns *were* [C]ten diadems, and on his heads *were* [D]blasphemous names. 2 And the beast which I saw was [A]like a leopard, and his feet were like *those* of [B]a bear, and his mouth like the mouth of [C]a lion. And the [D]dragon gave him his power and his [E]throne and great authority. 3 *I saw* one of his heads as if it had been [a]slain, and his [A]fatal wound was healed. And the whole earth [B]was amazed *and followed* after the beast; 4 they worshiped the [A]dragon because he [A]gave his authority to the beast; and they worshiped the beast, saying, "[B]Who is like the beast, and who is able to wage war with him?" 5 There was given to him a mouth [A]speaking [a]arrogant words and blasphemies, and authority to act for [B]forty-two months was given to him. 6 And he opened his mouth in blasphemies against God, to blaspheme His name and His tabernacle, *that is,* [A]those who [a]dwell in heaven.

7 It was also given to him to [A]make war with the [a]saints and to overcome them, and authority over [B]every tribe and people and tongue and nation was given to him. 8 All who [A]dwell on the earth will worship him, *everyone* [B]whose name has not been [a]written [C]from the foundation of the world in the [D]book of life of [E]the Lamb who has been slain. 9 [A]If anyone has an ear, let him hear. 10 [A]If anyone [a]*is destined* for captivity, to captivity he goes; [B]if anyone kills with the sword, with the sword he must be killed. Here is [C]the [b]perseverance and the faith of the [c]saints.

12:15 [a]Lit *threw* [A]Gen 3:1; 2 Cor 11:3; Rev 12:9; 20:2 12:16 [a]Lit *And* [b]Lit *threw* 12:17 [a]Lit *seed* [A]Rev 11:7; 13:7 [B]Gen 3:15 [C]1 John 2:3; Rev 14:12 [D]Rev 1:2; 6:9; 14:12; 19:10 13:1 [a]Lit *sea* [A]Dan 7:3; Rev 11:7; 13:14, 15; 15:2; 16:13; 17:8 [B]Rev 12:3 [C]Rev 12:3; 17:12 [D]Dan 7:8; 11:36; Rev 17:3 13:2 [A]Dan 7:6; Hos 13:7f [B]Dan 7:5 [C]Dan 7:4 [D]Rev 12:3; 13:4, 12 [E]Rev 2:13; 16:10 13:3 [a]Lit *slaughtered to death* [A]Rev 13:12, 14 [B]Rev 17:8 13:4 [A]Rev 12:3; 13:2, 12 [B]Ex 15:11; Is 46:5; Rev 18:18 13:5 [a]Lit *great things* [A]Dan 7:8, 11, 20, 25; 11:36; 2 Thess 2:3f [B]Rev 11:2 13:6 [a]Or *tabernacle* [A]Rev 7:15; 12:12 13:7 [a]Or *holy ones* [A]Dan 7:21; Rev 11:7 [B]Rev 5:9 13:8 [a]Or *written in the book...slain from the foundation of the world* [A]Rev 3:10; 13:12, 14 [B]Rev 3:5 [C]Matt 25:34; Rev 17:8 [D]Ps 69:28 [E]Rev 5:6 13:9 [A]Rev 2:7 13:10 [a]Or leads *into captivity* [b]Or *steadfastness* [C]Or *holy ones* [A]Is 33:1; Jer 15:2; 43:11 [B]Gen 9:6; Matt 26:52; Rev 11:18 [C]Heb 6:12; Rev 14:12

12:16 earth opened its mouth. A great army will come against Israel like a flood (v. 15; cf. Jer 46:8; 47:2), only to be swallowed up, perhaps in conjunction with one of the numerous earthquakes that occur during that period (6:12; 8:5; 11:13, 19; 16:18; Mt 24:7).

12:17 rest of her children. Satan will turn his frustrated rage against every follower of the Lamb he can find—Jew or Gentile. **commandments of God ... testimony of Jesus.** The revealed truth from God and Christ contained in Scripture. Obedience to God's Word always marks a genuine believer. Cf. Jn 8:32.

13:1 the dragon stood. Satan takes a position in the midst of the nations of his world, represented by the sand of the sea. **a beast.** Lit. "a monster" (cf. 11:7), which describes a vicious, killing animal. In this context, the term represents both a person (Antichrist) and his system (the world). The final satanic world empire will be inseparable from the demon-possessed man who leads it. For a discussion of Antichrist, *see notes on 2Th 2:3–11.* He is also described in Da 7:8, 21–26; 8:23–25; 9:24–27; 11:36–45. **coming up out of the sea.** The sea represents the abyss or pit, the haunt of demons (cf. 11:7; 17:8; 20:1; Lk 8:31). The picture is of Satan summoning a powerful demon from the abyss, who then activates and controls the beast (Antichrist) and his empire. **ten horns and seven heads.** This description is like that of Satan in 12:3. The heads may represent successive world empires—Egypt, Assyria, Babylon, Medo-Persia, Greece, Rome, and the final kingdom of Antichrist (*see notes on 17:9, 10*). The final one is made up of all the kingdoms represented by the horns (*see notes for 17:12*). Ten is a number that symbolizes the totality of human military and political power assisting the beast (Antichrist) as he controls the world. Horns always represent power, as in the animal kingdom—both offensive power (attack) and defensive power (protection). Daniel shows that the human Antichrist will rise up from these 10 kings (Da 7:16–24). John picks up the numerical imagery of Da 2:41, 42, which refers to the 10 toes on the statue's clay and iron feet. The apostle sees the beast as the final world government—the anti-Christ, anti-God coalition—headed by a revived Roman Empire, having the strengths of various world powers, yet mixed with weakness and ultimately crushed (cf. Da 2:32–45; 7:7, 8, 19–25; *see note on 12:3*). The crowns show the regal dominion of this confederate kingdom. **blasphemous names.** Throughout history, every time a monarch has identified himself as a god, he has blasphemed the true God. Each ruler who contributes to the beast's final coalition has an identity, wears a crown, exerts dominion and power, and therefore blasphemes God.

13:2 leopard. A metaphor for ancient Greece, alluding to the Greeks' swiftness and agility as their military moved forward in conquest, particularly under Alexander the Great (cf. Da 7:6). The leopard and subsequent animal symbols were all native wildlife in Syria and Israel, familiar to John's readers. **bear.** A metaphor for the ancient Medo-Persian Empire, depicting that kingdom's ferocious strength, combined with its great stability (cf. Da 7:5). **lion.** A metaphor for the ancient Babylonian Empire, referring to the Babylonians' fierce, all-consuming power as they extended their domain (cf. Da 7:4). **the dragon gave him his power.** *See notes on v. 1; 12:9.*

13:3 his fatal wound was healed. This statement could refer to one of the kingdoms that was destroyed and revived (i.e., the Roman Empire). But more likely it refers to a fake death and resurrection enacted by the Antichrist, as part of his lying deception. Cf. vv. 12, 14; 17:8, 11; 2Th 2:9. **earth was amazed.** People in the world will be astounded and fascinated when Antichrist appears to rise from the dead. His charisma, brilliance, and attractive but deluding powers will cause the world to follow him unquestioningly (v. 14; 2Th 2:8–12).

13:5 was given. The sovereign God will establish the limits within which Antichrist will be allowed to speak and operate. God will allow him to utter his blasphemies, to bring the rage of Satan to its culmination on earth for 3 1/2 years (v. 5; 11:2, 3; 12:6, 13, 14). **forty-two months.** The final 3 1/2 years—1,260 days—of the "time of Jacob's distress" (Jer 30:7) and Daniel's 70th week (Da 9:24–27), known as the Great Tribulation (*see notes on 11:2; 12:6*; cf. Da 7:25). This last half is launched by the abomination of desolations (*see note on Mt 24:15*).

13:6 His name. This identifies God and summarizes all His attributes (cf. Ex 3:13, 14). **His tabernacle.** This is symbolic of heaven (cf. Heb 9:23, 24). **those who dwell in heaven.** The angels and glorified saints who are before the throne of God and serve Him day and night.

13:7 make war with the saints. The Antichrist will be allowed to massacre those who are God's children (cf. 6:9–11; 11:7; 12:17; 17:6; Da 7:23–25; 8:25; 9:27; 11:38; 12:10; Mt 24:16–22). *See note on 17:6.*

13:8 from the foundation of the world. According to God's eternal, electing purpose before creation, the death of Christ seals the redemption of the elect forever (cf. Ac 2:23; 4:27, 28). Antichrist can never take away the salvation of the elect. The eternal registry of the elect will never be altered, nor will the saved in the Antichrist's day worship him. **book of life.** *See note on 3:5.* **Lamb ... slain.** The Lord Jesus who died to purchase the salvation of those whom God had chosen was fulfilling an eternal plan.

13:9 Cf. 2:7, 11, 17, 29; 3:6, 13, 22. This phrase omits "what the Spirit says to the churches" as in the 7 letters to the churches, perhaps because they have been raptured.

13:10 A call for believers to accept persecution from Antichrist with perseverance and endurance. God has chosen some believers

THE BEAST FROM THE EARTH

11 Then [A]I saw another beast coming up out of
the earth; and he had [B]two horns like a lamb and
he spoke as a [C]dragon. 12 He [A]exercises all the authority of the first beast [a,B]in his presence. And he
makes [C]the earth and those who dwell in it to [D]wor-
ship the first beast, whose [E]fatal wound was healed.
13 He [A]performs great signs, so that he even makes
[B]fire come down out of heaven to the earth in the
presence of men. 14 And he [A]deceives [B]those who
dwell on the earth because of [C]the signs which it
was given him to perform [a,D]in the presence of the
beast, telling those who dwell on the earth to make
an image to the beast who *had the [E]wound of the
sword and has come to life. 15 And it was given to
him to give breath to the image of the beast, so that
the image of the beast would even [a]speak and cause
[A]as many as do not [B]worship the image of the beast
to be killed. 16 And he causes all, [A]the small and the
great, and the rich and the poor, and the free men
and the slaves, [a]to be given a [B]mark on their right
hand or on their forehead, 17 and *he provides* that
no one will be able to buy or to sell, except the one
who has the [A]mark, *either* [B]the name of the beast
or [C]the number of his name. 18 [A]Here is wisdom. Let
him who has understanding calculate the number
of the beast, for the number is that [B]of a man; and
his number is [a]six hundred and sixty-six.

THE LAMB AND THE 144,000 ON MOUNT ZION

14 Then I looked, and behold, [A]the Lamb *was*
standing on [B]Mount Zion, and with Him [C]one
hundred and forty-four thousand, having [D]His name
and the [D]name of His Father written [E]on their foreheads. 2 And I heard a voice from heaven, like [A]the
sound of many waters and like the [B]sound of loud
thunder, and the voice which I heard *was* like *the*
sound of [C]harpists playing on their harps. 3 And they
*[a]sang [A]a new song before the throne and before the
[B]four living creatures and the [C]elders; and [D]no one
could learn the song except the [E]one hundred and

13:11 [A]Rev 13:1; 16:13 [B]Dan 8:3 [C]Rev 13:4 13:12 [a]Or *by his authority* [A]Rev 13:4 [B]Rev 13:14; 19:20 [C]Rev 13:8 [D]Rev 13:15; 14:9, 11; 16:2; 19:20; 20:4 [E]Rev 13:3 13:13 [A]Matt 24:24; Rev 16:14; 19:20 [B]1 Kin 18:38; Luke 9:54; Rev 11:5; 20:9 13:14 [a]Or *by the authority of* [A]Rev 12:9 [B]Rev 13:8 [C]2 Thess 2:9f [D]Rev 13:12; 19:20 [E]Rev 13:3 13:15 [a]One early ms reads *speak, and he will cause* [A]Dan 3:3ff [B]Rev 13:12; 14:9, 11; 16:2; 19:20; 20:4 13:16 [a]Lit *causes all,...that they give them a mark* [A]Rev 11:18; 19:5, 18 [B]Gal 6:17; Rev 7:3; 14:9; 20:4 13:17 [A]Gal 6:17; Rev 7:3; 14:9; 20:4 [B]Rev 14:11 [C]Rev 15:2 13:18 [a]One early ms reads 616 [A]Rev 17:9 [B]Rev 21:17 14:1 [A]Rev 5:6 [B]Ps 2:6; Heb 12:22 [C]Rev 7:4; 14:3 [D]Rev 3:12 [E]Ezek 9:4; Rev 7:3 14:2 [A]Rev 1:15 [B]Rev 6:1 [C]Rev 5:8 14:3 [a]Two early mss read *sing* something *like a new song* [A]Rev 5:9 [B]Rev 4:6 [C]Rev 4:4 [D]Rev 2:17 [E]Rev 7:4; 14:1

to be imprisoned and executed which they must not resist (cf. Mt 26:51–54; 2Co 10:4), but accept with patience such suffering as God ordains for them (cf. 1Pe 2:19–24).

13:11 another beast. This is the final false prophet (called such in 16:13; 19:20; 20:10) who promotes Antichrist's power and convinces the world to worship him as God. This companion beast will be the chief, most persuasive proponent of satanic religion (cf. 16:13; 19:20; 20:10). Antichrist will be primarily a political and military leader, but the false prophet will be a religious leader. Politics and religion will unite in a worldwide religion of worshiping the Antichrist (see 17:1–9, 15–17). **out of the earth.** Likely another reference to the abyss that lies below the earth. The false prophet will be sent forth and controlled by a powerful demon from below. The earth imagery, in contrast to that of the foreboding, mysterious sea in v. 1, may imply that the false prophet is subtler and more winsome than Antichrist. **two horns like a lamb.** This describes the relative weakness of the false prophet compared to Antichrist, who has 10 horns. A lamb has only two small bumps on its head, very inferior to the 10-horned beast. **like a lamb.** The lamb imagery may also imply that the false prophet will be also a false Christ masquerading as the true Lamb. Unlike Antichrist, the false prophet will come not as a killing, destroying animal, but as one who appears gentle and deceptively attractive. **spoke as a dragon.** The false prophet will be Satan's mouthpiece, and thus his message will be like the dragon, Satan—the source of all false religion (cf. 2Co 11:14).

13:12 exercises all the authority of the first beast. The false prophet exercises the same kind of satanic power as Antichrist because he is empowered by the same source. He, too, will have worldwide influence and a reputation as a miracle worker and speaker. **makes the earth ... to worship.** The phrase "he makes" or "he causes" is used several times of him. He wields influence to establish a false world religion headed by Antichrist and to entice people to accept that system. **whose fatal wound was healed.** *See notes on v. 3; 17:8.* This likely refers to the carefully crafted deception of a false resurrection, a false murder to inspire allegiance for the world.

13:13 great signs. The same phrase is used of Jesus' miracles (Jn 2:11, 23; 6:2), which indicates the false prophet performs signs that counterfeit Christ's. Satan, who has done supernatural works in the past (e.g., Ex 7:11; 2Ti 3:8), must use his strategy of false miracles to convince the world that Antichrist is more powerful than God's true witnesses (chap. 11), including Jesus Christ. **fire come down out of heaven.** The context indicates that the false prophet does counterfeit pyrotechnic signs continually to convince men of his power, and also in imitation of the two witnesses (11:5).

13:14 make an image. This refers to replication of Antichrist that is related to the throne he will erect during the abomination of desolation, halfway into the Tribulation period. This will happen in the Jerusalem temple when Antichrist abolishes the former false world religion and seeks to have people worship him alone as God (cf. Da 9:27; 11:31; 12:11; Mt 24:15; 2Th 2:4). The false prophet and Antichrist again will deceive the world with a clever imitation of Christ, who will later return and reign from the true throne in Jerusalem.

13:15 speak. The false prophet will give the image of Antichrist the appearance of life, and the image will seem to utter words—contrary to what is normally true of idols (cf. Ps 135:15, 16; Hab 2:19). **cause ... to be killed.** His gentleness is a lie, since he is a killer (7:9–17). Some Gentiles will be spared to populate the kingdom (Mt 25:31–40), and Jews will be protected (12:17).

13:16 a mark. In the Roman Empire, this was a normal identifying symbol, or brand, that slaves and soldiers bore on their bodies. Some of the ancient mystical cults delighted in such tattoos, which identified members with a form of worship. Antichrist will have a similar requirement, one that will need to be visible on the hand or forehead.

13:17 to buy or to sell. Antichrist's mark will allow people to engage in daily commerce, including the purchase of food and other necessities. Without the identifying mark, individuals will be cut off from the necessities of life. **number of his name.** The beast (Antichrist) will have a name inherent in a numbering system. It is not clear from the text exactly what this name and number system will be or what its significance will be.

13:18 his number is six hundred and sixty-six. This is the essential number of a man. The number 6 falls one short of God's perfect number, 7, and thus represents human imperfection. Antichrist, the most powerful human the world will ever know, will still be a man, i.e., a 6. The ultimate in human and demonic power is a 6, not perfect, as God is. The 3-fold repetition of the number is intended to reiterate and underscore man's identity. When Antichrist is finally revealed, there will be some way to identify him with this basic number of a man, or his name may have the numerical equivalent of 666. (In many languages, including Heb., Gr., and Lat., letters have numerical equivalents.) Because this text reveals very little about the meaning of 666, it is unwise to speculate beyond what is said.

14:1 the Lamb. *See note on 5:6.* **Mount Zion.** The city of Jerusalem, where Messiah will return and plant His feet (cf. Pss 2; 48:1, 2; Is 24:23). **one hundred and forty-four thousand.** *See note on 7:4.* **name.** The counterpart to the mark of the beast. It is the stamp that will identify the 144,000 as belonging to God (*see note on 13:6*).

14:2 harps. *See note on 5:8.*

14:3 new song. The song of redemption, which is being sung by all the redeemed saints in one gigantic choir. They are rejoicing over the accomplishment of God's entire redemptive work before Christ's return

forty-four thousand who had been [A]purchased from
the earth. 4 [A]These are the ones who have not been
defiled with women, for they [a]have kept themselves
chaste. These *are* the ones who [B]follow the Lamb
wherever He goes. These have been [C]purchased
from among men [D]as first fruits to God and to the
Lamb. 5 And [A]no lie was found in their mouth; they
are [B]blameless.

VISION OF THE ANGEL WITH THE GOSPEL

6 And I saw another angel flying in [A]midheaven,
having [B]an eternal gospel to preach to [C]those who
[a]live on the earth, and to [D]every nation and tribe
and tongue and people; 7 and he said with a loud
voice, "[A]Fear God, and [B]give Him glory, because
the hour of His judgment has come; worship Him
who [C]made the heaven and the earth and sea and
[D]springs of waters."
8 And another angel, a second one, followed, saying, "[a,A]Fallen, fallen is [B]Babylon the great, she who
has [C]made all the nations drink of the [D]wine of the
[b]passion of her immorality."

DOOM FOR WORSHIPERS OF THE BEAST

9 Then another angel, a third one, followed them,
saying with a loud voice, "If anyone [A]worships the
beast and his [B]image, and receives a [C]mark on his
forehead or on his hand, 10 he also will drink of the
[A]wine of the wrath of God, which is mixed [a]in full
strength [B]in the cup of His anger; and he will be
tormented with [C]fire and [b]brimstone in the presence of the [D]holy angels and in the presence of the
Lamb. 11 And the [A]smoke of their torment goes up
forever and ever; [B]they have no rest day and night,
those who [C]worship the beast and his [C]image, and
[a]whoever receives the [D]mark of his name." 12 Here
is [A]the [a]perseverance of the [b]saints who [B]keep the
commandments of God and [c,C]their faith in Jesus.
13 And I heard a voice from heaven, saying, "Write,
'[A]Blessed are the dead who [B]die in the Lord from now
on!' " "Yes," [C]says the Spirit, "so that they may [D]rest
from their labors, for their [E]deeds follow with them."

THE REAPERS

14 Then I looked, and behold, a [A]white cloud, and
sitting on the cloud *was* one [B]like [a]a son of man,

14:3 [A]Rev 5:9 14:4 [a]Lit *are chaste men* [A]Matt 19:12; 2 Cor 11:2; Eph 5:27; Rev 3:4 [B]Rev 3:4; 7:17; 17:14 [C]Rev 5:9 [D]Heb 12:23; James 1:18 14:5 [A]Ps 32:2; Zeph 3:13; Mal 2:6; John 1:47; 1 Pet 2:22 [B]Heb 9:14; 1 Pet 1:19; Jude 24 14:6 [a]Lit *sit* [A]Rev 8:13 [B]1 Pet 1:25; Rev 10:7 [C]Rev 3:10 [D]Rev 5:9 14:7 [A]Rev 15:4 [B]Rev 11:13 [C]Rev 4:11 [D]Rev 8:10 14:8 [a]Lit *Babylon…fell, fell, she who* [b]Or *wrath* [A]Is 21:9; Jer 51:8; Rev 18:2 [B]Dan 4:30; Rev 16:19; 17:5; 18:10 [C]Jer 51:7 [D]Rev 17:2, 4; 18:3 14:9 [A]Rev 13:12; 14:11 [B]Rev 13:14f; 14:11 [C]Rev 13:16 14:10 [a]Lit *unmixed;* in ancient times wine was usually diluted with water [b]I.e. burning sulphur [A]Is 51:17; Jer 25:15f, 27; Rev 16:19; 19:15 [B]Ps 75:8; Rev 18:6 [C]Gen 19:24; Ezek 38:22; 2 Thess 1:7; Rev 19:20; 20:10, 14f; 21:8 [D]Mark 8:38 14:11 [a]Lit *if anyone* [A]Is 34:8-10; Rev 18:9, 18; 19:3 [B]Rev 4:8 [C]Rev 13:12; 14:9 [D]Rev 13:17 14:12 [a]Or *steadfastness* [b]Or *holy ones* [c]Lit *the faith of* [A]Rev 13:10 [B]Rev 12:17 [C]Rev 2:13 14:13 [A]Rev 20:6 [B]1 Cor 15:18; 1 Thess 4:16 [C]Rev 2:7; 22:17 [D]Heb 4:9ff; Rev 6:11 [E]1 Tim 5:25 14:14 [a]Or *the Son of Man* [A]Matt 17:5 [B]Dan 7:13; Rev 1:13

(cf. Pss 33:1–3; 40:3; 96:1; 144:9, 10; 149; Lk 15:10; *see note on 5:9*). **the four living creatures and the elders.** *See notes on 4:4, 6.*

14:4 not been defiled with women. An illustration of God's ability to keep believers remarkably pure in the midst of great difficulty. This phrase indicates that the 144,000 Jewish evangelists will have not only resisted the perverse system of Antichrist, but they will have also resisted all temptations to illicit sex. Cf. 2Co 11:2. **follow the Lamb.** This indicates partisanship for Jesus Christ. The victorious 144,000 are unwaveringly loyal to Him, whatever the cost (cf. Mt 16:24; Mk 10:21; Lk 9:23; Jn 10:27; 12:26; 14:15). **first fruits.** Like the OT firstfruits offerings, these men will be set apart for special service to God (cf. Dt 26:1–11). Some see firstfruits as the first large group of redeemed Israel (*see note on 11:13*), saved much earlier, and representative of more converts to follow (cf. Ro 16:5; 1Co 16:15), the first fruits of a redeemed Israel (Ro 11:1–5, 11–15, 25–27).

14:5 no lie. The 144,000 speak God's truth accurately and precisely, with no exaggeration or understatement (cf. Zep 3:13). **blameless.** Not sinless, but sanctified (see Eph 1:4; 5:27; Col 1:22).

14:6 midheaven. From a Gr. term denoting the point in the noonday sky where the sun reaches its zenith. This is the highest and brightest point, where all can see and hear. **an eternal gospel.** The angel is preaching the good news concerning eternal life and entrance into the kingdom of God (cf. Mt 24:14; 1Co 15:1–10). He is urging the people of the world to change their allegiance from the beast to the Lamb. It is also called in the NT the gospel of God, the gospel of grace, the gospel of Christ, the gospel of peace, the glorious gospel, and the gospel of the kingdom. It is good news that God saves by the forgiveness of sin and opens His kingdom to all who will repent and believe. The whole world will hear this preaching by the angel as God graciously calls all to salvation.

14:7 Fear God. Not Satan, nor Antichrist. This is the theme of Scripture, calling people to give honor, glory, worship, and reverence to God (cf. Pr 23:17; 1Pe 2:17). *See notes on Ro 1:18–21.* **hour of His judgment has come.** The last moment arrives to repent and believe before God's wrath is poured out. This is the book's first use of the word judgment, a term that has the same meaning as wrath (see 6:17; 12:12). **Him who made the heaven and the earth.** Creation is the great proof of God, which preachers will appeal to as the ground for all people to believe in Him and worship Him (cf. 4:11; 10:6; Jn 1:9; Ac 14:15–17; 17:23–28).

14:8 fallen is Babylon. Lack of response to the first angel's message causes a second angel to pronounce this judgment. Babylon refers to the entire worldwide political, economic, and religious kingdom of Antichrist. (Cf. 16:17–19 for details of this fall.) The original city of Babylon was the birthplace of idolatry where the residents built the Tower of Babel, a monument to rebelliousness and false religion. Such idolatry was subsequently spread when God confounded man's language and scattered them around the world (cf. Ge 11:1–9). **wine of the passion of her immorality.** This pictures Babylon causing the world to become intoxicated with her pleasures and enter an orgy of rebellion, hatred, and idolatry toward God. Fornication is spiritual prostitution to Antichrist's false system, which will fall for such iniquity.

14:9 worships the beast. *See notes on 13:14, 15*; cf. 13:8.

14:10 cup of His anger. Anyone loyal to the Antichrist and his kingdom will suffer the outpouring of God's collected wrath, done with the full force of His divine anger and unmitigated vengeance (cf. Ps 75:8; Is 51:17; Jer 25:15, 16). Divine wrath is not an impulsive outburst of anger aimed capriciously at people God does not like. It is the settled, steady, merciless, graceless, and compassionless response of a righteous God against sin. **fire and brimstone.** These are two elements that are often associated in Scripture with the torment of divine punishment (Ge 19:24, 25; Is 34:8–10). Here the reference is to hell, the lake of fire (cf. 19:20; 20:10; 21:8). Brimstone is a fiery sulfur (*see note on 9:17*).

14:11 torment goes up forever and ever. A reference to the eternality of hell (cf. Mt 3:12; 13:41, 42; 25:41; Mk 9:48). Torment is the ceaseless infliction of unbearable pain (cf. Lk 16:23, 24), here prescribed for all who are loyal to Satan's leader.

14:12 This is excellent scriptural support for the doctrine of perseverance, which assures all true believers in Christ that they will never lose their faith. The regenerate will continually endure, right to the end, in obedience to the truth, no matter what may come against them (*see notes on Ro 8:31–39; Php 1:6*; cf. Jer 32:40; Mt 24:13; Jn 6:35–40; 10:27–30; 1Jn 5:4, 11–13, 20).

14:13 Blessed. *See note on 1:3.*

14:14 son of man. *See note on 1:13.* The imagery of the Lord on a cloud is from Da 7:13, 14 and emphasizes magnificent majesty (cf. 1:7; Mt 24:30; 26:64; Ac 1:9–11). **golden crown.** The victor's crown, a laurel wreath, worn by those who celebrated victory in war or athletic competition. Christ now wears this particular crown, in this case made of gold, as a triumphant conqueror coming out of heaven to prevail over His enemies. **sickle.** A harvesting tool with a razor-sharp, curved steel or iron blade and a wooden handle, commonly used by ancient farmers to cut grain. It represents swift and devastating judgment.

having a golden [C]crown on His head and a sharp
sickle in His hand. 15 And another angel [A]came out
of the [a]temple, crying out with a loud voice to Him
who sat on the cloud, "[b,B]Put in your sickle and reap,
for the hour to reap has come, because the [C]har-
vest of the earth [c]is ripe." 16 Then He who sat on
the cloud [a]swung His sickle over the earth, and the
earth was reaped.
17 And another angel [A]came out of the [a]temple
which is in heaven, and he also had a sharp sickle.
18 Then another angel, [A]the one who has power over
fire, came out from [B]the altar; and he called with a
loud voice to him who had the sharp sickle, saying,
"[a,C]Put in your sharp sickle and gather the clusters
[b]from the vine of the earth, [D]because her grapes are
ripe." 19 So the angel [a]swung his sickle to the earth
and gathered *the clusters from* the vine of the earth,
and threw them into [A]the great wine press of the
wrath of God. 20 And [A]the wine press was trodden
[B]outside the city, and [C]blood came out from the wine
press, up to the horses' bridles, [a]for a distance of
[b]two hundred miles.

A SCENE OF HEAVEN

15 Then I saw [A]another sign in heaven, great
and marvelous, [B]seven angels who had [C]seven
plagues, *which are* [D]the last, because in them the
wrath of God is finished.
2 And I saw something like a [A]sea of glass mixed
with fire, and those who had [B]been victorious [a]over the
[C]beast and [D]his image and the [E]number of his name,
standing on the [A]sea of glass, holding [F]harps of God.
3 And they *sang the [A]song of Moses, [B]the bond-servant
of God, and the [C]song of the Lamb, saying,

"[D]Great and marvelous are Your works,
[E]O Lord God, the Almighty;
Righteous and true are Your ways,
[F]King of the [a]nations!
4 "[A]Who will not fear, O Lord, and
glorify Your name?
For You alone are holy;
For [B]ALL THE NATIONS WILL COME
AND WORSHIP BEFORE YOU,
FOR YOUR [a,C]RIGHTEOUS ACTS
HAVE BEEN REVEALED."

5 After these things I looked, and [A]the [a]temple of
the [B]tabernacle of testimony in heaven was opened,
6 and the [A]seven angels who had the seven plagues
[B]came out of the [a]temple, clothed in [b]linen, clean *and*
bright, and [C]girded around their chests with golden

14:14 [C]Ps 21:3; Rev 6:2 14:15 [a]Or *sanctuary* [b]Lit *Send forth* [c]Lit *has become dry* [A]Rev 11:19; 14:17; 15:6; 16:17 [B]Joel 3:13; Mark 4:29; Rev 14:18 [C]Jer 51:33; Matt 13:39-41 14:16 [a]Lit *cast* 14:17 [a]Or *sanctuary* [A]Rev 11:19; 14:15; 15:6; 16:17 14:18 [a]Lit *Send forth* [b]Lit *of* [A]Rev 16:8 [B]Rev 6:9; 8:3 [C]Joel 3:13; Mark 4:29; Rev 14:15 [D]Joel 3:13 14:19 [a]Lit *cast* [A]Is 63:2f; Rev 19:15 14:20 [a]Lit *from* [b]Lit *sixteen hundred stadia;* a stadion was approx 600 ft [A]Is 63:3; Lam 1:15; Rev 19:15 [B]Heb 13:12; Rev 11:8 [C]Gen 49:11; Deut 32:14 15:1 [A]Rev 12:1, 3 [B]Rev 15:6-8; 16:1; 17:1; 21:9 [C]Lev 26:21 [D]Rev 9:20 15:2 [a]Lit *from* [A]Rev 4:6 [B]Rev 12:11 [C]Rev 13:1 [D]Rev 13:14f [E]Rev 13:17 [F]Rev 5:8 15:3 [a]Two early mss read *ages* [A]Ex 15:1ff [B]Josh 22:5; Heb 3:5 [C]Rev 5:9f, 12f [D]Deut 32:3f; Ps 111:2; 139:14 [E]Hos 14:9; Rev 1:8 [F]1 Tim 1:17 15:4 [a]Or *judgments* [A]Jer 10:7; Rev 14:7 [B]Ps 86:9; Is 66:23 [C]Rev 19:8 15:5 [a]Or *sanctuary* [A]Rev 11:19 [B]Ex 38:21; Num 1:50; Heb 8:5; Rev 13:6 15:6 [a]Or *sanctuary* [b]One early ms reads *stone* [A]Rev 15:1 [B]Rev 14:15 [C]Rev 1:13

14:15 harvest of the earth. The grain—in this case the ungodly people of the world—is ready to be gathered up and judged.

14:17 temple. *See note on 11:19.* This refers to the heavenly dwelling place of God, not the Tribulation temple in Jerusalem (cf. 11:1).

14:18 another angel … who has power over fire. This angel is associated with fire on the altar, which represents the prayers of the saints (6:9–11; 8:3–5). Fire refers to the constantly burning fire on the brass altar of the Jerusalem temple. Twice daily the priest would burn incense with that fire and offer the burning incense in the Holy Place as a symbol of the people's prayers (*see notes on 5:8; 6:9; 8:3*). This angel is coming from the heavenly altar to ensure that all the prayers of all the saints for judgment and the coming of the kingdom are answered. He calls for judgment to start. **sickle.** *See note on v. 14.*

14:19 wine press. This vivid imagery signifies a horrendous slaughter or bloodbath (cf. Is 63:2, 3; La 1:15; Joel 3:13). Here it refers to the slaughter of all the enemies of God who are still alive, facing the destruction at Armageddon, the final battle against God's enemies, staged on the Plain of Esdraelon. The bloody imagery comes from the fresh juice of stomped grapes splattering and running down a trough from the upper vat to the lower vat of a stone winepress.

14:20 outside the city. God will determine that this bloodbath will occur outside Jerusalem, as if God wants to protect the city from the carnage all around. Zechariah 14:1–5 makes clear that Jerusalem will be attacked, but will not be destroyed in the end, but spared for the glory of the kingdom, and the believing remnant will be saved as the Lord defends them and the city against the nations. They will escape through a newly created valley as the Lord finishes judgment and sets up His kingdom. **up to the horses' bridles.** The severity of the slaughter is indicated in the imagery of the blood of those killed in the Battle of Armageddon splattering as high (about 4 ft.) as the bridles of the horses involved. Equally likely, if the battle occurs near the central valley of Israel, the tremendous volume and flow of blood could easily form troughs 4 ft. deep in some places. This event clearly is described in 19:11–21. Ezekiel 39:8–16 may be describing the cleanup. **two hundred miles.** The approximate distance from Armageddon in the N of Israel to Edom in the S. The great battle will rage across that entire area and even slightly beyond.

15:1–8 Chapter 15 introduces the 7 bowls of wrath, God's final judgments at the end of the 7-year Tribulation period. The bowl judgments come in a rapid-fire, staccato fashion, each one stronger in fury and intensity. The bowls are the last plagues that issue from the blast of the seventh trumpet, and will conclude the seventh seal (*see note on 6:1*).

15:1 wrath of God. *See notes on 11:18; 14:10; 16:19; 19:15*; cf. Ro 1:18–21.

15:2 sea of glass. God's heavenly throne sits on a transparent crystal platform or pavement (*see note on 4:6*). **victorious over the beast.** All the saints from every nation, including Israel, ultimately triumph over Satan's Antichrist and his system because of their faith in Jesus Christ. **number of his name.** *See note on 13:17.* **harps.** *See note on 5:8.*

15:3 song of Moses. Sung by the people of Israel immediately after their passage through the Red Sea and their deliverance from the Egyptian armies (Ex 15:1–21; cf. Dt 32:1–43), this was a song of victory and deliverance that the redeemed who overcome Antichrist and his system will readily identify with. **song of the Lamb.** See 5:8–14. These two songs celebrate two great redemptive events: 1) deliverance of Israel by God from Egypt through Moses; and 2) deliverance of sinners by God from sin through Christ. **Great and marvelous are Your works.** This statement from the song of the Lamb extols God's powerful works in creation as He providentially upholds the universe (cf. Ps 139:14). **Almighty.** God is omnipotent (cf. Am 4:13). **King of the nations!** God is sovereign over the redeemed of every nation (cf. Jer 10:7).

15:4 God's holy and perfect character inevitably demands that He judge (cf. Ps 19:9; Na 1:3, 6). After God's righteous judgment is complete, He will set up Christ's millennial kingdom on earth, and the elect from every nation will come and worship Him (cf. Ps 66:4; Is 66:23; Php 2:9–11).

15:5 the temple of the tabernacle of testimony. This refers to the location of the ark of the covenant in the Holy of Holies where God dwells (*see note on 11:19*; cf. Nu 10:11).

15:6 seven plagues. The final, most severe judgments from God, described in chap. 16 (*see note on v. 1*). **linen … golden sashes.** The fabric represents holiness and purity (19:14). These are belts or girdles, running from the shoulder to the waist, that each of the 7 angels wear over his garments. The sashes demonstrate riches, royalty, and untarnished glory.

sashes. 7 Then one of the [A]four living creatures gave
to the [B]seven angels seven [C]golden bowls full of the
[D]wrath of God, who [E]lives forever and ever. 8 And
the [a]temple was filled with [A]smoke from the glory
of God and from His power; and no one was able
to enter the [a]temple until the seven plagues of the
seven angels were finished.

SIX BOWLS OF WRATH

16 Then I heard a loud voice from [A]the [a]temple,
saying to the [B]seven angels, "Go and [C]pour out
[b]on the earth the seven bowls of the wrath of God."
2 So the first *angel* went and poured out his bowl
[a,A]on the earth; and it became a loathsome and malignant [B]sore on the [b]people [C]who had the mark of
the beast and who worshiped his image.
3 The second *angel* poured out his bowl [A]into the
sea, and it became blood like *that* of a dead man;
and every living [a]thing in the sea died.
4 Then the third *angel* poured out his bowl into the
[A]rivers and the springs of waters; and they [B]became
blood. 5 And I heard the angel of the waters saying,
"[A]Righteous are You, [B]who are and who were, O [C]Holy
One, because You [D]judged these things; 6 for they
poured out [A]the blood of saints and prophets, and You
have given them [B]blood to drink. They [a]deserve it."
7 And I heard [A]the altar saying, "Yes, O [B]Lord God, the
Almighty, [C]true and righteous are Your judgments."
8 The fourth *angel* poured out his bowl upon [A]the
sun, [B]and it was given to it to scorch men with fire.
9 Men were scorched with [a]fierce heat; and they
[A]blasphemed the name of God who has the power
over these plagues, and they [B]did not repent so as
to [C]give Him glory.
10 Then the fifth *angel* poured out his bowl on
the [A]throne of the beast, and his kingdom became
[B]darkened; and they gnawed their tongues because
of pain, 11 and they [A]blasphemed the [B]God of heaven
because of their pains and their [C]sores; and they
[D]did not repent of their deeds.
12 The sixth *angel* poured out his bowl on the
[A]great river, the Euphrates; and [B]its water was dried
up, so that [C]the way would be prepared for the kings
[D]from the [a]east.

15:7 [A]Rev 4:6 [B]Rev 15:1 [C]Rev 5:8 [D]Rev 14:10; 15:1 [E]Rev 4:9 15:8 [a]Or *sanctuary* [A]Ex 19:18; 40:34f; Lev 16:2; 1 Kin 8:10f; 2 Chr 5:13f; Is 6:4 16:1 [a]Or *sanctuary* [b]Lit *into* [A]Rev 11:19 [B]Rev 15:1 [C]Ps 79:6; Jer 10:25; Ezek 22:31; Zeph 3:8; Rev 16:2ff 16:2 [a]Lit *into* [b]Gr *anthropoi* [A]Rev 8:7 [B]Ex 9:9-11; Deut 28:35; Rev 16:11 [C]Rev 13:15-17; 14:9 16:3 [a]Lit *soul* [A]Ex 7:17-21; Rev 8:8f; 11:6 16:4 [A]Rev 8:10 [B]Ex 7:17-20; Ps 78:44; Rev 11:6 16:5 [A]John 17:25 [B]Rev 11:17 [C]Rev 15:4 [D]Rev 6:10 16:6 [a]Lit *are worthy* [A]Rev 17:6; 18:24 [B]Is 49:26; Luke 11:49-51 16:7 [A]Rev 6:9; 14:18 [B]Rev 1:8 [C]Rev 15:3; 19:2 16:8 [A]Rev 6:12 [B]Rev 14:18 16:9 [a]Lit *great* [A]Rev 16:11, 21 [B]Rev 2:21 [C]Rev 11:13 16:10 [A]Rev 13:2 [B]Ex 10:21f; Is 8:22; Rev 8:12; 9:2 16:11 [A]Rev 16:9, 21 [B]Rev 11:13 [C]Rev 16:2 [D]Rev 2:21 16:12 [a]Lit *rising of the sun* [A]Rev 9:14 [B]Is 11:15f; 44:27; Jer 51:36 [C]Is 41:2, 25; 46:11 [D]Rev 7:2

15:7 four living creatures. *See notes on 4:6–8.* **seven golden bowls.** These are shallow saucers, familiar items often associated with various functions of the temple worship (1Ki 7:50; 2Ki 12:13; 25:15), such as wine (Am 6:6) and blood sacrifice (Ex 27:3). Their flat shallowness pictures how the divine judgments will be emptied instantly, rather than slowly poured, drowning those who refused to drink the cup of salvation. **wrath of God.** *See notes on 11:18; 14:10.*

15:8 filled with smoke. Cf. Ex 19:16–18; 40:34–35; 1Ki 8:10, 11; Is 6:4.

16:2 first ... bowl ... became a loathsome and malignant sore. The Septuagint (LXX) uses the same Gr. word to describe the boils that plagued the Egyptians (Ex 9:9–11) and afflicted Job (Job 2:7). In the NT, it describes the open sores that covered the beggar Lazarus (Lk 16:21). All over the world, people will be afflicted with incurable, open, oozing sores. **mark of the beast.** Only the worshipers of Antichrist will be afflicted (*see note on 13:16;* cf. 14:9–11).

16:3 second ... bowl ... every living thing in the sea died. This is reminiscent of the second trumpet (8:8, 9), and of the first plague against Egypt (Ex 7:20–25). This plague, however, will be far more widespread. The water in the world's oceans will become thick, dark, and coagulated, like the blood of a corpse. The death and decay of billions of sea creatures will only add to the misery of this judgment.

16:4 third ... bowl ... rivers and the springs of waters. Fresh water, already in short supply because of the prolonged drought (11:6), will now suffer the fate of the oceans (cf. Ex 7:19ff.). In addition to suffering from thirst, the worshipers of Antichrist will have no clean water with which to wash their sores.

16:5 who are and who were. This phrase expresses God's eternality (cf. 1:4, 8; 4:8; 11:17). Verse 6 says that the eternal God will judge justly because they have killed the believers and preachers of the gospel (6:9–11; 7:9–17; 11:18; 17:6; 18:20). This slaughter will have no parallel in history (Mt 24:21) and neither will the vengeance of God (cf. Ro 12:19–21).

16:6 given them blood to drink. The thick, blood-like substance which the fresh waters have become is all that is available to drink (cf. v. 4). **They deserve it.** The angel exonerates God from any charge that His judgments are too harsh. The unspeakably wicked generation then alive will shed more blood than any before it, including that of saints (6:9; 17:6) and prophets (11:7–10). God's judgment is fair and proper (cf. Ex 21:25–27; Lv 24:19, 20; Heb 10:26–31).

16:7 altar. The personified altar echoes the words of the angel, reinforcing the truth that God is just in all judgment (19:1, 2; cf. Ge 18:25; Ps 51:4; Ro 3:4).

16:8 fourth ... bowl ... scorch men with fire. The sun that normally provides light, warmth, and energy will become a deadly killer. With no fresh water to drink, earth's inhabitants will face extreme heat. The scorching heat will melt the polar ice caps, which some estimate would raise the level of the world's oceans by 200 ft., inundating many of the world's major cities and producing further catastrophic loss of life (cf. Am 9:5, 6). The resulting disruption of ocean transportation will make it difficult to distribute the dwindling resources of food and water.

16:9 they did not repent. Incredibly, sinners will still refuse to repent (cf. vv. 11, 21), and instead blaspheme God—the One they know has caused their afflictions.

16:10 fifth ... bowl ... throne of the beast. This refers to either Antichrist's actual throne, or his capital city, but extends to all his dominion. Regardless of where the darkness begins, it eventually covers Antichrist's entire kingdom. **darkened.** Worldwide darkness is elsewhere associated with the judgment of God (cf. Is 60:2; Joel 2:2; Mk 13:24, 25). **gnawed their tongues.** A futile attempt to alleviate the pain from their sores, the drought, and the fierce heat.

16:11 blasphemed the God of heaven. A sign of their continued loyalty to Antichrist and their anger at God for the cumulative miseries brought about by the first 5 bowls. "God of heaven," a frequent OT title for God, appears in the NT only here and in 11:13. **their sores.** The lingering effects of the first bowl are the chief cause of their blasphemy.

16:12 sixth ... bowl ... Euphrates. Called "the great river" 5 times in Scripture (cf. 9:14; Ge 15:18; Dt 1:7; Jos 1:4), it flows some 1,800 mi. from its source on the slopes of Mt. Ararat to the Persian Gulf (*see note on 9:14*). It forms the eastern boundary of the land God promised to Israel (Ge 15:18; Dt 1:7; 11:24; Jos 1:4). With its flow already reduced by the prolonged drought and intensified heat, God supernaturally will dry it up to make way for the eastern confederacy to reach Israel (Is 11:15). **the kings from the east.** God providentially draws these kings and their armies in order to destroy them in the battle of Armageddon (v. 14). Their reason for coming may be to rebel against Antichrist, whose failure to alleviate the world's suffering will no doubt erode his popularity. Or, this may be a final act of rabid anti-Semitism intent on destroying Israel, perhaps in retaliation for the plagues sent by her God. Since the sun may have melted the ice caps on Ararat, flooding the valley of the Euphrates as the river overflows its banks and bridges, the land will be swamped. God will have to dry it up miraculously for the eastern army to get to Armageddon.

ARMAGEDDON

13 And I saw *coming* out of the mouth of the
[A]dragon and out of the mouth of the [B]beast and out
of the mouth of the [C]false prophet, three [D]unclean
spirits like [E]frogs; 14 for they are [A]spirits of demons,
[B]performing signs, which go out to the kings of the
[C]whole [a]world, to [D]gather them together for the
war of the [E]great day of God, the Almighty. 15 ("Behold, [A]I am coming like a thief. [B]Blessed is the one
who stays awake and keeps his clothes, [C]so that he
will not walk about naked and men will not see his
shame.") 16 And they [A]gathered them together to the
place which [B]in Hebrew is called [a,C]Har-Magedon.

SEVENTH BOWL OF WRATH

17 Then the seventh *angel* poured out his bowl
upon [A]the air, and a [B]loud voice came out of the
[a,C]temple from the throne, saying, "[D]It is done."
18 And there were flashes of [A]lightning and sounds
and peals of thunder; and there was [B]a great earthquake, [C]such as there had not been since man came
to be upon the earth, so great an earthquake *was*
it, and so mighty. 19 [A]The great city was split into
three parts, and the cities of the [a]nations fell. [B]Bab-
ylon the great was [C]remembered before God, to
give her [D]the cup of the wine of [b]His fierce wrath.
20 And [A]every island fled away, and the mountains
were not found. 21 And [A]huge [a]hailstones, about [b]one
hundred pounds each, *came down from heaven
upon men; and men [B]blasphemed God because of
the [C]plague of the hail, because its plague *was
extremely [c]severe.

THE DOOM OF BABYLON

17 [A]Then one of the [B]seven angels who had the
[C]seven bowls came and spoke with me, saying, "Come here, I will show you [D]the judgment of
the [E]great harlot who [F]sits on many waters, 2 with
whom [A]the kings of the earth committed *acts of*
immorality, and [B]those who dwell on the earth were
[C]made drunk with the wine of her immorality." 3 And
[A]he carried me away [a,B]in the Spirit [C]into a wilderness; and I saw a woman sitting on a [D]scarlet beast,
full of [E]blasphemous names, having [F]seven heads

16:13 [A]Rev 12:3 [B]Rev 13:1 [C]Rev 13:11, 14; 19:20; 20:10 [D]Rev 18:2 [E]Ex 8:6 16:14 [a]Lit *inhabited earth* [A]1 Tim 4:1 [B]Rev 13:13 [C]Rev 3:10 [D]1 Kin 22:21-23; Rev 17:14; 19:19; 20:8 [E]Rev 6:17 16:15 [A]Matt 24:43f; Luke 12:39f; Rev 3:3, 11 [B]Luke 12:37 [C]Rev 3:18 16:16 [a]Two early mss read *Armagedon* [A]Rev 19:19 [B]Rev 9:11 [C]Judg 5:19; 2 Kin 23:29f; 2 Chr 35:22; Zech 12:11 16:17 [a]Or *sanctuary* [A]Eph 2:2 [B]Rev 11:15 [C]Rev 14:15 [D]Rev 10:6; 21:6 16:18 [A]Rev 4:5 [B]Rev 6:12 [C]Dan 12:1; Matt 24:21 16:19 [a]Or *Gentiles* [b]Lit *wrath of His anger* [A]Rev 11:8; 17:18; 18:10, 18f, 21 [B]Rev 14:8 [C]Rev 18:5 [D]Rev 14:10 16:20 [A]Rev 6:14; 20:11 16:21 [a]Lit *hail* [b]Lit *the weight of a talent* [c]Lit *great* [A]Rev 8:7; 11:19 [B]Rev 16:9, 11 [C]Ex 9:18-25 17:1 [A]Rev 1:1; 21:9 [B]Rev 15:1 [C]Rev 15:7 [D]Rev 16:19 [E]Is 1:21; Jer 2:20; Nah 3:4; Rev 17:5, 15f; 19:2 [F]Jer 51:13; Rev 17:15 17:2 [A]Rev 2:22; 18:3, 9 [B]Rev 3:10; 17:8 [C]Rev 14:8 17:3 [a]Or *in spirit* [A]Rev 21:10 [B]Rev 1:10 [C]Rev 12:6, 14; 21:10 [D]Matt 27:28; Rev 18:12, 16 [E]Rev 13:1 [F]Rev 12:3; 17:7, 9, 12, 16

16:13 **the dragon ... the beast ... the false prophet.** The "unholy trinity," composed of Satan (the dragon; *see note on 12:3*), the Antichrist (the beast; *see note on 11:7*), and Antichrist's associate (the false prophet; *see note on 13:11*), spew out this plague. **three unclean spirits.** A common NT designation for demons (cf. Mt 12:43; Mk 1:23; Lk 8:29). These are especially vile, powerful, and deceitful (v. 14). **like frogs.** This figure further emphasizes their vileness. Frogs were unclean animals according to OT dietary laws (Lv 11:10, 11, 41). Persian mythology viewed them as plague-inducing creatures. The demons are thus described as slimy, cold-blooded, loathsome beings.

16:14 **signs.** These are supernatural wonders (cf. 13:12–15) designed to deceive (cf. 19:20; 1Ki 22:20–23; Mk 13:22) the kings into invading Palestine. Their impact will be so great that the unclean spirits are able to induce the kings to make the journey to Palestine in spite of their sores, the intense heat, drought, and darkness. **kings of the whole world.** No longer just the eastern confederacy, but now all the world begins to gather in Palestine for the final, climactic battle (Ps 2:2, 3; Joel 3:2–4; Zec 14:1–3). **the war of the great day of God, the Almighty.** The Battle of Armageddon (v. 16). It is the great war with God and Christ (*see notes on 2Th 1:7–10*; cf. Joel 2:11; 3:2, 4). The war will end when Christ arrives (19:17–20).

16:15 **Blessed.** *See note on 1:3.* **stays awake and keeps his clothes.** Our Lord stresses the need for constant readiness for His return (cf. 1Jn 2:28). The imagery pictures a soldier ready for battle, or a homeowner watchful for the arrival of a thief (see also 3:3; 1Th 5:2, 4; 2Pe 3:10).

16:16 **Har-Magedon.** The Heb. name for Mt. Megiddo, 60 mi. N of Jerusalem. The battle will rage on the nearby plains, site of Barak's victory over the Canaanites (Jdg 4), and Gideon's victory over the Midianites (Jdg 7). Napoleon called this valley the greatest battlefield he had ever seen. But the Battle of Armageddon will not be limited to the Megiddo plains—it will encompass the length of Palestine (*see note on 14:20*).

16:17 **seventh ... bowl ... "It is done."** This bowl will complete God's wrath (except for final judgment on the rebellion at the end of the Millennium; 20:7–10) and immediately precedes the second coming of Christ. It will usher in the worst calamity in the history of the world. The voice from the temple in heaven is undoubtedly that of God Himself. "It is done" is best translated, "It has been and will remain done" (cf. Jn 19:30). God will punctuate the completion of His wrath with a devastating earthquake—the most powerful in earth's history (cf. vv. 19–21).

16:19 **The great city.** Cf. 11:13; 21:10; *see notes on Zec 14:1–8.* Jerusalem will be split into 3 parts (Zec 14:4), not as a judgment (cf. 11:13), but as an improvement. The additional water supply (Zec 14:8) and topographical changes (Zec 14:4, 5) will prepare the city for its central place in the millennial kingdom. Jerusalem is the only city to be spared the judgment (cf. 1Ch 23:25; Ps 125:1, 2; Mic 4:7) and will be made more beautiful (Ps 48:2), because of her repentance (see 11:13). **cities of the nations.** God's purpose is very different for the rest of the world's cities—they are to be destroyed. **Babylon.** The capital of the Antichrist's empire will receive a special outpouring of God's wrath as prophesied in Is 13:6–13. Chapters 17, 18 give details of its destruction.

16:20 **every island fled ... mountains were not found.** This powerful earthquake will radically alter all the earth's topography, preparing it for the coming millennial kingdom. Cf. 6:12–14; Is 40:4, 5; Jer 4:23–27.

16:21 **one hundred pounds.** The huge size of the hailstones indicates unparalleled atmospheric convulsions. Such massive chunks of ice will cause unimaginable devastation and death.

17:1 **seven angels.** The reference to these angels links chaps. 17, 18 with the bowl judgments (chap. 16), which extend to the second coming of Christ (*see note on 16:17*). Chapters 17, 18 focus on one aspect of those bowl judgments, the judgment of Babylon. The judgments already described are identified as targeting the final world system. **great harlot.** *See note on 14:8.* Prostitution frequently symbolizes idolatry or religious apostasy (cf. Jer 3:6–9; Eze 16:30ff.; 20:30; Hos 4:15; 5:3; 6:10; 9:1). Nineveh (Na 3:1, 4), Tyre (Is 23:17), and even Jerusalem (Is 1:21) are also depicted as harlot cities. **sits on many waters.** This picture emphasizes the sovereign power of the harlot. The picture is of a ruler seated on a throne, ruling the waters, which symbolize the nations of the world (see v. 15).

17:2 **kings ... committed *acts of* immorality.** The harlot will ally herself with the world's political leaders. Fornication here does not refer to sexual sin, but to idolatry (*see note on 14:8*). All the world rulers will be absorbed into the empire of Satan's false christ. **wine of her immorality.** The harlot's influence will extend beyond the world's rulers to the rest of mankind (cf. v. 15; 13:8, 14). The imagery does not describe actual wine and sexual sin, but pictures the world's people being swept up into the intoxication and sin of a false system of religion.

17:3 **in the Spirit.** Cf. 1:10; 4:2; 21:10. The Holy Spirit transports John into the wilderness (a deserted, lonely, desolate wasteland), perhaps to give him a better understanding of the vision. **a woman.** The harlot of v. 1, Babylon. **scarlet beast.** The Antichrist (cf. 13:1, 4; 14:9; 16:10), who for a time will support and use the false religious system to effect world unity. Then he will assume political control (cf. v. 16). Scarlet is the color of luxury, splendor, and royalty. **full of blasphemous names.** Because of his self-deification (cf. 13:1; Da 7:25;

and ten horns. 4 The woman [A]was clothed in purple
and scarlet, and [a]adorned with gold and precious
[b]stones and pearls, having in her hand [B]a gold cup
full of abominations and of the unclean things of
her immorality, 5 and on her forehead a name *was*
written, a [A]mystery,

"[B]BABYLON THE GREAT,
THE MOTHER OF HARLOTS
AND OF [C]THE ABOMINATIONS
OF THE EARTH."

6 And I saw the woman drunk with [A]the blood of the
[a]saints, and with the blood of the witnesses of Jesus.
When I saw her, I wondered [b]greatly. 7 And the angel
said to me, "Why [a]do you wonder? I will tell you the
[A]mystery of the woman and of the beast that carries
her, which has the [B]seven heads and the ten horns.
8 "[A]The beast that you saw [B]was, and is not, and
is about to [C]come up out of the [D]abyss and [a,E]go to
destruction. And [F]those who dwell on the earth,
[G]whose name has not been written in the book of
life [H]from the foundation of the world, will [I]wonder when they see the beast, that he was and is
not and will come. 9 [A]Here is the mind which has
wisdom. The [B]seven heads are seven mountains on
which the woman sits, 10 and they are seven [A]kings;
five have fallen, one is, the other has not yet come;
and when he comes, he must remain a little while.
11 The beast which [A]was and is not, is himself also
an eighth and is *one* of the seven, and he [B]goes to
destruction. 12 The [A]ten horns which you saw are
ten kings who have not yet received a kingdom, but
they receive authority as kings with the beast [B]for
one hour. 13 These have [A]one [a]purpose, and they give
their power and authority to the beast.

VICTORY FOR THE LAMB

14 These will wage [A]war against the Lamb, and the
Lamb will [B]overcome them, because He is [C]Lord of
lords and [C]King of kings, and [D]those who are with
Him *are the* [E]called and chosen and faithful."
15 And he *said to me, "The [A]waters which you
saw where the harlot sits, are [B]peoples and multitudes and nations and tongues. 16 And the [A]ten horns
which you saw, and the beast, these will hate the
harlot and will make her [B]desolate and [C]naked, and
will [D]eat her flesh and will [E]burn her up with fire.

17:4 [a]Lit *gilded* [b]Lit *stone* [A]Ezek 28:13; Rev 18:12, 16 [B]Jer 51:7; Rev 18:6 17:5 [A]2 Thess 2:7; Rev 1:20; 17:7 [B]Rev 14:8; 16:19 [C]Rev 17:2 17:6 [a]Or *holy ones* [b]Lit *with great wonder* [A]Rev 16:6 17:7 [a]Lit *have you wondered* [A]2 Thess 2:7; Rev 1:20; 17:5 [B]Rev 17:3 17:8 [a]One early ms reads *is going* [A]Dan 7:7 [B]Rev 13:3, 12, 14; 17:11 [C]Rev 11:7; 13:1 [D]Rev 9:1; 13:1 [E]Rev 13:10; 17:11 [F]Rev 3:10 [G]Ps 69:28; Rev 3:5 [H]Matt 25:34; Rev 13:8 [I]Rev 13:3 17:9 [A]Rev 13:18 [B]Rev 17:3 17:10 [A]Rev 10:11 17:11 [A]Rev 13:3, 12, 14; 17:8 [B]Rev 13:10; 17:8 17:12 [A]Dan 7:24; Rev 12:3; 13:1; 17:16 [B]Rev 18:10, 17, 19 17:13 [a]Or *mind* [A]Rev 17:17 17:14 [A]Rev 16:14 [B]Rev 3:21 [C]1 Tim 6:15; Rev 19:16 [D]Rev 2:10f [E]Matt 22:14 17:15 [A]Is 8:7; Jer 47:2; Rev 17:1 [B]Rev 5:9 17:16 [A]Rev 17:12 [B]Rev 18:17, 19 [C]Ezek 16:37, 39 [D]Rev 19:18 [E]Rev 18:8

11:36; 2Th 2:4). **having seven heads and ten horns.** This pictures the extent of Antichrist's political alliances (*see notes on vv. 9–12; 13:1*).

17:4 purple and scarlet. The colors of royalty, nobility, and wealth. The woman is portrayed as a prostitute who has plied her trade successfully and become extremely wealthy. **adorned.** Prostitutes often dress in fine clothes and precious jewels to allure their victims (cf. Pr 7:10). The religious harlot Babylon is no different, adorning herself to lure the nations into her grasp. **a gold cup.** Still another evidence of the harlot's great wealth (cf. Jer 51:7); but the pure gold is defiled by the filthiness of her immorality. Just as a prostitute might first get her victim drunk, so the harlot system deceives the nations into committing spiritual fornication with her.

17:5 forehead. It was customary for Roman prostitutes to wear a headband with their name on it (cf. Jer 3:3) parading their wretchedness for all to see. The harlot's forehead is emblazoned with a 3-fold title descriptive of the world's final false religious system. **mystery.** A NT mystery is truth once hidden, but in the NT revealed. *See notes on Mt 13:11; Eph 3:4, 5.* Spiritual Babylon's true identity is yet to be revealed. Thus, the precise details of how it will be manifested in the world are not yet known. **BABYLON THE GREAT.** This Babylon is distinct from the historical, geographical city of Babylon (which still existed in John's day). The details of John's vision cannot be applied to any historical city (*see note on 14:8*). **MOTHER OF HARLOTS.** All false religion stems ultimately from Babel, or Babylon (cf. Ge 11; *see note on 14:8*).

17:6 the blood of the saints ... witnesses of Jesus. Some see the first group as OT saints, and the second as NT saints—an unimportant distinction since this pictures the "witnesses," or martyrs, of the Tribulation. John's point is that the harlot is a murderer. False religion has killed millions of believers over the centuries, and the final false system will be far more deadly than any that preceded it.

17:7 mystery. Not that Babylon is a false system of religion, because that is already known, but that the beast will fully support the harlot and together exert vast influence over the whole earth.

17:8 The beast. Both a king and kingdom are referred to by this term. **was, and is not, and is about to come up.** A reference to the Antichrist's false resurrection (13:3, 4, 12–14; *see note on 13:3*). **out of the abyss.** After his "resurrection," the Antichrist will become possessed by a great demon from the abyss (*see notes on 13:1, 3*). **destruction.** Eternal destruction (cf. v. 11; Mt 7:13; Jn 17:12; Php 1:28; 3:19; 2Th 2:3; Heb 10:39; 2Pe 2:3; 3:7, 16). This is the lake of fire, the place of Antichrist's destruction (19:20). **book of life.** The roll of the elect, written in eternity past by God (*see note on 3:5*). Only the elect will escape the Antichrist's deception (Mt 24:24). **from the foundation of the world.** *See note on 13:8*; cf. 2Ti 1:9; Titus 1:2 ("long ages ago"). A frequent phrase (Mt 13:35; 25:34; Lk 11:50; Jn 17:24; Eph 1:4; Heb 4:3; 9:26; 1Pe 1:20) referring to God's pre-creation plan.

17:9 seven mountains. The Gr. word is often used of hills (Mt 5:1; 15:29; Jn 6:15; 8:1). Many commentators interpret this expression to mean Rome, which sits on 7 hills. It is true that the final worldwide system of false religion includes, but is not necessarily limited to, Rome; but specifically, the 7 mountains in context likely symbolize the 7 kingdoms and their kings of v. 10.

17:10 seven kings. Representatives of the 7 great world empires (Egypt, Assyria, Babylon, Medo-Persia, Greece, Rome, and that of the Antichrist). Cf. Daniel's image in Da 2:37–45. **five have fallen, one is, the other.** When John wrote, the Egyptian, Assyrian, Babylonian, Medo-Persian, and Greek empires had gone out of existence; Rome still existed; and the Antichrist's empire had not yet come. When it does, it will be brief (12:12; 13:5), and he will end in perdition (v. 11; *see note on v. 8*).

17:11 was and is not ... an eighth. The Antichrist's kingdom is said to be both the seventh and eighth kingdoms because of his supposed demise and resurrection. He is the seventh king before and the eighth king after his "resurrection" when he destroys the harlot's religious empire and demands exclusive worship of himself (v. 16).

17:12 ten kings. *See notes on 12:3; 13:1* (cf. Da 2:41, 42). These kings are sub-rulers under the Antichrist, whose empire will apparently be divided into 10 administrative districts. **not yet received a kingdom.** Thus, the kings cannot be identified with any historical figures. **one hour.** Symbolic of the brief 3 1/2 year period of time (cf. 11:2, 3; 12:6, 12, 14; 13:5; 18:10, 17, 19).

17:14 wage war. A reference to the battle of Armageddon (16:14–16), where the Lamb will utterly destroy the kings (19:17–21). **Lord of lords and King of kings.** A title for God (19:16; 1Ti 6:15; cf. Dt 10:17; Ps 136:3) that emphasizes His sovereignty over all other rulers to whom He has delegated authority.

17:15 *See note on v. 1.*

17:16 these will hate the harlot. After using the false religious system to unify the world kingdoms and gain control of all, the Antichrist—with the help of his 10 sub-rulers—will turn against the system, plunder and destroy it, and seize all power and worship for himself. They will be carrying out God's will (v. 17). Cf. Ge 50:20.

17 For [A]God has put it in their hearts to execute His
[a]purpose [b]by [B]having a common purpose, and by
giving their kingdom to the beast, until the [C]words
of God will be fulfilled. 18 The woman whom you
saw is [A]the great city, which [a]reigns over the kings
of the earth."

BABYLON IS FALLEN

18 After these things I saw another [A]angel
[B]coming down from heaven, having great
authority, and the earth was [C]illumined with his
glory. 2 And he cried out with a mighty voice, saying, "[a,A]Fallen, fallen is Babylon the great! She [B]has
become a dwelling place of demons and a [b]prison of
every [C]unclean spirit, and a [b]prison of every unclean
and hateful bird. 3 For all the nations [a]have drunk
of the [A]wine of the [b]passion of her immorality, and
[B]the kings of the earth have committed *acts of* immorality with her, and the [C]merchants of the earth
have become rich by the [c]wealth of her [d,D]sensuality."
4 I heard another voice from heaven, saying,
"[A]Come out of her, my people, so that you will not
participate in her sins and receive of her plagues;
5 for her sins have [a,A]piled up as high as heaven, and
God has [B]remembered her iniquities. 6 [A]Pay her back
even as she has paid, and [a]give back *to her* double
according to her deeds; in the [B]cup which she has
mixed, mix twice as much for her. 7 [A]To the degree
that she glorified herself and [B]lived [a]sensuously, to
the same degree give her torment and mourning;
for she says in her heart, '[C]I SIT *as* A QUEEN AND I AM
NOT A WIDOW, and will never see mourning.' 8 For
this reason [A]in one day her plagues will come, [a]pes-
tilence and mourning and famine, and she will be
[B]burned up with fire; for the Lord God who judges
her [C]is strong.

LAMENT FOR BABYLON

9 "And [A]the kings of the earth, who committed
acts of immorality and [B]lived [a]sensuously with her,
will [C]weep and lament over her when they [D]see the
smoke of her burning, 10 [A]standing at a distance
because of the fear of her torment, saying, '[B]Woe,
woe, [C]the great city, Babylon, the strong city! For
in [D]one hour your judgment has come.'
11 "And the [A]merchants of the earth [B]weep and
mourn over her, because no one buys their cargoes
any more— 12 cargoes of [A]gold and silver and precious
[a]stones and pearls and fine linen and purple and
silk and scarlet, and every *kind of* citron wood and
every article of ivory and every article *made* from
very costly wood and [b]bronze and iron and marble,
13 and cinnamon and [a]spice and incense and perfume
and frankincense and wine and olive oil and fine
flour and wheat and cattle and sheep, and *cargoes* of
horses and chariots and [b]slaves and [c,A]human lives.

17:17 [a]Or *mind* [b]Lit *even to do one mind and to give* [A]2 Cor 8:16 [B]Rev 17:13 [C]Rev 10:7 17:18 [a]Lit *has a kingdom* [A]Rev 11:8; 16:19 18:1 [A]Rev 17:1, 7 [B]Rev 10:1 [C]Ezek 43:2 18:2 [a]Lit *Babylon…fell, fell* [b]Or *haunt* [A]Is 21:9; Jer 51:8; Rev 14:8 [B]Is 13:21f; 34:11, 13-15; Jer 50:39; 51:37; Zeph 2:14f [C]Rev 16:13 18:3 [a]Two early ancient mss read *have fallen by* [b]Lit *wrath* [c]Lit *power* [d]Or *luxury* [A]Jer 51:7; Rev 14:8 [B]Rev 17:2; 18:9 [C]Ezek 27:9-25; Rev 18:11, 15, 19, 23 [D]1 Tim 5:11; Rev 18:7, 9 18:4 [A]Is 52:11; Jer 50:8; 51:6, 9, 45; 2 Cor 6:17 18:5 [a]Lit *joined together* [A]Jer 51:9 [B]Rev 16:19 18:6 [a]Lit *double* to her [A]Ps 137:8; Jer 50:15, 29 [B]Rev 17:4 18:7 [a]Or *luxuriously* [A]Ezek 28:2-8 [B]1 Tim 5:11; Rev 18:3, 9 [C]Is 47:7f; Zeph 2:15 18:8 [a]Lit *death* [A]Is 47:9; Jer 50:31f; Rev 18:10 [B]Rev 17:16 [C]Jer 50:34; Rev 11:17f 18:9 [a]Or *luxuriously* [A]Rev 17:2; 18:3 [B]1 Tim 5:11; Rev 18:3, 7 [C]Ezek 26:16f; 27:35 [D]Rev 14:11; 18:18; 19:3 18:10 [A]Rev 18:15, 17 [B]Rev 18:16, 19 [C]Rev 11:8; 16:19; 18:16, 18, 19, 21 [D]Rev 17:12; 18:8, 17, 19 18:11 [A]Ezek 27:9-25; Rev 18:3, 15, 19, 23 [B]Ezek 27:27-34 18:12 [a]Lit *stone* [b]Or *brass* [A]Ezek 27:12-22; Rev 17:4 18:13 [a]Gr *amomon* [b]Lit *bodies* [c]Lit *souls of people* (Gr *anthropoi*) [A]1 Chr 5:21; Ezek 27:13; 1 Tim 1:10

17:18 great city. Here is another identification of the capital city of Babylon, centerpiece of Antichrist's empire. Cf. 18:10, 18, 21.

18:1 earth was illumined with his glory. The fifth bowl (16:10) will have plunged the world into darkness. Against that backdrop, the sudden, blazing appearance of another angel (not the same as in 17:1, 7, 15) will certainly rivet the world's attention on him and his message of judgment on Babylon (cf. 14:8).

18:2 fallen is Babylon the great! Cf. 14:8; *see note on Is 21:9*, the verse from which these words come. The Gr. text views the results of this as if it had already taken place (*see note on 14:8*). But the seventh bowl is being referred to here, and it is yet to come at this point (16:17–21). When it comes, devastation and annihilation will take place, leaving the place to demons.

18:3 wine ... of her immorality. Religious Babylon (chap. 17) lures the nations into spiritual drunkenness and fornication with false gods (17:2, 4); commercial Babylon (chap. 18) seduces the unbelieving world into a materialistic stupor, so that the people of the world will become drunk with passion because of their relationship with Babylon. kings ... merchants. Political rulers and corporate leaders alike are swept up in this worldwide system of commerce (14:8; 17:2).

18:4 Come out of her, my people. God will call His own to disentangle themselves from this evil system. This may also be God's calling the elect to abandon the world system and come to faith in the Savior. In either case, the message is to abandon the system before it is destroyed (cf. 2Co 6:17; 1Jn 2:15). The judgment of God on that society living in sinful, arrogant self-indulgence can be avoided. Cf. Isaiah's and Jeremiah's message to their people to leave Babylon (Is 48:20; Jer 50:8; 51:6–9, 45).

18:5 remembered. See 16:19. God does not remember the iniquities of His people (Jer 31:34), but does remember to protect them (Mal 3:16–4:2). For unrepentant Babylon, there will be no such forgiveness, only judgment.

18:6, 7 Pay her back. The angel calls for God to recompense wrath to Babylon in her own cup to repay her according to her deeds (*see note on 17:4*). This is an echo of the OT law of retaliation (Ex 21:24) which will be implemented by God (Ro 12:17–21).

18:6 double. Has the sense of "full," or "overflowing." The punishment will fit the crime (cf. Jer 16:18). cup. The cup of wickedness from which so many have drunk (14:8; 17:2, 4, 6) will call for the cup of wrath (14:10; 16:19).

18:7b am not a widow. A proud, but empty, boast of self-sufficiency, also made by historical Babylon (Is 47:8). Cf. 1Co 10:12.

18:8 in one day. See vv. 10, 17, 19. The special judgments on Babylon take place in a brief period of time. Daniel 5:30 records that Babylon of old fell in one day. her plagues. These could include those of 16:1ff., but must be the special destruction of the city as well, described as "pestilence and mourning and famine."

18:9–20 This section records the lament over Babylon's destruction, not her sin, by those who were part of her system.

18:9 kings. The political leaders of the world will weep because the loss of his capital city will signal the doom of Antichrist's empire, and with it, the source of their power. Cf. v. 3; 17:2. weep and lament over her. "Weep" means "to sob openly." "Lament" translates the same Gr. word used to express the despair of the unbelieving world at the return of Christ (1:7).

18:10 one hour. Cf. vv. 8, 17, 19.

18:12, 13 Over half of their commodities appear in the list of Eze 27:12–22.

18:12 purple. This refers to garments laboriously dyed with purple dye extracted from shellfish. Lydia (Ac 16:14) was a seller of such expensive garments. A distinctive mark of the Caesars was their purple robes. citron wood. Wood from North African citrus trees, highly valued because of its color, which was used to make extremely expensive pieces of furniture. marble. Marble, imported from Africa, Egypt, and Greece, was widely used in Roman buildings.

18:13 perfume. Cf. Mt 26:7, 12; Jn 12:3. frankincense. A fragrant gum or resin imported from Arabia and used in incense and perfume (SS 3:6; Mt 2:11). slaves and human lives. The slave trade, long banned by the civilized nations of the world, will reappear in Antichrist's debauched commercial system.

14 The fruit [a]you long for has gone from you, and all
things that were luxurious and splendid have passed
away from you and *men* will no longer find them.
15 The [A]merchants of [B]these things, who became rich
from her, will [C]stand at a distance because of the fear
of her torment, weeping and mourning, 16 saying,
'[A]Woe, woe, [B]the great city, she who [C]was clothed
in fine linen and purple and scarlet, and [a]adorned
with gold and precious [b]stones and pearls; 17 for in
[A]one hour such great wealth has been laid [B]waste!'
And [C]every shipmaster and every [a]passenger and
sailor, and as many as make their living by the sea,
[A]stood at a distance, 18 and were [A]crying out as they
[B]saw the smoke of her burning, saying, '[C]What *city* is
like [D]the great city?' 19 And they threw [A]dust on their
heads and were crying out, weeping and mourning,
saying, '[B]Woe, woe, the great city, in which all who
had ships at sea [C]became rich by her [a]wealth, for in
[B]one hour she has been laid [D]waste!' 20 [A]Rejoice over
her, O heaven, and you [a]saints and [B]apostles and
prophets, because [C]God has [b]pronounced judgment
for you against her."
21 Then [a]a [A]strong angel [B]took up a stone like a
great millstone and threw it into the sea, saying,
"So will Babylon, [C]the great city, be thrown down
with violence, and [D]will not be found any longer.
22 And [A]the sound of harpists and musicians and
flute-players and trumpeters will not be heard in
you any longer; and no craftsman of any craft will
be found in you any longer; and the [B]sound of a
mill will not be heard in you any longer; 23 and the
light of a lamp will not shine in you any longer; and
the [A]voice of the bridegroom and bride will not be
heard in you any longer; for your [B]merchants were
the great men of the earth, because all the nations
were deceived [C]by your sorcery. 24 And in her was
found the [A]blood of prophets and of [a]saints and of
[B]all who have been slain on the earth."

THE FOURFOLD HALLELUJAH

19 After these things I heard something like a
[A]loud voice of a great multitude in heaven,
saying,
"[B]Hallelujah! [C]Salvation and [D]glory and power
belong to our God; 2 [A]BECAUSE HIS [B]JUDGMENTS
ARE [C]TRUE AND RIGHTEOUS; for He has judged the
[D]great harlot who was corrupting the earth with
her immorality, and HE HAS [E]AVENGED THE BLOOD
OF HIS BOND-SERVANTS [a]ON HER." 3 And a second
time they said, "[A]Hallelujah! [B]HER SMOKE RISES
UP FOREVER AND EVER." 4 And the [A]twenty-four
elders and the [B]four living creatures [C]fell down
and worshiped God who sits on the throne saying,
"[D]Amen. [E]Hallelujah!" 5 And a voice came from the
throne, saying,
"[A]Give praise to our God, all you His bond-servants, [B]you who fear Him, the small and the great."
6 Then I heard *something* like [A]the voice of a great
multitude and like [B]the sound of many waters and
like the [C]sound of mighty peals of thunder, saying,
"[A]Hallelujah! For the [D]Lord our God, the Almighty,
reigns.

MARRIAGE OF THE LAMB

7 Let us rejoice and be glad and [A]give the glory to
Him, for [B]the marriage of the Lamb has come and

18:14 [a]Lit *of your soul's desire* 18:15 [A]Rev 18:3 [B]Rev 18:12, 13 [C]Rev 18:10 18:16 [a]Lit *gilded* [b]Lit *stone and pearl* [A]Rev 18:10, 19 [B]Rev 18:10, 18, 19, 21 [C]Rev 17:4 18:17 [a]Lit *one who sails to a place* [A]Rev 18:10 [B]Rev 17:16; 18:19 [C]Ezek 27:28f 18:18 [A]Ezek 27:30 [B]Rev 18:9 [C]Ezek 27:32; Rev 13:4 [D]Rev 18:10 18:19 [a]Lit *costliness* [A]Josh 7:6; Job 2:12; Lam 2:10 [B]Rev 18:10 [C]Rev 18:3, 15 [D]Rev 17:16; 18:17 18:20 [a]Or *holy ones* [b]Lit *judged your judgment of her* [A]Jer 51:48; Rev 12:12 [B]Luke 11:49f [C]Rev 6:10; 18:6ff; 19:2 18:21 [a]Lit *one* [A]Rev 5:2; 10:1 [B]Jer 51:63f [C]Rev 18:10 [D]Ezek 26:21 18:22 [A]Is 24:8; Ezek 26:13; Matt 9:23 [B]Eccl 12:4; Jer 25:10 18:23 [A]Jer 7:34; 16:9 [B]Is 23:8; Rev 6:15; 18:3 [C]Nah 3:4; Rev 9:21 18:24 [a]Or *holy ones* [A]Rev 16:6; 17:6 [B]Matt 23:35 19:1 [A]Jer 51:48; Rev 11:15; 19:6 [B]Ps 104:35; Rev 19:3, 4, 6 [C]Rev 7:10 [D]Rev 4:11 19:2 [a]Lit *from her hand* [A]Ps 19:9 [B]Rev 6:10 [C]Rev 16:7 [D]Rev 17:1 [E]Deut 32:43; 2 Kin 9:7; Rev 16:6; 18:20 19:3 [A]Ps 104:35; Rev 19:1, 4, 6 [B]Is 34:10; Rev 14:11 19:4 [A]Rev 4:4, 10 [B]Rev 4:6 [C]Rev 4:10 [D]Ps 106:48; Rev 5:14 [E]Ps 104:35; Rev 19:3, 6 19:5 [A]Ps 22:23; 115:13; 134:1; 135:1 [B]Rev 11:18 19:6 [A]Jer 51:48; Rev 11:15; 19:1 [B]Ezek 1:24; Rev 1:15 [C]Rev 6:1 [D]Ps 93:1; 97:1; 99:1; Rev 1:8 19:7 [A]Rev 11:13 [B]Matt 22:2; 25:10; Luke 12:36; John 3:29; Eph 5:23, 32; Rev 19:9

18:17 shipmaster. Ship captains will mourn the loss of Babylon and the lucrative transport business that went with it.

18:19 threw dust on their heads. An ancient expression of grief (cf. Jos 7:6; 1Sa 4:12; 2Sa 1:2; 15:32; Job 2:12; La 2:10; Eze 27:30). **in one hour.** Not just 60 minutes, but one brief period of swift judgment (*see note on v. 8*).

18:20 God has pronounced judgment for you against her. The angel will exhort the tribulation martyrs (6:9–11) to rejoice, not over the deaths of those doomed to eternal hell, but, because God's righteousness and justice will have prevailed.

18:21 great millstone. Millstones were large, heavy stones used to grind grain. This metaphor portrays the violence of Babylon's overthrow. Cf. Jer 51:61–64; *see note on Mt 18:6*.

18:22, 23 The fall of Babylon ends whatever semblance of normalcy will still exist in the world after all the seals, trumpets, and bowls. Life will be totally disrupted and the end near. No more music, no industry, no preparing of food ("millstone"), no more power for light, and no more weddings because God will destroy the deceivers and deceived.

18:24 blood of prophets and of saints. The religious and commercial/political systems embodied in Babylon will commit unspeakable atrocities against God's people (cf. 6:10; 11:7; 13:7, 15; 17:6; 19:2). God will avenge that slaughter of His people (19:2).

19:1 After these things. This is a time key. After the destruction of Babylon at the end of the Great Tribulation, just before the kingdom is established (chap. 20). This section bridges the Tribulation and the millennial kingdom. **great multitude.** Probably angels, since the saints join in later (vv. 5ff.; cf. 5:11, 12; 7:11, 12). The imminent return of the Lord Jesus Christ prompts this outburst of praise.

19:1–6 Hallelujah! This Heb. word appears 4 times in the NT, all in this chapter (vv. 1, 3, 4, 6). This exclamation, meaning "Praise the Lord," occurs frequently in the OT (cf. Pss 104:35; 105:45; 106:1; 111:1; 112:1; 113:1; 117:1; 135:1; 146:1). Five reasons for their praise emerge: 1) God's deliverance of His people from their enemies (v. 1); 2) God's meting out of justice (v. 2); 3) God's permanent crushing of man's rebellion (v. 3); 4) God's sovereignty (v. 6); and 5) God's communion with His people (v. 7).

19:2 judgments. Saints long for the day of judgment (cf. 6:10; 16:7; Is 9:7; Jer 23:5). Godly people love righteousness and hate sin, for righteousness honors God and sin mocks Him. Believers long for a world of justice and it will come (v. 15; 2:27; 12:5).

19:3 smoke rises. This is because of the fire (cf. 17:16, 18; 18:8, 9, 18; 14:8–11).

19:4 twenty-four elders. Best understood as representatives of the church (*see note on 4:4*). **four living creatures.** A special order of angelic beings (*see note on 4:6*). These compose the same group as in 7:11 and are associated with worship frequently (4:8, 11; 5:9–12, 14; 11:16–18).

19:5 the small and the great. All distinctions and ranks are to be transcended.

19:6 the Almighty. Used 9 times in Revelation as a title for God (cf. v. 15; 1:8; 4:8; 11:17; 15:3; 16:7, 14; 21:22). The great praise of the multitude sounds like a massive crashing of waves.

19:7 marriage of the Lamb. Hebrew weddings consisted of 3 phases: 1) betrothal (often when the couple were children); 2) presentation (the festivities, often lasting several days, that preceded the ceremony); and 3) the ceremony (the exchanging of vows). The church was betrothed to Christ by His sovereign choice in eternity past (Eph 1:4; Heb 13:20) and will be presented to Him at the Rapture (Jn 14:1–3; 1Th 4:13–18). The final supper will signify the end of the

His [a,C]bride has made herself ready." 8 It was given to
her to clothe herself in [A]fine linen, bright *and* clean;
for the fine linen is the [B]righteous acts of the [a]saints.
9 Then [A]he *said to me, "[B]Write, '[C]Blessed are
those who are invited to the marriage supper of
the Lamb.' " And he *said to me, "[D]These are true
words of God." 10 Then [A]I fell at his feet to worship
him. [B]But he *said to me, "Do not do that; I am a
[C]fellow servant of yours and your brethren who
[D]hold the testimony of Jesus; worship God. For the
testimony of Jesus is the spirit of prophecy."

THE COMING OF CHRIST

11 And I saw [A]heaven opened, and behold, a [B]white
horse, and He who sat on it *is* called [C]Faithful and
True, and in [D]righteousness He judges and wages
war. 12 His [A]eyes *are* a flame of fire, and on His head
are many [B]diadems; and He has a [C]name written
on Him which no one knows except Himself. 13 *He
is* clothed with a [A]robe dipped in blood, and His
name is called [B]The Word of God. 14 And the armies
which are in heaven, clothed in [A]fine linen, [B]white
and clean, were following Him on white horses.
15 [A]From His mouth comes a sharp sword, so that
[B]with it He may strike down the nations, and He
will [a,C]rule them with a rod of iron; and [D]He treads
the [b]wine press of the fierce wrath of God, the Almighty. 16 And on His robe and on His thigh He has
[A]a name written,

"[B]KING OF KINGS, AND LORD OF LORDS."

17 Then I saw [a]an angel standing in the sun, and
he cried out with a loud voice, saying to [A]all the
birds which fly in [B]midheaven, "[C]Come, assemble
for the great supper of God, 18 so that you may [A]eat
the flesh of kings and the flesh of [a]commanders and
the flesh of mighty men and the flesh of horses and
of those who sit on them and the flesh of all men,
[B]both free men and slaves, and [C]small and great."

19:7 [a]Lit *wife* [C]Matt 1:20; Rev 21:2, 9 19:8 [a]Or *holy ones* [A]Rev 15:6; 19:14 [B]Rev 15:4 19:9 [A]Rev 17:1; 19:10 [B]Rev 1:19 [C]Matt 22:2f; Luke 14:15 [D]Rev 17:17; 21:5; 22:6 19:10 [A]Rev 22:8 [B]Acts 10:26; Rev 22:9 [C]Rev 1:1f [D]Rev 12:17 19:11 [A]Ezek 1:1; John 1:51; Rev 4:1 [B]Rev 6:2; 19:19, 21 [C]Rev 3:14 [D]Ps 96:13; Is 11:4 19:12 [A]Dan 10:6; Rev 1:14 [B]Rev 6:2; 12:3 [C]Rev 2:17; 19:16 19:13 [A]Is 63:3 [B]John 1:1 19:14 [A]Rev 19:8 [B]Rev 3:4; 19:8 19:15 [a]Or *shepherd* [b]Lit *wine press of the wine of the wrath of God's anger* [A]Rev 1:16; 19:21 [B]Is 11:4; 2 Thess 2:8 [C]Ps 2:9; Rev 2:27 [D]Is 63:3; Joel 3:13; Rev 14:19, 20 19:16 [A]Rev 2:17; 19:12 [B]Rev 17:14 19:17 [a]Lit *one* [A]Rev 19:21 [B]Rev 8:13 [C]1 Sam 17:44; Jer 12:9; Ezek 39:17 19:18 [a]I.e. chiliarchs, in command of one thousand troops [A]Ezek 39:18-20 [B]Rev 6:15 [C]Rev 11:18; 13:16; 19:5

ceremony. This symbolic meal will take place at the establishment of the millennial kingdom and last throughout that 1,000-year period (cf. 21:2). While the term "bride" often refers to the church, and does so here (2Co 11:2; Eph 5:22–24), it ultimately expands to include all the redeemed of all ages, which becomes clear in the remainder of the book.

19:8 righteous acts of the saints. Not Christ's imputed righteousness granted to believers at salvation, but the practical results of that righteousness in believers' lives, i.e., the outward manifestation of inward virtue.

19:9 Blessed. *See note on 1:3.* **those who are invited.** This is not the bride (the church), but the guests. The bride doesn't get invited, she invites. These are those saved before Pentecost, all the faithful believers saved by grace through faith up to the birth of the church (Ac 2:1ff.). Though they are not the bride, they still are glorified and reign with Christ in the millennial kingdom. It is really differing imagery rather than differing reality. The guests also will include tribulation saints and believers alive in earthly bodies in the kingdom. The church is the bride, pure and faithful—never a harlot, like Israel was (see Hos 2). So the church is the bride during the presentation feast in heaven, then comes to earth for the celebration of the final meal (the Millennium). After that event, the new order comes and the marriage is consummated (*see notes on 21:1, 2*). **true words of God.** This refers to everything since 17:1. *It is all true—the marriage* will take place after judgment.

19:10 fell at his feet. Overwhelmed by the grandeur of the vision, John collapsed in worship before the angel (cf. 1:17; 22:8). **Do not do that.** Cf. 22:8, 9. The Bible forbids the worship of angels (Col 2:18, 19). **the testimony of Jesus is the spirit of prophecy.** The central theme of both OT prophecy and NT preaching is the gospel of the Lord Jesus Christ.

19:11 heaven opened. The One who ascended to heaven (Ac 1:9–11) and had been seated at the Father's right hand (Heb 8:1; 10:12; 1Pe 3:22) will return to take back the earth from the usurper and establish His kingdom (5:1–10). The nature of this event shows how it differs from the Rapture. At the Rapture, Christ meets His own in the air—in this event He comes with them to earth. At the Rapture, there is no judgment; in this event it is all judgment. This event is preceded by blackness—the darkened sun, moon gone out, stars fallen, smoke—then lightning and blinding glory as Jesus comes. Such details are not included in Rapture passages (Jn 14:1–3; 1Th 4:13–18). **white horse.** In the Roman triumphal processions, the victorious general rode his white war horse up the Via Sacra to the temple of Jupiter on the Capitoline Hill. Jesus' first coming was in humiliation on a colt (Zec 9:9). John's vision portrays Him as the conqueror on His warhorse, coming to destroy the wicked, to overthrow the Antichrist, to defeat Satan, and to take control of the earth (cf. 2Co 2:14). **Faithful and True.** True to His word, Jesus will return to earth (Mt 24:27–31; *see note on 3:14*). **in righteousness He judges.** See 20:11–15; cf. Mt 25:31ff.; Jn 5:25–30; Ac 17:31. **wages war.** This startling statement, appearing only here and 2:16, vividly portrays the holy wrath of God against sinners (cf. Ps 7:11). God's patience will be exhausted with sinful, rebellious mankind.

19:12 His eyes *are* a flame of fire. Nothing escapes His penetrating vision, so His judgments are always just and accurate (*see note on 1:14*). **a name … no one knows.** John could see the name, but was unable to comprehend it (cf. 2Co 12:4). There are unfathomable mysteries in the Godhead that even glorified saints will be unable to grasp.

19:13 a robe dipped in blood. This is not from the battle of Armageddon, which will not have begun until v. 15. Christ's blood-spattered garments symbolize the great battles He has already fought against sin, Satan, and death and been stained with the blood of His enemies. **The Word.** Only John uses this title for the Lord (see Introduction: Author and Date). As the Word of God, Jesus is the image of the invisible God (Col 1:15); the express image of His person (Heb 1:3); and the final, full revelation from God (Heb 1:1, 2).

19:14 armies … in heaven. Composed of the church (v. 8), tribulation saints (7:13), OT believers (Jude 14; cf. Da 12:1, 2), and even angels (Mt 25:31). They return not to help Jesus in the battle (they are unarmed), but to reign with Him after He defeats His enemies (20:4; 1Co 6:2; 2Ti 2:12). Cf. Ps 149:5–9.

19:15 sharp sword. This symbolizes Christ's power to kill His enemies (1:16; cf. Is 11:4; Heb 4:12, 13). That the sword comes out of His mouth indicates that He wins the battle with the power of His word. Though the saints return with Christ to reign and rule, they are not the executioners. That is His task, and that of His angels (Mt 13:37–50). **rod of iron.** Swift, righteous judgment will mark Christ's rule in the kingdom. Believers will share His authority (2:26; 1Co 6:2; *see notes on 2:27; 12:5; Ps 2:9*). **wine press.** A vivid symbol of judgment (*see note on 14:19*). Cf. Is 63:3; Joel 3:13.

19:16 on His thigh. Jesus will wear a banner across His robe and down His thigh with a title emblazoned on it that emphasizes His absolute sovereignty over all human rulers (*see note on 17:14*).

19:17–21 These verses depict the frightening holocaust unparalleled in human history—the Battle of Armageddon, the pinnacle of the day of the Lord (*see note on 1Th 5:2*). It is not so much a battle as an execution, as the remaining rebels are killed by the Lord Jesus (v. 21; *see notes on 14:19, 20*; cf. Ps 2:1–9; Is 66:15, 16; Eze 39:1ff.; Joel 3:12ff.; Mt 24, 25; 2Th 1:7–9). This day of the Lord was seen by Isaiah (66:15, 16), Joel (3:12–21), Ezekiel (39:1–4, 17–20), Paul (2Th 1:6ff.; 2:8), and our Lord (Mt 25:31–46).

19:17, 18 great supper of God. Cf. Eze 39:17. Also called "the war of the great day of God, the Almighty" (16:14), it will begin with an angel summoning birds to feed on the corpses of those who will be slain (cf. Mt 24:27, 28). God will declare His victory before the battle even begins. The OT frequently pictures the indignity of carrion birds feasting on human dead (Dt 28:26; Ps 79:2; Is 18:6; Jer 7:33; 16:4; 19:7; 34:20; Eze 29:5).

19 And I saw [A]the beast and [B]the kings of the earth
and their armies assembled to make war against
Him who [C]sat on the horse and against His army.

DOOM OF THE BEAST AND FALSE PROPHET

20 And the beast was seized, and with him the
[A]false prophet who [B]performed the signs [a,C]in his
presence, by which he [D]deceived those who had
received the [E]mark of the beast and those who
[F]worshiped his image; these two were thrown alive
into the [G]lake of [H]fire which burns with [b]brimstone.
21 And the rest were killed with the sword which
[A]came from the mouth of Him who [B]sat on the horse,
and [C]all the birds were filled with their flesh.

SATAN BOUND

20 Then I saw [A]an angel coming down from
heaven, holding the [B]key of the abyss and
a great chain [a]in his hand. 2 And he laid hold of
the [A]dragon, the serpent of old, who is the devil
and Satan, and [B]bound him for a thousand years;
3 and he threw him into the [A]abyss, and shut *it* and
[B]sealed *it* over him, so that he would [C]not deceive the
nations any longer, until the thousand years were
completed; after these things he must be released
for a short time.
4 Then I saw [A]thrones, and [B]they sat on them,
and [C]judgment was given to them. And I *saw* [D]the
souls of those who had been beheaded because of
[a]their [E]testimony of Jesus and because of the word
of God, and those who had not [F]worshiped the beast
or his image, and had not received the [G]mark on
their forehead and on their hand; and they [H]came
to life and [I]reigned with Christ for a thousand years.
5 The rest of the dead did not come to life until the
thousand years were completed. [A]This is the first
resurrection. 6 [A]Blessed and holy is the one who has
a part in the first resurrection; over these the [B]sec-
ond death has no power, but they will be [C]priests

19:19 [A]Rev 11:7; 13:1 [B]Rev 16:14, 16 [C]Rev 19:11, 21 19:20 [a]Or *by his authority* [b]I.e. burning sulphur [A]Rev 16:13 [B]Rev 13:13 [C]Rev 13:12 [D]Rev 13:14 [E]Rev 13:16f [F]Rev 13:12, 15 [G]Rev 20:10, 14f; 21:8 [H]Is 30:33; Dan 7:11; Rev 14:10 19:21 [A]Rev 19:15 [B]Rev 19:11, 19 [C]Rev 19:17 20:1 [a]Lit *upon* [A]Rev 10:1 [B]Rev 1:18; 9:1 20:2 [A]Gen 3:1; Rev 12:9 [B]Is 24:22; 2 Pet 2:4; Jude 6 20:3 [A]Rev 20:1 [B]Dan 6:17; Matt 27:66 [C]Rev 12:9; 20:8, 10 20:4 [a]Lit *the* [A]Dan 7:9 [B]Matt 19:28; Rev 3:21 [C]Dan 7:22; 1 Cor 6:2 [D]Rev 6:9 [E]Rev 1:9 [F]Rev 13:12, 15 [G]Rev 13:16f [H]John 14:19 [I]Rev 3:21; 5:10; 20:6; 22:5 20:5 [A]Luke 14:14; Phil 3:11; 1 Thess 4:16 20:6 [A]Rev 14:13 [B]Rev 2:11; 20:14 [C]Rev 1:6

19:19 kings of the earth. See 17:12–17. **their armies.** See 16:13, 14. **His army.** Zechariah describes this army of the Lord as "all the holy ones" (Zec 14:5).

19:20 beast was seized, and … the false prophet. In an instant, the world's armies are without their leaders. The beast is Antichrist (*see notes on 13:1–8*); the false prophet is his religious cohort (*see notes on 13:11–17*). **thrown alive.** The bodies of the beast and the false prophet will be transformed, and they will be banished directly to the lake of fire (Da 7:11)—the first of countless millions of unregenerate men (20:15) and fallen angels (cf. Mt 25:41) to arrive in that dreadful place. That these two still appear there 1,000 years later (20:10) refutes the false doctrine of annihilationism (cf. 14:11; Is 66:24; Mt 25:41; Mk 9:48; Lk 3:17; 2Th 1:9). **lake of fire.** The final hell, the place of eternal punishment for all unrepentant rebels, angelic or human (cf. 20:10, 15). The NT says much of eternal punishment (cf. 14:10, 11; Mt 13:40–42; 25:41; Mk 9:43–48; Lk 3:17; 12:47, 48). **fire … brimstone.** *See note on 9:17.* These two are frequently associated with divine judgment (14:10; 20:10; 21:8; Ge 19:24; Ps 11:6; Is 30:33; Eze 38:22; Lk 17:29).

19:21 sword. See v. 15; cf. Zec 14:1–13. **birds were filled with their flesh.** All remaining sinners in the world will have been executed, and the birds will gorge themselves on their corpses.

20:1–22:21 Chapter 19 ends with the Battle of Armageddon and Christ's second coming—events that mark the close of the Tribulation. The events of chap. 20—the binding of Satan, Christ's 1,000-year earthly kingdom, Satan's final rebellion, and the Great White Throne Judgment—fit chronologically between the close of the Tribulation and the creation of the new heaven and the new earth described in chaps. 21, 22.

20:1 the abyss. The place where demons are incarcerated pending their final sentencing to the lake of fire (*see notes on 9:1; 2Pe 2:4*).

20:2 laid hold. This includes not only Satan, but the demons as well. Their imprisonment will dramatically alter the world during the kingdom, since their destructive influence in all areas of human thought and life will be removed. **dragon.** Likening Satan to a dragon emphasizes his ferocity, and cruelty (*see note on 12:3*). **serpent of old.** A reference to Satan's first appearance in the Garden of Eden (Ge 3:1ff.), where he deceived Eve (cf. 2Co 11:3; 1Ti 2:14). **devil … Satan.** *See note on 12:9.* **a thousand years.** This is the first of 6 references to the length of the millennial kingdom (cf. vv. 3, 4, 5, 6, 7). There are 3 main views of the duration and nature of this period: 1) Premillennialism sees this as a literal 1,000-year period during which Jesus Christ, in fulfillment of numerous prophecies (e.g., 2Sa 7:12–16; Ps 2; Is 11:6–12; 24:23; Hos 3:4, 5; Joel 3:9–21; Am 9:8–15; Mic 4:1–8; Zep 3:14–20; Zec 14:1–11; Mt 24:29–31, 36–44), reigns on the earth. Using the same general principles of interpretation for both prophetic and nonprophetic passages leads most naturally to premillennialism. Another strong argument supporting this view is that so many biblical prophecies have already been literally fulfilled, suggesting that future prophecies will likewise be fulfilled literally. 2) Postmillennialism understands the reference to a 1,000-year period as only symbolic of a golden age of righteousness and spiritual prosperity. It will be ushered in by the spread of the gospel during the present church age and brought to completion when Christ returns. According to this view, references to Christ's reign on earth primarily describe His spiritual reign in the hearts of believers in the church. 3) Amillennialism understands the 1,000 years to be merely symbolic of a long period of time. This view interprets OT prophecies of a Millennium as being fulfilled spiritually now in the church (either on earth or in heaven) or as references to the eternal state. Using the same literal, historical, grammatical principles of interpretation so as to determine the normal sense of language, one is left with the inescapable conclusion that Christ will return and reign in a real kingdom on earth for 1,000 years. There is nothing in the text to render the conclusion that "a thousand years" is symbolic. Never in Scripture when "year" is used with a number is its meaning not literal (*see note on 2Pe 3:8*).

20:3 the abyss. All 7 times that this appears in Revelation, it refers to the place where fallen angels and evil spirits are kept captive, waiting to be sent to the lake of fire—the final hell prepared for them (Mt 25:41). **released for a short time.** Satan will be released so God can make a permanent end of sin before establishing the new heaven and earth. All who survive the Tribulation and enter the kingdom will be believers. However, despite that and the personal presence and rule of the Lord Jesus Christ, many of their descendants will refuse to believe in Him. Satan will then gather those unbelievers for one final, futile rebellion against God. It will be quickly and decisively crushed, followed by the Great White Throne Judgment and the establishment of the eternal state.

20:4 the souls of those who had been beheaded. These are tribulation martyrs (cf. 6:9; 18:24; 19:2). The Gr. word translated "beheaded" became a general term for execution, not necessarily a particular method. **the mark.** *See note on 13:16.* Tribulation martyrs will be executed for refusing the mark of the beast. **reigned.** Tribulation believers, along with the redeemed from both the OT and NT eras, will reign with Christ (1Co 6:2; 2Ti 2:12) during the 1,000-year kingdom.

20:5 The rest of the dead. The bodies of unbelievers of all ages will not be resurrected until the Great White Throne Judgment (vv. 12, 13). **first resurrection.** Scripture teaches two kinds of resurrections: the "resurrection of life" and the "resurrection of judgment" (Jn 5:29; cf. Da 12:2; Ac 24:15). The first kind of resurrection is described as "the resurrection of the righteous" (Lk 14:14), the resurrection of "those who are Christ's at His coming" (1Co 15:23), and the "better resurrection" (Heb 11:35). It includes only the redeemed of the church age (1Th 4:13–18), the OT (Da 12:2), and the Tribulation (v. 4). They will enter the kingdom in resurrection bodies, along with believers who survived the Tribulation. The second kind of resurrection, then, will be the resurrection of the unconverted who will receive their final bodies suited for torment in hell.

20:6 Blessed. Those who die in the Lord

of God and of Christ and will [D]reign with Him for
a thousand years.

SATAN FREED, DOOMED

7 When the thousand years are completed, Satan
will be [A]released from his prison, 8 and will come
out to [A]deceive the nations which are in the [B]four
corners of the earth, [C]Gog and Magog, to [D]gather
them together for the war; the number of them is
like the [E]sand of the [a]seashore. 9 And they [A]came up
on the [a]broad plain of the earth and surrounded the
[B]camp of the [b]saints and the [C]beloved city, and [D]fire
came down from heaven and devoured them. 10 And
[A]the devil who [A]deceived them was thrown into the
[B]lake of fire and [a]brimstone, where the [C]beast and
the [C]false prophet are also; and they will be [D]tor-
mented day and night forever and ever.

JUDGMENT AT THE THRONE OF GOD

11 Then I saw a great white [A]throne and Him who
sat upon it, from whose [a]presence [B]earth and heaven
fled away, and [C]no place was found for them. 12 And
I saw the dead, the [A]great and the small, standing
before the throne, and [a,B]books were opened; and
another [b]book was opened, which is [C]*the book* of
life; and the dead [A]were judged from the things
which were written in the [a]books, [D]according to their
deeds. 13 And the sea gave up the dead which were
in it, and [A]death and Hades [B]gave up the dead which
were in them; and they were judged, every one *of*
them [C]according to their deeds. 14 Then [A]death and
Hades were thrown into [B]the lake of fire. This is the
[C]second death, the lake of fire. 15 And if [a]anyone's
name was not found written in [A]the book of life, he
was thrown into the lake of fire.

THE NEW HEAVEN AND EARTH

21 Then I saw [A]a new heaven and a new earth;
for [B]the first heaven and the first earth passed
away, and there is no longer *any* sea. 2 And I saw
[A]the holy city, [B]new Jerusalem, [C]coming down out of
heaven from God, [D]made ready as a bride adorned

20:6 [D]Rev 3:21; 5:10; 20:4; 22:5 20:7 [A]Rev 20:2f 20:8 [a]Lit *sea* [A]Rev 12:9; 20:3, 10 [B]Ezek 7:2; Rev 7:1 [C]Ezek 38:2; 39:1, 6 [D]Rev 16:14 [E]Heb 11:12 20:9 [a]Lit *breadth of the earth* [b]Or *holy ones* [A]Ezek 38:9, 16 [B]Deut 23:14 [C]Ps 87:2 [D]Ezek 38:22; 39:6; Rev 13:13 20:10 [a]I.e. burning sulphur [A]Rev 20:2f [B]Rev 19:20; 20:14, 15 [C]Rev 16:13 [D]Rev 14:10f 20:11 [a]Lit *face* [A]Rev 4:2 [B]Rev 6:14; 21:1 [C]Dan 2:35; Rev 12:8 20:12 [a]Or *scrolls* [b]Or *scroll* [A]Rev 11:18 [B]Dan 7:10 [C]Rev 3:5; 20:15 [D]Matt 16:27; Rev 2:23; 20:13 20:13 [A]1 Cor 15:26; Rev 1:18; 6:8; 21:4 [B]Is 26:19 [C]Matt 16:27; Rev 2:23; 20:12 20:14 [A]1 Cor 15:26; Rev 1:18; 6:8; 21:4 [B]Rev 19:20; 20:10, 15 [C]Rev 20:6 20:15 [a]Lit *anyone was* [A]Rev 3:5; 20:12 21:1 [A]Is 65:17; 66:22; 2 Pet 3:13 [B]2 Pet 3:10; Rev 20:11 21:2 [A]Is 52:1; Rev 11:2; 21:10; 22:19 [B]Rev 3:12; 21:10 [C]Heb 11:10, 16; Rev 21:10 [D]Is 61:10; Rev 19:7; 21:9; 22:17

(14:13) are blessed with the privilege of entering His kingdom (*see note on 1:3*). **second death.** The first death is only physical, the second is spiritual and eternal in the lake of fire, the final, eternal hell (v. 14). It could exist outside the created universe as we know it, outside of space and time, and be presently unoccupied (*see note on 19:20*). **a thousand years.** *See note on v. 2.*

20:7 Satan ... released. He is loosed to bring cohesive leadership to the world of rebels born to the believers who entered the kingdom at the beginning. He is loosed to reveal the character of Christ-rejecting sinners who are brought into judgment for the last time ever.

20:8 Gog and Magog. The name given to the army of rebels and its leader at the end of the Millennium. They were names of ancient enemies of the Lord. Magog was the grandson of Noah (Ge 10:2) and founder of a kingdom located N of the Black and Caspian Seas. Gog is apparently the leader of a rebel army known collectively as Magog. The battle depicted in vv. 8, 9 is like the one in Eze 38, 39; it is best to see this one as taking place at the end of the Millennium. For the difference, *see notes on Eze 38, 39.*

20:9 beloved city. Jerusalem (cf. Pss 78:68; 87:2), the capital city during Christ's millennial reign (Jer 3:17). The saints will be living around the city where Christ reigns (cf. Is 24:23; Jer 3:17; Zec 14:9–11). **fire.** Frequently associated in Scripture with divine judgment of wicked men (Ge 19:24; 2Ki 1:10, 12, 14; Lk 9:54; 17:29).

20:10 deceived. Just as his demons will entice the world's armies into the Battle of Armageddon, Satan will draw them into a suicidal assault against Christ and His people (16:13, 14). **lake of fire and brimstone.** *See note on 19:20.* **tormented day and night.** *See note on 14:11.* Continuous, unrelieved torment will be the final state of Satan, fallen angels, and unredeemed men.

20:11–15 These verses describe the final judgment of all the unbelievers of all ages (Mt 10:15; 11:22, 24; 12:36, 41, 42; Lk 10:14; Jn 12:48; Ac 17:31; 24:25; Ro 2:5, 16; Heb 9:27; 2Pe 2:9; 3:7; Jude 6). Our Lord referred to this event as the "resurrection of judgment" (Jn 5:29). This judgment takes place in the indescribable void between the end of the present universe (v. 11) and the creation of the new heaven and earth (21:1).

20:11 great white throne. Nearly 50 times in Revelation there is the mention of a throne. This is a judgment throne, elevated, pure, and holy. God sits on it as judge (cf. 4:2, 3, 9; 5:1, 7, 13; 6:16; 7:10, 15) in the person of the Lord Jesus Christ. See 21:5, 6; Jn 5:22–29; Ac 17:31. **earth and heaven fled away.** John saw the contaminated universe go out of existence. Peter described this moment in 2Pe 3:10–13 (*see notes there*). The universe is "uncreated," going into nonexistence (cf. Mt 24:35).

20:12 standing before the throne. In a judicial sense, as guilty, condemned prisoners before the bar of divine justice. There are no living sinners left in the destroyed universe since all sinners were killed and all believers glorified. **books.** These books record every thought, word, and deed of sinful men—all recorded by divine omniscience (*see note on Da 7:9, 10*, the verse that is the source of this text). They will provide the evidence for eternal condemnation. Cf. 18:6, 7. **book of life.** It contains the names of all the redeemed (Da 12:1; *see notes on 3:5*). **judged ... according to their deeds.** Their thoughts (Lk 8:17; Ro 2:16), words (Mt 12:37), and actions (Mt 16:27) will be compared to God's perfect, holy standard (Mt 5:48; 1Pe 1:15, 16) and will be found wanting (Ro 3:23). This also implies that there are degrees of punishment in hell (cf. Mt 10:14, 15; 11:22; Mk 12:38–40; Lk 12:47, 48; Heb 10:29).

20:13 death and Hades. *See note on 1:18.* Both terms describe the state of death. All unrighteous dead will appear at the Great White Throne Judgment; none will escape. All the places that have held the bodies of the unrighteous dead will yield up new bodies suited for hell.

20:14 second death. *See note on v. 6.*

20:15 lake of fire. *See note on 19:20.*

21:1 As the chapter opens, all the sinners of all the ages, both demons and men, including Satan, the beast, and false prophet, are in the lake of fire forever. The whole universe has been destroyed, and God creates a new universe to be the eternal dwelling place of the redeemed. **a new heaven and a new earth.** The entire universe as we now know it will be destroyed (2Pe 3:10–13) and be replaced by a new creation that will last forever. This is an OT reality (Ps 102:25, 26; Is 65:17; 66:22), as well as a NT one (Lk 21:33; Heb 1:10–12). *See note on 20:11–15.* **no longer *any* sea.** Currently three-fourths of the earth's surface is water, but the new environment will no longer be water-based and will have completely different climatic conditions. *See notes on 22:1, 2.*

21:2–22:5 By this point in the chronology of Revelation, OT saints, tribulation saints, and all those converted during the millennial kingdom will be incorporated into the ultimate redeemed bride and will dwell in the New Jerusalem. John described the consummation of all things in Christ and the New Jerusalem descending into the eternal state (cf. 19:7; 20:6; 1Co 15:28; Heb 12:22–24).

21:2 new Jerusalem. Cf. 3:12; Heb 11:10; 12:22–24; 13:14. This is the capital city of heaven, a place of perfect holiness. It is seen "coming down out of heaven," indicating it already existed; but it descends into the new heavens and new earth from its place on high. This is the city where the saints will live (cf. Jn 14:1–3). **bride.** An important NT metaphor for the church (cf. Mt 25:1–13; Eph 5:25–27). John's imagery here extends from the third part of the Jewish wedding, the ceremony. Believers (the bride) in the New Jerusalem

for her husband. 3 And I heard a loud voice from the
throne, saying, "Behold, [A]the tabernacle of God is
among men, and He will [a,B]dwell among them, and
they shall be His people, and God Himself will be
among them[b], 4 and He will [A]wipe away every tear
from their eyes; and [B]there will no longer be *any*
death; [C]there will no longer be *any* mourning, or
crying, or pain; [D]the first things have passed away."
5 And [A]He who sits on the throne said, "Behold, I
am [B]making all things new." And He *said, "Write,
for [C]these words are faithful and true." 6 Then He
said to me, "[a,A]It is done. I am the [B]Alpha and the
Omega, the beginning and the end. [C]I will give to
the one who thirsts from the spring of the [D]water of
life without cost. 7 [A]He who overcomes will inherit
these things, and [B]I will be his God and he will be
My son. 8 [A]But for the cowardly and [a]unbelieving
and abominable and murderers and immoral persons and sorcerers and idolaters and all liars, their
part *will be* in [B]the lake that burns with fire and
[b]brimstone, which is the [C]second death."
9 [A]Then one of the seven angels who had the
[B]seven bowls [a]full of the [C]seven last plagues came
and spoke with me, saying, "[A]Come here, I will show
you the [D]bride, the wife of the Lamb."

THE NEW JERUSALEM

10 And [A]he carried me away [a,B]in the Spirit to a
great and high mountain, and showed me [C]the holy
city, Jerusalem, coming down out of heaven from
God, 11 having [A]the glory of God. Her [a]brilliance was
like a very costly stone, as a [B]stone of [C]crystal-clear
jasper. 12 [a]It had a great and high wall, [a,A]with twelve
[B]gates, and at the gates twelve angels; and names
were written on them, which are *the names* of the
twelve tribes of the sons of Israel. 13 *There were* three
gates on the east and three gates on the north and
three gates on the south and three gates on the west.
14 And the wall of the city had [A]twelve foundation
stones, and on them *were* the twelve names of the
[B]twelve apostles of the Lamb.
15 The one who spoke with me had a [a]gold measuring [A]rod to measure the city, and its [B]gates and
its wall. 16 The city is laid out as a square, and its
length is as great as the width; and he measured
the city with the [a]rod, [b]fifteen hundred miles; its
length and width and height are equal. 17 And he
measured its wall, [a]seventy-two yards, *according
to* [A]human [b]measurements, which are *also* [B]an-
gelic *measurements*. 18 The material of the wall
was [A]jasper; and the city was [B]pure gold, like [a]clear
[C]glass. 19 [A]The foundation stones of the city wall
were adorned with every kind of precious stone.
The first foundation stone was [B]jasper; the second,
sapphire; the third, chalcedony; the fourth, [C]emer-
ald; 20 the fifth, sardonyx; the sixth, [A]sardius; the
seventh, chrysolite; the eighth, beryl; the ninth,
topaz; the tenth, chrysoprase; the eleventh, jacinth;

21:3 [a]Or *tabernacle* [b]One early ms reads, and be *their God* [A]Lev 26:11f; Ezek 37:27; 48:35; Heb 8:2; Rev 7:15 [B]John 14:23; 2 Cor 6:16 21:4 [A]Is 25:8; Rev 7:17 [B]1 Cor 15:26; Rev 20:14 [C]Is 35:10; 51:11; 65:19 [D]2 Cor 5:17; Heb 12:27 21:5 [A]Rev 4:9; 20:11 [B]2 Cor 5:17; Heb 12:27 [C]Rev 19:9; 22:6 21:6 [a]Lit *They are* [A]Rev 10:6; 16:17 [B]Rev 1:8; 22:13 [C]Is 55:1; John 4:10; Rev 7:17; 22:17 [D]Rev 7:17 21:7 [A]Rev 2:7 [B]2 Sam 7:14; Ps 89:26f; 2 Cor 6:16, 18; Rev 21:3 21:8 [a]Or *untrustworthy* [b]I.e. burning sulphur [A]1 Cor 6:9; Gal 5:19-21; Rev 9:21; 21:27; 22:15 [B]Rev 19:20 [C]Rev 2:11 21:9 [a]Lit *who were full* [A]Rev 17:1 [B]Rev 15:7 [C]Rev 15:1 [D]Rev 19:7; 21:2 21:10 [a]Or *in spirit* [A]Ezek 40:2; Rev 17:3 [B]Rev 1:10 [C]Rev 21:2 21:11 [a]Lit *luminary* [A]Is 60:1f; Ezek 43:2; Rev 15:8; 21:23; 22:5 [B]Rev 4:3; 21:18, 19 [C]Rev 4:6 21:12 [a]Lit *having* [A]Ezek 48:31-34 [B]Rev 21:15, 21, 25; 22:14 21:14 [A]Heb 11:10 [B]Acts 1:26 21:15 [a]Lit *measure, a gold reed* [A]Ezek 40:3; Rev 11:1 [B]Rev 21:12, 21, 25 21:16 [a]Lit *reed* [b]Lit *twelve thousand stadia;* a stadion was approx 600 ft 21:17 [a]Lit *one hundred forty-four cubits* [b]Lit *measure* [A]Deut 3:11; Rev 13:18 [B]Rev 21:9 21:18 [a]Lit *pure* [A]Rev 21:11 [B]Rev 21:21 [C]Rev 4:6 21:19 [A]Ex 28:17-20; Is 54:11f; Ezek 28:13 [B]Rev 21:11 [C]Rev 4:3 21:20 [A]Rev 4:3

come to meet Christ (the bridegroom) in the final ceremony of redemptive history (*see note on 19:7*). The whole city, occupied by all the saints, is called the bride, so that all saints must be finally included in the bride imagery and bridal blessing. God has brought home a bride for His beloved Son. All the saints live with Christ in the Father's house (a promise made before the church began; Jn 14:2).

21:3 the tabernacle of God. The word translated "tabernacle" means place of abode. This is God's house, the place where He lives (cf. Lv 26:11, 12; Dt 12:5).

21:4 wipe away every tear. Since there will never be a tear in heaven, nothing will be sad, disappointing, deficient, or wrong (cf. Is 53:4, 5; 1Co 15:54–57).

21:5 faithful and true. Cf. 3:14; 19:11. God always speaks truth (Jn 17:17).

21:6 the Alpha and the Omega. *See note on 1:8.* **the one who thirsts.** Heaven belongs to those who, knowing their souls are parched by sin, have earnestly sought the satisfaction of salvation and eternal life (cf. Ps 42:1, 2; Is 55:1, 2; Jn 7:37, 38). **water of life.** Cf. 7:17; 22:1, 17. The lasting spiritual water of which Jesus spoke (Jn 4:13, 14; 7:37, 38; cf. Is 55:1, 2).

21:7 He who overcomes. Cf. 1Jn 5:4, 5. Anyone who exercises saving faith in Jesus Christ (*see note on 2:7*). **inherit.** The spiritual inheritance all believers will receive (1Pe 1:4; cf. Mt 25:23) is the fullness of the new creation. Cf. Ro 8:16, 17.

21:8 A solemn, serious warning about the kinds of people who will be outcasts from the new heaven and the new earth in the lake of fire. The NT often goes beyond just citing unbelief in listing character and lifestyle traits of the outcast, so that believers can identify such people (1Co 6:9, 10; Gal 5:19; cf. Jn 8:31). **sorcerers.** *See note on 9:21.* **lake that burns with fire.** *See note on 19:20.* **brimstone.** *See note on 9:17.* **second death.** *See note on 20:6.*

21:9 seven bowls. *See note on 15:7.* **seven last plagues.** *See note on 15:1–8.*

21:9, 10 the wife of the Lamb. The New Jerusalem takes on the character of its inhabitants, the redeemed (*see notes on v. 2; 19:7–9*).

21:10 in the Spirit. *See note on 1:10.*

21:11 jasper. A transliteration, not a translation, of the Gr. word. Rather than the modern opaque jasper, the term actually refers to a completely clear diamond, a perfect gem with the brilliant light of God's glory shining out of it and streaming over the new heaven and the new earth (cf. 4:3).

21:12–14 wall. See v. 16 for the dimensions of the city and, thus, the length of the wall.

21:15 gold measuring rod. *See note on Eze 40:3.* This rod was about 10 ft. long, a standard for measure. **measure the city.** This action indicates that the capital of heaven belongs to God and He is measuring what is His (cf. 11:1; Eze 40:3).

21:16 fifteen hundred miles. This would be about two million square miles of ground space, offering plenty of room for all the glorified saints to live. **length and width and height.** The city has the symmetrical dimensions of a perfect cube, which parallels its closest earthly counterpart, the inner sanctuary in the tabernacle and temple (cf. 1Ki 6:20).

21:17 seventy-two yards. This is likely the width of the wall.

21:18 jasper. *See note on v. 11.* This is the material of the thick wall—diamond! **pure gold, like clear glass.** Unlike earth's gold, this gold will be transparent so the overpowering radiance of God's glory can refract and glisten through the entire city.

21:19, 20 Because some of the names of these gems have changed through the centuries, it is difficult to identify each one with certainty. Eight of the 12 stones are found in the breastpiece of the High Priest (Ex 28, 39), and the other 4 may also be related to the breastpiece. The gems picture a brilliant, indescribable panoply of beautiful colors that send forth the light of God's glory. The following are possible identifications for these gems.

21:19 chalcedony. This name derives from Chalcedon, an ancient name for a city in modern Turkey. The gem is a sky-blue agate stone with translucent, colored stripes.

21:20 sardonyx. A variety of chalcedony with parallel layers of red and white (*see note on v. 19*). **sardius.** A common stone from the quartz family, which ranged in color from orange-red to brownish-red to blood-red (4:3).

the twelfth, amethyst. 21 And the twelve [A]gates were
twelve [B]pearls; each one of the gates was a single
pearl. And the street of the city was [C]pure gold, like
transparent [D]glass.
22 I saw [A]no [a]temple in it, for the [B]Lord God the
Almighty and the [C]Lamb are its [a]temple. 23 And
the city [A]has no need of the sun or of the moon to
shine on it, for [B]the glory of God has illumined it,
and its lamp *is* the [C]Lamb. 24 [A]The nations will walk
by its light, and the [B]kings of the earth [a]will bring
their glory into it. 25 In the daytime (for [A]there will
be no night there) [B]its gates [C]will never be closed;
26 and [A]they will bring the glory and the honor of
the nations into it; 27 and [A]nothing unclean, and no
one who practices abomination and lying, shall
ever come into it, but only those [a]whose names are
[B]written in the Lamb's book of life.

THE RIVER AND THE TREE OF LIFE

22 Then [A]he showed me a [B]river of the [C]water
of life, [a]clear [D]as crystal, coming from the
throne of God and of [b]the Lamb, 2 in the middle of
[A]its street. [B]On either side of the river was [C]the tree
of life, bearing twelve [a]*kinds of* fruit, yielding its
fruit every month; and the leaves of the tree were
for the healing of the nations. 3 [A]There will no longer be any curse; and [B]the throne of God and of the
Lamb will be in it, and His bond-servants will [C]serve
Him; 4 they will [A]see His face, and His [B]name *will
be* on their [C]foreheads. 5 And [A]there will no longer
be *any* night; and they [a]will not have need [B]of the
light of a lamp nor the light of the sun, because the
Lord God will illumine them; and they will [C]reign
forever and ever.
6 And [A]he said to me, "[B]These words are faithful
and true"; and the Lord, the [C]God of the spirits of the
prophets, [D]sent His angel to show to His bond-servants the things which must soon take place.
7 "And behold, [A]I am coming quickly. [B]Blessed
is he who [a]heeds [C]the words of the prophecy of
this book."
8 [A]I, John, am the one who heard and saw these
things. And when I heard and saw, [B]I fell down to
worship at the feet of the angel who showed me
these things. 9 But [A]he *said to me, "Do not do that.
I am a [B]fellow servant of yours and of your brethren
the prophets and of those who [a]heed the words of
[C]this book. Worship God."

THE FINAL MESSAGE

10 And he *said to me, "[A]Do not seal up [B]the words
of the prophecy of this book, [C]for the time is near.
11 [A]Let the one who does wrong, still do wrong; and
the one who is filthy, still be filthy; and let the one
who is righteous, still practice righteousness; and
the one who is holy, still keep himself holy."

21:21 [A]Rev 21:12, 15, 25 [B]Rev 17:4 [C]Rev 21:18 [D]Rev 4:6 21:22 [a]Or *sanctuary* [A]Matt 24:2; John 4:21 [B]Rev 1:8 [C]Rev 5:6; 7:17; 14:4 21:23 [A]Is 24:23; 60:19, 20; Rev 21:25; 22:5 [B]Rev 21:11 [C]Rev 5:6; 7:17; 14:4 21:24 [a]Lit *bring* [A]Is 60:3, 5 [B]Ps 72:10f; Is 49:23; 60:16; Rev 21:26 21:25 [A]Zech 14:7; Rev 21:23; 22:5 [B]Rev 21:12, 15 [C]Is 60:11 21:26 [A]Ps 72:10f; Is 49:23; 60:16 21:27 [a]Lit *who have been* [A]Is 52:1; Ezek 44:9; Zech 14:21; Rev 22:14f [B]Rev 3:5 22:1 [a]Lit *bright* [b]Or *the Lamb. In the middle of its street, and on either side of the river, was* [A]Rev 1:1; 21:9; 22:6 [B]Ps 46:4; Ezek 47:1 [C]Zech 14:8; Rev 7:17; 22:17 [D]Rev 4:6 22:2 [a]Or *crops of fruit* [A]Rev 21:21 [B]Ezek 47:12 [C]Gen 2:9; Rev 2:7; 22:14, 19 22:3 [A]Zech 14:11 [B]Rev 21:3 [C]Rev 7:15 22:4 [A]Ps 17:15; 42:2; Matt 5:8 [B]Rev 14:1 [C]Rev 7:3 22:5 [a]Lit *do not have* [A]Zech 14:7; Rev 21:25 [B]Is 60:19; Rev 21:23 [C]Dan 7:18, 27; Matt 19:28; Rom 5:17; Rev 20:4 22:6 [A]Rev 1:1; 21:9 [B]Rev 19:9; 21:5 [C]1 Cor 14:32; Heb 12:9 [D]Rev 1:1; 22:16 22:7 [a]Lit *keeps* [A]Rev 1:3; 3:3, 11; 16:15; 22:12, 20 [B]Rev 1:3; 16:15 [C]Rev 1:11; 22:9, 10, 18f 22:8 [A]Rev 1:1 [B]Rev 19:10 22:9 [a]Lit *keep* [A]Rev 19:10 [B]Rev 1:1 [C]Rev 1:11; 22:10, 18f 22:10 [A]Dan 8:26; Rev 10:4 [B]Rev 1:11; 22:9, 18f [C]Rev 1:3 22:11 [A]Ezek 3:27; Dan 12:10

chrysolite. A gem with a transparent gold or yellowish tone. **beryl.** A mineral with several varieties of gems, ranging from the green emerald to the golden yellow beryl to the light blue aquamarine. **topaz.** Ancient topaz was a softer stone with a yellow or yellow-green color. **chrysoprase.** The modern form of this jewel is an apple-green variety of quartz. The Gr. name suggests a gold-tinted, green gemstone. **jacinth.** Today this stone is a transparent zircon, usually red or reddish-brown. The one John saw was blue or shining violet in color. **amethyst.** A clear quartz crystal that ranges in color from a faint purple tint to an intense purple.

21:21 a single pearl. Each of the gates of the city is a single, almost 1,400-mile-high pearl. Even as earthly pearls are formed in response to the wounding of oyster flesh, so these gigantic, supernatural pearls will remind saints throughout eternity of the magnitude of Christ's suffering and its eternal benefit.

21:22 no temple. Several passages affirm that there is a temple in heaven (3:12; 7:15; 11:19; 15:5). Here, it is clear there is none in eternity. How can this be? The temple is not a building; it is the Lord God Himself. Revelation 7:15 implies this when it says, "He who sits on the throne will spread His tabernacle over them." Verse 23 continues the thought of no temple, except God and the Lamb. The glory of God which illuminates all heaven defines it as His temple. There is no need for a temple in the eternal state since God Himself will be the temple in which everything exists. The presence of God lit. fills the entire new heaven and new earth (cf. v. 3). Going to heaven will be entering the limitless presence of the Lord (cf. Jn 14:3; 1Th 4:17).

21:24 The nations. Lit. "the peoples." Redeemed people from every nation and ethnic group will dwell in heaven's light. In the eternal city, there will be no more divisions, barriers, or exclusions because of race or politics. All kinds of peoples in eternity dissolve into the people of God, and they will move freely in and about the city.

21:27 Lamb's book of life. *See note on 3:5.*

22:1 river . . . of life. This river is unlike any on earth because no hydrological cycle exists. Water of life symbolizes the continual flow of eternal life from God's throne to heaven's inhabitants (*see note on 21:6*).

22:2 tree of life. A symbol of both eternal life and continual blessing (*see note on Ge 2:9*). The tree bears 12 fruits, one for each month, and is symbolic of the abundant variety in heaven. The Eng. word "therapeutic" comes from the Gr. word translated "healing." The leaves somehow enrich heavenly life, making it full and satisfying.

22:3 no longer be any curse. The curse on humanity and the earth as a result of Adam's and Eve's disobedience (Ge 3:16–19) will be totally finished. God will never have to judge sin again, since it will never exist in the new heaven and new earth. **His bond-servants will serve Him.** *See note on 7:15.*

22:4 see His face. No unglorified human could see God's face and live (Ex 33:20–23). But the residents of heaven can look on God's face without harm because they are now holy (cf. Jn 1:18; 1Ti 6:16; 1Jn 3:2). **His name.** They are God's personal possession (*see note on 3:12*).

22:5 they will reign. Heaven's citizens are more than servants (*see note on 3:21*).

22:6 His bond-servants. The members of the 7 churches of Asia Minor who received this letter (1:11), and then all believers who have read, or will read it since. **things which must soon take place.** This involves the entire revelation which John has just related (*see note on 1:1*).

22:7 I am coming quickly. Jesus' return is imminent (*see note on 3:11*). **Blessed.** *See note on 1:3.*

22:8 heard and saw. John resumes speaking for the first time since chap. 1 and confirms the veracity of the revelation with his own eyewitness testimony—the basis of any reliable witness. **fell down to worship.** *See note on 19:10.*

22:10 Do not seal up the words. Cf. 10:11. Previous prophecies were sealed up (Da 8:26; 12:4–10). These prophecies are to be proclaimed so they can produce obedience and worship. **the time is near.** This refers to imminency, which means that the end is next.

22:11 Those who reject God's warnings will fix their eternal destiny in hell, where they will retain their evil and filthy natures for all eternity. Those who respond to the warnings will fix their eternal destiny in glory and realize perfect righteousness and holiness in heaven.

12 "Behold, [A]I am coming quickly, and My [B]reward
is with Me, [C]to render to every man [a]according
to what he has done. 13 I am the [A]Alpha and the
Omega, [B]the first and the last, [C]the beginning and
the end."
14 Blessed are those who [A]wash their robes, so that
they may have the right to [B]the tree of life, and may
[C]enter by the [D]gates into the city. 15 [A]Outside are the
[B]dogs and the sorcerers and the immoral persons
and the murderers and the idolaters, and everyone
who loves and practices lying.
16 "[A]I, Jesus, have sent [B]My angel to testify to you
these things [a,C]for the churches. I am [D]the root and
the [E]descendant of David, the bright [F]morning star."
17 The [A]Spirit and the [B]bride say, "Come." And let
the one who hears say, "Come." And [C]let the one
who is thirsty come; let the one who wishes take
the [D]water of life without cost.
18 I testify to everyone who hears [A]the words of
the prophecy of this book: if anyone [B]adds to them,
God will add to him [C]the plagues which are written
in [D]this book; 19 and if anyone [A]takes away from the
[B]words of the book of this prophecy, God will take
away his part from [C]the tree of life and [a]from the
holy city, [D]which are written in this book.
20 He who [A]testifies to these things says, "Yes,
[B]I am coming quickly." Amen. [C]Come, Lord Jesus.
21 [A]The grace of the Lord Jesus be with [a]all. Amen.

22:12 [a]Lit *as his work is* [A]Rev 22:7 [B]Is 40:10; 62:11 [C]Ps 28:4; Jer 17:10; Matt 16:27; Rev 2:23 22:13 [A]Rev 1:8 [B]Is 44:6; 48:12; Rev 1:17; 2:8 [C]Rev 21:6 22:14 [A]Rev 7:14 [B]Gen 2:9; 3:22; Rev 22:2 [C]Rev 21:27 [D]Rev 21:12 22:15 [A]Matt 8:12; 1 Cor 6:9f; Gal 5:19ff; Rev 21:8 [B]Deut 23:18; Matt 7:6; Phil 3:2 22:16 [a]Or *concerning* [A]Rev 1:1 [B]Rev 1:1; 22:6 [C]Rev 1:4, 11; 3:22 [D]Rev 5:5 [E]Matt 1:1 [F]Matt 2:2; Rev 2:28 22:17 [A]Rev 2:7; 14:13 [B]Rev 21:2, 9 [C]Is 55:1; Rev 21:6 [D]Rev 7:17; 22:1 22:18 [A]Rev 22:7 [B]Deut 4:2; 12:32; Prov 30:6 [C]Rev 15:6-16:21 [D]Rev 22:7 22:19 [a]Lit *out of* [A]Deut 4:2; 12:32; Prov 30:6 [B]Rev 22:7 [C]Rev 22:2 [D]Rev 21:10-22:5 22:20 [A]Rev 1:2 [B]Rev 22:7 [C]1 Cor 16:22 22:21 [a]One early ms reads *the saints* [A]Rom 16:20

22:12 I am coming quickly. *See note on 3:11.* Again, imminence is the issue (cf. Mk 13:33–37). **according to what he has done.** Only those works which survive God's testing fire have eternal value and are worthy of reward (1Co 3:10–15; 4:1–5; 2Co 5:10).

22:13 the Alpha and the Omega. *See note on 1:8.*

22:14 Blessed are those who wash their robes. *See note on 1:3.* This symbolizes those who have been forgiven of their sins—who have been cleansed by the blood of the Lamb of God (Heb 9:14; 1Pe 1:18, 19; *see note on 7:14*). **tree of life.** *See notes on v. 2; Ge 2:9.*

22:15 dogs. Considered despicable creatures in NT times, the term when applied to people referred to anyone of low moral character. Unfaithful leaders (Is 56:10) and homosexual prostitutes (Dt 23:18) are among those who received such a designation. **sorcerers.** *See note on 9:21.*

22:16 My angel. See 1:1. **the churches.** The 7 churches of Asia Minor who were the book's original recipients (1:11). **the root and the descendant of David.** Christ is the source ("root") of David's life and line of descendants, which establishes His deity. He is also a "descendant" of David, which establishes His humanity. This phrase gives powerful testimony to Christ as the God-Man (cf. 2Ti 2:8). **bright morning star.** This is the brightest star announcing the arrival of the day. When Jesus comes, He will be the brightest star who will shatter the darkness of man's night and herald the dawn of God's glorious day (*see note on 2:28*).

22:17 Come. This is the Spirit's and church's answer to the promise of His coming. **let the one.** This is an unlimited offer of grace and salvation to all who desire to have their thirsty souls quenched. Cf. Is 55:1, 2. **water of life.** *See note on v. 1.*

22:18, 19 Jesus offers extended testimony on the authority and finality of the prophecy. He commissioned John to write it, but He was its author. These are not the first such warnings (cf. Dt 4:2; 12:32; Pr 30:6; Jer 26:2). These warnings against altering the biblical text represent the close of the NT canon. Anyone who tampers with the truth by attempting to falsify, mitigate, alter, or misinterpret it will incur the judgments described in these verses.

22:20 Yes, I am coming quickly. *See note on 3:11.* In light of this future expectation, what is now required of believers is outlined by Peter (see 2Pe 3:11–18).

APPENDICES

- The Character of Genuine Saving Faith
- Read Through the Bible in a Year
- Overview of Theology
- Monies, Weights, Measures
- Index to Key Bible Doctrines
- Concordance

THE
CHARACTER OF

GENUINE SAVING FAITH

2 CORINTHIANS 13:5

I. EVIDENCES THAT NEITHER PROVE NOR DISPROVE ONE'S FAITH

A. Visible Morality: Mt 19:16–21; 23:27.
B. Intellectual Knowledge: Ro 1:21; 2:17ff.
C. Religious Involvement: Mt 25:1–10
D. Active Ministry: Mt 7:21–24
E. Conviction of Sin: Ac 24:25
F. Assurance: Mt 23
G. Time of Decision: Lk 8:13, 14

II. THE FRUIT/PROOFS OF AUTHENTIC/TRUE CHRISTIANITY:

A. Love for God: Pss 42:1ff; 73:25; Lk 10:27; Ro 8:7
B. Repentance from Sin: Ps 32:5; Pr 28:13; Ro 7:14ff; 2Co 7:10; 1Jn 1:8–10
C. Genuine Humility: Ps 51:17; Mt 5:1–12; Jas 4:6, 9ff.
D. Devotion to God's Glory: Pss 105:3; 115:1; Is 43:7; 48:10ff.; Jer 9:23, 24; 1Co 10:31.
E. Continual Prayer: Lk 18:1; Eph 6:18ff.; Php 4:6ff.; 1Ti 2:1–4; Jas 5:16–18
F. Selfless Love: 1Jn 2:9ff; 3:14; 4:7ff.
G. Separation from the World: 1Co 2:12; Jas 4:4ff.; 1Jn 2:15–17; 5:5
H. Spiritual Growth: Lk 8:15; Jn 15:1–6; Eph 4:12–16
I. Obedient Living: Mt 7:21; Jn 15:14ff.; Ro 16:26; 1Pe 1:2, 22; 1Jn 2:3–5
J. Hunger for God's Word: 1Pe 2:1–3
K. Transformation of Life: 2Co 5:17

If List I is true of a person and List II is false, there is cause to question the validity of one's profession of faith. Yet if List II is true, then the top list will be also.

III. THE CONDUCT OF THE GOSPEL:

A. Proclaim it: Mt 4:23
B. Defend it: Jude 3
C. Demonstrate it: Php 1:27
D. Share it: Php 1:5
E. Suffer for it: 2Ti 1:8
F. Don't hinder it: 1Co 9:12
G. Be not ashamed: Ro 1:16
H. Preach it: 1Co 9:16
I. Be empowered: 1Th 1:5
J. Guard it: Gal 1:6–8

READ THROUGH THE

BIBLE IN A YEAR

JANUARY		
Date	MORNING	EVENING
	MT	**GE**
1	1	1, 2, 3
2	2	4, 5, 6
3	3	7, 8, 9
4	4	10, 11, 12
5	5:1–26	13, 14, 15
6	5:27–48	16, 17
7	6:1–18	18, 19
8	6:19–34	20, 21, 22
9	7	23, 24
10	8:1–17	25, 26
11	8:18–34	27, 28
12	9:1–17	29, 30
13	9:18–38	31, 32
14	10:1–20	33, 34, 35
15	10:21–42	36, 37, 38
16	11	39, 40
17	12:1–23	41, 42
18	12:24–50	43, 44, 45
19	13:1–30	46, 47, 48
20	13:31–58	49, 50
		EX
21	14:1–21	1, 2, 3
22	14:22–36	4, 5, 6
23	15:1–20	7, 8
24	15:21–39	9, 10, 11
25	16	12, 13
26	17	14, 15
27	18:1–20	16, 17, 18
28	18:21–35	19, 20
29	19	21, 22
30	20:1–16	23, 24
31	20:17–34	25, 26

FEBRUARY		
Date	MORNING	EVENING
	MT	**EX**
1	21:1–22	27, 28
2	21:23–46	29, 30
3	22:1–22	31, 32, 33
4	22:23–46	34, 35
5	23:1–22	36, 37, 38
6	23:23–39	39, 40
		LV
7	24:1–28	1, 2, 3
8	24:29–51	4, 5
9	25:1–30	6, 7
10	25:31–46	8, 9, 10
11	26:1–25	11, 12
12	26:26–50	13
13	26:51–75	14
14	27:1–26	15, 16

Date	MORNING	EVENING
15	27:27–50	17, 18
16	27:51–66	19, 20
17	28	21, 22
	MK	
18	1:1–22	23, 24
19	1:23–45	25
20	2	26, 27
		NU
21	3:1–19	1, 2
22	3:20–35	3, 4
23	4:1–20	5, 6
24	4:21–41	7, 8
25	5:1–20	9, 10, 11
26	5:21–43	12, 13, 14
27	6:1–29	15, 16
28	6:30–56	17, 18, 19
29	7:1–13	20, 21, 22

MARCH

Date	MORNING	EVENING
	MK	**NU**
1	7:14–37	23, 24, 25
2	8:1–21	26, 27
3	8:22–38	28, 29, 30
4	9:1–29	31, 32, 33
5	9:30–50	34, 35, 36
		DT
6	10:1–31	1, 2
7	10:32–52	3, 4
8	11:1–18	5, 6, 7
9	11:19–33	8, 9, 10
10	12:1–27	11, 12, 13
11	12:28–44	14, 15, 16
12	13:1–20	17, 18, 19
13	13:21–37	20, 21, 22

Date	MORNING	EVENING
14	14:1–26	23, 24, 25
15	14:27–53	26, 27
16	14:54–72	28, 29
17	15:1–25	30, 31
18	15:26–47	32, 33, 34
		JOS
19	16	1, 2, 3
	LK	
20	1:1–20	4, 5, 6
21	1:21–38	7, 8, 9
22	1:39–56	10, 11, 12
23	1:57–80	13, 14, 15
24	2:1–24	16, 17, 18
25	2:25–52	19, 20, 21
26	3	22, 23, 24
		JDG
27	4:1–30	1, 2, 3
28	4:31–44	4, 5, 6
29	5:1–16	7, 8
30	5:17–39	9, 10
31	6:1–26	11, 12

APRIL

Date	MORNING	EVENING
	LK	**JDG**
1	6:27–49	13, 14, 15
2	7:1–30	16, 17, 18
3	7:31–50	19, 20, 21
		RU
4	8:1–25	1, 2, 3, 4
		1SA
5	8:26–56	1, 2, 3
6	9:1–17	4, 5, 6
7	9:18–36	7, 8, 9
8	9:37–62	10, 11, 12

Date	MORNING	EVENING
9	10:1–24	13, 14
10	10:25–42	15, 16
11	11:1–28	17, 18
12	11:29–54	19, 20, 21
13	12:1–31	22, 23, 24
14	12:32–59	25, 26
15	13:1–22	27, 28, 29
16	13:23–35	30, 31
		2SA
17	14:1–24	1, 2
18	14:25–35	3, 4, 5
19	15:1–10	6, 7, 8
20	15:11–32	9, 10, 11
21	16	12, 13
22	17:1–19	14, 15
23	17:20–37	16, 17, 18
24	18:1–23	19, 20
25	18:24–43	21, 22
26	19:1–27	23, 24
		1KI
27	19:28–48	1, 2
28	20:1–26	3, 4, 5
29	20:27–47	6, 7
30	21:1–19	8, 9

MAY

Date	MORNING	EVENING
	LK	**1KI**
1	21:20–38	10, 11
2	22:1–20	12, 13
3	22:21–46	14, 15
4	22:47–71	16, 17, 18
5	23:1–25	19, 20
6	23:26–56	21, 22

Date	MORNING	EVENING
		2KI
7	24:1–35	1, 2, 3
8	24:36–53	4, 5, 6
	JN	
9	1:1–28	7, 8, 9
10	1:29–51	10, 11, 12
11	2	13, 14
12	3:1–18	15, 16
13	3:19–36	17, 18
14	4:1–30	19, 20, 21
15	4:31–54	22, 23
16	5:1–24	24, 25
		1CH
17	5:25–47	1, 2, 3
18	6:1–21	4, 5, 6
19	6:22–44	7, 8, 9
20	6:45–71	10, 11, 12
21	7:1–27	13, 14, 15
22	7:28–53	16, 17, 18
23	8:1–27	19, 20, 21
24	8:28–59	22, 23, 24
25	9:1–23	25, 26, 27
26	9:24–41	28, 29
		2CH
27	10:1–23	1, 2, 3
28	10:24–42	4, 5, 6
29	11:1–29	7, 8, 9
30	11:30–57	10, 11, 12
31	12:1–26	13, 14

JUNE

Date	MORNING	EVENING
	JN	**2CH**
1	12:27–50	15, 16
2	13:1–20	17, 18
3	13:21–38	19, 20

Date	MORNING	EVENING
4	14	21, 22
5	15	23, 24
6	16	25, 26, 27
7	17	28, 29
8	18:1–18	30, 31
9	18:19–40	32, 33
10	19:1–22	34, 35, 36
		EZR
11	19:23–42	1, 2
12	20	3, 4, 5
13	21	6, 7, 8
	AC	
14	1	9, 10
		NE
15	2:1–21	1, 2, 3
16	2:22–47	4, 5, 6
17	3	7, 8, 9
18	4:1–22	10, 11
19	4:23–37	12, 13
		EST
20	5:1–21	1, 2
21	5:22–42	3, 4, 5
22	6	6, 7, 8
23	7:1–21	9, 10
		JOB
24	7:22–43	1, 2
25	7:44–60	3, 4
26	8:1–25	5, 6, 7
27	8:26–40	8, 9, 10
28	9:1–21	11, 12, 13
29	9:22–43	14, 15, 16
30	10:1–23	17, 18, 19

JULY

Date	MORNING	EVENING
	AC	**JOB**
1	10:24–48	20, 21
2	11	22, 23, 24

Date	MORNING	EVENING
3	12	25, 26, 27
4	13:1–25	28, 29
5	13:26–52	30, 31
6	14	32, 33
7	15:1–21	34, 35
8	15:22–41	36, 37
9	16:1–21	38, 39, 40
10	16:22–40	41, 42
		PSS
11	17:1–15	1, 2, 3
12	17:16–34	4, 5, 6
13	18	7, 8, 9
14	19:1–20	10, 11, 12
15	19:21–41	13, 14, 15
16	20:1–16	16, 17
17	20:17–38	18, 19
18	21:1–17	20, 21, 22
19	21:18–40	23, 24, 25
20	22	26, 27, 28
21	23:1–15	29, 30
22	23:16–35	31, 32
23	24	33, 34
24	25	35, 36
25	26	37, 38, 39
26	27:1–26	40, 41, 42
27	27:27–44	43, 44, 45
28	28	46, 47, 48
	RO	
29	1	49, 50
30	2	51, 52, 53
31	3	54, 55, 56

AUGUST		
Date	MORNING	EVENING
	RO	**PSS**
1	4	57, 58, 59
2	5	60, 61, 62
3	6	63, 64, 65
4	7	66, 67
5	8:1–21	68, 69
6	8:22–39	70, 71
7	9:1–15	72, 73
8	9:16–33	74, 75, 76
9	10	77, 78
10	11:1–18	79, 80
11	11:19–36	81, 82, 83
12	12	84, 85, 86
13	13	87, 88
14	14	89, 90
15	15:1–13	91, 92, 93
16	15:14–33	94, 95, 96
17	16	97, 98, 99
	1CO	
18	1	100, 101, 102
19	2	103, 104
20	3	105, 106
21	4	107, 108, 109
22	5	110, 111, 112
23	6	113, 114, 115
24	7:1–19	116, 117, 118
25	7:20–40	119:1–88
26	8	119:89–176
27	9	120, 121, 122
28	10:1–18	123, 124, 125
29	10:19–33	126, 127, 128
30	11:1–16	129, 130, 131
31	11:17–34	132, 133, 134

SEPTEMBER		
Date	MORNING	EVENING
	1CO	**PSS**
1	12	135, 136
2	13	137, 138, 139
3	14:1–20	140, 141, 142
4	14:21–40	143, 144, 145
5	15:1–28	146, 147
6	15:29–58	148, 149, 150
		PR
7	16	1, 2
	2CO	
8	1	3, 4, 5
9	2	6, 7
10	3	8, 9
11	4	10, 11, 12
12	5	13, 14, 15
13	6	16, 17, 18
14	7	19, 20, 21
15	8	22, 23, 24
16	9	25, 26
17	10	27, 28, 29
18	11:1–15	30, 31
		ECC
19	11:16–33	1, 2, 3
20	12	4, 5, 6
21	13	7, 8, 9
	GAL	
22	1	10, 11, 12
		SS
23	2	1, 2, 3
24	3	4, 5
25	4	6, 7, 8
		IS
26	5	1, 2

Date	MORNING	EVENING
27	6	3, 4
	EPH	
28	1	5, 6
29	2	7, 8
30	3	9, 10

OCTOBER

Date	MORNING	EVENING
	EPH	IS
1	4	11, 12, 13
2	5:1–16	14, 15, 16
3	5:17–33	17, 18, 19
4	6	20, 21, 22
	PHP	
5	1	23, 24, 25
6	2	26, 27
7	3	28, 29
8	4	30, 31
	COL	
9	1	32, 33
10	2	34, 35, 36
11	3	37, 38
12	4	39, 40
	1TH	
13	1	41, 42
14	2	43, 44
15	3	45, 46
16	4	47, 48, 49
17	5	50, 51, 52
	2TH	
18	1	53, 54, 55
19	2	56, 57, 58
20	3	59, 60, 61
	1TI	
21	1	62, 63, 64
22	2	65, 66
		JER
23	3	1, 2
24	4	3, 4, 5
25	5	6, 7, 8
26	6	9, 10, 11
	2TI	
27	1	12, 13, 14
28	2	15, 16, 17
29	3	18, 19
30	4	20, 21
	TITUS	
31	1	22, 23

NOVEMBER

Date	MORNING	EVENING
	TITUS	JER
1	2	24, 25, 26
2	3	27, 28, 29
3	PHM	30, 31
	HEB	
4	1	32, 33
5	2	34, 35, 36
6	3	37, 38, 39
7	4	40, 41, 42
8	5	43, 44, 45
9	6	46, 47
10	7	48, 49
11	8	50
12	9	51, 52
		LA
13	10:1–18	1, 2
14	10:19–39	3, 4, 5
		EZE
15	11:1–19	1, 2

Date	MORNING	EVENING
16	11:20–40	3, 4
17	12	5, 6, 7
18	13	8, 9, 10
	JAS	
19	1	11, 12, 13
20	2	14, 15
21	3	16, 17
22	4	18, 19
23	5	20, 21
	1PE	
24	1	22, 23
25	2	24, 25, 26
26	3	27, 28, 29
27	4	30, 31, 32
28	5	33, 34
	2PE	
29	1	35, 36
30	2	37, 38, 39

DECEMBER

Date	MORNING	EVENING
	2PE	**EZE**
1	3	40, 41
	1JN	
2	1	42, 43, 44
3	2	45, 46
4	3	47, 48
		DA
5	4	1, 2
6	5	3, 4
7	**2JN**	5, 6, 7
8	**3JN**	8, 9, 10
9	**JUDE**	11, 12
	REV	**HOS**
10	1	1, 2, 3, 4
11	2	5, 6, 7, 8
12	3	9, 10, 11
13	4	12, 13, 14
14	5	**JOEL**
		AM
15	6	1, 2, 3
16	7	4, 5, 6
17	8	7, 8, 9
18	9	**OB**
19	10	**JON**
		MIC
20	11	1, 2, 3
21	12	4, 5
22	13	6, 7
23	14	**NA**
24	15	**HAB**
25	16	**ZEP**
26	17	**HAG**
		ZEC
27	18	1, 2, 3, 4
28	19	5, 6, 7, 8
29	20	9, 10, 11, 12
30	21	13, 14
31	22	**MAL**

OVERVIEW OF THEOLOGY

THE HOLY SCRIPTURES

We teach that the Bible is God's written revelation to man, and thus the 66 books of the Bible given to us by the Holy Spirit constitute the plenary (inspired equally in all parts) Word of God (1Co 2:7–14; 2Pe 1:20, 21).

We teach that the Word of God is an objective, propositional revelation (1Co 2:13; 1Th 2:13), verbally inspired in every word (2Ti 3:16), absolutely inerrant in the original documents, infallible, and God-breathed. We teach the literal, grammatical-historical interpretation of Scripture, which affirms the belief that the opening chapters of Genesis present creation in six literal days (Ge 1:31; Ex 31:17).

We teach that the Bible constitutes the only infallible rule of faith and practice (Mt 5:18; 24:35; Jn 10:35; 16:12, 13; 17:17; 1Co 2:13; 2Ti 3:15–17; Heb 4:12; 2Pe 1:20, 21).

We teach that God spoke in His written Word by a process of dual authorship. The Holy Spirit so superintended the human authors that, through their individual personalities and different styles of writing, they composed and recorded God's Word to man (2Pe 1:20, 21) without error in the whole or in the part (Mt 5:18; 2Ti 3:16).

We teach that, whereas there may be several applications of any given passage of Scripture, there is but one true interpretation. The meaning of Scripture is to be found as one diligently applies the literal, grammatical-historical method of interpretation under the enlightenment of the Holy Spirit (Jn 7:17; 16:12–15; 1Co 2:7–15; 1Jn 2:20). It is the responsibility of believers to ascertain carefully the true intent and meaning of Scripture, recognizing that proper application is binding on all generations. Yet the truth of Scripture stands in judgment of men; never do men stand in judgment of it.

GOD

We teach that there is but one living and true God (Dt 6:4; Is 45:5–7; 1Co 8:4), an infinite, all-knowing Spirit (Jn 4:24), perfect in all His attributes, one in essence, eternally existing in three Persons—Father, Son, and Holy Spirit (Mt 28:19; 2Co 13:14)—each equally deserving worship and obedience.

GOD THE FATHER

We teach that God the Father, the first person of the Trinity, orders and disposes all things according to His own purpose and grace (Ps 145:8, 9; 1Co 8:6). He is the Creator of all things (Ge 1:1–31; Eph 3:9). As the only absolute and omnipotent ruler in the universe, He is sovereign in creation, providence, and redemption (Ps 103:19; Ro 11:36). His fatherhood involves both His designation within the Trinity and His relationship with mankind. As Creator He is Father to all men (Eph 4:6), but He is Spiritual Father only to believers (Ro 8:14; 2Co 6:18). He has decreed for His own glory all things that come to pass (Eph 1:11). He continually upholds, directs, and governs all creatures and events (1Ch 29:11). In His sovereignty He is neither author nor approver of sin (Hab 1:13), nor does He abridge the accountability of moral, intelligent creatures (1Pe 1:17). He has graciously chosen from eternity past those whom He would have as His own (Eph 1:4–6); He saves from sin all those who come to Him through Jesus Christ; He adopts as His own all those who come to Him; and He becomes, upon adoption, Father to His own (Jn 1:12; Ro 8:15; Gal 4:5; Heb 12:5–9).

GOD THE SON

We teach that Jesus Christ, the second person of the Trinity, possesses all the divine excellencies, and in these He is coequal, consubstantial, and coeternal with the Father (Jn 10:30; 14:9).

We teach that God the Father created "the heavens and the earth and all that is in them" according to His own will, through His Son, Jesus Christ, by whom all things continue in existence and in operations (Jn 1:3; Col 1:15–17; Heb 1:2).

We teach that in the incarnation (God becoming man) Christ surrendered only the prerogatives of deity but nothing of the divine essence, either in degree or kind. In His incarnation, the eternally existing second person of the Trinity accepted all the essential characteristics of humanity and so became the God-man (Php 2:5–8; Col 2:9).

We teach that Jesus Christ represents humanity and deity in indivisible oneness (Mic 5:2; Jn 5:23; 14:9, 10; Col 2:9).

We teach that our Lord Jesus Christ was virgin born (Is 7:14; Mt 1:23, 25; Lk 1:26–35); that He was

God incarnate (Jn 1:1, 14); and that the purpose of the incarnation was to reveal God, redeem men, and rule over God's kingdom (Ps 2:7–9; Is 9:6; Jn 1:29; Php 2:9–11; Heb 7:25, 26; 1Pe 1:18, 19).

We teach that, in the incarnation, the second person of the Trinity laid aside His right to the full prerogatives of coexistence with God, assumed the place of a Son, and took on an existence appropriate to a servant while never divesting Himself of His divine attributes (Php 2:5–8).

We teach that our Lord Jesus Christ accomplished our redemption through the shedding of His blood and sacrificial death on the cross and that His death was voluntary, vicarious, substitutionary, propitiatory, and redemptive (Jn 10:15; Ro 3:24, 25; 5:8; 1Pe 2:24).

We teach that on the basis of the efficacy of the death of our Lord Jesus Christ, the believing sinner is freed from the punishment, the penalty, the power, and one day the very presence of sin; and that he is declared righteous, given eternal life, and adopted into the family of God (Ro 3:25; 5:8, 9; 2Co 5:14, 15; 1Pe 2:24; 3:18).

We teach that our justification is made sure by His literal, physical resurrection from the dead and that He is now ascended to the right hand of the Father, where He now mediates as our Advocate and High Priest (Mt 28:6; Lk 24:38, 39; Ac 2:30, 31; Ro 4:25; 8:34; Heb 7:25; 9:24; 1Jn 2:1).

We teach that in the resurrection of Jesus Christ from the grave, God confirmed the deity of His Son and gave proof that God has accepted the atoning work of Christ on the cross. Jesus' bodily resurrection is also the guarantee of a future resurrection life for all believers (Jn 5:26–29; 14:19; Ro 4:25; 6:5–10; 1Co 15:20, 23).

We teach that Jesus Christ will return to receive the church, which is His body, unto Himself at the Rapture and, returning with His church in glory, will establish His millennial kingdom on earth (Ac 1:9–11; 1Th 4:13–18; Rev 20).

We teach that the Lord Jesus Christ is the one through whom God will judge all mankind (Jn 5:22, 23):

a. Believers (1Co 3:10–15; 2Co 5:10);
b. Living inhabitants of the earth at His glorious return (Mt 25:31–46); and
c. Unbelieving dead at the Great White Throne (Rev 20:11–15).

As the mediator between God and man (1Ti 2:5), the head of His body the church (Eph 1:22; 5:23; Col 1:18), and the coming universal King who will reign on the throne of David (Is 9:6, 7; Eze 37:24–28; Lk 1:31–33), He is the final judge of all who fail to place their trust in Him as Lord and Savior (Mt 25:14–46; Ac 17:30, 31).

GOD THE HOLY SPIRIT

We teach that the Holy Spirit is a divine person, eternal, underived, possessing all the attributes of personality and deity, including intellect (1Co 2:10–13), emotions (Eph 4:30), will (1Co 12:11), eternality (Heb 9:14), omnipresence (Ps 139:7–10), omniscience (Is 40:13, 14), omnipotence (Ro 15:13), and truthfulness (Jn 16:13). In all the divine attributes He is coequal and consubstantial with the Father and the Son (Mt 28:19; Ac 5:3, 4; 28:25, 26; 1Co 12:4–6; 2Co 13:14; and Jer 31:31–34 with Heb 10:15–17).

We teach that it is the work of the Holy Spirit to execute the divine will with relation to all mankind. We recognize His sovereign activity in the creation (Ge 1:2), the incarnation (Mt 1:18), the written revelation (2Pe 1:20, 21), and the work of salvation (Jn 3:5–7).

We teach that a unique work of the Holy Spirit in this age began at Pentecost when He came from the Father as promised by Christ (Jn 14:16, 17; 15:26) to initiate and complete the building of the body of Christ. His activity includes convicting the world of sin, of righteousness, and of judgment; glorifying the Lord Jesus Christ and transforming believers into the image of Christ (Jn 16:7–9; Ac 1:5; 2:4; Ro 8:29; 2Co 3:18; Eph 2:22).

We teach that the Holy Spirit is the supernatural and sovereign agent in regeneration, baptizing all believers into the body of Christ (1Co 12:13). The Holy Spirit also indwells, sanctifies, instructs, empowers them for service, and seals them unto the day of redemption (Ro 8:9–11; 2Co 3:6; Eph 1:13).

We teach that the Holy Spirit is the divine teacher who guided the apostles and prophets into all truth as they committed to writing God's revelation, the Bible (2Pe 1:19–21). Every believer possesses the indwelling presence of the Holy Spirit from the moment of salvation, and it is the duty of all those born of the Spirit to be filled with (controlled by) the Spirit (Ro 8:9–11; Eph 5:18; 1Jn 2:20, 27).

We teach that the Holy Spirit administers spiritual gifts to the church. The Holy Spirit glorifies neither Himself nor His gifts by ostentatious displays, but He does glorify Christ by implementing His work of redeeming the lost and building up believers in the most holy faith (Jn 16:13, 14; Ac 1:8; 1Co 12:4–11; 2Co 3:18).

We teach, in this respect, that God the Holy Spirit is sovereign in the bestowing of all His gifts for the perfecting of the saints today and that speaking in tongues and the working of sign miracles in the beginning days of the church were for the purpose of pointing to and authenticating the apostles as revealers of divine truth, and were never intended to be characteristic of the lives of believers (1Co 12:4–11; 13:8–10; 2Co 12:12; Eph 4:7–12; Heb 2:1–4).

MAN

We teach that man was directly and immediately created by God in His image and likeness. Man was created free of sin with a rational nature, intelligence, volition, self-determination, and moral responsibility to God (Ge 2:7, 15–25; Jas 3:9).

We teach that God's intention in the creation of man was that man should glorify God, enjoy

God's fellowship, live his life in the will of God, and by this accomplish God's purpose for man in the world (Is 43:7; Col 1:16; Rev 4:11).

We teach that in Adam's sin of disobedience to the revealed will and Word of God, man lost his innocence; incurred the penalty of spiritual and physical death; became subject to the wrath of God; and became inherently corrupt and utterly incapable of choosing or doing that which is acceptable to God apart from divine grace. With no recuperative powers to enable him to recover himself, man is hopelessly lost. Man's salvation is thereby wholly of God's grace through the redemptive work of our Lord Jesus Christ (Ge 2:16, 17; 3:1–19; Jn 3:36; Ro 3:23; 6:23; 1Co 2:14; Eph 2:1–3; 1Ti 2:13, 14; 1Jn 1:8).

We teach that because all men were in Adam, a nature corrupted by Adam's sin has been transmitted to all men of all ages, Jesus Christ being the only exception. All men are thus sinners by nature, by choice, and by divine declaration (Ps 14:1–3; Jer 17:9; Ro 3:9–18, 23; 5:10–12).

SALVATION

We teach that salvation is wholly of God by grace on the basis of the redemption of Jesus Christ, the merit of His shed blood, and not on the basis of human merit or works (Jn 1:12; Eph 1:4–7; 2:8–10; 1Pe 1:18, 19).

ELECTION

We teach that election is the act of God by which, before the foundation of the world, He chose in Christ those whom He graciously regenerates, saves, and sanctifies (Ro 8:28–30; Eph 1:4–11; 2Th 2:13; 2Ti 2:10; 1Pe 1:1, 2).

We teach that sovereign election does not contradict or negate the responsibility of man to repent and trust Christ as Savior and Lord (Eze 18:23, 32; 33:11; Jn 3:18, 19, 36; 5:40; 2Th 2:10–12; Rev 22:17). Nevertheless, since sovereign grace includes the means of receiving the gift of salvation as well as the gift itself, sovereign election will result in what God determines. All whom the Father calls to Himself will come in faith and all who come in faith the Father will receive (Jn 6:37–40, 44; Ac 13:48; Jas 4:8).

We teach that the unmerited favor that God grants to totally depraved sinners is not related to any initiative of their own part nor to God's anticipation of what they might do by their own will, but is solely of His sovereign grace and mercy (Eph 1:4–7; Titus 3:4–7; 1Pe 1:2).

We teach that election should not be looked upon as based merely on abstract sovereignty. God is truly sovereign but He exercises this sovereignty in harmony with His other attributes, especially His omniscience, justice, holiness, wisdom, grace, and love (Ro 9:11–16). This sovereignty will always exalt the will of God in a manner totally consistent with His character as revealed in the life of our Lord Jesus Christ (Mt 11:25–28; 2Ti 1:9).

REGENERATION

We teach that regeneration is a supernatural work of the Holy Spirit by which the divine nature and divine life are given (Jn 3:3–8; Titus 3:5). It is instantaneous and is accomplished solely by the power of the Holy Spirit through the instrumentality of the Word of God (Jn 5:24) when the repentant sinner, as enabled by the Holy Spirit, responds in faith to the divine provision of salvation. Genuine regeneration is manifested by fruits worthy of repentance as demonstrated in righteous attitudes and conduct. Good works will be its proper evidence and fruit (1Co 6:19, 20; Eph 5:17–21; Php 2:12b; Col 3:12–17; 2Pe 1:4–11). This obedience causes the believer to be increasingly conformed to the image of our Lord Jesus Christ (2Co 3:18). Such a conformity is climaxed in the believer's glorification at Christ's coming (Ro 8:16, 17; 2Pe 1:4; 1Jn 3:2, 3).

JUSTIFICATION

We teach that justification before God is an act of God (Ro 8:30, 33) by which He declares righteous those who, through faith in Christ, repent of their sins (Lk 13:3; Ac 2:38; 3:19; 11:18; Ro 2:4; 2Co 7:10; Is 55:6, 7) and confess Him as sovereign Lord (Ro 10:9, 10; 1Co 12:3; 2Co 4:5; Php 2:11). This righteousness is apart from any virtue or work of man (Ro 3:20; 4:6) and involves the placing of our sins on Christ (Col 2:14; 1Pe 2:24) and the imputation of Christ's righteousness to us (1Co 1:2, 30; 6:11; 2Co 5:21). By this means God is enabled to "be just and the justifier of the one who has faith in Jesus" (Ro 3:26).

SANCTIFICATION

We teach that every believer is sanctified (set apart) unto God by justification and is therefore declared to be holy and is therefore identified as a saint. This sanctification is positional and instantaneous and should not be confused with progressive sanctification. This sanctification has to do with the believer's standing, not his present walk or condition (Ac 20:32; 1Co 1:2, 30; 6:11; 2Th 2:13; Heb 2:11; 3:1; 10:10, 14; 13:12; 1Pe 1:2).

We teach that there is also by the work of the Holy Spirit a progressive sanctification by which the state of the believer is brought closer to the likeness of Christ through obedience to the Word of God and the empowering of the Holy Spirit. The believer is able to live a life of increasing holiness in conformity to the will of God, becoming more and more like our Lord Jesus Christ (Jn 17:17, 19; Ro 6:1–22; 2Co 3:18; 1Th 4:3, 4; 5:23).

In this respect, we teach that every saved person is involved in a daily conflict—the new creation in Christ doing battle against the flesh—but adequate provision is made for victory through the power of the indwelling Holy Spirit. The struggle nevertheless stays with the believer all through this earthly life and is never completely ended. All claims to the eradication of sin in this life are unscriptural. Eradication of sin is not possible, but the Holy Spirit does provide for victory over sin (Gal 5:16–25; Php 3:12; Col 3:9, 10; 1Pe 1:14–16; 1Jn 3:5–9).

SECURITY

We teach that all the redeemed once saved are kept by God's power and are thus secure in Christ forever (Jn 5:24; 6:37–40; 10:27–30; Ro 5:9, 10; 8:1, 31–39; 1Co 1:4–9; Eph 4:30; Heb 7:25; 13:5; 1Pe 1:4, 5; Jude 24).

We teach that it is the privilege of believers to rejoice in the assurance of their salvation through the testimony of God's Word, which however, clearly forbids the use of Christian liberty as an excuse for sinful living and carnality (Ro 6:15–22; 13:13, 14; Gal 5:13, 16, 17, 25, 26; Titus 2:11–14).

SEPARATION

We teach that separation from sin is clearly called for throughout the Old and New Testaments, and that the Scriptures clearly indicate that in the last days apostasy and worldliness shall increase (2Co 6:14–7:1; 2Ti 3:1–5).

We teach that out of deep gratitude for the undeserved grace of God granted to us and because our glorious God is so worthy of our total consecration, all the saved should live in such a manner as to demonstrate our adoring love to God and so as not to bring reproach upon our Lord and Savior. We also teach that separation from any association with religious apostasy and worldly and sinful practices is commanded of us by God (Ro 12:1, 2; 1Co 5:9–13; 2Co 6:14–7:1; 1Jn 2:15–17; 2Jn 9–11).

We teach that believers should be separated unto our Lord Jesus Christ (2Th 1:11, 12; Heb 12:1, 2) and affirm that the Christian life is a life of obedient righteousness demonstrated by a beatitude attitude (Mt 5:2–12) and a continual pursuit of holiness (Ro 12:1, 2; 2Co 7:1; Heb 12:14; Titus 2:11–14; 1Jn 3:1–10).

THE CHURCH

We teach that all who place their faith in Jesus Christ are immediately placed by the Holy Spirit into one united spiritual body, the church (1Co 12:12, 13), the bride of Christ (2Co 11:2; Eph 5:23–32; Rev 19:7, 8), of which Christ is the head (Eph 1:22; 4:15; Col 1:18).

We teach that the formation of the church, the body of Christ, began on the day of Pentecost (Ac 2:1–21, 38–47) and will be completed at the coming of Christ for His own at the Rapture (1Co 15:51, 52; 1Th 4:13–18).

We teach that the church is thus a unique spiritual organism designed by Christ, made up of all born-again believers in this present age (Eph 2:11–3:6). The church is distinct from Israel (1Co 10:32), a mystery not revealed until this age (Eph 3:1–6; 5:32).

We teach that the establishment and continuity of local churches is clearly taught and defined in the New Testament Scriptures (Ac 14:23, 27; 20:17, 28; Gal 1:2; Php 1:1; 1Th 1:1; 2Th 1:1) and that the members of the one spiritual body are directed to associate themselves together in local assemblies (1Co 11:18–20; Heb 10:25).

We teach that the one supreme authority for the church is Christ (Eph 1:22; Col 1:18) and that church leadership, gifts, order, discipline, and worship are all appointed through His sovereignty as found in the Scriptures. The biblically designated officers serving under Christ and over the assembly are elders (males, who are also called bishops, pastors, and pastor-teachers; Ac 20:28; Eph 4:11) and deacons, both of whom must meet biblical qualification (1Ti 3:1–13; Titus 1:5–9; 1Pe 5:1–5).

We teach that these leaders lead or rule as servants of Christ (1Ti 5:17–22) and have His authority in directing the church. The congregation is to submit to their leadership (Heb 13:7, 17).

We teach the importance of discipleship (Mt 28:19, 20; 2Ti 2:2), mutual accountability of all believers to one another (Mt 18:15–17), as well as the need for discipline for sinning members of the congregation in accord with the standards of Scripture (Mt 18:15–22; Ac 5:1–11; 1Co 5:1–13; 2Th 3:6–15; 1Ti 1:19, 20; Titus 1:10–16).

We teach the autonomy of the local church, free from any external authority or control, with the right of self-government and freedom from the interference of any hierarchy of individuals or organizations (Titus 1:5). We teach that it is scriptural for true churches to cooperate with each other for the presentation and propagation of the faith. Local churches, however, through their pastors and their interpretation and application of Scripture, should be the sole judges of the measure and method of their cooperation (Ac 15:19–31; 20:28; 1Co 5:4–7, 13; 1Pe 5:1–4).

We teach that the purpose of the church is to glorify God (Eph 3:21) by building itself up in the faith (Eph 4:13–16), by instruction of the Word (2Ti 2:2, 15; 3:16, 17), by fellowship (Ac 2:47; 1Jn 1:3), by keeping the ordinances (Lk 22:19; Ac 2:38–42) and by advancing and communicating the gospel to the entire world (Mt 28:19; Ac 1:8).

We teach the calling of all saints to the work of service (1Co 15:58; Eph 4:12; Rev 22:12).

We teach the need of the church to cooperate with God as He accomplishes His purpose in the world. To that end, He gives the church spiritual gifts. First, He gives men chosen for the purpose of equipping the saints for the work of the ministry (Eph 4:7–12), and He also gives unique and special spiritual abilities to each member of the body of Christ (Ro 12:5–8; 1Co 12:4–31; 1Pe 4:10, 11).

We teach that there were two kinds of gifts given the early church: miraculous gifts of divine revelation and healing, given temporarily in the apostolic era for the purpose of confirming the authenticity of the apostles' message (Heb 2:3, 4; 2Co 12:12); and ministering gifts, given to equip believers for edifying one another. With the New Testament revelation now complete, Scripture becomes the sole test of the authenticity of a man's message, and confirming gifts of a miraculous nature are no longer necessary to validate a man or his message (1Co 13:8–12). Miraculous gifts can even be counterfeited by Satan so as to deceive even believers (Mt

24:24). The only gifts in operation today are those nonrevelatory equipping gifts given for edification (Ro 12:6–8).

We teach that no one possesses the gift of healing today but that God does hear and answer the prayer of faith and will answer in accordance with His own perfect will for the sick, suffering, and afflicted (Lk 18:1–8; Jn 5:7–9; 2Co 12:6–10; Jas 5:13–16; 1Jn 5:14, 15).

We teach that two ordinances have been committed to the local church: baptism and the Lord's Supper (Ac 2:38–42). Christian baptism by immersion (Ac 8:36–39) is the solemn and beautiful testimony of a believer showing forth his faith in the crucified, buried, and risen Savior, and his union with Him in death to sin, and resurrection to a new life (Ro 6:1–11). It is also a sign of fellowship and identification with the visible body of Christ (Ac 2:41, 42).

We teach that the Lord's Supper is the commemoration and proclamation of His death until He comes, and should be always preceded by solemn self-examination (1Co 11:23–32). We also teach that whereas the elements of communion are only representative of the flesh and blood of Christ, the Lord's Supper is nevertheless an actual Communion with the risen Christ who is present in a unique way, fellowshiping with His people (1Co 10:16).

ANGELS

HOLY ANGELS

We teach that angels are created beings and are therefore not to be worshiped. Although they are a higher order of creation than man, they are created to serve God and to worship Him (Lk 2:9–14; Heb 1:6, 7, 14; 2:6, 7; Rev 5:11–14).

FALLEN ANGELS

We teach that Satan is a created angel and the author of sin. He incurred the judgment of God by rebelling against his Creator (Is 14:12–17; Eze 28:11–19), by taking numerous angels with him in his fall (Mt 25:41; Rev 12:1–14), and by introducing sin into the human race by his temptation of Eve (Ge 3:1–15).

We teach that Satan is the open and declared enemy of God and man (Is 14:13, 14; Mt 4:1–11; Rev 12:9, 10), the prince of this world who has been defeated through the death and resurrection of Jesus Christ (Ro 16:20), and that he shall be eternally punished in the lake of fire (Is 14:12–17; Eze 28:11–19; Mt 25:41; Rev 20:10).

LAST THINGS (ESCHATOLOGY)

DEATH

We teach that physical death involves no loss of our immaterial consciousness (Rev 6:9–11), that there is a separation of soul and body (Jas 2:26), that the soul of the redeemed passes immediately into the presence of Christ (Lk 23:43; 2Co 5:8; Php 1:23), and that, for the redeemed, such separation will continue until the Rapture (1Th 4:13–17), which initiates the first resurrection (Rev 20:4–6), when our soul and body will be reunited to be glorified forever with our Lord (1Co 15:35–44, 50–54; Php 3:21). Until that time, the souls of the redeemed in Christ remain in joyful fellowship with our Lord Jesus Christ (2Co 5:8).

We teach the bodily resurrection of all men, the saved to eternal life (Jn 6:39; Ro 8:10, 11, 19–23; 2Co 4:14), and the unsaved to judgment and everlasting punishment (Da 12:2; Jn 5:29; Rev 20:13–15).

We teach that the souls of the unsaved at death are kept under punishment until the final resurrection (Lk 16:19–26; Rev 20:13–15), when the soul and the resurrection body will be united (Jn 5:28, 29). They shall then appear at the Great White Throne judgment (Rev 20:11–15) and shall be cast into hell, the lake of fire (Mt 25:41–46), cut off from the life of God forever (Da 12:2; Mt 25:41–46; 2Th 1:7–9).

THE RAPTURE OF THE CHURCH

We teach the personal, bodily return of our Lord Jesus Christ before the seven-year tribulation (1Th 4:16; Titus 2:13) to translate His church from this earth (Jn 14:1–3; 1Co 15:51–53; 1Th 4:15–5:11) and, between this event and His glorious return with His saints, to reward believers according to their works (1Co 3:11–15; 2Co 5:10).

THE TRIBULATION PERIOD

We teach that immediately following the removal of the church from the earth (Jn 14:1–3; 1Th 4:13–18), the righteous judgments of God will be poured out upon an unbelieving world (Jer 30:7; Da 9:27; 12:1; 2Th 2:7–12; Rev 16), and that these judgments will be climaxed by the return of Christ in glory to the earth (Mt 24:27–31; 25:31–46; 2Th 2:7–12). At that time the Old Testament and tribulation saints will be raised, and the living will be judged (Da 12:2, 3; Rev 20:4–6). This period includes the seventieth week of Daniel's prophecy (Da 9:24–27; Mt 24:15–31; 25:31–46).

THE SECOND COMING AND THE MILLENNIAL REIGN

We teach that after the tribulation period, Christ will come to earth to occupy the throne of David (Mt 25:31; Lk 1:32, 33; Ac 1:10, 11; 2:29, 30) and establish His messianic kingdom for a thousand years on the earth (Rev 20:1–7). During this time the resurrected saints will reign with Him over Israel and all the nations of the earth (Eze 37:21–28; Da 7:17–22; Rev 19:11–16). This reign will be preceded by the overthrow of the Antichrist and the False Prophet, and by the removal of Satan from the world (Da 7:17–27; Rev 20:1–6).

We teach that the kingdom itself will be the fulfillment of God's promise to Israel (Is 65:17–25; Eze 37:21–28; Zec 8:1–17) to restore them to the land which they forfeited through their disobedience (Dt 28:15–68). The result of their disobedience was that Israel was temporarily set aside (Mt 21:43; Ro 11:1–26) but will again be awakened through repentance to enter into the land of blessing (Jer 31:31–34; Eze 36:22–32; Ro 11:25–29).

We teach that this time of our Lord's reign will be characterized by harmony, justice, peace, righteousness, and long life (Is 11; 65:17–25; Eze 36:33–38), and will be brought to an end with the release of Satan (Rev 20:7).

THE JUDGMENT OF THE LOST

We teach that following the release of Satan after the thousand-year reign of Christ (Rev 20:7), Satan will deceive the nations of the earth and gather them to battle against the saints and the beloved city, at which time Satan and his army will be devoured by fire from heaven (Rev 20:9). Following this, Satan will be thrown into the lake of fire and brimstone (Mt 25:41; Rev 20:10), whereupon Christ, who is the judge of all men (Jn 5:22), will resurrect and judge the great and small at the Great White Throne judgment.

We teach that this resurrection of the unsaved dead to judgment will be a physical resurrection, whereupon receiving their judgment (Jn 5:28, 29), they will be committed to an eternal conscious punishment in the lake of fire (Mt 25:41; Rev 20:11–15).

ETERNITY

We teach that after the closing of the Millennium, the temporary release of Satan, and the judgment of unbelievers (2Th 1:9; Rev 20:7–15), the saved will enter the eternal state of glory with God, after which the elements of this earth are to be dissolved (2Pe 3:10) and replaced with a new earth wherein only righteousness dwells (Eph 5:5; Rev 20:15; 21–22). Following this, the heavenly city will come down out of heaven (Rev 21:2) and will be the dwelling place of the saints, where they will enjoy forever fellowship with God and one another (Jn 17:3; Rev 21, 22). Our Lord Jesus Christ, having fulfilled His redemptive mission, will then deliver up the kingdom to God the Father (1Co 15:23–28) that in all spheres the triune God may reign forever and ever (1Co 15:28).

MONIES, WEIGHTS, AND MEASURES

The Hebrews probably first used coins in the Persian period (500–350 B.C.). However, minting began around 700 B.C. in other nations. Prior to this, precious metals were weighed, not counted as money.

Some units appear as both measures of money and measures of weights. This comes from naming the coins after their weight. For example, the shekel was a weight long before it became the name of a coin.

It is helpful to relate biblical monies to current values. But we cannot make exact equivalents. The fluctuating value of money's purchasing power is difficult to determine in our own day. It is even harder to evaluate currencies used two- to three-thousand years ago.

Therefore, it is best to choose a value meaningful over time, such as a common laborer's daily wage. One day's wage corresponds to the ancient Jewish system (a silver shekel is four days' wages) as well as to the Greek and Roman systems (the drachma and the denarius were each coins representing a day's wage).

The monies chart below takes a current day's wage as thirty-two dollars. Though there are differences of economies and standards of living, this measure will help us apply meaningful value to the monetary units in the chart and in the biblical text.

MONIES			
Unit	**Monetary Value**	**Equivalents**	**Translations**
Jewish Weights			
Talent	gold—$5,760,000; silver—$384,0001	3,000 shekels; 6,000 bekas	talent, one hundred pounds
Shekel	gold—$1,920, silver—$128	4 days' wages (silver); 2 bekas: 20 gerahs	shekel
Beka	gold—$960, silver—$64	1/2 shekel; 10 gerahs	beka
Gerah	gold—$96, silver—$6.40	1/20 shekel	gerahs
Persian Coins			
Daric	gold—$1,2802, silver—$64	2 days' wages (silver); 1/2 Jewish silver shekel	daric, drachma
Greek Coins			
Tetradrachma	$128	4 drachmas	stater
Didrachma	$64	2 drachmas	two-drachma tax
Drachma	$32	1 day's wage	coin, silver coins
Lepton	$.25	1/2 of a Roman kodrantes	cents, small copper coin

Unit	Monetary Value	Equivalents	Translations
Roman Coins			
Aureus	$800	25 denarii	gold
Denarius	$32	1 day's wage	denarius
Assarius	$2	1/16 of a denarius	cent
Kodrantes	$.50	1/4 of an assarius	cent

[1]Value of gold is fifteen times the value of silver
[2]Value of gold is twenty times the value of silver

WEIGHTS			
Unit	**Weight**	**Equivalents**	**Translations**
Jewish Weights			
Talent	ca. 75 pounds for common talent, ca. 150 pounds for royal talent	60 minas; 3000 shekels	talent, one hundred pounds
Mina	1.25 pounds	50 shekels	maneh, mina
Shekel	ca. .4 ounce (11.4 grams) for common shekel, ca. .8 ounce for royal shekel	2 bekas; 20 gerahs	shekel
Beka	ca. .2 ounce (5.7 grams)	1/2 shekel; 10 gerahs	half-shekel
Gerah	ca. .02 ounce (.57 grams)	1/20 shekel	gerah
Roman Weight			
Litra	12 ounces		pound, pint

MEASURES OF LENGTH			
Unit	**Length**	**Equivalents**	**Translations**
Day's journey	ca. 20 miles		day's journey, day's walk
Roman mile	4,854 feet	8 stadia	mile
Sabbath day's journey	3,637 feet	6 stadia	a Sabbath day's journey
Stadion	606 feet	1/8 Roman mile	mile, stadion
Rod	9 feet (10.5 feet in Ezekiel)	3 paces; 6 cubits	measuring rod
Fathom	6 feet	4 cubits	fathom
Pace	3 feet	1/3 rod; 2 cubits	pace
Cubit	18 inches	1/2 pace; 2 spans	cubit, yards

Unit	Length	Equivalents	Translations
Span	9 inches	1/2 cubit; 3 handbreadths	span
Handbreadth	3 inches	1/3 span; 4 fingers	handbreadth
Finger	.75 inches	1/4 handbreadth	finger

DRY MEASURES

Unit	Measures	Equivalents	Translations
Homer	6.52 bushels	10 ephahs	homer
Kor	6.52 bushels	1 homer; 10 ephahs	kor, measure
Lethech	3.26 bushels	1/2 kor	a homer and a half
Ephah	.65 bushel, 20.8 quarts	1/10 homer	ephah
Modius	7.68 quarts		peck-measure, basket
Seah	7 quarts	1/3 ephah	measure, pecks
Omer	2.08 quarts	1/10 ephah; 1 4/5 kab	omer
Kab	1.16 quarts	4 logs	kab
Choenix	1 quart		quart
Xestes	11/16 pints		pitcher
Log	.58 pint	1/4 kab	log

LIQUID MEASURES

Unit	Measures	Equivalents	Translations
Kor	60 gallons	10 baths	kor
Metretes	10.2 gallons		gallon, measure
Bath	6 gallons	6 hins	measure, bath
Hin	1 gallon	2 kabs	hin
Kab	2 quarts	4 logs	kab
Log	1 pint	1/4 kab	log

INDEX TO

KEY BIBLE DOCTRINES

This Index to Key Bible Doctrines tells you where to find Bible passages that relate to the ten classical doctrines of the Christian faith: (1) the Holy Scriptures, (2) God the Father, (3) God the Son, (4) God the Holy Spirit, (5) Man, (6) Sin, (7) Salvation, (8) the Church, (9) Angels, and (10) Last Things.

Some of these major topics have subdivisions. For example, God the Father is organized under several subheads, arranged in alphabetical order. These subheads include Holiness of God, Mercy of God, Nature of God, Righteousness of God, etc. Under each major topic, look first for the subhead on "Nature of God," "Nature of Man," "Nature of Sin," etc. These are the best places to begin your research on these major Christian doctrines.

For a more extensive study of Bible topics beyond the doctrinal topics included below, you'll find the *The MacArthur Topical Bible* an invaluable resource. It is published as a separate volume by Thomas Nelson Publishers.

THE HOLY SCRIPTURES

Given by inspiration of God. 2Ti 3:16.
Given by inspiration of the Holy Spirit. Ac 1:16; Heb 3:7; 2Pe 1:21.
Christ sanctioned, by appealing to them. Mt 4:4; Mk 12:10; Jn 7:42.
Christ taught out of. Lk 24:27.
Are called the
- Book. Ps 40:7; Rev 22:19.
- Book of the Law. Ne 8:3; Gal 3:10.
- Book of the Lord. Is 34:16.
- Holy Scriptures. Ro 1:2.
- Law of the Lord. Ps 1:2; Is 30:9.
- Oracles of God. Ro 3:2.
- Sacred writings. 2Ti 3:15.
- Sword of the Spirit. Eph 6:17.
- Utterances of God. 1Pe 4:11.
- Word. Jas 1:21–23; 1Pe 2:2.
- Word of Christ. Col 3:16.
- Word of God. Lk 11:28; Heb 4:12.
- Word of truth. Jas 1:18.
- Writing of Truth. Da 10:21.

Contain the promises of the gospel. Ro 1:2.
Reveal the laws, statutes, and judgments of God. Dt 4:5, 14; Ex 24:3, 4.
Record divine prophecies. 2Pe 1:19–21.
Testify of Christ. Jn 5:39; Ac 10:43; 18:28; 1Co 15:3.
Are full and sufficient. Lk 16:29, 31.
Are an unerring guide. Pr 6:23; 2Pe 1:19.
Are able to make wise to salvation through faith in Christ Jesus. 2Ti 3:15.
Are profitable both for doctrine and practice. 2Ti 3:16, 17.
Described as
- Living and powerful. Heb 4:12.
- More desirable than gold. Ps 19:10.
- Perfect. Ps 19:7.
- Pure. Ps 12:6; 119:140.
- True. Ps 119:160; Jn 17:17.

Written for our instruction. Ro 15:4.
Intended for the use of all men. Ro 16:26.
Nothing to be taken from, or added to. Dt 4:2; 12:32.
One portion of, to be compared with another. 1Co 2:13.
Designed for
- Regenerating. Jas 1:18; 1Pe 1:23.
- Making alive. Ps 119:50, 93.
- Illuminating. Ps 119:130.
- Converting the soul. Ps 19:7.
- Making wise the simple. Ps 19:7.
- Sanctifying. Jn 17:17; Eph 5:26.
- Producing faith. Jn 20:31.
- Producing hope. Ps 119:49; Ro 15:4.
- Producing obedience. Dt 17:19, 20.
- Cleansing the heart. Jn 15:3; Eph 5:26.
- Cleansing the ways. Ps 119:9.
- Keeping from destructive paths. Ps 17:4.
- Supporting life. Dt 8:3; Mt 4:4.
- Promoting growth in grace. 1Pe 2:2.
- Building up in the faith. Ac 20:32.
- Admonishing. Ps 19:11; 1Co 10:11.
- Comforting. Ps 119:82; Ro 15:4.
- Rejoicing the heart. Ps 19:8; 119:111.

Work effectively in those who believe. 1Th 2:13.
The letter of, without the Spirit, kills. Jn 6:63; 2Co 3:6.
Ignorance of, a source of error. Mt 22:29; Ac 13:27.
Christ enables us to understand. Lk 24:45.
The Holy Spirit enables us to understand. Jn 16:13; 1Co 2:10–14.
No prophecy of, is of any private interpretation. 2Pe 1:20.
Everything should be tried by. Is 8:20; Ac 17:11.
Should be
- The standard of teaching. 1Pe 4:11.
- Believed. Jn 2:22.
- Appealed to. 1Co 1:31; 1Pe 1:16.
- Read. Dt 17:19; Is 34:16.
- Read publicly to all. Dt 31:11–13; Ne 8:3; Jer 36:6; Ac 13:15.
- Known. 2Ti 3:15.
- Received, not as the word of men, but as the Word of God. 1Th 2:13.
- Received with humility. Jas 1:21.
- Searched. Jn 5:39; 7:52.
- Searched daily. Ac 17:11.
- Laid up in the heart. Dt 6:6; 11:18.
- Taught to children. Dt 6:7; 11:19; 2Ti 3:15.
- Taught to all. 2Ch 17:7–9; Ne 8:7, 8.
- Talked of continually. Dt 6:7.
- Not handled deceitfully. 2Co 4:2.
- Not only heard, but obeyed. Mt 7:24; Lk 11:28; Jas 1:22.
- Used to answer spiritual enemies. Mt 4:4, 7, 10; Eph 6:11, 17.

All should desire to hear. Ne 8:1.
Mere hearers of, delude themselves. Jas 1:22.
Advantage of possessing. Ro 3:2.
Believers
- Love exceedingly. Ps 119:97, 113, 159, 167.
- Delight in. Ps 1:2.
- Regard, as sweet. Ps 119:103.
- Esteem, above all things. Job 23:12.
- Long after. Ps 119:82.
- Stand in awe of. Ps 119:161; Is 66:2.
- Keep, in remembrance. Ps 119:16.
- Grieve when men disobey. Ps 119:158.
- Hide, in their hearts. Ps 119:11.
- Hope in. Ps 119:74, 81, 147.
- Meditate in. Ps 1:2; 119:99, 148.
- Rejoice in. Ps 119:162; Jer 15:16.
- Trust in. Ps 119:42.
- Obey. Ps 119:67; Lk 8:21; Jn 17:6.
- Speak of. Ps 119:172.
- Esteem, as a light. Ps 119:105.
- Pray to be taught. Ps 119:12, 13, 33, 66.
- Pray to be conformed to. Ps 119:133.
- Plead the promises of, in prayer. Ps 119:25, 28, 41, 76, 169.

Those who search, are truly noble. Ac 17:11.
Blessedness of hearing and obeying. Lk 11:28; Jas 1:25.
Let them dwell richly in you. Col 3:16.
The wicked
 Corrupt. 2Co 2:17.
 Make, of no effect through their traditions. Mk 7:9–13.
 Reject. Jer 8:9.
 Stumble at. 1Pe 2:8.
 Do not obey. Ps 119:158.
 Frequently twist, to their own destruction. 2Pe 3:16.
Consequences for those who tamper with or destroy. Jer 36:29–31; Rev 22:18, 19.

GOD THE FATHER

Counsels and Purposes of God

Excellence of. Is 25:1; 28:29; Jer 32:19.
Immutability of. Ps 33:11; Pr 19:21; Is 14:24, 27; 46:11; Jer 4:28; Ro 9:11; Heb 6:17.
Sovereignty and eternality of. Is 40:13, 14; Da 4:35; Eph 3:11.
Sufferings and death of Christ were according to. Ac 2:23; 4:28.
Believers saved and united according to. Ro 8:28; Eph 1:9–11; 2Ti 1:9.
Should obey. Jer 49:20; 50:45.
Mystery of. Dt 29:29; Mt 24:36; Ac 1:7.
The wicked
 Do not understand. Mic 4:12.
 Despise. Is 5:19.
 Reject. Lk 7:30.

Faithfulness of God

Is part of His character. Is 49:7; 1Co 1:9; 1Th 5:24.
Declared to be
 Established. Ps 89:2.
 Everlasting. Ps 119:90; 146:6.
 Great. La 3:23.
 Incomparable. Ps 89:8.
 Infinite. Ps 36:5.
 Unfailing. Ps 89:33; 2Ti 2:13.
Should be pleaded in prayer. Ps 143:1.
Should be proclaimed. Ps 40:10; 89:1.
Manifested
 In His counsels. Is 25:1.
 In afflicting believers. Ps 119:75.
 In fulfilling His promises. 1Ki 8:20; Ps 132:11; Mic 7:20; Heb 10:23.
 In helping believers endure temptations. 1Co 10:13.
 In keeping His covenant. Dt 7:9; Ps 111:5.
 In executing His judgments. Jer 23:20; 51:29.
 In forgiving sins. 1Jn 1:9.
 To believers. Ps 89:24; 2Th 3:3.
Believers encouraged to depend on. 1Pe 4:19.
Will be praised. Ps 89:5; 92:2.

Glory of God

The supreme purpose of redemption. Eph 1:12.
Every tongue should confess Christ as Lord, to. Php 2:11.
Exhibited in Christ. Jn 1:14; 2Co 4:6; Heb 1:3.
Exhibited in
 His name. Dt 28:58; Ne 9:5.
 His majesty. Job 37:22; Ps 93:1; 104:1; 145:5, 12; Is 2:10.
 His power. Ex 15:1, 6; Ro 6:4.
 His works. Ps 19:1; 111:3.
 His holiness. Ex 15:11.
Described as
 Eternal. Ps 104:31.
 Great. Ps 138:5.
 Highly exalted. Ps 8:1; 113:4.
 Rich. Eph 3:16.
Exhibited to
 Moses. Ex 34:5–7; 33:18–23; Ac 7:2.
 Stephen. Ac 7:55.
 His people. Lv 9:23; Dt 5:24; Ps 102:16.
Enlightens the church. Rev 21:11, 23.
Believers desire to behold. Ps 63:2; 90:16.
Guarded by Him. Is 42:8.
Believers should
 Reverence. Is 59:19.
 Plead in prayer. Ps 79:9.
 Declare. 1Ch 16:24; Ps 96:3; 145:5, 11.
 Magnify. Ps 57:5.
The earth is full of. Is 6:3.
The knowledge of, shall fill the earth. Hab 2:14.

God in Three Persons (the Trinity)

Doctrine of, proved from Scripture. Is 11:2; 61:1; Mt 3:16, 17; 28:19; Lk 3:22; Ro 8:9; 1Co 12:3–6; 2Co 1:21, 22; 13:14; Eph 4:4–6; 1Pe 1:2; Jude 20, 21; Rev 1:4, 5.
Divine titles applied to the three persons in. Ex 20:2; Jn 20:28; Ac 5:3, 4.
Each person in, described as
 Author of all spiritual operations. 1Co 12:11; Col 1:29; Heb 13:21.
 Creator. Ge 1:1; Job 26:13; 33:4; Ps 148:5; Jn 1:3; Col 1:16.
 Eternal. Ro 16:26; Heb 9:14; Rev 22:13.
 Holy. Ac 3:14; 1Jn 2:20; Rev 4:8; 15:4.
 Inspiring the prophets, etc. Mk 13:11; 2Co 13:3; Heb 1:1.
 Omnipotent. Ge 17:1; Jer 32:17; Ro 15:19; Lk 1:35; Heb 1:3; Rev 1:8.
 Omnipresent. Ps 139:7; Jer 23:24; Eph 1:23.
 Omniscient. Jn 21:17; Ac 15:18; 1Co 2:10, 11.
 Raising Christ from the dead. 1Co 6:14; Jn 2:19; 1Pe 3:18.
 Sanctifier. Heb 2:11; 1Pe 1:2; Jude 1.
 Source of eternal life. Jn 10:28; Ro 6:23; Gal 6:8.
 Supplying ministers to the church. Jer 3:15; 26:5; Mt 10:5; Ac 13:2; 20:28; Eph 4:11.
 Teacher. Is 48:17; 54:13; Lk 21:15; Jn 14:26; Gal 1:12; 1Jn 2:20.
 True. Jn 7:28; Rev 3:7.
Salvation is work of. 2Th 2:13, 14; Titus 3:4–6; 1Pe 1:2.
Baptism administered in name of. Mt 28:19.
Benediction given in name of. 2Co 13:14.

Goodness of God

Is part of His character. Ps 25:8; Na 1:7; Mt 19:17.
Declared to be
 Abundant. Ex 34:6; Ps 33:5.
 Enduring. Ps 23:6; 52:1.
 Great. Ne 9:35; Zec 9:17.
 Rich. Ps 104:24; Ro 2:4.
 Satisfying. Ps 65:4; Jer 31:12, 14.
 Universal. Ps 145:9; Mt 5:45.
Ways It Is Manifested
 To His people. Ps 31:19; La 3:25.
 In doing good. Ps 119:68; 145:9.
 In supplying temporal wants. Ac 14:17.
 In providing for the poor. Ps 68:10.
 In forgiving sins. 2Ch 30:18; Ps 86:5.
Leads to repentance. Ro 2:4.
Recognize, in His dealings. Ezr 8:18; Ne 2:18.
Pray for the manifestation of. 2Th 1:11.
Do not despise. Ro 2:4.
Reverence. Jer 33:9; Hos 3:5.
Magnify. Ps 107:8; Jer 33:11.
Urge others to confide in. Ps 34:8.
The wicked disregard. Ne 9:35.

Holiness of God

Is incomparable. Ex 15:11; 1Sa 2:2.
Exhibited in His
 Character. Ps 22:3; Jn 17:11.
 Name. Is 57:15; Lk 1:49.
 Words. Ps 60:6; Jer 23:9.
 Works. Ps 145:17.
 Kingdom. Ps 47:8; Mt 13:41; 1Co 6:9, 10; Rev 21:27.
Is pledged for the fulfillment of
 His promises. Ps 89:35.
 His judgments. Am 4:2.
Believers are commanded to imitate. Lv 11:44; 1Pe 1:15, 16.
Believers should thank Him for. Ps 30:4.
Should produce reverential fear. Rev 15:4.
Heavenly hosts adore. Is 6:3; Rev 4:8.
Should be magnified. 1Ch 16:10; Ps 48:1; 99:3, 5; Rev 15:4.

Justice of God

Is a part of His character. Dt 32:4; Is 45:21.
Declared to be
 Abundant. Job 37:23.
 The foundation of His throne. Ps 89:14.
 Impartial. 2Ch 19:7; Jer 32:19.
 Incomparable. Job 4:1.
 Incorruptible. Dt 10:17; 2Ch 19:7.
 Undeviating. Job 8:3; 34:12.
 Unfailing. Zep 3:5.
Not to be sinned against. Jer 50:7.
Denied by the ungodly. Eze 33:17, 20.
Exhibited in
 Forgiving sins. 1Jn 1:9.
 Redemption. Ro 3:26.
 His government. Ps 9:4; Jer 9:24.
 His judgments. Ge 18:25; Rev 19:2.
 All His ways. Eze 18:25, 29.
 The final judgment. Ac 17:31.
Acknowledgment of. Ps 51:4; 98:9; Ro 3:4.
Should be praised. Ps 98:9; 99:3, 4.

Longsuffering of God

Is part of His character. Ex 34:6; Nu 14:18; Ps 86:15.
Should lead to repentance and salvation. Joel 2:13; Ro 2:4; 2Pe 3:9, 15.
Exercised toward
 His people. Is 30:18; Eze 20:17; Ro 3:25.
 The wicked. Ro 9:22; 1Pe 3:20.
Plead in prayer. Jer 15:15.
Limits set to. Ge 6:3; Jer 44:22.
The wicked
 Abuse. Ecc 8:11; Mt 24:48, 49.
 Disregard. Ro 2:4.
 Admonished for rejecting. Ne 9:30; Mt 24:48–51; Ro 2:5.
Illustrated. Lk 13:6–9.
Exemplified toward
 Manasseh. 2Ch 33:10–13.
 Israel. Ps 78:38; Is 48:9.
 Jerusalem. Mt 23:37.
 Paul. 1Ti 1:16.

- Special preservation and protection of believers. Ps 37:28; 91:3, 4, 11; 140:7; Is 3:5; Mt 10:30.
- Prospering believers. Ge 24:48, 56.
- Leading believers. Dt 8:2, 15; Is 31:5; 63:12.
- Bringing His words to pass. Nu 26:65; Jos 21:45; Lk 21:32, 33.
- Ordering the lives of men. 1Sa 2:7, 8; Ps 75:6, 7; Pr 16:9; 19:21; 20:24.
- Ordaining the lives of men. 1Sa 2:7, 8; Ps 75:6, 7; Pr 16:9; 19:21; 20:24.
- Determining the period of human life. Ps 31:15; 39:5; Ac 17:26.
- Defeating wicked designs. Ex 15:9–19; 2Sa 17:14, 15; Ps 33:10.
- Overruling wicked designs for good. Ge 45:5–7; 50:20; Php 1:12.
- Preserving the course of nature. Ge 8:22; Job 26:10; Ps 104:5–9.
- Directing all events. Jos 7:14; 1Sa 6:7–10, 12; Pr 16:33; Is 44:7; Ac 1:26.
- Ruling the elements. Job 37:9–13; Is 50:2; Jon 1:4, 15; Na 1:4.
- Ordering the minutest matters. Mt 10:29, 30; Lk 21:18.

Is righteous. Ps 145:17; Da 4:37.
Is ever watchful. Ps 121:4; Is 27:3.
Is all pervading. Ps 139:1–5.
Sometimes dark and mysterious. Ps 36:6; 73:16; 77:19; Ro 11:33.
All things are ordered by
- For His glory. Is 63:14.
- For good to believers. Ro 8:28.

The wicked sometimes made to further. Is 10:5–12; Ac 3:17, 18.
To be acknowledged
- In prosperity. Dt 8:18; 1Ch 29:12.
- In adversity. Job 1:21; Ps 119:15.
- In public calamities. Am 3:6.
- In our daily support. Ge 48:15.
- In all things. Pr 3:6.

Cannot be defeated. 1Ki 22:30, 34; Pr 21:30.
Man's efforts are useless without. Ps 127:1, 2; Pr 21:31.
Believers should
- Trust in. Mt 6:33, 34; 10:9, 29–31.
- Have full confidence in. Ps 16:8; 139:10.
- Commit their works to. Pr 16:3.
- Encourage themselves with. 1Sa 30:6.
- Pray in dependence upon. Ac 12:5.
- Pray to be guided by. Ge 24:12–14; 28:20, 21; Ac 1:24.

Result of depending upon. Lk 22:35.
Connected with the use of means. 1Ki 21:19; 22:37, 38; Mic 5:2; Lk 2:1–4; Ac 27:22, 31, 32.
Danger of denying. Is 10:13–17; Eze 28:2–10; Da 4:29–31; Hos 2:8, 9.

Righteousness of God

Is part of His character. Ps 7:9; 11:7; 116:5; 119:137.
Described as
- Abundant. Ps 48:10.
- Beyond computation. Ps 71:15.
- Enduring forever. Ps 111:3.
- Everlasting. Ps 119:142.
- The foundation of His throne. Ps 97:2.
- Very high. Ps 71:19.

Christ acknowledged. Jn 17:25.
Christ committed His cause to. 1Pe 2:23.
Angels acknowledge. Rev 16:5.
Exhibited in
- His testimonies. Ps 119:138, 144.
- His commandments. Dt 4:8; Ps 119:172.
- His judgments. Ps 19:9; 119:7, 62.
- His word. Ps 119:123.
- His ways. Ps 145:17.
- His acts. Jdg 5:11; 1Sa 12:7.
- His government. Ps 96:13; 98:9.
- The gospel. Ps 85:10; Ro 3:25, 26.
- The final judgment. Ac 17:31.
- The punishment of the wicked. Ro 2:5; 2Th 1:6; Rev 16:7; 19:2.

Shown to believers' descendants. Ps 103:17.
Shown openly before the nations. Ps 98:2.
He delights in the exercise of. Jer 9:24.
The heavens shall declare. Ps 50:6; 97:6.
Believers
- Ascribe, to Him. Job 36:3; Da 9:7.
- Acknowledge, in His dealings. Ezr 9:15.
- Acknowledge, though the wicked prosper. Jer 12:1; Ps 73:12–17.
- Recognize, in the fulfillment of His promises. Ne 9:8.
- Confident of seeing. Mic 7:9.
- Upheld by. Is 41:10.
- Do not conceal. Ps 40:10.
- Talk of. Ps 35:28; 71:15, 16, 24.
- Declare to others. Ps 22:31.
- Magnify. Ps 7:17; 51:14; 145:7.
- Plead in prayer. Ps 143:11; Da 9:16.

We should pray
- To be led in. Ps 5:8.
- To be revived in. Ps 119:40.
- To be delivered in. Ps 31:1; 71:2.
- To be answered in. Ps 143:1.
- To be judged according to. Ps 35:24.
- For its continued manifestation. Ps 36:10.

Redemption of His people designed to teach. Mic 6:4, 5.
The wicked have no interest in. Ps 69:27.
Illustrated. Ps 36:6.

Truth of God

Is one of His attributes. Dt 32:4; Ps 89:14; 146:6; Is 65:16.
Described as
- Abundant. Ex 34:6; Ps 86:15.
- Enduring to all generations. Ps 100:5.
- Great and endless. Ps 57:10.
- Inviolable. Nu 23:19; Titus 1:2.
- United with mercy in redemption. Ps 85:10.

Exhibited in His
- Counsels of old. Is 25:1.
- Ways. Rev 15:3.
- Works. Ps 11:7; 33:4; Da 4:37.
- Judgments. Ps 19:9; Ps 96:13.
- Word. Ps 119:160; Jn 17:17.
- Fulfillment of promises in Christ. 2Co 1:20.
- Fulfillment of His covenant. Mic 7:20.
- Preservation of believers. Ps 9:14; 25:10; 57:3; 98:3.
- Punishment of the wicked. Rev 16:7.

We should
- Confide in. Ps 31:5; Titus 1:2.
- Plead, in prayer. Ps 89:49.
- Pray for its manifestation to ourselves. 2Ch 6:17.
- Pray for its exhibition to others. 2Sa 2:6.
- Make known to others. Is 38:19.
- Magnify. Ps 71:22; 138:2.

Is denied by
- The devil. Ge 3:4, 5.
- The self-righteous. 1Jn 1:10.
- Unbelievers. 1Jn 5:10.

Exemplified toward
- Abraham. Ge 24:27.
- Jacob. Ge 32:10.
- Israel. Ps 98:3.

Unity of God

A ground for obeying Him exclusively. Dt 4:39, 40.
A ground for loving Him supremely. Dt 6:4, 5; Mk 12:29, 30.
Asserted by
- God Himself. Is 44:6, 8; 45:18, 21.
- Christ. Mk 12:29; Jn 17:3.
- Moses. Dt 4:39; 6:4.
- The apostles. 1Co 8:4, 6; Eph 4:6; 1Ti 2:5.

Consistent with the deity of Christ and of the Holy Spirit. Jn 10:30; 14:9–11; 1Jn 5:7.
Exhibited in
- His greatness and wonderful works. 2Sa 7:22; Ps 86:10.
- His works of creation and providence. Is 44:24; 45:5–8.
- His exclusive foreknowledge. Is 46:9–11.
- His exercise of uncontrolled sovereignty. Dt 32:39.
- His being the sole object of worship in heaven and earth. Ne 9:6; Mt 4:10.
- His being alone good. Mt 19:17.
- His being the only Savior. Is 45:21, 22.
- His being the only source of pardon. Mic 7:18; Mk 2:7.
- His unparalleled election and care of His people. Dt 4:32–35.

The knowledge of, necessary to eternal life. Jn 17:3.
All believers acknowledge, in worshiping Him. 2Sa 7:22; 2Ki 19:15; 1Ch 17:20.
All should know and acknowledge. Dt 4:35; Ps 83:18.
May be acknowledged without saving faith. Jas 2:19, 20.

Wisdom of God

One of His attributes. 1Sa 2:3; Job 9:4.
Described as
- Beyond human comprehension. Ps 139:6.
- Incomparable. Is 44:7; Jer 10:7.
- Infinite. Ps 147:5; Ro 11:33.
- Mighty. Job 36:5.
- Perfect. Job 36:4; 37:16.
- Underived. Job 21:22; Is 40:14.
- Universal. Job 28:24; Da 2:22; Ac 15:18.
- Unsearchable. Is 40:28; Ro 11:33.

The gospel contains treasures of. 1Co 2:7.
Wisdom of believers is derived from. Ezr 7:25.
All human wisdom derived from. Da 2:21.
Believers ascribe, to Him. Da 2:20.
Exhibited in
- His works. Job 37:16; Ps 104:24; 136:5; Pr 3:19; Jer 10:12.
- His counsels. Is 28:29; Jer 32:19.
- His foreshadowing events. Is 42:9; 46:10.
- Redemption. 1Co 1:24; Eph 1:8; 3:10.
- Searching the heart. 1Ch 28:9; Rev 2:23.
- Understanding the thoughts. 1Ch 28:9; Ps 139:2.

Exhibited in knowing
- The human heart. Ps 44:21; Pr 15:11; Lk 16:15.
- The actions of man. Job 34:21; Ps 139:2, 3.
- The words of man. Ps 139:4.

Wrath of God

GOD THE SON

Ascension of Christ

Character and Attributes of Christ

Compassion and Sympathy of Christ

Crucifixion of Christ

Death of Christ

Deity of Christ

Exaltation of Christ

Example of Christ

Excellency and Glory of Christ

Human Nature of Christ

Humility of Christ

Incarnation of Christ

Love of Christ

Ministry of Christ as Head of the Church

Preciousness of Christ

Prophecies Fulfilled in Christ

Resurrection of Christ

- The efficacy of preaching. 1Co 15:14.
- The efficacy of faith. 1Co 15:14, 17.
- The truth of the gospel. 1Co 15:14, 15.

A proof of His being the Son of God. Ps 2:7; Ac 13:33; Ro 1:4.

Effected by
- The power of God. Ac 2:24; 3:15; Ro 8:11; Eph 1:20; Col 2:12.
- His own power. Jn 2:19; 10:18.
- The power of the Holy Spirit. 1Pe 3:18.

On the first day of the week. Mk 16:9.

On the third day after His death. Lk 24:46; Ac 10:40; 1Co 15:4.

The apostles
- At first did not understand the predictions respecting. Mk 9:10; Jn 20:9.
- Very slow to believe. Mk 16:13; Lk 24:9, 11, 37, 38.
- Rebuked for their unbelief of. Mk 16:14.

He appeared after, to
- Mary Magdalene. Mk 16:9; Jn 20:18.
- The women. Mt 28:9.
- Simon. Lk 24:34.
- Two disciples. Lk 24:13–31.
- The apostles, except Thomas. Jn 20:19, 24.
- The apostles, including Thomas. Jn 20:26.
- The apostles (disciples) at the Sea of Tiberias. Jn 21:1.
- The apostles in Galilee. Mt 28:16, 17.
- About five hundred brethren. 1Co 15:6.
- James. 1Co 15:7.
- All the apostles. Lk 24:51; Ac 1:9; 1Co 15:7.
- Paul. 1Co 15:8.

Fraud impossible in. Mt 27:63–66.

He gave many infallible proofs of. Lk 24:35, 39, 43; Jn 20:20, 27; Ac 1:3.

Was attested by
- Angels. Mt 28:5–7; Lk 24:4–7, 23.
- Apostles. Ac 1:22; 2:32; 3:15; 4:33.
- His enemies. Mt 28:11–15.

Asserted and preached by the apostles. Ac 25:19; 26:23.

Believers
- Begotten to a living hope by. 1Pe 1:3, 21.
- Desire to know the power of. Php 3:10.
- Should keep, in remembrance. 2Ti 2:8.
- Shall rise in the likeness of. Ro 6:5; 1Co 15:49; Php 3:21.

Is an emblem of the new birth. Ro 6:4; Col 2:12.

The first fruits of our resurrection. Ac 26:23; 1Co 15:20, 23.

Followed by His exaltation. Ac 4:10, 11; Ro 8:34; Eph 1:20; Php 2:9, 10; Rev 1:18.

An assurance of the judgment. Ac 17:31.

Typified by
- Isaac. Ge 22:13; Heb 11:19.
- Jonah. Jon 2:10; Mt 12:40.

Titles and Names of Christ

Advocate. 1Jn 2:1.
Almighty. Rev 1:8.
Alpha and Omega. Rev 1:8; 22:13.
Amen. Rev 3:14.
Angel. Ge 48:16; Ex 23:20, 21.
Angel of the Lord. Ex 3:2; Jdg 13:15–18.
Angel of His [God's] presence. Is 63:9.
Apostle. Heb 3:1.
Arm of the Lord. Is 51:9; 53:1.
Author and perfecter of faith. Heb 12:2.
Author of salvation. Heb 2:10.
Beginning of the creation of God. Rev 3:14.
Blessed and only Sovereign. 1Ti 6:15.
Branch. Jer 23:5; Zec 3:8; 6:12.
Bread of life. Jn 6:35, 48.
Captain of the host of the Lord. Jos 5:14, 15.
Chief Shepherd. 1Pe 5:4.
Chosen one. Is 42:1.
Christ of God. Lk 9:20.
Commander. Is 55:4.
Consolation of Israel. Lk 2:25.
Cornerstone. Eph 2:20; 1Pe 2:6.
Counselor. Is 9:6.
David. Jer 30:9; Eze 34:23.
Deliverer. Ro 11:26.
Descendant of David. Rev 22:16.
Door. Jn 10:7.
Eternal life. 1Jn 1:2; 5:20.
Eternal Father. Is 9:6.
Faithful witness. Rev 1:5; 3:14.
First and the last. Rev 1:17; 2:8.
Firstborn of all creation. Col 1:15.
Firstborn of the dead. Rev 1:5.
Forerunner. Heb 6:20.
Glory of the Lord. Is 40:5.
God. Is 40:9; Jn 20:28.
God of the spirits of the prophets. Rev 22:6.
God's Associate. Zec 13:7.
Good shepherd. Jn 10:14.
Great High Priest. Heb 4:14.
Guarantee. Heb 7:22.
Head of the church. Eph 5:23; Col 1:18.
Heir of all things. Heb 1:2.
Holy One. Ps 16:10; Ac 2:27.
Holy One of God. Mk 1:24.
Holy One of Israel. Is 41:14.
Horn of salvation. Lk 1:69.
I AM. Ex 3:14; Jn 8:58.
Immanuel. Is 7:14; Mt 1:23.
Jesus. Mt 1:21; 1Th 1:10.
Judge of Israel. Mic 5:1.
King. Zec 9:9; Mt 21:5.
King of Israel. Jn 1:49.
King of the Jews. Mt 2:2.
King of Kings. 1Ti 6:15; Rev 17:14.
King of the nations. Rev 15:3.
Lamb. Rev 5:6, 12; 13:8; 21:22; 22:3.
Lamb of God. Jn 1:29, 36.
Last Adam. 1Co 15:45.
Lawgiver. Is 33:22.
Leader. Is 55:4.
Life. Jn 14:6; Col 3:4; 1Jn 1:2.
Light of the world. Jn 8:12.
Lion from the tribe of Judah. Rev 5:5.
Lord God, the Almighty. Rev 15:3.
Lord of all. Ac 10:36.
Lord of glory. 1Co 2:8.
Lord our righteousness. Jer 23:6.
Mediator. 1Ti 2:5.
Messenger of the covenant. Mal 3:1.
Messiah. Da 9:25; Jn 1:41.
Mighty God. Is 9:6.
Mighty One of Jacob. Is 60:16.
Morning star. Rev 22:16.
Nazarene. Mt 2:23.
Only begotten. Jn 1:14.
Our Passover. 1Co 5:7.
Prince of life. Ac 3:15.
Prince of Peace. Is 9:6.
Prophet. Lk 24:19; Jn 7:40.
Ransom. 1Ti 2:6.
Redeemer. Job 19:25; Is 59:20; 60:16.
Resurrection and the life. Jn 11:25.
Righteous One. Ac 7:52.
Rock. 1Co 10:4.
Root of Jesse. Is 11:10.
Ruler. Mt 2:6.
Ruler in Israel. Mic 5:2.
Ruler of the kings of the earth. Rev 1:5.
Savior. 2Pe 2:20; 3:18.
Servant. Is 42:1; 52:13.
Shepherd and Guardian of your souls. 1Pe 2:25.
Shiloh. Ge 49:10.
Son of the Blessed One. Mk 14:61.
Son of David. Mt 9:27.
Son of God. Lk 1:35; Jn 1:49.
Son of the Most High. Lk 1:32.
Son of Man. Jn 5:27.
Star. Nu 24:17.
Sunrise. Lk 1:78.
Sun of Righteousness. Mal 4:2.
True God. 1Jn 5:20.
True Light. Jn 1:9.
True vine. Jn 15:1.
Truth. Jn 14:6.
Way. Jn 14:6.
Wealth of all nations. Hag 2:7.
Wisdom. Pr 8:12.
Witness. Is 55:4.
Wonderful Counselor. Is 9:6.
Word. Jn 1:1, 14.
Word of God. Rev 19:13.
Word of Life. 1Jn 1:1.

Types of Christ

Aaron. Ex 28:1; Heb 5:4, 5; Lv 16:15.
Adam. Ro 5:14; 1Co 15:45.
Abel. Ge 4:8, 10; Heb 12:24.
Abraham. Ge 17:5; Eph 3:15.
Ark (Noah's). Ge 7:16; 1Pe 3:20, 21.
Ark of the covenant. Ex 25:16; Ps 40:8; Is 42:6.
Atonement, sacrifices offered on the day of. Lv 16:15, 16; Heb 9:12, 24.
Bronze altar. Ex 27:1, 2; Heb 13:10.
Bronze serpent. Nu 21:9; Jn 3:14, 15.
Burnt offering. Lv 1:2, 4; Heb 10:10.
Cities of refuge. Nu 35:6; Heb 6:18.
David. 2Sa 8:15; Eze 37:24; Ps 89:19, 20; Php 2:9.
Eliakim. Is 22:20–22; Rev 3:7.
Firstfruits. Ex 22:29; 1Co 15:20.
Gold altar. Ex 40:26, 27; Heb 13:15; Rev 8:3.
Gold lampstand. Ex 25:31; Jn 8:12.
Guilt offering. Lv 6:1–7; Is 53:10.
Isaac. Ge 22:1, 2; Heb 11:17–19.
Jacob. Ge 32:28; Jn 11:42; Heb 7:25.
Jacob's ladder. Ge 28:12; Jn 1:51.
Jonah. Jon 1:17; Mt 12:40.
Joseph. Ge 50:19, 20.
Joshua. Jos 1:5, 6; 11:23; Ac 20:32; Heb 4:8–9.
Laver of bronze. Ex 30:18–20; Zec 13:1; Eph 5:26, 27.
Leper's offering. Lv 14:4–7; Ro 4:25.
Manna (Bread from heaven). Ex 10:11–15; Jn 6:32–35.
Melchizedek. Ge 14:18–20; Heb 7:1–17.
Mercy seat. Ex 25:17–22; Ro 3:25; Heb 4:16.
Morning and evening offerings. Ex 29:38–41; Jn 1:29, 36.
Moses. Nu 12:7; Dt 18:15; Ac 3:20–22; Heb 3:2.
Noah. Ge 5:29.
Passover lamb. Ex 12:3–6, 46; Jn 19:36; 1Co 5:7.
Peace offerings. Lv 3:1; Eph 2:14, 16.
Red heifer. Nu 19:2–6; Heb 9:13, 14.
Rock at Horeb. Ex 17:6; 1Co 10:4.

Sacrifices offered on the day of Atonement. Lv 16:15, 16; Heb 9:12, 24.
Samson. Jdg 16:30; Col 2:14, 15.
Scapegoat. Lv 16:20–22; Is 53:6, 12.
Sin offering. Lv 4:2, 3, 12; Heb 13:11, 12.
Solomon. 2Sa 7:12, 13.
Tabernacle. Ex 40:2, 34; Col 2:9; Heb 9:11.
Table and showbread. Ex 25:23–30; Jn 1:16; 6:48.
Temple. 1Ki 6:1, 38; Jn 2:19, 21.
Tree of life. Ge 2:9; Jn 1:4; Rev 22:2.
Veil of the tabernacle and temple. Ex 40:21; 2Ch 3:14; Heb 10:20.
Zerubbabel. Zec 4:7–9; Heb 12:2, 3.

GOD THE HOLY SPIRIT

Anointing of the Holy Spirit
Is from God. 2Co 1:21.
That Christ should receive
  Foretold. Is 61:1; Da 9:24.
  Fulfilled. Lk 4:18, 21; Ac 4:27; 10:38; Heb 1:9.
God preserves those who receive. Ps 18:50; 20:6; 89:20–23.
Believers receive. 1Jn 2:20, 27.
Guides into all truth. 1Jn 2:27.

Baptism with the Holy Spirit
Is through Christ. Titus 3:6.
Christ administered. Mt 3:11; Jn 1:33.
Promised to believers. Ac 1:5; 2:38, 39; 11:16.
All believers partake of. 1Co 12:13.
Necessity for. Jn 3:5; Ac 19:2–6.
Renews and cleanses the soul. Titus 3:5; 1Pe 3:20, 21.
The Word of God instrumental to. Ac 10:44; Eph 5:26.
Typified. Ac 2:1–4.

Deity of the Holy Spirit
As Lord. Ex 17:7; Nu 12:6; Heb 3:7–9; 2Pe 1:21.
As Lord of hosts. Is 6:3, 8–10; Ac 28:25.
As Lord, Most High. Ps 78:17, 21; Ac 7:51.
Being invoked as Lord. Lk 2:26–29; Ac 1:16, 20; 4:23–25; 2Th 3:5.
Was called God. Ac 5:3, 4.
Part of the divine baptismal formula. Mt 28:19.
As eternal. Heb 9:14.
As omnipresent. Ps 139:7–13.
As omniscient. 1Co 2:10.
As omnipotent. Lk 1:35; Ro 15:19.
As the Spirit of glory and of God. 1Pe 4:14.
As Creator. Ge 1:26, 27; Job 33:4.
As equal to and one with the Father. Mt 28:19; 2Co 13:14.
As sovereign worker of all things. Da 4:35; 1Co 12:6, 11.
As author of the new birth. Jn 3:5, 6; 1Jn 5:4.
As raising Christ from the dead. Ac 2:24; Ro 1:4; Heb 13:20; 1Pe 3:18.
As inspiring Scripture. 2Ti 3:16; 2Pe 1:21.
As the source of wisdom. Is 11:2; Jn 16:13; 14:26; 1Co 12:8.
As the source of miraculous power. Mt 12:28; Lk 11:20; Ac 19:11; Ro 15:19.
As appointing and sending ministers. Ac 13:2, 4; 9:38; 20:28.
As directing where the gospel should be preached. Ac 16:6, 7, 10.
As dwelling in believers. Jn 14:17; 1Co 3:16; 6:19; 14:25.
As comforter of the church. Ac 9:31; 2Co 1:3.
As sanctifying God's people. Eze 37:28; Ro 15:16.
As the witness. Heb 10:15; 1Jn 5:9.
As convincing of sin, righteousness, and judgment. Jn 16:8–11.

Emblems of the Holy Spirit
Water. Jn 3:5; 7:38, 39.
  Cleansing. Eze 16:9; 36:25; Eph 5:26; Heb 10:22.
  Nourishing. Ps 1:3; Is 27:3, 6; 44:3, 4; 58:11.
  Refreshing. Ps 46:4; Is 41:17, 18.
  Abundant. Jn 7:37, 38.
  Freely given. Is 55:1; Jn 4:14; Rev 22:17.
Fire
  Purifying. Is 4:4; Mal 3:2, 3.
  Illuminating. Ex 13:21; Ps 78:14.
  Searching. Zep 1:12; 1Co 2:10.
Wind
  Independent. Jn 3:8; 1Co 12:11.
  Powerful. 1Ki 19:11; Ac 2:2.
  Sensible in its effects. Jn 3:8.
  Reviving. Eze 37:9, 10, 14.
Oil. Ps 45:7.
  Of joy. Ps 45:7.
  Illuminating. Mt 25:3, 4; 1Jn 2:20, 27.
  Consecrating. Ex 29:7; 30:30; Is 61:1.
Rain and dew. Ps 72:6.
  Fertilizing. Eze 34:26, 27; Hos 6:3; 10:12; 14:5.
  Refreshing. Ps 68:9; Is 18:5.
  Abundant. Ps 133:3.
  Imperceptible. 2Sa 17:12; Mk 4:26–28.
A dove. Mt 3:16.
  Gentle. Mt 10:16; Gal 5:22.
A voice. Is 6:8.
  Speaking. Mt 10:20.
  Guiding. Is 30:21; Jn 16:13.
  Warning. Heb 3:7–11.
A seal. Rev 7:2.
  Securing. Eph 1:13, 14; 4:30.
  Authenticating. Jn 6:27; 2Co 1:22.
Divided tongues. Ac 2:3, 6–11.

Gift of the Holy Spirit
By the Father. Ne 9:20; Lk 11:13.
By the Son. Jn 20:22.
To Christ without measure. Jn 3:34.
Given
  According to promise. Ac 2:38, 39.
  Upon the exaltation of Christ. Ps 68:18; Jn 7:39.
  Through the intercession of Christ. Jn 14:16.
  In answer to prayer. Lk 11:13; Eph 1:16, 17.
  For instruction. Ne 9:20.
  To help believers. Jn 14:16.
  To those who repent and believe. Ac 2:38.
  To those who obey God. Ac 5:32.
  To the Gentiles. Ac 10:44, 45; 11:17; 15:8.
Is abundant. Ps 68:9; Jn 7:38, 39.
Is permanent. Is 59:21; Hag 2:5; 1Pe 4:14.
Is fruit bearing. Is 32:15.
Received through faith. Gal 3:14.
An evidence of union with Christ. 1Jn 3:24; 4:13.
A guarantee of the inheritance of believers. 2Co 1:22; 5:5; Eph 1:14.
A pledge of the continued favor of God. Eze 39:29.

Indwelling of the Holy Spirit
In His church, as His temple. 1Co 3:16.
In the body of believers, as His temple. 1Co 6:19; 2Co 6:16.
Promised to believers. Eze 36:27; Ac 1:8.
Believers enjoy. Is 63:11; 2Ti 1:14.
As a helper to believers. Jn 14:16, 17.
A pledge of eternal salvation. Eph 1:13, 14.
Believers filled with. Ac 6:5; Eph 5:18; 2Ti 1:14; 1Jn 2:27.
Is the means of
  Receiving life. Ro 8:11.
  Guiding. Jn 16:13; Gal 5:18.
  Fruit bearing. Gal 5:22.
A proof of being Christ's child. Ro 8:9, 15; 1Jn 4:13.
A proof of adoption. Ro 8:15; Gal 4:5.
Those who do not have
  Are worldly minded. Jude 19.
  Are without Christ. Ro 8:9.
Opposed by the fleshly nature. Gal 5:17.

Inspiration of the Holy Spirit
Foretold. Joel 2:28; Ac 2:16–18.
All Scripture given by. 2Sa 23:2; 2Ti 3:16; 2Pe 1:21.
Purpose of
  To reveal future events. Ac 1:16; 28:25; 1Pe 1:11.
  To reveal the mysteries of God. Am 3:7; 1Co 2:10.
  To give power to ministers. Mic 3:8; Ac 1:8.
  To direct ministers. Eze 3:24–27; Ac 11:12; 13:2; 16:6.
  To testify against sin. 2Ki 17:13; Ne 9:30; Mic 3:8; Jn 16:8, 9.
Modes of
  Various. Heb 1:1.
  By secret impulse. Jdg 13:25; 2Pe 1:21.
  By a voice. Is 6:8; Ac 8:29; Rev 1:10.
  By visions. Nu 12:6; Eze 11:24.
  By dreams. Nu 12:6; Da 7:1.
Necessary to prophesying. Nu 11:25–27; 2Ch 20:14–17.
Is irresistible. Am 3:8.
Despisers of, punished. 2Ch 36:15, 16; Zec 7:12.

Ministry of the Holy Spirit as Helper
Proceeds from the Father. Jn 15:26.
Given by
  The Father. Jn 14:16.
  Christ. Is 61:3.
  Christ's intercession. Jn 14:16, 26.
Sent by Christ from the Father. Jn 15:26; 16:7.
Purposes of
  Communicates joy to believers. Ro 14:17; Gal 5:22; 1Th 1:6.
  Builds up the church. Ac 9:31.
  Testifies of Christ. Jn 15:26.
  Imparts the love of God. Ro 5:3–5.
  Imparts hope. Ro 15:13; Gal 5:5.
  Teaches believers. Jn 14:26.
  Dwells with and in believers. Jn 14:16, 17.
The world cannot receive. Jn 14:17.

Ministry of the Holy Spirit as Teacher
Promised. Pr 1:23.
As the Spirit of wisdom. Is 11:2; 40:13, 14.
Given
  In answer to prayer. Eph 1:16, 17.
  To believers. Ne 9:20; 1Co 2:12, 13.

- Does not receive the things of God. 1Co 2:14.
- Comes short of God's glory. Ro 3:23.
- Unteachable. Job 11:12.
- Separated from God. Ge 3:8; Ps 58:3; Eph 4:18; Col 1:21.
- In bondage to sin. Ro 6:19; 7:5, 23; Gal 5:17; Titus 3:3.
- In bondage to the devil. 2Ti 2:26; Heb 2:14, 15.
- Constant in evil. Ps 10:5; 2Pe 2:14.
- Conscious of guilt. Ge 3:7, 8, 10.
- Unrighteous. Ecc 7:20; Ro 3:10.
- Completely corrupt. Job 15:16; Ps 14:3.
- Turned to his own way. Is 53:6.
- Loves darkness. Jn 3:19.
- Corrupt, etc., in speech. Ro 3:13, 14.
- Devoid of the fear of God. Ro 3:18.
- Totally depraved. Ge 6:5; Ro 7:18; Eph 2:1; Col 2:13.

All men partake of the effects of. 1Ki 8:46; Gal 3:22; 1Jn 1:8; 5:19.

Man's punishment as a result of
- Banishment from paradise. Ge 3:24.
- Assigned difficult labor and troubles. Ge 3:16, 19; Job 5:6, 7.
- Temporal death. Ge 3:19; Ro 5:12; 1Co 15:22.
- Eternal death. Job 21:30; Ro 5:18, 21; 6:23.

Cannot be remedied by man. Pr 20:9; Jer 2:22; 13:23.

Remedy for, provided by God. Ge 3:15; Jn 3:16.

Nature of Man

Made for God. Pr 16:4; Rev 4:11.

Unworthy of God's favor. Job 7:17; 22:2; Ps 8:4; 16:2.

Created
- In successive generations. Job 10:8–11; 31:15.
- Marvelously. Ps 139:14.
- By God. Ge 1:27; Is 45:12.
- By Christ. Jn 1:3; Col 1:16.
- By the Spirit of God. Job 33:4.
- After consultation, by the Trinity. Ge 1:26.
- On the sixth day. Ge 1:31.
- Upon the earth. Dt 4:32; Job 20:4.
- From the dust. Ge 2:7; Job 33:6; 1Co 15:47.
- In the image of God. Ge 1:26, 27; 1Co 11:7.
- In the likeness of God. Ge 1:26; Jas 3:9.
- Male and female. Ge 1:27; 2:25; 5:2.
- A living being. Ge 2:7; 1Co 15:45.
- In uprightness. Ecc 7:29.
- In knowledge. Col 3:10.
- Under obligations to obedience. Ge 2:16, 17.
- A type of Christ. Ro 5:14.
- With purpose. Ge 2:5, 15.

Blessed by God. Ge 1:28, 31; 5:2.

Not good for, to be alone. Ge 2:18.

Described as having
- A body. Mt 6:25.
- A soul. Lk 12:20; Ac 14:22; 1Pe 4:19.
- A spirit. Pr 18:14; 1Co 2:11.
- Understanding. Eph 1:18; 4:18.
- Will. 1Co 9:17; 2Pe 1:21.
- Affections. 1Ch 29:3; Col 3:2.
- Conscience. Ro 2:15; 1Ti 4:2.
- Memory. Ge 41:9; 1Co 15:2.

Of every nation, made of one blood. Ac 17:26.

Made wise by the inspiration of the Almighty. Job 32:8, 9.

Inferior to angels. Ps 8:5; Heb 2:7.

Set apart from animals
- Different constitution. 1Co 15:39.
- More valuable than. Mt 6:26; 10:31; 12:12.
- Wiser than. Job 35:11.
- Received dominion over. Ge 1:28; 2:19, 20; Ps 8:6–8.

Intellect of, matured by age. 1Co 13:11.

Likened to
- An earthenware vessel. Is 45:9.
- A worm. Job 25:6.
- A foolish man. Job 11:12; Jas 2:20.
- Flesh. Ge 6:12; Joel 2:28.
- Grass. Is 40:6–8; 1Pe 1:24.
- Clay in the potter's hand. Is 64:8; Jer 18:2, 6.
- A shadow. Ps 144:4.
- A sleep. Ps 90:5.

The fall of
- Disobeyed God by eating the forbidden fruit. Ge 3:1–12.
- Filled with shame after. Ge 3:10.
- Punished for disobedience. Ge 3:16–19, 23, 24.
- Involved his descendants. Ro 5:12–19.

Born in sin after the Fall. Ps 51:5.

Days of, are limited. 1Ch 29:15; Job 7:1; Job 14:1; Ps 90:10.

Ignorant of what is best. Ps 39:6; Pr 20:24; Ecc 10:2, 14.

Relationship to God
- Instructed by Him. Ps 94:10.
- Guided by Him. Pr 5:21; 16:1; 20:24.
- Cared for by Him. Job 7:20; Ps 36:6; 145:15, 16.
- Life limited by Him. Job 14:19; 39:11; Ps 90:3.
- Made to praise Him. Ps 39:11; 76:10; 90:3.
- Made subordinate before Him. Job 9:2; 15:14; 25:4; Ps 143:2; Pr 16:2; Jer 2:22; Ro 3:20.

And Christ
- Nature of, known by Him. Jn 2:25.
- Nature of, taken by Him. Jn 1:14; Php 2:7, 8; Heb 2:14, 16.
- Dependent on Him as refuge and head. Is 32:2; 1Co 11:3.

Shall be recompensed according to his works. Ps 62:12; Ro 2:6.

Fragile existence. Job 2:4; Pr 18:14; Ecc 8:8.

No trust to be placed in. Ps 60:11; 118:8; Is 2:22.

The whole duty of. Ecc 12:13.

SIN

Characteristics of the Wicked

Abominable. Rev 21:8.

Alienated from God. Eph 4:18; Col 1:21.

Blasphemous. Lk 22:65; Rev 16:9.

Blinded. 2Co 4:4; Eph 4:18.

Boastful. Ps 5:5; 10:3; 49:6.

Conspiring against God's people. Ne 4:8; 6:2; Ps 38:12.

Deceitful. Ps 5:6; Ro 3:13.

Delighting in the iniquity of others. Pr 2:14; Ro 1:32.

Despising the works of the faithful. Ne 2:19; 4:2; 2Ti 3:3, 4.

Destructive. Is 59:7.

Disobedient. Ne 9:26; Titus 3:3; 1Pe 2:7.

Enticing to evil. Pr 1:10–14; 2Ti 3:6.

Envious. Ne 2:10; Titus 3:3.

Fearful. Pr 28:1; Rev 21:8.

Fierce. Pr 16:29; 2Ti 3:3.

Foolish. Dt 32:6.

Forgetting God. Job 8:13.

Fraudulent. Ps 37:21; Mic 6:11.

Glorying in their shame. Php 3:19.

Greedy. Mic 2:2; Ro 1:29.

Hard-hearted. Eze 3:7.

Hating the light. Job 24:13; Jn 3:20.

Headstrong and haughty. 2Ti 3:4.

Hostile to God. Ro 8:7; Col 1:21.

Hypocritical. Is 29:13; 2Ti 3:5.

Ignorant of God. Hos 4:1; 2Th 1:8.

Infidel. Ps 10:4; 14:1.

Loathsome. Pr 13:5.

Lovers of pleasure more than of God. 2Ti 3:4.

Lying. Ps 58:3; 62:4; Is 59:4.

Murderous. Ps 10:8; 94:6; Ro 1:29.

Prayerless. Job 21:15; Ps 53:4.

Persecuting. Ps 69:26; 109:16.

Perverse. Dt 32:5; Pr 21:8; Is 57:17; Ac 2:40.

Proud. Ps 59:12; Ob 1:3; 2Ti 3:2.

Rebellious. Titus 1:10.

Rejoicing in the affliction of believers. Ps 35:15.

Reprobate. 2Co 13:5; 2Ti 3:8; Titus 1:16.

Scheming. Pr 24:8; Mic 7:3.

Selfish. 2Ti 3:2.

Sold into sin. 1Ki 21:20; 2Ki 17:17.

Stiff-necked. Ex 33:5; Ac 7:51.

Stubborn and obstinate. Eze 2:4.

Uncircumcised in heart. Jer 9:26; Ac 7:51.

Unjust. Pr 11:7; Is 26:10.

Unmerciful. Ro 1:31.

Unholy. 2Ti 3:2.

Unprofitable. Mt 25:30; Ro 3:12.

Unthankful. Lk 6:35; 2Ti 3:2.

Unwise. Dt 32:6.

Without self-control. 2Ti 3:3.

Worldly minded. Php 3:19; Jude 19.

Worthless. Pr 16:27.

Ignorance of God

Ignorance of Christ is. Jn 8:19.

Darkness symbolizes. Ps 82:5.

Evidenced by
- Lack of love. 1Jn 4:8.
- Not keeping His commands. 1Jn 2:4.
- Living in sin. Titus 1:16; 1Jn 3:6.

Leads to
- Error. Mt 22:29.
- Idolatry. Is 44:19; Ac 17:29, 30.
- Alienation from God. Eph 4:18.
- Sinful lusts. 1Th 4:5; 1Pe 1:14.
- Persecution of believers. Jn 15:21; 16:3.

Is no excuse for sin. Lv 4:2; Lk 12:48.

The wicked, in a state of. Jer 9:3; Jn 15:21; 17:25; Ac 17:30; Ro 3:11.

The wicked choose. Job 21:14; Ro 1:28.

Punishment of. Ps 79:6; 2Th 1:8.

Ministers should
- Be compassionate to those in. Heb 5:2; 2Ti 2:24, 25.
- Labor to remove. Ac 17:23.

Illustrated by
- Pharaoh. Ex 5:2.
- The Israelites. Ps 95:10; Is 1:3.
- The false prophets. Is 56:10, 11.
- The Jews. Lk 23:34; Ro 10:3.
- Nicodemus. Jn 3:10.
- The Gentiles. Gal 4:8.
- Paul. 1Ti 1:13.

Nature of Sin

- Is the transgression of the law. 1Jn 3:4.
- Is of the devil. Jn 8:44; 1Jn 3:8.
- All unrighteousness is. 1Jn 5:17.
- Is the omission of what we know to be good. Jas 4:17.
- Whatever is not of faith is. Ro 14:23.
- The thought of foolishness is. Pr 24:9.
- All the imaginations of the unrenewed heart are. Ge 6:5; 8:21.
- Described as
  - An abomination to God. Pr 15:9; Jer 44:4, 11.
  - Blasphemes the Lord. Nu 15:30; Ps 74:18.
  - Coming from the heart. Mt 15:19.
  - Dead works. Heb 6:1; 9:14.
  - Deceitful. Heb 3:13.
  - Defiling. Pr 30:12; Is 59:3.
  - A disgrace. Pr 14:34.
  - The fruit of lust. Jas 1:15.
  - Like scarlet and crimson. Is 1:18.
  - Often mighty and many. Am 5:12.
  - Often presumptuous. Ps 19:13.
  - Often very great. Ex 32:20; 1Sa 2:17.
  - Reaching to heaven. Rev 18:5.
  - Rebellion against God. Dt 9:7; Jos 1:18.
  - Sometimes open and manifest. 1Ti 5:24.
  - Sometimes secret. Ps 90:8; 1Ti 5:24.
  - The sting of death. 1Co 15:56.
  - Works of darkness. Eph 5:11.
- Entered into the world by Adam. Ge 3:6, 7; Ro 5:12.
- All men are conceived and born in. Ge 5:3; Job 15:14; 25:4; Ps 51:5.
- Scripture concludes all under. Gal 3:22.
- No man is without. 1Ki 8:46; Ecc 7:20.
- Christ alone is without. 2Co 5:21; Heb 4:15; 7:26; 1Jn 3:5.
- God
  - Hates. Dt 25:16; Pr 6:16–19.
  - Takes note of. Job 10:14.
  - Remembers. Rev 18:5.
  - Is provoked to jealousy by. 1Ki 14:22.
  - Is provoked to anger by. 1Ki 16:2.
  - Alone can forgive. Ex 34:7; Da 9:9; Mic 7:18; Mk 2:7.
  - Recompenses those who live in. Jer 16:18; Rev 18:6.
  - Punishes. Is 13:11; Am 3:2.
- The Law
  - Is transgressed by every act of. Jas 2:10, 11; 1Jn 3:4.
  - Gives knowledge of. Ro 3:20; 7:7.
  - Shows exceeding sinfulness of. Ro 7:13.
  - Made to restrain. 1Ti 1:9, 10.
  - Arouses tendency toward. Ro 7:5, 8, 11.
  - Is the strength of. 1Co 15:56.
  - Curses those guilty of. Gal 3:10.
- No man can cleanse himself from. Job 9:30, 31; Pr 20:9; Jer 2:22.
- No man can atone for. Mic 6:7.
- God has opened a fountain for cleansing from. Zec 13:1.
- Christ was manifested to take away. Jn 1:29; 1Jn 3:5.
- Christ's blood redeems from. Eph 1:7; 1Jn 1:7.
- Believers
  - Made free from. Ro 6:18.
  - Dead to. Ro 6:2, 11; 1Pe 2:24.
  - Profess to have ceased from. 1Pe 4:1.
  - Cannot live in. 1Jn 3:9; 5:18.
  - Resolve against. Job 34:32.
  - Ashamed of having committed. Ro 6:21.
  - Abhor themselves because of. Job 42:6; Eze 20:43.
  - Have yet the remains of, in them. Ro 7:17, 23; Gal 5:17.
- The fear of God restrains. Ex 20:20; Ps 4:4; Pr 16:6.
- The Word of God keeps people from. Ps 17:4; 119:11.
- The Holy Spirit convinces of. Jn 16:8, 9.
- If we say that we have no, we make God a liar. 1Jn 1:10.
- Shame belongs to those guilty of. Da 9:7, 8.
- Should be
  - Confessed. Job 33:27; Pr 28:13.
  - Mourned over. Ps 38:18; Jer 3:21.
  - Hated. Ps 97:10; Pr 8:13; Am 5:15; Ro 12:9.
  - Put away. Job 11:14.
  - Departed from. Ps 34:14; 2Ti 2:19.
  - Avoided even in appearance. 1Th 5:22.
  - Guarded against. Ps 4:4; 39:1; Heb 12:4.
  - Put to death. Ro 8:13; Col 3:5; Ro 6:6.
- Especially strive against entangling. Heb 12:1.
- Aggravated by neglecting advantages. Lk 12:47; Jn 15:22.
- Guilt concerning. Job 31:33; Pr 28:13.
- We should pray to God
  - To search for, in our hearts. Ps 139:23, 24.
  - To make us know our. Job 13:23.
  - To forgive our. Ex 34:9; Lk 11:4.
  - To keep us from. Ps 19:13.
  - To deliver us from. Mt 6:13.
  - To cleanse us from. Ps 51:2.
- Prayer hindered by. Ps 66:18; Is 59:2.
- Blessings withheld on account of. Jer 5:25.
- The wicked
  - Are servants to. Jn 8:34; Ro 6:16.
  - Are dead in. Eph 2:1.
  - Are guilty of, in everything they do. Pr 21:4; Eze 21:24.
  - Plead necessity for. 1Sa 13:11, 12.
  - Excuse. Ge 3:12, 13; 1Sa 15:13–15.
  - Encourage themselves in. Ps 64:5.
  - Defy God in committing. Is 5:18, 19.
  - Boast of. Is 3:9.
  - Mock. Pr 14:9.
  - Expect God to overlook. Ps 10:11; 50:21; 94:7.
  - Cannot cease from. 2Pe 2:14.
  - Commit more and more. Ps 78:17; Is 30:1.
  - Are encouraged in, by prosperity. Job 21:7–15; Pr 10:16.
  - Are led by despair to continue in. Jer 2:25; 18:12.
  - Try to conceal, from God. Ge 3:8, 10; Job 31:33.
  - Throw the blame of, on God. Ge 3:12; Jer 7:10.
  - Throw the blame of, on others. Ge 3:12, 13; Ex 32:22–24.
  - Tempt others to. Ge 3:6; 1Ki 16:2; 21:25; Pr 1:10–14.
  - Delight in those who commit. Ps 10:3; Hos 7:3; Ro 1:32.
  - Shall bear the shame of. Eze 16:52.
- Shall find out the wicked. Nu 32:23.
- Ministers should warn the wicked to forsake. Eze 33:9; Da 4:27.
- Leads to
  - Shame. Ro 6:21.
  - Ill health. Ps 38:3.
  - Disease. Job 20:11.
- The ground was cursed on account of. Ge 3:17, 18.
- Toil and sorrow originated in. Ge 3:16, 17, 19; Job 14:1.
- Excludes from heaven. 1Co 6:9, 10; Gal 5:19–21; Eph 5:5; Rev 21:27.
- When finished brings forth death. Jas 1:15.
- Death is
  - The wages of. Ro 6:23.
  - The punishment of. Ge 2:17; Eze 18:4.

Rebellion Against God

- Forbidden. Nu 14:9; Jos 22:19.
- Provokes Him. Nu 16:30; Ne 9:26.
- Provokes Christ. Ex 23:20, 21; 1Co 10:9.
- Grieves the Holy Spirit. Is 63:10.
- Exhibited in
  - Contempt of God. Ps 107:11.
  - Departing from Him. Is 59:13; Da 9:5.
  - Departing from His instituted worship. Ex 32:8, 9; Jos 22:16–19.
  - Despising His law. Ne 9:26.
  - Despising His counsel. Ps 107:11.
  - Distrusting His power. Eze 17:15.
  - Injustice and corruption. Is 1:23.
  - Refusing to listen to Him. Dt 9:23; Eze 20:8; Zec 7:11.
  - Rejecting His government. Jos 1:18; 1Sa 8:7; 15:23.
  - Revolting against Him. Is 1:5; 31:6.
  - Sinning against spiritual light. Job 24:13; Jn 15:22; Ac 13:41.
  - Speaking against Him. Nu 20:3, 10.
  - Walking after our own thoughts. Is 65:2.
  - Stubbornness. Dt 31:27.
  - Unbelief. Dt 9:23; Ps 106:24, 25.
- Man is prone to. Dt 31:27; Ro 7:14–18.
- The heart is the seat of. Jer 5:23; Mt 15:18, 19; Heb 3:12.
- They who are guilty of
  - Aggravate their sin by it. Job 34:27.
  - Practice hypocrisy to hide it. Hos 7:14.
  - Persevere in it. Dt 9:7, 24.
  - Increase in it, though chastised. Is 1:5.
  - Warned not to exalt themselves. Ps 66:7.
  - Denounced. Is 30:1.
  - Have God as their enemy. 1Sa 12:15; Ps 106:26, 27; Is 63:10.
  - Impoverished because of it. Ps 68:6.
  - Brought low because of it. Ps 107:11, 12.
  - Delivered into the hands of enemies because of it. Ne 9:26, 27.
  - Cast out because of it. Ps 5:10; Eze 20:38.
  - Restored through Christ alone. Ps 68:18.
- Heinousness of. 1Sa 15:23.
- Guilt of
  - Aggravated by God's fatherly care and concern. Is 1:2; 65:2.
  - To be avoided. Jos 22:29.
  - To be confessed. La 1:18, 20; Da 9:5.
- God alone can forgive. Ne 9:17; Da 9:9.
- Religious instruction designed to prevent. Ps 78:5, 8.
- Promises to those who avoid. 1Sa 12:14. *Cf.* Dt 28:1–13.
- Forgiven upon repentance. Ne 9:26, 27.
- Ministers
  - Cautioned against it. Eze 2:8.
  - Often sent to people guilty of it. Eze 2:3–7; 3:4–9; Mk 12:4–8.
  - Should testify against it. Nu 14:9; Is 30:8, 9; Eze 17:12; 44:6.

Should remind their people of past occurrences. Dt 9:7; 31:27.
Punishment for. 1Sa 12:15; Is 1:20; Jer 4:16–18; Eze 20:8, 38.
Punishment for teaching. Jer 28:16.
Ingratitude of, illustrated. Is 1:2, 3.
Illustrated by
Pharaoh. Ex 5:1, 2.
Korah, etc. Nu 16:11.
Moses and Aaron. Nu 20:12, 24.
The Israelites. Dt 9:23, 24.
Saul. 1Sa 15:9, 23.
Jeroboam. 1Ki 12:28–33.
Zedekiah. 2Ch 36:13.
The kingdom of Israel. Hos 7:14; 13:16.

Spiritual Blindness

Explained. 1Co 2:14.
The effect of sin. Is 29:10; Mt 6:23; Jn 3:19, 20.
The effect of unbelief. Ro 11:8; 2Co 4:3, 4.
A proof of lack of love. 1Jn 2:9, 11.
A work of the devil. 2Co 4:4.
Leads to all evil. Eph 4:17–19.
Is inconsistent with communion with God. 1Jn 1:6, 7.
Of ministers, fatal to themselves and to the people. Mt 15:14.
The wicked are in. Ps 82:5; Is 26:11; Jer 5:21; Ro 1:19–24.
The self-righteous are in. Mt 23:19, 26; Rev 3:17.
Judicially inflicted. Ps 69:23; Is 29:10; 44:18; Mt 13:13, 14; Jn 12:40.
Pray for the removal of. Ps 13:3; 119:18.
Christ appointed to remove. Is 42:7; Lk 4:18; Jn 8:12; 9:39; 2Co 4:6.
Christ's ministers are lights to remove. Mt 5:14; Ac 26:18.
Believers are delivered from. Jn 8:12; Eph 5:8; Col 1:13; 1Th 5:4, 5; 1Pe 2:9.
Removal of, illustrated. Jn 9:7, 11, 25; Ac 9:18; Rev 3:18.
Examples of
Israel. Ro 11:25; 2Co 3:15.
Scribes and Pharisees. Mt 23:16, 24.
Church of Laodicea. Rev 3:17.

Spiritual Bondage

Is to the devil. 2Ti 2:26.
Is to the fear of death. Heb 2:14, 15.
Is to sin. Jn 8:34; Ac 8:23; Ro 6:16; 7:23; Gal 4:3; 2Pe 2:19.
Deliverance from, promised. Is 42:6, 7.
Christ delivers from. Lk 4:18, 21; Jn 8:36; Ro 7:24, 25; Eph 4:8.
The gospel, the instrument of deliverance from. Jn 8:32; Ro 8:2.
Believers are delivered from. Dt 4:20; Ro 6:18, 22.
Typified by Israel in Egypt. Ex 1:13, 14.

Temptation

Does not come from God. Jas 1:13.
Comes from
Lusts. Jas 1:14.
Greed. Pr 28:20; 1Ti 6:9, 10.
The devil is the author of. 1Ch 21:1; Mt 4:1; Jn 13:2; 1Th 3:5.
Evil associates, the instruments of. Pr 1:10; 7:6; 16:29.
Often arises through
Poverty. Pr 30:9; Mt 4:2, 3.
Prosperity. Pr 30:9; Mt 4:8.
Worldly glory. Nu 22:17; Da 4:30; 5:2; Mt 4:8.
Objectives of
To distrust God's providence. Mt 4:3.
Presumption. Mt 4:6.
Worshiping Satan. Mt 4:9.
Often strengthened by the perversion of God's Word. Mt 4:6.
Permitted as a trial of
Faith. 1Pe 1:7; Jas 1:2, 3.
Dedication. Job 1:9–12.
Always conformable to human nature. 1Co 10:13.
Often ends in sin and death. 1Ti 6:9; Jas 1:15.
Christ
Endured, from the devil. Mk 1:13.
Endured, from the wicked. Mt 16:1; 22:18; Lk 10:25.
Resisted it by the Word of God. Mt 4:4, 7, 10.
Overcame it. Mt 4:11.
Sympathizes with those under. Heb 4:15.
Is able to help those under. Heb 2:18.
Intercedes for His people under. Lk 22:31, 32; Jn 17:15.
Will not be greater than believers can endure. 1Co 10:13.
God delivers believers from. 2Pe 2:9.
Believers
May be in distress through. 1Pe 1:6.
Should resist, in faith. Eph 6:16; 1Pe 5:9.
Should guard against. Mt 26:41; 1Pe 5:8.
Should pray to be kept from. Mt 6:13; 26:41.
Should not cause, for others. Ro 14:13.
Should restore those overcome by. Gal 6:1.
Should avoid. Pr 4:14, 15.
The devil will renew. Lk 4:13.
Weakness of the flesh makes it stronger. Mt 26:41.
Nominal Christians fall away in time of. Lk 8:13.
Blessedness of those who meet and overcome. Jas 1:2–4, 12.
Those who encountered
Eve. Ge 3:1, 4, 5.
Joseph. Ge 39:7.
Balaam. Nu 22:17.
Achan. Jos 7:21.
David. 2Sa 11:2.
Jeroboam. 1Ki 15:30.
Peter. Mk 14:67–71.
Paul. 2Co 12:7; Gal 4:14.

Unbelief

Is defined as sin. Jn 16:9.
Defilement inseparable from. Titus 1:15.
All, by nature, committed to. Ro 11:32.
Proceeds from
An evil heart. Heb 3:12.
Slowness of heart. Lk 24:25.
Hardness of heart. Mk 16:14; Ac 19:9.
Not listening to the truth. Jn 8:45, 46.
Judicial blindness. Jn 12:39, 40.
Not being Christ's sheep. Jn 10:26.
The devil blinding the mind. 2Co 4:4.
The devil stealing the word out of the heart. Lk 8:12.
Seeking honor from men. Jn 5:44.
Makes God a liar. 1Jn 5:10.
Exhibited in
Rejecting Christ. Jn 16:9.
Rejecting the word of God. Ps 106:24.
Rejecting the gospel. Is 53:1; Jn 12:38.
Rejecting evidence of miracles. Jn 12:37.
Departing from God. Heb 3:12.
Questioning the power of God. 2Ki 7:2; Ps 78:19, 20.
Not believing the works of God. Ps 78:32.
Wavering at the promise of God. Ro 4:20.
Rebuked by Christ. Mt 17:17; Jn 20:27.
Was a hindrance to the performance of miracles. Mt 17:20; Mk 6:5.
Miracles designed to convince those in. Jn 10:37, 38; 1Co 14:22.
The Jews rejected because of. Ro 11:20.
Believers should have no fellowship with those in. 2Co 6:14.
They who are guilty of
Do not have the word of God in them. Jn 5:38.
Cannot please God. Heb 11:6.
Malign the gospel. Ac 19:9.
Persecute the ministers of God. Ro 15:31.
Excite others against believers. Ac 14:2.
Persevere in it. Jn 12:37.
Stiffen their necks. 2Ki 17:14.
Are condemned already. Jn 3:18.
Have the wrath of God abiding upon them. Jn 3:36.
Shall not be established. Is 7:9.
Shall die in their sins. Jn 8:24.
Shall not enter God's rest. Heb 3:19; 4:11.
Shall be condemned. Mk 16:16; 2Th 2:12.
Shall be destroyed. Jude 5.
Shall be cast into the lake of fire. Rev 21:8.
Warnings against. Heb 3:12; 4:11.
Pray for help against. Mk 9:24.
The portion of, awarded to all unfaithful servants. Lk 12:46.
Examples of
Eve. Ge 3:4–6.
Moses and Aaron. Nu 20:12.
The Israelites. Dt 9:23.
Naaman. 2Ki 5:12.
A Samaritan officer. 2Ki 7:2.
The disciples of Jesus. Mt 17:17; Lk 24:11, 25.
Zacharias. Lk 1:20.
The chief priests. Lk 22:67.
The Jews. Jn 5:38.
The brothers of Christ. Jn 7:5.
Thomas. Jn 20:25.
The Jews of Iconium. Ac 14:2.
The Thessalonian Jews. Ac 17:5.
The Ephesians. Ac 19:9.
Saul. 1Ti 1:13.
The people of Jericho. Heb 11:31.

SALVATION

Assurance of Believers

Produced by faith. Eph 3:12; 2Ti 1:12; Heb 10:22.
Made full by hope. Heb 6:11, 19.
Confirmed by love. 1Jn 3:14, 19; 4:18.
Is abundant in the understanding of the gospel. Col 2:2; 1Th 1:5.
Believers privileged to have, of
Their election. Ps 4:3; 1Th 1:4.
Their redemption. Job 19:25.
Their adoption. Ro 8:16; 1Jn 3:2.
Their salvation. Is 12:2.
Eternal life. 1Jn 5:13.

Election

Eternal Life

Faith

- A woman who was a sinner. Lk 7:50.
- Nathanael. Jn 1:49.
- The Samaritans. Jn 4:39.
- Martha. Jn 11:27.
- The disciples of Jesus. Jn 16:30.
- Thomas. Jn 20:28.
- Stephen. Ac 6:5.
- Priests. Ac 6:7.
- The Ethiopian. Ac 8:37.
- Barnabas. Ac 11:24.
- Sergius Paulus. Ac 13:12.
- The Philippian jailer. Ac 16:31, 34.
- The Roman believers. Ro 1:8.
- The Colossian believers. Col 1:4.
- The Thessalonian believers. 1Th 1:3.
- Lois. 2Ti 1:5.
- Paul. 2Ti 4:7.
- Abel. Heb 11:4.
- Enoch. Heb 11:5.
- Noah. Heb 11:7.
- Abraham. Heb 11:8, 17.
- Isaac. Heb 11:20.
- Jacob. Heb 11:21.
- Joseph. Heb 11:22.
- Moses. Heb 11:24, 27.
- Rahab. Heb 11:31.
- Gideon, etc. Heb 11:32, 33, 39.

Good Works

- Christ, an example of. Jn 10:32; Ac 10:38.
- Other names for
  - Fruit in keeping with repentance. Mt 3:8.
  - Fruit of righteousness. Php 1:11.
  - Good fruits. Jas 3:17.
  - Works of labor and love. Heb 6:10
- The Scripture designed to lead us to. 2Ti 3:16, 17; Jas 1:25.
- To be performed in Christ's name. Col 3:17.
- Heavenly wisdom is full of. Jas 3:17.
- Salvation unattainable by. Ro 3:20; Gal 2:16; Eph 2:8, 9; 2Ti 1:9; Titus 3:5.
- Believers
  - Will have, if they abide in Christ. Jn 15:4–5.
  - Wrought by God in them. Is 26:12; Php 2:13.
  - Created in Christ to. Eph 2:10.
  - Exhorted to put on. Col 3:12–14.
  - Should be equipped for. 2Ti 3:17.
  - Should be rich in. 1Ti 6:18.
  - Should be careful to maintain. Titus 3:8, 14.
  - Should be ready to engage frequently in. Ac 9:36; 2Co 9:8; Col 1:10; 2Th 2:17; 1Ti 6:18; 2Ti 2:21; Titus 2:14; 3:1; Heb 13:21.
  - Should encourage each other to. Heb 10:24.
  - Should avoid ostentation in. Mt 6:1–18; Jas 3:13.
  - Deeds are seen in light of the truth. Jn 3:21.
  - Follow believers when they die. Rev 14:13.
- Godly women should manifest. 1Ti 2:10; 5:10.
- God remembers. Ne 13:14; Heb 6:9, 10.
- Shall be brought into the judgment. Ecc 12:14; 2Co 5:10.
- In the judgment, will be an evidence of faith. Mt 25:34–40; Jas 2:14–20.
- Ministers should
  - Be examples of. Titus 2:7.
  - Exhort to. 1Ti 6:17, 18; Titus 3:1, 8, 14.
- God is glorified by. Jn 15:8.
- Designed to lead others to glorify God. Mt 5:16; 1Pe 2:12.
- A blessing attends. Jas 1:25.
- The unbelieving disqualified from. Titus 1:16.
- Illustrated. Jn 15:5.

Grace

- God is the source of all. Ps 84:11; 1Pe 5:10; Jas 1:17.
- God's throne, the throne of. Heb 4:16.
- The Holy Spirit is the Spirit of. Zec 12:10; Heb 10:29.
- Christ received it from. Lk 2:40; Jn 1:14; 3:24, 25.
- Christ spoke with. Ps 45:2; Lk 4:22.
- Came by Christ. Jn 1:17; Ro 5:15; 1Co 1:4.
- Foretold by the prophets. 1Pe 1:10.
- Riches of, exhibited in God's kindness through Christ. Eph 2:7.
- Glory of, exhibited in our acceptance in Christ. Eph 1:6.
- Descriptions of
  - Abundant. Ac 4:33.
  - Glorious. Eph 1:6.
  - Manifold. 1Pe 4:10.
  - Rich. Eph 1:7; 2:7.
  - Sovereign. Ro 5:21.
  - Surpassing. 2Co 9:14.
- The gospel, a declaration of. Ac 20:24, 32.
- Is the source of
  - Election. Ro 11:5.
  - The call of God. Gal 1:15.
  - Justification. Ro 3:24; Titus 3:7.
  - Faith. Ac 18:27.
  - Forgiveness of sins. Eph 1:7.
  - Salvation. Ac 15:11; Eph 2:5, 8.
  - Consolation. 2Th 2:16.
  - Hope. 2Th 2:16.
- Necessary to the service of God. Heb 12:28.
- God's work completed in believers by. 2Th 1:11, 12.
- The success and completion of the work of God to be attributed to. Zec 4:7.
- Inheritance of the promises is by. Ro 4:16.
- Justification by, opposed to that by works. Ro 4:4, 5; 11:6; Gal 5:4.
- Believers
  - Are heirs of. 1Pe 3:7.
  - Are under. Ro 6:14.
  - Receive, from Christ. Jn 1:16.
  - Are what they are by. 1Co 15:10; 2Co 1:12.
  - Abound in gifts of. Ac 4:33; 2Co 8:1; 9:8, 14.
  - Should mature in. Heb 13:9; 2Ti 2:1; 2Pe 3:18.
  - Should speak with. Eph 4:29; Col 4:6.
- Is especially given
  - To ministers. Ro 12:3, 6; 15:15; 1Co 3:10; Gal 2:9; Eph 3:7.
  - To the humble. Pr 3:34; Jas 4:6.
  - To those who walk uprightly. Ps 84:11.
- Not to be received in vain. 2Co 6:1.
- Pray for it
  - For yourselves. Heb 4:16.
  - For others. 2Co 13:14; Eph 6:24.
- Be careful not to fall short of. Heb 12:15.
- Manifestation of, in others, a cause of gladness. Ac 11:23; 1Jn 1:3, 4.
- Special manifestation of, at the second coming of Christ. 1Pe 1:13.
- Not to be abused. Ro 3:8; 6:1, 15.
- Lawless men will abuse. Jude 4.

Justification

- Promised in Christ. Is 45:25; 53:11.
- Is the act of God. Is 50:8; Ro 8:33.
- Under law
  - Requires perfect obedience. Lv 18:5; Ro 2:13; 10:5; Jas 2:10.
  - Man cannot attain to. Job 9:2, 3, 20; 25:4; Ps 130:3; 143:2; Ro 3:20; 9:31, 32.
- Under the gospel
  - Is not of works. Ac 13:39; Ro 8:3; Gal 2:16; 3:11.
  - Is not of faith and works united. Ro 3:28; 11:6; Gal 2:14–21; 5:4. *Cf.* Ac 15:1–29.
  - Is by faith alone. Jn 5:24; Ac 13:39; Ro 3:30; 5:1; Gal 2:16.
  - Is of grace. Ro 3:24; 4:16; 5:17–21.
  - In the name of Christ. 1Co 6:11.
  - By imputation of Christ's righteousness. Is 61:10; Jer 23:6; Ro 3:22; 5:18; 1Co 1:30; 2Co 5:21.
  - By the blood of Christ. Ro 5:9.
  - By the resurrection of Christ. Ro 4:25; 1Co 15:17.
  - Blessedness of. Ps 32:1, 2; Ro 4:6–8.
  - Frees from condemnation. Is 50:8, 9; 54:17; Ro 8:33, 34.
  - Entitles to an inheritance. Titus 3:7.
  - Ensures glorification. Ro 8:30.
- The wicked shall not attain to. Ex 23:7.
- By faith
  - Revealed under the Old Testament age. Hab 2:4; Ro 1:17.
  - Excludes boasting. Ro 3:27; 4:2; 1Co 1:29, 31.
  - Does not make void the law. Ro 3:30, 31; 1Co 9:21.
- Typified. Zec 3:4, 5.
- Illustrated. Lk 18:14.
- Exemplified in
  - Abraham. Ge 15:6.
  - Paul. Php 3:8, 9.

Nature of Salvation

- Is of God. Ps 3:8; 37:39; Jer 3:23; 1Th 5:9; 1Ti 2:4; 2Ti 1:9.
- Is by Christ. Is 45:21, 22; 59:16; 63:9; Ac 4:12; Eph 5:23.
- Is through faith in Christ. Mk 16:16; Ac 16:31; Ro 10:9; Eph 2:8; 1Pe 1:5.
- Confession of Christ necessary to. Ro 10:10.
- Announced after the Fall. Ge 3:15.
- Of Israel, predicted. Is 35:4; 45:17; Zec 9:16; Ro 11:26.
- Of the Gentiles, predicted. Is 45:22; 49:6; 52:10.
- Revealed in the gospel. Ro 1:16; 1Co 1:18; Eph 1:13; 2Ti 1:10.
- Came to the Gentiles through the fall of the Jews. Ro 11:11.
- Christ
  - The author of. Heb 2:10.
  - The source of. Heb 5:9.
  - Appointed for. Is 49:6.
  - Raised up for. Lk 1:69.
  - Brings, with Him. Is 62:11; Lk 19:9.
  - Came and died to bring. Is 63:1; Mt 18:11; Jn 3:14, 15; Gal 1:4; 1Ti 1:15; Heb 7:25.
  - Exalted to give. Ac 5:31.
- Described as
  - Common. Jude 3.
  - Eternal. Is 45:17; 51:6; Heb 5:9.
  - Glorious. 2Ti 2:10.
  - Great. Heb 2:3.

New Birth

Pardon

Perseverance of Believers

Privileges of Believers

Reconciliation with God

Redemption

Repentance

Exhortations to. Eze 14:6; 18:30; Ac 2:38; 3:19.
The wicked
- Averse to. Jer 8:6; Mt 21:32.
- Not led to, by the judgments of God. Rev 9:20, 21; 16:9.
- Not led to, by miraculous intervention. Lk 16:30, 31.
- Neglect the opportunity for. Rev 2:21.
- Condemned for neglecting. Mt 11:20.

Danger of neglecting. Mt 11:20–24; Lk 13:3, 5; Ro 2:5; Rev 2:5, 16, 22.
Denied to apostates. Heb 6:4–6.
Illustrated. Mt 21:29; Lk 15:18–21; 18:13; Gal 1:23.
True, illustrated by
- The Israelites. Jdg 10:15, 16.
- David. 2Sa 12:13.
- Manasseh. 2Ch 33:12, 13.
- Job. Job 42:6.
- Nineveh. Jon 3:5–8; Mt 12:41.
- Peter. Mt 26:75.
- Zaccheus. Lk 19:8.
- The thief on the cross. Lk 23:40, 41.
- The Corinthians. 2Co 7:9, 10.

False, illustrated by
- Saul. 1Sa 15:24–30.
- Ahab. 1Ki 21:27–29.
- Judas. Mt 27:3–5.

Righteousness Imputed to Believers
Predicted. Is 56:1; Eze 16:14.
Revealed in the gospel. Ro 1:17.
Is of the Lord. Is 54:17.
Described as
- Christ being the end of the law for righteousness. Ro 10:4.
- Christ being made righteousness for us. 1Co 1:30.
- Christ being "The LORD our righteousness." Jer 23:6.
- Christ bringing in an everlasting righteousness. Da 9:24.
- Our being made the righteousness of God, in Christ. 2Co 5:21.
- The righteousness of faith. Ro 4:13; 9:30; 10:6.
- The righteousness of God, apart from the law. Ro 3:21.
- The righteousness of God through faith in Christ. Ro 3:22.

Is a free gift. Ro 5:17.
God's righteousness never to be abolished. Is 5:16.
The promises made through. Ro 4:13.
Believers
- Receive, on believing. Ro 4:5, 11, 24.
- Clothed with the robe of righteousness. Is 61:10.
- Exalted in righteousness. Ps 89:16.
- Desire to be found in. Php 3:9.
- Glory in having. Is 45:24, 25.

The Gentiles attained to. Ro 9:30.
Blessedness of those who have. Ro 4:6.
The Jews
- Ignorant of. Ro 10:3.
- Stumble at the concept of. Ro 9:32.
- Do not submit to. Ro 10:3.

Exemplified by
- Abraham. Ro 4:9, 22; Gal 3:6.
- Paul. Php 3:7–9.

Sanctification
Is separation to the service of God. Ps 4:3; 2Co 6:17.
Effected by
- God. Eze 37:28; 1Th 5:23; Jude 1.
- Christ. Heb 2:11; 13:12.
- The Holy Spirit. Ro 15:16; 1Co 6:11; 2Th 2:13; 1Pe 1:2.

In Christ. 1Co 1:2, 30.
Through the atonement of Christ. Heb 10:10; 13:12.
Through the Word of God. Jn 17:17, 19; Eph 5:26.
All believers are growing in. Ac 20:32; 26:18; 1Co 6:11.
The church made glorious by. Eph 5:26, 27.
Described. Ro 13:14.
Purpose of. Eph 5:1.
Process of, working out salvation. Php 2:12.
Should lead to
- Mortification of sin. 1Th 4:3, 4.
- Fruitful living. Ro 6:22; Eph 5:7–9.

Believers fitted for the service of God by. 2Ti 2:21.
Ministers
- Set apart to God's service by. Jer 1:5.
- Should pray that their people may enjoy complete. 1Th 5:23.
- Should exhort their people to walk in. 1Th 4:1, 3.

None can inherit the kingdom of God without. 1Co 6:9–11.
Typified. Ge 2:3; Ex 13:2; 19:14; 40:9–15; Lv 27:14–16.

Spiritual Peace
God
- Is the God of. Ro 15:33; 2Co 13:11; 1Th 5:23; Heb 13:20.
- Ordains, for believers. Ps 85:8; Is 26:12.

Christ
- Is the Lord of. 2Th 3:16.
- Is the prince of. Is 9:6.
- Grants. Lk 1:79; Jn 14:27; 2Th 3:16.
- He is our. Eph 2:14.
- Comes through His atonement. Is 53:5; Eph 2:14, 15; Col 1:20.

Preached
- By Christ. Eph 2:17.
- Through Christ. Ac 10:36.
- By ministers. Is 52:7; Ro 10:15.
- By angels. Lk 2:14.

A fruit of the Spirit. Ro 14:17; Gal 5:22.
Divine wisdom is the way of. Pr 3:17.
Accompanies
- Justification. Ro 5:1.
- Faith. Ro 15:13.
- Righteousness. Is 32:17.
- Acquaintance with God. Job 22:21.
- The love of God's law. Ps 119:165.

Spiritual mindedness. Ro 8:6.
Established by covenant. Is 54:10; Eze 34:25; Mal 2:5.
Promised to
- The Gentiles. Zec 9:10.
- Believers. Ps 72:3, 7; Is 26:3; 55:12; 66:12.
- The humble. Ps 37:11.
- Returning backsliders. Is 57:18, 19.

Believers
- Have, in Christ. Is 27:5; Jn 16:33; Ro 5:1.
- Enjoy blessings of. Ps 4:8; 29:11; 119:165; Is 26:3.
- Governed by. Php 4:7; Col 3:15.
- Die in. Ps 37:37; Is 57:1; Lk 2:29.
- Wish, to each other. Gal 6:16; Php 1:2; Col 1:2; 1Th 1:1.
- Have much. Ps 72:7; 119:165; Is 54:13; Jer 33:6.
- Theirs is secure. Job 34:29.
- Theirs surpasses all comprehension. Php 4:7.
- Supports them under trials. Jn 14:27; 16:33.

The gospel is good news of. Ro 10:15.
The wicked
- Do not know. Is 57:2; Lk 19:42; Ro 3:17.
- Promise, to themselves. Dt 29:19.
- Are promised, by false teachers. Jer 6:14.
- There is none for. Is 48:22; 57:21.

Titles and Names of Believers
Attendants of the bridegroom. Mt 9:15.
Believers. Ac 5:14.
Beloved of God. Ro 1:7.
Beloved brethren. 1Co 15:58; Jas 2:5.
Beloved children. Eph 5:1.
Blessed of the Father. Mt 25:34.
Blessed of the Lord. Ge 24:31; 26:29.
Brethren, brothers. Mt 23:8; Lk 8:21; Jn 20:17; Ac 12:17.
Called of Jesus Christ. Ro 1:6.
Children of the free woman. Gal 4:31.
Children of God. Jn 1:12; 11:52; Php 2:15; 1Jn 3:1, 2, 10.
Children of light. Eph 5:8.
Children of promise. Ro 9:8; Gal 4:28.
Chosen instruments. Ac 9:15.
Chosen of God. Col 3:12; Titus 1:1.
Chosen ones. 1Ch 16:13.
Chosen race. 1Pe 2:9.
Christians. Ac 11:26; 26:28.
Consecrated people. Dt 26:19.
Disciples of Christ. Jn 8:31; 15:8.
Faithful, The. Ps 12:1.
Faithful brethren in Christ. Col 1:2.
Faithful of the land. Ps 101:6.
Fellow citizens with the saints. Eph 2:19.
Fellow heirs. Eph 3:6.
Fellow heirs with Christ. Ro 8:17.
Fellow servants. Rev 6:11.
Friends of Christ. Jn 15:15.
Friends of God. 2Ch 20:7; Jas 2:23.
Godly, The. Ps 4:3; 2Pe 2:9.
God's own possession. Ex 19:5; Ps 135:4.
Heirs of God. Ro 8:17; Gal 4:7.
Heirs of the grace of life. 1Pe 3:7.
Heirs of the kingdom. Jas 2:5.
Heirs of promise. Gal 3:29; Heb 6:17.
Heirs of salvation. Heb 1:14.
Holy brethren. Heb 3:1.
Holy nation. Ex 19:6; 1Pe 2:9.
Holy people. Is 62:12.
Holy priesthood. 1Pe 2:5.
Kingdom of priests. Ex 19:6.
Lambs. Is 40:11; Jn 21:15.
Letters of Christ. 2Co 3:3.
Lights of the world. Mt 5:14.
Little children. Jn 13:33; 1Jn 2:1.
Living stones. 1Pe 2:5.
Lord's freedmen. 1Co 7:22.
Majestic ones. Ps 16:3.
Members of Christ. 1Co 6:15; Eph 5:30.
Men of God. Dt 33:1; 1Ti 6:11; 2Ti 3:17.
Oaks of righteousness. Is 61:3.
Obedient children. 1Pe 1:14.
People for God's own possession. Dt 14:2; Titus 2:14; 1Pe 2:9.
People of God. Heb 4:9; 1Pe 2:10.
People near to God. Ps 148:14.
People saved by the Lord. Dt 33:29.
Pillars in the temple of God. Rev 3:12.
Priests to God. Rev 1:6.

Ransomed of the Lord. Is 51:11.
Righteous, The. Hab 2:4.
Royal priesthood. 1Pe 2:9.
Salt of the earth. Mt 5:13.
Servants (slaves) of Christ. 1Co 7:22; Eph 6:6.
Sheep of Christ. Jn 10:1–16; 21:16.
Slaves of righteousness. Ro 6:18.
Sojourners with God. Lv 25:23; Ps 39:12.
Sons of Abraham. Gal 3:7.
Sons of day. 1Th 5:5.
Sons of the Father. Mt 5:45.
Sons of Jacob. Ps 105:6.
Sons of the kingdom. Mt 13:38.
Sons of the Living God. Ro 9:26.
Sons of the Lord. Dt 14:1.
Sons of the resurrection. Lk 20:36.
Sons of Zion. Ps 149:2; Joel 2:23.
Vessels for honor. 2Ti 2:21.
Vessels of mercy. Ro 9:23.
Witnesses for God. Is 44:8.

Union with Christ

As head of the church. Eph 1:22, 23; 4:15, 16; Col 1:18.
Christ prayed that all believers might have. Jn 17:21, 23.
Described as
- Believers being in Christ. 2Co 12:2; 1Jn 5:20.
- Christ being in believers. Eph 3:17; Col 1:27.

Includes union with the Father. Jn 17:21; 1Jn 2:24.
Is of God. 1Co 1:30.
Maintained by
- Faith. Gal 2:20; Eph 3:17.
- Abiding in Him. Jn 15:4, 7.
- His word abiding in us. Jn 15:7; 1Jn 2:24; 2Jn 9.
- Feeding on Him. Jn 6:56.
- Obeying Him. 1Jn 3:24.

The Holy Spirit witnesses. 1Jn 3:24.
The gift of the Holy Spirit is an evidence of. 1Jn 4:13.
Believers
- Have, in mind. 1Co 2:16; Php 2:5.
- Have, in spirit. 1Co 6:17.
- Have, in love. SS 2:16; 7:10.
- Have, in sufferings. Php 3:10; 2Ti 2:12.
- Have, in His death. Ro 6:3–8; Gal 2:20.
- Have assurance of. Jn 14:20.
- Enjoy, in the Lord's Supper. 1Co 10:16, 17.
- Identified with Christ by. Mt 25:40, 45; Ac 8:1; 9:4.
- Are complete through. Col 2:10.
- Exhorted to maintain. Jn 15:4; Ac 11:23; Col 2:7.

Necessary to growth in grace. Eph 4:15, 16; Col 2:19.
Necessary for fruitfulness. Jn 15:4, 5.
Beneficial results of
- Righteousness imputed. 2Co 5:21; Php 3:9.
- Freedom from condemnation. Ro 8:1.
- Freedom from dominion of sin. 1Jn 3:6.
- Being created anew. 2Co 5:17.
- The spirit alive to righteousness. Ro 8:10.
- Confidence at His coming. 1Jn 2:28.
- Abundant fruitfulness. Jn 15:5.
- Answers to prayer. Jn 15:7.

They who have, ought to walk as He walked. 1Jn 2:6.
False teachers do not have. Col 2:18, 19.
Is indissoluble. Ro 8:35.
Punishment of those without. Jn 15:6.
Illustrated by
- Vine and branches. Jn 15:1, 5.
- Foundation and building. 1Co 3:10, 11; Eph 2:20, 21; 1Pe 2:4–6.
- Body and members. 1Co 12:12, 27; Eph 5:30.
- Husband and wife. Eph 5:25–32.

THE CHURCH

Baptism

As administered by John. Mt 3:5–12; Jn 3:23; Ac 13:24; 19:4.
Sanctioned by Christ's submission to it. Mt 3:13–15; Lk 3:21.
Adopted by Christ. Jn 3:22; 4:1, 2.
Appointed an ordinance of the Christian church. Mt 28:19, 20; Mk 16:15, 16.
To be administered in the name of the Father, Son, and Holy Spirit. Mt 28:19.
Water, the outward and visible sign in. Ac 8:36; 10:47.
Remission of sins, signified by. Ac 2:38; 22:16; Ro 6:3, 4.
Unity of the church effected by. 1Co 12:13; Gal 3:27, 28.
Confession of sin necessary to. Mt 3:6.
Repentance necessary to. Ac 2:38.
Faith necessary to. Ac 8:37; 18:8.
There is but one. Eph 4:5.
Administered to
- Individuals. Ac 8:38; 9:18.
- Households. Ac 16:15, 33; 1Co 1:16.
- Only to professing believers. Ac 2:38; Mt 3:6; Mk 16:16; Ac 8:12, 36, 37; 10:47, 48.

Administered by immersing the whole body of the person in water. Mt 3:16; Ac 8:38, 39.
Emblematic of the influences of the Holy Spirit. Mt 3:11; Titus 3:5.
Typified. 1Co 10:2; 1Pe 3:20, 21.

Church Discipline

Ministers authorized to establish. Mt 16:19; 18:18.
Consists in
- Maintaining sound doctrine. 1Ti 1:3; Titus 1:13.
- Ordering its affairs. 1Co 11:34; Titus 1:5.
- Rebuking offenders. 1Ti 5:20; 2Ti 4:2.
- Removing obstinate offenders. 1Co 5:3–5, 13; 1Ti 1:20.

Should be submitted to. Heb 13:17.
Is for edification. 2Co 10:8; 13:10.
Decency and order, the objects of. 1Co 14:40.
Exercise, in a spirit of charity. 2Co 2:6–8.
Prohibits women preaching. 1Co 14:34; 1Ti 2:12.

Church Leaders

Divinely called and protected. Mt 28:19; Ac 13:2, 4; 2Co 3:5, 6; Heb 5:4.
Have authority from God. 2Co 10:8; 13:10.
Described as
- Ambassadors for Christ. 2Co 5:20.
- Bond-servants for Jesus' sake. 2Co 4:5.
- Defenders of the faith. Php 1:7.
- Servants of Christ. 1Co 4:1.
- Stewards of the mysteries of God. 1Co 4:1.

Necessity for. Mt 9:37, 38; Ro 10:14.
Excellency of. Ro 10:15.
Labors of, vain, without God's blessing. 1Co 3:7; 15:10.
Should be
- Pure. 1Ti 3:9.
- Holy and devout. Titus 1:8.
- Humble. Ac 20:19.
- Patient. 2Co 6:4; 2Ti 2:24.
- Blameless. 1Ti 3:2; Titus 1:7.
- Willing. 1Pe 5:2.
- Unselfish. 2Co 12:14; 1Th 2:6.
- Impartial. 1Ti 5:21.
- Kind and gentle. 1Th 2:7; 2Ti 2:24.
- Devoted. Ac 20:24; Php 1:20, 21.
- Strong in grace. 2Ti 2:1.
- Self-denying. 1Co 9:27.
- Devout, just, and self-controlled. Titus 1:8.
- Hospitable. 1Ti 3:2; Titus 1:8.
- Able to teach. 1Ti 3:2; 2Ti 2:24.
- Studious, meditative, and prayerful. Eph 3:14; Php 1:4; 1Ti 4:13, 15.
- Diligent in ruling their own families. 1Ti 3:4, 12.
- Affectionate to their people. Php 1:7; 1Th 2:8, 11.
- Examples to the flock. Php 3:17; 2Th 3:9; 1Ti 4:12; 1Pe 5:3.

Should not be
- Lords over God's people. 1Pe 5:3.
- Greedy for money. Ac 20:33; 1Ti 3:3, 8; 1Pe 5:2.
- Quarrelsome. 1Ti 3:3; Titus 1:7.
- Crafty. 2Co 4:2.
- Men-pleasers. Gal 1:10; 1Th 2:4.
- Easily discouraged. 2Co 4:8, 9; 6:10.
- Entangled by cares. Lk 9:60; 2Ti 2:4.
- Addicted to wine. 1Ti 3:3; Titus 1:7.

Are responsible to
- Avoid giving unnecessary offense. 1Co 10:32, 33; 2Co 6:3.
- Fulfill their ministry. 2Ti 4:5.
- Preach the gospel to all. Mk 16:16; 1Co 1:17; 9:16; 10:33.
- Feed the church. Jn 21:15–17; Ac 20:28; 1Pe 5:2.
- Build up the church. 2Co 12:19; Eph 4:12.
- Have concern for their people. Lk 22:32; Ac 14:22; Col 1:9; Heb 13:17.
- Teach. 2Ti 2:2.
- Exhort. Titus 1:9; 2:15.
- Reprove. Titus 1:13; 2:15.
- Comfort. 2Co 1:4–6.
- Convince opponents of truth. Titus 1:9.
- Wage a good warfare. 1Ti 1:18; 2Ti 2:3; 4:7.

Should preach
- Christ only. Ac 8:5, 35; 1Co 2:2; 2Co 4:5.
- Repentance and faith. Ac 20:21.
- As spokesmen of God. 1Pe 4:11.
- Everywhere. Mk 16:20; Ac 8:4.
- Not with enticing words of man's wisdom. 1Co 1:17; 2:1, 4.
- Without deceitfulness. 2Co 2:17; 4:2; 1Th 2:3, 5.
- Fully and boldly. Mt 10:27, 28; Ac 5:20; 20:20, 27; Ro 3:12; 15:19; 1Th 2:8.
- With care and faithfulness. Ac 6:4; 2Co 1:18, 19; 1Ti 4:16; 2Ti 4:2; Php 1:15–17.
- Without charge, if possible. 1Co 9:18; 1Th 2:9.

When faithful
- Approve themselves as God's ministers. 2Co 6:4.

Thank God for His gifts to their people. 1Co 1:4; Php 1:3; 1Th 3:9.
Glory in their people. 2Co 7:4.
Rejoice in the faith and holiness of their people. 1Th 3:6–9.
Commend themselves to people's consciences. 2Co 4:2.
Are rewarded. Mt 24:47; 1Co 3:14; 9:17, 18; 1Pe 5:4.

False
- Described. Titus 1:10, 11.
- Deal treacherously with their people. Jn 10:12.
- Delude men. Mt 15:14.
- Seek gain. 2Pe 2:3.
- Shall be punished. Mt 24:48–51.

Flock responsible to
- Regard them as God's messengers. 1Co 4:1; Gal 4:14.
- Not to despise them. Lk 10:16; 1Ti 4:12.
- Listen to their instructions. Mt 23:3.
- Follow their holy example. 1Co 11:1; Php 3:17; Heb 13:7.
- Respect them. Php 2:29; 1Th 5:13; 1Ti 5:17.
- Love them. 2Co 8:7; 1Th 3:6.
- Pray for them. Ro 15:30; 2Co 1:11; Eph 6:19; Heb 13:18.
- Obey them. 1Co 16:16; Heb 13:17.
- Give them joy. 2Co 1:14; 2:3.
- Help and support them. Ro 16:2; 1Co 9:7–11; Gal 6:6; Php 4:3.

Pray for the increase of. Mt 9:38.

Faithful, exemplified by
- The eleven disciples. Mt 28:16–19.
- The seventy. Lk 10:1, 17.
- Matthias. Ac 1:26.
- Philip. Ac 8:5.
- Barnabas. Ac 11:23.
- Simeon, etc. Ac 13:1.
- Paul. Ac 28:31.
- Tychicus. Eph 6:21.
- Timothy. Php 2:22.
- Epaphroditus. Php 2:24.
- Archippus. Col 4:17.
- Titus. Titus 1:5.

Divisions in the Church
Are forbidden. 1Co 1:10–13; 11:18; 12:24, 25.

Are contrary to the
- Unity of Christ. 1Co 1:13; 12:13.
- Desire of Christ. Jn 17:21–23.
- Purpose of Christ. Jn 10:16.
- Spirit of the church. 1Co 11:16.

Are proof of a self-centered spirit. 1Co 3:3.
Believers should avoid those who cause. Ro 16:17.
Evil of, illustrated. Mt 12:25.

Excellency and Glory of the Church
Derived from Christ. Lk 2:34.

Consist in its
- Being the temple of God. 1Co 3:16, 17; Eph 2:21, 22.
- Being the body of Christ. Eph 1:22, 23.
- Being the bride of Christ. Rev 19:7, 8; 21:2.
- Members being righteous. Rev 19:8.
- Sanctification. Eph 5:26, 27.

Fellowship of Believers
God's will. Mt 18:20; Jn 17:20, 21.

Occurs
- With God. 1Jn 1:3.
- With believers in heaven. Heb 12:22–24.
- With each other. Gal 2:9; 1Jn 1:3, 7.
- In public and social worship. Ac 1:14; Heb 10:25.
- In the Lord's Supper. 1Co 10:17.
- In prayer for each other. 2Co 1:11; Eph 6:18.
- In exhortation. Col 3:16; Heb 10:25.
- In mutual comfort and edification. 1Th 4:18; 5:11.
- In mutual sympathy and kindness. Ro 12:15; Eph 4:32.
- In mutual love and concern. 1Co 12:26, 27.
- In mutual submission. Eph 5:21.
- In mutual sharing of life. Phm 6.

The delight of. Ro 15:32.
Exhortation to. Eph 4:1–3.
Opposed to communion with the wicked. 2Co 6:14–17; Eph 5:11.

Exemplified by
- The apostles. Ac 1:14.
- The local church. Ac 2:42; 5:12.
- Paul. Ac 20:36–38.

Lord's Supper
Prefigured. Ex 12:21–28; 1Co 5:7, 8.
Instituted. Mt 26:26; 1Co 11:23.
Purpose and character of. Mt 26:27; Lk 22:19; 1Co 10:16; 11:24, 26.
Qualifications to partake of. 1Co 5:7, 8; 10:21; 11:28, 31.
Was continually observed by the early church. Ac 2:42; 20:7.

Unworthy partakers of
- Are guilty of the body and blood of Christ. 1Co 11:27.
- Do not judge the Lord's body correctly. 1Co 11:29.
- Are visited with judgments. 1Co 11:30.

Missions
Commanded. Mt 28:19; Mk 16:15; Lk 10:2; Ro 10:14, 15.
Is according to the purpose of God. Lk 24:46, 47; Ac 13:2; Gal 1:15, 16; Col 1:25–27.
Christ engaged in. Mt 4:17, 23; 11:1; Mk 1:38, 39; Lk 8:1.
Apostles constrained to engage in. Mk 3:14; 6:7; Lk 10:1–11; Ac 4:19, 20; Ro 1:13–15; 1Co 9:16.
Excellency of. Ro 10:15.

Requirements for
- Wisdom and meekness. Mt 10:16.
- Aid others engaged in. Ro 16:1, 2; 2 Cor 11:9; 3Jn 5–8.
- Harmony of effort. Gal 2:9.
- Worldly concerns should not delay. Lk 9:59–62.

Success of
- To be prayed for. Eph 6:18, 19; Col 4:3.
- A cause of joy and praise. Ac 11:18; 15:3; 21:19, 20.

People should not limit. Mk 16:15; 1Co 16:9; Rev 14:6.

Exemplified by
- The Seventy. Lk 10:1, 17.
- The apostles. Mk 6:12; Ac 13:2–5.
- Philip. Ac 8:5.
- Paul, etc. Ac 13:2–4.
- Silas. Ac 15:40, 41.
- Timothy. Ac 16:3.
- Noah. 2Pe 2:5.

Nature of the Church
Belongs to God. Mt 16:18; Eph 3:21; 1Ti 3:15.
Purchased by the blood of Christ. Ac 20:28; Eph 5:25; Heb 9:12.
Displays the wisdom of God. Eph 3:10.
Elect. 1Pe 5:13.
Glorious. Eph 5:27.
Clothed in righteousness. Rev 19:8.
Believers continually added to, by the Lord. Ac 2:27; 5:14; 11:24.
Unity of. Ro 12:5; 1Co 10:17; 12:12; Gal 3:28.
Believers baptized into, by one Spirit. 1Co 12:13.
Ministers commanded to feed. Ac 20:28.
Is edified by the Word. 1Co 14:4, 13; Eph 4:15, 16.
The wicked persecute. Ac 8:1–3; 1Th 2:14, 15.
Not to be despised. 1Co 11:22.

Titles and Names of the Church
Body of Christ. Eph 1:22, 23; Col 1:24.
Bride of Christ. Rev 21:9.
Church of the firstborn. Heb 12:23.
Church of God. Ac 20:28.
Church of the Living God. 1Ti 3:15.
Dwelling of God. Eph 2:22.
Family in heaven and earth. Eph 3:15.
Flock of God. 1Pe 5:2, 3.
Fold of Christ. Jn 10:16.
God's building. 1Co 3:9.
God's field. 1Co 3:9.
Golden lampstand. Rev 1:20.
House of Christ. Heb 3:6.
House of God. Heb 10:21.
Household of God. Eph 2:19; 1Ti 3:15.
Lamb's wife. Rev 19:7.
Pillar and support of the truth. 1Ti 3:15.
Spiritual house. 1Pe 2:5.
Temple of God. 1Co 3:16, 17.
Temple of the living God. 2Co 6:16.

ANGELS

Nature of Holy Angels
Created by God and Christ. Ne 9:6; Col 1:16.
Worship God and Christ. Ne 9:6; Php 2:9–11; Heb 1:6.
Are ministering spirits. 1Ki 19:5; Ps 104:4; Lk 16:22; Ac 12:7–11; 27:23; Heb 1:7, 14.
Communicate the will of God and Christ. Da 8:16, 17; 9:21–23; 10:11; 12:6, 7; Mt 2:13, 20; Lk 1:19, 28; Ac 5:20; 8:26; 10:5; 27:23; Rev 1:1.
Obey the will of God. Ps 103:20; Mt 6:10.
Execute the purposes of God. Nu 22:22; Ps 103:21; Mt 13:39–42; 28:2; Jn 5:4; Rev 5:2.
Execute the judgments of God. 2Sa 24:16; 2Ki 19:35; Ps 35:5, 6; Ac 12:23; Rev 16:1.
Celebrate the praises of God. Job 38:7; Ps 148:2; Is 6:3; Lk 2:13, 14; Rev 5:11, 12; 7:11, 12.
The law given by the ministration of. Ac 7:53; Heb 2:2.

Announced
- The conception of Christ. Mt 1:20, 21; Lk 1:31.
- The birth of Christ. Lk 2:10–12.
- The resurrection of Christ. Mt 28:5–7; Lk 24:23.
- The ascension and second coming of Christ. Ac 1:11.
- The conception of John the Baptist. Lk 1:13, 36.

Minister to Christ. Mt 4:11; Lk 22:43; Jn 1:51.

Satan, a Fallen Angel

LAST THINGS

Antichrist

Eternal Death

The Final Judgment

Heaven

Second Coming of Christ

BOOK ABBREVIATIONS

USED IN THE CONCORDANCE

THE OLD TESTAMENT

Genesis	Ge
Exodus	Ex
Leviticus	Lv
Numbers	Nu
Deuteronomy	Dt
Joshua	Jos
Judges	Jdg
Ruth	Ru
First Samuel	1Sa
Second Samuel	2Sa
First Kings	1Ki
Second Kings	2Ki
First Chronicles	1Ch
Second Chronicles	2Ch
Ezra	Ezr
Nehemiah	Ne
Esther	Est
Job	Job
Psalms	Ps
Proverbs	Pr
Ecclesiastes	Ecc
Song of Solomon	SS
Isaiah	Is
Jeremiah	Jer
Lamentations	La
Ezekiel	Eze
Daniel	Da
Hosea	Hos
Joel	Joel
Amos	Am
Obadiah	Ob
Jonah	Jon
Micah	Mic
Nahum	Na
Habakkuk	Hab
Zephaniah	Zep
Haggai	Hag
Zechariah	Zec
Malachi	Mal

THE NEW TESTAMENT

Matthew	Mt
Mark	Mk
Luke	Lk
John	Jn
Acts	Ac
Romans	Ro
First Corinthians	1Co
Second Corinthians	2Co
Galatians	Gal
Ephesians	Eph
Philippians	Php
Colossians	Col
First Thessalonians	1Th
Second Thessalonians	2Th
First Timothy	1Ti
Second Timothy	2Ti
Titus	Titus
Philemon	Phm
Hebrews	Heb
James	Jas
First Peter	1Pe
Second Peter	2Pe
First John	1Jn
Second John	2Jn
Third John	3Jn
Jude	Jude
Revelation	Rev

CONCORDANCE

This concordance helps you locate occurrences of significant words, phrases and proper names of the Bible. Common words are followed by a simple definition or synonym. Underneath the key word are Scripture citations with the key word designated by an italic letter, followed by a Scripture reference for that occurrence. Occurrences of related forms of a key word, such as plurals and verb tenses, are usually grouped with the key word and are designated by an identifying suffix attached to the italic letter. Phrases are arranged in alphabetical order by the first word of the phrase, with the phrase in the Scripture citation designated by the italic first letter of the first word of the phrase.

With the proper names are given descriptive phrases and the important locations in Scripture. If a name applies to more than one person, place or group, the different identities are distinguished by a dash (——).

A

AARON
Ancestry and family of, Ex 6:16–20, 23
Helper and prophet to Moses, Ex 4:13–31; 7:1, 2
Appears before Pharaoh, Ex 5:1–4
Performs miracles, Ex 7:9, 10, 19, 20
Supports Moses' hands, Ex 17:10–12
Ascends Mt. Sinai; sees God's glory, Ex 19:24; 24:1, 9, 10
Judges Israel in Moses' absence, Ex 24:14
Chosen by God as priest, Ex 28:1
Consecrated, Ex 29; Lv 8
Duties prescribed, Ex 30:7–10
Tolerates Israel's idolatry, Ex 32
Priestly ministry begins, Lv 9
Sons offer profane fire; Aaron's humble response, Lv 10
Conspires against Moses, Nu 12:1–16
Rebelled against by Korah, Nu 16
Intercedes to stop plague, Nu 16:45–48
Rod buds to confirm his authority, Nu 17:1–10
With Moses, fails at Meribah, Nu 20:1–13
Dies; son succeeds him as priest, Nu 20:23–29
His priesthood compared:
with Melchizedek's, Heb 7:11–19
with Christ's, Heb 9:6–15, 23–28

ABADDON
Angel of the bottomless pit, Rev 9:11

ABANDON *leave*
LORD has *a-ed* us, Jdg 6:13
not *a* His people, 1Sa 12:22
a the remnant, 2Ki 21:14
not *a* my soul to, Ps 16:10
not *a* His people, Ps 94:14
a-ed My inheritance, Jer 12:7
a my soul to Hades, Ac 2:27

ABASE *humble*
man will be *a-d*, Is 2:11
lofty will be *a-d*, Is 10:33
a the haughtiness, Is 13:11
a-d before all, Mal 2:9

ABATED *decreased*
water was *a*, Ge 8:8
his vigor *a*, Dt 34:7

ABBA *father*
A! Father, Mk 14:36
we cry out, *A!*, Ro 8:15

ABED-NEGO
Babylonian name given to Azariah, a Hebrew captive, Da 1:7
Appointed by Nebuchadnezzar, Da 2:49
Refuses to serve idols; cast into furnace but delivered, Da 3:12–30

ABEL
Adam's second son, Ge 4:2
His offering accepted, Ge 4:4
Murdered by Cain, Ge 4:8
His sacrifice offered by faith, Heb 11:4

ABEL-BETH-MAACAH
Captured by Tiglath-pileser, 2Ki 15:29
Refuge of Sheba; saved from destruction, 2Sa 20:14–22
Seized by Ben-hadad, 1Ki 15:20

ABEL-MEHOLAH
A city a few miles east of Jabesh-gilead, Jdg 7:22; 1Ki 4:12
Elisha's native city, 1Ki 19:16

ABHOR *despise, detest*
associates *a* me, Job 19:19
greatly *a-red* Israel, Ps 78:59
nations will *a* him, Pr 24:24
To the One *a-red*, Is 49:7
A what is evil, Ro 12:9

ABHORRENT *detestable*
and they shall be *a* to you, Lv 11:11
his brother's wife, it is *a*, Lv 20:21
king's command was *a*, 1Ch 21:6
gold will become an *a* thing, Eze 7:19
I will make it an *a* thing, Eze 7:20

ABIATHAR
A priest who escapes Saul at Nob, 1Sa 22:20–23
Becomes high priest under David, 1Sa 23:6, 9–12
Remains faithful to David, 2Sa 15:24–29
Informs David about Ahithophel, 2Sa 15:34–36
Supports Adonijah's usurpation, 1Ki 1:7, 9, 25
Deposed by Solomon, 1Ki 2:26, 27, 35

ABIDE *remain, stay*
LORD *a-s* forever, Ps 9:7
a in Your tent, Ps 15:1
a in the shadow, Ps 91:1
wrath of God *a-s*, Jn 3:36
If you *a* in Me, Jn 15:7
a in My love, Jn 15:9
now faith...*a*, 1Co 13:13
love of God *a*, 1Jn 3:17
God *a-s* in us, 1Jn 4:12

ABIEZRITES
Relatives of Gideon; rally to his call, Jdg 6:11, 24, 34

ABIGAIL
Wise wife of foolish Nabal, 1Sa 25:3

Appeases David and becomes his wife, 1Sa 25:14–42
Mother of Chileab, 2Sa 3:3

ABIHU
Second son of Aaron, Ex 6:23
Offers profane fire and dies, Lv 10:1–7

ABIJAH
Samuel's second son; follows corrupt ways, 1Sa 8:2, 3
——— Descendant of Aaron; head of an office of priests, 1Ch 24:3, 10
Zacharias belongs to division of, Lk 1:5
——— Son of Jeroboam I, 1Ki 14:1–18
——— Another name for King Abijam, 2Ch 11:20

ABIJAM (or Abijah)
King of Judah, 1Ki 14:31
Follows the sins of his father, 1Ki 15:1–7
Defeats Jeroboam and takes cities, 2Ch 13:13–20

ABILENE
A province or tetrarchy of Syria, Lk 3:1

ABILITY *power, strength*
According to their *a*, Ezr 2:69
a for serving, Da 1:4
a to conceive, Heb 11:11

ABIMELECH
King of Gerar; takes Sarah in ignorance, Ge 20:1–18
Makes treaty with Abraham, Ge 21:22–34
——— A second king of Gerar; sends Isaac away, Ge 26:1–16
Makes treaty with Isaac, Ge 26:17–33
——— Gideon's son by a concubine, Jdg 8:31
Conspires to become king, Jdg 9

ABINADAB
A man of Kiriath-jearim in whose house the ark was kept, 1Sa 7:1, 2
——— The second of Jesse's eight sons, 1Sa 16:8
Serves in Saul's army, 1Sa 17:13
——— A son of Saul slain at Mt. Gilboa, 1Sa 31:1–8
Bones of, buried by men of Jabesh, 1Ch 10:1–12

ABIRAM
Reubenite who conspired against Moses, Nu 16:1–50

ABISHAG
A Shunammite employed as David's nurse, 1Ki 1:1–4, 15
Witnessed David's choice of Solomon as successor, 1Ki 1:15–31
Adonijah slain for desiring to marry her, 1Ki 2:13–25

ABISHAI
David's nephew; joins Joab in blood-revenge against Abner, 2Sa 2:18–24
Loyal to David during Absalom's and Sheba's rebellion, 2Sa 16:9–12; 20:1–6, 10
Rebuked by David, 2Sa 16:9–12; 19:21–23
His exploits, 2Sa 21:16, 17; 23:18; 1Ch 18:12, 13

ABLAZE *flaming*
brands you have set *a*, Is 50:11
throne *was a* with, Da 7:9
coming will set them *a*, Mal 4:1

ABLE *qualified*
chose *a* men out of all, Ex 18:25
not *a* to carry all this people, Nu 11:14
Who is *a* to stand, 1Sa 6:20
who is *a* to judge this great, 1Ki 3:9
so that I am not *a* to see, Ps 40:12
God whom we serve is *a*, Da 3:17
a to deliver you from the lions, Da 6:20
from these stones God is *a*, Mt 3:9
that I am *a* to do this, Mt 9:28
fear Him who is *a* to, Mt 10:28
Are you *a* to drink, Mt 20:22
no one is *a* to snatch, Jn 10:29
they were not *a* to haul, Jn 21:6
will be *a* to separate us, Ro 8:39
God is *a* to graft them, Ro 11:23
beyond what you are *a*, 1Co 10:13
be *a* to comprehend, Eph 3:18
Now to Him who is *a*, Eph 3:20
convinced that He is *a*, 2Ti 1:12
He is *a* to come to the aid, Heb 2:18
He is *a* also to save forever, Heb 7:25
is *a* to save your souls, Jas 1:21
a to keep you from, Jude 1:24
a to open, Rev 5:3

ABNER
Saul's cousin; commander of his army, 1Sa 14:50, 51
Rebuked by David, 1Sa 26:5, 14–16
Supports Ish-bosheth; defeated by David's men; kills Asahel, 2Sa 2:8–32
Makes covenant with David, 2Sa 3:6–21
Killed by Joab; mourned by David, 2Sa 3:22–39

ABOARD *on ship*
men, O Tyre, were *a*, Eze 27:8
we went *a* and set sail, Ac 21:2
Italy, and he put us *a* it, Ac 27:6

ABODE *habitation*
a of righteousness, Jer 31:23
Our *a* with him, Jn 14:23
their proper *a*, Jude 6

ABOLISH *annul, destroy*
I will *a* the bow, the sword, Hos 2:18
I did not come to *a* but, Mt 5:17
that will be *a-ed* is death, 1Co 15:26
the cross has been *a-ed*., Gal 5:11
a-ing in His flesh the, Eph 2:15
Jesus, who *a-ed* death, 2Ti 1:10

ABOMINABLE *detestable*
committed *a* deeds, Ps 14:1
your beauty *a*, Eze 16:25
a idolatries, 1Pe 4:3
unbelieving and *a*, Rev 21:8

ABOMINATION *hated thing*
a to the Egyptians, Ex 8:26
a into your house, Dt 7:26
seen their *a-s*, Dt 29:17
a to the LORD, Pr 3:32
all their *a-s*, Eze 33:29
a of desolation, Mt 24:15
a-s of the earth, Rev 17:5

ABOUND *excel, be plentiful*
make you *a* in prosperity, Dt 28:11
grain and new wine *a*, Ps 4:7
May your peace *a*!, Da 4:1
woman was *a-ing* with deeds, Ac 9:36
truth of God *a-ed* to His glory, Ro 3:7
Jesus Christ, *a* to the many, Ro 5:15
grace *a-ed* all the more, Ro 5:20
you will *a* in hope, Ro 15:13
always *a-ing* in the work, 1Co 15:58
righteousness *a* in glory., 2Co 3:9
a-s all the more toward, 2Co 7:15
to make all grace *a* to you, 2Co 9:8
your love may *a* still more, Php 1:9

ABOVE *over*
exalted *a* the heavens, Ps 57:5
disciple is not *a*, Mt 10:24
I am from *a*, Jn 8:23
a every name, Php 2:9
exalts himself *a*, 2Th 2:4
gift is from *a*, Jas 1:17

ABRAHAM
Ancestry and family, Ge 11:26–31
Receives God's call; enters Canaan, Ge 12:1–6
Promised Canaan by God; pitched tent near Bethel, Ge 12:7, 8
Deceives Egyptians concerning Sarai, Ge 12:11–20
Separates from Lot; inherits Canaan, Ge 13
Rescues Lot from captivity, Ge 14:11–16
Gives a tithe to Melchizedek; refuses spoil, Ge 14:18–24
Covenant renewed; promised a son, Ge 15
Takes Hagar as concubine; Ishmael born, Ge 16
Name changed from Abram; circumcision commanded, Ge 17
Entertains Lord and angels, Ge 18:1–15
Intercedes for Sodom, Ge 18:16–33
Deceives Abimelech concerning Sarah, Ge 20
Birth of Isaac, Ge 21:1–7
Sends Hagar and Ishmael away, Ge 21:9–14
Offers Isaac in obedience to God, Ge 22:1–19
Finds wife for Isaac, Ge 24
Marries Keturah; fathers other children; dies, Ge 25:1–10
Friend of God, 2Ch 20:7
Justified by faith, Ro 4:1–12
Father of true believers, Ro 4:11–25
In the line of faith, Heb 11:8–10
Eternal home of, in heaven, Lk 16:19–25

ABRAHAM'S BOSOM
Rabbinic terminology for Paradise, Lk 16:22

ABRAM
See ABRAHAM

ABROAD *extensively*
scattered *a* over the, Ge 11:4
sound His praise *a*, Ps 66:8
shed *a* a plentiful rain, Ps 68:9
springs be dispersed *a*, Pr 5:16
its spices be wafted *a*, SS 4:16
who are scattered *a*, Jn 11:52
A, he gave to the, 2Co 9:9

tribes who are dispersed *a*, Jas 1:1

ABRONAH
Israelite encampment, Nu 33:34

ABSALOM
Son of David, 2Sa 3:3
Kills Amnon for raping Tamar; flees from David, 2Sa 13:20–39
Returns through Joab's intrigue; reconciled to David, 2Sa 14
Attempts to usurp throne, 2Sa 15:1–18:8
Caught and killed by Joab, 2Sa 18:9–18
Mourned by David, 2Sa 18:19–19:8

ABSENT *being away*
we are *a* one from, Ge 31:49
a in body, 1Co 5:3
a from the Lord, 2Co 5:6
a from the body, 2Co 5:8

ABSTAIN *refrain from*
a from wine, Nu 6:3
a-ing from foods, 1Ti 4:3
a from wickedness, 2Ti 2:19
a from fleshly lusts, 1Pe 2:11

ABUNDANCE *plenty, surplus*
seven years of *a*, Ge 41:34
a of Your house, Ps 36:8
a of peace, Ps 72:7
a of counselors, Pr 24:6
he who loves *a*, Ecc 5:10
delight yourself in *a*, Is 55:2
one has an *a*, Lk 12:15
the *a* of grace, Ro 5:17

ABUNDANT *enough, plenteous*
come...find *a* water, 2Ch 32:4
a righteousness, Job 37:23
a in lovingkindness, Ps 86:5
comfort is *a*, 2Co 1:5

ABUNDANTLY
they may breed *a*, Ge 8:17
Populate the earth *a*, Ge 9:7
will prosper you *a*, Dt 30:9
drip upon man *a*, Job 36:28

ABUSE *(n) insulting speech*
hurling *a* at Him, Mt 27:39
was hurling *a*, Lk 23:39

ABUSE *(v) hurt, molest*
a-d her all night, Jdg 19:25
uncircumcised...*a* me, 1Ch 10:4

ABUSIVE *filthy, vulgar*
a speech from your, Col 3:8
strife, *a* language, 1Ti 6:4

ABYSS *deep, depth*
go away into the *a*, Lk 8:31
descend into the *a*, Ro 10:7
angel of the *a*, Rev 9:11
key of the *a*, Rev 20:1

ACCEPT *receive*
a the work of, Dt 33:11
a good from God, Job 2:10
a-ed no chastening, Jer 2:30
hear the word and *a*, Mk 4:20
God has *a-ed* him, Ro 14:3
a one another, Ro 15:7

ACCEPTABLE *pleasing*
my heart Be *a*, Ps 19:14
sacrifice, *a* to God, Ro 12:1
a to the saints, Ro 15:31
now is the *a* time, 2Co 6:2
to God an *a* service, Heb 12:28
sacrifices *a* to God, 1Pe 2:5

ACCEPTANCE *agreement*
will go up with *a* on My altar, Is 60:7
a be but life from the dead, Ro 11:15
statement, deserving full *a*, 1Ti 1:15
statement deserving full *a*, 1Ti 4:9

ACCESS *approach, entry*
grant you free *a*, Zec 3:7
our *a* in one Spirit, Eph 2:18

ACCOMPANY *attach to, follow*
who *a* my lord, 1Sa 25:27
a-ied the king, 2Sa 19:40
a-ied by trumpets, 2Ch 5:13
allowed no one to *a*, Mk 5:37
that *a* salvation, Heb 6:9

ACCOMPLISH *perform, realize*
a-ed deliverance, 1Sa 11:13
shall *a* my desire, 1Ki 5:9
God...*a-es all things*, Ps 57:2
has *a-ed* His wrath, La 4:11
a-ed redemption, Lk 1:68
a His work, Jn 4:34
I am *a-ing* a work, Ac 13:41
man can *a* much, Jas 5:16

ACCORD *agreement, union*
one *a* to fight, Jos 9:2
voices...with one *a*, Ac 4:24
one *a* in Solomon's, Ac 5:12
crowds with one *a*, Ac 8:6
one *a* they came, Ac 12:20

ACCORDANCE *in conformity*
in *a* with all these words, Ex 24:8
In *a* with the command, Jos 19:50
in *a* with all Your righteous, Da 9:16
Reap in *a* with kindness, Hos 10:12
in *a* with grace, Ro 4:16
not in *a* with knowledge, Ro 10:2
in *a* with the working of, Eph 1:19
in *a* with the eternal, Eph 3:11
a with the commandments, Col 2:22
in *a* to their own desires, 2Ti 4:3
in *a* with the teaching, Titus 1:9

ACCORDING *conforming*
a to your word, Ge 30:34
Moses did; *a* to all, Ex 40:16
a to our sins, Ps 103:10
a to his deeds, Mt 16:27
a to the revelation, Ro 16:25
heirs *a* to promise, Gal 3:29
a to His riches, Php 4:19

ACCORDING TO THE FLESH
You judge *a*, Jn 8:15
descendant of David *a*, Ro 1:3
Abraham, our forefather *a*, Ro 4:1
who do not walk *a*, Ro 8:4
who are *a* set their minds, Ro 8:5
not to the flesh, to live *a*, Ro 8:12
if you are living *a*, Ro 8:13
my kinsmen *a*, Ro 9:3
from whom is the Christ *a*, Ro 9:5
were not many wise *a*, 1Co 1:26
do I purpose *a*, 2Co 1:17
we have known Christ *a*, 2Co 5:16
we do not war *a*, 2Co 10:3
many boast *a*, 2Co 11:18
bondwoman was born *a*, Gal 4:23
who are your masters *a*, Eph 6:5

ACCORDING TO THE LAW
to do *a* which Moses, Jos 1:7
statutes *a* which I, 2Ki 17:13
to the LORD ... *a*, 2Ki 23:25
Jerusalem *a* of your God, Ezr 7:14
let it be done *a*, Ezr 10:3
a of the Medes and, Da 6:8
days for their purification *a*, Lk 2:22
and judge Him *a*, Jn 18:31
under Gamaliel, strictly *a*, Ac 22:3
We wanted to judge him *a*, Ac 24:6
who offer the gifts *a*, Heb 8:4
a, ... all things are, Heb 9:22

ACCORDING TO THE WORD OF THE LORD
Moses numbered them *a*, Nu 3:16
the sons of Israel *a*, Nu 36:5
of the LORD died ..., *a*, Dt 34:5
and went their way *a*, 1Ki 12:24
and mourned for him, *a*, 1Ki 14:18
household of Baasha, *a*, 1Ki 16:12
of oil become empty, *a*, 1Ki 17:16
barley for a shekel, *a*, 2Ki 7:16
to Ahab in Samaria ... *a*, 2Ki 10:17
David king over Israel, *a*, 1Ch 11:3
and went to Nineveh *a*, Jon 3:3

ACCORDINGLY *appropriately*
heard and has not acted *a*, Lk 6:49
A, whatever you have, Lk 12:3
exercise them a, Ro 12:6
A both gifts and sacrifices, Heb 9:9

ACCOUNT *(n) reckoning*
the *a* of the heavens, Ge 2:4
On whose *a has* this, Jon 1:8
settled *a-s* with, Mt 25:19
who will give an *a*, Heb 13:17

ACCOUNT *(v) reckon*
do not *a this* sin, Nu 12:11
I am *a-ed* wicked, Job 9:29
You have taken *a* of, Ps 56:8
are *a-ed* as nothing, Da 4:35

ACCOUNTABLE *answerable*
satraps might be *a*, Da 6:2
may become *a* to God, Ro 3:19

ACCURATELY *correctly*
teaching *a*...things, Ac 18:25
a handling...word, 2Ti 2:15

ACCURSED *damned*
camp of Israel *a*, Jos 6:18
be *thought a*, Is 65:20
Depart...*a* ones, Mt 25:41
he is to be *a*, Gal 1:8
in greed, *a* children, 2Pe 2:14

ACCUSATION *charge of wrong*
wrote an *a* against, Ezr 4:6
find a ground of *a*, Da 6:4
What *a* do you, Jn 18:29
a against my nation, Ac 28:19
Do not receive an *a*, 1Ti 5:19

ACCUSE *testify against*
has *a-ed* his brother falsely, Dt 19:18
a-s you in judgment, Is 54:17
at his right hand to *a* him, Zec 3:1
while He was being *a-ed*, Mt 27:12
began to *a* Him harshly, Mk 15:3
find *reason* to *a* Him, Lk 6:7
will *a* you before the Father, Jn 5:45
a-ing or else defending, Ro 2:15
not *a-ed* of dissipation, Titus 1:6

ACCUSER *complainant*
they act as my *a-s*, Ps 109:4
instructing his *a-s*, Ac 23:30
when the *a-s* stood, Ac 25:18
a of our brethren, Rev 12:10

ACCUSTOMED *by habit*
a to do so to you?", Nu 22:30
his men were *a* to go, 1Sa 30:31
Who are *a* to doing evil, Jer 13:23
governor was *a* to release, Mt 27:15
he had been *a* to do, Mk 15:8

ACHAIA
Visited by Paul, Ac 18:1, 12
Apollos preaches in, Ac 18:24–28
Gospel proclaimed throughout, 1Th 1:7, 8

ACHAN (or Achar)
Sin of, caused Israel's defeat, Jos 7:1–15
Stoned to death, Jos 7:16–25
Sin of, recalled, Jos 22:20
Also called Achar, 1Ch 2:7

ACHIEVE *attain*
a wealth in Ephrathah, Ru 4:11
sons *a* honor, but he does, Job 14:21
not *a* the righteousness, Jas 1:20

ACHIEVEMENTS *accomplishments*
trust in your own *a*, Jer 48:7

ACHISH
A king of Gath, 1Sa 21:10–15
David seeks refuge with, 1Sa 27:1–12
Forced by Philistine lords to expel David, 1Sa 29:1–11
Receives Shimei's servants, 1Ki 2:39, 40

ACHOR, VALLEY OF
Site of Achan's stoning, Jos 7:24–26
On Judah's boundary, Jos 15:7
Promises concerning, Is 65:10

ACHSAH
A daughter of Caleb, 1Ch 2:49
Given to Othniel, Jos 15:16–19
Given springs of water, Jdg 1:12–15

ACKNOWLEDGE *confess*
I *a-d* my sin, Ps 32:5
all your ways *a* Him, Pr 3:6
Pharisees *a* them all, Ac 23:8
see fit to *a* God, Ro 1:28

ACQUAINTANCE *friend*
a-s are...estranged, Job 19:13
dread to my *a-s*, Ps 31:11
removed my *a-s* far, Ps 88:8
relatives and *a-s*, Lk 2:44
And all His *a-s*, Lk 23:49

ACQUAINTED *become familiar*
a with all my ways, Ps 139:3
a with grief, Is 53:3

ACQUIRE *get, purchase*
a property in it, Ge 34:10
have *a-d* Ruth, Ru 4:10
a wise counsel, Pr 1:5
You have *a-d* riches, Eze 28:4
Do not *a* gold, Mt 10:9

ACQUISITION *something gained*
the *a* of wisdom is above, Job 28:18
a of treasures by, Pr 21:6

ACQUIT *declare innocent*
not *a* me of my guilt, Job 10:14
A me of hidden *faults*, Ps 19:12
You will not be *a-ted*, Jer 49:12

ACROSS *opposite side*
sent them *a* the stream, Ge 32:23
do not take us *a* the Jordan, Nu 32:5
Gilead remained *a*, Jdg 5:17
tendrils stretched *a* the sea, Jer 48:32
wanted to go *a* to Achaia, Ac 18:27
girded *a* His chest with a, Rev 1:13

ACT *(n) deed, work*
and mighty *a-s* as Yours?, Dt 3:24
committed a detestable *a*, Lv 20:13
not been caught in the *a*, Nu 5:13
every abominable *a* which, Dt 12:31
not commit this *a* of folly, Jdg 19:23
a-s of the LORD, 1Sa 12:7
rest of the *a-s* of Solomon, 1Ki 11:41
His wondrous *a-s* among, Ps 105:27
righteous *a-s* of the LORD, Mic 6:5
in adultery, in the very *a*, Jn 8:4
even so through one *a* of, Ro 5:18
by an *a* of human will, 2Pe 1:21
righteous *a-s* of the saints, Rev 19:8

ACT *(v) behave*
brothers, do not *a* wickedly, Ge 19:7
they also *a-ed* craftily, Jos 9:4
He *a-ed* valiantly, 1Sa 14:48
have *a-ed* very foolishly, 2Sa 24:10
be courageous and *a*, Ezr 10:4
they *a* as my accusers, Ps 109:4
for the LORD to *a*, Ps 119:126
a son who *a-s* wisely, Pr 10:5
prudent man *a-s* with, Pr 13:16
I will *a* on behalf of My, Is 65:8
he had *a-ed* shrewdly, Lk 16:8
he is *a-ing* unbecomingly, 1Co 7:36
a-ing like busybodies, 2Th 3:11
and so *a* as those who, Jas 2:12
A as free men, 1Pe 2:16

ACTION *behavior, work*
a-s are weighed, 1Sa 2:3
a-s of a...harlot, Eze 16:30
plan or *a* is, Ac 5:38
prepare your minds for *a*, 1Pe 1:13

ACTIVITY *action, pursuit*
seeking food in their *a*, Job 24:5
evil *a* that is done under, Ecc 4:3
the *a* of God who makes, Ecc 11:5
with the *a* of Satan, 2Th 2:9

ADAM
Creation of, Ge 1:26, 27; 2:7
Given dominion over the earth, Ge 1:28–30
Given a wife, Ge 2:18–25
Temptation, fall, and exile from Eden, Ge 3
Children of, Ge 4:1, 2; 5:3, 4
Transgression results in sin and death, Ro 5:12–14
——— Last or second Adam, an appellation of Christ, Ro 5:14, 15; 1Co 15:20–24, 45–48

ADAR
Twelfth month of Hebrew calendar, Ezr 6:15
Purim observed, Est 3:7; 9:19ff

ADD
a to your yoke, 1Ki 12:11
a-ing to the wrath, Ne 13:18
not *a* to His words, Pr 30:6
if anyone *a-s* to them, Rev 22:18

ADDICTED *dependent on*
not *a* to wine, 1Ti 3:3
or *a* to much wine, 1Ti 3:8
not quick-tempered, not *a*, Titus 1:7

ADDITION *besides, also*
marry a woman in *a*, Lv 18:18
its drink offering in *a*, Nu 28:15
In *a* to being a wise man, Ecc 12:9
a to all your abominations, Eze 44:7
a to all, taking up the, Eph 6:16

ADDRESS *direct; speak to*
a my verses to the King, Ps 45:1
are You *a-ing* this parable, Lk 12:41
release Jesus, *a-ed* them, Lk 23:20
a-ing them in the Hebrew, Ac 22:2
a-ed to you as sons, Heb 12:5
If you *a* as Father, 1Pe 1:17

ADEQUATE *sufficient*
who is *a* for these, 2Co 2:16
Not that we are *a*, 2Co 3:5
a as servants of a new, 2Co 3:6
man of God may be *a*, 2Ti 3:17

ADJURE *charge solemnly*
many times...I *a*, 1Ki 22:16
I *a* you, O daughters, SS 3:5
I *a* you by Jesus, Ac 19:13

ADMINISTRATION
a of the province, Da 3:12
healings, helps, *a-s*, 1Co 12:28
in our *a* of this, 2Co 8:20
a of the mystery, Eph 3:9

ADMONISH *warn*
prophets...had *a-ed*, Ne 9:26
How shall I *a* you, La 2:13
not cease to *a* each, Ac 20:31
able also to *a* one, Ro 15:14
a-ing one another, Col 3:16
a the unruly, 1Th 5:14
a him as a brother, 2Th 3:15

ADONIJAH
David's fourth son, 2Sa 3:2, 4
Attempts to usurp throne, 1Ki 1:5–53
Desires Abishag as wife, 1Ki 2:13–18
Executed by Solomon, 1Ki 2:19–25

ADONIRAM (or Adoram)
Official under David, Solomon, and Rehoboam, 2Sa 20:24; 1Ki 5:14; 12:18
Stoned by angry Israelites, 1Ki 12:18
Called Hadoram, 2Ch 10:18

ADONI-ZEDEK
An Amorite king of Jerusalem, Jos 10:1–5
Defeated and slain by Joshua, Jos 10:6–27

ADOPT *take as one's own*
a-ed other gods, 1Ki 9:9
will *a* no other view, Gal 5:10

ADOPTION *acceptance*
spirit of *a* as sons, Ro 8:15
to whom belongs...*a*, Ro 9:4
receive the *a* as sons, Gal 4:5
predestined us to *a*, Eph 1:5

ADORN *array, clothe*
A yourself with, Job 40:10
as a bride *a-s* herself, Is 61:10
a-ed with beautiful, Lk 21:5
women to *a*, 1Ti 2:9
a the doctrine of God, Titus 2:10
a-ed with gold, Rev 17:4
as a bride *a-ed*, Rev 21:2

ADULLAM
A town of Canaan, Ge 38:1, 12, 20; Jos 12:7, 15; 15:20, 35
David seeks refuge in the caves of, 1Sa 23:13–17

ADULTERER
a and the adulteress, Lv 20:10
eye of the *a* waits, Job 24:15
associate with *a-s*, Ps 50:18
a-s, nor effeminate, 1Co 6:9
a-s God will judge, Heb 13:4

ADULTERESS
a shall surely be, Lv 20:10
a who flatters with, Pr 2:16
mouth of an *a*, Pr 22:14
You *a* wife, who, Eze 16:32
they are *a-es*, Eze 23:45
shall be called an *a*, Ro 7:3

ADULTEROUS *unfaithful*
a woman is a narrow well, Pr 23:27
the way of an *a* woman, Pr 30:20
hurt by their *a*, Eze 6:9
a generation craves for, Mt 12:39
a generation seeks, Mt 16:4
in this *a* and sinful, Mk 8:38

ADULTERY
shall not commit *a*, Ex 20:14
man who commits *a*, Lv 20:10
a-ies of faithless, Jer 3:8
worn out by *a-ies*, Eze 23:43
committed *a* with her, Mt 5:28
woman commits *a*, Mt 5:32
Do not commit *a*, Lk 18:20
eyes full of *a*, 2Pe 2:14

ADVANCE *ahead, beyond*
old, *a-d* in age, Ge 24:1
a-d in years, 1Sa 17:12
have told you in *a*, Mt 24:25
both *a-d* in years, Lk 1:7
a-ing in Judaism, Gal 1:14

ADVANTAGE *benefit, profit*
lead surely to *a*, Pr 21:5
What *a* does man, Ecc 1:3
Wisdom has the *a*, Ecc 10:10
a that I go away, Jn 16:7
what *a* has the Jew, Ro 3:1
no *a* would be taken of us, 2Co 2:11
sake of *gaining an a*, Jude 16

ADVERSARY *foe, opponent*
an *a* to your *a-ies*, Ex 23:22
an *a* to Solomon, 1Ki 11:14
And my *a-ies* will rejoice, Ps 13:4
a-ies and my enemies, Ps 27:2
redeemed...from the *a*, Ps 78:42
crush his *a-ies*, Ps 89:23
there are many *a-ies*, 1Co 16:9
consume the *a-ies*, Heb 10:27
Your *a*, the devil, 1Pe 5:8

ADVERSITY *distress, misfortune*
death and *a*, Dt 30:15
not accept *a*, Job 2:10
relief from...*a*, Ps 94:13
falls into *a*, Pr 13:17
A pursues sinners, Pr 13:21

ADVICE *counsel*
forsook the *a*, 1Ki 12:13
a of the young, 2Ch 10:14
a of the cunning, Job 5:13
they took his *a*, Ac 5:40
have followed my *a*, Ac 27:21

ADVISE *counsel*
a you what this people, Nu 24:14
in charge of the women, *a*, Est 2:15
the one who had *a*, Jn 18:14
a you to buy from Me, Rev 3:18

ADVISER *counselor*
with his *a* Ahuzzath, Ge 26:26
Pharaoh's wisest *a-s*, Is 19:11

ADVOCATE *defender, witness*
my *a* is on high, Job 16:19
A with the Father, 1Jn 2:1

AENON
A place near Salim where John the Baptist baptized, Jn 3:22, 23

AFAR *distant*
against you from *a*, Dt 28:49
his fame spread *a*, 2Ch 26:15
Why do You stand *a* off, Ps 10:1
my kinsmen stand *a* off, Ps 38:11
haughty He knows from *a*, Ps 138:6
brings her food from *a*, Pr 31:14
I will save you from *a*, Jer 30:10
horsemen come from *a*, Hab 1:8

AFFAIR *matter, concern*
deceived you in the *a*, Nu 25:18
still speak of your *a-s*, 2Sa 19:29
a of God and of the king, 1Ch 26:32
regard to government *a-s*, Da 6:4
As to all my *a-s*, Tychicus, Col 4:7
the *a-s* of everyday life, 2Ti 2:4

AFFECTION *devotion, love*
set His *a* to love, Dt 10:15
in your own *a-s*, 2Co 6:12
a of Christ Jesus, Php 1:8
fond an *a* for you, 1Th 2:8

AFFLICT *(v) oppress, trouble*
a them with hard labor, Ex 1:11
not *a* any widow, Ex 22:22
Egyptians...*a-ed* us, Dt 26:6
bind him to *a* him, Jdg 16:5
the wicked *a* them, 2Sa 7:10
They *a-ed* his feet, Ps 105:18
He was *a-ed*, Is 63:9
will *a* you no longer, Na 1:12
were sick or *a-ed*, Ac 5:16
are a-ed in every, 2Co 4:8
those who *a* you, 2Th 1:6
a-ed, ill-treated, Heb 11:37

AFFLICTED *troubled*
save an *a* people, 2Sa 22:28
to catch the *a*, Ps 10:9
justice to the *a*, Ps 82:3
LORD supports the *a*, Ps 147:6
days of the *a*, Pr 15:15
O *a* one, Is 54:11
good news to the *a*, Is 61:1

AFFLICTION *oppression*
my *a* and the toil, Ge 31:42
the land of my *a*, Ge 41:52
the bread of *a*, Dt 16:3
LORD saw the *a*, 2Ki 14:26
You saw the *a*, Ne 9:9
afflicted in their *a*, Job 36:15
Look upon my *a*, Ps 25:18
a severe *a*, Ecc 6:2
a or persecution, Mk 4:17
healed of her *a*, Mk 5:29
a-s await me, Ac 20:23
out of much *a*, 2Co 2:4
great ordeal of *a*, 2Co 8:2
to suffer *a*, 1Th 3:4

AFFORD *bear the cost*
if he cannot *a* a lamb, Lv 5:7
if she cannot *a* a lamb, Lv 12:8
offer what he can *a*, Lv 14:31
what *else* he can *a*, Nu 6:21

AFLAME *burning*
Scorners set a city *a*, Pr 29:8
thickets of the forest *a*, Is 9:18
astonishment, Their faces *a*, Is 13:8
set *a* by such a small fire, Jas 3:5

AFRAID *dreading, fearful*
a because...naked, Ge 3:10
a to look at God, Ex 3:6
a and fainthearted, Dt 20:8
Whoever is *a*, Jdg 7:3
a of the terror, Ps 91:5
not *a* of the snow, Pr 31:21
a to swear, Ecc 9:2
a of man who dies, Is 51:12
a to take Mary, Mt 1:20
were *a* of Him, Mk 11:18
Do not be *a*, Mary, Lk 1:30
a of those who kill, Lk 12:4
a of the people, Lk 22:2
a that, as the serpent, 2Co 11:3
Do not be *a*, Rev 1:17

AFTERWARD *following*
A his brother came forth, Ge 25:26
A she bore a daughter, Ge 30:21
a Moses and Aaron came, Ex 5:1

AKRABBIM
An "ascent" on the south of the Dead Sea, Nu 34:4
One border of Judah, Jos 15:3

ALABASTER *whitish stone*
stones and *a*, 1Ch 29:2
pillars of *a*, SS 5:15
brought an *a* vial, Lk 7:37

ALARM *(n) danger, warning*
when you blow an *a*, Nu 10:5
The *a* of war, Jer 4:19
shout of *a* at noon, Jer 20:16
a on My...mountain, Joel 2:1

ALARM *(v) frighten, warn*
he is not *a-ed*, Job 40:23
interpretation *a* you, Da 4:19
thoughts *a-ed* him, Da 5:6
being much *a-ed*, Ac 10:4
in no way *a-ed* by, Php 1:28

ALARMING *disturbing*
visions in my mind kept *a*, Da 4:5
visions in my mind kept *a*, Da 7:15
a me and my face grew, Da 7:28

ALAS *exclamation of despair*
A, this people has, Ex 32:31
A, my daughter!, Jdg 11:35
A, sinful nation, Is 1:4
A, O Lord, the great and, Da 9:4
in all the streets they say, '*A*!, Am 5:16

ALERT *(n) watch*
be on the *a*, Mt 24:42
be *a* and sober, 1Th 5:6

ALERT *(v) be watchful*
keeping *a* in it, Col 4:2
let us be *a*, 1Th 5:6

ALEXANDER
A member of the high-priestly family, Ac 4:6
——— A Jew in Ephesus, Ac 19:33, 34
——— An apostate condemned by Paul, 1Ti 1:19, 20

ALEXANDRIA
Men of, persecute Stephen, Ac 6:9
Paul sails in ship of, Ac 27:6

ALIEN *foreigner, stranger*
love for the *a*, Dt 10:19
give it to the *a*, Dt 14:21
Our houses to *a-s*, La 5:2
a-s in a foreign land, Ac 7:6
no longer...*a-s*, Eph 2:19
he lived as an *a*, Heb 11:9
I urge you as *a-s*, 1Pe 2:11

ALIENATE *estrange*
Or I shall be *a-d*, Jer 6:8
a this choice *portion*, Eze 48:14
were formerly *a-d*, Col 1:21

ALIKE *equal; equally*
Darkness and light are *a*, Ps 139:12
wise man and the fool *a*, Ecc 2:16
baptized, men and women *a*, Ac 8:12

ALIVE
Is your father still *a*, Ge 43:7
down *a* to Sheol, Nu 16:33
go down *a* to Sheol, Ps 55:15
may keep *a* a heifer, Is 7:21
when He was...*a*, Mt 27:63
heard...He was *a*, Mk 16:11
presented Himself *a*, Ac 1:3
yet the spirit is *a*, Ro 8:10
all will be made *a*, 1Co 15:22
made us *a* together, Eph 2:5
a in the spirit, 1Pe 3:18
I am *a* forevermore, Rev 1:18

ALL THE DAYS OF HIS/YOUR/MY LIFE
a, and that your days, Dt 6:2
he shall read it *a*, Dt 17:19
they had revered Moses *a*, Jos 4:14
him to the LORD *a*, 1Sa 1:11
Samuel judged Israel *a*, 1Sa 7:15
and served Solomon *a*, 1Ki 4:21
I will make him ruler *a*, 1Ki 11:34
He commanded him *a*, 1Ki 15:5
presence regularly *a*, 2Ki 25:29
house of the LORD *a*, Ps 27:4

ALL THE EARTH
the cattle and over *a*, Ge 1:26
alive on the face of *a*, Ge 7:3
Judge of *a* deal justly?, Ge 18:25
famine was severe in *a*, Ge 41:57
My name through *a*, Ex 9:16
a will be filled with the, Nu 14:21
going the way of *a*, Jos 23:14
His judgments are in *a*, 1Ch 16:14
majestic is Your name in *a*, Ps 8:1
gone out through *a*, Ps 19:4
a fear the LORD, Ps 33:8
great King over *a*, Ps 47:2
Let Your glory be above *a*, Ps 57:5
Sing to the LORD, *a*, Ps 96:1
joyfully to the LORD, *a*, Ps 100:1
His judgments are in *a*, Ps 105:7
of His people from *a*, Is 25:8
Who is called the God of *a*, Is 54:5
a be silent before Him, Hab 2:20
LORD will be king over *a*, Zec 14:9
who dwell on the face of *a*, Lk 21:35
Spirits of God, sent out into *a*, Rev 5:6

ALL THE SAINTS
Olympas, and *a* who, Ro 16:15
a who are throughout, 2Co 1:1
A greet you, 2Co 13:13
and your love for *a*, Eph 1:15
comprehend with *a*, Eph 3:18
and petition for *a*, Eph 6:18
To *a* in Christ Jesus, Php 1:1
A greet you, Php 4:22
you have for *a*, Col 1:4
prayers of *a* on the golden, Rev 8:3

ALLEGIANCE *loyalty*
pledged *a* to King, 1Ch 29:24
he pledged his *a*, Eze 17:18

ALLIANCE *agreement*
formed a marriage *a*, 1Ki 3:1
after an *a* is made, Da 11:23

ALLIED *joined*
a...by marriage, 2Ch 18:1
throne of...*a*, Ps 94:20

ALLOT *apportion, divide*
only *a* it to Israel, Jos 13:6
a Him a portion, Is 53:12
a-ted to each...faith, Ro 12:3

ALLOTMENT *portion*
an *a* from Pharaoh, Ge 47:22
as a perpetual *a*, Nu 18:19
Jacob is the *a*, Dt 32:9
set apart the...*a*, Eze 48:20

ALLOW *permit*
not *a* the destroyer, Ex 12:23
whether his body *a-s*, Lv 15:3
a Your Holy One, Ps 16:10
Nor *a* Your Holy One, Ac 2:27
not be *a-ed* to live, Ac 22:22
a you to be tempted, 1Co 10:13
not *a* a woman, 1Ti 2:12

ALLOWANCE *allotment*
a was given him by, 2Ki 25:30
governor's food *a*, Ne 5:14
a regular *a* was given, Jer 52:34

ALMIGHTY *all-powerful*
I am God *A*, Ge 17:1
vision of the *A*, Nu 24:4
A has afflicted me, Ru 1:21
limits of the *A*, Job 11:7
A was yet with me, Job 29:5
destruction from...*A*, Joel 1:15
Lord God, the *A*, Rev 4:8
the *A*, reigns, Rev 19:6

ALMOND
a and plane trees, Ge 30:37
shaped like *a blossoms*, Ex 37:19
and it bore ripe *a-s*, Nu 17:8

ALMOST *nearly*
day was *a* gone, Jdg 19:11
My steps had *a* slipped, Ps 73:2
a destroyed me on earth, Ps 119:87
The night is *a* gone, Ro 13:12

ALMS *charity*
a to the *Jewish*, Ac 10:2
bring *a* to my nation, Ac 24:17

ALOES *fragrant trees*
a planted by the LORD, Nu 24:6
myrrh and *a*, Ps 45:8
myrrh, *a* and cinnamon, Pr 7:17
frankincense, myrrh and *a*, SS 4:14
mixture of myrrh and *a*, Jn 19:39

ALONE
So He let him *a*, Ex 4:26
Leave me *a*, for my, Job 7:16
not live on bread *a*, Mt 4:4
He was praying *a*, Lk 9:18
I am not *a in it*, Jn 8:16
receiving but you *a*, Php 4:15
and not by faith *a*, Jas 2:24

ALOOF *apart*
abhor me *and* stand *a*, Job 30:10
friends stand *a* from, Ps 38:11
and hold himself *a*, Gal 2:12

ALOUD *joyful, piercing*
crying *a* as she, 2Sa 13:19
read *a* from the book, Ne 13:1
I will cry *a*, Ps 77:1
Sing *a* with gladness, Jer 31:7
The king called *a*, Da 5:7

began to weep *a*, Ac 20:37

ALPHA
First letter of Gr. alphabet, Rev 1:8
Title of Jesus Christ, Rev 21:6
Expresses eternalness of God, Rev 22:13

ALREADY *prior to*
a laid at the root, Mt 3:10
with lust for her has *a*, Mt 5:28
that Elijah *a* came, Mt 17:12
whether He was *a* dead, Mk 15:44
wish it were *a* kindled, Lk 12:49
has been judged *a*, Jn 3:18
devil having *a* put into, Jn 13:2
You are *a* clean, Jn 15:3
You are *a* filled, 1Co 4:8
that I have *a* obtained, Php 3:12

ALTAR *place of sacrifice*
offerings on the *a*, Ge 8:20
Moses built an *a*, Ex 17:15
fire on the *a*, Lv 6:9
Gideon built an *a*, Jdg 6:24
erect an *a* to, 2Sa 24:18
go to the *a* of God, Ps 43:4
a-s may become waste, Eze 6:6
offering at the *a*, Mt 5:23
a that sanctifies, Mt 23:19
golden *a* of incense, Heb 9:4
we have an *a*, Heb 13:10
horns of the golden *a*, Rev 9:13

ALTOGETHER *completely*
fashioned and made me *a*, Job 10:8
they are righteous *a*, Ps 19:9
will be *a* destroyed, Ps 37:38
You are *a* beautiful, SS 4:7
speaking *a* for our sake, 1Co 9:10

ALWAYS *ever, forever*
fear the LORD...*a*, Dt 14:23
He will not *a* strive, Ps 103:9
fear of the LORD *a*, Pr 23:17
a loses his temper, Pr 29:11
will I *a* be angry, Is 57:16
I am with you *a*, Mt 28:20
you *a* have...poor, Mk 14:7
Rejoice in the Lord *a*, Php 4:4
a be with...Lord, 1Th 4:17
I will *a* be ready, 2Pe 1:12

AMALEK
Grandson of Esau, Ge 36:11, 12
A chief of Edom, Ge 36:16
First among nations, Nu 24:20

AMALEKITES
Destruction predicted, Ex 17:14; Dt 25:17–19
Defeated by Israel, Ex 17:8–13; Jdg 7:12–25; 1Sa 14:47, 48; 27:8, 9; 1Ch 4:42, 43
Overcome Israel, Nu 14:39–45; Jdg 3:13

AMASA
Commands Absalom's rebels, 2Sa 17:25
Made David's commander, 2Sa 19:13
Treacherously killed by Joab, 2Sa 20:9–12
Death avenged, 1Ki 2:28–34

AMAZED *astonished, astounded*
are *a* at His rebuke, Job 26:11
a at His teaching, Mk 1:22
heard Him were *a*, Lk 2:47
Do not be *a* that I said, Jn 3:7
were *a* and astonished, Ac 2:7
whole earth was *a*, Rev 13:3

AMAZEMENT *astonishment*
a came upon them, Lk 4:36
with wonder and *a*, Ac 3:10

AMAZIAH
King of Judah; kills his father's assassinators, 2Ki 14:1–6; 2Ch 25:1–4
Hires troops from Israel; is rebuked by a man of God; sends troops home, 2Ch 25:5–10
Defeats Edomites; worships their gods, 2Ch 25:11–16
Wars with Israel, 2Ki 14:8–14; 2Ch 25:17–24
Killed by conspirators, 2Ch 25:25–28

AMBASSADOR *envoy*
a-s of peace weep, Is 33:7
a-s for Christ, 2Co 5:20
an *a* in chains, Eph 6:20

AMBITION *design, intention*
out of selfish *a*, Php 1:17
a to lead a quiet, 1Th 4:11
jealousy...selfish *a*, Jas 3:14

AMBUSH *(n) cover, hiding place*
a for the city, Jos 8:2
rise from *your a*, Jos 8:7
Israel set men in *a*, Jdg 20:29
a...behind them, 2Ch 13:13
Place men in *a*, Jer 51:12

AMBUSH *(v) lie in wait*
going to *a* the city, Jos 8:4
a the innocent, Pr 1:11
a their own lives, Pr 1:18

AMEN *so be it*
people shall say, *A*, Dt 27:16
the LORD forever! *A*, Ps 89:52
glory forever...*A*, Php 4:20
the *A*, the faithful, Rev 3:14
A. Come, Lord Jesus, Rev 22:20

AMETHYST *purple quartz*
agate and an *a*, Ex 28:19
an agate, and an *a*, Ex 39:12
jacinth; the twelfth, *a*, Rev 21:20

AMMON
A nation fathered by Lot, Ge 19:36, 38

AMMONITES
Excluded from assembly for hostility to Israel, Dt 23:3–6
Propose cruel treaty; conquered by Saul, 1Sa 11:1–3, 11
Abuse David's ambassadors; conquered by his army, 2Sa 10:1–14
Harass postexilic Jews, Ne 4:3, 7, 8
Defeated by Israel and Judah, Jdg 11:4–33; 2Ch 20:1–25; 27:5, 6
Prophecies concerning, Ps 83:1–18; Jer 25:9–21; Eze 25:1–7; Am 1:13–15; Zep 2:9–11

AMNON
A son of David, 2Sa 3:2
Rapes his half sister, 2Sa 13:1–18
Killed by Absalom, 2Sa 13:19–29

AMON
King of Judah, 2Ki 21:18, 19
Follows evil, 2Ch 33:22, 23
Killed by conspiracy, 2Ki 21:23, 24
——— A governor of Samaria, 1Ki 22:10, 26

AMORITES
Defeated by Joshua, Jos 10:1–43
Not driven out of Canaan, Jdg 1:34–36
Put to forced labor under Solomon, 1Ki 9:20, 21

AMOS
A prophet of Israel, Am 1:1
Pronounces judgment against nations, Am 1:1–3, 15
Denounces Israel's sins, Am 4:1–7:9
Condemns Amaziah, the priest of Bethel, Am 7:10–17
Predicts Israel's downfall, Am 9:1–10
Foretells great blessings, Am 9:11–15

AMOUNT *measure*
daily *a* of bricks, Ex 5:19
a of your valuation, Lv 27:23
large *a* of bronze, 1Ch 18:8

AMPHIPOLIS
A city in Macedonia visited by Paul, Ac 17:1

AMRAM
Son of Kohath, Nu 3:17–19
The father of Aaron, Moses and Miriam, Ex 6:18–20; 1Ch 6:3

ANAKIM
A race of giants; very strong, Nu 13:28–33; Dt 2:10, 11, 21
Defeated
by Joshua, Jos 10:36–39; 11:21
by Caleb, Jos 14:6–15

ANANIAS
Disciple at Jerusalem; slain for lying to God, Ac 5:1–11
——— A Christian disciple at Damascus, Ac 9:10–19; 22:12–16
——— A Jewish high priest, Ac 23:1–5

ANATHOTH
A Levitical city in Benjamin, Jos 21:18
Jeremiah's birthplace; he buys property there, Jer 1:1; 32:6–15
To be invaded by Assyria, Is 10:30

ANCESTORS *forefathers*
blessings of my *a*, Ge 49:26
the *a* have set, Dt 19:14
iniquities of their *a*, Jer 11:10

ANCHOR
they weighed *a*, Ac 27:13
they cast four *a-s*, Ac 27:29
an *a* of the soul, Heb 6:19

ANCIENT *aged, old*
of the *a* mountains, Dt 33:15
the records are *a*, 1Ch 4:22
keep to the *a* path, Job 22:15
O *a* doors, Ps 24:9
A of Days, Da 7:9
the *a-s* were told, Mt 5:21
from *a* generations, Ac 15:21

not spare the *a* world, 2Pe 2:5

ANDREW
A disciple of John the Baptist, then of Christ, Mt 4:18, 19; Jn 1:40–42
Enrolled among the Twelve, Mt 10:2
Mentioned, Mk 13:3, 4; Jn 6:8, 9; 12:20–22; Ac 1:13

ANGEL *divine messenger*
send His *a* before, Ge 24:7
a-s…were ascending, Ge 28:12
an *a* to Jerusalem, 1Ch 21:15
bread of *a-s*, Ps 78:25
Praise Him, all His *a-s*, Ps 148:2
a of His presence, Is 63:9
a who was speaking, Zec 4:4
command His *a-s*, Mt 4:6
a Gabriel was sent, Lk 1:26
they are like *a-s*, Lk 20:36
two *a-s* in white, Jn 20:12
like the face of an *a*, Ac 6:15
as an *a* of light, 2Co 11:14
worship of the *a-s*, Col 2:18
entertained *a-s*, Heb 13:2
God did not spare *a-s*, 2Pe 2:4
a of the church, Rev 2:1

ANGEL OF GOD
See ANGEL OF THE LORD
a called to Hagar from, Ge 21:17
a said to me in the dream, Ge 31:11
a, who had been going, Ex 14:19
appearance of the *a*, Jdg 13:6
the *a* came again, Jdg 13:9
the wisdom of the *a*, 2Sa 14:20
king is like the *a*, 2Sa 19:27
clearly saw in a vision an *a*, Ac 10:3
received me as an *a*, Gal 4:14

ANGEL OF THE LORD
See ANGEL OF GOD
a found her by a spring, Ge 16:7
a called to him from, Ge 22:11
a appeared to him, Ex 3:2
a took his stand in, Nu 22:22
a came up from Gilgal, Jdg 2:1
a came and sat, Jdg 6:11
a appeared to the, Jdg 13:3
a was by the threshing, 2Sa 24:16
a said to Elijah, 2Ki 1:3
a went out and struck, 2Ki 19:35
a encamps around, Ps 34:7
With the *a* pursuing them, Ps 35:6
standing before the *a*, Zec 3:1
a appeared to him, Mt 1:20
a appeared to Joseph, Mt 2:13
a descended from heaven, Mt 28:2
a went down at certain, Jn 5:4
a opened the gates, Ac 5:19
a spoke to Philip, Ac 8:26
a suddenly appeared, Ac 12:7
a struck him because, Ac 12:23

ANGELIC *of angels*
a watcher, a holy one, Da 4:13
by the decree of the *a*, Da 4:17
they revile *a* majesties, 2Pe 2:10
and revile *a* majesties, Jude 1:8

ANGER *indignation, wrath*
My *a* will be kindled, Ex 22:24
Moses' *a* burned, Ex 32:19
from His burning *a*, Dt 13:17
a with their idols, 1Ki 16:13
not turn back His *a*, Job 9:13
not rebuke me in Your *a*, Ps 6:1
a is but for a moment, Ps 30:5
He who is slow to *a*, Pr 14:29
a man *given* to *a*, Pr 22:24
a of the LORD, Is 5:25
sun go down…*a*, Eph 4:26
put…aside: *a*, Col 3:8
slow to *a*, Jas 1:19

ANGER OF THE LORD
a burned against Moses, Ex 4:14
a was kindled greatly, Nu 11:10
a your God will be kindled, Dt 6:15
a burned against the sons, Jos 7:1
a burned against Israel, Jdg 2:20
through the *a* this came, 2Ki 24:20
fierce *a* has not turned, Jer 4:8

ANGRY *enraged, indignant*
Why are you *a*, Ge 4:6
king became very *a*, Est 1:12
that He not become *a*, Ps 2:12
a man stirs up strife, Pr 29:22
a beyond measure, Is 64:9
and *a* no more, Eze 16:42
a with his brother, Mt 5:22
Be *a*…do not sin, Eph 4:26
a with this generation, Heb 3:10

ANGUISH *distress, pain*
writhed in great *a*, Est 4:4
My heart is in *a*, Ps 55:4
land of distress and *a*, Is 30:6
A has seized us, Jer 6:24
and *a* of heart, 2Co 2:4

ANIMAL *beast, creature*
from man to *a-s*, Ge 6:7
lies with an *a*, Ex 22:19
the fat of the *a*, Lv 7:25
wild *a-s* of the field, Jer 27:6
a blemished *a*, Mal 1:14
four-footed *a-s*, Ac 10:12
like unreasoning *a-s*, 2Pe 2:12

ANNA
Aged prophetess, Lk 2:36–38

ANNAS
A Jewish high priest, Lk 3:2
Christ appeared before, Jn 18:12–24
Peter and John appeared before, Ac 4:6

ANNIHILATE *destroy*
to *a* all the Jews, Est 3:13
My enemy *a-d* them, La 2:22
to destroy and *a*, Da 11:44
let it be *a-d*, Zec 11:9

ANNOUNCE *proclaim*
Who *a-s* peace, Is 52:7
I will *a* My words, Jer 18:2
a-ing to…disciples, Jn 20:18
a-d…the Righteous, Ac 7:52

ANNUL *dismiss, make void*
he shall *a* her vow, Nu 30:8
husband has *a-led*, Nu 30:12
not *a* Your covenant, Jer 14:21
a-s one of the least, Mt 5:19

ANOINT *(v) sprinkle oil upon*
a them and ordain, Ex 28:41
a Aaron and his sons, Ex 30:30
LORD *a-ed* you king, 1Sa 15:17
a-ed my head with oil, Ps 23:5
a the most holy *place*, Da 9:24
has *a-ed* My body, Mk 14:8
did not *a* My head, Lk 7:46
and *a-ed* my eyes, Jn 9:11
a-ed…feet of Jesus, Jn 12:3
a-ed Him…Holy Spirit, Ac 10:38
a-ing him with oil, Jas 5:14

ANOINTED *(adj) consecrated*
if the *a* priest sins, Lv 4:3
not touch My *a*, 1Ch 16:22
a cherub who, Eze 28:14
the two *a* ones, Zec 4:14

ANOINTED *(n) consecrated one*
walk before My *a*, 1Sa 2:35
he is the LORD's *a*, 1Sa 24:10
against His *A*, Ps 2:2

ANOINTING *(adj) consecration*
spices for the *a* oil, Ex 25:6
shall be a holy *a* oil, Ex 30:31
for the LORD's *a* oil, Lv 10:7

ANOINTING *(n) consecration*
a will qualify them, Ex 40:15
a from the Holy, 1Jn 2:20
His *a* teaches you, 1Jn 2:27

ANOTHER *additional; distinct one*
a offspring in place, Ge 4:25
waited yet *a* seven days, Ge 8:10
Have you *a* brother?, Ge 43:7
Let me sow and *a* eat, Job 31:8
puts down one and exalts *a*, Ps 75:7
Let *a* take his office, Ps 109:8
glory I will not give to *a*, Is 48:11
own country by *a* way, Mt 2:12
that you love one *a*, Jn 13:34
will give you *a* Helper, Jn 14:16
Let a man take his office, Ac 1:20
to *a* the word of, 1Co 12:8
glory of the earthly is *a*, 1Co 15:40
are members of one *a*, Eph 4:25
speaking to one *a* in, Eph 5:19
regard one *a*, Php 2:3
Do not lie to one *a*, Col 3:9
admonishing one *a*, Col 3:16
comfort one *a*., 1Th 4:18
build up one *a*, 1Th 5:11
encourage one *a*, Heb 3:13
your sins to one *a*, Jas 5:16
love one *a* from the heart, 1Pe 1:22

ANSWER *(n) response*
consider what *a* I, 1Ch 21:12
the king sent an *a*, Ezr 4:17
Who gives a right *a*, Pr 24:26
amazed at…His *a-s*, Lk 2:47

ANSWER *(v) respond*
anyone who will *a* you, Job 5:1
The LORD *a-ed* me, Ps 118:5
Jesus *a-ing* said, Mt 3:15
who *a-s* back to God, Ro 9:20

ANT *insect*
to the *a*, O sluggard, Pr 6:6
a-s are not a strong, Pr 30:25

ANTELOPE *animal*
Like an *a* in a net, Is 51:20

ANTICHRIST *foe of Christ*
a-s have appeared, 1Jn 2:18
This is the *a*, 1Jn 2:22
the *spirit* of the *a*, 1Jn 4:3
deceiver and the *a*, 2Jn 7

ANTIMONY *a silver metal*
stones of *a* and, 1Ch 29:2
I will set your stones in *a*, Is 54:11

ANTIOCH
In Syria:
First Gentile church established, Ac 11:19–21
Disciples first called "Christians" in, Ac 11:26
Church commissions Paul, Ac 13:1–4; 15:35–41
Church troubled by Judaizers, Ac 15:1–4; Gal 2:11–21
——— In Pisidia:
Paul visits; Jews reject the gospel, Ac 13:14, 42–51

ANTIPATRIS
A city between Jerusalem and Caesarea, Ac 23:31

ANXIETY *sorrow*
a because of my sin, Ps 38:18
There is *a* by the sea, Jer 49:23
casting all your *a*, 1Pe 5:7

ANXIOUS *concern, worry*
and will become *a* for us, 1Sa 9:5
not be *a* in…drought, Jer 17:8
my spirit is *a* to, Da 2:3
Be *a* for nothing, Php 4:6

APART *separate*
So they set *a* Kedesh, Jos 20:7
tear their fetters *a*, Ps 2:3
a from your Father, Mt 10:29
a from Him nothing, Jn 1:3
a from Me you can, Jn 15:5
faith *a* from works, Ro 3:28

APHEK
A town in the Plain of Sharon, Jos 12:18
Site of Philistine camp, 1Sa 4:1; 29:1
——— A city in Jezreel, 1Ki 20:26–30
Syria's defeat prophesied here, 2Ki 13:14–19

APOLLONIA
A town between Amphipolis and Thessalonica, Ac 17:1

APOLLOS
An Alexandrian Jew; instructed by Aquila and Priscilla and sent to Achaia, Ac 18:24–28
Referred to as having ministered in Corinth, 1Co 1:12; 3:4, 22; 4:6; 16:12

APOLLYON
Angel of the bottomless pit, Rev 9:11

APOSTASY *faithlessness*
a-ies are numerous, Jer 5:6
Turned away in…*a*, Jer 8:5
I will heal their *a*, Hos 14:4
unless the *a* comes, 2Th 2:3

APOSTLE *sent with authority*
the twelve *a-s*, Mt 10:2
named as *a-s*, Lk 6:13
called *as an a*, Ro 1:1
an *a* of Gentiles, Ro 11:13
not fit to be called an *a*, 1Co 15:9
men are false *a-s*, 2Co 11:13
He gave some *as a-s*, Eph 4:11
Jesus, the *A* and, Heb 3:1
a-s of the Lamb, Rev 21:14

APOSTLESHIP *office of apostle*
received grace and *a*, Ro 1:5
seal of my *a*, 1Co 9:2
Peter in *his a* to, Gal 2:8

APPALLED *dismayed*
my beard, and sat down *a*, Ezr 9:3
upright will be *a*, Job 17:8
My heart is *a* within, Ps 143:4
Be *a*, O heavens, Jer 2:12
many peoples *a* at you, Eze 32:10
was *a* for a while, Da 4:19

APPAREL *clothing, garment*
of gold on your *a*, 2Sa 1:24
majestic in His *a*, Is 63:1
put on his royal *a*, Ac 12:21

APPEAL *ask, entreat*
standing and *a-ing*, Ac 16:9
I *a* to Caesar, Ac 25:11
Paul *a-ed* to be held, Ac 25:21
a-ed to…Emperor, Ac 25:25
a to *him* as a father, 1Ti 5:1
love's sake I…*a*, Phm 9

APPEAR *become visible*
LORD *a-ed* to Abram, Ge 12:7
glory of the LORD *a-ed*, Ex 16:10
and *a-ed* to many, Mt 27:53
first *a-ed* to Mary, Mk 16:9
who, *a-ing* in glory, Lk 9:31
a-ed to them tongues, Ac 2:3
we must all *a* before, 2Co 5:10
a-ing of the glory, Titus 2:13
will *a* a second time, Heb 9:28
Chief Shepherd *a-s*, 1Pe 5:4
not *a-ed* as yet, 1Jn 3:2

APPEARANCE *countenance*
handsome in…*a*, Ge 39:6
at the outward *a*, 1Sa 16:7
a is blacker than soot, La 4:8
lapis lazuli in *a*, Eze 1:26
they neglect their *a*, Mt 6:16
judge according to *a*, Jn 7:24
a of His coming, 2Th 2:8

APPEASE *moderate, mollify*
I will *a* him, Ge 32:20
wise man will *a* it, Pr 16:14
have *a-d* My wrath, Zec 6:8

APPETITE *desire, hunger*
our *a* is gone, Nu 11:6
a of the young lions, Job 38:39
man of *great a*, Pr 23:2
a is not satisfied, Ecc 6:7
enlarges his *a* like, Hab 2:5
whose god is *their a*, Php 3:19

APPIUS
A town about 40 miles south of Rome where Christians came to meet Paul, Ac 28:15

APPLE *fruit*
as the *a* of the eye, Ps 17:8
Like a-s of gold, Pr 25:11
Refresh me with *a-s*, SS 2:5
touches the *a* of His, Zec 2:8

APPLY *employ diligently*
a-ed myself to the work, Ne 5:16
A your heart to discipline, Pr 23:12
seen and *a-ed* my mind, Ecc 8:9
a-ed the clay to his eyes, Jn 9:6
figuratively *a-ed* to myself, 1Co 4:6
a-ing all diligence, 2Pe 1:5

APPOINT *assign, commission*
shall *a as a penalty*, Ex 21:23
who *a-ed* Moses, 1Sa 12:6
to *a* their relatives, 1Ch 15:16
a magistrates and, Ezr 7:25
there is a harvest *a-ed*, Hos 6:11
a-ed elders for them, Ac 14:23
For the Law *a-s* men, Heb 7:28

APPOINTED FEASTS
gladness and in your *a*, Nu 10:10
on the *a* of the LORD, 2Ch 2:4
festivals and your *a*, Is 1:14
no one comes to the *a*, La 1:4
My statutes in all My *a*, Eze 44:24
who grieve about the *a*, Zep 3:18

APPOINTED TIME
At the *a* I will return t, Ge 18:14
in his old age, at the *a*, Ge 21:2
the Passover at its *a*., Nu 9:2
aroma to Me, at their *a*, Nu 28:2
according to the *a* set by, 1Sa 13:8
When I select an *a*, Ps 75:2
For the *a* has come., Ps 102:13
an *a* for everything, Ecc 3:1
pertains to the *a* of the end, Da 8:19
know when the *a* will., Mk 13:33

APPORTION *distribute*
a the inheritance, Nu 34:29
a this land, Jos 13:7
He *a-s* our fields, Mic 2:4

APPROACH *come near*
a-ed the thick cloud, Ex 20:21
shall not *a* a woman, Lv 18:19
with me will *a* the city, Jos 8:5
it shall not *a* you, Ps 91:7
a-ing for His ascension, Lk 9:51
he *a-ed* Jesus to kiss Him, Lk 22:47

APPROPRIATE *suitable*
blessing *a* to him, Ge 49:28
eat at the *a* time, Ecc 10:17
a to repentance, Ac 26:20

APPROVAL *consent*
loved the *a* of men, Jn 12:43
give hearty *a* to, Ro 1:32
men of old gained *a*, Heb 11:2

APPROVE *accept, attest*
the Lord does not *a*, La 3:36
too pure to *a* evil, Hab 1:13
standing by *a-ing*, Ac 22:20

and *a-d* by men, Ro 14:18
present yourself *a-d*, 2Ti 2:15

AQUILA
Paul's host in Corinth, Ac 18:2, 3
Travels to Syria and Ephesus with Paul, Ac 18:18, 19
Instructs Apollos, Ac 18:24–26
Esteemed by Paul, Ro 16:3, 4

AR
A chief Moabite city, Nu 21:15
On Israel's route, Dt 2:18
Destroyed by Sihon, Nu 21:28
Destroyed by God, Is 15:1

ARAB
Town in Judah, Jos 15:52
Ethnic identity, 1Ki 10:15; Ne 2:19; Is 13:20

ARABAH
Desert steppe, Is 35:1, 6; Jer 52:7
Jordan rift valley, Dt 1:1; Jos 3:17
Dead Sea, Jos 3:16; 2Ki 14:25

ARABIA
Pays tribute to Solomon, 1Ki 10:14, 15
Plunders Jerusalem, 2Ch 21:16, 17
Defeated by Uzziah, 2Ch 26:1, 7
Denounced by prophets, Is 21:13–17

ARAMAIC
Semitic language, 2Ki 18:26; Ezr 4:7; Is 36:11; Da 2:4

ARARAT
Site of ark's landing, Ge 8:4
Assassins flee to, 2Ki 19:37; Is 37:38

ARAUNAH
See also ornan
A Jebusite, 2Sa 24:16–25

ARCHANGEL
voice of *the a*, 1Th 4:16
But Michael the *a*, Jude 9

ARCHELAUS
Son of Herod the Great, Mt 2:22

ARCHER *bowman*
the *a-s* hit him, 1Sa 31:3
a-s shot King Josiah, 2Ch 35:23
a-s equipped with bows, Ps 78:9
an *a* who wounds, Pr 26:10

AREOPAGUS
Paul preaches at, Ac 17:18–34

ARGUE *dispute, question*
I will *a* my ways, Job 13:15
hastily to *a your case*, Pr 25:8
Pharisees…*a* with, Mk 8:11
scribes *a-ing* with, Mk 9:14
a-ing with the…*Jews*, Ac 9:29

ARGUMENT *disagreement*
Please hear my *a*, Job 13:6
mouth are no *a-s*, Ps 38:14
a started among them, Lk 9:46

ARIEL
Ezra's friend, Ezr 8:15–17
——— Name applied to Jerusalem, Is 29:1, 2, 7

ARIMATHEA
Joseph from here was a disciple of Jesus, Mt 27:57; Mk 15:43; Lk 23:51; Jn 19:38
He asked for the body of Jesus, Mt 27:57–60

ARISE *rise, stand*
A, walk about the, Ge 13:17
will *a* and play, Dt 31:16
you have *a-n* early, 1Sa 29:10
when God *a-s*, Job 31:14
A, O LORD; save me, Ps 3:7
Though war *a*, Ps 27:3
A, my darling, SS 2:13
false prophets will *a*, Mt 24:11
arose from the dead, Ac 10:41
a from the dead, Eph 5:14

ARISTARCHUS
A Macedonian Christian, Ac 19:29
Accompanies Paul, Ac 20:1, 4
Imprisoned with Paul, Col 4:10

ARK *chest, vessel*
a of gopher wood, Ge 6:14
into the *a* to Noah, Ge 7:9
a of acacia wood, Ex 37:1
a of the covenant, Jos 4:7
Noah entered the *a*, Mt 24:38
a of His covenant, Rev 11:19

ARM *(n) part of body*
the everlasting *a-s*, Dt 33:27
a without strength, Job 26:2
His holy *a* have gained, Ps 98:1
a seal on your *a*, SS 8:6
be carried in the *a-s*, Is 60:4
took…in His *a-s*, Mk 10:16
with an uplifted *a*, Ac 13:17

ARM *(v) mobilize*
A men from among, Nu 31:3
a-ed for battle, Nu 32:29
a-ed with iron, 2Sa 23:7
a yourselves also, 1Pe 4:1

ARMED *(adj) mobilized*
the *a* men went, Jos 6:13
their *a* camps, 1Sa 28:1
So the *a* men left, 2Ch 28:14
like an *a* man, Pr 6:11

ARMOR *protective device*
a joint of the *a*, 1Ki 22:34
strip off his outer *a*, Job 41:13
all his *a* on which, Lk 11:22
put on…*a* of light, Ro 13:12
full *a* of God, Eph 6:11

ARMY *host, war*
not go out with the *a*, Dt 24:5
like the *a* of God, 1Ch 12:22
a ready for battle, 2Ch 26:11
officers of the *a*, Ne 2:9
forth with our *a-ies*, Ps 60:10
exceedingly great *a*, Eze 37:10
a-ies…in heaven, Rev 19:14
and against His *a*, Rev 19:19

ARNON
Boundary between Moab and Ammon, Nu 21:13, 26
Border of Reuben, Dt 3:12, 16
Ammonites reminded of, Jdg 11:18–26

AROER
A town in east Jordan; rebuilt by Gadites, Nu 32:34; Dt 2:36
Assigned to Reuben, Dt 3:12
Ruled by Amorites, Jos 12:2; 13:9, 10, 16

AROMA *odor*
the soothing *a*, Ge 8:21
his *a* has not changed, Jer 48:11
through us…sweet *a*, 2Co 2:14
a from life to life, 2Co 2:16
as a fragrant *a*, Eph 5:2

AROUSE *raise, stir*
A Yourself to help me, Ps 59:4
a-s for you the spirits, Is 14:9
a-d one from the north, Is 41:25
He will *a His* zeal, Is 42:13
LORD has *a-d* the spirit, Jer 51:11

ARPACHSHAD
A son of Shem, Ge 10:22, 24
Born two years after the flood, Ge 11:10–13
An ancestor of Christ, Lk 3:36

ARRANGE *set in order*
a what belongs on it, Ex 40:4
shall *a* the pieces, Lv 1:8
he *a-d* the wood, 1Ki 18:33
for so he had *a-d* it, Ac 20:13

ARRAY *(n) arrangement, order*
went up in martial *a*, Ex 13:18
in battle *a*, Jos 4:12
Worship…in holy *a*, 1Ch 16:29
holy *a*, from the womb, Ps 110:3

ARRAY *(v) adorn, clothe*
Israel *a-ed* for battle, Jdg 20:20
let them *a* the man, Est 6:9
A yourselves before, Job 33:5

ARREST *restrain*
he *a-ed* Jeremiah, Jer 37:13
Herod had John *a-ed*, Mt 14:3
and clubs to *a* Me, Mt 26:55
proceeded to *a* Peter, Ac 12:3

ARRIVE *come*
time *a-ed* when the saints, Da 7:22
your accusers *a* also, Ac 23:35
When I *a*, whomever, 1Co 16:3

ARROGANCE *pride*
your *a* has come, 2Ki 19:28
Pride and *a* and, Pr 8:13
a of the proud, Is 13:11
a, pride, and fury, Is 16:6
a of your heart, Jer 49:16
you boast in your *a*, Jas 4:16

ARROGANT *proud*
a men have risen up, Ps 86:14
But a fool is *a*, Pr 14:16
a toward the LORD, Jer 48:26
Knowledge makes *a*, 1Co 8:1
boastful, *a*, revilers, 2Ti 3:2
speaking…*a words*, 2Pe 2:18

ARROW *dart, missile*
shot an *a* past him, 1Sa 20:36
a-s of the Almighty, Job 6:4
make ready their *a*, Ps 11:2
broke the flaming *a-s*, Ps 76:3
sword and a sharp *a*, Pr 25:18
tongue is a deadly *a*, Jer 9:8
a-s of the evil *one*, Eph 6:16

ART *craft*
with their secret *a-s*, Ex 7:22
the perfumers' *a*, 2Ch 16:14

ARTAXERXES
Artaxerxes I, king of Persia (465–425 B.C.), authorizes Ezra's mission to Jerusalem, Ezr 7:1–28
Temporarily halts rebuilding program at Jerusalem, Ezr 4:7–23
Authorizes Nehemiah's mission, Ne 2:1–10
Permits Nehemiah to return, Ne 13:6

ARTEMAS
Sent by Paul to Titus, Titus 3:12

ARTICLE *object, vessel*
a-s of silver, Ge 24:53
any wooden *a*, Lv 11:32
of every precious *a*, Hos 13:15
every *a* of ivory, Rev 18:12

AS IT IS WRITTEN
a in the book of the law of, Jos 8:31
a in this book of the, 2Ki 23:21
a in the law of Moses, Ezr 3:2
the Feast of Booths, *a*, Ezr 3:4
LORD our God, *a*, Ne 10:34
just *a* of Him, Mt 26:24
A in Isaiah the prophet, Mk 1:2
a in the Law of the Lord, Lk 2:23
a, 'He gave them bread, Jn 6:31
a in the second Psalm, Ac 13:33
a, "But the righteous man, Ro 1:17
a, "There is none righteous, Ro 3:10
Israel will be saved; just *a*, Ro 11:26
a, "He scattered abroad, 2Co 9:9

ASA
Third king of Judah; restores true worship, 1Ki 15:8–15; 2Ch 14–15
Hires Ben-hadad against Baasha; rebuked by a prophet, 1Ki 15:16–22; 2Ch 16:1–10
Diseased, seeks physicians rather than the Lord, 2Ch 16:12
Death and burial, 2Ch 16:13, 14

ASAHEL
David's nephew; captain in his army; noted for valor, 2Sa 2:18; 23:24; 1Ch 2:16; 27:7
Killed by Abner, 2Sa 2:19–23
Avenged by Joab, 2Sa 3:27, 30

ASAPH
A Levite choir leader under David and Solomon, 1Ch 15:16–19; 16:1–7; 2Ch 5:6, 12
Twelve Psalms assigned to, 2Ch 29:30; Ps 50; 73–83

ASCEND *go up*
a into the hill, Ps 24:3
If I *a* to heaven, Ps 139:8
Who has *a-ed* into, Pr 30:4
breath of man *a-s*, Ecc 3:21
has *a-ed* into heaven, Jn 3:13
Son of Man *a-ing*, Jn 6:62
a-ed to the Father, Jn 20:17
who *a-ed* far above, Eph 4:10

ASCENSION
approaching for His *a*, Lk 9:51

ASCENT *hill, rise*
by the *a* of Heres, Jdg 8:13
a of the...Olives, 2Sa 15:30
Song of *A-s*, Ps 120–134

ASCRIBE *attribute*
have *a-d* to David, 1Sa 18:8
A to the LORD, 1Ch 16:28
a righteousness to, Job 36:3

ASENATH
Daughter of Potiphera and wife of Joseph, Ge 41:45
Mother of Manasseh and Ephraim, Ge 41:50–52; 46:20

ASH
but dust and *a-es*, Ge 18:27
from the *a* heap, 1Sa 2:8
a-es on her head, 2Sa 13:19
proverbs of *a-es*, Job 13:12
repent in dust and *a-es*, Job 42:6
garland instead of *a-es*, Is 61:3
sackcloth and *a-es*, Lk 10:13
a-es of a heifer, Heb 9:13

ASHAMED *embarrassed*
naked and were not *a*, Ge 2:25
Let me never be *a*, Ps 71:1
a of Me...My words, Mk 8:38
a...when He comes, Lk 9:26
not *a* of the gospel, Ro 1:16
a of the testimony, 2Ti 1:8
God is not *a*, Heb 11:16
he is not to be *a*, 1Pe 4:16

ASHDOD
One of five Philistine cities, Jos 13:3
Seat of Dagon worship, 1Sa 5:1–8
Opposes Nehemiah, Ne 4:7
Women of, marry Jews, Ne 13:23, 24
Called Azotus, Ac 8:40

ASHER
Jacob's second son by Zilpah, Ge 30:12, 13
Goes to Egypt with Jacob, Ge 46:8, 17
Blessed by Jacob, Ge 49:20
——— Tribe of:
Census of, Nu 1:41; 26:47
Slow to fight against Canaanites, Jdg 1:31, 32; 5:17
Among Gideon's army, Jdg 6:35; 7:23
A godly remnant among, 2Ch 30:11

ASHERAH
The female counterpart of Baal, Jdg 3:7; 1Ki 18:19
Image of, erected by Manasseh in the temple, 2Ki 21:7
Vessels of, destroyed by Josiah, 2Ki 23:4
——— Translated "wooden images," idols used in the worship of Asherah, Ex 34:13; Dt 12:3

ASHKELON
One of five Philistine cities, Jos 13:3; Jer 47:5, 7
Captured by Judah, Jdg 1:18
Men of, killed by Samson, Jdg 14:19, 20
Repossessed by Philistines, 1Sa 6:17; 2Sa 1:20
Doom of, pronounced by the prophets, Jer 47:5, 7; Am 1:8; Zep 2:4, 7; Zec 9:5

ASHTAROTH
A city in Bashan; residence of King Og, Dt 1:4; Jos 12:4
Captured by Israel, Jos 9:10
——— A general designation of the Canaanite female deities, 1Sa 7:3, 4; 31:10

ASHTORETH
A mother-goddess worshiped by the Philistines, 1Sa 31:10
Israel ensnared by, Jdg 2:13; 10:6
Worshiped by Solomon, 1Ki 11:5, 33
Destroyed by Josiah, 2Ki 23:13

ASIA
Paul forbidden to preach in, Ac 16:6
Paul's later ministry in, Ac 19:1–26
Seven churches of, Rev 1:4, 11

ASIDE
See TURN ASIDE

ASK *appeal, beg, inquire*
whatever you *a*, Ru 3:11
Two things I *a-ed*, Pr 30:7
A a sign for yourself, Is 7:11
A rain from the LORD, Zec 10:1
Give to him who *a-s*, Mt 5:42
A, and it will be, Mt 7:7
a...believing, Mt 21:22
pray and *a*, believe, Mk 11:24
let him *a* of God, Jas 1:5

ASLEEP *death, rest*
sound *a*...exhausted, Jdg 4:21
not died, but is *a*, Mt 9:24
in the stern, *a*, Mk 4:38
Lazarus...fallen *a*, Jn 11:11
said this, he fell *a*, Ac 7:60
fallen *a* in Jesus, 1Th 4:14

ASSAIL *attack*
will you *a* a man, Ps 62:3
Whoever *a-s* you, Is 54:15
storm was *a-ing* us, Ac 27:20

ASSEMBLE *gather*
A the people to Me, Dt 4:10
David *a-d* all Israel, 1Ch 13:5
peoples may be *a-d*, Is 43:9
A...on the mountains, Amos 3:9
whole city *a-d* to, Ac 13:44
a-d to make war, Rev 19:19

ASSEMBLY *congregation*
holy *a* on the seventh, Ex 12:16
a before the rock, Nu 20:10
Or calls an *a*, Job 11:10
a of the righteous, Ps 1:5
proclaim a solemn *a*, Joel 2:15
the *a* was divided, Ac 23:7
general *a* and church, Heb 12:23
comes into your *a*, Jas 2:2

ASSERT *declare positively*
A-ing in pride and in, Is 9:9
a-ing that these things, Ac 24:9
Paul *a-ed* to be alive, Ac 25:19
have *a-ed* our authority, 1Th 2:6

ASSHUR
One of the sons of Shem; progenitor of the Assyrians, Ge 10:22; 1Ch 1:17
——— The chief god of the Assyrians; seen in names like Ashurbanipal (Osnapper), Ezr 4:10
——— A city in Assyria or the nation of Assyria, Nu 24:22, 24

ASSIGN *appoint*
a each of them to his work, Nu 4:19
a men by it to guard, Jos 10:18
grave was *a-ed* with wicked, Is 53:9
cut him in pieces and *a*, Mt 24:51
a-ing to each one his, Mk 13:34
Lord has *a-ed* to each one, 1Co 7:17

ASSIST *help, aid*
a their brothers in, Nu 8:26
office is to *a* the sons, 1Ch 23:28
if she has *a-ed* those, 1Ti 5:10
a those who are widows, 1Ti 5:16

ASSOCIATE *(n) colleague*
All my *a-s* abhor me, Job 19:19
high priest and…*a-s*, Ac 5:21

ASSOCIATE *(v) identify with*
shall they *a* with, 1Ki 11:2
a with adulterers, Ps 50:18
not *a* with a man, Pr 22:24
but *a* with the lowly, Ro 12:16
not *a* with him, 2Th 3:14

ASSOS
A seaport of Mysia in Asia to which Paul walked, Ac 20:13

ASSURANCE *confirmation*
no one has *a* of life, Job 24:22
a of understanding, Col 2:2
full *a* of hope, Heb 6:11
full *a* of faith, Heb 10:22
a of *things* hoped for, Heb 11:1

ASSURE *confirm*
kingdom will be *a-d*, Da 4:26
I *a* you before God, Gal 1:20
will *a* our heart, 1Jn 3:19

ASSYRIA
See also asshur
Founded by Nimrod, Ge 10:8–12; Mic 5:6
Agent of God's purposes, Is 7:17–20; 10:5, 6
Attacks and finally conquers Israel, 2Ki 15:19, 20, 29; 17:3–41
Invades and threatens Judah, 2Ki 18:13–37
Hezekiah prays for help against; army miraculously slain, 2Ki 19:1–35
Prophecies concerning, Nu 24:22–24; Is 10:12–19; 14:24, 25; 19:23–25; Hos 10:6; 11:5; Na 3:1–19

ASTONISHED *amazed*
will be *a* and hiss, 1Ki 9:8
a at His teaching, Mt 22:33
listeners were *a*, Mk 6:2
they were all *a*, Lk 1:63

ASTONISHMENT *amazement*
at one another in *a*, Ge 43:33
look at one another in *a*, Is 13:8
trembling and *a*, Mk 16:8
a and *began* glorifying, Lk 5:26

ASTOUNDED *astonished*
prophets will be *a*, Jer 4:9
a at the vision, Da 8:27
were completely *a*, Mk 5:42

ASTRAY *erring, wandering*
a like a lost sheep, Ps 119:176
leading *them a*, Is 9:16
like sheep have gone *a*, Is 53:6
led My people *a*, Jer 23:32
lead *a*…the elect, Mk 13:22
a from the faith, 1Ti 6:21
go *a* in their heart, Heb 3:10

ATHALIAH
Daughter of Ahab and Jezebel, 2Ki 8:18, 26; 2Ch 22:2, 3
Kills royal children; usurps throne, 2Ki 11:1–3; 2Ch 22:10, 11
Killed in priestly uprising, 2Ki 11:4–16; 2Ch 23:1–21

ATHENS
Paul preaches in, Ac 17:15–34
Paul resides in, 1Th 3:1

ATONEMENT *expiation*
by which *a* was made, Ex 29:33
shall make *a* for him, Lv 4:35
how can I make *a*, 2Sa 21:3
make *a* for iniquity, Da 9:24

ATONEMENT, DAY OF
See DAY OF ATONEMENT

ATTACK *(n) assault*
at the first *a*, 2Sa 17:9
king ready for the *a*, Job 15:24
joined in the *a*, Ac 24:9

ATTACK *(v) assault, fall upon*
that he will come and *a*, Ge 32:11
and *a-ed* the camp, Jdg 8:11
a the Philistines, 1Sa 23:2
it *a-ed* the plant, Jon 4:7
no man will *a* you, Ac 18:10

ATTAIN *acquire*
I cannot *a* to it, Ps 139:6
woman *a-s* honor, Pr 11:16
a-ed righteousness, Ro 9:30
a to the resurrection, Php 3:11

ATTALIA
A seaport of Pamphylia from which Paul sailed to Antioch, Ac 14:25

ATTEND *pay attention to*
a to your priesthood, Nu 18:7
thousands were *a-ing*, Da 7:10
who *a* regularly, 1Co 9:13
a to…business, 1Th 4:11
ears *a* to their prayer, 1Pe 3:12

ATTENDANT *helper, servant*
the *a* of Moses, Nu 11:28
king's *a-s*, who served, Est 2:2
a-s of…bridegroom, Mk 2:19

ATTENTION *heed, regard*
no *a* to false words, Ex 5:9
gives *a* to the word, Pr 16:20
pays *a* to falsehood, Pr 29:12
pay *a* to myths, 1Ti 1:4
a to the…reading, 1Ti 4:13

ATTENTIVE *mindful, observant*
Your ears *a* to the prayer, 2Ch 6:40
Your ear now be *a*, Ne 1:6
be *a* to the voice, Ps 130:2
your ear *a* to wisdom, Pr 2:2

ATTIRE *covering, dress*
in his military *a*, 2Sa 20:8
cupbearers…*a*, 2Ch 9:4
Him in holy *a*, 2Ch 20:21

ATTITUDE *frame of mind*
see your father's *a*, Ge 31:5
a of the righteous, Lk 1:17
Have this *a* in, Php 2:5
have a different *a*, Php 3:15

AUTHOR *source*
a of their salvation, Heb 2:10
a…perfecter of faith, Heb 12:2

AUTHORITY *power, right*
submit…to her *a*, Ge 16:9
put…your *a* on him, Nu 27:20
Who gave Him *a*, Job 34:13
a over…day of death, Ecc 8:8
as *one* having *a*, Mt 7:29
a on earth to forgive, Mt 9:6
All *a*…given to Me, Mt 28:18
Son of Man has *a*, Lk 5:24
no *a* except from God, Ro 13:1
majesty, dominion…*a*, Jude 25

AVEN
A name contemptuously applied to Bethel, Hos 10:5, 8
——— Valley in Syria, Am 1:5

AVENGE *revenge*
He will *a* the blood, Dt 32:43
the LORD *a* me, 1Sa 24:12
Shall I not *a* Myself, Jer 5:9
I will *a* their blood, Joel 3:21
a-ing our blood, Rev 6:10

AVENGER *revenger*
The blood *a* himself, Nu 35:19
otherwise the *a* of blood, Dt 19:6
a of their *evil* deeds, Ps 99:8
God, an *a* who brings, Ro 13:4
Lord is *the a*, 1Th 4:6

AVOID *refuse*
A it, do not pass by, Pr 4:15
a-ing…empty chatter, 1Ti 6:20

AWAIT *wait*
afflictions *a* me, Ac 20:23
a-ing…the revelation, 1Co 1:7
who eagerly *a* Him, Heb 9:28

AWAKE *be attentive, watch*
Your likeness when I *a*, Ps 17:15
dream when one *a-s*, Ps 73:20
arouse or *a-n my* love, SS 2:7
He *a-ns* My ear, Is 50:4

A, a, put on strength, Is 51:9
A, drunkards…weep, Joel 1:5
that I may *a-n* him, Jn 11:11
hour for you to *a-n,* Ro 13:11

AWAKEN *become active, stir*
The lad has not *a-ed,* 2Ki 4:31
I will *a* the dawn, Ps 57:8
do not arouse or *a,* SS 2:7
not arouse or *a,* SS 8:4
I may *a* him out of sleep, Jn 11:11
for you to *a* from sleep, Ro 13:11

AWARE *know, understand*
the lad was not *a,* 1Sa 20:39
Will you not be *a,* Is 43:19
But Jesus, *a of this,* Mt 12:15
I was *a* that power, Lk 8:46

AWE *fear, reverence*
stand in *a* of Him, Ps 33:8
in *a* of Your words, Ps 119:161
in *a* of My name, Mal 2:5
feeling a sense of *a,* Ac 2:43

AWESOME *fearful*
How *a* is this place, Ge 28:17
angel of God, very *a,* Jdg 13:6
great and *a* God, Ne 1:5
God is *a* majesty, Job 37:22
As *a* as an army, SS 6:4
a day of the LORD, Joel 2:31

AWOKE *became active, stirred*
Noah *a* from his wine, Ge 9:24
Solomon *a,* and behold, 1Ki 3:15
I *a,* for the LORD sustains, Ps 3:5
Lord *a* as *if from* sleep, Ps 78:65
Joseph *a* from his sleep, Mt 1:24
When the jailer *a,* Ac 16:27

AXE *cutting tool*
his *a,* and his hoe, 1Sa 13:20
hammer nor *a,* 1Ki 6:7
a head fell into, 2Ki 6:5
a is already laid, Lk 3:9

AZARIAH
A prophet who encourages King Asa, 2Ch 15:1–8
——— Son of King Jehoshaphat, 2Ch 21:2
——— King of Judah, 2Ki 15:1
——— A high priest who rebukes King Uzziah, 2Ch 26:16–20
——— Chief priest in the time of Hezekiah, 2Ch 31:9, 10
——— The Hebrew name of Abed-Nego, Da 1:7

AZEKAH
Camp of Goliath, 1Sa 17:1, 4, 17
Besieged by Nebuchadnezzar, Jer 34:7

AZMAVETH
A village near Jerusalem, Ne 12:29
Also called Beth Azmaveth, Ne 7:28

AZOTUS
A city which Philip the evangelist visited, Ac 8:40

B

BAAL
See BAALS
Deities of Canaanite polytheism, Jdg 10:10–14
The male god of the Phoenicians and Canaanites; the counterpart of the female Ashtaroth, 2Ki 23:5
Nature of the worship of, 1Ki 18:26, 28; 19:18; Ps 106:28; Jer 7:9; 19:5; Hos 9:10; 13:1, 2
Worshiped by Israelites, Nu 25:1–5; Jdg 2:11–14; 3:7; 6:28–32; 1Ki 16:31, 32; 2Ki 21:3; Jer 11:13; Hos 2:8
Ahaz makes images to, 2Ch 28:1–4
Overthrown by Elijah, 1Ki 18:17–40
by Josiah, 2Ki 23:4, 5
Denounced by prophets, Jer 19:4–6; Eze 16:1, 2, 20, 21
Historic retrospect, Ro 11:4

BAAL OF PEOR
A Moabite god; worshiped by Israelites, Nu 25:1–9

BAALAH
A town also known as Kirjath Jearim, Jos 15:9, 10

BAAL-PERAZIM
Site of David's victory over the Philistines, 2Sa 5:18–20
Same as Perazim, Is 28:21

BAALS
Deities of Canaanite polytheism, Jdg 10:10–14
Ensnare Israelites, Jdg 2:11–14; 3:7
Ahaz makes images to, 2Ch 28:1–4

BAAL-ZEBUB
A Philistine god at Ekron, 2Ki 1:2
Ahaziah inquires of, 2Ki 1:2, 6, 16
Also called Beelzebub, Mt 10:25; 12:24

BAANAH
A murderer of Ishbosheth, 2Sa 4:1–12

BAASHA
Usurps throne of Israel; his evil reign; wars with Judah, 1Ki 15:16–16:7

BABBLER *one who speaks nonsense*
this idle *b* wish to say?, Ac 17:18

BABBLING *nonsensical*
a *b* fool will be ruined, Pr 10:8
a *b* fool will be ruined, Pr 10:10

BABEL, TOWER OF
A huge brick structure intended to magnify man and preserve the unity of the race, Ge 11:1–4
Objectives of, thwarted by God, Ge 11:5–9

BABES *infants*
From the mouth of…*b,* Ps 8:2
abundance to their *b,* Ps 17:14

BABY *infant*
woe…who are nursing *b-ies,* Mt 24:19
b leaped…her womb, Lk 1:41
b wrapped in cloths, Lk 2:12
b as He lay, Lk 2:16
like newborn *b-ies,* 1Pe 2:2

BABYLON
Built by Nimrod; Tower of Babel, Ge 10:8–10; 11:1–9
Descriptions of, Is 13:19; 14:4; Jer 51:44; Da 4:30
Jews carried captive to, 2Ki 25:1–21; 2Ch 36:5–21
Inhabitants of, described, Is 47:1, 9–13; Jer 50:35–38; Da 5:1–3
Prophecies concerning, Is 13:1–22; Jer 21:1–7; 25:9–12; 27:5–8; 29:10; Jer 50:1–46; Da 2:31–38; 7:2–4
The prophetic city, Rev 14:8; 16:19; 17:1–18:24

BACK *part of body*
you shall see My *b,* Ex 33:23
turned his *b* to leave, 1Sa 10:9
law behind their *b-s,* Ne 9:26
my sins behind Your *b,* Is 38:17

BACKSLIDER *lapsed*
b in heart will have his fill, Pr 14:14

BACKWARD *back first*
walked *b* and covered, Ge 9:23
Eli fell off the seat *b,* 1Sa 4:18
the shadow turn *b* ten, 2Ki 20:10
drove His adversaries *b,* Ps 78:66
to shame and turned *b,* Ps 129:5
may go and stumble *b,* Is 28:13
You keep going *b,* Jer 15:6

BAD *evil, wrong*
b report of the land, Nu 13:32
basket had very *b* figs, Jer 24:2
if your eye is *b,* Mt 6:23
b tree bears *b* fruit, Mt 7:17
B company corrupts, 1Co 15:33

BAG *sack*
fill their *b-s,* Ge 42:25
in the shepherd's *b,* 1Sa 17:40
silver in two *b-s,* 2Ki 5:23
carrying *his b* of seed, Ps 126:6
b of…weights, Mic 6:11
b for *your* journey, Mt 10:10
Carry no money belt, no *b,* Lk 10:4

BAGGAGE *bags, supplies*
stayed with the *b,* 1Sa 25:13
prepare…yourself *b,* Eze 12:3

BAGPIPE *a reed instrument*
lyre, trigon, psaltery, *b* and, Da 3:5
lyre, trigon, psaltery and *b,* Da 3:15

BAKE *cook*
b-d unleavened bread, Ge 19:3
b-d food for Pharaoh, Ge 40:17
they *b-d* the dough, Ex 12:39
B what you will *b,* Ex 16:23
grain offering *b-d,* Lv 2:4
b twelve cakes, Lv 24:5
taste of cakes *b-d,* Nu 11:8
fire to *b* bread, Is 44:15

BAKER *cook*
b for the king, Ge 40:1
cooks and *b-s,* 1Sa 8:13
from the *b-s'* street, Jer 37:21
oven heated by the *b,* Hos 7:4

BALAAM
Sent by Balak to curse Israel, Nu 22:5–7; Jos 24:9
Hindered by talking donkey, Nu 22:22–35; 2Pe 2:16
Curse becomes a blessing, Dt 23:4, 5; Jos 24:10
Prophecies of, Nu 23:7–10, 18–24; 24:3–9, 15–24
NT references to, 2Pe 2:15, 16; Jude 11; Rev 2:14

BALAK
A Moabite king, Nu 22:4
Hires Balaam to curse Israel, Nu 22–24

BALANCE *scale*
shall have just *b-s*, Lv 19:36
b-s...with my calamity, Job 6:2
False *b* is an, Pr 11:1
mountains in a *b*, Is 40:12

BALD *hairless*
If...head becomes *b*, Lv 13:41
every head is *b*, Jer 48:37
head was made *b*, Eze 29:18

BALDHEAD *hairless*
mocked him...you *b*, 2Ki 2:23

BALM *aromatic ointment*
b and myrrh, Ge 37:25
a present, a little *b*, Ge 43:11
no *b* in Gilead, Jer 8:22
Gilead and obtain *b*, Jer 46:11
Bring *b* for her pain, Jer 51:8
honey, oil and *b*, Eze 27:17

BALSAM *aromatic gum*
tops of the *b* trees, 2Sa 5:24
like a bed of *b*, SS 5:13

BAN *set apart to God*
city...under the *b*, Jos 6:17
destroy...under the *b*, Jos 7:12
who violated the *b*, 1Ch 2:7
consign Jacob to the *b*, Is 43:28

BAND *bond; group*
b-s shall be of silver, Ex 27:10
skillfully woven *b*, Ex 28:8
saw a marauding *b*, 2Ki 13:21
b of destroying angels, Ps 78:49
b-s of the yoke, Is 58:6

BANDAGE *give medical aid*
has but He will *b* us, Hos 6:1
him and *b* up his wounds, Lk 10:34

BANISH *exile*
b-ed one will not, 2Sa 14:14
assemble the *b-ed*, Is 11:12
gaiety...is *b-ed*, Is 24:11
where I will *b* them, Eze 4:13

BANK *slope*
b of the Nile, Ge 41:3
reeds by the *b*, Ex 2:3
b of the river, Eze 47:7
herd rushed down...*b*, Lk 8:33

BANNER *flag, standard*
set up our *b-s*, Ps 20:5
b to those who fear, Ps 60:4
b over me is love, SS 2:4
as an army with *b-s*, SS 6:4

BANQUET *dinner, feast*
b lasting seven days, Est 1:5
brought me to *his b*, SS 2:4
lavish *b* for all, Is 25:6
place of honor at *b-s*, Mt 23:6
Herod...gave a *b*, Mk 6:21

BAPTISM *symbolic washing*
Sadducees coming...*b*, Mt 3:7
b of repentance, Mk 1:4
b with which I am, Mk 10:38
with the *b* of John, Lk 7:29
a *b* to undergo, Lk 12:50
through *b* into death, Ro 6:4
one faith, one *b*, Eph 4:5
buried with Him in *b*, Col 2:12

BAPTIST *Jesus' precursor*
in those days John the *B*, Mt 3:1
greater than John the *B*!, Mt 11:11
the head of John the *B*, Mt 14:8
say John the *B*, Mt 16:14
John the *B* appeared in, Mk 1:4
B has risen from the dead, Mk 6:14
The head of John the *B*, Mk 6:24
head of John the *B*, Mk 6:25
John the *B* has sent us, Lk 7:20
John the *B* has come eating, Lk 7:33
John the *B*, and others, Lk 9:19

BAPTIZE *washing*
b...Holy Spirit, Mt 3:11
tax collectors...*b-d*, Lk 3:12
Jesus was also *b-d*, Lk 3:21
sent me to *b* in water, Jn 1:33
b-ing more disciples, Jn 4:1
b-d with the Holy, Ac 1:5
each of you be *b-d*, Ac 2:38
he got up and was *b-d*, Ac 9:18
household...been *b-d*, Ac 16:15
John *b-d* with the, Ac 19:4
b-d into Christ Jesus, Ro 6:3
b-d into Moses, 1Co 10:2
b-d into one body, 1Co 12:13
b-d for the dead, 1Co 15:29

BAR *metal; block*
b-s of your yoke, Lv 26:13
a *b* of gold, Jos 7:21
like *b-s* of iron, Job 40:18
earth with its *b-s*, Jon 2:6

BARABBAS
A murderer released in place of Jesus, Mt 27:16–26; Ac 3:14, 15

BARAK
Defeats Jabin, Jdg 4:1–24
A man of faith, Heb 11:32

BARBARIAN *non-Hellenic*
obligation...to *b-s*, Ro 1:14
who speaks a *b*, 1Co 14:11
b, Scythian, slave, Col 3:11

BARE *(adj) barren, uncovered*
to cover *their b* flesh, Ex 28:42
he went to a *b* hill, Nu 23:3
strips the forests *b*, Ps 29:9
were naked and *b*, Eze 16:7

BARE *(v) expose, uncover*
foundations...laid *b*, Ps 18:15
b-d His holy arm, Is 52:10
foundation is laid *b*, Eze 13:14
open and laid *b*, Heb 4:13

BAREFOOT *without sandals*
priests walk *b*, Job 12:19
gone naked and *b*, Is 20:3

BARGAIN *negotiate; agreement*
Will the traders *b* over him?, Job 41:6
you are *b-ing* for time, Da 2:8
And they strike *b-s* with, Is 2:6
make a *b* with my master, Is 36:8

BAR-JESUS
See ELYMAS
A Jewish false prophet, Ac 13:6–12

BAR-JONAH
Surname of Simon (Peter), Mt 16:17

BARLEY *grain*
land of wheat and *b*, Dt 8:8
beginning...*b* harvest, Ru 1:22
stinkweed instead...*b*, Job 31:40
has five *b* loaves, Jn 6:9

BARN *farm building*
b-s are torn down, Joel 1:17
seed still in the *b*, Hag 2:19
wheat into the *b*, Mt 3:12
nor gather into *b-s*, Mt 6:26
tear down my *b-s*, Lk 12:18

BARNABAS
A disciple from Cyprus; gives property, Ac 4:36, 37
Supports Paul, Ac 9:27
Ministers in Antioch, Ac 11:22–30
Travels with Paul, Ac 12:25; 13–15
Breaks with Paul over John Mark, Ac 15:36–39

BARRACKS *living quarters*
be brought into the *b*, Ac 21:34
to be brought into the *b*, Ac 22:24
and bring him into the *b*, Ac 23:10

BARREN *childless, sterile*
Sarai was *b*, Ge 11:30
but Rachel was *b*, Ge 29:31
wrongs the *b* woman, Job 24:21
Shout...O *b* one, Is 54:1
Blessed are the *b*, Lk 23:29

BARSABAS
Nominated to replace Judas, Ac 1:23
Sent to Antioch, Ac 15:22

BARTHOLOMEW
Called Nathanael, Jn 1:45, 46
One of the twelve apostles, Mt 10:3; Ac 1:13

BARTIMAEUS
Blind beggar healed by Jesus, Mk 10:46–52

BARUCH
Son of Neriah, Jer 32:12, 13
Jeremiah's faithful friend and scribe, Jer 36:4–32

BARZILLAI
Supplies David with food, 2Sa 17:27–29

Age restrains him from following David, 2Sa 19:31–39

BASE *dishonorable*
no *b* thought, Dt 15:9
b things of…world, 1Co 1:28

BASHAN
Conquered by Israel, Nu 21:33–35
Assigned to Manasseh, Dt 3:13
Conquered by Hazael, king of Syria, 2Ki 10:32, 33

BASIN *bowl, vessel*
blood…in the *b*, Ex 12:22
b-s…of pure gold, 1Ch 28:17
a *sacrificial b*, Zec 9:15
water into the *b*, Jn 13:5

BASKET *container*
got him a wicker *b*, Ex 2:3
b among the reeds, Ex 2:5
b of summer fruit, Am 8:1
lamp…under a *b*, Mt 5:15
not…put under a *b*, Mk 4:21
seven large *b-s* full, Mk 8:8
twelve *b-s full*, Lk 9:17
let down in a *b*, 2Co 11:33

BAT *winged mammal*
the hoopoe, and the *b*, Lv 11:19
the hoopoe and the *b*, Dt 14:18
to the moles and the *b-s*, Is 2:20

BATH *measure of capacity*
two thousand *b-s*, 1Ki 7:26
100 *b-s* of oil, Ezr 7:22
only one *b of wine*, Is 5:10
a tenth of a *b* from, Eze 45:14

BATHE *wash*
wash his clothes and *b*, Lv 15:5
b his body in water, Nu 19:7
saw a woman *b-ing*, 2Sa 11:2
B-d in milk, SS 5:12

BATHSHEBA
Wife of Uriah, taken by David, 2Sa 11
Her first child dies, 2Sa 12:14–19
Bears Solomon, 2Sa 12:24
Secures throne for Solomon, 1Ki 1:15–31
Deceived by Adonijah, 1Ki 2:13–25

BATTER *beat, strike*
And the gate is *b-ed* to ruins, Is 24:12
b-ed reed he will not, Mt 12:20
b-ed by the waves, Mt 14:24

BATTERING *beating*
b-ing rams against it, Eze 4:2
set *b-ing* rams against the, Eze 21:22
blow of his *b-ing* rams he, Eze 26:9

BATTLE *(n) conflict, war*
b is the LORD's, 1Sa 17:47
b is…God's, 2Ch 20:15
scents the *b* from afar, Job 39:25
with strength for *b*, Ps 18:39
noise of *b* is in, Jer 50:22
another king in *b*, Lk 14:31
horses prepared for *b*, Rev 9:7

BATTLE *(v) fight*
b against the sons, Jdg 20:14
drew near to *b*, 1Sa 7:10
about to go to *b*, 1Ch 12:19
nations…to *b*, Zec 14:2

BEACH *coast*
crowd…on the *b*, Mt 13:2
Jesus stood on the *b*, Jn 21:4
down on the *b*, Ac 21:5

BEADS *jewelry*
Your neck with strings of *b*, SS 1:10
of gold with *b* of silver, SS 1:11

BEAM *log*
like a weaver's *b*, 2Sa 21:19
one was felling a *b*, 2Ki 6:5
b-s, the thresholds, 2Ch 3:7
b-s of His…chambers, Ps 104:3

BEAR *(n) animal*
b came and took, 1Sa 17:34
b robbed of…cubs, Pr 17:12
the *b* will graze, Is 11:7
resembling a *b*, Da 7:5

BEAR *(v) sustain*
too great to *b*, Ge 4:13
bore you on eagles', Ex 19:4
not *b* false witness, Ex 20:16
Lord…*b-s* our burden, Ps 68:19
b their iniquities, Is 53:11
b the penalty, Eze 23:49
she will *b* a Son, Mt 1:21
it *b-s* much fruit, Jn 12:24
b-ing His own cross, Jn 19:17
b fruit for God, Ro 7:4
b the image of, 1Co 15:49
B…another's burdens, Gal 6:2
b the sins of many, Heb 9:28
bore our sins, 1Pe 2:24

BEAR FRUIT
take root downward and *b*, 2Ki 19:30
branch from his roots will *b*, Is 11:1
open up and salvation *b*, Is 45:8
bring forth boughs and *b*, Eze 17:23
b in keeping with repentance, Mt 3:8
tree that does not *b* is cut, Mt 3:10
tree that does not *b* is cut, Mt 7:19
word and accept it and *b*, Mk 4:20
hold it fast, and *b*, Lk 8:15
that *b-s* fruit, He prunes it, Jn 15:2
branch cannot *b* of itself, Jn 15:4
that you would go and *b*, Jn 15:16
that we might *b* for God, Ro 7:4
members of our body to *b*, Ro 7:5

BEARD *whiskers*
infection…on the *b*, Lv 13:29
seized *him* by…*b*, 1Sa 17:35
shaved…their *b-s*, 2Sa 10:4
until your *b-s* grow, 1Ch 19:5

BEARER *carrier*
the *b-s* of the ark, 2Sa 6:13
strength of…*b-s*, Ne 4:10
b of good news, Is 40:9

BEAST *animal, creature*
God formed every *b*, Ge 2:19
Noah and all the *b-s*, Ge 8:1
eliminate harmful *b-s*, Lv 26:6
b-s of the field, Lv 26:22
But now ask the *b-s*, Job 12:7
b of the forest, Ps 50:10
b also had four heads, Da 7:6
they worshiped the *b*, Rev 13:4
mark of the *b*, Rev 16:2

BEAT *hit, strike*
b-ing a Hebrew, Ex 2:11
b out what she, Ru 2:17
b-ing tambourines, Ps 68:25
B your plowshares, Joel 3:10
b Him with their, Mt 26:67
b-ing His head with, Mk 15:19
b-ing his breast, Lk 18:13
b-en us in public, Ac 16:37
stopped *b-ing* Paul, Ac 21:32
b-en with rods, 2Co 11:25

BEAUTIFUL *lovely, pleasing*
daughters…were *b*, Ge 6:2
Rachel was *b*, Ge 29:17
foliage of *b* trees, Lv 23:40
Most *b* among women, SS 1:8
Branch…will be *b*, Is 4:2
Your *b* sheep, Jer 13:20
enter the *B* Land, Da 11:41
How *b* are the feet, Ro 10:15

BEAUTIFUL GATE
See GATES OF JERUSALEM

BEAUTY
Your *b*…is slain, 2Sa 1:19
behold the *b* of the LORD, Ps 27:4
Zion…perfection of *b*, Ps 50:2
b is vain, Pr 31:30
see the King in His *b*, Is 33:17

BECOME *come to be*
and they shall *b* one flesh, Ge 2:24
man has *b* like one of Us, Ge 3:22
b a great and mighty, Ge 18:18
Israel will *b* a proverb, 1Ki 9:7
An idiot will *b* intelligent, Job 11:12
Son, that He not *b* angry, Ps 2:12
they have *b* corrupt;, Ps 14:3
I have *b* a reproach, Ps 31:11
You have *b* my salvation, Ps 118:21
Has *b* the chief corner, Ps 118:22
that these stones *b* bread, Mt 4:3
if the salt has *b* tasteless, Mt 5:13
converted and *b* like children, Mt 18:3
whoever wishes to *b* great, Mk 10:43
crooked will *b* straight, Lk 3:5
right to *b* children of God, Jn 1:12
the water which had *b* wine, Jn 2:9
have *b* united with, Ro 6:5
b as the scum of the world, 1Co 4:13
have *b* all things to all men, 1Co 9:22
might *b* the righteousness, 2Co 5:21
have *b* partakers of Christ, Heb 3:14
many *of you b* teachers, Jas 3:1

BECOMING *coming to be; fitting*
Praise is *b* to the upright., Ps 33:1
were *b* obedient to the faith., Ac 6:7
humbled Himself by *b*, Php 2:8
whatever is *b* obsolete nd, Heb 8:13

BED *pallet*
My *b* will comfort me, Job 7:13
make my *b* swim, Ps 6:6
remember…on my *b*, Ps 63:6
in *b* with a fever, Mt 8:14
pick up your *b*, Mt 9:6
lamp…under a *b*, Mk 4:21

BEDROOM *sleeping area*
and into your *b*, Ex 8:3
you speak in your *b*, 2Ki 6:12
his nurse in the *b*, 2Ch 22:11

BEELZEBUL
Jesus accused of serving, Mt 10:25; 12:24–27

BEER-LAHAI-ROI
Angel meets Hagar there, Ge 16:7–14
Isaac dwells in, Ge 24:62

BEERSHEBA
God appears there to Hagar, Ge 21:14–19
to Isaac, Ge 26:23–25
to Jacob, Ge 46:1–5
to Elijah, 1Ki 19:3–7
Oaths sworn there by Abraham, Ge 21:31–33
by Isaac, Ge 26:26–33

BEES *stinging insect*
and chased you as *b* do, Dt 1:44
swarm of *b* and honey, Jdg 14:8
surrounded me like *b*, Ps 118:12

BEFALL *happen*
afraid that harm may *b* him, Ge 42:4
No evil will *b* you, Ps 91:10
No harm *b-s* the righteous, Pr 12:21
that one fate *b-s* them both, Ecc 2:14

BEFOREHAND *prior*
do not worry *b*, Mk 13:11
anointed My body *b*, Mk 14:8
God announced *b*, Ac 3:18
prepared *b* for glory, Ro 9:23

BEG *appeal, ask*
children wander...*b*, Ps 109:10
b-s during...harvest, Pr 20:4
b You to look at, Lk 9:38
I am ashamed to *b*, Lk 16:3
who used to sit and *b*, Jn 9:8
b-ging them to leave, Ac 16:39

BEGET *bring into being, sire*
Rock who *begot*, Dt 32:18
whom you will *b*, 2Ki 20:18
begotten the...dew, Job 38:28
I have *begotten* You, Ps 2:7
have *begotten* You, Ac 13:33

BEGINNING *origin, starting*
In the *b* God created, Ge 1:1
from *b* to end, 1Sa 3:12
b was insignificant, Job 8:7
fear of the LORD...*b*, Ps 111:10
The *b* of the gospel, Mk 1:1
In the *b* was the Word, Jn 1:1
This b of His signs, Jn 2:11
He is the *b*, Col 1:18
the *b* and the end, Rev 21:6

BEGOTTEN *(adj) born one*
b from the Father, Jn 1:14
the only *b* God, Jn 1:18
gave His only *b* Son, Jn 3:16
only *b* Son of God, Jn 3:18
offering...only *b*, Heb 11:17
sent His only *b* Son, 1Jn 4:9

BEHALF *sake of*
atonement on his *b*, Lv 5:6
the Father on your *b*, Jn 16:26
I ask on their *b*, Jn 17:9
one man to die on *b*, Jn 18:14
be sin on our *b*, 2Co 5:21

BEHAVE *act*
David *b-d* himself, 1Sa 18:30
b-ing as a madman, 1Sa 21:14
b properly as in, Ro 13:13
blamelessly we *b-d*, 1Th 2:10

BEHAVIOR *conduct*
instruction in wise *b*, Pr 1:3
reverent in their *b*, Titus 2:3
holy...in all *your b*, 1Pe 1:15
the *b* of their wives, 1Pe 3:1

BEHEADED *cut off*
killed him and *b* him, 2Sa 4:7
John *b* in the prison, Mt 14:10
John, whom I *b*, Mk 6:16
b because of their, Rev 20:4

BEHEMOTH
Hippopotamus, Job 40:15

BEHOLD *look, see*
upright will *b* His face, Ps 11:7
b the works of the LORD, Ps 46:8
b-ing as in a mirror, 2Co 3:18
B, I stand at the door, Rev 3:20

BEING *existence, life*
man became a living *b*, Ge 2:7
a...*b* coming up, 1Sa 28:13
wisdom in the...*b*, Job 38:36
truth in the...*b*, Ps 51:6
four living *b-s*, Eze 1:5
resembled a...*b*, Da 10:16

BEL
Patron god of Babylon, Is 46:1; Jer 50:2; 51:44

BELIEVE *have faith, trust*
he *b-d* in the LORD, Ge 15:6
did not *b* in God, Ps 78:22
naive *b-s* everything, Pr 14:15
you *b* that I am able, Mt 9:28
ask in prayer, *b-ing*, Mt 21:22
repent and *b*, Mk 1:15
they *b-d*...Scripture, Jn 2:22
whoever *b-s* in Him, Jn 3:16
will you *b* My words, Jn 5:47
who *b-s* has eternal, Jn 6:47
men will *b* in Him, Jn 11:48
b in the Light, Jn 12:36
not see, and *yet b-d*, Jn 20:29
b-d were of one heart, Ac 4:32
B in the Lord Jesus, Ac 16:31
Abraham *b-d* God, Ro 4:3
How will they *b*, Ro 10:14
love...*b-s* all, 1Co 13:7
whom I have *b-d*, 2Ti 1:12
comes to God must *b*, Heb 11:6
demons also *b*, Jas 2:19
do not *b* every spirit, 1Jn 4:1

BELIEVERS *faithful ones*
all the circumcised *b*, Ac 10:45
example to all the *b*, 1Th 1:7
toward you *b*, 1Th 2:10

BELL
a *b*...a pomegranate, Ex 39:26
b-s of the horses, Zec 14:20

BELLY *stomach*
On your *b*...you go, Ge 3:14
crawls on its *b*, Lv 11:42
b of the sea monster, Mt 12:40

BELONG *be bound to*
interpretations *b* to God, Ge 40:8
males *b* to the LORD, Ex 13:12
Salvation *b-s* to the LORD, Ps 3:8
That power *b-s* to God, Ps 62:11
the Lord *b* escapes, Ps 68:20
plans of the heart *b* to man, Pr 16:1
wisdom and power *b* to Him, Da 2:20
Righteousness *b-s* to You, Da 9:7
b-ing to the number of the, Lk 22:3
anything *b* to him was his, Ac 4:32
to whom *b-s* the adoption, Ro 9:4
all things *b* to you, 1Co 3:22
and you *b* to Christ, 1Co 3:23
if you *b* to Christ, then you, Gal 3:29
to whom *b* the glory, 1Pe 4:11
glory and power *b-s* to our, Rev 19:1

BELOVED *dearly loved*
b of the LORD dwell, Dt 33:12
gives to His *b even*, Ps 127:2
b is like a gazelle, SS 2:9
This is My *b* Son, Mt 3:17
your upbuilding, *b*, 2Co 12:19
stand firm...my *b*, Php 4:1
faithful and *b* brother, Col 4:9
Luke, the *b* physician, Col 4:14
slave, a *b* brother, Phm 16
This is My *b* Son, 2Pe 1:17
the called, *b* in God, Jude 1

BELOVED SON
My *b*, in whom I am, Mt 3:17
My *b*, with whom I am, Mt 17:5
My *b*, in You I am, Mk 1:11
This is My *b*, listen to Him, Mk 9:7
a *b*; he sent him last of all, Mk 12:6
My *b*, in You I am pleased, Lk 3:22
send my *b*; perhaps they, Lk 20:13
us to the kingdom of His *b*, Col 1:13
Timothy, my *b*, 2Ti 1:2
My *b* with whom I am, 2Pe 1:17

BELOW *underneath*
waters which were *b*, Ge 1:7
above and on the earth *b*, Dt 4:39
keep away from Sheol *b*, Pr 15:24
gone *b* into the hold, Jon 1:5
Peter was *b* in the, Mk 14:66
You are from *b*, I am, Jn 8:23

BELSHAZZAR
King of Babylon; Daniel interprets his dream, Da 5

BELT *waistband*
the *b* of the strong, Job 12:21
leather *b* around his, Mt 3:4
no money in their *b*, Mk 6:8
Paul's *b* and bound, Ac 21:11

BELTESHAZZAR
Daniel's Babylonian name, Da 1:7

BENAIAH
The son of Jehoiada; a mighty man, 2Sa 23:20–23
Faithful to David, 2Sa 15:18; 20:23

Escorts Solomon to the throne, 1Ki 1:38–40
Executes Adonijah, Joab and Shimei, 1Ki 2:25, 29–34, 46
——— A Pirathonite; another of David's mighty men, 2Sa 23:30
Divisional commander, 1Ch 27:14

BEN-AMMI
Son of Lot; father of the Ammonites, Ge 19:38

BEND *turn from straight*
arms can *b* a bow of, 2Sa 22:35
the wicked *b* the bow, Ps 11:2
b their tongue, Jer 9:3
I will *b* Judah as My bow, Zec 9:13

BENEATH *under*
above or on the earth *b*, Ex 20:4
earth *b* or in the water, Dt 5:8
b every luxuriant tree, 1Ki 14:23
B Him crouch the helpers, Job 9:13
B the apple tree I, SS 8:5
Sheol from *b* is excited, Is 14:9
b their wings, Eze 10:21
are the dust *b* His feet, Na 1:3
enemies *b* your feet, Mt 22:44

BENEFIT *blessing, profit*
no return for the *b*, 2Ch 32:25
forget none of His *b-s*, Ps 103:2
His *b-s* toward me, Ps 116:12
the *b* of circumcision, Ro 3:1

BEN-HADAD
Ben-Hadad I, king of Damascus; hired by Asa, king of Judah, to attack Baasha, king of Israel, 1Ki 15:18–21
——— Ben-Hadad II, king of Damascus; makes war on Ahab, king of Israel, 1Ki 20
Falls in siege against Samaria, 2Ki 6:24–33; 7:6–20
Killed by Hazael, 2Ki 8:7–15
——— Ben-Hadad III, king of Damascus; loses all Israelite conquests made by Hazael, his father, 2Ki 13:3–25

BENJAMIN
Jacob's youngest son, Ge 35:16–20
Taken to Egypt against Jacob's wishes, Ge 42–45
Jacob's prophecy concerning, Ge 49:27
——— Tribe of:
Families of, Nu 26:38–41
Territory allotted to, Jos 18:11–28
Attacked by remaining tribes for condoning sin of Gibeah, Jdg 20:12–48
Wives provided for remnant of, Jdg 21:1–23
Tribe of Saul, 1Sa 9:1, 2
of Paul, Php 3:5

BENJAMIN GATE
See GATES OF JERUSALEM

BEN-ONI
Rachel's name for Benjamin, Ge 35:16–18

BENT *not straight*
has *b* His bow and made, Ps 7:12
straighten what He has *b*?, Ecc 7:13
she was *b* double, Lk 13:11

BEREA
A city of Macedonia; visited by Paul, Ac 17:10–15

BEREAVE *deprive, make sad*
be *b-d* of you both, Ge 27:45
b...of your children, Lv 26:22
I will *b them*, Jer 15:7
longer *b* your nation, Eze 36:14

BERNICE
Sister of Herod Agrippa II, Ac 25:13, 23
Hears Paul's defense, Ac 26:1–30

BERODACH-BALADAN
See MERODACH
A king of Babylon, 2Ki 20:12–19

BERYL *a hard mineral*
b and an onyx and, Ex 28:20
rods of gold Set with *b*, SS 5:14
like sparkling *b*, Eze 1:16
body also *was* like *b*, Da 10:6
chrysolite; the eighth, *b*, Rev 21:20

BESEECH *ask earnestly*
LORD, I *b* You, Ps 116:4
do save, we *b* You, Ps 118:25
leper came...*b-ing*, Mk 1:40
b the Lord of the, Lk 10:2

BESIDE *next to*
camped *b* Ebenezer, 1Sa 4:1
leads me *b* quiet waters, Ps 23:2
B them the birds, Ps 104:12
like doves *B* streams, SS 5:12
wheels rose close *b*, Eze 1:20
b the river Chebar, Eze 3:15
seeds fell *b* the, Mt 13:4
white clothing stood *b*, Ac 1:10
if we are *b* ourselves, 2Co 5:13

BESIDES *moreover; except*
B, she actually is my, Ge 20:12
other gods b Me, Ex 20:23
B the continual burnt, Nu 28:31
there is no other *b* Him, Dt 4:35
there is no one *b* You, 1Sa 2:2
is a rock, *b* our God?, 2Sa 22:32
I have no good *b* You, Ps 16:2
b You, I desire nothing, Ps 73:25
there is no savior *b* Me, Is 43:11
b women and children, Mt 14:21
one else *b* Him, Mk 12:32
b all this, between us, Lk 16:26
b our comfort, we, 2Co 7:13

BESIEGE *assail, surround*
When you *b* a city, Dt 20:19
enemies *b* them, 2Ch 6:28
was *b-ing* Jerusalem, Jer 32:2
b-d...with bitterness, La 3:5

BEST *superior*
Rebekah took the *b* garments, Ge 27:15
with the *b* things of Egypt, Ge 45:23
b of the fresh wine, Nu 18:12
Do what seems *b* to you, 1Sa 1:23
my *b* to maintain always, Ac 24:16
time as seemed *b*, Heb 12:10

BESTOWED *granted*
b...royal majesty, 1Ch 29:25
that the Spirit was *b*, Ac 8:18
which He freely *b*, Eph 1:6
b on Him the name, Php 2:9
love the Father has *b*, 1Jn 3:1

BETHANY
A town on the Mt. of Olives, Lk 19:29
A place beyond the Jordan where John baptized, Jn 1:28
Home of Lazarus, Jn 11:1
Home of Simon, the leper, Mt 26:6
Jesus visits there, Mk 11:1, 11, 12
Scene of the Ascension, Lk 24:50, 51

BETHEL
Abram settles near, Ge 12:7, 8
Site of Abram's altar, Ge 13:3, 4
Site of Jacob's vision of the ladder, Ge 28:10–19
Jacob returns to, Ge 35:1–15
Samuel judges there, 1Sa 7:15, 16
Site of worship and sacrifice, 1Sa 10:3
Center of idolatry, 1Ki 12:28–33
Josiah destroys altars of, 2Ki 23:4, 15–20
Denounced by prophets, 1Ki 13:1–10; Am 7:10–13; Jer 48:13; Hos 10:15

BETHESDA
Jerusalem pool, Jn 5:2–4

BETH-HORON
Twin towns of Ephraim, Jos 16:3, 5
Fortified by Solomon, 2Ch 8:3–5
Prominent in battles, Jos 10:10–14; 1Sa 13:18

BETHLEHEM
Originally called Ephrath, Ge 35:16
Rachel buried there, Ge 35:19
Home of Naomi and Boaz, Ru 1:1, 19; 4:9–11
Home of David, 1Sa 16:1–18
Predicted place of Messiah's birth, Mic 5:2
Christ born there, Mt 2:1; Lk 2:4–7; Jn 7:42
Infants of, killed by Herod, Mt 2:16–18

BETH-PEOR
Town near Pisgah, Dt 3:29
Moses buried near, Dt 34:6
Assigned to Reubenites, Jos 13:15, 20

BETHPHAGE
Village near Bethany, Mk 11:1
Near Mt. of Olives, Mt 21:1

BETHSAIDA
A city of Galilee, Mk 6:45
Home of Andrew, Peter and Philip, Jn 1:44; 12:21
Blind man healed there, Mk 8:22, 23
5, 000 fed nearby, Lk 9:10–17
Unbelief of, denounced, Mt 11:21; Lk 10:13

BETH-SHAN
A town in Issachar, Jos 17:11–16
Saul's corpse hung up at, 1Sa 31:10–13; 2Sa 21:12–14

BETH-SHEMESH
Ark brought to, 1Sa 6:12–19
Joash defeats Amaziah at, 2Ki 14:11
Taken by Philistines, 2Ch 28:18

BETRAY *break faith, disloyal*
do not *b* the fugitive, Is 16:3
wine *b-s* the haughty, Hab 2:5
b Him to you, Mt 26:15
how to *b* Him, Mk 14:11
one...will *b* Me, Mk 14:18
Judas, are you *b-ing*, Lk 22:48

BETROTH *promise to wed*
You shall *b* a wife, Dt 28:30
I will *b* you to Me, Hos 2:19
Mary had been *b-ed*, Mt 1:18
I *b-ed* you to one, 2Co 11:2

BETTER *more favorable*
b for us to return to Egypt?, Nu 14:3
last kindness to be *b* than, Ru 3:10
to obey is *b* than sacrifice, 1Sa 15:22
B is the little of the righteous, Ps 37:16
lovingkindness is *b* than life, Ps 63:3
wisdom is *b* than jewels, Pr 8:11
My fruit is *b* than gold, Pr 8:19
B is a little with the fear, Pr 15:16
b to be humble in spirit, Pr 16:19
B is a poor man, Pr 19:1
b to live in a corner of, Pr 21:9
Favor is *b* than silver, Pr 22:1
B is open rebuke, Pr 27:5
Two are *b* than one, Ecc 4:9
Sorrow is *b* than laughter, Ecc 7:3
b to listen to the rebuke of, Ecc 7:5
Wisdom is *b* than strength, Ecc 9:16
your love is *b* than wine, SS 1:2
death is *b* to me than life, Jon 4:3
b for you to lose one, Mt 5:29
it is *b* for you to enter life, Mt 18:8
it is *b* not to marry, Mt 19:10
is *b* to marry than to burn, 1Co 7:9
much *b* than the angels, Heb 1:4
guarantee of a *b* covenant, Heb 7:22
obtain a *b* resurrection, Heb 11:35

BEWARE *be careful, watch*
B of practicing, Mt 6:1
B of the scribes, Mk 12:38
B of the leaven, Lk 12:1
b...false circumcision, Php 3:2

BEYOND *over and above*
it was *b* measure, Ge 41:49
remove...*b* Babylon, Ac 7:43
tempted *b* what, 1Co 10:13
b their ability, 2Co 8:3
b all that we ask, Eph 3:20
and *b* reproach, Col 1:22

BEZALEL
Hur's grandson, 1Ch 2:20
Tabernacle builder, Ex 31:1–11; 35:30–35

BEZER
A city of refuge in the territory of Reuben, Dt 4:43; Jos 20:8

BIG *large*
on the *b* toes, Ex 29:20
Pharaoh...a *b* noise, Jer 46:17
gave a *b* reception, Lk 5:29

BILDAD
One of Job's friends, Job 2:11
Makes three speeches, Job 8:1–22; 18:1–21; 25:1–6

BILHAH
Rachel's maid, Ge 29:29
The mother of Dan and Naphtali, Ge 30:1–8
Commits incest with Reuben, Ge 35:22

BIND *fasten, secure*
bound his son Isaac, Ge 22:9
were *b-ing* sheaves, Ge 37:7
b them as a sign, Dt 6:8
b-s up their wounds, Ps 147:3
B up the testimony, Is 8:16
b up the brokenhearted, Is 61:1
b on earth, Mt 16:19
and *bound* Him, Jn 18:12
bound...a thousand, Rev 20:2

BIRD *fowl*
let *b-s* fly above the, Ge 1:20
the *b-s* after their kind, Ge 6:20
he did not cut the *b-s*, Ge 15:10
b-s will eat your flesh, Ge 40:19
let the live *b* go free, Lv 14:53
b that flies in the sky, Dt 4:17
may eat any clean *b*, Dt 14:11
wiser than the *b-s*, Job 35:11
Flee *as* a *b*, Ps 11:1
know every *b*, Ps 50:11
b also has found, Ps 84:3
Where the *b-s* build, Ps 104:17
soul has escaped as a *b*, Ps 124:7
b that wanders from, Pr 27:8
b of prey from the east, Is 46:11
Hunted me down like a *b*, La 3:52
a *b* fall into a trap on the, Am 3:5
Look at the *b-s*, Mt 6:26
b-s of the air *have*, Mt 8:20
b-s came and ate, Mt 13:4
the *b-s* of the air, Mk 4:32
you are than the *b-s*!, Lk 12:24
man and of *b-s*, Ro 1:23
b-s were filled with, Rev 19:21

BIRTH *act of being born*
A time to give *b*, Ecc 3:2
You gave me *b*, Jer 2:27
b of Jesus Christ, Mt 1:18
rejoice at his *b*, Lk 1:14
gave *b* to a son, Lk 1:57
a man blind from *b*, Jn 9:1
in pain to give *b*, Rev 12:2

BIRTHDAY *day of birth*
was Pharaoh's *b*, Ge 40:20
Herod's *b* came, Mt 14:6
his *b*...banquet, Mk 6:21

BIRTHRIGHT *first-born rights*
First sell me your *b*, Ge 25:31
He took away my *b*, Ge 27:36
sold his own *b*, Heb 12:16

BITE
serpent *bit* any man, Nu 21:9
it *b-s* like a serpent, Pr 23:32
if you *b*...one another, Gal 5:15

BITHYNIA
The Spirit keeps Paul from, Ac 16:7
Peter writes to Christians of, 1Pe 1:1

BITTER *painful, unpleasant*
b with hard labor, Ex 1:14
waters of Marah...*b*, Ex 15:23
b speech *as* their arrow, Ps 64:3
substitute *b* for sweet, Is 5:20
Strong drink is *b*, Is 24:9
fresh and *b water*, Jas 3:11

BITTERLY *severely*
Almighty has dealt very *b*, Ru 1:20
And Hezekiah wept *b*, 2Ki 20:3
he went out and wept *b*, Mt 26:75

BITTERNESS *unpleasantness*
in the *b* of my soul, Job 10:1
because of the *b*, Is 38:15
full of cursing and *b*, Ro 3:14
all *b*...be put away, Eph 4:31
no root of *b*, Heb 12:15

BLACK *dark*
sky grew *b* with, 1Ki 18:45
darkness and *b* gloom, Job 3:5
I am *b* but lovely, SS 1:5
behold, a *b* horse, Rev 6:5
sun became *b*, Rev 6:12

BLAME *fault, responsibility*
let me bear the *b*, Ge 43:9
bear the *b*...forever, Ge 44:32

BLAMELESS *faultless*
show Yourself *b*, 2Sa 22:26
just *and b man* is a, Job 12:4
His way is *b*, Ps 18:30
b will inherit good, Pr 28:10
a *b* conscience, Ac 24:16
holy and *b* before Him, Eph 1:4
in the Law, found *b*, Php 3:6
spotless and *b*, 2Pe 3:14
b with great joy, Jude 24

BLASPHEME *curse*
enemies...to *b*, 2Sa 12:14
name is continually *b-d*, Is 52:5
This *fellow b-s*, Mt 9:3
b-s...Holy Spirit, Mk 3:29
force them to *b*, Ac 26:11
name of God is *b-d*, Ro 2:24
taught not to *b*, 1Ti 1:20
b-d the God of, Rev 16:11

BLASPHEMOUS *profane*
heard him speak *b* words, Ac 6:11
on his heads *were b*, Rev 13:1
beast, full of *b* names, Rev 17:3

BLASPHEMY *cursing, profanity*
b against the Spirit, Mt 12:31
b-ies they utter, Mk 3:28
You...heard the *b*, Mk 14:64
man...speaks *b-ies*, Lk 5:21
stone You...for *b*, Jn 10:33
words and *b-ies*, Rev 13:5

BLAST *burst*
the *b* of Your nostrils, Ex 15:8
b with the ram's horn, Jos 6:5
a trumpet *b* of war, Jer 49:2

BLAZING *burning*
LORD...a *b* fire, Ex 3:2
furnace of *b* fire, Da 3:6
and to a *b* fire, Heb 12:18

BLEMISH *flaw*
two rams without *b*, Ex 29:1
And there is no *b* in you, SS 4:7
goat without *b*, Eze 43:22

BOASTING *bragging*
Where is your *b*, Jdg 9:38
Where then is *b*, Ro 3:27
our *b* about you, 2Co 9:3
all such *b* is evil, Jas 4:16

BOAT *watercraft*
slip by like reed *b-s*, Job 9:26
left the *b* and their, Mt 4:22
Peter got out of...*b*, Mt 14:29
filled both of the *b-s*, Lk 5:7
disciples into the *b*, Jn 6:22

BOAZ
A wealthy Bethlehemite, Ru 2:1, 4–18
Husband of Ruth, Ru 4:10–13
Ancestor of Christ, Mt 1:5
——— Pillar of the temple, 1Ki 7:21

BODILY *physical*
Him in *b* form like a dove, Lk 3:22
because of a *b* illness, Gal 4:13
Deity dwells in *b* form, Col 2:9
b discipline is only of little, 1Ti 4:8

BODY *corpse, flesh*
b cleaves to the earth, Ps 44:25
lamp of the *b*, Mt 6:22
perfume on My *b*, Mt 26:12
this is My *b*, Mk 14:22
did not find His *b*, Lk 24:23
b of sin...done away, Ro 6:6
redemption of our *b*, Ro 8:23
present your *b-ies*, Ro 12:1
b-ies are members, 1Co 6:15
b is a temple, 1Co 6:19
you are Christ's *b*, 1Co 12:27
b to be burned, 1Co 13:3
absent from the *b*, 2Co 5:8
one *b* and one Spirit, Eph 4:4
building up of the *b*, Eph 4:12
wives as...own *b-ies*, Eph 5:28
transform the *b*, Php 3:21
b be preserved, 1Th 5:23
bore...sins in His *b*, 1Pe 2:24

BODYGUARD *guard, protector*
captain of the *b* put, Ge 40:4
you my *b* for life, 1Sa 28:2

BOIL *(n) sore, swelling*
When...has a *b*, Lv 13:18
b-s of Egypt, Dt 28:27
smote Job with sore *b-s*, Job 2:7

BOIL *(v) cook, heat*
not *b* a young goat in its, Ex 34:26
we *b-ed* my son, 2Ki 6:29
fire causes water to *b*, Is 64:2
b the guilt offering, Eze 46:20

BOILING *seething*
while the meat was *b*, 1Sa 2:13
b pot and *burning*, Job 41:20
I see a *b* pot, facing, Jer 1:13
b places were made, Eze 46:23

BOISTEROUS *clamorous, loud*
woman of folly is *b*, Pr 9:13
of noise, You *b* town, Is 22:2
will drink *and* be *b*, Zec 9:15

BOLD *brave, fearless*
wicked man...*b* face, Pr 21:29
righteous are *b* as, Pr 28:1
I *need* not be *b*, 2Co 10:2

BOLDLY *with vigor*
mouth speaks *b*, 1Sa 2:1
spoken out *b* in the name, Ac 9:27
Barnabas spoke out *b*, Ac 13:46
b to you on some points, Ro 15:15

BOLDNESS *confidence*
word of God with *b*, Ac 4:31
b and...access, Eph 3:12
with *b* the mystery, Eph 6:19

BOND *band, restraint*
neither *b* nor free, 2Ki 14:26
b of the covenant, Eze 20:37
with *b-s* of love, Hos 11:4
he would break his *b-s*, Lk 8:29
in the *b* of peace, Eph 4:3
eternal *b-s* under, Jude 6

BONDAGE *servitude, slavery*
Israel sighed...*b*, Ex 2:23
the *b* of iniquity, Ac 8:23
sold into *b* to sin, Ro 7:14

BOND-SERVANT *servant, slave*
b-s of...Most High, Ac 16:17
Paul, a *b* of Christ, Ro 1:1
ourselves as your *b-s*, 2Co 4:5
b...be quarrelsome, 2Ti 2:24
b of God...apostle, Titus 1:1
His *b-s*...serve Him, Rev 22:3

BONDSLAVE *servant, slave*
state of His *b*, Lk 1:48
a *b* of Jesus Christ, Col 4:12
Urge b-s to be subject, Titus 2:9
use it as *b-s* of God, 1Pe 2:16

BONDWOMAN *female slave*
b and one by the free, Gal 4:22
the son by the *b* was born, Gal 4:23
cast out the *b* and her son, Gal 4:30
we are not children of a *b*, Gal 4:31

BONE *skeletal part*
now *b* of my *b-s*, Ge 2:23
carry my *b-s* up from, Ge 50:25
took the *b-s* of Joseph, Ex 13:19
buried the *b-s* of Joseph, Jos 24:32
your *b* and your flesh., 2Sa 5:1
and the *b-s* of Jonathan, 2Sa 21:12
man touched the *b-s*, 2Ki 13:21
touch his *b* and his flesh, Job 2:5
made all my *b-s* shake, Job 4:14
My *b* clings to my skin, Job 19:20
my *b-s* are out of joint, Ps 22:14
b-s which You have, Ps 51:8
My *b-s* cling to my flesh, Ps 102:5
refreshment to your *b-s*., Pr 3:8
spirit dries up the *b-s*, Pr 17:22
soft tongue breaks the *b*, Pr 25:15
give strength to your *b-s*;, Is 58:11
O dry *b-s*, Eze 37:4
b-s as you see that I, Lk 24:39
not a *b* of his, Jn 19:36
concerning his *b-s*, Heb 11:22

BOOK *scroll*
in a *b* as a memorial, Ex 17:14
blot me...from Your *b*, Ex 32:32
found the *b* of the, 2Ki 22:8
seal up the *b*, Da 12:4
not contain the *b-s*, Jn 21:25
names are in the *b*, Php 4:3
worthy to open the *b*, Rev 5:2
Lamb's *b* of life, Rev 21:27

BOOK OF LIFE
be blotted out of the *b*, Ps 69:28
whose names are in the *b*, Php 4:3
erase his name from the *b*, Rev 3:5
of the world in the *b*, Rev 13:8
been written in the *b* from, Rev 17:8
opened, which is the *b*, Rev 20:12
not found written in the *b*, Rev 20:15
written in the Lamb's *b*, Rev 21:27

BOOTH *shelters*
b-s for his livestock, Ge 33:17
live in *b-s* for seven, Lv 23:42
in *b-s* during the feast, Ne 8:14
sitting in the tax *b*, Lk 5:27

BOOTHS, FEAST OF
See FEASTS

BOOTY *loot, plunder*
b that remained, Nu 31:32
Swift is the *b*, Is 8:1
divide the *b* with, Is 53:12
have his *own* life as *b*, Jer 38:2

BORDER *boundary*
enlarge your *b-s*, Ex 34:24
b of...city of refuge, Nu 35:26
the Jordan as *a b*, Dt 3:17
God extends your *b*, Dt 12:20
peace in your *b-s*, Ps 147:14

BORN *brought into life*
man is *b* for trouble, Job 5:7
mountains were *b*, Ps 90:2
child will be *b* to us, Is 9:6
land be *b* in one day, Is 66:8
b King of the Jews, Mt 2:2
those *b* of women, Lk 7:28
b not of blood, Jn 1:13
unless one is *b* again, Jn 3:3
b of the Spirit, Jn 3:6
to one untimely *b*, 1Co 15:8
b...to a living hope, 1Pe 1:3
loves is *b* of God, 1Jn 4:7

BORN AGAIN
unless one is *b* he cannot, Jn 3:3
I said to you, 'You must be *b*, Jn 3:7
to be *b* to a living hope, 1Pe 1:3
b not of seed which is, 1Pe 1:23

BORNE *carried, took on*
have *b chastisement*, Job 34:31
for Your sake I have *b*, Ps 69:7
we who have *b* their iniquities, La 5:7
For the tree has *b* its fruit, Joel 2:22
who have *b* the burden, Mt 20:12
we have *b* the image, 1Co 15:49

BORROW *use temporarily*
if a man *b-s anything*, Ex 22:14
you shall not *b*, Dt 28:12
b-s and does not pay, Ps 37:21
wants to *b* from you, Mt 5:42

BOSOM *breast*
iniquity in my *b*, Job 31:33
take fire in his *b*, Pr 6:27
to Abraham's *b*, Lk 16:22
the *b* of the Father, Jn 1:18

reclining on Jesus' *b*, Jn 13:23

BOTHER *pester*
conscience *b-ed*, 1Sa 24:5
you *b* the woman, Mt 26:10
worried and *b-ed*, Lk 10:41
this widow *b-s* me, Lk 18:5

BOTTOMLESS *without bottom*
key of the *b* pit, Rev 9:1
he opened the *b* pit, Rev 9:2

BOUGH *branch*
Joseph is a fruitful *b*, Ge 49:22
b-s of leafy trees, Lv 23:40
cedars...with its *b-s*, Ps 80:10
nested in its *b-s*, Eze 31:6

BOUGHT *purchased*
Joseph *b* all the land of, Ge 47:20
Abraham *b* along with the, Ge 49:30
your Father who has *b* you, Dt 32:6
ground which Jacob had *b*, Jos 24:32
b from the hand of Naomi, Ru 4:9
David *b* the threshing floor, 2Sa 24:24
I *b* the field which was at, Jer 32:9
sold all that he had and *b*, Mt 13:46
b the Potter's Field, Mt 27:7
Joseph *b* a linen cloth, Mk 15:46
have *b* a piece of land, Lk 14:18
you have been *b* with, 1Co 6:20
You were *b* with a price;, 1Co 7:23
denying the Master who *b*, 2Pe 2:1

BOUND *(adj) fastened, tied*
Foolishness is *b* up, Pr 22:15
cast *b* into the...fire, Da 3:24
A wife is *b* as long, 1Co 7:39

BOUND *(n) boundary, limit*
utmost *b* of...hills, Ge 49:26
set *b-s* for the people, Ex 19:12
b-s...the mountain, Ex 19:23

BOUNDARY *border, limit*
b-ies of the peoples, Dt 32:8
b of light and, Job 26:10
the *b-ies* of the earth, Ps 74:17
set for the sea its *b*, Pr 8:29
the *b* of the widow, Pr 15:25

BOUNTIFUL *abundant*
He has dealt *b-ly* with me, Ps 13:6
Deal *b-ly* with Your servant, Ps 119:17
You will deal *b-ly* with me, Ps 142:7
delighted with her *b* bosom, Is 66:11
he who sows *b-ly* will also, 2Co 9:6

BOUNTY *generous gift*
to his royal *b*, 1Ki 10:13
crowned...with Your *b*, Ps 65:11
over the *b* of the LORD, Jer 31:12

BOW *(n) rainbow*
set My *b* in the cloud, Ge 9:13

BOW *(n) shooting device*
his *b* remained firm, Ge 49:24
a *b* of bronze, 2Sa 22:35
not trust in my *b*, Ps 44:6
b-s are shattered, Jer 51:56

BOW *(v) bend, worship*
nations *b* down to, Ge 27:29
Israel *b-ed* in, Ge 47:31
to Him you shall *b*, 2Ki 17:36
My soul is *b-ed* down, Ps 57:6
B Your heavens, O LORD, Ps 144:5
nations will *b* down, Zep 2:11
He *b-ed* His head, Jn 19:30
every knee shall *b*, Ro 14:11

BOWED DOWN/LOW
They *b* in homage, Ge 43:28
they *b* and worshiped, Ex 4:31
people *b* and worshiped, Ex 12:27
b and did homage, 1Ch 29:30
and *b* and worshiped, 2Ch 29:30
they *b* and worshiped, Ne 8:6

BOWELS *entrails, innards*
a disease of your *b*, 2Ch 21:15
smote him in his *b*, 2Ch 21:18

BOWL *dish, jug*
golden *b* is crushed, Ecc 12:6
from sacrificial *b-s*, Am 6:6
dips with Me in...*b*, Mk 14:20
b-s full of the wrath, Rev 15:7

BOX *container*
b with the golden, 1Sa 6:11
sashes, perfume *b-es*, Is 3:20
Judas had the...*b*, Jn 13:29

BOX *type of tree*
b tree and the cypress, Is 41:19

BOY *child, lad*
she left the *b*, Ge 21:15
let the *b-s* live, Ex 1:17
b will lead them, Is 11:6
Traded a *b* for a harlot, Joel 3:3
b was cured at once, Mt 17:18

BOZRAH
City of Edom, Ge 36:33
Destruction of, foretold, Am 1:12
Figurative of Messiah's victory, Is 63:1

BRACELETS *armlets*
two *b* for her wrists, Ge 24:22
armlets and *b*, Nu 31:50
earrings, *b*, veils, Is 3:19

BRAMBLE *briar*
trees said to the *b*, Jdg 9:14
fire...from the *b*, Jdg 9:15

BRANCH *bough*
David a righteous *B*, Jer 23:5
b-es fit for scepters, Eze 19:11
beautiful *b-es* and, Eze 31:3
birds...in its *b-es*, Lk 13:19
b-es of the palm, Jn 12:13
b...not bear fruit, Jn 15:2
you are the *b-es*, Jn 15:5
is holy, the *b-es*, Ro 11:16

BRANDISH *use threateningly*
b-ing weapons, He will, Is 30:32
I *b* My sword before, Eze 32:10
cypress *spears* are *b-ed*, Na 2:3

BRAND-MARKS *signs of ownership*
on my body the *b* of Jesus, Gal 6:17

BRASS *copper-zinc alloy*
18, 000 talents of *b*, 1Ch 29:7
gold, silver, *b* and iron, 2Ch 2:7
b and of stone and of wood, Rev 9:20

BREACH *break*
For every *b* of trust, Ex 22:9
LORD had made a *b*, Jdg 21:15
closed up the *b*, 1Ki 11:27
that no *b* remained, Ne 6:1
Heal its *b-es*, Ps 60:2

BREAD *food*
eat unleavened *b*, Ex 12:20
rain *b* from heaven, Ex 16:4
He will bless your *b*, Ex 23:25
b of the Presence, Ex 25:30
not live by *b* alone, Dt 8:3
ravens brought...*b*, 1Ki 17:6
b of heaven, Ps 105:40
satisfy...with *b*, Ps 132:15
b eaten in secret, Pr 9:17
eat the *b* of idleness, Pr 31:27
Cast your *b*...waters, Ecc 11:1
not live on *b* alone, Mt 4:4
Give us...daily *b*, Mt 6:11
gives you the true *b*, Jn 6:32
I am the *b* of life, Jn 6:35

BREADTH *width*
its *b* fifty cubits, Ge 6:15
discernment and *b* of mind, 1Ki 4:29
fill the *b* of your land, Is 8:8
the *b* and length and height, Eph 3:18

BREAK *divide, shatter*
See BROKE
b down your pride, Lv 26:19
never *b* My covenant, Jdg 2:1
broke the pitchers, Jdg 7:20
soft tongue *b-s* the, Pr 25:15
reed He will not *b*, Is 42:3
I *broke* your yoke, Jer 2:20
B...fallow ground, Hos 10:12
disciples *b* the, Mt 15:2
waves were *b-ing*, Mk 4:37
she *broke* the vial, Mk 14:3
their nets *began* to *b*, Lk 5:6
b his bonds, Lk 8:29
b-ing the Sabbath, Jn 5:18
did not *b* His legs, Jn 19:33
your *b-ing* the Law, Ro 2:23

BREAKERS *waves*
Your *b* and Your waves, Ps 42:7
the mighty *b* of the sea, Ps 93:4
b and billows passed over, Jon 2:3

BREAST *bosom*
orphan from the *b*, Job 24:9
upon my mother's *b-s*, Ps 22:9
b-s are like...fawns, SS 7:3
b-s...never nursed, Lk 23:29

BREASTPIECE *breast covering*
a *b* and an ephod, Ex 28:4
make a *b* of judgment, Ex 28:15
they bound the *b*, Ex 39:21

BREASTPLATE *breast armor*
righteousness like a *b*, Is 59:17
b of faith and love, 1Th 5:8
like *b-s* of iron, Rev 9:9

BREATH *air, spirit, wind*
the *b* of life, Ge 2:7
days are *but* a *b*, Job 7:16
man is a mere *b*, Ps 39:11

b came into them, Eze 37:10
give *b* to the image, Rev 13:15

BREATH OF LIFE
into his nostrils the *b*, Ge 2:7
all flesh in which is the *b*, Ge 6:17
all flesh in which was the *b*, Ge 7:15
regarding man, whose *b* is, Is 2:22
b from God came into, Rev 11:11

BREATHE *inhale and exhale*
Abraham *b-d* his last, Ge 25:8
such as *b* out violence, Ps 27:12
garden *b*...*fragrance*, SS 4:16
b on these slain, Eze 37:9
He *b-d* His last, Mk 15:39
He *b-d* on them, Jn 20:22

BRETHREN *brothers*
beating...his *b*, Ex 2:11
b from all the nations, Is 66:20
His *b* Will return, Mic 5:3
b, why do you injure, Ac 7:26
sinning against...*b*, 1Co 8:12
dangers...false *b*, 2Co 11:26
Peace be to the *b*, Eph 6:23
faithful *b* in Christ, Col 1:2
the love of the *b*, 1Th 4:9
b...not grow weary, 2Th 3:13
my *b*, do not swear, Jas 5:12
our lives for the *b*, 1Jn 3:16
accuser of our *b*, Rev 12:10

BRIAR *thistle, thorn*
b-s and thorns will come, Is 5:6
land will be *b-s*, Is 7:24
grapes from a *b* bush, Lk 6:44

BRIBE *illegal gift*
b blinds...clear-sighted, Ex 23:8
nor take a *b*, Dt 10:17
who hates *b-s* will, Pr 15:27
b corrupts the heart, Ecc 7:7
Everyone loves a *b*, Is 1:23

BRICK *clay block*
they used *b* for stone, Ge 11:3
straw to make *b* as, Ex 5:7
deliver...quota of *b-s*, Ex 5:18
burning incense on *b-s*, Is 65:3

BRIDE *newlywed*
as a *b* adorns herself, Is 61:10
the voice of the *b*, Jer 7:34
b out of her *bridal*, Joel 2:16
He who has the *b*, Jn 3:29
b...of the Lamb, Rev 21:9

BRIDEGROOM *newlywed*
a *b* of blood to me, Ex 4:25
As a *b* decks himself, Is 61:10
voice of the *b*, Jer 7:34
attendants of the *b*, Mt 9:15
out to meet the *b*, Mt 25:1

BRIDLE *(n) head harness*
My *b* in your lips, 2Ki 19:28
a *b* for the donkey, Pr 26:3
up to the horses' *b-s*, Rev 14:20

BRIDLE *(v) control*
not *b* his tongue, Jas 1:26
man, able to *b*, Jas 3:2

BRIEF *of short duration*
for a *b* moment grace has, Ezr 9:8
For a *b* moment I forsook, Is 54:7
as I wrote before in *b*, Eph 3:3
I have written to you *b-ly*, Heb 13:22
I have written to you *b-ly*, 1Pe 5:12

BRIGHT *shining*
b in the skies, Job 37:21
night is as *b* as, Ps 139:12
B eyes gladden, Pr 15:30
b cloud...them, Mt 17:5
b light...flashed, Ac 22:6
the *b* morning star, Rev 22:16

BRIGHTNESS *brilliance*
even the moon has no *b*, Job 25:5
the *b* before Him passed, Ps 18:12
b of a flaming fire by night, Is 4:5
righteousness goes forth like *b*, Is 62:1
And the stars lose their *b*, Joel 2:10
because of the *b* of that, Ac 22:11

BRIM *rim*
ten cubits from *b* to *b*, 1Ki 7:23
ten cubits from *b* to *b*, 2Ch 4:2
filled them up to the *b*, Jn 2:7

BRIMSTONE *sulfur*
b and fire from, Ge 19:24
b and burning wind, Ps 11:6
rained fire and *b*, Lk 17:29
tormented with...*b*, Rev 14:10
lake of fire and *b*, Rev 20:10

BRING *carry, lead*
will *b* forth children, Ge 3:16
Cain *brought*...offering, Ge 4:3
b two of every *kind*, Ge 6:19
B the ark of God, 1Sa 14:18
Kings will *b* gifts, Ps 68:29
B water for the thirsty, Is 21:14
B the whole tithe, Mal 3:10
brought...a paralytic, Mt 9:2
not...to *b* peace, Mt 10:34
I *b* you good news, Lk 2:10
Law *b-s* about wrath, Ro 4:15
b-ing salvation, Titus 2:11

BROAD *wide*
into a *b* place, 2Sa 22:20
land was *b* and, 1Ch 4:40
the sea, great and *b*, Ps 104:25
dark in *b* daylight, Am 8:9
way is *b* that leads to, Mt 7:13

BROKE *tore down; split*
See BREAK
you *b* faith with Me, Dt 32:51
b down the house of Baal, 2Ki 10:27
b the jaws of the wicked, Job 29:17
b the heads of the sea, Ps 74:13
b open springs and torrents, Ps 74:15
b the whole staff of bread, Ps 105:16
b it and gave, Mt 26:26
b the legs of the first man, Jn 19:32
He had given thanks, He *b*, 1Co 11:24
b down the barrier of, Eph 2:14
Lamb *b* one of the seven, Rev 6:1

BROKEN *crushed, separated*
My spirit is *b*, Job 17:1
A *b* and a contrite heart, Ps 51:17
they have *b* Your law, Ps 119:126
deeps were *b* up, Pr 3:20
silver cord is *b*, Ecc 12:6
bind up the *b*, Eze 34:16
Scripture...be *b*, Jn 10:35
Not a bone...*b*, Jn 19:36
Branches were *b* off, Ro 11:19

BROKENHEARTED *grieving*
LORD is near to the *b*, Ps 34:18
He heals the *b*, Ps 147:3
sent me to bind...*b*, Is 61:1

BROKENNESS *weak state*
b of My people, Jer 6:14
heal the *b* of the daughter, Jer 8:11
For the *b* of the daughter, Jer 8:21

BRONZE *metal*
implements of *b*, Ge 4:22
made a *b* serpent, Nu 21:9
bend a bow of *b*, 2Sa 22:35
as walls of *b*, Jer 1:18
third kingdom of *b*, Da 2:39
costly wood and *b*, Rev 18:12

BROOD *group, offspring*
b of sinful men, Nu 32:14
You *b* of vipers, Mt 3:7
hen *gathers* her *b*, Lk 13:34

BROOD OF VIPERS
"You *b*, who warned you, Mt 3:7
b, how can you, being evil, Mt 12:34
b, how will you escape, Mt 23:33
You *b*, who warned you to, Lk 3:7

BROOK *stream, wadi*
stones from the *b*, 1Sa 17:40
by the *b* Cherith, 1Ki 17:5
deer pants for...*b-s*, Ps 42:1
wisdom...bubbling *b*, Pr 18:4

BROTH *flavored liquid*
basket and the *b* in a pot, Jdg 6:19
and pour out the *b*, Jdg 6:20
the *b* of unclean meat, Is 65:4

BROTHER *male relative*
Am I my *b-'s*, Ge 4:9
b-s were jealous, Ge 37:11
b-s may redeem, Lv 25:48
b-s to dwell together, Ps 133:1
b is born for, Pr 17:17
closer than a *b*, Pr 18:24
b-s of a poor man, Pr 19:7
reconciled to your *b*, Mt 5:24
B will betray *b*, Mt 10:21
behold, His...*b-s*, Mt 12:46
not forgive his *b*, Mt 18:35
My *b* and sister, Mk 3:35
b of yours was dead, Lk 15:32
left...wife or *b-s*, Lk 18:29
not even His *b-s*, Jn 7:5
b will rise again, Jn 11:23
b goes to law with *b*, 1Co 6:6
my *b* to stumble, 1Co 8:13
yet hates his *b*, 1Jn 2:9

BROTHERHOOD
the covenant of *b*, Am 1:9
love the *b*, fear God, 1Pe 2:17

BROTHERLY *with fraternal affection*
one another in *b* love, Ro 12:10
harmonious, sympathetic, *b*, 1Pe 3:8
godliness, *b* kindness, 2Pe 1:7

BROTHER'S
Am I my *b* keeper, Ge 4:9
voice of your *b* blood, Ge 4:10
in to your *b* wife, Ge 38:8
nakedness of your *b* wife, Lv 18:16
not go to your *b* house, Pr 27:10
not gloat over your *b* day, Ob 1:12
speck that is in your *b* eye, Mt 7:3
stumbling block in a *b* way, Ro 14:13

BRUISE *(n) wound*
for wound, *b* for *b*, Ex 21:25
Only b-s, welts and raw, Is 1:6
the *b* He has inflicted, Is 30:26

BRUISE *(v) batter, crush*
b him on the heel, Ge 3:15
b-s me with a tempest, Job 9:17

BRUTAL *fierce, vicious*
hand of *b* men, Eze 21:31
b, haters of good, 2Ti 3:3

BUCKLER *small shield*
Take hold of *b* and shield, Ps 35:2
Line up the shield and *b*, Jer 46:3
b and shield and helmet, Eze 23:24

BUD *blossom, a sprout*
flax was in *b*, Ex 9:31
put forth *b-s*, Nu 17:8
the *b* blossoms, Is 18:5

BUILD *construct, form*
Noah *built* an altar, Ge 8:20
let us *b*...a city, Ge 11:4
b for Me a house, 1Ch 17:12
b-ing...house of God, 2Ch 3:3
built high places, 2Ch 33:19
has *built* up Zion, Ps 102:16
Unless the LORD *b-s*, Ps 127:1
a time to *b* up, Ecc 3:3
built his house on, Mt 7:24
I will *b* My church, Mt 16:18
able to *b you* up, Ac 20:32
being *built* together, Eph 2:22
stones...being *built*, 1Pe 2:5

BUILDER *fashioner, maker*
Solomon's *b-s*, 1Ki 5:18
b-s had laid the, Ezr 3:10
the *b-s* rejected, Mt 21:42
like a wise master *b*, 1Co 3:10
architect and *b* is, Heb 11:10

BUILDING *structure*
reconstructing this *b*, Ezr 5:4
b that *was* in front, Eze 41:12
what wonderful *b-s*, Mk 13:1
you are...God's *b*, 1Co 3:9
have a *b* from God, 2Co 5:1
whole *b*, being fitted, Eph 2:21

BULB *part of plant*
a *b* and a flower, Ex 25:33
b-s and their branches, Ex 25:36

BULL *animal*
b of the sin offering, Lv 4:20
b without blemish, Eze 45:18
blood of *b-s* and, Heb 10:4

BULRUSH *marsh plant*
b in a single day, Is 9:14
b-es by the Nile, Is 19:7
palm branch or *b*, Is 19:15

BUNDLE *package*
b...*was* in his sack, Ge 42:35
the *b* of the living, 1Sa 25:29
in *b-s* to burn, Mt 13:30

BURDEN *(n) load, weight*
b-s of the Egyptians, Ex 6:6
the *b* of the people, Nu 11:17
I am a *b* to myself, Job 7:20
who daily bears our *b*, Ps 68:19
My *b* is light, Mt 11:30
b-s hard to bear, Lk 11:46
Bear one another's *b-s*, Gal 6:2

BURDEN *(v) weigh down*
b-ed Me with your sins, Is 43:24
were *b-ed* excessively, 2Co 1:8
not *b* you myself, 2Co 12:16
the church must not be *b-ed*, 1Ti 5:16

BURDENSOME *heavy*
it is too *b* for me, Nu 11:14
things that you carry are *b*, Is 46:1
commandments are not *b*, 1Jn 5:3

BURIAL *interment*
give me a *b* site, Ge 23:4
even have a *proper b*, Ecc 6:3
to prepare Me for *b*, Mt 26:12
b custom of the Jews, Jn 19:40

BURN *(v) consume, kindle*
Jacob's anger *b-ed*, Ge 30:2
bush was *b-ing*, Ex 3:2
Your anger *b* against, Ex 32:11
Moses' anger *b-ed*, Ex 32:19
did not *b* any cities, Jos 11:13
jealousy *b* like fire, Ps 79:5
to *b* their sons, Jer 7:31
not to *b* the scroll, Jer 36:25
will *b* up the chaff, Lk 3:17
b-ed in their desire, Ro 1:27
my body to be *b-ed*, 1Co 13:3
works will be *b-ed*, 2Pe 3:10
lake of fire...*b-s*, Rev 19:20

BURNING *(adj)*
Your *b* anger, Ex 15:7
shall bewail the *b*, Lv 10:6
b lips and a wicked, Pr 26:23
b heat of famine, La 5:10
b anger of the LORD, Zep 2:2

BURNISHED *polished*
gleamed like *b* bronze, Eze 1:7
feet...like *b* bronze, Rev 1:15

BURNT OFFERINGS
See OFFERINGS

BURST *break*
great deep *b* open, Ge 7:11
wine will *b* the skins, Lk 5:37
he *b* open, Ac 1:18

BURY *place in earth*
b-ied at...old age, Ge 15:15
that I may *b* my dead, Ge 23:4
b-ied the bones of, Jos 24:32
go and *b* my father, Mt 8:21
dead to *b* their own, Mt 8:22
devout...*b-ied* Stephen, Ac 8:2
that He was *b-ied*, 1Co 15:4
b-ied...in baptism, Col 2:12

BUSH *shrub*
boy under...the *b-es*, Ge 21:15
the *b* was burning, Ex 3:2
who dwelt in the *b*, Dt 33:16
like a *b* in the desert, Jer 17:6

BUSINESS *occupation, work*
until I...told my *b*, Ge 24:33
carry on the *king's b*, Est 3:9
another to his *b*, Mt 22:5
a place of *b*, Jn 2:16
attend to your...*b*, 1Th 4:11
engage in *b*, Jas 4:13

BUSYBODIES *meddlers*
no work...like *b*, 2Th 3:11
gossips and *b*, 1Ti 5:13

BUT I SAY
B, "Woe to me, Is 24:16
B to you that everyone, Mt 5:22
b to you that everyone, Mt 5:28
b to you that everyone, Mt 5:32
B to you, make no oath, Mt 5:34
B to you, do not resist, Mt 5:39
B to you, love your, Mt 5:44
B to you that something, Mt 12:6
b to you that Elijah already, Mt 17:12
B to you, I will not drink, Mt 26:29
B to you that Elijah has, Mk 9:13
B to you in truth, there, Lk 4:25
B to you who hear, Lk 6:27
B to you truthfully, Lk 9:27
b these things so that you, Jn 5:34
B, surely they have, Ro 10:18
B, surely Israel did not, Ro 10:19
B to the unmarried and, 1Co 7:8
B, walk by the Spirit, Gal 5:16
B to you, the rest who, Rev 2:24

BUTTER *milk product; delight*
my steps were bathed in *b*, Job 29:6
smoother than *b*, Ps 55:21
churning of milk produces *b*, Pr 30:33

BUY *purchase*
b grain from Joseph, Ge 41:57
b the field from, Ru 4:5
of a fool to *b* wisdom, Pr 17:16
no money come, *b* and eat, Is 55:1
b food for themselves, Mt 14:15
b food for all these people, Lk 9:13
those who *b*, as though they, 1Co 7:30
b from Me gold, Rev 3:18

BUYER *purchaser*
Bad, bad, says the *b*, Pr 20:14
the *b* like the seller, Is 24:2
Let not the *b* rejoice, Eze 7:12

BYSTANDERS *onlookers*
b...said to Peter, Mt 26:73
the *b* heard it, Mk 15:35

BYWORD *term of derision*
b among all peoples, 1Ki 9:7
a proverb and a *b*, 2Ch 7:20
He has made me a *b*, Job 17:6
b among the nations, Ps 44:14

C

CAESAR
Augustus Caesar (31 B.C.–A.D. 14):
Decree of brings Joseph and Mary to Bethlehem, Lk 2:1
——— Tiberius Caesar (A.D. 14–37):
Christ's ministry dated by, Lk 3:1–23
Tribute paid to, Mt 22:17–21
Jews side with, Jn 19:12
——— Claudius Caesar (A.D. 41–54):
Famine in time of, Ac 11:28
Banished Jews from Rome, Ac 18:2
——— Nero Caesar (A.D. 54–68):
Paul appealed to, Ac 25:8–12
Christian converts in household of, Php 4:22
Paul tried before, 2Ti 4:16–18
Called Augustus, Ac 25:21

CAESAREA
Roman capital of Palestine, Ac 12:19; 23:33
Paul escorted to, Ac 23:23–33
Paul imprisoned at; appeals to Caesar, Ac 25:4, 8–13
Peter preaches at, Ac 10:34–43
Paul preaches at, Ac 9:26–30; 18:22; 21:8

CAESAREA PHILIPPI
A city in northern Palestine; scene of Peter's great confession, Mt 16:13–20

CAIAPHAS
Son-in-law of Annas; high priest, Jn 18:13
Makes prophecy, Jn 11:49–52
Jesus appears before, Jn 18:23, 24
Apostles appear before, Ac 4:1–22

CAIN
Adam's first son, Ge 4:1
His offering rejected, Ge 4:2–7; Heb 11:4
Murders Abel; is exiled; settles in Nod, Ge 4:8–17
A type of evil, Jude 11

CAKE *type of bread*
and make bread *c-s*, Ge 18:6
took one unleavened *c*, Lv 8:26
make me a…*c*, 1Ki 17:13

CALAMITY *adversity, trouble*
day of their *c* is near, Dt 32:35
c on us and strike, 2Sa 15:14
ease holds *c* in contempt, Job 12:5
reserved for the day of *c*, Job 21:30
also laugh at your *c*, Pr 1:26
his *c* will come suddenly, Pr 6:15
well-being and creating *c*, Is 45:7
have heard of my *c*;, La 1:21
comforted for the *c*, Eze 14:22
relents concerning *c*, Jon 4:2

CALCULATE *count*
shall *c* from the year, Lv 25:50
c the cost, Lk 14:28
c the…beast, Rev 13:18

CALEB
Sent as spy; gives good report; rewarded, Nu 13:2, 6, 27, 30; 14:5–9, 24–38
Inherits Hebron, Jos 14:6–15
Conquers his territory with Othniel's help, Jos 15:13–19

CALF *animal*
tender and choice *c*, Ge 18:7
into a molten *c*, Ex 32:4
made two golden *c-ves*, 1Ki 12:28
c and the young lion, Is 11:6
skip about like *c-ves*, Mal 4:2
bring the fattened *c*, Lk 15:23
blood of…*c-ves*, Heb 9:12

CALL *address, summon, name*
God *c-ed* the light day, Ge 1:5
c upon the name, Ge 4:26
c-s up the dead, Dt 18:11
LORD was *c-ing*…boy, 1Sa 3:8
c-ed fine gold my trust, Job 31:24
c upon the LORD, Ps 18:3
those who *c* evil good, Is 5:20
c His name Immanuel, Is 7:14
You shall *c* Me, Jer 3:19
who is *c-ed* the Messiah, Mt 1:16
to *c* the righteous, Mt 9:13
c-s his own sheep, Jn 10:3
c Me Teacher and, Jn 13:13
God has not *c-ed*, 1Th 4:7
c-s…a prophetess, Rev 2:20

CALLED BY MY NAME
people who are *c* humble, 2Ch 7:14
Everyone who is *c*, Is 43:7
this house, which is *c*, Jer 7:10
this city which is *c*, Jer 25:29
house which is *c*, Jer 34:15
nations who are *c*, Am 9:12
Gentiles who are *c*, Ac 15:17

CALLING *summoning*
the *c* of assemblies, Is 1:13
the *c* of God, Ro 11:29
For consider your *c*, 1Co 1:26
with a holy *c*, 2Ti 1:9
His *c* and choosing, 2Pe 1:10

CALM *still*
be *c*, have no fear, Is 7:4
sea may become *c*, Jon 1:11
it became perfectly *c*, Mt 8:26
you ought to keep *c*, Ac 19:36

CAMEL *animal*
I will water your *c-s* also, Ge 24:14
the *c*, for though it chews, Lv 11:4
the *c* and the rabbit and, Dt 14:7
ox and sheep, *c*, 1Sa 15:3
on mules and on *c-s*, Is 66:20
Rabbah a pasture for *c-s*, Eze 25:5
a garment of *c-'s* hair, Mt 3:4
gnat and swallow a *c*!, Mt 23:24
clothed with *c-'s* hair, Mk 1:6
is easier for a *c* to go, Mk 10:25

CAMP *(n) lodging area*
This is God's *c*, Ge 32:2
people out of the *c*, Ex 19:17
outside the *c* seven, Nu 31:19
pitch *c-s*, and place, Eze 4:2
the *c* of the saints, Rev 20:9

CAMP *(v) settle*
you shall *c* in front, Ex 14:2
they shall also *c*, Nu 1:50
Israel *c-ed* at Gilgal, Jos 5:10
I will *c* against you, Is 29:3
c around My house, Zec 9:8

CANA
A village of upper Galilee; home of Nathanael, Jn 21:2
Site of Christ's first miracle, Jn 2:1–11
Healing at, Jn 4:46–54

CANAAN
A son of Ham, Ge 10:6
Cursed by Noah, Ge 9:20–25
——— Promised Land, Ge 12:5
Boundaries of, Ge 10:19
God's promises concerning, given to Abraham, Ge 12:1–3
to Isaac, Ge 26:2, 3
to Jacob, Ge 28:10–13
to Israel, Ex 3:8
Conquest of, announced, Ge 15:7–21
preceded by spying expedition, Nu 13:1–33
delayed by unbelief, Nu 14:1–35
accomplished by the Lord, Jos 23:1–16
achieved only in part, Jdg 1:21, 27–36

CANAANITES
Israelites commanded to:
drive them out; not serve their gods, Ex 23:23–33
shun their abominations, Lv 18:24–30
not make covenants or intermarry with them, Dt 7:1–3

CANAL *water way*
c-s will emit a stench, Is 19:6
rivers *and* wide *c-s*, Is 33:21
the Nile *c-s* dry, Eze 30:12
in front of the *c*, Da 8:3

CANE *long-stemmed plant*
fragrant *c* two hundred, Ex 30:23
bought Me not sweet *c*, Is 43:24
sweet *c* from a distant land?, Jer 6:20

CAPERNAUM
Simon Peter's home, Mk 1:21, 29
Christ performs healings there, Mt 8:5–17; 9:1–8; Mk 1:21–28; Jn 4:46–54
preaches there, Mk 9:33–50; Jn 6:24–71
uses as headquarters, Mt 4:13–17
pronounces judgment upon, Mt 11:23, 24

CAPITAL *top part of column*
height of the other *c*, 1Ki 7:16
c on the top of each, 2Ch 3:15
c-s…were on top, 2Ch 4:12

CAPPADOCIA
Jews from, at Pentecost, Ac 2:1, 9
Christians of, addressed by Peter, 1Pe 1:1

CAPTAIN *leader*
c of the bodyguard, Ge 39:1
c of the host of, Jos 5:14
Sisera, *c* of the army, 1Sa 12:9
have a word for you, O *c*, 2Ki 9:5
c-s and all the mighty men, 2Ki 24:14
Nebuzaradan the *c* of the, Jer 39:9
c of the temple *guard*, Ac 4:1
the *c* of the ship, Ac 27:11

CAPTIVE *prisoner*
relative had been taken *c*, Ge 14:14
they took *c* the women, 1Sa 30:2

carried them *c* to Assyria, 2Ki 15:29
c-s who had been exiled, Est 2:6
restores his *c* people, Ps 14:7
led *c Your c-s*, Ps 68:18
back the *c* ones of Zion, Ps 126:1
proclaim liberty to *c-s*, Is 61:1
proclaim release to the *c-s*, Lk 4:18
every thought *c*, 2Co 10:5
that no one takes you *c*, Col 2:8
having been held *c*, 2Ti 2:26

CAPTIVITY *imprisonment*
the clothes of her *c*, Dt 21:13
c of the exiles, Ezr 2:1
had come from the *c*, Ezr 8:35
survived the *c* are in great, Ne 1:3
Restore our *c*, O LORD, Ps 126:4
your lovers will go into *c*, Jer 22:22
destined for *c*, Rev 13:10

CAPTURE *seize, take*
they *c-d* and looted, Ge 34:29
that Joshua had *c-ed* Ai, Jos 10:1
David *c-ed* the stronghold of, 2Sa 5:7
Samaria was *c-ed*, 2Ki 18:10
c-s the wise by their own, Job 5:13
c...with her eyelids, Pr 6:25
than he who *c-s* a city, Pr 16:32
have dug a pit to *c* me, Jer 18:22
c her spoil and seize her, Eze 29:19
to be *c-ed* and killed, 2Pe 2:12

CARAVAN *expedition*
a *c* of Ishmaelites, Ge 37:25
The *c-s* of Tema, Job 6:19
O *c-s* of Dedanites, Is 21:13

CARCASS *corpse*
down upon the *c-es*, Ge 15:11
one who touches...*c*, Lv 11:39
c-es will be food, Dt 28:26
c of the lion, Jdg 14:8
c-es of their...idols, Jer 16:18

CARE *(n) concern*
into the *c* of...sons, Ge 30:35
work is going on with great *c*, Ezr 5:8
friends and receive *c*, Ac 27:3
c for one another, 1Co 12:25

CARE *(v) have concern for*
God will surely take *c*, Ge 50:24
man that You *c* for him?, Ps 8:4
No one *c-s* for...soul, Ps 142:4
Take *c* and be calm, Is 7:4
tomorrow will *c* for itself, Mt 6:34
and did not take *c* of You?, Mt 25:44
So take *c* how you listen, Lk 8:18
and took *c* of him, Lk 10:34
take *c* that this liberty of, 1Co 8:9
take *c* that you are not, Gal 5:15
take *c* of the church, 1Ti 3:5
Take *c*, brethren, Heb 3:12
he *c-s* for you, 1Pe 5:7

CAREFUL *watchful, on guard*
Be *c* that you do not, Ge 31:24
c to observe all, Dt 6:25
c that you do not offer your, Dt 12:13
be *c* not to drink, Jdg 13:4
c how he builds on it, 1Co 3:10
be *c* how you walk, Eph 5:15
c to engage in good deeds, Titus 3:8

CAREFULLY *with concern*
observe *c* all this, Dt 15:5
Listen *c*, my daughter, Ru 2:8
Listen *c* to my speech, Job 13:17
you *c* fence *it* in, Is 17:11
search *c* for the Child, Mt 2:8
they *c* wash their hands, Mk 7:3
search *c* until she finds it?, Lk 15:8
examine everything *c*, 1Th 5:21

CARELESS *without concern*
fool is arrogant and *c*, Pr 14:16
food and *c* ease, Eze 16:49
every *c* word that people, Mt 12:36

CARGO *merchandise*
and they threw the *c*, Jon 1:5
to unload its *c*, Ac 21:3
no one buys...*c-es*, Rev 18:11

CARMEL
City of Judah, Jos 15:55
Site of Saul's victory, 1Sa 15:12
——— A mountain of Palestine, Jos 19:26
Scene of Elijah's triumph, 1Ki 18:19–45
Elisha visits, 2Ki 2:25

CARPENTER *craftsman*
c-s and stonemasons, 2Sa 5:11
to the masons and *c-s*, Ezr 3:7
this the *c-'s* son, Mt 13:55
c, the son of Mary, Mk 6:3

CARRY *bear*
sons of Israel *c-ied* their, Ge 46:5
came forward and *c-ied*, Lv 10:5
as a nurse *c-ies* a nursing, Nu 11:12
LORD...*c-ied* you, Dt 1:31
c-ied the ark came, Jos 3:15
Spirit...will *c* you, 1Ki 18:12
Nebuchadnezzar had *c-ied*, Ezr 1:7
we *c-ied* on the work with, Ne 4:21
chaff which the storm *c-ies*, Job 21:18
c them in His bosom, Is 40:11
And our sorrows He *c-ied*, Is 53:4
you will be *c-ied* on the hip, Is 66:12
c-ied away our diseases, Mt 8:17
paralytic, *c-ied* by four men, Mk 2:3
C no money belt, no bag, Lk 10:4
the cross to *c*, Lk 23:26
Sir, if you have *c-ied* Him, Jn 20:15
c-ied away by their hypocrisy, Gal 2:13
c-ied about by every wind, Eph 4:14
c-ied away and enticed by, Jas 1:14
c-ied along by winds;, Jude 12
c-ied me away in the Spirit, Rev 17:3

CART *wagon*
So Moses took the *c-s*, Nu 7:6
the cows to the *c*, 1Sa 6:7
sin as if with *c* ropes, Is 5:18
his c and his horses, Is 28:28

CARVE *(v) cut, fashion*
he *c-d* all the walls, 1Ki 6:29
who *c* a resting place, Is 22:16
c-d with cherubim, Eze 41:18
its maker has *c-d* it, Hab 2:18

CARVED *(adj) cut, etched*
with *c* engravings, 1Ki 6:29
c image of the idol, 2Ch 33:7
abdomen is *c* ivory, SS 5:14

CASE *legal hearing; circumstance*
c of both parties shall come, Ex 22:9
c that is too hard for you, Dt 1:17
If any *c* is too difficult for, Dt 17:8
in the *c* of Uriah the Hittite, 1Ki 15:5
his *c seems* right, Pr 18:17
Argue your *c* with your, Pr 25:9
let us argue our *c* together, Is 43:26
LORD has a *c*, Hos 4:1
In their *c* the prophecy of, Mt 13:14
down, I will decide your *c*, Ac 24:22
laid Paul's *c* before the king, Ac 25:14
has a *c* against his neighbor, 1Co 6:1
whose *c* the god, 2Co 4:4
in *c* I am delayed, 1Ti 3:15

CAST *throw*
one who *c-s* a spell, Dt 18:11
Joshua *c* lots for, Jos 18:10
c Your law behind, Ne 9:26
c lots for the orphans, Job 6:27
c My words behind, Ps 50:17
Do not *c* me away, Ps 51:11
c you out of My sight, Jer 7:15
will *c* out demons, Mk 16:17
c fire upon...earth, Lk 12:49
clothing they *c* lots, Jn 19:24
c-ing all your anxiety, 1Pe 5:7
but *c* them into hell, 2Pe 2:4
c their crowns before, Rev 4:10

CAST/CASTING OUT DEMONS
we not ... in Your name *c*, Mt 7:22
cleanse the lepers, *c*, Mt 10:8
by Beelzebul *c*, Mt 12:27
if I *c* by the Spirit of God, Mt 12:28
c; and He was not, Mk 1:34
preaching and *c-ing*, Mk 1:39
have authority to *c*., Mk 3:15
c-ing and were anointing, Mk 6:13
we saw someone *c-ing* in, Mk 9:38
in My name they will *c*, Mk 16:17
c-ing in Your name, Lk 9:49
say that I *c* by Beelzebul, Lk 11:18
if I by Beelzebul *c*, Lk 11:19
if I *c* by the finger of God, Lk 11:20
I *c* and perform cures, Lk 13:32

CATCH *seize, trap*
shall *c* his wife, Jdg 21:21
to *c* the afflicted, Ps 10:9
C the foxes for us, SS 2:15
caught in My snare, Eze 12:13
will be *c-ing* men, Lk 5:10
unable to *c* Him, Lk 20:26
caught in adultery, Jn 8:3
who *c-es* the wise, 1Co 3:19
if anyone is *caught*, Gal 6:1
child was *caught* up, Rev 12:5

CATTLE *domestic animals*
c and creeping things, Ge 1:24
the firstborn of *c*, Ex 12:29
defect from the *c*, Lv 22:19
c on a thousand hills, Ps 50:10
no *c* in the stalls, Hab 3:17

CAUSE *(n) purpose, reason*
the *c* of the just, Ex 23:8
to death without a *c*, 1Sa 19:5
place my *c* before God, Job 5:8
hate me without a *c*, Ps 69:4
wounds without *c*, Pr 23:29
hated...without a *c*, Jn 15:25

CAUSE *(v) make*
I *c* My name to be, Ex 20:24
c Israel to inherit, Dt 1:38
has *c-d* His name, Ezr 6:12
c His face to shine, Ps 67:1
speech *c* you to sin, Ecc 5:6
who *c* dissensions, Ro 16:17
was *c-ing* the growth, 1Co 3:6

CAVE *shelter*
buried him in the *c*, Ge 25:9
escaped to the *c*, 1Sa 22:1
by fifties in a *c*, 1Ki 18:4
mountains and *c-s*, Heb 11:38
hid...in the *c-s*, Rev 6:15

CEASE *stop*
day and night Shall not *c*, Ge 8:22
c from their labors, Ex 5:5
poor will never *c*, Dt 15:11
for the godly man *c-s* to be, Ps 12:1
He makes wars to *c*, Ps 46:9
C striving and know, Ps 46:10
How the oppressor has *c-d*, Is 14:4
c-d to kiss My feet, Lk 7:45
tongues, they will *c*, 1Co 13:8
do not *c* giving thanks, Eph 1:16
pray without *c-ing*, 1Th 5:17
in the flesh has *c-d* from sin, 1Pe 4:1
night they do not *c* to say, Rev 4:8

CEDAR *tree, wood*
with the *c* wood, Lv 14:6
c-s beside the waters, Nu 24:6
all the *c-s* of Lebanon, Is 2:13
the height of *c-s*, Am 2:9

CELEBRATE *rejoice*
may *c* a feast to Me, Ex 5:1
C the Passover, 2Ki 23:21
all Israel were *c-ing*, 1Ch 13:8
David leaping and *c-ing*, 1Ch 15:29
let us eat and *c*, Lk 15:23
c with my friends, Lk 15:29
let us *c* the feast, 1Co 5:8

CENCHREA
A harbor of Corinth, Ac 18:18
Home of Phoebe, Ro 16:1

CENSER *incense container*
c-s for yourselves, Nu 16:6
his *c* in his hand, Eze 8:11
holding a golden *c*, Rev 8:3
angel took the *c*, Rev 8:5

CENSUS *population roll*
c of...congregation, Nu 1:2
number of the *c*, 1Ch 21:5
c which...David, 2Ch 2:17
the first *c* taken, Lk 2:2
in the days of the *c*, Ac 5:37

CENT *money*
paid up the last *c*, Mt 5:26
sparrows...for a *c*, Mt 10:29
amount to a *c*, Mk 12:42

CENTER *middle*
strong tower in the *c*, Jdg 9:51
fire at the *c* of the city, Eze 5:2
the *c of the court*, Jn 8:9
like a voice in the *c*, Rev 6:6
in the *c* of the throne, Rev 7:17

CENTURION *captain*
Jesus said to the *c*, Mt 8:13
summoning the *c*, Mk 15:44
soldiers and *c-s*, Ac 21:32
gave orders to the *c*, Ac 24:23

CEPHAS
Aramaic for Peter, Jn 1:42

CERTAINLY *truly*
c she is your wife!, Ge 26:9
he will *c* die, 2Ki 8:10
lips *c* will not speak, Job 27:4
But *c* God has heard, Ps 66:19
c perform your vows, Jer 44:25
drink the cup will *c* drink, Jer 49:12
You are *c* God's Son, Mt 14:33
C this man also was with, Lk 22:59
Me I will *c* not cast out, Jn 6:37
This *c* is the Prophet, Jn 7:40
c we shall also be, Ro 6:5

CERTAINTY *sureness*
know with *c* that, Jos 23:13
c of the words, Pr 22:21
you know with *c*, Eph 5:5

CERTIFICATE *permit, record*
a *c* of divorce, Dt 24:1
a *c* of divorce, Mt 5:31
c of debt, Col 2:14

CHAFF *husk*
consumes them as *c*, Ex 15:7
c which the wind drives, Ps 1:4
make the hills like *c*, Is 41:15
c from the summer, Da 2:35
burn up the *c*, Mt 3:12

CHAIN *band*
bound...bronze *c-s*, Jdg 16:21
he drew *c-s* of gold, 1Ki 6:21
whose hands are *c-s*, Ecc 7:26
was bound with *c-s*, Lk 8:29
c-s fell off his hands, Ac 12:7
great *c* in his hand, Rev 20:1

CHALDEA
Originally, the southern portion of Babylonia, Ge 11:31
Applied later to all Babylonia, Da 3:8
Abram came from, Ge 11:28–31

CHALDEANS
Attack Job, Job 1:17
Nebuchadnezzar, king of, 2Ki 24:1
Jerusalem defeated by, 2Ki 25:1–21
Babylon, "the glory of," Is 13:19
Predicted captivity of Jews among, Jer 25:1–26
God's agent, Hab 1:6

CHAMBER *room*
entered his *c*, Ge 43:30
in his cool roof *c*, Jdg 3:20
c-s of the storehouse, Ne 10:38
bridegroom...his *c*, Ps 19:5
to the *c-s* of death, Pr 7:27
out of her *bridal c*, Joel 2:16
c-s in the heavens, Am 9:6

CHAMPION *fighter*
c, the Philistine, 1Sa 17:23
a Savior and a *C*, Is 19:20
like a dread *c*, Jer 20:11

CHANGE *(n) alteration*
gave *c-s* of garments, Ge 45:22
had a *c* of heart, Ex 14:5
two *c-s* of clothes, 2Ki 5:23
Until my *c* comes, Job 14:14
a *c* of law, Heb 7:12

CHANGE *(v) alter, transform*
and *c-d* my wages, Ge 31:7
He *c-s* a wilderness, Ps 107:35
c-d their glory, Jer 2:11
Ethiopian *c* his skin, Jer 13:23
He who *c-s* the times, Da 2:21
LORD *c-d* His mind, Am 7:6
I, the LORD, do not *c*, Mal 3:6
will all be *c-d*, 1Co 15:51

CHANNEL *furrow*
Who has cleft a *c*, Job 38:25
c-s of water appeared, Ps 18:15
heart is *like c-s*, Pr 21:1
sent out its *c-s*, Eze 31:4

CHANT *sing*
David *c-ed*...this, 2Sa 1:17
Jeremiah *c-ed* a, 2Ch 35:25
daughters...shall *c*, Eze 32:16

CHARACTER
and proven *c*, hope, Ro 5:4
Make sure...your *c* is free, Heb 13:5

CHARGE *(n) responsibility*
under Joseph's *c*, Ge 39:23
keep the *c* of the LORD, Lv 8:35
c of his household, Mt 24:45
allotted to your *c*, 1Pe 5:3

CHARGE *(n) accusation*
far from a false *c*, Ex 23:7
bring *c-s* against, Ac 19:38
c against God's elect, Ro 8:33

CHARGE *(n) cost*
gospel without *c*, 1Co 9:18

CHARGE *(v) command*
Abimelech *c-d* all, Ge 26:11
I *c-d* your judges, Dt 1:16
Moses *c-d* us with a, Dt 33:4
I solemnly *c* you, 1Ti 5:21

CHARGE *(v) exact a price*
not *c* him interest, Ex 22:25
c that to my account, Phm 18

CHARIOT *wagon*
Joseph prepared...*c*, Ge 46:29
appeared a *c* of fire, 2Ki 2:11
Some *boast* in *c-s*, Ps 20:7
c-s of God are myriads, Ps 68:17
Your *c-s* of salvation, Hab 3:8
I will cut off the *c*, Zec 9:10
and sitting in his *c*, Ac 8:28

CHARIOTEERS *warriors*
David killed 700 *c*, 2Sa 10:18
7, 000 *c* and 40, 000, 1Ch 19:18
with horses and *c*, Eze 39:20

CHARITY *alms*
give that...as *c*, Lk 11:41
and give to *c*, Lk 12:33
deeds of...*c*, Ac 9:36

CHARM *beauty*
A bribe is a *c*, Pr 17:8
C is deceitful, Pr 31:30
with *all* your *c-s*, SS 7:6

CHASE *drive, pursue*
Egyptians *c-d* after, Ex 14:9
will *c* your enemies, Lv 26:7
one *c* a thousand, Dt 32:30
c-ing...Philistines, 1Sa 17:53
be *c-d* like chaff, Is 17:13

CHASTE *pure*
c...behavior, 1Pe 3:2
kept themselves *c*, Rev 14:4

CHASTEN *discipline*
Man is also *c-ed*, Job 33:19
Nor *c* me in Your wrath, Ps 6:1
c-ed every morning, Ps 73:14
who *c-s* the nations, Ps 94:10

CHASTISE *punish*
You have *c-d* me, Jer 31:18
I will *c* all of them, Hos 5:2

CHATTER *babbling*
worldly...empty *c*, 1Ti 6:20
avoid...empty *c*, 2Ti 2:16

CHEAT *deceive*
your father has *c-ed*, Ge 31:7
c with...scales, Am 8:5

CHEBAR
River in Babylonia, Eze 1:3
Site of Ezekiel's visions, Eze 10:15, 20

CHEDORLAOMER
A king of Elam; invaded Canaan, Ge 14:1–16

CHEEK *part of face*
slapped me on the *c*, Job 16:10
Your *c-s* are lovely, SS 1:10
tears are on her *c-s*, La 1:2
hits you on the *c*, Lk 6:29

CHEERFUL
countenance and be *c*, Job 9:27
joyful heart...a *c*, Pr 15:13
c heart...feast, Pr 15:15
God loves a *c* giver, 2Co 9:7
Is anyone *c*, Jas 5:13

CHEMOSH
The god of the Moabites, Nu 21:29
Children sacrificed to, 2Ki 3:26, 27
Solomon builds altars to, 1Ki 11:7
Josiah destroys altars of, 2Ki 23:13

CHERISH *love*
or the wife you *c*, Dt 13:6
the wife he *c-es*, Dt 28:54
men *c* themselves, Ac 24:15
c-es it, just as Christ, Eph 5:29

CHERITH
God hides Elijah here and the ravens feed him, 1Ki 17:3–6

CHERUB *celestial being*
He rode on a *c*, 2Sa 22:11
one *c*...ten cubits, 1Ki 6:26
c stretched out his, Eze 10:7

CHERUBIM *plural of cherub*
He stationed the *c*, Ge 3:24
c had *their* wings, Ex 37:9
enthroned *above*...*c*, 2Sa 6:2
c appeared to have, Eze 10:8

CHEST *box*
the priest took a *c*, 2Ki 12:9
money in the *c*, 2Ki 12:10
levies...into the *c*, 2Ch 24:10

CHEW *eat*
which *c* the cud, Lv 11:4
before it was *c-ed*, Nu 11:33

CHIEF *head, prominent*
c-s of the sons of, Ge 36:15
the *c-s* of Edom, Ge 36:43
of the thirty *c* men, 2Sa 23:13
c of the magicians, Da 4:9
C Shepherd appears, 1Pe 5:4

CHILD
c grew...weaned, Ge 21:8
Train up a *c* in, Pr 22:6
discipline from the *c*, Pr 23:13
c will be born to us, Is 9:6
with *c* by the Holy, Mt 1:18
take the *C* and His, Mt 2:13
He called a *c* to, Mt 18:2
saying, *C*, arise, Lk 8:54
a woman with *c*, 1Th 5:3

CHILDBIRTH
multiply...pain in *c*, Ge 3:16
as of a woman in *c*, Ps 48:6
pains of *c* come, Hos 13:13
suffers the pains of *c*, Ro 8:22

CHILDLESS
I am *c*, and the heir, Ge 15:2
They will die *c*, Lv 20:20
c among women, 1Sa 15:33
and died *c*, Lk 20:29

CHILDREN
pain...bring forth *c*, Ge 3:16
Are these all the *c*, 1Sa 16:11
compassion on *his c*, Ps 103:13
c are a gift, Ps 127:3
c rise up and bless, Pr 31:28
c were dashed to, Na 3:10
slew all the male *c*, Mt 2:16
stones...to raise up *c*, Mt 3:9
c...against parents, Mt 10:21
and become like *c*, Mt 18:3
bringing *c* to Him, Mk 10:13
Being...the *c* of God, Ac 17:29
if *c*, heirs, Ro 8:17
C, obey your parents, Eph 6:1
My little *c*, 1Jn 2:1
kill her *c* with, Rev 2:23

CHILION
Elimelech's son, Ru 1:2
Orpah's deceased husband, Ru 1:4, 5
Boaz redeems his estate, Ru 4:9

CHINNERETH
Fortified city in Naphtali, Dt 3:17
Same as the plain of Gennesaret, Mt 14:34
——— The OT name for the Sea of Galilee, Nu 34:11
Also called Lake of Gennesaret, Lk 5:1

CHINNEROTH
A region bordering the Sea of Galilee, 1Ki 15:20; Jos 11:3, 12:3

CHISLEV
Ninth month of Hebrew calendar, Ne 1:1; Zec 7:1

CHOICE *option; best*
Saul, a *c*...*man*, 1Sa 9:2
c men of Israel, 2Sa 10:9
And eat its *c* fruits, SS 4:16
God made a *c* among, Ac 15:7
God's gracious *c*, Ro 11:5
His c of you, 1Th 1:4

CHOICEST *best*
c of every offering of My, 1Sa 2:29
rather than *c* gold, Pr 8:10
better than *c* silver., Pr 8:19
planted it with the *c* vine, Is 5:2
c valleys were full, Is 22:7
the *c* of your gifts, Eze 20:40
tenth of the *c* spoils, Heb 7:4

CHOIR *chorus*
c proceeded to the, Ne 12:38
two *c-s* took their, Ne 12:40

CHOKE *stifle*
wealth *c* the word, Mt 13:22
began to *c him*, Mt 18:28
thorns...*c-d* it, Mk 4:7
c-d with worries, Lk 8:14

CHOOSE *select, take*
C men for us, Ex 17:9
whom the LORD *c-s*, Nu 16:7
C wise...discerning, Dt 1:13
He *c-s* our inheritance, Ps 47:4
refuse evil and *c* good, Is 7:15
not God *c* the poor, Jas 2:5

CHOP *cut*
who *c-s* your wood, Dt 29:11
c-ped down...altars, 2Ch 34:7
C down the tree, Da 4:14

CHOSE *selected*
Lot *c* for himself, Ge 13:11
God has *c-n* you, Dt 7:6
I *c* David to be, 1Ki 8:16
when I *c* Israel, Eze 20:5
c twelve of them, Lk 6:13
has *c-n* the weak, 1Co 1:27
He *c* us in Him, Eph 1:4

CHOSEN *elected, selected*
Moses His *c* one, Ps 106:23
My *c one in whom*, Is 42:1
Israel My *c one*, Is 45:4
c ones shall inherit, Is 65:9
My Son, *My C* One, Lk 9:35
c of God, holy and, Col 3:12
of *His c* angels, 1Ti 5:21
you are a *c* race, 1Pe 2:9

CHRIST
See JESUS; LORD JESUS CHRIST; LOVE OF CHRIST; YOU ARE THE CHRIST
Preexistence of, Ps 2:7; Jn 8:58; Col 1:15–18
Birth of, from a virgin, Is 7:14; Mt 1:18–25
Deity of, Is 9:6; Jn 1:1, 14, 18; 20:28, 29; Ro 9:5; Heb 1:8

Humanity of, Ge 3:15; Mt 22:45; Lk 3:38; Jn 1:14; 1Co 15:45–47; Gal 4:4; Php 2:5–11; 1Ti 2:5
Character of:
omnipotent, Mt 28:18
omniscient, Col 2:3
omnipresent, Mt 18:20
eternal, Jn 1:1, 2, 15
holy, Lk 1:35
righteous, Is 53:11
just, Zec 9:9
guileless, 1Pe 2:22
sinless, 2Co 5:21
spotless, 1Pe 1:19
innocent, Mt 27:4
gentle, Mt 11:29
merciful, Heb 2:17
humble, Php 2:8
forgiving, Lk 23:34
Mission of:
do the Father's will, Jn 6:38
save sinners, Lk 19:10
destroy Satan's works, Heb 2:14; 1Jn 3:8
fulfill the O.T., Mt 5:17
give life, Jn 10:10, 28
complete revelation, Heb 1:1
Worshiped by:
O.T. saints, Jos 5:13–15
demons, Mk 5:2, 6
men, Jn 9:38
angels, Heb 1:6
disciples, Lk 24:52
saints in glory, Rev 7:9, 10
all, Php 2:10, 11
O.T. types of:
Adam, Ro 5:14
Abel, Heb 12:24
Moses, Dt 18:15
Passover, 1Co 5:7
manna, Jn 6:32
bronze serpent, Jn 3:14

CHRISTIAN *follower of Christ*
first called *C-s* in, Ac 11:26
me to become a *C*, Ac 26:28
suffers as a *C*, 1Pe 4:16

CHRONICLES *book of register*
1 Of kings of Israel, 1Ki 14:19; 15:31; 2Ki 14:28; 15:26
2 Of kings of Judah, 1Ki 14:29; 15:23; 2Ki 15:36; 24:5
3 Of kings of Media / Persia, Est 10:2

CHURCH *a called-out assembly*
I will build my *c*, Mt 16:18
tell it to the *c*, Mt 18:17
shepherd the *c*, Ac 20:28
c-es of the Gentiles, Ro 16:4
together as a *c*, 1Co 11:18
woman...speak in *c*, 1Co 14:35
to the *c-es* of Judea, Gal 1:22
Christ...head of the *c*, Eph 5:23
persecutor of the *c*, Php 3:6
c of the living God, 1Ti 3:15
Spirit says to the *c-es*, Rev 2:11

CILICIA
Paul's homeland, Ac 21:39
Students from, argued with Stephen, Ac 6:9
Paul labors in, Gal 1:21

CINNAMON *spice*
and of fragrant *c*, Ex 30:23
myrrh, aloes and *c*, Pr 7:17
and *c* and spice, Rev 18:13

CIRCLE *area*
sleeping inside...*c*, 1Sa 26:7
He has inscribed a *c*, Job 26:10
did not sit in the *c*, Jer 15:17

CIRCUIT *course*
on *c* to Bethel, 1Sa 7:16
its *c* to the other end, Ps 19:6

CIRCULATE *spread*
proclamation was *c-d*, Ex 36:6
LORD's people *c-ing*, 1Sa 2:24
to *c* a proclamation, 2Ch 30:5

CIRCUMCISE *be pure; cut off*
every male...be *c-d*, Ge 17:10
Abraham *c-d* his son, Ge 21:4
So *c* your heart, Dt 10:16
God will *c*...heart, Dt 30:6
C yourselves...LORD, Jer 4:4
came to *c* the child, Lk 1:59
c-d the eighth day, Php 3:5

CIRCUMCISION *act of purity*
because of the *c*, Ex 4:26
c is...of the heart, Ro 2:29
if you receive *c*, Gal 5:2
if I still preach *c*, Gal 5:11
we are the *true c*, Php 3:3
c made without hands, Col 2:11
those of the *c*, Titus 1:10

CIRCUMSTANCE *condition*
spoken in right *c-s*, Pr 25:11
may know...my *c-s*, Eph 6:21
peace in every *c*, 2Th 3:16
of humble *c-s*, Jas 1:9

CISTERN *reservoir*
a *c* collecting water, Lv 11:36
water from your...*c*, Pr 5:15
wheel at the *c* is, Ecc 12:6
prophet from the *c*, Jer 38:10

CITADEL *fortress*
c of the king's, 1Ki 16:18
c of Susa, Est 2:3
in the *c* of Susa, Da 8:2
c-s of Jerusalem, Am 2:5
Proclaim on the *c-s*, Am 3:9
tramples on our *c-s*, Mic 5:5

CITIES OF REFUGE
1 Kedesh in Naphtali, Jos 20:7
2 Shechem in Ephraim, Jos 20:7
3 Hebron (Kiriath-arba), Jos 20:7
4 Bezer in Reuben, Jos 20:8
5 Ramoth-gilead in Gad, Jos 20:8
6 Golan in Manasseh, Jos 20:8

CITIZEN *resident*
your fellow *c-s*, Eze 33:12
fellow *c-s* who talk, Eze 33:30
c-s hated him, Lk 19:14
c of no insignificant, Ac 21:39
fellow *c-s* with the, Eph 2:19

CITY
build...a *c*, Ge 11:4
burned...their *c-ies*, Nu 31:10
die in my own *c*, 2Sa 19:37
glad the *c* of God, Ps 46:4
LORD guards the *c*, Ps 127:1
the *C* of Destruction, Is 19:18
the *C* of Truth, Zec 8:3
a *c* called Nazareth, Mt 2:23
into the holy *c*, Mt 4:5
the *c* was stirred, Mt 21:10
c, shake the dust off, Lk 9:5
He has prepared a *c*, Heb 11:16
I saw the holy *c*, Rev 21:2

CITY OF DAVID
Zion, that is the *c*, 2Sa 5:7
called it the *c*, 2Sa 5:9
ark of the LORD into the *c*, 2Sa 6:10
of Obed-edom into the *c*, 2Sa 6:12
came into the *c*, 2Sa 6:16
and was buried in the *c*, 1Ki 2:10
brought her to the *c* until, 1Ki 3:1
from the *c*, which is Zion, 1Ki 8:1
of Zion (that is, the *c*), 1Ch 11:5
in the wall of the *c* were, Is 22:9
c which is called Bethlehem, Lk 2:4
in the *c* there has been born, Lk 2:11

CLAIM *demand*
Let darkness...*c* it, Job 3:5
Do not *c* honor in, Pr 25:6
c-ing to be someone, Ac 8:9

CLAN *family, tribe*
c of the household, Jdg 9:1
and by your *c-s*, 1Sa 10:19
among...*c-s* of Judah, Mic 5:2
I will make the *c-s*, Zec 12:6

CLAP *applaud*
c-ped their hands, 2Ki 11:12
c-s his hands among, Job 34:37
rivers *c* their hands, Ps 98:8
trees...will *c*, Is 55:12

CLAY *mud*
You have made me as *c*, Job 10:9
out of the miry *c*, Ps 40:2
Will the *c* say to the potter, Is 45:9
Father, We are the *c*, Is 64:8
c in the potter's hand, Jer 18:6
the *c* to his eyes, Jn 9:6
a right over the *c*, Ro 9:21

CLEAN *cleansed, washed*
animals that are not *c*, Ge 7:2
eat in a *c* place, Lv 10:14
pronounce him *c*, Lv 13:28
Create in me a *c* heart, Ps 51:10
make yourselves *c*, Is 1:16
You can make me *c*, Mt 8:2
things are *c* for you, Lk 11:41
c because of the word, Jn 15:3

CLEANSE *purify, wash*
To *c* the house then, Lv 14:49
c the house of the, 2Ch 29:15
I have *c-d* my heart, Pr 20:9
I am willing; be *c-d*, Mt 8:3
the lepers are *c-d*, Mt 11:5
not eat unless they *c*, Mk 7:4
let us *c* ourselves, 2Co 7:1
C...you sinners, Jas 4:8
blood...*c-s* us, 1Jn 1:7

CLEAR *make free; plain*
c-s away many nations, Dt 7:1
C the way for the LORD, Is 40:3
c His threshing floor, Mt 3:12

Christ has made *c*, 2Pe 1:14
river…*c* as crystal, Rev 22:1

CLEFT *crevice*
in the *c* of the rock, Jdg 15:8
the *c-s* of the cliffs, Is 2:21
who live in the *c-s*, Ob 3

CLEVER *smart*
c in their own sight, Is 5:21
cleverness of the *c*, 1Co 1:19

CLIFF *crag*
nest is set in the *c*, Nu 24:21
On the *c* he dwells, Job 39:28
c-s are a refuge, Ps 104:18

CLIMB *ascend*
I will *c* the palm tree, SS 7:8
the one who *c-s*, Jer 48:44
c-ed…a sycamore, Lk 19:4
c-s up…other way, Jn 10:1

CLING *cleave*
and *c* to Him, Dt 13:4
c to the LORD, Jos 23:8
My soul *c-s* to You, Ps 63:8
c to Your testimonies, Ps 119:31
Stop *c-ing* to Me, Jn 20:17
c to what is good, Ro 12:9

CLOAK *coat, mantle*
Give me the *c*, Ru 3:15
neither bread nor *c*, Is 3:7
fringe of His *c*, Mt 9:20
Wrap your *c* around, Ac 12:8

CLOSE *shut, stop*
and the LORD *c-d*, Ge 7:16
floodgates…were *c-d*, Ge 8:2
earth *c-d* over them, Nu 16:33
c your door…pray, Mt 6:6
have *c-d* their eyes, Ac 28:27
every mouth…*c-d*, Ro 3:19
c-s his heart, 1Jn 3:17

CLOTH *fabric*
spread over *it* a *c*, Nu 4:6
is wrapped in a *c*, 1Sa 21:9
with embroidered *c*, Eze 16:10
in the linen *c*, Mk 15:46

CLOTHE *array, dress*
Adam and his wife, and *c-d*, Ge 3:21
Saul *c-d* David with his, 1Sa 17:38
be *c-d* with salvation and, 2Ch 6:41
flesh is *c-d* with worms, Job 7:5
He is *c-d* with majesty, Ps 93:1
c-d with splendor and, Ps 104:1
I will *c* with salvation, Ps 132:16
c…with trembling, Eze 26:16
c-d Daniel with purple and, Da 5:29
Solomon in all his glory *c-d*, Mt 6:29
naked…you *c-d* Me, Mt 25:36
John was *c-d* with camel's, Mk 1:6
c-d with power, Lk 24:49
c-d yourselves with Christ, Gal 3:27
c…with humility, 1Pe 5:5
c-d with a robe dipped, Rev 19:13

CLOTHES *garments*
c of her captivity, Dt 21:13
your *c* have not worn, Dt 29:5
and worn-out *c* on, Jos 9:5
and changed his *c*, 2Sa 12:20
without wedding *c*, Mt 22:12
Tearing his *c*, Mk 14:63

CLOTHING *clothes, raiment*
reduce…her *c*, Ex 21:10
c did not wear out, Dt 8:4
purple are their *c*, Jer 10:9
and the body more than *c*, Mt 6:25
in sheep's *c*, Mt 7:15
c as white as snow, Mt 28:3
His *c became* white, Lk 9:29
men…in dazzling *c*, Lk 24:4
sister is without *c*, Jas 2:15

CLOUD *mist*
set My bow in the *c*, Ge 9:13
in a pillar of *c*, Ex 13:21
c where God *was*, Ex 20:21
c covered…mountain, Ex 24:15
c for a covering, Ps 105:39
voice came out…*c*, Mk 9:7
Son…coming in *c-s*, Mk 13:26
in a *c* with power, Lk 21:27
and a *c* received Him, Ac 1:9

CLUB *weapon*
went…with a *c*, 2Sa 23:21
C-s are…as stubble, Job 41:29
Like a *c* and a, Pr 25:18
with swords and *c-s*, Mt 26:47

CLUSTER *collection*
c-s produced ripe, Ge 40:10
c-s of raisins, 1Sa 25:18
breasts are…*c-s*, SS 7:7
gather the *c-s*, Rev 14:18

CNIDUS
City of Asia Minor on Paul's voyage, Ac 27:7

COAL *charcoal*
C-s were kindled by it, 2Sa 22:9
C-s were kindled by it, Ps 18:8
man walk on hot *c-s*, Pr 6:28
heap burning *c-s* on his, Pr 25:22
burning *c* in his hand, Is 6:6
heap burning *c-s*, Ro 12:20

COAST
c of the Great Sea, Jos 9:1
along the *c* of Asia, Ac 27:2

COASTLAND
inhabitants of this *c*, Is 20:6
to the *c-s* of Kittim, Jer 2:10
c-s shake at the, Eze 26:15
c-s of the nations, Zep 2:11

COAT *cloak*
have your *c* also, Mt 5:40
laid their *c-s* on them, Mt 21:7
spread their *c-s*, Mk 11:8
takes away your *c*, Lk 6:29
no sword is to sell his *c*, Lk 22:36

COBRA *snake*
deadly poison of *c-s*, Dt 32:33
To the venom of *c-s*, Job 20:14
tread upon the…*c*, Ps 91:13

COFFIN *bier*
in a *c* in Egypt, Ge 50:26
and touched the *c*, Lk 7:14

COHORT *military unit*
the whole *Roman c*, Mt 27:27
called the Italian *c*, Ac 10:1
of the Augustan *c*, Ac 27:1

COIN *money*
Show Me the *c*, Mt 22:19
woman…loses one *c*, Lk 15:8
He poured out…*c-s*, Jn 2:15

COLD *cool*
covering against the *c*, Job 24:7
Like the *c* of snow, Pr 25:13
cup of *c* water, Mt 10:42
love will grow *c*, Mt 24:12
neither *c* nor hot, Rev 3:15

COLLAPSE *fall*
grass *c-s* into the flame, Is 5:24
pathways will *c*, Eze 38:20
ancient hills *c-d*, Hab 3:6

COLLEAGUES *co-workers*
the rest of his *c*, Ezr 4:7
and your *c*, Ezr 6:6

COLLECT *exact, take*
c-ed his strength, Ge 48:2
cistern *c-ing* water, Lv 11:36
c captives like sand, Hab 1:9
C no more than, Lk 3:13
c-ed a tenth from, Heb 7:6

COLLECTION *acquisition*
let your *c of idols*, Is 57:13
no *c-s* be made, 1Co 16:2

COLORS *light spectra*
and stones of various *c*, 1Ch 29:2
high places of various *c*, Eze 16:16
full plumage of many *c*, Eze 17:3

COLOSSAE
A city in Asia Minor, Col 1:2
Evangelized by Epaphras, Col 1:7
Not visited by Paul, Col 2:1
Paul writes against errors of, Col 2:16–23

COLT *foal*
camels and their *c-s*, Ge 32:15
Even on a *c*, Zec 9:9
and a *c* with her, Mt 21:2
on a donkey's *c*, Jn 12:15

COLUMN *pillar, text*
in a *c* of smoke, Jdg 20:40
and marble *c-s*, Est 1:6
read three…*c-s*, Jer 36:23

COME
C, let us build, Ge 11:4
C, let us worship, Ps 95:6
All *came* from…dust, Ecc 3:20
your king is *c-ing*, Zec 9:9
Your kingdom *c*, Mt 6:10
C to Me, all who, Mt 11:28
children to *c* to Me, Mk 10:14
not *c*…temptation, Mk 14:38
Son of Man *c-ing*, Lk 21:27
Father…hour has *c*, Jn 17:1
His judgment has *c*, Rev 14:7
I am *c-ing* quickly, Rev 22:20

COMFORT *(n) consolation*
mourning without *c*, Job 30:28
c in my affliction, Ps 119:50
receiving your *c* in full, Lk 6:24
c of the Holy Spirit, Ac 9:31
and God of all *c*, 2Co 1:3
to *c* those who are, 2Co 1:4
joy and *c* in your love, Phm 1:7

COMFORT *(v) console, cheer*
he refused to be *c-ed*, Ge 37:35
you have *c-ed* me, Ru 2:13
David *c-ed* his wife, 2Sa 12:24
My bed will *c* me, Job 7:13
Your rod...they *c* me, Ps 23:4
When will You *c* me?, Ps 119:82
"*C*, O *c* My people,", Is 40:1
To *c* all who mourn, Is 61:2
she refused to be *c-ed*, Mt 2:18
mourn, for they shall be *c-ed*, Mt 5:4
God, who *c* the depressed, 2Co 7:6
he may *c* your hearts, Eph 6:22
c one another, 1Th 4:18

COMFORTER *consoler*
Sorry *c-s* are you all, Job 16:2
c-s, but I found none, Ps 69:20
She has no *c*, La 1:9
Where will I seek *c-s*, Na 3:7

COMING *(n) arrival*
Joseph's *c* at noon, Ge 43:25
the day of His *c*, Mal 3:2
be the sign of Your *c*, Mt 24:3
c of the Son of Man, Mt 24:37
Christ's at His *c*, 1Co 15:23
c of the Lord is, Jas 5:8
the promise of His *c*, 2Pe 3:4

COMMAND *(n) order*
the *c* of the LORD, Lv 24:12
disobeyed the *c*, 1Ki 13:21
to the king's *c*, 2Ch 35:10
no *c* of the Lord, 1Co 7:25
could not bear the *c*, Heb 12:20

COMMAND *(v) declare, order*
I *c-ed* you not to eat, Ge 3:11
may *c* his children, Ge 18:19
speak all that I *c* you, Ex 7:2
bring all that I *c*, Dt 12:11
the angel...*c-ed*, Mt 1:24
c that these stones, Mt 4:3
c-s even the winds, Lk 8:25
c-ing the jailer, Ac 16:23

COMMANDER *captain, general*
the *c-s* of Israel, Jdg 5:9
c of Saul's army, 2Sa 2:8
his chariot *c-s*, 1Ki 9:22
and Joab was the *c*, 1Ch 27:34
c for the peoples, Is 55:4
the *C* of the host, Da 8:11
and the flesh of *c-s*, Rev 19:18

COMMANDMENT *instruction*
and keep My *c-s*, Ex 20:6
the Ten *C-s*, Ex 34:28
and keep His *c-s*, Jos 22:5
c of the LORD is pure, Ps 19:8
the *c* of your father, Pr 6:20
which is the great *c*, Mt 22:36
A new *c* I give, Jn 13:34
will keep My *c-s*, Jn 14:15
I have kept...*c-s*, Jn 15:10
not writing a new *c*, 1Jn 2:7
keep the *c-s* of God, Rev 14:12

COMMEND *praise, present*
So I *c-ed* pleasure, Ecc 8:15
c-ed them to the Lord, Ac 14:23
food will not *c* us, 1Co 8:8
not again *c-ing* ourselves to, 2Co 5:12
those who *c* themselves, 2Co 10:12

COMMENDABLE *praiseworthy*
sought in a *c* manner, Gal 4:18

COMMENDABLY *praiseworthy manner*
eagerly seek you, not *c*, Gal 4:17

COMMENDATION *praise*
letters of *c* to you or, 2Co 3:1

COMMISSION *appoint*
c him in their sight, Nu 27:19
He *c-ed* Joshua, Dt 31:23
king has *c-ed* me, 1Sa 21:2
c it against the people, Is 10:6

COMMISSIONERS *supervisors*
and over them three *c*, Da 6:2
Then the *c* and satraps, Da 6:4

COMMIT *entrust, practice*
c-ted to Joseph's, Ge 39:22
shall not *c* adultery, Ex 20:14
have *c-ted* incest, Lv 20:12
I *c* my spirit, Ps 31:5
C your way to the LORD, Ps 37:5
weary...*c-ting* iniquity, Jer 9:5
Do not *c* adultery, Lk 18:20
I *c* My spirit, Lk 23:46
everyone who *c-s* sin, Jn 8:34
who *c-ted* no sin, 1Pe 2:22

COMMON *ordinary, shared*
anyone of...*c* people, Lv 4:27
place of the *c* people, Jer 26:23
iron...with *c* clay, Da 2:41
had all things in *c*, Ac 2:44
about our *c* salvation, Jude 3

COMMONWEALTH *nation*
from the *c* of Israel, Eph 2:12

COMMOTION *disturbance*
the noise of this *c*, 1Sa 4:14
great *c* out of the, Jer 10:22
Why make a *c* and, Mk 5:39

COMPANION *comrade, friend*
virgins, her *c-s* who follow, Ps 45:14
My *c* and my familiar, Ps 55:13
a *c* of all those who fear, Ps 119:63
falls, the one will lift up his *c*, Ecc 4:10
c-s of thieves, Is 1:23
hungry, he and his *c-s*, Mt 12:3
mother and His own *c-s*, Mk 5:40
seized him and all his *c-s*, Lk 5:9
Paul and his *c-s*, Ac 13:13
true *c*, I ask you also to, Php 4:3

COMPANY *assembly, group*
into three *c-ies*, Jdg 9:43
c of the godless, Job 15:34
c will stone them, Eze 23:47
Bad *c* corrupts, 1Co 15:33

COMPARE *contrast, like*
none to *c* with You, Ps 40:5
to what shall I *c*, Mt 11:16
c the kingdom of, Lk 13:20
be *c-d* with the glory, Ro 8:18

COMPASS
outlines it with a *c*, Is 44:13
four points of the *c*, Da 11:4

COMPASSION *concern, love*
whom I will show *c*, Ex 33:19
c on you and make, Dt 13:17
in Your great *c*, Ne 9:31
implore the *c* of the Almighty, Job 8:5
c and Your lovingkindnesses, Ps 25:6
Your *c* blot out, Ps 51:1
as a father has *c* on, Ps 103:13
His *c-s* never fail, La 3:22
I desire *c* and not, Mt 9:13
He felt *c* for them, Mt 9:36
c on whom, Ro 9:15
if any affection and *c*, Php 2:1

COMPASSIONATE *loving*
God, *c* and gracious, Ex 34:6
c, Slow to anger, Ne 9:17
LORD is gracious and *c*, Ps 111:4
Yes, our God is *c*, Ps 116:5
a gracious and *c* God, Jon 4:2

COMPEL *force, press*
Egyptians *c-led* the, Ex 1:13
c them to come in, Lk 14:23
c...to be circumcised, Gal 6:12

COMPETE *strive*
can you *c* with horses, Jer 12:5
everyone who *c-s*, 1Co 9:25
c-s as an athlete, 2Ti 2:5

COMPLAIN *murmur*
c-ed to Abimelech, Ge 21:25
c in the bitterness, Job 7:11
I will *c* and murmur, Ps 55:17
Do not *c*, brethren, Jas 5:9

COMPLAINT *grumbling*
c-s of...Israel, Nu 14:27
couch will ease my *c*, Job 7:13
today my *c* is rebellion, Job 23:2
hospitable...without *c*, 1Pe 4:9

COMPLETE *(adj) full, total*
a sabbath of *c* rest, Ex 35:2
be seven *c* sabbaths, Lv 23:15
not...a *c* destruction, Jer 5:10
you have been made *c*, Col 2:10
be perfect and *c*, Jas 1:4
joy may be made *c*, 1Jn 1:4

COMPLETE *(v) finish, fulfill*
God *c-d* His work, Ge 2:2
C the week of this, Ge 29:27
C your work quota, Ex 5:13
your days are *c*, 2Sa 7:12
house...was *c-d*, 2Ch 8:16
thousand years are *c-d*, Rev 20:7

COMPOSE *write*
c words against you, Job 16:4
have *c-d* songs for, Am 6:5
The first account I *c-d*, Ac 1:1

COMPOSE *make calm*
c-d and quieted my, Ps 131:2
I *c-d my soul*, Is 38:13

COMPREHEND *understand, overpower*
which we cannot *c*, Job 37:5
speech…no one *c-s*, Is 33:19
and they did not *c*, Lk 18:34
darkness did not *c*, Jn 1:5

COMPULSION *coercion*
under *c*…let them go, Ex 6:1
in effect, by *c*, Phm 14
not under *c*, but, 1Pe 5:2

CONCEAL *cover, hide*
man *c-s* knowledge, Pr 12:23
They do not *even c it*, Is 3:9
Do not *c it but*, Jer 50:2
was *c-ed* from them, Lk 9:45

CONCEIT *pride*
selfishness or empty *c*, Php 2:3
he is *c-ed*, 1Ti 6:4
c-ed, lovers of, 2Ti 3:4

CONCEIVE *become pregnant*
c-d and gave birth to Cain, Ge 4:1
to Hagar, and she *c-d*, Ge 16:4
Sarah *c-d* and bore a, Ge 21:2
LORD enabled her to *c*, Ru 4:13
after Hannah had *c-d*, 1Sa 1:20
c mischief and bring forth, Job 15:35
sin my mother *c-d* me, Ps 51:5
she *c-d* and gave birth, Is 8:3
c-d in her is of the Holy, Mt 1:20
you will *c* in your womb, Lk 1:31
when lust has *c-d*, Jas 1:15

CONCERN *(n) care*
with no *c* even for this, Ex 7:23
weights of the bag are His *c*, Pr 16:11
I had *c* for My holy name, Eze 36:21
you to be free from *c*, 1Co 7:32
c for all the churches, 2Co 11:28

CONCERN *(v) have care*
You are *c-ed* about, Job 7:17
c-d for the rights of the poor, Pr 29:7
not *c-d* about the sheep, Jn 10:13
c-ed about the poor, Jn 12:6
c-d about the things of the, 1Co 7:32
not *c-ed* about oxen, 1Co 9:9
of man, that You are *c-ed*, Heb 2:6

CONCERNING *regarding*
Joseph made it a statute *c*, Ge 47:26
God *c* you and me, Jos 14:6
come *c* your two sons, 1Sa 2:34
console him *c* his father, 2Sa 10:2
His angels charge *c* you, Ps 91:11
His angels *c* You, Mt 4:6
convict the world *c* sin, Jn 16:8
and *c* righteousness, Jn 16:10
things *c* the kingdom of God, Ac 1:3
all that was written *c* Him, Ac 13:29
c His Son, who was born, Ro 1:3
Now *c* spiritual *gifts*, 1Co 12:1

CONCUBINE *secondary wife*
Ephraim…took a *c*, Jdg 19:1
Now Saul had a *c*, 2Sa 3:7
king left ten *c-s*, 2Sa 15:16
three hundred *c-s*, 1Ki 11:3
in charge of the *c-s*, Est 2:14

CONDEMN *discredit, judge*
c-ing the wicked, 1Ki 8:32
my mouth will *c* me, Job 9:20
he who *c-s* Me, Is 50:9
will *c* Him to death, Mk 10:33
do not *c*, and you, Lk 6:37
you *c* yourself, Ro 2:1
he stood *c-ed*, Gal 2:11
our heart *c-s* us, 1Jn 3:20

CONDEMNATION *judgment*
receive greater *c*, Mk 12:40
same sentence of *c*, Lk 23:40
Their *c* is just, Ro 3:8
no *c*…in Christ, Ro 8:1
c upon themselves, Ro 13:2
c…by the devil, 1Ti 3:6

CONDITION *state, stipulation*
with you on this *c*, 1Sa 11:2
c-s were good in, 2Ch 12:12
c in which…called, 1Co 7:20
or adds *c-s* to it, Gal 3:15

CONDUCT *(n) behavior*
queen's *c*…known, Est 1:17
turn…*from his c*, Job 33:17
who are upright in *c*, Ps 37:14
sensual *c* of…men, 2Pe 2:7
holy *c* and godliness, 2Pe 3:11

CONDUCT *(v) behave*
c-s himself arrogantly, Job 15:25
c…same spirit, 2Co 12:18
C…with wisdom, Col 4:5
c yourselves in fear, 1Pe 1:17

CONDUIT *channel*
c of the upper pool, 2Ki 18:17
at the end of the *c*, Is 7:3

CONFESS *acknowledge*
that he shall *c*, Lv 5:5
c-ing the sins of, Ne 1:6
c my transgressions, Ps 32:5
c-es Me before men, Mt 10:32
c-ing their sins, Mk 1:5
c with your mouth, Ro 10:9
If we *c* our sins, 1Jn 1:9
I will *c* his name, Rev 3:5

CONFESSION *admission*
praying and making *c*, Ezr 10:1
your *c* of the gospel, 2Co 9:13
testified the good *c*, 1Ti 6:13
the *c* of our hope, Heb 10:23

CONFIDENCE *boldness, trust*
What is this *c*, 2Ki 18:19
they lost their *c*, Ne 6:16
LORD will be your *c*, Pr 3:26
proud *c* is this, 2Co 1:12
c in me may abound, Php 1:26
no *c* in the flesh, Php 3:3

CONFINE *imprison, limit*
who were *c-d* in jail, Ge 40:5
he does not *c* it, Ex 21:29
be *c-d* in prison, Is 24:22
c-d in the court, Jer 33:1

CONFINEMENT *imprisonment*
c in his master's, Ge 40:7
he put me in *c*, Ge 41:10

CONFIRM *establish, strengthen*
LORD *c* His word, 1Sa 1:23
c-ed Your inheritance, Ps 68:9
c the work of our, Ps 90:17
C-ing the word of His, Is 44:26
c-ed…by the signs, Mk 16:20
who will also *c* you, 1Co 1:8

CONFIRMATION *verification*
and *c* of the gospel, Php 1:7
an oath *given* as *c*, Heb 6:16

CONFLICT *contention*
one of great *c*, Da 10:1
in *c* with the LORD, Jer 50:24
experiencing…*c*, Php 1:30
source of…*c-s*, Jas 4:1

CONFORMED *being like*
c…image of His Son, Ro 8:29
not be *c* to…world, Ro 12:2
being *c* to His death, Php 3:10

CONFOUND *confuse*
LORD *c-ed* them, Jos 10:10
c their strategy, Is 19:3
c-ing the Jews, Ac 9:22

CONFRONT *challenge, face*
snares of death *c-ed*, 2Sa 22:6
Days of affliction *c*, Job 30:27
Arise, O LORD, *c* him, Ps 17:13
the elders *c-ed Him*, Lk 20:1

CONFUSE *perplex*
c their language, Ge 11:7
Send…and *c* them, Ps 144:6
They are *c-d* by wine, Is 28:7

CONFUSION *disorder*
into great *c*, Dt 7:23
Jerusalem was in *c*, Ac 21:31
not *a God* of *c*, 1Co 14:33

CONGREGATION *assembly*
all the *c* of Israel, Ex 12:3
c shall stone him, Nu 15:35
strife of the *c*, Nu 27:14
Bless God in the *c-s*, Ps 68:26
c of the godly ones, Ps 149:1
the *c* of the disciples, Ac 6:2
In the midst of the *c*, Heb 2:12

CONIAH
King of Judah, Jer 22:24, 28
Same as Jehoiachin, 2Ki 24:8

CONJURER *magician*
magician, *c* or, Da 2:10
wise men *and* the *c-s*, Da 5:15

CONQUER *be victorious*
c-ed all the country, Ge 14:7
but could not *c* it, Is 7:1
overwhelmingly *c* through, Ro 8:37
by faith *c-ed* kingdoms, Heb 11:33

CONSCIENCE *moral obligation*
David's *c* bothered, 1Sa 24:5
always a blameless *c*, Ac 24:16
also for *c'* sake, Ro 13:5
their *c* being weak is, 1Co 8:7
faith with a clear *c*, 1Ti 3:9

seared in their own *c*, 1Ti 4:2
keep a good *c*, 1Pe 3:16

CONSECRATE *(v) sanctify*
sons of Israel *c*, Ex 28:38
garments shall be *c-d*, Ex 29:21
c it and all its, Ex 40:9
C yourselves, Lv 11:44
c the fiftieth year, Lv 25:10
c-s his house as holy, Lv 27:14
he shall *c* his head, Nu 6:11
C yourselves, Jos 3:5
have *c-d* this house, 1Ki 9:3

CONSECRATED *(adj) sanctified*
touch any *c* thing, Lv 12:4
there is *c* bread, 1Sa 21:4
ate the *c* bread, Mt 12:4
ate the *c-d* bread, Mk 2:26
ate the *c-d* bread which, Lk 6:4

CONSECRATION *setting apart*
their ordination *and c*, Ex 29:33
the *c* of the anointing oil, Lv 21:12
they began the *c* on the, 2Ch 29:17

CONSENT *agree*
Do not listen or *c*, 1Ki 20:8
entice you, Do not *c*, Pr 1:10
If you *c* and obey, Is 1:19
c-s to live with him, 1Co 7:12

CONSIDER *observe, think*
were *c-ed* unclean, Ne 7:64
C my groaning, Ps 5:1
he who *c-s* the helpless, Ps 41:1
We are *c-ed* as sheep, Ps 44:22
day of adversity *c*, Ecc 7:14
c the work of His hands, Is 5:12
C the ravens, for, Lk 12:24
c your calling, 1Co 1:26
He *c-ed* me faithful, 1Ti 1:12
c how to stimulate, Heb 10:24
c-ed...God is able, Heb 11:19

CONSIST *composed of*
reverence for Me *c-s*, Is 29:13
life *c* of his, Lk 12:15
does not *c* in words, 1Co 4:20
c-ing of decrees, Col 2:14

CONSOLATION *comfort*
c-s of God too small, Job 15:11
Your *c-s* delight my, Ps 94:19
is any *c* of love, Php 2:1

CONSOLE *soothe*
Esau is *c-ing* himself, Ge 27:42
servants to *c* him, 2Sa 10:2
to lament or to *c* them, Jer 16:5
c them concerning, Jn 11:19

CONSPIRACY *plot, scheme*
the *c* was strong, 2Sa 15:12
found *c* in Hoshea, 2Ki 17:4
from the *c-ies* of man, Ps 31:20

CONSPIRE *plot against*
have *c-d* against me, 1Sa 22:8
c-d against my, 2Ki 10:9
c together against, Ps 83:3
Amos...*c-d* against, Am 7:10

CONSTELLATION *stars*
a *c* in its season, Job 38:32
c-s Will not flash, Is 13:10

CONSTRUCT *build*
c a sanctuary for Me, Ex 25:8
c siegeworks, Dt 20:20

CONSTRUCTION *structure*
c of the sanctuary, Ex 36:3
it has been under *c*, Ezr 5:16
the *c* of the ark, 1Pe 3:20

CONSULT *confer*
call the girl and *c* her, Ge 24:57
David *c-ed* with, 1Ch 13:1
I *c-ed* with myself, Ne 5:7
Without *c-ing* Me, Is 30:2
With whom did He *c*, Is 40:14
with the elders and *c-ed*, Mt 28:12
not...*c* with flesh, Gal 1:16

CONSULTATION *counsel*
had *c* with the elders, 2Sa 3:17
Philistines after *c* sent, 1Ch 12:19
Prepare plans by *c*, Pr 20:18
immediately held a *c*, Mk 15:1

CONSUME *destroy, devour*
c-d...purchase price, Ge 31:15
the bush was not *c-d*, Ex 3:2
c-d the burnt offering, Lv 9:24
great fire will *c* us, Dt 5:25
c the cedars, Jdg 9:15
You *c* as a moth, Ps 39:11
c-d by Your anger, Ps 90:7
c-s his own flesh, Ecc 4:5
fire *c-ing* the stubble, Joel 2:5
Zeal...will *c*, Jn 2:17
c your flesh like fire, Jas 5:3

CONSUMING *(adj) destroying*
glory...like a *c* fire, Ex 24:17
the flame of a *c* fire, Is 29:6
our God is a *c* fire, Heb 12:29

CONTAIN *hold*
cannot *c* You, 1Ki 8:27
c the burnt offering, 2Ch 7:7
c-ing twenty...gallons, Jn 2:6
not *c* the books, Jn 21:25
is *c-ed* in Scripture, 1Pe 2:6

CONTEMPT *scorn*
He pours *c* on nobles, Job 12:21
With pride and *c*, Ps 31:18
treating Him with *c*, Lk 23:11
your brother with *c*, Ro 14:10

CONTEND *strive*
c with him in battle, Dt 2:24
c-ed...vigorously, Jdg 8:1
c with the Almighty, Job 40:2
not *c*...without cause, Pr 3:30
Who will *c* with me, Is 50:8
I will not *c* forever, Is 57:16
he *c-ed* with God, Hos 12:3
c...for the faith, Jude 3

CONTENT *satisfied*
c with your wages, Lk 3:14
c with weaknesses, 2Co 12:10
have learned to be *c*, Php 4:11
c with what you have, Heb 13:5

CONTENTION *strife*
object of *c* to our, Ps 80:6
the *c-s* of a wife, Pr 19:13
Strife exists and *c*, Hab 1:3

CONTENTIOUS *quarrelsome*
a *c*...woman, Pr 21:19
with a *c* woman, Pr 25:24
inclined to be *c*, 1Co 11:16

CONTINUE *persevere, persist*
My covenant may *c*, Mal 2:4
c in My word, Jn 8:31
c in the grace of, Ac 13:43
Are we to *c* in sin, Ro 6:1
you *c* in the faith, Col 1:23
love of the brethren *c*, Heb 13:1

CONTRARY *against*
c to the command, Nu 24:13
for the wind was *c*, Mt 14:24
grafted *c* to nature, Ro 11:24
c to the teaching, Ro 16:17
a gospel *c* to what, Gal 1:8
c to sound teaching, 1Ti 1:10

CONTRIBUTE *give*
Josiah *c-d* to the, 2Ch 35:7
c yearly one third, Ne 10:32
c-ing to their support, Lk 8:3
c-ing to...the saints, Ro 12:13

CONTRIBUTION *gift, offering*
to raise a *c* for Me, Ex 25:2
as a *c* to the LORD, Lv 7:14
c-s, the first fruits, Ne 12:44
a *c* for the poor, Ro 15:26
liberality of your *c*, 2Co 9:13

CONTRITE *sorrowful*
broken and a *c* heart, Ps 51:17
humble and *c* of spirit, Is 66:2

CONTROL *(n) order, rule*
people were out of *c*, Ex 32:25
was it not under...*c*, Ac 5:4
children under *c*, 1Ti 3:4

CONTROL *(v) rule, subdue*
he *c-led* himself and, Ge 43:31
Joseph could not *c*, Ge 45:1
Haman *c-led* himself, Est 5:10

CONTROVERSY *dispute*
wise man has a *c*, Pr 29:9
LORD has a *c* with the, Jer 25:31
avoid foolish *c-ies*, Titus 3:9

CONVERSE *discuss*
Stoic...were *c-ing*, Ac 17:18
and *c* with him, Ac 24:26

CONVERSION *change*
c of the Gentiles, Ac 15:3

CONVERTED *changed*
sinners will be *c*, Ps 51:13
unless you are *c*, Mt 18:3
perceive...and be *c*, Jn 12:40

CONVICT *condemn, judge*
one of you *c-s* Me, Jn 8:46
c...concerning sin, Jn 16:8
he is *c-ed* by all, 1Co 14:24
to *c* all the ungodly, Jude 15

CONVINCED *persuaded*
c that John was a, Lk 20:6
c that neither death, Ro 8:38
c in the Lord Jesus, Ro 14:14
c of better things, Heb 6:9

CONVOCATION *conclave*
sabbath…a holy *c*, Lv 23:3
shall have a holy *c*, Nu 29:7

CONVULSION *paroxysm*
threw him into a *c*, Mk 9:20
a *c* with foaming, Lk 9:39

COOK *prepare food*
Jacob had *c-ed* stew, Ge 25:29
you shall *c* and eat, Dt 16:7

COOL *cold*
in the *c* of the day, Ge 3:8
in his *c* roof chamber, Jdg 3:20
who has a *c* spirit, Pr 17:27

COPPER *metal*
you can dig *c*, Dt 8:9
not acquire…*c*, Mt 10:9
widow…*c* coins, Lk 21:2

COPY *facsimile*
c of this law on a, Dt 17:18
c of…law of Moses, Jos 8:32
c of the edict, Est 8:13
mere c of the true, Heb 9:24

CORBAN *offering*
C (that is…), Mk 7:11

CORD *band, rope*
c-s of Sheol, 2Sa 22:6
c-s of affliction, Job 36:8
c-s of death, Ps 18:4
silver *c* is broken, Ecc 12:6
the *c-s* of falsehood, Is 5:18
a scourge of *c-s*, Jn 2:15

CORINTH
Paul labors at, Ac 18:1–18
Site of church, 1Co 1:2
Visited by Apollos, Ac 19:1

CORNELIUS
A religious Gentile, Ac 10:1–48

CORNER *angle, intersection*
the chief *c stone*, Ps 118:22
lurks by every *c*, Pr 7:12
on the street *c-s*, Mt 6:5
the chief *c stone*, Mk 12:10
four *c-s* of the earth, Rev 7:1

CORNER GATE
See GATES OF JERUSALEM

CORNERSTONE *support stone*
who laid its *c*, Job 38:6
the *c* of her tribes, Is 19:13
costly *c for* the, Is 28:16
From them…the *c*, Zec 10:4

CORPSE *dead body*
made unclean by a *c*, Lv 22:4
Their *c-s* will rise, Is 26:19
a mass of *c-s*, Na 3:3
boy…like a *c*, Mk 9:26

CORRECT *reprove*
c him with the rod, 2Sa 7:14
He who *c-s* a scoffer, Pr 9:7
C your son, and he, Pr 29:17
C me, O LORD, Jer 10:24
gentleness *c-ing*, 2Ti 2:25

CORRECTION *improvement*
Whether for *c*, or, Job 37:13
refused to take *c*, Jer 5:3
for reproof, for *c*, 2Ti 3:16

CORRUPT *(adj) evil, rotten*
the earth was *c*, Ge 6:11
detestable and *c*, Job 15:16
They are *c*, Ps 14:1
all of them, are *c*, Jer 6:28

CORRUPT *(v) make evil*
a bribe *c-s* the heart, Ecc 7:7
c-ed your wisdom, Eze 28:17
have *c-ed* the covenant, Mal 2:8
Bad company *c-s*, 1Co 15:33
harlot who was *c-ing*, Rev 19:2

CORRUPTION *decay, evil*
their *c* is in them, Lv 22:25
no negligence or *c*, Da 6:4
from the flesh reap *c*, Gal 6:8
c that is in the world, 2Pe 1:4
slaves of *c*, 2Pe 2:19

COSMETICS *beautifying aids*
provided her with…*c*, Est 2:9
the *c* for women, Est 2:12

COST *expense, price*
c of their lives, Nu 16:38
let the *c* be paid, Ezr 6:4
calculate the *c*, Lk 14:28
water…without *c*, Rev 21:6

COSTLY *expensive*
redemption…is *c*, Ps 49:8
gold, silver, *c* stones, Da 11:38
vial of…*c* perfume, Mk 14:3
pearls or *c* garments, 1Ti 2:9

COUCH *bed, pallet*
he went up to my *c*, Ge 49:4
falling on the *c*, Est 7:8
dissolve my *c* with my, Ps 6:6
sprawl on their *c-es*, Am 6:4

COUNCIL *assembly*
not enter into their *c*, Ge 49:6
the *c* of the holy ones, Ps 89:7
the *c* of My people, Eze 13:9
to their *c chamber*, Lk 22:66
conferred with his *c*, Ac 25:12

COUNCIL
Sanhedrin, Mt 26:59
Jewish governing body, Mk 15:1, 43; Lk 23:50

COUNSEL *(n) advice, opinion*
I will give you *c*, Ex 18:19
Take *c* and speak up, Jdg 19:30
To Him belong *c*, Job 12:13
not walk in the *c*, Ps 1:1
Listen to *c* and, Pr 19:20
the *c* of His will, Eph 1:11

COUNSEL *(v) advise*
he has *c-ed* rebellion, Dt 13:5
I *c* that all Israel, 2Sa 17:11
How do you *c me*, 1Ki 12:6
c you with My eye, Ps 32:8

COUNSELOR *adviser*
the king and his *c-s*, Ezr 7:15
c-s walk barefoot, Job 12:17
abundance of *c-s*, Pr 11:14
Wonderful *C*, Mighty, Is 9:6
who became His *c*, Ro 11:34

COUNT *consider, number*
c the stars, if you, Ge 15:5
could not be *c-ed*, 1Ki 8:5
If I should *c* them, Ps 139:18
my prayer be *c-ed*, Ps 141:2
was *c-ed* among us, Ac 1:17
I *c* all…loss, Php 3:8
as some *c* slowness, 2Pe 3:9

COUNTENANCE *appearance*
why has your *c* fallen, Ge 4:6
LORD lift up His *c*, Nu 6:26
light of Your *c*, Ps 4:6
an angry *c*, Pr 25:23

COUNTRY *land, region*
Go forth from your *c*, Ge 12:1
up into the hill *c*, Dt 1:24
go out into the *c*, SS 7:11
them from the *c-ies*, Eze 34:13
they are seeking a *c*, Heb 11:14

COUNTRYMAN
not hate…fellow *c*, Lv 19:17
among your *c-men*, Dt 17:15
a man and his *c*, Dt 25:11
my fellow *c-men* and, Ro 11:14

COURAGE *heart, valor*
he lost *c*, 2Sa 4:1
and do not lose *c*, 2Ch 15:7
let your heart take *c*, Ps 27:14
with justice and *c*, Mic 3:8
Take *c*, son, Mt 9:2
Take *c*, it is I, Mt 14:27
c; I have overcome, Jn 16:33
we are of good *c*, 2Co 5:8

COURAGEOUS *brave*
Be strong and *c*, Dt 31:6
be strong and very *c*, Jos 1:7
I propose to be *c*, 2Co 10:2

COURIER *messenger*
c-s went throughout, 2Ch 30:6
Letters…by *c-s*, Est 3:13
One *c* runs to meet, Jer 51:31

COURSE *area, extent, way*
strong man to run his *c*, Ps 19:5
on its circular *c-s*, Ecc 1:6
I have finished the *c*, 2Ti 4:7
the *c* of *our* life, Jas 3:6

COURT *area, hall, tribunal*
c of the tabernacle, Ex 27:9
c of the harem, Est 2:11
a day in Your *c-s*, Ps 84:10
c of the LORD's house, Jer 26:2
c of the guardhouse, Jer 39:15
if you have law *c-s*, 1Co 6:4
drag you into *c*, Jas 2:6

COURTYARD *compound*
a well in his *c*, 2Sa 17:18
c of the high priest, Mt 26:58
Peter...in the *c*, Mk 14:66

COVENANT *agreement*
establish My *c*, Ge 6:18
for a sign of a *c*, Ge 9:13
for an everlasting *c*, Ge 17:13
ark of the *c*, Nu 10:33
My *c* of peace, Nu 25:12
book of the *c*, 2Ki 23:2
Remember His *c*, 1Ch 16:15
who keep His *c*, Ps 103:18
I will make a new *c*, Jer 31:31
forsake the holy *c*, Da 11:30
a *c* with Assyria, Hos 12:1
the blood of *My c*, Zec 9:11
cup...is the new *c*, Lk 22:20
c which God made, Ac 3:25
this is My *c* with, Ro 11:27
servants of a new *c*, 2Co 3:6
strangers to the *c-s*, Eph 2:12
guarantee...better *c*, Heb 7:22
blood of the...*c*, Heb 13:20
ark of His *c*, Rev 11:19

COVER *(n)*
c of porpoise skin, Nu 4:14
the c of a couch, Am 3:12

COVER *(v) hide, protest*
and *c* up his blood, Ge 37:26
basket and *c-ed* it, Ex 2:3
Whose sin is *c-ed*, Ps 32:1
He will *c* you with, Ps 91:4
love *c-s* all, Pr 10:12
not *c* My face, Is 50:6
c-ed...with sackcloth, Jon 3:6
to the hills, *C* us, Lk 23:30
c a multitude of sins, Jas 5:20
love *c-s* a multitude, 1Pe 4:8

COVERING *canopy*
made...loin *c-s*, Ge 3:7
spread a cloud for a *c*, Ps 105:39
she makes *c-s* for, Pr 31:22
sackcloth their *c*, Is 50:3
given to her for a *c*, 1Co 11:15
freedom as a *c*, 1Pe 2:16

COVET *crave, desire*
not *c* your neighbor's, Ex 20:17
You shall not *c*, Dt 5:21
I *c-ed* them and took, Jos 7:21
They *c* fields and then, Mic 2:2
c-ed no one's silver, Ac 20:33

COVETOUS *desirous*
the *c* and swindlers, 1Co 5:10
c, nor drunkards, 1Co 6:10

COW *animal*
came up seven *c-s*, Ge 41:2
c calves and does not, Job 21:10
c and the bear will, Is 11:7
you *c-s* of Bashan, Am 4:1

CRAFTINESS *shrewdness*
the wise in their *c*, 1Co 3:19
not walking in *c*, 2Co 4:2
by *c* in deceitful, Eph 4:14

CRAFTSMAN *artisan*
the hands of the *c*, Dt 27:15
all the *c-men* and, 2Ki 24:14
idol, a *c* casts it, Is 40:19
business to...*c-men*, Ac 19:24
c of any craft will, Rev 18:22

CRAG *protrusion, rock*
sharp *c* on the one, 1Sa 14:4
Upon the rocky *c*, Job 39:28
clefts of the *c-s*, Is 57:5

CRAVE *covet, desire*
day long he is *c-ing*, Pr 21:26
fig *which* I *c*, Mic 7:1
generation *c-s* for, Mt 12:39
would not *c* evil, 1Co 10:6

CRAWLING *creeping*
venom of *c* things, Dt 32:24
beasts and the *c*, Ac 11:6
and *c* creatures, Ro 1:23

CREATE *form, make*
c-d the heavens, Ge 1:1
c-d man in His, Ge 1:27
C in me a clean, Ps 51:10
C-ing the praise of, Is 57:19
c new heavens, Is 65:17
one God *c-d* us, Mal 2:10
c-d...for good works, Eph 2:10
c-d in righteousness, Eph 4:24
You *c-d* all, Rev 4:11

CREATION
beginning of *c*, Mk 10:6
preach...to all *c*, Mk 16:15
whole *c* groans, Ro 8:22
beginning of *c*, 2Pe 3:4

CREATOR *Maker*
Remember...your *C*, Ecc 12:1
The *C* of Israel, Is 43:15
rather than the *C*, Ro 1:25
to a faithful *C*, 1Pe 4:19

CREATURE *created being*
every living *c* that, Ge 1:21
winged *c* will make, Ecc 10:20
and crawling *c-s*, Ro 1:23
in Christ...new *c*, 2Co 5:17
as *c-s* of instinct, 2Pe 2:12

CREDIT *(n) honor*
love you, what *c* is, Lk 6:32
one will *c* me with more, 2Co 12:6
what *c* is there if, when, 1Pe 2:20

CREDIT *(v) account*
c-ed to him as righteousness, Ro 4:3
written that it was *c-ed* to, Ro 4:23

CREDITOR *lender*
not to act as a *c* to, Ex 22:25
every *c* shall release, Dt 15:2
Let the *c* seize all, Ps 109:11
My *c-s* did I sell you, Is 50:1
Will not your *c-s* rise up, Hab 2:7

CREEP *crawl*
everything that *c-s*, Ge 1:25
that *c* on the earth, Eze 38:20

CREEPING *crawling*
cattle and *c* things, Ge 1:24
c things and fish, 1Ki 4:33
c locust has eaten, Joel 1:4
c locust strips and, Na 3:16

CRETE
Paul visits, Ac 27:7–21
Titus dispatched to, Titus 1:5
Inhabitants of, evil and lazy, Titus 1:12

CRIME *vice*
be a lustful *c*, Job 31:11
committed no *c*, Da 6:22
full of bloody *c-s*, Eze 7:23
not of such *c-s*, Ac 25:18

CRIMINAL *lawbreaker*
crucified...the *c-s*, Lk 23:33
imprisonment as a *c*, 2Ti 2:9

CRIMSON *deep red*
purple, *c* and violet, 2Ch 2:7
like *c*...be like wool, Is 1:18

CRIPPLED *lame*
a son *c* in his feet, 2Sa 4:4
enter life *c* or lame, Mt 18:8
bring...*c* and blind, Lk 14:21

CRISPUS
Chief ruler of synagogue of Corinth, Ac 18:8
Baptized by Paul, 1Co 1:14

CROOKED *evil, twisted*
and *c* generation, Dt 32:5
to their *c* ways, Ps 125:5
What is *c* cannot be, Ecc 1:15
make *c* the straight, Ac 13:10
c and perverse, Php 2:15

CROP *yield of produce*
old things from the *c*, Lv 25:22
c-s to the grasshopper, Ps 78:46
c began to sprout, Am 7:1
share of the *c-s*, 2Ti 2:6

CROSS *(n) execution device*
take his *c* and, Mt 10:38
down from the *c*, Mt 27:40
to bear His *c*, Mk 15:21
take up his *c* daily, Lk 9:23
standing by the *c*, Jn 19:25
hanging Him on a *c*, Ac 5:30
c of Christ would, 1Co 1:17
word of the *c* is, 1Co 1:18
boast, except in the *c*, Gal 6:14
even death on a *c*, Php 2:8
enemies of the *c*, Php 3:18
blood of His *c*, Col 1:20
endured the *c*, Heb 12:2

CROSS *(v) pass over*
you *c* the Jordan, Dt 12:10
c-ed opposite Jericho, Jos 3:16
kept *c-ing* the ford, 2Sa 19:18
Jesus had *c-ed* over, Mk 5:21
c-ing over to, Ac 21:2

CROUCH *bow, stoop*
sin is *c-ing* at the, Ge 4:7
Beneath Him *c* the, Job 9:13
Nothing...but to *c*, Is 10:4

CROWD *multitude*
send the *c-s* away, Mt 14:15
because of the *c*, Mk 2:4
He summoned the *c*, Mk 8:34

c of tax collectors, Lk 5:29
Him...a large *c*, Lk 23:27
they stirred up the *c*, Ac 17:8

CROWN *(n) royal emblem; top*
on the *c* of the head, Ge 49:26
the *c* of their king, 2Sa 12:30
he set the royal *c*, Est 2:17
wife is the *c* of, Pr 12:4
gray head is a *c*, Pr 16:31
c of the drunkards, Is 28:3
a *c* of thorns, Mt 27:29
receive the *c* of life, Jas 1:12
c-s before the throne, Rev 4:10
golden *c* on His head, Rev 14:14

CROWN *(v) to place crown on*
c him with glory, Ps 8:5
Who *c-s* you with, Ps 103:4
head *c-s* you like, SS 7:5
c-ed him with glory, Heb 2:7

CRUCIFY *to execute on a cross*
scourge and *c Him*, Mt 20:19
C Him, Mt 27:22
Jesus...been *c-ied*, Mt 28:5
c your King, Jn 19:15
Paul was not *c-ied*, 1Co 1:13
preach Christ *c-ied*, 1Co 1:23
not have *c-ied* the, 1Co 2:8
c-ied with Christ, Gal 2:20
world...*c-ied* to me, Gal 6:14
their Lord was *c-ied*, Rev 11:8

CRUEL *fierce, harsh*
their...*c* bondage, Ex 6:9
c man does...harm, Pr 11:17
compassion...is *c*, Pr 12:10
c and have no mercy, Jer 6:23
people has become *c*, La 4:3

CRUMBS *morsels*
dogs feed on the *c*, Mt 15:27
on the children's *c*, Mk 7:28

CRUSH *demolish, destroy*
a foot may *c* them, Job 39:15
saves...*c-ed* in spirit, Ps 34:18
lying tongue...*c-es*, Pr 26:28
by *c-ing* My people, Is 3:15
c-ed for our iniquities, Is 53:5
LORD was pleased To *c*, Is 53:10
who *c* the needy, Am 4:1
c Satan under...feet, Ro 16:20

CRY *(n) scream, sob*
great and bitter *c*, Ge 27:34
the *c* of triumph, Ex 32:18
c has come to Me, 1Sa 9:16
Hear my *c*, O God, Ps 61:1
the *c* of Jerusalem, Jer 14:2
Jesus uttered a...*c*, Mk 15:37

CRY *(v)*
do not *c* for help, Job 36:13
c aloud in the night, La 2:19
His elect, who *c*, Lk 18:7
stones will *c* out, Lk 19:40
Jesus stood and *c-ied*, Jn 7:37

CRYSTAL *glass*
awesome gleam of *c*, Eze 1:22
sea of glass, like *c*, Rev 4:6
water...clear as *c*, Rev 22:1

CUB *whelp, young*
robbed of her *c-s*, 2Sa 17:8
She reared her *c-s*, Eze 19:2
lioness, and lion's *c*, Na 2:11

CUBIT *linear measure*
ark three hundred *c-s*, Ge 6:15
length was nine *c-s*, Dt 3:11
gallows fifty *c-s* high, Est 5:14
the altar by *c-s*, Eze 43:13

CUD *previously swallowed food*
chews the *c*, Lv 11:3
not chew *c*, it is, Lv 11:7
chews the *c*, Dt 14:6

CULT *religious ritual*
be a *c* prostitute, Dt 23:17
male *c* prostitutes, 1Ki 14:24
male c prostitutes, 2Ki 23:7

CULTIVATE *till*
no man to *c* the, Ge 2:5
Eden to *c* it, Ge 2:15
and *c* vineyards, Dt 28:39
servants shall *c*, 2Sa 9:10
and *c* faithfulness, Ps 37:3

CUMMIN *plant for seasoning*
driven over *c*, Is 28:27
mint and dill and *c*, Mt 23:23

CUNNING *crafty*
he is very *c*, 1Sa 23:22
advice of the *c*, Job 5:13
harlot and *c* of heart, Pr 7:10

CUP *container*
into Pharaoh's *c*, Ge 40:11
My *c* overflows, Ps 23:5
the *c* of salvation, Ps 116:13
a *c* of consolation, Jer 16:7
c of cold water, Mt 10:42
let this *c* pass, Mt 26:39
washing of *c-s* and, Mk 7:4
gives you a *c* of, Mk 9:41
c...new covenant, Lk 22:20
c of blessing, 1Co 10:16
eat...drink the *c*, 1Co 11:26
c full of abominations, Rev 17:4

CUPBEARER *royal official*
c spoke to Pharaoh, Ge 41:9
his *c-s*, and his, 1Ki 10:5
c-s and their attire, 2Ch 9:4
c to the king, Ne 1:11

CURDS *butter, cheese*
he took *c* and milk, Ge 18:8
she brought him *c*, Jdg 5:25
with honey and *c*, Job 20:17

CURE *heal*
c him of his leprosy, 2Ki 5:3
c you of your wound, Hos 5:13
they could not *c* him, Mt 17:16
that...time He *c-d*, Lk 7:21

CURSE *(n) condemning oath*
upon myself a *c*, Ge 27:12
c on Mount Ebal, Dt 11:29
c to My chosen ones, Is 65:15
they will become a *c*, Jer 44:12
will no longer be a *c*, Zec 14:11
become a *c* for us, Gal 3:13

CURSE *(v) verbally condemn*
who *c-s* you I will *c*, Ge 12:3
You shall not *c* God, Ex 22:28
not *c* a deaf man, Lv 19:14
c-d the...anointed, 2Sa 19:21
c-d the day of his *birth*, Job 3:1
began to *c* and, Mk 14:71
bless and do not *c*, Ro 12:14
with it we *c* men, Jas 3:9

CURSED *(adj) under a curse*
C is the ground, Ge 3:17
C be Canaan, Ge 9:25
C is the man who, Dt 27:15
C...who trusts, Jer 17:5
C...who hangs, Gal 3:13

CURTAIN *covering, drape*
on the edge of the *c*, Ex 26:4
heaven like a *tent c*, Ps 104:2
c-s of your dwellings, Is 54:2
c-s of the land of, Hab 3:7

CUSH
Ham's oldest son, 1Ch 1:8–10
——— Another name for Ethiopia, Is 18:1

CUSHAN-RISHATHAIM
Mesopotamian king; oppresses Israel, Jdg 3:8
Othniel delivers Israel from, Jdg 3:9, 10

CUSTODY *prison, protection*
they put him in *c*, Nu 15:34
into the *c* of Hegai, Est 2:3
John...taken into *c*, Mt 4:12
holding Jesus in *c*, Lk 22:63

CUSTOM *manner; tax*
it became a *c* in, Jdg 11:39
not pay tribute, *c*, Ezr 4:13
c, He entered the, Lk 4:16
burial *c* of the Jews, Jn 19:40
c-s...not lawful, Ac 16:21
c-s of our fathers, Ac 28:17
whom tax *is due; c*, Ro 13:7

CUT *destroy, divide*
did not *c* the birds, Ge 15:10
c off from the earth, Ex 9:15
c down their Asherim, Ex 34:13
LORD *c* off...lips, Ps 12:3
tongue will be *c*, Pr 10:31
C off your hair and, Jer 7:29
were *c-ting* branches, Mt 21:8
and *c* off his ear, Mt 26:51
were *c* to the quick, Ac 7:54
you...will be *c* off, Ro 11:22

CYMBAL *musical instrument*
castanets and *c-s*, 2Sa 6:5
loud-sounding *c-s*, 1Ch 15:16
with loud *c-s*, Ps 150:5
or a clanging *c*, 1Co 13:1

CYPRESS *tree*
cedar and *c* timber, 1Ki 5:10
c and algum timber, 2Ch 2:8
Our rafters, *c-es*, SS 1:17
Wail, O *c*, for the, Zec 11:2

CYPRUS
Mentioned in prophecies, Nu 24:24; Is 23:1–12; Jer 2:10
Christians preach to Jews of, Ac 11:19, 20

Paul and Barnabas visit, Ac 13:4–13; 15:39

CYRENE
A Greek colonial city in North Africa; home of Simon the cross-bearer, Mt 27:32
Synagogue of, Ac 6:9
Christians from, become missionaries, Ac 11:20

CYRUS
King of Persia, referred to as God's anointed, Is 44:28–45:1

D

DAGON
The national god of the Philistines, Jdg 16:23
Falls before ark, 1Sa 5:1–5

DAILY *day by day*
d amount of bricks, Ex 5:19
d with her words, Jdg 16:16
LORD, who *d* bears our, Ps 68:19
Give us this day our *d* bread, Mt 6:11
take up his cross *d* and, Lk 9:23
He was teaching *d*, Lk 19:47
in the *d* serving *of food*, Ac 6:1
increasing in number *d*, Ac 16:5
examining the Scriptures *d*, Ac 17:11
Jesus our Lord, I die *d*, 1Co 15:31
in need of *d* food, Jas 2:15

DALMATIA
A region east of the Adriatic Sea; Titus departs for, 2Ti 4:10

DAMAGE *(n) destruction*
any *d* may be found, 2Ki 12:5
the *d-s* of the house, 2Ki 12:6
d and great loss, Ac 27:10
incurred this *d* and, Ac 27:21

DAMAGE *(v) destroy, hurt*
it will *d* the revenue, Ezr 4:13
and *d-ing* to kings, Ezr 4:15
enemy has *d-d*, Ps 74:3
So that no one...*d* it, Is 27:3

DAMASCUS
Capital of Syria; captured by David; ruled by enemy kings, 2Sa 8:5, 6; 1Ki 11:23, 24; 15:18
Elisha's prophecy in, 2Ki 8:7–15
Taken by Assyrians, 2Ki 16:9
Prophecy concerning, Is 8:3, 4
Paul converted on road to; first preaches there, Ac 9:1–22
escapes from, 2Co 11:32, 33
revisits, Gal 1:17

DAN
Jacob's son by Bilhah, Ge 30:5, 6
Prophecy concerning, Ge 49:16, 17
——— Tribe of:
Numbered, Nu 1:38, 39
Blessed, Dt 33:22
Receive their inheritance, Jos 19:40–47
Fall into idolatry, Jdg 18:1–31
——— Town, northern boundary of Israel, Jdg 20:1
Called Leshem; captured by Danites, Jos 19:47
Center of idolatry, 1Ki 12:28–30
Destroyed by Ben-Hadad, 1Ki 15:20

DANCE *(n) rhythmic movement*
timbrels...with *d-ing*, Ex 15:20
they sing in the *d-s*, 1Sa 29:5
will rejoice in the *d*, Jer 31:13
music and *d-ing*, Lk 15:25

DANCE *(v) move rhythmically*
from those who *d-d*, Jdg 21:23
David was *d-ing*, 2Sa 6:14
and a time to *d*, Ecc 3:4
Herodias *d-d* before, Mt 14:6

DANGER *peril*
not only is there *d*, Ac 19:27
often in *d* of death, 2Co 11:23
d-s from...Gentiles, 2Co 11:26

DANIEL
Taken to Babylon; refuses Nebuchadnezzar's foods, Da 1
Interprets dreams; honored by king, Da 2
Interprets handwriting on wall; honored by Belshazzar, Da 5:10–29
Appointed to high office; conspired against and thrown to lions, Da 6:1–23
Visions of four beasts, ram and goat, Da 7; 8
Intercedes for Israel, Da 9:1–19
Further visions, Da 9:20–12:13

DARE *presume, risk*
who *d-s* rouse him up, Ge 49:9
who would *d* to risk, Jer 30:21
d from that day, Mt 22:46
did not *d* pronounce, Jude 9

DARIUS
Darius the Mede, son of Ahasuerus; made king of the Chaldeans, Da 9:1
Succeeds Belshazzar, Da 5:30, 31
Co-ruler with Cyrus, Da 6:28
——— Darius Hystaspis (522–486 B.C.), king of all Persia; temple work dated by his reign, Ezr 4:5, 24
Confirms Cyrus's royal edict, Ezr 6:1–14
——— Darius the Persian (423–404 B.C.); priestly records kept during his reign, Ne 12:22

DARK *dim, shadow*
not in *d* sayings, Nu 12:8
d places of the land, Ps 74:20
live in a *d* land, Is 9:2
it was still *d*, Jn 20:1
shining in a *d* place, 2Pe 1:19

DARKEN *obscure*
the land was *d-ed*, Ex 10:15
this that *d-s* counsel, Job 38:2
the stars are *d-ed*, Ecc 12:2
sun will be *d-ed*, Mk 13:24
their eyes be *d-ed*, Ro 11:10

DARKNESS *gloom, shadow*
blind...gropes in *d*, Dt 28:29
are silenced in *d*, 1Sa 2:9
illumines my *d*, 2Sa 22:29
that stalks in *d*, Ps 91:6
those who dwelt in *d*, Ps 107:10
as light excels *d*, Ecc 2:13
people who walk in *d*, Is 9:2
light will rise in *d*, Is 58:10
into the outer *d*, Mt 22:13
those who sit in *d*, Lk 1:79
men loved the *d*, Jn 3:19
turn from *d* to light, Ac 26:18
has light with *d*, 2Co 6:14
unfruitful deeds of *d*, Eph 5:11
in Him there is no *d*, 1Jn 1:5
brother is in the *d*, 1Jn 2:9

DARLING *love*
you are, my *d*, SS 1:15
Arise, my *d*, SS 2:13
my *d*, My dove, SS 5:2

DATHAN
Joins Korah's rebellion, Nu 16:1–35
Swallowed up by the earth, Ps 106:17

DAUGHTER
d-s were born to them, Ge 6:1
if a man sells his *d*, Ex 21:7
inheritance to his *d*, Nu 27:8
Kings' *d-s* are among, Ps 45:9
d-s of song, Ecc 12:4
destruction of the *d*, Is 22:4
the *d* of my people, Jer 9:1
D rises up against, Mic 7:6
mother against *d*, Lk 12:53

DAUGHTER-IN-LAW
said to his *d* Tamar, Ge 38:11
nakedness of your *d*, Lv 18:15
said to Ruth her *d*, Ru 2:22
D against her, Mic 7:6

DAVID
Anointed by Samuel, 1Sa 16:1–13
Becomes royal harpist, 1Sa 16:14–23
Defeats Goliath, 1Sa 17
Makes covenant with Jonathan, 1Sa 18:1–4
Honored by Saul; loved by the people; Saul becomes jealous, 1Sa 18:5–16
Wins Michal as wife, 1Sa 18:17–30
Flees from Saul, 1Sa 19; 20; 21:10–22:5; 23:14–29
Eats the holy bread, 1Sa 21:1–6; Mt 12:3, 4
Saves Keilah from Philistines, 1Sa 23:1–13
Twice spares Saul's life, 1Sa 24:1–22; 26:1–25
Anger at Nabal appeased by Abigail; marries her, 1Sa 25:2–42
Allies with the Philistines, 1Sa 27:1–28:2
Rejected by them, 1Sa 29
Avenges destruction of Ziklag, 1Sa 30
Mourns death of Saul and Jonathan, 2Sa 1
Anointed king of Judah, 2Sa 2:1–7
War with Saul's house; Abner defects to David, 2Sa 3:1, 6–21
Mourns Abner's death, 2Sa 3:28–39
Punishes Ishbosheth's murderers, 2Sa 4
Anointed king of all Israel, 2Sa 5:1–5
Conquers Jerusalem; makes it his capital, 2Sa 5:6–16
Defeats Philistines, 2Sa 5:17–25
Brings ark to Jerusalem, 2Sa 6
Receives eternal covenant, 2Sa 7
Further conquests, 2Sa 8; 10
Shows mercy to Mephibosheth, 2Sa 9

Commits adultery and murder, 2Sa 11
Rebuked by Nathan; repents, 2Sa 12:1–23; Ps 32; 51
Absalom's rebellion, 2Sa 15–18
Mourns Absalom's death, 2Sa 18:33–19:8
Shows himself merciful, 2Sa 19:18–39
Sheba's rebellion, 2Sa 19:40–20:22
Avenges the Gibeonites, 2Sa 21:1–14
Song of deliverance, 2Sa 22
Sins by numbering the people, 2Sa 24:1–17
Buys threshing floor to build altar, 2Sa 24:18–25
Secures Solomon's succession, 1Ki 1:5–53
Instructions to Solomon, 1Ki 2:1–11
Last words, 2Sa 23:1–7
Inspired by Spirit, Mt 22:43
As prophet, Ac 2:29–34
Faith of, Heb 11:32–34

DAWN *(n) daylight*
at the approach of *d*, Jdg 19:25
caused the *d* to know, Job 38:12
rise before *d* and, Ps 119:147
wings of the *d*, Ps 139:9
As the *d* is spread, Joel 2:2

DAWN *(v) become light*
the day began to *d*, Jdg 19:26
when morning *d-s*, Ps 46:5
a Light *d-ed*, Mt 4:16
d toward the first, Mt 28:1
until the day *d-s*, 2Pe 1:19

DAY *light*
God called the light *d*, Ge 1:5
come on a festive *d*, 1Sa 25:8
d...LORD has made, Ps 118:24
what a *d* may bring, Pr 27:1
d-s of your youth, Ecc 12:1
a *d* of reckoning, Is 2:12
d of the LORD is near, Is 13:6
has despised the *d*, Zec 4:10
the *d* of His coming, Mal 3:2
Give us this *d*, Mt 6:11
raise...the last *d*, Jn 6:39
judge...the last *d*, Jn 12:48
the *d* of salvation, 2Co 6:2
perfect it until the *d*, Php 1:6
d of the Lord, 1Th 5:2
d is like a thousand, 2Pe 3:8
tormented *d*...night, Rev 20:10

DAY OF ATONEMENT
month is the *d*, Lv 23:27
for it is a *d*, Lv 23:28

DAY OF THE LORD
Wail, for the *d* is near, Is 13:6
stand in the battle on the *d*, Eze 13:5
Alas for the day! For the *d*, Joel 1:15
great and awesome *d*, Joel 2:31
For what purpose will the *d*, Am 5:18
d draws near on all the, Ob 15
For the *d* is near, Zep 1:7
the great and terrible *d*, Mal 4:5
great and glorious *d*, Ac 2:20
be saved in the *d* Jesus, 1Co 5:5
d will come like a thief, 2Pe 3:10

DAZZLING *blinding, bright*
My beloved is *d*, SS 5:10
Like *d* heat, Is 18:4
near...in *d* clothing, Lk 24:4

DEACONS *officer, server*
overseers and *d*, Php 1:1
D likewise *must be*, 1Ti 3:8
let them serve as *d*, 1Ti 3:10
D must be husbands, 1Ti 3:12
served well as *d*, 1Ti 3:13

DEAD *without life*
you are a *d* man, Ge 20:3
near to a *d* person, Nu 6:6
dealt with the *d*, Ru 1:8
forgotten as a *d* man, Ps 31:12
d do not praise, Ps 115:17
better than a *d* lion, Ecc 9:4
Your *d* will live, Is 26:19
not weep for the *d*, Jer 22:10
rising from the *d*, Mk 9:10
d will hear the, Jn 5:25
resurrection of the *d*, Ac 23:6
d in your trespasses, Eph 2:1
firstborn from the *d*, Col 1:18
living and the *d*, 2Ti 4:1
repentance...*d* works, Heb 6:1
to those who are *d*, 1Pe 4:6
I was *d*...I am alive, Rev 1:18
Hades gave up the *d*, Rev 20:13

DEAD SEA
Called the:
Salt Sea, Ge 14:3
Sea of the Arabah, Dt 3:17

DEADLY *fatal*
the *d* poison of cobras, Dt 32:33
prepared for Himself *d*, Ps 7:13
And from the *d* pestilence., Ps 91:3
Their tongue is a *d* arrow, Jer 9:8
drink any *d poison*, Mk 16:18
full of *d* poison, Jas 3:8

DEAF *without hearing*
makes *him* mute or *d*, Ex 4:11
not curse a *d* man, Lv 19:14
Like a *d* cobra, Ps 58:4
the *d* will hear, Is 29:18
and *the d* hear, Mt 11:5
the *d* to hear, Mk 7:37
d and mute spirit, Mk 9:25

DEAL *allot, barter, treat*
let us *d* wisely, Ex 1:10
have you *d-t* with us, Ex 14:11
nor *d* falsely, Lv 19:11
d-t with mediums, 2Ki 21:6
who *d* treacherously, Ps 25:3
has *d-t* bountifully, Ps 116:7
who *d* faithfully, Pr 12:22
Everyone *d-s* falsely, Jer 6:13
when I have *d-t*, Eze 20:44
has *d-t* with me, Lk 1:25

DEALINGS *actions, relations*
no *d* with anyone, Jdg 18:7
no *d* with Samaritans, Jn 4:9
of the Lord's *d*, Jas 5:11

DEAR *beloved*
Is Ephraim My *d* son, Jer 31:20
my life...as *d* to, Ac 20:24
had become very *d*, 1Th 2:8

DEATH *cessation of life*
d of the upright, Nu 23:10
d encompassed me, 2Sa 22:5
d for his own sin, 2Ch 25:4
D rather than my pains, Job 7:15
no mention of You in *d*, Ps 6:5
cords of *d* encompassed, Ps 18:4
the shadow of *d*, Ps 23:4
escapes from *d*, Ps 68:20
doomed to *d*, Ps 102:20
d of His godly ones, Ps 116:15
who hate me love *d*, Pr 8:36
love is as strong as *d*, SS 8:6
He will swallow up *d*, Is 25:8
D cannot praise You, Is 38:18
no pleasure in the *d*, Eze 18:32
d is better to me, Jon 4:3
is to be put to *d*, Mt 15:4
will not taste *d*, Mt 16:28
to the point of *d*, Mk 14:34
passed out of *d*, Jn 5:24
he will never see *d*, Jn 8:51
sickness is not to end in *d*, Jn 11:4
the agony of *d*, Ac 2:24
d by hanging Him, Ac 10:39
d reigned from Adam, Ro 5:14
wages of sin is *d*, Ro 6:23
the law of sin and of *d*, Ro 8:2
proclaim...Lord's *d*, 1Co 11:26
d, where...victory, 1Co 15:55
even *d* on a cross, Php 2:8
He might taste *d*, Heb 2:9
it brings forth *d*, Jas 1:15
passed out of *d*, 1Jn 3:14
Be faithful until *d*, Rev 2:10
had the name *D*, Rev 6:8
second *d*...no power, Rev 20:6

DEBATE *dispute*
d-d...themselves, Mk 1:27
dissension and *d*, Ac 15:2
had been much *d*, Ac 15:7

DEBIR
City of Judah; captured by Joshua, Jos 10:38, 39
Recaptured by Othniel; formerly called Kirjath Sepher, Jos 15:15–17; Jdg 1:11–13

DEBORAH
A prophetess and judge, Jdg 4:4–14
Composed song of triumph, Jdg 5:1–31

DEBT *obligation*
and pay your *d*, 2Ki 4:7
exaction of every *d*, Ne 10:31
guarantors for *d-s*, Pr 22:26
forgive us our *d-s*, Mt 6:12

DEBTOR *borrower*
restores to the *d*, Eze 18:7
forgiven our *d-s*, Mt 6:12
had two *d-s*, Lk 7:41
his master's *d-s*, Lk 16:5

DECAPOLIS
Multitudes from, follow Jesus, Mt 4:25
Jesus heals demon-possessed, preaches in, Mk 5:20

DECAY *corruption*
own eyes see his *d*, Job 21:20
Holy One to...*d*, Ac 2:27
did not undergo *d*, Ac 13:37

DECEASED *dead*
wife of the *d* shall, Dt 25:5
the widow of the *d*, Ru 4:5

the name of the *d*, Ru 4:10
the sister of the *d*, Jn 11:39

DECEIT *deception, falsehood, guile*
full of curses and *d*, Ps 10:7
in whose spirit...no *d*, Ps 32:2
your tongue frames *d*, Ps 50:19
D is in the heart, Pr 12:20
he lays up *d*, Pr 26:24
Offspring of *d*, Is 57:4
houses are full of *d*, Jer 5:27
house of Israel...*d*, Hos 11:12
d, sensuality, envy, Mk 7:22
in whom...is no *d*, Jn 1:47
full of envy...*d*, Ro 1:29
the lusts of *d*, Eph 4:22
all malice and all *d*, 1Pe 2:1
nor was any *d* found, 1Pe 2:22
lips from speaking *d*, 1Pe 3:10

DECEITFUL *false*
From a *d* tongue, Ps 120:2
the wicked are *d*, Pr 12:5
d are the kisses of, Pr 27:6
Charm is *d* and, Pr 31:30
The heart is more *d*, Jer 17:9
false apostles, *d*, 2Co 11:13

DECEIVE *cheat, mislead*
have you *d-d* me, Ge 29:25
Jacob *d-d* Laban, Ge 31:20
d-s his companion, Lv 6:2
both stolen and *d-d*, Jos 7:11
Do not *d* me, 2Ki 4:28
who *d-s* his neighbor, Pr 26:19
Do not *d* yourselves, Jer 37:9
your heart has *d-d* you, Ob 3
they keep *d-ing*, Ro 3:13
Let no one *d* you, Eph 5:6
d-ing and being *d-d*, 2Ti 3:13

DECEIVER *liar*
as a *d* in his sight, Ge 27:12
as *d-s* and yet true, 2Co 6:8
d and the antichrist, 2Jn 7

DECEPTION *falsehood*
their mind prepares *d*, Job 15:35
the hills are a *d*, Jer 3:23
last *d* will be worse, Mt 27:64
philosophy and empty *d*, Col 2:8
reveling in their *d-s*, 2Pe 2:13

DECEPTIVE *misleading*
wicked...*d* wages, Pr 11:18
Do not trust in *d* words, Jer 7:4
d stream With water, Jer 15:18

DECIDE *determine*
is too difficult for you to *d*, Dt 17:8
he has *d-d* on evil, 1Sa 20:7
d between you and me, 1Sa 24:15
Solomon *d-d* to build, 2Ch 2:1
d-s between the mighty, Pr 18:18
d with fairness for the, Is 11:4
lots for them *to d*, Mk 15:24
d-d to deliver such a one, 1Co 5:5
to *d* between his brethren, 1Co 6:5
d-d this in his own heart, 1Co 7:37

DECISION *judgment, resolution*
d is from the LORD, Pr 16:33
in the valley of *d*, Joel 3:14
My *d* is to gather, Zep 3:8
majority reached a *d*, Ac 27:12

DECLARE *explain, proclaim*
Moses *d-d* to...sons, Lv 23:44
d to Him the number, Job 31:37
d Your faithfulness, Ps 30:9
mouth...*d* Your praise, Ps 51:15
d Your lovingkindness, Ps 92:2
Who has *d-d this*, Is 41:26
d-s the LORD, Am 4:11
He will *d* all things, Jn 4:25
d-d the Son of God, Ro 1:4

DECLINE *decrease*
for the shadow to *d*, 2Ki 20:10
our days have *d-d*, Ps 90:9
for the day *d-s*, Jer 6:4

DECREASE *abate, subside*
the water *d-d* steadily, Ge 8:5
not let their cattle *d*, Ps 107:38
increase...I must *d*, Jn 3:30

DECREE *(n) judgment, order*
issued a *d* to rebuild, Ezr 5:13
and *d* of the king, Est 2:8
devises mischief by *d*, Ps 94:20
only one *d* for you, Da 2:9
delivering the *d-s*, Ac 16:4
to the *d-s* of Caesar, Ac 17:7

DECREE *(v) decide, determine*
been *d-d* against her, Est 2:1
will also *d* a thing, Job 22:28
And rulers *d* justice, Pr 8:15
Seventy weeks...*d-d*, Da 9:24

DEDICATE *consecrate, devote*
D yourselves today, Ex 32:29
I wholly *d* the silver, Jdg 17:3
d-d by...David, 1Ki 7:51
David...*d-d* these, 1Ch 18:11
d-d part...the spoil, 1Ch 26:27
d-ing it to Him, 2Ch 2:4

DEDICATION *consecration*
the *d* of the altar, 2Ch 7:9
celebrated the *d* of, Ezr 6:16
d of the wall, Ne 12:27
d of the image, Da 3:2
assembled for the *d*, Da 3:3

DEDICATION, FEAST OF
See FEASTS

DEED *action; document*
What is this *d*, Ge 44:15
for our evil *d-s*, Ezr 9:13
blot out...loyal *d-s*, Ne 13:14
abominable *d-s*, Ps 14:1
I...sealed the *d*, Jer 32:10
prophet mighty in *d*, Lk 24:19
their *d-s* were evil, Jn 3:19
d-s of the flesh are, Gal 5:19
for every good *d*, Titus 3:1
I know your *d-s*, Rev 2:2

DEEP *(adj) far ranging*
d sleep falls on men, Job 4:13
Your judgments are...*d*, Ps 36:6
casts into a *d* sleep, Pr 19:15
into *d* darkness, Jer 13:16
the well is *d*, Jn 4:11

DEEP *(n) abyss, depth*
fountains of the...*d*, Ge 7:11
the *d* lying beneath, Dt 33:13
surface of the *d* is, Job 38:30
D calls to *d*, Ps 42:7
The *d-s* also trembled, Ps 77:16
His wonders in the *d*, Ps 107:24
the springs of the *d*, Pr 8:28

DEER *animal*
besides *d*, gazelles, 1Ki 4:23
d pants for the water, Ps 42:1
lame will leap like a *d*, Is 35:6

DEFEAT *conquer, overthrow*
d-ed...and pursued, Ge 14:15
able to *d* them, Nu 22:6
sons of Israel *d-ed*, Jos 12:7
d the Arameans, 2Ki 13:17
d-ed the Philistines, 1Ch 18:1
d-ed the entire army, Jer 37:10

DEFECT *(n) blemish, spot*
No one who has a *d*, Lv 21:18
one ram without *d*, Nu 6:14
if it has any *d*, Dt 15:21
no *d* in him, 2Sa 14:25
in whom was no *d*, Da 1:4

DEFECT *(v) rebel, disobey*
d to his master, 1Ch 12:19
many *d-ed* to him, 2Ch 15:9
you have deeply *d-ed*, Is 31:6

DEFEND *protect*
LORD of hosts will *d*, Zec 9:15
d-ed him and took, Ac 7:24
or else *d-ing* them, Ro 2:15
are *d-ing* ourselves, 2Co 12:19

DEFENSE *protection*
d-s are *d-s* of clay, Job 13:12
the *d* of my life, Ps 27:1
You have been a *d*, Is 25:4
the *d*...of the gospel, Php 1:7

DEFILE *pollute, profane*
astray...*d-s* herself, Nu 5:29
d-d the high places, 2Ki 23:8
d-d the priesthood, Ne 13:29
d-d Your holy temple, Ps 79:1
your hands are *d-d*, Is 59:3
those *d* the man, Mt 15:18
is what *d-s* the man, Mk 7:20
conscience...is *d-d*, 1Co 8:7
d-s the entire body, Jas 3:6

DEFILEMENT *filth*
her *interest*, for *d*, Eze 22:3
from all *d* of flesh, 2Co 7:1

DEFRAUD *deprive, wrong*
whom have I *d-ed*, 1Sa 12:3
To *d* a man, La 3:36
Do not *d*, Mk 10:19
no one keep *d-ing*, Col 2:18

DEITY *God, gods*
of strange *d-ies*, Ac 17:18
fullness of *D* dwells, Col 2:9

DELAIAH
Son of Shemaiah; urges Jehoiakim not to burn Jeremiah's scroll, Jer 36:12, 25

DELAY *hinder, linger, stall*
Do not *d* me, Ge 24:56

Moses *d-ed* to come, Ex 32:1
shall not *d* to pay, Dt 23:21
bridegroom...*d-ing*, Mt 25:5
Do not *d* in coming, Ac 9:38
now why do you *d*, Ac 22:16
in case I am *d-ed*, 1Ti 3:15

DELICACIES *fancy foods*
eat of their *d*, Ps 141:4
Do not desire his *d*, Pr 23:3
Those who ate *d*, La 4:5

DELIGHT *(n) pleasure*
I have no *d* in you, 2Sa 15:26
Will he take *d*, Job 27:10
his *d* is in the law, Ps 1:2
commandments...*d*, Ps 119:143
my *d* in the sons of, Pr 8:31
a just weight is His *d*, Pr 11:1
the *d* of kings, Pr 16:13
I took great *d*, SS 2:3
call the sabbath a *d*, Is 58:13
My *d* is in her, Is 62:4

DELIGHT *(v) desire*
LORD *d-ed* over you, Dt 28:63
d in...offerings, 1Sa 15:22
d to revere Your name, Ne 1:11
d in the Almighty, Job 22:26
D yourself in the LORD, Ps 37:4
not *d* in sacrifice, Ps 51:16
Who *d* in doing evil, Pr 2:14
d in my ways, Pr 23:26
takes no *d* in fools, Ecc 5:4
I *d* in loyalty, Hos 6:6
d-s...unchanging love, Mic 7:18
d-ing...self-abasement, Col 2:18

DELIGHTFUL *pleasant*
d is a timely word, Pr 15:23
to find *d* words, Ecc 12:10
and how *d* you are, SS 7:6
Is he a *d* child, Jer 31:20

DELILAH
Deceives Samson, Jdg 16:4–22

DELIVER *give, rescue, save*
come down to *d* them, Ex 3:8
d the manslayer, Nu 35:25
My...power has *d-ed*, Jdg 7:2
can this one *d*, 1Sa 10:27
He will *d* you, Job 5:19
d-ed my soul from, Ps 56:13
none who can *d*, Is 43:13
mind on *d-ing* Daniel, Da 6:14
d us from evil, Mt 6:13
d-ed over to death, 2Co 4:11

DELIVERANCE *salvation*
by a great *d*, Ge 45:7
given this great *d*, Jdg 15:18
with songs of *d*, Ps 32:7
a God of *d-s*, Ps 68:20
d through...prayers, Php 1:19

DELIVERER *savior*
the LORD raised up a *d*, Jdg 3:9
gave them *d-s*, Ne 9:27
my fortress and my *d*, Ps 18:2
d-s...ascend Mount, Ob 21
D...come from Zion, Ro 11:26

DELUDE *lead astray*
they have *d-d* you, Is 47:10
no one will *d* you, Col 2:4
who *d* themselves, Jas 1:22

DEMAND *order, require*
husband may *d* of him, Ex 21:22
but I *d* one thing, 2Sa 3:13
captors *d-ed* of us, Ps 137:3
do not *d* it back, Lk 6:30
d-ing of Him a sign, Lk 11:16

DEMAS
Follows Paul, Col 4:14
Forsakes Paul, 2Ti 4:10

DEMETRIUS
A silversmith at Ephesus, Ac 19:24–31
——— A good Christian, 3Jn 12

DEMOLISH *destroy*
d all...high places, Nu 33:52
he *d-ed* its stones, 2Ki 23:15
to *d* its strongholds, Is 23:11

DEMON *devil*
sacrificed to *d-s*, Dt 32:17
daughters to the *d-s*, Ps 106:37
after the *d* was cast, Mt 9:33
sacrifice to *d-s*, 1Co 10:20
d-s also believe, Jas 2:19
not to worship *d-s*, Rev 9:20

DEMONIACS *possessed ones*
d, epileptics, Mt 4:24
what had happened to the *d*, Mt 8:33

DEMON-POSSESSED
many who were *d*, Mt 8:16
a mute, *d* man, Mt 9:32
to the *d* man, Mk 5:16
sayings of one *d*, Jn 10:21

DEMONSTRATE *show*
God *d-s* His own love, Ro 5:8
to *d* His wrath, Ro 9:22
d-d yourselves to be, 2Co 7:11
d His...patience, 1Ti 1:16

DEMONSTRATION *a showing*
for the *d*, *I say*, Ro 3:26
in *d* of the Spirit, 1Co 2:4

DEN *abode*
remains in its *d*, Job 37:8
From the *d-s* of lions, SS 4:8
the viper's *d*, Is 11:8
cast into the lions' *d*, Da 6:7
it a robbers' *d*, Mk 11:17

DENARIUS
Roman silver coin, Mt 20:2, 9
A day's wage, Lk 20:24
Denarii (pl), Jn 6:7; 12:5

DENOUNCE *accuse, slander*
And come, *d* Israel, Nu 23:7
the LORD has not *d-d*, Nu 23:8
let us *d* him, Jer 20:10
He...to *d* the cities, Mt 11:20

DENY *conceal, refuse*
Sarah *d-ied it*, Ge 18:15
so that you do not *d* your God, Jos 24:27
not *d-ied* the words, Job 6:10
and *d-ing* the LORD, Is 59:13
whoever *d-ies* Me, Mt 10:33
you have *d* three times, Lk 22:34
has *d-ied* the faith, 1Ti 5:8
deeds they *d Him*, Titus 1:16
us to *d* ungodliness, Titus 2:12
d-ies the Son, 1Jn 2:23

DEPART *leave*
scepter shall not *d*, Ge 49:10
sword...never *d*, 2Sa 12:10
to *d* from evil is, Job 28:28
His spirit *d-s*, Ps 146:4
his foolishness will not *d*, Pr 27:22
turned aside and *d-ed*, Jer 5:23
I never knew you; *d*, Mt 7:23
d from Me, all you, Lk 13:27
d and be with Christ, Php 1:23

DEPARTURE *death; leaving*
after their *d* from, Ex 16:1
speaking of His *d*, Lk 9:31
time of my *d* has, 2Ti 4:6
any time after my *d*, 2Pe 1:15

DEPEND *rely, rest*
d-ed on the weapons, Is 22:8
you did not *d* on Him, Is 22:11
d the whole Law, Mt 22:40

DEPORTATION *exile*
after the *d* to, Mt 1:12
to the *d* to Babylon, Mt 1:17

DEPORTED *exiled*
d...to Babylon, Ezr 5:12
d...entire population, Am 1:6

DEPOSE *release*
d you from your office, Is 22:19
d-d from his royal, Da 5:20

DEPOSIT *(n) security*
in regard to a *d*, Lv 6:2
d which was entrusted, Lv 6:4

DEPOSIT *(v) place, put*
d them in the tent, Nu 17:4
d it in your town, Dt 14:28
d...in the temple, Ezr 5:15
had *d-ed* the scroll, Jer 36:20

DEPRAVED *degenerate*
over to a *d* mind, Ro 1:28
men of *d* mind, 2Ti 3:8

DEPRIVE *take away*
d the needy of justice, Is 10:2
d-d of...my years, Is 38:10
d-ing one another, 1Co 7:5
d-d of the truth, 1Ti 6:5

DEPTH *abyss, deep*
d-s boil like a pot, Job 41:31
hand are the *d-s*, Ps 95:4
went down to the *d-s*, Ps 107:26
sins Into the *d-s*, Mic 7:19
drowned in the *d*, Mt 18:6
it had no *d* of soil, Mk 4:5
nor height, nor *d*, Ro 8:39
the *d* of the riches, Ro 11:33
even the *d-s* of God, 1Co 2:10

DEPUTY *proconsul*
he was the only *d*, 1Ki 4:19
Solomon's...*d-ies*, 1Ki 5:16
a *d* was king, 1Ki 22:47

DERBE
Paul visits, Ac 14:6, 20
Paul meets Timothy at, Ac 16:1

DERISION *laughingstock*
d among…enemies, Ex 32:25
d to those around us, Ps 44:13
reproach and *d* all, Jer 20:8
d to the rest of the, Eze 36:4

DESCEND *go down*
angels of God…*d-ing*, Ge 28:12
His glory will not *d*, Ps 49:17
breath of…*d-s*, Ecc 3:21
will *d* to Hades, Mt 11:23
Spirit *d-ing*…dove, Jn 1:32
d into the abyss, Ro 10:7
who *d-ed*…ascended, Eph 4:10

DESCENDANT *seed, offering*
your *d-s* I will give, Ge 12:7
will raise up your *d*, 2Sa 7:12
His *d-s* shall endure, Ps 89:36
So shall your *d-s* be, Ro 4:18
you are Abraham's *d-s*, Gal 3:29
to the *d* of Abraham, Heb 2:16
and the *d* of David, Rev 22:16

DESCENDANT OF DAVID
Christ comes from the *d-s*, Jn 7:42
a *d* according to the flesh, Ro 1:3
d, according to my gospel, 2Ti 2:8
d, the bright morning star, Rev 22:16

DESCENT *hill; heritage*
of Median *d*, Da 9:1
the *d* of the Mount, Lk 19:37
were of high-priestly *d*, Ac 4:6

DESCRIBE *explain*
you shall *d* the land, Jos 18:6
man, *d* the temple, Eze 43:10
who had seen it *d-d*, Mk 5:16

DESECRATE *defile*
d the sanctuary, Da 11:31
tried to *d* the temple, Ac 24:6

DESERT *(n) wilderness*
d plains of Jericho, Jos 5:10
grieved Him in the *d*, Ps 78:40
better to live in a *d*, Pr 21:19
in the *d* a highway, Is 40:3
Rivers in the *d*, Is 43:19
like a bush in the *d*, Jer 17:6
he lived in the *d-s*, Lk 1:80

DESERT *(v) abandon, forsake*
d-ed to the king, 2Ki 25:11
who had *d-ed* them, Ac 15:38
so quickly *d-ing* Him, Gal 1:6
but all *d-ed* me, 2Ti 4:16
I will never *d* you, Heb 13:5

DESERTERS *changers of loyalty*
d who had deserted, 2Ki 25:11
d who had gone over, Jer 39:9

DESERVE *earn, merit*
with him as he *d-d*, Jdg 9:16
done this *d-s* to die, 2Sa 12:5
He *d-s* death, Mt 26:66
receiving what we *d*, Lk 23:41

DESIGN *creation, plan*
d-s for work in gold, Ex 31:4
makers of *d-s*, Ex 35:35
execute any *d* which, 2Ch 2:14
All their deadly *d-s*, Jer 18:23

DESIGNATE *appoint*
if he *d-s* her for, Ex 21:9
one whom I *d* to, 1Sa 16:3
were *d-d* by name, 1Ch 16:41
being *d-d* by God, Heb 5:10

DESIRABLE *attractive*
the tree was *d*, Ge 3:6
d in your eyes, 1Ki 20:6
more *d* than gold, Ps 19:10
What is *d* in a man, Pr 19:22
every kind of *d* object, Na 2:9

DESIRE *(n) appetite, craving*
d…for your husband, Ge 3:16
poor from *their d*, Job 31:16
the *d-s* of your heart, Ps 37:4
d of the wicked will, Ps 112:10
d of the righteous, Pr 10:24
d of your eyes, Eze 24:16
great man speaks the *d*, Mic 7:3
d and my prayer, Ro 10:1
d-s of the flesh, Eph 2:3
d to depart and be, Php 1:23
evil *d*, and greed, Col 3:5

DESIRE *(v) crave, wish*
your heart *d-s*, Dt 14:26
as much as you *d*, 1Sa 2:16
I *d* to argue with God, Job 13:3
You *d* truth, Ps 51:6
not *d* his delicacies, Pr 23:3
all that my eyes *d-d*, Ecc 2:10
righteous men *d-d*, Mt 13:17
d the greater gifts, 1Co 12:31
d…a good showing, Gal 6:12
d a better *country*, Heb 11:16

DESOLATE *lonely, waste*
your sanctuaries *d*, Lv 26:31
sons of the *d* one, Is 54:1
high places will be *d*, Eze 6:6
d wilderness behind, Joel 2:3
loaves in *this d* place, Mt 15:33
homestead be made *d*, Ac 1:20
children of the *d*, Gal 4:27

DESOLATION *ruin, waste*
a *d* and a curse, 2Ki 22:19
a heap forever, a *d*, Jos 8:28
D is left in the city, Is 24:12
d-s of many generations, Is 61:4
an everlasting *d*, Eze 35:9
the abomination of *d*, Da 11:31
day of…*d*, Zep 1:15
her *d* is near, Lk 21:20

DESPAIR *(n) grief*
words of one in *d*, Job 6:26
my soul is in *d*, Ps 42:6
Why are you in *d*, Ps 43:5

DESPAIR *(v) grieve*
Saul then will *d*, 1Sa 27:1
I…*d-ed* of all, Ecc 2:20
we *d-ed* even of life, 2Co 1:8
but not *d-ing*, 2Co 4:8

DESPISE *reject, scorn*
d-d his birthright, Ge 25:34
those who *d* Me, 1Sa 2:30
d-d…in her heart, 2Sa 6:16
not *d* the discipline, Job 5:17
hate and *d* falsehood, Ps 119:163
Fools *d* wisdom and, Pr 1:7
wisdom…is *d-d*, Ecc 9:16
has *d-d* the day of, Zec 4:10
have we *d-d* Your name, Mal 1:6
not *d* one of these, Mt 18:10
be devoted to one and *d*, Lk 16:13
do you *d*…church, 1Co 11:22

DESPOIL *injure, lay waste*
d-ed all the cities, 2Ch 14:14
the wicked who *d* me, Ps 17:9
plundered and *d-ed*, Is 42:22

DESTINE *appoint*
is *d-d* for the sword, Job 15:22
d you for the sword, Is 65:12
things *d-d* to perish, Col 2:22
not *d-d* us for wrath, 1Th 5:9

DESTITUTE *deprived, in need*
prayer of the *d*, Ps 102:17
the land is *d*, Eze 32:15
being *d*, afflicted, Heb 11:37

DESTROY *abolish, ruin, waste*
to *d* all flesh, Ge 6:17
so that I do not *d* you, 1Sa 15:6
would You *d* me, Job 10:8
seek my life to *d* it, Ps 40:14
the wicked, He will *d*, Ps 145:20
that which *d-s* kings, Pr 31:3
one sinner *d-s* much, Ecc 9:18
stronghold is *d-ed*, Is 23:14
shepherds…are *d-ing*, Jer 23:1
He will *d* mighty men, Da 8:24
moth and rust *d*, Mt 6:19
who is able to *d*, Mt 10:28
You come to *d* us, Mk 1:24
seeking…to *d* Him, Mk 11:18
d the temple and, Mk 15:29
flood…*d-ed* them, Lk 17:27
D this temple, and, Jn 2:19
not for *d-ing* you, 2Co 10:8
to save and to *d*, Jas 4:12
heavens will be *d-ed*, 2Pe 3:12
d the works of the, 1Jn 3:8

DESTROYER *devastator*
d of our country, Jdg 16:24
of the *d-s* prosper, Job 12:6
d comes upon him, Job 15:21
d-s and devastators, Is 49:17
I will set apart *d-s*, Jer 22:7

DESTRUCTION *calamity, ruin*
the *d* of my kindred, Est 8:6
God apportion *d*, Job 21:17
Your tongue devises *d*, Ps 52:2
Pride *goes* before *d*, Pr 16:18
foolish son is *d* to, Pr 19:13
called the City of *D*, Is 19:18
d of the daughter of, La 2:11
broad that leads to *d*, Mt 7:13
whose end is *d*, Php 3:19
d will come, 1Th 5:3
penalty of eternal *d*, 2Th 1:9
bringing swift *d* upon, 2Pe 2:1

DETERMINE *decide*
to d whether he laid, Ex 22:8
his days are *d-d*, Job 14:5
d-d their appointed, Ac 17:26
but rather *d* this, Ro 14:13
d-d to know nothing, 1Co 2:2

DETEST *despise, loathe*
carcasses you shall *d*, Lv 11:11
not *d* an Egyptian, Dt 23:7
d his citadels, Am 6:8

DETESTABLE *abominable*
not eat any *d* thing, Dt 14:3
who is *d* and corrupt, Job 15:16
swine's flesh, *d*, Is 66:17
their *d* idols, Jer 16:18
remove all its *d*, Eze 11:18
d...sight of God, Lk 16:15

DEVASTATE *destroy, lay waste*
d-d the nations, 2Ki 19:17
Until cities are *d-d*, Is 6:11
the LORD...*d-s* it, Is 24:1
my tents are *d-d*, Jer 4:20
d...pride of Egypt, Eze 32:12

DEVASTATION *destruction*
d of the afflicted, Ps 12:5
Nor *d* or destruction, Is 60:18
raise up the former *d-s*, Is 61:4
d in their citadels, Am 3:10

DEVICE *plan, scheme*
By their own *d-s*, Ps 5:10
not promote his *evil d*, Ps 140:8
a man of evil *d-s*, Pr 14:17
in their *d-s* you walk, Mic 6:16

DEVIL *demon, Satan*
tempted by the *d*, Mt 4:1
one of you is a *d*, Jn 6:70
you son of the *d*, Ac 13:10
firm against...the *d*, Eph 6:11
render powerless...*d*, Heb 2:14
serpent...the *d*, Rev 12:9
d...into the lake, Rev 20:10

DEVIOUS *cunning*
who are *d* in their ways, Pr 2:15
the *d* are an abomination, Pr 3:32
put *d* speech far from you, Pr 4:24
he who is *d* in his ways, Pr 14:2

DEVISE *design, scheme, plot*
d-d against the Jews, Est 9:25
d-ing a vain thing, Ps 2:1
d-s mischief by decree, Ps 94:20
continually *d-s* evil, Pr 6:14
man who *d-s* evil, Pr 12:2
He *d-s* wicked schemes, Is 32:7
do not *d* evil in, Zec 7:10
d futile things, Ac 4:25

DEVOTE *commit, dedicate*
shall *d* to the LORD, Ex 13:12
d...to the law, 2Ch 31:4
d-d to one and despise, Mt 6:24
d-ing...to prayer, Ac 1:14
d-d to one another, Ro 12:10
D yourselves to prayer, Col 4:2

DEVOTED *set apart (to God)*
d to destruction, Lv 27:28
Every *d* thing in, Nu 18:14
d to destruction, 1Sa 15:21
d thing in Israel, Eze 44:29

DEVOTION *consecration*
his deeds of *d*, 2Ch 32:32
excessive *d to books*, Ecc 12:12
the *d* of your youth, Jer 2:2

DEVOUR *consume, swallow*
wild beast *d-ed* him, Ge 37:20
the sword *d* forever, 2Sa 2:26
is *d-ed* by disease, Job 18:13
fire from...*d-ed*, Ps 18:8
love all words that *d*, Ps 52:4
To *d* the afflicted, Pr 30:14
has *d-ed* your prophets, Jer 2:30
caterpillar was *d-ing*, Am 4:9
d widows' houses, Mk 12:40
bite...*d* one another, Gal 5:15

DEVOUT *God-fearing*
d men are taken away, Is 57:1
was righteous and *d*, Lk 2:25
d men, from every, Ac 2:5
the *d* women, Ac 13:50

DEW *drops of moisture*
God give...the *d*, Ge 27:28
d fell on the camp, Nu 11:9
d on the fleece only, Jdg 6:37
on him as the *d*, 2Sa 17:12
neither *d* nor rain, 1Ki 17:1
the *d* of Hermon, Ps 133:3
skies drip with *d*, Pr 3:20
Like a cloud of *d*, Is 18:4
drenched with the *d*, Da 4:15
sky has withheld its *d*, Hag 1:10

DIADEM *crown*
d to the remnant, Is 28:5
royal *d* in the hand, Is 62:3
heads *were* seven *d-s*, Rev 12:3
horns *were* ten *d-s*, Rev 13:1
His head *are* many *d-s*, Rev 19:12

DIALECT *language*
in the Hebrew *d*, Ac 21:40
the Hebrew *d*, Ac 22:2

DIAMOND *jewel*
a sapphire and a *d*, Ex 28:18
With a *d* point, Jer 17:1

DIANA
Worship of at Ephesus creates uproar, Ac 19:23–41

DIBON
Amorite town, Nu 21:30
Taken by Israel, Nu 32:2–5
Destruction of, foretold, Jer 48:18, 22

DICTATION *spoken words*
at the *d* of Jeremiah, Jer 36:4
written at the *d* of, Jer 36:27
book at Jeremiah's *d*, Jer 45:1

DIDYMUS
Another name for Thomas, Jn 11:16; 20:24; 21:2

DIE *decease, expire*
you will surely *d*, Ge 2:17
not eat...which *d-s*, Dt 14:21
Where you *d*, I will *d*, Ru 1:17
Curse God and *d*, Job 2:9
even wise men *d*, Ps 49:10
fools *d* for lack of, Pr 10:21
and the fool alike *d*, Ecc 2:16
soul who sins will *d*, Eze 18:4
to *d* with You, Mt 26:35
child has not *d-d*, Mk 5:39
live even if he *d-s*, Jn 11:25
grain of wheat...*d-s*, Jn 12:24
she fell sick and *d-d*, Ac 9:37
d-d for the ungodly, Ro 5:6
we who *d-d* to sin, Ro 6:2
for whom Christ *d-d*, Ro 14:15
I *d* daily, 1Co 15:31
I *d-d* to the Law, Gal 2:19
to *d* is gain, Php 1:21
Jesus *d-d* and rose, 1Th 4:14
to *d* once and after, Heb 9:27
these *d-d* in faith, Heb 11:13
who *d* in the Lord, Rev 14:13

DIFFICULT *hard*
too *d* for the LORD, Ge 18:14
test Solomon with *d*, 2Ch 9:1
anything too *d* for Me, Jer 32:27
speech or *d* language, Eze 3:5
solving of *d* problems, Da 5:12
last days *d* times, 2Ti 3:1

DIFFICULTY *impediment*
made them drive with *d*, Ex 14:25
deaf and spoke with *d*, Mk 7:32
with *d* does it leave him, Lk 9:39
with *d* had arrived, Ac 27:7
d that the righteous, 1Pe 4:18

DIG *excavate, till*
opens a pit, or *d-s*, Ex 21:33
you can *d* copper, Dt 8:9
they *d* into houses, Job 24:16
He has *dug* a pit, Ps 7:15
dug through the wall, Eze 8:8
dug a wine press, Mt 21:33
until I *d* around it, Lk 13:8

DIGNITY *majesty*
Preeminent in *d*, Ge 49:3
What honor or *d* has, Est 6:3
all godliness and *d*, 1Ti 2:2
must be men of *d*, 1Ti 3:8

DILIGENCE *effort*
carried out with all *d*, Ezr 6:12
Watch...with all *d*, Pr 4:23
lagging behind in *d*, Ro 12:11
show the same *d*, Heb 6:11

DILIGENT *persistent*
hand of the *d* makes, Pr 10:4
plans of the *d lead*, Pr 21:5
d to present, 2Ti 2:15
d to enter that rest, Heb 4:11
I will also be *d*, 2Pe 1:15

DILIGENTLY *with perseverance*
keep your soul *d*, Dt 4:9
teach them *d* to your, Dt 6:7
searched d for God;, Ps 78:34
They will seek me *d* but, Pr 1:28
who *d* seek me will find me., Pr 8:17
loves him disciplines him *d*., Pr 13:24
D help Zenas the lawyer, Titus 3:13

DIM *cloudy, dark*
eye was not *d*, Dt 34:7

eyesight...to grow *d*, 1Sa 3:2
d because of grief, Job 17:7
windows grow *d*, Ecc 12:3

DIMINISH *dwindle, reduce*
you shall *d* its price, Lv 25:16
d their inheritance, Nu 26:54
are *d-ed* and bowed, Ps 107:39

DINAH
Daughter of Leah, Ge 30:20, 21
Defiled by Shechem, Ge 34:1–24
Avenged by brothers, Ge 34:25–31

DINE *eat*
men are to *d* with, Ge 43:16
to *d* with a ruler, Pr 23:1
came and were *d-ing*, Mt 9:10

DINNER *meal*
I have prepared...*d*, Mt 22:4
because of...*d* guests, Mk 6:26
was giving a big *d*, Lk 14:16

DIONYSIUS THE AREOPAGITE
A believer in Athens, Ac 17:34

DIOTREPHES
Unruly church member, 3Jn 9, 10

DIP *plunge*
d-ped the tunic in, Ge 37:31
priest shall *d* his, Lv 4:6
d your piece of bread, Ru 2:14
d-ped...seven times, 2Ki 5:14
d-ped...with Me, Mt 26:23
who *d-s* with Me, Mk 14:20
robe *d-ped* in blood, Rev 19:13

DIRECT *arrange, guide, order*
LORD *d-s* his steps, Pr 16:9
d your heart in the, Pr 23:19
has *d-ed* the Spirit, Is 40:13
walks to *d* his steps, Jer 10:23
I *d-ed* the churches, 1Co 16:1
d their entire body, Jas 3:3

DIRECTION *path; order*
which turned every *d*, Ge 3:24
It changes *d*, Job 37:12
d of the daughter, Jer 4:11
of their four *d-s*, Eze 1:17

DIRGE *lament*
for you as a *d*, Am 5:1
we sang a *d*, Lk 7:32

DISAPPEAR *vanish*
For the faithful *d*, Ps 12:1
When the grass *d-s*, Pr 27:25
old is ready to *d*, Heb 8:13

DISAPPOINT *frustrate*
and were not *d-ed*, Ps 22:5
hope does not *d*, Ro 5:5

DISASTER *calamity*
d was close to them, Jdg 20:34
d on this people, Jer 6:19
because of all its *d-s*, Jer 19:8
In the day of their *d*, Ob 13

DISBELIEVE *doubt*
Jews who *d-d* stirred, Ac 14:2
for those who *d*, 1Pe 2:7

DISCERN *understand, recognize*
would *d*...future, Dt 32:29
king to *d* good, 2Sa 14:17
not *d* its appearance, Job 4:16
d-ed...the youths, Pr 7:7
d the...sky, Mt 16:3

DISCERNMENT *judgment*
blessed be your *d*, 1Sa 25:33
asked for yourself *d*, 1Ki 3:11
not a people of *d*, Is 27:11
knowledge and all *d*, Php 1:9

DISCHARGE *emission*
a *d* from his body, Lv 15:2
leper or who has a *d*, Lv 22:4
everyone having a *d*, Nu 5:2
d, or who is a leper, 2Sa 3:29
the *d* of your blood, Eze 32:6

DISCIPLE *student, learner*
to listen as a *d*, Is 50:4
His twelve *d-s*, Mt 10:1
d is not above his, Mt 10:24
d-s rebuked them, Mt 19:13
d-s left Him...fled, Mt 26:56
make *d-s* of all, Mt 28:19
Your *d-s* do not fast, Mk 2:18
Passover...My *d-s*, Mk 14:14
gaze toward His *d-s*, Lk 6:20
he cannot be My *d*, Lk 14:26
d-s believed in Him, Jn 2:11
His *d-s* withdrew, Jn 6:66
wash the *d-s'* feet, Jn 13:5
d whom He loved, Jn 19:26
d-s were first called, Ac 11:26

DISCIPLINE *(n) chastisement*
the *d* of the LORD, Dt 11:2
d of the Almighty, Job 5:17
The rod of *d*, Pr 22:15
to see your good *d*, Col 2:5
d...of little profit, 1Ti 4:8

DISCIPLINE *(v) chastise*
as a man *d-s* his son, Dt 8:5
d-d you with whips, 1Ki 12:11
D your son while, Pr 19:18
I *d* my body, 1Co 9:27
d-d by the Lord, 1Co 11:32
father does not *d*, Heb 12:7

DISCLOSE *reveal*
without *d-ing* it to, 1Sa 20:2
Esther had *d-d* what, Est 8:1
will *d* Myself to him, Jn 14:21
d the motives of, 1Co 4:5
secrets...are *d-d*, 1Co 14:25

DISCOURAGE *dishearten*
d-ing the sons of, Nu 32:7
people of the land *d-d*, Ezr 4:4
d-d with the work, Ne 6:9

DISCOVER *find, uncover*
strength was not *d-ed*, Jdg 16:9
d the depths of God, Job 11:7
man will not *d*, Ecc 7:14
shamed...he is *d-ed*, Jer 2:26

DISCRETION *understanding*
LORD give you *d*, 1Ch 22:12
sound wisdom and *d*, Pr 3:21
woman who lacks *d*, Pr 11:22
Daniel replied with *d*, Da 2:14

DISCUSS *converse, reason*
d matters of justice, Jer 12:1
d...among themselves, Mt 16:7
What were you *d-ing*, Mk 9:33
d-ed together what, Lk 6:11

DISEASE *sickness*
none of the *d-s* on you, Ex 15:26
harmful *d-s* of Egypt, Dt 7:15
d-d in his feet, 2Ch 16:12
d-d...not healed, Eze 34:4
heals all your *d-s*, Ps 103:3
various *d-s* and pains, Mt 4:24
power...to heal *d-s*, Lk 9:1

DISGRACE *reproach, shame*
a *d* to us, Ge 34:14
nakedness, it is a *d*, Lv 20:17
sin is a *d* to, Pr 14:34
not *d* the throne, Jer 14:21
and bear your *d*, Eze 16:52

DISGRACEFUL *shameful*
d thing in Israel, Ge 34:7
shameful and *d* son, Pr 19:26
d for a woman to, 1Co 11:6

DISGUISE *pretend*
d-d his sanity, 1Sa 21:13
Arise now, and *d*, 1Ki 14:2
king of Israel *d-d*, 1Ki 22:30
he *d-s* his face, Job 24:15
d-ing...as apostles, 2Co 11:13

DISH *bowl, plate*
prepare a savory *d*, Ge 27:7
was one silver *d*, Nu 7:43
as one wipes a *d*, 2Ki 21:13
30 gold *d-es*, Ezr 1:9

DISHEARTENED *discouraged*
not be *d* or crushed, Is 42:4
you *d* the righteous, Eze 13:22

DISHONEST *untruthful*
those who hate *d* gain, Ex 18:21
order to get *d* gain, Eze 22:27
cheat with *d* scales, Am 8:5

DISHONOR *(n) disgrace, shame*
to see the king's *d*, Ezr 4:14
Fill their faces with *d*, Ps 83:16
man conceals *d*, Pr 12:16

DISHONOR *(v) disgrace, shame*
who *d-s* his father, Dt 27:16
be ashamed and *d-ed*, Ps 35:4
and you *d* Me, Jn 8:49
bodies would be *d-ed*, Ro 1:24
do you *d* God, Ro 2:23

DISMAY *be troubled, fear*
d-ed at his presence, Ge 45:3
not tremble or be *d-ed*, Jos 1:9
d-ed and...afraid, 1Sa 17:11
or I will *d* you, Jer 1:17
are *d-ed* and caught, Jer 8:9
mighty men...be *d-ed*, Ob 9

DISMISS *release, send away*
d-ed the people, Jos 24:28
Solomon *d-ed*, 1Ki 2:27
priest did not *d any*, 2Ch 23:8
he *d-ed* the assembly, Ac 19:41

DISOBEDIENCE *rebellion*
the one man's *d*, Ro 5:19
in the sons of *d*, Eph 2:2
d received a just, Heb 2:2
same example of *d*, Heb 4:11

DISOBEDIENT *rebellious*
d and rebelled, Ne 9:26
hardened and *d*, Ac 19:9
d to parents, Ro 1:30
d...obstinate people, Ro 10:21

DISPERSE *spread*
d them in Jacob, Ge 49:7
d-d...the peoples, Est 3:8
d them among the, Eze 20:23
who are *d-d* abroad, Jas 1:1

DISPLAY *declare, show*
to *d* her beauty, Est 1:11
d-ed Your splendor, Ps 8:1
d their sin like, Is 3:9
works of God...*d-ed*, Jn 9:3

DISPLEASE *annoy, trouble*
if it is *d-ing* to you, Nu 22:34
d-ing in the sight, 1Sa 8:6
may not *d* the lords, 1Sa 29:7
d-ing in His sight, Is 59:15
it greatly *d-d* Jonah, Jon 4:1

DISPOSSESS *remove*
d-ed the Amorites, Nu 21:32
Esau *d-ed* them, Dt 2:12
He will assuredly *d*, Jos 3:10
d-ing the nations, Ac 7:45

DISPUTE *(n) controversy*
When they have a *d*, Ex 18:16
bring the *d-s* to God, Ex 18:19
d in your courts, Dt 17:8
a great *d* among, Ac 28:29

DISPUTE *(v) contend, debate*
wished to *d* with Him, Job 9:3
with Israel he will *d*, Mic 6:2
without...*d-ing*, Php 2:14
He *d-d* with the devil, Jude 9

DISSENSION *division*
great *d* and debate, Ac 15:2
d between the, Ac 23:7
those who cause *d-s*, Ro 16:17
without wrath and *d*, 1Ti 2:8

DISSIPATION *intemperance*
weighted...with *d*, Lk 21:34
wine, for that is *d*, Eph 5:18
not accused of *d*, Titus 1:6

DISSOLVE *melt*
d me in a storm, Job 30:22
I *d* my couch with, Ps 6:6
d-d in tears, Is 15:3
And the hills *d*, Na 1:5

DISTANCE *far away*
sister stood at a *d*, Ex 2:4
some *d* from the, Jdg 18:22
following...at a *d*, Mt 26:58
welcomed...from a *d*, Heb 11:13

DISTINCTION *difference*
the LORD makes a *d*, Ex 11:7
d between the holy, Lv 10:10
have made no *d*, Eze 22:26
He made no *d*, Ac 15:9
for there is no *d*, Ro 3:22
d-s among yourselves, Jas 2:4

DISTINGUISH *(v) discern*
I *d* between good, 2Sa 19:35
not *d* the sound, Ezr 3:13
d...the righteous, Mal 3:18
d-ing of spirits, 1Co 12:10

DISTINGUISHED *separated*
one *d* among his brothers., Ge 49:26
king of Israel *d* himself, 2Sa 6:20
d men of the foremost of, Am 6:1
someone more *d* than you, Lk 14:8
you are *d*, but we are, 1Co 4:10

DISTINGUISHING *(adj)*
became your *d* mark, Eze 27:7
this is a *d* mark, 2Th 3:17

DISTORT *pervert*
who *d-s* the justice, Dt 27:19
my garment is *d-ed*, Job 30:18
they *d* my words, Ps 56:5
d the gospel of Christ, Gal 1:7

DISTRESS *adversity, trouble*
day of my *d*, Ge 35:3
When you are in *d*, Dt 4:30
deliver me...*d*, 1Sa 26:24
I am in great *d*, 2Sa 24:14
cry to You in our *d*, 2Ch 20:9
refuge in the day of *d*, Jer 16:19
I am in *d*, La 1:20
d upon the land, Lk 21:23
d for every soul, Ro 2:9
assisted those in *d*, 1Ti 5:10
widows in their *d*, Jas 1:27

DISTRIBUTE *apportion*
d-d by lot in Shiloh, Jos 19:51
to *d* to their kinsmen, Ne 13:13
d it to the poor, Lk 18:22
d-ing to each one, 1Co 12:11

DISTRICT *area, province*
the *d* of Jerusalem, Ne 3:12
d around the Jordan, Mt 3:5
d of Galilee, Mk 1:28
the *d-s* of Libya, Ac 2:10

DISTURB *annoy, bother*
Why...*d-ed* me, 1Sa 28:15
no one *d* his bones, 2Ki 23:18
d them and destroy, Est 9:24
being greatly *d-ed*, Ac 4:2
one who is *d-ing* you, Gal 5:10

DISTURBANCE *turmoil*
to cause a *d* in it, Ne 4:8
hear of wars and *d-s*, Lk 21:9
d among the soldiers, Ac 12:18
arrogance, *d-s*, 2Co 12:20

DIVIDE *apportion, separate*
that *d-s* the hoof, Dt 14:6
D the living child, 1Ki 3:25
d my garments among, Ps 22:18
He will *d* the booty, Is 53:12
d-d up His garments, Mt 27:35
d-d his wealth, Lk 15:12

DIVINATION *witchcraft*
nor practice *d* or, Lv 19:26
witchcraft, used *d*, 2Ch 33:6
false vision, *d*, Jer 14:14
falsehood and lying *d*, Eze 13:6
a spirit of *d* met us, Ac 16:16

DIVINE *(adj) pertaining to deity*
in whom...*d* spirit, Ge 41:38
I see a *d* being, 1Sa 28:13
D Nature...gold, Ac 17:29
power and *d* nature, Ro 1:20
is the *d* response, Ro 11:4

DIVINE *(v) practice divination*
d-d that the LORD, Ge 30:27
they *d* lies for you, Eze 21:29
d-ing lies for them, Eze 22:28
prophets *d* for money, Mic 3:11

DIVINER *seer*
called for the...*d-s*, 1Sa 6:2
The *d* and the elder, Is 3:2
your *d-s* deceive you, Jer 29:8
d-s will be embarrassed, Mic 3:7
d-s see lying visions, Zec 10:2

DIVISION *dissension, segment*
d between My people, Ex 8:23
divided...into *d-s*, 1Ch 23:6
d...in the crowd, Jn 7:43
no *d-s* among you, 1Co 1:10
d of soul and spirit, Heb 4:12

DIVORCE *(n) separation*
a certificate of *d*, Dt 24:1
given her a writ of *d*, Jer 3:8
For I hate *d*, Mal 2:16

DIVORCE *(v) separate*
he cannot *d* her, Dt 22:19
husband *d-s* his wife, Jer 3:1
man to *d* his wife, Mt 19:3
Whoever *d-s* his, Mk 10:11

DIVORCED *(adj) separated*
woman *d* from her, Lv 21:7
or of a *d* woman, Nu 30:9
marries a *d* woman, Mt 5:32
marries...who is *d*, Lk 16:18

DO NOT BE AFRAID
D; for God has come, Ex 20:20
not be fainthearted. *D*, Dt 20:3
Stay with me; *d*, 1Sa 22:23
"Go down with him; *d*, 2Ki 1:15
D when a man becomes, Ps 49:16
D of sudden fear, Pr 3:25
Do not tremble and *d*, Is 44:8
D of the king of Babylon, Jer 42:11
D, Daniel, for from the, Da 10:12
D, O Zion; Do not let, Zep 3:16
d to take Mary as your wife, Mt 1:20
Take courage, it is I; *d*, Mt 14:27
said to the women, "*D*, Mt 28:5
D; go and take word to, Mt 28:10
D any longer, only, Mk 5:36
Take courage; it is I, *d*, Mk 6:50
D, Zacharias, for your, Lk 1:13
D, Mary; for you have, Lk 1:30
D; for behold, I bring you, Lk 2:10
d of those who kill the body, Lk 12:4
D, little flock, for your, Lk 12:32
He said to them, "It is I; *d*, Jn 6:20
D any longer, but go on, Ac 18:9

D; I am the first and the, Rev 1:17

DO NOT FEAR
D, Abram, I am a shield, Ge 15:1
D, for God has heard, Ge 21:17
your father Abraham; *D*, Ge 26:24
D! Stand by and see the, Ex 14:13
D or be dismayed, Dt 1:21
D him, for I have delivered, Dt 3:2
D or be dismayed, Dt 31:8
D or be dismayed!, Jos 10:25
my daughter, *d*. I will do, Ru 3:11
D, for those who are, 2Ki 6:16
D or be dismayed, 2Ch 20:15
Lift it up, *d*. Say to the cities, Is 40:9
"*D*, I will help you, Is 41:13
D, for I have redeemed, Is 43:1
Jacob My servant, *d*, Jer 46:27
D, O land, rejoice, Joel 2:21
is abiding in your midst; *d*, Hag 2:5
d them, for there is, Mt 10:26
d; you are more valuable, Mt 10:31
"*D*, from now on you will, Lk 5:10
d their intimidation, 1Pe 3:14
D what you are about, Rev 2:10

DOCTRINE *teaching*
Teaching as *d-s* the, Mt 15:9
every wind of *d*, Eph 4:14
to teach strange *d-s*, 1Ti 1:3
to exhort in sound *d*, Titus 1:9

DOCUMENT *manuscript*
the *d* which you sent, Ezr 4:18
And on the sealed *d*, Ne 9:38
Darius signed the *d*, Da 6:9

DOEG
An Edomite; chief of Saul's herdsmen, 1Sa 21:7
Betrays David, 1Sa 22:9, 10
Kills 85 priests, 1Sa 22:18, 19

DOER *workman*
recompenses the…*d*, Ps 31:23
d-s of the Law will, Ro 2:13
d-s of the word, Jas 1:22
not a *d* of the law, Jas 4:11

DOG *animal, scavenger*
Am I a *d*, 1Sa 17:43
d-s have surrounded, Ps 22:16
they howl like a *d*, Ps 59:6
live *d* is better than, Ecc 9:4
Beware of the *d-s*, Php 3:2
d-s and the sorcerers, Rev 22:15

DOMAIN *estate*
give You all this *d*, Lk 4:6
the *d* of darkness, Col 1:13
keep their own *d*, Jude 6

DOMINION *authority, rule*
Yours is the *d*, 1Ch 29:11
places of His *d*, Ps 103:22
d will be from sea, Zec 9:10
and power and *d*, Eph 1:21
thrones or *d-s* or, Col 1:16
glory and the *d* forever, Rev 1:6

DONKEY *ass*
a wild *d* of a man, Ge 16:12
Balaam…to the *d*, Nu 22:29
the foal of a *d*, Zec 9:9
you will find a *d*, Mt 21:2
and mounted on a *d*, Mt 21:5
a mute *d*, speaking, 2Pe 2:16

DOOM *ruin*
four kinds *of d*, Jer 15:3
Your *d* has come to you, Eze 7:7
time *of d* for the, Eze 30:3
to this *d* they were also, 1Pe 2:8

DOOMED *condemned*
d to eat their own dung, 2Ki 18:27
preserve those who are *d*, Ps 79:11
free those who were *d*, Ps 102:20
So I pastured the flock *d*, Zec 11:7

DOOR *entrance, opening*
crouching at the *d*, Ge 4:7
set the *d* of the ark, Ge 6:16
Uriah slept at the *d*, 2Sa 11:9
over the *d* of my lips, Ps 141:3
d turns on its, Pr 26:14
each had a double *d*, Eze 41:23
close your *d*…pray, Mt 6:6
I am the *d*, Jn 10:9
right at the *d*, Jas 5:9
before you an open *d*, Rev 3:8
I stand at the *d*, Rev 3:20

DOORKEEPER *guard*
d-s have gathered, 2Ki 22:4
the Levites, the *d-s*, 2Ch 34:9
eunuchs who were *d-s*, Est 6:2
commanded the *d*, Mk 13:34
To him the *d* opens, Jn 10:3

DOORPOST
put it on the two *d-s*, Ex 12:7
write them on the *d-s*, Dt 6:9
on the seat by the *d*, 1Sa 1:9
Waiting at my *d-s*, Pr 8:34

DOORWAY *entrance, opening*
the *d* of the tent, Jdg 4:20
d-s and doorposts, 1Ki 7:5
at my neighbor's *d*, Job 31:9
chamber with its *d*, Eze 40:38

DOR
City captured by Joshua and assigned to Manasseh, Jos 12:23; 17:11; Jdg 1:27

DORCAS
Disciple at Joppa, also called Tabitha; raised to life, Ac 9:36–42

DOTHAN
Ancient town where Joseph was sold, Ge 37:14–25
Elisha strikes Syrians at, 2Ki 6:8–23

DOUBT *(n) unbelief*
life shall hang in *d*, Dt 28:66
why do *d-s* arise, Lk 24:38

DOUBT *(v) disbelieve*
why did you *d*, Mt 14:31
not *d* in his heart, Mk 11:23
d-s is condemned, Ro 14:23
who *d-s* is like the, Jas 1:6

DOUGH *flour mixture*
people took their *d*, Ex 12:34
the first of your *d*, Nu 15:20
took *d*, kneaded *it*, 2Sa 13:8
knead *d* to make cakes, Jer 7:18

DOVE *bird*
he sent out a *d*, Ge 8:8
had wings like a *d*, Ps 55:6
eyes are *like d-s*, SS 1:15
descending as a *d*, Mt 3:16
descending as a *d*, Jn 1:32
selling the *d-s*, Jn 2:16

DOWNFALL *collapse*
became the *d* of, 2Ch 28:23
noise of their *d*, Jer 49:21

DOWNPOUR *rain*
the *d* and the rain, Job 37:6
d of waters swept, Hab 3:10

DOWRY *bequest*
must pay a *d* for her, Ex 22:16
to the *d* for virgins, Ex 22:17
d to his daughter, 1Ki 9:16

DRACHMA
Greek silver coin, Ne 7:70–72; Mt 17:24

DRAG *draw, pull*
grasshopper *d-s*, Ecc 12:5
D them off like sheep, Jer 12:3
the dogs to *d* off, Jer 15:3
Paul and *d-ged*, Ac 14:19
d you into court, Jas 2:6

DRAGON *monster, serpent*
d who *lives* in the sea, Is 27:1
Who pierced the *d*, Is 51:9
d stood before the, Rev 12:4
he laid hold of the *d*, Rev 20:2

DRAIN *empty*
blood is to be *d-ed*, Lv 1:15
he *d-ed* the dew, Jdg 6:38
must *d and* drink down, Ps 75:8
drink it and *d* it, Eze 23:34

DRAW *haul, pull*
out to *d* water, Ge 24:13
drew him out of the, Ex 2:10
but are *d-n* away, Dt 30:17
He *d-s* up the drops, Job 36:27
d near to my soul, Ps 69:18
They are *d-ing* back, Jer 46:5
redemption is *d-ing*, Lk 21:28
d all men to Myself, Jn 12:32
D near to God, Jas 4:8

DRAWERS *servants*
wood and *d* of water, Jos 9:21

DREAD *(n) fear*
in *d*…of Israel, Ex 1:12
in *d* night and day, Dt 28:66
d of the Jews, Est 8:17
they are in great *d*, Ps 14:5
d comes like a storm, Pr 1:27

DREAD *(v) fear*
what I *d* befalls me, Job 3:25
Whom shall I *d*, Ps 27:1
whose two kings you *d*, Is 7:16
are *d-ed* and feared, Hab 1:7

DREAM *(n) vision*
had a *d*, and behold, Ge 28:12
man was relating a *d*, Jdg 7:13
flies away like a *d*, Job 20:8
like a *d*, a vision, Is 29:7

visions and *d-s*, Da 1:17
to Joseph in a *d*, Mt 2:13

DREAM *(v) see a vision*
asleep and *d-ed*, Ge 41:5
like those who *d*, Ps 126:1
when a hungry man *d-s*, Is 29:8
Your old men will *d*, Joel 2:28

DREAMER *visionary*
Here comes this *d*, Ge 37:19
If a prophet or a *d*, Dt 13:1
your diviners, your *d-s*, Jer 27:9

DRENCH *soak, wet*
head is *d-ed* with dew, SS 5:2
d you with my tears, Is 16:9
d-ed with the dew, Da 4:33

DRESS *(n) clothing*
have taken off my *d*, SS 5:3
d was of fine linen, Eze 16:13
or putting on *d-es*, 1Pe 3:3

DRESS *(v) array, clothe*
d-ed in his military, 2Sa 20:8
D-ed as a harlot, Pr 7:10
you *d* in scarlet, Jer 4:30
d-ed Him...purple, Mk 15:17

DRINK *(n) refreshment*
gave the lad a *d*, Ge 21:19
or wine, or strong *d*, Dt 14:26
to desire strong *d*, Pr 31:4
gave Me *something* to *d*, Mt 25:35
My blood is true *d*, Jn 6:55
thirsty, give him a *d*, Ro 12:20

DRINK *(v)*
he *drank* of the wine, Ge 9:21
Do not *d* wine, Lv 10:9
d from the brook, 1Ki 17:6
they all *drank* from, Mk 14:23
after *d-ing* old *wine*, Lk 5:39
who eats and *d-s*, 1Co 11:29
ground that *d-s* the, Heb 6:7

DRIP *drop*
clouds...They *d*, Job 36:28
lips...*d* honey, SS 4:11
d-ped with myrrh, SS 5:5
D down, O heavens, Is 45:8

DRIVE *chase, defeat*
You have *d-n* me, Ge 4:14
and *drove* them away, Ex 2:17
angel...*d-ing them* on, Ps 35:5
d hard all your workers, Is 58:3
drove Him out of...city, Lk 4:29
drove them all out, Jn 2:15
to *d* the ship, Ac 27:39

DROP *(n) drip*
the *d-s* of water, Job 36:27
a *d* from a bucket, Is 40:15
like *d-s* of blood, Lk 22:44

DROP *(v) fall*
olives will *d* off, Dt 28:40
his bonds *d-ped*, Jdg 15:14
d off his unripe grape, Job 15:33
d-ped their wings, Eze 1:24

DROSS *metallic waste*
of the earth *like d*, Ps 119:119
Take away the *d*, Pr 25:4
silver has become *d*, Is 1:22
Israel has become *d*, Eze 22:18

DROUGHT *dryness*
Like heat in *d*, Is 25:5
in regard to the *d*, Jer 14:1
I called for a *d*, Hag 1:11

DROWNED *suffocated*
d in the Red Sea, Ex 15:4
to be *d* in the depth, Mt 18:6
were *d* in the sea, Mk 5:13

DRUNK *intoxicated*
arrows *d* with blood, Dt 32:42
d, but not with wine, Is 29:9
made...*d* in My wrath, Is 63:6
not get *d* with wine, Eph 5:18
I saw the woman *d*, Rev 17:6

DRUNKARD *intoxicated person*
a glutton and a *d*, Dt 21:20
song of the *d-s*, Ps 69:12
Awake, *d-s*, and weep, Joel 1:5
a reviler, or a *d*, 1Co 5:11

DRUNKEN *intoxicated*
stagger like a *d* man, Job 12:25
become like a *d* man, Jer 23:9

DRUNKENNESS *intoxicated*
and not for *d*, Ecc 10:17
weighted down...*d*, Lk 21:34
in carousing and *d*, Ro 13:13
envying, *d*, carousing, Gal 5:21

DRUSILLA
Wife of Felix; hears Paul, Ac 24:24, 25

DRY *(adj) parched, scorched*
let the *d* land appear, Ge 1:9
In a *d* and weary land, Ps 63:1
Better is a *d* morsel, Pr 17:1
O *d* bones, hear, Eze 37:4

DRY *(v) scorch, wither*
My strength is *dried*, Ps 22:15
dried up...streams, Ps 74:15
I *d* up the sea, Is 50:2
new wine *dries* up, Joel 1:10
dries up...rivers, Na 1:4

DUE *(adj) proper, right*
In *d* time their foot, Dt 32:35
food in *d* season, Ps 104:27
d penalty of their, Ro 1:27

DUE *(n) what is owed*
as *their d* forever, Lv 7:34
be the priests' *d*, Dt 18:3
Indeed it is Your *d*, Jer 10:7

DULL *heavy, stupid*
eyes are *d* from wine, Ge 49:12
Their ears *d*, Is 6:10
people...become *d*, Mt 13:15
become *d* of hearing, Heb 5:11

DUNG *waste*
sweeps away *d*, 1Ki 14:10
dove's *d* for five, 2Ki 6:25
give you cow's *d*, Eze 4:15
their flesh like *d*, Zep 1:17

DUNGEON *prison*
put me into the *d*, Ge 40:15
captive...in the *d*, Ex 12:29
prisoners from the *d*, Is 42:7
Jeremiah...into the *d*, Jer 37:16

DUST *dirt, earth*
God formed man of *d*, Ge 2:7
And *d* you will eat, Ge 3:14
the poor from the *d*, 1Sa 2:8
repent in *d* and ashes, Job 42:6
d before the wind, Ps 18:42
Will the *d* praise You, Ps 30:9
You who lie in the *d*, Is 26:19
shake the *d* off, Mt 10:14
the *d* of your city, Lk 10:11
d on their heads, Rev 18:19

DUTY *responsibility*
perform your *d*, Ge 38:8
d-ies of the sanctuary, Nu 3:38
charged with any *d*, Dt 24:5
the *d* of a husband's, Dt 25:7
d-ies according to their, 2Ch 31:16
his *d* to his wife, 1Co 7:3

DWELL *abide, live*
father of those who *d*, Ge 4:20
Behold, I am *d-ing*, 1Ch 17:1
No evil *d-s* with You, Ps 5:4
d on Your holy hill, Ps 15:1
I will *d* in the house, Ps 23:6
d among the wise, Pr 15:31
have *d-t* in Jerusalem, Jer 35:11
flesh, and *d-t* among, Jn 1:14
His Spirit who *d-s* in you, Ro 8:11
of God *d-s* in you, 1Co 3:16
Christ may *d* in your, Eph 3:17
d on these things, Php 4:8

DWELLING *habitation*
earth shall be your *d*, Ge 27:39
name there for His *d*, Dt 12:5
place for Your *d*, 1Ki 8:13
into the eternal *d-s*, Lk 16:9
might find a *d* place, Ac 7:46

DYED *colored*
rams' skins *d* red, Ex 25:5
A spoil of *d* work, Jdg 5:30

E

EAGER *keenly desiring*
the schemer is *e*, Job 5:5
lion that is *e* to tear, Ps 17:12
Do not be *e* in your heart, Ecc 7:9
e to corrupt all their deeds, Zep 3:7
e to preach the gospel, Ro 1:15
very thing I also was *e*, Gal 2:10
more *e* with great desire, 1Th 2:17

EAGERLY *with desire*
e waits for his wages, Job 7:2
to You and *e* watch, Ps 5:3
waited for You *e*, Is 26:8
Gentiles *e* seek all, Mt 6:32
waits *e* for the revealing, Ro 8:19
e for *our* adoption, Ro 8:23
awaiting *e* the revelation, 1Co 1:7
we *e* wait for a Savior, Php 3:20
he *e* searched for me, 2Ti 1:17

EAGLE *bird*
bore you on *e-s'* wings, Ex 19:4
the *e* swoops down, Dt 28:49
swifter than *e-s*, 2Sa 1:23
with wings like *e-s*, Is 40:31
the face of an *e*, Eze 1:10
was like a flying *e*, Rev 4:7

EAR *hearing*
heard with our *e-s*, 2Sa 7:22
the *e* test words, Job 12:11
And His *e-s* are *open*, Ps 34:15
and incline your *e*, Ps 45:10
He whose *e* listens, Pr 15:31
e of the wise seeks, Pr 18:15
e has not been open, Is 48:8
let your *e* receive, Jer 9:20
He who has *e-s* to, Mt 11:15
and cut off his *e*, Mt 26:51
fingers into his *e-s*, Mk 7:33
if the *e* says, 1Co 12:16
their *e-s* tickled, 2Ti 4:3
He who has an *e*, Rev 2:7

EARLY *beforetime, soon*
they arose *e* and, Ge 26:31
Let us rise *e*, SS 7:12
dew which goes away *e*, Hos 6:4
e on the first day, Mk 16:2
at the tomb *e*, Lk 24:22
the *e* and late rains, Jas 5:7

EARNEST *sincere*
will give *e* heed to the, Ex 15:26
being himself very *e*, 2Co 8:17
my *e* expectation, Php 1:20

EARNESTLY *with sincerity*
David *e* asked *leave*, 1Sa 20:6
I shall seek You *e*, Ps 63:1
seek your presence *e*, Pr 7:15
they will *e* seek Me, Hos 5:15
He *e* warned them, Mk 3:12
they *e* implored Him, Lk 7:4
I have *e* desired to eat, Lk 22:15
e desire the greater gifts, 1Co 12:31
laboring *e* for you in, Col 4:12
contend *e* for the faith, Jude 1:3

EARNESTNESS *sincerity*
behold what *e*, 2Co 7:11
your *e* on our behalf, 2Co 7:12
in all *e* and in the love, 2Co 8:7
same *e* on your behalf, 2Co 8:16

EARNINGS *gain, wages*
her *e* she plants, Pr 31:16
the *e* of a harlot, Mic 1:7

EARRING *ornament*
brought...*e-s*, Ex 35:22
e-s and necklaces, Nu 31:50
Like an *e* of gold, Pr 25:12
her *e-s* and jewelry, Hos 2:13

EARS TO HEAR
nor eyes to see, nor *e.*, Dt 29:4
e but do not hear, Eze 12:2
who has *e*, let him hear, Mt 11:15
who has *e*, let him hear, Mk 4:9
anyone has *e*, let him hear, Mk 4:23
anyone has *e*, let him hear, Mk 7:16
He who has *e*, let him hear, Lk 8:8
He who has *e*, let him hear, Lk 14:35
Eyes to see not and *e* not, Ro 11:8

EARTH *land, world*
God created the...*e*, Ge 1:1
Judge of all the *e*, Ge 18:25
the *e* is the LORD's, Ex 9:29
way of all the *e*, Jos 23:14
His stand on the *e*, Job 19:25
foundation of the *e*, Job 38:4
saints...in the *e*, Ps 16:3
the shields of the *e*, Ps 47:9
gave birth to the *e*, Ps 90:2
He established the *e*, Ps 104:5
wisdom founded...*e*, Pr 3:19
the *e* remains forever, Ecc 1:4
made the *e* tremble, Is 14:16
the circle of the *e*, Is 40:22
the ends of the *e*, Is 45:22
the *e* is My footstool, Is 66:1
e shone with His, Eze 43:2
make the *e* dark, Am 8:9
e will be devoured, Zep 3:8
shall inherit the *e*, Mt 5:5
you bind on *e*, Mt 16:19
on *e* peace among, Lk 2:14
glorified...on the *e*, Jn 17:4
man is from the *e*, 1Co 15:47
heavens and a new *e*, 2Pe 3:13
e and heaven fled, Rev 20:11

EARTHENWARE *pottery*
bird in an *e* vessel, Lv 14:5
holy water in an *e*, Nu 5:17
shatter them like *e*, Ps 2:9
buy a potter's *e* jar, Jer 19:1
vessels of...*e*, 2Ti 2:20

EARTHLY *physical*
e things and you do, Jn 3:12
heavenly bodies and *e*, 1Co 15:40
know that if the *e* tent, 2Co 5:1
their minds on *e* things, Php 3:19
worship and the *e* sanctuary, Heb 9:1
e fathers to discipline us, Heb 12:9
as long as I am in this *e*, 2Pe 1:13

EARTHQUAKE *tremor*
LORD *was* not...*e*, 1Ki 19:11
punished with...*e*, Is 29:6
be famines and *e-s*, Mt 24:7
will be great *e-s*, Lk 21:11
there was a great *e*, Rev 6:12
killed in the *e*, Rev 11:13

EARTHY *mortal*
man is...*e*, 1Co 15:47
those who are *e*, 1Co 15:48

EASE *free from difficulty, pain*
He who is at *e*, Job 12:5
at *e* and satisfied, Job 21:23
women who are at *e*, Is 32:9
Woe to those...at *e*, Am 6:1
nations who are at *e*, Zec 1:15

EASIER *less difficult*
will be *e* for you, Ex 18:22
Which is *e*, to say, Mt 9:5
is *e* for a camel to go, Mt 19:24
e, to say to the paralytic, Mk 2:9
It is *e* for a camel to go, Mk 10:25
is *e* for heaven and earth, Lk 16:17

EAST *direction of compass*
spread out...to the *e*, Ge 28:14
directed an *e* wind, Ex 10:13
sons of the *e* were, Jdg 7:12
men of the *e*, Job 1:3
With the *e* wind You, Ps 48:7
offspring from the *e*, Is 43:5
faces toward the *e*, Eze 8:16
Jerusalem on the *e*, Zec 14:4
saw His star in the *e*, Mt 2:2
lightning...the *e*, Mt 24:27
kings from the *e*, Rev 16:12

EAST GATE
See GATES OF JERUSALEM

EASY *without difficulty*
knowledge is *e* to one, Pr 14:6
My yoke is *e* and, Mt 11:30

EAT *consume, dine, feast*
shall not *e* from it, Ge 3:17
they *ate* every plant, Ex 10:15
not *e*...blood, Lv 19:26
that we may *e* him, 2Ki 6:28
e and be satisfied, Ps 22:26
not *e* the bread of, Pr 31:27
will *e* curds and honey, Is 7:15
words...I *ate* them, Jer 15:16
e this scroll, Eze 3:1
e-ing grass like cattle, Da 4:33
what you will *e*, Mt 6:25
e with unwashed, Mt 15:20
Take, *e;* this is My, Mt 26:26
sinners and *e-s* with, Lk 15:2
e...at My table, Lk 22:30
He took it and *ate*, Lk 24:43
e the flesh of...Son, Jn 6:53
Peter, kill and *e*, Ac 10:13
kingdom...not *e-ing*, Ro 14:17
ate...spiritual food, 1Co 10:3
e-s...judgment, 1Co 11:29

EBAL
Mountain in Samaria, Dt 27:12, 13
Stones of the law erected upon, Dt 27:1–8; Jos 8:30–35

EBED-MELECH
Ethiopian eunuch; rescues Jeremiah, Jer 38:7–13
Promised divine protection, Jer 39:15–18

EBENEZER
Site of Israel's defeat, 1Sa 4:1–10
Ark transferred from, 1Sa 5:1
Site of memorial stone, 1Sa 7:10, 12

EBER
Great-grandson of Shem, Ge 10:21–24; 1Ch 1:25
Progenitor of the:
Hebrews, Ge 11:16–26
Arabians and Arameans, Ge 10:25–30
Ancestor of Christ, Lk 3:35

EDEN
First home of mankind, Ge 2:8–15
Zion becomes like, Is 51:3
Called the "garden of God," Eze 28:13

EDICT *decree*
the king's *e-s*, Ezr 8:36
a royal *e* be issued, Est 1:19
king's command and *e*, Est 9:1
afraid of the king's *e*, Heb 11:23

EDIFICATION *building up*
his good, to his *e*, Ro 15:2

speaks to men for *e*, 1Co 14:3
all things…for *e*, 1Co 14:26

EDIFY *build up*
but love *e-ies*, 1Co 8:1
not all things *e*, 1Co 10:23
person is not *e-ied*, 1Co 14:17

EDOM
Name given to Esau, Ge 25:30
——— Land of Esau; called Seir, Ge 32:3
Called Edom and Idumea, Mk 3:8
People of, cursed, Is 34:5, 6

EDOMITES
Descendants of Esau, Ge 36:9
Refuse passage to Israel, Nu 20:18–20
Hostile to Israel, Ge 27:40; 1Sa 14:47; 2Ch 20:10; Ps 137:7
Prophecies concerning, Ge 27:37; Is 34:5–17; Eze 25:12–14; 35:5–7; Am 9:11, 12

EDREI
Capital of Bashan, Dt 3:10
Site of Og's defeat, Nu 21:33–35

EDUCATED *taught*
be *e* three years, Da 1:5
Moses was *e* in all, Ac 7:22
e under Gamaliel, Ac 22:3

EFFECTIVE *productive*
e service has opened, 1Co 16:9
e in the patient enduring, 2Co 1:6
your faith may become *e*, Phm 1:6
e prayer of a righteous man, Jas 5:16

EFFEMINATE *womanlike*
e, nor homosexuals, 1Co 6:9

EGG
in the white of an *e*, Job 6:6
gathers abandoned *e-s*, Is 10:14
hatch adders' *e-s* and, Is 59:5
is asked for an *e*, Lk 11:12

EGLON
King of Moab, Jdg 3:12
——— Philistine city, Jos 10:34

EGYPT
Abram visits, Ge 12:10
Joseph sold into, Ge 37:28, 36
Joseph becomes leader in, Ge 39:1–4
Hebrews move to, Ge 46:5–7
Hebrews persecuted in, Ex 1:15–22
Plagues on, Ex 7–11
Israel leaves, Ex 12:31–33
Army of, perishes, Ex 14:26–28
Prophecies concerning, Ge 15:13; Is 19:18–25; Eze 29:14, 15; 30:24, 25; Mt 2:15

EHUD
Son of Gera, Jdg 3:15
Slays Eglon, Jdg 3:16–26

EKRON
Philistine city, Jos 13:3
Captured by Judah, Jdg 1:18
Assigned to Dan, Jos 19:40, 43
Ark sent to, 1Sa 5:10
Denounced by the prophets, Jer 25:9, 20

ELAH
King of Israel, 1Ki 16:6, 8–10

ELAM
Descendants of Shem, Ge 10:22
Destruction of, Jer 49:34–39

ELAMITES
In Persian Empire, Ezr 4:9
Jews from, at Pentecost, Ac 2:9

ELATH
Seaport on Red Sea, 1Ki 9:26
Built by Azariah, 2Ki 14:21, 22
Captured by Syrians, 2Ki 16:6
Same as Ezion Geber, 2Ch 8:17

EL-BETHEL
Site of Jacob's altar, Ge 35:6, 7

ELDER *aged, older*
words of her *e* son, Ge 27:42
the *e-s* of Israel, Ex 17:6
sits among the *e-s*, Pr 31:23
Assemble the *e-s*, Joel 2:16
tradition of the *e-s*, Mt 15:2
chief priests and *e-s*, Mt 27:12
scribes…*e-s* came, Mk 11:27
Council of *e-s* of, Lk 22:66
e-s of the church, Ac 20:17
I saw twenty-four *e-s*, Rev 4:4

ELEAZAR
Son of Aaron; succeeds him as high priest, Ex 6:23, 25; 28:1; Lv 10:6, 7; Nu 3:32; 20:25–28; Jos 14:1; 24:33

ELECT *chosen*
sake of the *e*, Mt 24:22
to lead astray…the *e*, Mk 13:22
justice for His *e*, Lk 18:7
against God's *e*, Ro 8:33

ELEMENTARY *basic*
e principles of the, Col 2:8
e principles of the, Heb 5:12
e teaching about the, Heb 6:1

ELEMENTS *physical matter*
e will be destroyed, 2Pe 3:10
the *e* will melt with, 2Pe 3:12

ELI
Officiates in Shiloh, 1Sa 1:3
Blesses Hannah, 1Sa 1:12–19
Becomes Samuel's guardian, 1Sa 1:20–28
Samuel ministers before, 1Sa 2:11
Sons of, 1Sa 2:12–17
Rebukes sons, 1Sa 2:22–25
Rebuked by a man of God, 1Sa 2:27–36
Instructs Samuel, 1Sa 3:1–18
Death of, 1Sa 4:15–18

ELIAB
Brother of David, 1Sa 16:5–13
Fights in Saul's army, 1Sa 17:13
Discounts David's worth, 1Sa 17:28, 29

ELIAKIM
Son of Hilkiah, 2Ki 18:18
Confers with Rabshakeh, Is 36:4, 11–22
Sent to Isaiah, Is 37:2–5
Becomes type of the Messiah, Is 22:20–25
——— Son of King Josiah, 2Ki 23:34
Name changed to Jehoiakim, 2 Chr 36:4

ELIASHIB
High priest, Ne 12:10
Rebuilds Sheep Gate, Ne 3:1, 20, 21
Allies with foreigners, Ne 13:4, 5, 28

ELIHU
David's brother, 1Ch 27:18
Called Eliab, 1Sa 16:6
——— One who reproved Job and his friends, Job 32:2, 4–6

ELIJAH
Denounces Ahab; goes into hiding; fed by ravens, 1Ki 17:1–7
Dwells with widow; performs miracles for her, 1Ki 17:8–24
Sends message to Ahab; overthrows prophets of Baal, 1Ki 18:1–40
Brings rain, 1Ki 18:41–45
Flees from Jezebel; fed by angels, 1Ki 19:1–8
Receives revelation from God, 1Ki 19:9–18
Condemns Ahab, 1Ki 21:15–29
Condemns Ahaziah; fire consumes troops sent against him, 2Ki 1:1–16
Taken up to heaven, 2Ki 2:1–15
Appears with Christ in Transfiguration, Mt 17:1–4
Type of John the Baptist, Mal 4:5, 6; Lk 1:17

ELIMELECH
Naomi's husband, Ru 1:1–3; 2:1, 3; 4:3–9

ELIMINATE *remove*
e harmful beasts, Lv 26:6
I am going to *e*, Jer 16:9
stomach, and is *e-d*, Mk 7:19

ELIPHAZ
One of Job's friends, Job 2:11
Rebukes Job, Job 4:1, 5
Is forgiven, Job 42:7–9

ELISHA
Chosen as Elijah's successor; follows him, 1Ki 19:16–21
Witnesses Elijah's translation; receives his spirit and mantle, 2Ki 2:1–18
Performs miracles, 2Ki 2:19–25; 4:1–6:23
Prophesies victory over Moab; fulfilled, 2Ki 3:11–27
Prophesies end of siege; fulfilled, 2Ki 7
Prophesies death of Ben-Hadad, 2Ki 8:7–15
Sends servant to anoint Jehu, 2Ki 9:1–3
Last words and death; miracle performed by his bones, 2Ki 13:14–21

ELIZABETH
Barren wife of Zacharias, Lk 1:5–7
Conceives a son, Lk 1:13, 24, 25
Salutation to Mary, Lk 1:36–45
Mother of John the Baptist, Lk 1:57–60

ELIZAPHAN
Chief of Kohathites, Nu 3:30
Heads family, 1Ch 15:5, 8
Family consecrated, 2Ch 29:12–16

ELKANAH
Father of Samuel, 1Sa 1:1–23
——— Son of Korah, Ex 6:24
Escapes judgment, Nu 26:11

ELNATHAN
Father of Nehushta, 2Ki 24:8
Goes to Egypt, Jer 26:22
Entreats with king, Jer 36:25

ELOQUENT *persuasive*
I have never been *e*, Ex 4:10
Apollos...an *e* man, Ac 18:24

ELUL
Sixth month of Hebrew calendar, Ne 6:15

ELYMAS
Arabic name of Bar-Jesus, a false prophet, Ac 13:6–12

EMBALM *preserve*
to *e* his father, Ge 50:2
he was *e-ed* and, Ge 50:26

EMBARRASSED *ashamed*
e to lift up my face, Ezr 9:6
e at the gardens, Is 1:29
diviners will be *e*, Mic 3:7

EMBITTERED *resentful*
the people were *e*, 1Sa 30:6
e them against the, Ac 14:2

EMBRACE *clasp, hug*
Esau ran...and *e-d*, Ge 33:4
e...a foreigner, Pr 5:20
A time to *e*, Ecc 3:5
ran and *e-d* him, Lk 15:20

EMBROIDERED *woven*
spoil of dyed work *e*, Jdg 5:30
be led...in *e* work, Ps 45:14
silk, and *e* cloth, Eze 16:13
purple, *e* work, Eze 27:16

EMERALD *precious stone*
ruby, topaz and *e*, Ex 28:17
throne, like an *e*, Rev 4:3

EMINENT *renowned*
nor anything *e*, Eze 7:11
the most *e* apostles, 2Co 11:5
inferior to...*e*, 2Co 12:11

EMISSION *issuance*
man has a seminal *e*, Lv 15:16
nocturnal *e*, Dt 23:10

EMMAUS
Town near Jerusalem, Lk 24:13–18

EMPOWERED *authorized*
e him to eat from, Ecc 5:19
God has not *e* him, Ecc 6:2

EMPTY *(adj) containing nothing*
Now the pit was *e*, Ge 37:24
did not return *e*, 2Sa 1:22
sent widows away *e*, Job 22:9
deceive you with *e*, Eph 5:6
avoid...*e* chatter, 2Ti 2:16

EMPTY *(v) remove contents*
e-ing their sacks, Ge 42:35
they *e* the house, Lv 14:36
I *e-ied* them out as, Ps 18:42
therefore *e* their net, Hab 1:17
e the golden *oil*, Zec 4:12
but *e-ied* Himself, Php 2:7

EMPTY-HANDED *with nothing*
have sent me away *e*, Ge 31:42
you will not go *e*, Ex 3:21
shall appear before Me *e*, Ex 23:15
to your mother-in-law *e*, Ru 3:17
and sent him away *e*, Mk 12:3
And sent away the rich *e*, Lk 1:53

ENCAMP *abide, lodge*
the tabernacle *e-s*, Nu 1:51
and *e-ed* together, Jos 11:5
a host *e* against me, Ps 27:3
angel of the LORD *e-s*, Ps 34:7

ENCIRCLE *go around*
entirely *e-ing* the sea, 2Ch 4:3
he *e-d* the Ophel, 2Ch 33:14
cords...have *e-d* me, Ps 119:61
Who *e* yourselves with, Is 50:11

ENCOMPASS *surround*
waves of death *e*, 2Sa 22:5
e-ing the walls of, 1Ki 6:5
e-ed...with bitterness, La 3:5
Water *e-ed* me to the, Jon 2:5

ENCOURAGE *strengthen*
charge Joshua and *e*, Dt 3:28
e-d him in God, 1Sa 23:16
e them in the work, Ezr 6:22
Paul was *e-ing* them, Ac 27:33
e one another, 1Th 5:11
e the young women, Titus 2:4

ENCOURAGEMENT *support*
I arose to be an *e*, Da 11:1
God who gives...*e*, Ro 15:5
is any *e* in Christ, Php 2:1
we...would have strong *e*, Heb 6:18

END *(n) extremity, goal, result*
e of all flesh has, Ge 6:13
one *e* of the heavens, Dt 4:32
from beginning to *e*, 1Sa 3:12
what is my *e*, Job 6:11
very e-s of the earth, Ps 2:8
wicked come to an *e*, Ps 7:9
e is the way of death, Pr 14:12
no *e* to all his labor, Ecc 4:8
summer is *e-ed*, Jer 8:20
The *e* is coming, Eze 7:2
who endures to...*e*, Mt 24:13
to the *e* of the age, Mt 28:20
kingdom...no *e*, Lk 1:33
He loved...to the *e*, Jn 13:1
Christ...*e* of the law, Ro 10:4
beginning and the *e*, Rev 21:6

END *(v) complete, stop*
border *e-ed* at the sea, Jos 15:4
words of Job are *e-ed*, Job 31:40
days there were *e-ed*, Ac 21:5
it *e-s* up being burned, Heb 6:8

ENDLESS *limitless*
writing...is *e*, Ecc 12:12
and *e* genealogies, 1Ti 1:4

EN-DOR
Town of Manasseh which was the home of the witch whom Saul consulted, Jos 17:11; 1Sa 28:1–10; Ps 83:9, 10

ENDOW *provide a gift*
God has *e-ed* me, Ge 30:20
e-ed with discretion, 2Ch 2:12
to *e* those who love, Pr 8:21
e-ed with salvation, Zec 9:9

ENDURANCE *patience*
in much *e*, in, 2Co 6:4
you have need of *e*, Heb 10:36
let us run with *e*, Heb 12:1
of the *e* of Job, Jas 5:11

ENDURE *persevere*
will be able to *e*, Ex 18:23
that I should *e*, Job 6:11
while the sun *e-s*, Ps 72:5
May his name *e*, Ps 72:17
and your name will *e*, Is 66:22
Can your heart *e*, Eze 22:14
the one who has *e-d*, Mt 10:22
who *e-s* to the end, Mk 13:13
e-s all things, 1Co 13:7
discipline that you *e*, Heb 12:7
blessed who *e-d*, Jas 5:11
word...Lord *e-s*, 1Pe 1:25

ENEMY *foe*
delivered your *e-ies*, Ge 14:20
Your *e-ies* perish, Jdg 5:31
a man finds his *e*, 1Sa 24:19
consider me Your *e*, Job 13:24
make the *e*...cease, Ps 8:2
presence of my *e-ies*, Ps 23:5
e has persecuted my, Ps 143:3
If your *e* is hungry, Pr 25:21
kisses of an *e*, Pr 27:6
love your *e-ies*, and, Mt 5:44
e-ies with each other, Lk 23:12
e of all righteousness, Ac 13:10
e is hungry, feed, Ro 12:20
e...be abolished, 1Co 15:26
an *e* of God, Jas 4:4

ENGAGE *be involved, betroth*
virgin who is not *e-d*, Ex 22:16
the girl who is *e-d*, Dt 22:25
e-d in their work, 1Ch 9:33
e-d to...Joseph, Lk 1:27
to *e* in good deeds, Titus 3:8

ENGEDI
Assigned to Judah, Jos 15:61–63
David's hiding place, 1Sa 23:29
Noted for vineyards, SS 1:14

ENGRAVE *inscribe*
shall *e* the two stones, Ex 28:11
e-d on the tablets, Ex 32:16
e an inscription, Zec 3:9
letters *e-d* on stones, 2Co 3:7

ENGRAVINGS *carvings*
like the *e* of a seal, Ex 28:36
the *e* of a signet, Ex 39:30
carved *e* of cherubim, 1Ki 6:29

ENGULF *overwhelm, swallow*
water...to *e* them, Dt 11:4
sea *e-ed* their enemies, Ps 78:53
She has been *e-ed*, Jer 51:42

great deep *e-ed* me, Jon 2:5

EN-HAKKORE
Miraculous spring, Jdg 15:14–19

ENLARGE *extend, increase*
May God *e* Japheth, Ge 9:27
You will *e* my heart, Ps 119:32
Sheol has *e-d* its, Is 5:14
He *e-s* his appetite, Hab 2:5

ENLIGHTEN *illumine*
e-ing the eyes, Ps 19:8
eyes…may be *e-ed*, Eph 1:18
who have…been *e-ed*, Heb 6:4

ENMITY *hostility*
e Between you and, Ge 3:15
had everlasting *e*, Eze 35:5
sorcery, *e-ies*, strife, Gal 5:20
abolishing…the *e*, Eph 2:15

ENOCH
Father of Methuselah, Ge 5:21
Walks with God, Ge 5:22
Taken up to heaven, Ge 5:24
Prophecy of, cited, Jude 14, 15

ENRAGE *anger*
e-d and curse their, Is 8:21
jealousy *e-s* a man, Pr 6:34
he became very *e-d*, Mt 2:16
dragon was *e-d* with, Rev 12:17

ENRICH *make wealthy*
king will *e* the, 1Sa 17:25
You greatly *e*, Ps 65:9
You *e-ed* the kings, Eze 27:33

EN-ROGEL
Fountain outside Jerusalem, 2Sa 17:17
Seat of Adonijah's plot, 1Ki 1:5–9

ENROLLED *recorded*
were *e* by genealogy, 1Ch 7:9
people to be *e* by, Ne 7:5
e in heaven, Heb 12:23

ENSLAVE *subjugate*
you have been *e-d*, Is 14:3
e-d and mistreated, Ac 7:6
anyone *e-s* you, 2Co 11:20
e-d to various lusts, Titus 3:3

ENSNARE *catch*
An evil man is *e-d*, Pr 12:13
e him who adjudicates, Is 29:21

ENTANGLE *ensnare*
camel *e-ing* her ways, Jer 2:23
No soldier…*e-s*, 2Ti 2:4
sin which…*e-s* us, Heb 12:1

ENTER *go in*
you shall *e* the ark, Ge 6:18
He *e-s* into judgment, Job 22:4
E His gates with, Ps 100:4
E the rock and hide, Is 2:10
He *e-s* into peace, Is 57:2
Spirit *e-ed* me and, Eze 2:2
not *e* the kingdom, Mt 5:20
E through the narrow gate, Mt 7:13
to *e* life crippled, Mt 18:8
afraid as they *e-ed*, Lk 9:34
e into the kingdom, Jn 3:5
not *e* by the door, Jn 10:1
shall not *e* My rest, Heb 3:11

ENTERTAINED *provided for*
and he *e* them, Jdg 16:25
e us courteously three days, Ac 28:7
have *e* angels without., Heb 13:2

ENTHRONED *exalt, make king*
e above the cherubim, 2Sa 6:2
LORD who is *e above*, 1Ch 13:6
e upon the praises of, Ps 22:3
who sits *e* from of old, Ps 55:19
Who is *e* on high, Ps 113:5

ENTICE *deceive, seduce*
E your husband, Jdg 14:15
Who will *e* Ahab, 2Ch 18:19
if sinners *e* you, Pr 1:10
e-d by his own lust, Jas 1:14
e-ing unstable souls, 2Pe 2:14

ENTIRE *complete*
e vision will be to you, Is 29:11
deported an *e* population, Am 1:6
e crowd was rejoicing, Lk 13:17
made an *e* man well, Jn 7:23
the *e* nation of the Jews, Ac 10:22
from whom the *e* body, Col 2:19
we direct their *e* body, Jas 3:3

ENTIRELY *completely*
be *e* offered up in smoke, Lv 6:22
brings about an *e* new, Nu 16:30
You were born *e* in sins, Jn 9:34
Himself sanctify you *e*, 1Th 5:23

ENTRAILS *inner organs*
fat that covers the *e*, Ex 29:13
e and the lobe, Lv 8:16
also washed the *e*, Lv 9:14

ENTRANCE *doorway*
cloud…at the *e*, Ex 33:10
mark well the *e* of, Eze 44:5
stone against the *e*, Mt 27:60
e into the eternal, 2Pe 1:11

ENTREAT *appeal, ask*
E the LORD that he, Ex 8:8
Moses *e-ed* the LORD, Ex 32:11
Please *e* the LORD, 1Ki 13:6
gain if we *e* Him, Job 21:15
demons *began* to *e*, Mt 8:31

ENTRUST *assign, commit*
security *e-ed to him*, Lv 6:2
He *e-ed* the vineyard, SS 8:11
to whom they *e-ed*, Lk 12:48
not *e-ing* Himself to, Jn 2:24

ENVIOUS *covetous*
e of the arrogant, Ps 73:3
not be *e* of evil men, Pr 24:1
is your eye *e*, Mt 20:15
You are *e*, Jas 4:2

ENVIRONS *outskirts, suburbs*
the *e* of Jerusalem, Jer 32:44
devour all his *e*, Jer 50:32

ENVOY *agent, messenger*
e-s of the rulers, 2Ch 32:31
faithful *e brings*, Pr 13:17
sent your *e-s* a great, Is 57:9
his *e-s* to Egypt, Eze 17:15

ENVY *(n) jealousy*
full of *e*, murder, Ro 1:29
preaching…from *e*, Php 1:15
out of which arise *e*, 1Ti 6:4
life in malice and *e*, Titus 3:3
e and all slander, 1Pe 2:1

ENVY *(v) be discontent, jealous*
Philistines *e-ied* him, Ge 26:14
e a man of violence, Pr 3:31
not let your heart *e*, Pr 23:17
e-ing one another, Gal 5:26

EPAPHRAS
Leader of the Colossian church, Col 1:7, 8
Suffers as a prisoner in Rome, Phm 23

EPAPHRODITUS
Messenger from Philippi, Php 2:25–27
Brings a gift to Paul, Php 4:18

EPHAH
Bushel, measure of capacity, Lv 5:11; Nu 5:15

EPHES-DAMMIM
Philistine encampment, 1Sa 17:1
Called Pasdammim, 1Ch 11:13

EPHESUS
Paul visits, Ac 18:18–21
Miracles done here, Ac 19:11–21
Demetrius stirs up riot in, Ac 19:24–29
Elders of, addressed by Paul at Miletus, Ac 20:17–38
Letter sent to, Eph 1:1
Site of one of seven churches, Rev 1:11

EPHOD
1 Priestly garment, Ex 28:6; 1Sa 23:9; 2Sa 6:14
2 Father of Hanniel, Nu 34:23

EPHRAIM
Joseph's younger son, Ge 41:52
Obtains Jacob's blessing, Ge 48:8–20
——— Tribe of:
Predictions concerning, Ge 48:20
Territory assigned to, Jos 16:1–10
Assist Deborah, Jdg 5:14, 15
Assist Gideon, Jdg 7:24, 25
Quarrel with Gideon, Jdg 8:1–3
Quarrel with Jephthah, Jdg 12:1–4
Leading tribe of kingdom of Israel, Is 7:2–17
Provoke God by sin, Hos 12:7–14
Many of, join Judah, 2Ch 15:8, 9
Captivity of, predicted, Hos 9:3–17
Messiah promised to, Zec 9:9–13

EPHRAIM GATE
See GATES OF JERUSALEM

EPHRATHAH
Ancient name of Bethlehem, Ru 4:11
Prophecy concerning, Mic 5:2

EPHRON
Hittite who sold Machpelah to Abraham, Ge 23:8–20

EPICUREAN
A Greek philosophy, Ac 17:18

EPOCHS *ages, seasons*
the times and the *e*, Da 2:21
to know times or *e*, Ac 1:7

EQUAL *same*
shall eat *e* portions, Dt 18:8
a man my *e*, Ps 55:13
That I would be *his e*, Is 40:25
have made them *e*, Mt 20:12
Himself *e* with God, Jn 5:18

EQUIP *furnish, provide*
e-ped for war, Jos 4:13
e-ped for…work, 2Ti 3:17
e you in every good, Heb 13:21

EQUIPMENT *implements*
the *e* for the service, Ex 39:40
e for his chariots, 1Sa 8:12
e of a foolish, Zec 11:15

EQUITY *equality, fairness*
eyes look with *e*, Ps 17:2
have established *e*, Ps 99:4
justice and *e*, Pr 1:3
e and every good, Pr 2:9

ER
Son of Judah, Ge 38:1–7; 46:12

ERASTUS
Paul's friend at Ephesus, Ac 19:21, 22; 2Ti 4:20
Treasurer of Corinth, Ro 16:23

ERECT *(adj) straight*
rose up and also stood *e*, Ge 37:7
made you walk *e*, Lv 26:13
she was made *e* again, Lk 13:13

ERECT *(v) build*
he *e-ed* there an altar and, Ge 33:20
you shall *e* the tabernacle, Ex 26:30
e-ed over him, 2Sa 18:17
e an altar to the, 2Sa 24:18
places and *e* the Asherim, 2Ch 33:19
e-ed their siege towers, Is 23:13
about to *e* the tabernacle, Heb 8:5

ERROR *mistake, sin*
can discern *his e-s*, Ps 19:12
like an *e* which goes, Ecc 10:5
e against the LORD, Is 32:6
e of unprincipled, 2Pe 3:17
the spirit of *e*, 1Jn 4:6
rushed…into the *e*, Jude 11

ESARHADDON
Son of Sennacherib; king of Assyria (681–669 B.C.), 2Ki 19:36, 37

ESAU
Isaac's favorite son, Ge 25:25–28
Sells his birthright, Ge 25:29–34
Deprived of blessing; seeks to kill Jacob, Ge 27
Reconciled to Jacob, Ge 33:1–17
Descendants of, Ge 36

ESCAPE *(n) deliverance, refuge*
there will be no *e*, Job 11:20
is no *e* for me, Ps 142:4
Let there be no *e*, Jer 50:29
provide…*e*, 1Co 10:13

ESCAPE *(v) elude*
slave who has *e-d*, Dt 23:15
let no one *e or*, 2Ki 9:15
Our soul has *e-d*, Ps 124:7
tells lies will not *e*, Pr 19:5
how shall we *e*, Is 20:6
nothing at all *e-s*, Joel 2:3
had not *e-d* notice, Lk 8:47
how will we *e* if, Heb 2:3
it *e-s* their notice, 2Pe 3:5

ESHBAAL
Son of Saul, 1Ch 8:33

ESHCOL
Valley near Hebron, Nu 13:22–27; Dt 1:24

ESTABLISH *confirm, found*
I will *e* My covenant, Ge 17:19
how God *e-es* them, Job 37:15
e-es the mountains, Ps 65:6
my ways may be *e-ed*, Ps 119:5
e-ed in lovingkindness, Is 16:5
to *e* the heavens, Is 51:16
we *e* the Law, Ro 3:31
may *e* your hearts, 1Th 3:13
e-ed in the truth, 2Pe 1:12

ESTATE *domain; standard*
restore your…*e*, Job 8:6
us in our low *e*, Ps 136:23
squandered his *e*, Lk 15:13

ESTEEM *(n) honor*
man of high *e*, Da 10:11
held them in high *e*, Ac 5:13

ESTEEM *(v) have high regard*
I *e* right all *Your*, Ps 119:128
e-ed Him stricken, Is 53:4
e-ed among men, Lk 16:15
e them…in love, 1Th 5:13

ESTHER
Selected for harem, Est 2:7–16
Chosen to be queen, Est 2:17, 18
Agrees to intercede for her people, Est 4
Invites king to banquet, Est 5:1–8
Denounces Haman; obtains reversal of decree, Est 7:1–8:8
Establishes Purim, Est 9:29–32

ESTRANGED *separated*
completely *e* from me, Job 19:13
e from my brothers, Ps 69:8

ETAM
Rock where Samson took refuge, Jdg 15:8–19

ETERNAL *everlasting*
e God is a dwelling, Dt 33:27
E Father, Prince of, Is 9:6
An *e* decree, Jer 5:22
cast into the *e* fire, Mt 18:8
guilty of an *e* sin, Mk 3:29
to inherit *e* life, Lk 10:25
He may give *e* life, Jn 17:2
gift of God is *e* life, Ro 6:23
e weight of glory, 2Co 4:17
with the *e* purpose, Eph 3:11
Now to the King *e*, 1Ti 1:17
source of *e* salvation, Heb 5:9
through the *e* Spirit, Heb 9:14
kept in *e* bonds, Jude 6
an *e* gospel to preach, Rev 14:6

ETERNAL LIFE
that I may obtain *e*, Mt 19:16
as much, and will inherit *e*, Mt 19:29
but the righteous into *e*, Mt 25:46
what shall I do to inherit *e*, Mk 10:17
and in the age to come, *e*., Mk 10:30
what shall I do to inherit *e*, Lk 10:25
what shall I do to inherit *e*, Lk 18:18
and in the age to come, *e*, Lk 18:30
believes will in Him have *e*, Jn 3:15
shall not perish, but have *e*, Jn 3:16
believes in the Son has *e*, Jn 3:36
water springing up to *e*, Jn 4:14
that in them you have *e*, Jn 5:39
food which endures to *e*, Jn 6:27
he who believes has *e*, Jn 6:47
drinks My blood has *e*, Jn 6:54
You have words of *e*, Jn 6:68
His commandment is *e*, Jn 12:50
e, that they may know You, Jn 17:3
yourselves unworthy of *e*, Ac 13:46
had been appointed to *e*, Ac 13:48
by perseverance … *e*, Ro 2:7
e through Jesus Christ, Ro 5:21
free gift of God is *e*, Ro 6:23
will from the Spirit reap *e*, Gal 6:8
would believe in Him for *e*, 1Ti 1:16
take hold of the *e* to which, 1Ti 6:12
in the hope of *e*, Titus 1:2
according to the hope of *e*, Titus 3:7
the *e*, which was with the, 1Jn 1:2
no murderer has *e* abiding, 1Jn 3:15
God has given us *e*, 1Jn 5:11
may know that you have *e*, 1Jn 5:13
Lord Jesus Christ to *e*, Jude 21

ETERNITY *perpetuity*
set *e* in their heart, Ecc 3:11
from *e* I am He, Is 43:13
Jesus from all *e*, 2Ti 1:9
to the day of *e*, 2Pe 3:18

ETHAM
Israel's encampment, Ex 13:20

ETHIOPIA
See CUSH
Hostile to Israel and Judah, 2Ch 12:2, 3; 14:9–15; Is 43:3; Da 11:43
Prophecies against, Is 20:1–6; Eze 30:4–9

ETHIOPIAN
Skin of, unchangeable, Jer 13:23

EUNICE
Mother of Timothy, 2Ti 1:5

EUNUCH *chamberlain official*
seven *e-s* who served, Est 1:10
Nor let the *e* say, Is 56:3
children, and *the e-s*, Jer 41:16
made *e-s* by men, Mt 19:12
an Ethiopian *e*, Ac 8:27

EUPHRATES
River of Eden, Ge 2:14
Boundary of Promised Land, Ge 15:18; 1Ki 4:21, 24

Scene of battle, Jer 46:2, 6, 10
Angels bound there, Rev 9:14

EUTYCHUS
Sleeps during Paul's sermon, Ac 20:9
Restored to life, Ac 20:12

EVANGELIST *proclaimer*
house of Philip the *e*, Ac 21:8
and some *as e-s*, Eph 4:11
do the work of an *e*, 2Ti 4:5

EVENING *dusk, darkness*
cloud…from *e*, Nu 9:21
eats food before *e*, 1Sa 14:24
as the *e* offering, Ps 141:2
not be idle in the *e*, Ecc 11:6
When *e* came, Mt 8:16

EVENT *happening*
the *e-s* of the war, 2Sa 11:18
e became sin to the, 1Ki 13:34
recorded these *e-s*, Est 9:20
time for every *e*, Ecc 3:1

EVERLASTING *eternal*
e covenant between, Ge 9:16
the LORD, the *E* God, Ge 21:33
are the *e* arms, Dt 33:27
e to *e*, You are God, Ps 90:2
lovingkindness is *e*, Ps 106:1
From *e* I was, Pr 8:23
The *E* God, the LORD, Is 40:28
e name which will, Is 56:5
LORD for an *e* light, Is 60:20
loved you with an *e*, Jer 31:3

EVIDENCE *facts, testimony*
the *e* of witnesses, Nu 35:30
on the *e* of two, Dt 19:15
not able to give *e*, Ezr 2:59
and giving *e*, Ac 17:3

EVIDENT *obvious, plain*
the tares became *e*, Mt 13:26
for God made it *e*, Ro 1:19
work will become *e*, 1Co 3:13
Law before God is *e*, Gal 3:11
it is *e* that our Lord, Heb 7:14

EVIL *bad, wicked, wrong*
man's heart is *e*, Ge 8:21
keep…from every *e*, Dt 23:9
discern good and *e*, 2Sa 14:17
rebellious and *e* city, Ezr 4:12
I fear no *e*, Ps 23:4
repay me *e* for good, Ps 35:12
turn away from *e*, Pr 3:7
run rapidly to *e*, Pr 6:18
returns *e* for good, Pr 17:13
taken away from *e*, Is 57:1
committed two *e-s*, Jer 2:13
deliver us from *e*, Mt 6:13
what *e* has He, Mt 27:23
If you then, being *e*, Lk 11:13
who does *e* hates the, Jn 3:20
Never…*e* for *e*, Ro 12:17
love of money is…*e*, 1Ti 6:10
tongue…restless *e*, Jas 3:8

EVIL ONE
e comes and snatches, Mt 13:19
the sons of the *e*, Mt 13:38
to keep them from the *e*, Jn 17:15
flaming arrows of the *e*, Eph 6:16
protect you from the *e*, 2Th 3:3
you have overcome the *e*, 1Jn 2:13
you have overcome the *e*, 1Jn 2:14
the *e* does not touch him, 1Jn 5:18
lies in the power of the *e*, 1Jn 5:19

EVILDOER *wicked one*
LORD repay the *e*, 2Sa 3:39
e-s will be cut off, Ps 37:9
e listens to wicked, Pr 17:4
Offspring of *e-s*, Is 1:4
is godless and an *e*, Is 9:17
depart…you *e-s*, Lk 13:27
punishment of *e-s*, 1Pe 2:14

EVIL-MERODACH
Babylonian king (562–560 B.C.), 2Ki 25:27–30

EWE *female sheep*
seven *e* lambs, Ge 21:28
e lamb without, Lv 14:10
poor man's *e* lamb, 2Sa 12:4
e-s with suckling, Ps 78:71
like a flock of *e-s*, SS 6:6

EXACT *(adj) certain, correct*
e amount of money, Est 4:7
e meaning of all this, Da 7:16
know the *e* truth, Lk 1:4
a more *e* knowledge, Ac 24:22

EXACT *(v) collect*
let him *e* a fifth, Ge 41:34
he shall not *e* it, Dt 15:2
He *e-ed* the silver, 2Ki 23:35
You are *e-ing* usury, Ne 5:7
e a tribute of grain, Am 5:11

EXALT *extol, honor, lift*
He is highly *e-ed*, Ex 15:1
e-ed be God, 2Sa 22:47
He is *e-ed* in power, Job 37:23
let us *e* His name, Ps 34:3
e-ed far above all gods, Ps 97:9
city is *e-ed*, Pr 11:11
my God; I will *e* You, Is 25:1
E that which is low, Eze 21:26
humbles…be *e-ed*, Mt 23:12
e-ed to…right hand, Ac 2:33
be *e-ed* in my body, Php 1:20
He will *e* you, Jas 4:10

EXAMINE *investigate, search*
That You *e* him every, Job 7:18
E me, O LORD, and try, Ps 26:2
e my heart's *attitude*, Jer 12:3
e-ing the Scriptures, Ac 17:11
e-d by scourging, Ac 22:24
a man must *e* himself, 1Co 11:28

EXAMPLE *model, pattern*
the *e* of his father, 2Ch 17:3
I gave you an *e*, Jn 13:15
e of those who, 1Ti 4:12
e of disobedience, Heb 4:11
be *e-s* to the flock, 1Pe 5:3
made them an *e*, 2Pe 2:6

EXCEEDINGLY *very*
of Sodom were wicked *e*, Ge 13:13
And I will multiply you *e*, Ge 17:2
an *e* great and bitter cry, Ge 27:34
man became *e* prosperous, Ge 30:43
LORD shall be *e*, 1Ch 22:5
commandment is *e* broad, Ps 119:96
Nineveh was an *e* great city, Jon 3:3
rejoiced *e* with great joy, Mt 2:10
became radiant and *e* white, Mk 9:3

EXCEL *be superior*
e in…wickedness, Jer 5:28
wisdom *e-s* folly, Ecc 2:13
you *e*…more, 1Th 4:1

EXCELLENCE *perfection*
greatness of Your *e*, Ex 15:7
are a woman of *e*, Ru 3:11
if there is any *e*, Php 4:8
proclaim the *e-ies* of, 1Pe 2:9

EXCELLENT *outstanding*
e wife is the crown, Pr 12:4
E speech is not, Pr 17:7
He has done *e* things, Is 12:5
e governor Felix, Ac 23:26
a still more *e* way, 1Co 12:31
a more *e* name, Heb 1:4

EXCESS *too much*
he…had no *e*, Ex 16:18
are in *e* among them, Nu 3:48
same *e-es* of dissipation, 1Pe 4:4

EXCHANGE *trade, transfer*
shall *e it* for money, Dt 14:25
they *e-d* their glory, Ps 106:20
shall not sell or *e*, Eze 48:14
e-d the truth of God, Ro 1:25

EXCLUDE *refuse to admit*
e-d from…assembly, Ezr 10:8
e-d all foreigners, Ne 13:3
e you for My name's, Is 66:5
e-d from the life of, Eph 4:18

EXCUSE *justification*
began to make *e-s*, Lk 14:18
no *e* for their sin, Jn 15:22
they are without *e*, Ro 1:20

EXECUTE *carry out*
e-d the justice of, Dt 33:21
He has *e-d* judgment, Ps 9:16
e vengeance on the, Ps 149:7
Lord will *e* His word, Ro 9:28
e judgment upon all, Jude 15

EXERCISE *perform*
man has *e-d* authority, Ecc 8:9
e-s lovingkindness, Jer 9:24
e authority over, Mt 20:25
e-s self-control in all, 1Co 9:25

EXHAUSTED *used up, wearied*
sound asleep and *e*, Jdg 4:21
too *e* to follow, 1Sa 30:21
of flour was not *e*, 1Ki 17:16
Their strength is *e*, Jer 51:30

EXHORT *admonish, urge*
and kept on *e-ing*, Ac 2:40
e, with…patience, 2Ti 4:2
e in sound doctrine, Titus 1:9
e and reprove, Titus 2:15
e-ing and testifying, 1Pe 5:12

EXHORTATION *urging*
with many other *e-s*, Lk 3:18
given them much *e*, Ac 20:2

who exhorts, in his *e*, Ro 12:8
this word of *e*, Heb 13:22

EXILE *banishment; capture*
Israel away into *e*, 2Ki 17:6
people of the *e* were, Ezr 4:1
captivity of the *e-s*, Ne 7:6
into *e* from Jerusalem, Est 2:6
e will soon be set free, Is 51:14
Israel went into *e*, Eze 39:23

EXIST *be, live, occur*
they had never *e-ed*, Ob 16
Strife *e-s* and, Hab 1:3
live and move and *e*, Ac 17:28
authority...which *e*, Ro 13:1

EXODUS *departure*
e of...Israel, Heb 11:22

EXPANSE *firmament, vastness*
e of the heavens, Ge 1:20
e of the waters, Job 37:10
in His mighty *e*, Ps 150:1
from above the *e*, Eze 1:25

EXPECT *await*
never *e-ed* to see, Ge 48:11
e-ed good, then evil, Job 30:26
which we did not *e*, Is 64:3
lend, *e-ing* nothing, Lk 6:35

EXPECTATION *anticipation*
your *e* is false, Job 41:9
e of the wicked, Pr 10:28
to my earnest *e*, Php 1:20
e of judgment, Heb 10:27

EXPECTED *awaited*
Are You the *E* One, Mt 11:3
Are You the *E* One, Lk 7:20

EXPERIENCE *undergo*
all who had not *e-d*, Jdg 3:1
Your people *e* hardship, Ps 60:3
e-s Your judgments, Is 26:9
e-d mockings and, Heb 11:36

EXPERT *very skillful*
an *e* in warfare, 2Sa 17:8
be like an *e* warrior, Jer 50:9
an *e* in all customs, Ac 26:3

EXPLAIN *make clear*
no one who could *e*, Ge 41:24
he did not *e* to her, 2Ch 9:2
e its interpretation, Da 5:7
E the parable to us, Mt 15:15
e-ing the Scriptures, Lk 24:32
e-ed to him the way, Ac 18:26

EXPOSE *disclose, reveal*
shame...be *e-d*, Is 47:3
He will *e* your sins, La 4:22
deeds will be *e-d*, Jn 3:20
would *e* their infants, Ac 7:19
are *e-d* by the light, Eph 5:13

EXTEND *enlarge, stretch out*
God *e-s*...border, Dt 12:20
e-ed lovingkindness, Ezr 7:28
e-s her hand to the, Pr 31:20
I *e* peace to her, Is 66:12
boundary shall *e*, Eze 47:17

EXTENT *amount; degree*
the *e* of my days, Ps 39:4
e that you did it to, Mt 25:40
such an *e* that Jesus, Mk 1:45

EXTERMINATE *destroy*
planned to *e* us, 2Sa 21:5
He will *e* its sinners, Is 13:9

EXTERNAL *outward*
not with *e* service, Col 3:22
adornment must not be...*e*, 1Pe 3:3

EXTINGUISH *put out*
they will *e* my coal, 2Sa 14:7
not *e* the lamp of, 2Sa 21:17
my days are *e-ed*, Job 17:1
when *I e* you, Eze 32:7
e all the flaming, Eph 6:16

EXTOL *praise*
God, and I will *e* Him, Ex 15:2
I will *e* You, O LORD, Ps 30:1
I will *e* You, my God, Ps 145:1
We will *e* your love, SS 1:4

EXTORTION *stealing*
practicing...*e*, Jer 22:17
practiced *e*, robbed, Eze 18:18

EXTRAORDINARY *exceptional*
will bring *e* plagues, Dt 28:59
His *e* work, Is 28:21
insight, and *e* wisdom, Da 5:14
e miracles by, Ac 19:11
showed us *e* kindness, Ac 28:2

EXULT *rejoice*
heart *e-s* in the LORD, 1Sa 2:1
Let the field *e*, 1Ch 16:32
e-ed when evil befell, Job 31:29
let them *e* before God, Ps 68:3
I will *e* in the LORD, Hab 3:18
e in our tribulations, Ro 5:3

EXULTATION *jubilation*
e like the nations, Hos 9:1
joy or crown of *e*, 1Th 2:19
may rejoice with *e*, 1Pe 4:13

EYE *sight*
e-s are dull from, Ge 49:12
e for *e*, tooth for, Ex 21:24
be as *e-s* for us, Nu 10:31
his *e* was not dim, Dt 34:7
right in his own *e-s*, Jdg 17:6
open his *e-s* that he, 2Ki 6:17
e-s of the LORD, 2Ch 16:9
was *e-s* to the blind, Job 29:15
e-s...look to You, Ps 145:15
Haughty *e-s*, a lying, Pr 6:17
e...mocks a father, Pr 30:17
e is not satisfied, Ecc 1:8
To open blind *e-s*, Is 42:7
e-s will bitterly weep, Jer 13:17
have *e-s* to see but, Eze 12:2
I lifted my *e-s* and, Da 8:3
Your e-s...too pure, Hab 1:13
e for an *e*, and a, Mt 5:38
e...you to stumble, Mt 18:9
e is the lamp, Lk 11:34
the clay to his *e-s*, Jn 9:6
which *e* has not seen, 1Co 2:9
e-s of your heart may, Eph 1:18
e-s full of adultery, 2Pe 2:14
the lust of the *e-s*, 1Jn 2:16
God, who has *e-s* like, Rev 2:18
His *e-s are* a flame, Rev 19:12

EYEWITNESSES *observers*
e...of the word, Lk 1:2
e of His majesty, 2Pe 1:16

EZEKIEL
Sent to rebellious Israel, Eze 2; 3
Prophesies by symbolic action:
siege of Jerusalem, Eze 4
destruction of Jerusalem, Eze 5
captivity of Judah, Eze 12:1–20
destruction of the temple, Eze 24:15–27
Visions of:
God's glory, Eze 1:3–28
abominations, Eze 8:5–18
valley of dry bones, Eze 37:1–14
messianic times, Eze 40–48
river of life, Eze 47:1–5
Parables, allegories, dirges of, Eze 15; 16; 17; 19; 23; 24

EZION-GEBER
See ELATH
Town on the Red Sea, 1Ki 9:26
Israelite encampment, Nu 33:35
Seaport of Israel's navy, 1Ki 22:48

EZRA
Scribe, priest and reformer of postexilic times; commissioned by Artaxerxes, Ezr 7
Returns with exiles to Jerusalem, Ezr 8
Institutes reforms, Ezr 9
Reads the Law, Ne 8
Assists in dedication of wall, Ne 12:27–43

F

FACE *countenance*
sweat of your *f* You, Ge 3:19
Abram fell on his *f*, Ge 17:3
speak to Moses *f* to *f*, Ex 33:11
skin of his *f* shone, Ex 34:30
make His *f* shine, Nu 6:25
hide Your *f* from me, Ps 13:1
Who seek Your *f*, Ps 24:6
His *f* to shine upon us, Ps 67:1
f of Your anointed, Ps 84:9
makes a cheerful *f*, Pr 15:13
set My *f* against you, Jer 44:11
had the *f* of an eagle, Eze 1:10
Each...had four *f-s*, Eze 10:21
fast...wash your *f*, Mt 6:17
they spat in His *f*, Mt 26:67
like the *f* of an angel, Ac 6:15
natural *f* in a mirror, Jas 1:23
His *f* was like the sun, Rev 1:16

FACE TO FACE
I have seen God *f*, Ge 32:30
used to speak to Moses *f*, Ex 33:11
LORD spoke to you *f*, Dt 5:4
the LORD knew *f*, Dt 34:10
angel of the LORD *f*, Jdg 6:22
speak with him *f*, Jer 32:4
he will speak with you *f*, Jer 34:3
into judgment with you *f*, Eze 20:35
meets his accusers *f*, Ac 25:16
a mirror dimly, but then *f*, 1Co 13:12
am meek when *f* with you, 2Co 10:1

f, so that your joy may, 2Jn 12
we will speak *f*, 3Jn 14

FACT *truth*
f may be confirmed, Mt 18:16
are undeniable *f-s*, Ac 19:36
f is to be confirmed, 2Co 13:1

FACTIONS *divisions*
be *f* among you, 1Co 11:19
dissensions, *f*, Gal 5:20

FADE *wither*
it *f-s*, and withers, Ps 90:6
people...*f* away, Is 24:4
rich man...will *f*, Jas 1:11
will not *f* away, 1Pe 1:4

FAIL *be spent; fall short*
He will not *f* you, Dt 4:31
none of his words *f*, 1Sa 3:19
no man's heart *f*, 1Sa 17:32
not one word...*f-ed*, 1Ki 8:56
my strength *f-s* me, Ps 38:10
the olive should *f*, Hab 3:17
faith may not *f*, Lk 22:32
Love never *f-s*, 1Co 13:8

FAINT *languish, swoon*
has made my heart *f*, Job 23:16
soul *f-ed* within, Ps 107:5
grow *f* before Me, Is 57:16
I was *f-ing* away, Jon 2:7
men *f-ing* from fear, Lk 21:26
f when...reproved, Heb 12:5

FAINTHEARTED *weak*
Do not be *f*, Dt 20:3
encourage the *f*, 1Th 5:14

FAIR *attractive*
f are your tents, O Jacob, Nu 24:5
so *f* as Job's daughters, Job 42:15
It will be f weather, Mt 16:2
blaspheme the *f* name, Jas 2:7

FAIR HAVENS
Harbor of Crete at which Paul landed, Ac 27:8

FAIRER *more attractive*
are *f* than the sons of men, Ps 45:2

FAITH *believe, trust*
because you broke *f*, Dt 32:51
Will you have *f*, Job 39:12
Who keeps *f* forever, Ps 146:6
will live by his *f*, Hab 2:4
Seeing their *f*, Jesus, Mt 9:2
f the size of a mustard seed, Mt 17:20
Your *f* has saved you, Lk 7:50
Increase our *f*, Lk 17:5
your *f* may not fail, Lk 22:32
man full of *f*, Ac 6:5
of *f* to the Gentiles, Ac 14:27
sanctified by *f* in Me, Ac 26:18
justified by *f*, Ro 5:1
f...from hearing, Ro 10:17
if I have all *f*, 1Co 13:2
your *f* also is vain, 1Co 15:14
we walk by *f*, 2Co 5:7
live by *f* in the Son, Gal 2:20
saved through *f*, Eph 2:8
one Lord, one *f*, Eph 4:5
joy in the *f*, Php 1:25
stability of your *f*, Col 2:5
breastplate of *f*, 1Th 5:8
for not all have *f*, 2Th 3:2
fall away from the *f*, 1Ti 4:1
conduct, love, *f*, 1Ti 4:12
they upset the *f*, 2Ti 2:18
sound in the *f*, Titus 1:13
showing all good *f*, Titus 2:10
full assurance of *f*, Heb 10:22
By *f* Enoch was taken, Heb 11:5
perfecter of *f*, Heb 12:2
ask in *f*, Jas 1:6
prayer offered in *f*, Jas 5:15
power of God...*f*, 1Pe 1:5
the *f* of the saints, Rev 13:10

FAITHFUL *loyal, trustworthy*
the *f* God, who keeps, Dt 7:9
raise...a *f* priest, 1Sa 2:35
heart *f* before You, Ne 9:8
LORD preserves the *f*, Ps 31:23
commandments...*f*, Ps 119:86
the LORD who is *f*, Is 49:7
Well done...*f*, Mt 25:23
God is *f*, 1Co 1:9
F is He who calls, 1Th 5:24
He considered me *f*, 1Ti 1:12
entrust...to *f* men, 2Ti 2:2
souls to a *f* Creator, 1Pe 4:19
He is *f*...to forgive, 1Jn 1:9
Be *f* until death, Rev 2:10
called *F* and True, Rev 19:11

FAITHFULNESS *loyalty*
kindness and *f*, Ge 47:29
A God of *f*, Dt 32:4
make known Your *f*, Ps 89:1
f to all generations, Ps 100:5
and mercy and *f*, Mt 23:23
nullify the *f* of God, Ro 3:3
kindness, goodness, *f*, Gal 5:22

FAITHLESS *unbelieving*
what *f* Israel did, Jer 3:6
O *f* daughter, Jer 31:22
Their heart is *f*, Hos 10:2
If we are *f*, 2Ti 2:13

FALL *descend; fail*
deep sleep to *f* upon, Ge 2:21
devices let them *f*, Ps 5:10
I am ready to *f*, Ps 38:17
dread...had *f-en*, Ps 105:38
wicked will *f*, Pr 11:5
a righteous man *f-s*, Pr 24:16
whether a tree *f-s*, Ecc 11:3
Assyrian will *f*, Is 31:8
Babylon has *f-en*, Jer 51:8
f down and worship, Da 3:5
will *f* into a pit, Mt 15:14
f-ing on his knees, Mk 1:40
all may *f*...I will, Mk 14:29
appointed for the *f*, Lk 2:34
watching Satan *f*, Lk 10:18
house *divided*...*f-s*, Lk 11:17
f-ing headlong, Ac 1:18
sinned and *f* short, Ro 3:23
have *f-en* asleep, 1Co 15:6
f-en from grace, Gal 5:4
rich *f* into temptation, 1Ti 6:9
rocks, *F* on us, Rev 6:16

FALLOW *unproductive*
rest and lie *f*, Ex 23:11
f ground of the poor, Pr 13:23

FALSE *deceitful, dishonest*
not bear a *f* report, Ex 23:1
I hate every *f* way, Ps 119:104
But a *f* witness, Pr 12:17
f witness will not go, Pr 19:5
f scale is not good, Pr 20:23
F and foolish *visions*, La 2:14
And tell *f* dreams, Zec 10:2
not bear *f* witness, Mt 19:18
f Christs and *f*, Mt 24:24
men are *f* apostles, 2Co 11:13
the *f* circumcision, Php 3:2
and the *f* prophet, Rev 20:10

FALSE PROPHETS
Beware of the *f*, Mt 7:15
f will arise and will mislead, Mt 24:11
false Christs and *f*, Mt 24:24
false Christs and *f*, Mk 13:22
treat the *f* in the same way, Lk 6:26
f also arose among, 2Pe 2:1
f have gone out, 1Jn 4:1

FALSE WITNESS
You shall not bear *f*, Ex 20:16
You shall not bear *f*, Dt 5:20
f who utters lies, Pr 6:19
But a *f*, deceit, Pr 12:17
f will not go unpunished, Pr 19:5
f will perish, Pr 21:28
thefts, *f*, slanders, Mt 15:19
You shall not bear *f*, Mt 19:18
Do not bear *f*, Mk 10:19
Do not bear *f*, Lk 18:20

FALSEHOOD *deception*
lifted up his soul to *f*, Ps 24:4
delight in *f*, Ps 62:4
I hate and despise *f*, Ps 119:163
Bread obtained by *f*, Pr 20:17
trusted in *f*, Jer 13:25
prophesying *f* in My, Jer 14:14
laying aside *f*, Eph 4:25

FALSELY *with deception*
not deal *f* with me or, Ge 21:23
shall not steal, nor deal *f*, Lv 19:11
not dealt *f* with Your, Ps 44:17
Sons who will not deal *f*, Is 63:8
The prophets prophesy *f*, Jer 5:31
words in My name *f*, Jer 29:23
f say all kinds of evil, Mt 5:11
or accuse *anyone f*, Lk 3:14
of what is *f* called, 1Ti 6:20

FAME *greatness*
heard of Your *f*, Nu 14:15
Joshua, and his *f*, Jos 6:27
the *f* of Solomon, 1Ki 10:1
heard My *f*, Is 66:19
f in the things of, 2Co 8:18

FAMILY *household, relatives*
f-ies from the ark, Ge 8:19
all the *f-ies* of, Ge 12:3
f may redeem him, Lv 25:49
f-ies of the Levites, Nu 3:20
my *f* is the least, Jdg 6:15
f-ies like a flock, Ps 107:41
God of all the *f-ies*, Jer 31:1
f-ies of the earth, Am 3:2
every *f* in heaven, Eph 3:15
upsetting whole *f-ies*, Titus 1:11

FAMINE *shortage of food*
a *f* in the land, Ge 12:10
seven years of *f*, Ge 41:27
If there is *f*, 2Ch 6:28
In *f* He will redeem, Job 5:20
keep them alive in *f*, Ps 33:19
f and pestilence, Jer 14:12
f and wild beasts, Eze 5:17
f-s and earthquakes, Mt 24:7
plagues and *f-s*, Lk 21:11
Now a *f* came, Ac 7:11
mourning and *f*, Rev 18:8

FAMISHED *hungry, parched*
for I am *f*, Ge 25:30
strength is *f*, Job 18:12
honorable men are *f*, Is 5:13

FAMOUS *well-known*
f in Bethlehem, Ru 4:11
men of valor, *f* men, 1Ch 5:24

FAR *distant*
f from a false charge, Ex 23:7
come from a *f* country, Jos 9:6
Be not *f* from me, Ps 22:11
f above all gods, Ps 97:9
As *f* as the east, Ps 103:12
LORD is *f* from the, Pr 15:29
a God *f* off, Jer 23:23
heart is *f* away from, Mt 15:8
f from the kingdom, Mk 12:34
glory *f* beyond all, 2Co 4:17
f above all rule, Eph 1:21

FAR COUNTRY
have come from a *f*, Jos 9:6
a *f* for Your name's sake, 1Ki 8:41
from a *f*, from Babylon, 2Ki 20:14
f, from the farthest horizons, Is 13:5

FARM *agricultural land*
consume the *f* land, Am 7:4
one to his own *f*, Mt 22:5
or *f-s*, for My sake, Mk 10:29

FARMER *husbandman*
Does the *f* plow, Is 28:24
will be your *f-s*, Is 61:5
f-s...put to shame, Jer 14:4
the *f* to mourning, Am 5:16

FASHION *create, form*
f-ed into a woman, Ge 2:22
f us in the womb, Job 31:15
He who *f-s* the hearts, Ps 33:15
f a graven image, Is 44:9
I am *f-ing* calamity, Jer 18:11

FAST *(n) food abstinence*
Proclaim a *f*, 1Ki 21:9
you call this a *f*, Is 58:5
Consecrate a *f*, Joel 1:14
f was already over, Ac 27:9

FAST *(v) abstain from food*
and David *f-ed*, 2Sa 12:16
maidens also will *f*, Est 4:16
you *f* for contention, Is 58:4
had *f-ed* forty days, Mt 4:2
whenever you *f*, Mt 6:16
disciples do not *f*, Mk 2:18
I *f* twice a week, Lk 18:12
had *f-ed* and prayed, Ac 13:3

FASTING *food abstinence*
times of *f*, Est 9:31
weak from *f*, Ps 109:24
noticed...when they are *f*, Mt 6:16
by prayer and *f*, Mt 17:21
Pharisees were *f*, Mk 2:18

FAT *animal fat; obese*
f of the land, Ge 45:18
shall not eat any *f*, Lv 7:23
Go, eat of the *f*, Ne 8:10
their body is *f*, Ps 73:4
Good news puts *f*, Pr 15:30

FATE *destiny*
appalled at his *f*, Job 18:20
one *f* befalls them, Ecc 2:14
f for the righteous, Ecc 9:2
one *f* for all men, Ecc 9:3

FATHER *God; parent*
leave his *f*...mother, Ge 2:24
f of a multitude, Ge 17:4
Honor your *f*, Ex 20:12
who strikes his *f*, Ex 21:15
iniquity of the *f-s*, Dt 5:9
Is not He your *F*, Dt 32:6
your *f-'s* instruction, Pr 1:8
son makes a *f* glad, Pr 10:1
Eternal *F*, Prince of, Is 9:6
all have one *f*, Mal 2:10
F who sees...in secret, Mt 6:4
Our *F* who is in, Mt 6:9
does the will of My *F*, Mt 7:21
in My *F-'s* kingdom, Mt 26:29
in the glory of His *F*, Mk 8:38
be in my *F-'s house*, Lk 2:49
F, hallowed be Your, Lk 11:2
F, forgive them, Lk 23:34
begotten from the *F*, Jn 1:14
my *F-'s* house a, Jn 2:16
F...testifies, Jn 8:18
the *f* of lies, Jn 8:44
I and the *F* are one, Jn 10:30
In my *F-'s* house are, Jn 14:2
F is the vinedresser, Jn 15:1
ask the *F* for, Jn 16:23
I ascend to My *F*, Jn 20:17
one God and *F* of all, Eph 4:6

FATHER WHO IS IN HEAVEN
and glorify your *F*, Mt 5:16
sons of your *F*, Mt 5:45
no reward with your *F*, Mt 6:1
Our *F*, Hallowed, Mt 6:9
your *F* give what is good, Mt 7:11
will of My *F* will enter, Mt 7:21
confess him before My *F*, Mt 10:32
deny him before My *F*, Mt 10:33
will of My *F*, he is My, Mt 12:50
this to you, but My *F*, Mt 16:17
see the face of My *F*, Mt 18:10
will of your *F* that one, Mt 18:14
done for them by My *F*, Mt 18:19
your *F* will also forgive, Mk 11:25

FATHER-IN-LAW
she sent to her *f*, Ge 38:25
returned to Jethro his *f*, Ex 4:18
his *f*, the girl's, Jdg 19:4
f of Caiaphas, Jn 18:13

FATHERLESS *orphan*
father of the *f*, Ps 68:5
He supports the *f*, Ps 146:9
fields of the *f*, Pr 23:10
f and the widow, Eze 22:7

FATLING *young lamb; kid*
sacrificed...a *f*, 2Sa 6:13
f-s...in abundance, 1Ki 1:19
f-s of Bashan, Eze 39:18

FATNESS *abundance*
f of the earth, Ge 27:28
Shall I leave my *f*, Jdg 9:9
satisfied as with...*f*, Ps 63:5
eye bulges from *f*, Ps 73:7

FATTENED *well-fed*
woman had a *f* calf, 1Sa 28:24
f ox *served* with hatred, Pr 15:17
oxen and my *f* livestock, Mt 22:4
and bring the *f* calf, kill it, Lk 15:23
you have *f* your hearts in, Jas 5:5

FAULT *error, offense*
found no *f* in him, 1Sa 29:3
let no one find *f*, Hos 4:4
does He still find *f*, Ro 9:19
grumblers, finding *f*, Jude 16

FAVOR *kind regard*
Noah found *f*, Ge 6:8
I will grant...*f*, Ex 3:21
show no *f* to them, Dt 7:2
Why have I found *f*, Ru 2:10
surround him with *f*, Ps 5:12
showed *f* to Your land, Ps 85:1
obtains *f*...LORD, Pr 8:35
f is like a cloud, Pr 16:15
found *f* with God, Lk 1:30
in *f* with God and, Lk 2:52
seeking the *f* of men, Gal 1:10

FEAR *(n) awe, dread, reverence*
no *f* of God in, Ge 20:11
f of the LORD is clean, Ps 19:9
f...is the beginning, Ps 111:10
afraid of sudden *f*, Pr 3:25
f...prolongs life, Pr 10:27
f of man brings a, Pr 29:25
they cried out in *f*, Mt 14:26
guards shook for *f*, Mt 28:4
men fainting from *f*, Lk 21:26
for *f* of the Jews, Jn 7:13
no *f* of God before, Ro 3:18
in weakness and in *f*, 1Co 2:3
knowing the *f* of the, 2Co 5:11
with *f* and trembling, Eph 6:5
through *f* of death, Heb 2:15
love casts out *f*, 1Jn 4:18

FEAR *(v) be afraid, revere*
the midwives *f-ed* God, Ex 1:21
Moses said...Do not *f*, Ex 14:13
may learn to *f* Me, Dt 4:10
not *f* other gods, 2Ki 17:37
I *f* no evil, Ps 23:4
Whom shall I *f*, Ps 27:1
not *f* evil tidings, Ps 112:7
who *f-s* the LORD, Pr 31:30
Rather, *f* God, Ecc 5:7
Take courage, *f* not, Is 35:4
Do not *f*, for I am, Is 41:10
will *f* and tremble, Jer 33:9
do not *f* them, Mt 10:26
f-ed the crowd, Mt 14:5
who did not *f* God, Lk 18:2
slavery leading to *f*, Ro 8:15

I *f* for you, Gal 4:11
let us *f* if, Heb 4:1

FEAR OF THE LORD
let the *f* be upon you, 2Ch 19:7
the *f*, faithfully and, 2Ch 19:9
the *f*, that is wisdom, Job 28:28
f is clean, enduring forever, Ps 19:9
discern the *f* and discover, Pr 2:5
f is to hate evil, Pr 8:13
f is the beginning of wisdom, Pr 9:10
f is a fountain of life, Pr 14:27
Better is a little with the *f*, Pr 15:16
live in the *f* always, Pr 23:17
He will delight in the *f*, Is 11:3
going on in the *f*, Ac 9:31
knowing the *f*, we, 2Co 5:11

FEAR THE LORD
f-ed, and they believed, Ex 14:31
f our God for our good, Dt 6:24
f your God, to walk, Dt 10:12
f and serve Him in, Jos 24:14
who honors those who *f*, Ps 15:4
You who *f*, praise Him, Ps 22:23
Who is the man who *f-s*, Ps 25:12
O *f*, you His saints, Ps 34:9
blessed is the man who *f-s*, Ps 112:1
F and turn away from evil, Pr 3:7
f and the king, Pr 24:21
Who is among you that *f-s*, Is 50:10

FEARFUL *terrifying*
it is a *f* thing, Ex 34:10
were *f* and amazed, Lk 8:25
will be *f of sinning*, 1Ti 5:20

FEAST *celebration*
a *f* to the Lord, Ex 12:14
godless jesters at a *f*, Ps 35:16
hate…appointed *f-s*, Is 1:14
and cheerful *f-s*, Zec 8:19
refuse of your *f-s*, Mal 2:3
a wedding *f*, Mt 22:2
seeking Him at the *f*, Jn 7:11
celebrate the *f*, 1Co 5:8
f with you without, Jude 12

FEAST OF BOOTHS
F for seven days to the, Lv 23:34
at the *F*, and they shall, Dt 16:16
to celebrate the *F*, Zec 14:16
feast of the Jews, the *F*, Jn 7:2

FEAST OF DEDICATION
F took place at Jerusalem, Jn 10:22

FEAST OF HARVEST
observe the *F* of the first, Ex 23:16

FEAST OF INGATHERING
F at the end of the year, Ex 23:16

FEAST OF UNLEAVENED BREAD
shall also observe the *F*, Ex 12:17
the *F* and at the Feast, Dt 16:16
F seven days with joy, Ezr 6:22
F, which is called the, Lk 22:1

FEAST OF WEEKS
celebrate the *F*, Ex 34:22
the *F* and at the Feast, Dt 16:16

FEASTS
Alternate names in italics
1 Feast of Booths, Lv 23:24; Dt 16:16; 2Ch 8:13
Feast of Ingathering
2 Feast of Dedication, Jn 10:22
3 Feast of Harvest, Ex 23:16
Feast of Weeks, Feast of Pentecost
4 Feast of Ingathering, Ex 23:16
Feast of Booths
5 Feast of Passover, Ex 34:25; Lk 2:41
6 Feast of Unleavened Bread, Ex 23:15; Lk 22:1
7 Feast of Weeks, Ex 34:22; Dt 16:10, 16
Feast of Harvest, Feast of Pentecost
8 Feast of Pentecost, Ac 2:1; 20:16; 1Co 16:8
Feast of Harvest, Feast of Weeks

FEEBLE *weak*
when the flock was *f*, Ge 30:42
What are these *f* Jews, Ne 4:2
strengthen the *f*, Is 35:3
knees that are *f*, Heb 12:12

FEED *eat, supply*
fed you with manna, Dt 8:3
f him sparingly, 1Ki 22:27
F me with the food, Pr 30:8
He *f-s* on ashes, Is 44:20
f you on knowledge, Jer 3:15
He *fed* me this scroll, Eze 3:2
I will *f* My flock, Eze 34:15
dogs *f* on the, Mt 15:27
hungry, and *f* You, Mt 25:37
fed…the *crumbs*, Lk 16:21
enemy is hungry, *f*, Ro 12:20

FEEL *sense, touch*
I may *f* you, my son, Ge 27:21
Isaac…*felt* him and, Ge 27:22
Let me *f* the pillars, Jdg 16:26
He *felt* compassion, Mt 9:36
she *felt*…was healed, Mk 5:29
Jesus *felt* a love for, Mk 10:21
f-ing a sense of awe, Ac 2:43
f sensual desires, 1Ti 5:11

FELIX
Governor of Judea; letter addressed to, Ac 23:24–30
Paul's defense before, Ac 24:1–27

FELL *collapse, come upon*
wall *f* down flat, Jos 6:20
fire of the LORD *f*, 1Ki 18:38
the lot *f* on Jonah, Jon 1:7
seeds f beside the, Mt 13:4
He *f* asleep, Lk 8:23
he *f* to the ground, Ac 9:4
Holy Spirit *f* upon, Ac 10:44
star *f* from heaven, Rev 8:10

FELLOW *companion*
oil of joy above Your *f-s*, Ps 45:7
your *f* exiles, Eze 11:15
beat his *f* slaves, Mt 24:49
f heirs with Christ, Ro 8:17
f citizens with the, Eph 2:19
Gentiles are *f* heirs, Eph 3:6
brother and *f* worker, Php 2:25
f worker in the, 1Th 3:2
I am a *f* servant of, Rev 22:9

FELLOWSHIP *companionship*
had sweet *f* together, Ps 55:14
f…Holy Spirit, 2Co 13:14
right hand of *f*, Gal 2:9
f of His sufferings, Php 3:10
f is with the Father, 1Jn 1:3
f with one another, 1Jn 1:7

FEMALE *girl, woman*
and *f* He created, Ge 1:27
a *f* slave, Ex 21:7
f from the flock, Lv 5:6
likeness of male or *f*, Dt 4:16
neither male nor *f*, Gal 3:28

FERTILE *productive*
a *f* land, Ne 9:25
the *f* valley, Is 28:4
in *f* soil, Eze 17:5

FERVENT *ardent*
being *f* in spirit, Ac 18:25
f in spirit, serving, Ro 12:11
keep *f* in your love, 1Pe 4:8

FESTIVAL *celebration*
celebrate a great *f*, Ne 8:12
I reject your *f-s*, Am 5:21
turn your *f-s* into, Am 8:10
during the *f*, otherwise, Mt 26:5

FESTUS
Governor of Judea, Ac 24:27
Paul's defense made to, Ac 25:1–22

FETTERS *chains*
your feet put in *f*, 2Sa 3:34
they are bound in *f*, Job 36:8
tear their *f* apart, Ps 2:3
with *f* of iron, Ps 149:8

FEVER *inflammation*
bones burn with *f*, Job 30:30
in bed with a *f*, Mt 8:14
from a high *f*, Lk 4:38
He rebuked the *f*, Lk 4:39
the *f* left him, Jn 4:52

FIELD *productive land*
hail struck…the *f*, Ex 9:25
let me go to the *f*, Ru 2:2
glean in another *f*, Ru 2:8
f of the sluggard, Pr 24:30
Zion…plowed *as* a *f*, Jer 26:18
the lilies of the *f*, Mt 6:28
the *f* is the world, Mt 13:38
shepherds…in the *f-s*, Lk 2:8
Two men…in the *f*, Lk 17:36
f-s…white for, Jn 4:35
F of Blood, Ac 1:19

FIELD OF BLOOD
A field bought as a cemetery for Judas's burial, Mt 27:1–10

FIERCE *violent*
anger, for it is *f*, Ge 49:7
Wrath is *f*, Pr 27:4
see a *f* people, Is 33:19
a *f* gale of wind, Mk 4:37
scorched with *f* heat, Rev 16:9
f wrath of God, Rev 19:15

FIERCENESS *intensity*
f of His anger, Jos 7:26
the *f* of battle, Is 42:25

FLAME *fire*
ascended in the *f*, Jdg 13:20
f...the wicked, Ps 106:18
f of the LORD, SS 8:6
his Holy One a *f*, Is 10:17
crackling of a *f*, Joel 2:5
f of a burning thorn, Ac 7:30
eyes *are* a *f* of fire, Rev 19:12

FLAMING *burning*
the *f* sword, Ge 3:24
f fire by night, Is 4:5
eyes were like *f*, Da 10:6
angels in *f* fire, 2Th 1:7

FLASH *reflect, sparkle*
why do your eyes *f*, Job 15:12
lightning was *f-ing*, Eze 1:13
Polished to *f* like, Eze 21:10
He who *f-es* forth, Am 5:9
light suddenly *f-ed*, Ac 22:6

FLASK *utensil*
take this *f* of oil, 2Ki 9:1
took oil in *f-s*, Mt 25:4

FLATTER *falsely praise*
Nor *f any* man, Job 32:21
f with their tongue, Ps 5:9
adulteress who *f-s*, Pr 2:16
who *f-s* his neighbor, Pr 29:5

FLATTERING *with false praise*
With *f* lips and with a double, Ps 12:2
LORD cut off all *f* lips, Ps 12:3
With her *f* lips she seduces, Pr 7:21
their smooth and *f* speech, Ro 16:18
never came with *f* speech, 1Th 2:5

FLAX *plant*
the *f* was in bud, Ex 9:31
looks for wool and *f*, Pr 31:13
made from combed *f*, Is 19:9

FLEE *escape, run away*
arise, *f* to Haran, Ge 27:43
F as a bird, Ps 11:1
f from Your presence, Ps 139:7
rulers have *fled*, Is 22:3
f to Egypt, Mt 2:13
left Him and *fled*, Mt 26:56
fled from the tomb, Mk 16:8
f from idolatry, 1Co 10:14
f from youthful lusts, 2Ti 2:22
and heaven *fled*, Rev 20:11

FLEECE *wool*
put a *f* of wool, Jdg 6:37
dry only on the *f*, Jdg 6:39
warmed with the *f*, Job 31:20

FLEET *group of ships*
Solomon...built a *f*, 1Ki 9:26
sent...with the *f*, 1Ki 9:27

FLESH *body, meat*
f of my *f*, Ge 2:23
shall become one *f*, Ge 2:24
from my *f* I shall see, Job 19:26
heart and my *f* sing, Ps 84:2
All *f* is grass, Is 40:6
the *f* is weak, Mt 26:41
spirit...not have *f*, Lk 24:39
the Word became *f*, Jn 1:14
born of the *f* is *f*, Jn 3:6
who eats My *f*, Jn 6:56
children of the *f*, Ro 9:8
thorn in the *f*, 2Co 12:7
desires of the *f*, Eph 2:3
polluted by the *f*, Jude 23
filled with their *f*, Rev 19:21

FLESH AND BLOOD
f cannot inherit the, 1Co 15:50
immediately consult with *f*, Gal 1:16
struggle is not against *f*, Eph 6:12
the children share in *f*, Heb 2:14

FLESHLY *carnal*
not in *f* wisdom, 2Co 1:12
His *f* body, Col 1:22
abstain from *f* lusts, 1Pe 2:11

FLIES *insects*
sent...swarms of *f*, Ps 78:45
swarm of *f And* gnats, Ps 105:31
Dead *f* make a, Ecc 10:1

FLIGHT *departure*
F will perish from, Am 2:14
f will not be in, Mt 24:20
foreign armies to *f*, Heb 11:34

FLINT *stone*
Zipporah took a *f*, Ex 4:25
f into a fountain, Ps 114:8
hoofs...seem like *f*, Is 5:28
emery harder than *f*, Eze 3:9
hearts *like f*, Zec 7:12

FLOCK *goats, sheep*
a keeper of *f-s*, Ge 4:2
water their father's *f*, Ex 2:16
Your people like a *f*, Ps 77:20
He will tend His *f*, Is 40:11
scattered My *f*, Jer 23:2
over their *f* by night, Lk 2:8
will become one *f*, Jn 10:16
f of God among you, 1Pe 5:2

FLOOD *overflowing of water*
I am bringing the *f*, Ge 6:17
f came upon the earth, Ge 7:17
end...with a *f*, Da 9:26
the *f-s* came, Mt 7:25
f...destroyed, Lk 17:27

FLOOR *ground, level*
threshing *f* of Atad, Ge 50:11
go down to the...*f*, Ru 3:3
the *f*...with gold, 1Ki 6:30
f-s...full of grain, Joel 2:24
His threshing *f*, Mt 3:12
fell...from the third *f*, Ac 20:9

FLOUR *ground grain*
measures of fine *f*, Ge 18:6
only a handful of *f*, 1Ki 17:12
f...not exhausted, 1Ki 17:16

FLOURISH *blossom, thrive*
may the righteous *f*, Ps 72:7
who did iniquity *f-ed*, Ps 92:7
your bones will *f*, Is 66:14
make the dry tree *f*, Eze 17:24

FLOW *pour forth*
river *f-ed* out of Eden, Ge 2:10
f-ing with milk and, Ex 3:8
eyelids *f* with water, Jer 9:18
hills will *f* with milk, Joel 3:18
f of her blood, Mk 5:29
f...living water, Jn 7:38

FLOWER *blossom*
As a *f* of the field, Ps 103:15
f-s have *already*, SS 2:12
to the fading *f*, Is 28:1
glory like the *f*, 1Pe 1:24

FLUTE *musical instrument*
tambourine, *f*, and, 1Sa 10:5
playing on *f-s*, 1Ki 1:40
the *f* or on the harp, 1Co 14:7
musicians...*f-players*, Rev 18:22

FLY *soar*
let birds *f* above, Ge 1:20
a raven, and it *flew*, Ge 8:7
As sparks *f* upward, Job 5:7
f-ies away like a dream, Job 20:8
glory will *f* away, Hos 9:11
heard an eagle *f-ing*, Rev 8:13
the birds which *f*, Rev 19:17

FOAL *colt*
ties *his f* to the vine, Ge 49:11
f of a wild donkey, Job 11:12
f of a beast of burden, Mt 21:5

FODDER *animal food*
give his donkey *f*, Ge 42:27
eat salted *f*, Is 30:24

FOE *enemy*
before your *f-s*, 1Ch 21:12
A *f* and an enemy, Est 7:6
iniquity of my *f-s*, Ps 49:5
the evil to my *f-s*, Ps 54:5
avenge...His *f-s*, Jer 46:10

FOLD *animal pen*
goats out of your *f-s*, Ps 50:9
the peaceful *f-s*, Jer 25:37
cut off from the *f*, Hab 3:17
not of this *f*, Jn 10:16

FOLLOW *imitate, pursue*
not *f* other gods, Dt 6:14
turn back from *f-ing*, Ru 1:16
f the LORD your God, 1Sa 12:14
who *f*...wickedness, Ps 119:150
bloodshed *f-s*, Hos 4:2
He said to them, *F*, Mt 4:19
left...and *f-ed*, Mt 4:20
his cross, and *f* Me, Mt 16:24
crowd was *f-ing*, Mk 5:24
and they *f* Me, Jn 10:27
Peter...*f-ing* Jesus, Jn 18:15
f-ing after...lusts, Jude 16
ones who *f* the Lamb, Rev 14:4

FOLLOWERS *disciples*
His *f*...*began* asking, Mk 4:10

FOLLY *foolishness*
this act of *f*, Jdg 19:23
of fools spouts *f*, Pr 15:2
F is joy to him, Pr 15:21
devising of *f* is sin, Pr 24:9

FOOD *bread, meat*
shall be *f* for you, Ge 1:29
tree was good for *f*, Ge 3:6
in giving them *f*, Ru 1:6

tears have been my *f*, Ps 42:3
it is deceptive *f*, Pr 23:3
his *f* was locusts, Mt 3:4
life more than *f*, Mt 6:25
f is to do the will, Jn 4:34
My flesh is true *f*, Jn 6:55
milk...not solid *f*, 1Co 3:2

FOOL *unwise person*
The *f* has said in his, Ps 14:1
F-s despise wisdom, Pr 1:7
too exalted for a *f*, Pr 24:7
f multiplies words, Ecc 10:14
The prophet is a *f*, Hos 9:7
says, You *f*, Mt 5:22
f-s and blind men, Mt 23:17
wise, they became *f-s*, Ro 1:22
f-s for Christ's sake, 1Co 4:10

FOOLISH *silly, unwise*
O *f* and unwise, Dt 32:6
a *f* son is a grief, Pr 10:1
False and *f visions*, La 2:14
Woe to the *f*, Eze 13:3
f took their lamps, Mt 25:3
O *f* men and slow, Lk 24:25
he must become *f*, 1Co 3:18
You *f* Galatians, Gal 3:1
do not be *f*, Eph 5:17

FOOLISHNESS *folly*
The naive inherit *f*, Pr 14:18
folly of fools is *f*, Pr 14:24
mouth is speaking *f*, Is 9:17
f of God is wiser, 1Co 1:25
is *f* before God, 1Co 3:19

FOOT *part of body*
she lay at his *feet*, Ru 3:14
six toes on each *f*, 2Sa 21:20
pierced...my *feet*, Ps 22:16
the *f* of pride, Ps 36:11
lamp to my *feet*, Ps 119:105
their *feet* run to evil, Pr 1:16
signals with his *feet*, Pr 6:13
beautiful...your *feet*, SS 7:1
feet of the afflicted, Is 26:6
feet...polished bronze, Da 10:6
dust off your *feet*, Mt 10:14
Bind...hand and *f*, Mt 22:13
f causes you to, Mk 9:45
kissing His *feet*, Lk 7:38
anointed the *feet*, Jn 12:3
the disciples' *feet*, Jn 13:5
beautiful...the *feet*, Ro 10:15
Satan under...*feet*, Ro 16:20
worship at the *feet*, Rev 22:8

FOOTSTEPS *path*
make His *f* into a way, Ps 85:13
f of Your anointed, Ps 89:51
my *f* in Your word, Ps 119:133

FOOTSTOOL *foot support*
the *f* of our God, 1Ch 28:2
worship at His *f*, Ps 99:5
Your enemies a *f*, Ps 110:1
the earth is My *f*, Is 66:1
sit down by my *f*, Jas 2:3

FORBEARANCE *restraint*
By *f*...be persuaded, Pr 25:15
in the *f* of God, Ro 3:25

FORBID *prohibit*
if her father should *f*, Nu 30:5
f-ding to pay taxes, Lk 23:2
do not *f* to speak, 1Co 14:39
men who *f* marriage, 1Ti 4:3
he *f-s* those who, 3Jn 10

FORCE *(n) power, strength*
with a heavy *f*, Nu 20:20
captains of the *f-s*, 2Ki 25:23
use *f* against you, Ne 13:21
commanders of the *f-s*, Jer 43:5
with *f* and with, Eze 34:4

FORCE *(v) compel*
are *f-d* into bondage, Ne 5:5
man *f-d* to labor, Job 7:1
f-s you to go one mile, Mt 5:41
not take...by *f*, Lk 3:14
f them to blaspheme, Ac 26:11
f-d to appeal to, Ac 28:19

FORCED LABOR *work as tax*
Canaanites to *f*, Jos 17:13
was over the *f*, 2Sa 20:24
will be put to *f*, Pr 12:24

FORCED LABORERS
Solomon levied *f*, 1Ki 5:13
Solomon raised as *f*, 2Ch 8:8
men will become *f*, Is 31:8

FORD *shallow place*
the *f* of the Jabbok, Ge 32:22
the *f-s* of the Jordan, Jdg 12:5
f-s...been seized, Jer 51:32

FOREFATHER *ancestor*
iniquity of their *f-s*, Lv 26:40
Your first *f* sinned, Is 43:27
I swore to your *f-s*, Jer 11:5
Abraham, our *f*, Ro 4:1
the way my *f-s* did, 2Ti 1:3

FOREHEAD *brow*
on his bald *f*, Lv 13:42
stone...into his *f*, 1Sa 17:49
put a mark on the *f-s*, Eze 9:4
seal of God on their *f-s*, Rev 9:4
on her *f* a name, Rev 17:5

FOREIGN *alien, strange*
Put away the *f* gods, Ge 35:2
sojourner in a *f* land, Ex 2:22
sell her to a *f* people, Ex 21:8
drank *f* waters, 2Ki 19:24
married *f* women, Ezr 10:2
f armies to flight, Heb 11:34

FOREIGNER *alien, stranger*
no *f* is to eat of it, Ex 12:43
sell it to a *f*, Dt 14:21
charge...a *f*, Dt 23:20
since I am a *f*, Ru 2:10
a *f* in their sight, Job 19:15
f-s entered his gate, Ob 11

FOREKNEW *know beforehand*
whom He *f*, He also, Ro 8:29
people whom he *f*, Ro 11:2
He was *foreknown*, 1Pe 1:20

FOREKNOWLEDGE
plan and *f* of God, Ac 2:23
f of God the Father, 1Pe 1:2

FOREMOST *first*
f commandment, Mt 22:38
among whom I am *f*, 1Ti 1:15

FORERUNNER *goes before*
Jesus...as a *f* for, Heb 6:20

FORESKIN
the flesh of your *f*, Ge 17:11
cut off her son's *f*, Ex 4:25
a hundred *f-s*, 1Sa 18:25
the *f-s* of your heart, Jer 4:4

FOREST *woods*
f devoured more, 2Sa 18:8
the *f* of Lebanon, 1Ki 7:2
f will sing for joy, 1Ch 16:33
every beast of the *f*, Ps 50:10
the glory of his *f*, Is 10:18
beasts in the *f*, Come, Is 56:9
a *f* is set aflame, Jas 3:5

FORETOLD *predicted*
the Holy Spirit *f*, Ac 1:16
just as Isaiah *f*, Ro 9:29

FOREVER *always, eternal*
eat, and live *f*, Ge 3:22
not strive with man *f*, Ge 6:3
throne shall be...*f*, 1Ch 17:14
the LORD abides *f*, Ps 9:7
LORD sits as King *f*, Ps 29:10
glorify Your name *f*, Ps 86:12
riches are not *f*, Pr 27:24
One Who lives *f*, Is 57:15
Christ is to remain *f*, Jn 12:34
He...with you *f*, Jn 14:16
He is able...to save *f*, Heb 7:25
Son, made perfect *f*, Heb 7:28
they will reign *f*, Rev 22:5

FORFEIT *lose*
possessions...*f-ed*, Ezr 10:8
f-s his own life, Pr 20:2
f my head to the king, Da 1:10
and *f-s* his soul, Mt 16:26

FORGET *forsake, neglect*
God has made me *f*, Ge 41:51
that you do not *f* the LORD, Dt 6:12
f-got the God who, Dt 32:18
God *f-s*...iniquity, Job 11:6
nations who *f* God, Ps 9:17
needy...be *f-gotten*, Ps 9:18
Do not *f* the afflicted, Ps 10:12
They *f-got* His deeds, Ps 78:11
do not *f* my teaching, Pr 3:1
you will *f* the shame, Is 54:4
My people *f* My name, Jer 23:27
f-ting what *lies* behind, Php 3:13
f your work and, Heb 6:10

FORGIVE *pardon*
f the transgression, Ge 50:17
f their sin, Ex 32:32
f our sins, Ps 79:9
not *f* their iniquity, Jer 18:23
f us our debts, Mt 6:12
authority...to *f* sins, Mt 9:6
f-gave him the debt, Mt 18:27
can *f* sins but God, Mk 2:7
he who is *f-n* little, Lk 7:47
Father, *f* them, Lk 23:34
whom you *f*, 2Co 2:10
f-ing each other, Eph 4:32

f-n us all our, Col 2:13
righteous to *f* us, 1Jn 1:9

FORGIVENESS *pardon*
a God of *f*, Ne 9:17
there is *f* with You, Ps 130:4
poured out…for *f*, Mt 26:28
repentance for *f*, Lk 24:47
receives *f* of sins, Ac 10:43
f of our trespasses, Eph 1:7
the *f* of sins, Col 1:14
there is no *f*, Heb 9:22

FORK *instrument*
a three-pronged *f*, 1Sa 2:13
His winnowing *f*, Mt 3:12

FORM *(n) appearance, shape*
beautiful of *f* and, Ge 29:17
the *f* of the LORD, Nu 12:8
image in the *f*, Dt 4:23
like the *f* of a man, Is 44:13
in a different *f*, Mk 16:12
bodily *f* like a dove, Lk 3:22
f of corruptible man, Ro 1:23
existed in the *f* of God, Php 2:6

FORM *(v) fashion, shape*
f-ed man of dust, Ge 2:7
f-ed the dry land, Ps 95:5
f-ed my inward parts, Ps 139:13
One *f-ing* light, Is 45:7
who *f-s* mountains, Am 4:13
f-s the spirit of man, Zec 12:1
plot was *f-ed* against, Ac 20:3
Christ is *f-ed* in you, Gal 4:19

FORMATION *rank*
in *f* against, 1Ch 19:17
battle *f* in the, 2Ch 14:10

FORMLESS *without form*
earth was *f* and void, Ge 1:2
behold, *it was f*, Jer 4:23

FORNICATION
f-s, thefts, false, Mt 15:19
were not born of *f*, Jn 8:41
strangled and from *f*, Ac 15:29

FORNICATORS
neither *f*, nor, 1Co 6:9
f…God will judge, Heb 13:4

FORSAKE
Then he *f-sook* God, Dt 32:15
not fail you or *f* you, Jos 1:5
f-sook the law of the, 2Ch 12:1
f Him, He will *f* you, 2Ch 15:2
God has not *f-n* us, Ezr 9:9
why have You *f-n* me, Ps 22:1
not *f* your mother's, Pr 1:8
wicked *f* his way, Is 55:7
Your sons have *f-n* Me, Jer 5:7
f the idols of Egypt, Eze 20:8
have You *f-n* Me, Mt 27:46
persecuted…not *f-n*, 2Co 4:9
f-ing…assembling, Heb 10:25
nor will I ever *f* you, Heb 13:5

FORTIFICATIONS *stronghold*
the unassailable *f*, Is 25:12
your *f* are fig trees, Na 3:12

FORTIFIED *walled*
live in the *f* cities, Nu 32:17
f with high walls, Dt 3:5
strike every *f* city, 2Ki 3:19
f cities into, Is 37:26

FORTRESS *stronghold*
God is my strong *f*, 2Sa 22:33
my rock and my *f*, Ps 18:2
My refuge and my *f*, Ps 91:2
wealth is his *f*, Pr 10:15
f-es will be destroyed, Hos 10:14

FORTUNE *one's lot*
and the *f-s* of Israel, Jer 33:7
f-s of My people, Hos 6:11
restore their *f*, Zep 2:7

FORTY *number*
f days and *f* nights, Ge 7:4
flood…for *f* days, Ge 7:17
ate the manna *f* years, Ex 16:35
with the LORD *f* days, Ex 34:28
fasted *f* days and *f*, Mt 4:2
f days being tempted, Mk 1:13

FOUL *putrid, rotten*
Nile will become *f*, Ex 7:18
My wounds grow *f*, Ps 38:5
f with your feet, Eze 34:19

FOUNDATION *establishment*
f-s of heaven were, 2Sa 22:8
I laid the *f* of the, Job 38:4
the *f* of His throne, Ps 97:2
the earth upon its *f-s*, Ps 104:5
an everlasting *f*, Pr 10:25
cornerstone *for* the *f*, Is 28:16
a *f* on the rock, Lk 6:48
the firm *f* of God, 2Ti 2:19
laid the *f*, Heb 1:10
a *f* of repentance, Heb 6:1

FOUNDATION GATE
See GATES OF JERUSALEM

FOUNDED *established*
the day it was *f*, Ex 9:18
f it upon the seas, Ps 24:2
by wisdom *f* the earth, Pr 3:19
f His vaulted dome, Am 9:6
f on the rock, Mt 7:25

FOUNTAIN *spring, well*
f-s of the great deep, Ge 7:11
is the *f* of life, Ps 36:9
The *f* of wisdom, Pr 18:4
f of living waters, Jer 2:13

FOUNTAIN GATE
See GATES OF JERUSALEM

FOWL *bird*
and fattened *f*, 1Ki 4:23
things and winged *f*, Ps 148:10

FOX *small animal*
three hundred *f-es*, Jdg 15:4
f-es that are ruining, SS 2:15
like *f-es* among ruins, Eze 13:4
The *f-es* have holes, Mt 8:20
Go and tell that *f*, Lk 13:32

FRAGMENTS *pieces*
forth His ice as *f*, Ps 147:17
Gather up the…*f*, Jn 6:12
twelve baskets with *f*, Jn 6:13

FRAGRANCE *pleasant aroma*
oils have a pleasing *f*, SS 1:3
given forth *their f*, SS 2:13
f like *the cedars*, Hos 14:6
we are a *f* of Christ, 2Co 2:15

FRAGRANT *aromatic*
oil and for the *f* incense, Ex 25:6
burn *f* incense before, 2Ch 2:4
offerings and *f* incense, 2Ch 13:11
garments are *f with*, Ps 45:8
an offering and *f* incense., Da 2:46
to God as a *f* aroma, Eph 5:2
have sent, a *f* aroma, Php 4:18

FRAME *structure*
f-s of the tabernacle, Nu 3:36
with *artistic f-s*, 1Ki 6:4
He…knows our *f*, Ps 103:14
My *f* was not hidden, Ps 139:15

FRANKINCENSE *spice*
spices with pure *f*, Ex 30:34
f and the spices, 1Ch 9:29
trees of *f*, SS 4:14
gold, *f*, and myrrh, Mt 2:11

FREE *at liberty*
she is not to go *f*, Ex 21:7
be *f* from the oath, Jos 2:20
let the oppressed go *f*, Is 58:6
will make you *f*, Jn 8:32
who has died is *f-d*, Ro 6:7
the *f* gift of God, Ro 6:23
f from the law, Ro 8:2
Christ set us *f*, Gal 5:1
whether slave or *f*, Eph 6:8

FREEDOM *liberty*
proclaim…*f* to, Is 61:1
f of the glory, Ro 8:21
you were called to *f*, Gal 5:13
do not use your *f* as, 1Pe 2:16

FREEWILL *voluntary*
brought a *f* offering, Ex 35:29
your votive and *f* offerings, Lv 23:38
together with a *f* offering, Ezr 1:4
gold are a *f* offering to, Ezr 8:28
f offerings of my mouth, Ps 119:108
And proclaim *f* offerings, Am 4:5

FREEWILL OFFERINGS
See OFFERINGS

FRESH *new, recently prepared*
found a *f* jawbone, Jdg 15:15
anointed with *f* oil, Ps 92:10
f water from your, Pr 5:15
new wine into *f*, Mk 2:22
f and bitter *water*, Jas 3:11

FRIEND *companion, comrade*
man speaks to his *f*, Ex 33:11
f-s are my scoffers, Job 16:20
loved ones and my *f-s*, Ps 38:11
my familiar *f*, Ps 55:13
A *f* loves at all, Pr 17:17
Wealth adds…*f-s*, Pr 19:4
who blesses his *f*, Pr 27:14
confidence in a *f*, Mic 7:5
f of tax collectors, Mt 11:19

G

GAIUS
Companion of Paul, Ac 19:29
——— Convert at Derbe, Ac 20:4
——— Paul's host at Corinth, Ro 16:23; 1Co 1:14

GALATIA
Paul visits, Ac 16:6; 18:23
Paul writes to Christians in, Gal 1:1
Peter writes to Christians in, 1Pe 1:1

GALE *storm*
dust before a *g*, Is 17:13
a fierce *g* of wind, Mk 4:37

GALILEANS
Speech of, Mk 14:70
Faith of, Jn 4:45
Pilate's cruelty toward, Lk 13:1, 2

GALILEE
Prophecies concerning, Dt 33:18–23; Is 9:1, 2
Dialect of, distinctive, Mt 26:73
Herod's jurisdiction over, Lk 3:1
Christ's contacts with, Mt 2:22; 4:12–25; 26:32; 27:55; Jn 4:1, 3

GALILEE, SEA OF
Scene of many events in Christ's life, Mk 7:31
Called Chinnereth, Nu 34:11
Later called Gennesaret, Lk 5:1

GALL *bitter herb, bitterness*
gave me *g* for my food, Ps 69:21
drink...with *g*, Mt 27:34
the *g* of bitterness, Ac 8:23

GALLIO
Roman proconsul of Achaia, dismisses charges against Paul, Ac 18:12–17

GALLOWS *for hanging*
Have a *g*...made, Est 5:14
hanged...on the *g*, Est 7:10
his sons...on the *g*, Est 9:25

GAMALIEL
Famous Jewish teacher, Ac 22:3
Respected by people, Ac 5:34–39

GARDEN *planted area*
God walking in the *g*, Ge 3:8
from the *g* of Eden, Ge 3:23
Make my *g* breathe, SS 4:16
plant *g-s*, and eat, Jer 29:5
tabernacle like a *g*, La 2:6
in the *g* with Him, Jn 18:26
the *g* a new tomb, Jn 19:41

GARLAND *ornament*
a *g* instead of ashes, Is 61:3
brought...*g-s* to the, Ac 14:13

GARMENT *clothing, dress*
God made *g-s* of skin, Ge 3:21
caught him by his *g*, Ge 39:12
in *g-s* of fine linen, Ge 41:42
holy *g-s* for Aaron, Ex 28:2
divide my *g-s* among, Ps 22:18
on *g-s* of vengeance, Is 59:17
g-s of glowing colors, Is 63:1
g of camel's hair, Mt 3:4
I just touch His *g-s*, Mk 5:28
dividing up His *g-s*, Lk 23:34
put his outer *g* on, Jn 21:7
become old like a *g*, Heb 1:11
clothed in white *g-s*, Rev 3:5

GARRISON *defense*
g of the Philistines, 1Sa 13:4
the *g*...trembled, 1Sa 14:15
set *g-s* in the land, 2Ch 17:2

GATE *entry way*
is the *g* of heaven, Ge 28:17
oppressed in the *g*, Job 5:4
g-s with thanksgiving, Ps 100:4
enter the *g-s* of Sheol, Is 38:10
justice in the *g*, Am 5:15
Enter...narrow *g*, Mt 7:13
g-s of Hades will, Mt 16:18
did not open the *g*, Ac 12:14

GATEKEEPERS *guards*
g for the camp, 1Ch 9:18
divisions of the *g*, 1Ch 26:12
The sons of the *g*, Ezr 2:42
g, and the singers, Ne 10:39

GATES OF JERUSALEM
Alternate names in italics
1 Beautiful Gate, Ac 3:10
East Gate
2 Benjamin Gate, Jer 20:2; Zec 14:10
Gate of the Guard, Inspection Gate, Sheep Gate
3 Corner Gate, 2Ki 14:13; 2Ch 26:9
4 East Gate, Ne 3:29; Eze 10:19; 44:1
Beautiful Gate
5 Ephraim Gate, 2Ki 14:13; Ne 8:16
Middle Gate, Old Gate
6 First Gate, Zec 14:10
7 Fish Gate, 2Ch 33:14; Ne 3:3
8 Foundation Gate, 2Ch 23:5
Gate of Sur
9 Fountain Gate, Ne 2:14; 12:37
gate between two walls, 2Ki 25:4; Jer 39:4
10 Guard, Gate of the, Ne 12:39
Benjamin Gate, Inspection Gate, Sheep Gate
11 Horse Gate, 2Ch 23:15; Ne 3:28
12 Inspection Gate, Ne 3:31
Benjamin Gate, Gate of the Guard, Sheep Gate
13 Middle Gate, Jer 39:3
Ephraim Gate, Old Gate
14 Old Gate, Ne 3:6; 12:39
Ephraim Gate, Middle Gate
15 Refuse Gate, Ne 2:13; 12:31
16 Sheep Gate, Ne 3:1
Benjamin Gate, Gate of the Guard, Inspection Gate
17 Sur, Gate of, 2Ki 11:6
Foundation Gate
18 Valley Gate, 2Ch 26:9; Ne 3:13
19 Water Gate, Ne 3:26; 8:1, 3, 16

GATEWAY *entrance*
the *g* of the court, Ex 40:8
the *g* of the peoples, Eze 26:2

GATH
Philistine city, 1Sa 6:17
Ark carried to, 1Sa 5:8
David takes refuge in, 1Sa 21:10–15
David's second flight to, 1Sa 27:3–12
Captured by David, 1Ch 18:1
Destruction of, prophetic, Am 6:1–3
Name becomes proverbial, Mic 1:10

GATHER *assemble, collect*
g-ed to his people, Ge 25:8
g stubble for straw, Ex 5:12
He *g-s* the waters, Ps 33:7
G My godly ones, Ps 50:5
g all nations and, Is 66:18
hen *g-s* her chicks, Mt 23:37
elders...were *g-ed*, Mt 26:3
g...His elect, Mk 13:27
G up the leftover, Jn 6:12

GATH-HEPHER
Birthplace of Jonah, 2Ki 14:25

GAZA
Philistine city, Jos 13:3
Samson removes the gates of, Jdg 16:1–3
Samson taken there as prisoner; his revenge, Jdg 16:21–31
Sin of, condemned, Am 1:6, 7
Philip journeys to, Ac 8:26

GAZE *(n) view, glance*
Turn Your *g* away from, Ps 39:13
let your *g* be fixed, Pr 4:25
turning His *g* toward His, Lk 6:20

GAZE *(v) look, stare*
man...*g-ing* at her, Ge 24:21
and *g* after Moses, Ex 33:8
eye *g-s* on their, Job 17:2
LORD *g-d* upon the, Ps 102:19
g-ing...into the sky, Ac 1:10

GAZELLE *animal*
swift as the *g-s*, 1Ch 12:8
a *g* Or a young stag, SS 2:17
like a hunted *g*, Is 13:14

GEBA
Levite city in Benjamin, Jos 18:24; 21:17
Rebuilt by Asa, 1Ki 15:22

GEDALIAH
Made governor of Judah, 2Ki 25:22–26
Befriends Jeremiah, Jer 40:5, 6
Murdered by Ishmael, Jer 41:2, 18

GEHAZI
Elisha's servant; seeks reward from Naaman, 2Ki 5:20–24
Afflicted with leprosy, 2Ki 5:25–27
Relates Elisha's deeds to Jehoram, 2Ki 8:4–6

GENEALOGY *family record*
found the book of...*g*, Ne 7:5
g of Jesus the Messiah, Mt 1:1
and endless *g-ies*, 1Ti 1:4
whose *g* is not traced, Heb 7:6

GENERATION *age, period*
this evil *g*, Dt 1:35
the righteous *g*, Ps 14:5
faithfulness to all *g-s*, Ps 100:5
salvation to all *g-s*, Is 51:8
this *g* seek for a sign, Mk 8:12
g-s...not made known, Eph 3:5
and perverse *g*, Php 2:15

GENEROUS *bountiful*
g will be blessed, Pr 22:9
because I am *g*, Mt 20:15
g...ready to share, 1Ti 6:18

GENNESARET
A town on the northwestern shore of Lake Galilee, Mt 14:34; Mk 6:53

GENTILES *foreigners, non-Jews*
Galilee of the *G*, Mt 4:15
hand Him over to the *G*, Mt 20:19
revelation to the *G*, Lk 2:32
Why did the *G* rage, Ac 4:25
salvation...to the *G*, Ro 11:11
preach...among the *G*, Gal 1:16

GENTLE *compassionate, mild*
g answer turns away, Pr 15:1
I was like a *g* lamb, Jer 11:19
Blessed are the *g*, Mt 5:5
G, and mounted on, Mt 21:5
a *g* and quiet spirit, 1Pe 3:4

GENTLENESS *kindness*
and a spirit of *g*, 1Co 4:21
and *g* of Christ, 2Co 10:1
g, self-control, Gal 5:23
humility and *g*, with, Eph 4:2

GERAR
Town of Philistia, Ge 10:19
Visited by Abraham, Ge 20:1–18
Visited by Isaac, Ge 26:1–17
Abimelech, king of, Ge 26:1, 26

GERIZIM
See MOUNT GERIZIM

GERSHOM
Son of Moses, Ex 2:21, 22
Founder of Levite family, 1Ch 23:14–16

GESHUR
Inhabitants of, not expelled by Israel, Jos 13:13
Talmai, king of, grandfather of Absalom, 2Sa 3:3
Absalom flees to, 2Sa 13:37, 38

GETHSEMANE
Garden near Jerusalem, Mt 26:30, 36
Often visited by Christ, Lk 22:39
Scene of Christ's agony and betrayal, Mt 26:36–56; Jn 18:1–12

GEZER
Canaanite city, Jos 10:33
Inhabitants not expelled, Jos 16:10
Given as dowry of Pharaoh's daughter, 1Ki 9:15–17

GHOST *spirit*
resort to idols and *g-s*, Is 19:3
and said, It is a *g*, Mt 14:26
it was a *g*, Mk 6:49

GIANT
were born to the *g*, 2Sa 21:22
from the *g-s*, 1Ch 20:6

GIBEAH
Town of Benjamin; known for wickedness, Jdg 19:12–30
Destruction of, Jdg 20:1–48
Saul's birthplace, 1Sa 10:26
Saul's political capital, 1Sa 15:34
Wickedness of, long remembered, Hos 9:9

GIBEON
Sun stands still at, Jos 10:12
Location of tabernacle, 1Ch 16:39
Joab struck Amasa at, 2Sa 20:8–10
Joab killed at, 1Ki 2:28–34
Site of Solomon's sacrifice and dream, 1Ki 3:5–15

GIBEONITES
Trick Joshua into making treaty; subjected to forced labor, Jos 9:3–27
Rescued by Joshua, Jos 10
Massacred by Saul; avenged by David, 2Sa 21:1–9

GIDEON
Called by an angel, Jdg 6:11–24
Destroys Baal's altar, Jdg 6:25–32
Fleece confirms call from God, Jdg 6:36–40
Miraculous victory over the Midianites, Jdg 7
Takes revenge on Succoth and Penuel, Jdg 8:4–21
Refuses kingship; makes an ephod, Jdg 8:22–28
Fathers seventy-one sons; dies, Jdg 8:29–35

GIFT *present*
the sacred *g-s*, Nu 18:32
children are a *g*, Ps 127:3
to Him *g-s*, Mt 2:11
g of the Holy Spirit, Ac 2:38
impart...spiritual *g*, Ro 1:11
g of God is eternal, Ro 6:23
desire...greater *g-s*, 1Co 12:31
perfect *g* is from, Jas 1:17

GIHON
River of Eden, Ge 2:13
——— Spring outside Jerusalem, 1Ki 1:33–45
Source of water supply, 2Ch 32:30

GILBOA
Range of limestone hills in Issachar, 1Sa 28:4
Scene of Saul's death, 1Sa 31:1–9
Under David's curse, 2Sa 1:17, 21

GILEAD
Plain east of the Jordan; taken from the Amorites and assigned to Gad, Reuben, and Manasseh, Nu 21:21–31; 32:33–40; Dt 3:12, 13; Jos 13:24–31
Ishbosheth rules over, 2Sa 2:8, 9
David takes refuge in, 2Sa 17:21–26
Conquered by Hazael, 2Ki 10:32, 33
Balm of, figurative of national healing, Jer 8:22

GILGAL
Site of memorial stones, circumcision, first Passover in the Promised Land, Jos 4:19–5:12
Site of Gibeonite covenant, Jos 9:3–15
One location on Samuel's circuit, 1Sa 7:15, 16
Saul made king and later rejected, 1Sa 11:15; 13:4–15
Denounced for idolatry, Hos 9:15

GIRD *bind*
g him with the...band, Ex 29:5
g up your loins like, Job 38:3
g-ed me with gladness, Ps 30:11
g-s herself with, Pr 31:17
g-ed...with truth, Eph 6:14
g-ed across His chest, Rev 1:13

GIRDLE *belt, waistband*
man with a leather *g*, 2Ki 1:8
binds...with a *g*, Job 12:18

GIRGASHITE
Descendants of Canaan, Ge 10:15, 16
Land of, given to Abraham's descendants, Ge 15:18, 21
Delivered to Israel, Jos 24:11

GIRL *maiden*
the *g* and consult, Ge 24:57
sold a *g* for wine, Joel 3:3
boys and *g-s* playing, Zec 8:5
the *g* has not died, Mt 9:24

GITTITE
600 follow David, 2Sa 15:18–23

GIVE *bestow, yield*
g light on the earth, Ge 1:17
g-n you every plant, Ge 1:29
gave me from...tree, Ge 3:12
in the land...God *g-s*, Ex 20:12
I will *g* you rest, Ex 33:14
g him to the LORD, 1Sa 1:11
G ear to my prayer, Ps 17:1
gave me vinegar, Ps 69:21
G me neither poverty, Pr 30:8
a son will be *g-n*, Is 9:6
gave birth to a Son, Mt 1:25
G us this day, Mt 6:11
g-ing thanks, He, Mt 15:36
g you the keys, Mt 16:19
authority...been *g-n*, Mt 28:18
what will a man *g*, Mk 8:37
body which is *g-n*, Lk 22:19
gave His only...Son, Jn 3:16
not as the world *g-s*, Jn 14:27
gave up His spirit, Jn 19:30
what I do have I *g*, Ac 3:6
g-n among men, Ac 4:12
more blessed to *g*, Ac 20:35
was *g-n* me a thorn, 2Co 12:7
always *g-ing* thanks, Eph 5:20
who *gave* Himself, 1Ti 2:6
Every good thing *g-n*, Jas 1:17
g-s a greater grace, Jas 4:6
g-n us eternal life, 1Jn 5:11
to be *g-n* a mark, Rev 13:16

GLAD *pleased*
g in his heart, Ex 4:14
joy and a *g* heart, Dt 28:47
righteous see...are *g*, Job 22:19
Be *g* in the LORD, Ps 32:11
g when they said, Ps 122:1
son makes a father *g*, Pr 10:1
Rejoice, and be *g*, Mt 5:12
Be *g* in that day, Lk 6:23

GLADNESS *joy*
celebrate...with *g*, Ne 12:27

g...for the Jews, Est 8:17
Serve the LORD with *g*, Ps 100:2
g and sincerity of, Ac 2:46
With the oil of *g*, Heb 1:9

GLASS *crystal*
or *g* cannot equal, Job 28:17
sea of *g*, like crystal, Rev 4:6

GLEAM *brilliance*
awesome *g* of crystal, Eze 1:22
g of a Tarshish stone, Eze 10:9
g of polished bronze, Da 10:6

GLEAN *gather, pick*
Nor shall you *g*, Lv 19:10
Do not go to *g*, Ru 2:8
she *g-ed* in the field, Ru 2:17
g the vineyard, Job 24:6
g-ing ears of grain, Is 17:5

GLOOM *darkness*
cloud and thick *g*, Dt 4:11
The land of utter *g*, Job 10:22
darkness and *g* and, Heb 12:18
and your joy to *g*, Jas 4:9

GLORIFY *honor, worship*
g Your name forever, Ps 86:12
Let the LORD be *g-ied*, Is 66:5
g your Father, Mt 5:16
shepherds...*g-ing*, Lk 2:20
Jesus...not yet *g-ied*, Jn 7:39
Father, *g* Your name, Jn 12:28
God is *g-ied* in Him, Jn 13:31
were all *g-ing* God, Ac 4:21
Gentiles to *g* God, Ro 15:9
g God in your body, 1Co 6:20
did not *g* Himself, Heb 5:5

GLORIOUS *exalted, great*
g name be blessed, Ne 9:5
G things are spoken, Ps 87:3
resting place will be *g*, Is 11:10
the law great and *g*, Is 42:21
g gospel of...God, 1Ti 1:11

GLORY *(n) honor, splendor*
show me Your *g*, Ex 33:18
while My *g* is passing, Ex 33:22
Tell of His *g*, 1Ch 16:24
King of *g* may come, Ps 24:7
exchanged their *g*, Ps 106:20
earth is full of His *g*, Is 6:3
their *g* into shame, Hos 4:7
Solomon in all his *g*, Mt 6:29
g of the Lord shone, Lk 2:9
G...in the highest, Lk 2:14
He comes in His *g*, Lk 9:26
do not seek My *g*, Jn 8:50
short of the *g* of God, Ro 3:23
all to the *g* of God, 1Co 10:31
eternal weight of *g*, 2Co 4:17
body of His *g*, Php 3:21
crowned Him with *g*, Heb 2:7
unfading crown of *g*, 1Pe 5:4

GLORY *(v) exalt*
And *g* in Your praise, 1Ch 16:35
G in His holy name, Ps 105:3
in Him they will *g*, Jer 4:2
I...have reason to *g*, Php 2:16

GLORY OF GOD
heavens are telling of the *g*, Ps 19:1
g to conceal a matter, Pr 25:2
end in death, but for the *g*, Jn 11:4
you will see the *g*, Jn 11:40
saw the *g*, and Jesus, Ac 7:55
and fall short of the *g*, Ro 3:23
we exult in hope of the *g*, Ro 5:2
accepted us to the *g*, Ro 15:7
do all to the *g*, 1Co 10:31
he is the image and *g*, 1Co 11:7
Amen to the *g* through us, 2Co 1:20
the *g* in the face, 2Co 4:6
thanks to abound to the *g*, 2Co 4:15
Christ is Lord, to the *g*, Php 2:11
with smoke from the *g*, Rev 15:8
having the *g*, Rev 21:11
the *g* has illumined it, Rev 21:23

GLORY OF THE LORD
you will see the *g*, Ex 16:7
g appeared in the cloud., Ex 16:10
g rested on Mount Sinai, Ex 24:16
g filled the tabernacle., Ex 40:34
g appeared in the tent, Nu 14:10
g filled the house of, 1Ki 8:11
Let the *g* endure, Ps 104:31
g will be revealed, Is 40:5
the *g* has risen upon you, Is 60:1
the brightness of the *g*., Eze 10:4
g came into the house, Eze 43:4
g shone around them, Lk 2:9
as in a mirror the *g*, 2Co 3:18

GLUTTON *excessive eater*
g...come to poverty, Pr 23:21
a companion of *g-s*, Pr 28:7
evil beasts, lazy *g-s*, Titus 1:12

GNASH *grind*
They *g-ed* at me, Ps 35:16
He will *g* his teeth, Ps 112:10
They hiss and *g*, La 2:16
g-ing their teeth, Ac 7:54

GNAT *insect*
dust...became *g-s*, Ex 8:17
swarm of flies...*g-s*, Ps 105:31
strain out a *g* and, Mt 23:24

GO *move, proceed*
Let My people *g*, Ex 7:16
God who *g-es* before, Dt 1:30
where you *g*, I will *g*, Ru 1:16
the way he should *g*, Pr 22:6
g one mile, *g*...two, Mt 5:41
G into all...world, Mk 16:15
I *g* to prepare a, Jn 14:2
night is almost *gone*, Ro 13:12

GOADS *inducements*
wise men are like *g*, Ecc 12:11
kick against the *g*, Ac 26:14

GOAL *end, object*
press on toward the *g*, Php 3:14
g...is love, 1Ti 1:5

GOAT *animal*
a young *g* from the flock, Ge 38:17
curtains of *g-s' hair*, Ex 26:7
not boil a young *g*...milk, Ex 34:26
g for a sin offering, Nu 15:27
prepare a young *g* for you, Jdg 13:15
quilt of *g-s' hair*, 1Sa 19:13
g had a...horn, Da 8:5
shaggy *g represents*, Da 8:21
sheep from the *g-s*, Mt 25:32
never given me a young *g*, Lk 15:29
blood of *g-s*...bulls, Heb 9:13

GOD *Deity, Eternal One*
In the beginning *G*, Ge 1:1
G formed man of dust, Ge 2:7
G sent him out, Ge 3:23
G gave to Abraham, Ge 28:4
tablets were *G's* work, Ex 32:16
G is my...fortress, 2Sa 22:33
G of my salvation, Ps 18:46
In *G*...put my trust, Ps 56:4
Search me, O *G*, Ps 139:23
word of *G* is tested, Pr 30:5
servant of the living *G*, Da 6:20
I am *G* and not man, Hos 11:9
Will a man rob *G*, Mal 3:8
G descending...dove, Mt 3:16
they shall see *G*, Mt 5:8
What...*G* has joined, Mt 19:6
kingdom of *G* is at, Mk 1:15
My *G*, why have, Mk 15:34
You the Son of *G*, Lk 22:70
the Word was *G*, Jn 1:1
No one has seen *G*, Jn 1:18
the Lamb of *G*, Jn 1:29
G so loved the world, Jn 3:16
G is spirit, Jn 4:24
voice of...Son of *G*, Jn 5:25
obey *G* rather than, Ac 5:29
judgment of *G*, Ro 2:2
bear fruit for *G*, Ro 7:4
we are children of *G*, Ro 8:16
are a temple of *G*, 1Co 3:16
full armor of *G*, Eph 6:11
one *G*...one mediator, 1Ti 2:5
is inspired by *G*, 2Ti 3:16
word of *G* is...sharper, Heb 4:12
impossible...*G* to lie, Heb 6:18
G is love, 1Jn 4:8
great supper of *G*, Rev 19:17

GOD *false deity, idols*
no other *g-s* before Me, Ex 20:3
New *g-s* were chosen, Jdg 5:8
cast their *g-s* into, Is 37:19
bowed...to other *g-s*, Jer 22:9
no other *g* who is, Da 3:29
The voice of a *g*, Ac 12:22
g-s...become like, Ac 14:11
the *g* of this world, 2Co 4:4

GOD, SON OF
See SON OF GOD

GOD THE FATHER
Jesus Christ and *G*, Gal 1:1
from *G* and the Lord, Eph 6:23
to the glory of *G*, Php 2:11
G and the Lord Jesus, 1Th 1:1
peace from *G* and the, 2Th 1:2
mercy and peace from *G*, 1Ti 1:2
mercy and peace from *G*, 2Ti 1:2
Grace and peace from *G*, Titus 1:4
the foreknowledge of *G*, 1Pe 1:2
honor and glory from *G*, 2Pe 1:17
will be with us, from *G*, 2Jn 3
beloved in *G*, Jude 1

GOD WHO SEES
to her, "You are a *G*", Ge 16:13

GODDESS *female deity*
Ashtoreth the *g* of, 1Ki 11:5

great *g* Artemis, Ac 19:27
blasphemers of…*g*, Ac 19:37

GODLESS *pagan, without God*
hope of the *g* will, Job 8:13
joy of…*g* momentary, Job 20:5
g man destroys his, Pr 11:9
hands of *g* men, Ac 2:23
become of the *g*, 1Pe 4:18

GODLINESS *holiness*
in all *g* and dignity, 1Ti 2:2
the mystery of *g*, 1Ti 3:16
g is profitable, 1Ti 4:8
to a form of *g*, 2Ti 3:5
g, brotherly kindness, 2Pe 1:7

GODLY *holy*
keeps…His *g* ones, 1Sa 2:9
g man ceases to be, Ps 12:1
not forsake His *g* ones, Ps 37:28
and *g* sincerity, 2Co 1:12
to live *g* in Christ, 2Ti 3:12
rescue the *g* from, 2Pe 2:9

GOG
Prince of Rosh, Meshech, and Tubal, Eze 38:2, 3; Eze 39:1
——— Leader of the final battle, Rev 20:8–15

GOLAN
City of refuge, Jos 20:8; 21:27

GOLD *precious metal*
g of that land is good, Ge 2:12
mercy seat of pure *g*, Ex 25:17
Almighty…be your *g*, Job 22:25
more desirable than *g*, Ps 19:10
refine them like *g*, Mal 3:3
to Him gifts of *g*, Mt 2:11
Do not acquire *g*, Mt 10:9
Divine Nature…*g*, Ac 17:29
coveted no…*g*, Ac 20:33
city was pure *g*, Rev 21:18

GOLDSMITH *gold craftsman*
g-s and…merchants, Ne 3:32
g, and he makes it, Is 46:6

GOLGOTHA
Where Jesus died, Mt 27:33–35
Christ crucified there, Lk 23:33
Hebrew name for Calvary, Jn 19:17

GOLIATH
Giant of Gath, 1Sa 17:4
Killed by David, 1Sa 17:50
——— Brother of above; killed by Elhanan, 2Sa 21:19

GOMER
Son of Japheth, Ge 10:2, 3; 1Ch 1:5, 6
Northern nation, Eze 38:6
——— Wife of Hosea, Hos 1:2, 3

GOMORRAH
With Sodom, defeated by Chedorlaomer; Lot captured, Ge 14:8–12
Destroyed by God, Ge 19:23–29
Later references to, Is 1:10; Am 4:11; Mt 10:15

GOOD *complete, right*
God saw that it was *g*, Ge 1:18
knowledge of *g* and, Ge 2:9
Proclaim *g* tidings, 1Ch 16:23
Do not withhold *g*, Pr 3:27
joyful heart is *g*, Pr 17:22
planted in *g* soil, Eze 17:8
feed in…*g* pasture, Eze 34:18
Seek *g* and not evil, Am 5:14
how to give *g* gifts, Mt 7:11
Well done, *g* and, Mt 25:23
sown on the *g* soil, Mk 4:20
Salt is *g*, Mk 9:50
No one is *g* except, Lk 18:19
I am the *g* shepherd, Jn 10:11
men of *g* reputation, Ac 6:3
perseverance in…*g*, Ro 2:7
nothing *g*…in me, Ro 7:18
work together for *g*, Ro 8:28
who bring *g* news, Ro 10:15
overcome evil…*g*, Ro 12:21
is of *g* repute, Php 4:8
g hope by grace, 2Th 2:16
Fight the *g* fight, 1Ti 6:12
tasted the *g* word, Heb 6:5

GOOD WORKS
that they may see your *g*, Mt 5:16
I showed you many *g*, Jn 10:32
in Christ Jesus for *g*, Eph 2:10
g, as is proper for women, 1Ti 2:10
having a reputation for *g*, 1Ti 5:10
rich in *g*, to be generous, 1Ti 6:18

GOODNESS *excellence, value*
My *g* pass before you, Ex 33:19
Surely *g*…will follow, Ps 23:6
How great is Your *g*, Ps 31:19
kindness, *g*, Gal 5:22
every desire for *g*, 2Th 1:11

GOODS *possessions, supplies*
the *g* for yourself, Ge 14:21
have acquired…*g*, Eze 38:12

GORE *stab*
if an ox *g-s* a man, Ex 21:28
g the Arameans, 1Ki 22:11

GOSHEN
District of Egypt where Israel lived; the best of the land, Ge 45:10; 46:28, 29; 47:1–11

GOSPEL *good news*
proclaiming the *g* of, Mt 4:23
preach the *g* to all, Mk 16:15
not ashamed of the *g*, Ro 1:16
if our *g* is veiled, 2Co 4:3
or a different *g*, 2Co 11:4
distort the *g* of Christ, Gal 1:7
g of your salvation, Eph 1:13
g of peace, Eph 6:15
defense of the *g*, Php 1:16
the hope of the *g*, Col 1:23
eternal *g* to preach, Rev 14:6

GOSSIP *babbler*
associate with a *g*, Pr 20:19
malice; *they are g-s*, Ro 1:29
g-s and busybodies, 1Ti 5:13

GOVERN *rule*
light to *g* the day, Ge 1:16
light to *g* the night, Ge 1:16
when the judges *g-ed*, Ru 1:1

GOVERNMENT *authority, rule*
g…on His shoulders, Is 9:6
be no end to…*His g*, Is 9:7

GOVERNOR *ruler*
not offer it to your *g*, Mal 1:8
brought before *g-s*, Mt 10:18
g was quite amazed, Mt 27:14
Pilate was *g* of Judea, Lk 3:1
g over Egypt, Ac 7:10

GRACE *benevolence, favor*
G is poured upon Your, Ps 45:2
g to the afflicted, Pr 3:34
g of God was upon, Lk 2:40
full of *g* and truth, Jn 1:14
g abounded…more, Ro 5:20
g of our Lord Jesus, Ro 16:20
My *g* is sufficient, 2Co 12:9
by *g* you have been, Eph 2:8
justified by His *g*, Titus 3:7
to the throne of *g*, Heb 4:16
g to the humble, Jas 4:6

GRACIOUS *kind*
God be *g* to you, Ge 43:29
g to whom I will be, Ex 33:19
a *g* and…God, Ne 9:31
Be *g* to me, O LORD, Ps 6:2
and *g*, Slow to anger, Ps 86:15
g to a poor man, Pr 19:17
be *g* to…remnant, Am 5:15

GRACIOUSLY *with kindness*
God has *g* given your servant, Ge 33:5
And *g* grant me Your law, Ps 119:29
When he speaks *g*, do not, Pr 26:25
he *g* forgave them both, Lk 7:42

GRAFT *insert, join*
I might be *g-ed* in, Ro 11:19
God is able to *g*, Ro 11:23
g-ed into their own, Ro 11:24

GRAIN
Joseph stored up *g*, Ge 41:49
glean among the…*g*, Ru 2:2
g…for your enemies, Is 62:8
then the mature *g*, Mk 4:28
g of wheat falls, Jn 12:24

GRAIN OFFERING
See OFFERINGS

GRANDCHILDREN
G are the crown of, Pr 17:6
widow has…or *g*, 1Ti 5:4

GRANDDAUGHTER
g-s, and all his, Ge 46:7
g of Omri king of, 2Ki 8:26

GRANDSON
g might fear the LORD, Dt 6:2
sons and thirty *g-s*, Jdg 12:14
master's *g* shall eat, 2Sa 9:10

GRANT *give, provide*
g this people favor, Ex 3:21
have *g-ed* me life, Job 10:12
g us Your salvation, Ps 85:7
G that we may sit, Mk 10:37
Father has *g-ed* Me, Lk 22:29
g repentance to, Ac 5:31
g-ing…deliverance, Ac 7:25

GRAPE *fruit*
nor eat…dried *g-s*, Nu 6:3
of *g-s* you drank, Dt 32:14
when the *g* harvest is, Is 24:13
G-s are not gathered, Mt 7:16
g-s from a briar, Lk 6:44

GRASP *hold, seize*
hands *g* the spindle, Pr 31:19
He who *g-s* the bow, Am 2:15
a thing to be *g-ed*, Php 2:6

GRASS *vegetation*
g springs out, 2Sa 23:4
his days are like *g*, Ps 103:15
dry *g* collapses into, Is 5:24
g withers, the flower, Is 40:7
was given *g* to eat, Da 5:21
if God so clothes…*g*, Mt 6:30
All flesh is like *g*, 1Pe 1:24
not to hurt the *g*, Rev 9:4

GRASSHOPPER *insect*
the *g* in its kinds, Lv 11:22
we became like *g-s*, Nu 13:33
inhabitants are like *g-s*, Is 40:22

GRATITUDE *thankfulness*
overflowing with *g*, Col 2:7
is received with *g*, 1Ti 4:4
let us show *g*, Heb 12:28

GRAVE *sepulchre, tomb*
pillar of Rachel's *g*, Ge 35:20
throat is an open *g*, Ps 5:9
I will open your *g-s*, Eze 37:12
I will prepare your *g*, Na 1:14
made the *g* secure, Mt 27:66

GRAVEN *sculptured*
make…a *g* image, Dt 4:23
ashamed who serve *g*, Ps 97:7
praise to *g* images, Is 42:8

GRAY *color*
g hair…in sorrow, Ge 42:38
with the man of *g*, Dt 32:25
Both the *g-haired*, Job 15:10
when *I am* old and *g*, Ps 71:18
g head is a crown, Pr 16:31

GRAZE *feed*
cattle…*g-ing* in, 1Ch 27:29
wolf…shall *g*, Is 65:25
he will *g* on Carmel, Jer 50:19

GREAT *big, excellent, grand*
made…two *g* lights, Ge 1:16
make you a *g* nation, Ge 12:2
lovingkindness is *g*, Ps 57:10
your iniquity is *g*, Jer 30:15
g day of the LORD, Zep 1:14
rejoiced…with *g* joy, Mt 2:10
woman…faith is *g*, Mt 15:28
good news of *g* joy, Lk 2:10
reward is *g* in, Lk 6:23
because of His *g* love, Eph 2:4
so *g* a salvation, Heb 2:3
we have a *g*…priest, Heb 4:14
so *g* a cloud of, Heb 12:1
g supper of God, Rev 19:17
a *g* white throne, Rev 20:11

GREATEST *most important*
who is the *g* among, Lk 22:26
g of these is love, 1Co 13:13
least to the *g*, Heb 8:11

GREATNESS *magnitude*
Yours…is the *g*, 1Ch 29:11
g…lovingkindness, Ne 13:22
g of Your compassion, Ps 51:1
the *g* of His strength, Is 63:1
amazed at the *g* of, Lk 9:43
surpassing *g* of His, Eph 1:19

GREECE
Paul preaches in, Ac 17:16-31
Daniel's vision of, Da 8:21

GREED *excessive desire*
caught by *their*…*g*, Pr 11:6
every form of *g*, Lk 12:15
wickedness, *g*, evil, Ro 1:29
a pretext for *g*, 1Th 2:5
a heart trained in *g*, 2Pe 2:14

GREEDY *craving*
had *g* desires, Nu 11:4
g man curses, Ps 10:3
Everyone is *g* for, Jer 6:13

GREEKS
Natives of Greece, Joel 3:6; Ac 16:1
Spiritual state of, Ro 10:12
Some believe, Ac 14:1

GREEN *fertile, fruitful*
every *g* plant for, Ge 1:30
lie down in *g* pastures, Ps 23:2
dry up the *g* tree, Eze 17:24
nor any *g* thing, Rev 9:4

GREET *hail, welcome*
g no one on the way, Lk 10:4
G one another with, 1Pe 5:14

GRIEF *heartache, sorrow*
weeps because of *g*, Ps 119:28
foolish son is a *g*, Pr 17:25
acquainted with *g*, Is 53:3
our *g-s* He Himself, Is 53:4
g…turned into joy, Jn 16:20
joy and not with *g*, Heb 13:17

GRIEVE *distress, sorrow*
was *g-d* in His heart, Ge 6:6
Do not be *g-d*, Ne 8:10
g-d Him in the desert, Ps 78:40
g-d His Holy Spirit, Is 63:10
g-d at their hardness, Mk 3:5
Peter was *g-d*, Jn 21:17
not *g* the Holy Spirit, Eph 4:30

GRIEVOUS *severe*
g mourning for the, Ge 50:11
G punishment is for him, Pr 15:10
a *g* task *which* God, Ecc 1:13
his task is painful and *g*, Ecc 2:23
a *g* evil *which* I have, Ecc 5:13
and has incurred *g* guilt, Eze 25:12

GRIND *crush, press*
my wife *g* for another, Job 31:10
g-ing…the poor, Is 3:15
millstones and *g* meal, Is 47:2
women…*be g-ing*, Mt 24:41
and *g-s* his teeth, Mk 9:18

GROAN *cry, moan*
From the city men *g*, Job 24:12
man rules, people *g*, Pr 29:2
wounded will *g*, Jer 51:52
whole creation *g-s*, Ro 8:22

GROANING *crying*
God heard their *g*, Ex 2:24
O LORD, Consider my *g*, Ps 5:1
g of the prisoner, Ps 79:11
g-s of a wounded, Eze 30:24
g-s too deep for, Ro 8:26

GROPE *move about blindly*
you will *g* at noon, Dt 28:29
They *g* in darkness, Job 12:25
g…like blind men, Is 59:10
g for Him and find, Ac 17:27

GROUND *earth, land, soil*
man of dust from…*g*, Ge 2:7
Cursed is the *g*, Ge 3:17
crossed on dry *g*, Jos 3:17
a spirit from the *g*, Is 29:4
talent in the *g*, Mt 25:25
finger wrote on the *g*, Jn 8:6
standing is holy *g*, Ac 7:33
g that drinks the rain, Heb 6:7

GROUNDED *established*
hope…is firmly *g*, 2Co 1:7
rooted and *g* in love, Eph 3:17

GROW *develop, increase*
Moses had *g-n* up, Ex 2:11
You are *g-n* fat, Dt 32:15
my spirit *g-s* faint, Ps 77:3
youths *g* weary, Is 40:30
sun and moon *g* dark, Joel 3:15
lilies of the field *g*, Mt 6:28
love will *g* cold, Mt 24:12
Child continued to *g*, Lk 2:40
grew strong in faith, Ro 4:20
as your faith *g-s*, 2Co 10:15
not *g* weary of, 2Th 3:13
g in the grace, 2Pe 3:18

GROWTH *increase*
new *g* is seen, Pr 27:25
God who causes the *g*, 1Co 3:7

GRUDGE *hostile feeling*
Esau bore a *g*, Ge 27:41
nor bear any *g*, Lv 19:18
Herodias had a *g*, Mk 6:19

GRUMBLE *complain*
they *g-d* against Moses, Ex 17:3
the congregation *g*, Nu 14:36
g-d in their tents, Ps 106:25
scribes *began* to *g*, Lk 15:2
g among yourselves, Jn 6:43

GRUMBLING *complaint*
for He hears your *g-s*, Ex 16:7
g-s against Me, Nu 17:10
Do all…without *g*, Php 2:14

GUARD *(n) keeper*
set a *g* over me, Job 7:12
be a *g* for them, Eze 38:7
g-s shook for fear, Mt 28:4
Him away under *g*, Mk 14:44

GUARD *(v) keep watch*
g the way to the tree, Ge 3:24
g-ed the threshold, 2Ki 12:9
G-ing...justice, Pr 2:8
Discretion will *g* you, Pr 2:11
soldier...was *g-ing*, Ac 28:16
will *g* your hearts, Php 4:7
g...from idols, 1Jn 5:21

GUARDHOUSE *prison*
the court of the *g*, Jer 37:21
the court of the *g*, Jer 38:28

GUARDIAN *overseer*
g-s of *the children*, 2Ki 10:1
under *g-s* and, Gal 4:2
G of your souls, 1Pe 2:25

GUEST *visitor*
Herod and his...*g-s*, Mk 6:22
Where...My *g* room, Mk 14:14
to the invited *g-s*, Lk 14:7
g of a...sinner, Lk 19:7

GUIDANCE *counsel*
no *g*, the people fall, Pr 11:14
make war by wise *g*, Pr 20:18

GUIDE *(n) advisor, director*
The righteous is a *g*, Pr 12:26
Woe to...blind *g-s*, Mt 23:16
You blind *g-s*, who, Mt 23:24
are a *g* to the blind, Ro 2:19

GUIDE *(v) direct, lead*
LORD alone *g-d* him, Dt 32:12
He *g-s* me in the paths, Ps 23:3
g us until death, Ps 48:14
my mind was *g-ing me*, Ecc 2:3
blind...*g-s* a blind, Mt 15:14
g you into...truth, Jn 16:13
unless someone *g-s*, Ac 8:31

GUILT *offence*
be free from *g*, Nu 5:31
according to his *g*, Dt 25:2
charge me with a *g*, 2Sa 3:8
our *g* has grown, Ezr 9:6
land is full of *g*, Jer 51:5
must bear their *g*, Hos 10:2
I find no *g* in Him, Jn 18:38

GUILT OFFERING
See OFFERINGS

GUILTY *charged; condemned*
he sins and becomes *g*, Lv 6:4
murderer...*g* of, Nu 35:31
as one who is *g*, 2Sa 14:13
g by the blood, Eze 22:4
g of an eternal sin, Mk 3:29
has become *g* of all, Jas 2:10

GUSHED *burst, flowed*
so that waters *g* out, Ps 78:20
the rock...water *g*, Is 48:21
all his intestines *g* out, Ac 1:18

H

HABAKKUK
Prophet in Judah just prior to Babylonian invasion, Hab 1:1
Prayer of, in praise of God, Hab 3:1–19

HABITATION *abode, dwelling*
from Your holy *h*, Dt 26:15
a rock of *h*, Ps 71:3
h-s of violence, Ps 74:20
live in a peaceful *h*, Is 32:18
holy and glorious *h*, Is 63:15
laid waste his *h*, Jer 10:25
a *h* of shepherds, Jer 33:12

HACHILAH
Hill in the Wilderness of Ziph where David hid, 1Sa 23:19–26

HADAD
Prince of Edom, 1Ki 11:14–25
——— Son of Bedad, Ge 36:35–39
——— A son of Ishmael, 1Ch 1:30
——— King of Pai, 1Ch 1:50

HADADEZER
King of Zobah, 2Sa 8:3–13
Defeated by David, 2Sa 10:6–19

HADASSAH
Esther's Jewish name, Est 2:7

HADES *hell, place of dead*
will descend to *H*, Mt 11:23
in *H* he lifted up, Lk 16:23
abandoned to *H*, Ac 2:31
See also hell; sheol

HAGAR
Sarah's servant; bears Ishmael to Abraham, Ge 16
Abraham sends her away; God comforts her, Ge 21:9–21
Paul explains symbolic meaning of, Gal 4:22–31

HAGGAI
Postexilic prophet; contemporary of Zechariah, Ezr 5:1, 2; 6:14; Hag 1:1

HAGGITH
One of David's wives, 2Sa 3:4
Mother of Adonijah, 1Ki 1:5

HAIL *(n) pieces of ice*
rained *h* on the land, Ex 9:23
storehouses of the *h*, Job 38:22
gave them *h* for rain, Ps 105:32
plague of the *h*, Rev 16:21

HAIL *(v) greeting*
H, Rabbi, Mt 26:49
H, King of...Jews, Mt 27:29

HAILSTONES *pieces of ice*
who died from the *h*, Jos 10:11
H and coals of fire, Ps 18:13
you, O *h*, will fall, Eze 13:11
h...one hundred, Rev 16:21

HAIR
gray *h*...to Sheol, Ge 42:38
locks of his *h* and, Jdg 16:14
h...bristled, Job 4:15
h...like pure wool, Da 7:9
garment of camel's *h*, Mt 3:4
make one *h* white, Mt 5:36
h-s...all numbered, Mt 10:30
His feet with her *h*, Jn 11:2
not with braided *h*, 1Ti 2:9

HAIRY *having much hair*
all over like a *h* garment, Ge 25:25
a *h* man and I am a smooth, Ge 27:11
a *h* man with a leather, 2Ki 1:8
h crown of him who goes, Ps 68:21
a *h* robe in order to deceive, Zec 13:4

HAKELDAMA
Field called "Field of Blood," Ac 1:19

HAKKOZ
Descendant of Aaron, 1Ch 24:1, 10
Called Koz, Ezr 2:61, 62
Descendants of, kept from priesthood, Ne 7:63, 64

HALL *corridor*
h of pillars, 1Ki 7:6
h of judgment, 1Ki 7:7
wedding *h* was, Mt 22:10

HALLELUJAH *praise Yahweh*
H! Salvation and, Rev 19:1
H! Her smoke rises, Rev 19:3
Amen. *H*, Rev 19:4
H! For the Lord our, Rev 19:6

HALLOWED *consecrated, holy*
H be Your name, Mt 6:9

HAM
Noah's youngest son, Ge 5:32
Enters ark, Ge 7:7
His immoral behavior merits Noah's curse, Ge 9:22–25
Father of descendants of repopulated earth, Ge 10:6–20

HAMAN
Plots to destroy Jews, Est 3:3–15
Invited to Esther's banquet, Est 5:1–14
Forced to honor Mordecai, Est 6:5–14
Hanged on his own gallows, Est 7:1–10

HAMATH
Israel's northern boundary, Nu 34:8; 1Ki 8:65; Eze 47:16–20
Conquered, 2Ki 18:34; Jer 49:23
Israelites exiled there, Is 11:11

HAMMER *mallet, tool*
and seized a *h*, Jdg 4:21
neither *h* nor axe, 1Ki 6:7
smash with...*h-s*, Ps 74:6
like a *h* which, Jer 23:29

HAMOR
Sells land to Jacob, Ge 33:18–20; Ac 7:16
Killed by Jacob's sons, Ge 34:1–31

HANANI
Father of Jehu the prophet, 1Ki 16:1, 7
Rebukes Asa; confined to prison, 2Ch 16:7–10
——— Nehemiah's brother; brings news concerning the Jews, Ne 1:2
Becomes a governor of Jerusalem, Ne 7:2

HANANIAH
False prophet who contradicts Jeremiah, Jer 28:1–17
——— Hebrew name of Shadrach, Da 1:6, 7, 11

HAND *part of body*
cover you with My *h*, Ex 33:22
for tooth, *h* for *h*, Dt 19:21
sling was in his *h*, 1Sa 17:40
They pierced my *h-s*, Ps 22:16
buries his *h*, Pr 19:24
the hollow of His *h*, Is 40:12
clay in the potter's *h*, Jer 18:6
not let your left *h*, Mt 6:3
laying His *h-s* on, Mk 10:16
the right *h* of God, Mk 16:19
into the *h-s* of men, Lk 9:44
into Your *h-s* I, Lk 23:46
reach here your *h*, Jn 20:27
not made with *h-s*, 2Co 5:1
lifting up holy *h-s*, 1Ti 2:8
h-s of…God, Heb 10:31

HAND OF GOD
See HAND OF THE LORD
h was very heavy there, 1Sa 5:11
For the *h* has struck me, Job 19:21
seen that it is from the *h*, Ecc 2:24
their deeds are in the *h*, Ecc 9:1
sat down at the right *h*, Mk 16:19
been exalted to the right *h*, Ac 2:33
standing at the right *h*, Ac 7:55
who is at the right *h*, Ro 8:34
seated at the right *h*, Col 3:1
sat down at the right *h*, Heb 10:12
under the mighty *h*, 1Pe 5:6

HAND OF THE LORD
See HAND OF GOD
h will come with a very, Ex 9:3
the *h* is mighty, Jos 4:24
the *h* was against them, Jdg 2:15
the *h* was on Elijah, 1Ki 18:46
h, for His mercies are, 1Ch 21:13
h his God was upon him, Ezr 7:6
the *h* has done this, Job 12:9
right *h* does valiantly, Ps 118:15
channels of water in the *h*, Pr 21:1
crown of beauty in the *h*, Is 62:3
h was certainly with him, Lk 1:66
the *h* was with them, Ac 11:21

HANDLE *touch, lift*
could *h* shield and spear, 1Ch 12:8
h the law did not know Me, Jer 2:8
and Put, that *h* the shield, Jer 46:9
their virgin bosom was *h-d*, Eze 23:3
All who *h* the oar, Eze 27:29
Do not *h*, do not taste, Col 2:21
h-ing the word of truth, 2Ti 2:15

HANDMAID *servant, slave*
save the son of Your *h*, Ps 86:16
the son of Your *h*, Ps 116:16
her *h-s* are moaning, Na 2:7

HANDSOME *attractive*
a choice and *h man*, 1Sa 9:2
ruddy, with a *h*, 1Sa 17:42

HANG *attach, suspend*
h you on a tree, Ge 40:19
h up the veil, Ex 40:8
h-ed is accursed of, Dt 21:23
h-ing in an oak, 2Sa 18:10
they *h-ed* Haman, Est 7:10
he…*h-ed* himself, Mt 27:5
millstone were *hung*, Lk 17:2
h-ing Him on a cross, Ac 5:30
who *h-s* on a tree, Gal 3:13

HANNAH
Barren wife of Elkanah; prays for a son, 1Sa 1:1–18
Bears Samuel and dedicates him to the LORD, 1Sa 1:19–28
Magnifies God, 1Sa 2:1–10

HANUN
King of Ammon; disgraces David's ambassadors and is defeated by him, 2Sa 10:1–14

HAPPINESS *joy*
give *h* to his wife, Dt 24:5
eat your bread in *h*, Ecc 9:7
I have forgotten *h*, La 3:17

HAPPY *blessed, joyful*
Leah said, *H* am I, Ge 30:13
h…man whom God, Job 5:17
h…who keeps the, Pr 29:18

HARAN
Abraham's younger brother, Ge 11:26–31
City of Mesopotamia, Ge 11:31
Abraham leaves, Ge 12:4, 5
Jacob dwells at, Ge 29:4–35

HARD *difficult, firm*
bitter with *h* labor, Ex 1:14
case that is too *h*, Dt 1:17
made our yoke *h*, 2Ch 10:4
Water becomes *h*, Job 38:30
h for a rich man, Mt 19:23
h it is to enter, Mk 10:24
worked *h* all night, Lk 5:5

HARDEN *make hard, callous*
h Pharaoh's heart, Ex 7:3
dust *h-s* into a mass, Job 38:38
who *h-s his* neck, Pr 29:1
h-s whom He, Ro 9:18
minds were *h-ed*, 2Co 3:14
Do not *h* your hearts, Heb 3:15

HARDNESS *callousness*
give them *h* of heart, La 3:65
Because of your *h*, Mt 19:8
grieved at their *h*, Mk 3:5
unbelief and *h* of, Mk 16:14

HARDSHIP *difficulty*
H after *h* is with me, Job 10:17
people experience *h*, Ps 60:3
afflictions, in *h-s*, 2Co 6:4
our labor and *h*, 1Th 2:9
Suffer *h* with *me*, 2Ti 2:3

HAREM *royal wives' quarters*
best place in the *h*, Est 2:9
the court of the *h*, Est 2:11
from the *h* to the, Est 2:13
to the second *h*, Est 2:14

HARLOT *prostitute*
thought she *was* a *h*, Ge 38:15
the hire of a *h*, Dt 23:18
h whose name was, Jos 2:1
Dressed as a *h*, Pr 7:10
city has become a *h*, Is 1:21
also played the *h*, Eze 16:26
Traded a boy for a *h*, Joel 3:3
Mother of *H-s*, Rev 17:5

HARLOTRY *prostitution*
with child by *h*, Ge 38:24
profaned by *h*, Lv 21:7
uncovered her *h-ies*, Eze 23:18
children of *h*, Hos 1:2
spirit of *h*, Hos 5:4

HARM *(n) evil, hurt*
pillar to me, for *h*, Ge 31:52
h to this people, Ex 5:22
keep *me* from *h*, 1Ch 4:10
Do not devise *h*, Pr 3:29
great *h* to yourselves, Jer 44:7
the fire without *h*, Da 3:25
did me much *h*, 2Ti 4:14

HARM *(v) damage, hurt*
David seeks to *h*, 1Sa 24:9
planning to *h* me, Ne 6:2
have not *h-ed* me, Da 6:22
in order to *h* you, Ac 18:10
is there to *h* you, 1Pe 3:13

HAR-MAGEDON
See MEGIDDO
Possible site of final battle, Rev 16:16

HARMONY *agreement*
what *h* has Christ, 2Co 6:15
live in *h* in the, Php 4:2

HARP *musical instrument*
my *h* is turned to, Job 30:31
praises…with a *h*, Ps 33:2
Awake, *h* and lyre, Ps 57:8
gaiety of the *h* ceases, Is 24:8
each one holding a *h*, Rev 5:8
holding *h-s* of God, Rev 15:2

HARSH *difficult, hard*
man was *h* and evil, 1Sa 25:3
h word stirs up anger, Pr 15:1
A *h* vision, Is 21:2
under *h* servitude, La 1:3

HARVEST *reap and gather*
Seedtime and *h*, Ge 8:22
fruits of the wheat *h*, Ex 34:22
you reap your *h*, Dt 24:19
he who sleeps in *h*, Pr 10:5
snow…time of *h*, Pr 25:13
like rain in *h*, Pr 26:1
the gladness of *h*, Is 9:3
time of *h* will come, Jer 51:33
Lord of the *h*, Mt 9:38
h is the end of the, Mt 13:39
fields…white for *h*, Jn 4:35
h of the earth is, Rev 14:15

HARVEST, FEAST OF
See FEASTS

HASTE *hurrying*
shall eat it in *h*, Ex 12:11
Moses made *h* to bow low, Ex 34:8
Make *h* to help me, O LORD, Ps 38:22
who makes *h* to be rich, Pr 28:20
went in *h* to the lions' den, Da 6:19
Him saying to me, 'Make *h*, Ac 22:18

HASTEN *accelerate*
h-ed after deceit, Job 31:5
H to me, O God, Ps 70:5
they *h* to shed blood, Pr 1:16
bird *h-s* to the snare, Pr 7:23

eye *h-s* after wealth, Pr 28:22
h-ing...day of God, 2Pe 3:12

HATE *despise, loathe*
you *h* discipline, Ps 50:17
who *h* the LORD, Ps 81:15
I *h* every false way, Ps 119:104
fools *h* knowledge, Pr 1:22
withholds his rod *h-s*, Pr 13:24
a time to *h*, Ecc 3:8
H evil, love good, Am 5:15
For I *h* divorce, Mal 2:16
good to those who *h*, Lk 6:27
you will be *h-d*, Lk 21:17
he who *h-s* his life, Jn 12:25
the very thing I *h*, Ro 7:15
Esau I *h-d*, Ro 9:13
h-ing one another, Titus 3:3
yet h-s his brother, 1Jn 2:9

HATERS *those who hate*
slanderers, *h* of God, Ro 1:30
brutal, *h* of good, 2Ti 3:3

HATRED *hate, ill will*
h for my love, Ps 109:5
H stirs up strife, Pr 10:12
who conceals *h has*, Pr 10:18

HAUGHTY *proud*
nor my eyes *h*, Ps 131:1
H eyes, a lying, Pr 6:17
h spirit before, Pr 16:18
Proud, *H*, Scoffer, Pr 21:24
wine betrays the *h*, Hab 2:5
do not be *h* in mind, Ro 12:16

HAURAN
District southeast of Mt. Hermon, Eze 47:16

HAVE MERCY
I will surely *h* on him, Jer 31:20
h on the whole house of, Eze 39:25
H on us, Son of David, Mt 9:27
H on me, Lord, Son of, Mt 15:22
Father Abraham, *h* on, Lk 16:24
will *h* on whom I, Ro 9:15

HAVEN *harbor, shelter*
be a *h* for ships, Ge 49:13
to their desired *h*, Ps 107:30

HAWK *bird*
sea gull, and the *h*, Dt 14:15
h-s will be gathered, Is 34:15

HAZAEL
Anointed king of Syria by Elijah, 1Ki 19:15–17
Elisha predicts his taking the throne, 2Ki 8:7–15
Oppresses Israel, 2Ki 8:28, 29; 10:32, 33; 12:17, 18; 13:3–7, 22

HAZAR-ENAN
Village of north Palestine, Nu 34:9, 10

HAZEROTH
Scene of sedition of Miriam and Aaron, Nu 11:35–12:16

HAZOR
Royal Canaanite city destroyed by Joshua, Jos 11:1–13
Rebuilt and assigned to Naphtali, Jos 19:32, 36
Army of, defeated by Deborah and Barak, Jdg 4:1–24

HE WHO BELIEVES
H in Him is not judged, Jn 3:18
H in the Son has eternal, Jn 3:36
h in Me will never thirst, Jn 6:35
H in Me ... his innermost, Jn 7:38
h in Me, the works that I, Jn 14:12
h in Him will not be, Ro 9:33
h in Him will not be, 1Pe 2:6
overcomes the world, but *h*, 1Jn 5:5

HEAD *chief; part of body*
bruise you on the *h*, Ge 3:15
anointed my *h* with oil, Ps 23:5
h a garland of grace, Pr 4:9
gray *h* is a crown, Pr 16:31
coals on his *h*, Pr 25:22
h was made bald, Eze 29:18
had four *h-s*, Da 7:6
an oath by your *h*, Mt 5:36
nowhere to lay His *h*, Mt 8:20
h of John the Baptist, Mt 14:8
not a hair of your *h*, Lk 21:18
crown...on His *h*, Jn 19:2
God is the *h* of, 1Co 11:3
husband is the *h*, Eph 5:23

HEADLONG *headfirst*
He rushes *h* at Him, Job 15:26
falling *h*, he burst, Ac 1:18
h into the error, Jude 11

HEAL *make well, restore*
will *h* their land, 2Ch 7:14
h-s the brokenhearted, Ps 147:3
a time to *h*, Ecc 3:3
H me, O LORD, Jer 17:14
will *h* their apostasy, Hos 14:4
h-ed all who were, Mt 8:16
H the sick, raise, Mt 10:8
h him on...Sabbath, Mk 3:2
Physician, *h* yourself, Lk 4:23
you may be *h-ed*, Jas 5:16
fatal wound was *h-ed*, Rev 13:3

HEALING *health, wholeness*
be *h* to your body, Pr 3:8
h to the bones, Pr 16:24
sorrow is beyond *h*, Jer 8:18
There is no *h* for, Jer 46:11
their leaves for *h*, Eze 47:12
h every kind of, Mt 4:23
gifts of *h*, 1Co 12:9
h of the nations, Rev 22:2

HEALTH *soundness, wholeness*
no *h* in my bones, Ps 38:3
restore you to *h*, Jer 30:17
and be in good *h*, 3Jn 2

HEAP *(n) mound, pile*
stones and made a *h*, Ge 31:46
waters stood...like a *h*, Ex 15:8
made a refuse *h*, Ezr 6:11
needy from the ash *h*, Ps 113:7
Jerusalem a *h* of ruins, Jer 9:11
altars are...*h-s*, Hos 12:11

HEAP *(v) pile up, place*
h misfortunes on, Dt 32:23
will *h* burning coals, Pr 25:22
H on the wood, Eze 24:10
h up rubble to, Hab 1:10

HEAR *listen*
h-d the sound of, Ge 3:10
God *h-d* their groaning, Ex 2:24
H, O Israel, Dt 6:4
h the wisdom of, 1Ki 4:34
h in heaven, 1Ki 8:30
Will God *h* his cry, Job 27:9
who *h* prayer, Ps 65:2
h Your lovingkindness, Ps 143:8
poor *h-s* no rebuke, Pr 13:8
deaf will *h* words, Is 29:18
bones, *h* the word, Eze 37:4
ears to *h*, let him *h*, Mt 11:15
h of wars and, Mk 13:7
he who *h-s* My word, Jn 5:24
does not *h* sinners, Jn 9:31
sheep *h* My voice, Jn 10:27
we *h-d* of your faith, Col 1:4
anyone *h-s* My voice, Rev 3:20

HEARING *listening*
in the LORD's *h*, 1Sa 8:21
in the *h* of a fool, Pr 23:9
fulfilled in your *h*, Lk 4:21
I will give you a *h*, Ac 23:35
become dull of *h*, Heb 5:11

HEART *mind; seat of emotions*
intent of man's *h* is, Ge 8:21
I will harden his *h*, Ex 4:21
great searchings of *h*, Jdg 5:16
LORD looks at the *h*, 1Sa 16:7
fool has said in his *h*, Ps 14:1
meditation of my *h*, Ps 19:14
My *h* is like wax, Ps 22:14
in me a clean *h*, Ps 51:10
and a contrite *h*, Ps 51:17
Your word...in my *h*, Ps 119:11
Deceit is in the *h*, Pr 12:20
A joyful *h* is good, Pr 17:22
to a troubled *h*, Pr 25:20
bribe corrupts the *h*, Ecc 7:7
a new *h* and a new, Eze 18:31
uncircumcised in *h*, Eze 44:7
are the pure in *h*, Mt 5:8
adultery...in his *h*, Mt 5:28
and humble in *h*, Mt 11:29
h is far...from Me, Mt 15:8
pondering...in her *h*, Lk 2:19
pierced to the *h*, Ac 2:37
cleansing their *h-s*, Ac 15:9
who searches the *h-s*, Ro 8:27
tablets of human *h-s*, 2Co 3:3
not lose *h* in doing, Gal 6:9
melody with your *h*, Eph 5:19
intentions of the *h*, Heb 4:12
deceives his *own h*, Jas 1:26

HEAT *hotness, warmth*
the *h* of the day, Ge 18:1
and *h* consume, Job 24:19
hidden from its *h*, Ps 19:6
a shade from the *h*, Is 25:4
burning *h* of famine, La 5:10
scorching *h* of the, Mt 20:12
with intense *h*, 2Pe 3:10
scorched with fierce *h*, Rev 16:9

HEAVE OFFERING
See OFFERINGS

HEAVEN *place of God; sky*
God created the *h-s*, Ge 1:1
rain bread from *h*, Ex 16:4
shut up the *h-s*, Dt 11:17
thunder in the *h-s*, 1Sa 2:10
fire came…from *h*, 2Ki 1:14
make windows in *h*, 2Ki 7:2
walks…vault of *h*, Job 22:14
I consider Your *h-s*, Ps 8:3
h and earth praise, Ps 69:34
fixed patterns of *h*, Jer 33:25
lights in the *h-s*, Eze 32:8
open…windows of *h*, Mal 3:10
kingdom of *h* is at, Mt 3:2
voice out of the *h-s*, Mt 3:17
reward in *h* is great, Mt 5:12
Father who is in *h*, Mt 6:9
shall have been loosed in *h*, Mt 16:19
great signs from *h*, Lk 21:11
Him go into *h*, Ac 1:11
no…name under *h*, Ac 4:12
up to the third *h*, 2Co 12:2
citizenship is in *h*, Php 3:20
there was war in *h*, Rev 12:7
new *h* and a new, Rev 21:1

HEAVEN AND EARTH
Most High, Possessor of *h*, Ge 14:19
the LORD made *h*, Ex 31:17
call *h* to witness against, Dt 4:26
servants of the God of *h*, Ezr 5:11
LORD, Maker of *h*, Ps 115:15
LORD, Who made *h*, Ps 121:2
until *h* pass away, Mt 5:18
You, Father, Lord of *h*, Mt 11:25
H will pass away, Mt 24:35
easier for *h* to pass, Lk 16:17

HEAVENLY *related to God*
h Father is perfect, Mt 5:48
h Father knows that, Mt 6:32
h host praising God, Lk 2:13
I tell you *h* things, Jn 3:12
Him in the *h places*, Eph 2:6
partakers of a *h*, Heb 3:1
shadow of the *h*, Heb 8:5

HEAVENLY FATHER
as your *h* is perfect, Mt 5:4
your *h* will also forgive you, Mt 6:14
yet your *h* feeds them, Mt 6:26
h knows that you need, Mt 6:32
My *h* will also do the same, Mt 18:35
your *h* give the Holy Spirit, Lk 11:13

HEAVY *burdensome, hard to lift*
Moses' hands were *h*, Ex 17:12
servitude was *h* on, Ne 5:18
h drinkers of wine, Pr 23:20
A stone is *h*, Pr 27:3
Jerusalem a *h* stone, Zec 12:3
eyes were very *h*, Mk 14:40

HEBREW
Term applied to:
Abram, Ge 14:13
Israelites, 1Sa 4:6, 9
Jews, Ac 6:1
Paul, Php 3:5

HEBRON
Abram, Isaac, and Jacob dwell there, Ge 13:18; 23:2–20; 35:27
Visited by spies, Nu 13:21, 22
Defeated by Joshua, Jos 10:1–37
Caleb's inheritance, Jos 14:12–15
David's original capital; sons born there, 2Sa 2:1–3, 11; 3:2–5
Site of Absalom's rebellion, 2Sa 15:7–10

HEDGE *border; protection*
You not made a *h*, Job 1:10
as a *h* of thorns, Pr 15:19
along the *h-s*, and, Lk 14:23

HEED *(n) attention*
Give *h* to my speech, Ge 4:23
you will give earnest *h* to, Ex 15:26
give *h* to yourself and keep, Dt 4:9
Give *h* to my prayer., Ps 61:1
give *h* to the blameless way, Ps 101:2
Take *h* then to your spirit, Mal 2:15
Take *h*, keep on the alert, Mk 13:33
thinks he stands take *h*, 1Co 10:12
Take *h* to the ministry, Col 4:17

HEED *(v) give attention*
H the sound of my cry for help, Ps 5:2
H instruction and be wise, Pr 8:33
of life who *h-s* instruction, Pr 10:17
his words are not *h-ed*, Ecc 9:16
She *h-ed* no voice, Zep 3:2
did not all *h* the good news, Ro 10:16
Blessed is he who *h-s* the, Rev 22:7

HEEL *back of foot*
bruise him on the *h*, Ge 3:15
on to Esau's *h*, Ge 25:26
his *h* against Me, Jn 13:18

HEIFER *young cow*
unblemished red *h*, Nu 19:2
plowed with my *h*, Jdg 14:18
Egypt is a pretty *h*, Jer 46:20
Like a stubborn *h*, Hos 4:16

HEIGHT *elevation, heaven, sky*
in the *h* of heaven, Job 22:12
from His holy *h*, Ps 102:19
Praise Him in the *h-s*, Ps 148:1
As the heavens for *h*, Pr 25:3
ascend above the *h-s*, Is 14:14
nor *h*, nor depth, Ro 8:39

HEIR *person who inherits*
in my house is my *h*, Ge 15:3
has he no *h-s*, Jer 49:1
h-s also, *h-s* of God, Ro 8:17
an *h* through God, Gal 4:7
h-s of the kingdom, Jas 2:5

HELAM
Place between Damascus and Hamath where David defeated Syrians, 2Sa 10:16–19
Greek-speaking Jews, Ac 6:1
Hostile to Paul, Ac 9:29
Gospel preached to, Ac 11:20

HELL *place of dead*
go into the fiery *h*, Mt 5:22
soul and body in *h*, Mt 10:28
to be cast into *h*, Mk 9:47
set on fire by *h*, Jas 3:6
cast them into *h*, 2Pe 2:4
See also hades; sheol

HELLENISTIC JEWS
Greek speaking Jews, Ac 6:1; 9:29

HELMET *headpiece*
bronze *h* on his, 1Sa 17:5
h of salvation, Is 59:17
take the *h* of, Eph 6:17

HELP *(n) assistance, relief*
h is not within me, Job 6:13
He is our *h* and our, Ps 33:20
present *h* in trouble, Ps 46:1
I cried for *h*, Jon 2:2
gifts of…*h-s*, 1Co 12:28

HELP *(v) aid, assist*
h-ing the Hebrew, Ex 1:16
the LORD *h-ed* David, 2Sa 8:6
whence shall my *h*, Ps 121:1
I will *h* you, Is 41:13
Lord, *h* me, Mt 15:25
h my unbelief, Mk 9:24
must *h* the weak, Ac 20:35
Spirit also *h-s* our, Ro 8:26
earth *h-ed* the, Rev 12:16

HELPER *one who assists*
h of the orphan, Ps 10:14
be my *h*, Ps 30:10
Behold, God is my *h*, Ps 54:4
give you another *H*, Jn 14:16
H, the Holy Spirit, Jn 14:26

HELPLESS *weak*
the *h* has hope, Job 5:16
who considers the *h*, Ps 41:1
while we were still *h*, Ro 5:6

HEMAN
Composer of a Psalm, Ps 88:title

HEMORRHAGE *bleeding*
suffering from a *h*, Mt 9:20
a *h* for twelve years, Mk 5:25
her *h* stopped, Lk 8:44

HEN *fowl*
h gathers her, Mt 23:37
as a *h gathers* her, Lk 13:34

HERB *dried plant*
bread and bitter *h-s*, Ex 12:8
fade like the green *h*, Ps 37:2
h-s of…mountains, Pr 27:25
sweet-scented *h-s*, SS 5:13

HERD *cattle, flock*
firstborn of your *h*, Dt 12:6
h, or flock taste a, Jon 3:7
h of many swine, Mt 8:30

HERDSMEN *keepers of flocks*
h of Abram's livestock, Ge 13:7
between my *h* and, Ge 13:8
the *h* ran away, Mt 8:33

HERE AM I
See HERE I AM
Then I said, "*H*. Send me!, Is 6:8
'*H*, *h*,' To a nation, Is 65:1

HERE I AM
See HERE AM I
And he said, "*H*, Ge 22:1
And he said to him, "*H*, Ge 27:1
'Jacob,' and I said, '*H*, Ge 31:11
Moses!" And he said, "*H*, Ex 3:4
Samuel; and he said, "*H*, 1Sa 3:4

one who is speaking, '*H*', Is 52:6
And he said, "*H*, Ac 9:10

HERITAGE *what is inherited*
the *h* decreed to him, Job 20:29
my *h* is beautiful, Ps 16:6
their land as a *h*, Ps 136:21
inherit the desolate *h-s*, Is 49:8
you who pillage My *h*, Jer 50:11

HERMES
Paul acclaimed as, Ac 14:12

HERMON
Highest mountain (9, 166 ft.) in Syria; also called Sirion, Shenir, Dt 3:8, 9

HEROD
Herod the Great, procurator of Judea (37–4 B.C.), Lk 1:5
Inquires about Jesus' birth, Mt 2:3–8
Slays infants of Bethlehem, Mt 2:12–18
——— Herod Antipas, the tetrarch, ruler of Galilee and Perea (4 B.C.–A.D. 39), Lk 3:1
Imprisons John the Baptist, Lk 3:18–21
Has John the Baptist beheaded, Mt 14:1–12
Disturbed about Jesus, Lk 9:7–9
Jesus sent to him, Lk 23:7–11
——— Herod Agrippa I (A.D. 37–44), Ac 12:1, 19
Kills James, Ac 12:1, 2
Imprisons Peter, Ac 12:3–11, 19
Slain by an angel, Ac 12:20–23
——— Herod Agrippa II (A.D. 53–70); called Agrippa and King Agrippa, Ac 25:22–24, 26
Festus tells him about Paul, Ac 25:13–27
Paul makes a defense before, Ac 26:1–32

HERODIANS
Influential Jews favoring Herod, Mt 22:16; Mk 3:6

HERODIAS
Granddaughter of Herod the Great; plots John's death, Mt 14:3–12
Married her uncle, Mk 6:17, 18

HESHBON
Ancient Moabite city; taken by Moses, Nu 21:23–34
Assigned to Reubenites, Nu 32:1–37
Prophecies concerning, Is 15:1–4; 16:8–14; Jer 48:2, 34, 35

HETH
Son of Canaan, Ge 10:15
Abraham buys field from sons of, Ge 23:3–20
Esau marries daughters of, Ge 27:46

HEW *chop, cut*
h down their Asherim, Dt 7:5
H-n cisterns, vineyards, Ne 9:25
h-n out in the rock, Mk 15:46

HEZEKIAH
Righteous king of Judah; reforms temple and worship, 2Ch 29–31
Wars with Assyria; prayer for deliverance is answered, 2Ki 18:7–19:37
His sickness and recovery; thanksgiving, 2Ki 20:1–11; Is 38:9–22
Boasts to Babylonian ambassadors, 2Ki 20:12–19
Death, 2Ki 20:20, 21

HIDDEN *(adj) concealed*
Acquit me of *h faults*, Ps 19:12
h wealth of secret, Is 45:3
h snares for my feet, Jer 18:22
profound and *h*, Da 2:22
some of the *h* manna, Rev 2:17

HIDE *conceal, cover*
man and his wife *hid*, Ge 3:8
I *h* from Abraham, Ge 18:17
Moses *hid* his face, Ex 3:6
h me in Sheol, Job 14:13
h-ing my iniquity, Job 31:33
H me in the shadow, Ps 17:8
Do not *h* Your face, Ps 27:9
wrongs are not *h-den*, Ps 69:5
sees evil *and h-s*, Pr 27:12
hid your talent, Mt 25:25
nothing is *h-den*, Mk 4:22
Jesus *hid* Himself, Jn 8:59
h us from...Him, Rev 6:16

HIDING PLACE
Clouds are a *h*, Job 22:14
He lurks in a *h*, Ps 10:9
You are my *h*, Ps 32:7
uncovered his *h-s*, Jer 49:10

HIEL
Native of Bethel; rebuilds Jericho, 1Ki 16:34
Fulfills Joshua's curse in Jos 6:26

HIGH *elevated; heavenly*
it is still *h* day, Ge 29:7
the *h* places of Baal, Nu 22:41
h above all nations, Dt 26:19
h as the heavens, Job 11:8
my advocate is on *h*, Job 16:19
set him *securely* on *h*, Ps 91:14
or *h* as heaven, Is 7:11
to a very *h* mountain, Mt 4:8
the *h* priest, Mt 26:57
Son of the Most *H*, Mk 5:7
from a *h* fever, Lk 4:38
He ascended on *h*, Eph 4:8

HIGH PLACE
will destroy your *h-s*, Lv 26:30
and demolish all their *h-s*, Nu 33:52
a sacrifice on the *h* today, 1Sa 9:12
he came to the *h*, 1Sa 10:13
for that was the great *h*, 1Ki 3:4
a *h* for Chemosh, 1Ki 11:7
h which Jeroboam, 2Ki 23:15
h which was at Gibeon, 1Ch 16:39
Him with their *h-s*, Ps 78:58
offers sacrifice on the *h*, Jer 48:35
a *h* in every square, Eze 16:24
down and tread on the *h-s*, Mic 1:3

HIGH PLACES
And sets me on my *h*, 2Sa 22:34
And sets me upon my *h*, Ps 18:33
makes me walk on my *h*, Hab 3:19

HIGH PRIEST
king's scribe and the *h*, 2Ki 12:10
Eliashib the *h* arose, Ne 3:1
son of Jehozadak, the *h*, Hag 1:1
of the *h*, named Caiaphas, Mt 26:3
the time of Abiathar the *h*, Mk 2:26
Annas the *h* was there, Ac 4:6
The *h* Ananias commanded, Ac 23:2
a merciful and faithful *h*, Heb 2:17
Jesus, the Apostle and *H*, Heb 3:1
we have a great *h*, Heb 4:14
h forever according to the, Heb 6:20
Christ appeared as a *h*, Heb 9:11

HIGHWAY *road*
along the king's *h*, Nu 20:17
h from Egypt to, Is 19:23
the *H* of Holiness, Is 35:8
a *h* for our God, Is 40:3
Go out into the *h-s*, Lk 14:23

HILKIAH
Shallum's son, 1Ch 6:13
High priest in Josiah's reign, 2Ch 34:9–22
Oversees temple work, 2Ki 22:4–7
Finds the Book of the Law, 2Ki 22:8–14
Aids in reformation, 2Ki 23:4

HILL *mountain*
the everlasting *h-s*, Ge 49:26
the *h* of God, 1Sa 10:5
dwell on Your holy *h*, Ps 15:1
to Your holy *h*, Ps 43:3
cattle...thousand *h-s*, Ps 50:10
h-s, Fall on us, Hos 10:8
city set on a *h*, Mt 5:14
h...brought low, Lk 3:5
the brow of the *h*, Lk 4:29
h-s, Cover us, Lk 23:30

HINDER *delay, impede, restrain*
h meditation before, Job 15:4
do not *h* them, Mt 19:14
do not *h* them, Lk 18:16
h-ed you from obeying, Gal 5:7
prayers...not be *h-ed*, 1Pe 3:7

HINNOM, VALLEY OF THE SON OF
See TOPHETH
Place near Jerusalem used for human sacrifice, 2Ki 23:10; 2Ch 28:3; Jer 7:31, 32; 19:1–15

HIP *part of body*
the sinew of the *h*, Ge 32:32
curves of your *h-s* are, SS 7:1
h joints went slack, Da 5:6

HIRAM
King of Tyre; provided for David's palace and Solomon's temple, 2Sa 5:11; 1Ki 5:1–12; 9:10–14, 26–28; 10:11; 1Ch 14:1

HIRE *(n) wages*
it came for its *h*, Ex 22:15
the *h* of a harlot, Dt 23:18

HIRE *(v) engage for labor*
h...for bread, 1Sa 2:5
and *h-d* the Arameans, 2Sa 10:6
to *h*...chariots, 1Ch 19:6
he who *h-s* a fool, Pr 26:10
to *h* laborers for, Mt 20:1

HIRED *(adj) employed*
as a *h* man, as if, Lv 25:40
oppress a *h* servant, Dt 24:14
as one of your *h*, Lk 15:19

h hand…not a shepherd, Jn 10:12
because he is a *h* hand, Jn 10:13

HIS RIGHT HAND
At *H* there was flashing, Dt 33:2
the saving strength of *H*, Ps 20:6
H and His holy arm, Ps 98:1
sworn by *H* and by, Is 62:8
whom God exalted to *H*, Ac 5:31
H in the heavenly places, Eph 1:20
H He held seven stars, Rev 1:16

HISS *to show dislike*
h him from his place, Job 27:23
object of…h-ing, Jer 18:16
They *h* and shake, La 2:15
h And wave his hand, Zep 2:15

HITTITES
One of seven Canaanite nations, Dt 7:1
Israelites intermarry with, Jdg 3:5, 6; 1Ki 11:1; Ezr 9:1, 2

HIVITE, HIVITES
One of seven Canaanite nations, Dt 7:1
Esau intermarries with, Ge 36:2
Gibeonites belong to, Jos 9:7

HOLD *grasp, retain*
Moses *held* his hand, Ex 17:11
h fast to Him, Dt 11:22
h fast…evil purpose, Ps 64:5
heart *h* fast my words, Pr 4:4
Take *h* of instruction, Pr 4:13
h fast My covenant, Is 56:4
h to the tradition, Mk 7:8
h fast the word, 1Co 15:2
h-ing to the mystery, 1Ti 3:9
h of the eternal, 1Ti 6:12
He *held* seven stars, Rev 1:16

HOLE *opening*
the *h* of the cobra, Is 11:8
a *h* in the wall, Eze 8:7
a purse with *h-s*, Hag 1:6
foxes have *h-s*, Mt 8:20

HOLIDAY *period of leisure*
a feast and a *h*, Est 8:17
a h for rejoicing, Est 9:19
mourning into a *h*, Est 9:22

HOLINESS *sacredness*
majestic in *h*, Ex 15:11
H befits Your house, Ps 93:5
the Highway of *H*, Is 35:8
without blame in *h*, 1Th 3:13
we may share His *h*, Heb 12:10

HOLLOW *empty space*
the *h* of a sling, 1Sa 25:29
in the *h* of His hand, Is 40:12

HOLY *sacred, sanctified*
standing is *h* ground, Ex 3:5
sabbath…keep it *h*, Ex 20:8
you are a *h* people, Dt 7:6
ten thousand *h* ones, Dt 33:2
h like the LORD, 1Sa 2:2
Worship…*h* array, 1Ch 16:29
His *h* dwelling, 2Ch 30:27
Jerusalem, the *h* city, Ne 11:1
Zion, My *h* mountain, Ps 2:6
to His *h* land, Ps 78:54
bless His *h* name, Ps 145:21
H, H, H, is the LORD, Is 6:3
the *H* One of Israel, Is 30:15
what is *h* to dogs, Mt 7:6
righteous and *h* man, Mk 6:20
the *H* One of God, Lk 4:34
in the *h* Scriptures, Ro 1:2
and *h* sacrifice, Ro 12:1
with a *h* kiss, Ro 16:16
h both in body, 1Co 7:34
lifting up *h* hands, 1Ti 2:8
with a *h* calling, 2Ti 1:9
I saw the *h* city, Rev 21:2

HOLY CITY
live in Jerusalem, the *h*, Ne 11:1
call themselves after the *h*, Is 48:2
O Jerusalem, the *h*, Is 52:1
h, to finish the transgression, Da 9:24
devil took Him into the *h*, Mt 4:5
the *h* and appeared, Mt 27:53
saw the *h*, new Jerusalem, Rev 21:2
h, Jerusalem, coming, Rev 21:10
tree of life and from the *h*, Rev 22:19

HOLY NAME
not to profane My *h*, Lv 22:2
Glory in His *h*, 1Ch 16:10
a house for Your *h*, 1Ch 29:16
we trust in His *h*, Ps 33:21
give thanks to His *h*, Ps 97:12
bless His *h*, Ps 103:1
My *h* I will make known, Eze 39:7

HOLY OF HOLIES
See HOLY PLACE; MOST HOLY PLACE
the holy place and the *h*, Ex 26:33
the room of the *h*, 2Ch 3:8
doors for the *h*, 2Ch 4:22
which is called the *H*, Heb 9:3

HOLY ONE OF ISRAEL
Against the *H*, 2Ki 19:22
with the lyre, O *H*, Ps 71:22
pained the *H*, Ps 78:41
the *H* draw near, Is 5:19
eyes will look to the *H*, Is 17:7
your Redeemer is the *H*, Is 41:14

HOLY PLACE
See HOLY OF HOLIES; MOST HOLY PLACE
partition between the *h*, Ex 26:33
minister in the *h*, Ex 28:43
fragrant incense for the *h*, Ex 31:11
who may stand in His *h*, Ps 24:3
I dwell on a high and *h*, Is 57:15
standing in the *h*, Mt 24:15
way into the *h*, Heb 9:8
entered the *h* once for all, Heb 9:12
enter the *h* by the blood, Heb 10:19

HOLY SPIRIT
Third Person of the Godhead
See SPIRIT OF GOD; SPIRIT OF THE LORD, Mt 28:19; 2Co 13:14
Helper, Jn 14:16, 26
Giver of gifts, Ro 12:6–8; 1Co 12:8–11
Fruit of the Spirit, Gal 5:22
do not take Your *H*, Ps 51:11
put His *H* in the midst, Is 63:11
with child by the *H*, Mt 1:18
speaks against the *H*, Mt 12:32
and the Son and the *H*, Mt 28:19
H will come upon you, Lk 1:35
was filled with the *H*, Lk 1:41
baptize you with the *H*, Lk 3:16
H descended upon Him, Lk 3:22
give the *H* to those, Lk 11:13
Helper, the *H*, whom, Jn 14:26
"Receive the *H*, Jn 20:22
power when the *H*, Ac 1:8
filled with the *H*, Ac 2:4
seemed good to the *H*, Ac 15:28
H has made you, Ac 20:28
through the *H* who, Ro 5:5
peace and joy in the *H*, Ro 14:17
is a temple of the *H*, 1Co 6:19
men moved by the *H*, 2Pe 1:21

HOMAGE *act of reverence*
my people shall do *h*, Ge 41:40
did *h* to the LORD, 1Ch 29:20
and paid *h* to Haman, Est 3:2
did *h* to Daniel, Da 2:46

HOME *place of dwelling*
free at *h* one year, Dt 24:5
God makes a *h*, Ps 68:6
husband is not at *h*, Pr 7:19
to his eternal *h*, Ecc 12:5
Go *h* to your people, Mk 5:19
let him eat at *h*, 1Co 11:34
at *h* in the body, 2Co 5:6
at *h* with the Lord, 2Co 5:8

HOMER *measure of capacity*
a *h* of barley, Lv 27:16
a *h* of seed, Is 5:10
from a *h* of wheat, Eze 45:13

HOMESTEAD *family dwelling*
h forlorn and forsaken, Is 27:10
h be made desolate, Ac 1:20

HOMOSEXUALS
effeminate, nor *h*, 1Co 6:9
immoral men and *h*, 1Ti 1:10

HONEST *respectable, truthful*
we are *h* men, Ge 42:11
painful are *h* words, Job 6:25
an *h* and good heart, Lk 8:15

HONEY *sweetness*
with milk and *h*, Ex 3:8
swarm of bees and *h*, Jdg 14:8
is sweeter than *h*, Jdg 14:18
sweet as *h* in my, Eze 3:3
locusts and wild *h*, Mt 3:4

HONEYCOMB *honey storage*
drippings of the *h*, Ps 19:10
Pleasant words…a *h*, Pr 16:24

HONOR *(n) glory, great respect*
both riches and *h*, 1Ki 3:13
stripped my *h* from, Job 19:9
wise will inherit *h*, Pr 3:35
is not without *h*, Mt 13:57
glory and *h* and, Ro 2:10
Marriage…*be held* in *h*, Heb 13:4
blessing and *h* and, Rev 5:13

HONOR *(v) show respect*
H your father, Ex 20:12
h the aged, Lv 19:32
who *h* Me I will *h*, 1Sa 2:30
am *h-ed* in the sight, Is 49:5
A son *h-s his* father, Mal 1:6
may be *h-ed* by men, Mt 6:2

h-s Me with…lips, Mt 15:8
does not *h* the Son, Jn 5:23
fear God, *h* the king, 1Pe 2:17

HONORABLE *respectable*
the elder and *h* man, Is 9:15
one vessel for *h* use, Ro 9:21
whatever is *h*, Php 4:8

HOOF *part of animal foot*
which divide the *h*, Lv 11:4
with horns and *h-s*, Ps 69:31
h-s of beasts will, Eze 32:13
tear off their *h-s*, Zec 11:16

HOOK *fastener*
into pruning *h-s*, Is 2:4
My *h* in your nose, Is 37:29
h-s into your jaws, Eze 38:4

HOPE *(n) expectation*
Where now is my *h*, Job 17:15
h of the afflicted, Ps 9:18
My *h* is in You, Ps 39:7
You are my *h*, Ps 71:5
while there is *h*, Pr 19:18
the *h* of Israel, Jer 17:13
our *h* has perished, Eze 37:11
on trial for the *h*, Ac 23:6
h does not disappoint, Ro 5:5
rejoicing in *h*, Ro 12:12
may the God of *h*, Ro 15:13
ought to plow in *h*, 1Co 9:10
now faith, *h*, love, abide, 1Co 13:13
h of righteousness, Gal 5:5
the *h* of His calling, Eph 1:18
the *h* of the gospel, Col 1:23
the *h* of glory, Col 1:27
the *h* of salvation, 1Th 5:8
h of eternal life, Titus 3:7
to a living *h*, 1Pe 1:3
h that is in you, 1Pe 3:15

HOPE *(v) expect with confidence*
I will *h* in Him, Job 13:15
For I *h* in You, Ps 38:15
We *h* for justice, Is 59:11
are *h-ing* for light, Jer 13:16
Gentiles will *h*, Mt 12:21
h-s all things, 1Co 13:7
first to *h* in Christ, Eph 1:12
I *h* in the LORD Jesus, Php 2:19
of *things h-d* for, Heb 11:1
I *h* to come to you, 2Jn 12

HOPE OF GLORY
Christ in you, the *h*, Col 1:27

HOPHNI
Wicked son of Eli, 1Sa 1:3; 2:12–17, 22–25
Prophecy against, 1Sa 2:27–36; 3:11–14
Carries ark into battle; killed, 1Sa 4:1–11

HOR
Mountain of Edom; scene of Aaron's death, Nu 20:22–29; 33:37–39

HORDE *throng*
against Babylon A *h*, Jer 50:9
h-s of grasshoppers, Na 3:17

HOREB
See SINAI
God appears to Moses at, Ex 3:1–22
Water flows from, Ex 17:6
Elijah lodged here 40 days, 1Ki 19:8, 9

HORITE, HORITES
Inhabitants of Mt. Seir, Ge 36:20
Defeated by Chedorlaomer, Ge 14:5, 6
Driven out by Esau's descendants, Ge 36:20–29; Dt 2:12, 22

HORMAH
Destroyed by Israel, Nu 21:1–3

HORN
caught…by his *h-s*, Ge 22:13
h-s of the altar, Ex 29:12
you shall sound a *h*, Lv 25:9
with the ram's *h*, Jos 6:5
h of my salvation, 2Sa 22:3
the *h*, flute, lyre, Da 3:5
it had ten *h-s*, Da 7:7

HORROR *terror*
h overwhelms me, Is 21:4
object of *h*, Jer 49:13
clothed with *h*, Eze 7:27
cup of *h*, Eze 23:33

HORSE *animal*
bites the *h-'s* heels, Ge 49:17
h-s and chariots of, 2Ki 6:17
A *h* is a false hope, Ps 33:17
whip is for the *h*, Pr 26:3
slaves *riding* on *h-s*, Ecc 10:7
behold, a black *h*, Rev 6:5

HORSE GATE
See GATES OF JERUSALEM

HORSEMEN *cavalry, horse rider*
Pharaoh, his *h* and, Ex 14:9
chariots and *h*, 1Ki 10:26
h riding on, Eze 23:12
H charging, Swords, Na 3:3
armies of the *h*, Rev 9:16

HOSANNA *acclamation of praise*
H to the Son of, Mt 21:9
H in the highest, Mk 11:10
H! Blessed is He, Jn 12:13

HOSEA
Son of Beeri, prophet of the northern kingdom, Hos 1:1

HOSHEA
Original name of Joshua, the son of Nun, Dt 32:44; Nu 13:8, 16
——— Israel's last king; usurps throne, 2Ki 15:30
Reigns wickedly; Israel taken to Assyria during reign, 2Ki 17:1–23

HOSPITABLE *friendly*
h, able to teach, 1Ti 3:2
h, loving what is, Titus 1:8
h to one another, 1Pe 4:9

HOSPITALITY *open to guests*
practicing *h*, Ro 12:13
show *h* to strangers, Heb 13:2

HOST *army, multitude*
all the *h* of heaven, Dt 4:19
captain…Lord's *h*, Jos 5:15
LORD of *h-s*, He is, Ps 24:10
of the heavenly *h*, Lk 2:13

HOSTILE *antagonistic*
h to…Jesus, Ac 26:9
set on the flesh is *h*, Ro 8:7
h to all men, 1Th 2:15

HOSTILITY *warfare*
act with *h* against Me, Lv 26:21
because your *h* is, Hos 9:7
endured such *h* by sinners, Heb 12:3
the world is *h* toward God, Jas 4:4

HOT *very warm, violent*
when the sun grew *h*, Ex 16:21
and *h* displeasure, Dt 9:19
My heart was *h* within, Ps 39:3
man walk on *h* coals, Pr 6:28
neither cold nor *h*, Rev 3:15

HOUR *time*
add a *single h* to, Mt 6:27
watch…for one *h*, Mt 26:40
the *h* is at hand, Mt 26:45
ninth *h* Jesus cried, Mk 15:34
save Me from this *h*, Jn 12:27
the *h* has come, Jn 17:1
the *h* of testing, Rev 3:10

HOUSE *home; temple*
born in my *h* is my, Ge 15:3
passed over the *h-s*, Ex 12:27
the *h* of slavery, Ex 20:2
consecrates his *h*, Lv 27:14
as for me and my *h*, Jos 24:15
Set your *h* in order, 2Ki 20:1
h of God forsaken, Ne 13:11
h like the spider's, Job 27:18
Holiness befits Your *h*, Ps 93:5
LORD builds the *h*, Ps 127:1
Wisdom…built her *h*, Pr 9:1
in My *h* of prayer, Is 56:7
O *h* of Israel, Jer 18:6
his *h* on the rock, Mt 7:24
My *h*…a *h* of, Mt 21:13
devour widows' *h-s*, Mk 12:40
guards his own *h*, Lk 11:21
left *h* or wife or, Lk 18:29
In My Father's *h*, Jn 14:2
h not made…hands, 2Co 5:1
h for a holy, 1Pe 2:5

HOUSE OF DAVID
covenant with the *h*, 1Sa 20:16
rebellion against the *h*, 1Ki 12:19
be born to the *h*, Josiah, 1Ki 13:2
The thrones of the *h*, Ps 122:5
key of the *h*, Is 22:22
In the *h* His servant, Lk 1:69

HOUSE OF GOD / LORD
See TEMPLE
h was at Shiloh, Jdg 18:31
all the service of the *h*, 1Ch 28:21
of the LORD filled the *h*, 2Ch 5:14
work on the *h*, Ezr 4:24
in procession to the *h*, Ps 42:4
entered the *h*, and they, Mt 12:4
great priest over the *h*, Heb 10:21

HOUSE OF THE LORD
See LORD'S HOUSE; TABERNACLE
of your soil into the *h*, Ex 23:19
he came into the *h*, 2Sa 12:20
he began to build the *h*, 1Ki 6:1
had finished building the *h*, 1Ki 9:1
dwell in the *h* forever, Ps 23:6

in the *h* all the days, Ps 27:4
Planted in the *h*, Ps 92:13
"Let us go to the *h*.", Ps 122:1
serve by night in the *h*, Ps 134:1
who stand in the *h*, Ps 135:2
mountain of the *h*, Is 2:2
of thanksgiving to the *h*, Jer 17:26
burned the *h*, Jer 52:13
glory…filled the *h*, Eze 44:4
enemy comes against the *h*, Hos 8:1
go out from the *h*, Joel 3:18
mountain of the *h*, Mic 4:1
to the potter in the *h*, Zec 11:13

HOUSEHOLD *family, home*
herds and a great *h*, Ge 26:14
stole the *h* idols, Ge 31:19
each one with his *h*, Ex 1:1
to the ways of her *h*, Pr 31:27
like a head of a *h*, Mt 13:52
are of God's *h*, Eph 2:19
manages his own *h*, 1Ti 3:4
in the *h* of God, 1Ti 3:15

HOUSETOP *roof*
As grass on the *h-s*, 2Ki 19:26
lonely bird on a *h*, Ps 102:7
upon the *h-s*, Mt 10:27
Peter went…the *h*, Ac 10:9

HULDAH
Wife of Shallum, 2Ki 22:14
Foretells Jerusalem's ruin, 2Ki 22:15–17; 2Ch 34:22–25
Exempts Josiah from trouble, 2Ki 22:18–20

HUMBLE *(adj) gentle, modest*
Moses was very *h*, Nu 12:3
h will inherit, Ps 37:11
with the *h* is wisdom, Pr 11:2
H, and mounted on, Zec 9:9
gentle and *h* in, Mt 11:29
along with *h* means, Php 4:12
grace to the *h*, Jas 4:6

HUMBLE *(v) modest*
refuse to *h* yourself, Ex 10:3
He might *h* you, Dt 8:2
h…and pray, 2Ch 7:14
h-s…as this child, Mt 18:4
H yourselves, 1Pe 5:6

HUMBLE YOUR SOULS
shall *h* and not do any, Lv 16:29
rest … that you may *h*, Lv 16:31
shall *h* and present an, Lv 23:27
rest … you shall *h*, Lv 23:32

HUMILIATE *embarrass*
h-d who seek my hurt, Ps 71:24
do not feel *h-d*, Is 54:4
His opponents…*h-d*, Lk 13:17

HUMILIATION *embarrassment*
h has overwhelmed me, Ps 44:15
go away together in *h*, Is 45:16
let our *h* cover us, Jer 3:25
In *h* His judgment, Ac 8:33

HUMILITY *self-abasement*
before honor…*h*, Pr 15:33
with *h* of mind, Php 2:3
clothe…with *h*, 1Pe 5:5

HUNDRED *number; many*
Adam had lived one *h*, Ge 5:3
h of you will chase, Lv 26:8
captains of *h-s*, Nu 31:14
h pieces of money, Jos 24:32
went out by *h-s*, 2Sa 18:4
in groups of *h-s*, Mk 6:40

HUNGER *(n) craving, starvation*
in *h*, in thirst, Dt 28:48
lions…suffer *h*, Ps 34:10
man will suffer *h*, Pr 19:15
h is not satisfied, Is 29:8
faint because of *h*, La 2:19
sleeplessness, in *h*, 2Co 6:5

HUNGER *(v) crave, need food*
the righteous to *h*, Pr 10:3
are those who *h*, Mt 5:6
to Me will not *h*, Jn 6:35
They will *h* no longer, Rev 7:16

HUNGRY *empty, needing food*
let you be *h*, Dt 8:3
people are *h* and, 2Sa 17:29
h soul He has filled, Ps 107:9
If your enemy is *h*, Pr 25:21
when a *h* man dreams, Is 29:8
He then became *h*, Mt 4:2
disciples became *h*, Mt 12:1
For I was *h*, Mt 25:35
if your enemy is *h*, Ro 12:20

HUNT *pursue, seek*
to *h* for game, Ge 27:5
h-s a partridge, 1Sa 26:20
evil *h* the violent, Ps 140:11
H-ed me down like, La 3:52

HUNTER *seeker of game*
Nimrod a mighty *h*, Ge 10:9
became a skillful *h*, Ge 25:27

HUR
Man of Judah; of Caleb's house, 1Ch 2:18–20
Supports Moses' hands, Ex 17:10–12
Aids Aaron, Ex 24:14

HURAM
Master craftsman of Solomon's temple, 1Ki 7:13–40, 45; 2Ch 2:13, 14

HURRY *(n) haste*
Do not be in a *h* to leave him, Ecc 8:3
she came in a *h* to, Mk 6:25
Mary arose and went in a *h*, Lk 1:39
came in a *h* and found their, Lk 2:16

HURRY *(v) act in haste*
H, escape there, Ge 19:22
H, be quick, do not stay!, 1Sa 20:38
H, my beloved, And be, SS 8:14
Zaccheus, *h* and come down, Lk 19:5
h-ing to be in Jerusalem, Ac 20:16

HURT *(n) damage, harm, wound*
Who delight in my *h*, Ps 70:2
hoarded…to his *h*, Ecc 5:13
your brother is *h*, Ro 14:15

HURT *(v) cause pain, wound*
not allow him to *h*, Ge 31:7
may be *h* by them, Ecc 10:9
will not *h* or destroy, Is 11:9
their power to *h* men, Rev 9:10

HUSBAND *family head, spouse*
desire…your *h*, Ge 3:16
honor to their *h-s*, Est 1:20
crown of her *h*, Pr 12:4
is loved by *her h*, Hos 3:1
divorces her *h* and, Mk 10:12
have had five *h-s*, Jn 4:18
if her *h* dies, Ro 7:2
have her own *h*, 1Co 7:2
unbelieving *h* is, 1Co 7:14
h is the head of, Eph 5:23
H-s, love your wives, Eph 5:25
h-s of…one wife, 1Ti 3:12
adorned for her *h*, Rev 21:2

HUSHAI
Archite; David's friend, 2Sa 15:32–37
Feigns sympathy with Absalom, 2Sa 16:16–19
Defeats Ahithophel's advice, 2Sa 17:5–23

HYMENAEUS
False teacher excommunicated by Paul, 1Ti 1:19, 20

HYMN *song of praise*
h-s of thanksgiving, Ne 12:46
after singing a *h*, Mt 26:30
singing *h-s* of praise, Ac 16:25
psalms and *h-s* and, Eph 5:19

HYPOCRISY *pretense*
full of *h* and, Mt 23:28
love be without *h*, Ro 12:9
without *h*, Jas 3:17

HYPOCRITE *a pretender*
as the *h-s* do, Mt 6:2
and Pharisees, *h-s*, Mt 23:13
You *h,* first take, Lk 6:42

HYSSOP *fragrant plant*
bunch of *h* and dip it, Ex 12:22
scarlet string and *h*, Lv 14:4
Purify me with *h*, Ps 51:7
upon *a branch of h*, Jn 19:29

I

I AM
Related to name of God in Hebrew
I WHO I, Ex 3:14
I has sent me, Ex 3:14
I the LORD, Ex 6:2
I the LORD your God, Lv 19:3
I the first, Is 44:6
I the Son of God, Mt 27:43
Jesus said, *I*, Mk 14:62
believe that *I He*, Jn 8:24
will know that *I He*, Jn 8:28
before Abraham…*I*, Jn 8:58
believe that *I He*, Jn 13:19
I the Alpha and, Rev 1:8
I the first and, Rev 1:17

I AM WITH YOU
See I WILL BE WITH YOU
Do not fear, for *I*, Ge 26:24
I and will keep you, Ge 28:15
Do not fear, for *I*, Is 41:10
I to deliver you, Jer 1:19
For *I* to save you, Jer 15:20

and work; for *I*, Hag 2:4
I always, even to the, Mt 28:20
a little while longer *I*, Jn 7:33
I, and no man will attack, Ac 18:10

I WILL BE WITH YOU
See I AM WITH YOU
I and bless you, Ge 26:3
Certainly *I*, Ex 3:12
have been with Moses, *I*, Jos 1:5
I, and you shall defeat, Jdg 6:16
I and build you an, 1Ki 11:38
through the waters, *I*, Is 43:2

IBZAN
Judge of Israel; father of 60 children, Jdg 12:8, 9

ICE *frost*
turbid because of *i*, Job 6:16
womb has come…*i*, Job 38:29
casts forth His *i*, Ps 147:17

ICHABOD
Son of Phinehas, 1Sa 4:19–22

ICONIUM
City of Asia Minor; visited by Paul, Ac 13:51
Many converts in, Ac 14:1–6

IDDO
Leader of Jews at Casiphia, Ezr 8:17–20
——— Seer whose writings are cited, 2Ch 9:29

IDLE *unemployed, uninvolved*
i man will suffer, Pr 19:15
been standing here *i*, Mt 20:6
this *i* babbler, Ac 17:18

IDOL *false deity, image*
not make…an *i*, Ex 20:4
Do not turn to *i-s*, Lv 19:4
who makes an *i* or, Dt 27:15
the gods…are *i-s*, Ps 96:5
who blesses an *i*, Is 66:3
abstain from…*i-s*, Ac 15:20
guard…from *i-s*, 1Jn 5:21

IDOLATER *idol worshiper*
covetous, or an *i*, 1Co 5:11
Do not be *i-s*, 1Co 10:7
sorcerers and *i-s*, Rev 21:8

IDOLATRY *idol worship*
flee from *i*, 1Co 10:14
i, sorcery, enmities, Gal 5:20
and abominable *i-ies*, 1Pe 4:3

IDUMEA
Name used by Greeks and Romans to designate Edom, Mk 3:8

IGNORANCE *lack of knowledge*
you worship in *i*, Ac 17:23
i that is in them, Eph 4:18
silence the *i* of, 1Pe 2:15

IGNORANT *without knowledge*
I was senseless and *i*, Ps 73:22
not *i* of his schemes, 2Co 2:11
and *i* speculations, 2Ti 2:23

IJON
Town of Naphtali; captured by Ben-hadad, 1Ki 15:20
Captured by Tiglath-pileser, 2Ki 15:29

ILL *unhealthy, sick*
woman who is *i*, Lv 15:33
became mortally *i*, Is 38:1
lunatic and is…*i*, Mt 17:15
healed many…*i*, Mk 1:34

ILLEGITIMATE *bastard*
No one of *i* birth, Dt 23:2
borne *i* children, Hos 5:7
you are *i* children, Heb 12:8

ILLNESS *infirmity, sickness*
sick with the *i*, 2Ki 13:14
after his *i* and, Is 38:9
because of a bodily *i*, Gal 4:13

ILLUMINE *light up*
God *i-s* my darkness, Ps 18:28
fire to *i* by night, Ps 105:39
glory of God has *i-d*, Rev 21:23
God will *i* them, Rev 22:5

ILLYRICUM
Paul preaches in, Ro 15:19

IMAGE *copy, likeness*
make man in Our *i*, Ge 1:26
i of God He made, Ge 9:6
burn their graven *i-s*, Dt 7:5
worshiped a molten *i*, Ps 106:19
made an *i* of gold, Da 3:1
i and glory of God, 1Co 11:7
i of the invisible, Col 1:15
the *i* of the beast, Rev 13:15

IMITATORS *followers*
be *i* of me, 1Co 4:16
be *i* of God, Eph 5:1
i of the churches, 1Th 2:14

IMMANUEL
Son born to a virgin, Is 7:14
A sign to King Ahaz, Is 8:8
——— Title of Jesus, Mt 1:23

IMMORAL *lewd, unchaste*
with *i* people, 1Co 5:9
the *i* man sins, 1Co 6:18
i men…liars, 1Ti 1:10
i or godless person, Heb 12:16
and *i* persons, Rev 21:8

IMMORALITY *immoral acts*
no *i* in your midst, Lv 20:14
except for *i*, Mt 19:9
Flee *i*, 1Co 6:18
abstain from…*i*, 1Th 4:3
the wine of her *i*, Rev 17:2

IMMORTALITY *everlasting life*
must put on *i*, 1Co 15:53
alone possesses *i*, 1Ti 6:16
life and *i* to light, 2Ti 1:10

IMPATIENT *restless*
the people became *i*, Nu 21:4
should I not be *i*, Job 21:4
my soul was *i* with, Zec 11:8

IMPERISHABLE *indestructible*
wreath, but we an *i*, 1Co 9:25
will be raised *i*, 1Co 15:52
inheritance…*is i*, 1Pe 1:4

IMPLEMENTS *tools, utensils*
forger of all *i* of, Ge 4:22
the *i* of the oxen, 1Ki 19:21

IMPLORE *ask, beseech, entreat*
I *i* you, give glory, Jos 7:19
i-d him to avert, Est 8:3
i the compassion of, Job 8:5
centurion…*i-ing* Him, Mt 8:5
I *i* You by God, Mk 5:7
They were *i-ing* Him, Lk 8:31
I *i-d* the Lord, 2Co 12:8
i you to walk in a, Eph 4:1

IMPORTED *brought in*
chariot was *i* from, 1Ki 10:29
horses were *i*, 2Ch 1:16

IMPOSE *force upon*
i-d hard labor on us, Dt 26:6
whatever you *i* on, 2Ki 18:14
you *i* heavy rent, Am 5:11
i-d until a time of, Heb 9:10

IMPOSSIBLE *cannot be done*
nothing…will be *i*, Ge 11:6
With people this is *i*, Mt 19:26
i for God to lie, Heb 6:18
without faith it is *i*, Heb 11:6

IMPRISON *jail, restrict*
i-ed him at Riblah, 2Ki 23:33
i his princes at will, Ps 105:22
not *i* their survivors, Ob 14
I used to *i* and beat, Ac 22:19

IMPRISONMENT *confinement*
in *i-s*, in tumults, 2Co 6:5
Remember my *i*, Col 4:18
even to *i* as a, 2Ti 2:9

IMPURE *unclean*
her *i* discharge, Lv 15:25
eating…with *i* hands, Mk 7:2
no immoral or *i* person, Eph 5:5

IMPURITY *uncleanness*
menstrual *i* for seven, Lv 15:19
i-ies of the sons of, Lv 16:19
the *i* of the nations, Ezr 6:21
as slaves to *i*, Ro 6:19
of *i* with greediness, Eph 4:19

IN MY NAME
he shall speak *i*, Dt 18:19
i his horn will be exalted, Ps 89:24
prophesying falsehood *i*, Jer 14:14
receives one such child *i*, Mt 18:5
have gathered together *i*, Mt 18:20
perform a miracle *i*, Mk 9:39
Many will come *i*, Mk 13:6
Whatever you ask *i*, Jn 14:13
ask Me anything *i*, Jn 14:14

IN THE WORLD
Rejoicing *i*, Pr 8:31
He was *i*, and the world, Jn 1:10
While I am *i*, Jn 9:5
His own who were *i*, Jn 13:1
I you have tribulation, Jn 16:33

I am no longer *i*, Jn 17:11
until the Law sin was *i*, Ro 5:13
conducted ourselves *i*, 2Co 1:12
and without God *i*, Eph 2:12
you appear as lights *i*, Php 2:15
Believed on *i*, 1Ti 3:16
brethren who are *i*., 1Pe 5:9
nor the things *i*, 1Jn 2:15
than he who is *i*, 1Jn 4:4

INCENSE *fragrant substance*
burn fragrant *i* on, Ex 30:7
i as an offering, Lv 2:16
gold pans, full of *i*, Nu 7:86
My altar, to burn *i*, 1Sa 2:28
i on the high places, 2Ki 14:4
i before the LORD, 1Ch 23:13
golden altar of *i*, Heb 9:4
the smoke of the *i*, Rev 8:4

INCEST *illicit sexual relations*
they...committed *i*, Lv 20:12

INCITE *stir up*
i-d David against, 2Sa 24:1
Jezebel...*i-d* him, 1Ki 21:25
I will *i* Egyptians, Is 19:2
who *i-s* the people, Lk 23:14
Jews *i-d* the devout, Ac 13:50

INCLINE *bend, lean*
i your hearts to, Jos 24:23
I my heart to Your, Ps 119:36
i-s toward wickedness, Is 32:6
I Your ear, O LORD, Is 37:17
have not *i-d* your ear, Jer 35:15

INCOME *wages*
i of the wicked, Pr 10:16
i with injustice, Pr 16:8
abundance *with its i*, Ecc 5:10

INCORRUPTIBLE *not impure*
glory of the *i* God, Ro 1:23
Christ with *i love*, Eph 6:24

INCREASE *(n) multiplication*
the *i* of your herd, Dt 7:13
the *i* of your house, 1Sa 2:33
the LORD give you *i*, Ps 115:14
i of *His* government, Is 9:7

INCREASE *(v) multiply*
If riches *i*, do not, Ps 62:10
the righteous *i*, Pr 28:28
i-ing in wisdom, Lk 2:52
i-ing in...knowledge, Col 1:10
Lord cause...to *i*, 1Th 3:12

INCURABLE *fatal, without cure*
with an *i* sickness, 2Ch 21:18
sickliness and *i* pain, Is 17:11
Your wound is *i*, Jer 30:12

INDIA
Eastern limit of Persian Empire, Est 1:1

INDIGNANT *be angry*
i toward His enemies, Is 66:14
the ten became *i*, Mt 20:24
Jesus...was *i*, Mk 10:14
i because Jesus had, Lk 13:14

INDIGNATION *anger*
God who has *i*, Ps 7:11
Pour out Your *i*, Ps 69:24
lips are filled with *i*, Is 30:27
filled me with *i*, Jer 15:17
stand before His *i*, Na 1:6

INFANT *child*
carries a nursing *i*, Nu 11:12
an *i who lives*, Is 65:20
tongue of the *i*, La 4:4
the mouth of *i-s*, Mt 21:16
as to *i-s* in Christ, 1Co 3:1

INFECTION *disease*
an *i* of leprosy, Lv 13:2
with the scaly *i*, Lv 13:31
against an *i* of, Dt 24:8

INFERIOR *lower in status*
I am not *i* to you, Job 12:3
i against the honorable, Is 3:5
i to...apostles, 2Co 11:12

INFINITE *unlimited*
His understanding is *i*, Ps 147:5

INFLICT *strike, impose*
frogs...He had *i-ed*, Ex 8:12
i all these curses, Dt 30:7
i-s pain, and gives, Job 5:18

INGATHERING, FEAST OF
See FEASTS

INHABIT *dwell*
no one would *i*, Job 15:28
She shall be *i-ed*, Is 44:26
build houses and *i*, Is 65:21
those *i-ing* the desert, Jer 9:26
who *i* the coastlands, Eze 39:6
but not *i them*, Zep 1:13

INHABITANT *resident*
i-s of the cities, Ge 19:25
cities...without *i*, Is 6:11
ruins Without *i*, Jer 4:7
i-s of the seacoast, Zep 2:5
i-s of Jerusalem, Zec 12:10

INHERIT *receive a legacy*
shall *i it* forever, Ex 32:13
humble will *i* the land, Ps 37:11
wise will *i* honor, Pr 3:35
The naive *i* foolishness, Pr 14:18
gentle...*i* the earth, Mt 5:5
do to *i* eternal life, Lk 10:25
not *i* the kingdom, 1Co 6:9
might *i* a blessing, 1Pe 3:9
who overcomes will *i*, Rev 21:7

INHERITANCE *bequest, legacy*
Levites for an *i*, Nu 18:24
the LORD is his *i*, Dt 10:9
the nations as Your *i*, Ps 2:8
will He forsake His *i*, Ps 94:14
man leaves an *i*, Pr 13:22
I...abandoned My *i*, Jer 12:7
Your *i* a reproach, Joel 2:17
A man and his *i*, Mic 2:2
the *i* will be ours, Mk 12:7
we...obtained an *i*, Eph 1:11
the *i* of the saints, Col 1:12
i...imperishable, 1Pe 1:4

INIQUITY *injustice, wickedness*
bear...their *i-ies*, Lv 16:22
the *i* of the fathers, Dt 5:9
those who plow *i*, Job 4:8
O LORD, Pardon my *i*, Ps 25:11
my *i* I did not hide, Ps 32:5
blot out all my *i-ies*, Ps 51:9
sows *i* will reap, Pr 22:8
weighed down with *i*, Is 1:4
the workers of *i*, Is 31:2
die for his own *i*, Jer 31:30
Repent...so that *i*, Eze 18:30
the bondage of *i*, Ac 8:23
the *very* world of *i*, Jas 3:6
remembered her *i-ies*, Rev 18:5

INJUNCTION *decree*
establish the *i*, Da 6:8
that no *i* or statute, Da 6:15

INJURE *harm, wrong*
who seek to *i* me, Ps 38:12
i-d your neighbors, Eze 22:12
nothing will *i* you, Lk 10:19
do you *i* one another, Ac 7:26

INJURY *wound*
there is no *further i*, Ex 21:22
because of my *i*, Jer 10:19
no *i*...was found, Da 6:23

INJUSTICE *inequity, unfairness*
do no *i* in judgment, Lv 19:15
A God...without *i*, Dt 32:4
there *i* on my tongue, Job 6:30
They devise *i-s*, Ps 64:6
is no *i* with God, Ro 9:14

INK *writing liquid*
I wrote them with *i*, Jer 36:18
with pen and *i*, 3Jn 13

INN *lodge for travelers*
no room...in the *i*, Lk 2:7
brought him to...*i*, Lk 10:34

INNKEEPER *traveler's host*
gave them to the *i*, Lk 10:35

INNOCENCE *blamelessness*
wash my hands in *i*, Ps 26:6
be incapable of *i*, Hos 8:5

INNOCENT *blameless*
do not kill the *i*, Ex 23:7
the blood of the *i*, Dt 19:13
i before the LORD, 2Sa 3:28
the *i* mock them, Job 22:19
that shed *i* blood, Pr 6:17
and *i* as doves, Mt 10:16
betraying *i* blood, Mt 27:4
i of this Man's, Mt 27:24
holy, *i*, undefiled, Heb 7:26

INNOCENT BLOOD
i will not be shed, Dt 19:10
will you sin against *i*, 1Sa 19:5
And shed *i*, Ps 106:38
hands that shed *i*, Pr 6:17
do not shed *i*, Jer 7:6
sinned by betraying *i*, Mt 27:4

INQUIRE *ask, seek*
to *i* of the LORD, Ge 25:22
I of God, please, Jdg 18:5
David *i-d* of...Lord, 1Sa 23:2
you come to *i* of Me, Eze 20:3

i-d...where the Messiah, Mt 2:4
i-d of them the hour, Jn 4:52

INSANE *mad*
a demon and is *i*, Jn 10:20
I speak as if *i*, 2Co 11:23

INSCRIBE *carve, write*
were *i-d* in a book, Job 19:23
i it on a scroll, Is 30:8
and *i* a city on it, Eze 4:1
i it on tablets, Hab 2:2

INSCRIPTION *writing*
could not read the *i*, Da 5:8
I will engrave an *i*, Zec 3:9
Pilate...wrote an *i*, Jn 19:19
i, To An Unknown, Ac 17:23

INSECTS
all other winged *i*, Lv 11:23

INSIGHT *discernment*
a counselor with *i*, 1Ch 26:14
according to his *i*, Pr 12:8
i with understanding, Da 9:22
not gained any *i*, Mk 6:52
In all wisdom and *i*, Eph 1:8

INSIGNIFICANT *unimportant*
was *i* in Your eyes, 2Sa 7:19
your beginning was *i*, Job 8:7
citizen of no *i* city, Ac 21:39

INSOLENT *arrogant*
acts with *i* pride, Pr 21:24
haters of God, *i*, Ro 1:30

INSPECTION GATE
See GATES OF JERUSALEM

INSPIRED *stimulated*
the love we *i* in you, 2Co 8:7
All Scripture is *i*, 2Ti 3:16

INSTANT *point of time*
comes suddenly in an *i*, Is 30:13
in an *i* I will make him run, Jer 49:19

INSTANTLY *immediately*
I may consume them *i*, Nu 16:21
I he will be broken and, Pr 6:15
And it will happen *i*, Is 29:5

INSTINCT *natural tendency*
as creatures of *i*, 2Pe 2:12
they know by *i*, Jude 10

INSTRUCT *teach*
Your good Spirit to *i*, Ne 9:20
I will *i* you, Ps 32:8
the wise is *i-ed*, Pr 21:11
i-ed out of the Law, Ro 2:18
just as you were *i-ed*, Col 2:7
may *i* certain men, 1Ti 1:3

INSTRUCTION *teaching*
will walk in My *i*, Ex 16:4
Heed *i* and be wise, Pr 8:33
Get wisdom and *i*, Pr 23:23
i-s to His twelve, Mt 11:1
written for our *i*, Ro 15:4
i of the Lord, Eph 6:4
goal of our *i* is love, 1Ti 1:5
i about washings, Heb 6:2

INSTRUMENT *object, vessel*
cut...with sharp *i-s*, 1Ch 20:3
and *i-s* of music, 2Ch 5:13
with stringed *i-s*, Ps 150:4
he is a chosen *i*, Ac 9:15
i-s of unrighteousness, Ro 6:13

INSULT *(n) affront, indignity*
i-s of the nations, Eze 34:29
evil, or *i* for *i*, 1Pe 3:9

INSULT *(v) treat with scorn*
and do not *i* her, Ru 2:15
to *i* the LORD, 2Ch 32:17
times you have *i-ed*, Job 19:3
i-ing...with the same words, Mt 27:44
and *i* you, Lk 6:22
i-ed the Spirit of, Heb 10:29

INTEGRITY *honesty*
In the *i* of my heart, Ge 20:5
dealt in truth and *i*, Jdg 9:19
holds fast his *i*, Job 2:3
He who walks with *i*, Ps 15:2
have walked in my *i*, Ps 26:1
The *i* of the upright, Pr 11:3

INTELLIGENCE *mental ability*
He deprives of *i*, Job 12:24
gave them...*i*, Da 1:17
Paulus, a man of *i*, Ac 13:7

INTELLIGENT *bright, smart*
was *i* and beautiful, 1Sa 25:3
mind of the *i* seeks, Pr 15:14
from *the* wise and *i*, Mt 11:25

INTEND *purpose*
Are you *i-ing* to kill, Ex 2:14
I *i* to build a house, 1Ki 5:5
i to make My people, Jer 23:27
i-ing to betray Him, Jn 12:4
i-ing...to take Paul, Ac 20:13

INTENTION *aim, goal*
the *i-s* of the heart, 1Ch 29:18
i of your heart, Ac 8:22
kind *i* of His will, Eph 1:5

INTERCEDE *plead, mediate*
i-d for the people, Nu 21:7
who can *i* for him, 1Sa 2:25
And *i-d* for the, Is 53:12
do not *i* with Me, Jer 7:16
Spirit Himself *i-s*, Ro 8:26

INTERCOURSE *copulation*
not have *i* with, Lv 18:20
not have *i*...animal, Lv 18:23
husband has had *i*, Nu 5:20

INTEREST *concern; usury*
not charge him *i*, Ex 22:25
not take usurious *i*, Lv 25:36
i to a foreigner, Dt 23:20
his money at *i*, Ps 15:5
mind on God's *i-s*, Mt 16:23
money...with *i*, Mt 25:27
he has a morbid *i*, 1Ti 6:4

INTERMARRY
I with us, Ge 34:9
shall not *i* with, Dt 7:3
i with the peoples, Ezr 9:14

INTERPRET *explain, translate*
no one who could *i*, Ge 41:8
one who *i-s* omens, Dt 18:10
He *i* the message, Is 28:9
unless he *i-s*, 1Co 14:5
pray that he may *i*, 1Co 14:13

INTERPRETATION *explain*
i-s belong to God, Ge 40:8
the dream and its *i*, Jdg 7:15
make its *i* known, Da 5:16
the *i* of tongues, 1Co 12:10
of one's own *i*, 2Pe 1:20

INTIMATE *close*
my *i* friends have, Job 19:14
i with the upright, Pr 3:32
separates *i* friends, Pr 16:28

INTIMATELY *sexually; personally*
who has known man *i*, Nu 31:17
who have not known man *i*, Nu 31:18
i acquainted with all my, Ps 139:3

INVADE *attack*
king of Assyria *i-d*, 2Ki 17:5
nation has *i-d* my land, Joel 1:6
Assyrian *i-s* our land, Mic 5:5

INVALIDATE *nullify*
i-d the word of God, Mt 15:6
i-ing the word of, Mk 7:13
does not *i* a covenant, Gal 3:17

INVESTIGATE *examine*
the judges shall *i*, Dt 19:18
the plot was *i-d*, Est 2:23
i, and to seek wisdom, Ecc 7:25
having *i-d* everything, Lk 1:3

INVISIBLE *unseen*
His *i* attributes, Ro 1:20
image of the *i* God, Col 1:15
visible and *i*, Col 1:16
eternal, immortal, *i*, 1Ti 1:17

INVITE *request*
i-d us to impoverish, Jdg 14:15
you shall *i* Jesse, 1Sa 16:3
i-d all the king's, 2Sa 13:23
I am *i-d* by her, Est 5:12
did not *i* Me in, Mt 25:43
i the poor, Lk 14:13

IRON *metal*
was an *i* bedstead, Dt 3:11
whose stones are *i*, Dt 8:9
had *i* chariots, Jdg 1:19
made the *i* float, 2Ki 6:6
break them...rod of *i*, Ps 2:9
from the *i* furnace, Jer 11:4
as strong as *i*, Da 2:40
rule...rod of *i*, Rev 19:15

ISAAC
Promised heir of the covenant, Ge 17:16–21
Born and circumcised, Ge 21:1–7
Offered up as a sacrifice, Ge 22:1–19
Marries Rebekah, Ge 24:62–67
Prays for children; prefers Esau, Ge 25:21–28
Dealings with Abimelech, king of Gerar, Ge 26:1–31
Mistakenly blesses Jacob, Ge 27:1–28:5

Dies in his old age, Ge 35:28, 29
NT references to, Lk 3:34; Gal 4:21–31; Heb 11:9, 20

ISAIAH
Prophet during reigns of Uzziah, Jotham, Ahaz and Hezekiah, Is 1:1
Responds to prophetic call, Is 6:1–13
Prophesies to Hezekiah, 2Ki 19; 20
Writes Uzziah's biography, 2Ch 26:22
Writes Hezekiah's biography, 2Ch 32:32
Quoted in NT, Mt 1:22, 23; 3:3; 8:17; 12:17–21; Lk 4:17–19; Ac 13:34; Ro 9:27, 29; 10:16, 20, 21; 11:26, 27; 15:12; 1Pe 2:22

ISCARIOT, JUDAS
Listed among the Twelve, Mk 3:14, 19; Lk 6:16
Criticizes Mary, Jn 12:3–6
Identified as betrayer, Jn 13:21–30
Takes money to betray Christ, Mt 26:14–16
Betrays Christ with a kiss, Mk 14:43–45
Repents and commits suicide, Mt 27:3–10
His place filled, Ac 1:15–26

ISH-BOSHETH
One of Saul's sons; made king, 2Sa 2:8–10
Offends Abner, 2Sa 3:7–11
Slain; his assassins executed, 2Sa 4:1–12

ISHMAEL
Abram's son by Hagar, Ge 16:3, 4, 11–16
Circumcised, Ge 17:25
Scoffs at Isaac's feast; exiled with his mother, Ge 21:8–21
His sons; his death, Ge 25:12–18
——— Son of Nethaniah; kills Gedaliah, 2Ki 25:22–26

ISHMAELITE, ISMAELITES
Settle at Havilah, Ge 25:17, 18
Joseph sold to, Ge 37:25–28
Sell Joseph to Potiphar, Ge 39:1

ISLAND *surrounded by water*
the many *i-s* be glad, Ps 97:1
He lifts up the *i-s*, Is 40:15
i was called Malta, Ac 28:1
every *i* fled away, Rev 16:20

ISOLATE *set apart*
priest shall *i him*, Lv 13:4
i him for seven days, Lv 13:21
fortified city is *i-d*, Is 27:10

ISRAEL
Jacob, Ge 32:28–32; 35:10; 37:3
——— Line of Jacob, Ge 34:7
Tribal nation, Ex 1:7; 4:22; Nu 10:29
——— United kingdom, 1Sa 15:35; 1Ki 4:1
——— Northern kingdom, 1Ki 14:19; 15:9; 2Ki 10:29
——— Under Roman rule, Lk 2:32; Jn 1:49; Ro 9:6

ISRAELITES
Afflicted in Egypt, Ex 1:12–22
Escape from Egypt, Ex 12:29–42, 50; 13:17–22
Receive law at Sinai, Ex 19
Idolatry and rebellion of, Ex 32; Nu 13; 14
Wander in the wilderness, Nu 14:26–39
Cross Jordan; conquer Canaan, Jos 4; 12
Ruled by judges, Jdg 2
Saul chosen as king, 1Sa 10
Kingdom divided, 1Ki 12
Northern kingdom carried captive, 2Ki 17
Southern kingdom carried captive, 2Ki 24
70 years in exile, 2Ch 36:20, 21
Return after exile, Ezr 1:1–5
Nation rejects Christ, Mt 27:20–27
Nation destroyed, Lk 21:20–24

ISSACHAR
Jacob's fifth son, Ge 30:17, 18
——— Tribe of:
Genealogy of, 1Ch 7:1–5
Prophecy concerning, Ge 49:14, 15
Census at Sinai, Nu 1:28, 29
Inheritance of, Jos 19:17–23

ISSUE *(n) outflow, out go*
first *i* of the womb, Nu 3:12
offspring and *i*, Is 22:24
like the *i* of horses, Eze 23:20
concerning this *i*, Ac 15:2

ISSUE *(v) go forth, put forth*
Moses *i-d* a command, Ex 36:6
shall *i* from you, 2Ki 20:18
decree was *i-d* at, Est 3:15
i-d a proclamation, Da 5:29

IT IS WRITTEN
as *i* in the book of the law, Jos 8:31
i in this book of the, 2Ki 23:21
as *i* in the law of Moses, Ezr 3:2
scroll of the book *i* of me, Ps 40:7
"*I*, 'Man shall not live, Mt 4:4
i, 'Behold, I send My, Mt 11:10
"*I*, 'My house shall be, Mt 21:13
i, 'I will strike down the, Mt 26:31
i: 'This people honors Me, Mk 7:6
"*I*, 'You shall worship the, Lk 4:8
i, that the Christ would, Lk 24:46
For *i* in the book of Psalms, Ac 1:20
i, "But the righteous man, Ro 1:17
i, "There is none righteous, Ro 3:10
i, "Jacob I loved, but Esau, Ro 9:13
i, "How beautiful are the, Ro 10:15
i, "I will destroy the, 1Co 1:19
as *i*, "Let him who boasts, 1Co 1:31
i, "You shall be holy, 1Pe 1:16

ITALY
Jews expelled from, Ac 18:2
Paul sails for, Ac 27:1, 6
Christians in, Ac 28:14

ITHAMAR
Youngest son of Aaron, Ex 6:23
Consecrated as priest, Ex 28:1
Duty entrusted to, Ex 38:21
Jurisdiction over Gershonites and Merarites, Nu 4:21–33

ITURAEA
Region ruled by Herod Philip, Lk 3:1

IVORY *elephant tusk*
a great throne of *i*, 1Ki 10:18
silver, *i* and apes, 2Ch 9:21
Out of *i* palaces, Ps 45:8
every article of *i*, Rev 18:12

J

JABBOK
River entering the Jordan about 20 miles north of the Dead Sea, Nu 21:24
Scene of Jacob's conflict, Ge 32:22–32
Boundary marker, Dt 3:16

JABESH-GILEAD
Consigned to destruction, Jdg 21:8–15
Saul defeats the Ammonites at, 1Sa 11:1–11
Citizens of, rescue Saul's body, 1Sa 31:11–13
David thanks citizens of, 2Sa 2:4–7

JABEZ
City where scribes lived, 1Ch 2:55
——— A man of high character, 1Ch 4:9, 10

JABIN
Canaanite king of Hazor; leads confederacy against Joshua, Jos 11:1–14
——— Another king of Hazor; oppresses Israelites, Jdg 4:2
Defeated by Deborah and Barak, Jdg 4:3–24
Immortalized in poetry, Jdg 5:1–31

JACHIN
One of two pillars in front of Solomon's temple, 1Ki 7:21, 22

JACINTH *precious stone*
a *j*, an agate, Ex 28:19
the eleventh, *j*, Rev 21:20

JACKALS *wild dogs*
j in their...palaces, Is 13:22
ruins, A haunt of *j*, Jer 9:11
a lament like the *j*, Mic 1:8

JACOB
Son of Isaac and Rebekah; Rebekah's favorite, Ge 25:21–28
Obtains birthright, Ge 25:29–34
Obtains blessing meant for Esau; flees, Ge 27:1–28:5
Sees vision of ladder, Ge 28:10–22
Serves Laban for Rachel and Leah, Ge 29:1–30
Fathers children, Ge 29:31–30:24
Flees from, makes covenant with Laban, Ge 30:25–31:55
Makes peace with Esau, Ge 32:1–21; 33:1–17
Wrestles with God, Ge 32:22–32
Returns to Bethel; renamed Israel, Ge 35:1–15
Shows preference for Joseph, Ge 37:3
Mourns Joseph's disappearance, Ge 37:32–35
Sends sons to Egypt for food, Ge 42:1–5
Reluctantly allows Benjamin to go, Ge 43:1–15
Moves his household to Egypt, Ge 45:25–47:12
Blesses his sons and grandsons; dies, Ge 48; 49

Buried in Canaan, Ge 50:1–14

JACOB'S WELL
J was there, Jn 4:6

JAEL
Wife of Heber the Kenite; kills Sisera, Jdg 4:17–22
Praised by Deborah, Jdg 5:24–27

JAIL *place of confinement*
put him into the *j*, Ge 39:20
in *j* in the house, Jer 37:15
put them in…*j*, Ac 5:18

JAILER *warden*
sight of the chief *j*, Ge 39:21
chief *j* did not, Ge 39:23
the *j* to guard them, Ac 16:23

JAIR
Manassite warrior; conquers towns in Gilead, Nu 32:41; Dt 3:14
——— Eighth judge of Israel, Jdg 10:3–5

JAIRUS
Ruler of the synagogue; Jesus raises his daughter, Mk 5:22–24, 35–43

JAMES
Son of Zebedee, called as disciple, Mt 4:21, 22; Lk 5:10, 11
One of the Twelve, Mt 10:2; Mk 3:17
Zealous for the Lord, Lk 9:52–54
Ambitious for honor, Mk 10:35–45
Witnesses Transfiguration, Mt 17:1–9
Martyred by Herod Agrippa, Ac 12:2
——— Son of Alphaeus; one of the Twelve, Mt 10:3, 4
Called "the Less," Mk 15:40
——— Jesus' half brother, Mt 13:55, 56; Gal 1:19
Becomes leader of Jerusalem Council and Jerusalem church, Ac 15:13–22; Gal 2:9
Author of an epistle, Jas 1:1

JANNES AND JAMBRES
Two Egyptian magicians; oppose Moses, Ex 7:11–22; 2Ti 3:8

JANOAH
Town of Naphtali, 2Ki 15:29

JAPHETH
One of Noah's three sons, Ge 5:32
Receives blessing, Ge 9:20–27
His descendants occupy Asia Minor and Europe, Ge 10:2–5

JAR *container, jug*
and a *j* of honey, 1Ki 14:3
Bring me a new *j*, 2Ki 2:20
potter's earthenware *j*, Jer 19:1
j full of sour wine, Jn 19:29

JARED
Father of Enoch, Ge 5:15–20
Ancestor of Noah, 1Ch 1:2
Ancestor of Christ, Lk 3:37

JASHAR
Book quoted in Bible, Jos 10:13; 2Sa 1:18

JASON
Welcomes Paul at Thessalonica, Ac 17:5–9
Described as Paul's kinsman, Ro 16:21

JASPER *precious stone*
fourth row…a *j*, Ex 28:20
the onyx, and the *j*, Eze 28:13
was like a *j* stone, Rev 4:3
of crystal-clear *j*, Rev 21:11

JAVAN
Son of Japheth, Ge 10:2, 4
Descendants of, to receive good news, Is 66:19, 20

JAVELIN *spear*
Stretch out the *j*, Jos 8:18
j slung between his, 1Sa 17:6
flashing spear and *j*, Job 39:23
seize *their*…*j*, Jer 50:42

JAW *part of face*
j-s of the wicked, Job 29:17
cleaves to my *j-s*, Ps 22:15
j teeth *like* knives, Pr 30:14
hooks into your *j-s*, Eze 38:4

JAWBONE
j of a donkey, Jdg 15:15
threw the *j* from, Jdg 15:17

JEALOUS *envious, zealous*
brothers were *j* of, Ge 37:11
your God, am a *j* God, Ex 20:5
whose name is *J*, is, Ex 34:14
j with My jealousy, Nu 25:11
He is a *j* God, Jos 24:19
j and avenging God, Na 1:2
j for Jerusalem, Zec 1:14
Jews, becoming *j*, Ac 17:5
I will make you *j*, Ro 10:19
love is kind…not *j*, 1Co 13:4

JEALOUSY *envy; demanding exclusive loyalty*
spirit of *j* comes over him, Nu 5:14
This is the law of *j*, Nu 5:29
they provoked Him to *j*, 1Ki 14:22
And *j* kills the simple, Job 5:2
aroused His *j* with their, Ps 78:58
For *j* enrages a man, Pr 6:34
I have spoken in My *j*, Eze 36:6
and they were filled with *j*, Ac 5:17
I might move to *j* my, Ro 11:14
there is *j* and strife among, 1Co 3:3
you with a godly *j*, 2Co 11:2
sorcery, enmities, strife, *j*, Gal 5:20
where *j* and selfish ambition, Jas 3:16

JEBUS
Canaanite name of Jerusalem before captured by David, 1Ch 11:4–8

JEBUSITES
Descendants of Canaan, Ge 15:18–21; Nu 13:29
Defeated by Joshua, Jos 11:1–12
Not driven from Jerusalem; later conquered by David, Jdg 1:21; 2Sa 5:6–8
Put to forced labor under Solomon, 1Ki 9:20, 21

JECONIAH
See JEHOIACHIN
Variant form of Jehoiachin, 1Ch 3:16, 17
Abbreviated to Coniah, Jer 22:24, 28

JEDIDIAH
Name given to Solomon by Nathan, 2Sa 12:24, 25

JEDUTHUN
Levite musician appointed by David, 1Ch 16:41, 42
Heads a family of musicians, 2Ch 5:12
Name appears in Psalm titles, Ps 39; 62; 77

JEGAR-SAHADUTHA
Name given by Laban to memorial stones, Ge 31:46, 47

JEHOAHAZ
Son and successor of Jehu, king of Israel, 2Ki 10:35
Seeks the LORD in defeat, 2Ki 13:2–9
——— Son and successor of Josiah, king of Judah, 2Ki 23:30–34
Called Shallum, 1Ch 3:15
——— Another form of Ahaziah, youngest son of King Joram, 2Ch 21:17

JEHOASH
See JOASH

JEHOIACHIN
Son of Jehoiakim; next to the last king of Judah, 2Ki 24:8
Deported to Babylon, 2Ki 24:8–16
Liberated by Evil-Merodach, Jer 52:31–34

JEHOIADA
High priest during reign of Joash, 2Ki 11:4–12:16
Instructs Joash, 2Ki 12:2

JEHOIAKIM
Wicked king of Judah; son of Josiah; serves Pharaoh and Nebuchadnezzar, 2Ki 23:34–24:7
Taken captive to Babylon, 2Ch 36:6–8
Kills prophet Urijah, Jer 26:20–23
Destroys Jeremiah's scroll; cursed by God, Jer 36

JEHORAM (or Joram)
Wicked king of Judah; son of Jehoshaphat, 2Ki 8:16–24
Marries Athaliah, 2Ki 8:18, 19
Kills his brothers, 2Ch 21:2, 4
Elijah prophesies against him; prophecy fulfilled, 2Ch 21:12–20
——— Wicked king of Israel; son of Ahab, 2Ki 3:1–3
Counseled by Elisha, 2Ki 3; 5:8; 6:8–12
Wounded in battle, 2Ki 8:28, 29
Killed by Jehu, 2Ki 9:14–26

JEHOSHAPHAT
Righteous king of Judah; son of Asa, 1Ki 22:41–50
Goes to war with Ahab against Syria, 1Ki 22:1–36
Institutes reforms; sends out teachers of the Law, 2Ch 17:6–9; 19
His enemies defeated through his faith, 2Ch 20:1–30

JEHOZABAD
Son of a Moabitess; assassinates Joash, 2Ki 12:20, 21
Put to death, 2Ch 25:3

JEHOZADAK
Carried into exile, 1Ch 6:15
Father of Joshua the high priest, Hag 1:1

JEHU
Prophet; denounces Baasha, 1Ki 16:1–7
Rebukes Jehoshaphat, 2Ch 19:2, 3
——— Commander under Ahab; anointed king, 1Ki 19:16; 2Ki 9:1–13
Destroys the house of Ahab, 2Ki 9:14–10:30
Turns away from the LORD; dies, 2Ki 10:31–36

JEHUDI
Reads Jeremiah's scroll, Jer 36:14, 21, 23

JEPHTHAH
Gilead's son by a harlot, Jdg 11:1
Driven out, then brought back to command army against Ammonites, Jdg 11:2–28
Sacrifices his daughter to fulfill a vow, Jdg 11:29–40
Chastises Ephraim, Jdg 12:1–7

JEREMIAH
Prophet under Josiah, Jehoiakim, and Zedekiah, Jer 1:1–3
Called by God, Jer 1:4–9
Forbidden to marry, Jer 16:2
Imprisoned by Pashhur, Jer 20:1–6
Prophecy written, destroyed, rewritten, Jer 36
Accused of defection and imprisoned; released by Zedekiah, Jer 37
Cast into dungeon; rescued; prophesies to Zedekiah, Jer 38
Set free by Nebuchadnezzar, Jer 39:11–40:6
Forcibly taken to Egypt, Jer 43:5–7

JERICHO
City near the Jordan, Nu 22:1
Called the city of palm trees, Dt 34:3; 2Ch 28:15
Miraculously defeated by Joshua, Jos 6
Rebuilt by Hiel, 1Ki 16:34
Visited by Jesus, Mt 20:29–34; Lk 19:1–10

JEROBOAM
Son of Nebat; receives prophecy that he will be king, 1Ki 11:26–40
Made king; leads revolt against Rehoboam, 1Ki 12:1–24
Sets up idols, 1Ki 12:25–33
Rebuked by a man of God, 1Ki 13:1–10
Judgment on house of, 1Ki 13:33–14:20
——— Wicked king of Israel; son of Joash; successful in war, 2Ki 14:23–29
Prophecy concerning, by Amos, Am 7:7–13

JERUBBAAL
Name given to Gideon for destroying Baal's altar, Jdg 6:32

JERUSALEM
Originally called Salem, Ge 14:18
Jebusite city, Jos 15:8; Jdg 1:8, 21
King of, defeated by Joshua, Jos 10:5–23
Conquered by David; made capital, 2Sa 5:6–9
Ark brought to, 2Sa 6:12–17; 1Ki 8:1–13
Saved from plague, 2Sa 24:16
Temple built and dedicated here, 1Ki 6; 8:14–66
Suffers in war, 1Ki 14:25–27; 2Ki 14:13, 14; Is 7:1
Miraculously saved, 2Ki 19:31–36
Captured by Babylon, 2Ki 24:10–25:21; Jer 39:1–8
Exiles return and rebuild temple, Ezr 1:1–4; 2:1
Walls of, dedicated, Ne 12:27–47
Christ enters as king, Mt 21:4–11
Christ laments for, Mt 23:37; Lk 19:41–44
Church born in, Ac 2
Christians of, persecuted, Ac 4

JESHIMON
Wilderness west of the Dead Sea, 1Sa 23:19, 24

JESHUA (or Joshua)
Postexilic high priest; returns with Zerubbabel, Ezr 2:2
Aids in rebuilding temple, Ezr 3:2–8
Also called Joshua; seen in vision, Zec 3:1–10

JESHURUN
Poetic name of endearment for Israel, Dt 32:15

JESSE
Grandson of Ruth and Boaz, Ru 4:17–22
Father of David, 1Sa 16:1–13
Mentioned in prophecy, Is 11:1, 10

JEST *joke, mock*
appeared…be *j-ing*, Ge 19:14
Against whom do you *j*, Is 57:4

JESUS *the Lord is Salvation*
genealogy of *J* the Messiah, Mt 1:1
Mary, by whom *J* was born, Mt 1:16
and he called His name *J*., Mt 1:25
J was led up by the Spirit, Mt 4:1
J began to preach, Mt 4:17
When *J* saw the crowds, Mt 5:1
And *J* sternly warned them:, Mt 9:30
J summoned His twelve, Mt 10:1
knowing their thoughts *J*, Mt 12:25
J said, "Let the children, Mt 19:14
J touched their eyes, Mt 20:34
J entered the temple, Mt 21:12
when *J* was in Bethany, Mt 26:6
But *J* kept silent, Mt 26:63
J THE KING OF THE, Mt 27:37
J cried out with a loud, Mt 27:46
asked for the body of *J*, Mt 27:58
J met them and greeted, Mt 28:9
a leper came to *J*, Mk 1:40
J Himself was in the stern, Mk 4:38
J entered Jerusalem, Mk 11:11
and eating, *J* said, Mk 14:18
after having *J* scourged, Mk 15:15
J kept increasing in wisdom, Lk 2:52
J said, "Someone did touch, Lk 8:46
J rebuked the unclean, Lk 9:42
while *J* was praying, Lk 11:1
J, Son of David, have mercy, Lk 18:38
J entered the temple, Lk 19:45
Pilate, wanting to release *J*, Lk 23:20
J, remember me when, Lk 23:42
J Himself approached and, Lk 24:15
he saw *J* coming to him, Jn 1:29
J saw Nathanael coming, Jn 1:47
J said to them, "Fill the, Jn 2:7
His signs *J* did, Jn 2:11
J said to her, "Give Me, Jn 4:7
J went up on the mountain, Jn 6:3
saw *J* walking on the sea, Jn 6:19
J said to them, "I am the bread, Jn 6:35
J stooped down and with, Jn 8:6
J wept, Jn 11:35
anointed the feet of *J*, Jn 12:3
J said to him, "I am the way, Jn 14:6
when they had crucified *J*, Jn 19:23
J then saw His mother, Jn 19:26
they took the body of *J*, Jn 19:40
J said to her, "Mary!", Jn 20:16
may believe that *J* is the, Jn 20:31
now the third time that *J*, Jn 21:14
J said to him, "Tend My, Jn 21:17
"This *J* God raised up, Ac 2:32
Your holy servant *J*, Ac 4:27
J whom you are persecuting, Ac 9:5
peace through *J* Christ, Ac 10:36
Believe in the Lord *J*, Ac 16:31
the one who has faith in *J*, Ro 3:26
grace of the one Man, *J*, Ro 5:15
alive to God in Christ *J*, Ro 6:11
Spirit of Him who raised *J*, Ro 8:11
confess with your mouth *J*, Ro 10:9
put on the Lord *J* Christ, Ro 13:14
sanctified in Christ *J*, 1Co 1:2
nothing among you except *J*, 1Co 2:2
in the day of the Lord *J*, 1Co 5:5
Christ *J* neither circumcision, Ga 5:6
adoption as sons through *J*, Eph 1:5
J Himself being the corner, Eph 2:20
which was also in Christ *J*, Php 2:5
name of *J* every knee, Php 2:10
churches of God in Christ *J*, 1Th 2:14
J our Lord direct our way, 1Th 3:11
coming of our Lord *J*, 2Th 2:1
exhort in the Lord *J*, 2Th 3:12
J came into the world, 1Ti 1:15
consider *J*, the Apostle, Heb 3:1
body of *J* Christ once, Heb 10:10
covenant, *even J*, Heb 13:20
acceptable to God through *J*, 1Pe 2:5
J Christ has come in the, 1Jn 4:2
by water and blood, *J* Christ, 1Jn 5:6
The Revelation of *J* Christ, Rv 1:1
hold to the testimony of *J*., Rv 12:17
blood of the witnesses of *J*., Rv 17:6
I, *J*, have sent My angel, Rv 22:16
Amen. Come, Lord *J*, Rv 22:20

JETHER
Gideon's oldest son, Jdg 8:20, 21

JETHRO
Priest of Midian; becomes Moses' father-in-law, Ex 2:16–22
Blesses Moses' departure, Ex 4:18
Visits and counsels Moses, Ex 18
Also called Reuel, Nu 10:29

JEW(S)
Originally an inhabitant of Judah, a Judean, 2Ki 16:6
Judean shortened to Jew during exile, 2Ki 25:25
Synonym for Hebrew, Ezr 4:12, 23; Ne 4:1, 2; Est 4:3, 7; Jer 34:9

Later term for all Israelites in the land and in Diaspora, Mt 27:11; Mk 7:3; Lk 23:51; Jn 4:9; Ac 22:3; Ro 3:1; Gal 3:28; Rev 2:9

JEWEL *precious stone*
precious than *j-s*, Pr 3:15
better than *j-s*, Pr 8:11
adorns…her *j-s*, Is 61:10
the *J* of *his* kingdom, Da 11:20

JEWISH
Pertaining to Jews, Ne 5:1; Est 6:13; Jn 2:6; Ac 13:6

JEZEBEL
Ahab's idolatrous wife, 1Ki 16:31
Her abominable acts, 1Ki 18:4, 13; 19:1, 2; 21:1–16
Death prophesied; prophecy fulfilled, 1Ki 21:23; 2Ki 9:7, 30–37
——— Type of paganism in the church, Rev 2:20

JEZREEL
Ahab's capital, 1Ki 18:45; 21:1
Ahab's family destroyed at, 1Ki 21:23; 2Ki 9:30–37; 10:1–11

JOAB
David's nephew; commands his army, 2Sa 2:10–32; 8:16; 10:1–14; 11:1, 14–25; 20:1–23
Kills Abner, 2Sa 3:26, 27
Intercedes for Absalom, 2Sa 14:1–33
Remains loyal to David; kills Absalom, 2Sa 18:1–5, 9–17
Demoted; kills Amasa, 2Sa 19:13; 20:8–10
Opposes census, 2Sa 24:1–9; 1Ch 21:1–6
Supports Adonijah, 1Ki 1:7
Solomon orders his death in obedience to David's command, 1Ki 2:1–6, 28–34

JOANNA
Wife of Chuza, Herod's steward, Lk 8:1–3
With others, heralds Christ's resurrection, Lk 23:55, 56

JOASH (or Jehoash)
Son of Ahaziah; saved from Athaliah's massacre and crowned by Jehoiada, 2Ki 11:1–12
Repairs the temple, 2Ki 12:1–16
Turns away from the LORD and is killed, 2Ch 24:17–25
——— Wicked king of Israel; son of Jehoahaz, 2Ki 13:10–25
Defeats Amaziah in battle, 2Ki 14:8–15; 2Ch 25:17–24

JOB
Model of righteousness, Job 1:1–5
His faith tested, Job 1:6–2:10
Debates with his three friends; complains to God, Job 3–33
Elihu intervenes, Job 34–37
God's answer, Job 38–41
Humbles himself and repents, Job 42:1–6
Restored to prosperity, Job 42:10–17

JOB *occupation*
workmen…*j* to *j*, 2Ch 34:13

JOCHEBED
Daughter of Levi; mother of Miriam, Aaron, and Moses, Ex 6:20

JOEL
Preexilic prophet, Joel 1:1
Quoted in NT, Ac 2:16

JOGBEHAH
Town in Gilead, Nu 33:35; Jdg 8:11

JOHANAN
Military leader of Judah; warns Gedaliah of Ishmael's plot, Jer 40:13–16
Avenges Gedaliah; takes the people to Egypt, Jer 41:11–18

JOHN
The apostle, son of Zebedee; called as disciple, Mt 4:21, 22; Lk 5:1–11
Chosen as one of the Twelve, Mt 10:2
Especially close to Christ, Mt 17:1–9; Mk 13:3; Jn 13:23–25; 19:26, 27; 20:2–8; 21:7, 20
Ambitious and overzealous, Mk 10:35–41; Lk 9:54–56
Sent to prepare the Passover, Lk 22:8–13
With Peter, heals a man and is arrested, Ac 3:1–4:22
Goes on missionary trip with Peter, Ac 8:14–25
Exiled on Patmos, Rev 1:9
Author of Gospel, three epistles, and the Revelation, Jn 21:23–25; 1Jn; 2Jn; 3Jn; Rev 1:1
——— The Baptist; OT prophecy concerning, Is 40:3–5; Mal 4:5
His birth announced and accomplished, Lk 1:11–20, 57–80
Preaches repentance, Lk 3:1–20
Bears witness to Christ, Jn 1:19–36; 3:25–36
Baptizes Jesus, Mt 3:13–17
Jesus speaks about, Mt 11:7–19
Identified with Elijah, Mt 11:13, 14
Herod imprisons and kills, Mt 14:3–12
——— Surnamed Mark: *see* mark

JOIN *bring together, couple*
j-ed to his wife, Ge 2:24
do not *j* your hand, Ex 23:1
j field to field, Is 5:8
j…in hypocrisy, Da 11:34
God…*j-ed* together, Mt 19:6
j-ed him…believed, Ac 17:34
shall be *j-ed* to his wife, Eph 5:31
j…*me* in suffering, 2Ti 1:8

JOINT *juncture*
bones are out of *j*, Ps 22:14
together by the *j-s*, Col 2:19
both *j-s* and marrow, Heb 4:12

JOKTAN
See ARABIA
Descendant of Shem, Ge 10:21, 25

JONADAB (or Jehonadab)
David's nephew; encourages Amnon in sin, 2Sa 13:3–5, 32–36
——— Son of Rechab; father of the Rechabites, Jer 35:5–19
Helps Jehu overthrow Baal, 2Ki 10:15–28

JONAH
Prophet sent to Nineveh; rebels and is punished, Jon 1
Repents and is saved, Jon 2
Preaches in Nineveh, Jon 3
Becomes angry at God's mercy, Jon 4
Type of Christ's resurrection, Mt 12:39, 40

JONATHAN
King Saul's eldest son; his exploits in battle, 1Sa 13:2, 3; 14:1–14, 49
Saved from his father's wrath, 1Sa 14:24–45
Makes covenant with David; protects him from Saul, 1Sa 18:1–4; 19:1–7; 20:1–42; 23:15–18
Killed by Philistines, 1Sa 31:2, 8
Mourned by David; his son provided for, 2Sa 1:17–27; 9:1–8
——— Son of high priest Abiathar; faithful to David, 2Sa 15:26–36; 17:15–22
Informs Adonijah of Solomon's coronation, 1Ki 1:41–49

JOPPA
Scene of Peter's vision, Ac 10:5–23, 32

JORAM
See jehoram

JORDAN RIVER
Lot dwells near, Ge 13:8–13
Canaan's eastern boundary, Nu 34:12
Moses forbidden to cross, Dt 3:27
Miraculous dividing of, for Israel, Jos 3:1–17
by Elijah, 2Ki 2:5–8
by Elisha, 2Ki 2:13, 14
Naaman healed in, 2Ki 5:10–14
John baptizes in, Mt 3:6, 13–17

JOSEPH
Son of Jacob by Rachel, Ge 30:22–24
Loved by Jacob; hated by his brothers, Ge 37:3–11
Sold into slavery, Ge 37:12–36
Unjustly imprisoned in Egypt, Ge 39:1–23
Interprets dreams in prison, Ge 40:1–23
Wins Pharaoh's favor, Ge 41:1–44
Prepares Egypt for famine, Ge 41:45–57
Sells grain to his brothers, Ge 42–44
Reveals identity and reconciles with brothers; sends for Jacob, Ge 45:1–28
Settles family in Egypt, Ge 47:1–12
His sons blessed by Jacob, Ge 48:1–22
Blessed by Jacob, Ge 49:22–26
Buries his father; reassures his brothers, Ge 50:1–21
His death, Ge 50:22–26
——— Husband of Mary, Jesus' mother, Mt 1:16
Visited by angel, Mt 1:19–25
Takes Mary to Bethlehem, Lk 2:3–7
Protects Jesus from Herod, Mt 2:13–23
Jesus subject to, Lk 2:51
——— Secret disciple from Arimathea; donates tomb and assists in Christ's burial, Mk 15:42–46; Lk 23:50–53; Jn 19:38–42

JOSES
One of Jesus' half brothers, Mt 13:55

——— The name of Barnabas, Ac 4:36

JOSHUA
See JESHUA
Leader of Israel succeeding Moses, Nu 27:18–23
Leads battle against Amalek, Ex 17:8–16
Sent as spy into Canaan; reports favorably, Nu 13:16–25; 14:6–9
Assumes command, Jos 1:1–18
Sends spies to Jericho, Jos 2:1
Leads Israel across Jordan, Jos 3:1–17
Sets up commemorative stones, Jos 4:1–24
Circumcises the people, Jos 5:2–9
Conquers Jericho, Jos 5:13–6:27
Punishes Achan, Jos 7:10–26
Conquers Canaan, Jos 8–12
Divides the land, Jos 13–19
Addresses rulers, Jos 23:1–16
Addresses the people, Jos 24:1–28
His death, Jos 24:29, 30

JOSIAH
Righteous king of Judah; son of Amon, 2Ki 22:1, 2
Repairs the temple, 2Ki 22:3–9
Hears the Law; spared for his humility, 2Ki 22:10–20
Institutes reforms, 2Ki 23:1–25
Killed in battle, 2Ch 35:20–25

JOTHAM
Gideon's youngest son; escapes Abimelech's massacre, Jdg 9:5
Utters prophetic parable, Jdg 9:7–21
——— Righteous king of Judah; son of Azariah, 2Ki 15:32–38; 2Ch 27:1–9

JOURNEY *traveling, trip*
Let us take our *j*, Ge 33:12
day's *j* on the other, Nu 11:31
seek...a safe *j*, Ezr 8:21
a bag for *your j*, Mt 10:10
nothing for *your j*, Lk 9:3
Sabbath day's *j* away, Ac 1:12
on frequent *j-s*, 2Co 11:26

JOURNEYED *traveled*
about as they *j* east, Ge 11:2
Jacob *j* to Succoth, Ge 33:17
the sons of Israel *j*, Nu 22:1
j from the river, Ezr 8:31

JOY *delight, happiness*
raise sounds of *j*, 1Ch 15:16
shouted aloud for *j*, Ezr 3:12
see His face with *j*, Job 33:26
Restore to me the *j*, Ps 51:12
j at Your name, Ps 89:12
godly ones sing for *j*, Ps 132:9
Everlasting *j* will be, Is 61:7
their mourning into *j*, Jer 31:13
with great *j*, Mt 2:10
enter into the *j*, Mt 25:21
j in heaven over one, Lk 15:7
j in the Holy Spirit, Ro 14:17
love, *j*, peace, Gal 5:22
make my *j* complete, Php 2:2

JOYFUL *feeling gladness*
be altogether *j*, Dt 16:15
j with gladness, Ps 21:6
shall reap with *j*, Ps 126:5
j heart is good, Pr 17:22

JOYFULLY *full of joy, happy*
go *j* with the king, Est 5:14
Shout *j* to God, all, Ps 66:1
They shout *j* together, Is 52:8
to praise God *j*, Lk 19:37

JOYOUSLY *with joy*
The ostriches' wings flap *j*, Job 39:13
you will *j* draw water, Is 12:3
j living in splendor every, Lk 16:19
and patience; *j*, Col 1:11

JOZACHAR
Assassin of Joash, 2Ki 12:19–21

JUBAL
Son of Lamech, Ge 4:21

JUBILANT *elated*
no...*j* shouting, Is 16:10
Is this your *j city*, Is 23:7
because you are *j*, Jer 50:11
they may become *j*, Jer 51:39

JUBILEE, YEAR OF
Return of ancestral possessions every fiftieth year
Year of liberty, Lv 25:8ff

JUDAH
Son of Jacob and Leah, Ge 29:30–35
Intercedes for Joseph, Ge 37:26, 27
Fails in duty to Tamar, Ge 38:1–30
Offers himself as Benjamin's ransom, Ge 44:18–34
Jacob bestows birthright on, Ge 49:3–10
Ancestor of Christ, Mt 1:3, 16
——— Tribe of:
Prophecy concerning, Ge 49:8–12
Numbered at Sinai, Nu 1:26, 27
Territory assigned to, Jos 15:1–63
Leads in conquest of Canaan, Jdg 1:1–19
Makes David king, 2Sa 2:1–11
Loyal to David and his house, 2Sa 20:1, 2; 1Ki 12:20
Becomes leader of southern kingdom, 1Ki 14:21, 22
Taken to Babylon, 2Ki 24:1–16
Returns after exile, 2Ch 36:20–23

JUDAISM *Jewish way of life*
manner of life in *J*, Gal 1:13
advancing in *J*, Gal 1:14

JUDAS
Judas Lebbaeus, surnamed Thaddaeus, Mt 10:3
Half brother of Christ, Mt 13:55
One of Christ's apostles, Lk 6:13, 16
Offers a question, Jn 14:22
Becomes Christ's disciple, Ac 1:14
——— Judas Barsabas, a chief deputy, Ac 15:22–32
——— Betrayer of Christ: *see* iscariot

JUDE
See also judas
Writes an epistle, Jude 1

JUDEA
Christ born in, Mt 2:1, 5, 6
Hostile toward Christ, Jn 7:1
Gospel preached in, Ac 8:1, 4
Churches established in, Ac 9:31

JUDGE *(n) leader*
J of all the earth, Ge 18:25
prince or a *j* over us, Ex 2:14
LORD was with the *j*, Jdg 2:18
For God Himself is *j*, Ps 50:6
unrighteous *j* said, Lk 18:6
one Lawgiver and *J*, Jas 4:12

JUDGE *(v) pass judgment*
LORD *j* between you, Ge 16:5
Moses sat to *j* the, Ex 18:13
LORD will *j*...earth, 1Sa 2:10
coming to *j* the earth, Ps 98:9
He will *j* the poor, Is 11:4
Do not *j*...will not be *j-d*, Mt 7:1
Son...world to *j*, Jn 3:17
Law...not *j* a man, Jn 7:51
not come to *j* the, Jn 12:47
able to *j*...thoughts, Heb 4:12
adulterers God will *j*, Heb 13:4

JUDGMENT *condemnation*
I will execute *j-s*, Ex 12:12
partiality in *j*, Dt 1:17
let *j* be executed, Ezr 7:26
will not stand in the *j*, Ps 1:5
in the day of *j*, Mt 10:15
j, that the light, Jn 3:19
resurrection of *j*, Jn 5:29
My *j* is just, Jn 5:30
after this *comes j*, Heb 9:27
incur a stricter *j*, Jas 3:1
not fall under *j*, Jas 5:12
kept for the day of *j*, 2Pe 3:7
j of the great day, Jude 6
to execute *j* upon all, Jude 15
His *j-s* are true, Rev 19:2

JULIUS
Roman centurion assigned to guard Paul, Ac 27:1–44

JUMP *leap*
legs with which to *j*, Lv 11:21
if a fox should *j*, Ne 4:3
j-ed up, and came, Mk 10:50

JUNIPER *tree*
slept under a *j* tree, 1Ki 19:5
The *j*, the box tree, Is 60:13
like a *j* in the, Jer 48:6

JUST *fair, right*
shall have *j* balances, Lv 19:36
a man be *j* with God, Job 25:4
Hear a *j* cause, O LORD, Ps 17:1
He is *j* and endowed, Zec 9:9
My judgment is *j*, Jn 5:30
the j for *the* unjust, 1Pe 3:18

JUSTICE *fairness, righteousness*
shall not distort *j*, Dt 16:19
Does God pervert *j*, Job 8:3
j to the afflicted, Job 36:6
Righteousness and *j*, Ps 89:14
do not understand *j*, Pr 28:5
j is turned back, Is 59:14
let *j* roll down, Am 5:24
j and mercy and, Mt 23:23
acknowledged...*j*, Lk 7:29
grant to your slaves *j*, Col 4:1

JUSTIFICATION *vindication*
because of our *j*, Ro 4:25
j of life to all men, Ro 5:18

JUSTIFY *declare guiltless*
how...*j* ourselves, Ge 44:16
they *j* the righteous, Dt 25:1
he *j-ied* himself, Job 32:2
wishing to *j* himself, Lk 10:29
these...He also *j-ied*, Ro 8:30
God...*j-ies*, Ro 8:33
seeking to be *j-ied*, Gal 2:17

JUSTUS
Surname of Joseph, a disciple, Ac 1:23
——— Man of Corinth; befriends Paul, Ac 18:7

K

KADESH
Spies sent from, Nu 13:3, 26
Moses strikes rock at, Nu 20:1–13
Boundary in the new Israel, Eze 47:19

KADESH-BARNEA
Boundary of Promised Land, Nu 34:1–4
Limit of Joshua's military campaign, Jos 10:41

KARNAIM
Conquered region, Am 6:13

KEDESH
Town in south Judah, Jos 15:23
City of refuge, Jos 21:27, 32
——— Levite city in Issachar, 1Ch 6:72

KEDESH-NAPHTALI
Home of Barak, Jdg 4:6

KEEP *hold, guide, preserve*
k the way of the LORD, Ge 18:19
love Me and *k* My, Ex 20:6
shall *k* your sabbath, Lv 23:32
LORD bless you, and *k*, Nu 6:24
loved you and *k-t* the oath, Dt 7:8
I *k-t* myself...iniquity, 2Sa 22:24
k-t the ways of the LORD, Ps 18:21
who has *k-t* my soul from, Is 38:17
All these things I have *k-t*, Mt 19:20
to k the Passover, Mt 26:18
if anyone *k-s* My, Jn 8:51
he will *k* My word, Jn 14:23
k-t secret for long ages past, Ro 16:25
k-ing faith and a, 1Ti 1:19
k yourself free from, 1Ti 5:22
course, I have *k-t* the faith, 2Ti 4:7
k his tongue...evil, 1Pe 3:10

KEEPER *guard, protector*
Am I my brother's *k*, Ge 4:9
been *k-s* of livestock, Ge 46:32
The LORD is your *k*, Ps 121:5
I, the LORD, am its *k*, Is 27:3

KEILAH
Town of Judah; rescued from Philistines by David, 1Sa 23:1–5
Prepares to betray David; he escapes, 1Sa 23:6–13

KENITES
Canaanite tribe whose land is promised to Abraham's seed, Ge 15:19
Subjects of Balaam's prophecy, Nu 24:20–22
Settle with Judahites, Jdg 1:16
Spared by Saul in war with Amalekites, 1Sa 15:6

KENIZZITE
Canaanite tribe in S Palestine and Edom, Ge 15:19; Nu 32:12; Jos 14:14

KETURAH
Abraham's second wife, Ge 25:1
Sons of:
Listed, Ge 25:1, 2
Given gifts and sent away, Ge 25:6

KEY *unlocking tool*
k-s of the kingdom, Mt 16:19
the *k* of knowledge, Lk 11:52
k-s of death and of, Rev 1:18
k of the bottomless pit, Rev 9:1

KIBROTH-HATTAAVAH
Burial site of Israelites slain by God, Nu 11:33–35

KIDNEYS *innards*
two *k* and the fat, Ex 29:13
remove with the *k*, Lv 3:15
He splits my *k* open, Job 16:13

KIDRON
Valley near Jerusalem; crossed by David and Christ, 2Sa 15:23; Jn 18:1
Idols dumped there, 2Ch 29:16

KILL *take life*
for Cain *k-ed* him, Ge 4:25
k-ed every firstborn, Ex 13:15
who *k-s* a man shall, Lv 24:21
LORD *k-s* and makes, 1Sa 2:6
Am I God, to *k*, 2Ki 5:7
jealousy *k-s* the simple, Job 5:2
he *k-s* the innocent, Ps 10:8
A time to *k*, Ecc 3:3
unable to *k* the, Mt 10:28
k-ed, and be raised, Lk 9:22
do you seek to *k* Me, Jn 7:19
Get up, Peter, *k* and, Ac 10:13
the letter *k-s*, but, 2Co 3:6
who *k* their father, 1Ti 1:9
k a third of mankind, Rev 9:15

KIND *(adj) good, tender*
be *k* to this people, 2Ch 10:7
He Himself is *k*, Lk 6:35
love is *k*, 1Co 13:4
be *k* to one another, Eph 4:32

KIND *(n) group, variety*
fruit after their *k*, Ge 1:11
plant all *k-s* of trees, Lv 19:23
all *k-s* of evil, Mt 5:11
k-s of tongues, 1Co 12:28
every *k* of impurity, Eph 4:19

KINDLE *cause to burn*
anger...was *k-d*, Nu 11:10
His breath *k-s* coals, Job 41:21
man to *k* strife, Pr 26:21
all you who *k* a fire, Is 50:11
k-d a fire in Zion, La 4:11

KINDNESS *tenderness*
teaching of *k* is on, Pr 31:26
to love *k*, And to, Mic 6:8
with deeds of *k*, Ac 9:36
k and...of God, Ro 11:22
joy, peace, patience, *k*, Gal 5:22
compassion, *k*, Col 3:12
tasted the *k* of the, 1Pe 2:3
godliness, brotherly *k*, 2Pe 1:7

KINDRED *relative*
her people or her *k*, Est 2:10
destruction of my *k*, Est 8:6
no one...of *k* spirit, Php 2:20

KING *monarch, regent*
the *k-'s* highway, Nu 20:17
no *k* in Israel, Jdg 17:6
appoint a *k* for us, 1Sa 8:5
anointed David *k*, 2Sa 5:3
my *K* and my God, Ps 5:2
The LORD is *K* forever, Ps 10:16
Who is the *k* of glory, Ps 24:8
will shatter *k-s*, Ps 110:5
By me *k-s* reign, Pr 8:15
He will...before *k-s*, Pr 22:29
The Creator...your *K*, Is 43:15
O *K* of the nations, Jer 10:7
born *K* of the Jews, Mt 2:2
Are You the *K* of, Mt 27:11
your *K* is coming, Jn 12:15
no *k* but Caesar, Jn 19:15
K of *k-s* and Lord, 1Ti 6:15
God, honor the *k*, 1Pe 2:17

KING OF KINGS
the *K* and Lord of lords, 1Ti 6:15
Lord of lords and *K*, Rev 17:14
"*K*, AND LORD OF, Rev 19:16

KING OF THE JEWS
who has been born *K*, Mt 2:2
"Are You the *K*?", Mt 27:11
"Hail, *K*!", Mt 27:29
"THIS IS JESUS THE *K*", Mt 27:37
"Are You the *K*?", Mk 15:2
to release for you the *K*?, Mk 15:9
whom you call the *K*?, Mk 15:12
"Hail, *K*!", Mk 15:18
Him read, "THE *K*.", Mk 15:26
"Are You the *K*?", Lk 23:3
If You are the *K*, save, Lk 23:37
"THIS IS THE *K*", Lk 23:38
"Are You the *K*?", Jn 18:33
release for you the *K*?, Jn 18:39
"Hail, *K*!", Jn 19:3
NAZARENE, THE *K*, Jn 19:19

KINGDOM *domain, monarchy*
his *k* was Babel, Ge 10:10
to Me a *k* of priests, Ex 19:6
tear the *k* from, 1Ki 11:11
will establish his *k*, 1Ch 28:7
the *k* is the LORD's, Ps 22:28
Sing to God, O *k-s*, Ps 68:32
an everlasting *k*, Ps 145:13
k against *k*, Is 19:2
k of heaven is at, Mt 3:2
showed Him...*k-s*, Mt 4:8
Your *k* come, Mt 6:10
sons of the *k*, Mt 13:38
keys of the *k*, Mt 16:19
in My Father's *k*, Mt 26:29
enter the *k* of God, Mk 10:24
to give you the *k*, Lk 12:32
cannot see the *k* of, Jn 3:3
preaching the *k*, Ac 28:31
k of His beloved Son, Col 1:13
to His heavenly *k*, 2Ti 4:18
faith conquered *k-s*, Heb 11:33

heirs of the *k*, Jas 2:5

KINGDOM OF GOD
See KINGDOM OF HEAVEN
the *k* has come upon you, Mt 12:28
a rich man to enter the *k*, Mt 19:24
k is at hand; repent, Mk 1:15
the mystery of the *k*, Mk 4:11
k is like a man who casts, Mk 4:26
death until they see the *k*, Mk 9:1
k belongs to such, Mk 10:14
wealthy to enter the *k*!, Mk 10:23
not far from the *k*, Mk 12:34
was waiting for the *k*, Mk 15:43
poor, for yours is the *k*, Lk 6:20
is least in the *k* is greater, Lk 7:28
proclaim the *k* and to, Lk 9:2
proclaim everywhere the *k*, Lk 9:60
k has come near, Lk 10:9
at the table in the *k*., Lk 13:29
when the *k* was coming, Lk 17:20
again he cannot see the *k*, Jn 3:3
things concerning the *k*, Ac 1:3
we must enter the *k*, Ac 14:22
the *k* is not eating, Ro 14:17
will not inherit the *k*, 1Co 6:9
cannot inherit the *k*, 1Co 15:50

KINGDOM OF HEAVEN
See KINGDOM OF GOD
Repent, for the *k*, Mt 3:2
in spirit, for theirs is the *k*, Mt 5:3
'Lord, Lord,' will enter the *k*, Mt 7:21
saying, 'The *k* is at hand.', Mt 10:7
in the *k* is greater than, Mt 11:11
mysteries of the *k*, Mt 13:11
k may be compared to, Mt 13:24
k is like a mustard seed, Mt 13:31
keys of the *k*, Mt 16:19
greatest in the *k*?, Mt 18:1
for the sake of the *k*, Mt 19:12
k is like a landowner, Mt 20:1
k may be compared to, Mt 22:2
you shut off the *k*, Mt 23:13
k will be comparable to, Mt 25:1

KINSMAN *relative*
of my master's *k*, Ge 24:48
he took his *k-men*, Ge 31:23
a man has no *k*, Lv 25:26
Naomi had a *k* of her, Ru 2:1
k-men stand afar off, Ps 38:11
Herodion, my *k*, Ro 16:11

KIR-HARESETH
Fortified city of Moab, 2Ki 3:25; Is 15:1; 16:7

KIRIATH-ARBA
Ancient name of Hebron, Ge 23:2
Possessed by Judah, Jdg 1:10

KIRIATH-JEARIM
Gibeonite town, Jos 9:17
Ark taken from, 1Ch 13:5

KISH
Benjamite of Gibeah; father of King Saul, 1Sa 9:1–3

KISHON
River of north Palestine; Sisera's army swept away by, Jdg 4:7, 13
Elijah executes prophets of Baal at, 1Ki 18:40

KISS *(n) expression of affection*
threw a *k* from my, Job 31:27
the *k-es* of his mouth, SS 1:2
You gave Me no *k*, Lk 7:45
betraying…with a *k*, Lk 22:48
with a holy *k*, Ro 16:16
with a *k* of love, 1Pe 5:14

KISS *(v) expression of affection*
come close and *k*, Ge 27:26
let me *k* my father, 1Ki 19:20
I would *k* you, SS 8:1
Whomever I *k*, Mk 14:44
not…to *k* My feet, Lk 7:45

KITTIM
See CYPRUS
Descendants of Javan, Ge 10:4

KNEAD *work dough, clay*
took flour, *k-ed* it, 1Sa 28:24
the women *k* dough, Jer 7:18

KNEE *part of body*
strengthened feeble *k-s*, Job 4:4
k-s began knocking, Da 5:6
every *k* shall bow, Ro 14:11
every *k* will bow, Php 2:10

KNEEL *bend, rest on knee*
made the camels *k*, Ge 24:11
people *k-ed* to drink, Jdg 7:6
k before the LORD, Ps 95:6
knelt…before Him, Mt 27:29
man ran…*knelt*, Mk 10:17
He *knelt* down, Lk 22:41

KNIFE *cutting instrument*
k to slay his son, Ge 22:10
jaw teeth *like k-ves*, Pr 30:14
with a scribe's *k*, Jer 36:23

KNIT *joined together*
Jonathan was *k* to, 1Sa 18:1
k me together with, Job 10:11
his thighs are *k*, Job 40:17
His hand they are *k*, La 1:14
k together in love, Col 2:2

KNOCK *smite, strike*
his knees began *k-ing*, Da 5:6
k, and it will be, Mt 7:7
stand outside and *k*, Lk 13:25
he *k-ed* at the door, Ac 12:13
at the door and *k*, Rev 3:20

KNOW *experience, understand*
like one of Us, *k-ing*, Ge 3:22
make *k-n* the statutes, Ex 18:16
k that my Redeemer, Job 19:25
Make me *k* Your ways, Ps 25:4
He *k-s* the secrets, Ps 44:21
k that I am God, Ps 46:10
made *k-n* His salvation, Ps 98:2
Try me and *k* my, Ps 139:23
You *k* me, Jer 12:3
left hand *k* what, Mt 6:3
k…by their fruits, Mt 7:20
I never *knew* you, Mt 7:23
God *k-s* your hearts, Lk 16:15
you will *k* the truth, Jn 8:32
I *k* My own, Jn 10:14
k-ing that His hour, Jn 13:1
k that I love You, Jn 21:15
and *k* all mysteries, 1Co 13:2
who *knew* no sin, 2Co 5:21
k the love of Christ, Eph 3:19
value of *k-ing* Christ, Php 3:8
k…I have believed, 2Ti 1:12
k…eternal life, 1Jn 5:13
I *k* your deeds, Rev 2:2

KNOWLEDGE *information*
tree of the *k* of good, Ge 2:9
LORD is a God of *k*, 1Sa 2:3
anyone teach God *k*, Job 21:22
k is too wonderful, Ps 139:6
the beginning of *k*, Pr 1:7
fools hate *k*, Pr 1:22
Wise…store up *k*, Pr 10:14
k increases power, Pr 24:5
would He teach *k*, Is 28:9
in accordance with *k*, Ro 10:2
K makes arrogant, 1Co 8:1
k, it will be done, 1Co 13:8
have no *k* of God, 1Co 15:34
love…surpasses *k*, Eph 3:19
treasures of…*k*, Col 2:3
grow in…grace and *k*, 2Pe 3:18

KOHATH
Second son of Levi, Ge 46:8, 11
Brother of Jochebed, mother of Aaron and Moses, Ex 6:16–20

KOHATHITES
Numbered, Nu 3:27, 28
Duties assigned to, Nu 4:15–20
Leaders of temple music, 1Ch 6:31–38; 2Ch 20:19

KOR *measure of capacity*
k-s of fine flour, 1Ki 4:22
20, 000 *k-s* of barley, 2Ch 2:10
100 *k-s* of wheat, Ezr 7:22
a bath from *each k*, Eze 45:14

KORAH
Leads rebellion against Moses and Aaron; supernaturally destroyed, Nu 16:1–35
Sons of, not destroyed, Nu 26:9–11

L

LABAN
Son of Bethuel; brother of Rebekah; father of Leah and Rachel, Ge 24:15, 24, 29; 29:16
Agrees to Rebekah's marriage to Isaac, Ge 24:50, 51
Entertains Jacob, Ge 29:1–14
Substitutes Leah for Rachel, Ge 29:15–30
Agrees to division of cattle; grows resentful of Jacob, Ge 30:25–31:2
Pursues Jacob and makes covenant with him, Ge 31:21–55

LABOR *(n) work, childbirth*
fruits of your *l-s*, Ex 23:16
their *l* to the locust, Ps 78:46
bread of painful *l-s*, Ps 127:2
return for their *l*, Ecc 4:9
in *l* and hardship, 2Co 11:27
fruitful *l* for me, Php 1:22
faith and *l* of love, 1Th 1:3
cried out, being in *l*, Rev 12:2

LABOR *(v) toil, work*
Six days you shall *l*, Ex 20:9
l in vain who build, Ps 127:1
for whom am I *l-ing*, Ecc 4:8
l-ed over you in vain, Gal 4:11

LABORER *workman*
l-s for his vineyard, Mt 20:1
Call the *l-s* and pay, Mt 20:8
l-s into His harvest, Lk 10:2
l is worthy of his, Lk 10:7

LACHISH
Defeated by Joshua, Jos 10:3–33
Taken by Sennacherib, 2Ki 18:13–17; Is 36:1, 2; 37:8

LACK *(n) deficiency, need*
where there is no *l*, Jdg 18:10
for *l* of instruction, Pr 5:23
for *l* of a shepherd, Eze 34:5
l of self-control, 1Co 7:5

LACK *(v) be deficient, need*
will not *l* anything, Dt 8:9
l-ing in counsel, Dt 32:28
man *l-ing* sense, Pr 7:7
am I still *l-ing*, Mt 19:20
One thing you *l*, Mk 10:21
not *l-ing* in any gift, 1Co 1:7
if any…*l-s* wisdom, Jas 1:5

LAD *boy*
God heard the *l*, Ge 21:17
the *l* is not *with us*, Ge 44:31
the *l* was dead, 2Ki 4:32
a *l* here who has five, Jn 6:9

LADDER *steps*
l…set on the earth, Ge 28:12

LADY *woman*
Your noble *l-ies*, Ps 45:9
elder to the chosen *l*, 2Jn 1

LAISH
Called Leshem, Jos 19:47; Jdg 18:29
Taken by Danites, Jdg 18:7, 14, 27

LAKE *pool, water*
standing by the *l*, Lk 5:1
wind…on the *l*, Lk 8:23
into the *l* and was, Lk 8:33
into the *l* of fire, Rev 20:10

LAMB *young sheep*
l for the burnt, Ge 22:7
shall redeem with a *l*, Ex 34:20
l without defect, Lv 14:10
will dwell with the *l*, Is 11:6
l…led to slaughter, Is 53:7
wolf and the *l* will, Is 65:25
send you out as *l-s*, Lk 10:3
Behold, the *L* of God, Jn 1:29
Tend My *l-s*, Jn 21:15
l before its shearer, Ac 8:32
Worthy is the *L*, Rev 5:12
blood of the *L*, Rev 12:11

LAME *crippled, disabled*
was *l* in both feet, 2Sa 9:13
feet to the *l*, Job 29:15
Then the *l* will leap, Is 35:6
the l walk, Mt 11:5
l from his mother's, Ac 14:8

LAMECH
Son of Methushael, of Cain's race, Ge 4:17, 18
——— Son of Methuselah; father of Noah, Ge 5:25–31

LAMENT *(n) dirge, wail*
this *l* over Saul, 2Sa 1:17
chanted a *l*, 2Ch 35:25
I must make a *l*, Mic 1:8

LAMENT *(v) mourn, wail*
house of Israel *l-ed*, 1Sa 7:2
her gates will *l*, Is 3:26
fishermen will *l*, Is 19:8
And *l* over you, Eze 27:32
weep and *l* over her, Rev 18:9

LAMENTATION *weeping*
great…sorrowful *l*, Ge 50:10
in Ramah, *L and*, Jer 31:15
your songs into *l*, Am 8:10
made loud *l* over him, Ac 8:2

LAMP *light*
You are my *l*, 2Sa 22:29
l-s of pure gold, 2Ch 4:20
his *l* goes out, Job 18:6
Your word is a *l*, Ps 119:105
commandment is a *l*, Pr 6:23
l of the body, Mt 6:22
l-s are going out, Mt 25:8
l-s in the upper room, Ac 20:8
l shining in a dark, 2Pe 1:19
seven *l-s* of fire, Rev 4:5

LAMPSTAND *candlestick*
l of pure gold, Ex 25:31
and a chair and a *l*, 2Ki 4:10
puts it on a *l*, Lk 8:16
will remove your *l*, Rev 2:5

LAND *country, earth*
let the dry *l* appear, Ge 1:9
famine in the *l*, Ge 12:10
I have given this *l*, Ge 15:18
out of the *l* of Egypt, Ex 6:13
l flowing with milk, Dt 6:3
in to possess the *l*, Jos 1:11
l of their captivity, 2Ch 6:38
will heal their *l*, 2Ch 7:14
the *l* of the living, Job 28:13
will inherit the *l*, Ps 37:11
In a dry and weary *l*, Ps 63:1
l be born in one day, Is 66:8
again to this *l*, Jer 24:6
l is filled with blood, Eze 9:9
smite the *l* with a, Mal 4:6
darkness…all the *l*, Mt 27:45
owned a tract of *l*, Ac 4:37

LAND OF THE LIVING
of the LORD in the *l.*, Ps 27:13
the LORD In the *l*, Ps 116:9
My portion in the *l.*, Ps 142:5
He was cut off out of the *l*, Is 53:8

LANDOWNER *landlord*
slaves of the *l*, Mt 13:27
kingdom…like a *l*, Mt 20:1
l who planted a, Mt 21:33

LANGUAGE *speech, word*
according to his *l*, Ge 10:5
earth used the same *l*, Ge 11:1
speech or difficult *l*, Eze 3:5
in figurative *l*, Jn 16:25
speak in his own *l*, Ac 2:6
many kinds of *l-s*, 1Co 14:10

LANGUISH *faint*
l-ed because of the, Ge 47:13
My soul *l-es* for, Ps 119:81
never *l* again, Jer 31:12
refresh…who *l-es*, Jer 31:25

LAODICEA
Paul's concern for, Col 2:1; 4:12–16
Letter to church of, Rev 3:14–22

LAPIS LAZULI *precious stone*
polishing *was* like *l*, La 4:7
like *l* in appearance, Eze 1:26
the jasper; The *l*, Eze 28:13

LARGE *big, great, huge*
tears in *l* measure, Ps 80:5
a *l* upper room, Mk 14:15
a *l* crowd, Lk 7:11
what *l* letters, Gal 6:11

LAST *final, utmost*
breathed his *l*, Ge 25:8
In the *l* days, Is 2:2
first will be *l*, Mt 19:30
The *l* Adam, 1Co 15:45
at the *l* trumpet, 1Co 15:52
in these *l* days, Heb 1:2
it is the *l* hour, 1Jn 2:18
the first and the *l*, Rev 1:17

LAST DAY
See LAST DAYS; LATTER DAYS
but raise it up on the *l.*, Jn 6:39
will raise him up on the *l*, Jn 6:40
will raise him up on the *l*, Jn 6:44
will raise him up on the *l*, Jn 6:54
on the *l*, the great day, Jn 7:37
in the resurrection on the *l*, Jn 11:24
what will judge him at the *l*, Jn 12:48

LAST DAYS
See LAST DAY; LATTER DAYS
come about that in the *l*, Is 2:2
in the *l* you will, Jer 23:20
the *l* that I will restore, Jer 49:39
l that I will bring you, Eze 38:16
to His goodness in the *l.*, Hos 3:5
the *l* that the mountain, Mic 4:1
l,' God says, 'that I will, Ac 2:17
in the *l* difficult times, 2Ti 3:1
in these *l* has spoken, Heb 1:2
l that you have stored, Jas 5:3
in the *l* mockers will come, 2Pe 3:3

LATIN
language of the Roman Empire
one of three languages written on Jesus' cross, Jn 19:20

LATTER DAYS
See LAST DAY; LAST DAYS
in the *l* you will return, Dt 4:30
befall you in the *l*, Dt 31:29
blessed the *l* of Job, Job 42:12
the *l* you will understand, Jer 30:24
will take place in the *l*, Da 2:28
l, for the vision pertains, Da 10:14

LATTICE *trellis*
fell through the *l*, 2Ki 1:2
looked out…my *l*, Pr 7:6
peering through…*l*, SS 2:9

LAUGH *be amused, mock*
Why did Sarah *l*, Ge 18:13
will *l* at violence, Job 5:22
l at your calamity, Pr 1:26
weep, and a time to *l*, Ecc 3:4
began l-ing at Him, Mt 9:24

LAUGHINGSTOCK *derision*
l among the peoples, Ps 44:14
was not Israel a *l*, Jer 48:27
I have become a *l*, La 3:14

LAUGHTER *amusement*
God has made *l* for, Ge 21:6
Even in *l* the heart, Pr 14:13
Sorrow is better than *l*, Ecc 7:3

LAVER *wash basin*
make a *l* of bronze, Ex 30:18
set the *l* between, Ex 40:7
anoint the *l*, Ex 40:11

LAW *scripture, statute*
tablets with the *l*, Ex 24:12
Moses wrote this *l*, Dt 31:9
found the…*l*, 2Ki 22:8
walk in My *l*, 2Ch 6:16
l…is perfect, Ps 19:7
I delight in Your *l*, Ps 119:70
abolish the *L* or the, Mt 5:17
Our *L*…not judge, Jn 7:51
by that *l* He ought, Jn 19:7
by a *l* of faith, Ro 3:27
L brings…wrath, Ro 4:15
not under *l*, Ro 6:14
Is the *L* sin, Ro 7:7
the *L* is holy, Ro 7:12
L…become our tutor, Gal 3:24
thereby fulfill the *l*, Gal 6:2
L…nothing perfect, Heb 7:19

LAW AND THE PROPHETS
See LAW OF MOSES; LAW OF THE LORD; LAW/PROPHETS
for this is the *L*, Mt 7:12
depend the whole *L*, Mt 22:40
L were proclaimed until, Lk 16:16
the reading of the *L*, Ac 13:15
witnessed by the *L*, Ro 3:21

LAW OF MOSES
See LAW AND THE PROPHETS; LAW OF THE LORD; LAW/PROPHETS
the book of the *l*, Jos 8:31
the stones a copy of the *l*, Jos 8:32
according to all the *l*, 2Ki 23:25
scribe skilled in the *l*, Ezr 7:6
Remember the *l*, Mal 4:4
written about Me in the *L*, Lk 24:44
the *L* will not be broken, Jn 7:23
be freed through the *L*., Ac 13:39
Jesus, from both the *L*, Ac 28:23
has set aside the *L*, Heb 10:28

LAW OF THE LORD
See LAW AND THE PROPHETS; LAW OF MOSES; LAW/PROPHETS
l may be in your mouth, Ex 13:9
l, which He commanded, 1Ch 16:40
set his heart to study the *l*, Ezr 7:10
delight is in the *l*, Ps 1:2
l is perfect, restoring, Ps 19:7
who walk in the *l*, Ps 119:1
it is written in the *L*, Lk 2:23

LAW/PROPHETS
See LAW AND THE PROPHETS; LAW OF MOSES; LAW OF THE LORD
all the *L* prophesied, Mt 11:13
the *L*, Lk 24:44
whom Moses in the *L*, Jn 1:45
accordance with the *L*, Ac 24:14
both the *L*, Ac 28:23

LAWFUL *legal, right*
not *l* for him to eat, Mt 12:4
Is it *l* to heal, Mt 12:10
l…man to divorce, Mk 10:2
All things are *l*, 1Co 6:12

LAWGIVER *lawmaker*
The LORD is our *l*, Is 33:22
one *L* and Judge, Jas 4:12

LAWLESS *illegal, without law*
l one will be, 2Th 2:8
are *l* and rebellious, 1Ti 1:9
from every *l* deed, Titus 2:14

LAWYER *interpreter of law*
a *l*, asked Him, Mt 22:35
One of the *l-s* said, Lk 11:45
Woe to you *l-s*, Lk 11:52

LAY *place, put*
laid him on the altar, Ge 22:9
l My hand on Egypt, Ex 7:4
laid its cornerstone, Job 38:6
l my glory in the dust, Ps 7:5
he *l-s* up deceit, Pr 26:24
laid Him in a tomb, Mk 15:46
l-s down His life, Jn 10:11
I *l* down My life, Jn 10:15
have you *laid* Him, Jn 11:34
I *l* in zion a stone, Ro 9:33
l-ing aside falsehood, Eph 4:25

LAYMAN *non-ecclesiastic*
l shall not eat *them*, Ex 29:33
married to a *l*, Lv 22:12
l who comes near, Nu 3:10

LAZARUS
Beggar described in a parable, Lk 16:20–25
——— Brother of Mary and Martha; raised from the dead, Jn 11:1–44
Attends a supper, Jn 12:1, 2
Jews seek to kill, Jn 12:9–11

LAZY *idle, slothful*
Because they are *l*, Ex 5:8
You are *l*, *very l*, Ex 5:17
You wicked, *l* slave, Mt 25:26
beasts, *l* gluttons, Titus 1:12

LEAD (*n*) *metal*
They sank like *l*, Ex 15:10
an iron stylus and *l*, Job 19:24
l is consumed by, Jer 6:29
l in the furnace, Eze 22:18

LEAD (*v*) *direct, guide*
God *led* the people, Ex 13:18
cloud by day to *l*, Ex 13:21
l-s me beside quiet, Ps 23:2
L me in Your truth, Ps 25:5
led captive *Your*, Ps 68:18
little boy will *l*, Is 11:6
lamb that is *led* to, Is 53:7
not *l* us into, Mt 6:13
l astray…the elect, Mk 13:22
led Him…crucify, Mk 15:20
and *l-s* them out, Jn 10:3
led by the Spirit, Ro 8:14
led captive a host, Eph 4:8
that *l-s* to salvation, 2Ti 3:15

LEADER *director, guide*
Let us appoint a *l*, Nu 14:4
one *l* of every tribe, Nu 34:18
l over My people, 1Ki 14:7
the *l* like the servant, Lk 22:26
Obey your *l-s*, Heb 13:17

LEADING (*adj*) *chief, noted*
gathered *l* men, Ezr 7:28
number…*l* women, Ac 17:4
l men of the Jews, Ac 28:17

LEAF *foliage*
sewed fig *l-ves*, Ge 3:7
sound of a driven *l*, Lv 26:36
its *l* does not wither, Ps 1:3
puts forth its *l-ves*, Mt 24:32

LEAH
Laban's eldest daughter; given to Jacob deceitfully, Ge 29:16–27
Unloved by Jacob, but bears children, Ge 29:30–35; 30:16–21

LEAN (*adj*) *thin*
seven *l*…ugly cows, Ge 41:27
my flesh has grown *l*, Ps 109:24
and the *l* sheep, Eze 34:20

LEAN (*v*) *incline, rest*
may *l* against them, Jdg 16:26
l…own understanding, Pr 3:5
l on the God of Israel, Is 48:2

LEAP *jump, spring*
l-ing and dancing, 2Sa 6:16
I can *l* over a wall, Ps 18:29
baby *l-ed* in her, Lk 1:41
and *l for joy*, Lk 6:23
l-ed up and *began*, Ac 14:10

LEARN *get knowledge*
l to fear the LORD, Dt 31:13
I may *l* Your statutes, Ps 119:71
have I *l-ed* wisdom, Pr 30:3
will they *l* war, Is 2:4
l from Me, Mt 11:29
l-ed to be content, Php 4:11
He *l-ed* obedience, Heb 5:8

LEARNING (*n*) *knowledge*
increase *his l*, Pr 9:9
l of the Egyptians, Ac 7:22
great *l* is driving, Ac 26:24

LEAST *insignificant*
l of my master's, 2Ki 18:24
greatest to the *l*, 2Ch 34:30
l in the kingdom, Mt 5:19
the one who is *l*…is, Mt 11:11
l of the apostles, 1Co 15:9
very *l* of all saints, Eph 3:8

LEATHER *animal skin*
man with a *l* girdle, 2Ki 1:8
a *l* belt around his, Mt 3:4
and *wore* a *l* belt, Mk 1:6

LEAVE *abandon, depart, forsake*
shall *l* his father, Ge 2:24
arise, *l* this land, Ge 31:13
not *l* me defenseless, Ps 141:8
kindness and truth *l*, Pr 3:3
l the ninety-nine, Mt 18:12
Peace I *l* with you, Jn 14:27
I am *l-ing*...world, Jn 16:28
L your country, Ac 7:3

LEAVEN *yeast*
no *l* found in your, Ex 12:19
not be baked with *l*, Lv 6:17
seven days no *l* shall, Dt 16:4
heaven is like *l*, Mt 13:33
little *l* leavens the, 1Co 5:6

LEAVENED *raised by yeast*
whoever eats what is *l*, Ex 12:19
with cakes of *l* bread, Lv 7:13
not eat *l* bread, Dt 16:3
until it was all *l*, Mt 13:33

LEBANON
Part of Israel's inheritance, Jos 13:5–7
Not completely conquered, Jdg 3:1–3
Source of materials for temple, 1Ki 5:2–18; Ezr 3:7
Mentioned in prophecy, Is 10:34; 29:17; 35:2; Eze 17:3; Hos 14:5–7

LEBONAH
Town north of Shiloh, Jdg 21:19

LEG *part of body*
l-s are pillars of, SS 5:15
Uncover the *l*, Is 47:2
not break His *l-s*, Jn 19:33

LEGAL *lawful*
has a *l* matter, Ex 24:14
Give me *l* protection, Lk 18:3

LEGION *division, group*
twelve *l-s* of angels, Mt 26:53
My name is *L*, Mk 5:9
man who had...*l*, Mk 5:15
L; for many demons, Lk 8:30

LEHI
Samson kills Philistines at, Jdg 15:9–19

LEMUEL
King taught by his mother, Pr 31:1–31

LEND *loan*
l-ing them money, Ne 5:10
l-s...on interest, Eze 18:13
l, expecting nothing, Lk 6:35
l me three loaves, Lk 11:5

LENDER *loaner*
becomes the *l-'s* slave, Pr 22:7
l like the borrower, Is 24:2

LENGTH
the *l* of the ark, Ge 6:15
l of days and years, Pr 3:2
breadth and *l* and, Eph 3:18
l and width...equal, Rev 21:16

LEOPARD *animal*
l will lie down with, Is 11:6
Or the *l* his spots, Jer 13:23
Like a *l* I will lie, Hos 13:7
beast...was like a *l*, Rev 13:2

LEPER *one having leprosy*
As for the *l*, Lv 13:45
King Uzziah...a *l*, 2Ch 26:21
a *l* came to Him, Mt 8:2
cleanse *the l-s*, Mt 10:8
home of Simon the *l*, Mk 14:3

LEPROSY *infectious disease*
of *l* on the skin, Lv 13:2
mark of *l* on a, Lv 14:34
an infection of *l*, Dt 24:8
cure him of his *l*, 2Ki 5:3
his *l* was cleansed, Mt 8:3

LEPROUS *having leprosy*
hand was *l* like snow, Ex 4:6
is a *l* malignancy, Lv 13:51
ten *l*...met Him, Lk 17:12

LESS *fewer, smaller*
take *l* from the smaller, Nu 35:8
us l than our iniquities, Ezr 9:13
l are lying lips to a prince, Pr 17:7
the *l a part* of the body, 1Co 12:15
not *l* than sixty years old, 1Ti 5:9

LET *allow, permit*
L there be light, Ge 1:3
L My people go, Ex 5:1
L the children alone, Mt 19:14
l this cup pass from, Mt 26:39
Do not *l* your heart be, Jn 14:1

LETTER *epistle; symbol*
a *l* sent to Solomon, 2Ch 2:11
smallest *l* or stroke, Mt 5:18
You are our *l*, 2Co 3:2
l caused you sorrow, 2Co 7:8
large *l-s* I am writing, Gal 6:11

LEVEL *flat, plain*
lead me in a *l* path, Ps 27:11
path of the righteous *l*, Is 26:7
stood on a *l* place, Lk 6:17

LEVI
Third son of Jacob and Leah, Ge 29:34
Avenges rape of Dinah, Ge 34:25–31
Jacob's prophecy concerning, Ge 49:5–7
Ancestor of Moses and Aaron, Ex 6:16–27

LEVIATHAN
symbolic monster of the deep, Job 3:8; Ps 104:26; Is 27:1

LEVITES
Rewarded for dedication, Ex 32:26–29
Appointed over tabernacle, Nu 1:47–54
Substituted for Israel's firstborn, Nu 3:12–45
Consecrated to the Lord's service, Nu 8:5–26
Cities assigned to, Nu 35:2–8; Jos 14:3, 4; 1Ch 6:54–81
Organized for temple service, 1Ch 9:14–34; 23:1–26:28

LEVITICAL *Levite*
shall come to the *L* priest, Dt 17:9
L priests who carried the ark, Jos 8:33
all the *L* singers, Asaph, 2Ch 5:12
L priests shall never lack, Jer 33:18
through the *L* priesthood, Heb 7:11

LEVY *(n) payment, tax*
the LORD's *l*, Nu 31:38
l fixed by Moses, 2Ch 24:6

LEVY *(v) impose a tax*
l a tax for the LORD, Nu 31:28
l-ied forced laborers, 1Ki 9:21

LEWDNESS *lascivious, lust*
land...full of *l*, Lv 19:29
not commit this *l*, Eze 16:43
I will uncover her *l*, Hos 2:10

LIAR *one telling lies*
who...prove me a *l*, Job 24:25
a poor man than a *l*, Pr 19:22
I will be a *l* like, Jn 8:55
hypocrisy of *l-s*, 1Ti 4:2
we make Him a *l*, 1Jn 1:10

LIBATION
See OFFERINGS

LIBERALITY *generosity*
he who gives, with *l*, Ro 12:8
in the wealth of their *l*., 2Co 8:2
in everything for all *l*, 2Co 9:11
the *l* of your contribution, 2Co 9:13

LIBERTY *freedom*
I will walk at *l*, Ps 119:45
proclaim *l* to captives, Is 61:1
spy out our *l*, Gal 2:4
the *law* of *l*, Jas 1:25

LIBNAH
Canaanite city, captured by Joshua, Jos 10:29, 30
Given to Aaron's descendants, Jos 21:13

LIBYA
Mentioned in prophecy, Eze 30:5; Da 11:43
Jews from, present at Pentecost, Ac 2:1–10

LICK *lap up*
dogs will *l* up your, 1Ki 21:19
his enemies *l* the dust, Ps 72:9
dogs were...*l-ing*, Lk 16:21

LIE *(n) false statement*
speak *l-s* go astray, Ps 58:3
tells *l-s* will perish, Pr 19:9
prophesy a *l* to you, Jer 27:10
the father of *l-s*, Jn 8:44
truth of God for a *l*, Ro 1:25
no *l* is of the truth, 1Jn 2:21

LIE *(v) make false statement*
nor *l* to one another, Lv 19:11
l-d to Him with their, Ps 78:36
l-d about the LORD, Jer 5:12
l to the Holy Spirit, Ac 5:3
not *l* to one another, Col 3:9
impossible...God to *l*, Heb 6:18

LIE *(v) recline*
when you *l* down, Dt 11:19
she *lay* at his feet, Ru 3:14
Saul *lay* sleeping, 1Sa 26:7
makes me *l* down, Ps 23:2
lying in a manger, Lk 2:12

LIFE *living; salvation*
the breath of *l*, Ge 2:7
l for *l*, Ex 21:23
l...is in the blood, Lv 17:11
Our *l* for yours, Jos 2:14
my *l* is *but* breath, Job 7:7
Who redeems your *l*, Ps 103:4
the springs of *l*, Pr 4:23
way of *l* and...death, Jer 21:8
to everlasting *l*, Da 12:2
take my *l* from me, Jon 4:3
worried about your *l*, Mt 6:25
loses his *l* for My, Mt 16:25
His *l* a ransom for, Mt 20:28
to inherit eternal *l*, Mk 10:17
l is more than food, Lk 12:23
but have eternal *l*, Jn 3:16
out of death into *l*, Jn 5:24
I am the bread of *l*, Jn 6:35
lays down his *l*, Jn 10:11
resurrection and...*l*, Jn 11:25
truth, and the *l*, Jn 14:6
lay down his *l* for, Jn 15:13
walk in newness of *l*, Ro 6:4
the Spirit gives *l*, 2Co 3:6
Christ, who is our *l*, Col 3:4
an undisciplined *l*, 2Th 3:11
receive...crown of *l*, Jas 1:12
lay down our *l-ves*, 1Jn 3:16
book of *l* of the lamb, Rev 13:8

LIFEBLOOD
I will require your *l*, Ge 9:5
poured out their *l*, Is 63:6
l of the innocent, Jer 2:34

LIFETIME *length of life*
Throughout his *l*, 2Ch 34:33
His favor is for a *l*, Ps 30:5
my *l* of futility, Ecc 7:15
as the *l* of a tree, Is 65:22

LIFT *exalt, raise*
l up your eyes and, Ge 13:14
l up your staff and, Ex 14:16
l up your voice, Job 38:34
One who *l-s* my head, Ps 3:3
I will *l* up my eyes, Ps 121:1
will not *l* up sword, Is 2:4
Spirit *l-ed* me up, Eze 3:14
Son of Man be *l-ed*, Jn 3:14
He was *l-ed* up, Ac 1:9
l-ing up holy hands, 1Ti 2:8

LIGHT *brightness, lamp*
Let there be *l*, Ge 1:3
Israel had *l* in, Ex 10:23
l of the wicked, Job 18:5
LORD is my *l*, Ps 27:1
And a *l* to my path, Ps 119:105
like the *l* of dawn, Pr 4:18
walk in the *l* of the, Is 2:5
your *l* has come, Is 60:1
stars for *l* by night, Jer 31:35
the *l* of the world, Mt 5:14
body will be full of *l*, Mt 6:22
L of revelation to, Lk 2:32
There was the true *l*, Jn 1:9
I am the *L*, Jn 8:12
while you have...*L*, Jn 12:35
l of the gospel, 2Co 4:4
walk as children of *L*, Eph 5:8
Father of *l-s*, Jas 1:17
if we walk in the *L*, 1Jn 1:7

LIGHTNING *flash of light in sky*
thunder and *l* flashes, Ex 19:16
He spreads His *l*, Job 36:30
makes *l* for the rain, Jer 10:13
l...from the east, Mt 24:27
appearance...like *l*, Mt 28:3

LIKENESS *similarity*
according to Our *l*, Ge 1:26
an idol, or any *l*, Ex 20:4
the *l* of sinful flesh, Ro 8:3
made in the *l* of men, Php 2:7

LILY *flower*
The *l* of the valleys, SS 2:1
blossom like the *l*, Hos 14:5
l-ies of the field, Mt 6:28

LIMB *extremities*
or any deformed *l*, Lv 21:18
in twelve pieces, *l* by limb, Jdg 19:29
His *l* are like bars of iron, Job 40:18
When its *l* are dry, they are, Is 27:11
you will be torn *l* from limb, Da 2:5
Abed-nego shall be torn *l*, Da 3:29
l which is lame may, Heb 12:13

LIMIT *end, extent*
there is no *l*, 1Ch 22:16
no l to windy words, Job 16:3
set a *l* for the rain, Job 28:26
no *l* to the treasure, Na 2:9

LINE *boundary; cord*
draw your *border l*, Nu 34:7
ran from...battle *l*, 1Sa 4:12
a *l* into the Nile, Is 19:8
plumb *l* in the hand, Zec 4:10

LINEN *type of cloth*
makes *l* garments, Pr 31:24
buy...a *l* waistband, Jer 13:1
pulled free of the *l* sheet, Mk 14:52
wrapped Him...*l*, Mk 15:46
saw the *l* wrappings, Jn 20:5
clothed in fine *l*, Rev 19:14

LINTEL *horizontal crosspiece*
blood on the *l*, Ex 12:23
l and five-sided, 1Ki 6:31

LION *wild animal*
Judah is a *l-'s* whelp, Ge 49:9
a *l* or a bear, 1Sa 17:34
hunt me like a *l*, Job 10:16
tear my soul like a *l*, Ps 7:2
are bold as a *l*, Pr 28:1
cast into the *l-s'*, Da 6:16
like a roaring *l*, 1Pe 5:8

LIPS *part of mouth*
My *l* will praise, Ps 63:3
With her flattering *l*, Pr 7:21
Your *l*, *my* bride, SS 4:11
a man of unclean *l*, Is 6:5
honors Me with...*l*, Mt 15:8

LIQUOR *alcoholic drink*
concerning wine and *l*, Mic 2:11
drink no wine or *l*, Lk 1:15

LISTEN *hear, heed*
Pharaoh does not *l*, Ex 7:4
l to His voice, Dt 4:30
l...commandments, Dt 11:27
scoffer does not *l*, Pr 13:1
L to your father, Pr 23:22
draw near to *l*, Ecc 5:1
L to Me, O Jacob, Is 48:12
L...another parable, Mt 21:33
care what you *l* to, Mk 4:24
l-ing to the word, Lk 5:1
My Son...*l* to Him, Lk 9:35

LITERATURE *writings*
teach them the *l*, Da 1:4
every *branch of l*, Da 1:17

LITTLE *small quantity*
a *l* lower than God, Ps 8:5
a *l* boy will lead, Is 11:6
You of *l* faith, Mt 6:30
forgiven *l*, loves *l*, Lk 7:47
a *l* leaven leavens, 1Co 5:6
l children, abide, 1Jn 2:28

LITTLE CHILDREN
L, I am with you a little, Jn 13:33
My *l*, I am writing, 1Jn 2:1
l, because your sins, 1Jn 2:12
l, abide in Him, 1Jn 2:28
L, make sure no one, 1Jn 3:7
L, let us not love with, 1Jn 3:18
You are from God, *l*, 1Jn 4:4
L, guard yourselves, 1Jn 5:21

LIVE *(v) reside; be alive*
eat, and *l* forever, Ge 3:22
does not *l* by bread, Dt 8:3
my Redeemer *l-s*, Job 19:25
Let my soul *l*, Ps 119:175
Listen, that you may *l*, Is 55:3
can these bones *l*, Eze 37:3
righteous will *l* by, Hab 2:4
l-d in...Nazareth, Mt 2:23
not *l* on bread alone, Mt 4:4
l even if he dies, Jn 11:25
because I *l*, Jn 14:19
shall *l* by faith, Ro 1:17
Christ died and *l-d*, Ro 14:9
no longer I who *l*, Gal 2:20
to *l* is Christ, Php 1:21
worship Him who *l-s*, Rev 4:10

LIVER *internal organ*
the lobe of the *l*, Ex 29:13
l of the sin offering, Lv 9:10
pierces through his *l*, Pr 7:23
he looks at the *l*, Eze 21:21

LIVESTOCK *domestic animals*
was very rich in *l*, Ge 13:2
their *l* to Joseph, Ge 47:17
l of Egypt died, Ex 9:6
large number of *l*, Nu 32:1

LIVING *(adj) alive*
man became a *l* being, Ge 2:7
voice of the *l* god, Dt 5:26
Divide the *l* child, 1Ki 3:25
Son of the *l* God, Mt 16:16
given you *l* water, Jn 4:10

I am the *l* bread, Jn 6:51
l and holy sacrifice, Ro 12:1
became a *l* soul, 1Co 15:45
temple of the *l* God, 2Co 6:16
word of God is *l*, Heb 4:12

LIVING *(n) what is alive*
mother of all *the l*, Ge 3:20
land of the *l*, Job 28:13
that the *l* may know, Da 4:17
God…of the *l*, Mt 22:32
judge the *l* and the, 1Pe 4:5

LIVING CREATURE
with swarms of *l-s*, Ge 1:20
every *l* that moves, Ge 1:21
the man called a *l*, Ge 2:19
l that is with you, Ge 9:10
four *l-s* full of eyes, Rev 4:6
throne (with the four *l-s*), Rev 5:6
four *l-s* kept saying, Rev 5:14
heard one of the four *l-s*, Rev 6:1
the elders and the four *l-s*, Rev 7:11
before the four *l-s*, Rev 14:3
l-s gave to the seven, Rev 15:7
four *l-s* fell down, Rev 19:4

LOAD *burden*
in all their *l-s*, Nu 4:27
I alone bear the *l*, Dt 1:12

LOAF *portion of bread*
gave him a *l* of bread, Jer 37:21
asks for a *l*, Mt 7:9
five *l-ves* and two, Mt 14:17

LO-AMMI
Symbolic name of Hosea's son, Hos 1:8, 9

LOAN *something lent*
your neighbor a *l*, Dt 24:10
rich with *l-s*, Hab 2:6

LOATHE *despise, detest*
I *l-d that* generation, Ps 95:10
sated man *l-s* honey, Pr 27:7
I *l* the arrogance of, Am 6:8

LOATHSOME *detestable*
l to the Egyptians, Ge 46:34
like *l* food to me, Job 6:7
l and malignant sore, Rev 16:2

LOBE *projection*
the *l* of the liver, Ex 29:13
the *l* of Aaron's right ear, Ex 29:20

LOCK *(n) tuft of hair*
seven *l-s* of my hair, Jdg 16:13
flowing *l-s* of…head, SS 7:5
a *l* of my head, Eze 8:3

LOCK *(v) secure, shut*
l the door behind, 2Sa 13:17
l-ed quite securely, Ac 5:23
l up…the saints, Ac 26:10

LOCUST *grasshopper*
wind brought the *l-s*, Ex 10:13
you may eat: the *l*, Lv 11:22
come in like *l-s*, Jdg 6:5
leap like the *l*, Job 39:20
l-s have no king, Pr 30:27
like the swarming *l*, Na 3:17

food was *l-s* and wild, Mt 3:4

LODGE *dwell, spend the night*
where you *l*, I will *l*, Ru 1:16
drank and *l-d* there, Jdg 19:4
In his neck *l-s*, Job 41:22
l in the wilderness, Ps 55:7

LODGING *(adj) dwelling*
fodder at the *l* place, Ge 42:27
about at the *l* place, Ex 4:24
A wayfarers' *l* place, Jer 9:2

LOFTINESS *elevated, haughty*
l of man will be, Is 2:11
l of your dwelling, Ob 3

LOFTY *grand, high*
built You a *l* house, 1Ki 8:13
high and *l* mountain, Is 57:7

LOG *beam, wood*
he who splits *l-s*, Ecc 10:9
l out of your own eye, Mt 7:5

LOINS *lower back*
with your *l* girded, Ex 12:11
Gird up your *l*, 2Ki 4:29
l are full of anguish, Is 21:3
having girded your *l*, Eph 6:14

LONELY *alone, isolated*
I am *l* and afflicted, Ps 25:16
makes a home for the *l*, Ps 68:6
How *l* sits the city, La 1:1

LONG *(adj) extended*
there was a *l* war, 2Sa 3:1
L life is in her, Pr 3:16
you make *l* prayers, Mt 23:14
if a man has *l* hair, 1Co 11:14

LONG *(v) desire, want*
Who *l* for death, Job 3:21
my soul *l-s* for You, Is 26:9
l-ing to be fed, Lk 16:21
I *l* to see you, Ro 1:11
angels *l* to look, 1Pe 1:12
l for the pure milk, 1Pe 2:2

LOOK *see, stare*
Do not *l* behind you, Ge 19:17
afraid to *l* at God, Ex 3:6
LORD *l-s* at…heart, 1Sa 16:7
L upon my affliction, Ps 25:18
The sea *l-ed* and fled, Ps 114:3
not *l* on the wine, Pr 23:31
l eagerly for Him, Is 8:17
l to the Holy One, Is 17:7
l on Me…pierced, Zec 12:10
L at the birds of, Mt 6:26
l-ing up…heaven, Mt 14:19
plow and *l-ing* back, Lk 9:62
l on the fields, Jn 4:35
l on Him…pierced, Jn 19:37
l-ing for the blessed, Titus 2:13
l-ing for…heavens, 2Pe 3:13

LOOSE *release*
l the cords of Orion, Job 38:31
have *l-d* my bonds, Ps 116:16
l on earth shall have been, Mt 16:19
you *l* on earth, Mt 18:18

LORD *personal name of God*
Old Testament
Different Hebrew words are translated as Lord. English transliteration is in italics.
LORD *(Yahweh)*, Ge 4:1; Ex 3:2, 15; Ps 23:1; Is 40:31; Eze 11:23
Lord God *(Adonai Yahweh)*, Ge 15:2; 2Sa 7:18, 19; Is 1:24; Eze 28:6; Hab 3:19
LORD God *(Yahweh Elohim)*, Ge 2:4; Ps 59:5; 68:18; Jer 15:16; Jon 1:9
Lord *(Adonai)*, Ge 18:27; Ex 4:10; Jos 3:11; Ps 68:19; Mic 4:13
LORD God *(Yah Yahweh)*, Is 12:2
New Testament
Different Greek words are translated as Lord. English transliteration is in italics.
Lord (*Kyrios,* refers to either the Father or the Son), Mt 1:20; Jn 11:2; Ac 5:19; 2Co 5:6; 1Th 4:16
Lord (*Despotes,* refers to the Father), Lk 2:29; Ac 4:24; Rev 6:10
Lord God (*Kyrios Theos,* refers to either the Father or the Son), Lk 1:32; Rev 1:8; 11:17; 16:7; 18:8
Lord Jesus *(Kyrios Iesous)*, Mk 16:19; Lk 24:3; Ac 4:33; 7:59
Lord Jesus Christ *(Kyrios Iesous Christos)*, Ac 15:26; Ro 1:7; 5:1; 1Co 1:10; Eph 1:2, 3; 1Th 5:9; Jas 2:1

LORD *human master, ruler*
Hear us, my *l*, Ge 23:6
not my *l* be angry, Ge 31:35
Moses, my *l*, Nu 11:28
l-s of…Philistines, Jdg 16:27
counsel of my *l*, Ezr 10:3
l-s of the nations, Is 16:8
his *l* commanded, Mt 18:25
write to my *l*, Ac 25:26

LORD AND SAVIOR
See SAVIOR OF THE WORLD
kingdom of our *L*, 2Pe 1:11
knowledge of the *L*, 2Pe 2:20
commandment of the *L*, 2Pe 3:2
knowledge of our *L*, 2Pe 3:18

LORD APPEARED TO
L Abram, Ge 12:7
L Abram, Ge 17:1
L him by the oaks, Ge 18:1
L him the same night, Ge 26:24
glory of the *L* all the, Lv 9:23
glory of the *L* all the, Nu 16:19
L Solomon in a dream, 1Ki 3:5
L Solomon a second time, 1Ki 9:2

LORD COMMANDED
L the man, Ge 2:16
L Moses, Ex 16:34
which the *L* us, Ex 36:5
the *L* to apportion, Nu 34:29
ordinances which the *L*, Nu 36:13
L through Moses, Jos 14:2
not kept what the *L*, 1Sa 13:14
As the *L* them, Ps 106:34
L the blessing-life, Ps 133:3
L the fish, Jon 2:10

LORD GOD OF HOSTS
the *L* was with him., 2Sa 5:10
L … Awake to punish, Ps 59:5
L, How long will, Ps 80:4

A time to *l*, Ecc 3:8
Hate evil, *l* good, Am 5:15
do not *l* perjury, Zec 8:17
l your enemies, Mt 5:44
l to stand and pray, Mt 6:5
God so *l-d* the world, Jn 3:16
you *l* one another, Jn 13:34
l-s a cheerful giver, 2Co 9:7
Husbands, *l*...wives, Eph 5:25
Do not *l* the world, 1Jn 2:15
whom I *l*, I reprove, Rev 3:19

LOVE OF CHRIST
separate us from the *l*?, Ro 8:35
the *l* controls us, 2Co 5:14
l which surpasses, Eph 3:19

LOVE OF GOD
disregard justice and the *l*, Lk 11:42
do not have the *l*, Jn 5:42
the *l* has been poured, Ro 5:5
separate us from the *l*, Ro 8:39
l, and the fellowship, 2Co 13:14
your hearts into the *l*, 2Th 3:5
l has truly been perfected, 1Jn 2:5
how does the *l* abide, 1Jn 3:17
By this the *l* was, 1Jn 4:9
this is the *l*, 1Jn 5:3
keep yourselves in the *l*, Jude 21

LOVE ONE ANOTHER
l, even as I have, Jn 13:34
l, just as I have, Jn 15:12
to anyone except to *l*, Ro 13:8
taught by God to *l*, 1Th 4:9
fervently *l* from, 1Pe 1:22
we should *l*, 1Jn 3:11
l, just as He commanded, 1Jn 3:23
l, for love is from God, 1Jn 4:7
we also ought to *l*, 1Jn 4:11
if we *l*, God abides, 1Jn 4:12
beginning, that we *l*, 2Jn 5

LOVE THE LORD YOUR GOD
l with all your heart and, Dt 6:5
l, and always keep, Dt 11:1
l and to serve Him, Dt 11:3
l, to walk in all, Dt 11:22
l with all your heart, Dt 13:3
l, and to walk in, Dt 19:9
l with all your heart and, Dt 30:6
l, to walk in His, Dt 30:16
l and walk in all, Jos 22:5
heed to yourselves to *l*, Jos 23:11
l with all your heart, Mt 22:37
l with all your heart, Mk 12:30
l with all your heart, Lk 10:27

LOVE YOUR ENEMIES
l and pray for, Mt 5:44
l, do good, Lk 6:27
l, and do good, Lk 6:35

LOVE YOUR NEIGHBOR
l as yourself, Lv 19:18
l and hate your enemy, Mt 5:43
shall *l* as yourself, Mt 19:19
shall *l* as yourself, Mt 22:39
shall *l* as yourself, Mk 12:31
shall *l* as yourself, Ro 13:9
shall *l* as yourself, Gal 5:14
shall *l* as yourself, Jas 2:8

LOVELY *attractive*
How *l* are your dwelling, Ps 84:1
to His name, for it is *l*, Ps 135:3
"I am black but *l*, SS 1:5
sweet, And your form is *l*, SS 2:14
darling, As *l* as Jerusalem, SS 6:4
How *l* on the mountains, Is 52:7
he was *l* in the sight of God, Ac 7:20
is pure, whatever is *l*, Php 4:8

LOVERS *one who desires, loves*
l have been crushed, Jer 22:20
I called to my *l*, La 1:19
the hands of your *l*, Eze 16:39
I will go after my *l*, Hos 2:5
l of pleasure...*l* of, 2Ti 3:4

LOVINGKINDNESS *compassion*
His *l* is upon Israel, Ezr 3:11
abundant in *l* and, Ps 86:15
sing of the *l* of the, Ps 89:1
By *l* and truth, Pr 16:6
with everlasting *l*, Is 54:8

LOVINGKINDNESS IS EVERLASTING
For His *l*, 1Ch 16:34
LORD is good; His *l*, Ps 100:5
He is good, for His *l*, Ps 107:1
for He is good; for His *l*, Ps 118:1
He is good, for His *l*, Ps 136:1

LOW *downward*
bowed *l* and worshiped, Ge 24:26
Moses made haste to bow *l*, Ex 34:8
brought very *l* because, Jdg 6:6
He brings *l*, He also exalts, 1Sa 2:7
proud, and make him *l*, Job 40:11
confront him, bring him *l*, Ps 17:13
Men of *l* degree are only, Ps 62:9
us in our *l* estate, Ps 136:23
mountain and hill be made *l*, Is 40:4
hill will be brought *l*, Lk 3:5

LOWLAND *low hills*
country and in the *l*, Dt 1:7
the Negev and the *l*, Jos 10:40
sycamores in the *l*, 2Ch 1:15
the cities of the *l*, Jer 32:44
See also shephelah

LOWLY *humble, little*
He sets on high...*l*, Job 5:11
He regards the *l*, Ps 138:6
associate with the *l*, Ro 12:16

LOYALTY *faithfulness*
Is this your *l*, 2Sa 16:17
proclaims his own *l*, Pr 20:6
I delight in *l*, Hos 6:6

LUD
See LYDIA
A people descended from Shem, 1Ch 1:17

LUKE
"The beloved physician," Col 4:14
Paul's last companion, 2Ti 4:11

LUKEWARM *tepid*
because you are *l*, Rev 3:16

LUST *sexual desire*
looks at...woman with *l*, Mt 5:28
from youthful *l-s*, 2Ti 2:22
You *l* and do not, Jas 4:2
l of the eyes, 1Jn 2:16

LUXURIANT *lush, productive*
beneath...*l* tree, 1Ki 14:23
Israel is a *l* vine, Hos 10:1

LUXURY *extravagance*
L is not fitting for, Pr 19:10
clothed and live in *l*, Lk 7:25

LYCAONIA
District of Asia Minor where Paul preached, Ac 14:6, 11

LYCIA
Province of Asia Minor visited by Paul, Ac 27:5, 6

LYDDA
Aeneas healed at, Ac 9:32–35

LYDIA
Woman of Thyatira; Paul's first European convert, Ac 16:14, 15, 40
——— District of Asia Minor containing Ephesus, Smyrna, Thyatira, and Sardis, Rev 1:11

LYING *(adj) false*
with a *l* tongue, Ps 109:2
hatred *has l* lips, Pr 10:18
l pen of the scribes, Jer 8:8
and *l* divination, Eze 13:6

LYRE *stringed instrument*
play the *l* and pipe, Ge 4:21
prophesy with *l-s*, 1Ch 25:1
Awake, harp and *l*, Ps 57:8

LYSIAS
Roman commander who protected Paul, Ac 24:22–24, 26

LYSTRA
Paul visits; is worshiped by people of and stoned by Jews, Ac 14:6–20
Home of Timothy, Ac 16:1, 2

M

MAACAH
Small Syrian kingdom near Mt. Hermon, Dt 3:14
Not possessed by Israel, Jos 13:13
——— David's wife; mother of Absalom, 2Sa 3:3
——— Wife of Rehoboam; mother of King Abijah, 2Ch 11:18–21
Makes idol; is deposed as queen mother, 1Ki 15:13

MACEDONIA
Paul preaches in, Ac 16:9–17:14
Paul's troubles in, 2Co 7:5
Churches of, generous, Ro 15:26; 2Co 8:1–5

MACHIR
Manasseh's only son, Ge 50:23
Founder of the family of Machirites, Nu 26:29
Conqueror of Gilead, Nu 32:39, 40

MACHPELAH
Field containing a cave; bought by Abraham, Ge 23:9–18

Sarah and Abraham buried here, Ge 23:19; 25:9, 10
Isaac, Rebekah, Leah, and Jacob buried here, Ge 49:29–31

MAD *insane*
makes a wise man *m*, Ecc 7:7
nations are going *m*, Jer 51:7

MADMAN *insane person*
behaving as a *m*, 1Sa 21:14
m who prophesies, Jer 29:26

MADNESS *lunacy*
laughter, It is *m*, Ecc 2:2
consider...*m* and folly, Ecc 2:12

MAGADAN
A region of Galilee, Mt 15:39

MAGDALENE
See MARY

MAGI
wise men from Persia who visited Jesus, Mary, and Joseph, Mt 2:1, 7, 16

MAGIC *sorcery*
practicing *m*, Ac 8:9
who practiced *m*, Ac 19:19

MAGICIAN *sorcerer, wizard*
called for...*m-s*, Ge 41:8
the *m-s* of Egypt, Ex 7:11
of any *m*, conjurer or, Da 2:10
found a *m*, Ac 13:6

MAGISTRATE
appear before the *m*, Lk 12:58
to the chief *m-s*, Ac 16:20

MAGNIFY *extol, praise*
name...be *m-ied*, 2Sa 7:26
You *m* him, Job 7:17
O *m* the LORD with me, Ps 34:3
have *m-ied* Your word, Ps 138:2
Jesus was...*m-ied*, Ac 19:17
I *m* my ministry, Ro 11:13

MAGOG
People among Japheth's descendants, Ge 10:2
Associated with Gog, Eze 38:2
Representatives of final enemies, Rev 20:8

MAHANAIM
Name given by Jacob to a sacred site, Ge 32:2
Becomes Ishbosheth's capital, 2Sa 2:8–29
David flees to, during Absalom's rebellion, 2Sa 17:24, 27

MAHER-SHALAL-HASH-BAZ
Symbolic name of Isaiah's second son; prophetic of the fall of Damascus and Samaria, Is 8:1–4

MAHLON
Husband of Ruth; without child, Ru 1:2–5

MAID
Hagar, Sarai's *m*, Ge 16:8
gave my *m* to my, Ge 30:18
I am Ruth your *m*, Ru 3:9
way of a man...a *m*, Pr 30:19

MAIDENS *young woman*
at the Nile...her *m*, Ex 2:5
m...tambourines, Ps 68:25

MAIDSERVANT *female slave*
do...to your *m*, Dt 15:17
give Your *m* a son, 1Sa 1:11
let your *m* speak, 2Sa 14:12
while your *m* slept, 1Ki 3:20

MAINTAIN *keep*
and *m* their cause, 1Ki 8:45
You have *m-ed* my just, Ps 9:4
not *m* his position before, Ps 101:7
He will *m* his cause, Ps 112:5
m the cause of the, Ps 140:12
he *m-ed* his fury forever, Am 1:11
m always a blameless, Ac 24:16
m that a man is justified by, Ro 3:28
m-ing the same love, Php 2:2
which they had *m-ed*, Rev 6:9

MAJESTIC *dignified, grand*
Who is like You, *m*, Ex 15:11
with His *m* voice, Job 37:4
How *m* is Your name, Ps 8:1
They are the *m* ones, Ps 16:3
m is His work, Ps 111:3
by the *M* Glory, 2Pe 1:17

MAJESTY *grandeur*
Around God is...*m*, Job 37:22
He is clothed with *m*, Ps 93:1
The *m* of our God, Is 35:2
right hand of the *M*, Heb 1:3
revile angelic *m-ies*, Jude 8

MAKE *cause, create, do*
Let Us *m* man in, Ge 1:26
not *m* for...an idol, Ex 20:4
M me know Your ways, Ps 25:4
M ready the way of, Mt 3:3
m you fishers of men, Mt 4:19

MAKER *creator*
Where is God my *M*, Job 35:10
kneel before...our *M*, Ps 95:6
M of heaven and, Ps 115:15
I, the LORD, am the *m*, Is 44:24

MAKKEDAH
Canaanite town assigned to Judah, Jos 15:20, 41

MALACHI
Prophet and writer, Mal 1:1

MALCHI-SHUA
Son of King Saul, 1Sa 14:49
Killed at Gilboa, 1Sa 31:2

MALCHUS
Servant of the high priest, Jn 18:10

MALE
m and female He, Ge 1:27
lamb...unblemished *m*, Ex 12:5
likeness of *m* or, Dt 4:16
slew...*m* children, Mt 2:16
made...*m* and female, Mt 19:4
neither *m* nor female, Gal 3:28

MALICE *evil, mischief*
perceived their *m*, Mt 22:18
leaven of *m* and, 1Co 5:8
wrath, *m*, slander, Col 3:8
putting aside all *m*, 1Pe 2:1

MALICIOUS *harmful, spiteful*
to be a *m* witness, Ex 23:1
m gossips, without, 2Ti 3:3

MALTA
Paul's shipwreck, Ac 28:1–8

MAMRE
Town or district near Hebron, Ge 23:19
Abram dwells by the oaks of, Ge 13:18

MAN *male*
make *m* in Our image, Ge 1:26
God formed *m* of dust, Ge 2:7
Elisha the *m* of God, 2Ki 5:8
m is born for trouble, Job 5:7
blessed is the *m*, Ps 1:1
m is a mere breath, Ps 39:11
righteous *m* hates, Pr 13:5
Will a *m* rob God, Mal 3:8
light...before *men*, Mt 5:16
fishers of *men*, Mk 1:17
Sabbath...for *m*, Mk 2:27
rich *m* to enter, Mk 10:25
what is a *m* profited, Lk 9:25
a *m*, sent from God, Jn 1:6
How can a *m* be born, Jn 3:4
a *m* of Macedonia, Ac 16:9
through one *m* sin, Ro 5:12
as is common to *m*, 1Co 10:13
when I became a *m*, 1Co 13:11
m...leave his father, Eph 5:31

MAN OF GOD
Moses the *m* blessed, Dt 33:1
A *m* came to me, Jdg 13:6
a *m* came to Eli, 1Sa 2:27
is a *m* in this city, 1Sa 9:6
Shemaiah the *m*, 1Ki 12:22
came a *m* from Judah, 1Ki 13:1
to do with you, O *m*?, 1Ki 17:18
m came near and spoke, 1Ki 20:28
"O *m*, the king says, 2Ki 1:9
this is a holy *m*, 2Ki 4:9
Elisha the *m* heard, 2Ki 5:8
and the *m* wept, 2Ki 8:11
the *m* was angry, 2Ki 13:19
son of Igdaliah, the *m*, Jer 35:4
you *m*, and pursue, 1Ti 6:11
m may be adequate, 2Ti 3:17

MAN, SON OF
See SON OF MAN

MANAGER *one in charge*
a rich man who had a *m*, Lk 16:1
praised the unrighteous *m*, Lk 16:8
is under guardians and *m-s*, Gal 4:2
good *m-s* of their, 1Ti 3:12

MANASSEH
Joseph's firstborn son, Ge 41:50, 51
Adopted by Jacob, Ge 48:5, 6
Loses his birthright to Ephraim, Ge 48:13–20
——— Tribe of:
Numbered, Nu 1:34, 35
Half-tribe of, settle east of Jordan, Nu 32:33–42; Dt 3:12–15

Help Joshua against Canaanites, Jos 1:12–18
Land assigned to western half-tribe, Jos 17:1–13
Eastern half-tribe builds altar, Jos 22:9–34
Some of, help David, 1Ch 12:19–31
——— Wicked king of Judah; son of Hezekiah, 2Ki 21:1–18; 2Ch 33:1–9
Captured and taken to Babylon; repents and is restored, 2Ch 33:10–13
Removes idols and altars, 2Ch 33:14–20

MANDRAKES *love fruit*
found *m* in the field, Ge 30:14
m...fragrance, SS 7:13

MANGER *feeding trough*
spend...at your *m*, Job 39:9
the *m* is clean, Pr 14:4
laid Him in a *m*, Lk 2:7

MANIFEST *reveal*
I have *m-ed* Your name, Jn 17:6
became *m* to those, Ro 10:20
made *m* to God, 2Co 5:11
m-ed to His saints, Col 1:26

MANIFOLD *many and varied*
the *m* wisdom of God, Eph 3:10
stewards...*m* grace, 1Pe 4:10

MANKIND *the human race*
God...dwell with *m*, 2Ch 6:18
All *m* is stupid, Jer 51:17
His love for *m*, Titus 3:4
kill a third of *m*, Rev 9:15

MANNA *food of the desert*
Israel named it *m*, Ex 16:31
m was like coriander, Nu 11:7
m ceased on the day, Jos 5:12
He rained down *m*, Ps 78:24
Our fathers ate the *m*, Jn 6:31

MANNER *way*
Your *m* with those, Ps 119:132
spoke in such a *m*, Ac 14:1
m worthy of...saints, Ro 16:2
walk in a *m* worthy, Eph 4:1

MANOAH
Danite; father of Samson, Jdg 13:1–25

MANSLAYER
for the *m* to flee to, Nu 35:6
m might flee there, Dt 4:42
the *m* who kills any, Jos 20:3

MANTLE *cloak, garment*
threw his *m* on him, 1Ki 19:19
the *m* of Elijah, 2Ki 2:13
like a *m* You will roll, Heb 1:12

MAON
Village in Judah, Jos 15:55
David stays at, 1Sa 23:24, 25
Nabal's house here, 1Sa 25:2

MARA
Name chosen by Naomi, Ru 1:20

MARAH
First Israelite camp after passing through the Red Sea, Nu 33:8, 9

MARCH *pace, walk*
m around...seven times, Jos 6:4
m everyone in his path, Joel 2:8

MARDUK
chief Babylonian god, Jer 50:2

MARK (John)
Son of Mary of Jerusalem; travels with Barnabas and Saul, Ac 12:12, 25
Leaves Paul at Perga, Ac 13:13
Barnabas and Paul separate because of him, Ac 15:37–40
Later approved by Paul, Col 4:10; 2Ti 4:11
Companion of Peter, 1Pe 5:13
Author of the second Gospel, Mk 1:1

MARK *sign, spot*
make any tattoo *m-s*, Lv 19:28
m on the foreheads, Eze 9:4
m on his forehead, Rev 14:9
m of the beast, Rev 19:20

MARKET *selling; trading place*
was the *m* of nations, Is 23:3
coastlands were...*m*, Eze 27:15
idle in the *m* place, Mt 20:3
sold in the meat *m*, 1Co 10:25

MARRIAGE *wedlock*
a *m* alliance with, 1Ki 3:1
nor are given in *m*, Mt 22:30
M is to be held in honor, Heb 13:4
m supper of the Lamb, Rev 19:9

MARROW *pith*
the *m* of his bones is moist, Job 21:24
satisfied as with *m*, Ps 63:5
wine, choice pieces with *m*, Is 25:6
spirit, of both joints and *m*, Heb 4:12

MARRY *join in wedlock*
m-ied foreign wives, Ezr 10:10
m-ies a divorced, Mt 5:32
better not to *m*, Mt 19:10
neither *m* nor are, Mk 12:25
m-ied woman is bound, Ro 7:2
better to *m* than to, 1Co 7:9

MARTHA
Sister of Mary and Lazarus; loved by Jesus, Jn 11:1–5
Affirms her faith, Jn 11:19–28
Offers hospitality to Jesus, Lk 10:38; Jn 12:1, 2
Gently rebuked by Christ, Lk 10:39–42

MARVEL *be amazed, wonder*
Jesus heard...*m-ed*, Mt 8:10
the crowd *m-ed*, Mt 15:31
m-ed at the sight, Ac 7:31

MARVELOUS *extraordinary*
and see this *m* sight, Ex 3:3
It is *m* in our eyes, Ps 118:23
into His *m* light, 1Pe 2:9
m are Your works, Rev 15:3

MARY
Mother of Christ, Mt 1:16
Visited by angel, Lk 1:26–38
Visits Elizabeth and offers praise, Lk 1:39–56
Gives birth to Jesus, Lk 2:6–20
Flees to Egypt, Mt 2:13–18
Visits Jerusalem with Jesus, Lk 2:41–52
Entrusted to John's care, Jn 19:25–27
——— Mother of James and Joses; present at crucifixion and burial, Mt 27:55–61
Sees the risen Lord; informs disciples, Mt 28:1–10
——— Magdalene; delivered from seven demons; supports Christ's ministry, Lk 8:2, 3
Present at crucifixion and burial, Mt 27:55–61
First to see the risen Lord, Mk 16:1–10; Jn 20:1–18
——— Sister of Martha and Lazarus; loved by Jesus, Jn 11:1–5
Grieves for Lazarus, Jn 11:19, 20, 28–33
Anoints Jesus, Mt 26:6–13; Jn 12:1–8
Commended by Jesus, Lk 10:38–42
——— Mark's mother, Ac 12:12–17

MASSAH AND MERIBAH
First, at Rephidim, Israel just out of Egypt, Ex 17:1–7
Second, at Kadesh Barnea, 40 years later, Nu 20:1–13

MASTER *lord, ruler*
God of...*m* Abraham, Ge 24:12
m shall pierce his ear, Ex 21:6
can serve two *m-s*, Mt 6:24
death no longer is *m*, Ro 6:9
sin shall not be *m*, Ro 6:14
obedient to...your *m-s*, Eph 6:5
a *M* in heaven, Col 4:1

MATERIAL *(adj) physical*
minister to them also in *m*, Ro 15:27
we reap *m* things from, 1Co 9:11

MATERIAL *(n) cloth; substance*
blue, purple and scarlet *m*, Ex 25:4
two kinds of *m* mixed., Lv 19:19
and hyssop and scarlet *m*, Nu 19:6
not wear a *m* mixed of, Dt 22:11
m of the wall was jasper, Rev 21:18

MATTANIAH
King Zedekiah's original name, 2Ki 24:17

MATTHEW
Becomes Christ's follower, Mt 9:9
Chosen as one of the Twelve, Mt 10:2, 3
Called Levi, the son of Alphaeus, Mk 2:14
Author of the first Gospel, Mt (title)

MATTHIAS
Chosen by lot to replace Judas, Ac 1:15–26

MATURE *full grown; stable*
then the *m* grain, Mk 4:28
those who are *m*, 1Co 2:6
your thinking be *m*, 1Co 14:20
food is for the *m*, Heb 5:14

MATURITY *ripeness, adulthood*
bring no fruit to *m*, Lk 8:14
let us press on to *m*, Heb 6:1

MAY IT NEVER BE
heard it, they said, "*M*!", Lk 20:16
M! Rather, let God be, Ro 3:4
M! For otherwise, how will, Ro 3:6
Law through faith? *M*!, Ro 3:31

m on whom I have *m*, Ro 9:15
by the *m-ies* of God, Ro 12:1
God, being rich in *m*, Eph 2:4

MERCY SEAT
make a *m* of pure gold, Ex 25:17
put the *m* on the ark, Ex 26:34
m that is over the ark, Ex 30:6
made a *m* of pure gold, Ex 37:6
before the *m*, Lv 16:2
above the *m*, Nu 7:89
the room for the *m*, 1Ch 28:11
overshadowing the *m*, Heb 9:5

MERIB-BAAL
Another name for Mephibosheth, 1Ch 8:34

MERODACH
Supreme deity of the Babylonians, Jer 50:2
Otherwise called Bel, Is 46:1
Sends ambassadors to Hezekiah, Is 39:1–8
Also called Berodach-Baladan, 2Ki 20:12

MEROM
Lake along the Jordan River, in northern Palestine, Jos 11:5, 7

MEROZ
Town cursed for failing to help the LORD, Jdg 5:23

MERRY *joyful, lively*
wine makes life *m*, Ecc 10:19
eat, drink *and* be *m*, Lk 12:19

MESHACH
Name given to Mishael, Da 1:7
Advanced to high position, Da 2:49
Remains faithful in testing, Da 3:13–30

MESHECH
Son of Japheth, Ge 10:2
His descendants, mentioned in prophecy, Eze 27:13; 32:26; 38:2, 3

MESOPOTAMIA
Home of Abraham's relatives, Ge 24:4, 10, 15
Called Padan Aram and Syria, Ge 25:20; 31:20, 24
Israel enslaved to, Jdg 3:8–10
Jews from, present at Pentecost, Ac 2:9

MESSAGE *communication*
m from God for you, Jdg 3:20
m...with authority, Lk 4:32
m and my preaching, 1Co 2:4
the *m* of truth, Eph 1:13
m we have heard, 1Jn 1:5

MESSENGER *one sent*
My *m* whom I send, Is 42:19
m of the LORD of hosts, Mal 2:7
I send My *m* ahead, Mt 11:10
m-s of the churches, 2Co 8:23
m of Satan, 2Co 12:7

MESSIAH
anointed one, Da 9:25, 26; Jn 1:41; 4:25
Greek: Christ

METAL
like glowing *m*, Eze 1:4
their *m* images, Da 11:8

METHUSELAH
Oldest man on record, Ge 5:27

MICAH
Prophet, contemporary of Isaiah, Is 1:1; Mic 1:1

MICAIAH
Prophet who predicts Ahab's death, 1Ki 22:8–28
——— Contemporary of Jeremiah, Jer 36:11–13

MICHAEL
Chief prince, Da 10:13, 21
Disputes with Satan, Jude 9
Fights the dragon, Rev 12:7–9

MICHAL
Daughter of King Saul, 1Sa 14:49
Loves and marries David, 1Sa 18:20–28
Saves David from Saul, 1Sa 19:9–17
Given to Palti, 1Sa 25:44
David demands her from Abner, 2Sa 3:13–16
Ridicules David; becomes barren, 2Sa 6:16–23

MICHMASH
Site of battle with Philistines, 1Sa 13:5, 11, 16, 23
Scene of Jonathan's victory, 1Sa 14:1–16

MIDDAY *noon*
he was taking his *m* rest, 2Sa 4:5
from early morning until *m*, Ne 8:3
stumble at *m* as in the, Is 59:10
at *m*, O King, I saw, Ac 26:13

MIDDLE *midst*
the *m* of the garden, Ge 3:3
sun stopped in the *m*, Jos 10:13
m of the lampstands, Rev 1:13

MIDDLE GATE
See GATES OF JERUSALEM

MIDHEAVEN *directly overhead*
eagle flying in *m*, Rev 8:13
angel flying in *m*, Rev 14:6
birds which fly in *m*, Rev 19:17

MIDIAN
Son of Abraham by Keturah, Ge 25:1–4
——— Region in the Arabian desert occupied by the Midianites, Ge 25:6; Ex 2:15

MIDIANITES
Descendants of Abraham by Keturah, Ge 25:1, 2
Moses flees to, Ex 2:15
Join Moab in cursing Israel, Nu 22:4–7
Intermarriage with incurs God's wrath, Nu 25:1–18
Defeated by Israel, Nu 31:1–10
Oppress Israel; defeated by Gideon, Jdg 6; 7

MIDST *middle, within*
God is in the *m*, Ps 46:5
in the *m* of the fire, Da 3:25
Holy One in your *m*, Hos 11:9
I am...in their *m*, Mt 18:20

MIDWIFE *aids childbirth*
m...tied a scarlet, Ge 38:28
before the *m* can get, Ex 1:19

MIGDOL
Israelite encampment, Ex 14:2
Place Jews flee to in Egypt, Jer 44:1

MIGHT *strength*
my firstborn; My *m*, Ge 49:3
and with all your *m*, Dt 6:5
With Him are...*m*, Job 12:13
Not by *m* nor by, Zec 4:6
strength of His *m*, Eph 1:19

MIGHTY *powerful*
a *m* hunter before, Ge 10:9
m...awesome God, Dt 10:17
m men of valor, 1Ch 12:8
The LORD *m* in battle, Ps 24:8
a *m* king will rule, Is 19:4
m in the Scriptures, Ac 18:24
the *m* hand of God, 1Pe 5:6

MILCOM
Solomon went after, 1Ki 11:5
Altar destroyed by Josiah, 2Ki 23:12, 13

MILE *distance, measurement*
one *m*, go with him, Mt 5:41
m-s from Jerusalem, Lk 24:13

MILETUS
Paul meets Ephesian elders here, Ac 20:15–38
Paul leaves Trophimus here, 2Ti 4:20

MILK
land flowing with *m*, Ex 3:8
pour me out like *m*, Job 10:10
m produces butter, Pr 30:33
m to drink, not, 1Co 3:2
pure *m* of the word, 1Pe 2:2

MILK AND HONEY
to a land flowing with *m*, Ex 3:8
a land flowing with *m*, Ex 13:5
a land flowing with *m*, Lv 20:24
does flow with *m*, Nu 13:27
a land flowing with *m*, Dt 6:3
the land flowing with *m*, Dt 31:20
a land flowing with *m*, Jos 5:6
a land flowing with *m*, Jer 11:5
flowing with *m*, Eze 20:6

MILL *grinding stones*
sound of the...*m*, Ecc 12:4
at the grinding *m*, La 5:13
women...at the *m*, Mt 24:41

MILLO
Fort at Jerusalem, 2Sa 5:9
Prepared by Solomon, 1Ki 9:15
Strengthened by Hezekiah, 2Ch 32:5
Scene of Joash's death, 2Ki 12:20, 21

MILLSTONE *grinding stone*
upper *m* in pledge, Dt 24:6
woman threw...*m*, Jdg 9:53
m hung around, Mt 18:6
stone like a great *m*, Rev 18:21

MINA
measure of gold or silver coin, 1Ki 10:17; Ezr 2:69; Ne 7:71; Lk 19:13ff

MIND *memory, thought*
God tries the...*m-s*, Ps 7:9
Recall it to *m*, Is 46:8
I test the *m*, Jer 17:10
Let his *m* be changed, Da 4:16
He opened...*m-s*, Lk 24:45
with one *m* in the, Ac 2:46
to a depraved *m*, Ro 1:28
m set on the flesh, Ro 8:7
the *m* of Christ, 1Co 2:16
m-s were hardened, 2Co 3:14
with humility of *m*, Php 2:3

MINDFUL *aware*
LORD be *m* of me, Ps 40:17
He is *m* that we are, Ps 103:14
LORD has been *m*, Ps 115:12
m of the...faith, 2Ti 1:5

MINE *belonging to me*
and all that you see is *m*, Ge 31:43
and Manasseh shall be *m*, Ge 48:5
for all the earth is *M*, Ex 19:5
So the Levites shall be *M*, Nu 3:12
For all the firstborn are *M*, Nu 3:13
Vengeance is *M*, Dt 32:35
beast of the forest is *M*, Ps 50:10
Gilead is *M*, and Manasseh, Ps 60:7
My beloved is *m*, and I am, SS 2:16
these words of *M* and, Mt 7:24
this is not *M* to give, Mk 10:40
My teaching is not *M*, Jn 7:16
the Father has are *M*, Jn 16:15
Mine are Yours, and Yours are, Jn 17:10
vengeance is *M*, Ro 12:19
vengeance is *M*, Heb 10:30

MINISTER *(n) one who serves*
m-s before the ark, 1Ch 16:4
spoken of *as m-s*, Is 61:6
a *m* and a witness, Ac 26:16
a *m* of Christ Jesus, Ro 15:16
is Christ then a *m*, Gal 2:17
I was made a *m*, Eph 3:7
faithful *m* in the, Eph 6:21
His *m-s* a flame of, Heb 1:7
a *m* in the sanctuary, Heb 8:2

MINISTER *(v) give help, serve*
to *m* as priest to Me, Ex 28:1
the boy *m-ed* to, 1Sa 2:11
not stand to *m*, 1Ki 8:11
to the LORD, To *m*, Is 56:6
angels were *m-ing*, Mk 1:13
follow Him and *m*, Mk 15:41

MINISTRY *service*
He began His *m*, Lk 3:23
to the *m* of the word, Ac 6:4
m of the Spirit, 2Co 3:8
m of reconciliation, 2Co 5:18
fulfill your *m*, 2Ti 4:5
a more excellent *m*, Heb 8:6

MIRACLE *supernatural event*
Work a *m*, Ex 7:9
I will perform *m-s*, Ex 34:10
m-s had occurred, Mt 11:21
He could do no *m*, Mk 6:5
perform a *m* in My, Mk 9:39
this *m* of healing, Ac 4:22
works *m-s* among you, Gal 3:5
wonders and...*m-s*, Heb 2:4

MIRE *mud*
cast me into the *m*, Job 30:19
Deliver me from the *m*, Ps 69:14
wallowing in the *m*, 2Pe 2:22

MIRIAM
Sister of Aaron and Moses, Nu 26:59
Chosen by God; called a prophetess, Ex 15:20
Punished for rebellion, Nu 12:1–16
Buried at Kadesh, Nu 20:1

MIRROR *image reflector*
see in a *m* dimly, 1Co 13:12
natural face in a *m*, Jas 1:23

MISCARRIAGE *aborted fetus*
m-s of a woman, Ps 58:8

MISCHIEF *harm*
conceive *m* and bring forth, Job 15:35
m will return upon his, Ps 7:16
iniquity and *m* are, Ps 55:10
m of their lips cover them, Ps 140:9
conceive *m* and bring forth, Is 59:4

MISERABLE *bad, unhappy*
loathe this *m* food, Nu 21:5
m and chronic, Dt 28:59
Be *m* and mourn, Jas 4:9
m and poor and blind, Rev 3:17

MISERY *sorrow, suffering*
conscious of my *m*, Job 10:15
Destruction and *m*, Ro 3:16

MISFORTUNE *adversity*
M will not come, Jer 5:12
m which He has, Jer 26:13
The day of his *m*, Ob 12

MISLEAD *lead astray*
m-s a blind *person*, Dt 27:18
m-led My people, Eze 13:10
that no one *m-s* you, Mk 13:5
m-ing our nation, Lk 23:2

MISTREAT *treat badly, wrong*
not *m*...the stranger, Jer 22:3
slaves...*m-ed* them, Mt 22:6
pray for...who *m*, Lk 6:28
mocked and *m-ed*, Lk 18:32
m and to stone them, Ac 14:5

MISTRESS *woman in charge*
her *m* was despised, Ge 16:4
m of the house, 1Ki 17:17
the maid like her *m*, Is 24:2
the *m* of sorceries, Na 3:4

MITYLENE
Visited by Paul, Ac 20:13–15

MIZPAH
Site of covenant between Jacob and Laban, Ge 31:44–53
——— Town of Benjamin; outraged Israelites gather here, Jos 18:21, 26; Jdg 20:1, 3
Samuel gathers Israel, 1Sa 7:5–16; 10:17–25
Residence of Gedaliah, 2Ki 25:23, 25

MOAB
Son of Lot, Ge 19:33–37
——— Country of the Moabites, Dt 1:5

MOABITES
Descendants of Lot, Ge 19:36, 37
Join Midian in cursing Israel, Nu 22:4
Excluded from Israel, Dt 23:3–6
Kindred of Ruth, Ru 1:4
Subdued by Israel, 1Sa 14:47; 2Sa 8:2; 2Ki 3:4–27
Women of, lead Solomon astray, 1Ki 11:1–8
Prophecies concerning, Is 11:14; 15:1–9; Jer 48:1–47; Am 2:1–3

MOCK *ridicule, scorn*
lads...*m-ed* him, 2Ki 2:23
Fools *m* at sin, Pr 14:9
who *m-s* the poor, Pr 17:5
soldiers also *m-ed*, Lk 23:36
God is not *m-ed*, Gal 6:7

MOCKERY *object of ridicule*
a *m* of the Egyptians, Ex 10:2
made a *m* of me, Nu 22:29
a *m* of justice, Pr 19:28
m and insinuations, Hab 2:6

MOLECH
God of the Ammonites; worshiped by Solomon, 1Ki 11:7
Human sacrifice made to, Lv 18:21; 2Ki 23:10

MOLTEN *cast metal*
made it into a *m* calf, Ex 32:4
make...no *m* gods, Ex 34:17
destroy...*m* images, Nu 33:52
capitals of *m* bronze, 1Ki 7:16
his *m* images are, Jer 10:14

MONEY *currency*
take double *the m*, Ge 43:12
not sell her for *m*, Dt 21:14
time to receive *m*, 2Ki 5:26
loves *m* will not be, Ecc 5:10
no *m* in their belt, Mk 6:8
m in the bank, Lk 19:23
love of *m* is a root, 1Ti 6:10

MONEYCHANGERS
the tables of the *m*, Mt 21:12
coins of the *m*, Jn 2:15

MONSTER *enormous animal*
created...sea *m-s*, Ge 1:21
sea, or the sea *m*, Job 7:12
sea *m-s* in the waters, Ps 74:13
belly of the sea *m*, Mt 12:40

MOON
m and...were bowing, Ge 37:9
the *m* stopped, Jos 10:13
m and stars to rule, Ps 136:9
beautiful as...*m*, SS 6:10
the *m* into blood, Joel 2:31
m will not...light, Mt 24:29
signs in...and *m*, Lk 21:25

MORALS *principles*
Bad...good *m*, 1Co 15:33

MOUNTAIN OF GOD
came to Horeb, the *m*, Ex 3:1
met him at the *m*, Ex 4:27
Moses went up to the *m*, Ex 24:13
Horeb, the *m*, 1Ki 19:8
m is the mountain of, Ps 68:15
You were on the holy *m*, Eze 28:14

MOURN *grieve, lament*
m her father and, Dt 21:13
David m-ed…son, 2Sa 13:37
A time to *m*, Ecc 3:4
earth *m-s and* withers, Is 24:4
comfort all who *m*, Is 61:2
Blessed…who *m*, Mt 5:4
shall *m* and weep, Lk 6:25
Be miserable and *m*, Jas 4:9

MOUSE *rodent*
the mole, and the *m*, Lv 11:29
five golden *mice*, 1Sa 6:4
mice that ravage, 1Sa 6:5

MOUTH
has made man's *m*, Ex 4:11
m condemns you, Job 15:6
From the *m* of infants, Ps 8:2
Let the words of my *m*, Ps 19:14
fool's *m* is his ruin, Pr 18:7
your *m* is lovely, SS 4:3
out of the *m* of God, Mt 4:4
confess with your *m*, Ro 10:9

MOVE *change position, stir*
Spirit of God…*m-ing*, Ge 1:2
pillar of cloud *m-d*, Ex 14:19
I will not be *m-d*, Ps 10:6
all the hills *m-d*, Jer 4:24
m-d with compassion, Mk 1:41
He was deeply *m-d*, Jn 11:33
in Him we live…*m*, Ac 17:28
m-d by the…Spirit, 2Pe 1:21

MULE *animal*
mounted his *m*, 2Sa 13:29
Absalom…on *his m*, 2Sa 18:9
ride on the king's *m*, 1Ki 1:44
war horses and *m-s*, Eze 27:14

MULTIPLY *increase*
Be fruitful and *m*, Ge 1:22
the fool *m-ies* words, Ecc 10:14
He *m-ies* lies and, Hos 12:1
and peace be *m-ied*, 2Pe 1:2

MULTITUDE *crowd, number*
father of a *m* of, Ge 17:4
cover a *m* of sins, Jas 5:20
love covers a *m* of, 1Pe 4:8

MURDER *premeditated killing*
You shall not *m*, Ex 20:13
Whoever commits *m*, Mt 5:21
m-ed the prophets, Mt 23:31
full of envy, *m*, Ro 1:29

MURDERER *killer*
m shall be put to, Nu 35:30
m from…beginning, Jn 8:44
this man is a *m*, Ac 28:4
no *m* has eternal, 1Jn 3:15

MUSIC *harmony, melody*
instruments of *m*, 1Ch 15:16
m to the LORD, 2Ch 7:6
m upon the lyre, Ps 92:3
heard *m* and, Lk 15:25

MUSICIAN *skilled in music*
m, a mighty man, 1Sa 16:18
the *m-s* after *them*, Ps 68:25
harpists and *m-s*, Rev 18:22

MUSTARD *type of plant*
kingdom…like a *m*, Mt 13:31
faith the size of a *m* seed, Mt 17:20
It is like a *m* seed, Lk 13:19

MUTE *silent*
who makes *him m*, Ex 4:11
I was *m* and silent, Ps 39:2
a *m*…man, Mt 9:32
and the *m* to speak, Mk 7:37
astray to the *m* idols, 1Co 12:2

MUZZLE *gag*
shall not *m* the ox, Dt 25:4
guard…as with a *m*, Ps 39:1

MY RIGHT HAND
He is at *M*, Ps 16:8
have taken hold of *m*, Ps 73:23
"Sit at *M* Until I make, Ps 110:1
M spread out the, Is 48:13
signet ring on *M*, Jer 22:24
"Sit at *M*, Until I put, Mt 22:44
"Sit at *M*, Until I put, Mk 12:36
to my Lord, "Sit at *M*, Lk 20:42
He is at *M*, Ac 2:25
to my Lord, "Sit at *M*, Ac 2:34
"Sit at *M*, Until I make, Heb 1:13
which you saw in *M*, Rev 1:20

MYRA
Paul changes ships here, Ac 27:5, 6

MYRIADS *countless*
chariots…are *m*, Ps 68:17
m of angels, Heb 12:22
number…was *m*, Rev 5:11

MYRRH *spice*
aromatic gum…*m*, Ge 43:11
Dripping with…*m*, SS 5:13
frankincense and *m*, Mt 2:11
mixture of *m* and, Jn 19:39

MYRTLE *type of plant*
the *m*, and the olive, Is 41:19
among the *m* trees, Zec 1:11

MYSIA
Paul and Silas pass through here, Ac 16:7, 8

MYSTERY *hidden truth, secret*
no *m* baffles you, Da 4:9
God's wisdom in a *m*, 1Co 2:7
know all *m-ies*, 1Co 13:2
into the *m* of Christ, Eph 3:4
the *m* of the gospel, Eph 6:19
the *m* of the faith, 1Ti 3:9

MYTHS *fables*
to pay attention to *m*, 1Ti 1:4
will turn aside to *m*, 2Ti 4:4
attention to Jewish *m*, Titus 1:14

N

NAAMAN
Captain in the Syrian army, 2Ki 5:1–11
Healed of his leprosy, 2Ki 5:14–17
Referred to by Christ, Lk 4:27

NABAL
Refuses David's request, 1Sa 25:2–12
Escapes David's wrath but dies of a stroke, 1Sa 25:13–39

NABOTH
Murdered for his vineyard by King Ahab, 1Ki 21:1–16
His murder avenged, 1Ki 21:17–25

NADAB
Eldest of Aaron's four sons, Ex 6:23
Takes part in affirming covenant, Ex 24:1, 9–12
Becomes priest, Ex 28:1
Consumed by fire, Lv 10:1–7
——— King of Israel, 1Ki 14:20
Killed by Baasha, 1Ki 15:25–31

NAHASH
King of Ammon; makes impossible demands, 1Sa 11:1–15

NAHOR
Grandfather of Abraham, Ge 11:24–26
——— Son of Terah, brother of Abraham, Ge 11:17

NAHUM
Inspired prophet to Judah concerning Nineveh, Na 1:1

NAILED *(v) attached*
you *n* to a cross, Ac 2:23
n it to the cross, Col 2:14

NAILS *(n) finger ends; pins*
and trim her *n*, Dt 21:12
fasten it with *n*, Jer 10:4
imprint of the *n*, Jn 20:25

NAIN
Village south of Nazareth; Jesus raises widow's son here, Lk 7:11–17

NAIOTH
Prophets' school in Ramah, 1Sa 19:18, 19, 22, 23

NAIVE *simple, not suspicious*
prudence to the *n*, Pr 1:4
n believes everything, Pr 14:15
the *n* becomes wise, Pr 21:11
goes astray or is *n*, Eze 45:20

NAKED *unclothed*
n and…not ashamed, Ge 2:25
n I shall return there, Job 1:21
n…you clothed Me, Mt 25:36

NAKEDNESS *unclothed*
the *n* of his father, Ge 9:22
n of…father's sister, Lv 18:12
Your *n*…be uncovered, Is 47:3
shame of your *n*, Rev 3:18

NAME *designation, title*
man gave *n-s* to all, Ge 2:20

takes His *n* in vain, Ex 20:7
blot out his *n*, Dt 29:20
How majestic is Your *n*, Ps 8:1
sing praises to Your *n*, Ps 18:49
good n...desired, Pr 22:1
LORD, that is My *n*, Is 42:8
Hallowed be Your *n*, Mt 6:9
n-s of the twelve, Mt 10:2
such child in My *n*, Mt 18:5
n-s are recorded, Lk 10:20
will come in My *n*, Lk 21:8
baptized in the *n*, Ac 2:38
of faith in His *n*, Ac 3:16
other *n* under heaven, Ac 4:12
n-s are in the book, Php 4:3

NAOMI
Widow of Elimelech, Ru 1:1–3
Returns to Bethlehem with Ruth, Ru 1:14–19
Arranges Ruth's marriage to Boaz, Ru 3; 4

NAPHTALI
Son of Jacob by Bilhah, Ge 30:1–8
Receives Jacob's blessing, Ge 49:21, 28
——— Tribe of:
Numbered, Nu 1:42, 43
Territory assigned to, Jos 19:32–39
Joins Gideon's army, Jdg 7:23
Attacked by Ben-Hadad and Tiglath-Pileser, 1Ki 15:20; 2Ki 15:29
Prophecy of great light in; fulfilled in Christ's ministry, Is 9:1–7; Mt 4:12–16

NARD *fragrant ointment*
henna with *n* plants, SS 4:13
perfume of pure *n*, Jn 12:3

NARROW *limited*
stood in a *n* path, Nu 22:24
Enter through the *n* gate, Mt 7:13
the way is *n*, Mt 7:14

NATHAN
Son of David, 2Sa 5:14
Mary's lineage traced through, Zec 12:12
——— Prophet under David and Solomon, 1Ch 29:29
Reveals God's plan to David, 2Sa 7:2–29
Rebukes David's sin, 2Sa 12:1–15
Reveals Adonijah's plot, 1Ki 1:10–46

NATHANAEL
One of Christ's disciples, Jn 1:45–51

NATION *government, people*
make you a great *n*, Ge 12:2
priests and a holy *n*, Ex 19:6
scatter...the *n-s*, Lv 26:33
the *n-s* in an uproar, Ps 2:1
n-s...fear the name, Ps 102:15
N will not lift up sword, Is 2:4
sprinkle many *n-s*, Is 52:15
glory among the *n-s*, Is 66:19
n...rise against *n*, Mt 24:7
n not perish, Jn 11:50
men, from every *n*, Ac 2:5
tongue...people and *n*, Rev 5:9

NATIVE *indigenous*
or a *n* of the land, Ex 12:19
Or see his *n* land, Jer 22:10
the *n-s* showed us, Ac 28:2
n-s saw the creature, Ac 28:4

NATURAL *normal*
died a *n* death, Eze 44:31
n man...not accept, 1Co 2:14
is sown a *n* body, 1Co 15:44

NATURE *essence*
of the same *n* as you, Ac 14:15
n itself teach you, 1Co 11:14
We *are* Jews by *n*, Gal 2:15
of *the* divine *n*, 2Pe 1:4

NAVE *main room*
porch in front of the *n*, 1Ki 6:3
he brought me to the *n*, Eze 41:1

NAZARENE
Jesus to be called, Mt 2:23
Descriptive of Jesus' followers, Ac 24:5

NAZARETH
Town in Galilee; considered obscure, Jn 1:46
City of Jesus' parents, Mt 2:23
Early home of Jesus, Lk 2:39–51
Jesus rejected by, Lk 4:16–30

NAZIRITE
1 One consecrated to God, Nu 6:2, 19, 20
2 Religious vow, Jdg 13:5, 7; Am 2:11, 12

NEAPOLIS
Seaport of Philippi, Ac 16:11

NEBO
Moabite town, Nu 32:38
——— Mountain where Moses viewed promised land, Dt 32:49; 34:1
——— Babylonian god, Is 46:1
——— Town W of Jordan, Ezr 2:29; Ne 7:33
——— Jew whose sons married foreign wives, Ezr 10:43

NEBUCHADNEZZAR
Monarch of the Neo-Babylonian Empire (605–562 B.C.); carries Jews captive to Babylon, Da 1:1–3
Crushes Jehoiachin's revolt, 2Ki 24:10–17
Destroys Jerusalem; captures Zedekiah, Jer 39:5–8
Prophecies concerning, Is 14:4–27; Jer 21:7–10; 25:8, 9; 27:4–11; 32:28–36; 43:10–13; Eze 26:7–12

NEBUZARADAN
Nebuchadnezzar's captain at siege of Jerusalem, 2Ki 25:8–20
Protects Jeremiah, Jer 39:11–14

NECK *part of body*
you shall break its *n*, Ex 13:13
yoke on your *n*, Dt 28:48
stiffened their *n-s*, Jer 17:23
risked their own *n-s*, Ro 16:4

NECKLACE *neck ornament*
n around his neck, Ge 41:42
earrings and *n-s*, Nu 31:50
pride is their *n*, Ps 73:6

NECO
See PHARAOH

NEED *necessity, obligation*
sufficient for his *n*, Dt 15:8
ministered to...*n-s*, Ac 20:34
n-s of the saints, 2Co 9:12
supply all your *n-s*, Php 4:19

NEEDLE
the eye of a *n*, Mt 19:24
n than for a rich, Mk 10:25

NEEDY *destitute, poor*
to your *n* and poor, Dt 15:11
a father to the *n*, Job 29:16
n will not always be, Ps 9:18
the LORD hears the *n*, Ps 69:33
n will lie down in, Is 14:30

NEGLECT *disregard, ignore*
You *n-ed* the Rock, Dt 32:18
who *n-s* discipline, Pr 15:32
n so great a salvation, Heb 2:3
n to show hospitality, Heb 13:2
do not *n* doing good, Heb 13:16

NEHEMIAH
Jewish cupbearer to King Artaxerxes; prays for restoration of Jerusalem, Ne 1:4–11
King commissions him to rebuild walls, Ne 2:1–8
Overcomes opposition and accomplishes rebuilding, Ne 4–6
Appointed governor, Ne 5:14
Participates with Ezra in restored worship, Ne 8–10
Registers the people and the priests and Levites, Ne 11:1–12:26
Dedicates the wall, Ne 12:27–43
Returns to Jerusalem after absence and institutes reforms, Ne 13:4–31

NEIGHBOR *one living nearby*
not covet...*n's* wife, Ex 20:17
shall love your *n*, Lv 19:18
make your *n-s* drink, Hab 2:15
love your *n* and, Mt 5:43
And who is my *n*, Lk 10:29
love your *n* as, Gal 5:14

NEPHEW
and Lot his *n*, Ge 12:5
Lot, Abram's *n*, Ge 14:12

NEPHILIM
people of great stature, Ge 6:4; Nu 13:33

NEST
n is set in the cliff, Nu 24:21
n among the stars, Ob 4
birds...*have n-s*, Mt 8:20

NET *snare*
a *n* for my steps, Ps 57:6
an antelope in a *n*, Is 51:20
casting a *n* into, Mt 4:18
left their *n-s* and, Mk 1:18
n full of fish, Jn 21:8

NETHINIM
Servants of the Levites, Ezr 8:20
Possible origins of:
Gibeonites, Jos 9:23–27
Solomon's forced laborers, 1Ki 9:20, 21
Mentioned, 1Ch 9:2; Ezr 2:43–54; 7:24; 8:17; Ne 3:31; 7:46–60, 73; 10:28, 29; 11:21

NETWORK *artistic work*
a grating of *n* of bronze, Ex 27:4
nets of *n* and twisted, 1Ki 7:17
with *n* and pomegranates, Jer 52:22

NEW *fresh, recent*
nothing *n* under the, Ecc 1:9
Will gain *n* strength, Is 40:31
a *n* spirit within, Eze 11:19
n wine into old, Mk 2:22
A *n* commandment, Jn 13:34
he is a *n* creature, 2Co 5:17
a *n* and living way, Heb 10:20
making all things *n*, Rev 21:5

NEW COVENANT
I will make a *n*, Jer 31:31
is the *n* in My blood, Lk 22:20
"This cup is the *n*, 1Co 11:25
servants of a *n*, 2Co 3:6
I will effect a *n*, Heb 8:8
the mediator of a *n*, Heb 9:15
the mediator of a *n*, Heb 12:24

NEWBORN *just born*
like *n* babies, long, 1Pe 2:2

NEWNESS *freshness*
walk in *n* of life, Ro 6:4
in *n* of the Spirit, Ro 7:6

NEWS *report, tidings*
a day of good *n*, 2Ki 7:9
Good *n* puts fat on, Pr 15:30
the *n* about Jesus, Mt 14:1
n about Him spread, Mk 1:28
n of great joy, Lk 2:10
bring good *n* of good, Ro 10:15
n of your faith, 1Th 3:6

NICANOR
One of the first seven deacons, Ac 6:1–5

NICODEMUS
Pharisee; converses with Jesus, Jn 3:1–12
Protests unfairness of Christ's trial, Jn 7:50–52
Brings gifts to anoint Christ's body, Jn 19:39, 40

NICOLAITANS
Group teaching moral laxity, Rev 2:6–15

NICOLAS
One of the first seven deacons, Ac 6:5

NIGHT *darkness*
darkness He called *n*, Ge 1:5
pillar of fire by *n*, Ex 13:21
meditate…day and *n*, Jos 1:8
make *n* into day, Job 17:12
The terror by *n*, Ps 91:5
At *n* my soul longs, Is 26:9
over their flock by *n*, Lk 2:8
a thief in the *n*, 1Th 5:2
tormented day and *n*, Rev 20:10

NILE
Hebrew children drowned in, Ex 1:22
Moses hidden in, Ex 2:3–10
Water of, turned to blood, Ex 7:14–21
Mentioned in prophecies, Is 19:5–8; 23:3; 27:12; Jer 46:7–9; Am 9:5

NIMROD
Ham's grandson, Ge 10:6–12

NINEVEH
Capital of Assyria, 2Ki 19:36
Jonah preaches to; people repent, Jon 3:1–10; Mt 12:41
Prophecy against, Na 2:13–3:19; Zep 2:13–15

NISAN
first month of the Hebrew calendar, Ne 2:1; Est 3:7

NOAH
Son of Lamech, Ge 5:28–32
Finds favor with God; commissioned to build the ark, Ge 6:8–22
Fills ark and survives flood, Ge 7
Leaves ark; builds altar; receives God's promise, Ge 8
God's covenant with, Ge 9:1–17
Blesses and curses his sons; dies, Ge 9:18–29

NO-AMON
Nineveh compared to, Na 3:8

NOB
City of priests; David flees to, 1Sa 21:1–9
Priests of, killed by Saul, 1Sa 22:9–23

NOBLE *lofty* **or** *renowned one*
king's most *n* princes, Est 6:9
speak *n* things, Pr 8:6
all the *n-s* of Judah, Jer 39:6

NOBLEMAN *of high rank*
the house of the *n*, Job 21:28
A *n* went to, Lk 19:12

NOD
Place (east of Eden) of Cain's exile, Ge 4:16, 17

NOISE *loud sound*
You who were full of *n*, Is 22:2
Egypt *is but* a big *n*, Jer 46:17
from heaven a *n*, Ac 2:2

NOISY *clamorous*
head of the *n streets*, Pr 1:21
the crowd in *n* disorder, Mt 9:23
n gong or a clanging cymbal, 1Co 13:1

NOMADS *desert wanderers*
n of the desert bow, Ps 72:9

NONSENSE *foolishness*
a fool speaks *n*, Is 32:6
appeared…as *n*, Lk 24:11

NOON *midday*
you will grope at *n*, Dt 28:29
Baal from morning until *n*, 1Ki 18:26
grope at *n* as in the night., Job 5:14
and morning and at *n*, Ps 55:17

NOONDAY *midday*
life would be brighter than *n*;, Job 11:17
And your judgment as the *n*, Ps 37:6

NORTH *direction of compass*
stretches out the *n*, Job 26:7
Zion *in* the far *n*, Ps 48:2
king of the *N* will, Da 11:13
three gates on the *n*, Rev 21:13

NOSE *part of face*
the ring on her *n*, Ge 24:47
n-s…cannot smell, Ps 115:6
My hook in your *n*, Is 37:29

NOSTRILS *nose*
breathed into his *n*, Ge 2:7
breath of His *n*, 2Sa 22:16
breath of God…my *n*, Job 27:3

NOTHING *not a thing*
n which they purpose to do, Ge 11:6
n in common with us in, Ezr 4:3
Does Job fear God for *n*, Job 1:9
tested me and You find *n*, Ps 17:3
n hidden from its heat, Ps 19:6
besides You, I desire *n*, Ps 73:25
to be rich, but has *n*, Pr 13:7
there is *n* new under the sun, Ecc 1:9
N like this has ever been, Mt 9:33
n concealed that will not, Mt 10:26
n will be impossible to you, Mt 17:20
n is hidden, except to be, Mk 4:22
n will be impossible with God, Lk 1:37
the flesh profits *n*, Jn 6:63
apart from Me you can do *n*, Jn 15:5
n good dwells in me, Ro 7:18
Owe *n* to anyone except, Ro 13:8
do not have love, I am *n*, 1Co 13:2
Be anxious for *n*, but in, Php 4:6
brought *n* into the world, 1Ti 6:7
complete, lacking in *n*, Jas 1:4

NOTICE *attention, seen*
take *n* of me, Ru 2:10
not *n* the log, Mt 7:3
deeds to be *n-d* by, Mt 23:5

NOURISH *feed, sustain*
n-es and cherishes it, Eph 5:29
constantly n-ed on, 1Ti 4:6
she would be *n-ed*, Rev 12:6

NULLIFY *annul, make void*
LORD *n-ies* the counsel, Ps 33:10
unbelief will not *n*, Ro 3:3
the promise is *n-ied*, Ro 4:14
n the grace of God, Gal 2:21

NUMBER *(n) group, total*
their *n* according to, Nu 29:21
the *n* of the stars, Ps 147:4
increasing in *n* daily, Ac 16:5
his *n* is six hundred, Rev 13:18

NUMBER *(v) count, enumerate*
n…by their armies, Nu 1:3
You *n* my steps, Job 14:16
hairs…all *n-ed*, Mt 10:30

NURSE *(n) attendant*
Deborah, Rebekah's *n*, Ge 35:8
and call a *n* for you, Ex 2:7
n carries a nursing, Nu 11:12
n in the bedroom, 2Ki 11:2

NURSE *(v) suckle an infant*
Sarah…*n* children, Ge 21:7
the child and *n-d* him, Ex 2:9
morning to *n* my son, 1Ki 3:21
who are *n-ing* babies in, Mk 13:17
breasts…never *n-d*, Lk 23:29

O

OAK *type of tree*
by the *o-s* of Mamre, Ge 13:18
the diviners' *o*, Jdg 9:37
o-s of righteousness, Is 61:3
strong as the *o-s*, Am 2:9

OAR *pole used in rowing*
no boat with *o-s* will, Is 33:21
All who handle...*o*, Eze 27:29
straining at the *o-s*, Mk 6:48

OATH *declaration, vow*
confirm the *o* which, Dt 9:5
free from the *o*, Jos 2:20
make no *o* at all, Mt 5:34
priests without an *o*, Heb 7:21

OBADIAH
King Ahab's steward, 1Ki 18:3–16
——— Prophet of Judah, Ob 1

OBED
Son of Boaz and Ruth, Ru 4:17–22

OBED-EDOM
Philistine from Gath; ark of the Lord left in his house, 2Sa 6:10–12; 1Ch 13:13, 14

OBEDIENCE *submission*
the *o* of the peoples, Ge 49:10
pretend *o* to me, 2Sa 22:45
the *o* of the One, Ro 5:19
leading to *o* of faith, Ro 16:26
in *o* to the truth, 1Pe 1:22

OBEDIENT *willing to obey*
we will be *o*, Ex 24:7
o from the heart, Ro 6:17
o to the...death, Php 2:8
Children, be *o* to, Col 3:20

OBEY *follow commands, orders*
have *o-ed* My voice, Ge 22:18
o My voice and keep, Ex 19:5
o the LORD your God, Dt 27:10
to *o* is better than, 1Sa 15:22
O-ing...His word, Ps 103:20
and the sea *o* Him, Mt 8:27
o God rather than, Ac 5:29
o your parents, Eph 6:1
O your leaders, Heb 13:17
to *o* Jesus Christ, 1Pe 1:2

OBJECT *implement; goal*
struck...an iron *o*, Nu 35:16
an *o* of loathing to, Ps 88:8
o like a great sheet, Ac 10:11
god or *o* of worship, 2Th 2:4

OBLIGATION *duty*
o toward the LORD, Nu 32:22
for his daily *o-s*, 2Ch 31:16
under *o*, not to the, Ro 8:12
o to keep the...Law, Gal 5:3

OBSERVE *keep; notice*
surely *o* My sabbaths, Ex 31:13
o all My statutes, Lv 19:37
you may *o* discretion, Pr 5:2
the ant...*O* her ways, Pr 6:6
O how the lilies, Mt 6:28
o-ing the traditions, Mk 7:3
the word...*o* it, Lk 11:28
o days and months, Gal 4:10

OBSTACLE *hindrance*
Remove *every o* out of, Is 57:14
an *o* or a stumbling, Ro 14:13

OBSTINATE *stubborn*
you are an *o* people, Ex 33:3
made his heart *o*, Dt 2:30
Israel is...*o*, Eze 3:7
disobedient and *o*, Ro 10:21

OBTAIN *get possession of*
o children through, Ge 16:2
finds a wife...*o-s*, Pr 18:22
may *o* eternal life, Mt 19:16
o the gift of God, Ac 8:20
o-ed an inheritance, Eph 1:11
for *o-ing* salvation, 1Th 5:9

OCCASION *opportunity; happening*
seek *o* against us and, Ge 43:18
given *o* to the enemies of, 2Sa 12:14
become an *o* of stumbling, Eze 7:19
give the enemy no *o* for, 1Ti 5:14

OCCUPIED *busy*
he is *o* or gone aside, or, 1Ki 18:27
God keeps him *o* with the, Ecc 5:20
which they found me *o* in, Ac 24:18
who were so *o* were not, Heb 13:9

OCCUPY *inhabit; fill a position*
o, that you may possess, Dt 2:31
Who *o* the height of the hill., Jer 49:16
proceed to *o* the last place., Lk 14:9
o this ministry and, Ac 1:25

OCCUR *happen, take place*
this sign will *o*, Ex 8:23
will *o* at the final, Da 8:19
otherwise a riot might *o*, Mt 26:5
predestined to *o*, Ac 4:28

ODED
Prophet of Samaria, 2Ch 28:9–15

ODIOUS *offensive*
o in Pharaoh's sight, Ex 5:21
o to the Philistines, 1Sa 13:4

OF THE WORLD
See also of this world
foundations *o*, 2Sa 22:16
men *o*, whose portion is, Ps 17:14
utterances to the end *o*, Ps 19:4
all the inhabitants *o*, Ps 33:8
fill the face *o*, Is 14:21
inhabitants *o* learn, Is 26:9
all the kingdoms *o*, Mt 4:8
You are the light *o*, Mt 5:14
the beginning *o* until now, Mt 24:21
worries *o*, and the, Mk 4:19
nations *o* eagerly seek, Lk 12:30
takes away the sin *o*!, Jn 1:29
One is indeed the Savior *o*, Jn 4:42
for the life *o*, Jn 6:51
I am the Light *o*, Jn 8:12
I am the Light *o*, Jn 9:5
ruler *o* is coming, Jn 14:30
If you were *o*, Jn 15:19
not ask on behalf *o*, Jn 17:9
they are not *o*, Jn 17:14
since the creation *o*, Ro 1:20
the reconciliation *o*, Ro 11:15
foolish the wisdom *o*, 1Co 1:20
foolish things *o* to shame, 1Co 1:27
not the spirit *o*, 1Co 2:12
the things *o*, 1Co 7:33
sorrow *o* produces death, 2Co 7:10
elementary principles *o*, Col 2:8
a friend *o* makes himself, Jas 4:4
the defilements *o*, 2Pe 2:20
Son to be the Savior *o*, 1Jn 4:14
kingdom *o* has become, Rev 11:15

OF THIS WORLD
See also of the world
you are *o*, I am not, Jn 8:23
he sees the light *o*, Jn 11:9
ruler *o* will be cast, Jn 12:31
depart out *o*, Jn 13:1
ruler *o* has been judged, Jn 16:11
kingdom is not *o*, Jn 18:36
wisdom *o* is foolishness, 1Co 3:19
immoral people *o*, 1Co 5:10
form *o* is passing, 1Co 7:31
god *o* has blinded, 2Co 4:4
the course *o*, Eph 2:2
poor *o* to be rich, Jas 2:5

OFFEND *insult; violate*
I will not *o anymore*, Job 34:31
A brother *o-ed is*, Pr 18:19
Pharisees were *o-ed*, Mt 15:12

OFFENSE *anger; transgression*
of my *own o-s*, Ge 41:9
they took *o* at Him, Mt 13:57
of the *o* of Adam, Ro 5:14
and a rock of *o*, 1Pe 2:8

OFFER *(v) give, present*
o him...as a burnt, Ge 22:2
O to God a sacrifice, Ps 50:14
my mouth *o-s* praises, Ps 63:5
o both gifts and, Heb 5:1
o-ed Himself, Heb 9:14
prayer *o-ed* in faith, Jas 5:15
o...spiritual sacrifices, 1Pe 2:5

OFFERING *(n) contribution*
freewill *o* to the LORD, Ex 35:29
o of first fruits, Lv 2:12
your worthless *o-s*, Is 1:13
presenting your *o*, Mt 5:23
any o for sin, Heb 10:18

OFFERINGS
Alternate names in italics
1 Burnt Offering, Ge 22:13; Lv 1:17
2 Drink Offering, Php 2:17; 2Ti 4:6
Libation Offering
3 Freewill Offering, Ex 35:29; Lv 7:16
4 Grain Offering, Lv 9:4; Jos 22:29
Meal Offering
5 Guilt Offering, Lv 5:6; Nu 6:12
6 Heave Offering, Ex 29:27, 28
7 Libation Offering, Nu 6:15, 17; 28:9, 10
Drink Offering
8 Meal Offering, 2Ki 16:15; Ps 40:6
Grain Offering
9 Ordination Offering, Lv 8:28, 31
10 Peace Offering, Lv 4:31; Nu 6:14
11 Sin Offering, Ex 29:14; Eze 46:20
12 Thank Offering, 2Ch 33:16; Jer 33:11
13 Votive Offering, Dt 12:26; 23:18
14 Wave Offering, Lv 14:12; Nu 18:18

OFFICE *function; position*
wield the staff of *o*, Jdg 5:14
priests in their *o-s*, 2Ch 35:2
to the *o* of overseer, 1Ti 3:1

OFFICIAL *one in authority*
o-s in the palace, 2Ki 20:18
o of the synagogue, Lk 8:41

OFFSPRING *descendants*
o in place of Abel, Ge 4:25
bring forth *o* from, Is 65:9

OG
Amorite king of Bashan, Dt 3:1–13
Defeated and killed by Israel, Nu 21:32–35

OHOLAH
Symbolic name of Samaria, Eze 23:4, 5, 36

OIL
o for lighting, Ex 25:6
anointed my head...*o*, Ps 23:5
the *o* of joy, Ps 45:7
words...softer than *o*, Ps 55:21
prudent took *o* in, Mt 25:4
not anoint...with *o*, Lk 7:46

OINTMENT *salve*
a jar of *o*, Job 41:31
anointed...with *o*, Jn 11:2

OLD *aged, obsolete*
buried at a...*o* age, Ge 15:15
too *o* to have a, Ru 1:12
honor of *o* men, Pr 20:29
o men will dream, Joel 2:28
wine into *o* wineskins, Mt 9:17
be born when he is *o*, Jn 3:4
o self was crucified, Ro 6:6
o things passed away, 2Co 5:17
men of *o* gained, Heb 11:2
serpent of *o*...devil, Rev 12:9

OLD GATE
See GATES OF JERUSALEM

OLD MAN
an *o* and satisfied with life, Ge 25:8
an *o* of ripe age, Ge 35:29
o was coming out of the, Jdg 19:16
be an *o* in your house, 1Sa 2:31
"An *o* is coming up, 1Sa 28:14
Job died, an *o*, Job 42:17
o who does not live, Is 65:20
shatter *o* and youth, Jer 51:22
I am an *o* and my wife, Lk 1:18

OLIVE *tree; fruit*
freshly picked *o* leaf, Ge 8:11
land of *o* oil and, Dt 8:8
cherubim of *o* wood, 1Ki 6:23
children like *o* plants, Ps 128:3

OLIVES, MOUNT OF
David flees to, 2Sa 15:30
Prophecy concerning, Zec 14:4
Christ's triumphal entry from, Mt 21:1
Prophetic discourse delivered from, Mt 24:3
Christ's ascension from, Ac 1:9–12

OMEGA
last letter of Gr. alphabet, Rev 1:8
title of Jesus Christ, Rev 21:6
expresses eternalness of God, Rev 22:13

OMEN *foretells a future event*
who interprets *o-s*, Dt 18:10
took this as an *o*, 1Ki 20:33

OMER *dry measure*
take an *o* apiece, Ex 16:16
o is a tenth of an, Ex 16:36

OMRI
Made king of Israel by army, 1Ki 16:16, 21, 22
Builds Samaria; reigns wickedly, 1Ki 16:23–27

ON
City of Lower Egypt; center of sun worship, Ge 41:45, 50
Called Beth Shemesh, Jer 43:13

ONAN
Second son of Judah; slain for failure to give his brother an heir, Ge 38:8–10

ONE *single unit*
shall become *o* flesh, Ge 2:24
God, the LORD is *o*, Dt 6:4
Holy *O* of Israel, Ps 71:22
His chosen *o-s*, Ps 105:6
Are You the...*O*, Mt 11:3
joy...over *o* sinner, Lk 15:7
I...Father are *o*, Jn 10:30
they may all be *o*, Jn 17:21
o body in Christ, Ro 12:5
o died for all, 2Co 5:14
o Lord, *o* faith, Eph 4:5
o God...*o* mediator, 1Ti 2:5
husband of *o* wife, 1Ti 3:2

ONESIMUS
Slave of Philemon converted by Paul in Rome, Phm 10–17
With Tychicus, carries Paul's letters to Colosse and to Philemon, Col 4:7–9

ONESIPHORUS
Ephesian Christian commended for his service, 2Ti 1:16–18

ONLY BEGOTTEN SON
He gave His *o*, Jn 3:16
name of the *o*, Jn 3:18
offering up his *o*, Heb 11:17
God has sent His *o*, 1Jn 4:9

ONYX *precious stone*
bdellium and the *o*, Ge 2:12
o, and the jasper, Eze 28:13

OPEN *(adj) not shut, exposed*
throat is an *o* grave, Ps 5:9
Better is *o* rebuke, Pr 27:5
before you an *o* door, Rev 3:8

OPEN *(v) expose, free, unfasten*
eyes will be *o-ed*, Ge 3:5
Ezra *o-ed* the book, Ne 8:5
He *o-s* their ear, Job 36:10
O LORD, *o* my lips, Ps 51:15
O my eyes, that I, Ps 119:18
To *o* blind eyes, Is 42:7
o...windows of heaven, Mal 3:10
knock...will be *o-ed*, Mt 7:7
o-ed a door of faith, Ac 14:27
and *o-s* the door, Rev 3:20
worthy to *o* the book, Rev 5:2

OPHEL
Hill, southeast of Jerusalem, Ne 3:15–27
Fortified by Manasseh, 2Ch 27:3
Residence of Nethinim, Ne 3:26

OPHIR
Famous for gold, 1Ch 29:4

OPHRAH
Town in Manasseh; home of Gideon, Jdg 6:11, 15
Site of Gideon's burial, Jdg 8:32

OPPONENT *adversary*
friends...with your *o*, Mt 5:25
protection from my *o*, Lk 18:3

OPPORTUNITY *occasion*
o to betray Jesus, Mt 26:16
o for your testimony, Lk 21:13
an *o* for the flesh, Gal 5:13
not give...devil an *o*, Eph 4:27

OPPOSE *contend, resist*
o the Prince of, Da 8:25
o-d the ordinance of, Ro 13:2
men also *o* the truth, 2Ti 3:8
God is *o-d* to the, Jas 4:6

OPPOSITION *hostility*
you...know My *o*, Nu 14:34
these are in *o*, Gal 5:17
gospel...much *o*, 1Th 2:2

OPPRESS *(v) trouble, tyrannize*
enslaved and *o-ed*, Ge 15:13
Egyptians are *o-ing*, Ex 3:9
not *o* your neighbor, Lv 19:13
woman *o-ed* in, 1Sa 1:15
do not *o* the widow, Zec 7:10
healing all...*o-ed*, Ac 10:38
the rich who *o* you, Jas 2:6

OPPRESSED *(n) afflicted*
stronghold for the *o*, Ps 9:9
justice for the *o*, Ps 146:7
let the *o* go free, Is 58:6
devour...*o* in secret, Hab 3:14
vengeance for the *o*, Ac 7:24

OPPRESSION *affliction*
Do not trust in *o*, Ps 62:10
o makes a...man mad, Ecc 7:7
and water of *o*, Is 30:20
o of My people, Ac 7:34

OPPRESSOR *one who afflicts*
And crush the *o*, Ps 72:4
a great *o* lacks, Pr 28:16
punish all their *o-s*, Jer 30:20

ORACLE *revelation*
The *o* of Balaam, Nu 24:3
o concerning Babylon, Is 13:1
the *o* of the LORD, Jer 23:33
and misleading *o-s*, La 2:14
entrusted with the *o-s*, Ro 3:2

ORDAIN *invest, set apart*
anoint…and *o* them, Ex 28:41
o Aaron and his sons, Ex 29:9
o-ed His covenant, Ps 111:9
law as *o-ed* by angels, Ac 7:53

ORDEAL *difficulty, trial*
great *o* of affliction, 2Co 8:2
at the fiery *o*, 1Pe 4:12

ORDER *(n) arrangement*
Set your house in *o*, 2Ki 20:1
fixed *o* of the moon, Jer 31:35
the *o* of Melchizedek, Heb 5:6

ORDER *(v) command; request*
I will *o my prayer*, Ps 5:3
o-ed him to tell no, Lk 5:14
confidence…to *o* you, Phm 8

ORDINANCE *statute*
o of the Passover, Ex 12:43
they rejected My *o-s*, Lv 26:43
o-s of the heavens, Job 38:33
opposed the *o* of God, Ro 13:2

ORDINATION
Aaron's ram of *o*, Ex 29:26
and the *o* offering, Lv 7:37
period of your *o*, Lv 8:33

ORDINATION OFFERING
See OFFERINGS

ORIGIN *beginning, source*
of Jewish *o*, Est 6:13
o is from antiquity, Is 23:7
Your *o* and your, Eze 16:3

ORIGINATE *bring into being*
not *o* from woman, 1Co 11:8
all things *o*…God, 1Co 11:12

ORION
Brilliant constellation, Job 9:9

ORNAMENT *decoration*
put off your *o-s*, Ex 33:5
o of fine gold, Pr 25:12
beauty of His *o-s*, Eze 7:20

ORNAN
His threshing floor becomes site of temple, 1 Ch 21:18–28; 2Ch 3:1;

ORPAH
Ruth's sister-in-law, Ru 1:4, 14

ORPHAN *fatherless child*
not afflict any…*o*, Ex 22:22
justice for the *o*, Dt 10:18
helper of the *o*, Ps 10:14
may plunder the *o-s*, Is 10:2
Leave…*o-s* behind, Jer 49:11
visit *o-s* and widows, Jas 1:27

OSNAPPAR
Called "the great and noble," Ezr 4:10

OSTRICH *bird*
the *o* and the owl, Lv 11:16
a companion of *o-es*, Job 30:29
cruel Like *o-es*, La 4:3
mourning like the *o-es*, Mic 1:8

OTHNIEL
Son of Kenaz, Caleb's youngest brother, Jdg 1:13
Captures Kirjath Sepher; receives Caleb's daughter as wife, Jos 15:15–17
First judge of Israel, Jdg 3:9–11

OUTBURST *sudden release*
great *o* of anger, Dt 29:24
o of anger I hid My, Is 54:8
jealousy, *o-s* of anger, Gal 5:20

OUTCAST *rejected*
the *o-s* of Israel, Ps 147:2
Hide the *o-s*, Is 16:3
called you an *o*, Jer 30:17
o-s from…synagogue, Jn 16:2

OUTCOME *conclusion*
and know their *o*, Is 41:22
the officers to see the *o*, Mt 26:58
o of those things is death, Ro 6:21
and the *o*, eternal life, Ro 6:22
the *o* of the Lord's dealings, Jas 5:11
as the *o* of your faith, 1Pe 1:9

OUTCRY *strong cry; protest*
no *o* in our streets, Ps 144:14
o is heard among the, Jer 50:46
a *single o* arose, Ac 19:34

OUTSIDER *stranger*
o may not come near, Nu 18:4
toward *o-s*, 1Th 4:12

OUTSTRETCHED *extended*
redeem…with an *o* arm, Ex 6:6
war…with an *o* hand, Jer 21:5

OUTWARD *external*
at the *o* appearance, 1Sa 16:7
is *o* in the flesh, Ro 2:28

OVEN *baking, cooking vessel*
appeared a…*o*, Ge 15:17
make them as a fiery *o*, Ps 21:9

OVERCOME *conquer, master*
a man *o* with wine, Jer 23:9
I have *o* the world, Jn 16:33
but *o* evil with good, Ro 12:21
have *o* the evil one, 1Jn 2:13
who *o-s* will inherit, Rev 21:7

OVERFLOW *flood, inundate*
My cup *o-s*, Ps 23:5
waters will *o* the, Is 28:17
I am *o-ing* with joy, 2Co 7:4
o-ing with gratitude, Col 2:7

OVERLAID *decorate, spread*
o…with gold, 1Ki 6:28
vessel *o* with silver, Pr 26:23
o with gold…silver, Hab 2:19

OVERLOOK *ignore; view*
o a transgression, Pr 19:11
widows were…*o-ed*, Ac 6:1

OVERPOWER *subdue*
deceive you and *o* you, Ob 7
Hades will not *o*, Mt 16:18
attacks him and *o-s*, Lk 11:22

OVERSEER *director, leader*
o in the house of, Jer 29:26
the *o-s* and deacons, Php 1:1
the office of *o*, 1Ti 3:1
o…above reproach, Titus 1:7

OVERSHADOW *engulf, obscure*
Most High…*o* you, Lk 1:35
o-ing the mercy seat, Heb 9:5

OVERSIGHT *supervision*
o of the house of, 2Ki 12:11
having *o* at…gates, Eze 44:11
exercising *o* not, 1Pe 5:2

OVERTHREW *defeated*
He *o* those cities, Ge 19:25
the LORD *o* the, Ex 14:27
God *o* Sodom and, Jer 50:40

OVERTHROW *overcome*
You *o* those who rise up, Ex 15:7
city, to spy it out and *o* it, 2Sa 10:3
He *o-s* the words of the, Pr 22:12
man who takes bribes *o-s* it, Pr 29:4
I will *o* the thrones, Hag 2:22
o the chariots and their, Hag 2:22
not be able to *o* them, Ac 5:39

OVERTHROWN *destroyed*
had *o* Ziklag and burned it, 1Sa 30:1
wicked are *o* and are no, Pr 12:7
Sodom, Which was *o*, La 4:6
days and Nineveh will be *o*, Jon 3:4
is of men, it will be *o*;, Ac 5:38

OVERWHELM *crush, overcome*
humiliation has *o-ed*, Ps 44:15
darkness will *o* me, Ps 139:11
my spirit was *o-ed*, Ps 142:3
o-ed by…sorrow, 2Co 2:7

OWE *be indebted*
Pay…what you *o*, Mt 18:28
O nothing to anyone, Ro 13:8
that you *o* to me, Phm 19

OWL *bird*
the *o*, the sea gull, Dt 14:15
o of the waste places, Ps 102:6
houses…full of *o-s*, Is 13:21

OWN *(adj) belonging to*
man in His *o* image, Ge 1:27
led…His *o* people, Ps 78:52
calls his *o* sheep, Jn 10:3
in his *o* language, Ac 2:6

OWN *(n) belonging to*
He came to His *o*, Jn 1:11
provide for his *o*, 1Ti 5:8

OWNER *possessor*
restitution to its *o*, Ex 22:12
when the *o*…comes, Mt 21:40
who were *o-s* of land, Ac 4:34

OX *bull used as draft animal*
oxen and donkeys, Ge 12:16
servant or his *o*, Ex 20:17
horns of the wild *oxen*, Ps 22:21
An *o* knows its owner, Is 1:3
not muzzle the *o*, 1Ti 5:18

P

PACE *step, stride*
the *p* of the cattle, Ge 33:14
not slow down the *p*, 2Ki 4:24

PACT *agreement*
Sheol we…made a *p*, Is 28:15
p with Sheol will, Is 28:18

PADDAN-ARAM
Same as Mesopotamia, Ge 24:10; *see* mesopotamia
Home of Isaac's wife, Ge 25:20
Jacob flees to, Ge 28:2–7
Jacob returns from, Ge 31:17, 18
People of, called Syrians, Ge 31:24
Language of, called Aramaic, 2Ki 18:26

PAIN *discomfort, hurt*
multiply Your *p*, Ge 3:16
p-s came upon her, 1Sa 4:19
rejoice in unsparing *p*, Job 6:10
rest from your *p*, Is 14:3
Your *p* is incurable, Jer 30:15
bring *p* to my soul, La 3:51
no longer be…*p*, Rev 21:4

PAINFUL *hurting*
p are honest words, Job 6:25
the bread of *p* labors, Ps 127:2

PALACE *royal residence*
build…royal *p*, 2Ch 2:12
to the king's *p*, Est 2:8
Out of ivory *p-s*, Ps 45:8
A *p* of strangers, Is 25:2
luxury…royal *p-s*, Lk 7:25

PALE *colorless*
shall his face now turn *p*, Is 29:22
the king's face grew *p* and, Da 5:6
All faces turn *p*, Joel 2:6
all their faces are grown *p*, Na 2:10

PALLET *bed, mat*
they let down the *p*, Mk 2:4
pick up your *p* and, Mk 2:9

PALM *type of tree*
the city of *p* trees, Dt 34:3
flourish like the *p*, Ps 92:12
branches of the *p*, Jn 12:13

PALTI (or Paltiel)
Man to whom Saul gives Michal, David's wife, in marriage, 1Sa 25:44; 2Sa 3:15

PAMPHYLIA
People from, at Pentecost, Ac 2:10
Paul visits; John Mark returns home from, Ac 13:13; 15:38
Paul preaches in cities of, Ac 14:24, 25

PANGS *pains*
not *p* take hold of you, Jer 13:21
the beginning of birth *p*, Mt 24:8
the beginning of birth *p*, Mk 13:8

PANIC *fear*
P seized them there, Ps 48:6
P and pitfall have, La 3:47
great *p*…will fall, Zec 14:13

PANT *breathe rapidly*
deer *p-s* for the water, Ps 42:1
my soul *p-s* for You, Ps 42:1
I will both gasp and *p*, Is 42:14
beasts…*p* for You, Joel 1:20

PAPHOS
Paul blinds Elymas at, Ac 13:6–13

PAPYRUS *reed plant*
p…without a marsh, Job 8:11
Even in *p* vessels, Is 18:2

PARABLE *story for illustration*
speak a *p* to, Eze 17:2
p of the sower, Mt 13:18
heard His *p-s*, Mt 21:45
p from the fig tree, Mk 13:28
spoke by way of a *p*, Lk 8:4

PARADISE
abode of the righteous dead, Lk 23:43; 2Co 12:4; Rev 2:7
See also abraham's bosom

PARALYTIC *one with paralysis*
said to the *p*, Get up, Mt 9:6
p, carried by four, Mk 2:3

PARALYZED *with paralysis*
my servant is lying *p* at home, Mt 8:6
bed a man who was *p*, Lk 5:18
who had been *p* and lame, Ac 8:7
eight years, for he was *p*, Ac 9:33

PARAN
Residence of exiled Ishmael, Ge 21:21
Israelites camp in, Nu 10:12
Headquarters of spies, Nu 13:3, 26
Site of David's refuge, 1Sa 25:1

PARCHED *dry*
river becomes *p* and dried, Job 14:11
rebellious dwell in a *p* land, Ps 68:6
my throat is *p*, Ps 69:3
longs for You, as a *p*, Ps 143:6
the river will be *p* and dry, Is 19:5
it into a *p* and desolate land, Joel 2:20

PARDON *forgive, release*
he will not *p* your, Ex 23:21
May the…LORD *p*, 2Ch 30:18
O LORD, *P* my iniquity, Ps 25:11
He will abundantly *p*, Is 55:7
p, and you will be, Lk 6:37

PARENTS *father and mother*
rise up against *p*, Mt 10:21
left house or…*p*, Lk 18:29
evil, disobedient to *p*, Ro 1:30
Children, obey your *p*, Eph 6:1
disobedient to *p*, 2Ti 3:2

PARMENAS
One of the first seven deacons, Ac 6:5

PART *portion*
God…have no *p* in, 2Ch 19:7
formed my inward *p-s*, Ps 139:13
have no *p* with Me, Jn 13:8
no *p* or portion in, Ac 8:21
prophesy in *p*, 1Co 13:9
now I know in *p*, 1Co 13:12
tongue is a small *p*, Jas 3:5

PARTAKERS *participators*
do not be *p* with, Eph 5:7
become *p* of Christ, Heb 3:14
p of the Holy Spirit, Heb 6:4
p of *the* divine nature, 2Pe 1:4

PARTIAL *favoring*
not be *p* to the poor, Lv 19:15
you shall not be *p*, Dt 16:19
now be *p* to no one, Job 32:21
You are not *p*, Mt 22:16

PARTIALITY *favoritism*
show *p* in judgment, Dt 1:17
p is not good, Pr 28:21
God shows no *p*, Gal 2:6

PARTICIPATE *take part*
not *p*…deeds of, Eph 5:11
p-s in his evil deeds, 2Jn 11
will not *p* in her sins, Rev 18:4

PARTNER *comrade*
is a *p* with a thief, Pr 29:24
been *p-s* with them, Mt 23:30
regard me a *p*, Phm 17

PASHHUR
Official opposing Jeremiah, Jer 21:1; 38:1–13
——— Priest who puts Jeremiah in jail, Jer 20:1–6

PASS *proceed*
LORD will *p* over the, Ex 12:23
My glory is *p-ing* by, Ex 33:22
heaven and earth *p*, Mt 5:18
words will not *p*, Mt 24:35
this cup *p* from Me, Mt 26:39
p-ed out of death, Jn 5:24
old things *p-ed* away, 2Co 5:17
first earth *p-ed* away, Rev 21:1

PASSION *desire, lust*
p is rottenness to, Pr 14:30
over to degrading *p-s*, Ro 1:26
flesh with its *p-s*, Gal 5:24
dead to…*p*, Col 3:5
not in lustful *p*, 1Th 4:5

PASSOVER
Israel's firstborn protected from the plague of death prior to the exodus from Egypt, Ex 12:1–30
Feast commemorating Israelite exodus and protection from death, Ex 12:42, 43; Lv 23:5; Nu 9:2, 12, 14; Mt 26:2, 18; Jn 19:14; Ac 12:4
See also feasts

PASTORS *shepherds of people*
and some *as p*, Eph 4:11

PASTURE *(n) grazing field*
lie down in green *p-s*, Ps 23:2
sheep of Your *p*, Ps 79:13

PASTURE *(v) feed, graze*
Moses…*p-ing* the flock, Ex 3:1
They will *p* on it, Zep 2:7
So I *p-d* the flock, Zec 11:7

PATARA
Port of Lycia where Paul changes ships, Ac 21:1, 2

PATCH *mending cloth*
- *p* of unshrunk cloth, Mt 9:16
- *p* pulls away from it, Mk 2:21

PATH *way*
- snake in the *p*, Ge 49:17
- the *p* of life, Ps 16:11
- a light to my *p*, Ps 119:105
- *p* of the upright is, Pr 15:19
- Make His *p-s* straight, Mt 3:3

PATHROS
- Described as a lowly kingdom, Eze 29:14–16
- Refuge for dispersed Jews, Jer 44:1–15
- Jews to be regathered from, Is 11:11

PATIENCE *endurance*
- try the *p* of men, Is 7:13
- in *p*, in kindness, 2Co 6:6
- love, joy, peace, *p*, Gal 5:22
- exhort, with great *p*, 2Ti 4:2
- endure it with *p*, 1Pe 2:20

PATIENT *bearing, enduring*
- Love is *p*, love is, 1Co 13:4
- *p* when wronged, 2Ti 2:24
- Lord…is *p* toward, 2Pe 3:9

PATMOS
- John, banished here, receives the Revelation, Rev 1:9

PATRIARCH *father of clan*
- regarding the *p* David, Ac 2:29
- the twelve *p-s*, Ac 7:8
- Abraham, the *p*, gave, Heb 7:4

PATTERN *model, plan*
- fixed *p-s* of heaven, Jer 33:25
- walk according to…*p*, Php 3:17

PAUL
- Roman citizen from Tarsus; studied under Gamaliel, Ac 22:3, 25–28
- Originally called Saul; persecutes the church, Ac 7:58; 8:1, 3; 9:1, 2
- Converted on road to Damascus, Ac 9:3–19
- Preaches in Damascus; escapes to Jerusalem and then to Tarsus, Ac 9:20–30
- Ministers in Antioch; sent to Jerusalem, Ac 11:25–30
- First missionary journey, Ac 13; 14
- Speaks for Gentiles at Jerusalem Council, Ac 15:1–5, 12
- Second missionary journey, Ac 15:36–18:22
- Third missionary journey, Ac 18:23–21:14
- Arrested in Jerusalem; defense before Roman authorities, Ac 21:15–26:32
- Sent to Rome, Ac 27:1–28:31
- His epistles, Ro; 1 and 2Co; Gal; Eph; Php; Col; 1 and 2Th; 1 and 2Ti; Titus; Phm

PAULUS, SERGIUS
- Roman proconsul of Cyprus, Ac 13:4, 7

PAVEMENT *paved road*
- on a *p* of stone, 2Ki 16:17
- mosaic *p* of porphyry, Est 1:6
- place called The *P*, Jn 19:13

PAY *give what is due*
- thief…*p* double, Ex 22:7
- *p* You my vows, Ps 66:13
- *P* back what you, Mt 18:28
- Never *p* back evil, Ro 12:17
- *p* the penalty, 2Th 1:9

PAY MY VOWS
- I shall *p* before, Ps 22:25
- I may *p* day by day, Ps 61:8
- I shall *p*, Ps 66:13
- shall *p* to the LORD, Ps 116:14
- shall *p* to the LORD, Ps 116:18

PEACE *calmness, tranquility*
- grant *p* in the land, Lv 26:6
- made *p* with David, 1Ch 19:19
- Seek *p*, and pursue, Ps 34:14
- for the *p* of Jerusalem, Ps 122:6
- all her paths are *p*, Pr 3:17
- a time for *p*, Ecc 3:8
- Prince of *P*, Is 9:6
- *p*…like a river, Is 66:12
- have withdrawn My *p*, Jer 16:5
- not come to bring *p*, Mt 10:34
- on earth *p* among, Lk 2:14
- *P* I leave with you, Jn 14:27
- we have *p* with God, Ro 5:1
- love, joy, *p*, Gal 5:22
- He Himself is our *p*, Eph 2:14
- gospel of *p*, Eph 6:15
- *p* of God…surpasses, Php 4:7
- *p* through the blood, Col 1:20
- take *p* from the earth, Rev 6:4

PEACE OFFERING
- *See* OFFERINGS

PEACEABLE
- gentle, *p*, free from, 1Ti 3:3
- be *p*, gentle, Titus 3:2

PEACEMAKERS
- Blessed are the *p*, Mt 5:9

PEARL *precious gem*
- wisdom is above…*p-s*, Job 28:18
- *p-s* before swine, Mt 7:6
- one *p* of great value, Mt 13:46

PEKAH
- Son of Remaliah; usurps Israel's throne, 2Ki 15:25–28
- Forms alliance with Rezin of Syria against Ahaz, Is 7:1–9
- Alliance defeated; captives returned, 2Ki 16:5–9
- Territory of, overrun by Tiglath-Pileser, 2Ki 15:29
- Assassinated by Hoshea, 2Ki 15:30

PEKAHIAH
- Son of Menahem; king of Israel, 2Ki 15:22–26
- Assassinated by Pekah, 2Ki 15:23–25

PELEG
- Descendant of Noah, Ge 10:1–25
- Ancestor of Jesus, Lk 3:35

PENALTY *punishment*
- you will bear the *p*, Eze 23:49
- pay the *p* of eternal, 2Th 1:9
- received a just *p*, Heb 2:2

PENTECOST
- Jewish feast held 50 days after Passover, Ac 20:16; 1Co 16:8
- coming of the Holy Spirit, Ac 2:1
- *See also* feasts

PENUEL
- Place east of Jordan; site of Jacob's wrestling with angel, Ge 32:24–31
- Inhabitants of, slain by Gideon, Jdg 8:8, 9, 17

PEOPLE *group, nation*
- they are one *p*, Ge 11:6
- Let My *p* go, Ex 5:1
- You are an obstinate *p*, Ex 33:5
- blessed above all *p-s*, Dt 7:14
- Forgive Your *p* Israel, Dt 21:8
- LORD loves His *p*, 2Ch 2:11
- *p* who are called by, 2Ch 7:14
- restores His captive *p*, Ps 14:7
- *We are* His *p*, Ps 100:3
- LORD will judge His *p*, Ps 135:14
- *p* are unrestrained, Pr 29:18
- *p* whom I formed, Is 43:21
- do *p* say that I am, Mk 8:27
- they feared the *p*, Lk 20:19
- die for the *p*, Jn 11:50
- not rejected His *p*, Ro 11:2
- every tribe and *p*, Rev 13:7

PEOPLE OF GOD
- of the *p*, 400, 000, Jdg 20:2
- thing against the *p*?, 2Sa 14:13
- Sabbath rest for the *p*, Heb 4:9
- ill-treatment with the *p*, Heb 11:25
- now you are the *p*, 1Pe 2:10

PEOR
- Mountain of Moab opposite Jericho, Nu 23:28
- Israel's camp seen from, Nu 24:2
- ——— Moabite god called Baal of Peor, Nu 25:3, 5, 18
- Israelites punished for worship of, Nu 31:16

PERCEIVE *be aware, discern*
- *p-d* all the wisdom, 1Ki 10:4
- listening, but do not *p*, Is 6:9
- *p-ing* in Himself, Mk 5:30
- *p* with their heart, Jn 12:40

PERDITION *damnation*
- the son of *p*, Jn 17:12

PEREZ
- One of Judah's twin sons by Tamar, Ge 38:24–30

PERFECT *(adj) flawless*
- His work is *p*, Dt 32:4
- law of the LORD is *p*, Ps 19:7
- heavenly Father is *p*, Mt 5:48
- *p* bond of unity, Col 3:14
- be *p* and complete, Jas 1:4
- *p* love casts out, 1Jn 4:18

PERFECTED *completed*
- is *p* in weakness, 2Co 12:9
- love is *p* with us, 1Jn 4:17

PERFORM *carry out*
- I will *p* miracles, Ex 34:10
- *p* My judgments, Lv 18:4

p-s righteous deeds, Ps 103:6
p a miracle in My, Mk 9:39
John *p-ed* no sign, Jn 10:41
p-ing great wonders, Ac 6:8

PERFUME *fragrant oil*
and *p* make the heart, Pr 27:9
instead of sweet *p*, Is 3:24
p on My body, Mt 26:12
anointed...with *p*, Lk 7:46
prepared...*p-s*, Lk 23:56

PERGA
Visited by Paul, Ac 13:13, 14; 14:25

PERGAMUM
Site of one of the seven churches, Rev 1:11
Special message to, Rev 2:12–17

PERISH *be destroyed*
we *p*, we are dying, Nu 17:12
weapons...*p-ed*, 2Sa 1:27
if I *p*, I *p*, Est 4:16
hope...will *p*, Job 8:13
the wicked will *p*, Ps 1:6
rod of his fury will *p*, Pr 22:8
our hope has *p-ed*, Eze 37:11
little ones *p*, Mt 18:14
p by the sword, Mt 26:52
p, but have eternal, Jn 3:16
for any to *p*, 2Pe 3:9

PERIZZITES
One of seven Canaanite nations, Dt 7:1
Possessed Palestine in Abraham's time, Ge 13:7
Jacob's fear of, Ge 34:30
Many of, slain by Judah, Jdg 1:4, 5

PERMANENT *lasting*
it is a *p* ordinance, Lv 6:18
p right of redemption, Lv 25:32
use them as *p* slaves, Lv 25:46
p home for the ark, 1Ch 28:2

PERMISSION *consent*
p they had from Cyrus, Ezr 3:7
Jesus gave them *p*, Mk 5:13
he had given him *p*, Ac 21:40

PERMIT *allow*
not *p-ting*...demons, Mk 1:34
p the children, Mk 10:14
Spirit...did not *p*, Ac 16:7
if the Lord *p-s*, 1Co 16:7

PERPETUAL *lasting*
p incense before the, Ex 30:8
as a *p* covenant, Ex 31:16
for a *p* priesthood, Ex 40:15
may sleep a *p* sleep, Jer 51:39

PERPLEXED *puzzled*
and his nobles were *p*, Da 5:9
he was very *p*, Mk 6:20
she was very *p* at *this*, Lk 1:29
While they were *p* about, Lk 24:4
while Peter was greatly *p*, Ac 10:17
p, but not despairing, 2Co 4:8
for I am *p* about you, Gal 4:20

PERSECUTE *afflict, oppress*
Why do you *p* me, Job 19:22
has *p-d* my soul, Ps 143:3
pray for those who *p*, Mt 5:44
p you in one city, Mt 10:23
why are you *p-ing* Me, Ac 9:4
used to *p* the church, Gal 1:13

PERSECUTION *oppression*
p arises because of, Mk 4:17
p began against the, Ac 8:1
a *p* against Paul, Ac 13:50
distress, or *p*, or, Ro 8:35

PERSEVERANCE *persistence*
by *p* in doing good, Ro 2:7
tribulation brings...*p*, Ro 5:3
for your *p* and faith, 2Th 1:4
p of the saints, Rev 14:12

PERSON *human being*
If a *p* sins, Lv 4:2
hungry *p* unsatisfied, Is 32:6
p...be in subjection, Ro 13:1
hidden *p* of the heart, 1Pe 3:4

PERSUADE *convince, prevail on*
a ruler may be *p-d*, Pr 25:15
trying to *p* Jews and, Ac 18:4
p-s men to worship, Ac 18:13
you will *p* me, Ac 26:28

PERSUASIVE *convincing*
p words of wisdom, 1Co 2:4
delude you with *p*, Col 2:4

PERVERSE *corrupt*
a *p* and crooked, Dt 32:5
A *p* heart shall depart, Ps 101:4
mind will utter *p*, Pr 23:33
and *p* generation, Php 2:15

PERVERT *distort, misdirect*
not *p* the justice, Ex 23:6
Does God *p* justice, Job 8:3
have *p-ed* their way, Jer 3:21

PESTILENCE *epidemic, plague*
LORD sent a *p*, 2Sa 24:15
sword, famine, and *p*, Jer 27:13
p and mourning and, Rev 18:8

PETER
Fisherman; called to discipleship, Mt 4:18–20; Jn 1:40–42
Called as apostle, Mt 10:2–4
Walks on water, Mt 14:28–33
Confesses Christ's deity, Mt 16:13–19
Rebuked by Christ, Mt 16:21–23
Witnesses Transfiguration, Mt 17:1–8; 2Pe 1:16–18
Denies Christ three times, Mt 26:69–75
Commissioned to feed Christ's sheep, Jn 21:15–17
Leads disciples, Ac 1:15–26
Preaches at Pentecost, Ac 2:1–41
Performs miracles, Ac 3:1–11; 5:14–16; 9:32–43
Called to minister to Gentiles, Ac 10
Defends his visit to Gentiles, Ac 11:1–18
Imprisoned and delivered, Ac 12:3–19
Speaks at Jerusalem Council, Ac 15:7–14
Writes epistles, 1Pe 1:1; 2Pe 1:1

PETITION *request, supplication*
God...grant your *p*, 1Sa 1:17
p to any god or man, Da 6:7
p-s...be made, 1Ti 2:1

PHARAOH
Kings of Egypt, contemporaries of:
Abraham, Ge 12:15–20
Joseph, Ge 40; 41
Moses in youth, Ex 1:8–11
the Exodus, Ex 5–14
Solomon, 1Ki 3:1; 11:17–20
Other Pharaohs, 1Ki 14:25, 26; 2Ki 17:4; 18:21; 19:9; 23:29; Jer 44:30

PHARISEES
Jewish religious party, Mt 3:7; 23:13; Mk 2:18; 7:3; Lk 11:42; 16:14; Jn 3:1; 11:47

PHARISEES AND SCRIBES
See SCRIBES AND PHARISEES
P came to Jesus, Mt 15:1
P gathered around Him, Mk 7:1
P asked Him, Mk 7:5
P began grumbling at, Lk 5:30
P began to grumble, Lk 15:2

PHILADELPHIA
City of Lydia in Asia Minor; church established here, Rev 1:11

PHILEMON
Christian at Colosse to whom Paul writes, Phm 1
Paul appeals to him to receive Onesimus, Phm 9–21

PHILETUS
False teacher, 2Ti 2:17, 18

PHILIP
Son of Herod the Great, Mt 14:3
——— One of the twelve apostles, Mt 10:3
Brings Nathanael to Christ, Jn 1:43–48
Tested by Christ, Jn 6:5–7
Introduces Greeks to Christ, Jn 12:20–22
Gently rebuked by Christ, Jn 14:8–12
——— One of the first seven deacons, Ac 6:5
Called an evangelist, Ac 21:8
Preaches in Samaria, Ac 8:5–13
Leads the Ethiopian eunuch to Christ, Ac 8:26–40

PHILIPPI
City of Macedonia (named after Philip of Macedon); visited by Paul, Ac 16:12; 20:6
Paul writes letter to church of, Php 1:1

PHILIPPIANS
people of Philippi, Php 4:15

PHILISTIA
The land of the Philistines, Ge 21:32, 34; Jos 13:2; Ps 60:8

PHILISTINES
Not attacked by Joshua, Jos 13:1–3
Left to test Israel, Jdg 3:1–4
God delivers Israel to, as punishment, Jdg 10:6, 7
Israel delivered from, by Samson, Jdg 13–16
Capture, then return the ark of the LORD, 1Sa 4–6
Wars and dealings with Saul and David, 1Sa 13:15–14:23; 17:1–52; 18:25–27;

21:10–15; 27:1–28:6; 29:1–11; 31:1–13; 2Sa 5:17–25
Originally on the island of Caphtor, Jer 47:4
Prophecies concerning, Is 9:11, 12; Jer 25:15–20; 47:1–7; Eze 25:15–17; Zep 2:4–6

PHINEHAS
Aaron's grandson; executes God's judgment, Nu 25:1–18; Ps 106:30, 31
Settles dispute over memorial altar, Jos 22:11–32
——— Younger son of Eli; abuses his office, 1Sa 1:3; 2:12–17, 22–36
Killed by Philistines, 1Sa 4:11, 17

PHOENICIA
Mediterranean coastal region including the cities of Ptolemais, Tyre, Zarephath and Sidon; evangelized by early Christians, Ac 11:19
Jesus preaches here, Mt 15:21

PHRYGIA
Jews from, at Pentecost, Ac 2:1, 10
Visited twice by Paul, Ac 16:6

PHYLACTERIES *prayer bands*
as *p* on your forehead, Ex 13:16
they broaden their *p*, Mt 23:5
See also frontals

PHYSICIAN
all worthless *p-s*, Job 13:4
healthy who need a *p*, Mt 9:12
P, heal yourself, Lk 4:23
Luke, the beloved *p*, Col 4:14

PIECE *part, portion*
dip your *p* of bread, Ru 2:14
thirty *p-s* of silver, Mt 27:3
gave Him a *p*…fish, Lk 24:42
woven in one *p*, Jn 19:23

PIERCE *penetrate*
master shall *p* his ear, Ex 21:6
They *p-d* my hands, Ps 22:16
He was *p-d* through, Is 53:5
whom they have *p-d*, Zec 12:10
sword will *p*…soul, Lk 2:35
p-d His side, Jn 19:34
p-d to the heart, Ac 2:37

PIETY *reverence*
learn to practice *p*, 1Ti 5:4
because of His *p*, Heb 5:7

PI-HAHIROTH
Israel camps there before crossing the Red Sea, Ex 14:2, 9; Nu 33:7, 8

PILATE
Governor of Judea (A.D. 26–36), Lk 3:1
Questions Jesus and delivers Him to Jews, Mt 27:2, 11–26; Jn 18:28–19:16

PILLAR *column; memorial*
became a *p* of salt, Ge 19:26
p of fire by night, Ex 13:21
set up…a *p*, 2Sa 18:18
hewn…her seven *p-s*, Pr 9:1
feet like *p-s* of fire, Rev 10:1

PILOT *steersman*
sailors, and your *p-s*, Eze 27:27
the *p* and…captain, Ac 27:11
inclination of the *p*, Jas 3:4

PINION *wing*
p and plumage of, Job 39:13
cover you with His *p-s*, Ps 91:4

PINNACLE *highest point*
had Him…on the *p*, Mt 4:5
p of the temple, Lk 4:9

PISGAH
Balaam offers sacrifice upon, Nu 23:14
Moses views Promised Land from, Dt 3:27
Site of Moses' death, Dt 34:1–7

PISHON
One of Eden's four rivers, Ge 2:10, 11

PISIDIA
Twice visited by Paul, Ac 13:13, 14; 14:24

PIT *deep hole, dungeon*
full of tar *p-s*, Ge 14:10
Joseph…not in the *p*, Ge 37:29
redeems…from the *p*, Ps 103:4
harlot is a deep *p*, Pr 23:27
silenced me in the *p*, La 3:53
to *p-s* of darkness, 2Pe 2:4
the bottomless *p*, Rev 9:1

PITCH *(n) tar*
inside and out with *p*, Ge 6:14
covered it over…*p*, Ex 2:3

PITCH *(v) set up*
p-ed his tent in the, Ge 31:25
he will *p* the tents, Da 11:45
tabernacle…Lord *p-ed*, Heb 8:2

PITCHER *container*
torches inside the *p-s*, Jdg 7:16
Fill four *p-s*, 1Ki 18:33
carrying a *p* of, Mk 14:13

PITHOM
Egyptian city built by Hebrew slaves, Ex 1:11

PITY *(n) sympathy*
shall not show *p*, Dt 19:21
I will not show *p*, Jer 13:14
No eye looked with *p*, Eze 16:5

PITY *(v) have compassion*
she had *p* on him, Ex 2:6
eye shall not *p* them, Dt 7:16
P me, *p* me, O you, Job 19:21
take *p* on us, Mk 9:22
most to be *p-ied*, 1Co 15:19

PLACE *area, space*
waters…into one *p*, Ge 1:9
he enters the holy *p*, Ex 28:29
God is a dwelling *p*, Dt 33:27
a *p* for My people, 1Ch 17:9
earth out of its *p*, Job 9:6
You are my hiding *p*, Ps 32:7
love the *p* of honor, Mt 23:6
a *p* called Golgotha, Mt 27:33
I go to prepare a *p*, Jn 14:2

PLAGUE *contagious disease*
no *p* will befall you, Ex 12:13
Remove Your *p* from, Ps 39:10
p of the hail, Rev 16:21
the seven last *p-s*, Rev 21:9

PLAIN *flat area*
p in…Shinar, Ge 11:2
desert *p-s* of Jericho, Jos 4:13
the *p* of Megiddo, 2Ch 35:22
broad *p* of the earth, Rev 20:9

PLAN *design, scheme*
tabernacle…its *p*, Ex 26:30
P-s formed long ago, Is 25:1
follow our own *p-s*, Jer 18:12
p and foreknowledge, Ac 2:23

PLANT *(n) growth from soil*
every *p* yielding seed, Ge 1:29
eat the *p-s* of the, Ge 3:18
hail…struck every *p*, Ex 9:25
God appointed a *p*, Jon 4:6

PLANT *(v) put into soil*
God *p-ed* a garden, Ge 2:8
p…trees for food, Lv 19:23
shall *p* a vineyard, Dt 28:30
A time to *p*, Ecc 3:2
her earnings she *p-s*, Pr 31:16
p-ed a vineyard, Mk 12:1
I *p-ed*, Apollos, 1Co 3:6

PLATTER *shallow dish*
on a *p* the head of, Mt 14:8
his head on a *p*, Mk 6:28

PLAY *take part*
who *p* the lyre, Ge 4:21
man who can *p*, 1Sa 16:17
p-ed the fool, 1Sa 26:21
P skillfully with a, Ps 33:3
nursing child will *p*, Is 11:8
not *p* the harlot, Hos 3:3
We *p-ed* the flute, Mt 11:17

PLEAD *appeal, beseech*
p-ed with the LORD, Dt 3:23
man…*p* with God, Job 16:21
LORD…*p* their case, Pr 22:23
P for the widow, Is 1:17
Elijah…*p-s* with God, Ro 11:2

PLEASANT *pleasing*
despised the *p* land, Ps 106:24
P words are a, Pr 16:24
sleep…is *p*, Ecc 5:12
Speak to us *p* words, Is 30:10

PLEASE *satisfy*
it *p* You to bless, 2Sa 7:29
You are *p-d* with me, Ps 41:11
sacrifices…not *p* Him, Hos 9:4
how he may *p* his, 1Co 7:33
p all men in all, 1Co 10:33
striving to *p* men, Gal 1:10
to walk and *p* God, 1Th 4:1
impossible to *p*, Heb 11:6

PLEASING *agreeable, gratifying*
tree that is *p*, Ge 2:9
meditation be *p*, Ps 104:34
not as *p* men but, 1Th 2:4
p in His sight, 1Jn 3:22

PLEASURE *gratification*
old, shall I have *p*, Ge 18:12
p in His people, Ps 149:4
He who loves *p will*, Pr 21:17
work for *His* good *p*, Php 2:13
lovers of *p* rather, 2Ti 3:4
passing *p-s* of sin, Heb 11:25

PLEDGE *promise*
cloak as a *p*, Ex 22:26
those who give *p-s*, Pr 22:26
the Spirit as a *p*, 2Co 5:5
p of our inheritance, Eph 1:14

PLEIADES
Part of God's creation, Job 9:9; Am 5:8

PLENTIFUL *abundant*
shed abroad a *p* rain, Ps 68:9
harvest is *p*, Mt 9:37

PLOT *plan, scheme*
wicked *p-s* against, Ps 37:12
you have *p-ted evil*, Pr 30:32
Jews *p-ted* together, Ac 9:23

PLOW *dig the soil*
not *p* with an ox, Dt 22:10
those who *p* iniquity, Job 4:8
sluggard does not *p*, Pr 20:4
his hand to the *p*, Lk 9:62
ought to *p* in hope, 1Co 9:10

PLOWSHARES *blade of plow*
their swords into *p*, Is 2:4
your *p* into swords, Joel 3:10

PLUMB LINE *vertical line*
the *p* of emptiness, Is 34:11
p In the midst of My, Am 7:8
when they see the *p*, Zec 4:10

PLUNDER *(n) booty, loot*
took no *p* in silver, Jdg 5:19
You will become *p*, Hab 2:7
wealth will become *p*, Zep 1:13

PLUNDER *(v) rob*
will *p* the Egyptians, Ex 3:22
stouthearted were *p-ed*, Ps 76:5
he will *p* his house, Mt 12:29

POINT *particular time*
grieved, to the *p* of, Mt 26:38
obedient to the *p* of, Php 2:8
to the *p* of shedding, Heb 12:4

POISON *lethal substance*
P...under their lips, Ps 140:3
given us *p-ed* water, Jer 8:14
turned justice into *p*, Am 6:12

POLL-TAX *income and head tax*
collect customs or *p*, Mt 17:25
give a *p* to Caesar, Mt 22:17

POLLUTE *contaminate*
blood *p-s* the land, Nu 35:33
earth is also *p-d*, Is 24:5

POMEGRANATE *fruit*
golden bell and a *p*, Ex 28:34
p-s of blue and purple, Ex 39:24
juice of my *p-s*, SS 8:2
the fig tree, the *p*, Hag 2:19

PONDER *think deeply*
not *p* the path of life, Pr 5:6
Or *p* things...past, Is 43:18

PONTUS
Jews from, at Pentecost, Ac 2:5, 9
Home of Aquila, Ac 18:2
Christians of, addressed by Peter, 1Pe 1:1

POOL *pond*
of the upper *p*, 2Ki 18:17
rock into a *p*, Ps 114:8
land will become a *p*, Is 35:7
in the *p* of Siloam, Jn 9:7

POOR *impoverished, needy*
p will never cease, Dt 15:11
raises the *p* from the, 1Sa 2:8
or you will become *p*, Pr 20:13
not rob the *p*, Pr 22:22
are the *p* in spirit, Mt 5:3
a *p* widow came, Mk 12:42
you always have the *p*, Mk 14:7
sake He became *p*, 2Co 8:9
not God choose the *p*, Jas 2:5

POPULATE *increase number*
P the earth abundantly, Ge 9:7
whole earth was *p-d*, Ge 9:19

POPULATION *people*
with all *his* great *p*, Is 16:14
deported an entire *p*, Am 1:6

PORCIUS FESTUS
Paul stands trial before, Ac 25:1–22

PORPOISE SKIN
covering of *p-s* above, Ex 26:14
put sandals of *p* on, Eze 16:10

PORTICO *porch*
in the *p* of Solomon, Jn 10:23
one accord in...*p*, Ac 5:12

PORTION *part, share*
gather a day's *p*, Ex 16:4
LORD's *p* is...people, Dt 32:9
double *p* of...spirit, 2Ki 2:9
The LORD is my *p*, Ps 119:57
joy over their *p*, Is 61:7

POSSESS *control, take*
give...this land to *p*, Ge 15:7
are to *p* their land, Lv 20:24
go in and *p* the land, Dt 1:8
p-es all the nations, Ps 82:8
p-ed by Beelzebul, Mk 3:22
sell all you *p*, Mk 10:21
p-ed with demons, Lk 8:27
do not *p* silver and, Ac 3:6

POSSESSION *ownership*
for an everlasting *p*, Ge 17:8
you shall be My own *p*, Ex 19:5
people for His own *p*, Dt 4:20
full of Your *p-s*, Ps 104:24
charge of all his *p-s*, Mt 24:47
selling their...*p-s*, Ac 2:45

POSSIBLE *can be done*
all things are *p*, Mt 19:26
p with God, Lk 18:27

POSTERITY *descendants*
P will serve Him, Ps 22:30
p of the wicked, Ps 37:38

POT *container, vessel*
death in the *p*, 2Ki 4:40
refining *p* is for, Pr 17:3
I see a boiling *p*, Jer 1:13

POTIPHAR
High Egyptian officer, Ge 39:1
Puts Joseph in jail, Ge 39:20

POTIPHERAH
Egyptian priest of On (Heliopolis), Ge 41:45–50
Father of Asenath, Joseph's wife, Ge 46:20

POTSHERD *piece of pottery*
p to scrape himself, Job 2:8
is dried up like a *p*, Ps 22:15

POTTER *one who molds clay*
clay say to the *p*, Is 45:9
and You our *p*, Is 64:8
as it pleased the *p*, Jer 18:4
Throw it to the *p*, Zec 11:13

POTTER'S FIELD
burial place bought with Judas' money, Mt 27:3ff
also called *Field of Blood*

POUR *cause to flow*
p me out like milk, Job 10:10
I *p* out my soul, Ps 42:4
P out your heart, Ps 62:8
I will *p* out My Spirit, Is 44:3
P out Your wrath, Jer 10:25
p out...a blessing, Mal 3:10
p-ed it on His, Mt 26:7
p forth of My Spirit, Ac 2:17

POVERTY *destitution, want*
glutton...come to *p*, Pr 23:21
neither *p* nor riches, Pr 30:8
through His *p* might, 2Co 8:9

POWER *authority, strength*
to show you My *p*, Ex 9:16
from the *p* of Sheol, Ps 49:15
the *p* of His works, Ps 111:6
p of the tongue, Pr 18:21
the *p* of the sword, Jer 18:21
Not by might nor...*p*, Zec 4:6
Yours is...the *p*, Mt 6:13
the right hand of *p*, Mk 14:62
clothed with *p* from, Lk 24:49
you will receive *p*, Ac 1:8
gospel...*p* of God, Ro 1:16
the *p* of our Lord, 1Co 5:4
p of sin is the law, 1Co 15:56
p of Christ...dwell, 2Co 12:9
prince of the *p* of, Eph 2:2
p of His resurrection, Php 3:10
timidity, but of *p*, 2Ti 1:7
by the word of His *p*, Heb 1:3
quenched the *p* of, Heb 11:34
p-s...been subjected, 1Pe 3:22

POWER OF GOD
instruct you in the *p*, Job 27:11
Scriptures nor the *p*, Mt 22:29
Scriptures or the *p*?, Mk 12:24

right hand of the *p*.", Lk 22:69
is called the Great *P*, Ac 8:10
the *p* for salvation, Ro 1:16
being saved it is the *p*, 1Co 1:18
Christ the *p* and, 1Co 1:24
but on the *p*, 1Co 2:5
lives because of the *p*, 2Co 13:4
protected by the *p*, 1Pe 1:5

POWERLESS *without strength*
p before this great, 2Ch 20:12
He might render *p*, Heb 2:14

PRACTICE *(n) custom, habit*
evil of their *p-s*, Ps 28:4
disclosing their *p-s*, Ac 19:18
laid aside…*evil p-s*, Col 3:9

PRACTICE *(v) engage in*
keep…statutes and *p*, Lv 20:8
He who *p-s* deceit, Ps 101:7
Who *p* righteousness, Ps 106:3
p-ing hospitality, Ro 12:13
learn to *p* piety, 1Ti 5:4
the one who *p-s* sin, 1Jn 3:8

PRAETORIUM
Pilate's, in Jerusalem, Mk 15:16; Jn 18:28; Mt 27:27
——— Herod's palace at Caesarea, Ac 23:35

PRAISE *(n) acclamation, honor*
offering of *p*, Lv 19:24
sing *p-s* to Him, 1Ch 16:9
songs of *p*…hymns, Ne 12:46
From You…my *p*, Ps 22:25
sound His *p* abroad, Ps 66:8
makes Jerusalem a *p*, Is 62:7
his *p* is not from men, Ro 2:29
anything worthy of *p*, Php 4:8
a sacrifice of *p*, Heb 13:15
Give *p* to our God, Rev 19:5

PRAISE *(v) extol, glorify*
I will *p* Him, Ex 15:2
greatly to be *p-d*, 1Ch 16:25
Will the dust *p* You, Ps 30:9
My lips will *p* You, Ps 63:3
heavens will *p* Your, Ps 89:5
P Him, sun and moon, Ps 148:3
P Him with trumpet, Ps 150:3
Death cannot *p* You, Is 38:18
I *p* You, Father, Mt 11:25
heavenly host *p-ing*, Lk 2:13
disciples began to *p*, Lk 19:37
leaping and *p-ing* God, Ac 3:8

PRAISE THE LORD
I will *p*, Ge 29:35
thank and *p* God of, 1Ch 16:4
p according to the, Ezr 3:10
who seek Him will *p*, Ps 22:26
to be created may *p*, Ps 102:18
P! Praise, O servants, Ps 113:1
dead do not *p*, Ps 115:17
P, all nations, Ps 117:1
P, for the LORD is, Ps 135:3
that has breath *p*, Ps 150:6
P in song, Is 12:5
p! For He has delivered, Jer 20:13
"*P* all you Gentiles, Ro 15:11

PRAY *ask, worship*
Abraham *p-ed* to, Ge 20:17
For this boy I *p-ed*, 1Sa 1:27
found *courage* to *p*, 1Ch 17:25
For to You I *p*, Ps 5:2
P for…Jerusalem, Ps 122:6
p to a god who cannot, Is 45:20
We earnestly *p*, Jon 1:14
p for…persecute, Mt 5:44
by Himself to *p*, Mt 14:23
p and ask, believe, Mk 11:24
until I have *p-ed*, Mk 14:32
Lord, teach us to *p*, Lk 11:1
they ought to *p*, Lk 18:1
I have *p-ed* for you, Lk 22:32
p-ed with fasting, Ac 14:23
if I *p* in a tongue, 1Co 14:14
p without ceasing, 1Th 5:17
p for one another, Jas 5:16
p-ing in the…Spirit, Jude 20

PRAYER
I have heard your *p*, 2Ch 7:12
And my *p* is pure, Job 16:17
LORD receives my *p*, Ps 6:9
Give ear to my *p*, Ps 55:1
p of the righteous, Pr 15:29
joyful in My house of *p*, Is 56:7
ask in *p*, believing, Mt 21:22
you make long *p-s*, Mt 23:14
whole night in *p*, Lk 6:12
My house…of *p*, Lk 19:46
devoting…to *p*, Ac 1:14
offering *p* with joy, Php 1:4
but in everything by *p*, Php 4:6
p-s…not be hindered, 1Pe 3:7
p-s of the saints, Rev 5:8

PREACH *exhort, proclaim*
Jesus began to *p*, Mt 4:17
as you go, *p*, Mt 10:7
teach and *p* in their, Mt 11:1
p-ing…repentance, Mk 1:4
p the gospel to all, Mk 16:15
p the kingdom of, Lk 4:43
he *p-ed* Jesus to him, Ac 8:35
p…the good news, Ac 13:32
How will they *p*, Ro 10:15
we *p* Christ crucified, 1Co 1:23
He…*p-ed* peace, Eph 2:17
p the word, 2Ti 4:2

PREACH THE GOSPEL
all the world and *p*, Mk 16:15
He anointed Me to *p*, Lk 4:18
they continued to *p*, Ac 14:7
I am eager to *p*, Ro 1:15
p, not where Christ, Ro 15:20
p, not in cleverness, 1Co 1:17
p even to the regions, 2Co 10:16

PREACHER *one who proclaims*
hear without a *p*, Ro 10:14
appointed a *p* and an, 1Ti 2:7
Noah, a *p* of, 2Pe 2:5

PRECEPTS *commandments*
All His *p* are sure, Ps 111:7
meditate on Your *p*, Ps 119:15
as doctrines the *p* of, Mt 15:9

PRECIOUS *beloved; costly*
P in the sight of, Ps 116:15
like the *p* oil upon the, Ps 133:2
more *p* than jewels, Pr 3:15
p things…no profit, Is 44:9
more *p* than gold, 1Pe 1:7
with *p* blood, 1Pe 1:19

PREDESTINED *foreordained*
purpose *p* to occur, Ac 4:28
foreknew, He also *p*, Ro 8:29
God *p* before the ages, 1Co 2:7
p us to adoption, Eph 1:5
p according to His, Eph 1:11

PREDETERMINED
p plan…of God, Ac 2:23

PREEMINENT *foremost*
P in dignity, Ge 49:3

PREFECTS *Persian officials*
shatter governors…*p*, Jer 51:23
the satraps, the *p*, Da 3:3

PREGNANT *with child*
womb of…*p* woman, Ecc 11:5
And her womb ever *p*, Jer 20:17
ripped open…*p*, Am 1:13
Elizabeth…became *p*, Lk 1:24

PREPARATION *readiness*
distracted with…*p-s*, Lk 10:40
Jewish day of *p*, Jn 19:42
making *p-s*, he fell, Ac 10:10
p of the gospel of, Eph 6:15

PREPARE *make ready*
p a savory dish, Ge 27:4
mind *p-s* deception, Job 15:35
p a table before me, Ps 23:5
P to meet your God, Am 4:12
will *p* Your way, Mt 11:10
kingdom *p-d* for, Mt 25:34
to *p* Me for burial, Mt 26:12
p-d spices and, Lk 23:56
I go to *p* a place, Jn 14:2
worlds were *p-d* by, Heb 11:3
p your minds for, 1Pe 1:13

PRESENCE *appearance*
My *p* shall go *with*, Ex 33:14
in the *p* of my enemies, Ps 23:5
the light of Your *p*, Ps 44:3
tremble at Your *p*, Is 64:2
the *p* of His glory, Jude 24
the *p* of the Lamb, Rev 14:10

PRESENT *(n) gift*
a *p* for his brother, Ge 32:13
sent a *p* to the king, 2Ki 16:8
and a *p* to Hezekiah, Is 39:1

PRESENT *(v) give, offer*
p you with a crown of, Pr 4:9
you *p* the blind for, Mal 1:8
p Him to the Lord, Lk 2:22
p yourselves to God, Ro 6:13
p your bodies a, Ro 12:1
p you before Him holy, Col 1:22

PRESERVE *protect*
no son to *p* my, 2Sa 18:18
P me, O God, Ps 16:1
P my soul, Ps 86:2
LORD *p-s* the simple, Ps 116:6
p-d ones of Israel, Is 49:6
p the unity of the, Eph 4:3
be *p-d* complete, 1Th 5:23

PRESS *compel, force*
measure, *p-ed* down, Lk 6:38
I *p* on toward…goal, Php 3:14

PRETEND *deceive, feign*
p to be a mourner, 2Sa 14:2
p to be another, 1Ki 14:5
p-s to be poor, Pr 13:7
spies who *p-ed* to, Lk 20:20

PREVAIL *exist; triumph*
water *p-ed*…increased, Ge 7:18
not by might…man *p*, 1Sa 2:9
Iniquities *p* against me, Ps 65:3
overcome me and *p-ed*, Jer 20:7

PREVENT *stop*
has *p-ed* me from bearing, Ge 16:2
John tried to *p* Him, Mt 3:14
we tried to *p* him because, Mk 9:38
eyes were *p-ed* from, Lk 24:16
What *p-s* me from being, Ac 8:36
not to *p* any of his friends, Ac 24:23

PREY *what is hunted*
birds of *p* came, Ge 15:11
lion tearing the *p*, Eze 22:25
no longer be a *p* to, Eze 34:28

PRICE *cost, value*
shall increase its *p*, Lv 25:16
their redemption *p*, Nu 18:16
p of the pardoning of, Is 27:9
it is the *p* of blood, Mt 27:6
p of his wickedness, Ac 1:18
kept back *some*…*p*, Ac 5:2
bought with a *p*, 1Co 7:23

PRIDE *exaggerated self-esteem*
P goes before, Pr 16:18
you an everlasting *p*, Is 60:15
p of Israel testifies, Hos 5:5
envy, slander, *p*, Mk 7:22
boastful *p* of life, 1Jn 2:16

PRIEST *intermediary*
a *p* of God Most, Ge 14:18
a kingdom of *p-s*, Ex 19:6
Aaron's sons, the *p-s*, Lv 1:5
if the anointed *p* sins, Lv 4:3
p…make atonement, Lv 4:31
without a teaching *p*, 2Ch 15:3
You are a *p* forever, Ps 110:4
all the chief *p-s*, Mt 2:4
show yourself to the *p*, Mt 8:4
faithful high *p*, Heb 2:17
have a great high *p*, Heb 4:14
You are a *p* forever, Heb 5:6

PRIESTHOOD *office of priest*
for a perpetual *p*, Ex 40:15
have defiled the *p*, Ne 13:29
His *p* permanently, Heb 7:24
royal *p*, a holy nation, 1Pe 2:9

PRIME *fully mature period*
die in the *p* of life, 1Sa 2:33
p of life…fleeting, Ecc 11:10

PRINCE *ruler*
Who made you a *p*, Ex 2:14
p-s of the tribes, 1Ch 29:6
contempt upon *p-s*, Ps 107:40
Do not trust in *p-s*, Ps 146:3
Father, *P* of Peace, Is 9:6
p-s will rule justly, Is 32:1
to death the *P* of life, Ac 3:15
p of…the air, Eph 2:2

PRISCILLA (or Prisca)
Wife of Aquila, Ac 18:1–3
With Aquila, instructs Apollos, Ac 18:26
Mentioned by Paul, Ro 16:3; 1Co 16:19; 2Ti 4:19

PRISON *jail*
Put this man in *p*, 1Ki 22:27
my soul out of *p*, Ps 142:7
beheaded in the *p*, Mt 14:10
I was in *p*, and, Mt 25:36
opened…the *p*, Ac 5:19
spirits *now* in *p*, 1Pe 3:19

PRISONER *one who is confined*
sets the *p-s* free, Ps 146:7
a notorious *p*, Mt 27:16
p of the law of sin, Ro 7:23
Paul, a *p* of Christ, Phm 1

PRIVATE *not public*
show him his fault in *p*, Mt 18:15
but *I did so* in *p*, Gal 2:2

PRIZE *reward*
one receives the *p*, 1Co 9:24
p of the upward call, Php 3:14

PROCEED *go forth*
p from evil to evil, Jer 9:3
p-s out of the mouth, Mt 4:4
p-s from…Father, Jn 15:26

PROCHORUS
One of the first seven deacons, Ac 6:5

PROCLAIM *announce, declare*
p…name of the LORD, Ex 33:19
P good tidings, 1Ch 16:23
appointed…to *p*, Ne 6:7
p liberty to captives, Is 61:1
p justice to the, Mt 12:18
he *began* to *p* Jesus, Ac 9:20
first to *p* light, Ac 26:23
faith is being *p-ed*, Ro 1:8
p…eternal life, 1Jn 1:2

PROCLAMATION *declaration*
a *p* was circulated, Ex 36:6
made *p* to the spirits, 1Pe 3:19

PROCONSUL *Roman governor*
the *p*, Sergius Paulus, Ac 13:7
p-s are *available*, Ac 19:38

PRODUCE *(n) yield of the soil*
land will yield its *p*, Lv 25:19
tithe all the *p*, Dt 14:22
earth has yielded its *p*, Ps 67:6
precious *p* of…soil, Jas 5:7

PRODUCE *(v) bring forth*
milk *p-s* butter, Pr 30:33
cannot *p* bad fruit, Mt 7:18
they *p* quarrels, 2Ti 2:23
faith *p-s* endurance, Jas 1:3

PROFANE *defile, desecrate*
p My holy name, Lv 20:3
is *p-d* by harlotry, Lv 21:7
and *p-d* My sabbaths, Eze 22:8
p-d your sanctuaries, Eze 28:18
to *p* the covenant, Mal 2:10

PROFESS *confess, declare*
P-ing to be wise, Ro 1:22
They *p* to know God, Titus 1:16

PROFIT *(n) benefit, gain*
labor there is *p*, Pr 14:23
no *p* for the charmer, Ecc 10:11
not seeking my…*p*, 1Co 10:33
business…make a *p*, Jas 4:13

PROFIT *(v) reap an advantage*
p…my destruction, Job 30:13
what does it *p* a, Mk 8:36
the flesh *p-s* nothing, Jn 6:63
it *p-s* me nothing, 1Co 13:3

PROFITABLE *useful*
not all things are *p*, 1Co 6:12
godliness is *p*, 1Ti 4:8
p for teaching, 2Ti 3:16

PROMINENT *well-known*
a *p* member of the, Mk 15:43
of *p* Greek women, Ac 17:12
p men of the city, Ac 25:23

PROMISE *(n) agreement, pledge*
p of the Holy Spirit, Ac 2:33
the *p* made by God, Ac 26:6
the *p* is nullified, Ro 4:14
children of the *p*, Ro 9:8
commandment…a *p*, Eph 6:2
heirs of the *p*, Heb 6:17
precious…*p-s*, 2Pe 1:4
the *p* of His coming, 2Pe 3:4

PROMISED *made an agreement*
land which He had *p*, Dt 9:28
p to keep Your words, Ps 119:57
p long ages ago, Titus 1:2
He who *p* is faithful, Heb 10:23

PRONOUNCE *declare officially*
shall *p* him clean, Lv 13:23
I will *p* My judgments, Jer 1:16
Pilate *p-d* sentence, Lk 23:24
God…*p-d* judgment, Rev 18:20

PROOF *evidence*
furnished *p* to all, Ac 17:31
p of your love, 2Co 8:24
p of the Christ, 2Co 13:3

PROPER *suitable*
fulfilled…*p* time, Lk 1:20
is it *p* for a woman, 1Co 11:13
as is *p* among saints, Eph 5:3

PROPERTY *goods; land*
acquire *p* in it, Ge 34:10
p…too great, Ge 36:7
buys a slave as *his p*, Lv 22:11
who owned much *p*, Mt 19:22
selling their *p* and, Ac 2:45
things…common *p*, Ac 4:32

PROPHECY *proclamation*
seal up vision and *p*, Da 9:24
p…fulfilled, Mt 13:14
have *the gift of p*, 1Co 13:2
no *p*…of human will, 2Pe 1:21
the spirit of *p*, Rev 19:10

Many will be *p-d*, Da 12:10

PURIFICATION *cleansing*
Jewish custom of *p*, Jn 2:6
He...made *p* of sins, Heb 1:3

PURIFY *make clean*
p-ied these waters, 2Ki 2:21
P me with hyssop, Ps 51:7
p...a people, Titus 2:14
p your hearts, Jas 4:8
p-ied your souls, 1Pe 1:22

PURIM
Jewish festival, Est 9:26ff

PURITY *not corrupted*
who loves *p* of heart, Pr 22:11
love, faith *and p*, 1Ti 4:12
with p in doctrine, Titus 2:7

PURPLE *color*
a veil of blue and *p*, Ex 26:31
Those reared in *p*, La 4:5
clothed Daniel with *p*, Da 5:29
dressed Him...*p*, Mk 15:17
a seller of *p* fabrics, Ac 16:14
clothed in *p* and, Rev 17:4

PURPOSE *intention, reason*
p of shedding blood, Eze 22:9
rejected God's *p*, Lk 7:30
for this *p* I have, Ac 26:16
according to *His p*, Ro 8:28

PURSUE *chase, follow*
p the manslayer, Dt 19:6
They *p* my honor, Job 30:15
the enemy *p* my soul, Ps 7:5
Seek peace, and *p* it, Ps 34:14
Adversity *p-s*, Pr 13:21
p-s righteousness, Pr 21:21
may *p* strong drink, Is 5:11
p righteousness, 2Ti 2:22
P peace with...men, Heb 12:14

PURSUIT *effort to capture*
went in *p* as far as Dan, Ge 14:14
Egyptians took up the *p*, Ex 14:23
vapor, the *p* of death, Pr 21:6
who follows empty *p-s* will, Pr 28:19
man in the midst of his *p-s*, Jas 1:11

PUT
Country and people in Africa, Is 66:19

PUT *place*
p enmity Between, Ge 3:15
He *p* a new song, Ps 40:3
p a purple robe on Him, Jn 19:2
p on the Lord Jesus, Ro 13:14
p on the new self, Eph 4:24
P on the full armor, Eph 6:11

PUT OFF
p your ornaments from, Ex 33:5
shall *p* their garments, Eze 44:19

PUT ON
p her widow's garments, Ge 38:19
p Aaron the tunic, Ex 29:5
shall *p* the holy linen tunic, Lv 16:4
nor shall a man *p*, Dt 22:5
p your best clothes, Ru 3:3
p mourning garments now, 2Sa 14:2
Esther *p* her royal robes, Est 5:1
awake, *p* strength, Is 51:9
p righteousness like a, Is 59:17
do not *p* a gloomy face, Mt 6:16
what you will *p*, Mt 6:25
"Do not *p* two tunics.", Mk 6:9
p the armor of light., Ro 13:12
p the Lord Jesus, Ro 13:14
perishable must *p* the, 1Co 15:53
p the new self, Eph 4:24
having *p* the breastplate, Eph 6:14
p the new self, Col 3:10
p love, which is the, Col 3:14
p the breastplate of faith, 1Th 5:8

PUTEOLI
Seaport of Italy, Ac 28:13

Q

QUAIL *type of bird*
q-s came up and, Ex 16:13
q from the sea, Nu 11:31

QUAKE *shake, tremble*
The mountains *q-d*, Jdg 5:5
made the land *q*, Ps 60:2
The earth *q-d*, Ps 68:8
q at Your presence, Is 64:1

QUALITY *character*
test the *q* of each, 1Co 3:13
imperishable *q* of a, 1Pe 3:4

QUANTITY *amount*
large *q-ies* of cedar, 1Ch 22:4
a great *q* of fish, Lk 5:6

QUARANTINE *isolate*
shall *q* the article, Lv 13:50
q the house for, Lv 14:38

QUARREL *(n) altercation*
if men have a *q*, Ex 21:18
So abandon the *q*, Pr 17:14
are *q-s* among you, 1Co 1:11
the source of *q-s*, Jas 4:1

QUARREL *(v) contend, fight*
did not *q* over it, Ge 26:22
Why do you *q* with me, Ex 17:2
any fool will *q*, Pr 20:3
those who *q* with you, Is 41:12

QUARRY *rock mine*
of stone prepared at the *q*, 1Ki 6:7
q from which you were dug, Is 51:1

QUART *measure*
A *q* of wheat for a, Rev 6:6

QUEEN *female sovereign*
when the *q* of Sheba, 1Ki 10:1
king saw Esther the *q*, Est 5:2
The *q* of kingdoms, Is 47:5
The Q of the South, Mt 12:42
Candace, *q* of the, Ac 8:27

QUENCH *extinguish*
donkeys *q* their thirst, Ps 104:11
waters cannot *q* love, SS 8:7
not *q* the Spirit, 1Th 5:19
q-ed...power of fire, Heb 11:34

QUESTION *(n) inquiry, problem*
Was it not just a *q*, 1Sa 17:29
answered all her *q-s*, 2Ch 9:2
Jesus asked...a *q*, Mt 22:41
in controversial *q-s*, 1Ti 6:4

QUESTION *(v) ask*
q-ed the priests, 2Ch 31:9
Jeremiah and *q-ed*, Jer 38:27
He *began* to *q* them, Mk 9:33
to *q* Him closely on, Lk 11:53
Q those who have, Jn 18:21

QUICK *(adj) rapid*
is *q*-tempered exalts, Pr 14:29
q to hear, slow to, Jas 1:19

QUICK *(n) deepest feelings*
cut to the *q* and, Ac 5:33
were cut to the *q*, Ac 7:54

QUIET *(adj) calm, still*
he knew no *q* within, Job 20:20
me beside *q* waters, Ps 23:2
God, do not remain *q*, Ps 83:1
lead a...*q* life, 1Ti 2:2
gentle and *q* spirit, 1Pe 3:4

QUIET *(v) become calm, still*
and *q-ed* my soul, Ps 131:2
will be *q* in His love, Zep 3:17
Be *q*, and come out, Mk 1:25

QUIVER *case for holding arrows*
your *q* and your bow, Ge 27:3
man whose *q* is full, Ps 127:5
hidden Me in His *q*, Is 49:2
q is like an open grave, Jer 5:16
fill the *q-s*, Jer 51:11

QUOTA *portion assigned*
complete your work *q*, Ex 5:13
deliver the *q* of bricks, Ex 5:18

QUOTE *repeat a passage*
who *q-s* proverbs, Eze 16:44
will *q* this proverb, Lk 4:23

R

RAAMSES
Treasure city built by Hebrew slaves, Ex 1:11

RABBAH
Capital of Ammon, Am 1:14
Besieged by Joab; defeated and enslaved by David, 2Sa 12:26–31
Destruction of, foretold, Jer 49:2, 3

RABBI / RABBONI
Respectful form of address, Mt 23:7; 26:25; Mk 10:51
Master, teacher, Jn 1:49; 6:25; 11:8; 20:16

RABBONI
Mary addresses Christ as, Jn 20:16

RAB-MAG
Title applied to Babylonian prince, Jer 39:3, 13

RAB-SARIS
Title applied to:

Assyrian officials sent by Sennacherib, 2Ki 18:17
Babylonian prince, Jer 39:3, 13

RABSHAKEH
Sent by king of Assyria to threaten Hezekiah, 2Ki 18:17–37; Is 36:2–22
The LORD sends rumor to take him away, 2Ki 19:6–8; Is 37:6–8

RACE *(n) nation, people*
r has intermingled, Ezr 9:2
mongrel *r* will dwell, Zec 9:6
advantage of our *r*, Ac 7:19
you are a chosen *r*, 1Pe 2:9

RACE *(n) competition of speed*
r is not to…swift, Ecc 9:11
in a *r* all run, but, 1Co 9:24
r…set before us, Heb 12:1

RACHEL
Laban's younger daughter; Jacob's favorite wife, Ge 29:28–30
Supports her husband's position, Ge 31:14–16
Mother of Joseph and Benjamin, Ge 30:22–25
Prophecy concerning; quoted, Jer 31:15; Mt 2:18

RADIANCE *brightness*
a *r* around Him, Eze 1:27
His r is like, Hab 3:4
r of His glory, Heb 1:3

RADIANT *shining brightly*
looked to Him…were *r*, Ps 34:5
you will see and be *r*, Is 60:5
His garments…*r*, Mk 9:3

RAFTS *boats*
r to go by sea, 1Ki 5:9
bring it to you on *r*, 2Ch 2:16

RAGE *(n) violent anger*
Haman was filled…*r*, Est 3:5
with *r* as they heard, Lk 4:28

RAGE *(v) be very angry*
r-s against the LORD, Pr 19:3
foolish man…*r-s*, Pr 29:9
Why…Gentiles *r*, Ac 4:25

RAHAB
Prostitute in Jericho; helps Joshua's spies, Jos 2:1–21
Spared in battle, Jos 6:17–25
Mentioned in the NT, Mt 1:5; Heb 11:31; Jas 2:25
——— Used figuratively of Egypt, Ps 87:4

RAID *(n) robbery*
a *r* on the land, 1Sa 23:27
a *r* on the camels, Job 1:17

RAID *(v) make a sudden attack*
r at their heels, Ge 49:19
Bandits *r* outside, Hos 7:1

RAIN *(n)*
God had not sent *r*, Ge 2:5
r fell upon the earth, Ge 7:12
I shall give you *r-s*, Lv 26:4
LORD sent…*r*, 1Sa 12:18
no *r* in the land, 1Ki 17:7
the mountain *r-s*, Job 24:8
shed…a plentiful *r*, Ps 68:9
r is over *and* gone, SS 2:11
anger a flooding *r*, Eze 13:13
r on *the* righteous, Mt 5:45
ground…drinks the *r*, Heb 6:7

RAIN *(v) fall down, pour*
r bread from heaven, Ex 16:4
the LORD *r-ed* hail, Ex 9:23
it *r-ed* fire and, Lk 17:29
not *r*…for three, Jas 5:17

RAINBOW *colored arc in sky*
appearance of the *r*, Eze 1:28
a *r* around the throne, Rev 4:3
r was upon his head, Rev 10:1

RAISE *elevate, lift*
will *r* up a prophet, Dt 18:18
LORD *r-d* up judges, Jdg 2:16
r-s the poor from, 1Sa 2:8
eyelids are *r-d in*, Pr 30:13
r up shepherds over, Jer 23:4
He will *r* us up, Hos 6:2
Heal…*r the* dead, Mt 10:8
He will be *r-d* up, Mt 20:19
three days I will *r*, Jn 2:19
Jesus God *r-d* up, Ac 2:32
r-d a spiritual, 1Co 15:44
r-d us up with Him, Eph 2:6
God is able to *r people*, Heb 11:19

RAISED FROM THE DEAD
See RAISED … FROM THE DEAD
when He was *r*, Jn 2:22
whom Jesus had *r*, Jn 12:1
after He was *r*, Jn 21:14
one whom God *r*, Ac 3:15
whom God *r*, Ac 4:10
as Christ was *r*, Ro 6:4
r, in order that we, Ro 7:4
r, how do some, 1Co 15:12
r, the first fruits of, 1Co 15:20
He *r*, that is Jesus, 1Th 1:10

RAISED … FROM THE DEAD
See RAISED FROM THE DEAD
But God *r*, Ac 13:30
He *r*, no longer to return, Ac 13:34
believe in Him who *r*, Ro 4:24
Spirit of Him who *r*, Ro 8:11
in your heart that God *r*, Ro 10:9
God the Father, who *r*), Gal 1:1
when He *r* and seated, Eph 1:20
working of God, who *r*, Col 2:12
r and gave Him glory, 1Pe 1:21

RAISIN *dried grapes*
clusters of *r-s*, 2Sa 16:1
Sustain me with *r*, SS 2:5
and love *r* cakes, Hos 3:1

RAM *male sheep*
Abraham…took the *r*, Ge 22:13
a *r* without defect, Lv 5:15
the *r* of atonement, Nu 5:8
r which had two horns, Da 8:3

RAMAH
Fortress built, 1Ki 15:17–22
Samuel's headquarters, 1Sa 7:15, 17
David flees to, 1Sa 19:18–23

RAMOTH-GILEAD
City of refuge east of Jordan, Dt 4:43; Jos 20:8; 1Ch 6:80
Site of Ahab's fatal conflict with Syrians, 1Ki 22:1–39

RAMPART *bulwark, siege*
and *r-s* for security, Is 26:1
Whose *r was* the sea, Na 3:8
station myself on the *r*, Hab 2:1

RANK *position*
men of *r* are a lie, Ps 62:9
He…has a higher *r*, Jn 1:15
a Man…higher *r*, Jn 1:30

RANSOM *(n) payment*
give a *r* for himself, Ex 30:12
not take *r* for, Nu 35:31
wicked is a *r* for, Pr 21:18
His life a *r* for, Mt 20:28
gave Himself as a *r*, 1Ti 2:6

RANSOM *(v) redeem*
You have *r-ed* me, Ps 31:5
R me because of my, Ps 69:18
LORD has *r-ed* Jacob, Jer 31:11
Shall I *r* them from, Hos 13:14

RAVAGE *devastate*
famine will *r* the, Ge 41:30
mice that *r* the land, 1Sa 6:5
r-ing the church, Ac 8:3

RAVEN *type of bird*
he sent out a *r*, Ge 8:7
young *r-s* which cry, Ps 147:9
Consider the *r-s*, Lk 12:24

RAVENOUS *wildly hungry*
Benjamin is a *r* wolf, Ge 49:27
inwardly are *r* wolves, Mt 7:15

RAVINE *gorge*
settle on the steep *r-s*, Is 7:19
smooth *stones* of the *r*, Is 57:6
Every *r* will be filled, Lk 3:5

RAVISH *seize and take*
you may *r* them, Jdg 19:24
And their wives *r-ed*, Is 13:16
r-ed…women in Zion, La 5:11

RAZOR *instrument for shaving*
no *r* shall pass over, Nu 6:5
no *r* shall come upon, Jdg 13:5
A *r* has never come, Jdg 16:17
Like a sharp *r*, Ps 52:2

REACH *extend*
tower whose top *will r*, Ge 11:4
r-ed out her hand for the tent, Jdg 5:26
his loftiness *r-es* the heavens, Job 20:6
waters they will not *r* him, Ps 32:6
Your faithfulness *r* to the, Ps 36:5
Your truth *r* to the skies, Ps 108:4
strokes *r* the innermost, Pr 20:30
will *r* even to the neck, Is 8:8
its height *r-ed* to the sky, Da 4:11
sound of your greeting *r-ed*, Lk 1:44
R here with your finger, Jn 20:27
r-ing forward to *lies*, Php 3:13
r-ed the ears of the Lord., Jas 5:4

READ
you shall *r* this, Dt 31:11
r from the scroll, Jer 36:6
who *r-s* it may run, Hab 2:2
r-ing…Isaiah, Ac 8:28
prophets…are *read*, Ac 13:27
Moses is *read*, 2Co 3:15
Blessed is he who *r-s*, Rev 1:3

READY *equipped, prepared*
and *r* to forgive, Ps 86:5
Let Your hand be *r*, Ps 119:173
Make *r* the way, Mt 3:3
you also must be *r*, Mt 24:44
be *r* in season, 2Ti 4:2
r to make a defense, 1Pe 3:15

REALIZE *achieve; understand*
Desire *r-d* is sweet, Pr 13:19
r-d through Jesus, Jn 1:17
to *r*…assurance, Heb 6:11

REALM *area, kingdom*
ruler over the *r* of, Da 4:17
kingdom is not…*r*, Jn 18:36

REAP *cut, gather*
when you *r*…harvest, Lv 19:9
iniquity will *r* vanity, Pr 22:8
they *r* the whirlwind, Hos 8:7
not sow, nor *r*, Mt 6:26
neither sow nor *r*, Lk 12:24
sows…another *r-s*, Jn 4:37
r eternal life, Gal 6:8
your sickle and *r*, Rev 14:15

REAPER *harvester*
after the *r-s*, Ru 2:3
will overtake the *r*, Am 9:13
the *r-s* are angels, Mt 13:39

REASON *(n) explanation*
r a man shall leave, Mt 19:5
this *r* the Father, Jn 10:17
this *r* I found mercy, 1Ti 1:16
For this *r*, rejoice, Rev 12:12

REASON *(v) analyze, argue*
upright would *r* with, Job 23:7
let us *r* together, Is 1:18
Pharisees began to *r*, Lk 5:21
r-ing in…synagogue, Ac 17:17
like a child, *r* like a, 1Co 13:11

REBEKAH
Great-niece of Abraham, Ge 22:20–23
Becomes Isaac's wife, Ge 24:15–67
Mother of Esau and Jacob, Ge 25:21–28
Encourages Jacob to deceive Isaac, then to flee, Ge 27:1–29, 42–46

REBEL *(n) rebellious one*
Your rulers are *r-s*, Is 1:23
called a *r* from birth, Is 48:8
their princes are *r-s*, Hos 9:15

REBEL *(v) revolt*
not *r* against the, Nu 14:9
r-led against…words, Ps 107:11
r-led against Me, Eze 20:21

REBELLION *insurrection*
he has counseled *r*, Dt 13:5
I know your *r*, Dt 31:27
r is as the sin of, 1Sa 15:23
my *r* and my sin, Job 13:23
children of *r*, Is 57:4

REBELLIOUS *defiant*
r against the LORD, Dt 9:7
r generation, Ps 78:8
A *r* man seeks only, Pr 17:11
stubborn and *r* heart, Jer 5:23
there are many *r*, Titus 1:10

REBUILD *restore*
r the house of the, Ezr 1:3
let us *r* the wall, Ne 2:17
r the ancient ruins, Is 58:12
r it in three days, Mt 26:61
r the tabernacle, Ac 15:16

REBUKE *(n) reprimand*
amazed at His *r*, Job 26:11
At Your *r* they fled, Ps 104:7
the poor hears no *r*, Pr 13:8

REBUKE *(v) scold*
r me not in Your wrath, Ps 38:1
r the arrogant, Ps 119:21
LORD *r* you, Satan, Zec 3:2
r-d the winds, Mt 8:26
Jesus *r-d* him, Mt 17:18
He *r-d* the fever, Lk 4:39
Do not sharply *r*, 1Ti 5:1
reprove, *r*, exhort, 2Ti 4:2

RECEIVE *encounter, take*
The LORD *r-s* my prayer, Ps 6:9
r me to glory, Ps 73:24
man *r-s* a bribe, Pr 17:23
Freely you *r-d*, Mt 10:8
who *r-s* you *r-s* Me, Mt 10:40
the blind *r* sight, Mt 11:5
ask…you will *r*, Mt 21:22
r-d up into heaven, Mk 16:19
This man *r-s* sinners, Lk 15:2
as many as *r-d* Him, Jn 1:12
r you to Myself, Jn 14:3
R the Holy Spirit, Jn 20:22
you will *r* power, Ac 1:8
to give than to *r*, Ac 20:35
one *r-s* the prize, 1Co 9:24
r the crown of life, Jas 1:12
whatever…ask we *r*, 1Jn 3:22
r-d the mark of, Rev 19:20

RECHAB
Assassin of Ishbosheth, 2Sa 4:2, 6
——— Father of Jehonadab, founder of the Rechabites, 2Ki 10:15–23
Related to the Kenites, 1Ch 2:55

RECHABITES
Kenite clan fathered by Rechab, committed to nomadic life, Jer 35:1–19

RECKONED *accounted for*
r it to him as, Ge 15:6
r among the nations, Nu 23:9
r…as righteousness, Jas 2:23

RECLINE *lean, lie down*
r on beds of ivory, Am 6:4
r at the table in, Lk 13:29
r-ing on Jesus', Jn 13:23

RECOGNIZE *be aware, know*
he did not *r* him, Ge 27:23
Saul *r-d* David's, 1Sa 26:17
r that He is near, Mt 24:33
I did not *r* Him, Jn 1:31

RECOMPENSE *(n) reward*
the *r* of the wicked, Ps 91:8
r to the proud, Ps 94:2
r of God will come, Is 35:4

RECOMPENSE *(v) compensate*
LORD has *r-d* me, 2Sa 22:25
He will *r* the evil, Ps 54:5
But if you do *r* Me, Joel 3:4

RECONCILE *bring together*
r-d to your brother, Mt 5:24
be *r-d* to God, 2Co 5:20
r them both in one, Eph 2:16
r all…to Himself, Col 1:20

RECONCILIATION
now received the *r*, Ro 5:11
the *r* of the world, Ro 11:15
the ministry of *r*, 2Co 5:18
the word of *r*, 2Co 5:19

RECORD *(n) document, register*
the *r-s* are ancient, 1Ch 4:22
r-s of the kings, 2Ch 33:18
discover in…*r* books, Ezr 4:15
I found the…*r*, Ne 7:5

RECORD *(v) register, write*
r-ed their starting, Nu 33:2
R the vision, Hab 2:2
are *r-ed* in heaven, Lk 10:20

RECOVER *reclaim, become well*
did you not *r* them, Jdg 11:26
Will I *r* from this, 2Ki 8:8
and they will *r*, Mk 16:18

RED *color*
first came forth *r*, Ge 25:25
water…*r* as blood, 2Ki 3:22
they are *r* like crimson, Is 1:18
the sky is *r*, Mt 16:2
a great *r* dragon, Rev 12:3

RED SEA
Divided for Israelites, Ex 14:15–31
Boundary of Promised Land, Ex 23:31

REDEEM *buy back*
I will also *r* you, Ex 6:6
family may *r* him, Lv 25:49
wish to *r* the field, Lv 27:19
I will *r it*, Ru 4:4
God will *r* my soul, Ps 49:15
He will *r* Israel, Ps 130:8
Christ *r-ed* us, Gal 3:13
He might *r* those, Gal 4:5

REDEEMER *one who buys back*
left you without a *r*, Ru 4:14
know that my *R* lives, Job 19:25
my rock and my *R*, Ps 19:14
your *R* is the Holy, Is 41:14
our Father, Our *R*, Is 63:16
Their *R* is strong, Jer 50:34

REDEMPTION *deliverance*
r of the land, Lv 25:24
have my right of *r*, Ru 4:6
r of his soul is, Ps 49:8
r is drawing near, Lk 21:28

r...in Christ Jesus, Ro 3:24
r of our body, Ro 8:23
r through His blood, Eph 1:7
in whom we have *r*, Col 1:14
obtained eternal *r*, Heb 9:12

REED *tall marsh grass*
set *it* among the *r-s*, Ex 2:3
bruised *r* He will, Is 42:3
the *r*...to beat Him, Mt 27:30
and put it on a *r*, Mt 27:48

REEL *stagger, sway*
earth *r-s* to and fro, Is 24:20
r with strong drink, Is 28:7

REFINE *purify*
r-d seven times, Ps 12:6
in order to *r*, Da 11:35
R them as silver, Zec 13:9
r them like gold, Mal 3:3
gold *r-d* by fire, Rev 3:18

REFRAIN *abstain*
not *r* from spitting, Job 30:10
to *r* from working, 1Co 9:6
r from judging, Rev 6:10

REFRESH *renew, replenish*
you may *r* yourselves, Ge 18:5
R me with apples, SS 2:5
times of *r-ing* may, Ac 3:19
r my heart in Christ, Phm 20

REFUGE *protection, shelter*
in whom I take *r*, 2Sa 22:3
God is our *r*, Ps 46:1
r in the LORD, Ps 118:8
the *r* of lies, Is 28:17
r in...distress, Jer 16:19
who have taken *r*, Heb 6:18

REFUGE, CITIES OF
See CITIES OF REFUGE

REFUSE *(n) waste*
be made a *r* heap, Ezr 6:11
corpses lay like *r*, Is 5:25
its waters toss up *r*, Is 57:20
sell...*r* of the wheat, Am 8:6

REFUSE *(v) decline*
r you his grave, Ge 23:6
r to let My people go, Ex 10:4
his hands *r* to work, Pr 21:25
they *r* to know Me, Jer 9:6
r-d to be comforted, Mt 2:18
can *r* the water, Ac 10:47
not *r* Him who is, Heb 12:25

REFUSE GATE
See GATES OF JERUSALEM

REFUTE *prove wrong*
R me if you can, Job 33:5
he...*r-d* the Jews, Ac 18:28
to *r* those who, Titus 1:9

REGAIN *recover*
r-ed their sight, Mt 20:34
want to *r* my sight, Mk 10:51
he might *r* his sight, Ac 9:12

REGARD *(n) respect*
LORD had *r* for Abel, Ge 4:4
r to the prayer, 1Ki 8:28
have *r* for his Maker, Is 17:7
r for the humble, Lk 1:48

REGARD *(v) esteem, respect*
If I *r* wickedness, Ps 66:18
Yet He *r-s* the lowly, Ps 138:6
who *r-s* reproof, Pr 15:5
highly *r-ed* by him, Lk 7:2
r one another, Php 2:3
did not *r* equality, Php 2:6

REGENERATION *renewal*
r when the Son, Mt 19:28
the washing of *r*, Titus 3:5

REGION *area*
r of the Jordan, Jos 22:10
the *r-s* of Galilee, Mt 2:22
to the *r* of Judea, Mk 10:1
same *r*...shepherds, Lk 2:8

REGISTER *enroll, record*
r...people of Israel, 2Sa 24:4
to *r* for the census, Lk 2:3

REHOBOAM
Son and successor of Solomon; refuses reform, 1Ki 11:43–12:15
Ten tribes revolt against, 1Ki 12:16–24
Reigns over Judah 17 years, 1Ki 14:21–31; 2Ch 11:5–23
Apostasizes, then repents, 2Ch 12:1–16

REHOBOTH
Name of a well dug by Isaac, Ge 26:22

REIGN *rule*
LORD shall *r* forever, Ex 15:18
Shall Saul *r* over, 1Sa 11:12
David *r-ed* over all, 2Sa 8:15
The LORD *r-s*, Ps 93:1
By me kings *r*, Pr 8:15
will *r* righteously, Is 32:1
death *r-ed*...Adam, Ro 5:14
He must *r* until, 1Co 15:25
also *r* with Him, 2Ti 2:12
He will *r* forever, Rev 11:15
will *r* with Him, Rev 20:6

REJECT *decline, refuse*
have *r-ed* the LORD, Nu 11:20
will *r* you forever, 1Ch 28:9
not *r* the discipline, Pr 3:11
A fool *r-s* his, Pr 15:5
have *r-ed* this word, Is 30:12
He who *r-s* unjust gain, Is 33:15
r-ed My ordinances, Eze 20:13
have *r-ed* knowledge, Hos 4:6
they *r-ed* the law, Am 2:4
the builders *r-ed*, Mt 21:42
who *r-s* you *r-s* Me, Lk 10:16
He who *r-s* Me, Jn 12:48

REJOICE *be glad*
r before the LORD, Lv 23:40
R, O nations, Dt 32:43
I *r* in Your salvation, 1Sa 2:1
let the earth *r*, 1Ch 16:31
my soul shall *r*, Ps 35:9
king will *r* in God, Ps 63:11
Let us *r* and be glad, Ps 118:24
I *r* at Your word, Ps 119:162
R, young man, Ecc 11:9
God will *r* over you, Is 62:5
r-d exceedingly, Mt 2:10
r at his birth, Lk 1:14
crowd was *r-ing*, Lk 13:17
you would have *r-d*, Jn 14:28
r-ing in hope, Ro 12:12
yet always *r-ing*, 2Co 6:10
R in the Lord, Php 4:4
I *r* in my sufferings, Col 1:24
r, O heavens, Rev 12:12

REJOICE AND BE GLAD
r in Your lovingkindness, Ps 31:7
Let us *r* in it, Ps 118:24
Let us *r* in His salvation, Is 25:9
r, for the LORD has, Joel 2:21
R, for your reward in, Mt 5:12
r and give the glory to, Rev 19:7

REJOICE IN THE LORD
my soul shall *r*, Ps 35:9
r, You will glory, Is 41:16
their heart will *r*, Zec 10:7
my brethren, *r*, Php 3:1
R always; again I will, Php 4:4

REJOICING *(n) delight*
a holiday for *r*, Est 9:19
hills gird...with *r*, Ps 65:12
Jerusalem *for r*, Is 65:18

RELATIONS *sexual intercourse*
r with his wife Eve, Ge 4:1
had no *r* with a man, Jdg 11:39
we may have *r* with, Jdg 19:22
had *r* with Hannah, 1Sa 1:19

RELATIVE *kinsman*
and to my *r-s*, Ge 24:4
The man is our *r*, Ru 2:20
My *r-s* have failed, Job 19:14
among his *own r-s*, Mk 6:4
your *r* Elizabeth has, Lk 1:36

RELEASE *(n) liberation*
a *r* through the land, Lv 25:10
r for you the King, Mk 15:9
r to the captives, Lk 4:18

RELEASE *(v) set free*
he *r-d* Barabbas, Mt 27:26
wanting to *r* Jesus, Lk 23:20
efforts to *r* Him, Jn 19:12
you *r-d* from a wife, 1Co 7:27
r-d us from our sins, Rev 1:5
R the four angels, Rev 9:14

RELENT *yield*
I am tired of *r-ing*, Jer 15:6
r...the calamity, Jer 18:8
whether He will...*r*, Joel 2:14
God may turn and *r*, Jon 3:9

RELIEF *lessening of burden*
r and deliverance, Est 4:14
my *prayer for r*, La 3:56
r of the brethren, Ac 11:29

RELIGION *system of belief*
about their own *r*, Ac 25:19
sect of our *r*, Ac 26:5
pure and undefiled *r*, Jas 1:27

RELIGIOUS *devout, pious*
r in all respects, Ac 17:22
thinks...to be *r*, Jas 1:26

RELY *depend, trust*
r-ied on the LORD, 2Ch 16:8
who…*r* on horses, Is 31:1
r on his God, Is 50:10
You *r* on your sword, Eze 33:26
r upon the Law, Ro 2:17

REMAIN *abide, be left*
While the earth *r-s*, Ge 8:22
R…in his place, Ex 16:29
ark…not *r* with us, 1Sa 5:7
r-s yet…youngest, 1Sa 16:11
flee to Egypt, and *r*, Mt 2:13
dove…*r-ed* upon, Jn 1:32
not *r* in darkness, Jn 12:46
not *r* on the cross, Jn 19:31
she must *r* unmarried, 1Co 7:11
gospel would *r*, Gal 2:5
He *r-s* faithful, 2Ti 2:13

REMEMBER *recall, recollect*
God *r-ed* Noah, Ge 8:1
I will *r* My covenant, Ge 9:15
R the sabbath day, Ex 20:8
not *r* the sins of my, Ps 25:7
R also your Creator, Ecc 12:1
O LORD, *R* me, Jer 15:15
sin I will *r* no more, Jer 31:34
Peter *r-ed* the word, Mt 26:75
R Lot's wife, Lk 17:32
r the words of, Ac 20:35
to *r* the poor, Gal 2:10

REMEMBRANCE *memory*
Your *r*, O LORD, Ps 135:13
Put Me in *r*, Is 43:26
a book of *r* was, Mal 3:16
do this in *r* of Me, Lk 22:19
in *r* of Me, 1Co 11:25

REMIND *bring to mind*
r a man what is right, Job 33:23
points so as to *r* you again, Ro 15:15
I *r* you to kindle afresh, 2Ti 1:6
R them to be subject to, Titus 3:1
ready to *r* you of these, 2Pe 1:12
I desire to *r* you, though, Jude 1:5

REMINDER *remembrance*
as a *r* on your forehead, Ex 13:9
a *r* of sins year by year., Heb 10:3
to stir you up by way of *r*, 2Pe 1:13
sincere mind by way of *r*, 2Pe 3:1

REMNANT *remaining part*
preserve for you a *r*, Ge 45:7
prayer for the *r*, 2Ki 19:4
an escaped *r*, Ezr 9:8
A *r* will return, Is 10:21
the *r* of Israel, Jer 6:9
a *r* of the Spirit, Mal 2:15
r that will be saved, Ro 9:27

REMOVE *take away; off*
r your sandals, Ex 3:5
r-d all the idols, 1Ki 15:12
He *r-d* the high, 2Ki 18:4
r the heart of stone, Eze 36:26
not fit to *r* His, Mt 3:11
r this cup from Me, Lk 22:42
R the stone, Jn 11:39
as to *r* mountains, 1Co 13:2

REND *tear*
r the heavens, Is 64:1
r their garments, Jer 36:24
r your heart and not, Joel 2:13

RENDER *inflict, repay*
I will *r* vengeance, Dt 32:41
R recompense to the, Ps 94:2
r to Caesar the, Mt 22:21
R to all what is due, Ro 13:7

RENEW *make new, revive*
r a steadfast spirit, Ps 51:10
r-ed like the eagle, Ps 103:5
R our days as of old, La 5:21
inner man…*r-ed*, 2Co 4:16

RENOWN *fame*
men of *r*, Ge 6:4
a people, for *r*, Jer 13:11
shame into…and *r*, Zep 3:19

REPAIR *restore*
r the house of, 1Ch 26:27
r-ing…foundations, Ezr 4:12
r of the walls, Ne 4:7

REPAY *recompense*
He will *r* him to his face, Dt 7:10
I will *r* those who hate Me, Dt 32:41
LORD will *r* each man, 1Sa 26:23
to Me that I should *r*, Job 41:11
R them their recompense., Ps 28:4
They *r* me evil for good, Ps 35:12
Do not say, "I will *r* evil", Pr 20:22
r every man according, Mt 16:27
and I will *r* you everything, Mt 18:26
when I return I will *r* you, Lk 10:35
be *r-d* at the resurrection, Lk 14:14
vengeance is Mine, I will *r*, Ro 12:19
one *r-s* another with evil, 1Th 5:15
with my own hand, I will *r*, Phm 1:19

REPAYMENT *restitution*
he had, and *r* to be made, Mt 18:25
and *that* will be your *r*, Lk 14:12

REPENT *change mind*
that He should *r*, Nu 23:19
r in dust and ashes, Job 42:6
have refused to *r*, Jer 5:3
R, for the kingdom, Mt 3:2
r-ed long ago in, Mt 11:21
r and believe, Mk 1:15
one sinner who *r-s*, Lk 15:7
R…be baptized, Ac 2:38
all…should *r*, Ac 17:30
r and turn to God, Ac 26:20

REPENTANCE *penitence*
with water for *r*, Mt 3:11
baptism of *r*, Mk 1:4
r for forgiveness, Lk 24:47
appropriate to *r*, Ac 26:20
r without regret, 2Co 7:10
r from dead works, Heb 6:1
to come to *r*, 2Pe 3:9

REPHAIM
Valley near Jerusalem, 2Sa 23:13, 14
Scene of Philistine defeats, 2Sa 5:18–22

REPHIDIM
Israelite camp, Nu 33:12–15
Moses strikes rock at, Ex 17:1–7
Amalek defeated at, Ex 17:8–16

REPORT *account, statement*
not bear a false *r*, Ex 23:1
r concerning Him, Lk 7:17
has believed our *r*, Jn 12:38

REPRESENTATION *likeness*
exact *r* of His nature, Heb 1:3

REPRESENTATIVE *substitute*
people's *r* before God, Ex 18:19
the king's *r*, Ne 11:24

REPROACH (*n*) *dishonor*
taken away my *r*, Ge 30:23
a *r* on all Israel, 1Sa 11:2
I have become a *r*, Ps 31:11
with dishonor…*r*, Pr 18:3
not fear the *r* of, Is 51:7
the *r* of Christ, Heb 11:26

REPROACH (*v*) *accuse, rebuke*
to *r* the living God, 2Ki 19:4
My heart does not *r*, Job 27:6
foolish man *r-es* You, Ps 74:22
enemies have *r-ed* me, Ps 102:8
He *r-ed* them for, Mk 16:14

REPROOF *correction, rebuke*
spurned all my *r*, Pr 1:30
regards *r* is sensible, Pr 15:5
who hates *r* will, Pr 15:10
and *r* give wisdom, Pr 29:15
for teaching, for *r*, 2Ti 3:16

REPROVE *correct, rebuke*
r your neighbor, Lv 19:17
LORD loves He *r-s*, Pr 3:12
Do not *r* a scoffer, Pr 9:8
R the ruthless, Is 1:17
r, rebuke, exhort, 2Ti 4:2
whom I love, I *r*, Rev 3:19

REPTILE *snake*
and the sand *r*, Lv 11:30
r-s of the earth, Mic 7:17
r-s and creatures, Jas 3:7

REPUTATION *character*
seven men of good *r*, Ac 6:3
a *r* for good works, 1Ti 5:10

REQUEST *desire, petition*
my people as my *r*, Est 7:3
the *r* of his lips, Ps 21:2
He gave them their *r*, Ps 106:15
r-s be made known to, Php 4:6

REQUIRE *demand, insist*
r your lifeblood, Ge 9:5
God *r* from you, Dt 10:12
as each day *r-d*, Ezr 3:4
your soul is *r-d*, Lk 12:20
r-d of stewards, 1Co 4:2

REQUIREMENT *necessity*
r-s of the Lord, Lk 1:6
r of the Law, Ro 8:4
law of physical *r*, Heb 7:16

RESCUE *deliver, redeem*
O LORD, *r* my soul, Ps 6:4
R the weak and needy, Ps 82:4
He delivers and *r-s*, Da 6:27
The Lord will *r* me, 2Ti 4:18
r the godly from, 2Pe 2:9

RESERVE *retain, store up*
r-d a blessing for, Ge 27:36
darkness...in *r*, Job 20:26
lips may *r* knowledge, Pr 5:2
r-s wrath for, Na 1:2
r-d in heaven, 1Pe 1:4
r-d for fire, 2Pe 3:7

RESIDE *dwell, live*
stranger who *r-s*, Lv 19:34
a son of man *r* in it, Jer 49:18
those who *r* as aliens, 1Pe 1:1

RESIST *oppose, withstand*
not *r* an evil person, Mt 5:39
none...able to *r*, Lk 21:15
r-ing the Holy Spirit, Ac 7:51
whoever *r-s* authority, Ro 13:2
R the devil, Jas 4:7

RESPECT *(n) regard*
no *r* for the old, Dt 28:50
where is My *r*, Mal 1:6
please *Him* in all *r-s*, Col 1:10
to your masters...*r*, 1Pe 2:18

RESPECT *(v) esteem*
They will *r* my son, Mt 21:37
not fear God nor *r*, Lk 18:4
R what is right, Ro 12:17
wife...*r-s* her husband, Eph 5:33

RESPOND *answer, reply*
He will *r* to them, Is 19:22
r to the heavens, Hos 2:21
how you should *r*, Col 4:6
Peter *r-ed* to her, Ac 5:8

REST *(n) remainder*
r turned and fled, Jdg 20:45
the *r* of the exiles, Ezr 6:16
the *r* of your days, Pr 19:20
I will slay the *r*, Am 9:1
to the *r*...parables, Lk 8:10

REST *(n) tranquility*
r from our work, Ge 5:29
sabbath of solemn *r*, Lv 16:31
God gives you *r*, Jos 1:13
the weary are at *r*, Job 3:17
Return to your *r*, Ps 116:7
whole earth is at *r*, Is 14:7
there is no *r*, La 5:5
I will give you *r*, Mt 11:28
no *r* for my spirit, 2Co 2:13
not enter My *r*, Heb 3:11
no *r* day and night, Rev 14:11

REST *(v) settled, refresh*
the ark *r-ed* upon, Ge 8:4
glory...LORD *r-ed*, Ex 24:16
Spirit *r-ed* upon, Nu 11:25
R in the LORD, Ps 37:7
Wisdom *r-s* in, Pr 14:33
government will *r* on, Is 9:6
iniquity *r-ed* on, Eze 32:27
r-ed on the seventh, Heb 4:4
r from their labors, Rev 14:13

RESTING PLACE
dove found no *r*, Ge 8:9
This is My *r* forever, Ps 132:14
Do not destroy his *r*, Pr 24:15
r will be glorious, Is 11:10

RESTITUTION *reparation*
owner...make *r*, Ex 21:34
make *r* in full, Nu 5:7
r for the lamb, 2Sa 12:6

RESTORE *reestablish, replace*
son he had *r-d* to, 2Ki 8:1
they *r-d* Jerusalem, Ne 3:8
r His righteousness, Job 33:26
He *r-s* my soul, Ps 23:3
R to me the joy, Ps 51:12
O God, *r* us, Ps 80:3
the LORD *r-s* Zion, Is 52:8
R us to You, La 5:21
his hand was *r-d*, Mk 3:5
r-ing the kingdom, Ac 1:6

RESTRAIN *hold back*
the rain...was *r-ed*, Ge 8:2
who can *r* Him, Job 11:10
He *r-ed* His anger, Ps 78:38
who *r-s* his lips, Pr 10:19
Will You *r* Yourself, Is 64:12
R your voice from, Jer 31:16
r-ed the crowds, Ac 14:18

RESULT *(n) consequence, effect*
a *r* of the anguish, Is 53:11
not as a *r* of works, Eph 2:9
have *its* perfect *r*, Jas 1:4
as a *r* of the works, Jas 2:22

RESULT *(v) follow, happen*
r-ed In reproach, Jer 20:8
sin *r-ing* in death, Ro 6:16
proved to *r* in death, Ro 7:10
r-ing in salvation, Ro 10:10

RESURRECTION
who say...no *r*, Mt 22:23
r of the righteous, Lk 14:14
being sons of the *r*, Lk 20:36
r of judgment, Jn 5:29
the *r* and the life, Jn 11:25
r of the dead, Ac 24:21
if there is no *r*, 1Co 15:13
power of His *r*, Php 3:10
hope through the *r*, 1Pe 1:3
This is the first *r*, Rev 20:5

RETRIBUTION *punishment*
days of *r* have come, Hos 9:7
stumbling block...*r*, Ro 11:9
dealing out *r* to, 2Th 1:8

RETURN *go back; repay*
to dust you shall *r*, Ge 3:19
r-ed me evil for, 1Sa 25:21
clouds *r* after the, Ecc 12:2
a remnant...will *r*, Is 10:22
ransomed...will *r*, Is 51:11
r-ed to Galilee, Lk 4:14
repent and *r*, Ac 3:19
not *r-ing* evil for, 1Pe 3:9

REUBEN
Jacob's eldest son, Ge 29:31, 32
Lies with Bilhah; loses preeminence, Ge 35:22; 49:3, 4
Plots to save Joseph, Ge 37:21–30
Offers sons as pledge for Benjamin, Ge 42:37
——— Tribe of:
Numbered, Nu 1:20, 21; 26:5–11
Settle east of Jordan, Nu 32:1–42
Join in war against Canaanites, Jos 1:12–18
Erect memorial altar, Jos 22:10–34

REVEAL *expose, make known*
God had *r-ed* Himself, Ge 35:7
He *r-s* mysteries, Job 12:22
will *r* his iniquity, Job 20:27
do not *r* the secret, Pr 25:9
glory...will be *r-ed*, Is 40:5
r this mystery, Da 2:47
r-ed them to infants, Mt 11:25
blood did not *r this*, Mt 16:17
Son of Man is *r-ed*, Lk 17:30
glory...to be *r-ed*, Ro 8:18
r-ed with fire, 1Co 3:13
to *r* His Son in me, Gal 1:16
lawlessness is *r-ed*, 2Th 2:3
r-ed in the flesh, 1Ti 3:16

REVELATION *divine disclosure*
a *r* to Your servant, 2Sa 7:27
the *r* ended, Da 7:28
r to the Gentiles, Lk 2:32
r of...judgment, Ro 2:5
the *r* of the mystery, Ro 16:25
awaiting...the *r*, 1Co 1:7
through a *r* of Jesus, Gal 1:12
by *r*...made known, Eph 3:3
The *R* of Jesus, Rev 1:1

REVENGE *vengeance*
take our *r* on him, Jer 20:10
Never take...*r*, Ro 12:19

REVERE *adore, venerate*
r My sanctuary, Lv 19:30
nations will *r* You, Is 25:3

REVERENCE *respect, awe*
you do away with *r*, Job 15:4
Worship...with *r*, Ps 2:11
bow in *r* for You, Ps 5:7
in *r* prepared an ark, Heb 11:7
service with *r* and, Heb 12:28

REVILE *use abusive language*
Do you *r* God's high, Ac 23:4
are *r-d*, we bless, 1Co 4:12
r-d for the name of, 1Pe 4:14
r angelic majesties, Jude 8

REVIVE *bring back to life*
they *r* the stones, Ne 4:2
let your heart *r*, Ps 69:32
r us again, Ps 85:6
r me in Your ways, Ps 119:37
r-d your concern, Php 4:10

REVOLT *rebellion*
incited *r* within it, Ezr 4:15
Speaking...and *r*, Is 59:13
stirred up a *r*, Ac 21:38

REWARD *prize*
emptiness...his *r*, Job 15:31
r for the righteous, Ps 58:11
The *r* of humility, Pr 22:4
chases after *r-s*, Is 1:23
His *r* is with Him, Is 62:11
your *r* in heaven, Mt 5:12
not lose his *r*, Mt 10:42
looking to the *r*, Heb 11:26
receive a full *r*, 2Jn 8

REZIN
King of Damascus; joins Pekah against Ahaz, 2Ki 15:37
Confederacy of, inspires Isaiah's great messianic prophecy, Is 7:1–9:12

REZON
Son of Eliadah; establishes Syrian kingdom, 1Ki 11:23–25

RHEGIUM
City in Italy where Paul visits, Ac 28:13

RHODA
Servant girl, Ac 12:13–16

RHODES
Island off Asia Minor which Paul passes, Ac 21:1

RIB *bone*
took one of his *r-s*, Ge 2:21
r-s were in its mouth, Da 7:5

RIBLAH
Headquarters of:
Pharaoh Necho, 2Ki 23:31–35
Nebuchadnezzar, 2Ki 25:6, 20, 21
Zedekiah blinded here, Jer 39:5–7

RICH *(adj) wealthy*
Abram was very *r*, Ge 13:2
LORD makes poor…*r*, 1Sa 2:7
not a *r* man boast, Jer 9:23
woe to you who are *r*, Lk 6:24
a *r* man, Lk 16:1
being *r* in mercy, Eph 2:4
r in good works, 1Ti 6:18

RICH *(n) wealthy*
r shall not pay more, Ex 30:15
the *r* above the poor, Job 34:19
r among the people, Ps 45:12
The *r* and the poor, Pr 22:2

RICHES *wealth*
R do not profit, Pr 11:4
who trusts in his *r*, Pr 11:28
neither poverty nor *r*, Pr 30:8
choked with…*r*, Lk 8:14
abounding in *r*, Ro 10:12
r of His grace, Eph 1:7
r of Christ, Eph 3:8
His *r* in glory, Php 4:19
uncertainty of *r*, 1Ti 6:17
Your *r* have rotted, Jas 5:2

RIDDLE *puzzle*
propound a *r*, Jdg 14:12
my *r* on the harp, Ps 49:4
wise and their *r-s*, Pr 1:6
propound a *r*, Eze 17:2

RIDE *take transport*
r in his second chariot, Ge 41:43
Solomon *r* on King David's, 1Ki 1:38
majesty *r* on victoriously, Ps 45:4
made men *r* over our heads, Ps 66:12
Him who *r-s* through the, Ps 68:4
seen slaves *r-ing* on horses, Ecc 10:7
LORD is *r* on a swift, Is 19:1

RIDER *one who rides*
r He has hurled into the sea, Ex 15:1
laughs at the horse and his *r*., Jb 39:18
Both *r* and horse were cast, Ps 76:6
shatter the chariot and its *r*, Jer 51:21
the chariots and their *r-s*, Hag 2:22
the r-s had breastplates, Rev 9:17

RIGHT *(adj) correct; direction*
r in the sight of, Dt 12:25
r in his own eyes, Jdg 17:6
precepts…are *r*, Ps 19:8
r eye makes you, Mt 5:29
what your *r* hand is, Mt 6:3
Sit at My *r* hand, Mt 22:44
the *r* hand of God, Mk 16:19
at the *r* time Christ, Ro 5:6
r hand of fellowship, Gal 2:9
whatever is *r*, Php 4:8
forsaking the *r* way, 2Pe 2:15

RIGHT *(n) due, prerogative*
her conjugal *r-s*, Ex 21:10
r of redemption, Lv 25:32
r of the firstborn, Dt 21:17
the *r-s* of the poor, Pr 29:7
r-s of the afflicted, Pr 31:9
my *r* in the gospel, 1Co 9:18

RIGHT HAND
At His *r* there was flashing, Dt 33:2
my *r*, I will not be shaken, Ps 16:8
At Your *r* stands the queen, Ps 45:9
at the *r* of the needy, Ps 109:31
Sit at My *r* until I make, Ps 110:1
to go at the *r* of Moses, Is 63:12
Satan standing at his *r*, Zec 3:1
Sit at My *r*, until I put, Mt 22:44
Son of Man sitting at the *r*, Mt 26:64
sat down at the *r* of God, Mk 16:19
standing at the *r* of God, Ac 7:55
who is at the *r* of God, Ro 8:34
r in the heavenly places, Eph 1:20
He sat down at the *r* of, Heb 1:3
who is at the *r* of God, 1Pe 3:22

RIGHTEOUS *(adj) virtuous*
Noah was a *r* man, Ge 6:9
LORD is the *r* one, Ex 9:27
You are more *r*, 1Sa 24:17
God is a *r* judge, Ps 7:11
A *r* man hates, Pr 13:5
for David a *r* Branch, Jer 23:5
LORD our God is *r*, Da 9:14
ninety-nine *r*, Lk 15:7
coming of the *R* One, Ac 7:52
r man shall live by, Ro 1:17
none *r*, not even one, Ro 3:10
many will be made *r*, Ro 5:19
prayer of a *r* man, Jas 5:16

RIGHTEOUS *(n) moral one*
assembly of the *r*, Ps 1:5
LORD tests the *r*, Ps 11:5
LORD loves the *r*, Ps 146:8
the paths of the *r*, Pr 2:20
the *r* will flourish, Pr 11:28
joy for the *r*, Pr 21:15
way of the *r* is, Is 26:7
they sell the *r* for, Am 2:6
sends rain on *the r*, Mt 5:45
r into eternal life, Mt 25:46

RIGHTEOUS MAN
Noah was a *r*, blameless, Ge 6:9
men have killed a *r*, 2Sa 4:11
You who blesses the *r*, Ps 5:12
r will be glad, Ps 64:10
r will flourish like, Ps 92:12
Teach a *r* and he will, Pr 9:9
r has regard for the life, Pr 12:10
A *r* hates falsehood, Pr 13:5
r who walks in his integrity, Pr 20:7
r falls seven times, Pr 24:16
polluted well is a *r*, Pr 25:26
judge both the *r* and the, Ecc 3:17
a *r* who perishes, Ecc 7:15
not a *r* on earth who, Ecc 7:20
The *r* perishes, Is 57:1
warned the *r*, Eze 3:21
righteousness of a *r*, Eze 33:12
her husband, being a *r*, Mt 1:19
receives a *r* in the name, Mt 10:41
nothing to do with that *r*, Mt 27:19
Joseph …. good and *r*, Lk 23:50
the *r* shall live by faith, Ro 1:17
hardly die for a *r*, Ro 5:7
The *r* shall live by faith, Gal 3:11
put to death the *r*, Jas 5:6
effective prayer of a *r*, Jas 5:16
r, while living among them, 2Pe 2:8

RIGHTEOUSNESS
reckoned it…as *r*, Ge 15:6
will repay…his *r*, 1Sa 26:23
I put on *r*, Job 29:14
in the paths of *r*, Ps 23:3
judge the world in *r*, Ps 96:13
declare His *r*, Ps 97:6
His *r* endures forever, Ps 111:3
R exalts a nation, Pr 14:34
clouds pour down *r*, Is 45:8
wrapped me with…*r*, Is 61:10
The LORD our *r*, Jer 23:6
to rain *r* on you, Hos 10:12
to fulfill all *r*, Mt 3:15
and thirst for *r*, Mt 5:6
kingdom and His *r*, Mt 6:33
you enemy of all *r*, Ac 13:10
through one act of *r*, Ro 5:18
breastplate of *r*, Eph 6:14
pursue *r*, faith, 2Ti 2:22
the crown of *r*, 2Ti 4:8
peaceful fruit of *r*, Heb 12:11
not achieve the *r*, Jas 1:20
suffer for…*r*, 1Pe 3:14

RIGHTEOUSNESS OF GOD
r is revealed from faith, Ro 1:17
demonstrates the *r*, Ro 3:5
r has been manifested, Ro 3:21
themselves to the *r*, Ro 10:3
become the *r* in Him, 2Co 5:21
does not achieve the *r*, Jas 1:20

RING *jewelry, ornament*
make four gold *r-s*, Ex 25:26
took his signet *r*, Est 3:10
As a *r* of gold, Pr 11:22
finger *r-s*, nose *r-s*, Is 3:21

RIOT *tumult, uprising*
otherwise a *r* might occur, Mt 26:5
a *r* was starting, Mt 27:24
accused of a *r*, Ac 19:40

RIPE *fully developed*
old man of *r* age, Ge 35:29
produced *r* grapes, Ge 40:10
the harvest is *r*, Joel 3:13
harvest…is *r*, Rev 14:15

RISE *go up, issue forth*
mist used to *r* from, Ge 2:6
Cain *rose* up against, Ge 4:8
scepter shall *r*, Nu 24:17
witnesses *r* up, Ps 35:11
children *r* up, Pr 31:28
nation will *r*, Mt 24:7
r-n, just as He said, Mt 28:6
children will *r* up, Mk 13:12
Lord has really *r-n*, Lk 24:34

RIVER
r flowed out of Eden, Ge 2:10
the *r* Euphrates, Jos 1:4
r of Your delights, Ps 36:8
He changes *r-s* into, Ps 107:33
the *r-s* of Babylon, Ps 137:1
A place of *r-s* and, Is 33:21
r-s in the desert, Is 43:20
peace…like a *r*, Is 66:12
tears…like a *r*, La 2:18
baptized…Jordan *R*, Mk 1:5
r-s of living water, Jn 7:38
r of the water of life, Rev 22:1

RIZPAH
Saul's concubine taken by Abner, 2Sa 3:6–8
Sons of, killed, 2Sa 21:8, 9
Grief-stricken, cares for corpses, 2Sa 21:10–14

ROAD *path, way*
a lion in the *r*, Pr 26:13
the rough *r-s* smooth, Lk 3:5
coats on the *r*, Lk 19:36
the Lord on the *r*, Ac 9:27

ROAR *(n) loud deep sound*
the sound of the *r*, 1Ki 18:41
young lions' *r*, Zec 11:3
pass away with a *r*, 2Pe 3:10

ROAR *(v) utter a deep sound*
a voice *r-s*, Job 37:4
Let the sea *r*, Ps 96:11
LORD will *r* from, Jer 25:30
a lion *r* in the, Am 3:4

ROAST *cook*
grain *r-ed* in the fire, Lv 2:14
r-ed the…*animals*, 2Ch 35:13
lazy man…*r*, Pr 12:27

ROB *steal*
bear *r-bed* of her, Pr 17:12
Do not *r* the poor, Pr 22:22
Will a man *r* God, Mal 3:8
do you *r* temples, Ro 2:22
I *r-bed*…churches, 2Co 11:8

ROBBER *thief*
she lurks as a *r*, Pr 23:28
become a den of *r-s*, Jer 7:11
crucified two *r-s*, Mk 15:27
fell among *r-s*, Lk 10:30
a thief and a *r*, Jn 10:1
r-s of temples, Ac 19:37

ROBBERY *theft*
not vainly hope in *r*, Ps 62:10
I hate *r* in the, Is 61:8
they are full of *r*, Mt 23:25
you are full of *r*, Lk 11:39

ROBE *cloak, garment*
cut off…Saul's *r*, 1Sa 24:4
justice was like a *r*, Job 29:14
r of righteousness, Is 61:10
put a scarlet *r* on, Mt 27:28
walk…in long *r-s*, Mk 12:38
wearing a white *r*, Mk 16:5
bring…the best *r*, Lk 15:22
washed their *r-s*, Rev 7:14
a *r* dipped in blood, Rev 19:13

ROCK *stone*
the cleft of the *r*, Ex 33:22
struck the *r* twice, Nu 20:11
R of his salvation, Dt 32:15
LORD is my *r*, 2Sa 22:2
engraved in the *r*, Job 19:24
my *r* and my fortress, Ps 18:2
r and my Redeemer, Ps 19:14
set my feet upon a *r*, Ps 40:2
a *r* to stumble over, Is 8:14
an everlasting *R*, Is 26:4
his house on the *r*, Mt 7:24
upon this *r* I will, Mt 16:18
the *r-s* were split, Mt 27:51
hewn out in the *r*, Mk 15:46
a *r* of offense, Ro 9:33

ROD *staff, stick*
fresh *r-s* of poplar, Ge 30:37
r of Aaron, Nu 17:8
break them with a *r*, Ps 2:9
Your *r* and Your staff, Ps 23:4
who withholds his *r*, Pr 13:24
The *r* of discipline, Pr 22:15
r of My anger, Is 10:5
rule them with a *r*, Rev 19:15

RODE *took transport*
He *r* on a cherub and flew, 2Sa 22:11
r upon a cherub and flew, Ps 18:10
You *r* on Your horses, Hab 3:8

ROLL *move*
sky will be *r-ed* up, Is 34:4
let justice *r* down, Am 5:24
r-ed away the stone, Mt 28:2
Who will *r* away the, Mk 16:3

ROMANS
Citizens of Roman Empire, Jn 11:48; Ac 16:21, 37

ROME
Jews expelled from, Ac 18:2
Paul:
Writes to Christians of, Ro 1:7
Desires to go to, Ac 19:21
Comes to, Ac 28:14
Imprisoned in, Ac 28:16

ROOF
brought…to the *r*, Jos 2:6
r…woman bathing, 2Sa 11:2
removed the *r* above, Mk 2:4
r and let him down, Lk 5:19

ROOM *chamber*
the ark with *r-s*, Ge 6:14
go into your inner *r*, Mt 6:6
a large upper *r*, Mk 14:15
no *r* for them in, Lk 2:7
r for the wrath, Ro 12:19

ROOSTER *bird*
The strutting *r*, Pr 30:31
before a *r* crows, Mt 26:34
r will not crow, Jn 13:38

ROOT *(n) source*
the *r* of Jesse, Is 11:10
no *r*, it withered, Mk 4:6
if the *r* is holy, Ro 11:16
of money is a *r*, 1Ti 6:10
no *r* of bitterness, Heb 12:15
the *R* of David, Rev 5:5

ROOT *(v) establish; tear out*
r out your Asherim, Mic 5:14
r-ed and grounded in, Eph 3:17

ROPE *cord*
them down by a *r*, Jos 2:15
bound…two new *r-s*, Jdg 15:13
he snapped the *r-s*, Jdg 16:12
Instead of a belt, a *r*, Is 3:24

ROSE *(n) flower*
I am the *r* of Sharon, SS 2:1

ROT *decay*
their flesh will *r*, Zec 14:12
riches have *r-ted*, Jas 5:2

ROTTENNESS *decay*
passion is *r* to, Pr 14:30
r to the house of, Hos 5:12

ROUGH *jagged, uneven*
r ground become a, Is 40:4
the *r* places smooth, Is 45:2

ROUSE *stir up*
a lion, who dares *r* him up?, Ge 49:9
prepared to *r* Leviathan, Job 3:8
now He would *r* Himself for, Job 8:6
R yourself! Arise, O, Is 51:17
r the mighty men, Joel 3:9

ROYAL *kingly*
captured the *r* city, 2Sa 12:26
his *r* bounty, 1Ki 10:13
all the *r* offspring, 2Ki 11:1
put on her *r* robes, Est 5:1
And a *r* diadem, Is 62:3
roof of the *r* palace, Da 4:29
a *r* official, Jn 4:46
fulfilling the *r* law, Jas 2:8
a *r* priesthood, 1Pe 2:9

RUDDY *reddish in complexion*
he was *r*, 1Sa 16:12
a youth, and *r*, 1Sa 17:42
beloved is…and *r*, SS 5:10

RUHAMAH
symbolic for Israel, Hos 2:1

RUIN *(n) destruction*
shall be a *r* forever, Dt 13:16
become a heap of *r-s*, 1Ki 9:8
the perpetual *r-s*, Ps 74:3
Jerusalem in *r-s*, Ps 79:1
r of the poor is, Pr 10:15
fool's mouth is his *r*, Pr 18:7
rebuild its *r-s*, Ac 15:16

RUIN *(v) destroy*
to *r* him without, Job 2:3

S

and sowed it with *s*, Jdg 9:45
be eaten without *s*, Job 6:6
the *s* of the earth, Mt 5:13
seasoned with *s*, Col 4:6
can s water produce, Jas 3:12

SALVATION *deliverance*
For Your *s* I wait, Ge 49:18
He has become my *s*, Ex 15:2
scorned...his *s*, Dt 32:15
S belongs to the LORD, Ps 3:8
my light and my *s*, Ps 27:1
lift up the cup of *s*, Ps 116:13
My *s* will be forever, Is 51:6
helmet of *s* on His, Is 59:17
S is from the LORD, Jon 2:9
eyes have seen Your *s*, Lk 2:30
s in no one else, Ac 4:12
power of God for *s*, Ro 1:16
now is the day of *s*, 2Co 6:2
take the helmet of *s*, Eph 6:17
work out your *s* with, Php 2:12
s through our Lord, 1Th 5:9
that leads to *s*, 2Ti 3:15
who will inherit *s*, Heb 1:14
neglect so great a *s*, Heb 2:3
S to our God who, Rev 7:10

SAMARIA
Capital of Israel, 1Ki 16:24–29
Besieged by Ben-Hadad, 1Ki 20:1–21
Besieged again; miraculously delivered, 2Ki 6:24–7:20
Inhabitants deported by Assyria; repopulated with foreigners, 2Ki 17:5, 6, 24–41
——— District of Palestine in Christ's time, Lk 17:11–19
Disciples forbidden to preach in, Mt 10:5
Gospel preached there after the Ascension, Ac 1:8; 9:31; 15:3

SAMARITAN *a mixed race*
enter *any* city of the *S-s*, Mt 10:5
entered a village of the *S-s*, Lk 9:52
But a *S*, who was on a, Lk 10:33
And he was a *S*, Lk 17:16
have no dealings with *S-s*, Jn 4:9
many of the *S-s* believed, Jn 4:39
You are a *S* and have, Jn 8:48
to many villages of the *S-s*, Ac 8:25

SAMARITANS
People of mixed heredity, 2Ki 17:24–41
Christ preaches to, Jn 4:5–42
Story of "the good Samaritan," Lk 10:30–37
Converts among, Ac 8:5–25

SAMOS
Paul visits, Ac 20:15

SAMSON
Birth predicted and accomplished, Jdg 13:2–25
Marries Philistine; avenges betrayal, Jdg 14
Defeats Philistines singlehandedly, Jdg 15
Betrayed by Delilah; loses strength, Jdg 16:4–22
Destroys many in his death, Jdg 16:23–31

SAMUEL
Born in answer to prayer; dedicated to God, 1Sa 1:1–28
Receives revelation; recognized as prophet, 1Sa 3:1–21
Judges Israel, 1Sa 7:15–17
Warns Israel against a king, 1Sa 8:10–18
Anoints Saul, 1Sa 9:15–10:1
Rebukes Saul, 1Sa 15:10–35
Anoints David, 1Sa 16:1–13
Death of, 1Sa 25:1

SANBALLAT
Influential Samaritan; attempts to thwart Nehemiah's plans, Ne 2:10; 4:7, 8; 6:1–14

SANCTIFICATION *holiness*
resulting in *s*, Ro 6:22
righteousness and *s*, 1Co 1:30
will of God, your *s*, 1Th 4:3
s by the Spirit, 2Th 2:13
s without which no, Heb 12:14

SANCTIFY *set apart to God*
S to Me every, Ex 13:2
the LORD who *s-ies*, Lv 22:32
They will *s* My name, Is 29:23
will *s* the Holy One, Is 29:23
S My sabbaths, Eze 20:20
S them in the truth, Jn 17:17
s-ied by the...Spirit, Ro 15:16
husband is *s-ied*, 1Co 7:14
s Christ as Lord, 1Pe 3:15

SANCTUARY *place of worship*
construct a *s* for Me, Ex 25:8
revere My *s*, Lv 19:30
utensils of the *s*, 1Ch 9:29
into the *s* of God, Ps 73:17
Praise God in His *s*, Ps 150:1
beautify...My *s*, Is 60:13
a minister in the *s*, Heb 8:2

SAND
descendants as the *s*, Ge 32:12
treasures of the *s*, Dt 33:19
built...on the *s*, Mt 7:26
innumerable as the *s*, Heb 11:12

SANDAL *footwear*
s has not worn out, Dt 29:5
fit to remove His *s-s*, Mt 3:11
two coats, or *s-s*, Mt 10:10

SANHEDRIN
See COUNCIL

SAPPHIRA
Wife of Ananias; struck dead for lying, Ac 5:1–11

SAPPHIRE *precious stone*
a *s* and a diamond, Ex 28:18
Inlaid with *s-s*, SS 5:14
foundations...in *s-s*, Is 54:11

SARAH (or Sarai)
Barren wife of Abram, Ge 11:29–31
Represented as Abram's sister, Ge 12:10–20
Gives Abram her maid, Ge 16:1–3
Receives promise of a son, Ge 17:15–21
Gives birth to Isaac, Ge 21:1–8

SARDIS
Site of one of the seven churches, Rev 1:11

SASH *belt*
a turban and a *s*, Ex 28:4
and girded him with the *s*, Lv 8:7
headdresses, ankle chains, *s-s*, Is 3:20
tie your *s* securely about, Is 22:21
His chest with a golden *s*, Rev 1:13
their chests with golden *s-s*, Rev 15:6

SATAN
Titles:
Abaddon, Rev 9:11
accuser, Ps 109:6; Rev 12:10
adversary, 1Pe 5:8
Apollyon, Rev 9:11
Beelzebul, Mt 10:25; Mk 3:22
Belial, 2Co 6:15
deceiver of the world, Rev 12:9
devil, Mt 4:1, 5; 25:41; Jn 6:70; 13:2; Eph 4:27; 6:11; 1Ti 3:6, 7; Heb 2:14; 1Pe 5:8; Rev 2:10; 20:2, 10
dragon, Rev 12:9
enemy, Mt 13:28, 39
evil one, Mt 13:19, 38; Jn 17:15; Eph 6:16; 1Jn 2:13, 14; 5:18, 19
father of lies, Jn 8:44
god of this world, 2Co 4:4
liar, Jn 8:44
murderer, Jn 8:44
prince of the power of the air, Eph 2:2
ruler of the demons, Mt 9:34; Mk 3:22
ruler of this world, Jn 12:31; 14:30; 16:11
serpent of old, Rev 12:9

SATISFY *be content*
eat and not be *s-ied*, Lv 26:26
s-ied their desire, Ps 78:30
steals To *s* himself, Pr 6:30
Nor will he be *s-ied*, Pr 6:35
hunger is not *s-ied*, Is 29:8
to *s* the crowd, Mk 15:15

SATRAPS *Persian officials*
to the king's *s*, Ezr 8:36
the *s*, the governors, Est 8:9
commissioners and *s*, Da 6:4

SAUL
Becomes first king of Israel, 1Sa 9–11
Sacrifices unlawfully, 1Sa 13:1–14
Wars with Philistines, 1Sa 13:15–14:52
Disregards the LORD's command; rejected by God, 1Sa 15
Suffers from distressing spirits, 1Sa 16:14–23
Becomes jealous of David; attempts to kill him, 1Sa 18:5–19:22
Pursues David; twice spared by him, 1Sa 22–24; 26
Consults medium, 1Sa 28:7–25
Defeated, commits suicide; buried, 1Sa 31
——— of Tarsus, apostle to the Gentiles: *see* paul

SAVE *deliver, rescue*
s-d by the LORD, Dt 33:29
S with Your right hand, Ps 60:5
He will *s* you, Pr 20:22
Turn to Me, and be *s-d*, Is 45:22
s you from afar, Jer 30:10
he will *s* his life, Eze 18:27

will *s* His people, Mt 1:21
wishes to *s* his life, Mt 16:25
Son…has come to *s*, Mt 18:11
faith has *s-d* you, Lk 7:50
world might be *s-d*, Jn 3:17
Father, *s* Me from, Jn 12:27
by which we…be *s-d*, Ac 4:12
be *s-d* by His life, Ro 5:10
will *s* your husband, 1Co 7:16
Jesus came…to *s*, 1Ti 1:15
One who is able to *s*, Jas 4:12
the righteous is *s-d*, 1Pe 4:18

SAVIOR *one who saves*
My *s*, You, 2Sa 22:3
forgot God their *S*, Ps 106:21
send them a *S* and a, Is 19:20
no *s* besides Me, Is 43:11
righteous God and a *S*, Is 45:21
S, who is Christ, Lk 2:11
the *S* of the world, Jn 4:42
as a Prince and a *S*, Ac 5:31
S of all men, 1Ti 4:10
appearing of our *S*, 2Ti 1:10
our great God and *S*, Titus 2:13
kingdom of our…*S*, 2Pe 1:11

SAVIOR OF THE WORLD
See LORD AND SAVIOR
this One is indeed the *S*, Jn 4:42
sent the Son to be the *S*, 1Jn 4:14

SAVORY *appetizing*
prepare a *s* dish for, Ge 27:4
mother made *s* food, Ge 27:14

SAWS *cutting tools*
set *them* under *s*, 2Sa 12:31
cut *them* with *s*, 1Ch 20:3

SAY *pronounce, speak*
God blessed…*s-ing*, Ge 1:22
not *s* in your heart, Dt 9:4
to the wicked God *s-s*, Ps 50:16
Do not *s* to your, Pr 3:28
s-s the Preacher, Ecc 1:2
He will *s*, Here I am, Is 58:9
Many will *s* to Me, Mt 7:22
If we *s*…no sin, 1Jn 1:8

SAYINGS *statements*
utter dark *s* of old, Ps 78:2
s of understanding, Pr 1:2
s of the wise, Pr 24:23
anyone hears my *s*, Jn 12:47

SCALE *for measuring weight*
with accurate *s-s*, Job 31:6
false *s* is not good, Pr 20:23
been weighed on the *s-s*, Da 5:27
with dishonest *s-s*, Am 8:5
justify wicked *s-s*, Mic 6:11
a pair of *s-s* in his, Rev 6:5

SCAPEGOAT *for removal of sin*
lot for the *s* fell, Lv 16:10
released the goat…*s*, Lv 16:26

SCARLET *bright red*
tied a *s thread*, Ge 38:28
s thread…window, Jos 2:18
lips are like a *s*, SS 4:3
sins are as *s*, Is 1:18
put a *s* robe on Him, Mt 27:28

SCATTER *spread, sprinkle*
s among the nations, Lv 26:33
Brimstone is *s-ed* on, Job 18:15
storm will *s* them, Is 41:16
s-ing the sheep of, Jer 23:1
s him like dust, Mt 21:44
sheep…shall be *s-ed*, Mt 26:31

SCEPTER *symbol of authority*
s shall not depart, Ge 49:10
s…rise from Israel, Nu 24:17
A *s* of uprightness, Ps 45:6
The *s* of rulers, Is 14:5
s of His kingdom, Heb 1:8

SCHEME *plan, plot*
s…he had devised, Est 9:25
s brings him down, Job 18:7
carries out wicked *s-s*, Ps 37:7
ignorant of his *s-s*, 2Co 2:11
the *s-s* of the devil, Eph 6:11

SCOFF *mock, sneer*
s-ed…His prophets, 2Ch 36:16
The LORD *s-s* at them, Ps 2:4
s at all the nations, Ps 59:8
were *s-ing* at Him, Lk 16:14

SCOFFER *mocker*
My friends are my *s-s*, Job 16:20
sit in the seat of *s-s*, Ps 1:1
He who corrects a *s*, Pr 9:7
Behold, you *s-s*, Ac 13:41

SCORCHING *burning*
words are like *s* fire, Pr 16:27
s heat or sun strike, Is 49:10
appointed a *s* east wind, Jon 4:8
s heat of the day, Mt 20:12

SCORN *treat with contempt*
s-ed…his salvation, Dt 32:15
and *s-s* a mother, Pr 30:17

SCORPION *poisonous spider*
serpents and *s-s*, Dt 8:15
discipline…with *s-s*, 1Ki 12:11
tread on…*s-s*, Lk 10:19
not give him a *s*, Lk 11:12
s-s…have power, Rev 9:3

SCOURGE *(n) whip*
the *s* of the tongue, Job 5:21
arouse a *s* against, Is 10:26
He made a *s* of cords, Jn 2:15

SCOURGE *(v) flog, whip*
s and crucify *Him*, Mt 20:19
having Jesus *s-d*, Mt 27:26
lawful for you to *s*, Ac 22:25
He *s-s* every son, Heb 12:6

SCRAPE *rub, scratch*
plaster that they *s*, Lv 14:41
s-d the honey into, Jdg 14:9
potsherd to *s* himself, Job 2:8

SCREEN *conceal, separate*
s the ark with the veil, Ex 40:3
s-ed off the ark, Ex 40:21

SCRIBE *copier, writer*
and Sheva was *s*, 2Sa 20:25
then the king's *s*, 2Ch 24:11
Ezra the *s* stood, Ne 8:4
lying pen of the *s-s*, Jer 8:8
chief priests and *s-s*, Mt 2:4
and not as the *s-s*, Mk 1:22
Where is the *s*, 1Co 1:20

SCRIBES AND PHARISEES
See PHARISEES AND SCRIBES
surpasses that of the *s*, Mt 5:20
s said to Him, Mt 12:38
s have seated themselves, Mt 23:2
woe to you, *s*, Mt 23:13
s were watching Him, Lk 6:7
s began to be very hostile, Lk 11:53
s brought a woman caught, Jn 8:3

SCRIPTURE
understanding…*S-s*, Mt 22:29
fulfill…*S-s*, Mk 14:49
S has been fulfilled, Lk 4:21
You search the *S-s*, Jn 5:39
S cannot be broken, Jn 10:35
mighty in the *S-s*, Ac 18:24
what does the *S* say, Ro 4:3
S is inspired by God, 2Ti 3:16

SCROLL *parchment*
these curses on a *s*, Nu 5:23
Take a *s* and write, Jer 36:2
eat this *s*, and go, Eze 3:1
like a *s*…rolled, Rev 6:14

SEA *body of salt water*
waters He called *s-s*, Ge 1:10
s, or the *s* monster, Job 7:12
founded it upon the *s-s*, Ps 24:2
to the *s* in ships, Ps 107:23
the waters cover the *s*, Is 11:9
rebukes the *s* and, Na 1:4
walking on the *s*, Mt 14:26
s began to be stirred, Jn 6:18
dangers on the *s*, 2Co 11:26
s of glass, like crystal, Rev 4:6

SEA OF GALILEE
See GALILEE, SEA OF

SEACOAST *seashore*
remnant of the *s*, Eze 25:16
inhabitants of the *s*, Zep 2:5
s will be pastures, Zep 2:6

SEAL *(n) mark, stamp*
Your *s* and your cord, Ge 38:18
the engravings of a *s*, Ex 28:21
the *s* of perfection, Eze 28:12
testimony has set his *s*, Jn 3:33
s of God on their, Rev 9:4

SEAL *(v) mark, secure*
s-ed…his seal, 1Ki 21:8
s it…king's signet, Est 8:8
a spring *s-ed* up, SS 4:12
to *s* up vision, Da 9:24
s up the book until, Da 12:4

SEARCH *examine, inquire*
LORD *s-es* all hearts, 1Ch 28:9
S me, O God, and, Ps 139:23
LORD, *s* the heart, Jer 17:10
s for the Child, Mt 2:13
companions *s-ed* for, Mk 1:36
You *s* the Scriptures, Jn 5:39

SEASHORE *sea coast*
sand that is on the *s*, Jos 11:4

the *s* in abundance, 1Ki 4:20
the dragon stood on…*s*, Rev 13:1

SEASON *time of the year*
rains in their *s*, Lv 26:4
grain in its *s*, Job 5:26
its fruit in its *s*, Ps 1:3
in *s and* out of *s*, 2Ti 4:2

SEAT *(n) chair, stool*
mercy *s* of pure gold, Ex 25:17
sit in the *s* of scoffers, Ps 1:1
sit in the *s* of gods, Eze 28:2
s-s in the synagogues, Mt 23:6
before…judgment *s*, Ro 14:10

SEAT *(v) sit*
s-ed at the Lord's feet, Lk 10:39
coming, *s-ed*…colt, Jn 12:15
s-ed at the right hand, Col 3:1

SECLUDED *isolated*
The fountain of Jacob *s*, Dt 33:28
from there in a boat to a *s*, Mt 14:13
went away to a *s* place, Mk 1:35
away by yourselves to a *s*, Mk 6:31
Jesus left and went to a *s*, Lk 4:42

SECOND DEATH
not be hurt by the *s*, Rev 2:11
the *s* has no power, Rev 20:6
the *s*, the lake of fire, Rev 20:14
brimstone, which is the *s*, Rev 21:8

SECRET *what is hidden*
sets *it* up in *s*, Dt 27:15
the *s-s* of wisdom, Job 11:6
the *s-s* of the heart, Ps 44:21
bread *eaten* in *s*, Pr 9:17
A gift in *s* subdues, Pr 21:14
have not spoken in *s*, Is 45:19
giving will be in *s*, Mt 6:4
Father who sees…in *s*, Mt 6:4
God will judge the *s-s*, Ro 2:16

SECRETLY *in private*
Why did you flee *s* and, Ge 31:27
sent two men as spies *s*, Jos 2:1
she came *s*, and uncovered, Ru 3:7
off the edge of Saul's robe *s*, 1Sa 24:4
If you *s* show partiality, Job 13:10
they have *s* laid for me, Ps 31:4
Whoever *s* slanders his, Ps 101:5
planned to send her away *s*, Mt 1:19
Herod *s* called the magi, Mt 2:7
of the false brethren *s*, Gal 2:4
will *s* introduce destructive, 2Pe 2:1

SECT *faction, party*
s of the Sadducees, Ac 5:17
s of the Pharisees, Ac 15:5
s of the Nazarenes, Ac 24:5

SECURE *safe, stable*
overthrows the *s*, Job 12:19
be *s* on their land, Eze 34:27
s in the mountain, Am 6:1
made the grave *s*, Mt 27:66

SECURITY *certainty, safety*
Israel dwells in *s*, Dt 33:28
in it living in *s*, Jdg 18:7
provides them with *s*, Job 24:23
will lie down in *s*, Is 14:30
will dwell in *s*, Zec 14:11

SEDUCE *entice, persuade*
if a man *s-s* a virgin, Ex 22:16
s you from…LORD, Dt 13:10
s-d them to do evil, 2Ki 21:9
lips she *s-s* him, Pr 7:21

SEE *look, perceive*
I have *s-n* God face, Ge 32:30
No eye will *s* me, Job 24:15
s the works of God, Ps 66:5
the blind will *s*, Is 29:18
s the glory of the LORD, Is 35:2
to *s* but do not *s*, Eze 12:2
s your good works, Mt 5:16
and the blind *s-ing*, Mt 15:31
s the Son of Man, Mt 16:28
s-ing their faith, Mk 2:5
s-n Your salvation, Lk 2:30
we *saw* His glory, Jn 1:14
No one has *s-n* God, Jn 1:18
s the Son of Man, Jn 6:62
you will *s* Me, Jn 16:16
may *s* My glory, Jn 17:24
s in a mirror dimly, 1Co 13:12
of things not *s-n*, Heb 11:1
No one has *s-n*, 1Jn 4:12

SEED *descendant; plant*
sow your *s* uselessly, Lv 26:16
establish your *s*, Ps 89:4
O *s* of Abraham, Ps 105:6
s to the sower, Is 55:10
like a mustard *s*, Mt 13:31
went out to sow his *s*, Lk 8:5
s is the word of God, Lk 8:11
s which is perishable, 1Pe 1:23
His *s* abides in him, 1Jn 3:9

SEED OF DAVID
See DESCENDANT OF DAVID

SEEK *pursue, search for*
s the LORD your God, Dt 4:29
pray, and *s* My face, 2Ch 7:14
S peace, and pursue it, Ps 34:14
s me will find me, Pr 8:17
man *s-s* only evil, Pr 17:11
s wisdom and an, Ecc 7:25
I will *s* the lost, Eze 34:16
time to *s* the LORD, Hos 10:12
S good and not evil, Am 5:14
s first His kingdom, Mt 6:33
s, and you will find, Mt 7:7
s for a sign, Mk 8:12
he who *s-s*, finds, Lk 11:10
I do not *s* My glory, Jn 8:50
s-ing the favor of men, Gal 1:10
s-ing the things above, Col 3:1

SEEK THE LORD
you will *s* your God, Dt 4:29
those who *s* be glad, 1Ch 16:10
your soul to *s* your God, 1Ch 22:19
did not set his heart to *s*, 2Ch 12:14
the covenant to *s* God, 2Ch 15:12
who *s* shall not be in, Ps 34:10
heart of those who *s* be, Ps 105:3
who *s* understand all, Pr 28:5
S while He may be found, Is 55:6
s until He comes to rain, Hos 10:12
mankind may *s*, Ac 15:17

SEER *prophet*
prophets…every *s*, 2Ki 17:13
Who say to the *s-s*, Is 30:10
Go, you *s*, flee away, Am 7:12
s-s will be ashamed, Mic 3:7

SEIR
Home of Esau, Ge 32:3
Horites of, dispossessed by Esau's descendants, Dt 2:12
Desolation of, Eze 35:15

SEIZE *grasp, take*
mother shall *s* him, Dt 21:19
Babylon has been *s-d*, Jer 50:46
and *s* her plunder, Eze 29:19
fields and then *s them*, Mic 2:2
seeking to *s* Him, Jn 7:30

SELAH
musical or liturgical sign, Ps 3:2, 4, 8; 20:3; 60:4; 81:7; Hab 3:3, 9, 13

SELF-CONTROL
s and the judgment, Ac 24:25
your lack of *s*, 1Co 7:5
gentleness, *s*, Gal 5:23
without *s*, brutal, 2Ti 3:3
in *your* knowledge, *s*, 2Pe 1:6

SELFISH *self-centered*
the bread of a *s* man, Pr 23:6
s ambition in your, Jas 3:14

SELL *barter, trade*
s me your birthright, Ge 25:31
s me food for money, Dt 2:28
s the oil and pay, 2Ki 4:7
sold a girl for wine, Joel 3:3
sold all that he had, Mt 13:46
s-ing their property, Ac 2:45
sold into bondage, Ro 7:14

SELLER *merchant, trader*
the buyer like the *s*, Is 24:2
a *s* of purple, Ac 16:14

SENATE
Sanhedrin, Ac 5:21
See also council

SEND *convey, dispatch*
s rain on the earth, Ge 7:4
he *sent* out a raven, Ge 8:7
Whom shall I *s*, Is 6:8
LORD God has *sent* Me, Is 48:16
s-s rain on *the*, Mt 5:45
He has *sent* Me, Lk 4:18
s-ing His own Son, Ro 8:3
not *s* her husband, 1Co 7:13
s him…in peace, 1Co 16:11
God *sent* forth His Son, Gal 4:4

SENNACHERIB
Assyrian king (705–681 B.C.); son and successor of Sargon II, 2Ki 18:13
Death of, by assassination, 2Ki 19:36, 37

SENSUALITY
deceit, *s*, envy, Mk 7:22
promiscuity and *s*, Ro 13:13
themselves over to *s*, Eph 4:19
the wealth of her *s*, Rev 18:3

SENTENCE *judgment*
s is by the decree, Da 4:17
escape the *s* of hell, Mt 23:33
Pilate pronounced *s*, Lk 23:24

to the *s* of death, Lk 24:20

SEPARATE *divide, set apart*
God *s-d* the light, Ge 1:4
They *s* with the lip, Ps 22:7
s-s intimate friends, Pr 16:28
let no man *s*, Mt 19:6
Who will *s* us from, Ro 8:35

SEPARATION *division, isolation*
of his *s* to the LORD, Nu 6:6
his *s* he is holy, Nu 6:8
his *s* was defiled, Nu 6:12
have made a *s*, Is 59:2

SERAPHIM
celestial beings, Is 6:2, 6

SERGIUS PAULUS
Roman proconsul of Cyprus, converted by Paul, Ac 13:7–12

SERPENT *snake*
s was more crafty, Ge 3:1
they turned into *s-s*, Ex 7:12
viper and flying *s*, Is 30:6
be shrewd as *s-s*, Mt 10:16
will pick up *s-s*, Mk 16:18
Moses lifted up the *s*, Jn 3:14

SERVANT *helper, slave*
s of *s-s* He shall be, Ge 9:25
Your *s* is listening, 1Sa 3:9
to shine upon Your *s*, Ps 31:16
s-s of a new covenant, 2Co 3:6
they *s-s* of Christ, 2Co 11:23
s of Christ Jesus, 1Ti 4:6

SERVE *help, work for*
shall *s* the LORD, Ex 23:25
s Him with…heart, Jos 22:5
s-d as priests, 1Ch 24:2
you will *s* strangers, Jer 5:19
God whom we *s* is, Da 3:17
s God and wealth, Mt 6:24
If anyone *s-s* Me, Jn 12:26
s-ing the Lord, Ro 12:11
through love *s* one, Gal 5:13

SERVE THE LORD
that they may *s*, Ex 10:7
you shall *s* your God, Ex 23:25
love Him, and to *s*, Dt 10:12
and my house, we will *s*, Jos 24:15
S with gladness, Ps 100:2

SERVICE *ministry, work*
s of righteous, Is 32:17
spiritual *s* of worship, Ro 12:1
for the work of *s*, Eph 4:12
s with reverence, Heb 12:28

SET APART
s the land of Goshen, Ex 8:22
s from the peoples, Lv 20:26
Moses *s* three cities, Dt 4:41
LORD *s* the tribe of Levi, Dt 10:8
Aaron was *s* to sanctify, 1Ch 23:13
LORD has *s* the godly, Ps 4:3
Holy Spirit said, "*S* for Me, Ac 13:2
apostle, *s* for the gospel, Ro 1:1

SETH
Third son of Adam, Ge 4:25
In Christ's ancestry, Lk 3:38

SETTLED *arranged; inhabited*
Lot *s* in the cities, Ge 13:12
cloud *s* over the, Nu 9:18
assault shall be *s*, Dt 21:5
word is *s* in heaven, Ps 119:89
mountains were *s*, Pr 8:25
s in the lawful, Ac 19:39

SEVEN *number*
Jacob served *s* years, Ge 29:20
For *s* women…one man, Is 4:1
will be s weeks, Da 9:25
s other spirits more, Mt 12:45
forgive…*s* times, Mt 18:21
John to the *s* churches, Rev 1:4
s golden lampstands, Rev 1:12

SEVERE *difficult, hard*
famine was *s*, Ge 12:10
a very *s* pestilence, Ex 9:3
s and lasting plagues, Dt 28:59
s judgments against, Eze 14:21
a *s* earthquake had, Mt 28:2

SEW *fasten, join*
s-ed fig leaves together, Ge 3:7
s-ed sackcloth over, Job 16:15
a time to *s* together, Ecc 3:7
women who *s magic*, Eze 13:18

SEXUAL *of sex*
not in *s* promiscuity, Ro 13:13
from *s* immorality, 1Th 4:3

SHACKLES *fetters*
will tear off your *s*, Na 1:13
s broken in pieces, Mk 5:4
with chains and *s*, Lk 8:29

SHADE *protection*
cover him with *s*, Job 40:22
The LORD is your *s*, Ps 121:5
lived under its *s*, Eze 31:6
over Jonah to be a *s*, Jon 4:6
nest under its *s*, Mk 4:32

SHADOW *image of shade*
days…like a *s*, 1Ch 29:15
the *s* of Your wings, Ps 17:8
in the *s*…Almighty, Ps 91:1
the *s-s* flee away, SS 2:17
his *s* might fall on, Ac 5:15
s of the heavenly, Heb 8:5

SHADOW OF DEATH
the valley of the *s*, Ps 23:4
covered us with the *s*, Ps 44:19
in darkness and in the *s*, Ps 107:10
s, upon them a Light, Mt 4:16
s, to guide our feet, Lk 1:79

SHADRACH
Hananiah's Babylonian name, Da 1:3, 7
Cast into the fiery furnace, Da 3:1–28

SHAKE *quiver, tremble*
made all my bones *s*, Job 4:14
s my head at you, Job 16:4
peace will not be *s-n*, Is 54:10
s the dust off, Mt 10:14
A reed *s-n* by the, Mt 11:7
heavens will be *s-n*, Lk 21:26

SHALLUM
King of Israel, 2Ki 15:10–15

SHALMANESER
Assyrian king, 2Ki 17:3

SHAME *disgrace, dishonor*
wicked be put to *s*, Ps 31:17
my reproach and my *s*, Ps 69:19
s to his mother, Pr 29:15
wise men are put to *s*, Jer 8:9
unjust knows no *s*, Zep 3:5
worthy to suffer *s*, Ac 5:41
glory is in their *s*, Php 3:19
put Him to open *s*, Heb 6:6

SHAMGAR
Judge of Israel; strikes down 600 Philistines, Jdg 3:31

SHAMMAH
Son of Jesse, 1Sa 16:9
Called Shimea, 1Ch 2:13
——— One of David's mighty men, 2Sa 23:11
Also called Shammoth the Harorite, 1Ch 11:27

SHAPHAN
Scribe under Josiah, 2Ki 22:3–14

SHARE *(n) portion*
them take their *s*, Ge 14:24
s from My offerings, Lv 6:17
give me the *s*, Lk 15:12
I do my *s*, Col 1:24

SHARE *(v) partake, participate*
stranger does not *s*, Pr 14:10
s in the inheritance, Pr 17:2
s it…yourselves, Lk 22:17
s all good things, Gal 6:6
may *s* His holiness, Heb 12:10
s the sufferings of, 1Pe 4:13

SHARON
Coastal plain between Joppa and Mt. Carmel, 1Ch 27:29
Famed for roses, SS 2:1
Inhabitants of, turn to the Lord, Ac 9:35

SHARP *cutting*
their tongue a *s* sword, Ps 57:4
S…two-edged sword, Pr 5:4
Put in your *s* sickle, Rev 14:18

SHATTER *break, burst*
s-ed every tree of the, Ex 9:25
the mighty are *s-ed*, 1Sa 2:4
s them like earthenware, Ps 2:9
s the doors of bronze, Is 45:2
iron crushes and *s-s*, Da 2:40

SHAVE *cut; scrape*
he shall *s* his head, Lv 14:9
s off the seven, Jdg 16:19
s-d off half of, 2Sa 10:4
will *s* with a razor, Is 7:20

SHEAF *bundle of grain stalks*
s-ves in the field, Ge 37:7
s of the first fruits, Lv 23:10
among the *s-ves*, Ru 2:15

SHEALTIEL
Son of King Jeconiah and father of Zerubbabel, 1Ch 3:17

SHEARER *wool cutter*
silent before its *s-s*, Is 53:7
lamb before its *s*, Ac 8:32

SHEAR-JASHUB
Symbolic name given to Isaiah's son, Is 7:3

SHEBA
Land of, occupied by Sabeans, famous traders, Job 1:15; Ps 72:10
Queen of, visits Solomon; marvels at his wisdom, 1Ki 10:1–13
Mentioned by Christ, Mt 12:42

SHEBAT
eleventh month of Hebrew calendar, Zec 1:7

SHEBNA
Treasurer under Hezekiah, Is 22:15
Demoted to position of scribe, 2Ki 19:2
Man of pride and luxury, replaced by Eliakim, Is 22:19–21

SHECHEM
Son of Hamor; rapes Dinah, Jacob's daughter, Ge 34:1–31
——— Ancient city of Ephraim, Ge 33:18
Joshua's farewell address delivered at, Jos 24:1–25
Supports Abimelech; destroyed, Jdg 9
Rebuilt by Jeroboam I, 1Ki 12:25

SHED *pour out*
Whoever *s-s* man's, Ge 9:6
s streams of water, Ps 119:136
hasten to *s* blood, Pr 1:16
will not *s* its light, Is 13:10
bribes to *s* blood, Eze 22:12
swift to *s* blood, Ro 3:15
s-ding of blood, Heb 9:22

SHEEP *animal*
Rachel came with...*s*, Ge 29:9
not be like *s*, Nu 27:17
the fleece of my *s*, Job 31:20
s of His pasture, Ps 100:3
All of us like *s*, Is 53:6
a *s* that is silent, Is 53:7
will care for My *s*, Eze 34:12
lost *s* of...Israel, Mt 10:6
s from the goats, Mt 25:32
my *s* which was lost, Lk 15:6
His life for the *s*, Jn 10:11
s hear My voice, Jn 10:27
Tend My *s*, Jn 21:17
Shepherd of the *s*, Heb 13:20

SHEEP GATE
See GATES OF JERUSALEM

SHEEPFOLDS *enclosure*
s for the flocks, 2Ch 32:28
lie down among the *s*, Ps 68:13
took him from the *s*, Ps 78:70

SHEEPSKINS *coverings*
they went about in *s*, Heb 11:37

SHEET
hammered out gold *s-s*, Ex 39:3
s over *his* naked, Mk 14:51
object like a great *s*, Ac 10:11

SHELTER *cover, refuge*
under the *s* of my, Ge 19:8
in the *s* of Your wings, Ps 61:4
a *s* to *give* shade, Is 4:6
a *s* from the storm, Is 32:2
made a *s* for himself, Jon 4:5

SHEM
Oldest son of Noah, Ge 5:32
Escapes the flood, Ge 7:13
Receives a blessing, Ge 9:23, 26
Ancestor of Semitic people, Ge 10:22–32

SHEMAIAH
Prophet of Judah, 1Ki 12:22–24
Explains Shishak's invasion as divine punishment, 2Ch 12:5–8
Records Rehoboam's reign, 2Ch 12:15

SHEMER
Sells Omri the hill on which Samaria is built, 1Ki 16:23, 24

SHEOL
place of the dead, Ge 37:35; Job 7:9; Ps 49:15; Pr 15:11; Is 38:10; Eze 32:27; Hab 2:5
See also hades; hell

SHEPHELAH
low hill country, 1Ch 27:28; Ob 19
See also lowland

SHEPHERD *(n)*
sheep...have no *s*, Nu 27:17
The LORD is my *s*, Ps 23:1
Like a *s* He, Is 40:11
s-s after My own heart, Jer 3:15
for lack of a *s*, Eze 34:5
raise up a *s*, Zec 11:16
sheep without a *s*, Mt 9:36
strike down the *s*, Mt 26:31
s-s...in the fields, Lk 2:8
I am the good *s*, Jn 10:11
the great *S*, Heb 13:20
the Chief *S*, 1Pe 5:4

SHEPHERD *(v)*
s My people, 2Sa 5:2
s My people, Mt 2:6
S My sheep, Jn 21:16
to *s* the church, Ac 20:28
s the flock of God, 1Pe 5:2

SHESHACH
Symbolic of Babylon, Jer 25:26

SHESHBAZZAR
Prince of Judah, Ezr 1:8, 11

SHETHAR-BOZENAI
Official of Persia, Ezr 5:3, 6

SHIBBOLETH
Test word for identification, Jdg 12:6

SHIELD *protection*
Abram, I am a *s*, Ge 15:1
He is a *s* to all, 2Sa 22:31
My *s* is with God, Ps 7:10
faithfulness is a *s*, Ps 91:4
the *s* of faith, Eph 6:16

SHIHOR
Name given to the Nile, Is 23:3
Israel's southwestern border, Jos 13:3

SHILOH
Center of worship, Jdg 18:31
Headquarters for division of Promised Land, Jos 18:1, 10
Benjamites seize women of, Jdg 21:19–23
Ark of the covenant taken from, 1Sa 4:3–11
Punishment given to, Jer 7:12–15
——— Messianic title, Ge 49:10

SHIMEI
Benjamite; insults David, 2Sa 16:5–13
Pardoned, but confined, 2Sa 19:16–23
Breaks agreement; executed by Solomon, 1Ki 2:39–46

SHIMSHAI
Scribe opposing the Jews, Ezr 4:8–24

SHINAR
Tower built at, Ge 11:2–9

SHINE *be radiant, glow*
his face *shone*, Ex 34:29
His face *s* on you, Nu 6:25
Your face to *s upon us*, Ps 80:3
light *s* before men, Mt 5:16
s-s in the darkness, Jn 1:5
lamp *s-ing* in a dark, 2Pe 1:19
Light is...*s-ing*, 1Jn 2:8

SHIP *boat*
a haven for *s-s*, Ge 49:13
to the sea in *s-s*, Ps 107:23
like merchant *s-s*, Pr 31:14
escape from the *s*, Ac 27:30

SHIPHRAH
Hebrew midwife, Ex 1:15

SHISHAK
See PHARAOH

SHITTIM
Spies sent from, Jos 2:1
Israel's last camp before crossing the Jordan, Jos 3:1

SHOOK *trembled*
the earth *s* and quaked, 2Sa 22:8
the earth *s* and quaked, Ps 18:7
hearts of his people *s* as, Is 7:2
to bottom; and the earth *s*, Mt 27:51
guards *s* for fear of him, Mt 28:4
Moses *s* with fear, Ac 7:32
they *s* off the dust of their, Ac 13:51
he *s* the creature, Ac 28:5
voice *s* the earth, Heb 12:26

SHOOT *new growth*
s will spring from, Is 11:1
like a tender *s*, Is 53:2
His *s-s* will sprout, Hos 14:6

SHORT *lacking*
Is My hand so *s*, Is 50:2
days will be cut *s*, Mt 24:22
s of the grace, Heb 12:15

SHOULDER *part of body*
He bowed his *s*, Ge 49:15
turned a stubborn *s*, Ne 9:29

relieved his *s*, Ps 81:6
government...on His *s-s*, Is 9:6

SHOUT *cry out loudly*
s with a great *s*, Jos 6:5
the people *s-ed* with, Ezr 3:11
s for joy, Ps 35:27
S joyfully to God, Ps 66:1

SHOW *manifest, reveal*
land...I will *s* you, Ge 12:1
s me Your glory, Ex 33:18
s you the secrets, Job 11:6
s Your lovingkindness, Ps 17:7
s him his fault in private, Mt 18:15
S us the Father, Jn 14:9
God *s-s* no partiality, Gal 2:6
s hospitality, Heb 13:2
if you *s* partiality, Jas 2:9

SHOWBREAD
tables of *s*, 1Ch 28:16
s is *set*...table, 2Ch 13:11

SHOWER *abundant flow*
roar of a *heavy s*, 1Ki 18:41
Like *s-s* that water, Ps 72:6
be *s-s* of blessing, Eze 34:26
A *s* is coming, Lk 12:54

SHREWD *cunning*
frustrates...the *s*, Job 5:12
be *s* as serpents, Mt 10:16

SHRINE *object of worship*
built yourself a *s*, Eze 16:24
tear down your *s-s*, Eze 16:39
who made silver *s-s*, Ac 19:24

SHULAMMITE
Beloved of the bridegroom king, SS 6:13

SHUNAMMITE
Abishag, David's nurse, 1Ki 1:3, 15
——— Woman who cared for Elisha, 2Ki 4:8–12

SHUNEM
Town of Issachar, Jos 19:18

SHUR
Wilderness in south Palestine, to which Hagar flees, Ge 16:7
Israel went from Red Sea to, Ex 15:22

SHUT *close*
wilderness has *s* them, Ex 14:3
s the lions' mouths, Da 6:22
power to *s* up the sky, Rev 11:6

SIBBOLETH
Test word for identification, Jdg 12:6

SICK *unwell*
strengthen the *s*, Eze 34:16
lying *s* with a fever, Mk 1:30
Lazarus was *s*, Jn 11:2
anyone among you *s*, Jas 5:14

SICKLE *cutting tool*
who wields the *s*, Jer 50:16
sharp *s* in His hand, Rev 14:14
Put in your *s*, Rev 14:15

SICKNESS *illness*
remove from you...*s*, Dt 7:15
every kind of *s*, Mt 4:23
authority over...*s*, Mt 10:1
s is not to end in death, Jn 11:4

SIDON
Canaanite city; inhabitants not expelled, Jdg 1:31
Hostile relations with Israel, Jdg 10:12; Is 23:12; Joel 3:4–6
Jesus preaches to, Mt 15:21; Lk 6:17

SIEGE *encirclement*
throw up a *s* ramp, 2Ki 19:32
city came under *s*, 2Ki 24:10
their *s* towers, Is 23:13
s against Jerusalem, Jer 6:6
build a *s* wall, Eze 4:2

SIGHT *perception, vision*
pleasing to the *s*, Ge 2:9
acceptable in Your *s*, Ps 19:14
precious in My *s*, Is 43:4
blind receive *s*, Mt 11:5
three days without *s*, Ac 9:9
by faith, not by *s*, 2Co 5:7

SIGN *indication; wonder*
a *s* for Cain, Ge 4:15
s of the covenant, Ge 9:12
this shall be the *s*, Ex 3:12
blood shall be a *s*, Ex 12:13
His *s-s* in Egypt, Ps 78:43
Ask a *s* for yourself, Is 7:11
an everlasting *s*, Is 55:13
a *s* from You, Mt 12:38
s of Your coming, Mt 24:3
show *s-s* and, Mk 13:22
s-s in sun and moon, Lk 21:25
beginning of *His s-s*, Jn 2:11
s of circumcision, Ro 4:11
Jews ask for *s-s*, 1Co 1:22
tongues are for a *s*, 1Co 14:22
s-s...false wonders, 2Th 2:9

SIGNET *seal*
examine...whose *s*, Ge 38:25
engravings of a *s*, Ex 39:14
s rings of his nobles, Da 6:17

SIGNS AND WONDERS
See WONDERS AND SIGNS
great and distressing *s*, Dt 6:22
s against Pharaoh, Ne 9:10
s into your midst, O Egypt, Ps 135:9
s in Israel from the LORD, Is 8:18
good to me to declare the *s*, Da 4:2
s, so as to mislead, Mt 24:24
Unless you people see *s*, Jn 4:48
s God had done through, Ac 15:12
s, in the power of the, Ro 15:19
s and by various miracles, Heb 2:4

SIHON
Amorite king; defeated by Israel, Nu 21:21–32
Territory of, assigned to Reuben and Gad, Nu 32:1–38

SILAS (or Silvanus)
Leader in Jerusalem church; sent to Antioch, Ac 15:22–35
Travels with Paul, Ac 15:40, 41
Jailed and released, Ac 16:25–40
Mentioned in epistles, 2Co 1:19; 1Th 1:1; 2Th 1:1; 1Pe 5:12

SILENCE *quietness*
My soul *waits* in *s*, Ps 62:1
war will be *s-d*, Jer 50:30
s the ignorance, 1Pe 2:15
s in heaven, Rev 8:1

SILENT *quiet*
LORD, do not keep *s*, Ps 35:22
A time to be *s*, Ecc 3:7
But Jesus kept *s*, Mt 26:63
women...keep *s*, 1Co 14:34

SILOAM
Tower of, falls and kills 18 people, Lk 13:4
Blind man washes in pool of, Jn 9:1–11

SILVANUS
See SILAS

SILVER *precious metal*
rich in...*s*, Ge 13:2
took no plunder in *s*, Jdg 5:19
as *s* is refined, Ps 66:10
in settings of *s*, Pr 25:11
s has become dross, Is 1:22
The *s* is Mine, Hag 2:8
not acquire...*s*, Mt 10:9
thirty pieces of *s*, Mt 26:15

SIMEON
Son of Jacob by Leah, Ge 29:32, 33
Avenged his sister's dishonor, Ge 34:25–31
Held hostage by Joseph, Ge 42:18–20, 24
Rebuked by Jacob, Ge 49:5–7
——— Tribe of:
Numbered, Nu 1:23; 26:12–14
Receive inheritance, Jos 19:1–9
Fight Canaanites with Judah, Jdg 1:1–3, 17–20
——— Just man; blesses infant Jesus, Lk 2:25–35

SIMON
Simon Peter: *see* peter
——— One of the Twelve; called "the Cananite," Mt 10:4
——— One of Jesus' half brothers, Mt 13:55
——— Pharisee, Lk 7:36–40
——— Man of Cyrene, Mt 27:32
——— Sorcerer, Ac 8:9–24
——— Tanner in Joppa, Ac 9:43

SIMPLE *innocent; humble*
making wise the *s*, Ps 19:7
LORD preserves the *s*, Ps 116:6

SIN *(n) transgression*
please forgive my *s*, Ex 10:17
atonement for your *s*, Ex 32:30
purification from *s*, Nu 19:9
s will find you out, Nu 32:23
s of divination, 1Sa 15:23
the *s-s* of my youth, Ps 25:7
s my mother conceived, Ps 51:5
Fools mock at *s*, Pr 14:9
bore the *s* of many, Is 53:12
s-s of her prophets, La 4:13
an eternal *s*, Mk 3:29

forgive us our *s-s*, Lk 11:4
takes away the *s*, Jn 1:29
wash away your *s-s*, Ac 22:16
wages of *s* is death, Ro 6:23
died for our *s-s*, 1Co 15:3
Him who knew no *s*, 2Co 5:21
pleasures of *s*, Heb 11:25
confess your *s-s*, Jas 5:16
a multitude of *s-s*, Jas 5:20
confess our *s-s*, 1Jn 1:9
s is lawlessness, 1Jn 3:4

SIN *(v) transgress*
When a leader *s-s*, Lv 4:22
s against the LORD, 1Sa 14:34
Job did not *s*, Job 1:22
s against You, Ps 119:11
Father, I have *s-ned*, Lk 15:18
s no more, Jn 8:11
all have *s-ned*, Ro 3:23
that you may not *s*, 1Jn 2:1

SIN OFFERING
See OFFERINGS

SINAI
Mountain (same as Horeb) where the law was given, Ex 19:1–25
Used allegorically by Paul, Gal 4:24, 25

SINCERE *without deceit*
be *s* and blameless, Php 1:10
mindful of the *s* faith, 2Ti 1:5
s love…brethren, 1Pe 1:22

SINCERITY *genuineness*
serve Him in *s* and truth, Jos 24:14
gladness and *s* of heart, Ac 2:46
bread of *s* and truth, 1Co 5:8
word of God, but as from *s*, 2Co 2:17
men, but with *s* of heart, Col 3:22

SINEW *strength; tendon*
with bones and *s-s*, Job 10:11
neck is an iron *s*, Is 48:4
will put *s-s* on you, Eze 37:6

SINFUL *wicked*
a brood of *s* men, Nu 32:14
s generation, Mk 8:38
I am a *s* man, Lk 5:8
likeness of *s* flesh, Ro 8:3

SING
s to the LORD, Ex 15:1
s-ing and dancing, 1Sa 18:6
I will *s* praises, 2Sa 22:50
morning stars *sang*, Job 38:7
S to Him a new song, Ps 33:3
the righteous *s-s*, Pr 29:6
birds will *s*, Zep 2:14
after *s-ing* a hymn, Mk 14:26
s-ing…thankfulness, Col 3:16
sang a new song, Rev 5:9

SINGERS
these are the *s*, 1Ch 9:33
male and female *s*, Ecc 2:8

SINK *descend, fall*
do not let me *s*, Ps 69:14
so shall Babylon *s*, Jer 51:64

SINNED AGAINST THE LORD
I have *s* your God, Ex 10:16
s, and be sure your sin, Nu 32:23
Truly, I have *s*, Jos 7:20
"We have *s*." And Samuel, 1Sa 7:6
David said …, "I have *s*, 2Sa 12:13
s our God, we and our, Jer 3:25

SINNED AGAINST YOU
I *s*, that you have brought, Ge 20:9
have *s*, for indeed, Jdg 10:10
since he has not *s*, 1Sa 19:4
s, and they pray toward, 1Ki 8:35
Heal my soul, for I have *s*, Ps 41:4

SINNER *wrongdoer*
He instructs *s-s*, Ps 25:8
if *s-s* entice you, Pr 1:10
Adversity…*s-s*, Pr 13:21
one *s* destroys much, Ecc 9:18
a friend of…*s-s*, Mt 11:19
one *s* who repents, Lk 15:7
merciful to me…*s*, Lk 18:13
God…not hear *s-s*, Jn 9:31
while we were yet *s-s*, Ro 5:8
came…to save *s-s*, 1Ti 1:15

SION
See ZION
Name given to all or part of Mt. Hermon, Dt 4:48

SISERA
Canaanite commander of Jabin's army; slain by Jael, Jdg 4:2–22

SISTER
She is my *s*, Ge 12:19
We have a little *s*, SS 8:8
a *s* called Mary, Lk 10:39
commend…our *s*, Ro 16:1
younger women…*s-s*, 1Ti 5:2

SIT *recline, rest*
Moses *sat* to judge, Ex 18:13
Nor *s* in the seat, Ps 1:1
S at My right hand, Ps 110:1
lonely *s-s* the city, La 1:1
s down on the grass, Mt 14:19
who *s* in darkness, Lk 1:79
dead man *sat* up, Lk 7:15
where the harlot *s-s*, Rev 17:15

SIVAN
third month of Hebrew calendar, Est 8:9

SKILL *proficiency*
filled them with *s*, Ex 35:35
the heavens with *s*, Ps 136:5
work of *s-ed* men, Jer 10:9
s-ed in destruction, Eze 21:31

SKILLFUL *accomplished*
became a *s* hunter, Ge 25:27
s player on…harp, 1Sa 16:16
praises with a *s* psalm, Ps 47:7

SKIN *covering*
garments of *s*, Ge 3:21
s of his face shone, Ex 34:29
Clothe me with *s*, Job 10:11
My *s* turns black, Job 30:30
will burst the *s-s*, Mk 2:22

SKIP *hop, leap*
children *s* about, Job 21:11
Lebanon *s* like a calf, Ps 29:6
go forth and *s*, Mal 4:2

SKULL *bony framework of head*
head, crushing his *s*, Jdg 9:53
the *s* and the feet, 2Ki 9:35
Place of a *S*, Mt 27:33

SKY *heavens*
sun stopped in…*s*, Jos 10:13
the *s* grew black, 1Ki 18:45
witness in the *s*, Ps 89:37
s will be rolled up, Is 34:4
for the *s* is red, Mt 16:2
will appear in the *s*, Mt 24:30
s was shut up, Lk 4:25
gazing…into the *s*, Ac 1:10
s was split apart, Rev 6:14

SLANDER *(n) defamation*
spreads *s* is a fool, Pr 10:18
s-s, gossip, 2Co 12:20
and *s* be put away, Eph 4:31

SLANDER *(v) defame*
He does not *s*, Ps 15:3
Whoever secretly *s-s*, Ps 101:5
Do not *s* a slave, Pr 30:10

SLANDERER *defamer*
s separates…friends, Pr 16:28
s-s, haters of God, Ro 1:30

SLAUGHTER *(n) brutal killing*
great *s* at Gibeon, Jos 10:10
lamb led to the *s*, Jer 11:19
as a sheep to *s*, Ac 8:32
in a day of *s*, Jas 5:5

SLAUGHTER *(v) kill*
shall *s* the bull, Ex 29:11
shall *s* the lamb, Lv 14:25
Who *s* the children, Is 57:5
s-ed My children, Eze 16:21

SLAVE *bondservant*
The Hebrew *s*, Ge 39:17
s at forced labor, Ge 49:15
sold *in* a *s* sale, Lv 25:42
Is Israel a *s*, Jer 2:14
S-s rule over us, La 5:8
s above his master, Mt 10:24
good and faithful *s*, Mt 25:21
shall be *s* of all, Mk 10:44
is the *s* of sin, Jn 8:34
neither *s* nor free, Gal 3:28
as *s-s* of Christ, Eph 6:6

SLAVERY *servitude*
from the house of *s*, Ex 13:3
ransomed you from…*s*, Mic 6:4
received a spirit of *s*, Ro 8:15
to a yoke of *s*, Gal 5:1

SLAY *destroy, kill*
knife to *s* his son, Ge 22:10
s-s the foolish, Job 5:2
Though He *s* me, Job 13:15
Evil…*s* the wicked, Ps 34:21
s her with thirst, Hos 2:3
Lamb that was *slain*, Rev 5:12

SLEEP *(n) rest*
caused a deep *s*, Ge 2:21
Do not love *s*, Pr 20:13

not spare His own *S*, Ro 8:32
fellowship with His *S*, 1Co 1:9
if a *s*, then an heir, Gal 4:7
shall be a *S* to Me, Heb 1:5
abide in the *S*, 1Jn 2:24
He who has the *S*, 1Jn 5:12

SON OF DAVID
s had a beautiful sister, 2Sa 13:1
Solomon the *s* king, 1Ch 29:22
proverbs of Solomon the *s*, Pr 1:1
of the Preacher, the *s*, Ecc 1:1
Jesus the Messiah, the *s*, Mt 1:1
Joseph, *s*, do not be afraid, Mt 1:20
"Have mercy on us, *S*!", Mt 9:27
be the *S*, can he?", Mt 12:23
mercy on me, Lord, *S*, Mt 15:22
"Hosanna to the *S*, Mt 21:9
that the Christ is the *s*?, Mk 12:35
the son of Nathan, the *s*, Lk 3:31

SON OF GOD
"If You are the *S*, Mt 4:3
S? Have You come, Mt 8:29
If You are the *S*, Mt 27:40
of Jesus Christ, the *S*, Mk 1:1
this man was the *S*!", Mk 15:39
shall be called the *S*, Lk 1:35
the son of Adam, the *s*, Lk 3:38
"Are You the *S*, then?", Lk 22:70
testified that this is the *S*, Jn 1:34
of the only begotten *S*, Jn 3:18
S may be glorified by it, Jn 11:4
S; and that believing, Jn 20:31
Jesus Christ is the *S*, Ac 8:37
declared the *S* with, Ro 1:4
live by faith in the *S*, Gal 2:20
knowledge of the *S*, Eph 4:13
S, he remains a priest, Heb 7:3
S appeared for this, 1Jn 3:8
that Jesus is the *S*?, 1Jn 5:5
S, who has eyes like a, Rev 2:18

SON OF MAN
Nor a *s*, that He should, Nu 23:19
s that You care for him?, Ps 8:4
s, that You think of him?, Ps 144:3
the *s* who takes hold of it, Is 56:2
"*S*, stand on your feet, Eze 2:1
S, can these bones live, Eze 37:3
One like a *S* was coming, Da 7:13
S has nowhere to lay His, Mt 8:20
S has authority on earth, Mt 9:6
will the *S* be three days, Mt 12:40
say that the *S* is?", Mt 16:13
S has come to save, Mt 18:11
coming of the *S* will be, Mt 24:37
S is Lord even of the, Mk 2:28
S must suffer many, Mk 8:31
S did not come to be, Mk 10:45
S sitting at the right, Mk 14:62
S has come eating, Lk 7:34
S has nowhere to lay, Lk 9:58
S is coming at an hour, Lk 12:40
see the *S* coming, Lk 21:27
must the *S* be lifted up, Jn 3:14
flesh of the *S*, Jn 6:53
"Now is the *S* glorified, Jn 13:31
I saw one like a *s*, Rev 1:13

SONG *melody, music*
LORD is my…*s*, Ex 15:2
ministered with *s*, 1Ch 6:32
gives *s-s* in the night, Job 35:10
s-s of deliverance, Ps 32:7
Sing to Him a new *s*, Ps 33:3
A *s* of my beloved, Is 5:1
Praise the LORD in *s*, Is 12:5
not drink wine with *s*, Is 24:9
hymns…spiritual *s-s*, Eph 5:19

SON-IN-LAW
the *s* of the Timnite, Jdg 15:6
be the king's *s*, 1Sa 18:18
s of Sanballat, Ne 13:28

SONS OF GOD
s came in to the daughters, Ge 6:4
s came to present, Job 1:6
all the *s* shouted for joy, Job 38:7
they shall be called *s*, Mt 5:9
s, being sons of the, Lk 20:36
the revealing of the *s*, Ro 8:19
s through faith in Christ, Gal 3:26

SORCERER *witch*
interprets…or a *s*, Dt 18:10
witness against the *s-s*, Mal 3:5
immoral persons…*s-s*, Rev 21:8

SORCERY *witchcraft*
practiced *s*, 2Ch 33:6
idolatry, *s*, enmities, Gal 5:20
deceived by your *s*, Rev 18:23

SORDID *filthy*
fond of *s* gain, 1Ti 3:8
the sake of *s* gain, Titus 1:11
not for *s* gain, 1Pe 5:2

SORROW *grief, sadness*
down to Sheol in *s*, Ge 42:38
life is spent with *s*, Ps 31:10
man of *s-s*, Is 53:3
s is beyond healing, Jer 8:18
if I cause you *s*, 2Co 2:2

SORRY *regretful*
LORD was *s* that He, Ge 6:6
people were *s* for Benjamin, Jdg 21:15
S comforters are you all, Job 16:2
be *s* for Your servants., Ps 90:13
the king was very *s*, Mk 6:26

SORTS *kinds*
after its kind, all *s* of birds., Ge 7:14
all *s* of baked food for, Ge 40:17
in ten days all *s* of wine, Ne 5:18
money is a root of all *s* of, 1Ti 6:10

SOSTHENES
Ruler of the synagogue at Corinth, Ac 18:17
——— Paul's Christian brother, 1Co 1:1

SOUL *life, spirit*
her *s* was departing, Ge 35:18
humble your *s-s*, Lv 16:29
poured out my *s*, 1Sa 1:15
not abandon my *s*, Ps 16:10
He restores my *s*, Ps 23:3
my *s* pants for You, Ps 42:1
Bless…LORD, O my *s*, Ps 103:1
who is wise wins *s-s*, Pr 11:30
s who sins will die, Eze 18:4
unable to kill the *s*, Mt 10:28
exchange for his *s*, Mt 16:26
My *s* is…grieved, Mt 26:38
and forfeit his *s*, Mk 8:36
My *s* exalts the Lord, Lk 1:46
your *s* is required, Lk 12:20
one heart and *s*, Ac 4:32
an anchor of the *s*, Heb 6:19
able to save your *s-s*, Jas 1:21
save his *s* from, Jas 5:20
war against the *s*, 1Pe 2:11

SOUND *(adj) accurate, stable*
s wisdom…two sides, Job 11:6
I give you *s* teaching, Pr 4:2
the *s* doctrine, 1Ti 4:6

SOUND *(n) noise*
s of You in…garden, Ge 3:10
s of war in the camp, Ex 32:17
s of a great army, 2Ki 7:6
s of many waters, Eze 43:2

SOUND *(v) express*
s His praise abroad, Ps 66:8
s an alarm, Joel 2:1
trumpet will *s*, 1Co 15:52

SOUR *distasteful, tart*
eaten *s* grapes, Jer 31:29
offering…*s* wine, Lk 23:36

SOURCE *origin*
the *s* of sapphires, Job 28:6
s of eternal salvation, Heb 5:9
s of quarrels, Jas 4:1

SOVEREIGNTY *authority*
His *s* rules over all, Ps 103:19
s from Damascus, Is 17:3
s will be uprooted, Da 11:4

SOW *plant, spread*
you may *s* the land, Ge 47:23
s your seed uselessly, Lv 26:16
who *s* in tears, Ps 126:5
who *s-s* iniquity will, Pr 22:8
they *s* the wind, Hos 8:7
birds…do not *s*, Mt 6:26
s good seed, Mt 13:27
s-ed spiritual things, 1Co 9:11
whatever a man *s-s*, Gal 6:7

SOWER *planter*
seed to the *s*, Is 55:10
s went out to sow, Mt 13:3
s sows the word, Mk 4:14

SPARE *save; be lenient*
did not *s* their soul, Ps 78:50
No man *s-s* his brother, Is 9:19
not *s* His own Son, Ro 8:32
I will not *s anyone*, 2Co 13:2
God did not *s* angels, 2Pe 2:4

SPARROW *a songbird*
Like a *s* in *its* flitting, Pr 26:2
not two *s-s* sold for a cent, Mt 10:29
not five *s-s* sold for two cents, Lk 12:6

SPEAK *proclaim, tell*
God *spoke* to Noah, Ge 8:15
God *s-s* with man, Dt 5:24
S of all His wonders, 1Ch 16:9
He who *s-s* falsehood, Ps 101:7
and a time to *s*, Ecc 3:7
the mute to *s*, Mk 7:37
s of what we know, Jn 3:11
Never has a man *spoken*, Jn 7:46
s with other tongues, Ac 2:4

STAGGER *stumble*
them *s* like a drunken man, Job 12:25
to drink that makes us *s*, Ps 60:3
drunken man *s-s* in his vomit, Is 19:14
and *s* from strong drink, Is 28:7
s, but not with strong drink, Is 29:9
People will *s* from sea to, Am 8:12

STAIN *blemish*
s of your iniquity, Jer 2:22
without *s*...reproach, 1Ti 6:14

STAND *maintain position*
s before the LORD, Dt 10:8
O sun, *s* still, Jos 10:12
s before kings, Pr 22:29
word of our God *s-s*, Is 40:8
will *s* on the Mount, Zec 14:4
love to *s* and pray, Mt 6:5
s-ing by the cross, Jn 19:25
why do you *s* looking, Ac 1:11
s by your faith, Ro 11:20
s before...judgment, Ro 14:10
s firm in the faith, 1Co 16:13
foundation...*s-s*, 2Ti 2:19
I *s* at the door, Rev 3:20

STANDARD *banner; rule*
set up their own *s-s*, Ps 74:4
set up My *s*, Is 49:22
s of the Law, Ac 22:12
s of sound words, 2Ti 1:13

STAR *heavenly body*
He made the *s-s*, Ge 1:16
s shall come forth, Nu 24:17
morning *s-s* sang, Job 38:7
s of the morning, Is 14:12
s-s for light by night, Jer 31:35
His *s* in the east, Mt 2:2
morning *s* arises, 2Pe 1:19
wandering *s-s*, Jude 13
s fell from heaven, Rev 8:10
the bright morning *s*, Rev 22:16

STATE *position*
s of expectation, Lk 3:15
of our humble *s*, Php 3:21
s has become worse, 2Pe 2:20

STATEMENT *assertion*
let your *s* be, Mt 5:37
trap Him in a *s*, Mk 12:13
catch Him in...*s*, Lk 20:20
This is a difficult *s*, Jn 6:60

STATURE *height*
was growing in *s*, 1Sa 2:26
in wisdom and *s*, Lk 2:52
he was small in *s*, Lk 19:3
measure of the *s*, Eph 4:13

STATUTE *law, rule*
My *s-s* and My laws, Ge 26:5
a perpetual *s*, Ex 29:9
keep My *s-s*, Lv 18:5
Teach me Your *s-s*, Ps 119:26
not walked in My *s-s*, Eze 5:7

STEADFAST *established, firm*
be *s* and not fear, Job 11:15
renew a *s* spirit, Ps 51:10
My heart is *s*, Ps 57:7
s in righteousness, Pr 11:19
be *s*, immovable, 1Co 15:58

STEAL *rob, take*
You shall not *s*, Ex 20:15
be in want and *s*, Pr 30:9
thieves break in...*s*, Mt 6:19
Do not *s*, Mk 10:19

STEPHEN
One of the first seven deacons, Ac 6:1–8
Falsely accused by Jews; gives defense, Ac 6:9–7:53
Becomes first Christian martyr, Ac 7:54–60

STEPS *distance; movements*
number my *s*, Job 14:16
s...bathed in butter, Job 29:6
His *s* do not slip, Ps 37:31
s take hold of Sheol, Pr 5:5
in the *s* of the faith, Ro 4:12
follow in His *s*, 1Pe 2:21

STEWARD *supervisor*
and sensible *s*, Lk 12:42
s-s of the mysteries, 1Co 4:1
above reproach...*s*, Titus 1:7

STEWARDSHIP *responsibility*
a *s* entrusted to me, 1Co 9:17
s of God's grace, Eph 3:2

STIFFEN *make rigid*
s your neck no longer, Dt 10:16
do not *s* your neck, 2Ch 30:8
have *s-ed* their necks, Jer 19:15

STILL *motionless; quiet*
O sun, stand *s*, Jos 10:12
the storm to be *s*, Ps 107:29
Why are we sitting *s*, Jer 8:14
sea, Hush, be *s*, Mk 4:39

STIMULATE *excite*
how to *s* my body, Ecc 2:3
s one another to, Heb 10:24

STING *pain*
where is your *s*, 1Co 15:55
s of death is sin, 1Co 15:56

STIR *agitate*
S up Yourself, Ps 35:23
word *s-s* up anger, Pr 15:1
man *s-s* up strife, Pr 29:22
s-red up the water, Jn 5:4

STOCKS *confinement*
put my feet in the *s*, Job 13:27
Jeremiah from the *s*, Jer 20:3
their feet in the *s*, Ac 16:24

STOMACH *part of body*
s will be satisfied, Pr 18:20
s of the fish, Jon 1:17
Food is for the *s*, 1Co 6:13
s was made bitter, Rev 10:10

STONE *(n) rock*
they used brick for *s*, Ge 11:3
two *s* tablets, Ex 34:1
do these *s-s* mean, Jos 4:6
five smooth *s-s*, 1Sa 17:40
there was no *s* seen, 1Ki 6:18
Water wears...*s-s*, Job 14:19
foot against a *s*, Ps 91:12
in Zion a *s*, Is 28:16
take the heart of *s*, Eze 11:19
serving wood and *s*, Eze 20:32
foot against a *s*, Mt 4:6
will give him a *s*, Mt 7:9
rolled away the *s*, Mt 28:2
s-s will cry out, Lk 19:40
six *s* waterpots, Jn 2:6
first to throw a *s*, Jn 8:7
Remove the *s*, Jn 11:39
s-s, wood, hay, 1Co 3:12
as to a living *s*, 1Pe 2:4
A *s* of stumbling, 1Pe 2:8

STONE *(v) throw stones*
people will *s* us, Lk 20:6
seeking to *s* You, Jn 11:8
went on *s-ing* Stephen, Ac 7:59
they *s-d* Paul, Ac 14:19

STOP *cease*
the sun *s-ped*, Jos 10:13
And the oil *s-ped*, 2Ki 4:6
put a *s* to sacrifice, Da 9:27
s weeping for Me, Lk 23:28
s sinning, 1Co 15:34

STORE *accumulate*
s up the grain, Ge 41:35
His sin is *s-d* up, Hos 13:12
s up...treasures, Mt 6:20
place to *s* my crops, Lk 12:17
s-d up your treasure, Jas 5:3

STOREHOUSE *storage place*
s-s of the snow, Job 38:22
wind from His *s-s*, Jer 10:13
tithe into the *s*, Mal 3:10

STORK *bird*
the *s*, the heron, Lv 11:19
the *s* in the sky, Jer 8:7
wings of a *s*, Zec 5:9

STORM *tempest, whirlwind*
A refuge from the *s*, Is 25:4
will come like a *s*, Eze 38:9
a great *s* on the sea, Jon 1:4
a great *s* on the sea, Mt 8:24
mists driven by a *s*, 2Pe 2:17

STRAIGHT *direct*
Make Your way *s*, Ps 5:8
make your paths *s*, Pr 3:6
Make His paths *s*, Mt 3:3
Make *s* the way, Jn 1:23

STRANGE *foreign*
offered *s* fire, Lv 10:1
no *s* god among you, Ps 81:9
to teach *s* doctrines, 1Ti 1:3
went after *s* flesh, Jude 7

STRANGER *alien, sojourner*
s-s in a land, Ge 15:13
a *s* and a sojourner, Ge 23:4
shall not wrong a *s*, Ex 22:21
a *s* in the earth, Ps 119:19
LORD protects the *s-s*, Ps 146:9
violence to the *s*, Jer 22:3
I was a *s*, Mt 25:35
hospitality to *s-s*, Heb 13:2

STRAW *stalk of grain*
s to make brick, Ex 5:7
s for the horses, 1Ki 4:28

SWEAT *perspiration*
By the *s* of your face, Ge 3:19
s…like drops of, Lk 22:44

SWEET *fresh, pleasant*
waters became *s*, Ex 15:25
s psalmist of Israel, 2Sa 23:1
who had *s* fellowship, Ps 55:14
s are Your words, Ps 119:103
your sleep will be *s*, Pr 3:24
Stolen water is *s*, Pr 9:17
it was *s* as honey, Eze 3:3

SWIFT *fast, rapid*
horses and *s* steeds, 1Ki 4:28
s as the gazelles, 1Ch 12:8
race is not to the *s*, Ecc 9:11
riding on a *s* cloud, Is 19:1
s to shed blood, Ro 3:15

SWINDLER *cheater*
cursed be the *s*, Mal 1:14
a drunkard, or a *s*, 1Co 5:11
revilers, nor *s-s*, 1Co 6:10

SWINE *pig*
gold in a *s-'s* snout, Pr 11:22
Who eat *s-'s* flesh, Is 65:4
your pearls before *s*, Mt 7:6
Send us into the *s*, Mk 5:12

SWORD *long-bladed weapon*
flaming *s*…turned, Ge 3:24
by your *s* you shall, Ge 27:40
the *s* will bereave, Dt 32:25
A *s* for the LORD, Jdg 7:20
s devour forever, 2Sa 2:26
fell on his *s*, 1Ch 10:5
tongue a sharp *s*, Ps 57:4
as a two-edged *s*, Pr 5:4
teeth are *like s-s*, Pr 30:14
s against nation, Is 2:4
the power of the *s*, Jer 18:21
abolish…the *s*, Hos 2:18
s-s into plowshares, Mic 4:3
perish by the *s*, Mt 26:52
s of the Spirit, Eph 6:17
than any two-edged *s*, Heb 4:12
s of My mouth, Rev 2:16

SYCAMORE *tree*
olive and *s* trees, 1Ch 27:28
plentiful as *s-s*, 2Ch 1:15
grower of *s* figs, Am 7:14
climbed up into a *s*, Lk 19:4

SYCHAR
Town of Samaria where Jesus met woman at well, Jn 4:5–39

SYMPATHY *mutual feeling*
I looked for *s*, Ps 69:20
s to the prisoners, Heb 10:34

SYNAGOGUE *assembly*
pray in the *s-s*, Mt 6:5
He went into their *s*, Mt 12:9
flogged in *the s-s*, Mk 13:9
chief seats in…*s-s*, Lk 20:46
outcasts from the *s*, Jn 16:2
taught in *s-s*, Jn 18:20
reasoning in the *s*, Ac 17:17
but are a *s* of Satan, Rev 2:9

SYNAGOGUE OFFICIAL
s came and bowed down, Mt 9:18
of the *s-s* named Jairus, Mk 5:22
from the house of the *s*, Mk 5:35
from the house of the *s*, Lk 8:49
s, indignant because, Lk 13:14
s-s sent to them, saying, Ac 13:15

SYRACUSE
City visited by Paul, Ac 28:12

SYRIANS
Abraham's kindred, Ge 22:20–23; 25:20
Hostile to Israel, 2Sa 8:11–13; 10:6–19; 1Ki 20:1–34; 22:1–38; 2Ki 6:8–7:7
Defeated by Assyria, 2Ki 16:9
Destruction of, foretold, Is 17:1–3
Gospel preached to, Ac 15:23, 41

SYRO-PHOENICIAN
Daughter of, freed of demon, Mk 7:25–31

T

TABERAH
Israelite camp; fire destroys many there, Nu 11:1–3

TABERNACLE *assembly and area for sacrificial worship*
Dwelling place of God among the Israelites, Ex 25:8
Construction directed by God, Ex 25:9
Contained Ark of the Covenant, Ex 25:10
Other descriptive names of the tabernacle:
House of the LORD, Ex 23:19; 34:26; Dt 23:18
Tabernacle of the house of God, 1Ch 6:48
Tabernacle of the tent of meeting, Ex 39:40; 40:6, 29
Tabernacle of the testimony, Ex 38:21; Nu 1:50, 53
Tent of meeting, Ex 29:32; 30:26; 38:30; 39:43; 40:2, 6, 7

TABITHA
See DORCAS

TABLE *furniture*
gold t before the LORD, Lv 24:6
You prepare a *t*, Ps 23:5
crumbs…masters' *t*, Mt 15:27
t-s…moneychangers, Mt 21:12
dogs under the *t*, Mk 7:28
drink at My *t*, Lk 22:30
in order to serve *t-s*, Ac 6:2
t of the Lord, 1Co 10:21

TABLET *writing surface*
give you the stone *t-s*, Ex 24:12
t-s of the testimony, Ex 31:18
the *t* of their heart, Jer 17:1
t-s of human hearts, 2Co 3:3

TABOR
Scene of rally against Sisera, Jdg 4:6, 12, 14

TADMOR
Trading center near Damascus, 2Ch 8:4

TAHPANHES (or Tehaphnehes)
City of Egypt; refuge of fleeing Jews, Jer 2:16; 44:1; Eze 30:18

TAIL
grasp *it* by its *t*, Ex 4:4
the foxes t to *t*, Jdg 15:4
cuts off head and *t*, Is 9:14
t-s like scorpions, Rev 9:10

TAKE *get, grasp*
t…the tree of life, Ge 3:22
T My yoke upon, Mt 11:29
T, eat; this is My, Mt 26:26
t-s away the sin, Jn 1:29
day that He was *t-n*, Ac 1:22
to *t* hold of…hope, Heb 6:18

TAKE COURAGE
let your heart *t*, Ps 27:14
t, All you who hope, Ps 31:24
heart, "*T*, fear not, Is 35:4
t and be courageous, Da 10:19
you people of the land *t*, Hag 2:4
T, son; your sins are, Mt 9:2
t; your faith has made you, Mt 9:22
T, it is I; do not be afraid, Mt 14:27
T, stand up! He is calling, Mk 10:49
t; I have overcome the, Jn 16:33
at his side and said, "*T*, Ac 23:11

TAKE HEED
t to yourselves to love, Jos 23:11
sons *t* to their way to walk, 1Ki 8:25
T then to your spirit, Mal 2:15
t …. have told you, Mk 13:23
T, keep on the alert, Mk 13:33
who thinks he stands *t*, 1Co 10:12
T to the ministry which, Col 4:17

TALENT
Measure of weight, Ex 38:27; 2Sa 12:30; 2Ch 20:2
Measure of money, 1Ki 20:39; Mt 18:24; 25:15, 25

TALK *(n) conversation, speech*
argue with useless *t*, Job 15:3
no…silly *t*, Eph 5:4
their *t* will spread, 2Ti 2:17

TALK *(v) converse, speak*
God *t-ed* with him, Ge 17:3
lips *t* of trouble, Pr 24:2
who *t* about you, Eze 33:30
they were *t-ing*, Lk 24:15
Paul kept on *t-ing*, Ac 20:9

TALL *high*
cut…its *t* cedars, 2Ki 19:23
a nation *t* and smooth, Is 18:2
grew up, became *t*, Eze 16:7

TAMAR
Wife of Er and mother of Perez and Zerah, Ge 38:6–30
——— Absalom's sister, 2Sa 13:1–32

TAMARISK *tree*
a *t* tree at Beersheba, Ge 21:33
under the *t* tree, 1Sa 22:6

TAMBOURINE *musical instrument*
accompanied by…*t*, Is 5:12
gaiety of *t-s* ceases, Is 24:8

TAMMUZ
Mesopotamian god, Eze 8:14

TARES *weeds*
t among the wheat, Mt 13:25
gather up the *t*, Mt 13:30
parable of the *t*, Mt 13:36

TARSHISH
City at a great distance from Palestine, Jon 1:3
Ships of, noted in commerce, Ps 48:7

TARSUS
Paul's birthplace, Ac 21:39
Saul sent to, Ac 9:30
Visited by Barnabas, Ac 11:25

TARTAN
Sent to fight against Jerusalem, 2Ki 18:17

TASK *job*
the *t* is too heavy for you, Ex 18:18
a grievous *t which* God, Ecc 1:13
wisdom and to see the *t*, Ecc 8:16
to each one his *t*, Mk 13:34
may put in charge of this *t*, Ac 6:3

TASKMASTERS *overseers*
appointed *t* over them, Ex 1:11
Pharaoh commanded…*t*, Ex 5:6

TASTE *test flavor*
As the palate *t-s*, Job 34:3
O *t* and see, Ps 34:8
will not *t* death, Mt 16:28
t death for everyone, Heb 2:9
t-d…heavenly gift, Heb 6:4

TASTELESS *without taste*
Can something *t* be, Job 6:6
salt has become *t*, Mt 5:13

TATTENAI
Persian governor opposing the Jews, Ezr 5:3, 6

TAUNT *object of ridicule*
a *t* among all, Dt 28:37
I have become their *t*, Job 30:9

TAX *charge, tribute*
a *t* for the LORD, Nu 31:28
money for the king's *t*, Ne 5:4
sitting in the *t* collector's, Mt 9:9
pay *t-es* to Caesar, Lk 20:22
t to whom *t is due*, Ro 13:7

TAX COLLECTOR
See TAX COLLECTORS AND SINNERS
even the *t-s* do the same?, Mt 5:46
Matthew the *t*; James, Mt 10:3
as a Gentile and a *t*, Mt 18:17
t-s and prostitutes will get, Mt 21:31
t-s also came, Lk 3:12
a *t* named Levi sitting, Lk 5:27
t-s heard this, they, Lk 7:29
Pharisee and the other a *t*, Lk 18:10
Zaccheus; he was a chief *t*, Lk 19:2

TAX COLLECTORS AND SINNERS
See TAX COLLECTOR
t came, Mt 9:10
eating with the *t*?, Mt 9:11
friend of *t*, Mt 11:19
t were dining with, Mk 2:15
drink with the *t*?, Lk 5:30
friend of *t*, Lk 7:34
t were coming near, Lk 15:1

TEACH *instruct*
t you what…to say, Ex 4:12
t them the good way, 1Ki 8:36
Can anyone *t* God, Job 21:22
T me Your paths, Ps 25:4
T me to do Your will, Ps 143:10
would He *t* knowledge, Is 28:9
He…*began* to *t* them, Mt 5:2
t-ing…in parables, Mk 4:2
Lord, *t* us to pray, Lk 11:1
Spirit will *t* you, Lk 12:12
He will *t* you all, Jn 14:26
t strange doctrines, 1Ti 1:3
allow a woman to *t*, 1Ti 2:12
she *t-es* and leads, Rev 2:20

TEACHER *instructor*
will behold your *T*, Is 30:20
T, I will follow You, Mt 8:19
not above his *t*, Mt 10:24
why trouble the *T*, Mk 5:35
the *t* of Israel, Jn 3:10
call Me *T* and Lord, Jn 13:13
t of the immature, Ro 2:20
as pastors and *t-s*, Eph 4:11
t of the Gentiles, 1Ti 2:7
false *t-s* among you, 2Pe 2:1

TEACHING *(n) instruction*
t drop as the rain, Dt 32:2
your mother's *t*, Pr 1:8
amazed at His *t*, Mt 7:28
My *t* is not Mine, Jn 7:16
contrary to sound *t*, 1Ti 1:10

TEAR *crying*
have seen your *t-s*, 2Ki 20:5
my *t-s* in Your bottle, Ps 56:8
sow in *t-s* shall reap, Ps 126:5
drench you with my *t-s*, Is 16:9
eyes a fountain of *t-s*, Jer 9:1
His feet with her *t-s*, Lk 7:38
God…wipe every *t*, Rev 7:17

TEBETH
Name of the tenth month in Hebrew calendar, Est 2:16

TEETH *chewing instruments*
And his *t* white from milk, Ge 49:12
was still between their *t*, Nu 11:33
I take my flesh in my *t*, Job 13:14
by the skin of my *t*, Job 19:20
whose *t* are spears and, Ps 57:4
shatter their *t* in their mouth, Ps 58:6
Your *t* are like a flock of, SS 4:2
children's *t* are set on edge, Jer 31:29
gave you also cleanness of *t*, Am 4:6
weeping and gnashing of *t*, Mt 8:12
weeping and gnashing of *t*, Mt 24:51
and grinds his *t* and, Mk 9:18
their *t* were like, Rev 9:8

TEKOA
Home of a wise woman, 2Sa 14:2, 4, 9
Home of Amos, Am 1:1

TELL *relate, speak*
not *t* the riddle, Jdg 14:14
T of His glory, 1Ch 16:24
t of Your righteousness, Ps 71:15
t-s lies will perish, Pr 19:9
t you great and mighty, Jer 33:3
See that you *t* no one, Mt 8:4
t you about Me, Jn 18:34
t you the mystery, Rev 17:7

TEMPER *anger*
always loses his *t*, Pr 29:11
the ruler's *t* rises, Ecc 10:4

TEMPEST *storm*
bruises me with a *t*, Job 9:17
stormy wind *and t*, Ps 55:8
t of destruction, Is 28:2
on the day of *t*, Am 1:14

TEMPLE *structure for worship*
doorpost of the *t*, 1Sa 1:9
t is not for man, 1Ch 29:1
LORD is in His holy *t*, Ps 11:4
meditate in His *t*, Ps 27:4
t of the LORD, Jer 7:4
pinnacle of the *t*, Mt 4:5
will destroy this *t*, Mk 14:58
veil of the *t*, Lk 23:45
Destroy this *t*, and, Jn 2:19
you are a *t* of God, 1Co 3:16
t of the Holy Spirit, 1Co 6:19
his seat in the *t*, 2Th 2:4
the Lamb, are its *t*, Rev 21:22

TEMPT *test, try*
And *t-ed* God in the, Ps 106:14
being *t-ed* by Satan, Mk 1:13
so that Satan will not *t* you, 1Co 7:5
t-ed beyond what, 1Co 10:13
Himself does not *t*, Jas 1:13

TEMPTATION *testing, trial*
not lead us into *t*, Mt 6:13
not enter into *t*, Mt 26:41
time of *t* fall away, Lk 8:13
t has overtaken you, 1Co 10:13
the godly from *t*, 2Pe 2:9

TEN *number*
T Commandments, Dt 10:4
it had *t* horns, Da 7:7
has the *t* talents, Mt 25:28

TEND *take care of*
t his father's flock, 1Sa 17:15
He will *t* His flock, Is 40:11
T My lambs, Jn 21:15
T My sheep, Jn 21:17

TENDER *gentle, young*
t and choice calf, Ge 18:7
your heart was *t*, 2Ki 22:19
like a *t* shoot, Is 53:2
t mercy of our God, Lk 1:78

TENT *mobile shelter*
Abram moved his *t*, Ge 13:18
man, living in *t-s*, Ge 25:27
your *t-s*, O Israel, 1Ki 12:16
t-s of the destroyers, Job 12:6
dwell in Your *t* forever, Ps 61:4
grumbled in their *t-s*, Ps 106:25
Like a shepherd's *t*, Is 38:12

TENT OF MEETING
Perhaps the same as the Tabernacle or at certain periods a separate meeting place, Ex 33:7; Lv 1:1; Nu 7:5; Jos 18:1
See also tabernacle

TENT OF TESTIMONY
See TABERNACLE

TERAH
Father of Abram, Ge 11:26
Idolater, Jos 24:2
Dies in Haran, Ge 11:25–32

TERAPHIM
Household gods, idols, 2Ki 23:24; Zec 10:2

TERRIBLE *dreadful*
and *t* wilderness, Dt 8:15
t day of the LORD, Mal 4:5
into *t* convulsions, Mk 9:26

TERRIFY *frighten*
t-ied by the sword, 1Ch 21:30
t me by visions, Job 7:14
t them with Your storm, Ps 83:15
Him and were *t-ied*, Mk 6:50
t you by my letters, 2Co 10:9

TERRITORY *country, land*
smite your whole *t*, Ex 8:2
God enlarges your *t*, Dt 19:8
t of…inheritance, Jos 19:10
possess the *t*, Ob 19

TERROR *intense fear*
Sounds of *t* are in, Job 15:21
t-s of thick darkness, Job 24:17
t-s of Sheol came, Ps 116:3
meditate on *t*, Is 33:18
t-s and great signs, Lk 21:11

TERTULLUS
Orator who accuses Paul, Ac 24:1–8

TEST *(n) trial*
put God to the *t*, Ps 78:18
put Him to the *t*, Lk 10:25
you fail the *t*, 2Co 13:5

TEST *(v) try*
God *t-ed* Abraham, Ge 22:1
Why do you *t* the LORD, Ex 17:2
she came to *t* him, 1Ki 10:1
T my mind and my, Ps 26:2
word of God is *t-ed*, Pr 30:5
Spirit…to the *t*, Ac 5:9
fire itself will *t*, 1Co 3:13
t the spirits to see, 1Jn 4:1

TESTIFY *give witness*
nor shall you *t*, Ex 23:2
them *t* against him, 1Ki 21:10
I will *t* against you, Ps 50:7
our sins *t* against us, Is 59:12
John *t-ied*, Jn 1:15
John *t-ied*, Jn 1:32
Jesus Himself *t-ied*, Jn 4:44
If I *alone t*, Jn 5:31
t about Me, Jn 15:26
you *will t*, Jn 15:27
Spirit…*t-ies*, Ro 8:16
three that *t*, 1Jn 5:7

TESTIMONY *witness*
into the ark the *t*, Ex 25:16
two tablets of the *t*, Ex 31:18
t of the LORD is sure, Ps 19:7
t-ies are righteous, Ps 119:144
Bind up the *t*, Is 8:16
t to all the nations, Mt 24:14
t against Jesus, Mt 26:59
My *t* is true, Jn 8:14
t of two men is true, Jn 8:17
t concerning Christ, 1Co 1:6
ashamed of the *t*, 2Ti 1:8
This *t* is true, Titus 1:13
t of God is greater, 1Jn 5:9

TETRARCH
Governor of a region, Mt 14:1; Lk 3:1, 19; Ac 13:1

THADDAEUS
One of the Twelve, Mk 3:18

THANK *(v) express gratitude*
my song I shall *t* Him, Ps 28:7
God, I *t* You, Lk 18:11
I *t* my God always, 1Co 1:4

THANKS *(n) gratitude*
give *t* to the LORD, 1Ch 16:7
It is good to give *t*, Ps 92:1
giving *t*, He broke, Mt 15:36
a cup and given *t*, Mt 26:27
But *t* be to God, Ro 6:17
not cease giving *t*, Eph 1:16
always to give *t*, 2Th 1:3

THANKSGIVING *gratitude*
the sacrifice of *t*, Lv 7:12
with the voice of *t*, Ps 26:7
His presence with *t*, Ps 95:2
supplication with *t*, Php 4:6
t and honor and, Rev 7:12

THE LORD IS MY BANNER
altar and named it *T*, Ex 17:15

THE LORD IS PEACE
and named it *T*, Jdg 6:24

THE LORD WILL PROVIDE
name of that place *T*, Ge 22:14

THEFT *robbery*
be sold for his *t*, Ex 22:3
t-s, murders, Mk 7:21

THEOPHILUS
Luke addresses his writings to, Lk 1:3; Ac 1:1

THESSALONICA
Paul preaches in, Ac 17:1–13
Paul writes letters to churches of, 1Th 1:1

THICKET *underbrush*
ram caught in the *t*, Ge 22:13
the *t* of the Jordan, Jer 50:44

THIEF *robber*
that *t* shall die, Dt 24:7
partner with a *t*, Pr 29:24
companions of *t-ves*, Is 1:23
enter…like a *t*, Joel 2:9
t-ves break in and steal, Mt 6:19
t comes…to steal, Jn 10:10
nor *t-ves*, nor *the* covetous, 1Co 6:10
a *t* in the night, 1Th 5:2

THIGH *part of leg*
hand under my *t*, Ge 24:2
socket of Jacob's *t*, Ge 32:25
Your sword on *Your t*, Ps 45:3
on His *t*…a name, Rev 19:16

THIN *lean*
t ears scorched, Ge 41:27
t yellowish hair, Lv 13:30
streams…will *t* out, Is 19:6

THINK *ponder, reflect*
as he *t-s*…so he is, Pr 23:7
not *t*…to abolish, Mt 5:17
not to *t* more highly, Ro 12:3
t like a child, 1Co 13:11
t-s he is something, Gal 6:3
beyond all that we…*t*, Eph 3:20

THIRD *number*
morning, a *t* day, Ge 1:13
raised…the *t* day, Mt 16:21
raised on the *t* day, 1Co 15:4
to the *t* heaven, 2Co 12:2

THIRST *(n) craving, dryness*
for my *t*…vinegar, Ps 69:21
donkeys quench…*t*, Ps 104:11
not hunger or *t*, Is 49:10
in Me will never *t*, Jn 6:35
no longer…nor *t*, Rev 7:16

THIRST *(v) have a craving*
My soul *t-s* for God, Ps 42:2
Every one who *t-s*, come, Is 55:1
t for righteousness, Mt 5:6

THIRSTY *lacking water*
satisfied the *t* soul, Ps 107:9
In a dry and *t* land, Eze 19:13
I was *t*, and you, Mt 25:35
If anyone is *t*, Jn 7:37
one who is *t* come, Rev 22:17

THOMAS
Apostle of Christ, Mt 10:3
Ready to die with Christ, Jn 11:16
Doubts Christ's resurrection, Jn 20:24–29

THORN *sharp point*
Both *t-s* and thistles, Ge 3:18
as *t-s* in your sides, Nu 33:55
as a hedge of *t-s*, Pr 15:19
lily among the *t-s*, SS 2:2
have reaped *t-s*, Jer 12:13
fell among the *t-s*, Mt 13:7
a crown of *t-s*, Mt 27:29
a burning *t* bush, Ac 7:30
t in the flesh, 2Co 12:7

THOUGHT *concept, idea*
t-s of his heart, Ge 6:5
knows the *t-s* of man, Ps 94:11
My *t-s* are not your *t-s*, Is 55:8
Jesus knowing…*t-s*, Mt 9:4
heart come evil *t-s*, Mt 15:19
every *t* captive, 2Co 10:5

THREAD *string*
cord of scarlet *t*, Jos 2:18
lips…a scarlet *t*, SS 4:3

t-s of men…angels, 1Co 13:1
if I pray in a *t*, 1Co 14:14
every tribe and *t*, Rev 5:9

TOOL *work instrument*
among your *t-s*, Dt 23:13
nor any iron *t*, 1Ki 6:7
iron into a cutting *t*, Is 44:12

TOOTH
teeth white from, Ge 49:12
eye for eye, *t* for *t*, Ex 21:24
and a *t* for a *t*, Mt 5:38

TOPAZ *precious stone*
ruby, *t*, and emerald, Ex 39:10
t of Ethiopia, Job 28:19
the ninth, *t*, Rev 21:20

TOPHETH
See HINNOM, VALLEY OF THE SON OF
T has long been ready, Is 30:33
the high places of *T*, Jer 7:31
make this city like *T*, Jer 19:12
like the place *T*, Jer 19:13

TORE … CLOTHES
Jacob *t*, and put, Ge 37:34
they *t*, and when each, Ge 44:13
Joshua *t* and fell to the, Jos 7:6
When he saw her, he *t*, Jdg 11:35
David … *t*, and so also, 2Sa 1:11
king arose, *t* and lay, 2Sa 13:31
Ahab …*t* and put on, 1Ki 21:27
Elisha … *t* in two pieces, 2Ki 2:12
t and said, "Am I God, 2Ki 5:7
Hezekiah heard it, he *t*, 2Ki 19:1
book of the law, he *t*, 2Ki 22:11
Athaliah *t* and said, 2Ch 24:13
t and wept before Me, 2Ch 34:27
Mordecai …*t*, put on, Est 4:1
Hezekiah … *t*, covered, Is 37:1

TORMENT *(n) pain, torture*
this place of *t*, Lk 16:28
their *t* was like, Rev 9:5
the fear of her *t*, Rev 18:15

TORMENT *(v) annoy, harass*
long will you *t* me, Job 19:2
t us before the time, Mt 8:29
do not *t* me, Lk 8:28
Satan to *t* me, 2Co 12:7

TORRENT *flood*
The ancient *t*, Jdg 5:21
t-s of destruction, 2Sa 22:5
t-s of ungodliness, Ps 18:4
like an overflowing *t*, Is 30:28

TOUCH *feel, handle*
not eat…or *t* it, Ge 3:3
an angel *t-ing* him, 1Ki 19:5
evil will not *t* you, Job 5:19
not *t* My anointed, Ps 105:15
T nothing unclean, Is 52:11
t the fringe of His, Mt 14:36
not to *t* a woman, 1Co 7:1

TOWER *fortress structure*
t whose top *will reach*, Ge 11:4
Count her *t-s*, Ps 48:12
name…strong *t*, Pr 18:10
and built a *t*, Mt 21:33

TOWN *city, village*
many unwalled *t-s*, Dt 3:5
founds a *t* with, Hab 2:12
except in his home *t*, Mt 13:57

TRADE *(n) business, occupation*
abundance of your *t*, Eze 28:16
of the same *t*, Ac 18:3

TRADE *(v) buy; sell*
may *t* in the land, Ge 42:34
t-d with them, Mt 25:16

TRADERS *merchants*
Midianite *t* passed, Ge 37:28
king's *t* procured, 2Ch 1:16
in a city of *t*, Eze 17:4
increased your *t*, Na 3:16

TRADITION *custom*
sake of your *t*, Mt 15:3
hold to the *t* of men, Mk 7:8
hold…to the *t-s*, 1Co 11:2
my ancestral *t-s*, Gal 1:14

TRAIN *guide, instruct*
T up a child, Pr 22:6
will they *t* for war, Mic 4:3
t-ed to discern good, Heb 5:14
heart *t-ed* in greed, 2Pe 2:14

TRAMPLE *crush, hurt*
t-s down the waves, Job 9:8
let him *t* my life, Ps 7:5
t-d the nations, Hab 3:12
Jerusalem…*t-d*, Lk 21:24

TRANCE *daze, dream*
he fell into a *t*, Ac 10:10
in a *t* I saw a vision, Ac 11:5
fell into a *t*, Ac 22:17

TRANSFIGURED *changed*
He was *t* before them, Mt 17:2

TRANSFORM *change*
t-ed by the renewing, Ro 12:2
t-ed into the same, 2Co 3:18
who will *t* the body, Php 3:21

TRANSGRESS *break, overstep*
you *t* the covenant, Jos 23:16
rulers also *t-ed*, Jer 2:8
they *t-ed* laws, Is 24:5

TRANSGRESSION *trespass, sin*
forgives iniquity, *t*, Ex 34:7
I am pure, without *t*, Job 33:9
I know my *t-s*, Ps 51:3
removed our *t-s* from, Ps 103:12
love covers all *t-s*, Pr 10:12
pierced…for our *t-s*, Is 53:5
not forgive your *t-s*, Mt 6:15
dead in our *t-s*, Eph 2:5

TRANSGRESSOR *sinner*
teach *t-s* Your ways, Ps 51:13
numbered with the *t-s*, Is 53:12
a *t* of the law, Jas 2:11

TRANSLATED
t and read before me, Ezr 4:18
Immanuel…*t* means, Mt 1:23
Golgotha, which is *t*, Mk 15:22
Messiah…*t* means, Jn 1:41

TRAP *(n) snare*
a snare and a *t*, Jos 23:13
hidden a *t* for me, Ps 142:3
table become…a *t*, Ro 11:9

TRAP *(v) catch*
they might *t* Him, Mt 22:15
in order to *t* Him, Mk 12:13

TRAVAIL *intense pain*
t-ed nor given birth, Is 23:4

TRAVEL *journey*
t by day and by night, Ex 13:21
who *t* on the road, Jdg 5:10
Jesus…*began t-ing*, Lk 24:15

TREACHEROUS *traitorous*
I behold the *t*, Ps 119:158
t will be uprooted, Pr 2:22
way of the *t* is hard, Pr 13:15

TREAD *walk on*
They *t* wine presses, Job 24:11
as the potter *t-s* clay, Is 41:25
t on serpents, Lk 10:19
t-s the wine press, Rev 19:15

TREASURE *(n) valuable thing*
t-s of the sand, Dt 33:19
the LORD is his *t*, Is 33:6
opening their *t-s*, Mt 2:11
for where your *t* is, Mt 6:21
have *t* in heaven, Mt 19:21
t in earthen vessels, 2Co 4:7
stored up your *t*, Jas 5:3

TREASURE *(v) value greatly*
I have *t-d* the words, Job 23:12
Your word I have *t-d*, Ps 119:11
t my commandments, Pr 7:1

TREASURY *place of valuables*
t of the LORD, Jos 6:19
paid from the royal *t*, Ezr 6:4
fill their *t-ies*, Pr 8:21
into the temple *t*, Mt 27:6

TREAT *act toward*
Sarai *t-ed* her harshly, Ge 16:6
will *t* you worse than them, Ge 19:9
Why did you *t* me so badly, Ge 43:6
Me I will be *t-ed* as holy, Lv 10:3
t-ed us harshly and, Dt 26:6
you *t* us with contempt, 2Sa 19:43
I will not *t* the remnant, Zec 8:11
t people the same way, Mt 7:12
respect were you *t-ed* as, 2Co 12:13
sin and are harshly *t-ed*, 1Pe 2:20

TREATY *agreement, contract*
Let there be a *t*, 1Ki 15:19
go, break your *t*, 2Ch 16:3

TREE *woody plant*
fruit *t-s*…bearing, Ge 1:11
t of life, Ge 2:9
gave me from the *t*, Ge 3:12
hang him on a *t*, Dt 21:22
said to the olive *t*, Jdg 9:8
t firmly planted, Ps 1:3
she is a *t* of life, Pr 3:18
Beneath the apple *t*, SS 8:5
like a *t* planted by, Jer 17:8
under his fig *t*, Mic 4:4

U

USURY *interest*
leave off this *u*, Ne 5:10
by interest and *u*, Pr 28:8

UTENSILS *vessels*
table also and its *u*, Ex 31:8
u of the sanctuary, 1Ch 9:29

UTTER *express*
righteous *u-s* wisdom, Ps 37:30
Let my lips *u* praise, Ps 119:171
He *u-s* His voice, Jer 10:13
u words of…truth, Ac 26:25

UTTERANCE *expression*
was giving them *u*, Ac 2:4
in faith and *u*, 2Co 8:7
u may be given, Eph 6:19
through prophetic *u*, 1Ti 4:14

UZZAH
Son of Abinadab, struck down for touching the ark of the covenant, 2Sa 6:3–11

UZZIAH
King of Judah, called Azariah, 2Ki 14:21; 15:1–7
Reigns righteously, 2Ch 26:1–15
Usurps priestly function; stricken with leprosy, 2Ch 26:16–21
Life of, written by Isaiah, 2Ch 26:22, 23

V

VAIN *empty; profane*
name of…God in *v*, Ex 20:7
devising a *v* thing, Ps 2:1
labor in *v* who build, Ps 127:1
our preaching is *v*, 1Co 15:14

VALIANT *brave, strong*
these…*v* warriors, Jdg 20:46
be a *v* man for me, 1Sa 18:17
even all the *v* men, 1Ch 28:1
He drags off the *v*, Job 24:22

VALLEY *ravine*
v of the Jordan, Ge 13:10
the *v* of Aijalon, Jos 10:12
v of the shadow of, Ps 23:4
The lily of the *v-s*, SS 2:1
v of the dead bodies, Jer 31:40
v…full of bones, Eze 37:1
the *v* of decision, Joel 3:14

VALLEY GATE
See GATES OF JERUSALEM

VALOR *bravery*
mighty man of *v*, 1Sa 16:18
mighty men of *v*, 1Ch 12:8

VALUABLE *of worth*
not considered *v*, 1Ki 10:21
v articles of the house of, 2Ch 36:10
you are more *v*, Mt 10:31
How much more *v* then, Mt 12:12
more *v* than many sparrows, Lk 12:7

VALUE *worth*
one pearl of great *v*, Mt 13:46
v of knowing Christ, Php 3:8

VANISH *disappear*
When a cloud *v-es*, Job 7:9
sky will *v* like smoke, Is 51:6
v-ed from…sight, Lk 24:31

VANITY *futility, pride*
will reap *v*, Pr 22:8
V of *v-ies!* All is *v*, Ecc 1:2
arrogant *words* of *v*, 2Pe 2:18

VAPOR *smoke*
causes the *v-s* to, Ps 135:7
Is a fleeting *v*, Pr 21:6
You are *just* a *v*, Jas 4:14

VARICOLORED *multicolored*
made him a *v* tunic, Ge 37:3

VARIOUS *different*
v diseases and pains, Mt 4:24
led on by *v* impulses, 2Ti 3:6
encounter *v* trials, Jas 1:2
distressed by *v* trials, 1Pe 1:6

VASHTI
Queen of Ahasuerus, deposed and divorced, Est 1:9–22

VEGETABLE *plant*
like a *v* garden, Dt 11:10
Better…dish of *v-s*, Pr 15:17
weak eats *v-s only*, Ro 14:2

VEGETATION *plant life*
earth brought forth *v*, Ge 1:12
ate up all *v*, Ps 105:35
wither all their *v*, Is 42:15

VEIL *cover, curtain*
a *v* over his face, Ex 34:33
v of the sanctuary, Lv 4:6
Remove your *v*, Is 47:2
v of the temple, Mt 27:51
enters within the *v*, Heb 6:19

VENGEANCE *revenge*
not take *v*, Lv 19:18
V is Mine, Dt 32:35
God…executes *v*, 2Sa 22:48
LORD takes *v* on His, Na 1:2
V is Mine, I will, Heb 10:30

VESSEL *utensil*
Go, borrow *v-s*, 2Ki 4:3
I am like a broken *v*, Ps 31:12
v-s of wrath, Ro 9:22
treasure in…*v-s*, 2Co 4:7
be a *v* for honor, 2Ti 2:21
v-s of the potter, Rev 2:27

VESTURE *apparel*
v was like…snow, Da 7:9

VIAL *small container*
alabaster *v* of, Mt 26:7
she broke the *v*, Mk 14:3

VICTORIOUS *triumphant*
A *v* warrior, Zep 3:17
v over the beast, Rev 15:2

VICTORY *triumph*
LORD brought…*v*, 2Sa 23:10
had given *v* to Aram, 2Ki 5:1
the glory and the *v*, 1Ch 29:11
gained the *v* for Him, Ps 98:1
v belongs to…LORD, Pr 21:31
He leads justice to *v*, Mt 12:20
swallowed up in *v*, 1Co 15:54
v that has overcome, 1Jn 5:4

VIGOR *vitality*
nor his *v* abated, Dt 34:7
grave in full *v*, Job 5:26
his youthful *v*, Job 20:11

VILLAGE *small town*
land of unwalled *v-s*, Eze 38:11
Go into the *v*, Mt 21:2
entered a *v*, Lk 10:38

VINDICATE *justify*
will *v* His people, Dt 32:36
V the weak, Ps 82:3
wisdom is *v-d* by, Mt 11:19

VINE *stem of plant*
trees said to the *v*, Jdg 9:12
every man…his *v*, 1Ki 4:25
like a fruitful *v*, Ps 128:3
the *v-s* in blossom, SS 2:13
mother was like a *v*, Eze 19:10
Israel is a luxuriant *v*, Hos 10:1
The *v* dries up, Joel 1:12
fruit of the *v*, Mt 26:29
I am the true *v*, Jn 15:1

VINEDRESSER *gardener*
v-s and plowmen, 2Ki 25:12
My Father is the *v*, Jn 15:1

VINEGAR *sour liquid*
he shall drink no *v*, Nu 6:3
bread in the *v*, Ru 2:14
gave me *v* to drink, Ps 69:21
Like *v* to the teeth, Pr 10:26

VINE-GROWERS *tenders of vineyards*
rented it out to *v*, Mt 21:33
and destroy the *v*, Mk 12:9

VINEYARD *grapevines*
Noah…planted a *v*, Ge 9:20
Nor…glean your *v*, Lv 19:10
Hewn cisterns, *v-s*, Ne 9:25
shelter in a *v*, Is 1:8
ruined My *v*, Jer 12:10
laborers for his *v*, Mt 20:1
Who plants a *v*, 1Co 9:7

VIOLATE *assault; break*
shall not *v* his word, Nu 30:2
do not *v* me, 2Sa 13:12
who *v-d* the ban, 1Ch 2:7
If they *v* My statutes, Ps 89:31

VIOLENCE *destructive action*
earth was filled with *v*, Ge 6:11
implements of *v*, Ge 49:5
such as breathe out *v*, Ps 27:12
drink the wine of *v*, Pr 4:17
He had done no *v*, Is 53:9
not mistreat *or* do *v*, Jer 22:3

VIOLENT *destructive*
a wicked, *v* man, Ps 37:35
a *v*, rushing wind, Ac 2:2

VIPER *snake*
v-'s tongue slays him, Job 20:16

hand on the *v-'s* den, Is 11:8
v and flying serpent, Is 30:6
You brood of *v-s*, Mt 3:7

VIRGIN *unmarried maiden*
very beautiful, a *v*, Ge 24:16
if a man seduces a *v*, Ex 22:16
could I gaze at a *v*, Job 31:1
the *v* will rejoice, Jer 31:13
v shall be with child, Mt 1:23
kept her a *v*, Mt 1:25
comparable to ten *v-s*, Mt 25:1
v-'s name was Mary, Lk 1:27
if a *v* marries, 1Co 7:28

VIRGINITY *absence of sexual intercourse*
shall take a wife in her *v*, Lv 21:13
evidence of the girl's *v*, Dt 22:15
weep because of my *v*, Jdg 11:37

VISIBLE *manifest, seen*
He become *v*, Ac 10:40
becomes *v* is light, Eph 5:13
things which are *v*, Heb 11:3

VISION *dream, foresight*
to Abram in a *v*, Ge 15:1
v-s were infrequent, 1Sa 3:1
Where there is no *v*, Pr 29:18
prophets find No *v*, La 2:9
I saw *v-s* of God, Eze 1:1
in a night *v*, Da 2:19
young men…see *v-s*, Joel 2:28
Tell the *v* to no one, Mt 17:9
young men…see *v-s*, Ac 2:17

VISIT *come; go to see*
v-ing the iniquity of, Ex 20:5
You *v* the earth, Ps 65:9
you did not *v* Me, Mt 25:43
For He has *v-ed* us, Lk 1:68
v orphans…widows, Jas 1:27

VOICE *sound, speech*
have obeyed My *v*, Ge 22:18
listen to His *v*, Dt 4:30
v of singing men, 2Sa 19:35
You will hear my *v*, Ps 5:3
the *v* of my teachers, Pr 5:13
v of the turtledove, SS 2:12
Give ear…hear my *v*, Is 28:23
A *v* is calling, Is 40:3
v came from heaven, Da 4:31
v…heard in Ramah, Mt 2:18
v…out of the cloud, Mk 9:7
v of one crying in, Lk 3:4
v of the Son of God, Jn 5:25
v has gone out, Ro 10:18
v of *the* archangel, 1Th 4:16
His *v* shook…earth, Heb 12:26
if anyone hears My *v*, Rev 3:20
with a *v* of thunder, Rev 6:1

VOICE OF THE LORD
listen to the *v* your God, Dt 13:18
v is upon the waters, Ps 29:3
v, saying, "Whom shall, Is 6:8
there came the *v*, Ac 7:31

VOID *empty, invalid*
was formless and *v*, Ge 1:2
make *v* the counsel, Jer 19:7
faith is made *v*, Ro 4:14
cross…be made *v*, 1Co 1:17

VOMIT *throw up*
will *v* them up, Job 20:15
returns to its *v*, Pr 26:11
staggers in his *v*, Is 19:14
and it *v-ed* Jonah, Jon 2:10
returns to its own *v*, 2Pe 2:22

VOTIVE *dedicated*
his offering is a *v*, Lv 7:16
choice *v* offerings, Dt 12:11

VOW *solemn promise*
Jacob made a *v*, Ge 28:20
v of a Nazirite, Nu 6:2
I shall pay my *v-s*, Ps 22:25
not make false *v-s*, Mt 5:33
he was keeping a *v*, Ac 18:18

VOW TO THE LORD
When you make a *v*, Dt 23:21
Make *v-s* your God, Ps 76:11
I shall pay my *v-s*, Ps 116:14
shall fulfill your *v-s*., Mt 5:33

VOYAGE *journey*
v was now dangerous, Ac 27:9

VULTURE *bird*
not eat…the *v*, Dt 14:12
the *v-s* will gather, Mt 24:28
the *v-s* will be gathered, Lk 17:37

W

WAFER *thin cake of bread*
w-s with honey, Ex 16:31
one unleavened *w*, Nu 6:19

WAGE *salary*
God has given…*w-s*, Ge 30:18
w-s of the righteous, Pr 10:16
w is not credited, Ro 4:4
the *w-s* of sin, Ro 6:23
worthy of his *w-s*, 1Ti 5:18

WAIL *lament, mourn*
w with a broken spirit, Is 65:14
W, son of man, Eze 21:12
I must lament and *w*, Mic 1:8
W, O inhabitants of, Zep 1:11
weeping and *w-ing*, Mk 5:38

WAIST *midriff*
sheath fastened at his *w*, 2Sa 20:8
the belt about His *w*, Is 11:5
and put it around my *w*, Jer 13:2
whose *w* was girded, Da 10:5
a leather belt around his *w*, Mt 3:4

WAIT *expect*
For You I *w*, Ps 25:5
I *w* for Your word, Ps 119:81
who *w* for the LORD, Is 40:31
creation *w-s* eagerly, Ro 8:19
w-ing for the hope, Gal 5:5

WAIT FOR THE LORD
W; Be strong, Ps 27:14
who *w*, they will inherit, Ps 37:9
I *w*, my soul, Ps 130:5
My soul *w-s* more than, Ps 130:6
W, and He will, Pr 20:22
who *w* will gain new, Is 40:31

WAKE *rouse from sleep*
perpetual sleep And not *w*, Jer 51:39
W up, and strengthen, Rev 3:2
if you do not *w* up, I will, Rev 3:3

WALK *follow, go along*
w-ing in the garden, Ge 3:8
Enoch *w-ed* with God, Ge 5:22
W before Me, Ge 17:1
two of them *w-ed* on., Ge 22:6
w in My instruction, Ex 16:4
w in My statutes, Lv 26:3
to *w* in His ways, Dt 8:6
w-ed forty years, Jos 5:6
w before Me in truth, 1Ki 2:4
the man who does not *w*, Ps 1:1
though I *w* through, Ps 23:4
W about Zion, Ps 48:12
He *w-s* upon the wings, Ps 104:3
I will *w* at liberty, Ps 119:45
a man *w* on hot coals, Pr 6:28
fool *w-s* in darkness, Ecc 2:14
w in the light, Is 2:5
people who *w* in darkness, Is 9:2
w and not…weary, Is 40:31
w-ed with Me in peace, Mal 2:6
Get up, and *w*, Mt 9:5
and *the* lame *w*, Mt 11:5
w-ed on the water, Mt 14:29
like trees, *w-ing* around, Mk 8:24
pick up your pallet and *w*, Jn 5:8
anyone *w-s* in the day, Jn 11:9
W while you have the Light, Jn 12:35
w-ing and leaping and, Ac 3:8
w in newness of life, Ro 6:4
we *w* by faith, 2Co 5:7
w by the Spirit, Gal 5:16
that we would *w* in them, Eph 2:10
w in love, Eph 5:2
w as children of Light, Eph 5:8
you also once *w-ed*, Col 3:7
if we *w* in the Light, 1Jn 1:7
who *w-s* among the seven, Rev 2:1
w by its light, Rev 21:24

WALL *structure*
living on the *w*, Jos 2:15
So we built the *w*, Ne 4:6
I can leap over a *w*, Ps 18:29
w-s of Jerusalem, Jer 39:8
built a siege *w*, Jer 52:4
you whitewashed *w*, Ac 23:3
w-s of Jericho fell, Heb 11:30
a great and high *w*, Rev 21:12

WANDER *roam*
w in the wilderness, Nu 32:13
I would *w* far away, Ps 55:7
w…Your statutes, Ps 119:118
people w like sheep, Zec 10:2
w-ed…the faith, 1Ti 6:10
w-ing stars, for whom, Jude 13

WANDERER *roamer*
a *w* on the earth, Ge 4:12
an exile and a *w*, Is 49:21
w-s among…nations, Hos 9:17

WAR *battle, conflict*
when they see *w*, Ex 13:17
sound of *w* in…camp, Ex 32:17
land…rest from *w*, Jos 11:23
He makes *w-s* to cease, Ps 46:9
the weapons of *w*, Ps 76:3
A time for *w*, Ecc 3:8

will they learn *w*, Is 2:4
w-s...rumors of *w-s*, Mt 24:6
w against the law, Ro 7:23
w in your members, Jas 4:1
w against the soul, 1Pe 2:11
judges and wages *w*, Rev 19:11

WARM *heat*
could not keep *w*, 1Ki 1:1
the child became *w*, 2Ki 4:34
can one be *w alone*, Ecc 4:11
no one is *w enough*, Hag 1:6

WARN *give notice*
w the people, Ex 19:21
not...*w* the wicked, Eze 33:8
w-ed...in a dream, Mt 2:12
w you whom to fear, Lk 12:5
Moses was *w-ed*, Heb 8:5

WARRIOR *soldier*
The LORD is a *w*, Ex 15:3
O valiant *w*, Jdg 6:12
w from his youth, 1Sa 17:33
w-s will flee naked, Am 2:16

WARS OF THE LORD, BOOK OF
Ancient Hebrew literature, Nu 21:14

WASH *bathe, clean*
w your feet, and rest, Ge 18:4
w in the Jordan, 2Ki 5:10
w...in innocence, Ps 26:6
W...from my iniquity, Ps 51:2
w-ed off your blood, Eze 16:9
do not *w* their hands, Mt 15:2
ceremonially *w-ed*, Lk 11:38
w in the pool of, Jn 9:7
w the disciples' feet, Jn 13:5
w away your sins, Ac 22:16
w-ed...saints' feet, 1Ti 5:10
w-ed with pure, Heb 10:22
who *w* their robes, Rev 22:14

WASTE *(n) wilderness*
land was laid *w*, Ex 8:24
land into a salt *w*, Ps 107:34
lay *w* the mountains, Is 42:15
laid *w* like a desert, Jer 9:12
altars may become *w*, Eze 6:6
Egypt...become a *w*, Joel 3:19

WASTE *(v) destroy, use up*
he *w-d* his seed, Ge 38:9
w away the eyes, Lv 26:16
sick man *w-s* away, Is 10:18
perfume been *w-d*, Mk 14:4

WASTE PLACE *barren place*
w-s of the wealthy, Is 5:17
Seek Me in a *w*, Is 45:19
like the ancient *w-s*, Eze 26:20
w-s will be rebuilt, Eze 36:10

WATCH *(n) guard*
at the morning *w*, Ex 14:24
in the night *w-es*, Ps 63:6
His eyes keep *w*, Ps 66:7
keep *w* with Me, Mt 26:38
w over their flock, Lk 2:8
w over your souls, Heb 13:17

WATCH *(v) observe*
LORD *w* between you, Ge 31:49
w all my paths, Job 13:27
W over your heart, Pr 4:23
who *w-es* the wind, Ecc 11:4
w...for the LORD, Mic 7:7

WATCHMAN *one who guards*
w keeps awake in vain, Ps 127:1
w-men for...morning, Ps 130:6
W, how far gone is, Is 21:11
I set *w-men* over you, Jer 6:17
Ephraim *was* a *w*, Hos 9:8

WATER *(n) flood, liquid*
moving over...the *w-s*, Ge 1:2
flood of *w* came, Ge 7:6
w-s were like a wall, Ex 14:22
w of bitterness, Nu 5:18
the clouds dripped *w*, Jdg 5:4
W wears away stones, Job 14:19
poured out like *w*, Ps 22:14
beside quiet *w-s*, Ps 23:2
Stolen *w* is sweet, Pr 9:17
bread on the...*w-s*, Ecc 11:1
come to the *w-s*, Is 55:1
fountain of living *w-s*, Jer 2:13
eyes run...with *w*, La 1:16
knees...*like w*, Eze 7:17
baptize you with *w*, Mt 3:11
a cup of cold *w*, Mt 10:42
walked on the *w*, Mt 14:29
no *w* for My feet, Lk 7:44
one is born of *w*, Jn 3:5
given you living *w*, Jn 4:10
John baptized with *w*, Ac 1:5
of *w* with the word, Eph 5:26
formed out of *w*, 2Pe 3:5
by *w* and blood, 1Jn 5:6
sound of many *w-s*, Rev 19:6

WATER *(v) make moist*
to *w* the garden, Ge 2:10
I will *w* your camels, Ge 24:46
w their father's flock, Ex 2:16
that *w* the earth, Ps 72:6
Apollos *w-ed*, 1Co 3:6

WATER OF LIFE
to springs of the *w*, Rev 7:17
of the *w* without cost, Rev 21:6
river of the *w*, clear as, Rev 22:1
take the *w* without cost, Rev 22:17

WAVES *billows*
w of death, 2Sa 22:5
tramples down the *w*, Job 9:8
Your *w* have rolled, Ps 42:7
w were breaking, Mk 4:37
wild *w* of the sea, Jude 13

WAX *paraffin*
My heart is like *w*, Ps 22:14
Like *w* before the fire, Mic 1:4

WAY *manner; path*
guard the *w*, Ge 3:24
all His *w-s* are just, Dt 32:4
blameless...His *w*, 2Sa 22:33
from your evil *w-s*, 2Ki 17:13
joy of His *w*, Job 8:19
w of the righteous, Ps 1:6
Commit your *w* to, Ps 37:5
your *w-s* acknowledge, Pr 3:6
is the *w* of death, Pr 14:12
Clear the *w*, Is 40:3
w of the wicked, Jer 12:1
Make ready the *w*, Mt 3:3
Pray...in this *w*, Mt 6:9
w is broad that leads, Mt 7:13
teach...*w* of God, Mk 12:14
into the *w* of peace, Lk 1:79
I am the *w*, Jn 14:6
belonging to the *W*, Ac 9:2
the *w* of salvation, Ac 16:17
unfathomable...*w-s*, Ro 11:33
the *w* of escape, 1Co 10:13
new and living *w*, Heb 10:20
the *w* of the truth, 2Pe 2:2

WAY OF THE LORD
they will keep the *w*, Jdg 2:22
w is a stronghold, Pr 10:29
Make ready the *w*, Mt 3:3
Make ready the *w*, Mk 1:3
Make ready the *w*, Lk 3:4
Make straight the *w*., Jn 1:23
been instructed in the *w*, Ac 18:25

WEAK *feeble*
I will become *w*, Jdg 16:17
Rescue the *w*, Ps 82:4
but the flesh is *w*, Mt 26:41
must help the *w*, Ac 20:35
who is *w* in faith, Ro 14:1
God...chosen the *w*, 1Co 1:27

WEAKNESS *fault*
Spirit...helps our *w*, Ro 8:26
bear the *w-es*, Ro 15:1
w of God is stronger, 1Co 1:25
it is sown in *w*, 1Co 15:43
perfected in *w*, 2Co 12:9

WEALTH *riches*
power to make *w*, Dt 8:18
a man of great *w*, Ru 2:1
who trust in their *w*, Ps 49:6
Honor...from your *w*, Pr 3:9
W adds many friends, Pr 19:4
A *w* of salvation, Is 33:6
the *w* of all nations, Hag 2:7
serve God and *w*, Mt 6:24
deceitfulness of *w*, Mt 13:22
w of their liberality, 2Co 8:2
rich by her *w*, Rev 18:19

WEALTHY *having many possessions*
in the waste places of the *w*, Is 5:17
be for those who are *w*, Mk 10:23
it is for those who are *w*, Lk 18:24
become *w*, and have need, Rev 3:17

WEANED *no longer nursing*
The child grew and was *w*, Ge 21:8
until the child is *w*, 1Sa 1:22
Like a *w* child *rests*, Ps 131:2
the *w* child will put his hand, Is 11:8

WEAPON *armament*
girded on his *w-s*, Dt 1:41
flee from the iron *w*, Job 20:24
turn back the *w-s*, Jer 21:4
w-s of righteousness, 2Co 6:7

WEARY *tired*
the people were *w*, 1Sa 14:28
the *w* are at rest, Job 3:17
w with my crying, Ps 69:3
water to a *w* soul, Pr 25:25
and not become *w*, Is 40:31
sustain the *w* one, Is 50:4
all who are *w*, Mt 11:28

w of doing good, 2Th 3:13

WEAVE *interlace*
You *wove* me, Ps 139:13
w the spider's web, Is 59:5

WEB *woven work*
loom and the *w*, Jdg 16:14
trust a spider's *w*, Job 8:14

WEDDING *marriage*
had no *w* songs, Ps 78:63
day of his *w*, SS 3:11
come to the *w* feast, Mt 22:4
a *w* in Cana, Jn 2:1

WEEK *period of time*
Complete the *w* of, Ge 29:27
Seventy *w-s*, Da 9:24
first *day* of the *w*, Mt 28:1
I fast twice a *w*, Lk 18:12

WEEKS, FEAST OF
See FEASTS

WEEP *cry, sorrow*
sought *a place* to *w*, Ge 43:30
do not mourn or *w*, Ne 8:9
My eye *w-s* to God, Job 16:20
widows could not *w*, Ps 78:64
Let me *w* bitterly, Is 22:4
w day and night, Jer 9:1
Rachel *w-ing* for her, Mt 2:18
w-ing and gnashing, Mt 13:42
he...*wept* bitterly, Mt 26:75
saw the city...*wept*, Lk 19:41
w for yourselves, Lk 23:28
Jesus *wept*, Jn 11:35
why are you *w-ing*, Jn 20:13
w with...who *w*, Ro 12:15

WEIGH *measure out*
actions are *w-ed*, 1Sa 2:3
LORD *w-s* the motives, Pr 16:2

WEIGHT *heaviness*
a full and just *w*, Dt 25:15
w to the wind, Job 28:25
bag of deceptive *w-s*, Mic 6:11
eternal *w* of glory, 2Co 4:17

WELCOME *gladly receive*
no prophet is *w*, Lk 4:24
people *w-d* Him, Lk 8:40
who fears Him...*w*, Ac 10:35
she...*w-d* the spies, Heb 11:31

WELFARE *state of sufficiency*
see about the *w* of your, Ge 37:14
and asked him of his *w*, Jdg 18:15
one who spoke for the *w* of, Est 10:3
Do not pray for the *w* of, Jer 14:11
be concerned for your *w*, Php 2:20

WELL *water shaft*
sat down by a *w*, Ex 2:15
w of Bethlehem, 1Ch 11:17
Like...a polluted *w*, Pr 25:26
A *w* of fresh water, SS 4:15
Jacob's *w* was there, Jn 4:6

WELL KNOWN
name had become *w*, Mk 6:14
Christ has become *w*, Php 1:13

WELL-BEING *state of sufficiency*
w and creating calamity, Is 45:7
chastening for our *w fell*, Is 53:5
the *w* of your sons will be, Is 54:13

WELL-BELOVED
sing now for my *w*, Is 5:1

WELL-PLEASED *satisfied*
in whom I am *w*, Mt 3:17
in You I am *w*, Lk 3:22
God was not *w*, 1Co 10:5

WEST *direction*
very strong *w* wind, Ex 10:19
east is from the *w*, Ps 103:12
gather you from the *w*, Is 43:5

WHEAT *grain*
days of *w* harvest, Ge 30:14
first fruits of the *w*, Ex 34:22
plant *w* in rows, Is 28:25
gather His *w* into, Mt 3:12
to sift you like *w*, Lk 22:31
unless a grain of *w*, Jn 12:24

WHEEL *circular disk*
the *w*...is crushed, Ecc 12:6
w-s like a whirlwind, Is 5:28
one *w* were within, Eze 1:16
rattling of the *w*, Na 3:2

WHIRLWIND
take...Elijah by a *w*, 2Ki 2:1
comes like a *w*, Pr 1:27
chariots like the *w*, Jer 4:13
they reap the *w*, Hos 8:7

WHISPER *talk quietly*
who hate me *w*, Ps 41:7
w a prayer, Is 26:16
your speech will *w*, Is 29:4

WHISTLE *shrill sound*
And will *w* for it, Is 5:26
LORD will *w* for the fly, Is 7:18
I will *w* for them, Zec 10:8

WHITE *color*
teeth *w* from milk, Ge 49:12
w of an egg, Job 6:6
be as *w* as snow, Is 1:18
make one hair *w*, Mt 5:36
clothing *became w*, Lk 9:29
fields...*w* for harvest, Jn 4:35
clothed in *w* robes, Rev 7:9

WHITE AS SNOW
Miriam was leprous, as *w*, Nu 12:10
his presence a leper as *w*, 2Ki 5:27
as *w*; though they are red, Is 1:18
his clothing as *w*, Mt 28:3

WHITEWASHED *wall covering*
like *w* tombs, Mt 23:27
you *w* wall, Ac 23:3

WHO DO INIQUITY
See WORKERS OF INIQUITY
You hate all *w*, Ps 5:5
Depart from me, all you *w*, Ps 6:8
Deliver me from those *w*, Ps 59:2
From the tumult of those *w*, Ps 64:2
All *w* will be scattered, Ps 92:9
the snares of those *w*, Ps 141:9

WHOLE *entire*
water the *w* surface, Ge 2:6
w earth...populated, Ge 9:19
leavens the *w* lump, 1Co 5:6
keeps the *w* law, Jas 2:10

WICK *candle thread*
extinguished like a *w*, Is 43:17
a smoldering *w*, Mt 12:20

WICKED *evil, ungodly*
condemn the *w*, Dt 25:1
w ones are silenced, 1Sa 2:9
counsel of the *w*, Ps 1:1
the *w* spurned God, Ps 10:13
The *w* strut about, Ps 12:8
devises *w* plans, Pr 6:18
When a *w* man dies, Pr 11:7
no peace for the *w*, Is 48:22
turn from his *w* way, Jon 3:8
taking...some *w* men, Ac 17:5
righteous and the *w*, Ac 24:15

WICKEDNESS *evil*
w of man was great, Ge 6:5
If I regard *w*, Ps 66:18
eat the bread of *w*, Pr 4:17
inclines toward *w*, Is 32:6
w of My people, Jer 7:12
You have plowed *w*, Hos 10:13
repent of this *w*, Ac 8:22
spiritual *forces* of *w*, Eph 6:12

WIDOW *husband dead*
Remain a *w*, Ge 38:11
not afflict any *w*, Ex 22:22
sent *w-s* away empty, Job 22:9
judge for the *w-s*, Ps 68:5
Plead for the *w*, Is 1:17
devour *w-s'* houses, Mt 23:14
w put in more, Mk 12:43
Honor *w-s*, 1Ti 5:3
visit orphans...*w-s*, Jas 1:27

WIFE *married woman*
joined to his *w*, Ge 2:24
man and his *w* hid, Ge 3:8
shall not covet...*w*, Ex 20:17
w of your youth, Pr 5:18
An excellent *w*, Pr 31:10
who divorces his *w*, Mt 5:32
Remember Lot's *w*, Lk 17:32
have his own *w*, 1Co 7:2
head of the *w*, Eph 5:23
husband of one *w*, 1Ti 3:2
w-ves, be submissive, 1Pe 3:1
w of the Lamb, Rev 21:9

WILD *untamed*
w donkey of a man, Ge 16:12
horns of the *w* ox, Nu 23:22
locusts and *w* honey, Mk 1:6
being a *w* olive, Ro 11:17

WILDERNESS *barren area*
water in the *w*, Ge 16:7
journey into the *w*, Ex 5:3
to die in the *w*, Ex 14:11
forty years in the *w*, Dt 29:5
pastures of the *w*, Ps 65:12
roadway in the *w*, Is 43:19
Have I been a *w*, Jer 2:31
preaching in the *w*, Mt 3:1
into the *w*...tempted, Mt 4:1
crying in the *w*, Mk 1:3

manna in the *w*, Jn 6:31

WILL *attitude, purpose*
delight to do Your *w*, Ps 40:8
Your *w* be done, Mt 6:10
the *w* of My Father, Mt 7:21
not My *w*, but, Lk 22:42
nor of the *w* of man, Jn 1:13
who resists His *w*, Ro 9:19
what the *w* of God, Ro 12:2
knowledge of His *w*, Col 1:9
come to do Your *w*, Heb 10:9
an act of human *w*, 2Pe 1:21

WILL BE SAVED
shine upon us, and we *w*, Ps 80:3
endured to the end who *w*, Mt 10:22
on the name of the Lord *w*, Ac 2:21
the Lord Jesus, and you *w*, Ac 16:31
the remnant that *w*, Ro 9:27
Him from the dead, you *w*, Ro 10:9
the name of the Lord *w*, Ro 10:13
so all Israel *w*, Ro 11:26
w, yet so as through, 1Co 3:15

WILL OF GOD
whoever does the *w*, Mk 3:35
saints according to the *w*, Ro 8:27
prove what the *w*, Ro 12:2
Jesus Christ by the *w*, 1Co 1:1
doing the *w* from the heart, Eph 6:6
the *w*, your sanctification, 1Th 4:3
suffer according to the *w*, 1Pe 4:19

WIN *succeed*
wise *w-s* souls, Pr 11:30
we will *w* him over, Mt 28:14
that I might *w* Jews, 1Co 9:20
won without a word, 1Pe 3:1

WIND *air movement*
caused a *w* to pass, Ge 8:1
scorched by...*w*, Ge 41:27
will inherit *w*, Pr 11:29
prophets are *as w*, Jer 5:13
they sow the *w*, Hos 8:7
reed shaken by...*w*, Mt 11:7
w and the sea obey, Mk 4:41
He...rebuked the *w*, Lk 8:24
violent, rushing *w*, Ac 2:2
every *w* of doctrine, Eph 4:14
driven by strong *w-s*, Jas 3:4

WINDOW *opening*
enter through the *w-s*, Joel 2:9
open...*w-s* of heaven, Mal 3:10
sitting on the *w* sill, Ac 20:9
basket through a *w*, 2Co 11:33

WINE *strong drink*
eyes...dull from *w*, Ge 49:12
Do not drink *w*, Lv 10:9
overflow with new *w*, Pr 3:10
W is a mocker, Pr 20:1
love is better than *w*, SS 1:2
new *w* into old, Mt 9:17
gave Him *w* to, Mt 27:34
made the water *w*, Jn 4:46
full of sweet *w*, Ac 2:13
not get drunk with *w*, Eph 5:18
not addicted to *w*, 1Ti 3:3

WINESKINS *animal skin bag*
These *w*...were new, Jos 9:13
Like new *w*, Job 32:19
wine into fresh *w*, Mt 9:17

WINGS *flight; protection*
bore you on eagles' *w*, Ex 19:4
He spread His *w*, Dt 32:11
under whose *w*, Ru 2:12
under His *w*...refuge, Ps 91:4
with w like eagles, Is 40:31
healing in its *w*, Mal 4:2
chicks under her *w*, Mt 23:37

WINK *blink*
w maliciously, Ps 35:19
w-s with his eyes, Pr 6:13

WINNOW *scatter*
king *w-s* the wicked, Pr 20:26
You will *w* them, Is 41:16
His *w-ing* fork, Mt 3:12

WINTER *season*
And summer and *w*, Ge 8:22
the *w* is past, SS 2:11
even spend the *w*, 1Co 16:6

WIPE *pass over, rub*
God will *w* tears, Is 25:8
w-d His feet, Jn 11:2
sins...*w-d* away, Ac 3:19
w away every tear, Rev 21:4

WISDOM *discernment*
the spirit of *w*, Ex 28:3
w has two sides, Job 11:6
the beginning of *w*, Ps 111:10
Fools despise *w*, Pr 1:7
w to fear Your name, Mic 6:9
w given to Him, Mk 6:2
kept increasing in *w*, Lk 2:52
made foolish the *w*, 1Co 1:20
any of you lacks *w*, Jas 1:5

WISE *judicious, prudent*
not find a *w* man, Job 17:10
making *w* the simple, Ps 19:7
w in your own eyes, Pr 3:7
the words of the *w*, Pr 22:17
He is not a *w* son, Hos 13:13
Who...you is *w*, Jas 3:13

WISE MAN
See WISE MEN
I do not find a *w*, Job 17:10
w will hear and increase, Pr 1:5
Reprove a *w*, Pr 9:8
w is cautious and turns, Pr 14:16
a *w* will appease, Pr 16:14
w and the fool alike die, Ecc 2:16
w's heart directs him, Ecc 10:2
a *w* who built his house, Mt 7:24
Where is the *w*?, 1Co 1:20
not among you one *w*, 1Co 6:5

WISE MEN
See WISE MAN
of Egypt, and all its *w*, Ge 41:8
that even *w* die, Ps 49:10
W store up knowledge, Pr 10:14
w turn away anger, Pr 29:8
of *w* are like goads, Ecc 12:11
none of the *w*, Da 4:18
you prophets and *w*, Mt 23:34
speak as to *w*, 1Co 10:15

WISH *desire*
marry whom they *w*, Nu 36:6
does not *w* to redeem you, Ru 3:13
what *you w* Me to give, 1Ki 3:5
turns it wherever He *w-es*, Pr 21:1
done for you as you *w*, Mt 15:28
If anyone *w-es* to come, Mt 16:24
if you *w* to enter into life, Mt 19:17
What do you *w*, Mt 20:21
anyone *w-es* to come after, Mk 8:34
prophets and kings *w-ed*, Lk 10:24
how I *w* it were already, Lk 12:49
Do you *w* to get well, Jn 5:6
ask whatever you *w*, Jn 15:7
I *w* that all men were even, 1Co 7:7
a body just as He *w-ed*, 1Co 15:38
I could *w* to be present, Gal 4:20
not *w-ing* for any to perish, 2Pe 3:9
w that you were cold or hot, Rev 3:15

WITCHCRAFT *magic, sorcery*
who practices *w*, Dt 18:10
practiced *w* and, 2Ki 21:6

WITH ALL YOUR HEART
search for Him *w*, Dt 4:29
the LORD your God *w*, Dt 6:5
and serve Him *w*, Jos 22:5
Trust in the LORD *w*, Pr 3:5
Rejoice and exult *w*, Zep 3:14
love the Lord your God *w*, Mt 22:37
If you believe *w*, Ac 8:37

WITH CHILD
"Behold, you are *w*, Ge 16:11
were *w* by their father, Ge 19:36
she is also *w* by harlotry, Ge 38:24
strike a woman *w* so that, Ex 21:22
women *w* you will rip up, 2Ki 8:12
a virgin will be *w*, Is 7:14
to be *w* by the Holy Spirit, Mt 1:18
virgin shall be *w*, Mt 1:23
engaged to him, and was *w*, Lk 2:5
pains upon a woman *w*, 1Th 5:3
w; and she cried out, Rev 12:2

WITH ONE ACCORD
lifted their voices to God *w*, Ac 4:24
w in Solomon's portico, Ac 5:12
w were giving attention, Ac 8:6
w you may with one voice, Ro 15:6

WITHER *dry up*
its leaf does not *w*, Ps 1:3
w...like the grass, Ps 37:2
earth mourns *and w-s*, Is 24:4
the leaf will *w*, Jer 8:13
whose hand was *w-ed*, Mk 3:1
the fig tree *w-ed*, Mk 11:20

WITNESS *(n) testimony*
This heap is a *w*, Ge 31:48
not bear false *w*, Ex 20:16
is *w* between us, Jdg 11:10
my *w* is in heaven, Job 16:19
a *w* to the LORD, Is 19:20
He came as a *w*, Jn 1:7
you shall be My *w-es*, Ac 1:8
For God is my *w*, Php 1:8
Christ, the faithful *w*, Rev 1:5

WITNESS *(v) testify*
w against you today, Dt 4:26

WOLF *animal*
w will dwell with, Is 11:6
the midst of *w-ves*, Mt 10:16
w snatches them, Jn 10:12

WOMAN *female, lady*
She shall be called *W*, Ge 2:23
w...not wear man's, Dt 22:5
a *w* of excellence, Ru 3:11
Man...born of *w*, Job 14:1
gracious *w* attains, Pr 11:16
a contentious *w*, Pr 25:24
like a *w* in labor, Is 42:14
looks at a *w* with lust, Mt 5:28
W, behold, your son, Jn 19:26
not to touch a *w*, 1Co 7:1
w is the glory of, 1Co 11:7
w to speak in, 1Co 14:35
His Son, born of a *w*, Gal 4:4
w clothed with...sun, Rev 12:1

WOMB *uterus*
nations...in your *w*, Ge 25:23
LORD...closed her *w*, 1Sa 1:5
from *w* to tomb, Job 10:19
formed you from the *w*, Is 44:2
baby leaped in...*w*, Lk 1:41

WOMEN *female persons*
when *w* go out to draw, Ge 24:11
the Hebrew *w* are not as, Ex 1:19
Most blessed of *w* is Jael, Jdg 5:24
loved many foreign *w*, 1Ki 11:1
Esther more than all the *w*, Est 2:17
Most beautiful among *w*, SS 1:8
those born of *w* there, Mt 11:11
are you among *w*, Lk 1:42
w are to keep silent in, 1Co 14:34
w will be preserved through, 1Ti 2:15
may encourage the young *w*, Titus 2:4

WONDER *marvel, sign*
consider the *w-s* of, Job 37:14
tell of all Your *w-s*, Ps 9:1
His *w-s* in the deep, Ps 107:24
w-s in the sky, Joel 2:30
were filled with *w*, Ac 3:10

WONDERFUL *marvelous*
His *w* deeds, 1Ch 16:12
name will be called *W*, Is 9:6

WONDERS AND SIGNS
See SIGNS AND WONDERS
w which God performed, Ac 2:22
many *w* were taking place, Ac 2:43
was performing great *w*, Ac 6:8
w in the land of Egypt, Ac 7:36

WOOD *cut tree*
ark of gopher *w*, Ge 6:14
other gods, *w* and, Dt 28:36
children gather *w*, Jer 7:18
stones, *w*, hay, 1Co 3:12

WOOL *cloth; hair*
of *w* and linen, Dt 22:11
put a fleece of *w* on, Jdg 6:37
They will be like *w*, Is 1:18
hair...like pure *w*, Da 7:9
white like white *w*, Rev 1:14

WORD *message, speech*
to the *w* of Moses, Lv 10:7
declare to you the *w*, Dt 5:5
Joshua wrote...*w-s*, Jos 24:26
proclaim the *w* of, 1Sa 9:27
Your *w*...confirmed, 2Ch 6:17
no limit to windy *w-s*, Job 16:3
w-s of my mouth, Ps 19:14
Your *w* is a lamp, Ps 119:105
harsh *w* stirs up, Pr 15:1
w of God is tested, Pr 30:5
despised the *w*, Is 5:24
w-s of a sealed book, Is 29:11
speak My *w* in truth, Jer 23:28
conceal these *w-s*, Da 12:4
every *w* that proceeds, Mt 4:4
these *w-s* of Mine, Mt 7:24
sower sows the *w*, Mk 4:14
the *W* was God, Jn 1:1
the *W* became flesh, Jn 1:14
w-s of eternal life, Jn 6:68
continue in My *w*, Jn 8:31
glorifying the *w*, Ac 13:48
too deep for *w-s*, Ro 8:26
hearing by the *w*, Ro 10:17
the *w* of the cross, 1Co 1:18
fulfilled in one *w*, Gal 5:14
no unwholesome *w*, Eph 4:29
sanctified by...*w*, 1Ti 4:5
the *w* of truth, 2Ti 2:15
the faithful *w*, Titus 1:9
w of God is living, Heb 4:12
doers of the *w*, Jas 1:22
pure milk of the *w*, 1Pe 2:2
the *W* of Life, 1Jn 1:1
The *W* of God, Rev 19:13

WORD OF GOD
the *w* came to Nathan, 1Ch 17:3
Every *w* is tested, Pr 30:5
you invalidated the *w*, Mt 15:6
the *w* came to John, Lk 3:2
seed is the *w*, Lk 8:11
who hear the *w* and do it, Lk 8:21
neglect the *w* in order, Ac 6:2
w kept on spreading, Ac 6:7
also had received the *w*, Ac 11:1
peddling the *w*, 2Co 2:17
Spirit, which is the *w*, Eph 6:17
w is living and active, Heb 4:12
tasted the good *w*, Heb 6:5
the *w* abides in you, 1Jn 2:14
name is called The *W*, Rev 19:13

WORD OF TRUTH
w utterly out of my mouth, Ps 119:43
the *w*, in the power of God, 2Co 6:7
heard in the *w*, the gospel, Col 1:5
accurately handling the *w*., 2Ti 2:15
brought us forth by the *w*, Jas 1:18

WORK *(n) act, deed, labor*
God completed His *w*, Ge 2:2
You shall *w* six days, Ex 34:21
His *w* is perfect, Dt 32:4
the *w* of His hands, Ps 19:1
see the *w-s* of God, Ps 66:5
Commit your *w-s* to, Pr 16:3
let Him hasten His *w*, Is 5:19
His *w* on Mount Zion, Is 10:12
see your good *w-s*, Mt 5:16
the *w-s* of Christ, Mt 11:2
the *w* of the Law, Ro 2:15
faith apart from *w-s*, Ro 3:28
not...a result of *w-s*, Eph 2:9
for the *w* of service, Eph 4:12
began a good *w*, Php 1:6
fruit in...good *w*, Col 1:10
rich in good *w-s*, 1Ti 6:18
faith without *w-s*, Jas 2:20

WORK *(v) perform, produce*
has *w-ed* with God, 1Sa 14:45
those who *w* iniquity, Ps 28:3
Who...*w-s* wonders, Ps 72:18
not *w* for the food, Jn 6:27
w together for good, Ro 8:28
So death *w-s* in us, 2Co 4:12
w out your salvation, Php 2:12
anyone is not willing to *w*, 2Th 3:10

WORKER *laborer*
O *w* of deceit, Ps 52:2
w-s of iniquity, Pr 10:29
w is worthy of his, Mt 10:10
God's fellow *w-s*, 1Co 3:9
beware...evil *w-s*, Php 3:2
pure, *w-s* at home, Titus 2:5

WORKERS OF INIQUITY
See WHO DO INIQUITY
in company with the *w*, Job 34:8
Where the *w* may hide, Job 34:22
But ruin to the *w*, Pr 10:29
But is terror to the *w*, Pr 21:15
against the help of the *w*, Is 31:2

WORKMAN *craftsman*
a skillful *w*, Ex 38:23
approved...as a *w*, 2Ti 2:15

WORKMANSHIP *craftsmanship*
we are His *w*, Eph 2:10

WORKS OF THE LAW
by the *w* no flesh, Ro 3:20
faith apart from *w*, Ro 3:28
not justified by the *w*, Gal 2:16
receive the Spirit by the *w*, Gal 3:2
by the *w*, or by hearing, Gal 3:5
the *w* are under a curse, Gal 3:10

WORLD *earth, humanity*
foundations of...*w*, 2Sa 22:16
He will judge the *w*, Ps 9:8
first dust of the *w*, Pr 8:26
the light of the *w*, Mt 5:14
the field is the *w*, Mt 13:38
Go into all the *w*, Mk 16:15
gains the whole *w*, Lk 9:25
God so loved the *w*, Jn 3:16
Savior of the *w*, Jn 4:42
w cannot hate you, Jn 7:7
the Light of the *w*, Jn 8:12
overcome the *w*, Jn 16:33
have upset the *w*, Ac 17:6
sin entered...the *w*, Ro 5:12
reconciling the *w*, 2Co 5:19
unstained by the *w*, Jas 1:27
flood upon the *w*, 2Pe 2:5
Do not love the *w*, 1Jn 2:15

WORLDLY *earthly*
w fables fit only, 1Ti 4:7
avoid *w*...chatter, 2Ti 2:16

WORM *creeping animal*
But I am a *w*, Ps 22:6
w-s are your covering, Is 14:11
God appointed a *w*, Jon 4:7
their *w* does not die, Mk 9:48
he was eaten by *w-s*, Ac 12:23

WORMWOOD
1 A bitter plant, Dt 29:18
2 Used figuratively, Pr 5:4; Am 6:12; Rev 8:11

WORRY *anxious*
not be *w-ied* about your life, Mt 6:25
not *w* about tomorrow, Mt 6:34
do not *w* beforehand, Mk 13:11
w-ing can add a *single*, Lk 12:25

WORSHIP *bow, revere*
not *w* any other god, Ex 34:14
you shall *w* Him, Dt 6:13
W the LORD, Ps 2:11
earth will *w* You, Ps 66:4
in vain do they *w*, Mt 15:9
w in spirit and truth, Jn 4:24
w in the Spirit, Php 3:3
w Him who lives, Rev 4:10
who *w* the beast, Rev 14:11

WORTHLESS *useless*
all *w* physicians, Job 13:4
w man digs up evil, Pr 16:27
your *w* offerings, Is 1:13
your faith is *w*, 1Co 15:17
w for any good, Titus 1:16
man's religion is *w*, Jas 1:26

WORTHY *having merit*
sin *w* of death, Dt 21:22
w of his support, Mt 10:10
is not *w* of Me, Mt 10:37
is *w* of his wages, Lk 10:7
manner *w* of the, Ro 16:2
w of the gospel, Php 1:27
world was not *w*, Heb 11:38
W is the Lamb, Rev 5:12

WOUND *injury*
My *w* is incurable, Job 34:6
binds up their *w-s*, Ps 147:3
Your *w* is incurable, Jer 30:12
bandaged…his *w-s*, Lk 10:34
by His *w-s* you were, 1Pe 2:24
fatal *w* was healed, Rev 13:3

WRAPPINGS *cloth coverings*
bound…with *w*, Jn 11:44
linen *w* lying *there*, Jn 20:5

WRATH *anger, indignation*
and in great *w*, Dt 29:28
Nor chasten…in Your *w*, Ps 6:1
Pour out Your *w*, Ps 79:6
turns away *w*, Pr 15:1
Or else My *w* will go forth, Jer 4:4
spent My *w* upon, Eze 5:13
from the *w* to come, Mt 3:7
w of God abides on, Jn 3:36
God who inflicts *w*, Ro 3:5
children of *w*, Eph 2:3
w of God will come, Col 3:6
the *w* of the Lamb, Rev 6:16

WRATH OF GOD
See WRATH OF THE LORD
the *w* abides on him, Jn 3:36
w is revealed from, Ro 1:18
saved from the *w*, Ro 5:9
leave room for the *w*, Ro 12:19
w comes upon the sons, Eph 5:6
w will come upon the sons, Col 3:6
wine of the *w*, Rev 14:10
the *w* is finished, Rev 15:1
bowls full of the *w*, Rev 15:7
seven bowls of the *w*, Rev 16:1
press of the fierce *w*, Rev 19:15

WRATH OF THE LORD
See WRATH OF GOD
great is the *w*, 2Ki 22:13
the *w* was against Judah, 2Ch 29:8
w did not come on them, 2Ch 32:26
w, the rebuke of your God, Is 51:20
am full of the *w*, Jer 6:11
the day of the *w*, Eze 7:19

WRESTLED *struggled*
I have *w* with my sister, Ge 30:8
w with him until daybreak, Ge 32:24
he *w* with the angel and, Hos 12:4

WRESTLINGS *struggles*
mighty *w* I have wrestled, Ge 30:8

WRETCHED *miserable*
in to this *w* place, Nu 20:5
W man that I am, Ro 7:24

WRITE *enscribe*
Moses, *W* this in a, Ex 17:14
W them on the tablet, Pr 3:3
he *wrote* the dream, Da 7:1
w a certificate, Mk 10:4
with His finger *wrote*, Jn 8:6
w…King of the Jews, Jn 19:21
W in a book, Rev 1:11

WRITINGS *literary work*
not believe his *w*, Jn 5:47
known the sacred *w*, 2Ti 3:15

WRITTEN *enscribed*
w by…God, Ex 31:18
w in the law, 2Ch 23:18
remembrance was *w*, Mal 3:16
w by the prophet, Mt 2:5
about whom it is *w*, Mt 11:10
Law *w* in…hearts, Ro 2:15
name has not been *w*, Rev 13:8
w in the Lamb's, Rev 21:27

WRONG *do evil, harm*
not *w* a stranger, Ex 22:21
not *w* one another, Lv 25:14
I…have done *w*, 2Sa 24:17
Love does no *w*, Ro 13:10

WROUGHT *accomplished*
He *w* wonders, Ps 78:12
been *w* in God, Jn 3:21

YAHWEH
See YHWH; LORD

YEAR *period, time*
atonement…every *y*, Lv 16:34
fiftieth *y*…jubilee, Lv 25:11
the *y* of remission, Dt 15:9
crowned the *y* with, Ps 65:11
length of…*y-s*, Pr 3:2
favorable *y* of the LORD, Is 61:2
thirty *y-s* of age, Lk 3:23
y of the Lord, Lk 4:19
priest *enters*, once a *y*, Heb 9:7
sacrifices…*y* by *y*, Heb 10:1
y-s like one day, 2Pe 3:8
reign…thousand *y-s*, Rev 20:6

YEARLING *one year old*
a *y* ewe lamb, Lv 14:10
With *y* calves, Mic 6:6

YEARNS *deeply moved*
my flesh *y* for You, Ps 63:1
My heart *y* for him, Jer 31:20

YESTERDAY *past*
we are *only* of *y*, Job 8:9
thousand years…*y*, Ps 90:4
same *y* and today, Heb 13:8

YHWH
Hebrew tetragrammaton for name of God, probably pronounced Yahweh
Derived from Hebrew verb meaning "to be"
Translated usually as Lord
See also Lord
See also introductory material to NASB

YIELD *produce*
no longer *y* its, Ge 4:12
land…*y* its produce, Lv 25:19
Which *y-s* its fruit, Ps 1:3
y-ed up *His* spirit, Mt 27:50
not *y* in subjection, Gal 2:5
y-s the peaceful, Heb 12:11

YOKE *wooden bar*
break his *y* from, Ge 27:40
iron *y* on…neck, Dt 28:48
made our *y* hard, 1Ki 12:4
the *y* of their burden, Is 9:4
Take My *y* upon, Mt 11:29
to a *y* of slavery, Gal 5:1

YOU ARE THE CHRIST
Peter answered, "*Y*, Mt 16:16
Y, the Son of God, Mt 26:63
said to Him, "*Y*.", Mk 8:29
If *Y*, tell us, Lk 22:67
If *Y*, tell us, Jn 10:24
believed that *Y*, Jn 11:27

YOUNG *early age, youth*
he sent *y* men, Ex 24:5
or two *y* pigeons, Lv 15:29
glory of *y* men is, Pr 20:29
y men stumble, Is 40:30
like a *y* lion, Hos 5:14
finding a *y* donkey, Jn 12:14
y men…visions, Ac 2:17
urge the *y* men, Titus 2:6

YOUTH *young*
evil from his *y*, Ge 8:21
fresher than in *y*, Job 33:25
the sins of my *y*, Ps 25:7
confidence from my *y*, Ps 71:5
your *y* is renewed, Ps 103:5
the wife of your *y*, Pr 5:18
y-s grow weary, Is 40:30
the reproach of my *y*, Jer 31:19
life from my *y* up, Ac 26:4

Z

ZACCHEUS
Wealthy tax collector converted to Christ, Lk 19:1–10

ZACHARIAS
Father of John the Baptist, Lk 1:5–17

ZADOK
Co-priest with Abiathar; remains loyal to David, 2Sa 15:24–29; 20:25
Rebuked by David, 2Sa 19:11, 12
Does not follow Adonijah; anoints Solomon, 1Ki 1:8–45
Takes Abiathar's place, 1Ki 2:35

ZALMUNNA
Midianite king, Jdg 8:4–21

ZAREPHATH
Town of Sidon where Elijah revives widow's son, 1Ki 17:8–24; Lk 4:26

ZEAL *fervor, passion*
kill them in his *z*, 2Sa 21:2
my *z* for the LORD, 2Ki 10:16
z has consumed me, Ps 119:139
Your z for the people, Is 26:11
have a *z* for God, Ro 10:2
your *z* for me, 2Co 7:7

ZEALOT
member of radical Jewish nationalist party, Mt 10:4; Mk 3:18; Lk 6:15; Ac 1:13

ZEALOUS *fervent*
z for the LORD, 1Ki 19:10
all *z* for the Law, Ac 21:20
z of...*gifts*, 1Co 14:12
z for good deeds, Titus 2:14
be *z* and repent, Rev 3:19

ZEBAH
King of Midian killed by Gideon, Jdg 8:4–28

ZEBEDEE
Galilean fisherman; father of James and John, Mt 4:21, 22

ZEBULUN
Sixth son of Jacob and Leah, Ge 30:19, 20
Prophecy concerning, Ge 49:13
——— Tribe of:
Numbered, Nu 1:30, 31; 26:27
Territory assigned to, Jos 19:10–16
Joins Gideon in battle, Jdg 6:34, 35
Some respond to Hezekiah's reforms, 2Ch 30:10–18
Christ visits territory of, Mt 4:13–16

ZECHARIAH
King of Israel; last ruler of Jehu's dynasty, 2Ki 15:8–12
——— Postexilic prophet and priest, Ezr 5:1; Zec 1:1, 7

ZEDEKIAH
Last king of Judah; uncle and successor of Jehoiachin; reigns wickedly, 2Ki 24:17–19; 2Ch 36:10
Rebels against Nebuchadnezzar, 2Ch 36:11–13
Denounced by Jeremiah, Jer 34:1–22
Consults Jeremiah, Jer 37; 38
Captured and taken to Babylon, 2Ki 25:1–7; Jer 39:1–7

ZELOPHEHAD
Manassite whose five daughters secure female rights, Nu 27:1–7

ZEPHANIAH
Author of Zephaniah, Zep 1:1
——— Priest and friend of Jeremiah during Zedekiah's reign, Jer 21:1

ZERUBBABEL
Descendant of David, 1Ch 3:1–19
Leader of Jewish exiles, Ne 7:6, 7; Hag 2:21–23
Rebuilds the temple, Ezr 3:1–10; Zec 4:1–14

ZIBA
Saul's servant, 2Sa 9:9
Befriends David, 2Sa 16:1–4
Accused of deception by Mephibosheth, 2Sa 19:17–30

ZIKLAG
City on the border of Judah, Jos 15:1, 31
Held by David, 1Sa 27:6
Overthrown by Amalekites, 1Sa 30:1–31

ZILPAH
Leah's maid, Ge 29:24
Mother of Gad and Asher, Ge 30:9–13

ZIMRI
Simeonite prince slain by Phinehas, Nu 25:6–14
——— King of Israel for seven days, 1Ki 16:8–20

ZIN
Wilderness through which the Israelites passed, Nu 20:1
Border between Judah and Edom, Jos 15:1–3

ZION
Literally, an area in Jerusalem; called the City of David, 2Sa 5:6–9; 2Ch 5:2
Used figuratively of God's kingdom, Ps 125:1; Heb 12:22; Rev 14:1

ZIPPORAH
Daughter of Jethro; wife of Moses, Ex 18:1, 2

ZIV
Name of the second month in Hebrew calendar, 1Ki 6:1, 37

ZOAR
Ancient city of Canaan originally named Bela, Ge 14:2, 8
Spared destruction at Lot's request, Ge 19:20–23

ZOPHAR
Naamathite; friend of Job, Job 2:11

ZUZIM
Pre-Israelite tribe in Palestine, Ge 14:5